The New Schöffler-Weis German and English Dictionary

Comprehensive and Easy to Use

At last available in America, this widely acclaimed work will meet the needs of virtually anyone who has need for a German and English dictionary. A standard reference both in Germany and the United Kingdom, the Schöffler-Weis Dictionary has been highly praised for its accurate vocabulary, translations, examples of usage, and style of the German language. Because of its compact size (three columns per page) and ease of reference, this dictionary fits the varied needs of an American audience.

Contains a Variety of Modern Terms and Idioms

As a comprehensive bilingual lexicon with 150,000 entries, this dictionary is an invaluable reference source for current scientific and technological terms. Idioms and colloquialisms, from modern slang to classical expressions, are accurately rendered. An exceptionally large number of entries are drawn from the humanities and social sciences.

Labels Pinpoint Meanings

The entries are enriched with explanatory words and grammatical labels to pinpoint the exact equivalents the user is seeking. Common words and words with many meanings are given exhaustive treatment. Supplementary information in the introduction and the appendices includes irregular verb forms, important abbreviations, proper names, and the conversion to the metric system.

Source for Experts and Nonprofessionals

This dictionary is an indispensable reference work for the student, teacher, translator, traveler, scholar, scientist, and any professional or general reader who deals with the German language or people. It is a must for schools and libraries.

The New Schöffler-Weis German and English Dictionary

The New Schöffler-Weis German and English Dictionary

ENGLISH-GERMAN / GERMAN-ENGLISH

By

Dr. Herbert Schöffler

Late Professor of English Philology and Cultural History
at the University of Göttingen

Completely revised, greatly expanded, and fully updated by

Professor Erich Weis and Dr. Erwin Weis

in collaboration with

Dr. Heinrich Mattutat

Foreword by

Professor Kenneth J. Northcott

Chairman of the Department of Germanic Languages
and Literatures
The University of Chicago

FOLLETT PUBLISHING COMPANY · CHICAGO

Library of Congress Catalog Card Number: 73-90689

The ISBN of Follett Publishing Company is:
0-695-80458-8

The ISBN of Ernst Klett Verlag is:
3-12-5183-006 for Part 1
3-12-5184-002 for Part 2

3456789/8281807978

Contents

Foreword vii

Part I, English-German

Explanations xi-xii

List of Abbreviations xiii

Table of English Irregular Verbs xiv

List of Irregular German Verbs xv-xvi

Pronunciation Key xvii

English-German Dictionary 1-551

Abbreviations 552-558

Proper Names 559-562

Part II, German-English

Explanations iii-iv

List of Abbreviations v

Cardinal Numbers vi

Ordinal Numbers vi

Weights and Measures vii

German-English Dictionary 1-489

Abbreviations 491-495

Atlas 496-500

Foreword

For the student of language the availability of a new dictionary is a source of delight, for the everyday user, a necessity. I am particularly pleased that the Schöffler-Weis German Dictionary will now be readily available to the American public. This work, which is detailed enough to avoid the pitfalls of the "one-word-one-meaning" type of dictionary, yet compact enough to be published in one volume, reflects the learning and interests of its compilers. Herbert Schöffler was a man of many talents, interested in humanities, literature, history, religion, and philosophy, while Erich Weis has a more markedly pedagogic bent. These qualities combine to produce a dictionary with a very wide and pleasingly catholic vocabulary. The humanist, the social scientist as well as the physical and biological scientist will find their needs satisfied in everything but the most technical aspects of their vocabularies. In addition, the world of sport and entertainment is remarkably well represented.

One very important feature of the work is the fact that wherever possible the individual word is not only translated but also given in its idiomatic context.

The explanations of labels, grammatical abbreviations, and the layout of the dictionary will greatly enhance its value and they should be studied carefully by the user. Another valuable addition is the table of common abbreviations included at the end of each section.

Everyone who uses German in their daily life whether for profit or for pleasure will be well served by this work of reference.

Kenneth J. Northcott, Chairman
Department of Germanic Languages and Literatures
The University of Chicago

PART I

English — German

Revised by

Dr. Erich Weis

with the collaboration of

Dr. Heinrich Mattutat

EXPLANATIONS

1. Arrangement

Main headwords are placed in alphabetical order. Words with the same stem and in certain cases with the same prefix have been placed together in groups.

Example: **solemn**. . . .; ~ **ity** . . .; ~ **ize**. . .;
under|ground . . .; ~ **hand** . . .

Words with the same spelling but of different origin and different meaning—homonyms and their derivatives—are listed one after the other and are distinguished by a number in bold type.

Example: **date**. . . **1**. *s* Datum . . .; **2**. Dattel . . .

Derivatives and compounds therefore have to be looked up under the appropriate headword.

Example: **date-line** stands under **date 1**.
date-palm stands under **date 2**.

2. Tilde (~) and double tilde (~ ~)

The tilde (~) repeats the boldly printed main headword or its first part which is divided off by a vertical stroke (|).

Example: **car** . . .; ~ **aerial** . . .; ~ **body** . . .

The double tilde (~ ~) repeats the immediately preceding bold headword.

Example: **fo|cal**. . .; ~ ~ *distance, length* . . .

As the last example shows, the double tilde applies equally to a second word of the same meaning.

3. Hyphen(-)

In the phonetic transcription, a hyphen performs the same function as the tilde for the headword. It repeats the transcription of the headword.

Example: **counsel** [ˈkaunsəl] . . .; ~ **(l)or**
-ə] . . .

Note

Current usage has been taken into account in the use of the hyphen. However it must be pointed out that usage varies. In order to avoid mistakes resulting from the division of a hyphenated word at the point where the hyphen would occur if the word were not divided, the hyphen is repeated at the beginning of the new line.

Example: **freight-rate** appears as ~-
-rate

4. Layout of a group entry placed under one heading

A strict order is maintained within each entry which makes it easier to find the required meaning. The following order has been used:

(a) translations of the headword with references indicating the relevant area of usage. The first translation is the basic meaning, then follow the special, transferred and technical meanings;

(b) adverbial and prepositional phrases;
Example: for disposal;

(c) phrases in the infinitive;
Example: to be at s.o.'s disposal;

(d) idioms in the form of sentences;
Example: man proposes, God disposes.

Within this layout, the meanings are grouped together by using commas or semicolons. If two or more expressions have a common element, then it is not repeated but the variant part is indicated by a comma or the abbreviation od, *od* (oder). This is made to stand out by the use of a different type, except of course where *oder* is part of the sentence.

5. Grammatical details

The aim has been not only to find an exact translation or equivalent of the words and phrases, but also to show how they are incorporated in a sentence. For this purpose we have given grammatical details, which show the characteristic usage of phrases and thus eliminate difficulties. It is therefore stated whenever there could be any doubt what preposition a word takes, what preposition is used with an infinitive or whether it is used without a preposition.

The gender of German nouns is given in all cases. If there is a succession of German translations with the same gender, then the gender is only given with the last word. The next gender in the string of German nouns is that which applies.

Example: **bon|us** . . . Bonus, Sonderzuschlag
m . . .

The transitive and intransitive meanings of the English verb are always listed. Basic meanings are correspondingly subdivided.

Example: **sit** . . . *itr* sitzen . . .; *tr* setzen . . .

To make the division clear, numbers printed in bold type are used in the case of verbs that have numerous meanings and are used to form prepositional or adverbial phrases. This system is also used in the case of nouns that exist in the same form as a verb or an adjective, etc.

Example: **level** ... **1** *s* Ebene ... ;
2. *a* eben, flach ...;
3. *adv* auf gleicher Ebene ...;
4. *tr* planieren ...

If a verb can also be used reflexively or impersonally, then this usage follows the transitive and|or intransitive basic meaning.

The main forms of irregular verbs are placed immediately after the infinitive. Preterite and past participle are separated by a semicolon. In the case of compound verbs reference is made to the simplex.

Example: **take** ... *irr took* ..., *taken* ...

List of Abbreviations
Liste der Abkürzungen

a Adjektiv, Eigenschaftswort *adjective*
a. auch *also*
acc Akkusativ, Wenfall *accusative case*
adv Adverb, Umstandswort *adverb*
aero Luftfahrt *aeronautics*
agr Landwirtschaft *agriculture*
allg allgemein *commonly*
Am amerikanische Ausdrucksweise *Americanism*
anat Anatomie *anatomy*
arch Architektur *architecture*
astr Astronomie *astronomy*
attr als Attribut (Beifügung) gebraucht *attributively*
aux Hilfsverb, Hilfszeitwort *auxiliary (verb)*
bes. besonders *particular(ly)*
biol Biologie *biology*
bot Botanik *botany*
Br Britisches Englisch *in British usage only*
chem Chemie *chemistry*
com Handel *commerce*
conj Konjunktion, Bindewort *conjunction*
dat Dativ, Wemfall *dative case*
dial Dialekt *dialect*
e-e, *e-r*, *e-m*, *etc* eine, einer, einem etc. *(of, to) a(n)*
el Elektrizität *electricity*
etc. usw. *and so on*
etw etwas *something*
f weiblich *feminine*
fam familiär *familiar, colloquial*
fig bildlich *figuratively*
film Film *film*
fin Finanz *finance*
gen Genitiv, Wesfall *genitive case*
geog Geographie *geography*
geol Geologie *geology*
gram Grammatik, Sprachlehre *grammar*
hist Geschichte *history*
hum spaßhaft *humorously*
imp unpersönlich *impersonal*
inf Infinitiv, Nennform *infinitive*
interj Interjektion, Ausruf *interjection*
iro ironisch *ironical*
irr unregelmäßig *irregular*
itr intransitiv *intransitive*
jem, *jdm*, *jdn*, *jds* jemand(em, en, es) *someone, somebody*
jur Jurisprudenz, Rechtswissenschaft *jurisprudence*
lit literarisch *literary*
m männlich *masculine*
mar Schiffahrt *marine*
math Mathematik *mathematics*
med Medizin *medicine*
m-e, *m-m*, *m-n*, *m-s* meine(m, n, s) *to, of my*
metal Hüttenwesen *metallurgy*
mete Meteorologie, Wetterkunde *meteorology*
mil Militär *military*
min Bergbau *mining*
mot Kraftfahrwesen *motoring*
mus Musik *music*
n sächlich *neuter*
obs veraltet *obsolete*
od oder *or*
opt Optik *optics*
orn Ornithologie, Vogelkunde *ornithology*
o.s. sich *oneself*
parl parlamentarisch *parliamentary*
pej herabsetzend *pejorative*
pharm Pharmazie *pharmacy*
philos Philosophie *philosophy*
phot Photographie *photography*
phys Physik *physics*
physiol Physiologie *physiology*
pl Plural, Mehrzahl *plural*
poet dichterisch *poetical*
pol Politik *politics*
pp Partizip Perfekt, Mittelwort der Vergangenheit *past participle*
ppr Partizip Präsens, Mittelwort der Gegenwart *present participle*
pred prädikativ, aussagend *predicative*
pref Vorsilbe *prefix*
pret Präteritum, Vergangenheit *preterite*
prn Pronomen, Fürwort *pronoun*
prep Präposition, Verhältniswort *preposition*
prov Sprichwort *proverb*
psychol Psychologie *psychology*
radio Rundfunk *radio*
rail Eisenbahn *railway*
rel Religion *religion*
S Sache *thing*
s Substantiv, Hauptwort *substantive*
s. (d.) siehe (dort) *see (there)*
scient wissenschaftlich *scientific*
Scot schottisch *Scotish*
s-e, *s-em*, *s-en*, *s-r*, *s-es* seine(m, n, r, s) *(to) his, (to) one's*
sing Singular, Einzahl *singular*
s.o. jemand *someone*
sport Sport *sport*
s.th. etwas *something*
tech Technik *technics*
tele Telegraphie, Telephonie *telegraphy, telephony*
theat Theater *theatre*
tr transitiv *transitive*
u. und *and*
typ Buchdruck *printing*
v Verb, Zeitwort *verb*
vet Veterinärmedizin, Tierheilkunde *veterinary medicine*
video Fernsehen *television*
vulg vulgär *vulgar*
z. B. zum Beispiel *for example*
zoo Zoologie *zoology*
Zs.-, zs.- zusammen *together*
Zssg(en) Zusammensetzung(en) *compound word(s)*

Table of English irregular Verbs
Übersicht über die unregelmäßigen englischen Verben

* deutet an, daß das Verb auch in regelmäßiger Form vorkommt.
* indicates that the verb also exists in a regular form.

bear, bore, born(e) [ɛə, ɔ:] – (er)tragen; gebären
beat, beat, beaten [i:] – schlagen; besiegen
become, became, become [ʌ, ei, ʌ] – werden
begin, began, begun [i, æ, ʌ] – beginnen
bend, bent, bent [e] – (sich) beugen, biegen
bind, bound, bound [ai, au] – binden
bite, bit, bitten [ai, i] – beißen
blow, blew, blown [ou, u:, ou] – blasen
break, broke, broken [ei, ou] – brechen
breed, bred, bred [i:, e] – brüten; züchten; erziehen
bring, brought, brought [i, ɔ:] – (her)bringen
build, built, built [i] – bauen
burn, burnt*, burnt* [ə:] – (ver)brennen
burst, burst, burst [ə:] – bersten, platzen
buy, bought, bought [ai, ɔ:] – kaufen
cast, cast, cast [ɑ:] – werfen, gießen
catch, caught, caught [æ, ɔ:] – fangen
choose, chose, chosen [u:, ou] – wählen
come, came, come [ʌ, ei, ʌ] – kommen
cost, cost, cost [ɔ] – kosten
creep, crept, crept [i:, e] – kriechen
cut, cut, cut [ʌ] – schneiden
deal, dealt, dealt [i:, e] – handeln
dig, dug, dug [i, ʌ] – graben
draw, drew, drawn [ɔ:, u:, ɔ:] – ziehen; zeichnen
dream, dreamt*, dreamt* [i:, e] – träumen
drink, drank, drunk [i, æ, ʌ] – trinken
drive, drove, driven [ai, ou, i] – treiben; fahren
eat, ate, eaten [i:, e, i:] – essen
fall, fell, fallen [ɔ:, e, ɔ:] – fallen
feed, fed, fed [i:, e] – füttern
feel, felt, felt [i:, e] – fühlen
fight, fought, fought [ai, ɔ:] – kämpfen
find, found, found [ai, au] – finden
flee, fled, fled [i:, e] – fliehen
fling, flung, flung [i, ʌ] – schleudern; stürzen
forbid, forbad(e), forbidden [i, æ, i] – verbieten
forget, forgot, forgotten [e, ɔ] – vergessen
fly, flew, flown [ai, u:, ou] – fliegen
freeze, froze, frozen [i:, ou] – gefrieren
get, got, got [e, ɔ] – bekommen; werden
give, gave, given [i, ei, i] – geben
go, went, gone [ou, e, ɔ] – gehen
grow, grew, grown [ou, u:, ou] – wachsen; werden
hang, hung, hung [æ, ʌ] – hängen, (auf)hängen
hear, heard, heard [iə, ə:] – hören
hide, hid, hidden [ai, i] – verbergen
hit, hit, hit [i] – treffen; hauen
hold, held, held [ou, e] – halten
hurt, hurt, hurt [ə:] verletzen; weh tun
keep, kept, kept [i:, e] – (be)halten
know, knew, known [ou, nju:, ou] – kennen, wissen
lay, laid, laid [ei] – legen
lead, led, led [i:, e] – leiten, führen
leap, leapt*, leapt* [i:, e] – springen
learn, learnt*, learnt* [ə:] – lernen
leave, left, left [i:, e] – (ver)lassen
lend, lent, lent [e] – leihen
let, let, let [e] – lassen

lie, lay, lain [ai, ei] – liegen
lose, lost, lost [u:, ɔ] – verlieren
make, made, made [ei] – machen
mean, meant, meant [i:, e] – meinen; beabsichtigen
meet, met, met [i:, e] – begegnen, treffen
pay, paid, paid [ei] – bezahlen
put, put, put [u] setzen, stellen, legen
read, read, read [i:, e, e] – lesen
ride, rode, ridden [ai, ou, i] – reiten, fahren
ring, rang, rung [i, æ, ʌ] – läuten
rise, rose, risen [ai, ou, i] – aufstehen; aufgehen
run, ran, run [ʌ, æ, ʌ] – rennen, laufen [(Gestirne)
say, said, said [ei, e] – sagen
see, saw, seen [i:, ɔ:, i:] – sehen
seek, sought, sought [i:, ɔ:] – suchen
sell, sold, sold [e, ou] – verkaufen
send, sent, sent [e] – senden, schicken
set, set, set [e] – setzen; untergehen (Gestirne)
shake, shook, shaken [ei, u, ei] – schütteln
shine, shone, shone [ai, ɔ] – scheinen
shoot, shot, shot [u:, ɔ] – schießen
show, showed, shown [ou] – zeigen
shut, shut, shut [ʌ] – schließen
sing, sang, sung [i, æ, ʌ] – singen
sink, sank, sunk [i, æ, ʌ] – sinken, versenken
sit, sat, sat [i, æ] – sitzen
sleep, slept, slept [i:, e] – schlafen
slide, slid, slid [ai, i] – gleiten
smell, smelt, smelt [e] – riechen
speak, spoke, spoken [i:, ou] – sprechen
spend, spent, spent [e] – ausgeben; verbringen
split, split, split [i] – spalten; platzen
spread, spread, spread [e] – verbreiten, sich ausbreiten
spring, sprang, sprung [i, æ, ʌ] – springen
stand, stood, stood [æ, u] stehen
steal, stole, stolen [i:, ou] – stehlen
stick, stuck, stuck [i, ʌ] – (an)stecken, (an)kleben
sting, stung, stung [i, ʌ] – stechen
strike, struck, struck [ai, ʌ] – schlagen
swear, swore, sworn [ɛə, ɔ:] – schwören; fluchen
sweep, swept, swept [i:, e] – fegen, kehren
swim, swam, swum [i, æ, ʌ] – schwimmen
swing, swung, swung [i, ʌ] – schwingen
take, took, taken [ei, u, ei] – nehmen; fortbringen
teach, taught, taught [i:, ɔ:] – lehren
tear, tore, torn [ɛə, ɔ:] – zerreißen
tell, told, told [e, ou] – erzählen, sagen
think, thought, thought [i, ɔ:] – denken
throw, threw, thrown [ou, u:, ou] – werfen
thrust, thrust, thrust [ʌ] – stoßen, schieben
understand, -stood, -stood [æ, u] – verstehen
wake, woke*, woken* [ei, ou, ou] – (er)wecken, erwachen
wear, wore, worn [ɛə, ɔ:] – (an sich) tragen
weep, wept, wept [i:, e] – weinen
win, won, won [i, ʌ] – gewinnen
wind, wound, wound [ai, au] – winden
write, wrote, written [ai, ou, i] – schreiben

List of irregular German Verbs
Liste der starken, der unregelmäßigen und der Verben mit schwankender Konjugation

Sequence;
Infinitive – Imperfect –
Past Participle

backen – backte, buk – gebacken
befehlen – befahl – befohlen
beginnen – begann – begonnen
beißen – biß – gebissen
bergen – barg – geborgen
bersten – barst – geborsten
bewegen (= veranlassen) – bewog – bewogen
biegen – bog – gebogen
bieten – bot – geboten
binden – band – gebunden
bitten – bat – gebeten
blasen – blies – geblasen
bleiben – blieb – geblieben
braten – briet – gebraten
brechen – brach – gebrochen
brennen – brannte – gebrannt
bringen – brachte – gebracht
denken – dachte – gedacht
dingen – dingte, dang – gedungen
dreschen – drosch – gedroschen
dringen – drang – gedrungen
dünken – dünkte, deuchte – gedünkt, gedeucht
dürfen – durfte – gedurft
empfehlen – empfahl – empfohlen
essen – aß – gegessen
fahren – fuhr – gefahren
fallen – fiel – gefallen
fangen – fing – gefangen
fechten – focht – gefochten
finden – fand – gefunden
flechten – flocht – geflochten
fliegen – flog – geflogen
fliehen – floh – geflohen
fließen – floß – geflossen
fragen – fragte, frug – gefragt
fressen – fraß – gefressen
frieren – fror – gefroren
gären – gor, gärte – gegoren, gegärt
gebären – gebar – geboren
geben – gab – gegeben
gedeihen – gedieh – gediehen
gehen – ging – gegangen
gelingen – gelang – gelungen
gelten – galt – gegolten
genesen – genas – genesen
genießen – genoß – genossen
geschehen – geschah – geschehen
gewinnen – gewann – gewonnen
gießen – goß – gegossen
gleichen – glich – geglichen
gleiten – glitt – geglitten
glimmen – glomm, glimmte – geglommen, geglimmt
graben – grub – gegraben
greifen – griff – gegriffen
haben – hatte – gehabt
halten – hielt – gehalten
hängen *itr* – hing – gehangen
hauen – hieb – gehauen
heben – hob – gehoben
heißen – hieß – geheißen
helfen – half – geholfen
kennen – kannte – gekannt
klimmen – klomm, klimmte – geklommen, geklimmt
klingen – klang – geklungen
kneifen – kniff – gekniffen
kommen – kam – gekommen
können – konnte – gekonnt
kriechen – kroch – gekrochen
laden – lud – geladen
lassen – ließ – gelassen
laufen – lief – gelaufen
leiden – litt – gelitten
leihen – lieh – geliehen
lesen – las – gelesen
liegen – lag – gelegen
lügen – log – gelogen
mahlen – mahlte – gemahlt
meiden – mied – gemieden
melken – melkte, molk – gemelkt, gemolken
messen – maß – gemessen
mißlingen – mißlang – mißlungen
mögen – mochte – gemocht
müssen – mußte – gemußt
nehmen – nahm – genommen
nennen – nannte – genannt
pfeifen – pfiff – gepfiffen
preisen – pries – gepriesen
quellen *itr* – quoll – gequollen
reiben – rieb – gerieben
reißen – riß – gerissen
reiten – ritt – geritten
rennen – rannte – gerannt
riechen – roch – gerochen
ringen – rang – gerungen
rinnen – rann – geronnen
rufen – rief – gerufen
salzen – salzte – gesalzen, gesalzt
saufen – soff – gesoffen
schaffen (= erschaffen) – schuf – geschaffen
schallen – scholl – geschallt
scheinen – schien – geschienen
scheißen *vulg* – schiß – geschissen
schelten – schalt – gescholten
scheren – schor – geschoren
schieben – schob – geschoben
schießen – schoß – geschossen
schinden – schund – geschunden
schlafen – schlief – geschlafen
schlagen – schlug – geschlagen
schleichen – schlich – geschlichen
schleifen (= schärfen) – schliff – geschliffen
schleißen – schliß, schleißte – geschlissen, geschleißt

schließen – schloß – geschlossen
schlingen – schlang – geschlungen
schmeißen *fam* – schmiß – geschmissen
schmelzen – schmolz – geschmolzen
schnauben – schnaubte, schnob – geschnaubt, geschnoben
schneiden – schnitt – geschnitten
schreiben – schrieb – geschrieben
schweigen – schwieg – geschwiegen
schwellen *itr* – schwoll – geschwollen
schwimmen – schwamm – geschwommen
schwinden – schwand – geschwunden
schwingen – schwang – geschwungen
schwören – schwor, schwur – geschworen
sehen – sah – gesehen
sein – war – gewesen
senden – sandte – gesandt, gesendet
sieden – siedete, sott – gesiedet, gesotten
singen – sang – gesungen
sinken – sank – gesunken
sinnen – sann – gesonnen
sitzen – saß – gesessen
sollen – sollte – gesollt
spalten – spaltete – gespalten, gespaltet
speien – spie – gespie(e)n
spinnen – spann – gesponnen
spleißen – spliß – gesplissen
sprechen – sprach – gesprochen
sprießen – sproß – gesprossen
springen – sprang – gesprungen
stechen – stach – gestochen
stecken – stak, steckte – gesteckt
stehen – stand – gestanden
stehlen – stahl – gestohlen
steigen – stieg – gestiegen
sterben – starb – gestorben
stieben – stob, stiebte – gestoben, gestiebt
stinken – stank – gestunken
stoßen – stieß – gestoßen
streichen – strich – gestrichen
streiten – stritt – gestritten
tragen – trug – getragen
treffen – traf – getroffen
treiben – trieb – getrieben
treten – trat – getreten
triefen – triefte, troff – getrieft, getroffen
trinken – trank – getrunken
trügen – trog – getrogen
tut – tat – getan
verderben – verdarb – verdorben
verdrießen – verdroß – verdrossen
vergessen – vergaß – vergessen
verlieren – verlor – verloren
wachsen – wuchs – gewachsen
wägen – wog – gewogen
waschen – wusch – gewaschen
weben – wob, webte – gewoben
weichen (= nachgeben) – wich – gewichen
weisen – wies – gewiesen
wenden – wandte, wendete – gewendet, gewandt
werben – warb – geworben
werden – wurde – geworden, *aux* worden
werfen – warf – geworfen
wiegen – wog – gewogen
winden – wand – gewunden
winken – winkte – gewinkt
wissen – wußte – gewußt
wollten – wollte – gewollt
wringen – wrang – gewrungen
zeihen – zieh – geziehen
ziehen – zog – gezogen
zwingen – zwang – gezwungen

Pronunciation Key

Vowels and Diphthongs

[ɑ:] pl**a**nt, **a**rm, f**a**ther
[ai] l**i**fe
[au] h**ou**se
[æ] m**a**n, s**a**d
[e] g**e**t, b**e**d
[ei] n**a**me, l**a**me
[ə] **a**go, bett**er**
[ə:] b**ir**d, h**er**
[εə] th**ere**, c**are**
[ʌ] b**u**t, s**o**n
[i] **i**t, w**i**sh
[i:] b**ee**, s**ee**, m**e**, b**ea**t, bel**ie**f
[iə] h**ere**
[ou] n**o**, l**ow**
[o] m**o**lest, **o**bey
[ɔ] n**o**t, l**o**ng
[ɔ:] l**aw**, **a**ll
[ɔi] b**oy**, **oi**l
[u] p**u**sh, l**oo**k
[u:] y**ou**, d**o**
[uə] p**oor**, s**ure**

Consonants

[b] **b**een, **b**lind
[d] **d**o, ha**d**
[ð] **th**is, fa**th**er
[f] **f**ather, wol**f**
[g] **g**o, be**g**
[ŋ] lo**ng**, si**ng**
[h] **h**ouse
[j] **y**outh, Ind**i**an
[k] **k**eep, mil**k**
[l] **l**amp, oi**l**, i**ll**
[m] **m**an, a**m**
[n] **n**o, ma**nn**er
[p] **p**a**p**er, ha**pp**y
[r] **r**ed, d**r**y
[s] **s**tand, **s**and, ye**s**
[ʃ] **sh**ip, sta**ti**on
[t] **t**ell, fa**t**
[tʃ] **ch**ur**ch**, ca**tch**
[v] **v**oice, li**v**e
[w] **w**ater, **w**e, **wh**ich
[z] **z**eal, the**s**e, ga**z**e
[ʒ] plea**s**ure
[dʒ] **j**am, ob**j**ect
[θ] **th**ank, dea**th**
[ɑ̃] French **-an**
[ɔ̃] French **-on**
[x] Scottish lo**ch**

The English Alphabet

a [ei] b [bi:] c [si:] d [di:] e [i:] f [ef]
g [dʒi:] h [eitʃ] i [ai] j [dʒei] k [kei] l [el]
m [em] n [en] o[ou] p [pi:] q [kju:]
r [ɑ:] s [es] t [ti:] u [ju:] v [vi:]
w ['dʌblju:] x [eks] y [wai] z [zed]

Notes

1. The mark : indicates that the preceding vowel is long.
2. The mark ' precedes the accented syllable.
3. The transcription of the pronunciation is set in brackets.

The phonetic symbols of the International Phonetic Association (IPA) are used in the transcription of the pronunciation.

A

A, a [ei] *pl* **~'s** A, a; *mus* A, a *n*; *Am (Schule)* Eins *f*; *from ~ to Z* von A bis Z; gründlich; *A 1* [ei'wʌn] *mar (in Lloyds Register)* erstklassig; *fam* famos, prima, I a; *mil* k. v.
a [ə, *betont* ei] *vor gesprochenem Vokal* **an** [ən, *betont* æn] *unbestimmter Artikel* ein, eine, ein; *he is ~ mechanic* er ist Handwerker; *she is ~ German* sie ist Deutsche; *she is ~ Roman Catholic* sie ist Katholikin; *once ~ year* einmal im Jahr; *five pounds ~ week* fünf Pfund in der Woche; *as ~ boy* als Junge; *in ~ day or two* in ein paar Tagen; *~ Mr Myer* ein gewisser Herr Myer; *in ~ sense* in gewissem Sinn; *many ~ one* mancher, mancheiner; *of ~ size* von gleicher Größe; *60 miles an hour* 60 Meilen pro Stunde.
a- [ə] **1.** = on: *aback, aboard, aside, awake*; **2.** *obs mit gerund: the house is a-building = being built*; **3.** = not, without: *asymetrical*; [æ] in *amoral*; [ei, æ, ə] in *asexual.*
Aaron ['ɛərən] *(Bibel)* Aaron *m*; **~'s-beard** *bot* Großblumige(s) Johanniskraut *n*; Wuchernde(r) Steinbrech *m*; **~s rod** *bot* Königskerze; Goldrute *f*.
aback [ə'bæk] *adv mar* back; *to be taken ~* verblüfft, überrascht, bestürzt sein; *mar* back bekommen.
abacus ['æbəkəs] *pl a. -ci* [-sai] Rechenbrett *n*, -tafel *f*; *arch* Abakus *m*, Kapitelldeckplatte *f*.
abaft [ə'bɑ:ft] *adv mar* achteraus; nach hinten; *prp* hinter, achter.
abandon [ə'bændən] *tr* (vollständig) aufgeben, preisgeben, verzichten (*s.th.* auf etw); überlassen (*s.th. to s.o.* etw jdm); zurück-, verlassen; *jur* abandonnieren; *(Forderung)* fallenlassen, Abstand nehmen (*s.th.* von etw); *(Kind)* aussetzen; *(Verfolgung)* einstellen; *to ~ o.s.* sich hingeben, sich überlassen, sich ergeben (*to despair* der Verzweiflung); *s* Ungezwungenheit, Sorglosigkeit *f*; Sichgehenlassen *n*; Ausgelassenheit, Ungeniertheit *f*; *to ~ s.o. to his fate* jdn s-m Schicksal überlassen; **~ed** [-d] *a* verlassen; hemmungslos; verfallen, hingegeben; lasterhaft, verworfen, liederlich; **~ment** [-mənt] Verlassen, Aufgeben *n*; *jur* Abtretung, Preisgabe *f*, Verzicht *m*; Verlassensein; *fig* Sichgehenlassen *n*, Verzweiflung; *(Kind)* Aussetzung; *(Klage)* Zurücknahme *f*.
abase [ə'beis] *tr fig* erniedrigen, herabsetzen, demütigen; entmutigen; *to ~ o.s.* sich entwürdigen; **~ment** [-mənt] *fig* Erniedrigung; Demütigung *f*.
abash [ə'bæʃ] *tr* in Verlegenheit bringen; beschämen, demütigen; verblüffen; *to be, to stand, to feel ~ed* verlegen sein (*at, by* über); beschämt sein, sich schämen *(at über)*; die Fassung verlieren, verblüfft sein (*at* über).
abate [ə'beit] *tr* vermindern, reduzieren; *(Schmerz)* mildern, lindern, stillen; schwächen; *(Steuern)* ermäßigen, nachlassen; erlassen; *(Preis, Forderung)* herabsetzen, ermäßigen; erlassen; *(Stolz)* demütigen; mäßigen; abziehen; auslassen; *jur* aufheben, umstoßen; niederschlagen; abschaffen, beseitigen, abstellen; *(Prozeß)* einstellen; *itr* geringer werden, an Stärke verlieren, abnehmen; *(Wind, Flut)* abnehmen, abflauen, sich legen; *(Sturm)* nachlassen; *(Preise)* fallen; *jur (Gesetz)* ungültig werden; **~ment** [-mənt] Abnahme, Milderung, Verminderung; Beseitigung *f*; Abgang; *com* Rabatt, Abzug; (Preis-, Zahlungs-)Nachlaß *m*; *jur* Herabsetzung *(e-s Legats)*; Abschaffung, Beseitigung *f (e-s Übelstandes)*; Ungültigmachen *n*, Aufhebung *f*.
abattoir ['æbətwɑ:] (öffentliches) Schlachthaus *n*, Schlachthof *m*.
abb|acy ['æbəsi] Würde *f*, Amt *n* e-s Abtes; **~atial** [ə'beiʃəl] äbtlich; abteilich; **~é** ['æbei] Abbé *m (Frankreich)*; **~ess** ['æbəs, 'æbis] Äbtissin *f*; **~ey** ['æbi] Abtei *f*; **~ot** ['æbət] Abt *m*.
abbreviat|e [ə'bri:vieit] *tr math* kürzen; ab-, verkürzen; zs.ziehen; **~ion** [əbri:vi'eiʃən] Abkürzung, Kürzung *f*; Stummelwort *n*.
ABC ['ei'bi:'si:, --'-] Abc, Alphabet *n*; *fig* Anfangsgründe *pl*; *rail (England)* Kursbuch *n*.
abdicat|e ['æbdikeit] *tr (Amt)* niederlegen, aufgeben; *(auf ein Recht, e-n Anspruch)* verzichten; *(e-r Sache)* entsagen; *itr* abdanken; **~ion** [æbdi'keiʃən] *(Amt)* Niederlegung; Abdankung *f*; Verzicht *m* (*of* auf); Entsagung *f*.
abdom|en ['æbdəmen, æb'doumən] (Unter-)Leib, Bauch; *(Insekt)* Hinterleib *m*; **~inal** [æb'dəminl] *a* Bauch-, Leib-; ventral, abdominal.
abduc|t [æb'dʌkt] *tr (Frau, Kind)* entführen; *anat* abziehen; **~tion** [æb'dʌkʃən] Entführung; *anat (Muskeln)* Abziehung, Weg-, Auswärtsbewegung *f*; **~tor** [æb'dʌktə] Entführer *m*; **~~** *muscle* Abziehmuskel, Abduktor *m*.
abeam [ə'bi:m] *adv mar* dwars; *~ of us* gegenüber von uns, auf gleicher Höhe.
abed [ə'bed] *adv* im Bett; *to lie ~* bettlägerig sein.
abele [ə'bi:l, 'eibl] *bot* Weißpappel *f*.
aberr|ance, -cy [æ'berəns(i)] Abweichung; *fig* Verirrung *f*; **~ant** [æ'berənt] abirrend; irrend; *(von Sitte u. Moral)* abweichend; *zoo bot* anomal, außergewöhnlich; **~ation** [æbə'reiʃən] Abirrung, Abweichung *(vom rechten Weg, vom üblichen Standard)*; Verirrung *f*, Irrweg, Irrtum, Fehler *m*; *(mental ~~)* Geistesverirrung *f*, anomale(s) Verhalten *n*, Irrsinn *m*; *biol opt astr* Aberration *f*.
abet [ə'bet] *tr* anstiften, anreizen, aufhetzen; ermutigen; begünstigen, Beihilfe, Vorschub leisten; unterstützen, helfen; *to aid and ~ a criminal* e-n Täter begünstigen; **~ment** [ə'betmənt] Unterstützung, *jur* Beihilfe; Anstiftung; Aufreizung, Aufhetzung *f*; Vorschub *m*, Begünstigung *f*; **~tor, ~ter** [ə'betə] Anstifter, Helfershelfer, Begünstiger *m*.
abeyance [ə'beiəns] Schwebe, Unentschiedenheit *f*; *in ~* in der Schwebe; ruhend; noch nicht entschieden, (noch) umstritten; *(Arbeit)* unerledigt; *(Besitz)* herrenlos; *to hold, to keep in ~* ruhen lassen, suspendieren; *(Frage)* offen lassen; *to fall into ~ (Gesetze, Bestimmungen, Bräuche)* ruhen, zeitweilig außer Kraft treten.
abhor [əb'hɔ:] *tr* verabscheuen, hassen; verschmähen, verachten; **~rence** [əb'hɔrəns] Abscheu, Haß *m* (*of, from* vor, gegen), Abneigung *f*, Abscheu; Gegenstand *m* des Abscheues *od* Hasses; *to hold in ~~* verabscheuen; *flattery is my ~~* Schmeichelei ist mir ein Greuel; **~rent** [əb'hɔrənt] abstoßend; abscheulich; *~~ to* verhaßt, zuwider; unvereinbar mit; im Gegensatz zu.
abid|e [ə'baid] *irr abode, abode itr* verweilen, bleiben; *obs* wohnen; *to ~~ by* festhalten an; treu bleiben *dat*; verharren bei; sich zufrieden geben mit; *tr lit* erwarten, abwarten; *pej* ausstehen, aushalten, erdulden, ertragen; *she cannot ~~ dirt* sie kann Schmutz nicht ausstehen; *he can't ~~ that fellow* er kann den Kerl nicht riechen; **~ing** [-iŋ] dauernd; beständig, bleibend.
abigail ['æbigeil] Zofe, Kammerjungfer *f*.
ability [ə'biliti] Fähigkeit *f* (*for* für, zu); Talent *n*, Befähigung *f*, Können *n*; Qualifikation *f*; Vermögen *n*; *(~ to pay)* Zahlungsfähigkeit; Leistungsfähigkeit *f*; Geschick *n*, Geschicklichkeit *f (to do)*; *pl* geistige Anlagen *f pl*; *to the best of o.'s ~* nach besten Kräften.
abject ['æbdʒekt] elend; schauderhaft; verworfen, verächtlich; gemein; servil; *in ~ poverty* in tiefster Armut; *an ~ liar* ein gemeiner Lügner; **~ion** [æb'dʒekʃən] Verworfenheit, Gemeinheit *f*; Elend *n*; **~ness** ['-nis] Niedertracht, Gemeinheit *f*.
ab|juration [æbdʒuə'reiʃən] Abschwörung *f*; **~jure** [əb'dʒuə] *tr* abschwören; (feierlich) entsagen (*s.th.* dat); widerrufen, aufgeben.
ablation [æb'leiʃən] *med* Amputation; *geol* Abtragung *f*, Fortwaschen *n*, Ablation *f*; **~lative** ['æblətiv] *gram* Ablativ *m*.
ablaze [ə'bleiz] *adv pred a* in Flammen; brennend, lodernd; *fig* (sehr) zornig, (sehr) erregt (*with* vor); glänzend, funkelnd (*with* von, vor); *all ~* Feuer u. Flamme; *to set ~* entflammen.
able ['eibl] fähig; imstande; befähigt, talentiert, begabt; tüchtig, geschickt, gewandt; *jur* berechtigt, ermächtigt, bevollmächtigt; *(Rede)* klug; *(Unterstützung)* wirksam; *to be ~ to* können, vermögen, in der Lage sein zu, imstande sein zu; *~ to compete* konkurrenzfähig, wettbewerbsfähig; *~ to fly* flugfähig; *~ to pay* zahlungsfähig, solvent; *~ to work* arbeitsfähig; **~-bodied** ['eibl'bɔdid] (körperlich) kräftig, stark, rüstig, gesund, tauglich, arbeitsfähig, diensttauglich; *~~ seaman* Vollmatrose *m*.
abloom [ə'blu:m] *adv pred a* in Blüte, (er)blühend.
ablution [ə'blu:ʃən] (Ab-)Waschung, Abspülung *f*, Abwaschen *n*; *rel* Ablution *f*; *chem* Auswaschen; Wasch-, Spülwasser *n*; *to perform o.'s ~s* s-e Waschungen verrichten *(Ritual)*; *hum* sich waschen.
ably ['eibli] *adv* geschickt, gewandt.
abnegat|e ['æbnigeit] *tr* (ab-, ver-) leugnen, bestreiten; verzichten (*s.th.* auf etw); *(Recht)* aufgeben; entsagen (*s.th.* dat); *(Glauben)* abschwören (*s.th.* dat); **~ion** [æbni'geiʃən] (Ab-, Ver-) Leugnung *f*; Verzicht *m* (*of* auf), Aufgabe (*of* gen); Abschwörung *f*.
abnorm|al [æb'nɔ:məl] unregelmäßig, regelwidrig, normwidrig, anomal, abnorm; mißgestaltet, krankhaft; seltsam, sonderbar, ungewöhnlich; **~ality** [æbnɔ:'mæliti] Regelwidrigkeit, Unregelmäßigkeit; Mißbildung, Entartung *f*; **~ity** [æb'nɔ:miti] Unregelmäßigkeit, Regelwidrigkeit, Abnormität; Monstrosität, Ungeheuerlichkeit; Mißgestalt, Mißbildung *f*.
aboard [ə'bɔ:d] *adv prp* an Bord, *Am* im Zug, Omnibus, Flugzeug; entlang *(Schiffsbord, Küste)*; *(close, hard ~)* längsseits; *to go ~* an Bord gehen, sich einschiffen, *Am* einsteigen *(Zug, Bus,*

Flugzeug); *all ~! get ~!* alle Mann an Bord! *Am rail* alles einsteigen!

abode [ə'boud] *v s. abide*; *s* Verweilen, Bleiben *n*; Aufenthaltsort, Wohnort, Wohnsitz *m*; Wohnung, Behausung *f*; *to take up o.'s ~, to make o.'s ~* sich niederlassen, s-n Wohnsitz aufschlagen (*at* in); *fixed ~* feste(r) Wohnsitz *m*; *person with no fixed ~* Obdachlose(r) *m*.

abolish [ə'bɔliʃ] *tr* abschaffen, aufheben; vernichten, zerstören, beseitigen; *jur* außer Kraft setzen.

abolition [æbo'liʃən] Abschaffung, Aufhebung; *Am* Beseitigung *f* der Sklaverei; **~ist** [-ist] Abolitionist; *Am* Gegner *m* der Sklaverei.

A-bomb ['eibɔm] Atombombe *f*.

abomina|ble [ə'bɔminəbl] scheußlich, widerwärtig; *fam* furchtbar, schrecklich; **~te** [-eit] *tr* verabscheuen; *fam* ganz u. gar nicht gern haben; *I ~~ cold mutton* kalter Hammel ist mir höchst widerwärtig; *I ~~ it* es ist mir ein Greuel; **~tion** [-'neiʃən] Abscheu (*of, to* gegen, vor); Greuel *m*; Scheusal *n*; Schändlichkeit, Abscheulichkeit, Gemeinheit *f*; *to hold, to have s.th. in ~~* etw verabscheuen; *flattery is an ~~ to me* Schmeichelei ist mir ein Greuel.

aborigin|al [æbə'ridʒənl] *a* ureingeboren, ursprünglich; original, einheimisch; Ur-; *s* Ureinwohner *m*; **~es** [æbə'ridʒini:z] *pl* Ureinwohner *m*; die ursprüngliche Tier- *od* Pflanzenwelt *f* eines Gebietes.

abort [ə'bɔ:t] *itr* zu früh gebären; fehl-, mißgebären; verkümmern; *fig* fehlschlagen; **~ion** [ə'bɔ:ʃən] *med* Früh-, Fehlgeburt *f*, Abort *m*; Verkümmerung, Fehlbildung *f*; Fehlschlag *m*; *to procure ~~* abtreiben; *criminal ~~* Abtreibung *f*; **~ionist** [ə'bɔ:ʃənist] *Am* Abtreiber(in *f*) *m*; **~ive** [ə'bɔ:tiv] *a* zu früh geboren; mißgeboren, verkümmert, unvollständig; *med* abtreibend; *bot* unfruchtbar, taub; *fig* unreif, unvorzeitig; *fig* mißlungen, fruchtlos, verfehlt, fehlgeschlagen, erfolglos; *s* Abtreibungsmittel *n*; *to be, to prove ~~* mißlingen, fehlschlagen.

abound [ə'baund] *itr* im Überfluß vorhanden sein; reich sein (*in* an); reichlich versehen sein (*in* mit); Überfluß haben an, wimmeln (*with* von); *fish ~ in the ocean, the ocean ~s with fish* das Meer wimmelt von Fischen, ist reich an Fischen.

about [ə'baut] **I.** *prp* **1.** *(räumlich, örtlich)* um, um...herum, über...hin; auf allen Seiten; *a fence ~ the garden* ein Zaun um den Garten herum; **2.** nahe bei, nicht weit von; an; **3.** *(Zeit, Maß)* um, ungefähr, so ziemlich, etwa, gegen; *~ five o'clock, (fam) at ~ five o'clock* gegen fünf Uhr; *~ nightfall* gegen Abend; *~ ten* etwa zehn; *it is ~ the same* es ist ungefähr dasselbe; *~ the same height* ungefähr von derselben Höhe; *~ my size* etwa meine Größe; **4.** bei sich, an sich; *have you any money ~ you?* haben Sie Geld bei sich? **5.** in, an; *her hair is the worst thing ~ her* ihr Haar ist das Häßlichste an ihr; **6.** *(hinweisend, bezüglich)* von, über, in bezug auf, betreffend, wegen; *this book is ~ aeroplanes* dieses Buch handelt über Flugzeuge; *what do you know ~ him?* was wissen Sie über ihn? *what's she so angry ~?* worüber ist sie so zornig? *what is it all ~?* um was handelt es sich? *a quarrel ~ a trifle* ein Streit über (*od* wegen) e-r Kleinigkeit; *how ~ money?* wie steht es mit Geld? *what ~ dinner?* wie wär's mit Abendessen? **II.** *adv* **1.** herum, umher; **2.** rings herum, rund herum, im Kreise; in der Runde, um; im Umfang; **3.** ungefähr, fast, beinahe, nahezu; gleich; *~ full* nahezu voll; **4.** abwechselnd; **III.** *to be ~* sich handeln um, gehen um; im Begriffe sein; im Gange sein; nahe daran sein; auf sein, auf den Beinen sein, munter sein; im Umlauf sein, verbreitet sein; *rumours are ~* Gerüchte sind im Umlauf; *what is he ~?* was hat er vor? was macht er? *to bring ~* zuwege, zustande bringen; herbeiführen, verursachen; *to come ~* geschehen, sich ereignen, stattfinden, eintreffen, eintreten; *to go ~ s. th.* mit etw umgehen; etw angehen, anpacken; herumgehen; *go ~ your own business!* kümmern Sie sich um Ihre Sachen! *to hang ~ (fam)* herumstehen; *to lie ~* herumliegen; *to look ~* sich (nach allen Richtungen) umschauen (*for* nach); *to order ~* herumkommandieren; *to send s.o. ~ o.'s business* jdm heimleuchten, jdn heimschicken; *to set ~ s.th.* sich an etw machen; *to speak, to talk ~* sprechen über; *to think ~* nachdenken über; *to walk ~* umhergehen; auf u. ab gehen; *all ~* überall; *left ~!* linksum! *right ~!* rechtsum! *~ turn! ~ face! (Am)* ganze Abteilung kehrt! *round ~* ringsum; *turn and turn ~* abwechselnd, einer um den andern; *just ~ enough* gerade noch genug; *that will just ~ do* das reicht gerade noch; *a man ~ town* ein Lebemann; *a round-~ way, a long way ~* ein Umweg; *~ done? (Am)* sind Sie bald fertig? **~-face ,~-turn** *s* Kehrtwendung *f a. fig*; *fig* (völliger) Umschwung *m*.

above [ə'bʌv] **1.** *adv* oben, droben, oberhalb; weiter oben; aufwärts, hinauf; darüber, über; höher *(Rang, Bedeutung, Stellung)*; mehr als; im (am) Himmel; stromaufwärts *(there is good fishing ~)*; *the blue sky ~* der blaue Himmel droben; *green ~ and black below* oben grün und unten schwarz; *over and ~* obendrein; *as (mentioned) ~* wie oben erwähnt (*od* gesagt), wie früher; *the powers ~* die himmlischen Mächte; *the courts ~* die Gerichte höherer Instanz; **2.** *prp* über; erhaben über; höher als; mehr als; stärker als; vor; nördlicher als; früher (in der Geschichte) als; *~ all (things)* vor allem, vornehmlich, namentlich; *everything is ~ board* alles ist einwandfrei; *~ par* über pari; *~ praise* über alles Lob erhaben; *~ stairs* oben, in e-m höheren Stockwerk; bei den Herrschaften; *~ ten minutes* mehr als 10 Minuten; *~ a ton* über eine Tonne; *to be ~ s.o.* jdm überlegen sein, jdn übertreffen; *he is ~ it* er ist darüber weg, er steht darüber; *to be, to get ~ o.s.* überheblich sein; *it is ~ me* das geht über meinen Horizont; es ist mir zu hoch; *to fly ~ the earth* über der Erde fliegen; *to get ~* überflügeln; *the second corner ~ the cinema* die zweite Ecke oberhalb des Kinos; **3.** *a* obig; oben erwähnt; *s*: *the ~* das Obige; *the ~ is confirmed* Obiges wird bestätigt; *it follows from the ~* aus Vorstehendem ergibt sich; **~-board** *adv pred a* ehrlich, redlich, offen; **~-ground** *adv pred a Am* (noch) am Leben; *tech* über Erde; **-mentioned, -cited, -named, -said, -quoted** *a* vorerwähnt.

abracadabra [æbrəkə'dæbrə] Abrakadabra; *fig* Geschwätz *n*.

abra|de [ə'breid] *tr* abschaben, abkratzen; abschürfen, abhäuten; abschälen; abschleifen; (ab)reiben; abnutzen, angreifen; *fig (Ansehen)* vermindern, untergraben; *~~ with emery* abschmirgeln; *~~ with pumice* abbimsen; **~ded** [-id] *a* wund, aufgeschürft; **~sion** [ə'breiʒən] Abschaben; Abschabsel; Abschleifen *n*; Verschleiß *m*, Abnutzung *f*, Abrieb *m*; *med* Abschürfung, Schürfwunde *f*; *~~ resistance* Verschleißfestigkeit *f*; **~sive** [ə'breisiv] *s* Schleif-, Poliermittel *n*; Gebläsesand *m*; *a* abreibend, (ab)schleifend, schmirgelartig; *~~ cloth* Schmirgelleinen *n*; *~~ paper* Sand-, Schmirgelpapier *n*; *~~ wheel* Schleif-, Schmirgelscheibe *f*.

abreact [æbri'ækt] *tr psychol* abreagieren.

abreast [ə'brest] *adv* Seite an Seite; auf gleicher Höhe; nebeneinander; gegenüber; *fig* auf dem Niveau (*of* von); *to keep ~ of, with (fig)* Schritt halten mit; auf der Höhe bleiben *gen*; *to march three ~* in Dreierreihen marschieren.

abridg|e [ə'bridʒ] *tr* (ab-, ver)kürzen; *(Text, Buch)* zs.fassen, zs.ziehen; einschränken, beschränken; vermindern, schmälern, verringern; *to ~ s.o. of s.th.* jdn e-r Sache berauben; jdm etw entziehen, nehmen; **~(e)ment** [-mənt] (Ab-, Ver-)Kürzung *f*; *(Buch)* Auszug, Abriß *m*; Zs.fassung; Kurzausgabe; *(Rechte)* Beschränkung, Einschränkung, Schmälerung, Verminderung *f*.

abroad [ə'brɔ:d] *adv* **1.** außerhalb des Landes, auswärts; im *od* ins Ausland; *from ~* vom Ausland; *to go, to live, to travel ~* ins Ausland gehen *od* reisen, verreisen, im Ausland leben *od* wohnen, im Ausland reisen; **2.** weit umher, weit auseinander; überallhin, in allen Richtungen, (weit) verbreitet; *to get ~* bekannt, ruchbar werden; *to spread ~* verbreiten; *the news quickly spread ~* die Nachricht verbreitete sich rasch überallhin; *there's a rumour ~* es geht das Gerücht; *it is all ~* es ist allgemein bekannt; **3.** außerhalb des Hauses, der Wohnung; draußen, im Freien; *to be ~ early in the morning* e-n Frühspaziergang machen; *to walk ~* spazierengehen; *at home and ~* in und außer dem Hause; im In- u. Ausland; **4.** weit vom Ziel, weit von der Wahrheit, im Irrtum; *all ~* weit gefehlt, auf dem Holzweg.

abrogat|e ['æbrogeit] *tr* abschaffen, aufheben, widerrufen; *(Gesetz)* außer Kraft setzen; **~ion** [æbro'geiʃən] Abschaffung, Aufhebung *f*.

abrupt [ə'brʌpt] *a* abgebrochen; plötzlich, unerwartet; übereilt; unzeremoniell; *(Redeweise, Betragen, Verhalten)* kurz, schroff, hastig, rasch; unhöflich, barsch; *(Fels, Pfad)* sehr steil, schroff, jäh; *(Denk-, Sprechweise, Stil)* unzs.hängend, sprunghaft; abgebrochen, abgerissen; *bot* abgestumpft; *geol (Schicht)* plötzlich zutage tretend; **~ness** [-nis] Schroffheit; Plötzlichkeit; Steilheit; Übereilung *f*.

ab|scess ['æbsis] *med* Abszeß *m*, Geschwür *n*, Eiterbeule, Eitergeschwulst *f*; **~scind** [æb'sind] *tr* abschneiden; **~scissa** [æb'sisə] *pl a. -ae* [-i:] *geom* Abszisse, X-Koordinate *f*; **~scission** [æb'siʒən] Abschneiden *n*; Abtrennung; gewaltsame Lostrennung *f*.

abscond [əb'skɔnd] *itr* flüchten (*from* vor); sich davonmachen; durchbrennen; untertauchen, sich verbergen.

absen|ce ['æbsns] Abwesenheit *f* (*from* von); Fernbleiben, Ausbleiben, Nichterscheinen *n*; Mangel (*of* an); Fortfall *m*; Fehlen, Nichtvorhandensein *n*; *(~~ of mind)* Zerstreutheit, Unachtsamkeit, Unaufmerksamkeit *f*; *in ~~ of* mangels *gen*; *in the ~~ of evidence* aus Mangel an Beweisen; *on leave of ~~* auf Urlaub; *~~ without leave* unerlaubte Entfernung *f* (von der Truppe); **~t** ['æbsnt] *a* abwesend, fehlend; nicht zu Hause; nicht erschienen; geistesabwesend, unaufmerksam, zerstreut;

to be ~~ fehlen, abwesend sein; *v* [æb'sent]: *to* ~~ *o.s. from* sich fernhalten von, fernbleiben von, wegbleiben von; ausbleiben; **~tee** [æbsn'ti:] *n* Abwesende(r *m*) *f*; ~~ *landlord* der nicht auf seinem Besitztum lebende Inhaber *m*; ~~ *voting (Am)* Briefwahl *f*; **~teeism** [æbsən'ti:izm] (dauernde) Abwesenheit *f*, Fernbleiben *n*; Arbeitsausfall *m*, Feiern *n*, Fehlschicht *f*; *rate of* ~~ Abwesenheitssatz *m*; **~t-minded** zerstreut, geistesabwesend, unaufmerksam.

absinth(e) ['æbsinθ] *bot* Wermut; Absinth *m*.

absolu|te ['æbsəlu:t, -lju:t] völlig, vollständig, vollkommen, gänzlich, absolut; *chem* unvermischt, unverdünnt; *(Wahrheit)* rein, voll; positiv, wirklich, real; bedingungslos; unbedingt, unabhängig, unumschränkt, eigenmächtig; ~~ *alcohol* reine(r) Alkohol *m*; ~~ *ceiling (aero)* höchste Flughöhe, Gipfelhöhe *f*; ~~ *power* unumschränkte Macht *f*; ~~ *proof* eindeutige(r) Beweis *m*; ~~ *zero* absolute(r) Nullpunkt *m*; **~tely** ['æbsəlu:tli] *adv* völlig; gänzlich, durchaus; absolut, restlos; schlechthin; *fam* gewiß! unbedingt! *she is* ~~ *right* sie hat durchaus recht; **~tion** [æbsə'lu:ʃən] Loslösung; *rel* Absolution *f*; Sündenerlaß *m*; Los-, Freisprechung *f*; **~tism** ['æbsəlu:tizm] *pol* Absolutismus *m*; *rel* Prädestinationslehre *f*.

absolve [əb'zɔlv] *tr* los-, freisprechen (*from* von; *of sin* von Sünde); *(Pflicht, Versprechen)* entbinden (*from* von); Absolution erteilen (*s.o.* jdm).

ab|sorb [əb'sɔ:b, əb'zɔ:b] *tr* ein-, aufsaugen, aufnehmen; absorbieren, resorbieren; auf-, ein-, verschlucken; einverleiben; dämpfen; *(Geld)* abschöpfen; *fig* fesseln, ganz in Anspruch nehmen; **~sorbed** [-'sɔ:bd] *a fig* vertieft, versunken; gefesselt (*in* von); ~~ *in thought* in Gedanken vertieft; **~sorbent** [-'sɔ:bənt] *a* absorbierend; auf-, einsaugend; saugfähig; *s chem* Absorptionsmittel *n*, Schluckstoff *m*; ~~ *cotton(-wool)* (Verbands-)Watte *f*; **~sorbing** [-'sɔ:biŋ] aufnehmend, aufsaugend; *fig* fesselnd, interessant; ~~ *capacity* Aufnahmefähigkeit *f*; **~sorption** [-'sɔ:pʃən] Aufsaugung, Aufnahme *f*, Einsaugen; *n chem* Absorption *f*; Verlust *m*; *tech* Dämpfung *f*; *fig* Vertieftsein, Versunkensein *n*, Versunkenheit; eindringliche Beschäftigung *f* (*in* mit); ~~ *of energy* Kraftverbrauch *m*; ~~ *capacity* Aufnahmefähigkeit *f*, Aufsaugevermögen *n*; ~~ *of purchasing power* Abschöpfung *f* der Kaufkraft; **~sorptive** [-'sɔ:ptiv] aufnahmefähig, saugfähig, absorptionsfähig, absorbierend.

absquatulate [əb'skɔtjuleit] *itr fam* abhauen, verduften.

abstain [əb'stein] *itr* sich enthalten (*from s. th.* e-r S); sich zurückhalten; verzichten (*from* auf); **~er** [-ə] Abstinenzler *m*.

abstemious [æb'sti:miəs] mäßig; enthaltsam; zurückhaltend.

abstent|ion [æb'stenʃən] Enthaltung (*from* von); Stimmenthaltung *f*.

abstergent [əb'stə:dʒənt] *a* reinigend; *med* abführend; *s* Reinigungs-, *med* Abführmittel *n*.

abstinen|ce ['æbstinəns] Enthaltsamkeit; Enthaltung *f* (*from* von); **~t** ['-t] enthaltsam; mäßig; keusch.

abstract ['æbstrækt] *a* abstrakt, begrifflich, unwirklich, theoretisch; ideal; abgezogen, abgesondert; allgemein; *(Zahl)* unbenannt, rein, absolut; *fig* dunkel, schwer verständlich, schwierig; *s (Buch)* Auszug, Abriß, Überblick *m*, Analyse *f*, Verzeichnis *n*, Liste; Zs.fassung *f*; Inbegriff *m*; Gedachte(s) *n*; Abstraktion *f*; *gram* Begriffswort, Abstraktum *n*; *tr* [æb'strækt] trennen, absondern (*from* von); *(Aufmerksamkeit)* ablenken, abziehen; absehen (*from* von), für sich betrachten; e-n Auszug machen (*from* von), ausziehen, abkürzen; e-e Zs.fassung geben, zs.fassen; *fam* entwenden; *math* abstrahieren; *chem* destillieren; *in the* ~~ an sich; an u. für sich; im allgemeinen; theoretisch; ~ *of an account* Kontoauszug *m*; ~ *of title* Grundbuchauszug *m*; **~ed** [æb'stræktid] *a* abgesondert, abgezogen; *fig* unaufmerksam, zerstreut; **~ion** [æb'strækʃən] Abstraktion, Absonderung; Wegnahme; *fig* Zerstreutheit *f*; abstrakte(r) Begriff *m*; abstrakte Komposition *f*.

abstruse [æb'stru:s] schwerverständlich, dunkel, verworren; **~ness** [-nis] Schwerverständlichkeit; Dunkelheit, Verworrenheit *f*.

absurd [əb'sə:d] sinn-, vernunftwidrig, ungereimt, unsinnig, lächerlich; **~ity** [-iti] Unsinn *m*, Ungereimtheit *f*.

abundan|ce [ə'bʌndəns] Überfluß *m*, Fülle *f*, Reichtum *m* (*of* an); (große) Menge; Häufigkeit *f*; *to live in* ~~ alles haben, was das Herz begehrt; **~t** [-t] überreich, reich (*in* an); reichlich versehen (*with* mit); reichlich.

abus|e [ə'bju:z] *tr* mißbrauchen, mißbräuchlich verwenden, falsch anwenden; mißhandeln (*a child* ein Kind); beschimpfen, beleidigen, schmähen, heruntermachen; kränken; hintergehen; *(Geheimnis)* verraten; *(Frau)* schänden, verführen; *s* [ə'bju:s] Mißbrauch *m*, mißbräuchliche Verwendung *f*, Mißstand, Übelstand; Übergriff *m*; Mißhandlung; Schmähung, Beschimpfung, Schändung *f*; *to* ~~ *o.'s discretion* sein Ermessen mißbrauchen; *gross, crying* ~~ grobe(r) Mißbrauch *m*; ~~ *of authority, of power* Mißbrauch *m* der Amtsgewalt; ~~ *of confidence, of trust* Vertrauensmißbrauch, Parteienverrat *m*; **~ive** [-siv] mißbräuchlich, mißbrauchend, schmähend, beleidigend; Schimpf-, Schmäh-; *to become* ~~ ausfällig werden; ~~ *language* Schimpfworte *n pl*, Beschimpfungen *f pl*.

abut [ə'bʌt] *itr* (an)grenzen, (an)stoßen (*on, upon* an); auslaufen, (an)lehnen, enden, auftreffen (*on, against* an, auf); **~ment** [-mənt] Angrenzen, Aneinanderstoßen *n*; *arch* Stütz-, Strebepfeiler *m*; *(Brücke)* Widerlager *n*; **~ter** [-ə] (Grundstücks-)Anlieger, Angrenzer, Anrainer *m*; **~ting** [-iŋ] angrenzend; ~~ *face* Stoßfläche *f*.

ab|ysm [ə'bizm] *poet* Abgrund, Schlund *m*; **~ysmal** [-əl] abgrundtief, bodenlos; *fig* unergründlich, uferlos; abgründig; ~~ *ignorance* abgrundtiefe Unwissenheit; **~yss** [ə'bis] Abgrund *a. fig*, Schlund *m*; *fig* Unterwelt, Hölle *f*.

Abyssinia [æbi'sinjə] Abessinien *n*; **~n** [-n] *a* abessinisch; *s* Abessinier(in *f*) *m*.

*

acacia [ə'keiʃə] *bot* Akazie(nblüte); *Am (false* ~*)* falsche Akazie, Robinie *f*; Gummiarabikum *n*.

acade|mic [ækə'demik] *a* akademisch; wissenschaftlich, gelehrt, abstrakt, konventionell, formal; weltfremd, pedantisch, unpraktisch; *s* Akademiker *m*; *pl* akademische Tracht *f*; nur theoretische Argumente *n pl*; ~~ *year* Universitätsjahr *n*; **~mical** [ækə'demikəl] *a* akademisch; formal; *s pl* akademische Tracht *f*; **~mician** [əkædə'miʃən] Mitglied *n* e-r Akademie; **~my** [ə'kædəmi] Akademie; Unterrichts-, Bildungsanstalt; gelehrte Gesellschaft; *Br* Militärakademie; *(Schottland)* höhere Tagesschule; *Am* (*bes.* private) Internatsschule *f*; *military* ~~ Militärakademie *f*; *fencing* ~~ Fechtschule *f*; *riding* ~~ Reitschule *f*; ~~ *of music* Musikschule *f*.

acanthus [ə'kænθəs] *pl -es, -thi* [-θai] *bot* Bärenklau; *arch* Akanthus *m*.

accede [æk'si:d] *itr* hinzukommen; bei-, zustimmen (*to* dat); einwilligen (*to* in); nachgeben (*to* dat); beitreten, sich anschließen; *(zu e-m Amt)* gelangen; *to* ~ *to a convention, pact, party, treaty* e-m Abkommen, e-m Pakt, e-r Partei, e-m Vertrag beitreten; *to* ~ *to terms* Bedingungen annehmen; *to* ~ *to the throne* den Thron besteigen.

accelerat|e [æk'seləreit] *tr* beschleunigen; anregen; vorverlegen; *itr* schneller werden; **~ed** *service* Schnelldienst *m*; **~ion** [-reiʃən] Beschleunigung; *med* Frühreife *f*; *tech* Anzugsmoment *n*; Geschwindigkeitssteigerung *f*; ~~ *of fall, of gravity* Fall-, Erdbeschleunigung *f*; **~ive** [-iv] beschleunigend; **~or** [-eitə] *mot* Gaspedal *n*, -hebel; *tech* Förderer *m*, Spannstück *n (am Gewehr)*; *el* Beschleunigungsanode *f*; *anat* Sympathicus; *phot* Beschleuniger *m*.

accent ['æksənt] *s* Ton *m*; Betonung *f*; Akzent *m*; Betonungszeichen *n*; Tonfall; Stil, Ausdruck *m*; *pl* Rede, Äußerung *f*; *tr* [æk'sent] betonen, hervorheben; mit e-m Akzent versehen; **~ual** [æk'sentjuəl, *Am* -tʃuəl] *a* akzentuierend; Akzent-; **~uate** [æk'sentjueit, *Am* -tʃ-] *tr* betonen, heraus-, hervorheben, verstärken; **~uation** [æksentju'eiʃən, *Am* -tʃ-] Betonung, Akzentuierung *f*.

accept [ək'sept] *tr* annehmen, akzeptieren; entgegennehmen, in Empfang nehmen (*s.th., of s.th.* etw); übernehmen; zustimmen (*s.th.* dat), einverstanden sein (*s.th.* mit etw); glauben (*s.th.* an etw); *tech* abnehmen; *(Tatsache)* anerkennen, gelten lassen; *refusal to* ~ Annahmeverweigerung *f*; **~ability** [-ə'biliti] Annehmbarkeit *f*; angenehme(r), zufriedenstellende(r) Zustand *m*; Eignung; *mil* Tauglichkeit *f*; **~able** [-əbl] annehmbar, willkommen (*to* für); angenehm, zufriedenstellend; tragbar; *com* beleihbar, lombardfähig; **~ance** [-əns] Annahme, Entgegennahme; Übernahme *f*; Empfang *m*; Zustimmung, Genehmigung, Einwilligung, Billigung *f*; Vertrauen *n* (*of* auf); günstige Aufnahme; Zusage; *tech* Abnahme *f*; *com* (Wechsel-)Akzept *n*; *(~~ of persons)* Parteilichkeit *f*; *without* ~~ *of persons* ohne Ansehen der Person; *to find* ~~ gut aufgenommen werden; *to present a bill for* ~~ e-n Wechsel zum Akzept vorlegen; *collateral* ~~ Wechselbürgschaft *f*; *conditions, terms of* ~~ Annahmebedingungen *f pl*; *customer's* ~~ Kundenwechsel *m*; Tratte *f*; *refusal of* ~~ Annahmeverweigerung *f*; ~~ *bill* Dokumentenwechsel *m*; ~~ *credit* Wechselkredit *m*; ~~ *for hono(u)r* Ehrenakzept *n*; ~~ *list, report, run, test* Abnahmeliste *f*, -protokoll *n*, -lauf *m*, -prüfung *f*; ~~ *sampling* statistische Qualitätskontrolle *f*; **~ation** [æksep'teiʃən] (allgemein anerkannte) Bedeutung; Auffassung, Ansicht *f*; *in the full* ~~ in seiner ganzen Bedeutung; **~ed** [-id] *a* (allgemein) anerkannt, angenommen; *(Meinung)* herrschend, üblich; *(Wechsel)* akzeptiert; **~er, ~or** [-ə] Empfänger; *com* Akzeptant, Bezogene(r) *m*.

access ['ækses] Zutritt (*to* zu); *(~ road)* Zugang(sstraße *f*), Weg *m*; Zufahrt *f*; Zuwachs *m*, Zunahme *f*; *med* Ausbruch *(e-r Krankheit)*; (Wut-)Anfall *m*; *to be difficult, easy of ~* schwer, leicht zugänglich sein; *to have ~ to s.o.* Zutritt zu jdm haben; ~ **hatch** *(Panzer)* Einstiegluke *f*; **~ibility** [æksesi'biliti] Zugänglichkeit; Leutseligkeit; *(Gebiet)* Begehbarkeit *f*; **~ible** [æk'sesibl] zugänglich (*to* für); erreichbar (*by* mit); *(Preis)* erschwinglich; **~ion** [æk'seʃən] *s* Beitritt *m* (*to* zu); Zustimmung *f*; *(Amt)* Antritt; Zuwachs *m*, Vermehrung *f*; *Am (Bibliothek)* Zugang *m*, Neuerwerbung; Erreichung *f*; *~~ to power* Machtergreifung, -übernahme *f*; *~~ to the throne* Thronbesteigung *f*; **~ory** [æk'sesəri] *a* zusätzlich, hinzukommend, extra; nebensächlich, untergeordnet; *jur* mitschuldig (*to* an); Neben-, Zusatz-; Hilfs-; *s* Zubehörteil *m*; Hilfsgerät; Beiwerk; Ausrüstungsstück *n*; *jur* Mitschuldige(r) *m*; *pl* Zubehör *n*; *motor-car ~ories (pl)* Autozubehör *n*; *toilet ~ories (pl)* Toilettenartikel *m pl*; *~~ charges (pl)* Nebenkosten *pl*; *~~ chest, box* Zubehörkasten *m*; *~~ before, after the fact* Anstifter; Hehler *m*.

acciden|ce ['æksidəns] *gram* Formenlehre *f*; Grundlagen *f pl*, Anfangsgründe *m pl*; **~t** ['-t] Zufall *m*; unvorhergesehene(s) Ereignis *n*; Unglücksfall, Unfall *m*; nebensächliche, unwesentliche Eigenschaft; *geol* Störung *f*; *by ~~* zufällig; durch, aus Zufall; *in an ~~* bei e-m Unfall; *without ~~* unfallfrei; *to meet with an ~~* e-n Unfall erleiden; verunglücken; *railway, traffic, working ~~* Eisenbahn-, Verkehrs-, Betriebsunfall *m*; *~~ benefit* Unfallrente *f*; *~~ insurance* Unfallversicherung *f*; *~~ prevention* Unfallverhütung *f*; *~~-proneness* Unfallneigung *f*; *~~ report* Unfallmeldung *f*; **~tal** [æksi'dentl] *a* zufällig; unabsichtlich, versehentlich; nebensächlich, unwesentlich; *s* Nebensache; zufällige Eigenschaft *f*; *mus* Versetzungszeichen *n*; *~~ hit* Zufallstreffer *m*.

accl|aim [ə'kleim] *tr* freudig begrüßen, zujubeln (*s.o.* jdm), durch Beifall zustimmen (*s.th.* dat); *s* Beifall *m*, Zustimmung, laute Begrüßung *f*; **~amation** [æklə'meiəʃn] laute(r) Beifall *m*, Zustimmung *f*; *pol* Zuruf *m*; *to elect by ~~* durch Zuruf wählen.

acclimat|e, *Br* **~ize** [ə'klaimət, 'æklimeit; ə'klaimətaiz] *tr* (an)gewöhnen, anpassen (*to* an); akklimatisieren; einführen, heimisch machen; **~ion,** *Br* **~ization**[ækli'meiʃən; əklaimətai'zeiʃən, -ti-] Angewöhnung, Akklimatisierung *f* (*to* an); Heimischmachen *n*.

acclivity [ə'kliviti] Steigung, Böschung, Anhöhe.

*

accommodat|e [ə'kɔmədeit] *tr* anpassen (*to* an), abstimmen (*to* auf); versorgen (*with* mit); e-n Dienst, e-e Gunst, e-n Gefallen erweisen (*s.o.* jdm); gefällig sein (*with* mit); beherbergen, unterbringen, einquartieren; versöhnen; *(Streit)* beilegen, schlichten, ausgleichen; ausrüsten, ausstatten; *itr* sich anpassen; **~ing** [-iŋ] willig, fügsam; gefällig, entgegen-, zuvorkommend; *(Bedingungen)* günstig; *~~ power* Anpassungsfähigkeit *f*; **~ion** [əkɔmə'deiʃən] Anpassung (*to* an), Abstimmung (*to* auf); Schlichtung *f*, Ausgleich *m*, Beilegung *f*; Abkommen *n*, Kompromiß *m*; Gefälligkeit *f*, Gefallen *m*; (Aus-)Hilfe, Unterstützung; praktische Sache, Bequemlichkeit; Unterkunft, Unterbringung; *com* Anleihe, geldliche Unterstützung *f*; *(~~ bill)* Gefälligkeitswechsel *m*; *(Auge)* Akkomodation *f*; *(Am pl)* Unterbringung(smöglichkeit), Unterkunft, *mil* Einquartierung *f*; Hotelzimmer *n*, (Schiffs-, Schlafwagen-) Platz *m*; *~~ ladder (mar)* Fallreepstreppe *f*; *~~ requirement* Raumbedarf *m*; *~~ train (Am)* Bummelzug *m*; *~~ unit* Wohneinheit *f*.

accompan|iment [ə'kʌmpənimənt] Begleiterscheinung *f*, -umstand *m*; gleichzeitige(s) Vorkommen *n*; *mus* Begleitung *f* (*to, for* zu); **~ist** [-ist] *mus* Begleiter *m*; **~y** [-i] *tr* begleiten *a. mus* (*by* von; *with s.th.* von etw; *on* auf); beifügen, beilegen; zugesellen; geleiten; *~ying artillery, letter, tank* Begleitartillerie *f*, -brief, -panzer *m*; *~ying phenomenon* Begleiterscheinung *f*.

accomplice [ə'kɔmplis] Helfershelfer, Mittäter, Komplize; Mitschuldiger *m*.

accomplish [ə'kɔmpliʃ] *tr* vollenden; vollbringen, ausrichten, zustande bringen; erfolgreich erledigen, tun, schaffen; leisten; aus-, durchführen, bewerkstelligen; *(Entfernung)* zurücklegen; *(Zweck, Aufgabe)* erfüllen; *(Plan)* verwirklichen, ausführen; *(Arbeit)* verrichten; **~ed** [-t] *a* vollendet *a. fig*; ausgebildet; gewandt; kultiviert, gebildet; *mission ~~* Befehl ausgeführt; **~ment** [-mənt] Vollendung; Erfüllung, Durchführung, Realisierung; vollendete Arbeit *f*, Werk *n*; Leistung *f*; *pl* Fähigkeiten, Fertigkeiten *f pl*, vielseitige Ausbildung *f*; *he has many ~~s* er ist sehr gebildet.

accord [ə'kɔ:d] *itr* übereinstimmen, harmonisieren, im Einvernehmen, im Einklang stehen (*with* mit); *tr* aufea. abstimmen; einräumen, gewähren, zugestehen, zuerkennen; zustimmen; bewilligen; *(Bitte)* erfüllen; *s* Übereinstimmung *f*; Einklang *m*, Eintracht, Einigkeit; *(Farben)* Harmonie *f*; *mus* Akkord, Gleichklang *m*; *jur* Abkommen *n*, Abmachung *f*, Vergleich *m*; *in ~ with* in Einklang mit; *of o.'s own ~* freiwillig, aus eigenem Antrieb, von sich aus; *with one ~* einstimmig; übereinstimmend, einmütig; **~ance** [-əns] Übereinstimmung; Zustimmung; Gewährung *f*; *in ~~ with, (Am) to* gemäß, in Übereinstimmung, gleichlautend mit; laut *gen*; *in ~~ with o.'s duty* pflichtgemäß; *in ~~ with instructions* weisungsgemäß; *to be in ~~ with s.th.* etw entsprechen; **~ant** [-ənt] übereinstimmend (*to, with* mit); entsprechend, gemäß; **~ing** [-iŋ] *adv* gemäß, laut, entsprechend (*to* dat); *~~ as (conj)* je nachdem, wie; sofern; *~~ to all appearances* allem Anschein nach; *~~ to orders* auftragsgemäß; *~~ to plan* planmäßig; *~~ to scale* maßstabgerecht; *~~ to schedule* fahrplanmäßig; **~ingly** [-iŋli] *adv* demgemäß, dementsprechend; folglich, danach; **~ion** [ə'kɔ:diən] *s mus* Akkordeon *n*, Ziehharmonika *f*; *a* Harmonika-, Falt-; *~~ player* Akkordeonspieler *m*; *~~ pleats (pl)* Ziehharmonikafalten *f pl*.

accost [ə'kɔst] *tr* ansprechen; zuerst grüßen.

accouch|ement [ə'ku:ʃmã:] *med* Entbindung *f*; **~eur** [æku:'ʃə:] Geburtshelfer *m*; **~euse** [æku:'ʃə:z] Hebamme *f*.

account [ə'kaunt] *s* (Ab-)Rechnung, Faktur; Berechnung *f*; Konto, Guthaben *n* (*with* bei); Rechenschaft, ausführliche Darlegung, Erklärung *f*; Bericht *m*, Erzählung *f*; *(Bestand)* Nachweis(ung *f*) *m*; Bedeutung, Wichtigkeit *f*; Grund *m*, Ursache *f*; Verzeichnis *n*; Gewinn, Nutzen *m*; *pl com* Buchhaltung, -führung *f*; Bücher *n pl*; *itr* abrechnen (*to* mit); erklären (*for s.th.* etw); Rechenschaft ablegen (*for* für); ausreichende Gründe angeben, verantwortlich sein (*for* für), sich rechtfertigen (*for* wegen); Bericht erstatten (*for* über); *sport* erledigen, außer Gefecht setzen, töten, schießen (*for s.o.* jdn); *tr* erachten, halten für, erklären; ansehen, betrachten als; *as per ~ rendered* laut Rechnung *od* Aufstellung; *by order and ~ of* im Auftrag u. auf Rechnung *gen*; *of no ~* unwichtig, unbedeutend; wertlos; *not... on any ~, on no ~* auf keinen Fall, unter keinen Umständen; *on ~ (com)* auf Abschlag *od* Konto; *on ~ of* wegen, auf Grund *gen*; *on this ~* aus diesem Grunde; *on my ~* meinetwegen, wegen mir, im Hinblick auf mich; *on o.'s own ~* zum eigenen Nutzen; für eigene Rechnung; *taking everything into ~* unter Berücksichtigung aller Umstände; *to call to ~* zur Rechenschaft ziehen (*for* wegen); *to carry forward to a new ~* auf neue Rechnung vortragen; *to debit an ~* ein Konto belasten; *to give, to render, to make an ~ of s.th.* von etw Bericht erstatten; über etw Rechenschaft ablegen; *to have in o.'s ~* auf dem Konto (stehen) haben; *to keep ~s* Bücher führen; *to open an ~ with the bank* ein Bankkonto eröffnen; *to pay into an ~* auf ein Konto einzahlen; *to pay on ~* anzahlen; *to place, to put s.th. into ~* etw in Rechnung stellen; *to settle ~s with s.o.* mit jdm abrechnen; *to square ~s* Rechnungen begleichen; *to take (no) ~ of s.th.* etw berücksichtigen, in Betracht ziehen; etw beachten; etw unberücksichtigt lassen; *to take into ~* in Betracht ziehen, Rechnung tragen (*s.th.* dat), berücksichtigen; *to turn s.th. to ~* sich etw zunutze machen, aus etw Vorteil ziehen, etw ausnutzen; *that ~s for it* das ist die Erklärung dafür; *there's (no) ~ing for tastes* über den Geschmack läßt sich (nicht) streiten; *balance of ~* Rechnungsabschluß *m*; *blocked ~* Sperrkonto *n*; *current ~* Kontokorrent; Girokonto *n*; *debit ~* Debitorenkonto *n*; *opening of an ~* Kontoeröffnung *f*; *outstanding ~* Außenstände *m pl*; *payment on ~* Abschlagszahlung *f*; *savings(-bank) ~* Sparkonto *n*; *statement of ~* Kontoauszug *m*; *yearly ~* Jahresabrechnung *f*; *~ of charges* Unkostenkonto *n*; Kosten-, Gebührenrechnung *f*; *~ of expenses* Spesenrechnung *f*; *~ of settlement* Schluß-(ab)rechnung *f*; **~ability** [əkauntə'biliti] Verantwortlichkeit *f*; **~able** [-əbl] verantwortlich; erklärlich; nachweisbar, -pflichtig; *to hold s.o. ~~ for s.th.* jdn für etw verantwortlich machen; *~~ stores (pl)* Gebrauchsgüter *n pl*; *Br* Inventar *n*; **~ancy** [-ənsi] Buchführungs-, Rechnungswesen *n*; Buchhaltung *f*; **~ant** [-ənt] Buchhalter *m*; *(Am) certified public ~~, (Br) chartered ~~* Buch-, Wirtschaftsprüfer *m*; **~book** Kontobuch *n*; *pl* Geschäftsbücher *n pl*; **~ classification** Kontengliederung *f*; **~ current** Kontokorrent *n*; Rechnungsauszug *m*; **~ deposits** *pl* Kontoeinlagen *f pl*; **~ distribution** Kontierung *f*; **~ing** [-iŋ] Buchführung, -haltung *f*; *~~ clerk* Buchhalter *m*; *~~ department* Buchhaltung(sabteilung) *f*; *~~ form* Kontenblatt *n*; *~~ machine* Buch(halt)ungsmaschine *f*; *~~ period* Abrechnungszeitraum *m*, Wirtschaftsperiode *f*; *~~ system* Buchführungssystem *n*; **~ sales** Verkaufs(ab)rechnung *f*; **~s payable** Verbindlichkeiten, Schulden *f pl*; **~s receivable** Außenstände *pl*, Forderungen *f pl*; ~ **year** Rechnungs-, Wirtschaftsjahr *n*.

accoutre, *Am* **-er** [ə'ku:tə] *tr* ausrüsten *bes. mil*; **~ments** [-mənts] *pl* Ausrüstung *f a. mil.*

accredit [ə'kredit] *tr* beglaubigen, *pol* akkreditieren (*to* bei); zuschreiben (*s.o. with s.th.* jdm etw); zu allgemeiner Anerkennung verhelfen (*s.th.* e-r S); anerkennen; (amtlich) zulassen.

accret|e [ə'kri:t] *itr* zs.wachsen, verbinden (*to* mit); e-n Zuwachs erfahren; *a bot* zs.gewachsen; **~ion** [æ'kri:ʃən] Zuwachs *m*; Zs.wachsen *n*; Zunahme *f*.

accrue [ə'kru:] *itr* an-, zufallen (*to s.o.* jdm); *(Zinsen)* auflaufen; entstehen, herkommen (*from* aus).

accumulat|e [ə'kju:mjuleit] *tr* auf-, anhäufen; ansammeln, speichern; zs.-bringen; *itr* sich (an)sammeln, anwachsen, sich häufen; *com* auflaufen; *~ed dividend* rückständige Dividende *f*; **~ion** [əkju:mju'leiʃən] Anhäufung, Ansammlung *f*; *~~ of capital* Kapitalbildung, -anhäufung *f*; *~~ of heat* Wärmestauung *f*; **~ive** [-lətiv] *a* (sich) anhäufend, (sich) steigernd; angehäuft; **~or** [-ə] Sammler *a. tech*; *tech* Akku(mulator) *m*; *Br (~~ battery)* Akkumulatorenbatterie *f*; *~~ container* Batteriekasten *m*.

accura|cy ['ækjurəsi] Genauigkeit, Exaktheit; Sorgfalt; Fehlerlosigkeit *f*; *~~ landing* Ziellandung *f*; *~~ of fire* Zielsicherheit, Treffgenauigkeit *f*; **~te** ['-it] genau, exakt; richtig, fehlerlos; sorgfältig.

accurs|ed, ~t [ə'kə:sid, -t] *a* verflucht; verdammenswert, abscheulich.

accus|ation [ækju'zeiʃən] Anklage; An-, Beschuldigung *f*; *to be under an ~~* unter Anklage stehen; *to bring an ~~ against s.o.* gegen jdn Anklage erheben; *the ~~ is murder* die Anklage lautet auf Mord; **~ative** [ə'kjuzətiv] *gram* Akkusativ *m*; **~atory** [ə'kju:zətəri] anklagend; Anklage-; **~e** [ə'kju:z] *tr* anklagen, beschuldigen, bezichtigen (*of a crime* (wegen) e-s Verbrechens; *of having done* etw getan zu haben); vorwerfen (*of being s.th.* etw zu sein); **~ed** [ə'kju:zd] *s sing u. pl* Angeklagte(r); Angeschuldigte(r) *m*.

accustom [ə'kʌstəm] *tr* gewöhnen (*to* an); **~ed** [-d] *a* gewohnt (*to doing s.th.* etw zu tun); gewöhnlich, üblich; *to be ~~* gewohnt sein (*to* an); *to get ~~* sich gewöhnen (*to* an).

ace [eis] *s* Eins *f (auf Würfeln)*; *(Spielkarten)* As; *aero* (Flieger-)As *n*; *(Tennis)* Punkt; *fam* Pfundskerl *m*; *a fam* erstklassig, hervorragend, sehr anständig; *tr* e-n Punkt gewinnen; *to be within an ~ of doing s.th.* beinahe, um Haaresbreite etw tun; *to have an ~ up o.'s sleeve, (Am) in the hole* e-n Trumpf in Reserve haben.

acerbity [ə'sə:biti] Herbheit; *fig* Schärfe, Strenge, Bitterkeit *f*.

acet|ate ['æsitit, -eit] *chem* Azetat *n*; *cellulose ~~* Zelluloseazetat *n*; **~ic** [ə'si:tik, ə'setik] *chem* essigsauer; *~~ acid, ether* Essigsäure *f*, -äther *m*; **~one** ['æsitoun] *chem* Azeton *n*; **~ous** ['æsitəs] essigsauer; **~ylene** [ə'setili:n] *chem* Azetylen *n*; *~~ welding* Azetylen-, Autogenschweißung *f*.

ache [eik] *itr* (dauernd) schmerzen; Schmerz empfinden (*all over* am ganzen Körper); wehtun; *fam* sich sehnen (*for* nach); *s* (dauernder, dumpfer) Schmerz *m*.

achieve [ə'tʃi:v] *tr* vollbringen, vollenden; durch-, ausführen, zustande bringen; erreichen; erlangen; *(Ziele)* verwirklichen; *(Erfolg)* erzielen; *to ~ distinction* sich auszeichnen; **~ment** [-mənt] Vollendung, Ausführung, Bewerkstelligung, Verwirklichung; Erzielung *f*; Werk *n*, Tat; Groß-, Heldentat; *(Schule)* Leistung *f*.

achromat|ic [ækro'mætik] achromatisch, farblos; **~opsia** [ækromə'tɔpsia] *med* Farbenblindheit *f*.

acid ['æsid] *a* sauer, herb, scharf, beißend; *s* Säure *f*; ~ **bath** Säurebad *n*; ~ **content** Säuregehalt *m*; ~ **drops** *pl* saure Fruchtbonbons *n pl*; **~-fast, -proof, -resistant** säurefest, -beständig; ~ **formation** Säurebildung *f*; **~ic** [ə'sidik] säurehaltig, sauer; **~ification** [əsidifi'keiʃən] Säurebildung *f*; **~ify** [ə'sidifai] *tr chem* ansäuern; **~imeter** [æsi'dimitə] Säuremesser *m*; ~ **intensity** Säurewert *m*; **~ity** [ə'siditi] Säuregehalt, -grad *m*; ~ **lining** säurefeste(r) Belag *m*; ~ **test** Säurebestimmung; *fig* Feuerprobe, Prüfung (*of* für); **~ulate** [ə'sidjuleit] *tr* ansäuern; **~ulous** [ə'sidjuləs] säuerlich *a. fig*, leicht sauer.

ack|-ack ['æk'æk] *mil sl* Flak *f*; **~-emma** *mil sl* Vormittag *m*.

acknowledg|e [ək'nɔlidʒ] *tr* anerkennen (*s.o. to be s.th.* als etw); zugeben, (ein)gestehen; bestätigen; quittieren; sich erkenntlich zeigen (*s.th. to s.o.* jdm für etw); *this is to ~~ receipt of* ich bestätige hiermit den Empfang *gen*; **~(e)ment** [-mənt] Anerkennung *f*; Eingeständnis *n*; Bestätigung; Quittung, Empfangsbestätigung; *jur* Schuldanerkenntnis; Erkenntlichkeit *f* (*of* für); *in ~~ of* zum Zeichen der Anerkennung für.

acme ['ækmi] Gipfel, Höhepunkt *m*.

acne ['ækni] *med* Pickel *m*, Hautfinne *f*.

acolyte ['ækəlait] *rel* Altardiener; Ministrant; Helfer; Anhänger *m*.

aconite ['ækənait] *bot* Eisenhut *m*.

acorn ['eikɔ:n] *bot* Eichel *f*.

acoustic [ə'ku:stik, ə'kau-] *a* akustisch; *s pl* Akustik *f*; ~ **nerve** Hörnerv *m*; ~ **power** Schallstärke *f*; ~ **sounding** Echolotung *f*; ~ **tile** *arch* Dämmplatte *f*.

acquaint [ə'kweint] *tr* bekannt, vertraut machen (*with* mit); benachrichtigen, in Kenntnis setzen (*that* daß); *to be ~ed with s.th.* mit etw bekannt, vertraut sein; *to become, to get ~ed with s.o.* mit jdm bekannt werden, sich kennenlernen; **~ance** [-əns] (praktische) Kenntnis; Bekanntschaft *f*; Bekannte(r *m*) *f*; Bekanntenkreis *m*; *to make s.o.'s ~~* jds Bekanntschaft machen.

acquiesce [ækwi'es] *itr* sich fügen, einwilligen (*in* in); zustimmen (*in* dat); sich abfinden (*in* mit); **~nce** [-ns] Einwilligung, (wortlose) Zustimmung; Ergebung *f* (*in* in); **~nt** [-nt] fügsam, nachgiebig; ergeben.

acquir|e [ə'kwaiə] *tr* erreichen, erlangen; erwerben, in den Besitz kommen; *(Sprache)* erlernen; *(Kenntnisse)* sich aneignen; *to ~~ by purchase* käuflich erwerben; **~ement** [-mənt] Erwerb(ung *f*) *m*, Erlangung; erworbene Fähigkeit *od* Kenntnis *f*; *pl* Kenntnisse *f pl*, Bildung *f*; **~er** [-rə] Erwerber *m*.

acquisi|tion [ækwi'ziʃən] Erwerb *m*, Erwerbung *f*; *fig* Gewinn *m*, Bereicherung, Errungenschaft *f*; *~~ of land, of property* Land-, Eigentumserwerb *m*; **~tive** [ə'kwizitiv] habsüchtig, gierig (*of* auf); *fig* begierig (*of* nach).

acquit [ə'kwit] *tr (Schuld)* begleichen, regeln, tilgen; *(Anspruch)* befriedigen; freistellen, entbinden (*of a duty* e-r Pflicht); *jur* freisprechen, entlasten (*of a charge* von e-r Anklage); *to ~ o.s.* sich verhalten; seine Schuldigkeit tun; **~tal** [-l] *jur* Freisprechung *f*, Freispruch *m*; *(Pflicht)* Erfüllung; *(Rechnung)* Begleichung, Regelung *f*; **~tance** [-əns] Bezahlung, Regelung, Tilgung; Quittung, Empfangsbestätigung *f*; *sum of ~~* Abfindungssumme *f*; *~~ roll* Lohnliste *f*.

acre ['eikə] Morgen *m* (*= 160 square poles = 43 560 square feet = 0,40467 ha*); *pl* Ländereien *n pl*, Gut *n*; *God's ~* Friedhof *m*; **~age** ['eikəridʒ] Fläche *f*, Umfang *m* an Morgen.

acrid ['ækrid] scharf, ätzend, beißend *a. fig*; **~ity** [æ'kriditi] Schärfe *f a. fig*.

acrimon|ious [ækri'mounjəs] *fig* scharf, bitter, beißend; **~y** ['ækriməni] Schärfe, Bitterkeit, bissige Art *f*.

acrobat ['ækrobæt] Akrobat *m*; **~ic** [ækro'bætik] *a* akrobatisch; *s pl* Akrobatik *f*; *aero* Kunstflug *m*.

across [ə'krɔ(:)s] *adv* kreuzweise; quer über, quer durch; jenseits; drüben; *prp* quer über, quer durch; auf der anderen Seite, jenseits; über; *to come ~* stoßen auf; *s.o.* jdm begegnen; *to put ~ (Am)* durchbringen, -drücken; *just ~* gerade gegenüber; *right ~* quer durch.

acrostic [ə'krɔstik] Akrostichon *n*.

act [ækt] *s* Handlung, Tat *f*, Akt; *theat* Akt, Aufzug, Auftritt *m*; *jur* Gesetz *n*, Rechtshandlung *f*; Akten-, Schriftstück *n*; *tr theat (e-e Rolle)* spielen, darstellen; *(Stück)* aufführen; so tun (*a child* wie ein Kind), simulieren; *itr* e-e Rolle spielen, als Schauspieler auftreten; sich benehmen, sich verhalten (*like* wie); vorgeben, aussehen; sich in Szene setzen; tätig sein, dienen (*as* als); handeln, tun, in Aktion treten, tätig werden; (ein)wirken (*on* auf), beeinflussen (*on s.th.* etw); *(Maschine)* arbeiten, laufen, funktionieren; *to ~ for s.o.* jdn vertreten; in jds Namen, für jdn handeln; *to ~ on* (be)folgen; sich richten, handeln nach; einwirken auf; *to ~ up (fam)* sich aufspielen; *to s.th.* sich e-r S gemäß benehmen, sich richten nach; *in the ~* auf frischer Tat; gerade dabei (*of doing s.th.* etw zu tun); *to ~ in cold blood* nach reiflicher Überlegung handeln; *to ~ the goat* sich töricht benehmen; *don't put on an ~!* spiel doch nicht Komödie! *the A~s (of the Apostles)* Apostelgeschichte *f*; *~ of aggression* Angriffshandlung *f*; *~ of bankruptcy* Konkursdelikt *n*; *~ of grace* Gnadenakt *m*; *~ of force* Gewaltakt *m*; *A~ of God* höhere Gewalt *f*; unabwendbare(s) Ereignis *n*; *~ of oblivion* Amnestie *f*; **~able** ['-əbl] *theat* aufführbar; **~ing** ['-iŋ] *a* Bühnen-; *tech* funktionierend, wirksam, aktiv; stellvertretend, geschäftsführend; *s* Theaterspielen *n a. fig*; Schauspielkunst *f*.

actin|ia [æk'ti:niə] *pl -ae* [-i:] Seeanemone *f*; **~ic** [-ik] aktinisch; **~ometer** [ækti'nɔmitə] Aktinometer *n*.

action ['ækʃən] Handlung, Tätigkeit *f*; Handeln *n*; Tat; Wirkung *f*; *tech* Funktionieren *n*, Gang *m*, Wirkungsweise *f*; Mechanismus *m*; *jur* Klage *f*, Prozeß *m*; *mil* Gefecht *n*, Kampf(handlung *f*) *m*, Unternehmen *n*, *aero* Feindflug *m*; *(Kunst)* Leben; *pl* Verhalten *n*, Führung, Handlungsweise *f*; *for further ~* zur weiteren Veranlassung; *in full ~* in vollem Betrieb; *out of ~ (tech)* außer Betrieb; *mil* außer Gefecht; *to break off an ~* ein Gefecht abbrechen; *to bring s.th. into ~, to put s.th. in ~* etw in Gang setzen; *to come, to go into ~ (mil)* eingreifen; in Tätigkeit treten; *to put out of ~* außer Gefecht, außer Betrieb setzen; *to see ~ (Am)* (an der Front) kämpfen; *to take ~* Schritte unternehmen, Maßnahmen ergreifen; mit der Arbeit beginnen; *to* *take, to bring an ~ against* gegen jdn e-e Klage einreichen, anhängig machen, klagen; *cause of ~* Klagegrund *m*; *clear for ~ (mar)* gefechtsklar; *defence to an ~* Klagbeantwortung *f*; *enemy ~* Feindeinwirkung *f*; *field, sphere of ~* Tätigkeitsbereich *m*, Betätigungsfeld *n*; *killed in ~ (mil)* gefallen; *libel ~* Beleidigungsklage *f*; *man of ~* Mann *m* der Tat; *nullity ~* Nichtigkeits-, Anfechtungsklage *f*; *ready for ~* einsatzbereit; *right of ~* Klagrecht *n*; *~ for annulment* Anfechtungs-, Nichtigkeitsklage *f*; *~ for damages* Schadenersatzklage *f*; *~ for declaratory judg(e)ment* Feststellungsklage *f*; *~ for ejection* Räumungsklage *f*; *~ for permanent injunction* Unterlassungsklage *f*; *~ for maintenance* Unterhaltsklage *f*; *~ for payment* Klage *f* auf Zahlung; *~ for restitution* Klage *f* auf Herausgabe; **~able** ['-ʃnəbl] (ein)klagbar; verfolgbar; *~* **committee** Aktionskomitee *n*; *~* **station** Gefechts-, Alarmstation *f*.

activ|ate ['æktiveit] *tr* aktivieren *a. chem*, in Tätigkeit setzen; *(Büro)* organisieren, auf die Beine stellen, aufbauen; radioaktiv machen; *(Truppen)* aufstellen; *(Zünder)* scharfmachen; **~ation** [ækti'veiʃən] Aktivierung *f a. chem*; *(Organisation)* Aufbau *m*; *(Truppen)* Aufstellung *f*; **~ator** ['æktiveitə] Katalysator, Aktivator *m*, Koenzym *n*; **~e** ['æktiv] *a* tätig, aktiv, handelnd; betriebsam, rührig, regsam, rege; wirksam; *(Hilfe)* praktisch, greifbar; *(Greis)* rüstig; *(Geist)* beweglich, lebendig; *(Umsatz)* lebhaft; *(Geld)* zins-, gewinnbringend; *gram* aktiv; *chem* radioaktiv, spaltbar; *s* aktive(s), tätige(s) Mitglied; *(~~ voice) gram* Aktiv *n*; *to be on the ~~ list, on ~~ service (mil)* aktiv dienen; *to take an ~~ part in s.th.* an etw tätigen Anteil nehmen; *~~ balance* Aktivsaldo *n*; *~~ component* Wirkkomponente *f*; *~~ current* Nutz-, Wirkstrom *m*; *~~ debts (pl)* Außenstände *pl*; *~~ electrode* Sprühelektrode *f*; *~~ force* Wucht, lebendige Kraft *f*; *~~ funds (pl)* zins-, gewinnbringend angelegte Kapitalien *n pl*; *~~ service allowance* Frontzulage *f*; *~~ service pay* Wehrsold *m*; *~~ voltage* Wirkspannung *f*; *~~ waste* radioaktive(r) Abfall *m*; **~ity** [æk'tiviti] Tätigkeit; Regsamkeit, Geschäftigkeit, Rührigkeit; Wirksamkeit; Aktivität, Energie; Betätigung *f*; *there is little ~~* es ist wenig los; *in full ~~* in voller Tätigkeit, in vollem Gang; *building, business ~~* Bau-, Geschäftstätigkeit *f*; *classroom ~ities (pl)* Arbeiten *f pl* im Rahmen des Unterrichts in der Klasse.

act|or ['æktə] Täter; *theat* Schauspieler *m*; **~ress** ['-tris] Schauspielerin *f*.

actu|al ['æktjuəl] wirklich, tatsächlich (vorhanden); eigentlich; faktisch; gegenwärtig, derzeitig; *~~ assets (pl)* Reinvermögen *n*; *~~ cash value* Barwert *m*; *~~ cost* Ist-Kosten *pl*; *~~ inventory* Istbestand *m*; *~~ order* feste(r) Auftrag *m*; *~~ power* Wirk-, Effektivleistung *f*; *~~ price* Tagespreis *m*; *~~ report* Iststärkemeldung *f*; *~~ strength* Iststärke *f*; *~~ value* Effektiv-, Marktwert *m*; *~~ working* Funktionieren *n*; **~ality** [æktju'æliti] Wirklichkeit; *pl* Tatsachen *f pl*; tatsächliche(r) Zustand *m*; **~alize** ['æktjuəlaiz] *tr* in die Tat umsetzen, verwirklichen; realistisch darstellen; **~ly** ['æktjuəli] *adv* tatsächlich, wirklich, in Wirklichkeit; jetzt; **~arial** [æktju'ɛəriəl] versicherungsmathematisch; Versicherungs-; **~ary** ['æktjuəri] Versicherungsmathematiker *m*; **~ate** ['æktjueit] *tr* in Bewegung setzen, in Gang bringen, antreiben; beeinflussen, bewegen; auslösen, betätigen; **~ation** [æktju'eiʃən] Antrieb *m*; Betätigung *f*.

acuity [ə'kju(:)iti] Schärfe *f*.

acum|en [ə'kju:mən] Scharfsinn *m*; **~inate** [ə'kju:minit] *a bot* spitz, zugespitzt; *tr* [-eit] *Am* zuspitzen.

acupuncture [ækju:'pʌŋktʃə] *med* Akupunktur *f*.

acute [ə'kju:t] *a* spitz; scharf; scharfsinnig; empfindlich; *(Schmerz)* stechend; *(Sinne)* scharf; *(Eifersucht)* heftig; *(Frage)* brennend; *(Ton)* schrill; *(Freude)* groß; *(Winkel)* spitz; *(Depression)* stark; *med* akut, hitzig; *s (~ accent)* Akut *m*; **~ness** [-nis] Schärfe; Spitze *f*; Scharfsinn; schrille(r) Klang *m*; *med* akute(s) Stadium *n*, Heftigkeit *f*; *~~ of vision* Sehschärfe *f*.

ad [æd] *Am sl* Zeitungsanzeige *f*; *to put in an ~ (Am)* e-e Anzeige aufgeben; **~-card** Reklameschild *n*; **A~ Club** Vereinigung *f* der Werbefachleute; **~-lib** *s* Improvisation *f*; *a* Stegreif-; *itr* aus dem Stegreif reden; e-e kluge Bemerkung machen; **~man** ['-mən] Anzeigen-, Werbefachmann *m*; **~mass** leicht beeinflußbare(s) Massenpublikum *n*; **~-rate** Anzeigenpreis *m*; **~-writer** Texter *m*.

adage ['ædidʒ] Sprichwort *n*.

adagio [ə'dɑ:dʒiou] *s* Adagio *n*; *adv* adagio.

Adam ['ædəm] Adam *m*; *not to know s.o. from ~* jdn überhaupt nicht kennen; *~* **-and-Eve** *Am* zwei Spiegeleier *n pl (on a raft* auf Toast); **~'s apple** Adamsapfel *m*;

adamant ['ædəmənt] sehr hart; *fig* unnachgiebig (*to* gegenüber); **~ine** [ædə'mæntain] *fig* hart, fest, unnachgiebig.

adapt [ə'dæpt] *tr* anpassen (*to* an); zweckentsprechend verändern; *(Roman)* bearbeiten; *to be well ~ed* sehr geeignet sein (*for* für); **~ability** [ədæptə'biliti] Anpassungsfähigkeit, Wendigkeit *f*; **~able** [-əbl] anpassungsfähig (*to* an); **~ation, ~ion** [ædæp'teiʃən, ə'dæpʃən] Anpassung (*to* an); *theat* Bearbeitung *f*; **~er, ~or** [-ə] Bearbeiter *m*; *tech* Verbindungs-, Zwischenstück *n*, Zwischenteil *m*, Paßstück *n*; *el (~~ plus)* Zwischen-, Schraubstecker *m*; Vorsatzgerät *n*; **~ive** [-iv] anpassungsfähig.

add [æd] *tr* hinzusetzen, -tun, -fügen (*to* zu); *chem* zusetzen, beimischen; *tech* auftragen; *math (to ~ up)* zs.zählen, addieren; *to ~ up to (Am)* hinauslaufen auf; sich belaufen auf; *itr fig* beitragen (*to* zu), vermehren (*to s.th.* etw); **~ed** ['-id] *a* verstärkt, erhöht; *~~ metal* Zusatzmetall *n*; **~endum** [ə'dendəm] *pl -a* [-ə] Zusatz, Nachtrag; *tech* Zahnkopf *m*; **~ing machine** Addier-, Rechenmaschine *f*.

adder ['ædə] *zoo* Natter *f*.

addict [ə'dikt] *tr* widmen; *to ~ o.s. to s.th.* sich e-r S hingeben; *s* ['ædikt] Süchtige(r *m*) *f*; *drug ~* Rauschgiftsüchtige(r *m*) *f*; **~ed** [-id] *a* ergeben, verfallen (*to* dat); **~ion** [-ʃən] Neigung *f*, Hang *m* (*to* zu).

addition [ə'diʃən] Bei-, Zugabe, Beifügung, Zutat; Erweiterung *f*, Zusatz *m*; *com* Zulage *f*; *com* Zugang *m*; *math* Addition *f*; *arch* Erweiterungsbau; *(Familie)* Zuwachs; Nachtrag *m*; *in ~* außerdem (noch); dazu; *in ~ to* (zusätzlich) zu, neben, außer; **~al** [-l] zusätzlich, hinzukommend; weiter; ergänzend; nachträglich; Zusatz-; *~~ agreement* Nebenabrede *f*; *~~ allowance* Zulage *f*; *~~ charge* Preiszuschlag *m*; *pl* Nebenkosten *pl*; *~~ income* Nebeneinnahmen *f pl*; *~~ insurance* Zusatzversicherung *f*; *~~ payment* Nachzahlung *f*; *~~ postage* Nachporto *n*; *~~ purpose* Nebenabsicht *f*; *~~ strain* zusätzliche Anstrengung, Mehrarbeit *f*; *~~ time* Aufschub *m*; **~ally** [-ʃnəli] *adv* zusätzlich; in verstärktem Maße; als Zugabe, als Zusatz, als Nachtrag.

additive ['æditiv] *a* zusätzlich; *s tech* Zusatzmittel, Additiv *n*.

addle ['ædl] *a* verwirrt; *(Ei)* faul; *tr* verwirren; *itr* verderben; durchea.kommen, verwirrt werden; **~-brained, ~-pated** *a* verschroben; töricht; hohl im Kopf; **~-head** Hohlkopf *m*.

address [ə'dres] *tr (Worte)* richten (*to* an); *(Brief)* adressieren; absenden, schicken (*to* an); *(Person)* anreden, ansprechen; reden zu, e-e Ansprache halten an (*a meeting* e-e Versammlung); *(Anfrage)* richten (*to* an); *to ~ o.s. to* sich wenden an; sich (be)mühen um; seine Anstrengungen richten auf; *s* Anrede, Ansprache; *Am* ['ædres] Anschrift, Adresse; Geschicklichkeit, Gewandtheit *f*; Anstand *m*, Benehmen *n*; *to deliver an ~* e-e Ansprache halten; *to pay o.'s ~es to s.o.* jdm den Hof machen; *business ~* Geschäftsadresse *f*; *home, private ~* Privatanschrift *f*; *inaugural ~* Antrittsrede *f*; *radio ~* Rundfunkansprache *f*; *~ of thanks* Dankschreiben *n*; **~ee** [ædre'si:] Empfänger, Adressat *m*; **~ing** [-iŋ] Adressieren *n*; *~~ machine* = **~ograph** [-əgrɑ:f] *(Schutzmarke)* Adressiermaschine *f*.

adduc|e [ə'dju:s] *tr (Beispiel)* anführen, zitieren; *(Beweis)* erbringen; *(Zeugen)* stellen.

adenoid ['ædinɔid] *a* drüsenartig; *s pl med* Rachenmandelwucherung *f*, Polypen *m pl*.

adept ['ædept, *a.* ə'dept] *s* Kenner, Sachverständige(r) *m*; *a* [*Am* ə'dept] erfahren, fachkundig, sehr geschickt (*in* in; *at doing s.th.* etw zu tun).

adequa|cy ['ædikwəsi] Angemessenheit; ausreichende Zahl, Qualität; Eignung *f*; **~te** ['-it] angemessen, ausreichend (*to* für); entsprechend; noch genügend, annehmbar.

adhere [əd'hiə] *itr* haften, kleben (*to* an); anhängen, hängenbleiben; *fig* festhalten (*to* an), bleiben (*to* bei); *(Anspruch)* aufrechterhalten; *(Bestimmung)* einhalten, befolgen; *(Versprechen)* halten; *(Form)* beachten; *(e-r Partei)* treu bleiben; Mitglied sein (*to* von); *to ~ to an opinion* bei e-r Meinung bleiben; **~nce** [-rəns] Anhänglichkeit *f* (*to* an); Festhalten *n* (*to* an); *(Vertrag)* Beitritt *m* (*to* zu); *(Partei)* Mitgliedschaft, Zugehörigkeit *f* (*to* zu); *bot* Verwachsensein *n*; **~nt** [-rənt] *a* anhaftend, festklebend (*to* an); *bot* verwachsen; *fig* festhaltend (*to* an); *s* Anhänger(in *f*) *m*, (Partei-)Mitglied *n*; *pl* Gefolgschaft *f*.

adhes|ion [əd'hi:ʒən] *phys* Adhäsion *f*, Haftvermögen *n*, -fähigkeit; Bindekraft; *fig* Anhänglichkeit; Mitgliedschaft *f*; Beitritt *m* (*to a contract* zu e-m Vertrag); *med* Adhäsion *f*; **~ive** [-siv] *a* klebend, klebrig, haftend; gummiert; *s* Klebstoff, Kleister *m*; *~~ plaster* Heftpflaster *n*; *~~ power* Haftvermögen *n*; *~~ tape* Klebeband *n*, -streifen *m*; Leukoplast *n*.

adieu [ə'dju:] *pl -s, -x s* Lebewohl *n*; *interj* lebewohl! adieu! *to bid, to make, to take o.'s ~x* Lebewohl sagen.

adipos|e ['ædipous] *a* fett; *s* (tierisches) Fett *n*; *~~ tissue* Fettgewebe *n*; **~ity** [ædi'pɔsiti] Dick-, Fettleibigkeit *f*.

adit ['ædit] Zugang, Zutritt; *min* (waagrechter) Stollen *m*.

adjacen|cy [ə'dʒeisənsi] unmittelbare Nachbarschaft *f*, Angrenzen *n*; **~t** [-t] angrenzend, anliegend, anstoßend (*to* an); benachbart; nebenea.liegend; *to be ~~ to* angrenzen an; *~~ angle, sector* Nebenwinkel, -abschnitt *m*; *~~ sheet (Karte)* Anschlußblatt *n*.

adjective ['ædʒiktiv] *s* Adjektiv, Eigenschaftswort *n*; *a* adjektivisch; Adjektiv-; **~ law** formelle(s) Recht *n*.

adjoin [ə'dʒɔin] *tr* angrenzen an; sehr nahe liegen bei; an-, bei-, hinzufügen, verbinden (*to* mit); *itr* nahe beiea.liegen, anea.grenzen; eng mitea. in Verbindung stehen; **~ing** [-iŋ] benachbart, anliegend, anstoßend.

adjourn [ə'dʒə:n] *tr itr* verschieben, vertagen (*for a week* um e-e Woche); *(Debatte)* schließen; *itr* die Sitzung schließen *od* vertagen; *fam* sich begeben (*to* nach, in, zu); **~ment** [-mənt] Vertagung, Verschiebung; Aussetzung *f*.

adjudge [ə'dʒʌdʒ] *tr* entscheiden, für Recht erkennen, gerichtlich zusprechen, zuerkennen; verurteilen (*to* zu); *to ~ s.o. a bankrupt* das Konkursverfahren über jdn eröffnen.

adjudicat|e [ə'dʒu:dikeit] *tr* Recht sprechen; zuerkennen, zusprechen; *(Versteigerung)* zuschlagen (*to the highest bidder* dem Meistbietenden); *itr* entscheiden (*in, on* über); **~ion** [ədʒudi'keiʃən] Urteil *n*, Beschluß *m*; Zuerkennung *f*; Zuschlag *m*; *~~ of bankruptcy* Eröffnung *f* des Konkursverfahrens; **~or** [ə'dʒu:dikeitə] (Schieds-)Richter *m*.

adjunct ['ædʒʌŋkt] *s* Zusatz, Anhang; Gehilfe, Beigeordnete(r) *m*; Attribut *n*; *tech* Zubehörteil *m*; **~ive** [ə'dʒʌŋktiv] beigefügt; verbunden (*to* mit).

adjur|ation [ædʒuə'reiʃən] Beschwörung; eidliche Bindung *f*; **~e** [ə'dʒuə] *tr* beschwören; inständig bitten; eidlich, unter Strafandrohung verpflichten.

adjust [ə'dʒʌst] *tr* anpassen, passend machen, verstellen; abstimmen (*to* auf); *tech* einstellen, justieren, einrichten, regulieren; berichtigen; eichen; *el* abgleichen; *(Gerät)* verpassen; *(Streit)* beilegen, in Ordnung bringen, regeln, erledigen; schlichten; *(Rechnung)* berichtigen, richtigstellen; *(Konto)* ausgleichen; *itr* sich einfügen; *to ~ o.s. to* sich anpassen, sich gewöhnen an; sich einrichten, sich einstellen auf; **~able** [-əbl] regulierbar; ein-, verstellbar, justierbar; *el* abgleichbar; veränderlich; *~~ spanner (tech)* Engländer *m*; **~er, ~or** [-ə] *com* Dispacheur, Schiedsmann; *tech* Einstellmechanismus *m*; **~ing** [-iŋ] Stell-, Einstell-; *~~ lever, ring, screw* Stellhebel, -ring *m*, -schraube *f*; **~ment** [-mənt] Anpassung, Angleichung; Regelung; Einstellung, Regulierung, Justierung; Eichung *f*; *el* Abgleich; Ausgleich *m*; *(~~ device)* Einstellvorrichtung; *(Streit)* Schlichtung; *(Rechnung)* Richtigstellung, Berichtigung; *~~ of damages* Schadensregulierung *f*; *~~ screw* Stell-, Justierschraube *f*.

adjutan|cy ['ædʒutənsi] *mil* Adjutantur *f*; **~t** ['-t] Adjutant *m*; *~~ general* erste(r) Generalstabsoffizier; *Am* Kommandeur *m* der Miliz e-s Staates.

ad-lib [æd'lib] *tr itr Am fam* improvisieren.

administ|er [əd'ministə, æd-] *tr* verwalten, leiten, lenken, führen; *(Amt)* versehen; *(Trost)* spenden; *(Vergnügen)* geben; *(Medizin)* eingeben, verabreichen; *itr* verwalten, amtieren; beisteuern, beitragen (*to* zu); *to ~~ justice* Recht sprechen; *to ~~ an oath* e-n Eid abnehmen, vereidigen; *the oath was ~~ed to him* er wurde vereidigt; **~rate** [-reit] *tr Am* verwalten, kontrollieren; **~ration** [ədminis'treiʃən] Verwaltung; Amtsführung, *Am* -zeit; Administration, Behörde; Regierung; Leitung *f*; Tätigkeitsbereich *m* der Betriebsführung; *(Medizin)* Eingeben, Einflößen *n*; *(Sakrament)* Austeilung *f*, Spenden *n*; *(Eid)* Abnahme *f*; *branch of ~~* Verwaltungszweig *m*; *council of ~~* Verwaltungsrat *m*; *municipal ~~* Stadtverwaltung *f*; *~~ building* Verwaltungsgebäude *n*; *~~ of an estate* Nachlaßverwaltung *f*; *~~ of justice* Justizverwaltung; Rechtspflege *f*; *~~ of an oath* Beeidigung *f*; **~rative** [əd'ministrətiv, æd-] verwaltungsmäßig; Verwaltungs-; innerbetrieblich, -dienstlich; *through ~~ channels* auf dem Verwaltungswege; *~~ body, court* Verwaltungsbehörde *f*, -gericht *n*; *~~ expense* Verwaltungskosten *pl*; *~~ regulation* Verwaltungsvorschrift *f*; **~rator** [əd'ministreitə, æd-] Verwalter; Leiter; *(~~ of an estate)* Testamentsvollstrecker, Nachlaßverwalter *m*.

admirable ['ædmirəbl] wunderbar, bewundernswert, herrlich.

admiral ['ædmərəl] *mar zoo* Admiral *m*; Admiralsschiff *n*; *~ of the fleet* Großadmiral *m*; *rear ~* Konteradmiral *m*; *vice ~* Vizeadmiral *m*; **A~ty** ['-ti] *Br* Marineministerium; *(~~ Division)* Seeamt *n*; *First Lord of the ~~ (Br)* Marineminister *m*.

admir|ation [ædmə'reiʃən] Bewunderung *f* (*of, for* für); Gegenstand *m* der Bewunderung; **~e** [əd'maiə] *tr* bewundern (*for* wegen); hochschätzen; *Am fam* wünschen, gerne wollen (*to do* zu tun); **~er** [əd'maiərə] Bewunderer; Verehrer *m*.

admiss|ibility [ədmisi'biliti] Zulässigkeit, Statthaftigkeit *f*; **~ible** [-'misibl] zulässig, statthaft; berechtigt; **~ion** [əd'miʃən] Einlaß, Eintritt, Zutritt *m*; Zulassung; Aufnahme *f* (*to* in); *(~~ charge)* Eintrittspreis *m*, -geld; Ein-, Zugeständnis *n*, Anerkenntnis, Einräumung; Aufnahmegebühr *f*; *tech* Einlaß *m*, Einströmung *f*; *to make an ~~ of o.'s guilt* s-e Schuld eingestehen, ein Schuldbekenntnis ablegen; *~~ free* Eintritt frei! *no ~~!* Eintritt verboten! *condition of ~~* Aufnahmebedingung *f*; *price of ~~* Eintrittspreis *m*; *~~ of guilt* Geständnis *n*; *~~ valve* Einlaßventil *n*.

admit [əd'mit] *tr* herein-, vor-, zulassen, Zutritt gewähren; zum Eintritt berechtigen; aufnehmen (*to a club* in e-n Klub); *(Saal)* fassen, Raum haben für; (als wahr) anerkennen, zugeben, ein-, zugestehen; *itr* den Zugang gestatten (*to* zu); gestatten, erlauben (*of no doubt* keinen Zweifel); *to ~ to the Bar* als Rechtsanwalt zulassen; *to ~ o.'s guilt* ein Geständnis ablegen; *to ~ of no other meaning* keinen anderen Sinn, keine andere Bedeutung zulassen; **~tance** [-əns] Einlaß, Zutritt *m*; Zulassung *f*; *el* Leitwert *m*; *no ~~* Zutritt verboten! *no ~~ except on business* kein Zutritt für Unbefugte! **~tedly** [-idli] *adv* zugegebenermaßen.

admix [æd-, əd'miks] *tr* mischen; beimengen, zu-, versetzen; **~ture** [-tʃə] Beimischung, Beimengung *f*; Zusatz *m*.

admonish [əd'mɔniʃ] *tr* ermahnen; warnen (*of* vor); verwarnen.

admonit|ion [ædmo'niʃən] Ermahnung; Warnung; Verwarnung *f*; **~ory** [əd'mɔnitəri] ermahnend; (ver)warnend.

ado [ə'du:] Lärm *m*, Aufregung *f*, Umtrieb *m*; *much ~ about nothing* viel Lärm um nichts; *without more ~* ohne weitere Umstände.

adobe [ə'doubi] (Haus *n* aus) Luftziegel(n) *m*.

adolescen|ce [ædo'lesns] Jugend *f*; Jünglingsalter *n*; **~t** [-t] *a* jugendlich; *s* Jugendliche(r *m*) *f*.

adopt [ə'dɔpt] *tr jur* adoptieren, an Kindes Statt annehmen; *(Bericht)* billigen; *(Gedanken)* übernehmen, annehmen, sich zu eigen machen, sich aneignen; *(Einteilung)* wählen; *(Methode)* einführen; *(Maßnahmen)* ergreifen; *(Rat)* befolgen; *(Richtung)* einschlagen; *Br* als Kandidat aufstellen; *to ~ a motion by a vote of 10 to 5* e-n Antrag mit 10:5 Stimmen annehmen; *to ~ as a rule* zum Grundsatz machen; *to ~ the view* der Meinung sein; **~ion** [-ʃən] Adoption, Annahme *f* an Kindes Statt; Annahme, Billigung, Einführung *f*; **~ive** [-iv] angenommen; Adoptiv-.

ador|able [ə'dɔ:rəbl] anbetungswürdig; *fam* reizend, entzückend; **~ation** [ædo'reiʃən] Anbetung; Verehrung *f*; **~e** [ə'dɔ:] *tr* anbeten; verehren; *fam* wundervoll finden, sehr gern haben; **~er** [-rə] Anbeter(in *f*); Verehrer(in *f*) *m*.

adorn [ə'dɔ:n] *tr* (ver)zieren, schmücken, verschönern; **~ment** [-mənt] Schmuck *m*, Verzierung, Verschönerung *f*.

adrenal [ə'dri:nl] *a* Nebennieren-; *s (~ gland)* Nebennierendrüse *f*; **~in** [ə'drenəlin] Adrenalin *n*.

adrift [ə'drift] *adv pred a mar* treibend; *to go ~* (ab)treiben; *he is all ~ (fig)* er läßt sich ganz gehen.

adroit [ə'drɔit] gewandt, geschickt; geistig wendig.

adulat|e ['ædjuleit, *Am* 'ædʒə-] *tr* übermäßig loben; niedrig schmeicheln (*s.o.* jdm); **~ion** [ædju'leiʃən] übermäßige(s) Lob *n*; Speichelleckerei *f*; **~or** [-ə] Speichellecker *m*; **~ory** [-əri] schmeichlerisch.

adult ['ædʌlt, *Am* ə'dʌlt] *a* erwachsen; *fig* reif; *(Tier)* ausgewachsen; *s* Erwachsene(r *m*) *f*; ausgewachsene(s) Tier *n od* Pflanze *f*; **~ education** Erwachsenenbildung *f*.

adulter|ant [ə'dʌltərənt] Verfälschungsmittel *n*; **~ate** [-eit] *tr* verfälschen; *a* [-it] verfälscht; ehebrecherisch; **~ation** [ədʌltə'reiʃən] (Ver-)Fälschung *f*, Verschnitt *m*; **~ator** [-eitə] Fälscher *m*; **~er** [-ə] Ehebrecher *m*; **~ess** [-is] Ehebrecherin *f*; **~ous** [-əs] ehebrecherisch; **~y** [-i] Ehebruch *m*.

adumbrat|e ['ædəmbreit] *tr* skizzieren, roh entwerfen; andeuten, ahnen lassen; beschatten; **~ion** [-breiʃən] Skizze *f*, schwache(r) Umriß *m*; Andeutung *f*; Beschatten *n*; **~ive** [-iv] andeutend.

advance [əd'vɑ:ns] *tr* vorrücken (lassen); vorverlegen; befördern; fördern, vorantreiben, unterstützen; *tech* vorschieben, -stellen; *(Meinung)* vorbringen, äußern; *(Grund)* anführen, vortragen; *(Preis)* heraufsetzen, erhöhen, steigern; *(Geld)* vorschießen, -strecken, leihen; bevorschussen; im voraus bezahlen; *itr* vorrücken, an-, aufrücken, vorgehen, -stoßen, -dringen; anmarschieren; fortschreiten, Fortschritte machen, besser werden; sich entwickeln; *(Preise)* steigen, e-e Erhöhung erfahren; *(Qualität)* besser werden; *(Beamter)* befördert werden, aufrücken; *s* Vorrücken *n*; An-, Vormarsch *m*, Vorgehen; *(Alter)* Voranschreiten *n*; Fortschritt *m*, Besserung, Aufwärtsentwicklung; (Preis-)Erhöhung; (Wert-)Steigerung *f*; Vorschuß *m*; An-, Vorauszahlung *f*; Darlehen *n*, Kredit *m*; *(~ money)* Handgeld *n*; *(Beamter)* Beförderung *f*, Aufrücken *n*; *pl* Annäherungsversuche *m pl*, Entgegenkommen *n*, erste Schritte *m pl*; *a* Vor(aus)-; vorherig; *mil* vorgeschoben; *in* ~ im voraus, zuvor; *to be in* ~ *of o.'s times* s-r Zeit voraus sein; *to be on the* ~ *(com)* im Steigen begriffen sein; *to book in* ~ vorausbestellen, -belegen; *to make* ~*s to s.o. (fig)* jdm entgegenkommen; ~ **booking** Vorausbestellung *f*; Vorverkauf *m*; ~**d** [-t] *a* vorgeschoben, vorgeschritten; fortschrittlich, modern; *com* im voraus bezahlt; ~~ *in age* in vorgerücktem Alter; ~~ *airfield* Feldflugplatz *m*; ~~ *element, detachment* Vorausabteilung, Spitzengruppe *f*; ~~ *ignition* Frühzündung *f*; ~~ *post* Außenposten *m*; ~ **guard** *mil* Vorhut, Vorausabteilung *f*; ~**ment** [-mənt] Vorwärtsbewegung; Beförderung *f*; Fortschritt *m*, Förderung *f*; ~ **notice** Voranzeige, Voranmeldung, -kündigung *f*; ~ **payment** Vorauszahlung *f*.

advantage [əd'vɑ:ntidʒ] *s* Vorteil, Nutzen, Gewinn; Vorzug; Vorsprung *m*; Überlegenheit (*over, of* über); günstige Gelegenheit *f*; *tech* Nutzeffekt *m*; *tr* nutzen (*s.o.* jdm); fördern (*s.th.* etw); *to* ~ vorteilhaft; *to s.o.'s* ~ zu jds Gunsten; *to the best* ~ so günstig, vorteilhaft wie möglich; *to be of* ~ von Nutzen, nützlich sein; *to gain, to win an* ~ *over s.o.*, *to have an* ~ *over, to have the* ~ *of s.o.* jdm gegenüber im Vorteil sein; *to set off to* ~ vorteilhaft tragen; zur Geltung bringen; *to take* ~ *of* ausnutzen, übervorteilen (*s.o.* jdn); benutzen, wahrnehmen, ausnutzen (*s.th.* etw); *to turn to* ~ Vorteil, Nutzen ziehen aus; ~**ous** [ædvɑ:n'teidʒəs, -vən-] vorteilhaft, günstig, nützlich; einträglich.

advent ['ædvənt] Ankunft *f*, Erscheinen *n*; *A*~ Advent *m*; ~**itious** [ædven'tiʃəs] zufällig; zusätzlich, weiter.

adventure [əd'ventʃə] *s* Abenteuer *n*; *com* Spekulation *f*, Risiko *n*; *tr* wagen, riskieren; *itr* sich wagen (*on* an); ein Risiko auf sich nehmen; ~**r** [-rə] Abenteurer; *mil* Reisgänger; Spekulant; Hochstapler *m*; ~**some**, ~**ous** [-səm, -rəs] abenteuerlich; gewagt, riskant; waghalsig.

adverb ['ædvə:b] Adverb, Umstandswort *n*; ~**ial** [əd'və:biəl] adverbial.

advers|ary ['ædvəsəri] Gegner, Widersacher *m*; ~**ative** [əd'və:sətiv] gegensätzlich; *gram* adversativ; ~**e** ['ædvə:s, əd'və:s] feindlich, gegnerisch; entgegengesetzt; ungünstig, nachteilig; *(Umstände)* widrig; *(Bemerkung)* abfällig; ~~ *balance* Unterbilanz *f*; ~~ *party* Gegenpartei *f*; ~~ *weather* Schlechtwetter *n*; ~**ity** [əd'və:siti, æd-] Unglück, Mißgeschick; Elend *n*, Not *f*; *pl* Ungunst *f* der Verhältnisse.

advert [əd'və:t, æd-] *itr* hinweisen (*to* auf).

advertis|e, -ize ['ædvətaiz, *Am a.* ædvə'taiz] *tr* anzeigen, ankündigen; öffentlich anschlagen; werben für; *itr* inserieren; annoncieren, e-e Anzeige, ein Inserat aufgeben; Reklame, Propaganda machen, Werbung betreiben; *to* ~ *for* inserieren nach; durch e-e Zeitungsanzeige suchen; ~**ment** [əd'və:tismənt, *Am a.* ædvə'taizmənt] (Zeitungs-)Anzeige *f*, Inserat *n*, Annonce; Ankündigung, Bekanntmachung; Reklame, Propaganda, Werbung *f*; ~**er** [-ə] Inserent *m*; Anzeigenblatt *n*; ~**ing** [-iŋ] *s* Werbung, Reklame, Propaganda *f*; *a* werbend; Werbung-, Reklame-; *to spend money on* ~~ Geld für Reklame ausgeben; *direct mail* ~~ Kundenwerbung *f* durch Postversand; *newspaper, radio* ~~ Zeitungs-, Rundfunkreklame *f*; ~~ *agency* Werbe-, Reklamebüro *n*, Werbeagentur; Anzeigenannahme *f*; ~~ *agent* Anzeigenvertreter *m*; ~~ *campaign* Werbefeldzug *m*; ~~ *consultant* Werbeberater *m*; ~~ *costs, expenses (pl)* Reklame-, Werbekosten *pl*; ~~ *expert* Werbefachmann *m*; ~~ *hoarding* Reklametafel *f*; ~~ *lights (pl)* Lichtreklame *f*; ~~ *literature* Werbematerial *n*; ~~ *manager* Werbeleiter *m*; ~~ *media* Werbemittel *n pl*; ~~ *operator* Vermieter *m* von Reklameflächen; ~~ *paper* Anzeigenblatt *n*; ~~ *pillar* Litfaß-, Anschlagsäule *f*; ~~ *rates, charges (pl)* Anzeigentarif *m*; ~~ *service* Anzeigendienst *m*; ~~ *slogan* Werbeschlagwort *n*; ~~ *space* Reklamefläche; *(Zeitung)* Inseratenteil *m*.

advice [əd'vais] Rat(schlag) *m*; Auffassung, Meinung *f*; Gutachten *n*; Mitteilung, Benachrichtigung *f*; *com* Avis *n*; *pl* Nachrichten *f pl* (*from* von); *a piece, a bit of* ~ ein Rat; *as per* ~ *(com)* laut Avis; *to act on s.o.'s* ~ jds Rat befolgen; *to ask s.o.'s* ~ sich bei jdm Rat holen; jdn um Rat fragen; *to take s.o.'s* ~ *on a matter* sich in e-r S beraten lassen; *to take medical* ~ e-n Arzt aufsuchen; *letter of* ~ Ankündigungsschreiben *n*; ~ *of dispatch* Versandanzeige *f*; ~ *of receipt* Empfangsbestätigung *f*; ~ **note** Benachrichtigungsschreiben *n*.

advis|ability [əd'vaizəbiliti] Ratsamkeit *f*; ~**able** [-əbl] ratsam, empfehlenswert, klug, vernünftig; zweckmäßig; ~**e** [əd'vaiz] *tr* raten, empfehlen; beraten; *com* benachrichtigen, Bescheid geben, avisieren; *itr* sich beraten (*with* mit); Rat erteilen; *to* ~~ *s.o. against s.th.* jdm von etw abraten; *to be well* ~~*d* wohlberaten sein; *to keep s.o. well* ~~*d of s.th.* jdn gut auf dem laufenden halten; ~**ed** [-d] *a* durchdacht, überlegt; *as* ~~ laut Avis; *ill-, well-*~~ schlecht, gut beraten; ~**edly** [-zidli] *adv* mit Überlegung; übersichtlich; ~**er**, ~**or** [-ə] Berater, Ratgeber; *Am (Schule)* Studienberater *m*; *my legal* ~~ mein Rechtsanwalt *m*; *my medical* ~~ mein (Haus-)Arzt *m*; ~**ory** [-əri] beratend; *in an* ~~ *capacity* in beratender Eigenschaft; ~~ *board, committee* Beratungsausschuß *m*.

advoca|cy ['ædvəkəsi] Verteidigung *f*, Eintreten *n* (*of* für); *jur* Anwaltstätigkeit *f*; ~**te** [-'it] *s* Anwalt, Verteidiger; Fürsprecher, Verfechter *m*; *tr* [-'eit] verteidigen; eintreten (*s.th.* für etw), befürworten, verfechten.

adz(e) [ædz] Dechsel *f*, Querbeil *n*.

*

(a)egis ['i:dʒis] *fig* Schutz, Schirm *m*.

aeon ['i:ən, 'i:ɔn] Äon *m*; Ewigkeit *f*.

aerat|e ['eiəreit] *tr* lüften; aus-, belüften; mit Kohlensäure versetzen; ~**ion** [eiə'reiʃən] (Be-)Lüftung; *min* Bewetterung *f*; ~**or** ['-ə] Belüfter *m*.

aerial ['ɛəriəl] *a* luftig; atmosphärisch; *fig* wesenlos, ungreifbar; fliegerisch; *(Kabel)* oberirdisch; Luft-; *s* Antenne *f*; ~ **cable** Luftkabel *n*; ~~ *way* Seilschwebebahn *f*; ~ **camera** Luftbildgerät *n*; ~ **combat** Luftkampf *m*; ~ **conductor** Freileitung *f*; ~ **corridor** Flugschneise *f*; ~ **coverage** Luftsicherung *f*; ~ **current** Antennenstrom *m*; ~ **defence** Luftabwehr *f*; ~ **delivery** Versorgung *f* aus der Luft; ~ **map** Luftbildkarte *f*; ~ **navigation** Luftnavigation *f*; ~ **photo(graph)** Luftbild *n*; ~~ *interpretation* Luftbildauswertung *f*; ~ **railway** Schwebebahn *f*; ~ **reconnaissance** Luftaufklärung *f*; ~ **ropeway** Drahtseilbahn *f*; ~ **supply** Versorgung *f* aus der Luft; ~ **surveying** Luftbildmessung *f*; ~ **terminal** Antennenklemme *f*; ~ **traffic** Luftverkehr *m*; ~ **transport** Lufttransport *m*; ~ **view** Luftbild *n*; ~ **warfare** Luftkrieg *m*.

aerie ['ɛəri] Raubvogelnest *n*; (Adler-) Horst *m*; Brut *f*.

aero ['ɛərou] *a* Luft-; Flug-, Aero-; ~**batic** [ɛərə'bætik] *a* Kunstflug-; *s pl mit sing* Kunstflug *m*; ~~ *figure* Kunstflugfigur *f*; ~**drome** ['ɛərədroum] Flughafen *m*; *alternative* ~~ Ausweichhafen *m*; ~~ *beacon* Flughafen-Leuchtfeuer *n*; *pl* Platzbefeuerung *f*; ~~ *control (Br)* Flugleitung *f*; ~~ *control tower* Flugsicherungs-Kontrollturm *m*; ~~ *traffic circuit* Platzrunde *f*; ~**dynamic** ['ɛəro(u)dai'næmik] *a* aerodynamisch; *s pl mit sing* Aerodynamik *f*; ~~ *drag* Luftwiderstand *m*; ~**dyne** ['ɛəro(u)dain] Luftfahrzeug *n* schwerer als Luft; ~**foil** ['ɛərəfɔil] *s* Tragflügel *m*; *a* stromlinienförmig; ~**gram** ['ɛərəgræm] Funkspruch; Luftpost(leicht)-brief *m*; ~**lite** ['ɛərəlait] Meteorstein *m*; ~**meter** [ɛə'rɔmitə] Aerometer *n*; ~**naut** ['ɛərənɔ:t] Aeronaut *m*; ~**nautic(al)** [ɛərə'nɔ:tik(əl)] aeronautisch; ~~ *chart* Fliegerkarte *f*; ~~ *engineering* Luftfahrttechnik *f*; ~~ *medicine* Luftfahrtmedizin *f*; ~~ *station* Bodenfunkstelle *f*; ~~ *weather service* Flugwetterdienst *m*; ~**nautics** [ɛərə'nɔ:tiks] *pl mit sing* Aeronautik *f*, Flugwesen *n*; ~**plane** ['ɛərəplein] Flugzeug *n*; ~**sol** ['ɛərəsɔl] Aerosol *n*; ~**stat** ['ɛərostæt] Luftfahrzeug *n* leichter als Luft; Ballon *m*; ~**static** [ɛəro'stætik] *a* aerostatisch; *s pl mit sing* Aerostatik *f*; ~**-tow-flight** Schleppflug *m*.

aesthet|e ['i:sθi:t, 'es-] Ästhet *m*; ~**ic(al)** [i(:)s'θetik(əl), es-] *a* ästhetisch; ~**icism** [i(:)s'θetisizm, es-] Ästhetizismus *m*; ~**ics** [i(:)s'θetiks, es-] *pl mit sing* Ästhetik *f*.

aestiva|l [i:s'taivəl, *Am* 'estəvəl] sommerlich; ~**te** ['i:stiveit, 'es-] *itr* den Sommerschlaf halten.

aether ['i:θə] Äther *m*; ~**eal** [i'θiəriəl] ätherisch.

aetiology [i:ti'ɔlədʒi] Ätiologie, Ursachenforschung *f*.

afar [ə'fɑ:] *adv poet* weit, entfernt.

affab|ility [æfə'biliti] Leutseligkeit, Ansprechbarkeit *f*; ~**le** ['æfəbl] leutselig, umgänglich, ansprechbar.

affair [ə'fɛə] Geschäft *n*; Angelegenheit, Sache; Veranstaltung *f*; *(love* ~*)* Liebesverhältnis *n*; *to have an* ~ ein Verhältnis haben (*with* mit); *foreign* ~*s (pl pol)* auswärtige Angelegenheiten *f pl*; *Secretary of State for Foreign A*~*s* Außenminister *m*.

affect [ə'fekt] *tr* **1.** beeinflussen, in Mitleidenschaft ziehen, einwirken (*s.th.* auf etw); *med* angreifen; angehen, betreffen; e-n tiefen Eindruck machen (*s.o.* auf jdn), bewegen, (be)rühren, *fam* mitnehmen; **2.** gerne haben, Gefallen finden (*s.th.* an etw); vorgeben, so tun, als ob, heucheln, den Anschein zu erwecken suchen; *(e-e Gestalt)* annehmen; ~**ation** [æfek'teiʃən] Verstellung, Heuchelei *f*, Schein *m*; unnatürliche(s) Wesen *n*, Künstelei, Affektation *f*; ~**ed** [-id] *a* **1.** geziert, affektiert, unnatürlich; **2.** bewegt, beeinflußt; in Mitleidenschaft gezogen; angegriffen, erkrankt, verletzt; *com* belastet; ~**ing** [-iŋ] ergreifend, rührend, pathetisch; ~**ion** [-ʃən] (Zu-)Neigung *f*, Gefühl *n* (der Herzlichkeit); Liebe *f* (*for, towards* zu); Sinn *m* (*for* für); *med* Erkrankung *f*; ~**ionate** [-ʃ(ə)nit] liebevoll, herzlich, zärtlich; *yours* ~~*ly* mit herzlichen Grüßen.

affian|ce [ə'faiəns] *s* Vertrauen *n*; Verlobung *f*; *tr* verloben; *to be* ~~*d* verlobt sein (*to* mit); **~t** [-t] *Am* Aussteller *m* e-r eidesstattlichen Erklärung.

affidavit [æfi'deivit] *jur* eidesstattliche Versicherung *f*; *to swear an ~* e-e eidesstattliche Versicherung abgeben.

affiliat|e [ə'filieit] *tr* eng verbinden; angliedern; verschmelzen; *(Mitglied)* aufnehmen (*to, (Am) with* in); herleiten (*upon* von); *jur* die Vaterschaft zuschreiben (*upon s.o.* jdm); *itr* eng verbunden sein (*to, (Am) with* mit); sich anschließen (*to, (Am) with* an); ein Mitglied sein (*to, (Am) with* bei); *s* [-iit] *Am* Tochter(gesellschaft) *f*; Mitglied *n*; **~ed** [-id] *a* angegliedert, angeschlossen; Zweig-, Tochter-; *~~ firm* Zweigniederlassung *f*; **~ion** [əfili'eiʃən] Verbindung *f*, Anschluß *m*; Aufnahme; Angliederung; Mitgliedschaft; *jur* Feststellung *f* der Vaterschaft; *~~ case* Vaterschaftsklage *f*.

affinity [ə'finiti] Verwandtschaft (durch Heirat), Verschwägerung; enge Verbindung, Ähnlichkeit; Anziehungskraft; *chem* Affinität *f*.

affirm [ə'fə:m] *tr* (nachdrücklich) erklären, behaupten; versichern, bestätigen; *itr jur* feierlich versichern; **~ation** [æfə:'meiʃən] Bestätigung, Bekräftigung, Versicherung; Behauptung; *jur* Erklärung *f* an Eides Statt; **~ative** [-ətiv] *a* bejahend; bestätigend; *s* Bejahung *f*; *in the ~~* bejahendenfalls.

affix [ə'fiks] *tr* befestigen, anheften (*to* an); an-, beifügen; ankleben; *(Stempel)* auf-, beidrücken; *s* ['æfiks] Anhang *m*; *gram* Affix *n*.

afflatus [ə'fleitəs] Eingebung *f*.

afflict [ə'flikt] *itr* betrüben, kränken; **~ed** *a* betrübt (*at* über); leidend (*with* an); **~ion** [-ʃən] Leiden *n*, Not, Pein *f*; Kummer *m*, Betrübnis *f*; Leiden *n*, Heimsuchung *f*.

affluen|ce ['æfluəns] Zustrom; Reichtum *m*; Fülle *f*, Überfluß *m*; *to live in ~~* im Gelde schwimmen; **~t** ['-t] *a* reich, wohlhabend (*in, of, with* an); reichlich; *s* Nebenfluß *m*.

afflux ['æflʌks] Zustrom, Zufluß; *(Blut)* Andrang *m*.

afford [ə'fɔ:d] *tr* sich erlauben, sich leisten *(in Verbindung mit can, could, be able to)*; *(Vergnügen)* geben, gewähren; *(Gewinn)* einbringen; *(Schatten)* spenden; *I can't ~ it* ich kann es mir nicht leisten; *you can ~ to laugh* Sie haben gut lachen.

afforest [ə'fɔrist] *tr* aufforsten; **~ation** [əfɔris'teiʃən] Aufforstung *f*.

affranchise [ə'fræntʃaiz] *tr* befreien.

affray [ə'frei] Schlägerei *f*, Raufhandel *m*, Rauferei *f*; *jur* Landfriedensbruch *m*.

affricate ['æfrikeit] *gram* Affrikata *f*.

affright [ə'frait] *tr poet* erschrecken.

affront [ə'frʌnt] *tr* (absichtlich) beleidigen, verletzen; gegenüberstellen; trotzen (*s.o.* jdm); *s* Beleidigung *f*, Schimpf *m*.

afield [ə'fi:ld] *adv* auf dem Felde, ins Feld; fort, weg; *far ~* weit weg.

afire [ə'faiə] *adv pred a* in Flammen, in Brand, brennend *a. fig*.

aflame [ə'fleim] *adv pred a* in Flammen.

afloat [ə'flout] *adv pred a* flott, schwimmend; über Wasser; an Bord; treibend; vom Wasser bedeckt, überflutet; *fig* in Umlauf; *to get ~* flottmachen; *to keep ~* sich über Wasser halten; *to set rumours ~* Gerüchte ausstreuen.

afoot [ə'fut] *adv pred a* zu Fuß; im Gang; in Umlauf.

afore|mentioned [ə'fɔ:menʃnd], **~said** [-sed] *a* vorher erwähnt; **~thought** [-θɔ:t] *a* vorbedacht; **~time** [-taim] *adv* früher, einstmals.

afoul [ə'faul] *adv Am* in Schwierigkeit; *to run ~ of s.th.* mit etw zs.stoßen; mit etw in Schwierigkeiten geraten.

afraid [ə'freid] *pred a* erschrocken, bange; besorgt; *to be ~* (sich) fürchten, Angst haben (*of* vor); *I am ~ I have to go* ich muß leider gehen; *don't be ~ to...* scheuen Sie sich nicht zu...

afresh [ə'freʃ] *adv* wieder, erneut, von neuem, abermals.

Africa ['æfrikə] Afrika *n*; **~n** ['-ən] *s* Afrikaner (in *f*) *m*; *a* afrikanisch.

Afrika|ans [æfri'kɑ:ns] Afrikaans, Kapholländisch *n*; **~nder** [-ændə] Afrikander, Bure *m*.

aft [ɑ:ft] *a adv mar* achter(aus), achtern.

after ['ɑ:ftə] *adv* hinterher, darauf, danach, nachher; hinterdrein, hintennach; *prp (räumlich)* hinter, nach, hinter ... her; *(zeitlich)* nach; *(Reihenfolge)* nächst; hinter; *(Verhältnis)* gemäß, in der Art wie, entsprechend; *(Grund)* auf Grund von, infolge; bei; *(Gegensatz)* trotz; *conj* nachdem; *a* später, zukünftig; *mar* achter; *day ~ day* Tag für Tag; *day ~ tomorrow* übermorgen; *one ~ another* einer nach dem andern; *time ~ time* immer wieder; *~ all* schließlich, eben, doch; schließlich u. endlich, letzten Endes; *~ hours* nach Geschäftsschluß; *~ that* danach, nachher, daraufhin; **~birth** ['-bə:θ] Nachgeburt *f*; **~-care** *med* Nachbehandlung *f*; **~cost** ['-kɔst] *Am* zusätzliche Kosten *pl*; **~damp** ['-dæmp] *min* Nachschwaden *m*; **~deck** ['-dek] Achterdeck *n*; **~ dinner** nach Tisch; *~~ speech* Tischrede *f*; **~-effect** Nachwirkung *f*; **~-glow** Nachleuchten; Abendrot *n*; **~-hold** Achterladeraum *m*; **~hours** ['-auəz] *pl Am* Überstunden *f pl*; **~-image** *psychol* Nachempfindung *f*; **~-life** spätere(s) Leben; Leben *n* nach dem Tode; *in ~~* in späteren Jahren; **~math** ['-mæθ] Spätheu *n*; *fig* (unangenehme) Folgen, Nachwirkungen *f pl*; *fig* Nachwehen *f pl*, Nachspiel *n*; **~most** ['-moust] hinterst, letzt; **~noon** [-'nu:n] *s* Nachmittag *m*; *adv* u. *in the ~~* nachmittags, am Nachmittag (*at* um); *this ~~* heute nachmittag; *~~ performance* Nachmittagsvorstellung *f*; **~pains** ['-peinz] *pl* Nachwehen *f pl*; **~taste** ['-teist] Bei-, Nachgeschmack *m a. fig*; **~thought** ['-θɔ:t] nachträgliche Überlegung *f*; **~time** ['-taim] Folgezeit, Zukunft *f*; **~treatment** ['-tri:tmənt] Nachbehandlung; *tech* Weiterbearbeitung *f*; **~ward(s)** ['-wəd(z)] *adv* danach, darauf; nachher, später.

again [ə'gein, ə'gen] *adv* wieder, noch einmal, nochmals; *as much ~* noch einmal soviel; *as far ~* noch einmal soweit; *never ... ~* nie wieder, nie mehr; *now and ~* dann u. wann; *over and over ~, time and (time) ~, ~ and ~* immer wieder; *to be o.s. ~* wieder der alte, wieder auf der Höhe sein.

against [ə'genst, *bes. Br* ə'geinst] *prp* gegen, wider; entgegen(gesetzt zu); unmittelbar bei; an; für; *over ~* gegenüber; im Vergleich zu; *to be for or ~ s.th.* für oder gegen etw sein; *I'm not ~ it* ich habe nichts dagegen; *it goes ~ the grain* es geht mir gegen den Strich (*to do s.th.* etw zu tun); *he's saving money ~ a rainy day* er spart für seine alten Tage.

agape [ə'geip] *adv a* mit offenem Munde, gaffend; weit offen.

agaric ['ægərik, ə'gærik] *bot* Blätterpilz *m*.

agate ['ægit] Achat *m*; *typ Am* $5\frac{1}{2}$-Punkt-Schrift *f*; *Am fig* Zwerg *m*, Glasmurmel *f*.

age [eidʒ] *s* Alter; Lebensalter; reifere(s) Alter *n*; Generation *f*; Zeitalter *n*; Epoche; *oft pl* lange Zeit *f*; *itr* alt, reif werden; altern; *tr tech* altern, ablagern, aushärten, veredeln; *(Textil)* dämpfen; *at the ~ of* im Alter von; *in ~s* seit e-r Ewigkeit, seit Ewigkeiten, ewig; *in ~s to come* in künftigen Zeiten; *of ~* mündig, volljährig; *over ~* über der Altersgrenze; *under ~* unter 21; minderjährig, unmündig; *to come of ~* mündig, volljährig werden; *the Ice A~* die Eiszeit; *president by ~* Alterspräsident *m*; *the Stone A~* die Steinzeit; *the Middle A~s* das Mittelalter; *~ of consent* Mündigkeitsalter *n*; *~ of discretion* Strafmündigkeit *f*; **~ bracket, group** Jahrgang *m*; **~ class** Altersklasse *f*; **~ coating** Altersschicht *f*; **~d** ['-id] *a* bejahrt, betagt; sehr alt; ['-d] im Alter von; *the ~~* die Alten, die alten Leute; **~ determination** Altersbestimmung *f*; **~-in-grade** *Am* Dienstalter *n*; **~less** ['-lis] ewig; nicht alternd; **~ limit** Altersgrenze *f*; **~-long** ewig dauernd; **~-worn** *a* altersschwach.

agency ['eidʒənsi] Tätigkeit; Kraft; Vermittlung; Geschäftsstelle; Vertretung *f*, Büro *n*; Agentur, Nebenstelle, Filiale; *(government-~)* Behörde, Dienststelle; *jur* Beauftragung, Stellvertretung *f*; *by, through the ~ of* durch Vermittlung *gen*; *advertising ~* Inseratenannahme; Annoncenexpedition *f*; *debt-collecting ~* Inkassobüro *n*; *employment ~* Stellenvermittlung *f*; *news ~* Nachrichtenagentur *f*; *power of ~* Vertretungsbefugnis *f*; *sole ~* Alleinvertretung *f*; *tourist, travel(ling) ~* Reisebüro *n*; **~ business, trade** Kommissionsgeschäft *n*.

agenda [ə'dʒendə] Tagesordnung *f*; Notizbuch *n*; *to be on the ~* auf der Tagesordnung stehen; *to place, to put on the ~* auf die Tagesordnung setzen; *item on the ~* Punkt *m* der Tagesordnung.

agent ['eidʒənt] Mittel, Agens *n*, wirkende Kraft *f*; *chem* Wirkstoff; *mil* Kampfstoff; Vertreter, Repräsentant, Beauftragte(r), Agent, Bevollmächtigte(r), Mandatar; *Am fam* Handelsreisende(r); *(Polizei)* Agent, V-Mann; *Br* Wahlleiter *m*; *advertising ~* Anzeigenvertreter *m*; *commission ~* Kommissionsagent *m*; *estate ~* Grundstücksmakler *m*; *forwarding ~* Spediteur *m*; *house ~* Vermietungen *f pl*; *insurance ~* Versicherungsagent, -vertreter *m*; *putrefactive ~* Fäulniserreger *m*; *secret ~* Geheimagent *m*; *sole ~* Alleinvertreter *m*.

agglomerat|e [ə'glɔməreit] *tr itr* zs.ballen, (sich) anhäufen; [-it] *a* an-, aufgehäuft; zs.geballt; *s* Anhäufung *f*; *geol* Agglomerat *n*; **~ion** [-'reiʃən] Zs.ballung, Anhäufung; *geol* Anlagerung *f*.

agglutinate [ə'glu:tinit] *a* verklebt; *gram* agglutinierend; [-eit] *tr* zs.leimen, verkleben; agglutinieren; **~ation** [əglu:ti'neiʃən] Zs.leimen, Verkleben *n*; Agglutination *f*; **~ative** [-ətiv] verklebend; agglutinierend.

aggrandize ['ægrəndaiz, ə'grændaiz] *tr* vergrößern, erhöhen; **~ment** [ə'grændizmənt] Vergrößerung, Erhöhung *f*.

aggravat|e ['ægrəveit] *tr* verschlimmern, verschärfen; erschweren; *fam* ärgern, auf die Palme bringen; **~ed** ['-id] *a jur* schwer; erschwerend; **~ion** [ægrə'veiʃən] Verschlimmerung, Verschärfung; Erschwerung *f*; *jur* erschwerende(r) Umstand; *fam* Ärger *m*.

aggregat|e ['ægrigit] *a* gesamt, ganz; *bot* gehäuftblütig; *geol* Aggregat-;

s Aggregat n a. *geol*; Menge, Summe, Masse; Gesamtheit; Gesamtsumme *f*; *tech* Zuschlagstoff *m*; *v* ['-eit] *tr* anhäufen, vereinigen, verbinden (*to* mit); sich belaufen (£ *10* auf £10), ergeben; *itr* sich anhäufen; *in the* ~~ insgesamt; alles in allem; ~~ *amount* Gesamtbetrag *m*; ~~ *area* Gesamtfläche *f*; ~~ *volume* Gesamtumfang *m*; ~~ *weight* Gesamtgewicht *n*; **~ion** [ægri'geiʃən] Ansammlung, Anhäufung *f*; Aggregatzustand *m*.
aggress|ion [ə'greʃən] Angriff; Überfall *m*; *war of* ~~ Angriffskrieg *m*; **~ive** [ə'gresiv] angreifend, angriffslustig, aggressiv; unternehmend, energisch; **~or** [-sə] Angreifer *m*; ~~ *nation* Angreiferstaat *m*.
aggrieve [ə'gri:v] *tr* kränken; benachteiligen, beeinträchtigen, beschweren.
aghast [ə'gɑ:st] *pred a* entsetzt, entgeistert, bestürzt (*at* über).
agil|e ['ædʒail] flink, gewandt, behend, beweglich *a. fig*; **~ity** [ə'dʒiliti] Behendigkeit, Gewandtheit *f*.
agio ['ædʒou] *pl -os* Aufgeld, Agio *n*.
agitat|e ['ædʒiteit] *tr* schütteln, rütteln; auf-, erregen, beunruhigen (*about* wegen); aufwiegeln; *itr* agitieren, hetzen; sich öffentlich einsetzen (*against* gegen; *for* für); **~ion** [-'teiʃən] Auf-, Erregung; Beunruhigung; Agitation, Hetze, Aufwiegelung; (heftige) Bewegung; *tech* Umwälzung *f*; **~or** ['-ə] Aufrührer, Aufwiegler, Agitator; *tech* Rührapparat *m*, Umwälzeinrichtung *f*.
aglow [ə'glou] *pred a adv* glühend; *fig* erregt (*with* von, vor).
agnate ['ægneit] *s jur* Agnat *m*; *a* von väterlicher Seite verwandt.
agnostic [æg'nɔstik] *s* Agnostiker *m*; *a* agnostisch; **~ism** [-sizm] Agnostizismus *m*.
ago [ə'gou] *a adv* vor; *three months* ~ vor drei Monaten; *a long time* ~ schon lange her; *(just) a moment* ~ eben noch; *not long* ~ vor kurzem, unlängst; *a while* ~ vor e-r Weile; *how long* ~? wie lange ist es her?
agog [ə'gɔg] *pred a adv* eifrig; begierig (*about* auf); *sl* neugierig (*for* auf); *to be all* ~ ganz aus dem Häuschen sein (*to* um zu).
agon|ize ['ægənaiz] *itr* verzweifelte Anstrengungen machen; mit dem Tode ringen; Qualen erleiden; *fig* sich quälen; *tr* martern; **~izing** ['-iŋ] quälend, qualvoll; **~y** ['-i] verzweifelte Anstrengung *f*; furchtbare(r) Schmerz *m*, Marter *f*; Todeskampf *m*; Qual *f*; ~~ *column (Zeitung)* Seufzerspalte *f*, Familiennachrichten *f pl*.
agoraphobia [ægərə'foubiə] *med* Platzangst *f*.
agrarian [ə'grɛəriən] landwirtschaftlich; Land-, Agrar-; ~ **policy** Agrar-, Landwirtschaftspolitik *f*; ~ **reform** Bodenreform *f*.
agree [ə'gri:] *itr* zustimmen (*to* zu), einverstanden sein (*to* mit), einwilligen (*to* in); ja sagen; übereinstimmen, übereinkommen; Übereinstimmung, ein Übereinkommen erzielen (*with* mit); sich einigen, einig sein (*on* über); verabreden, vereinbaren (*on s.th.* etw); zuträglich sein (*with* für), (gut) bekommen (*with s.o.* jdm); zs.passen, harmonieren; *tr* (als richtig) anerkennen; **~able** [-iəbl] angenehm; liebenswürdig; *to be* ~~ einverstanden sein (*to* mit); **~ment** [-mənt] Vereinbarung *f*, Übereinkommen *n*, Übereinkunft *f*, Abkommen *n*, Abmachung *f*; Vertrag *m*; Zustimmung, Verständigung, Einigung *f*, Einverständnis, Einvernehmen *n*; Einklang *m*, Harmonie *f*; *as per* ~~ wie vereinbart; *by mutual* ~~ in gegenseitigem Einverständnis; *to be in* ~~ sich einig sein (*on* über); übereinstimmen (*with* mit); einig gehen (*with* mit); sich anschließen (*with* an); *to come to an* ~~ zu e-m Übereinkommen gelangen, sich einig werden, sich verständigen (*with* mit); *to reach an* ~~ e-e Vereinbarung treffen; *additional* ~~ Nebenabrede *f*; *arbitration* ~~ Schiedsvertrag *m*; *collective* ~~ Tarif-, Kollektivvertrag *m*; *hire-purchase* ~~ Abzahlungsvertrag *m*; *lease* ~~ Mietvertrag *m*; *monetary* ~~ Währungsabkommen *n*; *service* ~~ Dienstvertrag *m*; *supplementary* ~~ Zusatzabkommen *n*; *verbal* ~~ mündliche Vereinbarung *f*; ~~ *clause* Vertragsbestimmung *f*; ~~ *draft* Vertragsentwurf *m*.
agricultur|al [ægri'kʌltʃərəl] landwirtschaftlich; Ackerbau-; ~~ *college* landwirtschaftliche Hochschule *f*; ~~ *machinery* Landmaschinen *f pl*; ~~ *worker* Landarbeiter *m*· **~alist, ~ist** [-(əl)ist] Landwirt; Agronom *m*; **~e** ['ægrikʌltʃə] Landwirtschaft *f*, Ackerbau *m*; ~~ *and forestry* Land- u. Forstwirtschaft *f*.
agrimony ['ægriməni] *bot* Ackermennig *m*.
agronom|ic [ægrə'nɔmik] landwirtschaftlich; Ackerbau-; **~ist** [ə'grɔnəmist] Agronom, Diplomlandwirt *m*; **~y** [ə'grɔnəmi] (praktische) Ackerbaukunde, Landwirtschaft *f*.
aground [ə'graund] *adv pred a* gestrandet; *to run* ~ *(itr)* stranden; *tr* auf den Strand setzen.
agu|e ['eigju:] *med* Malaria *f*; Schüttelfrost *m*; **~ish** ['-iʃ] fieberhaft.
ah [ɑ:] *interj* ach! ah! **~a** [ɑ:'hɑ:] *interj* aha!
ahead [ə'hed] *pred a adv* vor, voran, voraus; vorn, nach vorn zu, vorwärts; vorn dran; im voraus; ~ *of* vor; *for some time* ~ einige Zeit lang; *full speed* ~ volle Kraft voraus; ~ *of time* vorzeitig; *to be* ~ *of s.o.* jdm voraus sein; *to get* ~ vorwärtskommen; *of s.o.* jdn überflügeln; *to go* ~ voran-, vorausgehen; weitermachen, fortfahren; vorankommen; *(Schiff)* an Fahrt gewinnen; schneller werden; *go* ~ *and tell her* sag's ihr doch! *to look* ~ sich vorsehen; an die Zukunft denken; *next* ~ Vordermann *m*; *straight* ~ gerade aus; *way* ~ *(Am)* weit voraus.
ahem [ə'hem] *interj* hm!
ahoy [ə'hɔi] *interj mar* ahoi!
aid [eid] *tr* helfen, beistehen, Beistand leisten (*s.o.* jdm; *in* bei); unterstützen; *el* verstärken; *s* Hilfe, Unterstützung *f*, Beistand; Gehilfe, Helfer *m*; Hilfsmittel *n*; *mil* Adjutant *m*; *by the* ~ *of* mit Hilfe *gen*; *in* ~ *of* zugunsten, zur Unterstützung *gen*; *to give first* ~ Erste Hilfe leisten; *to* ~ *and abet (jur)* begünstigen, Vorschub leisten; *grant in* ~ staatliche Subvention *f*; *legal* ~ Rechtshilfe *f*; *medical* ~ ärztliche Betreuung *f*; **~(e)-de-camp** ['-də'kɑ:, *Am* -kæmp] *pl ~(e)s-~ mil* Adjutant *m*; ~ **station** Truppenverbandsplatz *m*.
aigret(te) ['eigret, ei'gret] Feder-, Reiherbusch *m*; Büschel *n*; weiße(r) Reiher *m*.
ail [eil] *tr* schmerzen; *itr* krank, unpäßlich sein; *what ~s him?* was fehlt ihm? **~ing** ['-iŋ] unpäßlich, leidend; krank; **~ment** ['-mənt] Unpäßlichkeit *f*.
aileron ['eilərən] *aero* Querruder *n*.
aim [eim] *itr tr* zielen (*at* auf, nach); *(Gewehr)* anschlagen, anlegen; *(Anstrengungen)* richten (*at* auf; *to do* zu tun); *(Gegenstand)* werfen, schleudern; beabsichtigen, bezwecken (*at doing, (Am) to do* zu tun); zielen, münzen, absehen (*at* auf); *s* Ziel *n*; Zweck *m*, Absicht *f*; *to take* ~ zielen, aufs Korn nehmen; *(Gewehr)* anlegen, anschlagen; *(Gegenstand)* anvisieren; *his* ~ *was good* er zielte gut; *you are ~ing too high* du willst zu hoch hinaus; ~ *in life* Lebenszweck *m*; **~ing** ['-iŋ] zielend; ~~ *accuracy* Zielgenauigkeit *f*; ~~ *error* Zielfehler *m*; ~~ *mechanism* Zielvorrichtung *f*; ~~ *position (Gewehr)* Anschlag *m*; ~~ *silhouette* Kopfscheibe *f*; ~~ *target* Zielscheibe *f*; **~less** ['-lis] ziellos, zwecklos, planlos.

*

air [ɛə] **1.** *s* Arie; Weise *f*; Lied *n*; **2.** *s* Aussehen, Äußere(s) *n*, Miene *f*; Gebaren, Verhalten *n*; Art *f* (u. Weise); *to put on ~s, to give o.s. ~s* sich aufspielen, sich wichtig machen, angeben; **3.** *s* Luft *f*; Himmel *m*; Atmosphäre *f a. fig*; Lufthauch, leichte(r) Wind *m*; *min* Wetter *n*; *a* Luft-, Flieger-; *tr* (aus-, durch)lüften; *(Wäsche)* trocknen; kühlen, erfrischen; *fig* bekanntmachen, an die große Glocke hängen; *radio tele Am* senden; *itr* an der Luft trocknen, kühlen; frische Luft schöpfen; *by* ~ auf dem Luftwege; *in the* ~ in der Schwebe, unentschieden; unbestimmt; ruchbar, allgemein bekannt; in der Luft liegend; *in the open* ~ unter freiem Himmel; *on the* ~ über den Rundfunk; im Radio(programm); durch Fernsehen; *to be on the* ~ im Rundfunk sprechen; *to clear the* ~ die Luft reinigen *a. fig*; reinen Wein einschenken; den Kopf zurechtrücken; *to get the* ~ *(Am fam)* entlassen, auf die Straße gesetzt werden; *to give the* ~ *(Am fam)* entlassen, sitzenlassen; *to go by* ~ fliegen; *to take* ~ an die Öffentlichkeit dringen; ruchbar werden; *to take the* ~ *(aero)* abfliegen, starten; frische Luft schöpfen; *Am sl* abhauen; *my plans are still in the* ~ meine Pläne haben noch keine feste Gestalt angenommen; *there's an* ~ *of mystery about the whole affair* die Sache ist in ein geheimnisvolles Dunkel gehüllt; *there are rumours in the* ~ es heißt; angeblich soll(en); man behauptet; *castles in the* ~ Luftschlösser *n pl*; *hot* ~ *(Am)* Fantasterei *f*; *open-~ theatre* Freilichtbühne *f*; *open-~ swimming pool* Freibad *n*; ~ **action** Luftwaffeneinsatz *m*; ~ **activity** Fliegertätigkeit *f*; Flugbetrieb *m*; ~ **admission** *tech* Luftzutritt *m*; ~ **alert** Fliegeralarm *m*; Alarmbereitschaft *f*; ~ **attaché** Luft(waffen)attaché *m*; ~ **attack** Luft-, Fliegerangriff *m*; ~ **barrage** Luftsperre *f*; ~ **base** Luftstützpunkt; *Am* Fliegerhorst *m*; ~~ *commander* (Flieger-)Horstkommandant *m*; ~ **battle** Luftschlacht *f*; ~ **bath** Luftbad *n*; ~ **bladder** *anat* Luftblase *f*; **~blast** Luftstrom *m*; ~ **blower** Gebläse *n*; ~ **bomber** Bombenschütze *m*; **~borne** *a* in, aus der Luft; Luftlande-; Bord-; ~~ *attack* Angriff *m* mit Luftlandetruppen; ~~ *division* Luftlandedivision *f*; ~~ *operation* Luftlandeunternehmen *n*; ~~ *radar* Bordfunkmeßgerät *n*; ~~ *supply* Versorgung *f* auf dem Luftweg; ~~ *troops (pl)* Luftlandetruppen *f pl*; ~~ *unit* Luftlandeeinheit *f*; ~ **brake** Luftdruckbremse; *aero* Bremsklappe; ~ **brick** Hohlziegel *m*; ~ **bridge** Luftbrücke *f*; **~-brush** Spritzpistole *f*; ~ **bubble** Luftblase *f*; ~ **bump** Luftloch *n*; **~cast** ['-kɑ:st] *tr Am* durch Radio übertragen; ~ **cannon** Flugzeugkanone *f*; ~ **carriage** Lufttransport *m*; ~ **chamber** Windkessel *m*; Gasschleuse *f*; ~ **chart** Luftkarte *f*; ~ **chief marshal** *aero Br* Generalmajor *m*; ~ **commodore** *aero* Brigadegeneral *m*; ~ **cleaner** Luftreinigungsfilter *n*; ~ **cock** Lufthahn *m*, -ventil *n*; ~ **compressor** Luftkompressor *m*; ~ **company** Luftverkehrsgesellschaft *f*; ~-**condition** *tr* mit e-r Klimaanlage versehen; ~-**conditioned** *a* klimatisiert; ~-**conditioning** Klimatisierung; *(~~ plant)* Klimaanlage *f*; ~ **container** Luftbehälter *m*; ~ **cooled** *a* luftgekühlt; ~ **cooling** Luftkühlung *f*; ~ **corridor** Luftkorridor *m*; ~ **cover(age)** Luftsicherung *f*; ~**craft** ['-krɑ:ft] Flugzeug *n*; ~~ *carrier* Flugzeugträger *m*; ~~ *designer* Flugzeugkonstrukteur *m*; ~~ *engine* Flugmotor *m*; ~~ *factory, plant* Flugzeugfabrik *f*; ~~ *fuselage* Flugzeugrumpf *m*; ~~ *industry* Flugzeugindustrie *f*; ~~-*man (Br aero)* Flieger *m*; ~~-*man 2nd class* Gefreiter *m*; ~~ *marking (aero)* Kennzeichen *n*; ~~ *mechanic* Bordwart *m*; ~~ *reporting system* Flugmeldenetz *n*; ~~ *tail (aero)* Leitwerk *n*; ~~ *towing* Flugzeugschlepp *m*; ~~ *warning net* Flugmelde-, Luftwarnnetz *n*; ~~ *wireless operator (Br)* Bordfunker *m*; ~**crew** (Flugzeug-)Besatzung *f*; ~~ *man* Mitglied *n* der Besatzung; ~ **current** Luftstrom *m*, -strömung *f*; ~-**cushion** Luftkissen *n*; ~ **defence** Luftverteidigung, Flugabwehr *f*; ~~ *command* Luftverteidigungskommando *n*; ~ **density** Luftdichte *f*; ~ **display** Flugschau *f*; Schaufliegen *n*; ~ **district (command)** Luftabschnitt *m*; ~ **division** Fliegerdivision *f*; ~-**driven** *a* mit Preßluftantrieb; ~**drome** ['-droum] *Am* Flughafen *m*; ~**drop** *tr Am* mit dem Fallschirm abwerfen, versorgen; *s* Versorgung *f* aus der Luft; ~-**dry** *tr* an der Luft trocknen; ~ **eddy** Luftwirbel *m*; ~ **engineer** *Br* Bordmechaniker *m*; ~-**escape** Luftaustritt *m*; ~ **fee** Luftpostgebühr *f*; ~**field** Flugplatz; *mil aero* Horst *m*; ~~ *lighting* Flugplatzbefeuerung *f*; ~ **fight** Luftkampf *m*; ~-**filled** *a* luftgefüllt; ~ **filter** Luftfilter *m*; ~ **fleet** Luftflotte *f*; ~ **flow** Luftströmung *f*; ~**foil** *aero* Tragflügel *m*; ~~ *section* Tragflügelprofil *n*; ~**force** Luftflotte *f*; *A~ F~* Luftstreitkräfte *f pl*; ~**frame** Flugzeuggerippe *n*; ~ **freight** Luftfracht *f*; ~ **freighter** Transportflugzeug *n*; ~**graph** ['-grɑ:f] *Br* Mikroluftpostbrief *m*; ~-**gun** Luftgewehr *n*; ~ **gunner** Bordschütze *m*; ~ **head** Luftlandekopf *m*; ~**heater** Lufterhitzer *m*; ~-**hole** Luftloch *n*; ~ **hose** Luftschlauch *m*; ~-**hostess** Luftstewardeß *f*; ~ **humidity** Luftfeuchtigkeit *f*; ~**ing** ['-riŋ] (Ent-, Be-) Lüftung *f*; Trocknen *n*; Spaziergang *m*; Luftschnappen *n*; *to give an ~~ to s.th.* etw gründlich trocknen; *to go for, to take an ~~* an die frische Luft gehen; ~ **inlet** Lufteinlaßöffnung *f*; ~ **intake** Luftaufnahme *f*; ~ **interception** *aero* Jagdverteidigung *f*; ~ **jacket** *Br* Rettungsweste *f*; ~ **lag** Luftwiderstand *m*; ~ **lane** Luftschneise *f*; ~ **layer** Luftschicht *f*; ~**less** ['-lis] windstill; ohne frische Luft; ~ **letter** Luftpostbrief *m*; ~ **liaison officer** Luftwaffenverbindungsoffizier *m*; ~-**lift** Luftbrücke *f*; ~ **pump** Druckluftpumpe *f*; ~**line** Fluglinie, -gesellschaft *f*; ~**liner** Verkehrsflugzeug *n*; ~ **lock** Gasschleuse *f*; ~**mail** *tr* mit Luftpost senden; *s* Luftpost *f*; ~~ *edition (Zeitung)* Luftpostausgabe *f*; ~~ *letter, package* Luftpostbrief *m*, -paket *n*; ~**man** Flieger, Flugzeugführer *m*; ~ **map** Fliegerkarte *f*; ~ **marshal** *aero* Generalleutnant *m*; ~ **mass** Luftmasse *f*; ~-**mechanic** Flugzeugmechaniker *m*; ~**men** *aero Am* Unteroffiziere u. Mannschaften; ~-**minded** *a* flugbegeistert; **A~ Ministry** *Br* Luftfahrtministerium *n*; ~ **navigation** Flugnavigation *f*, -wesen *n*; ~ **observer** Luftbeobachter *m*; ~ **offensive** Luftoffensive *f*; **A~ Officer Commanding** Geschwaderkommodore *m*; ~ **operated** *a* pneumatisch; ~**park** *Am* kleine(r) Privatflugplatz *m*; ~ **photo(graph)** Luftbild *n*, -aufnahme *f*; ~**plane** *Am* Flugzeug *n*; *by ~~* mit dem Flugzeug; ~~ *ticket* Flugschein *m*; ~-**pocket** Luftloch *n*; ~ **police** Luftpolizei *f*; ~**port** Lufthafen *m*; ~~ *traffic control tower* Flughafen-Kontrollturm *m*; ~ **post** *Br* Luftpost *f*; ~ **power** Luftmacht; *tech* Druckluft *f*; ~ **pressure** Luftdruck *m*; ~-~ *brake* Druckluftbremse *f*; ~**proof** luftdicht; ~-**pump** Luftpumpe *f*; ~ **raid** Luft-, Fliegerangriff *m*; ~-~ *alarm* Flieger-, Luftalarm *m*; ~-~ *alert* Luftwarnung *f*; ~-~ *damage* Bombenschaden *m*; ~-~ *danger* Luftgefahr *f*; ~-~ *precautionary measures (pl)* Luftschutzmaßnahmen *f pl*; ~-~ *protection* Luftschutz *m*; ~-~ *shelter* Luftschutzkeller, -bunker *m*; ~-~ *warden* Luftschutzwart *m*; ~ **reconnaissance** Luftaufklärung *f*; ~ **region** Luftraum *m*; ~ **resistance** Luftwiderstand *m*; ~ **rifle** Luftgewehr *n*; ~ **root** *bot* Luftwurzel *f*; ~ **route** Flugstrecke, Luftverkehrslinie *f*; ~ **safety** Flugsicherheit *f*; ~**screw** *Br* Luftschraube *f*; ~-**seasoned** *a* lufttrocken; ~ **service** Luft-, Flug(linien)verkehr *m*; *Am* Luftwaffe *f*; ~-**shaft,** ~-**well** *min* Luftschacht *m*; ~**ship** Luftschiff *n*; ~~ *dock* Luftschiffhalle *f*; ~**sick** luftkrank; ~**sickness** Luftkrankheit *f*; ~ **signaller** *Br* Bordfunker *m*; ~ **sovereignty** Lufthoheit *f*; ~ **space** Luftraum *m*; *tech* Luftspalt, -zwischenraum *m*; ~ **speed** Fluggeschwindigkeit, Fahrt *f*; ~~ *indicator* Fahrtmesser *m*; ~**staff** Generalstab *m* der Luftwaffe; ~ **station** *Br* (Flieger-)Horst; Flugstützpunkt *m*; ~**stop** Hubschrauber-Landeplatz *m*; ~ **stratum** Luftschicht *f*; ~ **stream** Fahrtwind *m*; ~ **strip** Feldflugplatz *m*; Rollbahn *f*; ~ **superiority, supremacy** Luftüberlegenheit *f*; ~ **supply** Versorgung *f* aus der Luft; ~ **support** Luftunterstützung *f*; ~ **surveillance** Luftüberwachung *f*; ~ **switch** Luftschalter *m*; ~ **terminal** Flughafen (-abfertigungsgebäude *n*) *m*; ~ **ticket** Flugschein *m*; ~-**tight** luftdicht; *fig Am* undurchdringlich; ~-**to**-~ **rocket** Luftkampf-Rakete *f*; ~-**to-ground** Bord-Boden-; ~ **traffic** Flugverkehr *m*; ~~ *control service* Flugsicherung *f*; ~ **transport(ation)** Lufttransport *m*; ~~ *company* Luftverkehrsgesellschaft *f*; ~ **tube** Luftschlauch *m*; ~ **tunnel** Luftschneise *f*; ~ **vent** Entlüfterstutzen *m*; ~ **war (-fare)** Luftkrieg *m*; ~ **warning** Luftwarnung *f*; ~**way** Flugstrecke *f*; *anat* Luftweg *m*; *pl* Fluglinie *f*; ~~ *lighting* Streckenbefeuerung *f*; ~ **weather service** Flugwetterdienst *m*; ~**worthiness** ['-wə:ðinis] Lufttüchtigkeit *f*; ~**worthy** lufttüchtig; ~**y** ['-ri] luftig; leicht; dünn; hoch in der Luft; *fig* lebhaft, lustig; leichtfüßig; unwirklich, phantastisch.

aisle [ail] *(Wald)* Schneise *f*; *arch* Seitenschiff *n*; Gang *m (zwischen Sitzreihen)*.

ajar [ə'dʒɑ:] *adv* **1.** halboffen; angelehnt; **2.** im Widerstreit.

akimbo [ə'kimbou] *adv (with arms ~)* mit in die Seite gestemmten Armen.

akin [ə'kin] *pred a* (bluts-)verwandt (*to* mit); *fig* ähnlich, gleich.

alabaster ['æləbɑ:stə] *s* Alabaster *m*; *a* alabastern.

alacrity [ə'lækriti] Lebendigkeit, Munterkeit; Bereitwilligkeit *f*.

alarm [ə'lɑ:m] *s* Alarm *m*; Warnung *f*; *(~ signal)* Alarmsignal *n*; Beunruhigung *f*, Schreck *m*; Alarmvorrichtung, Warneinrichtung *f*; *(~ clock)* Wecker *m*; *tr* alarmieren; aufscheuchen; beunruhigen, erschrecken (*at* über); *to give, to sound, to ring the ~* Alarm schlagen, blasen, geben; *false*~blinde(r) Alarm *m*; ~ **bell** Warnglocke *f*; ~ **cord** Notleine *f*; ~**ing** beunruhigend, alarmierend; ~**ist** Schwarzseher *m*; ~ **readiness** Alarmbereitschaft *f*; ~ **whistle** Alarm-, Trillerpfeife *f*.

alas [ə'lɑ:s] *interj* ach! leider!

alb [ælb] Albe *f*, Meßgewand *n*.

albatross ['ælbətrɔs] *zoo* Albatros *m*.

albeit [ɔ:l'bi:it] *conj* obgleich, ungeachtet.

albino [æl'bi:nou] *pl -os biol* Albino *m*.

Albion ['ælbjən] *poet* England *n*.

album ['ælbəm] Album; Schallplattenalbum *n*; *Am* Langspielplatte *f* mit mehreren Musikstücken; *Am* Gästebuch *n*.

album|en ['ælbjumin] Eiweiß; *chem* Albumin; *bot* Endosperm *n*; ~**in** ['-in] *chem* Albumin *n*; ~~ *requirement* Eiweißbedarf *m*; ~**inous** [æl'bju:minəs] albumin-, eiweißhaltig.

alchem|ist ['ælkimist] Alchimist *m*; ~**y** ['-i] Alchimie *f*.

alcohol ['ælkəhɔl] Alkohol; Spiritus *m*; ~**ic** [ælkə'hɔlik] *a* alkoholisch; *s* Alkoholiker *m*; ~**ism** ['-izm] Alkoholismus *m*; Trunksucht *f*.

alcove ['ælkouv] Alkoven *m*; Nische, Laube *f*; Sommer-, Gartenhaus *n*.

aldehyde ['ældihaid] Aldehyd *m*.

alder ['ɔ:ldə] *bot* Erle *f*; ~**man** ['-mən] Ratsherr *m*.

*

ale [eil] Ale, *Art* Bier *n*; ~**house** Wirtschaft *f*; ~ **wife** Wirtin *f*.

alee [ə'li:] *adv pred a* unter dem Winde, in Lee.

alembic [ə'lembik] Destillierkolben, -apparat *m*.

alert [ə'lə:t] *a* wachsam; munter, lebhaft; aufgeweckt; *mil* auf Draht; *s* Alarm *m*, -signal *n*, -bereitschaft *f*; Fliegeralarm *m*; *tr* alarmieren, in Alarmbereitschaft versetzen; *to be on the ~* auf der Hut, alarmbereit sein; sich bereithalten; ~**ness** [-nis] Wachsamkeit; Alarmbereitschaft; Aufgewecktheit *f*; ~ **phase** Alarmstufe *f*; sich bereithalten; ~ **stand-by** Alarmbereitschaft *f*.

alfalfa [æl'fælfə] Alfalfa, Luzerne *f*.

al fresco [æl'freskou] *a adv* im Freien.

alga ['ælgə] *pl -ae* ['ældʒi:] *bot* Alge *f*.

algebra ['ældʒibrə] Algebra *f*; ~**ic(al)** [ældʒi'breiik(əl)] algebraisch.

alias ['eiliæs] *adv* sonst...genannt; *s* angenommene(r) Name *m*.

alibi ['ælibai] *s jur* Alibi *n*; *fam* Ausflucht, Entschuldigung *f*; *itr fam* e-e Ausrede vorbringen; *to establish, to prove o.'s ~* sein Alibi nachweisen.

alien ['eiljən] *s* Ausländer; Außenseiter, Fremde(r) *m*; *a* ausländisch; fremd, unbekannt (*to* dat); *tr jur* übertragen; ~**able** ['-əbl] übertragbar, veräußerlich; ~**ate** ['-eit] *tr* entfremden (*from* dat); abspenstig machen; *jur* übertragen, veräußern; ~**ation** [-'neiʃən] Entfremdung (*from* von); *(Eigentum)* Übertragung; Veräußerung; *(~~ of mind)* Geistesgestörtheit *f*; ~**ist** ['-ist] *jur* Irrenarzt, Psychiater *m*.

alight [ə'lait] **1.** *pred a* brennend, in Flammen; erleuchtet; *tech* gezündet; *(Gesicht)* glühend, strahlend; *to be ~* strahlen, glühen (*with* vor); *to catch ~* aufflammen; **2.** *itr (a. irr alit, alit)* ab-, aussteigen; *(Vogel)* sich setzen (*on* auf); *aero* landen, niedergehen, wassern; zufällig stoßen, treffen (*upon* auf).
ali(g)n [ə'lain] *tr* in e-e Linie bringen, (aus)richten *a. fig* (*with* nach); an-, abgleichen; begradigen; fluchten, eintrimmen; *(Vermessung)* abstecken; *fig* abstimmen (*with* auf); *itr* e-e Linie bilden; *to ~ o.s.* sich orientieren (*with* nach); sich anschließen (*with* an); **~ment** [-mənt] Ausrichtung *a. fig*; An-, Abgleichung; Begradigung, Eintrimmung; Absteckung *f*; *tech* Gleichlauf *m*; *(~~ of houses)* Fluchtlinie; *fig* Orientierung, Gruppierung *f*.
alike [ə'laik] *pred a* ähnlich, gleich; *adv* in gleicher Weise, ebenso, ohne Unterschied; *to treat ~* gleich behandeln.
aliment ['ælimənt] *s* Nahrungsmittel *n*; Unterhalt *m*; *tr* ernähren; mit Nahrungsmitteln versorgen; **~ary** [æli'mentəri] nährend, nahrhaft, Nahrungs-; *~~ canal* Nahrungskanal *m*; **~ation** [ælimen'teiʃən] Ernährung *f*; Unterhalt *m*.
alimony ['æliməni] Unterhalt *m*; Alimente *pl*; *obligation to pay ~* Unterhaltspflicht *f*.
alive [ə'laiv] *a, meist pred* lebend(ig), am Leben; wimmelnd, voll (*with* von); bewußt; munter, tätig, unternehmend; *jur* in Kraft; *el* spannungsführend; *to be ~* leben, am Leben sein; *to be ~ to s.th.* sich e-r S bewußt sein; *to be ~ with s.th.* von etw wimmeln; *to keep ~* am Leben bleiben; *s.o.* jdn über Wasser halten; *look ~* auf! beeil dich!
alkal|i ['ælkəlai] *chem* Alkali *n*, Lauge *f*; **~ine** ['-ain] alkalisch, laugenhaft; **~oid** ['ælkəlɔid] Alkaloid *n*.
all [ɔ:l] **1.** *a* ganz, gesamt; alle *pl*; allein, einzig, nur; **2.** *prn* alle, alles; jeder einzelne; **3.** *s* Gesamtheit *f*; das Ganze; Alles *n*; **4.** *adv* gänzlich; ganz u. gar; für das Stück; **5.** *above ~* vor allem, vor allen Dingen; *after ~* trotzdem; schließlich (und endlich); *and ~* und alles andere; *at ~* überhaupt; *beyond ~ doubt, question* ohne jeden Zweifel, ohne jede Frage; *for ~ that* trotzdem; *for good and ~* endgültig, für immer; *from ~ over* von überall her; *in ~* insgesamt, im ganzen; *not at ~* keineswegs; überhaupt nicht; nicht im geringsten, gar nicht; keine Ursache! nichts zu danken! *once (and) for ~* ein für allemal; *on ~ fours* auf allen vieren; *with* auf der gleichen Stufe mit; völlig gleich wie; *with ~ speed* so schnell wie möglich; **6.** *~ in ~* alles in allem; im ganzen genommen; *~ alone* ganz allein; auf sich angewiesen; *~ along* schon immer; *~ but* beinahe, nahezu; *~ day, night long* den ganzen Tag, die ganze Nacht hindurch; *~ the more difficult* um so schwieriger; *~ the go (fam)* in Mode, im Schwang; *~ gone* gänzlich verschwunden, weg; *(Nahrungsmittel)* aufgegessen, alle; *~ at once* plötzlich; zugleich; *~ right* in Ordnung; wohl; schön; einverstanden; *~ the same* ganz gleich, ganz einerlei; trotzdem; *~ of a sudden* auf einmal, plötzlich, mit einem Mal(e); *~ the time* die ganze Zeit andauernd; *~ told* alles zs.genommen; alles in allem; *~ over* zu Ende; über ganz; durch ganz; ganz u. gar; *~ over (the place)* überall; *~ over the world* in der ganzen Welt; **7.** *to be ~-in-~ to s.o.* jdm sehr am Herzen liegen; *to be ~ attention* sehr gespannt sein; *to be ~ eyes, ears* ein wachsames Auge haben; ganz Ohr sein; *to be ~ in* ganz erledigt, fertig, kaputt sein; *to be ~ of a piece with* in engem Zs.hang stehen mit; *to be ~ at sea* ganz verwirrt sein; *fam* schwimmen; *to be ~ there* auf Draht, schlau, gewitz(ig)t sein; *not to be ~ there* dumm, beschränkt sein; *to go on ~ fours* auf allen vieren kriechen; gleichmäßig voranschreiten; *to tremble ~ over* an allen Gliedern, am ganzen Körper zittern; *to wait ~ day* den ganzen Tag warten; **8.** *he isn't ~ there* er ist nicht richtig im Oberstübchen; *is that ~ right with you?* ist Ihnen das recht? *it's ~ one to me* es ist mir egal; *it's ~ over od up with him* er ist erledigt, fertig, ruiniert; *don't worry, it'll be ~ right* mach dir keine Sorgen, es kommt schon alles in Ordnung; *~ hands on deck!* alle Mann an Deck! *~ aboard! (Am)* alles einsteigen! *if that's ~ there is to it* wenn's weiter nichts ist; *that's ~ I needed* das hat mir gerade noch gefehlt; *our plans are ~ set* unsere Pläne sind völlig ausgearbeitet, liegen fest; **~-American** *a* gesamtamerikanisch; nur aus amerikanischem Material hergestellt; *s* amerikanische Nationalmannschaft *f*; amerikanische(r) Nationalspieler *m*; **~-around** *Am* vielseitig; gewandt; *~~ defence (mil)* Rundumverteidigung *f*; **~-automatic** vollautomatisch; **~-clear** *mil* Entwarnung *f*; *to sound the ~~* entwarnen; **~-electric** vollelektrisch; **~-embracing** alles umfassend; **A~ Fools Day** 1. April *m*; **A~hallow(ma)s** Allerheiligen *n*; **~-important** wesentlich; entscheidend; *to be ~~* von größter Wichtigkeit, von entscheidender Bedeutung sein; **~-in** *Br* einschließlich, gesamt, global; *~~ wrestling* Freistilringen *n*; **~-inclusive** alles umfassend; **~ a-jump** *Am sl* erregt, nervös; **~-mains** Allstrom-; *~~ radio* Allstromempfänger *m*; *~~ set* Allstromgerät *n*; **~-metal** Ganzmetall-; *~~ construction* Ganzmetallbauweise *f*; **~-out** *Am fam* umfassend, total; radikal; *~~ effort* e-e alle Kräfte beanspruchende Anstrengung *f*; **~-outer** Radikale(r) *m*; **~-purpose** Allzweck-; *~~ adhesive* Alleskleber *m*; *~~ tractor* Allzweckschlepper *m*; **~-right** *a sl* anständig, zuverlässig; ausgezeichnet; **~-round** *a Br* vielseitig; gewandt; Rundum-; *~~ businessman* sehr erfahrene(r) Geschäftsmann *m*; *~~ education* umfassende Bildung *f*; *~~ estimate* Gesamtüberschlag *m*; *~~ improvement* Verbesserung *f* insgesamt; *~~ properties (pl)* Gesamteigenschaften *f pl*; *~~ price* Globalpreis *m*; **A~ Saints' Day** Allerheiligen *n*; **~ shook (up)** *Am sl* erregt, aus der Fassung; **~ shot** *Am sl* erledigt, erschossen; **A~ Souls' Day** Allerseelen *n*; **~-steel** Ganzstahl-; *~~ body* Ganzstahlkarosserie *f*; **~-time high** *das* höchste je erzielte Ergebnis; **~-time low** absolute(r) Tiefstand *m*; **~-up** *aero* Gesamt-; *~~ weight* Gesamtgewicht *n*; **~-weather** Allwetter-; *~~ flying* Allwetterfliegen *n*; *~~ hood* Allwetterverdeck *n*; **~ wet** *Am sl* erledigt; besoffen; krank; **~-wheel** Allrad-; *~~ drive* Allrad-, Geländeantrieb *m*; **~-wing** Nurflügel-; *~~ airplane* Nurflügelflugzeug *n*; **~-wood** Ganzholz-.
allay [ə'lei] *tr* beruhigen; verringern.
allegation [æle'geiʃən] Angabe, Aussage; Behauptung *f*.
allege [ə'ledʒ] *tr* angeben, vorbringen, anführen, erklären; behaupten; einwenden; vorschützen; **~d** [-d] *a* angeblich; vermeintlich.
allegiance [ə'li:dʒəns] Bürgerpflicht, Treue zum Staat; Treue, Anhänglichkeit *f*; *oath of ~* Treueid *m*.
allegor|ic(al) [æle'gɔrik(əl)] allegorisch, sinnbildlich; **~ize** ['æligəraiz] *tr* sinnbildlich darstellen; **~y** ['æligəri] Allegorie *f*, Sinnbild *n*.
allegro [ə'leigrou] *s pl -os mus* Allegro *n*; *a adv* lebhaft.
alleluia [æli'lu:jə] Hallelujah *n*.
allerg|ic(al) [ə'lə:dʒik(əl)] *med* allergisch (*to* gegen); *to be ~~ to s.o. (fam)* jdn nicht ausstehen können; **~y** ['ælədʒi] *med* Allergie; *fam* Abneigung *f*.
alleviat|e [ə'li:vieit] *tr* erleichtern; lindern, mildern; **~ion** [əli:vi'eiʃən] Erleichterung; Linderung(smittel *n*), Milderung *f*.
alley ['æli] **1.** Gasse *f*, Gäßchen *n*; schmale(r) Gang *m*; Allee *f*; *min* Gang *m*; *(bowling ~)* Kegelbahn; **2.** große Murmel *f*; *up o.'s ~ (Am sl)* nach Geschmack, passend; *blind ~* Sackgasse; *fig* ausweglose Lage *f*; hoffnungslose(s) Unternehmen *n*; **~ cat** herumstreunende Katze *f*; **~way** Gäßchen *n*; schmale(r) Gang *m*.
alliance [ə'laiəns] Bündnis *n*; *(Familien)* Verbindung, Verschwägerung *f*; Zs.schluß *m*; Arbeitsgemeinschaft *f*; *to form an ~* ein Bündnis schließen (*with* mit); *defensive, military ~* Schutz-, Militärbündnis *n*.
allied [ə'laid, 'ælaid] *a* verbündet, alliiert; verwandt (*to* mit); *com* assoziiert.
alligator ['æligeitə] *zoo* Alligator *m*.
alliterat|ion [əlitə'reiʃən] Alliteration *f*, Stabreim *m*; **~ive** [ə'litəreitiv] alliterierend.
allocat|e ['æləkeit] *tr* an-, zuweisen, zuteilen; zur Verfügung stellen; **~ion** [ælo'keiʃən] Zuteilung, An-, Zuweisung; Verteilung, Umlage; Quote *f*; zugeteilte(r) Betrag *m*; *~~ of funds* Mittelzuweisung *f* (*to* für).
allopathy [ə'lɔpəθi] Allopathie *f*.
allot [ə'lɔt] *tr* zu-, anweisen; verteilen; zubilligen, zumessen, bestimmen; **~ment** [-mənt] Zu-, Verteilung; An-, Zuweisung *f*; Anteil *m*; *Br* Parzelle *f*; *on ~~* bei Zuteilung; *~~ garden* Schrebergarten *m*; **~ter** [-ə] Vorwähler *m*.
allotropy [ə'lɔtrəpi] Allotropie *f*.
allow [ə'lau] *tr* erlauben, gestatten *(s.o. to do, doing s.th.)*; zulassen; geben, bewilligen; anerkennen; *(Betrag)* anrechnen (*for* für); *(Ausgaben)* ansetzen (*for* für); *itr* erlauben, gestatten, zulassen (*of s.th.* etw); *Am fam* erklären, behaupten (*that* daß); *to ~ for (o.'s being s.th.)* berücksichtigen, in Betracht ziehen; berechnen; einkalkulieren, vorsehen; Platz, Zeit lassen; *will you ~ me?* darf ich? **~able** [-əbl] statthaft, zulässig; *~~ variation (tech)* Toleranz *f*; **~ance** [-əns] *s* Erlaubnis; Bewilligung, Genehmigung; Zuteilung; Berücksichtigung *f*; Zuschuß *m*, Taschengeld *n*; Vergütung; Rente; Beihilfe, Unterstützung *f*; Nachlaß, Abzug, Rabatt *m*; *tech* Toleranz, Zugabe *f*, Spielraum *m*; *sport* Vorgabe *f*; *mil* Ausstattungssoll *n*; *tr* rationieren, wirtschaftlich einteilen; *to grant an ~~* e-n Zuschuß bewilligen; *to make ~~(s) for s.th.* etw berücksichtigen, zugute halten; einkalkulieren, vorsehen; für etw Platz, Zeit lassen; *to make an ~~ on s.th.* auf etw e-n Nachlaß, e-n Rabatt gewähren; *active service ~~ (mil)* Frontzulage *f*; *additional, supplementary ~~* Nachbewilligung *f*; *children's ~~* Kindergeld *n*; *clothing monetary ~~ (mil)* Kleidergeld *n*;

daily ~~ Tagessatz *m*; *dress* ~~ Nadelgeld *n*; *extra* ~~ Sondervergütung *f*; *family* ~~ Familienzulage *f*; *tax* ~~ Steuerabzug *m*; *travel* ~~ Reisekostenentschädigung *f*; ~~ *for dependents* Familienunterstützung *f*; ~~ *for quarters* Wohnungsgeld *n*; ~~ *for subsistence* Unterhaltszuschuß *m*.

alloy ['æləi, ə'ləi] *s* Legierung; Beigabe, Mischung *f*; *tr* [ə'ləi] *tr* legieren; mischen; verschlechtern; *(Glück)* trüben; schmälern; ~ **steel** legierte(r) Stahl *m*.

allude [ə'l(j)u:d] *itr* anspielen (*to* auf), sich beziehen (*to* auf).

allur|e [ə'ljuə] *tr* ködern, (an)locken, verführen, verleiten, versuchen; *s* Reiz, Zauber *m*; ~**ement** [-mənt] Verlockung, Verführung *f*; Reiz, Köder; Bann *m*; ~**ing** [-riŋ] verlockend, verführerisch, faszinierend.

allus|ion [ə'lu:ʒən, -lju:-] Anspielung (*to* auf); zufällige Erwähnung (*to* von); Andeutung *f*; *to make an* ~~ *to* auf etw anspielen; ~**ive** [-siv] anspielend (*to* auf); voller Anspielungen.

alluv|ial [ə'l(j)u:viəl] *a geol* alluvial; angeschwemmt, angespült; *s (*~~ *soil)* Schwemmland *n*; ~~ *cone (geol)* Schuttkegel *m*; ~~ *stone* Schwemmstein *m*; ~**ium** [-iəm] *geol* Alluvium *n*; Ablagerung *f*; Schwemmland *n*.

ally ['ælai, ə'lai] *s* Bundesgenosse, Verbündete(r), Alliierte(r); *fig* Helfer *m*; *bot zoo* verwandte Gattung *f*; *tr* [ə'lai] verbünden, vereinigen (*to, with* mit); *to be allied to* eng verbunden, verwandt sein mit.

almanac ['ɔ:lmənæk] Kalender *m*, Jahrbuch *n*.

almighty [ɔ:l'maiti] *a* allmächtig; *sl* sehr, gewaltig; *the A*~ der Allmächtige.

almond ['ɑ:mənd] *bot* Mandel(baum *m*) *f*; ~-**eyed** *a* mit mandelförmigen Schlitzaugen.

almoner ['ɑ:mənə] (Sozial-)Fürsorger *m*.

almost ['ɔ:lmoust] *adv* fast, beinahe.

alms ['ɑ:mz] *meist pl* Almosen *n*; ~**giver** Almosenspender *m*; ~ **house** Altersheim für Bedürftige; *Am* Armenhaus *n*.

aloe ['ælou] *bot* Aloe, Agave *f*; *pl* Aloesaft *m*; ~ **hemp** Sisalhanf *m*.

aloft [ə'lɔft] *adv* droben, hoch oben; *mar* in der Takelage.

alone [ə'loun] *adv, a (meist nachgestellt)* allein; nur, bloß; *leave, let it* ~*!* lassen Sie es sein *od* bleiben! *leave, let me* ~*!* laß mich in Ruhe! *let* ~ ganz abgesehen von; geschweige denn.

along [ə'lɔŋ] *prp* entlang, längs; an ... entlang; *adv* geradeaus, weiter; vorwärts; der Länge nach; *all* ~ die ganze Zeit, schon immer; von Anfang an; die ganze Strecke entlang; überall; ~ *here* in dieser Richtung; ~ *with* zusammen mit; dazu, außerdem; *to come* ~ mitkommen; *to get* ~ weg-, weitergehen; Fortschritte machen (*with* mit); auskommen, fertig werden (*with* mit); durchkommen, leben; *to take* ~ mitnehmen; *how are you getting* ~*?* wie geht es Ihnen denn? *get* ~ *with you!* das glaubt kein Mensch! scher dich! ~**shore** *adv* der Küste entlang; ~**side** *adv* Seite an Seite; *mar* Bord an Bord; längsseits; ~~ *of* neben, ganz in der Nähe von; *prp* neben.

aloof [ə'lu:f] *adv* abseits, entfernt, von weitem, fern; *pred a* uninteressiert, zurückhaltend; *to stand, to hold o.s.* ~ *from s.th.* mit etw nichts zu tun haben wollen, sich von etw zurückhalten.

aloud [ə'laud] *adv* laut; vernehmlich; *to read* ~ vorlesen.

alp [ælp] Alpe, Alm *f*; *the Alps* die Alpen; ~**ine** ['-ain] alpin; sehr hoch.

alpaca [æl'pækə] *zoo* Alpaka *n*; *(Textil)* Alpakastoff *m*, -wolle *f*.

alpha ['ælfə] Alpha *n*; ~**bet** ['-bit] Alphabet, Abc *n*; ~**betical** [ælfə'betikəl] alphabetisch.

already [ɔ:l'redi] *adv* schon, bereits.

Alsatian [æl'seiʃiən] *s* Elsässer(in *f*) *m*; *a* elsässisch; ~ **dog** Schäferhund *m*.

also ['ɔ:lsou] *adv* auch, ebenfalls, gleichfalls; ferner, auch noch, dazu; ~-**ran** *s sl fig* Blindgänger, Versager *m*; *a* minderwertig; *among the* ~~*s* unter „ferner liefen".

altar ['ɔ:ltə] Altar *m*; *to lead to the* ~ zum Traualtar führen, heiraten; ~ **boy** Ministrant *m*; ~ **piece** Altargemälde *n*.

alter ['ɔ:ltə] *tr* (ab-, um-, ver)ändern, modifizieren, variieren; verwandeln; umbauen; *itr* sich wandeln, sich (ver-) ändern; ~**able** ['-rəbl] veränderlich; ~**ation** [ɔ:ltə'reiʃən] Ab-, (Ver-)Änderung, Verwandlung *f*; *subject to* ~~*s* Änderungen vorbehalten; ~~ *of course* Kurswechsel *m*.

altercat|e ['ɔ:ltəkeit] *itr* (heftig) streiten; ~**ion** [ɔ:ltə'keiʃən] (heftiger) Streit; Wortwechsel *m*, hitzige Auseinandersetzung *f*.

alternat|e [ɔ:l'tə:nit, *Am* 'ɔ:ltənit, 'ælt-] *a* abwechselnd; *bot* wechselständig; *s* Stellvertreter, Ersatzmann *m*; *v* ['ɔ:ltəneit] *tr* abwechseln lassen; umschichtig erledigen; *itr* abwechseln (*with* mit); abwechselnd, umschichtig stattfinden; *on* ~ *days* einen Tag um den andern; ~~ *angles (pl)* Wechselwinkel *m pl*; ~**ely** [-li] *adv* abwechselnd, umschichtig; ~**ing** ['ɔ:ltəneitiŋ] abwechselnd; Wechsel-; ~~ *current* Wechselstrom *m*; ~**ion** [ɔ:ltə'neiʃən] Wechsel *m*, Abwechslung, Wechselfolge; abwechselnde Betätigung *f*; ~**ive** [ɔ:l'tə:nətiv] *a* abwechselnd; sich gegenseitig ausschließend; verschieden; *s* Alternative, Doppelwahl, mehrfache Möglichkeit *f*; *there is no* ~~ es gibt keine andere Möglichkeit; ~~ *airfield, target* Ausweichflugplatz *m*, -ziel *n*; ~**or** ['ɔ:ltəneitə] Wechselstromgenerator *m*.

altho(ugh) [ɔ:l'ðou] *conj* obgleich, wenn auch, obschon.

altimeter [æl'timitə] Höhenmesser *m*.

altitude ['æltitju:d] Höhe; Höhenlage *f*; *to fly at an* ~ *of* in e-r Höhe von ... fliegen; ~ *above sea level* Höhe *f* über dem Meeresspiegel, über Normalnull; ~ **bracket** Höhenschicht *f*; ~ **chamber, depression box** Unterdruckkammer *f*; ~ **determination** Höhenbestimmung *f*; ~ **difference** Höhenunterschied *f*; ~ **indication** Höhenangabe *f*; ~ **range** *(Geschoß)* Steighöhe *f*.

alto ['æltou] *pl -s, -ti* [-ti:] *mus* Alt *m*; Altstimme *f*; ~-**relievo** ['-ri'li:vou] Hochrelief *n*.

altogether [ɔ:ltə'geðə] *adv* gänzlich, ganz und gar, völlig; alles in allem, insgesamt, im ganzen; *in the* ~ *(fam)* im Adamskostüm; *taken* ~ alles in allem genommen.

altruis|m ['æltruizm] Altruismus *m*, Uneigennützigkeit *f*; ~**t** ['-st] Altruist, selbstlose(r) Mensch *m*; ~**tic** [æltru'istik] altruistisch, selbstlos.

alum ['æləm] *chem* Alaun *m*; ~**ina** [ə'lju:minə] *chem* Tonerde *f*; ~**inate** [ə'lju:mineit] *chem* Aluminat *n*; ~**in(i)um** [ælju'min(j)əm] Aluminium *n*; ~~ *acetate* essigsaure Tonerde *f*; ~~ *foil* Aluminiumfolie *f*; ~**inous** [ə'lju:minəs] tonerdehaltig.

alumn|a [ə'lʌmnə] *pl -ae* [-i:], ~**us** [-əs] *pl -i* [-ai] *Am* Alte(r) Herr *m*.

alveol|ar [æl'viələ] alveolar; ~**us** [-ləs] *pl -i* [-ai] *anat* Alveole *f*.

always ['ɔ:lwəz, -iz, -eiz] *adv* immer, stets, (be)ständig, zu allen Zeiten, bei jeder Gelegenheit; von jeher, schon immer.

*

amalgam [ə'mælgəm] *chem* Amalgam *n*; *fig* Mischung *f*; ~**ate** [-eit] *tr* amalgamieren; vermischen; vereinigen, verschmelzen; *itr* sich vereinigen, verschmelzen; *com* fusionieren, sich zs.-schließen; ~**ation** [əmælgə'meiʃən] Amalgamierung; Vereinigung, Verschmelzung, Fusionierung *f*; Zs.schluß *m*, Fusion *f*.

amanuensis [əmænju'ensis] *pl -ses* [-si:z] Sekretär *m*.

amaranth ['æməræn θ] *bot* Amarant, Fuchsschwanz *m*; Purpurrot *n*.

amaryllis [æmə'rilis] *bot* Narzissenlilie *f*.

amass [ə'mæs] *tr* an-, aufhäufen; zs.-tragen, -bringen.

amateur ['æmətə:] *s* Amateur; Dilettant; Bastler *m*; *a* Liebhaber-; ~**ish** [æmə'tə:riʃ, 'æm-] dilettantisch.

amatory ['æmətəri] erotisch; Liebes-.

amaz|e [ə'meiz] *tr* verblüffen, sehr überraschen; *to be* ~*ed at* erstaunt sein über; ~**ement** [-mənt] Erstaunen *n*, Verblüffung *f*; ~**ing** [-iŋ] erstaunlich, verblüffend.

amazon ['æməzən] Amazone *f*; ~**ian** [æmə'zounjən] amazonenhaft.

ambassad|or [æm'bæsədə] Botschafter *m*; ~**orial** [æmbæsə'dɔ:riəl] Botschafter-; ~**ress** [-dris] Botschafterin *f*.

amber ['æmbə] *s* Bernstein *m*; *a* bernsteinfarben; ~**gris** ['-gri:s] Ambergris *m*.

ambidext|erity ['æmbideks'teriti] Beidhändigkeit; ungewöhnliche Geschicklichkeit; *pej* Unaufrichtigkeit *f*; ~**rous** ['æmbi'dekstrəs] beidhändig; sehr geschickt; *pej* hinterhältig, unaufrichtig.

ambient ['æmbient] umgebend; ~ **noise** Neben-, Raumgeräusch *n*.

ambigu|ity [æmbi'gju:iti] Mehr-, Doppeldeutigkeit; Unklarheit; Zweideutigkeit *f*; ~**ous** [æm'bigjuəs] mehr-, doppel-, zweideutig; unklar.

ambit ['æmbit] *oft pl* Umfang, Umkreis *m*; Gebiet *n*.

ambit|ion [æm'biʃən] Ehrgeiz *m*; *to be filled with* ~ ehrgeizig sein; *political* ~~*s (pl)* politische Ambitionen *f pl*; ~~ *for power* Streben *n* nach Macht; ~**ious** [-əs] ehrgeizig; begierig (*of* nach); eifrig, strebsam.

ambivalen|ce ['æmbi'veiləns] Ambivalenz *f*, widerstreitende Gefühle *n pl*; Zweiwertigkeit *f*; ~**t** [-t] ambivalent.

amble ['æmbl] *s* Paßgang; *fig* zwanglose(r) Gang *m*; *itr* im Paßgang reiten; *fig* zwanglos dahinschlendern.

ambrosia [æm'brouziə] Ambrosia, Götterspeise *f*; ~**l** [-l] ambrosisch.

ambul|ance ['æmbjuləns] Kranken-, Sanitätswagen *m*; *Br* Feldlazarett; *(*~~ *aircraft)* Sanitätsflugzeug *n*; ~~ *box* Verbandkasten *m*; ~~ *driver* Fahrer *m* e-s Sanitätswagens; ~~ *dog* Sanitätshund *m*; ~~ *station* Unfallstation *f*; ~~ *truck (mot)* Krankenwagen *m*; ~**ant** ['-ənt] wandernd; gehfähig; ~**atory** ['-ətəri] *a* umherziehend; gehfähig, beweglich; *med* ambulant; *jur* veränderlich; *s* Wandelgang *m*, -halle *f*.

ambuscade [æmbəs'keid], **ambush** ['æmbuʃ] *s* Hinterhalt *m*, Lauerstellung *f*; *tr* in den Hinterhalt legen; aus dem Hinterhalt überfallen; *itr* im Hinterhalt liegen.

ameliorat|e [ə'mi:liəreit] *tr* verbessern; *itr* besser werden; ~**ion** [əmi:liə'reiʃən] Verbesserung *f*; ~**ive** [-iv] verbessernd.

amen ['ei'men, 'ɑ:'men] Amen *n.*
amenab|ility [ə'mi:nəbiliti] Zugänglichkeit (*to* für); Verantwortlichkeit *f* (*to* gegenüber); **~le** [-l] zugänglich (*to* für); verantwortlich (*to* gegenüber), abhängig (*to* von), unterworfen (*to the law* dem Gesetz); bedroht (*to* mit).
amend [ə'mend] *tr* verbessern, berichtigen, richtigstellen; (ab)ändern; ergänzen; *itr* sich bessern, besser werden; *motion to ~ (parl)* Ergänzungsantrag *m*; **~ment** [-mənt] Verbesserung, Berichtigung, Richtigstellung; Änderung; Ergänzung(santrag *m*) *f*; Zusatzantrag *m*; *to bring forward, to move an ~~* e-n Abänderungsantrag einbringen; **~s** [-z] *pl* Entschädigung, Wiedergutmachung *f*; Ersatz *m*; Buße *f*; *to make ~~* Schadenersatz leisten.
amenity [ə'meniti, -'mi:-] Annehmlichkeit; Anmut *f*; *pl* höfliche(s) Betragen *n*, Höflichkeiten *f pl.*
American [ə'merikən] *s* Amerikaner(in *f*) *m*; *a* amerikanisch; **~ aloe** Yucca *n*; **~ cloth** Wachstuch *n*; **~ism** [-izm] amerikanische Ausdrucksweise *f*; **~ize** [-aiz] *tr* amerikanisieren; **A~ Legion** Vereinigung *f* der Kriegsteilnehmer.
amethyst ['æmiθist] *min* Amethyst *m.*
amiab|ility [eimjə'biliti] Freundlichkeit, Liebenswürdigkeit; Gutherzigkeit *f*; **~le** ['eimjəbl] liebenswürdig, freundlich; gutherzig.
amicable ['æmikəbl] freundschaftlich, friedlich; gütlich.
amid, ~st [ə'mid(st)] *prp* mitten unter; **~ship(s)** *adv* mittschiffs.
amino acids [ə'mi:nou 'æsidz] *chem* Aminosäuren *f pl.*
amiss [ə'mis] *pred a, adv* in Unordnung, schlecht, übel; mangelhaft, fehlerhaft; falsch; *to take s.th. ~* etwas übelnehmen; *there's not much ~ with it* es ist alles in Ordnung.
amity ['æmiti] Freundschaft *f*, gute(s) Einvernehmen *n*, freundschaftliche Beziehungen *f pl.*
ammeter ['æmitə] *el* Amperemeter *n*, Strommesser *m.*
ammoni|a [ə'mounjə] *chem* Ammoniak; *(~~ water)* Ammoniakwasser *n*; *~~ solution* Salmiakgeist *m*; **~ac(al)** [-k(əl)] ammoniakalisch; **~te** ['æmənait] *geol* Ammonit *m*; **~um** [-m] *chem* Ammonium *n*; *~~ chloride* Ammoniumchlorid *n*; Salmiak *m.*
ammunition [æmju'niʃən] Munition *f*; **~ bearer, handler** *(MG)* Munitionsschütze *m*; **~ belt** *(MG)* Patronen-, Munitionsgurt *m*; **~ box** Patronen-, Munitionskasten *m*; **~ clip** *(Gewehr)* Ladestreifen *m*; **~ container** Munitionsbehälter *m*; **~ depot** Munitionsdepot *n*; **~ drum** *(MG)* Trommelmagazin *n*; **~ dump** Munitionslager *n*; **~ factory** Munitionsfabrik *f*; **~ pocket, pouch** Patronentasche *f*; **~ shortage** Munitionsmangel *m*; **~ supply** Munitionsversorgung *f.*
amnesia [æm'ni:ziə] *med* Gedächtnisschwund *m.*
amnesty ['æmnisti] *s* Amnestie *f*, Straferlaß *m*; *tr* amnestieren, begnadigen.
amoeb|a [ə'mi:bə] *zoo* Amöbe *f*; **~ic** [-ik] *a* Amöben-; *~~ dysentery* Amöbenruhr *f.*
among(st) [ə'mʌŋ(st)] *prp* unter, zwischen; in; bei; *~ other things* unter anderem; neben anderem, neben anderen Dingen; *they agreed ~ themselves* sie kamen untereinander überein.
amoral [æ'mɔrəl, *Am* ei-] amoralisch.
amorous ['æmərəs] verliebt (*of* in); liebevoll.
amorphous [ə'mɔ:fəs] *chem min* amorph; unkristallinisch; gestaltlos, formlos; anomal.
amortiz|ation, ~ement [əmɔ:ti'zeiʃən, ə'mɔ:tizmənt] Amortisation, Tilgung; Rückzahlung *f*; **~e, amortise** [ə'mɔ:taiz] *tr* amortisieren, tilgen.
amount [ə'maunt] *s* Betrag *m*, Summe; Menge *f*, Umfang *m*; Bedeutung, Auswirkung *f*; *itr* sich belaufen (*to* auf), (den Betrag) erreichen (*to* von), betragen, ausmachen (*to s.th.* etw); hinauslaufen (*to* auf); bedeuten (*to s.th.* etw); *any ~ of (fam)* viel; *up to the ~ of* bis zum Betrage von, nicht mehr als; im Werte von; *to be large in ~* dem Umfang nach groß sein; *to ~ to nothing* belanglos sein; *he doesn't ~ to much* mit ihm ist nicht viel anzufangen; *aggregate, total ~* Gesamtbetrag *m*; *nominal ~* Nennwert *m*; *~ of damages* Höhe *f* des Schadensersatzes; *~ of the debt* Schuldsumme *f*; *~ of indemnification* Entschädigungssumme *f*; *~ of punishment* Strafmaß *n*; *~ of security* Kautionssumme *f*; **~ carried forward, over** *com* Übertrag *m.*
amper|age [æm'pɛəridʒ] Stromstärke *f*; **~e** ['æmpɛə] Ampere *n*; *~~ hour* Amperestunde *f*; *~~-meter* Amperemeter *n.*
amphibi|an [æm'fibiən] *s zoo* Amphibie *f*; *aero* Amphibienflugzeug *n*; *a* amphibisch; Amphibien-; *~~ tank* Amphibienkampfwagen *m*; **~ous** [-əs] amphibisch; Amphibien-; *~~ operation (mil)* Landungsunternehmen *n.*
amphitheatre ['æmfiθiətə] Amphitheater *n*; Arena *f*; große(r) Hörsaal *m* (mit ansteigenden Sitzreihen).
ample ['æmpl] geräumig, ausgedehnt; reichlich; ausreichend, genügend.
amplif|ication [æmplifi'keiʃən] Erweiterung, Ausdehnung; *el* Verstärkung *f*; zusätzliche Einzelheiten, weitere Ausführungen *f pl* (*upon* über); ausführliche Darstellung; *pej* Übertreibung *f*; **~ier** ['æmplifaiə] *el* Verstärker *m*; *(~~ tube)* Verstärkerröhre *f*; Lautsprecher *m*; Vergrößerungslinse *f*; **~y** ['æmplifai] *tr* verstärken *a. el*; erweitern, ausdehnen, vergrößern; *(Thema)* näher ausführen, ausführlich darstellen; *itr* sich ausführlich, weitschweifig auslassen (*upon* über).
amplitude ['æmplitju:d] Weite, Größe *f*, Umfang *m*; Fülle; *phys* Amplitude, Schwingungsweite *f*; *tech* Größt-, Scheitelwert *m.*
ampoule ['æmpu:l] *med* Ampulle *f.*
amputat|e ['æmpjuteit] *tr* amputieren, abnehmen; abschneiden; **~ion** [æmpju'teiʃən] *med* Amputation *f*; **amputee** [æmpju'ti:] *Am* Amputierte(r) *m.*
amuck [ə'mʌk] *adv*: *to run ~* Amok laufen; *fig* außer Kontrolle geraten.
amulet ['æmjulet] Amulett *n.*
amus|e [ə'mju:z] *tr* belustigen, amüsieren, erheitern; unterhalten, erfreuen; *to ~~ o.s.* sich die Zeit vertreiben (*by doing s.th.* mit); **~ement** [-mənt] Belustigung, Unterhaltung *f*; Zeitvertreib *m*, Vergnügen *n* (*at* über); *pl* Vergnügungen *f pl*; *to do s.th. for ~~* etw zum Zeitvertreib tun; **~ing** [-iŋ] unterhaltend, belustigend, amüsant (*to* für).
amyl ['æmil] *chem* Amyl *n*; **~ acetate** Fruchtäther *m*; **~oid** ['-ɔid] *a* stärkeartig, -haltig; *s* stärkehaltige(s) Nahrungsmittel *n.*
an [ən, æn] *unbest. Artikel s. a.*
anabatic [ænə'bætik] *(Wind)* steigend; **~ wind** Aufwind *m.*
anachronism [ə'nækrənizm] Anachronismus *m*; **~chronistic** [ənækrə'nistik] anachronistisch; **~conda** [ænə'kɔndə] Anakonda *f.*
an(a)emi|a [ə'ni:miə] *med* Anämie, Blutarmut *f*; **~c** [-k] anämisch, blutarm; bleichsüchtig.
an(a)esthe|sia [æni:s'θi:ziə] Unempfindlichkeit; *med* Narkose *f*; **~tic** [-'θetik] *a* unempfindlich; betäubend; *s* Betäubungsmittel *n*; **~tize** [æ'ni:sθətaiz] *tr* betäuben.
anagram ['ænəgræm] Anagramm *n.*
anal|ects ['ænəlekts] *pl* Auswahl, Blumenlese *f*; **~gesia** [ænæl'dʒi:ziə] Gefühllosigkeit, Schmerzunempfindlichkeit *f*; **~gesic** [ænæl'dʒi:sik, -'dʒe-] schmerzunempfindlich.
analog|ic(al) [ænə'lɔdʒik(əl)] analogisch; **~ous** [ə'næləgəs] analog, entsprechend; ähnlich, vergleichbar; **~ue** ['ænəlɔg] Analogon *n*; **~y** [ə'nælədʒi] Analogie, Ähnlichkeit *f*; Vergleich *m*; *on the ~~ of* analog, gemäß *gen.*
analy|se, ~ze ['ænəlaiz] *tr* analysieren, zergliedern, zerlegen; bestimmen; *fig* untersuchen; *(Bericht)* auswerten; *math* mit Gleichungen lösen; berechnen; **~sis** [ə'næləsis] *pl -ses* [-si:z] Analyse, Zerlegung; *math* Analysis; Berechnung; Untersuchung, Auswertung *f*; *(~~ of an account)* Rechnungs-, Kontenauszug *m*; **~st** ['ænəlist] Analytiker; *Am* Psychotherapeut *m*; *food ~~* Lebensmittelchemiker *m*; **~tic(al)** [-'litik(əl)] analytisch; *~~al geometry* analytische Geometrie *f.*
anapaest ['ænəpi:st] Anapäst *m.*
anarch|ic(al) [æ'nɑ:kik(əl)] anarchisch; anarchistisch; staatsfeindlich; **~ism** ['ænəkizm] Anarchismus *m*; **~(ist)** ['ænək(ist)] Anarchist *m*; **~istic** [ænə'kistik] anarchistisch; **~y** ['ænəki] Anarchie, Gesetzlosigkeit *f.*
anathema [ə'næθimə] Kirchenbann; Fluch; Gebannte(r), Verfluchte(r) *m.*
anatom|ic(al) [ænə'tɔmikəl] anatomisch; **~ist** [ə'nætəmist] Anatom *m*; **~ize** [ə'nætəmaiz] *tr* sezieren; zerlegen; *fig* Einzelheiten prüfen; **~y** [ə'nætəmi] Anatomie; *fig* genaue Analyse *f.*
ancest|or ['ænsistə] Vorfahre, Ahn *m*; **~ral** [æn'sestrəl] angestammt; Ur-, Stamm-; **~ry** ['-ri] Ahnen, Vorfahren *m pl.*
anchor ['æŋkə] *s* Anker; *fig* Halt *m*, Zuflucht *f*; *tr* verankern; befestigen; *itr* ankern, vor Anker liegen; *at ~* vor Anker; *to cast ~* Anker werfen; *to ride at ~* vor Anker liegen; *to weigh ~* (den) Anker lichten; *as if ~ed to the spot (fig)* wie angenagelt; **~age** ['-ridʒ] Liege-, Ankerplatz *m*, -gebühr; Verankerung *f*; *fig* feste(r) Halt *m*; Einsiedelei *f*; **~ bolt** Ankerbolzen *m*; **~ buoy** Ankerboje *f*; **~ cable** Ankertau *n*; **~ clamp** Abspannklemme *f*; **~ess** ['-ris] Einsiedlerin *f*; **~et, ~ite** ['-ret, '-rait] Anachoret, Einsiedler *m*; **~ ice** Bodeneis *n*; **~ pole, tower** Ankermast *m.*
anchovy [æn'tʃouvi] Anschovis, Sardelle *f.*
ancient ['einʃənt] *a (Gegenstand)* sehr alt, uralt, aus alter Zeit; antik; *(Mensch)* bejahrt; *s* bejahrte(r) Mann *m*; *the ~s* die alten Griechen u. Römer.
ancillary [æn'siləri] Hilfs-, Zusatz-; zusätzlich, ergänzend (*to* für).

*

and [ænd, ənd, ən] *conj* und; und auch; und dazu; *fam* um zu; *for days ~ days* tagelang; *years ~ years* unzählige Jahre; *nice ~ warm* schön warm; *~ so forth, on* usw.; *~ sundry* u. dergleichen; *try ~ do it* versuch's doch mal! *wait ~ see* abwarten (u. Tee trinken)!
andante [æn'dænti] *s mus* Andante *n.*
andiron ['ændaiən] Feuerbock *m.*
anecdot|al [ænek'doutl] anekdotisch; **~e** ['ænikdout] Anekdote *f.*
anemometer [æni'mɔmitə] Anemometer *n*, Windstärkemesser *m.*

anemone [ə'neməni] *bot* Anemone *f*, Windröschen *n*.
aneroid ['ænərɔid] *(~ barometer)* Aneroid-, Dosenbarometer *n*.
anew [ə'nju:] *adv* wieder, von neuem; auf neue Weise.
angel ['eindʒəl] *s* Engel *a. fig*; Geist; *sl* Geldgeber *m*; *Am sl aero* 1000 Fuß; *tr sl* finanzieren; *guardian* ~ Schutzengel *m*; **~-fish** Engelhai *m*; ~ **food** *Am Art* Gebäck *n*; **~ic** [æn'dʒelik] engelhaft; **~ica** [æn'dʒelikə] *bot* Angelika, Engelwurz *f*; **~us** ['ændʒiləs] Angelus-Läuten *n*.
anger ['æŋgə] *s* Ärger, Zorn *m*, Wut *f*; *tr* erzürnen, wütend machen; *in (a moment of)* ~ im Zorn.
angina [æn'dʒainə] *med* Angina, Halsentzündung *f*; ~ **pectoris** Angina pectoris, Herzbräune *f*, -krämpfe *m pl*.
angle ['æŋgl] **1.** *itr* angeln (*for* nach) *a. fig*; *fig* listig zu erreichen versuchen (*for s.th.* etw); **~r** ['-ə] Angler; *fig* Schlauberger; *zoo* Seeteufel *m*; ~ **worm** *zoo* Regenwurm *m*; **2.** *s* Winkel *m*, Ecke *f*; *tech* Knie *n*; *Am* Gesichtspunkt *m*, Auffassung, Stellungnahme *f*, persönliche(r) Vorteil *m*; *tr fam* e-e andere Richtung geben, entstellen, verdrehen; *tech* bördeln, umbiegen; *to be at an ~ to* e-n Winkel bilden mit; *to consider s.th. from all ~s* etw von allen Seiten betrachten; *acute, right, obtuse ~* spitze(r), rechte(r), stumpfe(r) Winkel *m*; *~ of attack* Anstellwinkel *m*; *~ of elevation* Höhenwinkel *m*; *~ of impact, incidence* Auftreff-, Einfallwinkel *m*; *~ of refraction* Brechungswinkel *m*; *~ of slope* Böschungswinkel *m*; *~ of vision* Gesichtswinkel *m*; ~ **bar, iron** Winkeleisen *n*.
Anglican ['æŋglikən] *s* Anglikaner *m*; *a* anglikanisch; *Am* englisch; **~ism** ['-izm] Anglikanismus *m*.
anglici|sm ['æŋglisizm] Anglizismus *m*; typisch englische Ausdrucksweise *f*; **~st** ['-st] Anglist *m*; **~ze** ['-aiz] *tr* englisch machen.
Anglo ['æŋglo(u)] *a* Anglo-; englisch; **~-American** angloamerikanisch; **~-French** anglofranzösisch; **a~mania** [-'meiniə] übertriebene Vorliebe *f* für englisches Wesen; **~-Norman** anglonormannisch; **a~phile** ['-fail] Freund *m* Englands; **a~phobe** ['-foub] Feind *m* Englands; **a~phobia** ['foubiə] Haß *m* gegen England; **~-Saxon** *s* Angelsachse *m*; *a* angelsächsisch.
angora [æŋ'gɔrə] Angorawolle *f*; ~ **cat, goat, rabbit** Angorakatze, -ziege *f*, -kaninchen *n*.
angry ['æŋgri] ärgerlich, zornig (*at s.th.* über etw; *with s.o.* auf jdn); *(Meer)* stürmisch; wild; *med* entzündet u. schmerzhaft; *to be ~* sich ärgern, ärgerlich sein; böse sein (*at, with* auf, mit); *what are you ~ about?* worüber ärgern Sie sich?
anguish ['æŋgwiʃ] große(r) Schmerz *m*, Qual *f*; *to be in ~* Qualen ausstehen *a. fig*.
angular ['æŋgjulə] wink(e)lig; eckig, spitzig, kantig; *(Mensch)* knochig; *fig* steif, hölzern; schroff; Winkel-; **~ity** [æŋgju'læriti] Eckigkeit; Winkellage; *fig* Steifheit *f*.

*

anhydr|id(e) [æn'haidrid, -aid] *chem* Anhydrid *n*; **~ous** [-əs] *chem* (kristall-) wasserfrei; Dörr-.
anil ['ænil] Indigo *n*; **~in(e)** ['-i:n, '-ain] Anilin *n*; *~~ dye* Anilinfarbstoff *m*.
animadver|sion [ænimæd'və:ʃən] Tadel *m*, Kritik (*on* an), absprechende Bemerkung *f* (*on* über); **~t** [-t] *tr* tadeln, kritisieren, ungünstig beurteilen.
animal ['æniməl] *s* Tier, (tierisches) Lebewesen *n*; *fig* rohe(r) Kerl *m*; *the ~* das Tierische; *a* tierisch, animalisch; *fig* grob, bestialisch, sinnlich; ~ **charcoal** Tierkohle *f*; **~cule** [æni'mælkju:l] mikroskopisch kleine(s) Tierchen *n*; ~ **fat** Tierfett *n*; ~ **glue** Tierleim *m*; ~ **hair** Tierhaar *n*; ~ **husbandry** Viehzucht *f*; **~ism** ['-izm] Animalismus *m*; Lebenskraft *f*; ~ **kingdom** Tierreich *n*; ~ **products** *pl* tierische Rohprodukte *n pl*; ~ **spirits** *pl* Lebensgeister *m pl*, -kraft; unbekümmerte Heiterkeit *f*.
animat|e ['ænimeit] *tr* beleben, mit Leben erfüllen; animieren, anregen; aufmuntern, ermutigen, begeistern; *(Sache)* bewegen; *a* ['-it] belebt, lebendig; *fig* lebendig, kraftvoll, frohgemut; **~ed** ['-id] *a* lebendig, voller Leben; lebhaft, kraftvoll, heiter; beseelt (*by, with* von); *~~ cartoon* Trickfilm *m*; **~ion** [æni'meiʃən] Belebung *f*; Leben *n*; Aufmunterung; Lebhaftigkeit; Munterkeit *f*; **~or** ['-ə] Trickfilmzeichner *m*.
animism ['ænimizm] Animismus *m*.
anim|osity [æni'mɔsiti] Haß *m*, Feindseligkeit; starke Abneigung *f* (*against* gegen; *between* zwischen); **~us** ['æniməs] Absicht *f*, Beweggrund *m*; Einstellung; Abneigung *f*, Haß *m*.
anis|e ['ænis] *bot* Anis *m*; **~eed** ['-i:d] Anissamen *m*.
ank|le ['æŋkl] Fußknöchel *m*; *to sprain o.'s ~~* sich den Fuß verstauchen; *~~ bone* Fußknochen *m*; **~let** ['-lit] Band *n*, Fessel *f* um den Knöchel; (Frauen-)Söckchen *n*; **~ylosis** [æŋki'lousis] *med* Gelenkversteifung, -verwachsung *f*.
annal|ist ['ænəlist] Chronist *m*; **~s** ['-z] *pl* Jahrbücher *n pl*.
anneal [ə'ni:l] *tr* anlassen, (aus)glühen, tempern; *~ed copper* Weichkupfer *n*; **~ing** [-iŋ] (Aus-)Glühen, Härten *n*.
annex ['æneks] *s arch a. ~e* Anbau *m*, Nebengebäude *n*; Anhang *m*, Anlage *f*; Nachtrag, Zusatz *m* (*to* zu); *tr* [ə'neks] *pol* annektieren, einverleiben, eingliedern (*to* in); anhängen, beifügen; *as ~ed* laut Anlage; **~ation** [ænek'seiʃən] *pol* Annexion, Eingliederung (*to* in); Anlage, Beifügung *f*.
annihilat|e [ə'naiəleit] *tr* vernichten, ausrotten; ausmerzen; **~ing fire** *mil* Vernichtungsfeuer *n*; **~ion** [ənaiə'leiʃən] Vernichtung, Zerstörung *f*.
anniversary [æni'və:səri] Jahrestag *m*; *wedding ~* Hochzeitstag *m*.
annotat|e ['æno(u)teit] *tr* mit Anmerkungen versehen, kommentieren; *itr* Anmerkungen machen (*on* zu); **~ion** [æno(u)'teiʃən] Anmerkung *f*, Kommentar *m*, Erläuterung *f*; **~or** ['-ə] Kommentator *m*.
announce [ə'nauns] *tr* ankündigen, (an)melden; ansagen, durchgeben; bekanntgeben, -machen, anzeigen; **~ment** [-mənt] Ankündigung, Anzeige, Bekanntmachung; *radio* Durchsage *f*; **~r** [-ə] *radio* Ansager *m*.
annoy [ə'nɔi] *tr* belästigen, stören; ärgern; quälen, plagen; verletzen; *to be ~ed* sich ärgern (*at s.th.* über etw; *with s.o.* über jdn); **~ance** [-əns] Ärger *m*, Störung *f*; Verdruß *m*, Verstimmung; Belästigung; lästige Person *f*; **~ing** [-iŋ] lästig, störend; ärgerlich.
annual ['ænjuəl] *a* jährlich; *bot* einjährig; Jahres-; *s* Jahrbuch *n*; einjährige Pflanze *f*; Jahresgehalt; Jahresgedächtnis(messe *f*) *n*; ~ **amount** Jahresbetrag *m*; ~ **balance** Jahresabschluß *m*; ~ **consumption** Jahresverbrauch *m*; ~ **estimates** *pl* Jahresvoranschlag *m*; ~ **fee** Jahresbeitrag *m*, -gebühr *f*; ~ **financial statement** Jahresabschluß *m*; ~ **income** Jahreseinkommen *n*; **~ize** ['-aiz] *tr* auf Jahresbasis umrechnen; **~ly** ['-i] *adv* jährlich, Jahr für Jahr; ~ **meeting** Jahres-, Hauptversammlung *f*; ~ **proceeds** *pl* Jahresertrag *m*; ~ **production** Jahreserzeugung *f*; ~ **profit** Jahresgewinn *m*; ~ **receipts** *pl* Jahreseinnahmen *f pl*; ~ **rent** Jahresmiete *f*; ~ **report** Jahresbericht *m*; ~ **result** Jahresergebnis *n*; ~ **revenue** Jahreseinkommen *n*; ~ **ring** *bot* Jahresring *m*; ~ **salary** Jahresgehalt *n*; ~ **subscription** Jahresabonnement *n*; ~ **turnover** Jahresumsatz *m*; ~ **wage** Jahreslohn *m*.
annuit|ant [ə'nju(:)itənt] Rentenempfänger, Rentner *m*; **~y** [-i] Jahresrente, Annuität *f*; *to settle an ~~ on s.o.* jdm e-e Rente aussetzen; *government ~~* Staatsrente *f*; *invalidity ~~* Invalidenrente *f*; *life ~~* Lebens-, Leibrente *f*; *~~ agreement* Leibrentenvertrag *m*; *~~ bank* Rentenbank *f*; *~~ bond* Rentenpapier *n*; *~~ charge* Rentenschuld *f*; *~~ insurance* Rentenversicherung *f*.
annul [ə'nʌl] *tr* annullieren, aufheben, für ungültig erklären, außer Kraft setzen; abschaffen, auflösen; *(Vertrag)* kündigen; *(Verfügung)* aufheben; **~ment** [-mənt] Annullierung, Aufhebung, Auflösung, Nichtigkeitserklärung; Abschaffung *f*; *action for ~~* Anfechtungsklage *f*.
annul|ar ['ænjulə] ringförmig; *~~ body* Ringkörper *m*; **~et** ['-et] kleine(r) Ring *m*; *arch* schmale Ringverzierung *f*; **~us** ['-əs] Ring(raum) *m*.
annunciat|e [ə'nʌnsieit, -ʃi-] *tr* ankündigen; **~ion** [ənʌnsi'eiʃən] Verkündigung *f*; *A~~* Mariae Verkündigung *(25. März)*; **~or** [ənʌnsi'eitə] Ankündiger *m*; Meldeanlage *f*.
anod|e ['ænoud] *el* Anode *f*; *~~ battery* Anodenbatterie *f*; *~~ circuit* Anodenkreis *m*; *~~ current* Anodenstrom *m*; *~~ slime* Anodenschlamm *m*; *~~ voltage* Anodenspannung *f*; **~ize** ['ænədaiz] *tr* eloxieren; **~yne** ['ænədain] schmerzstillend(es Mittel *n*).
anoint [ə'nɔint] *tr* salben *a. rel*.
anomal|ous [ə'nɔmələs] unregelmäßig; anomal; **~y** [-i] Unregelmäßigkeit, Anomalie; *biol* Mißbildung *f*.
anon [ə'nɔn] *adv* bald, in Kürze; ein andermal; wieder; *ever and ~* von Zeit zu Zeit.
anonym|ity [ænə'nimiti] Anonymität *f*; **~ous** [ə'nɔniməs] anonym, ungenannt, ohne Namensnennung.
ano|pheles [ə'nɔfəli:z] *zoo* Anopheles *f*; **~rak** ['ɑ:norɑ:k] Anorak *m*.
another [ə'nʌðə] *a prn* ein anderer; noch ein; ein zweiter, -s; *at ~ time* zu e-r anderen Zeit; *in ~ place* an e-m anderen Ort; *one ~* einander, sich.
answer ['ɑ:nsə] *s* Antwort; Entgegnung, Erwiderung *f*; Bescheid *m* (*to* auf); *(Problem)* Lösung *f*, Resultat *n*; *jur* Replik, Gegenschrift, Verteidigung *f*; *itr* antworten, erwidern, entgegnen; verantwortlich sein, haften, bürgen (*for* für); einstehen, die Verantwortung übernehmen (*for* für); dienen (*for a purpose* e-m Zweck); entsprechen (*to a description* e-r Beschreibung); übereinstimmen (*to* mit); reagieren (*to* auf); *(Plan)* Erfolg haben; *tr* beantworten; e-e Antwort geben (*s.o.* jdm); entsprechen (*a purpose* e-m Zweck); erfüllen (*s.th.* etw); *(Wechsel)* einlösen; *(Verpflichtungen)* nachkommen; *(Anforderungen)* ge-

nügen; *(Schuld)* bezahlen; *in ~ to* in Beantwortung *gen*, als Antwort auf; *to ~ back* unverschämt antworten; *to ~ up* sofort, laut antworten; e-e Antwort bereit haben (*to s.o.* für jdn); *to ~ the bell, door* (auf ein Klingelzeichen) die Tür öffnen; *to ~ the helm* dem Steuer gehorchen; *to ~ to the name of* ... auf den Namen ... hören; *to ~ a summons (jur)* e-r Ladung Folge leisten; *to ~ the (tele)phone* ans Telephon gehen; *he knows all the ~s (fam)* er ist ein schlauer Bursche; *pej* er ist abgebrüht; **~able** ['-rəbl] beantwortbar; *(Problem)* lösbar; *jur* verantwortlich; *to be (held) ~ ~ to s.o. for s.th.* für etw gegenüber jdm verantwortlich sein.

ant [ænt] Ameise *f*; **~-bear** Ameisenbär *m*; **~-eater** Ameisenfresser *m*; **~-hill** Ameisenhaufen *m*.

antacid ['ænt'æsid] *a* säurebindend, neutralisierend; *s* Mittel *n* gegen Magensäure.

antagoni|sm [æn'tægənizm] Gegensatz *m*; Feindseligkeit *f*; Widerspruch *m*; *to be in ~ ~ with* im Gegensatz stehen zu; **~st** [-st] Gegner, Widersacher *m*; **~stic** [æntægə'nistik] gegensätzlich, widerstreitend, feindlich; **~ze** [-aiz] *tr* zu s-m Gegner machen; entfremden; den Widerstand hervorrufen (*s.o.* jds); *Am* bekämpfen, Widerstand leisten (*s.th.* gegen etw), ablehnen.

antarctic [ænt'ɑ:ktik] *s* Antarktis *f*; *a* antarktisch; **~ circle** Südpolarkreis *m*.

ante ['ænti] *s (Poker)* Einsatz *m*; *tr Am (s-n Einsatz, Anteil)* bezahlen.

anteceden|ce [ænti'si:dəns] Vortritt, Vorrang *m*; *astr* Rückläufigkeit *f*; **~t** [-t] *a* früher (*to* als); vorangehend; *s* frühere(s) Ereignis *n*; Voraussetzung, Vorstufe *f*; *math* Vorderglied *n*; *gram* Vordersatz *m*, Bezugswort *n*; *pl* Vorleben *n*, Vergangenheit *f*.

antechamber ['æntitʃeimbə] Vorzimmer *n*; *tech* Vorkammer *f*.

antedate ['ænti'deit] *tr* vordatieren; e-r früheren Zeit zuweisen; vorausnehmen.

antediluvian ['æntidi'lu:viən] *a* vorsintflutlich *a. fig*; altmodisch; *s* altmodische(r) Mensch *m*, *fam* Fossil *n*.

antelope ['æntiloup] *zoo* Antilope *f*.

antenatal ['ænti'neitəl] vor der Geburt (liegend).

antenna [æn'tenə] *pl -ae* [-i:] *zoo* Fühler *m*; *pl -s tech* Antenne *f*; **~ mast, pole** Funkmast *m*; **~ power** Antennenleistung *f*.

antenuptial ['ænti'nʌpʃəl] vorehelich.

anterior [æn'tiəriə] *a (Ort)* vorder; *(Zeit)* vorhergehend, früher (*to* als).

anteroom ['æntirum] Vor-, Wartezimmer *n*.

anthem ['ænθəm] (National-)Hymne *f*.

anther ['ænθə] *bot* Staubbeutel *m*.

anthology [æn'θɔlədʒi] Anthologie *f*.

anthracite ['ænθrəsait] *min* Anthrazit *m*, Glanzkohle *f*.

anthrax ['ænθræks] *med* Milzbrand *m*.

anthropo|id ['ænθrəpɔid] *a* menschenähnlich; *s* Menschenaffe *m*; **~logical** [ænθropo'lɔdʒikəl] anthropologisch; **~logy** [ænθro'pɔlədʒi] Anthropologie *f*; **~metry** [ænθro'pɔmitri] Anthropometrie *f*; **~morphism** [ænθropo'mɔ:fizm] Anthropomorphismus *m*, Vermenschlichung *f*; **~morphous** [ænθropo'mɔ:fəs] von menschenähnlicher Gestalt; **~phagous** [ænθrou'pɔfəgəs] menschenfressend, kannibalisch; **~phagy** [ænθrou'pɔfədʒi] Menschenfresserei *f*.

anti|aircraft ['ænti'εəkrɑ:ft] *a* Flugabwehr-; *~ ~ artillery* Flak *f*; *~ ~ balloon* Sperrballon *m*; *~ ~ barrage* Flaksperre *f*; *~ ~ defence* Fliegerabwehr *f*; *~ ~ gun* Flugabwehrgeschütz *n*; *~ ~ rocket* Flugabwehrrakete *f*; **~biosis** ['-bai'ousis] *biol* Antibiose *f*, schädliche(s) Zs.leben *n*; **~biotic** ['-bai'ɔtik] *a* antibiotisch; *s* Antibiotikum *n*; **~body** ['-bɔdi] Antikörper, Schutz-, Abwehrstoff *m*.

antic ['æntik] *s meist pl* dumme(r) Streich *m*, Posse *f*.

Antichrist ['æntikraist] Antichrist *m*.

anticipat|e [æn'tisipeit] *tr* erwarten; *(zeitlich)* vorwegnehmen, zuvorkommen; verhindern; voraussehen; ahnen; im voraus bezahlen; im voraus verbrauchen, genießen; vorgreifen; beschleunigen; **~ion** [-'peiʃən] Erwartung, Voraussicht, Ahnung; Vorwegnahme *f*; Zuvorkommen *n*; Abschlagszahlung *f*; Verbrauch *m* im voraus; *in ~ ~* im voraus; in Erwartung (*of* gen); **~ory** [-peitəri, *Am* -pətɔ:ri] erwartend; vorgreifend; vorwegnehmend.

anti|clerical ['ænti'klerikəl] antiklerikal; **~climax** ['-'klaimæks] plötzliche(r) Abfall *od* Übergang *m*; **~cline** ['-klain] *geol* Sattel *m*; **~clockwise** ['-'klɔkwaiz] entgegen dem Uhrzeigersinn; **~corrosive** ['-kə'rousiv] korrosionsfrei; **~cyclone** ['-'saikloun] Hoch(-druckgebiet) *n*; **~-dazzle lamp** Blendschutzlampe *f*; **~dim glass** Klarscheibe *f*; **~dotal** ['-'doutəl] als Gegenmittel dienend; **~dote** ['-dout] Gegenmittel, -gift *n* (*against, for, to* gegen); **~-fading device** *radio* Schwundausgleich *m*; **~febrile** ['-'fi:brail] *a* das Fieber vermindernd; *s* Fiebermittel *n*; **~-freeze** ['-'fri:z] Frostschutzmittel *n*; **~gas** ['-'gæs] Gasschutz *m*; *~ ~ canvas, tarpaulin* Gasplane *f*, **~gen** ['-dʒen] *biol* Abwehrstoff *m*; **~glare** ['-'glεə] blendsicher; *~ ~ goggles (pl)* Blendschutzbrille *f*; **~halation** ['-hæ'leiʃən] *phot* Lichthoffreiheit *f*; **~-icer** Enteiser *m*; **~jamming** ['-dʒæmiŋ] *radio* Entstörung *f*; **~knock** ['-'nɔk] *(Benzin)* klopffest; *~ ~ fuel* klopffeste(r) Kraftstoff *m*; **~logarithm** ['-lɔgəriθm] *math* Numerus *m*; **~macassar** ['-mə'kæsə] Schonerdeckchen *n*.

antimon|ial [ænti'mounjəl] antimonhaltig; **~y** ['æntiməni] Antimon *n*.

anti|nomy [æn'tinəmi] Widerspruch *m*; **~pathetic** [æntipə'θetik] e-e Abneigung empfindend (*to* gegen); gegensätzlich; **~pathy** [æn'tipəθi] Antipathie, Abneigung *f*; Widerwillen *m* (*to, towards, against* gegen); **~personnel** [æntipə:sə'nel] gegen Menschen gerichtet; *~ ~ bomb* Splitterbombe *f*; *~ ~ mine* Tretmine *f*; **~phon** ['æntifən] Antiphon; Wechselgesang *m*; **~podal** [æn'tipədl] antipodisch; genau entgegengesetzt, gegenüberstehend; **~podes** [æn'tipədi:z] *pl* entgegengesetzte Stelle *f* auf der Erde; *mit sing* Gegensatz *m*; **~pope** ['æntipoup] Gegenpapst *m*; **~pyretic** ['æntipai'retik] *a* fieberhemmend; *s* Fiebermittel *n*; **~pyrin(e)** [ænti'paiəri(:)n] Antipyrin *n*.

antiqu|arian [ænti'kwεəriən] *a* Altertums-, Antiquar-; altertümlich; *s* Altertumsforscher; Altkunsthändler *m*; **~ary** ['æntikwəri] Antiquar; Altertumsforscher *m*; **~ated** ['æntikweitid] *a* altmodisch, veraltet; rückständig; **~e** [æn'ti:k] *s* Antike; *typ* Antiqua *f*; alte(r) (Kunst-)Gegenstand *m*; *a* alt, ehrwürdig; antik; *~ ~ dealer* Antiquitätenhändler *m*; **~ity** [æn'tikwiti] Altertum *n*; *pl* Altertümer *pl*; Antiquitäten *pl*.

anti|rachitic ['antirə'kitik] antirachitisch; **~rust** ['-'rʌst] *a* rostfrei; Rostschutz-; *~ ~ agent* Rostschutzmittel *n*; **~-Semite** ['-semait] Antisemit *m*; **~-Semitic** ['-sə'mitik] antisemitisch; **~-Semitism** ['-'semitizm] Antisemitismus *m*; **~sepsis** ['-'sepsis] *med* Antisepsis *f*; **~septic** ['-'septik] *a med* antiseptisch, keimtötend; *s* keimtötende(s) Mittel *n*; **~skid** ['-'skid] *a* Gleitschutz-; **~social** ['-'souʃəl] gegen die Gesellschaft gerichtet; **~spasmodic** ['-spæz'mɔdik] krampflösend; **~splinter cover** ['-'splintə] Splitterschutz *m*; **~submarine** ['-'sʌbməri:n] *a* U-Boot-Abwehr-; *~ ~ barrier, net* U-Boot-Sperre *f*, -Netz *n*; **~tank** [-'tæŋk] *a* Panzerabwehr-; *~ ~ battalion* Panzerjägerbataillon *n*; *~ ~ concrete cone* Hökersperre *f*; *~ ~ defence* Panzerabwehr *f*; *~ ~ ditch* Panzergraben *m*; *~ ~ gun* Panzerabwehrgeschütz *n*; *~ ~ mine* Panzermine *f*; *~ ~ obstacle* Panzersperre *f*; *~ ~ rifle* Panzerbüchse *f*; *~ ~ rocket* Panzerabwehrrakete *f*; **~thesis** [æn'tiθisis] *pl -ses* [-si:z] Antithese *f*, Gegensatz *m*; **~thetic(al)** [-'θetik(əl)] gegensätzlich; **~toxin** ['-'tɔksin] Gegengift *n*; **~trust** ['-'trʌst] *a* Antitrust-.

antler ['æntlə] Geweihsprosse *f*.

antonym ['æntənim] Antonym, Wort *n* gegenteiliger Bedeutung.

anus ['einəs] *anat* After *m*.

anvil ['ænvil] Amboß *m a. anat.*

anxi|ety [æŋ'zaiəti] Besorgnis, Angst(-gefühl *n*) (*for, about* um); Beklemmung *f*; (dringender) Wunsch *m*, Verlangen, Streben *n* (*for* nach); *with ~ ~* angstvoll, besorgt; **~ous** ['æŋkʃəs] besorgt, unruhig, beunruhigt (*about* wegen); begierig (*for* nach); gespannt (*for* auf); *to be ~ ~* gespannt, darauf aus sein (*to do s.th.* etw zu tun); besorgt sein, sich Sorgen machen (*about* um).

any ['eni] **1.** *adv* irgend(wie); überhaupt; ein wenig; *it isn't ~ good* es ist zu gar nichts nütze, es nützt nichts; *~ more?* noch mehr? *~ longer* noch länger; **2.** *a prn (in fragenden, bedingenden, zweifelnden, verneinenden Sätzen)* irgendein(e, s), irgendwelche(r, s); *not ... ~* kein; *pl* alle; *have you ~ other questions* haben Sie noch e-e Frage? *do you have ~ money with you?* haben Sie Geld bei sich? *there isn't ~ water* es ist kein Wasser da; *(in positiven Sätzen)* jede(r, s) beliebige; irgendein(e, s); *come at ~ time* kommen Sie zu jeder (beliebigen) Zeit, jederzeit; *~ policeman can direct you* jeder Polizist kann dir den Weg sagen; *~ child knows that* jedes Kind weiß das; *if ~* wenn überhaupt; *in ~ case, at ~ rate* auf jeden Fall; *in ~ place* überall; *under ~ circumstances* unter allen Umständen; **~body** ['-bɔdi] *s prn* **1.** irgend jemand; *is ~ ~ ill?* ist jemand krank? **2.** *(in positiven Sätzen)* jeder (beliebige), jedermann; *I can't take just ~ ~* ich kann nicht den ersten besten nehmen; *~ ~ can do that* jeder kann das machen; *~ ~ would be better than nobody* irgendeiner wäre besser als keiner; *~ ~ else* (irgend)ein anderer; *if ~ ~* wenn überhaupt jemand; *not ~ ~* niemand; keine(r, s); **~how** ['-hau] *adv* **1.** irgendwie, gleichgültig wie; ohne besondere Sorgfalt; so obenhin; *he does his work ~ ~* er erledigt seine Arbeit schlecht u. recht; **2.** auf jeden Fall, trotzdem, gleichwohl, doch, sowieso, ohnehin; *he did it ~ ~* er tat es doch; *I'm going ~ ~* ich gehe trotzdem; *I would have gone ~ ~* ich wäre sowieso gegangen; **~one** ['-wʌn] *s. ~body*; **~place** ['-pleis] *adv Am* irgendwo; **~thing** ['-θiŋ] *s prn* (irgend) etwas, jedes beliebige; alles; *adv* irgendwie, in irgendeiner Art, überhaupt; *is there ~ ~ new?* gibt es etwas Neues? *is ~ ~ left over?* ist noch was übrig? *can't ~~ be done?* kann man nichts tun? *is it ~~ like mine?* hat es mit meinem überhaupt e-e Ähnlichkeit? *if ~~* womöglich, noch; eher, sogar; *not... ~~* nichts; *for ~~ I know* soviel ich weiß; *not for ~~* um keinen Preis; *scarcely ~~* fast nichts; kaum etwas; *~~ but* alles andere als; nichts weniger als; *~~ else* noch etwas, sonst etwas; **~time** ['-taim] *adv Am* zu jeder Zeit; **~way(s)** ['-wei(z)] *adv* irgendwie, in irgendeiner Weise; ohnehin, sowieso, doch; trotzdem; *(Satzanfang) fam* auf jeden Fall; *I didn't want to go ~~* ich wollte sowieso nicht gehen; *I did it ~~* ich tat es trotzdem; **~where** ['-wɛə] *adv* irgendwo(hin); wo... auch(immer); wohin man will; überall(hin); *fam* überhaupt; *are you going ~~ tomorrow?* gehen Sie morgen irgendwohin? *~~ you go* wohin Sie auch gehen; *he'll never get ~~* er kommt nie auf e-n grünen Zweig; *that won't get you ~~* damit erreichen Sie gar nichts; *if ~~* wenn überhaupt (irgendwo); *not ~~* nirgendwo(hin); nirgends; *scarcely ~~* fast nirgends; *~~ else* irgendwo anders(hin); *~~ from (fam)* beliebig zwischen *(five to six* fünf u. sechs); **~wise** ['-waiz] *adv* irgendwie.

aorta [ei'ɔ:tə] *anat* Aorta *f*.

apace [ə'peis] *adv* schnell, eilig, geschwind.

apart [ə'pɑ:t] *adv* auseinander, getrennt; abseits *(from* von), für sich, abgesondert; *a pred* besonders; *~ from* abgesehen von; *to know ~* ausea.halten können; *to live ~* getrennt leben; *to set ~* beiseite legen; *to stand ~* beiseite, abseits stehen *(from* von); *to take ~* ausea.-nehmen, zerlegen; beiseite nehmen; *to tell ~* ausea.halten, unterscheiden; *joking ~* Scherz beiseite; *viewed ~* für sich betrachtet; **~heid** [-heit] Apartheid, Rassentrennung *f (in Südafrika)*; **~ment** [-mənt] *Am* (Miet-)Wohnung, Etagenwohnung *f*; *Br* Zimmer *n*; *~~ house (Am)* Rente-, Mietshaus *n*; *~~ house aerial* Gemeinschaftsantenne *f*.

apath|etic [æpə'θetik] apathisch, teilnahmslos; **~y** ['æpəθi] Apathie, Teilnahmslosigkeit *f (to* gegen).

ape [eip] *s* Affe *m a. fig*; *tr* nachäffen.

aper|ient, ~itive [ə'piəriənt, ə'peritiv] *a* abführend; *s* Abführmittel *n*; **~ture** ['æpətjuə, 'æpətʃə] Öffnung *f*, Loch; *mil* Visierloch *n*; *phot* Blende *f*.

apex ['eipeks] *pl a. apices* ['-pisi:z] Spitze *f a. fig*; *fig* Gipfel, Höhepunkt; *math* Scheitel(punkt) *m*.

aph|asia [ə'feiziə] *med* Aphasie, Sprechunfähigkeit *f*; **~elion** [æ'fi:liən] Aphel *n*, Sonnenferne *f*; **~id, ~is** ['eifid, -s] *pl aphides* ['-di:z] *zoo* Blattlaus *f*; **~orism** ['æfərizm] Aphorismus *m*; **~oristic** [æfə'ristik] aphoristisch.

api|arist ['eipiərist] Bienenzüchter, Imker *m*; **~ary** ['-i] Bienenhaus *n*; **~culture** ['eipikʌltʃə] Bienenzucht *f*.

apiece [ə'pi:s] *adv* je Stück; pro Kopf, für jeden.

apish ['eipiʃ] affenartig; nachäffend; töricht.

aplenty [ə'plenti] *adv fam* in Menge, reichlich viel.

apoc|alypse [ə'pɔkəlips] Apokalypse, Offenbarung *f*; **~alyptic(al)** [əpɔkə'liptik(əl)] apokalyptisch; **~ope** [ə'pɔkəpi] *gram* Apokope *f*; **~rypha** [ə'pɔkrifə] *pl* apokryphe Schriften *f pl*; **~ryphal** [-l] apokryph, unecht; nachgemacht.

apogee ['æpədʒi:] *astr* Apogäum *n*, Erdferne *f*; *fig* höchste(r), entfernteste(r) Punkt *m*.

apolog|etic(al) [əpɔlə'dʒetik(əl)] rechtfertigend; entschuldigend, bedauernd; *~~ letter* Entschuldigungsschreiben *n*; **~etics** [-s] *pl mit sing rel* Apologetik *f*; **~ize, ~ise** [ə'pɔlədʒaiz] *itr* sich entschuldigen *(to s.o. for s.th.* bei jdm wegen etw); um Entschuldigung bitten; sein Bedauern ausdrücken; Abbitte leisten; *jur* e-e Verteidigungsschrift verfassen; **~y** [ə'pɔlədʒi] Entschuldigung; Abbitte; Rechtfertigung; Verteidigung(sschrift) *f*; Ersatz, Notbehelf *m*.

apo|(ph)thegm ['æpoθem] Maxime *f*, Denkspruch *m*; **~plectic** [æpə'plektik] *a med* apoplektisch, am Schlagfluß leidend; *s* Apoplektiker *m*; **~plexy** ['æpəpleksi] *med (attack of ~~)* Schlaganfall *m*; **~stasy** [ə'pɔstəsi] *rel pol* Abtrünnigkeit *f*; **~state** [ə'pɔsteit, -it] *s* Abtrünnige(r) *m*; *a* abtrünnig; **~statize** [ə'pɔstətaiz] *itr* abfallen *(from* von).

apost|le [ə'pɔsl] Apostel; *fig* Verfechter *m*; *the A~s* die (zwölf) Apostel; **~olic** [æpəs'tɔlik] apostolisch.

apo|strophe [ə'pɔstrəfi] Apostroph *m*, Auslassungszeichen *n*; Apostrophe, Anrede *f*; **~strophize** [-aiz] *tr* apostrophieren, anreden; **~thecary** [ə'pɔθikəri] *obs* Apotheker *m*; **~theosis** [əpɔθi'ousis] Vergötterung; Verherrlichung *f*.

*

appal(l) [ə'pɔ:l] *tr* erschrecken; entsetzen, bestürzen; **~ling** [-iŋ] schrecklich, furchtbar, entsetzlich.

ap(p)anage ['æpənidʒ] *hist* Apanage *f*; Leibgedinge *n*; Anteil *m*; abhängige(s) Gebiet, Protektorat *n*.

apparatus [æpə'reitəs] *pl a. ~* Apparat *m*, Gerät *n*, Vorrichtung *f*.

apparel [ə'pærəl] *s poet* Kleidung, Tracht *f*; *tr* (be)kleiden.

appar|ent [ə'pærənt] *a* offenbar, offensichtlich, sichtbar; einleuchtend; scheinbar; vermeintlich; *~~ death* Scheintod *m*; **~ently** [-li] *adv* anscheinend; allem Anschein nach; **~ition** [æpə'riʃən] Erscheinung *f*; Auftauchen *n*; Geist *m*; *astr* Sichtbarkeit *f*.

appeal [ə'pi:l] *s* Appell *m*, dringende Bitte *(for* um); Anrufung *f*; *fig* Reiz *m*, Anziehungskraft; *jur* Berufung, Revision *f*, Rekurs *m (from* gegen); *tr jur Am (~~ the case)* verweisen *(to* an); *itr* sich berufen *(to* auf); sich wenden, appellieren *(to* an); anrufen *(to s.o.* jdn); *fig* zusagen, gefallen, liegen; Anklang finden *(to* bei); *jur* Berufung einlegen *(against* gegen); *without further ~* in letzter Instanz; *to dismiss an ~* e-e Berufung verwerfen; *to lodge an ~* Berufung, Revision einlegen *(with* bei); **~ing** [-iŋ] flehentlich; reizvoll, ansprechend; *~* **judg(e)ment** Berufungsurteil *n*.

appear [ə'piə] *itr* erscheinen, zum Vorschein kommen, sichtbar werden, auftauchen; sich zeigen; (an)kommen; hervorgehen *(from* aus); scheinen, den Anschein haben; auftreten; *(Zeitung)* erscheinen, veröffentlicht werden; *(Buch)* herauskommen; stehen *(in the list* auf der Liste); *jur* vor Gericht erscheinen; *to ~ for s.o.* jdn als Anwalt vor Gericht vertreten; *to summon s.o. to ~* jdn vorladen; *to ~ before a court, in court* vor Gericht erscheinen; *to ~ for the defence* als Verteidiger für den Angeklagten auftreten; *failure to ~* Nichterscheinen *n* (vor Gericht); **~ance** [-rəns] Erscheinen, Auftauchen, Sichtbarwerden; Auftreten *n*; Anschein *m*; Aussehen *n*; Äußere(s) *n*; Anblick *m*; *(Buch)* Veröffentlichung *f*; Gespenst *n*; *pl* Anzeichen *n pl*, Schein *m*; *by his ~~* s-m Aussehen, s-m Äußeren nach; *by, to all ~~s* allem Anschein nach; *in ~~* anscheinend; *to assume an ~~* sich den Anschein geben *(of being* zu sein); *to enter an ~~* vor Gericht erscheinen; *to judge by ~~s* nach dem äußeren Schein urteilen; *to keep up ~~s* den äußeren Schein wahren; **~ing** [-riŋ] *Am* aussehend.

appease [ə'pi:z] *tr* beruhigen, beschwichtigen, besänftigen; *(Hunger)* stillen; *(Durst)* löschen; *(Neugier)* befriedigen; **~ment** [-mənt] Beruhigung, Beschwichtigung; Befriedung *f*; *~~ policy* Beschwichtigungs-, Befriedungspolitik *f*; **~r** [-ə] Beschwichtigungspolitiker *m*.

appell|ant [ə'pelənt] *s jur* Berufungskläger; Bittsteller *m*; *a* appellierend; Appellations-; **~ate** [-it] *a* Berufungs-, Appellations-; *to have final ~~ jurisdiction* in letzter Instanz zuständig sein; *~~ court* Berufungsgericht *n*; **~ation** [æpe'leiʃən] Benennung, Bezeichnung *f*; (Bei-)Name *m*; **~ative** [-ətiv] *a* benennend, bezeichnend; *s* Bezeichnung, Benennung *f*; *gram* Gattungsname *m*.

append [ə'pend] *tr* anhängen; beifügen, beigeben; *(Siegel)* beidrücken; **~age** [-idʒ] Beifügung *f*; Anhang *m*, Anhängsel; Zubehör *n*; *pl biol* Extremitäten *f pl*; **~ectomy** [æpən'dektəmi] *med* Blinddarmoperation *f*; **~icitis** [əpendi'saitis] Blinddarmentzündung *f*; **~ix** [-iks] *pl -ices* [-isi:s] Anhang; Zusatz *m (to* zu); *anat (vermiform ~~)* Wurmfortsatz, Blinddarm *m*.

appertain [æpə'tein] *itr* gehören *(to* zu), ein Teil sein *(to* von); zustehen, zukommen; sich beziehen *(to* auf).

appet|ence, -cy ['æpətens(i)] Verlangen *n*, Begierde; Sehnsucht *f (for* nach); Hang *m (for* zu); innere Verwandtschaft *f*; **~ite** ['æpitait] Appetit *m*, Lust *f (for* auf); Verlangen *n*, Trieb *m*; *to lose o.'s ~~* keinen Appetit haben; **~izer** ['æpitaizə] Appetithappen; Aperitif *m*; **~izing** ['æpitaiziŋ] appetitanregend; appetitlich; *fig* lecker, reizvoll.

applau|d [ə'plɔ:d] *itr* Beifall klatschen; *tr* Beifall spenden, applaudieren *(s.o.* jdm); loben, preisen; **~se** [-z] Beifall *m*; Zustimmung *f*, Lob *n*.

apple ['æpl] Apfel *m*; *~ of discord* Zankapfel *m*; *~ of the eye* Augapfel *m a. fig*; *~* **butter** *Art* Apfelmus *n*; **~-cart**: *to upset s.o.'s ~~* jds Pläne über den Haufen werfen; jds Absichten vereiteln; *~* **dumpling** Apfel *m* im Schlafrock; **~-jack** Apfelbranntwein *m*; **~-juice** Apfelsaft *m*; **~-pie** Apfelpastete *f*; *~~ order* tadellose, einwandfreie Ordnung *f*; *~* **polisher** *sl* Schmeichler *m*; **~-sauce** Apfelmus *n*; *Am sl* Quatsch, Unsinn *m*, Geschwätz *n*; *that's a lot of ~~* das ist alles Quatsch; **~-tart** Apfelkuchen *m*; **~-tree** Apfelbaum *m*.

appli|ance [ə'plaiəns] Gerät *n (for doing s.th.* um etw zu tun), Apparat *m*, Vorrichtung, Einrichtung *f*; Mittel *n*; Anwendung *f*; *pl* Zubehör *n*; *domestic ~~s (pl)* Haushaltgeräte *n pl*; *office ~~s (pl)* Bürobedarf *m*; *safety ~~* Sicherheitsvorrichtung *f*; **~cability** [æplikə'biliti] Anwendbarkeit *f (to* auf); **~cable** ['æplikəbl] zutreffend, anwendbar *(to* auf); *not ~~* nicht zutreffend; **~cant** ['æplikənt] *s* Bewerber *(for* um); Antragsteller: Kandidat; *com* Zeichner *m*; *list of ~~s* Bewerberliste *f*; **~cation** [æpli'keiʃən] An-, Verwendung *f*, Gebrauch *m (to* für, auf); Auftragung, Handhabung *f*; *tech* Anlegen; (aufzutragendes) Mittel *n*, Umschlag *m*, Kompresse *f*; Antrag *m (for* auf); Gesuch, Ansuchen *n*, Anmeldung, Bewerbung *f (for* um); Bewerbungsschreiben *n*; Fleiß, Eifer *m* (*in* bei); gespannte Aufmerksamkeit; *com* Zeichnung *f*; *mil* Belegen *n* (*of fire* mit Feuer); *by* ~~ auf (Grund e-s) Antrag(s); *on* ~~ *to* auf Antrag, auf Ansuchen an; *to file an* ~~ e-e Bewerbung, e-n Antrag, e-e Anmeldung einreichen (*with* bei); *to make an* ~~ e-n Antrag stellen; sich bewerben (*for* um); *to send, to put, to mail (Am) in an* ~~ e-n Antrag einschicken *od* einreichen; *for external* ~~ *(med)* äußerlich; *this has no* ~~ *to* dies findet keine Anwendung auf; *field of* ~~ Anwendungsgebiet *n*, -bereich *m*; *letter of* ~~ Bewerbungsschreiben *n*; ~~ *of funds* Mittelverwendung *f*; ~~ *blank, form* Bewerbungs-, Antragsformular *n*; ~~ *range* Anwendungsgebiet *n*; **~ed** [ə'plaid] *a* angewandt; *(Spannung)* angelegt; ~~ *aerodynamics* Strömungstechnik *f*; ~~ *graphics* Gebrauchsgraphik *f*.

appliqué [æ'pli:kei] *s* Applikations-, Aufnäharbeit *f*; *tr* aufnähen; *a* aufgenäht.

apply [ə'plai] *tr itr* anwenden (*to* auf); anlegen (*to* an); *(Mittel)* benutzen, verwenden; *(Farbe)* auftragen; *(Pflaster) med* auflegen; *(Kraft)* an-, aufwenden; *(Bremse)* betätigen, ziehen; *(Spannung) el* anlegen (*across* zwischen); *itr* sich beziehen, zutreffen (*to* auf), gelten (*to* für), angehen (*to all* alle); sich wenden (*to* an); anrufen (*to the court* das Gericht); sich bewerben (*for* um); beantragen (*for s.th.* etw); bitten, nachsuchen (*for* um); anmelden (*for a patent on an invention* ein Patent auf e-e Erfindung); *to* ~ *o.s. to* sich (be)mühen um; sich befleißigen, sich angelegen sein lassen; sich stürzen (*to o.'s. work* in die Arbeit); *to* ~ *a compress* sich e-n Umschlag machen; ~ *to* Näheres bei; ~ *within* Auskunft hier; *the information doesn't* ~ die Auskunft stimmt nicht.

appoint [ə'pɔint] *tr* ernennen, bestellen, berufen (*s.o. judge* jdn zum Richter); anstellen; *(Ausschuß)* einsetzen; festlegen, -setzen, bestimmen; anordnen, anweisen; *(Arbeit)* zuteilen; *(Termin)* anberaumen; verabreden; vereinbaren; *(e-n Erben)* benennen; **~ed** [-id] *a* vereinbart, verabredet; bevollmächtigt; bestellt; *at the* ~~ *time* zum vereinbarten Zeitpunkt; *on* ~~ *days* an festgelegten Tagen; *well-*~~ gut ausgestattet; ~~ *by the court* gerichtlich bestellt; **~ee** [əpɔin'ti:] Ernannte(r), Bestellte(r) *m*; **~ment** [-mənt] Ernennung; Bestellung, Bestallung, Einsetzung; Stelle *f*, Amt *n*, Anstellung (*in a firm* bei e-r Firma); Festsetzung, Bestimmung; Verabredung *f*, Stelldichein *n*, Vereinbarung; *jur* Namhaftmachung *f (e-s Erben)*; *meist pl* Ausstattung, Ausrüstung(sgegenstände *m pl*) *f*; Mobiliar *n*; *to have an* ~~ e-e Verabredung haben (*with* mit); bestellt sein (*at the dentist's* zum Zahnarzt); *to keep an* ~~ e-e Verabredung einhalten; *to make an* ~~ e-e Verabredung treffen (*with* mit); sich anmelden (*with* bei); *document of* ~~ Anstellungsurkunde *f*; *power of* ~~ *(jur)* Verfügungsrecht *n*.

apportion [ə'pɔ:ʃən] *tr* gleichmäßig, anteilmäßig zu-, verteilen; umlegen; zuweisen; austeilen; **~ment** [-mənt] (anteilmäßige) Zuteilung; Umlage; Verteilung *f*; ~~ *of indirect cost* Gemeinkostenumlage *f*.

appos|ite ['æpəzit] passend; schicklich; geeignet (*to* für); sachdienlich; *(Bemerkung)* treffend; **~ition** [æpə'ziʃən, æpə-] Nebenea.stellen, -legen *n*; *gram* Apposition, Beifügung *f*; *to be in* ~~ *to* als Apposition stehen zu.

apprais|al [ə'preizəl] Schätzung, Bewertung *f*; ~~ *fees (pl)* Schätzgebühren *f pl*; **~e** [ə'preiz] *tr* abschätzen, den Wert ermitteln *gen*; bewerten, taxieren (*to* auf); *~ed value* Schätzwert *m*; **~ment** [-mənt] (Ab-)Schätzung *f*; Schätz-, Taxwert *m*; **~er** [-ə] Schätzer, Taxator *m*.

appreci|able [ə'pri:ʃəbl] fühlbar, merkbar, -lich; *com* taxierbar; **~ate** [-ieit] *tr* schätzen, zu schätzen wissen, (zu) würdigen (wissen); gut verstehen, gut begreifen; anerkennen; dankbar sein (*s.th.* für etw); richtig einschätzen; *com* abschätzen, taxieren; *com* den Wert steigern, erhöhen, in die Höhe treiben *gen*; *itr* im Wert steigen, e-e Wertsteigerung erfahren; *I would* ~~ *it, if* es wäre mir lieb, wenn; *I quite* ~~ *that* ich verstehe ganz gut, daß; **~ation** [əpri:ʃi'eiʃən] Ab-, Einschätzung; Schätzung, Würdigung *f*; Verständnis *n* (*of* für); Dank *m*, Anerkennung *f*; *com* Wertzuwachs *m*, -steigerung *f*; **~ative** [ə'pri:ʃiətiv] empfänglich, verständnisvoll (*of* für); anerkennend; dankbar.

apprehen|d [æpri'hend] *tr* festnehmen, verhaften; begreifen, erfassen; (be-)fürchten, erwarten, voraussehen; **~sible** [-səbl] begreiflich, faßlich; **~sion** [-ʃən] Verhaftung, Ergreifung, Festnahme; Fassungskraft *f*, Auffassungsvermögen, Verständnis *n*; Meinung, Auffassung, Ansicht; *oft pl* Furcht, Besorgnis, Befürchtung *f*; *rather slow of* ~~ ziemlich schwer von Begriff; *warrant of* ~~ Haftbefehl *m*; **~sive** [-siv] besorgt (*for* um; *of* wegen); angstvoll, bange, unruhig; leicht begreifend, rasch auffassend.

apprentice [ə'prentis] *s* Lehrling *m* *a. fig*; *tr* als Lehrling annehmen; in die Lehre tun (*to* bei); **~ship** [-ʃip] Lehrzeit; Lehre *f*; *to serve o.'s* ~~ in der Lehre sein (*with s.o.* bei jdm); ~~ *deed* Lehrvertrag *m*.

apprise [ə'praiz] *tr com* benachrichtigen, in Kenntnis setzen (*of* von); *Am s. appraise*.

approach [ə'proutʃ] *itr* sich nähern, näher kommen, anrücken, (heran-)nahen; *(Wetter)* aufziehen; *tr* (an-)nähern; näherbringen (*to* an); sich wenden, herantreten (*s.o. about s.th.* an jdn wegen etw); reden (*s.o.* mit jdm); anpacken, anfassen, herangehen (*a problem* an ein Problem); ähnlich sein, nahekommen (*s.th.* dat); *aero* anfliegen; *s* Annäherung *f*, Herankommen, Nahen *n*; Zugang *m*, (~ *road)* Zufahrt(straße) *f*; *mil* Anmarsch(weg) *m*; Auf-, Anfahrt *f*; *aero* Anflug (*to* auf); *fig* Weg *m*, Methode, Hin-, Einführung (*to* zu); Einstellung *f* (*to* zu); *oft pl* Annäherungsversuch *m*; *pl aero* Vorfeld *n*; *easy, difficult of* ~ leicht, schwer zugänglich; *fig* leicht, schwer ansprechbar; **~able** [-əbl] zugänglich, erreichbar; ~ **flight** Zielanflug *m*; ~ **lane, path** Anflugschneise *f*; ~ **march** Anmarsch *m*; ~ **route** Anmarschweg *m*; ~ **trench** Laufgraben *m*.

approbation [æpro'beiʃən, æprə-] Billigung, Zustimmung, Genehmigung *f*; *on* ~ zur Ansicht.

appropria|ble [ə'proupriəbl] anwendbar (*to* auf); **~te** [ə'proupriit] *a* geeignet, zweckdienlich, passend, angemessen (*to, for* dat); *(Bemerkung)* angebracht; *tr* [-eit] sich aneignen, in Besitz nehmen; *(Geld)* bestimmen, anweisen; bewilligen, aussetzen, auswerfen (*for* für); **~tion** [əproupri'eiʃən] Aneignung, Besitzergreifung; Verwendung; (~~ *of funds)* (Geld-)Zuteilung, Zuwendung, Zuweisung, Bereitstellung *f*; *Am* Betrag *m*, Summe *f*; ~~ *committee* Bewilligungsausschuß *m*.

approv|able [ə'pru:vəbl] löblich, annehmbar; **~al** [-əl] Zustimmung, Einwilligung, Billigung, Genehmigung *f* (*of s.th.* für, zu etw); *on* ~~ zur Ansicht, auf Probe; *upon* ~~ *by* mit Zustimmung *gen*; *to nod in* ~~ zustimmend nicken; *does it meet with your* ~~*?* findet es Ihre Zustimmung? sind Sie damit einverstanden? **~e** [ə'pru:v] *tr* billigen, gutheißen, genehmigen; anerkennen, empfehlen; *itr* zustimmen (*of* dat), einverstanden sein (*of* mit), billigen (*of s.th.* etw); *to* ~~ *o.s.* sich erweisen, sich zeigen, sich bewähren (*as* als); *to be ~ed of* Anerkennung, Anklang finden bei; **~ed** [-d] *a* bewährt, anerkannt; wohlbekannt; erwiesen, notorisch; *read and* ~~ gelesen u. genehmigt; **~er** [-ə] Zustimmende(r); *Br* V-Mann, Kronzeuge *m*; **~ingly** [-iŋli] *adv* zustimmend, billigend.

approximat|e [ə'prɔksimit] *a* annähernd (gleich), ungefähr, überschlägig; *v* [-eit] *tr itr* nahekommen, sich nähern; näherbringen; *(Summe)* ungefähr betragen, fast erreichen; *math* auf-, abrunden; **~ely** [-li] *adv* ungefähr, zirka, etwa; **~ion** [əprɔksi'meiʃən] Annäherung *f* (*to* an); (~~ *value)* Näherungswert *m*.

appurtenan|ce [ə'pə:tinəns] *meist pl* Zubehör *n*; **~t** [-t] zugehörig, akzessorisch (*to* zu).

apricot ['eiprikɔt] Aprikose *f*; (~ *tree)* Aprikosenbaum *m*.

April ['eipril] April *m*; *to make an* ~ *fool of s.o.* jdn in den April schicken; ~ **Fools' Day** 1. April.

apron ['eiprən] *s* Schürze *f*, Schurz *m*; Schurzfell, -leder *n*; *tech* Schutzvorrichtung *f*; *aero* Hallenvorfeld *n*, Abstellplatz; *mar* Dockboden *m*; *(Fluß)* Schutzschicht *f* gegen Unterspülung, Vorlage *f*; *tech* Transportband *n*; *theat* Plattform; *(screen* ~*)* (Kartoffel-)Schar *f*; *geol (frontal* ~*)* Sand(e)r *m*, glaziale Schwemmebene *f*; *tr* e-e Schürze umbinden (*s.o.* jdm); **~-strings** *pl* Schürzenbänder *n pl*; *tied to his wife's* ~~ unter dem Pantoffel.

apse [æps] *arch* Apsis *f*.

apt [æpt] fähig, geeignet, tauglich, geschickt (*at* in); *(Bemerkung)* passend, treffend; geneigt, willig; begabt, gescheit; *to be* ~ *to do s.th.* geneigt sein, etw zu tun; *I'm* ~ *to be out (Am)* es kann sein, daß ich nicht da bin; möglicherweise bin ich nicht zu Hause; **~itude** ['-itju:d] Fähigkeit, Tauglichkeit, Eignung; Geschicklichkeit; Neigung *f*, Hang *m*; Begabung *f*, Talent *n* (*for* für); *language* ~~ Sprachbegabung *f*; ~~ *test* Eignungsprüfung *f*.

apterous ['æptərəs] *zoo* flügellos.

aqua ['ækwə, 'eikwə] *chem* Wasser *n*; *pharm* Flüssigkeit *f*; **~(-)fortis** Scheidewasser *n*; **~lung** ['-lʌŋ] Taucherlunge *f*; **~marine** [ækwəmə'ri:n] *s min* Aquamarin *m*; *a* blaugrün; **~plane** ['-plein] Gleitbrett *n*; **~relle** [ækwə'rel] Aquarell *n*; **~rium** [ə'kwεəriəm] Aquarium *n*; **A~rius** [ə'kwεəriəs] *astr* Wassermann *m*; **~tic** [ə'kwætik] *a* im Wasser lebend; Wasser-; *s* Wasserpflanze *f*; im Wasser lebende(s) Tier *n*; *pl* u. ~~ *sports (pl)* Wassersport(arten *f pl*) *m*; **~tint** ['-tint] Aquatinta *f*; **~(-)vitae** ['-'vaiti:] Aquavit, Branntwein *m*.

aque|duct ['ækwidʌkt] Aquädukt *m*; Wasserleitung *f*; *med* Kanal *m*; **~ous** ['eikwiəs] wäss(e)rig; Wasser-; *geol* aquatisch; Sediment-; ~~ *humo(u)r (med)* wässerige Flüssigkeit *f*; ~~ *rocks (pl)* Sedimentgesteine *n pl*.

aquiline ['ækwilain] *a* Adler-; gekrümmt; ~ **nose** Adlernase *f*.

Arab ['ærəb] *s* Araber; *Am sl* Straßenhändler *m*; *a* arabisch; *street* ~ Straßenjunge *m*; **a~esque** [ærə'besk] Arabeske *f*; **~ian** [ə'reibjən] *a* arabisch; *the ~~ Nights* Tausendundeine Nacht; **~ic** ['-ik] *s* arabische Sprache *f*; *a* arabisch; ~~ *numerals (pl)* arabische Zahlen *f pl*; **~ist** ['-ist] Arabist *m*.

arable ['ærəbl] *a* anbaufähig, kultivierbar; *s* Ackerland *n*; ~ **acreage** Anbaufläche *f*.

araucaria [ærɔ:'kɛəriə] *bot* Zimmertanne, Araukarie *f*.

arbit|er ['ɑ:bitə] Schiedsrichter, Unparteiische(r) *m* (*of* über); **~rage** [ɑ:bi'trɑ:ʒ] *com* Arbitrage *f*; **~ral** ['-rəl] Schiedsrichter-; schiedsgerichtlich; ~~ *jurisdiction* Schiedsgerichtsbarkeit *f*; ~~ *tribunal* Schiedsgericht *n*; **~rament** [ɑ:'bitrəmənt] Schiedsspruch *m*; Entscheidungsgewalt *f*; **~rary** ['-rəri] willkürlich, eigenmächtig; eigenwillig; tyrannisch; beliebig; ~~ *address* Deckadresse *f*; ~~ *government* Willkürherrschaft *f*; **~rate** ['-reit] *tr* schlichten, schiedsrichterlich entscheiden (lassen); *itr* als Schiedsrichter tätig sein; **~ration** [ɑ:bi'treiʃən] Schiedsspruch *m*, schiedsgerichtliche Entscheidung; Schiedsgerichtsbarkeit *f*, -verfahren *n*; *com* Arbitrage *f*; *court of* ~~ Schiedsgericht(shof *m*) *n*; ~~ *agreement* Schiedsvertrag *m*; ~~ *award* Schiedsspruch *m*; ~~ *board* Schlichtungsausschuß *m*; ~~ *clause* Schiedsgerichtsklausel *f*; ~~ *procedure* Schiedsgerichtsverfahren *n*; **~rator** ['-reitə] Schiedsrichter, Schlichter *m*.

arb|or ['ɑ:bə] *tech* Welle, Spindel, Achse *f*, Dorn *m*; **~oraceous** [-ə'reiʃəs] baumähnlich; bewaldet; **~oreal** [ɑ:'bɔriəl] baumartig; auf Bäumen lebend; Baum-; **~orescent** [ɑ:bə'resnt] baumförmig; **~oretum** [ɑ:bə'ri:təm] botanische(r) Garten; mit Bäumen bestandene(r) öffentliche(r) Park *m*; **~or vitae** ['-'vaiti:] Lebensbaum *m*; **~o(u)r** ['ɑ:bə] Laube *f*; *Arbor Day (Am)* Tag *m* des Baumes; **~utus** [ɑ:'bju:təs] *bot* Erdbeerbaum *m*.

arc [ɑ:k] *s* Bogen; Kreis-, Lichtbogen *m*; *itr* e-n Lichtbogen bilden; ~ **lamp** Bogenlampe *f*; ~ **lighting** Bogenlicht *n*; ~ **welding** Lichtbogenschweißen *n*.

arcade [ɑ:'keid] Arkade *f*, Bogengang *m*; Passage *f*, Durchgang *m*; *Am* Allee *f*.

arch [ɑ:tʃ] *s arch* Bogen *m*; Gewölbe (-bogen *m*) *n*; Wölbung *f*; *(triumphal ~)* Triumphbogen; *(~ of the foot)* Fußrücken, Spann, Rist; *(~way)* Bogengang *m*; *tr* wölben; *itr* sich wölben; *a* hauptsächlich, wichtigst; größt; Haupt-, Erz-; schelmisch, schalkhaft, durchtrieben, *to look* ~ schelmisch blicken; *dental* ~ Zahnbogen *m*; *fallen ~es (pl)* Senkfüße *m pl*; ~ **support** Senk-, Plattfußeinlage *f*.

archa|ean [ɑ:'ki:ən] *geol* archäisch; frühzeitlich; **~ological** [ɑ:kiə'lɔdʒikəl] archäologisch; **~ologist** [ɑ:ki'ɔlədʒist] Archäologe *m*; **~ology** [ɑ:ki'ɔlədʒi] Archäologie *f*.

archa|ic [ɑ:'keiik] altertümlich; veraltet, altmodisch; **~ism** ['ɑ:keiizm] veraltete(r) Ausdruck, Archaismus *m*.

archangel ['ɑ:keindʒəl] Erzengel *m*.

arch|bishop ['ɑ:tʃ'biʃəp] Erzbischof *m*; **~bishopric** Erzbistum; Amt *n*, Stellung *f* e-s Erzbischofs; **~deacon** Archidiakon *m*; **~diocese** Erzdiözese *f*; **~ducal** erzherzoglich; **~duchess** Erzherzogin *f*; **~duchy** Erzherzogtum *n*; **~duke** Erzherzog *m*.

archer ['ɑ:tʃə] Bogenschütze *m*; **~y** ['-ri] Bogenschießen *n*; Pfeil *m* u. Bogen *m*; Bogenschützen *m pl*.

archetype ['ɑ:kitaip] Urbild, Vorbild *n*; *psych* Archetyp *m*.

archfiend ['ɑ:tʃ'fi:nd] Erzfeind; Teufel, Satan *m*.

archiepiscopal [ɑ:kii'piskəpəl] erzbischöflich.

archipelago [ɑ:ki'peligou] *pl -(e)s* Archipel *m*, Inselgruppe *f*.

architect ['ɑ:kitekt] Architekt; Erbauer, Baumeister; *fig* Urheber *m*; *naval* ~ Schiffsbauingenieur *m*; **~onic** [ɑ:kitek'tɔnik] *a* architektonisch; planvoll gestaltet; überwachend, kontrollierend; systematisch; *pl mit sing* Lehre *f* von der Baukunst; *fig* Aufbau *m*, Struktur; Systematisierung *f*; **~ural** [ɑ:ki'tektʃərəl] architektonisch, baulich; **~ure** ['-ʃə] Baukunst, Architektur *f*; Baustil *m*; Gebäude *n*, Bau (-körper) *m*.

architrave ['ɑ:kitreiv] *arch* Architrav *m*.

archiv|al [ɑ:'kaivəl] archivalisch; **~es** ['ɑ:kaivz] *pl* Archiv *n*; **~ist** ['ɑ:kivist] Archivar *m*.

archness ['ɑ:tʃnis] Schalkhaftigkeit *f*.

archway ['ɑ:tʃwei] *arch* Bogengang; gewölbte(r) Eingang *m*; Eingangstor *n*.

arctic ['ɑ:ktik] *a* arktisch; Polar-; sehr kalt; *s* Arktis *f*; *pl* gefütterte Überschuhe *m pl*; **A~ Circle** Polarkreis *m*; ~ **fox** Polarfuchs *m*; **A~ Ocean** Nördliche(s) Eismeer *n*.

arden|cy ['ɑ:dənsi] Glut *a. fig*; *fig* Wärme, Inbrunst *f*; **~t** ['-] brennend, heiß, glühend, feurig; eifrig; enthusiastisch, begeistert; inbrünstig, sehnsüchtig.

ardo(u)r ['ɑ:də] Eifer *m*, Leidenschaft; Wärme, Glut; große Begeisterung (*for* für); Inbrunst *f*.

arduous ['ɑ:djuəs] steil, abschüssig; schwer ersteigbar; anstrengend; mühsam, schwierig; energisch, arbeitsam, eifrig.

area ['ɛəriə] Gebiet *n*, Bereich *a. fig*, Teil; Raum *m*; (Grund-, Boden-) Fläche *f*; Flächenraum, -inhalt *m*; Areal, Gelände *n*, Zone *f*; Bezirk; *(Haus)* umschlossene(r) Hof, Vorraum; *fig* Sektor, Umfang; *mil* (Unter-) Abschnitt *m*; *min* Feld *n*; *to cover an ~ of, to be ... in area* ein Gebiet umfassen von; ... groß sein; *city* ~ Stadtgebiet *n*; *combat* ~ Kampfgebiet *n*; *depressed* ~ Notstandsgebiet *n*; *distribution, trading* ~ Absatzgebiet *n*; *electoral* ~ Wahlkreis *m*; *goal, penalty* ~ Tor-, Strafraum *m (Fußball)*; *industrial* ~ Industriegebiet *n*; *postal* ~ Postbezirk *m*; *production* ~ Produktionsgebiet *n*; *safety* ~ Sicherheitszone *f*; *suburban* ~ Vorstadtgebiet *n*; ~ *of attack* Angriffsraum *m*; ~ *of authority, of responsibility* Verantwortungsbereich *m*; ~ *of contact* Berührungsfläche *f*; ~ *of dispersion* Trefferkreis *m*; ~ *of operations (mil)* Operationsgebiet *n*; ~ *of power* Machtbereich *m*; ~ *of study* Studiengebiet *n*; ~ *of war* Kriegsgebiet *n*; ~ **bombing** Bombenflächenwurf *m*; ~ **command** *Am* Militärbereich *m*; ~ **forecast** Gebietswettervorhersage *f*; ~ **target** *mil aero* Flächenziel *n*; **~way** ['-wei] *Am* tiefgelegene(r) Vorraum, Zugang; Durchgang *m*.

arena [ə'ri:nə] Arena *a. fig*; *sport* Kampfbahn *f*; *boxing-~* Boxkampfarena *f*; ~ *of politics* politische Arena *f*; **~ceous** [æri'neiʃəs] sandig.

arête [æ'reit] *geogr* (Berg-)Grat *m*.

argentiferous [ɑ:dʒən'tifərəs] silberhaltig.

Argentin|a [ɑ:dʒən'ti:nə] Argentinien *n*; **~e, ~ean** ['ɑ:dʒentain, -'tiniən] *a* argentinisch; *s* Argentinier(in *f*) *m*.

argil ['ɑ:dʒil] Ton *m*; Töpfererde *f*; **~laceous** [ɑ:dʒi'leiʃəs] tonartig; *geol* tonig; ~~ *earth* Tonerde *f*.

argo|l [ɑ:gɔl] *chem* Weinstein *m*; **~n** ['ɑ:gɔn] *chem* Argon *n*; **~sy** ['ɑ:gəsi] *poet* große(s) (Handels-)Schiff *n*.

argue ['ɑ:gju:] *itr* diskutieren, argumentieren, sich ausea.setzen (*with* mit; *about* über; *against* gegen); sich streiten (*about* über), sprechen, Zeugnis ablegen (*for* für; *against* gegen); *tr* überreden (*s.o. into doing s.th.* jdn etw zu tun); bestreiten; er-, beweisen, zeigen (*to be s.th.* als etw); *(Gesichtspunkt)* ausführen, vortragen, darlegen, erörtern; folgern, behaupten (*that* daß); *to ~ away* wegdisputieren; *to ~ s.o. out of s.th.* jdn von etw abbringen; **~fy** ['-fai] *itr fam* herumstreiten, -nörgeln; **~ment** ['-mənt] Argument *n* (*in his favour* zu s-n Gunsten; *against* gegen); Beweisgrund *m*; Beweisführung, Erörterung, Debatte (*about* über), Argumentation *f*, Ausführungen *f pl*; Ausea.setzung *f*; Wortwechsel, Auftritt *m*; Thema *n*, Gegenstand *m*; Zs.fassung, Inhaltsangabe *f*; *jur* Vorbringen *n*, Verhandlung, Verteidigungsrede *f*, Vortrag; *math* Ansatz *m*, Behauptung *f*; *to advance, to bring forward, to set forth an ~~* ein Argument vorbringen; **~mentation** [ɑ:gjumen'teiʃən] Beweisführung, Argumentation; Diskussion, Ausea.setzung, Debatte *f*; **~mentative** [ɑ:gju'mentətiv] *(Person)* streitsüchtig, rechthaberisch; *(Arbeit)* logisch, überlegt, folgerichtig.

aria ['ɑ:riə] *mus* Arie *f*.

arid ['ærid] trocken, dürr; wasserarm; unfruchtbar; *fig* langweilig, uninteressant; **~ity** [æ'riditi] Trockenheit, Dürre; Unfruchtbarkeit; *fig* Leblosigkeit, Interesselosigkeit, Stumpfheit *f*.

Aries ['ɛərii:z] *astr* Widder *m*.

aright [ə'rait] *adv* recht, richtig.

arise [ə'raiz] *irr arose, arisen itr* hervorkommen, -gehen, entspringen; entstehen (*from, out of* aus); *(Schwierigkeiten)* sich zeigen; *(Problem)* aufkommen, auftauchen; herrühren (*from* von); *fig* aufstehen, sich erheben.

aristocra|cy [æris'tɔkrəsi] Aristokratie *f*, Adel *m*; Elite *f*; *landed ~~* Landadel *m*; **~t** ['æristəkræt] Aristokrat *m*; **~tic(al)** [æristə'krætik(əl)] aristokratisch; adlig.

arithmetic [ə'riθmətik] Arithmetik *f*, Rechnen *n*; *(~ book)* Rechenbuch *n*; **~al** [æriθ'metikəl] arithmetisch; ~~ *progression* arithmetische Reihe *f*.

ark [ɑ:k] *rel* Arche *f*; *allg* Kasten *m*, Lade *f*; *this is s.th. out of the ~* das hat e-n Bart; *Noah's ~* Arche *f* Noah; *A~ of the Covenant* Bundeslade *f*.

arm [ɑ:m] **1.** Arm *m*; *(Tier)* Vorderbein *n*; *(Polyp)* Fangarm; Ärmel; *(~ of the sea)* (Meeres-)Arm; *(Baum)* dicke(r) Ast *m*; *(Stuhl)* Seitenlehne; *(Rad)* Speiche; Abzweigung *f*; *tech* Hebelarm, Ausleger; Signalflügel; Brückenzweig; *(Waage)* Balken *m*; *mil (Zangenbewegung)* Zange *f*; *mar* Ankersplint *m*; ~ *in* ~ Arm in Arm; *on the ~ (Am sl)* umsonst; *to hold, to keep s.o. at ~'s length* sich jdn vom Leibe halten; *to receive, to welcome s.o. with open ~s* jdn mit offenen Armen empfangen; *child, infant in ~s* Säugling *m*; *secular ~* weltliche Obrigkeit *f*; *~ of the* *law* Arm *m* des Gesetzes; **~-band** Armbinde *f*; **~chair** ['-tʃɛə] Lehnstuhl *m*; *~~ strategist* Bierhausstratege *m*; **~ful** ['-ful] Armvoll *m*; **~ hole** Ärmelloch *n*; **~let** ['-lit] Armband *n*, -binde *f*; schmale(r) Meeresarm *m*; **~-pit** Achselhöhle *f*; **~-rest, -support** Armstütze *f*; **2.** *s* Waffe; Truppen-, Waffengattung; *pl* militärische Laufbahn *f*; *pl* Wappen *n*; *tr* bewaffnen; ausrüsten; *(Magnet)* armieren; *(Balken)* verstärken; *tech* mit e-r Schutzschicht versehen; *mil* scharf machen; *itr* sich bewaffnen; *allg* sich versehen (*with* mit); *to ~ o.s. with* sich bewaffnen mit; *to be under ~s* unter Waffen stehen; *to appeal to ~s* die Waffen entscheiden lassen; *to be up in ~s* empört sein (*against* gegen); *to bear ~s (mil)* dienen; *to call to ~s* zum Wehrdienst einberufen; *to carry ~s* Waffen tragen; *to lay down ~s* die Waffen strecken; *to take up ~s* zu den Waffen greifen; *fig* nachdrücklich eintreten (*for* für); *coat of ~s* Wappen *n*; *companion in ~s* Waffengefährte *m*; *fire ~* Feuerwaffe *f*; *side-~s (pl)* Seitenwaffen *f pl*; *small ~s (pl)* Handfeuerwaffen *f pl*; *~s container* Waffenbehälter *m*; *~s depot* Waffenlager *n*; *~s inspection*, Waffenappell *m*; *~s race* Wettrüsten *n*; **A~ada** [ɑ:'mɑ:də] *mar* Armada *f*; **~adillo** [ɑ:mə'dilou] *zoo* Armadill, Gürteltier *n*; **A~ageddon** [ɑ:mə'gedən] *fig* Endkampf *m*; **~ament** ['ɑ:məmənt] Bewaffnung, Ausrüstung, Bestückung; Armierung; Aufrüstung *f*; Streitkräfte *f pl*; *~~ industry* Rüstungsindustrie *f*; *~~ limitation* Rüstungsbeschränkung *f*; **~ature** ['ɑ:mətjuə] *tech* Anker *m*, Armatur *f*; *zoo* Panzer, Schutzschild *m*; *~~ coil* Ankerspule *f*; *~~ core* Ankerkern *m*; *~~ shaft* Ankerwelle *f*; *~~ winding* Ankerwicklung *f*; **~ed** [-d] *a* bewaffnet; gerüstet; ausgestattet (*with* mit); *tech* armiert; *(Revolver)* entsichert; *(Geschütz)* geladen; *(Munition)* scharf; *~~ forces (pl)* Streitkräfte *f pl*; bewaffnete Macht *f*; **~ing** ['-iŋ] Bewaffnung, Ausrüstung *f*; *tech mil* Scharfmachen *n*; **~istice** ['ɑ:mistis] Waffenstillstand *m*; *to enter into negotiations for an ~~* Waffenstillstandsverhandlungen aufnehmen (*with* mit); *A~~ Day* Waffenstillstandstag *m (11.Nov.)*; *~~ terms (pl)* Waffenstillstandsbedingungen *f pl*; **~orial** [ɑ:'mɔriəl] Wappen-; *~~ bearings (pl)* Wappen *n*; **~o(u)r** ['ɑ:mə] *s* Panzer(ung *f*) *m*, *hist* Rüstung *f*, Harnisch *m*; *mil* Panzertruppe *f*; *mar* Taucheranzug *m*; Wappen *n*; *tech* Armierung, Bewehrung; *bot zoo* Schutzdecke *f*; *tr itr* panzern; armieren, bewehren; *~~-bearer (hist)* Schildknappe *m*; *~~-clad (a)* gepanzert; *~~-piercing* panzerbrechend; *~~-plate* Panzerplatte *f*; **~oured** ['ɑ:məd] *a* gepanzert, bewehrt; *~~ attack* Panzerangriff *m*; *~~ cable* armierte(s) Kabel *n*; *~~ car* Panzerkampfwagen, Panzerspähwagen *m*; *~~ personnel carrier* Schützenpanzerwagen *m*; *~~ corps* Panzerkorps *n*; *~~ cupola* Panzerkuppel *f*; *~~ division* Panzerdivision *f*; *~~ force* Panzertruppe *f*; *~~ glass* Drahtglas *n*; *~~ infantry* Panzergrenadiere *m pl*; *~~ support* Panzerunterstützung *f*; *~~ thrust* Panzervorstoß *m*; *~~ turret* Panzerturm *m*; *~~ unit* Panzereinheit *f*; **~o(u)rer** ['-ərə] *mil* Waffenmeister *m*; **~o(u)ry** ['-əri] *mil* Waffenmeisterei, -kammer *f*; Arsenal *n*; *Am* Exerzierhalle; *Am* Waffenfabrik *f*; **~y** ['-i] Armee *f*; Heer; Militär *n*; *A~~* Landstreitkräfte *f pl*; *fig* Menge, große Zahl *f*, Heer *n*, Schwarm *m*; *to go into, to enter, to join the ~~* zum Militär gehen; *to serve in the ~~* im Heer dienen; *Salvation A~* Heilsarmee *f*; *~~ of occupation* Besatzungsheer *n*; *~~ area* Armeegebiet *n*; *~~ contract* Heereslieferung *f*; *~~ boot* Kommißstiefel *m*; *~~ bread* Kommißbrot *n*; *~~ clothing depot* Armeebekleidungsamt *n*; *~~ contractor* Heereslieferant *m*; *~~ corps* Armeekorps *n*; *~~ group* Heeresgruppe *f*; *~~ headquarters* Armeeoberkommando *n*; *~~ kitchen* Feldküche *f*; *~~ manual* Heeresdienstvorschrift *f*; *A~~ Ordnance* Heereswaffenamt *n*; *~~ pay* Wehrsold *m*; *~~ postal service* Feldpost *f*; *~~ supply station* Nachschubbahnhof *m*.

arnica ['ɑ:nikə] *bot* Arnika *f*.

aroma [ə'roumə] Aroma *n*, Duft(stoff) *m*; **~tic** [ærə'mætik] aromatisch, würzig; wohlriechend; *~~ vinegar* Gewürz-, Kräuteressig *m*; **~tize** [-taiz] *tr* würzen.

around [ə'raund] *adv* ringsherum, rundherum; nach, auf allen Seiten; überall; *Am* hier u. da; *fam* in der Nähe; *prp* um...herum, rings um; am Rande; *Am* ungefähr, etwa um; *somewhere ~ here* irgendwo hier herum; *to fool ~ (fam)* die Zeit vertrödeln; *to look ~* sich umsehen (*for* nach); *to turn ~* sich umdrehen.

arouse [ə'rauz] *tr* (auf)wecken; aufrütteln, anstacheln; *to ~ suspicion* Verdacht erregen.

arraign [ə'rein] *tr* anklagen, vor Gericht stellen; *(Angeklagten)* vernehmen; *(Behauptung)* bezweifeln; kritisieren, tadeln; **~ment** [-mənt] *jur* Anklage; Beschuldigung *f*; Tadel *m*, heftige Kritik *f*.

arrange [ə'reindʒ] *tr* (an)ordnen; veranlassen; ausmachen, festlegen, einrichten; festsetzen; regeln, ordnen; arrangieren (*to do s.th., for doing s.th.* daß etw getan wird); *(Zimmer)* einrichten; *(Versammlung)* veranstalten; *(Haar)* in Ordnung bringen; *(Rechnung)* ausgleichen; *(Streit)* schlichten; *(Anspruch)* befriedigen; *(Treffen)* verabreden, vereinbaren; *mus* umsetzen; bearbeiten; *itr* ein Übereinkommen treffen, sich verständigen (*with* mit; *about* über); Vorsorge treffen (*for s.th. to be done* daß etw getan wird); *mus* Musikstücke bearbeiten; *as ~d* wie abgesprochen, laut Abrede; *to ~ amicably* gütlich beilegen; *~ it so that* richten Sie es so ein, daß; **~ment** [-mənt] Ordnung; Anordnung, Gruppierung *f*, Arrangement *n*, Einteilung, Gliederung, Einordnung *f*; *tech* Einbau *m*; Vorbereitung, Vorsorge, Vorkehrung; Abmachung, Abrede, Vereinbarung, Verständigung, Übereinkunft; *(Streit)* Beilegung *f*, Vergleich *m*; Erledigung, Regelung; *mus* Bearbeitung *f*; *fam* Ding, Gerät *n*, Apparat *m*; *by ~~* nach Vereinbarung; *to come to an ~~* zu e-r Einigung kommen; *to make ~~s* Vorkehrungen, Vorbereitungen treffen; *to make an ~~* ein Abkommen, e-e Vereinbarung treffen; e-n Vergleich schließen.

arrant ['ærənt] durchtrieben; *(Unsinn)* komplett; *(Lügner)* notorisch.

array [ə'rei] *s* (An-)Ordnung, Aufstellung *f*; Aufgebot *n*; Truppen, Mannschaften *f pl*; Kleidung *f*, Putz, Staat *m*; Zurschaustellen *n*; *tr* (an)ordnen; bereitstellen; *(Truppen)* aufstellen; *to ~ o.s.* sich kleiden, sich schmücken (*in* mit); *to form in battle ~* in Schlachtordnung aufstellen; *to ~ a panel (jur)* die Liste der Geschworenen aufstellen.

arrear|age [ə'riəridʒ] *fin* Rückstände *m pl*, unbezahlte(r) Restbetrag *m*, Schulden *f pl*; **~s** [-z] *pl* rückständige Zahlungen, Schulden *f pl*; *allg* Rückstände *m pl*; unerledigte Sachen *f pl*; *to be in ~(s)* Rückstände haben; im Verzug sein; *to work off ~s* Rückstände aufarbeiten; *~s of work* Arbeitsrückstände *m pl*.

arrest [ə'rest] *tr* auf-, anhalten; verhindern, hemmen; *tech* ab-, feststellen, arretieren; *jur* festnehmen, verhaften; einsperren; *(Sache)* beschlagnahmen; die Vollstreckung aussetzen (*judg(e)ment* e-s Urteils); *(Aufmerksamkeit)* fesseln; *s* Verhaftung, Inhaftierung, Festnahme *f*; *mil* Arrest *m*; *(Urteil)* Aussetzung *f* der Vollstreckung; *tech* Arretierung, Hemmung *f*; *under ~* in Haft, in Gewahrsam; in Beschlag; *to ~ under strong suspicion* wegen dringenden Verdachts verhaften (*of* gen); *to grant a warrant of ~* e-n Haftbefehl erlassen; *to make ~s* Verhaftungen durchführen; *to place, to put s.o. under close, open ~* gegen jdn strengen, gelinden Arrest verhängen; *~ in development* Entwicklungsstillstand *m*; *~ in quarters* Stubenarrest *m*; **~er** [-ə] *el* Ableiter *m*; *(~~ cable)* Fangkabel *n*; *(dust ~~)* Staubabscheider *m*; *~~ hook (aero)* Fanghaken *m*; *lightning-~~* Blitzableiter *m*; **~ing** [-iŋ] *a* fesselnd, auffallend, interessant.

arriv|al [ə'raivəl] Ankunft *f*; Eintreffen *n*; *(Waren)* Eingang *m*; *(Ziel)* Erreichung *f*; Ankömmling; *(Hotel)* neue(r) Gast *m*; *pl com* eingegangene Waren *f pl*; *on ~~* bei Ankunft; *late, new ~~* Spät-, Neuankömmling *m*; *~~s and departures (rail)* Ankunfts- u. Abgangszeiten *f pl*; **~e** [ə'raiv] *itr* ankommen (*at, in* in); *fig* gelangen, kommen (*at a decision* zu e-r Entscheidung); erlangen (*at s.th.* etw); *fam* arrivieren, Erfolg haben; *to ~~ at an agreement* zu e-r Einigung kommen.

arrog|ance ['ærəgəns] Anmaßung, Frechheit *f*; Hochmut *m*, Einbildung *f*; **~ant** ['-ənt] anmaßend, frech; hochmütig, eingebildet; **~ate** ['ærogeit] *tr* (unrechtmäßig) fordern, beanspruchen (*to* für); zuschreiben (*s.th. to s.o.* jdm etw); *to ~~ to o.s.* sich anmaßen; **~ation** [ærə'geiʃən] Anmaßung *f*; unbegründete(r) Anspruch *m*.

arrow ['ærou] *s* Pfeil; Richtungspfeil; *tech* Zählstab *m*; *tr* mit e-m Pfeil bezeichnen; *returning ~ (fig)* Bumerang *m*; **~head** Pfeilspitze *f*; **~root** *bot* Pfeilwurz *f*.

arroyo [ə'rɔiou] *Am* ausgetrocknete(s) Flußbett *n*; Bach *m*.

arse [ɑ:s] *vulg* Hinterteil *n*.

arsenal ['ɑ:sinl] Zeugamt; *mar* Arsenal *n*; Waffen-, Munitionsfabrik *f*.

arsen|ate ['ɑ:sinit, -eit] *chem* arseniksaure(s) Salz *n*; **~ic** ['ɑ:snik] *s chem* Arsen(ik) *n*; *a* [ɑ:'senik] arsensauer; *~~ poisoning* Arsenvergiftung *f*;

arson ['ɑ:sn] Brandstiftung *f*.

*

art [ɑ:t] **1.** *s. to be*; **2.** Kunst; Kunstfertigkeit; Geschicklichkeit *f*; Grundsätze *m pl*, Methode *f*; Verfahren *n*, Technik *f*; Handwerk, Gewerbe *n*; Kenntnisse *f pl*; Fachgebiet *n*; Verschlagenheit, List *f*; *pl* Geisteswissenschaften *f pl*; *pl* Kniffe, Schliche *m pl*; *~s and crafts* Kunstgewerbe *n pl*; *fine, liberal, useful ~s (pl)* schöne, freie, angewandte Künste *f pl*; *work of ~* Kunstwerk *n*; *~ of printing* Buchdruckerkunst *f*; *~ of war* Kriegskunst *f*; *~ collection, critic, dealer, gallery, school* Kunstsammlung *f*, -kritiker, -händler *m*, -galerie, -schule *f*.

arter|ial [ɑ:'tiəriəl] *med* Arterien-, Schlagader-; *~~ road* Hauptverkehrsstraße *f*; **~iosclerosis** [ɑ:'ti:əriouskliə'rousis] Arterienverkalkung *f*; **~y** ['ɑ:təri] *med* Arterie, Schlagader; Verkehrsader *f*.

artesian [ɑ:'ti:ʒən, -zjən] *a* artesisch; **~ well** artesische(r) Brunnen *m*.

artful ['ɑ:tful] verschlagen, listig; gewandt, geschickt; sinnreich; künstlich; nachahmend.

arthriti|c [ɑ:'θritik] *med* arthritisch; **~s** [-'θraitis] Gelenkentzündung, Arthritis *f*; *rheumatoid ~~* Gelenkrheuma(tismus *m*) *n*.

artichoke ['ɑ:titʃouk] *bot* Artischocke *f*.

artic|le ['ɑ:tikl] Artikel *a. gram jur com*; Aufsatz; *(newspaper ~~)* Zeitungsartikel *m*; Objekt *n*, Gegenstand *m*; *gram* Geschlechtswort *n*; *com* Ware *f*, *(~ of commerce)* Handelsartikel, Warenposten *m*; *jur* Klausel, Bestimmung *f*, Abschnitt, Paragraph; *(Vertrag)* Punkt *m*; *pl (ship's ~~s)* Schiffsmusterrolle *f*; *tr* in die Lehre geben (*to* bei); in Artikel einteilen; anklagen (*for* wegen); *itr* e-e Anklageschrift verfassen (*against* gegen; *for* wegen); *in the ~~ of death* im Augenblick des Todes; *to serve o.'s ~~s* s-e Lehre durchmachen; *leading ~~* Leitartikel *m*; *~~s of apprenticeship* Lehrvertrag *m*; *~~s of association* Satzungen *f pl*; *~~ of clothing* Bekleidungsstück *n*; *~~ of consumption* Bedarfsgegenstand *m*; *~~ of luggage* Gepäckstück *n*; *~~s of partnership* Gesellschaftsvertrag *m* (e-r OHG); *~~ of value* Wertsache *f*; *~~ of war* Kriegsartikel *m*; **~ular** [ɑ:'tikjulə] Gelenk-; *~~ rheumatism* Gelenkrheumatismus *m*; **~ulate** [ɑ:'tikjulit] *a* durch ein Gelenk verbunden; gegliedert; unterteilt; deutlich, artikuliert; *tr* [ɑ:'tikjuleit] durch ein Gelenk verbinden; zs.passen; gliedern; artikulieren; artikuliert, deutlich aussprechen; *~~d coupling* Gelenkkupplung *f*; **~ulation** [ɑ:tikju'leiʃən] Gelenkverbindung; Zs.fügung; Gliederung; *(Sprache)* Artikulation *f*.

artifact ['ɑ:tifækt] Artefakt *n*.

artific|e ['ɑ:tifis] gewandte(r) Trick, Kniff, Dreh *m*; List; *pej* Gewandtheit, Geschicklichkeit *f*; **~er** [ɑ:'tifisə] *tech* (geschickter) Handwerker; Mechaniker; *mil* Feuerwerker; Erfinder *m*; **~ial** [ɑ:ti'fiʃəl] künstlich; nachgemacht, unecht; unnatürlich; gesucht, affektiert, geziert; *(Lächeln)* gezwungen; *(Zähne)* falsch; *chem* synthetisch; *~~ draught* Belüftung *f*; *~~ fibre* Kunstfaser *f*; *~~ ice* Kunsteis *n*; *~~ insemination* künstliche Befruchtung *f*; *~~ leather* Kunstleder *n*; *~~ leg* Beinprothese *f*; *~~ light* Kunstlicht *n*; *~~ manure* Kunstdünger *m*; *~~ person* juristische Person *f*; *~~ resin* Kunstharz *n*; *~~ respiration* künstliche Atmung *f*; *~~ silk* Kunstseide *f*; *~~ stone* Kunststein *m*; *~~ sun* Höhensonne *f*; *~~ wood* Kunstholz *n*; *~~ wool* Kunstwolle *f*; *~~ work* Kunstbau *m*; **~iality** [ɑ:tifiʃi'æliti] künstliche(r) Charakter *m*; Unechtheit; Unnatürlichkeit *f*.

artillery [ɑ:'tiləri] Artillerie *f*; **~ fire** Artilleriefeuer *n*; **~ group** Artillerieregiment *n*; **~man** Artillerist *m*; **~ observer** Artilleriebeobachter *m*; **~ officer** Artillerieoffizier *m*; **~ position** Artilleriestellung *f*; **~ protection** Feuerschutz *m*; **~ range** Artillerieschießplatz *m*.

artisan [ɑ:ti'zæn] Handwerker *m*.

artist ['ɑ:tist] Künstler(in *f*); Maler(in *f*); Könner *m*; **~e** [ɑ:'ti:st] Artist(in *f*); Sänger(in *f*), Tänzer(in *f*) *m*; **~ic** [ɑ:'tistik] künstlerisch; kunstvoll, geschmackvoll; Kunst-; **~ry** ['-ri] Kunstsinn *m*; Kunstfertigkeit *f*; künstlerische Fähigkeiten, Eigenschaften *f pl*.

art|less ['ɑ:tlis] einfach, natürlich; harmlos, naiv; kunstlos, kulturlos; ungeschickt, linkisch; **~lessness** ['-nis] Kunstlosigkeit; Schlichtheit; Naivität *f*; **~y** ['-i] *fam* gewollt künstlerisch.

arum ['ɛərəm] *bot* gemeine(r) Aronsstab *m*; **~ lily** weiße Gartenlilie *f*.

Aryan ['ɛəriən] *a* arisch; *s* Arier *m*; arische Sprachengruppe *f*.

as [æz, əz] **1.** *adv* wie, als; wie zum Beispiel; *~ ... ~* (eben)so ... wie; *not so ... ~* nicht so ... wie; *~ long ~* so lange wie; *~ much, many ... ~* ebensoviel(e)... wie; bis zu ...; *~ yet* bis jetzt; bisher, soweit; *not ~ yet* noch nicht; *~ well* auch; *~ well ~* dazu, außerdem; *~ far ~* bis (zu); soviel; soweit; *~ soon ~ not, (just) ~ soon* ebenso gern; *I thought ~ much* das war meine Ansicht; **2.** *conj* da, weil; als, während; (in der Art) wie, genauso wie; wie, als; obgleich; als (ob); *~ is (com)* im gegenwärtigen Zustand; *~ it is* in Wirklichkeit; ohnehin; *~ it were* gleichsam; gewissermaßen; sozusagen; *~ if, though* als ob; *~ ... so* wie ... so; *~ soon ~* sobald (als), sowie; *~ a rule* gewöhnlich, üblicherweise; *~ and when received (com)* je nach Eingang; *everything stands ~ it was* alles bleibt beim alten; **3.** *prp* als; in der Eigenschaft als; *~ for, ~ to* was ... anbetrifft; hinsichtlich; *~ to whether* ob; *so ... ~ to* so ... um zu; *so ~ to be sure* um sicher zu sein; **4.** *prn* welche(r, s); was; wie; *in proportion ~* in dem Maße wie.

asbestos [æz'bestɔs] Asbest *m*; **~board roofing** Asbestpappe *f*.

ascend [ə'send] *itr* auf-, ansteigen, sich erheben (*from* von); *(zeitlich)* zurückgehen (*to* bis auf); *(Ton)* steigen; *(Weg)* ansteigen, nach aufwärts führen; *astr* aufgehen; *tr* be-, ersteigen; erklettern; *(e-n Fluß)* hinauffahren; *(e-e Leiter)* hinaufsteigen; *(Thron)* besteigen; **~ance, ~ence, ~cy** [-əns(i)] *fig* Übergewicht *n*, Überlegenheit *f*; beherrschende(r) Einfluß *m* (*over* auf); *to rise to ~~* an die Macht kommen; **~ant, ~ent** [-ənt] *a* aufsteigend; *fig* überragend, beherrschend, überlegen; *astr* aufgehend; *bot* aufwärts gerichtet; *s fig* beherrschende Stellung, Überlegenheit *f* (*over* über); *(Astrologie)* Horoskop *n*; *to be in the ~~ (fig)* im Steigen sein; **~ing** [-iŋ] aufsteigend; *~~ current* Aufwind *m*; *~~ gust* Steigbö *f*.

ascen|sion [ə'senʃən] Aufsteigen *n*, Aufstieg *m*; *A~~ Day* Himmelfahrtstag *m*; **~t** [ə'sent] Aufsteigen *n*; Auf-, Anstieg; Aufgang *m*; Steigung *f*; *(im Rang)* Steigen; *(zeitlich)* Zurückgehen *n* (*to, into* bis auf); *(Berg)* Besteigung *f*.

ascertain [æsə'tein] *tr* feststellen, ermitteln, herausfinden; (nach)prüfen; in Erfahrung bringen (*s.th. from s.o.* etw von jdm); **~ment** [-mənt] Feststellung, Ermittlung; *(Schaden, Recht)* Festlegung *f*.

ascetic [ə'setik] *a* asketisch; *s* Asket *m*; **~ism** [-sizm] Askese *f*.

ascri|bable [əs'kraibəbl] zuzuschreiben; **~be** [əs'kraib] *tr* zuschreiben, beimessen (*to s.o.* jdm); **~ption** [əs'kripʃən] Beimessung, Zumessung *f* (*of* gen; *to s.o.* jdm).

asep|sis [ə'sepsis, ei-] Asepsis, keimfreie Wundbehandlung *f*; **~tic** [-tik] aseptisch, keimfrei.

asexual [ei'seksjuəl] geschlechtslos.

ash [æʃ] **1.** *bot (~ tree)* Esche *f*; **~en** ['-ən] eschen; **~ wood** Eschenholz *n*; **2.** Asche *f*; *pl* Asche *f (a. d. Menschen)*, sterbliche Überreste *m pl*; *to burn to ~es* niederbrennen; **~-bin,** *Am* **-can** Kehrichtkasten, -eimer *m*; **~ content** Aschengehalt *m*; **~en** ['-ən] aschfarben; **~-grey** aschgrau; **~man** *Am* Arbeiter *m* der Müllabfuhr; **~ pan** Aschenkasten, -behälter *m*; **~ pit** Aschengrube *f*; **~ removal** Beseitigung *f* der Asche; Entaschung *f*; **~ tray** Aschenbecher *m*; **A~Wednesday** Aschermittwoch *m*; **~y** ['-i] aschen; aschfarben, -fahl.

ashamed [ə'ʃeimd] *pred a* beschämt; *to be ~* sich schämen (*of s.th.* e-r S; *to do s.th.* etw zu tun); *you ought to be ~ of yourself* du solltest dich schämen.

ashlar, -er ['æʃlə] *arch* Quaderstein *m*.

ashore [ə'ʃɔ:] *adv* ans Ufer; am Ufer; *to go ~* an Land gehen; landen.

Asia ['eiʃə] Asien *n*; **~ Minor** Kleinasien *n*; **~n, ~tic** ['-n, eiʃi'ætik] *a* asiatisch; *s* Asiate *m*.

aside [ə'said] *adv* beiseite; abseits; auf die Seite; weg, fort; *s theat* Aparte *n*; *~ from (Am)* abgesehen von; außer; zusätzlich zu; *all joking ~* Spaß beiseite; *to lay ~* beiseite legen; *(Gewohnheit)* ablegen, aufgeben; *to put ~* auf die Seite legen, beiseite legen; *(Waren, Geld)* zurücklegen; *to set ~* weg-, beiseite legen; *(Geld)* beiseite -, zurücklegen; *(Anspruch)* abweisen; *(Einwand)* verwerfen; *(Urteil)* aufheben; *to speak ~ (theat)* beiseite sprechen; *allg* leise mitea. reden; *to stand, to step ~* zur, auf die Seite gehen *od* treten; *to turn ~* sich wegwenden (*from* von); *(Straße)* verlassen.

asinine ['æsinain] Esel-; *fam* dumm, blöde, töricht.

ask [ɑ:sk] *tr* erfragen; fragen (*s.o. for s.th., s.o. s.th.* jdn nach etw); *(Frage)* stellen; bitten (*s.th. of s.o.* jdn um etw; *s.o. to do s.th.* jdn etw zu tun); erbitten; erwarten, fordern, verlangen; brauchen; einladen (*to s.th.* zu etw); auffordern, ersuchen; *(to ~ the banns)* das Aufgebot bestellen; *itr* fragen (*for* nach); sich erkundigen (*about, after, for* nach); sich informieren (*about* über); *to ~ for it (sl)* herausfordernd wirken; *to ~ of, from s.o.* von jdm erbetteln; *to ~ how to do s.th.* danach fragen, wie etw getan werden soll; *to ~ s.o.'s advice* jdn um Rat fragen; sich bei jdm Rat holen; *to ~ s.o. his name* jdn nach s-m Namen fragen; *to ~ for permission* um Erlaubnis bitten; *to ~ to be allowed to speak* um das Wort bitten; *to ~ for trouble* zu Schwierigkeiten führen; Schwierigkeiten heraufbeschwören; **~ed** [-t] *a* gefragt; *price ~~* Briefkurs *m*; *~~ and bid* Brief u. Geld; **~ing** ['-iŋ] Fragen, Bitten *n*; *it's yours for the ~~* Sie brauchen nur darum zu bitten (u. erhalten es); *~(~) price* Angebotspreis *m*.

askance, askant [əs'kæns, -t] *adv* von der Seite, schief; scheel; auf e-e Seite; *to look ~ at s. th.* etw mißtrauisch, mißbilligend betrachten.

askew [əs'kju:] *adv pred a* auf der Seite; verschoben, schief, quer.

aslant [ə'slɑ:nt] *adv pred a* schief, schräg; *prp* quer über, quer durch.

asleep [ə'sli:p] *pred a* schlafend; eingeschlafen; *fig* untätig, rückständig; tot; *adv* im Schlaf; *to be ~* schlafen; *to fall ~* einschlafen.

aslope [ə'sloup] *pred a adv* abschüssig, schief.

asp [æsp] **1.** *s bot* Espe *f*; *a* aus Espenholz; **2.** *zoo* Natter *f*.

asparagus [əs'pærəgəs] Spargel; *(~-fern)* Asparagus *m*; **~ tips** *pl* Spargelköpfe *m pl*.

aspect ['æspekt] Aussehen *n*, Erscheinung *f*; Anblick, Gesichtsausdruck *m*; Aussicht *f*, Ausblick *m*; Richtung; *(e-s Problems)* Seite *f*, Aspekt, Stand-, Gesichtspunkt *m*; Betrachtungsweise *f*; *astr gram* Aspekt *m*; *(Haus)* Seite, Front, Fläche *f*; *phys* Verhältnis *n*; *from a higher* ~ von höherer Warte aus; *to be of good* ~ gut, günstig aussehen; *to see s.th. in its true* ~ etw in s-m wahren Licht sehen; *facial* ~ Gesichtsausdruck *m*; *general* ~ Gesamteindruck *m*; ~ *of a disease* Krankheitsbild *n*; ~ **ratio** *tele* Bildverhältnis *n*; *aero* (Flügel-)Streckung *f*.

aspen ['æspən] *s* Espe *f*; *a* aus Espenholz; *fig* zitternd, bebend; *to tremble like an* ~ *leaf* wie Espenlaub zittern.

asper|ity [æs'periti] Rauheit, Unebenheit; *fig* Schroffheit, Strenge, Härte; *(Klima)* Unwirtlichkeit *f*; ~**se** [æs'pə:s] *tr* besprengen, bespritzen (*with* mit); *fig* verleumden; ~**sion** [æs'pə:ʃən] Besprengung *f*, Bespritzen *n*; *fig* Verleumdung *f*.

asph|alt ['æsfælt] *s* Asphalt *m*; *tr* asphaltieren; ~ ~ *board, cement* od *mastic, concrete, pavement* Asphaltpappe *f*, -kitt *m* od -masse *f*, -beton *m*, -pflaster *n*; ~**odel** ['æsfədel] *bot* Affodillwurz; *poet* gelbe Narzisse *f*; ~**yxia** [æs'fiksiə] Erstickung; Bewußtlosigkeit (durch Sauerstoffmangel), Asphyxie *f*; ~**yxiate** [æs'fiksieit] *tr* ersticken; ~**yxiation** [æsfiksi'eiʃən] Erstickung *f*.

aspic ['æspik] *(Küche)* Aspik *m*; *poet* (giftige) Natter *f*.

aspidistra [æspi'distrə] *bot* Aspidistra *f*.

aspir|ant [əs'pairənt, 'æspirənt] *s* Bewerber (*to, after* um); Anwärter *m* (*to, after* auf); ~**ate** ['æspireit] *tr gram* aspirieren; *med* einatmen; aufsaugen; ['æspirit] *a* aspiriert; *s* Hauchlaut *m*; ~**ation** [æspi'reiʃən] Wunsch *m*, Verlangen, Streben *n*, Sehnsucht *f* (*after, for* nach); Einatmen *n*, Atemzug *m*; ~**ator** ['æspireitə] Ansauger *m*, Saug-, Strahlpumpe *f*; *med* Aspirator *m*; ~**e** [əs'paiə] *itr* streben, trachten (*after, at, to* nach); ~**in** ['æspirin] Aspirin *n*; ~ ~ *tablets (pl)* Aspirintabletten *f pl*; ~**ing** [əs'pairiŋ] ehrgeizig; strebend (*after, to* nach).

*

ass [æs] Esel *a. fig*; *fig* Dummkopf *m*; *Am sl* Hinterteil *n*; *to make an* ~ *of s.o.* jdn zum Narren halten; *of o.s.* sich lächerlich machen; ~-**foal** Eselsfüllen *n*; ~'**s milk** Eselsmilch *f*.

assail [ə'seil] *tr* angreifen, überfallen; *(Aufgabe)* in Angriff nehmen; *(e-r Schwierigkeit)* begegnen; *to* ~ *s.o. with questions* jdn mit Fragen bestürmen; *to be* ~*ed with doubts* von Zweifeln geplagt sein; ~**able** [-əbl] angreifbar; anfechtbar; ~**ant** [-ənt] Angreifer *m*.

assassin [ə'sæsin] (gedungener) Mörder *m*; ~**ate** [-eit] *tr* ermorden; ~**ation** [əsæsi'neiʃən] Ermordung *f*.

assault [ə'sɔ:lt] *s* (Sturm-)Angriff, Überfall (*upon* auf); Anschlag *m*, Attentat *n*; *jur* tätliche Beleidigung, Bedrohung, Tätlichkeit, *a. (criminal* ~*)* Vergewaltigung *f*; *tr* angreifen, überfallen; bestürmen, berennen; *jur* tätlich beleidigen; bedrohen; vergewaltigen; *to take by* ~ erstürmen, im Sturm nehmen; *bayonet* ~ Bajonettangriff *m*; *indecent* ~ Sittlichkeitsverbrechen *n*; ~ ~ **and battery** schwere tätliche Beleidigung; Schlägerei *f*; **artillery** Sturmartillerie *f*; ~ **boat** Sturmboot *n*; ~**er** [-ə] Angreifer *m*; ~ **gun** Sturmgeschütz *n*; ~ **tank** Sturmpanzer *m*; ~ **troops** *pl* Stoßtruppen *f pl*; ~ **wave** Sturm-, Angriffswelle *f*; ~ **wire** *tele* Feldkabel *n*.

assay [ə'sei, 'æsei] *s chem* (Metall-) Probe, Analyse; *allg* Prüfung *f*, Test, Versuch *m*; *v* [ə'sei] *tr* prüfen, erproben; analysieren; *fig* versuchen (*to* zu); *itr* e-n Gehalt haben (*in gold* an Gold); titrieren; ~ **balance, crucible, spoon** Probierwaage *f*, -tiegel, -löffel *m*.

assembl|age [ə'semblidʒ] Versammlung *f*; Treffen *n*, Zs.kunft; Sammlung *f*; *tech* Zs.setzen *n*, Montage *f*; ~**e** [-] *tr* versammeln; zs.bringen, -tragen, -stellen; *(Parlament)* einberufen; *tech* zs.setzen, -bauen, montieren; *(Truppen)* bereitstellen; *itr* sich versammeln, zs.kommen, sich treffen; *mil* aufmarschieren; ~**er** [-ə] *agr* Aufkäufer *m*; ~**y** [-i] Versammlung; Zs.kunft; Veranstaltung; Gesellschaft; *pol* gesetzgebende Körperschaft *f*, *Am a.* Repräsentantenhaus *n (einzelner Staaten)*; *tech* Montage, -halle, -gruppe *f*, -teile *m pl*; *(Maschine)* Aufstellen *n*; Aufbau, Zs.bau *m*; Anordnung *f*; *mil* Sammelsignal, Sammeln *n*, Bereitstellung *f*, Aufmarsch *m*; ~ ~ *area (mil)* Bereitstellungsraum *m*; ~ ~ *drawing* Montageplan *m*; ~ ~ *error* Montagefehler *m*; ~ ~ *jig* Montagegerüst *n*; ~ ~ *hangar (aero)* Montagehalle *f*; ~ ~ *line* Fließ-, Montageband *n*; ~ ~-*line work* Fließbandarbeit *f*; ~ ~ *order (mil)* Bereitstellungsbefehl *m*; ~ ~ *plant* Montagewerk *n*; ~ ~ *point, position (mil)* Bereitstellungsort; *allg* Sammelpunkt *m*; ~ ~ *room* Festsaal, Versammlungsraum *m*; *tech* Fertigbau-, Montagehalle *f*; ~ ~ *shop* Montagewerkstatt, -halle *f*; ~ ~ *stand* Montagebock *m*.

assent [ə'sent] *itr* einwilligen (*to* in), zustimmen (*to* dat); billigen (*to s.th.* etw); *(e-r Meinung)* beipflichten; *s* Zustimmung, Einwilligung, Billigung *f*; *with one* ~ einmütig; *to nod* ~ zustimmend nicken; ~**er** [-ə] Jasager; *pol Br* Unterstützer *m* e-s Wahlvorschlags.

assert [ə'sə:t] *tr* feststellen; bestehen auf, behaupten; vorbringen; *(Recht)* verteidigen, geltend machen; beanspruchen, e-n Anspruch erheben auf; *(Forderung)* durchsetzen; *to* ~ *o.s.* sich durchsetzen; auf s-m Recht bestehen; *pej* sich herausstreichen, sich in den Vordergrund drängen; ~**ion** [ə'sə:ʃən] Erklärung *f*; Vorbringen *n*; Behauptung, Feststellung; *(Rechte)* Geltendmachung *f*; *to make an* ~ ~ e-e Behauptung aufstellen; ~**ive** [-iv] zustimmend, bejahend; *pej* übertrieben selbstsicher; ~**or** [-ə] Verfechter *m*.

assess [ə'ses] *tr* bewerten, den Wert feststellen (*s.th.* e-r S); besteuern, veranlagen; *(Schadenssumme)* festsetzen, feststellen (*at* auf); (ab)schätzen, veranschlagen; *(Unkosten)* aufteilen, umlegen; e-e Zahlung, Geldstrafe festsetzen; ~**able** [-əbl] bewertbar, festsetzbar; steuerpflichtig; abschätzbar; umlegbar; ~**ed** [-t] *a* veranschlagt; ~ ~ *value* Einheitswert *m*; ~**ment** [-mənt] Feststellung, Festsetzung; Ab-, Einschätzung; Besteuerung, Veranlagung; *(Schaden)* Bewertung; Umlage; *(Strafe)* Zumessung *f*; festgelegte(r) Betrag *m*; *notice of* ~ ~ Steuerbescheid *m*; *period of* ~ ~ Veranlagungszeitraum *m*; *rate of* ~ ~ Steuersatz *m*; *tax* ~ ~ Steuerveranlagung *f*; ~ ~ *roll* Steuerliste *f*; ~**or** [-ə] *fin* Schätzer, *(*~ ~ *of taxes)* Steuerbeamte(r); *jur* Beisitzer *m*.

asset ['æset] Gut *n*, Vorteil *m*, Plus *n*; *fig* Trumpf; *com* Vermögenswert, Aktivposten *m*; *pl* Aktivposten *m pl*, Aktiva *pl*, Vermögensstand *m*, Aktivvermögen *n*; *capital* ~*s (pl)* Anlagevermögen; unbewegliche(s) Vermögen *n*; *trading, working* ~*s (pl)* Betriebskapital, -vermögen *n*; ~ **account** Aktivkonto *n*; ~**s and liabilities** *pl* Aktiva u. Passiva *pl*.

asseverat|e [ə'sevəreit] *tr* beteuern, versichern; ~**ion** [əsevə'reiʃən] Beteuerung, Versicherung *f*.

assidu|ity [æsi'djuiti] Fleiß, Eifer *m*; Beharrlichkeit; Gefälligkeit *f*; ~**ous** [ə'sidjuəs] fleißig, eifrig; beharrlich, ausdauernd; gefällig.

assign [ə'sain] *tr* festlegen, festsetzen, bestimmen; besteuern; an-, zuweisen; zuteilen; *(Aufgabe)* stellen, beauftragen mit; *(Schule)* aufgeben; *(Ursache)* zuschreiben, bezeichnen (*as* als); *(Bedeutung)* beilegen; *jur* übertragen, abtreten, zedieren; ernennen (*to a post* auf e-n Posten); *mil* abkommandieren, versetzen, unterstellen; e-n Anspruch, Eigentum übertragen; *s meist pl* Rechtsnachfolger; Beauftragte(r) *m*; ~**able** [-əbl] *jur* übertragbar, zedierbar; *allg* zuschreibbar; ~**ation** [æsig'neiʃən] Festlegung, Festsetzung, Bestimmung; *jur* Abtretung, Zession, Übertragung; Zuweisung, Zuteilung *f*; Stelldichein *n*; ~**ee** [æsi'ni:] Rechtsnachfolger, (Vertrags-)Begünstigte(r), Zessionar *m*; ~ ~ *in bankruptcy* Konkursverwalter *m*; ~**ment** [-mənt] Zuteilung; An-, Zuweisung; Verwendung; zugewiesene Aufgabe *f*, Auftrag *m*; *(Gründe)* Vorbringen *n*; *(Schule)* Hausaufgabe; Ernennung; Stellung *f*, Posten *m*; *jur* Übertragung, Abtretung, Zession; Besteuerung; *(deed of* ~ ~*)* Übertragungsurkunde; *mil* Abkommandierung, Versetzung, Unterstellung, Eingliederung *f*; ~**or** [æsi'nɔ:] Abtretende(r), Zedent *m*.

assimila|ble [ə'similəbl] assimilierbar; ~**te** [-eit] *tr* aufnehmen, einverleiben; angleichen, assimilieren; (geistig) verdauen; vergleichen (*to* mit); *itr* sich assimilieren, sich einverleiben; aufgehen (*in* in); sich anpassen (*to* an); ähnlich werden; ~**tion** [əsimi'leiʃən] Angleichung, Assimilation; Übereinstimmung (*to* mit); *med* Nahrungsaufnahme *f*; ~**tive** [-eitiv] assimilierend.

assist [ə'sist] *tr* helfen (*s.o.* jdm), unterstützen, beistehen (*s.o.* jdm); mitwirken (*in doing s.th.* etw zu tun; *in* bei); *itr* anwesend, zugegen sein (*at* bei); beiwohnen; teilnehmen (*at* an); helfen; *s Am* Hilfe *f*, Beistand *m*; Anwesenheit *f*; *sport* Zuspiel *n*; ~*ed by* unter Mitwirkung *gen*; ~**ance** [-əns] Hilfe, Unterstützung; Mitwirkung *f*, Beistand *m*; *with the* ~ ~ *of s.o.* unter jds Mitwirkung; *of s.th.* mit Hilfe *gen*; *public* ~ ~ öffentliche Fürsorge *f*; ~**ant** [-ənt] *s* Assistent, Helfer, Gehilfe, Mitarbeiter; *jur* Stellvertreter, Assessor *m*; *tech* Zusatzgerät *n*; *a* behilflich (*to s.o.* jdm); Hilfs-; *chemist's* ~ ~ Apothekergehilfe *m*; *shop* - ~ ~ Verkäufer(in *f*) *m*; ~ ~ *accountant* Hilfsbuchhalter *m*; ~ ~ *director, manager, superintendent* stellvertretende(r) Direktor *m*; ~ ~ *physician* Assistenzarzt *m*; ~ ~ *professor* (etwa) außerplanmäßige(r) Professor *m*.

assizes [ə'saiziz] *pl* Schwurgerichtssitzungen *f pl* des *High Court of Judges*.

associat|e [ə'souʃiit] *s* Mitarbeiter, Kollege, Freund; Gefährte; *com* Partner, Teilhaber, Gesellschafter *m*; *(Institut)* außerordentliche(s) Mitglied *n*; *jur* Beisitzer; *jur* Mittäter, -schuldige(r) *m*; *a* verbündet, verbunden, begleitend, assoziiert; eng zs.gehörig; nicht hauptamtlich angestellt; *v* [-eit] *tr* vereinigen, verbinden, assoziieren; hinzufügen; zuordnen; in Verbindung bringen (*with* mit); *itr* verkehren (*with s.o.* mit jdm); sich zs.tun, sich zs.schließen (*with* mit); *chem* zs. vorkommen (*with* mit); eng zs.gehören; *he never did ~~ with us very much* er war nie mit uns besonders befreundet; *~~ professor (Am)* außerordentliche(r) Professor *m*; **~ed** [ə'souʃieitid] *a* vereinigt; gemeinsam; *el* angeschlossen; Assoziations-; *~~ company* Tochter(gesellschaft) *f*; **~ion** [əsousi'eiʃən, -ʃi-] Vereinigung *f*, Verein *m*; Gesellschaft *f*; Verband *m*, Syndikat, Konsortium *n*, Genossenschaft; Vergesellschaftung *f*; Umgang, Verkehr *m*, Verbindung (*with* mit), Beziehung (*with* zu); Assoziation, Gedankenverbindung *f*; *(~~ football)* (europäisches) Fußballspiel *n*; *to call up ~s* Erinnerungen wachrufen; *to establish, to form an ~~* e-e Gesellschaft, e-n Verein gründen; *articles of ~~* Gründungsvertrag *m* (e-r AG); Satzung *f*; *bar ~~* Rechtsanwaltskammer *f*; *co-operative ~~* Genossenschaft *f*; *credit ~~* Kreditverein *m*, -genossenschaft *f*; *employers' ~~* Arbeitgeberverband *m*; *member of an ~~* Gesellschafter *m*; *miners' ~~* Knappschaft *f*; *parent-teacher ~~* Eltern-Lehrer-Vereinigung *f*; *Young Men's Christian A~~* (= Y.M.C.A.) Christliche(r) Verein *m* Junger Männer; *~~ of ideas* Ideenassoziation *f*; *~~ test* Assoziationstest *m*; **~ive** [ə'souʃieitiv] assoziativ, gesellig; sich vereinigend.

assonance ['æsənəns] *gram* Assonanz *f*.

assort [ə'sɔ:t] *tr* (aus)sortieren, aussuchen; sichten; klassifizieren, ordnen, gruppieren; *com* mit e-m Warensortiment ausstatten; *itr* zs.passen (*with* mit); derselben Gruppe angehören; sich verbinden, sich zs.schließen, sich verstehen, verkehren (*with* mit); **~ed** [-id] *a com* sortiert; von verschiedenen Arten, verschiedenartig; geordnet, klassifiziert; zs.passend; *ill-~~* schlecht zs.passend; *(Waren)* schlecht zs.gestellt; *well-~~* gut zs.passend; *com* reich sortiert; **~ment** [-mənt] Sortieren, Klassifizieren *n*; Gruppe, Klasse, Klassifizierung; Auswahl, Zs.-stellung *f*, Sortiment *n*, Kollektion *f*; *sample ~~* Musterkollektion *f*.

assuage [ə'sweidʒ] *tr (Schmerz)* lindern; *(Zorn)* besänftigen; beruhigen; *(Durst)* löschen; *(Hunger)* stillen; *(Wunsch)* erfüllen.

assum|e [ə'sju:m] *tr* annehmen; übernehmen; als sicher annehmen; voraussetzen, annehmen, vermuten; vorgeben, sich den Schein geben, unterstellen; *(Macht)* an sich reißen, sich anmaßen; *(Amt)* antreten; *fig* in die Hand nehmen, ergreifen; *(Verantwortung)* übernehmen; *(Erbschaft)* antreten; *(Namen)* beilegen, annehmen; *(Kleider)* anziehen; *~ing that it is true* angenommen, es stimme; **~ed** [-d] *a* vorausgesetzt; angenommen; fiktiv; *(Name)* falsch; **~ing** [-iŋ] eingebildet, anmaßend, überheblich; **~ption** [ə'sʌmpʃən] An-, Übernahme; Aneignung; Vermutung, Annahme, Voraussetzung; Anmaßung; Überheblichkeit *f*, Dünkel *m*; *A~~* (Mariä) Himmelfahrt *f*; *on the ~~ that* unter der Annahme, Voraussetzung, daß; *~~ of power* Machtübernahme *f*.

assur|ance [ə'ʃuərəns] Versicherung, Beteuerung, Zusicherung *f*, Versprechen *n*; Sicherheit, Gewißheit *f*, Vertrauen *n*; Garantie; Selbstsicherheit, Zuversicht; Überheblichkeit, Einbildung; *com* Versicherung *f*; *life ~~* Lebensversicherung *f*; *~~ company* Versicherungsgesellschaft *f*; **~e** [ə'ʃuə] *tr* überzeugen (*of s.th.* von e-r S); beruhigen; versichern (*s.o. of s.th.* jdn e-r S), beteuern; garantieren; zusichern; *com* versichern; *to ~ o.'s life with* e-e Lebensversicherung abschließen bei; **~ed** [-d] *a* sicher; zuversichtlich; keck; *com* versichert; *s* Versicherte(r), Versicherungsnehmer *m*; **~edly** [-dli] *adv* sicherlich, unzweifelhaft; selbstbewußt, kühn; **~er** [-rə] *Br* Versicherungsnehmer *m*.

astatic [æ'stætik] *phys* astatisch.

aster ['æstə] *bot* Aster *f*.

asterisk ['æstərisk] *s typ* Sternchen *n*; *tr* mit e-m Sternchen versehen.

astern [əs'tə:n] *a adv mar* achter(n); rückwärts; zurück; *prp: ~ of* hinter; *full speed ~* volle Kraft zurück.

asteroid ['æstərɔid] *astr* Asteroid *m*.

asthma ['æsmə] *med* Asthma *n*, Kurzatmigkeit *f*; *cardiac ~* Herzasthma *n*; **~tic** [æs'mætik] *a* asthmatisch, kurzatmig; *s* Asthmatiker *m*.

astigmat|ic [æstig'mætik] *phys* astigmatisch; **~ism** [æ'stigmətizm] *phys* Astigmatismus *m*.

astir [ə'stə:] *adv pred a* in Bewegung, auf den Beinen; aufgeregt, erregt, in Aufregung; aufgeschreckt (*with* durch).

astonish [əstɔniʃ] *tr* in Erstaunen setzen; *to be ~ed* erstaunt, überrascht sein, sich wundern (*at* über); **~ing** [-iŋ] erstaunlich, verwunderlich, verblüffend; *it's ~~ to me* das überrascht mich; **~ment** [-mənt] Erstaunen, Verwunderung, Verblüffung *f* (*at* über).

astound [əs'taund] *tr* bestürzen, erschrecken; aus der Fassung bringen.

astraddle [əs'trædl] *adv pred a* rittlings.

astragal ['æstrəgəl] *anat* Sprungbein *n*; *arch* Rundstab *m*.

astrakhan, -chan [æstrə'kæn] *(Textil, Fell)* Astrachan, Krimmer *m*.

astral ['æstrəl] gestirnt; sternförmig; astral; *~* **body** Astralkörper.

astray [ə'strei] *adv pred a* vom rechten Weg ab; *to go, to lead ~* in die Irre gehen, vom rechten Weg abführen.

astride [ə'straid] *adv prp pred a* rittlings (*of* auf); mit gespreizten Beinen.

astringen|cy [əs'trindʒənsi] *med* Adstringenz *f*; **~t** [-t] *s* zs.ziehende(s) Mittel *n*; *a* zs.ziehend.

astro|dome ['æstrədoum] *aero* Astronavigationskuppel *f*; **~labe** ['-leib] Astrolabium *n*; **~loger** [əs'trɔlədʒə] Astrologe *m*; **~logical** [æstrə'lɔdʒikəl] astrologisch; **~logy** [əs'trɔlədʒi] Astrologie *f*; **~naut** ['æstronɔ:t] Astronaut *m*; **~nautics** [-'nɔ:tiks] *pl mit sing* Astronautik, Raumfahrt *f*; **~nomer** [əs'trɔnəmə] Astronom *m*; **~nomic(al)** [æstrə'nɔmik(əl)] astronomisch; *~~ chart, clock* Sterntafel, -uhr *f*; **~nomy** [əs'trɔnəmi] Astronomie; Sternkunde *f*; **~physical** [æstrou'fizikəl] astrophysisch; **~physics** [æstrou'fiziks] *pl mit sing* Astrophysik *f*.

astute [əs'tju:t] schlau; scharfsinnig; **~ness** [-nis] Schlauheit, List *f*; Scharfsinn *m*.

asunder [ə'sʌndə] *adv* auseinander; *to break ~* ausea.brechen; *to come ~* uneins werden; *to drive ~* trennen.

asylum [ə'sailəm] Asyl *n*; *fig* Zufluchtsort *m*; *lunatic ~* Irrenanstalt *f*; *~ for the blind* Blindenanstalt *f*.

asymmetr|ic(al) [æsi'metrik(əl)] asymmetrisch; **~y** [æ'simitri] Asymmetrie *f*.

asymptote ['æsimtout] *math* Asymptote *f*.

at [æt, ət] *prp* **1.** *(Ort)* in, bei, an, auf, zu; *~ Oxford* in Oxford; *~ a distance* in e-r Entfernung; *~ school* in der Schule; *~ the office* im Büro; *~ the dentist's* beim Zahnarzt; *~ work* bei der Arbeit; *~ the sight* beim Anblick (*of* gen); *~ the next corner* an der nächsten Ecke; *~ the station* auf dem Bahnhof; *~ home* zu Hause; **2.** *(Art u. Weise)* in, zu; *~ a trot* im Trab; *to be ~ a loss* in Verlegenheit sein; *(Veranlassung)* auf ... hin; *~ his request* auf s-e Bitte (hin); **3.** *(zeitlich)* um; in; zu; *~ midnight* um Mitternacht; *~ night* in der Nacht; *~ a snail's pace* im Schneckentempo; *~ a moment's notice* sofort; *~ the age of* im Alter von; *~ Christmas* zu Weihnachten; **4.** *(Zustand)* in; *~ peace* im Frieden; *~ rest* in Ruhe; *I feel ~ ease* mir ist wohl zumute; *he is ~ it again* er beschäftigt sich wieder damit; er arbeitet wieder; **5.** *(Richtung)* nach, gegen, zu, an, auf; über; *to aim ~* zielen nach; *to arrive ~ a decision* zu e-r Entscheidung kommen; *to be astonished ~* erstaunt sein über; *he is mad ~ me* er ist wütend auf mich; **6.** *(bei Zahlangaben)* zu; *to buy ~ a shilling* zu (je) e-m Schilling kaufen; *~* **all** überhaupt; *~ all costs* um jeden Preis; *not ~ all* gar nicht, durchaus nicht; nichts zu danken, keine Ursache; *~* **best** bestenfalls; im besten Fall(e); *~* **first** zuerst; *~* **last** endlich; *~* **least** mindestens, wenigstens; *~* **most** höchstens; *~* **noon** mittags; *~* **once** sofort, sogleich; auf einmal; *~* **that** dabei; *(even) ~ that* sogar so; trotzdem; überdies; *~* **times** manchmal, zeitweise; *~* **will** nach Belieben.

ata|brine ['ætəbri:n] *med* Atebrin *n*; **~vism** ['-vizm] Atavismus; (Entwicklungs-)Rückschlag *m*; **~vistic** [ætə'vistik] atavistisch; **~xia** [ə'tæksiə] *med* Ataxie *f*.

atheis|m ['eiθiizm] Atheismus *m*; **~t** ['-st] Atheist *m*; **~tic(al)** [eiθi'istik(əl)] atheistisch.

athirst [ə'θə:st] *pred a* durstig; begierig (*for* nach).

athlet|e ['æθli:t] Athlet *m*; **~ic** [æθ'letik] *a* athletisch; *s pl a. mit sing* (Leicht-)Athletik *f*.

athwart [ə'θwɔ:t] *prp* quer über; gegenüber; *adv* kreuzweise; quer; *mar* dwars.

atilt [ə'tilt] *pred a adv* vornübergeneigt; *hist* mit eingelegter Lanze.

atishoo [ə'tiʃu:] *interj* hatzi!

Atlantic [ət'læntik] *s* Atlantische(r) Ozean, Atlantik *m*; *a* atlantisch.

atlas ['ætləs] *geogr anat* Atlas; *fig* Hauptträger *m*, -stütze *f*; Atlasformat *n*; *(Textil)* Atlas *m*.

atmospher|e ['ætməsfiə] Atmosphäre *a. phys (= 14.69 pounds per square inch = 1 kp/cm²)*; Lufthülle *f*, -raum *m*; *fig* Atmosphäre, Umgebung *f*, Milieu *n*, Stimmung *f*; **~ic(al)** [ætməs'ferik(əl)] *a* atmosphärisch; Luft-; *s pl* atmosphärische Störungen *f pl*; *~~ conditions (pl)* Witterung(sbedingungen *f pl*) *f*; *~~ corrosion* Verwitterung *f*; *~~ electricity* Luftelektrizität *f*; *~~ layer* Luftschicht *f*; *~~ moisture* Luftfeuchtigkeit *f*; *~~ noise* atmosphärische(r) Störpegel *m*; Rauschen *n*; *~~ oxygen* Luftsauerstoff *m*; *~~ pollution* Verunreinigung *f* der Luft; *~~ pressure* Luftdruck *m*; *~~ reflection* Luftspiegelung *f*; *~~ resistance* Luftwiderstand *m*.

atoll ['ætɔl, ə'tɔl] *geogr* Atoll *n*.

atom ['ætəm] *chem* Atom *n*; *fig* winzige Kleinigkeit, Spur *f*; *to blow to ~s* durch e-e Explosion völlig vernichten; in tausend Stücke zerreißen; *~* **bomb** Atombombe *f*; *~* **disintegration** Atomzerfall *m*; *~* **explosion** Atomexplosion *f*; ~ **gun** Atomgeschütz *n*; ~ **pile** Atommeiler *m*.

atomic [ə'tɔmik] atomar; Atom-; ~ **artillery** Atomartillerie *f*; ~ **body** Atomkörper *m*; ~ **bomb** Atombombe ; ~ **bombardment** atomare Beschießung *f*; ~ **canon** Atomgeschütz *n*; ~ **charge** Kernladung *f*; ~ **chart** Atomgewichtstafel *f*; ~ **decay** Atomzerfall *m*; ~ **clock** Atomuhr *f*; ~ **disintegration** Atomzerfall *m*; ~ **dust** Atomstaub *m*; ~ **energy** Atomenergie *f*; *A~ E~ Commission (Am)* Atomenergiebehörde *f*; *~-~ generation* Atomenergieerzeugung *f*; **~fall-out** radioaktive(r) Niederschlag *m*; ~ **fission** Atomspaltung, -zertrümmerung *f*; ~ **force** Atomkraft *f*; ~ **fuel** Kern-, Atombrennstoff *m*; ~ **furnace** Kernreaktor *m*; ~ **group** Atomgruppe *f*; ~ **heat** Atomwärme *f*; **~-hydrogen welding** Arcatomschweißung *f*; ~ **nucleus** Atomkern *m*; *~ ~ explosion* Atomkernsprengung *f*; ~ **number** Ordnungs-, Kernladungszahl *f*; ~ **physics** *pl mit sing* Atomphysik *f*; ~ **pile** Atombrenner, -meiler *m*; ~ **power** Atomkraft *f*; *~ ~ plant, station* Atomkraftwerk *n*; ~ **race** Wettlauf *m* um die Atomrüstung; ~ **reactor** Atomreaktor *m*; ~ **research** Atom-, Kernforschung *f*; ~ **smashing** Atomzertrümmerung *f*; ~ **structure** Atomaufbau *m*, -gitter *n*; ~ **symbol** Atomzeichen *n*; ~ **valence** Atomwertigkeit *f*; **~warfare** Atomkriegführung *f*; **~warhead** Atomsprengkopf *m*; ~ **weapon** atomare Waffe *f*; ~ **weight** Atomgewicht *n*.

atom|istic [ætə'mistik] atomistisch; **~ize** ['ætəmaiz] *tr* atomisieren, feinst verteilen, zerstäuben; **~izer** ['ætəmaizə] Zerstäuber *m*; Spritzdüse *f*; *~ ~ cone* Spritzkegel *m*; *~ ~ valve* Einspritzventil *n*; **~y** ['ætəmi] Atom *n*; *fig* Kleinigkeit *f*; Zwerg *m*.

atonal [ei-, æ'tounəl] *mus* atonal.

atone [ə'toun] *itr* sühnen (*for* für); wiedergutmachen (*for s.th.* etw); **~ment** [-mənt] Sühne, Buße, Wiedergutmachung *f*; *rel* Sühnopfer *n*.

atop [ə'tɔp] *adv* oben, zuoberst; *prp* auf.

atrabilious [ætrə'biljəs] griesgrämig, reizbar; melancholisch.

atroc|ious [ə'trouʃəs] grausam; roh, brutal; *fam* abscheulich, scheußlich; **~ity** [ə'trɔsiti] Grausamkeit; Roheit; Greueltat; Scheußlichkeit *f*; *fam* üble(s) Stück *n*, Geschmacklosigkeit *f*; Mißgriff, grobe(r) Fehler *m*.

atrophy ['ætrəfi] *s med* Atrophie *f*, Schwund *m*, Schrumpfung *f*; *itr* verkümmern, schrumpfen, absterben; *tr* verkümmern lassen; *muscular ~* Muskelatrophie *f*.

atropine ['ætrəpi:n] *pharm* Atropin *n*.

attaboy ['ætəbɔi] *interj Am sl* bravo!

attach [ə'tætʃ] *tr* anheften, anbringen, anschließen, anbauen, anhängen, befestigen (*to* an); *(e-m Schriftstück)* beifügen; *(Bedeutung)* beilegen, beimessen, verbinden; *fig* fesseln, für sich gewinnen; *jur* verhaften, festnehmen; *(Gegenstand)* pfänden (lassen); beschlagnahmen; *mil* abkommandieren, zuteilen, *(vorübergehend)* unterstellen; *itr* haften (*to* an); verknüpft, verbunden sein (*to* mit); *(Versicherung)* zu laufen beginnen; *to ~ o.s. to* sich anschließen an; *(Partei)* beitreten *dat*; *to be ~ed* eng verbunden sein (*to* mit); hängen (*to* an); abkommandiert sein (*to* zu); *to ~ value to* Wert legen auf; **~able** [-əbl] pfändbar; mit Beschlag belegbar; **~é** [ə'tæʃei, ætə'ʃei] *pol* Attaché *m*; *~ ~ case* Aktentasche *f*; *air, commercial, military, naval, press ~ ~* Luft-, Handels-, Militär-, Marine-, Presseattaché *m*; **~ed** [-t] *a* beigefügt, anliegend; zugehörig (*to* zu); *mil* abkommandiert; **~ment** [-mənt] Befestigung, An-, Beifügung; Bei-, Anlage; *fig* Anhänglichkeit, Zuneigung; *tech* Zusatzvorrichtung *f*, -gerät *n*; Anschluß *m* (*to* an); *anat (Muskel)* Ansatzstelle; *jur* Verhaftung; *(Sache)* Beschlagnahme, Pfändung *f*; *(Versicherung)* Inkrafttreten *n*; *mil* Abkommandierung, Zuteilung, Unterstellung *f*; *pl* Zubehör(teile *m pl*) *n*.

attack [ə'tæk] *tr* angreifen *a. chem*; vorgehen (*s.o.* gegen jdn); sich stürzen (*s.th.* auf etw); *(Aufgabe)* in Angriff nehmen, anpacken; *(Krankheit)* befallen; kritisieren, beschimpfen; *itr* e-n Angriff unternehmen, *aero* fliegen; *s* Angriff *m* (*on* auf, gegen); Attacke *a. fig*; *(Arbeit)* Inangriffnahme *f*; *(Krankheit)* Anfall *m*, Kolik *f*; *chem* Angriff; *mus* Einsatz *m*; *to launch, to start an ~* angreifen; *air ~* Luftangriff *m*; *bilious ~* Gallenkolik *f*; *front of ~* Angriffsfront *f*; *heart ~* Herzanfall *m*; *low-flying ~* Tiefangriff *m*; *surprise ~* Überraschungsangriff *m*; *zone of ~* Angriffsfeld *n*; *~ of fever* Fieberanfall *m*.

attain [ə'tein] *tr* erreichen, erlangen, fertigbringen, vollenden; *itr* gelangen (*to* bis zu); *to ~ to man's estate* in die Mannesjahre kommen; *to ~ power* an die Macht gelangen; **~able** [-əbl] erreichbar; **~der** [-də] *jur* Ehrverlust u. Vermögenseinziehung *f*; *bill of ~ ~* Verordnung *f* über Vermögenseinziehung u. Ehrverlust; **~ment** [-mənt] Errungenschaft; Leistung *f*; *(Ziel)* Erreichen *n*; Erlangung *f*; *pl* Kenntnisse, Fähigkeiten, Fertigkeiten *f pl*; Bildung, Kultur *f*; *previous ~~s (pl)* Vorbildung *f*; **~t** [-t] *tr* entehren, beflecken; *jur* zum Tode u. zu dauerndem Ehrverlust verurteilen.

attar ['ætə] Essenz *f*; *~ of roses* Rosenöl *n*.

attempt [ə'tempt] *tr* versuchen, unternehmen; wagen; sich bemühen (*to do, at doing s.th.* etw zu tun); *s* Versuch *m* (*at* mit); Attentat *n*, Anschlag *m* (*upon, against* auf); *to make an ~ on s.o.'s life* auf jdn e-n Anschlag verüben; *~ed murder* Mordversuch *m*.

attend [ə'tend] *tr (Schule)* besuchen; beiwohnen (*a meeting* e-r Versammlung); *(Vorlesung)* hören; betreuen, bedienen, pflegen; *(Arzt)* behandeln; begleiten; s-e Aufwartung machen (*s.o.* jdm); das Ergebnis sein *(s.th.* von etw); *tech* bedienen; *obs* erwarten; *itr* anwesend, zugegen sein (*at* bei); aufpassen, sich konzentrieren, hören, achtgeben (*to* auf); beachten, einhalten (*to s.th.* etw); sich befassen (*to* mit); sorgen (*to* für), sich kümmern (*to* um), besorgen, erledigen (*to s.th.* etw); erfüllen (*to o.'s duties* s-e Pflicht); ausführen (*to an order* e-n Auftrag); berücksichtigen (*to a recommendation* e-e Empfehlung); bedienen (*to a customer* e-n Kunden); aufwarten (*upon s.o.* jdm); die Folge sein (*on* von); *to ~ church* in die Kirche gehen; **~ance** [-əns] Anwesenheit *f*, Besuch *m*, Erscheinen *n*; (Zu-)Hörerschaft (*at* bei), Teilnahme, Beteiligung (*at* bei, an); Begleitung, Aufwartung, Bedienung; *tech* Wartung; *med* Behandlung *f* (*on s.o.* jds); *in ~ ~* wartend; diensttuend; *to be in ~ ~* Dienst haben; anwesend sein (*at* bei); *to dance ~ ~ on s.o.* hinter jdm her sein; sich sehr um jdn bemühen; *the ~ ~ at the meeting was poor* die Versammlung war schwach besucht; *hours of ~ ~* Dienststunden *f pl*; Besuchszeit *f*; *medical ~ ~* ärztliche Behandlung *f*; *~ ~ at school* Schulbesuch *m*; *~ ~ card* Anwesenheitskarte *f*; *~ ~ fees (pl)* Präsenzgelder *n pl*; *~ ~ list, book* Anwesenheitsliste *f*; *~ ~ recorder* Stechuhr *f*; **~ant** [-ənt] *a* begleitend; anwesend; folgend (*on* auf); diensttuend (*on* bei); *s* Diener(in *f*); Wärter(in *f*); Aufseher(in *f*); Begleiter (in *f*) *m*; Anwesende(r *m*); *theat* Logenschließerin *f*; *pl* Dienerschaft *f*; *~ ~ circumstances (pl)* Begleitumstände *m pl*.

attent|ion [ə'tenʃən] Aufmerksamkeit; Berücksichtigung, Beachtung, Gefälligkeit; *med* Pflege, Behandlung; *tech* Aufsicht, Wartung; *mil* Grund-, Habachtstellung *f*; *(in Briefen)* zu Händen von; *~! (mil)* Stillgestanden! *without attracting ~ ~* unauffällig; *to attract ~ ~* Aufmerksamkeit erregen; *to be all ~ ~ (fam)* ganz Ohr sein; *to call, to draw s.o.'s ~ ~ to s.th.* jdn auf etw hinweisen; *to come to, to stand at ~ ~ (mil)* Haltung annehmen; stillstehen; *to command s.o.'s ~ ~* jds Aufmerksamkeit in Anspruch nehmen; *to give s.o. ~ ~* jdm Aufmerksamkeit, Gehör schenken; *to pay ~ ~* achtgeben, aufpassen; *to s.o.* jdm aufmerksam zuhören; *to s.th.* etw beachten, auf etw achten; *to pay o.'s attentions to s.o.* jdm den Hof machen; *to receive ~ ~* berücksichtigt, erledigt werden; Beachtung finden; *med* versorgt werden; *to turn o.'s ~ ~ to s.th.* auf etw s-e Aufmerksamkeit richten; **~ive** [-tiv] aufmerksam (*to* auf); besorgt (*to* um); zuvorkommend, gefällig (*to* gegenüber).

attenuat|e [ə'tenjueit] *tr* verdünnen; schwächen, dämpfen; verkleinern, verringern; *fig* abschwächen, mildern; *a* [-it] verdünnt; abgemagert; spitz zulaufend; **~ion** [ətenju'eiʃən] Dämpfung; Schwächung; Verdünnung; Abmagerung; *fig* Abschwächung, Milderung *f*; **~or** [-ə] *tech* Dämpfer *m*.

attest [ə'test] *tr* bezeugen, bestätigen; beweisen; klarlegen; beglaubigen, bescheinigen, beurkunden; unter Eid aussagen; legalisieren; *mil* vereidigen (*s.o.* jdn); *itr* bezeugen (*to s.th.* etw); **~ation** [ætes'teiʃən] Bescheinigung, Bestätigung *f*; Zeugnis *n*; Beurkundung, Beglaubigung; *mil* Vereidigung *f*; **~er, ~or** [-ə] Zeuge *m*.

attic ['ætik] *s* Dachkammer *f*; *a A~* attisch; *fig* vornehm, elegant; klassisch.

attire [ə'taiə] *s* Kleidung; Tracht *f*; *tr* kleiden; schmücken; *to ~ o.s. in* sich schmücken mit; sich kleiden in.

attitud|e ['ætitju:d] Stellung, Haltung *f*; Verhalten *n*, Einstellung (*towards* gegenüber); *aero* Fluglage *f*; *to strike an ~ ~* sich affektiert benehmen; *~ ~ of mind* Geisteshaltung *f*; **~inize** [æti'tju:dinaiz] *itr* sich aufspielen.

attorney [ə'tə:ni] *jur Am (~ at law)* Bevollmächtigte(r); Rechtsanwalt *m*; *power of ~ ~* Vollmacht *f*; *~ for the defense (jur)* Verteidiger *m*; **A~-General** *Br* erste(r) Kronanwalt; *Am etwa* Justizminister *m*.

attract [ə'trækt] *tr* anziehen *a. fig*; *(Aufmerksamkeit)* erregen, auf sich lenken; *fig* fesseln, reizen, anlocken; *without ~ing attention* unauffällig; **~ion** [-ʃən] Anziehung *a. phys*; *(power of ~ ~)* Anziehungskraft *f*; Reiz, Zauber *m*; Attraktion, Zugnummer *f*; *~ ~ of gravity* Schwerkraft *f*; **~ive** [-iv] fesselnd, anziehend; Anziehungs-; *fig* günstig, vorteilhaft, verlockend.

attribut|able [ə'tribjutəbl] entfallend (*to* auf); zuzuschreiben; **~e** [ə'tribju:t]

tr zuschreiben, beimessen (*to s.th.* e-r S); *s* ['ætribju:t] Eigenschaft *f*, Merkmal, Attribut *n a. gram*; **~ive** [-iv] *a gram* attributiv; *s* Attribut *n*.
attrition [ə'triʃən] Abnutzung *f*, Verschleiß *m*; *med* Wundreiben *n*; *war of* ~ Zermürbungskrieg *m*.
attune [ə'tju:n] *tr* in Einklang bringen (*to* mit); *mus* stimmen; *tech* einstellen.
auburn ['ɔ:bən] kastanienbraun.
auction ['ɔ:kʃən] *s* Auktion, (öffentliche) Versteigerung *f*; *(~ bridge) Art* Bridge *n*; *tr (to ~ off)* versteigern; *to buy by ~* ersteigern; *to hold an ~* e-e Versteigerung abhalten; *to sell by ~* im Wege der Versteigerung verkaufen; *to put up to (Am at)* ~ versteigern; *Dutch ~* Auktion *f*, bei der der Preis so lange herabgesetzt wird, bis sich ein Käufer findet; ~ **day** Versteigerungstermin *m*; **~eer** [ɔ:kʃə'niə] *s* Versteigerer, Auktionator *m*; *tr* versteigern; ~ **market, room** Versteigerungslokal *n*; **~-sale** Verkauf *m* im Wege der Versteigerung.
audaci|ous [ɔ:'deiʃəs] kühn, wagemutig; *pej* frech, dreist; **~ty** [ɔ:'dæsiti] Kühnheit *f*; Wagemut *m*, Tollkühnheit; *pej* Frechheit, Dreistigkeit *f*.
audib|ility [ɔ:di'biliti] Hörbarkeit, Vernehmbarkeit; Verständigung *f*; **~le** ['ɔ:dəbl] hörbar; vernehmlich.
audience ['ɔ:djəns] Hören *n*; Zuhörer (-schaft *f*) *m pl*; Publikum *n*, Besucher, Anwesende *m pl*; Gelegenheit *f*, gehört zu werden; Audienz *f* (*of, with* bei); *radio* Hörer *m pl*; *tele* Fernsehpublikum *n*; Leser *m pl*; *to give s.o. ~* jdn anhören (*to* um zu); ~ **room** Audienz-, *jur* Verhandlungssaal *m*.
audio ['ɔ:dio(u)] Ton-, Radio-, Hör-; ~ **frequency** Tonfrequenz *f*; *~~ current* Sprechstrom *m*; *~~ transformer* Übertrager *m*; **~meter** [ɔ:di'ɔmitə] Audiometer *m*; ~ **monitor** Tonüberwachung *f*; **~phile** ['-fail] Schallplattennarr *m*; **~-visual aids** *pl (Schule)* Anschauungsmaterial *n*; *mar* akustisch-optische Hilfsmittel *n pl*.
audit ['ɔ:dit] *s* Buchprüfung; *(~ of accounts)* Rechnungsprüfung *f*; *itr* Rechnungen, Bücher prüfen; *Am* als Gasthörer teilnehmen; *tr* prüfen; **~ion** [ɔ:'diʃən] *s* (Zu-, An-)Hören *n*; *theat* Sprech-, Hörprobe *f*; *itr* e-e Hörprobe abnehmen; *tr* zur Probe vortragen lassen; ~ **officer** Rechnungsprüfer *m*; **~or** ['ɔ:ditə] Wirtschafts-, Buchprüfer; Hörer; *Am (Universität)* Gasthörer *m*; **~orium** [ɔ:di'tɔ:riəm] Hörsaal *m*, Auditorium *n*; Vortrags-, Konzert-, Theatersaal *m*; *(Kirche)* Schiff; *(Kloster)* Sprechzimmer *n*; **~ory** ['ɔ:ditəri] *s* Auditorium *n*; große(r) Saal *m*; Zuhörerschaft *f*; *a* Hör-; *~~ acuity* Hörschärfe *f*; *~~ duct* Gehörgang *m*; *~~ impression* Gehöreindruck *m*; *~~ nerve* Gehörnerv *m*; *~~ ossicles (pl)* Gehörknöchelchen *n pl*; *~~ tube* Eustachische Röhre *f*.
auger ['ɔ:gə] *s tech* Erd-, Löffelbohrer *m*; *itr Am fam aero (to ~ in)* e-e Bruchlandung, Kleinholz machen.
aught [ɔ:t] *s* (irgend) etwas; Null *f*; *adv* in irgendeiner Art; überhaupt; *for ~ I know* soviel ich weiß.
augment [ɔ:g'ment] *tr* vermehren, vergrößern; *itr* zunehmen, sich steigern, sich vergrößern; *s* ['ɔ:gmənt] Zunahme *f*; *gram* Augment *n*; **~ation** [ɔ:gmen'teiʃən] Vermehrung, Steigerung, Vergrößerung, Erhöhung *f*; Wachstum *n*, Zunahme *f*.
augur ['ɔ:gə] *s* Augur, Wahrsager *m*; *tr* weissagen, vorhersagen; *itr* ein Vorzeichen sein; *to ~ ill, well* ein schlechtes, ein gutes Vorzeichen sein (*for* für); **~y** ['ɔ:gjuri] Weissagung, Ahnung, Vorbedeutung *f*; Vorzeichen, Omen *n*.
August ['ɔ:gəst] *s* August *m*; *a*: *a~* erhaben, ehrfurchtgebietend; erlaucht.
auk [ɔ:k] *zoo* Alk *m*.
auld [ɔ:ld] *Scot* alt; ~ **lang syne** [læŋ'sain] vor langer Zeit.
aunt [ɑ:nt] Tante *f*; **A~ Sally** *fam* Wurfbude *f* auf Jahrmärkten; **~y, ~ie** ['-i] Tantchen *n*.
aur|a ['ɔ:rə] *pl a. -ae* ['-ri:] Aura *f*; *med* Vor-, Angstgefühl; *phys* Gasleuchten *n*; **~al** ['-l] Ohr-; *~~ reception* Hörempfang *m*; *~~ surgeon* Ohrenarzt *m*; **~eole** ['ɔ:rioul] Glorie *f*, Heiligenschein; *astr* Hof *m*, Aureole *f*; **~eomycin** [ɔ:rio'maisin] *pharm* Aureomycin *n*; **~icle** ['ɔ:rikl] *(Herz)* Vorhof *m*; äußere(s) Ohr *n*; **~icular** [ɔ:'rikjulə] Ohr-; *~~ confession* Ohrenbeichte *f*; *~~ witness* Ohrenzeuge *m*; **~iferous** [ɔ:'rifərəs] goldhaltig; **~ist** ['ɔ:rist] Ohrenarzt *m*; **~ochs** ['ɔ:rɔks] *zoo* Auerochse *m*; **~ora** [ɔ:'rɔ:rə] Aurora; Morgenröte *f*; *~~ australis, borealis* Süd-, Nordlicht *n*; **~oral** [ɔ:'rɔrəl] rosig; hell, leuchtend; Morgen-.
auscultat|e ['ɔ:skəlteit] *tr itr med* abhorchen, auskultieren; **~ion** [ɔ:skʌl'teiʃən] Abhorchen *n*, Auskultation *f*.
auspic|e ['ɔ:spis] (günstiges) Vorzeichen, Anzeichen, Omen *n*; *pl* Schirmherrschaft *f*; Schutz *m*; *under the ~~s of s.o.* unter jds Schirmherrschaft; **~ious** [ɔ:s'piʃəs] günstig, erfolgversprechend; erfolgreich.
auster|e [ɔ:s'tiə] streng; ernst; schmucklos, einfach, herb; asketisch, enthaltsam; **~ity** [ɔ:s'teriti] Strenge *f*; Ernst *m*; Schmucklosigkeit, Herbheit, strenge Einfachheit *f*; *pl* Kasteiungen *f pl*; Sparmaßnahmen *f pl*.
austral ['ɔ:strəl] südlich.
Australia [ɔ:s'treiljə] Australien *n*; **~n** [-n] *a* australisch; *s* Australier(in *f*) *m*.
Austria ['ɔ:striə] Österreich *n*; **~n** *a* österreichisch; *s* Österreicher(in *f*) *m*.
autar|chy ['ɔ:tɑ:ki] Autokratie; *Am* Autarkie *f*; **~ky** [-] Autarkie *f*.
autar|chy ['ɔ:tɑ:ki] absolute Herrschaft; *Am* Autarkie *f*; **~ky** [-] Autarkie *f*.
authentic [ɔ:'θentik] authentisch, zuverlässig; echt; glaubwürdig; verbürgt; **~ate** [-eit] *tr* beglaubigen; die Echtheit nachweisen (*s.th.* gen); **~ation** [ɔ:θenti'keiʃən] Beglaubigung; Feststellung *f* der Echtheit; **~ity** [ɔ:θen'tisiti] Echtheit; Glaubwürdigkeit *f*; **~ator** [ɔ:'θentikeitə] Kennziffer(n) *f (pl)*.
author ['ɔ:θə] *s* Autor, Verfasser; Schriftsteller; Urheber; Schöpfer *m*; *tr Am* verfassen; **~ess** ['-ris] Verfasserin, Schriftstellerin *f*.
authorit|arian [ɔ:θɔri'tεəriən] *a* autoritär; *s* autoritäre(r) Mensch *m*; **~arianism** [-izm] Führerprinzip *n*; **~ative** [ɔ:'θɔriteitiv] maßgebend, maßgeblich, autoritativ; kompetent; gebieterisch; **~y** [ɔ:'θɔriti] (Amts-, Befehls-)Gewalt, (Macht-)Befugnis; Machtvollkommenheit, Autorität *f*; Recht *n*, Vollmacht, Genehmigung *f*; Ansehen *n*, Einfluß *m*; Behörde, Dienststelle *f*; Sachverständige(r) *m*, Kapazität, Autorität (*on* auf dem Gebiet *gen*); zuverlässige Quelle *f*, Nachweis; Ratgeber, Gewährsmann *m*; *jur* Rechtsquelle *f*, Präzedenzfall *m*; Rechtskraft *f*; *pl* Behörde(n) *f pl*, Obrigkeit *f*; *from competent ~~* von maßgebender Seite; *on o.'s own ~~* auf eigene Verantwortung; *on good ~~* aus guter Quelle; *on legal ~~* auf gesetzlicher Grundlage; *under the ~~ of* im Auftrag *gen*; *without ~~* unbefugt, unberechtigt; *to apply to the proper ~~* sich an die zuständige Stelle wenden; *to exercise ~~* Einfluß ausüben *od* haben (*over* auf); *to have ~~* befugt, ermächtigt sein (*to do* zu tun); *assumption of ~~* Amtsanmaßung *f*; *court, judicial ~ies (pl)* Gerichtsbehörden *f pl*; *governmental ~~* Staatsbehörde *f*; *local ~~* Lokalbehörde *f*; *municipal ~~* Stadtbehörde *f*; *parental ~~* elterliche Gewalt *f*; *port ~~ (mar)* Hafenamt *n*; *power of ~~* Ermächtigung *f*; *~~ of command* Befehlsgewalt *f*.
author|ization [ɔ:θərai'zeiʃən] Bevollmächtigung, Ermächtigung; Genehmigung, Einwilligung *f*; *to give s.o. ~~* jdm die Ermächtigung erteilen, jdn ermächtigen (*to do* zu tun; *for* zu); **~ize** ['ɔ:θəraiz] *tr* bevollmächtigen, ermächtigen; die Befugnis erteilen (*s.o.* jdm), berechtigen; genehmigen, billigen (*to do* zu tun); *(Zahlung)* anweisen; **~ized** ['ɔ:θəraizd] *a* befugt, bevollmächtigt, berechtigt; *through ~~ channels* auf dem Dienstweg; *to be ~~* befugt, ermächtigt, autorisiert sein (*to* zu); *~~ agent* Bevollmächtigte(r) *m*; *~~ capital* Stamm-, Grundkapital *n*; *~~ maximum load* zulässige Höchstbelastung *f*; *~~ recipient* Zustellungsbevollmächtigte(r) *m*; *~~ to sign* zeichnungsberechtigt; *~~ strength* Sollstärke *f*; *A~~ Version* amtliche englische Bibelübersetzung von 1611; **~less** ['ɔ:θəlis] *a* ohne Angabe des Verfassers; **~ship** ['ɔ:θəʃip] Verfasserschaft; Schriftstellerei *f*; Schriftstellerberuf *m*.
auto ['ɔ:tou] *pl -os s Am fam* Auto *n*; *~- (pref)* selbst(tätig); Auto-, auto-; **~-alarm device** *(Radar)* selbsttätige(s) Alarmgerät *n*.
autobiograph|er [ɔ:to(u)bai'ɔgrəfə] Selbstbiograph *m*; **~ic(al)** [ɔ:to(u)baiə'græfik(əl)] autobiographisch; **~y** [ɔ:to(u)bai'ɔgrəfi] Selbstbiographie *f*.
autochthonous [ɔ:'tɔkθənəs] autochthon; ursprünglich.
autoclave ['ɔ:toukleiv] Dampfkochtopf *m*.
autocra|cy [ɔ:'tɔkrəsi] Autokratie, Selbstherrschaft *f*; **~t** ['ɔ:təkræt] Autokrat, Selbstherrscher *m*; **~tic(al)** [ɔ:tə'krætik(əl)] autokratisch, selbstherrlich.
autogiro, -gyro ['ɔ:tou'dʒaiərou] *pl -os aero* Drehflügelflugzeug *n (Schutzmarke)*.
autograph ['ɔ:təgræf, -ɑ:f] *s* Autogramm *n*; eigenhändige Unterschrift; Vervielfältigung; Originalhandschrift *f*; *tr* eigenhändig unterschreiben; vervielfältigen, umdrucken; **~ic(al)** [ɔ:tə'græfik(əl)] eigenhändig geschrieben; hektographisch vervielfältigt.
automat ['ɔ:təmæt] (Nahrungsmittel-) Automat *m*, Automatenbüfett *n*; **~ed** ['-meitid] *a* automatisiert; **~ic** [ɔ:tə'mætik] *a* automatisch selbsttätig; *fig* mechanisch; *s* Selbstladepistole *f*, -gewehr *n*; Automat *m*; *~~ control* Selbststeuerung *f*; *~~ cut-in, cut-out* Selbstein-, -ausschalter *m*; *~~ drive* Selbstantrieb *m*; *~~ exchange (tele)* Wählamt *n*; *~~ engine control* Kommandogerät *n*; *~~ lubrication* Selbstschmierung *f*; *~~ pencil* Druckbleistift *m*; *~~ pilot* Steuerautomatik *f*, Selbststeuergerät *n*; *~~ release* Selbstauslösung *f*; *~~ rifle* automatische(s) Gewehr, Sturmgewehr *n*; *~~ transmitter (tele)* Maschinengeber *m*; *~~ tuning (Radio)* Druckknopfeinstellung *f*; *~~ volume control* Schwundausgleich *m*, Lautstärkeregelung *f*; *~~ weapon* Maschinenwaffe *f*; *~ welding* Automatenschweißung *f*; **~ion** [ɔ:tə'meiʃən] Automation *f*;

~ism [ɔ:'tɔmətizm] *psychol* Automatismus *m*; **~on** [ɔ:'tɔmətən, -tɔn] *pl a. -ta* [-tə] Automat *m*; Gliederpuppe *f*.

automo|bile ['ɔtəməbi:l, -'bi:l, ɔ:tə'moubi:l] *s Am* Auto(mobil) *n*, Kraftwagen *m*; *a* [ɔ:tə'moubil] selbstbeweglich; mit eigenem Antrieb (versehen); *~~ body* Karosserie *f*; *~~ club* Automobilklub *m*; *~~ flag* Standarte *f*; *~~ manufacture* Kraftfahrzeugbau *m*; *~~ spares and accessories (pl)* Kraftfahrzeugersatz- u. -zubehörteile *m pl*; **~bilist** [ɔ:təmou'bi:list, ɔ:tə'moubilist] *Am* Autofahrer *m*; **~tive** [ɔ:tə'moutiv] *Am* Auto-; Automobil-; selbstbeweglich; *~~ engineering* Kraftfahrzeugtechnik *f*; *~~ equipment, supplies (pl)* Autozubehör *n*; *~~ gas oil* Dieselöl *n*; *~~ industry* Kraftfahrzeugindustrie *f*; *~~ maintenance* Kraftfahrzeuginstandhaltung *f*; *~~ mechanic* Kraftfahrzeugmechaniker *m*.

autonom|ic, ~ous [ɔ:tə'nɔmik, ɔ:'tɔnəməs] autonom, unabhängig, selbständig; mit eigener Verwaltung; **~y** [ɔ:'tɔnəmi] Autonomie, Selbstverwaltung, -regierung *f*; *administrative ~~* Verwaltungsautonomie *f*.

autopsy ['ɔ:təpsi] *med* Autopsie, Obduktion, Leichenschau *f*.

auto|suggestion [ɔ:to(u)sə'dʒestʃən] Selbstsuggestion *f*; **~truck** ['ɔ:toutrʌk] *Am* Lastkraftwagen *m*; **~type** ['ɔ:tətaip] *s* Faksimile *n*; Autotypie *f*.

autumn ['ɔ:təm] *s* Herbst *m a. fig*; *a* herbstlich; Herbst-; *in ~* im Herbst; **~nal** [ɔ:'tʌmnəl] herbstlich *a. fig*; Herbst-.

auxiliary [ɔ:g'ziljəri] *a* Hilfs-, Not-, Neben-; behelfsmäßig; zusätzlich; *s (~ verb)* Hilfszeitwort *n*; Hilfsgröße *f*; *pl* Hilfskräfte, -truppen *f pl*; *to be ~ to s.th.* e-r S dienlich sein; *~* **antenna** Behelfsantenne *f*; *~* **apparatus** Zusatzgerät *n*; *~* **causes** *pl jur* Nebenursachen *f pl*; *~* **cruiser** Hilfskreuzer *m*; *~* **engine** Hilfsmotor *m*; *~* **equipment** Hilfs-, Zusatzgerät *n*; *~* **frequency** *tele* Hilfsfrequenz *f*; *~* **fuel tank** *mot* Reservetank *m*; *~* **gear** *mot* Geländegang *m*; *~* **hospital** *mil* Ausweichlazarett *n*; *~* **means** Behelf *m*, Hilfsmittel *n pl*; *~* **material** Behelfsmaterial *n*; *~* **personnel** Hilfspersonal *n*; *~* **police** Hilfspolizei *f*; *~* **rocket** Zusatzrakete *f*; *~* **seat** Notsitz *m*; *~* **service** Hilfsdienst *m*; *~* **set** Zusatzgerät *n*; *~* **target** Hilfsziel *n*.

*

avail [ə'veil] *itr tr* helfen, nützen, von Nutzen sein; *to ~ (o.s.) of s.th.* sich e-r S bedienen; etw benutzen; Gebrauch von etw machen; *(Gelegenheit)* ergreifen; *s* Nutzen, Vorteil *m*, Hilfe *f*; *of no ~* nutzlos; *without ~* vergeblich; *to be of little ~* von geringem Nutzen sein (*to* für); **~ability** [əveilə'biliti] Verfügbarkeit, Verwendbarkeit *f* (*for* für); Vorhandensein *n*; *jur* Gültigkeit, -sdauer *f*; **~able** [-əbl] verfügbar, greifbar, vorhanden; brauchbar; *com* lieferbar, erhältlich; *jur* gültig (*for* für); *by all ~~ means* mit allen verfügbaren Mitteln; *no longer ~~ (Buch)* vergriffen; *(Ware)* nicht mehr lieferbar; *jur* nicht mehr gültig, ungültig; *to be ~~* zur Verfügung stehen, erhältlich sein; zugänglich, *(Person)* zu sprechen sein; *to make ~~ to s.o.* jdm zur Verfügung stellen.

avalanche ['ævəlɑ:nʃ] Lawine *f a. fig*.

avaric|e ['ævəris] Gier, Habsucht *f*; Geiz *m*; **~ious** [ævə'riʃəs] gierig, habsüchtig; geizig.

avast [ə'vɑ:st] *interj mar* stop!

avatar [ævə'tɑ:] Inkarnation (e-s Gottes), Menschwerdung *f*.

avenge [ə'vendʒ] *tr* rächen; strafen, ahnden; *to be ~d on* Rache nehmen, Vergeltung üben an; *to ~ o.s. on* sich rächen an.

avenue ['ævinju:] Zugang *m*, Anfahrt; Allee; *Am* Durchgangs-, Hauptstraße *f*.

aver [ə'və:] *tr* behaupten, als Tatsache hinstellen; bekräftigen; *jur* beweisen.

average ['ævəridʒ] *s* Durchschnitt, Mittelwert *m*; *mar* Havarie *f*, Seeschaden *m*; *a* durchschnittlich; Durchschnitts-; üblich, normal; *mar* Havarie-; *tr itr* im Durchschnitt betragen *od* rechnen; den Durchschnitt nehmen von, mitteln; im Durchschnitt ausmachen, *mot* zurücklegen, fahren; im Mittel ergeben; durchschnittlich verdienen *od* leisten; *Am* gleichmäßig verteilen (*among* unter); *to ~ up to* sich im Durchschnitt belaufen auf; *on the (an) ~* durchschnittlich, im Durchschnitt; *to be above (below) the ~* überdurchschnittlich sein; über (unter) dem Durchschnitt liegen; *to strike, to take an (the) ~* den Durchschnitt nehmen; *adjustment of ~* Schadensregulierung *f*; *annual, monthly ~* Jahres-, Monatsdurchschnitt *m*; *~* **adjuster** Havariedispacheur *m*; *~* **age** Durchschnittsalter *n*; *~* **amount, sum** Durchschnittsbetrag *m*; *~* **consumption** Durchschnittsverbrauch *m*; *~* **cost** Durchschnittskosten *pl*; *~* **damage** Havarieschaden *m*; *~* **income** Durchschnittseinkommen *n*; *~* **life** mittlere Lebensdauer *od* Nutzungsdauer *f*; *~* **load** Durchschnittsbelastung *f*; *~* **output** Durchschnittsproduktion, -ausbringung *f*, -ausstoß *m*; *~* **price** Durchschnittspreis *m*; *~* **proceeds** *pl* Durchschnittsertrag *m*; *~* **quality** Durchschnittsqualität *f*; *~* **result** Durchschnittsergebnis *n*; *~* **speed, velocity** Durchschnittsgeschwindigkeit *f*; *~* **value** Durchschnittswert *m*; *~* **wage** Durchschnittslohn *m*; *~* **yield** Durchschnittsertrag *m*.

avers|e [ə'və:s] abgeneigt (*to* gegen); unwillig; **~ion** [ə'və:ʃən] Widerwille *m*, Abneigung *f* (*to, from* gegen); Greuel *m*; Widerstreben *n*.

avert [ə'və:t] *tr* abwenden (*from* von); verhindern, verhüten, abwehren, vermeiden.

aviary ['eiviəri] Vogelhaus *n*.

aviat|e ['eivieit, 'æ-] *itr aero* (ein)fliegen; **~ion** [eivi'eiʃən] Luftfahrt *f*, Fliegen, Flugwesen *n*; *civil, commercial ~~* Zivil-, Verkehrsluftfahrt *f*; *~~ allowance* Fliegerzulage *f*; *~~ badge* Fliegerabzeichen *n*; *~~ company* Luftverkehrsgesellschaft *f*; *~~ field* Flugfeld *n*; *~~ fuel, petrol, spirit, (Am) gasoline* Flugbenzin *n*; *~~ medicine* Luftfahrtmedizin *f*; *~~ meeting* Flugtag *m*; *~~ school* Fliegerschule *f*; **~or, ~trix** ['-ə, -triks] Flieger(in *f*) *m*.

avid ['ævid] gierig (*for, of* nach); begierig (*for, of* auf); **~ity** [ə'viditi] Begierde; Gier *f* (*of, for* nach).

avocation [ævo(u)'keiʃən] Nebenbeschäftigung *f*; Steckenpferd, Hobby *n*; *a.* Beschäftigung *f*, Beruf *m*.

avoid [ə'vɔid] *tr* meiden, aus dem Wege gehen (*s.o.* jdm); ausweichen; vermeiden (*doing s.th.* etw zu tun); *(Schaden)* verhüten; *jur* für ungültig, nichtig erklären; *(Vertrag)* auflösen, aufheben; **~able** [-əbl] vermeidbar; **~ance** [-əns] (Ver-)Meiden *n*, Abwendung, Verhütung; *jur* Aufhebung *f*, Widerruf *m*; Anfechtung; Umgehung *f*.

avoirdupois [ævədə'pɔiz] *(~ weight)* englische(s) Handelsgewicht *n*; *fam* Körpergewicht *n*.

avouch [ə'vautʃ] *itr* sich verbürgen, einstehen (*for s.th.* für etw); *tr* garantieren; bestätigen, versichern.

avow [ə'vau] *tr* anerkennen, zugeben, eingestehen; freimütig bekennen, gestehen; **~al** [-əl] Eingeständnis, Bekenntnis *n*; **~edly** [-idli] *adv* zugegebener-, eingestandenermaßen.

avuncular [ə'vʌŋkjulə] Onkel-.

*

await [ə'weit] *tr* erwarten, warten auf; abwarten.

awake [ə'weik] *a. irr awoke, awoke*; *tr* aufwecken; *itr* aufwachen; *pred a* wach, munter; *to be ~* wach sein; *to s.th.* sich e-r S bewußt sein; *wide ~* hellwach; **~n** [-n] *tr* aufwecken; *itr* aufwachen; **~ning** [-niŋ] Erwachen, Erwecken *n a. fig*.

award [ə'wɔ:d] *s* Preis *m*, Prämie; Verleihung; Auszeichnung *f*; *jur* Urteilsspruch *m*; Zuerkennung, Zubilligung *f*; Schadenersatz *m*; (Sachverständigen-)Gutachten *n*; *(auf ein Angebot)* Zuschlag *m*; *Am* Stipendium *n*; *tr* zuerkennen, zusprechen; zubilligen; entscheiden; *(Preis)* verleihen; *~ of punishment* Strafzumessung *f*.

aware [ə'wɛə] *pred a* gewahr, bewußt; unterrichtet; *I'm ~ of that* ich bin mir dessen bewußt.

awash [ə'wɔʃ] *adv pred a* vom Wasser bespült.

away [ə'wei] *adv a interj* weg, fort; entfernt, abseits; abwesend; weit; sofort; unaufhörlich; *far ~* weit weg; *far and ~* bei weitem; *out and ~* unvergleichlich; *right, straight ~* auf der Stelle; sofort, gleich; *to do ~ with* abschaffen; beseitigen; *to give ~* verschenken; *to go ~* weg-, fortgehen; *to sleep ~ the day* den Tag verschlafen; *to put ~* wegschaffen; beseitigen; klassifizieren; *to take ~* weg-, fortnehmen; *to work ~* durcharbeiten; ohne Unterbrechung arbeiten; *fire ~!* leg los! fang an! **~match** *sport* auswärtige(s) Spiel *n*.

awe [ɔ:] *s* Ehrfurcht; Furcht, Scheu *f*; *tr* Ehrfurcht einflößen; *to keep s.o. in ~* jdm imponieren; *to stand in ~ of s.o.* jdn fürchten; *to strike s.o. with ~* jdm Furcht einflößen; **~-commanding, -inspiring** ehrfurchtgebietend; **~-some** ['-səm] eindrucksvoll, imponierend; erschreckend, furchtbar; **~-stricken, -struck** *a* tief beeindruckt; vor Schreck wie gelähmt.

awful ['ɔ:ful] furchtbar, schrecklich; fürchterlich, entsetzlich; *fam* ['ɔ:fl] scheußlich; **~ly** ['-li] *adv* schrecklich; *fam* ['ɔ:fli] äußerst, sehr.

awhile [ə'wail] *adv* für kurze Zeit; eine Weile, eine Zeitlang.

awkward ['ɔ:kwəd] linkisch, unpraktisch, unbeholfen, ungeschickt; unhandlich; *(Situation)* peinlich, unangenehm; *(Stil)* schwerfällig; *~* **age** Flegeljahre *n pl*; *~* **customer** *fam* schwieriger Bursche *m*; **~ness** ['-nis] Ungeschicklichkeit; Unannehmlichkeit *f*.

awl [ɔ:l] Ahle *f*, Pfriem(en) *m*.

awn [ɔ:n] *bot* Granne *f*; **~ing** ['-iŋ] Plane *f*; Zeltdach; Verdeck; *mar* Sonnensegel *n*; Markise *f*.

awry [ə'rai] *pred a adv* schief, verkehrt, krumm; *to go ~* schiefgehen; *(Plan)* ins Wasser fallen.

axe, *Am* ax [æks] *s* Axt *f*; Beil *n*; Hacke; *fam* Entlassung *f*, Abbau *m*, Amtsenthebung *f*, Sitzenlassen *n*; *tr* mit e-r Axt behauen; *fig* stark beschneiden, kürzen, abbauen; *to get the*

~ *(fam)* entlassen, herausgeworfen, sitzengelassen werden; *to give the* ~ *(fam)* entlassen, 'rauswerfen; sitzenlassen; *to have an* ~ *to grind (fam)* persönliche Interessen verfolgen; etw auf dem Herzen haben; **~man** Holzhauer *m*.
axial ['æksiəl] axial; achsenförmig; ~ **load** Achsdruck *m*.
axil ['æksil] *bot* Blattwinkel *m*; **~la** [æk'silə] *pl -ae* [-i:] *anat* Achselhöhle *f*; **~lary** ['æksiləri] Achselhöhle-; *bot* achselständig.
axiom ['æksiəm] Axiom *n*, Grundsatz *m*; **~atic** [æksiə'mætik] axiomatisch.
axis ['æksis] *pl axes* ['æksi:z] *phys pol* Achse; *math* Mittellinie; *fig* wichtige Verbindungslinie *f*.
axle ['æksl] (Rad-)Achse, Welle *f*; **~-tree** Achse *f*.
ay(e) [ei] **1.** *adv* immer, stets; **2.** [ai] *adv* ja; *s* Ja *n*; *pl* Jastimmen *f pl*; *the ~s have it* die Mehrzahl ist dafür.
azalea [ə'zeiljə] *bot* Azalie *f*.
azimuth ['æzimәθ] Azimut *m* od *n*.
azur|e ['æʒə, 'ei-] *s* Azur *m*, Himmelblau *n*; *a* himmelblau.

B

B [bi:] *s pl ~s, ~'s*, A, a; *mus* H, h *n*; *(Schule)* gut; *a* zweitklassig, -rangig; ~ **flat** *mus* B, b *n*; *hum* (Bett-)Wanze *f*; **~-girl** *Am sl* Bardame *f*; ~ **sharp** His, his *n*.
baa [bɑ:] *itr (Schaf)* blöken; *s* Blöken, Geblök(e) *n*.
babbitt ['bæbit] *tr* mit Weißmetall ausgießen; *s (B~-metal)* Weiß-, Lager-(weiß)metall *n*; *Am* Spießbürg(er) *m*.
babble ['bæbl] *tr itr* stammeln, lallen; plappern; schwatzen, *fam* babbeln; nachplappern; ausplaudern; *itr (Wasser)* murmeln, plätschern; *s* Lallen; Geplapper; Geschwätz; *(Wasser)* Murmeln *n*; *tech* Diaphonie *f*, **~r** ['-ə] Schwätzer *m*.
babe [beib] *poet* Kind; (großes) Kind *n*; Kindskopf; *sl* nette(r) Käfer *m*, saubere(s) Ding *n*; *~s in the woods (Am)* krasse Anfänger *m pl*; **~l** ['beibl] Wirrwarr *m*, Durcheinander, Tohuwabohu, Stimmengewirr *n*; *Tower of B~~* Turm *m* zu Babel.
baboon [bə'bu:n] *zoo* Pavian; *sl* Mensch, *Am sl* Tolpatsch *m*.
baby ['beibi] *s* Säugling *m*, (Klein-, kleines) Kind; Kindchen *n*; Kindskopf; Jüngste(r) *(e-r Gruppe)*, Benjamin; *sl* Liebling *m*, Schätzchen *n*; *sl* Sache *f*; *a* Kinder-; Klein-, Miniatur-; kindlich; kindisch; *tr* verzärteln, verhätscheln; *to carry, to hold the* ~ *(fam)* die Verantwortung (dafür) tragen (müssen); ~ **bonds** *pl* Kleinobligationen *f pl*; ~ **car** Kleinwagen *m*; **~-carriage,** ~ **buggy** *Am* Kinderwagen *m*; **~-farm** *pej* Kinderbewahranstalt *f*; Säuglingsheim *n*; ~ **grand** *mus* Stutzflügel *m*; **~hood** ['-hud] Säuglingsalter *n*; **~house** Puppenhaus *n*; **~ish** ['-iʃ] kindisch; dumm; **~like** ['-laik] kindlich; **~linen** Babywäsche *f*; **~(-)sitter** Babysitter, Aufpasser(in *f*) *m* bei Kindern; **~-snatching** Kindsentführung *f*.
bacc|alaureate [bækə'lɔ:riit] Bakkalaureat *n (unterster akad. Grad)*; *Am* Predigt *f* anläßlich des B.; **~ara(t)** ['-rɑ:] Bakkarat *n (Kartenglücksspiel)*.
bacchanal ['bækənl] *a* bacchantisch; trunken, ausgelassen; *s* Bacchant(in *f*); Zecher(in *f*) *m*; *pl* u. **~ia** [-'neiljə] Bacchanal *n*, Orgie, Schwelgerei *f*, Zechgelage *n*; **~ian** [-'neiljən] *a s.* ~; **bacchant** ['bækənt] *s* Bacchant *m*; *a* bacchantisch; **Bacchus** ['bækəs] Bacchus *m*.
baccy ['bæki] *fam* Tabak *m*.
bach [bætʃ] *s Am sl* Junggeselle *m*; *itr (to ~ it)* als J. e-n eigenen Haushalt führen; **~elor** ['bætʃələ] Bakkalaureus *(unterster akad. Grad)*; Junggeselle *m*; *~~'s button* Patentknopf; *bot* Blütenknopf *m*; *bot* scharfe(r) Hahnenfuß *m*, Kornblume *f*; *~~ girl* Junggesellin *f*; *~~hood* Junggesellenleben, -dasein; Bakkalaureat *n*; *~~ tax* Junggesellen-, Ledigensteuer *f*.
bacillus [bə'siləs] *pl -li* [-lai] Bazillus *m*; ~ **carrier** Bazillenträger *m*.
back [bæk] *s* Rücken *m a. allg* u. *fig*; Kreuz, Rückgrat *n*; Rücklehne *f*; *mot* Rücksitz *m*; Rückseite *f*; Hintergrund *m*; *fig* Kehrseite; körperliche Kraft, Stärke *f*; *(Fußball)* Verteidiger *m*; *(Kleid)* Rückenteil *n*; *(Stoff)* linke Seite; *min* Firste *f*; *a* rückseitig, -wärtig, -läufig; hinter; Nach-, Hinter-, Rück-; *(Betrag)* rückständig; abgelegen, fern; *adv* rückwärts; zurück (*from* von); hinten; wieder; *tr* (unter)stützen; tragen; *(to ~ up)* den Rücken decken, beistehen, beispringen (*s.o.* jdm); billigen; decken, begünstigen; zurückschieben, -fahren, -stellen; *mot* zurückstoßen; *jur com* gegenzeichnen; bürgen (*s.o.* für jdn); indossieren; wetten (*s.th.* auf etw); *tech* auf der Rückseite versehen (*with s.th.* mit etw); *(Pferd)* aufsitzen (auf), besteigen; *(Segel)* backlegen; mit e-m Rücken versehen; den Rücken bilden (*s.th.* von etw); *itr (to ~ up)* zurücktreten, -gehen, -fahren; *(Wind)* umspringen *(entgegen dem Uhrzeigersinn)*; *at the ~ of* hinter; *fig* hinter dem Rücken *gen*; *behind o.'s ~ (fig)* hinter jds Rücken; *on o.'s ~* auf dem Rükken (liegen); *(als Kranker)* auf der Nase (liegen); *on the ~ of it* außerdem; *there and ~* hin u. zurück; *with o.'s ~ to the wall (fig)* in der Klemme; *5 years ~* fünf Jahre früher, vor fünf Jahren; *~ to ~* Rücken an Rücken; *~ and forth (Am)* hin u. her; *to answer ~* frech antworten; *to be on s.o.'s ~ (fam)* von jdm abhängig sein; jdn necken, reizen, ärgern; *to break s.o.'s ~* jdn überlasten; *to break the ~* den größten Teil, die Hauptsache erledigen (*of s.th.* e-r S); *to get, to put, to set s.o.'s ~ up* jdn ärgerlich machen, *fam* auf die Palme bringen; *to get off s.o.'s ~* jdn in Ruhe lassen; *to give, to make a ~* den Rücken krumm, e-n Buckel machen; *to go ~ from* od *upon o.'s word* sein Wort zurücknehmen; *on o.'s promise* sein Versprechen nicht halten; *on s.o.* jdn im Stich lassen; *to pay ~* zurückbezahlen; *to take a ~ seat* e-e untergeordnete Stellung einnehmen od Rolle spielen; *to turn o.'s ~ (up)on* den Rücken kehren *dat*; *to ~ away* zurücktreten (*from* von); *to ~ down (fam)* nach-, klein beigeben; von s-n Ansprüchen Abstand nehmen; verzichten (*from* auf); *to ~ the wrong horse* auf das falsche Pferd setzen; *to ~ off (fam)* in Ruhe lassen; *mot* Gas wegnehmen; *to ~ out (of) (fam)* sich zurückziehen (aus); ausreißen; kneifen, e-n Rückzieher machen, absagen; *to ~ s.o. up* jdn unterstützen; *stand* od *keep ~!* zurück (-bleiben)! *don't ~ down on what you said* bleib bei deinem Wort! *~ of a book, hill* Buch-, Bergrücken *m*; *~ of the hand* Handrücken *m*; **~-bencher** *parl* Hinterbänkler *m*; **~bite** *irr tr* verleumden, schlecht sprechen (*s.o.* über jdn); **~biting** Verleumdung, üble Nachrede *f*; **~board** Rückenlehne *f*; **~bone** Rückgrat *n a. fig*; *fig* Stütze *f*, Rückhalt; Hauptteil *m*; *to the ~~* durch u. durch; bis aufs Mark; **~-chat** scharfe, unverschämte Entgegnung *f*; **~cross** *biol* Rückkreuzung *f*; **~door** *a* Hintertür-; *fig* heimlich, verstohlen; **~-drop** *theat* Hintergrund(vorhang) *m*; **~er** ['-ə] Helfer, Förderer, *com* Hintermann; Wettende(r) *m*; **~field** *sport (Fußball) Am* hintere(s) Feld *n*; **~-fire** *s mot* Rückschlag *m*, Fehlzündung *f*; *(bei e-m Waldbrand)* Gegenfeuer *n*; *itr* (zu)rückknallen, -schlagen; *fig* schief-, *fam* ins Auge gehen; e-e gegenteilige Wirkung haben; **~-formation** *gram* Rückbildung *f*; **~gammon** ['-gæmən] Puff, Tricktrack *n (Spiel)*; *~~ board* Puffbrett *n*; **~ground** Hintergrund *m a. fig*, Umwelt *f*, Milieu *n*; *fig* berufliche Erfahrung, Aus-, Vorbildung *f*; zugrundeliegende Ursachen *f pl*, Beweggründe *m pl*; Voraussetzungen *f pl*, nähere Umstände *m pl*, Vorgeschichte *f*; *film radio* Tonkulisse *f*; *with a good family ~~* aus gutem Hause; *to keep in the ~~* im Hintergrund bleiben; *financial ~~* finanzielle(r) Rückhalt *m*; *~~ job (theat)* Statistenrolle *f*; *~~ noise (radio)* Neben-, Störgeräusch *n*; *~~ research* Grundlagenforschung *f*; **~hand** *s (Tennis)* Rückhand; nach links geneigte Handschrift *f*; *a (~~ed)* Rückhand-; *(Schrift)* nach links geneigt; *fig* doppeldeutig, unaufrichtig; spöttisch; schwerfällig, ungeschickt; *tech (Kabel)* verkehrt gedreht; **~hander** Rückhandschlag *m*; **~ing** ['-iŋ] Stütze, Unterstützung, Hilfe *f*; Rückhalt *m*; *com* Indossierung; *(Währung)* Deckung; *tech* Unterlage *f*; Träger *m*; Rückwärtsgehen, -fahren, -laufen, *mot* -stoßen; *(Wind)* Zurück-, Linksdrehen *n*; **~-lash** *tech* tote(r) Gang, Leergang *m*, Spiel *n*; **~log** *s* große(r) Holzklotz *m* als Unterlage bei e-m Holzfeuer; *com* Rückstände, unerledigte Aufträge *m pl*; versandbereite Güter *n pl*; *allg* Reserve *f*; *tr* beiseite, zurücklegen, reservieren; *~~ demand* Nachholbedarf *m*; **~-number** *(Zeitung)* alte Nummer *f*; *fam* altmodische(r), rückständige(r) Mensch; *sl* Dreh *m*, alte Leier *f*; ~ **pay** rückständige(r) Lohn *m*;

Nachzahlung *f*; **~-pedalling brake** Rücktrittbremse *f*; **~rest** Stützlager *n*; Lünette *f*; **~-room boy** *fam* Hintermann; Spitzel; Forscher *m*, der an kriegswichtigen Vorhaben arbeitet; **~ seat** Rücksitz *m*; *fig* untergeordnete Stellung *f*; *~-seat driver (mot)* Mitfahrende(r) *m*, der unerwünschte Ratschläge gibt; *fig* Besserwisser *m*; **~set** *fig* Rückschlag *m*; *(Wasser)* Gegenströmung *f*, Strudel *m*; **~side** Rückseite *f*; Hintern *m*; **~sight** *(Visier)* Kimme *f*; **~slapper** *fam* jem, der sich gern anbiedert; **~slide** *irr itr* abfallen, abtrünnig, *rel* rückfällig werden; zurücksacken; **~slider** *rel* Rückfällige(r), Abtrünnige(r) *m*; **~sliding** Ab-, Rückfall *m*; **~ spacer (key)** *(Schreibmaschine)* Rücktaste *f*; **~spin** *(Ball)* Rückwärtseffetball *m*; **~stage** hinter der Bühne (gelegen); *fig* verborgen; **~stair(s)** *a* Hintertreppen-; heimlich; heimtückisch; unehrlich, krumm; **~s** *s* Geheim-, Hintertreppe *f*; *fig* krumme Wege *m pl*; **~stay** Verstrebung *f*; Abspanndraht; Backstag *m*; *pl mar* Pardunen *f pl*; **~stitch** Steppstich *m*; **~stroke** Rückschlag, -stoß *m*; Rückenschwimmen *n*; *tech* Rückhub, -gang; *(Ball)* Rückschlag *m*; **~swept** *a* nach hinten verjüngt **~talk** *Am* unverschämte Antwort *f*; **~track** *tr* zurückverfolgen; *itr Am* umkehren; sich zurückziehen; **~ward** ['-wəd] *a* rückwärtig; rückwärts gerichtet *od* gehend; *fig* widerstrebend, zögernd; scheu, schüchtern; zurückgeblieben, rückständig, spät entwickelt; *~~ation* [-'deiʃən] *com* Deportgeschäft *n*; Kursabschlag *m*; Konventionalstrafe *f*; *~~ness* ['-nis] Rückständigkeit; Spätreife; Schüchternheit, Zurückhaltung *f*; Zögern *n*; *~~ position* rückwärtige Stellung *f*; *~~ roll (sport)* Rückwärtsrolle *f*; *~~(s) adv* rückwärts, zurück *a. fig;* verkehrt; rücklings; in früheren Zeiten; *~~s and forwards* hin u. her; *~~ somersault* Rückwärtssalto *m*; *~~ travelling (tech)* rückläufig; **~wash** Rückstau *m*; zurücklaufende (Luft-) Strömung *f*; *aero* Luftschraubenstrahl *m*; *fig* Rückwirkung *f*; *fig* Wellen *f pl*, die etw schlägt; **~water** *s* Rückstau *m*; Stauwasser *n*; *fig* Stillstand *m*, Stagnation *f*; *a fig* stagnierend; zurückgeblieben; **~ wind** Rücken-, *aero* Schiebewind *m*; **~woods** *a a. ~wood* hinterwäldlerisch; *s pl* Urwaldgebiete *n pl*; abgelegene Gegend *f*; *~~man* Hinterwäldler; Urwaldbewohner *m*; **~yard** Hinterhof; Garten *m* hinter dem Haus.

bacon ['beikən] (Schweine-)Speck *m*; *to bring home the ~ (fam)* es schaffen, den Vogel abschießen; s-n Lebensunterhalt verdienen; *to save o.'s ~* mit heiler Haut davonkommen; *flitch of ~* Speckseite *f*; **~ pig,** *Am* **hog** Fett-, Speckschwein *n*; **~y** ['-i] speckartig; *~~ liver (med)* Leberverfettung *f*.

bacteri|al [bæk'tiəriəl] bakteriell; Bakterien-; **~ological** [-tiəriə'lɔdʒikl] *a*: *~~ warfare* Bakterienkrieg *m*; **~ologist** [-'ɔlədʒist] Bakteriologe *m*; **~ology** [-'ɔlədʒi] Bakteriologie *f*; **~um** [bæk'tiəriəm] *pl -a* [-iə] *a. sing* Bakterie *f*, Bakterium *n*, Spaltpilz *m*.

bad [bæ(:)d] *a (fam a. adv)* schlecht, übel; böse, schlimm; *(Fehler)* schwer; armselig, *fam* mies; minderwertig, mangelhaft; dürftig, unzulänglich, -reichend; *jur* nichtig, ungültig, *(Anspruch)* unbegründet; *(Risiko)* zweifelhaft; falsch; schädlich, gefährlich, nachteilig (*for* für); widerlich, -wärtig; ärgerlich; unanständig; ungezogen; verdorben; *(Ei)* faul; unpäßlich, krank; *(Krankheit, Schmerz)* stark, heftig; *the ~* das Böse, Schlechte; die Bösen, Schlechten; *from ~ to worse* immer schlimmer; *in ~ (Am fam)* in der Klemme *od* Patsche; in Ungnade (*with* bei); *in ~ faith* wider Treu u. Glauben; *in a ~ sense* im schlechten Sinne; *not (half) ~ (fam)* nicht übel, ganz ordentlich; *to the ~* zum Nachteil; ... Schulden; *with ~ grace* ungern, widerwillig; *to feel ~(ly)* sich ärgern, sich Sorgen machen (*about* über); *to go ~* schlecht werden, verderben *itr*; *to go to the ~* zugrunde gehen; völlig versacken; auf Abwege geraten; *to take the ~ with the good* das Böse wie das Gute hinnehmen; *I am ~* es geht mir schlecht, mir ist unwohl; *at it* ich verstehe davon nichts; *that is ~!* das ist schlecht, böse, arg! *that is too ~!* das ist zu dumm! *it's ~ form* es gehört sich nicht; *a ~ shot!* fehlgeschossen! falsch geraten! **~ blood** *fig* böse(s) Blut *n*; **~ debt** uneinbringliche Forderung *f*; **~ debtor** zahlungsunfähige(r) Schuldner *m*; **~ egg, hat, lot** *sl* Lump *m*; Weibsbild *n*; **~lands** *pl* durch Erosion zerstörtes Land *n*; **~ language** Anzüglichkeiten *f pl*; Fluchen *n*; **~ luck** Unglück, *fam* Pech *n*; **~ mark, point** Strafpunkt *m*; **~tempered** *a* reizbar, übellaunig; **~weather (zone)** Schlechtwetter(gebiet) *n*.

badg|e [bædʒ] Abzeichen; *allg* Kennzeichen, Sinnbild, Merkmal *n*; *~~ of office, party, proficiency, rank, society* Dienst-, Partei-, Leistungs-, Dienstgrad-, Vereinsabzeichen *n*; **~er** ['-ə] *s* Dachs; Pinsel *m* (aus Dachshaar); künstliche Fliege *f (als Angelköder)*; *tr fig* hetzen, jagen; plagen, quälen; reizen, ärgern; *~~ hole* Dachsbau *m*.

bad|ly ['bædli] *adv fam* sehr, schwer, stark; arg, dringend; *to come off ~~* schlecht ausgehen, fehlschlagen; *to be ~~ off* finanziell schlecht dran sein; *to want ~~* dringend gebrauchen *od* benötigen; *~~ beaten* entscheidend geschlagen; *he is doing ~~* s-e Geschäfte gehen schlecht; **~ness** ['-nis] schlechte Qualität; Minderwertigkeit, Dürftigkeit; Unzulänglichkeit; Schlechtheit, Bösartigkeit, Verdorbenheit *f*.

badminton ['bædmintən] Federballspiel *n*.

baffl|e ['bæfl] *tr* vor den Kopf stoßen; aus dem Konzept bringen; stutzig machen; verblüffen, verwirren, täuschen; enttäuschen; *(Pläne)* durchkreuzen, vereiteln, zunichte machen; vernichten, zerschlagen; *tech* drosseln; *itr* sich vergeblich abmühen; *s* Verwirrung, Enttäuschung *f*; *(~~ plate) tech* Sperre, Stauscheibe, Unterbrecherklappe; Schall-, Zwischenwand *f*; Widerstandskörper *m*; *mot* Leitblech *n*; **~ing** verwirrend; unverständlich; hinderlich, vereitelnd; *(Person)* undurchsichtig; *mar (Wind)* umspringend.

bag [bæ(:)g] *s* Beutel, Sack *m*; *(paper ~)* Tüte *f*; *(money ~)* Geldbeutel *m*; Handtasche; *(game-~, (Am) hunting-~)* Jagdtasche, Jagdbeute, Strecke; *zoo* Tasche *f*; Kuheuter *n*; *med* Beutel *m*; Blase; *tech (Luftschiff)* Gaszelle; *Am sl* Uniform *f*; *pl* Geld *n* (wie Heu); *sl pl* Hose, Büx *f*; *sl* Fallschirm *m*; *sl* Weibsstück *n*; *sl mil* Zahl *f* der abgeschossenen Flugzeuge; *~s of (fam)* e-e Menge; [bæg] *tr* in den Beutel *od* Sack stecken; *fig* einstecken; *sl pej* sich unter den Nagel reißen, organisieren; *mil sl* abschießen, herunterholen; *Am sl* entlassen, verhaften, *(Schule)* schwänzen; *(Jäger)* erbeuten, erlegen; *itr* sich bauschen, aufschwellen; sich (aus)beulen; *(Kleid)* lose herunterhängen, sackartig sitzen; *in the ~ (fam fig)* in der Tasche, (so gut wie) sicher; erfolgreich erledigt; *in the bottom of the ~* als letzte Reserve; *~ and ~gage* mit Sack u. Pack; völlig; *to hold the ~* mit leeren Händen ausgehen; die Folgen tragen müssen; *to let the cat out of the ~ (fig)* die Katze aus dem Sack lassen; *a ~ of bones* Haut u. Knochen; **~atelle** [bægə'tel] Kleinigkeit; Bagatelle, *fam* Lappalie *f*; **~gage** ['bægidʒ] *Am* (Reise-)Gepäck *n*; *mil* Troß *m*, Gepäck; *fam* freche(s) Ding *n*; *~~ animal* Lasttier *n*; *~~ car (Am)* Gepäckwagen *m*; *~~-check (Am)* Gepäckschein *m*; *~~ compartment* Gepäckraum *m*; *~~hold (Am aero)* Gepäck-, Frachtraum *m*; *~~ insurance* Gepäckversicherung *f*; *~~ office* Gepäckabfertigung *f*; *~~ rack* Gepäcknetz *n*; *~~-room (Am)* Gepäckraum *m*; *~~ slip* Gepäckadresse *f*; *~~-smasher (Am)* Gepäckträger *m*; *~~ truck (Am)* Gepäckkarren *m*; **~ging** ['bægiŋ] Sack-, Packleinen *n*; **~gy** ['bægi] bauschig; ausgebeult; sackartig (erweitert); *(Hosen)* ungebügelt; **~man** *com* Reisende(r) *m*; **~pipe,** *Am Scot a.* *~~s* Dudelsack *m*, Sackpfeife *f*; **~piper** Dudelsackpfeifer *m*.

bah [bɑ:] *interj* pah! bah!

bail [beil] **1.** *s jur* Bürgschaft, Kaution, Sicherheitsleistung *f*; Bürge *m*; Haftentlassung *f* gegen Sicherheitsleistung; *tr* hinterlegen, deponieren; gegen Bürgschaft freilassen; bürgen, gutsagen (*s.o.* für jdn); *out on ~* auf freiem Fuß gegen Sicherheitsleistung; *to forfeit o.'s ~* s-e Kaution durch Nichterscheinen verwirken; *to go ~ for* Bürgschaft leisten, bürgen für; sich verbürgen für; **2.** *s (Pferdestall)* Trennstange *f*; *(Kricket)* Querholz *n*; **3.** *s* Bügel, Henkel, Griff *m*; **4.** *(a.* **bale***) v itr* Wasser aus e-m Boot schöpfen; *tr (Boot)* leer schöpfen; *s* Schöpfeimer *m*, -kelle *f*; *to ~ out (mit dem Fallschirm)* abspringen, *sl aero* aussteigen; *sl aero fig* sich aus der Schlinge ziehen; **~able** ['-əbl] kautionsfähig; **~ee** [-'li:] Depositar, Verwahrer *m*; **~ey** ['-i] Ring *m* e-r Verteidigungsanlage; Außenhof *m* e-r Burg; *Old B~~* Schwurgericht *n* in London; **~iff** ['-if] Gerichtsvollzieher; Amts-, Gerichtsdiener, Wachtmeister; (Guts-) Verwalter *m*; *hist* Amtmann, (Land-) Vogt; **~iwick** ['-iwik] Vogtei *f*, Amtsbezirk *m*; *fig* Interessen-, Arbeitsgebiet *n*; **~ment** ['-mənt] Verpfändung, Hinterlegung; Freilassung gegen Kaution; Bürgschaft *f*; **~or, ~er** ['-ə] Deponent, Hinterleger *m*.

bairn [bɛən] *Scot* Kind *n*.

bait [beit] *tr* (mit Hunden) hetzen; *(Menschen)* quälen, reizen, ärgern; *(Pferd)* füttern (u. tränken); mit e-m Köder versehen; *fig* ködern, locken, in Versuchung führen; *itr* einkehren, rasten; *(Tier)* fressen; *s* Köder *m*; *fig* (Ver-)Lockung, Versuchung *f*; Reiz *m*; (Pferde-)Futter *n*; Imbiß *m*; Erfrischung; Einkehr, Rast *f*.

baize [beiz] Flaus, Fries *m (rauher Wollstoff)*.

bak|e [beik] *tr* backen; *(durch Hitze)* härten; dörren; *(Ziegel)* brennen; *(Früchte)* zur Reife bringen; *(Haut)* bräunen; *(Erdboden)* austrocknen, -dörren; *itr* backen; *(durch Hitze)* hart *od* braun werden; *half ~ed (fam)* blöde; *~~-house* Backhaus *n*, -stube *f*, Bäckerei *f*; **~elite** ['-əlait] Bakelit *n*; **~er** [-'ə] Bäcker *m*; Trockenkammer *f*; *a ~~'s dozen* dreizehn; **~ery** ['-əri] Bäckerei *f*; *Am* Bäckerladen *m*; **~ing** ['-iŋ] *s* Bakken; Dörren; Brennen, Sintern *n*; Ofenvoll, Schub *m*; *a* u. *adv*: *~~hot* brennend, glühend heiß; *~~ oven* Backofen *m*; *~~ powder* Backpulver *n*; *~~ soda* Natron *n*; *~~ trough* Backtrog *m*.

balanc|e ['bæləns] *s* Waage *a. fig; (Uhr) (~~ wheel)* Unruhe *f*; *fig* (Ab-, Er-) Wägen; schwankende(s) Glück *n*; Entscheidung *f*, Ausschlag *m*; Gleichgewicht *n*; (innere) Ausgeglichenheit *f*; Gleichmut *m*, Ruhe; *(Kunst)* Ausgewogenheit, Harmonie *f*; Gegengewicht; Übergewicht *n*; *com* Ausgeglichenheit *f*; Unterschied *m*, Differenz *f*; Mehr *n*, Überschuß; Saldo *m*; Guthaben *n*; Bilanz *f*, Rechnungs-, Kontenabschluß; Ausgleich *m*; *tech* Auswuchtung; *astr B~~* Waage *f*; *Am u. fam* Rest, Überschuß *m*; *tr* wiegen, wägen; (gegenea.) abwägen; erwägen; (mitea.) ausgleichen; ins Gleichgewicht bringen, im G. halten; die Waage, das Gleichgewicht halten (*s.th.* e-r S); *com* ausgleichen; saldieren; *(Rechnung)* abschließen; *tech* abstimmen, auslasten, auswuchten, symmetrieren; die Bilanz ziehen (*s.th.* gen); *itr* sich im Gleichgewicht halten *a. fig*; *fig* schwanken, unschlüssig sein; sich ausgleichen, sich gegenseitig aufheben *(to ~ each other)*; *com* ausgeglichen sein; *in the ~~* in der Schwebe; *on ~~* zieht man die Bilanz; alles in allem; *to be (thrown) off o.'s ~~* sehr aufgeregt, *fam* ganz aus dem Häuschen sein; *to draw, to make up, to strike the ~~* die Bilanz ziehen *od* aufstellen; *to hold the ~~* die Entscheidung (in der Hand) haben; *to keep o.'s ~~* das Gleichgewicht halten; *fig* die Ruhe bewahren; *to lose o.'s ~~* das Gleichgewicht, *fig* den Kopf verlieren; *to show a ~~* e-n Saldo aufweisen (*of* von); *to ~~ the books* Bilanz machen; *to ~~ the budget* den Haushalt ausgleichen; *to ~~ the cash* Kasse machen, die Kasse abrechnen; *active* od *credit ~~* Kredit-, Haben-, Aktivsaldo *m*; *annual, final ~~* Jahres-, Schlußbilanz *f*; *cash ~~* Kassenbestand *m*; *favo(u)rable, unfavo(u)rable trade ~~, ~~ of trade* aktive, passive Handelsbilanz *f*; *opening ~~* Eröffnungsbilanz *f*; *passive* od *debit ~~* Debet-, Soll-, Passivsaldo *m*; *rough, trial ~~* Rohbilanz *f*; *~~ in, at (the) bank, bank ~* Bankguthaben *n*; *~~ of the bank* Bankausweis *m*; *~~ bill* Saldowechsel *m*; *~~ of the books* Abschluß *m* der Bücher; *~~ in* od *of cash, hand* Kassen-, Barbestand *m*; *~~ of mind* seelische(s) Gleichgewicht *n*; *~~ of payments* Zahlungsbilanz *f*; *~~ of power (pol)* Gleichgewicht *n* der Mächte; *~~(-)sheet* Bilanzbogen, Rechnungsabschluß, Kassenbericht *m*; **~ed** ['-t] *a* ab-, ausgeglichen, ausgewogen, symmetrisch, entlastet; *(Motor)* ausgewuchtet; *(Antenne)* entkoppelt; *~~ condition* Gleichgewichtszustand *m*; *~~ diet* ausgeglichene Kost *f*; *~~ position* Gleichgewichts-, Ruhelage *f*; *~~ stock(s)* ausreichende Bestände *od* Vorräte *m pl*; **~er** ['-ə] *tech* Stabilisator, Schwinghebel *m*, Ausgleichsmaschine *f*; Äquilibrist *m*; *ent* Flügelkölbchen *n*; **~ing** ['-iŋ] *com* Abrechnung, Saldierung *f*; Ausgleich; *tech* Abgleich(ung *f*) *m*, Auswuchtung, Zentrierung *f*.

balcony ['bælkəni] Balkon; *theat meist* 2. Rang, *Am* 1. Rang *m*.

bald [bɔ:ld] *(Kopf)* kahl *(a. Baum, Berg)*, kahlköpfig; unbehaart; nackt *a. fig*; *(Land)* ohne Vegetation; *(Tier)* mit e-m weißen Fleck auf dem Kopf; *fig* dürftig, ärmlich, armselig; schmucklos: nichtssagend; offen, ungeschminkt; *~ as a coot* ratzekahl; **~head, ~pate** Kahlkopf *m*, Glatze *f*; **~headed** ['-'-, *attr* '--] *a* kahlköpfig; *adv sl* blindlings; **~ly** ['-li] *adv* offen, frei heraus, unverblümt; ungeschminkt; nüchtern, trocken; **~ness** ['-nis] Kahlheit; *fig* Dürftigkeit, Ärmlichkeit, Armseligkeit *f*.

baldachin, baldaquin ['bɔ:ldəkin] Baldachin *m*.

balderdash ['bɔ:ldədæʃ] Geschwätz *n*, Unsinn *m*.

baldric ['bɔ:ldrik] Schulter-, Wehrgehänge *n*.

bale [beil] *s. a. bail* 4; **1.** *s com* Ballen *m*, Bündel *n*; Pack *m*; *tr* in Ballen verpacken; **2.** *s obs poet* Unheil, Weh, Leid *n*; **~-fire** große(s) Feuer im Freien; Leucht-, *a.* Freudenfeuer *n*; **~ful** ['-ful] unheilvoll; übel, böse.

balk, baulk [bɔ:k] *s* (Feld-, Furchen-) Rain; (rohbehauener) Balken; *(Haus)* Anker-, Tragbalken; Klotz *m* (im Weg); Hindernis *n*, Hemmschuh *m*; Enttäuschung *f*; Fehler, Schnitzer, Bock *m*; *(Billard)* Quartier *n*; *tr* (be-, ver)hindern, durchkreuzen, vereiteln; hemmen, aufhalten; enttäuschen; *(Gelegenheit)* (absichtlich) verpassen, vorbeigehen, entgehen lassen; *(Pflicht)* versäumen, vernachlässigen; *(Thema)* verfehlen; *itr* stutzen, stocken; plötzlich stehenbleiben; *(Pferd)* scheuen; nicht weitergehen wollen; **~line** *sport* Sperrlinie *f*; **~y** ['-i] störrisch; *mot* mit Fehlzündung.

Balkan ['bɔ:lkən] *a* Balkan-; *s pl* Balkan(länder *n pl*, -staaten *m pl*) *m*; **b~ize** ['-aiz] *tr pol* balkanisieren.

ball [bɔ:l] **1.** Kugel *f*; Kloß *m*; Knäuel *m* od *n*; *(~ of the thumb, of the foot)* Hand-, Fußballen; *sport* (Spiel-, *a.* Schnee-)Ball; Erdball; *bot* Wurzelballen *m*; (Kanonen-, Gewehr-)Kugel *f*; *(~ of the eye)* Augapfel *fig*; Unsinn *m*; *pl vulg* Hode(n *m*) *m* od *f*; **2.** Ball *m (Tanzfest)*; *at a ~* auf e-m Ball; *on the ~ (fam)* auf Draht; *to give a ~* e-n Ball geben *od* veranstalten; *to have the ~ at o.'s feet (fig)* e-n guten Start haben, voran-, vorwärtskommen *(im Leben)*; *to have a lot on the ~ (Am)* sehr tüchtig sein; *to keep up the ~, to keep the ~ rolling* das Gespräch im Gang halten, nicht einschlafen lassen; *to open the ~* den Ball eröffnen; *fig* s-e Tätigkeit aufnehmen; die Diskussion eröffnen; den Streit beginnen; *to play ~ (Am)* mitmachen, zs.arbeiten; *to set the ~ rolling* die Sache in Gang bringen; *fancy(-dress) ~* Kostümball *m*, -fest *n*; *~ of fire (Atombombe)* Feuerball *m*; **~-bearing(s)** *tech* Kugellager *n*; **~ field** *Am* Baseballplatz *m*; **~ game** Ballspiel, *Am* Baseballspiel *n*; **~ (-point) pen** Kugelschreiber *m*; **~ player** Ball-, *Am* Baseballspieler *m*; **~-room** Ballsaal *m*.

ball|ad ['bæləd] Ballade *f*; *~~ concert* Liederabend *n*; *~~-monger* Bänkelsänger *m*; *~~-opera* Singspiel *n*; **~ast** ['bæləst] *s* Ballast; Schotter *m*; *rail* Bettung *f*; *fig* Halt *m*, Stütze *f*; (be-) schottern; *fig* Halt geben; *~~ pit* Kiesgrube *f*; *~~ tank* Tauchtank *m*; *~~ weight (mot)* Leergewicht *n*; **~et** ['bælei] Ballett *n*; Ballettanz *m*; **~~-dancer, -skirt** Ballettänzer(in *f*) *m*, -röckchen *n*; **~istic** [bə'listik] *a* ballistisch; Wurf-, Flug-; *s pl meist mit sing* Ballistik *f*; *~~ curve* Flug-, Geschoßbahn *f*; **~ocks** ['-ks] *pl vulg* Hoden *pl*; Unsinn *m*; **~oon** [bə'lu:n] *s* Ballon; *chem* (Glas-)Ballon, (Destillier-)Kolben *m*; *arch* Kugel *f*; *(Spielzeug)* Luftballon *m*; *a* Ballon-; *(Karikatur)* die in den Mund gelegten Worte *n pl*; *itr* im B. aufsteigen; *aero* bumslanden; sich (auf)blähen, anschwellen; *tr Am (Kurse)* in die Höhe treiben; *captive, registering ~~* Fessel-, Registrierballon *m*; *sounding ~~, ~~ sonde (Meteorologie)* Ballonsonde *f*; *~~ ascent, barrage, observer, pilot, race, shed, tyre* Ballonaufstieg *m*, -sperre *f*, -beobachter, -führer *m*, -rennen *n*, -halle *f*, *mot* -reifen *m*; *~~ silk* Ballonseide *f*; **~oonist** Ballonfahrer *m*; **~ot** ['bælət] *s* Wahlkugel *f*; Stimmzettel *m*; Kugelung; (Geheim-)Abstimmung *f*; Wahlgang *m*; Stimmen(zahl *f*) *f pl*; *Am* Wahlvorschlag *m*; *itr* (geheim) abstimmen (*for* über); losen (*for* um); *to ~~ for s.o.* jdn (durch Geheimabstimmung) wählen; *to take a ~~* (geheim) abstimmen; *second, final ~~* Stichwahl *f*; *~~-box* Wahlurne *f*; **~y** ['bæli] *a u. adv sl* verdammt, verflucht; *(in Fragen)* denn eigentlich; **~yhoo** [-i'hu] *sl* marktschreierische Reklame *f*, Reklamerummel; Schmus; Tumult *m*, laute(s) Palaver *n*; **~yrag** ['-iræg] *sl tr* durch den Kakao ziehen, verhohnepipeln.

balm [bɑ:m] Balsam; *allg* Duft, Wohlgeruch *m*; *bot* Melisse *f*; *fig* Trost *m*; Linderung *f*; **~-cricket** *zoo* Zikade *f*; **~y** ['-i] balsamisch; weich, sanft; lindernd, heilend; *sl* bekloppt, meschugge.

baln|eal ['bælniəl] *a med* Bade-; **~eology** [-i'ɔlədʒi] *med* Bäderkunde *f*.

baloney [bə'louni] *Am sl* Quatsch, Unsinn, Stuß *m*.

balsam ['bɔ:lsəm] Balsam *a. fig*; *fig* Trost *m*; Linderung; *bot* Gartenbalsamine *f*; Rührmichnichtan *n*; **~ic** [bɔ:l'sæmik] balsamisch; erquickend, lindernd.

Baltic ['bɔ:ltik] *a* baltisch; *s u. ~ Sea* Ostsee *f*.

balust|er ['bæləstə] Baluster *m*, Geländerdocke, -stütze *f*; **~rade** [-'treid] Geländer *n*, Balustrade *f*.

bamboo [bæm'bu:] Bambus(rohr *n*) *m*; **~zle** [-u:zl] *tr sl* beschwindeln, betrügen (*out of s.th.* um etw); verleiten, verführen (*into doing s.th.* etw zu tun); aus dem Konzept bringen.

ban [bæn] *s* (Kirchen-)Bann, Bannfluch, -strahl *m*; (Reichs-)Acht; Verbannung; (gesellschaftliche) Ächtung *f*; Verbot *n*; Sperre; Ablehnung, Mißbilligung *f*; *tr* verbieten; *sport* sperren; *hist* verbannen, ächten; *to place, to put under a ~* mit dem Bann belegen.

banal ['beinl, bə'nɑ:l] banal, abgedroschen; **~ity** [bə'næliti] Banalität *f*; abgedroschene(s) Zeug *n*, Gemeinplatz *m*.

banana [bə'nɑ:nə] Banane *f*; **~ oil** *Am sl* Quatsch, Blödsinn *m*; **~ plug** Bananenstecker *m*; **~ split** (aufgeschnittene u.) mit Eiskrem gefüllte B.

band [bænd] *s* Band *n*; Ring, Streifen *m*; Leiste; Binde *f*; Gurt; *tech* Riemen; Bund, Leibriemen, Gürtel; Hemdenhalsbesatz *m*; Faßband *n*; (Rad-) Reifen *m*; Türband *n*, Angel; *min* dünne Schicht; *(Buchbinderei)* Heftschnur *f*; *radio anat* Band *n*; Bande, Schar *f*, Trupp *m*; (Musik-, *bes.* Blas-) Kapelle *f*; *pl* Beffchen *n*; *tr* mit e-m Band, mit Streifen versehen; *tr itr* (anea.-, zs.)binden *a. fig*; *fig (to ~ together)* zs.bringen, vereinen, vereinigen; **~age** ['-idʒ] *s* Bandage, Binde *f*; Verbandsstoff *m*, -zeug *n*;

Verband *m*; *tr* bandagieren, verbinden; ~ **adjustment** *radio* Bandbreitenregler *m*; ~**an(n)a** [-'dænə, -'dɑ:nə] große(s), farbige(s) (Kopf-, Taschen-)Tuch *n*; ~**box** Hutschachtel *f*; *he looks as if he had just come out of a* ~~ er sieht aus wie aus dem Ei gepellt; ~ **conveyer** Bandförderer *m*; ~**eau** ['-ou] *pl -x* ['-ouz] Haar-, Kopf-, Stirnband *n*; (schmaler) Büstenhalter *m*; ~**erol(e)** ['-əroul] Wimpel *m*; (Meß-, Lanzen-)Fähnlein; Spruchband *n*; ~ **iron** Bandeisen *n*; ~**it** ['-it] *pl a. -ti* Bandit, Straßenräuber *m*; ~**itry** ['-ri] Straßenräuberei *f*; ~**master** Kapellmeister *m*; ~-**pass filter** Bandpaßfilter *n*; ~ **pulley** *tech* Riemenscheibe *f*; ~ **saw** Bandsäge *f*; ~ **shell** *Am* halbkreisförmige(r) Musikpavillon *m*; ~**sman** Mitglied *n* e-r Musikkapelle; ~**stand** Musikpodium *n*, -pavillon *m*; ~**wagon** *Am* Festwagen *m* mit Musikkapelle; *fig* siegreiche Partei *f*, Gewinner *m pl*, Mehrheit *f*; *to get on the* ~~ zur siegreichen Partei, zur Mehrheit übergehen; ~-**width** *radio* Bandbreite *f*; ~**y** ['-i] **1.** *tr (Worte, Blicke, Schläge)* tauschen, wechseln; *(Ball)* sich zuwerfen; *to* ~~ *about (Nachricht)* weitergeben, verbreiten *(a. Gerücht)*, unter die Leute bringen; **2.** *s* Hockey(schläger *m*) *n*; **3.** *a (Beine)* krumm; ~~-*legged (a)* krumm-, O-beinig.

bane [bein] *(außer in Zssgen) lit poet* Gift *a. fig*; *fig* Verhängnis *n*, Verderb(en *n*) *m*; ~**ful** ['-ful] unheil-, verhängnisvoll, tödlich, verderblich.

bang [bæŋ] *s* (heftiger) Schlag; (lauter) Knall; *pl* Pony(frisur *f*) *m*; *tr* heftig schlagen; *(to* ~ *up)* prügeln, durchhauen; *(to* ~ *about)* herumstoßen *(s.o.* jdn); *(Tür)* zuknallen, zuschlagen; *(Stirnhaar)* zu e-r Ponyfrisur schneiden; *itr* (laut) knallen; heftig stoßen *(against* gegen); *adv* heftig, laut, mit lautem Knall; *fig* plötzlich; *interj* peng! bums! *with a* ~ *(Am)* mit e-m Bombenerfolg; *he* ~*ed his fist on the table* er schlug mit der Faust auf den Tisch; ~**er** ['-ə] *sl* Wurst *f*; Knallfrosch *m*; ~-**up** *Am sl* blendend, knorke, tipptopp.

bangle ['bæŋgl] Arm-, Fußring *m*.

banish ['bæniʃ] *tr* ausweisen, verbannen *a. fig (from* aus); *fig* verscheuchen; *fig* sich frei machen von; sich aus dem Kopf schlagen; ~**ment** ['-mənt] Verbannung, Ausweisung; Entlassung *f*.

banisters ['bænistəz] *pl* Treppengeländer *n*.

banjo ['bændʒou] *pl -o(e)s mus* Banjo *n*; ~**ist** ['-ist] Banjospieler *m*.

bank [bæŋk] **1.** *s* (Fluß-, Kanal-, See-) Ufer *n*; (Ufer-)Hang *m*, Böschung *f*; Abhang *m*; Aufschüttung *f*; Damm, Deich *m*; Bankett *n*, Berme; Untiefe, *(sand~)* (Sand-)Bank; *(~ of snow)* (Schnee-)Verwehung; *(cloud ~)* (Wolken-)Bank; *min* Hängebank; *aero* Quer-, Seitenneigung; *(Kurve)* Überhöhung; Ruderbank; *tech* Reihe *f*, Aggregat *n*, Satz *m*, Schaltung *f*; *tr* aufschütten, anhäufen, massieren; *(Feuer)* aufdämmen; *itr aero* in die Schräglage gehen, sich in die Kurve legen; sich schief legen; *to* ~ *up (tr)* (auf)stauen; eindämmen; *(Kurve)* überhöhen; *itr (Sand)* sich aufschichten; *(Schnee)* verwehen; *(Wolken)* sich auftürmen, sich massieren; **2.** *s* Bank(haus, -geschäft *n*); *(Spiel)* Bank; *med* (Blut-)Bank *f*; *allg* Vorratsraum *m*, Reserven *f pl*; *tr (Geld)* auf die Bank bringen; *itr* ein Bankkonto haben; Bankgeschäfte machen; *with s.o.* mit jdm in Bankverbindung stehen; *(Spiel)* die Bank halten; e-e Bank leiten; *(to* ~ *on s.o.) fam* auf jdn vertrauen, sich auf jdn verlassen; *tr (Geld)* auf e-r Bank einzahlen; *to open a* ~ *account* ein Bankkonto eröffnen *od* einrichten; *to overdraw o.'s* ~ *account* sein Bankkonto überziehen; *annuity* ~ Rentenbank *f*; *blood* ~ Blutbank *f*; *clearing* ~ Abrechnungsstelle *f*; *return (statement) of a* ~ Bankausweis *m*; *savings-bank* Sparkasse *f*; ~ *of circulation* Noten-, Zettelbank *f*; ~ *of discount, discount* ~, ~ *of exchange* Diskont-, Wechselbank *f*; ~ *of issue, issuing* ~ Emissionsbank *f*; ~**able** diskontfähig, diskontierbar; ~ **acceptance** Bankakzept *n*, -wechsel *m*; ~**account** Bankkonto *n*; ~-**bill** *Br* Bankwechsel *m*, -akzept *n*; *Am* Banknote *f*; ~-**book** Bankbuch *n*; ~ **building** Bankgebäude *n*; ~ **clerk** Bankangestellte(r) *m*; ~ **deposit** Bankguthaben *n*, *pl* -einlagen *f pl*; ~ **discount** Bankdiskont *m*; ~ **draft** Bankwechsel *m*; ~**er** ['-ə] Bankier, Bankmann *m*; *pl (mit Possessivprn)* Bankverbindung *f*; *group of* ~~*s* Bankenkonsortium *n*; Finanzgruppe *f*; ~ **guarantee, security** Banksicherheit *f*; ~ **holiday** Bankfeiertag *m* ~**ing** ['-iŋ] Bankwesen, -fach; Bankgeschäft *n*, -verkehr *m*; *aero* Schräglage *f*, Kurvenflug *m*; *min* Hängebankarbeiten *f pl*; *(Hochofen)* Dämpfen *n*; ~~ *expert* Bankfachmann *m*; ~~-*house* Bankhaus *n*; ~-**note** Banknote *f*; ~-**rate** Wechseldiskontsatz; Diskontsatz *m (der Bank von England)*; ~ **reserve** Bankreserve *f*; ~ **robbery** Bankraub, -überfall *m*; ~**rupt** ['-rʌpt] *s* Bankrotteur *a. fig*; Gemein-, Konkursschuldner *m*; *a* bankrott, zahlungsunfähig, insolvent, *fam* pleite; *fig* unfähig, völlig ohne *(of s.th.* etw), völlig ...los; *tr* zugrunde richten *(s.o.* jdn); *to declare o.s.* ~~ Konkurs anmelden; *to go, to become* ~~ in Konkurs gehen, s-e Zahlungen einstellen, *fam* pleite machen; ~~*'s estate* Konkursmasse *f*; ~**ruptcy** ['-rəp(t)si] Bankrott, Konkurs *m*, Zahlungseinstellung, Insolvenz, *fam* Pleite *f*; Konkursverfahren *n*; *fig* Schiffbruch, Ruin *m*; ~~ *act, law, proceedings, trustee* Konkursordnung *f*, -recht, -verfahren *n*, -verwalter *m*; ~~ *petition* Antrag *m* auf Konkurseröffnung; Konkursanmeldung *f*.

banner ['bænə] *s* Banner *n*, Fahne *f a. fig*, Panier *n a. fig*; *(getragene)* Spruch-, Reklametafel *f*; *(bei Umzügen mitgeführtes)* Spruchband *n*; *(~ headline) (Zeitung)* (Haupt-)Schlagzeile *f*; *a Am* ins Auge fallend, hervorstechend; hervorragend, glänzend; Haupt-; Rekord-; *to join, to follow the* ~ *of s.o.* jds Fahne folgen; sich um jds Fahne scharen.

banns [bænz] *pl* (kirchliches) Aufgebot *n*; *to call, to put up the* ~ kirchlich aufbieten; *to have o.'s* ~ *called* das Aufgebot bestellen.

banquet ['bæŋkwit] *s* Bankett, Festessen; *Am* Essen *n*; *tr* festlich bewirten; *itr* schwelgen, schlemmen, schmausen; ~-**hall** Speise-, Festsaal *m*, Festhalle *f*; ~**er** ['-ə] Teilnehmer *m* an e-m Festessen; Schlemmer; Schwelger *m*; ~**te** [bæŋ'ket] Böschungsabsatz; *mil* Schützenauftritt; *Am* Gehweg *m*; gepolsterte Sitzbank *f*.

bant|am ['bæntəm] *s* Zwerg-, Bantamhuhn *n*; *fig* Zwerg, Knirps *m*, Giftkröte *f*; *a* winzig, zwergenhaft; angriffslustig, händelsüchtig; ~~ *weight (Boxen)* Bantamgewicht *n*; ~**er** ['-ə] *s* (harmloser) Scherz, Spaß, Ulk *m*; *tr* sich lustig machen, scherzen über; *itr* Spaß, Ulk machen, scherzen *(with* mit); ~**erer** ['-ərə] Spaßmacher, -vogel, Bruder *m* Lustig; ~**ling** ['-liŋ] Balg *m*, Gör, Kind *n*.

baobab ['beiobæb] Affenbrotbaum *m*.

bapt|ism ['bæptizm] Taufe *f a. fig*; *certificate of* ~~ Taufschein *m*; ~~ *of fire* Feuertaufe *f*; ~**ismal** [-'tizməl] *a* Tauf-; ~~ *font* Taufstein *m*; ~**ist** ['-ist] Täufer; *B*~~ Baptist *m*; ~**ist(e)ry** ['-ist(ə)ri] Taufkapelle *f*, Baptisterium *n*; ~**ize** [-'taiz] *tr* taufen *a. fig*.

*

bar [bɑ:] *s* Stange; Barre *f*; Barren; Riegel *(Schokolade)*; Querriegel *m*; Gitterstange *f*; Schlagbaum *m*, Schranke, Barriere; (Straßen-)Sperre; Flußbarre, Sandbank; *(Pferd)* Kandare *f*; *fig* Hindernis *n (to* für), Schranke *f*, Verbot *n*; Ausschluß; Hinderungsgrund; Querstrich; (waagerechter) Querstreifen; (Licht-, Farb-)Streifen; *mus* Taktstrich, Takt *m*; *el* Lamelle *f*; *tech* Bügel *m*, Breiteisen *n*; Gerichtsschranke *f*; Gericht *n*; *jur* Verjährung, prozeßhindernde Einrede *f*; Einwand *m*; *the B*~ Advokatur *f*, Anwaltsberuf, Stand *m* der Barrister; *parl (England)* Schranke *f*; *fig* Richterstuhl *m*, Entscheidungsgewalt *f*; Forum *n (of public opinion* der öffentlichen Meinung); Ausschank, Schanktisch *m*, Büfett *n*, Bar, *fam* Theke; *mil* Ordensspange *f*; *mete* Bar; *US* Rangabzeichen *n*; *mar* Brandungsgürtel *m*; *tr (Tür, Fenster)* verriegeln, ab-, ver-, zusperren, zumachen, schließen; *(Person)* aussperren, ausschließen *a. fig*; *(Weg)* (ver)sperren; *fig* verbieten, untersagen; *(Person)* hindern *(from* an), abhalten *(from* von), aufhalten, erschweren, unmöglich machen *(s.o. from s.th.* jdm etw); *jur* e-e prozeßhindernde Einrede erheben; mit Streifen versehen; *adv* abgesehen von, außer; ~ *none* ohne Ausnahme; ~ *one* außer einem; *at the B*~ vor Gericht; *to be* ~*red* verjährt sein; *to be a* ~ *to s.th.* e-r S hindernd im Wege stehen; *to go to the B*~, *to be called to the B*~ Barrister werden; als B. zugelassen werden; *to read for the B*~ sich auf den Anwaltsberuf vorbereiten; *parallel* ~*s (pl) (sport)* Barren *m*; *toll* ~ Zollschranke *f*; ~ *of rest (mus)* Pause *f*; ~-**keep(er)** *Am fam* Büfettier; Schankwirt *m*; ~ **magnet** Stabmagnet *m*; ~**maid** Kellnerin; Bardame *f*; ~**man** Kellner *m*; ~ **parlour, -room** Gastzimmer *n*, Schankstube *f*; ~-**tender** *Am* Büfettier *m*.

barb [bɑ:b] *s (Angel, Pfeil)* Widerhaken *m*; *(Feder)* Fahne *f*; *(Fisch)* Bartfäden *m pl*; *bot* Bart *m*; Kinnstück *n* (des Nonnenschleiers); *(Haube)* Barbe; *fig* Schärfe, Spitze *f*; *lit* Berber *m (Pferd)*; *tr* mit Widerhaken versehen; *pp*: ~*ed wire (entanglement)* Stacheldraht(verhau) *m*; ~**arian** [-'bɛəriən] *s* Barbar(in *f*); Wilde(r); rohe(r), ungesittete(r), ungebildete(r), geistig uninteressierte(r) Mensch *m*; *a* barbarisch; roh, ungesittet, ungebildet, uninteressiert; ~**aric** [-'bærik] roh, ungebildet, ohne Geschmack; unverbildet; ~**arism** ['-ərizm] Barbarei, Unkultur; Grobheit, Roheit; Ungebildetheit *f*; falsche(r) *od* schlechte(r) Sprachgebrauch, Barbarismus *m*; ~**arity** [-'bæriti] Unkultur, Barbarei; Unmenschlichkeit, Roheit, Wildheit, Grausamkeit; rohe Tat *f*; Barbarismus; schlechte(r) Geschmack *m*;

~arize *tr* verballhornen, roh umgehen mit; *itr* verrohen; **~arous** ['-ərəs] barbarisch, unmenschlich, grausam, roh, wild; ungesittet, ungebildet, geschmacklos; **B~ary** ['-əri]: *~~ ape (zoo)* Magot *m*; **~ate** ['-eit] *zoo bot* mit Barthaaren, -fäden, Grannen (versehen); **~ecue** ['-ikju:] *s* Bratrost *m*; am Spieß gebratene(s) Fleisch *od* Tier; *Am* Fest *n*, Ausflug *m*, bei dem Fleisch am offenen Feuer gebraten wird; *tr (Ochsen etc)* im Ganzen auf dem Rost braten; **~el** ['-əl] *zoo* Barbe *f*; Bartfäden *m pl*; **~er** ['-ə] Barbier, Friseur *m*; *~~'s itch (med)* Bartflechte *f*; *~~('s) pole* spiralig bemalte Stange *f* als Ladenschild; *~~shop (Am)* (Herren-) Frisörsalon *m*.

bard [bɑ:d] Barde *m a. fig*.

bare [bεə] *a* nackt, bloß; kahl; ohne, entblößt (*of* von); leer, öde; *(Raum)* unmöbliert, leer; ärmlich, dürftig; fadenscheinig; schmucklos; ungeschützt; unbehaart; entlaubt; ohne Hut; *fig* unverhüllt, offen; *(Tatsachen)* nackt; *(Mehrheit)* knapp; *tech* ohne Zubehör; *(Draht)* blank; bloß, nur..., ... allein; *tr* entblößen; aufdecken; berauben; *fig* enthüllen, bloßlegen; *on his ~ word* auf sein bloßes Wort (hin); *to lay ~* entblößen; aufdecken, offen darlegen; **~back** *a adv (Pferd)* ohne Sattel; auf ungesatteltem Pferd; **~faced** *a* unverhüllt *bes. fig*; unverschämt; **~foot** *a adv*, *~~ed (a)* barfuß; **~headed** *a* barhäuptig; **~ly** ['-li] *adv* unverhüllt, offen; dürftig, wenig; kaum, gerade (genug), gerade so eben; **~ness** ['-nis] Nacktheit, Blöße; Ärmlichkeit, Dürftigkeit; Schmucklosigkeit *f*.

bargain ['bɑ:gin] *s* Handel *m*, Geschäft(sabschluß *m*) *n*, Kauf(vertrag) *m*; Übereinkunft *f*, Vertrag; gute(r) Kauf *m*, gute(s) Geschäft *n*, Gelegenheitskauf *m*; *fam* gefundene Sache *f*; *(-sale)* Gelegenheits-, Ausverkauf *m*; *itr* handeln, feilschen (*with s.o., s.o. for s.th.* mit jdm um etw); verhandeln; abmachen (*with s.o. for s.th., to do* mit jdm etw, zu tun); *tr: to ~ away* mit Verlust verkaufen; zu billig abgeben; verschachern; *to ~ for* handeln, feilschen um; rechnen mit, zählen auf, erwarten *(meist mit Negation od more than)*; *to ~ over s.th.* um etw feilschen; *into the ~* obendrein, noch dazu, zusätzlich, außerdem, auch; *to close, to conclude, to settle, to strike a ~~* ein Geschäft abschließen, e-n Kauf tätigen; handelseinig werden; *to drive a hard ~* s-n Vorteil rücksichtslos wahren; *to make the best of a bad ~ (fig)* sich mit e-m Übel, Mißgeschick abfinden; *to make a good ~* ein gutes Geschäft machen; billig einkaufen; *it's a ~* abgemacht! *it's a ~ at that price* das ist geschenkt zu dem Preis! *a ~'s a ~* abgemacht ist abgemacht! *chance ~* Gelegenheitskauf *m*; *collective ~* Kollektiv(arbeits)vertrag *m*; *Dutch, wet ~* begossene(r) Kauf, Abschluß *m*; *firm ~* feste(r) Abschluß *m*; *good, bad ~* gute(s), schlechte(s) Geschäft *n*; günstige(r), ungünstige(r) Abschluß *od* Vertrag *m*; *hard ~* ungünstige(r) Vertrag *m*; *time ~* Termingeschäft *n*; **~ basement, counter** *(Warenhaus)* Abteilung *f* mit verbilligten Artikeln; **~ing** ['-iŋ] Vertrag(sabschluß) *m*; Verhandeln; Feilschen *n*; **~ money** An-, Hand-, Draufgeld *n*; **~ price** Vorzugs-, Ausverkaufspreis *m*; **~ work** Kontraktarbeit *f*.

barge [bɑ:dʒ] *s* Last-, Schleppkahn *m*; Barke *f*; Leichter *m*; Schute *f*; *Am* Vergnügungsschiff *n*, -bus *m*; Hausboot; Hotelschiff *n*; *sl* schwerfällige(r) Kahn *m*; *sl* Auseinandersetzung *f*; *itr fam* taumeln, torkeln, stürzen; hereinstolpern (*into* in; *against* gegen); *(to ~ in)* mit der Tür ins Haus fallen; sich einmischen; *a arch* Giebel-; *I would not touch him with a ~-pole* ich kann ihn nicht riechen, nicht ausstehen; **~e** [-'dʒi:], **~man** Kahnfahrer, Lastschiffer, Bootsmann *m*; *to swear like a ~~* wie ein Kutscher fluchen.

bar|ic ['bεərik] *a chem* Barium-; barometrisch; **~itone, ~ytone** ['bæritoun] Bariton *m (Stimme u. Sänger)*; **~ium** ['bεəriəm] *chem* Barium *n*.

bark [bɑ:k] **1.** *s (Baum)* Rinde, Borke; *(Gerberei)* Lohe *f*; *pharm* Chinin *n*; *sl* Pelle *f*, Fell *n*, Haut *f*; *itr* ab-, entrinden; gerben; *fam* abpellen, wundreiben, -scheuern; *with the ~ on (Person)* noch ungeschliffen; **~ beetel** Borkenkäfer *m*; **~-pit** Lohegrube *f*; **~-tree** China-, Fieberrindenbaum *m*; **2.** (*a.* **barque**) *s mar* Dreimaster *m*, Bark *f (meist barque)*; *poet allg* Schiff, Boot *n*, Barke *f (meist ~)*; **3.** *s* Bellen, Gebell, Kläffen; *fig (Kanone)* Donnern; Gekrächz, Gehuste *n*, Husten *m*; Gebelfer *n*; *itr* bellen, kläffen; *fam* husten; ausschimpfen, abkanzeln, anfahren (*at s.o.* jdn); *tr sl* marktschreierisch anpreisen; *to ~ up the wrong tree (fam)* auf dem Holzweg sein; **~er** ['-ə] Ausrufer; lästige(r) Mensch *m*; *fam* Schießeisen *n*; *tech* Schälmaschine *f*; Schäler *m*.

barley ['bɑ:li] Gerste *f*; *pearl ~* (Perl-) Graupen *f pl*; **~-broth** *Art* Starkbier *n*; **~corn** Gerstenkorn *n*, -saft; Whisky *m*; *(Gewehr)* Korn *n*; $^1/_3$ Zoll *m*; *John B~~* Gerstensaft *m (personifiziert)*; **~ sugar** Malzbonbon *m* od *n*; **~(-)water** Gerstenschleim *m (für Kranke)*.

barm [bɑ:m] (Bier-)Hefe, Bärme *f*; **~y** ['-i] hefig; schaumig; *fig fam* verrückt, blöd(e).

barn [bɑ:n] Scheune, Scheuer *f*; *Am* Stall *m*; *Am (car~)* Straßenbahndepot *n*; **~acle** ['-əkl] **1.** *(Pferd)* Nasenklemme; *pl sl* Brille *f*; **2.** Ringelgans; Entenmuschel; *fig* Drohne, Klette *f*; **~-door** Scheunentor *n a. fig*; *Am* Stalltüre; *theat* Lichtblende *f*; **~-floor** Tenne *f*; **~-owl** Schleiereule *f*; **~-storm** *itr* auf dem Land (Wahl-)Reden halten *od* Theaterstücke aufführen; **~-stormer** Wanderredner; Schmierenkomödiant; Kunstflieger *m*; **~-swallow** Rauchschwalbe *f*; **~-yard** (Bauern-)Hof *m*.

baro|graph ['bærogrɑ:f] Höhenschreiber, Barograph *m*; **~meter** [bə'rɔmitə] Barometer *n a. fig*; *~~ reading* Barometerstand *m*; **~metric(al)** [bærə'metrik(l)] barometrisch; Barometer-; *~~ pressure* Luftdruck *m*.

baron ['bærən] Baron *a. fig*, Freiherr; *fig* Magnat, König, Schlotbaron *m*; *beer ~* Bierkönig, -magnat *m*; *~ of beef* (Rinds-)Keulen u. Filetstücke *pl*; **~age** ['-idʒ] Kronvasallen *m pl*; Rang *m* e-s Barons; Adelsbuch *n*, -liste *f*; *die* Barone; **~ess** ['-is] Baronin *f*; **~et** ['-it] *s* Baronet *m*; *tr* in den Baronetsstand erheben; **~etage** ['-itidʒ] (Gesamtheit der) Baronets *m pl*; Baronetsbuch *n*, -liste *f*; **~etcy** ['-itsi] Baronetsbrief *m*, -würde *f*; **~ial** [bə'rouniəl] freiherrlich; Barons-; großartig, prächtig; **~y** ['bærəni] Baronie *f*; Besitz *m* e-s Barons; Freiherrnstand *m*, -würde *f*; *(Irland)* B. *(Teil e-r Grafschaft)*; *(Schottland)* Herrensitz *m*, große(s) Herrenhaus *n*.

bar|oque [bə'rouk] *a (Kunst)* barock; überladen; *fig* sonderbar, eigenartig; *s* Barock(stil *m*) *s* od *m*; **~ouche** [bə'ru:ʃ] Landauer *m*.

barque [bɑ:k] *s. bark* 2.

barr|ack ['bærək] *s meist pl mit sing mil* Mannschaftsgebäude *n*, Truppenunterkunft, Kaserne; *allg* Massenunterkunft; *pej* (Miets-)Kaserne *f*; *tr* kasernieren; *sport* auszischen; *confinement to ~~s* Kasernenarrest *m*; *~~(s) yard, square* Kasernenhof *m*; **~age** ['bærɑ:ʒ] Damm *m*, Wehr; Stauwerk *n*, Talsperre; *mil* Sperre *f*; *(~~ fire)* Sperrfeuer *n*, Feuerschutz, -riegel, -vorhang *m*; *mar* Minensperre; *fig* Flut *f* (*of questions* von Fragen); Hagel *m* (*of blows* von Schlägen); *~~ balloon* Sperrballon *m*; **~el** ['bærəl] *s* Faß, Gebinde *n*, Tonne *(a. als Maß: Br 36 imperial gallons, Am $31^1/_2$ gallons)*; Walze *f*, Zylinder, zylindrische(r) Gegenstand *m*; *tech* Trommel *f*; (Geschütz-, Kanonen-)Rohr *n*, (Gewehr-)Lauf; *(Trommel)* Kasten *m*; *(Objektiv)* Fassung; *(Kolben)* Führung; Drehbankspindel *f*; (Pumpen-) Stiefel; (Feder-)Kiel; *(Füllfederhalter)* Tintenraum; (Tier-)Körper, Rumpf; *Am fam* Haufen *m*, Menge *f*; *sl pol* Wahlgelder *n pl*; *tr* in ein Faß *od* in Fässer abfüllen; verstauen; *itr sl Am mot* rasen; *to have s.o. over a ~~ (Am)* jdn in der Gewalt haben; *~~-maker* Faßbinder *m*; *~~-organ* Drehorgel *f*, Leierkasten *m*; *~~ roll (aero)* Rolle *f*; *~~-vault (arch)* Tonnengewölbe *n*; **~en** ['bærən] *(Land, Pflanzen, Tiere, Frau)* unfruchtbar, ertragsunfähig; wüst, dürr, karg; steril *a. fig*; *fig* dürftig, mager, ärmlich; *fig* unergiebig, unproduktiv, unrentabel; unschöpferisch, ohne Einfälle; langweilig, uninteressant; *com (Kapital)* tot; *min* taub; **~enness** ['-ənnis] Unfruchtbarkeit; *fig* Dürftigkeit; Unergiebigkeit; (geistige) Armut, Leere *f*; Mangel *m* (*of* an); **~icade, ~icado** [bæri'keid, -'keidou] *s* Barrikade; Wege-, Straßensperre *f*; *tr (Straße)* mit e-r Barrikade sperren, verrammeln; verbarrikadieren; **~ier** ['bæriə] Schranke, Sperre; Barriere *f*, Damm *m*, Aufschüttung *f*; Schlagbaum *m*, Zollschranke; *fig* Schranke *f*, Hindernis *n* (*to* für); Trennwand; Grenze *f*; **~ing** ['bɑ:riŋ] *prp* außer *dat*, ausgenommen *acc*, mit Ausnahme *gen*, abgesehen von, ohne; *~~ errors* Irrtum vorbehalten; **~ister** ['bæristə] *(~~-at-law)* vor Gericht auftretende(r) Anwalt *m*; *revising-~~* Wählerlistenprüfer *m*; **~ow** ['bærou] **1.** kleine(r) Hügel; Grabhügel *m*, Hügelgrab *n*; **2.** *(hand-~~)* Trage, (Trag-)Bahre *f*; *(wheel-~~)* Schubkarren; *(coster's ~~)* (zweirädriger) (Hand-)Karren *m*; *~~-boy, -man* Straßenhändler *m* mit Gemüse.

barter ['bɑ:tə] *tr* (aus-, ein)tauschen, in Tausch geben (*against, for* gegen); *itr* Tauschhandel treiben; *s* Tausch (-handel); *fig* (Aus-)Tausch *m*; *by way of ~* im Tauschwege; *to ~ s.th. away* verschachern; verschleudern; **~ agreement, contract** Tauschabkommen *n*, -vertrag *m*; **~er** ['-rə] Tauschhändler *m*.

barytone *s. baritone*.

basal ['beisl] an der Basis befindlich; grundsätzlich, prinzipiell; fundamental; Grund-, Ausgangs-; **~t** ['bæsɔ:lt, bə'sɔ:lt] *geol* Basalt *m*; **~tic** [bə'sɔ:ltik] basaltisch; Basalt-.

bascule ['bæskju:l]: **~ bridge** Klappbrücke *f (z. B. Tower Bridge, London)*.

base [beis] *s* Grundlinie, -fläche *a. math*, -zahl; Basis *f a. math*, Fundament *n*; untere(r) Teil; *arch* Fuß, Sockel *m*; *(~ plate)* Grundplatte *f*;

Grund(lage *f*) *m*, Basis *f* ; Grundsatz *m*, Prinzip *n*; Ausgangspunkt *m*; *(Landmessung)* Standlinie *a. sport*; *mil* (Operations-)Basis *f*, Stützpunkt *m*; Ausgangsstellung *f*; *sport* Mal *n*; *mus* Baßstimme *f*; *(Mischung)* Hauptbestandteil; *tech* Grundstoff *m*, -metall *n*; *chem* Base *f*; *gram* Stamm; *radio* Röhrensockel; *(air ~) US* Fliegerhorst; *(Munition)* Boden *m*; *(Wolken)* Untergrenze *f*; *a* Grund-; niedrig, untergeordnet; gewöhnlich, gemein, unedel, unfein, unwürdig, verächtlich, unrühmlich, niederträchtig; gering-, minderwertig, dürftig, schäbig; *(Münze)* falsch, unecht; *(Metall)* unedel; *jur* dienstbar; auf Dienstleistungen beruhend; *mil* Etappen-; *(Stimme)* tief, Baß-; *(Sprache)* korrumpiert; *tr* basieren, gründen, stützen (*on* auf); auf-, hinstellen; sichern (*on* durch); *itr (to ~ at, upon)* stationiert sein; *to ~ o.s. on* sich stützen auf; *to get to the first ~ (Am sl)* sein Ziel mühelos erreichen; *naval ~* Flottenstützpunkt *m*, -basis *f*; *~ of supply, supply ~* Versorgungsbasis *f*; **~ball** Baseball *m (Am, Nationalspiel)*; **~baller** Baseballspieler *m*; **~board** Bodenbrett *n*; *Am* Scheuerleiste *f*; **~-born** *a* von niedriger Herkunft; unehelich; gewöhnlich; **~less** ['-lis] grundlos, unbegründet; **~man** *sport* am Mal stehende(r) Spieler *m*; **~ment** ['-mənt] *arch* Fundament; Kellergeschoß *n*; **~ness** ['-nis] Niedrigkeit; Gemeinheit, Verächtlichkeit, Niedertracht, -trächtigkeit; Minderwertigkeit, Dürftigkeit; Unechtheit; *(Sprache)* Entartung *f*; **~plate** *(Gebiß)* Gaumenplatte; *allg* Unterlage *f*; **~ price** Grundpreis *m*; **~ runner** *sport (Baseball)* Spieler *m*, der das erste Mal erreicht.

bash [bæʃ] *tr fam* heftig schlagen; *s* heftige(r) Schlag *m*; *to ~ in* einschlagen, zertrümmern; *to have a ~ at s.th. (sl)* etw versuchen; **~ful** ['-ful] scheu; schüchtern, verlegen, befangen, zaghaft; **~fulness** ['-fulnis] Schüchternheit; Verlegenheit, Befangenheit *f*.

basic ['beisik] Grund-, Ausgangs-; grundsätzlich (wichtig), prinzipiell; fundamental, (von) grundlegend(er Bedeutung) maßgebend; *chem* basisch; **~ idea** Grund-, Leitgedanke *m*; **~ industry** Grundstoffindustrie *f*; **~ iron** od **pig, steel, slag** Thomasroheisen *n*, -stahl *m*, -schlacke *f*; **~ material** Ausgangswerkstoff *m*; **~ pay** Grundgehalt *n*; **~ research** Grundlagenforschung *f*; **~ training** Grundausbildung *f*; **~ trait** Grundzug *m*; **~ wage(s)** Grundlohn *m*.

basil ['bæzl, 'bæzil] *bot* Basilikum, Basili(k)en-, Hirnkraut *n*; **~ica** [bə'silikə] *arch* Basilika *f*; **~isk** ['bæzilisk] *zoo* Basilisk *m*; *~~ glance* Basiliskenblick *m*.

bas|in ['beisn] (Wasser-, Wasch-)Bekken *n a. geol geog*; Schale, Schüssel; (Tal-)Mulde, Wanne *f*; *(river ~~)* Fluß-, Stromgebiet *n*; Bucht *f*; Hafenbecken; (Wasser-)Bassin *n*, Teich *m*; **~is** ['beisis] *pl -ses* [-i:z] Basis, Grundlage *f*, Fundament *n*, Unterlage *f*; *mil* Stütz-, Ausgangspunkt *m*; *on the ~~ of* auf Grund *gen*, auf der Grundlage, unter Zugrundelegung *gen*; *to serve as a ~* als Grundlage dienen.

bask [bɑ:sk] *itr* sich be-, anstrahlen lassen; sich sonnen *a. fig (in her favour* in ihrer Gunst); **~et** ['-it] Korb; Korbvoll; *aero* Ballonkorb *m*; *clothes-~~* Wäschekorb *m*; *the pick of the ~~* das Beste davon; *~~-ball (sport)* Basket-, Korbball *m*; *~~ case* Arm- u. Beinamputierte(r) *m*; *~~-hilt (Fechten)* Korb *m (des Korbschlägers)*; *~~-maker* Korbmacher *m*; *~~ work* Korbwaren *f pl*, -geflecht *n*.

bas-relief ['bɑ:rili:f, 'bæs-] *(Kunst)* Basrelief *n*.

bass [bæs] **1.** *zoo* Flußbarsch; Gemeine(r) Seebarsch *m*; **2.** Bast *m*; Bastmatte, -tasche *f*; **3.** [beis] *a mus* tief; Baß-; *s* Baß *(Stimme u. Sänger)*; Bassist; *(~ clef)* Baßschlüssel *m*; **~ drum** große Trommel *f*; **~-viol** Viola da gamba, Kniegeige *f*; (Violon-) Cello *n*; **~et** ['-it] **1.** Dackel *m*; **2.**: *~~-horn (mus)* Alt-, Baritonklarinette *f*; **3.** *min* Ausgehende(s) *n*; **~inet** ['-inet] Korbwiege *f*, -kinderwagen *m*; **~o** ['bæsou] Baß, Bassist *m*; **~oon** [bə'su:n, -z-] *mus* Fagott *n*.

bast [bæst] Bast *m*; Bastseil *n*, -matte *f*; **~ard** ['-əd] *s* Bastard *m a. bot zoo*; un-*od* außereheliche(s) Kind *n*; *fig* Nachahmung, -bildung *f*; Abklatsch; *sl* Schweinehund *m*; *a* un-, außerehelich; Bastard-; *fig* unecht, falsch; minderwertig; *(Gegenstand)* abnorm, ungewöhnlich, aus dem Rahmen fallend; *~~ file* Bastard-, Vorfeile *f*; *~~ title (typ)* Schmutztitel *m*; **~ardize** ['-ədaiz] *tr* für un-, außerehelich erklären; *fig* korrumpieren; *(Sprache)* verballhornen; **~ardy** ['-ədi] un-, außereheliche Geburt *f*; **~e** [beist] **1.** *tr* (zs.-, an)heften; **2.** *tr (bratendes Fleisch)* mit Fett begießen; **3.** *tr* verprügeln; beschimpfen; **~inado** [bæsti'neidou] *pl -oes s u. tr* Stockstreiche *m pl* auf die Fußsohlen (geben (*s.o.* jdm)); **~ion** ['bæstiən] Bastion, Bastei *f*.

bat [bæt] **1.** *s* Fledermaus *f*; *to have ~s in the belfry* nicht alle Tassen im Spind haben, verrückt sein; *~-blind, ~-eyed, blind as a ~* stockblind; **2.** *s* Schlagholz *n*, Schläger; *a. fam* Schlag, Hieb; *Br* Kricketschläger; Klotz, Klumpen *m*; *fig fam* Geschwindigkeit *f*, Tempo *n*, Schwung; rasche(r) Schritt *m*; *Am sl* Sauferei, Besäufnis *f*; fidele(r) Abend *m*; *tr* (mit dem Schlagholz) schlagen; prügeln; *itr* am Schlagen, dran sein; *fig* eintreten, kämpfen (*for* für); *at ~ (sport)* an der Reihe, dran; *off o.'s own ~ (Spiel u. fig)* allein, ohne Hilfe; *right off the ~* sofort, augenblicklich; *to carry o.'s ~* am Spiel, dran bleiben; *to go to ~ for s.o.* jdm helfen, unter die Arme greifen; *to ~ around (itr)* herumreisen; *tr (Plan)* diskutieren; **3.** *s fam* Umgangssprache, Sprechweise *f*; **4.** *itr fam* zwinkern *(mit den Augen)*; *not to ~ an eye lid* kein Auge zutun; mit keiner Wimper zucken; **~-horse** ['bæthɔ:s] Packpferd *n*; **~man** *mil* Putzer *m*; **~sman** *sport* Schläger; *aero* Einwinker *m*.

batch [bætʃ] *(Bäckerei)* Schub *m*; *tech* Füllung, Speisung; *tech* Ladung; *allg* Reihe, Serie, Partie *f*, Quantum *n*, Haufen, Satz, Stoß, *fam* Schwung *m*; **~y** ['-i] *sl* bekloppt, plemplem.

bate [beit] **1.** *itr* nachlassen; geringer, schwächer werden; *tr (den Mut, die Hoffnung)* sinken lassen; *(den Atem)* anhalten; *(meist mit Negation)* vermindern, herab-, heruntersetzen; **2.** *s* Alkalilauge, Beize *f (zum Gerben)*; **3.** *a. bait sl* Wut *f*.

bath [bɑ:θ] *s* Bad *n a. chem phot*, Waschung *f*; Bad(ewasser) *n*, Lösung; Badewanne *f*, -zimmer *n*, -anstalt *f*; (Stadt-)Bad; *pl* [bɑ:ðz] Heilbad *n*, Kurort *m*; *(Hochofen)* geschmolzene(s) Metall *n*; *tr (Kind, Kranken)* baden; *to have, to take a ~* ein Bad nehmen; *air-, foot-, mud-, sitz-, sun-, vapour-~* Luft-, Fuß-, Schlamm- *od* Moor-, Sitz-, Sonnen-, Dampfbad *n*; *swimming ~* Hallen(schwimm)bad *n*; *water-, sand-~ (chem)* Wasser-, Sandbad *n*; **~ bonnet** *Am* Badehaube *f*; **B~ brick** *Art* Metallreiniger *m*; **B~ bun, Oliver** *Art* Früchtebrot *n*; **~ chair** Kranken-, Rollstuhl *m*; **~e** [beið] *tr u. itr* baden; *tr* bespülen, befeuchten, benetzen; *(Fluß)* vorbeifließen an; *allg* einhüllen, -tauchen; *s Br* Baden *n* im Freien, Schwimmen *n*; *to go ~ing* schwimmen, baden gehen; **~er** ['beiðə] Badende(r *m*) *f*; **~house** *Am* Bad *n*, -eanstalt *f*; Umkleideräume *m pl*; **~inette** [-i'nεt] *(Warenzeichen)* zs.klappbare Gummibadewanne *f* für Kinder; **~ing** ['beiðiŋ] Baden *n*; Bade-; *~~-cap* Badehaube *f*; *~~-costume, -dress, -suit* Badeanzug *m*; *~~-drawers, trunks (pl)* Badehose *f*; *~~ fatality* Badeunfall *m*; *~~-gown, -wrap* Bademantel *m*; *~~ resort* Badeort *m*; **~ mat** Badematte *f*; **~os** ['beiθɔs] Alltäglichkeit, Flachheit, Banalität *f*; Umschlagen *n* vom Erhabenen ins Gemeine, Banale, Lächerliche; **~robe, wrap** Bademantel *m*; **~room** Badezimmer *n*; **~ towel** Badetuch *n*; **~tub** Badewanne *f*; **~ymetry** [bæ'θimitri] Tiefseelotung *f*; **~ysphere, ~yscaphe** ['bæθisfiə, -skeif] Tiefsee-Taucherkugel *f*.

bat|ik ['bætik] *(Textil)* Batik(druck) *m*; **~ing** ['beitiŋ] *prp obs* ausgenommen, abgesehen von; **~iste** [bæ'ti:st] Batist *m*; **~on** ['bætən] Kommando-, Marschallstab; (Polizei-)Knüppel; Dirigentenstab, Taktstock; Tambourstock *m*; **~rachian** [bə'treikjən] *a* froschartig; Frosch-; *s* Froschlurch *m*.

batt|alion [bə'tæljən] Bataillon *n*; Abteilung *f*; *pl* Streitkräfte *f pl*; *~~ aid station, commander, command post, sector* Bataillonsverbandsplatz, -kommandeur, -gefechtsstand, -abschnitt *m*; **~els** ['bætlz] *pl (Oxford)* College-Rechnung *f* für Verpflegung und sonstige Auslagen; **~en** ['bætn] **1.** *s* Brett *n*, Planke, Diele, Bohle; Latte, Leiste *f*; *(Seidenwebstuhl)* Schlag *m*, Lade *f*; *tr (to ~ up, down)* mit Brettern, Bohlen benageln, versehen, verstärken; **2.** *itr* sich gütlich tun (*on* an), schwelgen (*on* in); fett, dicker werden (*on* von).

batter ['bætə] *tr itr* heftig u. wiederholt schlagen; zerschlagen, zerschmettern; *(to ~ down, in)* nieder-, einschlagen; trommeln (*at the door* gegen die Tür); mit Trommelfeuer belegen, beschießen; *(to ~ down)* zs.schießen; zs.hauen; zerfetzen; beschädigen, verbeulen; abnützen, verschleißen, strapazieren; *fig* streng umgehen, verfahren mit; böse zurichten; *typ (Letter)* abnutzen; *arch* sich verjüngen; *s (Spiel)* Schläger *(Person)*; geschlagene(r) Teig *m (aus Eiern, Milch u. Mehl)*; *arch* Abschrägung, Verjüngung, Ausbauchung *f*; defekte Type *f*; **~ed** ['-d] *a* stark mitgenommen, abgenutzt; *fig* ausgemergelt, abgezehrt, elend; *(Gewinde)* verdrückt; **~ing** ['-riŋ] *a* Sturm-, Belagerungs-; *s* Ausloten *n*; Ausbauchung *f*; Zerschlagen *n*; *~~-ram (hist)* Sturmbock, Mauerbrecher *m*; *~~ wall* ausgebauchte Mauer *f*; **~y** ['-ri] tätliche(r) Angriff *m*, Schlägerei *f*, Tätlichkeiten, Realinjurie *f pl (assault and ~~)*; *allg* Reihe, Serie; *mil el allg* Batterie *f*; *el* Akkumulator, Sammler *m*; *opt* Linsen- u. Prismensystem *n*; Test(reihe *f*) *m*; *mus* Schlaginstrumente *n pl*; *in ~~* in Feuerstellung; *to boost, to change, to load, to run* *down a ~~* e-e B. verstärken, auswechseln, aufladen, erschöpfen; *~~ cell (el)* Batterieelement *n*; *~~ charger (el)* Ladesatz *m*; *~~ charging-station (el)* Ladestation *f*; *~~ circuit, current* Batteriestrom *m*; *~~ commander (mil)* Batteriechef *m*; *~~ commutator (el)* Polwechsler *m*; *~~ ignition (mot)* Batteriezündung *f*; *~~(-operated) set (radio)* Batterieempfänger *m*.

batting ['bætiŋ] *(Baseball, Kricket)* Schlagen *n*; *(Textil)* (Baumwoll-)Watte *f*; ~ **average** *fam* Durchschnittsleistung *f*.

battle ['bætl] *s* Schlacht *f* (*of* bei), Gefecht, Treffen *n a. fig* (*for* um); (See-, Luft-)Schlacht *f*; *fig* Kampf (*for* um); Sieg, Erfolg *m*; *itr* kämpfen, streiten (*for* um; *with* mit); *to accept, to refuse ~* die Schlacht annehmen, verweigern; *to do* od *to give, to offer ~* e-e Schlacht liefern *od* schlagen, anbieten; *to join ~* sich in e-e Schlacht einlassen; *a good start is half the ~ (prov)* frisch gewagt ist halb gewonnen; *the ~ is to the strong (prov)* dem Mutigen gehört die Welt; *pitched ~* regelrechte Schlacht *f*; *~ of annihilation, of encirclement* Vernichtungs-, Kesselschlacht *f*; *~ of life* Lebenskampf *m*; *~ of material* Materialschlacht *f*; ~ **alarm** Gefechtsalarm *m*; ~ **area** Gefechtszone *f*; **~-array, -order, line of ~** Schlachtordnung, Gefechtsgliederung *f*; **~-ax(e)** Streitaxt *f*; *sl* Ripp *n*, Hausdrachen *m*; ~ **casualty** Schwerverwundete(r); Gefallene(r) *m*; *pl* Gefechtsverluste *m pl*; **~-cruiser** *mar* Schlachtkreuzer *m*; **~(-)cry** Schlachtruf *m*; **~dore** *sport* Racket *n*; ~ **dress** Kampf-, Feldanzug *m*; **~-experience** Kampferfahrung *f*; ~ **fatigue** Frontneurose *f*; **~field, -ground** Schlachtfeld, Kampfgelände *n*; **~front** Hauptkampflinie, Frontstellung *f*; ~ **jacket** Feldbluse *f*; **~-line** Kampffront *f*; **~ment** *arch mil hist* Zinne *f*; **~-noise** Schlacht-, Kampflärm *m*; **~-piece** *(Kunst)* Schlachtenbild *n*, *lit* Schlachtschilderung *f*; ~ **royal** große Schlacht *f*; Großkampf *m*; allgemeine heftige Auseinandersetzung *f*; **~ship,** *sl* **wagon** Schlachtschiff *n*; **~-song** Kampflied *n*; **~-tested, -tried** *a* kampferprobt; **~-weary** kampfmüde.

batt|ue [bæ'tu:] Treibjagd *f*; geschossene(s) Wild *n*, Strecke *f*; Gemetzel *n*; **~y** ['bæti] *sl* hirnverbrannt, verrückt; überspannt.

bauble ['bɔ:bl] Flitter *m*; *hist* Narrenzepter *n*.

baulk [bɔ:k] *s. balk.*

bauxite ['bɔ:ksait] *min* Bauxit *m*.

Bavaria [bə'vɛəriə] Bayern *n*; **~n** [-n] *a* bay(e)risch; *s* Bayer(in *f*) *m*.

bawd [bɔ:d] Kupplerin; Bordellmutter *f*; **~iness** ['-inis] Zotenhaftigkeit *f*; **~ry** ['-ri] Kuppelei; Zotenhaftigkeit, Unflätigkeit; Zote *f*; **~y** ['-i] kupplerisch; zotenhaft, zotig; obszön; *s* Zote *f*; *~~-house* Bordell *n*.

bawl [bɔ:l] *tr (a. ~ out), itr* brüllen, schreien; *(Waren)* ausrufen; *itr fam* das Maul aufreißen; *fam* laut schluchzen, plärren; *to ~ out (Am sl)* anschnauzen, e-e Zigarre verpassen (*s.o.* jdm), abkanzeln, fertigmachen; *s* Schrei *m*; *fam* laute(s) Schluchzen, Plärren *n*.

bay [bei] **1.** *(~-tree, laurel)* Edle(r) Lorbeer; *allg* Lorbeer(baum); *meist pl* Lorbeer(kranz); *fig* Ruhm *m*, Ehre *f*; **~leaf** Lorbeerblatt *n*; ~ **rum** Bayrum *(Kopfwaschmittel)*; **2.** Bai, Bucht *f a. tech*, Meerbusen *m*; *(Gebirgszug)* Einbuchtung *f*, Einschnitt *m*; *arch* Mauerfläche *(zwischen zwei Vorsprüngen)*; Fensteröffnung *f*, -joch *n*; Erker *m*; Box; (Tür-)Nische *f*; Brückenglied *n*; *allg* Zwischenraum *m*, Kassette *f*, Feld, Fach *n*; Lücke, Öffnung *f*; Abschnitt *m*; *mil* Hindernislücke *f*; tote(r) Winkel *m*; *agr* (Heu-, Getreide-)Banse *f*; *rail* Nebenbahnsteig *m*; Funkstille *f*; *mar* Lazarett *n*; *aero (bomb ~)* (Bomben-)Schacht *m*; **~-line** *rail* Stichbahn *f*; **~-salt** Seesalz *n*; ~ **window** Erkerfenster *n*; *Am sl* Dickbauch, Fettwanst *m*; **3.** *tr itr* (an)bellen (*at s.o.* jdn); *(Wild)* stellen; *s* Bellen, Gebell *n*; *at ~ (Wild)* gestellt *a. fig*; *fig* ohne Ausweg; *to hold, to keep at ~* in Schach halten; **4.** *a u. s* rotbraun(es Pferd *n*); **~berry** ['-beri] *bot* Pimentbaum *m*; **~onet** ['beiənit] *s* Bajonett, Seitengewehr *n*; *a. pl* bewaffnete Macht, Waffengewalt *f*; *pl* (*mit Zahl*) Mann Infanterie; *tr* mit dem Seitengewehr erstechen; *mil* zwingen (*into* zu) *a. allg*; *to fix ~~s* das Seitengewehr aufpflanzen; *~~ charge* Bajonettangriff *m*; **~ou** ['baiu:] *Am geog* Altwasser *n*.

baz|a(a)r [bə'zɑ:] Basar *m (oriental. Markt)*; Kaufhaus *n*; (Wohltätigkeits-)Basar *m*; **~ooka** [bə'zu:kə] *mil* Panzerbüchse *f*, *sl* Ofenrohr *n*.

be [bi(:)] **1.** *aux u. itr* sein, existieren, leben, vorhanden sein; sich befinden; *(Zustand)* herrschen; bleiben; *(bes. beruflich)* werden; stattfinden, geschehen, sich ereignen; gehören; betragen, ausmachen; kosten; bedeuten; gelten (*to s.o.* jdm); müssen, sollen (*to do* tun); *(verneint)* nicht dürfen; *(Passiv)* werden; **2.** *to ~ about* in der Nähe sein; *to do s.th.* im Begriff sein, etw zu tun; *to ~ after s.th.* hinter etw her sein; *to ~ along* da, hier sein; *to ~ at s.th.* bei, an etw sein; *s.o.* an jdm herumnörgeln; *to ~ before o.'s time* zu früh dran sein; *to ~ behind* im Rückstand, zu spät dran sein; *to ~ by s.o.* jdm zur Seite stehen; *to ~ in contact with s.o.* mit jdm in Verbindung stehen; *to ~ doing* gerade tun; *to ~ down* schlecht dran sein; *(in e-m Examen)* durchgefallen sein; *to ~ down on s.o.* jdn nicht leiden können; *to ~ for* eintreten für; *mar* bestimmt sein nach; *(Strafe)* dran sein; *to ~ in* zu Hause sein; *parl* e-n Sitz im Parlament haben; *fig* am Ruder sein; *to ~ in for* sich beteiligen an; zu erwarten haben; *to ~ long* lange machen, viel Zeit brauchen; *to ~ of* gehören zu; *to ~ off* weggehen, *fam* abhauen; *to ~ on* lasten auf; *to ~ on to s.o.* es mit jdm haben, e-n Pick auf jdn haben; *to ~ out* nicht zu Hause sein; *parl* s-n Sitz im Parlament verlieren; Unrecht haben, auf dem Holzweg sein; *to ~ out of s.th.* etw nicht mehr haben; außerhalb sein; *to ~ out of step* falschen Tritt haben; *to ~ out for s.th.* auf der Suche nach etw sein; hinter etw her sein; *to ~ right* Recht haben; *to ~ in ruins* in Trümmern liegen; *to ~ up* auf(gestanden) sein; sein Glück gemacht haben; *to ~ up to s.o.* jds Aufgabe sein; *s.th.* etw im Schilde führen; gekommen sein bis zu; **3.** *it is I, (fam) me* das bin ich; *is that you?* bist Du, sind Sie das? *it was not to* es hat nicht sein sollen; *you are out of it* du hast verloren; *as it is* wie die Dinge liegen; *here you are!* nun ist's in Ordnung! siehst du! *how is he?* wie geht es ihm? *how is this?* wie kommt es? *how is it that?* wie kommt es, daß ...? *how much will that ~?* wieviel macht das? *let it ~* laß sein! *that is his* das gehört ihm; *that is to say* das heißt; *there is, are* es gibt; *there you are* da haben Sie's! da sind Sie ja! *when is that to ~?* wann soll das sein? *~ that as it may!* wie dem auch sei! *I have been to London* ich bin in L. gewesen; *~ off with you!* fort mit euch! raus! *the ~-all* das Ganze; *a has-been* e-e gesunkene Größe *(Mensch)*; *might-have-beens* versäumte Gelegenheiten *f pl*; *the to-~* die Zukunft; *his wife (that is) to ~* s-e Zukünftige; *a would-~* ein Möchtegern *m*; *the would-~* das Wenn.

beach [bi:tʃ] *s* (flacher) Strand *m*, *poet* Gestade *n*; Küstenstreifen, -strich *m*; flache(s) (Meeres-)Ufer *n*; *mil mar* Ausbootungsstelle *f*; *tr (Schiff)* auf den Strand setzen *od* ziehen; *on the ~* am Strand; *fig Am* arbeitslos; **~-comber** Strandwelle *f*; Strandguträuber *m*; **~head** *mil* Landekopf *m*; **~-la-mar** *Art* Pidgin-Englisch *n* in der Südsee; **~-shoe, -suit, umbrella, -wear** Strandschuh, -anzug, -schirm *m*, -kleidung *f*; ~ **wagon** *Am* Kombiwagen *m*.

beacon ['bi:kn] *s* Leuchtfeuer *a. aero*, Lichtsignal *n*; Signalanlage *f*; Leuchtturm *m*; *aero mar* Bake *f*; Verkehrs-, Warnsignal *n*; *fig* Leitstern *m*, Leuchte *f*; *tr* mit Leuchtfeuern versehen; lenken, leiten; *fig* als Vorbild dienen (*s.o.* jdm); *itr* (hell) leuchten; ~ **tower** Signalturm *m*.

bead [bi:d] *s* (*bes.* durchbohrtes) Kügelchen *n*, (Glas-, Isolier-)Perle *f*; Schaumbläschen *n*; (Tau-, Schweiß-) Perle *f*, Tropfen *m*; *(Gewehr)* (Perl-) Korn; Ziel *n*; Wulst *m*; Schweißraupe *f*; isolierte(r) Rand *m*; *arch* Schurleiste; *pl* Perlenschnur *f*; *pl* Rosenkranz *m*; *tr* mit Perlen versehen *od* verzieren; *(Kügelchen auf e-e Schnur, e-n Draht)* aufreihen; *tech* bördeln, einrollen; *(Blech)* sicken; *itr* Perlen, Tropfen bilden; *to draw a ~ upon s.th.* sorgfältig auf etw zielen; *to tell, to say, to count o.'s ~s* s-n Rosenkranz beten, s-e Gebete hersagen; *~ of sweat* Schweißperle *f*; *~ of tyre (mot)* Laufdeckenwulst *m*; **~ing** ['-iŋ] Perlstikkerei *f*, *arch* -stab *m*; *tech* Durchführungs-, Einschmelzperle *f*; Wulst *m*; **~le** ['bi:dl] Kirchendiener, Küster; Pedell *m*; **~ledom** kleinliche(r) Bürokratismus *m*, behördliche Schulmeisterei *f*; **~-roll** (Namens-)Liste *f*; **~sman, ~woman** Almosenempfänger(in *f*) *m*; ~ **work** Perlstickerei *f*, *arch* -stab *m*; **~y** ['-i] perlenförmig; mit Perlen übersät; *~~ eyes (pl)* Kulleraugen *n pl*.

beagl|e ['bi:gl] *fig* Spürnase *f*, Spion; *(Jagd)* Spürhund *m*.

beak [bi:k] Schnabel *m (bes. d. Raubvögel) a. fig*; *allg* Spitze *f*; *(Gefäß)* Ausguß *m*, Tülle, Schneppe, Schnauze *f*; (Schiffs-)Schnabel *m*; *bot* Lippe; *arch* (Haken-)Nase *f*; *(Amboß)* Hörnchen *n*; *fam* Friedensrichter; *sl* Federfuchser; Pauker *m*; **~ed** [-t] *a* mit (e-m) Schnabel; schnabelartig, spitz; **~er** ['-ə] *obs lit* Humpen, große(r) Trinkbecher *m*; *chem* Becherglas *n*.

beam [bi:m] *s* Balken *m*; *tech* Schwelle *f*; Holm *m*; (Wagen-)Deichsel *f*; *(~ of balance)* Waagebalken; Pflugsterz; Kett-, Weberbaum; *(Schiff)* Deck-, Querbalken *m*; *mar aero* (größte) Breite; *(Geweih)* Stange *f*; *arch* Träger, Tragebalken; *(~ of light)* (Licht-) Strahl *m*, *(~ of rays)* (Strahlen-)Bündel *n*; Wärme *f*; Glanz; strahlende(r) Blick *m*, leuchtende Augen *n pl*; *radio* Leit-, Richtstrahl; *(~ angle)* Keulenwinkel *m*; *tr (Licht, Wärme)* (aus-) strahlen; *(Kette)* (auf)bäumen; *(Strah-*

len) bündeln, richten; *itr* (übers ganze Gesicht) strahlen, ein frohes Gesicht machen; *tech* Strahlen aussenden; mit Radar feststellen; *off the ~ (aero)* vom Leitstrahl abgekommen; *sl* falsch, unrichtig; nicht funktionierend; *(Mensch)* nicht beieinander; *on the ~ (aero)* dem Leitstrahl entlang; *sl fig* einwandfrei (funktionierend), genau richtig; erfolgreich; *to be on her, o.'s ~('s)-ends (Schiff)* auf der Seite liegen, *fig* aus dem letzten Loch pfeifen; *to fly, to ride the ~* auf dem Leitstrahl fliegen; *to kick the ~ (fig)* sich als der Schwächere erweisen, unterliegen; *radio ~* Funkstrahl *m*; *(radio bearing) ~* Peilstrahl *m*; *starboard, port ~ (Schiff)* rechte, linke Seite *f*; **~ing** ['-iŋ] *s (Strahlen)* Bündelung *f*; *a (Mensch)* freudestrahlend (*with* vor); **~y** ['-i] strahlend; *(Schiff)* breit; *(Hirsch)* mit Geweihsprossen; *poet (von länglichen Gegenständen)* gewaltig, massiv.

bean [bi:n] *s* Bohne *f a. allg*; *pl* Kohlengrus *m*; *Am sl* Rübe *f*, Kopf *m*; *tr sl* auf den Kopf schlagen; *to give s.o. ~s (sl)* jdn *(mit Worten* od *Schlägen)* fertigmachen *a. sport*; *not to know ~s about s.th. (Am)* von etw keinen blassen Dunst haben; *to spill the ~s (Am sl)* das Geheimnis ausplaudern, nicht dicht halten; *I haven't a ~ (sl)* ich bin ohne e-n Pfennig Geld, (völlig) abgebrannt; *coffee-~* Kaffeebohne *f*; *full of ~s*, *~-fed* in guter Laune, guter Dinge; gute(r) Kasse; wohlgenährt; *old ~ (sl)* altes Haus *n*, alter Junge *m*; **~-feast** Festessen; *allg* Gelage *n*; **~o** ['-ou] Freudenfest *n*; **~-pole, -stick** Bohnen-, *fig* Hopfenstange *f*; **~ stalk** Bohnenstengel *m*; **~-straw** Bohnenstroh *n*; **~y** ['-i] *sl* gutgelaunt, munter; *Am* bekloppt.

bear [bɛə] **1.** *s* Bär; *fig* (grober) Klotz *(Mensch)*, *fam* sture(r) Bock; *com* Baissespekulant; *com* Schwarzseher; *tech* Rammbär *m*, Ramme *f*; *tech* Härtling *m*; *itr* auf Baisse spekulieren; *tr* e-n Preissturz bewirken (*s.th.* bei e-r S); *(Preise)* drücken; *Great, Little B~ (astr)* Große(r), Kleine(r) Bär, Wagen *m*; **~baiting** Bärenhatz *f*; **~ garden** Bärenzwinger *m*; *fig* Tohuwabohu *n*, Wirrwarr *m*; **~ish** ['-riʃ] rauh, grob; ıoh *(Mensch)*; *(Börse)* auf Baisse gerichtet; **~leader** Bärenführer *m a. fig*; **~'s-breech** *bot* Bärenklau *f* od *m*; **~'s-ear** *bot* Aurikel *f*; **~'s foot** *bot* stinkende Nieswurz *f*; **~skin** Bärenfell (-mütze *f*) *n*; *Art* grobe(r) Mantelstoff *m*; **~wood** *bot* Wegdorn *m*.

bear [bɛə] **2.** *irr bore, borne* **1.** *tr* tragen *(Namen, Waffe)* führen, tragen; *(Zeichen)* tragen; *(Amt)* ausüben, innehaben; *(Titel)* führen; *(Gefühl)* hegen (*against* gegen); *(Gerücht)* verbreiten; *(Frucht)* tragen, (hervor)bringen; *(Zinsen, Geld)* (ein-) bringen, eintragen; gebären; *fig* Frucht tragen; (v)ertragen, aushalten, erdulden, leiden; *fam* mit ansehen; *(meist fragend* od *verneint)* ertragen, dulden, zulassen, gewähren, gestatten; in e-m Verhältnis stehen (*to* zu); *(Menschen)* ausstehen, leiden (können); **2.** *itr* sich wenden, sich halten (*to the right* nach rechts, rechts); e-e Richtung einschlagen (*to* nach); sich stützen, drücken; *fig* lasten (*on* auf); e-n Einfluß haben (*on* auf); sich beziehen (*on* auf); **3.** *to bring pressure to ~* Druck ausüben (*on* auf); *to ~ o.s.* sich verhalten, auftreten, sich benehmen; *to ~ against* angreifen; *to ~ arms* Waffen tragen, bewaffnet sein; *to ~ away (mar)* abfahren; *to be borne away* mitgerissen werden *a. (fig)*; *to ~ (away) the palm* (den Preis) gewinnen; *to ~ back* zurücktragen, -bringen, -treten; *to ~ the blame* die Schuld auf sich nehmen; *to ~ on s.o.'s books (com)* jdm zu Lasten schreiben; *to ~ s.o. company* jdm Gesellschaft leisten; *to ~ comparison* e-n Vergleich aushalten (*with* mit); *to ~ the date January 1st* das Datum des 1. Januar tragen; *to ~ down* nieder-, über den Haufen werfen, überwinden; *to ~ down on* losgehen, sich stürzen auf; sich (mit Gewalt) drängen gegen; in Richtung kommen auf; *to ~ fruit (fig)* erfolgreich sein; *to ~ a grudge against s.o.* jdm grollen, *fam* böse sein; *to ~ a hand* helfen (*s.o.* jdm); *to ~ interest* Zinsen tragen, abwerfen; *to ~ a meaning* bedeuten; *to ~ (s.o.) in mind* sich (an jdn) erinnern (*that* daß); berücksichtigen (*s.th.* etw); *to ~ off, away* davontragen, gewinnen; sich entfernen (*towards the left* nach links); *to ~ (s.o.) out* (jdn) hinaustragen; (jds) Aussagen bestätigen; *to ~ a part in s.th.* an e-r S Anteil haben; *to ~ resemblance to* gleichen; ähneln, ähnlich sehen *dat*; *to ~ up (itr)* sich tapfer zeigen, sich wacker, den Kopf hoch halten; standhaft bleiben; *tr* (unter-) stützen; *to ~ up for, towards (mar)* nach ..., auf ... zu fahren; *to ~ upon* Bezug haben auf; in Beziehung stehen zu; Bedeutung haben für; *to ~ with* Geduld, Nachsicht haben mit, üben gegenüber; *to ~ witness* Zeugnis ablegen; **~able** ['-rəbl] erträglich, zu ertragen(d); **~er** ['bɛərə] Träger; *com* Überbringer, Vorzeiger, Inhaber; fruchttragende(r) Baum *m*, blütentragende Pflanze *f*; *(pall ~~)* Leichenträger *m*; *cheque to ~~ (com)* Inhaber-, Überbringerscheck *m*; *~~ clause* Inhaberklausel *f*; *~~ securities (pl)* Inhaberpapiere *n pl*; *~~share* Inhaberaktie *f*; **~ing** ['-riŋ] *s* Tragen *n (a. von Früchten)*; *agr* Ertrag *m*; Fähigkeit *f* des Tragens, des Hervorbringens; Entbindung, Geburt *f*; Ertragen, Dulden, Aushalten; Verhalten, Auftreten, Benehmen *n*; Beziehung *f*, Bezug (*on* auf); Zs.hang (*on* mit); Sinn *m*, Bedeutung; Tragweite; Wirkung *f*, Einfluß *m* (*on* auf); (ausgepeilte) Richtung, *pl* Lage *f*; Kompaßkurs; Azimut *m*; *pl mar aero* Peilung, Ortung *f*; *tech* Lager(ung *f*), Auflager *n*; *arch* Spann-, Tragweite *f*; *(Schicht)* Streichen; Wappenbild *n*; *a* bezüglich; tragend; *min* enthaltend; *beyond, past all ~~* nicht auszuhalten(d), unerträglich; *to consider s.th. from all its ~~s (fig)* etw von allen Seiten betrachten; *to have a ~~ upon* von Bedeutung sein für, Einfluß haben auf; *to have lost, to be out of o.'s ~~s* sich verlaufen haben, *fig* nicht mehr aus noch ein, nicht mehr weiter wissen; *to take ~~s (mar aero)* peilen, orten; *to take o.'s ~~s* sich orientieren; *~~ metal* Lagermetall *n*.

beard [biəd] *s* Bart *m a. zoo*; *bot* Grannen *f pl*; *(Pfeil)* Widerhaken *m pl*; *typ* Fleisch *n*; *tr* am Bart packen *od* zupfen; mit e-m Bart versehen; *fig* offen entgegentreten (*s.o.* jdm), herausfordern; *to ~ the lion in his den (fig)* sich in die Höhle des Löwen wagen; **~ed** ['-id] *a* bärtig; mit Grannen versehen; mit Widerhaken; **~less** ['-lis] bartlos; *fig* unreif, jugendlich.

beast [bi:st] *(vierfüßiges)* (*bes.* wildes) Tier *n*; *agr* Stück *n* Rindvieh, *pl* Rindvieh; *fig* Biest *n*, viehische(r) Mensch *m*; *the ~* das Tier im Menschen; *the B~* der Antichrist; *~ of burden, of prey* Last-, Raubtier *n*; **~liness** ['-linis] Bestialität, Roheit; Gier(igkeit), Gefräßigkeit; Trunkenheit *f*, *sl* Suff *m*; Gemeinheit; Schweinigelei, Unanständigkeit *f*; **~ly** ['-li] *a* viehisch; dreckig; bestialisch, brutal; schweinisch, säuisch; *fam* gräßlich, abscheulich, scheußlich; widerlich, unangenehm; *adv fam* mächtig, fürchterlich, äußerst.

beat [bi:t] *irr beat, beat(en)* **1.** *tr (bes. wiederholt)* schlagen; *(Pfad)* trampeln; *(Weg)* bahnen; *(Teppich)* klopfen; *(Kleider)* ausklopfen; *(Regen)* peitschen (*the trees* gegen die Bäume); schlagen (*the windows* an die Fenster); *(Eier, Feind)* schlagen; *(Trommel)* rühren; *(Flachs)* schwingen; *(Wild)* aufstöbern; *(den Takt)* schlagen; hauen; verhauen, prügeln, *fam* verdreschen; *(Gegend)* absuchen; *mil sport (Wettstreit)* schlagen, besiegen; *(Rivalen)* ausstechen; ermatten, *fam* fertig machen; stampfen; treiben; *(~ out)* schmieden; *sl* hereinlegen, beschwindeln; *sl* täuschen; **2.** *itr* schlagen (*on* an, gegen); klopfen *(a. Herz)*, pochen (*at* an); stürmen, tosen; siegen, gewinnen; *(Regen)* prasseln, klatschen (*on* an, auf); *(Trommeln)* dröhnen; *mar* lavieren, kreuzen; **3.** *s* Schlag(en *n*) *m*; Klopfen, Pochen *n*; (Trommel-, Herz-, Puls-)Schlag *m*; Taktschlagen *n*; Takt(strich) *m*; *mus* Schwebung *f*; Rundgang *m*, Runde *f*; (Jagd-)Revier *n*; *phys* Interferenz *f*; (Zeiger-)Ausschlag; *Am* Wahlbezirk *m*; *Am fam der, die, das* Beste, Phänomen *n (Person* od *Sache)* (*of* gen); *Am (Zeitung)* Knüller *m*; *sl* Schwindler *m*; **4.** *a sl* ausgepumpt, erschossen, fertig; *Am* verblüfft; *Am sl* illusionslos; **5.** *on the ~* im Takt; *to be on o.'s ~* s-e Runde machen, auf s-m Rundgang sein; *to be ~-up* abgenutzt, ausgeleiert sein; *to ~ about, (Am) around the bush* wie die Katze um den heißen Brei gehen; *to ~ about (mar)* gegen den Wind (an)kämpfen *od* segeln; *allg* suchen (*for* nach); *to ~ the air (fig)* leeres Stroh dreschen; sich vergeblich abmühen; *to ~ all (fam)* alles schlagen, in den Schatten stellen; *to ~ away, off* wegtreiben, verjagen; *to ~ back* zurückschlagen; *to ~ black and blue* braun u. blau schlagen; *to ~ the bounds* die Grenze abstecken; *to ~ o.'s brains (fig)* sich den Kopf zerbrechen; *to ~ o.'s breast* sich an die Brust schlagen; *to ~ down* ein-, niederschlagen, umhauen; *(bes. Preis)* drücken; *s.o. (in price)* bei jdm e-n niedrigeren Preis durchsetzen; *to ~ in (Tür, Wand)* einschlagen, -stoßen; *to ~ s.th. into s.o.* jdm etw einbleuen; *to ~ it (sl)* abhauen, türmen (gehen); *to ~ s.o. to it (fam)* jdn abhängen, jdm zuvorkommen; *to ~ off* abschlagen, -hauen; abwehren; *to ~ on* sich stürzen auf; *to ~ the rap (sl)* der Strafe entgehen; *to ~ a retreat* zum Rückzug blasen; *fig* das Weite suchen; *to ~ time* den Takt schlagen; *to ~ to s.th.* aufrufen, -fordern; *to ~ up (Küche)* kräftig verrühren, schlagen; *(Menschen)* verdreschen; zs.trommeln, -bringen; *mil sl* mit Bordwaffen beschießen; **6.** *~ it!* hau ab! *that ~s it! (Am sl)* da hört doch alles auf! das ist ein starkes Stück! *dead ~ (fam) (Mensch)* völlig erledigt, ganz kaputt; *heart-~* Herzschlag *m*; **~en** ['-n] *a* geschlagen; *(Weg)* ausgetreten; *fig* abgedroschen; erschöpft, erledigt; besiegt; *fam* verwirrt; *mil* bestrichen, unter Feuer; *off the ~~-track (fig)* aus dem Rahmen fallend, außergewöhnlich; *~~ path* Trampelpfad *m*; *~~ silver* Blattsilber *n*; *~~ zone (mil)*

bestrichene(s) Gelände *n*; **~er** ['-ə] Schläger, Klopfer *(Gegenstand)*; Holländer *m*, Schlageisen *n*, -wolf *m*; Ramme *f*; *(Jagd)* Treiber *m*; **~ing** ['-iŋ] Schlagen, Klopfen; Verdreschen *n*, Prügel *m pl*; Niederlage *f*; *to give a good ~~* e-e tüchtige Tracht Prügel geben; *~* **music** Beatjazz *m*; *~* **reception** Überlagerungsempfang *m*.
beati|fic [biə'tifik] glücklich, (glück-)selig, (freude)strahlend; **~fication** [biætifi'keiʃən] *rel* Seligsprechung, *allg* -preisung; Glückseligkeit *f*; **~fy** [bi'ætifai] *tr* (glück)selig machen; *rel* seligsprechen; **~tude** [bi'ætitju:d] (Glück-)Seligkeit *f*; *the B~~s (rel)* die (7) Seligpreisungen *f pl*.
beatnik ['bi:tnik] *Am* zornige(r) junge(r) Mann *m*.
beau [bou] *pl -x, a. -s* [-z] Geck, Stutzer; Liebhaber *(e-r Frau)*; Schürzenjäger *m*; *~* **geste** [-'ʒest] große Geste *f*; *~* **ideal** (Schönheits-)Ideal, Idealbild *n*, ideale(r) Typ *m*; *~* **monde** [-'mɔnd] vornehme Welt, Hautevolee *f*; **~t** [bju:t] *Am fam (oft iro)* Schönheit *f (Person* od *Sache)*; **~teous** ['bju:tiəs] *poet* schön; **~tician** [bju'tiʃən] Kosmetiker(in *f*) *m*; **~tification** [bjutifi'keiʃən] Verschönerung *f*; **~tifier** ['bju:tifaiə] Verschönerer *m*; **~tiful** ['bju:tiful] schön; herrlich, wundervoll; ausgezeichnet, vortrefflich; *the ~~* das Schöne; die Schönen, Schönheiten; **~tify** ['bju:tifai] *tr* verschönern; *itr* schön werden; **~ty** ['bju:ti] Schönheit *f (a. Person* od *Sache, oft iro)*; *das* Schöne; Schön, Prachtexemplar *n*; *pl* schöne Eigenschaften *f pl od* Züge; *pl* Reize *m pl*; *a ~~* etw Schönes; *the Sleeping B~~* Dornröschen *n*; *~~ contest* Schönheitswettbewerb *m*; *~~ culture* Schönheitspflege *f*; *~~ doctor* Kosmetiker(in *f*) *m*; *~~ parlo(u)r, salon, shop* Schönheitssalon *m*; *~~-queen* Schönheitskönigin *f*; *~~(-)sleep* Schlaf *m* vor Mitternacht; *~~(-)spot* Schönheitspflästerchen *n*; schöne Stelle, Gegend *f*.
beaver ['bi:və] *zoo* Biber *m*; Biberfell *n*, -pelz; Hut *m* aus Biberfell; *Am fam* Kerl; *sl* Bart *m*; *fam* Arbeitstier *n*, -biene, Ameise *f*; *(Ritterrüstung)* Kinnreff, Visier *n*; *(Textil)* Biber *m*; **~board** *(Warenzeichen)* Hartfaserplatte *f*; **~-lodge** Biberbau *m*.
bebop ['bi:bɔp] Bebop *m (Art Jazzmusik)*.
becalm [bi'kɑ:m] *tr (die See)* beruhigen; *(Wogen)* glätten; den Wind nehmen (*a ship* e-m Schiff).
because [bi'kɔz] *conj* weil, da; *adv* deswegen, darum, aus dem Grunde; *~ of (prp)* wegen, infolge *gen*; *~ of her, him* ihret-, seinetwegen.
beck [bek] *s* **1.** *Br* (Wild-)Bach *m*; **2.** Zeichen *n*, Wink; *to be at s.o.'s ~ and call* nach jds Pfeife tanzen (müssen); *v poet* = **~on** ['bekən] *tr* (zu)winken, ein Zeichen geben (*s.o.* jdm); verlocken; *itr* nicken; winken; *to ~~ to s.o.* jdm zuwinken.
becloud [bi'klaud] *tr* be-, umwölken; *fig* verschleiern.
becom|e [bi'kʌm] *irr became, become itr* werden; *tr* (gut) stehen (*s.o.* jdm), kleiden, passen (*s.o.* jdm); sich passen, schicken für; **~ing** [-iŋ] *a* kleidsam; passend; schicklich, geziemend; *s das* Werden; *to be ~~ to s.o.* jdm sehr gut stehen, jdn sehr gut kleiden.
bed [bed] *s* Bett; Bettgestell *n*; Liege-, Lagerstatt *f*, Lager; (Blumen-, Gemüse-)Beet; *(river ~)* Flußbett *n*; Sohle *f*; Seebecken *n*; Meeresboden *m*; *geol* Schicht *f*, Flöz; *min* Lager *n*; *tech* Bettung *f*, Unterbau *m*, -lage; *rail (~ of ballast)* Bettungssohle *f*; Bohrtisch *m*; (Austern-)Bank; *fig* eheliche Gemeinschaft *f*; *tr (to ~ down)* ein Lager herrichten für; *tech* betten, lagern, e-e feste Unterlage geben (*s.th.* e-r S); *(Bürsten)* einschleifen; in ein Beet pflanzen; in die Erde legen; ins Bett legen, zu Bett bringen; *itr* zu Bett gehen; *geol* e-e Schicht bilden; *to be brought to ~ of (Frau)* entbunden werden von; *to get out of ~* aufstehen; *to get out of ~ on the wrong side* mit dem verkehrten Fuß aufstehen; *to go to ~* zu Bett, schlafen gehen; *to keep o.'s ~* das Bett hüten; *to lie in the ~ one has made (fig)* die Suppe (,die man sich eingebrockt hat,) auslöffeln; *to make the ~* das Bett machen; *to put to ~* zu Bett bringen; *to take to o.'s ~* sich ins Bett legen (müssen) *(wegen Krankheit)*; *to ~ down level (tech)* in die Waage richten; *to ~ in* einbetten; *to ~ out* verpflanzen; *as a man makes his ~ he must lie (prov)* wie man sich bettet, so liegt man; *double ~* zweischläfige(s), Doppelbett *n*; *flower ~* Blumenbeet *n*; *sick-~* Krankenbett *n*; *single ~* einschläfige(s) Bett *n*; *~ of clay* Tonschicht *f*; *~ of concrete* Betonunterbau *m*; *~ of onions* Zwiebelbeet *n*; *~ of straw* Strohlager *n*, -schütte *f*; *~* **and board** freie Station, Unterkunft u. Verpflegung *f*; *fig* das Zuhause, der heimische Herd; *~* **bug** Bettwanze *f*; **~clothes** *pl* Bettwäsche *f*, -zeug *n*; **~cover** Bettdecke *f*; **~ding** ['-iŋ] Bettzeug *n*, -wäsche; Streu; *tech* Bettung, Auflage, Lagerung *f*; *(Rohre)* Verlegen *n*; *geol* Schicht(ung) *f*; **~fast** *Am* bettlägerig; **~fellow** Schlafkamerad; Mitarbeiter, Gefährte *m*; **~(-)linen** Bettwäsche *f*; **~pan** Schieber *m (für Kranke)*; **~plate** Boden-, Sohlenplatte; Bettung *f*, Fundament *n*; **~post** Bettpfosten *m*; *between you and me and the ~~ (fig)* unter uns; **~rail** Seitenbrett *n* des Bettgestells; **~(-)rest** Bettruhe *f*; *med* Stellkissen *n*; **~rid(-den)** *a* bettlägerig, ans Bett gefesselt *fig*; **~rock** *geol* gewachsene(r) anstehende(r) Fels, Felsuntergrund *m*; *allg* feste Unterlage; *fig Am* Grundlage *f*; **~roll** Schlafsack *m*; **~room** Schlafzimmer *n*; **~side** *s* Bettrand *m*, -kante *f*; *to have a good ~~ manner (Arzt)* gut mit Kranken umzugehen verstehen; *to sit at o.'s ~~* an jds Bett sitzen; *~~ lamp* Nacht(tisch)lampe *f*; *~~ table* Nachttisch *m*; **~-sitting-room, ~-sitter** Wohn-Schlaf-Zimmer *n*; **~sore**: *to be ~~* sich durchgelegen haben; **~spread** *(Bett)* Tagesdecke *f*; **~spring** Sprungfedern *f pl (für e-e Matratze)*; **~stead** Bettstelle *f*; **~straw** *bot* Labkraut *n*; **~tick** Inlett *n*; **~time** Schlafenszeit *f*; **~wetter** Bettnässer *m*.
be|dabble [bi'dæbl] *tr* bespritzen; **~daub** [bi'dɔ:b] *tr* beschmieren; mit Zierat überladen; **~dazzle** [bi'dæzl] *tr* blenden; verwirren.
be|deck [bi'dek] *tr* (übermäßig) schmücken, zieren; **~del(l)** [be'del, *Am* 'bi:dl] *(Universität)* Pedell *m*; **~devil** [-'devl] *tr* be-, verhexen, verzaubern; verderben; mißhandeln, -brauchen; **~dew** [-'dju:] *tr* betauen, (be)netzen.
be|dim [bi'dim] *tr fig* trübe machen, trüben; **~dizen** [-'dizn, -'daizn] *tr* herausputzen, ausstaffieren.
bedlam ['bedləm] *obs* Irrenhaus; *fig* Tollhaus *n*; **~ite** ['-ait] Irre(r), Verrückte(r) *m*.
Bedouin ['beduin] *s* Beduine *m*; *a* beduinisch.
bedraggle [bi'drægl] *tr (Kleider)* durch den Schmutz ziehen, beschmutzen.
bee [bi:] Biene *f*; *bes. Am* Arbeitskreis; Zirkel *m*, Kränzchen *n*; *busy as a ~* fleißig wie e-e Biene; *to have a ~ in o.'s bonnet* e-n Sparren zuviel haben; verrückte Ansichten haben (*about* über); *queen ~* Bienenkönigin *f*; *spelling ~* Wettbewerb *m* im Rechtschreiben; *swarm of ~s* Bienenschwarm *m*; *worker ~* Arbeitsbiene *f*; **~-bread** Bienenbrot *n*, Blütenstaub, Pollen *m*; **~-eater** *orn* Bienenfresser *m*; **~hive** ['bi:haiv] Bienenstock *m*; *mil* Hohlladung *f*; **~line** Luftlinie *f*; *to make a ~~ for* gerade(swegs) zugehen auf; **~-master, -mistress, ~keeper** Imker(in *f*), Bienenzüchter *m*; **~swax** ['bi:zwæks] *s* Bienenwachs *n*; *tr* wachsen, bohnern.
beech [bi:tʃ] Buche(nholz *n*) *f*; *copper-~* Blutbuche *f*; **~en** ['-ən] buchen; Buchen-; *~* **marten** Steinmarder *m*; **~mast** ['-mɑ:st] Bucheckern *f*; *~* **nut** Buchecker *f*; **~-oil** Buchöl *n*.
beef [bi:f] *s pl beeves* Rindfleisch *n*; Ochse *m*, Rind *n (zum Schlachten)*; *fam (Mensch)* (Muskel-)Kraft *f*; *fam* (Körper-)Gewicht *n*, Schwere *f*; *Am sl* Gemecker *n (pl ~s)*; *itr Am sl* herummeckern, -schimpfen (*about* über); *corned-~* Büchsen-Rindfleisch *n*; *roast-~* Rinderbraten *m*; **~cattle** Schlachtvieh *n*; *~* **cube** Bouillonwürfel *m*; **~eater** Königliche(r) Leibgardist; Tower-Wärter *m*; **~ing** ['-iŋ] *Am sl* Herummeckern, -schimpfen *n*; **~steak** *(Küche)* Beefsteak *n*; **~-tea** Fleisch-, Kraftbrühe *f*; **~y** ['-i] fleischig; kräftig, stark, sehnig; schwerfällig, stur.
beer [biə] Bier *n*; verdünnte(r) Pflanzensaft *m*; nichtalkoholische(s) Getränk *n*; *to think no small ~ of* viel halten von; *small ~* Dünnbier *n*; *fig* Null *f*; Nichts *n*; *ginger, root ~* Ingwersprudel; Pflanzensaft *m*; **~-barrel, -engine, -garden, -house, -pull** Bierfaß *n*, -leitung *f*, -garten *m*, -lokal *n*, -hahn *m*; **~-jug, -mug** Bierkrug *m*, Bierseidel *n*; **~y** ['-ri] bierartig; nach Bier riechend; in Bierlaune.
beet [bi:t] *pl -roots, Am a. -s*: *red ~* Rote Rübe, Be(e)te *f*; *silver ~* Mangold *m*; *sugar ~* Zuckerrübe *f*; **~root** Runkelrübe *f*; **~-sugar** Rübenzucker *m*; **~le** ['bi:tl] **1.** *s* Ramme *f*, Rammbär; Schlägel; *(Textil)* Stoßkalander *m*; *tr* (fest)stampfen; (zer)stoßen; *(Textil)* schlagen; *~~-brain, ~~head* Dummkopf *m*; **2.** *s* Käfer *m*; *black-~~* (Küchen-)Schabe *f*; Kakerlak *m*; *~~-crusher (fam)* große(r) Schuh *od* Fuß, Quadratlatschen *m*; **3.** *a* vorstehend, überhängend; *itr* überhängen, hervorragen, überstehen; *to ~~ off(sl)* abhauen; *~~-browed (a)* mit vorstehenden Augenbrauen; *fig* mürrisch, verdrießlich.
be|fall [bi'fɔ:l] *irr -fell, -fallen tr* zustoßen (*s.o.* jdm); *itr* sich ereignen, geschehen; **~fit** [-'fit] *tr* geeignet, angebracht, passend sein, passen (*the occasion* für die Gelegenheit); **~fitting** angemessen, schicklich; **~fog** [-'fɔg] *tr* in Nebel hüllen, einnebeln, verdunkeln *a. fig*; *fig* verwirren; **~fool** [-'fu:l] *tr* täuschen, anführen, hereinlegen.
before [bi'fɔ:] **1.** *prp (zeitlich, räumlich, fig)* vor; *the day ~ yesterday* vorgestern; *~ my very eyes* vor meinen Augen; *~ long* bald, in Bälde, in absehbarer Zeit; *to sail ~ the mast* als einfacher Matrose dienen; *to sail ~ the wind* mit dem Winde segeln, den Wind im Rücken haben; *business ~ pleasure* erst die Arbeit, dann das Vergnügen; **2.** *adv* vorn; voran; voraus; (schon) früher, vorher, zuvor;

ehemals; *the day* ~ am Tage vorher, am Vortage; *long* ~ lange vorher, viel früher; **3.** *conj* bevor, eher; als; lieber..., als *od* ehe; **~hand** *adv* im voraus, (schon) vorher; *to be* ~~ *with s.th.* etw vorher, rechtzeitig tun; **~-mentioned** *a* oben-, vorerwähnt.

be|foul [bi'faul] *tr* beschmieren, -schmutzen; verpesten; *fig* besudeln, verunglimpfen; *to* ~~ *o.'s own nest (fig)* sein eigenes Nest beschmutzen; **~friend** [-'frend] *tr* als Freund, bevorzugt behandeln; liebevoll, gütig sein (*s.o.* zu jdm); helfen, unterstützen; **~fuddle** [-'fʌdl] *tr* benebelt, betrunken machen; *fig* durchea.bringen, verwirrt machen.

beg [beg] *tr* erbitten, ersuchen; erbetteln, erflehen; (inständig) bitten, flehen um; *itr* bitten (*for* um), *(to go ~ging)* betteln(gehen)(*for* um); *(Hund)* Männchen machen; *to* ~ *to differ* sich nicht einverstanden erklären können (*from s.o.* mit jdm); *to* ~ *a favour of s.o.* jdn um etw bitten; *to* ~ *leave to* um Erlaubnis bitten, zu; *to* ~ *off* sich entschuldigen, absagen; *to* ~ *the question* e-r Entscheidung ausweichen; *I* ~ *your pardon* Verzeihung! wie bitte? *it is going ~ging* niemand will es haben; *we* ~ *to inform you (com)* wir gestatten uns, Ihnen mitzuteilen.

beget [bi'get] *irr begot, begot(ten) tr* (er)zeugen, hervorbringen, (er-) schaffen; **~ter** [-ə] Erzeuger; *fig* Urheber *m*.

beggar ['begə] *s* Bettler(in *f*) (*at the door* an, vor der Tür); *fam* Bursche *m*, Bürschchen *n*, Kerl(chen *n*) *m*; *tr* an den Bettelstab bringen, ruinieren; *fig* unmöglich machen; nutzlos erscheinen lassen; übertreffen, übersteigen; *no ~s allowed* Betteln verboten! *~s cannot be choosers* in der Not frißt der Teufel Fliegen; **~ly** ['-li] bettelhaft, ärmlich, arm(selig), dürftig *a. fig*; *fig* niedrig, schmutzig; **~y** ['-ri] Bettel-, äußerste Armut *f*; *to reduce to* ~~ an den Bettelstab bringen.

begin [bi'gin] *irr began, begun* (*mit to od* -ing); *tr itr* beginnen, anfangen; einleiten; *(Reise)* antreten; *Am* im mindesten etw tun *od* sein; *itr* s-n Anfang nehmen; entstehen; ausgehen (*at* von); *to* ~ *again* (wieder) von vorn anfangen; *to* ~ *(up)on s.th.* etw in Angriff nehmen; *to* ~ *with* erstens; vorab; von vornherein; *he began by saying* zuerst sagte er; **~ner** [-ə] Anfänger *m*; **~ning** [-iŋ] Beginn; Anfang; *(Reise)* Antritt; Ausgangspunkt, Ursprung; Einsatz *m*; *pl* erste Anfänge *m pl*, Anfangsstadium *n*; *at the very* ~~ ganz am Anfang; *from the* ~~ von Anfang an; *from* ~~ *to end* von Anfang bis zu Ende; *in the* ~~ anfangs, im Anfang.

be|gird [bi'gə:d] *tr* umgürten, umgeben, einschließen; **~gone** [-'gɔn] *interj* (geh) weg! fort (mit dir)! **~gonia** [-'gounjə] *bot* Begonie *f*, Schiefblatt *n*; **~grime** [-'graim] *tr* beschmieren, schwarz machen; **~grudge** [-'grʌdʒ] *tr* beneiden (*s.o. s.th.* jdn um etw), nicht gönnen, mißgönnen; ungern geben; **~guile** [-'gail] *tr* täuschen, betrügen (*(out) of* um); verführen, verleiten (*into doing s.th.* etw zu tun); *(Sache)* kurzweilig machen; *(Zeit)* verkürzen, schnell vergehen lassen, hinbringen, vertreiben.

behalf [bi'hɑ:f]: *on, in* ~ *of* im Interesse, zugunsten, im Sinne *gen*; für; im Namen *gen*; als Vertreter *gen*.

behav|e [bi'heiv] *itr (meist mit adv)* sich verhalten, sich aufführen, sich betragen, sich (gut) benehmen; *(Sache)* gehen, laufen, funktionieren, *fam* klappen; *to* ~~ *o.s.* sich gut, ordentlich benehmen; ~ *yourself!* benimm dich! *he doesn't kow how to* ~~ er weiß sich nicht zu benehmen; **~io(u)r** [-'heivjə] Verhalten, Betragen, Benehmen *n* (*to, towards* gegen); Anstand *m*; *(Sache)* Funktionieren, Laufen, Betriebsverhalten *n*; *to be on o.'s good, best* ~~ sich tadellos benehmen; ~~ *pattern* Verhaltensweise *f*; **~iourism** [-rizm] Behaviorismus *m (psychol. Richtung)*.

be|head [bi'hed] *tr* enthaupten; **~hemoth** [-'hi:məθ] große(s) Tier *n Am a. fig*; **~hest** [-'hest] *poet lit* Geheiß, Gebot *n*.

behind [bi'haind] *prp* hinter *(a. zeitlich, Reihenfolge)*; *(Rangfolge)* unter; *adv* hinten; nach hinten, zurück; dahinter *a. fig*, hinterher; rückständig (*with, in* mit); *s fam* Hintern *m*, Hinterteil *n*; *to be on o.'s* ~ (auf dem Hintern) sitzen; *to be* ~ *in, with s.th.* mit e-r S zurück, im Rückstand sein *(a. mit Zahlungen)*; *to be* ~ *the eight ball (Am sl)* in der Patsche sitzen; *to fall od to stay, to leave* ~ zurückbleiben, -lassen; *to leave* ~ *one* zurücklassen; *to put* ~ *one* zur Seite legen, nicht beachten; *he has s.o.* ~ *him* hinter ihm steht jem *(ein Gönner)*; *my watch is ten minutes* ~ meine Uhr geht zehn Minuten nach; *who's* ~ *that scheme?* wer steckt hinter dem Plan? ~ *s.o.'s back* hinter jds Rücken, ohne jds Wissen; ~ *the scenes* im geheimen, heimlich; ~ *time* zu spät; ~ *the times* (*fam* hinter dem Monde) zurück, veraltet, altmodisch; **~hand** *adv* zurück, im Rückstand (*with* mit).

be|hold [bi'hould] *irr -held, -held, obs poet lit tr* sehen, schauen, betrachten; **~holden** *a* (zu Dank) verpflichtet; **~holder** [-'houldə] Betrachter *m*; **~hoof** [-'hu:f] *lit* Vorteil, Nutzen *m*; **~ho(o)ve** [-'houv, -'hu:v] *imp lit: it does not* ~~ *you to* es kommt Ihnen nicht zu, zu; Sie dürfen nicht *inf*.

beige [beiʒ] *s* Beige *f*; *a* beige, sandfarben.

being ['bi:iŋ] *s* (Da-)Sein; Wesen *n*, Natur, Art; Existenz *f*; (Lebe-)Wesen, Geschöpf *n*; *a* gegenwärtig, vorhanden, da; *in* ~ existierend, vorhanden; *this* ~ *so* da dies (nun einmal) so ist; *the time* ~ im gegenwärtigen Zeitpunkt, zur Zeit; *for the time* ~ einstweilen; ~ *that* da (nun einmal); *to come into* ~ entstehen, ins Leben gerufen werden; *human* ~ Menschen-, menschliche(s) Wesen *n*; Mensch *m*; *the Supreme* ~ das Höchste Wesen *(Gott)*.

be|labo(u)r [bi'leibə] *tr* (ver)prügeln, verdreschen, mit Schlägen bearbeiten; *fig* herumreiten (*s.th.* auf etw); **~lated** [-'leitid] *a* verspätet; zu spät kommend *od* gekommen; **~lay** [-'lei] *tr mar* belegen; befestigen; anbinden; *s* Befestigen *n* (e-s Kletterseils); ~~ *there! (fam)* halt! genug! ~~*ing pin (mar)* Belegnagel *m*.

belch [beltʃ] *itr* rülpsen, aufstoßen; *tr* von sich geben, ausstoßen, auswerfen; *lit (Vulkan, Geschütz)* speien; *s* Aufstoßen, Rülpsen *n*; Auswurf; *(Vulkan)* Ausbruch; *(Geschütz)* Donner *m*.

beldam(e) ['beldəm] *obs* alte(s) Weib *n*; Hexe; Xanthippe *f*.

beleaguer [bi'li:gə] *tr* belagern; *fig* heimsuchen; belästigen.

belfry ['belfri] Glockenturm, -stuhl *m*.

Belgi|an ['belʒən] *a* belgisch; *s* Belgier(in *f*) *m*; **~um** ['-əm] Belgien *n*.

belie [bi'lai] *tr* belügen, hintergehen, täuschen; *(Versprechen)* nicht halten; *(Hoffnung)* nicht erfüllen; *Am* Lügen strafen; als falsch erweisen.

belie|f [bi'li:f] Glaube(n) *m* (*in* an) *a. rel*, Vertrauen *n* (*in* zu), Zuversicht; Meinung, Überzeugung *f*; *rel* Glaubenssatz *m*; *pl rel* Lehre *f*; *beyond, past all* ~~ unglaublich; *to the best of o.'s* ~~ nach bestem Wissen u. Gewissen; *worthy of* ~~ glaubwürdig; **~vable** [-'li:vəbl] glaubhaft, glaublich; **~ve** [-'li:v] *itr* glauben (*in* an); vertrauen (*in, on* auf); überzeugt sein (*in* von); der Meinung sein (*that* daß); viel halten (*in* von), schwören (*in* auf); *tr* glauben; denken, meinen; halten für; *to make* ~~ behaupten; *I* ~~ meines Wissens; *I* ~~ *so* ich glaube, ja; *I* ~~ *not* ich glaube, nein; *would you* ~~ *it!* hätten Sie das für möglich gehalten! **~ver** [-'li:və] Gläubige(r *m*) *f*; *he is a great* ~~ er glaubt fest (*in* an); er hält viel (*in* von); er ist strenggläubig.

Belisha [bə'li:ʃə]: ~ *beacon* Pfosten *m* mit gelber Kugel (zur Kennzeichnung e-s Fußgänger-Überwegs).

belittl|e [bi'litl] *tr* verkleinern, herabsetzen, -würdigen, schmälern.

bell [bel] **1.** *s* Glocke, Schelle, Klingel *f*; Glockenschlag, -ton *m*, Klingelzeichen; *mar* Glas; *tech (a. pl)* Läutewerk *n*, Wecker *m*; *allg* Glocke *f (glockenförmiger Gegenstand)*; (Blüten-)Kelch *m*; *tr* glockenförmig gestalten; *to answer the* ~ an die Glastür gehen; die Tür öffnen; *to ring the ~s* die Glocken läuten; *to* ~ *the cat (fig)* der Katze die Schelle umhängen, sein Leben einsetzen; *the* ~ *rings* die Glocke läutet; *diving-*~ Taucherglocke *f*; *hand-*~ Tischglocke *f*; *sound as a* ~ gesund u. munter, kerngesund; **2.** *itr (Hirsch)* röhren; *s* Röhren *n*; **~-bird** Glockenvogel *m*; **~-boy,** *(Am sl)* **~-hop** Hotelboy, Page *m*; ~ **buoy** *mar* Glockenboje *f*; **~-button, push** Klingelknopf *m*; **~-flower** Glockenblume *f*; **~-founder, -founding, -foundry** Glockengießer, -guß *m*, -gießerei *f*; **~-metal** Glockenmetall, -gut *n*, -speise *f*; **~-pull** Glocken-, Klingelzug *m*; **~-ringer** Glöckner *m*; **~-ringing** Glockenspiel *n*; **~-rope** Glockenstrang *m*; **~-shaped** *a* glockenförmig; **~-tent** Rundzelt *n*; **~-tower** Glockenturm *m*; **~-wether** Leithammel *a. fig*; *fig* Rädels-, Anführer *m*.

bell|adonna [belə'dɔnə] *bot* Belladonna, Tollkirsche *f*; **~e** [bel] Schönheit *(Frau)*, (Dorf-)Schöne *f*; **~es-lettres** [-'letr] *pl* schöne Literatur *f*; **~icose** ['-ikous] kriegerisch, kriegslustig; **~icosity** [-i'kɔsiti] Kriegslust *f*, kriegerische(s) Wesen *n*; **~ied** ['-id] *a* bauchig, ausgebaucht; **~igerence, -cy** [bi'lidʒərens(i)] Status *m* e-r kriegführenden Nation; kriegerische(s) Wesen *n*; **~igerent** [bi'lidʒərənt] *a u.s* kriegführend(e Nation *f*); *the* ~~ *Powers(pl)* die kriegführenden Mächte *f pl*; **~ow** ['belou] *itr* brüllen; *(vor Schmerz)* heulen; *(vor Wut)* schreien, brüllen; *(Geschütz)* donnern; *(Donner)* (g)rollen; *tr (to* ~ *forth)* herausbrüllen; *s* Gebrüll; Geheul; Geschrei *n*; *(a. Geschütz-)* Donner *m*; **~ows** ['-ouz] *sing u. pl (pair of ~~s)* Blasebalg; *phot* Balg(en) *m*; Lunge *f*; **~y** ['beli] *s* Bauch(höhle *f*); Magen; Unterleib; *allg* Bauch *m*, Ausbauchung *f*; Mutterleib *m*; Innere(s) *n*; *tech* Unterseite *f*; *fig* Appetit *m*, Gier *f*; *(Violine)* Resonanzboden *m*; *aero sl* Fahrwerk *n*; *tr itr (~~ out) (bes. Segel)* schwellen; *with an empty* ~~ mit hungrigem Magen; *to ~~-land, to land on the ~~ (aero)* bauchlanden; *~~-ache(s)* Leibschmerzen *m pl*, *fam* Bauchweh *n*; *itr sl* mächtig jammern, klagen; *~~-band (Pferd)* Bauchgurt *f*; *~~button (coll)* Nabel *m*;

~~*ful* Überfluß *m*; ~~ *landing (aero), (sl)* ~~ *flop* Bauchlandung *f*; ~~ *tank (aero)* Abwurfbehälter *m*.
belong [bi'lɔŋ] *itr* gehören (*to s.o.* jdm), das Eigentum sein (*to s.o.* jds); *(e-r Gemeinschaft)* angehören (*to* dat); dazugehören; gehören (*to, (Am) in, on* in, auf); *to ~ here* hergehören, am rechten Platz sein; *to ~ under, in* gehören zu *(e-r Klasse, Abteilung)*; zukommen, gebühren (*to s.o.* jdm); *I ~ here* ich bin von hier; *where does that ~? (fam)* wohin gehört das? **~ings** [-iŋz] *pl* Eigentum *n*, Habe *f*, Sachen *f pl*; Zubehör *n od* Teile *n pl (e-r Sache)*; *my ~~* meine Habseligkeiten *f pl*.
beloved [bi'lʌv(i)d] *a* (innig-, heiß)geliebt (*of, by* von); *s* Geliebte(r *m*) *f*, Liebling *m*.
below [bi'lou] *prp (Ort, Rang, Wert)* unter; unterhalb *gen*; niedriger; geringer; *adv* unten; nach unten, abwärts, hinunter, hinab; niedriger im Rang; *(im Buch)* weiter unten *od* hinten; als Fußnote; flußabwärts; im Schiffsinnern; *(down) ~* in der Hölle; *(here) ~ (obs poet)* hienieden; *~ o.'s breath* ganz leise, im Flüsterton; *~ his dignity, ~ him* unter s-r Würde; *~ ground* unter der Erde; *min* unter Tage; *~ the mark, ~ par* von geringer Qualität, nicht viel wert; nichts Besonderes; *(gesundheitlich)* nicht auf der Höhe, nicht auf dem Posten.
belt [belt] *s* Gürtel *a. allg*, Leibriemen *m*; *mil* Koppel *n*; Riemen; Streifen; Gurt(band *n*) *m*; *sport* Gürtellinie; (Landbau-)Zone *f*, (Anbau-)Gebiet *n*; *tech* Treibriemen *m*; *tr* um-, anschnallen; *(Munition)* gurten; mit e-m (farbigen) Streifen umgeben; (mit e-m Riemen) verdreschen, verprügeln; *sl* abhauen: *to ~ up(sl)* die Klappe halten; *to hit below the ~* e-n Tiefschlag versetzen (*s.o.* jdm); *allg* unfair kämpfen; *to tighten o.'s ~* den Gürtel enger schnallen *a. fig*; *cotton, wheat ~* Baumwoll-, Weizengebiet *n*; *green ~* Grüngürtel *m (e-r Stadt)*; *safety ~* Anschnall-, Sicherheitsgurt *m*; *~ of high pressure* Hochdruckzone *f*; *~* **conveyor** Förderband *n*; **~ing** [-iŋ] Riemen(leder *n*) *m pl*; *fig fam* Dresche *f*; *~* **line** *Am* Ringbahn, -straße *f*; *~* **loader** Bandlader *m*.
be|moan [bi'moun] *tr* beklagen, bedauern; **~muse** [-'mju:z] *tr* verwirren, durchea.bringen; *(mit Alkohol)* benebelt machen.
ben [ben] *adv scot* binnen; *s* innere(r) Raum *m (e-r Wohnhütte)*; *but and ~* das ganze Haus.
bench [bentʃ] *s* (Sitz-)Bank *f*; Arbeitstisch *m*, Werkbank; Berme *f*, Bankett *n*; *geogr* Leiste, *Am* Flußterrasse *f*; Richterstuhl *m*, -amt; Gericht(shof *m*) *n (King's, Queen's B~)*; Richter(kollegium *n*); Gerichtsbeamte *m pl*, -personen *f pl*; *parl* Sitz *m*, (Minister-) Bank *f*; Ausstellungstisch m *(bei e-r Hundeausstellung)*; *tr* mit Bänken ausstatten; auf e-e Bank setzen; *(Hunde)* ausstellen; *Am (Spieler)* hinausstellen; *(Blumen)* im Gewächshaus ziehen; *to be on the ~* Richter sein; *Am sport* zur Reserve gehören; *to be raised to the ~* zum Richter ernannt werden; *carpenter's ~* Hobelbank *f*; *testing ~* Prüfstand *m*; **~er** ['-ə] Vorstandsmitglied *n* e-s der vier 'Inns of Court' in England; *~* **mark** Festpunkt *m*; *~* **test** Prüfstandversuch *m*; **~-warrant** richterliche(r) Haftbefehl *m*.
bend [bend] *irr bent, bent tr* biegen, beugen, knicken, krümmen; *(to ~ o.'s steps)* abbiegen (*from* von); *(Bogen)* spannen; *(Kopf)* wenden, neigen (*towards us* uns zu); *mar (Tau, Segel)* anknoten; zwingen, gefügig machen, *fig* lenken, richten (*to* auf); unterwerfen (*s.o. to o.'s will* jdn seinem Willen); *itr* sich biegen, sich beugen, sich neigen; sich krümmen; *fig* sich unterwerfen; *(Fluß, Straße, Bahn)* um-, abbiegen; sich wegwenden; *s* Biegung, Krümmung; Kurve; *fig* Wendung, Richtung *f (d. Geistes)*; *mar* (Kreuz-, Weber-)Knoten *m*; *tech* Kurvenstück, Knie *n*, Krümmer *m*; *pl* Höhen-, Tiefdruckkrankheit *f*; *pl mar* Krummhölzer *n pl*; *to be bent on doing* entschlossen sein zu tun; *to ~ back* sich zurückbiegen; *to ~ before s.th.* sich beugen, nachgeben vor etw; *to ~ down* sich bücken; *to ~ every effort* alle Kräfte anspannen; *to ~ to it* sich an die Arbeit machen; *to ~ o.'s mind to* s-n Sinn, s-e Aufmerksamkeit richten auf; *to ~ o.'s steps* die Schritte lenken (*homeward* nach Hause); **~ed** *a* gebeugt; *on ~~ knees* kniefällig; **~er** ['-ə] Flachzange; *sl, bes. Am* Sauferei *f*; **~ing** ['-iŋ] Biegung *f*, Krümmen *n*; *(~~ at angles)* Abkröpfung *f*; *~~ press* Biegepresse *f*; *~~ strength, stress* Biegefestigkeit, -spannung *f*; **~-leather** Sohlenleder *n*; *~* **test** Biegeprobe *f*.
beneath [bi'ni:θ] **1.** *prp (Ort u. Rang)* unter, unterhalb; *fig* niedriger als, tiefer; *~ contempt, notice* nicht der Beachtung wert; *to marry ~ one* unter s-m Stande heiraten; *that's ~ him* das ist unter s-r Würde; **2.** *adv* (weiter) unten, tiefer; *on the earth ~* auf Erden, *obs* hienieden.
bene|dicite [beni'daisiti] Bitte *f* um Segen; Tischgebet *n*; **~dick** ['-dik] junge(r), *fam* frischgebackene(r) Ehemann *m*; **B~dictine** [-'dikt(a)in] *rel* Benediktiner(in *f*); *b~~* [-'dikti:n] Benediktiner(likör) *m*; **~diction** [-'dikʃən] Segen(sspruch) *m*; Dankgebet *n*; (Ein-) Segnung *f*; *fig* Segen *m*; **~faction** [-'fækʃən] Wohltat; (Geld-)Spende *f*; **~factor, -tress** ['-fæktə, '-fæktris] Wohltäter(in *f*); Spender(in *f*), Förderer *m*; **~fice** ['-fis] *rel* Pfründe *f*; *hist* Lehen *n*; **~ficence** [bi'nefisns] Mildtätigkeit, Wohltätigkeit *f*; **~ficent** [bi'nefisnt] wohltätig; günstig wirkend; **~ficial** [beni'fiʃəl] gut, nützlich, vorteilhaft, *lit* heilsam (*to* für); wohltuend, gesund; *jur* den Vorteil genießend; *to be ~ to s.o.* jdm guttun, (gut) bekommen; *~~ owner* materielle(r) Eigentümer *m*; **~ficiary** [beni'fiʃəri] *a* Lehns-; Nutzungs-; *s jur* Begünstigte(r *m*) *f*, Nutznießer(in *f*), Erbe *m*, Erbin *f*; **~fit** ['-fit] *s* Wohltat; Gunst; (Bei-)Hilfe *f*; Nutzen, Vorteil, Gewinn *m*; *(finanzielle)* Unterstützung, Beihilfe; (Versicherungs-)Leistung; *theat* Benefizvorstellung; *(~~ of law)* Rechtswohltat *f*; *tr* fördern; nutzen, nützen, Gewinn bringen (*s.o.* jdm); von Nutzen, Vorteil, vorteilhaft, gut, gesund sein (*s.o.* für jdn); *itr* Nutzen ziehen (*by* aus), begünstigt sein, Gewinn, Vorteil haben (*by* durch); e-n Rechtsvorteil herleiten (*by* aus); *for the ~~ of* zum Nutzen *gen*, für; *to be of ~~* nützen, Nutzen bringen; *for pecuniary ~~* in gewinnsüchtiger Absicht; *for the public ~~* im öffentlichen Interesse; *to o.'s own ~~* seines Vorteils wegen; *maternity ~~* Wochengeld *n*, -hilfe *f*; *medical ~~* freie ärztliche Behandlung *f*; *sickness ~~* Krankengeld *n*, -unterstützung *f*; *unemployment ~~* Arbeits-, Erwerbslosenunterstützung *f*; *unjustified ~~* ungerechtfertigte Bereicherung *f*; *~~ clause* Begünstigungsklausel *f*; **~volence** [bi'nevələns] Güte *f*, Wohlwollen *n*; Wohltätigkeit *f*; **~volent** [bi'nevələnt] wohlwollend; wohltätig, hilfreich, hilfsbereit; *~~ fund* Unterstützungsfonds *m*; *~~ institution, society* Wohltätigkeitseinrichtung *f*, -verein *m*.
benighted [bi'naitid] *a* von der Nacht, Dunkelheit überrascht; *fig* unwissend.
benign [bi'nain] gütig, gutmütig, hilfsbereit, zuvorkommend, gefällig; *(Sache)* günstig; glücklich; dankbar; wohltuend, angenehm; zuträglich; *(Klima)* mild, günstig, gesund; *(Boden)* fruchtbar, ertragreich; *med* gutartig; **~ant** [-'nignənt] gütig, gutmütig; umgänglich, leutselig; *(Herrscher)* huldvoll; *(Einfluß)* wohltätig; *med* gutartig; **~ity** [-'nigniti] Güte, Gutmütigkeit; gute Tat, Wohltat *f*.
bent [bent] **1.** *s* Biegung, Krümmung; Kurve *f*; *tech* Knie *n*; *fig* Neigung *f*, Hang *m*; Begabung *f* (*for* zu, für); *a* versessen (*on* auf); gekrümmt; *(Röhre)* abgeknickt; *(Nagel)* verbogen; *sl* unehrlich, geklaut; *to (at) the top of o.'s ~* aus Leibeskräften; nach Herzenslust; *to follow o.'s ~* s-n Neigungen nachgehen; *~ out of shape* verbogen; **2.** *(~ grass)* Riedgras *n*.
benumb [bi'nʌmb] *tr (bes. Kälte)* erstarren lassen; *fig* betäuben, lähmen, widerstandslos machen; **~ed** *a* steif(gefroren), (er)starr(t) (*with cold* vor Kälte); *fig* benommen, wie gelähmt.
benz|ene ['benzi:n] *chem* Benzol *n*; *~~ ring (chem)* Benzolring *m*; **~ine** [-] Benzin *n (bes. a. Reinigungsmittel, a. aero)*; **~(o)-, ~oic** [-'zouik] *a chem* Benzoe-; **~oin** ['-ouin] Benzoe(harz *n*) *f*; **~ol(e)** ['benzəl, -oul] Benzol *n*.
beque|ath [bi'kwi:ð] *tr* vererben, vermachen; hinterlassen (*to s.o.* jdm) *a. fig*; **~st** [-est] Vermächtnis *n*, Hinterlassenschaft *f*.

*

be|rate [bi'reit] *tr bes. Am* ausschimpfen, schelten, herunterputzen; **~reave** [-'ri:v] *a. irr bereft, bereft bes. fig tr* berauben, (*s.o. of his life, hope* jdm das Leben, die Hoffnung) nehmen, rauben; **~reaved** [-'ri:vd] *a* leidtragend, hinterblieben; *fig* verwaist; **~reavement** [-'ri:vmənt] Trauerfall; schmerzliche(r), herbe(r) Verlust *m*.
beret ['berei, -ət] Baskenmütze *f*.
berg [bə:g] Eisberg; *(Südafrika)* Berg *m*.
beriberi ['beri'beri] *med* Beriberi *f (Mangelkrankheit)*.
Ber|kshire ['bɑ:kʃiə] *(engl. Grafschaft)*; **~lin** [bə:'lin] Berlin *n*; *hist* Berline *f (Reisewagen)*; *~~ black* schwarze(r) Eisenlack *m*; *~~ blue* Berliner Blau *n*; *~~ gloves (pl)* Strickhandschuhe *m pl*; *~~ wool* (feine, gefärbte) Strickwolle *f*.
berm [bə:m] *Am* Berme *f*, Böschungsabsatz; *mil* Schützenauftritt *m*.
berry ['beri] *s bot* Beere *f*; (Getreide-) Korn; *zoo* Hummerei *n*; *itr (Pflanze)* Beeren ansetzen; Beeren sammeln.
berth [bə:θ] *mar s* Anlege-, Liege-, Ankerplatz *m*; *mar* Helling; *mar* Offiziersmesse; *mar* Koje *f*; *mar rail aero* Liegeplatz *m*, Bett *n*; *fam* Stelle, (An-) Stellung *f*, Job *m*; *tr (Schiff)* festmachen; docken; unterbringen (*s.o.* jdn); *to give s.th. a wide ~* sich etw vom Halse halten; um etw e-n weiten Bogen machen; **~-deck** Zwischendeck *n*.
beryl ['beril] *min* Beryll *m*; **~lium** [be'riljəm] *chem* Beryllium *n*.
be|seech [bi'si:tʃ] *irr besought, besought, Am a.~~ed*; *tr (Person)* ersuchen, anflehen (*for* um); *(Gunst)* erflehen; **~seeching** *a* flehentlich; **~seem** [-'si:m] *itr imp* sich ziemen, sich schicken (*to s.o.* für jdn); **~set** [-'set] *irr beset, beset tr* umgeben, einschließen; *mil* belagern; besetzen (*with gems* mit Edelsteinen); *(Platz)*

einnehmen; *(Straße)* blockieren; *(Menschen)* einengen, bedrängen; einstürmen auf, bestürmen (*with* mit); *(Schwierigkeiten)* sich häufen, sich türmen bei, um; **~setting** immer wiederkehrend, unausrottbar; *~~ sin* Gewohnheitssünde *f*.

beside [bi'said] *prp (örtlich)* neben, (nahe) an, bei, dicht bei, in der Nähe *gen*; außer, dazu; weit entfernt von; *fig* neben, verglichen mit; *adv* außerdem, dazu; *to be ~ o.s. with rage* vor Wut außer sich sein; *that is ~ the mark, point, question* das hat nichts mit der Sache zu tun; **~s** [-z] *prp* außer, neben; abgesehen von; *adv* außerdem, ferner, (noch) dazu, des weiteren, überdies, sonst.

be|siege [bi'si:dʒ] *tr mil* belagern *a. fig*; sich drängen (*s.o.* um jdn); *fig* bestürmen (*with questions* mit Fragen); **~smear** [-'smiə] *tr* beschmieren; beschmutzen, besudeln; **~smirch** [-'smə:tʃ] *tr* beschmutzen, besudeln *(meist fig)*.

besom ['bi:zəm] *s* u. *tr* (mit e-m) (Reiser-)Besen *m* (fegen); *scot pej* Weib(sbild, -stück) *n*.

be|sot [bi'sɔt] *tr* den Verstand rauben *od* nehmen (*s.o.* jdm), verdummen; e-n Rausch anhängen (*s.o.* jdm); *lit* betören; **~sotted** *a* betrunken, betäubt; betört; vernarrt (*on* in); **~spatter** [-'spætə] *tr* bespritzen; *fig* überschütten; verleumden; **~speak** [-'spi:k] *irr bespoke, bespoke(n) tr* absprechen, festmachen, vergeben; *Br* (vor)bestellen, vormerken (lassen), belegen; erscheinen lassen, ausweisen als; zeigen, verraten, weisen auf; ahnen lassen; **~spoke** [-'spouk] *a Br* Maß-; *~~ tailor* Maßschneider *m*; **~sprinkle** [-'spriŋkl] *tr* besprengen, bestreuen, bespritzen (*with* mit).

Bess|(y) [bes(i)] Lieschen *n*; **~emer** ['besimə]: *~~ converter, process, steel (tech)* Bessemerbirne *f*, -verfahren *n*, -stahl *m*.

best [best] **1.** *a (Superlativ von good)* best; *s der, die, das* Beste; *the ~* die Besten; *the ~ of s.th.* das Beste an e-r S; *at ~* bestenfalls, höchstens; *at the ~ hand* aus erster Hand, günstig; *for the ~* in bester Absicht; *in o.'s (Sunday) ~* im Sonntagsstaat; *to the ~ of o.'s belief, of o.'s knowledge* nach bestem Wissen; *to the ~ of o.'s power, ability* so gut man kann; *with the ~* so gut wie nur einer; *to be at o.'s ~* ganz auf der Höhe sein, sich von s-r besten Seite zeigen; *to do o.'s (level) ~* sein Bestes, möglichstes tun; tun, was man kann; *to get the ~ of s.o. (Am)* jdm überlegen sein; jdn übers Ohr hauen; *to have, to get the ~ of it (fig)* den Vogel abschießen; am besten wegkommen; *to make the ~ of it* den Kopf oben behalten, sich nicht unterkriegen lassen; das Beste aus der Sache herausholen; sich damit abfinden; *to put o.'s ~ foot* od *leg foremost* od *forward* gehen, so schnell man kann; *fig* sein Bestes tun; tun, was man kann; *the ~ is the enemy of the good (prov)* das Bessere ist der Feind des Guten; *the very ~* der, die, das Allerbeste; *the ~ girl (sl)* die Liebste; *~ man* Brautführer *m*; *the ~ part of s.th.* das meiste von e-r S; *~-seller* Bestseller *m*, Erfolgsbuch *n*; *allg* Kassenschlager *m*; *the ~ thing to do* das Beste, was man tun kann; **2.** *adv (Superlativ von well)* am besten, aufs beste, bestens, auf die beste Weise; am meisten; *to like ~* am liebsten mögen; *you had ~ (inf)* du würdest am besten, du solltest *inf*; **3.** *tr fam* übertreffen, übertrumpfen; hereinlegen.

bestial ['bestjəl] tierisch; unmenschlich; bestialisch, roh, wild; triebhaft, animalisch; **~ity** [-i'æliti] Bestialität, Brutalität, Roheit, Wildheit; Triebhaftigkeit *f*; **~ize** ['-jəlaiz] *tr* vertieren, verrohen lassen.

be|stir [bi'stə:] *tr* aufmuntern, Leben bringen (*s.o.* in jdn); *to ~~ o.s.* sich rühren, sich regen, sich ermuntern; **~stow** [-'stou] *tr* geben, schenken, verleihen (*s.th. on s.o.* jdm etw); widmen (*much time on s.th.* e-r S viel Zeit); an-, verwenden, benutzen; *(Wohltat)* erweisen (*upon s.o.* jdm); *(Bedeutung)* beilegen; **~stowal** [-'stouəl] Verleihung, Übertragung *f*; **~strew** [-'stru:] *irr bestrewed, bestrewed* od *bestrewn tr* bestreuen (*with* mit); verstreut liegen (*the street* auf der Straße); **~stride** [-'straid] *irr bestrode, bestridden* od *bestrid, bestrode tr* zwischen die Beine nehmen, zwischen den Beinen haben; mit gespreizten Beinen stehen auf; sich rittlings setzen auf; *(Pferd)* besteigen, reiten; hinüberschreiten, e-n Schritt machen über.

bet [bet] *a. irr bet(ted), bet(ted) tr* wetten, setzen (*on* auf; *against* gegen); *itr* e-e Wette machen *od* abschließen (*on* auf; *against* gegen; *with* mit); *s* Wette *f*; Wettbedingungen *f pl*; Wetteinsatz, gewettete(r) Betrag; Gegenstand *m*, Tier *n*, Person *f*, auf die gewettet wird; *to lay* od *make, to hold* od *take (up), to lose a ~* e-e Wette machen *od* abschließen, annehmen, verlieren; *you ~ (sl), you can ~ your bottom dollar (fam)* darauf können Sie Gift nehmen! sicherlich! *I ~ you (ten to one) that* ich wette mit Ihnen (zehn gegen eins), daß; *heavy ~* hohe Wette *f*.

be|take [bi'teik] *irr betook, betaken tr*: *to ~~ o.s.* sich begeben; s-e Zuflucht nehmen (*to* zu), sich wenden (*to* an); sich zuwenden (*to s.th.* e-r S); (*to ~~ o.s. to o.'s heels* Reißaus nehmen, das Weite suchen; **~tatron** ['bi:-, *Am* 'beitətrɔn] Betatron *n*, Elektronenschleuder *f*; **~think** [-'θiŋk] *irr bethought, bethought tr*: *to ~~ o.s.* sich bedenken, überlegen; *that* daran denken, daß; *of* sich besinnen auf, sich erinnern an; vorhaben, ins Auge fassen; **~tide** [-'taid] *tr* geschehen (*s.o.* jdm); *(fast nur noch in:) woe ~~ me* wehe mir, dir! *itr: whate'er ~~!* was immer geschieht! **~times** [-'taimz] *adv* beizeiten, (recht)zeitig, früh(zeitig); bald; **~token** [-'touken] *tr* be-, andeuten, anzeigen, -künden, voraussagen.

be|tray [bi'trei] *tr* verraten (*a. unabsichtlich*) (*to* an); *(Geheimnis)* preisgeben; *(Mängel)* sichtbar machen, sehen lassen, hinweisen auf; zeigen; irre-, verführen, -leiten (*into* zu); enttäuschen; *(Vertrauen)* mißbrauchen; *(Versprechen)* nicht halten; untreu werden (*s.o.* jdm); *to ~~ o.s.* sich verraten; zeigen, was e-r ist; **~trayal** [-'treiəl] Verrat, Treubruch *m* (*of* an); *~~ of confidence* Vertrauensbruch *m*; *~~ of trust* Untreue *f*; **~troth** [-'trouð] *tr lit* verloben (*to* mit); **~trothal** [-'trouðəl] Verlobung *f*, Verlöbnis *n*; **~trothed** [-'trouðd] *a* verlobt; *s* Verlobte(r *m*) *f*.

bett|er, ~or ['betə] Wettende(r) *m*; **~ing** ['-iŋ] Wetten *n*; *~~-book* Wettbuch *n*; *~~-man* (gewohnheitsmäßig *od* Berufs-)Wettende(r) *m*; *~~-office* Wettbüro *n*; *~~-slip* Wettschein *m*.

better ['betə] **1.** *a (Komparativ von good)* besser; über, mehr (*than* als); **2.** *s das* Bessere; *one's ~s* die Höherstehenden; *for ~ for worse* in Freud u. Leid; gleich wie, *fam* so oder so; *to change for the ~* sich zum Besseren wenden; *to do, to be ~ than o.'s word* über sein Versprechen hinausgehen; *to feel ~* sich besser, wohler fühlen; *to get the ~ of* besiegen; übertreffen; übervorteilen, übers Ohr hauen; *to have seen ~ days* bessere Tage gesehen haben; *I am getting ~ now* es geht mir *(gesundheitlich)* (wieder) besser; *he is my ~* er ist mir überlegen; *he is ~ off* es geht ihm *(wirtschaftlich)* besser; *I know ~* das weiß ich besser; da lasse ich mir nichts vormachen; *no ~ than* nicht(s) Besser(es) als; im Grunde; *o.'s ~ feelings* das bessere Ich; *o.'s ~ half (hum)* die bessere Hälfte, (Ehe-)Frau *f*; *~ and ~* immer besser; *all the ~, so much the ~* um so, desto besser; *~ off* besser daran; wohlhabender, reicher; *the longer the ~* je länger, je lieber; *the sooner the ~* je eher, desto besser; *the ~ part, half of* der größere Teil *gen*, mehr als die Hälfte; **3.** *adv (Komparativ von well)* besser; *fam* mehr; *~ and ~* mehr u. mehr; *to like ~* lieber haben, vorziehen; *you had ~ go, you ~ go now* du tätest besser, jetzt zu gehen; es wäre besser für dich, wenn du jetzt gingest; geh lieber; *you had ~ not!* das will ich dir nicht geraten haben! **4.** *tr* (ver)bessern; steigern; vervollkommnen; (es) besser machen als, übertreffen; *to ~ o.s.* sich (beruflich) verbessern; vorwärtskommen; **~ment** ['-mənt] (Ver-)Besserung; (Wert-)Steigerung *f*, Zuwachs *m*; *Am* Melioration *f*.

between [bi'twi:n], *obs lit* **betwixt** [-'twikst] *prp (zeitlich, der Menge* u. *dem Grade nach)* zwischen, unter; *adv* dazwischen, darunter; *betwixt and ~ (fam)* halb u. halb; *far ~* in großen Abständen; *few and far ~ (fig)* dünn gesät; *in ~ (prp)* (in der Zeit) zwischen; inmitten; *adv* dazwischen, darunter; mitten drin; *~ us, you, them* zusammen, gemeinschaftlich; *~ you and me, ~ ourselves* unter uns (gesagt); *to stand ~* e-e vermittelnde Rolle spielen, vermitteln; *there's often a slip ~ the cup and the lip (prov)* es kommt oft anders, als man denkt; *go-~* Vermittler(in *f*) *m*; *something ~* ein Zwischending; **~times** *Am*, **~whiles** *adv* dann u. wann.

bev|el ['bevəl] *s tech* Schrägfläche, Abschrägung, schräg geschliffene Kante, Fase, Gehrung; Schmiege *f*, Schrägmaß *n*, Schräg-, Stellwinkel *m (Gerät)*; *a* schiefwinkelig; schräg; *tr (Kante)* abschrägen, schräg schleifen, abkanten; *~~ wheel* Kegelrad, Ritzel *n*; **~erage** ['-əridʒ] Getränk *n*; **~y** ['bevi] Gesellschaft *(bes. von Frauen)*, Schar *(Mädchen)*; *(Gegenstände)* Sammlung *f*; *(Vögel)* Schwarm *m*, Volk *n*, Kette *f*, Flug *m*.

be|wail [bi'weil] *tr* beklagen, bejammern; *itr* (weh)klagen, trauern (*for* um); **~ware** [-'wɛə] *(nur Imperativ u. inf)*: *~~ what you say* gib acht auf das, was du sagst; *~~ of the dog!* Achtung, bissiger Hund! *~~ of imitations!* vor Nachahmungen wird gewarnt! *~~ of pickpockets!* vor Taschendieben wird gewarnt! **~wilder** [-'wildə] *tr* verwirren, verwirrt, verlegen machen, durchea.-, in Verlegenheit bringen; **~wildered** *a* verwirrt; verblüfft; **~wildering** [-riŋ] verwirrend, verblüffend; **~wilderment** [-mənt] Verwirrung, Verlegenheit; Verblüffung *f*; *in ~~* verwirrt, verlegen; **~witch** [-'witʃ] *tr* verzaubern, verhexen; *fig* bezaubern, ganz (für sich) einnehmen, faszinieren; **~witching** [-iŋ] bezaubernd, hinreißend, unwiderstehlich.

beyond [bi'jɔnd] *prp* jenseits *gen*, über ... hinaus *a. fig*; außerhalb *gen*; weiter als; *(örtlich)* nach; *(zeitlich)* länger als (bis), später als; mehr als; außer, neben; *adv* jenseits; darüber hinaus; *s the* ~ das Jenseits; *at the back of* ~ *(fam)* am Ende der Welt; ~ *belief* unglaublich, unglaubwürdig; ~ *compare* über jeden Vergleich erhaben; unvergleichlich; ~ *control* unkontrollierbar; ~ *dispute* über jeden Zweifel erhaben; ~ *endurance* unerträglich; ~ *hope* hoffnungslos; ~ *imagination* unvorstellbar; ~ *measure* maßlos; unermeßlich; ~ *the memory of men* in unvordenklichen Zeiten; ~ *all praise* über alles Lob erhaben; ~ *reason* unvernünftig; *to be* ~ *s.o.* jdn übertreffen; *to live* ~ *o.'s income* über s-e Verhältnisse leben; *he is* ~ *help* ihm ist nicht (mehr) zu helfen; *that is* ~ *a joke* das ist kein Spaß mehr; *that is* ~ *me* das ist mir zu hoch, das geht über meine Fassungskraft, *fam* meinen Horizont.

bezel ['bezl] *(Meißel)* Schneide; *(geschliffener Edelstein)* Facette; Rille *f* *(in Fassungen)*; *tech* Fenster *n*.

bi [bai] *pref* Zwei-, Doppel-; **~annual** halbjährlich; **~monthly** alle zwei Monate (erscheinend); **~weekly** zweimal wöchentlich *od* alle 14 Tage (erscheinend).

bias ['baiəs] *s* schräge Linie *od* Fläche *f*, Schrägstreifen *m*; Schräge, Abschrägung, Neigung; *el* Vorspannung, Vorbelastung *f*; *(Kegelkugel)* schiefe(r) Lauf *m*; *fig* Neigung *f*, Hang *m* (*towards* zu), Vorliebe *f* (*towards* für); Befangenheit, Parteilichkeit; Abneigung *f*, Vorurteil *n* (*against* gegen); *a* schräg, schief; quer verlaufend; *(Textil)* mit Schrägstreifen; *tr* beeinflussen, in e-e bestimmte Richtung lenken; einnehmen (*to* für); *el* vorspannen, vorbelasten; *free from* ~, *without* ~ unvoreingenommen, unparteiisch; **~(s)ed** ['-t] *a fig* voreingenommen, parteiisch (*against* gegen), befangen; *to be* ~~ ein Vorurteil haben (*against* gegen).

bib [bib] **1.** *itr* viel trinken; **2.** *s* (Schlabber-)Lätzchen *n (für Kinder)*; (Schürzen-)Latz *m*; *best* ~ *and tucker (fam)* Sonntagsstaat *m*; **~ber** ['-ə] (Gewohnheits-)Trinker *m (bes. in Zssgen)*; *wine-*~~ Weintrinker *m*; **~bing** ['-iŋ] Trinken *n (bes. in Zssgen)*; *beer-*~~ Biertrinken *n*; **~cock** Zapfhahn *m*.

Bibl|e ['baibl] Bibel *f a. fig*; *~~-Christian, -reader, -society* Bibelchrist, -leser *m*, -gesellschaft *f*; **b~ical** ['biblikəl] biblisch; Bibel-.

biblio ['biblio] *pref* Buch-; Bibel-; **~grapher** [-'ɔgrəfə] Bibliograph, Bücherkenner *m*; **~graphic(al)** [-o'græfik(əl)] bibliographisch; **~graphy** [-'ɔgrəfi] Bibliographie, Bücherkunde *f*; **~mania** [-o'meinjə] Bibliomanie *f*; **~maniac** [-o'meinjæk] Bibliomane, Büchernarr *m*; **~phil(e)** ['-ofail, -fil] Bibliophile, Bücherfreund *m*.

bibulous ['bibjuləs] trunksüchtig.

bicarbonate [bai'kɑ:bənit] Bikarbonat *n*; ~ *of soda* (doppeltkohlensaures) Natrium *n*.

bicenten|ary [baisen'ti:nəri] *s* Zweihundertjahrfeier *f*; *a* Zweihundertjahr-; **~nial** [-'tenjəl] zweihundertjährig.

biceps ['baiseps] *anat* Bizeps *m*.

bi|chloride [bai'klɔ:raid] *chem* Bichlorid *n*; **~chromate** [-'kroumit] *chem* Dichromat *n*; ~~ *of potash* doppeltchromsaure(s) Kali *n*.

bicker ['bikə] *itr* (sich herum)zanken, keifen; rasseln, rascheln; *(Wasser)* plätschern; *(Flamme)* lodern, flakkern; *(Licht)* blinken; *s* u. **~ing** ['-riŋ] Gezänk *n*.

bicycl|e ['baisikl] *s* (Fahr-)Rad *n*; *itr* radfahren, radeln = *to ride (on) a* ~~; ~~ *frame, tyre, tube* Fahrradgestell *n*, -decke *f*, -schlauch *m*; **~ist** [-'ist] Radfahrer(in *f*) *m*.

bid [bid] *irr bad(e), bidden (in der Bedeutung befehlen, entbieten)*; *sonst*: *bid, bid*; *tr itr (Preis)* bieten; *(Kartenspiel)* bieten, melden, reizen; *itr* ein (Preis-An-)Gebot machen; *tr lit* gebieten, befehlen (*s.o. do* jdm zu tun), heißen (*s.o. do* jdn tun); *(Gruß)* entbieten; *obs* einladen; *s (Auktion)* Gebot; *(Börse)* Geld; Lieferungs-, Preisangebot *n*; *Am fam* Einladung *f*; *(Karten)* Reizen *n*; Versuch *m*, Bewerbung, Bemühung *f* (*for* um); *to* ~ *against s.o.* jdn überbieten; *(Kartenspiel)* reizen; *to make a* ~ bieten, ein Gebot machen; *for s.th.* auf etw bieten; etw zu erlangen, für sich etw zu sichern suchen; sich um etw bewerben; *fair* (viel) versprechen, zu (großen) Hoffnungen berechtigen; *to* ~ *up (Ware im Preis)* hochtreiben; *to* ~ *s.o. welcome* jdn willkommen heißen; *nearest, highest, lowest* ~ Nächst-, Höchst-, Mindestgebot *n*; **~dable** ['-əbl] willig, gehorsam; *(Bridge)* bietbar; **~der** ['-ə] *(Auktion)* Bieter; Bewerber *m*; **~ding** ['-iŋ] *(Auktion)* Gebot; Gebot, Geheiß *n*, Befehl *m*; Lieferungsangebote *n pl*; *to do s.o.'s* ~~ jdm gehorchen, jds Befehl ausführen; **~dy** ['-i] *Am* Küken, Hühnchen *n*.

bide [baid] *tr irr bode (in der Bedeutung* ertragen, *obs)*; *obs poet für abide*; *to* ~ *o.'s time* s-e Zeit, Gelegenheit abwarten.

biennial [bai'enjəl] *a* zweijährig; alle zwei Jahre stattfindend; *s* zweijährige Pflanze *f*.

bier [biə] (Toten-)Bahre *f*.

biff [bif] *s sl* tüchtige(r) Schlag, Hieb, Denkzettel *m*; *tr* e-n Denkzettel verpassen (*s.o.* jdm), verprügeln; schlagen.

bi|filar ['bai'failə] *tech* bifilar, doppelfädig, -adrig; **~focal** ['-'fouk(ə)l] Bifokal-; mit doppeltem Brennpunkt, mit zwei Brennweiten; ~~ *spectacles* u. *s pl* Bifokalgläser *n pl*; **~furcate** ['-fə:keit] *tr itr* (sich) gabeln; sich verzweigen; *a* ['-it] gegabelt; **~furcation** [-fə:'keiʃən] Gabel(ung) *f allg.*

big [big] *a* groß, dick; groß, erwachsen; laut; groß, bedeutend, wichtig; großzügig, -mütig, edel(mütig), vornehm; hochmütig, anmaßend, hochfahrend; schwanger, trächtig; *Am fam* großartig, gewaltig, trefflich; ~ *with* voller, voll von; *adv* aufgeblasen, großspurig; ~ *with young (Tier)* trächtig; ~ *with child (Frau)* schwanger; ~ *with fate (fig)* unheilschwanger; ~ *with importance, significance* bedeutungsvoll; ~ *with pride* aufgeblasen; *to look* ~ *(fig)* von oben herab sehen; die Nase hoch tragen; *to talk* ~ angeben, den Mund voll nehmen; große Töne reden; *he has grown, got too* ~ *for his boots (sl)* ihm ist was in den Kopf gestiegen; ~ **bug, noise** *(sl)*, *(Am sl)* **dog, fish, shot** hohe(s) Tier *n*; ~ **business** Großindustrie *f*; ~ **game** Hochwild; *sport* Entscheidungsspiel *n*; ~ **head** *Am* Großkopfete(r) *m*; *fam* Einbildung *f*; **~-hearted** *a* großherzig; ~ **horn** (amerik.) Dickhornschaf *n*; ~ **idea** *Am fam* gute, großartige Idee *f*; **~ness** ['-nis] Größe; Dicke *f*; Umfang *m*; *fig* Aufgeblasenheit *f*; ~ **stick** *Am* die nötigen Mittel *n pl*, Macht *f*; **~(-)time** *attr Am fam* groß, gewaltig; einflußreich; ~~ *operator (Am)* Großschieber, Konjunkturritter *m*; ~ **toe** große Zehe *f*; ~ **top** *Am (Zirkus)* Hauptzelt *n*; ~ **wheel** Riesenrad *n*; **~wig** *fam fig* große(s) Tier *n*.

bigam|ist ['bigəmist] Bigamist *m*; **~ous** [-əs] bigamisch; **~y** ['-i] Bigamie, Doppelehe *f*.

bight [bait] *geog* Bucht; *(Tau)* Bucht; *(Fluß)* Schleife *f*.

bigot ['bigət] engstirnige(r) Mensch; Fanatiker; blinde(r) Anhänger; *rel* Frömmler *m*; **~ed** ['-id] *a* engstirnig; fanatisch; scheinheilig; **~ry** ['-ri] Engstirnigkeit *f*; Fanatismus *m*; Frömmelei *f*.

bike [baik] *s fam* (Fahr-)Rad *n*; *itr* radeln.

bikini [bi'ki:ni] Bikini, zweiteilige(r) Badeanzug *m*.

bi|labial [bai'leibiəl] *gram* bilabial; **~labiate** [-ət] *bot* zweilippig; **~lateral** [-'lætərəl] bilateral, zweiseitig *(bes. a. pol)*; gegenseitig, wechselseitig; ~~ *trade agreement* zweiseitige(s) Handelsabkommen *n*.

bilberry ['bilbəri] Heidel-, Blaubeere *f*; *red* ~ Preiselbeere *f*.

bile [bail] *physiol* Galle *f*; *fig* bittere(s) Gefühl *n*, Ärger *m*; schlechte Laune *od* Stimmung *f*; **~-duct** *anat* Gallengang *m*.

bilge [bildʒ] *s mar* Bilge *f*, Kiel-, Lagerraum; Faßbauch *m*; *(Schiff)* Bilgenwasser *n* (*~-water*); *sl fig* Quatsch, Blödsinn *m*; *tr (Schiff)* leck machen; *itr* leck werden; *tr (itr* sich) ausbauchen.

bili|ary ['biljəri] *scient* Gallen-; **~ous** [-əs] Gallen-; *fig (Mensch)* gallig, reizbar; übellaunig; trübsinnig; ~~ *attack* Gallenanfall *m*, -kolik *f*.

bilingual [bai'liŋgwəl] zweisprachig.

bilk [bilk] *tr* betrügen; täuschen, beschwindeln; *(Rechnung)* nicht bezahlen; *s* Betrug, Schwindel; Betrüger, Schwindler *m*; **~er** ['-ə] (Zech-)Preller, Betrüger *m*.

bill [bil] **1.** *s* Schnabel *m (bestimmter Vögel)*; Landzunge; *mar* Spitze *f* (des Ankerflügels); *agr* Hippe *f*, Gartenmesser *n*; *itr* sich schnäbeln; *to* ~ *and coo (fig)* mitea. liebkosen; **2.** *s* Rechnung; Faktur(a), Nota; Mitteilung, Benachrichtigung *f*; Schein *m*, Bescheinigung *f*; Anschlag(zettel) *m*, Plakat *n*, (Hand-)Zettel *m*, Flugblatt; (Theater-, Konzert-)Programm; Verzeichnis *n*, Liste *f*; *jur* Schriftsatz, Antrag *m*, Eingabe; *bes.* Klageschrift *(~ of indictment)*; Gesetzesvorlage *f*, -entwurf; *com (~ of exchange)* Wechsel *m*, Tratte; Anweisung *f*; *Am (bank, Treasure ~)* Banknote *f*, Geldschein *m*; *pl* Wechselbestand *m*; *tr* durch Anschlag *od* Plakate bekanntmachen, -geben; anschlagen; mit Plakaten, Anschlägen bekleben; *(Liste)* aufstellen; in e-e Liste eintragen; *(to* ~ *for)* in Rechnung stellen, fakturieren; *to accept a* ~ e-n Wechsel akzeptieren; *to cash, to honour a* ~ e-n Wechsel einlösen; *to draw a* ~ *on s.o.* e-n Wechsel auf jdn ziehen; *to fill the* ~ *(fam)* alle Erwartungen erfüllen; *to foot the* ~ *(fam)* aufkommen für; *to issue, to negotiate a* ~ e-n Wechsel begeben, in Umlauf setzen; *to pass a* ~ ein Gesetz verabschieden; e-n Gesetzentwurf annehmen; *to refer a* ~ *to a committee* e-n Gesetzentwurf e-m Ausschuß überweisen; *to reject a* ~ e-n Gesetzentwurf ablehnen; *to table a* ~ e-n Gesetzentwurf einbringen; *to stick a* ~ e-n Zettel, ein Plakat ankleben; *post, stick no* ~*s* Ankleben verboten; *the* ~, *please* bitte, zahlen!

drawing, drawer, drawee of a ~ Wechselausstellung *f*, -aussteller, -bezogene(r) *m*; *hotel* ~ Hotelrechnung *f*; *pay-* ~ Lohnliste *f*; *theatre* ~ *(theat)* Spielplan *m*; *Treasury* ~ Schatzanweisung *f*; ~ *of carriage, of freight* Frachtbrief, Ladeschein *m*; ~ *of charges* Kosten-, Gebührenrechnung *f*; ~ *in circulation* laufende(r), in Umlauf befindliche(r) Wechsel *m*; ~ *of consignment, of lading, shipping* ~ Seefrachtbrief, -ladeschein *m*, Konnossement *n*; ~ *of costs* Kosten-, Spesenrechnung *f*; ~ *of credit* Kreditbrief *m*, Akkreditiv *n*; ~ *of debt* Schuldbrief *m*, -anerkennung *f*; ~ *of delivery* Lieferschein *m*; ~ *of entry* Zolleinfuhrerklärung, -deklaration *f*; ~ *of fare* Speisekarte; Speisenfolge *f*, Menü; *fig* Programm *n*; ~ *of health* Gesundheitsbescheinigung *f*, -paß *m*, Attest *n*; ~ *of quantities (arch)* Kostenvoranschlag *m*; ~ *of review (jur)* Berufung *f*; ~ *of rights (pol)* verfassungsmäßig garantierte Grundrechte *n pl*; ~ *of sale* Kaufvertrag *m*; Übertragungsurkunde *f*; ~ *at sight, sight* ~ Sichtwechsel *m*; **~board** Anschlag-, Plakattafel *f*; ~ **book** Wechseljournal, Akzeptbuch *n*; *Am* Brieftasche *f*; ~ **broker** Wechsel-, Diskontmakler; Geldwechsler, -makler *m*; ~ **debt(or)** Wechselschuld(ner *m*) *f*; ~ **discount (rate)** Wechseldiskont(satz) *m*; ~ **fold** *Am* Brieftasche *f*; ~ **forger** Wechselfälscher *m*; ~ **forgery** Wechselfälscherei *f*; ~ **holder** Wechselinhaber *m*; **~ing** ['-iŋ] Fakturierung *f*, Ausstellen *n* der Rechnung; Zettelankleben *n*; Liste, Reihenfolge *f* der Schauspieler auf e-m Anschlag; ~ **jobbing** Wechselreiterei *f*; ~ **poster, sticker** Plakat-, Zettelankleber *m*; ~ **posting** Plakatankleben *n*; ~ **protest** Wechselprotest *m*; ~ **rate** Wechselkurs *m*; ~ **surety** Wechselbürgschaft *f*; ~ **wallet** (Geld-)Brieftasche *f*; Wechselbestand *m*.

billet ['bilit] **1.** *s mil* Quartierschein *m*; (Privat-)Quartier *n*; (Orts-)Unterkunft, Unterbringung *f*; Bestimmungsort *m*; Gebiet *n*, Raum *m*; *fam* Stellung, Arbeit *f*; *tr* einquartieren, unterbringen (*on s.o.* bei jdm; *in, at* in); ein Quartier stellen (*s.o.* jdm); *(Haus, Ort)* belegen; *to* ~ *out* ausquartieren; **~-command** Quartiermacherkommando *n*; **~ee** [-'ti:] Einquartierte(r) *m*; *pl* Einquartierung *f*; **~ing** ['-iŋ] Einquartierung; Belegung; Unterbringung *f*; ~~ *area* Unterkunftsbereich *m*; ~~ *office* Quartieramt *n*; ~~ *order, paper, slip* Quartierschein *m*; ~~ *strength* Belegungsstärke *f*; **2.** (Holz-)Scheit *n*; Knüppel, (kleiner) Metallbarren *m*.

billhook ['bilhuk] *agr* Hippe *f*; *mil* Faschinenmesser *n*.

billiard ['biljəd] *a* Billard-; *s pl mit sing* Billard(spiel) *n*; *a game of* ~*s* e-e Partie Billard; **~-ball** Billardkugel *f*; **~-cloth** Billardtuch *n*; ~ **cue** Queue *n*, Billardstock *m*; **~-marker** Markör *m* **~-table** Billard(tisch *m*) *n*.

billingsgate ['biliŋzgit] gemeine Schimpfwörter *n pl*, schwere Beleidigung *f*.

billion ['biljən] Billion; *Am* Milliarde *f*; **~aire** ['-ɛə] *Am* Milliardär *m*.

billow ['bilou] *s* Woge, (Sturz-)Welle *f a. fig*; *(Rauch)* Schwaden *m*; *poet* Meer *n*, See *f*; *itr* wogen; sich (auf-)türmen; in Schwaden aufsteigen; **~y** ['-i] *a* wogend; *(Flammen)* flackernd; *(Rauch)* in Schwaden aufsteigend.

Billy ['bili] Willi; *b*~ *(Australien)* Zinnkessel *(zum Abkochen)*; *Am* Gummiknüppel *m*; **b~cock** *fam* Melone *f* *(Hut)*; **b~-goat** *fam* Ziegenbock *m*; *b~-o*: *like* ~~ *(fam)* sehr kräftig.

bimetal ['baimetl] Bimetall *n*; **~lic** [-mi'tælik] Bimetall-; bimetallisch; Doppelwährungs-; ~~ *wire* Manteldraht *m*; **~lism** [-'metəlizm] Bimetallismus *m*, Doppelwährung *f*.

bi|monthly ['bai'mʌnθli] *a* alle zwei Monate (stattfindend); zweimal im Monat, halbmonatlich; **~motored** [bai'moutəd] *a aero* zweimotorig.

bin [bin] Behälter; Kasten *m*, Kiste *f*; Silo *m*; Weinregal *n*.

bin|ary ['bainəri] *scient* binär, binar(isch), aus zwei Einheiten, *chem* Stoffen bestehend; Doppel-; ~~*-compound (chem)* binäre Verbindung *f*; ~~ *scale (math)* dyadische(s), Zweiersystem *n*; ~~ *star* Doppelstern *m*; ~~ *system* binäre(s) System *n*; **~ate** ['-eit] *scient* paarig; **~aural** [bi'nɔ:rəl] binaural; stereophonisch; ~~ *effect* Raumtoneffekt *m*.

bind [baind] *irr bound, bound tr* binden *(a. Buch)*; befestigen (*to, on* an); binden *(a. Küche)*, fest, hart machen; umwinden; einfassen (*with* mit), mit e-m Saum, Rand, e-r Kante versehen; *fig* binden, verpflichten *a. itr*; *(Vertrag, Geschäft)* abschließen; *(Passiv)* verpflichtet sein (*to* zu); *itr* fest, hart werden; *(Schnee)* pappen; *(Zement)* abbinden; *mil sl* sich zu Tode langweilen; *to* ~ *o.s. to s.th.* sich zu etw verpflichten; *s* Bindemittel *n*; *mus* Bindung(szeichen *n*); *bot* Ranke *f*; *sl* Unfug, Blödsinn, *m*; *to* ~ *(out) (as an) apprentice* in die Lehre geben; *to* ~ *down* festbinden; *fig* fest verpflichten; zwingen; *to* ~ *over* rechtlich verpflichten; *to* ~ *together* zs.-, *fig* verbinden; *to* ~ *up* an-, hoch-, zu-, zs.binden; verheilen lassen; *I'll be bound* ich stehe dafür ein, Sie können sich darauf verlassen; **~er** ['-a] (Buch-)Binder *m*; Band *n*; Binde *f*; Aktendeckel *m*; *(Zigarre)* Deckblatt *n*; *agr* Mähbinder; *(~~ agreement)* Vorvertrag *m*; *tech* Bindemittel *n*, Binder *m*; Heftklammer; *aero sl* Bremse *f*; *tech* Fressen *n*; **~ery** ['-əri] *Am* Buchbinderei *f*; **~ing** ['-iŋ] *a* bindend, verbindlich, verpflichtend (*on* für); *s (Buch)* Einband; Besatz *m*, Einfassung *f*, Saum *m*; *(Schi)* Bindung *f*; *to be* ~~ *on s.o.* jdn verpflichten; für jdn rechtsverbindlich sein; *legally* ~~ rechtsverbindlich; *not* ~~ unverbindlich; ~~ *force* Klebkraft; *jur* bindende Kraft *f*; ~~ *nut* Gegenmutter *f*; ~~ *wire* Bindedraht *m*; **~weed** *bot* Winde *f*.

bing|e [bindʒ] *sl* Sauferei *f*, Kneipabend *m*, Bierreise *f*; **~o** ['biŋgo] *sl* Schnaps *m*; Bingo *n (Spiel)*.

binnacle ['binəkl] *mar* Kompaßhaus *n*.

bino|cular [bai'nɔkjulə] *a* binokular, für beide Augen (zugleich); *s pl* [bi-] Feldstecher *m*; Opernglas; Doppelmikroskop *n*; **~mial** [bai'noumiəl] *a math* binomisch, zweigliederig; *s* Binom *n*; ~~ *theorem* binomische(r) Lehrsatz *m*.

bio ['baio(u)] *pref scient* Bio-, Lebens-; **~bibliography** Biobibliographie *f*; **~chemic(al)** ['baio'kemikəl] biochemisch; **~chemist** [-'kemist] Biochemiker *m*; **~chemistry** [-'kemistri] Biochemie *f*; **~dynamic** [baiodai'næmik] biodynamisch; *pl mit sing* Biodynamik *f*; **~genesis** [baio'dʒenisis] Biogenesis *f*; **~genetic** [baiodʒi'netik] biogenetisch; *pl mit sing* Biogenetik *f*; **~geography** [baiodʒi'ɔgrəfi] Biogeographie *f*; **~grapher** [bai'ɔgrəfə] Biograph *m*; **~graphic(al)** [baio'græfik(əl)] biographisch; **~graphy** [bai'ɔgrəfi] Biographie, Lebensbeschreibung *f*; **~logic(al)** [baio'lɔdʒik(əl)] biologisch; ~~*al shield* Strahlenschutz *m*; ~~*al warfare* biologische(r) Krieg *m*; **~logist** [bai'ɔlədʒist] Biologe *m*; **~logy** [bai'ɔlədʒi] Biologie, Lehre *f* vom Leben; **~metry** [bai'ɔmetri] Biometrie, biologische Statistik *f*; **~physics** [baio'fiziks] *pl mit sing* Biophysik *f*.

biparous ['bipərəs] *zoo* zwei Junge zur Welt bringend.

bi|partisan [bai'pɑ:tizn] *a pol* Zweiparteien-; **~partite** [-'pɑ:tait] *bot* zweiteilig; *pol (Vertrag)* zweiseitig; in zwei Ausfertigungen; **~ped** ['baiped] *s zoo* Zweifüßler *m*; **~plane** ['baiplein] *aero* Doppeldecker *m*; **~pod** ['baipod] *tech* Gabelstütze *f*; **~polar** [bai'poulə] zwei-, doppelpolig.

birch [bə:tʃ] *s* Birke(nholz *n*) *f*; *(~-rod)* (Birken-)Rute *f*; *tr* mit der Rute züchtigen; **~en** ['-n] birken, aus Birkenholz.

bird [bə:d] *s* Vogel *m*; *sl* Mädchen *n*; *sl* Kauz *m*; *Am sl* Kumpel *m*, Marke; *sport* Tontaube *f*; Rebhuhn *n*; Zischen, Pfeifen *n to give the* ~ *to s.o.* jdn; auspfeifen; *to kill two* ~*s with one stone (fig)* zwei Fliegen mit einer Klappe schlagen; *they are* ~*s of a feather (fig)* sie sind zum Verwechseln ähnlich; *fine feathers make fine* ~*s (prov)* Kleider machen Leute; ~*s of a feather flock together* gleich und gleich gesellt sich gern; *a* ~ *in the hand is worth two in the bush* ein Spatz in der Hand ist besser als eine Taube auf dem Dach; *the early* ~ *catches the worm* Morgenstunde hat Gold im Munde; *early* ~ Frühaufsteher *m*; *old* ~ *(fig)* alte(r) Fuchs *m*; *song-*~ Singvogel *m*; ~ *of ill omen* Unglücksrabe *m*; ~ *of paradise* Paradiesvogel *m*; ~ *of passage* Zugvogel *m a. fig (Mensch)*; ~ *of prey* Raub-, Greifvogel *m*; **~-cage** Vogelkäfig *m*, -bauer *n*, a. *m*; **~-call** Lockpfeife *f*; Vogelruf *m*; **~-catcher** Vogelfänger, -steller *m*; **~-cherry, ~'s cherry** Traubenkirsche *f*; ~ **dog** Hühnerhund *m*; **~-fancier** Vogelzüchter *m*; **~ie** ['-i] Vögelchen *n*; **~-lime** Vogelleim; Langfinger, Dieb *m*; **~man** Geflügelzüchter; Vogelkenner; *sl* Flieger *m*; **~-net** Vogelnetz *n*; **~-seed** Vogelfutter *n*; **~'s-eye view** Vogelschau *f*; *fig* allgemeine(r) Überblick *m*; **~'s nest** Vogelnest *n*; *to go* ~*'s-nesting* Vogelnester ausnehmen.

birth [bə:θ] Geburt *f a. fig*; Gebären *n*, Entbindung, Niederkunft *f*; *(Tier)* Wurf *m*; Erzeugnis *n*, Frucht *f*; Abstammung, Herkunft *f*, Ursprung *m*; Entstehung *f*, Aufkommen *n*, Auftakt, Ausgangspunkt, Anbruch *m*; *pref* angeboren; *at* ~ bei der Geburt; *by* ~ von Geburt; *from his* ~ von s-r Geburt an; *of good* ~ aus gutem Hause; *to give* ~ *to* zur Welt bringen; *fig* ins Leben rufen, schaffen; *date, place of* ~ Geburtsdatum *n*, -ort *m*; *new* ~ *(rel)* Wiedergeburt *f*; *premature* ~ Frühgeburt *f*; **~-certificate,** *certificate of* ~ Geburtsurkunde *f*; **~-control** Geburtenregelung, -beschränkung *f*; **~day** Geburtstag *m*; ~~ *party* Geburtstagsfeier *f*; ~~ *present* Geburtstagsgeschenk *n*; ~~ *suit (hum)* Adamskostüm *n*; **~-mark** Muttermal *n*; **~-place** Geburtsort *m*, -haus *n*; **~-rate** Geburtenziffer *f*; *falling* ~~ Geburtenrückgang *m*; **~right** Geburtsrecht *n*.

biscuit ['biskit] Biskuit, Keks *m*; Biskuitporzellan *n*; *mil sl* kleine Matratze *f*; *Am* Brötchen *n*; *ship's* ~ Schiffszwieback *m*.

bi|sect [bai'sekt] *tr* in zwei (*meist* gleiche) Teile teilen, halbieren; *itr* sich

teilen; ~**section** [-'sekʃən] Zweiteilung, Halbierung *f*; ~**sector** [-'sektə] *math* Halbierende *f*; ~**sectrix** [-'sektriks] Winkelhalbierende *f*; ~**sexual** [-'seksjuəl] zweigeschlechtig, zwitterig.
bishop ['biʃəp] *rel* Bischof; *(Schach)* Läufer; Bischof(swein) *m*; ~*'s cap (bot)* Bischofsmütze *f*; ~**ric** ['-rik] Bistum *n*, Diözese *f*; Bischofsamt *n*, -würde *f*.
bismuth ['bizməθ] *chem* Wismut *n*, *a. m.*
bison ['baisn] *pl* ~ *zoo* Wisent; Bison *m*.
bisque [bisk] **1.** *sport* Vorgabe *f*; **2.** Biskuitporzellan *n*; **3.** *Am, Br* **bisk** Kraft-, *bes.* Fischsuppe *f*; Nußeis *n*.
bissextile [bi'sekstail] *a* Schalt-; *s* Schaltjahr *n*.
bist|ort ['bistɔ:t] *bot* Wiesenknöterich *m*; ~**oury** ['-uri] *med* Bistouri *m od s*; ~**re,** *Am* ~**er** ['-ə] *s* Bister *m od n*, braune Farbe *f*; *a* braun.
bisulph|ate [bai'sʌlfeit] *chem* Bisulfat *n*; ~~ *of potash* doppelschwefelsaure(s) Kalium *n*; ~**ite** [-ait] Bisulfit *n*.
bit [bit] *s* Bissen, Happen *m*, Stückchen, Bißchen *n*; *(Gegend, Buch)* Stelle *f*; (ein) bißchen, kurze Zeit; *film* kleine Rolle *f*; *(Pferdegeschirr)* Gebiß *n*; *tech* Schneide, Schneidkante *f*, -werkzeug; Bohreisen *n*, Bohrerspitze *f*; Bohreinsatz; Kloben, (Löt-)Kolben(kopf) *m*; *(Zange)* Backe *f*; Schlüsselbart *m*; *fam* threepenny, *Am fam* 12½ Cent; *sl* Mädel *n*; *tr (Pferd)* aufzäumen; mit e-r Schneide versehen; an den Zaum gewöhnen; *fig* zügeln, hemmen, zurückhalten; *tech* e-n Schlüsselbart verfertigen; *a* klein, unbedeutend; *a* ~ *(of)* ein bißchen; *a* ~ *of a* so etwas wie; *every* ~ *as* ganz genauso; *a* ~ *at a time,* ~ *by* ~ Stück für Stück, schrittweise, allmählich, nach u. nach; *not a* ~ nicht ein, kein bißchen, nicht im geringsten; *to do o.'s* ~ sein Teil tun; *to give s.o. a* ~ *of o.'s mind* jdm die *od* s-e Meinung sagen; *to smash to* ~*s* kurz u. klein schlagen; *a nice* ~ *of money* ein schönes Stück Geld.
bitch [bitʃ] *s* Fähe; Hündin; *vulg* Hure *f*; *sl* Gemecker *n*; *itr Am sl mil* meckern, schimpfen; *tr sl* verpfuschen, zs.stümpern; ~ **fox** Füchsin *f*; ~ **wolf** Wölfin *f*.
bit|e [bait] *irr bit, bit(ten) tr* beißen; schneiden; stechen; brennen; durchbohren; verletzen; schnappen; *tech* ätzen, zerfressen, sich hineinfressen (*s.th.* in etw); *(Feile)* angreifen; fassen, packen; *fig* hereinlegen, betrügen; *fig* tief beeindrucken; wirken (*s.th.* auf etw); *itr* (hinein-, zu)beißen (*into, at* in); schnappen (*at s.th.* nach etw); brennen, stechen; *(to* ~~ *into)* sich hineinfressen in; *tech* eingreifen (*in* in); *(Fisch)* anbeißen *a. fig*; *tech* festhalten, fassen; *(Passiv)* hereinfallen, beschwindelt werden; *s* Biß(wunde *f*) *m*; Stich; Bissen; beißende(r) *od* stechende(r) Schmerz; *(Angeln)* Anbiß; Imbiß *m*; *agr* Grünfutter *n*; *tech* Eingreifen, Ätzen, Fassen *n*; *fig* Schärfe, Bitterkeit *f*; *to* ~~ *the dust, ground* ins Gras beißen, daran glauben müssen; *to* ~~ *o.'s lips* sich *(in verhaltener Wut)* auf die Lippen beißen; *to* ~~ *o.'s nails* an den Nägeln kauen; *to* ~~ *off* abbeißen; *to* ~~ *out of* herausbeißen aus; *he has* ~*ten off more than he can chew (fig)* s-e Augen sind größer als sein Mund; ~**er** ['-ə] Schwindler *m*; ~**ing** ['-iŋ] *(Wind, Kälte)* schneidend; *(Speise)* scharf; *fig (Worte)* scharf, beißend, bitter, sarkastisch; ~**ten** *a* durchdrungen, angesteckt (*with* von); verschossen, vernarrt (*with* in); *once* ~~ *twice shy* gebranntes Kind scheut das Feuer; ~**ts** *pl mar* Beting *m od f*.
bitter ['bitə] *a* bitter *a. fig*; *fig* schmerzlich, hart, schwer; erbittert; sarkastisch, scharf, heftig; *(Wind)* scharf, rauh; *(Kälte)* streng, scharf; *poet lit* grimmig; *s* bittere(s) Bier *n*; *pl* Bittere(r), Magenbitter *m*; *to the* ~ *end* bis zum bitteren Ende; ~**ly** ['-li] *adv* bitterlich; ~**n** ['-n] **1.** *chem* Mutterlauge *f*; **2.** *orn* Rohrdommel *f*; ~**ness** ['-nis] Bitterkeit, Herbheit *f*.
bitum|en ['bitjumin] Bitumen, Erdpech *n*; Asphalt *m*; ~~ *cable* Massekabel *n*; ~**inize** [bi'tjuminaiz] *tr* bituminieren, mit Erdpech bestreichen; asphaltieren; ~~*d road* Asphaltstraße *f*; ~**inous** [bi'tju:minəs] *geol (Schiefer)* bituminös; Asphalt-; ~~ *coal* Bituminit *n*, Flamm-, Fettkohle *f*; ~~ *schist* Ölschiefer *m*.
bival|ent ['bai'veilənt] *chem* zweiwertig; ~**ve** ['baivælv] *a bot* zweiklappig; *a* u. *s zoo* zweischalig(e Muschel *f*).
bivouac ['bivuæk] *s mil* Biwak, Feldlager *n*; *itr mil* biwakieren.
biz [biz] *fam (= business)* Geschäft *n*; ~**arre** [bi'zɑ:] bizarr, seltsam, eigenartig, phantastisch, grotesk.

*

blab [blæb] *itr* schwatzen, plappern; *tr* ausplaudern; *s* Schwätzer *m*; Schwätzerei *f*; ~**ber** ['-ə] *itr tr* lallen; gurgeln; plappern.
black [blæk] *a* schwarz; dunkel, düster, finster; trüb(e); schmutzig, dreckig; dunkel(häutig); dunkel-, schwarzgekleidet; *fig* unheimlich, unheilvoll, drohend; ärgerlich, mürrisch; böse, abscheulich; schrecklich, furchtbar, scheußlich; eingefleischt; *(~ as thunder)* wütend; *Am* Neger-; *(~ in the face)* hochrot *(vor Ärger od Anstrengung)*; *s* Schwarz *n*, schwarze Farbe, Schwärze *f*; schwarze(r) Fleck *m*; Rußkörnchen; Schwarz *n*, schwarze(r) Stoff *m*, Trauerkleidung *f*; Schwarze(r *m*) *f (Neger)*; *tr* schwarz machen, schwärzen; *(schwarze Schuhe)* wichsen; *(to ~ out)* verdunkeln; *(Zensur)* streichen; *radio* stören; *itr* schwarz werden; *(to ~ out)* vorübergehend ohnmächtig werden; *in the* ~ bei Kasse; *to give a* ~ *look to s.o.* jdn finster anblikken; *to have s.th. down in* ~ *and white* etw schwarz auf weiß haben; *he is not so* ~ *as he is painted* er ist nicht so schlecht wie sein Ruf; ~**amoor** ['-əmuə] *fam* Mohr, Neger *m*; *the* ~ **art** die Schwarze Kunst, Magie *f*; ~**ball** *parl s* schwarze Kugel; Ablehnung *f*; *tr* dagegen stimmen; *(e-n Kandidaten)* ablehnen; ~~**beetle** *ent fam* Küchenschabe *f*; ~**berry** Brombeere *f*; ~**bird** Amsel, Schwarzdrossel *f*; ~**board** Wandtafel *f*; *to write on the* ~~ an die Tafel schreiben; ~ **book** *fig* schwarze Liste *f*; *to be in o.'s* ~~*s* bei jdm auf der schwarzen Liste stehen; es mit jdm verdorben haben; ~**cap**: ~~ *warbler (orn)* Mönchsgrasmücke *f*; ~~**cock** *orn* Birkhahn *m*; ~ **currant** Schwarze Johannisbeere *f*; ~ **damp** *min* böse(s) Wetter *n*; ~**en** ['-n] *tr* schwarz machen, schwärzen; *fig* anschwärzen, schlecht sprechen von; *itr* schwarz, dunkel werden; ~**eteer** ['-ətiə] *Am* Schwarzhändler *m*; ~ **eye** blaue(s) Auge *n*; *fam* Schandfleck *m*; ~**face** *typ* Fettdruck *m*; ~ **fellow** *(Australien)* Eingeborene(r) *m*; *the* **B~ Forest** der Schwarzwald; ~ **friar** Dominikaner *m*; ~ **game, grouse** *orn* Birkhuhn *n*; ~**guard** ['blægɑ:d] *s* Schuft, Schurke, Lump *m*; *a* schuftig, gemein; *tr* schlecht-, heruntermachen (*s.o.* jdn); ~**head** *med* Mitesser *m*; ~**ing** ['-iŋ] schwarze Schuhkrem, -wichse; *tech* Schwärze *f*; ~**ish** ['-iʃ] schwärzlich; ~**jack** *Am* Totschläger *(Waffe)*; große(r) (Bier-)Krug *m*; ~~**lead** Graphit *n*; ~ **leg** *Br* Streikbrecher; *Am* Falschspieler, Betrüger *m*; Klauenseuche *f*; ~ **letter** *typ* Fraktur *f*; ~*-letter day* Unglückstag *m*; ~ **light** infrarote(s) Licht *n*; ~ **list** schwarze Liste *f*; ~*-list tr* auf die schwarze Liste setzen; ~**mail** *s* Erpressung *f*; erpreßte(s) Geld *n*; *tr* erpressen; ~**mailer** Erpresser *m*; ~ **Maria** [mə'raiə] Grüne Minna *f*, Polizeigefangenenwagen; *mil* dicke(r) Brocken *m*; ~ **mark** *fig* Minuspunkt *m*, schlechte Note *f*; ~ **market** schwarze(r) Markt *m*; ~ **marketeer** Schwarzhändler *m*; **B~ Monday** Unglückstag; *sl* erste(r) Schultag *m* nach den Ferien; ~ **monk** Benediktiner *m*; ~**ness** ['-nis] Schwärze; *fig* Verderbtheit, Schlechtigkeit *f*; ~**out** ['-aut] *s* Verdunk(e)lung; Benommenheit, *fam* Mattscheibe; Bewußtlosigkeit; *(Zensur)* Streichung, Nachrichtensperre *f*; ~ **pudding** Blutwurst *f*; **the B~ Sea** das Schwarze Meer; ~ **sheep** *fig* schwarze(s) Schaf *n*; ~**smith** (Grob-) Schmied *m*; ~**snake** *Am* Natter; geflochtene Lederpeitsche *f*; ~ **spruce** *(amerik.)* Schwarzfichte *f*; ~**thorn** *bot* Schwarzdorn *m*; ~ **widow** *ent* Schwarze Witwe *f*.
bladder ['blædə] *anat* Blase *f a. allg*; *fig* Schaumschläger *m*; *air-, gall-, rubber, swimming-, urinary* ~ Luft-, Gallen-, Gummi-, *(Fische)* Schwimm-, Harnblase *f*; ~ **trouble** Blasenleiden *n*; ~ **worm** *zoo* Finne *f*, Blasenwurm *m*; ~ **wort** *bot* Wasserschlauch *m*.
blade [bleid] *bot* (*bes.* langes, schmales) Blatt *n*; Halm *m*; (Ruder-, Säge-)Blatt *n*; (Turbinen-)Schaufel *f*; (Propeller-) Flügel *m*; *(Messer)* Klinge *f*, Blatt; *(shoulder-~)* (Schulter-)Blatt *n*; *(meist mit a)* (lustiger) Bursche, (netter) Kerl *m*; *in the* ~ *(Getreide)* auf dem Halm.
blah [blɑ:] *fam* Geschwätz, Gewäsch, Gefasel *n*; Unsinn, Quatsch *m*, Blech *n*.
blain [blein] *med* Pustel *f*, Pickel *m*, Stippe *f*.
blam|able ['bleiməbl] tadelnswert; ~**e** [bleim] *tr* tadeln (*for doing* für, wegen); die Schuld geben (*s.o. for s.th., s.th. on s.o.* jdm an e-r S); Vorwürfe machen (*s.th. on s.o.* jdm wegen etw); vorwerfen (*s.th. on s.o.* jdm etw); übelnehmen (*s.o. for doing s.th.* jdm etw); *to be to* ~ *(for)* (die) Schuld (an e-r S) haben; schuld sein an; Tadel verdienen (für); *s* Tadel *m*, Rüge *f*, Verweis *m*; Schuld *f* (*on, for* an); *to bear the* ~ Schuld haben, die S. tragen; *to lay the* ~ *for s.th. on s.o.* jdm die Schuld an e-r S geben; *to take the* ~ *for s.th.* die Schuld für etw auf sich nehmen; ~**ed** *a fam* verflixt; ~**less** ['-lis] untadelig, makellos; ~**lessness** ['-lisnis] Untadeligkeit, Makellosigkeit *f*; ~**worthy** tadelnswert.
blanch [blɑ:ntʃ] *tr* weiß machen, bleichen; *(durch Brühen)* schälen, enthülsen; *(Küche)* blanchieren; *(Metall)* weiß sieden; *(Menschen)* erbleichen lassen; *itr* erbleichen, erblassen, bleich, blaß werden (*with cold, fear* vor Furcht, Kälte); *to* ~ *over (fig)* abschwächen, verharmlosen, beschönigen.
blancmange [blə'mɔnʒ] *(Küche)* Blancmanger *m (milchige Gallerte)*.
bland [blænd] freundlich, umgänglich, angenehm, nett; sanft; einschmeichelnd; *(Klima)* mild; *med* beruhigend; ~**ish** ['-iʃ] *tr* schmeicheln (*s.o.* jdm), liebkosen; ~**ishment** ['-iʃmənt] Schmeichelei; Liebkosung *f*; ~**ness** ['-nis] Freundlichkeit *f*, angenehme(s) Wesen *n*; Sanftmut, Milde *f*.

blank [blæŋk] *a* weiß, leer, unbeschrieben, unausgefüllt; *com* Blanko-; *com* ungedeckt; stumpf, dumpf, ausdruckslos, langweilig; vergeblich, ergebnislos; ereignislos, inhaltleer; unfruchtbar, unergiebig; einfallslos; verblüfft, bestürzt; bloß, rein; völlig, vollständig; *(Absage)* unmißverständlich; *(Schweigen)* tief; *poet* reimlos; *s (Buch, Blatt Papier)* leere Stelle *f*, freie(r) Raum *m*; unbeschriebene(s) Blatt (Papier); *Am* Formblatt, Formular *n* zum Ausfüllen, Vordruck; Gedankenstrich *m (für ein Schimpfwort)*; (Sprech-)Pause *f*; *(Zielscheibe) das* Schwarze; Ziel *n*; *allg* Lücke, Leere, Unausgefülltheit; *mil(~cartridge)* Platzpatrone; Niete *f (Lotterielos)*; *typ* Durchschuß; *tech* Rohling, Preßling *m*; *tech* Stanzstück *n*; Münzplatte *f*; *tr tech* stanzen; *Am sport (den Gegner)* zu keinem Pluspunkt kommen lassen, haushoch schlagen; *to ~ out* verbergen, verdecken; ausstreichen; *tech* ausstanzen; *video* austasten; *to draw a ~* e-e Niete ziehen; *fam fig* Pech haben; *to fill out a ~ (Am)* ein Formular ausfüllen; *to fill in the ~s* die leeren Stellen ausfüllen; *(drawn) in ~ (com)* blanko; *~* **cheque,** *Am* **check** Blankoscheck *m*; Scheckformular *n*; *fig* freie Hand *f*; **~et** ['blæŋkit] *s* (Woll-, wollene) Decke *f a. allg*; *typ* Druckfilz *m*, -tuch *n*; *mil* Nebelwand *f*; *a* allgemein, umfassend; Gesamt-, General-; *tr* be-, über-, zudecken; *(Vorschriften)* er-, umfassen; einnebeln, abschirmen; *radio* stören; *mar* den Wind abfangen *dat*; *fig Am* den Wind aus den Segeln nehmen; *fig* vertusche(l)n, verheimlichen; *wet ~~* kalte Dusche *f*, Dämpfer; Spiel-, Spaßverderber *m*; *~~ clause* Generalklausel *f*; *~~ insurance* Kollektivversicherung *f*; *~~ of snow* Schneedecke *f*; *~~ travel order (mil)* allgemeine Reisegenehmigung *f*; **~eting** ['blæŋkitiŋ] *radio* Störung, Überlagerung, Überdeckung *f*; *~~smoke (mil)* Tarnnebel *m*; *~* **form** unausgefüllte(s) Formular *n*, Vordruck *m*; **~ing** ['-iŋ] *video* Austasten; *tech* Schneiden *n*; *~~ tool* Stanzwerkzeug *n*; *~* **policy** Generalpolice *f*; *~* **signature** Blankounterschrift *f*; *~* **space** freie(r) Raum *m*, freigelassene Stelle *f*; *~* **verse** Blankvers *m*; *~* **voting paper** leere(r) Stimmzettel *m*; *to return a ~~* e-n leeren Stimmzettel abgeben.

blare [blɛə] *tr itr (Trompete)* schmettern; grölen; *fig* laut verkünden; *s* Schmettern *n*; Lärm *m*.

blarney ['blɑ:ni] *s* Schmeichelei *f*; *tr itr* schmeicheln (*s.o.* jdm).

blasphem|e [blæs'fi:m] *tr (Gott)* lästern; schmähen, schimpfen (*s.o.* über jdn); *itr* fluchen; lästern (*against* gegen); **~er** [-ə] (Gottes-)Lästerer *m*; Lästermaul *n*; **~ous** ['-fiməs] *(Mensch)* lästernd; *(Rede)* lästerlich; **~y** ['-fimi] Gotteslästerung *f*; Fluchen *n*.

blast [blɑ:st] (plötzlicher, heftiger) Windstoß, Luftzug; heiße(r), sengende(r) Wind *m*; *tech* Gebläse *n*; *(~ air)* Gebläsewind; Preßluftstrom; Knall, Luftdruck *m*, Druckwelle, Explosion; Sprengladung *f*; Trompetenstoß *m*; Hornsignal *n*; *bot* Brand, Meltau; *fig* verderbliche(r) Einfluß *m*; *tr (in heißer Luft)* verbrennen; versengen, verdorren, erfrieren lassen; vernichten; sprengen; *fig* zum Schwinden bringen; verderben, ruinieren; *itr* welken, zugrunde gehen; *in ~ (Hochofen, a. allg tech)* in Betrieb; *in, at full ~* in vollem Betrieb *od* Gange, auf vollen Touren, auf Hochtour *a. fig*; *out of ~* außer Betrieb; *to be ~ed (fig)* (dahin-)schwinden, vergehen; *to be going full ~* auf Hochtouren laufen; *~ it!* verflucht! *~* **box** *tech* Windkessel *m*; **~ed** ['-id] *a* verflixt, verdammt; *~* **effect** Luftdruckwirkung *f*; **~er** ['-ə] Sprengmeister *m*; *~* **flame** Stichflamme *f*; *~* **furnace** Hochofen *m*; *~~ gas* Gichtgas *n*; **~ing** ['-iŋ] Sprengung; *radio* Verzerrung *f*; *fig* Verderben *n*; *danger! ~~ in progress!* Achtung! Sprengarbeiten! *~~ charge* Bohr-, Sprengladung *f*; **~oderm** ['blæstodə:m] *anat* Keimhaut *f*; **~-off** *(Rakete)* Abschuß *m*; **~-pipe** *tech* Windleitung *f*; *~* **wave** (Luft-)Druckwelle *f*.

blat [blæt] *fam itr* blöken; *tr (to ~ out)* ausplaudern; **~ancy** ['bleitənsi] lärmende(s) Benehmen *n*; *das* Auffallende; **~ant** ['bleitənt] geräuschvoll, laut; aufdringlich; *(Unrecht)* kraß, schreiend, offensichtlich.

blather ['blæðə] *s* törichte(s) Gerede *n*; *tr itr* (dummes Zeug) reden; **~skite** ['-skait] *fam* Schwätzer *m*.

blaz|e [bleiz] **1.** *s* (helle, lodernde) Flamme, Glut, Lohe *f*; Feuer *n*, Brand; helle(r) Schein; (Lichter-)Glanz *m (~~ of light)*; (Farben-)Pracht *f (~~ of colour)*; *fig* Ausbruch, Anfall *m*, Auflodern *n*; *pl* Hölle *f*; *itr* flammen, lodern; glänzen, leuchten, strahlen; *fig* wütend *od* Feuer u. Flamme sein; loslegen; *(Augen)* aufflammen; *in a ~~ of publicity* im Scheinwerferlicht der Öffentlichkeit; *(to be) in a ~~* in Flammen (stehen); *to be ~ing with fury* vor Zorn funkeln; *to ~~ away (mil)* Feuer geben, feuern (*at* gegen); *fig* loslegen (*at* gegen); herangehen (*at* an); *to ~~ up* auflodern, entflammen; *fig* in Zorn geraten; **2.** *s (Pferd, Rind)* Blesse *(weißer Stirnfleck)*; *(Baum)* Markierung; Wegmarke *f*, Schalm *m (Ausschnitt in der Rinde)*; *tr (Baum)* markieren; *(Weg)* bezeichnen; *to ~~ a trail* e-n Weg bezeichnen; *fig* Pionierarbeit leisten; **3.** *tr* ausposaunen; **~er** ['-ə] leichte, farbige Sportjacke *f*; *fam* strahlende(r) Tag *m*; **~ing** ['-iŋ] hell, lodernd; offenkundig; *(Fährte)* warm; *fam* verflucht; *in the ~~ sun* in der prallen Sonne; *~~ hot* glühend heiß; *~~ star* Phänomen *n (Person)*.

blazon ['bleizn] *s* Wappen, Banner *n*; aufwendige Darstellung *f*; *tr* verzieren, ausmalen; prächtig gestalten; (in) glänzend(en Farben) schildern; *(to ~ out, forth, abroad)* ausposaunen; **~ry** ['-ri] Wappen(kunde *f*) *n pl*, Heraldik *f*; Farben *f pl*; Prachtentfaltung, prächtige Schau *f*.

bleach [bli:tʃ] *s* Bleichen; Bleichmittel *n*; Chlorlauge *f*; *tr* bleichen; *itr* verbleichen; **~er** ['-ə] Bleicher(in *f*); Bleichkessel *m*; Bleichmittel *n*; *pl Am sport* Zuschauersitze *m pl (im Freien)*; **~ing** ['-iŋ] Bleichen *n*; *~~-powder* Chlor-, Bleichkalk *m*; *~~ resistance* Farb-, Waschechtheit *f*.

bleak [bli:k] *a* bleich; kahl, öde; kalt, rauh; *fig* unfreundlich, trostlos, niederdrückend; *s zoo* Weißfisch *m*.

blear [bliə] *tr* trüb(e), unscharf, undeutlich, verschwommen machen; *a* trüb(e); **~-eyed** ['-raid] *a* triefäugig; *fig* einfältig; **~y** ['-ri] trübe; *(Bild)* verschwommen.

bleat [bli:t] *itr (Schaf)* blöken; *(Ziege)* meckern; *(Kalb)* schreien; *tr* weinerlich sagen; *s* Blöken, Meckern, Schreien *n*.

bleb [bleb] Bläschen *n*; Pustel *f*.

bleed [bli:d] *irr bled, bled itr* bluten; *bot* Saft verlieren; *fig* Geld lassen müssen; *(Herz)* bluten, wehtun; *tr* zur Ader lassen (*s.o.* jdn); *(Bremse)* entlüften; *(Blut, Saft)* abzapfen; entnehmen; *(Flüssigkeit)* ausfließen lassen; entleeren; *fig (finanziell)* schröpfen; *(to ~ off) el* abführen; *to ~ to death* verbluten; *to ~ white (fig)* zum Weißbluten bringen; **~er** ['-ə] *med* Bluter; *sl* Schmarotzer; *tech* Muster-, Ölstandshahn; *el* Entladewiderstand *m*; **~ing** ['-iŋ] *a* blutend; mitleidig; *sl* verflixt; *s* Bluten *n*, Blutung *f*; Aderlaß *m*; *tech* Entnehmen, Anzapfen, Ablassen, Entlüften, Auslaufen *n*; *~~ heart (bot)* Tränende(s) Herz *n*.

bleep [bli:p] *s* Sputnik(funksignal *n*) *m*; *itr (Sputnik)* funken.

blemish ['blemiʃ] *s* Fehler, Mangel, Makel, Defekt; *fig* (Schand-)Fleck *m*; *tr* entstellen, verunstalten, beschmutzen, beflecken; *without ~* untadelig, makellos, fehlerfrei.

blench [blentʃ] **1.** *itr* zurückschrecken, -fahren, ausweichen; *tr fig* die Augen schließen vor; **2.** *itr* bleich werden; *tr* bleichen.

blend [blend] *a. irr blent, blent tr (Tee, Kaffee, Tabak)* mischen; (ver)mengen; *(Wein, Spirituosen)* verschneiden; übergehen lassen (*into* in); *itr* sich (ver)mischen (*with* mit); *(bes. Farben)* inea. übergehen; zs.laufen; zs.passen, harmonieren (*with* mit); *s* Mischung *f*; *(Wein, Spirituosen)* Verschnitt *m*; **~e** [-] *min* Blende *f*.

bless [bles] *poet a irr blest, blest tr* segnen; das Kreuzeszeichen machen (*s.o.* über jdm); (lob)preisen; beglückwünschen; beglücken (*with* mit); *to ~ o.s.* sich glücklich preisen; *to be ~ed with* gesegnet sein mit *(bes. iro)*; *~ me, ~ my soul, I'm blest* verflixt! *I'm blest if* der Teufel soll mich holen, wenn; **~ed,** *poet* **blest** ['blesid, blest] *a* gesegnet, (glück)selig, gnadenvoll, -reich; glücklich; glückbringend, glück-, freudespendend; *(euphemistisch)* verdammt, verflucht, verflixt; *the ~~ (rel)* die Seligen; *the Isles of the Blest* die Inseln *f pl* der Seligen; *the B~~ Virgin* die Heilige Jungfrau; **~edness** ['-idnis] Segen(sspruch) *m*; Glück(seligkeit *f*) *n*; **~ing** ['-iŋ] Segen *m*; Gnade *f a. fig* (*to* für); Tischgebet *n*; Gottessegen *m*, wahre Wohltat *f*, Glück *n*; *iro* Fluch *m*; *~~ in disguise* Glück *n* im Unglück.

blether ['bleðə] *s. blather*.

blight [blait] *s bot* Brand, Meltau; Dunst *m*, feuchte, ungesunde Luft *f*; *allg* Gifthauch; schädliche(r) Einfluß *m*; *tr fig* enttäuschen, vereiteln, zunichte machen; **~er** ['-ə] Schädling; *sl* Ekel *n*; *sl* Kerl *m*; **~ing** ['-iŋ] schädlich; vernichtend; **~y** ['-i] *mil sl* Heimat(urlaub, -schuß *m*) *f*.

blimey ['blaimi] *interj sl* verdammt und zugenäht!

blimp [blimp] **1.** (unstarres) Kleinluftschiff *n*; **2.** *(Colonel B~)* Stockkonservative(r) *m*.

blind [blaind] *a* blind *a. fig* (*to* für); *fig* uneinsichtig, verständnislos (*to* gegenüber); planlos; sinnlos, unüberlegt; ohne Öffnung *od* Ausgang; *(Kurve)* unübersichtlich; *(Tür, Fenster)* ver-, zugemauert; undeutlich, schwer lesbar; *(Winkel)* tot; verdeckt, unsichtbar; *mil* getarnt; *(Brief)* unzustellbar; *bot* taub, ohne Blüte; *adv sl (~ drunk, ~ to the world)* sinnlos besoffen; *s* Blende *f*; Rouleau *n*, Rolljalousie, Markise; *(Pferd)* Scheuklappe *f*; *fig* Vorwand *m*, Ausrede *f*; *mil* Blindgänger; Deckname *m*; Tarnung *f*; Lockspitzel *m*; Versteck *n*; Hinterhalt *m*; Gelage *n*; *pl die* Blinden *m pl*; *tr* blind machen (*to* für); blenden; *fig* verblenden; verdunkeln; verbergen; *itr aero* blindfliegen; *sl* blind drauflos, rücksichtslos fahren; *to be ~ of, in one eye* auf e-m Auge blind sein; *to turn a* od *o.'s ~ eye to s.th.* so tun, als sähe man etw nicht; beide Augen zudrücken; **~ alley** Sackgasse *f a. fig*; *fig* tote(s) Geleise *n*; *that's leading up a ~~* das führt in e-e Sackgasse *f*; **~ approach beacon system** (= BABS) Blindlandeverfahren *n*; **~ bombing** Blindabwurf *m*; **~ coal** Glanzkohle, Anthrazit *m*; **~er** ['-ə] *Am* Scheuklappe *f*; **~ flying** *aero* Blind-, Instrumentenflug *m*; *~-flying equipment* Blindfluggerät *n*; **~fold** ['-fould] *tr* die Augen verbinden (*s.o.* jdm); *fig* irreführen, blenden; *a adv* mit verbundenen Augen; *fig* rücksichtslos; blindlings; **~ing** ['-iŋ] *opt* Blenden; *(Straßenbau)* Abdecken, Absplitten; *(Sieb)* Verstopfen *n*; *(~~ sand)* Walzsand *m*; **~ landing** *aero* Blindlandung *f*; **~ly** ['-li] *adv* blind; blindlings, unbesonnen; **~ man** Blinde(r) *m*; *~~'s buff* Blindekuh(spiel *n*) *f*; **~ness** ['-nis] Blindheit *f a. fig* (*to* gegen) **~ side** schwache Seite *f*, wunde(r) Punkt *m*; **~ spot** *mil aero* tote(r) Winkel; Totpunkt *m*; *radio* tote Zone *f*; *anat* blinde(r) Fleck; *fig* wunde(r) Punkt *m*; **~ take-off** *aero* Blindstart *m*; **~ window** *arch* Blendnische *f*; **~-worm** *zoo* Blindschleiche *f*.

blink [bliŋk] *tr itr* blinzeln, zwinkern (*o.'s eyes* mit den Augen; *at the light* in das Licht); *(Licht, Stern)* blinken; flackern; *(Licht)* schnell ein- u. ausschalten; *(Milch)* sauer werden; *fig* nicht sehen wollen, übergehen (*at s.th.* e-e S); *s* Aufleuchten, -blitzen *n*; Blick; Augenblick *m*; Blinzeln *n*; *on the ~ (sl)* in Unordnung; **~er** ['-ə] Scheuklappe; *(~~ lamp)* Blinklampe *f*; *sl* Auge *n*; *pl* Schutzbrille *f*; *~~ light* Blinkfeuer, Flackerlicht *n*; **~ing** ['-iŋ] *a* blinzelnd, blinkend; *sl* verflixt, verdammt; *sl* dämlich.

blip [blip] *itr mot* ständig Gas geben u. wieder wegnehmen; *s* Leucht-, Echozeichen *n (auf d. Radarschirm)*.

bliss [blis] große Freude, Wonne, (Glück-)Seligkeit *f*; **~ful** ['-ful] (glück-)selig, überglücklich; **~fulness** ['-fulnis] Wonne, Seligkeit *f*.

blister ['blistə] *s med* Blase; *allg* Blase *f*, Bläschen *n*; *fam* widerliche(r) Kerl; *aero sl* Bordwaffenstand *m*; *pharm* blasenziehende(s) Mittel; Zugpflaster *n*; *attr* Blasen hervorrufend, ätzend; *tr* Blasen ziehen auf; *fig* die Hölle heiß machen (*s.o. with* jdm mit); scharf kritisieren; auf die Nerven fallen (*s.o.* jdm); *itr* Blasen bekommen, *tech* werfen; abblättern.

blithe [blaið], *a.* **~some** *meist poet* heiter, froh, fröhlich, lustig; **~ring** ['bliðəriŋ] *a fam* schwatzhaft, geschwätzig; voll(kommen), völlig, komplett, total; blöde, dämlich; *a ~~ idiot* ein Vollidiot.

blitz [blits] *s* schwere(s) Bombardement *n*, heftige(r) Luftangriff; Blitzkrieg *m*; *tr* heftig bombardieren; vernichten; *~ed town* zerbombte Stadt *f*.

blizzard ['blizəd] Schneesturm *m*.

*

bloat [blout] *tr* aufblähen, aufschwellen, dick machen; *(Hering)* salzen u. räuchern; *fig* eingebildet machen; *itr* dick werden; (an)schwellen, auflaufen; *s Am sl* Kerl, Betrunkene(r) *m*; *vet* Blähung *f*; **~ed** ['-id] *a* aufgebläht, (an)geschwollen, aufgedunsen (*with* mit); *fig* übertrieben; aufgeblasen, dünkelhaft; (schnell) reich geworden; **~er** ['-ə] Bückling *m*.

blob [blɔb] *s* Tropfen *m*, Klümpchen, Kügelchen *n*; (Farb-)Fleck, Spritzer *m*; *itr* klecksen; **~ber** ['-ə]: *~~-lipped (a)* mit wulstigen Lippen.

bloc [blɔk] *parl* (Regierungs-)Block; *pol* (Staaten-)Block *m*; *sterling ~* Sterling-Block *m*.

block [blɔk] *s* (Holz-)Klotz; (Stein-, Fels-)Block; (Baum-)Stumpf; Hack-, Hauklotz; Richtblock; Bremsklotz *m*; *Br* (großes) Gebäude *n*, Bau *m*; Baugruppe *f*; *Am* Häuserblock *m*; *(Formular)* Feld *n*; *(writing ~)* Schreibblock *m*; *(Australien)* elegante Promenade *f*; (Verkehrs-)Hindernis *n*, Sperre, Stokkung, Verstopfung; *parl* Obstruktion *f*; *(Aktien)* Paket *n*, Partie *f*; *tech* Flaschenzug, Rollenkloben; Mauerblock *m*; *rail* Blockstrecke *f*; *typ* (Druck-)Stock *m*, Klischee *n*; Führungs-, Farbstein *m*; *mil* geballte Ladung *f*; *(Spielzeug)* Bauklotz *m*; Hutform *f*; *fig* Block *m*, geschlossene Gruppe *f*, Satz *m*; Siedlerstelle *f*; Dummkopf; hartherzige(r) Mensch; *sl* Kopf *m*; *tr* zu Blöcken verarbeiten; blockieren, einschließen, verstopfen, aufhalten, (ver)sperren *a. fig*, hemmen; *(to ~ off)* ver-, abriegeln; *chem* abbinden; *typ* aufklotzen; *(Hut)* pressen, formen; *parl* Obstruktion treiben gegen, verschleppen; *(Ball)* abfangen; *a* blockförmig; umfassend, gesamt; ohne Unterteilung; *on the ~* zur Versteigerung, zum Verkauf; *to go, to be sent to the ~ (hist)* das Schafott besteigen; *com* versteigert werden; *to put on ~* aufbocken; *to ~ off* abschirmen, absperren; *to ~ out, in* skizzieren, entwerfen; über den Daumen peilen; *to ~ up* einsperren; zumauern; versperren; *a chip of the old ~ (Kind)* ganz der Vater, der ganze Vater; *date-~* Notizblock *m*; *erratic ~* Findling, erratische(r) Block *m*; *traffic ~* Verkehrsstauung *f*; *~ of flats* Mietskaserne *f*; *~ of stone* Steinblock *m*; *~ of wood* Holzklotz *m*; **~ade** [blɔ'keid] *s mar* Blockade; Verkehrssperre, -verstopfung *f*; *tr* blockieren, (ver)sperren; *to impose, to raise, to run the ~~* e-e Blockade verhängen, aufheben, brechen; *economic ~~* Wirtschaftsblockade *f*; *~~-runner* Blokkadebrecher *m*; **~age** ['-idʒ] Blokkierung *f*; **~ antenna** Gemeinschaftsantenne *f*; **~ brake** Backenbremse *f*; **~-buster** Luftmine *f*; **~head** Dummkopf, Esel *m*; **~house** Blockhaus *n*; **~ing** ['-iŋ] Blockierung, Sperrung *f*; Festklemmen *n*; Block-, Sperr-; *~~ condenser* Blockkondensator *m*; *~~ effect (Wetter)* Stauwirkung *f*; *~~ layer* Sperrschicht *f*; *~~ position (mil)* Riegelstellung *f*; **~ish** ['-iʃ] blockförmig; *fig* dumm; schwerfällig; **~ lava** Schollenlava *f*; **~ letters** *pl* Blockschrift *f*; **~-making** *typ* Klischieren *n*; **~-pavement** *Am* Steinpflaster *n*, Pflasterung *f*; **~ printing** *typ* Holz-, Handdruck *m*; **~ section, signal, station, system** *rail* Blockabschnitt *m*, -signal *n*, -stelle *f*, -system *n*.

bloke [blouk] *sl* Kerl, Bursche *m*.

blond *m*, **blonde** *f* [blɔnd] *a* blond; *s* blonde(r) Mann *m*; Blondine *f*; *(~-lace)* Blonde, Seidenspitze *f*; **~ine(d)** [-'din(d)] *a Am* blondiert.

blood [blʌd] *s* Blut *a. fig*; Blutvergießen *n*, Mord *m*; Abstammung, Herkunft, Geburt *f*, Geblüt *n*; Verwandtschaft, Familie; Rasse; Leidenschaft *f*; Temperament, Gefühl; Leben *n*; *fig* (Trauben-)Saft *m*, Blut *n*; Draufgänger; Stutzer *m*; *(full-~)* Vollblut (-pferd) *n*; *in cold ~* kaltblütig; *in hot ~* im Zorn; *to make bad ~ between* gegenea. aufbringen, Unfrieden stiften zwischen; *my ~ ran cold, froze* ich war starr vor Schrecken; *his ~ was up* er war sehr erregt; *it made my ~ boil* ich kochte vor Wut; *blue ~* blaue(s) Blut *n*; *circulation of the ~* Blutkreislauf *m*; *flesh and ~* ein Mensch, die menschliche Natur; *my own flesh and ~* mein eigenes Fleisch u. Blut; *full-~ (attr)* Vollblut-; *loss of ~* Blutverlust *m*; *prince of the ~ (royal)* Prinz *m* von königlichem Geblüt; **~ bank** *med* Blutbank *f*; **~ brother** Blutsbruder *m*; **~ clot** Blutgerinnsel *n*; **~ count** Blutbild *n*; **~-curdling** haarsträubend; **~-donor** Blutspender *m*; **~ed** ['-id] *a* blütig; *(full-~~)* reinrassig, vollblütig; **~ feud** *hist* offene Fehde *f*; **~ group** *biol* Blutgruppe *f*; **~-guilt(iness)** Blutschuld *f*; **~-guilty** blutbefleckt, mit Blutschuld beladen; **~-heat** Körpertemperatur *f*; **~-horse** Vollblutpferd *n*; **~ hound** Bluthund, Bullenbeißer; *sl* Detektiv *m*; **~less** ['-lis] blutleer; bleich; gefühllos; schwunglos; unblutig; **~-letting** Aderlaß *m*; **~mobile** fahrbare Blutbank *f*; **~-money** Blutgeld *n*; **~ orange** Blutorange *f*; **~ plasma** Blutflüssigkeit *f*; **~-poisoning** Blutvergiftung *f*; **~-pressure** Blutdruck *m*; **~-pudding** Blutwurst *f*; **~-red** blutrot; **~-relation** Blutsverwandte(r *m*) *f*; **~ revenge** Blutrache *f*; **~shed** Blutvergießen *n*; **~shot** *a* blutunterlaufen; **~-stain** Blutfleck *m*, -spuren *f pl*; **~-stained** *a* blutbefleckt *a. fig*; **~stock** Vollblutpferde *n pl*; **~stone** *min* Blutjaspis, Heliotrop; Roteisenstein *m*; **~-sucker** *zoo u. fig (Mensch)* Blutsauger *m*; **~ sugar** Blutzucker *m*; **~test** Blutprobe, -untersuchung *f*; **~-thirstiness** Blutdurst *m*; **~-thirsty** blutdurstig; **~ transfusion** Blutübertragung *f*; **~-vessel** *anat* Blutgefäß *n*; **~wort** *bot* Blutwurz *f*; **~y** ['-i] *a* blutig, blutend; *(~-minded)* blutdürstig, -rünstig, grausam; *vulg* verdammt, verflucht, Scheiß-; *adv vulg* sehr.

bloom [blu:m] *s* Blüte *f a. fig*; Flaum, Reif *(auf Früchten)*; Hauch *m* der Frische *(auf den Wangen)*, Schmelz *m*; *tech* Luppe *f*, Deul *m*; Bramme *f*; *itr* blühen *a. fig*, in Blüte stehen; *tr tech* vorhämmern, -walzen; *(die Luppen)* auswalzen; vergüten; *in (full) ~* in (voller) Blüte; *in the ~ of youth* in der Blüte der Jugend; **~er** ['-ə] Blütenpflanze *f*; *sl* Bock, Schnitzer *m*; **~ery** ['-əri] *tech* Luppen-, Rennfeuer *n*; **~ers** ['-əz] *pl Am* Schlüpfer *m*; **~ing** ['-iŋ] *a* blühend *a. fig*; *sl* verflixt, verteufelt; *s tech* Vorwalzen *n*; Vergütung *f*; *~~ mill* Block-, Grobwalzwerk *n*; *~~ train* Vorstraße *f*; **~y** ['-i] blühend; flaumbedeckt.

blossom ['blɔsəm] *s* (*bes.* Baum-) Blüte *f*; *itr* zur Blüte kommen, aufblühen; blühen; *(to ~ out into) fig* erblühen, sich entwickeln, sich entfalten zu, sich herausmachen; *(Fallschirm) sl* sich öffnen; **~y** ['-i] blühend *a. fig*; voller Blüten.

blot [blɔt] *s* Fleck, Klecks *m*; ausradierte Stelle *f*; *fig* Makel, Schandfleck; Mangel *m*, Schwäche *f*; *(ink ~)* Tintenklecks *m*; *tr* e-n Fleck, Klecks machen (*s.th.* auf etw); *(Papier)* beschmieren, besudeln; *typ* unsauber abziehen; *(Ehre)* beflecken; *(to ~ out)* (aus)streichen, ausradieren; verbergen, -decken, -sperren; (aus)tilgen, aufheben, vernichten; auslöschen; wegnehmen; *(to ~ up)* (ab)löschen, *(Tinte)* aufsaugen; *itr (Tinte, Feder)* klecksen; mit Flecken bedeckt werden; aufsaugen; **~ch** [blɔtʃ] *s* große(r)

(Tinten-)Klecks; (Farb-)Fleck; *med* Pickel *m*, Stippe *f*; *tr* beflecken; **~chy** ['blɔtʃi] fleckig; **~ter** ['-ə] Löschblatt *n*; Löscher *m*; *Am* Eintrags-, Wachbuch *n*; *Am* Kladde *f*; **~ting** ['-iŋ]: *~~-book* Block *m* Löschpapier; Kladde *f*; *~~-pad* Schreibunterlage *f* (mit Löschblatt); *~~-paper* Löschpapier *n*; **~to** ['-ou] *sl* besoffen.

blouse [blauz] Bluse; *mil* Feldbluse *f*; (Arbeits-)Kittel *m*.

blow [blou] **1.** *v irr blew, blown itr (Wind)* wehen, blasen, pfeifen; stürmen; *(im Wind)* wegfliegen; weggetrieben, -gefegt werden; *(Blasinstrument)* blasen, ertönen; heftig atmen, keuchen, *fam* aus der Puste sein; *(Wal)* Luft ausstoßen; *(Fliegen)* Eier legen; *el (Sicherung)* durchbrennen; *sl Am* angeben, große Bogen spucken; *sl* abhauen, verduften; *tr* blasen, wehen, fegen; in die Luft blasen; *(Feuer)* anblasen, anfachen; *(Röhre)* aus-, hindurchblasen; *(Blasebalg, Bälge der Orgel)* treten; aufblähen; *mus (Instrument)* blasen; *s.th. on, with an instrument* etw auf e-m Instrument blasen; *(Nachricht)* ausposaunen, verbreiten, veröffentlichen; *(Fliege)* beschmeißen; *(Sicherung)* durchbrennen; *sl* beschwindeln, anführen; *sl* verfluchen, verdammen *(pp: blowed)*; *sl (Geld)* zum Fenster hinauswerfen *fig*; *Am sl (mit gutem Essen)* traktieren; *o.s.* sich etw Gutes gönnen *od* leisten; *sl* sitzen lassen, im Stich lassen; *s* frische (Atem-)Luft *f*, Lufthauch, -zug; Windstoß, Sturm; Atemzug, *fam* Schnaufer *m*; Blasen, Schnauben, Schnupfen *n*; *fig* Prahlerei *f*; *sl* Angeber *m*, Großmaul *n*; *to have, to go for a ~* an die (frische) Luft gehen, *fam* Luft schnappen; *to ~ down, over (Sturm)* umwerfen; *to ~ the horn (mot)* hupen; *to ~ hot and cold* nicht wissen, was man will; *to ~ in (sl) (Mensch)* hereinstürmen, -schneien; sein ganzes Geld vertun; *(e-e Tür)* eindrücken; *to ~ o.'s nose* sich die Nase putzen; *to ~ off, away (itr) (im Winde)* wegfliegen; *tr* wegwehen, -blasen, -fegen; *to ~ off (tr) (Gas)* ablassen; abblasen; *itr Am sl* Schluß machen, es aufgeben; *to ~ the lid off (Am sl)* den Schleier fallen lassen; *to ~ off steam* sich abreagieren, sich austoben; *to ~ out (itr el) (Sicherung)* durchbrennen; *(Reifen)* platzen; *(Dampf)* ausströmen; *(Maschine)* versagen; *tr (Kerze, Streichholz)* ausblasen; *to ~ out o.'s brains* jdm, *meist* sich e-e Kugel durch den Kopf jagen; *to ~ over* vorbei-, vorübergehen; aus dem Gedächtnis verschwinden; *to ~ taps* den Zapfenstreich blasen; *to ~ o.'s (own) top* in die Höhe gehen, aufbrausen, in Zorn geraten; *to ~ o.'s own trumpet* sein eigenes Lob singen; *to ~ up (tr)* aufblasen, -pumpen; sprengen, in die Luft jagen; *phot* vergrößern; *itr* explodieren, in die Luft fliegen; *fig* in die Höhe gehen, wild werden; *(Sturm)* stärker werden; *fam* herunterlaufen lassen; *to ~ upon s.th. (fig)* auf etw pfeifen; *s.o.* jdn verpfeifen; *to be ~n upon* ramponiert werden; *to ~ a whistle* pfeifen; *~ it!* verdammt noch mal! *~ the expense!* egal was es kostet! **2.** *itr* (auf-, er)blühen; *a. fig*; *in full ~* in voller Blüte; **3.** *s* Schlag, Hieb, Streich, Stoß; *fig* (harter, schwerer) Schlag *m* (*to* für); *at a, one ~* auf einen Schlag, auf einmal; *without striking a ~* ohne e-n Schwertstreich, kampflos *adv*; *to come to ~s* handgemein werden, sich in die Haare geraten; *to exchange ~s* sich in den Haaren liegen; *to strike a ~* e-n Schlag führen (*at* gegen); *for s.o.* für jdn e-e Lanze brechen, sich für jdn einsetzen; **~back** *(Feuerwaffe)* Rückstoß, Gasdruck *m*; **~ball** *(Löwenzahn)* Pusteblume *f*; **~er** ['-ə] Bläser *m*; Gebläse *n*; Lüfter; *mot* Vorverdichter *m*; *(Ofen, Kamin)* Schiebeblech *n*; *aero* Lader; *sl* Telephon, Radio *n*; **~fly** Schmeißfliege *f*, Brummer *m*; **~gun** Spritzpistole *f*; Blasrohr *n*; **~-hard** *sl* Großschnauze *f*; **~hole** *(Wal)* Nasen-, Spritzloch; Luftloch *n*; *tech* Gas-, Gußblase *f*; Fehler *m*, **~ing** ['-iŋ] *(Sicherung)* Ab-, Durchschmelzen *n*; Frischung *f*; **~lamp** Lötlampe *f*; **~n** [-n] *a* aufgeblasen *a. fig*; außer Atem, atemlos; *tech* blasig; *(Sicherung)* durchgebrannt; verdorben, schal; **~-off** *(Dampf)* Ablassen *n*; *(~~ cock)* Ablaßhahn *m*, Luftventil *n*; *sl* Angeber, aufgeblasene(r) Mensch *m*; **~-out** *el* Durchbrennen, Durchschmelzen *n*; *Am* Reifenpanne *f*, Plattfuß *m*; *sl* Fresserei, Festivität *f*; **~pipe** Lötrohr *n*, Schweißbrenner *m*; Blasrohr; *mil sl* Düsenflugzeug *n*; **~post** Rohrpost *f*; **~torch** *Am* Lötlampe *f*; **~-up** Explosion *f*; *fam* Zornesausbruch, Anfall *m*; *phot* Vergrößerung *f*; *fam* ausgearbeitete(r) Plan *m*; **~wash** Düsenabgas *n*; **~y** ['-i] *tech* blasig; windig, luftig.

blowzy ['blauzi] *(meist von Frauen)* unordentlich, schlampig, schmutzig, schmudd(e)lig.

blubber ['blʌbə] *s* Speck von Walen *od* Robben; Wal-, Fischtran *m*; *zoo* Meduse, Qualle *f*; *a (Lippen)* schwulstig; *(Backen)* an-, aufgeschwollen; gedunsen; *tr* unter Tränen, Schluchzen sagen;

bludgeon ['blʌdʒən] *s* Knüppel *m*; *tr* (ver)prügeln; bedrohen, tyrannisieren; zwingen (*into doing s.th.* etw zu tun).

blue [blu:] *a* blau; *(Haut)* leichen-, bleifarben, fahl; *fig* ängstlich, angstvoll, besorgt; verstimmt; trübsinnig, schwermütig, niedergeschlagen; unanständig, zweideutig; *Am* puritanisch, streng; *s* Blau *n*; blaue Farbe *f*; Wäscheblau *n*; Himmel *m*; Meer *n*, See *f*; *pol* Konservative(r) *m*; *(~ stocking)* Blaustrumpf *m*; *the ~s (Am) (~ devils)* Trübsinn *m*, Schwermut *f*; Blues *m (mod. Tanz)*; *tr* blau färben; mit Waschblau behandeln; *sl (Geld)* verprassen; *itr* blau werden; *like ~ murder (fam)* wie der Wind, im Nu; *once in a ~ moon* alle Jubeljahre (einmal); *out of the ~* aus heiterem Himmel, unerwartet; *to be in the ~s (Am)* Trübsal blasen; *to look ~* ein trübseliges Gesicht machen; *a bolt from the ~ (fig)* ein Blitz aus heiterem Himmel; *dark, light ~* dunkel-, hellblau; *dark ~s and light ~s* Mannschaften *f pl* von Oxford und Cambridge; *Navy, Prussian ~* Marine-, Preußischblau *n*; *true ~* treu; **B~beard** Blaubart *m*; **~bell** *(Schottland)* blaue Glockenblume *f*; **~berry** Blau-, Heidelbeere *f*; **~-black** blauschwarz; **~ blood** blaue(s) Blut *n*; *~-blooded (a)* blaublütig; **~-book** *pol* Blaubuch; Register *n* der Regierungsbeamten der USA; *Am* Liste *f* der Prominenz; *Am* Heft *n* für Examensarbeiten; **~bottle** Kornblume; Schmeißfliege *f*; *sl* Schupo *m*; **~-eyed** *a* blauäugig; *sl* geliebt; **~ funk** schreckliche Angst *f*; *to be in a ~ ~* e-n Bammel haben; **~ glow** Glimmlicht *n*; **~-grass** *Am* Blaugras *n*; **~ish** ['-iʃ] bläulich; **~-jacket** Blaujacke *f*, Matrose *m*; **~ jay** *orn (amerik.)* Blauhäher *m*; **~ laws** *pl Am* strenge Bräuche *m pl*, Sittengesetze *n pl*; **~ pencil** Blaustift *m*; *to ~-pencil* ausstreichen, korrigieren; zensieren; **~-print** *s* Blaupause *f*; *allg* Plan, Entwurf *m*; *tr* durchpausen; entwerfen; *~~ paper* Lichtpauspapier *n*; **~ ribbon** Band des Hosenbandordens; Abstinenzlerabzeichen *n*; erste(r) Preis *m* bei e-m Wettbewerb.

bluff [blʌf] **1.** *s* Steilufer *n*, Klippe *f*; Vorgebirge *n*; *a (Klippe, Schiffsbug)* breit u. steil, schroff, abschüssig; *fig* rauh, aber herzlich; freimütig derb; **2.** *tr* bluffen; irreführen; einschüchtern; ins Bockshorn jagen; durch Bluffen erreichen; *itr* sich aufspielen, *fam* angeben; *s* Bluff *m*; Einschüchterung(sversuch *m*) *f*; Schreckschuß *m*; *fam* Angabe *f*; Angeber *m*; *I'd call his ~* ich würde ihn auf die Probe stellen; **~er** ['-ə] Bluffer, Angeber; Schwindler *m*; **~ line** Steilabfall *m (e-r Hochfläche)*; **~ness** ['-nis] Steilheit; *fig* rauhe Herzlichkeit *f*, derbe(r) Freimut *m*.

bluish ['bluiʃ] bläulich.

blunder ['blʌndə] *tr* durchea.bringen, verwechseln; schlecht erledigen, zs.-stümpern, pfuschen; *(to ~ out)* herausplatzen (*s.th.* mit etw); *itr* herumirren, stolpern (*on, against* gegen; *into* in); zufällig geraten (*upon* auf); e-n dummen Fehler, Schnitzer machen, *fam* e-n Bock schießen; *s* (dummer) Fehler, Schnitzer; Mißgriff *m*; *to make a ~* e-e Dummheit machen; *to ~ away* verwirtschaften; **~buss** ['-bʌs] *hist* Donnerbüchse *f*; **~er** ['-rə] Tölpel, ungeschickte(r) Mensch.

blunt [blʌnt] *a* stumpf; *fig* (abge-)stumpf(t) (*to* gegen); offen, frei(mütig); derb, barsch; *tr* stumpf machen; *fig* abstumpfen; *itr* stumpf werden; *s sl* Geld, Moos *n*; **~ly** ['-li] *adv* ganz offen, frei heraus, unverblümt; **~ness** ['-nis] Stumpfheit; *fig* Derbheit, Unverblümtheit *f*.

blur [blə:] *tr itr* trüben, trübe, undeutlich, unscharf, verschwommen machen *od* werden; verwischen, verschmieren; *s* undeutliche(s), verschwommene(s) Bild *n*; Trübung, Verschwommenheit *f*; Fleck; *fig* Schandfleck, Makel *m*; **~red** [-d] *a* verschwommen, unscharf.

blurb [blə:b] Waschzettel, Klappentext *m*; Bauchbinde *f*; *Am allg* Reklame(text *m*) *f*.

blurt [blə:t] *tr*: *to ~ out* herausplatzen (*s.th.* mit e-r S).

blush [blʌʃ] *itr* erröten; (scham)rot werden (*at* bei; *with* od *for* vor); *s* Schamröte *f*, Erröten, Rotwerden *n*; *at the first ~* auf den ersten Blick; *to put to the ~* erröten lassen; **~ing** ['-iŋ] errötend; *fig* bescheiden.

bluster ['blʌstə] *itr (Sturm, See, Mensch in Wut)* toben; poltern; leere Drohungen ausstoßen; *tr* tyrannisieren; *s* Toben, Heulen (des Sturmes); Wutgeheul, -geschrei; Getöse *n*; Prahlerei *f*; *to ~ o.s. into* sich hineinsteigern in; *to ~ out, forth* (wütend) ausstoßen, schreien; **~er** ['-rə] Tobende(r) *m*; **~ing** ['-riŋ] tobend; lärmend; prahlend; drohend; **~ous, ~y** ['-rəs, '-ri] wild, tobend, heftig.

bo [bou] *interj s. boh*; *s Am sl* Vagabund *m*; *(Anrede)* alter Junge!

boa ['bouə] *zoo (Mode)* Boa; Riesenschlange *f*; **~ constrictor** *zoo* Königs-, Abgottschlange *f*.

boar [bɔ:] Eber; Keiler *m*; *wild ~* Wildschwein *n*; **~'s head** *(Küche)* Schweinskopf *m*.

board [bɔ:d] **1.** *s.* Brett *n*, Diele, Planke *f*; Pappdeckel, Karton *m*, Pappe; (Anschlag-, Wand-)Tafel *f*; Spielbrett *n*; (Tisch-)Platte *f*; Eßtisch *m*; Kost, Verpflegung; Pension *f*; Beratungstisch *m*;

Versammlung *f*, Ausschuß, Rat *m*, Körperschaft; Behörde, Verwaltung *f*, Amt; Ministerium *n*; *mar* Bord *m*, Deck *n*; *Am* Börse(nnotierungen *f pl*) *f*; *the ~s (theat)* die Bretter *n pl (Bühne)*; **2.** *tr* verschalen, dielen; mit Brettern verkleiden, täfeln; beköstigen, verpflegen, in Pension haben *od* geben; *med* untersuchen, mustern; an Bord gehen (*a ship* e-s Schiffes); *(Fahrzeug)* besteigen, einsteigen (*the train* in den Zug); *(Schiff)* entern; **3.** *itr* essen, s-e Mahlzeiten einnehmen, in Pension sein (*with* bei); *mar* lavieren; **4.** *above ~* offen, ehrlich *adv*; *free on ~, f.o.b.* frei Schiff; *in ~s (Buch)* in Pappe, Pappband; *in cloth ~s (Buch)* in(Ganz-)Leinen, Leinenband; *on ~ (a) ship* an Bord e-s Schiffes; *on even ~* quitt; *to be a member of the ~* Mitglied des Vorstandes sein; *to be represented on the ~* im Vorstand vertreten sein; *to go by the ~* über Bord gehen; *fig* s-n Plan fallenlassen, s-e Hoffnung aufgeben; scheitern; *to go on ~ ship* sich einschiffen; *to go on ~ the train (Am)* in den Zug einsteigen; *to sweep the ~* alles erledigen; *(Spiel u. allg)* den ganzen Gewinn einstreichen, -stecken; *to ~ out (itr)* auswärts essen; *tr* ausmustern; *to ~ up* (mit Brettern) zu-, vernageln; *advisory, arbitration* od *conciliation ~* Beratungs-, Schlichtungsausschuß *m*; *bed and ~* Tisch u. Bett *(ehel. Gemeinschaft)*; *bulletin ~ (Am)* Schwarze(s) Brett *n*; *chess-~* Schachbrett *n*; *examination ~* Prüfungskommission *f*; *groaning ~* üppige Mahlzeit *f*; *ironing ~* Bügelbrett *n*; *meeting of the ~* Vorstandssitzung *f*; *Road-B~* Straßenbauamt *n*; *school ~* Schulbehörde *f*; *shipping ~* Seeamt *n*; *switch ~* Schalttafel *f*; *B~ of Admiralty, of Trade* Marine-, Wirtschaftsministerium *n*; *~ of audit* Rechnungsausschuß *m*; *~ of control* Kontroll-, Aufsichtsbehörde *f*; Überwachungsausschuß *m*; *~ of directors* Aufsichtsrat *m*; *~ of elections* Wahlausschuß *m*; *~ of inquiry* Untersuchungsausschuß *m*; *~ of review* Überprüfungs-, Berufungsausschuß *m*; *~ of supervisors* Verwaltungs-, Aufsichtsrat *m*; *member of the ~* ~Aufsichtsratmitglied *n*; *~ of trade (Am)* Handelskammer *f*; *B~ of Trade regulations (pl)* Sicherheitsvorschriften *f pl*; **~ed** ['-id] *a* abgedeckt; *(Diele)* getäfelt; **~er** ['-ə] Kostgänger; zahlende(r) Pensionsgast; Internatsschüler *m*; **~fence, floor, shack** *Am* Bretterzaun, -boden *m*, -bude *f*; **~ing** ['-iŋ] Bretterzaun, -verschlag *m*, -verkleidung; Täfelung; Verschalung *f*; Dielen *f pl*; Verpflegung, Beköstigung *f*; Pensionsessen; *mar aero* Anbordgehen; *mar* Entern *n*; *~~-house* Pension *f*; *~~ kennel* Hundeasyl *n*; *~~-out* Auswärtsessen *n*; Unterbringung *f* in e-r Familie; *~~-school* Internat *n*; *~~ stable (Am)* Stall *m*, in dem Pferde gegen Bezahlung gefüttert u. gepflegt werden; **~ and lodging** Unterkunft u. Verpflegung, volle Pension; freie Station *f*; **~ meeting** Ausschußsitzung; Sitzung *f* des Verwaltungsrats; **~-money, -wages** *pl* Verpflegungsgeld *n*, Verpflegung *f* in bar; **~walk** *Am* Lattenrost *m*; Uferpromenade *f*.

boast [boust] *s* Prahlerei *f*, überhebliche Worte *n pl*, Eigenlob *n*; Stolz *m (Gegenstand)*; *itr* prahlen (*of* mit), sich rühmen (*of s.th.* e-r S), den Mund vollnehmen; *tr* stolz sein (*s.th.* auf e-e S); **~er** ['-ə] Prahlhans, *fam* Angeber *m*; **~ful** ['-ful] prahlerisch; überheblich.

boat [bout] *s* Boot *n*, Kahn, Nachen *m*; Schiff *n*; Dampfer *m*; *(gravy ~)* Sauciere, Soßenschüssel *f*; *aero* Flugboot *n (flying ~)*; *itr* in e-m Boot fahren, rudern, segeln; *in the same ~ (fig)* in der gleichen Lage *od* Gefahr; *to burn o.'s ~s (fig)* alle Brücken hinter sich abbrechen; *cargo ~* Frachtdampfer *m*; *life-~* Rettungsboot *n*; *motor-~* Motorboot *n*; *passenger ~* Passagierdampfer *m*; *~s for hire* Bootsverleih *m*; **~-fly** Wasserwanze *f*; **~-hook** Bootshaken *m*; **~-house** Bootshaus *n*; **~ing** ['-iŋ] Rudern, Segeln *n*; Segel-, Rudersport *m*; **~-race** Bootsrennen *n*; (Ruder-)Regatta *f*; **~-shaped** *a* kahnförmig; **~(s)man** Bootsverleiher, -verkäufer; Bootsmann, Ruderer *m*; **~swain** ['bousn] *mar* Bootsmann *m*; Bootszug *m*; **~ train** Schiffszug *m*; **~ trip** Schiffsreise *f*.

bob [bɔb] *s* (hängendes) Gewicht *(an Pendel, Lot, Drachen)*; Senkblei *n*; (Haar-)Knoten *m*; Hänge-, kurze Locke *f*; Haarbüschel; Knäuel *n*; *(Pferd)* Stutzschwanz; *(Frauen)* kurzer Haarschnitt *m*; *(ear ~)* Ohrgehänge *n*; Kehrreim; Klaps; Ruck, Stoß; Knicks *m*; *Art* Glockengeläut *n*; schottische(r) Tanz; *(Angeln)* Schwimmer; *inv sl* Schilling; *B~* Robert *m*; *(~-sled, -sleigh)* Bobsleigh, Rennschlitten; *Am* Langholzschlitten *m*; *itr* sich auf u. ab *(up and down) od* hin u. her *(to and fro)* bewegen; sich ruckartig bewegen; e-n Knicks machen (*to* vor); linkisch tanzen; mit dem Munde schnappen (*for s.th.* nach etw); mit e-m Schwimmer fischen; *tr (Haar e-r Frau)* kurz schneiden; *(Schwanz)* stutzen; leicht anstoßen (*s.th.* an etw); e-n Klaps geben; ruckartig bewegen; *on the ~ (Am fam)* auf den Beinen, in Bewegung; *to ~ up* plötzlich, unerwartet auftauchen *od* erscheinen; **~bed hair** Bubikopf *m*; **~bin** ['bɔbin] (Garn-)Spule *f*, Klöppel *m*, Haspel, Garnwinde; *allg* Rolle; *el* Draht-, Induktionsrolle; Trommel *f*; *~~ lace* Klöppelspitze *f*; *~~ net* Tüll *m*; **~bish** *(pretty ~~) sl* lebhaft, quicklebendig, munter, aufgeweckt; **~ble** ['bɔbl] *Am fam* Bock, Fehler; Versager *m*; **~by** ['-i] *fam* Schupo, Polizist *m*; *~~-dazzler (sl)* etw Knalliges; *~~-soxer* Backfisch, Teenager *m*; **~cat** *Am* Luchs *m*; **~olink** ['bɔbəliŋk] Reisstar, Boblink *m (amerik. Singvogel)*; **~stay** *mar* Wasserstag *n*; **~tail** *s (Pferd, Hund)* Stutzschwanz *m*; *tr* (den Schwanz) stutzen; beschneiden; *rag-tag and ~~* Krethi u. Plethi *pl*, Lumpenpack, Gesindel *n*.

bock [bɔk] Bockbier; Glas *n* Bier.

bode [boud] *tr* bedeuten, ahnen, vermuten lassen; *itr (well, ill)* ein (gutes, schlechtes) (Vor-)Zeichen sein (*for* für).

bodi|ce ['bɔdis] *(Kleid)* Oberteil *m* od *n*, Taille *f*; Mieder, Leibchen *n*; **~ed** [-id] *a* in Zssgen: *able-~~ (mil)* dienstfähig; *big-~~* von großem Wuchs; *full-~~ (Wein)* stark; **~less** ['-lis] unkörperlich, körperlos, wesenlos; **~ly** ['-li] *a* körperlich, leiblich; *adv* in Person, persönlich; leibhaftig; wie ein Mann, geschlossen; im ganzen, als Ganzes; *~~ harm, injury* Körperverletzung *f*; *~~ search* Leibesvisitation *f*.

bodkin ['bɔdkin] Schnür-, Packnadel *f*; Pfriemen *m*, Ahle; (lange) Haarnadel *f*.

body ['bɔdi] *s* Körper, Leib; Rumpf *m*; *(dead ~)* Leiche *f*, Leichnam *m*; *fam* Person *f*, Mensch *m*; *jur* Korporation, Körperschaft *f*, Gremium; Organ *n*; Gesellschaft *f*, Bund; *mil* (Truppen-) Verband *m*; (Geschoß-)Hülle *f*; *bot* (Pflanzen-)Stengel *m*; (Menschen-) Gruppe, Ansammlung, Masse; Sammlung *f (von Vorschriften, Nachrichten usw)*; Hauptteil *m*, -masse, Mehrheit *f*; Inhalt, Stamm, Kern; *(Brief)* Text *m*; *tech* Gehäuse; Hauptgebäude *n*; *typ (~ of a letter)* Schriftgrad, -kegel; *(Schiff, Flugzeug)* Rumpf *m*; *mot* Karosserie *f*, Aufbau; Körper, Gegenstand *m*; Mieder *n*, Taille *f*; Material *n*, Materie, Substanz, Masse *f*; *das* Ganze; *fig* Festigkeit, Kompaktheit, Massigkeit, Dichte *f*, Gehalt *m*, Stärke; Güte *f*; *tr* gestalten, Gestalt geben (*s.th.* e-r S); verkörpern; *(Öl)* eindicken; *in a ~* im ganzen, zusammen, insgesamt, geschlossen; *to keep ~ and soul together* am Leben bleiben, das Leben fristen, sich durchschlagen; *to ~ forth* verkörpern, darstellen, symbolisieren; *all-steel ~* Ganzstahlkarosserie *f*; *governing ~* Direktion, Leitung *f*; *heavenly ~* Himmelskörper *m*; *heir of o.'s ~* Leibeserbe *m*; *legislative ~* gesetzgebende Körperschaft *f*; *main ~* Gros *n*, Kern *m* der Truppe; *wine of good ~* starke(r) Wein *m*; *~ of Christ* Leib *m* des Herrn *(Hostie)*; **~-building** Körperschulung *f*; **~-colo(u)r** *a* undurchsichtig; *s* Deckfarbe, Grundierung; *fig* Undurchsichtigkeit *f*; **~ corporate** Körperschaft, juristische Person *f*; **~ design** Karosserieform *f*; **~-guard** Leibwache *f*; **~ politic** Staat(swesen *n*) *m*; politische Organisation *f*; **~-servant** Leib-, Kammerdiener *m*; **~-snatcher** Leichenräuber; *mil sl* Sani(täter) *m*.

Boer ['buə, 'bouə] Bure *m*.

boffin ['bɔfin] *sl* Spezialist *m*.

bog [bɔg] *s* Sumpf, Morast *m*, Moor *n*; *tech* Senkgrube *f*; *itr* im Sumpf, Moor versinken, *tr* versenken; *to ~ down* steckenbleiben (*in the mud* im Schlamm); *peat ~* Torfmoor *n*; **~gle** ['bɔgl] *itr* erschrecken, zs.fahren; stutzen (*at* vor); Angst haben, ängstlich sein; zögern, schwanken (*at, about* bei); schlampern; Ausflüchte machen; nervös mit den Fingern spielen; *tr* zs.schustern, schlampig machen; **~gy** ['-i] sumpfig; **~ie, ~y** ['bougi] *rail* Drehgestell *n*; Laufrolle *f*, -rad *n*; *~~ wheel* (Ketten-)Laufrad *n*; **~le** ['bougl], **~y, ~ey, ~ie** ['bougi] Kobold; Popanz *m*, Schreckgespenst *n*, Butzemann *m*; Vogelscheuche *f*; *(~ey, ~ie) aero* unbekannte(s) Flugzeug *n*; **~-trotter** Sumpfbewohner; *pej* Ire *m*; **~us** ['bougəs] falsch; Schein-; nachgemacht, unecht; Schwindel-; *~~ firm* Schwindelunternehmen *n*; *~~ money* Falschgeld *n*.

bo(h) [bou] *interj* hu(hu)! buh! *he can't say ~ to a goose* er ist etwas ängstlich.

Bohemia [bou'hi:mjə] Böhmen; Zigeunertum *n*; Boheme *f*; **~n** [-n] *a* böhmisch; zigeunerhaft, ungebunden, frei, locker; *s* Böhme *m*, Böhmin *f*; Bohemien *m*.

boil [bɔil] **1.** *itr tr v* kochen, sieden; *itr fig (vor Wut)* kochen, schäumen (*with* vor); *(Fluten)* wogen, toben; *tr* zum Sieden bringen; *s* Siedepunkt *m*; Kochen, Sieden *n*; **2.** *s* Furunkel *m*; *to make o.'s blood ~* jdn rasend machen; *to ~ away* verkochen, verdampfen; *to ~ down* einkochen, -dicken; *fig* zs.drängen, -fassen (*into* in); *to ~ over (bes. Milch)* überkochen; *fig* überschäumen (*with rage* vor Wut); *to ~ up (fam)* auf die Palme gehen; **~ed**: *~~ shirt (sl)* Hemd *n* mit gestärkter Brust; *fig* eingebildete(r), hochnäsige(r) Mann *m*; **~er** ['-ə] (Heiz-, Dampf-, Wasch-)Kessel; Warmwasserbereiter, -speicher *m*; *(Färberei)* Küpe *f*; *~~ pressure* Kesseldruck *m*; *~~ scale, incrustation* Kesselstein *m*; *~~ suit* Overall *m*; *~~ tube* Kesselrohr *n*; **~ing** ['-iŋ] *a* kochend, siedend; *fig* sehr erregt; *s* Kochen, Sieden; Brodeln *n*; *to keep the pot ~~ (fig)* für den Lebensunterhalt sorgen; etw im Schwung halten; *the whole ~~ (sl)* die ganze Blase, Bande, Sippschaft, Gesellschaft; *~~ (hot) (fam)* kochend, siedend, glühend heiß; *~~ point* Siedepunkt *m a. fig.*

boisterous ['bɔistərəs] heftig, stürmisch; polternd, lärmend, laut, ausgelassen; **~ness** ['-nis] Heftigkeit *f*; Ungestüm *n*; Ausgelassenheit *f*.

boko ['boukou] *sl* Zinken *m*, Nase *f*.

bold [bould] kühn, tapfer, mutig, *fam* forsch; selbstsicher, -bewußt, keck; gewagt; dreist, frech, ungehörig; *(Handschrift)* kräftig, deutlich; in die Augen fallend, hervortretend; *(Vorstellung, Bild)* klar, deutlich; fest umrissen; *(Küste)* steil; *to make (so) ~ as* sich anheischig machen, es wagen *(to* zu); sich erkühnen; **~face, ~-face type** Fettdruck *m*; *to be in ~~* fett gedruckt sein; **~-faced** *a* frech, dreist, unverschämt; *typ* in Fettdruck, fett; **~ness** ['-nis] Kühnheit, Tapferkeit *f*, (Wage-)Mut *m*; Frechheit, Dreistigkeit; freche Bemerkung *f*.

bole [boul] **1.** (Baum-)Stamm; (runder) Pfeiler, Pfosten *m*; Rolle, Walze *f*.

bol|ection [bou'lekʃən] *arch* vorspringende Verzierung *f*; **~ero** [bə'lɛərou] Bolero *(Tanz)*; ['bɔlərou] Bolero(jäckchen *n*) *m*; **~etus** [bo'li:təs] *bot* Röhrenpilz *m*; **~ide** ['boulaid] Feuerkugel *f* *(Meteor)*.

Bolivia [bə'liviə] Bolivien *n*; **~n** *a* bolivianisch; *s* Bolivianer(in *f*) *m*.

boll [boul] *bot* Samen(kapsel *f*) *m*; **~ard** ['bɔləd] *mar* Poller *m*; **~ix** ['-iks] *tr sl* durchea.bringen; zs.schustern, -stümpern *(to ~~ up)*; **~-weevil** *ent* Baumwollkapselkäfer, Baumwollrüßler *m*.

boloney [bə'louni] *sl* Stuß, Quatsch, Blödsinn; *Am fam* Bologneser Wurst *f*; *Am sl* Autoreifen *m*.

Bolshev|ik ['bɔlʃivik] *s* Bolschewist *m*; *pl* Bolschewiken *m pl*; *a* bolschewistisch; **~ism** ['-izm] Bolschewismus *m*; **~ist**, *sl* **Bolshy** ['-ist, 'bɔlʃi] *s* Bolschewist *m*; *a* bolschewistisch.

bolster ['boulstə] *s* Kissen, Polster *n*, *bes.* Schlummerrolle; *tech* Unterlage *f*, Kissen *n*; *tr* wattieren, polstern; *(to ~ up)* stützen, absteifen, *fig* zuhalten versuchen; *fam* mit Kissen bewerfen.

bolt [boult] **1.** *s* (Tür-)Riegel; Bolzen; *tech* Dorn; *(screw ~)* Schraubenbolzen *m*; *(Gewehr)* Schloß *n*; Bolzen, (kurzer, starker) Pfeil; Blitz(strahl) *a. fig*; Schlag *m*, Unvorhergesehene(s) *n*; *fam* Satz, plötzliche(r) Sprung; *Am (Partei)* Austritt *m*; *(Stoff, Papier)* Satz *m*; Rolle *f*, Ballen *m*; *itr* davonstürzen, Reißaus nehmen, weg-, *fam* losrennen, abhauen; e-n Satz machen; Speisen hinunterschlingen; *(Pferd)* durchgehen; *Am* aus e-r Partei austreten; *bot* verfrüht Samen bilden; *tr (Speise)* hinunterstürzen, -würgen, -schlingen; verriegeln; ver-, festschrauben; an-, verbolzen, mit Schraubenbolzen verbinden; *Am (Partei)* im Stich lassen; austreten *(a group* aus e-r Gruppe); *(Pfeil)* abschießen; *(Tuch, Papier)* zs.rollen; *(to ~ out)* herausplatzen *(s.th.* mit etw); *adv* pfeilgeschwind, wie der Wind; *to shoot o.'s ~* tun, was man kann; die letzten Reserven einsetzen; *to ~ in, out* ein-, aussperren; *a ~ from the blue* ein Blitz aus heiterem Himmel; **2.** *tr* sieben; *fig* durchsieben, (aus-)mustern, sichten, sorgfältig prüfen; **~ed** *a* verschraubt; *~~ joint* Schraubenverbindung *f*; **~er** ['-ə] **1.** Ausreißer *m*; durchgehende(s) Pferd *n*; *Am pol* Abtrünnige(r) *m*; **2.** Sieb *n*; Sichtmaschine *f*; (Mehl-)Beutel *m*; **~head** Schraubenkopf; *chem* Destillierkolben *m*; **~-hole** Schlupfloch *n a. fig*; **~ing** ['-iŋ] **1.** (Bolzen-)Verschraubung *f*; **2.** Sieben *n*; **~ nut** Bolzenmutter *f*; **~ position** *mil* Riegelstellung *f*; **~rope** *mar* Liek *n*; **~ upright** kerzengerade.

bolus ['bouləs] *pharm* große Pille *f*.

bomb [bɔm] *s* (Hand-)Granate *f*; (Werfer-)Geschoß *n*; Bombe *f*; Sprengkörper *m*; *itr* Bomben (ab)werfen; Bomben laden; *tr* bombardieren, mit Bomben belegen, *(Flugzeug)* beladen; zerbomben; *to ~ out* ausbomben; *to ~ up* mit Bomben beladen; *time ~* Zeitbombe; Höllenmaschine *f*; **~ aimer** Bombenschütze *m*; **~ard** [-'bɑ:d] *tr* mit Granatfeuer belegen, bombardieren, beschießen, unter Feuer nehmen; *(Atomkern)* beschießen; *fig (mit Fragen)* bestürmen, überschütten, bombardieren; **~ardier** [-bə'diə] *Br* Artillerie-Unteroffizier; *aero* Bombenschütze *m*; **~ardment** [-'bɑ:dmənt] Beschießung *f*, Bombardement *n*, Bombardierung *f*, Beschuß *m*; **~ast** ['-bæst] Schwulst, Bombast; (Rede-)Schwall *m*; **~astic** [-'bæstik] bombastisch, schwülstig, geschwollen; **~ bay** Bombenschacht *m (im Flugzeug)*; **~ burst** Bombeneinschlag *m*; **~ carpet** Bombenteppich *m*; **~ crater** Bombenkrater *m*; **~ damage** Bombenschaden *m*; **~ disposal unit** Bombenspreng- *od* -räumkommando *n*; **~ door** Bombenklappe *f*; **~ dropping** Bombenabwurf *m*; **~ dump** Bombenlager *n*; **~e** [bõ:b] *(Küche)* (Eis-)Bombe *f* *(a. aus anderen Speisen)*; **~ed** ['-d] *a*: *~~ area* Luftnotstandsgebiet *n*; *~~ site* Trümmergrundstück *n*; **~er** ['-ə] Bomber *m*, Bombenflugzeug *n*; *fighter ~~* Jagdbomber, Jabo *m*; *~~ aircraft* Bombenflugzeug *n*; *~~ crew* Besatzung *f* e-s Bombenflugzeugs; *~~ group (Br)* Bombergeschwader *n*, *Am* -gruppe *f*; *~~ pilot* Bombenflieger *m*; *~~ squadron* Bomberstaffel *f*; *~~ wing (Br)* Bombergruppe *f*, *Am* -geschwader *n*; **~ fuse** Bombenzünder *m*; **~ing** ['-iŋ] Bombardierung *f*, Bombenwurf *m*; *pattern ~~* Flächenbombardierung *f*; *pinpoint, precision ~~* gezielte(r) Bombenwurf *m*; *~~ (air)plane* Bombenflugzeug *n*; *~~ attack, raid* Bombenangriff *m*; *~~ range* Bombenwurfübungsplatz *m*; Einsatzbereich *m* e-s Bombers; *~~ run* Bombenzielanflug *m*; **~-load** Bombenlast *f*; **~-proof** bombensicher; *~~ shelter* bombensichere(r) Unterstand *m*; **~ release** Bombenabwurf *m*, -auslösevorrichtung *f*; **~-shell** Bombe *a. fig*; *fig* plötzliche Überraschung *f*; **~-sight** Bombenzielgerät *n*; **~ splinter** Bombensplitter *m*.

bona fide ['bounə'faidi] *a jur* ehrlich, aufrichtig, gutgläubig; *adv* in gutem Glauben; **~s** [-i:z] *pl* Ehrlichkeit, Aufrichtigkeit, Gutgläubigkeit *f*.

bonanza [bo(u)'nænzə] *s fam* Glück(sfall *m*) *n*; *min* Ergiebigkeit; Goldgrube *f* *fig*, blendende(s) Geschäft *n*; *a* ergiebig, ertragreich, gewinnbringend, blühend.

bonce [bɔns] große Marmel *f*; Marmelspiel *n*; *sl* Rübe *f*, Kopf *m*.

bond [bɔnd] *s das* Verbindende, (Ver-)Bindung, Zs.gehörigkeit(sgefühl *n*) *f*, Band *n (pl* Bande), Fessel *f*; *tech* Bindemittel *n*; *(Bauwerk)* Verband *m*; *chem* Bindung; *com* Verbindlichkeit, Verpflichtung *f*, Übereinkommen *n*, Abmachung; Bürgschaft *f*; Schuldschein *m*, -verschreibung *f*; Garantieschein; Pfandbrief *m*, Obligation *f*; Zollverschluß *m*; *pl* festverzinsliche Wertpapiere *n pl*; *pl* Fesseln *f pl*; *pl* Haft *f*, Gefängnis *n*; *tr* verpfänden; unter Zollverschluß nehmen *od* legen; *tech* abbinden; *in ~* unter Zollverschluß; *in ~s* unfrei; in Fesseln, *lit* in Banden; *to be under ~* unter Kontrakt stehen; *~ of security, indemnity* Garantie-, Bürgschaftsschein *m*; *baby ~* Kleinobligation *f*; *matrimonial ~* Band *n* der Ehe; *mortgage ~* Hypothekenbrief *m*; *treasury ~* Schatzanweisung *f*; *warehouse ~* Zollverschlußschein *m*; **~age** ['-idʒ] Knechtschaft, Sklaverei; Unfreiheit, Gebundenheit *f*; **~-creditor, -holder** Pfandbrief-, Obligationsgläubiger, -inhaber *m*; **~-debt(or)** Pfandbrief-, Obligationsschuld(ner *m*) *f*; **~ed** ['-id] *a (~~ goods* Waren *f pl)* unter Zollverschluß; *tech* verbunden; *~~ port* Zollhafen *m*; *~~ shed* Zollschuppen *m*; *~~ warehouse* Zollspeicher *m*, -depot *n*; **~ing** ['-iŋ] Bindung *f*; Abbinden *n*; *~~ agent, capacity, power* Bindemittel, -vermögen *n*, -fähigkeit *f*; **~ market** Pfandbriefmarkt *m*; **~ note** Zollpassierschein *m*; **~(s)man** *hist* Leibeigene(r) *m*; **~sman** *fin* Bürge *m*.

bone [boun] *s* Knochen *m (a. pl)*; *(Fisch)* Gräte *f*; Bein *(Knochensubstanz)*; Fischbein *n*; Zahnschmelz *m*, Elfenbein *n*; *fig (~ of contention)* Zankapfel; *Am sl* Büffler *m*; *pl* Gebein(e *pl*) *n*; *pl* Körper *m*; *pl fam* Würfel *m pl*; *pl* Kastagnetten; *pl* Korsettstangen *f pl*; *tr* die Knochen entfernen aus, ablösen von; *(Fisch)* entgräten; *sl* klauen, mopsen; *itr Am sl* büffeln, ochsen; *to ~ up on s.th. (Am sl)* etw durcharbeiten; *to the ~* bis auf die Knochen, völlig; *to be nothing but skin and ~s* nur noch Haut u. Knochen sein; *to feel in o.'s ~s (fam)* (s-r S) ganz sicher sein; in den Knochen spüren; *to have a ~ to pick with s.o.* mit jdm ein Hühnchen zu rupfen haben; *to make no ~s about s.th.* nicht viel Federlesens machen; keine Gewissensbisse haben; *to make old ~s* alt werden; *bred in the ~* unausrottbar; *as dry as ~, ~-dry* knochentrocken; **~ ash** Knochenasche *f*; **~ black** Knochenkohle *f*; **~-dust, meal** Knochenmehl *n*; **~er** *Am sl* Schnitzer *m*; *to pull a ~~* e-n Bock schießen; **~ fracture** Knochenbruch *m*; **~ glass** Milchglas *n*; **~ glue** Knochenleim *m*; **~-head** *sl* Dummkopf *m*; **~-lace** Klöppelspitzen *f pl*; **~less** ohne Knochen *od* Gräten; **~ oil** Knochenöl *n*; **~-spavin** *vet (Pferd)* Piephacke *f*; **~-yard** *Am* Abdeckerei *f*; *sl* Autofriedhof *m*.

bonfire ['bɔnfaiə] Freudenfeuer; Feuer *n* im Freien; *to make a ~ of s.th.* etw vernichten.

bonn|et ['bɔnit] *s (bes.* Kapott-)Hut *m*; *Scot* Mütze; *tech* Haube *f*, Schutzkorb *m*; *mot* Motorhaube *f*; *(Indianer)* Kopf-, Federschmuck; *sl fig* Komplize, Helfershelfer *m*; *tr* e-n Hut, e-e Mütze aufsetzen; **~y** ['bɔni] *a bes. Scot* gut, gesund aussehend, frisch; *~~-clabber (Am)* dicke Milch *f*.

bon|us ['bounəs] Bonus, Sonderzuschlag *m*, Gratifikation, Prämie; *com* Sonderdividende; Vergütung, Entschädigung *f*; Zuschlag *m*; *Christmas ~~* Weihnachtsgratifikation *f*; *cost-of-living ~~* Teuerungszulage *f*; *production ~~* Leistungsprämie *f*; *~~ share* Gratisaktie *f*; **~y** ['bouni] voller Knochen *od* Gräten; *(big-boned)* (grob)knochig; knochenhart, knochig, knöchern; mager, ausgemergelt.

boo [bu:] *interj (Verachtung)* bah! pah! buh! *(um Tiere zu verscheuchen)* sch! *tr* auszischen, -pfeifen; *(Tier)* (ver-)scheuchen; *itr* buh machen.
boob [bu:b] *sl* Simpel, (Einfalts-)Pinsel, Idiot *m*; **~y** ['-i] Tölpel, Trottel, Gimpel; letzte(r) Sieger; *orn* Tölpel *m*; *~~ hatch (Am sl)* Irrenhaus *n*; *mar* Niedergangstreppe *f*; *~~ prize* Trostpreis *m*; *~~ trap* Falle *f fig*; Streich; Budenzauber *m*; *mil* getarnte(r) Explosivkörper *m*; Todesfalle *f*.
boodle ['bu:dl] *Am sl* Pack *n*, Mob *m*, Bagage *f*; (Falsch-)Geld *n*; Bestechungsgelder *n pl*; Bestechung; Beute *f*; *the whole ~~* der ganze Kram, Dreck, Betrag; alle(s).
boogie-woogie ['bu:giwu:gi] Boogie-Woogie *m (Tanz, Musik)*.
boohoo [bu:'hu:] *s* Huhu, laute(s) Weinen *n*; *itr* laut weinen.

*

book [buk] *s* Buch; Heft *n*; Block *m*; *(Bridge)* Buch *n*; Aufzeichnungen *f pl*; Liste *f*; *(Tabakblätter)* Stoß *m*; *mus* Textbuch, Libretto; *theat* Rollenbuch *n*; Wettliste *f*; *pl* Studium *n*, Unterricht *m*; *the B~* die Bibel; *(~ of matches)* (Streichholz-)Heftchen *n*; *the ~s (com)* die Bücher; *the ~ (fam)* die maßgeblichen Vorschriften *f pl*, die offizielle Lesart; *tr* buchen; auf-, niederschreiben; *(to ~ in)* eintragen, notieren; vormerken; *(Platz)* (vor)bestellen, buchen, belegen; *tele (Gespräch)* anmelden; *(Karte)* lösen; *(Polizei)* in ein Protokollbuch eintragen *(s.o. on a charge of* jdn wegen); *(Person)* in Anspruch nehmen, engagieren; *by (the) ~* gut unterrichtet, informiert; offiziell; einwandfrei; *on the ~s* in der Liste; aufgeschrieben; *without ~* inoffiziell, informell; aus dem Gedächtnis; *to balance the ~s* die Bilanz ziehen; die Bücher abschließen; *to be in s.o.'s black* od *bad, good ~s* bei jdm schlecht, gut angeschrieben sein; *to be ~ed (fig)* festgenagelt sein; *for s.th.* etw zu erwarten haben; *up* belegt sein; *to bring to ~* verbuchen; *for s.th.* wegen etw zur Rechenschaft ziehen; *to close the ~s* die Bücher abschließen; *to keep ~s* Bücher führen; *to speak like a ~* wie ein Buch reden; *to suit s.o.'s ~* jdm recht kommen; gut, *fam* in den Kram passen; *to take a leaf out of s.o.'s ~* es jdm nachmachen; jdm nacheifern; es machen wie jem; *to take s.o.'s name off the ~s* jdn aus der Liste streichen; *to ~ through to* direkt bis ... lösen *~ of acceptance* Akzeptbuch; Wechseljournal *n*; *~ of account* Kontobuch *n*; *~ of commissions* Bestellbuch *n*; *~ of printed forms* Formularbuch *n*; *~ of reference* Nachschlagewerk *n*; *~ of stamps* Briefmarkenheft *n*; *~ of tickets* Fahrscheinheft *n*; **~able** ['-əbl] im Vorverkauf erhältlich; **~binder** Buchbinder *m*; **~bindery** Buchbinderei *f*; **~binding** Buchbinderei *f*, Buchbinderhandwerk *n*; **~-case** Bücherschrank *m*; **~ club** Buchklub *m*; **~-end, -rest** Bücherstütze *f*; **~ie** ['-i] *sl* Buchmacher *m*; **~ing** ['-iŋ] Buchung *f*; Vorverkauf *m*; Vorbestellung, Reservierung *f*; *~~-clerk* Fahrkartenverkäufer *m*; *~~-machine* Buchungsmaschine *f*; *~~-office* Fahrkartenschalter *m*; (Theater-)Kasse; Vorverkaufsstelle *f*; **~ish** ['-iʃ] lesefreudig; literarisch, gelehrt; *(Stil)* papieren; **~ishness** ['-iʃnis] Stubengelehrsamkeit *f*; **~ jacket** *Am* Schutzumschlag *m*; **~-keeper** Buchhalter *m (Person)*; **~-keeping** Buchhaltung, -führung *f*; *~~ by double, single entry* doppelte, einfache Buchführung *f*; *~~ machine* Buchhaltungsmaschine *f*; **~-learning** Bücherweisheit; *fam* schulische Erziehung *f*; **~let** ['-lit] Broschüre *f*; **~-maker** Bücherschreiber (*a.* *~-wright*); *(Pferderennen)* Buchmacher *m*; **~man** *Am* Gelehrter; Buchhändler, Verleger *m*; **~-mark** Lesezeichen *n*; **~ market** Büchermarkt *m*; **~-mate** Schulkamerad, -freund *m*; **~mobile** ['-məbi:l] *Am* fahrbare Leihbücherei *f*; **~-plate** Exlibris, Bücherzeichen *n*; **~-post** Drucksachen *f pl* zu ermäßigter Gebühr; *by ~~* Drucksache! **~-rack** Büchergestell *n*; **~ review** Buchbesprechung *f*; **~ reviewer** Kritiker *m*; **~ room** Leseraum *m (e-r Bibliothek)*; **~seller** Buchhändler *m*; *~~'s (shop)* Buchhandlung *f*; **~selling** Buchhandel *m*; **~shelf** Bücherregal, -bord *n*; **~shop** Buchhandlung *f*; **~stack** Bücherregal *n*; **~stall** Buchverkaufsstand; *Br* Zeitungskiosk *m*; Bahnhofsbuchhandlung *f*; **~stand** Büchergestell, Regal *n*; Bücherauslage *f (im Laden)*; Buchverkaufsstand *m*; **~store** *Am* Buchhandlung *f*; **~-token** Büchergutschein *m*; **~ trade** Buchhandel *m*; **~-value** *com* Buchwert *m*; **~work** Bücherstudium *n*; **~worm** *ent* u. *fig* Bücherwurm *m*; **~-wrapper** Buchhülle *f*.
boom [bu:m] **1.** *s mar* Baum, Ausleger, Ladebaum *m*, (Back-)Spiere; (Fluß-, Hafen-)Sperre; *(Brücke)* Gurtung *f*; *Am radio video* (beweglicher) Galgen *m* für Mikrophon *(mike ~)* *od* Kamera *(camera ~)*; *(Tankflugzeug)* Füllschlauch *m*; **2.** *s com* (Hoch-)Konjunktur *f*; wirtschaftliche(r) Aufschwung *m*; geschäftliche Aufwärtsentwicklung; *com* Hausse; *com* Vogue, Beliebtheit *f (e-r Ware)*; *itr* e-e Hochkonjunktur haben *od* erleben; e-n (großen) wirtschaftlichen Aufschwung nehmen; sich großer Beliebtheit erfreuen; *tr com* lancieren, laute Reklame machen für; e-e Hochkonjunktur herbeiführen in; *to be ~ing* im Aufschwung begriffen sein; *building ~* Hochkonjunktur *f* im Bauwesen; **3.** *itr* dröhnen, hallen, brausen, brummen; *tr* dröhnend verkünden; *s* Dröhnen, Hallen; Brummen *n*; **~-and-bust** *Am* Hochkonjunktur *f* u. nachfolgende Depression; **~er** ['-ə] *Am* Reklamemacher, tatkräftige(r) Förderer; Bombenerfolg *m*; **~erang** ['bumeræŋ] Bumerang *m a. fig*; **~ing** ['-iŋ] Hochkonjunktur; Stimmungsmache *f*; **~ prices** *pl* Konjunktur-, Höchstpreise *m pl*.
boon [bu:n] *s* Wohltat *f*, Segen *m*; *obs* Gunst, Gnade *f*; *a* lustig; *poet* gütig; wohltuend; **~ companion** lustige(r) Bruder, Zechkumpan *m*; **~doggle** ['-dɔgl] *itr Am sl* die Zeit vertrödeln.
boor ['buə] (Bauern-)Lümmel, Rüpel *m*; **~ish** ['buriʃ] rüpel-, lümmelhaft; **~ishness** ['-riʃnis] Rüpel-, Lümmelhaftigkeit *f*.
boost [bu:st] *tr fam* hochschieben, -heben; beim Klettern nachhelfen *(s.o.* jdm); *(Preise)* in die Höhe treiben; (unter)stützen; sich einsetzen, lebhafte Reklame machen für, lancieren; *el (Strom, Leistung)* verstärken; *(Batterie)* aufladen; *(Spannung)* erhöhen; *s* Propaganda, Stimmungsmache, Reklame; Preistreiberei *f*; Aufschwung *m*, Konjunktur; *el* Zusatzspannung; *tech* Steigerung, Erhöhung *f*; *(~ pressure) el* Ladedruck *m*; **~er** ['-ə] Trommler, unermüdliche(r) Reklamemacher *od* Förderer; *tech* Hilfs-, Servomotor *m*; Aufladegebläse *n*; *el* Spannungserhöher, Zusatzdynamo; Übertragersatz *m*; *~~ amplifier* Zusatzverstärker *m*; *~~ injection* Wiederholungsimpfung *f*; *~~ rocket* Startrakete *f*.
boot [bu:t] **1.** *s* Stiefel; *Am* Schaftstiefel; *hist* Spanische(r) Stiefel *(Folterinstrument)*; *hist* Wagenkasten; Knieschutz *(für Kutscher)*; *mot Br* Kofferraum *m*; *(Autoreifen)* Einlage *f*; *Am mar sl* Rekrut; Stoß; *sl* Rausschmiß *m*; *pl mit sing* Hoteldiener *m*; *tr* Stiefel anziehen *(s.o.* jdm); stoßen; *sl* 'rauswerfen, -schmeißen, entlassen; *like old ~s (sl) (übertreibend)* furchtbar, schrecklich *adv*; *to die with o.'s ~s on* in den Sielen sterben; *to get the ~ (sl)* 'rausgeschmissen werden, fliegen; *to give the ~ to s.o.* jdn 'rausschmeißen; *the ~ is on the other leg (fig)* es ist gerade andersherum; *bet your ~s (sl)* verlaß dich drauf; *high ~s (pl)* hohe Stiefel, Langschäfter *m pl*; **~black** *Am* Schuhputzer *m*; **~ed** *a* gestiefelt; **~ee** [bu:'ti:] Halbstiefel, Überschuh *(für Frauen u. Kinder)*; gestrickte(r) *od* gehäkelte(r) Babyschuh *m*; **~jack** Stiefelknecht *m*; **~lace** Schuhriemen, Schnürsenkel *m*; **~leg** *Am tr (Alkohol)* schmuggeln; *a* ungesetzlich; *s* geschmuggelte(r) Alkohol; Stiefelschaft *m*; **~legger** *Am* Alkoholschmuggler *m*; **~legging** *Am* Alkoholschmuggel *m*; **~less** ['-lis] nutz-, zwecklos; **~lick** *Am sl itr* niedrig schmeicheln; *tr* Honig ums Maul schmieren *(s.o.* jdm); **~licker** Speichellecker *m*; **~-maker** Schuhmacher *m*; **~-tree** (Schuh-)Spanner *m*; **2.** *v imp* nützen, dienlich sein *(s.o.* jdm); *s*: *to ~* obendrein, zusätzlich, noch dazu.
booth [bu:ð] *(bes.* Markt-)Bude *f*; Messestand; Verschlag *m*; Nische *f (in e-m Kaffee)*; *polling, voting ~* Wahlzelle *f*; *telephone ~* Fernsprech-, Telephonzelle *f*.
booty ['bu:ti] (Kriegs-)Beute *f*; Raub; *allg* Gewinn *m*, Erwerbung *f*.
booz|e [bu:z] *itr fam* saufen, picheln; *s fam* Alkohol *m (als Getränk)*; *(Am sl ~~ fight)* Sauferei *f*, Besäufnis *n*; *~~ fighter (Am sl)*, **~er** ['-ə] Säufer *m*; **~y** ['-i] *fam* be- *od* versoffen.

*

bor|acic [bə'ræsik] *a chem* Bor-; *~~ acid* Borsäure *f*; **~age** ['bɔridʒ] *bot (Küche)* Borretsch *m*; **~ax** ['bɔræks] Borax *m*; *attr Am sl* in die Augen fallend, kitschig.
border ['bɔ:də] *s* Kante *f*, Rand(streifen), Saum *m*; Einfassung *f*; Ufer *n*; Rabatte; *typ* Zierleiste; (Landes-)Grenze *f*; Grenzgebiet *n*; *the B~* das englisch-schottische Grenzgebiet; *tr* begrenzen; einfassen; *itr* grenzen *(on* an); *within, out of the ~s* inner-, außerhalb der Grenzen; *to ~ (up)on* ähneln *(s.th.* e-r S), nahekommen *(s.th.* e-r S), streifen; **~er** ['-rə] Grenzbewohner *m*; **~ incident** Grenzzwischenfall *m*; **~ing** ['-riŋ] angrenzend *(on* an), dicht *(on* bei); **~land** Grenzland; *fig scient psychol* Grenzgebiet *n*; **~line** Grenzstreifen *m*, *fig* -gebiet *n*; *attr* Grenz-; *on the ~~ (psychol)* an der Grenze des Normalen.
bore [bɔ:] **1.** *tr* ausbohren, -höhlen; *(Insekten, Würmer)* nagen, fressen, graben; *(to ~ through)* durchbohren; *(Zylinder)* ausschleifen; *itr* bohren *a. min*; sich bohren lassen; *s* Kaliber *n*, lichte Weite *f*, Durchmesser *m*, (Rohr-)Seele *f*; *(~-hole)* Bohrloch *n*; Bohrung *f*; *to ~ o.'s way* sich e-n Weg bahnen; **2.** *tr* langweilen; *to be ~d* sich langweilen; *s* langweilige(r) Mensch *m*, Nervensäge *f*; **3.** Springflut *f*.
borea|l ['bɔriəl] nördlich; Nord(wind)-; **B~s** ['bɔriæs] Nordwind *m*.
boredom ['bɔ:dəm] Langeweile; Lästigkeit *f*, lästige(s) Wesen *n*.

borer ['bɔːrə] Bohrer *m (Mensch* od *Gerät)*; Bohrmaschine *f*; *zoo* Bohr-, Pfahlwurm; *ent* Holzwurm *m*.

boric ['bɔrik] Bor-; ~ **acid** Borsäure *f*; ~ **acid ointment** Borsalbe *f*.

boring ['bɔːriŋ] *a* langweilig, lästig; *s* Bohrloch *n*; *pl* Bohrmehl *n*, Drehspäne *m pl*.

born [bɔːn] geboren; *to be ~ with a silver spoon in o.'s mouth* reiche Eltern haben; *he was ~ in the year 1940* er ist im Jahre 1940 geboren; *he was ~ before his time* er war s-r Zeit weit voraus; *he was ~ blind* er ist von Geburt blind.

borne [bɔːn] *pp von to bear*.

boron ['bɔːrɔn] *chem* Bor *n*.

borough ['bʌrə] Stadt(gemeinde); Stadt *f* mit Parlamentsvertretung; Wahlbezirk; Stadtbezirk *m (in New York)*.

borrow ['bɔrou] *tr* borgen, (aus-, ent-) leihen, entlehnen *a. fig (of, from* von); *to ~ trouble* sich unnütze Sorgen machen; ~ **area, pit** Entnahmestelle *f (für Baumaterial)*; ~**ed light** *arch* Innenfenster *n*; ~**er** ['-ə] Borger, (Ent-) Leiher *m*; ~~*'s ticket* Entleihkarte *f*; ~**ing** ['-iŋ] Lehnwort *n*; Kreditaufnahme *f*.

bos [bɔs] *s sl (~-shot)* Fehlschuß *m*; falsche Annahme; Pfuscherei *f*, Mist *m*; *itr* daneben schießen; vorbeiraten; *tr* verpfuschen, -murksen, -masseln.

bosh [bɔʃ] **1.** *s sl* Quatsch, Blöd-, Unsinn *m*; *tr sl (Schule)* ärgern, auf die Palme bringen; **2.** *tech* Rast *f (e-s Hochofens)*.

bosky ['bɔski] buschig, buschbewachsen, -bestanden, waldig; schattig; *sl* besoffen.

bosom ['buzəm] *s* Innere(s); Herz *n fig*; Busen, Schoß *m fig*; *obs* (Hemd-) Brust *f*, Vorhemd *n*; *(See)* Oberfläche *f*; *obs poet* Busen *m*, Brust *f*; *tr (Geheimnis)* bewahren; nicht vergessen; verbergen; ans Herz drücken; ~ **friend** Busenfreund *m*.

boss [bɔs] **1.** *s* Buckel, Knauf, Knopf *m*; erhabene Verzierung *f*; *tech* Gesenk *n*, Nabe, Warze *f*; Wellenende *n*; *tr* bossieren; **2.** *s. bos*; **3.** *s fam* Chef, Meister; Arbeit-, Brötchengeber; Vorgesetzte(r); Parteiführer, -chef; Meister, überlegene(r) Mann, führende(r) Kopf *m*; *attr* Haupt-, Ober-, Über-; *a* besonder, erstklassig, -rangig; *tr* arrangieren; dirigieren, lenken, leiten; beherrschen; der Chef, führende Kopf, Hauptmacher sein (*s.th.* e-r S); *to ~ around* herumkommandieren; *to ~ it* der führende Kopf sein; ~ **rule** Herrschaft *f* der Parteiführer; ~**iness** ['-inis] *Am fam* Herrschsucht *f*; ~**y** ['-i] **1.** mit erhabenen Verzierungen; **2.** *Am fam* herrschsüchtig; rechthaberisch.

bosun ['bousn] *mar* Bootsmann *m*.

bot, bott [bɔt] *zoo* Dassellarve *f*; ~**-bee, -fly** Dasselfliege *f*; ~**s** [bɔts] *sing vet* Dasselbeulen *f pl*, -plage *f*.

botan|ic(al) [bə'tænik(əl)] botanisch, pflanzenkundlich; *B~ical Garden* Botanische(r) Garten *m*; ~**ist** ['bɔtənist] Botaniker *m*; ~**ize** ['-aiz] *itr* botanisieren; ~**y** ['-i] Botanik, Pflanzenkunde *f*.

botch [bɔtʃ] **1.** *dial* Schwäre *f*, Geschwür *n*; **2.** *s* Flickwerk *n*, Pfuscherei *f*; Flicken, Lappen *m*; Füllwort *n*; *itr* stümpern; *tr* zs.flicken; verpfuschen; ~**er** ['-ə] **1.** Stümper; Flickschneider, -schuster *m*; **2.** junge(r) Lachs *m*.

both [bouθ] *a u. prn* beide; beides; ~ *(the) brothers, (Am) ~ of the brothers* beide Brüder; *adv* zusammen, miteinander; *conj ~ ... and* sowohl ... als auch; *on ~ sides* auf beiden Seiten.

bother ['bɔðə] *s* Mühe (u. Not), Schererei, Schwierigkeit; Belästigung *f*; Umstände *m pl*; ärgerliche Sache *f*, Ärger, Verdruß *m*; *tr* lästig sein *od* fallen (*s.o.* jdm), belästigen; plagen, quälen; aufregen, in Aufregung versetzen, aus der Ruhe bringen; *itr* sich Umstände, Sorgen (*about* um), Gedanken (*about* über) machen; sich abgeben, sich befassen (*with* mit); ~ *(it)! ~ you! ~ the flies!* zum Kuckuck! verdammt noch mal! *don't ~* bemühen Sie sich nicht! machen Sie sich keine Umstände! ~**ation** [-'reiʃən] *interj* verflixt! *s fam* Belästigung *f*; ~**some** ['-sʌm] lästig; mühevoll; ärgerlich.

bottle ['bɔtl] **1.** *s* Flasche *f*; *tr* auf, in Flaschen füllen; *sl* schnappen; erwischen; *(to ~ up) (fig)* zurückhalten *(o.'s anger* s-n Ärger, Zorn), aufhalten; *over a ~* beim Trinken; *to bring up on the ~ (Kind)* mit der Flasche aufziehen; *to hit the ~ (sl)* sich dem Suff ergeben; *~ it! (sl mil)* (halt die) Schnauze! *hot-water ~* Wärmflasche *f*; ~**-brush** Flaschenbürste *f*; ~**d** ['-d] *a* in Flaschen; *(Ärger) fig* aufgestaut; *fam* beschwipst; ~**ful** ['-ful] Flaschevoll *f*; ~**-glass** (dunkelgrünes) Flaschenglas *n*; ~**-green** dunkelgrün; ~**-holder** *fig* Helfershelfer; Sekundant *m*; ~**-neck** Flaschenhals *m*; Straßenverengung; *tech* Stauung, Stockung *f*; *fig* Engpaß *m*; *Am* Hindernis *n*; ~**-nose** *(Boxen)* geschwollene Nase *f*; *zoo* Entenwal *m*; ~**-party** gesellige(s) Beisammensein *n*, bei dem jeder sein Getränk mitbringt; ~**r** ['-ə] Küfer *m*; ~**-rack** Flaschengestell *n*; ~**-washer** *fam* Faktotum *n*; **2.** *obs* u. *dial* Bund, Bündel *n (Heu, Stroh)*; **3.** *s*: *Blue B~* Kornblume *f*; *White, Yellow B~* Wucherblume *f*.

bottom ['bɔtəm] *s* Boden, Grund *m (a. e-s Gewässers)*; Basis *f*; untere(s) Ende *n*, Fuß *m (bes. e-s Berges)*; Tal-, Grabensohle *f*; erste(r) Gang; *Am* Talgrund; Schiffsboden *m*; Schiff *n*; Sitz *m*; *fam* Gesäß *n*, Hintern; Hintergrund; *fig* Grund(lage *f*); Kern *m (e-r S)*; Ursache *f*, Anlaß *m*, Triebfeder *f*; *das* Wichtigste, Wesentlichste; Ausdauer, Standfestigkeit *f*; *attr* letzt, unterst, niedrigst; grundlegend; *tr* mit e-m Boden versehen; *fig* gründen (*upon* auf); ergründen; *itr* den Boden berühren, auf den Grund stoßen; *at ~ (fig)* im Grunde (genommen); *from top to ~* von oben bis unten; *from the ~ of my heart* im Grunde meines Herzens, zutiefst, aufrichtig; *~ left, right (Buch)* unten links, rechts; *~ up* auf dem Kopf, verkehrt herum; kieloben; *to be at the ~ of s.th.* der Anlaß zu e-r S sein, etw verursachen, zugrunde liegen; *to bet o.'s ~ dollar (sl)* s-n Kopf wetten; todsicher sein; *to get, to search to the ~ of s.th.* e-r S auf den Grund gehen; *to go to the ~ (Schiff)* sinken; *to knock the ~ out of s.th.* etw zerschlagen, *fig* als falsch erweisen; ~ **face** Grundfläche *f*; ~ **gear** *mot* erste(r) Gang *m*; ~**less** ['-lis] grundlos, ohne Boden; *fig* unergründlich; *~~ pit (sl)* Hölle *f*; ~**most** *a* allerunterst; ~ **price** niedrigste(r), äußerste(r) Preis *m*; *at ~~s* billigst; ~**ry** ['-ri] *s* Bodmerei, Schiffsverpfändung *f*, -darlehen *n*, -hypothek *f*; *tr (Schiff)* verpfänden, beleihen.

botulism ['bɔtjulizm] Wurstvergiftung *f*.

bough [bau] (Haupt-)Ast, (großer) Zweig *m*.

boulder ['bouldə] rund(gespült)er Stein, Kopfstein; Fels-, erratische(r) Block, Findling *m*; ~**-clay** Geschiebelehm *m*; ~**-period** Eiszeit *f*.

bounc|e [bauns] *itr* aufschlagen, auf-, zurückprallen; springen; stürzen; sich auf u. ab bewegen; hochschnellen; *(to ~ about)* herumhupfen; prahlen, aufschneiden; *sl (Scheck)* platzen; *(to ~~ into)* hineinstürmen; *tr* auf u. ab bewegen, in schnelle Bewegung versetzen; werfen; aufprallen lassen; ausschimpfen; überreden; *Am sl (to ~~ out)* 'rauswerfen, -schmeißen *(aus e-r Stelle)*, an die Luft setzen; *s* Rückprall, -stoß *m*; Elastizität *f*; Sprung; heftige(r) Schlag *m*; Prahlerei; *sl* Frechheit; *Am sl* Energie *f*, Rückgrat *n*, Mut; *Am sl* Rausschmiß *m*; *adv* mit e-m plötzlichen Knall; *interj* bums! *to get the ~~* entlassen, hinausgeworfen werden; ~**er** ['-ə] große(s) Ding *n*, gewaltige Sache; freche Lüge *f*; Aufschneider; ungedeckte(r) Scheck; *sl* Rausschmiß; *sl* Hinauswerfer *m (in e-m Restaurant)*; ~**ing** ['-iŋ] groß; stramm, drall; gesund; stark; munter, lebhaft; geräuschvoll, lärmend, laut; *(Lüge)* faustdick; ~**y** ['-i] elastisch; *fig* überheblich.

bound [baund] **1.** *pp von to bind a* angebunden *a. fig*; gebunden, verpflichtet; *(Buch)* gebunden; *med* an Verstopfung leidend; *to be ~ up with* od *in* eng verbunden sein mit; ganz in Anspruch genommen sein von; *to be ~ to do* ganz bestimmt tun; entschlossen sein, zu tun; *to be (in) hono(u)r ~ to* moralisch verpflichtet sein, zu; *I'm ~ to (inf)* ich muß; *I'll be ~* darauf kannst du Gift nehmen; *he's ~ to be late* er kommt bestimmt zu spät; *it was ~ to happen sooner or later* es mußte früher oder später so kommen; **2.** fertig, bereit, im Begriff (*for* zu); bestimmt, unterwegs (*for, to* nach); *where are you ~ for?* wo geht ihr hin? *homeward ~* auf der Heimreise, -fahrt; *outward ~* auf der Ausreise; **3.** *itr* hüpfen (*with joy* vor Freude); e-n Satz machen; springen; (auf)prallen *(against* gegen); *s* Sprung, Satz; (Auf-, Rück-)Prall *m*; *by leaps and ~s* in großer Eile; in raschem Tempo; sprunghaft; **4.** *s* Grenze *f*; Maß *n*; *pl* Grenzgebiet *n*; *tr* begrenzen; einschränken; *itr* angrenzen (*on* an); *in, out of ~s (Lokal)* Betreten erlaubt, verboten; *within, beyond the ~s of* innerhalb, jenseits der Grenzen *gen*, im Bereich, außerhalb des Bereiches *gen*; ~**ary** ['baundəri] Grenze, Umgrenzung; Trennungslinie *f*; *~~ crossing* Grenzübergang *m*; *~~ dispute, litigation* Grenzstreit(igkeiten *f pl*) *m*; *~~ stone* Grenzstein *m*; ~**en** ['-n] *a*: *my ~~ duty* meine Pflicht u. Schuldigkeit; ~**er** ['-ə] *sl* Prolet, Rowdy; ungebildete(r) Mensch *m*; ~**less** ['-lis] grenzen-, maßlos; unbeschränkt.

bount|eous ['bauntiəs], ~**iful** ['-iful] freigebig, großzügig; *(Sache)* ergiebig; reichlich (vorhanden); ~**y** ['-i] Freigebigkeit, Großzügigkeit; großzügige Gabe *f*, Geschenk *n*; (Staats-)Prämie *f*; Bonus *m*; Handgeld *n*; Zulage; Gratifikation *f*; *child ~~* Kinderzulage *f*; *~~ on exports, imports* Ausfuhr-, Einfuhrprämie *f*; *~~ on production* Produktionsprämie *f*; *~~-fed (a)* subventioniert.

bouquet ['bukei, bu'kei] Bukett *n*, (Blumen-)Strauß *m*; Bukett *n*, Blume *f*, Duft *m (des Weines)*.

bourgeois ['buəʒwɑː] **1.** *s* (Spieß-)Bürger; Philister *m*; *pl* Bürgertum *n*; *a* (spieß)bürgerlich; spießig, philisterhaft; **2.** [bəː'dʒɔis] *s typ* Borgis *f*.

bourn(e) [buən, bɔːn] **1.** (Gieß-)Bach *m*; **2.** *obs* Grenze *f*; Ziel *n*.

bout [baut] (Arbeits-, Waffen-)Gang *m*; (Tanz-)Tour; Reihe; Runde *(Boxen)*; Lage *(beim Zechen)*; Periode, Zeitspanne *f*; *med* Anfall *m*; *this* ~ diesmal; *coughing* ~ Hustenanfall *m*; *drinking* ~ Trinkgelage *n*; ~ *of fighting* Waffengang *m*.

bov|id ['bouvid] *scient* Rinder-; **~ine** [-ain, -in] *a* Rind(er)-, Ochsen-; *fig* blöd(e), doof, dumm; *s* Ochse *m*, Rind *n*.

bow 1. [bou] *s* Bogen *(Waffe)*; *pl* Bogenschützen *m pl*; *(saddle-~)* Geigenbogen; *(rain~)* Regenbogen; *tech* Bügel *m*; Masche *f*; Knoten *m*, Schleife *f*; Bogen *m*, Kurve, Krümmung *f*; *itr* sich bogenförmig krümmen; Geige spielen, fiedeln; *to draw the long ~ (fig)* aufschneiden, *fam* angeben; *to have two strings to o.'s ~ (fig)* zwei Eisen im Feuer haben; **~-compasses** *pl* Nullenzirkel *m*; **~-head** Nord-, Grönlandwal *m*; **~-legged** *a* O-beinig; **~-man** Bogenschütze *m*; **~-saw** Bügelsäge *f*; **~shot** Bogenschuß *m (Entfernung)*; **~-string** *s* Bogensehne; seidene Schnur *(zum Erdrosseln)*; *tr* erdrosseln; **~-window** Erkerfenster *n*; **2.** [bau] *tr itr* (sich) verbeugen, verneigen (*to, before* vor); sich fügen (*to s.th.* etw); grüßen (*to s.o.* jdn); *tr* biegen; beugen, krümmen, niederdrücken *a. fig*; *s* Verbeugung, Verneigung *f* (*to* vor); *to ~ down* sich (ver-) neigen (*to* vor); *to ~ out (tr)* hinauskomplimentieren; *itr* sich geschickt zurückziehen; *to have a ~ing acquaintance* sich nur flüchtig kennen; *to make o.'s ~* sich zurückziehen; mit e-r Verbeugung eintreten; **3.** [bau] *mar* Bug *m*; **~-heavy** *aero* kopf-, buglastig; ~ **wave** Bugwelle *f*.

bowdlerize ['baudləraiz] *tr (Buch)* von anstößigen Stellen säubern.

bowel ['bauəl] *scient* Darm *m*; *pl* Eingeweide *pl*, Innere(s) *n (des Körpers)*; *pl obs* Mitgefühl *n*, Gefühle *n pl*; *to open o.'s ~s* sich entleeren.

bower ['bauə] **1.** (Garten-)Laube *f*; Gartenhaus; *poet* Gemach; Damenzimmer *n*; **2.** *mar* Buganker *m*; **3.** *(Kartenspiel)* Bube *m*; **~y** ['-ri] belaubt, schattig; voller Lauben.

bowie-knife ['boui'naif] *Am* Hirschfänger *m*.

bowing ['bauiŋ] **1.** Verbeugung, Verneigung *f*; *to be on ~ terms with s.o.* jdn nur flüchtig kennen; **2.** ['bouiŋ] *mus* Bogenführung *f*.

bowl [boul] **1.** *s* Schüssel *f*, Napf *m*, Schale; Trinkschale *f*; starke(s) alkoholische(s) Getränk; Trinkgelage *n*; Höhlung *f*; Pfeifenkopf *m*, Waagschale *f*; *Am* Sportplatz *m*, Stadion *n*; *punch-~* Punschbowle *f*; *salad-~ (Br)* Salatschüssel *f*; **~-fire** *el* Heizsonne *f*; **~ful** ['-ful] Schüssel-, Schalevoll *f*; **2.** *s* (schwere) Holzkugel, Kegelkugel; *tech* Walze *f*; *pl Art* Rasenkegelspiel; *dial* Kegeln *n*; *tr sport (bes. Kricket) (Ball)* werfen; *(Kugel)* schieben, rollen; *itr* kegeln; *allg (to ~ along)* rollen; *to ~ out (Kricket) (gegnerischen Schläger)* durch Treffen des Dreistabes *(wicket)* aus dem Spiel bringen; *fig* schlagen, besiegen; *to ~ over* umwerfen, -stoßen, -hauen; *fig* aus dem Konzept bringen, hilflos machen; *to be ~ed over* sprachlos, *fam* platt sein; **~er** ['-ə] *(Kricket)* Ballmann, Werfer *m*; *(~~ hat)* Melone *f (Hut)*.

bowline ['boulain, -in] *mar* Bulin(e) *f*.

bowling ['bouliŋ] Bowlingspiel; *Am* Kegeln; *(Kricket)* Werfen *n* des Balles; **~-alley** Kegelbahn *f*; **~-green** Rasenplatz *m* zum Bowlingspiel.

bowsprit ['bousprit] *mar* Bugspriet *m*.

bow-wow ['bau'wau] *interj* wauwau! *s* ['--] *(Kindersprache)* Wauwau *m*.

box [bɔks] **1.** *bot* Buchsbaum; *(~wood)* Buchsbaum *m (Holz)*; **2.** *s* Schachtel *f*, Kasten, Behälter *m*; Etui, Futteral *n*; Kiste *f*, Koffer; *(Wagen)* Kofferraum; Kutschbock *m*; (Wahl-)Urne *f*; *(letter-~)* Briefkasten *m*; *(money-~)* Kasse, Geldkassette *f*; *tech* Gehäuse *n*, Kapsel, Muffe, Dose, Büchse *f*; *tech* Führerstand; *(Zeitung)* kurze(r), eingerahmte(r) Artikel *m*; *theat* Loge *f*; *jur* Stand *m*; *(Stall, Garage)* Box; Zelle *f*; Abteil *n*; Unterstand *m*, Hütte *f*; *Am* Postfach *n*; *Am* Wagen-, Schlittenkasten *m*; *mil* (taktische) Riegelstellung *f*; *tr* in e-e Schachtel, e-n Kasten tun *od* stecken *od* packen; *(to ~ off) (Raum)* unterteilen; *to ~ in* einschließen; *sport* behindern; *mil* abriegeln; *to ~ up* einschließen; *sl* zs.schustern; *to be in the same ~* in der gleichen Lage sein; *witness-~ (jur)* Zeugenstand *m*; ~ **barrage** *s mil* Sperrfeuer *n*, Feuerriegel *m*; *tr* (taktisch) abriegeln; ~ **barrow, cart** Kastenwagen *m*; **~-calf** Boxkalf *n (Leder)*; ~ **car** *Am rail* gedeckte(r) Güterwagen *m*; *pl sl (Würfel)* Zwölfer *m*; **~-keeper** *theat* Logenschließer *m*; **~kite** Kastendrachen *m*; **~-number** Chiffre(-nummer) *f*; **~-office** (Theater-) Kasse *f*; *Am sl* Kassen-, Publikumserfolg *m*; *the actress got a big ~~ on her show* die Schauspielerin hatte bei ihrem Auftreten e-n Bombenerfolg; *~~ life (Am) theat film* Spielzeit *f*; *~~ value (Am) theat film* Zugkraft *f*; ~ **seat** Logenplatz *m*; ~ **section** *tech* Kastenprofil *n*; ~ **spanner, wrench** Steckschlüssel *m*; **~-type delivery van** Kastenwagen *m*; **~-up** *sl* Schlamassel *n*; **3.** *tr itr* boxen; *tr*: *to ~ s.o.'s ear(s)* jdn ohrfeigen; *s* Stoß, Schlag *m*; *(~ on the ear)* Ohrfeige *f*; **~er** Boxer *m (a. Hunderasse)*; *~~ engine* Boxermotor *m*; **~ing** ['-iŋ] **1.** Boxen *n*, Boxsport *m*; *~~-gloves (pl)* Boxhandschuhe *m pl*; *~~-match* Boxkampf *m*; **2.** *B~~-Day* erste(r) Wochentag *m* nach Weihnachten, an dem die Weihnachtsgeschenke *(Christmas ~es)* verteilt werden.

boy [bɔi] Knabe, Junge, Bub; Bursche, Diener, Bote *m*; *my ~! (fam)* mein Lieber! *old ~! (fam)* alter Junge! *oh, ~!* o prima! toll! **~cott** ['bɔikət] *s com pol* Boykott *m*, Verruf(serklärung *f*) *m*, Ächtung, Aussperrung *f*; *tr* boykottieren, ächten, aussperren; ~ **friend** Freund, Liebste(r) *m*; **~hood** ['-hud] Knabenalter *n*, Kindheit; Jugend *f*; **~ish** ['-iʃ] knaben-, jungenhaft; ~ **scout** Pfadfinder *m*.

bra [brɑ:] *fam* Büstenhalter, BH *m*.

brac|e [breis] *s* Klammer; *tech* Strebe, Stütze *f*, Stützbalken *m*, Versteifung *f*, Verband; Gurt *m*, Band *n*, Aufhängeriemen *m*; *mar* Brasse *f*; *(Tiere, pej Menschen)* Paar *n*; *(Hunde)* Koppel *f*; *(~~ and bit)* Brustbohrer *m*; *pl Br (pair of ~s)* Hosenträger *m pl*; *(Zahnkorrektur)* Spange *f*; *med* Suspensorium *n*; *typ* geschweifte Klammer *f*; *tr* verklammern, befestigen; (ver)spannen; ver-, absteifen, (ab)stützen, verstreben; festigen, stärken *a. fig*; *fig (körperlich)* kräftigen, stärken; *mar* brassen; *sl* anpumpen; *to ~~ up, to take a ~~ (fam)* sich am Riemen reißen, sich zs.reißen, -nehmen; **~elet** ['-lit] Armband(uhr *f*) *n*; *fam* Handschelle *f*; **~er** ['-ə] Armschiene *f*, -schutz *m*; Tonikum, Stärkungsmittel *n*; *Am fam* Schnaps *m (zum Aufwärmen)*; **~ing** ['-iŋ] *a* stärkend, kräftigend; erfrischend; *s tech* Verspannung, Verstrebung, Versteifung *f*.

brach|ial ['bræk-, 'breikiəl] *a scient* Arm-; **~y** ['bræki] *pref scient* Kurz-; **~ycephalic** [-ike'fælik] kurzköpfig.

bracken ['brækən] *bot* Farnkraut *n*.

brack|et ['brækit] *s* Träger, (Wand-) Arm, Ausleger *m*, Stütze *f*, Ständer *m*, Unterlage *f*, Lagerbock *m*; Knagge *f*, Kragstein *m*, Krage; Konsole *f*; Bügel *m*; *mil (Artillerie)* Gabel *f*; Tragebaum *m*; Lafettenwand; *gram math* (eckige) Klammer; (Einkommens-) Klasse, Gruppe, Schicht *f*; *tr tech mil (Artillerie)* eingabeln; *gram* einklammern, in Klammern setzen *a. math*; (zu e-r Gruppe *od* Klasse) zs.stellen; gleichzeitig erwähnen, gleichstellen (*with* mit); *in ~~s (gram)* in Klammern; *income ~~* Einkommensgruppe *f*; *round, square ~~* runde, eckige Klammer *f*; **~ish** ['-iʃ] *(Wasser)* brackig, mit Salzwasser gemischt; *fig* widerlich, ekelerregend.

bract [brækt] *bot* Deckblatt *n*.

brad [bræd] Stift, dünne(r) Nagel *m*; **~awl** ['-ɔ:l] Bindeahle *f*, Vorstecker *m*.

brag [bræg] *tr* herausstreichen, rühmend hervorheben; *itr* prahlen (*of, (Am) about s.th.* mit e-r S; *that* daß); sich rühmen (*of s.th.* e-r S); den Mund voll nehmen, angeben; *s u.* **~gadocio** [brægə'doutʃiou] Prahlerei *f*; Prahler *m*; **~gart** ['-ət], **~ger** ['-ə] Prahler, Prahlhans, Aufschneider; (vor)laute(r) Mensch *m*.

brahm|an ['brɑ:mən] *rel* Brahmane *m*.

braid [breid] *s* Litze, Kordel, Tresse, Borte, Paspel *f*, Besatz *m*; (Band-, Haar-)Flechte *f*; Zopf *m*; eingeflochtene(s) Haarband *n*; *tr* mit Litze, Tresse besetzen, umklöppeln, einfassen; *(Litze, Haar in Zöpfe)* flechten; *~ed wire* umsponnene(r) Draht *m*; **~ing** ['-iŋ] Einfassung, Paspelung, Umklöppelung *f*.

brail [breil] *s mar* Geitau *n*; *tr (to ~ up) (Segel)* aufgeien; **~le** [-] Blindenschrift *f*.

brain [brein] *s* (Ge-)Hirn *n*; *fig (meist pl)* Geist, Verstand *m*, Intelligenz *f*, Fähigkeiten *f pl*, *fam* Grips *m*, Grütze *f*; *tr* den Schädel einschlagen (*s.o.* jdm); *to beat, to cudgel, to rack o.'s ~(s)* sich den Kopf zerbrechen; *to blow out o.'s ~s* sich e-e Kugel durch den Kopf jagen; *to have s.th. on the ~* nach etw verrückt, auf etw versessen, erpicht sein; *to pick s.o.'s ~s* jds Ideen stehlen; *to turn s.o.'s ~* jdn verrückt machen, jdm den Kopf verdrehen; *I have it on the ~* es geht mir immerzu im Kopf herum ~ **box, case, pan** Hirnschale *f*, Schädel *m*; **~-fag** geistige Erschöpfung *f*; ~ **fever** Gehirnentzündung *f*; **~less** ['-lis] gedankenlos; dumm; **~-sick** geisteskrank, irre, verrückt; **~-storm** verrückte Idee *f*; Tobsuchtsanfall; *Am fam* Geistesblitz *m*; ~ **trust** *Am pol* Gehirntrust *m*; **~-tunic** Hirnhaut *f*; ~ **twister** *Am* harte Nuß, schwierige Aufgabe *f*; **~washing** Gehirnwäsche *f*; **~-wave** *fam* glänzende Idee *f*, Geistesblitz *m*; *pl* Elektroenzephalogramm *n*; **~-work** Kopf-, geistige Arbeit *f*; **~-worker** Kopf-, Geistesarbeiter *m*; **~y** ['-i] *fam* klug.

braise [breiz] *tr (Küche)* schmoren.

brak|e [breik] **1.** Farnkraut *n*; **2.** Dikkicht, Unterholz, Gebüsch *n*; **3.** *s* (Flachs-, Hanf-)Breche; Teigknetmaschine; (schwere) Egge *f*; *tr (Flachs, Hanf)* brechen; *(Teig)* kneten; eggen; **4.** Hebelarm; Pumpenschwengel *m*; **5.** *s tech* Bremse, Bremsvorrichtung *f*; *(~-cabin) rail* Bremserhäuschen *n*; *tr itr* bremsen; *tr* abbremsen; *tech* anhalten, feststellen, sperren; *to put on the ~s* die Bremsen betätigen, bremsen; *~~ action* Bremswirkung, Hemmung *f*; *~~ block, cheek, shoe* Bremsklotz *m*, -backe *f*, -schuh *m*; *~~ drum* Bremstrommel *f*; ~~ *horsepower* Brems-PS *pl*, -leistung *f*; ~~ *lever* Bremshebel *m*; ~~ *lining* Bremsbelag *m*; ~~ *pedal* Bremspedal *n*; -fußhebel *m*; ~~*(s)man*, *Am* ~*man* Bremser *m*; ~~*-wheel* Bremsrad *n*; ~**ing** ['-iŋ] Bremsen *n*; Brems-; ~~ *controller*, *current*, *distance*, *effect*, *force* Bremsschalter, -strom, -weg *m*, -wirkung, -kraft *f*.

brambl|e ['bræmbl] Dorn-, *bes.* Brombeerstrauch *m*; ~~*-berry* Brombeere *f*; ~~*-flower*, *-rose* Heckenrose *f*; ~**ing** ['-iŋ] Bergfink *m*; ~**y** ['-i] voller Dornen, dornig.

bran [bræn] Kleie *f*.

branch [brɑ:ntʃ] *s* Zweig, Ast; *allg* (Seiten-)Zweig; (Fluß-)Arm; *Am* Bach *m*; *(Straße, rail)* Abzweigung, Nebenstrecke *f*; (Höhen-)Zug *m*; (Geweih-)Sprosse *f*; *fig* Zweig, Teil *m*; (Unter-)Abteilung *f*, Fach *n*, Abschnitt *m*; Zweiggeschäft, -büro *n*, -stelle, Filiale; *com* Branche *f*, Zweig *m*; *pol* Ortsgruppe; Truppengattung *f*; *el* Stromkreis *m*; *(Stammbaum)* Linie *f*, Zweig *m*; *attr* Zweig-, Filial-, Neben-; *tr* abzweigen; *itr (to ~ out, forth)* sich verzweigen, sich ausbreiten; *(to ~ off)* abzweigen, ausea.gehen; *to ~ out* ein neues Geschäft beginnen; sein Geschäft erweitern, vergrößern; *root and ~ (fig)* gründlich; ~ *of commerce* od *trade*, *of industry* Handels-, Industriezweig *m*; ~ **bank** Bankfiliale, Zweig-, Nebenstelle *f* (e-r Bank); ~ **circuit** Nebenstromkreis *m*; ~**line** *rail* Zweigbahn, -linie, Nebenstrecke; *el* Zweigleitung *f*; ~**-off** Abzweigung *f*; ~ **office** Zweigstelle, -niederlassung *f*, -geschäft *n*, Filialbetrieb *m*, Filiale *f*; ~ **switchboard** *el* Verteilertafel *f*; ~**y** *(Baum, Strauch)* dicht; *allg* weitverzweigt.

brand [brænd] *s* Feuerbrand *m*; *poet* Fackel *f*; Brandmal, -zeichen, -eisen *n*; *fig* Schande *f*, Verruf *m*; *com* Warenzeichen *n*; Güteklasse; Sorte *f*; *bot* Getreidebrand *m*; *Am* Viehherde *f* (mit eigenem Brandzeichen); *tr* brandmarken *a. fig*, brennen, ein Zeichen einbrennen (*the cattle* dem Vieh); mit dem Waren- *od* Gütezeichen versehen; *fig* einprägen (*s.o. with s.th.* jdm etw); ~**ish** ['-iʃ] *tr* schwingen; ~**-new** (funkel)nagelneu; ~**y** ['-i] Weinbrand; Likör; Schnaps *m*; *cherry* ~~ Kirschlikör *m*; ~~ *glass* Branntweinglas *n*; ~~ *snap* Ingwerwaffel *f*.

brant [brænt], ~**-goose** Ringel-, Brandgans *f*.

brash [bræʃ] Regenschauer *m*; Trümmergestein *n*; Eistrümmer *pl*; Trümmer *pl*, Schutt *m*, (Über-)Reste *m pl*, Abfall *m*; *a (bes. Holz)* brüchig, spröde; mürbe, morsch; *fam* quecksilberig, wild; *fam* keck, frech, vorwitzig, unverschämt; *water-~* Sodbrennen *n*.

brass [brɑ:s] *s* Messing *n*; Gelbguß *m*; Geschützbronze *f*; Metallfutter *n*, Lagerschale; beschriftete Messingplatte, Grabplatte *f*; *(the ~) mus* Blasinstrumente *n pl*; *pl* Messinggegenstände *m pl*; *sl* Geld, Moos *n*, Zaster *m*; *fam* Unverschämtheit, Frechheit *f*; *Am sl* hohe Offiziere *m pl*; *a* Messing-, aus Messing; *red ~* Rotguß, Tombak *m*; ~ **band** Blaskapelle *f*; ~ **farthing** rote(r) Heller *m*, wertlose(s) Zeug *n*, *fam* Dreck *m*; *I don't care a ~~* das ist mir völlig gleich(gültig), egal, *fam* schnuppe, Wurst; ~ **foil** Messingfolie *f*, Rauschgold *n*; ~ **foundry** Gelbgießerei *f*; ~ **hat** *sl mil* hohe(r) Offizier *m*, hohe(s) Tier *n*; ~**iness** ['-inis] Unverschämtheit, Frechheit *f*; ~ **knuckles** *pl Am* Schlagring *m*; ~ **mounting** Messingfassung *f*; ~ **plate** Messingblech; Türschild *n*; ~ **rolling mill** Messingwalzwerk *n*; ~**-tacks** *pl sl* Hauptsache *f*, Kern *m* der Sache; *to get down to ~~* zur Sache kommen; ~**-ware, articles** *pl* Messingwaren *f pl*; ~ **wind instruments,** ~ **winds** *pl* Blechblasinstrumente *n pl*; ~ **wire** Messingdraht *m*; ~**y** ['-i] messingartig; bronzen, ehern; mit Messing überzogen; *fig* grell, unnatürlich; *(Ton)* blechern; protzig, kitschig; *fam* frech, unverschämt, pampig.

brass|ard ['bræsɑ:d] Armbinde *f*; ~**ière** ['bræsiεə] Büstenhalter *m*.

brat [bræt] *pej* Balg *m*, Gör *n*, Göre, Range *f*, Bengel *m*.

brav|ado [brə'vɑ:dou] *pl -o(e)s* forsche(s), übermütige(s) Auftreten *n*, *fam* Angabe *f*; herausfordernde(s) Wesen *n*, Herausforderung *f*; ~**e** [breiv] *a* tapfer, mutig, unerschrocken, furchtlos; *s* tapfere(r) Mann *m*; *tr* mutig entgegentreten, trotzen (*s.th.* e-r S), herausfordern; Widerstand leisten, standhalten (*s.th.* e-r S); ~**ery** ['breivəri] Tapferkeit *f*, (Wage-)Mut *m*, Furchtlosigkeit, Unerschrockenheit; Pracht(entfaltung) *f*, prunkvolle(s) Auftreten *n*, Prunk *m*; ~**o** ['brɑ:'vou] *interj* bravo! *s pl -o(e)s* Bravo *n*; gedungene(r) Meuchelmörder; Bandit *m*.

brawl [brɔ:l] *s* laute(r), Streit, Zank *m*; lärmende Gesellschaft *f*; *itr* sich laut, lärmend zanken, streiten; *(Fluß)* rauschen, tosen; ~**er** ['-ə] Zankhahn, -teufel *m*; ~**ing** ['-iŋ] zänkisch.

brawn [brɔ:n] Muskel(fleisch *n*) *m*; *fig* (Muskel-)Kraft *f*; Pökelfleisch *n*, Sülze *f (vom Schwein)*; ~**iness** ['-inis] muskulöse Beschaffenheit; (Muskel-)Kraft *f*; ~**y** ['-i] muskulös, kräftig, kraftvoll, stark.

bray [brei] **1.** *tr (bes. im Mörser)* zerstoßen, zerreiben; dünn auftragen; **2.** *s* Schrei *m* des Esels, Iahen *n*; Trompetenstoß *m*; *itr (Esel)* schreien, iahen; *(Trompete)* schmettern.

braz|e [breiz] *tr* **1.** aus Messing machen; mit Messing überziehen; *fig* hartmachen; **2.** hartlöten; ~**en** ['breizn] *a* ehern; metallen; metallisch (klingend); *(~~-faced)* schamlos, unverschämt, frech, dreist; *tr (to ~~ it out, through)* frech wie Oskar sein; ~**ier** ['breiziə] Gelbgießer *m*; Kohlenbecken *n*.

Brazil [brə'zil] Brasilien *n*; ~**ian** [-iən] *a* brasilianisch; *s* Brasilianer(in *f*) *m*; ~ **nut** Paranuß *f*.

*

breach [bri:tʃ] *s fig* Bruch *m*; *(Gesetz)* Übertretung *f*, Verstoß *m*; *(Pflicht)* Verletzung *f*; Abbruch *m* der Beziehungen, Trennung *f*; Streit, Zwist *m*; Lücke; *mil* Bresche *f*, Einbruch(stelle *f*) *m*; *tr* u. *to make a ~ in* e-e Bresche schlagen in, durchbrechen; *to commit ~ of contract* vertragsbrüchig werden; *to stand in the ~*, *to step into the ~* in die Bresche springen; ~ *of discipline* Disziplinarvergehen *n*; ~ *of duty* Pflichtverletzung *f*; ~ *of law* Gesetzesübertretung *f*; ~ *of the peace* Friedensbruch; grobe(r) Unfug *m*; ~ *of promise* Verlöbnisbruch *m*; ~ *of trust* Untreue; Verletzung *f* der Treuepflicht.

bread [bred] *s* Brot *n*; Lebensunterhalt *m*; *tr* panieren; *Am* (mit Brot) versorgen; *to earn o.'s ~* s-n Lebensunterhalt verdienen, sein Auskommen haben; *to know which side o.'s ~ is buttered* wissen, wo man s-n Vorteil hat; *to take the ~ out of s.o.'s mouth* jdn s-s Lebensunterhalts, s-r Existenzmittel berauben; *the daily ~* das tägliche Brot; *a loaf, a slice, a piece of ~* ein Laib, e-e Scheibe, ein Stück Brot; ~ **and butter** Butterbrot *n*; Lebensunterhalt *m*, Brot *n*; ~**-and-butter** *a fam* unreif, jugendlich; alltäglich, prosaisch; ~~ *letter (fam)* Dankbrief *m* für genossene Gastfreundschaft; ~ **and cheese** Lebensunterhalt *m*, Auskommen *n*; ~**-basket** Brotkorb; *sl* Magen *m*; Kornkammer *f*; ~ **board** *Am* (Teig-)Knetbrett; Brett *n*, um Brot zu schneiden; ~ **bowl** *Am* Teigschüssel *f*; ~ **box, bin** Brotkapsel *f*; ~**-crumb** Brotkrume *f*; Paniermehl *n*; ~**-crust** Brotrinde *f*; ~**-knife** Brotmesser *n*; ~**less** ['-lis] brot-, erwerbslos, ohne Einkommen; ~**-line** Schlange *f* von Bedürftigen bei e-r Verteilung von Lebensmitteln; ~**-mould** Brotform *f*; ~**-stuffs**, *Am* ~**stuff** Brotgetreide, Mehl *n*; ~**-winner** Ernährer *m*.

breadth [bredθ] Breite; Weite; Ausdehnung, Größe *f*, Ausmaß *n*; *in ~* breit, in der Breite; *of full ~* in voller Breite; *to a hair's ~* um Haaresbreite, haargenau, -scharf; ~ *of mind*, *of view* Weitherzigkeit, Weite *f* des Gesichtskreises; ~**ways,** ~**wise** *adv* in der Breite; der Breite nach.

break [breik] **1.** *v broke, broken tr* (zer-)brechen, zerreißen, zerstoßen, aufschlagen; *fam* kaputt machen; *(Fensterscheibe)* einschlagen; *(Siegel)* erbrechen; *(Bank)* sprengen; *(Banknote)* in Kleingeld einwechseln; *(Angriff)* abschlagen; *(die Haut)* aufstoßen, auf-, wundscheuern; *fig (Gesetz)* übertreten; *(sein Wort, Versprechen)* nicht halten; *(Verabredung)* nicht einhalten; *(Vertrag)* verletzen; *(Verlobung)* auflösen; unter-, abbrechen; *(Rekord)* brechen; *el* abschalten; (ab)schwächen, mindern; ruinieren, zugrunde richten; entlassen; *mil* degradieren; *(Tier)* zähmen, abrichten, dressieren; abgewöhnen (*s.o. of s.th.* jdm etw); *(Weg)* bahnen; *(Fahne)* entfalten, hissen; mitteilen, eröffnen, *lit* kundtun; *fam* beibringen; aufs Tapet bringen; *with s.o.* mit jdm brechen; *itr* (zer)brechen, *fam* kaputtgehen, zu Bruch gehen; zerreißen; zerkleinern; aufgehen, sich öffnen; ausea.-gehen; *fam* sich ereignen, geschehen, laufen; *(Zeit)* anbrechen, beginnen; *(Unwetter)* aus-, los-, hereinbrechen; *(Wetter)* sich ändern, wechseln; aufhören, zu Ende gehen; bank(e)rott werden; *to be broken* kaputt, ruiniert sein; *to ~ camp* das Lager abbrechen; *to ~ even* gerade die Unkosten decken; *to ~ o.'s neck* sich den Hals brechen, ums Leben kommen; *to ~ the news* die Mitteilung machen, die Nachricht eröffnen; *to ~ the ranks (fig)* aus der Reihe tanzen; *mil* wegtreten; *~ step!* Ohne Tritt! *my heart ~s* mir bricht das Herz, es tut mir in der Seele weh; **2.** *s* Bruch(stelle *f*); Sprung, Riß, Durchbruch, Knick *m*; Lücke; Nische; Lichtung *f*; *el* Leitungsfehler *m*; Unterbrechung; Pause *f*; Urlaub *m*; Fortführungspunkte *m pl*; Absatz *m (in Schrift u. Druck)*; Unregelmäßigkeit *f*; Anbruch, Beginn; (Wetter-)Umbruch *m*; *(Kricket)* Abspringen *n* (des Balles); (Billard-)Serie *f*; *sl* Schnitzer, Fehltritt; *Am* Versuch *m*, (große) Anstrengung *f*; Fluchtversuch; *Am (~ in prices)* Preis-, Börsensturz; *Am fam* Fehler, Irrtum, Versager; *Am* entscheidende(r) Punkt *od* Augenblick *m*; *fam* Chance *f*, Glück(sfall *m*); Wagengestell *n (zum Einfahren junger Pferde)*; Kremser *m*; *without a ~* ohne Unterbrechung, ununterbrochen *adv*; *to get the ~s (Am)* Glück haben; *to make a clean ~* jede Verbindung abbrechen (*with* mit); *bad, tough* ~ (großes) Pech *n*; ~ *of day* Tagesanbruch *m*; *to* ~ **apart into** *tr* zerlegen in; *to* ~ **away** *itr* ab-, ausbrechen; abreißen; sich losreißen, sich trennen, sich lossagen (*from* von); *mil* sich absetzen (*from* von); *aero* abdrehen; *(Gewohnheiten)* aufgeben (*from s.th.* etw); *el* abschalten; *to* ~ **down** *tr* abbrechen, zs.schlagen; ausea.nehmen, abmontieren; *fig (Widerstand)* brechen; *(Kosten, Rechnung)* aufgliedern; *itr* aufhören zu funktionieren *od fam* zugehen; den Dienst versagen; betriebsunfähig werden, kaputt gehen; *mot* e-e Panne haben; *fig* versagen, ausfallen; zs.brechen; in Tränen ausbrechen; *(in der Rede)* steckenbleiben; ungültig werden; *to* ~ **forth** *itr* ausbrechen (*in cheers* in Hochrufe); hervorbrechen; *to* ~ **free** *itr* ausbrechen, sich befreien; *to* ~ **in** *tr* einbrechen, -stoßen; abrichten, dressieren; *(Lehrling)* anlernen; *(Schuhe)* einlaufen; *itr* einbrechen; unterbrechen; *to* ~ **in on** *itr* hineinplatzen in, unterbrechen; *to* ~ **into** *itr* einbrechen in; *fig* Fuß fassen; fallen (*into a gallop* in e-n Galopp); plötzlich beginnen mit; *to* ~ **loose** *tr* los-, abbrechen; *itr* ausbrechen, sich befreien, sich losreißen; *to* ~ **off** *tr* abbrechen; *fig (Verlobung)* aufheben, lösen; *itr (in der Rede)* aufhören, abbrechen; *to* ~ **open** *tr* auf-, erbrechen; *to* ~ **out** *itr (Gefangener, Feuer, Krieg)* ausbrechen; *med* e-n Ausschlag bekommen; *to* ~ *out into itr* ausbrechen in *(Gelächter, Schimpfereien)*; *to* ~ **through** *tr* durchstoßen; *to* ~ **up** *tr* auf-, er-, zerbrechen; *tech* ausea.nehmen; verschrotten; aufgraben; *fig (Veranstaltung)* abbrechen, aufheben; *(Versammlung)* auflösen, *(durch Gegner)* sprengen; unterteilen (*into* in), aufschlüsseln, aufgliedern; *fam* aus der Fassung bringen, kränken; *itr* in Stücke gehen, zerschellen; *fig* nachlassen, abnehmen, zs.fallen; zu Ende gehen, aufhören; ~ *it up!* auseinandergehen! ~**able** ['-əbl] zerbrechlich; ~**age** ['-idʒ] (Zer-)Brechen *n*; Bruch(stelle *f*); Bruch(schaden) *m*; ~**away** *(Fußball)* Durchbruch *m*; *(Boxen)* Trennen *n*; *sport* Fehlstart *m*; *pol* Absplitterung *f*; ~**down** ['-daun] Versagen *n*, Ausfall *m*; (Betriebs-)Störung; *mot* Panne *f*, Maschinenschaden *m*; *fig* Versagen *n*; Niedergang *m*; Scheitern *n*; Zs.bruch *m*; *tech* Kippen *n*; *el* Durchschlag *m*; listenmäßige Aufführung, Aufstellung; Aufgliederung, Detaillierung, Aufschlüsselung *f (e-r Rechnung, der Kosten)*; *Am Art* Negertanz *m*; ~~*van, lorry* Abschleppwagen *m*; ~~ *service* Stördienst *m*; ~**er** ['-ə] (Zer-)Brecher; (Gesetzes-)Übertreter; (Wort-, Vertrags-) Brüchige(r); (Rekord-)Brecher; Dresseur *m*; *mar* Wasserfaß *n*; Brecher *m*, Sturzwelle, -see; *pl* Brandung *f*; *el* Schalter *m*; ~**fast** ['brekfəst] *s* Frühstück *n*; *to have* ~~ u. *itr* frühstücken; ~~ *food* Hafergrütze *f etc*; ~-**in** Einbruch *m*; *tech* Einlaufen *n*; ~**ing** ['-iŋ] *s* (Zer-)Brechen, Zerkleinern *n*, Bruch *m*; Zerreißen; *el* Abschalten *n*; *a* (zer)brechend; Bruch-; ~~ *current* Abschaltstrom *m*; ~~-*off* Abbruch *m*; ~~-*test* Bruch-, Zerreißprobe *f*; ~~-*weight* Bruchlast *f*; ~**jaw** schwer auszusprechende(s) Wort *n*; ~**neck** halsbrecherisch; ~-**out** Ausbruch *m*; ~-**through** *mil* Durchbruch *m a. fig*; Preis-, Wertsteigerung; Sensation *f*; ~-**up** Auf-, Zerbrechen, Zerreißen *n*; Zerfall *m*, Auflösung *f a. fig*; Zs.bruch; (Wetter-)Umschwung, Wechsel *m*; Ende *n*, Schluß *m*; ~**water** Wellenbrecher *m*.

bream [bri:m] Brassen, Brachsen *m (Flußfisch)*.

breast [brest] *s* (*bes.* weibliche) Brust *f*, Busen *m*; Oberteil *n*; *fig* Nährboden *m*; *fig* Herz, Innere(s) *n*, Seele *f*, Gemüt *n*; *(Meer)* Spiegel; *min* Ort *m*; *tr* die Stirn bieten, trotzen (*s.th.* etw); vorgehen (*s.th.* gegen etw), losgehen (*s.th.* auf etw); *to make a clean* ~ *of s.th.* sich etw vom Herzen reden, etw frei bekennen; ~-**band** Brustband *n*; ~**bone** *anat* Brustbein *n*; ~ **collar** *(Pferdegeschirr)* Brustblatt *n*; ~**ed** ['-id] *a* -brüstig; *double-*~~ *(Jacke, Mantel)* zweireihig; *narrow-*~~ eng-, schmalbrüstig; *single-*~~ einreihig; ~-**fed** *a*: ~~ *child* Brustkind *n*; ~-**fin** Brustflosse *f*; ~-**high** *a* brusthoch; *adv* bis an die Brust *(im Wasser)*; ~**pin** Busen-, Krawattennadel; *Am* Brosche, Spange *f*; ~**plate** *hist* Bruststück *n*, -panzer; *(Schildkröte)* Bauchpanzer *m*; Inschrifttafel *f (an e-m Sarg)*; *(Pferd)* Brustriemen; *(Fallschirm)* Brustgurt *m*; ~ **pocket** Brusttasche *f*; ~-**stroke** Brustschwimmen *n*; ~-**wall** Stützmauer *f*; ~**work** *mil* Brustwehr *f*.

breath [breθ] Atem(zug *m*, -luft *f*); (Luft-)Hauch *m*; Atmung *f*; *fig* Augenblick *m*; *fig* Spur; *gram* Stimmlosigkeit *f*; *below, under o.'s* ~ leise, flüsternd; *in a* ~ im Nu; *in one, in the same* ~ in einem Atem, im gleichen Augenblick; *out of* ~ außer Atem, atemlos; *to catch o.'s* ~ Atem holen *od* schöpfen; verschnaufen; *to draw* ~, *to get o.'s* ~ Atem holen; *to gasp for* ~ nach Luft schnappen; *to hold o.'s* ~ den Atem anhalten; *to lose o.'s* ~ außer Atem kommen; *to save o.'s* ~ sich s-e Worte sparen; *to spend, to waste o.'s* ~ in den Wind reden, s-e Worte verschwenden; *to take* ~ Atem, Luft schöpfen; *to take a deep* ~ tief Atem, Luft holen; *to take s.o.'s* ~ *away* jdn sprachlos machen; ~**e** [bri:ð] *tr itr* (ein-, aus)atmen; hauchen; *itr* Luft holen; duften (*of* nach); e-n Ton von sich geben; leben; ausruhen; *(Wind)* wehen; *tr* (leise) sagen, aussprechen, flüstern; leise singen; *(Duft)* von sich geben, ausdünsten; *fig* atmen, ausstrahlen, an den Tag legen; verschnaufen lassen; stimmlos aussprechen; *mot* entlüften; *to allow to* ~~ verschnaufen lassen; *to force to* ~~ nicht zur Ruhe kommen lassen, keine Ruhe lassen (*s.o.* jdm); *to* ~~ *again, freely* tief aufatmen; von e-r Last befreit sein; *to* ~~ *hard* schwer Luft holen; *to* ~~ *in, out* ein-, ausatmen; *to* ~~ *o.'s last (*~*)* den letzten Atemzug tun; *don't* ~ *a word* verrate kein Wort (*on* über); ~**er** ['bri:ðə] Atmende(r) *m*; Atemübung; Atempause; *tech* Entlüftungsvorrichtung *f*; Atemgerät *n*; *fam* körperliche Anstrengung *f*; ~**ing** ['bri:ðiŋ] *s* Atmen *n*; Atemzug; Augenblick; Hauch *a. gram, gram* Spiritus *m*; Wehen *n*; Äußerung *f*; *a* lebenswahr, -echt; ~~ *apparatus* Sauerstoffgerät *n*; ~~-*space* Atem-, Ruhepause *f*; ~~-*tube (U-Boot)* Schnorchel *m*; ~**less** ['-lis] außer Atem, atemlos; ohne ein Lebenszeichen; *(Luft)* ruhig; windstill; ~-**taking** ['-teikiŋ] atemberaubend; ~ **test** *med* Atemtest *m*.

breech [bri:tʃ] Gesäß, Hinterteil *n*; *tech* Verschluß(stück *n*) *m*; *(Geschütz)* Ladeöffnung, -klappe *f*; *pl* Kniehose; *dial* Hose *f*; *to wear the* ~*es (Frau)* die Hosen anhaben; ~**es-buoy** *mar* Hosenboje *f*; ~**ing** ['-iŋ] *(Pferdegeschirr)* Umgang *m*; ~-**loader** Hinterlader *m (Gewehr)*.

breed [bri:d] *irr bred, bred itr* sich fortpflanzen, sich vermehren; Junge bekommen *od* werfen; (legen u.) brüten; erzeugt werden; *fig* entstehen; wachsen (*in* aus); *tr* tragen, werfen; ausbrüten; gebären; *agr* züchten; auf-, erziehen (zu); *allg u. fig* hervorbringen, erzeugen, die Ursache sein *gen*; *s* Brut *f*, *die* Jungen *pl*; Wurf *m*, Hecke; Zucht; Rasse; (Wesens-)Art *f*; ~**er** ['-ə] Erzeuger; Züchter; *phys* Brüter *m*; *fig* Quelle *f*, Ursprung *m*; *to be a good* ~~ ein gutes Zuchttier sein; *cattle* ~~ Viehzüchter *m*; ~**ing** ['-iŋ] Werfen; Brüten *n a. phys*; *agr* Zucht *a. fig*; Erziehung, Gesittung, Bildung *f*; ~~ *cage* Nistkasten *m*; ~~ *cattle* Zuchtvieh *n*; ~~ *ground* Nährboden *m*; ~~ *place (fig)* Brutstätte *f*.

breez|e [bri:z] **1.** *s* Brise *f*, (sanfter) Wind *m*, Lüftchen *n*; *fam* Zank *m*; schlechte Laune *f*; *itr sl* ('rum)sausen, -spritzen; *to* ~~ *by* vorbeiflitzen; *to* ~~ *in* frisch u. vergnügt hereinkommen; *there's not a* ~~ *stirring* es weht kein Lüftchen; **2.** *ent* Bremse *f*; **3.** (Koks-) Lösche *f*, Kohlenklein *n*, feine(r) Koks *m*, Kohlenschlacke *f*; Grus *m*; ~~ *block* Leichtbauplatte *f*; ~**y** ['-i] *(Wetter)* (leicht) windig; *(Platz)* luftig; *fig* lebhaft, forsch, flott; *tech* grusig.

brent [brent], ~-**goose** *s. brant(-goose)*.

brethren ['breðrin] *s. brother*.

Breton ['bretən] *a* bretonisch; *s* Bretone *m*, Bretonin *f*; *das* Bretonische.

brev|e [bri:v] amtliche(s), *bes.* päpstliche(s) Schreiben, Breve; *gram* Kürzezeichen *n*; *mus* Brevis, doppelganze Note *f*; ~**et** ['brevit] *s* Titularoffizierspatent *n*; *attr* Titular-; *tr* zum Titularoffizier ernennen; ~**iary** ['bri:vjəri] *rel* Brevier *n*; ~**ier** [brə'viə] *typ* Petit *f (Schriftgrad)*; ~**ity** ['breviti] Kürze (des Ausdrucks); Gedrängtheit, Bündigkeit; kurze (Zeit-)Spanne *f*.

brew [bru:] *tr (Bier, sonst fam)* brauen; *(Getränk)* kochen, mischen, zubereiten; *fig* zustande bringen, ins Werk setzen, *pej* ausbrüten, -hecken; *itr (Getränk)* brauen; *fig* sich zs.brauen, im Anzug sein, in der Luft liegen; *s* (Ge-)Bräu; Brauen *n*, Brauvorgang *m*; Braumenge, -qualität *f*; ~**age** ['-idʒ] Gebräu; *lit fig* Sich-Zs.brauen *n*; (schlimme) Folgen *f pl*; ~**er** ['-ə] Brauer *m*; ~~*'s grains* Treber *m*; ~**ery** ['-əri] Brauerei *f*; ~**ing** ['-iŋ] Bierbrauen *n*; Sud *m*; Gebräu *n*.

briar ['braiə] *s. brier*.

brib|e [braib] *s* Schmier-, Bestechungsgeld(er *pl*), -geschenk *n*; *tr* bestechen, *fam* schmieren; verleiten, -führen; ~**(e)able** ['-əbl] bestechlich, käuflich; ~**ery** ['-əri] Bestechung *f*; *attempt at* ~~ Bestechungsversuch *m*; *(not) open to* ~~ (un)bestechlich.

bric-à-brac ['brikəbræk] Antiquitäten *f pl*; Nippsachen *f pl*.

brick [brik] *s* Ziegel, Ziegel-, Bau-, Backstein; Block, Riegel *m*, Stück *n (Seife)*; Bauklotz *(Spielzeug)*; *sl* Pfundskerl *m*; *a* Backstein-; ziegelförmig; *tr* mit Ziegeln bauen, auslegen *od* pflastern; ziegelartig bemalen; *to* ~ *in, up* (mit Ziegelsteinen) zu-, vermauern; *to come down like a ton of* ~*s* heftig tadeln (*on s.o.* jdn); *to drop a* ~ *(sl)* sich vorbeibenehmen; *to make* ~*s without straw* nicht das nötige Handwerkszeug haben; *to swim like a* ~ wie e-e bleierne Ente schwimmen; ~**bat** *s* Ziegelbrocken *m*, Stück Ziegelstein *(als Wurfgeschoß)*; *fam* Schimpfwort *n*, Beleidigung *f*; ~ **dust** Ziegelmehl *n*; ~ **edging** Backsteineinfassung *f*; ~ **facing, veneer** Verkleidung *f* mit Blendsteinen; ~-**field, -kiln** Ziegelbrennerei *f*, -ofen *m*; ~ **foundation** Backsteinfundament *n*; ~**layer** Maurer *m*; ~ **machine** Strang-, Ziegelpresse *f*; **~-masonry** Backsteinbau *m*; **~-pavement** Klinkerpflaster *n*; **~-wall** Ziegelmauer *f*; *to talk to a ~~* tauben Ohren predigen; **~work** Backsteinbau *m*; (Aus-)Mauerung; Maurerarbeit *f*; *~~ base* Untermauerung *f*; *~* **works** *pl Am*, **~yard** *Br* Ziegelei *f*; **~y** ['-i] Backstein-, Ziegel-; ziegelrot; ziegelartig.

brid|al ['braidl] *a* bräutlich; hochzeitlich; Braut-; *s meist poet* Hochzeit(s-feier *f*, -fest *n*) *f*; *~~ bouquet, couple, wreath* od *garland, gown, veil* Brautstrauß *m*, -paar *n*, -kranz *m*, -kleid *n*, -schleier *m*; **~e** [braid] Braut; Neu-, Jungvermählte *f*; *~~cake* Hochzeitskuchen *m*; *~~groom* ['-grum] Bräutigam; Neu-, Jungvermählte(r) *m*; *~~smaid* Brautjungfer *f*; *~~sman* Brautführer *m*; *~~well* Arbeits-, Zuchthaus *n*, Strafanstalt *f*, Gefängnis *n*.

bridg|e [bridʒ] *s* Brücke *a. el sport*; *mar* Kommandobrücke *f*; *(Geige, Brille)* Steg; Nasenrücken *m*; *(a. ~~work)* Brücke *(Zahnprothese)*; *(Ofen)* Feuerbrücke *f*, -bock *m*; Bridge *n (Kartenspiel)*; *tr* e-e Brücke schlagen *od* bauen über; *(to ~~ over)* überbrücken *a. fig*; *railway ~~* Eisenbahnbrücke *f*; *suspension ~~* Hängebrücke *f*; *weigh-~~* Brückenwaage *f*; *~~ of boats* Schiffs-, Pontonbrücke *f*; *~~-head (mil)* Brükken-, Landekopf *m*; *~~ toll* Brückenzoll *m*; *~~-train (mil)* Brückentrain *m*; **~ing** ['-iŋ] Überbrückung *f*; Brückenbau *m*.

bridle ['braidl] *s* Zaum(zeug *n*); Zügel; *el* Spanndraht *m*; *tr* (auf)zäumen; *fig* im Zaum halten, zügeln; *itr (a. to ~ up) fig* sich brüsten; den Kopf hoch tragen; ärgerlich, böse werden (*at* über); **~-path, -road, -way** Reitweg *m*; **~-rein** Zügel *m*.

bridoon [bri'du:n] Trense *f* (u. Zügel *m pl*).

brief [bri:f] *s* Breve *n (päpstl. Schreiben)*; zs.fassende Darstellung *f* der Tatsachen u. rechtlichen Gegebenheiten e-s Falles; *jur* Schriftsatz *m*; *jur* Vollmacht *f (of the attorney* des Anwalts); *mil* Einsatzbefehl *m*; *mil aero* Flugbesprechung *f*; *pl fam* (Damen-)Schlüpfer *m*; *tr* e-n Auftrag geben (*s.o.* jdm); einweisen, instruieren, unterrichten; *jur (Fall)* zs.fassend darstellen; *mil* e-n genauen Lagebericht geben (*s. o.* jdm); *a* kurz, flüchtig, von kurzer Dauer; kurzgefaßt, knapp, gedrängt; *in ~* in Kürze, kurz *adv*; *to be ~* sich kurz fassen; *to hold a ~ for s.o.* jdn, jds Sache (vor Gericht) vertreten; *s.th.* etw billigen; **~-bag, -case** Aktentasche, -mappe *f*; **~ing** ['-iŋ] *mil* Befehlsausgabe *(für Kampfeinsatz)*; Einsatzbesprechung; *aero* Flugbesprechung; Einweisung *f*; *~~ room* Flugvorbereitungsraum *m*; **~ly** ['-li] *adv* kurz, in Kürze, mit wenigen Worten; **~ness** ['-nis] Kürze, Gedrängtheit *f*.

brier, briar ['braiə] **1.** Dornstrauch *m*, *bes.* Heckenrose *f (~-rose)*; Dornen, Dornsträucher *m pl*; **2.** Baumheide; Bruyèrepfeife *f*.

brig [brig] *mar* Brigg *f*; *Am mar mil* Arrestlokal *n*, -anstalt *f*; **~ade** [bri'geid] *s mil* Brigade; *allg* Kolonne *f*, Trupp *m*; *tr* zu e-r Brigade zs.fassen; einteilen, klassifizieren; *fire ~~* Feuerwehr *f*; **~adier** [brigə'diə], *(Am) ~~ general* Brigadegeneral *m*; **~and** ['brigənd] Räuber, Bandit *m*; **~andage** ['-idʒ] Räuberei *f*; Banditentum *n*.

bright [brait] *a* leuchtend, scheinend; strahlend, glänzend; klar, hell, heiter; *(Stahl)* blank; glücklich, freudestrahlend, freudig; lebhaft; *fam* aufgeweckt, gescheit, klug; *adv* glänzend; *~ and early* in aller Frühe; *B~'s disease (med)* Nierenschrumpfung *f*; **~en** ['braitn] *tr* hell, glänzend machen, (auf)polieren; blankmachen; aufheitern, heiter stimmen, froh, glücklich machen; *itr (Himmel)* sich aufhellen, sich aufklären; *fig* aufleuchten; **~ener** ['-nə] *film* Stativscheinwerfer, Aufheller *m*; *~* **light** *Am mot* Fernlicht *n*; **~ness** ['-nis] Glanz *m*, Klarheit, Helligkeit; *tech* Leuchtdichte, Beleuchtungsstärke; *fig* Heiterkeit; Lebhaftigkeit; Aufgewecktheit *f*.

brill [bril] *zoo* Glattbutt *m*; **~iance, -cy** ['briljəns(i)] helle(r) Glanz *m*, Leuchtkraft *f*; *(Edelstein)* Feuer *n*; *(Ton)* Brillanz; *fig* große Klugheit, geistige Wendigkeit *f*; **~iant** ['-jənt] *a* hell leuchtend; blendend, funkelnd, strahlend, glänzend; glanzvoll; *fig* sehr klug; aufsehenerregend; *s* Brillant *m a. typ*; **~iantine** [briljən'ti:n] Brillantine *f*.

brim [brim] *s* Rand *m (e-s Gefäßes)*; *(Hut)* Krempe *f*; *tr* bis an den Rand füllen, *itr* voll sein; *to ~ over (Gefäß)* überfließen; *fig* übersprudeln (*with* von); *full to the ~* voll bis an den Rand; **~ful** ['-ful] randvoll; *he is ~~ of new ideas* er steckt voller Ideen *od* Pläne; **~less** ['-lis] randlos; **~med** [-d] *a* : *broad ~~* breitrandig; **~mer** ['-ə] bis an den Rand gefüllte(r, s), volle(r, s) Becher *m*, Glas *n*; Humpen *m*; **~stone** ['-stən] *obs* Schwefel *m*; *~~ butterfly (ent)* Zitronenfalter *m*.

brindle(d) ['brindl(d)] *a (Haustier)* scheckig, bunt.

brine [brain] *s* Salzwasser *n*, Lake, Sole *f*; *meist poet* Meer *n*, See *f*; *poet* Tränen, Zähren *f pl*; *tr (Küche)* einpökeln, einsalzen; **~-pan** Salzpfanne *f*.

bring [briŋ] *irr brought, brought tr (Personen u. Sachen)* (mit-, her)bringen; holen; tragen; mitführen, bei sich haben; mit sich bringen, im Gefolge haben; verschaffen, schenken, geben; *(Preis)* erzielen; *(Person)* dazu bringen, veranlassen, bewegen; *to ~ upon o.s.* sich zuziehen; *to ~ to account* in Rechnung stellen; *to ~ an action against s.o.* gegen jdn e-e Klage einreichen; *to ~ to bear* anwenden (*on* auf), anbringen (*on* bei); geltend machen; *mil* einsetzen (*on* gegen); *to ~ to an end* zu Ende bringen, beenden; *to ~ to a head (fig)* auf die Spitze treiben; *to ~ to light* ans Licht bringen, an den Tag legen; *to ~ into play* ins Spiel bringen, einsetzen; ins Feld führen, auffahren; *to ~ s.o. to reason, to ~ s.o. to his senses* jdn zur Vernunft bringen; *to ~ to a stop* abstoppen; *to ~ to terms* auf die Knie zwingen; *to ~ into the world* zur Welt bringen; *to ~* **about** verursachen, veranlassen, herbeiführen; zustande, zuwege bringen; umdrehen, -kippen; to ~ **again** wieder-, zurückbringen; to ~ **along** mitbringen; erziehen; *to ~* **away** wegbringen, fortschaffen; *to ~* **back** ins Gedächtnis (zurück)rufen; *(Gegenstand)* zurückbringen; erbrechen; *to ~* **down** herunterbringen, -holen *(a. Flugzeug)*; umlegen, zur Strecke bringen; *(Preis)* herabsetzen, senken, (herunter)drükken; *fig* bescheidener werden lassen; fortführen, -setzen (*to* bis zu); *tech* übertragen; *to ~ down the house (theat)* die Zuschauer mitreißen; *to ~* **forth** zur Welt, hervorbringen, ins Leben rufen; enthüllen, ans Licht der Öffentlichkeit bringen; *to ~* **forward** aufweisen, vorbringen; zur Sprache, *fam* aufs Tapet bringen, anschneiden; *com* über-, vortragen; *to ~* **home** überzeugen (*s.th. to s.o.* jdn von e-r S); klar, deutlich machen, zu Gemüte führen (*s.th. to s.o.* jdm etw); einsehen lassen (*to s.o.* jdn); *to ~ home the bacon, the groceries* erfolgreich sein; genügend verdienen; *to ~* **in** *(finanziell)* einbringen, abwerfen; aufbringen; hereinbringen; vorlegen, -weisen; *(Waren)* einführen; *(Bericht)* vorlegen; *(Gesetzesvorlage)* einbringen; zu bedenken geben; anführen; *to ~ in (not) guilty (jur fam)* für (nicht) schuldig erklären; *to ~* **off** wegbringen, -führen, fortschaffen; *(Schiffbrüchige)* retten; *fam* zustande, zuwege bringen; verwirklichen; zu e-m günstigen Abschluß bringen; *to ~* **on** verursachen, bewirken, zur Folge haben, herbeiführen, führen zu ; an-, zur Sprache bringen; fördern, vorwärts-, weiterbringen; *to ~* **out** herausbekommen; herauslocken; *(Leitung)* herausführen; klar, deutlich machen, aufdecken; *(Standpunkt)* vorbringen, vertreten; anwenden, aufbringen; *(Buch)* herausbringen, veröffentlichen; *(Ware)* auf den Markt bringen; *(junges Mädchen)* in die Gesellschaft einführen; *(Pflanzen, Blätter, Blüten)* treiben, zur Entwicklung bringen *a. fig*; *to ~* **over** umstimmen; *(für e-e andere Ansicht, Überzeugung, für e-n andern Glauben)* gewinnen, *fam* 'rumkriegen; *(Besucher)* mitbringen; *to ~* **round,** *Am* **around** *(nach e-m Anfall* od *e-r Ohnmacht)* wieder zu sich bringen; wieder auf die Beine bringen; aufheitern; *fam (Besucher)* mitbringen; umstimmen, überzeugen, überreden, *fam* 'rumkriegen; *to ~* **through** *(Kranken)* durchbringen, helfen (*s.o.* jdm); *to ~* **to** *tr (Ohnmächtigen)* wieder zu sich bringen; *tr itr* anhalten; *itr mar* beidrehen; *to ~* **under** unterwerfen, untertan machen; *to ~ under control* unter Kontrolle bringen; *to ~* **up** *tr* heraufbringen, -holen; auf-, erziehen; gerichtlich belangen; zum Schweigen bringen; servieren, auftragen; *(Truppen)* einsetzen; *(Schiff)* vor Anker legen; zum Stillstand bringen, anhalten; (wieder) aufmerksam machen auf, zur Sprache, *fam* aufs Tapet bringen, vorbringen; *parl* das Wort erteilen (*s.o.* jdm); fortführen, -setzen; erbrechen; *itr* (plötzlich) anhalten, aufhören; *(Schiff)* vor Anker gehen; *to ~ up the rear* als letzter kommen; *mil* die Nachhut bilden; **~down** *Am sl s* Murks; Trauerkloß *m*; *a* unerfahren, grün; unbefriedigend; niederdrückend; **~er** ['-ə] (Über-)Bringer *m*; **~ing** ['-iŋ]: *~~-up* Aufziehen *n*; Erziehung *f*.

brink [briŋk] Rand *m (e-s Steilhangs)*; (steiles) Ufer *n*; *on the ~ of disaster, of ruin (fig)* am Rande des Abgrunds; *to be on the ~ of the grave* mit einem Fuß im Grabe stehen.

briny ['braini] salz(halt)ig.

briquet(te) [bri'ket] Brikett *m*.

brisk [brisk] *a* lebhaft, munter, schnell, rasch, flott; belebend, anregend, feurig; *v (meist to ~ up) tr* anregen, beleben, anfeuern; *itr* lebhaft, feurig werden; **~et** ['-it] *(Küche)* Brust(stück *n*) *f*; **~ness** ['-nis] Lebhaftigkeit, Munterkeit *f*.

bristl|e ['brisl] *s* Borste *f*; *tr itr (Haar)* (sich) sträuben, zu Berge stehen (lassen) *(oft to ~ up)*; *itr* strotzen *a. fig* (*with* von); *fig* stecken (*with* voller); *fig* die Zähne zeigen; **~ed, ~y** ['-d, '-li] *a* borstig, stach(e)lig; *fig* kratzborstig, widerhaarig.

bris(t)ling ['brisliŋ] Brisling *m*, Sprotte *f*.

Brit|ain ['britən] *hist* Britannien *n*; *Great* ~~ Großbritannien *n*; *North* ~~ Schottland *n*; **~annia** [-'tænjə] *poet* Großbritannien, England *n*; ~~ *metal* Neusilber *n*; **~annic** [-'tænik] britisch *(hauptsächlich in:) Her (His)* ~~ *Majesty* Ihre (Seine) Majestät die Königin (der König) von England; **~icism** ['-isizm] *Am s. -ishism (Br)*; **~ish** ['-iʃ] *a* britisch, englisch; *s*: *the* ~~ die Briten; *the* ~~ *Isles (geog)* die Britischen Inseln; **~isher** Brite *m*; **~ishism** ['-iʃizm] britisch-englische Spracheigentümlichkeit *f*; **~on** ['-ən] *hist* Britannier; Brite *n*; *North* ~~ Schotte *m*; **~(t)any** ['-əni] die Bretagne.

brittle ['britl] *a* zerbrechlich, spröde, brüchig; *fig* hin-, anfällig, schwach, wenig widerstandsfähig; reizbar; *s Art* Bonbon *n*; **~ness** ['-nis] Zerbrechlich-, Sprödigkeit *f*.

*

broach [broutʃ] *s* Bratspieß *m*; (Räum-, Reib-)Ahle; Kirchturmspitze; Brosche *f*; *tr* anzapfen, -stechen; anbrechen; *fig (Thema)* anschneiden; *(Frage)* aufrollen; zur Sprache, aufs Tapet bringen.

broad [brɔ:d] *a* breit; weit; groß; voll, völlig; spürbar, merklich, offen(kundig), klar, deutlich, unmißverständlich; *(Sprache)* breit, gewöhnlich; kunstlos, ungekünstelt, derb, anzüglich; dreist, frech; allgemein; umfassend, weit, verständnisvoll, nachsichtig, duldsam; *adv* voll(ständig, -kommen), völlig, ganz; *s* breite(r) Teil *m*; *Am sl* Weib *n*; Nutte *f*; *as* ~ *as it is long* so breit wie lang, Jacke wie Hose, gleichgültig, egal; *in* ~ *outline* im Umriß, in groben Zügen; *~ly speaking* im allgemeinen; ~ **ax(e)** Breit-, Richtbeil *n*; ~ **bean** Pferdebohne *f*; **B~ Church** liberale(r) Teil *m* der (Anglikanischen) Kirche; **~cloth** feine(r), *bes.* schwarze(r) Anzugstoff; *Am* feine(r) Wäschestoff *m*; **~en** ['-n] *tr itr* (sich) verbreitern, (sich) erweitern; **~-faced** *a* mit breitem, vollem Gesicht; **~-gauge** *a (a.* ~*~d) rail* breitspurig; Breitspur-; *Am fam* in großem Maßstab; großzügig, verständnisvoll; *s* Breitspur *f*; ~ **hint** deutliche(r) Wink *m*; **~ish** ziemlich breit; ~ **jump** *Am* Weitsprung *m*; **~-minded** *a* weitherzig, verständnisvoll, großzügig; **~sheet** einseitig bedruckte(r) Bogen *m*; Plakat; Querformat *n*; **~side** *s mar* Breitseite *f*; *fam* Großangriff *m*; einseitig bedruckte(r) Bogen *m*, Plakat *n*; *fam* gemeine Schmähung *f*; ~~ *on, to* mit der Breitseite nach; *adv* mit der Breitseite (*to* gegen); querab; **~sword** Säbel *m* mit breiter Klinge; **~tail** Breitschwanzschaf, Karakul *n*; **~ways, ~wise** *adv* seitlich, -wärts, der Breite nach, in die Breite.

broadcast ['brɔ:dkɑ:st] *s* Rundfunk *m*, Radio *n*; Sendung, (Rundfunk-, Funk-) Übertragung, Durchgabe *f*; *v irr* ~, ~; *radio a.* ~*ed*, ~*ed tr* senden, übertragen, funken; im Rundfunk, Radio übertragen, durchgeben; durch den, im, über den Rundfunk verbreiten; weit verbreiten; an die große Glocke hängen, ausposaunen; *itr* ein Rundfunkprogramm ausstrahlen; *a (Saat)* breitwürfig *a. adv*, mit der Hand (aus)gesät; *fig* weit ausholend, in die Breite gehend, umfassend; weitverbreitet; *adv* in die Breite; nach allen Seiten; *facsimile* ~*(ing)* Bildfunk *m*; *radio* ~*(ing)* Rundfunk; Hörfunk *m*; Hörsendung *f*; *television* ~*(ing)* Bildfunk *m*; Fernsehsendung *f*; **~er** ['-ə] Rundfunksprecher; *news* ~~ Nachrichtensprecher *m*; **~ing** ['-iŋ] Funken, Senden *n*; (Rund-)Funk *m*, Radio *n*; *attr* (Rund-)Funk-, Radio-; *B~~ Corporation* Rundfunkgesellschaft *f*; ~~ *engineering* Funktechnik *f*; ~~ *range* Hörbereich *n*; ~~ *station* (Rundfunk-) Sender *m*; Sendestation, -stelle *f*; Funkhaus *n*; ~~ *studio* Senderaum *m*; ~~ *time* Sendezeit *f*; ~ **receiver** Rundfunkempfänger *m*; ~ **reception** Rundfunkempfang *m*; **station** (Rund-) Funk-, Sendestation, -stelle *f*, Funkhaus *n*; ~ **studio** Rundfunkstudio *n*, -aufnahmeraum *m*.

brocade [brə'keid] *s* Brokat *m*; *tr (Gewebe)* broschieren, mit Brokatmuster versehen.

broc(c)oli ['brɔkəli] Brokkoli *pl*, Spargelkohl *m*.

brochure ['brou-, brə'ʃjuə] Broschüre *f*.

brock [brɔk] Dachs; *fig* stinkende(r) Kerl *m*; **~et** ['-it] Spießer *m (Hirsch im 2. Jahr)*.

brodie ['broudi] *Am sl s* Schnitzer, Mißerfolg, Reinfall *m*; *itr* versagen; Selbstmord begehen.

brogue [broug] derbe(r) (Arbeits-) Schuh; Golfschuh; irische(r) Akzent *m*; *fishing* ~*s (pl)* Wasserstiefel *m pl*.

broil [brɔil] **1.** *s* Tumult, Aufruhr *m*, Unruhe *f*, Lärm; Zank, Streit *m*; **2.** *tr* an offenem Feuer *od* auf dem Rost braten, rösten; *tr itr (Mensch)* (in der Sonne) braten, schmoren; *s* Hitze *f*; (Rost-)Braten *m*; **~er** ['-ə] **1.** Unruh(e)stifter, Aufrührer *m*; **2.** Bratrost *m*; Brathuhn *n*; *Am sl* Backfisch, Teenager, Flapper *m*; *sl (~ing hot day)* glühendheiße(r) Tag *m*, Backofen-, Bullenhitze *f*.

brok|e [brouk] *pp obs zu break a sl* abgebrannt, pleite, ruiniert; bank(e)rott, *fam* kaputt; *to go* ~~ ruiniert sein; pleite gehen; *I am dead* ~~ *(sl)* ich bin vollständig blank, ohne einen Pfennig (Geld), **~en** ['-ən] *pp zu break a* unvollständig, lückenhaft; unvollkommen; ge-, zerbrochen, zerrissen, *fam* kaputt; *(Stimmung)* gedrückt; *(Gesundheit)* zerrüttet; *(Tier)* gezähmt; *(Pferd)* zugeritten; *mil* degradiert; *(Gelände)* uneben; *(Linie)* punktiert, gestrichelt; *~~-down (Pferd)* abgearbeitet; *(Maschine)* nicht in Ordnung, nicht betriebs-, gebrauchsfähig; abgenutzt, verbraucht, *fam* hin(über); *(Mensch) (gesundheitlich)* angegriffen, *fam* heruntergekommen, mitgenommen; krank; ~~ *English* gebrochene(s) Englisch *n*; ~~ *ground* unebene(s) Gelände *n*; *~~-hearted (a)* mit gebrochenem Herzen; ~~ *lots (pl)* Gelegenheitskäufe *m pl*; ~~ *man* Ruinierte(r), Verzweifelte(r) *m*; ~~ *meat, bread* Fleisch-, Brotrest(e *m pl*) *m*; ~~ *money* Klein-, Wechselgeld *n*; ~~ *number* Bruch(zahl *f*) *m*; ~~ *sleep* unterbrochene(r) Schlaf *m*; ~~ *stones (pl)* Steinschlag *m*; ~~ *time* Kurzarbeit *f*, Arbeits-, Lohnausfall *m*; ~~ *water* See *f* mit kurzen, heftigen Wellen; ~~ *weather* unbeständige(s) Wetter *n*; *~~-winded (a) (Pferd)* dämpfig; **~er** ['-ə] Makler, Agent, Vermittler; Gerichtsvollzieher *m*; *to act as an honest* ~~ vermitteln; *exchange* ~~ Börsenmakler *m*; *insurance* ~~ Versicherungsagent, -vertreter *m*; *real estate* ~~ Grundstücksmakler *m*; *ship(ping)* ~~ Schiffsmakler *m*; *~~'s office* Maklerbüro *n*, Agentur *f*; **~erage** ['-əridʒ] Maklergeschäft *n*; Maklergebühr, (Makler-)Provision, Courtage *f*; **~ing** ['-iŋ] Maklergeschäft *n*, Vermittlung, Agentur *f*.

brolly ['brɔli] *sl* Musspritze *f*, Schirm; *sl* Fallschirm *m*.

brom|ate ['broumeit] *chem* Bromat, Salz *n* der Bromsäure; **~ide** ['-aid] *chem* Bromid *n*; *Am sl* Phrasendrescher *m*; Nervensäge *f*; abgedroschene(s) Zeug *n*, Banalität, Phrase *f*.

bronchi|(a) ['brɔŋkai, -iə] *pl anat* Bronchien *f pl*; **~al** ['-iəl] *a* Bronchial-; **~tis** [-'kaitis] Bronchitis *f*, Bronchialkatarrh *m*.

bronc(h)o ['brɔŋkou] kalifornische(s) (halb)wilde(s) Pferd *n*; ~ **buster** *Am* Zureiter *m*.

Bronx [brɔŋks] *Stadtteil von New York*; *Am Art* Cocktail *m (~ cocktail)* aus Gin, Wermut u. Orangensaft; ~ **cheer** *Am sl* verächtliches Zischen, Buhrufen *n*; spöttische Bemerkung *f*; ~ **vanilla** *Am sl* Knoblauch *m*.

bronz|e [brɔnz] *s* Bronze; Bronze(arbeit) *f*; *a* bronzen, aus Bronze, Bronze-; bronzefarben; *tr* bronzieren; *tr itr (in der Sonne)* bräunen; *B~ Age* Bronzezeit *f*; **~y** ['-i] bronzen.

brooch [broutʃ] Brosche, Vorstecknadel *f*.

brood [bru:d] *s* Brut *a. pej*; *pej* Sippschaft *f*; Schwarm, Haufen *m*; *attr* Brut-, Zucht-; *itr* brüten *a. fig (on, over* über); schwer lasten (*over, on* auf); **~er** ['-ə] Wärmekasten *m*; Schirmglucke *f*; **~-mare** Zuchtstute *f*; **~y** ['-i] *(Henne)* brütig; *fig* niedergedrückt.

brook [bruk] **1.** *s* Bach *m*; **~lime** *bot* Bachbunge *f*; ~ **trout** Bachforelle *f*; **2.** *tr (meist verneint)* ertragen, aushalten; gestatten.

broom [bru(:)m] *s bot* Ginster; Besen *m*; *tr* fegen, kehren; *a new* ~ *sweeps clean* neue Besen kehren gut; ~ **corn** *Am* Mohrenhirse *f*; ~ **cupboard** Besenschrank *m*; **~stick** Besenstiel *m*.

broth [brɔ(:)θ] (Fleisch-)Brühe *f*; *a* ~ *of a boy (irisch)* ein guter Kerl; ~ **cube** Brühwürfel *m*; **~el** ['brɔθl] Bordell *n*; **~er** ['brʌðə] Bruder *m a. fig rel (pl rel brethren)*; *pl com* Gebrüder *m pl*; *attr* Mit-; *~~(s) and sister(s)* Geschwister *pl*; **~erhood** Brüderschaft; Berufsgenossenschaft; *Am fam* Gewerkschaft; Brüderlichkeit *f*; **~er-in-law** Schwager *m*; **~erly** *a* brüderlich.

brougham ['bruəm, bru:m] einspännige(r), geschlossene(r), zweisitzige(r) Wagen *m*, Coupé *n*.

brow [brau] Augenbraue *f*; Augenbrauenbogen *m*; Stirn *a. fig*; *poet* Miene *f*, Gesichtsausdruck; Rand *(e-s Abhangs)*, Vorsprung *m*; (Berg-)Kuppe *f*; *to knit o.'s* ~*s* die Stirn runzeln; **~beat** ['-bi:t] *irr s. beat tr* einschüchtern; *to* ~~ *s.o. into doing s.th.* jdn so einschüchtern, daß er etw tut.

brown [braun] *a* braun; braungebrannt; dunkelhäutig; *poet* dunkel, düster *a. fig*; *fig* ernst; *s* Braun *n*, braune Farbe *f*, braune(r) Farbstoff *m*; *sl* Kupfermünze *f*; *tr* bräunen; brünieren; braun braten *od* backen; *itr* braun werden, sich bräunen; *to* ~ *off (sl mil)* anscheißen, -pfeifen; erledigen; *to be in a* ~ *study* völlig in Gedanken verloren sein; *to do* ~ *(sl)* 'reinlegen, anführen; *to do up* ~ *(sl)* völlig erledigen; *I'm ~ed off (sl)* das hab' ich satt, das hängt mir zum Halse 'raus, das steht mir bis oben; ~ **betty** *Art* Apfelpudding *m*; ~ **bread** Graubrot *n*; ~ **coal** Braunkohle *f*; ~ **ie** ['-i] Heinzelmännchen *n*; *phot (billige)* Box; junge Pfadfinderin *f*; *Am Art* Schokoladengebäck *n*; **~ish** ['-iʃ] bräunlich; **~out** *Am* Teilverdunkelung *f*; ~ **paper** Packpapier *n*; **~stone** *Am* Sandstein *m*; ~ **sugar** Rohzucker *m*.

browse [brauz] *s* Weiden *n*; *tr* abweiden, abfressen; *itr* weiden; *fig (in Bü-*

chern) (herum)schmökern, flüchtig lesen, durchblättern.

bruin ['bru:in] Meister Petz *m.*

bruise [bru:z] *s med* Quetschung *f,* braune(r) *od* blaue(r) Fleck *m;* braune Stelle *f (an Obst); tr* quetschen, stoßen *(a. Obst);* braun u. blau schlagen; *(Knie)* aufschlagen; *(Malz)* schroten; zerkleinern, -stoßen, -quetschen; verbeulen; *(Gefühle)* verletzen; *itr* gequetscht, gestoßen werden, braune u. blaue Flecke bekommen; **~r** ['-ə] *fig fam* Bulle; (Berufs-)Boxer *m; tech* Schleifschale *f.*

bruit [bru:t] *tr obs (Gerücht)* verbreiten.

Brummagem ['brʌmədʒəm] *s dial pej* Birmingham; *sl* Ramsch *m;* falsche(s) Geldstück *n;* unechte(r) Schmuck *m; a* falsch, unecht; billig.

brunch [brʌntʃ] *fam* Frühstück u. Mittagessen *n* zugleich.

brunet(te) [bru:'net] *a* brünett; *s* Brünette *f.*

brunt [brʌnt] Hauptangriff, -stoß; Anprall *m;* Hitze *f* des Gefechts *a. fig; fig* Hauptarbeit *f,* Haupt-, Stoßgeschäft *n; to bear the ~ of s.th.* die Hauptlast e-r S tragen.

brush [brʌʃ] *s* Bürste *f;* Pinsel; Pinselstrich *m,* Malweise; Quaste *f;* Abbürsten *n;* leichte Berührung *f;* (*bes.* Fuchs-)Schwanz *m;* Gestrüpp, Gebüsch *n,* Busch *m,* Unterholz *n; fig* unkultivierte Gegend *f;* Lichtbündel, -büschel *n; el* Schleifbürste; *el (~ discharge)* Büschelentladung *f;* Ansturm, kurze(r) heftige(r) Kampf; Zs.stoß *m,* Scharmützel *n; pl mus Art* Trommelschlegel *m pl; tr* (ab)bürsten, -kehren, -fegen; reinigen, leicht berühren, streifen; *Am* erzwingen; *itr* vorbeistreichen, -fliegen, -sausen, -fegen; stürmen, eilen; *attr Am sl* ländlich; Bauern-; *to ~ aside, away* beiseite schieben, übergehen, ignorieren, sich nicht kümmern um, zur Tagesordnung übergehen (*s.th.* über etw); *to ~ by* vorbeieilen, -stürmen, -sausen; *to ~ off (Am) tr* abbürsten, (auf)polieren; *fig* übergehen, beiseite schieben; e-e Abfuhr erteilen; *itr sl* entkommen; *to ~ over* abbürsten; streifen; auf die Leinwand werfen; *to ~ up* (auf)polieren, abbürsten, reinigen; *fig (Erinnerung, Kenntnisse)* auffrischen (*s.th., (Am) on s.th.* etw); *to give s.o. a ~* jdn abbürsten; **~-off** *sl* Abfuhr, Absage *f; to give the ~~* abfahren lassen; *to get the ~~* e-e Abfuhr einstecken (müssen); **~-pencil** Haar-, Malerpinsel *m;* **~wood** Unterholz, Dickicht *n;* **~-work** Pinselstrich *m;* Malweise *f;* **~y** ['-i] mit Gestrüpp, Gebüsch bedeckt; büschelartig, zottig.

brusque [brusk, brʌsk] brüsk, barsch, grob, *fam* kurz angebunden; **~ness** ['-nis] schroffe(s) Wesen *n.*

Brussels ['brʌslz] Brüssel *n;* **~ lace, net** Brüsseler Spitzen *f pl,* Tüll *m;* **~ sprouts** *pl* Rosenkohl *m.*

brut|al ['bru:tl] roh, brutal; grausam; viehisch; gierig; dumm; **~ality** [-'tæliti] Roheit, Brutalität *f;* **~alize** ['-əlaiz] *tr* roh, brutal machen; brutalisieren, brutal, roh behandeln; **~e** [bru:t] *s* niedere(s) Tier; Vieh *n;* rohe(r), gefühllose(r) Mensch, Rohling *m; a* viehisch, grausam, brutal, roh; stumpf, gefühllos, unverständig; *(Materie)* unbelebt, unbewußt; *(Kraft)* roh; **~ish** ['bru:tiʃ] tierisch, viehisch; dumm, roh, gierig.

bub [bʌb] *Am fam* Bub, Junge *m.*

bubbl|e ['bʌbl] *s* (Luft-, Seifen-)Blase *f;* Sprudeln *n; fig* Schaum *m;* Luftschloß *n;* Schwindel *m; attr* Schwindel-; *itr* Blasen werfen, sprudeln, blubbern, schäumen; *to ~~ over* überfließen, -sprudeln; *fig* außer Rand u. Band sein; *to prick the ~~* den Schwindel auffliegen lassen; *soap-~~* Seifenblase *f;* *~~ bath* Schaumbad *n;* *~~-car (mot)* Kabinenroller *m;* *~~ gum* Ballongummi *m;* *~~ head (Am sl)* blöde(r) Kerl *m;* **~er** ['-ə] Trinkfontäne *f;* **~ing** ['-iŋ] Blasenbildung *f;* **~y** ['-i] *a* voller Blasen; sprudelnd; *s sl* Champagner *m.*

bubo ['bju:bou] *pl -oes med* Achsel- *od* Leistendrüsenschwellung; Leistengeschwulst *f;* **~nic** [-'bɔnik] *a: ~~ plague* Beulenpest *f;* **~nocele** [-'bɔnosi:l] *med* Leistenbruch *m.*

buccan|eer, ~ier [bʌkə'niə] *s* Seeräuber, Pirat, Freibeuter *m.*

buck [bʌk] *s* Bock *(Männchen von Reh u. Steinwild);* Rammler *(männl. Hase); Am* (Schaf-)Bock; *(old ~)* Geck, Stutzer; *Am sl* Neger, Indianer; *Am fam* junge(r) Mann; *(saw-~)* Sägebock; Bock *m (Turngerät);* Aalreuse *f; Am sl* Dollar *m; Br* Prahlerei, *fam* Angabe *f; Am (Fußball)* Angriff *m; itr (Pferd)* bocken; *Br* prahlen, angeben; *Am (Mensch)* bocken, bockig sein, sich sträuben, nicht wollen, sich widersetzen; *fam* Theater machen; *Am* ruckweise fahren; *tr Am* losgehen (*s.o.* auf jdn); sich widersetzen (*s.o.* jdm); *sport* angreifen; *to ~ for (sl)* sich mächtig ins Zeug legen; *to ~ off (Pferd)* abwerfen; *to ~ up (itr)* sich beeilen, sich sputen; stark, munter *od* vergnügt werden; sich zs.reißen; *tr* stark machen, stärken, kräftigen; ermutigen, er-, aufmuntern, aufheitern; *in the ~s (Am sl)* bei Geld; *as hearty as a ~ (Am)* gesund u. munter, munter wie ein Fisch im Wasser; *to pass the ~* die Verantwortung abschieben (*to* auf); den Schwarzen Peter weitergeben (*to* an); **~-bean** *bot* Sumpfklee *m;* **~board** *Am hist Art* einfache(r) einsitzige(r) Wagen *m;* **~ed** [-t] *a* munter, vergnügt, lustig; **~er** ['-ə] *Am sl* Streber; *Am* Cowboy *m;* bockige(s) Pferd *n;* **~eye** amerik. Roßkastanie *f;* **~ fever** *fam* Jagdfieber *n;* **~-handled** *a* mit Horngriff *m;* **~-horn** Hirschhorn *n (Material);* **~-hound** Parforcehund *m;* **~-jump** Bocksprung *m;* **~ naked** *a sl* splitternackt; **~o** ['-ou] *pl -oes Am sl s* Kerl; Bulle *m; a* stark, kräftig; **~ private** *Am sl* Muschkote, einfache(r) Soldat *m;* **~ram** ['-rəm] Steifleinen *n; fig* Steifheit *f,* steife(s) Wesen *n;* **~saw** *Am* Steifsäge *f;* **~seat** *Am* Notsitz *m;* **~shot** Rehposten *m;* **~skin** Wildleder *n;* **~slip** Schriftstück *n,* das e-e Aufgabe zuständigkeitshalber weitergibt; **~stick** *sl* Angeber, Aufschneider, Prahlhans *m;* **~thorn** Gemeine(r) Kreuz-, Hirschdorn *m;* **~-tooth** Raffzahn *m;* **~wheat** Buchweizen *m; Am* Buchweizenmehl *n,* -teig *m,* -gericht *n; (~~ cake)* Buchweizenkuchen *m.*

bucket ['bʌkit] *s* Eimer, Kübel; Pumpenkolben *m;* Schaufel, Zelle *f (e-s Wasserrades, e-r Turbine);* (Bagger-)Eimer; *min* Förderkübel; *sl* Abort *m; sl* Hinterteil *n; tech* Dose, Hülse, Fassung; *Am sl mot* alte Klapperkiste, Mühle *f;* altes Schiff *n; sl* unangenehme(s) Frauenzimmer *n; tr (Pferd)* müde reiten, erschöpfen; *itr sl* Wasser schöpfen; drauflosreiten, -rudern; *to kick the ~ (sl)* ins Gras beißen (müssen); **~ful** ['-ful] Eimer-, Kübelvoll *m;* **~-seat** Kübelsitz *m;* **~-shop** Winkelbörse *f.*

buckle ['bʌkl] *s* Schnalle, Spange *f; tr* an-, um-, zuschnallen; *tech* (ver-)biegen, krümmen, verziehen; knikken; *itr tech* sich werfen; sich verziehen; *to ~ down to s.th.* sich eifrig an e-e S machen, etw ernsthaft in Angriff nehmen; *to ~ to* sich beeilen; *to ~ under* zs.brechen; *to ~ up* ausea.brechen, kaputt gehen; **~r** ['-ə] (runder) Schild; *fig* Schutz, (Be-)Schützer *m.*

buckshee ['bʌkʃi:] *sl* umsonst.

bucolic [bju'kɔlik] *a lit* Hirten-; *s* Hirtengedicht *n.*

bud [bʌd] **1.** *s* Knospe *f a. zoo,* Auge *n,* Keim *m a. fig;* Blüten-, *fig* Mädchenknospe *f; fig* Anfangsstadium *n; Am* Debütantin *f; itr* knospen, keimen *a. fig;* ausschlagen; *fig* im Werden begriffen, im Entstehen sein, aufblühen; *zoo* durch Knospung entstehen, *tr* hervorbringen; *itr u. tr* pfropfen, okulieren; *in (the) ~* voller Knospen; *to nip in the ~ (fig)* im Keim ersticken; **2.** *fam* Bruder *a. allg;* Kamerad, Genosse, Kumpel *(a. als Anrede);* Junge, Bub *m; Am* Kind, junge(s) Mädchen *n;* **~ding** ['-iŋ] *fig* angehend; *~~ knife* Okuliermesser *n; a ~~ lawyer, poet* ein angehender Rechtsanwalt, Dichter *m;* **~dy** ['-i] *s Am sl* Kumpel *m; itr: to ~~ up* eng befreundet sein; mitea. zs.wohnen; sich anbiedern; *~~ seat (mot sl)* Beiwagen *m; sl* einflußreiche Stellung *f.*

Buddh|ism ['budizm] Buddhismus *m;* **~ist** ['-ist] *a, a.* **~istic** [bu'distik] buddhistisch; *s* Buddhist(in *f*) *m.*

budge [bʌdʒ] **1.** *s* Lammfell *n; a* mit Lammfell besetzt; *fig* prahlerisch, wichtigtuerisch; **2.** *(nur negiert) itr* sich rühren, sich bewegen; *tr* (fort)bewegen, von der Stelle bringen; **~rigar** ['-ərigɑ:] Wellensittich *m.*

budget ['bʌdʒit] *s* Vorrat *m,* Sammlung *f (meist fig);* Voranschlag; Haushalt(splan) *m,* Budget *n,* Etat *m; tr* in den Voranschlag einsetzen; im Haushaltsplan vorsehen; einteilen, genau planen; *itr* den Haushaltsplan aufstellen; *to ~ for s.th.* etw im Etat vorsehen; *to balance the ~* den (Staats-)Haushalt ausgleichen; *to introduce, to open the ~* den Haushalt, das Budget vorlegen; *to make up the ~* den Haushaltsplan, den Etat aufstellen; *to pass the ~* den Etat annehmen; **~ary** ['-əri] *a* Haushalt-, Budget-; etatmäßig; *extra-~~* außer-, nicht etatmäßig; *~~ appropriations (pl)* (bewilligte) Haushaltsmittel *n pl; ~~ commission* Haushaltsausschuß *m; ~~ control* Haushaltskontrolle *f; ~~ deficit* Haushaltfehlbetrag *m;* **~-priced** *a* preisgünstig.

buff [bʌf] *s* dicke(s), weiche(s) Büffel- *od* Rindleder; *hist* Lederkoller *n; fam* bloße Haut *f; fam* begeisterte(r) Anhänger *m;* stumpfe(s) Gelbbraun *n; tech* Polierscheibe *f; a* beige, leder-, sandfarben; *tr* schwabbeln; *(Leder)* weich machen; *in ~* im Adamskostüm, nackt; **~alo** ['bʌfəlou] *pl -o(e)s s* Büffel; Wisent; Bison *m;* Büffelfleisch *n; Am sl* Nigger *m; Am sl* dicke Frau *f; tr Am sl* einschüchtern, bange machen; *~~ hide* Büffelhaut *f; ~~ robe* Büffelfell *n;* **~er** ['-ə] **1.** *tech* Puffer, Prellbock *m; el* Trennstufe *f;* **2.** Polierer; **3.** komische(r), alte(r) Kauz; **4.** *Am sl* (Wach-)Hund *m; ~~ state* Pufferstaat *m; ~~ stop (rail)* Prellbock *m;* **~et** ['bʌfit] **1.** *s* Schlag (mit der Hand); *fig* (Schicksals-, harter) Schlag *m, tr* schlagen, hauen, boxen; umherwerfen; *(fig) (Schlag)* treffen; (an-)kämpfen gegen *(a. itr: to ~~ with); itr* sich durchkämpfen, -schlagen; **2.** [-] Büfett *(Möbel);* ['bufei] Büfett *n,* Theke, Bar *f;* (Verkaufs-)Stand *m (mit Erfrischungen);* kalte(s) Büfett *n; ~~ car (rail)* Büfettwagen *m; ~~ supper* Abendessen *n* mit Selbstbedienung; **~oon** [bʌ'fu:n] Possenreißer, Clown *m;*

~oonery [bəˈfu:nəri] Possenreißerei *f*; grobe(r) Scherz, derbe(r) Spaß *m*.

bug [bʌg] *s* Wanze *f*; *Am* (*bes.* kriechendes) Insekt *n*, Käfer, Wurm *(Larve)*; Bazillus *f*; *Am sl* Besessene(r), Verrückte(r); *Am sl* Anfänger-Jokkey *m Am sl mot* (Volks-)Wagen; *Am sl* Bock, Fehler, Defekt *m*; *Am sl* Einbildung *f*; *typ sl* Sternchen *n*; *tr Am (Pflanze)* von Schädlingen befreien; *Am* e-e Abhörvorrichtung einbauen; ärgern, auf die Palme bringen; *itr Am fam (Augen)* 'rausstehen; wütend sein (*at* auf); *to have a ~ on (Am sl)* schlechter Laune sein; *to be a ~ on s.th. (Am sl)* nach etw verrückt, auf etw scharf, versessen sein; *to put a ~ in o.'s ear (Am sl)* jdm e-n Floh ins Ohr setzen; *bed~* Bettwanze *f*; *big ~ (sl)* hohe(s) Tier *n*; **~aboo** [ˈ-əbu:], **~bear** [ˈ-bɛə] Butzemann *(Kinderschreck)*; Popanz *m*, Schreckgespenst *n*; Komplex *m*; **~-catcher, -hunter** *hum* Entomologe *m*; **~ger** [ˈ-ə] *s jur* Homosexuelle(r); Sodomit; *sl* schlaue(r) Kerl, Strolch, Lump *m*; *tr itr* Unzucht treiben (mit); *to ~~ off* abhauen; **~gery** [ˈ-əri] *jur* widernatürliche Unzucht *f*; **~gy** [ˈ-i] *s* leichte(r) ein- *od* zweisitzige(r) Wagen *m*; Bremserhäuschen *n*; *Am sl* Kinderwagen; *mot* Schlitten *m*; *a* verwanzt; *Am sl* verrückt, bekloppt; **~house** *s Am sl* Irrenanstalt *f*; *a* verrückt, bekloppt; **~s** *a sl* verrückt, bekloppt.

bugle [ˈbju:gl] **1.** *s (~-horn)* Wald-, *mil mar* Signalhorn *n*; *tr itr* (das Horn) blasen; **2.** (schwarze, längliche) Glasperle *f (auf Stoffen)*; **~r** [ˈe,ə] Hornist *m*.

buhl [bu:l] Einlegearbeit *f*.

build [bild] *irr built, built tr* bauen (*of* aus) *a. fig*; auf-, erbauen, errichten; *(Brücke)* schlagen; *fig* gründen, anlegen; *Am fam* übertreiben, planen; *itr* (ein Haus) bauen; im Baugewerbe tätig sein; e-n Plan aufbauen (*on, upon* auf); *Am sl* zunehmen; *s* Bauart, -weise *f*; Körperbau *m*, *fam* Figur *f*; *theat fam* zugkräftige(s) Theaterstück *n*; *to ~ in* einbauen; *to ~ over* über-, verbauen; *to ~ up* (allmählich) aufbauen; um ... herum bauen, mit Häusern, Gebäuden umgeben; *(Gelände)* verbauen; *(Baulücke)* ausfüllen; *fig* propagandistisch herausstreichen; moralisch stützen; *fig (Geschäft, System)* aufbauen; *(Vorräte, Reserven)* ansammeln, vermehren; *(Vermögen)* erwerben; *(s-e Gesundheit)* wiederherstellen; *(Truppen)* aufstellen; *tech* auftragschweißen; *sl* durchverbinden; *to ~ (up)on (fig)* bauen, sich stützen, sich verlassen auf; *(Hoffnung)* setzen auf; **~er** [ˈ-ə] Erbauer, Baumeister; *fig* (Be-)Gründer; *chem* Zusatz *m*; *empire ~~* Staaten-, Reichsgründer *m*; *master-~~* Baumeister, Architekt *m*; *~~'s hoist* Bauaufzug *m*; *~~-upper (Am fam)* moralische(r) Rückhalt *m*; **~ing** [ˈ-iŋ] Bau(-en *n*) *m*; Baukunst; Konstruktion *f*; Bau(werk *n*) *m*, Gebäude *n*; Bautätigkeit *f*; *attr* Bau-; *~~ block* Baustein *m*, -element *n*; *~~-contractor* Bauunternehmer *m*; *~~-costs (pl)* Baukosten *pl*; *~~ cradle (aero)* Helling *f*; *~~-credit* Baukredit *m*; *~~ elevator (Am)* Bauaufzug *m*; *~~-enterprise* Bauunternehmung *f*; *~~ estimate* Baukostenanschlag *m*; *~~ expenses (pl)* Baukosten *pl*; *~~-ground, -lot, -site* Baugrundstück *n*, -platz *m*; *~~ inspector* Beamte(r) *m* der Baupolizei; *~~ joiner* Bautischler, -schreiner *m*; *~~ land* Bauland *n*; *~~-line* Baufluchtt, Fluchtlinie *f*; *~~-manager* Bauführer *m*; *~~ material* Baumaterial *n*, -stoffe *m pl*; *~~-office* Baubüro *n*; *~~ permit* Bauerlaubnis *f*; *~~ plan* Bauplan *m*; *~~ programme, project* Bauvorhaben *n*; *~~ regulations (pl)* Bauvorschriften *f pl*; *~~-restriction* Bausperre *f*; *~~ slip* Helling *f*; *~~ in series* Serien-, Reihenbau *m*; *~~-society* Baugesellschaft, -genossenschaft; Bausparkasse *f*; *~~ trade* Baugewerbe *n*; *~~-up (fig)* Aufbau *m (e-s Systems)*; *tech* Selbsterregung *f*, Anspringen *n*; **~-up, ~up** *sl* Propaganda *f*; *mil* Aufbau *m*, Aufstellung *f*; *to give s.o. a ~~* jdn propagandistisch herausstellen.

built [bilt] *pp zu build a* gebaut; *German ~* in Deutschland gebaut; *well-~* gutgebaut; **~-in** *a* umbaut; eingebaut; Einbau-; **~-on** *a* angebaut; **~-up** *a* bebaut; aufgebaut; zs.gesetzt bestehend (*by* aus); *tech* montiert; Aufbau-; *~~ area* bebaute(s) Gelände *n*; *(Verkehr)* geschlossene Ortschaft *f*.

bulb [bʌlb] *s* (Blumen-)Zwiebel, Knolle *f*; Kolben, Wulst *m*; *(electric lamp~)* (Glüh-)Birne; *(~ of a hair)* (Haar-)Wurzel *f*; *itr* sich kolbenförmig erweitern; e-n Wulst bilden; *bot* Knollen bilden; **~ed, ~iferous** [-d, -ˈbifərəs] *a* kolbenförmig erweitert; **~ous** [ˈbʌlbəs] *a bot* mit e-r Zwiebel, Zwiebel-; zwiebelförmig.

Bulgaria [bʌlˈgɛəriə] Bulgarien *n*; **~n** [-n] *a* bulgarisch; *s* Bulgare *m*, Bulgarin; bulgarische Sprache *f*.

bulg|e [bʌldʒ] *s* Ausbuchtung, Ausbauchung; (An-)Schwellung; Wölbung; Beule *f*; Wulst; *mil* Frontvorsprung; *(Schiff)* Schutzwulst; *sl* Vorteil, Vorsprung, vorspringende(r) Teil *m*; *tr* ausbauchen; anschwellen lassen; *itr* anschwellen; e-e Ausbauchung haben; e-n Wulst bilden; **~ing** [-iŋ] zum Besten voll (*with* von); **~y** [ˈ-i] geschwollen; ausgebaucht.

bulk [bʌlk] *s* Last, Ladung; *mar* Schiffsladung; (große) Menge, Masse *f*; (großer) Umfang *m*, Volumen *n*, Größe *f*; Hauptteil *m*, Mehrzahl *f* (*of* gen); *attr* Pauschal-; *itr* erscheinen, aussehen (*large* groß, bedeutend); *tr* anhäufen, (auf)stapeln; das Gewicht prüfen (*s.th.* e-r S); *a* gesamt; lose; *by the ~* in Bausch u. Bogen; *in ~* unverpackt, lose; in Menge; *to ~ up* e-e große Menge *od* Summe bilden; sich belaufen (*to* auf); *to break ~ (mar)* mit dem Löschen beginnen; *to load in ~* lose, mit Massengütern (ver)laden; **~ articles, goods** *pl* Massengüter *n pl*; **~ bargain, deal** Pauschalabschluß *m*, -abkommen *n*; **~ breaking point** *Br* Umschlagstelle *f*; **~head** *mar* Schott *n*; Kabine(ndecke) *f*; *aero* Spant; *arch* Überbau *m (über e-r Treppe)*; **~iness** [ˈ-inis] große(r), gewaltige(r) Umfang *m*; **~y** [ˈ-i] groß, umfangreich, massig; schwer zu bewegen(d), unhandlich; sperrig, hinderlich; *~~ goods (pl)* Sperrgut *n*.

bull [bul] **1.** *s* Stier, Bulle *m a. fig*; *Am* Bulldogge *f*; *fin* Haussier, Haussespekulant; *astr* Stier; *Am sl* Schupo, Polizist *m*; *rail sl Am* Lokomotive *f*; *sl* Quatsch, Unsinn *m*; *mil sl* sinnlose Routine *f*; *Am sl* dumme(s) Geschwätz, alberne(s) Gerede, dumme(s) Zeug *n*, Angabe *f*; *mar* Bullauge *n*; *itr fin* auf Hausse spekulieren; *sl* quasseln; *tr* die Kurse in die Höhe treiben; *sl* bluffen; *a sl* groß, gewaltig, kräftig; **2.** *(päpstliche)* Bulle *f*; **3.** *(Irish ~)* innere(r) Widerspruch *m*; (unbeabsichtigtes) Wortspiel *n*; *like a ~ in a china shop* wie ein Elefant im Porzellanladen *m*; *to shoot the ~ (sl)* Unsinn reden, quatschen; *to take the ~ by the horns (fig)* den Stier an den Hörnern packen; *to throw, to sling the ~ (fig sl)* aufschneiden, übertreiben; **~-baiting** Stierhetze *f*; **~ bitch** *sl* Mannweib *n*; **~-calf** Bullenkalb *n*; *fig* Dummkopf, Esel *m*, Kamel *n*; **~dog** [ˈ-dɔg] *s* Bulldogge; *tech* Dörner-, Puddelschlacke *f*; *Art* Revolver; *Br* Pedell *m*; *itr sl* sich herausstreichen; *~~ edition (Zeitung)* Früh-, Landausgabe *f*; **~doze** [ˈ-douz] *tr Am sl* (durch Drohungen) einschüchtern; *Am* (mit der Planierraupe) einebnen, räumen; *Am mil* niederwalzen; **~dozer** [ˈ-douzə] Planiermaschine, -raupe *f*, Fronträumer *m*; *(~~ blade)* Planierschild *n*; *Am sl* rabiate(r) Mensch *m*; **~ elephant** Elefantenbulle *m*; **~et** [ˈ-it] Gewehrkugel *f*; Geschoß *n*; *~~-headed (a)* mit dickem Kopf; *Am fig* dickköpfig, -schädelig, halsstarrig; *~~ mark* Einschuß *m*; *~~-proof* kugel-, schußsicher; *~~-proof glass* Panzerglas *n*; **~etin** [ˈ-itin] amtliche(r) Bericht; Tages-, Krankenbericht *m*; Nachrichten-, Vereinsblatt *n*; *~~ board (Am)* Nachrichten-, *Am mil* Befehls-, Anschlagtafel *f*, Schwarze(s) Brett *n*; **~ fiddle** *Am fam* Bratsche *f*; **~-fight** Stierkampf *m*; **~-fighter** Stierkämpfer *m*; *Am sl* leere(r) Güterwagen *m*; **~finch** *orn* Dompfaff *m*; Grenzhecke *f*; **~frog** Ochsenfrosch *m*; **~head** Ochsenkopf; Kaulkopf *(Fisch)*; *Am* Dummkopf, Dussel *m*; **~headed** *a* starrsinnig, hartnäckig; draufgängerisch, stürmisch; tölpelhaft, ungeschickt; **~ion** [ˈ-jən] Gold- *od* Silberbarren; Edelmetallbestand *m*, -reserve; Gold-, Silberfranse *f*; **~ish** [ˈ-iʃ] bullenhaft; *fin* preissteigernd, -treibend; **~neck** Stiernacken *m*; **~ock** [ˈ-ək] Ochse *m*; **~pen** *Am sl* Gefängnis(-raum *m*); Schlafraum *n*; **~-puncher** *Am, Australien* Ochsentreiber *m*; **~ring** Stierkampfarena *f*; **~roarer** (Kinder-)Klapper *f*; **~ session** *Am sl* Herrengesellschaft; lang(weilig)e Diskussion *f* über Lebensfragen; *Am mil (dienstliche)* allgemeine Aussprache *f*; **~shit** *Am sl s* Schwindel *m*; *itr* schwindeln; aufschneiden; klönen; **~'s-eye** *mar* Bullauge; *arch* Ochsenauge; Schießscheibenzentrum *n*, *das* Schwarze; Treffer *m a. fig*; **~-terrier** Kreuzung *f* zwischen Bulldogge u. Terrier; Vorarbeiter *m*; **~y** [ˈbuli] brutale(r) Kerl, Angeber; Tyrann; Zuhälter, Lude *m*; *(~~ beef)* Büchsenfleisch *n*; *a fam* großartig, glänzend, phantastisch, prächtig, famos; *tr* (mit Drohungen) einschüchtern; bange machen; jagen, treiben, hetzen; *mil* zs.stauchen, fertigmachen; *interj* famos, hervorragend; *~~ (for you)! (Am)* großartig! bravo! **~ying** unverschämt; **~yrag** [ˈ-ræg] *tr* einschüchtern; schikanieren piesacken.

bul|rush [ˈbulrʌʃ] *bot* Rohrkolben *m*; **~wark** [ˈ-wək] Bollwerk *n*, Schutzwehr *f*; Mole *f*, Schutzdamm *m*; *pl mar* Reling *f*; *fig* Schutz *m*, Stütze *f*.

bum [bʌm] **1.** *s Br sl* Gesäß *n*, Hintern *m*; *itr (auf e-m Schiff)* Proviant liefern, ausgeben; **2.** *Am s sl* Bummler, Vagabund, Landstreicher, Stromer, Strolch; *Am sl* Säufer *m*; *a* mies, mau, elend, jämmerlich, erbärmlich, schlecht; falsch, unzuverlässig; verdorben; energielos; *itr* (herum)bummeln, vagabundieren, stromern; (herum)saufen, nassauern; *tr* schnorren; *on the ~ (sl)* kaputt; in schlechtem Zustand; auf der Walze; *to give s.o. the ~'s rush (Am sl)* jdn hinauswerfen; **~(-bailiff)** Gerichtsdiener *m*; **~-boat** Proviantboot *n*; **~-fodder** *sl* Klosettpapier *n*; **~mer** ['-ə]*sl Am* Nichtsnutz, Blindgänger *m*; **~my** ['-i] *Am sl* unwohl; *(Nahrungsmittel)* verdorben; **~ steer** *Am sl* falsche(r) Tip *m*.

bumb|ershoot ['bʌmbəʃu:t] *Am sl* Musspritze *f*, Regenschirm *m*; **~le-bee** Hummel *f*; **~ledom** Wichtigtuerei *f*.

bumf [bʌmf] *sl s. bum-fodder.*

bump [bʌmp] *tr* stoßen (*s.th.* gegen etw); wuchten; rammen; *(Boot beim Wettrudern)* überholen; *sl* wegschubsen, verdrängen; *sl (Gehalt)* erhöhen; *itr* stoßen (*against, into* gegen, an); in die Arme laufen (*into s.o.* jdm); *(Wagen)* rumpeln, holpern; *(Bootsrennen)* beim Überholen anstoßen; *(Kricketball beim Aufschlag)* hochspringen; *s* Stoß, Puff, (dumpfer) Schlag *m*; Beule (*on the head* am Kopf); Schädelausweitung *f*; *fig* Anlagen, Fähigkeiten *f pl*; Anstoß *(beim Bootsrennen)*; *aero* Windstoß *m*, Steig-, Aufwindbö; *(Straße)* Unebenheit, Querrinne; *sl* Gehaltserhöhung *f*; *sl* Mord *m*; *adv u.*: *with a ~* mit e-m Ruck, *fam* Wuppdich, bums, plötzlich; *to ~ off (sl)* umlegen, abmurksen; *(Gegenstand)* herunterwerfen; **~er** ['-ə] *s* volle(s) Glas *n*; *sl* Riesending *n*, gewaltige Menge, Unmasse; *(~~ crop)* Rekordernte *f*, *theat(~~ house)* volle(s) Haus *n*; *Am rail* Puffer *m*; *mot* Stoßstange *f*; *attr fam* gewaltig, ungeheuer, Riesen-, Rekord-; *tr* bis an den Rand füllen; **~iness** ['-inis] holp(e)rige *od* böige Beschaffenheit *f*; **~kin** ['-kin] Tölpel, Tolpatsch, linkische(r) Mensch *m*; **~off** Mord *m*; **~tious** ['-ʃəs] überheblich, anmaßend, eingebildet, aufgeblasen; **~y** ['-i] holp(e)rig; böig.

bun [bʌn] **1.** *(England) Art* kleine(r) runde(r) Kuchen; *(Schottland)* Rosinenstollen *m*; *sl* Hinterteil *n*; *sl* Zakken *m* in der Krone; *fam* Kaninchen *n*; *to take the ~ (sl)* den Vogel abschießen; sich lächerlich machen; **2.** *a.* **~n** (Haar-)Knoten *m*.

bunch [bʌntʃ] *s* Büschel, Bündel, Bund; *(Elektronen)* Paket *n*; *(Blumen)* Strauß; Bausch *m*; *fam* Bande, Gesellschaft, Gruppe *f*, Trupp, Schwarm; *allg* Haufen *m*, Masse *f*; *tr* bündeln; *(Kleid)* raffen; *(Elektronen)* paketieren; *itr* sich bauschen; sich zs.drängen; zs.stehen, ein Knäuel bilden; *the best of the ~* das Beste an der ganzen Sache; *~ of flowers* Blumenstrauß *m*; *~ of fruit (bot)* Fruchtstand *m*; *a ~ of girls* ein (ganzer) Schwung *m* Mädchen; *~ of grapes* Weintraube *f*; *~ of keys* Schlüsselbund *n*; **~y** ['-i] büschelig, in Büscheln.

bun|co, bunko ['bʌŋkou] *s Am sl* Schwindel, Betrug *m*; *tr* beschwindeln, betrügen, beschummeln; *~~ game* falsche(s) Spiel *n*; **~combe, bunkum** ['-əm] Geschwätz, dumme(s) Gerede *n*; Quatsch, Unsinn *m*.

bundle ['bʌndl] *s* Bündel; Paket *n*; *(Papier)* Rolle *f*; *tr* (zs.)bündeln, zs.binden; (unordentlich) (hinein-) stopfen (*into* in); *(Menschen)* verfrachten; *to ~ away* od *off, out* (schnell) weg- *od* fort-, hinausschicken, *fam* -befördern; *itr*: *to ~ away, off, out* sich fortmachen, sich packen, sich trollen, *fam* abhauen, -ziehen; *to ~ up* sich einmummeln, sich warm anziehen; *~ of nerves* Nervenbündel *n*; *~ of rays* Strahlenbündel *n*; *~ of straw* Strohbündel *n*; *~ of twigs* Reisigbündel *n*.

bung [bʌŋ] *s* Spund *m*; *tr* verspunden; *sl* schmeißen; *to ~ up* verstopfen; *sl* grün u. blau schlagen; *~ed-up* geschwollen; verstopft; **~alow** ['bʌŋgəlou] einstöckige(s) (Sommer-)Haus *n*; **~-hole** Spundloch *n*.

bungl|e ['bʌŋgl] *itr* pfuschen, stümpern; *tr* verpfuschen; durchea.bringen; *(Aufgabe)* verfehlen; *s* Pfuscherei, Stümperei, Pfuscharbeit *f*; **~er** ['-ə] Pfuscher, Stümper *m*; **~ing** ['-iŋ] stümperhaft.

bunion ['bʌnjən] entzündete(r) Fußballen *m*.

bunk [bʌŋk] **1.** *s* Schlafstelle; *mar* Koje *f*; *itr* in e-r Koje schlafen; *fam* sich schlafen legen; **~ house** *Am* Arbeiterwohnbaracke *f*; **~ inspection** *Am* Stubenappell *m*; **~ mate** *Am* Schlafkamerad, -genosse *m*; **2.** *itr sl* ausreißen, abhauen, türmen (gehen); *s*: *to do a ~* Reißaus nehmen; **3.** *s. buncombe*; **~er** ['-ə] *mar* Kohlenbunker; *mil* Bunker *m*; *(Golf)* Sandgrube *f*; Hindernis *n*; **~ered** ['-əd] *a fam* in der Klemme; **~ie** ['-i] *Am fam* Kumpel *m*; **~o, ~um** *s. bunco, buncombe.*

bunny ['bʌni] *(Kindersprache)* Kaninchen; *Am a.* Eichhörnchen *n*; *Am sl* Jammerlappen *m*.

bunt [bʌnt] **1.** *s* Wölbung, Ausweitung; *(Fischnetz)* sackartige Erweiterung *f*; *(Aalreuse)* bauchige(r) Teil *m*; *(Segel)* (sich blähendes) Mittelstück *n*; *tr itr (Segel)* (sich) blähen; **2.** *tr (bes. dial)* schlagen, stoßen, schieben; **3.** *s* (Weizen-)Brand *m (Krankheit)*; **~ing** ['-iŋ] **1.** *orn* Ammer *f*; **2.** Fahnentuch *n*; Fahnen(schmuck *m*) *f pl*; *Art* Steckkissen *n* mit Kapuze; **~ line** *mar* Gording *f*.

buoy [bɔi] *s* Boje, Bake *f*; *(life-~)* Rettungsring *m*; *fig* Weisung, Warnung *f*; Schutz *m*; *tr (a. to ~ out)* durch Bojen bezeichnen; *(meist to ~ up)* über Wasser halten *a. fig*; *(gesunkenes Schiff)* heben, wieder flottmachen; *fig* die Stimmung heben, Mut zusprechen (*s.o.* jdm); **~age** ['-idʒ] Betonnung *f*; **~ancy** ['-ənsi] *(Wasser)* Tragfähigkeit; *(Gegenstand)* Schwimmfähigkeit *f*; *phys* Auftrieb *m a. fig*; *fig* Spannkraft *f*, innere(r) Schwung, Lebensmut *m*; *fin* steigende Tendenz *f*; **~ant** ['-ənt] *(Wasser)* tragend; *(Gegenstand)* schwimmend; *fig* schwungvoll.

bur *a.* **burr** [bə:], *bot* Klette *a. fig*; stach(e)lige Schale *f (e-r Frucht)*.

Burb|erry ['bə:bəri] *Art* wasserdichte(r) Stoff *m*, Kleidung *f*, *bes.* Regenmantel *m (Schutzmarke)*; **b~le** ['bə:bl] *tr itr* murmeln, brumme(l)n; gurgeln; *fam* daherquasseln; *s aero* Wirbel *m*; **b~ot** ['bə:bət] Quappe *f*.

burd|en ['bə:dn] *s* (schwere) Last *a. fig*, Ladung; *(Schiff)* Tragkraft *f*, Tonnengehalt *m*; *min* Beschickungsgut *n*; *fig* Verantwortlichkeit, Verpflichtung *f*; Kehrreim, Refrain; Leitgedanke *m*; *mus* Baßbegleitung *f*; *tr* belasten *a. fig*; *to be a ~~ on s.o.* jdm zur Last fallen; *beast of ~~* Lasttier *n*; *testamentary ~~ (jur)* Auflage *f*; *~~ of care* Unterhaltspflicht *f*; *~~ of debts* Schuldenlast *f*; *~~ of proof* Beweislast *f*; *~~ of sorrow* Sorgenlast *f*; *~~ of taxation* Steuerlast *f*; **~ensome** ['-səm] lästig, beschwerlich; **~ock** ['bə:dək] *bot* Große Klette *f*.

bureau [bjuə'rou, 'bjuərou], *pl a.* *-x* [-z] *Br* Schreibtisch *m*; Geschäftszimmer; Büro *n*; Geschäfts-, Dienststelle *f*, Am Amt *n*; *Am* Kommode *f*; *information ~* Auskunftsstelle, Auskunftei *f*; *press ~* Nachrichten-, Presseagentur *f*; *publicity ~* Werbebüro *n*; Anzeigen-, Inseratenannahme *f*; *statistical ~* Statistische(s) Amt *n*; *B~ of Internal Revenue (Am)* Steuerbehörde *f*; *B~ of Standards (Am)* Amt *n* für Maße u. Gewichte; *B~ of Vital Statistics (Am)* Standesamt *n*; **~cracy** [bjuə'rɔkrəsi] Bürokratie *f*; **~crat** ['bjuəro(u)kræt] Bürokrat *m*; **~cratic** [bjuəro(u)'krætik] bürokratisch; **~ lamp** *Am* Schreibtischlampe *f*; **~ telephone** *Am* Tischtelephon *n*; **~ trunk** *Am* Schrank *m*.

burg [bə:g] *hist* Burg; (befestigte) Stadt; *fam* Stadt; Siedlung *f*; **~ee** [bə:'dʒi:] Stander *m*; **~eon** ['bə:dʒən] *s* Knospe *f*, Keim, Sproß, Schößling, Trieb *m*; *itr* knospen, keimen, sprießen; **~ess** ['bə:dʒis] wahlberechtigte(r) Bürger; *hist* Parlamentsvertreter, Abgeordnete(r) *m* e-r Stadt *od* Universität; **~h** ['bʌrə] *Scot* Stadt *f (mit Stadtrechten)*; **~her** ['bə:gə] Bürger *m (e-r Stadt)*; **~lar** ['bə:glə] Einbrecher *m*; *~~-proof* einbruchsicher; **~larize** ['-raiz] *tr fam Am* einbrechen (*a house* in ein Haus); **~lary** ['-ləri] Einbruch(sdiebstahl) *m*; **~le** ['bə:gl] *itr* einbrechen; **~omaster** ['bə:gəma:stə] *(holländischer* od *deutscher)* Bürgermeister *m*; **B~undy** ['bə:gəndi] Burgund *n*; *b~~* Burgunder *m (Wein)*.

burial ['beriəl] Begräbnis *n*, Bestattung, Beerdigung *f*; **~ case, casket** *Am* Sarg *m*; **~-ground** Begräbnisplatz, Friedhof *m*; **~ lot** *Am*, **place** Begräbnisstätte *f*; **~ service** Trauerfeier *f*.

burke [bə:k] *tr fig* geheimhalten, verheimlichen, vertuschen; *(Nachricht, Buch)* unterdrücken.

burl [bə:l] Knoten *(im Garn* od *Stoff)*; *Am* Knorren, Ast *m (im Holz)*; **~ap** ['bə:læp] grobe Leinwand; *Am sl* Entlassung *f*; **~esque** [bə:'lesk] *s* Parodie; Karikatur; Burleske, Posse; *Am* Tingeltangelvorführung *f*; *a* parodistisch, karikaturenhaft; *tr* parodieren; **~y** ['-i] stämmig, kräftig, vierschrötig, untersetzt.

Burm|a ['bə:mə] Burma, Birma *n*; **~ese** [bə:'mi:z] *a* birmanisch; *s* Birmane *m*, Birmanin *f*.

burn [bə:n] *irr burnt, burnt, a. ~ed tr* verbrennen; anbrennen, anzünden, in Brand stecken; *(ein Loch in e-e S)* brennen; *(Licht, Kerzen, Gas)* brennen; *(Kohle)* verfeuern; *(Ziegel, Kalk, Kohlen im Meiler)* brennen; *(Uran im Atommeiler)* brennen; *(Haut)* braun brennen, bräunen; sich *(den Mund, die Finger)* verbrennen *a. fig*; *(Speise)* anbrennen lassen; *(Hitze)* versengen, verdorren lassen, ausdörren; *(Säure, mit Säure)* ätzen; *fig (Leidenschaft)* verzehren; *Am sl* hinausekeln, auf dem el. Stuhl hinrichten, umbringen, unter Druck setzen; *itr* brennen, in Flammen stehen; *poet* lodern; *(Licht)* brennen, eingeschaltet, *fam* an sein; *(Speise)* anbrennen; *(Haut)* braun werden, bräunen; *fig* darauf brennen (*to* zu); *(in Liebe)* entbrennen, (er)glühen, sich verzehren; brennen (*with curiosity* vor Neugierde); *fam* davonrasen; *(vor Wut)* kochen, schäumen, beben; *Am sl* enttäuscht, entmutigt sein, keinen Mumm mehr haben, auf dem el. Stuhl hingerichtet werden; *s* Brandwunde, Verbrennung *f*; *to ~ away (tr)* ab-, aus-, verbrennen; *to ~ down (tr)* ab-, *itr* niederbrennen; *Am sl* fertigmachen, niederknallen; *to ~ in(to)* einbrennen (in); *fig* fest, unauslöschlich einprägen (in); *to ~ out (tr itr)* völlig aus-, verbrennen; *el* durchbrennen; *tr (Feuer)* verzehren; *(Feinde)* durch Feuer vertreiben, ausräuchern; *to ~ through* durchbrennen; *to ~ up (tr)* ganz verbrennen; *fam* in Harnisch bringen; *fam* herunterputzen; *sl* mit aller Energie betreiben; *(Rekord)* brechen; *itr* sich entzünden, Feuer fangen, in Flammen aufgehen; wieder aufflammen; *to be ~t up (fam)* Gift u. Galle speien, wütend sein; *to ~ o.'s boats, o.'s bridges behind o. (fig)* alle Brücken hinter sich abbrechen, sich den Rückweg versperren; *to ~ brown* braun brennen; *to have money, time to ~ (Am)* Geld wie Heu haben; nicht wissen, was man mit s-r Zeit anfangen soll; **~able** ['-əbl] brennbar; **~ed-out** *a* ausgebrannt; *fig fam* völlig erschöpft; *sl* gelangweilt; **~er** ['-ə] Brenner *m*; *~~ nozzle* Brennerdüse *f*; **~ing** ['-iŋ] *a* brennend *a. fig*, glühend; *fig* leidenschaftlich, feurig; *(Schmach)* empörend; *s* (Ver-)Brennen *n*, Brand *m*; *~~-glass* Brennglas *n*; *~~ hour* Brennstunde *f*; *~~ hot* glühend heiß; *~~ time* Brenndauer *f*; **~ish** ['-iʃ] *tr* polieren, schleifen; *(Hirschgeweih)* fegen; *itr* glänzen; **~isher** ['-iʃə] Polierer, Bossierer; Polierstahl, -stein *m*; **~-out** *(Rakete)* Brennschluß *m*; **~t** [bə:nt] *a* verbrannt; *to have a ~~ taste* angebrannt schmecken; *~~ child dreads fire (prov)* gebranntes Kind scheut das Feuer; *sun-~~* sonn(en)verbrannt; *~~ almond* gebrannte Mandel *f*; *~~ clay, lime, ochre, sienna* gebrannte(r) Ton, Kalk, Ocker *m*, Siena *f*; *~~ gas (mot)* Auspuffgas *n*; *pl tech* Abgase *n pl*; *~~ offering (rel)* Brandopfer *n*.

bournouse [bə:'nu:z] Burnus *m*.

burp [bə:p] *itr Am sl* rülpsen; *s* Rülpser *m*; **~gun** *Am sl mil* Maschinengewehr *n*, -pistole *f*.

burr [bə:] **1.** *s. bur*; **2.** *s* Hof *(um den Mond)*; Mühl-, Schleifstein; *Art* kieselhaltige(r) Kalkstein; *tech* (Bohr-, Walz-)Grat *m*; Vertiefung; Gußnaht *f*; Bohrer *m (des Zahnarztes)*; Surren *(sich drehender Maschinenteile)*; Zäpfchen-R *n*; *tr tech* abgraten, verdrücken; *tr itr* (ein Zäpfchen-R) sprechen; **~ow** ['bʌrou] *s* Erdloch *n*, -höhle *f*; (Fuchs-, Kaninchen-)Bau *m*; *min* Halde *f*; *tr (Bau)* graben; *fig* zu ergründen suchen, erforschen; *itr* sich einwühlen, -graben, sich vergraben, eindringen *a. fig* (*into* in); **~y** ['-ri] voller Kletten; rauh, stechend.

bursar ['bə:sə] Schatzmeister (e-s College); *Scot* Stipendiat *m*.

burst [bə:st] *irr burst, burst itr* bersten, (zer)platzen, reißen, zerspringen, brechen, ausea.-, in die Luft fliegen, explodieren, krepieren, detonieren; *(Knospe)* aufbrechen; (her)einbrechen; *(Sturm)* ausbrechen, lostoben; *(Gewitter)* sich entladen; brechend, zum Bersten, zum Platzen voll sein (*with* von); bersten, platzen (*with* vor) *a. fig*; *tr* sprengen; bersten, platzen, ausea., in die Luft fliegen lassen; *to ~ o.s.* sich umbringen, sich alle erdenkliche Mühe geben; *s* Bersten, Zerspringen, Zerreißen *n*, Explosion, Detonation *f*; *mil (~ of fire)* Feuerstoß *m*; *(~ cloud)* Sprengwolke *f*; Aufschlag; Sprengpunkt; Knall *m*; *mot* Reifenpanne *f*; *sport* Spurt; *fig* (plötzlicher) Ausbruch; (Lach-, Wein-) Krampf *m*; plötzliche Anstrengung *f*; *to ~ forth* ausbrechen (*into* in); *to ~ from* sich losreißen von; *to ~ in(to) (itr)* (her)einbrechen, *fig* hereinplatzen, -stürzen; *tr* einbrechen, -schlagen, sprengen, zertrümmern; *fig* unterbrechen; *to ~ open (tr)* auf-, erbrechen; aufsprengen; *to ~ out* ausbrechen in, ausrufen, (plötzlich) schreien; *to ~ out crying* in Weinen ausbrechen; *to ~ out laughing* sich vor Lachen nicht halten können; *to ~ up (itr fam)* in die Luft fliegen; völlig zs.brechen (*tr* lassen); *to ~ upon* einbrechen in, herfallen über; *to ~ (o.'s sides) with laughing* vor Lachen platzen; *to ~ into tears* in Tränen ausbrechen; *ready to ~* aufs äußerste erregt; *a ~ tyre* ein geplatzter Reifen *m*; *~ of applause* Beifallssturm *m*; **~ing** ['-iŋ] platzend, krepierend; **~-up** (völliger) Zs.bruch *m*.

burton ['bə:tn] *mar* (leichte) Talje *f*.

bury ['beri] *tr* begraben, beerdigen, bestatten; ein-, vergraben; verbergen; *tech* versenken; *fig* begraben, vergessen, auf sich beruhen lassen; *Am sl (e-n Freund)* verraten, verpfeifen; *to ~ o.s. in o.'s books* sich in s-n Büchern vergraben; *to ~ o.'s face in o.'s hands, o.'s hands in o.'s pockets* sein Gesicht in den Händen, s-e Hände in den Taschen vergraben; *to ~ o.'s head in the sand (fig)* den Kopf in den Sand stecken; nichts sehen wollen; *to ~ the hatchet (fig)* das Kriegsbeil begraben, sich versöhnen; *to be buried in thoughts*; in Gedanken versunken sein; **~ing** ['-iŋ]: *~~-ground, -place* Friedhof *m*.

bus [bʌs] *pl bus(s)es* [-iz] *s* Bus, Omnibus, Autobus *m*; *tech* Sammelschiene; *mot aero fam* Kiste *f*; *tr Am sl* abräumen (*dishes* Geschirr); *to go by ~* mit dem Bus fahren; *to miss the ~ (sl)* den Anschluß, e-e Gelegenheit verpassen, Pech haben; **~ bar** Sammel-, Stromzuführungsschiene *f*; **~ boy, girl** *Am* Kellnerlehrling *m*; **~by** *mil* Bärenfellmütze *f*; **~car** *Am sl* gute(r) Freund, Kumpel *m*; unerwartete(s) Vergnügen *n*; **~-conductor** Omnibusschaffner *m*; **~-driver, ~man** Omnibusfahrer *m*; **~ stop** Omnibushaltestelle *f*; **~ line, route** Omnibuslinie *f*; **~load** ['-loud] Omnibusvoll *m*; **~man's holiday** Fortsetzung *f* der Berufsarbeit in den Ferien; **~ service** Busverkehr *m*; **~ terminal** Omnibusendstation *f*, -bahnhof *m*.

bush [buʃ] *s* Busch, Strauch *m*; Gebüsch, Gesträuch, Gestrüpp, Buschwerk *n*; Busch *(Wald-* od *Ödland bes. in Übersee)*; Besen *(als Zeichen am Winzerhaus)*; üppige(r), starke(r) Haar-, Bartwuchs *m*; *tech* Lagerfutter *n*, -schale; (Lager-)Buchse, Hülse *f*, Ring(muffe *f*) *m*; *Am sl* Mädchen *n*; *pl* Provinzstädte *f pl*; *a sl* rückständig, einfach, unkompliziert, zweitrangig; *tr Am fam* ermüden, erschöpfen; *tech* ausfüttern, ausbüchsen; *to beat about (Am around) the ~ (fig)* wie die Katze um den heißen Brei herumgehen; **~-bean** *Am* Busch-, Zwergbohne *f*; **~ country** unbewohnte(s) Gebiet, Ödland *n*; **~el** ['buʃl] *s* Scheffel *m (= 4 pecks = 32 quarts = Am 8 gallons = 33,35 l)*; *tr Am (Kleider)* abändern, ausbessern; *to hide o.'s light under a ~~ (fig)* sein Licht unter den Scheffel stellen; **~el(l)er, ~elman** *Am* Schneider *m*; **~er** ['-ə] *Am fam sport* zweitrangige(r) Spieler; *fig* Versager, Blindgänger *m*; **~-harrow** *agr* Rahmenegge *(für Wiesen)*; **~ing** ['-iŋ] *tech* Lagerschale, -buchse, -hülse; *el* Durchführung *f*; **~ knife** *Am* Buschmesser *n*; **~ league** *Am a* zweitrangig, provinziell; *s sport* schlechte Mannschaft *f*; **~man** Buschmann *m*; **~-ranger** Buschklepper, Strauchdieb *m*; **~-sniper** Heckenschütze *m*; **~wa(h)** ['-wa] *Am sl* Geschwätz *n*, Unsinn *m*; **~whack** ['-wæk] *s Am* Buschmesser *n*; *itr* sich e-n Weg bahnen; im Wald hausen; **~whacker** ['-wækə] *Am* Hinterwäldler, Grenz(bewohn)er; *(rebel ~~)* Guerillakämpfer *m*; Buschmesser *n*; **~y** ['-i] buschig, buschbestanden.

busily ['bizili] *adv* geschäftig, eifrig.

business ['biznis] Geschäftsleben *n*, Handel *m*, Gewerbe; geschäftliche(s) Unternehmen *n*, Geschäfts-, gewerbliche(r) Betrieb *m*; Firma, Handelsgesellschaft *f*; Abschluß, Umsatz *m*; geschäftliche(s) Verhalten; Geschäft(slokal) *n*, Laden(geschäft *n*) *m*; Beschäftigung, Arbeit *f*, Broterwerb, Beruf *m*, Gewerbe, Geschäft *n*, geschäftliche Tätigkeit; Pflicht, Obliegenheit, Aufgabe; Angelegenheit, Sache; *theat* Geste, Bewegung *f (des Schauspielers)*; *in ~* im Geschäftsleben; *on ~* geschäftlich, in geschäftlichen Angelegenheiten; *to be in ~* im Geschäftsleben stehen; *to come, to get (down) to ~* sich an die Arbeit machen; *to do ~, a ~, good ~* Geschäfte, ein G., gute G. machen; *to do o.'s ~ (sl)* jdn erledigen, umlegen, umbringen; *to have no ~ to* kein Recht haben zu; *to make it o.'s own ~ to do* es über-, auf sich nehmen, etw zu tun; *to mean ~ (fam)* es ernst meinen, ernste Absichten haben; *to open a ~* ein Geschäft eröffnen; *to retire from ~* sich aus dem Geschäftsleben zurückziehen; *to send s.o. about his ~* jdn weg-, hinausschicken; *to set up in ~* ein Geschäft anfangen; *to wind up a ~* ein Geschäft auflösen; *mind your own ~* kümmern Sie sich um Ihre eigenen Angelegenheiten! *no ~ done* kein, ohne Umsatz; *that's no ~ of yours, that's none of your ~* das geht Sie nichts an; *what's his ~?* was macht, treibt, arbeitet, wovon lebt er? *what's your ~ (with me)?* was führt Sie zu mir? was wollen Sie von mir? *what ~ is he in?* in welcher Branche arbeitet er? *~ is ~* Geschäft ist Geschäft; **~ address** Geschäftsadresse *f*; **~ agent** Handels-, Geschäftsvertreter *m*; **~ area** Geschäftsviertel *n*; **~ capital** Betriebskapital *n*; **~ card** Geschäftskarte *f*; **~ centre, quarter, street** Geschäftszentrum, -viertel *n*, -straße *f*; **~ connections** od **connexions, relations** *pl* Geschäftsbeziehungen *f pl*; **~ correspondence, letter** Geschäftskorrespondenz *f*, -brief *m*; **~ cycle** Konjunkturzyklus *m*; **~ end** *sl* vordere(r) Teil *m*; **~ enterprise** geschäftliche(s) Unternehmen *n*; **~ executive** *Am* Geschäftsführer *m*; **~ experience** Geschäftserfahrung *f*; **~ friend** Geschäftsfreund *m*; **~ hours** *pl* Geschäftszeit *f*; **~ house** Handels-, Geschäftshaus *n*; **~ interests** *pl* Geschäftsinteressen *n pl*; **~ journey** Geschäftsreise *f*; **~like** ['-laik] geschäftstüchtig; praktisch (veranlagt), gewandt; geschäftsmäßig; **~ letter** Geschäftsbrief *m*; **~ loss** Geschäftsverlust *m*; **~man** Geschäftsmann *m*; **~ management** Geschäftsleitung *f*; **~-manager** Geschäftsführer *m*; **~ matter** Geschäftssache, -angelegenheit *f*; **~ name** Handelsname *m*; **~ office** Büro *n*; **~ outlook** Geschäftslage *f*; **~ papers** *pl* Geschäftspapiere *n pl*; **~ place, town** Handelsplatz *m*, -stadt *f*; **~ premises** *pl* Geschäftsräume *m pl*; **~ training** Geschäftserfahrung; Ausbildung *f* als Kaufmann; **~ transaction** Geschäftsabschluß *m*; *pl* Geschäfte *n pl*; **~ turnover** Geschäftsumsatz *m*; **~woman** Geschäftsfrau *f*; **~ world** *Am* Geschäftswelt *f*; **~ year** Geschäfts-, Rechnungsjahr *n*.

busk [bʌsk] *s* Korsettstange *f*, Blankscheit *n*; *itr* beschleunigen; *sl* als Straßensänger sein Geld verdienen; **~er** ['-ə] Straßensänger *m*; **~in** ['-in] (hoher *od* Halb-)Stiefel; *hist theat* Kothurn *m*; *fig* Tragödie *f*.

buss [bʌs] **1.** *s* Büse *f*, Fahrzeug *n* für den Heringsfang; **2.** *dial s* Kuß *m*; *tr* küssen.

bust [bʌst] **1.** *s (bes. weibliche)* Brust *f*, Busen *m*; *(Kunst)* Büste *f*; *film (~ shot)* Nah-, Großaufnahme *f*; **2.** *s fam* Zs.bruch; Bank(e)rott *m*, Pleite *f*; Versager, Reinfall *m*; Sauferei *f*; Schlag *m*; *itr fam (to go ~)* Bank(e)rott machen, pleite gehen; herumsaufen; e-n Fehler begehen; *(beim Aufsagen)* steckenbleiben; *(im Examen)* durchfallen; *tr (= burst)* zerbrechen; *(= break)* zähmen, dressieren, abrichten; *(Pferd)* einreiten; (durch)fallen lassen; *mil* degradieren; *sl* aufbrechen; *a sl* pleite; *to ~ out (sl)* relegiert werden; *to go on the ~* e-n Lokalbummel machen; *to ~ a gut, to ~ o.'s conk (Am sl)* alles dransetzen; **~ard** ['-əd] *orn* Große Trappe, Trappgans *f*; **~-bodice, -support** Büstenhalter *m*; **~ed** ['-id] *a sl* ruiniert, pleite; *Am mil sl* degradiert; *Am sl* eingesperrt; **~er** ['-ə] *Am sl* Pfundsding *n*, große Sache *f*; Pfundskerl; *Am sl* Radaubruder; Brecher, Sprenger *(Person)*; Einreiter; heftige(r), scharfe(r) Wind *m*; **~-up** *sl* Krach, Streit *m*.

bustle ['bʌsl] **1.** *s* Turnüre *f*; **2.** *itr* sich geschäftig bewegen, sich tummeln, (*fam* sich ab)hetzen; *tr* auf den Trab bringen, Beine machen (*s.o.* jdm); *s* Geschäftigkeit, Eile, Hetze, Aufregung *f*; *to ~ about* herumsausen, sehr geschäftig tun; *to ~ up* sich beeilen, hetzen.

busy ['bizi] *a* fleißig, arbeitsam; geschäftig, tätig; beschäftigt (*at, in, with* mit; *doing* damit beschäftigt zu *od* daß); *pej* aufdringlich, lästig; *(Straße)* verkehrsreich, belebt; *(Laden)* voll; *(Tag)* voll ausgefüllt; *(Mensch)* ausgelastet; *Am tele* besetzt; *s sl* Detektiv *m*; *v*: *to ~ o.s.* sich beschäftigen, tätig, beschäftigt sein (*with* mit); **~body** ['-bɔdi] Gschaftlhuber, Wichtigtuer; aufdringliche(r) Mensch *m*; **~ hours** *pl* Hauptverkehrszeit *f*; **~ idle** sich in nebensächlichen Dingen verlierend; **~ signal, tone** *tele* Besetztzeichen *n*.

but [bʌt, bət] *conj* aber, dennoch, (je-)doch, indessen, nichtsdestoweniger, and(e)rerseits; sondern; außer daß; ohne daß, ohne zu; wenn nicht; *(nach Verneinung, verneintem Zweifeln) (a. ~ that)* daß; *~ that* außer daß, ohne daß; *not ~ that* nicht als ob; *not only ... ~ also* nicht nur ... sondern auch; *~ for all that* trotz alledem; *prp* außer; *anything ~* nichts weniger als; *nothing ~* nichts als; *the last ~ one* der vorletzte; *all ~ one* alle bis auf einen; *~ for* ohne; *adv* nur, bloß; *Am sl* sehr; *all ~* beinahe, fast, nahezu; *~ then* dafür aber; *prn (nach verneintem Hauptsatz)* der, die, das, welcher, e, es, nicht; *there was not one ~ was wounded* es war nicht einer da, der nicht verwundet war; *s* Aber *n*, Einwand *m*.

butane ['bjutein] Butan(gas) *n*.

butcher ['butʃə] *s* Metzger, Fleischer, Schlächter, Schlachter; *fig pej* Menschenschlächter, Henker, Bluthund *m*; *Am bes. rail (~ boy, candy ~)* Obst-, Süß- u. Tabakwarenverkäufer; *tr (Menschen)* (hin)schlachten, niedermachen, -metzeln; *fig* entstellen, verzerren, verhunzen; verpfuschen; *(durch Kritik)* heruntermachen; **~-bird** *orn* Große(r), Raubwürger *m*; **~ knife** *Am* Tranchiermesser *n*; **~ly** ['-li] *a adv* roh, brutal, blutdürstig; **~'s meat** Rind-, Schweine- u. Hammelfleisch *n (im Gegensatz zu Wild u. Geflügel)*; **~'s (shop)**, *Am* **~ shop** Metzgerei, Schlächterei *f*, Fleischer-, Schlachterladen *m*; **~y** ['-ri] (kleineres) Schlachthaus *n*; Metzgerei *f*; *fig* Gemetzel, Blutbad *n*.

butler ['bʌtlə] Kellermeister; erste(r) Diener *m*.

butt [bʌt] **1.** große(s) Faß *n (von etwa 500—700 l Fassungsvermögen)*; Butte *f* (*= 126 gallons = 2 hogsheads =* 480 l); **2.** *(~-end)* stumpfe(s), dicke(s) Ende; *(Fleisch)* dicke(s) Stück *n*; (Gewehr-)Kolben; untere(r) Teil *m* e-s Baumstammes *od* Blattstieles; Nadelfuß; Rest *m*, Überbleibsel *n*; Butt *m*, Flunder, Scholle *f (Fisch)*; (dickeres) Rücken- u. Seitenleder *n*; Zigaretten-, Zigarrenstummel *m*; *sl* Zigarette *f*; **3.** (Schießscheibe *f* mit) Geschoßfang *m*; *fig* Zielscheibe *f (des Spottes)*; Ziel *n*, Zweck, Gegenstand; *pl* Schießstand *m*; **4.** *s* Stoß *m (mit dem Kopf)*; *tr* (mit dem Kopf) stoßen; e-n Kopfstoß versetzen (*s.o.* jdm); *itr* stoßen (*against, upon, on* gegen, auf); zufällig treffen (*against s.o.* jdn); *tr itr (to ~ against, upon) (Balken)* mit dem flachen Ende stoßen (lassen) auf; *to ~ in(to) fam* sich (ungefragt) einmischen (in); dazwischenfahren, -treten; **~e** [bju:t] *bes. Am* einzelne(r) (steiler) Berg *m*; **~-in** *fam* Eindringling *m*.

butter ['bʌtə] *s* Butter *f*; *allg* Aufstrich *m*; *fig* Schmeichelei *f*; *tr* mit Butter bestreichen, anrichten, zubereiten *od* herstellen; *fig (a. to ~ up) fam* Honig ums Maul schmieren, schmeicheln (*s.o.* jdm); *to know on which side o.'s bread is ~ed* wissen, wo der Vorteil liegt; *to look as if ~ would not melt in o.'s mouth* aussehen, als ob man kein Wässerchen trüben könnte; *peanut-~* Erdnußbutter *f*; **~-bird** *Am* Reisstar, Boblink *m*; **~-boat** (kleine) Sauciere *f (für zerlassene Butter)*; **~ churn** Süßrahmbutterungsanlage *f*; **~cup** Butterblume *f*, Hahnenfuß *m*; **~-dish** Butterdose *f*; **~ed roll** Buttersemmel *f*; **~flower** *bot* scharfe(r) Hahnenfuß *m*; **~fat** Butterfett *n*; **~fingers** *sing fam* ungeschickte(r) Mensch *m*; **~fly** Schmetterling *m a. fig*; *pl Am fam* Nervosität *f*; *~~ collection* Schmetterlingssammlung *f*; *~~ nut* Flügel(schrauben)mutter *f*; *~~ stroke (Schwimmen)* Schmetterlingsstil *m*; *~~ valve (mot)* Drosselklappe *f*; **~-knife** Buttermesser *n*; **~ milk** Buttermilch *f*; **~nut** graue Walnuß *f*; **~-scotch** Butterbonbon *m od n*; **~wort** ['-wə:t] *bot* Fettkraut *n*; **~y** ['-ri] **1.** *a* butterartig, -haltig; butterbestrichen; *fig* schmeichlerisch; **2.** *s* Speisekammer *f*, Vorratsraum *m*; *~~-hatch* Durchreiche *f*.

buttock ['bʌtək] Hinterbacke *f*; *meist pl* Hinterteil *n*, Hintern *m*, Gesäß *n*; *sport* Hüftschwung *m*.

button ['bʌtn] *s* Knopf *m*; Knospe *f*, Auge *n*; *el* Klingel-, Schaltknopf, Taster; (Degen-)Knopf *m*, Arretspitze; *(Ruder)* Belederung *f*; (kleiner drehbarer) Türriegel *m*; *Am sl* Kinn *n*; *pl fam (boy in ~s)* Page *m (in Livree)*; *pl Am sl* Verkaufsprämie *f*; *tr* mit Knöpfen versehen, besetzen; *(Fechten)* mit dem Knopf berühren; *itr* (zu-)geknöpft werden; sich knöpfen lassen; *on the ~ (Am fam)* pünktlich; haargenau; *to ~ down (Am sl)* richtig einschätzen; *(Zimmer)* aufräumen, abschließen; *to ~ up* (zu)knöpfen; *Am sl (Aufgabe)* erledigen, fertigbringen; *(Zimmer)* abschließen; *(Maschine)* abstellen; *to ~ up o.'s lips* den Mund halten; *to have all o.'s ~s (fam)* alle fünf Sinne beieinander haben; *to press, to touch the ~* auf den Knopf drücken *a. fig*; *to sew the ~ on* den Knopf annähen; **~-boy** Page *m*; **~-control** Druckknopfsteuerung *f*; **~-fastening** Knopfverschluß *m*; **~-fish** Seeigel *m*; **~hole** *s* Knopfloch(blume *f*); Sträußchen *n*; *tr* Knopflöcher machen; *fig* fest-, zurückhalten; *~~ machine* Knopflochmaschine *f*; *~~ scissors (pl)* Knopflochschere *f*; *~~ stitch* Knopfloch-, Schlingstich *m*.

buttress ['bʌtris] *s arch* Strebepfeiler *m*; *fig* Stütze *f*, Halt *m*; *tr lit fig (oft to ~ up)* stützen; *flying ~* Strebebogen *m*.

butty ['bʌti] *min* Steiger; *fam* Kumpel, Kamerad *m*.

butyr|aceous, ~ic [bju:ti'reiʃəs, -'tirik] *a chem* Butter-; **~ic acid** Buttersäure *f*.

buxom ['bʌksəm] *(Frau)* drall, frisch u. blühend, von Gesundheit strotzend.

buy [bai] *irr bought, bought tr* kaufen; erwerben, erstehen, einhandeln; an-, einkaufen; bestechen; *(Fahrkarte)* lösen; *fig* erkaufen (*with* mit); *Am sl* schlucken, glauben, einverstanden sein (*a plan* mit e-m Plan); *Am sl* erreichen, anheuern; *itr* als Käufer auftreten; *s* Kauf *m*; *Am fam (Br good ~)* (gutes) Geschäft *n*, gute(r) Kauf *m*; *to ~ ahead* auf spätere Lieferung kaufen; *to ~ back* zurückkaufen; *to ~ in* (in größerer Menge) einkaufen; *(auf e-r Auktion)* durch höheres Gebot zurückhalten; *sl* sich einkaufen; *to ~ off* auszahlen; los-, freikaufen; bestechen; *to ~ out* auszahlen, ablösen; *to ~ over* bestechen, kaufen; *to ~ up* aufkaufen; *to ~ at an auction* ersteigern; *to ~ against, for cash* (gegen) bar, gegen Barzahlung, gegen Kasse kaufen; *to ~ on commission* auf Kommission kaufen; *to ~ firm* fest, auf feste Rechnung kaufen; *to ~ at a loss, profit* mit Verlust, Gewinn kaufen; *to ~ a pig in a poke (fig)* die Katze im Sack kaufen; *I'll ~ it* ich höre; *(beim Raten)* ich gebe es auf; *that's a good ~* das ist preiswert, ein guter Kauf; **~able** ['-əbl] käuflich; **~er** ['-ə] Käufer, Abnehmer; Einkäufer *m (e-s großen Handelshauses)*; *(Börse)* Geld *n*; *~'s market, strike* Käufermarkt, -streik *m*; **~ing** ['-iŋ] Kaufen *n*, Kauf, Erwerb; An-, Einkauf *m*; *~~-back* Rückkauf *m*; *~~ capacity, power* Kaufkraft *f*; *~~ commission* Einkaufsprovision *f*; *~~ order* Kaufauftrag *m*, -order *f*; *~~-up* Aufkaufen *n*; *~~ value* Kaufwert *m*.

buzz [bʌz] *itr* summen, surren, schwirren, brausen, brummen; (in den Bart) murmeln, durchea.-, zs. reden; *(Gerücht)* sich verbreiten; *Am sl* sich ankündigen; *mil sl* sich betrinken; *tr (Gerücht)* verbreiten; summen lassen; *tele radio* durch Summer übermitteln; *fam* telephonieren; *aero* dicht vorbeisausen an, niedrig fliegen (*a field* über ein Feld); *Am sl* im Vertrauen sagen, klauen, ausfragen; *s* Summen, Brausen, Brummen *n*; (Volks-)Gemurmel, Durchea.reden, allgemeine(s) Gerede *n*; *tele fam* Anruf *m*; *Am sl* Vergnügen *n*; Aufregung *f*; *Am sl* Kuß *m* (auf die Wangen); *to ~ about (fam)* herumsausen; *to ~ along (fam)* sich dünne machen, abhauen; *to*

~ *off (sl)* lossausen, abhauen; *tele* einhängen; ~**ard** ['-əd] *orn* (Mäuse-)Bussard; *mil sl* Adler *m (Abzeichen)*; *Am sl* Hühnchen *n*; ~-**bomb** *fam* V-1-Bombe *f*; ~**er** ['-ə] *tele radio* Summer *m*; *fam* Sirene *f*; *Am fam* Polizeiabzeichen *n*; *sl mil* Agent, V-Mann *m*; ~~ *signal, sound* Summerton *m*, -zeichen *n*; ~**ing** ['-iŋ] *radio* Summen *n*; ~-**saw** *Am* Kreissäge *f*.

*

by [bai] *prp* **1.** *(örtlich)* bei, an, neben; ~ *the sea* an der See; *close* ~ *the river* dicht am Fluß; *sit* ~ *me* setz dich zu mir, neben mich; **2.** *(örtlich)* durch, über; *I went* ~ *Paris* ich bin über Paris gefahren; **3.** *(örtlich)* an ... vorbei; *I walked* ~ *the post-office* ich bin an der Post vorbeigegangen; **4.** *(zeitlich)* während, in, an; ~ *day* bei, am Tage, tagsüber; **5.** *(zeitlich)* vor, bis(zu), spätestens an, um; ~ *to-morrow* bis morgen; ~ *now* bisher, bis jetzt; ~ *then* bis dahin; ~ *the time* unterdessen, inzwischen; **6.** *(zeitlich)* ~ *the day* am Tage, täglich, pro Tag; ~ *the month* im Monat, monatlich, pro Monat; **7.** *(Ausdehnung) four feet* ~ *six* vier zu sechs Fuß; **8.** von, durch, mit, (ver)mittels, an; *a tragedy* ~ *Shakespeare* e-e Tragödie von S.; ~ *car, rail, train, tram, bus, boat, plane* mit dem Wagen, der Bahn, dem Zug, der Straßenbahn, dem Bus, dem Schiff, im Flugzeug; ~ *land, sea, air* zu Lande, zu Wasser, auf dem Luftwege; ~ *the pound* pfundweise; *to live* ~ *bread* von Brot leben; **9.** nach *(e-r S urteilen)*; *to judge* ~ *appearances* nach dem Äußeren urteilen; **10.** *(Ausdrücke) (all)* ~ *o.s.* (ganz) allein; ohne Hilfe; *day* ~ *day* Tag für Tag, täglich; *little* ~ *little* nach u. nach, langsam, allmählich, stufen-, schrittweise; *one* ~ *one* einer nach dem andern; *step* ~ *step* Schritt für Schritt, schrittweise; ~ *chance* zufällig; ~ *degrees* stufenweise; ~ *the dozen* dutzendweise; im Dutzend; ~ *far* bei weitem, (sehr) viel; ~ *God* bei Gott; ~ *a hair* um ein Haar; ~ *all, no means* auf jeden, keinen Fall; ~ *name* dem Namen nach; ~ *the name of* unter dem Namen *gen*; ~ *nature* von Natur (aus); ~ *right* von Rechts wegen; ~ *turns* wechselweise; ~ *the way,* ~ *the by(e)* beiläufig, nebenbei (gesagt); **11.** *to swear* ~ *s.th. (fig)* auf etw schwören; *what do you mean* ~ *that?* was meinen Sie damit, was wollen Sie damit sagen? **12.** *adv* vorbei; *I can't get* ~ ich kann, komme nicht vorbei; *in days gone* ~ in vergangener-früherer Zeit; *to stand* ~ in der Nähe, fertig *od* bereit sein; *to put, to lay* ~ auf die Seite legen, sparen; ~ *and* ~ nach und nach; gleich; bald; ~ *and large* im ganzen (gesehen).

by|(e) [bai] *a,* ~- *pref* Neben-, Seiten-; ~-**and**-~ Zukunft *f*; ~**e** *s* etw Unwichtig(er)e(s), Nebensächliche(s) *n*; *(Kricket)* angerechnete(r) Lauf *m* für e-n vorbeigelassenen Ball; *(Golf)* beim Spiel übrigbleibende Löcher *n pl*; *(Tennis)* überzählige(r) Spieler *m*; ~(~)-*blow* uneheliche(s) Kind *n*; ~~-~~ ['baibai] *(Kindersprache)* Heia *f*, Bettchen *n*; Schlaf *m*; *interj* ['bai'bai] *fam* tjüs! auf Wiedersehen! *to go to* ~~-~~ zu Bett gehen.

by|-blow ['baiblou] *lit fig* Seitenhieb *m*; uneheliche(s) Kind *n*, Bastard *m*; ~-**election** *parl* Nachwahl *f*; ~**gone** *a* vergangen, gewesen; *pred* vorbei, vorüber; *s pl das* Vergangene, Vergangenes *n*, *bes.* vergangene Unbill *f*; *to let* ~~*s be* ~~*s* die Vergangenheit begraben sein lassen, vergeben u. vergessen; ~**(e)-law** (Gemeinde- *od* Vereins-)Statut *n*, Satzung *f*; Ausführungsbestimmungen *f pl*; ~**pass** *s* (Gas-)Kleinsteller *m*; Umgehung(sstraße); *el* Überbrückung; Nebenleitung *f*; Nebenschluß-; *tr* e-e Umgehungsstraße anlegen, bauen um; umfahren, herumfahren um; seitlich liegenlassen; *fig* umgehen; *el* umleiten, überbrücken; ~**path** Neben-, Seitenweg *m a. fig*; ~**play** Nebenhandlung; *theat* Pantomime *f*; ~-**product** Nebenprodukt *n*; ~**stander** (bloßer) Zuschauer *m*; ~**street** (stillere) Neben-, Seitenstraße *f (in e-r Stadt)*; ~**way** abgelegene (Land-)Straße *f*; Richtweg *m*; *fig* Nebengebiet *n*.

byre ['baiə] Kuhstall *m*.

Byzantin|e [bai'zæntain, bi-] *a* byzantinisch; *s* Byzantiner *m*; ~**ism** [bi'zæntinizm] Byzantinismus *m*.

C

C [si:] *pl* ~'*s*, ~*s s* C, c *n*; *mus* c *n (Moll)*, C *n (Dur)*; *chem* Kohlenstoff *m*; *phys* Coulomb *n*; *Am (Schule)* Befriedigend *n*; **C 3** *mil* untauglich; *fig* völlig unbrauchbar; ~ **flat** Ces *n*; ~ **major** C-Dur; ~ **minor** c-Moll; ~ **sharp** Cis *n*.

cab [kæb] **1.** *s (horse-~)* Droschke; *(taxi-~)* Taxe *f*, Taxi *n*; *rail* Führerstand *m (a. Kran, Bagger)*; *(Lastkraftwagen)* Führerhaus *n*; *aero mil* Kanzel *f*; ~-**driver,** ~**man** Droschkenkutscher; Taxifahrer *m*; ~**ette** [kə'bet] *Am* Taxifahrerin *f*; ~-**rank, -stand** Droschken-, Taxenstand *m*; **2.** *s sl* Klatsche *f*, Schmöker; Schlauch *m*.

cab|al [kə'bæl] *s* Kabale, Intrige *f*, Ränke(spiel *n*) *m pl*; Clique *f*, Klüngel *m*; *itr* Ränke schmieden, intrigieren; ~**aret** ['kæbərei] Kabarett *n*, Kleinkunstbühne *f*; *Am* Trinklokal *n* mit Vorführungen; ~~ *performer* Ansager *m*; ~~ *singer* Chansonette, Diseuse *f*.

cabbage ['kæbidʒ] *s* Kohl *m*, Kraut; *Am fam* Geld; *Am sl* junge(s) Mädchen *n*; *Br (Schule) s. cab 2*; *itr (Kohl)* e-n Kopf ansetzen; *tr fam* sich unter den Nagel reißen, stibitzen; *turnip* ~ Kohlrabi *m*; ~ **butterfly** *ent* Kohlweißling *m*; ~-**head** Kohlkopf; *Am* Dummkopf *m*; ~-**lettuce** Kopfsalat *m*; ~-**rose** Zentifolie *f (Rose)*.

cab(b)ala ['kæbələ] *rel* Kabbala; *allg* Geheimlehre *f*.

cabby ['kæbi] *fam* Droschkenkutscher; Taxifahrer *m*.

cabin ['kæbin] (Bau-)Hütte *f*; *Am* kleine(s) Häuschen, Wochenendhaus *n*; Badezelle, -kabine; *mar* Kabine, Kajüte *f*; *Br* Stellwerk *n*; *aero* Kabine *f*, Fluggastraum *m*; ~-**boy** *mar* Offiziersbursche; Logisjunge *m*; ~ **car, scooter** Kabinenroller *m*; ~-**class** *mar* 2. Klasse *f*; ~ **trunk** Kabinenkoffer *m*; ~ **wall** *aero* Kabinenschott *n*, -wand *f*.

cabinet ['kæbinit] *s* Glasschrank *m*, Vitrine *f*; Schrank *m*; Truhe *f*, Kasten *m*; *(bes. radio)* Gehäuse *n*; Geräteschrank *m*; kleine(s) Zimmer *n*, Nebenraum *m*; *pol (meist C~)* Kabinett, Ministerium *n*, Regierung *f*; *a* privat, vertraulich; kostbar; Kabinett-; *filing* ~ Aktenschrank *m*; *shadow* ~ Schattenkabinett *n*, Führer *m pl* der Opposition; ~ **council** Kabinetts-, Ministerrat *m (beratende Versammlung)*; ~ **crisis** Kabinetts-, Regierungskrise *f*; ~ **factory** *Am* Möbelfabrik *f*; ~**maker (-making)** Möbeltischler(ei *f*), -schreiner(ei *f*) *m*; ~ **minister** Staats-, amtierende(r) Minister *m*; ~ **photograph** Kabinettbild *n*; ~ **pudding** *Art* (warmer) Gebäckpudding *m*; ~**work** Kunsttischlerarbeit *f*.

*

cable ['keibl] *s bes. mar* Tau; Seil; *(chain ~)* Ankertau *n*, -kette; *mar* Trosse; Kabellänge *f* ($^1/_{10}$ *Seemeile)*; *tele* Kabel *n*; Kabelnachricht *f*; *el* Kabel *n*; Leitung *f*; *tr mar* vertäuen, mit Tauen festmachen; *tr itr tele* kabeln; *by* ~ durch Kabel, telegraphisch; *aerial, air, overhead* ~ Luftkabel *n*, Freileitung *f*; ~-**address** Telegrammadresse, Drahtanschrift *f*; ~-**car** Wagen *m* e-r (Draht-)Seilbahn; ~ **clamp** Seil-, Kabelklemme *f*; ~-**code** Telegraphenkode *m*; ~ **company** Telegraphengesellschaft *f*; ~ **connection** Kabelverbindung *f*; ~ **core** Kabelader *f*, -kern *m*, -seele *f*; ~ **ferry** Seilfähre *f*; ~**gram** ['-græm] Kabelnachricht *f*; ~ **railway, tramway** Drahtseilbahn *f*; ~ **reel** Kabeltrommel *f*; ~**se** ['-li:z] Telegrammstil *m*; ~-**ship** Kabelleger *m (Schiff)*.

cab|oodle [kə'bu:dl]: *the whole* ~~ *(fam)* alle(s) zs., der ganze Haufen; ~**oose** [kə'bu:s] Kombüse *f (Schiffsküche)*; *Am rail* Bremserhaus *n*; *(~~ car)* Bremserwagen *m*; ~**otage** ['kæbətɑ:ʒ] Küstenschiffahrt *f*, -handel *m*; *aero* Flugverkehr *m* innerhalb der Landesgrenzen; ~**riolet** [kæbrio'lei] zweirädrige(r) Einspänner *m*; *mot* Kabriolett *n*; ~~ *hood* aufklappbare(s) Verdeck *n*.

ca'canny [kɑ:'kæni] passive(r) Widerstand; Bummelstreik, Streik *m* durch zu genaue Anwendung der Vorschriften.

cacao [kə'kɑ:ou] *(~bean)* Kakaobohne *f*; *(~-tree)* Kakaobaum *m*.

cach|alot ['kæʃəlɔt, -lou] *zoo* Pottwal *m*; ~**e** [kæʃ] *s* Versteck *n*; versteckte(r) Vorrat *m*; *tr* verstecken, verbergen; ~**ectic** [kæ'kektik] *med* kachektisch, krankhaft (verändert); ~**et** ['kæʃei] Siegel *n*, (Qualitäts-, Herkunfts-) Stempel *m*; *pharm* Kapsel *f*; ~**exia** ['kækeksia, kə'keksia], ~**exy** ['kækeksi] *med* Kachexie *f*, Kräfteverfall *m*; ~**innate** ['kækineit] *itr* schallend lachen.

cackle ['kækl] *s (Huhn)* Gegacker; *(Gans)* Geschnatter *a. fig*; *fig* Geplapper, Geschwätz; Gekicher; *Am sl* Ei *n*;

itr (Huhn) gackern; *(Gans)* schnattern *a. fig*; *fig* plappern, schwatzen; prahlen; kichern; **~r** ['-ə] gackernde Henne; schnatternde Gans *f a. fig*; *Am sl* Bürohengst *m*.
caco ['kæko] *pref scient* Miß-; häßlich, schlecht; krank(haft); **~phonic(al)**, **~phonous** [-ə'fɔnik(l), -'kɔfənəs] schlecht klingend; **~phony** [-'kɔfəni] Mißklang *m*, Kakophonie *f*.
cactus ['kæktəs] *pl a. -ti* [-tai] *bot* Kaktus *m*.
cad [kæd] *fam* Flegel, Lümmel, Rüpel; *(~dy) Am* Cadillac *m*; **~astral** [kə'dæstrəl] *a* Kataster-, Grundbuch-; *~~ survey*, **~astre** [kə'dæstə] Kataster *m od n*, Grundbuch *n*; **~aver** [kə'deivə] *bes. tech* Kadaver *m*, Leiche *f*; **~averous** [kə'dævərəs] leichenhaft; leichenblaß, totenbleich; **~die, ~dy** ['kædi] Golfjunge *f*; **~dis fly** *zoo* Köcherfliege *f*; **~dish** ['kædiʃ] *fam* flegel-, rüpelhaft, unfein, ungebildet; **~dy** ['kædi] Teebüchse *f*.
cad|ence ['keidəns] Kadenz *f*; Rhythmus, Takt *m*; Intonation *f*, Tonfall *m*, Betonung *f*; *Am mil* Gleichschritt *m*; **~et** [kə'det] *mil* Kadett, Offiziersanwärter; jüngere(r) *od* jüngste(r) Sohn *od* Bruder *m*; *~~ ship (mar)* Schulschiff *n*; *~~ teacher* Junglehrer *m*.
cadge [kædʒ] *itr* betteln (*for* um); hausieren; *tr* erbetteln; **~r** ['-ə] Hausierer, Straßenhändler; Schmarotzer; Bettler, Landstreicher *m*; *tech* Ölkännchen *n*.
cadmium ['kædmiəm] *chem* Kadmium *n*; **~ cell** Normalelement *n*.
cadre ['kɑ:dr, *Am mil* 'kædri] Rahmen *m*, Schema *n*; *mil* Kader *m*, Stammtruppe, -einheit *f*; **~ personnel** Rahmen-, Stammpersonal *n*; **~ unit** Stamm-, Rahmeneinheit *f*.
caduc|ity [kə'dju:siti] Hinfälligkeit, Vergänglichkeit, Kurzlebigkeit *f*; **~ous** [-kəs] hinfällig, vergänglich, kurzlebig, vorübergehend.

*

ca(e)cum ['si:kəm] *anat* Blinddarm *m*.
Caesar ['si:zə] Caesar *m*; **~ean, ~ian** [-'zɛəriən]: *~~ birth, operation, section (med)* Kaiserschnitt *m*.
caes|ious ['si:zjəs] *bot* blau- *od* graugrün; **~ium** ['-əm] *chem* Zäsium *n*; **~ura** [si'zjuərə] Zäsur *f*, (Vers-)Einschnitt *m*.
caf|é ['kæfei, *Am* kə'fe, kæ'fe] *(England)* Café, Kaffeehaus; *(Festland, US)* Restaurant *n*, Bar *f*; **~eteria** [kæfi'ti(ə)riə] Selbstbedienungsrestaurant *n*; Automat(enbüfett *n*) *m*; **~fein(e)** ['kæfii(:)n] Koffein *n*.
cage [keidʒ] *s* Käfig *m*; (Vogel-)Bauer *n* od *m*; Aufzug-, *min* Förderkorb; eingezäunte(s) Kriegsgefangenenlager *n*; *allg* Drahtbehälter *m*, Lattenkiste *f*, Verschlag; *(Korbball)* Korb *m*; *(Hockey)* Tor; *(Baseball)* Übungsfeld *n*; *lit fig* Gefängnis *n*, Kerker *m*; *tr* in e-n Käfig sperren; **~y, cagy** ['-i] *fam* zurückhaltend; *Am sl* schlau, vorsichtig, auf Draht.
cahoot [kə'hu:t] *Am sl*: *to be, to go in ~(s), to go ~s with s.o.* mit jdm unter einer Decke stecken.
caiman ['keimən] *s. cayman*.
Cain [kein] Kain; (Bruder-)Mörder *m*; *what in ~ (Am fam)* was in aller Welt; *to raise ~ (Am fam)* Unruhe stiften.
cairn ['kɛən] Hügelgrab *n*; Steinpyramide *f*.
caisson ['keisn] Munitionskiste *f*, -wagen; *arch* Senkkasten; *(Schiffbau)* Verschlußponton *m*; **~ disease** Caisson(arbeiter)krankheit *f*.
caitiff ['keitif] *s obs poet* Schurke *m*.
cajole [kə'dʒoul] *tr* schmeicheln (*s.o.* jdm); *s.o. into* od *out of doing s.th.* jdn dazu verleiten, verführen, etw zu tun *od* zu (unter)lassen; *s.th. out of s.o.* jdm etw abschmeicheln; **~ry** [-əri] Schmeichelei *f*.
cake [keik] *s* Kuchen *m*; Stück Kuchen, Törtchen *n*; *allg* Stück *n*, Riegel *m* (*~ of soap* Seife), Tafel; *tech* Masse *f*, Klumpen *m*; *Am sl* hübsche(s) Mädchen *n*; *tr* (in e-e Form) pressen; *itr* zs.backen, e-n Klumpen bilden; brikettieren; tablettieren; *to be ~d with mud* vor Dreck, Schmutz starren; *to take the ~ (fam)* den Vogel abschießen; *you cannot eat your ~ and have it (prov)* man kann nicht auf zwei Hochzeiten tanzen; *piece of ~* Stück *n* Kuchen; *fig fam* einfache *od* schöne Sache *f*; **~s and ale** Wohlleben *n*; **~-walk** *Art* amerik. Negertanz *m*.
calab|ash ['kæləbæʃ] Flaschenkürbis *m*; **~oose** [kælə'bu:s] *Am sl* Kittchen *n*.
calam|ary ['kæləməri] Kalmar *m (Tintenfisch)*; **~ine** ['-ain] Galmei *m (Zinkerz)*; **~itous** [kə'læmitəs] unglücklich, unglückselig, verhängnisvoll; **~ity** [kə'læmiti] (großes) Unglück *n*; Schicksalsschlag *m*; große Not *f*, Elend *n*, Jammer *m*, Trübsal *f*; *~~ howler, prophet, shouter (Am sl)* Unglücksprophet *m*; **~us** ['kæləməs] *pl -mi* [-mai]: *Sweet C~ (bot pharm)* Kalmus *m*.
calc [kælk] *pref* Kalk-; **~areous** [-'kɛəriəs] kalkartig, Kalk-; **~ic** ['kælsik] *a* Kalzium-; **~iferous** [-'sifərəs], **~ific** [-'sifik] kohlensauren Kalk enthaltend *od* bildend; **~ification** [-sifi'keiʃən] *med* Verkalkung *f*; **~ify** ['kælsifai] *tr itr* verkalken; **~imine** ['-simain] *s* Kalkmilch *f (zum Tünchen)*; *tr* weißen, tünchen; **~ination** [-si'neiʃən] Kalkbrennen; Austrocknen *n*; Veraschung *f*; **~ine** ['kælsain, -in] *tr (itr* Kalk) brennen; austrocknen; veraschen, kalzinieren; entwässern; *fig* von den Schlacken befreien; *itr (Kalk)* gebrannt werden; **~ite** ['-sait] Kalzit, Kalkspat *m*; **~ium** ['-siəm] Kalzium *n*; *~~ carbide* Kalziumkarbid *n*; *~~ phosphate* Kalziumphosphat *n*; **~~spar** ['-spɑ:] Kalkspat *m*.
calcul|able ['kælkjuləbl] berechenbar; zuverlässig; **~ate** ['-eit] *itr* rechnen (*on* mit) *a. fig*; *fig* sich verlassen (*on* auf); *tr* aus-, be-, errechnen; überschlagen, veranschlagen, kalkulieren; zählen; *(im Passiv)* planen, einrichten, bedenken, berechnen, ausdenken; *Am fam* denken, meinen, annehmen; *to be ~~d to* darauf berechnet, zugeschnitten sein, zu, daß; **~ated** ['-leitid] *a* berechnet, ausgedacht, vorbedacht, absichtlich; eingerichtet, vorgesehen; **~ating** ['-eitiŋ] *(Mensch)* berechnend; überlegt; *~~ error* Rechenfehler *m*; *~~-machine* Rechenmaschine *f*; **~ation** [-'leiʃən] Rechnen *n*; Zählung; Kalkulation, (Be-)Rechnung *f*; Überschlag *m*, Veranschlagung *f*, Plan *m*; *~~ of cost* Kostenberechnung *f*; **~ator** ['-eitə] (Be-)Rechner; Planer *m*; Rechentabelle, -maschine *f*; **~us** ['-əs] *pl -i* [-ai] *med* Stein *m*; *math* Rechnungsart, *bes.* Differentialrechnung *f*.
caldron ['kɔ:ldrən] *s. cauldron*.
calefact|ion [kæli'fækʃən] *scient* Erwärmung *f*; **~ory** [-təri] wärmeerzeugend.
calend|ar ['kælində] *s* Kalender *m*; Verzeichnis, Register *n*, Liste *f*; Programm; Brief-, Urkundenregister *n*; *jur (~~ of cases)* Terminkalender *m*; *jur* Geschäftsverteilung *f*; *tr* registrieren, in e-e Liste eintragen, aufführen; katalogisieren; ein Register anlegen zu *(Briefen, Urkunden)*; *~~ call (Am)* Aufruf *m* der Streitsache; *~~ clock* Kalenderuhr *f*; *~~ day, month* Kalendertag, -monat *m*; **~er** [-] *s (Textil)* Kalander *m*, Glätt-, Prägemaschine *f*; *tr* kalandern; glätten; prägen.
calf [kɑ:f] *pl calves* [kɑ:vz] Kalb *n*; *(Mensch)* Ochse, Esel *m*, Schaf; *(~-leather, -skin)* Kalbleder *n*; Eisberg *m*, -scholle; Wade *f*; *in, with ~ (Kuh)* trächtig; *to kill the fatted ~ (fig)* ein Kalb schlachten; *the golden ~* das Goldene Kalb, der Mammon; **~ love** jugendliche Liebe *f*; **~'s tooth** Milchzahn *m*.
calibr|ate ['kælibreit] *tr* kalibrieren, das Kaliber messen (*a gun* e-r Schußwaffe); *(Meßgerät)* eichen; **~ation** [-'breiʃən] Kalibrierung; Eichung *f*; *~~ scale* Einstellskala *f*; **~e,** *Am* **caliber** ['kælibə] Kaliber *n*; Schublehre *f*; *(Faden)* Titer *m*; *fig* Gewicht *n*, Bedeutung *f*, Kaliber *n (e-s Menschen)*.
calico ['kælikou] *pl -o(e)s* Kaliko *(weißer Baumwollstoff)*; *Am* Kattun *m*.
California [kæli'fɔ:niə] Kalifornien *n*; **~n** [-n] *a* kalifornisch; *s* Kalifornier(in *f*) *m*.
caliph, calif ['keilif, 'kælif] *rel hist* Kalif *m*.
calk [kɔ:k] **1.** *s* Eisstollen, -nagel *m (am Hufeisen, unter den Schuhsohlen)*; *tr* scharf beschlagen; **2.** *s caulk*; **3.** *tr* durchpausen.
call [kɔ:l] **1.** *tr* rufen *a. radio*; anrufen *a. tele*; *(Namen)* aufrufen; *(Schauspieler vor den Vorhang)* herausrufen; *(e-n Arzt, e-e Taxe)* holen, rufen; wecken; nennen (*in German* auf deutsch); bezeichnen, betrachten, ansehen als, halten für; *(in ein Amt)* berufen; *jur* anberaumen; *(Versammlung)* einberufen; *(Pause)* einlegen; *(Wild)* locken; *itr* rufen; heißen; *meist pret (zu e-m Besuch)* vorsprechen, da sein; *to be ~ed* heißen, genannt werden (*after s.o.* nach jdm); *to ~ to account* zur Rechenschaft ziehen; *to ~ to arms (mil)* einberufen; *to ~ attention to* aufmerksam machen auf; *to ~ into being* ins Leben rufen; *to ~ o.'s bluff (Am)* gegen jdn auftreten; *to ~ over the coals* ausschimpfen; *to ~ it a day* Feierabend machen; *to ~ a halt* Halt gebieten; aufhören (*to* mit), beenden (*to s.th.* etw); *to ~ s.o. names* jdn be-, ausschimpfen; *to ~ to order* zur Ordnung rufen; *to ~ o.'s own* sein eigen nennen; *to ~ in question* in Frage stellen; *to ~* **at** vorsprechen bei, in *(e-m Hause)*; halten in *(e-m Ort) a. rail*; *(Schiff e-n Hafen)* anlaufen; *aero* anfliegen, zwischenlanden in; *to ~* **away** *tr* ab-, wegrufen; *to ~* **back** *tr itr* zurückrufen; *to ~* **down** *tr* herunterrufen; *Am fam* ausschimpfen, fertigmachen, herunterputzen; *to ~* **for** *tr* fragen nach, rufen um, (dringend) verlangen; benötigen; erfordern; *(Konferenz)* einberufen, ansetzen; *(Menschen)* abholen; *to be ~ed for* postlagernd; *to ~* **forth** *tr* einsetzen, anwenden, zur Anwendung bringen; hervorzaubern, -bringen; erfordern; *all o.'s energy* s-e ganze Kraft zs.nehmen; *to ~* **from** *tr* abrufen, wegholen; *to ~* **in** *tr* hereinrufen; herbeirufen, -holen; *(e-n Arzt)* holen, zuziehen, zu Rate ziehen; zurückfordern; ein-, aus dem Umlauf ziehen *(bes. Geldsorten)*; *to ~* **off** *tr* ab-, wegrufen; *(Veranstaltung, Unternehmen)* absagen, *fam* abblasen, abbrechen; *to ~* **on** *tr* auf-, besuchen (*at o.'s home, office* in jds Heim, Büro);

vorsprechen bei; sich wenden an; *to* ~ **out** *tr* herausrufen; in Tätigkeit setzen, in Aktion bringen; *(Name)* aufrufen; *(Haltestelle)* ausrufen; *(zum Duell) obs* herausfordern; *(Truppen)* einsetzen; *Am (Schauspieler vor den Vorhang)* herausrufen; *(Feuerwehr)* herbeirufen; zum Streiken auffordern; *itr* (laut) aufschreien; *to* ~ **over** *tr (Namen)* verlesen; *to* ~ **together** *tr* zs.rufen; *to* ~ **up** *tr* aufrufen; *tele* anrufen, anläuten; ins Gedächtnis rufen; aufwecken; *mil* einberufen, einziehen *(a. Geldsorten)*; **2.** *s* Ruf *a. zoo, bes. orn*; *tele* Anruf *m*, (Telephon-)Gespräch *n*; (dringende) Bitte, Aufforderung *f*; Abruf; Aufruf *m*; Zahlungsaufforderung; An-, Nachfrage *f* (*for* nach); Anspruch *m* (*for, on* auf); Signal(pfeife *f*) *n*; *theat fig* Vorhang; *jur* Aufruf *m* (*of a case* e-r Sache); (kurzer) Besuch; *(Fahrzeug a. rail)* (Aufent-)Halt *m*; *mar aero* Zwischenlandung *f*; *fig* Hang *m*, Neigung, (innere) Berufung (*of* zu); Pflicht; *(meist verneint)* Notwendigkeit, Gelegenheit *f*, Grund *m*, Ursache *f* (*for, to* zu); *at* ~ bereit; verfügbar, greifbar; *at, on* ~ *(fin)* auf tägliche Kündigung; *on* ~ auf Abruf, auf Anforderung; *within* ~ in Ruf-, Hörweite; *to book a* ~ *(tele)* ein Gespräch anmelden; *to give s.o. a* ~ *(tele)* jdn anrufen; *local* ~ *(tele)* Ortsgespräch *n*; *official* ~ *(tele)* Dienstgespräch *n*; *roll* ~ namentliche(r) Aufruf; *mil* Anwesenheitsappell *m*; *trunk* ~, *long distance* ~ Ferngespräch *n*; ~ *for help* Hilferuf *m*; ~ *to order* Ordnungsruf *m*; ~**-box** Telephonzelle *f*; ~**-boy** *theat* Inspizientengehilfe; Hotelpage *m*; ~**ed** [-d] *a* berufen; genannt; *many are* ~~ viele sind berufen; *so-*~~ sogenannt; ~**er** ['-ə] Besucher; *tele* Anrufer, Sprecher; (Einbe-)Rufer *m*; ~**-girl** Prostituierte *f (auf Abruf)*; ~**ing** ['-iŋ] Rufen *n*; Aufruf *m*; *(Versammlung)* Einberufung *f*; *mar* Anlaufen *n*; (innere) Berufung *f*; Pflichtgefühl, -bewußtsein *n*; Beruf *m*, Gewerbe *n*; Berufsgruppe *f*, Stand *m*; *X.* ~~ *(tele)* hier spricht X.; ~~ *card (Am)* Visiten-, Besuchskarte *f*; ~~ *current* Rufstrom *m*; ~~ *dial* Ruf-, Wählerscheibe *f*; ~~ *hours (pl)* Besuchszeit *f*; ~~ *station* anrufende Station *f*; ~**-loan, -money** täglich fällige(s) Geld *n*; ~**-office** Fernsprechamt *n*; ~**-sign(al)** *radio* Rufzeichen *n*; ~**-up** Einberufung *f*.

calli|graphy [kə'ligrəfi] Schönschreibkunst, Kalligraphie *f*; ~**per** ['kælipə] *meist pl* u. a.: ~ *compasses (pl)* Taster, Tast-, Greifzirkel *m*; ~**sthenics** [kælis'θeniks] *pl* Freiübungen *f pl*; Gymnastik *f*.

call|osity [kæ'lɔsiti] (*oft* hornige) Verdickung (der Haut); Schwiele *f*; ~**ous** ['kæləs] schwielig; *fig* gefühllos, abgestumpft (*to* gegen); ~**ousness** ['kæləsnis] Gefühllosigkeit, Abgestumpftheit *f*; ~**ow** ['kælou] ungefiedert; *fig* unreif, unerfahren.

calm [kɑ:m] *s* Unbewegtheit, Ruhe, Stille; Windstille, *mar* Flaute; *fig* (innere, Gemüts-)Ruhe *f*, (Seelen-)Frieden *m*; soziale *od* politische Befriedung *f*; *a* unbewegt, ruhig, (wind)still; *fig* ruhig, friedlich, friedfertig; *fam* unverschämt; *v* (sich) beruhigen; *to* ~ *down* sich beruhigen; *(Wind)* abflauen; ~**ative** ['-ətiv, 'kælmətiv] *pharm* Beruhigungsmittel *n*; ~**ness** ['-nis] (*bes.* innere) Ruhe *f*.

calor|escence [kælə'resns] *phys* Verwandlung *f* von Wärme- in Lichtstrahlen; ~**ic** [kə'lɔrik] *s phys* Wärme *f*; *a* Wärme-; ~~ *unit(phys)* Wärmeeinheit *f*; ~**ie** ['kæləri] Kalorie, Wärmeeinheit *f*; ~**ific** [kælə'rifik] wärmeerzeugend; ~~ *effect* Wärme-, Heizwirkung *f*; ~~ *value* Heiz-, Brennwert *m*; ~**imeter** [kælə'rimitə] Kalorimeter *n*, Wärmemesser *m*.

calotte [kə'lɔt] Käppchen *n (bes. d. kath. Priester)*.

caltrop ['kæltrɔp], *a.* **caltrap** *hist* Fußangel *f*; *mot* Autonagel *m*; *bot meist pl* Stolperpflanze, *bes.* Sternflockenblume *f*.

calumet ['kæljumet] Friedenspfeife *f*.

calumn|iate [kə'lʌmnieit] *tr* verleumden; ~**iation** [kəlʌmni'eiʃən], ~**y** ['kæləmni] Verleumdung *f*; ~**iator** [-ieitə] Verleumder *m*; ~**iatory** [-əri], ~**ious** [kə'lʌmniəs] verleumderisch.

Calvary ['kælvəri] *rel* Golgatha; Kalvarienberg *m*.

calv|e [kɑ:v] *itr* kalben *(a. vom Gletscher* od *Eisberg)*; *tr (Kalb)* gebären.

Calvin ['kælvin] Kalvin *(Reformator)*; ~**ism** ['-izm] Kalvinismus *m*; ~**ist** ['-ist] Kalvinist(in *f*) *m*; ~**istic(al)** [-'nistik(l)] kalvinistisch.

calx [kælks] *pl -ces* ['-si:z] Oxyd, Verbrennungsprodukt *n*.

caly|c(i) ['kælik, -si] *pref bot* Kelch-; ~**x** ['-ks, 'keiliks] *pl -ces, -xes* [-si:z, -ksiz] *bot* Kelch *m*.

cam [kæm] *tech* Nocken, Mitnehmer, Daumen *m*, Nase *f*; Steuer-, Hebenocken, -daumen *m*; (Steuer-, Leit-, Arbeits-)Kurve *f*; ~ **gear** Nocken-, Kurvengetriebe *n*, -steuerung *f*; ~**shaft** Nocken-, Steuerwelle *f*.

camb|er ['kæmbə] *s* Wölbung, Biegung nach oben; Schweifung *f*; *bes. mot (*~~ *of wheel)* Radsturz *m*; *tr* wölben, nach oben biegen, durchdrücken; *(Straße)* überhöhen; ~**ist** ['-ist] (Geld-)Wechsler; Wechselmakler, -agent *m*; ~**ric** ['keimbrik] Batist *m*.

Cambrian ['kæmbriən] *a* walisisch; *s* Waliser(in *f*) *m*; *geol* Kambrium *n*.

camel ['kæməl] Kamel *n a. mar*; ~ **caravan** Kamelkarawane *f*; ~**-hair** Kamelhaar *n*; ~**lia** [kə'mi:ljə] *bot* Kamelie *f*.

cameo ['kæmiou] Kamee *f*.

camera ['kæmərə] Kamera *f*, Fotoapparat *m*; (Film-)Aufnahmegerät *n*; *jur* Richterzimmer *n*; *in* ~ *(jur)* unter Ausschluß der Öffentlichkeit; *allg* hinter den Kulissen; ~ **man, operator** *film* Kameramann; Bildberichter *m*.

cami|-knickers, ~**knicks** [kæmi'nikəz, -'niks] *pl* Damenhemdhose *f*; ~**sole** ['kæmisoul] (Damen-)Untertaille *f*.

camomile ['kæməmail] *bot* Kamille *f*; ~ **tea** Kamillentee *m*.

camouflage ['kæmuflɑ:ʒ] *s mil* Tarnung, Deckung, Maskierung; *biol* Schutzfärbung *f*; *tr mil* tarnen, maskieren, *allg* verschleiern, vertuschen; ~ **netting, screen** Tarnnetz *n*; ~ **paint(ing)** Tarnanstrich *m*; ~ **suit** Tarnanzug *m*.

camp [kæmp] *s* (Zelt-)Lager *n*; Lagerplatz *m*; *(holiday* ~*)* Ferienkolonie *f*; *fig* (Partei-)Lager *n*; *tr* in e-m Lager unterbringen; lagern lassen; *itr* lagern; kampieren; *mil* biwakieren; *in the same* ~ in Übereinstimmung, einer Meinung; *to* ~ *out* zelten; *to break up, to strike* ~ das Lager abbrechen; *summer* ~ Sommerlager *n*; *training* ~ Ausbildungslager *n*; ~**-bed(stead)** Feldbett(stelle *f*) *n*; ~**-chair, -stool** Feldstuhl *m*; ~**er** ['-ə] Zeltler, Zeltwanderer *m*; ~**-fever** Typhus *m*; ~**-fire** Lagerfeuer *n*; ~**-follower** Schlachtenbummler *m*; ~ **ground** *Am* Lager-, Zeltplatz *m*; ~**ing** ['-iŋ] Zelten; Camping, (Zelt-, Wochenend-, Ferien-)Lager *n*; *to go* ~~ zelten, in ein Zeltlager gehen; ~~*-ground* Camping-, Zeltplatz *m*; ~~ *trailer* Wohnwagen *m*; ~ **meeting** *Am* Zeltmission *f*; ~**oree** [kæmpə'ri:] Pfadfindertreffen *n* (e-s Bezirks); ~**us** ['-əs] *Am* Universitätsgelände *n*.

campaign [kæm'pein] *s* Feldzug *a. fig, bes. pol*; *(electoral* ~*)* Wahlfeldzug *m*; *tech* Kampagne *f*; *itr* an e-m Feldzug teilnehmen; e-n Feldzug, e-e Werbung durchführen; *publicity, press* ~ Werbe-, Pressefeldzug *m*; ~ **badge, button** *Am* Wahl-, Parteiabzeichen *n*; ~**er** [-ə] Feldzugsteilnehmer; Veteran, alte(r) Krieger *m*; ~ **speech** Wahl-, Werberede *f*.

campanula [kəm'pænjulə] Glockenblume *f*; ~**te** [-ət] *a zoo bot* glockenförmig.

camphor ['kæmfə] *pharm* Kampfer *m*; ~**ate** ['-reit] *tr* mit K. behandeln; ~ **ball** Mottenkugel *f*.

can 1. [kæn] *s* Kanne *f*; Becher *m a. tech*; Büchse; *tech* Kartusche, Hülse *f*; *el* Metallmantel, Abschirmbecher *m*, Abschirmung; *Am* Konservenbüchse, -dose *f*; Kanister *m*; *pl* Kopfhörer *m pl*; *Am sl* Kittchen, Gefängnis *n*; Lokus *m*, Klosett; Hinterteil *n*; *(tin* ~*) mil* Zerstörer; *rail* Tankwagen *m*; *tr Am* (in Konservenbüchsen *od* Gläser) einmachen, -kochen, -wecken; *Am sl* aufhören mit; in Ruhe lassen; in Ordnung bringen; *(Schüler, Angestellten)* schassen, 'rausschmeißen, an die Luft setzen; einsperren; *to carry the* ~ *(sl)* den Kopf hinhalten; ~ *it! (Am sl)* halt's Maul! *ash-*~ Ascheneimer *m*; *milk-, oil-*~ Milch-, Ölkanne *f*; ~ **opener** *Am* Büchsenöffner *m*; **2.** [kæn, kən] *(nur Präsens Indikativ u. pret* **could**) können; *as brave as* ~ *be* überaus, sehr tapfer; *you can't go* du darfst nicht gehen; *I* ~*not but do it* ich kann nicht anders, als es zu tun; *I* ~ *no more* ich kann nicht mehr, ich bin am Ende meiner Kraft; *could I look at it?* darf ich es mir ansehen?

Canad|a ['kænədə] Kanada *n*; ~**ian** [kə'neidjən] *a* kanadisch; *s* Kanadier(in *f*) *m*.

canal [kə'næl] *s* Kanal; Bewässerungsgraben *m*; *anat* Röhre *f*, Gang *m*; *bot* Leitbündel *n*; *tr (Land mit e-m Kanal)* durchstechen; mit Bewässerungsgräben versehen; ~ **bottom** Kanalsohle *f*; ~ **dues** *pl* Kanalgebühren *f pl*; ~ **entrance** Kanaleinfahrt *f*; ~**ization** [kænəlai'zeiʃən] Kanalisation, Kanalisierung *a. fig*, Schiffbarmachung *f*; ~**ize** ['kænəlaiz] *tr (Fluß)* kanalisieren, schiffbar machen; e-n Ausfluß verschaffen *a. fig*; *fig* lenken in; ~ **lift** Schiffshebewerk *n*; ~ **lock** Kanalschleuse *f*; ~ **system** Kanalnetz *n*.

canard [kə'nɑ:(d)] (Zeitungs-)Ente *f*; Jägerlatein, Seemannsgarn; *aero* Vorderschwanzflugzeug *n*, *sl* Ente *f*.

Canar|ies, the [kə'nɛəriz], ~**y**: *the* ~~ *Isles* od *Islands* die Kanarischen Inseln *f pl*; *c*~~*(-bird)* *s* Kanarienvogel *m*; *Am sl* Mädchen *n*, Sängerin *f*; *sl* V-Mann, Spitzel *m*; *tr Am sl* als Sängerin auftreten; *c*~~*-seed* (Kanarien-)Vogelfutter *m*.

canasta [kə'næstə] *Art* Kartenspiel *n*.

cancel ['kænsəl] *tr* (aus-, durch)streichen; ungültig machen, *(bes. Briefmarke)* entwerten; rückgängig machen, abbestellen, widerrufen, annullieren, für ungültig erklären, aufheben, löschen; *com* stornieren; *(Veranstaltung)* absetzen, absagen; *(Schuld)* erlassen; *(Vertrag)* lösen; *(Anordnung)* zurückziehen; *math (in e-m Bruch, e-r Gleichung)* streichen, kürzen; *(Urteil)* aufheben; *(Kosten)* niederschlagen; *itr* sich (gegenseitig) aufheben; *s typ* Streichung, Berichtigung *f*; *(pair of) ~s (pl)* Lochzange *f (des Schaffners)*; **~lation** [kænsə'leiʃən] Streichung, Löschung; Entwertung; Auflösung, Kündigung; Annullierung, Aufhebung *f*; Widerruf *m*; Abbestellung; *com* Stornierung; Kraftloserklärung *f*; *~~ clause* Rücktrittsklausel *f*; **~led** ['-d] *a* ungültig, annulliert, aufgehoben; *until ~~* bis auf Widerruf; *to be ~~* erloschen sein; **~ling** ['-iŋ] Annullierung; Entwertung *f*; *~~ key* Löschtaste *f*; *~~ stamp* Entwertungsstempel *m*.

cancer ['kænsə] *med* Krebs *m*, Karzinom; *fig* Krebsgeschwür, schleichende(s) Übel *n*; *C~ (astr)* Krebs *m*; *the Tropic of C~ (geog)* der Wendekreis des Krebses; **~ cell** Krebszelle *f*; **~ous** ['-rəs] krebsartig; Krebs-; *~~ ulcer* Krebsgeschwür *n*; **~-producing** krebserregend; **~ research** Krebsforschung *f*.

cand|elabrum [kændi'leibrʌm] *pl -bra* [-brə] Kandelaber *m*; **~ent** ['kændənt], **~escent** [-'desnt] weißglühend; **~escence** [-'desns] Weißglut *f*; **~id** ['kændid] *a* aufrichtig, ehrlich, offen; *s film sl* (ungestellte) Momentaufnahme *f*; **~idacy** ['-dəsi], **~idature** ['-ditju:ə, '-ditʃə] Bewerbung, Kandidatur *f*; **~idate** ['-dit, '-eit] *s* Kandidat, Bewerber, Anwärter; Prüfling *m*; *itr Am* kandidieren, Kandidat, Bewerber sein *(bes. für e-e Pfarrstelle)*; *to put up a ~~* e-n Kandidaten aufstellen; *to stand as ~~* kandidieren (*for* für); **~ied** ['-id] *a (Früchte)* kandiert, überzuckert.

candle ['kændl] *s* Kerze *f*; *tr (Eier)* durchleuchten, prüfen; *to light a ~* e-e Kerze anzünden; *not to be able* od *fit to hold a ~ to s.o. (fig)* jdm das Wasser nicht reichen können; *to burn the ~ at both ends (fig)* sich keine Ruhe gönnen; das Geld mit vollen Händen ausgeben; *to hide o.'s ~ under a bushel (fig)* sein Licht unter den Scheffel stellen; *not worth the ~* lohnt sich nicht! **~-light** Kerzenlicht *n*; Dämmerung *f*, Zwielicht *n*; **C~mas** ['-məs] *rel* Lichtmeß *f*; **~-power** Licht-, Kerzenstärke *f (Lichteinheit)*; **~-stick, holder** Leuchter *m*; **~wick** Kerzendocht *m*.

cand|o(u)r ['kændə] Aufrichtigkeit, Offenheit, Ehrlichkeit *f*; **~y** ['-i] *s (sugar-~)* Kandis(zucker) *m*; *Am* Bonbon *m* od *n*; *pl* Süßigkeiten, Süßwaren *f pl*; *Am sl* Kokain *n*; *tr (Früchte)* kandieren, überzuckern; *tr itr* (sich) kristallisieren; *~~ store (Am)* Süßwarenhandlung *f*, Schokoladengeschäft *n*.

cane [kein] *s bot* (Schilf-, Zucker-)Rohr *n*; (Spazier-, Rohr-)Stock *m*; *tr* (ver-)prügeln; *s.th. into s.o.* jdm etw einbleuen; das Rohr einziehen in *(e-n Stuhlrahmen)*; *sugar ~* Zuckerrohr *n*; **~-sugar** Rohrzucker *m*.

can|icular [kə'nikjulə]: *~~ days (pl)* Hundstage *m pl*; **~ine** ['keinain, 'kæn-] *a* Hunde-; *s* Hund; *(~~ tooth)* Eckzahn *m (des Menschen)*; *~~ appetite, hunger* Bären-, Wolfshunger *m*; **~ister** ['kænistə] Kanister *m*, Blechbüchse, -dose; *(~~-shot)* Kartätsche *f*; *(Gasmaske)* Atemeinsatz *m*.

canker ['kæŋkə] *s med* Krebs *m*, Lippengeschwür *n*; *(Pferd)* Huf-, Strahlkrebs; *bot* Brand *m*; *fig* Krebsgeschwür *n*, -schaden *m*; *tr* anfressen; *fig* verderben; **~ed** ['-d] *a fig* gehässig, mißgünstig, übellaunig; **~ous** ['-rəs] krebsartig; *fig* zersetzend; **~worm** (Spanner-)Raupe *f*.

cann|a ['kænə] *bot* Kanna *f*; **~ed** [kænd] *a* eingemacht, eingedost; Büchsen-; *Am sl* mechanisch hergestellt *od* konserviert, Konserven-; gefilmt; auf Schallplatte, Band aufgenommen; *Am sl* geschaßt, 'rausgeschmissen, an die Luft gesetzt; *sl* besoffen; *~~ meat* Büchsenfleisch *n*; *~~ milk* Büchsenmilch *f*; *~~ music (sl)* Musikkonserve, Schallplatten- *od* Radiomusik *f*; *~~ vegetable* Büchsengemüse *n*; **~er** ['kænə] *Am* Konservenfabrikant, -arbeiter *m*; **~ery** ['-əri] Konservenfabrik *f*; *Am sl* Kittchen *n*; **~ing** ['-iŋ] *s* Einmachen, -kochen, Konservieren *n*; *attr* Konserven-; *~~ factory* Konservenfabrik *f*; *~~ industry* Konservenindustrie *f*.

cannibal ['kænibəl] Kannibale *m a. zoo*; *a* u. **~istic** [-'listik] kannibalisch; **~ism** ['-izm] Kannibalismus *m*; *fig* barbarische Grausamkeit *f*; **~ize** ['-aiz] *tr mot* ausschlachten; *mil (Einheit)* aufteilen; *tech* demontieren.

can(n)ikin ['kænikin] Kännchen *n*.

cannon ['kænən] *s kollektiv meist sing* Kanone *f*, Geschütz *n*; *Am sl* Revolver, (Taschen-)Dieb; *tech* Glas-, Hohlzylinder *m*; *Br (Billard)* Karambolage *f*; *itr* karambolieren; *fig* zs.stoßen; (*into s.th.* mit etw); **~ade** [-'neid] Kanonade *f*; **~-ball** *hist* Kanonenkugel *f*; *Am sl* Kassiber; *Am sl rail* D-Zug *m*; **~-barrel** Kanonenrohr *n*; **~-bone** *(Pferd)* Mittelfuß *m*, Röhre *f*; **~ cracker** Kanonenschlag *m (Feuerwerk)*; **~eer** [-'niə] *Am* Kanonier *m*; **~-fodder** Kanonenfutter *n*; **~-shot** Kanonenschuß(weite *f*) *m*.

cannula ['kænjulə] *pl -lae* [-li:] *med* Kanüle *f*.

canny ['kæni] schlau, pfiffig; vorsichtig; umsichtig, sorgfältig; wirtschaftlich, haushälterisch, sparsam.

canoe [kə'nu:] *s* Kanu, Paddelboot *n*; *itr* Kanu fahren; paddeln; **~ist** [-ist] Kanufahrer; Paddler *m*.

canon ['kænən] *rel* Kanon *m*, Regel *f*, Maßstab *m*, Richtschnur *f*; Domherr, Kanonikus; *mus* Kanon *m a. typ*; **~ess** ['-nis] Stiftsdame *f*; **~ical** [kə'nɔnikl] *a rel* kanonisch; *s pl* Meßgewand *n*; **~ist** ['kænənist] Kenner *m* d. kanonischen Rechts; **~ization** [kænənai'zeiʃən] Heiligsprechung *f*; **~ize** ['-aiz] *tr* heiligsprechen; **~ law** Kirchenrecht *n*; **~ry** ['-ri] (*a.* **~icate** [kə'nɔnikit]) Stiftspfründe *f*; Kanonikat *n*.

canon *s. canyon*.

canoodle [kə'nu:dl] *tr itr sl* knutschen, liebkosen.

canopy ['kænəpi] *s* Baldachin; Betthimmel *m*; *arch* Vordach; *fig* Himmels-, Laubgewölbe *n*; *(Tankstelle)* Überdachung *f*; *aero* durchsichtige(s) Kanzel-, Kabinendach *n*; Verkleidung; (Fallschirm-)Kappe; *el* Lampenfassung *f*; *tr* überdachen.

cant [kænt] **1.** *s* Schrägung, geneigte Fläche; Verkantung, Schräglage; *(Straße)* Kurvenüberhöhung *f*; Ruck, Stoß *m*; *tr* abschrägen; zur Seite, beiseite stoßen; umstoßen, -kippen; auf den Kopf stellen; verkanten; *itr* sich verkanten, umkippen; schräg liegen, e-e geneigte Fläche bilden; **2.** *s* Zunftsprache *f*; Jargon *m*; (beliebte) Redensarten *f pl*; Geschwätz *n*; Heuchelei; Scheinheiligkeit *f*; *attr* Mode-*(Wort)*; *a* abgedroschen; scheinheilig; *itr* Jargon reden; Phrasen dreschen; scheinheilig reden, heucheln; **~ hook** Kanthaken *m*.

can't [kɑ:nt] *fam* = *cannot*.

cant|aloup(e) ['kæntəlu:p] Kantalupe *f (Melonenart)*; **~ankerous** [kən'tæŋkərəs] zänkisch, streitsüchtig, rechthaberisch; **~ata** [kæn'tɑ:tə] *mus* Kantate *f*; **~een** [-'ti:n] Kantine; Feldflasche *f*; *allg* (Eß-)Geschirr-, Besteckkasten *m*; Büfett *n (bei Veranstaltungen im Freien)*; *~~ cup* Feldbecher *m*; **~er** ['kæntə] **1.** Heuchler, Scheinheilige(r), Frömmler *m*; **2.** *s* Handgalopp *m*; *itr* Handgalopp reiten; *to win in a ~~* mühelos gewinnen *od* siegen; **~ing** ['-iŋ] *s (Schi)* Kanten *n*; *a* scheinheilig.

Canterbury ['kæntəbəri] *Stadt in England*; *c~* Notenständer *m*, -pult *n*; **~ bell** Glockenblume *f*.

cantharides [kæn'θæridi:z] *pl pharm* Spanische Fliegen *f pl*.

cant|icle ['kæntikl] *rel* (Lob-)Gesang *m*; *C~~s (pl)*, *a. C~~ of C~~s* das Hohelied (Salomos); **~ilever** ['-li:və], *a.* **~alever** ['-tələvə] *s arch* Frei-, Konsol-, Kragträger; *(Brückenbau)* Ausleger *m*; *a* freitragend; *itr* auskragen; *~~ bridge* Auslegerbrücke *f*; *~~ crane* Turmdrehkran *m*; **~o** ['-ou] *pl -s* Gesang *m (als Teil e-s Epos)*; *Am sport sl* Runde *f*.

canton *s* ['kæntɔn, -tən, -'tɔn] Bezirk, Kanton *m*; *(Wappen)* ['-tən] viereckige(s) Feld *n*; *tr* [kən'tɔn, *a.* -'tu:n] *tr* in Kantone, Bezirke einteilen; [-'tu:n] *tr mil* einquartieren; **~ment** [-'tɔnmənt, -'tu:n-] Quartier *n*, (Orts-)Unterkunft *f*.

Canu(c)k [kə'nʌk] *Am sl* (französischer) Kanadier *m*.

canvas ['kænvəs] *s* Kanevas *m*; Segeltuch *n*; Zeltbahn *f*, -tuch *n*; Sack-, Packleinwand *f*; Drillich *m*; *(Malerei)* Leinwand *f*; *tr* mit Kanevas herrichten, be-, überziehen, einfassen; *under ~ (mil)* in Zelten; *mar* unter Segel.

canvass ['kænvəs] *tr* diskutieren, (eingehend) erörtern; gründlich untersuchen, prüfen; *(Kunden, Wähler)* bearbeiten, besuchen; *Am (Wahlstimmen)* zählen; *itr com pol* werben (*for* für); sich um Aufträge bemühen; e-n Wahlfeldzug führen; sich bewerben (*for* um); *s* Erörterung, Untersuchung, Prüfung; (Stimmen-, Kunden-)Werbung *f*; Werbe-, Wahlfeldzug *m*; Propaganda; *Am* Wahlprüfung *f*; **~er** ['-ə] (Kunden-, Abonnenten-)Werber; Platzreisender; *pol* Propagandist; *Am* Wahlprüfer *m*; **~ing** ['-iŋ] (Stimmen-, Kunden-)Werbung; (Wahl-)Propaganda *f*; *~~ for votes* Stimmenfang *m*.

canyon, canon ['kænjən] Cañon *n*; Schlucht, Klamm *f*.

caoutchouc ['kautʃuk] Kautschuk *m*, (Roh-)Gummi *m* od *n*.

*

cap [kæp] *s* Mütze, Kappe, Haube *f*, Barett *n*; *Br mil* Feldmütze *f*; *tech* Aufsatz, Deckel *m*, Kappe, Haube, Kapsel *f (a. e-r Flasche)*, Verschluß *m*; Spreng-, Zündkapsel *f*; Knauf, (Balken-)Kopf *m*; *(Zahn)* Krone *f*; *(Pilz)* Hut; *(Orgel)* Vorschlag *m*; *mot* neue Lauffläche *f (e-s Reifens)*; Papierformat *(14×17 inches)*; *typ* Initial *n*; *tr* e-e Mütze aufsetzen (*s.o.* jdm); abdecken, mit e-m Deckel, e-r Kappe versehen; *allg* bedecken; *tech* sockeln; *fig* übertreffen; e-n akad. Grad verleihen; *itr (to ~ it)* die Mütze abnehmen (*to s.o.* vor jdm); *to ~ everything* alles übertreffen; *to set o.'s ~ at s.o. (fam)* jdn angeln; *~ in hand* unterwürfig, demütig *adv*; *those the ~ fits, let them wear it (fig)* wen's kratzt, der jucke sich; *that's a feather in your ~* darauf können Sie stolz sein; **~ and gown** Barett *n* u. Talar *m*; akade-

mische(s) Leben *n*; ~ **strap, visor** Mützenriemen, -schirm *m*.
capab|ility [keipə'biliti] Fähigkeit (*of* zu; *to do* zu tun); *pl (schlummernde)* Fähigkeiten, Möglichkeiten *f pl*, Begabung *f*; **~le** ['keipəbl] fähig, tüchtig, begabt; befähigt; geeignet; *pej* fähig (*of* zu); *~~ of earning* erwerbsfähig; *~~ of work* arbeitsfähig.
capac|ious [kə'peiʃəs] geräumig; weiträumig; umfassend *a. fig*; **~iousness** [-ʃəsnis] große(s) Fassungsvermögen *n*; Geräumigkeit; Weiträumigkeit *f*; **~itance** [kə'pæsitəns] *el* Kapazität *f*, kapazitive(r) Widerstand *m*; *~~ current* Ladestrom *m*; **~itate** [kə'pæsiteit] *tr* ermächtigen, befähigen (*for* zu; *to do* zu tun); **~itive** [kə'pæsitiv] *el* kapazitiv; **~itor** [kə'pæsitə] Kondensator *m*; **~ity** [kə'pæsiti] Inhalt *m*, Volumen *n*, Fassungskraft *f*, -vermögen *n a. fig*; *fig* Umfang *m*; geistige Fähigkeiten *f pl*; *tech* Leistung(sfähigkeit); Tragkraft *f*; Produktionsvermögen *n*; *el* Kapazität; *(relative)* Eigenschaft; *jur* Handlungsfähigkeit; *allg* Funktion, Aufgabe, Stellung *f*; *Am* Höchstmaß *n*; *in my ~~ as* (in meiner Eigenschaft) als; *in a civil ~~* als Zivilist; *buying ~~* Kaufkraft *f*; *carrying ~~* Tragfähigkeit *f*; *(Schiff)* Laderaum, Tonnengehalt *m*; *tele* Belastungsfähigkeit *f (e-r Leitung)*; *filled to ~~ (theat)* voll (besetzt); *measure of ~~* Raummaß *n*; *seating ~~*: *to have a seating ~~ of 600* 600 Sitzplätze haben; *~~ of disposing (jur)* Geschäftsfähigkeit *f*; *~~ for reaction* Reaktionsfähigkeit *f*.
cap-à-pie [kæpə'pi:] *adv* von Kopf bis Fuß, vollständig, völlig.
caparison [kə'pærisn] *s* Schabracke; *fig* Kleidung *f*, Putz *m*; *tr (Pferd)* mit e-r Schabracke bedecken; *fig* kleiden, aufputzen.
cape [keip] **1.** Umhang *m*, Cape *n* *(lose* od *festsitzend)*; Schalkragen *m*; **2.** Kap, Vorgebirge *n*; *the C~ (of Good Hope, the C~ Colony)* das Kap (der Guten Hoffnung), die Kapkolonie.
caper ['keipə] **1.** *s* Kapernstrauch *m*; *pl* Kapern *f pl (Gewürz)*; **2.** *s* Luftsprung *m*; *fig meist pl* Kapriolen *f pl*; *tr (to cut ~s, a ~)* Luftsprünge machen, herumtollen; *fig* Kapriolen machen; **~caillie, ~cailye, ~cailzie** [kæpə'keilji, -zi] Auerhahn *m*.
capillar|ity [kæpi'læriti] *phys* Kapillarität, Haarröhrchenwirkung *f*; **~y** [kə'piləri] *a* Haar-; haarfein; Kapillar-; *s anat* Kapillargefäß *n*; *(~~ tube)* Kapillare *f*.
capital ['kæpitl] **1.** *s arch* Kapitell *n*; **2.** *a* Todes- *(Strafe, Urteil)*; *(Verbrechen)* todeswürdig, schwer; folgenschwer, verhängnisvoll; hauptsächlich; Haupt-; groß(artig), gewaltig, ausgezeichnet, *fam* glänzend, prächtig, tadellos, famos; *s* Kapital, Vermögen *n*; Fonds *m*; Einlage; Geldaristokratie *f*, Unternehmertum *n*; Hauptstadt *f*; Groß-, große(r) Anfangs-, Blockbuchstabe *m*; *C~ das* (Groß-)Kapital; *to make ~ out of s.th. (fig)* aus e-r S Kapital schlagen; *demand for ~* Kapitalbedarf *m*; *federal ~* Bundeshauptstadt *f*; *fixed ~* Anlagekapital *n*; *floating, rolling, circulating ~* Umlaufs-, Betriebskapital *n*; ~ **assets** *pl* Kapitalguthaben, Anlagevermögen *n*; ~ **bonus** Gratisaktien *f pl*; ~ **crime** Kapitalverbrechen *n*; ~ **expenditure** Kapitalausgabe *f*, -aufwand *m*; Anlagekosten *pl*; ~ **goods** *pl* Produktionsgüter, -mittel, Investitionsgüter *n pl*; Anlagewerte *m pl*; ~ **investment** Kapitalanlage *f*; **~ism** ['-izm] Kapitalismus *m*; **~ist** ['-ist] Kapitalist; Geldmann, -geber *m*; **~istic** [-'listik] kapitalistisch; **~ization** [kæpitəlai'zeiʃən] Kapitalisierung *f*; Großschreibung *f*; **~ize** ['kæp-, kə'pitəlaiz] *tr* kapitalisieren, zu Kapital machen; ausnutzen; (mit) groß(en Anfangsbuchstaben) schreiben; ~ **letter** Groß-, große(r) Anfangsbuchstabe *m*; ~ **levy** Vermögensabgabe *f*; **~ly** *adv* ausgezeichnet, famos; ~ **punishment** Todesstrafe *f*; ~ **ship** Schlachtschiff *n*, -kreuzer *m*; ~ **stock** *Am* Aktienkapital *n*; Stammaktien *f pl*; ~ **yields** *pl* Kapitalerträge *m pl*; *~~ tax* Kapitalertragssteuer *f*.
capitation [kæpi'teiʃən] *hist* Schätzung *f*, Zensus *m*; Kopfsteuer *f*.
Capitol, the ['kæpitl] das Kapitol, *bes.* das Kongreßgebäude *(in Washington)*.
capitulat|e [kə'pitjuleit] *itr* kapitulieren (*to* vor); sich ergeben; **~ion** [-'leiʃən] Kapitulation, Übergabe, Waffenstreckung *f*; *(Festung)* Fall *m*; *pl* Übergabebedingungen *f pl*.
capon ['keipən] Kapaun *m*.
capr|iccio [kə'pritʃiou] *mus* Kapriccio *n*; **~ice** [-'pri:s] Laune *f*; (lustiger, launiger) Einfall *m*; *mus* Kapriccio *n*; **~icious** [-'priʃəs] launisch, launenhaft; wechselnd, wechselhaft, unberechenbar, unzuverlässig; unmotiviert; **~iciousness** [-'priʃəsnis] Launenhaftigkeit; Unberechenbarkeit *f*; **C~icorn** ['kæprikɔ:n] *astr* Steinbock *m*; *the Tropic of C~~ (geog)* der Wendekreis des Steinbocks; **~iole** ['kæpri oul] Luftsprung *m*.
caps|icum ['kæpsikəm] Spanische(r) Pfeffer *m*; **~ize** [-'saiz] *tr itr (Schiff)* kentern (lassen); **~tan** ['-stən] *mar* Gangspill *n*, Ankerwinde *f*; *~~ lathe* Revolverdrehbank *f*; *~~ wheel* Speichenrad *n*; **~ular** ['-sjulə] kapselartig; Kapsel-; **~ule** ['-sju:l] *s anat bot pharm* Kapsel; *bot* Hülse; (Flaschen-)Kapsel; Dose *f*; *a fig* zs.gefaßt.
captain ['kæptin] *s mil* Hauptmann *(a. Am Feuerwehr, Polizei)*; *mar (mil u. com)* Kapitän; *aero* Flugzeugführer, -kapitän; *allg* Führer, Leiter; Vorarbeiter, Rottenführer; *sport* Spiel-, Mannschaftsführer; *(Schule)* Primus, Sprecher(in *f*) *m*; *tr sport (die Mannschaft)* führen; *industry ~* Wirtschaftsführer *m*; **~cy** ['-si], **~ship** ['-ʃip] Hauptmanns-, Kapitänsrang *m*, -stelle *f*.

*

capt|ion ['kæpʃən] *s jur* Einleitungsformel *f*, Rubrum *n*; *(Buch)* Kapitel-, *(Zeitung)* Beitrags-, Artikelüberschrift *f*, Titel, Kopf *m*, Schlagzeile; (Bild-)Erklärung *f*; *film* Untertitel, (erläuternder) Zwischentext *m*; *tr Am* mit e-r Überschrift, Erklärung, Erläuterung versehen; **~ious** ['-əs] verfänglich, spitzfindig; wortklauberisch; tadelsüchtig, nörg(e)lig, kleinlich; **~ivate** ['kæptiveit] *tr* einnehmen, hinreißen, fesseln, faszinieren, bezaubern; **~ivation** [-'veiʃən] Faszination, Bezauberung *f*; **~ive** ['-iv] *a* gefangen, eingesperrt; *s* Gefangene(r *m*) *f*; *to hold ~~* gefangenhalten; *to take ~~* gefangennehmen, festsetzen, einsperren; *~~ balloon* Fesselballon *m*; **~ivity** [kæp'tiviti] Gefangenschaft *f*; **~or** *m*, **~ress** *f* ['-ə, -tris] Fänger(in *f*) *m*; **~ure** ['-ʃə] *s* Fest-, Gefangennahme; Besitzergreifung, Wegnahme *f*, Raub *m*; *mar* Aufbringung; Prise *f*; Gefangene(r *m*); Beute *f*, Raub; *(Tier)* Fang *m*; *tr* gefangennehmen; *(Tier)* einfangen; wegnehmen, rauben, erbeuten; kapern.
Capuchin ['kæpjuʃin] *rel* Kapuziner *m*; *c~* Damenmantel *m* mit Kapuze; ~ **monkey** Kapuzineraffe *m*.
car [kɑ:] *s* (niedriger, zweirädriger) Karren; (Kraft-)Wagen *m*, Auto(mobil) *n*; (Straßenbahn-)Wagen; *Am* (Eisenbahn-)Wagen, Waggon *m*; *(Ballon, Luftschiff)* Gondel *f*; *(Aufzug)* Fahrstuhl; *min* Förderwagen; *poet* Wagen *m*; *the ~s (Am rail)* der Zug; *by ~* mit dem Wagen; *to put a ~ into the garage* ein Auto in die Garage fahren; *to take the ~s (Am)* mit der Bahn fahren; ~ **aerial** Autoantenne *f*; **~-body** (Wagen-)Aufbau *m*, Karosserie *f*; *~~ designer* Karosseriekonstrukteur *m*; ~ **door** Wagentür *f*; **~-driver** (Kraft-)Fahrer *m*; ~ **dump** Autofriedhof *m*; ~ **ferry** Autofähre *f*; ~ **hoist** Wagenheber *m*, Hebebühne *f*; **~hop** *Am* Kellner(in *f*) *m*, der (die) Gäste in parkenden Wagen bedient; ~ **maintenance** Wagenpflege *f*; **~man** Fuhrmann, Kärrner; *mot* Fahrer, Chauffeur; *(Straßenbahn)* (Wagen-)Führer *m*; ~ **owner** Kraftfahrzeughalter *m*; **~-park** Parkplatz *m*; ~ **polish** Wagenpflegemittel *n*.
cara|cal ['kærəkæl] *zoo* Karakal, Wüstenluchs *m*; **~col(e)** ['-koul, '-kɔl] *s* (halbe) Wendung; *arch* Wendeltreppe *f*; *itr (Reiter)* e-e Wendung ausführen; **~fe** [kə'rɑ:f] Karaffe *f*; **~mel** ['kærəmel] Karamel(zucker) *m*; Karamelle *f*, Karamelbonbon *m* od *n*; Karamelfarbe *f*, Hellbraun *n*; **~pace** ['-peis] *zoo* Rückenschild *m*; **~t** ['-ət] Karat *n (= 3,17 grains = 205 mg)*; **~van** ['kærəvæn, -'væn] Karawane *f*; *mot* Wohnwagen; Zirkus-, Wanderschauwagen *m*; *gipsy ~~* Zigeunerwagen *m*; **~vansera(i)** [-'vænsərai], **~vansary** ['-vænsəri] Karawanserei *f*; *Am* große(s) Hotel *n*; **~vel(le)** ['kærəvel], **carvel** ['kɑ:vl] *mar hist* Karavelle *f*; **~way** ['kærəwei] *bot* Kümmel *m*, Karve *f*; *~~-seeds (pl)* Kümmel *m (Gewürz)*.
carb|ide ['kɑ:baid] (Kalzium-)Karbid *n*; **~ine** ['-ain], **carabine** ['kærəbain] Karabiner *m*; **~ohydrate** [kɑ:bo(u)-'haidreit] *chem* Kohlenwasserstoff(verbindung *f*) *m*; *physiol* Kohlehydrat *n*; **~olic** [kɑ:'bɔlik] *a* Karbol-; *~~ acid* Karbolsäure *f*, Phenol *n*; **~olize** ['-bəlaiz] *tr* mit Karbol behandeln.
carbon ['kɑ:bən] *chem* Kohlenstoff; *el* Kohlenstift *m (für Bogenlicht)*; *(~ paper)* Kohlepapier *n*; *(~copy)* Durchschlag *m*, -schrift *f*; **~aceous** [kɑ:bə'neiʃəs] kohlen(stoff)haltig; ~ **anode** Kohlenanode *f*; **~ate** *s* ['kɑ:bənit] Karbonat, kohlensaure(s) Salz *n*; *tr* ['-eit] mit Kohlensäure behandeln *od* sättigen lüften; **~-copy** Durchschlag *m*; ~ **dioxide** Kohlendioxyd *n*; **~ic** [kɑ:'bɔnik] Kohlen-; *~~ acid* Kohlensäure *f*; *~~ oxide* Kohlenoxyd *n*; **~iferous** [kɑ:bə'nifərəs] *a = ~aceous*; *s C~~ (geol)* Karbon *n*; **~ization** [kɑ:bənai'zeiʃən] Verkohlung, Inkohlung; *(Textil)* Karbonisation; *(Kohle)* Verkokung *f*; **~ize** ['kɑ:bənaiz] *tr* verkohlen, inkohlen; *(Textil)* karbonisieren; *(Kohle)* verkoken; ~ **lamp, light** Bogenlampe *f*, -licht *n*; ~ **microphone, transmitter** Kohlemikrophon *n*; ~ **monoxide** Kohlenoxyd *n*; **~-paper** Kohlepapier *n*; **~yl** ['kɑ:bənil] Karbonyl *n*; *~~ chloride* Karbonylchlorid *n*.
carb|orundum [kɑ:bə'rʌndəm] Karborundum, Siliziumkarbid *n*; **~oy** ['kɑ:bɔi] Korbflasche *f*, (*bes.* Säure-)

Ballon *m*; **~uncle** ['kɑ:bʌŋkl] *min* Karfunkel; *med* Karbunkel *m*; **~uret** ['kɑ:bjuret] *tr chem* karburieren, mit Kohlenstoff aufsättigen *od* verbinden; *mot* vergasen; **~uret(t)ed** ['-id] *a* mit Kohlenstoff verbunden *od* aufgesättigt; *~~ air* Gas-, Luftgemisch *n*; **~uretting** ['-iŋ] Karburierung; *mot* Vergasung *f*; **~uret(t)or, ~uret(t)er** ['-ə] *mot* Vergaser *m*; *down-draught ~~* Fallstromvergaser *m*; *~~ adjustment* Vergasereinstellung, -regulierung *f*; **~urization** [kɑ:bjurai'zeiʃən] Aufkohlen *n*; **~urize** ['kɑ:bju:raiz] *tr* karburieren, aufkohlen.

carcass, carcase ['kɑ:kəs] Tierleiche *f*, tote(s) Tier, Aas *n*, *(pej a. vom Menschen)* Kadaver; *(Fleischerei)* Tierkörper, Rumpf *m*; *(Haus, Schiff)* Gerippe *a. pej*, Skelett *n*, Rohbau *m*; *(Reifen)* Karkasse *f*; *el* Stator *m*; *Am* Brandbombe *f*.

carcinoma [kɑ:si'noumə] *med* Karzinom *n*, Krebs *m*.

card [kɑ:d] **1.** *s* Wollkratze *f*, Krempel *m*, Kardätsche *f*; *tr* krempeln, kardätschen, streichen; **~ed wool** Streichwolle *f*; **~-thistle** *bot* Karde(ndistel) *f*; **~ing-machine** Streichmaschine *f*; **2.** *s* (Spiel-, Post-, Besuchs-)Karte; Windrose *f*; Programm (-nummer *f*); Schild *n (in e-m Schaufenster)*; *fam* (komischer) Kerl *m*; *tr Am* e-e Karte schreiben (*s.o.* jdm); auf e-e Karte schreiben; *in, on the ~s* wahrscheinlich, möglich, zu erwarten; *to have a ~ up o.'s sleeve* etw in petto haben; *to play (at) ~s* Karten spielen; *to play o.'s ~s well, badly* s-e Sache gut, schlecht machen; *to put, to lay o.'s ~s on the table, to show, to throw up o.'s ~s (fig)* s-e Karten aufdecken, mit offenen Karten spielen; *game of ~s* Kartenspiel *n*; *house of ~s (fig)* Kartenhaus *n*; *picture post-~* Ansichtskarte *f*; *reply ~* Antwortkarte *f*; *visiting-~, Am a. calling-~* Besuchs-, Visitenkarte *f*; *voting ~* Stimmzettel *m*; *wedding ~* Heiratsanzeige *f*; **~board** ['-bɔ:d] Pappe *f*; *~~ box* Pappschachtel *f*, -karton *m*; **~-case** Kartei-, Zettelkasten *m*; Visitenkartentasche *f*; **~-index** *s* Kartei, Kartothek *f*; *tr* verzetteln; katalogisieren; e-e Kartei anlegen von; *~~ cabinet* Karteischrank *m*; *~~ guide* Leitkarte *f*; *~~ number* Karteinummer *f*; **~-sharper,** *Am* **~-sharp** Falschspieler *m*; **~ table** Bridgetisch *m*; **~-vote** *pol* Stimme *f* e-s Wahlmannes.

cardam|ine [kɑ:'dæmini:, 'kɑ:dəmain] Wiesenschaumkraut *n*; **~om** ['-əməm] Kardamom *m* od *n (Gewürz)*.

cardan ['kɑ:dən] *a*: **~ joint** Kardangelenk *n*; **~ shaft** Kardan-, Gelenkwelle *f*.

cardi|ac ['kɑ:diæk] *a bes. med* Herz-; *a u. s* herzstärkend(es Mittel *n*); *~~ apoplexy, gland, probe, sound, valve* Herzschlag *m*, -drüse, -sonde *f*, -ton *m*, -klappe *f*; **~algy, ~algia** ['-ældʒi, kɑ:di'ældʒiə] Sodbrennen *n*; **~gan** ['-gən] Wolljacke, -weste *f*.

cardinal ['kɑ:dinl] *a* hauptsächlich; Haupt-; hochrot; *s rel* Kardinal *m a. zoo*; Kardinalsrot *n*; Bischof *m (Getränk)*; Kardinalzahl *f*; **~ate, ~ship** ['-eit, '-ʃip] Kardinalswürde *f*; **~ bird, grosbeak** *Am orn* Rote(r) Kardinal *m*, Virginische Nachtigall *f*; **~-flower** *bot* Scharlachrote Lobelie *f*; **~ number** Grund-, Kardinalzahl *f*; **~ point** Hauptpunkt *m*; Himmelsrichtung *f*; **~'s hat** Kardinalshut *m*; **~ virtue** Kardinaltugend *f*.

cardio ['kɑ:dio, -ə] *(in Zssgen) scient* Herz-; **~gram** ['-græm] Kardiogramm *n*; **~neurosis** ['-nju:'rousiz] Herzneurose *f*.

carditis [kɑ:'daitis] *med* Herzentzündung *f*.

cardoon [kɑ:'du:n] *bot* Kard(on)e, Spanische Artischocke *f*.

care [kɛə] *s* Sorgfalt, Achtsamkeit; Obhut; Behandlung; Pflege, Fürsorge, Wartung; Sorge, Besorgnis, Besorgtheit; Anteilnahme *f*; *meist pl* Sorgen *f pl*, Not *f*, Kummer *m*; *itr* sich Sorgen, sich Gedanken machen (*about* über); *to ~ about* Interesse haben an, Lust haben zu; *to ~ for* sorgen für, aufpassen, sich kümmern um; pflegen; *(fragend u. verneint)* gern haben, mögen, Interesse haben an; wünschen, haben wollen; *to be ~d for* versorgt, aufgehoben sein; *to ~ to (fragend u. verneint)* Lust haben zu; *free from ~s* ohne Sorgen, sorgenfrei, sorglos; *in, under o.'s ~* in jds Obhut; *(in) ~ of* (= c./o.) bei, per Adresse; *not to ~ a rap* od *fig* sich keinen Deut kümmern (*whether* ob; *for* um); *to take ~* vorsichtig sein, sich hüten, aufpassen; sorgen (*of* für), sich kümmern (*of* um); schonen, achtgeben (*of* auf; *to* inf; *that* daß); erledigen (*of s.th.* etw); aufbewahren (*of s.th.* etw); *to take ~ of o.s.* sich pflegen; *I don't ~* das ist mir gleich, *fam* egal; meinetwegen! mir liegt nichts daran (*to* zu); *what do I ~!* was geht's mich an! *who ~s?* wen interessiert das schon? *I couldn't ~ less* das macht mir nichts; *for all I ~* meinetwegen; *would you ~ to ...?* macht es Ihnen was aus zu *od* wenn ...? *have a ~* paß auf! *that takes ~ of that* damit wäre das erledigt; **~ful** ['-ful] sorgfältig; achtsam, bedacht(sam), um-, vorsichtig; *to be ~~* vorsichtig sein, aufpassen; *I was ~~ not to go* ich habe mich gehütet, zu gehen; *be ~~ to write* vergiß nicht zu schreiben; **~fulness** ['-fulnis] Sorgfalt; Achtsamkeit, Um-, Vorsicht *f*; **~free** ['-fri:] ohne Sorgen, sorglos; **~less** ['-lis] sorglos; gleichgültig, gedankenlos; achtlos; unachtsam (*of* gegen); unvorsichtig; nachlässig; **~lessness** ['-lisnis] Sorglosigkeit; Fahrlässigkeit; Unachtsamkeit; Nachlässigkeit *f*; **~taker** Wärter, Aufpasser; Hausmeister, -besorger *m*; *~~ government* Übergangsregierung *f*; **~worn** *a* erschöpft, ausgemergelt.

careen [kə'ri:n] *tr* kielholen; *itr* krängen.

career [kə'riə] *s* Lebensgeschichte *f*, -lauf *m*; Laufbahn, Karriere *f*; Beruf; Lauf, Galopp *m*; *itr* laufen, eilen, stürmen, sausen; *to ~ about, along, over, through* umher-, entlang-, hinüber-, hindurchlaufen; *in full ~* in vollem Lauf, in großer Eile; *to enter upon a ~* e-e Laufbahn einschlagen; **~ diplomat** Berufsdiplomat *m*; **~ girl, woman** Berufstätige *f*; **~ism** [-rizm] Streberei *f*; **~ist** [kə'riərist] Karrieremacher, Postenjäger, Streber *m*.

caress [kə'res] *s* Liebkosung *f*; Kuß *m*, Umarmung *f*; *tr* liebkosen, streicheln; küssen; umarmen; **~ing** [-iŋ] liebkosend, einschmeichelnd.

caret ['kærət] *typ* Fehlzeichen *n*.

cargo ['kɑ:gou] *pl -(e)s aero mar* Fracht, (Schiffs-)Ladung *f*; **~ aircraft, plane,** Transportflugzeug *n*; **~ boat, ship, vessel** Frachtschiff *n*; **~ capacity** Laderaum *m*; **~ door,** *aero* **bay, hatch** Ladeluke *f*; **~checker** Tallymann *m*; **~ glider** Lastensegler *m*; **~ insurance** Frachtversicherung *f*; **~ (para)chute** Lastenfallschirm *m*; **~ space** *aero* Laderaum *m*; **~ steamer** Frachtdampfer *m*.

Carib ['kærib] *a* karibisch; *s pl* Kariben *m pl*; **~bean** [-'bi(:)ən, -'ribiən]: *the ~~ Sea* das Karibische Meer.

caricatur|e [kærikə'tjuə] *s* Karikatur *f*, Zerrbild *n*; *tr* karikieren; **~ist** [kærikə'tjuərist, *Am* 'kærikətʃərist] Karikaturist, Karikaturenzeichner *m*.

cari|es ['kɛərii:z] *med* Knochenfraß *m*, Karies *f*; *dental ~~* Zahnfäule, (Zahn-)Karies *f*; **~ous** ['kɛəriəs] kariös, zerfressen.

carking ['kɑ:kiŋ] *nur in*: *~ care* lästige Sorge *f*.

Carl|ovingian, Carolingian [kɑ:lo(u)'vindʒiən, kærə'l-] *a hist* karolingisch; *s pl* Karolinger *m pl*.

Carmelite ['kɑ:məlait] *rel* Karmeliter(in *f*) *m*.

carmine ['kɑ:main] *s* Karmin(rot) *n*; *a* karminrot.

carn|age ['kɑ:nidʒ] Gemetzel, Blutbad *n*; **~al** ['kɑ:nl] leiblich, fleischlich; sinnlich, geschlechtlich; weltlich; **~ality** [kɑ:'næliti] Sinnlichkeit; Weltlichkeit *f*; **~ation** [kɑ:'neiʃən] *bot* Gartennelke *f*; **~elian** [kə'ni:ljən] *min* Karneol *m*; **~ival** ['kɑ:nivəl] Karneval, Fasching *m*; Lustbarkeit *f*, (Fest-)Rummel *m*; **~ivora** [kɑ:'nivərə] *pl* Raubtiere *n pl*; **~ivore** ['kɑ:nivɔ:] Raubtier *n*; fleischfressende Pflanze *f*; **~ivorous** [kɑ:'nivərəs] *zoo bot* fleischfressend.

carob ['kærəb] *(~-bean, -pod)* Johannisbrot *n*; **~-tree** Johannisbrotbaum *m*.

carol ['kærəl] *s* lustige(s), frohe(s) Lied *n (a. d. Vögel)*; Jubel-, Lobgesang *m*; *(Christmas ~)* Weihnachtslied *n*; *itr* jubilieren; *tr* singen; **~ler** ['-ə] (Weihnachtslieder-)Sänger *m*.

carotid [kə'rɔtid] Halsschlagader *f*.

carous|al [kə'rauzəl], **~e** [-z] *s* Trink-, Zechgelage *n*, Zecherei *f*; *itr (to ~e)* zechen.

carp [kɑ:p] **1.** *s* Karpfen *m*; **2.** *itr* herumschimpfen (*at* mit), herumnörgeln, etw auszusetzen haben (*at* an); **~al** ['-əl] *a* Handwurzel-; *~~ bone* Handwurzelknochen *m*; **~ing** ['-iŋ]: *~~ criticism* bissige Kritik *f*; *~~ tongue* scharfe Zunge *f*.

carpent|er ['kɑ:pintə] *s* Zimmermann, Tischler *m*; *tr itr* zimmern; **~ry** ['-tri] Zimmerhandwerk *n*, -arbeit, Zimmerei *f*; Balkenwerk, Gebälk *n*.

carpet ['kɑ:pit] *s* Teppich *m a. fig*, Brücke *f*, Läufer *m*; *tr* mit e-m Teppich, e-m Läufer belegen; *to be ~ed with* dicht bedeckt sein mit; *to be on the ~* zur Debatte, zur Diskussion stehen; *to have s.o. on the ~ (fam)* sich jdn vorknöpfen, -nehmen; **~-bag** Reisetasche *f*; **~bagger** *Am* politische(r) Abenteurer; nicht ansässige(r) Agitator *od* Kandidat *m*; **~-bed** Teppichbeet *n*; **~ bombing** Flächenbombardierung *f*; **~ing** ['-iŋ] Belegen *n* mit Teppichen; Teppichstoff *m*; **~-sweeper** Teppichkehrmaschine *f*.

carpus ['kɑ:pəs] *pl -pi* [-pai] Handwurzel *f*.

carriage ['kæridʒ] *(Personen-, bes. Güter)* Transport *m*, Beförderung; Fracht; Transportgebühr *f*, Frachtkosten *pl*, Fuhrlohn *m*, Rollgeld *n*; (Last-)Wagen; Waggon; (Eisenbahn-, Personen-)Wagen *m*; Wagengestell, Laufwerk *n*, -katze; *mil (gun-~)* Lafette *f*; *tech* Wagen *(a. d. Schreibmaschine)*, Schlitten *m*; *aero (under ~)* Fahrgestell *n*; Ausführung, Verwaltung, Leitung, Führung; (Körper-)Haltung *f*; Auftreten; Verhalten, Betragen *n*; *~-forward (adv)* unter

Frachtnachnahme; ~-*free, -paid (adv)* frachtfrei; ~ *by air, by rail, by sea* Luft-, Bahn-, Seetransport *m*; ~ *of goods* Gütertransport *m*; ~ *of parcels* Paketbeförderung *f*; ~-**drive** Fahrweg *m (auf e-m Grundstück, in e-m Park)*; ~-**horse** Zugpferd *n*; ~ **release** Wagenlöser *m (Schreibmaschine)*; ~-**road, -way** Fahrweg *m*; ~**stock** *rail* Wagenpark *m*.

carrier ['kæriə] (Last-, Gepäck-, Aus-) Träger *a. el*, Bote; Fuhrmann; Fuhrunternehmer, Spediteur *m*; Speditionsgesellschaft *f*; *med* Keimträger; *tech* Mitnehmer, Rahmen, Schlitten, Transport *m*; *radio* Trägerwelle *f*; *(Fahrrad)* Gepäckständer, -träger; *(aircraft* ~*)* Flugzeugträger *m*; *(*~*-pigeon)* Brieftaube *f*; *mail-*~ *(Am)* Briefträger *m*; ~-**bag** Tragebeutel *m*.

carrion ['kæriən] *s* Aas *n*; *allg* Abfall, Dreck, *fam* Mist *m*; *a* verfault; ~ **beetle, crow, vulture** Aaskäfer *m*, -krähe *f*, -geier *m*.

carrot ['kærət] Mohrrübe, Möhre *f*; *pl sl* rote Haare *n pl*; Rotkopf *m*; *the stick and the* ~ *(fig)* Zuckerbrot u. Peitsche; ~**y** ['-i] rötlich, rot(haarig).

car(r)ousel [kæru(:)'zel] *Am* Karussell *n*.

carry ['kæri] **1.** *tr* tragen *a. fig*, fahren, befördern, transportieren; (über)bringen; leiten, führen; (bei sich) haben, (*about one* mit sich) führen, tragen; *(Kopf, Körper)* halten; *arch tech* halten, stützen, tragen; *(Gewicht, Last)* aushalten; fort-, weiterführen, ausdehnen, fortsetzen; *(Buchung)* über-, vortragen; *mil* ein-, gefangennehmen, stürmen, erobern, besetzen; *(den Sieg)* davontragen; *(Preis)* gewinnen; (erfolgreich) behaupten; *(Menschen)* für sich einnehmen, gewinnen, überzeugen, mitreißen; *parl (Antrag)* durchbringen; *to be carried (Antrag)* durchgehen, angenommen werden; *(Ertrag)* bringen; *(Geld)* einbringen; *Am (Ware)* führen, auf Lager haben, zurückhalten; *Am (in den Büchern)* führen; *Am (finanziell)* (unter)stützen, tragen; *Am (Zeitung, Ztschr.)* bringen; *Am mus (Melodie)* tragen; **2.** *itr (bis zu e-r bestimmten Entfernung)* reichen, gehen, tragen, dringen; schwanger sein; *Am* das Boot (u. die Last) tragen; *to* ~ *o.s* sich *(körperlich)* halten, sich bewegen; **3.** *s* Trag-, Reichweite *f*; *(Golf)* Flug(strecke *f*) (des Balles); Wolkenzug *m*; *(Lochkarten)* Zehnerübertragung *f*; *Am* Tragen *n* bei e-r Unterbrechung des Wasserweges; *to* ~ *all before one* erfolgreich sein, Erfolg haben; *to* ~ *the baby (fig)* etw ausbaden müssen; *to* ~ *coals to Newcastle (fig)* Eulen nach Athen tragen; *to* ~ *consequences* Folgen haben; *to* ~ *conviction* überzeugen, überzeugend wirken; *to* ~ *current* Strom führen; *to* ~ *into effect* zur Wirkung bringen; *to* ~ *interest* Zins(en) tragen *od* bringen; *to* ~ *it, the day* siegen, Sieger sein; *to* ~ *o.'s point* s-e Ansicht durchdrücken; *to* ~ *the torch (sl)* Trübsal blasen (*for s.o.* wegen jdm); *to* ~ *weight (fig)* Gewicht haben, von (ausschlaggebender) Bedeutung sein; *to* ~ **away** wegtragen, -bringen, -schaffen; abbrechen, ab-, wegreißen; *fig* mitreißen, begeistern (*a. to* ~ **along**); *to* ~ **back** zurücktragen, -bringen; *(in Gedanken)* zurückversetzen; *to* ~ **forward** fortsetzen; *(Buchung)* vor-, übertragen; *(amount) carried forward* Übertrag *m*; *to* ~ **off** wegschleppen, weg-, mitnehmen, entführen; *(Preis)* gewinnen; *(Rolle)* spielen; *to* ~ *it off well* e-e Schwierigkeit glänzend meistern; *to* ~ **on** *tr* fortsetzen, weiterführen; *(Gespräch, Krieg)* führen; *(Geschäft)* betreiben; *(Beruf)* ausüben; *itr* weitermachen; *fam* sich aufregen, die Nerven verlieren; verrückt spielen, den wilden Mann markieren; es haben (*with* mit), herumpoussieren, poussieren (*with* mit); ~ *on! (mil)* weitermachen! *to* ~ **out** aus-, durchführen; *to* ~ **over** *(Buchung)* vor-, übertragen; *(Effekten)* vortragen; überzeugen; *to* ~ **through** durchführen, zu Ende bringen; durchhelfen (*s.o.* jdm); *to* ~ **up** *(Gebäude)* aufführen; *(zeitlich)* zurückverfolgen; ~-**all** ['-ɔ:l] *s* große Tasche *f*; *Am* leichte(r) Einspänner; *allg* (Pferde-)Wagen; *mot* (Personen-)Wagen *m* mit Sitzreihen an den Seiten; *a* Allzweck-, Mehrzweck-; ~~ *truck* Kombiwagen *m*; ~-**cot** Tragbettchen *n*; ~-**forward** *com* Saldovortrag *m*; ~**ing** ['-iŋ] *s* Beförderung *f*, Transport *m*, Fracht; Spedition *f*; *(*~~ *fees)* Transportkosten *pl*, Fracht; *(Gesetzesvorlage)* Annahme *f*; *attr* Transport-, Fuhr-; ~~*-agent* Spediteur *m*; ~~ *of arms* Waffentragen *n*; ~~ *cable* Tragseil *n*; ~~*-capacity* Tragfähigkeit, Belastbarkeit *f*; Ladegewicht *n*, Nutzlast; Platzzahl *f*; ~~ *container* Transportbehälter *m*; ~~*-out laws (pl) (Am)* Ausführungsgesetze *n pl*; ~~ *roller(tech)* Führungsrolle *f*; ~~ *rope* Tragseil *n*; ~~*s -on (pl fam)* kindische(s) Benehmen *n*; ~~ *strap* Tragriemen, -gurt *m*; ~~*-trade* Fuhrunternehmen; Speditionsgeschäft *n*; ~~*-traffic (rail)* Güterverkehr *m*; ~~ *value* Buchwert *m*; ~-**over** *com* Übertrag, Verlustvortrag; Rest *m*.

cart [kɑ:t] *s* Karren, *(a. schwerer)* (zweirädriger) Wagen *m*; *tr* befördern, transportieren; *in the* ~ *(sl)* in der Tinte, im Eimer; *to push a* ~ e-n Karren schieben; *to put the* ~ *before the horse (fig)* das Pferd am Schwanz aufzäumen; ~**age** ['-idʒ] Fahren *n*, Fuhre *f*; Fuhrlohn *m*, Rollgeld *n*; ~**er** ['-ə] Fuhrmann, Kärrner *m*; ~**ful** ['-ful] *s.* ~*-load*; ~-**horse** (schweres) Zugpferd *n*; ~-**load** Fuhre, Wagen-, Karrenladung *f*; ~ **rut** Wagenspur *f*; ~-**track** unbefestigte(r) Weg *m*; ~-**wheel** Wagenrad *n*; *fam Br* Krone *f*, *Am* Dollar *m*; *fam* Radschlagen *n*.

cartel ['kɑ:tel, -'-] *fin* Kartell *n*, Ring; *(*~ *agreement)* Kartellvertrag *m*; Abkommen *n* über den Austausch von Kriegsgefangenen; Herausforderung *f* zum Duell; ~**ization** [-ai'zeiʃən, -li-] Kartellierung *f*; ~**ize** ['-aiz] *tr* kartellieren.

cartilag|e ['kɑ:tilidʒ] Knorpel *m*; ~**inous** [-'lædʒinəs] knorpelig; Knorpel-; ~~ *fishes (pl)* Knorpelfische *m pl*.

carto|grapher [kɑ:'tɔgrəfə] Kartograph *m*; ~**graphic(al)** [kɑ:to'græfik(l)] kartographisch; ~**graphy** [kɑ:'tɔgrəfi] Kartographie *f*.

cart|on ['kɑ:tən] Karton *m*, Pappschachtel; Pappe *f*; *das Weiße (im Zentrum e-r Schießscheibe)*; ~**oon** [kɑ:'tu:n] *s (Kunst)* Karton *m*; *typ* (*bes.* ganzseitige) Illustration; (*bes.* politische) Karikatur; Trickzeichnung *f*, -bild *n*; Entwurf *m*; *tr itr* karikieren; *animated* ~~ Trickfilm *m*; ~**oonist** [-'tu:nist] (Karikaturen-, Trickfilm-)Zeichner *m*.

cartouch(e) [kɑ:'tu:ʃ] *arch* Kartusche *f*, Rollwerk *n*, *bes.* Umrahmung *f*.

cartridge ['kɑ:tridʒ] *mil* Kartusche, Patrone; *phot* (Film-)Patrone *f*; ~-**belt** Patronen-, *(MG)* Ladegurt *m*; ~-**case** Patronenhülse *f*; ~-**paper** (starkes) Zeichenpapier *n*.

carv|e [kɑ:v] *tr* (*on* od *in(to), out of wood* in, aus Holz) schnitzen; (*on, in(to) stone* in Stein) meißeln, (*out of stone* aus Stein) hauen; (*o.'s name on a tree* s-n Namen in e-n Baum) (ein-) ritzen, (ein)schneiden; *(zubereitetes Fleisch)* (zer)schneiden, tranchieren, zerlegen; *(meist to* ~~ *up)* einteilen; in Stücke schneiden; *Am sl* lebhaft interessieren; *to* ~~ *out (fig)* erkämpfen, erarbeiten; *to* ~~ *a way through s.th.* sich durch etw e-n Weg bahnen; ~**er** ['-ə] Bildschnitzer, -hauer; Vorschneider *m (bei Tisch)*; Vorlegemesser *n*; *pl u. pair of* ~~*s* Vorlegebesteck *n*; ~**ing** ['-iŋ] Bildschnitzen, -hauen *n*; Schnitzerei *f*, Bildwerk *n*, Skulptur *f*; Tranchieren *n*; ~~*-fork, -knife* Tranchier-, Vorlegegabel, -messer *n*.

caryatid [kæri'ætid] *arch* Karyatide *f*.

cascade [kæs'keid] Kaskade *f*, Wasserfall *m*; *tech (*~ *connection)* Stufen-, Kaskadenschaltung *f*; *(Kleid)* Volant *m*.

case [keis] **1.** *s* (Einzel-)Fall; *gram* Fall, Kasus; (Rechts-)Fall *m*, Sache *f*; Prozeß; (Krankheits-)Fall; Kranke(r), Patient; Betroffene(r); *Am fam* eigenartige(r), sonderbare(r) Mensch *m*; *Am sl* (Liebes-)Verhältnis *n*, Verliebtheit *f*; *tr sl* inspizieren, genau ansehen; *in* ~ *(conj)* im Falle, für den Fall daß; damit nicht; *in (the)* ~ *of (prp)* im Fall *gen*; *in* ~ *of doubt* im Zweifelsfall; *in* ~ *of fire* bei Feuer; *in any* ~ in jedem, auf jeden Fall; jedenfalls; *in this, that* ~ in d(ies)em Fall; *in your* ~ in Ihrem Fall; *to* ~ *out (Am sl)* sich zs.tun, zs.arbeiten; *to close the* ~ die Beweisaufnahme schließen; *to come down to* ~*s (Am fam)* zur Sache kommen; *to hear a* ~ über e-e Sache verhandeln; *to put (the)* ~ den Fall setzen, annehmen; den Fall vortragen; *to state o.'s* ~ s-e Sache darlegen; *that's (not) the* ~ das ist (nicht) der Fall; *if that's the* ~ wenn das der Fall, wenn das so ist; *as the* ~ *may be* nach Lage des Falles, der Sache; *as the* ~ *stands* so wie die Dinge liegen; *should the* ~ *occur* sollte der Fall eintreten, eintretendenfalls; *dismissal of a* ~ Klagabweisung *f*; *merits (pl) of the* ~ *(jur)* Tatbestandsmerkmale *n pl*; *petty* ~ Bagatellsache *f*; ~ *of emergency* Dringlichkeitsfall *m*; ~ **history, record** Krankengeschichte; Personalakte *f*; Erfahrungs-, Tatsachenbericht *m*; ~-**law** Präzedenzrecht *n*; ~ **work** Fürsorge(tätigkeit) *f*; ~ **worker** Fürsorger(in *f*) *m*; **2.** *s* Behälter *m*; Hülle, Hülse, Kapsel *f*; Etui, Futteral *n*, Scheide *f*; Gehäuse; Fach *n*; Tasche *f*, Beutel, Sack *m*; Mappe; Schachtel *f*, Kästchen *n*, Kasten *m*, Kiste *f*; Blumenkasten; *(glass* ~*)* Glas-, Schaukasten; *typ* Setzkasten *m*; *(Buchbinderei)* Einbanddecke; *tech* Be-, Umkleidung *f*, Einsatz, Mantel *m*; *mil s.* ~*-shot*; *tr* ein-, in e-n Behälter stecken; *(to* ~ *up, over) tech* überziehen, be-, umkleiden; *to* ~ *in plaster (med)* in Gips legen; ~ *of instruments (med)* Besteck *n*; ~**book** *med* Patientenregister *n*; ~-**harden** *tr* hartgießen, im Einsatz härten, stählen; ~-**hardening** Hart-, Schalen-, Kokillenguß *m*; Einsatzhärtung *f*; ~-**knife** Finnenmesser *n*; Hirschfänger *m*; ~-**law** Fallrecht *n*; ~-**shot** *mil* Schrapnell *n*; ~ **stand** *typ* Setzregal *n*; ~-**weed** *bot* Hirtentäschel *n*.

case|mate ['keismeit] *mil* Kasematte *f*; ~**ment** ['keismənt] Fensterflügel *m*;

poet Fenster *n*; ~~ *curtain* Scheibengardine *f*; ~~ *cloth* Gardinen-, Vorhangstoff *m*; **~ous** ['keisiəs] käs(eart)ig.

cash [kæʃ] *s* Bargeld *n*, Kasse *f*; *attr* Bar-; *tr* einwechseln, zu Geld machen; *(to ~ up)* bezahlen, einlösen; *(to ~ up)* (ein-)kassieren, einziehen; *to ~ down, over (Am fam)* das Geld auf den Tisch legen für; *to ~ in (sl)* abkratzen, ins Gras beißen (müssen); *Am fam* zu Gelde, flüssig machen; *to ~ in on* gewinnen, profitieren an; nützen, nach besten Kräften ausnutzen; *against, for, in ~, in ready ~, ~ down* (gegen, in) bar; *in ~* bei Kasse; *out of ~* nicht bei Kasse, ohne Geld; *~ and carry (Am)* nur gegen Barzahlung u. eigenen Transport; *~ on delivery* gegen, per Nachnahme; *~ with order* zahlbar bei Auftragserteilung; *to buy for ~* (gegen) bar kaufen; *to make up the ~* Kasse(nsturz) machen; *to pay (in) ~* bar (be-)zahlen; *to pay in hard ~* in barer Münze bezahlen; *to turn into ~* zu Geld machen; *I have no ~ with me* ich habe kein Bargeld bei mir; *balance in, of ~, stock in ~* Kassen-, Barbestand *m*; *discount for ~* Diskont *m* bei Barzahlung; **~able** ['-əbl] einziehbar, (ein)kassierbar; **~ account** Kassakonto *n*; **~ advance** Barvorschuß *m*; **~ amount** Kassenbetrag *m*; **~ assets** *pl* Barwerte *m pl*, -vermögen *n*; **~ audit** Kassenprüfung, -kontrolle, -revision *f*; **~ balance** Kassenbilanz *f*, -bestand *m*; *adverse ~~ (Am)* Kassendefizit *n*; **~ at, in bank, on deposit** Bankguthaben *n*; **~ bill** Kassenzettel *m*; **~ book** Kassenbuch *n*; **~ box** Kasse; (Geld-)Kassette *f*; Kassenschalter *m*; **~ discount** Kassakonto *n*, Barzahlungsrabatt *m*; **~-expenditure, expenses** *pl* Barausgabe *f*; **~ in, on hand** Bar-, Kassenbestand *m*; **~ier** [kæ'ʃiə] *s* Kassierer(in *f*); Kassenbeamte(r); Kassenführer, -wart *m*; *tr* [kə'ʃiə] *(Beamten)* entlassen, *fam* kassieren; *~~'s desk* Kassenschalter *m*; *~~'s office* Kasse(nabteilung) *f*; **~ keeper** *Am* Kassenführer, Kassierer *m*; **~ keeping** *Am* Kassenführung *f*; **~ price** Preis *m* bei Barzahlung, Kassapreis *m*; **~ receipts** *pl* Kasseneinnahme *f*; **~ register** Registrierkasse *f*; **~ remittance** Barüberweisung *f*; **~ surrender value** Rückkaufswert *m*; **~ system** Barzahlungssystem *n*; **~ turnover** Kassenumsatz *m*; **~ value** Barwert *m*; **~ voucher** Kassenbeleg *m*; **~ withdrawal** Barentnahme, -abhebung *f*.

cash|ew [kæ'ʃu:] *(~~-tree)* Kaschubaum *m*; **~mere** [kæʃ'miə] Kaschmir(schal, -stoff) *m*.

casing ['keisiŋ] *tech* Be-, Umkleidung, Umhüllung, Hülle *f*, Futteral *n*, Mantel; Überzug *m*; Gehäuse *n*; Nutleiste; Verrohrung; *arch* (Ver-)Schalung; Auskleidung *f*; *min* Schachtausbau *m*; *(Textil)* Futter *n*; *Am* Tür-, Fensterrahmen *m*; *Am mot* (Reifen-)Decke *f*, Mantel *m*; *pl Am* Därme *m pl (als Wursthüllen)*.

casino [kə'si:nou] *pl* -*os* Kasino *n*.

cask [kɑ:sk] Faß *n*; Tonne *f*; **~et** ['-it] (Schmuck-)Kästchen *n*; *Am* Sarg *m*.

cass|ation [kæ'seiʃən] *jur* Aufhebung, Annullierung *f (e-s Urteils)*; **~ava** [kə'sɑ:və] Kassawastrauch *m*; Tapioka(stärke) *f*; *~~ root* Maniokwurzel *f*; **~erole** ['kæsəroul] feuerfeste Schüssel *f*; **~ia** ['kæsiə] *bot* Kassia, Kassie(nbaum *m*); *(~~ bark)* Kassienrinde *f*, gemeine(r) Zimt *m*; **~ock** ['kæsək] *rel* Soutane *f*; **~owary** ['kæsəwɛəri] *orn* Kasuar *m*.

cast [kɑ:st] *irr cast, cast tr* (ab-, aus-, fort-, hin-, weg)werfen; hinfallen lassen; *(Zahn, Huf)* verlieren; *(Kuh)* zu früh gebären; *(Frucht)* zu früh abwerfen; *tech* gießen; *(~ up)* zs.zählen, -rechnen; aus-, berechnen; *jur* verwerfen; entlassen; in e-e Form bringen, formen, gestalten; *(Schauspieler)* einteilen (*for* für); *(Rolle)* besetzen (*to* mit); *itr (Holz)* sich werfen, sich verziehen, arbeiten; sich gießen lassen; würfeln; zs.zählen; sich erbrechen; planen; *s* Wurf(weite *f*) *m*, Auswerfen *n (der Angel, des Netzes, des Lotes)*; Wurf *m (beim Würfeln)*; *zoo das* Abgeworfene; *(Raubvogel)* Gewölle *n*; *tech obs* Guß *m*; *tech* Gußform; Gußprobe *f*; Abguß *m*, Gußstück *n*; *(plaster ~)* Gipsverband *m*; Aus-, Zs.rechnen *n*, Berechnung; *theat* (Rollen-)Besetzung *f*; Ensemble *n*; *fig* Neigung, Anlage, Eigenart; (Farb-)Nuance, Schattierung *f*, Schimmer, Anstrich *m*; Eigenschaft *f*, Charakter, Wesenszug *m*; *(~ of features)* Gesichtszüge *m pl*; Wesen *n*, Natur, Art, Prägung *f*, Gepräge *n*, Typ *m*; *(~ of mind)* Geistes-, Wesensart *f*; *attr* Guß-; *to ~ anchor* Anker werfen; *to ~ dice* würfeln; *to ~ an eye, a glance, a look at, on, over s.th.* e-n Blick auf etw werfen; *to ~ a horoscope, a nativity* ein Horoskop stellen; *to ~ light, a shadow on* Licht, s-n Schatten werfen auf; *to ~ lots* Lose ziehen; das Los entscheiden lassen; *to ~ pearls before swine* Perlen vor die Säue werfen; *to ~ into prison* ins Gefängnis werfen, einsperren; *to ~ o.'s skin (zoo)* sich häuten; *to ~ a spell on* verhexen; *to ~ s.th. in s.o.'s teeth* jdm etw unter die Nase reiben, vorhalten, -werfen; *to ~ a vote, a ballot* s-e (Wahl-)Stimme abgeben; *to put in a ~* in Gips legen, e-n Gipsverband anlegen; *to ~* **about** (herum)suchen (*for* nach); (hin u. her) überlegen (*to* inf; *how* wie); *to ~* **aside, away** wegwerfen; *to be ~ away (Schiff)* untergehen; schiffbrüchig sein; *to ~* **back** abweisen, zurückgeben; *to ~* **down** niederwerfen, zerschmettern; *fig* niederschmettern, -drücken, deprimieren; *~ down (a)* niedergeschlagen, traurig; *to ~* **in** *fig* teilen (*o.'s lot with s.o.* sein Los mit jdm); *to ~* **loose** sich losmachen, -reißen; *to ~* **off** *tr (alte Kleider)* ablegen; *(Masche beim Stricken)* abnehmen; *mar (Tau)* abrollen; *typ (Manuskript)* be-, ausrechnen *(in Druckseiten)*; *fig* verstoßen; *itr* in See stechen; *to ~* **on** *(Masche)* aufnehmen; *to ~* **out** hinauswerfen; *lit fig* vertreiben; aus-, *itr* erbrechen *a. fig*, (wieder) von sich geben; *to ~* **up** in die Höhe, hochwerfen; *(die Augen)* auf-, *(den Kopf)* hochwerfen; zs.-, ausrechnen, zs.zählen; **~ iron** *s* Gußeisen *n*; **~-iron** *a* gußeisern; *fig* hart, unbeugsam; *(Wille)* eisern; **~ mo(u)ld** Blockform, Kokille *f*; **~-off** *s* Verstoßene(r *m*) *f*; Weggeworfene(s) *n*; *a* abgelegt; **~ scrap** Gußbruch, -schrott *m*; **~ seam** Gußnaht *f*; **~steal** Gußstahl *m*; **~ strength** Gußfestigkeit *f*.

castanet ['kæstə'net, -'net] *meist pl* Kastagnette *f*.

castaway ['kɑ:stəwei] *s* Verworfene(r), Ausgestoßene(r); Schiffbrüchige(r), Gestrandete(r) *m*; *a* verworfen, ausgestoßen; überflüssig, unnütz; schiffbrüchig, gestrandet *a. fig*.

caste [kɑ:st] *rel* Kaste *a. allg*; *allg* exklusive Gesellschaft(sschicht); soziale Stellung *f*, Rang *m*; **~ feeling** Kastengeist *m*.

castell|an ['kæstələn] Kastellan, Schloßverwalter *m*; **~ated** ['-eleitid] *a* burgartig, wie e-e Burg (gebaut), mit Zinnen (versehen); *(Land)* burgenreich.

caster ['kɑ:stə] Werfer; *tech* Gießer; Berechner *m*; *a.* **castor** [-] Möbelrolle *f*; *(Salz-, Pfeffer-, Zucker-)* Streuer *m*; *pl (~,* **castor stand** *Am)* Menage *f*; *china ~* Porzellangießer *m*; **~ sugar** Puder-, Staubzucker *m*.

castigat|e ['kæstigeit] *tr* züchtigen; heftig tadeln, heruntermachen; *(Buch)* durchsehen, verbessern; **~ion** [-'geiʃən] Züchtigung *f*; heftige(r) Tadel *m*; *(Buch)* kritische Durchsicht *f*; **~or** ['-tə] Tadler *m*.

casting ['kɑ:stiŋ] *s* Wurf; Guß *m*; Berechnung *f*; *(~ up)* Zs.zählen; *a. pl* Gußeisen, -stück *n*; Abguß *m*; *(~ of votes)* Stimmabgabe *f*; *a* entscheidend; *case-hardened, chilled ~* Hart-, Kokillenguß *m*; **~ defect** Gußfehler *m*; **~ net** Wurfnetz *n*; **~ ~-vote** *parl* entscheidende Stimme *f*, Zünglein *n* an der Waage; *the chairman has the ~~* die Stimme des Vorsitzenden entscheidet.

castle ['kɑ:sl] *s* Burg *f*; (festes) Schloß *n*; *(Schach)* Turm *m*; *itr* rochieren, die Rochade ausführen; *~ in the air, in Spain* Luftschloß *n*; **~-builder** Träumer *m*; **~-guard** Kastellan *m*.

castor ['kɑ:stə] **1.** *obs zoo* Biber *m*; Bibergeil *n*; Bibermütze *f*; *sl* Deckel, Hut *m*; **~-oil** Rizinusöl *n*; **2.** *s. caster*; **3.** *vet (Pferd)* Spat *m*.

castrat|e [kæs'treit] *tr* kastrieren, verschneiden; *fig* ausmerzen; *(Text)* verstümmeln; *(Buch)* die anstößigen Stellen entfernen aus; **~ion** [-ʃən] Kastration, Verschneidung; *fig* Verstümmelung *f*.

casual ['kæʒ(j)uəl] *s* zufällig Anwesende(r); Gelegenheitsarbeiter; *pl mil* Durchgangspersonal *n*; Hausanzug *m*, Slipper *pl*; *a* zufällig, unerwartet, unvorhergesehen; gelegentlich, beiläufig; *(Bekanntschaft, Bemerkung)* flüchtig; unabsichtlich Freizeit-; Gelegenheits-; **~ clothes** *pl* Haus-, Sportkleidung *f*; **~ employment, labo(u)r** Gelegenheitsarbeit *f*; **~ income** Nebenverdienst *m*, -einkommen *n*; **~ labour(er), work(er** Ge-)legenheitsarbeit(er *m*) *f*; **~ly** ['-li] *adv* zufällig, durch Zufall; gelegentlich, beiläufig; **~ty** ['kæʒjuəlti] Un(glücks)fall; Verunglückte(r), Verletzte(r), Verwundete(r) *m*, (Todes-)Opfer *n*; *pl mil* Ausfälle, Verluste *m pl*; *(~~ list)* Verlustliste *f*; *~~ insurance* Unfallversicherung *f*; *~~ report* Verlustmeldung *f*; *~~ ward* Unfallstation *f (in e-m Krankenhaus)*; **~ ward** Obdachlosenasyl *n*.

casuist ['kæzjuist] Kasuist *m*; **~ic(al)** [-'istik(l)] kasuistisch; **~ry** ['-ri] Kasuistik; Haarspalterei, Spitzfindigkeit *f*.

cat [kæt] *s zoo* Katze *f*; *Am* Luchs *m*; *Am s. ~fish*; *Am* Swingenthusiast, Jazzmusiker *m*; *mar (~head)* (Anker-)Katt *f*; *tech* Traktor *m*; *(~-o'-nine-tails)* neunschwänzige Katze *f*; *pej* giftige(s) Weib *n*; *sl* Frauenjäger *m*; *tr mar (Anker)* katten; auspeitschen; *itr sl* kotzen; freche Bemerkungen machen; herumlungern; *to lead a ~ and dog life* wie Hund u. Katze mitea. leben; *to let the ~ out of the bag (fig)* die Katze aus dem Sack lassen; *to see, to watch which way the ~ jumps (fig)* sehen, wohin der Hase läuft; *there is not room to swing a ~* man kann sich dort nicht umdrehen; *it's raining ~s and dogs* es regnet in Strömen; *when the ~'s away,* *the mice will play* wenn die Katze weg ist, tanzen die Mäuse; ~ **burglar** Fassadenkletterer *m*; ~**call** *s theat* Pfeifen, Zischen *n*; *tr* auspfeifen, -zischen; ~**fish** *zoo* Zwerg-, Katzenwels; Seewolf *m*; ~-**mint** *bot* (Gemeine) Katzenminze *f*; ~-**nap** leichte(r) Schlaf *m*; ~'**s-eye** Rückstrahler *m (an Fahrzeugen)*; *Art* Murmel *f*; ~'**s-paw** Katzenpfote *f*; (als) Werkzeug *n* (mißbrauchter Mensch *m*); *mar* leichte Brise *f*; ~'**s sleep** leichte(r) Schlaf *m*; ~-**walk** Laufplanke *f*; schmale(r) Steg *m*; ~**y**, ~**ish** ['-i, '-iʃ] katzenartig; katzenhaft; *fig* giftig.

cata|clysm ['kætəklizm] *geol* Flutkatastrophe; *(politische* od *soziale)* Umwälzung *f*; ~**comb** ['-koum] Katakombe *f*; ~**falque** ['-fælk] Katafalk *m*.

cata|lepsy ['kætəlepsi] Starrsucht *f*, -krampf *m*; ~**leptic** [-'leptik] kataleptisch, starrsüchtig; Krampf-; ~**log(ue)** ['-lɔg] *s* Katalog *m*, Verzeichnis *n*; *(price(d)* ~~*)* Preisliste *f*; Prospekt *m*; *Am* Vorlesungsverzeichnis *n*; *tr* katalogisieren; *library* ~~ Bibliothekskatalog *m*; ~~ *price* Katalogpreis *m*; ~~ *wholesaler* Versandgroßhändler *m*; ~**log(u)ing** Katalogisierung *f*.

catalpa [kə'tælpə] *bot* Trompetenbaum *m*.

cataly|sis [kə'tælisis] *chem* Katalyse *f*; ~**st** ['kætəlist] *chem* Katalysator(masse *f*) *m*; ~**tic** [kætə'litik] *chem* katalytisch.

cata|maran [kætəmə'ræn] Floß; Auslegerboot *n*; *fam fig* Kratzbürste *f*; ~**menia** [-'mi:niə] *med* Menstruation *f*.

cata|plasm ['kætəplæzm] *med* Breiumschlag *m*; ~**pult** ['-pʌlt] *s* Wurf-, Schleudermaschine *f*, Katapult *m* od *n a. aero*; Schleuder *f*; *tr (*~~ *off) aero* katapultieren, (ab)schleudern; ~~ *aircraft, plane* Katapultflugzeug *n*; ~~ *launching, take-off (aero)* Katapult-, Schleuderstart *m*; ~~ *seat (aero)* Schleuder-, Katapultsitz *m*; ~**ract** ['-rækt] Wasserfall *m*; Stromschnelle *f*; starke(r) Regenguß; *med* graue(r) Star; *tech* Regulator *m*; *fig* Flut *f*.

catarrh [kə'tɑ:] Katarrh *m*, Erkältung *f*, Schnupfen *m*; ~**al** [-rəl] katarrhalisch.

catastroph|e [kə'tæstrəfi] Katastrophe *f a. theat geol*, Schicksalsschlag *m*, große(s) Unglück *n*; *geol* Umwälzung *f*; ~**ic(al)** [kætəs'trɔfik(l)] katastrophal, verhängnisvoll, niederschmetternd; Unglücks-; katastrophenartig.

catch [kætʃ] **1.** *irr caught, caught tr* (auf-, ein)fangen, ergreifen, packen, schnappen; *fig* betrügen, hereinlegen; (fest-)halten; *(Finger)* einklemmen; treffen (*on* auf); einholen, erreichen; überholen; *(Ball)* abfangen; *(Menschen, Zug, Bahn, Bus)* (noch) erreichen, *fam* kriegen, erwischen; ertappen, erwischen (*at* bei); hängenbleiben (*a coat* mit e-m Mantel); erlangen, erhalten, bekommen, *fam* kriegen; *(Krankheit)* sich holen, sich zuziehen; *(Gewohnheit)* annehmen; mitkriegen, hören, verstehen, begreifen; auf sich ziehen *od* lenken; für sich gewinnen, bezaubern; *itr* (fest)gehalten werden, sich verfangen (*on a nail* an e-m Nagel), sich einklemmen, eingeklemmt werden; *(Schloß, Riegel)* fassen, einschnappen, einrasten, (inea.)greifen, halten; *(Schlag)* treffen (*on the nose* auf die Nase); in Brand geraten, Feuer fangen; zufrieren; *med* anstecken(d sein); **2.** *s* Fang *m*; *(Ball)* Fangen *n*; Beute *f*, Fang *(bes. Fische)*, Gewinn; *sport* Fangball; *phot* Verschluß; *tech* Anschlag *m*, Arretierung, Sperre *f*; Mitnehmer; Haken *m (zum Befestigen)*; (Tür-)Klinke *f*; (Fenster-)Griff *m*; *(Stimme)* Stocken *n*; *fig* Haken, Nachteil, Kniff, Trick *m*; *(*~ *question)* Fangfrage *f*; Blickfang *m*; *(Frau)* Partie *f*; *mus* Kanon *m*; *fig* Bruchstück *n*, Fetzen *m*; *to* ~ *in the act, redhanded* auf frischer Tat ertappen; *to* ~ *(a) cold* sich erkälten, sich e-n Schnupfen holen; *to* ~ *s.o.'s eye* jds Blick, Aufmerksamkeit auf sich ziehen *od* lenken; jdm ins Auge fallen; *to* ~ *fire* Feuer fangen; *to* ~ *hold of* ergreifen, packen, anfassen; *to* ~ *it (fam)* eins abkriegen; geschimpft, bestraft werden; *to* ~ *sight, a glimpse of* erblicken, e-n Augenblick zu Gesicht bekommen; *to* ~ *the Speaker's eye (parl)* das Wort erhalten; *I caught my breath* mir stockte der Atem, mir blieb die Luft weg; ~ *me!* denkste! das fällt mir gar nicht, nicht im Traum ein! *to* ~ **at** greifen, fassen, haschen nach; *to* ~ **away** wegschnappen; *to* ~ **on(to)** *tr* begreifen, verstehen; *(Gelegenheit)* beim Schopf ergreifen; *itr* Anklang finden, Mode werden; *to* ~ **out** *(beim Kricket den Schläger)* aus dem Spiel bringen; *fig* (bei e-m Fehler) ertappen; erwischen; *to* ~ **up** auftreiben, *fam* ergattern; *(Redensart)* aufschnappen, *(Gewohnheit)* annehmen; *(Redenden)* unterbrechen, kritisieren; nachkommen (*with* mit); (*s.o.* u. *with s.o.* jdn) ein-, überholen; ~**able** ['kætʃəbl] zu fangen(d), zu kriegen(d); einzuholen(d), erreichbar; ~**all** *Am* Rumpelkammer *f*; ~-**as**-~-**can** Freistilringen *n*; ~ **basin** Auffangschale; Senkgrube *f*; ~ **crop** dritte Ernte *f*; ~-**drain** Wasserauffanggraben *m*; ~**er** ['-ə] Fänger *a. sport*; Häscher *m*; *tech* Auskopplungsglied *n*, Schnapper, Auffänger *m*; ~**ing** ['-iŋ] anziehend, einnehmend; *med* ansteckend; unsicher, verfänglich; täuschend, trügerisch; ~-**line** Schlagzeile *f*; ~**ment** ['-mənt] (Wasser-)Stauung *f*; *(*~~ *aerea)* Einzugsgebiet *n*; ~~-*basin* Staubecken *n*, -see *m*; ~-**net** Schutz-, Fangnetz *n*; ~**penny** *s* Lockartikel, Verkaufsschlager, Ramsch *m*; *a* billig, wertlos; ~-**phrase** Schlagwort *n*; ~**up** *Am s. ketchup*; ~**weed** *bot* Klebkraut *n*; ~**word** Schlagwort; *(Lexikon, theat)* Stichwort; *poet* Reimwort *n*; ~**y** ['-i] anziehend, einnehmend, sich einschmeichelnd, gefällig; verfänglich; schwierig.

catech|etic(al) [kæti'ketik(əl)] *a* katechetisch; Katechismus-; *s pl* Katechetik *f*; ~**ism** ['-kizm] *rel* Katechismus(unterricht); Religionsunterricht *m*; *to put s.o. through his* ~~ *(fig)* jdn genau ausfragen; ~**ize** ['-kaiz] *tr* katechisieren, Religionsunterricht erteilen (*s.o.* jdm); *fig* ausfragen; ~**umen** [-'kju:men] *rel* Konfirmand; *fig* Neuling *m*.

categor|ic(al) [kæti'gɔrik(əl)] kategorisch, absolut, keinen Widerspruch duldend; ~**y** ['kætigəri] Kategorie; Klasse; Begriffs-, Anschauungsform *f*.

catena|ry [kə'ti:nəri] *a* Ketten-; *s math* Kettenlinie *f*; ~~ *bridge* Kettenbrücke *f* ~**tion** [-'neiʃən] Verkettung *f*.

cater ['keitə] *itr (Lebensmittel)* be-, heranschaffen, liefern (*for* für); für Verpflegung sorgen; etw bringen, beschaffen, geben (*to* dat); *to* ~ *for* beliefern; betreuen; sorgen für; ~**er** ['-rə] Lebensmitteleinkäufer, -lieferant *m*; ~**ing** ['-riŋ] Verpflegung(swesen *n*), Lebensmittelbeschaffung *f*; ~~ *officer (Br)* Verpflegungsoffizier *m*; ~**pillar** ['kætəpilə] *zoo tech* Raupe *f*; Raupenschlepper *m*; ~~ *drive* Raupen-, Gleiskettenantrieb *m*; ~~ *glue* Raupenleim *m*; ~~ *track* Raupen-, Gleiskette *f*; ~~ *tractor (Firmenbezeichnung)* Raupenschlepper *m*; ~**waul** ['kætəwɔ:l] *itr* miauen; *s* Miauen *n*; *fig* Katzbalgerei, Katzenmusik *f*.

catgut ['kætgʌt] Darmsaite *f*; *mus* Saiteninstrumente *n pl*.

catharsis [kə'θɑ:sis] *psychol* Entspannung *f*, Abreagieren *n*; Sublimierung *f*.

cathedral [kə'θi:drəl] Kathedrale *f*, Dom *m*, Bischofskirche *f*.

Catherine ['kæθərin] Katharina, Katharine *f*; ~-**wheel** *arch* Rosette *f*; *(Feuerwerk)* Feuerrad *n*; *to turn a* ~~ ein Rad schlagen.

cathe|ter ['kæθitə] *med* Katheter *n*; ~**tron** [kə'θi:trən] Gleichrichter *m* mit Außengittersteuerung; ~**xis** [kə'θeksis] *psychol* Besetzung *f*; Gefühlswert *m*.

cathod|e ['kæθoud] *el* Kathode *f*; ~~ *current* Kathodenstrom *m*; ~~ *filament* Glühkathode *f*; ~~ *ray* Kathodenstrahl *m*; ~~ *ray tube* Braunsche Röhre *f*; ~**ic** [kə'θɔdik] kathodisch.

catholic ['kæθəlik] *a rel* katholisch; *allg* universal, allgemein; (all)umfassend, weitgespannt, vielseitig; vorurteilslos, weitherzig, aufgeschlossen, frei(sinnig), verständnisvoll, tolerant; *s* Katholik(in *f*) *m*; *Roman C*~ römisch-katholisch; *the C*~ *Church* die katholische Kirche; **C**~**ism** [kə'θɔlisizm] Katholizismus *m*; ~**ity** [kæθɔ'lisiti] Universalität, Allgemeinheit; Vorurteilslosigkeit, Weitherzigkeit, Aufgeschlossenheit *f*, Freisinn *m*, Toleranz *f*; ~**ize** [kə'θɔlisaiz] *tr itr* katholisch machen *od* werden.

cation ['kætaiən] *phys* Kation *n*.

catkin ['kætkin] *bot* Kätzchen *n*.

cattle ['kætl] Vieh; Groß-, Rindvieh *n*; *in Zssgen* Rinder-, Vieh-; *to raise* ~ Vieh züchten; ~ **barn, shed** Viehstall *m*; ~-**breeder** Viehzüchter *m*; ~-**breeding** Rinderzucht *f*; ~ **broker** *Am* Viehhändler *m*; ~-**car, -truck, -van, -wag(g)on** *rail* Viehwagen *m*; ~-**dealer** Viehhändler *m*; ~-**feeder** (Stall-)Schweizer; Futterverteiler *m (Gerät)*; ~-**fodder**, *Am* **feed** Viehfutter *n*; ~-**lifter, -rustler, -thief** Viehdieb *m*; ~-**lorry** Viehtransporter *m*; ~ **man** *Am* Viehzüchter *m*; ~-**pen** Viehhürde *f*; ~-**plague** *vet* Rinderpest *f*; ~ **puncher** *Am* Rinderhirt *m*; ~ **ranch** *Am* Rinderfarm *f*; ~ **range** *Am* Weidegründe *m pl*, Viehweiden *f pl*; ~ **salt** Viehsalz *n*; ~-**wire** Schutzdraht *m*; ~**yard** Schlachthof *m*.

*

Caucas|ian [kɔ:'keiʃən, -ziən] *a obs* kaukasisch; europid; *s* Kaukasier, Weiße(r) *m*; ~**us** ['kɔ:kəsəs] Kaukasus *m*.

caucus ['kɔ:kəs] *Am s* Parteiführerversammlung; Wahlvorversammlung *f*; Partei-, Wahlausschuß; *Br* örtliche(r) Parteiausschuß *m*; *itr* sich zu e-r politischen Konferenz versammeln; intrigieren, e-e Clique bilden; *tr (Partei)* durch e-e Gruppe beherrschen; *the* ~, ~ *system* Gruppenbildung; Cliquenwirtschaft *f*.

caud|al ['kɔ:dl] schwanzartig; Schwanz-; ~~ *fin* Schwanzflosse *f*; ~**ate** ['-eit] geschwänzt; *to be* ~~ e-n Schwanz haben.

caudle ['kɔ:dl] Glühwein *m*; Haferflockensuppe *f* mit Wein.

caul [kɔ:l] *hist* Netzhaube *f*; Haarnetz *n*; *physiol* innere Embryonalhülle *f*, Amnion *n*; Glückshaube *f*.

ca(u)ldron ['kɔ:ldrən] große(r) (Koch-) Kessel *m.*
cauliflower ['kɔliflauə] Blumenkohl *m*; ~ **cloud** Kumulus *m*, Quellwolke *f*; ~ **ear** Boxerohr *n.*
ca(u)lk [kɔ:k] *tr* dicht machen, abdichten; *(Dampfkessel)* verstemmen; *mar* kalfatern; *to* ~ *off (Am sl)* schlafen gehen, sich ausruhen; ~**er** ['-ə] *tech* Stemmer; *mar* Kalfaterer *m.*
caus|al ['kɔ:zəl] ursächlich; kausal; *gram* Kausal-; ~~ *nexus* ursächliche(r), Kausalzs.hang *m*; ~**ality** [kɔ:'zæliti] Ursächlichkeit, Kausalität *f*; ~**ative** ['kɔ:zətiv] verursachend, ursächlich; *gram* kausativ; ~**e** [kɔ:z] *s* Ursache; Veranlassung *f*; Grund, Anlaß *m* (*for* zu); Sache, Angelegenheit *f*; *jur* Prozeß, Streitfall *m*; *tr* verursachen; *(Schaden)* anrichten, bewirken; veranlassen; *(Überraschung)* hervorrufen, erregen; *to be the* ~~ *of s.th.* Anlaß zu etw sein; *to make common* ~~ *with s.o.* mit jdm gemeinsame Sache machen; *to plead a* ~~ e-e Sache *(vor Gericht)* vertreten; ~~ *of action (jur)* Klagegrund *m*; ~~ *of divorce* Scheidungsgrund *m*; ~~ *of trouble* Fehlerquelle *f*; ~~-*list (jur)* Terminliste *f*; ~**eless** ['-lis] grundlos.
cause(wa)y ['kɔ:z(w)ei] (Straßen-) Damm *m*; Chaussee, Landstraße *f.*
causti|c ['kɔ:stik] *a* ätzend; *fig* beißend, scharf, sarkastisch; *chem* kaustisch, Brenn-; *s* Ätzmittel *n*; ~~ *lime, potash, soda* Ätzkalk *m*, -kali, -natron *n*; ~**city** [kɔ:s'tisiti] ätzende, Ätzwirkung *f*; *fig* Schärfe *f*, Sarkasmus *m.*
cauter|ization [kɔ:tərai'zeiʃən] *med* Ausbrennen *n*, Ätzung *f*; *tech* Brennschneiden *n*; ~**ize** ['kɔ:təraiz] *tr med* kauterisieren, ausbrennen, ätzen; *tech* brennschneiden; *fig* abstumpfen; ~**y** ['kɔ:təri] *med (~~ burner)* Thermokauter, Brenner *m*; Ätzmittel; *tech* Brennschneiden *n.*
cauti|on ['kɔ:ʃən] *s* Vorsicht, Achtsam-, Bedachtsamkeit, Umsicht; Vorsichtsmaßregel, -maßnahme; *fin* Bürgschaft, Sicherheit, Kaution, Garantie; Warnung *f*, Warn-, Alarmzeichen *n*; *jur* Verwarnung *f*, Verweis *m*; (Rechtsmittel-, Eides-)Belehrung *f*; *mil* Ankündigungskommando *n*; *Br* ulkige Nummer; *Am sl* (ganz) große, phantastische, tolle Sache *f*; *tr* warnen (*against* vor); *jur* verwarnen, e-n Verweis erteilen (*s.o.* jdm); *jur* belehren; ~**onary** ['-ʃnəri] *a* Warn-; *jur* Sicherheits-; ~~ *command (Br)* Ankündigungskommando *n*; ~**ous** ['kɔ:ʃəs] vorsichtig, umsichtig, achtsam, bedachtsam; ~**ousness** Vorsicht, Umsicht, Bedachtsamkeit *f.*
caval|cade [kævəl'keid] Reiterzug *m*; ~**ier** [-'liə] *s* Reiter, Ritter; Kavalier; *C~~ (17. Jhdt.)* Royalist *m*; *a* sorglos, unbeschwert, heiter, froh (-gemut); hochmütig, -näsig; ~**ry** ['kævəlri] Reiterei, Kavallerie *f*; ~~*man* Kavallerist, Reiter *m.*
cav|e 1. [keiv] *s* Höhle *f*, Hohlraum; *sl* (fensterloser) Raum *m*; *Br pol* Parteispaltung *f*; Abtrünnige, Spalter *m pl*; *tr* aushöhlen; ausbeulen, eindrücken; *itr pol* sich abspalten, die Partei spalten; *Am fam* zs.sacken; *to* ~~ *down (Am fam) tr* unterwühlen; zs.hauen; *itr* zs.sacken; *to* ~~ *in (itr) (Erde über e-m Hohlraum)* nachgeben, einsinken, -stürzen; *fig fam* nachgeben, sich fügen, klein beigeben; *Am fam* zs.sacken; *tr* zum Einsturz bringen; ~~-*bear* Höhlenbär *m*; ~~-*dweller (hist)* Höhlenbewohner *m*; ~~-*in* eingebrochene Stelle *f*; ~~-*man (hist)* Höhlenmensch; *fig* primitive(r) Mensch, Wilde(r); *Am* Draufgänger *m*; ~~ *painting* Höhlenmalerei *f*; **2.** ['-i] *sl (Schule)* Achtung! der Alte kommt!
~**eat** ['keiviæt] *s jur* Warnung *f*; Einspruch *m*; *Am* vorläufige Patentanmeldung *f*; *to enter, to put in a* ~~ *against s.th.* gegen e-e S Einspruch erheben; ~**ern** ['kævən] *s bes. lit* (große) Höhle *f*; *tr* aushöhlen; ein-, umschließen; ~**ernous** ['-əs] höhlenreich; porös; *fig* hohl, tief(liegend), eingefallen; *(Dunkelheit)* groß.
caviar(e) ['kævia:] Kaviar *m*; ~ *to the general (fig)* Kaviar fürs Volk.
cavil ['kævil] *s* Nörgelei; Spitzfindigkeit *f*; *itr* (herum)kritteln, etw auszusetzen haben, (herum)nörgeln (*at, about* an); ~**(l)er** ['-ə] Nörgler *m.*
cavity ['kæviti] Hohlraum *m*, Höhlung, Mulde *f*; *(Zahn)* Loch *n*; *(im Metall)* Lunker *m.*
cavort [kə'vɔ:t] *itr Am sl* sich aufplustern; *fam* herumtollen.
cavy ['keivi] Meerschweinchen *n.*
caw [kɔ:] *itr (Rabe, Krähe)* krächzen; *s* Krächzen *n.*
cay [kei] Sandbank *f*; Riff *n*; Klippe *f*; ~**enne** [-'en] *(~~ pepper)* Kayennepfeffer *m*; ~**man, caiman** ['-mən] Kaiman *m.*

*

cease [si:s] *itr* aufhören (*doing, to do* zu tun); ablassen (*from* von); *tr* einstellen, aufhören mit; *to* ~ *fire (mil)* das Feuer einstellen; *to* ~ *payment (fin)* die Zahlungen einstellen; *to* ~ *work* die Arbeit(en) einstellen; ~-**fire** *mil* Feuereinstellung *f*; ~**less** ['-lis] unaufhörlich, pausenlos.
cedar ['si:də] *bot* Zeder *f*; *(~-wood)* Zedernholz *n*; ~-**bird** *Am orn* Seidenschwanz *m.*
cede [si:d] *tr* aufgeben, abtreten, überlassen, zedieren (*to* an); zugeben.
ceil [si:l] *tr (Zimmerdecke)* täfeln; verputzen; ~**ing** ['-iŋ] (Zimmer-)Decke *f*, Plafond *m*; *(Schiffbau)* Innenbeplankung, Wegerung; *aero* untere Wolkengrenze; *aero* Steig-, Gipfelhöhe; höchste Steigmöglichkeit; *fin* oberste Grenze *f*; Höchstpreis *m*, -miete *f*, -lohn *m*, -gehalt *n*; *attr* Höchst-; *to hit the* ~~ *(sl)* rasend werden, platzen.
celandine ['seləndain] *bot (Common* od *Greater C~)* Schell-, Schöllkraut *n*; *(Small* od *Lesser C~)* Scharbocks-, Feigwarzenkraut *n*, Feig(en)wurz(el) *f.*
celebr|ant ['selibrənt] Zelebrant *m*; ~**ate** ['-eit] *tr rel* zelebrieren; feiern; *itr fam* es sich wohl sein lassen; ~**ated** [-id] *a* gefeiert; berühmt; weit u. breit bekannt; ~**ation** [-'breiʃən] Feier *f*; (Freuden-)Fest *n*; ~**ity** [si'lebriti] Berühmtheit *f (a. Person).*
celer|iac [si'leriæk] Knollensellerie *m* od *f*; ~**ity** [-iti] Geschwindigkeit *f*; ~**y** ['seləri] *bot* Sellerie *m* od *f.*
celestial [si'lestjəl] *astr* Himmels-; *rel poet* himmlisch; ~ **body** Himmelskörper *m*; ~ **globe** Himmelsglobus *m*; ~ **map** Sternkarte *f.*
celib|acy ['selibəsi] Ehelosigkeit *f*, Zölibat *n* od *m*; ~**ate** [-ət, -eit] *a bes. rel* ehelos; *s* Ehelose(r *m*) *f.*
cell [sel] Zelle *(in e-m Kloster, e-m Gefängnis, e-r Bienenwabe) a. biol pol*; *poet* Hütte *f*; *poet* Grab *n*; *el* Element *n*; ~ **body** Zellkörper *m*; ~**cleavage, division** Zellspaltung, -teilung *f*; ~ **nucleus** Zellkern *m*; ~ **wall** Zellwand *f*; ~ **wool** Zellwolle *f*; ~-*wool factory* Zellwollfabrik *f.*
cellar ['selə] *s* Keller *m*; *tr* einkellern; im Keller lagern; *to keep a good* ~ e-n guten Tropfen (im Keller) haben; ~**age** ['-ridʒ] Kellergeschoß *n*; Kellermiete *f*; ~**er** ['-rə] Kellermeister *m.*
cello ['tʃelou] *pl -os mus* Cello *n.*
cell|ophane ['seləfein] Zellophan *n*, Glashaut *f*; ~**ular** ['seljulə] *a biol* zellular, aus Zellen gebildet; zellenartig, netzförmig; Zellular-, Zell-; Netz-; ~~ *pathology (med)* Zellularpathologie *f*; ~~ *tissue* Zellengewebe *n*; ~**ulation** [selju'leiʃən] *biol* Zellbildung *f*; ~**uloid** ['seljulɔid] Zelluloid; *fig* Kino *n*; ~**ulose** ['seljulous] Zellulose *f*, Zellstoff *m.*
Celt [selt, kelt] Kelte *m*; ~**ic** ['-ik] keltisch.
cement [si'ment] *s* Zement *(als Baustoff u. Zahnfüllung)*; Kitt *m*; *geol* Bindemittel; *fig* Band *n*; *tr* (aus-) zementieren; (ver)kitten, kleben; *fig* binden, zs.halten; ~**ation** [si:men'teiʃən] Zementieren *n*; Verkittung *f*; ~ **block, clinker, conveyor** Zementblock, -klinker, -förderer *m*; ~ **fibre slab** Zementfaserplatte *f.*
cemetery ['semitri] Friedhof *m.*
cenotaph ['senəta:f] Ehrenmal *n.*
cens|e [sens] *tr* weihräuchern, Weihrauch streuen (*s.o.* jdm); ~**er** ['-ə] *rel* Weihrauchfaß *n*; Räucherpfanne *f*; ~**or** ['-ə] *s* Zensor; bösartige(r) Kritiker *m*; *tr* zensieren; prüfen; ~**orious** [-'sɔ:riəs] tadelsüchtig, sehr kritisch, schwer zufriedenzustellen(d); ~**orship** Amt *n* e-s Zensors; Zensur *f*; ~~ *office* Zensurstelle *f*; ~**urable** ['senʃərəbl] tadelnswert; ~**ure** ['senʃə] *s* Tadel *m* (*of* an); Mißbilligung *f*; *tr* tadeln, rügen; mißbilligen; ~**us** ['sensəs] (Volks-) Zählung *f*, Zensus *m*; ~~ *paper* Hausliste *f.*
cent [sent] *Am* Cent *m* ($^1/_{100}$ *Dollar)*; *I don't care a* ~ das ist mir völlig egal; *per*~Prozent *n*; vom Hundert(%); ~**aur** ['sentɔ:] Kentaur *m a. astr (C~~us)*; ~**aury** ['-ɔ:ri] *bot* Flockenblume *f*; ~**enarian** [senti'nɛəriən] *a (Mensch)* hundertjährig; *s* Hundertjährige(r *m*) *f*; ~**enary** [sen'ti:nəri, 'sentinəri] *a* hundertjährig; *s* Jahrhundert *n*; hundertste(r) Jahrestag *m*, Hundertjahrfeier *f*; ~**ennial** [sen'tenjəl] *a* hundertjährig; Hundertjahrs-; *s* hundertste(r) Jahrestag *m*, Hundertjahrfeier *f*; ~**er** ['-ə] *Am s. centre*; ~**esimal** [-'tesiməl] hundertteilig; Zentesimal-; ~**igrade** ['sentigreid] *(Thermometer)* hundertgradig, Celsius-; ~**igram(me)** ['-græm] Zentigramm *n*; ~**imetre,** *Am* ~**imeter** ['-imi:tə] Zentimeter *n*; ~**ipede** ['-ipi:d] *zoo* Tausendfuß, -füß(l)er *m.*
centr|al ['sentrəl] *a* in der Mitte gelegen, die Mitte bildend, zentral *a. fig*; Mittel-, Zentral-; *fig* führend, leitend, Haupt-; *s Am tele* Zentrale, Vermittlung *f*; *Am* Vermittler(in *f*) *m*; *Am* (Rohr-)Zuckerfabrik *f*; ~~ *adjusting (tech)* Zentralanstellung *f*; *C~~ America* Mittelamerika *n*; *C~~ Asia* Zentralasien *n*; ~~ *corridor, gangway (rail)* Mittelgang *m*; ~~ *depot* Sammelstelle *f*; *C~~ Europe* Mitteleuropa *n*; *C~~ European* mitteleuropäisch; *C~~ European time* mitteleuropäische Zeit (MEZ); ~~ *heating* Zentralheizung *f*; ~~-*heating plant* Heizanlage *f*; ~~ *lubrication* Zentralschmierung *f*; ~~ *nave (arch)* Mittelschiff *n*; ~~ *position* Mittellage, -stellung *f*; ~~ *post office* Hauptpostamt *n*; ~~ *power-plant* Kraftzentrale *f*; ~~ *reserve* Mittel-, Grünstreifen *m (bei d. Autobahn)*; ~~ *station* Hauptbahnhof *m*; *el* Kraftwerk *n*; ~~ *water-works* Wasserwerk *n*, Pumpstation *f*; ~**alization** [sentrəlai'zeiʃən] Zentralisation, Zentralisierung *f*; ~**alize** ['sentrəlaiz] *tr* zentralisieren,

zs.fassen; ~e, *Am* **center** ['sentə] Mitte(lpunkt *m*) *f*, Zentrum *n a. mil*, Brennpunkt *m*; Zentrale, Zentralstelle; Achse, *(Rad)* Nabe; *tech* Spitze *f*; Körner; *arch* Lehrbogen; *fig* Kern. Ausgangspunkt *m*, Innerste(s) *n*; *das* Schwarze *(der Schießscheibe)*; *(~~ forward) sport* Mittelstürmer *m*; *the C~~ (pol)* die Mitte(lparteien *f pl*) *f*; *pl tech* Mittelpunktsabstand *m*; *itr* s-n Mittelpunkt finden *od* haben (*in* in), beruhen (*on* auf); sich drehen (*round* um); sich konzentrieren; *tr* in die Mitte, in Mittelstellung bringen, in der M. anbringen, in den Mittelpunkt stellen; mitten, zentrieren; *opt* fokussieren; *tech* ankörnen; *sport* zur Mitte spielen; sammeln, zs.bringen, konzentrieren (*in* in); *to be ~ed on* sich drehen, kreisen um; *business ~~* Geschäftszentrum *n*; *industrial, economic ~~* Industrie-, Wirtschaftszentrum *n*; *~~ of attraction (phys)* Anziehungspunkt *m*; *~~ of disturbance* Störungszentrum *n*; *~~ of the earth* Erdmittelpunkt *m*; *~~ of gravity, of mass* Schwerpunkt *m*; *~~ of gyration, of motion* Drehpunkt *m*; *~~ of resistance (mil)* Widerstandskern *m*; *~~-bit* Zentrumsbohrer *m*; *~~-board (mar)* Schwert *n*; *~~ distance* Achsabstand, Radstand *m*; *~~ forward* Mittelstürmer *m*; *~~ half (sport)* Mittelläufer *m*; *~~-lathe* Spitzendrehbank *f*; *~~-line* Mittellinie *f*; *(Kompaß)* Richtstrich *m*; *~~-piece* Tafelaufsatz *m*; *~~-rail (rail)* Mittelschiene *f*; *~~ strip* Mittelstreifen *m*; **~ic(al)** ['sentrik(l)] zentral, zentrisch, mittig; **~ing** *arch* Lehrbogen *m*; Zentrierung *f*; **~ifugal** [sen'trifjugəl, 'sentrifjugəl] zentrifugal; Zentrifugal-; *~~ casting* Schleuderguß *m*; *~~ drying machine* Trockenschleuder *f*; *~~ force, tendency* Zentrifugal-, Fliehkraft *f*; *~~ pump* Kreiselpumpe *f*; **~ifuge** ['sentrifju:dʒ] *s* Zentrifuge, Schleuder *f*; *tr tech* schleudern, zentrifugieren; **~ipetal** [sen'tripitl] mittelpunktstrebig, zentripetal; Zentripetal-.

cent|uple ['sentjupl] *a* hundertfach; *s das* Hundertfache; *tr* verhundertfachen; **~ury** ['sentʃuri, -əri] Jahrhundert *n*; *(Kricket)* 100 Läufe; *Am sl* 100 Dollar.

cephal|ic [ke-,se'fælik] Schädel-, Kopf-; *~~ index* Schädelindex *m*; **~ometry** [sefə'ləmitri] Schädelmessung *f*; **~opod** ['sefələpəd] *zoo* Kopffüßler *m*; **~othorax** [sefələ(u)'θəræks] Kopfbruststück *n (der Spinnentiere)*.

ceram|ic [si'ræmik] *a* keramisch, Töpfer-; *s pl mit sing* Keramik, (Kunst-)Töpferei *f*; **~ist** ['serəmist] Keramiker(in *f*), Kunsttöpfer *m*.

Cerberus ['sə:bərəs] Zerberus, Höllenhund *m*; *a sop to ~* e-e Beruhigungspille.

cereal ['siəriəl] *a* Getreide-; *s pl* Getreide *n*, Brotfrucht *f*; *Am* Nährmittel *n pl*; *(breakfast) ~ (bes. Am)* Hafergrütze *f*, Getreideflocken *f pl*.

cereb|ellum [seri'beləm] *scient* Kleinhirn *n*; **~ral** ['seribrəl] *a* Gehirn-, Großhirn-; *~~ apoplexy* Gehirnschlag *m*; **~ration** [-'breiʃən] Gehirntätigkeit *f*; **~rum** ['-brəm] *scient* Großhirn *n*.

cere|cloth ['siəkləθ] Wachstuch *n*; **~ment** ['-ment] *meist pl* Leichentücher *n pl*, Totenhemd *n*.

ceremon|ial [seri'mounjəl] *a* zeremoniell, feierlich, förmlich; *s* Zeremoniell *n*; **~ious** [-jəs] zeremoniös, steif, gemessen, feierlich; **~y** ['seriməni] Zeremonie; Feierlichkeit *f*; *without ~~* zwanglos, ungezwungen; *to stand (up) on ~~* auf Äußerlichkeiten Wert legen; *no ~~ please!* bitte, keine Umstände! *master of ~ies* Zeremonienmeister *m*.

cerise [sə'ri:z] *a* kirschrot; *s* Kirschrot *n*.

cert [sə:t] *sl* todsichere Sache *f*.

cert|ain ['sə:tn] bestimmt; gewiß; sicher, verläßlich, zuverlässig; überzeugt (*of doing*; *to do*; *that* daß), sicher (*of* gen; *that* daß); *a ~~* ein(e) gewisse(r, s); *for ~~* bestimmt, (ganz) sicher *adv*; *to a ~~ extent* bis zu e-m gewissen Grade; *under ~~ circumstances* unter bestimmten Bedingungen; *to make ~~* sich vergewissern; **~ainly** ['-li] *adv* sicher(lich), gewiß, wirklich, bestimmt, ja, aber; *I ~~ won't do it* ich tue es gerade nicht; **~ainty** ['-ti] Gewißheit, Sicherheit, Bestimmtheit; unbestrittene Tatsache *f*; *to, for a ~~* ohne jeden Zweifel; **~ifiable** ['ifaiəbl] feststellbar; *fam* geisteskrank; **~ificate** *s* [sə'tifikit] Zeugnis *n*, Bescheinigung *f*, Attest *n*; Urkunde *f*; *tr* [-keit] bescheinigen, beurkunden; e-e Bescheinigung, e-e Urkunde ausstellen (*s.o.* jdm); *~~ of deposit* Hinterlegungsschein *m*; *~~ of incorporation (com)* Gründungsurkunde *f*; *~~ of origin* Ursprungszeugnis *n*; *~~d (a)* staatlich genehmigt, anerkannt; **~ification** [sə:tifi'keiʃən] Bescheinigung, Beglaubigung, Beurkundung *f*; **~ifier** ['sə:tifaiə] Aussteller *m* e-r Urkunde *od* Bescheinigung; **~ify** ['-ifai] *tr* bezeugen; beglaubigen; bestätigen; bescheinigen, beurkunden; bekräftigen, versichern (*s.o.* jdm); benachrichtigen; amtlich zulassen; *jur* wegen Geisteskrankheit entmündigen; *this is to ~~* hiermit wird bescheinigt; *~ified copy* beglaubigte Abschrift *f*; *~ified milk* den (behördlichen) Vorschriften entsprechende Milch *f*; *~ified public accountant (Am)* Wirtschaftsprüfer *m*; **~itude** ['-tju:d] Gewißheit; feste Überzeugung *f*.

ceru|lean [si'ru:liən] *meist poet* himmel-, tiefblau; **~men** [-men] Ohrenschmalz *n*; **~se** ['siəru:s, si'ru:s] Bleiweiß *n*.

cerv|ical ['sə:vikəl] *a scient* Hals-, Nacken-; **~ine** ['-ain] *a scient* Hirsch-.

cess|ation [se'seiʃən] Aufhören, Anhalten *n*, Stillstand *m*; Unterbrechung, Pause *f*; **~ion** ['seʃən] Aufgabe *f*, Verzicht *m* (*of* auf); Überlassung, Abtretung, Zession (*to* an); **~pit** ['sespit], **~pool** ['-pu:l] Senkgrube *f*; *fig* (Sünden-)Pfuhl *m*.

cetace|an [si'teiʃiən] *scient a* Wal-; *s* Wal, Delphin *m*; **~ous** [-iəs] *a* Wal-.

Ceylon [si'lən] Ceylon *n*.

*

chaf|e [tʃeif] *tr* (warm)reiben; wundreiben, -scheuern; reizen, ärgern, in Erregung, aufbringen; *itr* sich reiben (*on, against* an); sich wundscheuern; sich auf-, erregen, sich ärgern, aufgeregt, -gebracht sein, toben; *s* Reibung; Schürfwunde, wundgeriebene, -gescheuerte Stelle *f*, Wolf *m*; Gereiztheit *f*, Ärger *m*, Wut *f*; *to ~~ at the bit* die Geduld verlieren; **~er** ['-ə] (Mai-)Käfer; *(rose-~~)* Rosenkäfer *m*; **~ing dish** Wärmplatte *f*.

chaff [tʃa:f] *s agr* Spreu *f*, Kaff *n*; Häcksel *m* od *n*; Abfall, Plunder *m*; *fam* Neckerei *f*, (harmloser) Spaß *m*, Späßchen *n*; *(~ anti-radar)* Düppel (-streifen) *m pl*; *tr fam* necken; **~-cutter** Häckselmaschine *f*; **~er** ['tʃæfə] *itr* handeln, feilschen (*about, for* um); *s* Handeln, Feilschen *n*; **~ grains** *pl* Spelzen *f pl*; **~inch** ['tʃæfin(t)ʃ] Buchfink *m*; **~y** ['-i] voller Spreu; *fig* wertlos; spaßig.

chagrin ['ʃægrin] *s* Ärger, Kummer *m*; *tr* ärgern, Kummer machen (*s.o.* jdm); *to be, to feel ~ed* sich ärgern (*at, by* über).

chain [tʃein] *s* Kette; Schmuck-, Hals-, Uhrkette; *fig* (Gedanken-)Kette, Folge, Reihe *f*; *meist pl* Ketten, Fesseln *f pl a. fig*; Meßkette *f (66 u. 100 ft)*; *tr* (an)ketten, fesseln *a. fig*; *to ~ up* anketten, *(Hund)* an die Kette legen; *in ~s* in Ketten, in Fesseln, unfrei; *~ of mountains* Bergkette *f*; **~ armour, mail** *hist* Panzerhemd *n*; **~ bridge** Kettenbrücke *f*; **~-drive** Kettenantrieb *m*; **~ insulator** Kettenisolator *m*; **~-gang** Kettensträflinge *m pl*; **~less** ['-lis] kettenlos; **~-letter** Kettenbrief *m*; **~ reaction** *chem phys* Kettenreaktion *f*; **~-smoker** Kettenraucher *m*; **~-stitch** *(Näherei)* Kettenstich *m*; **~-store** *Am* Kettenladen *m*, Filiale *f*, Filialgeschäft *n*.

chair [tʃɛə] *s* Stuhl; *fig* Amtssitz; Lehrstuhl *m*; Bürgermeisteramt *n*; Vorsitz(ender) *m (bei e-r Versammlung, Veranstaltung)*, *parl* Präsidium *n*; *Am* Zeugenstand; *Am (electric ~)* elektrische(r) Stuhl *m*; *tr* bestuhlen; auf e-n Stuhl setzen; zum Vorsitzenden wählen; *(in ein Amt)* einsetzen; *Br* im Triumph umhertragen; *itr fam* den Vorsitz führen; *with Mr. X. in the ~* unter dem Vorsitz von Herrn X.; *to address, to appeal to the ~* sich an den Vorsitzenden wenden; *to leave the ~* die Sitzung beenden, die Versammlung schließen; *to leave, to vacate the ~* das Amt des Vorsitzenden abgeben; *to take a ~* sich setzen, Platz nehmen; *to take the ~* den Vorsitz übernehmen, die Sitzung, die Verhandlungen eröffnen; *~! (parl)* zur Ordnung! **~ lift** Sesselbahn *f*; **~man, ~woman** Vorsitzende(r *m*) *f*; *to act as ~~* den Vorsitz führen; *~~ of the board (of directors)* Aufsichtsratvorsitzende(r) *m*; **~manship** Amt *n* des Vorsitzenden; **~o'plane** Kettenkarussell *n*.

chaise longue [ʃeiz'lɔ:ŋ] Chaiselongue *f* od *n*.

chalc|edony [kæl'sedəni] *min* Chalzedon *m*; **~ographer** [-'kɔgrəfə] Kupferstecher *m*; **~ography** [-'kɔgrəfi] (Kunst *f* des) Kupferstich(s) *m*; **~opyrite** [kælkə'pairait] Kupferkies *m*.

chal|et ['ʃælei] Sennhütte *f*; Schweizerhaus *n*; Villa *f* im Schweizer Stil; Bedürfnisanstalt *f*; **~ice** ['tʃælis] (Abendmahls-)Kelch; (Blumen-, Blüten-) Kelch *m*.

chalk [tʃɔ:k] *s* Kreide *f*; Schuldposten; *(Spiel)* Punkt; *Am* Favorit *m (Pferd)*; *tr* mit Kreide zeichnen, markieren, schreiben; *agr* mit Kalk düngen; *(to ~ up)* ankreiden, anschreiben, notieren; *to ~ out* skizzieren, entwerfen; *com* auszeichnen; *to ~ up (Am fam)* im Preis erhöhen, heraufsetzen; *as like as ~ and cheese* grundverschieden, sehr ungleich; *by a long ~, by long ~s* bei weitem; *to walk a ~ line (Am fam)* sich vorschriftsmäßig benehmen; linientreu sein; **~-bed** *geol* Kreideschicht *f*; **~-drawing** Kreidezeichnung *f*; **~-pit, -quarry** Kreidegrube *f*, -bruch *m*; **~-stone** *med* Gichtknoten *m*; **~ talk** *Am* Vortrag *m* mit Tafelanschrieb; **~y** ['-i] (stark) kreidehaltig, -artig; *fig* kreidig, kreideweiß, -bleich; mit Gichtknoten behaftet.

challenge ['tʃælindʒ] *s* Aufforderung *f*; Anruf *m (durch e-n Posten)*; *(Jagd)* Anschlagen *n (der Hunde)*; Herausforderung; *(Duell)* Forderung *f*; Anzweifeln, Infragestellen *n*; Ablehnung *f (of a juror* e-s Geschworenen); Einwand *m* gegen e-e Wahlstimme; Anfechtung *f* des Stimmrechts e-s Wählers; *tr* auffordern; *(Posten)* anrufen; herausfordern, hervorrufen, führen zu; fordern, beanspruchen, verlangen; in Frage stellen, streitig machen, bezweifeln, bestreiten, anfechten, Einwendungen machen gegen, e-n Einwand erheben gegen; *jur* (als befangen) ablehnen; *(Duell)* fordern; *I ~ anybody else to do that* das soll mir jemand nachmachen! **~able** ['-əbl] bestreitbar; **~-cup** *sport* Wanderpokal *m*; **~r** ['-ə] Herausforderer; *jur* Ablehnende(r) *m*.

chalybeate [kə'libiit] *(Quelle, Mineralwasser)* eisenhaltig.

chamber ['tʃeimbə] *s obs* Kammer *f*, (Schlaf-)Zimmer *n*, Raum *m*; *pol* Kammer, gesetzgebende Körperschaft; (Handels-)Kammer *f*; *pl jur* Richterzimmer *n*; *anat bot tech (bes. Schußwaffe)* Kammer; *mil* Sprengkammer *f*; *pl Br* möblierte Zimmer *n pl*, Wohnung *f*; *pl jur* Rechtsanwaltskanzlei *f*; *tr (Patrone)* in den Lauf einführen; *to sit in ~s* unter Ausschluß der Öffentlichkeit verhandeln; *C~ of Agriculture, of Commerce* Landwirtschafts-, Handelskammer *f*; **~ concert** Kammerkonzert *n*; **~ counsel** (beratender) Rechtsanwalt *m*; **~lain** ['-lin] Kämmerer; Schatzmeister; Kammerherr *m*; **~maid** Zimmermädchen *n (im Hotel)*; **~ music** Kammermusik *f*; **~ orchestra** Kammerorchester *n*; **~-pot** Nachttopf *m*.

chameleon [kə'mi:ljən] *zoo* Chamäleon *n*; *fig* wetterwendische(r) Mensch *m*.

chamfer ['tʃæmfə] *s* Schrägkante, Fase, Auskehlung *f*; *tr* abschrägen, -fasen, -kanten; ein-, auskehlen.

chamois ['ʃæmwa:] *pl ~* ['-z] Gemse *f*; ['ʃæmi] *(~-leather)* Sämisch-, Fensterleder *n*.

champ [tʃæmp] *tr itr* geräuschvoll kauen; *itr* schmatzen; beißen (*at* auf); sich ungeduldig gebärden; *s* Schmatzen *n*; *Am sl* Sportskanone *f*; **~agne** [ʃæm'pein] Champagner *m*; **~aign** ['tʃæmpein] *s* flache(s), offene(s) Gelände; flache(s) Land *n*, Ebene *f*; freie(s) Feld *n*; *a (Land)* offen; **~ion** ['tʃæmpjən] *s* (Vor-)Kämpfer, Verfechter; *sport* Meister, Sieger *m*; *a* Meister-; Preis-; best, erst; *tr* kämpfen, sich einsetzen für, verfechten; verteidigen, (be)schützen; **~ionship** *(sport)* Meisterschaft *f*.

chance [tʃa:ns] *s* Zufall *m*; Möglichkeit, Aussicht, Chance; Gelegenheit *f*; Glück(sfall *m*); *Am* Wagnis, Risiko; *Am* Los *n*; *Am fam* Anzahl *f (of)*; *a* zufällig; *itr* zufällig geschehen; *tr to ~ it* es riskieren, wagen; es darauf ankommen lassen; *to ~ (up)on* stoßen auf, zufällig finden; *by ~* zufällig, durch Zufall; *on the ~ of* im Falle *gen*; in der Hoffnung auf, zu; *to give a ~ to s.o.* jdm e-e Chance geben; *to give a fair ~ to s.o.* jdm jede Möglichkeit geben; *to stand a (good, fair) ~* Aussichten, Chancen haben; *to take o.'s, a ~* die Gelegenheit wahrnehmen; sein Glück versuchen; es riskieren; *to ~ o.'s arm (fam)* es drauf ankommen lassen; *the ~s are against it* da ist nichts zu machen; *I ~d to be* zufällig war ich; *not a ~!* keine Spur! *~ of winning* Gewinnaussichten, -chancen *f pl*; **~ acquaintance** Zufallsbekanntschaft *f*; **~ bargain** Gelegenheitskauf *m*; **~-comer** *fam* Hereinschneiende(r) *m*; **~ customers** *pl* Laufkundschaft *f*; **~ event** zufällige(s) Ereignis *n*; **~ hit** Zufallstreffer *m*.

chancel ['tʃa:nsəl] *arch rel* Chor *m*.

chancell|ery, ~ory ['tʃa:nsələri] Kanzlerschaft *f*, -amt *n*; Kanzlei *f (e-s Konsulats, e-r Botschaft)*; **~or** ['-ə] Kanzler; *(Universität)* Rektor; *Am* Richter; Oberste(r) Richter *m (e-s Staates)*; *Am* erste(r) Sekretär *m* e-r Botschaft *od* Gesandtschaft; *Lord (High) C~, C~ of England* Oberste(r) Richter *m (in England)*; *vice-~ (Universität)* Prorektor *m*; *C~ of the Exchequer* Schatzkanzler *m*; **~~ship** ['-ʃip] Amt *n*, Würde *f* e-s Kanzlers.

chancery ['tʃa:nsəri] Kanzleigericht *n*; Gericht *n* für Einzelfälle *(court of equity)*; (Staats-)Archiv *n*; Kanzlei *f*; *(Ringkampf)* Schwitzkasten *m*; *to be in ~ (fig)* sich in e-r mißlichen Lage befinden; **~ securities** *pl* mündelsichere Wertpapiere *n pl*.

chancre ['ʃæŋkə] *med* Schanker *m*; *hard, soft ~* harte(r), weiche(r) S.

chancy ['tʃa:nsi] *fam* kipp(e)lig, riskant.

chand|elier [ʃændi'liə] Kronleuchter *m*; **~ler** ['tʃa:ndlə] Lichtzieher; (Klein-)Händler; *oft pej* Krämer, Höker *m*.

change [tʃeindʒ] **1.** *s* (Ab-, Um-, Ver-)Änderung; (Ab-, Um-, Ver-)Wandlung *f*; Wandel, Wechsel, Umschwung, Umschlag *m*; Abwechs(e)lung; Schwankung, Variation *f*; Unterschied *m*; frische Wäsche, Kleidung *f*; (Aus-, Um-)Tausch *m*; Kleingeld, Wechselgeld *n*, -kurs *m*; *rail* Umsteigen *n*; *astr* Mondwechsel *m*; *C~* Börse *f*; **2.** *tr* (ab-, um-, ver)ändern; um-, verwandeln (*into* in); (aus-, um)tauschen; *(Geld)* (um)wechseln; *tech radio* umschalten; **3.** *itr* sich (ver)ändern, anders werden, sich (ver)wandeln; wechseln, umschlagen; variieren, schwanken; *to ~ (trains, buses)* umsteigen; sich umziehen; *to ~ over* die Stellung wechseln; *to ~ up, down (mot)* e-n höheren, niederen Gang einschalten; **4.** *for a ~* zur Abwechs(e)lung; *on C~* auf der Börse; *to bring about a ~* Wandel schaffen; *to get sixpence ~* e-n halben Schilling herausbekommen; *to get no ~ out of s.o.* mit jdm nicht fertig werden, gegen jdn nicht ankommen; *to give ~ for* herausgeben auf; *to make a ~* e-e Veränderung vornehmen; *to need a ~* Luftveränderung brauchen; *to ring the ~s (fig)* dasselbe immer wieder in anderer Form tun *od* sagen; *to take o.'s ~ (the ~ out of)* sich schadlos halten (an); *to ~ o.'s address* umziehen; *to ~ for the better* sich verbessern; *to ~ (o.'s clothes)* sich umziehen; *into a new suit* e-n neuen Anzug anziehen; *to ~ front* e-n Frontwechsel vornehmen; *to ~ gear(s) (mot)* umschalten; *to ~ hands* den Besitzer wechseln; in andere Hände übergehen; *to ~ o.'s mind* sich e-s anderen besinnen; s-e Meinung ändern; *to ~ o.'s note, tune, tone* klein beigeben, bescheidener werden; e-n anderen Ton anschlagen; *to ~ places* den Platz wechseln (*with* mit); *to ~ o.'s position* sich (beruflich) verändern; *to ~ for the worse* sich verschlechtern; *many ~s have taken place* es hat sich viel verändert; *I've ~d my mind* ich hab's mir anders überlegt; *can you give me ~ (for a pound note)* können Sie (e-e Pfundnote) wechseln? *all ~! (rail)* alles aussteigen! **5.** *~ for the better* Besserung *f*; *~ of clothes* ein Anzug, ein Kleid zum Wechseln; *~ of direction* Richtungsänderung *f*; *~ of life* Wechseljahre *n pl*; *~ of position (mil)* Stellungswechsel *m*; *~ of prices* Preisschwankung *f*; *~ of speed (mot)* Gangwechsel *m*; *~ of state* Zustandsänderung *f*; *~ in the, of weather* Wetterwechsel, -umschlag *m*; **~ability, ~ableness** [tʃeindʒə'biliti, '-əblnis] Unregelmäßigkeit, Unbeständigkeit, Veränderlichkeit *f*; **~able** ['-əbl] unregelmäßig; unbeständig; veränderlich, wandelbar; wechselnd, schillernd; **~ful** ['-ful] *meist poet* sich (ewig) wandelnd, (ständig) wechselnd, unbeständig; **~less** ['-lis] unveränderlich, unwandelbar; **~ling** ['-liŋ] Wechselbalg *m*; **~-over** Umstellung, -schaltung *f*; Übergang, Wechsel; Schichtwechsel *m*; *~~ panel* Schalttafel *f*; *~~ sheet (typ)* Deckblatt *n*; *~~ switch* Umschalter *m*; **~r** ['-e] Wechsler *a. tech*; *el* Umsetzer *m*.

channel ['tʃænl] *s mar* Kanal *m*; Fluß-, Kanalbett *n*; Fahrrinne *f*, -wasser *n*; Rinne, Gosse *f*, Graben *m*; Gerinne *n*, offene Wasserleitung; *arch* Hohlkehle *f*; *el* Übertragungsweg *m*; *radio* Frequenzband *n*, Kanal *m*; *tech* U-Profil *n*; *fig* Weg *m*, Verbindung, Vermitt(e)lung, Übertragung *f*; *the (English) C~* der (Ärmel-)Kanal; *tr (Rinne)* graben; *(Flußbett)* vertiefen; *arch* auskehlen, kannelieren, riffeln; hinleiten (*to* zu); *through proper, official ~s* auf dem Dienst-, Instanzenweg; *~ of communication* Nachrichtenverbindung *f*; Verbindungsweg; Dienstweg *m*; *~ of distribution* Absatzweg *m*; **~ (bar), ~ (iron)** U-Eisen; **~ marks** *pl mar* Fahrwasserzeichen *n*; **~ section** U-Profil *n*, U-Querschnitt *m*; **~ selector** *radio* Kanalwähler *m*; **~ switch** *radio* Kanalschalter *m*.

chant [tʃa:nt] *s* Gesang *m*; Psalmodie *f*; Rezitativ *n*; Singsang *m*; *tr itr* singen; psalmodieren; *pej* (herunter-, her-)leiern; **~erelle** [tʃæntə'rel] Pfifferling, Eierschwamm *m*; **~icleer** [tʃænti'kliə] *poet* (Haus-)Hahn *m*; **~ress** ['-rəs] *poet* Sängerin *f*; **~ry** ['-ri] *rel* Stiftung *f* zum Lesen von Totenmessen; zum Lesen von Totenmessen gestiftete Kapelle *f*; **~y** ['tʃa:nti] Matrosenlied *n*.

chao|s ['keiɔs] Chaos, völlige(s) Durcheinander *n*, Verwirrung *f*, Drunter u. Drüber *n*, Wirrwarr *m*; **~tic** [kei'ɔtik] chaotisch, (völlig) durchea.gebracht, wirr, verworren.

chap [tʃæp] **1.** *s* Riß, Sprung *m*; *tr* rissig machen; *itr* rissig werden, Risse, Sprünge bekommen; **2.** (*a.* **chop**) *meist pl* Kinnbacken *m (bes. d. Tiere)*; *(Küche)* (Schweine-)Schnauze *f*; *to lick o.'s ~s* sich den Mund ablecken; **~-fallen** *(a)* mit langem Gesicht, trübselig, niedergeschlagen, hoffnungslos; **3.** *fam* Kerl, Bursche, Junge *m*; **~-book** *hist lit* Volksbuch *n*; Traktat *m*; **~el** ['tʃæpəl] *rel* Kapelle *f*; (nichthochkirchliches) Gotteshaus *n (in Großbritannien)*; **~eron(e)** ['ʃæpəroun] *s* Anstandsdame *f*; *tr* (als Anstandsdame) begleiten; **~iter** ['tʃæpitə] *arch* Kapitell *n*; **~lain** ['tʃæplin] (Haus-)Kaplan; Feldkaplan, -geistliche(r) *m*; **~let** ['tʃæplit] Kranz *(als Kopfschmuck)*; *rel* Rosenkranz *m*; *tech* Kernstütze *f*; *arch* Perlstab *m*; **~man** Hausierer *m*; **~py** ['tʃæpi] rissig, voller Sprünge; **~s** [tʃæps] *pl Am* Cowboylederhose *f*.

chapter ['tʃæptə] *s* Kapitel *(Teil e-s Buches, des Lebens)*; *fig* Stück *(e-r Erzählung)*, (ausgewähltes) Kapitel, Thema; *(cathedral ~) rel* Domkapitel *n*; *Am* Ortsgruppe *f (e-r Organisation, Gesellschaft, Vereinigung)*; *tr* in Kapitel einteilen; tadeln, rügen; *to the end of the* ~ bis ans Ende; *to give* ~ *and verse for s.th.* etw genau belegen, nachweisen; ~ *of accidents* Reihe *f* unglücklicher Zufälle; ~ *and verse* Angabe *f* der Bibelstelle; Autorität *f*; *fam* alle Einzelheiten, Regeln, Bestimmungen; **~-house** Domstift; *Am* Klubhaus *n*.

char [tʃɑ:] **1.** *zoo* See-, *Am* Bachsaibling *m*; **2.** *tr* verkohlen; (an-)sengen; in Rauch schwärzen; *s* Verkohlte(s) *n*; Asche; *(~ coal)* Holzkohle *f*; **3.** *sl* Tee *m*; **4.** *a.* **chare** *itr* (stundenweise) Hausarbeit verrichten; reinemachen, putzen *itr*; *s* (stundenweise verrichtete) Hausarbeit; *(~woman, (sl) ~lady)* Reinemache-, Scheuer-, Putz-, Stundenfrau *f*.

char-à-banc ['ʃærəbæŋ] Kremser; Ausflugsautobus *m*.

character ['kæriktə] Kennzeichen *n*; Beschaffenheit, Anlage, Natur, Art *f*, Wesen(sart *f*) *n*; Charakter *m*; *psychol* Verhaltensweise; Persönlichkeit, Person *f*; *fam* Sonderling *m*, Unikum *n*; *lit* Person, Figur; *theat* (handelnde) Person, Rolle *f*; Stand *m*; Zeugnis *n*, Empfehlung *f (e-s Arbeitgebers)*; Name, Ruf (*of, for* gen), gute(r) Ruf *m*; Schriftzeichen *n*, Buchstabe *m*; Ziffer *f*; *by* ~ dem Rufe nach; *in the* ~ *of* in der Eigenschaft als; *in (out of)* ~ s-r Rolle (nicht) entsprechend; s-m Wesen (nicht) gemäß; ~ **actor** *theat* Charakterdarsteller *m*; **~istic** [-'ristik] *a* charakteristisch, be-, kennzeichnend, typisch (*of* für); *tech* Eigen-; *s* Charakteristikum, Kennzeichen, Merkmal *n*, Besonderheit; *math* Vorzahl *f*, Numerus *m*; Kennlinie *f*, -wert *m*; *pl* Leistungsmerkmale *n pl*, Daten *pl*; **~ization** [-rai'zeiʃən] Charakterisierung, Beschreibung, Schilderung *f*; **~ize** ['-aiz] *tr* charakterisieren; beschreiben (als), schildern; kennzeichnen; **~less** ['-lis] charakterlos.

charade [ʃə'rɑ:d, *Am* -'reid] Scharade *f*.

charcoal ['tʃɑ:koul] Holzkohle *f*; *(~ crayon)* Kohlestift *m*, Zeichenkohle; *(~ drawing)* Kohlezeichnung *f*; ~ **burner** Köhler *m*; ~ **filter** Kohlenfilter *m*; ~ **pile** Kohlenmeiler *m*.

charg|e [tʃɑ:dʒ] **1.** *s* (Trag-)Last; Ladung *(a. e-r Feuerwaffe)*; *tech* Beschickung, Füllung *f*, Einsatz *m*; *(oft pl)* Lasten *f pl*, Kosten *pl*, Preis *m*; *(Konto)* Belastung; Lastschrift; Gebühr, Taxe *f*; Amt *n*, Pflicht, Verpflichtung, Obliegenheit, Aufgabe, Verantwortung *f*; Auftrag, Befehl *m*; (*a.* Polizei-)Aufsicht *f*, Gewahrsam *m*; Überwachung, Obhut, Fürsorge; anvertraute Person *od* Sache *f*; Schützling *m*, Mündel *n*; *rel* Schafe *n pl*, Herde *f*; anvertraute(s) Gut *n*; Ermahnung, Anweisung *f*; Vorwurf *m*, Beschuldigung, Anklage(punkt *m*); *jur* Rechtsbelehrung *f* (der Geschworenen); *mil* Angriff(ssignal *n*), Sturm *m*; *(Geschoß)* Füllung *f*; Wappenbild *n*; *pl* Unkosten, Spesen *pl*; *Am sl* Dosis *f* Marihuana; *Am sl* plötzliche Erregung *f*; **2.** *tr* (be)laden; *(Schußwaffe, el)* laden; *(Batterie)* aufladen; *chem (Flüssigkeit, Gas)* sättigen; *tech* beschicken, einsetzen; *com* fordern, verlangen, rechnen für *(e-e Ware, Arbeit)*; berechnen (*too much* zu viel); *(to ~~ upon, against s.o.)* jdm aufrechnen; *(Abnehmer)* belasten mit, zu Lasten schreiben (*s.o.* jdm); *(to ~~ off)* abschreiben, abbuchen; anvertrauen, zur Pflicht machen (*s.o. with s.th.* jdm etw); anweisen, beauftragen, befehlen (*s.o.* jdm); ermahnen; zur Last legen, vorwerfen (*s.o. with, s.th. on s.o.* jdm etw), beschuldigen, anklagen; *Am* die Anklage vorbringen, behaupten (*that* daß); angreifen (*s.o., at s.o.* jdn); *sport* (an)rempeln; *Am (to ~~ off)* zuschreiben; **3.** *itr* berechnen (*for s.th.* etw); sich stürzen (*into* in); *(Hund)* sich kuschen; angreifen (*at s.o.* jdn); **4.** *at s.o.'s ~~* zu jds Lasten, auf jds Kosten; *in ~~* aufsichtführend; verantwortlich; *Br* in Gewahrsam; *on a ~~ of* unter der Anklage *gen*; *under s.o.'s ~~* unter jds Aufsicht; *without ~~* unentgeltlich *adv*; *to ~~ to s.o.'s account* auf jds Rechnung setzen; *to ~~ s.o. up for s.th.* jdm etw draufschlagen; *to be in ~~ of s.th.* etw unter s-r Aufsicht, die Aufsicht über, die Verantwortung für etw haben; etw leiten; *to bring a ~~ against s.o.* jdn anklagen; *to have ~~ of s.th.* für etw verantwortlich sein; etw leiten; *to lay s.th. to s.o.'s ~~* etw jdm zur Last legen; *to make a ~~ for s.th.* etw in Rechnung stellen; *to take ~~ of s.th.* etw in s-e Obhut nehmen; für etw die Verantwortung, die Leitung übernehmen; *there's no* ~ es kostet nichts; Eintritt frei; **5.** *additional ~~* Gebührenzuschlag, Aufschlag *m*; *bishop's ~~ (rel)* Hirtenbrief *m*; *free of ~~* gebührenfrei; kostenfrei, -los; gratis; *overhead ~~s (pl)* allgemeine Unkosten *pl*; *rate of ~~s* Gebührensatz *m*; *statement of ~~s* Kostenrechnung *f*; *travelling ~~s (pl)* Reisekosten *pl*; *~~ account (Am)* Lastenkonto *n*; *~~ for delivery* Zustellgebühr *f*; *~~ sales (pl)* Kreditverkäufe *m pl*; *~~ sheet* polizeiliche Einvernahmliste *f*; **~eable** ['-əbl] zu berechnen(d), zu Lasten (*to* von); *fig* zur Last zu schreiben(d), zuzuschreiben(d); (mit e-r Lastschrift, e-r Gebühr) zu belasten(d); allgemein verantwortlich; e-m Vorwurf, e-r Anklage, e-m Angriff ausgesetzt; *to be ~~* zu Lasten gehen (*to s.o.* gen); **~é d'affaires** ['ʃɑ:ʒeidæ'fɛə] *pol* Geschäftsträger; **~ed** [-d] *a jur* angeklagt (*with* wegen); *el* stromführend; **~er** ['-ə] *mil* Ladestreifen *m*; Offizierspferd *n*; Platte, Schale, flache Schüssel *f*; *tech* Gichtmann *m*; *el* Ladeaggregat *n*; **~ing** ['-iŋ] (Auf-)Laden *n*; *com* Berechnung; Besteuerung; *el* Ladung; *tech* Beschickung, Begichtung *f*; *~~ voltage (el)* Ladespannung *f*.

chariness ['tʃɛ(ə)rinis] Vorsicht, Besorgtheit, Behutsamkeit, Scheu, Zurückhaltung *f*.

chariot ['tʃæriət] *hist (zweirädriger)* (Streit-, Renn-, Triumph-)Wagen *m a. poet*; *(im 18. Jh.) (vierrädrige) Art* Kutsche *f*; *sun's ~ (hist)* Sonnenwagen *m*; **~eer** [-'tiə] *s* Wagenlenker *m*.

charit|able ['tʃæritəbl] wohl-, mildtätig; mild(herzig), gütig; wohlmeinend, nachsichtig, nachsichtsvoll; **~ableness** ['-nis] Wohltätigkeit; Milde, Güte; Nachsicht(igkeit) *f*; **~y** ['-i] (christliche) Nächstenliebe; Güte; Nachsichtigkeit; Wohl-, Mildtätigkeit *f*; Almosen *n pl*; Almosengeben *n*; wohltätige Zwecke *m pl*; Wohlfahrtseinrichtung *f*; *~~ begins at home* jeder ist sich selbst der Nächste; *Brother, Sister of C~* Barmherzige(r) Bruder *m*, Schwester *f*.

charivari ['ʃɑ:ri'vɑ:ri] Lärm *m*, Getöse *n*.

charlatan ['ʃɑ:lətən] Quacksalber; *allg* Scharlatan, Marktschreier *m*; **~ry** ['-ri] Quacksalberei *f*.

Charl|emagne, ~emain ['ʃɑ:lə'main] Karl *m* der Große; **~es** ['tʃɑ:lz] Karl *m*; *~~'s Wain (astr)* der Große Bär; **~ey** ['-i] Karlchen *n*; *~~ horse (Am fam)* Muskelkater *m*; **c~otte** ['ʃɑ:lət] Apfelpudding *m* mit Brot; *~~ russe* Eierkrem *f* od *m* in Biskuitkuchen.

charm [tʃɑ:m] *s* Zauber(spruch *m*, -wort *n*) *m*; Amulett *n*, Glücksbringer; Anhänger *m*; Anmut *f*, Reiz, Zauber, Scharm *m*; *pl* Reize *m pl*, bezaubernde(s) Wesen *n*; *tr* verzaubern; gefangennehmen, bezaubern, entzücken; *itr* reizend sein; *to ~ away* wegzaubern; *to ~ s.th. out of s.o.* jdm etw entlocken; *under a ~* wie verzaubert; **~ed** [-d] *a* bezaubert, entzückt, berauscht (*with* von); **~er** ['-ə] Zauberer *m*; reizende(s) Geschöpf *n*, bezaubernde Frau *f*; *snake ~~* Schlangenbeschwörer *m*; **~euse** ['ʃɑ:mə:z] *(Textil)* Charmeuse *f*; **~ing** ['-iŋ] berückend, betörend; bezaubernd, entzückend, reizend, reizvoll, charmant; *Prince C~~* Märchenprinz *m*.

charnel ['tʃɑ:nl]: **~-house** Leichen-, Beinhaus *n*.

chart [tʃɑ:t] *s mar* Seekarte; (Übersichts-)Karte *f*; Schaubild *n*, graphische Darstellung *f*, Diagramm *n*; Tabelle, tabellarische Übersicht *f*; Registrierstreifen *m*; *tr* in e-r Karte, graphisch *od* tabellarisch darstellen; ~ **clip** Kartenhalter *m*; ~ **diagram** Nomogramm *n*; ~ **house** *mar* Kartenhaus *n*; **~room** Kartenraum *m*; *mil* Feuerleitstelle *f*.

charter ['tʃɑ:tə] *s* Charta *f*; Grundgesetz *n*, Verfassungsurkunde; Gründungsurkunde; (Urkunde über e-e) Landverleihung, -übertragung, Rechtsbewilligung *f*; Statut; bewilligte(s) Recht, Vorrecht, Privileg *n*; *mar aero* Charter(vertrag) *m*; *tr* ein Grundgesetz geben, ein (Vor-)Recht verleihen (*s.o.* jdm); *(Schiff, Flugzeug)* chartern; **~ed** ['-d] *a* privilegiert, bevorrechtet; konzessioniert; *~~ accountant* (beeidigter) Buch-, Wirtschaftsprüfer *m*; **~er** ['-rə] Charterer, Befrachter *m*; ~ **member** Gründungsmitglied *n*; **~-party** *mar aero* Chartepartie *f*, Chartervertrag *m*.

chary ['tʃɛəri] scheu (*of* gegenüber); vorsichtig, besorgt, behutsam; zurückhaltend (*of* gegenüber), sparsam (*of* mit); *to be ~ of s.th.* mit etw geizen.

*

chase [tʃeis] **1.** *s* Verfolgung; Jagd *f*; *Br* Gehege, Jagdrevier *n*; *Br* Jagdschein *m*; gehetzte(s) Wild; verfolgte(s) Schiff *n*; *fig Am* Hetze *f*; *tr* verfolgen; (nach)jagen, (herum)hetzen; *(to ~ away)* weg-, verjagen, vertreiben; *Am sl (Speisen)* auftragen; *itr* herrennen (*after s.o.* hinter jdm), nachlaufen (*after s.o.* jdm); herumrennen; *to ~ o.s. (Am sl)* abhauen, weggehen; *to give ~* die Verfolgung aufnehmen (*to* gen); *wild-goose ~ (fig)* vergebliche Liebesmüh *f*; **2.** *tr* treiben, punzen, ziselieren; *s* Rinne, Furche *f*; *typ* Formrahmen *m*; *(Kanone)* Feld *n*; **~r** ['-ə] **1.** Jäger *a. aero*; Verfolger; *(bow-, stern-~~) mar mil* Bug-, Heckgeschütz; Verfolgerschiff *n*; U-Boot-Jäger; *fam* Schnaps *m* auf Kaffee; *fam* Schluck *m* Wasser auf scharfen Schnaps; Glas *n* Wasser; *sl* Schürzenjäger; *Am sl* Antreiber; *Am fam* Rausschmeißer *m (Musikstück, bes. Marsch nach Programmschluß)*; **2.** Ziselierer, Strehler *m*; *~~ tool* Grabstichel *m*.

chasm ['kæzm] (Erd-)Spalt *m*, Schlucht *f*, Abgrund *m*; *fig* Lücke, Unterbrechung; *fig* Kluft *f*.

chassis ['ʃæsi] *pl* ~ [-iz] *mot* Fahrgestell *n*; *radio* Rahmen *m (des Empfängers)* ~ **clearance** *mot* Bodenfreiheit *f*; ~ **(serial) number** Fahrgestellnummer *f*; ~ **washing** *mot* Unterwäsche *f*.

chast|e [tʃeist] keusch, rein; *fig* zuchtvoll, zurückhaltend, streng, schmucklos, einfach; ~**en** ['tʃeisn] *tr* züchtigen *fig*; mäßigen; in Zucht nehmen, reinigen, vereinfachen; ~**ise** [tʃæs'taiz] *tr (körperlich)* züchtigen, streng strafen; ~**isement** ['tʃæstizmənt] Züchtigung, strenge Strafe *f*; ~**ity** ['tʃæstiti] Keuschheit; Reinheit; Jungfräulichkeit; *fig* Einfachheit, Strenge, Schmucklosigkeit *f*.

chasuble ['tʃæzjubl] *rel* Kasel *f (Meßgewand)*.

chat [tʃæt] **1.** *s* Geplauder, Schwätzchen *n*, kleine Unterhaltung *f*; *itr* plaudern, sich unterhalten; **2.** *s orn (meist in Zssgen)* Schmätzer *m*; *stone-*~ Steinschmätzer *m*; ~**elaine** ['ʃætəlein] Gürtelkette; Schloßherrin *f*; ~**tel** ['tʃætl] *meist pl* bewegliche Habe *f*, Vermögen *n*; *goods and* ~~*s (pl)* Hab u. Gut *n*; ~~ *loan* Mobiliarkredit *m*; ~~ *mortgage* Sicherungsübereignung *f*; ~**ter** ['tʃætə] *itr (Vögel)* zwitschern; *(Menschen)* schnattern, plappern, quasseln; *(Zähne)* klappern *a. tech*; rasseln; *tech* flattern; *s* Gezwitscher; Geschnatter, Geplapper, Gequassel, Geschwätz; (Zähne-)Klappern, Geklapper, Gerassel *n*; ~~*box* Plappermaul *n*; *fam* Quasseltüte, -strippe; *sl* Schreibmaschine *f*; *sl* (Auto-)Radio; *sl mil* Maschinengewehr, MG *n*; ~**terer** ['-ərə] Schwätzer(in *f*); *orn* Seidenschwanz *m*; ~**ty** ['-i] redselig, geschwätzig; familiär, formlos.

chauff|er ['tʃɔ:fə] Kohlenbecken *n*; ~**eur** ['ʃoufə] *s* Chauffeur, (Kraftwagen-)Fahrer *m (als Beruf)*.

chauvini|sm ['ʃouvinizm] Chauvinismus, Hurrapatriotismus *m*; ~**st** ['-st] Hurrapatriot *m*.

chaw [tʃɔ:] *tr vulg* kauen, schmatzen, mümmeln; *to* ~ *up (Am sl)* kaputt-, fertigmachen; *s Am sl* Priem *f* (Kautabak).

cheap [tʃi:p] *a* u. *adv* billig; preiswert, verbilligt; minderwertig, schlecht; gewöhnlich, gemein, ordinär; *Am fam* knauserig; *on the* ~ auf bequeme Weise, leicht; *to feel* ~ *(sl)* nicht auf der Höhe, nicht in Stimmung sein; beschämt sein; *to get* ~ billig erstehen; *to get off* ~ billig davonkommen; *to hold* ~ geringschätzen, verachten; *to make, to render o.s.* ~ *(fig)* sich wegwerfen; *(fam) dirt, dog* ~ spottbillig; ~**en** ['-ən] *tr* verbilligen, herabsetzen; den Wert herabsetzen *od* mindern (*s.th.* e-r S); *itr* billiger werden; ~**ie** ['-i] *Am fam* billige(r) Gegenstand *m*; ~**-jack** ['-dʒæk] Hausierer, Marktschreier *m*; ~~ *goods (pl)* Plunder *m*; **C**~ **John** *Am a* billig, unansehnlich; *s* üble Kneipe *f*; ~**ly** ['-li] *adv* billig; leicht; ~**ness** ['-nis] Billigkeit, Wohlfeilheit; Minderwertigkeit *f*, geringe(r) Wert *m*; Gewöhnlichkeit *f*; ~**skate** ['-skeit] *Am sl* Knicker, Knauser *m*.

cheat [tʃi:t] *tr* betrügen, täuschen; *fam* anschmieren, bemogeln; übervorteilen; *(die Zeit, Müdigkeit)* vertreiben; *itr* mogeln; betrügen; *to* ~ *s.o. out of s.th.* jdn um etw bringen, betrügen, prellen; *s* Betrug, Schwindel *m*, Mogelei *f*; Betrüger, Schwindler *m*; Mogeln *n*.

check [tʃek] **1.** *tr* zum Stehen, Stillstand bringen, Einhalt gebieten (*s.th.* e-r S); hindern, zurückhalten, in Grenzen halten; verhindern, unterbinden, *fam* abbremsen; eindämmen, hemmen, *tech* drosseln; tadeln, e-n Verweis erteilen (*s.o.* jdm); (nach-, über-) prüfen, kontrollieren, revidieren, nach~, durchsehen, nachrechnen; kollationieren, (prüfend) vergleichen (*by* mit); anstreichen, markieren, abhaken; *Am (Geld auf der Bank)* mit e-m Scheck abheben; *Am (Gepäck)* ab-, aufgeben, gegen Bescheinigung in Verwahrung geben *od* nehmen; Schach bieten *a. fig* (*s.o.* jdm) *a. itr*; **2.** *itr* Schach sagen; übereinstimmen; *(Farbe)* absplittern; *(Jagdhund)* die Spur aufnehmen; *Am* e-n Scheck ausstellen (*for, against an amount* über e-n Betrag; *upon s.o.* auf jdn); *Am* sich durch Vergleich als übereinstimmend erweisen; *a* Prüf-, Kontroll-; kariert; **3.** *s* Schach(ankündigung *f*) *n*; Stillstand, Aufschub, Rückschlag *a. mil*; *mil* Mißerfolg *m*, *fam* Schlappe *f*; An-, Festhalten; Hindernis *n*, Widerstand; *aero* Luftwiderstand *m*; (Nach-, Über-)Prüfung; Kontrolle (*on* über); Probe *f*; (prüfender) Vergleich *m*; Prüf-, Kontrollzeichen *n*, -marke *f*, Haken; Gepäckschein *m*; Garderobenmarke *f*; *(Textil)* Karo *n (Muster)*; karierte(r) Stoff *m*; *Am* Rechnung *(in e-m Restaurant) Am s. cheque*; *Am sl* Dosis *f*; *interj* Schach! *fam* einverstanden! **4.** *to* ~ *in (Am fam)* ins Gras beißen (müssen); sich melden; *(Hotel)* sich eintragen, ankommen; *to* ~ *off* abhaken, ankreuzen; *to* ~ *out (Am) (Hotel)* abreisen; *(Gepäck)* abholen; weggehen; *to* ~ *through (Am rail) (Gepäck)* aufgeben; *to* ~ *up* genau überprüfen, im einzelnen nachprüfen, genau vergleichen (*on s.th.* etw); Erkundigungen einziehen (*on* über); *to* ~ *with* übereinstimmen mit; sich besprechen mit; *to act as a* ~ *on* behindern; hemmend, nachteilig wirken auf; *to draw a* ~ e-n Scheck ausstellen (*for* über); *to keep, to hold in* ~ *(fig)* in Schach halten; *spot* ~ *(Am)* Stichprobe *f*; ~ **analysis** Kontrollanalyse *f*; ~**-back** Rückfrage *f*; ~**book** *Am* Scheckbuch *n*; ~**bouncer** ['-baunsə] *Am sl* Scheckbetrüger *m*; ~ **crew** *Am* Gruppe *f* schwarzer u. weißer Arbeiter; ~**er** ['-ə] *s* karierte(s) Muster *n*; Brettstein; Prüfer *m*; Aufsicht *f*; *pl* Damespiel *n*; *tr* karieren, mustern; sprenkeln; *itr* sich oft ändern; *fig* auf u. ab gehen; *s. chequer*; ~**erboard** Schach-, Damebrett *n*; ~**eroo** ['-əru:] *Am sl* karierte(s) Kleidungsstück *n*; ~**ing** ['-iŋ] Hemmung *f*, Widerstand *m*; Abbremsen *n*; Nach-, Überprüfung, Kontrolle *f*; ~~ *account (Am)* Girokonto *n*; ~~ *copy* Belegexemplar *n*; ~~ *form, slip* Kontrollzettel, -abschnitt *m*; ~~ *of luggage (Am baggage) rail* Gepäckaufgabe *f*; ~~ *room, office Am s.* ~ *room*: ~ **girl** *Am* Garderobenfrau *f*; ~ **lamp** Kontrollampe *f*; ~ **letter** *Am* Kontrollbuchstabe *m*; ~ **lever** Sperrhebel *m*; ~ **list** *Am* Kontrolliste; *pol* Wahlliste *f*; ~ **mark** Prüf-, Kontrollzeichen *n*; ~**mate** *interj* Schach u. matt! *s* (Schach-)Matt *n*; *fig* hoffnungslose Lage *f*; *tr* mattsetzen; ~ **nut** *tech* Gegenmutter *f*; ~**-point** (Verkehrs-)Überwachungs-, Kontrollstelle *f*; Orientierungs-, Anhaltspunkt *m*; ~ **room** *Am* Garderobe; *rail* Gepäckaufbewahrung *f*, -schalter; *(Hotel)* Gepäckraum; *tech* Prüfraum, -stand *m*; ~ **test** Kontrollversuch *m*; ~**-up** genaue Prüfung, Kontrolle; *med* gründliche Untersuchung; *tech* Nachuntersuchung *f*.

Cheddar ['tʃedə] *(~ cheese)* Cheddarkäse *m*.

cheek [tʃi:k] *s* Backe, Wange *a. tech*; (Tür-)Wange *f*; *tech* Scherblatt *n*; Seitenfläche; *fig fam* Unverschämtheit, Frechheit, Anmaßung *f*; *tr* frech sein gegen; ~ *by jowl* dicht an dicht, dicht beisammen; intim, eng vertraut; *he said that with his tongue in his* ~ das hat er nicht im Ernst gemeint; ~ *of a brake* Bremsbacke *f*; ~**-bone** Wangen-, Jochbein *n*; ~**ed** [-t] *a* -wangig; ~**iness** ['-inis] *fam* Frechheit, Dreistigkeit *f*; ~ **pouch** Backentasche *f*; ~**y** ['-i] *fam* frech, unverschämt; dreist, keck.

cheep [tʃi:p] *s* Piepen *n*; *itr* piepen.

cheer [tʃiə] *s* (gute) Stimmung *f*; Frohsinn *m*, Freude; Hoffnung *f*; Hoch, Hurra(ruf *m*) *n*, Aufmunterung *f*; Jubel, Beifall(sruf) *m*; Essen *n*; *tr* in gute Stimmung versetzen, erfreuen; auf-, ermuntern, ermutigen; zujubeln (*s.o.* jdm); laut Beifall zollen (*s.o.* jdm); *(Nachricht)* freudig begrüßen *od* entgegennehmen; *itr* hurra schreien, jubeln (*at the news* bei der Nachricht); *interj pl* zum Wohl! prima! bestens! *with good* ~ herzlich *adv*; *to* ~ *on* anfeuern, durch Zurufe ermuntern; *to* ~ *up (itr)* froh werden; Mut fassen, Hoffnung schöpfen; *tr* aufmuntern; *to be of good* ~ guten Mutes, frohgelaunt, voller Freude, voller Hoffnung sein; *to give three* ~*s for s.o.* ein dreifaches Hoch auf jdn ausbringen; *to give s.o. a* ~ jdn hochleben lassen; *three* ~*s* ein dreifaches Hoch (*for* für); ~**ful** ['-ful] froh, freudig; gut aufgelegt, aufgeräumt; hoffnungsvoll, zuversichtlich; glücklich, erfreulich, angenehm, schön; gefällig, anregend, belebend, aufmunternd; entgegenkommend; ~**fulness,** ~**iness** ['-nis, '-rinis] Heiterkeit *f*, Frohsinn *m*, Freude *f*; ~**io(h)** ['tʃiəri'ou] *interj fam* mach's gut! alles Gute! ~ **leader** *Am* Leiter(in *f*) *m* des organisierten Beifalls bei College-Sportwettkämpfen; ~**less** ['-lis] freudlos; ungemütlich, unbehaglich; ~**y** ['-ri] aufgeräumt, heiter; gewollt herzlich.

chees|e [tʃi:z] *s* Käse *m*; *a* ~~ ein (ganzer) Käse *(in s-r Rinde)*; *the* ~~ *(sl)* das einzig Richtige, Vernünftige, Gescheite; *Am sl* Schwindel *m*, Übertreibung *f*; *Am sl* Geld, Moos *n*; *v (nur)*: ~~ *it! (sl)* halt! langsam! hau (ja) ab! hör auf! *to make* ~~*s* sich schnell im Kreise drehen; ~~*-cake (s)* Käsekuchen *m*; *sl* leichtbekleidete(s) Mädchen *n (als Bild)*; *sl* aufreizende Kleidung *f*; *a* aufreizend; ~~ *cloth (Am)* Musselin *m*; ~~*-cutter* Käsemesser *n*; ~~*-fly* Käsefliege *f*; ~~*-hopper, -maggot* Käsemade *f*; ~~*-monger* Butter- u. Käsehändler *m*; ~~*-paring (a)* knauserig, filzig, geizig; *s* Käserinde; *fig* Knauserei *f*, Geiz; Plunder *m*, wertlose(s) Zeug *n*; ~~*-rennet (bot)* Labkraut *n*; ~**eburger** ['-bə:gə] belegte(s) Brot *n* mit Käse u. Frikadellen; ~**ed off** *a sl* angeödet, gelangweilt; ~**y** ['-i] käsig; käseartig; *sl* richtig, in Ordnung; *Am sl* wertlos, kläglich, unzureichend.

chef [ʃef] Küchenchef *m*.

chem|ical ['kemikəl] *a* chemisch; *mil* Gas-, Kampfstoff-; *s pl* Chemikalien *f pl*; ~~ *warfare* Gas-, chemische(r) Krieg *m*; ~~ *works, plant* chemische Fabrik *f*; ~**ise** [ʃi'mi:z] Damenhemd *n*; ~**ist** ['kemist] Chemiker; *Br* Drogist; *(dispensing* ~~*)* Apotheker *m*; ~~*'s shop* Drogerie; Apotheke *f*; ~**istry** ['-istri] Chemie *f*; *applied, practical* ~~ Chemotechnik *f*.

cheque, *Am* **check** [tʃek] Scheck *m*, Zahlungsanweisung *f* (*for* auf); *to cash a* ~ e-n Scheck einlösen; *to give a blank* ~ *to s.o.* jdm Blankovollmacht geben, (völlig) freie Hand lassen; *to make out a* ~ e-n Scheck ausstellen; *crossed* ~ Verrechnungsscheck *m*; *traveller's* ~ Reisescheck, -kreditbrief *m*; **~-account** Scheckkonto *n*; **~-book** Scheckbuch *n*; **~-form** Scheckformular *n*.

chequer, *Am* **checker** ['tʃekə] *s* Schachbrett *(als Wirtshausschild)*; *oft pl* Karo *(Muster)*; Schachbrettmuster *n*; *pl dial Am* Damespiel *n*; *tr* karieren, schachbrettartig mustern; abwandeln, *fig* abwechslungsreich gestalten; **~-board** Schach-, Damebrett *n*; **~ed** ['-d] *a* kariert, schachbrettartig gemustert; bunt, mannigfaltig, abwechslungsreich; veränderlich, unbeständig, schwankend; **~ work** *arch* Fachwerk *n*.

cherish ['tʃeriʃ] *tr* pflegen, hegen (u. pflegen); hängen an, (großen) Wert legen auf; *(Gefühle, Gedanken)* hegen; *(e-r Hoffnung)* sich hingeben.

cheroot [ʃə'ru:t] Stumpen *m (Zigarre)*.

cherry ['tʃeri] *s* Kirsche *f*; *(~-tree, -wood)* Kirschbaum *m*, -holz *n*; *a* kirschrot; Kirsch-; *to make two bites at a* ~ nicht recht wissen, was man will; **~-blossom** Kirschblüte *f*; **~ brandy** Kirschlikör *m*; **~-cheeked** *a* rotwangig, -bäckig; **~-laurel, -bay** Kirschlorbeer *m*; **~ pie** *Art* Kirschkuchen *m*; *bot* Heliotrop *n*; *Am sl* Kinderspiel *n*; **~-stone** Kirschkern *m*.

cherub ['tʃerəb] *pl -im rel* Cherub *m (Engel)*; *pl -s (Kunst)* Putte *f*; Engelskopf; *fig* Pausback *m*; **~ic** [tʃə'ru:bik] cherubinisch; Engels-; pausbäckig.

chervil ['tʃə:vil] *bot* Kerbel *m*.

*

Cheshire ['tʃeʃə]: *to grin like a* ~ *cat* übers ganze Gesicht grinsen; **~ cheese** Chesterkäse *m*.

chess [tʃes] Schach(spiel) *n*; *to play (at)* ~ Schach spielen; **~-board** Schachbrett *n*; **~man** Schachfigur *f*.

chest [tʃest] *s* Kiste *f*, Kasten *m*, Truhe *f*, Koffer, Behälter; Gerätekasten *m*; Kasse *f a. fig*; Fonds *m*, Geldmittel *n pl*; Brust(kasten *m*) *f*; *tr* in e-e Kiste tun *od* packen; *to get s.th. off o.'s* ~ *(sl)* mit etw herausplatzen; *that's a load off my* ~ da fällt mir ein Stein vom Herzen; *community* ~ Gemeindekasse *f*; ~ *of drawers* Kommode *f*; **~y** ['-i] *Am sl* eingebildet, aufgeblasen; *to be* ~~ *(Br fam)* es auf der Lunge haben.

chesterfield ['tʃestəfi:ld] einreihige(r) Mantel *m*; Sofa *n* mit Rücken- u. Seitenlehnen.

chestnut ['tʃes(t)nʌt] *(bes.* Eß-, *a.* Roß-)Kastanie; *(~-tree, -wood)* Kastanie(nbaum *m*, -nholz *n*) *f*; Braune(r) *m (Pferd)*; *fam* alte Geschichte *f*, Witz *m* mit Bart; *a* kastanienbraun; *to pull s.o.'s ~s out of the fire (fig)* für jdn die Kastanien aus dem Feuer holen; *horse-~* Roßkastanie *f*.

cheval|-de-frise [ʃə'vældə'fri:z] *meist pl chevaux-de-frise* [ʃəvou-] *mil* spanische(r) Reiter *m (pl)*; **~-glass** große(r) Drehspiegel *m*; **~ier** [ʃevə'liə] Ritter *m (e-s Ordens)*; ~~ *of industry, of fortune* Hochstapler *m*.

cheviot ['tʃeviət] Cheviot *m (Wollstoff)*.

chevron ['ʃevrən] *arch mil* Winkel *m*; Dienstgradabzeichen *n*; *(Wappen)* Sparren *m*; *~s of rank* Rangabzeichen *n*; **~-mo(u)lding** *arch* Zickzackleiste *f*.

chevy, chivy ['tʃevi, 'tʃivi] *s* (Hetz-) Jagd; *fig* Hetze *f*; *tr* jagen, hetzen; *itr fig* (sich ab)hetzen.

chew [tʃu:] *tr itr* kauen; *itr* Tabak kauen; *Am sl* essen, quasseln; überdenken *(upon, over s.th.* etw), nachdenken, -sinnen *(upon, over* über); *to* ~ *s.o. out (sl)* jdn ausschimpfen, zur Sau machen; *s* Kauen *n*; Priem *m (Stück Kautabak)*; *to* ~ *the cud* wiederkäuen; *fig* hin u. her überlegen *(of s.th.* etw); *to* ~ *the rag, fat (sl)* herumdebattieren, -nörgeln; *Am sl* viel schwätzen, quasseln *(about* über); Mund; **~ed** [-d] *a sl* wütend; ~~ *up* am Ende, erschöpft; **~ing** ['-iŋ]: *~~-gum, -tobacco* Kaugummi, -tabak *m*.

chic [ʃi(:)k] *s* Schick; Geschmack *m*; Kunstfertigkeit, Geschicklichkeit *f*; *a* schick, elegant; *Am fam* hell, klug, auf Draht; nett, hübsch.

chicane [ʃi'kein] *s* Schikane *f*; *tr* schikanieren; die Hölle heißmachen *(s.o.* jdm); **~ry** [-əri] Schikane *f*, Schikanieren *n*; Kleinlichkeit, Spitzfindigkeit *f*.

chick [tʃik] Küken *n*; junge(r) Vogel *m*; Kind(chen) *n*; *(~abiddy)* kleine(r) Liebling *m*; *sl* hübsche(s) Mädchen *n*; **~adee** ['-ədi:] Weidenmeise *f*; **~aree** ['-əri:] *Am* rotbraune(s) Eichhörnchen *n*; **~en** ['-in] *s* Küken, Hähnchen, Hühnchen, (junges) Huhn *(als Fleisch)*; *Am* Huhn *n (jeden Alters)*; *Am* junge(r) Vogel *m*; Kind; dumme(s) Kind, Gänschen *n*; *sl* Feigling, Milchbart, Grünschnabel *m*; *sl* hübsche(s) Mädchen; *Am mil sl* US-Abzeichen *n*; Unfug, Schwindel *m*; *Am pl* Federvieh; Geflügel *n (a. als Fleisch)*; *a* zart; *Am sl* feige, kleinlich, unüberlegt, sich aufspielend; *I'm no* ~~ ich bin (doch) kein Kind mehr; *~~-breast* Hühnerbrust *f (Deformation beim Menschen)*; *~~-broth, -soup* Hühnersuppe *f*; *~~-cholera (vet)* Hühnerpest *f*; *~~-farm* Hühnerfarm *f*; *~~-feed* Hühnerfutter *n*; *fig fam* kleine Fische *m pl*; lächerliche Summe, Lappalie *f*; *~~-head (Am)* dumme(r) Kerl *m*; *~~-heart (fig)* Hasenherz *n*, -fuß *m*; *~~-hearted, -livered (a)* bange, feige; ~~ *money (Am)* Lappalie *f*; *~~-pox* Windpocken *pl*; *~~-run (Br), -yard (Am)* Hühnerhof *m*; ~~ *shit (Am sl)* Schwindel *m*, Angeberei, widerliche Geschichte *f*; *~~wort (bot)* Vogelmiere *f*; ~~ *tracks (pl Am)* Krickelzeichen *n*; *~(~)wire* Drahtnetz *n*; **~ling** ['-liŋ] *bot* Kicherling *m*, Saatplatterbse *f*; **~-pea** *bot* Kichererbse *f*; **~weed** *bot* Vogelmiere *f*.

chicle ['tʃikl] *Am (~gum)* Kaugummi *m* od *n* (aus Sapotillsaft).

chicory ['tʃikəri] *bot* Zichorie *f*.

chide [tʃaid] *irr chid* od *chided, chid(den)* od *chided*; *tr lit* schelten, tadeln.

chief [tʃi:f] *s* Chef *m*, (Ober-)Haupt *n*, Erste(r); (An-)Führer, Leiter, Kommandeur; Abteilungsleiter, -chef *(e-r Dienststelle)*; Vorgesetzte(r); Häuptling *m (e-s Stammes)*; *a* Haupt-, Ober-, erst, oberst; führend, leitend; *~(est) of all* vor allem, insbesondere; ~ *of naval operations (Am)* Chef *m* des Admiralstabs; ~ *of police (Am)* Polizeipräsident *m*; ~ *of staff* Chef *m* des Stabes, Stabschef *m*; **~ clerk** erste(r) Buchhalter; Büro-, Kanzleivorsteher *m*; **~ designer** Chefkonstrukteur *m*; **~ editor** Hauptschriftleiter, verantwortliche(r) Redakteur *m*; **~ engineer** Ober-, leitende(r) Ingenieur *m*; **~ justice** Gerichtspräsident *m*; *Lord C~~* Lord Oberrichter *m*; **~ly** ['-li] *adv* hauptsächlich, besonders; **~tain** ['-tən] Häuptling; Gruppen-, Bandenführer; (An-)Führer *m*; **~taincy** ['-si] Stellung *f* e-s Häuptlings.

chiffon ['ʃifɔn] Chiffon *m*; *pl* Besatz *m*; **~ batiste** Wollbatist *m*; **~ette** [ʃifə'nɛt] sehr feine(s) Chiffongewebe *n*; **~ net** *Br* Seidentüll *m*; **~ velvet** Chiffonsamt *m*.

chilblain ['tʃilblein] Frostbeule *f*.

child [tʃaild] *pl children* ['tʃildrən] Kind *n a. fig*; *pl (Bibel)* Kinder *n pl*, Nachkommen *m pl*; *from a* ~ von klein auf, von Kindheit an, von Jugend auf; *with* ~ schwanger; *to give birth to a* ~ ein Kind zur Welt bringen; *burnt* ~ *dreads fire (prov)* gebranntes Kind scheut das Feuer; *grand-~* Enkel *m*; *children's allowance, book, clothing, drawing, games, newspaper, nurse, playground, playroom* Kinderzulage *f*, -buch *n*, -kleidung, -zeichnung *f*, -spiele *n pl*, -zeitung, -schwester *f*, -spielplatz *m*, -zimmer *n*; **~-bearing, -bed, -birth** Entbindung, Niederkunft *f*, Kindbett *n*; **~hood** ['-hud] Kindheit *f*; **~ish** ['-iʃ] kindlich; kindisch; **~ishness** Kindlichkeit *f*; kindische(s) Wesen *n*; **~ labo(u)r** Kinderarbeit *f*; **~less** ['-lis] kinderlos, ohne Kinder; **~like** ['-laik] kindlich; einfach; unschuldig; zutraulich; vertrauensselig; **~ psychology** Kinderpsychologie *f*; **~'s play** Kinderspiel *n*, leichte Sache *f*; **~ welfare** Jugendfürsorge *f*.

Chil|e, ~i ['tʃili] Chile *n*; *s. chilli*; **~ean** [-'liən] *a* chilenisch; *s* Chilene *m*, Chilenin *f*.

chill [tʃil] *s* Frost *m*, Kälte *f*; Kältegefühl, Frösteln *n*; Fieberschauer, Schüttelfrost *m*; *fig* Gedrücktheit, Mutlosigkeit, Niedergeschlagenheit, Hoffnungslosigkeit; *tech* Gußform, -schale, Kokille *f*; *a* unangenehm kühl, frisch; fröstelnd, frierend; *fig* (gefühls)kalt, kühl, frostig; niederdrückend; *tr* kalt stellen; erstarren lassen; *fig* niederdrücken, deprimieren, entmutigen, mutlos machen; *tech* in Kokillen gießen, abschrecken; *Am sl (Problem)* lösen, *(Mensch)* umbringen; *itr* kalt werden, abkühlen, erstarren; *Am sl* sich ausnutzen, sich verhaften lassen; *to cast a* ~ *over s.o.* jdn deprimieren, mutlos machen; *to put on the* ~ *(Am fam)* kühl behandeln *(on s.o.* jdn); *sl* kalt machen; **~-casting** Hart-, Schalen-, Kokillenguß *m*; **~ed** [-d] *a (Mensch)* durchfroren; niedergedrückt, -geschlagen, deprimiert, entmutigt, mutlos; *tech* hart gegossen, schalenhart; ~~ *cast iron* Hartguß *m*; ~~ *meat* Kühlhausfleisch *n*; **~er(-diller)** ['-ə-dilə] *fam* Reißer *m*, Revolvergeschichte *f*; **~(i)ness** ['-inis] unangenehme Kälte; *fig* Frostigkeit *f*; **~ing** ['-iŋ] *tech* Abkühlung, Abschreckung *f*; **~y** ['-i] unangenehm kalt; fröstelnd, frierend; kälteempfindlich; *fig* kühl, frostig; *to feel* ~~ frösteln.

chilli, chilly, *Am* **chile, chili** ['tʃili] Paprikaschote *f*; Paprika, Cayenne-, Guineapfeffer *m*; **~ con carne** *Am* Fleisch *n* mit weißen Bohnen u. Paprika; **~ sauce** *Am* Tomatensoße mit Zwiebeln u. Paprika.

Chiltern Hundreds ['tʃiltən 'hʌndrədz]: *to apply for, to accept the* ~ s-n Sitz im Unterhaus aufgeben.

chime [tʃaim] *s* Melodie *f*, Rhythmus, Wohlklang *m*, Harmonie *f*; Einklang *m*, Übereinstimmung, Eintracht *f*; *radio* Pausenzeichen; *pl* Geläut, Glockenspiel *n*; *tr (die Glocke(n))* läuten; *(Stunde)* schlagen; *(Ton)* anschlagen; *itr* das Glockenspiel ertönen lassen; *(Glocke)* schlagen, läuten; *(Glockenspiel)* ertönen; sich reimen; *(to ~ in, together)* harmonisieren, in Einklang sein, übereinstimmen (*with* mit); *to ~ in (on a talk) fam* sich in ein Gespräch einschalten, einmischen; beipflichten (*with s.o.* jdm).

chimer|a, chimaera [kai'miərə] Trugbild; Monstrum, Ungeheuer; Hirngespinst *n*; **~ic(al)** [kai'merik(əl)] unwirklich, trügerisch; monströs; phantastisch.

chimney ['tʃimni] Rauchfang, Kamin *(a. im Hochgebirge)*; Schornstein *m*; Esse *f*, Schlot; *geol* Schlot, Eruptionskanal; (Lampen-)Zylinder; *fig* Ausweg *m*; **~-corner** Kaminecke *f*, warme(r) Ofenplatz *m*; **~-piece** Kaminsims *m*; **~-pot** Schornsteinaufsatz *m*; *fam* Angströhre *f*, Zylinder *m*; **~-stack** Fabrikschornstein, Schlot *m*; **~-sweep(er)** Schornsteinfeger *m*.

chimpanzee [tʃimpən'zi:] Schimpanse *m*.

chin [tʃin] *s* Kinn; *Am sl* Gerede, Geschwätz, Gequassel *n*; *tr Am sl* anquasseln, anquatschen; *itr Am sl* quasseln, quatschen, schwätzen; *to ~ o.s.* e-n Klimmzug machen; *up to the ~ (fig)* bis über die Ohren; *to take it on the ~ (Am fam fig)* völlig ausgepunktet sein; *~-~! sl* prost! tjüs! *~ up!* Kopf hoch! **~-wag** *itr fam* schwätzen; **~-whiskers** *pl Am* Kinnbart *m*.

china ['tʃainə] *s (~-ware)* Porzellan *n*; *Am sl* Zähne *m pl*; *C~* China *n*; *a* Porzellan-; **~-clay** Porzellanerde *f*, Kaolin *n*; **~-closet** Porzellanschrank *m*, -vitrine *f*; **C~man** ['-mən] *fam pej* Chinese *m*; *Am mar sl* in der Wäscherei beschäftigte(r) Matrose *m*; **C~town** ['-taun] Chinesenviertel *n*.

chinch [tʃintʃ] *Am* Bett-, *(~bug)* Kornwanze *f*; **~illa** [tʃin'tʃilə] Chinchilla *f* od *n*.

chine [tʃain] Rückgrat *n*, Wirbelsäule *f*; *(Küche)* Lendenstück *n*; *fig* Bergkamm, (Fels-)Grat *m*.

Chinese ['tʃai'ni:z] *a* chinesisch; *s pl ~* Chinese *m*, Chinesin *f*; (das) Chinesisch(e); **~ lantern** Lampion *m*; **~puzzle** verzwickte Geschichte *f*; **~ Wall** Chinesische Mauer *f*.

chink [tʃiŋk] **1.** *s* Ritze *f*, Spalt, Schlitz *m*; Guckloch *n*; **2.** *s (Metall-, Gläser-)* Klang *m*; *sl* Geld *n* (in der Tasche); *tr* klingen lassen, *fam* klimpern mit; *(Gläser)* anstoßen; *itr* klingen, klimpern; **3. C~** *(sl pej)* Chinese *m*; *pl* chinesische Gerichte *n pl*.

chin|ning ['tʃiniŋ] *Am* Klimmzug *m*; **~o** ['-ou] *Am* olivenfarbige(s) Baumwollgewebe *n*.

chintz [tʃints] Chintz *m*; **~y** ['-i] *Am sl* unmodern, nicht elegant; doof.

chip [tʃip] *s* (abgebrochenes) Stück (-chen) *n*, Ecke *f*, Eckchen *n*; Splitter, Span *m*; *(Porzellan, Glas)* lädierte Stelle *f*; (Apfel-, Kartoffel-) Schnitzel *n*; Bast *m*; Spielmarke *f*; Geldstück *n*; *pl (potato-~s)* Chips *pl*; *sl* Geld, Moos *n*; *mar sl* Schiffszimmermann *m*; *tr (Holz)* zerhacken, spalten; *(Geschirr)* auszacken, anstoßen; abbrechen (*off, from* von), ausbrechen (*off, from* aus); *(Obst, Kartoffeln)* zerkleinern, zerschneiden, in Scheiben, Stückchen schneiden; *(to ~ out)* herausschnitzen; *(Inschrift)* einritzen; *(Ei)* aufschlagen; *(to ~ at) fam* zum besten haben, verpflaumen; *itr (Porzellan, Glas)* (leicht) angestoßen, beschädigt werden; *to ~ in (fam)* ins Wort fallen (*s.o.* jdm); *Am fam* Geld (her)geben *(für e-e Sache)*; mitmachen *(bei e-r Sache)*; beitragen zu; *in the ~s (fam)* bei Kasse, bei Geld; *dry as a ~* langweilig, uninteressant; stock-, knochentrocken; *to carry a ~ on o.'s shoulder (fam)* leicht gereizt sein; *he is a ~ of the old block (fig)* der Apfel fällt nicht weit vom Stamm; **~-basket** Spankorb *m*; **~-bonnet, -hat** Basthut *m*; **~muck, ~munk** ['-mʌk, -mʌŋk] *zoo* Chipmunk *m (nordamerik. Erdhörnchen)*; **~ped** [-pt] *a (Porzellan, Glas)* angestoßen, angeschlagen; **~piness** ['-inis] Trockenheit; Langweiligkeit, Reizbarkeit *f*; **~ping** ['-iŋ] *Am* Einschnitt *m*; *pl* Späne, Splitter *m pl*; **~py** ['-i] *a* trocken, langweilig, uninteressant; (müde u.) reizbar; *s Am (~ping sparrow)* Spatz, Sperling *m*; *sl* Nutte *f*; *s. ~muck*; *he is ~~* es ist nichts (mehr) mit ihm anzufangen.

chipper ['tʃipə] **1.** *a Am* lebendig, lebhaft; lustig; gesprächig, geschwätzig; **2.** *dial Am itr* zwitschern, schwatzen, plaudern; *tr* aufmuntern.

chirk [tʃə:k] *tr itr Am fam* in Stimmung kommen, *(to ~ up)* bringen; *a Am fam* lebhaft, in gehobener Stimmung.

chiro|graph ['kaiərəgra:f] Handschrift, handschriftliche Urkunde *f*; **~mancer** ['-mænsə] Chiromant, Handliniendeuter *m*; **~mancy** ['-mænsi] Handliniendeutung, Chiromantie *f*; **~-podist** [ki'rɔpədist] Hühneraugenoperateur, Fußpfleger *m*; **~pody** [ki'rɔpədi] Fußpflege *f*.

chirp [tʃə:p] *itr* zirpen, zwitschern; lustig plaudern, schwatzen, flüstern; *Am sl (Frau)* singen; *tr (Lied)* trällern; *Am sl* verpfeifen; *s* Gezirp, Gezwitscher, Geträller *n*; **~er** ['-ə] *Am sl* Sängerin *f*, Agent *m*; **~iness** ['-inis] Munterkeit *f*; **~y** ['-i] lebhaft, munter.

chirr [tʃə:] *itr* zirpen; **~up** ['tʃirʌp] *itr* zwitschern, (t)schilpen, zirpen; *theat sl* als Claqueur fungieren; *s* Gezwitscher *n*.

chisel ['tʃizl] *s* Meißel, Stechbeitel *m*; *sl* Gaunerei *f*, Betrug *m*; *the ~ (sculptor's ~)* Bildhauerei *f*; *tr* (aus)meißeln; *sl* begaunern, beschummeln, betrügen; *(Zigarette)* schnorren; **~led** ['-d] *a (fig* wie) gemeißelt; **~ler** ['-lə] *sl* Gauner, Betrüger; Nassauer *m*.

chit [tʃit] **1.** *fam* kleine(s) Ding, Kind; *pej* junge(s), freche(s) Ding *n*, Rotznase *f*; **2.** Notiz *f*, *(beschriebener)* Zettel *m*, Unterlage *f*; Bon *m*; Rechnung *f (bes. des Kellners)*; *(Dienstboten-)* Zeugnis *n*; **3.** *dial bot* Schößling, Trieb *m*; **~-chat** ['-tʃæt] Geplauder *n*.

chitin ['kaitin] Chitin *n*.

chitterlings ['tʃitəliŋz] *pl* Kaldaunen *f pl*, Innereien *pl*, Gekröse *n*; *(Küche)* Kutteln *f pl*.

chivalr|ic ['ʃivəlrik] *poet*, **~ous** ['-əs] ritterlich; **~y** ['-ri] Rittertum *n*; Ritterlichkeit *f*, ritterliche(s) Wesen *n*.

chive, cive [tʃaiv, s-] *bot* Schnittlauch *m*; kleine Zwiebel *f*.

chiv(v)y ['tʃivi] *s. chevy.*

*

chlor|al ['klɔ:rəl] *chem* Chloral *n*; **~ate** ['-it] Chlorat, chlorsaure(s) Salz *n*; *~~ of potash, sodium* Kalium-, Natriumchlorat *n*; **~ic** ['-ik] *a*: *~~ acid* Chlorsäure *f*; **~ide** ['klɔ:raid] Chlorid *n*, Chlorverbindung *f*; **~inate** ['-ineit] *tr* chlorieren, (ver)chloren; **~ination** [klɔ:ri'neiʃən] Chlorierung, (Ver-)Chlorung *f*; **~ine** ['-i:n] Chlor *n*; *~~ water* Chlorwasser *n*; **~oform** ['klɔrəfɔ:m] *s* Chloroform *n*; *tr* chloroformieren; **~ophyll** ['klɔrəfil] Chlorophyll, Blattgrün *n*; **~osis** [klɔ'rousis] *med* Bleichsucht *f*; **~otic** [klɔ'rɔtik] bleichsüchtig; **~ous** ['klɔ:rəs] chlorig.

choc [tʃɔk] *fam* Schokolade *f*; *pl* Pralinen *f pl*; **~-ice** Schokoladeneis *n*.

chock [tʃɔk] *s (~-block)* Bremsklotz, -schuh; Riegel *m*; *mar* Klampe *f*; *tr* verkeilen, -klemmen, -riegeln, blockieren, bremsen; **~-a-block, -full** [-'-] *a fam* gerammelt, gedrängt voll (*with* von).

chocolate ['tʃɔkəlit] *s* Schokolade; Praline; Schokoladenfarbe *f*, -braun *n*; *a* schokoladenbraun, -farben; *bar of ~* Tafel *f*, Riegel *m* Schokolade; **~ cream** Krem-, gefüllte Schokolade *f*.

choice [tʃɔis] *s* (Aus-)Wahl *f*; *das* Beste, *die* Auslese; *a* vorzüglich, ausgezeichnet, erstklassig; (aus)gewählt, ausgesucht; *at ~* nach Belieben, nach Wunsch; *by, for, of ~* Lieblings-; *to have the ~* die (Aus-)Wahl haben; *to have no ~* keine andere Wahl haben; *to make a ~* e-e (Aus-)Wahl treffen; *to take ~, to make o.'s ~* es sich aussuchen; *I have no ~* es bleibt mir nichts anderes übrig; *he is my ~* ich habe ihn gewählt (*for* als); *a large ~* e-e große Auswahl; *Hobson's ~* keine Wahl; *ladies' ~* Damenwahl *f*; **~ness** ['-nis] Vorzüglichkeit; *com* hervorragende Qualität *f*.

choir ['kwaiə] *s mus* (Kirchen-)Chor; *arch* Chor *m (e-r Kirche)*; *tr itr* im Chor singen; **~-boy** Chorknabe *m*; **~master** Chordirigent *m*.

choke [tʃouk] *tr* (er)würgen, ersticken *a. fig*; *(to ~ up)* verstopfen, versperren, vollpfropfen (*with* mit); *(Gefühl)* unterdrücken, ersticken; *tech* (ab)drosseln; *itr* (zu) ersticken (drohen), keine Luft bekommen, würgen; kein Wort herausbringen (können) (*with* vor); *s* Würgen *n*; *tech* Verengung, Einschnürung *f*; *mot* Drossel-, Starterklappe; *el* Drossel(spule) *f*; *sl* Kittchen *n*; *to ~ back* unterdrücken, herunterschlucken (*the tears* die Tränen); *to ~ to death* erwürgen, erdrosseln; *to ~ down* hinunterwürgen *a. fig*; *(Gefühl)* unterdrücken; *to ~ off* anschnauzen; abschrecken, -halten; ein Ende machen; *to ~ up (tr)* verstopfen; zu voll machen; *itr fam* den Tränen nahe sein, kein Wort herausbringen; *~ up!* hör auf! **~-circuit** *el* Sperrkreis *m*; **~-coil** *el* Drosselspule *f*; **~-damp** *min* Grubengas *n*; **~-pear** *fig* bittere Pille *f*; *it is a ~~ to him* er hat schwer daran zu schlucken; **~r** ['-ə] Drosselspule *f*; *fam* Schlips *m*, Halstuch *n*, *obs* Stehkragen *m*; *Am sl* große(s) Stück *n* (Brot); **~ shot** *sl* Nahaufnahme *f*; **choky** ['tʃouki] *s sl* Kittchen *n*; *a* erstickend.

choking ['tʃoukiŋ] *s tech* Verstopfung; Verengung, Einschnürung *f*; *a* erstickend.

choler ['kɔlə] Wut *f*, Zorn *m*; **~a** ['kɔlərə] *med* Cholera *f*; **~ic** ['-rik] cholerisch, jähzornig, aufbrausend; **cholesterol** [kə'lestərɔl] Cholesterin, Gallenfett *n*.

choose [tʃu:z] *irr chose, chosen tr* (aus-) wählen, aussuchen; vorziehen, lieber wollen, sich entscheiden für; erwählen (zu) *a. rel*; *Am fam* haben wollen, wünschen; *itr* wählen; s-e Wahl treffen; *to have to ~ between* die Wahl haben zwischen; *to pick and ~* sehr wählerisch sein; *I cannot ~ but* ich muß, mir bleibt nichts anderes übrig als zu; **choos(e)y** ['tʃu:zi] *fam* wählerisch.

chop [tʃɔp] **1.** *tr* (zer)hacken, zerschneiden; *(Holz)* spalten; *(to ~ up)* zerkleinern; *fig (Wort, Satz)* zerhacken;

itr hacken, hauen, schlagen (*at* nach); *s* Hieb, Schnitt *m*; Hacken *n*; (Fleisch-)Schnitte *f*, Schnitzel, *(meist)* Kotelett *n*; *(Haut)* Schrunde *f*; kabbelige(r) Wellenschlag *m*; *to ~ away* wegschneiden, -hacken; *to ~ down* umhakken, -legen; *(Baum)* fällen; *to ~ in* (in e-e Unterhaltung) hineinplatzen; *to ~ off* abhacken, -schneiden, -hauen; *to ~ out, up (geol)* an die Oberfläche treten; *to ~ o.'s teeth (Am sl)* Unsinn reden; *~-~! interj sl* dalli! beeil Dich! **~-house** billige(s) Speiselokal *n*; **~ped** *a: ~~ meat* Hackfleisch *n*; *~~ straw* Häcksel *m*; **~per** ['-ə] Hackmesser *n*; *tech* Zerhacker *m*; *sl* Ohrfeige *f*; *mil sl* MG *n*, Hubschrauber; *Am sl* Fahrkarten-, Eintrittskartenkontrolleur *m*; **~ping** ['-iŋ] *a* groß u. stark, kräftig; *s (~~ sea)* kabbelige(r) Wellenschlag *m*; *el* Amplitudenbegrenzung *f*; **~py** ['-i] zerschnitten, rissig; *(See)* kabbelig; *(Worte, Sätze)* abgehackt; **~-sticks** *pl* Eßstäbchen *n pl*; **~-suey** [-'su:i] *chinesisches Gericht*; **2.** *s. chap 2.*; **3.** *s meist pl* Kinnbacken *m pl*; *meist pej* od *hum* Rachen, Schlund *m*; *(Hund)* Maul *n*; *fig* Eingang *m*, Mündung *f (e-s Tales, e-r Schlucht)*; *to lick o.'s ~s* sich die Lippen lecken; *he licked his ~s* ihm lief das Wasser im Munde zusammen; **4.** *itr (~ and change)* wechseln, schwanken, unbeständig sein; *s (~s and changes)* Veränderungen *f pl*, ständige(r) Wechsel *m*; *to ~ round, about (Wind)* umschlagen, -springen; **~py** unbeständig, wechselhaft; **5.** *(Indien, China)* Siegel *n*, Stempel *m*; Erlaubnis(schein *m*) *f*; Paß *m*; Sorte, Qualität, Güte *f*; *(China)* Warenzeichen *n*, Handelsmarke *f*; *first-, second-~* erste(r), zweite(r) Güte *od* Qualität.

choral *a* ['kɔ:rəl] Chor-; *s (a. ~e)* [kɔ'rɑ:l] Choral *m*; **~-society** Gesangverein *m*.

chord [kɔ:d] *anat* Band *n*; *math* Sehne; *mus poet fig* Saite *f*; *mus* Akkord *m*; *tech* Gurt(ung *f*) *m*; Profiltiefe; harmonische Farbenzs.stellung *f*; *to touch the right ~ (fig)* den rechten Ton finden; *spermatic ~ (anat)* Samenstrang *m*; *spinal ~* Rückenmark *n*; *vocal ~* Stimmband *n*.

chore [tʃɔ:] *meist pl* Gelegenheitsarbeit; unangenehme, schwere Arbeit *f*.

choreograph|er [kɔri'ɔgrəfə] Choreograph; Ballettmeister *m*; **~ic** [-ə'græfik] choreographisch; Ballett-, Tanz-; **~y** [-'ɔgrəfi] Choreographie; Tanz-, Ballettkunst *f*.

chor|ine ['kɔ:ri:n] *Am fam* Chorsängerin; Ensembletänzerin *f*, (Tanz-)Girl *n*; **~ister** ['kɔristə] Chorsänger(in *f*), Chorist(in *f*) *m*; Chorknabe; *Am* Chorleiter *m*; **~us** ['kɔ:rəs] *s* (Sing-, Sprech-)Chor *a. theat*; *theat* (Prolog-)Sprecher; Chorgesang; Refrain *m*; *(Revue)* Tanzgruppe *f*; *tr* im Chor singen, (auf)sagen, sprechen; *in ~~* im Chor, alle zusammen, gleichzeitig; *~~ girl* Revuetänzerin *f*.

chose [ʃouz] *jur* Gegenstand *m*; **~n** ['-n] *s meist pl rel die* Auserwählten.

chough [tʃʌf] *orn* (Stein-)Dohle *f*.

chouse [tʃaus] *s fam* Schwindel *m*; *tr* prellen, betrügen.

chow [tʃau] *s sl (Australien)* Chinese *m*; *(~-~)* Chow-Chow *m (Hunderasse)*; *sl* Futter *n*, Fraß *m*; *tr (to ~ down) sl* (fr)essen; *~-~ (Küche)* Gemischte(s), Mischgericht *n*; **~der** *Am* ['tʃaudə] *Art* Fischgericht *n*; **~ hall** *Am sl* Kantine, Messe *f*, Speisesaal *m*; **~ hound** *sl mil* Fresser *m*; **~-line** *sl mil* Essenholerschlange; Essenausgabe *(Einrichtung)*; Clique *f*; *to join the ~~* sich zum Essenfassen anstellen; **~ mein** [-'mein] Huhn *n* in gebratenen Nudeln, Pilzen u. Zwiebeln *(chines. Gericht)*; **~mobile** ['-məbi:l] *Am* fahrbare(r) Imbißstand *m*; **~ time** *sl* Essenszeit *f*.

chris|m ['krizm] Salböl *n*; Salbung *f*; **~om** [-] Taufkleid *n*; *(~~-child, -babe)* Täufling *m*; unschuldige(s) Kind *n*.

Christ [kraist] Christus *m*; **~ child** Christkind; **~'s thorn** *bot* Christusdorn *m*.

christen ['krisn] *tr* taufen *(a. Schiffe)*; nennen, den Namen geben (*s.o.* jdm); **C~dom** ['-dəm] die Christenheit; **~ing** ['-iŋ] *s* Taufe *f*; *attr* Tauf-.

Christian ['kristjən, 'kristʃən] *a* christlich; *fam* menschlich, anständig; *s* Christ(in *f*) *m*; **~ burial** kirchliche(s) Begräbnis *n*; **~ era** christliche Zeitrechnung *f*; **~ity** [kristi'æniti] Christentum *n*; **~ization** [kristjənai'zeiʃən, kristʃ-] Bekehrung, Christianisierung *f*; **~ize** ['-aiz] *tr* (zum Christentum) bekehren, christianisieren; **~ name** Vorname *m*; **~ Science** *rel* Christliche Wissenschaft *f*.

Christmas, Xmas ['krisməs] Weihnacht(en *n* od *f pl*) *f*, Weihnachtsfest *n*; *Am sl* auffallende(s) Kleidungsstück *n*, aufgedonnerte Angelegenheit *f*; *Father ~* der Weihnachtsmann; **~ book, card** Weihnachtsglückwunsch *m*, -karte *f*; **~-box** Weihnachtsgeld, -geschenk *n*; **~-carol** Weihnachtslied *n*; **~ catalog(ue)** Weihnachtskatalog *m*; **~-day** der 1. Weihnachtstag *(25. Dez.)*; **~ eve** der Heilige Abend *(24. Dez.)*; **~-flower, rose** *bot* Christrose *f*; **~ present** Weihnachtsgeschenk *n*; **~ pudding** Weihnachtspudding *m*; **~(s)y** ['-si] *fam* weihnachtlich; **~-tide** die Weihnachtszeit; **~-tree** Weihnachts-, Christ-, Tannenbaum *m*; *Am* Bohrgerüst *n*.

chrom|ate ['kroumət, '-eit] *chem* Chromat *n*; **~atic** [krə'mætik] *a* farbig, Farben-; *phys mus* chromatisch; *s pl mit sing* Farbenlehre *f*; *~~ printing* Buntdruck *m*; *~~ scale* chromatische Tonleiter *f*; *~~ spectrum* Farbenspektrum *n*; **~atin** ['kroumətin] *biol* Chromatin *n*; **~e** [kroum] *chem* Chrom; Chromgelb *n*; *~~ (steel)* Chromstahl *m*; *~~ tanning* Chromgerbung *f*; **~ic** ['-ik] *a* Chrom-; *~~ acid* Chromsäure *f*; **~ite** ['-ait], *~e iron (ore)* Chromit *n*, Chromeisenstein *m*; **~ium** ['-iəm] *chem* Chrom *n*; *~~ plated* verchromt; **~o(lithograph)** ['kroumou('liθəgrɑ:f)] (einzelner) lithographische(r) Farbendruck *m*; **~olithography** [-o(u)li'θɔgrəfi] lithographische(r) Farbendruck *m (als Verfahren)*; **~osome** ['krouməsoum] *biol* Chromosom *n*.

chron|ic(al) ['krɔnik(əl)] *med* chronisch; *allg* dauernd, (be)ständig; *vulg* schlimm, böse; **~icle** ['krɔnikl] *s* Chronik *f*; *tr* aufzeichnen; **~icler** ['-iklə] Chronist *m*; **~ograph** [krɔnə'grɑ:f] Zeitschreiber *m (Gerät)*; **~ologer, ~ologist** [krə'nɔlədʒə, -ist] Chronologe *m*; **~ologic(al)** [krɔnə'lɔdʒik(əl)] chronologisch; *in ~~ order* in zeitlicher Folge; *~~ chart* Zeittafel *f*; **~ologize** [krə'nɔlədʒaiz] *tr* chronologisch, zeitlich ordnen; **~ology** [krə'nɔlədʒi] Chronologie; chronologische Übersicht, Zeitfolge *f*; **~ometer** [krə'nɔmitə] Chronometer *n*; **~ometry** [krə'nɔmitri] Zeitmessung *f*; **~oscope** ['krɔnəskoup] Chronoskop *n*, Zeitzeichenschreiber *m*.

chrys|alid, ~alis ['krisəlid, -s] *ent* Puppe, Larve *f*; *fig* Vor-, Übergangsstadium *n*; **~anthemum** [-'sænθəməm] *bot* Chrysantheme *f*; **~oprase** ['-əpreiz] *min* Chrysopras *m*.

chub [tʃʌb] Döbel *m (Fisch)*; **~by** ['-i] pausbäckig; dick, *fam* mollig.

chuck [tʃʌk] **1.** *s* Glucken *n (Lockruf der Glucke)*; *itr (Henne)* glucken; *(Glucke, Mensch)* locken *itr*; *interj* put! put! put! **2.** *tr (unter dem Kinn)* kraulen (*s.o.* jdn); hätscheln, tätscheln; achtlos wegwerfen; loswerden; *(Gewohnheit)* ablegen; *itr* e-n Ball werfen *(Baseball)*; *sl* den Mund halten; *s* sanfte(r) Schlag, Klaps *m* unters Kinn; Kraulen *n*; Wurf; *sl* Fraß *m*; *Am* Rindfleisch *n* geringer Qualität, Kamm *m*; *to ~ away (Gelegenheit)* verpassen, versäumen; *to ~ out (Menschen)* hinauswerfen; *to ~ up* weit wegwerfen; *(Arbeitsplatz)* aufgeben; *to ~ up the sponge* den Versuch aufgeben; *to ~ o.'s. weight about* sich aufspielen; *to give s.o. the ~ (sl)* jdn 'rausschmeißen, an die Luft setzen; *~ it! (fam)* laß das! halt den Mund! **3.** *s* Spann-, Klemm-, Bohrmaschinen-, Bohrfutter *n*; (Ein-)Spannvorrichtung; Spannschraube; Klemme *f*, Klemmkonus *m*; *tr tech* (ein)spannen; **~er-out** *sl* Rausschmeißer *m*.

chuckle ['tʃʌkl] *itr* kichern; *(to ~ to o.s.)* in sich hineinlachen, sich im stillen, insgeheim freuen, sich ins Fäustchen lachen (*at, over* über); glucksen; *s* Gekicher, Glucksen *n*; **~head** Dummkopf *m*; **~headed** *a* dumm, doof.

chuffed [tʃʌft] *a sl* hingerissen.

chug [tʃʌg] *s* Stampfen, Blubbern, Tuckern *n*; *itr (Motor)* blubbern, tuckern; *(Maschine)* stampfen; *to ~ along (Zug)* vorbeirattern; **~-a-lug** *tr Am sl* glucksend trinken.

chukker ['tʃʌkə] *(Polo)* Spielgang *m*.

chum [tʃʌm] *s* (Schul-)Kamerad; (Stuben-, Schlaf-)Genosse; Kumpan, *fam* Kumpel; (Busen-)Freund, Intimus; *pej* Trottel, Gimpel *m*; *itr* zs.wohnen, -leben (*with* mit); eng, intim (mitea.) befreundet sein (*with* mit); *(to ~ up (Am around) with (fam)* sich (eng) anschließen an, intim werden mit; **~-buddy** *Am fam* Busenfreund *m*; **~my** ['-i] *fam* eng befreundet, intim; *to be (very) ~~* ein Herz u. eine Seele sein.

chump [tʃʌmp] (Holz-)Klotz *m*; Keule *(bes. Küche)*; *sl* Birne *f*; *fam* Schafskopf *m*; *off o.'s ~ (sl)* aus dem Häuschen, nicht ganz bei Trost.

chunk [tʃʌŋk] Klumpen; (Holz-)Klotz *m*; dicke(s) Stück *n*; Ranken *(Brot)*; untersetzte(r) Mensch *m*; stämmige(s) Tier *n*; **~y** ['-i] *fam* untersetzt; dick.

church [tʃə:tʃ] Kirche *f*, *(in England nur anglikanisches)* Gotteshaus *n*; Kirche *f*, Gottesdienst *m*; *die* Christen *m pl*; Geistlichkeit *f*; *at, in ~* in der Kirche, beim Gottesdienst; *in the ~* im Gotteshaus, in der Kirche; *poor as a ~ mouse* arm wie eine Kirchenmaus; *to go to ~* in die Kirche gehen, den Gottesdienst besuchen; *to go into, to enter the C~* Geistlicher werden; *Established C~* Staatskirche *f*; *the primitive C~* die Urkirche; **~-goer** Kirchgänger *m*; **~ing** ['-iŋ] erste(r) Kirchgang *m (e-r Wöchnerin)*; **~man** Geistlicher *m*; Mitglied *n* der engl. Staatskirche; **~ parade** *mil* Kirchgang *m*; **~-rate** Kirchensteuer *f*; **~ tower** Kirchturm *m*; **~warden** ['-wɔ:dn] Kirchenvorsteher, -älteste(r) *m*; *sl* lange Tonpfeife *f*; **~woman**

['-'wumən] Kirchenmitglied *n*; e-e in der kirchlichen Arbeit tätige Frau *f*; **~y** ['-i] *Am* (streng) kirchlich (gesinnt); **~yard** ['-'jɑ:d] Kirchhof *m*.
churl [tʃə:l] grobe(r) Klotz, Flegel; Knauser, Knicker *m*; **~ish** ['-iʃ] flegelhaft; filzig, knauserig; störrisch.
churn [tʃə:n] *s* Butterfaß *n*; Zentrifuge; *Br* große Milchkanne *f*; *tr* kirnen, zu Butter machen, verarbeiten; *(to ~ up)* auf-, umwühlen; *itr* buttern; schäumen.
chute, shute [ʃu:t] Wasserfall *m*, Stromschnelle *f*; Wehr *n*; *Am* Lachsleiter; Gleitbahn, -rinne, Schütte, Rutsche; *sport* Rodelbahn *f*; *fam* Fallschirm *m*; *~-~ (Am)* Rutschbahn *f (auf Rummelplätzen)*.
chyle [kail] Milch-, Speisesaft *m*.
chyme [kaim] *physiol* Speisebrei *m*.
cica|da [si'keidə] *pl a. -ae* [-i:], **~la** [si'kɑ:lə] *ent* Zikade, Zirpe *f*.
cicatri|ce ['sikətris], **~x** ['-iks] Narbe *f a. bot*; **~zation** [-'zeiʃən] Vernarbung, Narbenbildung *f*; **~ze** ['sikətraiz] *tr itr* vernarben (lassen).
cicely ['sisili, 'saisli] *bot* Kerbel *m*.
cicerone [tʃitʃə-, sisə'rouni] *pl -ni* [-ai] Fremdenführer *m*; *itr* [-'roun] als Fremdenführer dienen (*s.o.* jdm).
cider ['saidə] Apfelwein, Most *m*; **~-press** Mosterei, Mostpresse *f*.
cigar [si'gɑ:] Zigarre *f*; **~-box** Zigarrenkiste *f*; **~-case** Zigarrenetui *n*; **~-cutter** Zigarrenabschneider *m*; **~et(te)** [sigə'ret] Zigarette *f*; *~~-box* Zigarettenschachtel *f*; *~~-case* Zigarettenetui *n*; *~~-end, -stub, Am -butt* Zigarettenstummel *m*, Kippe *f*; *~~-holder* Zigarettenspitze *f*; *~~ paper* Zigarettenpapier *n*; *~~ tip* Mundstück *n*; *~~ tray* Bauch-, Tragladen *m*; **~illo** [sigə'rilou] Zigarillo *m* od *n*, *fam a. f*; **~ lighter** Zigarrenanzünder *m*.
cilia ['siljə] *pl scient* (Ränder *m pl* der) Augenlider *n pl*; Wimpern *f pl a. ent bot*; *zoo bot* Flimmer(härchen *n pl*) *m pl*, Zilien *f pl*; **~ry** ['-ri] Wimper-.
cinch [sintʃ] *s Am* Sattelgurt *m*; *sl* Kinderspiel *n*; *(a.: dead ~)* todsichere Sache *f*; *tr (Sattel)* mit e-m Sattelgurt befestigen; *fig sl* sicherstellen; Schwierigkeiten machen, e-n Stein in den Weg legen (*s.o.* jdm).
cinchona [siŋ'kounə] Chinarindenbaum *m*; *(~ bark)* China-, Fieberrinde *f*.
cincture ['siŋktʃə] *s* Gürtel, Gurt; *arch* Saum, Gurt; (Säulen-)Kranz *m*, Riemchen *n*; *tr* umgürten, -zäunen.
cinder ['sində] verkohlte(s) Stück *n* Holz; Schlacke *f*; *sl* Schuß *m* Rum *(im Tee)*; *(~-path, -track) sport* Aschenbahn; *pl* Asche *f*; **~ cone** *geol* Aschenkegel *m*; **C~ella** [-'relə] Aschenbrödel, -puttel *n*.
cine ['sini] *(in Zssgen)* Film-, Kino-; **~-camera** Filmkamera *f*; **~-film** Kinofilm *m*; **~ma** ['sinimə] Kino, Film-, Lichtspieltheater *n*; *the ~~* der Film; *~~ goer* (regelmäßiger) Kinobesucher *m*; *~~ poster* Filmplakat *n*; **~mactor, ~mactress** [-'mæktə, -tris] *Am* Filmschauspieler(in *f*) *m*; **~mascope** [-mə'skoup] Breit(lein)wand *f*; **~matic** [-'mætik] *a* Film-; *s pl mit sing* Filmkunst *f*; **~matograph** [sini'mætəgrɑ:f] Kinematograph *m*; **~matographer** [sinimə'təgrəfə] Kameramann *m*; **~matographic** [sinimætə'græfik] kinematographisch; Film-; **~matography** [sinimə'təgrəfi] Kinematographie, Lichtbildkunst *f*; **~ photomicrography** Filmaufnahme *f* durch Mikroskop; **~-projector** Vorführapparat *m*; **~rama** [sini'rɑ:mə] Cinerama *n (Schutzmarke)*.
ciner|aria [sini'rɛəriə] *bot* Aschenkraut *n*, Zinerarie *f*; **~arium** [-'rɛəriəm] *pl -ia* [-iə] Urnenhalle *f*, Kolumbarium *n*; **~ary** ['sinərəri] Aschen-; *~~ urn* Aschenurne *f*.
cinna|bar ['sinəbɑ:] *s* Zinnober *m*; *a* zinnoberrot; **~mon** ['-mən] *s* Zimt *m*; *a* zimtfarben, -braun.
cinq(ue) [siŋk] *(Spielkarten, Würfel)* Fünf *f*; **~foil** ['-fɔil] *bot* Fünffingerkraut *n*; *arch* Fünfblatt *n*, -paß *m*; **Cinque Ports** [-'pɔ:ts] *Br* (ursprüngl. fünf) privilegierte Häfen *m pl*.
cipher, cypher ['saifə] *s math* Null (-zeichen *n*); *fig* Null *f*, völlig unbedeutende(r) Mensch *m*, völlig belanglose Sache; *(arabische)* Ziffer; Chiffre; Geheimschrift *f*; chiffrierte(s) Schreiben; Chiffrierverfahren *n*; *(~-key)* Schlüssel *m (e-r Geheimschrift)*; *fig* Geheimnis; Monogramm; *(Orgelpfeife)* fehlerhafte(s) Nachklingen *n*; *tr* ausrechnen; chiffrieren, verschlüsseln; *Am fam* ausknobeln, -tüfteln; **~ code** Chiffrierschlüssel *m*; **~ disk** Chiffrierscheibe *f*; **~ed** ['-d] *a* chiffriert, verschlüsselt, in Geheimschrift; *~~ message* Chiffriertext *m*, verschlüsselte Meldung *f*; **~ group** Schlüsselgruppe *f*; **~ing machine** Chiffrier-, Schlüsselmaschine *f*; **~ office** Chiffrierstelle *f*; **~ text** Chiffriertext *m*.

*

circle ['sə:kl] *s math* Kreis *a. allg*; Kreisumfang *m*, -linie *f*, -bogen *m*; *astr* Kreisbahn *f*, Umlauf; Kreislauf *m (des Jahres)*, Periode *f*; Ring; (Stirn-)Reif; *sport* Rundlauf; *theat* Rang; Kreis, Bezirk *m*, Gebiet *n*; *(~ of friends)* Freundes-, Bekanntenkreis; Wirkungskreis *m*, (Einfluß-)Sphäre *f*; Spielraum, Bereich *m*; *tr poet* umgeben, einschließen; *astr* umkreisen, sich bewegen um; umfahren, -schiffen, -segeln, -fliegen; *itr* fahren, segeln, fliegen *(round, about s.th.* um etw); sich im Kreis, auf e-r Kreisbahn bewegen; *(Vogel, aero)* kreisen; *full ~* rund herum, im Kreise; *Arctic, Antarctic ~* Nördliche(r), Südliche(r) Polarkreis *m*; *dress ~ (theat)* 1. Rang *m*; *Polar ~* Polarkreis *m*; *squaring the ~* Quadratur *f* des Kreises; *upper, family ~ (theat)* 2. (od *höherer*) Rang *m*; *vicious ~* Teufelskreis, Circulus vitiosus *m*; **~t** ['-it] kleine(r) Kreis; Stirnreif *m*, -band *n*, Kranz *m*.
circs [sə:ks] *pl sl* Umstände *m pl*.
circuit ['sə:kit] *s* Umkreis, Umfang *m*; (eingeschlossenes) Gebiet *n*, Bezirk *m*; Runde *f*, Rundgang *m*, -fahrt *f*, -flug *m (of* um); Rundreise, Tournee; *jur* Rundreise *f* (e-s Richters), Gerichtsbezirk *m*; (reisende) Gerichtskommission *f*; *Am (methodistischer)* (Kirchen-)Sprengel; Ring, Kreislauf *m*, Periode *f*; Theater-, Kinoring *m*; *aero* Platzrunde *f*; *el* Stromkreis *m*; Schaltung; *radio* Koppelung *f*; *tr* umfahren, -schiffen, -segeln, -fliegen; *itr* e-e Runde, Rundfahrt, -reise machen; sich im Kreis bewegen; *to put in ~ (el)* einschalten; *short ~ (el)* Kurzschluß *m*; **~ous** [sə'kjuitəs] weitschweifig, umständlich; indirekt.
circular ['sə:kjulə] *a* kreisförmig, rund; Kreis-, Rund(reise)-; zirkulierend; sich *(beim Denken)* im Kreise bewegend; *s* Rundschreiben *n*; *court ~* Hofnachrichten *f pl*; **~ize** ['-raiz] *tr* ein Rundschreiben versenden an; **~ letter** Rundschreiben *n*; Umlauf *m*; **~ note** Reisekreditbrief, Reisescheck *m*; **~ railway** Ringbahn *f*; **~ saw** Kreissäge *f*; **~ ticket** Rundreisebillett *n*; **~ tour, trip** Rundreise, -fahrt *f*.
circulat|e ['sə:kjuleit] *itr* zirkulieren *(a. Blut)*, kursieren, umlaufen; herumkommen; die Runde machen, sich verbreiten; *math* periodisch wiederkehren; *tr* in Umlauf setzen; *Am* durch Umlauf bekanntgeben; *tech* umwälzen, -pumpen; *to ~~ about* sich drehen um; **~ing** ['-iŋ] *math* periodisch; Umlauf-; *fin* umlaufend; im Umlauf (befindlich); *~~ capital* Umlaufskapital *n*; *~~ library* Leihbibliothek, -bücherei *f*; *~~ medium* (im Umlauf befindliche) Zahlungsmittel *n pl*; **~ion** [-'leiʃən] (*bes.* Blut-)Zirkulation *f*, Kreislauf *m*; Luft-, atmosphärische Strömungen *f pl*; Ventilation *f*, Durchzug *m*; Verbreitung *(e-r Nachricht, e-r Zeitung)*; Auflage(nhöhe, -ziffer) *f*; (Geld-)Umlauf, (Zahlungs-)Verkehr *m*; *out of ~~* außer Kurs; *with a wide ~~* mit hoher Auflage; *to be in ~~* sich in, im Umlauf befinden, in Umlauf sein; *to put into ~~* in Umlauf setzen, in Verkehr bringen; *to withdraw from ~~* außer Kurs setzen; *(un)covered ~~* (un)gedeckte(r) Notenumlauf *m*; *forced ~~ (fin)* Zwangskurs, -umlauf *m*; *withdrawal from ~~* Außerkurssetzung *f*; *~~ of the blood* Blutkreislauf *m*; *~~ of capital* Kapitalumlauf *m*; *~~ file* Umlaufmappe *f*; *~~ of money* Geldumlauf *m*; **~ory** ['-lətəri] umlaufend, zirkulierend; *~~ disease* Kreislaufkrankheit *f*; *~~ lubrication* Umlaufschmierung *f*.
circum ['sə:kəm] *(in Zssgen)* (her)um-; Um-; **~adjacent** [sə:kəmə'dʒeisənt] (unmittelbar) angrenzend; **~ambient** [-'æmbiənt] umgebend, um-, einhüllend, einschließend; **~ambulate** [-'æmbjuleit] *tr itr* herumgehen (um); *itr* umhergehen; *fig* auf den Busch klopfen; **~cise** ['-saiz] *tr rel med* beschneiden; *fig* läutern, veredeln; **~cision** [-'siʒən] Beschneidung *f*; *C~~* Fest *n* der Beschneidung des Herrn *(1. Jan.)*; **~ference** [sə'kʌmfərəns] *math* Umfang *m a. allg*; *allg* Peripherie *f*, Rand *m*; **~flex** ['-fleks] *a anat* einschließend, -hüllend; *s u. ~~ accent (gram)* Zirkumflex *m*; **~jacent** [-'dʒeisənt] umliegend; **~locution** [-lə'kju:ʃən] Umschreibung *f*; lange(s) Reden *f pl (n)*, Weitschweifigkeit *f*, viele Worte *n pl*, Umschweife *pl*; **~navigate** [-'nævigeit] *tr* umschiffen, -segeln; **~navigation** ['-'geiʃən] Umschiffung, Umsegelung *f*; **~polar** [-'poulə] *geog* zirkumpolar; *~~ star (astr)* Zirkumpolarstern *m*; **~scribe** ['-skraib] *tr math (Figur)* um-, (be)schreiben; *math* legen um *(e-e Figur)*; begrenzen, einschränken; definieren; **~scription** [-'skripʃən] *math* Umschreibung; Ab-, Begrenzung, Beschränkung; Grenze *f*; (abgegrenzter) Bezirk *m*; Definition; *(Münze)* Umschrift *f*.
circumspect ['sə:kəmspekt] umsichtig; bedachtsam, sorgsam, sorgfältig; behutsam, vorsichtig; **~ion** [-'spekʃən] Umsicht, Bedachtsamkeit; Vorsicht *f*.
circumstan|ce ['sə:kəmstəns] Umstand *m*, Tatsache *f*; Sachverhalt *m*; Einzelheit *f*; Umstände *m pl (die man sich macht)*; *pl* (nähere) Umstände *m pl*, Einzelheiten, Gegebenheiten *f pl*, Verhältnisse *n pl*; Fall *m*; *in, under the ~~s* unter diesen Umständen, in diesem Fall; *in, under no ~~s* unter keinen Umständen, in keinem, auf keinen Fall; *in all ~~s* unter allen Umständen; *in easy, good* od *flourishing ~~s* in angenehmen, guten Verhältnissen; *in bad, reduced* od *straitened ~~s* in schlechten, beschränkten Verhältnissen; *without ~~* ohne Umstände (zu machen); *the ~~ that* der Umstand,

daß; *that depends on ~~s* das kommt darauf an; *attendant, concomitant ~~s (pl)* Begleitumstände *m pl*; *aggravating, extenuating ~~s (pl) (jur)* erschwerende, mildernde Umstände *m pl*; **~tial** [-'stænʃəl] genau, eingehend, ausführlich; zufällig; *jur* sich aus den Umständen ergebend; *~~ evidence* Indizienbeweis *m*; *on ~~ evidence* auf Grund der Indizien; **~tiality** [-ʃi'æliti] Ausführlichkeit; Zufälligkeit *f*; **~tiate** [-'stænʃieit] *tr* ausführlich beschreiben *od* angeben; genau belegen *od* beweisen.

circum|vallate [sə:kəm'væleit] *tr* mit e-m Wall, mit Befestigungsanlagen umgeben; **~vallation** [-'leiʃən] Umwallung *f*; **~vent** [-'vent] *tr* herumgehen um; Fallen stellen (*s.o.* jdm); hereinlegen, überlisten, hintergehen, überspielen; (daran) hindern (*from doing* zu tun); *(Sache)* umgehen, verhindern, vereiteln, verhüten; **~vention** [-'venʃən] Überlistung; Verhinderung, Vereitelung *f*; **~volution** [-'lu:ʃən] (Um-)Drehung, Umwälzung *f a. fig*; Windung; *arch* Rolle, Schnecke; Umlaufzeit, Periode *f*.

cir|cus ['sə:kəs] Zirkus *m*; Arena *f*; *Br* runde(r) Platz, Stern *m*; Bergrund *n*; *Am sl* Schau *f*, Nackttanz *m*; **~que** [sə:k] *geol* Hochtal *n*.

cirr|hosis [si'rousis] *med* Leberzirrhose, -schrumpfung, *fam* Säuferleber *f*; **~ocumulus** ['sirou'kju:mjuləs] Schäfchenwolke *f*; **~o-stratus** ['sirou-'streitəs] fedrige Schicht-, Schleierwolke *f*; **~ous** ['sirəs] rankenförmig, -tragend; **~us** ['sirəs] *pl -i* [-ai] *bot* Ranke *f*; *zoo* Anhang *m*; *(~~ cloud)* Zirrus(wolke *f*) *m*, Faser-, Federwolke *f*; *~~ stripe* Zirrusstreifen *m*.

cissy ['sisi] *s. sissy*.

cist [sist] *hist* Ziste, Zista *f (Behälter)*; (prähistorisches) Steingrab *n*.

Cistercian [sis'tə:ʃiən] *rel* Zisterzienser *m*.

cistern ['sistən] Zisterne *f*; Wasser-, Hochbehälter; Tank *m*, Reservoir *n*.

citadel ['sitədl] Zitadelle; *fig* Zuflucht *f*.

cit|ation [s(a)i'teiʃən] *jur* (Vor-)Ladung *f* (vor Gericht); Zitieren *n*, Anführung *f*; Zitat *n*; *mil Am* ehrenvolle, lobende Erwähnung *f*; **~e** [sait] *tr* (vor Gericht) laden, vorladen (*before* vor); zitieren, anführen, sich berufen (*s.th.* auf etw).

citizen ['sitizn] Bürger, Städter, (Stadt-)Bewohner, Einwohner; Zivilist; Staatsangehörige(r), -bürger *m*; *honorary ~* Ehrenbürger *m*; *~ of the world* Weltbürger *m*; *~ by birth* Staatsangehörige(r) *m* kraft Geburt; **~ship** ['-ʃip] Bürgerrecht *n*; Staatsangehörigkeit *f*.

citr|ic ['sitrik] *a chem* Zitronen-; *~~ acid* Zitronensäure *f*; **~on** ['-ən] *s* Zitronenbaum *m*; Zitronat; Zitronengelb *n*; *a* zitronengelb; **~us** ['-əs] Citrus *m*, Agrume; *(~~ fruit)* Zitrusfrucht *f*.

city ['siti] (große, bedeutende) Stadt, *Am* Stadtgemeinde *f*; Zentrum *n*, Stadtkern *m*, Altstadt *f*, Geschäftsviertel *n*, City *f*; *(auf Briefen:)* hier; *the C~* die (Londoner) City; *freedom of the ~* Ehrenbürgerschaft *f*; *freeman of the ~* Ehrenbürger *m*; *garden ~* Gartenstadt, Siedlung *f*; *the Holy C~* (das Himmlische) Jerusalem; **C~-article** *(Zeitung)* Börsen-, Marktbericht *m*; **~-authorities** *pl* Stadtverwaltung *f*, -behörden *f pl*; Städtische Ämter *n pl*; **~-bound traffic** einstrahlende(r) Verkehr *m*; **~-boundary** Stadtgrenze *f*; **~ centre** Stadtzentrum *n*; **~ council** Stadtparlament *n*, Gemeindevertretung *f*, -rat *m*; **~-editor** Schriftleiter, Redakteur *m* des Handels-, *Am* des Lokalteils *(e-r Zeitung)*; **~-father** Stadtvater *m (Magistratsbeamter* od *Ratsherr)*; **~ gate** Stadttor *n*; **~ hall, building** *Am* Rathaus *n*; **~ life** Großstadtleben *n*; **~man** Finanz- *od* Geschäftsmann *m*; **~ manager** *Am* Stadtdirektor *m*; **~ news** *pl mit sing* Handelsnachrichten *f pl*; **~ planner** *Am* Stadtplaner *m*; **~ prices** *pl* Großhandelspreise *m pl*; **~ railway** Stadtbahn *f*; **~ slicker** *Am sl* Asphaltmensch, Städter *m*; **~-state** Stadtstaat *m*; **~ wall** Stadtmauer *f*.

civet ['sivit] *(~-cat)* Zibetkatze *f*.

civic ['sivik] *a* (staats)bürgerlich, Bürger-; städtisch, Stadt-; *s pl mit sing* Staatsbürger-, Gemeinschaftskunde *f*.

civil ['sivl] menschlich, Menschen-; (staats)bürgerlich, (Staats-)Bürger-; zivil(rechtlich), Zivil-; zivil, bürgerlich, Zivil-; höflich, gesittet, entgegenkommend, freundlich; **~ aircraft, airplane** Zivilflugzeug *n*; **~ air defence** Luftschutz *m*; **~ aviation** Zivilluftfahrt *f*; **~ case** Zivilprozeß *m*; **~ desobedience** passive(r) Widerstand *m*; **~ engineer** Bauingenieur *m*; **~ engineering** Ingenieurbau *m*; **~ guard** Einwohner-, Bürgerwehr *f*; **~ian** [si'viljən] *s* Zivilist *m*, Zivilperson *f*; Zivilrechtslehrer, -rechtler *m*; *a* Zivil-; *~~ occupation* Zivilberuf *m*; **~ity** [-'viliti] Höflichkeit *f*; **~ization** [sivilai'zeiʃən] Zivilisation, Kultur, Gesittung *f*; **~ize** ['sivilaiz] *tr* zivilisieren; bilden; zu e-m gesitteten Menschen machen; **~ jurisdiction** Zivilgerichtsbarkeit *f*; **~ law** bürgerliche(s) Recht *n*; **C~ Law** das Römische Recht; **~ liberties** *pl* die bürgerlichen Freiheiten *f pl*; **~ marriage** standesamtliche Trauung *f*; **~ population** Zivilbevölkerung *f*; **~ procedure** Zivilprozeß *m*; **~ rights** *pl* Bürgerrechte, die bürgerlichen Ehrenrechte *n pl*; **C~ Servant** (Staats-) Beamte(r) *m*; **C~ Service** Staatsdienst *m*; *the C~ Service* die Zivilverwaltung; **~ war** Bürgerkrieg *m*.

civ(v)ies ['siviz] *pl fam* Zivilklamotten *f pl*; Zivilisten *m pl*.

clabber ['klæbə] *Am s* dicke, gestandene Milch *f*; *itr (Milch)* dick werden.

clack [klæk] *s* Klappern, Rasseln; Plappern *n*; Ventil(klappe *f*); *(~ valve)* Klappenventil *n*; *itr* klappern, rasseln; *fam* schwatzen; *(Henne)* gackern.

clad [klæd] *a* bekleidet, angezogen; *tech* umkleidet; plattiert.

claim [kleim] *s* Anspruch *m (to* auf); Forderung *(on s.o.* gegen jdn); *Am* Behauptung *f*; Anrecht *n*; *(~ of right)* Rechtstitel *m*; *min* (beanspruchte) Parzelle; Mutung *f*; Kux *m*; *jur* Schadenssumme, Klage, Mängelrüge, Reklamation *f*; *tr (Person)* Anspruch erheben *od* machen auf; verlangen, fordern, geltend machen; *Am* behaupten, versichern; *to lay ~ to, to make, to set up a ~ to, to put in a ~ for s.th. against s.o.* gegenüber jdm Anspruch erheben auf; *to lodge a ~ against s.o.* gegen jdn e-e Forderung einklagen; *to stake out a ~* e-e Parzelle abstecken; *a ~ for s.th. against s.o.* Anspruch erheben auf; *to ~ compensation* e-e Entschädigung verlangen; *to waive a ~* auf e-n Anspruch verzichten, von e-m Anspruch zurücktreten; *where do I ~ my baggage? (Am)* wo bekomme ich mein Gepäck? *outstanding ~s (pl)* Außenstände *pl*; *wage ~s (pl)* Lohnansprüche *m pl*; *~ for damages* Schadensanspruch *m*; *~ of indemnification* Entschädigungsanspruch *m*; *~ for maintenance* Unterhaltsanspruch *m*; **~able** ['-əbl] zu beanspruchen(d), zu fordern(d); **~ant, ~er** ['-ənt, '-ə] Antragsteller; Anspruchsberechtigte(r), Kläger *m*.

clairvoyan|ce [klɛə'vɔiəns] Hellsehen *n*; tiefe Einsicht *f*; **~t** [-t] *(f a. ~~e) s* Hellseher(in *f*) *m*; *a* hellseherisch; hellsichtig.

clam [klæm] *s* (eßbare) Muschel *f*; *Am sl* maulfaule(r) Mensch; Stiesel, Döskopf; *Am sl* Dollar; *Am sl* Schnitzer, Fehler *m*; *itr Am* Muscheln suchen; *to ~ up (Am sl)* die Schnauze, das Maul halten; **~bake** ['-beik] *Am* Picknick *n* mit e-m Muschelgericht; *Am sl* lärmende Versammlung *f*; Reinfall, Fehlschlag *m*; Jazzkonzert *n*.

clamant ['kleimənt] *lit* laut, lärmend, lärmvoll, schreiend; *fig* dringend (Abhilfe verlangend).

clamber ['klæmbə] *itr* (mühsam) klettern.

clamm|iness ['klæminis] Feuchtigkeit; Klebrigkeit *f*; **~y** ['-i] feucht(-kalt), schleimig, klebrig; *(Brot)* teigig.

clamo|rous ['klæmərəs] laut, lärmend, schreiend; stürmisch fordernd; **~(u)r** ['-ə] *s* Geschrei *n*, Lärm *m*; *(Wind)* Heulen *n*; laute Forderung *od* Klage *f*; *itr* schreien, lärmen; *itr tr* laut fordern, rufen nach (*s.th., for s.th.* etw); laut protestieren (*s.th., against s.th.* gegen etw).

clamp [klæmp] **1.** *s* (Eisen-)Klammer, Krampe; (Spannfutter-)Klemme, (Schraub-)Zwinge, *(Kabel)* Schelle *f*; *(Schi)* Strammer *m*; *tr* (ver)klammern; festklemmen; (ein)spannen; *to ~ down (fam)* unter Druck setzen (*on s.o.* jdn); **2.** *s Br* Haufen, Stoß, Stapel *m*; (Kartoffel-, Rüben-)Miete *f*; *tr* (auf-) stapeln; einmieten; **3.** *meist dial* schwere(r) Tritt *m*.

clan [klæn] *(Schottland)* Sippe(nverband *m*) *f*, Stamm *m*; Sippschaft; *fig* Clique; Art, Klasse *f*; **~nish** ['-iʃ] stammesbewußt; **~sman** Sippenangehörige(r) *m*.

clandestine [klæn'destin] heimlich, geheim; **~ trade** Schleichhandel *m*.

clang [klæŋ] *s* (lauter) Klang *m*, Klirren, Rasseln *n*; Schrei *m (der Kraniche)*; *itr tr* klingen, klirren, rasseln (lassen); *(Trompeten)* schmettern; **~orous** ['-gərəs] laut, schallend, klirrend, rasselnd; **~o(u)r** ['-gə] Klirren *n*, Schall *m*; *(Trompete)* Geschmetter; *(Glocken)* Geläut *n*.

clank [klæŋk] *s* Klirren, Geklirr, Rasseln, Gerassel *n*; *pl Am sl* Säuferwahnsinn *m*, nervöse Erschöpfung *f*; *itr tr* klirren, rasseln (lassen).

clap [klæp] **1.** *tr* (zs.)schlagen; klopfen, klapsen, e-n Klaps geben (*s.o.* jdm); beklatschen, Beifall spenden (*s.o.* jdm); *(die Sporen)* geben; *(ins Gefängnis)* werfen, sperren; *(Zoll auf e-e Ware)* schlagen; *itr* (Beifall) klatschen; *s* (lauter) Schlag *m*; (Hände-)Klatschen *n*, Beifall, Applaus; *obs* Klaps, leichte(r) Schlag *m*; *to ~ on (Segel)* setzen; *to ~ over* befestigen, legen auf; *to ~ up (Handel, Frieden)* in Eile abschließen; laut klatschen; *to ~ eyes on s.o.* jdn erblicken, sehen; unerwartet treffen; *to ~ o.'s hands* in die Hände klatschen; *to ~ hold of s.o. (fam)* jdn festnehmen; zu fassen kriegen; *to ~ s.o. on the shoulder* jdm (freundschaftlich) auf die Schulter klopfen; *~ of thunder* Donnerschlag *m*; **2.** *vulg* Tripper *m*; **~board** *Am* Schalbrett *n*; *Br* (Wand- *od* Dach-)Schindel, Faßdaube *f*; **~net** Vogel-, Schmetterlingsnetz *n*; **~per** ['-ə] (Beifall-)Klatschende(r); *(Glokke)* Klöppel *m*; (Vogel-)Klapper;

Br sl Zunge *f*; **~trap** ['-træp] *s* Effekthascherei *f*; Geschmus(e), Gerede, Geschwätz *n*; Schwindel; Klimbim *m*; *a* effekthaschend, aufgemacht.
claque [klæk] *theat* Claque *f*; *pol* Gefolge *n*, Gefolgschaft *f*.
claret ['klærət] französische(r) Rotwein, *bes.* Bordeaux *m*; Weinrot *n*; *(künstliche)* rote Angelfliege *f (für Lachse)*; *sl* Blut *n*.
clari|fication [klærifi'keiʃən] Klärung *a. fig*; Klarstellung, Verdeutlichung *f*; **~fy** ['-fai] *tr* abklären, läutern *a. fig*; reinigen; *itr* klar werden, sich klären *a. fig*; sich läutern; *~~ing bath* Klärbad *n*; **~ty** ['-ti] Klarheit *f a. fig*.
clari|(o)net [klæri'net, 'klæriənet] *mus* Klarinette *f*; **~on** ['klæriən] *s poet* Trompetenschall *m*; *mus* Zinke *f*; *a* laut u. hell; schmetternd.
clash [klæʃ] *itr* klirren, rasseln; (zs.-, aufea.)prasseln, -prallen (*with* mit); anea.-, zs.stoßen, kollidieren *a. fig*; *fig* (zeitlich) zs.fallen; sich widersprechen, nicht zs.-, zuea. passen (*with* mit); *to ~ into s.o.* auf jdn stoßen; *s* Klirren *n*; Zs.prall, -stoß *a. fig*; *fig* Widerstreit *m*; Disharmonie, Diskrepanz; Kollision *f*, Zs.treffen *n*.
clasp [klɑ:sp] *tr* fest-, an-, ein-, zuhaken; (mit e-m Haken) befestigen; umklammern, umfassen; fassen, (er-)greifen; fest drücken (*to* an); *s* Haken *m* (u. Öse); Haspe, Klammer; Schnalle; Spange *(a. als Auszeichnung)*; (Buch-)Schließe; Umklammerung; Umarmung *f*; feste(r) Griff; (fester) Händedruck *m*; *by ~ of hands* durch Handschlag; *to ~ s.o. in o.'s arms* jdn in die Arme schließen; *to ~ s.o.'s hand* jdm die Hand drücken; *to ~ o.'s hands* die Hände falten; **~-knife** Klappmesser *n*.
class [klɑ:s] *s allg (a. Wert-)*Klasse; (Gesellschafts-)Klasse, Schicht *f*, Stand, Rang *m*; (*rail* u. Schul-)Klasse; Unterrichts-, Schulstunde; Vorlesung *f*, Kolleg *n*, Kurs *m*; *Br (Universität)* Klassifizierung *f* im Examen; Jahrgang *m*; *sl* hohe Qualität, Klasse, Eleganz *f*; *pl* Unterricht *m*; *the ~es* die oberen Klassen, die höheren Stände; *tr* einstufen, klassieren, in Gruppen einteilen, (in e-e Klasse) einordnen; *itr* eingeordnet sein; *to ~ with* auf e-e Stufe stellen mit, gleichstellen *dat*; *in a ~ by itself* von besonderem Rang, von besonderer Qualität; einzigartig; *in the same ~* derselben Art, Gruppe; *not to be in the same ~ with* sich nicht messen können mit; *first-, second-, third-~ matter (Am)* Briefpost *f*, Zeitungen, Drucksachen *f pl*; *middle ~* Mittelstand *m*; *no ~ (sl)* Mist, Dreck *m*, miese(s) Zeug *n*; *top of the ~* Klassenbester *m*; **~able** ['-əbl] klassierbar, einzuordnen(d); **~-book** Schulbuch; *Am* Klassen-, Erinnerungsbuch *n*; **~-conscious** klassenbewußt; **~-consciousness** Klassenbewußtsein *n*; **~-distinctions** *pl* Klassenunterschiede *m pl*; **~-fellow, -mate** Klassen-, Schulkamerad, Schulfreund *m*; **~-hatred** Klassenhaß *m*; **~-interest** Klasseninteresse *n*; **~less** ['-lis] klassenlos; **~ record** Klassenbestleistung *f*; **~-room** Klassenzimmer *n*; **~-war** Klassenkampf *m*; **~y** ['-i] *sl* Klasse, prima, (schwer) in Ordnung.
classic ['klæsik] *a* erstklassig, -rangig; anerkannt; *bes. lit (Kunst)* klassisch; ausgewogen, klar, einfach; *fam* (alt-)bekannt, berühmt; *s* Klassiker; antike(r) Autor *od* Schriftsteller; Alt-, Klassische(r) Philologe *m*; klassische(s) Werk, Spiel *n*; *the C~s* die Alten Sprachen *(Latein u. Griechisch)*; die antike Literatur; **~al** ['-əl] erstklassig, -rangig; *bes. mus* klassisch; *lit* antik; humanistisch (gebildet); *(Stil)* einfach, schlicht, klar, harmonisch, vollendet, in sich (ab)gerundet; *~~ education* humanistische Bildung *f*; **~ism** ['-sizm] Klassik *f*; **~ist** ['-sist] klassische(r) Philologe *m*.
classi|fiable ['klæsifaiəbl] klassifizierbar; einzuteilen(d); **~fication** [klæsifi'keiʃən] Klassifizierung, Einteilung, (An-, Ein-)Ordnung, Eingruppierung, Sortierung; *tech* Klassierung *f*; **~ficatory** [-'keitəri] klassifizierend; Einteilungs-; **~fied** ['-faid] *a Am mil* geheim; *~~ ad(vertising) (Zeitung)* Klein-, Suchanzeige *f*; *~~ document, matter (Am mil)* Verschlußsache; geheime Kommandosache *f*; **~fier** ['-faiə] Klassifizierer *m*; **~fy** ['klæsifai] *tr* klassifizieren, (in Klassen, Gruppen) einteilen, (an-, ein)ordnen, sortieren, sichten; *tech* klassieren.
clatter ['klætə] *s* Klappern, Rasseln, Rattern; Stimmengewirr *n*; Lärm, Tumult *m*; *tr itr* klappern, rasseln, rattern (lassen); *itr* lärmen, Lärm machen; *to ~ along* dahinrattern, -rasseln; *to ~ down* herunterpoltern.
clause [klɔ:z] kurze(r) Satz *m*; Zitat *n*; *jur* Vertragsbestimmung, Klausel *f*, Vorbehalt; Absatz, Paragraph *m*; *arbitration, currency, escape, jurisdiction ~* Schiedsgerichts-, Währungs-, Rücktritts-, Gerichtsstandklausel *f*; *main, subordinate ~* Haupt-, Nebensatz *m*; *most favo(u)red nation ~* Meistbegünstigungsklausel *f*; *penalty ~* Vertrags-, Konventionalstrafe *f*.
claustr|al ['klɔ:strəl] klösterlich; Kloster-; **~ophobia** [-'foubiə] Platzangst *f*.
clavichord ['klævikɔ:d] Klavichord *n*.
clavicle ['klævikl] *anat* Schlüsselbein *n*.
claw [klɔ:] *s* Kralle, Klaue *a. tech*; Tatze, Pratze, Pfote *a. pej*; (Krebs-)Schere *f*; *tech* Haken *m*, Drahtzange *f*; *tr* packen, zerren; zerkratzen, zerkrallen; *(juckende Stelle)* kratzen; *to ~ off* von der Küste ab-, wegtreiben, -getrieben werden; *to put the ~ on s.o. (Am sl)* jdn anpumpen; jdn festnehmen; **~-hammer** Klauen-, Splitthammer *m*; **~-hatchet** Klauenbeil *n*.
clay [klei] *s* Lehm, Ton *m*; Steingut *n*; *allg* (feuchte) Erde *f*, Schlamm, Schmutz, Dreck *m*; *poet (Bibel)* Erde *f*, Staub; (Menschen-)Leib *m*; *(~ pipe)* Tonpfeife *f*; *tr* mit Lehm bedecken *od* mischen; *to bake, to mo(u)ld, to tread the ~* den Lehm brennen, streichen, treten; *to wet, to moisten o.'s ~ (fig)* einen hinter die Binde gießen; **~brick** Tonziegel *m*; **~ey** ['-i] lehmig, tonig; *~(~) marl* Tonmergel *m*; **~ pigeon** Tontaube; *Am sl* Kleinigkeit *f*; **~ pit** Lehm-, Tongrube *f*; **~ slate, shale** Tonschiefer *m*; **~ soil** Lehmboden *m*; **~ware** Ton-, Töpferwaren *f pl*.

*

clean [kli:n] **1.** *a* rein, sauber *a. fig*; reinlich; frisch, neu, unbenutzt; *(Papier)* weiß, unbeschrieben; *fig* einwandfrei, tadellos; unschuldig; vorbehaltlos, uneingeschränkt; *(Wechsel)* einwandfrei; *(~-cut)* klar, scharf(geschnitten), wohlgeformt, -gestaltet; geschickt, gewandt, *fam* gekonnt; *tech* rauchfrei; **2.** *adv* vollkommen, -ständig, völlig, ganz; **3.** *tr* reinigen, säubern, putzen; schrubben, abwischen; blank machen; *(Fisch, Geflügel)* ausnehmen; *(to ~ out) Am sl (Gegner)* fertigmachen; *to ~ down* abwischen, -bürsten; gründlich abwaschen; *to ~ out* beseitigen, aufräumen; *(Geld)* aufbrauchen; *s.o. (fam)* jdn ausnehmen; *to be ~ed out (fam)* blank sein, kein Geld mehr haben; *to ~ up (tr)* reine-, saubermachen, aufräumen, aufwischen; *fam* fertigmachen; *tech* absorbieren; *sl (als Gewinn)* ein-, in die Tasche stecken; viel verdienen; *itr* s-e Arbeit zu Ende bringen; sich zurechtmachen, sich waschen; **4.** *to come ~ (sl)* alles gestehen; *to give s.o. a ~ bill of health (fig)* jdm bescheinigen, daß er e-e reine Weste hat; *to have ~ hands, a ~ slate (fig)* e-e reine Weste haben; *to have a ~ record* e-e tadellose Vergangenheit haben; *to keep ~* sauberhalten; *to make a ~ breast of s.th.* sich etw vom Herzen reden, etw frei u. offen bekennen; *to make a ~ copy of s.th.* etw ins reine schreiben; *to make a ~ sweep of s.th.* mit e-r S vollständig aufräumen; *to show a ~ pair of heels* das Weite suchen; *to win by a ~ sweep* e-n überwältigenden Sieg davontragen; **~-bred** *a* rein(rassig); **~-cut** scharf umrissen; *fig* klar; **~er** ['-ə] Reiniger *m*, Reinigungsmittel *n*; Reinigungs-, Waschanstalt; Putzfrau *f*; *dry-~~'s* chemische Reinigung *f*; **~-handed** *a fig* mit reiner Weste; **~ing** ['-iŋ] Reinigung, Säuberung *f*; **~-limbed** *a (Mensch)* gutgebaut; **~liness** ['klenlinis] Reinlichkeit, Sauberkeit *f*; **~ly** *adv* ['kli:nli] sauber; tadellos; gewandt; *a* ['klenli] reinlich, sauber; **~ness** ['-nis] Sauberkeit *f*; **~se** [klenz] *tr lit obs* reinigen, säubern, *(Bibel) (vom Aussatz)* heilen, rein machen; *fig* läutern; *(von Sünde)* frei machen; **~ser** ['klenzə] Reinigungsmittel *n*; **~-shaven** *a* glattrasiert; **~-up** Reine-, Saubermachen *n*; *sl* Profit, Gewinn *m*.
clear [kliə] **1.** *a* klar; hell, rein; deutlich, scharf, fest umrissen; ersichtlich, verständlich; zweifelsfrei, eindeutig; *(Straße)* frei; *(Weg)* offen; frei (*of* von); sicher, zuversichtlich, entschlossen (*of, on* in, hinsichtlich); frei von Schuld, unschuldig; *(Zeit, Summe)* voll; Steuern u. Unkosten abgezogen; schuldenfrei; *(Gewinn)* Rein-; Netto-; *(Himmel)* wolkenlos; **2.** *adv* (voll u.) ganz, völlig, vollkommen, vollständig; abseits; *fam* geradeswegs, mitten durch; **3.** *s* Klartext *m*; *Am* leere Stelle *f*, freie(r) Platz *m*, Lichtung *f*; **4.** *tr* klar, hell, deutlich machen; auf-, erhellen; *(Straße)* frei machen; räumen; (ent-)leeren; *(Wald)* roden; *(Weg)* bahnen; *(Konto)* ausgleichen; *(Schuld)* bereinigen, begleichen; säubern; *(Tisch)* abräumen; aufräumen; klären; *com (Lager)* räumen; überholen, springen über, vorbeikommen an *(ohne zu berühren)*; *fig* freimachen, befreien (*of, from* von); verständlich machen; *jur* entlasten, freisprechen (*of* von); für unbedenklich erklären; genehmigen; freigeben; *fin* bezahlen, begleichen; einlösen; *(Grundstück)* von Belastungen freimachen; (rein) gewinnen, einnehmen, (wieder) hereinbekommen; die Erlaubnis zur Veröffentlichung erhalten (*s.th.* für etw); *radio (Sendezeit)* kaufen; *(Ware)* verzollen; zollamtlich abfertigen; *tech* entstören, *(Störung)* beseitigen; *(Aufnahme)* löschen; **5.** *itr* klar, hell, deutlich werden; *(Himmel) (to ~ up)* aufklaren; *(Schiff)* absegeln, -fahren; klarkommen; *(to ~ in, out)* Hafengebühren bezahlen; **6.** *in ~* im Klartext,

unverschlüsselt; *in the* ~ unbehindert; schuldenfrei; *tech* im Lichten; *to come out of a* ~ *sky* aus heiterem Himmel kommen; *to be* ~ *about* im klaren sein über; *to get* ~ *of s.th.* etw loswerden; *to have a* ~ *head* e-n klaren Kopf haben; *to keep* ~ *of* sich frei machen, sich frei halten von; *to make o.s.* ~ sich verständlich machen, sich verständlich ausdrücken; *to* ~ *expenses* auf s-e Kosten kommen; *to* ~ *the hurdle (Am)* die Schwierigkeiten überwinden; *to* ~ *o.'s throat* sich räuspern; *all* ~*!* Gefahr vorbei! ~ *the decks! (mar)* klar Deck! ~ *of charges* kostenfrei; *a* ~ *conscience* ein reines, gutes Gewissen; *the* ~ *contrary* genau das Gegenteil, das genaue G.; *three* ~ *days* drei volle, volle drei Tage; ~ *of debt* schuldenfrei; **7.** *to* ~ **away** *tr* ab-, wegräumen *(bes. vom Tisch)*; *fig (Zweifel)* beseitigen; *(Schwierigkeiten)* überwinden; *itr* nachlassen, aufhören; *(Wolken)* sich verziehen, verschwinden; *to* ~ **off** *tr* wegbringen, beseitigen, weg-, fortschaffen, sich vom Halse schaffen; *(Waren)* abstoßen; *itr* weg-, fortgehen, sich entfernen, sich (auf u.) davon machen; verschwinden; *fam* abhauen, türmen; *to* ~ **out** *tr* säubern, reinigen, ausräumen; *itr* sich aus dem Staub machen, verduften; ausziehen; *to be* ~*ed out* blank sein, kein Geld mehr haben; *to* ~ **up** *tr* aufräumen; ins reine, in Ordnung bringen; fertig machen, abschließen; (auf)klären; *itr (Wetter)* sich aufklären, sich aufheitern; **8.** *all* ~ Entwarnung *f*; ~**-cut** *a* scharf geschnitten; *fig* klar, unzweideutig, eindeutig; ~**-eyed** *a lit fig* mit klarem Blick; ~ **gain, profit** Reingewinn *m*; ~**-headed** *a* einsichtig, verständig, verständnisvoll; ~**ness** ['-nis] Klarheit; Deutlichkeit *f*; ~**-sighted** *a* klarsehend, scharfsichtig; ~ **space** freie(r), leere(r) Raum *m*; ~ **span** *(Brücke)* lichte Weite *f*; ~**-starch** *tr (Wäsche)* stärken; ~**-voiced** *a* mit heller Stimme; ~ **width** lichte Weite *f*.

clearance ['kliərəns] Freimachung, (Auf-)Räumung(sarbeiten *f pl*), Entfernung, Beseitigung, Reinigung; *com* Räumung *f* des Lagers; *fin* Tilgung; Rodung; *(Brücke)* lichte Höhe *f*; *tech* Spiel(raum *m*) *n*, Abstand, Zwischenraum, freie(r) Raum *m*, Luft; Überprüfung, Genehmigung, Erlaubnis; Verzollung, Zollabfertigung, Freigabe, Abfertigung *f a. aero*; *(bill of* ~*)* Zoll(abfertigungs)schein *m*; *aero* Starterlaubnis *f*; *aero* Flug *m* über Hindernisse; *ground* ~ *(mot)* Bodenfreiheit *f*; ~ **certificate** Unbedenklichkeitsbescheinigung *f*; ~ **charges, papers** *pl* Verzollungskosten *pl*, -papiere *n pl*; ~ **order** Räumungsbefehl *m*; ~**-sale** Räumungs-, (Total-)Ausverkauf; *Am* Schlußverkauf *m*; ~ **space** *tech* Toleranzfeld *n*; Kompressions-, Verdichtungsraum; schädliche(r) Raum *m*.

clearing ['kliəriŋ] Freimachung, Räumung, Säuberung; (Briefkasten-)Leerung; Entlastung, Rechtfertigung; Bezahlung, Begleichung; Einlösung; Ab-, Verrechnung *f*, Clearing *n*; zollamtliche Abfertigung, Verzollung; Rodung *f*; gerodete(s) Land *n*; Lichtung *f (im Walde)*; *mar* Aufklaren *n*; *com (*~ *of goods)* Ausverkauf *m*; *phot* Abschwächung *f*; ~ **agreement** Verrechnungs-, Clearingabkommen *n*; ~ **bank** Girobank, -kasse *f*; ~ **certificate** Zollabfertigungsschein *m*; ~ **hospital** Feldlazarett *n*, Verwundetensammelstelle *f*; ~ **house** (Bank-)Abrechnungsstelle, Verrechnungskasse *f*; ~ **inwards** *mar* Einklarierung *f*; *certificate of* ~~ Zolleinfuhrbescheinigung *f*; ~ **office** Ausgleichs-, Ab-, Verrechnungsstelle *f*; ~ **outwards** *mar* Ausklarierung *f*; *certificate of* ~~ Ausfuhrbescheinigung *f*; ~ **papers** *pl* Verzollungspapiere *n pl*; ~ **sheet** Abrechnungsbogen *m*; ~**-up** Aufklärung *f*; Aufräumungsarbeiten *f pl*.

cleat [kli:t] *s* Dübel, Keil *m*; *mar* Klampe *f*, Kreuzholz *n*; *dial* Schuhnagel *m*.

cleav|age ['kli:vidʒ] Spalte; (Auf-)Spaltung *a. fig*; *fig* Uneinigkeit; *(line, plane of* ~~*)* Spaltlinie, -fläche; *biol* Zellteilung; *min* Spaltbarkeit *f*; ~**e** [kli:v] **1.** *irr clove, cloven* od *cleft, cleft a. regelmäßig*; *tr* (auf)spalten, zerhacken, ausea.-, zerbrechen; durchstoßen; *(Wasser, Luft)* teilen; *(Weg)* bahnen; *(Menschen)* trennen; *itr* sich spalten, (auf)platzen, ausea.fallen; springen, bersten; sich teilen; sich e-n Weg bahnen; ~**er** ['-ə] Spalter *m*; Hackmesser *n*; **2.** ~*ed*, ~*ed*, *pret a. obs. clave itr* anhaften *(to* an); *fig* halten *(to* zu), ergeben, treu sein *(to* dat); ~**ers** *pl bot* Klebkraut *n*.

cleek [kli:k] große(r) Haken; *(Golf)* Löffler *m*.

clef [klef] *s mus* (Noten-)Schlüssel *m*; *tr Am sl* komponieren.

cleft [kleft] Spalt(e *f*), Riß, Sprung *m*.

clematis ['klemətis, klə'meitis] *bot* Klematis; Waldrebe *f*.

clemen|cy ['klemənsi] Milde *(a. d. Wetters)*; Gnade; Nachsicht *f*; Mitgefühl *n*; ~**t** ['-t] milde *(a. Wetter)*; mitfühlend; gnädig; nachsichtig.

clench [klentʃ] *tr* (fest) zs.drücken, -pressen; ergreifen, packen; verklammern; *(Niete)* stauchen; *fig (s-n Geist, Willen)* anspannen; *(Sache)* festlegen, regeln; bestätigen; *s* Zs.drükken, -pressen *n*; Bestätigung *f*; *s. a. clinch*; *to* ~ *o.'s fist* die Faust ballen; *to* ~ *o.'s teeth* die Zähne aufea.beißen.

clepsydra ['klepsidrə] *hist* Wasseruhr *f*.

clerestory ['kliəstəri] *arch rel* Lichtgaden *m*.

clergy ['klə:dʒi] *sing mit pl* Klerus *m*, Geistlichkeit *f*; ~**man** *(bes. anglikanischer)* Geistliche(r), Seelsorger; Kleriker *m*.

clerical ['klerikəl] *a* klerikal, geistlich; Pfarrers-, Pastoren-; Schreib(er)-; *s* Kleriker; *pol* Klerikale(r) *m*; *pl* Kleider *n pl* e-s Geistlichen; ~ **error** (Ab-)Schreibfehler *m*; ~**ism** ['-izm] Klerikalismus *m*; ~ **staff** Büropersonal *n*, Schreibkräfte *f pl*; ~ **work** Schreibarbeit(en *pl*); Büroarbeit *f*.

clerk [kla:k, *Am* klə:k] *s* Büroangestellte(r); Schreiber, Sekretär; Buchhalter; Kontorist; *Am* Verkäufer(in *f*); *(parish* ~*) rel* Gemeindeschreiber; Geistliche(r) *m*; *itr fam* als Verkäufer tätig sein; ~ *of the court* Gerichtsschreiber; Urkundsbeamte(r) *m*; ~ *of (the) works* Bauaufseher *m*.

clever ['klevə] klug, gescheit *(a. Rede, Schrift)*; begabt, talentvoll, talentiert; geschickt, gewandt *(at* in); tüchtig; gewiegt, raffiniert; ~**ness** ['-nis] Klugheit; Geschicklichkeit, Gewandtheit *f*.

clew [klu:] *s* Knäuel *n*; *fig* (roter) Faden *m*; *mar* Schothorn *n*; *v*: *to* ~ *down (Segel)* herunterholen; *to* ~ *out* herausfinden, ausfindig machen; *to* ~ *up* aufwickeln; *mar* aufgeien; *fig* erledigen *f*; ~**-garnet, -line** *mar* Geitau *n*.

cliché ['kli:ʃei] *typ* Klischee *n*; Abklatsch *m*; *fig* (abgedroschene) Redensart *f*, Gemeinplatz *m*, Phrase *f*.

click [klik] *s* Klicken; Schnalzen; *tele* Knacken, Knackgeräusch *n*, -ton; Sperrhaken *m*, -klinke; Schaltklinke *f*; *Am sl* kommerzielle(r) Erfolg, Schlager *m*; *itr* klicken; *tele* knacken; zuschnappen; *sl* zs.passen, erfolgreich ankommen *(for* bei); sich verknallen; *mil* abkommandiert werden *(for* nach); *tr* schnalzen mit *(o.'s tongue* der Zunge); *to* ~ *o.'s heels* die Hacken zs.schlagen

client ['klaiənt] Klient(in *f*), Mandant(in *f*) *(e-s Rechtsanwalts)*; *allg* Kunde *m*, Kundin *f*; ~**ele** [kli:ɔn'te(i)l] Anhänger(schaft *f*) *m pl*; Kundschaft; *jur* Klientel *f*; *med* Patienten *m pl*.

cliff [klif] Klippe *f*; Felshang *m*, -wand *f*; ~**-hanging** *fam* haarsträubend.

climacteric [klai'mæktərik] *a* kritisch, entscheidend; *physiol* klimakterisch; *s psychol* Stufenjahr *n*, Wechseljahre *n pl*; *fig* kritische(r) Punkt *m od* Zeit *f*.

climat|e ['klaimit] Klima *n a. fig*; Himmelsstrich *m*; Klimagebiet *n*; *fig* Stimmung, Atmosphäre *f*; ~**ic** ['-mætik] klimatisch; ~~ *zone* Klimazone *f*; ~**ology** [klaimə'tɔlədʒi] Klimakunde, Klimatologie *f*.

climax ['klaimæks] *s* Gipfel-, Scheitel-, Höhepunkt *m*; *(Stil)* Steigerung *f*; *tr itr* s-n Höhepunkt erreichen (lassen).

climb [klaim] *tr* ersteigen, erklimmen *a. fig*, erklettern; steigen, klettern *(the tree* auf den Baum); *itr* klettern; (empor-, auf)steigen; *fig (sozial)* aufsteigen; *s* Klettern; Steigen *n*, Aufstieg; *aero* Steigflug *m*; *(*~ *power)* Steigleistung *f*; *to* ~ *down* hinab-, hinunterklettern, -steigen; *fig* nachgeben; zurücktreten; *to* ~ *up* hinaufklettern (auf); *to* ~ *stairs* Treppen steigen; ~**able** ['-əbl] ersteigbar; ~**-down** Abstandnahme *f*, Zurücktreten *n*; ~**er** ['-ə] Kletterer; Bergsteiger *m*; Steigeisen *n*; *fig* Streber *m*, Kletterpflanze *f*; *pl* Klettervögel *m pl*; ~**ing** ['-iŋ] Klettern *n*; *aero* Steigflug *m*; *mountain-*~~ Bergsteigen *n*; ~~ *ability, capability, capacity (aero)* Steigfähigkeit *f*, -vermögen *n*; ~~ *altitude (aero)* Steighöhe *f*; ~~*-irons (pl)* Steigeisen *n*; ~~*-rope* Kletterseil *n*; ~~ *shoe* Kletterschuh *m*.

clime [klaim] *poet* Himmelsstrich *m*, Land *n*.

clinch [klintʃ] *tr (den Gegner im Boxkampf)* umklammern; festhalten; festnageln; *(a. clench)* (ver)nieten, stauchen; *mar (Tau)* festmachen; *fig* bestätigen; entscheiden; fest abmachen, abschließen; *sl* umarmen; *itr (Boxen)* sich umklammern; *fig (a. clench)* den Ausschlag geben; *Am sl* sich umarmen; *s (Boxen)* Clinch *m*, Umklammerung *f*, Nahkampf *m*; *(a. clench)* Vernietung; Haspe(n *m*); *fig* Bestätigung, Entscheidung *f*, Ausschlag *m*; Abmachung *f*, Abschluß *m*; *sl* Umarmung *f*; ~**ed** [-t] *a*: ~~ *and riveted* niet- u. nagelfest; ~**er** ['-ə] *(a. clencher)* Klammer; Krampe, Haspe(n *m*) *f*; *fam das* Ausschlaggebende, entscheidende(s) Argument *n*; *pl Am sl mot* Bremsen *f pl*; *that's a* ~~ damit ist der Fall erledigt.

cling [kliŋ] *irr clung, clung itr* haften, sich klammern *(to* an); *fig* hängen, festhalten *(to* an), treu sein *(to* dat); *to* ~ *on* fest haften *(to* an); *to* ~ *together* (fest) zs.halten; ~**ing** ['-iŋ] *a (Kleidung)* enganliegend; *fig* (sehr)anhänglich; ~**y** ['-i] klebrig, zäh; eng.

clinic ['klinik] *s med* klinische(s) Praktikum *n*; *(Instituts- od Privat-)* Klinik; *Am* ärztliche Beratungsstelle, Poliklinik *f*; *children's* ~ Kinderklinik *f*; *speech* ~ Beratungsstelle *f* für Sprachgestörte; **~(al)** *a* klinisch; *~~ history* Krankengeschichte *f*; *~~ record* Krankenblatt *n*; *~~ thermometer* Fieberthermometer *n*; **~ian** [-'niʃən] Kliniker *m*.

clink [kliŋk] *itr tr* klirren, klinge(l)n (lassen); (sich) reimen; *s* Klirren *n*; *sl* Gefängnis, Kittchen *n*; *pl Am sl* Geld, Moos; *pl Am sl* Eisstückchen *n pl*; *to ~ glasses* (mit den Gläsern) anstoßen; **~er** ['-ə] **1.** Klinker *m*; **2.** *sl* Prachtexemplar, -stück; Ding *n*, das hinhaut; *sl* Schlag, Schwindel *m*, Lüge *f*; *Am sl tele* Nebengeräusch *n*, *mus* falsche Note *f*, *allg* Schund *m*, olle Kamelle *f*, Schnitzer *m*; **~ing** ['-iŋ] *sl* prima.

clinometer [kl(a)i'nɔmitə] Neigungsmesser; Winkelquadrant *m*.

clip [klip] **1.** *s* Halter *m*, Klemme, Klammer *f*; Klipp *m*, Spange, Brosche; *(paper ~)* Brief-, Heft-, Büroklammer; *(laundry ~)* Wäscheklammer; *(trouser-, bicycle-~)* Hosen-, Fahrradklammer; *(Weberei)* Kluppe; *(Rohr)* Schelle; *rail* (Stoß-)Lasche *f*; *tele* Bügel; *mil* Ladestreifen; *film* Auszug *m*; *tr* umfassen, umklammern; festklammern, -klemmen, -halten; *(to ~ together)* zs.klammern, -heften, -klemmen, -halten; **2.** *tr (Haar)* schneiden; *(Hund)* scheren; abzwicken; stutzen; kappen; *(Hecke)* beschneiden; *tech* abschroten; *(Fahrschein, -karte)* knipsen; *(aus e-r Zeitung)* ausschneiden; *fig (Laut, Silbe)* verschlucken; *(in der Rede)* unterbrechen; *fam* e-n heftigen Schlag versetzen (*s.o.* jdm); *Am sl* hereinlegen, stehlen, umbringen; *s* Schnitt *m*, Schur *f*; *fam* heftige(r) Schlag, Hieb *m*; rasche Bewegung *f*; *Am* Tempo *n*; *Am sl* Schlaumeier, Dieb *m*; *at one ~ (Am)* auf einen Schlag; *to ~ away, off, out* weg-, ab-, ausschneiden; *to ~ s.o.'s wings (fig)* jdm die Flügel stutzen, beschneiden, jdn kurzhalten; **~ artist** *Am sl* berufsmäßige(r) Betrüger *m*; **~ joint** *sl* Kneipe, Räuberhöhle *f*; **~per** ['-ə] Karabinerhaken; *mar* Schnellsegler *m*; *aero* Großverkehrs-, Langstreckenflugzeug *n*; *tele* Amplitudenbegrenzer *m*; *sl* Pfundsding *n*, -sache; *f*, -exemplar *n*; *pl* (Hecken-)Schere; *(hair-~~s)* Haarschneidemaschine *f*; *nail-~~s* Nagelschere *f*; **~ping** ['-iŋ] *s* (Zeitungs-)Ausschnitt *m*; *tele* Begrenzung *f*; *Am sl* heftige(r) Schlag *m*; *pl* Abfälle *m pl*; *a sl* pfundig, ganz groß, Klasse; *~~ bureau* Büro *n* für Zeitungsausschnitte; **~py, ~pie** ['-i] *fam* (Bus-)Schaffnerin *f*.

cliqu|e [kli:k] Clique *f*, Grüppchen *n*, Sippschaft *f*, Klüngel *m*; **~(e)y, ~ish** ['-i, '-iʃ] *a* Cliquen-, Klüngel-.

clitoris ['kl(a)itəris] *anat* Kitzler *m*.

cloaca [klo(u)'eikə] *pl -ae* [-i:] Kloake *f a. fig.*

cloak [klouk] *s* Umhang, (weiter, ärmelloser) Mantel *m*; *allg* Hülle, Decke *f*; *fig* Deckmantel, Vorwand *m* (*for* für); *tr fig* verbergen, nicht zeigen; bemänteln; *under the ~ of* unter dem Vorwand, im Schutz *gen*; **~-room** Garderobe, Kleiderabgabe, -ablage; Toilette; *rail* Gepäckaufbewahrung *f*; *~~ ticket* Garderobemarke *f*; Gepäckaufbewahrungsschein *m*.

clobber ['klɔbə] *s Br sl* Plunder *m*; *tr fam* zerstören; (vollkommen) erledigen, fertigmachen; herunterlaufen lassen, ankotzen; **~ed** *a Am sl* besoffen.

clock [klɔk] **1.** *s (Wand-, Turm-)* Uhr *f*; *tr* mit der Stoppuhr messen, abstoppen; *(Zeit)* registrieren; *to ~ in* od *on, off* od *out* den Arbeitsanfang, das Arbeitsende an der Kontrolluhr stechen; *to punch the ~* die Kontrolluhr stechen; *it is ten o'~* es ist 10 Uhr; *alarm ~* Wecker *m*, Weckuhr *f*; *control ~* Kontrolluhr *f*; *cuckoo ~* Kuckucksuhr *f*; **~-tower** Uhrturm *m*; **~wise** im Uhrzeigersinn; *counter-~~* gegen den Uhrzeigersinn; **~work** Uhrwerk *n*; *attr (Spielzeug)* aufziehbar; *like ~~ (fig)* wie aufgezogen, wie am Schnürchen; **2.** *s* Seitenverzierung *f* (am Strumpf); **3.** *itr (Henne)* brüten.

clod [klɔd] *s* Scholle *f*, Erdklumpen *m*; *(~hopper, ~pole)* (Bauern-)Tölpel; schwere(r) Stiefel *m*; *mot* alte Mühle *f*.

clog [klɔg] *s* (Holz-)Klotz, Pflock; *fig* Klotz *m* am Bein, Fessel, Last *f*, Hindernis *n*, Behinderung *f*, Hemmnis *n*; *tech* Verstopfung, Verkleisterung, Verschmierung *f*; Holzschuh *m*, Pantine *f*; *tr fig* belasten, behindern, hemmen; *tech* verstopfen, verkleistern, verschmieren; *itr* sich (zs.)ballen; stocken, gehemmt, behindert werden; **~-dance** Holzschuhtanz *m*; **~ged** [-d] *a tech* verstopft, verkleistert, verschmiert; **~ging** ['-iŋ] *tech* Verstopfung, Verkleisterung, Verschmierung *f*.

cloist|er ['klɔistə] *s* Kloster *n*; Kreuzgang *m*; *tr* ins Kloster stecken; *allg fig* einsperren; sich von der Welt verschließen; **~ral** ['-rəl] klösterlich; Kloster-; zurückgezogen, abgeschlossen.

close 1. [klous] *a* (ab-, ein)geschlossen *a. gram*; eingeengt, beengt, eng (anliegend); knapp; *(Deckel)* dicht schließend; *(Gelände)* bedeckt, bewachsen; *fig* beschränkt, begrenzt; nah; dicht(gedrängt), eng(stehend), eng anea.gerückt; *mil (Ordnung)* geschlossen; *(Fahrzeuge)* aufgeschlossen; *fig* scharf, streng (bewacht); vertraut, eng befreundet; (eng) zs.hängend; *(Beweis)* lückenlos; *(Schrift)* gedrängt; voll(ständig), völlig, vollkommen, genau, sparsam, sorgfältig; geizig; sorgsam, genau bedacht; schwer erhältlich; beharrlich, beständig; verborgen, geheim; zurückhaltend, verschlossen; *pol* in scharfem Wettbewerb befindlich; *(Luft)* verbraucht, schlecht, stickig, drückend, schwül; *(Übersetzung)* getreu, genau; *(Aufmerksamkeit)* gespannt; *Am fam* tüchtig; *adv* dicht, nahe (*by* dabei); dicht, eng zusammen; genau, streng, scharf; *~ on* nahezu; *~ to (prp)* dicht, nahe bei; *~ up to* dicht heran an; *s* geschlossene(r), eingefriedigte(r), ummauerte(r), umzäunte(r) Platz; Hof; Domplatz; Schulhof; *Br* Ein-, Durchgang *m*; *~ together* dicht zu-, beisammen; *~ to the ground* dicht am Boden; *after ~ consideration* nach reiflicher Überlegung; *at ~ proximity, quarters* in nächster Nähe; *from ~ up* in der Nähe; *in ~ confinement* unter strenger Bewachung, in Einzelhaft; *in ~ formation (aero)* in geschlossenem Verband; *in ~ contact* in enger Berührung; *in ~ order (mil)* in geschlossener Ordnung *od* Formation; *to come ~r together* zs.-rücken; *to cut ~* glatt abschneiden, scheren; *to drive up ~* dicht heranfahren; *to have a ~ shave* scharf ausrasieren; *fig* mit knapper Not davonkommen; *to live ~* sehr eingeschränkt, sparsam leben; *to press s.o.~* jdn streng halten *od* behandeln; *to run s.o. ~* jdm nahekommen, jdm fast, beinahe, nahezu, ziemlich gleich sein; *to sit ~* eng beiea.sitzen; *to stick ~ to s.o.* sich eng an jdn halten, anschließen; *that was a ~ call (Am)* das ist noch einmal gut abgegangen; *there was a ~ contest, game* die Wettkämpfer, Spieler waren ziemlich gleich; *he is a ~ friend of mine* wir sind eng mitea. befreundet; **~-bodied** *a* enganliegend; **~-fisted** *a* geizig; **~-grained** *a* feinkörnig; **~-knit** *a* engmaschig; **~ly** *adv* dicht, eng; streng; genau; **~-mouthed** *a fig* verschlossen; **~ness** ['-nis] Abgeschlossenheit; Beengtheit, Enge, Knappheit; Nähe, Dichte; Schärfe, Strenge; Lückenlosigkeit; Vollständigkeit; Genauigkeit, Sorgfalt; Beharrlichkeit; Verborgenheit; Schwüle *f*; **~ price** scharf kalkulierte(r) Preis *m*; **~ quarters** *pl* Handgemenge *n*; überfüllte(r) Raum *m*; **~ range** *phot* Naheinstellung *f*; **~ reconnaissance** *mil* Nahaufklärung *f*; **~ season, time** *(Jagd)* Schonzeit *f*; **~-stool** Nachtstuhl *m*; **~-tongued** *a* verschwiegen, wortkarg; **~ touch, interval** *mil* Tuchfühlung *f*; **~-up** *film* Nah-, Großaufnahme; Lebensbeschreibung *f*; *~~ view* Nahansicht *f*; **2.** [klouz] *tr* (zu-, ver)schließen, zumachen; einfriedigen; *(Straße)* (für den Verkehr) sperren; in Verbindung, Berührung bringen, vereinigen; *el (Stromkreis)* schließen, einschalten; beenden, ab-, beschließen; *(Versammlung, Sitzung)* schließen; *(Fabrik)* stillegen; *com* abschließen, saldieren, liquidieren; *(Hypothek)* löschen; *itr* (sich) schließen, zugehen; mitea. in Berührung kommen, sich berühren; *(Wasser)* zs.schlagen (*over* über); aufhören, zu Ende gehen *od* sein, ein Ende finden, nehmen; handgemein werden (*with* mit); zs.kommen; zu-, übereinstimmen, einverstanden sein; **3.** *s* [klouz] (Ab-, Be-)Schluß *m*, Ende *n*, Ausgang *m*; Handgemenge *n*; (Ton-)Schluß *m*; Kadenz *f*; *to bring to a ~* zu Ende bringen; *to draw to a ~* dem Ende zu-, zu Ende gehen; *to ~ a bargain* ein Geschäft abschließen; *to ~ o.'s days* sein Leben beschließen; *to ~ the ranks (mil)* die Reihen schließen, aufrücken, -schließen; *to ~* **about** umschließen, -geben, einhüllen; *to ~* **down** die Arbeit niederlegen, den Betrieb stillegen, das Geschäft schließen; *to ~* **in** *(on, upon) tr* einschließen *a. mil*, *mil* abriegeln; hereinbrechen über; sich zs.ziehen um, sich schließen um; *itr* sich nähern, (heran)nahen, hereinbrechen; *(Tage)* kürzer werden; *with* sich anschließen *dat*; *to ~* **off** ab-, ver-, wegschließen; *to ~* **on, upon** sich schließen um; *(Augen)* sich schließen vor; *to ~* **out** *Am* ausverkaufen, liquidieren; *to ~* **up** *tr* (ver)schließen, zumachen; (ver) sperren, verstopfen, blockieren; *(Stromkreis)* schließen; übergehen (*into* in); *itr* sich schließen; sich nähern, näherrücken; *mil* aufschließen, -rücken; *sl* den Mund halten; *to ~* **with** *mil* heranrücken an, sich nähern *dat*; in Gefechtsberührung kommen, handgemein werden mit; *to ~ with an offer* ein Angebot annehmen; **~d** [klouzd] *a* geschlossen, zu; gesperrt; *tech* geblockt; *el* eingeschaltet, geschlossen; *to declare (a debate, a meeting) ~~* (e-e Aussprache, e-e Versammlung *od* Sitzung) für geschlossen erklären; *road ~~!* Straße gesperrt! *~~* geschlossene(r) Stromkreis *m*; *~~ circuit current* Ruhestrom *m*; *~~ corporation (Am) etwa* GmbH *f*; *~~ display* Waren *f pl* unter Glas; *~~ season (Am) (Jagd)* Schonzeit *f*; *~~ shop* Betrieb *m*, in dem nur Mitglieder e-r (bestimmten) Gewerkschaft arbeiten; *~~-shop system* Gewerkschaftszwang *m*; *~~ truck* gedeckte(r) Güterwagen *m*; *~~ union*

Gewerkschaft *f* mit begrenzter Mitgliederzahl; **~-down** Betriebsstillegung *f*; *radio* Ende *n* (der Sendung); **~-out** ['klouzaut] Räumungsausverkauf *m*; **~r** ['-zə] Schlußlinie *f*, *fam* Schlußlicht *n*.

closet ['klɔzit] *s fast obs* Kabinett *n*; große(r), eingebaute(r) (Wand-)Schrank *m*; *(water-~)* WC *n*, Abort *m*; *v*: *to ~ o.s.* sich zurückziehen (*with* mit); *to be ~ed* e-e vertrauliche Besprechung haben; **~ play** Buch-, Lesedrama *n*.

closing ['klouziŋ] Schließen *n*, Schließung, Beendigung, Einstellung *f*, (Ab-)Schluß *m*; *early ~ day* Tag *m* mit frühem Ladenschluß; *~ of an account, of the books* Abschluß *m* e-s Kontos *od* e-r Rechnung, der Bücher; *~ of a business* Schließung *f* e-s Geschäftes; *~ of a factory* Stillegung *f* e-r Fabrik; *~ of a road* Straßensperrung *f*; *~ of the shops* Ladenschluß *m*; **~ bid** letzte(s), Höchstgebot *n*; **~ date** Schlußtermin; Redaktionsschluß *m*; **~ price** *(Börse)* Schlußkurs *m*; **~ session, speech** Schlußsitzung, -ansprache *f*; **~ time, hour** Geschäfts-, Ladenschluß *m*; Polizeistunde *f*; Schluß *m*.

closure ['klouʒə] *s* (Ver-)Schließen *n*; Schließung *f*; *tech* (Ver-)Schluß; *parl* Schluß *m* der Debatte; *tr* u. *to apply (the) ~ to a debate* e-e Aussprache schließen; *to move the ~* Antrag auf Schluß der Debatte stellen.

clot [klɔt] *s* Klümpchen *n (geronnener Flüssigkeit)*; *Br sl* Dussel, Depp *m*; *itr* Klümpchen bilden; *itr tr* gerinnen (lassen); **~ted** ['-id] *a (Haar)* verklebt; *(Blut)* geronnen.

cloth [klɔ(:)θ, *pl a.* klɔ:ðz] Tuch *n*, Stoff *m*, Zeug, Gewebe; Leinen; Tuch *n*, Lappen *m*; Amtstracht *(bes. d. Geistlichen)*; Geistlichkeit *f*; *to cut o.'s coat according to o.'s* od *the ~ (fig)* sich nach der Decke strecken; *to lay the ~* den Tisch decken; *to make s.th. out of whole ~ (Am fam)* sich etwas aus den Fingern saugen; *dish-, wash-~* Spültuch *n*, -lappen *m*; **~-binding** *(Buch)* (Ganz-)Leineneinband *m*; **~ making, manufacturing** Tuchfabrikation *f*.

clothe [klouð] *obs lit irr clad, clad tr* kleiden, mit Kleidung versorgen; ankleiden, anziehen; *fig* (ein)hüllen in, überziehen mit; *(Gedanken)* einkleiden.

clothes [klouðz] *pl (nie mit Zahlwort)* Kleider *n pl*, Kleidung *f*, *fam* Sachen *f pl*, Zeug *n*, (Bett-)Wäsche *f*; *in plain ~* in Zivil; *bed-~* Bettwäsche *f*; **~-bag** Wäschebeutel *m*; **~-basket** Wäschekorb *m*; **~-brush** Kleiderbürste *f*; **~-dryer** Wäschetrockner *m*; **~ hanger** Kleiderbügel *m*; **~ hook** Kleiderhaken *m*; **~-horse** Wäscheständer; *fam* Kleidernarr *m*; **~-line, -rope** Wäscheleine; *Am fam fig* schmutzige Wäsche *f*; **~-moth** *ent* Kleidermotte *f*; **~-peg,** *Am* **-pin** Wäscheklammer *f*; **~(-)press** Wäscheschrank *m*; **~ rack, tree** *Am* Kleiderständer *m*; Kleiderablage, Garderobe *f*.

clothier ['klouðiə] Tuch-, Kleiderhändler; *obs u. Am* Tuchmacher *m*.

clothing ['klouðiŋ] Kleidung *f*, Kleider *n pl*, Anzug *m allg*; (Stoff-)Hülle; *fig* Einkleidung *f*; **~ allowance** *mil* Kleidergeld *n*; **~ bag** Kleidersack *m*; **~ depot** *mil* Bekleidungsamt *n*; **~ money** Kleidergeld *n*; **~ store** Bekleidungsgeschäft, *mil* -amt *n*.

cloture ['kloutʃə] *Am s. closure parl.*

cloud [klaud] *s* Wolke *a. fig*; (Rauch-, Staub-)Wolke *f*; trübe(r) Fleck, Schleier; *(Vögel, Insekten, Reiter)* Schwarm; *(Pfeile)* Hagel; *fig* Schatten *m*, Drohung *f*, Schreckgespenst *n*; *tr itr (to ~ over, up)* (sich) bewölken; *tech* trüben, flammen, ädern; *fig* (sich) umwölken, (sich) umschatten, (sich) verdüstern; *(Ruf)* besudeln; *on a ~ (fam)* im siebenten Himmel; *under the ~ of the night* im Dunkel, im Schutz der Nacht; *to be in the ~s, to have o.'s head in the ~s (fig)* in den Wolken schweben, (mit den Gedanken) ganz woanders sein; *to be under a ~* in Verdacht stehen; in Ungnade gefallen sein; *~ of dust* Staubwolke *f*; *~ of flies* Fliegenschwarm *m*; *~ of words* Wortschwall *m*; **~-burst** Wolkenbruch *m*; **~-capped, -covered** *a (Berggipfel)* in Wolken gehüllt; **~ ceiling** Wolkenhöhe *f*; **~ cover** Wolkendecke *f*; **~ droplet** Nebeltropfen *m*; **~ed** ['-id] *a* bewölkt, bedeckt, wolkig; *fig* trübe; **~ formation** Wolkenbildung; Trübung *f*; **~iness** ['-inis] Umwölkung; *fig* Unklarheit *f*; **~ layer** Wolkenschicht *f*; **~less** ['-lis] wolkenlos; ungetrübt; **~lessness** ['-lisnis] Wolkenlosigkeit *f*; **~let** ['-lit] Wölkchen *n*; **~-rack, ~shred** Wolkenfetzen *m pl*; **~wards** *adv* himmelwärts; **~y** ['-i] wolkig, bewölkt, trübe *(a. Flüssigkeit u. Gedanken)*; *~~ with sleep (Augen)* müde, schläfrig.

clout [klaut] *s* Lappen; *fam* Schlag *m*; *tr fam* schlagen; *fam* ausbessern; *Am sl* klauen, stehlen.

clove [klouv] **1.** (Gewürz-)Nelke *f*; Gewürznelkenbaum *m*; *(~-pink, -gillyflower)* Nelke *f (Blume)*; **2.** *bot* Brutzwiebel *f*.

cloven [klouvn] *a* gespalten, (der Länge nach) geteilt; Spalt-; **~ hoof,** gespaltene(r) Huf *m*; *to show the ~ hoof (fig)* sein wahres Gesicht zeigen.

clover ['klouvə] Klee *m*; *to be, to live in ~* wie die Made im Speck, wie Gott in Frankreich leben; **~-leaf** ['-li:f] *tech* Kleeblatt *n*.

clown [klaun] *s* Spaßmacher, dumme(r) August; dumme(r) Kerl, Tölpel, Tolpatsch *m*; *itr (Clown)* s-e Späße machen; **~ish** ['-iʃ] tölpelhaft, ungeschliffen; blöd(e).

cloy [klɔi] *tr* übersättigen, überfüttern (*with* mit); *I am ~ed with that* das ekelt, widert mich an.

*

club [klʌb] *s* Keule *f (Waffe)*; (Golf-)Schläger; (Gummi-)Knüppel; Klub, Verein *m*, Gesellschaft *f*; *(~-house, -rooms)* Klub-, Vereinshaus *n*, Klubräume *m pl*; *pl (Spielkarten)* Kreuz, Treff *n*, Eichel(n *pl*) *f*; *tr* mit der Keule, mit dem Gewehrkolben schlagen; verprügeln; beisteuern, -tragen; *itr* zs.kommen, sich (an)sammeln; *(to ~ together)* sich zs.tun, -schließen (*with* mit); *Indian ~s (pl) (sport)* Keulen *f pl*; **~ car** *Am rail* Salonwagen *m* mit Bar; **~-foot** Klumpfuß *m*; **~-footed** *a* klumpfüßig; **~-law** Faustrecht, Recht *n* des Stärkeren; **~-man** Klubmitglied; eifrige(r) Besucher *m* e-s Klubs; **~ membership** Mitgliedschaft *f* in e-m Verein; **~ moss** *bot* Bärlapp *m*; **~ sandwich** *Am* dick mit Schinken, Huhn, Tomaten belegtes Brot *n*; **~ steak** *Am* kleine(s) Rindslendenstück *n*; **~ woman** (weibliches) Klubmitglied *n*.

cluck [klʌk] *itr (Henne)* glucken, locken; *Am sl* ein gutes Examen ablegen; *s* Glucken *n*; *Am sl* doofe Nuß *f*.

clue [klu:] Anhaltspunkt, Schlüssel (*to* zu); (roter) Faden, Gang *(e-r Erzählung, Handlung)*, Verlauf *m (des Geschehens, der Ereignisse)*; *he hasn't a ~* er hat keine Ahnung; **~less** ['-lis] ohne Anhaltspunkte; *sl* ahnungslos.

clump [klʌmp] *s* (Erd-)Klumpen; Haufen *m*, Ansammlung *f*; (Holz-)Klotz *m*; (Baum-)Gruppe; *(~-sole)* Doppelsohle *f*; schwere(r) Tritt; heftige(r) Schlag *m*; *itr* schwer auftreten; *tr* zu e-m Klumpen ballen; anhäufen; *(Bäume, Büsche)* massieren; *(Schuhe)* doppelt sohlen; *fam* schlagen.

clums|iness ['klʌmzinis] Plumpheit, Schwerfälligkeit; Ungeschicktheit *f*; **~y** ['-i] plump, schwerfällig; unelegant; ungeschickt; unpassend.

clunk [klʌŋk] *Am sl tr* schlagen; bar bezahlen, auf den Tisch legen; *s* Dummkopf, Blödian; Schlag; alte(r) Karren; Fuß; schwere(r) Gegenstand *m*; **~er** ['-ə] *Am sl mot* alte(r) Schlitten; ungeschickte(r) Mensch *m*.

cluster ['klʌstə] Traube *f*, Büschel, Bündel *n*; Gruppe *f*, Schwarm *m*; *itr* in Trauben, Büscheln wachsen; Trauben, Büschel bilden; sich scharen, (herum)schwärmen (*round* um).

clutch [klʌtʃ] *s* feste(r) Griff, (Zu-)Griff; *tech* Haken *m*, Klaue; *mot* Kupp(e)lung *f*; Nest *n (Eier)*, Brut *f*; *pl* Hände, Klauen *f pl*, Gewalt; *Am sl* Klemme, Schwierigkeit *f*; entscheidende(r) Augenblick *m*; *tr* (er)greifen, packen, festhalten, umklammern; *itr* greifen, schnappen (*at* nach); *to fall into s.o.'s ~es* jdm in die Hände, in jds Hände fallen; *to let in, to disengage the ~ (mot)* ein-, auskuppeln; *to make a ~ at s.th.* nach etw greifen; *to ~ the gummy (Am sl)* die Suppe auslöffeln müssen; *to ~ at a straw* sich an e-n Strohhalm klammern; **~ disk, plate** Kupplungsscheibe *f*; **~-pedal** Kupp(e)lungspedal *n*.

clutter ['klʌtə] *s* Durcheinander *n*, Wirrwarr *m*, Unordnung *f*; *tr* anhäufen; *(to ~ up)* in Unordnung bringen; *itr* aufgeregt hin- u. herlaufen; durchea.reden.

coach [koutʃ] *s* Kutsche; *(stage-~)* Postkutsche *f*; (Eisenbahn-)Wagen; Reise-, Gesellschafts(omni)bus *m*; *Am* Limousine; *mar* Kapitänskajüte *f*; Einpauker, Repetitor; *sport* Trainer *m*; *itr* Kutsche fahren, *fam* kutschieren; *hist* mit der Postkutsche reisen; bei e-m Repetitor fürs Examen pauken; als Repetitor tätig sein; *tr* aufs Examen vorbereiten; *sport* eintrainieren; *to drive ~-and-four* vierspännig fahren; **~-box** Kutschbock *m*; **~builder** Karosseriebauer *m*; **~-horse** Kutschpferd *n*; **~-house** (Wagen-)Remise *f*; **~-maker** Stellmacher, Wagner *m*; **~-man** ['-mən] Kutscher; künstliche(r) Köder *m*; **~-work** *mot* Karosserie *f*; **~-wrench** Engländer *m (Werkzeug)*.

coact|ion [ko(u)'ækʃən] Zs.wirken *n*; **~ive** [-tiv] zs.-, mitwirkend.

coadjutor [ko(u)'ædʒutə] Gehilfe, Assistent; *rel* Koadjutor *m*.

coagulat|e [ko(u)'ægjuleit] *itr tr* gerinnen (lassen); **~ion** [-'leiʃən] Gerinnen; Festwerden *n*, Verdichtung *f*.

coal [koul] *s* (Stein-)Kohle(n *pl*) *f*; *tr (Holz)* zu Kohle brennen; *mar* mit Kohlen versorgen; *itr mar* Kohlen einnehmen; *to blow the ~s (fig)* Öl ins Feuer gießen; *to call, to haul s.o. over the ~s* jdm die Leviten lesen; *to carry ~s to Newcastle (fig)* Eulen nach Athen tragen; *to heap ~s of fire on s.o.'s head (fig)* feurige Kohlen auf jds Haupt sammeln; **~-bearing** *geol* kohleführend; **~-bed, -seam** Kohlenflöz *n*; **~bin** ['-bin]

Kohlenkasten, -bunker *m*; **~-black** kohlrabenschwarz; **~-box, -scuttle,** *sl* **-vase** Kohlenkasten *m*; **~-bunker** Kohlenbunker *m*; **~-cellar** Kohlenkeller *m*; **~ depot** Kohlenlager *n*; **~er** ['-ə] *rail* Kohlenwagen; *mar* Kohlentransporter *m*; **~ face** *min* Streb *m*; **~-field** Kohlenrevier, -gebiet *n*; **~-gas** Steinkohlengas *n*; **~-heaver,** *Am* **-handler,** *fam* **~ie** Kohlenträger, *fam* -mann *m*; **~ hod** *Am* Kohlenkorb *m*; **~-hole** kleine(r) Kohlenkeller; *Am* Kohlenkellerhals *m*; **~ing** ['-iŋ] *mar* Kohleneinnehmen *n*; **~ liquefaction** Kohleverflüssigung *f*; **~-measures** *pl geol* Kohlengebirge *n*; **~-mine, -pit** Kohlenbergwerk *n*, -grube, Zeche *f*; **~-mining** Kohlenbergbau *m*; **~-mouse, -tit** *orn* Kohlmeise *f*; **~-output** Kohlenförderung *f*; **~-pile** (Kohlen-)Halde *f*; **~-tar** Steinkohlenteer *m*; *~~ burner* Teerschweler *m*; *~~ dye* Teerfarbstoff *m*; **~y** ['-i] kohlenreich; kohlen(stoff)haltig; kohlrabenschwarz; **~-yard** Kohlenplatz *m*, -lager *n*.

coalesce [ko(u)ə'les] *itr* zs.wachsen; sich vereinigen *a. fig*; *pol* e-e Koalition bilden; **~nce** [-ns] *biol* Zs.wachsen *n*; Vereinigung; Einheit *f*; **~nt** [-nt] zs.wachsend; sich vereinigend, e-e Einheit bildend.

coalition [ko(u)ə'liʃən] Vereinigung, Verschmelzung; *pol* Koalition *f*, Bündnis *n*; **~ government, party** Koalitionsregierung, -partei *f*.

coarse [kɔːs] rauh, grob, (ganz) gewöhnlich, sehr einfach; grob(körnig), dick, klobig; *fig* roh, ungebildet, unfein, unzart, gewöhnlich, gemein, unanständig; **~ bread** grobe(s), dunkle(s) Brot *n*; **~-fibred, -grained** *a* grobkörnig; **~-meshed** *a* grobmaschig; **~n** ['-n] *tr itr* grob machen *od* werden; **~ness** ['-nis] Grobheit, Roheit *f*; **~ setting, adjustment** Grobeinstellung *f*.

coast [koust] *s* Küste; *Am* Talfahrt *f* mit dem Rodelschlitten *m*; *the C~* Küste *f* am Pazifischen Ozean; *itr mar* an der Küste entlang fahren; Küstenhandel treiben; (hinunter)rodeln; *mot* im Leerlauf fahren, ausrollen; im Freilauf, (mit dem Fahrrad) bergab fahren; *Am* mühelos bekommen; ein Examen mit Leichtigkeit bestehen; nicht wissen, was man will; im siebenten Himmel sein; *on the ~* an der Küste; *the ~ is clear* die Luft ist rein; **~al** ['-əl] *a* Küsten-; *~~ navigation, trade* Küstenschiffahrt *f*, -handel *m*; *~~ region, zone, area* Küstengebiet *n*, -zone *f*; *~~ waters (pl)* Küstengewässer *n pl*; **~ defence** Küstenverteidigung *f*; **~er** ['-ə] *mar* Küstenfahrzeug *n*; *Am* Rodelschlitten; *(Glas)* Untersetzer *m*; *Am* Berg-u.-Tal-Bahn *f*; *~~ brake (Am)* Rücktrittbremse *f*; **~guard(sman)** Küstenwacht(mann *m*) *f*; **~ing** ['-iŋ] Küstenschiffahrt *f*, -handel *m*; *mot* Ausrollen; *Am* Rodeln *n*; *~~ trade* Küstenhandel *m*; **~land** *Am* Land *n* entlang der Küste; **~line** Küstenlinie *f*; **~ward(s)** *adv* auf die Küste zu; **~wise** *a adv mar* die, an der Küste entlang.

coat [kout] *s* Jacke *f*, Rock; Damenmantel *m*; Kostümjacke *f*; *zoo* Haarkleid, Fell *n*, Pelz *m*; Federkleid, Gefieder *n*; *anat* Haut *(e-s inneren Organs)*; *bot* (Zwiebel-)Schale; Rinde; *allg* Haut, Hülle *f*, Überzug *m*, Decke *f*; Anstrich *m*; *tr* überziehen, bestreichen (*with* mit); mit e-r Hülle, e-m Überzug versehen *od* belegen; (ein)hüllen (*with* in); umkleiden; *tech* *(Linse)* vergüten; anstreichen, verputzen; *to turn o.'s ~* die Partei wechseln; *~ of arms* Wappen *n*; *~ of mail (hist)* Panzerhemd *n*; *~(ing) of paint* Anstrich *m*; *~ and skirt* (Damen-)Kostüm *n*; **~ed** *a* überzogen, mit e-r Hülle versehen; bedeckt (*with* mit); *tech (Linse)* vergütet; *tech* umhüllt; *med* belegt; **~ee** ['-iː, -'-] kurze(r) Rock *m*; **~-hanger** Kleiderbügel *m*; **~ing** ['-iŋ] Jacken-, Rockstoff *m*, -tuch *n*; Überzug *m*, Hülle; Umhüllung; (äußere) Schicht; Streichmasse; *(Linse)* Vergütung *f*; Belag; Anstrich; (Ver-)Putz *m*; *~~ colo(u)r* Deckfarbe *f*; *~~ of ice* Eisbelag *m*; *~~ of paint* Farbanstrich *m*; **~-tail** Rockschoß *m*; *to trail o.'s ~-tails (fig)* Streit suchen.

coax [kouks] *tr* überreden, im guten dazu, dahin bringen (*s.o. to do, into doing s.th.* daß jem etw tut); beschwatzen; schmeicheln (*s.o.* jdm); *to ~ s.th. out of* od *from s.o.* jdm etw abschmeicheln, entlocken; *itr* schmeicheln; gut zureden.

coax(i)al [kou'æks(i)əl] koaxial, konzentrisch.

cob [kɔb] **1.** *s* (männlicher) Schwan *m*; kräftige(s), aber gedrungen gebaute(s), kurzbeinige(s) Pferd; *(~-nut)* (große) Haselnuß *n*; (runder) Kern *m*; Stück, Klümpchen *n*; *bot* Spindel *f (der Ähre)*; *Am* Maiskolben *m*; *tr fam* werfen, schlagen; **2.** *arch* Weller *m (Lehm mit Stroh)*; **3.** *orn* Mantelmöwe *f a. cobb.*

cobalt [kə'bɔːlt, ko(u)'bɔ(ː)lt, 'koubɔːlt] *chem* Kobalt; *(~-blue)* Kobaltblau *n*.

cobble ['kɔbl] **1.** *s (~-stone)* Kiesel (-stein); Kopfstein *m*; *pl* Eier-, Nußkohlen *f pl*; *tr* mit Kieselsteinen, Kopfstein pflastern; **2.** *tr* roh ausbessern, *(bes. Schuhe)* flicken; zs.pfuschen, -stümpern; **~r** ['-ə] **1.** Flickschuster; Pfuscher, Stümper *m*; **2.** *(sherry-~)* Cobbler *m*; *Am Art* Fruchttorte *f*; **~stone** ['-stoun] Pflaster-, Kopfstein *m*; *~~ pavement* Kopfsteinpflaster *n*.

cobra ['koubrə] *zoo* Kobra *f*.

cobweb ['kɔbweb] Spinn(en)gewebe *n*, -faden *m*; *to blow (away) the ~s from o.'s brain* (ein bißchen) frische Luft schnappen.

coca ['koukə] *bot* Koka(strauch *m*) *f*; Koka *n*; **~-cola** ['-'koulə] Coca-Cola *n*, *fam f (Warenzeichen)*; **~in(e)** [kə-, ko'kein, 'koukein] Kokain *n*; **~inism** [ko'keinizm] Kokainvergiftung *f*.

cochineal ['kɔtʃiniːl] Koschenille *f*.

cochlea ['kɔkliə] *anat* Schnecke *f*.

cock [kɔk] **1.** *s* (Haus-)Hahn; Hahn *m*; (Vogel-)Männchen *n*; *(~ of the walk, bes. ~ of the school)* (An-)Führer, Erste(r); Rädels-, Wortführer; (Wasser-)Hahn, Kran; *(Gewehr)* Abzug *m*; *(Waage)* Zunge *f*; *(Sonnenuhr)* Gnomon, Sonnenzeiger *m*; *(weather ~)* Wetterfahne *f*; Emporrichten; *(Gewehr)* Spannen; *(Augen)* Aufschlagen *n*; *tr (to ~ up)* aufrichten; *(Gewehr)* spannen; *itr* aufrecht stehen; *to go off at half ~* ohne genügende Vorbereitung tun; *to live like fighting ~s* wie die Made im Speck leben; *to knock into a ~ed hat (fam)* verreißen; zu Brei schlagen; *to ~ o.'s ears* die Ohren spitzen; *to ~ o.'s eye at s.o.* jdm e-n verständnisvollen Blick zuwerfen; *to ~ o.'s hat* den Hut schief aufsetzen *od* zurückschieben; *to ~ o.'s nose* die Nase rümpfen; *this beats ~-fighting* das ist (ja) großartig, phantastisch, prima; *that ~ won't fight* das hat keinen Sinn, ist zwecklos; das zieht nicht; *fighting ~* Kampfhahn *m*; *old ~ (fam, Anrede)* alter Junge *od* Knabe; *~-a-doodle-doo* Kikeriki *n*; *(Kindersprache)* Hahn *m*; *~-a-hoop (a adv)* voller, außer sich vor Freude; jubelnd, frohlockend; *~-and-bull story* Jägerlatein, Seemannsgarn *n*, Räuberpistole *f*; *~ of the north* Bergfink *m*; *~ of the wood* Auerhahn *m*; **~chafer** ['-tʃeifə] Maikäfer *m*; **~-crow(ing)** Hahnenschrei *m*, erste (Morgen-)Dämmerung *f*; **~ed** ['-t] *a* aufgerichtet, hochgestülpt; *~~ hat* Dreispitz *m (Hut)*; **~erel** ['-ərəl] Hähnchen *n*; *fig* Kampfhahn, Rowdy, Halbstarke(r) *m*; **~-eyed** *a* schielängig; (krumm u.) schief; doof; *sl* besoffen, verrückt, nicht normal, falsch, schief; **~-fight(ing)** Hahnenkampf *m*; **~-horse** *adv* rittlings; **~iness** ['-inis] Keckheit, Frechheit, Arroganz *f*; **~-loft** Dachkammer *f*; **~pit** ['-pit] (Hahnen-)Kampfplatz *m*, Arena *f*; Schlachtfeld *n*; *mil* Gefechtsverbandsplatz *m*; *mar* Schiffslazarett *n*; *aero* Führersitz, -raum *m*, Kabine, Kanzel *f*; **~scomb** ['-skoum] Kamm *(des Hahnes)*; *bot* Hahnenkamm *m*; *s.a. coxcomb*; **~sure** ['-ʃuə] *fam* todsicher; felsenfest überzeugt (*of, about* von); von sich überzogen, -zeugt; **~tail** ['-teil] Cocktail *m (alkohol. Mischgetränk)*; **~-up** *typ* Initiale *f*; aufgebogene(r) Rand *od* Hut *m*; **~y, ~sy, coxy** ['kɔk(s)i] keck, dreist, frech, *fam* keß; anmaßend, arrogant; **2.** *s* Heuhaufen *m*; *tr (Heu)* in Haufen legen.

cockade [kɔ'keid] Kokarde *f*.

Cockaigne, Cockayne [kɔ'kein] das Schlaraffenland; *hum* London *n*.

cockalorum [kɔkə'lɔːrəm] *fam* kleine(r) Angeber *m*.

cockatoo [kɔkə'tuː] *orn* Kakadu *m*.

cockatrice ['kɔkətr(a)is] *zoo* Basilisk *m*.

cocker ['kɔkə] *tr (meist: to ~ up)* verhätscheln, verzärteln, verwöhnen; *s (~ spaniel)* Cocker-Spaniel *m*.

cockle ['kɔkl] **1.** *(corn-~) bot* Kornrade *f*; Flugbrand *m* des Weizens; **2.** *(~-shell) zoo* Herzmuschel *f*; *(~boat)* kleine(s) Boot *n*, Nußschale *f*; *to warm, to delight the ~s of s.o.'s heart* jdn erfreuen, jdm e-e Freude machen, jdn aufmuntern; **3.** *s* Falte *f*; *tr itr* faltig machen, werden, (sich) fälteln; **4.** *(~-stove)* Kachelofen *m*.

cockney ['kɔkni] *s* (gebürtiger) Londoner *m*, *bes. pej* der unteren Klassen; *a* Cockney-; **~ism** ['-izm] Mundart *f od* (das) Benehmen *n* e-s C.

cockroach ['kɔkroutʃ] *ent* Küchenschabe *f*.

cockswain *s. coxswain.*

coco ['koukou], **coker** ['koukə] *(~(nut) tree)* Kokospalme *f*; **~a** ['koukou] Kakao(pulver *n*) *m*; **~a bean** Kakaobohne *f*; **~(a)nut** ['-kənʌt] Kokosnuß; *s* Birne *f*, Kürbis, Kopf *m*; *that accounts for the milk in the ~~* da haben wir's (ja)! das ist des Pudels Kern! *~(~) butter* Kokosöl, -fett *n*, -butter *f*; Palmin *n (Warenzeichen)*; *~~ matting* Kokosmatte *f*; *~~ milk* Kokosmilch *f*.

cocoon [kə'kuːn] *s zoo* Kokon *m*; Schutzhülle *f*; *tr mil (Gerät)* einmotten.

cod [kɔd] **1.** *pl ~ (~fish)* Kabeljau, Dorsch *m*; *cured ~* Laberdan *m*; *dried ~* Stock-, Klippfisch *m*; **~-liver oil** Lebertran *m*; **2.** *sl dial tr* foppen, verulken, veräppeln; *itr* Spaß, Blödsinn machen.

coddle ['kɔdl] *tr* verzärteln, verweichlichen; verhätscheln, verwöhnen.

code [koud] *s* Kodex *m*, Gesetzbuch *n*; ungeschriebene Gesetze *n pl*, Sittenkodex; Kode, Schlüssel (zu Geheimschriften), Telegraphenschlüssel *m*; *tr* (ver)schlüsseln, chiffrieren; *~ of honour* Ehrenkodex *m*; *C~ of Civil,*

Criminal Procedure Zivil-, Strafprozeßordnung *f*; ~ **light** Blink-, Kennfeuer *n*; ~ **name** Deckname *m*; ~ **number, sign, word** Kodenummer *f*, -zeichen, -wort *m*.

codex ['koudeks] *pl codices* ['koudisi:z] Kodex *m*.

codger ['kɔdʒə] *fam (old* ~*)* alte(r) Knacker *m*.

codicil ['kɔdisil] *jur* Kodizill *n*, Zusatz, Nachtrag *m*.

codif|ication [kɔdifi'keiʃən] Systematisierung; Kodifikation, Kodifizierung, Sammlung *f (von Gesetzen)*; ~**y** ['kɔdifai] *tr* kodifizieren, in ein System bringen; *(Gesetze)* sammeln.

codling ['kɔdliŋ] **1.** kleine(r) Kabeljau *m*; **2.** Kochapfel *m*; *hot* ~ Bratapfel *m*.

co-ed, coed ['kou'ed] *Am s* Studentin, Schülerin *f*; ~**ucation** ['ko(u)edju:'keiʃən] Koedukation, gemeinsame Erziehung *f* beider Geschlechter.

coefficient [ko(u)i'fiʃənt] *math phys* Koeffizient, Beiwert *m*, Kennzahl *f*.

c(o)eliac ['s:iliæk] *a scient* Unterleibs-.

coequal [ko(u)'i:kwəl] *lit* gleich; ~**ity** [ko(u)i(:)'kwɔliti] *lit* Gleichheit *f*.

coerc|e [ko(u)'ə:s] *tr (Person)* zwingen, nötigen *(into doing* zu tun); *(Verhalten)* erzwingen; unterdrücken; ~**ible** [-ibl] erzwingbar; ~**ion** [-'ə:ʃən] (moralischer) Zwang *m*, Gewalt, Nötigung *f*; *under* ~~ unter Zwang *od* Druck, gezwungenermaßen, zwangsweise; ~**ive** [-iv] *a* Zwangs-; *tech* koerzitiv; ~~ *measure* Zwangsmaßnahme, -maßregel *f*.

coessential [ko(u)i'senʃəl] einsseiend; wesensgleich.

coeval [ko(u)'i:vəl] gleichzeitig; gleich alt; gleichaltrig, im gleichen Alter.

coexist ['ko(u)ig'zist] *itr* gleichzeitig, zs. (vorhanden)sein, bestehen, existieren *(with* mit); ~**ence** [-əns] gleichzeitige(s), Mitvorhandensein, -bestehen *n*; *pol* Koexistenz *f*; ~**ent** [-ənt] gleichzeitig (bestehend, vorhanden).

coffee ['kɔfi] Kaffee; Kaffeestrauch, -baum *m*; Kaffeebraun *n*; *ground* ~ gemahlene(r) Kaffee *m*; ~ *and cakes (Am sl)* kleine(s) Gehalt *n*; ~**-bean, -berry** Kaffeebohne *f*; ~ **break** *Am* Kaffeepause *f*; ~ **cream** Kaffeekreme *f*; ~**-cup** Kaffeetasse *f*; ~**-extract** Kaffee-Extrakt *m*; ~**-grinder, -mill** Kaffeemühle *f*; ~**-grounds** *pl* Kaffeesatz *m*; ~**-machine** Kaffeemaschine *f*; ~**-percolator** Kaffeefilter *m*; ~**-pot** Kaffeekanne *f*; *Am* kleine(s) Restaurant *n*; ~**-roaster** Kaffeebrenner *m*, -röstmaschine *f*; ~**-room, shop** Gast-, Frühstückszimmer *n (im Hotel)*; ~**-set** Kaffeeservice *n*; ~**-stall** Kaffeestand *m (auf d. Straße)*; ~ **table** Kaffee-, Teetisch *m*.

coffer ['kɔfə] *s* Koffer *m*, Kiste *f*, Kasten *m (bes. für Wertsachen)*; Kasse *f*, Geldschrank; *tech* Caisson *m*, Schleuse; *pl arch* Nische *f*; *pl* Tresor (-raum) *m*; *pl* Gelder, (Geld)-Mittel *n pl*; Kapital, Vermögen *n*; *tr* verwahren, zurücklegen, horten; *tech* abdichten; ~**-dam** *tech* Senkkasten; Caisson, Fangdamm *m*.

coffin ['kɔfin] *s* Sarg *m*; *tr* wegschließen, gut weglegen; *to drive a nail into o.'s* ~ s-e Gesundheit untergraben; ~ **corner** *Am (Fußballplatz)* Ecke *f*; ~**-nail** *fam* Sargnagel *m (Zigarette)*.

cog [kɔg] **1.** *s tech* (Rad-)Zahn *m*, Nase *f*, Daumen *m*; *fig* Rädchen *n (Mensch)*; *tr tech* mit Zähnen versehen; aufkämmen, auswalzen; *min* mit Bergen versetzen; *to slip a* ~ *(fig)* e-n Fehler machen; ~ **wheel** Zahnrad *n*; ~ **(-wheel) railway** Zahnradbahn *f*; **2.** *v*: *to* ~ *the dice* beim Würfeln betrügen.

cogen|cy ['koudʒənsi] Stichhaltigkeit, Beweiskraft *f (e-s Argumentes)*; ~**t** ['-t] *(Beweis)* zwingend, schlagend, überzeugend, unwiderlegbar; *(Grund)* triftig.

cogit|able ['kɔdʒitəbl] denkbar, mit dem Verstand erfaßbar; ~**ate** ['-eit] *itr* (tief) nachdenken, nachsinnen *(upon* über); gründlich durchdenken *(upon s.th.* etw); ~**ation** [-'teiʃən] (Nach-)Denken, Nachsinnen *n*; *pl* Überlegungen *f pl*.

cognac ['koun-, 'kɔnjæk] Kognak; *allg* Weinbrand *m*.

cognate ['kɔgneit] *a* verwandt *a*. *fig (bes. Sprachen)*; *s* Verwandte(r) *m*; verwandte(s) Wort *n*.

cognition [kɔg'niʃən] *scient* Erkenntnis(vermögen *n*) *f*.

cogniz|able ['kɔgnizəbl, 'kɔn-] erkennbar; *jur* der Zuständigkeit (e-s Gerichts) unterliegend; ~**ance** [-əns] Kenntnis *f*, Wissen *n*; Erkenntnisbereich *m*; *jur* Anerkennung; *jur* Zuständigkeit *f*; Erkennungs-, Abzeichen *n*; *to have* ~~ *of (bes.* amtlich) Kenntnis haben von; *to take* ~~ *of* zur Kenntnis nehmen, K. nehmen von; ~**ant** ['-ənt] in Kenntnis *(of* gen), unterrichtet *(of* über); *philos* erkennend.

cognomen [kɔg'noumən] Zu-, Bei-, Spitzname *m*.

cohabit [ko(u)'hæbit] *itr* ehelich zs.wohnen; beiwohnen, -schlafen; ~**ation** [-'teiʃən] eheliche(s) Zs.wohnen *n*; Beiwohnung *f*, Beischlaf *m*.

coheir, ~ess ['kou'ɛə, -ris] Miterbe *m*, -erbin *f*.

coher|e [ko(u)'hiə] *itr* (mitea.) verbunden sein, zs.hängen; zs.halten; *tech* haften, kohärieren; ~**ence, -cy** [-rəns(i)] Zs.hang, -halt *m*; ~**ent** [-rənt] zs.hängend, mitea., innerlich verbunden; klar gegliedert u. verständlich; ~**er** [-rə] *el* Kohärer, Fritter *m*.

cohes|ion [ko(u)'hi:ʒən] *phys* Kohäsion *f*; *fig* Zs.halt *m*; ~**ive** [-'hi:siv] zs.haltend; Kohäsions-.

cohort ['kouhɔ:t] *hist* Kohorte; Schar, Gruppe *f*.

coiff|eur [kwɑ:'fə:] Friseur *m*; ~**ure** [-'fjuə] Frisur *f*.

coil [kɔil] *s* Spirale, Spule, Rolle; Windung; *(~ of a pipe)* Schlange(nrohr *n*), Rohrschlange; *el* Spule *f*; (Haar-)Wikkel *m*; *tr (to* ~ *up)* (auf)wickeln, -rollen, spulen; *itr* sich winden, sich (auf-) wickeln.

coin [kɔin] *s* Münze *f*; Metall-, Hartgeld; *Am fam* Geld *n*; *tr (Geld, Wort)* prägen; *fig* ausdenken, ersinnen, *bes. pej* aushecken; *Am fam* verdienen; *to pay s.o. back in his own* ~ *(fig)* jdm mit gleicher Münze heimzahlen; *to* ~ *money (fig fam)* viel Geld machen, das Geld scheffeln; *false* ~ Falschgeld *n*; *fig* Fälschung *f*; *small* ~ Kleingeld *n*; ~**age** ['-idʒ] Prägen *(des Geldes)*, Ausmünzen; Geld *n*; Währung *f*; Münzrecht *n*; *fig* Erfindung, *bes.* Schaffung, Bildung, Prägung *(neuer Wörter)*; Neubildung, Neuprägung *f*; neue(s) Wort *n*, Neologismus *m*; ~**-box telephone** Münzfernsprecher *m*; ~**er** *(bes.* Falsch-) Münzer; Präger *m* (e-s neuen Wortes).

coincid|e [ko(u)in'said] *itr (räumlich)* sich decken; *(zeitlich)* zs.fallen, -treffen; *fig* übereinstimmen, zs.passen; passen *(with* zu), harmonieren *(with* mit); ~**ence** [-'insidəns] (zufälliges) Zs.-treffen *n*; Gleichzeitigkeit; Übereinstimmung *f*; ~**ent** [-'insidənt] gleichzeitig; zs.treffend, zs.fallend; übereinstimmend; ~**ental** [-'dentl] zufällig übereinstimmend.

coir ['kɔiə] Kokosfaser *f*, -bast *m*.

coition [kou'iʃən], **coitus** ['ko(u)itəs] Beischlaf, Koitus *m*.

coke [kouk] *s* Koks *m*; *sl* Kokain *n*; *Am fam* Coca-Cola *n*, *fam f*; *tr* verkoken; *broken* ~ Bruchkoks *m*; ~**-oven** Kokereiofen *m*; ~~ *battery* Koksofenbatterie *f*; ~~ *coke* Zechenkoks *m*; ~~ *plant* Kokerei *f*; ~**rnut** *fam* Kokosnuß *f*; **coking** ['koukiŋ] Verkokung *f*.

*

cola ['koulə] Kolabaum *m*; *(~-nut, -seed)* Kolanuß *f*.

colander, cullender ['kʌləndə] Durchschlag *m*, (Küchen-)Sieb *n*.

cold [kould] *a* kalt; *fig* kühl, leidenschaftslos; ruhig, zurückhaltend; *(Empfang)* eisig, frostig; *sl* besinnungslos; *s* Kälte *f*, *das* Kalte; Erkältung *f*, Schnupfen *m*; *in* ~ *blood* kaltblütig, mit voller Überlegung; *(shivering) with* ~ (zitternd) vor Kälte; *to be, to feel* ~ *(Mensch)* frieren; *(on s.th.) Am sl* e-r S völlig sicher sein; *to be left out in the* ~ links liegen gelassen werden; *to catch (a)* ~ sich erkälten, sich e-n Schnupfen holen; *to get* ~ *feet (fam)* es mit der Angst kriegen; *to give s.o. the* ~ *shoulder* jdm die kalte Schulter zeigen, e-e Abfuhr erteilen; *to make s.o.'s blood run* ~ jdn erschau(d)ern lassen; *to suffer from the* ~ unter der Kälte (zu) leiden (haben); *to throw* ~ *water on (fig)* e-e kalte Dusche geben *dat*; *I am* ~ ich friere, mir ist kalt; ~**-blooded** *a zoo fig* kaltblütig; *fig* gefühl-, herzlos; ~ **chisel** Kaltmeißel *m*; ~**-cock** *tr Am sl* bewußtlos schlagen; ~ **cream** *Art* Hautcreme *f*; ~ **cuts** *pl* kalte(r) Aufschnitt *m*, kalte Platte *f*; ~**-deck** *Am sl* gezinkte Karten *f pl*; ~**-drawn** *a (Stahl)* kaltgezogen; ~ **front** *mete* Kaltfront *f*; ~ **glue** Kaltleim *m*; ~**-hammer** *tr tech* kalthämmern, -schmieden; ~ **haul** *tr Am sl* mit der linken Hand, nachlässig tun; *itr* abhauen; ~**-hearted** *a* gefühl-, herzlos; kaltherzig; ~**ish** ['-iʃ] etwas kalt, kühl; ~**ly** ['-li] *adv* kalt, teilnahmslos; unfreundlich; ~**ness** ['-nis] Kälte *f*; ~ **news** *pl mit sing* schlechte Nachrichten *f pl*; ~ **pig** kalte Dusche *f* (zum Wecken); ~**-resistant** kältebeständig; ~**-rivet** *tr* kaltnieten; ~**-roll** *tr* kaltwalzen; ~~*ing mill* Kaltwalzwerk *n*; ~**-short** *tech* kaltbrüchig; ~**-shoulder** *tr* die kalte Schulter zeigen *(s.o.* jdm); ~ **snap** *mete* plötzliche Kälte *f*; ~ **steel** blanke Waffe *f*; ~**-storage** Lagerung *f* im Kühlraum; *to put in* ~~ *(fig)* auf Eis legen; ~~ *room* Kühlraum *m*; ~~ *ship* Kühlschiff *n*; ~ **store** Kühlhaus *n*; ~ **turkey** *Am sl* sachlich, offenherzig; ohne Ankündigung; ~ **war** kalte(r) Krieg *m*; ~ **wave** *mete* Kältewelle; *(Frisur)* Kaltwelle *f*; ~**-work** *tr tech* kaltverformen.

cole [koul] Kohl; Raps, Rübsen *m*; ~**-seed** Rübsame(n), Rübsen *m*; ~**-slaw** ['-slɔ:] *Am* Kraut-, Kohlsalat *m*; ~**-wort** ['-wə:t] Kohl ohne Kopf; Grünkohl *m*.

coleoptera [kɔli'ɔptərə] *pl scient* Käfer *m pl*.

col|ic ['kɔlik] Kolik *f*, Leibschmerzen *m pl*, Bauchgrimmen *n*; ~**icky** ['-i] kolikartig; ~**itis** [ko(u)'laitis] Dickdarmkatarrh *m*.

collaborat|e [kə'læbəreit] *itr* zs.arbeiten *(with* mit); mitarbeiten; ~**ion** [-'reiʃən] Zs.-, Mitarbeit *f*; ~**or** [-ə] Mitarbeiter; *pol* Kollaborateur *m*.

collaps|e [kə'læps] *s* Einsturz *m*, Zs.-brechen *n*; *fig* Zs.bruch *a. med psychol*; Kollaps, Nervenzs.bruch; *(Börse)* Krach, Sturz *m*; *itr* zs.-, einstürzen, zs.brechen *a. fig*, umfallen; e-n (Nerven-)Zs.bruch haben *od* erleiden; **~ible** [-ibl] zs.legbar, zs.klappbar; Falt-; *~~ boat, canoe* Faltboot *n*; *~~ roof* Klappdach *n*; *~~ top (mot)* Klappverdeck *n*.

collar ['kɔlə] *s* Kragen *m*; Ordenskette *f*; *zoo* Halsstreifen *m*; *(Hund)* Halsband; *(Pferd)* Kum(me)t *n*; *tech* Kragen, Ring, Reif(en) *m*, Manschette *(a. bei e-m Glas Bier)*, Muffe *f*; *arch* Kranz, Saum *m*; *(Küche)* Roulade *f*; *mar* Stagkragen *m*; *Am sl* Verhaftung *f*; *tr* beim Kragen nehmen *od* packen; festhalten; *s.o.* jdn anhalten u. mit ihm reden; *fam* wegnehmen; *sl* sich unter den Nagel reißen; *Am sl* verhaften; *Am sl* gründlich verstehen; *(Fleisch)* rollen; *against the ~ (fig)* angestrengt; *hot under the ~ (fam)* aufgeregt; *white ~ worker* Büroangestellte(r)*m*; **~-beam** Querbalken *m*; **~-bearing** *tech* Halslager *n*; **~-bone** *anat* Schlüsselbein *n*; **~-stud,** *Am* **~ button** Kragenknopf *m*.

collat|e [kɔ'leit] *tr* zs.tragen; *(Schriftstücke, Bücher)* genau vergleichen, kollationieren; **~ion** [-ʃən] Vergleichung; Kollationierung; *hist* Übertragung, Verleihung *f (e-r Pfründe)*; Imbiß *m*, leichte Mahlzeit *f*.

collateral [kɔ'lætərəl] *a* Seiten-, Parallel-; parallel; Neben-, Ersatz-; zusätzlich; entsprechend; *s* (Seiten-) Verwandte(r) *m*; *(~ security) fin* weitere, zusätzliche Sicherheit *od* Dekkung, Ausfallbürgschaft *f*; (Ersatz-) Pfand *n*; **~ acceptance** Wechselbürgschaft *f*; **~ agreement** Nebenabreden *f pl*; **~ circumstances** *pl* Begleitumstände *m pl*; **~ insurance** Zusatzversicherung *f*; **~ly** [-li] *adv* in der Seitenlinie; zusätzlich.

colleague ['kɔli:g] Kollege *m*.

collect [kə'lekt] *tr* (ein)sammeln, auflesen; zs.tragen, zs.fassen; beschaffen; abholen, mitnehmen; einkassieren; eintreiben, -ziehen; *(Steuern)* einnehmen; *(Briefmarken, s-e Gedanken)* sammeln; *(Strom)* abnehmen; *fam* holen; *tech* auf-, abfangen; montieren; *itr* sich (an)sammeln, sich (an)häufen, zs.kommen; Geld einziehen; *s* ['kɔlekt] *rel* Kollekte *f (kurzes liturgisches Gebet)*; *pl* Stoßgebete *n pl*; *to telephone ~ (Am)* ein R-Gespräch führen; *to ~ information* sich orientieren; *to ~ the mail* den Briefkasten, die Briefkästen leeren; *~ on delivery (C.O.D.) (Am)* gegen Nachnahme *f*; **~able, ~ible** [kə'lektəbl,-ibl] eintreib-, einziehbar; **~ call** *Am* R-Gespräch *n*; **~ed** [-id] *a* (innerlich) gesammelt, gefaßt; **~edness** Gefaßtheit, Fassung *f*; **~ing** [-iŋ] Sammeln *n*; Einziehung, Eintreibung *f*, Einkassieren *n*; Abholung *f*; *attr* Inkasso-; *~~ charges (pl)* Inkassospesen *pl*; *~~ office* Inkassobüro *n*; (Ein-)Hebestelle *f*; *~~ pipe* Auffangrohr *n*; *~~ point* Auffang-, Sammelstelle *f*; *~~ ring* Schleifring *m*; *~~ service (com)* Abholdienst *m*; **~ion** [kə'lekʃən] Sammeln *n*; Ansammlung, Anhäufung *f*, Zs.kommen *n*; Abholung; (Briefkasten-)Leerung; Eintreibung, Einziehung *f*, Einkassieren *n*; *(Steuer)* Erhebung; *(Nachrichten)* Beschaffung; *com* Kollektion; (Geld-, Spenden-)Sammlung, *rel* Kollekte; *pl* Schlußprüfung; *stamp ~~* Briefmarkensammlung *f*; *~~ agent* Inkassovertreter *m*; **~ive** [kə'lektiv] *a* gemeinsam, gemeinschaftlich, geschlossen; Gemeinschafts-, Kollektiv-; Gesamt-; Sammel-; *s (~~ idea, noun)* Sammelbegriff *m*, -wort; *pol* Kollektiv *n*; *~~ agreement* Kollektivvertrag *m*; *~~ bargaining* Tarifverhandlungen *f pl*; *~~ consignment* Sammelladung *f*; *~~ employment regulation* Tarifordnung *f*; *~~ farm* Kolchose *f*; *~~ guilt* Kollektivschuld *f*; *~~ number (tele)* Sammelnummer *f*; *~~ ownership* Kollektiveigentum *n*; *~~ passport* Sammelpaß *m*; *~~ penalty* Gesamtstrafe *f*; *~~ security (pol)* kollektive Sicherheit *f*; *~~ training (mil)* geschlossene Ausbildung *f*; **~ivism** [-ivizm] Kollektivismus *m*; **~ivist** [-ivist] Kollektivist *m*; **~ivity** [kɔlek'tiviti] Allgemeinheit, Gesamtheit *f*; **~ivization** [-vai'zeiʃən] Kollektivisierung *f*; **~or** [-ə] Sammler; Einsammler; Kassierer, (Zoll-, Steuer-)Einnehmer; *tech* Sammelapparat; *el* Stromabnehmer, Kollektor *m*; *~~ of customs* Zolleinnehmer *m*; *~~ ring (el)* Schleifring *m*.

colleg|e ['kɔlidʒ] College *n (Teil e-r Universität)*, *Art* Fakultät; (kleinere) Universität, Akademie; (Fach-)Hochschule, höhere (Fach-)Schule; höhere Lehr-, Bildungsanstalt; höhere (Privat-)Schule *f*; Universitäts-, Schulgebäude; Kolleg(ium) *n*; *Electoral ~ (Am)* Wahlkollegium *n* für die Präsidentenwahl; *Sacred C~~*, *~~ of cardinals (rel)* Kardinalskolleg(ium) *n*; *technical ~~* höhere technische Lehranstalt *f*; *~~-pudding* kleine(r) Plumpudding *m*; **~ian** [kə'li:dʒən] höhere(r) Schüler *(e-s College)*, Student *m*; **~iate** *a* [kə'li:dʒiit] College-, Universitäts-, (Hoch-)Schul-; akademisch; *~~ church* Stifts-, Kollegiatkirche *f*.

collet ['kɔlit] *tech* Zwinge *f*, Klemmring *m*, Metallband *n*; Konushülse *f*; Futter *n*.

collid|e [kə'laid] *itr* kollidieren, zs.-stoßen, -prallen *a. fig (with* mit); *fig* ea. entgegengesetzt sein, in Widerspruch stehen *(with* zu); **~ing** [-iŋ] *(Interessen)* widerstreitend; *(Fahrzeuge)* an e-m Zs.stoß beteiligt.

collie, colly ['kɔli] Collie, schottische(r) Schäferhund *m*.

collier ['kɔliə] Bergmann, Grubenarbeiter, Kumpel *m*; (Seemann *m* auf e-m) Kohlenschiff *n*; **~y** ['kɔljəri] Kohlenbergwerk *n*, (Kohlen-)Grube, Zeche *f*.

collision [kə'liʒən] Zs.stoß, -prall *a. fig*; *fig* Widerspruch, -streit *m*; *in ~* in Widerspruch *(with* zu); *to come into ~ with* in Widerspruch geraten zu.

collocat|e ['kɔləkeit] *tr* zs.stellen, (an)ordnen, arrangieren, verteilen; an s-n Platz bringen; **~ion** [-'keiʃən] Zs.stellung, (An-)Ordnung, Verteilung *f*.

collodion [kə'loudiən] *chem pharm* Kollodium *n*.

collogue [kə'loug] *itr* sich vertraulich besprechen.

colloid ['kɔlɔid] *s chem* Kolloid *n*; *a.* **~al** [-'lɔidl] kolloid(al).

collop ['kɔləp] Fleischschnitte *f*.

colloqu|ial [kə'loukwiəl] Gesprächs-; umgangssprachlich, familiär; **~ialism** [-izm] familiäre(r) Ausdruck(sweise *f*) *m*, Umgangssprache *f*; **~y** ['kɔləkwi] Gespräch *n*, Konferenz *f*; Kolloquium *n*.

collu|sion [kə'lu:ʒən] geheime(s) Einverständnis *n*; **~sive** [kə'lu:siv] verabredet, abgekartet.

colly *s. collie.*

collywobbles ['kɔliwɔblz] *pl fam* Magenknurren; Bauch-, Leibweh *n*.

Cologne [kə'loun] Köln *n*; Kölnischwasser *n*.

colon ['koulən] **1.** *anat* Dickdarm; **2.** *gram* Doppelpunkt *m*.

colonel ['kə:nl] Oberst *m*; *lieutenant-~* Oberstleutnant *m*; **~cy** ['-si] Oberstenstelle *f*.

colon|ial [kə'lounjəl] *a* Kolonial-; *s* Einwohner *m* e-r Kolonie; *C~~ Office* Kolonialamt, -ministerium *n*; **~ialism** [-izm] Kolonialismus *m*; **~ist** ['kɔlənist] Siedler *m*; **~ization** [kɔlənai'zeiʃən] Kolonisation, Kolonisierung, Besiedlung *f*; **~ize** ['kɔlənaiz] *tr* kolonisieren, besiedeln; *itr* e-e Kolonie gründen; sich niederlassen, (sich an)siedeln; **~izer** ['kɔlənaizə] Kolonisator *m*; **~y** ['kɔləni] Kolonie, Niederlassung, (An-) Siedlung; Kolonie *f (e-r Landsmannschaft, e-r Berufsgruppe)*; *zoo* Kolonie *a. bot*, Volk *n*; *~~ of ants* Ameisenvolk *n*; *~~ of artists* Künstlerkolonie *f*.

colonnade [kɔlə'neid] Säulengang *m*, Kolonnade *f*.

colophony [kə'lɔfəni] Kolophonium, Geigenharz *n*.

Colorado [kɔlə'rɑ:dou]: **~ beetle** Kartoffelkäfer *m*.

color|ation, colouration [kʌlə'reiʃən] Färbung *f*; **~ific** [kɔlə'rifik] färbend; farbkräftig; **~imeter** [-'rimitə] Kolorimeter *n*, Farbmesser *m*.

coloss|al [kə'lɔsl] *fam* kolossal, gewaltig, gigantisch; **~us** [-'lɔsəs] *pl a.* -*i* [-ai] Koloß *m*.

colo(u)r ['kʌlə] *s* Farbe *f*; Farbstoff *m*; Haut-, Gesichtsfarbe *f*; (Farb-)Ton *m*, Färbung, Farbgebung, (Farb-)Schattierung, Farbwirkung *f*, Kolorit *n a. mus*; *mus* Ausdruckskraft; *lit* Bildhaftigkeit *f*, *das* Malerische; *allg* Ton *m*, Färbung, Schattierung, Eigenart, Eigentümlichkeit *f*, Charakter; Anstrich, (An-)Schein; Vorwand *m*, Ausrede, -flucht *f*; *pl (bestimmte)* Farben *f pl (als Kennzeichen)*; *pl* Fahne, Flagge; *pl fig* Überzeugung *f*; *tr* färben, farbig machen; (an-, be)malen, (an-) streichen, tönen, schattieren, kolorieren; *fig* glaubhaft machen; abfärben *(s.th.* auf etw); *itr* sich (ver)färben; erröten; *of ~ (Mensch)* farbig; *under ~ of* unter dem Vorwand *gen*; *with flying ~s* höchst erfolgreich; *to be off ~ (fam)* sich nicht wohl fühlen; schlechte Laune haben; *to change ~* die Farbe *(im Gesicht)* wechseln; rot werden; *to come off with flying ~s* großen Erfolg haben; *to get o.'s ~s (sport)* in die Schulmannschaft aufgenommen werden; *to give, to lend ~ to (fig)* unterstreichen, wahrscheinlich, glaubhaft machen; *to give a false ~ to* in ein falsches Licht rükken, entstellen; *to have a high ~* wie das blühende Leben aussehen; *to join the ~s* Soldat werden; *to lose ~* die Farbe im Gesicht verlieren; blaß werden; *to lower o.'s ~s* nachgeben; *to nail o.'s ~s to the mast* sich festlegen; *to paint in bright, dark ~s (fig)* in glänzenden, trüben Farben malen; *to put false ~s upon s.th.* ein falsches Licht auf etw werfen; *to sail under false ~s (fig)* unter falscher Flagge segeln; *to see s.th. in its true ~s (fig)* etw im rechten Licht sehen; *to show o.'s true ~s* Farbe bekennen; *to stick to o.'s ~s* s-r Überzeugung, s-r Partei treu bleiben; **~able** ['-rəbl] glaubhaft; scheinbar richtig; angeblich; **~ bar** Rassenschranke *f*; **~-blind** farbenblind; **~-blindness** Farbenblindheit *f*; **~-box** Farb-, Mal-, Tuschkasten *m*; **~cast** ['-kɑ:st] Farbfernsehsendung *f*; **~ chart** Farbtafel *f*; **~ed** ['-d] *a* farbig; bunt; *(angehängt)* -farben; *fig* gefärbt, beschönigt; *Am* Neger-; *~~ pencil* Farbstift *m*; *~~ people* (die) Farbige(n) *m pl*; **~ filter** Farbfilter *m*; **~ful** ['-ful] farbenreich, -prächtig *a. fig*; *fig* farbig, lebhaft, lebendig; **~ing**

['-riŋ] Färbung *f*, Farbton *m*, Schattierung; (Gesichts-, Augen-, Haar-) Farbe *f*; Farben *f pl (zum Malen)*; Mal-, *allg* Darstellungsweise *f*; Schein *m*; **~ist** ['-rist] Kolorist *m*; **~istic** [-'ristik] koloristisch; **~less** ['-lis] farblos, blaß *a. fig*; *fig* matt, kraftlos, uninteressant, nichtssagend; **~ line** *Am* Rassentrennung *f*; *to draw the ~~* Rassenunterschiede machen; **~-man** Farbenhändler *m*; **~-photography** Farbphotographie *f*; **~-printing** Bunt-, Farbendruck *m*; **~ rendition** *Am* Farbwiedergabe *f*; **~-sensitive** farbempfindlich; **~-sensitivity** Farbempfindlichkeit *f*; **~-sergeant** Kompanie-, Hauptfeldwebel *m*; **~-shot** *phot* Farbaufnahme *f*; **~ slide** Farbdia(positiv) *n*; **~ television** Farbfernsehen *n*; **~ vision** *physiol* Farbensehen *n*; **~-wash** Temperafarben *f pl*.

colt [koult] Fohlen *n*; *fig* junge(r) Dachs; Neuling *m*; *mar* Tauende *n (als Prügel)*; Colt *m (Revolver)*; **~ish** ['-iʃ] lebhaft, ausgelassen; unerfahren; **~sfoot** ['-sfut] *bot* Huflattich *m*.

colter ['koultə] *s. coulter.*

columb|arium [kɔləm'bɛəriəm] *pl -ria* Urnenhalle *f*; **~ine** ['-ain] *bot* Akelei *f*.

column ['kɔləm] Säule *a. fig*; *fig* Stütze; *typ* Spalte; Rubrik *f*; regelmäßig erscheinende(r) Zeitungsartikel *m*; *Am* Feuilleton(abteilung *f*) *n*; *mil* Kolonne *a. math*; *geol* Schichtenfolge *f*; *to dodge the ~ (fam)* sich drücken; *spinal ~ (anat)* Wirbelsäule *f*; *~ of figures* Zahlenreihe *f*; *~ of march, of route* Marschkolonne *f*; *~ of mercury* Quecksilbersäule *f*; *~ of smoke* Rauchsäule *f*; *~ of water* Wassersäule *f*; **~ar** [kə'lʌmnə] säulenartig, -förmig; von Säulen getragen; in Spalten gedruckt; **~ base** Säulenfuß *m*; **~ed** ['kɔləmd] *a* mit Säulen verziert; auf Säulen ruhend; in Spalten eingeteilt; **~ heading** Tabellen-, Spaltenkopf *m*; **~ist** ['kɔləm(n)ist] Feuilletonist; *Am* Leitartikler *m*.

colza ['kɔlzə] *bot* Raps, Rübsen *m*.

coma ['koumə] **1.** *med* Koma *n*, tiefe Bewußtlosigkeit *f*; **~tose** ['-tous] komatös, in tiefer Bewußtlosigkeit (befindlich); **2.** *pl -ae* ['-i:] *bot* Haarbüschel *n*; *astr* Koma *n*; *phot* Lichthof *m*.

comb [koum] *s* Kamm; *(horse ~)* Striegel *m*; *tech (Textil)* (Hechel-)Kamm *m*, Hechel; Kämmaschine *f*; *(~ collector)* Spitzenabnehmer; *zoo, bes. orn* (Hahnen-)Kamm; *fig* (Berg-, Wellen-)Kamm *m*; *(honey~)* Honigwabe *f*; *tr* kämmen; *(Pferd)* striegeln; *(Textil)* hecheln, (aus)kämmen; *fig* durchkämmen, -suchen; *itr* sich kämmen; *(Welle)* sich brechen; *to ~ out* auskämmen; *fig mil (Gelände)* aus-, durchkämmen, absuchen; (aus)sieben; *mil sl* erfassen; *to ~ up (Am fam)* sich (über)kämmen; **~er** ['-ə] Kämmer, Hechler *m*; Kämmaschine *f*; Brecher *m*, Sturzwelle *f*; **~ing** ['-iŋ] Kämmen *n*; *pl* ausgekämmte Haare *n pl*; *(Textil)* Kammabfall, Kämmling *m*; *~~ wool* Kammwolle *f*.

combat ['kɔm-, 'kʌmbət] *s* Kampf *m*, Gefecht *n*; (Kampf-, Front-)Einsatz *m*; *itr* kämpfen; *tr* bekämpfen, kämpfen gegen; *close ~* Nahkampf *m*; **~ant** ['-ənt] *a* kämpfend; Front-; kämpferisch; *s* Kämpf(end)er *m*; *non-~~ (a)* nichtkämpfend; *s* Nichtkämpfer *m*; *~~ value* Kampfwert *m*; **~ area** Kampfgebiet *n*; **~ car** Kampfwagen *m*; **~ fatigue** *Am* Frontneurose *f*; **~ group** Kampfgruppe *f*; **~ive** ['-iv] zank-, streitsüchtig; kampfbereit; *~~ instinct* Kampfgeist *m*; **~ pay, allowance** Frontzulage *f*; **~ patrol** Stoßtrupp *m*; **~ practice, training** Gefechtsausbildung *f*; **~-ready** einsatzbereit; **~ reconnaissance** Gefechtsaufklärung *f*; **~ report** Gefechtsbericht *m*; **~ section, sector** Kampf-, Frontabschnitt *m*; **~ team** *Am* Kampfgruppe *f*; **~ training** Gefechtsausbildung *f*; **~ unit** Kampfeinheit *f*, -verband *m*; **~ zone** Kampfzone *f*.

combin|able [kəm'bainəbl] kombinierbar; vereinbar; **~ation** [kɔmbi'neiʃən] Zs.setzung, -stellung, -legung, Verbindung *a. chem*, Vereinigung, Zs.fassung *f*, -schluß *m*, Verschmelzung, Vermischung; Kombination *a. math*; *el* Schaltung *f*; gemeinsame(s) Handeln *n*, Aktion *f*; Zs.wirken *n*; *pol com* (Interessen-)Verband *m*; Kartell *n*; Gewerkschaft *f*; *(~~ lock)* Kombinations-, Vexierschloß; Motorrad *n* mit Beiwagen; *pl* Hemdhose; Garnitur *f* (Unterwäsche); *in ~~ with* in Verbindung mit; *~~ pliers (pl)* Kombinationszange *f*; **~e** *v* [kəm'bain] *tr* zs.stellen, -setzen, -legen; (mitea.) verbinden, vereinigen; zs.schließen, -fassen, -ziehen; verknüpfen; vermischen; chemisch verbinden; kombinieren; *(verschiedene Eigenschaften)* in sich vereinigen; *itr* sich verbinden *a. chem*, e-e Verbindung eingehen, sich vereinigen, sich zs.schließen (*with* mit); sich mischen, mitea. verschmelzen; gemeinsam handeln, zs.arbeiten, zs.-wirken; *s* ['kɔmbain] Verband, Ring *m*, Kartell *n*, Trust *m*; Finanzgruppe *f*; *Am* Mähdrescher *m*; *to ~~ in parallel (el)* parallel schalten; *~~ of producers* Erzeugerverband *m*; **~ed** *a* zs.gefaßt, gemeinsam; *chem* gebunden; *~~ action, effect* Gesamtwirkung *f*; *~~ board* vermischte(r) Ausschuß *m*.

combo ['kʌmbou] *Am sl* Mischung; Gruppe *f*; kleine(s) (Jazz-)Orchester; Kombinationsschloß *n*.

combust|ibility [kəmbʌstə'biliti] Brennbarkeit *f*; **~ible** [-'bʌstibl] *a* (ver)brennbar; entzündlich, Feuer fangend; *fig* erregbar, reizbar, leicht erregt; *s meist pl* brennbare(s) Material; Brennmaterial *n*; *fig* Zündstoff *m*; *highly ~~* leicht Feuer fangend, leicht entzündlich; **~ion** [-'bʌstʃən] Verbrennung *f*, Brand *m*; *chem physiol* Verbrennung, Oxydation *f*; *fig* Aufruhr *m*; *(internal) ~~ engine* Verbrennungsmotor *m*; *~~ chamber (mot)* Verbrennungsraum *m*; *(Rakete)* Brennkammer *f*; *~~ fuse* Brennzünder *m*; *~~ heat* Verbrennungswärme *f*; *~~ residue* Verbrennungsrückstand *m*; *~~ temperature* Verbrennungstemperatur *f*.

come [kʌm] *irr came* [keim], *come itr* (an-, her-, herbei)kommen; erreichen (*to s.th.* etw), sich belaufen (*to* auf), hinauslaufen (*to* auf); *(der Ordnung nach)* kommen, folgen; werden; geschehen, sich ereignen, stattfinden; die Folge sein (*of doing* davon daß, wenn man tut); sich zeigen, sich erweisen als; erhältlich sein; *Am sl* im Kommen sein, sich erregen; *to have ~* da sein, *to do* tun müssen, zu tun pflegen; *to ~* (zu)künftig, kommend; *to ~ of age* mündig werden; *to ~ to an agreement* zu e-r Vereinbarung kommen *od* gelangen; *to ~ into blossom, flower* auf-, erblühen; *to ~ to blows* anea., sich in die Haare geraten; *to ~ off with flying colours (fam)* erfolgreich sein; *to ~ clean (fam)* gestehen, die Wahrheit sagen; *to ~ a cropper (fam)* e-e Dummheit machen, e-n Fehler begehen; *to ~ to a decision* sich entscheiden; *to ~ to s.o.'s ear(s)* jdm zu Ohren kommen; *to ~ into effect, force* in Kraft treten; *to ~ to an end* zu Ende kommen, aufhören; *to ~ into existence* entstehen; beginnen; *to ~ into fashion, style* Mode, modern werden; *to ~ to grief, harm* zu Schaden kommen, Schaden (er)leiden *od* nehmen; *to ~ to grips* zu tun haben mit; *to ~ to hand* zu Händen kommen; *to ~ to a head* zur Entscheidung kommen; *to ~ into s.o.'s head* jdm in den Kopf kommen, einfallen; *to ~ home* heim-, nach Haus(e) kommen, *to s.o.* jdm einleuchten; *to ~ down off o.'s high horse* vom hohen Roß steigen; *to ~ before (the) judge* vor den Richter, vor Gericht kommen; *to ~ to s.o.'s knowledge, notice* jdm zur Kenntnis gelangen; *to ~ into leaf* grün werden, ergrünen, ausschlagen; *to ~ to light* ans Licht kommen *od* treten, bekanntwerden; *to ~ naturally to s.o.* jdm liegen; *to ~ to nothing* ins Wasser fallen, zu Wasser werden, fehlschlagen; *to ~ under notice* bekanntwerden; *to ~ to pass* sich ereignen, geschehen; *to ~ to pieces* in Stücke gehen, zerbrechen; *to ~ to a point* spitz zulaufen; *fig* e-n Höhepunkt erreichen; *to ~ up to scratch (fam)* s-n Mann stellen; *to ~ and see, to ~ to see* besuchen; *to ~ to o.'s senses, to o.s.* zu sich, zum Bewußtsein kommen; zur Vernunft kommen; *to ~ short* zu kurz kommen, *of* nicht erreichen, nicht befriedigen, hinter den Ansprüchen zurückbleiben; *to ~ into sight* in Sicht kommen, auftauchen; *to ~ to a standstill od stop* zum Stillstand kommen; *to ~ it strong (sl)* zeigen, was man kann; *to ~ it too strong (sl)* mächtig übertreiben, schaurig angeben; *to ~ to terms with s.o.* mit jdm einig werden; *to ~ true* wahr, Wirklichkeit werden, sich verwirklichen; in Erfüllung gehen; *to ~ into use* auf-, in Gebrauch kommen; *to ~ into the world* auf die Welt kommen; *how ~s it that ...?* wie kommt es, daß ...? *that ~s of doing* das kommt daher, davon, daß man tut; *I'm coming 16* ich werde 16 (Jahre alt); *~ what may!* komme, was (da) wolle! *let'em all ~! (sl)* es kann losgehen, ich bin fertig; *I don't know whether I'm coming or going* ich weiß nicht, wo mir der Kopf steht; *~!* hör mal! hör zu! *~, ~!* komm, mach keinen Unsinn! komm, mach mir nichts vor! sei so gut!; *light ~ light gone (prov)* wie gewonnen, so zerronnen; *to ~* **about** sich ereignen, geschehen, passieren; *to ~* **across** *(upon)* (zufällig) treffen, begegnen (*s.o.* jdm); stoßen auf; *with (fam)* blechen für, bezahlen; *sl* bestechen; *to ~* **after** *s.th.* hinter etw her, auf etw aus sein, nach etw fragen, etw (ab)holen wollen; *to ~* **again** wieder-, zurück-, noch (ein)mal kommen; *~ again!* sag es nochmal! *to ~* **along** *fam* schnellmachen, sich sputen, sich (be)eilen; mitkommen, -gehen (*with s.o.* mit jdm); vorwärtsgehen, gedeihen; *~ along!* los! mach zu! vorwärts! *everything's coming along fine* alles geht gut; *to ~* **amiss** zu unpassender Zeit, ungelegen kommen; *to ~* **apart, asunder** ausea.-, in Stücke gehen, zerbrechen, -reißen; *to ~* **at** kommen, gelangen zu, erreichen; herfallen über, anfallen, -greifen; *to ~* **away** weg-, abhanden kommen; sich loslösen; *to ~* **back** zurückkehren, wiederkommen; wieder einfallen; *fam* sich erholen; *sl* es heimzahlen, Rache nehmen; die passende Antwort geben;

to ~ **by** *tr* erhalten, erreichen; erwerben, kommen zu; *itr* vorbei-, vorübergehen; fahren mit; *to* ~ **down** herunterkommen; heruntergehen, -reichen (*to* bis); mit dem Preis heruntergehen; *(durch Überlieferung)* kommen auf; (ein)stürzen, fallen; *fig (sozial)* (ab-) sinken; *(up)on s.o.* jdn tadeln, bestrafen, zur Rechenschaft ziehen; sich auf jdn stürzen; *with (Geld)* hergeben, herausrücken; *Am fam (Krankheit)* sich holen; sich ins Bett legen müssen; *to* ~ *down handsomely* sich freigebig, großzügig zeigen; *to* ~ **for** *s.th.* um etw, wegen e-r S kommen; kommen, um etw zu holen; *to* ~ **forward** vortreten; Folge leisten; sich freiwillig melden; *to* ~ **from** (her)kommen von; abstammen von; *to* ~ **in** hereinkommen, nähertreten; *(Geld)* einkommen; sich zeigen, sich erweisen als; liegen in; aufkommen, Mode, modern werden; *to* ~ *in for (fam)* erhalten; *to* ~ *in handy, useful* zustatten kommen; *to* ~ *in second (sport)* Zweiter werden, den zweiten Platz belegen; *where do I* ~ *in?* wie steht es in meiner Angelegenheit? ~ *in!* herein! *to* ~ **into** kommen an, zu; beitreten; erben; *o.'s own* bekommen, was e-m zusteht, zu s-m Recht kommen; *to* ~ **near** sich nähern; beinahe tun *(doing s.th.)*; *to* ~ **of** die Folge sein *gen*; werden aus; *to* ~ **off** *(Knopf)* ab-, *(Haare)* ausgehen; abblättern, sich ablösen; loskommen, sich losreißen, davonkommen; weggehen, herausgehen; daraus hervorgehen; sich ereignen, stattfinden; eintreten, in Erfüllung gehen; Erfolg haben, ins Schwarze treffen; ~ *off (it)!* das ist doch nicht dein Ernst! *to* ~ **on** weiterkommen, vorrücken; fortschreiten, gedeihen; sich stürzen, hereinbrechen auf; stoßen auf; *(Frage)* sich erheben, sich ergeben; *theat* auftreten; *(Tag)* fallen auf; ~ *on!* los! vorwärts! *to* ~ **out** herauskommen *(a. etw Geheimgehaltenes)*; *(Fleck)* herausgehen; hervorgehen *(a. aus e-m Examen)*; an den Tag treten, sich zeigen, bekannt-, offenkundig werden, herauskommen, sich herausstellen; enden; *(Zeitung, Druckschrift)* erscheinen, herauskommen, veröffentlicht werden; *(junge Dame)* in die Gesellschaft eingeführt werden; in Streik treten; *to* ~ *out against* sich erklären gegen; *to* ~ *out in the open* die Katze aus dem Sack lassen; *to* ~ *out with* gestehen; herausrücken mit; veröffentlichen; auf den Markt bringen; hinausgehen, -fahren mit; ~ *out of that (sl)* hau, zieh ab! laß das (sein)! *he came out third* er wurde dritter; *to* ~ **over** herüberkommen; *radio tele* herauskommen; s-e Ansicht ändern, die Partei wechseln; sich ereignen; *(Gefühle)* überkommen; *what's* ~ *over you?* was ist in dich gefahren? *to* ~ **round,** *Am* **around** (bei Gelegenheit, zufällig) vorbeikommen, hereinschauen; gelegentlich wiederkommen; *(e-r Auffassung)* sich anschließen (*to* an); nachgeben, einlenken; hereinlegen, täuschen; sich wieder erholen, wieder auf die Beine kommen, wieder der alte sein; *to* ~ **through** durchkommen, das Ziel erreichen; überstehen; *Am fam* bekennen; herausrücken (*with* mit); den Erwartungen entsprechen; sein Herz ausschütten; sich durchscheuern; *to* ~ **to** dazu kommen (*to do* zu tun); führen zu; *s.o.* jdm zustoßen; einwilligen, einverstanden sein; (wieder) zu sich kommen, sich (wieder) erholen; sich belaufen auf; *mar* ankern; *to* ~ **under** fallen unter; unter die Herrschaft, Aufsicht kommen *gen*; *to* ~ **up** heraufkommen; *(Gewitter)* im Anzug sein; in die Stadt kommen; die Universität beziehen; *bot* keimen, aufgehen; *fig (Mode)* aufkommen; *(Gedanke)* auftauchen; zur Sprache kommen; *to* ~ *up to* sich belaufen auf, gleichkommen, erreichen; *(den Erwartungen)* entsprechen; *(s-n Platz)* ausfüllen; *to* ~ *up with* erreichen, ein-, überholen; vorschlagen, zur Sprache bringen; sich einfallen lassen; *something has* ~ *up* es ist etw dazwischengekommen; *to* ~ **upon** überfallen, überraschen; *(die Gedanken)* einnehmen; in Anspruch nehmen; lästig fallen; zufällig treffen, stoßen auf; **~-at-able** [-'ætəbl] *fam* erreichbar, zugänglich; **~-back** ['--] Wieder-, Rückkehr *f*; *theat film* Comeback *n*; *sl* schlagfertige Antwort *f*; **~-down** ['--] Niedergang, Sturz *m*; Enttäuschung *f*, *fam* Reinfall *m*; **~-hither** *a fam fig* aufreizend; **~-off** ['--] Ausgang *m*, Ende *n*; Ausrede, -flucht *f*; **~-on** ['--] *Am sl* Werbegeschenk, Lockmittel *n*; Einladung, Aufforderung *f*; Dummkopf *m*.

comed|ian [kə'mi:diən] Komödiant; Lustspiel-, Komödiendichter *m*; Spaßmacher, -vogel, Komiker *m*; **~y** ['kɔmidi] Lustspiel *n*, Komödie; komische Szene(n *pl*) *f (e-s Dramas)*; Spaß *m*; komische Geschichte *od* Sache *f*; *to cut the* ~~ *(Am sl)* mit dem Unsinn aufhören; *drawing-room* ~~ Salonstück *n*; ~~ *of manners* Sittenkomödie *f*.

comel|iness ['kʌmlinis] Anmut *f*; angenehme(s), gefällige(s) Äußere(s) *n*; Anstand *m*; **~y** ['-li] *(Mensch)* gutaussehend, hübsch; *(Äußeres)* gefällig, angenehm; *(Benehmen)* gut, artig; *(Umgangsformen)* gewinnend; *(Wesen)* einnehmend, nett.

comer ['kʌmə](An-)Kommende(r) *m*; *Am sl der* kommende Mann; *all* ~*s* jedermann, all u. jeder; *the first* ~ der zuerst Kommende; der erste beste.

comestible [kə'mestibl] *a* eßbar; *s pl* Lebensmittel *n pl*, Eßwaren *f pl*; *hum* Fressalien *pl*.

comet ['kɔmit] *astr* Komet *m*.

comfit ['kʌmfit] kandierte Frucht, *bes.* Pflaume *f*; Konfekt *n*.

comfort ['kʌmfət] *s* Trost *m*, Beruhigung *f* (*to* für); Tröster *m*, Stütze, Hilfe; Genugtuung; Zufriedenheit, Ausgeglichenheit, (innere) Ruhe; Behaglichkeit, Bequemlichkeit *f*, Komfort *m*; *Am* Steppdecke *f*; *tr* trösten, beruhigen; aufheitern, erfreuen; das Leben leicht, angenehm machen (*s.o.* jdm); *to live in* ~ in angenehmen, guten Verhältnissen leben; *aid and* ~ Hilfe u. Unterstützung; *creature* ~*s (pl)* alles, was man zum Leben braucht; **~able** ['-əbl] *a* bequem, behaglich, gemütlich; komfortabel, gut eingerichtet; *fam* auskömmlich, -reichend; sorgenfrei; *s Am* Steppdecke *f*; *make yourself* ~~ machen Sie sich's bequem! **~ably** ['-əbli] *adv*: *to be* ~~ *off* in angenehmen Verhältnissen leben; ~~ *warm* angenehm warm; **~er** ['-ə] Tröster; *Br* Schnuller *m*, wollene(s) Halstuch *n*; Steppdecke *f*; *the C*~~ der Heilige Geist; *Job's* ~~ schlechte(r) Tröster *m*; **~ing** ['-iŋ] tröstend, trostbringend, -reich, tröstlich; **~less** ['-lis] schlecht eingerichtet, ohne Komfort; unbehaglich, ungemütlich; ~ **room, station** *Am fam* öffentliche Bedürfnisanstalt *f*.

comfrey ['kʌmfri] *bot pharm* Schwarz-, Wallwurz *f*, Gemeine(r) Beinwell *m*.

comfy ['kʌmfi] *fam* gemütlich, behaglich.

comic ['kɔmik] *a* Komödien-, Lustspiel-; komödienhaft; komisch; spaßig, spaßhaft, lustig, drollig, amüsant; *s (a. comique) fam* Komiker *m*; *pl Am* Witzecke, lustige Seite, Bildgeschichte *f (e-r Zeitung)*; **~al** ['-əl] amüsant, lustig, heiter; drollig, komisch; sonderbar, eigenartig, merkwürdig; ~ **book** *Am* Heft *n* mit Bildgeschichten; ~ **strip** (lustige) Bildgeschichte *f*.

coming ['kʌmiŋ] *a* kommend, (zu-) künftig; *(zeitlich)* nächst; *fam* vielversprechend; *s* Kommen *n*; Ankunft *f*; *interj* ja! (ich) komme! gleich! sofort! *during the* ~ *summer* (im) nächsten Sommer; ~ *of age* Mündigwerden *n*; ~ *to power* Machtübernahme, -ergreifung *f*; **~s-in** *pl* Einnahmen *f pl*; **~-out party** Empfang *m*, um ein junges Mädchen in die Gesellschaft einzuführen.

comity ['kɔmiti] Höflichkeit *f*; ~ *of nations* Achtung *f* fremder Gesetze u. Sitten im Zs.leben d. Völker.

*

comma ['kɔmə] Komma *n*; Pause *f*; *inverted* ~*s (pl)* Anführungszeichen, Gänsefüßchen *n pl*; ~ **bacillus** Kommabazillus *m (Erreger d. Cholera)*; ~ **counter** *Am* Kleinigkeitskrämer *m*.

command [kə'mɑ:nd] *s* Befehl *m*; Kommando *n*; Befehlsgewalt *f*, Oberbefehl *m*, Kommando *n*, Führung, Leitung; Beherrschung *f*; Überblick *m*, Übersicht; Herrschaft *f* (*of* über); *mil* Befehlsbereich, Führungsstab *m*; Kommando *n (Einheit, a. aero)*; *el* Steuerung *f*; *tr* befehlen, den Befehl erteilen (*to* zu); kommandieren (*s.o. to do s.th.* jdn etw zu tun); den Befehl haben über, befehligen, (an)führen; zur, zu s-r Verfügung haben, verfügen über; beherrschen, herrschen über; *fig (Gefühl)* beherrschen, im Zaum halten, in der Gewalt haben; *(Achtung)* fordern, gebieten; *(Mitgefühl)* verdienen; *(Preis)* erzielen; übersehen, -schauen; *mil (Gelände)* beherrschen; *(Rakete)* steuern; *itr* den Oberbefehl, das Kommando haben; herrschen, e-e beherrschende Stellung innehaben; *at my* ~ zu meiner Verfügung; *by* ~ auf Befehl (*of* gen); *under s.o.'s* ~ unter jds Befehl; *to be in* ~ die Befehlsgewalt, das Kommando haben (*of* über); *to have a good* ~ *of s.th.* etw beherrschen; *to take* ~ *of* die Befehlsgewalt, das Kommando übernehmen über; *to* ~ *a high price* e-n hohen Preis erzielen; ~ *of the air* Luftherrschaft *f*; ~ *of execution* Ausführungskommando *n*; **~ant** [kɔmən'dænt] *(Lager)* Kommandant; Befehlshaber; *(Schule)* Kommandeur *m*; ~ **car** Führer-, Befehlswagen *m*; ~ **centre** Befehlskopf *m*; ~ **channel** Befehlsweg *m*; Unterstellungsverhältnis *n*; **~eer** [kɔmən'diə] *tr* zum Militärdienst pressen; dienstverpflichten; beitreiben, requirieren, mit Beschlag belegen; *fam* gewaltsam wegnehmen; **~er** [kə'mɑ:ndə] Kommandeur; Befehlshaber; *(Kompanie)* Chef; (Truppen-, Einheits-)Führer; Dienststellenleiter; *mar* Fregattenkapitän; *(Panzer, aero)* Kommandant; (Ordens-) Komtur *m*; *wing-*~~ *(aero)* Oberstleutnant *m*; ~~*-in-chief* Oberbefehlshaber; ~~ *of the fleet* Flottenchef *m*; ~~ *of the guard* Wachhabende(r) *m*; ~~ *of a station* Ortskommandant *m*; **~ing** [-iŋ] kommandierend; *(Anhöhe, Stellung)* beherrschend; *fig* überragend, eindrucksvoll; ~~ *officer* Einheitsführer *m*; ~ **jurisdiction** Befehlsbereich *m*; ~**ment** [-mənt] Gebot *n*, Vorschrift *f*; *the Ten C~~s* die Zehn Gebote *pl*; ~**o** [-ou] *pl -os* (Truppen-) Kommando; Expeditionskorps *n*; *Br* Sabotagetrupp *m*; *pl* Kommando-, Schocktruppen *f pl*; ~ **post** Befehlsstelle *f*; Gefechtsstand *m*; *Am* Hauptquartier *n*; ~ **tank** Befehls-, Führungspanzer *m*; ~ **vehicle** Befehlswagen *m*.

commemor|ate [kə'meməreit] *tr* gedenken (*s.o., s.th.* jds, e-r S); feiern; *(Sache)* erinnern an; ~**ation** [kəmemə'reiʃən] Gedenken *n* (*of* an); Gedenk-, Gedächtnisfeier *f a. rel*; *in ~~ of* zur Erinnerung an, zum Gedächtnis, zum Gedenken *gen*; ~**ative** [kə'memərəitiv, -rətiv] Erinnerungs-, Gedenk-; erinnernd (*of* an).

commence [kə'mens] *tr itr* beginnen, anfangen (*to do* od *doing s.th.* etw zu tun); ~**ment** [-mənt] Anfang, Beginn *m*; Promotion(stag *m*, -feier) *f*.

commend [kə'mend] *tr* anvertrauen; (an)empfehlen, herausstreichen; loben, preisen, rühmen; ~**able** [-əbl] empfehlens-, lobenswert, rühmlich; ~**ation** [kɔmen'deiʃən] Empfehlung *f*; Lob *n*, Preis *m*, Würdigung *f*; Inverwahrunggeben *n*; ~**atory** [kə'mendətəri] *a* Empfehlungs-; empfehlend, lobend; *~~ letter* Empfehlungsschreiben *n*.

commensal [kə'mensəl] *s* Tischgenosse; *bot zoo* Schmarotzer *m*.

commensur|able [kə'menʃərəbl] kommensurabel; mit dem gleichen Maß, nach dem gleichen Maßstab zu messen(d), meßbar (*with, to* wie); *math* durch die gleiche Zahl teilbar; vergleichbar (*with, to* mit, *dat*); angemessen (*to* dat); ~**ate** [-rit] angemessen, entsprechend (*with, to* dat); im richtigen, rechten Verhältnis (*with, to* zu).

comment ['kɔment] *s* Kommentar *m*, Stellungnahme; Erklärung, Erläuterung, Auslegung; Kritik *f*; Gerede *n*, Klatsch *m*; Bemerkung, Äußerung *f*; *itr* [*a.* kə'ment] kommentieren (*on s.th.* etw); sich, s-e Meinung äußern (*on* über); erklären, erläutern (*on s.th.* etw); (*bes.* kritische, abfällige) Bemerkungen machen (*on* über); *to make no ~s* sich jeder Stellungnahme enthalten; ~**ary** ['-əri] Kommentar *m* (*on* zu), Anmerkungen *f pl*; *running ~~* (Rundfunk-)Reportage *f*; ~**ation** [-'teiʃən] Kommentieren *n*; ~**ator** ['-eitə] Kommentator, Kritiker; *(news, network ~~)* Rundfunkkommentator *m*.

commerc|e ['kɔmə(:)s] (*bes.* Groß-, Zwischen-)Handel; (Geschäfts-)Verkehr *m*, -leben *n*; *fig* gesellschaftliche(r) Verkehr, Umgang *m*; *trade and ~~* Handel u. Verkehr *m*; ~**ial** [kə'mə:ʃəl] *a* geschäftlich, kaufmännisch, kommerziell; Handels-, Geschäfts-; *s Am* Werbefunk *m*, -fernsehen *n*; Funk-, Fernsehwerbung *f*; lobende(r) Hinweis; *fam* Reisende(r) *m*; *sl* auf Verlangen gespielte(s) Musikstück *n*; *~~ academy, college* Handelshochschule *f*; *~~ agency* Handelsvertretung; *Am* Auskunftei *f*; *~~ agent, broker, representative* Handelsvertreter *m*; *~~ articles (pl)* Handelsartikel *m pl*; *~~ art(ist)* Gebrauchsgraphik(er *m*) *f*; *~~ aviation* Verkehrsluftfahrt *f*; *~~ bank* Handels-, Kommerzbank *f*; *~~ building* Geschäftsgebäude *n*; *~~ clerk* Handlungsgehilfe *m*; *C~~ Code* Handelsgesetzbuch *n*; *~~ company* Handelsgesellschaft *f*; *~~ correspondence* Handelskorrespondenz *f*; *~~ court* Handelsgericht *n*; *~~ credit, debt* Warenkredit *m*, -schuld *f*; *~~ crisis* Handelskrise *f*; *~~ firm, house* Handelshaus *n*; *~~ harbo(u)r* Handelshafen *m*; *~~ interests (pl)* Geschäftsinteressen *n pl*; *~~ law, legislation* Handelsrecht *n*, -gesetzgebung *f*; *~~ line* Handels-, Geschäftszweig *m*, Branche *f*; *~~ manager* kaufmännische(r) Leiter *m*; *~~ marine* Handelsmarine *f*; *~~ mark* Warenzeichen *n*; *~~ name* Firmenbezeichnung *f*; *~~ navigation* Handelsschiffahrt *f*; *~~ paper* Handelswechsel *m*; Handelsblatt *n*; *pl (Post)* Geschäftspapiere *n pl*; *~~ policy* Handelspolitik; *~~ register* Handelsregister *n*; *~~ relations (pl)* Handels-, Geschäftsbeziehungen *f pl*; *~~ report* Handels-, Marktbericht *m*; *~~ school* Handelsschule *f*; *~~ stagnation* Geschäftsstockung *f*; *~~ street* Geschäftsstraße *f*; *~~ tariff* Handelstarif *m*; *~~ television* Werbefernsehen *n*; *~~ traveller (Br)* Handlungsreisende(r) *m*; *~~ value* Handels-, Marktwert *m*; *the ~~ world* die Geschäftswelt; ~**ialism** [kə'mə:ʃəlizm] Handels-, Geschäftsgeist *m*; ~**ialization** [kəmə:ʃəlai'zeiʃən] Kommerzialisierung *f*; ~**ialize** [kə'mə:ʃəlaiz] *tr* kommerzialisieren; geschäftlich (aus)nutzen; in den Handel bringen.

comminat|ion [kɔmi'neiʃən] Drohung; *rel* Androhung *f* göttliche(r) Strafen; ~**ory** ['kɔminətəri] drohend, Droh-; denunzierend.

commingle [kə'miŋgl] *tr itr* (sich) (ver)mischen, (sich) (ver)mengen.

comminut|e ['kɔminju:t] *tr* fein (zer-) mahlen, zer-, verreiben, pulverisieren; ~**ed** *a*: *~~ fracture (med)* Splitterbruch *m*; ~**ion** [kɔmi'nju:ʃən] Pulverisierung *f*; *med* Splitterbruch *m*; *fig* Zermürbung *f*.

commiser|ate [kə'mizəreit] *tr* bemitleiden; bejammern, beklagen; ~**ation** [-'reiʃən] Mitleid *n*; (Äußerung *f* des) Mitgefühl(s) *n*.

commissar [kɔmi'sɑ:] (sowjetischer) Kommissar *m*; ~**ial** [kɔmi'sɛəriəl] kommissarisch; ~**iat** [-'sɛəriət] Kommissariat *a. pol*; *mil* Intendantur *f*; Nachschub *m*; *~~ officer* Intendanturbeamte(r) *m*; ~**y** ['kɔmisəri] Beauftragte(r), Kommissar *m*.

commission [kə'miʃən] *s* Übertragung *f*; Auftrag *m*, Instruktion *f*; Amt *n*, Funktion; Indienststellung *f (e-s Schiffes)*; (Offiziers-)Patent *n*; Kommission *f*, (Untersuchungs-)Ausschuß *m*; *com* Bestellung *f*, Auftrag *m*, Order; Kommission(sgebühr); Provision; *jur* Begehung, Verübung *f*; *tr* beauftragen, den Auftrag erteilen (*s.o.* jdm); ermächtigen, bevollmächtigen; *(Schiff)* in Dienst stellen; *mil* (zum Offizier) befördern; *com* bestellen; *by ~* im Auftrag; *in ~ (Kriegsschiff)* auslaufbereit; *fam* in Ordnung, in Butter; gebrauchsfähig; *in, on ~ (com)* gegen Provision, provisionsweise; *on ~, by way of ~ (com)* in Kommission, im Auftrag; *out of ~* nicht gebrauchs- *od* dienstfähig; außer Betrieb; *to appoint a ~* e-e Kommission einsetzen; *to buy and sell on ~* Kommissionsgeschäfte machen, Kommissionshandel treiben; *to carry out a ~* e-n Auftrag ausführen *od* erledigen; *to give, to take in ~ (com)* in Kommission geben, nehmen; *to put out of ~ (Schiff)* außer Dienst stellen; *to resign o.'s ~* den Dienst quittieren, s-n Abschied nehmen; *arbitration ~* Schlichtungsausschuß *m*; *~ of inquiry* Untersuchungsausschuß *m*; *~ of Parliament* Parlamentsausschuß *m*; *~ on turnover* Umsatzprovision *f*; ~ **agent** Kommissionär *m*; ~**aire** [kəmiʃə'nɛə] Portier; Dienstmann; Bürodiener *m*; ~ **business, trade** Kommissionsgeschäft *n*, -handel *m*; ~**ed** [-d] *a* beauftragt, bevollmächtigt; *(Schiff)* in Dienst gestellt; *~~ officer* Offizier *m*; ~**er** [-ʃnə] Beauftragte(r), Bevollmächtigte(r) *m*; Kommissions-, Ausschußmitglied *n*; Regierungsvertreter, leitende(r) Beamte(r); *Am* Untersuchungsrichter *m*; *Government ~~* Regierungskommissar *m*; *High C~~* Hochkommissar *m*; *police ~~, ~~ of police* Polizeikommissar *m*; *~~ for oaths (Br)* Urkundsbeamte(r) *m*; ~ **fee** Kommissionsgebühr *f*; ~ **house** Maklerfirma *f*; ~ **rates** *pl* Provisionssätze *m pl*; ~ **traveller** Provisionsreisende(r) *m*.

commissure ['kɔmisjuə, -iʃuə] Verbindungsstelle; Naht *f*; *anat* Band *n*, Kommissur *f*.

commit [kə'mit] *tr* übergeben, anvertrauen; e-m Ausschuß überweisen; *(Verbrechen)* begehen, verüben; *to ~ o.s.* sich verraten, sich bloßstellen; sich festlegen, sich binden, sich verpflichten (*to do* od *to doing s.th.* etw zu tun); *to ~ to earth, to the flames* der Erde, den Flammen übergeben; *to ~ to memory* dem Gedächtnis einprägen; *to ~ to paper, to writing* niederschreiben; *to ~ to prison* ins Gefängnis einliefern, inhaftieren, festnehmen; *to ~ for trial* dem Gericht überweisen, in den Anklagezustand versetzen; ~**ment** [-mənt] Verpflichtung, Bindung; *fin* Verbindlichkeit; Überweisung (*parl* an e-n Ausschuß); Einlieferung (ins Gefängnis), Inhaftierung, Festnahme; Einweisung *f* (*to* in); *(warrant of ~~)* Haftbefehl *m*; ~**tal** [kə'mitl] Überweisung (an e-n Ausschuß); Inhaftierung, Festnahme; Verübung, Begehung *f*; *~~ for trial* Versetzung *f* in den Anklagezustand; Untersuchungshaft *f*; ~**ted** [-tid] *a* verpflichtet, gebunden; ~**tee** [kə'miti] Ausschuß *m*, Kommission *f*; Komitee *n*; *Br* [kɔmi'ti:] Vormund *m (e-s Entmündigten)*; *to appoint, to set up a ~~* e-n Ausschuß, e-e Kommission einsetzen; *to be, to sit on a ~~* e-m Ausschuß, e-r Kommission angehören; *to refer to a ~~* e-m Ausschuß, an e-n A. überweisen; *the matter is in ~~* die Sache liegt dem Ausschuß vor; *action ~~* Aktionsausschuß *m*; *arbitration ~~* Schlichtungsausschuß *m*; *joint ~~* gemischte(r) Ausschuß *m*; *permanent, standing ~~* ständige(r) Ausschuß *m*; *special ~~* Sonderausschuß *m*, -kommission *f*; *supervisory ~~* Überwachungsausschuß; Aufsichtsrat *m*; *working ~~* Arbeitsausschuß *m*; *~~ man, woman* Ausschußmitglied *n*; *~~ meeting* Ausschußsitzung *f*; *~~ of experts* Sachverständigenkommission *f*, -ausschuß *m*; *~~ of inquiry* Untersuchungskommission *f*, -ausschuß *m*; *~~ of Parliament* Parlamentsausschuß *m*.

commod|e [kə'moud] Kommode *f*; Nähtischchen *n*; *Am* Waschtisch; *(night-~~)* Nachtstuhl *m*; *Am* Toilette *f*, WC *n*; ~**ious** [-iəs] geräumig, bequem; ~**ity** [-'mɔditi] (Gebrauchs-) Artikel; *pl* Grund-, Rohstoffe *m pl*; *bes. pl* Waren *f pl*; Produkte; Verbrauchsgüter *n pl*; Lebensmittel *n pl*; *~~ credits (pl)* Warenkredite *m pl*; *~~ exchange* Rohproduktenbörse *f*; *~~ market* Waren-, Rohstoffmarkt *m*; *~~ prices (pl)* Produktenpreise *m pl*.

commodore ['kɔmədɔ:] *mar* Flottillenadmiral; *(dienstältester)* Kapitän *(a. e-r Schiffahrtslinie)*; *aero* Brigadegeneral *m*; Präsident *m* e-s Jachtklubs.

common ['kɔmən] *a* gemein(sam, -schaftlich); Gemein-; *math* gemeinsam; Gemeinde-; öffentlich; allgemein, (weit)verbreitet, häufig, alltäglich, abgedroschen, Allerwelts-; gemein *a. zoo bot*, ordinär, vulgär, niedrig; schlecht, gering(wertig), billig; *s* Gemeindeland *n*, -weide *f*; Mitbenutzungsrecht *n* (*of* an); Gerechtsame *f*; *pl das* gewöhnliche Volk, *die* Gemeinen, *die* Bürgerlichen *pl (im Gegensatz zum Adel)*; *(mit sing)* Gemeinschaftsverpflegung *f*; *the C~s (fam)* das Unterhaus; *at ~ expense* auf Kosten der Allgemeinheit; *by ~ consent* mit Zustimmung aller; *for the ~ good* im allgemeinen Interesse; für das allgemeine Wohl; *in ~ with* in Übereinstimmung mit, (ebenso, so) wie; *out of the ~* ungewöhnlich; *to be on short ~s* nicht viel zu beißen haben; *to be ~ practice* allgemein üblich sein; *to be ~ talk* Stadtgespräch, in aller Munde sein; *to have in ~* gemein(sam) haben (*with* mit); *to have interests in ~* gemeinsame Interessen haben; *to make ~ cause with* gemeinsame Sache machen mit; *it is ~ knowledge that* es ist allgemein bekannt, daß; *the House of C~s* das (Britische) Unterhaus; *~ or garden (sl)* nichts Besonderes, nichts Aufregendes; *~ of pastur(ag)e* Weide(mitbenutzungs)recht *n*, -gerechtsame *f*; *~ of wood* Gemeindewald *m*; **~alty** ['-əlti] *das* gemeine, gewöhnliche Volk; *die* Allgemeinheit *(der Menschen)*; **~ chord** Dreiklang *m*; **~ council** Gemeinde-, Stadtrat *m (Gremium)*; **~ debtor** Gemeinschuldner *m*; **~ denominator** *math* gemeinsame(r) Nenner *m*; **~er** ['-ə] Gemeine(r), Bürgerliche(r), Nichtadlige(r) *m*; *(selten)* Mitglied *n* des (Britischen) Unterhauses; *First C~~* Sprecher *m* (des Unterhauses); **~ fraction** *math* gemeine(r) Bruch *m*; **~ funds** *pl* öffentliche Gelder *od* Mittel *n pl*; **~ ground** gemeinsame, Diskussions-, Verhandlungsgrundlage *f*; **~ household** häusliche Gemeinschaft *f*; **~ informer** Denunziant *m*; **~ land** Gemeindeland *n*; **~ law** *(engl.)* Gewohnheitsrecht *n*; **~ly** ['-li] *adv* gewöhnlich; (im) allgemein(en); *the* **~ man** der gemeine Mann, der Durchschnittsmensch; **C~ Market** Gemeinsame(r) Markt *m*, EWG; **~ market value** gemeine(r) Handelswert *m*; **~ nuisance** allgemeine(s), öffentliche(s) Ärgernis *n*; *the* **~ people** die kleinen Leute *pl*; **~place** ['-pleis] *s* Gemeinplatz *m*, Binsenwahrheit, Banalität; alltägliche Sache *f*; *a* gewöhnlich, alltäglich; abgedroschen; alt; uninteressant; nichtssagend; **~ property** Gemeineigentum *n*; Gütergemeinschaft *f*; **~ rights** *pl* Menschenrechte *n pl*; **~ room** Gemeinschaftsraum *m*; *the* **~ run** die große Masse; **~ school** *Am (öffentliche)* Volks-, Grundschule *f*; **~ sense** *s* gesunde(r) Menschenverstand *m*; *a*: *~-sense* vernünftig; **~ stock** *fin* Stammaktien *f pl*, -kapital *n*; **~ wall** Brandmauer *f*; *the* **~ weal** das (All-)Gemeinwohl, der Gemeinnutz, das allgemeine Wohl, der Nutzen aller; **~wealth** ['-welθ] Gemeinwesen *n*, (Frei-)Staat *m*, Republik *f a. fig*; *Am* Bundesstaat *m*; *the C~~ of Nations* das Commonwealth; *the C~ of Australia* der Australische Staatenbund; *~~ of learning* Gelehrtenrepublik *f*.

commotion [kə'mouʃən] (heftige) Erregung, Erschütterung *f*; Aufruhr *m*; innere Erregung, Erregtheit *f*.

communal ['kɔmjunl] Gemeinde-, Kommunal-; kommunal; gemeindeeigen; Gemeinschafts-; öffentlich; **~ize** [kə'mju:nəlaiz] *tr* kommunalisieren, in Gemeindebesitz *od* -verwaltung überführen; **~ life** Gemeinschaftsleben *n*; **~ tax** Gemeindeumlage *f*.

commune [kə'mju:n, 'kɔmju:n] *itr* sich vertraulich besprechen *od* unterhalten; vertraulich verkehren, vertraut sein (*with* mit; *together* mitea.); *Am rel* kommunizieren, die Kommunion empfangen; *s* ['kɔmju:n] vertrauliche Besprechung; *Am rel* Kommunion; Gemeinde *f*.

communic|able [kə'mju:nikəbl] mitteilbar; *med* übertragbar, ansteckend; **~ant** [-'mju:nikənt] Informant; *rel* Kommunikant *m*; **~ate** [-'mju:nikeit] *tr* mitteilen; übertragen *a. phys med* (*to* auf); (aus)tauschen, teilen (*with* mit); *itr rel* die Kommunion, das Abendmahl empfangen; in Verbindung stehen, verkehren (*with* mit); *(Zimmer)* durch e-e Tür mitea. verbunden sein; **~ation** [kəmju:ni'keiʃən] Mitteilung (*to* an); *phys med* Übertragung *f*; Zs.hang *m*, Verbindung *f*, Verkehr, Umgang, Austausch *m*; Unterredung, Besprechung; Mitteilung, Nachricht, Zuschrift; Verbindung(sweg *m*) *f*, Verkehr(sweg *m*, -mittel *n*) *m*; Verbindungstür *f*; Fernmeldewesen *n*; *pl mil* Nachschublinien *f pl*, -verkehr *m*; Fernmeldeeinrichtungen *f pl*; *channel of ~~* Dienstweg; *tele* Fernmeldekanal *m*; *zone of ~~s*, *~~s zone (mil)* rückwärtige(s) Gebiet *n*; *~~(s) centre (mil)* Nachrichtensammelstelle; Fernmeldezentrale *f*; *~~ cord (rail)* Notleine, -bremse *f*; *~~ engineering* Schwachstromtechnik *f*; *~~ line* Verbindungslinie *f*; *~~ traffic* Fernmeldeverkehr *m*; *~~ trench (mil)* Lauf-, Verbindungsgraben *m*; **~ative** [kə'mju:nikeitiv, -kətiv] mitteilsam, gesprächig; Verbindungs-; **~ator** [kə'mju:nikeitə] Verbindung(smann, -weg *m*, -mittel *n*) *f*; Radiosprecher; *tele* Fernmelder *(Person)*; Zeichengeber *m (Gerät)*; *rail* Notleine *f*.

commun|ion [kə'mju:njən] (enge) Gemeinschaft, Gemeinschaftlichkeit, Gemeinsamkeit *f*, enge Beziehungen *f pl*, Gedankenaustausch *m*; Glaubensgemeinschaft; *(Holy C~~)* (Heilige) Kommunion *f*, Abendmahl *n*; *to go to ~~* zum Abendmahl gehen; *to hold ~~ with o.s.* mit sich zu Rate, in sich gehen; **~iqué** [-nikei, -'kei] Kommuniqué *n*, amtliche, offizielle Mitteilung *f*; **~ism** ['kɔmjunizm] Kommunismus *m*; **~ist** ['kɔmjunist] Kommunist(in *f*) *m*; **~ist(ic)** ['-ist, -'nistik] kommunistisch; *the C~~ Manifesto* das Kommunistische Manifest; **~ity** [kə'mju:niti] Gemeinschaft, Gemeinsamkeit; Gemeinschaft *f*, -wesen *n*, Gesellschaft, Öffentlichkeit *f*, Staat *m*; Gemeinde *a. rel*; Übereinstimmung, Ähnlichkeit; *biol* Lebensgemeinschaft *f*; *the ~~* die Allgemeinheit, die Öffentlichkeit, der Staat; *~~ centre* Gemeindehaus *n*; *~~ chest, fund (Am)* Wohltätigkeitsfonds *m*; *~~ of goods* Gütergemeinschaft *f*; *~~ of heirs* Erbengemeinschaft *f*; *~~ of interests* Interessengemeinschaft *f*; *~~ service* Dienstleistungen *f pl* für die Gemeinschaft; *~~ singing* gemeinschaftliche(s) Liedersingen *n*.

communize ['kɔmjunaiz] *tr* sozialisieren; kommunistisch machen.

commut|ability [kəmju:tə'biliti] Austauschbarkeit *f*; **~able** [kə'mju:təbl] austauschbar; ersetzbar; **~ate** ['kɔmju(:)teit] *tr el* kommutieren; **~ation** [kɔmju(:)'teiʃən] (Aus-, Um-)Tausch *m*; Ablösung(ssumme); (Straf-)Umwandlung, Herabsetzung, Milderung; *el* Kommutierung; *Am* regelmäßige Fahrt zur Arbeitsstätte; Benutzung *f* e-r Zeitkarte; *~~ of sentence* Änderung *f* des Strafmaßes; *~~ passenger (Am)* Zeitkarteninhaber *m*; *~~ pole (el)* Wendepol *m*; *~~ ticket (Am)* Zeitkarte *f*; **~ative** [kə'mju:tətiv, -eitiv] auswechselbar; gegenseitig; Ersatz-; *el* kommutativ; **~ator** ['kɔmju(:)teitə] *el* Kommutator, Stromwender, Kollektor *m*; **~e** [kə'mju:t] *tr* (aus-, ein-, um-)tauschen (*for* gegen), ersetzen; *fin* ablösen; *jur (Strafe)* umwandeln, herabsetzen (*to, into* in); *itr* als Ersatz dienen (*for* für); e-e Ablösung(ssumme) zahlen; *Am* auf Zeitkarte fahren, e-e Z. benutzen; pendeln; **~er** [kə'mju:tə] *Am* Zeitkarteninhaber; Pendler *m*; *~~ train (Am)* Vorortzug *m*.

*

compact ['kɔmpækt] *s* (zweiseitiger) Vertrag *m*, Abkommen *n*, Pakt *m*; Übereinkunft, Vereinbarung; Puderdose *f*; *a* [kəm'pækt] eng, fest gepackt; dicht (gepreßt), fest; fest gefügt; knapp; kurz(gefaßt), gedrängt; bestehend (*of* aus); *tr* fest zs.packen; fest zs.fügen; pressen, zs.drängen, verdichten; **~ car** *Am* Kompaktwagen *m*; **~ness** [kəm'pæktnis] Knappheit; Gedrängtheit; Festigkeit, Dichte *f*; *for ~~* um Platz zu sparen.

companion [kəm'pænjən] **1.** *s* Begleiter(in *f*); Genosse *m*, Genossin *f*, Gefährte *m*, Gefährtin *f*; Gesellschafter; Umgang *(Person)*; Ritter *m (e-s Ordens)*; *(lady ~) (angestellte)* Gesellschafterin *f*; Gegenstück, Pendant; Vademekum *n*, Ratgeber, Leitfaden *m (Buch)*; *tr* begleiten; *itr* Gesellschaft leisten (*with s.o.* jdm); *travel(l)er's ~* Reisehandbuch *n*; *travel(l)ing ~* Reisebegleiter, -gefährte, Mitreisende(r) *m*; *~ in arms* Waffenbruder *m*; **2.** *mar* Kajütkappe *f*, Deckfenster *n*; **~able** [-əbl] gesellig, umgänglich; *to be ~~* ein guter Gesellschafter sein; **~ate** [-it] *Am, Br obs* Kameradschafts-; *~~ marriage* Kameradschaftsehe *f*; **~ship** [-ʃip] Gesellschaft *f*; Umgang *m*; *typ* (Setzer-)Kolonne *f*; **~way** [-wei] Kajütentreppe *f*.

company ['kʌmpəni] Gesellschaft *f*, Umgang, Verkehr *m (a. Personen)*; Gesellschaft *f*, Gäste *m pl*, Besuch *m*; (Menschen-)Gruppe, Ansammlung; (*bes.* Handels-)Gesellschaft, Firma; Innung; (Schauspieler-)Truppe; *(ship's ~)* (Schiffs-)Besatzung; *mil* Kompanie *f*; *for ~* zur Gesellschaft; *in ~* zusammen, gemeinsam; *to be good, bad* od *poor ~* ein guter, schlechter Gesellschafter sein; *to bear, to keep s.o. ~* jdm Gesellschaft leisten; *to get into bad ~* in schlechte Gesellschaft geraten; *to keep ~ with* verkehren, Umgang haben mit; *to keep good, bad ~* guten, schlechten Umgang haben; *to part ~* sich trennen (*with* von); *to receive ~* Besuch empfangen; *affiliated, associated ~* Tochter(gesellschaft) *f*; *assurance, insurance ~* Versicherungsgesellschaft *f*; -firma *f*; *broadcasting ~* Rundfunkgesellschaft *f*; *holding ~* Holding-, Dachgesellschaft *f*; *(joint) stock ~* Aktiengesellschaft *f*; *limited liability ~* Gesellschaft *f* mit beschränkter Haftung (GmbH); **~ clerk,** *Am* **stooge** Kompanieschreiber *m*; **~commander** Kompaniechef *m*; **~ law** Gesellschaftsrecht *n*; **~ leader** Kompanieführer *m*; **~ meeting** *com* Generalversammlung *f*; **~ office** *mil* Schreibstube *f*; **~ officer** Kompanieoffizier *m*; **~ punishment** *Am* Disziplinarstrafe *f*; **~ sergeant-major** Hauptfeldwebel, *sl* Spieß *m*; **~'s water** Leitungswasser *n*; **~'s year** Geschäfts-, Rechnungsjahr *n*.

compar|able ['kɔmpərəbl] vergleichbar; ähnlich; gleichwertig; entsprechend; **~ative** [kəm'pærətiv] *a scient* vergleichend; verhältnismäßig, relativ; Vergleichs-; *s (~~ degree) gram* Komparativ *m*; **~atively** [kəm'pærətivli] *adv* vergleichsweise; verhältnismäßig; **~e** [kəm'pɛə] *tr (prüfend)* vergleichen (*with* mit); e-n Vergleich ziehen (*to* mit); gleichstellen, auf eine Stufe stellen (*to* mit); *gram* steigern; *itr* sich vergleichen (lassen) (*with* mit); *s poet* Vergleich *m*; *beyond, past, without ~~* unvergleichlich *adv*; *to ~~ favo(u)rably with* bei e-m Vergleich günstig abschneiden mit; *to ~~ notes* in Gedankenaustausch treten; sich aussprechen; **-ison** [kəm'pærisn] Vergleich *m* (*to, with* mit); Gegenüberstellung; *gram* Steigerung *f*; *by ~~* vergleichsweise, verhältnismäßig *adv*; *in ~~ with* im Vergleich zu; *to bear, to stand ~~ with* sich vergleichen lassen, den Vergleich aushalten mit; *there is no ~~ between them* sie lassen sich nicht vergleichen; *that's a lame ~~* der Vergleich hinkt.

compartment [kəm'pɑ:tmənt] Abteilung *f*; Fach, Feld *n*; *aero* Kabine *f*; *rail* Abteil, *Am* Einzelabteil *n* mit Schlafgelegenheit; *mar* Abteilung *f*.

compass ['kʌmpəs] *s* Umfang, -kreis *m*; Um-, Einfassung, Begrenzung *f*; Bezirk *m*, Gebiet *n*, Bereich *m* od *n*; Ausdehnung, Reichweite; *fig* Fassungskraft *f*, Begriffs-, Vorstellungsvermögen *n*, *fam* Horizont; Stimmumfang; (*mariner's ~*) (Schiffs-)Kompaß *m*; *pl (pair of ~es), Am a. sing (drawing ~)* Zirkel *m (Gerät)*; *tr* herumgehen um; umgeben; um-, einfassen, säumen; *fig* (geistig) erfassen, begreifen, verstehen; vollenden; *(Ziel)* erreichen, durchsetzen; im Schilde führen, anzetteln; *point of the ~* Himmelsrichtung *f*; **~ bearing** (Kompaß-)Peilung *f*; **~ card** Windrose, Kompaßscheibe *f*; **~ needle** Kompaßnadel *f*; **~ point** Kompaßstrich *m*; **~ saw** Stich-, Laubsäge *f*.

compassion [kəm'pæʃən] Mitleid, -gefühl *n* (*for* mit); *to have, to take ~ on* Mitleid haben mit; **~ate** [-it] *a* mitleidig, mitleid(s)voll, mitfühlend; *~~ allowance* Zulage *f* in Härtefällen; *~~ leave (mil Br)* Sonderurlaub *m* aus familiären Gründen.

compatib|ility [kəmpætə'biliti] Vereinbarkeit; Verträglichkeit; Umgänglichkeit *f*; **~le** [kəm'pætəbl] vereinbar, verträglich (*with* mit); in Übereinstimmung (*with* mit); angemessen (*with s.th.* e-r S); *(Mensch)* verträglich, umgänglich.

compatriot [kəm'pætriət, *Am meist* -pei-] Landsmann *m*, -männin *f*.

compeer [kɔm'piə] Gleichstehende(r); Kollege, Genosse; Kamerad *m*.

compel [kəm'pel] *tr* zwingen, nötigen (*to do* zu tun); erzwingen (*from* von); *Am* überwältigen; **~ling** [-iŋ] zwingend; *fig* verlockend; unwiderstehlich.

compend ['kɔmpend] *s ~ium*; **~ious** [kəm'pendiəs] kurz(gefaßt), gedrängt; **~ium** [kəm'pendiəm] *pl a. -dia* [-diə] Zs.fassung *f*, Auszug *m*, Übersicht *f*; Ab-, Grundriß, Leitfaden *m*.

compensat|e ['kɔmpenseit] *tr* ausgleichen, ersetzen; aufwiegen; abgelten; *phys tech* kompensieren; *psychol* sublimieren; *fin* entschädigen; *(Schaden)* ersetzen; *Am* bezahlen, entlohnen, vergüten; *itr* ausgleichen (*for s.th.* etw), e-n Ausgleich gewähren (*for* für), e-n Schaden vergüten, wiedergutmachen (*for s.th.* etw); e-e Entschädigung zahlen, Ersatz leisten, e-e Wiedergutmachung gewähren; **~ion** [-'seiʃən] Ausgleich, Ersatz *m*; *phys tech biol* Kompensierung; *psychol* Sublimierung; *fin* Entschädigung *f*, Schadenersatz *m*; Vergütung; *Am* (Be-)Zahlung; Entlohnung *f*; Lohn *m*, Gehalt *n*; *as ~~, by way of ~~ for* als Ersatz, als Entschädigung für; *to demand full ~~* volle Entschädigung verlangen; **~ive** ['kɔmpenseitiv, kəm'pensətiv] als Ausgleich, Ersatz, Entschädigung dienend; Ausgleichs-, Ersatz-, Entschädigungs-; **~or** ['-ə] *tech* Entzerrer, Kompensator, Ausgleicher; Spartransformator *m*; **~ory** [kəm'pensətəri] *a* Ausgleichs-, Ersatz-, Entschädigungs-.

compete [kəm'pi:t] *itr* sich mitbewerben (*for* um); teilnehmen (*in a contest* an e-m Wettbewerb); im Wettbewerb stehen, wetteifern (*with s.o. for s.th.* mit jdm um etw); konkurrieren, sich messen (*against s.o. in a race* mit jdm bei e-m Rennen).

competen|ce, -cy ['kɔmpitəns(i)] Auskommen; Können, Geschick *n*; Fähigkeit, Befähigung, Qualifikation (*for s.th.* zu etw); *jur* Zuständigkeit, Kompetenz, Befugnis *f*; *to be within the ~~ of* unter die Zuständigkeit fallen *gen*; *~~ of a court* Gerichtsstand *m*; **~t** ['-t] geschickt, fähig, befähigt, qualifiziert (*for s.th.* zu etw; *to do* zu tun); genügend, ausreichend, entsprechend; passend, angebracht (*to s.o.* für jdn; *in, at doing* zu tun); erlaubt (*to s.o.* jdm); *jur* zuständig; zurechnungsfähig.

competit|ion [kɔmpi'tiʃən] Wettbewerb, -streit, -kampf (*for* um); Konkurrenz(kampf *m*); Rivalität *f*; Preisausschreiben *n*; *to be in ~~ with* im Wettbewerb stehen mit; *to enter into ~~ with* in Wettbewerb treten mit; *to stand, to sustain ~~* es mit der Konkurrenz aufnehmen (können), sich gegen die Konkurrenz behaupten; *defying all ~~, without ~~* konkurrenzlos; *free, open ~~* freie(r) Wettbewerb *m*; *keen ~~* scharfe(r) Wettbewerb, heftige(r) Konkurrenzkampf *m*; **~ive** [kəm'petitiv] *a* Wettbewerbs-, Konkurrenz-; *~~ game* Kampfspiel *n*; *~~ power* Wettbewerbs-, Konkurrenzfähigkeit; *sport* Kampfkraft *f*; *~~ price* Wettbewerbspreis *m*; **~or** [-'petitə] Mitbewerber(in *f*), Konkurrent(in *f*), Rivale *m*, Rivalin *f*; *sport* Wettkämpfer, Wettbewerbsteilnehmer *m* (*for* um).

*

compil|ation [kɔmpi'leiʃən] Auf-, Zs.-stellung; Kompilation *f*; **~e** [kəm'pail] *tr (Material zu e-m Buch)* zs.tragen, zs.stellen; *(Buch)* kompilieren; **~er** [kəm'pailə] Kompilator *m*.

complacen|ce, -cy [kəm'pleisns(i)] (stille, ruhige) Behaglichkeit, Beschaulichkeit; Selbstzufriedenheit, -gefälligkeit *f*; **~t** [-t] selbstzufrieden, -gefällig.

complain [kəm'plein] *itr* klagen, sich beklagen (*of* über); sich beschweren (*of, about* über; *to* bei); *com* bemängeln, reklamieren; **~ant** [-ənt] *bes. jur* Kläger (-in *f*); Beschwerdeführer(in *f*) *m*; **~t** [-t] Klage, Beschwerde, Beanstandung, Reklamation, Mängelrüge *f*; Grund zur Klage, Beschwerdegrund *m*; *jur* Klage, Strafanzeige (*against* gegen); *(bill of ~~)* Klag-, Beschwerdeschrift *f*; *med* Beschwerden *f pl*, Leiden *n*; *on ~~ by* auf e-e Beschwerde *gen*; *to make, to lodge a ~~ against s.o.* sich über jdn beschweren; *~~ book* Beschwerdebuch *n*; *~~ regulations (pl)* Beschwerdeordnung *f*.

complaisan|ce [kəm'pleizəns] Gefälligkeit, Höflichkeit, Umgänglichkeit *f*; angenehme(s), nette(s) Wesen *n*; **~t** [-t] gefällig, höflich; entgegenkommend, willfährig.

complement ['kɔmplimənt] *s* Ergänzung *f a. math*; volle(r) Betrag; *math* Ergänzungswinkel *m*; *gram (~~ of the predicate)* Prädikatsnomen *n*; *mar* Bemannung; *mil* Sollstärke; *aero* volle Besatzung *f*; *tr* ['-ment] ergänzen, vollständig machen; **~al, ~ary** [-'mentl, -'mentəri] *a* Ergänzungs-; zusätzlich; *~ary colo(u)rs (pl)* Komplementärfarben *f pl*.

complet|e [kəm'pli:t] *a* vollständig, -kommen, völlig, ganz; *(Untersuchung)* eingehend; komplett; voll besetzt; vollendet, fertig(gestellt), zu Ende (gebracht), abgeschlossen; *obs (Mensch)* perfekt; *tr* vervollständigen, vollständig machen, abschließen; *(Formular)* ausfüllen; beenden, fertigstellen, -machen, vollenden; ergänzen; *(Vergessenes)* nachtragen; *fig (Glück)* vollkommen machen; **~ely** [-li] *adv* völlig, ganz (u. gar), vollständig, vollkommen; **~eness** [-nis] Vollständigkeit; Vollkommenheit, Vollendetheit *f*; **~ion** [-'pli:ʃən] Vervollständigung *f*; Abschluß *m*, Beendigung; Erledigung, Fertigstellung, Vollendung *a. jur*; Ergänzung, Vervollständigung; Ausfüllung *(e-s Formulars)*; *(Vertrag)* Erfüllung; Vervollkommnung; Vollständigkeit; Vollkommenheit *f*; *on ~~ of* bei Beendigung *gen*; *to be nearing ~~* vor dem Abschluß stehen.

complex ['kɔmpleks] *a* zs.gesetzt; kompliziert, schwierig, verwickelt, verworren; *s* (aus Teilen zs.gesetztes) Ganze(s) *n*; *math* komplexe Zahl *f*; *psychol* Komplex *m*; *fam* unbegründete Abneigung *od* Angst *f*; *guilt, inferiority* Schuld-, Minderwertigkeitskomplex *m*; **~ion** [kəm'plekʃən] (Haut-, *bes.* Gesichts-)Farbe *f*, Aussehen *n*; *fig* Erscheinung, Art *f*, Charakter *m*, Wesen *n*; Aspekt, Anblick *m*; **~ity** [kəm'pleksiti] Kompliziertheit, Verworrenheit, Schwierigkeit; verwickelte Lage *f*.

complian|ce [kəm'plaiəns] Einwilligung (*with* in), Zustimmung (*with* zu); *(Bedingung, Wunsch)* Erfüllung (*with* gen); *(Gesetz)* Befolgung, Beobachtung; Nachgiebigkeit *a. tech*, Bereitwilligkeit, Willfährigkeit *f*; *in ~~ with* in Übereinstimmung mit; entsprechend, gemäß *dat*; **~t** [-t] nachgiebig; bereitwillig, willfährig.

complicat|e ['kɔmplikeit] *tr* komplizieren, (noch) verwickelter, schwieriger machen; *that ~es matters* das macht die Sache noch schwieriger; *a* [-it] *bot zoo* längs gefaltet; **~ed** [-id] *a* kompliziert; verzwickt, verwickelt, schwierig; **~ion** [kɔmpli'keiʃən] Verwick(e)lung; Komplizierung, neue Schwierigkeit; *med* Komplikation *f*.

complicity [kəm'plisiti] Mitschuld (*in* an), Mittäterschaft *f* (*in* bei).

compliment ['kɔmplimənt] *s* Kompliment *n*, Artigkeit; Anerkennung *f*, Lob *n*; Höflichkeitsbezeigung, Ehrenerweisung *f*; *pl (in Briefen)* Grüße *m pl*, Gruß *m*; Empfehlung *f*; *tr* ['-ment, -'ment] ein Kompliment machen (*s.o.* jdm), beglückwünschen (*on* zu); beschenken (*with* mit); schenken (*s.o. with s.th.* jdm etw); *to fish for ~s* Komplimente hören wollen; *to pay a ~ to s.o.* jdm ein Kompliment machen; *with the ~s of the season* mit den besten Wünschen zum Fest; **~ary** [-'mentəri] höflich, artig;

Ehren-, Gratis-; ~~ *copy* Widmungs-, Freiexemplar *n*; ~~ *ticket* Frei-, Ehrenkarte *f*.

comply [kəm'plai] *itr* nachgeben, sich fügen, Folge leisten; einwilligen (*with* in); zustimmen (*with* zu), stattgeben (*with s.th.* dat); *(Wunsch, Bedingung, Bitte)* erfüllen (*with s.th.* etw); *(Regeln, Bestimmungen)* sich halten (*with* an), befolgen (*with s.th.* etw), nachkommen, entsprechen (*with s.th.* dat); *(Frist)* einhalten (*with s. th.* etw).

component [kəm'pounənt] *a* einzeln, Einzel-, Teil-; *s* (notwendiger, wesentlicher) Bestandteil *m*; *phys* Komponente *f*; Einzelteil, Ingrediens *n*; *tech* Baugruppe *f*, Bau-, Maschinenteil *m*; ~ **layout** Bauplan *m*; ~ **parts** *pl* Zubehör-, Einzelteile *m pl*.

comport [kəm'pɔ:t] *itr* übereinstimmen, harmonieren (*with* mit), passen (*with* zu); *to ~ o.s.* sich benehmen, sich betragen, sich verhalten.

compos|e [kəm'pouz] *tr* zs.setzen, zs.stellen; (an)ordnen, bilden, (er-)schaffen; ab-, verfassen, aufsetzen; dichten; komponieren, vertonen; *typ* setzen; *(Streit)* (gütlich) beilegen, schlichten, (glücklich) beenden; *(s-e Gedanken)* sammeln; *(s-e Gesichtszüge)* glätten; *itr (literarische Werke)* schreiben; dichten; komponieren; setzen; *to ~~ o.s.* sich beruhigen, sich fassen; sich anschicken (*to* zu); *to be ~ed of* sich zs.setzen, zs.gesetzt sein, bestehen aus; **~ed** [-d] *a* gefaßt, beruhigt, ruhig, gelassen; *(Gesicht)* unbewegt; **~edness** [-idnis] Gefaßtheit, Ruhe, Gelassenheit *f*; **~er** [-ə] Komponist; Verfasser *m*; **~ing** [-iŋ] Komponieren; Dichten; *typ* Setzen *n*; ~~ *draught* Schlaftrunk *m*; ~~*-frame, -stand (typ)* Setzpult *n*; ~~*-machine* Setzmaschine *f*; ~~*-room* Setzerei *f*; ~~*-stick (typ)* Winkelhaken *m*; **~ite** ['kɔmpəzit] *a* zs.gesetzt; *arch (Säulenkapitell)* komposit; vielfältig; *tech* Verbund-; *bot* Korbblütler *m*, Komposite *f*; ~~ *construction* Gemischtbauweise *f*; ~~ *photograph* Fotomontage *f*; **~ition** [kɔmpə'ziʃən] Zs.setzung, (An-)Ordnung, Anlage, Bildung; *(Kunst)* Gliederung, Raumaufteilung; Abfassung; Komposition *f*; *typ* (Schrift-)Satz *m*; Fassung *f*; (Musik-)Stück; Schriftstück *n*, (*bes.* Schul-)Aufsatz *m*; Übersetzung *f*; Bildwerk *n*; *scient* Zs.setzung *f*, (Auf-)Bau; Kunststoff *m*; *psychol* Anlage, Art *f*, Wesen *n*; *jur* Verständigung *f*, Vergleich *m*, gütliche Abmachung *f*, Kompromiß *m* od *n*; Vergleichs-, Abfindungssumme *f*; ~~ *book (Am)* Schreibheft *n*; ~~ *costs (pl)* Satzkosten *pl*; ~~ *sole* Kunstledersohle *f*; **~itor** [kəm'pɔzitə] (Schrift-)Setzer *m*; **~ure** [kəm'pouʒə] Gefaßtheit, Fassung, Gelassenheit, (Gemüts-)Ruhe *f*.

compost ['kɔmpəst] Kompost, Kompost-, Menge-, Streudünger *m*.

compote ['kɔmpout] eingelegte, eingemachte Früchte *f pl*; Kompott *n*; *Am* Obstschale *f*.

compound ['kɔmpaund] *a* zs.gesetzt; aus einzelnen, verschiedenen Teilen bestehend; gemischt; *tech* Verbund-, Kompound-; *s* Zs.setzung; Mischung; *(chemische)* Verbindung; *tech* (Verguß-, Kabel-)Masse *f*; *gram (~ word)* Kompositum, zs.gesetzte(s) Wort *n*; eingefriedigte(r) Platz *m*, Lager *n*; *v* [kəm'paund] *tr* zs.setzen; verbinden; mischen; *(Streit)* beilegen; *(Schuld)* tilgen; *(Zinsen)* kapitalisieren; *tech* mit Masse füllen, kompoundieren; *itr* sich vergleichen, sich einigen, sich verständigen (*with* mit); pauschalieren (*for s.th.* etw); *chemical ~* chemische Verbindung *f*; ~ **engine** Verbundmaschine *f*; ~ **interest** Zinseszins(en *pl*) *m*.

comprehend [kɔmpri'hend] *tr* verstehen, einsehen, begreifen; umfassen, einschließen, enthalten.

comprehens|ibility [kɔmprihensi'biliti] Verständlichkeit *f*; **~ible** [-'hensəbl] verständlich, begreiflich; **~ion** [-'henʃən] Verstehen, Begreifen; Verständnis *n* (*of* für), Einsicht *f*, Fassungs-, Begriffsvermögen *n*; Einschluß *m*, Enthaltensein *n*; (Bedeutungs-, Begriffs-)Umfang *m*; *of wide ~~* umfassend; **~ive** [-'hensiv] umfassend; übersichtlich; verständnisvoll, einsichtig; ~~ *school* Einheits-, Sammelschule *f*; **~iveness** [-nis] umfassende(r) Charakter *m*, Reichhaltigkeit; Ausdehnung, Weite; gedrängte Kürze *f*.

compress [kəm'pres] *tr* zs.drücken, (zs.)pressen, verdichten, komprimieren; *tech* drücken, druckvergüten; *s* ['kɔmpres] *med* Kompresse *f*, Kompressions-, feste(r) Verband, Umschlag *m*; Baumwollballenpresse *f*; **~ed** [-'prest] *a* zs.gedrückt; *zoo* platt; *tech* unter Druck stehend; Druck-, Preß-; ~~ *air* Druck-, Preßluft *f*; ~~ *air brake* Druckluftbremse *f*; **~ible** [-'presəbl] zs.drückbar, -preßbar, verdichtbar; **~ion** [kəm'preʃən] Zs.drücken *n*, (Zs.-)Pressung, Verdichtung, Kompression *f*, Druck *m*; ~~ *chamber (mot)* Kompressionsraum *m*; ~~ *gauge* Manometer *n*; ~~ *pump* Druck-, Kompressionspumpe *f*; ~~ *spring* Druckfeder *f*; ~~ *strength* Druckfestigkeit *f*; ~~ *stress* Druckspannung *f*; **~ive** [-iv] drückend; Druck-; ~~ *bandage* Druckverband *m*; ~~ *strength* Druckfestigkeit *f*; ~~ *stress* Druckbeanspruchung *f*; **~or** [-'presə] *tech* Kompressor *m*, Druckpumpe *f*, Verdichter *m*; *med* Klemme *f*; *anat* Schließmuskel *m*.

comprise [kəm'praiz] *tr* umfassen; einschließen (*within* in); enthalten; bestehen aus.

compromise ['kɔmprəmaiz] *s* Kompromiß *m* od *n*; Übereinkunft *f*, Vergleich *m*; Kompromittierung *f*; Risiko *n*, Preisgabe *f*; *itr* e-n Kompromiß, e-n Vergleich schließen, sich vergleichen (*on* über); *tr* durch e-n Vergleich beilegen; kompromittieren, bloßstellen; gefährden, preisgeben; *to come to a ~* e-n Vergleich schließen.

comptroller [kən'troulə] Rechnungsprüfer *m*.

compuls|ion [kəm'pʌlʃən] Zwang *m*; Zwangslage; Nötigung *f*; *psychol* Zwang(santrieb) *m*, Zwangshandlung *f*; *under ~~* unter Zwang; **~ive** [-siv] Zwangs-; zwingend; ~~ *action (psychol)* Zwangshandlung *f*; **~ory** [-səri] gezwungen, Zwangs-; obligatorisch; zwingend, bindend; ~~ *administration* Zwangsverwaltung *f*; ~~ *auction* Zwangsversteigerung *f*; ~~ *education, school attendance, schooling* Schulpflicht *f*; ~~ *execution* Zwangsvollstreckung *f*; ~~ *insurance* Pflichtversicherung; Versicherungspflicht *f*; ~~ *labo(u)r* Arbeits-, Dienstverpflichtung *f*; ~~ *labo(u)r service* Arbeitsdienstpflicht *f*; ~~ *loan* Zwangsanleihe *f*; ~~ *(military) service* (allgemeine) Wehrpflicht *f*; ~~ *purchase* Enteignung *f*; ~~ *rate of exchange (fin)* Zwangskurs *m*; ~~ *registration* Meldepflicht *f*; ~~ *sale* Zwangsvollstreckung *f*; ~~ *subject (Schule)* Pflichtfach *n*; ~~ *vaccination* Impfzwang *m*.

compunct|ion [kəm'pʌŋkʃən] Schuldgefühl, -bewußtsein *n*; Gewissensbisse *m pl*; Reue *f*; Bedenken *n*.

comput|ability [kəmpju:tə'biliti] Berechenbarkeit *f*; **~able** [-'pju:təbl] berechenbar, zählbar; **~ation** [-'teiʃən] (Be-, Er-)Rechnung *f*; Überschlag *m*, Schätzung; (Aus-)Zählung; Rechenmethode *f*; (Rechen-)Ergebnis *n*, Summe *f*, Betrag *m*; **~e** [kəm'pju:t] *tr itr* (aus-, be-, er)rechnen; überschlagen, schätzen, veranschlagen (*at* auf); zählen; auswerten; **~er** [-'pju:tə] Berechner, Auswerter *m*; Rechengerät *n*; *(~ing machine)* Rechenmaschine *f*; *electronic ~* Elektronenrechner *m*.

comrade ['kɔm-, 'kʌmrid, 'kɔmreid] Kamerad(in *f*); Genosse *m*, Genossin *f*; **~ship** ['-ʃip] Kameradschaft *f*.

con [kɔn] **1.** *tr (to ~ over)* sorgfältig durchlesen, lernen, (ein)studieren, einüben; auswendig lernen; **2.** *a.* **conn** *tr mar* (durch Anweisung) steuern, lenken, leiten; *s* Steuerung *f*; *(~ning tower)* Kommandoturm *m*; **3.** (von *contra*) *adv*: *pro and ~* für u. wider; *s* Gegenargument *n*, -stimme *f*; Gegner *m*; *the pros and ~s* das Für u. Wider; **4.** *a Am sl* Vertrauens-, Schwindel-; betrügerisch; *tr* beschwindeln, 'reinlegen, betrügen; ~ **man** Schwindler *m*.

conat|ion [kou'neiʃən] *psychol* Strebung *f*; **~ive** ['kounətiv] strebend.

concatenat|e [kɔn'kætineit] *tr* (mitea.) verketten, verbinden *fig*; *a* verkettet, verbunden; ~~*d motor* Kaskadenmotor *m*; **~ion** [-'neiʃən] Verkettung; Kette, Folge *f*.

concav|e ['kɔn'keiv] *a* konkav, nach innen gewölbt; *s* ['kɔnkeiv] nach innen gewölbte Fläche *f*; *tr* nach innen wölben; ~~ *glass, mirror* Hohlglas *n*, -spiegel *m*; **~ity** [kɔn'kæviti] Höhlung, Wölbung *f* nach innen; **~o-convex** [kɔn'keivou-kɔn'veks] konkavkonvex.

conceal [kən'si:l] *tr* verstecken, verbergen, verdecken, verheimlichen, verhehlen; verschleiern; geheimhalten (*from* vor); *mil* tarnen; *jur* unterdrücken; *~ by smoke* vernebeln; *~ed pit (mil)* Fall(grub)e *f*; **~ment** [-mənt] Verbergen *n*, Verheimlichung; Geheimhaltung; Verborgenheit *f*; Versteck *n*; *mil* Deckung; Tarnung; Maskierung, Verschleierung *f*; *jur (Tatsachen)* Unterdrücken *n*.

concede [kən'si:d] *tr* einräumen, zugeben, anerkennen (*that* daß); zugestehen; nachgeben (*a point* in e-m Punkt); *(Recht)* bewilligen; *sport (Punkte)* vorgeben; *sport sl* verlieren; *itr* nachgeben, Konzessionen machen; *fam* sich geschlagen geben; **~dly** [-idli] *adv Am* nach allgemeiner Ansicht.

conceit [kən'si:t] *s* Selbstgefälligkeit, Einbildung, Eingebildetheit, Überheblichkeit *f*, Dünkel, Hochmut; Einfall *m*, Laune *f*; geistreiche(r) Gedanke *od* Ausdruck *m*; witzige Bemerkung *f*; *in o.'s own ~* nach s-r eigenen Überzeugung; *out of ~ with* nicht mehr zufrieden mit; **~ed** [-id] *a* eingebildet (*about, of* auf); *dial* einfalls-, geistreich, witzig.

conceiv|able [kən'si:vəbl] erdenklich, denkbar, vorstellbar; **~e** [kən'si:v] *tr* aus-, erdenken, ersinnen; *(Gedanken)* fassen, haben; in Worte fassen; sich denken, sich vorstellen, meinen; begreifen, verstehen (*a. itr: of s.th.* etw) *(Abneigung)* fassen; *(Kind)* empfangen; *itr* schwanger werden, empfangen (*with* acc); sich e-e Vorstellung bilden (*of* von); *to be ~ed* ausgedrückt, formuliert werden.

concentrat|e ['kɔnsentreit] *tr* zs.ziehen, zs.ballen, konzentrieren; *(Trup-*

pen) massieren; *(Feuer)* zs.fassen; *chem* verdichten, eindicken, eindampfen, kondensieren, sättigen, anreichern; *a. min*; *(Strahlen)* bündeln; *itr* sich sammeln; sich konzentrieren (*upon, on* auf); seine Gedanken zs.nehmen; *s* Konzentrat *n*; *a* konzentriert; **~ed** [-id] *a chem el* konzentriert; *mil (Feuer)* zs.gefaßt; *min* angereichert; *fig* stark; *~~ charge (Am)* geballte Ladung *f*; **~ion** [-'treiʃən] Anhäufung, Ansammlung, Zs.ziehung, Zs.fassung; Konzentration *a. fig chem*; *mil* Zs.ballung, Massierung, Bereitstellung; Schwerpunktbildung; *chem* Verdichtung; Eindampfung, Kondensierung *f*; Gehalt *m*, Dichte, Sättigung(sgrad *m*); *min* Anreicherung *f*; *~~ area (mil)* Aufmarschgebiet *n*, Bereitstellungsraum *m*; *~~ camp* Konzentrationslager *n*; *~~ (of) fire (mil)* Feuervereinigung *f*.

concentr|e [kən'sentə] *tr itr* (sich) konzentrieren, (sich) vereinigen; *itr* zs.kommen; konvergieren; **~ic(al)** [-trik(əl)] konzentrisch; *~~ charge (Br)* geballte Ladung *f*; **~icity** [kənsen'trisiti] Rundlauf *m*, Mittigkeit *f*.

concept ['kənsept] Begriff *m*, Vorstellung, Idee *f*; **~ion** [kən'sepʃən] (geistige) Gestaltungskraft *f*; Vorstellungsvermögen *n*, Fassungskraft *f*; Begriff *m*; Auffassung, Vorstellung, Idee *f*, Gedanke; Plan, Entwurf; Beginn, Anfang *m*; *physiol* Empfängnis, Befruchtung *f*; *~~ control* Empfängnisverhütung *f*; **~ual** [-'septjuəl] Begriffs-.

concern [kən'sə:n] *tr* betreffen, angehen, berühren; interessieren; wichtig sein für; besorgt machen, beunruhigen; *to be ~ed about* sich Gedanken, Sorgen machen um; in Unruhe, in Sorge sein um; *to be ~ed in* zu tun haben, beschäftigt sein mit, verwickelt sein in; *to ~ o.s. about, in* sich bemühen, sich Mühe machen um; *to ~ o.s. with* sich befassen, zu tun haben, sich abgeben mit, *fam* s-e Nase stecken in; *s* Beziehung *f*, Bezug *m*; Interesse *n*, Anteil *m*; Sorge, Besorgnis, Beunruhigung, Unruhe, Angst, Befürchtung (*over* wegen); (wichtige) Angelegenheit, Sache *f*; Geschäft, Unternehmen *n*, Betrieb; *fam* Kram, Plunder, Dreck *m*; *pl* Belange *pl*; *as ~s* was ... betrifft, betreffend, betreffs; *as far as I am ~ed* soweit die Sache für mich von Interesse, Wichtigkeit ist; was mich angeht, von mir aus; *to whom it may ~* an die zuständige Stelle; *with deep ~* sehr besorgt *adv*; *to have a ~ in* interessiert sein, Anteil haben an; *that is no ~ of yours* das geht Sie nichts an; *business ~s (pl)* Geschäftsinteressen *n pl*; *flourishing, paying ~* gutgehende(s) Geschäft, Unternehmen *n*; *industrial ~* Industriebetrieb *m*, gewerbliche(s) Unternehmen *n*; **~ed** *a* betroffen (*in* von), beteiligt (*in* an); besorgt, in Unruhe (*at, for s.o.* um jdn; *about s.th.* wegen e-r S); *all ~~* alle Beteiligten; *the persons ~~* die Interessenten *m pl*; **~ing** [-iŋ] *prp* betreffend, betreffs; bezüglich, wegen, in bezug auf.

concert ['kənsət] *s* Einverständnis, Einvernehmen *n*; Übereinstimmung *f*; Einklang *m*, Harmonie *f*; Konzert *n*; *a* Konzert-; *v* [kən'sə:t] *tr* vereinbaren, verabreden; planen, einrichten, arrangieren; *(Kräfte)* vereinigen; *itr* gemeinsam handeln, zs.arbeiten; *in ~* zusammen, gemeinsam; im Einvernehmen, Einverständnis (*with* mit); *to work in ~* zs.arbeiten (*with* mit); **~ed** [kən'sə:tid] *a* verabredet, abgemacht; überlegt, ausgedacht; gemeinsam; *mus* mehrstimmig; für mehrere Instrumente; **~ grand (piano)** Konzertflügel *m*; **~ina** [kənsə'ti:nə] Ziehharmonika *f*, *fam* Schifferklavier *n*; *mil* zs.legbare(s) Stacheldrahthindernis *n*; **~ master** Konzertmeister *m*; **~o** [kən'tʃə:tou] *pl -os* Konzert(stück) *n*; **~ pitch** *mus* Kammerton *m*; *at ~~ (fig)* auf der Höhe.

concess|ion [kən'seʃən] (behördliche) Bewilligung, Genehmigung, Verleihung; Einräumung *f*, Zugeständnis, Entgegenkommen *n*; Zulassung; Konzession *f*; *to grant a ~~* e-e Konzession erteilen; *to make ~~s* Zugeständnisse machen; *to withdraw the ~~ to s.o.* jdm die Konzession entziehen; *~~ to build* Baugenehmigung *f*; **~ion(n)aire** [-seʃə'nεə] Konzessionär, Inhaber *m* e-r Konzession; **~ionary** [-'seʃnəri] *a* Konzessions-; *s* Konzessionär *m*; **~ive** [-'sesiv] bereitwillig, entgegenkommend; *gram* einräumend, konzessiv.

conch [kəŋk] (See-)Muschel *f*; *hist rel* Tritonshorn *n*; *arch* Halbkuppel, Apsis *f*; **~a** ['-ə] *pl -ae* [-i] Ohrmuschel *f*; **~ology** [kəŋ'kələdʒi] Muschelkunde *f*.

conchy ['kənʃi] *sl* Kriegsdienstverweigerer *m*.

conciliat|e [kən'silieit] *tr* beschwichtigen, besänftigen; in Übereinstimmung, in Einklang bringen; *to ~~ s.o.* jds Achtung, Gunst, Wohlwollen, Freundschaft gewinnen; **~ion** [-'eiʃən] Ausgleich *m*; Einigung; Schlichtung *f*; *~~ board, court* Schlichtungsausschuß *m*; Schiedsamt *n*; *~~ hearing (jur)* Sühnetermin *m*; **~ive** [-eitiv], **~ory** [-ətəri] versöhnlich, nachgiebig, konziliant; vermittelnd, ausgleichend.

concis|e [kən'sais] kurz (u. bündig), knapp, gedrängt, prägnant, lapidar, scharf formuliert; **~eness** [-nis], **~ion** [-'siʒən] Kürze, Knappheit, Prägnanz, scharfe Formulierung *f*.

conclave ['kənkleiv] *rel* Konklave *n*; *allg* Geheimsitzung *f*; *to sit in ~* e-e Geheimsitzung abhalten.

conclud|e [kən'klu:d] *tr* beenden, (be-, ab)schließen, zu Ende führen; zum Schluß sagen; herbeiführen, in die Wege leiten, zustande bringen; *(Vertrag)* (ab)schließen, eingehen; *bes. Am* beschließen, entscheiden, bestimmen; *itr* schließen, den Schluß ziehen, folgern (*that* daß; *from* aus); *jur* beantragen; ausschließen; zu Ende gehen, sein Ende finden; enden, aufhören, schließen; zu e-m Entschluß, zu e-m Ergebnis kommen; *jur* e-e Einrede bringen; **~ing** [-iŋ] abschließend; Schluß-.

conclus|ion [kən'klu:ʒən] Beendigung *f*; (Ab-)Schluß *m*, Ende; Ergebnis *n*, Folge; Herbeiführung *f*; Abschluß *(e-s Vertrages)*; Beschluß, Entscheid (-ung *f*); Schluß(folgerung *f*) *m*, Folgerung *f*; *jur* Klagantrag *m*; Einrede *f*; *in ~~* zuletzt, am Ende, schließlich; zum Schluß; *to bring to a ~~* zum Abschluß bringen, zu Ende führen; *to come to a ~~* zu e-r Ansicht, Überzeugung kommen *od* gelangen; *to draw the ~~ from* den Schluß, die Folgerung ziehen, folgern aus; *to jump at (to) ~~s* voreilige Schlüsse ziehen; *to try ~~s with s.o.* sich mit jdm messen; **~ive** [-siv] abschließend, Schluß-; endgültig; überzeugend; entscheidend; beweiskräftig; *(Beweis)* schlüssig, zwingend; *to be ~~ against s.o. (jur)* gegenüber jdm wirksam sein.

concoct [kən'kəkt] *tr* zs.brauen; *fig* austüfteln, *fam* -knobeln, -klamüsern, -hecken, -brüten; *(Plan)* schmieden; **~ion** [-'kəkʃən] Zs.brauen; Gebräu *n*; *pharm* Mischung *f*; *fig* Tüfteln, Aushecken *n*; Erfindung, Idee *f*.

concomitan|ce, -cy [kən'kəmitəns(i)] Mitea.verbundensein *n*; *rel* Konkomitanz *f*; **~t** [-t] *a* verbunden (*with* mit); Begleit-; *s* Begleitumstand *m*, -erscheinung *f*.

concord ['kəŋkə:d] Übereinstimmung *a. gram*, Eintracht, Harmonie; Übereinkunft *f*, Abkommen *n*, Vertrag; *mus* Akkord *m*; **~ance** [kən'kə:dəns] Übereinstimmung, Harmonie; *scient* Konkordanz *f*, Wörterverzeichnis *n*; *in ~~ with* in Übereinstimmung mit; **~ant** [-ənt] übereinstimmend (*with* mit), einträchtig, harmonisch; gleichlaufend; einstimmig, -hellig; *geol* gleichförmig gelagert; **~at** [kən'kə:dæt] *rel* Konkordat *n*.

concourse ['kəŋkə:s] Zs.treffen, Aufea.prallen *n*, Zs.stoß; (Menschen-) Auflauf *m*, Gewühl, Gedränge *n*; Menge, Masse *f*; *Am* Aufmarschplatz *m*, -gelände *n*; (großer) freie(r) Platz *m*, breite Straße, Durchfahrt; *Am rail* Bahnhofshalle *f*.

concrete ['kənkri:t] *a* fest(geworden), (ver)dicht(et), kompakt; real, wirklich; konkret, gegenständlich, dinghaft; einzeln, besonder, speziell; *(Zahl)* benannt; Beton-; *s* Beton, Zement *m*; *v* [kən'kri:t] *tr itr* fest werden (lassen), (sich) verdichten, sich kristallisieren (lassen); ['kənkri:t] *tr* aus Beton herstellen *od* bauen; betonieren; mit Beton verkleiden; *armoured, reinforced ~* Eisenbeton *m*; **~d steel work** Stahlskelettbau *m*; **~ foundation** Betonfundament *n*; Zementsockel *m*; **~ mixer** Betonmischer *m*, -mischmaschine *f*; **~ paving, road surface** *(Straße)* Betondecke *f*; **~ pillar** Betonpfeiler *m*; **~ pole** Betonmast *m*; **~r** [-ə] Betonarbeiter *m*; **~ slab** Betondiele *f*.

concret|ion [kən'kri:ʃən] Festwerden *n*, Verdichtung; feste Masse; *geol* Konkretion; *min* Schwiele *f*; *med* Konkrement *n*, Stein *m*; **~ize** ['kənkri(:)taiz] *Am tr* konkretisieren, e-e feste Form geben.

concubin|age [kən'kju:binidʒ] außereheliche(r) Verkehr *m*; Konkubinat *n*, wilde Ehe *f*; **~e** ['kəŋkjubain] Konkubine, Geliebte; Nebenfrau *f*.

concupiscen|ce [kən'kju:pisns] (geschlechtliche) Begierde, Begehrlichkeit, Sinnlichkeit, Geilheit *f*; **~t** [-snt] lüstern, sinnlich.

concur [kən'kə:] *itr* zs.kommen, -treffen, -fallen, gleichzeitig geschehen; zs.-, mitwirken, (mit) dazu beitragen (*to do s.th.* etw zu tun); beipflichten, -stimmen (*with s.o.* jdm); einer Meinung, sich einig sein, übereinstimmen (*with* mit); **~rence, -cy** [-'kʌrəns(i)] Zs.treffen, -fallen *n*, Gleichzeitigkeit *f*; Zs.wirken *n*, Mitwirkung *f*, Beitrag *m*; Übereinstimmung *f*, Einverständnis *n*, gleiche Meinung *f od* Ansichten *f pl*, Einigkeit *f*; *math* Schnittpunkt; *jur* gleiche(r) Anspruch *m*; **~rent** [-'kʌrənt] *a* gleichzeitig, -laufend, zs.treffend, -fallend; mitwirkend, mit dazu beitragend; übereinstimmend, gleicher Meinung, einig; *math* sich schneidend; *s* Begleitumstand *m*, -ursache *f*; *to be ~~ (math)* sich schneiden; *jur* ideell konkurrieren (*with* mit).

concuss [kən'kʌs] *tr* erschüttern *bes. fig*; einschüchtern, durch Drohungen bringen (*into* zu), veranlassen, dazu bringen (*to do* zu tun), erpressen; **~ion** [-'kʌʃən] *med psychol* Erschütterung *f*; Stoß *m*; ~~ *of the brain* Gehirnerschütterung *f*.

condemn [kən'dem] *tr* verurteilen, verwerfen, mißbilligen, ablehnen, verdammen; *jur* für schuldig erklären, schuldig sprechen; verurteilen (*to* zu); (amtlich) für ungeeignet *od* baufällig erklären; *(im öffentlichen Interesse)* enteignen; *(Arzt e-n Kranken)* aufgeben; *(Umstände e-n Schuldigen)* verraten; *to ~ to death* zum Tode verurteilen; **~able** [-nəbl] verwerflich, verdammenswert; abzulehnen(d); **~ation** [kɔndem'neiʃən] Mißbilligung, Ablehnung, Verdammung; *jur* Verurteilung; Mißbilligung; Verurteilung; Enteignung *f*; **~atory** [kən'demnətəri] ablehnend, mißbilligend; Verdammungs-.

condens|ability [kəndensə'biliti] Verdichtbarkeit *f*; **~able** [-'densəbl] kondensierbar, verdichtbar; **~ate** ['-denseit] Kondensat *n*, Niederschlag(wasser *n*) *m*; **~ation** [kɔnden'seiʃən] Verdichtung, Kondensation; *(Gase)* Verflüssigung *f*; Kondensat *n*, Niederschlag *m*; *fig* Zs.fassung, Straffung *f* *(e-s Gedankens, e-s Textes)*; ~~ *trail (aero)* Kondensstreifen *m*; **~e** [kən'dens] *tr itr* (sich) verdichten; *tr* kondensieren, eindicken; *(Gas)* verflüssigen; *opt* sammeln; *el* verstärken; *fig* zs.fassen, straffen, komprimieren; *itr (Wasserdampf)* sich niederschlagen; sich verdichten; **~ed** [-t] *a*: ~~ *milk* kondensierte, Büchsenmilch *f*; **~er** [-'densə] *chem* Kühler; *opt el radio* Kondensator; Kondenser, Verdichter *m*.

condescen|d [kɔndi'send] *itr* sich herablassen, geruhen (*to do* zu tun); leutselig sein; herablassend tun; so tief sinken (*to* daß); **~dence** [-dəns] *s.* *~sion*; **~ding** [-diŋ] herablassend; leutselig; *fam* von oben herab; **~sion** [-ʃən] Herablassung; Leutseligkeit *f*; herablassende(s) Wesen *n*.

condign [kən'dain] *(bes. Strafe)* verdient, angemessen, angebracht.

condiment ['kɔndimənt] Gewürz *n*, Würze; Zutat *f*.

condition [kən'diʃən] *s* Bedingung, Voraussetzung *f* (*of* für), Erfordernis *n*; Zustand *m*, Verfassung, Beschaffenheit, Lage *f*; Stand *m*, Stellung *f*, Rang; Personenstand *m*; *sport* gute Form *f*; *gram* Bedingungssatz; *jur* Vorbehalt *m*, Klausel; *Am (Schule)* Auflage *f*; *pl* Umstände *m pl*, Gegebenheiten *f pl*, Lage *f*; *tr* ausbedingen, ausmachen; zur Bedingung machen (*to do* zu tun); an e-e Bedingung, an Bedingungen knüpfen; e-e Bedingung, Voraussetzung sein für; in e-n guten Zustand versetzen, *fam* in Form bringen; regeln, bestimmen; *psychol* e-n bedingten Reflex hervorrufen in; gewöhnen (*to* an); *Am (Schule)* e-e Auflage machen (*s.o.* jdm); *com* prüfen, den Zustand feststellen (*s.th.* e-r S); *tech* konditionieren, klimatisieren; *itr* über die Bedingungen verhandeln; Bedingungen stellen; *in good ~* in gutem Zustand; *sport fam* in Form; *on ~ (that)* unter der Voraussetzung *od* Bedingung (, daß); *on, under no ~* unter keinen Umständen, auf keinen Fall; unter keiner Bedingung; *out of ~* in schlechter Verfassung, *sport* Form; *tech* nicht gebrauchsfähig; *under existing ~s* so wie die Dinge liegen; *under favo(u)rable ~s* unter günstigen Umständen; *to answer, to comply with, to fulfil a ~* e-e Bedingung erfüllen; *to be in good ~* gut erhalten sein; *sport* in Form sein; *to be in no ~ to* nicht in der Lage sein zu; *to change o.'s. ~* (sich ver)heiraten; *to keep in good ~* gut im Stande halten; *to make s.th. a ~* etw zur Voraussetzung machen; *to make, to lay down ~s* Bedingungen stellen; *he is in (out of) ~* es geht ihm gesundheitlich (nicht) gut; *it is ~ed* es hängt ab (*by* von); *basic ~* Grundbedingung *f*; *dependant ~* Abhängigkeitsverhältnis *n*; *main, principal ~* Hauptbedingung *f*; *married ~* Ehe (-stand *m*) *f*; *operating, working ~* Betriebsfähigkeit *f*; **~al** [-l] *a* an e-e Bedingung geknüpft; bedingt (*on* durch), abhängig (*on* von); e-e Bedingung enthaltend; *com* freibleibend; Kopp(e)lungs-; *s (~~ clause)* Bedingungssatz *m*; *(~~ mood)* Konditional *m*; **~ally** [-ʃnəli] *adv* bedingt, unter gewissen Bedingungen *od* Voraussetzungen; *com* unter Vorbehalt; **~ed** [-d] *a* bedingt; abhängig (*upon* von); in e-m (bestimmten *od* in gutem) Zustand; beschaffen, geartet; vorgeplant; *psychol* mit e-m bedingten Reflex; gewöhnt (*to* an); *tech* klimatisiert.

condol|atory [kən'doulətəri] *a* Beileids-; ~~ *card* Beileidskarte *f*; **~e** [kən'doul] *itr* sein Beileid bezeigen *od* aussprechen (*with s.o. upon the loss of s.o.* jdm zu jds Tode); **~ence** [-əns] *a. pl* Beileid *n*; *letter of ~~* Beileidsbrief *m*; *visit of ~~* Beileidsbesuch *m*.

condom ['kɔndəm] Präservativ *n*.

condon|ation [kɔndo(u)'neiʃən] Verzeihung, Vergebung *f*; **~e** [kən'doun] *tr* verzeihen, vergeben; (mit Absicht) übersehen, nicht beachten.

condor ['kɔndɔ:] *orn* Kondor *m*.

conduc|e [kən'dju:s] *itr* beitragen, dienen, führen (*to, toward* zu); **~ive** [-iv] dienlich, förderlich, zuträglich, von Nutzen (*to* für).

conduct [kən'dʌkt] *tr* führen; (ge-) leiten; *(Unternehmen)* (durch)führen, leiten; *(Geschäft)* führen; *(Prozeß)* betreiben; *(Orchester, Chor)* leiten; dirigieren; *(Experiment)* durchführen; *phys (Wärme) el* leiten; *to ~ o.s.* handeln, sich verhalten, sich aufführen, sich betragen, sich benehmen; *itr* die Führung innehaben; als Dirigent tätig sein; *s* ['kɔndʌkt] Führung, Leitung, Verwaltung; Durchführung, Handhabung; Handlungsweise *f*, (Art *f* des) Verhalten(s), Betragen, Benehmen *n*, Führung *f*; *~ of the affairs* Geschäftsführung, -leitung *f*; *~ of a case* Führung *f* e-s Prozesses; *~ of war* Kriegführung *f*; **~ance** [kən'dʌktəns] *el* Leitwert *m*; *~* **book** *mil* Führungs-, *Br* Strafbuch *n*; **~ibility** [-i'biliti] *phys el* Leitfähigkeit *f*; **~ible** [-əbl] *phys el* leitfähig; zu leiten(d), zu führen(d); **~ing** [-iŋ] *a* Leit-; Leitungs-; Führungs-; ~~ *wire* Leitungsdraht *m*; **~ion** [kən'dʌkʃən] Leitung *f*, Durchgang *m*; *phys* Übertragung *f*; **~ive** [-iv] *phys el* leitend, leitfähig; Leit(ungs)-; **~ivity** [-'tiviti] *phys el* Leitfähigkeit *f*; *~* **money** Reisegeld *n*, -kostenvorschuß *m*; **~or** [kən'dʌktə] Führer, Leiter; Direktor; *mus* Dirigent, Chorleiter; Schaffner *(in Bus u. Straßenbahn, Am rail)*; *phys el* (Wärme-)Leiter *m*; *(Kabel)* Ader *f*; *Am obs* Blitzableiter *m*; ~~ *rail* Stromschiene *f*; **~ress** [-ris] Schaffnerin *f*; *~* **sheet** *mil* Strafliste *f*.

conduit ['kɔndit, *(el)* 'kɔnd(j)uit, 'kɔndwit] Wasserrohr *n*, Rohrleitung *f*; Rohrnetz *n*; (Kabel-)Kanal; *geol* Vulkanschlot; *fig* Weg *m*; *el* Leitungs-, Isolierrohr *n*; *~ of water* Wasserleitung *f*; *~* **box** *el* Abzweigdose *f*; *~* **cable, wire** Rohrkabel *n*, -draht *m*; *~* **connection** Leitungsanschluß *m*.

cone [koun] *s math* Kegel, Konus; *allg* Kegel, Trichter; (Berg-, *bes.* Vulkan-) Kegel *m*; Schlechtwettersignal *n*; Eistüte *f*; *(Scheinwerfer)* Strahlenbündel *n*; *bot* Zapfen *m (der Koniferen)*; *tr* kegelförmig gestalten; *itr bot* Zapfen tragen; *alluvial ~ (geol)* Schuttkegel *m*; *truncated ~* Kegelstumpf *m*; *~ of blast* Sprengkegel *m*; *~ of dispersion* Streu(ungs)kegel *m*; *~ of fire* Geschoß-, Feuergarbe *f*; *~ of light* Lichtkegel *m*; *~ of rays* Strahlenbündel *n*; *~* **bearing** *tech* Kegellager *n*; *~* **belt** Keilriemen *m*; **~-shaped** *a* kegelförmig; *~* **speaker** *radio* Trichterlautsprecher *m*; *~* **surface** Kegelmantel *m*.

coney *s. cony.*

*

confab ['kɔnfæb] *fam* = *~ulate* od *~ulation*; **~ulate** [kən'fæbjuleit] *itr* plaudern, sich (zwanglos) unterhalten; **~ulation** [kɔnfæbju'leiʃən] Unterhaltung *f*, Geplauder *n*.

confection [kən'fekʃən] *s* Zs.setzung, Mischung; Zubereitung, Herstellung; Süßigkeit *f*, Bonbon *m* od *n*, Praline, kandierte Frucht; (*bes.* Damen-)Konfektion; Konfektionsware *f*; Modeartikel *m*; *tr* zubereiten; *(Konfekt)* machen; (*bes.* fabrik-, serienmäßig) herstellen; **~er** [-'fekʃnə] Süßwarenfabrikant, -händler, Konditor *m*; *~~'s sugar* Puderzucker *m*; **~ery** [-'fekʃnəri] Konfekt, Zuckerwerk *n*, Süßwaren *f pl*; Süßwarenhandlung *f*, Schokoladengeschäft *n*, Konditorei *f*.

confeder|acy [kən'fedərəsi] Bund *m*, Bündnis *n*, Allianz, Liga; Verschwörung *f*, Komplott *n*; *the C~~* die KonföderiertenStaaten; **~ate** [-it] *a* verbündet; *s* Bundesgenosse, Alliierte(r); Komplice, Verschwörer; *hist* Konföderierte(r), Südstaatler *m*; *v* [-eit] *tr itr* (sich) verbünden; *itr* sich verschwören; **~ation** [-'reiʃən] Bund *m*, Bündnis *n*; Staatenbund, Bundesstaat *m*.

confer [kən'fə:] *tr* geben, erteilen, verleihen, übertragen; *itr* sich beraten, beratschlagen, verhandeln, konferieren; **~ee** [kɔnfə'ri:], **conferree** *Am* Konferenzteilnehmer *m*; *Am* derjenige, dem e-e Würde *od* ein Recht verliehen wird; **~ence** ['kɔnfərəns] Tagung, Konferenz, Besprechung, Unterredung, Beratung, Verhandlung *f*; Zs.schluß *m*; *to declare a ~~ open* e-e Konferenz für eröffnet erklären; *to hold a ~~* e-e Konferenz abhalten; *to meet in ~~* zu e-r Besprechung zs.-kommen; *the ~~ is held* die Konferenz findet statt; *news, press ~~* Pressekonferenz *f*; *peace ~~* Friedensverhandlung *f*; **~ment** [-mətn] Erteilung, Verleihung, Übertragung *f* (*upon* an).

confess [kən'fes] *tr* bekennen, (ein-, zu)gestehen *(to have, to having* zu haben); sich bekennen zu; *poet* bekunden, an den Tag legen; *rel* beichten; die Beichte abnehmen (*s.o.* jdm); *itr* s-e Schuld, s-n Fehler eingestehen; ein Geständnis ablegen; sich bekennen (*to* zu); *to stand ~ed as* sich enthüllen, herausstellen, erweisen als; **~edly** [-idli] *adv* zugestandenermaßen; **~ion** [-'feʃən] Bekenntnis, Geständnis; (Glaubens-) Bekenntnis *n*; *jur* Anerkenntnis; *rel* Beichte *f*; Heiligenschrein *m*, Märtyrergrab *n*; *to go to ~~* zur Beichte gehen; *to make a full ~~* ein volles Geständnis ablegen; ~~ *of faith* Glaubensbekenntnis *n*; **~ional** [-'feʃnl] *a* Beicht-; *s* Beichte *f*; Beichtstuhl *m*; *secret of the ~~* Beichtgeheimnis *n*; **~or** [-'fesə] Bekenner; Beichtvater *m*.

confetti [kən'feti(:)] *pl mit sing* Konfetti *pl*.
confid|ant, ~ante [kɔnfi'dænt, 'kən-] Vertraute(r *m*) *f*; **~e** [kən'faid] *tr* anvertrauen (*to s.o.* jdm); *itr* vertrauen (*in s.o.* jdm); sich verlassen (*in s.o.* auf jdn); **~ence** ['kɔnfidəns] Vertrauen (*in* auf), Zutrauen *n* (*in* zu); Zuversicht, Gewißheit, feste Überzeugung; Selbstsicherheit *f*, sichere(s) Auftreten *n*; vertrauliche Mitteilung *f*, Geheimnis *n*; *(told) in ~~* im Vertrauen (gesagt); *to have, to put ~~ in* Glauben schenken *dat*; *to place ~~ in s.o.* in jdn Vertrauen setzen; *to take s.o. into o.'s ~~* jdn ins Vertrauen ziehen; *question of ~~ (pol)* Vertrauensfrage *f*; *vote of ~~* Vertrauensvotum *n*; *~~ trick, (Am) game* Bauernfängerei *f*, Schwindel, Betrug *m*; Hochstapelei *f*; *~~ vote* Abstimmung *f* über die Vertrauensfrage *f*; **~ent** ['kɔnfidənt] sicher, überzeugt (*of* von); zuversichtlich, voller Zuversicht; sicher (im Auftreten), selbstsicher; überheblich; **~ential** [kɔnfi'denʃəl] *(Mitteilung)* vertraulich, geheim; vertrauensvoll, -selig; vertraut, eingeweiht; *~~ agent* Vertrauensmann *m*; *~~ clerk* Privatsekretär; *com* Prokurist *m*; **~entially** [kɔnfi'denʃəli] *adv* im Vertrauen, vertraulich, im geheimen, (ins)geheim; im Vertrauen gesagt; **~ing** [kən'faidiŋ] vertrauensvoll, -selig; arglos.
configuration [kənfigju'reiʃən] Anordnung, Gestaltung, Bildung; Struktur, Gestalt *f a. psychol*; Umriß; *astr* Planetenstand *m*; **~ism** [-izm] *Am* Gestaltpsychologie *f*.
confine *s* ['kɔnfain] *meist pl* Grenze, Grenzlinie *f*, -streifen *m*, -gebiet *n fig*; *tr* [kən'fain] begrenzen, beschränken (*to* auf); einsperren, eingesperrt, gefangen halten (*in, to* in); *to be ~d* niederkommen, entbunden werden, *to o.'s bed* ans Bett, *to o.'s room* ans Zimmer gefesselt sein; *to ~ o.s. to* sich beschränken auf; *to ~ to, within limits* in Grenzen halten; **~ment** [kən'fainmənt] Einschränkung, Beschränkung, Begrenzung; Haft; Bettlägerigkeit; Niederkunft *f*, Wochenbett *n*; *(being) in ~~* in Haft (befindlich); *solitary ~~* Einzelhaft *f*; *~~ to barracks* Kasernenarrest *m*; *~~ to o.'s room, to quarters* Stubenarrest *m*.
confirm [kən'fə:m] *tr* bestätigen, bekräftigen (*in* in); erhärten; (unter-)stützen, (be)stärken, festigen; ratifizieren, rechtskräftig machen; *rel* konfirmieren, einsegnen; firmen; **~ation** [kɔnfə'meiʃən] Bestätigung, Bekräftigung, Erhärtung; Unterstützung, Bestärkung, Festigung; Ratifizierung, Ratifikation; *rel* Konfirmation, Einsegnung, Firm(el)ung *f*; *in ~~ of* zur Bestätigung *gen*; *~~ by oath* Beeidigung *f*; **~ative** [kən'fə:mətiv], **~atory** [-ətəri] bestätigend; *~~ test* Kontrollversuch *m*; **~ed** [-d] *a* bestätigt; bestimmt, fest; endgültig; *(Kredit)* unwiderruflich; *mil* erkannt; eingewurzelt, eingefleischt, Gewohnheits-; *med* chronisch; *rel* konfirmiert; *~~ bachelor* eingefleischte(r) Junggeselle *m*; *~~ drunkard* Gewohnheitstrinker, -säufer *m*; *~~ by oath* eidlich.
confisc|ate ['kɔnfiskeit] *tr* beschlagnahmen, konfiszieren; einziehen; **~ation** [-'keiʃən] Beschlagnahme, Einziehung, Konfiskation *f*; *~~ of property* Vermögensbeschlagnahme *f*; **~atory** [kən'fiskətəri, '-keitəri] Beschlagnahme-.
conflagration [kɔnflə'greiʃən] Feuersbrunst *f*, Schadenfeuer *n*, Brandkatastrophe *f*; (großer) Brand *m a. fig*.
conflict ['kɔnflikt] *s* Zs.stoß, Kampf *m*, Gefecht *n*, Schlacht *f*; Streit, Konflikt *m*; Meinungsverschiedenheit *f*; Widerstreit *(der Gefühle)*; Widerspruch *m*; *itr* [kən'flikt] entgegenstehen, widerstreiten (*with* dat); im Widerspruch stehen, sich im W. befinden (*with* zu); nicht übereinstimmen, kollidieren (*with* mit), widersprechen (*with* dat); *in ~ with* im Widerspruch zu; *labo(u)r ~* Arbeitsstreitigkeit *f*; *~ of authority* Kompetenzstreit(igkeiten *f pl*) *m*; *~ of evidence (jur)* Beweiskonflikt *m*; *~ of interests* Interessenkonflikt *m*; **~ing** [kən'fliktiŋ] *(Gefühle)* widerstreitend; widersprechend.
conflu|ence ['kɔnfluəns] *geog* Zs.fluß *m*; Zs.strömen *n (von Menschen)*, Zustrom, -lauf *m*; Menschenansammlung, -menge *f*; **~ent** [-ənt] *a* zs.fließend, -strömend, -treffend; *bot med* verwachsen; *s* Zu-, Nebenfluß *m*; **~x** ['-flʌks] = *~ence*.
conform [kən'fɔ:m] *tr* in Übereinstimmung bringen (*to* mit), anpassen (*to* an); *itr* übereinstimmen, sich in Übereinstimmung befinden (*to* mit); entsprechen (*to* dat); sich anpassen (*to* an), sich fügen, gehorchen, sich unterwerfen (*to* dat); **~able** [-əbl] übereinstimmend, in Übereinstimmung (*to* mit); entsprechend, gemäß (*to* dat), passend (*to* zu); nachgiebig, fügsam, gehorsam, unterwürfig; *geol* gleich gelagert; **~ance** [-əns], **~ity** [-iti] Übereinstimmung (*with* mit); Anpassung (*to* an); Zugehörigkeit *f* zur Anglikanischen Kirche; *in ~ity with* gemäß, übereinstimmend mit, laut, zufolge; **~ation** [kɔnfɔ:'meiʃən] Form *f*, (Auf-)Bau *m*, Gestalt, Struktur *f*; *anat* Bau *m*; **~ist** [kən'fɔ:mist] Angehörige(r) *m* der Anglikanischen Kirche.
confound [kən'faund] *tr* verwechseln (*with* mit); durchea.bringen, -werfen; verwirren, aus der Fassung bringen, in Erstaunen versetzen, überraschen; *lit* beschämen, in Verlegenheit bringen; zunichte machen, über den Haufen werfen; *~* ['kɔn'faund] *it!* verdammt (noch mal)! **~ed** [-id] *a fam* verdammt, verflixt; abscheulich.
confraternity [kɔnfrə'tə:niti] *bes. rel* Bruderschaft *f*.
confrère, *Am* **confrere** ['kɔnfrɛə] Kollege *m*.
confront [kən'frʌnt] *tr* gegenüberstellen (*with* dat), konfrontieren (*with* mit); *jur (Urkunden)* vergleichen (*with* mit), gegenea.halten; gegenüber-, entgegentreten (*s.th.* e-r S), ins Auge sehen (*danger* der Gefahr); gegenüberstehen (*s.th.* e-r S); **~ation** [kɔnfrən'teiʃən] *jur* Gegenüberstellung; Vergleichung *f (von Urkunden)*.
confus|e [kən'fju:z] *tr* durchea.bringen, -werfen, verwechseln (*with* mit); in Verwirrung bringen, verwirren; *meist Passiv*: *to be, to become, to get ~ed* in Verwirrung, aus der Fassung geraten, bestürzt, in Verlegenheit sein; **~ed** [-d] *a* durchea.(gebracht), verwirrt, in Verwirrung, in Verlegenheit; verworren, unklar; **~ion** [-'fju:ʒən] Verwirrung *f*, Durcheinander *n*, verworrene Lage *f*, Tumult *m*; Verworrenheit; Verwirrtheit, Bestürzung, Fassungslosigkeit, Verlegenheit; Verwechs(e)lung *f*.
confut|able [kən'fju:təbl] widerlegbar; **~ation** [kɔnfju'teiʃən] Widerlegung *f*; **~e** [kən'fju:t] *tr* widerlegen; *(Person)* e-s Irrtums überführen, e-n Irrtum nachweisen (*s.o.* jdm).
congé ['kɔ̃:ʒei] Abschied *m*, Verabschiedung *f*.
congeal [kən'dʒi:l] *tr (Kälte)* erstarren lassen; *itr* (vor Kälte) erstarren, steif werden; *(Flüssigkeit)* fest werden, (ge-)frieren; gerinnen; *(Küche)* zu Gallerte werden; *fig (to be ~ed)* (vor Schreck) starr werden, erstarren; **~able** [-əbl] gefrier-, gerinnbar; **~ment** [-mənt], **congelation** [kɔndʒi'leiʃən] Gefrieren; Gerinnen *n*; Erstarrung *a. fig*; geronnene, erstarrte Masse *f*.
congen|er ['kɔndʒinə] Mensch gleichen Schlages; gleichartige(r), verwandte(r) Gegenstand *m*, ähnliche Sache *f* (*of* wie); **~ial** [kən'dʒi:niəl] geistesverwandt (*with, to s. o.* jdm); mit gleichen Interessen (*with, to* wie); freundlich, sympathisch; *(Sache)* angenehm, zusagend; passend, angemessen (*to* dat); **~iality** [kəndʒi:ni'æliti] geistige Verwandtschaft, Interessengleichheit; Angemessenheit *f*; **~ital** [kən'dʒenitl] angeboren (*with s.o.* jdm); **~itally** [-təli] *adv* von Geburt (an).
conger ['kɔŋgə] Meer-, Seeaal *m*.
congeries [kən'dʒiəri:z] *pl ~* ungeordnete(r) Haufen *m (von Sachen)*.
congest [kən'dʒest] *itr tr meist Passiv* verstopfen; *(Straßen)* überfüllen, *(Land)* übervölkern, *(Markt)* überschwemmen; *itr med* sich ansammeln; **~ed** [-id] *a* überfüllt; übervölkert, sehr dicht besiedelt; **~ion** [-ʃən] Blutandrang *m*, -wallung *f*; Überfüllung; *(~~ of traffic)* (Verkehrs-)Stauung, Stockung, Verstopfung; *(~~ of population)* Übervölkerung *f*.
conglobat|e ['kɔŋ-, kɔŋ'glo(u)beit, -gləb-] *tr itr* (sich) zs.ballen (*into* zu); *a* zs.geballt; **~ion** [-'beiʃən] Zs.ballung *f*.
conglomerat|e [kən'glɔməreit] *tr itr* (sich) (zs.)ballen; [kən'glɔmərit] *a* (zs.)geballt, (an)gehäuft, massiert; *s* bunte Masse *f*, Konglomerat *n a. geol*; **~ion** [kəŋglɔmə'reiʃən] Zs.ballung, Anhäufung *f*; bunte(r) Haufen *m*, Konglomerat *n*.
conglutinat|e [kən'glu:tineit] *tr* zs.-, anea.kleben, -leimen; *fig* zs.fügen, verein(ig)en; *itr lit fig* zs.hängen; **~ion** [-'neiʃən] Zs.kleben *n*; *fig* Vereinigung *f*.
congratul|ate [kən'grætjuleit] *tr* beglückwünschen, Glück wünschen (*s.o.* jdm), gratulieren (*s.o.* jdm; *on* zu); *to ~~ o.s. on s.th.* sich über etw freuen, über etw froh sein; **~ation** [-'leiʃən] *meist pl* Glückwunsch *m*, Gratulation *f*; **~ator** [-'grætjuleitə] Gratulant *m*; **~atory** [-əri] *a* Glückwunsch-; beglückwünschend.
congregat|e ['kɔŋgrigeit] *tr (Menschen)* zs.bringen; versammeln; *itr* zs.-kommen, sich an-, versammeln; *a* ['kɔŋgrigit] versammelt; Sammel-; **~ion** [-'geiʃən] Ansammlung; Zs.-kunft *f*, Treffen *n*, Versammlung; *rel* Gemeinde(versammlung); Ordens-, Kardinalskongregation *f*; **~ional** [-'geiʃnl] *rel* Gemeinde-, Versammlungs-; kongregationalistisch; **~ionalism** [-'geiʃnəlizm] *rel* Kongregationalismus *m*.
congress ['kɔŋgres] Zs.kunft, Tagung *f*, Kongreß *m*; Versammlung; Gesellschaft *f*; gesellschaftliche(r) Verkehr; Geschlechtsverkehr *m*; *C~ (Am)* der Kongreß *(Senat u. Repräsentantenhaus)*; **~ional** [kɔŋ'greʃnl] *a (pol C~~)* Kongreß-; **~man, ~woman** *pol* Kongreßmitglied *n, bes.* Abgeordnete(r *m*) *f* des Repräsentantenhauses.
congru|ence, -cy ['kɔŋgruens(i)] Übereinstimmung *a. gram* (*of ... with* zwischen ... und; *between* zwischen); Richtigkeit, Vernünftigkeit; Angebrachtheit, Angemessenheit; *math* Kongruenz *f*; **~ent** ['-ənt] in Überein-

stimmung, übereinstimmend *a. gram* (*with* mit); angemessen, entsprechend, gemäß (*with* dat), passend (*with* zu); *math* kongruent, deckungsgleich; **~ity** [-'gru(:)iti] Übereinstimmung; Angebrachtheit, Angemessenheit; *math* Kongruenz, Deckungsgleichheit *f*; **~ous** ['-əs] übereinstimmend, in Übereinstimmung (*with* mit); angemessen (*with* dat), passend (*with* zu; *to* für); richtig, recht, vernünftig.

conic ['kɔnik] *s* Kegelschnitt *m*; *pl mit sing* Lehre *f* von den Kegelschnitten; **~, ~al** ['-əl] konisch, kegelförmig; **~ section** Kegelschnitt *m*.

conifer ['kounifə] Nadelbaum *m*, Konifere *f*; **~ous** [kou'nifərəs] *bot* zapfentragend; *~~ tree* Nadelbaum *m*; *~~ wood* Nadelwald *m*.

conjectur|able [kən'dʒektʃərəbl] zu vermuten(d), konjizierbar; **~al** [-əl] mutmaßlich; **~e** [-ʃə] *s* Vermutung, Mutmaßung; *scient* Konjektur *f*; *tr* mutmaßen, vermuten; *scient* konjizieren; *itr* Vermutungen anstellen.

conjoin [kən'dʒɔin] *tr itr* (sich) verbinden,(sich) vereinigen; **~t** ['kɔndʒɔint, -'-] verbunden, vereinigt; gemeinsam; **~tly** *adv* gemeinschaftlich, gemeinsam, zusammen (*with* mit).

conjug|al ['kɔndʒugəl] ehelich; Ehe-, Gatten-; *~~ community, duty, faith* eheliche Gemeinschaft, Pflicht, Treue *f* *~~ happiness* Eheglück *n*; *~~ life* eheliche(s) Zs.leben *n*; **~ate** [-eit] *tr gram* konjugieren, *(Zeitwort)* beugen; *itr biol* sich paaren; [-it] *a* (*bes.* ehelich) verbunden, verein(ig)t, gepaart; *bot* paarig; *gram* vom gleichen Stamm; *math* konjugiert; *s* [-it] *gram* Wort *n* vom gleichen Stamm; *math* konjugierte Zahl *f*; **~ation** [-'geiʃən] Verbindung, Vereinigung; *biol* Paarung, Verschmelzung *(der Zellen)*; *gram* Konjugation, Beugung *f*.

conjunct [kən'dʒʌŋkt, 'kɔndʒʌŋkt] verbunden, verein(ig)t; **~ion** [kən'dʒʌŋkʃən] Verbindung, Vereinigung *f*; Zs.-treffen, -fallen *n*; *gram astr* Konjunktion *f*; *in ~~ with* in Verbindung mit; **~iva** [-'taivə] *anat* Bindehaut *f*; **~ival** [-əl] *a* Bindehaut-; **~ive** [-'dʒʌŋktiv] *a* verbindend; Binde-; *(Logik, gram)* konjunktiv; *s (~~ mood) gram* Konjunktiv *m*, Möglichkeitsform *f*; *(~~ word)* Bindewort *n*, Konjunktion *f*; *~~ tissue (anat)* Bindegewebe *n*; **~ively** *adv* vereint, gemeinsam; **~ivitis** [-'vaitis] *med* Bindehautentzündung *f*; **~ure** [kən'dʒʌŋktʃə] Umstände *m pl*, Gegebenheiten *f pl*; Lage, Konjunktur; kritische Lage, Krise *f*.

conjur|ation [kɔndʒuə'reiʃən] (Geister-) Beschwörung *f*; Zauber *m*; **~e** [kən'dʒuə] *tr* beschwören, anflehen, flehentlich, inständig bitten; ['kʌndʒə] *tr itr (to ~~ up) (Geist)* beschwören *a. fig*; *fig* heraufbeschwören; zaubern, hexen; Zauberkunststücke machen *od* aus-, vorführen; *to ~ out* od *up, away* hervor-, wegzaubern; **~er, ~or** ['kʌndʒərə] Zauberkünstler, Taschenspieler *m*; [kən'dʒuərə] Beschwörende(r), Flehende(r); **~ing** ['kʌndʒəriŋ] Zaubern *n*, Hexerei, Zauberei *f*; *~~-trick* Zauberkunststück *n*, Taschenspielertrick *m*.

conk [kɔŋk] **1.** *itr fam (to ~ out)* nicht mehr tun, nicht mehr mitmachen, aussetzen, -fallen, versagen; *mot* stehenbleiben, bocken; mit der Arbeit aufhören; sterben; *to ~ off (Am sl)* nicht arbeiten; sich aufs Ohr legen; **2.** *s sl Br* Zinken *m*, Gurke, Nase; *Am* Rübe *f*, Kopf; Schlag *m* auf den Kopf; *tr Am* einen Schlag auf den Kopf verpassen (*s.o.* jdm); **~er** ['-ə] Roßkastanie *f*; **~y** ['-i] *a s sl Am* (Mensch *m*) mit e-m großen Zinken.

conn [kɔn] *s. con* **2**.

connat|e ['kɔneit] angeboren; gleichzeitig entstanden, stammverwandt, gleichartig; *zoo bot* mitea. verwachsen; **~ural** [kə'nætʃrəl] angeboren, natürlich (*to* dat); gleichartig; verwandt.

connect [kə'nekt] *tr* verbinden (*with* mit) *a. fig tele*; anschließen (*with* an) *a. tele*; verknüpfen; *tech* koppeln, kuppeln, in Eingriff bringen (*with* mit); *el* schalten, anschließen (*to* an); an-, einschalten; *chem* ketten; *fig* mitea. in Verbindung, in Zs.hang bringen, *fam* zs.reimen; *itr* zs.hängen, Verbindung haben, in V. stehen (*with* mit); *(Zug)* Anschluß haben (*with* an); *Am fam* als Gesprächsgegenstand dienen; *sl* (gut) hinkriegen; *(Sache)* hinhauen, klappen; landen (*with a blow* e-n Schlag); *to ~ through (tele)* durchschalten; *to be ~ed with* in Verbindung stehen mit; *to be (well) ~ed* (gute) Verbindungen, Beziehungen haben; *to ~ in series* hinterea.schalten; **~ed** *a* verbunden; verwickelt (*with* in); *tech* gekoppelt; *el* geschaltet; verwandt; *fig* zs.hängend, logisch aufgebaut; *~~ in parallel* parallelgeschaltet; **~er, ~or** [-ə] *rail* Kopp(e)lung; *el* Anschluß-, Verbindungsklemme *f*, Stekker *m*; **~ing** [-iŋ] *a* Verbindungs-, Binde-, Zwischen-; *tech meist* Verbindungs-, Anschluß-; *~~ cord, flex (tele)* Verbindungsschnur *f*; *~~ link* Zwischen,- Bindeglied *n*; *~~ pipe, tube* Anschluß-, Verbindungsrohr *n*; *~~ train* Anschlußzug *m*; **~ion,** *Br* **connexion** [kə'nekʃən] Verbindung *f a. tele*, Anschluß *a. tele rail*; Zs.hang *m*; *(a. pl)* Beziehungen (*with* zu), Verbindungen *f pl*; Kundschaft; Bekanntschaft *f*, Bekanntenkreis *m*, Verwandtschaft *f*; Geschlechtsverkehr *m*; Kirchengemeinschaft, Religionsgesellschaft; politische *od* wirtschaftliche Vereinigung *od* Gruppe *f*; *el* Anschluß *m*, Schaltung *f*; *tech* Anschlußleitung *f*; *in this ~~* in diesem Zs.hang; *in ~~ with* im Zs.hang mit; in bezug auf; *with good ~~s* mit guten Beziehungen; *to establish a ~~* sich e-n Kundenkreis schaffen; *to make ~~s* den Anschluß erreichen; Anschluß haben (*at* bei); *to open a ~~* in Verbindung treten (*with* mit); *what is the ~~ between ...* welcher Zs.hang besteht zwischen, wie hängen ... zs.? *rail, train ~~* Bahn-, Zugverbindung *f*; *series ~~* Reihenschaltung *f*; *telephone ~~* Fernsprechverbindung *f*; *trunk ~~* Ferngespräch *n*; *~~ by air, by sea* Flug-, Schiffsverbindung *f*; *~~ box* Anschlußdose *f*; *~~ cable* Anschlußkabel *n*; *~~ diagram* Schaltbild *n*; **~ive** [-iv] verbindend, verknüpfend; Verbindungs-, Binde-; *~~ tissue (anat)* Bindegewebe *n*.

conning-tower *s. con* 2.

conniption [kə'nipʃən] *(~ fit) Am fam* Wut-, hysterische(r) Anfall *m*.

conniv|ance [kə'naivəns] (sträfliche) Nachsicht (*at, in* mit), Zustimmung (*at, in* zu); Begünstigung *f*; Gewährenlassen; (strafbares) geheime(s) Einverständnis, Einvernehmen *n* (*with* mit); *to be in ~~ with* in strafbarem Einvernehmen stehen mit; **~e** [kə'naiv] *itr (Unrecht)* nicht sehen wollen, mit Absicht übersehen (*at s.th.* etw), ein Auge zudrücken (*at* bei); stillschweigend dulden (*at s.th.* etw); in geheimem Einverständnis sein (*with* mit).

connoisseur [kɔni'sə:] (Kunst-)Kenner *m*; *~ of (in) wine* Weinkenner *m*.

connot|ation [kɔno(u)'teiʃən] Mit-, Neben-, weitere Bedeutung *f*; Attribut *n*, Eigenschaft *f*, Merkmal *n*; Begriffsinhalt, Bedeutungsumfang *m*; Bedeutung *f*; **~e** [kə'nout] *tr* zugleich bedeuten *od* bezeichnen; (mit)einschließen, einbegreifen; *fam* bedeuten.

connubial [kə'nju:biəl] ehelich; Ehe-; verheiratet; **~ity** [-'æliti] Ehe(stand), eheliche Gemeinschaft *f*; Eherecht *n*.

conoid ['kounɔid] *a* kegelförmig, konisch; *s math* Konoid *n*; *med* Zirbeldrüse *f*.

conquer ['kɔŋkə] *tr* erobern; besiegen, unterwerfen, überwältigen, überwinden *a. fig (Schwierigkeit)*; *fig* Herr werden über *(e-e Leidenschaft)*; *(Gewohnheit)* ablegen; *itr* siegen, siegreich sein, gewinnen; **~ing** ['-riŋ] siegreich; **~or** ['-rə] Eroberer; Sieger, Überwinder *m*.

conquest ['kɔŋkwest] Eroberung *a. fig*; Unterwerfung *f*; eroberte(s) Land; unterworfene(s) Volk *n*; Beute; *jur* Errungenschaft *f*; *to make a ~ of s.o.* jdn erobern.

consanguin|eous [kɔnsæŋ'gwiniəs] blutsverwandt; **~ity** [-iti] Blutsverwandtschaft; nahe Verwandtschaft *f*.

conscience ['kɔnʃəns] Gewissen *n*; *for ~(') sake* um das Gewissen zu beruhigen; *in all ~ (fam)* alles, was recht ist; *in all ~, in, upon my ~ (fam)* sicher, bestimmt; *to have on o.'s. ~* auf dem Gewissen haben; *his ~ is bothering him* er macht sich Gewissensbisse; **~ money** bezahlte Gewissensschuld *f*; **~-smitten, -stricken** *a* schuldbewußt.

conscientious [kɔnʃi'enʃəs] gewissenhaft, pflichtbewußt; *(Arbeit)* sorgfältig; **~ness** [-nis] Gewissenhaftigkeit *f*; **~ objector** Kriegs-, Wehrdienstverweigerer *m*.

conscious ['kɔnʃəs] *a* bewußt; bei (vollem) Bewußtsein; absichtlich, wissentlich; vorsätzlich; selbstbewußt, überzeugt; *s*: *the ~ (psychol)* das bewußte Seelenleben; *with ~ superiority* im Bewußtsein s-r Überlegenheit; *to be ~ of s.th.* sich e-r S bewußt, sich über etw im klaren sein; *to be ~ that* überzeugt sein, daß; **~ness** ['-nis] Bewußtheit *f*; Bewußtsein *n* (*of* gen; *that* daß); *class ~~* Klassenbewußtsein *n*; *~~ of guilt* Schuldbewußtsein *n*.

conscript [kən'skript] *tr mil* ausheben, einziehen, einberufen; ['kɔnskript] *a* einberufen, eingezogen, ausgehoben; *s* Eingezogene(r), Einberufene(r), Wehrdienstpflichtige(r) *m*; **~ee** [-'i:] *Am fam* Rekrut *m*; **~ion** [kən'skripʃən] Einberufung, Aushebung; Wehrpflicht *f*; *universal ~~* allgemeine Wehrpflicht *f*; *~~ of labo(u)r* Arbeits-, Dienstpflicht *f*; *~~ law* Wehrgesetz *n*; *~~ list* (Wehr-)Stammrolle *f*, -blatt *n*.

consecrat|e ['kɔnsikreit] *tr rel* weihen, konsekrieren; *allg* widmen; heiligen; **~ion** [-'kreiʃən] *rel* Weihe, Konsekration; *allg* Hingabe *f* (*to* an).

consecut|ion [kɔnsi'kju:ʃən] (Aufea.-, Reihen-)Folge; (logische) Folge, Folgerung *f*; **~ive** [kən'sekjutiv] aufea.-folgend, fortlaufend; nach-, hinterea. *attr*; folgerichtig; *~~ clause (gram)* Konsekutivsatz *m*; *~~ interpreting* Konsekutivdolmetschen *n*; **~ively** [-'sekjutivli] *adv* fortlaufend.

consensus [kən'sensəs] Übereinstimmung; *(~ of opinion)* übereinstimmende Meinung, allgemeine Ansicht.

consent [kən'sent] *itr* einwilligen (*to* in), einverstanden sein (*to* mit); beipflichten, zustimmen (*to s.th.* e-r S), billigen (*to s.th.* etw); *s* Einwilligung *f* (*to* in); Einverständnis, Einvernehmen *n* (*to* mit); Zustimmung (*to* zu); Billigung *f* (*to* gen); *by mutual* ~ in gegenseitigem Einvernehmen; *with one* ~ einstimmig, -mütig; *to give o.'s* ~ *to* s-e Einwilligung geben in, s-e Zustimmung erteilen zu; *silence gives* ~ *(prov)* wer schweigt, gibt zu.

consequen|ce ['kɔnsikwəns] Folge, Konsequenz *f*, Ergebnis *n*, Wirkung; Folgerung *f*, Schluß *m*; Bedeutung, Wichtigkeit *f*, Einfluß *m*; *in* ~~ folglich; *in* ~~ *of* infolge *gen*; *of* ~~ bedeutend, wichtig (*to* für); *of no* ~~ unwichtig, unbedeutend, belanglos, ohne Bedeutung; *to be the* ~~ *of s.th.* die Folge e-r S sein; *to have serious* ~~*s* ernste Folgen haben *od* nach sich ziehen; *to take, to bear the* ~~*s* die Folgen auf sich nehmen *od* tragen; *that's of no further* ~~ das fällt nicht weiter ins Gewicht; **~t** ['-t] *a* folgend (*upon* auf), sich ergebend (*upon* aus); folgerichtig, konsequent; *s* Folge, Konsequenz *f*, Ergebnis *n*; **~tial** [kɔnsi'kwenʃəl] daraus folgend, sich ergebend (*on* aus); dünkelhaft, eingebildet; *Am* einflußreich; **~tly** ['-tli] *adv* folglich.

conserv|able [kən'sə:vəbl] konservierbar; **~ancy** [-ənsi] Erhaltung *(der Natur)*; Unterhaltung (von Anlagen, Einrichtungen); (Forst-, Fischerei-, Hafen-)Verwaltung *f*; *river-*~~ Flußbauamt *n*; **~ation** [kɔnsə(:)'veiʃən] Erhaltung, Bewahrung *f*, Schutz *m*; sachgerechte Verwendung; Melioration; Pflege *f*; *soil* ~~ Bodenmelioration *f*; ~~ *of energy (phys)* Erhaltung *f* der Energie; **~atism** [-'sə:vətizm] *bes. pol* Konservat(iv)ismus *m*; **~ative** [-iv] *a* konservativ *a. pol*; erhaltend; *fam* vorsichtig, zurückhaltend, mäßig, bescheiden; *s pol* Konservative(r) *m*; Schutzmittel *n*; **~atoire** [kən'sə:vətwɑ:] *Br* Musikhochschule *f*; **~ator** ['kɔnsə(:)veitə] Erhalter, Bewahrer, Schützer; *Am jur* Pfleger *m*; [kən'sə:vətə] (Museums-, Landes-)Konservator, Museumsdirektor, -leiter; *Br* (Ober-)Aufseher, Inspektor *m*; **~atory** [kən'sə:vətri] *a* erhaltend; Schutz-; *s* Treibhaus *n*; Wintergarten *m*; *Am mus* Konservatorium *n*, Musik(hoch)schule *f*; **~e** [kən'sə:v] *tr* erhalten, bewahren, schützen; konservieren, einmachen, -kochen; *s* [*a.* 'kɔnsə:v] *meist pl* Konserven *f pl*, Eingemachte(s) *n*.

consider [kən'sidə] *tr* betrachten, erwägen, bedenken; reiflich überlegen, prüfen; berücksichtigen, Rücksicht nehmen auf; ansehen, betrachten als, halten für; *to* ~ *that* der Ansicht sein, daß; für annehmbar, möglich halten (*doing s.th.* etw zu tun); *to be* ~*ed* gelten als; *itr* nachdenken, überlegen; *all things* ~*ed* wenn man alles in Betracht zieht; bei dieser Sachlage; *what do you* ~ *me to be?* wofür halten Sie mich? *I* ~~ ich bin der Auffassung (*that* daß); **~able** [-rəbl] bedeutend *(a. Person)*, beachtlich, beträchtlich, erheblich, merklich; *Am* sehr viel; **~ate** [-rit] rücksichtsvoll, aufmerksam, zuvorkommend (*of* gegen); *to be* ~~ *of* Rücksicht nehmen auf; **~ation** [-'reiʃən] Überlegung, Erwägung *f*; Gesichtspunkt; Beweggrund, Anlaß; Umstand *m*; Rücksicht(nahme), Aufmerksamkeit, Zuvorkommenheit (*of* gegenüber); Bedeutung; Belohnung, Vergütung *f*, Entgelt *n*, Entschädigung, Gegenleistung *f*, Gegenwert *m*; *com* Deckung *f*; *after long* ~~ nach reiflicher Überlegung; *in* ~~ *of* in Anbetracht *gen*, im Hinblick, mit Rücksicht auf; *for a* ~~ entgeltlich; *of no* ~~ *(at all)* (völlig) belanglos, unerheblich; *on, under no* ~~ auf keinen Fall, unter keinen Umständen; *on further* ~~ bei näherer Überlegung; *out of* ~~ *for* mit Rücksicht auf; in Anbetracht *gen*; *to be (still) under* ~~ noch nicht entschieden sein; *to come into* ~~ in Frage, in Betracht kommen; *to give careful* ~~ *to s.th.* etw sorgfältig berücksichtigen; *to leave out of* ~~ unberücksichtigt, außer acht lassen; *to take into* ~~ in Betracht, in Erwägung ziehen; berücksichtigen; *the case under* ~~ der vorliegende Fall; *time for* ~~ Bedenkzeit *f*; **~ed** [-d] *a* (wohl)überlegt; geachtet, geschätzt; **~ing** [-riŋ] *prp* in Anbetracht *gen*, in Hinblick auf; ~~ *(adv fam)* unter Berücksichtigung aller Umstände; nach reiflicher Überlegung.

consign [kən'sain] *tr* (ver)senden, (ver)schicken; über-, zusenden, zustellen, übergeben, ausliefern, aushändigen, überlassen (*to* für); einweisen (*to* in); anvertrauen; *lit (Gott)* anbefehlen, in die Hände legen (*to* gen); hinterlegen, deponieren; in Kommission geben; konsignieren; *to be* ~*ed to (fig)* ausgeliefert, überlassen sein; **~ee** [kɔnsai'ni:] Empfänger, Adressat, Depositar *m*; **~er, ~or** [kən'sainə] Absender; Deponent; Konsignant *m*; **~ment** [-mənt] Verschickung *f*, Versand *m*, Zustellung, Aushändigung; (Waren-)Sendung; Hinterlegung, Deposition; Kommission; Konsignation *f*; *to take on* ~~ in Kommission nehmen; ~~ *note* Frachtbrief, Ladeschein *m*; ~~ *for (inspection and) approval* Ansichtssendung *f*; ~~ *in part* Teilsendung, -lieferung *f*.

consist [kən'sist] *itr* bestehen, sich zs.-setzen, gebildet sein (*of* aus); *to* ~ *in* bestehen in; *to* ~ *with* übereinstimmen, im Einklang stehen mit; **~ence, -cy** [-əns(i)] Dichte, Festigkeit, Konsistenz *f*; Dichte-, Festigkeitsgrad *m*; **~ency** Übereinstimmung; logische Folge *f*, Zs.hang *m*, Folgerichtigkeit; Beständigkeit *f*; **~ent** [-ənt] in Übereinstimmung, in Einklang, vereinbar (*with* mit); beständig, gleichbleibend, konsequent, folgerichtig (*about s.th.* in etw); **~ory** [-əri] *rel* Konsistorium *n*.

consol|ation [kɔnsə'leiʃən] Trost *m*; ~~ *prize* Trostpreis *m*; **~atory** [kən'sɔlətəri], **~ing** [-'souliŋ] tröstend, trostreich; Trost(es)-; **~e** [kən'soul] *tr* trösten (*for* über); **~er** [-ə] Tröster *m*.

console ['kɔnsoul] Konsole; Krage *f*, Kragträger, -stein *m*; Wandgestell *n*; Instrumentenbank; Musiktruhe *f*; Gehäuse *n*; ~ **table** Konsol-, Wandtisch *m*.

consolidate [kən'sɔlideit] *tr itr* (sich) stärken, (sich) festigen; *tr* mitea. verbinden, vereinigen, zs.schließen; zs.-legen *a. fin*; *fin* fundieren, konsolidieren; *mil (Stellung)* ausbauen; **~ated** *a fin* fundiert, konsolidiert; *com Am* gemeinsam, für mehrere Betriebe arbeitend; ~~ *annuities s. consols*; ~~ *debt* fundierte, konsolidierte Schuld *f*; ~~ *school (Am)* Sammel-, Bezirksschule *f*; **~ation** [-'deiʃən] Stärkung, Festigung; Verbindung, Vereinigung *f*, Zs.schluß *m*, Fusion; Zs.legung *a. fin*; *fin* Verschmelzung; Fundierung, Konsolidierung *f*.

consols [kən-, kən'sɔlz, 'kɔnsɔlz] *pl fin* Konsols *m pl*, konsolidierte Staatsanleihen, -renten *f pl*, -papiere *n pl*.

consommé [kən'sɔmei, *Am* kɔnsə'mei] (klare) Fleischbrühe *f*.

consonan|ce ['kɔnsənəns] Übereinstimmung *f*, Ein-, Zs.klang *m*, Konsonanz *f*; Wohlklang; *mus* Akkord *m*; *gram* Mitlaut-, Konsonantenfolge *f*; **~t** ['-t] *a* übereinstimmend, in Einklang (*with* mit); harmonisch; rhythmisch; gereimt; *gram* konsonantisch, Konsonanten-; *s gram* Konsonant, Mitlaut *m*; ~~ *shift* Lautverschiebung *f*; **~tal** [-'næntl] konsonantisch.

consort [kən'sɔ:t] *itr* Umgang haben, verkehren (*with* mit); in Einklang stehen, harmonieren (*with* mit), passen (*with* zu); *tr* verbinden; *s* ['kɔnsɔ:t] Gemahl(in *f*) *m*; *mar* Begleitschiff *n*; *prince* ~ Prinzgemahl *m*; **~ium** [kən'sɔ:tjəm, *Am* -'sɔ:ʃjəm] *fin* Konsortium, Syndikat *n*; eheliche Gemeinschaft *f*.

conspectus [kən'spektəs] (allgemeine) Übersicht *f*, Überblick *m*; Zs.fassung *f*.

conspicuous [kən'spikjuəs] gut zu sehen(d), deutlich sichtbar, bemerkbar; (klar) ersichtlich, offensichtlich, -bar; auffällig, hervorragend, auffallend, bemerkenswert (*by, for* durch, wegen); *to be* ~ *by o.'s absence* durch Abwesenheit glänzen; *to make o. s.* ~ sich auffällig benehmen; **~ness** [-nis] Deutlichkeit, Auffälligkeit *f*.

conspir|acy [kən'spirəsi] Verschwörung; Verschwörergruppe *f*; *fig* Zs.-wirken *n*; **~ator** [-ətə] Verschwörer *m*; **~e** [kən'spaiə] *itr* sich verschwören (*against* gegen) *a. fig*; *fig* zs.wirken; *tr* (heimlich) planen.

constab|le ['kʌnstəbl] *(police* ~~*)* Schutzmann, Polizist *m*; *Chief C*~~ Polizeichef, -direktor *m*; *to outrun the* ~~ Schulden machen; **~ulary** [kən'stæbjuləri] *s* städtische *od* Bezirkspolizei *f*; *a* Polizei-.

constan|cy ['kɔnstənsi] Standhaftigkeit, Beständigkeit, Unwandelbarkeit, Treue; Festigkeit, Stabilität; Dauerhaftigkeit; Regelmäßigkeit *f*; **~t** [-t] *a* standhaft, beständig, unwandelbar, treu, fest; beständig, ununterbrochen, fortwährend, dauernd; gleichbleibend, regelmäßig, konstant; *s math phys* Konstante *f*, Festwert *m*; *el* Schaltelement *n*; **~tly** *adv* (be)ständig, immer(zu), dauernd, unaufhörlich, fortwährend; wiederholt, oft.

constellation [kɔnstə'leiʃən] *astr* Sternbild *n*; *(Astrologie)* Planetenstellung *f*, Aspekte *m pl*; *fig* Konstellation *f*, Aussichten *f pl*; *fig* glänzende(r) Kreis *m*; *psychol* Komplex *m* von Gedanken u. Gefühlen.

consternat|ion [kɔnstə'neiʃən] Entsetzen *n*, Bestürzung *f*; völlige Fassungslosigkeit, Verwirrung *f*.

constipat|e ['kɔnstipeit] *tr med* verstopfen; **~ion** [-'peiʃən] Verstopfung *f*.

constituen|cy [kən'stitjuənsi] Wähler (-schaft *f*) *m pl (e-s Wahlbezirks)*; Wahlbezirk, -kreis *m*; Anhängerschaft *f*; Kundenkreis *m*, Abnehmer *m pl*; **~t** [-t] *a* wählend, Wahl-; verfassunggebend; wesentlich; Bestand-; *s* Wähler; Auftrag-, Vollmachtgeber, Mandant *m*; *(*~~ *part)* wesentliche(r), Haupt-, Grundbestandteil; Bauteil *m*, Komponente *f*; *el* Schaltelement *n*; ~~ *assembly* verfassunggebende Versammlung *f*.

constitute ['kɔnstitju:t] *tr (Person)* einsetzen, ernennen, bestellen; beauftragen, bevollmächtigen; *(Körperschaft)* konstituieren, begründen, ein-, errichten; *(Ausschuß)* bilden, einsetzen; *(Einrichtung)* schaffen; *(Gesetz)* in Kraft setzen; *(ein Ganzes)* ausmachen, bilden, darstellen; *(Summe)* betragen; *to* ~ *o.s. a judge of* sich zum Richter aufwerfen über.

constitution [kɔnsti'tju:ʃən] Ernennung, Bestellung; Ein-, Errichtung, Begründung, Konstituierung, Einsetzung, Schaffung, Bildung *f*, (Auf-)Bau *m*, Struktur, Organisation, Beschaffenheit; *(Mensch)* Konstitution; Wesensart *f*, Charakter *m*; Gesellschafts-, Staats-, Regierungsform; Verfassung *f*, (Staats-)Grundgesetz *n*; *to give a* ~ e-e Verfassung geben; **~al** [-nl] *a* konstitutionell, in der Natur *od* im Wesen begründet; wesentlich; natürlich, der Veranlagung entsprechend, Veranlagungs-; gesundheitsfördernd; *pol* verfassungsmäßig, -gemäß, Verfassungs-; *s fam* Verdauungsspaziergang *m*; *to take a* ~~ ein bißchen an die (frische) Luft gehen; ~~ *charter* Verfassungsurkunde *f*; ~~ *crisis, reform* Verfassungskrise, -reform *f*; ~~ *monarchy* konstitutionelle Monarchie *f*; **~alism** [-ʃnəlizm] verfassungsmäßige Regierung *f*; Konstitutionalismus *m*; **~alist** [-ʃnəlist] *pol* Konstitutionelle(r) *m*.

constitutive ['kɔnstitju:tiv] konstitutiv, konstituierend, rechtsbegründend; *(Bestandteil)* wesentlich, Grund-; e-n Bestandteil bildend (*of* gen).

constrain [kən'strein] *tr* (er)zwingen; nötigen; **~ed** [-d] *a* verwirrt, verlegen, befangen; gezwungen, unnatürlich; *to find o.s.* ~~ sich gezwungen, genötigt sehen; **~edly** [-idli] *adv* gezwungenermaßen; **~t** [-t] Zwang, Druck *m*, Nötigung; Haft; Verlegenheit, Befangenheit *f*; *under* ~~ unter Zwang, zwangsweise; *to be under* ~~ sich in e-r Zwangslage befinden; *to put under* ~~ unter Druck setzen.

constrict [kən'strikt] *tr* zs.ziehen, -drücken; einengen; abschnüren; *(Muskel, Ader)* zs.schnüren, verenge(r)n; *fig* hemmen; **~ed** [-id] *a* eingeengt, begrenzt; **~ion** [-kʃən] Zs.ziehung; Zs.schnürung, Vereng(er)ung; Beklemmung *f*, (beklemmendes) Druckgefühl *n*; **~or** [-ər] *anat* Schließmuskel *m*; *boa* ~~ Abgott-, Königsschlange *f*.

constringent [kən'strindʒənt] zs.-schnürend, verenge(r)nd.

construct [kən'strʌkt] *tr* (auf-, er-)bauen, errichten; konstruieren; *fig* aus-, erdenken, ersinnen; *gram (Satz)* bauen, konstruieren; *(Kunstwerk)* aufbauen; *(Argument, Theorie)* aufstellen; *s* ['kɔnstrʌkt] Konstruktion *f a. gram*; **~ion** [kən'strʌkʃən] Bau *m*, Erbauung, Errichtung, Gestaltung, Konstruktion; Bauart, -weise, Ausführung *f*; Gebäude *n*, Bau(werk *n*) *m*, Anlage; *fig* Deutung, Erklärung, Auslegung; Bedeutung; *gram* Konstruktion *f*, Satzbau; *(Wort)* Gebrauch *m*; *under* ~~, *in the course of* ~~ im Bau; *to bear the* ~~ die Bedeutung haben; *to put a (good, wrong)* ~~ *on* (günstig, falsch) auslegen; e-e Bedeutung beilegen; ~~ *battalion, company (mil)* Baubataillon *n*, -kompanie *f*; ~~ *of bridges* Brückenbau *m*; ~~ *cost* Bau-, Anlagekosten *pl*; ~~ *drawing* Konstruktionszeichnung *f*; ~~ *engineering* Bauwesen *n*; ~~ *laborer (Am)* Gleisbauarbeiter *m*; ~~ *material* Baumaterial *n*; ~~ *office* Konstruktionsbüro *n*; ~~ *programme, schedule* Bauprogramm *n*; ~~ *series* Baureihe, -serie *f*; ~~ *squad, unit, crew* Bautrupp *m*, Kolonne *f*; ~~ *supervision* Bauaufsicht *f*; ~~ *train* Bauzug *m*; ~~ *worker* Bauarbeiter *m*; **~ional** [-'strʌkʃənl] baulich, konstruktiv; Bau-, Konstruktions-; ~~ *competition* Bauwettbewerb *m (mit Modellen)*; ~~ *detail* Einzelheit *f* der Konstruktion; ~~ *drawing* Konstruktionszeichnung *f*; ~~ *element* Bauelement *n*; ~~ *engineering* Maschinenbau *m*; ~~ *sketch* Bauskizze *f*; ~~ *work* Baukonstruktion *f*; **~ive** [-iv] Bau-, Konstruktions-; *fig* aufbauend, konstruktiv, positiv, fördernd; *(Mensch)* schöpferisch, erfinderisch; *jur* präsumptiv, hypothetisch; **~or** [-ə] Erbauer; Konstrukteur *m*.

construe [kən'stru:] *tr (Satz)* konstruieren, grammatisch erklären; übersetzen; *(Worte od Handlung)* erklären, deuten, auslegen; ableiten, folgern; *(Wort)* gebrauchen, konstruieren; *itr (Satz)* sich konstruieren lassen; *s fam* Übersetzungsaufgabe *f*.

consubstanti|al [kɔnsəb'stænʃəl] *rel* wesensgleich; **~ality** [-ʃi'æliti] *rel* Wesensgleichheit *f*; **~ate** [-'stænʃieit] *tr* wesensgleich machen; *itr* sich zu e-m Wesen vereinigen; **~ation** [-'eiʃən] Konsubstantiation *f*.

consuetud|e ['kɔnswitju:d] *bes. jur* Gewohnheit *f*; **~inary** [-'tju:dinəri] gewohnheitsmäßig; Gewohnheits-.

consul ['kɔnsəl] Konsul *m a. hist*; *honorary* ~ Wahlkonsul *m*; **~ar** ['-sjulə] konsularisch; Konsular-, Konsulats-; *the* ~~ *corps* das konsularische Korps; ~~ *officer* Konsulatsbeamte(r); ~~ *representation* konsularische Vertretung *f*; **~ate** ['-sjulit] Konsulat *n a. hist*; ~~ *general* Generalkonsulat *n*; ~ **general** Generalkonsul *m*; **~ship** ['-ʃip] Amt *n* e-s Konsuls.

consult [kən'sʌlt] *tr* um Rat fragen, zu Rate ziehen, konsultieren, sich beraten lassen von; *(Buch)* nachschlagen, nachsehen in; Rücksicht nehmen auf, denken an, beachten, berücksichtigen, bedenken; *itr* sich beratschlagen (*with s.o. about s.th.* mit jdm über etw); **~ant** [-ənt] Spezialist, Berater; (Rechts-)Konsulent; beratende(r) Arzt *m*; *industrial, technical* ~~ Industrie-, technische(r) Berater *m*; **~ation** [kɔnsəl'teiʃən] Befragung, Konsultation, Berat(schlag)ung (*with* mit); Konferenz *f* (*on* über), Treffen *n*, Sitzung *f*; Nachschlagen *n*; *on* ~~ *with* nach Rücksprache mit; ~~ *room* Sprechzimmer *n*; **~ative** [kən'sʌltətiv] beratend, konsultativ; ~~ *assembly, voice* beratende Versammlung, Stimme *f*; **~ing** [-iŋ] *a* beratend; *s* Beratung *f*; ~~ *barrister, engineer, physician* beratende(r) Anwalt, Ingenieur, Arzt *m*; ~~*-hours (pl) (med)* Sprechstunden *f pl*, -zeit *f*; ~~*-room (med)* Sprechzimmer *n*.

consum|able [kən'sju:məbl] *a* verzehrbar, genießbar; abnutzbar, verschleißbar; zerstörbar; *s pl* Nahrungsmittel *n pl*; ~~ *item* Verbrauchsartikel *m*; **~e** [kən'sju:m] *tr* verzehren, genießen, konsumieren; ver-, aufbrauchen *(a. Geld)*; *(Geld, Zeit, Kraft)* verbrauchen, verschwenden, vergeuden; *(Zeit)* gänzlich in Anspruch nehmen; verbrauchen, abnutzen, verschleißen; zerstören, vernichten; *(Feuer)* verzehren; *(Strom)* aufnehmen; *itr* sich abnutzen, sich verbrauchen; *(to* ~~ *away)* sich verzehren, vergehen (*with grief* vor Kummer); *to be ~ed with* von *(Haß, Neid, Kummer)* erfüllt sein; **~er** [-ə] Verbraucher, Konsument, Abnehmer *m*; *ultimate* ~~ Endverbraucher *m*; ~~*'s acceptance* bereitwillige Aufnahme *f* durch den Verbraucher; ~~ *advertising* Verbraucherwerbung *f*; ~~*(s') goods, durables (pl)* Verbrauchsgüter *n pl*; ~~ *income* Verbrauchereinkommen *n*, ~~ *research* Marktforschung *f*; ~~ *resistance* Kaufunlust *f*; ~~ *spending* Verbraucherausgaben *f pl*; ~~*s' surplus* Konsumentenrente *f*; **~ing** *a*: ~~ *desire* brennende Begierde *f*; ~~ *power* Kaufkraft *f*.

consummat|e ['kɔnsʌmeit] *tr* vollenden; *com* perfekt machen; *jur (Ehe)* vollziehen; *a* [kən'sʌmit] vollständig, vollkommen, vollendet; *(im negativen Sinn)* ausgemacht, Erz-; **~ion** [-'meiʃən] Vollendung; Erfüllung, Krönung *f (des Lebens)*; Abschluß *a. com*, Ende *n*; *jur* Vollziehung *f (d. Ehe)*.

consumpt|ion [kən'sʌmpʃən] Verbrauch, Konsum (*of* an); Absatz *m*; Verschwendung, Vergeudung; Abnutzung *f*, Verschleiß *m*; Vernichtung, Zerstörung; *med* Auszehrung, Schwindsucht *f*; *increase of* ~~ Absatzsteigerung *f*; *power of* ~~ Kaufkraft *f*; ~~ *area* Absatzgebiet *n*; ~~ *of current, energy, fuel, materials, water* Strom-, Energie-, Brennstoff-, Material-, Wasserverbrauch *m*; **~ive** [-iv] *a* verbrauchend (*of* acc); *com* Verbrauchs-; schwindsüchtig, tuberkulös; *s* Schwindsüchtige(r *m*) *f*.

*

contact ['kɔntækt] *s* Berührung *f a. el*; *tech* Eingriff; *el* Kontakt; *phot* Kontaktabzug *m*; *fig* Verbindung (*with* mit), Beziehung (*with* zu); *mil* Fühlung *f*, Anschluß; Meinungsaustausch (*with* mit); *Am* gesellige(r) Verkehr, Umgang *m* (*with* mit); *med* Kontaktperson *f*; *tr Am* Verbindung aufnehmen *od* herstellen; Fühlung nehmen, in Verbindung treten mit; in Verbindung setzen; *to be in* ~ *with* in Verbindung stehen mit; *to be in* ~ *with the enemy (mil)* Feindberührung haben; *to break* ~ *(el)* den Strom unterbrechen; *to bring, to come into* ~ *with* in Berührung bringen, kommen mit; *to make* ~ Verbindung anknüpfen (*with* mit); *el* Kontakt herstellen; *to* ~ *by telephone* sich telefonisch in Verbindung setzen mit, anrufen; ~ *with the enemy* Feindberührung *f*; ~ **area** *tech* Berührungsfläche *f*; ~ **breaker** *el* Unterbrecher, Schalter *m*; ~ **fuse** *(Bombe)* Aufschlagzünder *m*; ~ **glass, lens** *opt* Haftschale *f*; ~ **landing** Landung *f* mit Bodensicht; ~ **(man)** Verbindungsmann, Vermittler *m*; ~ **manager** *Am* Pressevertreter *m*; ~ **mine** *mil* Fladder-, Tret-, Stoßmine *f*; ~ **print** *phot typ* Kontaktabzug *m*; ~ **rail** Stromschiene *f*.

contagi|on [kən'teidʒən] *med* Ansteckung, Übertragung; ansteckende, übertragbare Krankheit, Seuche *f*; *fig* Einfluß *m*, Vergiftung *f*; **~ous** [-əs] ansteckend *a. fig*, übertragbar.

contain [kən'tein] *tr* enthalten, (um-)fassen, einschließen, in sich begreifen; *(Gefühl, Leidenschaft)* in Schranken, im Zaum halten, beherrschen, zügeln, unterdrücken; *mil* fesseln, binden, abriegeln; *math* enthalten, teilbar sein durch; begrenzen, einschließen; *to* ~ *o.s.* sich beherrschen, sich in der Gewalt haben, sich fassen, sich mäßigen, sich zurückhalten; **~er** [-ə] Behälter; (Benzin-)Kanister *m*; **~ment** [-mənt] Mäßigung, Zurückhaltung; *pol* Eindämmung *f*, In-Grenzen-Halten *n*.

contaminat|e [kən'tæmineit] *tr* verschmutzen, verunreinigen; *med* verseuchen *a. mil (Gelände)*; (radioaktiv) verseuchen; *gram* kontaminieren; *fig* beflecken, besudeln, vergiften, anstecken, e-n verderblichen Einfluß ausüben auf, verderben; **~ion** [-'neiʃən] Verschmutzung, Verunreinigung; (*a.* radioaktive) Verseuchung; Besudelung; Ansteckung *f*; verderbliche(r)

Einfluß; Schmutz *m*, Unreinigkeit; *gram* Kontamination *f*.

contango [kən'tæŋgo] *s fin* Reportgeschäft *n*, -kurs *m*, -prämie *f*, Aufgeld *n*; *itr* reportieren, Reportgeschäfte machen; ~ **days** *pl* Reporttage *m pl*.

contemn [kən'tem] *tr lit* verachten.

contemplat|e ['kɔntempleit] *tr* betrachten, beschauen; nachdenken, (nach)sinnen über; ins Auge fassen, im Auge haben, vorhaben, beabsichtigen; erwarten, rechnen mit; *itr* (nach)sinnen, meditieren (*on* über); **~ion** [-'pleiʃən] Betrachtung *f*; Nachdenken, (Nach-)Sinnen *n*; Beschaulichkeit; Absicht; Erwartung *f*; *to be in ~~* geplant werden; **~ive** ['kɔntempleitiv, kən'templətiv] nachdenklich, besinnlich, beschaulich.

contempor|aneity [kən-, kɔntempərə'ni:iti] Gleichzeitigkeit *f*; **~aneous** [-'reinjəs] gleichzeitig (*with* mit); **~aneousness** Gleichzeitigkeit *f*; **~ary** [kən'tempərəri] *a* gleichzeitig (*with* mit); zeitgenössisch; gleichaltrig; *fam* modern; *s* Zeit-, Altersgenosse *m*; **~ize** [-'tempəraiz] *tr* synchronisieren; *itr* gleichzeitig stattfinden.

contempt [kən'tempt] Verachtung, Geringschätzung; Schande *f*; *(~ of court)* Mißachtung *f* des Gerichts; *to bring into ~* der Verachtung preisgeben; *to fall into ~* der Verachtung anheimfallen; **~ible** [-ibl] verachtenswert, verächtlich; **~uous** [-juəs] verächtlich, geringschätzig; **~uousness** [-juəsnis] Geringschätzigkeit *f*; anmaßende(s) Wesen *n*.

contend [kən'tend] *itr* kämpfen, ringen, sich bewerben (*for* um); streiten, disputieren (*with s.o. about s.th.* mit jdm über etw); *tr* verfechten; behaupten (*that* daß).

content 1. ['kɔntent] Rauminhalt *m*, Volumen, Fassungsvermögen *n*; *math* (Flächen-)Inhalt; Gehalt, Anteil; *lit* Inhalt *m (im Gegensatz zur Form)*; ['kɔntent, kən'tent] *meist pl* Inhalt; Inneneinrichtung *f*; *table of ~s (Buch)* Inhaltsverzeichnis *n*; **2.** [kən'tent] *a* zufrieden (*with* mit); geneigt, bereit, gewillt (*to do* zu tun); *s* Zufriedenheit *f*; *pl parl* Jastimmen *f pl*; *tr* zufriedenstellen, befriedigen; *to ~ o.s. with* zufrieden sein, sich begnügen mit; *to o.'s heart's ~* nach Herzenslust; *~, not ~ (parl, nur im Br Oberhaus)* ja! nein! **~ed** [-'tentid] *a* zufrieden (*with* mit); **~edness** [-'tentidnis], **~ment** [-'tentmənt] Zufriedenheit *f*.

contenti|on [kən'tenʃən] Streit, Zank, Disput *m*, Wortgefecht *n*, Kontroverse *f*; Streitpunkt *m*; *(verfochtene)* Meinung, Ansicht; Behauptung, Feststellung *f*; *obs* u. *Am* Kampf, Streit *m allg*; *bone of ~* Zankapfel *m*; **~ous** [-əs] streit-, zanksüchtig, rechthaberisch; *jur* streitig; *(Sache)* strittig, umstritten; **~ousness** [-əsnis] Streit-, Zanksucht *f*.

contermin|al, ~ous [kən'tə:minəl, -əs] angrenzend (*to, with* an), anea.stoßend, ea. berührend; sich deckend, gleichzeitig, gleichbedeutend (*with* mit).

contest [kən'test] *tr* umkämpfen, kämpfen um; sich bemühen, sich bewerben, wetteifern um; streitig machen, bestreiten, in Frage stellen, nicht gelten lassen; *(Wahl)* anfechten; debattieren über; *itr* streiten, kämpfen (*with, against s.o.* mit jdm); *s* ['kɔntest] Kampf, Streit; Wettkampf, -streit, -bewerb, -eifer (*for* um); Wortwechsel *m*; Ausea.setzung *f*; Preisausschreiben *n*; **~able** [-əbl] bestreitbar, anfechtbar; **~ant** [-ənt] Wettkämpfer; Kandidat; Bewerber *m*; streitende Partei *f*; **~ation** [kɔntes'teiʃən] Streit, Disput *m*.

context ['kɔntekst] (Satz-, Sinn-)Zs.hang; Wortlaut, Text *m*; Milieu *n*; *fam* Gehalt *m*; *in this ~* in diesem Zs.hang; *out of its ~* aus dem Zs.hang (gerissen), zs.hanglos *adv*; **~ual** [kən'tekstjuəl] *a* Kontext-; **~ure** [-'tekstʃə] Gewebe *n*; (Auf-)Bau *m*, Struktur *f*, Gefüge *n*, Zs.setzung, Gliederung *f*.

contigu|ity [kɔnti'gju(:)iti] Berührung *f*, Angrenzen *n* (*to* an); unmittelbare Nähe, Nachbarschaft *f*; **~ous** [kən'tigjuəs] berührend (*to s.th.* etw), in Berührung (*to* mit); angrenzend (*to* an), benachbart (*to* dat).

continen|ce, -cy ['kɔntinəns(i)] Enthaltsamkeit, Genügsamkeit, Mäßigkeit; Keuschheit *f*; **~t** [-t] *a* beherrscht, zurückhaltend; enthaltsam, genügsam, mäßig; keusch, tugendsam; *s* Festland *n*, Kontinent *m*; **~tal** [kɔnti'nentl] *a* kontinental, Land-; Kontinental-, Festlands-; *hist* amerikanisch; *s* Bewohner *m* des Kontinents; *~~ climate* Landklima *n*; *C~~ Divide* Wasserscheide *f* zwischen Atlantischem u. Stillem Ozean; *~~ drift (geol)* Kontinentalverschiebung *f*; *~~ shelf* Festlandssockel *m*.

contingen|ce, -cy [kən'tindʒəns(i)] Möglichkeit; Unsicherheit, Ungewißheit, Zufälligkeit *f*; Zufall *m*, Ereignis *n*, Eventualität *f*; *pl* unvorhergesehene Ausgaben *f pl*; **~t** [-t] *a* möglich, eventuell; unsicher, ungewiß; zufällig; abhängig (*on, upon* von); bedingt; eingeschränkt zutreffend *od* gültig; unwesentlich, unerheblich; *s* Kontingent *n*, Quote *f*, Anteil *m*; Gruppe, Anzahl *f*; *~~ fee* Erfolgshonorar *n*; *~~ reserve (com)* Rücklage *f* für unvorhergesehene Verluste.

continu|able [kən'tinjuəbl] *Am* fortsetzbar; **~al** [-əl] wiederholt, immer wiederkehrend; fortwährend, beständig, dauernd; unaufhörlich, ununterbrochen; **~ally** *adv* immer wieder; ohne Unterbrechung; **~ance** [-əns] *nur sing* Dauer, Zeit (*of* gen); Fortdauer, *f*, -bestehen *n*; Fortführung *f*, Fortbestand *m*; Bleiben *n* (*in a place* an e-m Ort), (weiterer) Aufenthalt *m*; Folge; *jur* Vertagung *f*; **~ation** [-'eiʃən] Fortsetzung, Weiterführung, Wiederaufnahme; Fortdauer *f*, -bestehen *n*, -bestand *m*; Ausdehnung; Ergänzung, Erweiterung *f*, Zusatz *m*; Verlängerung, *com* Prolongation *f*; *~~ school* Fortbildungs-, Abendschule *f*; **~e** [kən'tinju:] *tr* fortsetzen, fortfahren mit; verlängern, ausdehnen; (bei)behalten; *jur* vertagen; *itr* fortfahren, weitermachen, fortdauern, anhalten; (ver)bleiben; weiterhin sein, sich weiterhin befinden; weitergehen, nicht abge-, nicht unterbrochen werden, fortgesetzt, fortgeführt werden; sich fortsetzen, sich (weiter) erstrecken; wieder anfangen, fortfahren; *to ~~ on (o.'s way)* weiterfahren, -reisen; *to ~~ to do s.th.* weiterhin etw tun; *to ~~ to work, to ~~ working* weiterarbeiten; *to be ~ed* Fortsetzung folgt; *~~! mil* weitermachen! **~ity** [kɔnti'nju(:)iti] (Fort-)Dauer, Beständigkeit, Stetigkeit; natürliche Folge *f*, Zs.hang *m*; *film* Drehbuch *n*; *radio* verbindende Worte *n pl*, Ansage *f*, (Sende-)Manuskript *n*; *el* Durchgang *m*; *in ~~* im Zs.hang, in der richtigen Reihenfolge; *out of ~~* nicht im Zs.hang, nicht in der natürlichen *od* gegebenen Reihenfolge; *~~ of programme* Sendefolge *f*; **~ous** [-'tinjuəs] zs.hängend, durchgehend, -laufend, *scient* kontinuierlich; stetig, beständig, fortlaufend, ununterbrochen; *~~ current (el)* Gleichstrom *m*; *~~ operation* Dauerbetrieb *m*; *~~ output* Dauerleistung *f*; *~~ performance (film)* ununterbrochene Vorstellung *f*; **~um** [-əm] *pl -ua* zs.hängende Reihe *f*, einheitliche(s) Ganze(s) *n*.

contort [kən'tɔ:t] *tr* verdrehen, verzerren *a. fig*; *tech* verformen; *~ed with anger, pain* wut-, schmerzverzerrt; **~ion** [-'tɔ:ʃən] Verzerrung, Verdrehung *(bes. des Körpers)*; *tech* Verformung *f*; **~ionist** [-'tɔ:ʃnist] Schlangenmensch; *fig pej* Verdrehungskünstler, Wortverdreher *m*.

contour ['kɔntuə] *tr* umreißen; *tech* formen, profilieren; *geog* e-r Höhenlinie folgen lassen; *s* Rand(linie *f*); Umriß(linie *f*) *m*; Kontur *f*; ~ **farming** Pflügen *n* entlang den Höhenlinien; ~ **line** *geog* Isohypse, Schicht-, Höhenlinie; *tech* Profillinie *f*; ~ **map** Höhenschichtkarte *f*.

contra ['kɔntrə] *adv* dagegen; im Gegensatz dazu, im Gegenteil; *s* Gegenteil *n*; *com* Haben-, Kreditseite *f*; *tr com* zurückbuchen, stornieren.

contraband ['kɔntrəbænd] *s* Schmuggel, Schleichhandel *m*; Schmuggelware, Konterbande *f*; *a* Schmuggel-.

contrabass ['kɔntrə'beis] *mus* Kontrabaß *m*.

contracept|ion [kɔntrə'sepʃən] Empfängnis-, Schwangerschaftsverhütung *f*; **~ive** [-tiv] *a* u. *s* empfängnisverhütend(es Mittel *n*).

contract [kən'trækt] *tr* zs.ziehen *a. physiol (Muskel)*, verkürzen; enger machen, einengen; erwerben, erlangen; *(Gewohnheit)* annehmen; *(Krankheit)* bekommen, sich zuziehen, *fam* kriegen, sich holen; *(Freundschaft)* schließen; *(Ehe)* eingehen; *(Bekanntschaft)* machen; *(Verpflichtung)* übernehmen; *(Schulden)* machen, eingehen; *(Anleihe)* aufnehmen; *a.* ['kɔntrækt] *(Vertrag)* (ab)schließen, eingehen; *itr* sich zs.ziehen; zs.schrumpfen, einlaufen; enger werden, sich verenge(r)n; *fig* (ein-, ver-) schrumpfen; *a.* ['kɔntrækt] e-n Vertrag abschließen, sich vertraglich verpflichten, kontrahieren; *to ~~ for s.th.* etw vertraglich übernehmen; *to ~ out of s.th.* sich von etw freimachen; *s* ['kɔntrækt] Vertrag *m*, Abkommen *n*, Kontrakt *m*, Übereinkunft, Vereinbarung *f*; Akkord; Abschluß; (Liefer-, Werk-)Vertrag *m*; *com* Submission *f*; vereinbarte(r) Preis; *com* Schlußschein *m*, -note; *rail (~ ticket)* Zeitkarte *f*; *according to, as agreed by, per, under ~* wie vereinbart, laut Vertrag *od* Vereinbarung, vertragsgemäß; *by ~* vertraglich; *to accede to a ~* e-m Vertrag beitreten; *to be under an obligation of ~* vertraglich verpflichtet sein; *to bind o.s. by ~* sich vertraglich binden *od* festlegen; *to break a ~* e-n Vertrag brechen; *to buy on ~* fest kaufen; *to cancel, to annul a ~* e-n Vertrag annullieren, aufheben; *to come under a ~* unter e-n Vertrag fallen; *to execute, to fulfil, to perform a ~* e-n Vertrag erfüllen; *to give out by ~* in Submission vergeben; *to invalidate a ~* e-n Vertrag für nichtig, ungültig erklären; *to make, to pass a ~* e-n Vertrag abschließen; *to ratify a ~* e-n Vertrag ratifizieren; *to violate a ~* e-n Vertrag verletzen; *to withdraw, to recede from, to repudiate a ~* von e-m Vertrag zurücktreten;

article of a ~ Vertragsbestimmung *f*; *breach of* ~ Vertragsbruch *m*; *collective labo(u)r* ~ Tarifvertrag *m*; *conclusion, consummation of a* ~ Vertragsabschluß *m*; *draft (of a)* ~ Vertragsentwurf *m*; *labo(u)r* ~ Arbeits-, Dienstvertrag *m*; *marriage* ~ Ehevertrag *m*; *party to a* ~ Vertragspartei *f*; *preliminary* ~ Vorvertrag *m*; *verbal* ~ mündliche Vereinbarung *f*; *violation of a* ~ Vertragsverletzung *f*; ~ *of apprenticeship* Lehrvertrag *m*; ~ *of arbitration* Schiedsvertrag *m*; ~ *of carriage* Frachtvertrag *m*; ~ *for delivery* Lieferungsvertrag *m*; ~ *of employment* Arbeits-, Anstellungsvertrag *m*; ~ *of hiring* Mietvertrag *m*; ~ *of insurance* Versicherungsvertrag *m*; ~ *of purchase* Kaufvertrag *m*; ~ *of sale* Kaufvertrag *m*; ~ *of service* Dienst-, Arbeitsvertrag *m*; ~ *of tenancy, of lease* Pachtvertrag *m*; ~ *of warranty* Garantievertrag *m*; ~ **clause** Vertragsklausel, -bestimmung *f*; ~**ed** [-id] *a* zs.gezogen, verkürzt; (ein)geschrumpft; verengt; *fig* engstirnig, -herzig; erworben; ~~ *price* vereinbarte(r), Lieferpreis *m*; ~**ibility** [kəntrækti'biliti] Zs.ziehbarkeit *f*; ~**ible** [kən'træktibl] zs.ziehbar; ~**ility** [kɔntræk'tiliti] Fähigkeit *f*, sich zs.zuziehen; ~**ile** [kən'træktail, -il] zs.ziehbar; Zs.ziehung bewirkend; ~**ing** [-iŋ] vertragschließend, kontrahierend; *capable of* ~~ geschäftsfähig; ~**ion** [kən'trækʃən] Zs.ziehung, Verkürzung; Einengung; *fig* Schrumpfung; *gram* Kontraktion *f*, zs.gezogene(s) Wort *n*; ~**ive** [-iv] zs.ziehend; ~ **note** Schlußschein *m*, -note *f*; ~**or** [kən'træktə, *Am* 'kɔntræktə] Vertragschließende(r), Kontrahent; Lieferant, (Bau-)Unternehmer *m*; *anat* Schließmuskel *m*; ~**ual** [kən'træktjuəl] vertraglich; vertragsmäßig; Vertrags-; ~~ *obligations (pl)* Vertragspflichten *f pl*; ~ **work** Akkordarbeit *f*.

contradict [kɔntrə'dikt] *tr* widersprechen (*s.o.* jdm), Lügen strafen; für falsch, unrichtig erklären, leugnen; im Widerspruch stehen (*s.o., s.th.* zu jdm, zu e-r S), unvereinbar sein (*s.th.* mit e-r S); ~**ion** [-kʃən] Widerspruch *m*, Widerrede *f*; Leugnen *n*; Unvereinbarkeit *f*; innere(r) Widerspruch *m*; ~**ious** [-kʃəs] zu Widerspruch neigend, streitsüchtig, rechthaberisch; ~**ive** [-iv], ~**ory** [-əri] (sich) widersprechend, widerspruchsvoll; zu Widerspruch neigend; ~**oriness** [-ərinis] Widersprüchlichkeit *f*, Widerspruch *m* (*to* zu); Unvereinbarkeit *f* (*to* mit).

contradistinction [kɔntrədis'tiŋkʃən] Gegensatz *m*, Gegenüberstellung *f*; *in* ~~ *to* im Gegensatz zu.

contrail ['kɔntreil] *aero* Kondensstreifen *m (e-s Strahltriebwerks)*.

contralto [kən'træltou] *pl* -*os* Alt(stimme *f*) *m*; Altistin *f*.

contraption [kən'træpʃən] *fam hum pej* komische(s), ulkige(s) Ding(s) *n*; komische(r) Apparat *m*, ulkige Kiste *f*, Monstrum, Mords-, tolle(s) Ding *n*.

contrapuntal [kɔntrə'pʌntl] *mus* kontrapunktisch.

contrar|iety [kɔntrə'raiəti, -iti] Gegensätzlichkeit *f*; Gegensatz, Widerspruch *m* (*to* zu); Widrigkeit *f*, Hindernis, Hemmnis *n*; ~**ily** ['kɔntrərili] *adv* entgegen; andererseits; ~**iness** ['kɔntrərinis] Gegensätzlichkeit; Widrigkeit, Ungunst; Andersartigkeit, Eigenart *f* [*a.* kən'trɛərinis] *fam* Eigensinn *m*; ~**iwise** ['kɔntrəriwaiz] *adv* ander(er)seits; im Gegenteil; (ganz) anders; ~**y** ['kɔntrəri] *a* entgegengesetzt; widrig, ungünstig, hinderlich, hemmend; [*a.* kən'trɛəri] *fam* verbohrt; bockig; widerspenstig; *s* Gegenteil *n*; (*to* von); *adv*: ~~ *to* entgegen *dat*, gegen; *on the* ~~ im Gegenteil; *to the* ~~ im entgegengesetzten Sinn, in entgegengesetzter Absicht; *proof to the* ~~ Gegenbeweis *m*; ~~ *to expectations* wider Erwarten; ~~ *to order, to rule* befehls-, regelwidrig.

contrast [kən'træst, -trɑ:st] *tr (Gegensätzliches)* vergleichen (*with* mit); gegenüberstellen (*with* dat), in Gegensatz stellen (*with* zu); *itr* sich (stark) abheben (*with* von), abstechen (*with* von, gegen), kontrastieren; im Widerspruch stehen (*with* zu); *s* ['kɔntræst, -trɑ:st] Gegenüberstellung, Kontrastierung *f*; (großer) Unterschied, Gegensatz (*to* zu); Kontrast *m*; (~ *effect)* Kontrastwirkung *f*; *by* ~ *with* im Vergleich zu; *in* ~ *to* im Gegensatz zu; ~**y** [-'træsti, -'trɑ:sti] *phot* kontrastreich, hart.

contraven|e [kɔntrə'vi:n] *tr* zuwiderhandeln (*s.th.* e-r S); *(Gesetz)* übertreten, verstoßen (*a law* gegen ein Gesetz); *(Bestimmung, Vorschrift)* nicht beachten; widersprechen (*s.th.* e-r S), in Abrede stellen, Stellung nehmen (*s.th.* gegen etw); widerstreiten (*s.th.* e-r S), im Widerspruch stehen (*s.th.* zu e-r S); ~**tion** [-'venʃən] Zuwiderhandlung *f*, Verstoß *m*, Zuwiderhandlung (*of* gegen), Nichtbeachtung *f*; Widerspruch; Widerstreit *m*.

contribut|e [kən'tribju:t] *tr* geben (*to* für), beitragen, zuschießen, beisteuern *a. fig*; *(e-n Beitrag)* liefern; *(Energie)* abgeben, zuführen; *itr* mitwirken, helfen (*to* bei); spenden; unterstützen, fördern (*to s.th.* etw); *com* in ein Geschäft einbringen; *to* ~~ *to a newspaper* an e-r Zeitung mitarbeiten; ~**ion** [kɔntri'bju:ʃən] Mitwirkung *f*; Beitrag *m* (*to* zu) *(a. lit, Zeitung)*; Einlage; Spende; Beitragsleistung, Beisteuer; Zwangsauflage; (Kriegs-)Kontribution, Kriegssteuer *f*; eingebrachte(s) Gut *n*; ~~ *of capital* Kapitaleinlage *f*; ~~ *in kind* Naturalleistung *f*; ~~ *period* Beitragsabschnitt *m*; ~**ive** [-tiv] mitwirkend, beitragend; ~**or** [-ə] Beitragende(r); *(Buch, Zeitung)* Mitarbeiter *m*; ~**ory** [-əri] *a* beitragend (*to* zu); mitwirkend (*to* an); mitverursachend; Beitrags-; Kontributions-; *s* Miturheber *m*, -ursache *f*; Beitragspflichtige(r) *m*.

contrit|e ['kɔntrait] zerknirscht, schuldbewußt; reumütig, bußfertig; ~**ion** [kən'triʃən] Zerknirschung *f*, Schuldbewußtsein *n*; Reue, Bußfertigkeit *f*.

contriv|ance [kən'traivəns] Erfindung(sgabe); Findigkeit *f*; Plan, Entwurf, Gedanke *m*, Idee *f*, Kunstgriff, Kniff, Dreh *m*; Erfindung *(Sache)*, Vorrichtung *f*, Apparat *m*; ~**e** [kən'traiv] *tr* ausdenken, ersinnen, ausklügeln, -tüfteln; erfinden; planen, entwerfen; zustande, zuwege bringen, bewerkstelligen, einrichten (*to do, that* mit Konj.); *itr* es dahin, es soweit, es fertigbringen; (gut) haushalten, wirtschaften; Pläne schmieden; e-e Erfindung machen; *I* ~*ed to meet him* es gelang mir, ihn zu treffen; ~**er** [-ə] erfinderische(r) Mensch, findige(r) Kopf; haushälterische(r) Mensch *m*, (gute) Hausfrau *f*; *to be a good* ~~ gut wirtschaften können.

control [kən'troul] *tr* beherrschen, in s-r Gewalt haben, die Gewalt haben über; in Händen haben; e-n beherrschenden, entscheidenden Einfluß haben auf; leiten, lenken, dirigieren, bewirtschaften, steuern; in Schranken, zurückhalten; zügeln, mäßigen, eindämmen, einschränken; beaufsichtigen, überwachen; prüfen, kontrollieren; *tech* regulieren, regeln, steuern; schalten; *aero* führen, steuern; *s* Herrschaft, Gewalt, Macht (*of* über); Beherrschung *f*, beherrschende(r), entscheidende(r) Einfluß *m* (*of* auf); Leitung, Lenkung, Führung, Steuerung, Regulierung, Regelung; Bewirtschaftung; Zurückhaltung, Zügelung, Mäßigung, Einschränkung; Aufsicht (*of, over* über), Beaufsichtigung, Überwachung; Kontrolle *f*, Kontrollorgan, Mittel *n* zur Kontrolle; *tech* Regulierung, Steuerung, Betätigung, Bedienung; Schaltung *f*, Regler *m*; *aero* Führung, Steuerung; *pl tech aero* Steuerung; *el* Armatur *f*; *aero* Leitwerk *n*; *out of* ~ herren-, führerlos (geworden); der Steuerung entzogen, ungesteuert; *under* ~ unter Aufsicht *od* Kontrolle; *under government* ~ unter staatlicher Aufsicht; *without* ~ uneingeschränkt; *to gain, to get* ~ *of, over* in s-e Gewalt bekommen, die Herrschaft gewinnen über; *to get, to bring under* ~ unter Kontrolle bringen; *to lose* ~ *of, over* die Gewalt, die Herrschaft verlieren über; *to relax, to tighten the* ~ die Kontrolle lockern, verschärfen; *to* ~ *from a distance* fernsteuern; *parental* ~ elterliche Gewalt *od* Aufsicht *f*; *price* ~ Preisüberwachung *f*; *remote* ~ Fernlenkung *f*; *volume* ~ *(radio)* Lautstärkeregler *m*; ~ *of the air, sea (mil)* Luft-, Seeherrschaft *f*; ~ **board** Kontroll-, Bewirtschaftungsstelle; *tech* Überwachungs-, *el radio* Schalttafel *f*; ~ **cabin** Führerstand *m*, *aero* -kanzel *f*; ~ **cable** *aero* Steuerseil *n*, Bowdenzug *m*; ~ **clock** Kontrolluhr *f*; ~ **column** *aero* Steuersäule *f*; ~ **desk** Steuer-, Schaltpult *n*; ~ **experiment** Kontrollversuch *m*; ~ **fund** Ausgleichsfonds *m*; ~ **gear** Steuergetriebe, -gestänge *n*; ~ **knob, switch** Bedienungs-, Betätigungsknopf, -schalter *m*; ~**lability** [-ə'biliti] Lenkbarkeit; Kontrollierbarkeit; Steuerfähigkeit *f*; ~**lable** [-əbl] lenkbar; regulierbar; kontrollierbar; *(Luftschraube)* verstellbar; ~**led** [-d] *a* überwacht, kontrolliert; bewirtschaftet; *state*-~~ unter staatlicher Kontrolle *od* Aufsicht; ~~ *company* Tochter(gesellschaft) *f*; ~~ *distribution* Absatzlenkung *f*; ~~ *economy* gelenkte Wirtschaft *f*; ~**ler** [-ə] Leiter; Aufseher, Aufsichtsbeamte(r), Inspektor, Überwacher, Aufsichtführende(r); Geschäftsführer; *Am* Leiter des Rechnungswesens; Kontrolleur; *mil* Leitoffizier; *aero* Flugsicherungslotse; *el* Steuer-, Fahrschalter, Regler *m*; Steuergerät *n*; ~ **lever** Schalt-, Bedienungs-, Betätigungshebel *m*; ~ **light** Kontrollampe *f*; ~ **officer** Kontroll-, Aufsichtsbeamte(r) *m*; ~ **panel** Bedienungsanlage *f*; Schaltbrett *n*, -tafel *f*; ~ **point** Orientierungs-, Kontrollpunkt *m*; *mil* Meldestelle *f*; ~ **post** Befehlsstelle *f*; Kontrollposten *m*; ~ **room** *aero* Kommando-, *radio* Regieraum *m*; Befehlszentrale *f*; Prüfraum *m*; ~ **sheet** Kontrollzettel *m*; ~ **station** Kommando-, Bedienungsstand *m*; *mar* Zentrale *f*; ~ **stick** *aero* Steuerknüppel *m*; ~ **surface** Steuerfläche *f*, Ruder *n*; ~ **system** Kontrollsystem *n*; *aero* Steuerung(sanlage) *f*, Fliegerleitverfahren *n*; ~ **test** Prüfmessung *f*; ~ **tower** *aero* Kontroll-, Flugleitungsturm *m*; ~ **valve** *aero* Regelventil *n*; *radio* Steuerröhre *f*.

controvers|ial [kɔntrə'vəːʃəl] strittig, streitig, umstritten; Streit-; polemisch, streitlustig; rechthaberisch; *to be highly* ~~ stark umstritten sein; **~ialist** [-ist] Polemiker; streitsüchtige(r) Mensch *m*; **~y** ['kɔntrəvəːsi] Streitfrage *f*, -punkt, -fall *m*; strittige Frage, Kontroverse *f*; (Wort-) Streit, Disput *m*, (erregte) Debatte; Polemik *f*; *beyond* ~~ über jeden Streit *od* Zweifel erhaben; feststehend.
controvert ['kɔntrəvəːt] *tr* bestreiten, in Frage stellen; zu widerlegen suchen; argumentieren gegen; widersprechen (*s.th.* e-r S); diskutieren, debattieren; **~ible** [-'vəːtəbl] bestreitbar, anfechtbar, widerlegbar.
contumac|ious [kɔntju(ː)'meiʃəs] widerspenstig, halsstarrig; widersetzlich, unbotmäßig; *jur* trotz (Vor-)Ladung nicht erschienen; **~y** ['kɔntjuməsi] Widersetzlichkeit, Unbotmäßigkeit *f*; (vorsätzliches) Nichterscheinen *n* (vor Gericht) trotz (Vor-)Ladung.
contumel|ious [kɔntju(ː)'miːliəs] unverschämt, anmaßend; höhnisch; beleidigend; **~y** ['kɔntju(ː)mli] Unverschämtheit *f*, anmaßende(s) Wesen *n*; Hohn *m*, Verhöhnung, Beleidigung *f*.
contus|e [kən'tjuːz] *tr med* quetschen, prellen; **~ion** [-'tjuːʒən] Quetschung, Prellung *f*.
conundrum [kə'nʌndrəm] (Scherz-) Rätsel *n*, Scherzfrage; knifflige Frage *f*, Problem *n*.
conurbation [kɔnəː'beiʃən] Groß(siedlungs)raum *m*; gesamte(s) Siedlungsgebiet *n* e-r Großstadt.

*

convalesc|e [kɔnvə'les] *itr* genesen, (wieder) gesund werden; *he is ~ing* es geht ihm (wieder) besser; **~ence** [-ns] Genesung(szeit), Rekonvaleszenz *f*; **~ent** [-nt] *a* genesend; Genesungs-; *s* Genesende(r *m*) *f*, Rekonvaleszent(in *f*) *m*; ~~ *home, hospital* Genesungsheim *n*; ~~ *leave* Genesungsurlaub *m*.
convect|ion [kən'vekʃən] *phys (Wärme) el* Leitung, Übertragung, Fortpflanzung, Strömung, Konvektion *f*; **~ive** [-tiv] leitend; Konvektions-; **~or** [-tə] *el* Leiter; Konvektionsofen *m*.
conven|e [kən'viːn] *itr* zs.kommen, -treten, sich versammeln; *tr* zs.kommen lassen; *(e-e Versammlung)* einberufen; *jur* (vor)laden (*before the court* vor Gericht); **~er** [-ə] Versammlungsteilnehmer; Einberufende(r) *m*.
convenien|ce [kən'viːnjəns] Geeignetheit; Bequemlichkeit, Annehmlichkeit; Erleichterung *f*; Vorteil *m*; *meist pl* praktische Dinge *n pl*, Komfort *m*; Waschgelegenheit *f*; Klosett *n*; *at your earliest* ~~ möglichst bald; *at your (own)* ~~ wann es Ihnen recht ist *od* paßt; *to make a ~~ of s.o.* jdn ausnutzen; *marriage of* ~~ Verstandesheirat *f*; *(public)* ~~ Bedürfnisanstalt *f*; ~~ *goods (pl)* Waren *f pl* des täglichen Bedarfs; **~t** [-t] passend, geeignet; angebracht; vorteilhaft; genehm, bequem; *(Zeit)* gelegen; *(Ort)* bequem gelegen *od* zu erreichen(d); *(Werkzeug, Gerät)* praktisch, leicht zu handhaben(d); *if it is ~~ for you* wenn es Ihnen paßt *od* recht ist.
convent ['kɔnvənt] (*meist* Nonnen-) Kloster *n*; *to go into a ~ (Mädchen)* ins Kloster gehen; **~icle** [kən'ventikl] Konventikel *n*, (außerkirchliche) Betstunde *f*; **~ion** [kən'venʃən] Zs.kunft, Versammlung *f*, Treffen *n*; *bes. Am* Tag(ung *f*), Kongreß; *Am pol* Parteitag *m*; Übereinkommen, Abkommen *n*, Vereinbarung, Konvention *f*, Vertrag *m*; (allgemeine) Übereinkunft; Sitte *f*, Brauch *m*, Gewohnheit *f*; Herkommen *n*, Tradition *f*; **~ional** [-'venʃənl] konventionell, förmlich; üblich, gewöhnlich, gebräuchlich, herkömmlich, traditionell; vereinbart, vertraglich, vertragsgemäß; ~~ *sign* Kartenzeichen, Symbol *n*; **~ionalism** [-'venʃnəlizm] Hängen, Festhalten *n* am Hergebrachten; Förmlichkeit *f*; **~ionality** [kənvenʃə'næliti] förmliche(s) Wesen *n*, Traditionsgebundenheit *f*; förmliche(s) Verhalten *n*, Förmlichkeit; *a. pl* Form, Sitte *f*, Brauch *m*; Umgangsformen *f pl*; **~ionalize** [-'venʃnəlaiz] *tr* konventionell gestalten; *(Kunst)* in der üblichen, hergebrachten Form darstellen.
converg|e [kən'vəːdʒ] *itr math* konvergieren, zs.laufen; *allg* aufea., auf einen Punkt zustreben, sich näher kommen; sich schneiden (*at* bei); *tr* zs.laufen lassen; **~ence, -cy** [-əns(i)] *math* Konvergenz(punkt *m*); *allg* Annäherung *f*; **~ent** [-ənt] konvergierend, zs.laufend; aufea. zustrebend; *tech* sich verjüngend; **~ing** [-iŋ]: ~~ *lens (opt)* Sammellinse *f*.
convers|able [kən'vəːsəbl] um-, zugänglich, leutselig; gesprächig, redselig, unterhaltsam; Gesprächs-; **~ance, -cy** [kən'vəːsəns(i), 'kɔnvəsəns(i)] Vertrautheit, Bekanntschaft, Erfahrung *f* (*with* mit); **~ant** [kən'vəːsənt, 'kɔnvəsənt] vertraut, bekannt (*with* mit); erfahren (*with* in); *to be* ~~ auf dem laufenden sein (*with* mit); **~ation** [kɔnvə'seiʃən] Gespräch *n*, Unterhaltung *f*; *obs* Umgang, Verkehr *m*; *obs u. Am* Vertrautheit, Erfahrung *f*; *by way of* ~~ gesprächsweise; *to enter into a* ~~ ein Gespräch anknüpfen; *criminal ~~ (jur)* Ehebruch *m*; ~~ *piece* Genrebild; *allg* interessante(s) Möbelstück *n*; **~ational** [-(ə)l] gesprächig, unterhaltsam, redselig; Gesprächs-, Unterhaltungs-; Umgangs-; ~~ *style* Umgangssprache *f*; **~ation(al)ist** [-'seiʃn(əl)ist] unterhaltsame(r), gesprächige(r) Mensch *m*; **~ationally** [-ʃnəli] *adv* in der Unterhaltung, gesprächsweise; **~e** *itr* [kən'vəːs] sprechen, sich unterhalten (*with s.o. on, about s.th.* mit jdm über etw); ['kɔnvəːs] *a* entgegengesetzt, umgekehrt; *s* Unterhaltung *f*; Umgang; Gegensatz *m*, Umkehrung *f*; **~ion** [kən'vəːʃən] Umwandlung (*from* von; *into* in); Umstellung; *tech* Umformung; *rel* Bekehrung, Konversion *f*, Übertritt *m*; *fin* Konvertierung *f*, Umtausch *m*; Ablösung; Umschuldung; *math* Umkehrung; *jur* widerrechtliche Aneignung *f*; ~~ *rate* Umrechnungskurs *m*; ~~ *stocks (pl)* Wandelanleihen *f pl*; ~~ *table* Umrechnungstabelle *f*; ~~ *training* Umschulung *f*.
convert [kən'vəːt] *tr* ver-, umwandeln (*into* in); umbauen, -formen; umrechnen (*to* auf); umschulen; *rel allg* bekehren (*to* zu); *fin* umtauschen, wechseln, konvertieren, umstellen, einlösen; zu Geld machen; sich (unrechtmäßig) aneignen, unterschlagen; *tech* umformen, umsetzen (*into* in), windfrischen; *s* ['kɔnvəːt] *rel* Konvertit, Übergetretene(r), Bekehrte(r) *m*; *(~ brother, sister)* Laienbruder *m*, -schwester *f*; **~er, ~or** [kən'vəːtə] Bekehrer; *tech* Konverter *m*, Bessemerbirne *f*; *el* Umformer; *el* Überlagerer *m*; Chiffriermaschine *f*; *mil* Umwertegerät *n*; *com* Kaufmann *m*, der die Ware noch bearbeitet; ~~ *plant, station* Umformeranlage *f*, -werk *n*; ~~ *process* Bessemerverfahren *n*; ~~ *tube, valve* Mischröhre *f*; **~ibility** [kənvəːtə'biliti] Umwandelbarkeit; *fin* Konvertierbarkeit, Einlösbarkeit *f*; **~ible** [kən'vəːtəbl] *a* umwandelbar; *fin* konvertierbar; einlösbar; *s mot* Kabrio(-lett) *n*; ~~ *bonds (pl)* Wandelschuldverschreibungen *f pl*; ~~ *husbandry* Fruchtwechselwirtschaft *f*.
convex ['kɔn'veks] *bes. opt a* konvex, erhaben, (nach außen) gewölbt; **~ity** [kən'veksiti] konvexe Form *f*.
convey [kən'vei] *tr* befördern, transportieren, verfrachten, (über-, weg-) bringen, hinschaffen; *(el Strom)* leiten; mitteilen; *(Nachricht)* übermitteln; *(Sinn, Gedanken)* vermitteln; *(Trost)* spenden; *(Eigentum, Vermögen)* übertragen, abtreten, übereignen (*to* an), *to ~ movement to s.th.* etw in Bewegung setzen; **~ance** [-əns] Beförderung *f*, Transport *m*, Spedition; *tech* Zuführung, Leitung; Übermitt(e)lung, Mitteilung; *jur* Übertragung, Abtretung, Übereignung, Auflassung; Fahrgelegenheit *f*; Beförderungsmittel, Fahrzeug *n*; *(deed of ~~)* Übertragungsurkunde *f*; ~~ *by agreement (jur)* Auflassung *f*; ~~ *insurance* Transportversicherung *f*; ~~ *of passengers* Personenbeförderung *f*; ~~ *of property* Eigentumsübertragung *f*; **~ancer** [-ənsə] Notar *m* für Eigentumsübertragungen; **~er, ~or** [kən'veiə] Übermittler, Beförderer; Fuhrunternehmer, Spediteur; *tech* Förderer *m*, Förderband *n*, -streifen *m*, -anlage *f*; ~~ *belt* laufende(s) Band, Fließ-, Förderband *n*; **~ing** [-iŋ] *s* Beförderung *f*, Transport *m*; *tech* Förderung *f*; *a* Förder-, Transport-; ~~ *capacity* Förderleistung *f*; ~~ *plant* Förderanlage *f*.
convict ['kɔnvikt] *s* Verurteilte(r); Sträfling, Strafgefangene(r), Zuchthäusler *m*; *tr* [kən'vikt] überführen (*of a crime* e-s Verbrechens); für schuldig befinden *od* erklären; verurteilen (*on a criminal charge* wegen e-r strafbaren Handlung; *of murder* wegen Mords); *Am (fälschlich)* überzeugen; *former ~* Rückfällige(r), Vorbestrafte(r) *m*; **~ion** [kən'vikʃən] *jur* Überführung; Schuldigsprechung, Verurteilung; (feste) Überzeugung *f*; *by ~~* aus Überzeugung; *in the (full) ~~ that* in der (vollen) Überzeugung, daß; *(up)on ~~ (jur)* nach Überführung; *to be open to ~~* sich überzeugen lassen; *to carry* ~~ überzeugend wirken; *to have a previous* ~~ vorbestraft sein (*for* wegen); *former, previous* ~~ Vorstrafe *f*.
convinc|e [kən'vins] *tr* überzeugen (*of* von); *to be ~~d (of)* überzeugt sein (von); *to ~~ o.s. (of)* sich überzeugen (von); **~ible** [-ibl] überzeugbar, zu überzeugen(d); **~ing** [-iŋ] überzeugend, schlagend; beweiskräftig.
convivial [kən'viviəl] festlich; Fest-; gesellig(keitsliebend), unterhaltend, -haltsam; heiter, fröhlich, lustig; *fam* angesäuselt; *to be ~* gern in Gesellschaft sein; **~ity** [-'æliti] Geselligkeit; Unterhaltsamkeit; Fröhlichkeit *(bei Tisch)*; Festesfreude *f*; Tafelfreuden *f pl*.
convocation [kɔnvə'keiʃən] Einberufung *(e-r Versammlung)*; Zs.kunft, Versammlung; (Kirchen-)Synode *f*; *(Universität)* Konzil *n*.
convoke [kən'vouk] *tr* zs.rufen, zs.-kommen lassen; *(Versammlung)* einberufen.
convol|ute ['kɔnvəl(j)uːt] *tr itr* (sich) ein-, (sich) zs.rollen; *a (a. ~uted)* ein-, zs.gerollt *bes. bot*; **~ution** [-'luːʃən] Ein-, Zs.rollen, -wickeln *n*; Windung; Einrollung *f*, Eingerollte(s) *n*; *(~~ of the brain)* Gehirnwindung *f*; **~ve** [kən'vɔlv] *s. ~ute tr itr*; **~vulus** [kən'vɔlvjuləs] *bot* Winde *f*.

convoy [kən'vɔi] *tr bes. mar (Kriegsschiff)* geleiten, eskortieren; *s* ['kɔnvɔi] (Schutz-)Geleit *n*; *mil* (LKW-)Kolonne; *mil* Eskorte *f*; Geleitschiffe *n pl*, -mannschaften *f pl*; Geleitzug, Konvoi *m*;
convuls|e [kən'vʌls] *tr lit* in Zuckungen versetzen; erschüttern *a. fig*; *(Gesicht)* verzerren; *to be ~ed with pain, laughter* sich vor Schmerzen, Lachen krümmen; sich verzerren (*with rage* vor Wut); **~ion** [-'vʌlʃən] Erschütterung *a. fig*; (Nerven-)Zuckung, (Muskel-)Zerrung, Verkrampfung *f*; (Lach-, Schüttel-)Krampf *m*; *to be in ~~s* sich vor Lachen biegen; *~~ of laughter* Lachanfall, -krampf *m*; **~ive** [-iv] krampfhaft, konvulsivisch; *fig* erschütternd.
cony, coney ['kouni] Kaninchen; (gefärbtes) Kanin(chenfell) *n*.

*

coo [ku:] *itr (Taube)* girren, gurren; *tr (Worte)* girren; *s* Gurren *n*; *interj Br* Mensch! *to bill and ~* zärtlich tun *od* mitea. sein; *~-~ (Am sl)* wahnsinnig, verrückt; unrealistisch.
cook [kuk] *tr itr* kochen; *tr (Essen)* zubereiten; braten, backen; *(to ~ up) fam* zs.brauen, aushecken, -brüten; *fam* verfälschen, (auf)frisieren; *(Konten)* verschleiern; *sl* kaputt machen, erledigen, verderben; *Am* auf dem elektrischen Stuhl hinrichten; *itr* sich kochen lassen; als Koch arbeiten; *Am sl* vor die Hunde gehen; *s* Koch *m*, Köchin *f*; *to ~ s.o.'s goose* jdn ruinieren; *what's ~ing? (fam Am)* was gibt's Neues? *too many ~s spoil the broth* viele Köche verderben den Brei; **~book** *Am* Kochbuch *n*; **~ee** [-'ki:] *Am fam* Lagerkoch; Küchengehilfe, -bulle *m*; *Am sl* pfundige(r) Kerl, hübsche(r) Käfer *m*; **~er** ['-ə] Kocher, Kochapparat; (Gas-, Elektro-)Herd *m*; *pl* Kochobst *n*; **~ery** ['-əri] Kochen *n*, Kochkunst, Küche *f*; *~~-book (Br)* Kochbuch *n*; **~-general** Mädchen *n* für alles; **~-house** Lagerküche, Küchenbaracke; *mar* Kombüse *f*; **~ie, ~y** ['kuki] *Am* (gefülltes) Plätzchen *n*; *mil sl* schwere(r) Brocken *m*; *Scot* süße(s) Brötchen *n*; *Am sl* Pfundskerl, hübsche(r) Käfer *m*; *~~-cutter (Am sl) (Polizei)* Knüppel; Schwächling *m*; **~ing** ['-iŋ] Kochen *n*, Küche *f*; *attr* Koch-; *~~ range, Am* **~stove** Koch-, Küchenherd *m*; **~out** ['kukaut] *Am* Abkochen *(im Freien)*; Picknick *n*; **~-shop** Speisehaus, -lokal *n*.
cool [ku:l] *a* kühl, frisch; *fig* kühl, frostig; zurückhaltend, ablehnend; kaltblütig; dreist, frech, unverschämt; *a ~ (fam) (vor e-r Zahlenangabe)* lausige, lumpige, bloß(e), nur; rund; *Am sl* verächtlich, gefühllos, intellektuell, geschmackvoll; *s* Kühle *f*; *tr itr (to ~ off)* abkühlen (lassen); *itr* kühl werden; *as ~ as a cucumber* ohne e-e Miene zu verziehen, ruhig, gelassen; *to get ~* sich abkühlen; *to keep ~* Ruhe bewahren, gelassen bleiben; *to ~ o.'s heels (fam)* sich *(bei langem Warten)* die Beine in den Leib stehen; *to ~ down, off (fig)* abkühlen, ruhiger werden; *a ~ cheek* e-e große Frechheit, e-e Unverschämtheit; *a ~ customer* ein unverschämter Kerl; **~er** ['-ə] Kühlgefäß *n*, Kühler *m*; *sl* Gefängnis *n*, Bau *m*; *wine ~~* Sektkühler *m*; **~-headed** *a* besonnen; **~ing** ['-iŋ] (Ab-)Kühlung *f*; *~~ by air* Luftkühlung *f*; *~~ rib, water* Kühlrippe *f*, -wasser *n*; *~~-off period* Stillhaltezeit *f*; **~ness** ['-nis] Kühle, Frische *f*; *fig* innere(r) Abstand *m*; Entfremdung; ruhige Sicherheit *f*.
cool|ie, ~y ['ku:li] Kuli, Tagelöhner *m (in Süd- u. Ostasien)*.
coomb, comb(e) [ku:m] enge(s) Tal *n*, Schlucht *f*.
coon [ku:n] Waschbär; *Am sl* doofe(r) Bursche; *sl pej* Nigger, Neger *m*; *a gone ~ (sl)* ein hoffnungsloser Fall, e-e verpfuschte *od* verkrachte Existenz *(Mensch)*; *a ~'s age (fam)* e-e Ewigkeit; **~ song** Negerlied *n (d. amerik. Neger)*; **~y** ['-i] *Am sl* schlau.
coop [ku:p] *s* Vogel-, *bes.* Hühnerkäfig; Kaninchenstall *m*; *sl* üble Behausung *f*, Loch *n*, Bude *f*; *sl* Kittchen *n*, Knast *m*; *aero sl* Kanzel *f*; *Am sl* Kabrio *n*; *tr (to ~ in, up)* in e-m Käfig halten; einsperren, einschließen; *to fly the ~ (Am sl)* entwischen.
co-op, coop ['kouɔp, ko(u)'ɔp] *fam (von: co-operative)* Konsum(verein) *m*.
cooper ['ku:pə] Küfer, Böttcher *m*; **~age** ['-ridʒ], **~y** ['-ri] Küferei, Böttcherei; Küfer-, Böttcherarbeit *f*.
co-operat|e [ko(u)'ɔpəreit] *itr* zs.arbeiten (*with* mit); mitarbeiten, -wirken, -helfen (*in* an); *fig* (gemeinsam) beitragen (*to* zu); hinwirken (*to* auf); **~ion** [-'reiʃən] Zs.arbeit, Mitwirkung *f*; genossenschaftliche(r) Zs.schluß *m*; Genossenschaft, Kooperative *f*; *in ~~ with* in Zs.arbeit mit; **~ive** [-'ɔpərətiv] *a* zs.arbeitend, mitwirkend; zur Zs.-arbeit bereit; genossenschaftlich; *s (~~ association, society)* Genossenschaft, Kooperative *f*; Konsum *m*; *building ~~* Baugenossenschaft *f*; *credit ~~* Kreditgenossenschaft *f*; *distributive, marketing ~~* Absatzgenossenschaft *f*; *~~ advertising* Gemeinschaftswerbung *f*; *~~ bank* Genossenschaftsbank *f*; *~~ movement* Genossenschaftsbewegung *f*; *~~ shop, store(s)* Konsum(-vereinsladen) *m*; **~or** [-ə] Mitarbeiter *m*; Genossenschafts-, Konsumvereinsmitglied *n*.
co-opt [ko(u)'ɔpt] *tr* hinzuwählen, kooptieren; **~ation** [-'teiʃən] Zu-, Ergänzungswahl, Kooptation *f*.
co-ordinat|e [ko(u)'ɔ:dinit] *a* gleichrangig, -gestellt, -geordnet; bei-, zugeordnet; *s* Beigeordnete(r) *m*; Zugeordnete(s) *n*; *math* Koordinate *f*; *tr* [ko(u)'ɔ:dineit] gleichstellen; bei-, zuordnen, koordinieren, (aufea.) abstimmen, ea. angleichen; **~ion** [ko(u)-ɔ:di'neiʃən] (rangmäßige) Gleichstellung; Zuordnung; Koordinierung, Angleichung, Abstimmung *f*.
coot [ku:t] Wasserhuhn *n*; *Am fam* Esel *m*; *as bald as a ~ (fam)* ratzekahl; **~ie** ['-i] *sl mil* (Kleider-)Laus *f*.
co-owner [ko(u)'ounə] Miteigentümer, -inhaber *m*; **~ship** [-ʃip] Miteigentum; Gemeinschaftseigentum *n*.
cop [kɔp] **1.** *(Spinnerei)* Kötzer, Garnwickel *m*; **2.** *s sl* Schupo, Polizist *m*; *tr sl* erwischen, schnappen (*at* bei); stibitzen, mausen; kapieren; *no great ~* wertlos; *to ~ the needle* auf die Palme gehen; *to ~ it* Prügel bekommen; bestraft werden; *it's a fair ~* man hat mich erwischt.
copal ['koupəl, ko(u)'pæl] Kopal *m*.
copartner ['kou'pɑ:tnə] Teilhaber; Mitbeteiligte(r) *m*; **~ship** [-ʃip] Teilhaberschaft *f*; Gesellschafts-, Genossenschaftsverhältnis *n*; Beteiligung *f*.
cope [koup] **1.** *itr* sich messen (können) (*with* mit); Herr werden *od* bleiben (*with* gen, über); gewachsen sein (*with* dat); es aufnehmen, fertigwerden (*with* mit); **2.** *rel* Chorrock; *fig* Mantel *m*, Decke, Hülle *f*; (Himmels-)Gewölbe *n*; *arch* Mauerkappe *f*; *tr* mit dem Chorrock bekleiden; *fig* bedecken, wölben; *itr* sich wölben; **~lessness** ['-lisnis] Lebensuntüchtigkeit *f*; **~-stone** *arch* Deck-, Schlußstein *a. fig*; *fig* Schlußstrich, Höhepunkt *m*.
copier ['kɔpiə] (Ab-)Schreiber, Kopist; Plagiator, Nachahmer *m*.
co-pilot ['koupailət] Kopilot, zweite(r) Flugzeugführer *m*.
coping ['koupiŋ] (Mauer-)Abdeckung; *(Talsperre)* Krone *f*; **~-stone** Abdeckplatte; *fig* Krönung *f*.
copious ['koupjəs] reich(lich), massenhaft, in Mengen; *(Stil)* wortreich, weitschweifig; **~ly** ['-li] *adv* in reichem Maße, in (Hülle u.) Fülle; **~ness** ['-nis] Fülle *f*, Reichtum *m*, Menge, Masse(nhaftigkeit); Weitschweifigkeit *f*.
copper ['kɔpə] *s* Kupfer *n*; Kupfermünze *f*; Kupferkessel *m*; Kupferfarbe *f*; *sl* Schupo, Polizist *m*; *pl* Kupferwerte *m pl*, -münzen *f pl*; *a* kupfern; kupferfarben; *tr* verkupfern; *sl* wetten (*s.th.* gegen etw); *to cool o.'s ~s* e-n hinter die Binde kippen; **~as** ['-rəs] Kupfervitriol *n*; **~-bearing** kupferhaltig; **~-beech** Blutbuche *f*; **~-bottomed** *a mar* mit Kupferboden; seetüchtig; *fig* todsicher; **~head** ['-hed] *zoo* Mokassinschlange *f*; **~-mine** Kupfermine *f*, -bergwerk *n*; **~-nose** Kupfernase *f*; **~-ore** Kupfererz *n*; **~plate** ['-pleit] *typ* Kupferplatte *f*; (Kunst *f* des) Kupferstich(s) *m*; **~-plate** *tr* verkupfern; *a (Handschrift)* wie gestochen; **~ pyrites** *min* Kupferkies *m*; **~-smith** Kupferschmied *m*; **~ sulfate** *chem* Kupfersulfat *n*; **~-top** *sl* Rothaarige(r *m*) *f*; **~ y** ['-ri] kupferig.
coppice ['kɔpis], **copse** [kɔps] Dikkicht; *(~ wood)* Unterholz *n*, (dichter) junge(r) Wald *m*.
copra ['kɔprə] Kopra *f*.
Copt [kɔpt] Kopte *m*, Koptin *f*; **~ic** ['-ik] koptisch.
copula ['kɔpjulə] Band *a. anat*, Bindeglied *n*; *gram* Kopula *f*; **~te** ['kɔpjuleit] *itr* sich paaren; **~tion** [-'leiʃən] Verbindung; Paarung, Begattung *f*; **~tive** ['kɔpjulətiv, -leit-] *a* verbindend, kopulativ *a. gram*; Binde-, Begattungs-; *s* Kopula *f*.
copy ['kɔpi] *s* Nachbildung, -ahmung; Kopie, Abschrift *f*, Abdruck *m*; Durchschrift *f*, -schlag *m*; Ausfertigung *f*; *phot* Abzug *m*; (Druck-)Manuskript; *(Buch, Druck)* Exemplar *n*; *(Zeitung, Zt.schrift)* Nummer *f*; Muster, Modell *n*; Stoff *m*, Material *n (für ein Buch, e-e Zeitung)*; *Br fam* (schriftliche) Schulaufgabe *f*; *tr itr* nachahmen, -machen; imitieren; nachbilden; *(to ~ down)* kopieren, abschreiben; vervielfältigen; durchpausen; *(to ~ out)* ins reine schreiben; ab-, nachzeichnen; *phot* abziehen, *to ~ after s.th.* etw folgen; *s.o.* in jds Fußstapfen treten; *by way of ~* abschriftlich; *to make, to take a ~ of s.th.* e-e Abschrift von e-r S machen *od* anfertigen; *certified true ~* für die Richtigkeit; *attested, certified, exemplified, legalized, official ~* beglaubigte Abschrift *f*; *clean, fair, final ~* Reinschrift *f*; *conformed, exact, true ~* gleichlautende, genaue, wörtliche Abschrift *f*; *duty ~* Pflichtexemplar *n*; *foul, rough ~* Kladde *f*, Konzept *n*; *specimen ~* Probenummer *f*; *voucher ~* Belegstück *n*; **~-book** *s* (Schön-)Schreibheft; *Am* Durchschreibbuch *n*; *a* abgedroschen, alltäglich, gewöhnlich; **~-cat** *fam* Nachahmer(in *f*), Plagiator *m*; **~ chief** *Am* Chefredakteur *m*; **~ desk** *(Zeitung)* Schreibtisch *m* des Redakteurs; **~hold** ['-hould] *hist (England)* Lehnsgut *n*; **~holder** *hist* Eigentümer e-s Zinsgutes; *(Schreib-*

maschine) Stenogrammhalter; Korrektorgehilfe *m*; **~ing** ['-iŋ] Kopieren *n*; *attr* Kopier-; *~~ apparatus* Vervielfältigungsapparat *m*; *~~ book* Durchschreibbuch *n*; *~~ ink* Kopiertinte *f*; *~~ machine* Kopiermaschine *f*; *~~ pencil* Kopierstift *m*; *~~ press* Kopierpresse *f*; **~ist** ['-ist] Abschreiber; Nachahmer, Imitator *m*; **~reader** *Am* Redakteur *m*; **~right** *s* Urheber-, Verlagsrecht, literarische(s) Eigentum *n* *(in* an); *a (protected by ~~)* urheberrechtlich geschützt; *tr* urheberrechtlich schützen; *to be ~~ (Br: ~~ed)* urheberrechtlich geschützt sein; *~~ reserved* Nachdruck verboten; *~~ on designs* Geschmacksmusterrecht *n*; **~writer** Texter *m*.

coquet, ~te [ko(u)'ket] *itr* kokettieren, flirten *(with* mit); *fig* tändeln, spielen *(with* mit); **~ry** ['koukitri] Gefallsucht; Koketterie; Tändelei *f*; **~te** [ko(u)-, kə'ket] Kokette *f*; **~tish** [-iʃ] kokett, gefallsüchtig; gefällig; hübsch.

coracle ['kɔrəkl] Fischerboot *n* aus Weidengeflecht.

coral ['kɔrəl] *s* Koralle *f*; Hummerrogen *m*; Kinderklapper *f*; *a (~-red)* korallenrot; **~ island** Koralleninsel *f*; **~line** ['-ain], **~loid(al)** ['-ɔid(əl)] korallenartig; **~ reef** Korallenriff *n*.

corbel ['kɔ:bəl] *s arch* Kragstein *m*; Knagge *f*; Balkenträger *m*; *tr* durch Kragsteine stützen.

cord [kɔ:d] *s* Seil *n*, Strick; Bindfaden, *(Österreich)* Spagat *m*; Leine, Kordel; Litze; *el* Schnur *f*, Kabel; *anat* Band *n*, Strang *m*; *fig* Band *n*, Bindung; Klafter *f (3,63 cbm)*; Kord, Rippsamt *m*; Kordrippe *f*; *pl* Kordhose *f*; *tr* verschnüren; *(to ~ up)* festbinden; *(Holz)* klaftern; **~age** ['-idʒ] Faserseil; *mar* Tauwerk *n*; **~ed** ['-id] *a* verschnürt; angeseilt; *(Stoff)* gerippt; *(Holz)* geklaftert.

cord|ate ['kɔ:dit, -deit] herzförmig; **~ial** ['-iəl] *a* herzlich, herzerfrischend; aufrichtig, tiefgefühlt; (herz)stärkend; Stärkungs-; *s* herzstärkende(s) Mittel *n*; Kräuterlikör *m*; *to give a ~~ welcome* e-n herzlichen Empfang bereiten; **~iality** [kɔ:di'æliti] Herzlichkeit *f*; **~ite** ['-ait] rauchlose(s) Pulver *n*.

cordon ['kɔ:dən] *s* Schiffs-, Truppen-, Polizei-, Posten-, Absperrkette *f*, Kordon *m*; Litze *f*; Ordensband *n*; *arch* Mauerkranz; Spalierbaum; *(sanitary ~)* Sperrgürtel *m*; *tr* einschließen, umzingeln; *to ~ off* absperren, -riegeln.

corduroy ['kɔ:dərɔi, -dju-] *s* Kord, Rippsamt *m*; *pl* Kordhose *f*; *a* Kord-; gerippt; *tr (Straße)* mit Knüppeln, Bohlen befestigen; **~ road** Knüppeldamm, Bohl(en)weg *m*.

core [kɔ:] *s (Apfel)* Kerngehäuse, -haus *n*; *tech* Formkern; *el* Eisenkern *m*; (Kabel-)Ader, Seele *f*; *fig* Kern (-stück *n*) *m*, Herz, Mark, Inner(st)e(s) *n*; *tr (Apfel)* entkernen; *tech* mit e-m Kern versehen; *at the ~* im Inner(ste)n; *to the ~* durch u. durch, voll u. ganz, völlig, vollkommen; bis ins Innerste.

corelation ['kouri'leiʃən] *s. correlation.*

co-religionist ['kouri'lidʒənist] Glaubensgenosse *m*.

co-respondent ['kouris'pɔndənt] Mitbeklagte(r *m*) *f (bes. in e-m Scheidungsprozeß)*.

corf [kɔ:f] *pl corves (min)* Hund, Förderwagen; Fischkorb *m*.

coriaceous [kɔri'eiʃəs] ledern; lederartig; zäh.

coriander [kɔri'ændə] *bot* Koriander *m*.

Corinthian [kə'rinθiən] *a* korinthisch; *s* Korinther(in *f*) *m*.

cork [kɔ:k] *s* Kork *m (~ oak)* Korkeiche; (Baum-)Rinde *f*; Pfropfen, Stöpsel; Angel-, Netzkork *m*; *a* Kork-; *tr (to ~ up)* ver-, zukorken; *fig* in Schach, zurückhalten, unterdrücken; mit e-m gebrannten Kork schwärzen; *to be like a ~ (fig)* sich nicht unterkriegen lassen; **~age** ['-idʒ] Ver- *od* Entkorken; Pfropfengeld *n*; **~ed** [-t] *a* verkorkt; *fig* verschlossen; mit e-m Korkgeschwärzt; *(Wein)* mit Korkgeschmack; *fam fig* verdorben, ruiniert; *sl* besoffen; **~er** [-ə] *s sl* unwiderlegbare(s) Argument *n*; unbestreitbare Tatsache; verblüffende Geschichte; tolle Lüge *f*; *sl* Mords-, Pfundskerl *m*; prima, Pfundssache *f*; **~ing** ['-iŋ] *s* Verkorken *n*; *a sl* prima, pfundig, Pfunds-, Klasse-; **~ jacket** Schwimmweste *f*, -gürtel *m*; **~-oak, -tree** Korkeiche *f*; **~screw** *s* Kork(en)zieher *m*; *a* spiralig; *tr itr* (sich) in e-r Spirale bewegen; *fig* mühsam herausziehen; sich hindurchwinden; *~~ curl* Kork(en)zieherlocke *f*; *~~ staircase* Wendeltreppe *f*; **~-sole** Kork(einlege)sohle *f*; **~y** ['kɔ:ki] aus Kork, Kork-; korkartig; *fig fam* locker, lose, leicht; quecksilb(e)rig, lebhaft; bockig; *(Wein)* nach dem Kork schmeckend.

cormorant ['kɔ:mərənt] *orn* Seerabe, Kormoran *m*, Scharbe *f*; *fig* Nimmersatt, Vielfraß *m*.

corn [kɔ:n] **1.** *s* Korn, Getreide *n*; *(England) meist* Weizen; *(Schottland, Irland) meist* Hafer; *(Am) meist* Mais *(Indian ~)*; Whisky *m* aus Mais, Korn(schnaps); körnige(r) Schnee *m*; *fam* Rührseligkeit, abgedroschene Geschichte *f*; *tr* körnen, granulieren; einsalzen, (ein-)pökeln; **~-ball** *Am* süße(s) Puffkorn *n*; *sl* altmodische(r), sentimentale(r) Mensch *m*; **~-beetle** *zoo* Kornkäfer, -wurm *m*; **C~-Belt, the** *geog* der Maisgürtel *(im Mittelwesten der US)*; **~-bind** *bot* Ackerwinde *f*; **~brash** ['-bræʃ] Kalksandstein *m*; **~ bread** *Am* Maisbrot *n*; **~-chandler, -dealer, -factor, -merchant** Getreide-, Samenhändler *m*; **~-cob** Maiskolben *m*; **~-cockle** *bot* Kornrade *f*; **~-crake** *orn* Wiesenknarrer *m*; **~ed** [-d] *a* gekörnt, granuliert; gesalzen, gepökelt; *sl* besoffen; *~~ beef* Büchsen(rind)fleisch *n*; **~ exchange** Getreidebörse *f*; **~fed** ['-fed] *a Am* mit Körnern gefüttert; *sl* bäuerisch, simpel; *sl* fett, plump; **~field** Korn-, *(Schottland)* Hafer-, *Am* Maisfeld *n*; **~-flakes** *pl* Weizen-, Hafer- *od* Maisflocken *f pl*; **~-flour** Mais-, Reismehl *n*; **~-flower** Kornblume; Kornrade *f*; **~-harvester** (Getreide-)Mähmaschine *f*; **~husk** ['-hʌsk] *Am* Hüllblätter *n pl* des Maises, Lieschen *pl*; **~-juice** *Am* Maisschnaps *m*; **~-market** Getreidemarkt *m*; **~ picker** *Am* Entkolbe-, Entlieschmaschine *f*; **~ pone** *Am* (viereckiges) Maisbrot *n*; **~-poppy** Klatschmohn *m*; **~-rose** Klatschmohn *m*; Kornrade *f*; **~ salad** Ackersalat *m*; **~ shock** Garbe *f*; *Am* aufgeschichtete Maisstengel *m pl*; **~ silk** *Am* Maisgrannen *f pl*; **~ sirup** Stärkesirup *m*; **~ smut** Getreidebrand *m (Pilzkrankheit)*; **~stalk** ['-stɔ:k] Getreidehalm; *Am* Maisstengel; *fam* lange(r) Laban, Lulatsch *m*, Hopfenstange *f*; **~y** ['-i] *a* Korn-; kornreich; *sl* altmodisch, abgedroschen; rührselig; kitschig; simpel; **2.** *med* Hühnerauge *n*; *to tread on s.o.'s ~s (fig)* jdm auf die Füße treten, auf jds Gefühlen herumtrampeln; **~ea** ['kɔ:niə] Hornhaut *f (d. Auges)*; **~-plaster** Hühneraugenpflaster *n*.

cornel ['kɔ:nəl] *bot* Hartriegel, Hornstrauch *m*, Kornelkirsche *f*.

cornelian [kɔ:'ni:ljən] *min* Karneol *m*.

corner ['kɔ:nə] *s* Ecke *f*, Winkel *m*; *(street-~)* (Straßen-)Ecke; *mot* Kurve *f*; (finsterer, heimlicher) Winkel *m*, (abgelegene) Gegend *f*, Ende *n*; *(tight ~)* Klemme, schwierige Lage; Verlegenheit, *fam* Patsche, Klemme; *fam* Kante, Ecke *f*, Stückchen *n*; *com* (spekulative) Aufkäufergruppe *f*; *(~ kick) sport* Eckball; *(~ protection)* Kantenschutz *m*; *tr* in die Enge treiben *a. fig*; *com* aufkaufen; *itr* e-e Ecke bilden; *mot* um die Ecke biegen; *Am* sich an e-r Ecke treffen; *in every nook and ~ (Am)* in allen Ecken u. Winkeln; *in every ~, in the (four) ~s of the world* an allen Enden der Welt, an allen Ecken u. Enden; *to cut ~s* den Weg abschneiden; *fig* Ausgaben, Löhne, Zeit einsparen; *to cut off a ~* e-e Ecke *(des Weges)* abschneiden; *fig* den Preis drücken; *to drive, to force, to put s.o. into a ~ (fig)* jdn in die Enge treiben; *to keep a ~* e-n freien Platz lassen; *to turn the ~* um die Ecke biegen; *fig* (gut) davonkommen, es überstehen, über den Berg kommen; **~-boy** Faulenzer *m*; **~ed** ['-d] *a* eckig, wink(e)lig; *fig* in der Klemme; **~ house** Eckhaus *n*; **~ iron** Winkeleisen *n*; **~-room** Eckzimmer *n*; **~ seat** Eckplatz *m*; **~-stone** Eck-, Grundstein *m*; *fig* Grundlage *f*, Fundament *n*; **~-wise** ['-waiz] *adv* schräg; diagonal.

cornet ['kɔ:nit] *mus* Kornett *n*; Tüte; *Br (Speiseeis)* Eistüte *f*; Cremetörtchen *n*; Schwesternhaube *f*; *mil hist* Kornett, Fahnenjunker *m*.

cornice ['kɔ:nis] *arch* Karnies *n*, Sims *m od n*, Gesimse *n*; Zierleiste; Gardinen-, Vorhangleiste; Schneewächte; *tech* Kehlung *f*.

cornucopia [kɔ:nju'koupjə] Füllhorn *n*; (Papier-)Tüte; *fig* Fülle *f*, Überfluß *m*.

corolla [kə'rɔlə] Blumenkrone *f*; **~ry** [-ri] *philos* Folgesatz *m*; Folgerung, Ableitung; *allg* (natürliche) Folge, Folgeerscheinung *f*, Ergebnis *n*.

coron|a [kə'rounə] *pl a. -ae* [-i:] Krone *f a. anat*; Kron-, Radleuchter *(bes. in e-r Kirche)*; *arch* Kranz *m*; (Zahn-)Krone; *astr* Korona *f*, Hof *m*; *el (~~ discharge)* Glimmentladung *f*; **~al** ['kɔrənl] *s* Diadem *n*; Kranz *m*; Stirnbinde *f*; *a* Kronen-, Kranz-, Koronar-; *~~ suture* Kranznaht *f*; **~ary** ['kɔrənəri] *med* koronar; Kranz-; *~~ artery (anat)* Kranzarterie *f*; *~~ thrombosis* Koronarthrombose *f*; **~ation** [kɔrə'neiʃən] Krönung(sfeierlichkeiten *f pl*) *f*; *~~ oath* Krönungseid *m*; **~er** ['kɔrənə] (amtlicher) Leichenbeschauer *n*; *~~'s inquest* (amtliche) Leichenschau *f*; **~et** ['kɔrənit] Adelskrone *f*; Diadem *n*; *(Pferd)* Hufkrone *f*.

corpor|al ['kɔ:pərəl] **1.** *a* körperlich, leiblich; Leibes-; persönlich; *s rel* Meßtuch *n*; *~~ punishment* Prügelstrafe, körperliche Züchtigung *f*; **2.** Unteroffizier *m (im engeren Sinn)*; *lance-~~* Ober-, Hauptgefreite(r) *m*; **~ality** [-'ræliti] Körperlichkeit, Materialität, körperliche Existenz *f*; **~ate** ['kɔ:pərit] vereinigt, zs.geschlossen; körperschaftlich, gesellschaftlich, korporativ; gemeinsam, gemeinschaftlich; *~~ assets (pl)* Gesellschaftsvermögen *n*; *~~ name* Firmenname *m*; *~~ income tax* Körperschaftssteuer *f*; **~ation** [kɔ:pə'reiʃən] Körperschaft; juristische Person; Innung, Gilde; Gemeindevertretung *f*, -rat *m*; *Am* Gesellschaft *f* mit beschränkter Haftung *(GmbH)*, Aktiengesellschaft *f*; *fam* Dick-, Fettwanst, Schmerbauch *m*; ~~ *law (Am)* Aktienrecht *n*; ~~ *tax* Körperschaftssteuer *f*; **~ative** ['kɔːpərətiv] körperschaftlich, korporativ; **~eal** [kɔː'pɔːriəl] körperlich, physisch, sinnlich (wahrnehmbar), greifbar, konkret; **~e(al)ity** [kɔːpɔ'riːiti, -ri'æliti] Körperlichkeit, körperliche, physische Existenz *f*.

corposant ['kɔːpəzənt] St.-Elms-Feuer *n*.

corps [kɔː, *pl* kɔːz] *mil* (Armee-)Korps *n*; Truppe *f*; *allg* Korps *n*; *medical* ~ Sanitätstruppe *f*; ~ *de ballet* ['kɔːdə'bælei] Ballettgruppe *f*; *C* ~ *of Engineers* Pionierkorps *n*; *the C~ Diplomatique* ['kɔːdiplo(u)mæ'tiːk] das Diplomatische Korps; ~ **headquarters staff** Korpsstab *m*; **~man** ['-mən] *Am* Sanitäter, Sanitätssoldat *m*.

corpse [kɔːps] Leiche *f*, Leichnam *m*.

corpulen|ce, -cy ['kɔːpjuləns(i)] Beleibtheit, Korpulenz, Fettleibigkeit *f*; **~t** ['-t] beleibt, korpulent, fettleibig, stark, dick, *fam* fett.

corpus ['kɔːpəs] *pl -pora* ['-pərə] Körper; Hauptteil; *fin* Kapitalbetrag *m*; geschlossene(s) Ganze(s); Korpus *n*, (Gesetzes-)Sammlung; *typ* Korpus *f*; **C~ Christi** ['kristi] *rel* Fronleichnam(sfest *n*) *m*.

corpusc|le ['kɔːpʌsl], **~ule** [-'pʌskjuːl] *phys* Korpuskel, Massenteilchen *n*; *allg* sehr kleine(r) Teil *m*; *pl physiol (red, white ~s)* (rote, weiße) Blutkörperchen *n pl*; **~ular** [kɔː'pʌskjulə] *a phys* Korpuskular-.

corral [kɔː'rɑːl] *s* Umzäunung *f*; Pferch, Korral *m*; Wagenburg *f*; *tr (Vieh)* in e-n Korral einschließen, -sperren, -pferchen; *sl* sich unter den Nagel reißen, organisieren.

correct [kə'rekt] *a* richtig, korrekt, genau; *(Antwort)* zutreffend; *(Verhalten)* einwandfrei; *(bes. Kleidung)* vorschriftsmäßig, korrekt; *tr* (ver)bessern, korrigieren, richtigstellen; *(Uhr)* stellen; *(Fehler)* ausschalten, abstellen; richtig einstellen; zurechtweisen, tadeln, (be)strafen, züchtigen; abstellen, heilen, entfernen; aufheben, ausgleichen, aufwiegen; *phot* entzerren; *(Ladehemmung)* beheben; *to do the ~ thing* richtig handeln, sich richtig verhalten; *to prove ~* zutreffen; *to ~ proofs (typ)* Korrektur lesen; **~ion** [-kʃən] Verbesserung, Korrektur, Berichtigung, Richtigstellung; richtige Einstellung *f*; Ausgleich *m*; Zurechtweisung *f*, Tadel *m*, Strafe, Züchtigung; *phot* Entzerrung; Beseitigung *f (e-r Ladehemmung)*; *subject to ~~, under ~~* unter Irrtumsvorbehalt; ohne Gewähr; *to make ~~s* Verbesserungen vornehmen; **~ional** [-ʃənl] *a* Besserungs-, *jur* Straf-; ~~ *court* Strafkammer *f*; **~itude** [kə'rektitjuːd] Korrektheit *f*; **~ive** [-iv] *a* verbessernd, berichtigend; ausgleichend; *s* Abhilfe (*of*, *Am for* für) *f*; Ausgleich *m*; ~~ *exercises (pl)* Ausgleichsübungen *f pl*; **~ly** [-li] *adv* mit Recht; **~ness** [-nis] Richtigkeit, Korrektheit, Genauigkeit *f*; **~or** [-tə] Verbesserer *m*; Abhilfe *f*; *typ* Korrektor; *tech* Entzerrer *m*.

correlat|e ['kərileit] *tr* in Wechselbeziehung setzen (*with* zu); (mitea.) in Beziehung, in Zs.hang bringen; aufea. abstimmen; *itr* in Wechselbeziehung stehen (*to, with* zu), sich wechselgegenseitig bedingen; verknüpft sein (*to* mit); *s* Korrelat *n*, Wechselbegriff *m*, Ergänzung *f*; *a* in enger Beziehung, in Wechselbeziehung stehend; **~ion** [kəri'leiʃən] Wechselbeziehung *f*; Vergleich *n*, Korrelation *f*; Inbeziehungsetzen *n*; **~ive** [kɔ'relətiv] *a* in Wechselbeziehung stehend, zs.hängend; *gram* korrelativ; *s* Wechselbegriff *m*, Gegenstück *n*.

correspond [kɔris'pɔnd] *itr* entsprechen (*to* dat); übereinstimmen, in Einklang stehen (*with, to* mit); den Anforderungen genügen (*to* gen); in Briefwechsel stehen, korrespondieren (*with* mit); **~ence,** *a.* **-cy** [-əns(i)] Übereinstimmung *f*, Einklang *m* (*with* mit; *between* zwischen); Entsprechung; Verbindung *f*; Zs.hang; Schriftverkehr, Briefwechsel *m*, Korrespondenz; Post (-sachen *f pl*) *f*; *(Zeitung)* Briefkasten *m*, Leserbriefe *m pl*; *(~~ column)* Eingesandt *n*; *to attend to the ~~, to take care of the ~~* die Post erledigen; *to carry on a wide ~~* e-n großen Briefwechsel haben; *to be in ~~ with* in Briefwechsel stehen, korrespondieren mit; ~~ *clerk* Korrespondent *m*; ~~ *course* Fernunterricht *m*; ~~ *school* Fernlehrinstitut *n*; **~ent** [-ənt] *a* entsprechend; *s* Briefpartner; *(com, Zeitung)* Korrespondent; Berichterstatter; Einsender; Kunde, Geschäftsfreund *m*; *foreign ~~* Auslandskorrespondent *m*; *war ~~* Kriegsbericht(erstatt)er *m*; **~ing** [-iŋ] entsprechend (*to* dat); übereinstimmend, in Einklang (*with* mit); korrespondierend, im Briefwechsel (*with* mit); *to apply ~~ly* entsprechend anwenden; ~~ *member* korrespondierende(s), auswärtige(s) Mitglied *n*.

corridor ['kɔridɔː] Gang, Korridor, *a. pol*, Flur; Luftkorridor *m*, Flugschneise *f*; ~ **train** D-Zug *m*.

corrig|endum [kɔri'dʒendəm] *pl -da* [-də] Berichtigung *f*; Druckfehler *m*; *pl* Druckfehlerverzeichnis *n*; **~ible** ['kɔridʒibl] verbesserlich; fügsam.

corrobor|ant [kə'rɔbərənt] *a* bestätigend; stärkend, tonisch; Stärkungs-; *s* Bestätigung *f*; *pharm* Stärkungsmittel, Tonikum *n*; **~ate** [-eit] *tr* bestätigen, bekräftigen, erhärten, stützen; festigen; **~ation** [kərɔbə'reiʃən] Bestätigung, Erhärtung, Bekräftigung; Stärkung *f*; **~ative** [kə'rɔbərətiv] bestätigend, bekräftigend.

corro|de [kə'roud] *tr* zerfressen, -nagen, -setzen; angreifen, ätzen *a. fig*; zerstören; *fig* verderben, schädigen, beeinträchtigen; *itr* sich zersetzen; korrodieren, rosten; **~dible** [-əbl] korrosionsempfindlich; **~sion** [kə'rouʒən] Zerfressen, Ätzen *n*, Korrosion *f*, Rosten *n*; Zersetzung, Zerstörung *f*; ~~ *resistant* korrosionsfest; **~sive** [-siv] *a* zerfressend, -setzend, ätzend, beizend; *fig* zersetzend; nagend, bohrend, quälend; *s* Korrosions-, Ätzmittel *n*.

corrugat|e ['kɔrugeit] *tr* runzeln; wellen; furchen, riefe(l)n, mit Rillen versehen; **~ed** ['-id] *a* gerillt, geriefelt, gewellt; ~~ *cardboard, paper* Wellpappe *f*; ~~ *sheet steel, iron* Wellblech *n*; **~ion** [kɔru'geiʃən] Welle; Rippe; Riefelung; Runzel, Falte *f*.

corrupt [kə'rʌpt] *a* verdorben, verrottet, faul; *fig* (sittlich) verkommen; schlecht, böse; unredlich, unehrenhaft; bestechlich, käuflich; korrupt; *(Text)* verderbt, entstellt, verfälscht; *tr* verderben; anstecken, ungünstig beeinflussen, untergraben; bestechen; *(Text)* entstellen; verfälschen; *itr* verderben, (ver)faulen; **~ibility** [kərʌptə'biliti] Verderblichkeit; Bestechlichkeit, Käuflichkeit *f*; **~ible** [-əbl] verderblich *(im passiven Sinn)*, vergänglich, verweslich; bestechlich, käuflich; **~ion** [kə'rʌpʃən] Fäulnis *f*, Verfall *m*, Verwesung *f*; Sittenverfall *m*, (Sitten-)Verderbnis; Verkommenheit, Verdorbenheit; Verführung; Bestechung; Bestechlichkeit, Käuflichkeit; Korruption; *(Text)* Entstellung, Verfälschung *f*; *electoral ~~* Wahlbestechung *f*; ~~ *of witnesses* Zeugenbestechung *f*; **~ive** [-iv] verderblich *(im aktiven Sinn)*; ansteckend; **~ness** [-nis] Verdorbenheit, Verkommenheit; Bestechlichkeit, Käuflichkeit *f*; ~ **practices** *pl* Bestechung(saffäre) *f*, Durchstechereien *f pl*.

corsage [kɔː'sɑːʒ, *Am* 'kɔːsidʒ] Oberteil (e-s Damenkleides); (Blumen-) Sträußchen *n* zum Anstecken.

corsair ['kɔːsɛə] Seeräuber(schiff *n*), Korsar *m*.

cors(e)let ['kɔːslit] (Brust-)Harnisch *m*; *zoo* Brustschild *m*; *Am* [kɔːs'lɛt] Korselett *n*.

corset ['kɔːsit] *a. pl (pair of ~s)* Korsett *n*, Hüfthalter, -former *m*.

cortege [kɔː'teiʒ, -ɛːʒ] Gefolge *n*; feierliche(r) Zug *m*.

cort|ex ['kɔːteks] *pl -ices* [-isiːz] *bot anat* Rinde; *(brain ~~)* Großhirnrinde *f*; **~ical** ['-ikəl] *scient* Rinden-; kortikal.

corundum [kə'rʌndəm] Korund *m*.

corusc|ant [kə'rʌskənt] funkelnd, glitzernd; **~ate** ['kɔrəskeit] *itr* funkeln, glitzern; *fig (Geist)* sprühen; **~ation** [kɔrəs'keiʃən] Funkeln, Glitzern; Flimmern *n*; Licht-, *fig* Geistesblitz *m*.

corvée ['kɔːvei, kɔrve] *hist* Fron(arbeit) *f a. fig*.

corvette [kɔː'vet] *mar* Korvette *f*.

corvine ['kɔːvain, -in] *scient* rabenartig; Raben-.

corymb ['kɔ(ː)rim(b)] *bot* Doldentraube *f*.

coryphee [kɔri'fei] Primaballerina *f*.

coryza [kə'raizə] Schnupfen; Katarrh *m*.

*

cosecant ['kou'siːkənt] *math* Kosekante *f*.

cosey *s. cosy*.

cosh [kɔʃ] *s* Totschläger, Knüppel *m*; *math* Hyperbelcosinus *m*; *tr* mit e-m Knüppel, bewußtlos schlagen; **~er** ['-ə] *tr* verhätscheln, verwöhnen.

cosh [kɔʃ] *s* Totschläger *m (Waffe)*; *math* Hyperbelcosinus *m*; *tr* mit dem T. treffen; **~er** ['-ə] *tr* verhätscheln, verwöhnen.

co-signatory ['kou'signətəri] *a* mitunterzeichnend; *s* Mitunterzeichner *m*.

cosine ['kousain] *math* Kosinus *m*.

cosiness ['kouzinis] Gemütlichkeit *f*.

cosmet|ic(al) [kɔz'metik(əl)] *a* kosmetisch; *s* Schönheitsmittel *n*; *a. pl* Kosmetik *f*; **~ician** [kɔzmə'tiʃən] Kosmetiker(in *f*) *m*.

cosmic(al) ['kɔzmik(əl)] kosmisch; Welt(en)-; riesig, gewaltig, ungeheuer; (wohl)geordnet, harmonisch; ~ **rays** *pl* kosmische Strahlen *m pl*.

cosmo|gonic [kɔzmo(u)-, kɔzmə'gɔnik] kosmogonisch, Weltentstehungs-; **~gony** [kɔz'mɔgəni] Kosmogonie, (Theorie der) Weltentstehung *f*; **~grapher** [kɔz'mɔgrəfə] Kosmograph *m*; **~graphic(al)** [kɔzmo(u)-, kɔzmə'græfik(əl)] kosmographisch; **~graphy** [kɔz'mɔgrəfi] Kosmographie, Weltbeschreibung *f*; **~logical** [kɔzmə-, kɔzmo(u)'lɔdʒikəl] kosmologisch; **~logy** [kɔz'mɔlədʒi] Kosmologie *f*; **~politan** [kɔzmə-, kɔzmo(u)'pɔlitən] *a* über die ganze Erde verbreitet; weltbürgerlich, kosmopolitisch; *s* Weltbürger *m*; **~politanism** [kɔzmə'pɔlitənizm] Weltbürgertum *n*; **~s** ['kɔzmɔs] Kosmos *m*, Weltall *n*; Harmonie, Ordnung *f*.

Cossack ['kɔsæk] Kosak *m*.

cosset ['kɔsit] *tr* verhätscheln, verwöhnen.
cost [kɔst] *irr cost, cost itr* kosten *a. fig,* zu stehen kommen; *fig (Zeit, Mühe)* (er)fordern; *(Schaden, Ärger)* einbringen, machen; *tr com* kalkulieren, berechnen, den Kostenpreis festsetzen; *s* Preis *m,* (Un-)Kosten *pl;* Kostenbetrag; Einkauf-, Kauf-, Selbstkostenpreis *m;* Ausgaben, -lagen *f pl; fig* Einsatz; Schaden, Nachteil, Verlust *m,* Opfer *n; pl* Gerichtskosten, Kosten des Verfahrens; Anwaltskosten; Spesen *pl;* Gestehungskosten *pl; at ~* zum Selbstkostenpreis; *at the ~ of* auf Kosten *gen; at all ~s, at any ~* um jeden Preis; *at great ~ of blood* unter großen Blutopfern; *to o.'s ~* zu jds Schaden; *under ~* mit Verlust; *with ~s* kostenpflichtig; *without ~* kostenlos, gratis; *to bear, to pay the ~* die Kosten tragen; *to carry ~s* Kosten nach sich ziehen; *to count the ~ (fig)* alles in Anschlag bringen; *to dismiss with ~s* kostenpflichtig abweisen; *to spare no ~* keine Kosten scheuen; *to ~ a pretty penny* e-e schöne Stange Geld kosten; *that will ~ him dearly* das wird ihm teuer zu stehen kommen; *advance on ~* Kostenvorschuß *m; overhead, operating, running, working ~s (pl)* Betriebs(un)kosten *pl; ~ of labo(u)r* Lohnkosten *pl; ~ of living* Lebenshaltungskosten *pl; ~-of-living bonus* Teuerungszulage *f; ~-of-living index, escalator* Lebenshaltungsindex *m; ~ of maintenance* Unterhaltungskosten *pl; ~ of operation* Betriebskosten *pl; ~ of packing* Verpackungskosten *pl; ~ of printing* Druckkosten *pl; ~ of production* Herstellungskosten *pl; ~ of repair* Reparaturkosten *pl; ~ of storage* Lagerkosten *pl,* -geld *n; ~ of transportation* Transportkosten *pl;* **~ accounting, calculation** Kostenberechnung *f;* **~ing** ['-iŋ] Kostenberechnung; Kalkulation *f; ~~ department* Kalkulationsabteilung *f;* **~liness** ['-linis] Kostspieligkeit *f;* **~ly** ['-li] kostspielig, teuer; **~-plus** Kosten *pl* plus Gewinn; **~ price** Einkaufs-, Selbstkostenpreis *m,* Gestehungskosten *pl;* **~ reduction** Kostensenkung *f;* **~ saving** Kosteneinsparung *f.*
costal ['kɔstl] *scient* Rippen-, Seiten-.
co-star ['kou'stɑ:] *theat film s* zweite(r) *od* weitere(r) Hauptdarsteller(in *f*) *m; tr itr* e-e zweite *od* weitere Hauptrolle spielen (lassen).
coster(monger) ['kɔstəmʌŋgə] *Br* Straßen-, Obst- u. Gemüsehändler(in *f*), Höker(in *f*) *m.*
costive ['kɔstiv] *med* verstopft, hartleibig; *fig* langsam, schwerfällig.
costum|e ['kɔstju:m] *s* Tracht *f;* (historisches, Theater-, Masken- *od* Damen-)Kostüm *n;* Ornat *m; tr* [kɔs'tju:m] kostümieren; *~~ ball* Kostümfest *n,* -ball *m; ~~ designer* Gewandmeister *m; ~~ film, piece* Kostümfilm *m,* -stück *n;* historische(r) Film *m; ~~ jewel(le)ry* Modeschmuck *m;* **~(i)er** [kɔs'tju:m(i)ə] Kostümschneider, -händler, -verleiher *m.*
cosy, cosey, cozy ['kouzi] *a* gemütlich, behaglich, mollig; *s (tea-~)* Tee-, Kaffeewärmer; gemütliche(r) Platz *m,* Sitzecke *f; egg-~* Eierwärmer *m.*
cot [kɔt] **1.** Unterstand *m,* Schutzdach *n;* (Schutz-)Hülle *f,* Fingerling *m; poet* Häuschen *n,* Kate, Hütte *f;* **2.** Klapp-, Feld-, Krankenhaus-, Kinderbett *n; mar* Hängematte *f.*
cotangent ['kou'tændʒənt] *math* Kotangente *f.*
cote [kout] Schutzdach *n (für Vieh),* Stall *m; dove-~* Taubenschlag *m.*
coterie ['koutəri] Gruppe, Clique *f,* Klüngel *m.*
cottage ['kɔtidʒ] Hütte *f,* Häuschen *n;* Siedlungs-, kleine(s) Landhaus; Ferien-, Sommerhaus *n;* **~-cheese** *Am* Quark *m;* **~ industry** Heimindustrie *f;* **~-loaf** *Art* Doppelbrot *n;* **~-piano** Pianino *n;* **~-pie** Kartoffelpastete *f* mit Fleischfüllung; **~-pudding** Kuchen *m* mit süßem Aufguß; **~r** ['-ə] *Br* Häusler; *Br* Landarbeiter; *Am* Eigentümer *m* e-s Sommerhauses.
cotter ['kɔtə] *s tech (~ pin)* Splint; Vorsteck-, Sicherungsstift, Vorsteck-, Schließkeil *m; tr* versplinten.
cotton ['kɔtn] *s* Baumwolle *f (als Pflanze, Rohstoff u. Gewebe);* Kattun *m; (~ yarn, ~ thread, sewing-~)* Baumwollgarn *n,* -zwirn *m; Am (absorbent ~)* Watte *f; a* Baumwoll(en)-; baumwollen; *tr (to ~ up)* in B. kleiden; mit B. ausstatten, versehen, füttern; *itr fam (to ~ together)* dicke Freunde, ein Herz u. e-e Seele sein (*with* mit); *to ~ on* sich (eng) anschließen (*to* an), sympathisieren (*to* mit); *to ~ up* Freundschaft schließen (*to* mit); **C~ Belt** Baumwollgürtel *m (in den USA);* **~-cake** *Am* Baumwollsamenkuchen *m (Viehfutter);* **~-gin** Egreniermaschine *f;* **~-grass** *bot* Wollgras *n,* Binsenweide *f;* **~-grower** Baumwollpflanzer *m;* **~ mill** Baumwollspinnerei *f;* **~mouth** Mokassinschlange *f;* **~-picker** Baumwollpflücker(in *f*); Baumwollrupper *m;* **~-seed** Baumwollsamen *m; ~~ meal, oil* Baumwollsamenkuchen *m,* -öl *n;* **~-tail** amerik. (Wild-)Kaninchen *n;* **~ waste** Putzwolle *f;* **~wood** *bot* Balsampappel *f;* **~-wool** *Br* Watte *f; Am* Rohbaumwolle *f;* **~y** ['-i] Baumwoll(en)-; baumwollartig; flauschig, weich.

*

couch [kautʃ] *s* Couch *f,* Liege-, Ruhesofa *n; allg* Ruheplatz *m; obs* Lager *n (e-s wilden Tieres); (Farbe)* Schicht, Lage *f; poet* Lager(statt *f*), Bett *n; (Mälzerei)* Haufen *m,* Beet *n,* Malzscheibe; *tech* Gautschpresse *f; tr* (nieder)legen; *(Lanze)* einlegen; *(Kopf)* senken; *(Gedanken)* ausdrücken, (ein-)kleiden, hüllen, abfassen (*in* in); besticken; *(Gerste in der Mälzerei)* in Haufen aufschütten; *tech* gautschen; *med (grauen Star)* stechen; *itr (bes. Tiere)* sich (nieder)ducken, (nieder-)kauern; sich lagern; (auf)lauern, im Hinterhalt liegen; (ausgestreckt) liegen; ausgebreitet, geschichtet liegen; **~ grass** Schnürgras *n;* **~ing** ['-iŋ] Plattstickerei *f; tech* Gautschen *n.*
cougar ['ku:gə] *zoo* Kuguar, Puma *m.*
cough [kɔ(:)f] *s* Husten *m; itr* husten; *tr: to ~ out, up* aushusten; *sl (Geld)* 'rausrücken; *to give a (slight) ~* sich durch Husten bemerkbar machen; **~-drop, -lozenge, sweet** Hustenbonbon *n,* -pastille *f;* **~ mixture** Hustentröpfchen *n.*
coulee ['ku:li] *geol* Lavastrom *m; Am* Schlucht, Klamm *f;* Gebirgsbach *m.*
coulisse [ku(:)'li:s] *theat* Kulisse *f.*
co(u)lter ['koultə] *(Pflug)* Kolter, Sech *n.*
council ['kauns(i)l] Rat(sversammlung *f*) *m;* beratende Versammlung; Beratung *f; (church ~)* Kirchenrat *m; rel* Konzil *n;* Gewerkschaftsrat *m; in ~* bei der Beratung; zur Beratung versammelt; *to be in ~, to hold ~* beraten; *cabinet ~* Kabinetts-, Ministerrat *m; security ~* Sicherheitsrat *m; shop, workers' ~* Betriebsrat, -ausschuß *m; supervisory ~* Kuratorium *n; ~ of action* Aktionsausschuß *m; ~ of elders* Ältestenrat *m; C~ of Europe* Europarat *m; ~ of ministers* Ministerrat *m; ~ of war* Kriegsrat *m;* **~ committee** Ratsausschuß *m;* **~ elections** *pl* Ratswahlen *f pl;* **~ house** *Br* städtische(s) *od* staatliche(s) Wohngebäude *n;* **~(l)or** ['kaunsilə] Rat(smitglied *n*) *m;* **~man** ['-mən] *Am* Ratsherr, Stadtrat, Stadtverordnete(r) *m.*
counsel ['kaunsəl] *s* Beratung *f;* Ratsbeschluß *m,* Entschließung, Empfehlung *f;* Plan *m,* Absicht, Meinung *f;* Rat *m (den man gibt);* (Rechts-)Anwalt, Rechtsbeistand, -berater; Syndikus *m; pl (ohne s)* Anwaltschaft *f; tr (Sache)* raten, empfehlen; *(Person)* beraten; den Rat geben, raten (*s.o. to do* jdm zu tun); *itr* beraten; sich Rat holen, Rat suchen; *to keep o.'s own ~* schweigen; s-e Gedanken, s-e Absichten für sich behalten; *to take, to hold ~ (lit)* zu Rate gehen, sich beraten; Rat suchen (*with* bei); *King's, Queen's C~* Kronanwalt *m; ~ for the defence* Prozeßbevollmächtigte(r); Verteidiger *m; ~ for the prosecution* Anklagevertreter *m;* **~(l)or** [-ə] Berater, Ratgeber; *(Irland, US)* (Rechts-)Anwalt *m.*
count [kaunt] **1.** *tr* zählen; *(to ~ up)* zs.zählen, -rechnen; *(Geld)* (nach-)zählen; nach-, berechnen; *(to ~ in)* (mit)rechnen, einschließen; halten für, ansehen als; in Rechnung stellen; *itr* (mit)zählen; ins Gewicht fallen, wichtig sein; *phys* die Radioaktivität (mit e-m Geigerzähler) feststellen; *s* (Zs.-)Zählung; (Be-)Rechnung; Gesamtzahl; Summe *f,* Ergebnis *n; jur* Klag(e)punkt, *(~ of an indictment)* Anklagepunkt *m; (~-out) Br parl* Vertagung *f* wegen Beschlußunfähigkeit; *(Garn)* Feinheitsnummer; *tech* Impulszahl *f; (Boxen)* Auszählen *n; on all ~s* in jeder Beziehung; *to ~ against s.o.* sich gegen jdn auswirken; *to ~ as, for* zählen, angesehen werden, gelten als; *to ~ the cost* die Kosten veranschlagen; *to ~ for* wert sein; *to ~ off* abzählen; *to ~ out* übersehen, auslassen; nicht rechnen mit; *(Geldstücke)* zs.zählen; *(Boxen)* auszählen; *Am (Stimmzettel)* unterschlagen, verschwinden lassen; *Br parl* wegen Beschlußunfähigkeit vertagen; *to ~ (up)on* rechnen mit, zählen, sich verlassen auf; *to keep ~* (richtig) zs.zählen; *to lose ~* falsch zs.zählen, sich verrechnen, sich verzählen, den Überblick verlieren; *to take no ~ of s.th.* etw nicht berücksichtigen; *to take the ~ (Boxen)* ausgezählt werden; *that doesn't ~* das macht nichts; das gilt nicht; *~ me in* ich mache mit; **~-down** letzte Überprüfung *f* (e-r Rakete vor d. Abschuß); **~-out** *parl Br* Vertagung *f* wegen Beschlußunfähigkeit; **2.** (ausländischer) Graf *m.*
countenance ['kauntinəns] *s* Gesicht(sausdruck *m*) *n,* Miene *f;* innere Haltung, Fassung, innere Ruhe; Billigung, Unterstützung, Ermunterung *f,* Beistand *m,* Gunst *f; tr* billigen, gutheißen, zulassen, *fam* durchgehen lassen; begünstigen, unterstützen, ermutigen; *in ~* gefaßt, ruhig; *out of ~* fassungslos; *to change (o.'s) ~* den Gesichtsausdruck wechseln; *to give, to lend ~ to* billigen, unterstützen; *to keep (o.'s) ~* Haltung, die Fassung bewahren; *to lose ~* die Fassung verlieren, *fam* aus dem Häuschen geraten; *to put out of ~* jdn aus der Fassung bringen.
counter ['kauntə] **1.** Zähler *m;* Zählgerät *n,* -apparat *m,* -werk *n;* Spiel-

marke *f*; Laden-, Zahltisch *m*; Theke *f*, Büfett *n*; (Bank-)Schalter *m*; *sl* Geldstück *n*; *at the* ~ an der Theke; *over the* ~ außerbörslich, im Freiverkehr; gegen bar; *under the* ~ unter dem Ladentisch, heimlich; *Geiger* ~ *(phys)* Geigerzähler *m*; **~-clerk** *Am* Schalterbeamte(r) *m*; **2.** *adv* entgegen, zuwider; *a* entgegengesetzt; *s* Gegenteil *n*; *(Pferd)* Bug *m*, Vorbrust *f*; *(Schuh)* Fersenleder *n*; *(Schiff)* Gilling *f*; *sport* Gegenschlag *m*; *(Fechten)* Parade; *mus* Gegenstimme *f*; *tr (to* ~ *s.o.)* gegen jds Willen handeln, jdm entgegenarbeiten; entgegnen (*s.o.* jdm); *(Angriff)* abfangen; *(to* ~ *s.th.)* e-r S entgegen-, zuwiderhandeln, etw durchkreuzen; *itr (Boxen)* kontern; e-n Gegenschlag führen; widersprechen; *to run* ~ *to s.th.* gegen etw verstoßen, etw zuwiderlaufen.

counteract [kauntə'rækt] *tr* entgegen-, zuwiderhandeln, entgegenarbeiten *(s.o.* jdm; *s.th.* e-r S); *(to* ~ *s.o.)* gegen jdn arbeiten; durchkreuzen, verhindern, hintertreiben, unterbinden, verhüten, unterdrücken; aufheben, unwirksam machen; entgegenwirken (*s.th.* e-r S); **~ion** [-kʃən] Zuwiderhandeln *n*; Widerstand *m*; Gegenwirkung *f*; **~ive** [-tiv] *a* entgegenwirkend; *s* Widerstand *m*, Gegenmittel *n*.

counter|-agent [kauntə'reidʒənt] Gegenmittel *n*, -wirkung *f*; **~-attack** ['kauntərətæk] *s* Gegenangriff, -stoß *m*; *tr itr* [kauntərə'tæk] e-n Gegenangriff machen (auf); **~-~** *division* Eingreifdivision *f*; **~balance** ['kauntəbæləns] *s* Gegengewicht *a. fig* (*to* gegen); *com* Gegensaldo *m* ; *tr* [-'bæləns] ein Gegengewicht bilden (*s.th.* gegen etw); entgegenwirken (*s.o.* jdm); das Gleichgewicht halten (*s.th.* e-r S); aufwiegen, aufheben, ausgleichen, kompensieren; *tech* auswuchten; **~blast** ['kauntəblɑ:st] *fig* heftige Entgegnung, Widerrede *f*; **~charge** ['-] *s* Gegenbeschuldigung, Widerklage *f*; Gegenangriff *m*; *tr* Gegenklage erheben (*with* wegen); *mil* e-n Gegenstoß ausführen gegen; **~check** ['-] *s* Gegenstoß *m*, -wirkung *f*; Widerstand *m*, Hindernis *n*; *(Schach)* Gegenzug *m*; Gegenprüfung, -kontrolle *f*; *tr* [-'tʃek] entgegenwirken (*s.th.* e-r S); gegenprüfen; **~-claim** ['-] *s jur* Gegenforderung, Widerklage *f*; *tr itr* [-'kleim] e-e Gegenforderung, e-e Widerklage erheben; Gegenansprüche stellen (*for* auf); **~-clockwise** ['-'klɔkwaiz] *a adv* gegen den Uhrzeigersinn; **~-espionage** (Spionage-)Abwehr *f*.

counter|feit ['kauntəfit] *a* nachgeahmt, -gemacht, unecht, falsch; vorgetäuscht, geheuchelt; *s* Nachahmung, Fälschung *f*; *tr* nachmachen, -ahmen, fälschen; vortäuschen, -schützen, heucheln; **~~** *money* Falschgeld *n*; **~feiter** ['-fitə] Fälscher; Falschmünzer *m*; **~foil** ['-] (Kontroll-)Abschnitt, Kupon; Gepäckschein *m*; **~~** *book* Abreiß-, Quittungsblock *m*; **~fort** ['-] Strebepfeiler; *(Brücke)* Eisbrecher *m*; **~-intelligence** ['-rin'telidʒəns] (Spionage-)Abwehr *f*; *C~~ Corps (Am)* Spionageabwehrdienst *m*; **~jumper** ['-] *fam* Heringsbändiger, Ladenschwengel *m*; **~mand** [-'mɑ:nd] *tr (Befehl)* widerrufen; *(Anordnung)* aufheben; *(Bestellung)* zurückziehen; abbestellen; absagen; *s* Gegenbefehl, Widerruf *m*; Aufhebung; Zurückziehung; Abbestellung *f*; *unless* **~~***ed* bis auf Widerruf; **~march** ['-] *s* Rückmarsch, Rückzug *m*; *itr* zurückmarschieren, sich zurückziehen; **~mark** ['-] Gegenzeichen *n*; **~measure** ['-] Gegenmaßnahme; Repressalie, Vergeltung *f*; **~mine** ['-] *s mil mar* Gegenmine *f*; *pol* Gegenschlag *m*; *tr* durch e-e Gegenmine abfangen; *(Verschwörung)* auffliegen, *fam* platzen lassen; **~-motion** ['-] Gegenantrag *m*; **~-move** ['-] Gegenzug, -schlag *m*; **~-offensive** [-rə-'fensiv] Gegenoffensive *f*, -angriff *m*; **~-order** ['-] Gegenbefehl *m*, -order; Abbestellung *f*.

counter|pane ['kauntəpein] Bett-, Steppdecke *f*; **~part** ['kauntəpɑ:t] Gegenstück *n* (*of* zu), Kopie *f*, Duplikat *n*; Ergänzung *f* (*of* gen); Ebenbild *n*; *mus* Gegenstimme *f*; **~~** *funds (pl)* Gegenwertmittel *n pl*; **~plot** ['-] Gegenschlag *m*; **~point** ['-] *mus* Kontrapunkt *m*; **~poise** ['-] *s* Gegengewicht *n* *a. fig*; Gleichgewicht(szustand *m*, -lage *f*) *n*; *tr* ein Gegengewicht bilden zu; das Gleichgewicht, die Waage halten (*s.th.* e-r S); aufwiegen, ausgleichen, aufheben; austarieren, durch Gegengewichte ausbalancieren; **C~ Reformation** ['-] *hist* Gegenreformation *f*; **~-revolution** ['-] Gegenrevolution *f*; **~sign** ['-] *s* Gegenzeichnung *f*; *mil* Kennwort *n*, Losung, Parole *f*; *tr* gegenzeichnen; *fig* bestätigen; **~sink** [-'siŋk] *irr -sunk, -sunk tr tech* versenken; ausfräsen; *s* ['-] Versenker, Versenkbohrer *m*; **~stroke** ['-] Gegenschlag, -stoß; Rückschlag *m*; **~-tenor** ['-'tenə] *mus* hohe(r) Tenor *m*; Altstimme *f*; **~vail** ['-] *tr* ausgleichen, aufwiegen; aufkommen gegen; *itr* gleich stark sein (*against* wie).

countess ['kauntis] Gräfin *f*.

counting ['kauntiŋ] *s* Zählen, Rechnen *n*; *attr* Zähl-, Rechen-; **~-house,** *Am* **-room** Büro, Kontor *n*, Buchhalterei, Buchhaltung *f*; **~ mechanism** Zählwerk *n*.

countless ['kauntlis] zahllos, unzählig.

country ['kʌntri] *s* Land *n*; Heimat (-land *n*) *f*, Vaterland *n*; Staat *m*; *ohne pl* Land(strich *m*) *n*, Gegend(en *pl*) *f*, Gebiet *n a. fig*; *the* ~ das Land *(im Gegensatz zur Stadt)*, die Provinz; *Am jur* Jury *f*, Geschworene(n) *m pl*; *a* Land-, ländlich, Bauern-, bäuerlich, Dorf-, dörflich; Provinz-; *from all over the* ~ aus allen Teilen des Landes; *in the* ~ auf dem Lande; *into the* ~ aufs Land; *out of the* ~ im Ausland; *to go to the* ~ *(Br parl)* Neuwahlen ausschreiben; *this is strange* ~ *to me (fig)* das sind mir böhmische Dörfer; *agricultural* ~ Agrarland *n*; *God's (own)* ~ die Vereinigten Staaten; *industrial* ~ Industriestaat *m*; *member* ~ Mitgliedstaat *m*; ~ *of destination (Post)* Bestimmungsland *n*; ~ *of origin* Herkunfts-, Ursprungsland *n*; **~ club** Sportklub *m* auf dem Lande (für Städter); **~ cousin** Vetter *m*, Base, *fig* Unschuld *f* vom Lande; **~-dance** Ländler *m (Tanz)*; **~fied, countrified** ['-faid] *a* ländlich; bäurisch; **~ folk** Landvolk *n*; **~ gentleman** Landedelmann; Großgrundbesitzer *m*; **~-house** Landhaus *n*; **~ life** Landleben *n*; **~man, ~woman** Landmann *m*, -frau *f*; Landsmann *m*, -männin *f*; **~ party** Bauernpartei *f*; **~ people** Landbewohner *m pl*, -leute *pl*; **~ road** Landstraße *f*; **~-seat** Landsitz *m*; **~side** : *the* **~~** das Land *(im Gegensatz zur Stadt)*; *in the* **~~** auf dem Lande; **~ squire** Landjunker *m*; **~ town** Landstadt *f*; **~-wide** *a* über das ganze Land hin.

county ['kaunti] *s* Grafschaft *f*, *etwa* (Land-)Kreis *m*; *Am* (Verwaltungs-, Regierungs-)Bezirk *m (e-s Staates)*; *a* Grafschafts-, Kreis-, Bezirks-; *fam* vornehm, exklusiv; **~ borough, corporate** *etwa* kreisfreie Stadt *f*, Stadtkreis *m*; **~ college** *Br* Fortbildungsschule *f*; **~ council** *etwa* Kreis-, Bezirkstag *m*; **~ court** *etwa* Amtsgericht *n*; **~ family** alteingesessene Familie *f*; **~ seat** *Am* Kreisstadt *f*; **~ town** *Br* Bezirkshauptstadt *f*.

coup [ku:] Schlag, Streich *fig*, Coup *m*; **~ d'état** [ku:dei'tɑ:] *pol* Staatsstreich *m*; **~ de grâce** ['ku:də'grɑ:s] Gnadenstoß *m*; **~ de main** ['ku:də'mæn] *mil* Handstreich *m*.

coupé ['kupei, kupe], *Am* **coupe** [ku:p] Coupé *n* (*mot* u. *hist Kutsche*); *rail* Halbabteil *n*.

coupl|e ['kʌpl] *s* Paar; *(married~)* Ehepaar *n*; Koppel *f*, Band *n*, Verbindung *f*; *phys* Kräfte-, Zugpaar *n*; *tr* (ver)koppeln; verheiraten; *fig* verbinden, in Verbindung bringen (*with* mit); *tech* kuppeln, koppeln, einrücken; auskoppeln (*from* aus); *rail (to* ~ *up)* ankuppeln, -hängen (*with* an); *mot* kuppeln, schalten; *radio chem* koppeln; *itr* sich paaren; heiraten; *a* ~ *of (fam)* zwei; ein paar; **~er** ['-ə] *(~~ plug)* Gerätestecker *m*; **~ing** ['-iŋ] Verbindung; *tech rail mot* Kupp(e)lung; *radio chem* Kopp(e)lung; *(Pferd)* Kruppe *f*.

couplet ['kʌplit] Reimpaar *n*.

coupon ['ku:pɔn] Abschnitt, Coupon, Zettel; Zinsschein; Gutschein *m*; *fin* Sparmarke *f*; *book of travel* **~s** Fahrscheinheft *n*; *reply* ~ Antwortschein *m*; **~ bonds** *pl Am* festverzinsliche Schuldverschreibungen *f pl*.

courage ['kʌridʒ] Mut *m*; Unerschrockenheit, Furchtlosigkeit; Tapferkeit *f*; *to have the* ~ *of o.'s convictions, opinions* nach s-r Überzeugung handeln, *fam* Zivilcourage haben; *to lose* ~ den Mut verlieren; *to pluck up, to muster up, to take* ~ Mut, sich ein Herz fassen; *to take o.'s* ~ *in both hands* allen Mut zs.nehmen; *Dutch* ~ angetrunkene(r) Mut *m*; **~ous** [kə'reidʒəs] mutig, tapfer, furchtlos, unerschrocken.

courier ['kuriə] Kurier, (Eil-)Bote; Reiseführer *m*; *by* ~ durch Boten.

course [kɔ:s] *s* Gang, Lauf *m a. fig*, Fahrt *f*; *fig (zeitl.)* Verlauf; Fortschritt; Verlauf *(e-r Linie, e-r Straße)*; *(Fluß)* Lauf; Kurs *m*, Richtung, Strecke *f*; *fig* Weg *m*, Möglichkeit; (Verhaltens-, Lebens-)Weise *f*; *(Mahlzeit)* Gang *m*; Reihe, Folge *f*; *(~ of instruction)* Kurs(us), Lehrgang *m*; Rennen *n*; Rennbahn *f*, Sportplatz *m*; *arch (Stein-)* Lage *f*; *mar* Untersegel *n*; *pl* Menstruation *f*; *tr* jagen; *(Hund)* hetzen; überqueren; *itr* laufen, rennen, jagen, schießen; *in the* ~ *of* im Verlauf *gen*, während *gen*; *in due* ~ zu seiner, zu gegebener Zeit, wenn es soweit ist; *in* ~ *of construction* im Bau (befindlich); *in* ~ *of organization* in der Bildung begriffen; *in the* ~ *of time* im Laufe der Zeit; *of* ~ natürlich, selbstverständlich; gewiß, sicher *adv*; *to run its* ~ s-n Gang gehen, s-n Verlauf nehmen; *to set the* ~ *for s.th.* etw ansteuern; *to stay the* ~ *(lit fig)* das Rennen nicht aufgeben; *to take, to hold, to change o.'s* ~ Kurs nehmen, halten, den Kurs wechseln; *a matter of* ~ e-e Selbstverständlichkeit; *as a matter of* ~ selbstverständlich *adv*; ~ *of business* Geschäftsgang *m*; ~ *of a disease* Krankheitsverlauf *m*; *the* ~ *of events* der Gang der Ereignisse, der Hergang; ~ *of indoctrination* Schulungskurs *m*; *the* ~ *of life* der Lauf des Lebens; *the* ~ *of nature* der Lauf der Welt; **~ light** *aero* Streckenfeuer *n*; **~r**

['-ə] *poet* Rennpferd *n*; *Am* Jagdhund *m*; **coursing** ['-iŋ] Hetzjagd *f a. fig.*

court [kɔ:t] *s* Hof; Lichthof *m*; Sackgasse *f*, Hof; (Tennis-)Platz *m*; Spielfeld *n*; (Fürsten-)Hof; Hofstaat *m*, -gesellschaft, -veranstaltung *f*, Empfang *m* bei Hof; Aufwartung, Aufmerksamkeit *f*; Werben *n*, Werbung *f*; Gericht(shof *m*); Gerichts-, Justizgebäude *n*; Gerichtsversammlung, -sitzung *f*; *a* Hof-; hoffähig; *tr* den Hof machen (*s.o.* jdm), werben um; *fig* sich bemühen um; *(Gelegenheit)* erspähen; *(Gefahr, Unheil)* heraufbeschwören; *at ~* bei Hof; *by action in a ~* gerichtlich; *by order of the ~* auf Grund richterlicher Verfügung; *in ~* vor, bei Gericht; *in open ~* in öffentlicher Verhandlung; *out of ~* nicht dazugehörig; außergerichtlich; *to appear before the ~* vor Gericht erscheinen; *to assert in ~* gerichtlich geltend machen; *to bring, to lay before the ~* vor Gericht bringen; *to pay ~ to s.o.* jdm den Hof machen, um jdn werben; *to represent s.o. in ~* jdn vor Gericht vertreten; *to seize through the ~* gerichtlich beschlagnahmen; *to settle out of ~* gütlich beilegen; *to take to ~* vor Gericht bringen; *that is out of ~* das kommt nicht in Frage, nicht in Betracht; *the ~ is sitting* das Gericht tagt; *appellate, appeal ~* Berufungsgericht *n*; *hearing of the ~* Gerichtssitzung *f*; *High, Supreme C~ of Justice* Oberste(r) Gerichtshof *m*; *juvenile ~* Jugendgericht *n*; *labo(u)r, industrial ~* Arbeitsgericht *n*; *probate ~* Nachlaßgericht *n*; *~ of administration* Verwaltungsgericht *n*; *~ of arbitration* Schiedsgericht *n*; *~ of assizes* Schwurgericht *n*; *~ of commerce* Handelsgericht *n*; *~ of conciliation* Schiedsamt *n*; *~ of finances* Rechnungshof *m*, -kammer *f*; *~ of guardianship* Vormundschaftsgericht *n*; *~* **circuit** Gerichtsbezirk *m*; *~* **circular** Hofnachrichten *f pl (in der Zeitung)*; *~* **costs** *pl* Gerichtskosten *pl*; *~* **day** Gerichtstag *m*; *~* **decision, judg(e)ment** Gerichtsentscheidung *f*; **~-dress** Hofanzug *m*, -kleid *n*; **~eous** ['kə:t-, 'kɔ:tjəs] höflich, gesittet; aufmerksam, gefällig, freundlich, nett; **~eousness** ['-nis] Höflichkeit; Freundlichkeit *f*; **~esan, ~ezan** [kɔ:ti'zæn] Kurtisane *f*, Freudenmädchen *n*; **~esy** ['kə:tisi, 'kɔ:təsi] Höflichkeit, Freundlichkeit; Aufmerksamkeit, Gefälligkeit *f*; Entgegenkommen *n*; Genehmigung *f*; *s. curtsy*; *as a matter of ~~* aus Höflichkeit; *by ~~ of* mit freundlicher Genehmigung *gen*; *~~ call* Höflichkeitsbesuch *m*; **~-hand** Kanzleischrift *f*; *~* **hearing** Gerichtstermin *m*; *~* **house** Gerichts-, Justizgebäude; *Am* Regierungsgebäude, Kreishaus *n*; **~ier** ['kɔ:tjə] Höfling, Hofmann *m*; **~ly** ['kɔ:tli] *a* höfisch; würdevoll, fein, elegant; höflich; schmeichlerisch; *~* **martial** *s* Kriegsgericht *n*; **~-martial** *tr* vor ein K. stellen; *to be ~~led and shot* standrechtlich erschossen werden; **~-plaster** Heftpflaster *n*; *~* **room** Gerichtssaal *m*; **~ship** ['-ʃip] Hofmachen *n*, Werbung *f*; **~yard** Hof(raum) *m*; *in the ~~* auf dem Hof.

cousin ['kʌzn] Vetter *m*, Base *f*, Cousin(e *f*) *m*; (entfernte(r)) Verwandte(r *m*) *f*; *pl* Geschwisterkinder *n pl*; *boy, girl ~* Vetter *m*, Base *f*; *first ~, ~ german* Vetter *m*, Base *f* 1. Grades; *second ~* Vetter *m*, Base *f* 2. Grades; **~ship** Vetter(n)schaft; Verwandtschaft *f*.

cove [kouv] **1.** *s* kleine Bucht; Einbuchtung; Höhle *f*; geschützte Wiese *f*; Schlupfwinkel, Unterschlupf *m*; *arch* Deckenkehle; Wölbung *f*; *tr* auskehlen; (über)wölben; **2.** *Br sl* Kerl, Bursche *m*.

covenant ['kʌvinənt] *s* (feierlicher) Vertrag, Pakt *m*; Ab-, Übereinkommen *n*, Vereinbarung, Abmachung; Vertragsklausel; Schadenersatzklage *f* wegen Vertragsverletzung; *rel* Bund *m*; *tr itr* e-n Vertrag schließen; übereinkommen, vereinbaren, abmachen (*with* mit); sich (vertraglich) verpflichten (*with s.o.* jdm gegenüber); *Ark of the C~ (rel)* Bundeslade *f*; *the Land of the C~* das Gelobte Land *(Palästina)*; *the Old and the New C~ (rel)* der Alte u. der Neue Bund; *C~ of the League of Nations* Völkerbundssatzungen *f pl*; **~er** ['-ə] Verbündete(r), Bündnispartner; Vertragspartner, Kontrahent *m*; *C~~* schottische(r) Presbyterianer *m*.

Coventr|y ['kɔvəntri] *(Stadt in Mittelengland) to send s.o. to ~* jdn schneiden.

cover ['kʌvə] *tr* be-, zudecken, be-, überziehen (*with* mit), ausbreiten über; sich verbreiten, sich erstrecken über; *(Land)* einnehmen, besetzen; bespritzen; einschlagen, einwickeln, ver-, bekleiden, umhüllen (*with* mit), einhüllen (*with* in), verbergen; abschirmen, schützen, decken; *(mit Stoff)* beziehen; *(finanziell)* sichern, decken, ausreichen für; *(Strecke)* zurücklegen; *(Wette)* den gleichen Betrag setzen, die Bedingungen annehmen; *mil* bestreichen, beherrschen; *(Radar)* erfassen; *(mit Feuer)* belegen; *(Waffe)* richten auf (*with s.th.* etw), in Schach halten (*with* mit); *(Kartenspiel)* stechen; *(Tier)* decken, bespringen; *(Eier)* ausbrüten; *fig* umfassen, einbeziehen, einschließen, decken; *(Gebiet)* bearbeiten; *Am (Berichterstatter)* aufnehmen; e-n Bericht zs.stellen, berichten über; *to ~ o.s. (fig)* sich bedecken *(with glory* mit Ruhm*)*; *s* Decke *f*; Deckel; Überzug *m*; (Schutz-)Hülle *f*, Umschlag *m*, Futteral *n*; *(Buch)* Einband(decke *f*, -deckel); (Brief-)Umschlag *m*; Verpackung; Deckung *f*, Schutz *m (vor dem Feinde, vor Verfolgern)*; Zuflucht *f*, Unterschlupf *m*, Obdach; *bes.* Gebüsch, Dickicht, Unterholz *n*; *fig* Schutz-, Deckmantel, Vorwand *m*; *fin* Deckung, Sicherheit *f*; Gedeck *n (für e-e Mahlzeit, a. der Preis dafür)*; *to ~ in (mit Erde)* auffüllen; *to ~ over* abdecken, -dichten; zudecken; *(Anleihe)* überzeichnen; *to ~ up* (warm) anziehen, (gut) zudecken, (dicht) verhüllen, (gut) verpacken; *fam* verbergen; *s.o.* jdn decken; *from ~ to ~ (Buch)* von Anfang bis zu Ende *(lesen)*; *under ~* in Deckung, versteckt; heimlich; zum Schein; *under ~ of* im Schutz *gen*; unter dem Deckmantel, Vorwand *gen*; *under the same ~* beiliegend, in der Anlage; *under separate ~* mit gleicher Post; *without ~ (fin)* ungedeckt; *to break ~* die Deckung verlassen; *to take ~* in Deckung gehen, Schutz suchen; *~!* Deckung! *~ off!* Vordermann! *cloud ~, ~ of clouds* Wolkendecke *f*; *sufficient ~ (fin)* ausreichende Sicherheit *f*; *~* **address** Deckadresse *f*; **~age** ['-ridʒ] Geltungs-, Anwendungsbereich; Umfang *m* des Versicherungsschutzes; *(Zeitung)* (Zs.-stellung *f* e-s) Bericht(s) *m*, Berichterstattung; Erfassung *f*; *tele* Empfangs-, Sendebereich *m*, Reichweite; Verbreitung(sgebiet *n*) *f*; *phot aero* Geländeausschnitt *m*; *mil* Sicherung *f*; **~all** [-rɔ:l] *Am meist pl* Arbeitsmantel, -kittel *m*; *~* **belt** *mil* Sicherungsgürtel *m*; *~* **charge** *Am* (Preis *m* e-s) Gedeck(s) *n*; *~* **crop** *Am* Schutzbepflanzung *f*; *~* **detachment** *mil* Sicherungstrupp *m*; **~ed** ['-d] *a* bedeckt; gesichert; überdacht; *mil* gedeckt, angelehnt; *tech* umsponnen, umhüllt, isoliert; *to be ~~ in file* auf Vordermann stehen; *period ~~* Berichtszeit *f*; *~~ wagon (Am)* Planwagen; *Br* geschlossener Güterwagen *m*; *~~ wire* isolierte(r) Draht *m*; *~* **girl** Titelbildmädchen *n (auf Illustrierten)*; Reklameschönheit *f*; Fotomodell *n*; **~ing** ['-riŋ] *s* Decke, Hülle; Verkleidung; Überdachung; *tech* Verschalung *f*; Überzug *m*, Futteral *n*; *mil* Deckung, Abschirmung, Sicherung *f*; *~~ letter* Begleitbrief *m*, -schreiben *n*; *~~ position (mil)* Aufnahmestellung *f*; **~let** [-lit], **~lid** [-lid] Bett-, Steppdecke *f*; **~name** Deckname *m*; *~* **note** vorläufige(r) Versicherungsschein *m*; **~-up** *Am fam* Alibi *n*, Vorwand *m*.

covert ['kʌvət, *mil Am* 'kouvə:t] *a fig* versteckt, verborgen, verhüllt, verschleiert, heimlich, verstellt, irreführend; geheim, getarnt; *jur (Frau)* verheiratet; *s* Zuflucht(sort *m*) *f*, Unterschlupf *m*; Dickicht, Unterholz, Gebüsch *n*; *pl* Deckfedern *f pl*; *to draw a ~ (Jagd)* ein Gebüsch absuchen; *a ~ threat* e-e versteckte Drohung; **~-coat** *Br* kurze(r), leichte(r) Mantel *m*; **~ure** ['-juə, '-tʃuə]; *(Frau)* Ehestand *m*.

covet ['kʌvit] *tr* (heftig) begehren, verlangen nach, unbedingt haben wollen, versessen sein auf, *fam* verrückt sein nach; **~ous** ['-əs] begierig (*of* nach), versessen (*of* auf); gierig, habsüchtig, geizig; **~ousness** ['-əsnis] Begierde, Gier; Habsucht *f*, Geiz *m*.

covey ['kʌvi] *(Vögel)* Brut, Hecke *f*; Trupp *m*; *(Rebhühner)* Kette *f*, Volk *n*; *(Menschen)* Gruppe, Schar *f*.

*

cow [kau] **1.** *s* Kuh *f*; Weibchen *n*; *sl* Hexe *f*; *till the ~s come home* e-e Ewigkeit; **2.** *tr* einschüchtern, verängstigen; *~* **bell** Kuhglocke *f*; *~* **berry** ['-beri] Preiselbeere *f*; **~boy** *Am* Cowboy *m*; **~-cage** *Am rail* Viehwagen *m*; **~-catcher** *Am rail* Schienenräumer *m*; **~-dung** Kuhmist *m*; **~-fish** Seekuh *f*; Tümmler; Kofferfisch *m*; **~girl** *Am* weibliche(r) Cowboy *m*; **~hand** *Am* Cowboy; Schweizer *m*; **~-heel** *(Küche)* (Rinder-)Hesse *f*, Kalbsfuß *m* (in Gelee); **~herd** Kuhhirt *m*; **~hide** *s* Kuhhaut *f*, -leder *n*; *Am* Lederpeitsche *f*, Ochsenziemer *m*; *tr* mit dem Ochsenziemer schlagen; **~lick** ['-lik] (Haar-)Strähne *f*; **~man** *Am* Rinder-, Viehzüchter *m*; **~-milker** Melkmaschine *f*; **~-parsley, -weed** *bot* Wiesenkerbel *f*, Kälberrohr *n*; **~-parsnip** *bot* Bärenklau *m*; **~-pea** *bot* Vignabohne, Kuherbse *f*; **~-pox** *vet med* Kuhpocken *pl*; **~puncher** *Am fam* Cowboy *m*; **~shed** Kuhstall *m*; **~slip** Schlüsselblume, Primel; *Am* Sumpfdotterblume *f*.

coward ['kauəd] *s* Feigling, *fam* Angsthase *m*; *a (a. ~ly)* feige, bange, ängstlich; **~ice** ['-is], **~liness** ['-linis] Feigheit, Angst *f*.

cower ['kauə] *itr* (nieder-, zs.)kauern, sich ducken; *Am (erschrocken)* zs.fahren, (er)zittern, -beben.

cowl [kaul] Kapuze; Schornstein-, Kaminkappe; *mot* Haube; *(Kühler)* Verkleidung *f*; **~ing** ['-iŋ] *aero mot* (Hauben-)Verkleidung *f*.

co-work [kou'wə:k] Zs.arbeit *f*; **~er** [-ə] Mitarbeiter *m*.

cowr|ie, ~y ['kauri] *zoo* Kaurimuschel *f*; Kauri *m* od *n*, Muschelgeld *n*.

coxcomb ['kɔkskoum] Narrenkappe *f*; *bot* Hahnenkamm; *fig* Laffe, Geck *m*.
cox(swain) ['kɔks(wein), *mar* 'kɔksn] Boots-, Steuermann; Bootsführer *m*.
coy [kɔi] scheu, schüchtern, zurückhaltend; *(Frau)* spröde, zimperlich; **~ness** ['-nis] Schüchternheit; Sprödigkeit *f*.
coyote ['kɔiout] *zoo* Prärie-, Steppenwolf *m*.
cozen ['kʌzn] *tr itr lit* betrügen, prellen (*of, out of* um); täuschen, hintergehen; betören, verführen (*into doing* zu tun).
coz(e)y *s. cosy*.
crab [kræb] **1.** *s* Krabbe *f*, Taschenkrebs *m*; *tech* Hebezeug *n*; Winde; Laufkatze *f*; *aero* Schieben *n (im Seitenwind)*; *C~ (astr)* Krebs *m*; *pl (Würfelspiel)* Pasch eins *m*; *itr* Krabben fischen; *tr aero* schieben; *to catch a ~* e-n falschen Ruderschlag tun; *to turn out ~s (fam)* schiefgehen, scheitern; **~-louse** Filzlaus *f*; **2.** *s (~ apple)* Holzapfel *m*; *fam* Miesmacher; Nörgler, Meckerer; Querkopf *m*; *a* Holzapfel-; *tr itr fam* meckern, nörgeln, schimpfen (*s.o., s.th.* od *about s.th.* über jdn, über etw); *to ~ o.'s act (Am fam)* sich die Sache vermasseln; *to ~ the deal (Am fam)* e-n Strich durch die Rechnung machen; **~bed** ['-id] *a* mürrisch, griesgrämig; kompliziert, schwierig; schwer verständlich, schlecht lesbar; **~by** ['-i] mürrisch, sauertöpfisch; querköpfig; **~-pot** Krebsreuse *f*; **~-tree** Holzapfel *m (Baum)*.
crack [kræk] *itr* rissig werden; *(Glas)* springen, e-n Sprung bekommen; (auf)platzen, bersten, brechen; knallen, krachen; *(Stimme)* rauh werden *(bes. beim Stimmwechsel)*; umschlagen, überschnappen; *Am (Tag)* anbrechen; *sl* zs.klappen, -brechen, rasen; *sl* Witze reißen, *sl* scharfe Bemerkungen machen; *tr* (zer)brechen; beschädigen, zerstören; *(Nuß, sl: Geldschrank)* knacken; *(Ei)* aufschlagen; *(Öl)* kracken; knallen lassen, *(die Peitsche)* knallen; herausschreien; *(die Stimme)* überschnappen lassen; *fam* eine knallen (*s.o.* jdm); *fam* 'rauskriegen, klären, lösen; *fam (Stellung)* bekommen, erringen; *Am fam* ohne Eintrittskarte, uneingeladen besuchen; *(Geld)* wechseln; *s* Sprung, Riß, Spalt *m*; Ritze *f*; Knall, Krach, (Donner-)Schlag; Schlag, Stoß *m*; *(Stimme)* Überschnappen; *(Peitsche)* Knallen *n*; *sl* Vorstoß, Versuch *m*; *sl* Angabe, Vorspiegelung *f* falscher Tatsachen; *fam* Moment, Augenblick *m*, Sekunde *f*; *sl* Pfunds-, Prachtkerl *m*; Prachtpferd, -stück *n*; Favorit; hervorragende(r) Spieler; *sl* Einbruch; Einbrecher; *sl* Witz, Spaß *m*, bissige Bemerkung *f*; *a fam* großartig, glänzend, blendend, prachtvoll, phantastisch, prima, Pracht-; *adv* krachend; *interj* krach! *to ~ back (Am fam)* scharf erwidern; *to ~ down (fam)* fest anpacken, scharf anfassen (*on s.o.* jdn), was unternehmen, vorgehen, (*on* gegen); *to ~ up (fam) itr* zs.sacken, -klappen, gewaltig nachlassen; *tr fam* herausstreichen, in den Himmel heben; *aero fam* e-e Bruchlandung machen; *at day ~, at the ~ of dawn* bei Tagesanbruch; beim Morgengrauen; *in a ~* im Nu; *on the ~ (Am) (Tür)* angelehnt; *to take a ~ at s.th.* etw versuchen; *to ~ a bottle* e-r Flasche den Hals brechen; *to ~ a crib (in ein Haus)* einbrechen; *to ~ a joke (sl)* e-n Witz reißen; *to ~ wise (Am sl)* e-e witzige Bemerkung machen; *he didn't ~ a smile* er verzog keine Miene; *get ~ing!* los! voran! *a dry ~ (Am sl)* e-e kurze bissige Bemerkung; *~ of the door (Am sl)* Türspalt *m*; *~ of thunder* Donnerschlag *m*; *~ of a whip* Peitschenknall *m*; **~ajack, ~erjack** ['krækə(:)dʒæk] *Am sl a* pfundig, großartig, Klasse; *s* Pfundssache *f*, -kerl *m*; **~-brained** *a* verrückt, wahnsinnig; **~down** ['-daun] *Am fam* schnelle(s) Eingreifen *n*; **~ed** [-t] *a* gesprungen, rissig; *(Stimme)* übergeschnappt, rauh, schrill; *fam* verrückt, übergeschnappt; **~er** ['-ə] Knall-, Feuerwerkskörper, Schwärmer *m*; *(Christmas ~~)* Knallbonbon *m* od *n*; *(dünner, harter)* Keks *m*; *fam* Angabe, Lüge *f*; *meist pl (nut-~~s)* Nußknacker *m*; *~~-barrel (Am fam) s* Biertisch *m*; *a* einfach, simpel, spießig; **~ers** ['-əz] *fam* plemplem; **~-jaw** Zungenbrecher *m*; **~ing** ['-iŋ] *s tech* Kracken *n*; *a fam* rasend schnell; *~~ plant* Kracking-, Fraktionierungsanlage *f*; *~~ process* Krackverfahren *n*; **~le** ['krækl] *itr* knistern, prasseln, knattern; *s* Knistern, Geknister; Geprassel; Geknatter *n*; *(~~ ware)* Craquelée *f* od *n*; **~ling** ['-liŋ] *s* Geknitter, Geprassel *n*; knusprige Schwarte *f (des Schweinebratens)*; *pl (Speck-)* Grieben *f pl*; *a* knisternd; *~~ noise (tele)* Nebengeräusch *n*; **~nel** ['-nl] harte(r) Keks *m*; *pl (Am) (frische, knusprige)* Speckgrieben *f pl*; **~pot** ['-pɔt] *s* Verrückte(r) *m*; *a* verrückt; **~ shot** *Am fam* Meisterschuß *m*; **~sman** *sl* Einbrecher *m*; **~ troops** *pl mil* Kerntruppen *f pl*; **~-up** Zs.bruch, Kollaps; *(Fahrzeuge)* Aufprall, Zs.stoß, -prall; *aero* Absturz, Bruch *m*; **~y** ['-i] rissig; brüchig; *fam* verrückt, wahnsinnig; *by ~~! (Am)* verdammt! verflixt!
cradle ['kreidl] *s* Wiege *a. fig*; *fig* Kindheit *f*; *fig* Ursprungsland, -gebiet; *tech* Gestell *n*; Schlitten *m*; *mar* Ab-, *aero* Anlaufgestell *n*; Telefongabel; *(miner's ~)* Wiege *f*, Schwingtrog *m*; *tr (Kind)* in die Wiege legen; (in den Schlaf) wiegen; aufziehen; *tech* auflegen; *min* wiegen; *from the ~* von klein auf; *in the ~* in frühester Jugend; *to ~ in o.'s arms* auf den Armen wiegen; **~song** Wiegenlied *n*.
craft [krɑ:ft] Geschick(lichkeit *f*) *n*, (Hand-, Kunst-)Fertigkeit; *fig* Schlauheit, Verschmitztheit *f*; Handwerk, Gewerbe *n*; *(~-guild)* Zunft, Gilde, Innung *f*; Schiff(e *pl*); Flugzeug(e *pl*) *n*; **~iness** ['-inis] Schlauheit, Gerissenheit, Durchtriebenheit *f*; **~sman** Handwerker; Künstler *m*; **~smanship** Handwerk(skunst *f*) *n*, Kunst *f*; fachliche(s) Können *n*; **~y** ['-i] schlau, verschmitzt, listig, gerissen.
crag [kræg] Felsspitze *f*, -zacken, -vorsprung *m*; Klippe *f*; **~ged** ['-id], **~gy** ['-i] *a* zackig, ausgezackt, zerklüftet; steil, schroff; **~sman** ['-zmən] erfahrene(r) Bergsteiger *m*.
crake [kreik] *s. corn-crake*.
cram [kræm] *tr* hineinstopfen; (voll-) stopfen, vollpfropfen (*s.th. into s.th.* etw mit e-r S); stopfen, nudeln, mästen; *fam* einpauken; mit (Wissens-)Stoff überladen; *sl* belügen; *itr fam* pauken, ochsen, büffeln; verschlingen; *s* Überfülle; *fam* Paukerei *f*; Wissensballast; Büffler, Bücherwurm *m*; Lehrbuch *n*; *sl* Lüge *f*; **~-full** vollgepropft, übervoll; **~mer** ['-ə] Examenskandidat; Repetitor; *sl* Lügner *m*; Lüge *f*.
cramp [kræmp] *s med* (Muskel-)Krampf *m*; *pl (Magen-)* Krämpfe *m pl*; *sing tech* Krampe, Haspe, (Eisen-)Klammer; Schraubzwinge; *fig* Fessel *f*, Hindernis *n*; Zwang *m*; Behinderung; Enge, Beengtheit, Eingeengtheit *f*; *tr* verkrampfen, krampfhaft verzerren; *tech* verklammern; *fig* hindern, hemmen, be-, einengen, in Schranken halten; *a* behindert, gehemmt, eingeengt; schwer verständlich, schwer lesbar, unleserlich; *writer's ~* Schreibkrampf *m*; **~ed** [-d] *a* verkrampft, steif; gehemmt; eng, be-, eingeengt; engstirnig; *(Schrift)* kritz(e)lig, unleserlich; **~-fish** *zoo* Zitterrochen *m*; **~-iron** Krampe, Haspe, Klammer *f*; **~on** ['-ən] eiserne(r) Haken *m*; *meist pl* Steigeisen *n (pl)*.
cran|age ['kreinidʒ] Krangeld *n*, -gebühren *f pl*; **~e** [krein] *s orn* Kranich; *tech* Kran *m*; Winde *f*; Hebezeug *n*; Ladebaum *m*; *tr itr* (den Hals) recken (*for* nach); *tr* mit e-m Kran heben *od* bewegen; hochwinden, -heben; *~~ beam* Ausleger, Ladearm *m*; *~~ driver, operator* Kranführer *m*; *~~-fly (ent)* Schnake *f*; *~~'s bill (bot)* Storchschnabel *m*; *~~ truck (mot)* Kranwagen *m*.
cranberry ['krænbəri] Preisel-, Kronsbeere *f*.
cran|ial ['kreiniəl] *a scient* Schädel-, Kopf-; *~~ index* Schädelindex *m*; *~~ nerve* Gehirnnerv *m*; **~iology** [kreini'ɔlədʒi] Schädellehre *f*; **~iometry** [-'ɔmətri] Schädelmessung *f*; **~iotomy** [-'ɔtəmi] Schädeleröffnung *f*; **~ium** ['kreiniəm] *pl -ia* Schädel *m*.
crank [kræŋk] *s tech* Kurbel *f*; Schwengel *m*; Knie(stück) *n*; *fig* (witziger) Einfall *m*, verrückte Idee *f*; (toller) Streich; *fam* komische(r) Kauz *m*, Original *n*, Sonderling; Nörgler, Querulant *m*; *a tech* wack(e)lig, locker, lose, nicht in Ordnung; *mar* rank; *tr (to ~ up) (Motor)* (an)kurbeln, anwerfen; drehen *(a. film)*; krümmen, biegen, kröpfen; *itr* kurbeln, drehen; **~case** Kurbelgehäuse *n*, -wanne *f*; **~iness** ['-inis] Reizbarkeit; schlechte Laune *f*; komische(s) Wesen *n*; **~le** ['-l] *itr* sich winden, sich schwankend bewegen; *s* Windung *f*; **~pin** Kurbel-, Treibzapfen *m*; *~~ box* Pleuelkopf *m*; **~shaft** Kurbelwelle *f*; **~y** ['-i] *tech* nicht in Ordnung, *fam* kaputt; wack(e)lig, lose; *fam* komisch; *fam* schlecht-, übelgelaunt; *mar* rank.
crann|ied ['krænid] *a* rissig; **~y** ['-i] Riß *m*, Ritze *f*, Spalt(e *f*) *m*.
crap [kræp] *s meist pl* Crapsspiel *(mit zwei Würfeln)*; *sl* Unsinn, Schwindel; Schund *m*; *sl* Kacke *f*; *tr Am sl* beschummeln; *to shoot ~s* Craps spielen, würfeln; *to ~ out (Am sl) (Geld)* verlieren; sich drücken, kalte Füße kriegen; **~per** ['-ə] *Am sl* Klo *n*; **~ shooter** Crapsspieler *m*; **~py** ['-i] *Am sl* wertlos, häßlich, widerlich.
crape [kreip] *s* Krepp, Flor; *(~ of mourning)* Trauerflor *m*; *tr* drapieren; **~hanger** *Am sl* Schwarzseher, Pessimist *m*.
crapulence ['kræpjuləns] Trunk(sucht *f*) *m*; Ausschweifung *f*; Katzenjammer *m*, *fam* Kater *m*.
crash [kræʃ] **1.** *itr* (ein)stürzen, zs.brechen, *fam* (zs.)krachen; herab-, -unterstürzen, -poltern; *aero* abstürzen, Bruch machen, *sl* abschmieren; krachen, stürzen (*against* gegen); brechen (*through* durch); einbrechen (*into* in); (wirtschaftlich, finanziell) zs.brechen; *tr* zerschmettern; *aero* zum Absturz bringen, bruchlanden; *sl* eindringen, sich einschleichen in *(e-e Gesellschaft, e-e Veranstaltung)*; *s* Krachen *n*; Krach *m*; Zs.Brechen *n*, (Ein-)Sturz; Aufprall, Zs.stoß; *aero* Absturz, Bruch; Aufschlag *(auf den Boden)*; *fin* Zs.bruch, Bankrott; *(bank ~)* Bankkrach *m*; *Am fam* Schwärmen *n*; **2.** Drillich *m (grobes Leinen)*; *to ~ in, out, through*

ein-, aus-, durchbrechen; **~-dive** *mar* Alarmtauchen *n*; **~-helmet** *mot* Sturzhelm *m*; **~ing** ['-iŋ] *fam* völlig, gänzlich; **~-land** *itr aero* bruchlanden; **~-landing** *aero* Bruchlandung *f*; **~out** *Am* Ausbruch *m* aus dem Gefängnis; **~ truck, vehicle** Bergungsfahrzeug *n*; **~ wagon** *Am* Kranken-, Unfallwagen *m*.

crass [kræs] grob; kraß; *fam* absolut.

crate [kreit] *s* Lattenkiste *f*, Verschlag *m*; Flechtwerk *n*; *mot aero sl* (alte) Kiste *f*; *tr* in Kisten verpacken.

crater ['kreitə] *geol* Krater; Granat-, Bombentrichter *m*.

cravat [krə'væt] Halstuch *n*; *hist* Halsbinde; Krawatte *f*, Binder *m*.

crav|e [kreiv] *tr* erbitten, erflehen; sehnlichst wünschen; dringend benötigen *od* gebrauchen; *itr* sich sehnen (*for* nach); sehnlichst wünschen (*for s.th.* etw); **~ing** ['-iŋ] heiße(s), heftige(s), starke(s) Verlangen *n*, Sehnsucht *f* (*for* nach).

craven ['kreivn] *a* feig(e); *s* Feigling *m*; *to cry ~* um Gnade flehen.

craw [krɔ:] *orn* Kropf; *allg* Magen *m*; *to stick in the ~, in o.'s ~ (fig Am)* (e-m) im Halse steckenbleiben.

crawfish ['krɔ:fiʃ] *s bes. Am* = *crayfish*; *Am fam* Drückeberger *m*; *itr Am fam* kneifen, sich drücken.

crawl [krɔ:l] *itr* kriechen *a. fig* (*to* vor); krabbeln; schleichen; *mil* robben; *(Ort)* wimmeln (*with* von); *(Haut)* kribbeln; *sport* kraulen; *s* Kriechen; *sport* Kraul *n*; *sl* Sauftour *f*; *to go at a ~* im Schneckentempo gehen; **~er** ['-ə] Kriechtier *n*; *sport* Kraulstilschwimmer; *fig* Kriecher, Speichellecker *m*; *pl* Krabbelanzug *m*; *tech* Raupenkette *f*; *~~ tractor* Raupenschlepper *m*; **~y** ['-i] krabb(e)lig.

crayfish ['kreifiʃ] (Fluß-)Krebs *m*; *(sea ~)* Languste *f*.

crayon ['kreiən, '-ɔn] *s* Zeichen-, Farb-, (Öl-)Kreidestift; Pastellstift *m*; *(~-drawing)* Kreidezeichnung *f*; Pastell *n*; *tr* mit Kreide zeichnen; mit Pastell malen; skizzieren.

craz|e [kreiz] *tr* den Verstand rauben (*s.o.* jdm) *(Glasur)* rissig machen, krakelieren; *itr* den Verstand verlieren; *s* große Begeisterung, Vorliebe (*for* für), Manie, fixe Idee *f*; Hobby *n*; Modetorheit *f*; Sprung, feine(r) Riß *m (in Glasur)*; *to be the ~~* sehr beliebt sein; *the latest ~~* der letzte Schrei; **~ed** [-d] *a* irre, geistesgestört, wahnsinnig, verrückt (*with* vor); *(Glasur)* rissig, krakeliert; *to be ~~ about* verrückt sein nach; **~iness** ['-inis] Irresein *n*, Geistesgestörtheit *f*, Wahnsinn *m*, Verrücktheit *f*; **~y** ['-i] rissig; wack(e)lig; baufällig, altersschwach; wahnsinnig; außer sich; verrückt (*with* vor; *about* nach), versessen (*about* auf), wild (*about* nach); aufregend, neu; *like ~~ (adv Am fam)* wie verrückt, wie wahnsinnig, wie ein Irrer; *~~ bone (Am)* Musikantenknochen *m*; *~~ paving* mit unregelmäßigen Platten belegte(r) Gartenweg *m*.

creak [kri:k] *itr* knarren; quietschen; *s* Knarren; Quietschen *n*; **~y** ['-i] knarrend; quietschend.

cream [kri:m] *s* Sahne *f*, Rahm *m*, *(Österreich)* Obers *n*; Krem, Schaum-, Süßspeise *f*, Pudding, Flammeri *m*; Püree, Mark *n*; (dickflüssiger) Likör *m*; (Haut-)Creme *od* Krem *f*; *(the ~)* das Beste, die Besten, die Spitze, die Auslese, die Pointe; Cremefarbe *f*; *a* sahnig; Sahne-; cremefarben; *itr* sahnig *od* schaumig werden; *tr* entrahmen; *fig* das Beste abschöpfen von; Sahne tun an, in; mit Sahne zubereiten; schaumig schlagen; *Am fam* leicht u. mit Erfolg erledigen, übertrumpfen, hereinlegen; *chocolate ~* Schokoladenkrem *f*; *the ~ of the crop* das Feinste vom Feinen; *~ of tartar (chem)* (gereinigter) Weinstein *m*; **~ cheese** Sahnekäse *m*; **~-colo(u)r** Cremefarbe *f*; **~-colo(u)red** *a* cremefarben; **~er** ['-ə] Milchschüssel, -schale; Zentrifuge *f*; *Am* Sahnekännchen *n*; **~ery** ['-əri] Molkerei *f*; Milchgeschäft *n*, Butter- u. Käsehandlung *f*; **~-laid, ~-wove** *a*: *~~ paper (Art)* feine(s) Briefpapier *n*; **~y** ['-i] sahn(ehalt)ig; *fig* salbungsvoll.

creas|e [kri:s] **1.** *s* Falte *f*; Kniff *m*; Bügelfalte *f (in der Hose)*; Eselsohr *n (in Papier)*; *sport* Linie *f (auf dem Spielfeld)*; *tr* falten; *(Hose)* bügeln; zerknittern; *itr* knittern; *~~-proof* knitterfrei; **2.** *s. creese*; **~y** ['-i] faltig, wellig.

creat|e [kri'eit] *tr* (er)schaffen, erzeugen, hervorbringen, herstellen, machen; erfinden; ins Leben rufen; hervorrufen, verursachen, bewirken; *(to ~~ s.o. s.th.)* machen zu, ernennen; gründen, errichten; *(Stiftung)* einsetzen; *(Verpflichtung)* begründen; *(Prokura)* erteilen; *(Hypothek, Pfandrecht)* bestellen; *theat (Rolle)* zum erstenmal spielen; *itr sl* Theater, Tamtam machen (*about* um); **~ion** [-'eiʃən] Erschaffung; Schöpfung; Welt *f*, Universum, All; Werk *n (a. in d. Kunst)*; Modeschöpfung; Erzeugung, Hervorbringung, Herstellung; Erfindung; Hervorrufung, Verursachung, Bewirkung; Schaffung, Bildung, Gestaltung; (Be-)Gründung, Errichtung; Ernennung *f*; *theat* Kreieren *n (e-r Rolle)*; *the C~~ (rel)* die Schöpfung; *~~ of capital* Kapitalbildung *f*; **~ive** [-iv] schöpferisch; produktiv (*of* in); erfinderisch; **~iveness** [-ivnis] Schöpfer-, Erfindungsgabe *f*; **~or** [-ə] Schöpfer, Erschaffer, Erzeuger, Hersteller; Erfinder; Modeschöpfer *m*; *the C~~* der Schöpfer, Gott *m*.

creature ['kri:tʃə] Geschöpf *n*, Kreatur *f*, (Lebe-)Wesen, Tier; *meist pej (Mensch)* Geschöpf *n*, Kreatur *f*; *living ~* Lebewesen *n*; **~ comfort(s** *pl) die* Annehmlichkeiten *f pl* des Lebens.

crèche [kreiʃ] Krippe *f*, Tagesheim *n* für Kleinkinder.

creden|ce ['kri:dəns] Glaube(n) *allg*; *rel* Kredenztisch *m*; *to give ~~ to* Glauben schenken *dat*; *letter of ~~* Empfehlungs-, Beglaubigungsschreiben *n*; **~tial** [kri'denʃəl] *s meist pl* Empfehlungs-, Beglaubigungsschreiben *n*; Zeugnisse; (Ausweis-)Papiere *n pl*.

credib|ility [kredi'biliti] Glaubwürdigkeit, Glaubhaftigkeit, Zuverlässigkeit *f*; **~le** ['kredəbl, -ibl] glaubwürdig, -haft, zuverlässig.

credit [kredit] Glaube(n) *m*, Vertrauen *n*; Glaubens-, Vertrauenswürdigkeit *f*; Ansehen *n*, Geltung *f*, (guter) Name, (guter) Ruf *m*; Verdienst *n*, Ehre *f*, Ruhm; Einfluß *m*; Namensnennung, Quellenangabe *f*, Hinweis *m a. radio*; *Am (~ point)* Gutpunkt *m*; *fin* Kredit *m*; Guthaben *n*, -schrift *f*; *pl* Ausgabemittel *n pl*; *com* Haben *n*; *mil* Zuteilung *f* auf Abruf; *tr* glauben, Glauben schenken; (ver)trauen (*s.o., s.th.* jdm, e-r S); Anerkennung bringen (*s.o.* jdm); (ehrenvoll) erwähnen; *Am (Universität)* testieren, bescheinigen; *fin* Kredit geben (*s.o.* jdm); *com* gutschreiben, -bringen, kreditieren; erkennen (*for a sum* für e-e Summe); *to ~ s.th. to s.o., to ~ s.o. with s.th.* jdm etw zutrauen, -schreiben; *on ~* auf Kredit, auf Ziel, *fam* auf Pump; *to s.o.'s ~* zu jds Ehre, Gunsten; *to allow, to give, to grant, to open ~ to s.o.* jdm Kredit gewähren, einräumen, eröffnen; *to be to s.o.'s ~* jds Verdienst sein; *to do ~ to s.o.* jdm Ehre machen; *to give ~ to, to put, to place ~ in* Glauben schenken *dat*; *to give s.o. ~ for s.th.* jdm etw zutrauen, -schreiben; jdm etw zugute halten; *to give s.th. on ~* etw auf Kredit geben, kreditieren; *to take ~ for* sich als Verdienst anrechnen; *debit and ~* Soll u. Haben *n*; *~ with the bank* Bankguthaben *n*, -einlage *f*; *~ on mortgage* Hypothekarkredit *m*; *~ with the savings bank* Sparguthaben *n*, -einlage *f*; *~ on security* gedeckte(r), gesicherte(r) Kredit *m*; **~able** ['-əbl] ansehnlich, beachtlich (*to* für); achtbar; **~ advice, note** Gutschriftsanzeige *f*; **~ balance** Guthaben *n*, Aktivsaldo *m*; **~ bank** Kreditbank, -anstalt *f*; **~ department** Kreditabteilung *f*; **~ line** *(Zeitung) Am* Quellenangabe; Nennung *f* der Mitarbeiter; *fin* Kreditlinie *f*; **~or** [-ə] Gläubiger *m*; *(~~ side)* Haben(seite *f*) *n*; *(~~ account)* Kreditorenkonto *n*; *judg(e)ment ~~* Urteils-, Vollstrekkungsgläubiger *m*; *~~ in bankruptcy* Konkursgläubiger *m*; *~~s' meeting* Gläubigerversammlung *f*; **~ slip** Einzahlungs-, Gutschein *m*; **~ society** Kreditverein *n*, -genossenschaft *f*; **~ standing** Kreditwürdigkeit *f*; **~ union** *Am* Kreditgenossenschaft *f*; **~-worthy** kreditwürdig.

credo ['kri:dou] *pl -os* Kredo, Glaubensbekenntnis *n*.

credul|ity [kri'dju:liti] Leichtgläubigkeit *f*; **~ous** ['kredjuləs] leichtgläubig.

creed [kri:d] (Glaubens-)Bekenntnis, Kredo *n*; *allg* Überzeugung *f*, Grundsätze *m pl*, Prinzipien *n pl*.

creek [kri:k] Bucht, Einbuchtung *f*; kleine(r) Hafen *m*; Bach *m*, Flüßchen *n*; *up the ~ (sl)* in der Klemme.

creel [kri:l] Fischkorb *m (der Angler)*.

creep [kri:p] *itr irr crept, crept* kriechen, krabbeln; sich langsam (fort)bewegen *od* wandern, schleichen *a. fig (Zeit)*; *(to ~ on) (Zeit)* vergehen; *(Pflanze)* sich ranken; *(Haut)* kribbeln; *to ~ into (fig)* sich einschleichen in; *to ~ up* heranschleichen, sich heranarbeiten (*to* an); *s* Kriechen *n*; *(mountain ~)* Bergrutsch; *min* Sohlenauftrieb *m*; *rail* Sichverschieben *n* der Gleise (in der Längsrichtung); niedrige Öffnung *f*; *fam* unangenehme(r), widerliche(r) Mensch *m*; *pl* Kribbeln *n*, Schauder; *pl* Säuferwahnsinn *m*; *it made my flesh ~, (fam) it gave me the ~s (s pl)* es überlief mich (eis)kalt, ich bekam e-e Gänsehaut; **~er** ['-ə] Kriecher *m a. fig fam*; Kriechtier *n*; Klettervogel *m*; Schling-, Kletterpflanze *f*; Enterhaken *m*; *tech* Transportschnecke *f*; *mot* erste(r) Gang *m*; *pl* Steigeisen *n pl*; *pl* Schuhe *m pl* mit Gummi- *od* Kreppsohlen; Strampelhöschen *n*; **~ing** ['-iŋ] *a (Krankheit)* schleichend; *~~ barrage (mil)* Feuerwalze *f*; **~y** ['-i] schaudernd; gruselig.

cremat|e [kri'meit, *Am a.* 'kri:meit] *tr (Leiche)* einäschern; **~ion** [-'meiʃən] Einäscherung, Feuerbestattung *f*; **~orium** [kremə'tɔ:riəm] *bes. Br* Krematorium *n*; **~ory** ['kremətəri, *Am a.* 'kri:mətəri] *a* Verbrennungs-; *s bes. Am* Krematorium *n*.

crenat|e ['kri:neit], **~ed** [-id] *a bot zoo* gekerbt; **~ion** [-'neiʃən] Kerbung *f*.

crenel|(l)ate ['krenileit] *tr* mit Zinnen, Schießscharten versehen.

Creol|e ['kri:oul] *s* Kreole *m*, Kreolin *f*; *a* kreolisch.

creosote ['kriəsout] *s chem pharm* Kreosot *n*; *tr* mit Kreosot behandeln.

crepe, crêpe [kreip] *(Textil)* Krepp, Flor *m*; *(~ paper)* Kreppapier *n*; *(~ rubber)* Kreppgummi *m*.
crepitat|e ['krepiteit] *itr* knistern, prasseln, rattern, knattern, rasseln, knacken; **~ion** [-'teiʃən] Knistern, Knattern, Rasseln, Knacken *n*.
crepuscular [kri'pʌskjulə] dämmerig; trüb(e), düster; *bes. zoo* Dämmerungs-.
crescent ['kresnt] *s* Mondsichel *f*; *pol* Halbmond *m*; *Br* bogenförmig geschwungene Häuserreihe *f*; *mus* Schellenbaum *m*; *Am* Hörnchen *n* *(Gebäck)*; *a* sichelförmig; *poet* zunehmend, wachsend.
cress [kres] *bot* Kresse *f*; *garden, water ~* Garten-, Brunnenkresse *f*.
crest [krest] *s* *(Hühner)* Kamm *m*; *orn* Feder-, *zoo* Haarbüschel *n (auf dem Kopf)*; *orn* Haube *f*; *zoo* Schopf *m*; *(Pferd, Löwe)* Mähne *f*; Helmbusch, *poet* Helm; (Wappen-)Helm; *(mountain ~)* Bergkamm, -rücken; *(~ of a wave)* Wellenkamm *m*; *arch* Bekrönung *f*; *fig* Höchst-, Scheitelwert; *tech* Kranz *m*, Spitze *f*; *tr* erklimmen; bekrönen *a. fig*; *on the ~ of the wave (fig)* auf dem Gipfel des Glücks; **~ed** ['-id] *a* mit e-m Kamm *usw* (versehen); **~fallen** ['-fɔ:lən] *a fig* enttäuscht, hoffnungslos, entmutigt.
cretaceous [kri'teiʃəs] *a* kreidig; Kreide- *a. geol*; *s geol* Kreidezeit *f*.
cretin ['kre-, 'kri:tin] Kretin, Schwachsinnige(r) *m*; **~ism** ['kre-, 'kritinizm] Kretinismus, Schwachsinn *m*.
cretonne [kre'tɔn, 'kretɔn] Cretonne *f*.
crev|asse [kri'væs] tiefe(r) Riß, Spalt(e *f*) *m*, *bes.* Gletscherspalte *f*; *tech* Resonanzloch *n*; **~ice** ['krevis] enge(r) Spalt(e *f*) *m*, Ritze *f*, Sprung, (Mauer-)Riß *m*.
crew [kru:] *mar aero* Besatzung; *mar* Mannschaft *(ohne Offiziere)*; Belegschaft; (Arbeiter-)Kolonne; Gruppe, Gesellschaft; *pej* Bande; *(gun ~)* (Geschütz-)Bedienung *f*; **~ cut** Borsten-, Igel-, Meckifrisur *f*; **~ member** Besatzungsmitglied *n*; **~ space** Kabine *f*.
crewel [kru(:)il, -əl] Stick-, Krüwellwolle *f*; **~ yarn** Perlgarn *n*.
crib [krib] *s* Krippe, Raufe *f*, Trog *m*; Box, Bucht *f*, Stand *m (im Stall)*; Hütte *f*; Kinderbett *n*; Lachsreuse *f*; *min* Kranz *m*; *Am* Lagergestell *n*, Behälter *m (bes. für Mais)*; *fam* Plagiat *n*; *(Schule)* Eselsbrücke *f*, Spickzettel; kleine(r) Diebstahl *m*; *Br sl* Wohnung *f*, Haus; *Am sl* billige(s) Lokal, Nachtlokal *n*; *Am sl* Panzerschrank *m*; *Am rail* Bremserhäuschen *n*; *tr* einsperren; mit Krippen *od* Hürden versehen; *fam* plagiieren; *(Schule)* abschreiben; *fam* mausen, stibitzen; *itr* Spickzettel benutzen; **~bage** ['-idʒ] *(Kartenspiel)* Kribbage *n*; **~-biter** Krippenbeißer *m (Pferd)*; **~bing** ['-iŋ] *fam* Abschreiben *n*.
crick [krik] *s med* (Muskel-)Krampf *m*; *tr* verkrampfen; *(Hals)* verrenken; *~ in the neck* steife(r) Hals *m*.
cricket ['krikit] **1.** *zoo* Grille *f*; *(house-~)* Heimchen *n*, Hausgrille *f*; **2.** *s* Kricket *n (Spiel)*; *fam* sportliche Haltung *f*; *Am* niedere(r) Holzstuhl, Hocker *m*; *itr* K. spielen; *a*: *not ~ (fam)* unfair, unkameradschaftlich; **~-bat** (Kricket-)Schläger *m*, Schlagholz *n*; **~er** ['-ə] Kricketspieler *m*; **~-field, -ground** Kricketplatz *m*; **~-match** Kricketspiel *n*, -partie *f*; **~-pitch** Raum *m* zwischen den Dreistäben.
crier ['kraiə] Schreier, *(bes. Kind)* Schreihals; *(town-~)* (öffentlicher) Ausrufer; Marktschreier *m*.
crikey ['kraiki] *inter fam* herrje!
crime [kraim] strafbare Handlung *f*, Vergehen, Verbrechen *n a. fig*; *lit* Missetat; Verfehlung *f*; Frevel *m*; *to commit, to perpetrate a ~* ein Verbrechen begehen; *~ against humanity* Verbrechen *n* gegen die Menschlichkeit; **~ prevention** Verbrechensverhütung, -bekämpfung *f*; **~ rate** *(Statistik)* Kriminalität *f*.
crimin|al ['kriminl] *a* verbrecherisch, kriminell; strafbar; strafrechtlich; Kriminal-, Straf-; *s* Verbrecher(in *f*) *m*; *with ~~ intent* in verbrecherischer Absicht; *habitual ~~* Gewohnheitsverbrecher *m*; *~~ act, offence* strafbare Handlung *f*; *~~ assault* Sittlichkeitsverbrechen, -vergehen *n*; Vergewaltigung, Notzucht *f*; *~~ case* Strafsache *f*; *~~ conversation* Ehebruch *m*; *~~ court* Strafkammer *f*, Kriminalgericht *n*; *~~ investigation department, ~~ police* Kriminalpolizei, Kripo *f*; *~~ jurisdiction* Strafgerichtsbarkeit, -rechtspflege *f*; *~~ law* Strafrecht *n*; *~~ proceedings (pl)* Strafprozeß *m*, -verfahren *n*; *to take ~~ proceedings against s.o.* gegen jdn ein Strafverfahren einleiten; *~~ record* Strafregister *n*; **~ality** [krimi'næliti] Kriminalität, Strafbarkeit, Schuld *f*; Verbrechertum *n*; **~ally** ['-li] *adv* strafrechtlich; **~ate** ['krimineit] *tr* e-s Verbrechens bezichtigen; **~ology** [-'nɔlədʒi] Kriminologie *f*.
crimp [krimp] **1.** *tr* fälteln; riffeln, wellen; *(Haar)* kräuseln; *(Fisch, Fleisch)* schlitzen; *Am sl* hindern; *(Oberleder)* formen; *tech* umbördeln, -nieten; *s* Fälteln *n*; Falte(n *pl*) *f*; *fam* Hindernis *n*; *meist pl* gekräuselte Haare *n pl*; *a (~y)* gekräuselt, kraus; brüchig; *to put s.o. a ~ in (Am)* jdm e-n Stein in den Weg legen; **2.** *s* Werber *m*; *tr* (an)werben, pressen.
crimson ['krimzn] *a* karm(es)inrot; blutrot; *Am* blutig; *s* Karm(es)in *(Farbstoff)*; Karm(es)inrot *n*; *tr* rot färben; *itr* rot werden; erröten.
cringe [krindʒ] *itr* sich (ängstlich) ducken (*to* vor); kriechen, liebedienern, katzbuckeln; *s* kriecherische(s) Benehmen *n*.
cringle ['kriŋgl] *mar* Legel *m*.
crinkl|e ['kriŋkl] *tr itr* wellig, faltig, kraus machen *od* werden; *tr* (zer-)knittern; *s* Kräuselung *f*; **~y** ['-i] wellig, faltig, kraus.
crinoline ['krinəli:n] Krinoline *f*, Reifrock *m*.
cripple ['kripl] *s* Krüppel, Körperbehinderte(r) *m*; *tr* zum Krüppel machen; lähmen; verletzen; *fig* (be)schädigen, schwächen, behindern.
crisis ['kraisis] *pl -ses* ['-i:z] Krise, Krisis *f*; Wendepunkt, entscheidende(r) Augenblick *m*; ernste, schwierige Lage *od* Situation *f*; *to bring to a ~* der Entscheidung entgegenführen; *to overcome, to pass a ~* e-e Krise überwinden; *to pass through a ~* e-e Krise durchmachen; *financial ~* Finanzkrise *f*.
crisp [krisp] *a* knusprig; frisch, fest; klar; frisch, belebend, kräftig(end); lebendig, lebhaft, belebt, angeregt; kraus; wellig, faltig; *s pl Br* Kartoffelchips *pl*; *tr itr* knusprig machen *od* werden; *tr* kräuseln; *itr* kraus werden; **~y** ['-i] knusperig; kraus.
criss-cross ['kriskrɔs] *s* Kreuz(zeichen); Kreuzmuster *n*; *tele* gitterartige Störung *f*; *a* sich kreuzend, gekreuzt, Kreuz-; *adv* kreuzweise; schief; *tr* kreuzweise schraffieren; *itr* sich kreuzen.
crit|erion [krai'tiəriən] *pl -ria* [-'tiəriə] Kriterium, Merkmal, Kennzeichen *n*;
~ic ['kritik] Kunstkenner, -sachverständige(r); Kritiker; Splitterrichter, Tadler *m*; **~ical** ['kritikəl] kritisch; *(Augenblick, Punkt)* entscheidend; ernst, bedenklich, gefahrvoll; tadelsüchtig (*of s.o.* jdm gegenüber); anspruchsvoll; *(Waren)* mangelnd, fehlend, rationiert; *at the ~~ moment* im entscheidenden Augenblick; *in a ~~ situation* in e-r schwierigen Lage; *~~ case* Grenzfall *m*; *~~ load* Belastungsgrenze *f*; *~~ point* Grenz-, Wende-, Gefahren-, Höhe-, Schlüsselpunkt *m*; *~~ supplies (pl)* Mangelgüter *n pl*; *~~ value* Grenzwert *m*; **~icism** ['kritisizm] Kritik (*of* an, über); Besprechung; negative Beurteilung *f*; *philos* Kritizismus *m*; *open to ~~* der Kritik ausgesetzt; *to lay o.s. open to ~~* sich der Kritik aussetzen; *textual ~~* Textkritik *f*; **~icize** ['kritisaiz] *tr* kritisieren, bemängeln, sich kritisch äußern über, zu; tadeln; **~ique** [kri'ti:k] Kritik, Besprechung *f*.
croak [krouk] *s* Quaken, Krächzen *n*; *itr (Frosch)* quaken; *(Rabe)* krächzen; *fig* düster in die Zukunft blicken; *sl* abkratzen; *tr* krächzend sagen; *sl* abmurksen; **~er** ['-ə] Miesmacher *m*; **~y** ['-i] krächzend, heiser.
crochet ['krouʃei, *Am* -'-] *tr itr* häkeln; *sl (~-work)* Häkelarbeit *f*; **~-hook** Häkelnadel *f*.
crock [krɔk] **1.** *s* Topf *m*, -scherbe *f*; **~ery** ['-əri] Töpferware *f*, Steingut *n*; **2.** *s fam* alte(r) Klepper *m*; *mot* alte Kiste *f*; *(Mensch)* Klappergestell *n*; *tr* kaputtmachen, erledigen; *itr (to ~ up)* zs.brechen; **~y** ['-i] *fam* völlig erledigt.
crocodile ['krɔkədail] *zoo* Krokodil *n*; *fam* Schulmädchen *n pl* in Zweierreihen; **~ tears** *pl* Krokodilstränen *f pl*.
crocus ['kroukəs] *bot* Krokus *m*.
croft [krɔft] eingefriedete(s) Feld *n*; kleine(r) Bauernhof *m*; **~er** ['-ə] Kleinpächter *m*.
cromlech ['krɔmlek] Kromlech *m*.
cron|e [kroun] alte(s) Weib *n*; **~y** ['-i] (Busen-)Freund *m*.
crook [kruk] *s* Haken; Hirten-, *rel* Krummstab *m*; *(Fluß)* Krümmung, Biegung *f*; *fam* Schwindler, Gauner *m*; *tr itr* (sich) krümmen, sich biegen; *a fam* unehrlich; *(Austr.)* krank; *on the ~ (sl)* unehrlich; **~ed** ['-id] *a* gekrümmt, gebeugt; schief; buck(e)lig; *fig (Wege)* krumm; unehrlich; **~edness** ['-idnis] Krümmung; *fig* Unehrlichkeit *f*.
croon [kru:n] *tr itr* schmalzig singen; **~er** ['-ə] Schnulzensänger *m*.
crop [krɔp] *s orn* Kropf *m*; Feldfrüchte *m pl*; Getreide *n*; Ertrag *m*, Ernte *f*; *(~ping result)* Ernteergebnis *n*; Ausbeute *f*; *allg* Haufen *m*, Menge *f*; gegerbte(s) Tierfell *n*, -haut *f*; Peitschenstiel *m*; *(riding-~)* Reit-, *(hunting-~)* Jagdpeitsche *f*; (ganz) kurze Haare *n pl*; *agr* Eigentumszeichen *n* am Ohr e-s Tieres; *tr* kurz abschneiden, stutzen, scheren; ab-, kahlfressen, abgrasen; (ab)ernten; *(Feld)* bestellen; *itr agr* e-n guten Ertrag bringen; das Feld bestellen; *to ~ out, up* auftauchen; *fam* aufkreuzen; *geol* zutage treten; *land under ~* Anbaufläche *f*; **~-eared** *a* mit Stutzohren; mit ganz kurzen Haaren; **~per** ['-ə] Kropftaube *f*; Scherer *m*; Schermaschine *f*, Schneidemesser *n*; *Am* Farmer *m*, der das Land e-s andern anbaut u. in Naturalien entlohnt wird; *fam* furchtbare(r) Sturz; *fam* Mißerfolg, Reinfall, Zs.bruch *m*; *to be a good, bad ~~ (agr)* gut, schlecht

tragen; *to come a ~~ (fam)* furchtbar (hin)fallen; versagen; *(im Examen)* durchsausen, -rasseln; **~ rotation** Fruchtwechsel *m.*

croquet ['kroukei] *s* Krocket *n (Kugelspiel)*; *tr* krockieren.

crosier ['krouʒə] Bischofs-, Krummstab *m.*

cross [krɔs] *s* Kreuz *n*; Querstrich *m (e-s Buchstabens)*; *the C~* das Kreuz *(Christi)*, *fig* das Christentum; *fig* Kreuz, Leiden; Ordenskreuz *n*; *biol* (Rassen-)Kreuzung; *el* Überbrückung *f*; *tech* Kreuzstück *n*; *sl* Gemeinheit, Schweinerei *f*; *a* querliegend, quer verlaufend, schräg; kreuzend; gekreuzt; Quer-; entgegengesetzt, widrig, Gegen-;gegenseitig; *biol* gekreuzt, Kreuzungs-; *fam* mißgestimmt, schlecht-, übelgelaunt; gereizt, ärgerlich, böse; launisch, reizbar; *sl* gemein, schuftig; *tr* kreuzen, durch-, überqueren, überschreiten; *lit* durchmessen; das Kreuz machen *(s.th.* über etw); *(die Arme, die Beine)* kreuzen, überea.schlagen; hinüberbefördern; *(Brücke)* überspannen, hinüberführen *(s.th.* über); mit e-m Querstrich versehen; übersetzen *(s.th.* über); überfliegen; verschränken; *(to ~ off, to ~ out)* (durch-) streichen; *(Scheck)* mit Verrechnungsvermerk versehen; *(Plan)* durchkreuzen, vereiteln; *sl* hereinlegen; *(Person)* in den Weg, entgegentreten *(s.o.* jdm); begegnen *(s.o.* jdm); *biol (Rassen)* kreuzen; *itr* hinüberfahren *(from...to* von...nach); sich treffen, sich begegnen, sich kreuzen; sich überschneiden; *(Briefe)* sich kreuzen; *to ~ o.s. (rel)* sich bekreuzen; *to ~ over* hinübergehen; *as ~ as two sticks* in e-r üblen Laune; *on the ~* schräg, diagonal; *to bear, to take up o.'s ~ (fig)* sein Kreuz auf sich nehmen; *to ~ s.o.'s hand with money* jdm Geld in die Hand drücken; *to ~ o.'s mind* in den Sinn kommen, einfallen; *to ~ s.o.'s palms* jdn bestechen, jdm Schmiergelder zahlen; *to ~ s.o.'s path* jds Weg kreuzen, jdm begegnen; *to ~ o.'s t's and dot o.'s i's (fig)* es (ganz) genau nehmen, (sehr) genau sein; *no ~, no crown* ohne Fleiß kein Preis; *~ your heart!* Hand aufs Herz! *I'll keep my fingers ~ed* ich halte den Daumen! **~-action, -suit** *jur* Gegenklage *f*; **~-bar** Querholz *n*, -balken *m*, -stange; *sport* Torlatte *f*; **~beam** Quer-, Tragbalken, Träger *m*; **~-bencher** *pol* Unabhängige(r) *m*; **~bill** *orn* Kreuzschnabel *m*; **~-bill** *fin* Gegen-, Rückwechsel *m*; **~-bow** *hist* Armbrust *f*; **~-bred** *a biol* Kreuzungs-; **~-breed** *s* Kreuzung *(Individuum)*; Mischrasse *f*, -ling *m*; *tr* kreuzen; **~-check** *tr* doppelt kontrollieren; **~-country** *a* querfeldein verlaufend; *~~ driving* Geländefahren *n*; *~~ flight (aero)* Überlandflug *m*; *~~ mobility* Geländegängigkeit *f*; *~~ race* Geländelauf *m*; *~~ vehicle* geländegängige(r) Wagen *m*; **~-cut** Querschnitt *m*; Schrotsäge *f*; Abkürzungsweg *m*; **~ed** [-t] *a*: *~~ cheque* Verrechnungsscheck *m*; **~-examination** Kreuzverhör *n*; **~-examine** *tr* ins Kreuzverhör nehmen; **~-eyed** *a* schielend; **~fade** *tr (Radar)* einblenden; **~-fertilization** Kreuzbefruchtung *f*; **~-fire** *mil* Kreuzfeuer *n a. fig*; **~-grained** *a* unregelmäßig gemasert; *fig* übelgelaunt; widerborstig; **~-hatch** *tr* kreuzweise schraffieren; **~-head** *tech* Kreuzkopf *m*; **~-heading** Schlagzeile *f*; **~ing** ['-iŋ] Kreuzung *f*, Kreuz-, Schnittpunkt *m*; Überquerung *f*, -gang *m*, -fahrt; *rail* Überführung *f*; (Fußgänger-)Überweg *m*; *biol* Kreuzung *m*; *arch* Vierung *f*; *fig* Durchkreuzen *n*; *level, (Am) grade ~~* schienengleiche(r) Bahnübergang *m*; *~~-out* Ausstreichen *n*; **~-legged** *a* mit übergeschlagenen Beinen; **~ level** *tech* Libelle *f*; **~-light** Seitenlicht *n a. fig*; **~-line** *biol* aus e-r Kreuzung hervorgegangen; **~-link** *Am* Querverbindung *f*; **~ness** ['-nis] schlechte Laune; Gereiztheit; Reizbarkeit *f*; **~-over** Kreuzungsstelle *f*; Überschneidungspunkt; Nulldurchgang *m*; **~-patch** *fam* Querkopf, übellaunige(r) Mensch *m*; **~-piece** Querstück *n*; **~-purposes** *pl* Frage-u.-Antwort-Spiel *n*; *to be at ~~ with s.o.* mit jdm e-e Meinungsverschiedenheit haben; *to talk at ~~* anea.vorbeireden; **~-rail** Querschiene, Traverse *f*; **~-reference** *(Buch)* (Kreuz-)Verweisung *f*; **~-road, -street, -way** Querstraße *f*, -weg *m*; **~-roads** *sing* Wege-, Straßenkreuzung, Wegspinne *f*; Treffpunkt *m*; *Am* Gemeinde *f*, Weiler *m*; *at the ~~ (fig)* am Scheideweg; **~-section** Durch-, Querschnitt *m a. fig*, Profil *n*; *~~ paper* karierte(s) Papier *n*; **~-stitch** *(Handarbeit)* Kreuzstich (-arbeit *f*) *m*; **~ talk** *tele* Übersprechen *n*; **~-tie** *Am rail* Schwelle; Querstrebe *f*; **~-town** *Am* quer durch die Stadt (führend); **~-trees** *pl sport* Querbalken *m pl*; *mar* Saling *f*; **~-up** *Am sl* Irreführung, Betrügerei *f*; **~-walk** *Am* Überweg *m* für Fußgänger; **~ways, ~wise** *adv* quer hinüber; kreuzweise; **~ wind** *aero* Seitenwind *m*; **~word (puzzle)** Kreuzworträtsel *n.*

crotch [krɔtʃ] Gabel(ung); Astgabel *f*; *anat* Schritt *m.*

crotchet ['krɔtʃit] Häkchen *n*, Haken *m*; *mus* Viertelnote *f*; *fig* Marotte, Schrulle, fixe Idee *f*; **~y** ['-i] schrullenhaft; exzentrisch.

crouch [krautʃ] *itr* sich ducken, sich (nieder)kauern; sich (tief) verbeugen, sich verneigen *(to* vor); *s* geduckte Stellung; Verneigung *f.*

croup [kru:p] **1.** *med* Krupp *m*, Kehlkopfdiphtherie *f*; *vet* Bräune *f*; **2.** *(Pferd)* Kruppe *f*, Kreuz *n.*

croupier ['kru:piə] Croupier *m.*

crow [krou] *s* Krähe *f*; Krächzen, Krähen; *(Kind)* Juchzen; *(~-bar)* Brecheisen *n*, -stange *f*, Kuhfuß *m*; *itr (crowed od crew, crowed)* krächzen, krähen; jubeln, frohlocken, triumphieren *(over* über); *(Kind, vor Wonne)* krähen, juchzen; *as the ~ flies, in a ~ line* (in) gerade(r Linie); *to eat ~ (Am fam)* klein beigeben; *to have a ~ to pluck, to pick with s.o.* mit jdm ein Hühnchen zu rupfen haben; *a white ~* ein weißer Rabe, e-e ganz große Seltenheit; **~-foot** ['-fut] *bot* Hahnenfuß; *mar* Hahnepot *m*; **~'s feet** Krähenfüße *m pl (im Gesicht)*; **~'s nest** *mar* Mastkorb *m.*

crowd [kraud] *s* (Menschen-)Menge *f*, Menschenmassen *f pl*; Gedränge, Gewühle, Gewimmel *n*; *die* große Masse, *das* gemeine Volk; *fam* Gruppe *f*, Haufen, Verein *m*, Gesellschaft *f*; Haufen, Berg, Stoß, Stapel *m (Sachen)*; *itr (to ~ round)* sich ansammeln, zs.-strömen; (sich) drängen *(round* um; *into* in); wimmeln, stoßen *(through* durch); *(to ~ forward)* vorwärtsdrängen, -stürmen; *tr* drängen, stoßen, schieben; vollstopfen, -pfropfen; zum Brechen füllen; *Am fam (Menschen)* unter Druck setzen, auf den Leib rücken *(s.o.* jdm); *sport (Gegner)* abdecken; *to ~ out* ausschließen; *to ~ up (Am) (Preise)* in die Höhe treiben; *to be ~ed with* wimmeln von; *to follow the ~ (fig)* dem Haufen folgen, mitlaufen; *to ~ in, out* hinein-, hinausdrängen; *to ~ in upon (fig)* einstürmen auf, jdn bestürmen; *to ~ (on) sail* alle Segel beisetzen; **~ed** ['-id] *a* gedrängt, zum Brechen voll *(with* von); zs.gepfercht; *~~ to capacity* bis auf den letzten Platz gefüllt.

crown [kraun] *s* Krone *f a. fig pol*; *the C~* die Krone, der König; (Sieger-) Kranz *m*; Krone *f*, Fünfschillingstück *n*, 5 Schilling; obere(r) Teil *m*, Krone *f*, Gipfel; Scheitel, Schädel *m*; Kappe *f*, Aufsatz; Hutkopf *m*; (Zahn-)Krone; (Blüten-, Baum-)Krone *f*; *mar* Ankerkreuz *n*; *arch* Schlußstein; *fig* Höhepunkt *m*, höchste (Entwicklungs-) Stufe, Krone *f*, Gipfel *m*, Krönung, Vollendung *f*; *tr* krönen *a. fig*; *fig* bekrönen, die Krone aufsetzen *(s.th.* e-r S); vollenden; *(Zahn)* mit e-r Krone versehen; *sl* eins aufs Dach geben *(s.o.* jdm); *to ~ all* um das Faß vollzumachen, um der Sache die Krone aufzusetzen; *to ~ s.o. king* jdn zum König krönen; **~ glass** *tech* Kronglas *n*; **~ing** ['-iŋ] *s* Krönung; *fig* Bekrönung, Vollendung, Erfüllung *f*; *a* (be)krönend, höchst, oberst, letzt; **~ jewels** *pl* Kronjuwelen *n pl.*

cruc|ial ['kru:ʃiəl] entscheidend, kritisch, ernst; *Am* mißlich, streng, schwierig; *anat* kreuzförmig; *to put to a ~~ test* e-r entscheidenden Prüfung unterziehen, -werfen; **~ible** ['-sibl] Schmelztiegel; *(Hochofen)* Tiegel *m*; *fig* Feuer-, Bewährungsprobe *f*; *~~ steel* Tiegelstahl, -guß *m*; **~ifix** ['kru:sifiks] *rel* Kruzifix *n*; **~ifixion** [-'fikʃən] Kreuzigung *f (a. Kunst)*; **~iform** ['-fɔ:m] kreuzförmig; **~ify** ['-fai] *tr* kreuzigen *a. fig*; kränken, quälen.

crud|e [kru:d] roh *a. fig*; unreif; unbearbeitet; *fig* ungeformt, unfertig; primitiv, einfach, schlicht, schmucklos, kahl, nackt; *(Sitten)* rauh; *(Bemerkung)* plump; *(Mensch)* grob, ungeschliffen, ungebildet; *~~ iron, oil, rubber* Roheisen, -öl *n*, -gummi *m*; **~eness** ['-nis], **~ity** ['-iti] Roheit; Unreife; Unfertigkeit; Einfachheit, Schmucklosigkeit *f.*

cruel ['kruəl] grausam; unmenschlich, erbarmungs-, mitleid(s)los, herzlos, hart, streng *(to* gegen); schmerzvoll, -lich; *fig* heftig, schwer, stark; **~ty** ['-ti] Grausamkeit; Unmenschlichkeit, Herzlosigkeit; Erbarmungslosigkeit *f*; *~~ to animals* Tierquälerei *f.*

cruet ['kruit] *(Essig-, Öl-)* Fläschchen *n (auf dem Tisch)*; *(~-stand)* Menage *f.*

cruis|e [kru:z] *itr mar* kreuzen; (planlos) umherfahren; *aero* fliegen; *(Taxi)* fahren (u. Fahrgäste suchen); *s* Kreuz-, See-, Vergnügungsfahrt, Schiffsreise *f*; Reiseflug *m*; *round-the-world ~~* (Schiffs-)Weltreise *f*; **~er** ['-ə] *mar* Kreuzer *m*; Jacht *f*, Segler *m*; Motorboot *n*; *Am* Funkstreifenwagen *m*; Flugzeug *n*; **~ing** ['-iŋ] Reise-; *~~ flight* Reiseflug *m*; *~~ order* Marschordnung *f*; *~~ radius (mot)* Fahrbereich *m*; *~~ range (aero)* Aktionsradius *m*; *~~ speed (mot)* Marsch-, *aero* Reisegeschwindigkeit *f.*

crumb [krʌm] *s* Stück(chen) *n*, Krume *f*, Krümel, Brösel *m*; (Brot-)Krume *f*; *fig* Fetzen *m*, Stück *n*, Brocken *m*; *Am sl* widerliche(r) Kerl *m*; *pl Am sl* kleine Geldsumme *f*; *a ~ of* ein bißchen, ein wenig; *tr itr* zerbröckeln, zerkrümeln; *tr (Küche)* panieren; *fam* die Krümel entfernen von; **~le** ['krʌmbl] *tr itr* zerkrümeln, zerbröckeln; *itr* zer-, verfallen; *fig* einstürzen, zs.brechen; *(Preise)* abbröckeln; **~bly** ['-bli] krüm(e)lig; bröck(e)lig; **~by** ['krʌmi] voller Krümel, weich; *Am sl* verlaust.

crummy ['krʌmi] *sl (Frau)* mollig, üppig, dick, fett; *sl* mies(epet(e)rig), mau, lausig, schäbig, dürftig, elend.

crump [krʌmp] *sl mil* dicke(r), schwere(r) Brocken *m*.

crumpet ['krʌmpit] *Art* Pfannkuchen *m*; *Br sl* Birne, Rübe *f*, Kopf *m*; *to be barmy on the ~, off o.'s ~ (sl)* e-e weiche Birne, nicht alle Tassen im Spind haben.

crumple ['krʌmpl] *tr* zerknittern, zerknüllen, faltig machen; *itr* faltig werden, knittern; *(to ~ up) fam* zs.brechen, zs.sacken; *to ~ up (tr)* zs.knüllen; *(Feind)* zs.hauen, -schlagen; *itr* zs.-schrumpfen; *s* Falte *f*.

crunch [krʌntʃ] *tr* knacken, zerbeißen; *tr itr* knirschen (lassen); *s* Knacken, Knirschen *n*; *sl* Krise *f*.

crupper ['krʌpə] *(Pferdegeschirr)* Schweifriemen *m*; *(Pferd)* Kruppenhöhe *f*.

crural ['kruərəl] *a anat* Schenkel-.

crusade [kru:'seid] *s hist* Kreuzzug *m a. fig*; *fig* Unternehmen *n*, Kampf *m* (*against* gegen; *for* für); *itr* sich an e-m Kreuzzug beteiligen; **~r** [-ə] Kreuzfahrer *m*.

cruse [kru:z] *obs* Krug *m*; *widow's ~ (fig)* unerschöpfliche Quelle *f*.

crush [krʌʃ] *tr* (zer-, zs.)drücken, pressen, (zer)quetschen, zermalmen, zerschmettern; zerkleinern; (zer)knautschen, (zer)knüllen, zerknittern; aus der Fasson bringen; *fig* zerstören, vernichten, überwältigen, niederschmettern; nieder-, zu Boden werfen, unterdrücken, *fam* erledigen; *fam* austrinken, leeren, vernichten; *itr* sich drängen, sich stürzen, stürmen; zerquetscht werden; *s* (starker) Druck, Stoß *m*; Gedränge *n*, (Menschen-)Menge *f*, Massen *f pl*; *fam* große Gesellschaft *f*, Haufen *m*; *sl* große Liebe; Verknalltheit *f*; *to ~ down* niederdrücken; zerkleinern; *fig* niederwerfen, unterdrücken; *to ~ out (Frucht)* auspressen, -drücken; *fig* auslöschen, völlig vernichten; *to ~ up* zermahlen, zerstampfen; *to get, to have a ~ on (sl)* sich wahnsinnig verlieben, bis über die Ohren verliebt sein in; *~ed stone* Steinschotter, Split *m*; *~ed sugar* gestoßene(r) Zucker *m*; **~ barrier** Absperrung *f*; **~er** ['-ə] *tech* (Vor-)Brecher, Zerkleinerer *m*, Zerkleinerungsmaschine *f*; *fam* Knüller; *Am sl* hübsche(r) Junge *m*; **~ing** ['-iŋ] *a* überwältigend, erdrückend; *s tech* Zerkleinerung *f*; **~-room** *theat fam* Foyer *n*.

crust [krʌst] *s* (Brot-)Kruste, Rinde *f*; Stück *n* hartes, trockenes Brot; Pastete; *allg* Kruste *f a. med geol*; *med* Schorf *m*; *geol* Rinde; *bot zoo* Schale *f*; Harsch *m*; Ablagerung; *sl* Unverschämtheit *f*; *tr itr* (sich) mit e-r Kruste überziehen; *to ~ over* überfrieren; *~ of ice* Eisdecke *f*; **~acea** [-'teiʃjə] Krebs-, Krustentiere *n pl*; **~acean** [-'teiʃjən] *a* Krebs(tier)-; *s* Krebs-, Krustentier *n*; **~aceous** [-'teiʃjəs] krustenartig; mit e-r Kruste *od* Schale versehen; *zoo* krebsartig, Krebs-, Krusten-; **~ed** ['-id] *a* verkrustet, mit e-r Kruste überzogen; *fig* veraltet, antiquiert; altmodisch; *~~ snow* Harsch; verharschte(r) Schnee *m*; **~y** ['-i] verkrustet; krustig; *fig* verdrießlich, mürrisch; barsch, grob.

crutch [krʌtʃ] *s* Krücke *a. fig*; *fig* Stütze; *mar* Stützgabel, Piek *f*; *anat* Schritt *m*; *to go on ~es* an Krücken gehen.

crux [krʌks] *pl -es* ['-iz] harte Nuß *f*, schwierige(s) Problem *n*; *fig* Haken *m*.

cry [krai] *itr* schreien (*with* vor; *for* nach); verlangen (*for* nach); weinen (*for* um), heulen, jammern (*over* über); *(Tier)* rufen, schreien; *tr* (aus)rufen, schreien; verkünden, ankündigen, *fam* ausposaunen; *s* Schrei, Ruf *m*, Geschrei (*for* nach); Ausrufen, Verkünden *n*, Verkündung *f*; Gerücht *n*; dringende Bitte *f*; (allgemeiner) Aufschrei *m*; Parole *f*, Schlachtruf *m*, Schlagwort *n*; Weinen, Heulen, Geheul *n*; *(Tier)* Ruf, Schrei, Laut *m*, Gebell *n*; *(Jagdhunde)* Anschlag *m*; Koppel, Meute *f*; *to ~ down* herabsetzen, -würdigen, schlechtmachen; niederschreien; *to ~ for* dringend gebrauchen, benötigen; verlangen nach; *to ~ off* widerrufen, sein Wort zurücknehmen; es sich anders überlegen, sich besinnen; sich zurückziehen, zurücktreten, sich lossagen; *to ~ out* aufschreien, laut schreien, jammern; *against* scharf protestieren gegen; *to ~ up* in den Himmel heben, (laut) rühmen, preisen; *(Preis)* in die Höhe treiben; *in full ~* in vollem Eifer; *within ~* in Rufweite (*of* gen); *to follow in the ~* mit der großen Masse mitlaufen; *to have a good ~* sich ausweinen; *to ~ o.'s eyes, heart out* sich die Augen aus dem Kopf weinen; *to ~ for the moon* Unmögliches verlangen; *to ~ quits* nachgeben; *to ~ o.s to sleep, asleep* sich in den Schlaf weinen; *to ~ over spilt milk* Vergangenem nachweinen; *to ~ stinking fish* herummäkeln; Übles nachsagen; *to ~ (for) vengeance* nach Rache schreien; *much ~ and little wool (prov)* viel Geschrei u. wenig Wolle, viel Lärm um nichts; *a far ~* e-e große Entfernung, ein weiter Weg (*from* von); **~-baby** Schreihals *m*; **~ing** ['-iŋ] (himmel)schreiend; dringend.

crypt [kript] *arch* Krypta; Gruft *f*; *med* Hohlraum *m*; **~ic(al)** ['-ik(l)] geheim, verborgen, versteckt; zwei-, mehrdeutig; *zoo* Schutz-; **~o** ['-ou] *pol fam* Heimliche(r), *bes.* heimliche(r) Kommunist *m*; **~ocentre** ['-o(u)sentə] Schlüsselzentrale *f*; **~ogam** ['kripto(u)gæm] *bot* Bedecktsamer *m*, Kryptogame *f*; **~ogamic** [-ə'gæmik], **~ogamous** [-'tɔgəməs] *bot* bedecktsamig, kryptogam; **~ogram** [-ə'græm], **~ograph** [-ə'grɑ:f] chiffrierte(s) Schreiben *n*, verschlüsselte(r) Text *m*; **~ographer** [krip'tɔgrəfə] Schlüßler *m*; **~ography** [-'tɔgrəfi] Geheimschrift *f*; Ver- u. Entschlüsseln *n*.

crystal ['kristl] *s min chem phys* Kristall; Quarz *m*; *(~ glass)* Kristall(glas); Kristallgefäß(e *pl*), -geschirr; *Am* Uhrglas *n*; *(~ detector) radio* Kristalldetektor *m*; *a* kristallen *a. fig*; **~ gazing** Deutung *f* der Zukunft mittels e-r Kristallkugel; **~line** ['kristəlain] kristallinisch; kristallen; Kristall-; kristallklar; *~~ lens (anat)* Kristallinse *f*; **~lization** [kristəlai'zeiʃən] Kristallisation, Kristallbildung; Kristallisierung *f*; **~lize** ['kristəlaiz] *tr* die Kristallbildung anregen (*s.th.* e-r S); *fig* e-e endgültige Gestalt geben (*s.th.* e-r S); *(Küche)* mit Zuckerguß überziehen; *itr* Kristalle bilden; *fig* sich herauskristallisieren; **~lography** [kristə'lɔgrəfi] Kristallographie *f*.

cub [kʌb] Junge(s) *n (e-s Raubtieres)*; (junger) Bursche, Tolpatsch; *(Pfadfinder)* Wölfling; *Am* Neuling, Anfänger *m*; *fam (~ reporter)* junge(r), unerfahrene(r) Berichter *m*.

cub|age ['kju:bidʒ] Kubik-, Rauminhalt *m*, Volumen *n*; **~e** [kju:b] *s* Würfel, Kubus *m*; Kubikzahl, dritte Potenz *f*; *tr math* kubieren, zur dritten Potenz erheben; in Würfel schneiden; den Rauminhalt berechnen; *~~ root (math)* Kubikwurzel *f*; *~~ sugar* Würfelzucker *m*; **~ic** ['-ik] würfelförmig, kubisch; *math* Kubik-; *~~ capacity* Rauminhalt; *mot* Hubraum *m*; **~icle** ['-ikl] (Schlaf-, Umkleide-, Dolmetscher-, Bade-)Kabine; *tech* Zelle *f*; **~ism** ['-izm] *(Kunst)* Kubismus *m*; **~it** ['-it] Elle *f (Maß)*.

cubby-hole ['kʌbihoul] gemütliche(s) Stübchen; *mot* Handschuhfach *n*.

cuckold ['kʌkəld] Hahnrei *m*.

cuckoo ['kuku] *s* Kuckuck(sruf); *sl* Einfaltspinsel *m*; *a sl* verrückt, blöd(e); **~-clock** Kuckucksuhr *f*; **~-flower** Kuckucksblume *f*, Wiesenschaumkraut *n*; **~-pint** *bot* Aronsstab *m*; **~-spit(tle)** *ent* Kuckucksspeichel *m*; Schaumzikade, -zirpe *f*.

cucumber ['kju:kʌmbə] Gurke *f*; *cool as a ~* ruhig und beherrscht; kalt wie e-e Hundeschnauze; **~ tree** *Am* Magnolienbaum *m*.

cucurbit|(e) [kju'kə:bit] Kürbis *m*.

*

cud [kʌd] wiedergekäute(s) Futter *n*; *to chew the ~* wiederkäuen *a. fig*; *fig* (hin u. her, gründlich, gut) überlegen.

cuddle ['kʌdl] *tr* liebevoll umarmen, hätscheln, liebkosen; *itr (to ~ up)* sich *(im Bett)* (zs.)kuscheln; wohlig anea.geschmiegt liegen; *s* Kuscheln *n*; Umarmung *f*.

cudgel ['kʌdʒəl] *s* Keule *f*, Knüppel *m*, Prügel *m*; *tr* (ver)prügeln; *to take up the ~s for s.o.* für jdn Partei ergreifen, sich für jdn einsetzen; *to ~ o.'s brains* sich den Kopf zerbrechen (*about* über; *for* wegen).

cue [kju:] **1.** *theat* Stichwort *n*; Fingerzeig, Hinweis, Wink, Vorschlag *m*; *theat* Rolle *f*; (Handlungs-)Verlauf, Ablauf (des Geschehens); *mus* Einsatz *m*; Denkart, -weise; Stimmung *f*; Temperament *n*; *psychol* zusätzliche(r) Anreiz *m*; *to give s.o. his ~* jdm nahelegen, was er zu tun hat; *to take o.'s ~ from s.o.* sich von jdm anregen lassen; sich nach jdm richten; **2.** (Billard-)Queue *n*; Zopf *m*; Schlange *f (Anstehender)*.

cuff [kʌf] **1.** *s* Manschette *f*; Ärmel-, *Am* Hosenaufschlag *m*; Handschelle *f*; *tr Am sl* anpumpen; *off the ~ (sl)* (frisch) drauflos; ohne Konzept; Stegreif-; inoffiziell; *on the ~ (sl)* auf Pump; gratis; vertraulich; **~-link** *Br*, **~-button** *Am* Manschettenknopf *m*; **2.** *s* Ohrfeige, Backpfeife *f*; *tr* ohrfeigen, backpfeifen.

cuirass [kwi'ræs] *hist* Panzer *m a. zoo*; Korsett *n*; **~ier** [kwirə'siə] Kürassier *m*.

cuisine [kwi(:)'zi:n] Küche; Kochkunst *f*; Essen *n*.

cuke [kju:k] *Am* Gurke *f*.

cul-de-sac ['kuldə'sæk, kyldəsak] Sackgasse *f a. fig*; *fig* ausweglose Situation *f*.

culinary ['kju:linəri] kulinarisch; Küchen-, Tafel-.

cull [kʌl] *tr (Blumen, Obst)* pflücken; *fig* auslesen, -suchen, -wählen; sortieren; *s* Ausschuß *m*.

cullet ['kʌlit] *tech* Bruchglas *n*, Glasbruch *m*.

cully ['kʌli] *Br sl* (Einfalts-)Pinsel, Esel; Kumpel, Kumpan, Kerl *m*.

culm [kʌlm] **1.** Kohlenstaub, -grus *m*; Steinkohlenklein *n*; *geol* Kulm *m*; **2.** (*bes.* Gras-)Halm *m*.

culmin|ant ['kʌlminənt] *astr fig* kulminierend, auf dem höchsten Punkt (befindlich); *fig* den Höhepunkt, den Gipfel, die Spitze bildend; **~ate** ['-eit] *itr astr fig* kulminieren; *astr* durch den Meridian gehen; *fig* s-n Höhepunkt erreichen, gipfeln (*in* in); **~ation**

[-'neiʃən] Kulminieren *n*; Höhepunkt, Gipfel; *astr* Meridiandurchgang *m*.

culp|ability [kʌlpə'biliti] Tadelnswürdigkeit; *obs* Straffälligkeit, Schuld *f*; **~able** ['-əbl] tadelnswert; strafbar, schuldhaft; **~~** *negligence* sträfliche(r) Leichtsinn *m*; *jur* grobe Fahrlässigkeit *f*; **~rit** ['-rit] Angeklagte(r), Angeschuldigte(r); Missetäter, Übeltäter *m*.

cult [kʌlt] *rel* Kult(us) *m a. allg*; Verehrung; Mode(torheit) *f*; Anhänger *m pl*; **~ivable** ['-ivəbl] *(Land)* anbaufähig; **~ivate** ['-iveit] *tr agr* kultivieren, an-, bebauen; *fig* kultivieren, pflegen, unterhalten; (be)fördern; **~ivated** *a agr* bebaut; gezüchtet, Zucht-; *fig* gebildet; **~ivation** [-'veiʃən] *agr* Kultur, Urbarmachung *f*, Anbau *m*; Pflege, Förderung; Kultiviertheit *f*; *under* **~~** *(Land)* bebaut; *to bring under* **~~** in Kultur nehmen; **~ivator** ['-iveitə] Landwirt; *agr* Kultivator *m*; **~ural** ['kʌltʃərəl] kulturell; Kultur-; **~~** *lag* Nachhinken *n* auf einem Gebiet der Kultur; **~ure** ['kʌltʃə] *s agr* Kultur, Bebauung *f*, Anbau *m*; Zucht; *fig* Pflege, Unterhaltung, (Be-)Förderung; Bildung, Kultur; Zivilisation; *biol* (Bakterien-)Kultur *f*; *tr* kultivieren, pflegen; *(Bakterien)* züchten; *physical* **~~** Körperkultur *f*, Leibesübungen *f pl*; **~~** *broth* Kulturlösung *f*; **~~** *medium* Nährboden *m*; **~~** *pearl* Zuchtperle *f*; **~ured** ['-tʃəd] *a* gebildet.

culvert ['kʌlvət] Durchlaß, Abzugskanal *m*; Kabelrohr *n*.

*

cumb|er ['kʌmbə] *tr* (unnütz) beladen, -lasten, überladen, -lasten (*with* mit); (be)hindern, versperren; **~ersome** ['-səm], **~rous** ['-rəs] lästig, beschwerlich, mühsam; sperrig, schwerfällig.

cum(m)in ['kʌmin] Kümmel *m*.

cumul|ative ['kju:mjulətiv] sich (an-) häufend, zunehmend; kumulativ; **~~** *process* Kettenreaktion *f*; **~~** *voting (parl)* Stimmenhäufung *f*, Kumulieren *n*; **~o-cirrus** Schäfchenwolke *f*; **~o-nimbus** Gewitterwolke *f*; **~o-stratus** Haufenschichtwolke *f*; **~us** ['-ləs] *pl -i* ['-ai] Haufenwolke *f*; Haufe *m*.

cune|ate(d) ['kju:niit, -eitid], **~iform** ['-niifɔ:m] keilförmig; *~iform characters (pl)* Keilschrift *f*.

cunning ['kʌniŋ] *a* schlau, listig, *fam* gerissen; *obs u. Am* geschickt, tüchtig; *Am* gekonnt, gut gemacht; *Am fam* nett; reizend, entzückend; wohlschmeckend; *s* Schlauheit, List *f*.

cup [kʌp] *s* (Ober-)Tasse *f*; Becher; Behälter *m*; Tasse(voll) *f*; Pokal *m a. sport*; *tech* Kalotte *f*; *rel fig* Kelch *(des Leidens)*; Wein, (guter) Trunk *m*, Trinken *n*; gewürzte(r) Wein; *med* Schröpfkopf; *bot* Blumenkelch *m*; *tr med* schröpfen; becherförmig gestalten; aufstülpen; aushöhlen; *in o.'s ~s* betrunken; *~ of sorrow (fig)* Kelch *m* des Leidens; *~ of tea* Tasse *f* Tee; *that's not my ~ of tea (fam)* das ist nicht nach m-m Geschmack; **~-bearer** *hist* Mundschenk *m*; **~board** ['kʌbəd] Schrank *m*; Büfett *n*; **~~** *love* Bratkartoffelverhältnis *n*; **~ final** Pokal-Endspiel *n*; **~ful** ['-ful] Tasse-, Bechervoll *f, m*; **~ping** ['-iŋ] *med* Schröpfen *n*; **~-tie** *sport* Pokalspiel *n*.

Cupid *(Mythologie)*, **c~** *(Kunst)* ['kju:pid] Amor *m*; **c~ity** [kju(:)'piditi] Begierde, Gier *f*.

cupola ['kju:pələ] *s arch* Kuppel; *arch* Laterne *f*; *tech (~ furnace)* Kupol-, Schachtofen *m*; *mil* Panzerkuppel *f*; *tr* mit e-r Kuppel versehen, kuppelartig wölben.

cupr|eous ['kju:priəs] kupfern, kupferhaltig, -artig, -farben; **~ic** ['-ik] *a chem* Kupfer- *(zweiwertig)*; **~~** *acetate, oxide* Kupferazetat, -oxyd *n*; **~ous** ['-əs] *a chem* Kupfer- *(einwertig)*.

cur [kə:] Köter; *fig* gemeine(r) Kerl, Lump, Schuft, Schurke *m*.

cura|bility [kjuərə'biliti] Heilbarkeit *f*; **~ble** ['kjuərəbl] heilbar; **~cy** ['kjuərəsi] Stelle *f* e-s Hilfsgeistlichen, e-s Vikars; **~te** ['kjuərit] Hilfsgeistliche(r), Vikar *m*; **~tive** ['kjuərətiv] *a* heilend; Heil-; *s* Heilmittel *n*; **~~** *value* Heilwirkung *f*; **~tor** [kjuə'reitə] Konservator, Museumsdirektor; Pfleger, Verwalter *m*;

curaçao, curaçoa [kjuərə'sou] Curaçao *m (Likör)*.

curb [kə:b] *s (Pferd)* Zaum(zeug *n*) *m*; Kandare *f*; *fig* Zügel *m pl*; Rahmen (-werk *n*) *m*; *arch* Mauerlatte *f*, Spannring; Brunnenrand; *Am* Bordstein *m*; *(~ market) fin* Freiverkehr *m*; *tr* an die Kandare nehmen; *bes. fig (to put, to keep a ~ on)* zügeln, im Zaum halten; bändigen; *to ~ o.'s temper* sich im Zaum halten; **~-market** *Am com* Freiverkehr(smarkt) *m*; **~-roof** Mansardendach *n*; **~stone** ['-stoun] *Am* Bordstein; *sl* Zigarettenstummel *m*.

curd [kə:d] *oft pl* dicke Milch *f*, Quark *m*; *tr itr* u. **~le** ['kə:dl] *tr itr* gerinnen (lassen); *itr* sauer werden; *my blood ~led* es durchlief mich eiskalt, mir standen die Haare zu Berge.

cure [kjuə] *med* Heilung(sprozeß *m*) *f*; Heilmittel, -verfahren *n*, -methode, Kur (*for* gegen); Heilung, Genesung *f*; geheilte(r) Fall *m*; *fig* Mittel *n* (*for* gegen), Abhilfe (*for* für); Pfarrstelle *f*; Pökeln, Räuchern *n*; *tr* heilen, *fam* kurieren; *fig* abhelfen (*s.th.* e-r S), beheben; pökeln, einsalzen; räuchern; trocknen, dörren; konservieren, haltbar machen; *tech* vulkanisieren, aushärten; *past ~* unheilbar; *~ of souls* Seelsorge *f*; *there is no ~ for* es gibt kein Mittel gegen; **~-all** Allheilmittel *n*.

curfew ['kə:fju:] *hist* Abendläuten *n*, -glocke *f*; Sperrstunde, -zeit *f*; Ausgehverbot *n*, -sperre *f*; *mil* Zapfenstreich *m*.

curio ['kjuəriou] *pl -os* Seltenheit, Rarität *f*; **~sity** [-'ɔsiti] Neugier(de) *f*, Wissensdurst *m*; Seltenheit, Rarität *f*; **~~** *shop* Antiquitätengeschäft *n*; **~us** ['-əs] neugierig; wißbegierig; seltsam, eigenartig, ungewöhnlich, unbegreiflich, geheimnisvoll; *to be ~~ about s.th.* gar zu gerne wissen wollen; auf etw gespannt sein.

curl [kə:l] *s* Locke; Kräuselung; *(Welle)* Schaumkrone; *bot* Kräuselkrankheit *f*; *tr* kräuseln; *itr* sich in Locken legen, sich kräuseln *a. fig*; Curling spielen; *to ~ up (tr itr)* (sich) zs.-rollen, (sich) aufrollen, (sich) umbiegen; mit angezogenen Beinen liegen; hocken; *fam* zs.brechen (lassen); *in ~* gekräuselt; *a ~ of the lips* verzogene Lippen *f*; *pl ~ of smoke* Rauchwölkchen *n pl*; **~ing** ['-iŋ] Kräuselung *f*; *sport* Curling *n*; *~~-tongs, ~(~)-irons (pl)* Brennschere *f*; **~ers** ['-əz] *pl*, **~-papers** *pl* Lockenwickel *m pl*; **~y** ['-i] gewellt, gekräuselt, gelockt; lockig.

curlew ['kə:lju:] *orn* Brachvogel *m*.

curmudgeon [kə:'mʌdʒən] Griesgram, Brummbär; Knicker, Filz *m*.

currant ['kʌrənt] Korinthe; Johannisbeere *f*; Johannisbeerstrauch *m*.

curren|cy ['kʌrənsi] *fin* (Geld-, Noten-) Umlauf; Kurs *m*; Laufzeit, Gültigkeitsdauer; Währung *f*, Zahlungsmittel *n*, Geldsorte, Valuta; *allg* Geltung, (Allgemein-)Gültigkeit, (allgemeine) Anerkennung *f*, Gebrauch *m*; Lebensdauer, -zeit *f*; *in common ~~* in allgemeinem Gebrauch, gebräuchlich, üblich; *to have short ~~* e-e kurze Lebensdauer haben; *to gain ~~* in Umlauf, in Gebrauch kommen; *to give ~~ to* in Umlauf setzen *od* bringen; **~~** *agreement* Währungsabkommen *n*; **~~** *area* Währungsgebiet *n*; **~~** *block* Währungsblock *m*; **~~** *control* Devisenkontrolle *f*; **~~** *depreciation, devaluation* Geldent-, abwertung *f*; **~~** *law* Münzgesetz *n*; **~~** *reform* Währungsreform *f*; **~~** *restrictions (pl)* Devisenbewirtschaftung *f*; **~~** *stability, stabilization* Währungsstabilität, -stabilisierung *f*; **~t** ['-t] *a* laufend; im Umlauf befindlich, umlaufend; gebräuchlich, üblich, gangbar, marktgängig, anerkannt; (allgemein)gültig, landläufig; *s* Strom *m*, Strömung *f*; Luftzug; *el* Strom; Ab-, Verlauf *m*; *fig* Tendenz, Richtung *f*; *alternating ~~ (el)* Wechselstrom *m*; *direct ~~ (el)* Gleichstrom *m*; *generation of ~~* Stromerzeugung *f*; *down-, up-~~* Ab-, Aufwind *m*; **~~** *account* laufende (Ab-)Rechnung *f*, Kontokorrent; Scheckkonto *n*; **~~** *carrying* stromführend; **~~** *consumption* Stromverbrauch *m*; **~~** *demand* Strombedarf *m*; **~~** *events (pl)* Tagesgeschehen *n*; **~~** *expenses (pl)* laufende Ausgaben *f pl*; **~~** *intensity, strength* Stromstärke *f*; **~~** *issue (Zeitschrift)* letzte Nummer *f*; **~~** *market value, price* Marktwert, -preis *m*; **~~** *opinion* öffentliche Meinung *f*; **~~** *rate* (Tages-, laufender) Kurs *m*; **~tly** ['-tli] *adv* gegenwärtig, jetzt.

curriculum [kə'rikjuləm] *pl a. -la* [-lə] Lehrplan *m*; **~ vitae** ['vaiti:] Lebenslauf *m*.

currier ['kʌriə] (Leder-, Pferde-)Zurichter; Gerber *m*.

currish ['kə:riʃ] *fig* knurrig, gemein; ungezogen.

curry ['kʌri] **1.** *s (~ powder)* Curry *m* od *n (Gewürzpulver)*; Currysoße *f*; mit C. gewürzte(s) Ragout *n*; *tr* mit C. zubereiten; **2.** *tr (Pferd)* striegeln; *(Leder)* zurichten, gerben; schlagen, prügeln, (aus)peitschen; *to ~ favour with s.o.* sich bei jdm einzuschmeicheln suchen; **~-comb** Striegel *m*.

curse [kə:s] *s* (Ver-)Fluch(ung *f*) *m*, Verwünschung *f*; Fluch, Unsegen *m*, Unglück *n* (*to* für); *tr* verfluchen, verdammen, fluchen (*s.o.* jdm, auf jdn); *itr* fluchen, lästern; *to mutter a ~ under o.'s breath* e-n Fluch vor sich hinmurmeln; **~d** ['-id, -t] *a* verflucht, *fam* verflixt; eigensinnig.

cursive ['kə:siv] *a (Handschrift u. typ)* kursiv; *s* Kursivschrift; *typ* Kursive *f*.

cursor|iness ['kə:sərinis] Flüchtigkeit, Oberflächlichkeit, Nachlässigkeit *f*; **~y** ['-i] flüchtig, oberflächlich, nachlässig.

curt [kə:t] kurz, knapp; barsch (*to* gegen); **~ail** [kə:'teil] *tr* beschneiden, (ab)kürzen, schmälern, verkleinern (*of* um); verstümmeln *fig*; *(Lohn)* herabsetzen; **~ailment** [-'teilmənt] Beschneidung, (Ab-)Kürzung, Verkleinerung, Be-, Einschränkung, Schmälerung *f*.

curtain ['kə:tn] *s* Gardine *f*, Vorhang *a. theat*; *allg* Schleier *m fig*; *arch (~ wall)* Abschirmwand *f*; *mil* Zwischenwall *m*; *pl sl* Ende, Unglück *n*, Tod *m*; *tr* mit e-m Vorhang versehen; verhüllen, verhängen; verschleiern; *to ~ off* mit e-m Vorhang abteilen; *behind the ~ (fig)* hinter den Kulissen; *to draw the ~* den Vorhang zuziehen; *to draw a ~ over s.th. (fig)* den Vorhang über e-r S zuziehen, über etw nicht mehr sprechen; *to lift the ~* den Vorhang aufziehen; *fig* den Schleier lüften; *the ~ rises, falls* od *drops (theat)* der

Vorhang geht auf, fällt; *iron-~ (pol), fireproof, safety-~ (theat)* eiserne(r) Vorhang *m*; *~ of fire* Feuervorhang *m*; *~ of smoke* Rauchschleier *m*; **~-call** *theat fig* Vorhang *m*; **~-lecture** Gardinenpredigt *f*; **~-raiser** *theat* Eröffnungseinakter; *film* Vorspann *m*; **~-rod** Gardinenstange *f*.

curts(e)y ['kə:tsi] *s* Knicks *m*; *itr u. to make, to drop a ~* e-n Knicks machen, knicksen (*to* vor).

curv|aceous [kə:'veiʃəs] *fam (Frau)* kurvenreich, vollschlank; **~ature** ['kə:vətʃə] Biegung, Krümmung *a. math*; *med* Verkrümmung *f*; *~~ of the spine* Rückgratverkrümmung *f*; *~~ radius* Krümmungsradius *m*; **~e** [kə:v] *s* Kurve *a. math*, Biegung, Krümmung *f*, Bogen; *(Ball)* Drall *m*; *tr itr* (sich) biegen, e-n Bogen machen; (sich) wölben, (sich) krümmen, (sich) winden; *tech* schweifen; kurven; *to enter, to take a ~~* in e-e Kurve gehen, e-e K. nehmen; *~~ sheet, tracer* Kurvenblatt *n*, -zeichner *m*; **~ed** [-d] *a* bogenförmig, gebogen, gewölbt, gekrümmt; krumm; **~et** [kə:'vet] *s (Pferd)* Bogensprung *m*; *itr* e-n Bogensprung machen; herumhupfen; **~ilinear** [kə:vi'liniə] krummlinig.

cushion ['kuʃən] *s* Kissen *a. tech*, Polster *n a. fig*; *tech* Puffer *m*; *(Billard)* Bande *f*; *mot (~tyre)* Halbluftreifen *m*; *Am rail pl* Zug *m*; *Am sl* Rücklage, Gewinnspanne *f*; *tr* polstern; auf ein Kissen setzen *od* legen; abschirmen, -decken; *tech* (ab)federn; *(Stoß)* abfangen; *(Billard)* auf Bande spielen; *air ~* Luftkissen *n*.

cushy ['kuʃi] *a sl* gemütlich, bequem, leicht; *s* Geld, Moos *n*.

cusp [kʌsp] Spitze *f*, Scheitelpunkt *m*; *arch* Bogenspitze *f*; *(Mond)* Horn *n*; *(Herzklappe)* Zipfel *m*; *(Zahn)* Höcker *m*; **~id** ['-id] *s* (menschlicher) Eckzahn *m*; *a u.* **~idal** ['-idl], **~idate(d)** ['-ideit(id)] (zuge)spitz(t); **~idor** ['-idɔ:] *Am* Spucknapf *m*.

cuss [kʌs] *s fam* Fluch; (komischer) Kauz, (verrückter) Kerl *m*; dumme(s) Tier *n*; *tr itr fam* (ver)fluchen; *not worth a tinker's ~* keinen Heller wert; *he doesn't care a ~* er kümmert sich e-n Dreck darum; **~ed** ['-id] *fam* verflucht, verdammt; **~edness** ['-idnis] *fam* Bosheit, -haftigkeit *f*; zänkische(s) Wesen *n*; **~-word** *fam* Fluch *m*, Schimpfwort *n*.

custard ['kʌstəd] Eiermilch, -krem *f*.

custod|ial [kʌs'toudjəl] *a* vormundschaftlich, Aufsichts-; treuhänderisch; *s* Reliquienschrein *m*; **~ian** [-jən] Verwahrer, Pfleger, Kurator, Konservator; Aufseher; Treuhänder; (Haus-) Verwalter, Hausmeister *m*; *~~ country* Treuhänderstaat *m*; **~y** ['kʌstədi] Obhut, Verwahrung *f*, Gewahrsam *m*; Aufsicht(spflicht), Vormundschaft; (*bes.* Schutz-, Untersuchungs-)Haft *f*; *to release from ~~* aus der Haft entlassen; *to take into ~~* in Verwahrung nehmen; in Haft nehmen, verhaften; *preventive ~~* Untersuchungshaft *f*; *protective ~~* Schutzhaft *f*.

custom ['kʌstəm] *s* Sitte *f*, Brauch *m*, Herkommen *n*, Gewohnheit, Gepflogenheit *f*; Gewohnheitsrecht *n*; *(commercial, trade ~)* Handelsbrauch *m*, Usance; *com* Kundschaft *f*; Kundenkreis *m*; Klientel *f*; *pl* Zoll(verwaltung *f*, -gebühren *f pl*) *m*; *a Am (Kleidung)* Maß-; *to get, to pass through the ~s* den Zoll passieren, beim Zoll durchgehen; *to pay ~s on s.th.* für etw Zoll bezahlen; *it is his ~ to do* er pflegt zu tun; **~ary** ['-əri] üblich, gebräuchlich, gewöhnlich, herkömmlich, landläufig; Gewohnheits-; *not ~~* ungebräuchlich; *~~ law* Gewohnheitsrecht *n*; **~ clothes** *pl Am* Maßkleidung *f*; **~er** ['-ə] Kunde, Verbraucher, Abnehmer; Teilnehmer; Auftraggeber; *fam* Kauz, Kunde, Kerl *m*; *pl* Kundschaft *f*, Kundenkreis *m*; *an awkward ~~ (fam)* ein schwieriger Mensch; *list of ~~s* Kundenkartei *f*; *a queer ~~ (fam)* ein komischer Kauz; *regular ~~* Stammkunde *m*; *stray ~~* Laufkunde *m*; **~-house** Zollamt *n*; **~-made** *a Am* nach Maß angefertigt; *fam* teuer; **~s** *pl*: *~~ agent* Zollagent *m*; *~~ barrier* Zollschranke *f*; *~~ clearance* Zollabfertigung *f*; *~~ declaration* Zollerklärung *f*; *~~ district* Zollbezirk *m*; *~~ dues, duties (pl)* Zollgebühren *f pl*; *~~ examination* Zollrevision *f*; *~~ office* Zollamt *n*; *~~ officer, official* Zollbeamte(r) *m*; *~~ regulations (pl)* Zollvorschriften *f pl*; *~~ tariff* Zolltarif *m*; *~~ territory* Zollgebiet *n*; *~~ union* Zollunion *f*; *~~ warehouse* Zollspeicher *m*; *~~ warrant* Zollauslieferungsschein *m*.

cut [kʌt] *irr cut cut* **1.** *tr* (ab-, an-, auf-, aus-, be-, durch-, ein-, zer)schneiden; (sich) schneiden in; *math (Linie)* schneiden; stutzen; (ab)mähen; scheren; spalten, trennen, (zer)teilen, (auf)schlitzen; zer-, abhauen; *mar* kappen; verschneiden, kastrieren; *(Stoff)* zuschneiden; *(Film)* schneiden; schnitzen, (ein)gravieren; *(Karten)* abheben; *sport (Ball)* schneiden; *(alkohol. Getränk)* verschneiden, verdünnen; *fig* beschneiden, verringern, verkleinern; *(Gehalt)* kürzen; *(Preise)* herabsetzen, ermäßigen, reduzieren; *fam (Menschen)* schneiden, nicht sehen wollen; *fam (Schule)* schwänzen; sich drücken vor; *sl* stoppen, Schluß machen, aufhören mit; **2.** *itr* scharf sein, schneiden; sich schneiden lassen; *(Wind)* schneiden, *(to ~ through)* pfeifen durch; *fam* abhauen; *(Schule)* schwänzen; *(Karten)* abheben; **3.** *a* (ab-, aus-, ein)geschnitten; be-, zerschnitten; behauen; beschnitten, kastriert; *fig* verkleinert, verringert, reduziert, gekürzt; *sl* besoffen; **4.** *s* Schnitt, Hieb, Schlag, Stoß, Stich; (Ein-)Schnitt *m*, (Schnitt-) Wunde; Schnittfuge *f*; Ab-, Aus-, Einschnitt *m*; *(Fleisch)* abgeschnittene(s) Stück *n*, Scheibe; *(Schafe)* Schur *f*; Durchstich, Graben *m*; (Druck-)Platte *f*; (Kupfer-, Stahl-) Stich, Holzschnitt; *tech* Schliff, Span(stärke *f*); *(Kleidung)* (Zu-)Schnitt *m*, Fasson *f*; *(Karten)* Abheben *n*; *(short~)* Richtweg *m*, (Weg-)Abkürzung; *fig* Verringerung, Verkleinerung, Verminderung, Kürzung *f (a. d. Gehaltes)*, Abstrich *m*; Nachlassen *n*, Abnahme *f*; Schneiden, Ignorieren, verletzende(s) Verhalten *n od* Worte *n pl*, Hieb (*at* auf); *fam* Rüffel, Anschnauzer *m*; *fam* Schwänzen *n*, Drückebergerei *f*; *sl* (Gewinn-)Anteil *m*; *sl* soziale Stufe *f*; **5.** *a ~ above (fam)* ein bißchen, etwas besser als; *to ~ a caper (vor Freude)* e-n Luftsprung machen; *to ~ o.'s coat according to o.'s cloth (fig)* sich nach der Decke strecken; *to ~ and come again* tüchtig (drauflos) essen; *to ~ corners (Am)* einsparen (*on* bei); *to ~ a dash* sich von s-r besten Seite zeigen; *to ~ a figure* Eindruck schinden *od* machen; *to ~ it fine (fam)* es (*bes. zeitl.*) gerade (so) schaffen; *to ~ the ground from under s.o., s.o.'s feet (fig)* jdm den Boden unter den Füßen wegziehen; *to ~ no, not much ice (fam)* nicht viel ausrichten; niemanden überzeugen; *to ~ it out (fam)* Schluß machen, aufhören; *to ~ s.o. to the quick (fig)* jdn tief verletzen; *to ~ the record* den Rekord brechen; *to ~ a record, a take* e-e Schallplattenaufnahme machen (*of* von); *to ~ and run (fam)* schleunigst das Weite suchen; *to ~ o.'s teeth* zahnen; *on* sich früh gewöhnen an; *to ~ in two, in half, into halves* mitten durchschneiden, halbieren; *to ~ both ways (fig)* ein zweischneidiges Schwert sein; *~!* hau ab! zieh ab! mach, daß du wegkommst! *~ it out!* halt den Mund! hören Sie damit auf; **6.** *salary ~* Gehaltskürzung *f*, -abbau *m*; *wage ~* Lohnkürzung *f*; *~ in prices* Preissenkung *f*, -nachlaß *m*; **7.** *to ~* **across** quer gehen, laufen über, überqueren; *to ~* **after** her sein hinter, auf den Fersen sein *dat*, verfolgen; *to ~* **at** schlagen, ausholen nach, gegen; *to ~* **away** *tr* weg-, abschneiden, entfernen; *itr fam* auskneifen, türmen; *to ~* **back** *tr* zurück-, beschneiden, (ab)kürzen; einschränken; ab-, unterbrechen; *itr* in der Erzählung zurückgehen; *film* zurückblenden; *sport* e-n Haken schlagen; *to ~* **down** ab-, umhauen, *(Baum)* fällen; *(Wald)* abholzen; niederhauen, -schlagen; *fig (to ~ down on)* kleiner machen, verkleinern, (ver-)kürzen, verringern, herabsetzen, einschränken; *(Text)* beschneiden; *to ~* **in** einfallen, dazwischentreten, unterbrechen, in die Rede fallen; *mot* nach dem Überholen einbiegen; sich *(durch e-e Lücke)* durchschlängeln; einkerben; *(beim Tanzen)* abklatschen; *to ~* **into** unterbrechen, einfallen in *(e-e Rede)*; *to ~* **loose** *tr* abtrennen; *itr (Schiff)* den Anker kappen; *fam* (frisch) drauflos reden; sich keine Hemmungen auferlegen; außer Rand u. Band geraten; *to ~* **off** abschneiden, -hauen, -trennen; plötzlich unterbrechen, *tele* trennen; *(Gas, el Strom)* abschneiden, wegnehmen, abstellen; *mot* stillsetzen; abschneiden, -fangen; *(Truppen)* absprengen; ausschließen, verstoßen; *(Zuwendung)* streichen; *to ~ (off) a corner* (auf dem Weg) e-e Ecke abschneiden; *to ~ off from (fig)* abschneiden von; *to ~ off o.'s nose to spite o.'s face* sich ins eigene Fleisch schneiden; *to ~ off with a shilling* enterben; *to ~* **on** losstürmen; *to ~* **open** aufschneiden, -schlitzen, -schlagen; *to ~* **out** *tr* ausschneiden; wegschneiden, entfernen, streichen, weg-, auslassen; *(Weg)* bahnen; *(Stoff)* zuschneiden; *(Rivalen)* ausstechen; übertrumpfen, verdrängen; *(Licht)* ausschalten, -machen; *(Radio)* abschalten, -stellen; *fam* weg-, auslassen, unterbinden; *(das Rauchen)* aufgeben; *to be ~ out for* geschaffen sein für; *itr tech* aussetzen; *mot* scharf ausbiegen; *(Karten)* ausscheiden; *to ~* **short** abkürzen, unterbrechen; das Wort abschneiden (*s.o.* jdm); *to ~* **through** durchschneiden; durchqueren; *to ~* **under** *fam* unterbieten; *to ~* **up** *tr* zerschneiden, -legen; vernichten; Verletzungen beibringen; *(seelisch)* mitnehmen, aufwühlen, *fam* fertigmachen; heftig kritisieren, herunterreißen, *fam* fertigmachen; *Am sl* dumme Witze machen, schwätzen, diskutieren; *itr* viel ab-, hergeben; *to ~ up rough* aufbrausen, wütend werden, (los)poltern; *to ~ up well* reich sterben; **8. ~-and-come-again** Fülle *f*, Überfluß *m*; **~-and-dry, -dried** *a* fix und fertig; *(Mei-*

nung) vorgefaßt; angestaubt *fig*; **~-and-thrust weapon** Hieb- u. Stichwaffe *f*; **~away** ['-əwei] *s* Cut (-away) *m (Herrenrock)*; *a tech* aufgeschnitten; *~~ drawing* Schnittzeichnung *f*; *~~ model* Schnittmodell *n*; **~-back** Zurück-, Beschneiden *n*; Kürzung, Verminderung; Einschränkung; Unterbrechung *f*; Personalabbau; Rückgang *m*, Nachlassen; Zurückgreifen *n* (in der Erzählung); *film* Rückblende; *sport* plötzliche Wendung *f*; **~ face** Schnittfläche *f*; **~ flowers** *pl* Schnittblumen *f pl*; **~-in** *film* Zwischentitel *m*; *el* automatische Einschaltung; Eingriffstellung *f*; *Am sl* Anteil *m*; **~-off** *Am* Richtweg *m*, (Weg-)Abkürzung *f*; *(Fluß)* Durchbruch *m*; *tech* Schieber *m*; Abschalten *n*; Ausschaltung *f*; *(Rakete)* Brennschluß; Seitenkanal *m*; *rail* Anschlußgleis *n*; *mil* Stellungsriegel *m*; **~-out** Ausschnitt *m*, Aussparung *f*; *mot* Auspuff; *el* Schalter; *(~~ switch)* Unterbrecher; Auslöser *m*; **~over** ['-ouvə] *Am a s* gerodet(es Land *n*); *tech* Überleitung *f*; **~throat** ['-θrout] *s* Mörder *m*; *a* mörderisch; halsabschneiderisch; **~up** ['-ʌp] *Am sl* Witzbold; freche(r) Kerl; Angeber; Saufbruder *m*.

cutaneous [kju(:)teinjəs] *a scient* Haut-.

cut|e [kju:t] *fam* gewitzt, hell(e); *Am fam* nett, hübsch, reizend, entzückend, süß; **~ie, ~(e)y** ['-i] *Am sl* fesche(s) Mädel *n*; Schlauberger *m*.

cuticle ['kju:tikl] *anat bot* Oberhäutchen *n*, Kutikula *f*.

cutlass ['kʌtləs] Hirschfänger *m*, *bes.* Entermesser *n*.

cutler ['kʌtlə] Messerschmied *m*; **~y** ['-ri]; Stahlwaren(handel *m*) *f pl*; Besteck, Tafelsilber *n*.

cutlet ['kʌtlit] Kotelett; Schnitzel *n*; *Am* Fleisch- *od* Fischklops *m*.

cutter ['kʌtə] Schneidende(r), Schneider *(bes. in Zssgn)*; Zuschneider; Schnitzer; Hauer; *film* Schnittmeister, Cutter; *(Schallplatte)* Schreiber *m*; *tech* Messer *n*, Schneide *f*, Schneidwerkzeug *n*, -apparat *m*, -maschine *f*; Fräser; (Löffel-)Bohrer; *min* Häuer, Gesteinshauer *m*; Münz-, Pappschere *f*; *mar* Kutter *m*; Beiboot *n*; *Am* kleine(r) Schlitten *m*, Küstenschutzboot *n*; **~-head** Fräskopf *m*; Schneidedose *f*.

cutting ['kʌtiŋ] *s* Schneiden *n*, Schnitt; *(Holz)* Einschlag *m*; Fräsen *n*; Einschnitt, Durchstich (für e-e Straße *od* Bahnlinie); *film* Schnitt; *Br* (*bes.* Zeitungs-)Ausschnitt *m*; *agr* Reis *n*, Steckling *m*; *fin com* Herabsetzung, Kürzung *f*; *pl* Schneid-, Drehspäne; *pl* Abfälle *m pl*; *a tech* Schneid-, Fräs-; spanabhebend; *(Kälte, Wind)* schneidend; *fig* beißend, verletzend; **~-burner, -torch** Schneidbrenner *m*; **~ room** *film* Schneideraum *m*; **~ tool** Drehstahl *m*.

cuttle ['kʌtl] *(~-fish)* Tintenfisch *m*, Sepia, Sepie *f*; *(~-bone)* Schulp *m*.

*

cyan|ic [sai'ænik] *a* :*~~ acid* Zyansäure *f*; **~ate** ['saiəneit] *chem* Zyanat, Salz *n* der Zyansäure; **~ide** ['saiənaid] *chem* Zyanid, blausaure(s) Salz *n*; *~~ of hydrogen* Blausäure *f*; **~ogen** [sai'ænədʒin] *chem* Zyan *n*.

cybernetics [saibə:'netiks] *pl mit sing* Kybernetik *f*.

cyclamen ['sikləmən] *bot* Alpenveilchen *n*.

cycl|e ['saikl] *s* Kreis(lauf), Zyklus *m*, Periode *f*; Arbeitsgang *m*; *astr* (Kreis-)Bahn *f*; Zeitalter *n*; *lit* Sagen-, Legendenkreis *m*; *fam* (Fahr-)Rad *n*; *itr* sich in e-m Kreislauf bewegen, periodisch wiederkehren; *fam* radfahren, radeln; **~ic(al)** ['-ik(l)] zyklisch, periodisch; zu e-m Sagenkreis gehörig; **~ist** ['-ist] Radfahrer(in *f*) *m*; **~oid** ['-ɔid] *math* Zykloide *f*; *a* kreisförmig; *med* zyklothym; **~oidal** [-'klɔidl] *math* zykloidal; **~ometer** [-'klɔmitə] Zyklometer, Wegmesser, Kilometerzähler *m*; **~one** ['-oun] Wirbelsturm, Zyklon *m*; **~op(a)edia** [-ə'pi(:)djə] Enzyklopädie *f*, Konversationslexikon *n*; **C ~opean** [-klo(u)'pi:ən, -'-] gigantisch, gewaltig, ungeheuer; **C~ops** ['-ɔps] Zyklop *m*; **~otron** ['-ətrɔn] Zyklotron *m*.

cygnet ['signit] junge(r) Schwan *m*.

cylind|er ['silində] *math tech mot* Zylinder *m*; *tech* Walze, Trommel, Rolle *f*; *(Papierfabrikation)* Holländer *m*; Mangel-, Rollholz *n*; *attr tech* Zylinder-; *~~ block* Zylinder-, Motorblock *m*; *~~ capacity (mot)* Hubraum *m*; *~~ head* Zylinderkopf *m*; **~ric(al)** [-'lindrik(əl)] zylindrisch, walzenförmig.

cymbals ['simbəlz] *pl mus* Becken *n*.

Cymric ['kimrik] *a* kymrisch; *s* Kymrisch *n*.

cynic ['sinik] *s* Zyniker *m*; *a* zynisch; **~al** ['-əl] zynisch, sarkastisch; höhnisch; verächtlich; griesgrämig; **~ism** ['-sizm] Zynismus *m*; zynische Bemerkung *f*.

Cynosure ['sinəzjuə, '-ʃuə] *astr* Kleine(r) Bär *od* Wagen; Polarstern *m*; *c~ (fig)* Leitstern; Anziehungspunkt, Mittelpunkt *m* des Interesses.

cypher *s. cipher.*

cypress ['saipris, -əs] *bot* Zypresse *f*.

Cypr|ian ['sipriən], **~iot** ['-ət, -ət] *a* zyprisch; *s* Zypriot(in *f*) *m*; **~us** ['saiprəs] Zypern *n*.

cyst [sist] *bot zoo* Beutel *m*; *anat* (Harn-)Blase; *med* Zyste, Sackgeschwulst *f*; *synovial ~ (med)* Überbein *n*; **~itis** [-'taitis] *med* Blasenentzündung *f*; **~olith** ['sistəliθ] *med* Blasenstein *m*; **~oscope** ['-əskoup] Blasenspiegel *m*; **~otomy** [-'tɔtəmi] Blasenschnitt *m*.

czar, ~ina *s. tsar.*

Czech [tʃek] *s* Tscheche *m*, Tschechin *f*; Tschechisch *n*; *a* tschechisch; **~o-Slovakia** ['-o(u)slo(u)vɑ:kjə, -vækiə] die Tschechoslowakei; **~o-Slovakian** *s* Tschechoslowake *m*, Tschechoslowakin *f*; *a* tschechoslowakisch.

D

D, d [di:] *pl ~'s, ~s s* D, d *n a. mus*; *Am (Schule)* ausreichend; **~ flat** Des, des *n*; **~ sharp** Dis, dis *n*.

dab [dæb] **1.** *tr* leicht, sanft schlagen, berühren; (leicht) abklopfen; *fam* antippen, klapsen; ab-, betupfen (*with s.th.* mit etw); *typ* klischieren; *(to ~ on)* auftragen *(Farbe)*; *itr* tippen; tupfen; betupfen (*at s.th.* etw); *s* leichte(r), sanfte(r) Schlag, *fam* Klaps *m*; Betupfen *n*; Spritzer, Tupfen, Klecks *m*; *(Butter)* Klümpchen *n*; *fig* Schlampe *f*; *pl sl* Fingerabdrücke *m pl*; **2.** *zoo* Flunder, Scholle *f*, Butt *m*; **3.** *s fam* Kenner, Könner *m*, As *n*, Kanone *f* (*at s.th* in etw); *to be a ~ (hand)* viel loshaben; *at doing s.th.* in e-r S (sehr) beschlagen, bewandert sein, etw aus dem ff können; *adv*: *right ~ in the middle (Am fam)* haargenau in die Mitte; **~ber** ['-ə] Tupfen *m*; *typ* Filzwalze *f*.

dabble ['dæbl] *tr* bespritzen, benetzen, naß machen; *itr* herumspritzen, (herum)plätschern, plan(t)schen; *fig* sich ein bißchen befassen, abgeben (*at, in* mit); (hinein)pfuschen, (herum)stümpern (*at, in* in); als Hobby betreiben (*at, in s.th.* etw); **~r** ['-ə] *fig* Stümper, Pfuscher; Dilettant, Liebhaber *m*.

dabchick ['dæbtʃik] *orn* Zwergsteißfuß *m*, Tauchentchen *n*.

dabster ['dæbstə] *fam* Alleskönner, Tausendsasa; *Am fam* Stümper *m*.

dace [deis] Weißfisch *m*.

dactyl ['dæktil] Daktylus *m (Versfuß)*; *zoo* Finger *m*, Zehe *f*; **~ic** [dæk'tilik] daktylisch; **~ogram** ['-əgræm, -'ti-] Fingerabdruck *m*; **~ology** [-'lɔlədʒi] Finger-, Taubstummensprache *f*.

*

dad(dy) ['dæd(i)], **dad(d)a** ['dædə], **da** [dɑ:] *fam* Papa, Pappi, Vati *m*.

daddy-long-legs ['dædi'lɔŋlegz] Bachmücke, (Bach-)Schnake *f*; *Am* Kanker, Weberknecht *m*.

dado ['deidou] *pl -oes* Sockel, Würfel *(e-s Postaments)*; untere(r) Wandteil *m*.

daemon ['di:mən] *s. demon.*

daffodil ['dæfədil] *bot* Narzisse *f*; (Blaß-, Hell-)Gelb *n*.

daffy ['dæfi] *Am fam* verrückt, wahnsinnig; albern; *sl* verliebt (*about* in).

daft [dɑ:ft] albern, dumm, blöd(e); schwachsinnig; verrückt, wahnsinnig.

dagger ['dægə] *s* Dolch *m*; *typ* Kreuz *n*; *tr* erdolchen, -stechen; *to be at ~s drawn with s.o.* mit jdm auf (sehr) gespanntem Fuß stehen; *to look ~s at* feindselige Blicke werfen, schleudern auf; *to speak ~s at s.o.* jdm verletzende, beleidigende Worte sagen; **~s** ['-z] *bot* Wasserschwertlilie *f*.

dago ['deigou] *pl -o(e)s Am sl pej* Italiener, Spanier *od* Portugiese *m*.

dahlia ['deiljə] *bot* Dahlie, Georgine *f*.

Dail Eireann [dail-, dɔil'ɛərən] *parl* das Irische Unterhaus.

daily ['deili] *a adv* täglich, Tag(e, es)-; werktäglich; alltäglich, Alltags-; *s (~ paper)* Tageszeitung; *(~ help) fam* Stunden-, Zugehfrau *f*; *o.'s ~ bread* das tägliche Brot; **~ allowance** Tagegeld *n*; **~ consumption** Tagesverbrauch *m*; **~ dozen** *fam* tägliche Gymnastik *f*; **~ money** tägliche(s) Geld; Tagesgeld *n*; **~ output** Tagesleistung *f*; **~ pay, wages** *pl* Tag(e)-lohn *m*; **~ quantity, rate, scale**

Tagessatz *m*; ~ **report, return** Tagesmeldung *f*.

daint|iness ['deintinis] Zierlichkeit, Zartheit *f*; Fein-, Zartgefühl *n*, Verfeinerung; Verwöhntheit, Leckerhaftigkeit; Feinheit, Köstlichkeit *f*; **~y** ['deinti] *a (Person)* niedlich, hübsch, lieblich, zierlich, zart; fein-, zartfühlend, verfeinert; verwöhnt, wählerisch (*about* in); lecker, schmackhaft; *(Sache)* fein, ausgesucht, köstlich, delikat; *s* Leckerbissen *m*, Leckerei *f*; *pl* Leckerbissen *m pl*.

dairy ['deiri] *(~ing, ~ farming)* Milchwirtschaft; *(~ farm) (einzelne)* Milchwirtschaft, Meierei; Molkerei *f*; Milchgeschäft *n*; ~ **cattle** Milchkühe *f pl*; **~maid** ['-meid] Milchmädchen *n*; **~man** ['-mən] Milchhändler, *fam* -mann; Schweizer *m*; ~ **produce** Milchprodukte, Molkereierzeugnisse *n pl*.

dais ['dei(i)s] Podium *n*; erhöhte(r) Platz *m (für e-n Thron* od *Ehrensitz)*.

daisy ['deizi] Maßliebchen, Gänseblümchen; *(double ~)* Tausendschön *n*; *(ox-eye, Ox-eye D~)* Margerite *f*; *Am Art* Käse *m*; *sl* Pfundsding *n*, -sache *f*, -kerl *m*; *fig* Perle *f*; *to push up the daisies (sl)* die Radieschen von unten begucken; ~ **chain** Gänseblumenkränzchen *n*.

dale [deil] *(nordengl. dial u. poet)* Tal *n*.

dall|iance ['dæliəns] Tändelei *f*, Flirt *m*, Techtelmechtel *n*, Liebelei; Spielerei *f*; Trödeln *n*; **~y** ['-i] *itr* tändeln, flirten (*with* mit); *fig* spielen, liebäugeln (*with* mit); die Zeit verplempern *od* vertrödeln (*over o.'s work* bei der Arbeit).

daltonism ['dɔ:ltənizm] Farbenblindheit *f (bes. rotgrün)*.

*

dam [dæm] **1.** *s* Damm *m*, Wehr *n*; Talsperre *f*; Stauwasser, -becken *n*; *fam* Wasserbehälter *m*; *tr (to ~ in, up)* (durch e-n Damm, ein Wehr) (auf-) stauen, eindämmen; *to ~ up (fig) (Gefühl)* unterdrücken, zurückhalten mit; **2.** Muttertier *n*.

damage ['dæmidʒ] *s* Schaden *m*, Beschädigung *f*, Verlust *m*, Einbuße *f (to* an); Nachteil *m*; *(Bombe)* Wirkung *f*; *sl* Preis *m*, Kosten *pl*; *pl* Entschädigung *f*, Schaden(s)ersatz *m*; *tr* (be)schädigen; Schaden zufügen (*s.o.* jdm); herabsetzen, (herab)mindern, beeinträchtigen, verletzen; *to his ~* zu s-m Schaden, Nachteil; *to be liable for the ~* für den Schaden haften; *to claim ~s* Schadenersatz fordern; *to pay ~s* Schadenersatz leisten; *to sue s.o. for ~s* jdn auf Schadenersatz verklagen; *to suffer ~* Schaden erleiden *od* nehmen, zu Schaden kommen, be-, geschädigt werden; *what's the ~ (sl)* was kostet's? *adjustment of ~s* Schadensregelung *f*; *appraisal of the ~* Schadensfeststellung *f*; *claim for ~s* Schadensersatzanspruch *m*; *material ~* Sachschaden *m*; *war ~* Kriegsschaden *m*; *~ caused by fire, game, hail, sea, water* Feuer-, Wild-, Hagel-, See-, Wasserschaden *m*; **~able** ['-əbl] *(Sache)* empfindlich; **~ assessment** Schadensfeststellung *f*; **~d** ['-d] *a* beschädigt, zu Schaden gekommen; *fig* angeschlagen; **~ report** Schadensbericht *m*, -aufstellung *f*.

damask ['dæməsk] *s* Damast *(Gewebe)*; Damaszenerstahl *m*; Damaszierung *f*; Rosenrot *n*; *a* Damast-; Damaszener-; rosenrot; *tr* rosenrot machen; damastartig weben; *tr u.* **~een** [-'i:n], **damascene** ['-si:n, *a.* -'si:n] *tr (Stahl)* damaszieren.

dame [deim] *obs poet hum* Frau, Dame; (Titel *m* e-r) Witwe von Stand (*od* e-r) Ordensinhaberin *f*; *sl* Weib(sbild) *n*.

damn [dæm] *tr* verdammen *a. rel*, verfluchen, verwünschen; tadeln, verurteilen, heruntermachen; ruinieren, zuschanden machen; *theat* auspfeifen; *s* Fluch *m*, Verwünschung *f*; *a sl* verdammt, verflucht, verwünscht; *not care, not give a ~* sich e-n Dreck machen aus; *~ it (all)!* verdammt (noch mal)! verflixt (u. zugenäht)! *~ you!* hol dich der Teufel! **~able** ['-nəbl] verdammenswert; abscheulich; schändlich; *fam* verdammt, verflixt, Dreck-; **~ation** [-'neiʃən] *s* Verdammung *a. rel*; *rel* Verdammnis *f*; *interj* verdammt! verflucht! **~ed** [-d] *a* verdammt; verflucht; verflixt; verwünscht; abscheulich, widerlich; *adv* äußerst, sehr; *the ~~* die Verdammten; *to suffer the tortures of the ~~ (fam)* Höllenqualen leiden müssen.

damp [dæmp] *a* feucht; dunstig; *s* Feuchtigkeit *f*; Dunst *m*, Luftfeuchtigkeit *f*; *(fire ~)* Grubengas *n*, Schwaden *m*, schlagende Wetter *n pl*; *fig* gedrückte Stimmung, Niedergeschlagenheit, Mut-, Hoffnungslosigkeit *f*; *tr* an-, befeuchten, benetzen; *(to ~ down) phys tech* drosseln, bremsen; *el* dämpfen *a. fig*; *fig* drücken, herabsetzen, mindern; entmutigen, den Mut, die Hoffnung nehmen *(s.o.* jdm); *to ~ off (agr)* in Fäulnis übergehen (vor Nässe); *to cast, to strike a ~ over, into (fig)* e-n Schatten werfen auf, die Stimmung *gen* drücken; **~-course** *arch* Isolierschicht *f*; **~en** ['-ən] *tr* an-, befeuchten; mindern, einschränken, bremsen, drosseln; dämpfen; *(to ~~ s.o.'s spirits)* entmutigen; **~er** ['-ə] Dämpfer *(Person u. Sache, a. fig phys tech)* (*to* für); *mot* Stoßdämpfer; Anfeuchter *m*; (Ofen-) Klappe *f*, Zugregler *m*; *Am fam* Ladenkasse *f*; *(~~ of a radiator)* Kühlerjalousie *f*; *to put the ~~ on* e-n Dämpfer aufsetzen (*s.o.* jdm); entmutigen; die Freude verderben an; **~ing** ['-iŋ] Dämpfung *f*; **~ish** ['-iʃ] etwas feucht; dumpfig; **~ness** ['-nis] Feuchtigkeit *f*; Dunst *m*.

damsel ['dæmzəl] *obs poet* Jungfer, Jungfrau *f*.

damson ['dæmzən] Damaszener Pflaume *f*.

danc|e [dɑ:ns] *itr* tanzen (*with* mit); tänzeln; (fröhlich) umherspringen; hüpfen (*for, with* vor); schaukeln; *s* Tanz; *tr (Tanz)* tanzen; schaukeln; *s* Tanz; *mus* Tanz(weise *f*) *m*; Tanzparty *f*, -abend, Ball *m*; *to lead s.o. a pretty ~~* jdm Scherereien machen; jdn an der Nase herumführen; *to ~~ attendance on s.o.* sich um jdn unablässig bemühen; *to ~~ to s.o.'s pipe, tune* nach jds Pfeife tanzen; *to ~~ to another tune (fig)* s-n Mantel nach dem Winde hängen; *St Vitus's ~~ (med)* Veitstanz *m*; *~~-band* Tanzkapelle *f*; *~~ of death (Kunst)* Totentanz *m*; *~~ floor* Tanzboden *m*; *~~ frock* Tanzkleid *n*; *~~ hall* Tanz-, Ballsaal *m*; *sl* Todeszelle *f*; *~~ music* Tanzmusik *f*; *~~ record (Am)* Tanzplatte *f*; **~er** ['-ə] Tänzer(in *f*) *m*; **~ing** ['-iŋ] Tanzen *n*; *~~-girl* Tanzgirl *n*; *~~-lesson* Tanzstunde *f*, -unterricht *m*; *~~-master* Tanzlehrer *m*; *~~-partner* Tanzpartner *m*; *~~-party* Tanzabend *m*; *~~-room* Tanzsaal *m*; *~~-school* Tanzschule *f*; *~~ shoes (pl)* Ballschuhe *m pl*.

dandelion ['dændilaiən] *bot* Löwenzahn *m*.

dander ['dændə] *fam bes. Am* Ärger *m*; Laune *f*; *to get o.'s ~ up* ärgerlich werden, in Rage kommen; *to get s.o.'s ~ up* jdn auf die Palme bringen.

dandify ['dændifai] *tr* stutzer-, geckenhaft heraus-, aufputzen.

dandle ['dændl] *tr (Kind)* wiegen, schaukeln; hätscheln, liebkosen.

dandruff ['dændrəf] Kopfschuppen *f pl*.

dandy ['dændi] *s* Stutzer, Geck; leichte(r) Wagen; *mar* Treiber *m*; *sl* Pfundsding *n*, -sache *f*; *a* gecken-, stutzerhaft; *sl* pfundig, phantastisch, prima, Klasse; *adv* bestens, glänzend; *fine and ~ (fam)* in Form, auf der Höhe; **~ish** ['-iʃ] stutzer-, geckenhaft; **~ism** ['-izm] geckenhafte(s) Wesen *n*.

Dan|e [dein] Däne *m*, Dänin *f*; *Great ~~* Deutsche Dogge *f*; **~ish** ['-iʃ] *a* dänisch; *s* (das) Dänisch(e).

danger ['deindʒə] Gefahr *f* (*to* für); *at ~ (Signal)* auf Halt; *in ~* in Gefahr; *out of ~* außer Gefahr; *to avert, to ward off a ~* e-e Gefahr abwenden *od* beseitigen; *to be a ~ to* e-e Gefahr bilden, bedeuten für; *to be in ~ of losing* Gefahr laufen, zu verlieren; *caution! ~!* Achtung! Lebensgefahr! *war ~, ~ of war* Kriegsgefahr *f*; *~ of fire, to life* Feuer-, Lebensgefahr *f*; ~ **area** Gefahrenzone *f*; ~ **money** Gefahrenzulage *f*; **~ous** ['-dʒrəs] gefährlich, gefahrvoll (*to* für); ernst; ~ **point** Gefahrenpunkt *m*, -moment *n*; ~ **signal** *rail* Warn-, Haltesignal *n*; ~ **zone** Gefahrenzone *f*, *mar* Warngebiet *n*.

dangle ['dæŋgl] *itr tr* baumeln, schlenkern (lassen); *tr fig* vor Augen, *fam* vor die Nase halten (*before s.o.* jdm); *to ~ about, after, round s.o.* jdm nachlaufen.

dank [dæŋk] unangenehm feucht, feuchtkühl, naßkalt.

Danube, the ['dænju:b] die Donau.

daphne ['dæfni] Lorbeerbaum; Seidelbast *m*.

dapper ['dæpə] nett, fein, hübsch, niedlich; behende, gewandt, flink.

dapple ['dæpl] *tr* sprenkeln; **~d** ['-d] *a (Tier)* gesprenkelt, scheckig, gefleckt, bunt; **~-grey**: *~~ horse* Apfelschimmel *m*.

darbies ['dɑ:biz] *pl sl* Handschellen *f pl*.

Darby and Joan ['dɑ:bi ən(d) 'dʒoun] glückliche(s) alte(s) Ehepaar *n*.

dare [dɛə] *v aux (meist in verneinten, fragenden, Bedingungs-* od *e-n Zweifel ausdrückenden Sätzen)* es wagen, können, dürfen (*do s.th.* etw zu tun); *tr* wagen, sich getrauen, riskieren (*to do s.th.* etw zu tun); ins Auge sehen, trotzen (*s.th.* e-r S); heraus-, auffordern; *I ~ say* ich darf wohl sagen, ich stehe nicht an zu sagen; doch wohl, vermutlich, wahrscheinlich; *don't you ~* unterstehen Sie sich! *s fam* wagemutige Tat *f*; **~-devil** *s* Wagehals *m*; *a* wagehalsig, tollkühn.

daring ['dɛəriŋ] *a* (toll)kühn, wagehalsig, -mutig, unerschrocken; dreist, frech; *s* Wagemut, Unternehmungsgeist *m*; Dreistigkeit, Frechheit *f*.

dark [dɑ:k] *a* dunkel, finster; schwärzlich; *(Farbe, Haut, Haare)* dunkel; brünett; *fig* verborgen, versteckt; geheim(nisvoll); unklar, unverständlich, unerklärlich; unheilvoll, böse, übel; hoffnungs-, mutlos, niedergeschlagen, traurig; trüb(e), finster; unheimlich; unwissend, unaufgeklärt; *Am sl theat sport* geschlossen; *s* Dunkelheit, Finsternis; (Einbruch *m* der) Nacht; Verborgenheit; dunkle Färbung *f*; *at ~* beim Dunkelwerden; *before, after ~* vor, nach Einbruch der Dunkelheit *od* Nacht; *in the ~* im Dunkeln, in der Dunkelheit, bei Nacht;

fig im dunkeln; nicht auf dem laufenden; *to be in the* ~ *about s.th.* über etw im ungewissen sein; *to keep* ~ *(fig)* im ungewissen lassen; geheimhalten; *to look on the* ~ *side of things (fig)* alles von der Schattenseite sehen; *leap in the* ~ Sprung *m* ins Ungewisse; *the* ~ *side of things* die Schatten-, Kehrseite; *the* **D~ Ages** *pl* das (Früh-)Mittelalter; **~-blue, -brown, -colo(u)red** *a* dunkelblau, -braun, -farbig; **~en** ['-ən] *tr itr* dunkel machen *od* werden; ver-, abdunkeln; (sich) verdunkeln, (sich) verfinstern, (sich) verdüstern; ~ **horse** *(Rennpferd, a. Mensch)* Außenseiter *m*; **~ish** ['-iʃ] etwas dunkel, trübe; schwärzlich; ~ **lantern** Blendlaterne *f*; **~ling** ['-liŋ] *adv* im Dunkel(n); *a poet* dunkel(nd), düster, finster, trüb(e); **~ness** ['-nis] Dunkelheit, Finsternis; Schwärze *f*; das Geheime; Unverständlichkeit; Unwissenheit; Blindheit *f*; das Böse, Übel *n*; ~ **room** *phot* Dunkelkammer *f*; **~-skinned** *a* dunkelhäutig; ~ **slide** *phot* Kassette *f*; **~some** ['-səm] *poet* dunkel *a. fig*, trüb(e); finster, unheimlich; **~y, ~ey, ~ie** ['-i] *fam u. pej* Nigger, Neger *m*.

darling ['dɑ:liŋ] *s* Liebling *m*; *a* lieb, (heiß, innig) geliebt, teuer; allerliebst; Lieblings-.

darn [dɑ:n] **1.** *tr (Strümpfe)* stopfen; ausbessern; *s* Stopfen, Ausbessern *n*; Stopfstelle *f*; **2.** *fam (euph für damn) tr fam* verdammen; *s* Verwünschung *f*, Fluch *m*; *a adv interj* verdammt, verflixt; *not to know a* ~ *thing* gar nichts wissen; völlig im dunkeln tappen; *I don't give a* ~ *about it!* ich pfeife darauf! ~ *it!* zum Kuckuck nochmal! **~er** ['-ə] Stopfer(in *f*) *m*; Stopfnadel *f*; Stopfei *n*, -pilz *m*; **~ing** ['-iŋ] Stopfen, Ausbessern *n*; auszubessernde Sachen *f pl*; **~~** *needle* Stopfnadel; *zoo Am* Libelle *f*; **~~** *yarn* Stopfgarn *n*.

dart [dɑ:t] *tr* schießen, schleudern, werfen, schnellen; *(Strahlen)* aussenden; *itr* schießen, sausen, fliegen, flitzen, schnellen; (los)stürmen (*at* auf, zu); herfallen (*on* über); *to* ~ *away* fortstürmen, davonstürzen; *s* Wurfspieß; Pfeil; *zoo* Stachel; *fig* Stich *m*; Schleudern, Werfen, Schießen *n*; Sprung, Sturz (auf etw); *(Textil)* Abnäher *m*; *pl* Pfeilwerfen *n (Spiel)*; *to make a* ~ *at* sich stürzen auf; **~-board** Zielscheibe *f*; **~er** ['-ə] Schlangenhalsvogel; Weißfisch *m*.

dash [dæʃ] *tr* schmettern, schlagen, stoßen; (aus-, be-, ver)spritzen, versprühen, (aus)gießen, (aus-, ver-) schütten; (ver)mischen (*with* mit); zerschlagen (*to pieces* in Stücke); vernichten; zuschanden, zunichte machen; entmutigen, verwirren, verlegen machen, beschämen; *sl* (= *damn*) verdammen; *itr* schlagen, prallen (*against* gegen); laufen, (sich) stürzen, stürmen, jagen, rasen, sausen; patschen; *s* (heftiger) Schlag, Stoß *m*; Klatschen *n*, Guß, Spritzer *m*; Prise, Messerspitze *f*; Schuß *m*, Beimischung *f*; Schwung, Sturz, Sturm; Vorstoß, Sturmangriff; *fig* Schwung, Elan *m*, Feuer *n*, Schneid; Überschwang *m*, Begeisterung *f*, (Gefühls-)Ausbruch, (Gedanken-)Flug; Gedankenstrich; *(Morsealphabet)* Strich *m*; *mot* Armaturenbrett *n*; *sport* Kurzstreckenlauf *m*; *at a* ~ wie der Wind, im Sturm; *at one* ~ in e-m Zug; *at (the) first* ~ auf Anhieb; *to cut a* ~ Aufsehen erregen, auffallen; *to make a* ~ *at, for s.th.* sich auf etw stürzen, auf etw losstürmen; ~ *it! (sl)* verdammt! verflixt! *to* ~ **aside** beiseite werfen, -schleudern; *to* ~ **away** wegwerfen, -schleudern; *to* ~ **down** niederwerfen, zu Boden schleudern; *to* ~ **into** hineinstürzen; *to* ~ **off** *tr* wegwerfen, -schleudern; schnell erledigen, abtun, *fam* hinhauen, -werfen; schnell zu Papier bringen, schreiben; *itr* wegsausen, losrasen, davonstürzen, *fam* (schnell) abhauen; *to* ~ **out** aus-, zerschlagen; hinausstürzen; *to* ~ **over** ausstreichen; *to* ~ **with** verdünnen mit; sprenkeln mit; **~board** ['-bɔ:d] Spritzbrett, -leder *n*; *mot* Armaturenbrett *n*; Schalttafel *f*; **~~** *light* Instrumentenleuchte *f*; **~er** ['-ə] Schläger, Stürmer *m*; Rührholz *n*, -flügel *m*; *Am* Spritzleder *n*; *fam* imposante Erscheinung *f*; **~ing** ['-iŋ] schwungvoll, überschwenglich, begeistert; gefühl- *od* geistvoll; lebhaft; feurig, schneidig; aufsehenerregend, auffällig.

dastard ['dæstəd] Feigling, feige(r) Schuft *m*; *a u.* **~ly** ['-li] *a* feige, hinterhältig, gemein.

data ['deitə] *pl Am oft sing* Einzelheiten, Tatsachen, Gegebenheiten *f pl*; *das* Bekannte; (Tatsachen-)Material *n*, Daten *n pl*, Unterlagen, Angaben *f pl*; Meßwerte *m pl*; Versuchsergebnisse *n pl*; *personal* ~ Personalangaben *f pl*; ~ **processing** Datenverarbeitung *f*; ~ **sheet** Unterlagenliste *f*; Lebenslauf *m* in Stichwörtern; ~ **transmission** Meßwertübertragung *f*.

date [deit] **1.** *s* Datum *n*, Zeitangabe *f*; (bestimmter) Tag; Termin, Zeitpunkt *m*; Frist, Zeit(raum *m*, -alter *n*); *fam* Verabredung *f*, Stelldichein, Rendezvous *n*; *fam* jem, mit dem man e-e Verabredung hat; *tr* datieren; zeitlich festlegen, bestimmen; die Zeit festlegen (*s.th.* e-r S); *to* ~ *s.o. (Am)* sich mit jdm verabreden, mit jdm ausgehen; *itr Am fam* sich verabreden; datiert sein (*from* von); sich herleiten (*from* aus); veralten; *to* ~ *from, to* ~ *back to* stammen aus, zurückgehen auf; zählen von; *at an early* ~ bald, in Bälde, in Kürze; *at long* ~ auf lange Sicht; *at short* ~ kurzfristig; *at that* ~ zu jener Zeit; damals; *bearing* ~ *of* unter dem Datum des, datiert vom; *of recent* ~ neueren Datums; *out of* ~ aus der Mode (gekommen); *(up) to* ~ bis jetzt, noch; *under (the)* ~ *of* unter dem Datum des; *up to* ~, *(attr a) up-to-*~ auf der Höhe (der Zeit), zeitgemäß, modern, in Mode; auf dem laufenden; *without* ~ ohne Datum, undatiert; *to become, to get out of* ~ aus der Mode kommen, veralten; *to fix, to set a* ~ e-e Frist festlegen; den Zeitpunkt bestimmen; *to have, to make a* ~ sich verabreden; *what is the* ~ *of ...?* wann war ...? *what is the* ~ *to-day?* welches Datum, den wievielten haben wir heute? *critical, crucial* ~ Stichtag *m*; *effective* ~ Tag *m* des Inkrafttretens; *to-day's* ~ das heutige Datum; ~ *of acceptance* Annahmetag *m*; ~ *of birth* Geburtsdatum *n*, -tag *m*; ~ *of delivery* Liefertermin *m*; ~ *of dispatch* Aufgabe-, Absende-, Abgangstag *m*; ~ *of issue* Ausgabe-, Ausstellungs-, Ausfertigungstag *m*, -datum *n*; ~ *of maturity* Verfall(s)tag *m*; ~ *of the postmark* Datum *n* des Poststempels; ~ *of publication* Bekanntmachungs-, *(Buch)* Erscheinungstag *m*; ~ *of receipt* Eingangsdatum *n*; ~ **bait** *Am* hübsche(s), gerngesehene(s) Mädchen *n*; **~-block** Abreißkalender *m*; **~d** ['-id] *a* datiert; antiquiert, aus der Mode, altmodisch; *to be* ~ datiert sein vom; **~ing** ['-iŋ] Datierung *f*; **~less** ['-lis] undatiert, ohne Datum; unbegrenzt; zeitlich nicht mehr festzulegen(d); immer noch brauchbar *od* interessant; **~-line** *geog* Datumsgrenze *f*; *(Zeitung)* Datum *n (e-r Nachricht)*; **~-stamp** Datums-,Tages-, Poststempel *m*; **2.** Dattel *f*; **~-palm** Dattelpalme *f*.

dative ['deitiv] *gram* Dativ *m*.

datum ['deitəm] *pl -ta* ['-tə] gegebene *od* angenommene Größe *f*; Meßwert *m*; Gegebenheit, Tatsache; Annahme; Grundlage *f*; *(~ point)* Ausgangs-, Bezugs-, Nullpunkt *m*; *attr* gegeben, Ausgangs-, Null-; ~ **line** Bezugs-, *mil* Stand-, Grundlinie *f*.

daub [dɔ:b] *tr itr* (be)schmieren; (be-) sudeln, (be)pinseln; bekleckern; *arch* grob auftragen; *s* schmierige(s) Zeug *n*, Überzug; Lehm-, Gipsbewurf *m*; *a.* **~ery** ['-əri] Geschmiere *n*, Sudelei; Pinselei, Kleckserei *f*; *(Kunst)* Schinken *m*; **~(st)er** ['-(st)ə] Schmierfink; Farbenkleckser *m*.

daughter ['dɔ:tə] Tochter *f a. fig*; ~ *of Eve* Evastochter *f*; **~-in-law** Schwiegertochter *f*; **~ly** ['-li] *a* töchterlich.

daunt [dɔ:nt] *tr* schrecken, ängstigen, Angst machen (*s.o.* jdm); entmutigen, den Mut nehmen (*s.o.* jdm); *nothing ~ed* unverzagt; **~less** ['-lis] furchtlos, unerschrocken; mutig, tapfer.

davenport ['dævnpɔ:t] *Br* (kleiner, Klapp-)Schreibtisch, Sekretär *m*; *Am* Sofa *n*; (Schlaf-)Couch *f*.

davit ['dævit] Davit, Schiffskran *m*.

Davy ['deivi]: ~ **Jones** *mar hum* Neptun, der Seegeist; ~ *Jones's locker* der Meeresgrund, das feuchte Grab.

davy ['deivi] *sl* Eid *m*; *to take o.'s* ~ schwören; *on my* ~*!* Ehrenwort!

daw [dɔ:] *orn* Dohle *f*.

dawdle ['dɔ:dl] *itr* (herum)trödeln, -bummeln; *tr (to* ~ *away) (Zeit)* vertrödeln, -bummeln; *to* ~ *over o.'s work* saumselig arbeiten; **~r** ['-ə] Trödler, Bummler, Bummelant, Tagedieb *m*.

dawn [dɔ:n] *s* (Morgen-)Dämmerung *f*, Tagesanbruch *m*; *fig* Morgenröte *f*, Anfang, Beginn *m (e-r neuen Zeit)*; *fig* Erwachen *n*; *itr* dämmern, tagen, Tag werden; *fig* heraufkommen, dämmern, beginnen, anbrechen; *(Sinn)* aufgehen, dämmern (*on, upon s.o.* jdm); *at* ~ beim Morgengrauen.

day [dei] Tag *(a. Zeitraum)*; Wochentag *m*; Tageslicht *n*; entscheidende(r) Tag; Termin *m*; Epoche, Zeit; (Blüte-)Zeit *f*; *(at-home* ~*)* Empfangstag *m*; *astr* Umdrehungszeit *f*; *pl* Tage *m pl*, Zeiten *f pl*; Leben *n*; *(three times) a* ~ (dreimal) täglich, am Tage; *all (the)* ~ *long* den ganzen Tag (über); *at, by* ~ am Tag(e), bei Tage; *at the present* ~ gegenwärtig; *at this time of* ~ augenblicklich; *before* ~ vor Tage(sanbruch); *by the* ~ tageweise; *every* ~ jeden Tag, täglich; *from* ~ *to* ~ von Tag zu Tag; *in my boyhood ~s* als ich (noch) ein Junge war; *in a few ~s time* in ein paar, in wenigen Tagen; *in these ~s* heute, heutzutage; *in those ~s* damals; *in ~s of old* in vergangenen Zeiten, früher; *in ~s to come* in Zukunft; *of a* ~ Tages-; kurz(lebig); *one* ~ eines Tages; einmal, *lit* dereinst; *one of these ~s* in den nächsten Tagen; nächstens; eines Tages; *some* ~ einmal, *lit* dereinst; *the other* ~ kürzlich, neulich, vor ein paar Tagen; unlängst; *the present* ~ die Gegenwart; *the* ~ *after to(-)morrow* übermorgen; *the* ~ *before yester*~ vorgestern; *the* ~ *before, after the fair* zu früh, zu spät; *this* ~ heute; *this* ~ *week, month, year* heute in acht Tagen, vier Wochen, einem Jahr; *these ~s* heutzutage; *up to this* ~ bis heute, bis auf den heutigen Tag; *the* ~ *after* der, am folgende(n) Tag; ~ *after* ~, ~ *by* ~ Tag für Tag; von Tag zu Tag; ~ *and night, night and* ~ Tag u. Nacht, ununterbrochen; *the* ~ *before* der, am Vortag; ~ *in*, ~ *out* tagein, tagaus; *to call it a* ~ *(fam)* Feierabend, Schluß machen; *to carry* od *to win, to lose the* ~ siegen *od* gewinnen, verlieren; *to end o.'s* ~*s* sein Leben beschließen; *to fix a* ~ e-n Tag festlegen; e-n Termin anberaumen; *to have o.'s* ~*(s)* s-e (Blüte-) Zeit haben; *to keep o.'s* ~*s* den Termin einhalten; *to know the time of* ~ wissen, was los ist, Bescheid wissen; *to pass the time of* ~ *with s.o.* jdm (kurz) guten Tag sagen, jdn (kurz) begrüßen; *what* ~ *of the week is it?* welchen Wochentag haben wir? *business* ~ Werk-, Arbeitstag; Markt-, Börsentag *m*; *eight-hour* ~ Achtstundentag *m*; *election* ~ Wahltag *m*; *the Last D*~ der Jüngste Tag; *market* ~ Markt-, Börsentag *m*; *order of the* ~ Tagesordnung *f*; *pay-*~ Zahltag *m*; *present-*~ heutig, von heute; *rainy* ~ Regentag *m*; *fig* schlechte Zeiten *f pl*; *red-letter* ~ (gesetzlicher) Feiertag *m*; *wedding* ~ Hochzeitstag *m*; *work(ing)* ~ Arbeitstag *m*; ~ *of arrival* Ankunftstag *m*; ~ *of birth, of death* Geburts-, Sterbetag *m*; ~ *in court* Gerichtstag *m*; ~ *of expiration (fin)* Verfall(s)tag *m*; ~ *of grace (fin)* Respektstage *m pl*; Gnadenfrist *f*; ~ *of issue* Ausgabe-, Erscheinungstag *m*; *D*~ *of Judg(e)ment (rel)* Tag des Gerichts, Jüngste(r) Tag *m*; ~ *of maturity* Verfalltag *m*; ~ *of payment* Zahlungstermin *m*; ~ *of rest* Ruhetag *m*; ~*-to-*~ *matters (pl)* laufende Angelegenheiten *f pl*; ~*-to-*~ *money (Bank)* Tagesgeld *n*; ~**-bed** Schlafsofa *n*, -couch *f*; ~**-boarder** *(Schule)* Halbpensionär *m*; ~**book** Tagebuch; *com* Journal *n*; ~**-boy, -girl, -pupil** Tagesschüler(in *f*) *m*, Externe(r *m*) *f*; ~**break** ['-breik] Tagesanbruch *m*; *at* ~~ bei Tagesanbruch; ~ **coach** *Am rail* Personenwagen *m*; ~**-dream** *s* Wachtraum *m*; Wunschvorstellungen *f pl*; *itr* mit offenen Augen träumen; ~**-labourer** Tag(e)löhner *m*; ~ **letter** *Am* Brieftelegramm *n*; ~**light** ['-lait] Tageslicht *n a. fig*; Öffentlichkeit *f*; Zwischen-, Hohlraum *m*; Lücke *f*; *Am* Bewußtsein; *(Problem)* Lösung *f*; *Am sl* Augen *n pl*; *by* ~~ bei Tageslicht; *from* ~~ *till dark* den ganzen Tag (über); *in broad* ~~ am hellichten Tage; *to see* ~~ *(fam)* kapieren; das Ende absehen; ~~ *exposure* Tageslichtaufnahme *f*; ~~*-saving time (Am)* Sommerzeit *f*; ~**long** *a* einen (ganzen) Tag dauernd, *adv* lang; ~ **nursery** Tagesheim *n* für Kleinkinder, Kinderbewahranstalt *f*; ~**-off** dienstfreie(r) Tag *m*; ~**-out** freie(r) Tag, Ausgang *m*; ~**'s receipts, takings** *pl* Tageseinnahme, -kasse *f*; ~**-shift** Tag(es)-schicht *f*; ~**-school** Tagesschule *f*, Externat *n*; ~**spring** *poet* Tagesanbruch *m*; ~**-star** Morgenstern *m*; *poet* Sonne *f*; ~**-ticket** *rail* Tagesrückfahrkarte *f*; ~**time** Tag *m*; *during, in the* ~~ bei Tage.

daze [deiz] *tr* vor den Kopf stoßen, betäuben *fig*, völlig überraschen; *(vorübergehend)* blenden; *fam* verwirren; *s* Benommenheit, Betäubung; Bestürzung, Verwirrung *f*; ~**dly** ['-zidli] *adv* benommen; verwirrt; bestürzt.

dazzl|e ['dæzl] *tr* (vorübergehend) blenden *a. fig*; *fig* ungeheuer beeindrucken, überwältigen *fig*, überraschen, verwirren; *(Schiff)* tarnen; *itr* geblendet sein; blenden, e-n gewaltigen Eindruck machen, überwältigend wirken; *s* Blenden; Geblendetsein *n*; gewaltige(r) Eindruck *m*, große Überraschung *f*; *(*~~ *paint) mil* Schutz-, Tarnanstrich *m*; ~**ing** ['-iŋ] *a* blendend; schimmernd, grell; *s* Blendung *f*.

deacon ['di:kən] *rel* Diakon(us) *m*; ~**ess** ['-is] Diakonisse, Diakonissin *f*; ~**ry** ['-ri] Diakonat, Diakonenamt *n*.

dead [ded] **1.** *a* tot, ge-, verstorben; *(Pflanze(nteil))* abgestorben, dürr, trocken; *(Materie)* tot, leblos, unbelebt; *min* taub; außer Gebrauch (gekommen), abgekommen, überlebt, veraltet; *(Sprache)* tot; *(Maschine)* nicht in Betrieb; unempfindlich (*to* gegen), gefühl-, kraft-, energie-, bewegungs-, reg(ungs)los, wie abgestorben, wie tot; *fam* todmüde, ausgepumpt; öde, langweilig, leblos; *(Schlaf)* tief; *(Wasser)* stehend, still; *(Feuer)* erloschen; *(Zigarre)* ausgegangen; *(Flasche)* leer; *arch* blind, Blend-, Schein-; *el* spannungslos; unfruchtbar, unproduktiv, unergiebig; unwirksam; unbrauchbar, unbenutzbar; unbenutzt, abgestellt; unverkäuflich; *(Plan)* abgelehnt, erledigt; (toten)still, einsam, öde, leer; kalt, matt, farb-, glanzlos, blind, stumpf, schal; uninteressant, reizlos; (tod-) sicher, unfehlbar, unzweifelhaft; vollständig, völlig, total, absolut; unveränderlich; unverlangt; unentschieden; der bürgerlichen Ehrenrechte beraubt; **2.** *adv* (voll u.) ganz, völlig, vollständig; absolut, total; zutiefst, außerordentlich, aufs äußerste, tödlich; direkt, genau; **3.** *s* Tiefpunkt *m*; Toten-, absolute Stille *f*; *the* ~ die Toten *m pl*; **4.** *in the* ~ *of night* mitten in der Nacht, in tiefer Nacht; *in the* ~ *of winter* mitten im Winter, in tiefem Winter; **5.** ~ *against* genau entgegen (-gesetzt) *dat*; ~ *from the neck up (Am sl)* strohdumm; ~ *to rights (Am sl)* sicher; absolut; ~ *on the target* genau ins Ziel; ~ *to the world (fam)* tief eingeschlafen; betrunken; ~ *as a doornail* mausetot; ~ *and gone* unwiderruflich dahin; **6.** *to be in* ~ *earnest about s.th.* in etw keinen Spaß verstehen; *to be a* ~ *failure* (völlig) schiefgehen; ein völliger Versager sein; *to be a* ~ *man* ein Kind des Todes sein; keine Chancen haben; *to come to a* ~ *stop* plötzlich stehenbleiben; *to declare legally* ~ für tot erklären; *that has been* ~ *and buried (for) a long time* darüber ist längst Gras gewachsen; ~ *men tell no tales (prov)* ein Toter redet nicht; ~ *slow!* Schritt fahren! ~**-alive** mehr tot als lebendig, halbtot; *fig* sterbenslangweilig; ~ **ball** *sport* Ball *m* außer Spiel; ~ **bargain**: *at a* ~~ spottbillig; *that's a* ~~ das ist (halb) geschenkt; ~**-beat** *a phys* aperiodisch; *fam (körperlich)* kaputt, erledigt, völlig erschöpft; ~ **beat** *Am sl* Nassauer, Schmarotzer; Zechpreller; *Am sl* Nichtstuer, Tagedieb *m*; ~ **broke** *a fam* völlig abgebrannt, pleite; ~ **calm** Totenstille; *mar* Windstille, Flaute *f*; ~ **capital, money** tote(s) Kapital *n*; ~ **centre** *tech* Totpunkt *m*; ~ **certain, sure** todsicher; ~ **colo(u)r** Grundierung *f*; ~ **drunk** *a* sternhagelvoll; ~**en** ['dedn] *tr* abtöten, unempfindlich machen; abstumpfen (*to* gegen); abschwächen, dämpfen; *tech* mattieren; ~ **end** *s* Endpunkt *m*, -station *(e-r Zweigbahn)*; Sackgasse *f*; *fig* tote(s) Geleise *n*; ~**-end** *a* nicht weiterführend, blind, tot; *fam* Elends-; ~~ *kid* Straßenjunge, (kleiner) Rowdi *m*; ~~ *siding* tote(s) Gleis *n*; ~~ *station* Kopfbahnhof *m*; ~~ *street* Sackgasse *f*; ~**fall** Wildfalle *f*; *(Wald)* Windbruch; gestürzte(r) Baum *m*; *Am sl* Räuberhöhle *f*, Nachtlokal *n*; ~ **files** *pl* abgelegte Akten *f pl*; ~ **fire** Elmsfeuer *n*; ~ **freight** Leerfracht *f*; ~ **gold** Mattgold *n*; ~ **ground** *mil* tote(r) Winkel *m*; ~**head** Inhaber *m* e-r Freikarte *od* e-s Freifahr(t)scheins; Schwarzhörer; blinde(r) Passagier; nicht beladene(r) Wagen; Dummkopf *m*; ~ **heat** *sport* tote(s) Rennen *n* ~ **horse** etw, das man am besten vergißt; Ladenhüter *m*; ~ **hours** *pl* Nachtstunden; *(Schule)* Hohlstunden *f pl*; ~**-house** Leichenhalle *f*; ~ **letter** tote(r) Buchstabe *m*; nicht mehr beachtete(s) Gesetz *n*; nicht zustellbare(r) Brief *m*; ~~ *office* Abteilung *f* für unbestellbare Briefe (bei e-m Postamt); ~ **level** glatte Fläche; *fig* Eintönigkeit, Monotonie *f*; ~ **lift** Kraftanstrengung; schwierige Aufgabe *f*; ~ **light** *arch* Oberlicht *n*; ~**-line** Absperr-, Grenzlinie; äußerste Grenze *f*; letzte(r) Termin; Redaktionsschluß; Stichtag *m*; ~**liness** ['-linis] Tödlichkeit *f*; ~ **load** Eigen-, Leergewicht *n*; ~ **loan** verlorene Anleihe *f*; ~**lock** völlige(r) Stillstand *m*; ausweglose Situation *od* Lage *f*; *at a* ~~ auf dem toten Punkt, festgefahren; *to come to a* ~~ sich festfahren, auf den toten Punkt gelangen; ~ **loss** völlige(r), Totalverlust *m*; ~**ly** ['-li] *a adv* tödlich; giftig; fatal, unheilvoll; Tod-, Toten-, Leichen-; bis zum Äußersten, Letzten; übermäßig, stark; *fam* unerträglich, schrecklich; *Am* **sl** ausgezeichnet; ~~ *nightshade (bot)* Tollkirsche *f*; ~~ *pale* leichenblaß; ~~ *sin* Todsünde *f*; ~ **man** Tote(r) *m*; ~**man** ['-mən] *(Zelt)* Hering; *mar el* Abspannpfahl; Verankerungspflock *m*; ~ **march** *mus* Trauermarsch *m*; ~ **marines** *pl fam* leere Flaschen *f pl*; ~ **matter** tote Materie *f*; ~**ness** ['-nis] Abgestorbenheit; Leblosigkeit; Überlebtheit; Unempfindlichkeit; Regungslosigkeit; Unwirksamkeit; Unbrauchbarkeit; Totenstille, Einsamkeit, Leere; Kälte, Mattheit, Farb-, Glanzlosigkeit; Stumpfheit, Schalheit *f*; ~**-nettle** *bot* Taubnessel *n*; ~ **pan** *s Am sl* ausdruckslose(s), nichtssagende(s) Gesicht *n*; ~**-pan** *a sl* mit e-m ausdruckslosen, nichtssagenden Gesicht; ~ **point** tote(r) Punkt *m*; ~**reckoning** *mar* Koppelkurs *m*; ~ **ringer** *Am sl* Doppelgänger *m*; *the* **D**~ **Sea** das Tote Meer; ~ **season** *com* Sauregurkenzeit, Flaute *f*; ~ **set** *s* heftige(r) Angriff *m*, große Anstrengung *f*; *a fam* versessen (*on* auf); ~ **stock** tote(s) Kapital *n*; *agr* landwirtschaftliche Maschinen *f pl*, tote(s) Inventar *n*; unverkäufliche Ware *f*; ~ **tired** *a* todmüde; ~ **wagon** *Am sl* Totenwagen *m*; ~ **weight** tote(s) Gewicht *n*; schwere Last *f*; Eigengewicht *n (e-s Fahrzeugs)*; *mar* Nutzlast, Tragfähigkeit *f*; ~ **wind** *mar* Gegenwind *m*; ~**wood** trockene Äste, Zweige *m pl (am Baum)*; *fig* Plunder *m*, wertlose(s) Zeug *n*; *sport* unfähige(r) Spieler *m*, Flasche *f*; *gram* überflüssige Wörter *n pl*; ~ **work** vorbereitende Arbeit *f*.

de-aerat|e ['di'ɛəreit] *tr* entlüften; ~**ion** [-'reiʃən] Entlüftung *f*; ~**or** [diɛə'reitə] Entlüfter *m*.

deaf [def] taub *a. fig* (*to* für, gegen); schwerhörig; *to be* ~ *of (in) one ear* auf e-m Ohr taub sein; *to turn a* ~ *ear to* nichts hören wollen von; ~ *and dumb* taubstumm; ~ **aid** Hörapparat *m*; ~**en** ['-n] *tr* taub machen; betäuben; übertönen, -schreien; schalldicht machen; ~**ening** ['-niŋ] *a* taubmachend; (ohren-)

betäubend, lärmend; schalldicht (machend); *s* schalldichte(s) Material *n*; **~-mute** Taubstumme(r) *m*; *a* taubstumm; **~ness** ['-nis] Taubheit *f a. fig* (*to* für, gegen).

deal [di:l] **1.** *v irr dealt, dealt tr (to ~ out)* aus-, verteilen; ausgeben; *(Karten)* geben; *(Schlag)* versetzen; *itr* handeln (*in* mit); kaufen (*at, with* bei); in Geschäftsverbindung, -verkehr stehen (*with* mit); in Verbindung stehen, Umgang, zu tun haben, verkehren (*with* mit); fertigwerden (*with* mit); handhaben, einrichten, in Ordnung bringen, erledigen (*with s.th.* etw); umgehen (*with* mit), behandeln (*with s.o.* jdn), sich verhalten (*by, with s.o.* gegenüber jdm); sich befassen (*with* mit); *(Buch)* handeln (*with* von), behandeln (*with s.th.* etw); *s* Handel *m*, Geschäft *n*; (Geschäfts-)Abschluß *m*, Abmachung *f*; Plan *m*, Programm *n*; Menge *f*, Teil, Betrag *m*; *Am* unsaubere(s) Geschäft *n*, Schiebung, Manipulation, *fam* krumme Tour *f*; (Karten-)Geben *n*; *a good, great ~ (of), (sl) a ~* recht, sehr viel, e-e Menge; *to give s.o. a square ~ (fam)* jdn fair behandeln; *who's ~ is it?* wer ist am Geben? *he got a raw ~ (fam)* man hat ihm übel mitgespielt; **~er** ['-ə] Händler (*in* mit); Vertreter; Lieferant; Kartengeber *m*; *retail, wholesale ~~* Klein-, Großhändler, Grossist *m*; *second-hand ~~* Altwarenhändler, Trödler *m*; *share ~~, ~~ in securities* Effektenhändler *m*; *~~ in furs* Pelzhändler *m*; **~ing** ['-iŋ] Verhalten(sweise *f*), Verfahren *n*, Handlungsweise *f* (*with* gegenüber); geschäftliche(s) Verhalten; Geschäft(sgebaren *n*, -verkehr *m*) *n*, Handel *m* (*in* mit); *pl* Geschäft(sabschlüss)e *pl*, Transaktionen *f pl*; Beziehungen (*with* zu), Verbindungen (*with* mit) *f pl*; Umsatz *m*; *to have ~~s with s.o.* mit jdm in (Geschäfts-)Verbindung stehen; *option ~~* Prämien-, Distanzgeschäft *n*; *volume of ~~s* Geschäftsumsatz *m*; *~~-out* Verteilung *f*; **2.** (Diele *f*, Brett *n*, Planke *f* aus) Tannen-, Fichten-, Kiefernholz *n*.

dean [di:n] *(rel, Univ., College)* Dekan *m*; *pol* Doyen *m*; *fig* Haupt *n*; **~ery** ['-əri] Dekanat *n*; Stellung *f* e-s Dekans.

dear [diə] *a* teuer *a. fig*; kostspielig; lieb; *fam* reizend; *(in der Briefanrede)* liebe(r); (sehr) geehrt; *s* Liebling, Schatz *m*; *(in der Anrede) (my ~)* mein Lieber; *adv* teuer; *interj: oh, ~! ~ me! ~, ~!* ach herrje! du liebe Zeit! verwünscht! Donnerwetter! *to get ~er* sich verteuern; **~ly** ['-li] *adv* teuer; sehr; **~ness** ['-nis] hohe(r) Preis *m*; Verteuerung; Kostspieligkeit *f*; **~y, ~ie** ['-ri] *fam* Liebling *m*.

dearth [də:θ] Lebensmittelknappheit; Hungersnot *f*; Mangel *m* (*of* an).

death [deθ] Tod *m*, Hinscheiden, Sterben *n*; Todesfall *m (pl nur in dieser Bedeutung)*; *fig* Ende, Aufhören *n*, Vernichtung, Zerstörung *f*, Untergang; Tod(esursache *f*); Mord *m*, Blutvergießen *n*; *at ~'s door* an der Schwelle des Todes; *in ~* im Tode; *till ~* auf Lebenszeit; *under pain, penalty of ~* bei Todesstrafe; *(on) to ~* zu Tode; (bis) auf den Tod; *(up)on ~* beim Tode, im Todesfall, bei Eintritt des Todes; *to be burnt, frozen, starved to ~* verbrennen *itr*, erfrieren, verhungern lassen; *to be in at the ~ (Jagdhund)* beim Verenden des Wildes dabeisein; *fig* das Ende erleben; *to be ~ on* schnell fertigwerden mit; glänzend verstehen; versessen sein auf; nicht riechen können; *to catch o.'s ~* sich den Tod holen; *of cold* sich auf den Tod erkälten; *to condemn to ~* zum Tode verurteilen; *to die a natural, a violent ~* e-s natürlichen, e-s gewaltsamen Todes sterben; *to do to ~* töten; *to put to ~* töten; hinrichten; *to work o.s. to ~* sich totarbeiten; *that will be my ~* das wird (noch) mein Tod sein; *he'll be the ~ of me yet* er bringt mich noch ins Grab; *the Black D~ (hist med)* der Schwarze Tod, die Pest; *declaration of ~* Todeserklärung *f*; *hour of ~* Sterbe-, Todesstunde *f*; *pale as ~* leichenblaß; *register of ~s* Sterberegister *n*; *sure as ~* todsicher; *time of ~* Zeitpunkt *m* des Todes; **~ agony** Todeskampf *m*; **~-bed** Totenbett *n a. fig*; *~~ confession* Geständnis *n* auf dem Totenbett *n*; *~~ repentance* (zu) späte Reue *f*; *~~ will* letzte(r) Wille *m*; **~-bell** Totenglocke *f*; **~-benefit** Sterbegeld *n*; **~-blow** Todesstoß *m* (*to* für); **~-cell,** *(Am)* **~-house** *(Gefängnis)* Todeszelle *f*; **~-certificate** Sterbe-, Totenschein *m*; **~-chamber** Sterbezimmer *n*; *Am* Hinrichtungsraum *m*; **~-duties** *pl* Erbschaftssteuer *f*; **~less** unsterblich, unvergänglich; **~like** totenähnlich; **~ly** *a adv* tödlich; verhängnis-, unheilvoll; **~-mask** Totenmaske *f*; **~-notice** Todesanzeige *f*; **~ penalty** Todesstrafe *f*; **~-rate** Sterblichkeit(sziffer) *f*; **~-rattle** Todesröcheln *n*; **~-ray** Todesstrahl *m*; **~-roll** Verlust-, Gefallenenliste *f*; **~'s head** Totenkopf *m*; *~~ moth (ent)* Totenkopf *m*; Todes-; **~ sentence, - warrant** Todesurteil *n*, Hinrichtungsbefehl *m*; **~-struggle, -throes** *pl* Todeskampf *m*; **~-trap** Todesfalle *f*; *fig* gefährliche(r) Stelle *f*, Ort *m*, Lage, *mot* Kreuzung *f*; **~-watch** *zoo* Totenuhr; Totenwache *f*.

deb [deb] *Am* = *debutante*.

debacle [dei'bɑ:kl] Eisbruch, -gang *m*; *geol* Mure *f*; *fig* Umsturz, Zs.bruch, Untergang *m*.

debar [di'bɑ:] *tr* ausschließen (*from doing s.th.* etw zu tun); versagen, verbieten (*s.o. from s.th.* jdm etw); hindern (*from doing s.th.* etw zu tun).

debark [di'bɑ:k] *tr* ausschiffen, ausbooten; *(aus e-m Schiff)* ausladen; *itr* das Schiff verlassen, an Land gehen; landen; **~ation** [di:bɑ:'keiʃən] Ausschiffung, Ausbootung; Landung *f*.

debase [di'beis] *tr* entwerten, im Wert herabsetzen; entwürdigen, erniedrigen, herabsetzen; verringern, verschlechtern, verderben; verfälschen; **~ment** [-mənt] Entwertung; Erniedrigung, Entwürdigung; Verschlechterung; Verfälschung *f*.

debat|able [di'beitəbl] fraglich; strittig, unentschieden; **~e** [di'beit] *s* Debatte, Aussprache *bes. parl*, Diskussion; Besprechung, Erörterung, Beratung *f*; *itr* diskutieren (*with s.o. on s.th.* mit jdm über etw); zur Diskussion stehen; beraten (*on* über); *tr* debattieren, diskutieren; erörtern, besprechen; beraten, beratschlagen über; erwägen, be-, durch-, überdenken, (sich hin u. her) überlegen (*with o.s., in o.'s own mind* bei sich); *after much ~~* nach langem Hin u. Her; *to open the ~~ (parl)* die Debatte eröffnen; **~er** [-ə] Debattierer, Redner *m* (in e-r Aussprache); *to be a good ~~* ein guter Diskussionsredner sein; **~ing society** Debattierklub *m*.

debauch [di'bɔ:tʃ] *s* Ausschweifung *f*; ausschweifende(s) Leben *n*; *tr* verführen, -leiten, auf Abwege führen; verderben; **~ed** [-t] *a* verführt, verdorben; ausschweifend, liederlich; **~ee** [debɔ:'(t)ʃi:] Wüstling, ausschweifende(r) Mensch *m*; **~ery** [di'bɔ:tʃəri] Ausschweifung *f*.

debenture [di'bentʃə] Schuldschein *m*; *(~ bond, certificate)* festverzinsliche Schuldverschreibung, Obligation *f*, Pfandbrief; Zollrückschein *m*; **~ stock** Schuldverschreibungen, Obligationen *f pl*, Pfandbriefe *m pl*.

debilit|ate [di'biliteit] *tr* schwächen, entkräften, entnerven, verbrauchen, abnutzen; *to be ~ating to s.o.* für jdn entnervend sein; **~ation** [-'teiʃən] Schwächung, Entkräftung, Abnutzung *f*; **~y** [di'biliti] Schwäche *f a. fig*.

debit ['debit] *s* Debet, Soll *n*, Lastschrift *f*; Debetposten *m*; Debet-, Sollseite *f*; *tr* debitieren, belasten; ins Soll, Debet eintragen; *to ~ s.o.'s account with s.th., to ~ s.th. against* od *to s.o.'s account* jds Konto mit etw belasten; *~ and credit* Soll und Haben *n*; **~ account** Debet-, Debitorenkonto *n*; **~ balance** Debetsaldo *n*; Restschuld *f*; **~ entry** Lastschrift *f*; **~ note** Lastschriftzettel *m*; **~ side** Soll-, Debet-, Passivseite *f*; **~ voucher** Lastschriftbeleg *m*.

debonair(e) [debə'nɛə] gutmütig, umgänglich, freundlich, nett; heiter, aufgeräumt, munter, lustig.

debouch [di'bautʃ, -'bu:ʃ] *itr mil* hervorbrechen, ausfallen; auftauchen, in Erscheinung treten; *(Fluß)* einmünden; sich ergießen; **-é** ['debuʃe] *mil* Lücke *f*; *com* Absatzgebiet *n*, -markt *m*; **~ment** [-mənt] (Fluß-) Mündung *f*.

debris, débris ['de-, 'deibri(:)] Trümmer *pl*, Schutt *m*; *geol* Gesteinstrümmer *pl*.

debt [det] *fin com* Schuld *f*; *in ~* verschuldet; *out of ~* schuldenfrei; *to acknowledge a ~* e-e Schuld anerkennen; *to be in ~* verschuldet sein, Schulden haben; *to be head over heels* od *up to o.'s ears in ~* bis an den Hals, bis über die Ohren in Schulden stekken; *to be in s.o.'s ~* jds Schuldner, jdm verpflichtet sein; *to be out of s.o.'s ~* jdm nichts mehr schuldig sein; *to call in, to collect, to recover a ~* e-e Schuld beitreiben, einziehen; *to contract, to incur ~s* Schulden machen; *to pay off a ~* e-e Schuld abzahlen, abtragen, tilgen; *to pay the ~ of nature* das Zeitliche segnen, sterben; *to remit a ~ to s.o.* jdm e-e Schuld erlassen; *to run into ~* Schulden machen; *to settle a ~* e-e Schuld begleichen; *action for ~* Forderungsklage *f*; *active ~* ausstehende Forderung *f*; *pl* Außenstände *m pl*; *amount of a ~* Schuldsumme *f*; *bad ~s (pl)* uneinbringliche Außenstände *pl*; *balance of ~* Restschuld *f*; *burden of ~s* Schuldenlast *f*; *collection of ~s* Einziehung *f* von Außenständen, Inkasso *n*; *floating ~* schwebende Schuld *f*; *outstanding ~s (pl)* Außenstände *m pl*; *war ~* Kriegsschuld *f*; *~ of gratitude, of honour* Dankes-, Ehrenschuld *f*; **~-collecting agency** Inkassobüro *n*; **~-collector** Inkassobeauftragte(r) *m*; **~or** ['detə] Schuldner *m*; Soll, Debet *n*; *(~~ side)* Soll-, Debetseite *f*; *principal ~~* Hauptschuldner *m*; *~~ account* Debetkonto *n*; *~~ country, nation* Schuldnerland *n*, -staat *m*; *~~ relief* Entschuldung *f*; **~ service** Schuldendienst *m*; **~ settlement** Schuldenregelung *f*.

debunk ['di:'bʌŋk] *tr Am fam* den Nimbus rauben, den Zauber nehmen (*s.o.* jdm); das Geheimnis lüften (*s.o.* jds), entlarven; *(Schleier, Geheimnis)* lüften;

die Binde von den Augen nehmen *fig*, die Illusion nehmen *od* zerstören (*s.o.* jdm).
debus [di:'bʌs] *tr mot* aussteigen lassen, ausladen; *itr* aussteigen.
debut ['deibu:, dei'bu:] Debüt *n (e-r jungen Dame in der Gesellschaft)*; erste(s) öffentliche(s) Auftreten *n (e-s Künstlers)*; **~ant, ~ante** ['debju(:)tɑ̃ŋ, -ɑ:nt] junge(r) Künstler(in *f*) *m (beim ersten Auftreten)*; Debütantin *f*.
decad(e) ['dekeid, -əd, di'keid] Dekade; Zehnergruppe, -stufe *f*; Jahrzehnt *n*.
decadenc|e, -cy ['dekədəns(i), di-, de'keidəns(i)] Verfall *m*, Dekadenz *f*; **~t** ['-t] *a* verfallen(d); angekränkelt; entartet, dekadent; *s (Kunst)* Dekadente(r) *m*.
deca|gon ['dekəgən] *math* Zehneck *n*; **~ gram(me)** ['-græm] Dekagramm *n*.
decalcify [di:'kælsifai] *tr* entkalken.
Decalogue, the ['dekəlɔg] der Dekalog, die Zehn Gebote *n pl*.
decamp [di'kæmp] *itr* das Lager abbrechen *od* verlassen; sich (auf und) davon-, sich aus dem Staube machen, das Weite suchen, ausreißen, verschwinden; **~ment** [-mənt] Abbrechen *n* des Lagers; (schneller) Aufbruch *m*.
decant [di'kænt] *tr* dekantieren, (vorsichtig) abgießen, abklären; umfüllen; **~er** [-ə] Karaffe *f*; *tech* Abklärgefäß *n*, Schlammabscheider *m*.
decapitat|e [di'kæpiteit] *tr* enthaupten, köpfen; *Am fam fig* absägen, -schießen; **~ion** [-'teiʃən] Enthauptung; *Am fam* Entlassung *f*.
decarboniz|ation [di:kɑ:bənai'zeiʃən] *chem* Entkohlung *f*; **~e** [di:'kɑ:bənaiz] *tr* entkohlen; *sl* reinigen.
decartelization [di:kɑ:təlai'zeiʃən] Konzernentflechtung, Entkartellisierung *f*.
decasyllabic [dekəsi'læbik] *a* zehnsilbig; *s* Zehnsilbler *m*.
decathlon [də'kæθlən] *sport* Zehnkampf *m*.
decay [di'kei] *itr* sich zersetzen, verderben, verrotten, verfaulen, verwesen, verwittern; verkommen, verfallen *a. fig*; *(Schönheit, Pflanze)* verblühen, vergehen; *fig* nachlassen, abnehmen; *(Hoffnung)* schwächer werden; vergehen; *tech* abklingen, ausschwingen; *(Zahn)* Karies bekommen; *s* Zersetzung *f*, Verderb *m*, Verfaulen *n*, Verwesung *f*; Niedergang, Verfall *m*; Nachlassen *n*, Abnahme; *arch* Baufälligkeit; *fig* (Alters-)Schwäche *f*; *phys* Zerfall; Abklang *m*; *in* **~** im Verfall; *to fall into* **~** in Verfall geraten; *tooth-***~** Zahnfäule, Karies *f*; **~ed** [-d] *a* verdorben, verrottet, verfault, schlecht; hinfällig; verfallen; *phys* abklingend; *med* kariös.
decease [di'si:s] *itr* verscheiden, (ver-)sterben; *s* Ableben *n*, Tod *m*; **~d** [-t] *a* verstorben; *the* **~~** der, die Verstorbene.
decedent [di'si:dənt] *Am jur* Verstorbene(r *m*) *f*; Erblasser *m*.
deceit [di'si:t] Täuschung, Irreführung *f*, Betrug, *fam* Schwindel *m*; **~ful** [-ful] unaufrichtig, unehrlich, hinterlistig, -hältig; irreführend; (be)trügerisch, unwahr, falsch; **~fulness** [-fulnis] Unaufrichtigkeit, Falschheit, Hinterlist; Unwahrheit *f*.
deceiv|able [di'si:vəbl] leicht zu täuschen(d), zu hintergehen(d), irrezuführen(d); **~e** [di'si:v] *tr* täuschen, irreführen, hintergehen; *fam* hinters Licht führen; verführen, verleiten (*into* zu); *itr* lügen; sich e-r Täuschung bedienen; *to* **~~** *out of* betrügen, bringen um; *to* **~~** *o.s.* sich etwas vormachen (*in* über), sich täuschen (*with* von); **~er** [-ə] Betrüger; Verführer *m*.
decelerat|e [di:'seləreit] *tr* verlangsamen; verzögern; *(Geschwindigkeit)* drosseln, (ab)bremsen; *itr mot* das Gas wegnehmen; sich verlangsamen, langsamer werden; **~ion** [-'reiʃən] Verzögerung, Geschwindigkeitsabnahme, Verlangsamung *f*; Abbremsen *n*.
December [di'sembə] Dezember *m*; *in* **~** im Dezember.
decency ['di:snsi] Anstand *m*, Schicklichkeit *f*, gute(s) Betragen *od* Benehmen *n*; Zurückhaltung, Bescheidenheit *f*; *pl* Anstandsformen *f pl*.
decenn|ary [di'senəri] *s* Jahrzehnt *n*; *a u.* **~ial** [-jəl] zehnjährig; alle zehn Jahre stattfindend; **~ial** *s* zehnte(r) Jahrestag *m*; **~ium** [-jəm] *pl -ia* [-jə] Jahrzehnt *n*.
decent ['di:snt] passend; anständig, schicklich, ordentlich; achtbar, geachtet; bescheiden, zurückhaltend; *fam* ganz nett, (ganz) ordentlich; annehmbar; *fam* recht nett, freundlich (*to* zu, gegenüber).
decentraliz|ation [di:sentrəlai'zeiʃən] Dezentralisation *f*; **~e** [di:'sentrəlaiz] *tr* dezentralisieren.
decept|ion [di'sepʃən] Irreführung, Täuschung, Illusion *f*; Betrug, Trick *m*; *mil* Verschleierung *f*; *to practise* **~~** *on s.o.* jdn irreführen; **~ive** [-iv] täuschend, trügerisch, irreführend.
decibel ['desibel] *el* Dezibel; Phon *n*.
decid|e [di'said] *tr* entscheiden (*between* zwischen; *for, in favour of* zugunsten; *against* gegen); *itr* sich entscheiden *(a. Sache)*, sich entschließen, beschließen (*on* über, für); **~ed** [-id] *a* bestimmt, entschieden, endgültig; unbestreitbar; klar (erkennbar), merklich, deutlich; (fest) entschlossen; **~edly** [-idli] *adv* fraglos; endgültig; entschieden; **~er** [-ə] *sport* Entscheidungsspiel *n*, -kampf *m*.
deciduous [di'sidjuəs] *bot zoo* ab-, ausfallend; jährlich die Blätter abwerfend, Laub-; *fig* kurzlebig, vorübergehend, vergänglich; **~ tree** Laubbaum *m*, **~ wood** Laubwald *m*.
decim|al ['desiməl] *a* Dezimal-; *s u.* **~~** *fraction* Dezimalbruch *m*; *recurring* **~~** periodische Dezimalzahl *f*; **~~** *point* Komma *n* (e-s Dezimalbruches); **~~** *system* Dezimalsystem *n*; **~ate** ['-eit] *tr* dezimieren; die Reihen *gen* lichten; **~ation** [-'meiʃən] Dezimierung *f*; **~etre** ['desimi:tə] Dezimeter *m*.
decipher [di'saifə] *tr* entziffern; entschlüsseln, dechiffrieren; **~able** [-rəbl] entzifferbar, zu entziffern(d); **~er** [-rə] Entzifferer; Dechiffrierer *m*; **~ment** [-mənt] Entzifferung *f*; Entschlüsselung *f*; entschlüsselte(r) Text *m*.
decis|ion [di'siʒən] Entscheidung *f* (*over* über); Entschluß; Beschluß *m*; *jur* Urteil *n*; *(Verwaltung)* Bescheid *m*; Entschlußkraft; Entschlossenheit; Bestimmtheit; Festigkeit, Unbeirrbarkeit *f*; *to appeal against a* **~~** gegen ein Urteil Berufung einlegen; *to bring about a* **~~** e-e Entscheidung herbeiführen; *to come to a* **~~**, *to make a* **~~**, *to reach a* **~~** e-e Entscheidung treffen; e-n Beschluß fassen; *arbitral* **~~** Schiedsspruch *m*; *provisional* **~~** Vorentscheidung *f*; **~ive** [-'saisiv] entscheidend, ausschlaggebend (*for* für); schlüssig; *(Maßnahme)* einschneidend; entschieden, entschlossen; bestimmt, fest, unbeirrbar; **~~** *battle* Entscheidungsschlacht *f*; **~iveness** [-'saisivnis] Entschiedenheit, Entschlossenheit, Festigkeit *f*.
deck [dek] *s mar* Deck; Verdeck *n*; *allg* Decke *f*, Boden *m*; *Am* Stockwerk *n*; Fahrbahn; *aero* Tragfläche; *aero sl* Erde *f*, Boden *m*; *Am* Spiel *n* Karten; *Am sl* Schachtel *f (Zigaretten)*; *tr* mit e-m Deck versehen; schmücken, verzieren; *to* **~** *o.s. out* herausputzen (*with* mit); *on* **~** auf Deck; *fig fam* bereit, fertig; *to clear the* **~***s (for action)* das Schiff klar zum Gefecht machen; *fig* sich bereitmachen; *to hit the* **~** *(Am sl)* auf die Bretter müssen *(Boxen)*; *mil* aufstehen; **~-cargo, -load** Deckladung *f*, -güter *n pl*; **~-chair** Deck-, Liegestuhl *m*; **~-hand** Decksmann; *theat Am sl* Bühnenarbeiter *m*; **~-landing** *aero* Trägerlandung *f*; **~~** *aircraft* Trägerflugzeug *n*; **~-passenger** Deckpassagier *m*; **~ runway** Decklandebahn *f*.
declaim [di'kleim] *tr* auf-, hersagen, deklamieren; *itr* (daher-, drauflos)reden; losziehen (*against* gegen), schimpfen (*against* auf).
declamat|ion [deklə'meiʃən] Aufsagen *n*, Deklamation; Vortragskunst; öffentliche Rede; schwungvolle, begeisterte Rede *f*; **~ory** [di'klæmətəri] deklamatorisch; pathetisch; Vortrags-; rhetorisch, Rede-.
declar|able [di'klɛərəbl] steuer-, zollpflichtig; **~ation** [deklə'reiʃən] Erklärung, Feststellung, Aussage; Deklaration; Anmeldung; *jur* Klageschrift; *com* Zollinhaltserklärung *f*; *to give, to make a* **~~** e-e Erklärung abgeben, sich erklären; *export, import* **~~** Aus-, Einfuhrerklärung *f*; **~~** *of abandonment* Verzicht(erklärung *f*) *m*; **~~** *of accession* Beitritt(serklärung *f*) *m*; **~~** *of approval, of consent* Zustimmungserklärung *f*; **~~** *of bankruptcy* Konkurseröffnung *f*; **~~** *of a dividend* Dividendenausschüttung *f*; **~~** *of income* Steuererklärung *f*; *the D***~~** *of Independence* die Unabhängigkeitserklärung *(der USA 1776)*; **~~** *of legitimation* Ehelichkeitserklärung *f*; **~~** *of love* Liebeserklärung *f*; **~~** *of majority* Volljährigkeitserklärung *f*; **~~** *of nullity* Nichtigkeitserklärung *f*; **~~** *upon oath* eidesstattliche Erklärung *od* Versicherung *f*; **~~** *of the poll* Verkündigung *f* des Abstimmungsergebnisses; **~~** *of value* Wertangabe *f*; **~~** *of war* Kriegserklärung *f*; **~~** *in writing* schriftliche Erklärung *f*; **~ative** [di'klærətiv] erklärend; *gram* Aussage-; **~~** *sentence* Aussagesatz *m*; **~atory** [di'klærətəri] erklärend; *jur* Feststellungs-; **~~** *action, judg(e)ment* Feststellungsklage *f*, -urteil *n*; **~e** [di'klɛə] *tr* erklären; versichern, ausdrücklich erklären, feststellen, behaupten; (öffentlich) bekanntmachen, -geben, verkündigen; ausbieten; zur Verzollung erklären, deklarieren; *(Wert)* angeben; anmelden; *itr* sich erklären, sich entscheiden (*against, for* gegen, für); *to* **~** *off* zurücktreten (*from* von); *I* **~~!** tatsächlich! *to* **~~** *(o.'s) adherence* den (s-n) Beitritt erklären; *to* **~~** *null and void* für null u. nichtig erklären; *to* **~~** *a state of emergency* den Ausnahmezustand verhängen; *to* **~~** *a strike* e-n Streik ausrufen; *to* **~~** *war* den Krieg erklären (*on* dat); **~ed** [-d] *a* deklariert; **~edly** [-ridli] *adv* offen; formell.
declassify [di:'klæsifai] *tr* zur Veröffentlichung freigeben; *mil* die Geheimhaltungsstufe aufheben.
declension [di'klenʃən] Neigung *f*, Gefälle *n*; Niedergang, Verfall *m*, Verschlechterung; Abweichung (*from* von); *gram* Deklination, Beugung *f*.
declin|able [di'klainəbl] *gram* deklinierbar; **~ation** [dekli'neiʃən] Neigung, Schräge; Abweichung *(von e-r Richtung, a. d. Kompaßnadel)*; *(Kompaß)* Mißweisung; *astr* Deklination *f*; **~e** [di'klain] *itr* sich neigen, abfallen, sich

senken; *(Sonne)* sinken; schwächer werden, nachlassen, abnehmen, verfallen; *(Preise)* zurückgehen, sinken, fallen; ablehnen; *tr* e-e Neigung geben (*s.th.* e-r S); ablehnen, ausschlagen (*doing, to do* zu tun); *gram* deklinieren, beugen; *s* Abhang *m*; Abnahme *f*, Absinken *n*, Abstieg, Niedergang, Verfall *m*; Verfallszeit *f*, Ende; Versagen, Nachlassen *n*, Schwächung *(der Gesundheit)*; Schwindsucht *f*; *astr* Untergang *m*; *to be on the* ~~ abnehmen, nachlassen, sinken; *(Preise)* fallen, zurückgehen; zur Neige gehen; ~~ *of the birth-rate* Geburtenrückgang *m*; ~~ *of business* Geschäftsrückgang *m*; ~~ *in prices* Preisrückgang *m*, Fallen, Sinken *n* der Preise; ~~ *in strength* Kräfteverfall *m*; ~~ *in value* Wertminderung, Entwertung *f*.

decliv|ity [di'kliviti] Abschüssigkeit *f*; Abhang *m*; Gefälle *n*; Abdachung *f*.

declutch ['di:'klʌtʃ] *itr tech, bes. mot* auskuppeln.

decoct [di'kɔkt] *tr* (ab-, aus)kochen; **~ion** [-kʃən] (Ab-, Aus-)Kochen *n*; Absud *m*.

decode ['di:'koud] *tr* dechiffrieren, entschlüsseln; **~r** ['-ə] Dechiffrierer *m*; Dechiffriermaschine *f*; *tech* Rufumsetzer *m*.

decohe|re [dikou'hiə] *tr el* entfritten; **~rer** [-rə] Entfritter *m*; **~sion** [-'hi:ʒən] Entfrittung *f*.

decollet|age [dei'kɔltɑ:ʒ] Dekolleté *n*; Dekolletierung *f*; Kleid *n* mit tiefem Ausschnitt; **~é(e)** [dei'kɔltei] *a (Kleid)* tief ausgeschnitten; *(Frau)* mit tief ausgeschnittenem Kleid.

decolo(u)r|(ize) [di:'kʌlə(raiz)] *tr* entfärben; bleichen; **~ant** [-rənt] *a* Bleich-; *s* Bleichmittel *n*.

decompos|e [di:kəm'pouz] *tr* zerlegen, zergliedern, aufspalten; analysieren; *itr* sich zersetzen, zerfallen; (ver)faulen, verwesen; verwittern; **~ition** [di:kɔmpə'ziʃən] Zerlegung, Aufspaltung *f*, Abbau *m*; Zersetzung, Fäulnis, Verwesung; Verwitterung *f*; ~~ *product* Zersetzungs-, Verfallprodukt *n*.

decompress ['di:kəm'pres] *tr* entspannen; **~ion** [-ʃən] Druckentlastung, Entspannung *f*; ~~ *chamber* Unterdruckkammer *f*.

decontaminat|e ['di:kən'tæmineit] *tr* entgiften, entseuchen; *(Radioaktivität)* entstrahlen; **~ion** [-'neiʃən] Entseuchung, Entgiftung; Entstrahlung *f*; ~~ *squad, station (mil)* Entgiftungstrupp *m*, -station *f*.

decontrol ['di:kən'troul] *tr* die Kontrolle, (Zwangs-)Bewirtschaftung, Preisüberwachung aufheben (*s.th.* e-r S); freigeben; *s* Aufhebung der (Zwangs-) Bewirtschaftung *od* Preisüberwachung *od* Kontrolle; Freigabe *f*; **~led** ['-d] *a* nicht mehr bewirtschaftet.

decorat|e ['dekəreit] *tr* schmücken, (ver)zieren; dekorieren; *(Wände)* bemalen, tapezieren; *(mit e-m Orden)* auszeichnen (*with* mit); **~ion** [-'reiʃən] Ausschmückung *f*; Schmuck *m*, Verzierung; Dekoration *f*; Ehrenzeichen *n*; Auszeichnung *f*, Orden *m*; *D~~ Day amerik. Gedenktag (30. Mai) für die Gefallenen*; **~ive** ['dekərətiv, -eit-] dekorativ; Dekorations-, Schmuck-, Zier-; **~or** ['dekəreitə] (Dekorations-) Maler, Tapezierer, Dekorateur; *(interior* ~~*)* Raumgestalter, Innenarchitekt *m*.

decorous ['dekərəs] anständig, ordentlich, geschmackvoll, dezent.

decorticat|e [di'kɔ:tikeit] *tr* abrinden, schälen, enthülsen.

decorum [di'kɔ:rəm] *pl a. -ra* [-rə] Anstand *m*, Schicklichkeit *f*; gute(s), gesittete(s) Benehmen *n*; geschmackvolle, dezente Kleidung *f*; *pl* Höflichkeiten *f pl*.

decoy [di'kɔi, 'di:kɔi] *s* Fangstelle *f (für Vögel)*; Lockvogel *m a. fig*; *mil* Scheinanlage *f*; *(~ ship)* U-Boot-Falle *f*; *fig* Köder; Spitzel *m*; *tr itr* [di'kɔi] (sich) ködern, (ver)locken (lassen); *fig* verleiten, (ver)locken (*into* in; *out of* aus).

decrease [di:'kri:s] *itr* abnehmen, nachlassen, sich vermindern, sich verringern, zurückgehen; abflauen; *tr (nach u. nach)* verringern, vermindern, verkleinern, einschränken; reduzieren, herabsetzen; *s* ['di:kri:s] Abnahme, Verringerung, Verminderung *f*, Rückgang *m (in* an); *on the* ~ in der Abnahme begriffen, im Abnehmen; *to be decreasing (fig)* zurückgehen, abnehmen; *to show a* ~ e-n Rückgang aufweisen; ~ *in output* Leistungsrückgang *m*; ~ *in population* Bevölkerungsrückgang *m*; ~ *of price* Preisrückgang *m*; ~ *in value* Wertminderung *f*; ~ *in weight* Gewichtsabnahme *f*.

decree [di'kri:] *s* Erlaß *m*, Dekret *n*; Verordnung, Verfügung *f*; Gerichtsbeschluß, -entscheid; *rel* Ratschluß *m*; *tr itr* ver-, anordnen, verfügen, beschließen; gerichtlich anordnen, durch Gerichtsbeschluß verfügen; *by ~s* im, auf dem Verordnungswege; *to issue, to pass a* ~ e-e Verordnung erlassen; ~ **nisi** vorläufige(s) (Scheidungs-)Urteil *n*.

decrement ['dekrimənt] Verminderung, Verringerung, Abnahme *f*, Rückgang; Verlust *m*.

decrepit [di'krepit] altersschwach, abgelebt; (durch Krankheit) heruntergekommen, gebrechlich; verbraucht, abgenutzt; **~ude** [-ju:d] Hinfälligkeit, Gebrechlichkeit; Entkräftung, (Alters-)Schwäche *f*.

decrescent [di'kresnt] *(Mond)* abnehmend.

decretal [di'kri:təl] Verordnung *f*, Erlaß *m*; *pl rel* Dekretal(i)en *n pl*.

decry [di'krai] *tr* (offen, öffentlich) anprangern, herabsetzen; in den Schmutz ziehen, in Mißkredit, in Verruf bringen; verleumden; verurteilen.

decuple ['dekjupl] *a* zehnfach; *s* Zehnfache(s) *n*; *tr itr* verzehnfachen.

decussate [di'kʌseit] *tr itr* (sich) schneiden, (sich) kreuzen; *a* [*a.* -sit] sich schneidend, sich kreuzend; kreuzweise.

dedicat|e ['dedikeit] *tr rel* weihen *a. fig*; *fig* widmen *(a. ein Buch)*; zueignen, dedizieren; *(Gebäude)* einweihen; *Am* (feierlich) dem Verkehr übergeben; *Am* (feierlich) eröffnen; *(Eigentum)* der Öffentlichkeit übergeben, zur Verfügung stellen; **~ion** [-'keiʃən] Weihe, Einweihung; Hingabe (*to* an); *(Buch)* Widmung, Zueignung; *Am* Eröffnung *f*; ~~ *copy* Widmungsexemplar *n*; **~ive** ['-iv], **~ory** ['-əri, -kətəri, *(Am)* dedikə'tɔ:ri] Weih-, Einweihungs-, Widmungs-; **~or** ['-ə] (Ein-)Weihende(r); Zueigner, Widmende(r) *m*.

deduc|e [di'dju:s] *tr* ab-, herleiten (*from* von); folgern, schließen (*from* aus); **~ible** [-ibl] ableitbar.

deduct [di'dʌkt] *tr (Summe, Punktzahl)* abziehen, in Abzug bringen (*for* wegen); *(Betrag)* einbehalten; **~ible** [-ibl] absetzbar; abzugsfähig; **~ibility** [-i'biliti] Abzugsfähigkeit *f*; **~ing** [-iŋ] abzüglich; **~ion** [-kʃən] Abzug *m*, Kürzung; Einbehaltung *f*; einbehaltene(r) Betrag; *com* Rabatt *m*; Folgerung *f*, Schluß *m*, Schlußfolgerung *f*; *after* ~~ *of* nach Abzug *gen*; *without* ~~ ungekürzt; *payroll* ~~ Gehalts-, Lohnabzug *m*, -kürzung *f*; **~ive** [-iv] zu folgern(d), sich ergebend; folgernd.

deed [di:d] *s* Tat; Heldentat, (große) Leistung *f*; Handeln, Tun *n*; (*bes.* Notariats-)Urkunde *f*, Schriftstück, Dokument *n*; Vereinbarung *f*, Vertrag *m*; *tr Am (Eigentum)* notariell übertragen, überschreiben; *in* ~ in Wirklichkeit; *in word and* ~ in Wort u. Tat; *to draw up a* ~ e-e Urkunde aufsetzen; ~ *of appointment* Bestallungsurkunde *f*; ~ *of consent* Beitrittserklärung *f*; ~ *of conveyance* Übertragungsurkunde *f*; ~ *of donation, of gift* Schenkungsurkunde *f*; ~ *of foundation* Stiftungsurkunde *f*; ~ *of sale* Kaufvertrag *m*; ~ **poll** einseitige Erklärung *f*.

deem [di:m] *tr* halten für, ansehen, betrachten als; beurteilen; *itr* denken (*of* von), meinen, glauben, urteilen (*of* über).

deep [di:p] *a* tief, *(Schnee a.:)* hoch; *fig* tief *(z. B. Schlaf)*, stark, groß; tief(sinnig), tiefgründig; gründlich; schwierig, schwerverständlich, dunkel; tief(empfunden), innig, herzlich; weise; scharfsinnig, klug, schlau, listig; *(Farbe)* tief, satt; *(Ton)* tief; *adv* tief; *s* Tiefe *f a. fig*; Abgrund *m*; *poet* Meer *n*, See *f*; ~ *in debt, thought* tief in Schulden, Gedanken; ~ *in love* sehr verliebt; ~ *in mud* tief im Dreck, Schmutz; *in* ~ *array* tief gestaffelt; *in the* ~ *of night* tief in der Nacht; ~ *in the night* bis tief in die Nacht, bis in die tiefe Nacht; *to go off the* ~ *end* sich mitten hineinstürzen; hochgehen, aufbrausen; *to play* ~ hoch spielen; *to take a* ~ *breath* tief atmen; *still waters run* ~ *(prov)* stille Wasser sind tief; *that's too* ~ *for me (fam)* das geht über meinen Horizont; **~-breathing** Atemübung *f*; **~-dyed** *a* durchgefärbt; *fig* vollendet; **~en** ['-ən] *tr* vertiefen; dunkler machen; *(Farben)* verdunkeln; *itr* tiefer, dunkler werden; **~-felt** *a* tiefempfunden; ~ **foundation** *tech* Tiefgründung *f*; **~-freeze** ['-fri:z] *(Warenzeichen) tr* tiefkühlen; *s* Tiefkühlschrank *m*; **~-fry** *tr* im Fett schwimmend braten; **~-laid** *a (Plan)* schlau, raffiniert angelegt, ausgedacht; **~ly** ['-li] *adv* (zu)tief(st); sehr, stark; ~~ *hurt (fig)* schwer gekränkt; **~ness** ['-nis] Tiefe *f*; Scharfsinn *m*, Schlauheit *f*; **~-rooted** *a* tief ver-, eingewurzelt; **~-sea** *a* Tiefsee-; Hochsee-; ~~ *cable* Tiefseekabel *n*; ~~ *fishing* Hochseefischerei *f*; **~-seated** *a* tief (-sitzend); *fig* fest verankert; **~-set** *a* tief, gut befestigt, verankert; *(Augen)* tiefliegend; ~ **shelter** Tiefbunker *m*.

deer [diə] *pl* ~ Hirsch(e *pl*) *m (als Familie)*; *fallow* ~ Damhirsch *m*; *red* ~ Hirsch *m (als Gattung)*, Rotwild *n*; *small* ~ Kleingetier *n*; Kleinkram *m*; **~-hound** (Schottischer) Jagdhund *m*; **~-lick** Salzlecke *f*; **~skin** Wildleder *n*; **~-stalker** pirschende(r) Jäger *m*; Jagdmütze *f*; **~-stalking** Pirsch *f* (auf Hochwild).

deface [di'feis] *tr* entstellen *a. fig*, verunstalten, verunzieren, verschandeln; *fig* verderben; unkenntlich, unleserlich machen; streichen, löschen; abstempeln, entwerten; **~ment** [-mənt] Entstellung; Streichung, Löschung; Entwertung *f*.

defalcat|e ['di:fælkeit] *itr* unterschlagen, Gelder veruntreuen; **~ion** [-'keiʃən] Unterschlagung, Veruntreuung *f*; unterschlagene(s) Geld(er *pl*) *n*.

defam|ation [defə'meiʃən, di:-] Verleumdung, üble Nachrede, Ehrabschneidung; Schmähung *f*; **~atory** [di'fæmətəri] verleumderisch, ehrenrührig, beleidigend, diffamierend; Schmäh-; **~e** [di'feim] *tr* verleumden, schmähen, verunglimpfen.

defatted [di:'fætid] *a* entfettet.

default [di'fɔ:lt] *s* Unterlassung, Nichteinhaltung, Nichterfüllung *f*; *fin* Verzug *m*, Versäumnis *n*; Zahlungseinstellung, Insolvenz *f*; Nichterscheinen, Ausbleiben *n*; *itr* s-e Verpflichtungen nicht erfüllen *od* nicht einhalten, s-n Verbindlichkeiten nicht nachkommen; (mit s-n Zahlungen) in Verzug kommen; die Zahlungen einstellen, zahlungsunfähig werden; vor Gericht *od* bei e-m Entscheidungsspiel nicht erscheinen; *sport* durch Nichterscheinen verlieren; *tr* nicht erfüllen, nicht einhalten, nicht nachkommen (*s.th.* e-r S); *(Zahlung)* nicht leisten; *sport* nicht erscheinen bei; durch Nichterscheinen verlieren; *by ~ (jur)* im Versäumnisverfahren; *in ~ of* mangels *gen*; *to be in ~* in, im Verzug sein; *to make ~* nicht erscheinen, ausbleiben; nicht bezahlen; *judg(e)ment by ~* Versäumnisurteil *n*; *~ in paying* Zahlungsverzug *m*; Nichtzahlung *f*; **~er** [-ə] säumige(r) Zahler; Nichterschienene(r); Veruntreuer; *mil Br* Delinquent *m*; *~~ (book mil Br)* Strafbuch *n*.

defeat [di'fi:t] *tr* besiegen, schlagen; vereiteln, zum Scheitern bringen, zunichte machen; *(Antrag)* ablehnen; *(Gläubiger)* benachteiligen; *jur* aufheben, annullieren, für nichtig erklären; anfechten; *(Hoffnung)* enttäuschen; *parl* überstimmen; *s* Niederlage, Schlappe *f*; Unterliegen *n*; Mißerfolg *m*, Scheitern *n*; Vereitelung; *jur* Ungültigerklärung, Aufhebung, Annullierung *f*; *parl* Überstimmen *n*; *to be ~ed, to suffer, to sustain, to receive a ~* e-e Niederlage erleiden; verlieren, unterliegen; *parl* überstimmt werden; *to ~ s.o.'s plans* jds Pläne durchkreuzen; *~ at the polls* Wahlniederlage *f*; **~ism** [-izm] Defätismus *m*, Miesmacherei *f*; **~ist** [-ist] Defätist, Miesmacher *m*.

defecat|e ['defikeit] *tr* klären, läutern; *(Zucker)* raffinieren; *itr* Stuhlgang haben; **~ion** [defi'keiʃən] Reinigung, Klärung, Läuterung; *med* Darmentleerung *f*, Stuhl *m*.

defect [di'fekt] *s* Fehler, Defekt *m*, Störung *f* (*in* an); schadhafte Stelle *f*; Mangel *m* (*of* an); Gebrechen *n*; *itr* (von e-r Partei, Sache) abfallen; *constructional ~* Konstruktions-, Formfehler *m*; *free from ~s* fehlerfrei, tadellos; *mental ~* Geistesstörung *f*; **~ion** [-kʃən] Versagen *n*; Treu-, Gewissenlosigkeit *f*; Abfall *m* (*from* von); **~ive** [-iv] *a* fehlerhaft, schadhaft, defekt, mangelhaft; gebrechlich; unvollkommen, unvollständig *a. gram*; *s (mental ~~)* Schwachsinnige(r) *m*; **~iveness** [-ivnis] Fehlerhaftigkeit, Schadhaftigkeit *f*; mangelhafte(r) Zustand *m*; Unvollständigkeit *f*.

defen|ce, *Am* **~se** [di'fens] Verteidigung(sanlage); Abwehr *f*; Widerstand *m*, Gegenwehr *f*; Schutz(mittel *n*) *m*; *jur* Verteidigung; *(statement of ~~)* Klageerwiderung; Einrede *f*, (Rechts-) Einwand *m* (*to an action* gegen e-e Klage); Rechtfertigung; Verteidigung, Angeklagte(r *m*) *f* u. Verteidiger *m*; *pl* Befestigungsanlagen *f pl*; Abwehrstellung *f*; *in (the) ~~ of* zur Verteidigung *gen*; *in s.o.'s ~~* zu jds Rechtfertigung, Entlastung; *to come to s.o.'s ~~* jdn in Schutz nehmen; *to conduct o.'s own ~~* sich selbst (vor Gericht) vertreten; *to make a ~~* sich verteidigen; *to speak, to say in s.o.'s ~~* für jdn sprechen, plädieren; jdn verteidigen; *all-round ~~* Rundumverteidigung *f*; *lawful, legitimate ~~* Notwehr *f*; **~celess** [-lis] wehr-, schutzlos; offen; **~celessness** Schutz-, Wehrlosigkeit *f*; **~d** [di'fend] *tr* verteidigen (*against* gegen); (be-) schützen (*against, from* vor), sichern (*against* gegen); rechtfertigen; *jur* verteidigen; **~dant** [-dənt] Ange-, Beklagte(r *m*) *f*; **~der** [-də] Verteidiger *a. jur*; Beschützer *m*; **~sible** [-səbl] zu verteidigen(d), zu schützen(d); verfechtbar, vertretbar; **~sive** [-siv] *a* Defensiv-, Verteidigungs-, Schutz-; *s* Defensive, Verteidigung; Abwehr *f*; *on the ~~* in der Verteidigung; *to act on the ~~* sich (nur) verteidigen; *~~ fire* Abwehrfeuer *n*; *~~ measures (pl)* Verteidigungs-, Schutzmaßnahmen *f pl*; *~~ warfare* Verteidigungs-, Defensivkrieg *m*; *~~ weapon* Verteidigungswaffe *f*.

defer [di'fə:] **1.** *tr* auf-, hinaus-, verschieben; hinaus-, verzögern (*doing s.th.* etw zu tun); vertagen; zurückstellen *(a. vom Wehrdienst)*; *jur (Urteil)* aussetzen; *itr* zögern, warten; **~ment** [-mənt] Verschiebung *f*, Aufschub *m*, Vertagung; Zurückstellung *f (a. vom Wehrdienst)*; **~red** [-d] *a* aufge-, verschoben, vertagt; nicht dringlich; *fin* nach e-r bestimmten Zeit fällig werdend; gestundet; befristet; *mil* zurückgestellt; *on ~~ terms* auf Raten, auf Abzahlung; *~~ payment* gestundete *od* Ratenzahlung *f*; **2.** *itr* nachgeben, sich unterwerfen (*to* dat); sich *(e-r Meinung)* anschließen; **~ence** ['defərəns] Nachgiebigkeit, Unterwerfung; Achtung *f*, Respekt *m*, Ehrerbietung *f* (*to* für); *in, out of ~~ to* aus Achtung vor; aus Rücksicht gegen; *with all due ~~* mit der gebührenden Hochachtung (*to* vor); *to pay, to show ~~ to s.o.* jdm Achtung erweisen; **~ential** [defə'renʃəl] ehrerbietig, achtungsvoll (*to* gegenüber).

defian|ce [di'faiəns] Herausforderung; (Gehorsamsver-)Weigerung *f*; Widerstand *m*; *in ~~ of* trotz, ungeachtet *gen*; entgegen *dat*; *(e-m dat nachgestellt)* zum Trotz; *to bid ~~ to, to set at ~~* sich widersetzen, Widerstand leisten *dat*; *(Gesetz)* mißachten, verletzen; **~t** [-t] herausfordernd, trotzig; frech, dreist.

deficien|cy [di'fiʃənsi] Mangelhaftigkeit, Unvollständigkeit; Unzulänglichkeit *f*, Fehler; Mangel *m*; *fin u. fam* Manko *n*, Ausfall *m*, Defizit *n*, Fehlbetrag, -bestand *m*; *~~ of blood* Blutarmut *f*; *~~-disease* Mangelkrankheit *f*; *~~ report* Fehlmeldung *f*; *~~ in weight* Mindergewicht *n*; **~t** [-t] mangelhaft, ungenügend, arm (*in* an); nicht vollwertig, unvollkommen, unvollständig; Unter-; *to be ~~ in* Mangel haben an; *mentally ~~* schwachsinnig.

deficit ['defisit] Defizit *n*, Fehlbetrag; Ausfall *m*; *to meet a ~* e-n Fehlbetrag decken; *to show a ~* ein Defizit, e-n Fehlbetrag aufweisen; *~ in taxes* Steuerausfall *m*, Minderaufkommen *n* an Steuern; *~* **account** Verlustkonto *n*.

defilade [defi'leid] *tr itr mil* decken; *s* [*a.* 'defileid] *mil* Deckung *f* gegen Sicht; *area in ~* nicht einzusehendes Gelände *n*.

defile [di'fail] **1.** *tr* beschmutzen, schmutzig, dreckig machen; *fig* beflecken, in den Schmutz ziehen, schänden; *rel* entweihen, profanieren; verderben; **2.** *itr* vorbeimarschieren, defilieren; *s* ['di:fail] Vorbeimarsch; Gänsemarsch; Engpaß *m*.

defin|able [di'fainəbl] *a* abgrenzbar; bestimmbar; definierbar; **~e** [di'fain] *tr* genau, scharf abgrenzen; näher bestimmen, festlegen, -setzen; präzisieren, klarlegen, -stellen; definieren, (genau) erklären; kennzeichnen (*as* als); *to be ~ed against* sich abheben von, gegen; **~ite** ['definit] *a* fest umrissen, scharf; klar, deutlich, genau, eindeutig, unmißverständlich; bestimmt, sicher, fest; *tech* unabhängig; *it's ~~ that* es ist sicher, daß; **~itely** ['-li] *adv fam* sicherlich, zweifellos; **~iteness** ['definitnis] Deutlichkeit; Eindeutigkeit; Bestimmtheit *f*; **~ition** [defi'niʃən] Erklärung; Definition, (Begriffs-)Bestimmung; Bezeichnung; Festlegung; genaue, scharfe Abgrenzung; *opt phot* (Bild-)Schärfe; *video* Zeilenzahl, Fernsehnorm; *radio fam* Ton-, Lautschärfe *f*; *by ~~* definitionsgemäß; **~itive** [di'finitiv] *a* abgrenzend, unterscheidend; genau festgelegt; entscheidend, endgültig, definitiv; *biol* fertig, voll entwickelt; *s gram* Bestimmungswort *n*.

deflat|e [di'fleit] *tr* (die) Luft lassen aus *(e-m Ballon, Reifen)*; *(bes. Notenumlauf)* verringern, vermindern; *fig fam* am Boden zerstören (*s.o.* jdn); *itr* (die) Luft ablassen; im Wert abnehmen; **~ion** [-ʃən] *fin* Deflation *f*; **~ionary** [-ʃnəri] deflationistisch, deflatorisch; Deflations-.

deflect [di'flekt] *tr* um-, ablenken, ableiten; beugen; *itr* abweichen (*from* von); *(Zeiger)* ausschlagen; *mar (vom Kurs)* abweichen; *tech* sich verbiegen; *(Räder)* ausschlagen; **~ion, deflexion** [-'flekʃən] Abweichung; Um-, Ablenkung *f*; *phys el* (Zeiger-)Ausschlag *m*; *tech* Ab-, Durchbiegung; *(Geschoß)* Seitenabweichung *f*.

deflorat|e [di:'flɔ:rit] *bot* verblüht; **~ion** [-'reiʃən] *physiol* Defloration, Entjungferung *f*.

deflower [di:'flauə] *tr physiol* deflorieren, entjungfern; *fig* der Blüte berauben, den Reiz nehmen (*s.th.* e-r S), verderben; schänden.

defoliat|e [di:'foulieit] *tr* entblättern; **~ion** [di:fouli'eiʃən] Entblätterung *f*.

deforest [di'fɔrest] *s. disforest*.

deform [di'fɔ:m] *tr* deformieren, aus der Fasson bringen, verformen; entstellen, verunstalten; **~ation** [di:fɔ:'meiʃən] Deformation; Entstellung; *tech* Deformierung, Formänderung, Verformung *f*; **~ed** [di'fɔ:md] *a* deformiert, aus der Fasson, verformt; entstellt, häßlich, abstoßend; **~ity** [-iti] Deformation *f*, Körperfehler *m*, Gebrechen *n*; Mißgestalt, Mißbildung; Entstellung; Häßlichkeit; Scheußlichkeit; Verderbtheit *f*.

defraud [di'frɔ:d] *tr* betrügen (*of s.th., s.th.* um etw); unterschlagen; *(Zoll, Steuer)* hinterziehen; *with intent to ~* in betrügerischer Absicht; **~ation** [-'deiʃən] Betrug *m*; Unterschlagung; Hinterziehung *f*; *~~ of the customs, of the revenue* Zoll-, Steuerhinterziehung *f*; **~er** [-ə]: *tax ~~* Steuerhinterzieher *m*.

defray [di:'frei] *tr* bezahlen; *(Kosten)* bestreiten, tragen, decken; *to ~ s.o.'s expenses* jdn freihalten.

defrock ['di:'frɔk] *tr* den Priesterrock ausziehen (*s.o.* jdm); des Priesteramtes entkleiden.

defrost ['di:'frɔst] *tr* enteisen; ab-, auftauen; *itr* von Eis freiwerden, auftauen; **~er** ['-ə] *mot aero* Entfroster *m*, Enteisungsanlage *f*.

deft [deft] gewandt, geschickt, flink, fix; **~ness** ['-nis] Gewandtheit *f*.

defunct [di'fʌŋkt] *a* verstorben; ausgestorben, erloschen; *s*: *the* ~ der, die Verstorbene.
defy [di'fai] *tr* herausfordern (*to do* etw zu tun); den Gehorsam verweigern, sich widersetzen, trotzen (*s.o.* jdm); mißachten; widerstehen, trotzen, Trotz bieten, spotten (*s.th.* e-r S).
degas(ify) [di'gæs(ifai)] *tr* entgasen; entseuchen; **~ifier** [-ifaiə] Entgaser *m.*
degauss ['di:'gaus] *tr* entmagnetisieren.
degener|acy [di'dʒenərəsi] Entartung; Verkommenheit *f*; **~ate** [-rit] *a biol* degeneriert, entartet *a. allg*; *allg* verkommen; *s* Entartete(r *m*); Geistesschwache(r *m*), sittlich Minderwertige(r *m*) *f*; *itr* [-reit] *biol* degenerieren, entarten (*into* in, zu); *allg* (herab-) sinken, verkommen; *tech* gegenkoppeln; **~ation** [didʒenə'reiʃən] *biol* Entartung, Degeneration *(a. med e-s Gewebes* od *Organs)*; *tech* Gegenkopplung *f.*
degrad|ation [degrə'deiʃən] Degradierung, Absetzung *f*, Rangverlust *m*; Erniedrigung; Herabwürdigung, Verächtlichmachung, Entehrung; *geol* Abtragung; *biol* Entartung *f*; **~e** [di'greid] *tr* degradieren, absetzen; abbauen; *fig* erniedrigen; (sittlich) verderben; herabwürdigen, verächtlich machen, entehren; *(im Wert, im Preis, in der Qualität)* herabsetzen; niedriger einstufen; *geol* abtragen; *itr* auf e-e niedrigere Stufe zurückfallen; entarten; **~ed** [di'greidid] *a* erniedrigt, verdorben; entehrt; **~ing** [di'greidiŋ] herabwürdigend, entehrend.
degreas|e [di'gri:s] *tr* entfetten, -ölen; **~ing** [-iŋ] Entfettung, Entölung *f.*
degree [di'gri:] *math phys* Grad *m a. allg*; *allg* Stufe *f*; (Aus-)Maß *n*; Stand, Rang *m*, (soziale) Stellung; Ordnung, Klasse *f*; *(~ of consanguinity, of relationship)* Verwandtschaftsgrad; (akademischer) Grad *m*, Würde; *gram* Steigerungsform *f*; *math* (Winkel-)Grad *m*; *mus* Tonstufe *f*, Intervall *n*; *by ~s* stufenweise, Schritt für Schritt, nach und nach, allmählich; *in some ~* einigermaßen; *in its ~* in s-r, auf s-e Art, Weise; *to a ~ (fam)* außerordentlich, in hohem Maße; *to a certain ~* bis zu e-m gewissen Grade; *to a high, to a very large, to the last ~* in hohem Maße, besonders, außerordentlich; *to some ~* gewissermaßen; *to such a ~* in solchem Maße, dermaßen; *to drop five ~s* um fünf Grad fallen; *to stand at ten ~s* auf zehn Grad stehen; *to take o.'s ~* promovieren *itr*, *fam* s-n Magister, Doktor machen; *murder in the first, second ~* Mord; Totschlag *m*; *~ of classification* Geheimhaltungsgrad *m*; *~ of development* Entwicklungsstufe *f*; *~ of heat* Hitzegrad *m*; *~ of latitude, longitude* Breiten-, Längengrad *m*; *~ of priority* Dringlichkeitsstufe *f*; *~ of saturation* Sättigungsgrad *m*; *~* **mark** Gradstrich *m.*
degress|ion [di'greʃən] Abnahme *f*, Geringerwerden, Nachlassen *n*; *fin Am* Degression, gestufte Steuerermäßigung *f*; **~ive** [-'gresiv] *(Steuer)* degressiv.
dehisce [di'his] *itr bot (Samenkapsel)* aufspringen; *med* platzen; **~nce** [-əns] Platzen; Aufspringen *n.*
dehumanize [di:'hjumənaiz] *tr* entmenschlichen.
dehumidify [di:hju'midifai] *tr* lüften; entfeuchten, trocknen lassen.
dehydrat|e [di:'haidreit] *tr* dehydrieren, das Wasser entziehen (*s.th.* e-r S), entwässern; trocknen; **~ed** [-id] *a* getrocknet; *~~ eggs (pl)* Eipulver *n*; *~~ potatoes (pl)* Trockenkartoffel *f pl*; *~~ vegetables (pl)* Trocken-, Dörrgemüse *n*; **~ion** [-'dreiʃən] Dehydrierung, Entwässerung *f*; Trocknen *n.*
deice, de-ice ['di:'ais] *tr aero* enteisen; **~r** [-ə] Enteisungsanlage *f*, Enteiser *m.*
deif|ication [di:ifi'keiʃən] Vergötterung; göttliche Verehrung *f*; **~y** ['di:ifai] *tr* zum Gott erheben; göttliche Verehrung erweisen (*s.o.* jdm); vergöttern *a. fig*, verehren, anbeten.
deign [dein] *tr* sich herablassen zu; *itr* geruhen (*to do* zu tun); sich herablassen (*to* zu).
deioniz|ation [di:aiənai'zeiʃən] *phys* Entionisierung *f*; **~e** [di:'aiənaiz] *tr* entionisieren.
dei|sm ['di:izəm] *hist philos* Deismus, Vernunftglaube *m*; **~st** ['di:ist] Deist *m*; **~stic(al)** [di:'istik(əl)] deistisch, vernunftgläubig; **~ty** ['-iti] Gottheit *f*; *the D~~* die Gottheit, Gott *m.*
dejam ['di:'dʒæm] *tr tele* entstören.
deject|ed [di'dʒektid] *a* bedrückt, niedergeschlagen; mut-, hoffnungslos; **~ion** [-ʃən] Bedrücktheit, Niedergeschlagenheit; Mut-, Hoffnungslosigkeit *f*; *physiol* Stuhlgang *m.*
dekko ['dekou] *sl* Blick *m.*
delat|e [di'leit] *tr* denunzieren; publik machen; **~ion** [-ʃən] Denunziation *f.*
delay [di'lei] *tr* ver-, hinauszögern (*doing s.th.* etw zu tun); auf-, ver-, hinausschieben; verschleppen; auf-, hin-, zurückhalten; *(Zahlung)* stunden; *itr* zögern, zaudern; Zeit verlieren *od* vertrödeln; *to be ~ed* sich verzögern, sich verspäten; aufgehalten werden (*on the way* unterwegs); *s* Verzögerung, Verspätung, Verschleppung *f*; Verzug, Aufschub; Zeitverlust *m*; Frist, Stundung *f*; *without (any) ~* ohne (jeden) Aufschub, sofort, unverzüglich; *to admit, to permit of no ~* keinen Aufschub dulden; *to grant a ~* e-e Frist bewilligen; Stundung gewähren; *don't ~!* verliere keine Zeit! nicht aufhalten! *~ of payment* Zahlungsaufschub *m*; *~ of proceedings* Prozeßverschleppung *f*; **~ed** [-d]: *~~ action fuse* Verzögerungs-, Zeitzünder *m*; *el* träge Sicherung *f*; **~ing** [-iŋ] hinhaltend; *~~ tactics* Verzögerungstaktik *f.*
dele ['di:li(:)] *tr typ* tilgen, streichen; *meist Imperativ*: zu tilgen! *s* Deleatur *n.*
delect|able [di'lektəbl] *Br meist iro* ergötzlich, erfreulich; *Am* reizend, entzückend; **~ation** [di:lek'teiʃən] Vergnügen *n*, Belustigung, Unterhaltung *f.*
delega|cy ['deligəsi] Abordnung *f*; **~te** ['deligeit] *tr* bevoll-, ermächtigen; abordnen, delegieren; als Abgeordneten, Delegierten, Vertreter (ent)senden *od* schicken; *(Vollmacht)* erteilen; *(Befugnisse)* übertragen (*to s.o.* jdm); *s* ['deligit] Abgeordnete(r) *Am a. pol*, Bevollmächtigte(r), Delegierte(r), Vertreter *m*; *~~ conference* Delegiertenversammlung *f*; **~tion** [-'geiʃən] Abordnung, Delegation, Vertretung; Übertragung *f (von Vollmachten, Rechten)*; *(Am) die* Abgeordneten *(e-s Staates im Kongreß).*
delet|e [di'li:t] *tr* ausradieren, (aus-) streichen; *typ* tilgen; löschen; **~erious** [deli'tiəriəs] schädlich, ungesund; nachteilig; **~ion** [di'li:ʃən] Streichung, Tilgung *f.*
delf(t), delftware ['delf(t)wεə)] Delfter Fayence *f*, Delft *n.*
deliberat|e [di'libəreit] *itr* be-, nachdenken, mit sich zu Rate gehen; beratschlag(en (*upon* über); *tr* (sich) (genau) überlegen, bedenken, erwägen, sich durch den Kopf gehen lassen; *a* [di'libərit] bedächtig, besonnen, behutsam, vorsichtig; (wohl-) überlegt, beabsichtigt, bewußt, absichtlich; planmäßig; *jur* vorsätzlich; *~~ action* mit Vorsatz begangene Tat *f*; **~ely** [-ritli] *adv* mit Überlegung, mit (Vor-)Bedacht; mit Vorsatz, vorsätzlich; mit Absicht, absichtlich; **~eness** [-ritnis] Bedächtigkeit, Besonnenheit; Absichtlichkeit *f*; **~ion** [dilibə'reiʃən] Überlegung, Erwägung; Beratung; Bedächtigkeit, Besonnenheit, Behutsamkeit, Vorsicht *f*; *pl* Verhandlungen *f pl*; *after due ~~* nach reiflicher Überlegung; **~ive** [di'libəreitiv, -ətiv] beratend; (wohl)überlegt; *~~ assembly (parl)* beratende Versammlung *f.*
delica|cy ['delikəsi] Feinheit, Zartheit, Zerbrechlichkeit; Empfindlichkeit, Anfälligkeit; Schwächlichkeit, Gebrechlichkeit *f*; *(~~ of feeling)* Zart-, Feingefühl; feine(s) Empfinden, Fingerspitzengefühl *n*, Takt *m*; Empfindsamkeit *f*; Leckerbissen *m*, Delikatesse *f*; *of great ~~* heikel, schwierig; *~~ of hearing* feine(s) Gehör *n*; **~te** ['delikit] schmackhaft, köstlich, delikat, lecker; fein, zart; weich, sanft, mild; empfindlich, schwach, schwächlich, anfällig, gebrechlich; *(Situation)* heikel, schwierig; *(Instrument)* empfindlich; feinfühlig, zartfühlend, -besaitet, empfindsam; behutsam, taktvoll, geschickt; sich leicht ekelnd; lecker; **~tessen** [delikə'tesn] *pl* Delikatessen(geschäft *n*) *f pl*; *sing* Feinkosthaus *n.*
delicious [di'liʃəs] köstlich; herrlich, prachtvoll, wunderbar, ausgezeichnet, schmackhaft, delikat; **~ness** [-nis] Köstlichkeit; Schmackhaftigkeit *f.*
delict ['di:likt, di'likt] *jur* Vergehen, Delikt *n.*
delight [di'lait] *tr* erfreuen, entzücken; *itr* Freude, Spaß machen; sich erfreuen, s-e Freude, s-n Spaß haben (*in* an); *s* (große) Freude *f*, Vergnügen, Entzücken *n*, Lust, Wonne *f*; *to the ~ of* zur (großen) Freude *gen*; *to take ~* Freude, Spaß haben (*in doing s.th.* etw zu tun); **~ed** [-id] *a* (hoch)erfreut, sehr froh (*with, at* über), entzückt (*with, at* von); *I shall be ~ed* mit größtem Vergnügen; **~ful** [-ful] (hoch-) erfreulich, (sehr) angenehm; köstlich, entzückend, reizend, bezaubernd.
delimit|(ate) [di(:)'limit(eit)] *tr* abgrenzen; die Grenzen *gen* festlegen; **~ation** [dilimi'teiʃən] Abgrenzung; Grenzlinie *f*, Grenzen *f pl.*
delineate [di'linieit] *tr* zeichnen, skizzieren, entwerfen, umreißen; *(mit Worten)* schildern, beschreiben; darstellen, wiedergeben; **~ion** [-'eiʃən] Zeichnung, Skizze *f*, Entwurf *m*; Schilderung, Beschreibung *f.*
delinquen|cy [di'liŋkwənsi] Pflichtvergessenheit; Unterlassung, (Ver-) Säumnis *f (n)*; Fehler *m*, Schuld *f*, Vergehen *n*; *(juvenile ~~)* (Jugend-) Kriminalität *f*; *~~ report* Tatbericht *m*; **~t** [-kwənt] *a* pflichtvergessen; säumig; schuldig; *(Steuern)* rückständig; *s (bes.* jugendlicher) Straffällige(r), Missetäter, Verbrecher, Delinquent *m.*
deliquesc|e [deli'kwes, di:-] *itr* (zer-) schmelzen; sich aufspalten, sich verzweigen; *chem* flüssig werden, sich verflüssigen; **~ence** [-əns] Flüssigwerden *n*, Verflüssigung *f*; **~ent** [-ənt] schmelzend, zerfließend; hygroskopisch; *bot* sich verzweigend.
delir|ious [di'liriəs] im Delirium, geistesabwesend, phantasierend, im Wahn; außer sich (*with* vor); **~ium** [-iəm] Delirium *n*, (Fieber-, Säufer-)

Wahn; (Freude-, Begeisterungs-)Taumel *m*, Verzückung *f*; *~~ tremens* ['-tri:mənz] Säuferwahn *m*.

deliver [di'livə] *tr* befreien, frei machen; (er)retten, erlösen (*from* von); (ab-, aus)liefern, ab-, übergeben, -reichen, aushändigen (*to* dat); *com* schicken, liefern; *(Post)* verteilen, austragen, zustellen; *(Nachricht)* übermitteln, -bringen; *(Rede, Vortrag)* halten (*to* vor); vortragen; *(to ~ o.s. of)* äußern, ausdrücken, von sich geben; *(Schlag)* austeilen; *(Schlacht)* liefern; *(Ball)* werfen; *(Urteil)* fällen, verkünden; *(Gutachten)* abgeben, erstatten; *(Besitz)* aufgeben; (von sich, her)geben, ausstoßen, e-e Leistung haben von; *Am pol fam* beeinflussen; Geburtshilfe leisten bei *(e-m Kinde)*; *to be ~ed of (Frau)* entbunden werden von *(e-m Kinde)*; *to ~ over* übertragen, abtreten; überantworten; *to ~ up* heraus-, über-, zurückgeben; *to ~ o.s. up* sich ergeben, sich stellen; **~able** [-rəbl] zu liefern(d), abzuliefern(d); lieferbar; **~ance** [-rəns] Befreiung, Freilassung, (Er-)Rettung (*from* von, aus); Äußerung, Aussage, Feststellung *f*; *jur* verkündete(s) Urteil *n*; **~ed** [-d]: *when ~~* bei Lieferung; *~~ free of charge* Lieferung kostenfrei; *~~ free at the station* Lieferung frei Bahnhof; **~er** [-rə] Befreier, Retter; Überbringer; Verteiler *m*; **~ing** [-riŋ] Ablieferung, Aushändigung, Zustellung *f*; *~~ area* Zustellbezirk *m*; *~~ office* Zustellpostamt *n*; *~~ station* Bestimmungsbahnhof *m*; **~y** [-ri] *physiol* Entbindung; (Ab-, Aus-)Lieferung, Übergabe, Überreichung, Aushändigung, Überbringung, Verteilung, Zustellung; *(Abschrift)* Ausfertigung; Aus-, Heraus-, Übergabe; Errettung, Befreiung; Äußerung, Aussage *f*; Vortrag(sweise *f*) *(a. e-s Sängers, Schauspielers)*; Schlag; Wurf *m (e-s Balles)*; *jur* Übertragung; *(Urteil)* Verkündung *f*; *tech* Ausstoß *m*, Zuleitung *f*; *for immediate ~~* sofort, kurzfristig lieferbar; *ready for ~~* lieferbereit; auf Abruf; *on ~~* bei Lieferung; *to refuse ~~* die Herausgabe verweigern; *to refuse to take ~~* die Annahme verweigern; *advice of ~~* Rückschein, Lieferavis *m*; *cash on ~~* gegen Nachnahme; zahlbar bei Empfang; *date, day of ~~* Liefertag *m*; *free ~~* Zustellung *f* frei Haus; *General D~~ (Am)* postlagernd; *non-~~* Unzustellbarkeit *f*; *notice of ~~* Empfangsschein *m*; *parcel(s) ~~, parcel-post ~~* Paketzustellung *f*; *place of ~~* Liefer-, Erfüllungsort *m*; *port of ~~* Bestimmungshafen *m*; *postal ~~* Postzustellung *f*; *special ~~* Zustellung *f* durch Eilboten; *by special ~~* durch Eilboten; *term of ~~* Lieferzeit, -frist *f*; *pl* Lieferbedingungen *f pl*; *~~ area* Liefer-, Zustellbezirk *m*; *~~ charge, fee* Zustellgebühr *f*; *~~ note, ticket* Lieferschein, -zettel *m*; *~~ office* Ausgabestelle *f*; Zustellpostamt *n*; *~~ order* Lieferauftrag; Lieferschein *m*; *~~ pipe* Zuleitung *f*; *~~ room* Kreißsaal *m*; *~~ service* Zustelldienst *m*; *~~ sheet* Empfangs-, Rückschein *m*; *~~ of telegrams* Telegrammzustellung *f*; *~~ truck, van* Lieferwagen *m*.

dell [del] enge(s) (Wald-)Tal *n*, *(baumbestandene)* Schlucht *f*.

delous|e ['di:'lauz, -s] *tr* entlausen; **~ing** [-iŋ] Entlausung *f*; *~~ centre, station* Entlausungsanstalt *f*.

delphinium [del'finiəm] *bot* Rittersporn *m*.

delt|a ['deltə] (Fluß-)Delta *n*; *~~-connection (el)* Dreieck-, Sternschaltung *f*; *~~-wing aeroplane* Deltaflugzeug, fliegende(s) Dreieck *n*; **~oid** ['deltɔid] *a* dreieckig; *s u. ~~ muscle* Deltamuskel *m*.

delude [di'lu:d] *tr* täuschen, irreführen; verleiten (*into* zu); *to ~ o.s.* sich selbst etwas vormachen (*regarding* über).

deluge ['delju:dʒ] *s* Überschwemmung, (große) Flut *f*; heftige(r) Regen; *fig (Wort-)*Schwall *m*; große Menge, Flut *f (von Briefen)*; Strom *m (von Besuchern)*; *the D~* die Sintflut; *tr* überfluten, überschwemmen (*with* mit) *a. fig*; *fig* überwältigen.

delus|ion [di'l(j)u:ʒən] Täuschung, Irreführung; Verblendung, Selbsttäuschung *f*; *psychol med* Wahn *m*; *~~ of grandeur* Größenwahn *m*; **~ive** [-siv] täuschend, irreführend.

delve [delv] *tr obs dial* (um)graben; *itr* sich vertiefen (*into* in), er-, durchforschen, untersuchen (*into s.th.* etw).

demagnetiz|ation ['di:mægnitai'zeiʃən] Entmagnetisierung *f*; **~e** ['di:'mægnitaiz] *tr* entmagnetisieren.

demagog|ic(al) [deməˈgɔgik(əl), -dʒik-] demagogisch, aufwieglerisch, hetzerisch; Hetz-; **~(ue)** ['deməgɔg] Demagoge, Aufwiegler, Hetzer, Volksverführer *m*; **~y** ['deməgɔgi, -dʒi] Demagogie, Volksverhetzung *f*.

demand [di'mɑ:nd] *tr (Person)* fordern, verlangen, beanspruchen; ersuchen um; auffordern; fragen nach; *(Sache)* erfordern, erforderlich machen, bedürfen *gen*, nötig haben, benötigen; anfordern, verlangen, beanspruchen; *s* (An-)Forderung *f*; Verlangen *n*, Anspruch *m* (*on, upon* auf); Begehren *n*; Inanspruchnahme *f* (*on s.th.* gen); Ersuchen *n*, Antrag; *com* Bedarf *m* (*for* an), Nachfrage *f* (*for* nach); Absatz; *jur* Rechtsanspruch *m*, Forderung *f*; Erfordernis *n*; *tech* Leistungsbedarf *m*; *on ~* auf Verlangen; bei Vorzeigung, bei Sicht; *to be in poor ~* nicht gefragt sein; *to make ~s* Ansprüche stellen; *to meet, to supply the ~* den Bedarf decken *od* befriedigen; *he's in great ~* man reißt sich um ihn; *ever increasing ~* e-e (sich) steige(r)nde Nachfrage *f*; *~ for capital* Kapitalbedarf *m*; *~ for exemption, for extension, for extradition* Befreiungs-, Verlängerungs-, Auslieferungsantrag *m*; *~ for payment* Zahlungsaufforderung *f*; *(the law of) supply and ~* (das Gesetz von) Angebot u. Nachfrage; *~* **bill, draft** *fin* Sichtwechsel *m*; *~* **deposit** Sichteinlage *f*; *~* **note** *Am* Sichtwechsel; *Br* Steuerbescheid *m*.

demarcat|e ['di:mɑ:keit] *tr* abgrenzen (*from* von, gegen); die Grenzen *gen* abstecken *od* ziehen; **~ion** [-'keiʃən] Abgrenzung, Grenzziehung; *(line of ~~)* Demarkations-, Grenzlinie, Grenze; (Ab-)Trennung *f*.

demean [di'mi:n] **1.** *tr* erniedrigen, demütigen; *to ~ o.s.* sich herabwürdigen, sich erniedrigen (*to do, by doing* zu tun); **2.** *to ~ o.s.* sich benehmen, sich betragen, sich aufführen; **~o(u)r** [-ə] Benehmen, Betragen, Verhalten, Auftreten *n*; Haltung *f*.

dement|ed [di'mentid] *a* wahnsinnig, irr(e), geisteskrank; *fam* ganz durcheinander, völlig fertig; **~ia** [-'menʃ(i)ə] Schwach-, Blödsinn *m*; Geistesschwäche *f*.

demerit [di:'merit] Fehler *m*; Unwürdigkeit *f*; Versehen *n*, Schuld; *(Schule)* schlechte Zensur *f*.

demesne [di-, də'mein, -mi:n] (selbstbewirtschaftetes) (Erb-)Gut, Grundeigentum *n*; Herrensitz *m*; Domäne *f*; *fig* Bereich *m* od *n*, Gebiet *n*.

demi ['demi] *pref* Halb-, halb; **~god** ['-gɔd] Halbgott *m*; **~john** ['-dʒɔn] Korbflasche *f*, Ballon *m*.

demilitariz|ation ['di:militərai'zeiʃən] Entmilitarisierung *f*; **~e** ['di:'militəraiz] *tr* entmilitarisieren.

demis|able [di'maizəbl] übertragbar, zu verpachten(d); **~e** [di'maiz] *s* Übertragung, Übergabe *f (e-s Gutes)*; Thron-, Regierungswechsel; Tod *m*, Ableben *n*; *tr (Gut)* übertragen; vermachen; hinterlassen; verpachten; *(Gut, Regierung)* übergeben.

demission [di'miʃən] Abdankung *f*, Rücktritt *m*, Demission *f*.

demist ['di:'mist] *tr mot* klar halten *(der Windschutzscheibe)*; **~er** [-ə] Klartuch *n*.

demitasse ['demitɑ:s] *Am* Mokkatasse *f*.

demobiliz|ation ['di:moubilai'zeiʃən] Demobilmachung, Demobilisierung; Auflösung *f (e-r Einheit)*; *~~ centre* Entlassungsstelle *f*; **~e** ['di:'moubilaiz], *Br sl* **demob** ['di:'mɔb] *tr (Truppen, Soldaten)* entlassen; *(Wehrmacht)* demobilisieren, auflösen.

democra|cy [di'mɔkrəsi] Demokratie *f*; demokratische(s) Verhalten *n*; *the D~~ (Am)* die Demokratische Partei; **~t** ['deməkræt] Demokrat *m*; *D~~ (Am)* (Mitglied *n* der) Demokrat(ischen Partei) *m*; **~tic(al)** [demə'krætik(əl)] demokratisch; **~tization** [dimɔkrətai'zeiʃən] Demokratisierung *f*; **~tize** [di'mɔkrətaiz] *tr* demokratisieren.

demodulate ['di:'mɔdjuleit] *tr tech* entmodulieren, rückmodeln.

demographer [di:'mɔgrəfə] Bevölkerungsstatistiker, Demograph *m*; **~ic** [demə'græfik] demographisch; **~y** [di:'mɔgrəfi] Bevölkerungsstatistik, Demographie *f*.

demol|ish [di'mɔliʃ] *tr (Gebäude)* abbrechen, abtragen, ab-, ein-, niederreißen; abbauen; demolieren, zertrümmern, zerstören; sprengen; **~ition** [demə'liʃən] Abbruch *m*, Abbrechen, Niederreißen *n*; Zerstörung *f*; zerstörte(s) Haus *n*; *~~ bomb* Sprengbombe *f*; *~~ chamber* Sprengkammer *f*; *~~ detail* Sprengkommando *n*.

demon, daemon ['di:mən] Dämon; (böser) Geist; Teufel *m*; **~iac(al)** [di'mouniæk, di:mə'naiəkəl] *a* dämonisch, teuflisch; rasend, von Sinnen; (von e-m bösen Geist) besessen; *s* Besessene(r *m*) *f*; **~ic** [di(:)'mɔnik] dämonisch; besessen; begeistert; **~ism** ['di:mənizm] Dämonen-, Geisterglaube *m*.

demonstr|able [di'mɔnstrəbl, 'demən-] be-, nachweisbar; **~ably** [di'mɔnstrəbli] *adv* nachweislich; **~ate** ['demənstreit] *tr* be-, nachweisen; dartun, -legen, aufzeigen; erklären, klar-, verständlich machen; vorführen, demonstrieren; offenzeigen, an den Tag legen, kundtun; *itr pol* demonstrieren, e-e Kundgebung veranstalten; **~ation** [deməns'treiʃən] Beweis(führung *f*) *m* (*of* gen, für); Darlegung; Erklärung; Vorführung *f* (*to* vor); Zeigen *n*; *pol* Kundgebung, Demonstration; (Militär-)Parade *f*; *mil* Täuschungsmanöver, Scheinunternehmen *n*, -angriff *m*; *~~ car* Vorführwagen *m*; **~ative** [di'mɔnstrətiv] *a* beweiskräftig; *(Beweis)* überzeugend, schlagend; ausdrucksvoll; *(Mensch)* offen; offenherzig, überschwenglich; *gram* Demonstrativ-; *s (~~ pronoun)* Demonstrativpronomen, hinweisende(s) Fürwort *n*; *~~ geometry* darstellende Geometrie *f*; **~ativeness** [di'mɔnstrətivnis] Beweis-, Ausdruckskraft; Überschwenglichkeit *f*; **~ator** ['demənstreitə] Erklärer; *com* Vorführer(in *f*); *chem* wissenschaftliche(r) Assistent; *med* Prosektor; *pol* Demonstrant *m*.

demoraliz|ation [dimɔrəlai'zeiʃən,-li-] Sittenverderbnis; schlechte, gedrückte Stimmung *f*; **~e** [di'mɔrəlaiz] *tr* (sittlich) verderben; demoralisieren, zermürben; die Kampfmoral untergraben (*an army* e-s Heeres); entmutigen; verwirren, durchea.bringen.

demot|e [di:'mout] *tr* degradieren (*to* zu); *(Schule)* zurückversetzen; **~ion** [-ʃən] Degradierung; Zurückversetzung *f*.

demount [di:'maunt] *tr* zerlegen, abnehmen, ausbauen; **~able** [-əbl] zerlegbar, abnehmbar, ausbaubar.

demur [di'mə:] *itr* zögern, zaudern, schwanken, unschlüssig sein; Bedenken tragen (*at* gegen); Einwände machen *od* erheben (*at, to* gegen); *s* Zögern *n*, Unschlüssigkeit *f*; Zweifel *m*, Bedenken *n pl*; Einwand *m*, Einwendung *f*, Widerspruch *m* (*at* gegen).

demure [di'mjuə] ruhig, bescheiden, gesetzt, ernst, nüchtern; *pej* spröde, geziert, zimperlich; **~ness** [-nis] Bescheidenheit, Gesetztheit; Geziertheit *f*.

demurr|age [di'mʌridʒ] *fin* Überliegezeit *f*, -geld *n*; **~er** [-ə] *jur* Einwand *m* (*to* gegen).

demy [di'mai] Papierformat *n* 15½ × 20 *(als Schreibpapier)* od 18 × 23 Zoll *(als Druckpapier)*; Stipendiat *m* des Magdalen College in Oxford.

den [den] *s* Höhle *f*, Bau *m (e-s wilden Tieres)*; Käfig *m*; (Räuber-)Höhle *f*; Loch *n*; *fam* Bude *f*.

denationalize [di:'næʃnəlaiz] *tr* wieder ausbürgern, die Staatsangehörigkeit aberkennen (*s.o.* jdm); die Verstaatlichung rückgängig machen (*an industry* e-r Industrie), reprivatisieren.

denature [di:'neitʃə] *tr chem* denaturieren; *(Spiritus)* ungenießbar machen, vergällen.

dendr|iform ['dendrifɔ:m] baumförmig; **~ology** [den'drɔlədʒi] Baumkunde *f*.

deni|able [di'naiəbl] zu leugnen(d), bestreitbar; **~al** [-əl] (Ab-)Leugnung, Bestreitung; Verneinung *f*; Dementi *n*; Absage, Ablehnung, Verweigerung *f*; *to give an official* **~~** dementieren (*to s.th.* etw); in Abrede stellen; **~~** *of justice* Rechtsverweigerung *f*.

denigrat|e ['denigreit] *tr* schwarz machen; *fig* anschwärzen, verunglimpfen, verleumden, diffamieren; **~ion** [-'greiʃən] Schwarzmachen *n*; Verunglimpfung *f*, Anschwärzen *n*, Verleumdung *f*.

denim ['denim] Zwil(li)ch, Drell *m*.

denizen ['denizn] *s* Bewohner *m a.zoo bot.*

denominat|e [di'nɔmineit] *tr* (be)nennen, e-n Namen geben (*s.th.* e-r S), bezeichnen; **~ion** [dinɔmi'neiʃən] Benennung, Bezeichnung *f*, Name *m*; Klasse, Kategorie; Konfession *f*, Bekenntnis *n*, Kirche, Sekte *f*; *math* Nenner *n*; (Maß-)Einheit *f*; *(Banknote)* Nennwert *m*; *to reduce to the same* **~~** *(math)* auf e-n Nenner bringen; **~ional** [dinɔmi'neiʃnl] konfessionell; Konfessions-; Kirchen-, Sekten-; **~~** *school* Konfessionsschule *f*; **~or** [-ə] *math* Nenner *m*; *common* **~~** Hauptnenner *m*.

denotat|ion [di:no(u)'teiʃən] Bezeichnung *f*, (Kenn-)Zeichen *n*; Bedeutung *f*; Begriffsumfang *m*; **~ative** [di'noutətiv] bezeichnend; kennzeichnend; **~e** [di-'nout] *tr* be-, kennzeichnen, benennen; bedeuten; (an)zeigen.

denounce [di'nauns] *tr* heftig kritisieren, öffentlich brandmarken; *jur* anzeigen, melden, denunzieren (*to* bei); *(Vertrag, Abkommen)* kündigen; **~ment** [-mənt] Anzeige, Meldung; öffentliche Anklage; Denunziation *f*.

dens|e [dens] dicht, eng(gepreßt), dick, fest, undurchdringlich; *phot* gut belichtet; *fig* schwerfällig, schwer von Begriff (*about* in); **~eness** ['-nis] Dichte, Undurchdringlichkeit; *fig* Beschränktheit *f*; **~imeter** ['-imi:tə] Dichtemesser *m*; **~ity** ['-iti] Dichte *f*; *(Fahrzeugkolonne)* Abstand *m*; *fig* Dummheit *f*; *phys* spezifische(s) Gewicht *n*; Porenfreiheit; *el* Stromdichte *f*; **~~** *of population* Bevölkerungsdichte *f*; **~~** *of traffic* Verkehrsdichte *f*.

dent [dent] **1.** *s* Kerbe, Beule, Delle *f*; Einschnitt *m*; Vertiefung, Einbuchtung; hohle Stelle *f*, Loch *n*; *tr* einkerben, -drücken, -beulen; zer-, verbeulen; zacken; *itr* sich vertiefen, eingedrückt werden; *to make a* **~** e-e Beule machen (*in* in); **2.** *tech* Zahn, Zacken *m*; **~al** ['-l] *a* Zahn-; *gram* dental; *s* Dental-, Zahnlaut *m*; **~~** *enamel* Zahnschmelz *m*; **~~** *hospital* Zahnklinik *f*; **~~** *nerve* Zahnnerv *m*; **~~** *plate* Zahnprothese *f*; **~~** *surgeon* Zahnarzt *m*; **~~** *treatment* Zahnbehandlung *f*; **~ate** ['-eit] *bot zoo* gezähnt; **~icle** ['-ikl] Zähnchen, Zäckchen *n*; *arch* Zahn *m* (e-s Zahnfrieses); **~iculate(d)** ['-tikjulit, -eit(id)] *a* gezähnelt; **~iculation** ['-leiʃən] Auszackung *f*; **~iform** ['-ifɔ:m] zahnförmig; **~ifrice** ['-ifris] Zahnpasta *f*, -pulver *n*; **~il(e)** ['-il] *arch* Zahn *m (e-s Frieses)*; **~ine** ['-i:n] *anat* Zahnbein, Dentin *n*; **~ist** ['-ist] Zahnarzt *m*; **~istry** ['-istri] Zahnheilkunde *f*; **~ition** ['-tiʃən] Zahnen; *(natürliches)* Gebiß *n*; Zahnformel *f*; **~ure** ['dentʃə] (künstliches) Gebiß *n*.

denud|ation [di:nju'deiʃən] Entblößung, Bloß-, Freilegung; *geol* Abtragung *f*; **~e** [di'nju:d] *tr* entblößen, bloßlegen (*of* von), freilegen; *fig* berauben (*of* gen); *geol* abtragen.

denunciat|ion [dinʌnsi'eiʃən, -ʃi-] Drohung, Warnung *f*; scharfe(r) Tadel *m* (*of* für); *jur* Meldung, Anzeige, Anklage, Denunziation; Kündigung *f (e-s Vertrages, Abkommens)*; **~or** [di'nʌnsieitə] Denunziant, Angeber *m*; **~ory** [di'nʌnsiətəri] anklägerisch, verleumderisch; Denunzianten-.

deny [di'nai] *tr* (ver)leugnen, ab-, bestreiten, verneinen, in Abrede stellen (*having done s.th.* etw getan zu haben); dementieren; ablehnen, -schlagen, verweigern, ab-, versagen (*to* zu); *(Unterschrift)* nicht anerkennen; *to* **~** *o.s.* sich versagen, sich abgehen lassen, verzichten auf; sich verleugnen lassen; nicht empfangen (*to visitors* Besucher); *to* **~** *the door to s.o.* jdn nicht empfangen; *to* **~** *all responsibility* jede Verantwortung ablehnen; *I don't* **~** *that* ich leugne nicht, daß.

deodor|ant [di:'oudərənt] *a* desodor(i-s)ierend(es Mittel *n*); **~ization** [-rai'zeiʃən, -ri-] Desodor(is)ierung *f*; **~ize** [-aiz] *tr* desodor(is)ieren.

deoxidate, -ize [di:'ɔksideit, -aiz] *tr* desoxydieren, reduzieren.

*

depart [di'pɑ:t] *itr* sich entfernen, aufbrechen; abreisen, -fahren, -gehen, -segeln, -fliegen (*from* von; *for* nach); *mil* ab-, ausmarschieren, ausrücken; verlassen (*from s.th.* etw); abweichen, sich trennen (*from* von); aufgeben (*from s.th.* etw); *obs* verscheiden, sterben; *to* **~** *from o.'s customs, principles* von s-n Gewohnheiten, Grundsätzen abweichen; *to* **~** *(from) this life* aus dem Leben scheiden; *to* **~** *from o.'s word, promise* sein Wort brechen, sein Versprechen nicht halten; *the* **~***ed* die Toten *m pl*; **~ment** [-mənt] Abteilung *f*, Zweig *m*, Linie, Seite, Branche *f*; Fach, Gebiet, Ressort *n*; (Dienst-)Stelle *f*; *D***~~** *(Am)* Ministerium *n*; *head of a* **~~** Abteilungsleiter *m*; *men's clothing* **~~** Abteilung *f* für Herrenkleidung; *research, experimental* **~~** Forschungsabteilung *f*; **~~** *store* Waren-, Kaufhaus *n*; **~mental** [-'mentl] *a* Abteilungs-; Fach-; Ministerial-; **~ure** [di'pɑ:tʃə] Aufbruch *a. fig*; Weg-, Abgang *m*; Abreise, -fahrt *f*, -flug (*from* von; *for* nach); *mil* Ab-, Ausmarsch *m*, Ausrücken *n*; Abwendung *f*, Abweichen *n* (*from* von); Aufgabe (*from* gen); *mar* Abweichung *f*; *mar* Ausgangspunkt; *fig* neue(r) Anfang, Start *m*; Richtung, Tendenz *f*; *to make a new* **~~** *(fig)* e-n neuen Weg einschlagen; *to take o.'s* **~~** aufbrechen, weggehen; *notice of* **~~** Abmeldung *f*; *port of* **~~** Abgangshafen *m*; **~~** *platform* Abfahrtsbahnsteig *m*.

depend [di'pend] *itr* abhängen, abhängig sein (*on* von); bedingt sein (*on* durch); sich verlassen, angewiesen sein (*on, upon* auf); *jur* in der Schwebe, noch unentschieden sein; **~** *upon it* verlassen Sie sich darauf! *that* **~***s, it all* **~***s* das kommt drauf an; das hängt davon ab; **~ability** [-ə'biliti] Verläßlichkeit, Zuverlässigkeit, Vertrauenswürdigkeit *f*; **~able** [-əbl] verläßlich, zuverlässig, vertrauenswürdig; **~ant** [-ənt] *(bes. s)*, **~ent** *(bes. a)* *a* abhängig (*on* von); bedingt (*on* durch); sich verlassend (*on* auf); *gram* untergeordnet; *s* Abhängige(r); Untergebene(r); Bedienstete(r), Diener; (Familien-)Angehörige(r), Unterhaltsberechtigte(r), Hinterbliebene(r) *m*; *to be* **~~** *on* abhängen von; abhängig sein von; **~~***s allowance* Familienbeihilfe *f*; **~~***s relief* Hinterbliebenenfürsorge *f*; **~~** *clause (gram)* Nebensatz *m*; **~ence, ~ance** [-əns] Abhängigkeit (*on* von); Bedingtheit; Unterordnung *f* (*on* unter); Verlaß *m*, Vertrauen *n* (*on* auf); Zuversicht *f* (*on* in); *to put* **~~** *on* Vertrauen setzen in; **~ency, ~ancy** [-ənsi] Schutzgebiet *n*, Kolonie *f*; **~~** *exemption (fin. Am)* Unterhaltsfreibetrag *m*; **~encies** *pl* Zubehör *n, a. m.*

depersonaliz|ation ['di:pə:sənəlai-'zeiʃən] Entpersönlichung, Vermassung *f*; **~e** [di'pə:sənəlaiz] *tr* entpersönlichen, vermassen.

depict [di'pikt] *tr* (ab)zeichnen, (ab-)malen; abbilden; *(mit Worten)* schildern, beschreiben; veranschaulichen; **~ion** [-kʃən] Abbildung, Darstellung; Schilderung, Beschreibung *f*.

depilat|e ['depileit] *tr* enthaaren; **~ory** [-'pilətəri] *a* Enthaarungs-; *s* Enthaarungsmittel *n*.

deplane [di:'plein] *itr* (aus dem Flugzeug) aussteigen; *tr* aus-, ent-, abladen.

deplet|e [di'pli:t] *tr* (aus-, ent)leeren; erschöpfen; *med (von Flüssigkeit)* erleichtern; **~ed** [-id] *a* ausgebraucht, erschöpft; *(Säure)* matt; **~ion** [-ʃən] Aus-, Entleerung; *med* Erschöpfung(szustand *m*) *f*; *fin* Substanzverzehr *m*; *(Atom)* Abreicherung *f*; **~ive** [-iv], **~ory** [-əri] *a med* entleerend, erleichternd; *s* Erleichterungsmittel *n*.

deplor|able [di'plɔ:rəbl] bedauerns-, beklagens-, bejammernswert; jämmerlich, kläglich, armselig, unglücklich; **~e** [di'plɔ:] *tr* bedauern, beklagen, bejammern, beweinen.

deploy [di'plɔi] *tr itr mil* sich entwickeln (*for action* zum Gefecht), ausea.ziehen, sich entfalten (lassen); ausschwärmen, aufmarschieren (lassen); **~ment** [-mənt] *mil* Entwick(e)lung *f*; Ausea.ziehen *n*, Entfaltung *f*, Aufmarsch *m*.

depon|e [di'poun] *itr jur* schriftlich unter Eid aussagen; eidlich aussagen;

~**ent** [-ənt] *s* vereidigte(r) Zeuge *m*; *gram (~~ verb)* Deponens *n*.

depopulat|e [di:'pɔpjuleit] *tr itr* (sich) entvölkern; ~**ion** [-'leiʃən] Entvölkerung; Bevölkerungsabnahme *f*.

deport [di'pɔ:t] *tr* verbannen; *(Ausländer)* aus-, des Landes verweisen; abschieben; *to ~ o.s.* sich verhalten, sich betragen, sich aufführen, sich benehmen; ~**ation** [di:pɔ:'teiʃən] Deportation, Verbannung; Aus-, Landesverweisung; Zwangsverschickung *f*; ~**ee** [di:pɔ:'ti:] Ausgewiesene(r) *m*; ~**ment** [di'pɔ:tmənt] Führung *f*, Verhalten, Betragen, Benehmen *n*; Haltung *f*.

depos|able [di'pouzəbl] absetzbar; ~**e** [di'pouz] *tr* aus dem Amt entfernen, absetzen (*from* von); entthronen; *itr jur* e-e (eidliche) Aussage machen (*to s.th.* etw); zu Protokoll erklären.

deposit [di'pɔzit] *tr* deponieren, zur Aufbewahrung, in Depot geben (*with* bei); einlagern; *com* einzahlen, hinterlegen, deponieren (*at the bank* bei der Bank); *(Kaution)* stellen; bezahlen; anzahlen, als An-, Handgeld geben; *(Urkunde)* vorlegen, einreichen; niederlegen, -setzen, -stellen; *(Eier)* legen; *(vor Gericht)* niederlegen; *geol* ablagern (*on* auf); *chem* ausscheiden, niederschlagen; *s* Aufbe-, Verwahrung; Einlagerung *f*; Depot *n*; Hinterlegung; Kaution *f*, Einsatz *m*, Pfand; eingezahlte(s) Geld *n*, Einzahlung, Einlage *f*, Guthaben *n* (*at the bank* auf der Bank); Anzahlung *f*, An-, Handgeld *n*; *geol* Ablagerung *f*, Lager *n*; *chem* Niederschlag, Bodensatz, Rückstand *m*; *against a ~ of* gegen Hinterlegung *gen*; *to leave, to pay a ~* e-e Anzahlung machen; *money on ~* Bank-, Spareinlage *f*, -konto *n*; *savings-bank ~* Spareinlage *f*; *sum on ~* Hinterlegungssumme *f*; ~**ary** [-əri] *a* Hinterlegungs-, Depot-; *s* Verwahrer, Depositar *m*; ~ **bank** Depositenbank *f*; ~ **book** Einlagen-, Sparbuch *n*; ~**ion** [depə'siʃən] Niederlegen *n*; Absetzung, Amtsenthebung; Entthronung; *jur* (Zeugen)Aussage; Aufbewahrung; Hinterlegung *f*; Pfand *n*; *geol* Ablagerung *f*, Lager *n*; *chem* Abscheidung, Niederschlag; *rel (Kunst)* Kreuzabnahme *f*; *tech* Auftrag *m*; ~**or** [di'pɔzitə] Hinter-, Einleger, Depositeninhaber; Einzahler *m*; *(savings-) bank ~~* (Spar-)Konteninhaber *m*; ~**ory** [di'pɔzitəri] Aufbewahrungs-, Hinterlegungsort *m*; Lagerhaus *n*; ~ **receipt**, *Am* **slip** Einzahlungsbeleg *m*.

depot ['depou] (Waren-)Lager *n*, Niederlage *f*, Depot, Lagerhaus, Magazin; *mil* Nachschublager *n*, Park *m*; *Br mil (~ troop)* Ersatzeinheit *f*, -truppenteil; Regimentsstab; *rail* Schuppen *m*; *Am* ['di:pou] Bahnhof *m*; ~ **battalion** *Br* Ersatz-Bataillon *n*.

deprav|ation [deprə'veiʃən] Verführung, -leitung; Verderbtheit *f*; ~**e** [di'preiv] *tr* verführen, -leiten, verderben; ~**ed** [di'preivd] *a* verdorben, sittenlos, lasterhaft; ~**ity** [di'præviti] Verderbtheit, Verworfenheit, Sittenlosigkeit; Schlechtigkeit *f*.

deprec|ate ['deprikeit] *tr* mißbilligen, tadeln; verurteilen; ablehnen; verabscheuen, hassen; ~**ation** [-'keiʃən] Mißbilligung *f*, Tadel; Abscheu, Widerwillen *m*; ~**atory** ['-kətəri] mißbilligend, tadelnd; Entschuldigungs-.

depreciat|e [di'pri:ʃieit] *tr* (im Preis) herabsetzen; im Wert mindern, ent-, abwerten; *fin* amortisieren, abschreiben; *fig* herabsetzen, geringschätzen; *itr* (im Preis) fallen; an Wert verlieren; ~**ing** [-iŋ] geringschätzig, verächtlich; ~**ion** [-'eiʃən] Entwertung, Wertminderung *f*, -verlust, Minderwert *m*; Abschreibung, Amortisation *f*; *(~~ of money)* Geldab-, -entwertung *f*; Sinken, Nachlassen *n*, Rückgang *m*; Geringschätzung, Verachtung *f*; *~~ of coinage* Münzverschlechterung *f*; ~**ory** [-ʃətəri] geringschätzig, verächtlich; herablassend.

depredation [depri'deiʃən] Plünderung *f*, Raub *m*.

depress [di'pres] *tr* nieder-, herunterdrücken, -ziehen; senken, niedriger machen; mindern, schwächen; mäßigen; abflauen lassen; *(im Preis, in der Leistung)* herabsetzen; im Wert mindern; *tech* betätigen, drücken; *mus* tiefer singen *od* spielen; *fig* niederdrücken, deprimieren, traurig stimmen; ~**ant** [-ənt] *a med* beruhigend, hemmend, herabsetzend; *s* Beruhigungsmittel *n*; ~**ed** [-t] *a fig* deprimiert, niedergeschlagen, (in) gedrückt(er Stimmung), traurig; *com* flau; *tech* flach gedrückt; *~~ area* Notstandsgebiet *n*; ~**ing** [-iŋ] bedrückend; erbärmlich; ~**ion** [-'preʃən] Druck *m*, Senkung; Senke, Druckstelle; Minderung, Schwächung; Abnahme *f*, Nachlassen, Abflauen *n*, Abspannung; *(Gelände)* Vertiefung, Senkung, Mulde; *fin med* Depression; *com* Flaute, Krise *f*, Rückgang *m*; *mete* Tief(druckgebiet); *(Barometer)* Fallen *n*; *phys* Unterdruck; Sattelpunkt *m*; *fig* Niedergeschlagenheit, gedrückte Stimmung *f*.

depriv|ation [depri'veiʃən] Beraubung *f*, Verlust *m*; *rel* Amtsenthebung *f*; ~**e** [di'praiv] *tr* berauben (*of s.th.* e-r S), nehmen (*s.o. of s.th.* jdm etw); entziehen, aberkennen (*s.o. of s.th.* jdm etw); *(bes. rel)* s-s Amtes entheben; *he didn't ~~ himself of anything* er ließ sich nichts abgehen.

depth [depθ] Tiefe; Höhe; *fig* Stärke, Kraft, Tiefe *(des Schweigens, des Tones)*; *(Farben)* Leuchtkraft, Sattheit; *(~ of thought)* Gedankentiefe, Unergründlichkeit, Unerforschlichkeit; *(~ of feeling, of emotion)* Stärke (des Gefühls); Begabung, Begabtheit; Klugheit, Weisheit; *mil* Tiefengliederung, -staffelung; *min* Teufe *f*; *meist pl* (Meeres-)Tiefe *f*, (Erd-)Innere(s) *n*; *in ~ (fig)* gründlich; tief; *in the ~(s) of* mitten in; *in the ~(s) of despair, of misery* in tiefer Verzweiflung, in tief(st)em Elend; *in the ~(s) of o.'s heart* im Grunde s-s Herzens; *in the ~ of winter* mitten im Winter; *of great ~* (sehr) tief veranlagt, begabt, klug, weise; *to be out of, beyond o.'s ~ (im Wasser)* keinen Grund mehr haben; *fig* den Boden unter den Füßen verlieren, *~ of focus (phot)* Tiefenschärfe *f*; *~ of column (mil)* Marschtiefe *f*; ~ **psychology** Tiefenpsychologie *f*.

deput|ation [depju'teiʃən] Abordnung *f*; ~**e** [di'pju:t] *tr* abordnen, bevollmächtigen; beauftragen, anweisen; *(Vollmachten, Befugnisse)* übertragen; ~**ize** ['depjutaiz] *tr* abordnen, zu s-m Stellvertreter ernennen; *itr* vertreten (*for s.o.* jdn); ~**y** ['depjuti] *pol* Abgeordnete(r), Deputierte(r); *jur* Stellvertreter, Bevollmächtigte(r) *m*; *attr* stellvertretend, geschäftsführend; Vize-; *~~ chairman, (party) leader* stellvertretende(r) Vorsitzende(r), Parteiführer *m*; *~~ consul* Vizekonsul *m*; *~~ judge* Hilfsrichter *m*.

deracinate [di'ræsineit] *tr* entwurzeln; *fig* (ver)tilgen, ausrotten, -löschen.

derail [di'reil] *tr itr* entgleisen (lassen); ~**ment** [mənt] Entgleisen *n*.

derange [di'reindʒ] *tr* in Unordnung, durchea.bringen, *fam* über den Haufen werfen; verwirren; stören; ~**d** [-d] *a* in Unordnung, nicht in Ordnung, durcheinander; *(Magen)* verdorben; *(mentally ~~)* geistesgestört; zerrüttet; ~**ment** [-mənt] Unordnung *f*, Durcheinander *n*; Verwirrung; Zerrüttung *f*; *(mental ~~)* Geistesgestörtheit *f*.

derate [di:'reit] *tr (Gemeindesteuern)* herabsetzen, aufheben.

Derby ['dɑ:bi] Derby(rennen) *n*; *d~* ['də:bi] *Am* Melone *f (Hut)*.

derelict ['derilikt] *a (bes. Schiff)* herrenlos; *Am* pflichtvergessen, nachlässig; *s* herrenlose(s) Gut; Strandgut; Wrack *n a. fig*; *Am* pflichtvergessene(r) Mensch *m*; ~**ion** [-'likʃən] (Besitz-)Aufgabe; Preisgabe; Verlassenheit *f*; Landgewinn *m*; vom Meer freigegebene(s) Land *n*; *Am* Pflichtvergessenheit *f*; Vertrauensbruch *m*; Nachlässigkeit *f*.

deride [di'raid] *tr* aus-, verlachen; verspotten; Witze machen über; lächerlich machen.

deris|ion [di'riʒən] Spott *m*, Verspottung, Verhöhnung *f*, Hohn *m*, Verächtlichmachung *f*, Gespött *n*; *to be held in ~* Zielscheibe des Spottes sein; ~**ive** [-'raisiv], ~**ory** [-əri] spottlustig; spöttisch, höhnisch.

deriv|able [di'raivəbl] ableitbar, abzuleiten(d) (*from* von); ~**ation** [deri'veiʃən] Ableitung; Herkunft *f*; Ursprung *m*, Wurzel, Quelle; *(Wort)* Etymologie *f*; ~**ative** [di'rivətiv] *a* abgeleitet; nicht ursprünglich, sekundär; *s* Ableitung *f*; abgeleitete(s) Wort; *chem* Derivat *n*; *math* Differentialkoeffizient *m*; ~**e** [di'raiv] *tr* ab-, herleiten (*from* von), zurückführen (*from* auf); gewinnen, erhalten (*from* von); *itr u. to be ~ed* herrühren, stammen (*from* von); *to ~~ benefit, profit from* Nutzen, Vorteile ziehen aus.

derm(a, ~is) ['də:m(ə, -is)] *scient* Haut; Lederhaut *f*; ~**al** ['-əl], ~**ic** ['-ik] *a* Haut-; ~**atitis** [-'taitis] Hautentzündung *f*; ~**atologist** [də:mə'tɔlədʒist] Dermatologe, Hautarzt *m*; ~**atology** [-'tɔlədʒi] Dermatologie *f*.

derogat|e ['derəgeit] *itr* beeinträchtigen (*from s.th.* etw), schaden (*from s.o.* jdm); Abbruch tun (*from s.th.* e-r S); ~**ion** [-'geiʃən] Schwächung, Schmälerung, Beeinträchtigung; Herabsetzung, Herabwürdigung, Verleumdung; Verschlechterung *f*, Verfall *m*; *to the ~~ of* auf Kosten *gen*; ~**ory** [di'rɔgətəri] nachteilig, abträglich; herabwürdigend.

derrick ['derik] (beweglicher) (Lade-) Kran, Ausleger; *mar* Ladebaum; *Am* Bohrturm *m*.

derring-do ['deriŋ'du:] *obs* Heldentat *f*; Heldenmut *m*.

dervish ['də:viʃ] Derwisch *m*.

descant ['deskænt] mehrstimmige(r) Gesang *m*; Sopran-, Oberstimme *f*; *tr* [des-, dis'kænt] *mus* kontrapunktisch begleiten; *itr* sich (lobend) auslassen (*on, upon* über), (lang u. breit) reden (*on, upon* über); *mus* Sopran singen.

descen|d [di'send] *itr* herab-, hinabsteigen, herabkommen, hinabgehen, -gleiten, -fallen, -sinken; *aero* landen, niedergehen; *(Straße)* hinabführen, -gehen; kommen, greifen, übergehen (*to* zu); *(Fluß)* fließen (*to the sea* in das Meer); *(to be ~ded)* ab-, herstammen (*from* von); sich vererben (*to* auf); sich stürzen (*on* auf), herfallen (*on to* über); heimsuchen, überfallen (*on s.o.* jdn); einfallen, hereinbrechen (*on, upon* in); *mus* tiefer werden; *tr* herabsteigen, hinabgehen; *to ~~ to details* in die Einzelheiten gehen; ~**dant** [-ənt] Nachkomme, Abkömmling *m*; *pl* Nachkommenschaft *f*; ~**t** [di'sent] Abstieg *m*, Hinabgleiten, Sinken *n*, Fall *m*; *aero* Landung *f*; *(Fallschirm)* Absprung; Abhang; hinabführende(r) Weg *m*; Abstammung, Herkunft; Nachkommen (-schaft *f*) *m pl*; Erbfolge *f*; Sturm, Überfall (*on, upon* auf), Einfall (*on, upon* in); *fig* Niedergang, Verfall *m*.

describ|able [dis'kraibəbl] zu beschreiben(d); ~**e** [dis'kraib] *tr* beschreiben; (mit Worten) schildern, darstellen; *(e-n Kreis)* beschreiben; *(Kurve)* durchlaufen; *to* ~~ *o.s. as* sich ausgeben als.

descript|ion [dis'kripʃən] Beschreibung; Schilderung, Darstellung; Personalbeschreibung; Titelaufnahme; Gebrauchsanweisung; Bezeichnung, Angabe *f*; nähere Angaben, Einzelheiten *f pl*; *fam* Art, Sorte *f*; *beyond* ~~ unbeschreiblich; *to answer to a* ~~ e-r Beschreibung entsprechen; ~**ive** [-tiv] beschreibend, darstellend; kennzeichnend; erläuternd.

descry [dis'krai] *tr* erblicken, wahrnehmen; erkennen, unterscheiden; erspähen, entdecken.

desecrat|e ['desikreit] *tr rel* entweihen, profanieren, schänden; ~**ion** [-'kreiʃən] Entweihung, Schändung *f*.

desegregat|e ['di:'segrəgeit] *tr* die Rassentrennung aufheben in; ~**ion** ['-'geiʃən] Aufhebung *f* der Rassentrennung.

desert 1. [di'zə:t] Verdienst *n*; *meist pl* Lohn *m (a. als Strafe)*; *to get o.'s just* ~*s* s-n gerechten Lohn empfangen; **2.** *v* [di'zə:t] *tr* (böswillig) verlassen, im Stich lassen, aufgeben, abfallen von, untreu werden (*s.th.* e-r S); *(Frau)* sitzenlassen; *itr* desertieren, fahnenflüchtig werden, Fahnenflucht begehen; überlaufen; ~**er** [di'zə:tə] Deserteur, Fahnenflüchtige(r), Überläufer *m*; ~**ion** [di'zə:ʃən] Imstichlassen, (böswilliges) Verlassen *n*; Aufgabe *f*; Abfall *m*; Fahnenflucht, Desertion *f*; **3.** ['dezət] *s* Wüste; Einöde *f*; *a* wüst, öde, unfruchtbar; unbewohnt, verlassen.

deserv|e [di'zə:v] *tr* verdienen, wert sein; Anspruch haben auf; *itr* sich verdient machen (*of s.th.* um etw); ~**ed** [-d] *a* (wohl)verdient (*of* um); ~**edly** [-idli] *adv* verdientermaßen, nach Verdienst, gebührend; ~**ing** [-iŋ] *a* verdienstvoll, -lich; wert (*of s.th.* etw), würdig (*of s.th.* etw).

desicc|ant ['desikənt] *a* austrocknend; *s* Trockenmittel *n*, -puder *m*; ~**ate** ['-eit] *tr* (aus)trocknen; *(bes. Lebensmittel)* dörren; *itr* Wasser entziehen; austrocknen, -dörren; ~**ation** [-'keiʃən] (Aus-)Trocknen, (Aus-)Dörren *n*; ~**ator** ['-eitə] Trockenapparat, Entfeuchter *m*.

desideratum [dizidə'reitəm] *pl -ta* [-tə] Bedürfnis; Erfordernis *n*; (Gegenstand des) Wunsch(es) *m*.

design [di'zain] *s* Zeichnung, Skizze *f*; Entwurf, Plan *m*; Planung, Anlage *f*, (Auf-)Bau *m*; Gestaltung, Formgebung; Ausführung, Konstruktion *f*; Auf-, Abriß *m*; Absicht *f*, Vorhaben *n*; Vorsatz *m*; Ziel *n*; Zweck *m*; Ausführung *f*; Modell; Muster; Musterzeichnen *n*, Zeichenkunst *f*; *pl* (geheime) Absichten *f pl*, Anschläge *m pl*; *tr* zeichnen, skizzieren; entwerfen, planen, ausdenken, ersinnen; ausführen, konstruieren; beabsichtigen, vorhaben; auswählen, ausersehen, bestimmen (*for* zu); *by* ~ = ~*edly*; *in the* ~ *stage* im Stadium der Planung; *with this* ~ in dieser Absicht; zu diesem Zweck; *to be under* ~ geplant sein; *to have* ~*s on, against* Absichten, es abgesehen haben auf; etw im Schilde führen gegen; *to work on a* ~ an e-m Entwurf arbeiten; *protection of* ~*s* (Gebrauchs-)Musterschutz *m*; *registered* ~ Gebrauchsmuster *n*; ~ **data** Konstruktionsdaten *n pl*; ~**edly** [-idli] *adv* absichtlich, mit Absicht; nach vorgefaßtem Plan, vorsätzlich; mit Vorbedacht, mit Überlegung, wohlüberlegt; ~**er** [-ə] (Muster-)Zeichner; Formgestalter; Konstrukteur; *theat* Dekorateur; *fig* Ränkeschmied, Intrigant *m*; ~**ing** [-iŋ] *a* intrigant; listig, verschlagen, durchtrieben; *s* (Muster-)Zeichnen, Entwerfen; Planen, Konstruieren *n*; ~~ *department* Zeichenatelier *n*; Konstruktionsabteilung *f*; ~ **stress** zulässige Belastung *f*.

designat|e ['dezigneit] *tr* be-, kennzeichnen, erkennen lassen; beschriften; aus-, erwählen, ausersehen, bestimmen, ernennen (*to, for* zu); einsetzen (*to, for, as* als); *(mil)* ansprechen (*a target* ein Ziel); *a* [-nit] auser-, vorgesehen, (aus)erwählt, designiert, bestimmt, ernannt; ~**ion** [-'neiʃən] Bezeichnung *f*; Name *m*; Kennzeichnung; Kenntlichmachung; Bestimmung, Be-, Ernennung; Beschriftung *f*; ~~ *of origin* Herkunftsbezeichnung *f*.

desir|ability [dizairə'biliti] Anziehungskraft; Annehmlichkeit *f*; ~**able** [di'zairəbl] wünschens-, begehrens-, erstrebenswert; erwünscht, günstig, angenehm, schön, gut; ~**e** [di'zaiə] *tr* wünschen, begehren, erstreben, verlangen nach (*to do* zu tun; *od* Konj); wünschen, bitten, ersuchen, auffordern; *s* Wunsch *m*, Verlangen *n*, Begehr(en *n*) *m* od *n* (*for doing, to do* etw zu tun; *for* nach); Bitte *f*, Ersuchen *n*, Aufforderung *f*; *das* Gewünschte, Gegenstand *m* des Wunsches; *at s.o.'s* ~~ auf jds Wunsch, Ersuchen; *by* ~~ auf Wunsch; *to leave (much) to be* ~*ed* (viel) zu wünschen übriglassen; ~**ous** [-'zaiərəs]: *to be* ~~ *of* den Wunsch haben zu; beabsichtigen.

desist [di'zist] *itr* abstehen, Abstand nehmen, ablassen (*from* von; *from doing* zu tun).

desk [desk] (Lese-, Schreib-, Zeichen-) Pult *n*; Schreibtisch *m*; Katheder *n* od *m*; Schulbank *f*; *mus* Notenständer *m*; *Am (~ job)* Platz *m*, Stelle im Büro; *Am* Redaktion *f*; Schalter *m*; *pay* ~ Kasse *f*; *information* ~ Auskunft(sstelle) *f*; ~ **clerk** Büroangestellte(r) *m*; ~ **man, jockey** *Am* Redakteur *m*, Redaktionsmitglied *n*; ~ **pad** Schreibtischunterlage *f*; ~ **switchboard** Schaltpult *n*; ~ **work** Schreib-, Büroarbeit *f*.

deskill ['di:'skil] *tr (Arbeit durch Teilung od Mechanisierung)* vereinfachen.

desolat|e ['desəleit] *tr* verwüsten, verheeren; *(Menschen)* verlassen, sich selbst, s-m Schmerz überlassen; betrüben, traurig, untröstlich machen; *a* [-it] wüst, öde, menschenleer, verlassen, trostlos; *(Mensch)* einsam, verlassen, elend, traurig, ohne Hoffnung; ~**ion** [-'leiʃən] Verwüstung, Verheerung *f*; wüste(r) Zustand *m*, Öde, Trostlosigkeit; Verlassenheit, Einsamkeit *f*, Elend *n*, Hoffnungslosigkeit *f*.

despair [dis'pɛə] *itr* verzweifeln (*of* an; *of doing* zu tun); die Hoffnung aufgeben (*of* auf); *s* Verzweiflung, Hoffnungslosigkeit *f* (*at* über); *in* ~ verzweifelt *adv*; *to give up in* ~ verzweifeln an, aufgeben; *he is my* ~ ich verzweifle an ihm; ~**ing** [-riŋ] verzweifelt; hoffnungslos.

despatch *s. dispatch.*

desperado [despə'ra:dou] *pl -o(e)s* Bandit *m*.

desperat|e ['despərit] verzweifelt; vor nichts zurückschreckend, rasend, verwegen, tollkühn, alles auf eine Karte setzend; *(Lage)* hoffnungslos; *(a. Krankheit)* gefährlich, ernst; *(übertreibend)* furchtbar, schrecklich; gewaltig, enorm, riesig, ganz groß; ~**ion** [-'reiʃən] Verzweiflung, Raserei, Verwegenheit, Tollkühnheit *f*; *in* ~~ verzweifelt; *to drive to* ~~ *(fam)* zur Verzweiflung treiben.

despicable ['despikəbl] verächtlich, verachtenswert, niedrig, gemein.

despise [dis'paiz] *tr* verachten, geringachten, -schätzen; verschmähen.

despite [dis'pait] *s* Bosheit, Gehässigkeit *f*; *prp u. (in)* ~ *(of)* trotz, ungeachtet *gen*.

despoil [dis'pɔil] *tr* berauben (*of s.th.* e-r S); ausrauben, (aus)plündern; ~**ment** [-mənt], **despoliation** [dispouli'eiʃən] Be-, Ausraubung, Plünderung *f*.

despond [dis'pɔnd] *itr* verzagen (*of* an); ~**ence, -cy** [-əns(i)] Verzagtheit, Mut-, Hoffnungslosigkeit *f*; ~**ent** [-ənt], ~**ing** [-iŋ] verzagt, mut-, hoffnungslos.

despot ['despɔt] *pol* Gewaltherrscher, -haber, Tyrann *m a. fig*; ~**ic(al)** [des-, dis'pɔtik(əl)] despotisch, tyrannisch; ~**ism** ['despətizm] Gewaltherrschaft, Despotismus *m*; Diktatur, Tyrannei *f*.

desquamate ['deskwəmeit] *itr (Haut)* sich abschuppen.

dessert [di'zə:t] *(~-service)* Nachtisch *m*, Dessert *n*; ~**-knife, -spoon** Dessertmesser *n*, -löffel *m*.

destin|ation [desti'neiʃən] Bestimmung(sort *m*) *f*; Zweck *m*, Ziel *n*; Adresse, Anschrift *f*; *port of* ~~ Bestimmungshafen *m*; ~**e** ['destin] *tr* bestimmen, ausersehen (*for* für, zu; *to be* zu sein); *(it) was* ~*ed to (happen)* (es) sollte (so kommen); ~**y** ['destini] *(persönliches)* Schicksal, Geschick; Verhängnis *n*; *the D~ies (pl)* die Parzen *f pl*.

destitut|e ['destitju:t] *a* hilflos, in Not, notleidend; mittellos, ohne Mittel, arm, (unterstützungs)bedürftig; ~~ *of* ohne; bar *gen*; *to be* ~~ *of* entbehren *gen*; ~**ion** [-'tju:ʃən] Armut, (bittere) Not *f*, Elend *n*; Bedürftigkeit *f*; Mangel *m* (*of* an).

destroy [dis'trɔi] *tr* abbrechen, nieder-, einreißen; zertrümmern; zerstören, vernichten, vertilgen, *fam* kaputtmachen, ruinieren; *(Gesundheit)* zerrütten; *mil (Truppen)* aufreiben; ein Ende machen mit (*s.th.* e-r S); töten; unwirksam, unschädlich, unbrauchbar machen; *to* ~ *o.s.* Selbstmord begehen; ~**er** [-ə] Zerstörer *m a. mar mil.*

destruct|ibility [distrʌkti'biliti] Zerstörbarkeit *f*; ~**ible** [-'trʌktibl] zerstörbar; ~**ion** [-'trʌkʃən] Abbruch *m (e-s Gebäudes)*; Zertrümmerung, Verwüstung; Zerstörung, Vernichtung; Tötung; *mil* Niederkämpfung *f*; Untergang, Verderb(en *n*) *m*; *self-*~~ Selbstmord *m*, -vernichtung *f*; ~~ *squad* Abbruchkommando *n*; ~**ive** [-iv] zerstörerisch, verderblich, zersetzend; zerstörend; *(Kritik)* vernichtend; niederreißend; negativ; ~~ *fire* Vernichtungsfeuer *n*; ~**iveness, ~ivity** [-'trʌktivnis, -'tiviti] zerstörende Gewalt; Zerstörungswut, -lust *f*; ~**or** [-ə] *Br* Müllofen *m*.

desuetude [di'sju(:)itju:d] *s*: *to fall into* ~ außer Gebrauch kommen.

desulfur(ize) [di:'sʌlfəraiz] *tr* entschwefeln.

desulto|riness ['desəltərinis] Zs.hanglosigkeit; Flüchtigkeit; Plan-, Ziellosigkeit *f*; **~y** ['desəltəri] zs.hanglos, unzs.hängend, abgerissen, abgehackt; zufällig, hin- u. herspringend, plan-, ziellos; flüchtig; unmethodisch, unsystematisch.

detach [di'tætʃ] *tr* losmachen; los-, ablösen, abtrennen, abreißen; absondern *a. fig*; *rail (Wagen)* ab-, aussetzen; *fig* abspenstig machen; *mil* (ab)kommandieren, abstellen; *to ~ o.s.* sich trennen, sich losreißen; **~able** [-əbl] ablösbar, abtrennbar, abnehmbar (*from* von); **~ed** [-t] *a* abgelöst, abgetrennt; abgesondert; lose; *(Haus)* freistehend, einzeln(stehend); *fig* unabhängig, unbeeinflußt, selbständig; unvoreingenommen, unbeschwert; sachlich, objektiv; unparteiisch; gleichgültig (*about* gegenüber); *mil* (ab)kommandiert; *~~ pieces (pl)* Einzelteile *m pl*; *~~ service* Abkommandierung *f*; *~~ unit* Kommando *n*; **~ment** [-mənt] Ablösung *a. med*, Abtrennung; Absonderung *f* (*from* von); *rail* Ab-, Aussetzen *n*; *mil* (Ab-)Kommandierung *f*; Kommando *n*; Abteilung *f*, Trupp *m*; Unabhängigkeit, Selbständigkeit; Unvoreingenommenheit, Sachlichkeit, Objektivität; Gleichgültigkeit *f* (*from* gegenüber); *on ~~* abkommandiert, abgestellt; *~~ of police* Polizeiaufgebot *n*.

detail ['di:teil] Einzelteil *m*; Einzelheit *f*; *(Kunst)* Detail *n*; Detaillierung, genaue Aufzählung, Wiedergabe *f* im einzelnen; eingehende(r), ins Einzelne gehende(r) Bericht *m*; Beiwerk *n*; *mil* Kommando *n*, Gruppe, Abteilung *f*; (Sonder-)Einsatz *m*, -aufgabe *f*; *pl* (nähere) Einzelheiten *f pl*, Einzelumstände *m pl* (*of* über); *tr a.* [di'teil] einzeln aufführen, genau aufzählen, detaillieren; im einzelnen wiedergeben, eingehend berichten über, schildern; *mil* abstellen, abkommandieren (*for* um zu); *in ~* im einzelnen, bis in die Einzelheiten, genau, ausführlich; *in every ~* Punkt für Punkt; *to go, to enter into ~s* ins Einzelne, (bis) in die Einzelheiten gehen; **~drawing** Teilzeichnung *f*; **~ed** [di'teild] *a* eingehend, ausführlich.

detain [di'tein] *tr (Person)* ab-, fest-, zurückhalten, nicht gehen lassen; warten lassen; *(Sache)* (ein-)behalten, nicht zurückgeben; vorenthalten; verwahren; verzögern, aufschieben; *(Schüler)* nachsitzen lassen; *jur* in Haft (be)halten; **~ed** [-d] *a* inhaftiert, in Haft; **~ee** [di:tei'ni:] Häftling *m*.

detect [di'tekt] *tr* auf-, entdecken; feststellen, herausfinden, ausfindig machen, ermitteln; entlarven; ertappen; bemerken, sehen, erfassen; *chem* nachweisen; *(Gas)* spüren; **~able, ~ible** [-əbl, -ibl] feststellbar; *chem* nachweisbar; **~aphone** [-əfoun] Abhörapparat *m*; **~ion** [-ʃən] Auf-, Entdeckung; Ermitt(e)lung; Ortung *f*; *chem* Nachweis *m*; *tele* Gleichrichtung *f*; **~ive** [-iv] *s* Geheimpolizist, Detektiv *m*; *a* Detektiv-; *~~ story* Kriminalroman *m*; **~or** [-ə] Entdecker; *tech* Anzeiger *m*; Spürgerät *n*; *mar* Ortungsgerät *n*; Sucher; *radio* Detektor, Gleichrichter *m*; Nullinstrument *n*.

detent [di'tent] *tech* Rast-, Sperrklinke; Arretierung *f*.

detention [di'tenʃən] Fest-, Zurückhalten; (Ein-)Behalten, Vorenthalten *n*; Verzögerung *f*; Aufschub *m*; *jur* Haft *f*; *mil* Arrest *m*; Beschlagnahme *f*; *(Schule)* Nachsitzen *n*; *to hold under ~* in Haft halten; *~ awaiting trial* Untersuchungshaft *f*; **~-barracks** *pl Br* Arrestlokal, -gebäude, Militärgefängnis *n*; **~-camp** Internierungslager *n*; **~ centre** *Br* Jugendhaftanstalt *f*.

deter [di'tə:] *tr* abschrecken, zurückhalten (*from* von); hindern (*from* an)

detergent [di'tə:dʒənt] *a* reinigend; *s* Reinigungsmittel *n*; *pl* Detergentien *pl*.

deteriorat|e [di'tiəriəreit] *tr* verschlechtern, verschlimmern; im Wert mindern, abwerten; *itr* sich verschlechtern, sich verschlimmern; verderben; an Wert verlieren; entarten; **~ion** [-'reiʃən] Verschlechterung, Verschlimmerung; (Wert-)Minderung *f*; Verderb *m*.

determin|able [di'tə:minəbl] bestimmbar; **~ant** [-ənt] *a* entscheidend, bestimmend; *s* entscheidende(r) Faktor *m*; *math* Determinante *f*; **~ate** [-it] be-, abgegrenzt, festgelegt, endgültig, genau; entschieden; entscheidend, bestimmend; entschlossen; *math* determiniert; **~ation** [-'neiʃən] Bestimmung, Festsetzung, -legung *f*, Entscheid(ung *f*), Beschluß, Entschluß *m* (*on doing* zu tun); Bestimmtheit, Entschiedenheit; Entschlossenheit; *jur* Auflösung *f*; Ablauf *m*, Ende *n*; *(~~ of direction)* (Richtungs-)Bestimmung *f*; **~ative** [di'tə:minətiv] *a* entscheidend, bestimmend, einschränkend, begrenzend; *s* entscheidende(r) Faktor *m*; *gram* Determinativpronomen *n*; **~e** [di'tə:min] *tr* bestimmen, entscheiden (über), beschließen, festlegen, -setzen (*to* auf); berechnen; zur Folge haben; veranlassen, verursachen, herbeiführen; dazu bringen; beenden, beschließen; *(Vertrag)* (auf)lösen; *itr* sich entschließen, sich entscheiden, sich festlegen (*on* auf); *jur* ablaufen, zu Ende gehen; zum Abschluß kommen; *to be ~~d* entschlossen sein (*to do, on doing* zu tun); bestimmt werden (*by* von).

deterr|ence [di'terəns] Abschreckung(smittel *n*) *f*; **~ent** [-ənt] *a* abschreckend, entmutigend; *s* Abschreckungsmittel *n*.

detest [di'test] *tr* verabscheuen, hassen; **~able** [-əbl] verabscheuens-, hassenswert; abscheulich, scheußlich; **~ation** [di:tes'teiʃən] Verabscheuung *f*, Abscheu (*of* vor); Haß *m*.

dethrone [di'θroun] *tr* entthronen; absetzen; *fig* stürzen; **~ment** [-mənt] Entthronung, Absetzung *f*.

detonat|e ['de-, 'di:to(u)neit] *tr itr* explodieren, platzen, krepieren; knallen, detonieren (lassen); verpuffen; *mot* klopfen; **~ing** [-iŋ] *a* Zünd-; *~~ cap* Zündhütchen *n*; *~~ gas* Knallgas *n*; *~~ power* Sprengkraft *f*; *~~ wave* Detonationswelle *f*; **~ion** [-'neiʃən] Explosion; Detonation *f*, laute(r) Knall *m*; Sprengung *f*; **~or** [-ə] Zündkapsel *f*, -satz; Sprengkörper *m*; *rail* Knallsignal *n*.

detour ['deituə, dei-, di(:)'tuə] *s* Umweg *m*; Umleitung *f*; Abstecher *m*; *to make a ~* e-n Umweg, e-n Abstecher machen; *tr itr* e-n Umweg machen (lassen); umleiten.

detract [di'trækt] *tr* abziehen, abwegnehmen (*from* von); *itr* Abbruch tun (*from s.th.* e-r S), beeinträchtigen (*from s.th.* etw); **~ion** [-kʃən] Abzug *m*, Wegnahme; Ablenkung; Herabsetzung, -würdigung, Schmälerung *f*; **~or** [-ə] Lästerer, Verleumder *m*.

detrain [di:'trein] *tr rail* ab-, ausladen *(a. Truppen)*; *itr* ausgeladen werden; aussteigen; **~ment** [-mənt] Ausladen *n*.

detriment ['detrimənt] Nachteil, Schaden *m* (*to* für); *to s.o.'s ~* zu jds Nachteil, Schaden; *without ~ to* unbeschadet *gen*; **~al** [detri'mentl] nachteilig, ungünstig, schädlich (*to* für); *(Bemerkung)* abfällig.

detrit|al [di'traitl] *a* Geröll-; **~ion** [-'triʃən] *geol* Erosion *f*; **~us** [-'traitəs] Geröll *n*, Flußschotter *m*, Geschiebe (-masse *f*) *n*; Rest *m*.

deuce [dju:s] *s (Spielkarten, Würfel)* Zwei *f*; *(Tennis)* Einstand *m*; *interj u. what the ~* was (zum) Teufel! *to play the ~ with* Schindluder treiben mit; *there will be the ~ to pay* das dicke Ende kommt noch; **~d** [dju:st, 'dju:sid] *a adv fam* verteufelt, verflixt, verflucht, verdammt.

deuter|ium [dju:'tiəriəm] Deuterium *n*, schwere(r) Wasserstoff *m*; **D~onomy** [dju:tə'rɔnəmi] *rel* 5. Buch *n* Mose.

devalu|(at)e [di:'vælju(eit):] *tr (Geld)* ab-, entwerten; **~ation** [di:vælju'eiʃən] *fin* Abwertung *f*.

devastat|e ['devəsteit] *tr* verwüsten, zerstören, verheeren; **~ing** [-iŋ] *fig* verheerend, vernichtend; **~ion** [-'teiʃən] Zerstörung, Verwüstung *f*.

develop [di'veləp] *tr* entwickeln *a. phot u. fig*; entfalten, ausweiten, vergrößern; stärken, kräftigen; nutzbar machen, fördern, erschließen; ausarbeiten, auswerten, ausbauen *fig*; *(Krankheit)* sich zuziehen; *(Gewohnheit)* annehmen; *math* abwickeln; (nach u. nach) aufdecken, enthüllen, bekanntgeben; deutlicher, genauer erklären, ausführlich darlegen; zu Tage, ans Licht bringen; *itr* sich entwickeln (*from* aus; *into* zu); sich entfalten, größer, stärker, kräftiger werden; entstehen; heranwachsen; *(Krankheit)* ins akute Stadium treten, zum Ausbruch kommen; sich herausstellen, sich zeigen, bekanntwerden; **~er** [-ə] Entwickler *m a. phot*; **~ing** [-iŋ] Entwicklungs-; **~ment** [-mənt] Entwick(e)lung, Entfaltung *f*; Wachstum *n*; Ausweitung, Vergrößerung *f*, Ausbau *m*; Stärkung, Kräftigung; Nutzbarmachung, Erschließung *f*, Ausbau *m*; Ausarbeitung, Auswertung *f*; *(Krankheit)* Ausbruch *m*; Enthüllung, Bekanntgabe *f*, -werden *n*; Entwicklungsstufe *f*, -stadium *n*; Verlauf; Fortschritt *m*; Ereignis *n*; Tatsache *f*; Entwicklungsergebnis *n*; *pl* Gang *m* der Ereignisse; *ribbon ~~* Stadtrandsiedlung *f*; *~~ area* Notstands-, Förderungsgebiet *n*; **~mental** [diveləp'mentl] *a* Entwicklungs-, Ausbau-.

deviat|e ['di:vieit] *itr* abweichen, abgehen, sich entfernen *fig* (*from* von); *(vom Kurs)* abkommen; **~ion** [di:vi'eiʃən] *fig phys* Abweichung *f*, Abgehen; *(vom Kurs)* Abkommen *n*; *(Kompaß)* Ablenkung; *aero* Versetzung *f*; **~ionism** [di:vi'eiʃənizm] *pol* Mangel *m* an Linientreue; **~ionist** [di:vi'eiʃənist] *pol* Abtrünnige(r), Spalter *m*.

device [di'vais] Absicht *f*, Vorhaben *n*; Plan *m*, Schema *n*, Entwurf; Kunstgriff, Trick *m*; *tech* Vorrichtung, Erfindung *f*, Ding, Gerät *n*; Zeichnung *f*, Muster, Ornament; Sinnbild, Wappen *n*; Wahlspruch *m*, Motto *n*, Devise *f*; *to leave s.o. to his own ~s* jdn sich selbst überlassen.

devil ['devl] *s* Satan; Teufel *a. fig*; böse(r) Geist, Teufelskerl *m*; verteufelte Angelegenheit, dumme Sache *f*; Handlanger, *jur* Anwaltsgehilfe *m*; Würzfleisch *n*; *tech* Wolf *m*; *the D~* der Teufel; *tr* mit viel Gewürz zubereiten; *(im Wolf)* zerreißen; *Am fam* belästigen, behelligen, ärgern, necken; *itr* (als) Anwaltsgehilfe (tätig) sein; Handlangerdienste tun (*for* für);

between the ~ and the deep sea in der Klemme; *like the ~* wie ein Wilder, Verrückter, Kümmeltürke; *to give the ~ his due* jdm sein Recht werden lassen; *to go to the ~ (sl)* vor die Hunde gehen, versumpfen; *to play the ~ with (fam)* Schindluder treiben mit; auf die Palme bringen; *to raise the ~, to talk of the ~ (fig)* den Teufel an die Wand malen; *the ~! (fam)* zum Teufel! *go to the ~* geh, scher dich zum Teufel! *that's the ~* das ist ärgerlich, dumm; *blue ~s (fig)* Bedrücktheit *f*; *printer's ~* Laufjunge, -bursche *m* in e-r Druckerei; *the ~ of* ein(e) verdammte(r), tolle(r); *the ~ a one* nicht einer; *the ~ to pay* das dicke Ende (, das hinterherkommt); **~-fish** *zoo* Seeteufel *m*; **~ish** ['-iʃ] *a* teuflisch, satanisch; niederträchtig, gemein; *adv fam* verdammt, mächtig, sehr; **~-may-care** *a* rücksichtslos; sorglos, unbekümmert; draufgängerisch, verwegen, burschikos; **~ment** [-mənt] Teufelei; Gehässigkeit *f*; **~(t)ry** ['-(t)ri] Teufelswerk *n*; Teufelei, Niederträchtigkeit, Gemeinheit; Rücksichtslosigkeit *f*; Übermut *m*.

devious ['di:vjəs] vom (geraden) Wege abweichend, indirekt, gewunden, weitschweifig; irrig, unrichtig, falsch; unrechtmäßig; *(Mensch)* zwielichtig, unaufrichtig; *by ~ ways (fig)* auf krummen Wegen, (auf) unrechtmäßig(e Weise); auf Abwegen; **~ step** Fehltritt *m*.

devis|able [di'vaizəbl] erdenkbar; *jur* vererbbar; **~e** [di'vaiz] *tr* aus-, erdenken, ersinnen; planen; erfinden; zuwege bringen, bewerkstelligen; *jur (Grundbesitz)* vermachen; *s* letztwillige Verfügung *f* über Grundbesitz; **~ee** [devi'zi:, divai'zi:] Erbe, Legatar, Vermächtnisnehmer *m*; **~er** [di'vaizə] Erfinder *m*; **~or** [devi'zɔ:, divai'zɔ:, -'vaizɔ:] Erblasser *m*.

devitalize [di:'vaitəlaiz] *tr* abtöten; schwächen, entkräften, erschöpfen.

devoid [di'vɔid]: *~ of* (völlig) ohne; entblößt von; frei, leer von; ohne, bar... *~ of fear* furchtlos, unerschrocken; *~ of sense* dumm, töricht.

devol|ution [di:və'lu:ʃən] *fig* Ab-, Verlauf; *jur* Heimfall; Erbfall, -gang; Übergang *m*, Übertragung; *parl* Überweisung; Dezentralisation *f* der Verwaltung; *biol* Entartung *f*; **~ve** [di'vɔlv] *tr* übertragen, abwälzen (*on* auf); *itr* übergehen (*to, (up)on* auf); zufallen (*upon s.o.* jdm).

Devonian [de'vounjən] *s geol* Devon *n*; *a* Devon-.

devot|e [di'vout] *tr* widmen, weihen, hingeben, opfern; **~ed** [-id] *a* geweiht, gewidmet; voller Hingabe (*to* an), ergeben, treu; *to be ~~ to s.o.* sehr an jdm hängen; **~ee** [divo(u)'ti:] (leidenschaftlicher) Verehrer, treue(r) Anhänger; tiefreligiöse(r) Mensch; religiöse(r) Eiferer, Fanatiker *m*; **~ion** [di'vouʃən] Weihe; Hingebung (*to* an); Hingabe, Ergebenheit (*for* für); Treue (*to* zu); Frömmigkeit *f*; religiöse(r) Eifer *m*; religiöse Verehrung *f*; *pl* Gebete *n pl*, Andacht *f*; **~ional** [-ʃən(ə)l] *a* andächtig, fromm; Andachts-, Gebets-.

devour [di'vauə] *tr* ver-, hinunterschlingen; *fig (mit den Augen, Buch)* verschlingen; *fig* völlig in Anspruch nehmen; vernichten, zerstören; *(Feuer)* verzehren; *to be ~ed by* erfüllt sein von; **~ing** [-riŋ] *fig* verzehrend.

devout [di'vaut] fromm, religiös, andächtig; ehrfürchtig; ernst(haft), aufrichtig, echt, tiefempfunden, innig, herzlich; **~ness** [-nis] Frömmigkeit, Religiosität; Innigkeit *f*.

dew [dju:] *s* Tau *m a. fig*; *tr* betauen; *allg* be-, anfeuchten; *wet with ~* feucht von Tau; **~-berry** *bot* Gemeine Kratzbeere *f*; **~-claw** *(Hund)* Afterklaue *f*; **~-drop** Tautropfen *m*; **~-fall** Taubildung *f*; **~-lap** *zoo* Wamme *f*; **~-point** *mete* Taupunkt *m*; **~-worm** Regenwurm *m*; **~y** ['-i] taufeucht, -frisch; glänzend; erfrischend.

dext|erity [deks'teriti] Geschicklichkeit, Gewandtheit *a. fig*; Fertigkeit, Übung; (geistige) Beweglichkeit, Klugheit *f*; **~(e)rous** ['dekst(ə)rəs] geschickt, gewandt; (geistig) beweglich; klug (*in doing s.th.* wenn er etw tut).

dextr|in(e) ['dekstrin] Dextrin *n*, (Klebe-)Stärke *f*; **~ose** ['-ous] Traubenzucker *m*, Dextrose *f*.

diabet|es [daiə'bi:ti(:)z] *med* Zuckerkrankheit, -harnruhr *f*; **~ic** [-ik, -'betik] *a* zuckerkrank; *med* Zucker-; *s* Diabetiker, Zuckerkranke(r) *m*.

diabol|ic(al) [daiə'bɔlik(əl)] teuflisch, satanisch, **~ism** [dai'æbəlizm] Teufelsglaube *m*, -unwesen *n*.

diaconal [dai'ækənl] *a rel* Diakons-, Diakonen-; **~ate** [dai'ækənit, -eit] Diakonat *n*.

diacritic [daiə'kritik] *a* diakritisch; *(Geist)* scharf, durchdringend; *med* diagnostisch; *s gram* diakritische(s), Unterscheidungszeichen *n*; **~al** [-əl] unterscheidend; Unterscheidungs-; *~~ mark* Unterscheidungszeichen *n*.

diadem ['daiədem] Diadem *n*; Krone *f*; Blütenkranz *m*; *fig* Herrschaft, Hoheit, Würde *f*.

diagnos|e [daiəg'nouz, 'daiə-] *tr med* diagnostizieren; **~is** [-'nousis] *pl -es* Diagnose *f*; **~tic** [-'nɔstik] *a* diagnostisch; *s* Diagnose *f*; Symptom *n*; *pl mit sing* Diagnostik *f*; **~tician** [-nɔs'tiʃən] Diagnostiker *m*.

diagonal [dai'ægənl] *a* diagonal; schräg; quer; *s math* Diagonale *f*; *(~ cloth)* diagonal gestreifte(r) Stoff *m*.

diagram ['daiəgræm] *s* graphische Darstellung *f*, Schaubild, Diagramm *n*; Übersichtsskizze *f*, Schema *n*, Plan *m*, Zeichnung *f*; *tr* graphisch, schematisch darstellen; skizzieren; **~matic (-al)** [daiəgrə'mætik(əl)] graphisch; schematisch; skizzenhaft; *~~ layout, view* schematische Darstellung *f*.

dial ['daiəl] *s (sun~)* Sonnenuhr *f*; *(~-plate)* Zifferblatt *n*, Skalen-, Nummernscheibe; *(Kompaß)* Rose; *tech* Zeigerplatte, Skalen-, Einstell-, Wähl-, Drehscheibe; *radio* Rundskala; *sl* Fresse *f*, Gesicht *n*; *tr tele* drehen, wählen; *radio* einstellen, abstimmen; **~ illumination** Skalenbeleuchtung *f*; **~ knob** Schaltknopf *m*; **~(l)ling** *tele* Wählen *n* der Nummer; **~ pointer** Skalenzeiger *m*; **~ reading** Skalenablesung *f*; **~-tone** *tele* Amtszeichen *n*.

dialect ['daiəlekt] Dialekt *m*, Mundart *f*; **~al** [-'lektəl] mundartlich; Dialekt-; **~ic(al)** [-'lektik(əl)] *philos* dialektisch; mundartlich; **~ic(s** *pl*) [-lektik(s)] *philos* Dialektik *f*; **~ician** [-'tiʃən] *philos* Dialektiker *m*.

dialogue, *Am a.* **dialog** ['daiəlɔg] Unterhaltung *f*, Gespräch *n*; Wechselrede *f*; *lit* Dialog *m*.

dia|meter [dai'æmitə] Durchmesser *m*; Dicke, Stärke *f*; **~metric(al)** [-æ'metrik(əl)] diametral; genau entgegengesetzt.

diamond ['daiəmənd] *s* Diamant; *(glazier's, cutting ~)* Glaserdiamant; glitzernde(r) Punkt; *math* Rhombus *m*; *(Spielkarten)* Karo *n*, Schellen *n od f pl*; *typ* Diamant *f (Schriftgrad)*; *(Baseball)* (Innen-)Spielfeld *n*; *a* diamanten, mit Diamanten besetzt; *tr* mit Diamanten besetzen; *~ cut ~* es gibt keiner dem andern etw nach; *rough ~* ungeschliffene(r) Diamant; *fig* Mensch *m* mit gutem Kern in rauher Schale; **~-anniversary, -jubilee** 60jährige(s) Jubiläum *n*; **~-cutter** Diamantschleifer *m*; **~-dust** Diamantstaub *m*; **~-point** Diamantspitze; *rail* Kreuzungsweiche *f*; **~-shaped** *a* rautenförmig; **~-stylus** Saphir *m* (e-s Grammophons); **~-wedding** diamantene Hochzeit *f*.

diapason [daiə'peisn] Umfang *(e-s Musikinstrumentes)*, Stimmumfang *m*; Melodie; *(Orgel)* Mensur *f*; Kammerton *m*; Stimmgabel, -pfeife *f*; *normal ~* Pariser Kammerton *m*.

diaper ['daiəpə] *s* (Handtuch *n od* Serviette *f* aus) rautenförmig gemusterte(r) Leinwand *od* Baumwolle *f*; Rautenmuster *n*; Windel *f*; *tr* rautenförmig mustern; *(Kind)* trockenlegen, wickeln.

dia|phanous [dai'æfənəs] durchscheinend, -sichtig; **~phoretic** [-æfə'retik] schweißtreibend(es Mittel *n*).

diaphragm ['daiəfræm, -frəm] *anat* Zwerchfell *n*; *allg* Trennwand; *phys tele* Membran; *phot* Blende *f*; Pessar *n*, Mutterring *m*; **~ setting** Blendeneinstellung *f*.

diar|ist ['daiərist] Tagebuchschreiber *m*; **~ize** ['-raiz] *itr* Tagebuch führen; *tr* ins Tagebuch eintragen; **~y** ['-ri] Tagebuch *a. com*; *com* Journal *n*, Agenda *f*; *(pocket) ~~* Taschenkalender *m*; *travel(l)ing ~~* Reisetagebuch *n*.

diarrh(o)ea [daiə'riə] *med* Durchfall *m*.

dia|stole [dai'æstəli] *physiol* Ausdehnung *f* des Herzens; **~thermy** [-ə'θə:mi] *med* Diathermie *f*; **~thesis** [-'æθisis] Diathese; **~tom** ['daiətəm, -tɔm] *bot* Kieselalge, Diatomee *f*; **~tonic** [-ə'tɔnik] *mus* diatonisch; **~tribe** ['daiətraib] Schmähung, Verleumdung; heftige Kritik (*on* an); Schmähschrift *f*.

dib [dib] Spielmarke *f*; *pl* Kinderspiel *n* mit Kieselsteinen *od* Knöchelchen; *pl sl* Moos, Geld *n*.

dibble ['dibl] *s* Pflanz-, Setzholz *n*; *tr itr* (junge Pflanzen) setzen, stecken.

dice [dais] *s pl (sing: die)* Würfel *m pl*, *(als sing gebraucht)* Würfelspiel *n*; *itr* würfeln, *fam* knobeln; *tr* verspielen; in Würfel schneiden; würfeln, karieren, schachbrettartig mustern; **~-box** Würfel-, *fam* Knobelbecher *m*; **~r** ['ə] Würfelspieler *m*; *sl* Melone *f (Hut)*; **~y** ['-i] *fam* riskant.

dich|otomy [di'kɔtəmi] *bot zoo* Zweiteilung, Gabelung *f*; *fig* Zwiespalt *m*; **~romatic** [daikro(u)'mætik] zweifarbig.

dick [dik] Bursche, Kerl; *Am sl* Detektiv, Schupo *m*; *to take o.'s ~ (sl)* steif u. fest, felsenfest behaupten.

dickens ['dikinz] *fam* Teufel *m*; *what the ~!* was zum Teufel!

dicker ['dikə] *s* zehn (Stück) *(bes. Häute)*; *Am* (Tausch-)Handel *m*; *sl* Wörterbuch *n*; *itr Am* handeln, schachern; (Tausch-)Handel treiben.

dick(e)y ['diki] *s fam* Esel *m*; *(~-bird)* Vöglein, Vögelchen *n*; Hemdbrust *f*; (Blusen-)Einsatz *m*; Lätzchen *n*; Schürze *f*; *(~box)* Kutschbock; Bedientensitz; *mot* Notsitz *m*; *a sl (dicky)* kränklich; *fig* wackelig.

dicotyledon ['daikɔti'li:dən] *bot* Dikotyledone *f*, Blattkeimer *m*.

dictaphone ['diktəfoun] Diktaphon *n*.

dictat|e [dik'teit] *tr (Text, Worte)* diktieren; ausdrücklich befehlen, vorschreiben, auferlegen; *itr* diktieren; befehlen; *s* ['dikteit] Diktat *n*, Befehl *m*, Gebot *n*, Vorschrift, (strikte) Anordnung, Anweisung *f*; **~ion** [-'teiʃən] Diktat *n*; Herumkommandieren *n*; (Erteilung *f* e-s) Befehl(s) *m*, (Erlaß *m* e-r) Vorschrift, (Geben *n* e-r) Anordnung *f*; *to take a* ~~ ein Diktat aufnehmen; *to write at s.o.'s* ~~ nach jds Diktat schreiben; **~or** [-'teitə] Diktator *m*; **~orial** [-tə'tɔriəl] diktatorisch, autoritär, autoritativ, gebieterisch, befehlend; ~~ *power* diktatorische Gewalt *f*; **~orship** [-'teitəʃip] Diktatur *f*.

diction ['dikʃən] Ausdruck(sweise *f*) *m*, Redeweise *f*, Stil *m*, Sprachform, Sprache *f*; *poetic* ~ dichterische Sprache *f*; **~ary** [-(ə)ri, *Am* -nɛəri] Wörterbuch, Lexikon *n*; *pocket* ~~ Taschenwörterbuch *n*.

dictum ['diktəm] *pl a. -ta* [-tə] (Aus-)Spruch *m*; Redensart; amtliche Verlautbarung; *jur* richterliche Feststellung *f*.

didactic|(al) [di'dæktik(əl)] *a* belehrend, unterrichtend, didaktisch; Lehr-, Unterrichts-; lehrhaft *a. pej*; *pej* schulmeisterlich, pedantisch; *s pl mit sing* Didaktik *f*.

diddle ['didl] *fam itr* schwindeln; *Am sl* zappeln; *tr* beschwindeln, anführen; *(Menschen)* ruinieren; *(Zeit)* verplempern, vertrödeln.

dido ['daidou] *Am fam* (übler) Streich *m*, Posse(n *m*) *f*, Trick *m*.

didy, didie ['daidi] *Am fam* Windel *f*.

die [dai] **1.** *itr ppr dying, pret, pp died* sterben (*of* an; *from, of, through* an, durch; *by* durch; *with, of* vor; *for* für, um ... willen); versterben, verscheiden, das Zeitliche segnen; sein Leben lassen *od* hingeben (*for* für); dahinschwinden, nachlassen, schwächer werden, vergehen; verwelken, verdorren, absterben; erlöschen, eingehen; zu Ende gehen, aufhören, untergehen; gleichgültig werden (*to s.o.* jdm); *fam* den sehnlichen Wunsch haben (*to* zu); vor Sehnsucht vergehen, verschmachten (*for* nach); *fam* vergehen, umkommen (*of, for* vor); *rel (geistig)* sterben; *(Motor)* absterben; *to* ~ *in o.'s bed* e-s natürlichen Todes sterben; *to* ~ *a beggar* als Bettler sterben; *to* ~ *in o.'s boots, shoes* e-s gewaltsamen Todes sterben; *to* ~ *a dog's death* wie ein Hund krepieren; *to* ~ *in the last ditch* nach verzweifelter Gegenwehr fallen; *to* ~ *game* im Kampf fallen; *to* ~ *hard* sich bis zum äußersten wehren; ein zähes Leben haben; *to* ~ *in harness (fig)* in den Sielen sterben; *to* ~ *(of) laughing, with laughter* sich totlachen (wollen), sich biegen vor Lachen; *to* ~ *young* jung sterben; *never say* ~*!* nur nicht verzweifeln! nicht unterkriegen lassen! *I'm dying to* ich brenne darauf, zu; ich möchte furchtbar gern; *to* ~ **away** nachlassen, schwächer werden, (ver)schwinden, vergehen, verhallen; *to* ~ **back** *(Pflanze)* absterben, verdorren, (ver)welken; *to* ~ **down** schwächer werden, allmählich erlöschen, nachlassen; *(Pflanze)* absterben; *(Feuer)* verlöschen, ausgehen; *(Aufregung)* sich legen; *to* ~ **off** weg-, aus-, einer nach dem andern sterben; *to* ~ **out** aussterben, erlöschen; **~-away** *a* schmachtend, sehnsuchtsvoll; **~-hard** zähe(r), *fig* verbissene(r), hartnäckige(r) Mensch; zähe(r), unnachgiebige(r) Politiker; *pol* Unentwegte(r), Extremist; Konservative(r) *m*; **2.** *s pl dice* Würfel *m (bes. zum Spielen)*; *pl dies arch* Platte *f*; *tech* (Präg-)Stempel *m*; Kokille; Schneidbacke; Prägeplatte; Matrize; Gußform *f*; Gesenk *n*; *tr (ppr dieing)* stempeln, formen, schneiden; *to be upon the* ~ auf dem Spiel stehen; *the* ~ *is cast* die Würfel sind gefallen, die Sache ist entschieden; *straight as a* ~ kerzengerade; ~ **casting** *tech* Kokillen-, Spritzguß *m*; ~ **steel** Werkzeugstahl *m*.

dielectric [daii'lektrik] *a el* dielektrisch, isolierend; *s* Dielektrikum *n*; ~ **resistance** Isolationswiderstand *m*; ~ **strength** Durchschlagsfestigkeit *f*; ~ **test** Spannungsprüfung *f*.

Diesel ['di:zəl]: ~ **engine, motor** Dieselmotor *m*; ~ **fuel** Dieselkraftstoff *m*; ~ **locomotive** Diesellokomotive *f*; ~ **oil** Schwer-, Dieselöl *n*; ~ **tractor** Dieselschlepper *m*.

diet ['daiət] **1.** *s* Speise, Kost, Nahrung, Ernährung(sweise); (geregelte) Lebensweise; Diät, Kranken-, Schonkost *f*; Heilfasten *n*; *itr* diät leben; *tr* auf Diät setzen; *to keep to a strict* ~ strenge Diät einhalten; *he is on a* ~ er lebt diät; **2.** Versammlung, Konferenz *f*, Konvent *m*, Tagung *f*; Parlament *n*, Land-, Bundes-, Reichstag *m*; **~ary** ['-əri] *s* Diät, geregelte Lebensweise *f*; Diätzettel *m*, -vorschrift *f*; Tagessatz *m*, Ration *f*; Speisezettel *m*; *a u.* **~etic(al)** [daii'tetik(əl)] diätetisch, Diät-; **~etics** [daii'tetiks] *pl mit sing* Ernährungswissenschaft, Diätetik *f*; **~itian, ~ician** [daii'tiʃən] Diätfachmann; Diätkoch *m*, -köchin; Diätschwester *f*; ~ **kitchen** Diätküche *f*.

differ ['difə] *itr* verschieden sein (*in* in); sich unterscheiden, abweichen (*from* von); sich widersprechen; verschiedener, entgegengesetzter Meinung sein (*on* über; *from, with* als); nicht übereinstimmen (*with* mit); ausea.gehen; (sich) streiten; *to agree to* ~ bei s-r Meinung bleiben; *I beg to* ~ Verzeihung, da bin ich anderer Ansicht; **~ence** ['difrəns] Unterschied *m*, Differenz *a. math*; Verschiedenheit, Unterschiedlichkeit *f*; Unterscheidungsmerkmal *n*; Meinungsverschiedenheit *f*; Streit, Konflikt *m*; *with the* ~~ *that* mit dem Unterschied, daß; *to make a* ~~ e-n Unterschied machen (*between* zwischen); *to make up, to settle a* ~~ e-n Streit beilegen *od* schlichten; *to split the* ~~ den Rest teilen; e-n Kompromiß schließen; *I can't see much* ~~ ich sehe keinen großen Unterschied; *it's the same* ~~ *(Am)* das ist Jacke wie Hose; *it won't make much* ~~, *whether* es macht keinen großen Unterschied, nicht viel aus, ob; *does it make any* ~~ *if* macht es was aus, wenn; *what's the* ~~*? (fam)* was macht das schon? ~~ *in age* Altersunterschied *m*; ~~ *of opinion* Meinungsverschiedenheit *f*; ~~ *in price* Preisunterschied *m*; **~ent** ['-rənt] ander, anders (*from, to, (obs u. Am) than* als), verschieden (*from, to, (obs u. Am) than* von); mannigfach, -faltig; andersartig; *fam* nicht alltäglich, ungewöhnlich; *in a* ~~ *way than* anders als; **~ential** [-'renʃəl] *a* unterschiedlich, verschieden; gestaffelt; differenziert; unterscheidend, Unterscheidungs-; *math tech* Differential-; *s math* Differential; *(*~~ *gear) mot* Differential-, Ausgleichsgetriebe *n*; ~~ *calculus, coefficient* od *quotient, equation (math)* Differentialrechnung *f*, -quotient *m*, -gleichung *f*; ~~ *connection* Differentialschaltung *f*; ~~ *cost* Grenzkosten *pl*; ~~ *price* Preisspanne *f*; ~~ *tariff* Differential-, Staffeltarif *m*; **~entiate** [-'renʃieit] *tr* verschieden, anders machen *od* gestalten; differenzieren *a. math*; unterscheiden (*from* von); *itr* sich unterscheiden, abweichen; sich verschieden, anders (weiter)entwickeln, sich entfernen (*from* von); **~entiation** [-renʃi'eiʃən] Differenzierung, Abstufung; Unterscheidung, Abweichung; *biol* getrennte, abweichende Entwick(e)lung *f*; *math* Differenzieren *n*.

difficult ['difikəlt] schwer, schwierig *(zu tun)*; *(Mensch)* schwierig, anspruchsvoll, nicht leicht zu befriedigen(d), zu lenken(d); eigensinnig; *(Lage)* schwierig, heikel; ~ *of access* schwer zugänglich; **~y** ['-i] Schwierigkeit (*in walking* beim Gehen); schwierige Angelegenheit, Verlegenheit; *pl* Notlage *f*; *with* ~~ mit Mühe; *without much* ~~ unschwer, leicht *adv*; *to be in* ~*ies* Schwierigkeiten haben; in Verlegenheit, in Geldnöten sein; *to bridge, to overcome, to surmount* ~*ies* Schwierigkeiten überwinden; *to make* ~*ies* Schwierigkeiten machen *od* bereiten; Einwände erheben; *to work under* ~*ies* unter schwierigen Umständen arbeiten.

diffiden|ce ['difidəns] Mangel *m* an Selbstvertrauen (*in* zu); Schüchternheit, (zu große) Bescheidenheit *f* (*in doing* zu tun); **~t** [-t] ohne Selbstvertrauen; zaghaft, schüchtern, (zu) bescheiden; *to be* ~~ kein Selbstvertrauen haben (*about doing s.th.* etw zu tun).

diffract [di'frækt] *tr* zerbrechen; *(Licht)* zerlegen, brechen, beugen; **~ion** [-kʃən] *phys* Farbenzerstreuung, Dispersion; Zerlegung, Beugung, Brechung *f*.

diffus|e [di'fju:z] *tr* ausgießen; aus-, ver-, zerstreuen; aus-, verbreiten; *phys chem* mischen; *itr* sich zerstreuen, sich aus-, verbreiten; diffundieren (*through* durch; *to* nach); weitschweifig reden; *a* [-s] weitschweifig, langatmig, wortreich; unscharf, diffus; wirr; **~eness** [-snis] Weitschweifigkeit *f*; **~ion** [-ʒən] Zerstreuung, Aus-, Verbreitung; *phys chem* Mischung, gegenseitige Durchdringung; *opt* Diffusion; Streuung, Unschärfe *f*; Wortreichtum *m*, Weitschweifigkeit, Langatmigkeit; *fig* Zersplitterung *f (der Kräfte)*; **~ive** [-siv] sich aus-, verbreitend; zerstreut, ausgebreitet, verbreitet; diffundierend; streuend; weitschweifig, langatmig.

dig [dig] *irr dug, dug tr* (aus-, um)graben, (durch-, um)wühlen; *(Graben)* ausheben; ernten (*potatoes* Kartoffeln); stoßen, drücken, bohren, wühlen; puffen, knuffen, stoßen, schubsen; *fig* stöbern, suchen nach, heraussuchen; herausarbeiten; herausbekommen, *fam* -kriegen, ausfindig machen, aufdecken; *sl* kapieren, begreifen, verstehen; *sl* verhohnepipeln; *sl* bemerken, (gespannt) zuhören (*s. th.* dat); *itr* graben, wühlen; *min* schürfen, muten; ein Loch machen (*into* in); stöbern, suchen (*for* nach); *fam* wohnen, hausen; *Am* schuften, pauken, ochsen, büffeln; *to* ~ *s.o. the most (fam)* sich mit jdm glänzend verstehen; *s* Graben, Wühlen *n*; *fam* Puff, Stoß; *Am sl* Büffler; *fam* (Seiten-)Hieb (*at* auf), Stich *m*, bissige, boshafte Bemerkung (*at* gegen); *Am sl* Büffler *m*; *pl fam Br* Bude *f*, möblierte(s) Zimmer *n*; ~ *in the ribs* Rippenstoß *m*; *to* ~ **in** ein-, vergraben; *Am fam* schuften; *(Dünger)* untergraben; *(beim Essen)* zugreifen, zulangen; *mil (to* ~ *o.s. in)* sich eingraben, sich verschanzen; *fig* sich vergraben in; *to* ~ **into** eindringen in; *fig fam* sich hineinwühlen, sich hineinarbeiten in; *to* ~ **out** ausgraben; herausbekommen, aufdecken; *to* ~ **up** um-, ausgraben *a. fig*; aufstöbern, aufdecken, ausfindig machen, herausbekommen.

digest [di-, dai'dʒest] *tr* verdauen; *chem* digerieren, auslaugen -ziehen; *fig*, ganz, völlig durchdenken, geistig verarbeiten, in sich aufnehmen; ertragen, aushalten, verwinden, hinnehmen; ordnen, (systematisch) zs.fassen; *itr* verdauen; sich verdauen lassen; die Verdauung fördern; *chem* sich auflösen; *s* ['daidʒest] Zs.fassung *f*, Abriß *m*; Besprechung; Zs.stellung, Übersicht, Synopse *f*; Kompendium *n*; Sammlung *f* von Gerichtsentscheidungen; *the D~(s pl)* die Digesten, die Pandekten *pl*; **~ible** [-ibl] (leicht)verdaulich; **~ion** [-ʃən] Verdauung; *chem* Digestion; Aufnahme *(e-s Gedankens)*, (geistige) Verarbeitung *f*; *easy of ~~* leichtverdaulich; **~ive** [-iv] *a* Verdauungs-; auslaugend, digestiv; *a s* verdauungsfördernd(es Mittel *n*); *~~ tract* Verdauungsapparat *m*; *~~ trouble* Verdauungsstörungen *f pl*.

digg|er ['digə] Gräber *m*; Grabwerkzeug *n*; Bagger *m*; *(~~ wasp) zoo* Grabwespe *f*; *Am sl* Taschendieb; *sl* Kumpan; *sl* Australier *m*; *gold-~~* Goldgräber *m*; **~ings** ['-iŋz] *pl* Ausgegrabene(s) *n*, Bodenfunde *m pl*; Grabungsstelle *f*; Erdarbeiten *f pl*; (*bes.* Gold-)Mine *f*, Bergwerk *n (oft mit sing)*; *sl* Hütte, Bude *f*, Bau *m*.

digit ['didʒit] Finger *m*, Zehe; Fingerbreite; Dezimalstelle, Ziffer *f*, Einer; astronomische(r) Zoll *m* ($^1/_{12}$ *Sonnen- od Monddurchmesser)*; **~al** ['-l] *a* Finger-; mit Fingern versehen; fingerartig; *s* Finger *m*; Taste *f*; *~~ computer* Ziffernrechner *m*; **~alis** [-'teilis] *bot* Fingerhut *m*; *pharm* Digitalis *f*; **~ate** ['-it, '-eit], **ated** ['-eitid] *a zoo* mit Fingern *od* Zehen versehen; fingerartig; *bot* fingerförmig (geteilt); **~igrade** ['-igreid] *s zoo* Zehengänger *m*; *a* auf (den) Zehen gehend.

dignif|ied ['dignifaid] *a* würdig; würdevoll, erhaben; stattlich, ansehnlich; **~y** ['-ai] *tr* mit e-r Würde bekleiden, auszeichnen, ehren; e-n hochtrabenden Namen geben (*s.th.* e-r S); herausstreichen, beschönigen; *fam* schmükken, verzieren, verschönern (*with* mit).

dignit|ary ['dignitəri] (*bes.* kirchlicher) Würdenträger *m*; **~y** ['-i] Würde *f*, hohe(r) Rang; Adel *m*, Erhabenheit *f*; würdevolle(s) Auftreten *n*; *beneath s.o.'s ~~* unter jds Würde; *to stand (up)on o.'s ~~* sich nichts vergeben.

digress [dai-, di'gres] *itr (vom Thema, in der Rede)* abschweifen (*from* von; *into* in); **~ion** [-ʃən] Abschweifung *f*; **~ive** [-iv] ausweichend, abschweifend.

dihedral [dai'hi:drəl] zweiseitig, diedrisch; V-förmig; **~ angle** V-Winkel *m*.

dike [daik] *s* (Wasser-)Graben; Deich; Damm; *(niedriger)* (Erd-, Stein-) Wall *m*; Schranke *f*, Hindernis *n*; *geol* Ader *f*, Gangstock *m*; *tr* eindeichen, -dämmen; **~-reeve** Deichgraf *m*.

dilapidat|e [di'læpideit] *tr itr* verfallen, baufällig werden (lassen); herunterkommen (lassen); einreißen; *tr fig* zerrütten, vergeuden; **~ed** [-id] *a* (halb) verfallen, baufällig; **~ion** [-'deiʃən] Verfall *m*; Baufälligkeit; *fig* Zerrüttung, Vergeudung *f (e-s Vermögens)*.

dilat|ability [daileitə'biliti, di-] Dehnbarkeit *f*; **~able** [dai'leitəbl] dehnbar; **~ation** [dailei'teiʃən, -lət-] (Aus-) Weitung, Erweiterung, (Aus-)Dehnung, (An-)Schwellung; *med* Erweiterung *f*; *cardiac ~~* Herzerweiterung *f*; **~e** [dai'leit, di-] *tr* weiten, erweitern, weiter machen, (aus)dehnen; *itr* sich weiten, sich erweitern, weiter werden; sich (aus)dehnen, (an)schwellen; weitläufig reden, sich weitläufig verbreiten, viel sagen *od* schreiben (*upon, on* über); **~ed** [dai'leitid] *a med* aufgetrieben; **~ion** [dai'leiʃən, di-] = *~ation*; **~or** [dai'leitə] Ausweiter; *anat* Dilatator *m (Dehnmuskel)*; *med* Erweiterungssonde *f*.

dilator|iness ['dilətərinis] Säumigkeit, Saumseligkeit, Langsamkeit *f*; **~y** ['-i] hinhaltend, dilatorisch, verzögernd, aufschiebend; säumig, saumselig.

dilemma [di'lemə, dai-] Dilemma *n*, Zwangslage, Verlegenheit, *fam* Klemme *f*; *on the horns of a ~* in der Klemme, vor e-r schwierigen Entscheidung.

dilettant|e [dili'tænti] *pl a.* *-i* [-i:] *s* (Kunst-)Liebhaber; Dilettant, Stümper *m*; *a u.* **~ish** [-iʃ] dilettantisch; stümperhaft; **~ism** [-izm] Dilettantismus *m*; Stümperei *f*.

diligen|ce ['dilidʒəns] Fleiß *m*; Sorgfalt, -samkeit, Gewissenhaftigkeit; Beharrlichkeit *f*; dauernde Bemühungen *f pl*; *hist* Postkutsche *f*; **~t** ['-ənt] fleißig, sorgfältig, -sam, emsig; gewissenhaft.

dill [dil] *bot* Dill *m*; **~ pickle** (mit Dill gewürzte) saure Gurke *f*.

dilly [dili] *Am sl* Pfundssache; Schönheit *f*, Star *m*; **~-dally** ['dilidæli] *itr fam* (herum)trödeln, bummeln, zögern.

diluent ['diljuənt] *a s* verdünnend(es), auflösend(es Mittel *n*).

dilut|e [dai'l(j)u:t, di-] *tr* verdünnen (*to* auf); verwässern *a. fig*; *fig* abschwächen, verringern, mildern; *a u.* **~ed** [-id] *a* verdünnt; verwässert *a. fig*; *(Farbe)* abgestumpft; *fig* abgeschwächt, verringert; **~ee** [-'ti:] Aushilfe *f*; angelernte(r) Arbeiter *m*; **~ion** [dai'l(j)u:ʃən, di-] Verdünnung; Verwässerung *a. fig*; *fig* Abschwächung, Verringerung *f*.

diluvi|al [dai'l(j)u:viəl, di-], **~an** [-ən] *a* (Sint-)Flut-; *geol* diluvial; **~um** [-əm] *geol* Diluvium *n*.

dim [dim] *a* trübe, matt; düster; *(Licht, Augen, Sehkraft)* schwach; undeutlich, verschwommen; *(Erinnerung)* blaß, dunkel, unklar; *fam fig* schwer von Begriff; *fig* blaß; *itr* trübe, dunkel, undeutlich, *(Licht)* schwächer werden; *tr* trüben; verdunkeln; *(Licht)* abblenden; *(Scheibe)* sich beschlagen; *to ~ o.'s lights (mot)* abblenden; *to take a ~ view of s.th.* in e-r S (sehr) schwarzsehen; pessimistisch, skeptisch sein; **~mer** ['-ə] Abblendschalter *m*, -vorrichtung *f*; **~ness** ['-nis] Mattheit; Undeutlichkeit, Verschwommenheit; Dunkelheit *f*; **~-out** *Am* Teilverdunkelung *f*; **~wit** ['-wit] *sl* Dussel, Depp *m*; **~witted** *a sl* doof, blöd(e).

dime [daim] *Am* Zehncentstück *n*; *attr* Spar-, billig; *a ~ a dozen (fam)* in rauhen Mengen, massenhaft; (spott-) billig; **~ edition** billige, Taschenbuch-Ausgabe *f*; **~ novel** (billiger) Schundroman *m*; **~ store** Einheitspreisgeschäft *n*.

dimension [di'menʃən, dai-] *s* Dimension *a. math*, Abmessung; Ausdehnung *f*, Umfang *m*, Größe *f*, Ausmaß *n*, Grad *m*; Bedeutung *f*; *pl* (Aus-)Maße *n pl*, Größe *f*; *tr* bemessen, dimensionieren; *of great ~s* von großen Dimensionen, sehr groß; **~al** [-l] ausgedehnt; dimensional; *three-~~* dreidimensional.

dimin|ish [di'miniʃ] *itr* sich vermindern, sich verringern; kleiner, weniger werden; abnehmen (*in* an); nachlassen; *tr* vermindern, verringern; kleiner machen, herabsetzen; *tr itr* *arch* (sich) verjüngen; **~ution** [-'nju:ʃən] Verminderung, Verringerung, Verkleinerung; Abnahme *f* (*in* an), Nachlassen *n*; *arch* Verjüngung *f*; **~utive** [di'minjutiv] *a* sehr klein, winzig; verkleinernd; *gram* Diminutiv-, Verkleinerungs-; *s* kleine(s) Kerlchen; winzige(s) Ding *n*; *gram* Verkleinerungsform *f*, Diminutivum *n*.

dimissory [di'misəri] *a* Entlassungs-.

dimity ['dimiti] geköperte(r) Barchent *m*.

dimpl|e ['dimpl] *s* Grübchen *n (in der Haut)*; flache Mulde *f (im Boden)*; *(Wasser)* Kräuseln *n*; kleine Welle *f*; *tr itr (Boden)* uneben machen, werden; *(Wasserfläche)* (sich) kräuseln; *itr* Grübchen bekommen; **~ed, ~y** ['-d, '-i] *a* mit flachen Vertiefungen, mit Grübchen.

din [din] *s* Lärm *m*, Getöse *n*, Tumult *m*; *tr fig* dauernd wiederholen, unausgesetzt vorpredigen, einhämmern, eintrichtern, einbleuen (*into s.o.* jdm); *itr* lärmen, tosen, toben; *(in den Ohren)* tönen, klingen; *to ~ s.th. into s.o.'s ears* jdm mit etw dauernd in den Ohren liegen; *to kick up a ~ (fam)* Krach schlagen.

din|e [dain] *itr* (zu) Mittag essen, speisen, dinieren; *(Gäste)* fassen; *tr* zum (Mittag-)Essen einladen, *(mit e-m Mittagessen)* bewirten; *to ~~ off, on s.th.* etw zu Mittag essen; *to ~~ out* außer (dem) Haus(e), auswärts (zu Mittag) essen; *to ~~ with Duke Humphrey* nichts zu essen haben; **~er** ['-ə] Mittags-, Tischgast; *Am rail* Speisewagen *m*; *Am* kleine(s) Speiselokal *n*; *~~-out* jem, der oft auswärts ißt *od* zum Essen eingeladen wird; Schmarotzer *m*; **~ette** [-'net] *Am* Eßnische, -ecke *f*; **~ing** ['-iŋ]: *~~-car (rail)* Speisewagen *m*; *~~-room* Eß-, Speisezimmer *n*; *~~-table* Eßtisch *m*.

ding [diŋ] *itr (Glocke)* schlagen, läuten; *fam* dauernd vorpredigen; *Am sl* betteln; *tr fam* einzureden suchen (*s.th. into s.o.* jdm etw); *Am sl (to ~ s.o.)* gegen jdn stimmen; *s* Glockenschlag *m*, -läuten *n*; **~bat** ['-bæt] *Am sl* Dingsda *n*, Vorrichtung *f*; Gegenstand; Bettler *m*; **~-dong** ['diŋ'dɔŋ] *interj* bimbam; *s* Bimmeln, Geläut, Läuten *n*; (dreieckiger) Gong *m*; *a fam (Kampf)* umstritten, heiß, mit wechselndem Glück; *adv* absichtlich; heftig; **~ how** *Am sl adv* in Ordnung.

dinghy, dingey, *a.* **dingy** ['diŋgi] Beiboot *n*; *collapsible ~* Faltboot *n*; *rubber ~* Schlauchboot *n*.

ding|iness ['dindʒinis] schmutzige(s) Farbe *f od* Aussehen *n*; **~y** ['-i] schmutzfarben, schmutzig(braun, -gelb), schmierig, trüb(e).

ding|le ['diŋgl] Waldtal *n*, *(baumbestandene)* Schlucht *f*; **~o** ['-ou] australische(r) Wildhund *m*; **~us** ['-əs] *Am sl* Dingsda *n*; (Herr) Soundso *m*.

dink|ey ['diŋki] *Am* Boot *n*; (Rangier-)Lokomotive *f*; kleine(r) Straßenbahnwagen *m*; **~um** ['-əm] *a (Australien)* zuverlässig, anständig; hübsch; *s* australische(r) Soldat *m*.

dinky ['diŋki] *a fam* hübsch, nett, süß, reizend, entzückend; *Am sl* puppig, klein; nebensächlich, unwichtig.

dinner ['dinə] (Mittag-, Abend-)Essen *n*, Hauptmahlzeit *f*; Diner; Festessen *n*; *after ~* nach Tisch; *at ~* beim (Mittag-) Essen, bei Tisch; *for ~* zum (Mittag-) Essen; *to ask to ~* zum (Mittag-)Essen einladen, zu Tisch laden; *~ is served* bitte, zu Tisch! **~-bell** Tischglocke *f*; **~ card** Tischkarte *f*; **~-dress** Nachmittags-, Cocktailkleid *n*; **~-hour,**

-time Essenszeit *f*; **~-jacket** Smoking *m*; **~-pail** *Am* Essenträger *(der Arbeiter)*, Eß-, *fam* Picknapf *m*; **~-party** Tisch-, Abendgesellschaft *f*; **~-service, -set,** *(Am)* **~-ware** Eßservice, Tafelgeschirr *n*; **~-suit** Gesellschaftsanzug *m*; **~-table** Eßtisch *m*; **~-wag(g)on** Tee-, Servierwagen *m*.

dinosaur ['dainəsɔ:] *zoo* Dinosaurier *m*.

dint [dint] *s* Druckstelle, Beule, Einkerbung, Kerbe *f*; *tr* eindrücken, einbeulen, (ein)kerben; *by ~ of* (ver)mittels, mit Hilfe, kraft *gen*, durch.

dioces|an [dai'ɔsisən] *a rel* Diözesan-; *s* (Diözesan-)Bischof *m*; **~e** ['daiəsi(:)s] Diözese *f*.

diode ['daioud] Diode, Zweipolröhre *f*; **~ detector, rectifier** Gleichrichterdiode *f*.

diopt|er [dai'ɔptə] *opt* Dioptrie *f*.

diorama [daiə'rɑ:mə] Diorama, Schaubild *n*, Guckkasten(bild *n*) *m*.

diorite ['daiərait] *geol* Diorit *m*.

dioxide [dai'ɔksaid] *chem* Dioxyd *n*; *carbon ~* Kohlendioxyd *n*.

dip [dip] *tr* (kurz) (ein-, unter)tauchen, (ein)tunken (*in* in); stecken (*into* in); durch Untertauchen taufen; *(Schafe)* in e-r desinfizierenden Flüssigkeit waschen; *(in e-m Farbbad)* färben; *(Kerzen)* ziehen; *(Fahne)* senken, *mar* dippen; galvanisieren; *mot (Licht)* abblenden; *(to ~ up)* schöpfen, heraus-, hervorholen; *fam* in Schulden stürzen; *itr* (kurz) (ein-, unter)tauchen; (plötzlich) fallen, (ab)stürzen, purzeln; *geol* einfallen; *(to ~ down)* sich neigen, sich senken; greifen (*into s.th.* in etw; *for s.th.* nach etw); herumstöbern, -suchen, *fam* -schnuppern (*into* in); durchblättern, flüchtig lesen (*into a book* ein Buch); *s* (Ein-, Unter-)Tauchen; Bad; (Wasser-, Farb-)Bad; Tauch-, Schöpfgerät *n*; gezogene Kerze *f*; flüchtige(r) Blick *m* (*into* in); *aero* Durchsacken *n*; Neigung; Senke, Mulde; *geol* Neigung(swinkel *m*) *f*; *min* Einfallen *n*; *phys* Inklination; *(Feldmessung, mar)* Kimmtiefe; *fam* Tunke, Soße *f*; *sl* Taschendieb *m*; *at the ~* auf Halbmast; *to have, to take, to go for a ~* baden gehen; *to ~ into o.'s savings* die Ersparnisse angreifen; *to ~ o.'s hand into o.'s purse* tief in die Tasche greifen, viel Geld ausgeben; **~per** ['-ə] Taucher *a. orn*; Wiedertäufer, Baptist; Färber; Schöpfer *(Arbeiter)*; Schöpflöffel *m*, -kelle *f*; *mot* Ölschöpfer; *mot* Abblendschalter *m*; *orn* Tauchente *f*; *the Big, Little D~~ (Am astr)* der Große, Kleine Bär; **~ping** ['-iŋ] *s* Eintauchen *n*; **~py** ['-i] *sl* plemplem, meschugge, verrückt; **~~dro** ['-drou] *Am sl fig* Wetterfahne *f*; **~stick** *mot* Ölmeßstab *m*.

diphtheria [dif'θiəriə, dip-] *med* Diphtherie *f*.

diphthong ['difθɔŋ, dip-] Diphthong, Doppel-, Zwielaut *m*; **~al** [dif'θɔŋgəl] diphthongisch; **~ize** ['-aiz] *tr* diphthongieren.

diploma [di'ploumə] Diplom *n*; Urkunde *f*; Befähigungsnachweis *m*; **~cy** [-əsi] *pol* Diplomatie *f a. allg*; **~t** ['dipləmæt, -plo(u)m-] *pol* Diplomat *m a. allg*; **~tic** [diplə'mætik] *adv ~~ally pol allg* diplomatisch; gewandt, geschickt, taktvoll; *through ~~ channels* auf diplomatischem Wege; *to break off, to sever ~~ relations* die diplomatischen Beziehungen abbrechen; *the ~~ body, corps* das diplomatische Korps; *~~ copy* originalgetreue Abschrift *f*; *~~ representation* diplomatische Vertretung *f*; *~~ service* Auswärtige(r) Dienst *m*; **~tics** *s pl mit sing* Diplomatik, Urkundenlehre *f*; **~tist** [di'ploumətist] Diplomat.

dipsomania [dipso(u)'meinjə] Trunksucht *f*; **~c** [-iæk] Trunksüchtige(r) *m*.

dipter|al, ~ous ['diptərəl, -əs] *bot zoo* zweiflügelig.

diptych ['diptik] *(Kunst)* Diptychon *n*.

dire ['daiə], **~ful** ['-ful] schrecklich, gräßlich, scheußlich, furchtbar, fürchterlich *a. fam*; *fam* gewaltig, mächtig, groß, stark; *to be in ~ need of help* Hilfe dringend brauchen.

direct [di'rekt, də-, dai-] *a* g(e)rade, fortlaufend, ununterbrochen; unmittelbar; ohne Umweg; direkt *(a. math, Steuer)*; gerade, offen, klar, deutlich; genau, völlig, vollkommen; *adv* direkt, gerade, unmittelbar; *tr* richten (*towards* auf); steuern, weisen; lenken, leiten, führen, einweisen; den Weg zeigen (*to* nach, zu); anweisen, anordnen, befehlen; verwalten; belehren; *(Verkehr)* regeln; *(Aufmerksamkeit, Worte)* richten (*to* an); *(Brief)* adressieren, schicken (*to* an); *(Orchester)* dirigieren, leiten; *itr* befehlen, anordnen; dirigieren; *as ~ed* laut Verfügung; *in a ~ line* in gerader Linie; *to ~ a play* Regie führen, die Spielleitung haben; **~ action** Selbsthilfe *f bes. pol*; Streik *m*, Demonstration *f*; **~ current** *el* Gleichstrom *m*; **~ hit** Volltreffer *m*; **~ion** [di'rekʃən, də-, dai-] Richtung; Gegend *f*; Gebiet *n a. fig*; Sinn *m*; Beziehung, Hinsicht; Leitung, Führung; Verwaltung, Geschäftsleitung, Direktion *f*, Vorstand *m*; *theat film* Regie; Anordnung, Anweisung, Anleitung, Einweisung; Führung, Instruktion *f*; *pl* Richtlinien *f pl*; *pl* Gebrauchsanweisung *f*; *meist pl* Adresse, Anschrift; *(Artillerie)* Seitenrichtung *f*; *by ~~ of* auf Anweisung, Anordnung *gen*; *in the ~~ of* in Richtung auf; *in many ~~s* in vieler Hinsicht; *in a northerly ~~* in nördlicher Richtung; *in the opposite ~~* in entgegengesetzter Richtung; *in this, in every ~~* in dieser, in jeder Beziehung, Hinsicht; *under the ~~ of* unter Leitung *gen*; *sense of ~~* Ortssinn *m*; *~~ of firing, flight, march* Schuß-, Flug-, Marschrichtung *f*; *~~ of rotation* Dreh-, Umlaufsinn *m*; *~~ finder* Funkpeiler *m*; *~~ indicator (mot)* Fahrtrichtungsanzeiger, Winker; *aero* Kursweiser *m*; *~~-post* Wegweiser *m*; *~~(s) for use* Gebrauchsanweisung *f*; **~ional** [-ʃənl] *a* Richt(ungs)-; *radio* gerichtet, Richt-; *~~ aerial, antenna* Richtstrahler *m*, -antenne *f*; *~~ controls (aero pl)* Seitensteuerung *f*; **~ive** [-iv] *a* Richt(ungs)-; leitend, führend, maßgebend, -geblich; *s* (allgemeine An-) Weisung, Richtschnur, Direktive *f*; *~~ idea* Leitgedanke *m*; **~ labo(u)r cost** Fertigungslohn *m*; **~ly** [-li] *adv* direkt, geradewegs; unmittelbar; sofort, gleich; geradeheraus; *conj fam Br* ['drekli] in dem Augenblick, Moment, wo, wie, als; sobald als; **~ness** [-nis] *lit fig* Geradheit, Offenheit *f*; **~ object** *gram* Akkusativobjekt *n*; **~or** [-ə] Direktor, Leiter; Geschäftsführer, Produktionsleiter *m*; Verwaltungs-, Aufsichtsratsmitglied *n*; *theat film* Regisseur; *mus* Dirigent; *mil* Richtkreis *m*, Kommandogerät *n*; *mil* Manöverleiter *m*; *tech* Leitantenne *f*; *tech* Nummernspeicher *m*; *board of ~~s* Verwaltungs-, Aufsichtsrat; Vorstand *m*; *managing ~~* Generaldirektor *m*; *operating ~~* Betriebsleiter *m*; *regional ~~* Bezirksleiter *m*; *~~ general* Generaldirektor *m*; *~~'s fees (pl)* Aufsichtsratsvergütungen *f pl*; **~orate** [-ərit] Stellung *f* als Direktor, Direktorenstelle; (Geschäfts-)Leitung *f*, Direktorium *n*, Vorstand, Verwaltungs-, Aufsichtsrat *m*; **~orial** [-'tɔriəl] *a* Direktoren-; **~orship** [-əʃip] Direktorenstelle *f*, Amt *n*, Stellung *f* als Direktor; *under s.o.'s ~~* unter jds Leitung; **~ory** [-əri] Adreßbuch; Direktorium *n*, Vorstand, Aufsichtsrat *m*; *(telephone ~~)* Telefonbuch, Fernsprechverzeichnis *n*; *trade, commercial ~~* Handels-, Branchenadreßbuch *n*; **~ress** [di'rektris, dai-] Direktorin, Leiterin, Vorsteherin, Direktrice *f*; **~ train** durchgehende(r) Zug *m*.

dirge [də:dʒ] Grabgesang *m*; Totenklage; Klage(lied *n*) *f*.

dirigible ['diridʒəbl] *a* lenkbar; *s* lenkbare(s) Luftschiff *n*, Zeppelin *m*.

dirk [də:k] *s* Dolch(messer *n*) *m*; *tr* erdolchen.

dirt [də:t] Schmutz, Dreck, Kot *m*; *Am* (*bes.* Garten-)Erde *f*; *pej* Land *n*; *fig pej* Dreck, Mist; (Schmutz u.) Schund *m*; Schmutzigkeit, Gemeinheit *f*; schmutzige, gemeine Reden *f pl*; *min (Gold)* Waschberge *m pl*; *sl* Moos *n*, Moneten *pl*, Geld *n*; *Am sl* geheime Information *f*, Tip *m*; *to do s.o. ~ (Am sl fig)* jdn durch den Dreck ziehen; *to eat ~* was einstecken, 'runterschlucken (müssen); *to fling, to throw ~ at s.o.* jdn in den Schmutz ziehen; *yellow ~* Gold *n*; **~-cheap,** *cheap as ~* spottbillig; **~ farmer** *Am fam* kleine(r) Farmer *m*; **~iness** ['-inis] Schmutzigkeit, Dreckigkeit *f*; **~ road** *Am* Feldweg *m*; unbefestigte Straße *f*; **~-track** *sport* Aschenbahn *f*; *~~ racing* Aschenbahnrennen *n*; **~y** ['-i] *a* schmutzig *(a. Wetter, Farbe, Bombe)*, dreckig; unflätig, zotig; böse, gemein; *(Wetter)* stürmisch, windig, scheußlich; *tr* schmutzig, dreckig machen, beschmutzen, besudeln; *to do the ~~ on s.o. (Br sl)* jdn gemein behandeln; *to play a ~~ trick on s.o.* jdm e-n üblen Streich spielen; *that's a ~~ shame! (Am)* das ist e-e Gemeinheit! *~~ green* schmutziggrün; *~~ neck (Am sl)* Farmer; Einwanderer *m*; *~~ wash (Am sl) fig* schmutzige Wäsche *f*.

disab|ility [disə'biliti] Unfähigkeit *f*, Unvermögen *n*; Arbeits-, Erwerbs-, *jur* Geschäftsunfähigkeit; Invalidität *f*; *~~ benefit od pension, insurance* Invalidenrente, -versicherung *f*; **~le** [dis'eibl, di'z] *tr* unfähig, untauglich, unbrauchbar machen, außerstand setzen; verstümmeln; *jur* für unfähig erklären (*from doing s.th.* etw zu tun); **~led** [dis'eibld] *a* verkrüppelt, schwer(kriegs)beschädigt, körperbehindert; arbeits-, erwerbs-, dienstunfähig; betriebsunfähig, außer Betrieb; *mil* abgeschossen; *mar* manövrierunfähig; *seriously ~~* schwerbeschädigt; *~~ soldier* Schwerkriegsbeschädigte(r), Kriegsversehrte(r) *m*; **~lement** [-mənt] Invalidität, Arbeits-, Erwerbs-, Dienstunfähigkeit; *mil* Kampfunfähigkeit *f*; *degree of ~~* Invaliditätsgrad *m*; *~~ pension* Invalidenrente *f*.

disabuse [disə'bju:z] *tr* von s-m Irrtum befreien; von s-n falschen Vorstellungen, Ansichten abbringen; e-s Besseren belehren; aufklären (*of* über).

disaccord [disə'kɔ:d] *itr* nicht übereinstimmen (*with* mit); *s* mangelnde Übereinstimmung, Meinungsverschiedenheit *f*.

disaccustom [disə'kʌstəm] *tr* entwöhnen (*to s.th.* e-r S), abgewöhnen (*s.o. to s.th.* jdm etw).

disadvantage [disəd'vɑ:ntidʒ] Nachteil *m*, Hindernis *n*, Behinderung *f*;

Schaden, Verlust *m*; ungünstige Lage *f*; *at a ~* im Nachteil; *to s.o.'s ~* zu jds Nachteil; *under ~s* unter ungünstigen Bedingungen; *to be at a ~* im Hintertreffen, im Nachteil sein; *to put at a ~* benachteiligen; *to sell at a ~* mit Verlust verkaufen; *to take s.o. at a ~* jds ungünstige Lage ausnützen; **~ous** [disædvɑ:n'teidʒəs] nachteilig, ungünstig, unvorteilhaft (*to* für).

disaffect|ed [disə'fektid] *a* unfreundlich (*to* gegenüber); unzufrieden (*to* mit) *bes. pol*; widerspenstig; **~ion** [-'fekʃən] Abneigung, Unfreundlichkeit (*to* gegen); *(bes. pol)* Unzufriedenheit, Unzuverlässigkeit *f*.

disaffirm [disə'fə:m] *tr (Aussage)* zurücknehmen; *(Urteil)* aufheben; *(Vertrag)* zurücktreten von, anfechten.

disagree [disə'gri:] *itr* nicht übereinstimmen (*with* mit; *about* über); verschieden sein, vonea. abweichen; im Widerspruch mitea. stehen; verschiedener Ansicht, Meinung sein; nicht einverstanden, anderer Ansicht, Meinung sein (*with* als); uneins sein, streiten; schlecht *od* nicht bekommen, unzuträglich sein (*with s.o.* jdm); **~able** [-əbl] unangenehm, widerwärtig; *(Wetter)* häßlich; *(Mensch)* unleidlich, wenig umgänglich, zänkisch, streitsüchtig; *(Sache)* unzuträglich; *(Speise)* unbekömmlich; **~ment** [-mənt] mangelnde Übereinstimmung, Verschiedenheit; Unstimmigkeit, Mißhelligkeit; Meinungsverschiedenheit *f*, Streit *m*.

disallow [disə'lau] *tr* nicht erlauben, nicht gestatten, verweigern; *jur* nicht zulassen; nicht anerkennen, verwerfen; zurückweisen, ablehnen; *(Forderung)* bestreiten; **~ance** [-əns] Ablehnung, Zurückweisung *f*.

disappear [disə'piə] *itr* ent-, verschwinden (*from* von, aus); **~ance** [-rəns] Verschwinden *n*; *tech* Schwund *m*.

disappoint [disə'pɔint] *tr* enttäuschen; *s.o.* jds Erwartungen nicht erfüllen; sein Wort, sein Versprechen nicht halten (*s.o.* jdm gegenüber); im Stich lassen, *fam* e-n Strich durch die Rechnung machen (*s.o.* jdm); *(Absicht, Plan)* durchkreuzen, zunichte, zuschanden machen, vereiteln; **~ed** [-id] *a* enttäuscht (*in s.o.* von jdm); vereitelt; betrübt, traurig; *to be ~~* enttäuscht sein (*at, with s.th.* über etw; *in s.o.* über jdn); *I am ~~ of it* es ist mir entgangen, ich habe darauf verzichten müssen; **~ing** [-iŋ] enttäuschend; **~ment** [-mənt] Enttäuschung *f* (*at s.th.* über etw; *in s.o.* über jdn); Fehlschlag; Verdruß *m*.

disapprobation [disæpro(u)'beiʃən] = *disapproval*.

disapprov|al [disə'pru:vəl] Mißbilligung; ungünstige Meinung, Abneigung *f*; Mißfallen *n* (*of* über); **~e** ['disə'pru:v] *tr itr (~~ of)* mißbilligen, tadeln; ablehnen, verwerfen, zurückweisen; e-e ungünstige, schlechte Meinung haben von; **~ingly** [-iŋli] *adv* mißbilligend, ablehnend.

disarm [dis'ɑ:m] *tr* entwaffnen *a. fig*; *(Bombe)* entschärfen; *fig* milde stimmen; *itr* abrüsten; **~ament** [-əment] Entwaffnung; Abrüstung *f*; *~~ conference* Abrüstungskonferenz *f*; **~ing** [-iŋ] *a fig* entwaffnend.

disarrange ['disə'reindʒ] *tr* in Unordnung, durchea.bringen; **~ment** [-mənt] Unordnung *f*, Durcheinander *n*, Verwirrung *f*.

disarray ['disə'rei] *tr* in Unordnung, durchea.bringen; *s* Unordnung; Verwirrung *f*.

disassembl|e [disə'sembl] *tr* ausea.-nehmen, zerlegen, demontieren; **~y** [-i] Ausbau *m*, Demontage *f*.

disast|er [di'zɑ:stə] Unheil, Verderben, große(s) *od* plötzliche(s) Unglück *n*, Katastrophe *f* (*to* für); *air, railway ~~* Flugzeug-, Eisenbahnunglück *n*; **~rous** [-rəs] verheerend, schrecklich (*to* für); katastrophal, vernichtend; unglücklich, unheilvoll, verhängnisvoll (*to* für).

disavow ['disə'vau] *tr* (ab-, ver)leugnen, abstreiten; nicht gelten lassen (wollen), ablehnen, nicht anerkennen; **~al** [-əl] (Ver-)Leugnung; Ablehnung, Nichtanerkennung *f*; Dementi *n*.

disband [dis'bænd] *tr (Organisation, Gesellschaft)* auflösen; zerstreuen; *mil* entlassen, verabschieden; *itr* sich auflösen, sich zerstreuen; **~ment** [-mənt] Auflösung; Entlassung *f*.

disbar [dis'bɑ:] *tr (Rechtsanwalt)* aus der Anwaltschaft ausschließen.

disbelie|f ['disbi'li:f] Unglaube *m*, Zweifel *m pl* (*in* an); **~ve** [-i:v] *itr (to ~~ in)* nicht glauben (wollen) (an); *tr* an-, bezweifeln; **~ver** [-və] Ungläubige(r), Zweifler *m*.

disburden [dis'bə:dn] *tr* entlasten, erleichtern (*to s.o.* gegenüber jdm); befreien, freimachen (*of* von); *to ~ o.'s mind* sein Herz erleichtern.

disburs|e [dis'bə:s] *tr* auszahlen, -geben; auslegen, verauslagen, vorstrecken, vorschießen; *(Einnahmen)* verwenden; **~ement** [-mənt] Auszahlung *f*; Vorschuß *m*; Verauslagung *f*; *pl* Auslagen, Aufwendungen *f pl*; *cash ~~s (pl)* Barauslagen *f pl*; *dividend ~~s (pl Am)* Dividendenausschüttungen *f pl*; **~ing** [~iŋ]: *~~ office (Am)* Zahlstelle, Kasse *f*; *~~ officer* Zahlmeister *m*.

disc *s. disk.*

discard [dis'kɑ:d] *tr (Karte, Kleider)* ablegen, abwerfen; *allg* wegwerfen, ablegen, aufgeben, beiseite legen, abtun, *fam* ausrangieren; sich lossagen, sich trennen von; *s* ['diskɑ:d] *(Karte)* Ablegen, Abwerfen; Wegwerfen *n*, Aufgabe; abgelegte Karte(n *pl*) *f*; *fam* etwas Abgelegtes, *fam* Ausrangiertes; *Am* Abfall(-), Schutt(haufen) *m*; *in ~ (Am)* abgelegt, ausrangiert; *to throw into the ~ (fig Am)* zum alten Eisen werfen, *fam* ausrangieren.

discern [di'sə:n, di'z-] *tr* deutlich sehen, wahrnehmen; klar erkennen, unterscheiden; *itr* unterscheiden (*between* zwischen; *from* von); **~ible** [-əbl] wahrnehmbar; deutlich sichtbar, klar erkennbar; unterscheidbar, merkbar, -lich; **~ing** [-iŋ] scharfsinnig, verstandesscharf, tiefdringend, einsichtig; **~ment** [-mənt] Unterscheidung *f*; Scharfsinn *m*, Verstandesschärfe, Urteilskraft, -fähigkeit; Einsicht *f*, tiefe(s) Verständnis *n*.

discharg|e [dis'tʃɑ:dʒ] **1.** *tr* e-e Last abnehmen (*s.o.* jdm); *(Fahrzeug)* entladen; *(Ladung, Last)* ab-, ausladen; *mar* löschen; *(el, Feuerwaffe)* entladen; *(Gewehr)* abdrücken; *(Schuß)* abschießen, -feuern; abwerfen, ab-, ausstoßen; von sich geben, ausströmen lassen, abblasen; *(Eiter)* ausscheiden; *chem* ätzen; *arch (durch Druckverteilung)* entlasten; (aus dem Dienst) entlassen, abbauen; freilassen, -machen, auf freien Fuß setzen; *mil* verabschieden; ausmustern; *(des Amtes)* entheben; *mar* abmustern; *(Angeklagten)* entlasten; freisprechen; *(in e-r Kartei)* streichen; sich freimachen, befreien (*from* von); (ab)bezahlen, begleichen, tilgen; *(Wechsel)* einlösen; *(Konto)* ausgleichen; *(Vertrag)* beenden; *(Gläubiger)* befriedigen; *(Pflicht)* erfüllen; *jur (von e-r Schuld)* freisprechen; entlasten (*a bankrupt* e-n Gemeinschuldner); *(von e-r Verpflichtung)* befreien; (*from* von); *(Beschluß)* aufheben; **2.** *itr (Feuerwaffe)* sich entladen, losgehen; entströmen; *(Fluß)* sich ergießen, einmünden (*into* in); *(Wunde)* eitern; *(frische Farbe)* sich verwischen; **3.** *s* Ab-, Entladen; *mar* Löschen *n*; *(Feuerwaffe)* Entladung *f a. el*, (Ab-)Schuß *m*, (Ab-)Feuern, Feuer *n*, Salve; Explosion, Sprengung *f*; Aus-, Entströmen *n*; Ab-, Ausfluß *m*, Schüttmenge; *chem* Ätze; Ausscheidung *f*, Eiter(ung *f*) *m*; *mil* Abschied *m*; Ausmusterung; Entlassung; Entlastung; Entbindung *f*; Freispruch; *(~~ certificate)* Entlassungsschein *m*; Bezahlung, Begleichung; Tilgung; Einlösung; Quittung; *(Vertrag)* Beendigung; *(Pflicht)* Erfüllung *f*; *in ~ of* zur Begleichung *gen*; in Erfüllung *gen*; *~~ centre* Entlassungsstelle *f*; *~~ pipe, tube* Abfluß(rohr *n*) *m*; *~~ spark* Entladungsfunke *m*; *~~ velocity* Ausflußgeschwindigkeit *f*; **~er** [-ə] *tech radio* Entlader; *el* Widerstandszünder; *mil aero* Abwurfbehälter *m*; **~ing** [-iŋ]: *~~ current* Entladestrom *m*; *~~ point* Entladestelle *f*.

disciple [di'saipl] Anhänger; Schüler; Jünger *m*; **~ship** [-ʃip] Anhängerschaft; Jüngerschaft *f*.

disciplin|able ['disiplinəbl] disziplinierbar; **~arian** [-'nɛəriən] *a* = *~ary*; *s* strenge(r) Zuchtmeister *m*; **~ary** [-əri] disziplinarisch; Disziplinar-; *~~ board, case, committee, court, power, proceedings* od *action* Disziplinar(straf)kammer *f*, -fall, -ausschuß *m*, -gericht *n*, -gewalt *f*, -verfahren *n*; *~~ jurisdiction* Disziplinar-, Ehrengerichtsbarkeit *f*; *~~ measures (pl), punishment* disziplinarische Maßnahmen *f pl*, Strafe *f*; *~~ offence* Disziplinarvergehen *n*, Dienstpflichtverletzung *f*; *~~ transfer* Strafversetzung *f*; **~e** ['disiplin] *s* Wissenszweig *m*, (Lehr-)Fach *n*; Zucht, Disziplin, (Zucht u.) Ordnung; Züchtigung, Bestrafung, Strafe; Lehr-, Unterrichtsmethode *f*; *tr* disziplinieren; *mil* drillen; schulen; *to keep, to maintain ~~* die Disziplin aufrechterhalten, die Ordnung bewahren; *breach of ~~* Disziplinarvergehen *n*; Dienstpflichtverletzung *f*; *party ~~ (pol)* Parteidisziplin *f*; *self-~~* Selbstdisziplin *f*.

disclaim [dis'kleim] *tr* verzichten auf, den Anspruch aufgeben auf; (ver-)leugnen; nicht anerkennen (wollen), ab-, bestreiten, ablehnen, zurückweisen; *(Erbschaft)* ausschlagen; *(Vertrag)* anfechten; **~er** [-ə] Verzicht(leistung *f*) *m*; Aufgabe *f* e-s Anspruches; Einspruch *m*; Ablehnung, Zurückweisung, Weigerung *f*; Widerruf *m*, Dementi *n*; *(Erbschaft)* Ausschlagung *f*.

disclos|e [dis'klouz] *tr* freilegen, enthüllen, aufdecken, ans Tageslicht bringen, an den Tag legen; bekanntmachen, mitteilen, verbreiten; zeigen; **~ure** [-ʒə] Freilegung, Enthüllung, Aufdeckung; Bekanntmachung, Mitteilung *f*; Aufschluß *m*.

disco|graphy [dis'kɔgrəfi] Schallplattenverzeichnis *n*; **~phile** ['disko(u)fail] Schallplattensammler *m*.

discolo(u)r [dis'kʌlə] *tr* ent-, verfärben; fleckig machen; *itr* die Farbe verlieren; verschießen; sich verfärben; fleckig werden; **~ation** [-'reiʃən] Ent-, Verfärbung *f*; Fleck *m*.

discomfit [dis'kʌmfit] *tr*: *to* ~~ *s.o.* jds Pläne durchkreuzen, jdsErwartungen zuschanden machen; jdn durchea., aus der Fassung, in Verwirrung, in Verlegenheit bringen, verwirren; ~**ure** [-ʃə] Enttäuschung; Verwirrung, Verlegenheit, Fassungslosigkeit *f*; Mißerfolg *m*, Niederlage *f*.

discomfort [dis'kʌmfət] *s* Un-, Mißbehagen *n*; Verdruß *m*; unangenehme Sache *f*; *pl* Beschwerden, Beschwerlichkeiten *f pl*.

discommode [diskə'moud] *tr* belästigen, Unannehmlichkeiten bereiten (*s.o.* jdm).

discompos|e [diskəm'pouz] *tr* in Unruhe versetzen, beunruhigen; verwirren; in Unordnung, durchea.bringen; ~**ure** [-'pouʒə] Unruhe, Auf-, Erregung, Verwirrung; Unordnung *f*.

disconcert [diskən'sə:t] *tr* aus der Fassung, in Verlegenheit bringen, verwirrt machen; *(Plan)* durchkreuzen.

disconnect ['diskə'nekt] *tr* trennen (*from, with* von) *a. tele*; *tech* aus-, entkuppeln, ausrücken; *tele* unterbrechen; *rail* abhängen; *(Tau)* kappen; *(Segelflugzeug)* ausklinken; *el* aus-, abschalten; *(Wasser)* abstellen; ~**ed** [-id] *a* getrennt; unzs.hängend; isoliert; ~**ing** [-iŋ] Ab-, Ausschalten *n*; ~~ *switch* Trennschalter *m*; ~**ion, disconnexion** [-kʃən] Trennung; *tech* Ausrückung; *el* Abschaltung, Unterbrechung; *tele* Sperre *f*; *fig* mangelnde(r) Zs.hang *m*.

disconsolate [dis'kɔnsəlit] untröstlich; mutlos, ohne Hoffnung; (tief-) betrübt, (tief)traurig; *(Sache)* trost-, freudlos; unfreundlich.

discontent ['diskən'tent] *s* Unzufriedenheit *f* (*at, with* mit); *tr* unzufrieden machen; ~**ed** [-id] *a* unzufrieden, mißmutig, mißgestimmt (*with* mit, über); ~**ment**[-mənt]Unzufriedenheit*f*.

discontinu|ance [diskən'tinjuəns], *a.* ~**ation** [-'eiʃən] Unterbrechung; Beendigung, Einstellung; *jur (Verfahren)* Aussetzung *f*; Aufhören *n*; *(Zeitung)* Abbestellung *f*; ~*ance of work* Arbeitseinstellung *f*; ~**e** ['diskən'tinju(:)] *tr* ab-, unterbrechen, aussetzen mit, beenden, aufhören (*doing* zu tun); *(Geschäft)* aufgeben; *(Zeitung)* abbestellen; *(Verbindung)* lösen; *jur (Klage)* zurückziehen, fallenlassen; *(Prozeß)* unterbrechen; *itr* aufhören, anhalten; ~**ity** ['diskɔnti'nju(:)iti] Zs.hanglosigkeit; Unstetigkeit; mangelnde Folgerichtigkeit *f*; Abreißen *n*, Unterbrechung, Lücke *f*; ~**ous** ['diskən'tinjuəs] zs.hanglos; diskontinuierlich; unstetig, ruckweise; abge-, unterbrochen; *(Welle)* gedämpft.

discord ['diskɔ:d] Zwietracht, Uneinigkeit; Meinungsverschiedenheit *f*; *mus* Mißklang *m*, Dissonanz *f*; Lärm *m*, Getöse *n*; *to sow the seeds of* ~ Zwietracht säen; ~**ance** [dis'kɔ:dəns] Uneinigkeit *f*, Mißklang *m*; ~**ant** [-'kɔ:dənt] nicht übereinstimmend, widersprechend; uneinig, uneins; nicht zs.-passend; mißtönend, disharmonisch.

discount ['diskaunt] *s* (Preis-)Abschlag, Nachlaß, Skonto, Rabatt (*on* auf); (Zahlungs-)Abzug; Diskont; (~ *rate, rate of* ~) Diskontsatz *m*; *tr* abziehen; diskontieren; e-n Rabatt gewähren (*s.th.* für etw); herabsetzen; *fig* von vornherein Abstriche machen (*s.th.* bei etw); vorwegnehmen; berücksichtigen; *at a* ~ unter pari, mit Verlust; *no* ~ feste Preise; *to allow a* ~ Rabatt gewähren; *to be at a* ~ wenig gefragt, leicht zu haben sein; *to give on* ~ zum Diskont geben, diskontieren lassen; *to lower* od *to reduce, to raise the* ~ den Diskont senken, erhöhen; *to take on* ~ in Diskont nehmen, diskontieren; *bank* ~ Bankdiskont *m*; *dealer* ~ Händlerrabatt *m*; *quantity* ~ Mengenrabatt *m*; *retail, wholesale* ~ Klein-, Großhandelsrabatt *m*; ~**ability** [-'biliti] Diskontierbarkeit *f*; ~**able** [-'kauntəbl] diskontierbar, diskontfähig; ~ **bank** Diskontbank *f*; ~ **broker, credit** Wechselmakler, -kredit *m*; ~ **department** Wechselabteilung *f*; ~**er** ['-ə] Diskontgeber *m*; ~**ing** ['-iŋ] Diskontierung *f*; Diskontgeschäft; Einkalkulieren, Inrechnungstellen *n*; ~~ *of bills* Wechseldiskontierung *f*; ~ **rate** Diskontsatz *m*; ~ **ticket** Rabattmarke *f*.

discountenance [dis'kauntinəns] *tr* aus der Fassung, in Verlegenheit bringen, verlegen machen, beschämen; entmutigen; mißbilligen, ablehnen.

discourag|e [dis'kʌridʒ] *tr* entmutigen; abraten (*s.o. from s.th.* jdm von e-r S); abhalten, abbringen, abschrecken (*from* von; *from doing s.th.* etw zu tun); vereiteln, verhindern; Steine in den Weg legen (*s.o.* jdm); *to get* ~*ed* den Mut verlieren, sinken lassen; ~**ement** [-mənt] Entmutigung; Mutlosigkeit; Abschreckung(smittel *n*); Schwierigkeit *f*, Hindernis *n* (*to* für); ~**ing** [-iŋ] entmutigend; abschreckend.

discourse [dis'kɔ:s, 'dis-] *s* Ausführung, Rede (*to* an); Vorlesung; Predigt; Abhandlung *f*; *itr* [dis'kɔ:s] sich (lange) unterhalten; sprechen, reden, sich äußern; e-n Vortrag, e-e Vorlesung halten; schreiben (*of, upon* über); erörtern, abhandeln (*of, upon s.th.* etw).

discourte|ous [dis'kə:tjəs] unhöflich, grob; ungeschliffen; ~**sy** [-'kə:tisi] Unhöflichkeit, Grobheit *f*; schlechte(s) Benehmen *n*.

discover [dis'kʌvə] *tr* entdecken, herausbekommen, -finden, ausfindig machen, ermitteln, aufdecken; gewahr werden, erkennen; ~**able** [-rəbl] herauszubekommen(d), erkennbar, ersichtlich; ~**er** [-rə] Entdecker; Erfinder *m*; ~**y** [-ri] Entdeckung; Erfindung; *jur* Pflicht *f* zur Vorlage von Urkunden; Versicherungsanzeige; *theat* Lösung *f* (des Knotens); *to resist* ~~ *(jur)* die Aussage verweigern.

*

discredit [dis'kredit] *tr* an-, bezweifeln, in Zweifel ziehen; anfechten, bestreiten; in Verruf, in schlechten Ruf, in Mißkredit bringen(*with* bei); *s.o.* jds Ruf schaden; *s* Unglaube, Zweifel *m*, Mißtrauen *n*; Mißkredit *m*; Unehre, Schande *f* (*to* für); schlechte(r) Ruf; Schandfleck *m*; *to fall into* ~ in Mißkredit kommen; *to throw* ~ *on* in Zweifel ziehen; ~**able** [-əbl] unehrenhaft, schändlich,schimpflich; *(Ruf)* schlecht.

discreet [dis'kri:t] um-, vorsichtig, klug, besonnen, bedächtig; rücksichtsvoll, verschwiegen, diskret.

discrepan|cy [dis'krepənsi] Unterschied *m*, Verschiedenheit, Abweichung *f*; Gegensatz, Widerstreit, -spruch *m*, Gegensätzlichkeit *f*.

discrete [dis'kri:t] getrennt, (ab)gesondert, einzeln; nicht zs.hängend, nicht stetig; *philos* abstrakt.

discretion [dis'kreʃən] Um-, Vorsicht *f*, Bedacht *m*, Klugheit, Besonnenheit; Verschwiegenheit, Diskretion *f*, Takt *m*, Rücksicht(nahme) *f*; (freies, eigenes) Ermessen, Gutdünken, Belieben *n*; *at* ~ nach Belieben; *to leave to s.o.'s* ~ jdm anheimstellen, jdm freie Hand lassen; *to use* ~ Rücksicht nehmen od üben; *it is within your own* ~ es liegt bei Ihnen; *the age, the years of* ~ Strafmündigkeit *f*; ~**ary** [-ʃnəri] dem (freien, eigenen) Ermessen überlassen; dem freien Willen unterworfen; willkürlich, beliebig; ~~ *clause* Kannvorschrift *f*.

discriminat|e [dis'krimineit] *tr* unterscheiden (*from* von); ausea.halten; *itr* unterscheiden (*between* zwischen); unterschiedlich behandeln, e-n Unterschied machen; *to* ~~ *in favour of s.o.* jdn bevorzugen; *to* ~~ *against s.o.* jdn benachteiligen, zurücksetzen; ~**ing** [-iŋ] unterscheidend;umsichtig,urteilsfähig, scharfsinnig; anspruchsvoll; *(Tarif)* Differential-; *(Kritik)* scharf; *el* Rückstrom-; ~**ion** [-'neiʃən] Unterscheidung *f*; Scharfsinn *m*, Unterscheidungsvermögen *n*, -gabe; unterschiedliche Behandlung; Bevorzugung, Begünstigung; Benachteiligung, Diskriminierung *f*; *pl* Handelsbeschränkungen *f pl*; *racial* ~~ Rassendiskriminierung *f*; ~**ive**[dis'kriminətiv, -neit-], ~**ory** [dis'krimineitəri] unterscheidend; unterschiedlich; nachteilig; ~*ory law* Ausnahmegesetz *n*.

discursive [dis'kə:siv] unstet, abschweifend; unzs.hängend; *philos* diskursiv.

discus ['diskəs] *sport* Diskus *m*, Wurfscheibe *f*; (~ *throw*) Diskuswerfen *n*; ~ **thrower** Diskuswerfer *m*.

discuss [dis'kʌs] *tr* diskutieren, debattieren, beraten über; *(mündlich)* erörtern, besprechen; *(schriftlich)* ab-, behandeln; *fam (Speise* od *Getränk)* verdrücken, sich zu Gemüt führen; *to* ~ *s.th. at great length* über etw des langen u. breiten diskutieren; ~**ion** [-'kʌʃən] Diskussion, Debatte, Aussprache, Besprechung, Beratung *f*, Meinungsaustausch *m*; Erörterung; Abhandlung *f*; *fam* Verdrücken *n (e-r Speise)*; *to open, to close a* ~~ e-e Aussprache eröffnen, schließen; *it is still under* ~~ es wird noch darüber beraten; *panel* ~~ Forumsdiskussion *f*; *preliminary* ~~ Vorbesprechung *f*; *subject for* ~~ Diskussionsthema *n*.

disdain [dis'dein, diz-] *tr* verachten, herabsehen auf; geringschätzig behandeln; verschmähen, ablehnen (*doing, to do* zu tun); *s* Verachtung, Geringschätzung; Geringschätzigkeit *f*, Hochmut *m*; *with* ~ von oben herab; ~**ful** [-ful] verächtlich, geringschätzig.

disease [di'zi:z] *s* Krankheit; Erkrankung *f*, Leiden *n*; *occupational* ~ Berufskrankheit *f*; *venereal* ~ Geschlechtskrankheit *f*; ~**d** [-d] *a* krank; ungesund, in Unordnung.

disembark ['disim'bɑ:k] *tr* ausschiffen, ausbooten, ausladen, löschen; *itr* an Land gehen, landen; *aero* das Reiseziel erreicht haben; ~**ation** [disembɑ:'keiʃən] Ausbootung, Ausschiffung *f*; Löschen *n*; Landung *f*; *aero* Ende *n* der Reise.

disembarrass ['disim'bærəs] *tr* freimachen, befreien, erleichtern (*of, from* von); aus der Verlegenheit ziehen; ~**ment** [-mənt] Befreiung, Erleichterung *f*.

disembod|ied ['disim'bɔdid] *a* entkörperlicht, entstofflicht, immateriell; ~**iment** [-'bɔdimənt] Entkörperlichung, Entstofflichung *f*; ~**y** ['disim'bɔdi] *tr* entkörperlichen, entstofflichen.

disembogue [disim'boug] *itr (to* ~ *o.s.) (Fluß)* sich ergießen *a. fig*.

disembowel [disim'bauəl] *tr* ausweiden, -nehmen.

disenchant ['disin'tʃɑ:nt] *tr* desillusionieren, ernüchtern, enttäuschen; be-

freien (*from* von); **~ment** [-mənt] Ernüchterung, Enttäuschung *f* (*with* über).
disencumber ['disin'kʌmbə] *tr* entlasten, freimachen, befreien (*from* von); entschulden.
disenfranchise ['disin'fræntʃaiz] *s.* *disfranchise.*
disengag|e ['disin'geidʒ] *tr itr* (sich) lösen, (sich) los-, freimachen, (sich) befreien, (sich) losreißen (*from* von); *(von e-r Verpflichtung)* entbinden; *tr tech* auskuppeln, -rücken, -klinken; *rail* loskuppeln, abhängen; *itr mil* sich absetzen, sich loslösen; **~ed** [-d] *a* (ge)locker(t), lose; frei, ungebunden, unbeschäftigt, ohne Verpflichtung; *tele (Leitung)* frei, nicht besetzt; **~ement** [-'geidʒmənt] (Los-)Lösung, Befreiung; *jur* Entlobung *f*; *pol* Ausea.rücken *n*; *tech* Abschaltung; Freiheit, Ungebundenheit, Muße *f*; *mil* Absetzen *n*; **~ing** [-'iŋ]: *~~ action (mil)* Absetzbewegung *f*.
disentangle ['disin'tæŋgl] *tr* los-, freimachen, befreien (*from* von); herauslösen (*from* aus); entwirren, ordnen; *itr* sich entwirren, sich freimachen; **~ment** [-mənt] Entwirrung; Befreiung *f*.
disentomb ['disin'tu:m] *tr (Leiche* od *archäologischen Fund)* ausgraben *a. fig.*
disequilibrium [disekwi'libriəm] Störung *f* des Gleichgewichts.
disestablish ['disis'tæbliʃ] *tr (die Kirche)* vom Staat trennen; **~ment** [-mənt]: *~~ of the Church* Trennung *f* von Kirche u. Staat.
disfavour ['dis'feivə] *s* Mißfallen *n*; Mißbilligung, Ablehnung, ablehnende Haltung; Ungnade *f*; *tr* mißbilligen, ablehnen; zurücksetzen, ungnädig behandeln; *to fall into ~~ with* in Ungnade fallen bei; *to look with ~ on s.th.* etw mißbilligend betrachten.
disfigur|ation [disfigjuə'reiʃən], **~ement** [dis'figəmənt] Entstellung, Verunstaltung *f*; **~e** [dis'figə] *tr* deformieren; entstellen, verunstalten.
disfranchise ['dis'fræntʃaiz] *tr* die bürgerlichen Ehrenrechte, *bes.* das Wahlrecht entziehen (*s.o.* jdm); entrechten; **~ment** [-'fræntʃizmənt] Entzug, Verlust *m* der bürgerlichen Ehrenrechte; Wahlunfähigkeit *f*.
disgorge [dis'gɔ:dʒ] *tr* ausspeien, ergießen, entladen (*into* in); herausrücken, (widerwillig) herausgeben; *itr* sich leeren; *(Fluß)* sich ergießen (*into* in).
disgrace [dis'greis] *s* Ungnade; Schande (*to* für); Unehre *f*, Schimpf; Schandfleck *m*; *tr* Schande bringen über, Unehre machen (*s.o.* jdm); unwürdig, nicht würdig sein (*s.o.* jds); zurücksetzen, demütigen; *to be ~d* in Ungnade fallen; *there is no ~ in doing s.th.* es ist keine Schande etw zu tun; **~ful** [-ful] schändlich, schimpflich; unehrenhaft, entehrend.
disgruntled [dis'grʌntld] *a* mißgestimmt, übelgelaunt, mürrisch; unzufrieden (*at* mit); verstimmt (*at* über).
disguise [dis'gaiz] *tr* verkleiden *(a. Möbel, Wand)*; *(Stimme)* verstellen; verhehlen, verbergen; *to ~ o.s.* sich verkleiden (*in* in; *as* als); sich verstellen; *s* Verkleidung, Maske; Verstellung *f*; *in ~* verkleidet, maskiert; *to make no ~ of* kein(en) Hehl machen aus, nicht verhehlen.
disgust [dis'gʌst] *s* Ekel (*at, for, towards, against* vor), Widerwille *(gegen)*; *tr* anekeln, -widern; abstoßen, verärgern; *in ~* voller Ekel, angewidert; *to ~ s.o. with s.th.* jdm etw verleiden; *I'm ~ed with everything* mir hängt alles zum Halse heraus; **~ing** [-iŋ] ekelhaft, widerlich, widerwärtig, abstoßend, abscheulich, scheußlich.
dish [diʃ] *s* Schüssel, Schale *f*, Napf *m*; Platte; Schüsselvoll *f*; Gericht *n*, Speise; Portion *f (Eis)*; *pl* Geschirr *n*; *Am sl* Pfundskerl *m*, phantastische Frau; *Am sl* Vorliebe *f*; *tr (Speise)* anrichten; *(to ~ up)* auftragen, servieren; *fig* schmackhaft, mundgerecht machen; *(to ~ out)* (flach aus)höhlen, vertiefen; *fam* austeilen; *sl* 'reinlegen, *pol* erledigen, schlagen, *(Plan)* verpatzen; *to wash, (fam) to do the ~es* das Geschirr spülen; *standing ~* Stammessen *n*; **~-cloth,** *Am* **-towel** Geschirr-, Tellertuch *n*; Abwaschlappen *m*; **~-drainer** *Am*, **-rack** Abtropfkörbchen *n*; **~ed** [-t] *a* konkav; *arch* gewölbt; *(Radscheiben)* gepreßt; *fam* erledigt, kaputt; **~ful** ['-ful] Schüsselvoll *f*; **~-pan** *Am* Spül-, Abwaschschüssel *f*; **~-rag** Spül-, Abwaschlappen *m*; **~-warmer** Wärmplatte *f*; **~-wash, -water** Spül-, Abwaschwasser *n*; **~-washer** Abwaschfrau; Geschirrspülmaschine *f*.
dishabille [disæ'bi:l, disə-] Morgenrock *m*; Hauskleid *n*; *in ~* im Negligé.
disharmon|ious ['dishɑ:'mounjəs] dis-, unharmonisch; **~y** ['dis'hɑ:məni] Disharmonie *f*; Mißklang *m*.
dishearten [dis'hɑ:tn] *tr* entmutigen; *to be ~ing to s.o.* für jdn entmutigend sein.
dishevel [di'ʃevəl] *tr* in Unordnung, durchea.bringen; *(Haare)* zerzausen; **~(l)ed** *a (Kleidung)* in Unordnung, durcheinander; *(Haare)* wirr, zerzaust.
dishonest [dis'ɔnist, di'z-] unredlich, unehrlich, unaufrichtig; betrügerisch; *fig* unsauber; *(Geschäft)* unreell; **~y** [-i] Unredlichkeit, Unehrlichkeit, Unaufrichtigkeit *f*; Betrug, Schwindel *m*.
dishono(u)r [dis'ɔnə, di'z-] *s* Unehre *f*, Schimpf *m*, Schande *f* (*to* für); *tr* beleidigen; Schande bringen über, entehren; *(Mädchen, Frau)* schänden; *(Wort)* nicht einlösen, brechen; *fin (Wechsel)* nicht einlösen, nicht honorieren; **~able** [-rəbl] unehrenhaft, ehrenrührig, schimpflich, schändlich; ehrlos; **~ed** [-d] *a* entehrt; *(Scheck)* nicht eingelöst; *(Wechsel)* notleidend.

*

disillusion [disi'l(j)u:ʒən] *tr u.* **~ize** [-aiz] ernüchtern, desillusionieren, enttäuschen; *to be ~ed with s.th.* über etw die Illusion verloren haben; *s u.* **~ment** [-mənt] Ernüchterung (*with* durch); Enttäuschung *f* (*with* über).
disincentive [disin'sentiv] *s* Abschreckung *f* (*to* von); *a* abschreckend.
disinclin|ation [disinkli'neiʃən] Abneigung (*for* gegen); Abgeneigtheit *f* (*to* gegen); *~~ to buy* Kaufunlust *f*; **~e** ['disin'klain] *tr itr* abgeneigt machen, sein; **~ed** [-d] *a* abgeneigt (*for, to* gegen); nicht willens (*to* zu).
disinfect [disin'fekt] *tr med* desinfizieren, entwesen; **~ant** [-ənt] *a* desinfizierend; *s* Desinfektionsmittel *n*; **~ion** [-fekʃən] Desinfektion *f*.
disinfest ['disin'fest] *tr* entwesen, von Ungeziefer befreien; **~ation** ['-'teiʃən] Entwesung *f*.
disingenuous [disin'dʒenjuəs] nicht offen, unaufrichtig; unredlich.
disinherit ['disin'herit] *tr* enterben; **~ance** [-əns] Enterbung *f*.
disintegr|ate [dis'intigreit] *tr itr* (sich) auflösen, (sich) zersetzen *a. fig*; *itr* zerfallen, sich in s-e Bestandteile auflösen; *geol* verwittern; **~ation** [disinti'greiʃən] Auflösung, Zersetzung *f*, Zerfall; *fig* Verfall *m*; *geol* Verwitterung *f*; *~~ product* Zerfallsprodukt *n*.
disinter ['disin'tə:] *tr* (wieder) ausgraben, exhumieren; *fig* ans Licht bringen, aufdecken; **~ment** [-mənt] Ausgrabung *f*.
disinterested [dis'intristid] *a* uneigennützig, selbstlos; unparteiisch, unvoreingenommen; *fam* uninteressiert, gleichgültig; **~ness** [-nis] Uneigennützigkeit, Selbstlosigkeit; Unvoreingenommenheit, Unparteilichkeit *f*.
disjoint [dis'dʒɔint] *tr* ausrenken *a. med*; zerlegen, zergliedern; ausea.-nehmen; (zer)trennen; den Zs.hang stören (*s.th.* e-r S), durchea.bringen; **~ed** [-id] *a* ausgerenkt, aus den Fugen; ausea.gegangen, -gefallen; *(bes. Reden)* unzs.hängend, zs.hanglos, wirr.
disjunct [dis'dʒʌŋkt] *a* getrennt, gesondert, auseinander; **~ion** [-kʃən] Trennung, Sonderung *f*; **~ive** [-iv] trennend, Trenn-; *gram philos* disjunktiv.
disk [disk] Scheibe *a. med*; (runde) Platte, runde Fläche *f*; *bot* (scheibenförmiges) Blütenlager *n*; *med* Papille *f*, Sehfleck *m*; Schallplatte; *tele* Nummernscheibe *f*; *tech* Teller *m*, Lamelle *f*; *identity ~ (mil)* Erkennungsmarke *f*; *~* **brake, clutch** Scheibenbremse, -kupplung *f*; **~-jockey** *sl radio* (Schallplatten-)Ansager *m*.
dislike [dis'laik] *tr* nicht mögen, nicht leiden können, nicht gern haben; e-e Abneigung, etwas haben gegen (*doing s.th.* dagegen etw zu tun); *s* Abneigung *f*, Widerwille *m*, Antipathie *f* (*of, for* gegen); *to have a strong ~ for s.o.* jdn nicht riechen können; *full of likes and ~s* ['-s] mit zahlreichen Vorurteilen.
dislocat|e ['disləkeit, -lo(u)-] *tr bes. med* aus-, verrenken; durchea.-, in Unordnung bringen; verlagern; *fig* verwirren; *(bes. den Verkehr)* (empfindlich) stören; **~ion** [-'keiʃən] Verrenkung; Störung; Unordnung *f*, Durcheinander *n*; Verlagerung, Verschiebung; *fig* Verwirrung; *geol* Dislokation *f*.
dislodg|e [dis'lɔdʒ] *tr* verlagern, verlegen; umquartieren; vertreiben, verjagen, verdrängen; *(Elektronen)* befreien.
disloyal ['dis'lɔiəl] untreu, treulos (*to* gegen); verräterisch, hinterhältig; pflichtvergessen; **~ty** ['-ti] Untreue, Treulosigkeit *f* (*to* gegenüber).
dismal ['dizməl] *a* düster, trübe, traurig, trübselig; pessimistisch; niederdrückend; niedergedrückt, elend, jammervoll; *s pl* gedrückte Stimmung *f*.
dismantl|e [dis'mæntl] *tr* frei-, bloßlegen; leermachen, ausräumen; ausea.nehmen, zerlegen; *(Gebäude)* niederreißen, abbrechen; aus-, abbauen, demontieren; *mar* abtakeln, abwracken; *(Festung)* schleifen; unbrauchbar machen; *(Kontrollen)* abbauen, aufheben; **~ing** [-iŋ] Demontage *f*; Abbau *m*.
dismay [dis'mei, diz-] *s* Bestürzung (*at* über); Angst *f*, Schrecken *m*, Entsetzen *n* (*at* vor); *tr* erschrecken; in Angst, in Aufregung versetzen; bestürzt machen.
dismember [dis'membə] *tr* zerreißen, zerschneiden; zerstückeln; *(Gebiet)* aufteilen; **~ment** [-mənt] Zerstückelung, Aufteilung; *med* Amputation *f*.
dismiss [dis'mis] *tr* weg-, fortschicken; (weg)gehen lassen; freilassen; *(aus dem Dienst, e-r Stellung, e-m Amt)* entlassen, s-s Amtes entheben, beurlauben, verabschieden; abbauen; *(Versammlung)* aufheben, -lösen; *(Thema)* fallenlassen; *jur* ab-, zurück-

weisen, ablehnen; sich *(Gedanken)* aus dem Kopf, aus dem Sinn schlagen; abtun (*as* als; *with a shrug of the shoulder* mit e-m Achselzucken); übergehen, hinweggehen über; ablegen; *mil* wegtreten lassen; *~! (mil)* wegtreten! **~al** [-əl] Freilassung; Entlassung, Amtsenthebung; Schließung *(e-r Versammlung)*; *jur* Ab-, Zurückweisung, Ablehnung *f*; *~~ without notice* fristlose Entlassung *f*.

dismount ['dis'maunt] *tr* aus dem Sattel heben, abwerfen; abmontieren; ausea.nehmen; ab-, ausbauen; *itr* absteigen, absitzen; aussteigen *(from* von).

disobedien|ce [disə'bi:djəns] Ungehorsam *m* (*to* gegen); Befehlsverweigerung; Unbotmäßigkeit, Widersetzlichkeit, Widerspenstigkeit *f*; **~t** [-t] ungehorsam (*to* gegen); unbotmäßig.

disobey ['disə'bei] *tr* nicht gehorchen, ungehorsam sein, den Gehorsam verweigern (*s.o.* jdm); sich widersetzen (*an order* e-m Befehl).

disoblig|e ['disə'blaidʒ] *tr* ungefällig, unhöflich sein (*s.o.* jdm gegenüber); kränken, verletzen, beleidigen; **~ing** [-iŋ] ungefällig, unhöflich; verletzend; **~ingness** [-iŋnis] Ungefälligkeit, Unhöflichkeit *f*.

disorder [dis'ɔ:də, di'z-] *s* Unordnung *f*, Durcheinander *n*; Tumult, Aufruhr *m*; Unregelmäßigkeit *f*; (gesundheitliche) Störung(en *pl*) *f*; *pl pol* Unruhen *f pl*; *tr* in Unordnung, durchea.-bringen; stören; verwirren; *(körperlich* od *geistig)* zerrütten; *in ~* in Unordnung; durcheinander; *mental ~* Geistesgestörtheit *f*; **~ed** [-d] *a* durcheinander, unordentlich; *(Magen)* verdorben; *(Geist)* zerrüttet; **~ly** [-li] *a adv* unordentlich, unaufgeräumt; ungeordnet; unruhig, aufsässig, aufrührerisch; liederlich, zuchtlos; *~~ conduct* unsittliche(r) Lebenswandel *m*; Ungebührlichkeit *f*; *~~ house* Bordell *n*; Spielhölle *f*.

disorganiz|ation [disɔ:gənai'zeiʃən] Unordnung, Desorganisation, Zerrüttung, Auflösung *f*; **~e** [dis'ɔ:gənaiz] *tr* stören, durchea.-, in Unordnung, in Verwirrung bringen; desorganisieren, zerrütten, auflösen.

disorient(ate) [dis'ɔ:riənt(eit)] *tr fig* desorientieren, verwirren.

disown [dis'oun] *tr* ab-, verleugnen, abstreiten, nicht anerkennen, nicht gelten lassen wollen; nichts zu tun haben wollen mit; *(Kind)* verstoßen.

disparag|e [dis'pæridʒ] *tr* herabsetzen, -würdigen, verkleinern, diskreditieren, verunglimpfen, in Verruf bringen; **~ement** [-mənt] Herabsetzung, -würdigung, Verunglimpfung; Beeinträchtigung *f*; **~ing** [-iŋ] *a* herabsetzend, -würdigend, verunglimpfend.

dispar|ate ['dispərit, -eit] *a* ungleich-, verschiedenartig; (völlig) verschieden; *s pl* völlig verschiedene, ganz andere Dinge *n pl*; **~ity** [dis'pæriti] Ungleichheit *f* (*in* in, bei); *~~ in, of age, rank* Alters-, Rangunterschied *m*.

dispassionate [dis'pæʃnit] leidenschaftslos, ohne Erregung, ruhig; unparteiisch.

dispatch [dis'pætʃ] *tr* abschicken, -senden, befördern; *(Person)* entsenden; *(Zug)* abfertigen; schnell erledigen, abmachen, abtun; *mil* in Marsch setzen; ein Ende machen (*s.th.* e-r S); töten, hinrichten, erledigen; *fam (Essen)* verdrücken; *s* Abschicken, -senden *n*; Versand *m*, Verschickung, Beförderung; Abfertigung, (schnelle) Erledigung; Eile; Tötung, Hinrichtung *f*; Telegramm *n*, Depesche; Mitteilung, Nachricht *f*, Bericht *m*; Nachrichtenbüro *n*; Spedition *f*; *with ~* in Eile, eilig, schnell; **~-box, -case** Kuriergepäck *n*; Meldetasche *f*; **~er** [-ə] Absender, Expedient; *rail* Fahrdienstleiter; *aero* Abfertigungsbeamte(r) *m*; **~-goods** *pl* Eilgut *n*; **~ing** [-iŋ]: *~~ of goods* Waren-, Güterbeförderung *f*, -transport *m*; *~~ point* Absendestelle *f*; **~-note, -order** Versandschein, -auftrag *m*; **~-office** Versandstelle *f*; **~-rider** *mil* Meldereiter, -fahrer *m*; *~* **tube** Rohrpost *f*.

dispel [dis'pel] *tr* vertreiben, zerstreuen, auflösen, zum Verschwinden bringen *a. fig*.

dispens|able [dis'pensəbl] entbehrlich, nicht (unbedingt) notwendig; nicht bindend; *(Sünde)* läßlich; **~ary** [-əri] Apotheke; Arzneiausgabe(stelle) *f*; *mil* Krankenrevier *n*; **~ation** [-'seiʃən] Aus-, Verteilung; Verwaltung; Führung, Leitung, Regierung; Befreiung *f*, Dispens *m* (*from* von); Schickung, Fügung *f (des Schicksals)*; Rechts- *od* Glaubenssystem *n*; **~e** [dis'pens] *tr* ausgeben, aus-, verteilen; *(Arznei)* herstellen u. ausgeben; anwenden, handhaben, verwalten; *rel* spenden; *(Recht)* sprechen; befreien, dispensieren (*from* von); *itr*: *to ~~ with* überflüssig machen, ab-, wegtun; einsparen, auskommen ohne; verzichten auf; außer acht, unberücksichtigt lassen; *I can ~~ with* ich kann entbehren, verzichten auf; **~er** [-ə] Verteiler; Verwalter; Apotheker(gehilfe) *m*; **~ing** [-iŋ] Rezeptur *f*; *~~-chemist* Apotheker *m*.

dispers|al [dis'pə:səl] Zerstreuung, Aus-, Verbreitung (*over* über); weite Verteilung, Auflockerung *f*; *mil* Abmarsch *m*; *tech* Dispersion, Zerstreuung *f*; *~~ point* Abstellplatz *m*, Verteilungsstelle *f*; **~e** [dis'pə:s] *tr* ver-, zerstreuen; aus-, verbreiten; (weit, fein) verteilen; verzetteln; *tech* dispergieren; *(Nebel, Wolken)* zerstreuen, auflösen; *(Licht)* zerlegen; *(Fahrzeuge, Truppen)* ausea.ziehen, auflockern; *mil* ver-, ausea.sprengen; *itr* sich zerstreuen, ausea.gehen, -laufen; **~ed** [-t] *a* aufgelockert; fein verteilt; **~ion** [-'pə:ʃən] Zerstreuung, Aus-, Verbreitung; *mil* Auflockerung *f*, Ausea.ziehen *n*; *opt el* Dispersion, Aufteilung, Zerstreuung; Streuung *f*; *(Diamant)* Feuer *n*.

dispirit [di'spirit] *tr* entmutigen; **~ed** [-id] *a* mutlos, niedergedrückt.

displace [dis'pleis] *tr* versetzen, -legen, -lagern, -schieben, -schleppen; absetzen, (aus dem Amt) entfernen; an die Stelle setzen *od* treten (*s.o.* jds; *s.th.* e-r S), ablösen, ersetzen; *mar (Wasser)* verdrängen; *~d person* Verschleppte(r) *m*; **~ment** [-mənt] Versetzung, Verschiebung; Verlagerung; Absetzung, Entfernung (aus dem Amt); anderweitige Verwendung; Ablösung *f*, Ersatz *m*; *psychol* Verdrängung; *mar* Wasserverdrängung *f*, Tonnengehalt *m*, Tonnage; *geol* Verstellung *f*; *piston ~~* Hubraum *m*.

display [dis'plei] *tr* entfalten, aufrollen, -decken; ausbreiten; hervorkehren, -heben; (offen) zeigen, zur Schau stellen; ausstellen; *fig* entfalten, entwickeln, an den Tag legen, enthüllen; *typ* hervorheben; *(Radar)* wiedergeben; *s* Entfaltung; Zurschaustellung; (Schaufenster-)Auslage; Ausstellung, Vorführung, Schau(stellung), Darbietung *f*; Prunk, Aufwand *m*, Prachtentfaltung *f*, Pomp *m*, *fam* Angabe; *typ* Hervorhebung; *(Radar)* Wiedergabe *f*, Bildschirm *m*; *to be on ~* ausgestellt sein; *to make (a) ~ of* auffällig zur Schau tragen; viel Aufhebens machen von; *to ~ a flag* flaggen; *~ of power* Machtentfaltung *f*; *~* **board** Anschlagbrett *n*; Schautafel *f*; *~* **case** Schau-, Auslagekasten *m*; *~* **compositor** *typ* Akzidenzsetzer *m*; *~* **poster** Aushang *m*, Plakat *n*; *~* **room** Ausstellungsraum *m*; *~* **stand** Auslagestand *m*; *~* **type** Plakatschrift *f*; *~* **window** Auslage-, Schaufenster *n*; *~* **work** Schaufenstergestaltung, -dekoration *f*; *typ* Akzidenzarbeiten *f pl*.

displeas|e [dis'pli:z] *tr* mißfallen (*s.o.* jdm); lästig fallen *od* sein (*s.o.* jdm); ärgerlich machen; *obs* beleidigen; **~ed** [-d] *a* ärgerlich, ungehalten, verstimmt (*at, with* über); **~ing** [-iŋ] unangenehm, lästig; mißfällig; **~ure** [-'pleʒə] Mißvergnügen *n*, -stimmung; Verstimmung *f*, Verdruß, Unwille, Ärger *m*; Mißfallen *n*, Unzufriedenheit *f* (*at, over* mit).

disport [dis'pɔ:t] *itr u. to ~ o.s.* sich belustigen, sich amüsieren, Scherze, Späße machen; herumtollen.

dispos|able [dis'pouzəbl] (frei) verfügbar, zur Verfügung stehend, greifbar; *(Geld)* flüssig; verwendbar; zur einmaligen Benutzung, zum Wegwerfen; *~~ income* Nettoverdienst *m*; *~~ tissue* Zellstoff *m*; **~al** [-'pouzəl] (An-)Ordnung, Einrichtung; Regelung, Erledigung; Verwendung *f*, Gebrauch *m*, Nutzbarmachung; Verfügung(sgewalt) (*of* über); Leitung; Beseitigung, Weggabe; Übergabe *f*; Verkauf *m*, Veräußerung *f*; *for ~~* zum Verkauf; *to be at s.o.'s ~~* zu jds Verfügung stehen; *to have the ~~ of s.th.* etw zur Verfügung, die Verfügung(sgewalt) über e-e S haben; **~e** [dis'pouz] *tr* (an)ordnen, ein-, verteilen, einrichten; *(Angelegenheit)* regeln; *(Sache)* erledigen, abmachen; benutzen, gebrauchen, verwenden, verwerten; geneigt machen, dazu bringen, bewegen, veranlassen (*to* zu); *med* anfällig machen (*to catching cold* für e-e Erkältung); *itr*: *to ~~ of* verfügen über, regeln, erledigen; loswerden; beseitigen, wegwerfen, -geben; abschaffen; verkaufen, veräußern, abgeben, absetzen; erledigen, abmachen; *(Frage)* beantworten, erledigen; *(Behauptung)* widerlegen; aus dem Felde schlagen; *(Gegner)* erledigen, aus dem Wege räumen, ungefährlich machen; aufessen; austrinken; *to ~~ of o.'s time* über s-e Zeit verfügen, Herr s-r Zeit sein; *man proposes, God ~es* der Mensch denkt, Gott lenkt; **~ed** [-d] *a* geneigt, bereit, aufgelegt (*for s.th.* zu etw; *to do* zu tun); veranlagt (*to* für); *easily ~~ of* leicht verkäuflich; *well, ill ~~ towards* wohlgesinnt *dat*, kritisch eingestellt gegen; *to feel ~~ for, to* Lust haben zu; *~~ to think* geneigt, anzunehmen; **~ition** [dispə'ziʃn] (An-)Ordnung, Aufstellung *f*; Plan *m*; Verwendung, Einteilung, Einrichtung; Vorkehrung; Erledigung; Weggabe; Verfügung(sgewalt) (*of* über); Entscheidung; Bestimmung, Klausel; Natur *f*, Wesen *n*, Art; Gemütsverfassung, Veranlagung; Anlage, Neigung *f*, Hang *m* (*to* zu); *mil* Aufstellung, Gliederung *f*; *pl* Vorkehrungen, Dispositionen *f pl*; *power of ~~* Verfügungsgewalt *f*.

dispossess ['dispə'zes] *tr* enteignen, verdrängen, vertreiben; berauben (*of*

s.th. e-r S); **~ion** ['-'zeʃən] (Zwangs-) Enteignung, Verdrängung, Räumung *f*.
dispraise [dis'preiz] *tr* herabwürdigen, tadeln; mißbilligen, ablehnen; *s* Tadel, Vorwurf *m*; Mißbilligung *f*.
disproof ['dis'pru:f] Widerlegung *f*.
disproportion ['disprə'pɔ:ʃən] Mißverhältnis *n*; Unproportioniertheit *f*; **~ate** [-ʃnit] un-, disproportioniert; unverhältnismäßig (groß) (*to* im Vergleich zu).
disprov|al [dis'pru:vəl] Widerlegung *f*; **~e** ['dis'pru:v] *tr* widerlegen.
disput|able [dis'pju:təbl, 'dis-] anfechtbar; nicht sicher, zweifelhaft; **~ant** [dis'pju:tənt] Disputierende(r), Disputant; Gegner *m (im Gespräch)* **~ation** [dispju:'teiʃən] Streitgespräch *n*; gelehrte(r) Meinungsaustausch *m*; Disputation, Kontroverse *f*; Wortstreit *m*, -gefecht *n*, Debatte *f*, Disput *m*; **~atious** [-'teiʃəs] streitsüchtig, rechthaberisch; **~e** [dis'pju:t] *itr* disputieren, streiten (*with, against* mit; *on, about* über); *tr* disputieren, streiten über; bestreiten; widerstreben, -stehen (*s.o.* jdm); streitig machen (*s.th. to s.o.* jdm etw); *s* (Wort-)Streit *m*, Kontroverse, Meinungsverschiedenheit *f*; *beyond, past, without ~~* unbestritten, fraglos, ganz sicher, ganz gewiß *adv*; *in ~~* strittig; fraglich; *to settle a ~~* e-n Streit beilegen; *labo(u)r ~~* Arbeitsstreitigkeit *f*; *wage ~~* Lohnstreitigkeit *f*; **~ed** [-id] *a* strittig; *~~ claims office* Rechtsabteilung *f*.
disqualif|ication [diskwɔlifi'keiʃən] Disqualifizierung, Untauglichkeit, Unfähigkeit *f*; *sport* (Grund zum) Ausschluß *m*; **~ied** [dis'kwɔlifaid] *a* untauglich, unfähig; *sport* disqualifiziert; **~y** [dis'kwɔlifai] *tr* untauglich (*for* für), unfähig (*for* zu) machen; für ungeeignet erklären; *sport* ausschließen, disqualifizieren; den Führerschein entziehen (*s.o.* jdm).
disquiet [dis'kwaiət] *tr* beunruhigen; *s* Unruhe, Aufregung, Sorge, Besorgnis *f*; **~ing** [-iŋ] beunruhigend, besorgniserregend, aufregend; **~ude** [dis'kwaiitju:d] Ruhelosigkeit, Besorgtheit, Aufgeregtheit *f*.
disquisition [diskwi'ziʃən] (längere mündliche *od* schriftliche) Ausführungen *f pl* (*on* über).
disregard ['disri'gɑ:d] *tr* nicht beachten, ignorieren, in den Wind schlagen, sich hinwegsetzen (*s.th.* über etw); mißachten, geringachten, -schätzen; *s* Nichtbeachtung, Nichteinhaltung; Geringschätzung *f* (*of, for* gen).
disrelish [dis'reliʃ] *s* Widerwille, Ekel *m*; Abneigung *f* (*for* gegen); *tr* e-e starke Abneigung haben gegen.
disrepair ['disri'pɛə] Verfall *m*, Baufälligkeit; Reparaturbedürftigkeit *f*; *in (bad) ~* in (sehr) schlechtem (Erhaltungs-)Zustand; reparaturbedürftig; *to fall into ~* verfallen.
disreput|able [dis'repjutəbl] in schlechtem Ruf stehend; *(Lokal)* verrufen; anrüchig; unansehnlich; **~e** ['disri'pju:t] schlechte(r) Ruf, Verruf *m*; Schande *f*; Mißkredit *m*; *to bring, to fall into ~~* in Verruf bringen, kommen.
disrespect ['disris'pekt] Nichtachtung, Unehrerbietigkeit, Respektlosigkeit, Unhöflichkeit *f* (*to* gegenüber); **~ful** [-ful] respektlos, unehrerbietig; unhöflich, grob (*to* gegen).
disrobe ['dis'roub] *tr* ausziehen, -kleiden; *fig* entkleiden; *itr u. to ~ o.s.* sich auskleiden, sich ausziehen.
disroot [dis'ru:t] *tr* entwurzeln; *fig* verdrängen, vertreiben.
disrupt [dis'rʌpt] *tr* zerbrechen, spalten, auf-, zersplittern; (gewaltsam) unterbrechen; *itr el* durchschlagen; **~ion** [-'rʌpʃən] Bruch, Riß *m*, Spaltung, Zersplitterung; gewaltsame Unterbrechung *f*; **~ive** [-iv] zum Bruch, zur Spaltung führend; *(Sprengstoff)* brisant.
dissatis|faction ['dissætis'fækʃən] Unzufriedenheit (*with* mit); **~factory** [-'fæktəri] unbefriedigend; **~fied** ['dis'sætisfaid] *a* unbefriedigt; unzufrieden (*with* mit); **~fy** ['dis'sætisfai] *tr* nicht befriedigen, nicht genügen (*s.o.* jdm); mißfallen (*s.o.* jdm).
dissect [di'sekt] *tr anat* sezieren; zergliedern; im einzelnen, genau prüfen, untersuchen, studieren; *(Konten)* aufgliedern; **~ion** [-kʃən] Zerlegung; *anat* Sektion *f*; (seziertes) Präparat *n*; Zergliederung, genaue Untersuchung *f*.
disseise, disseize ['dis'si:z] *tr* widerrechtlich aus dem Besitz verdrängen.
dissembl|e [di'sembl] *tr (Gedanken, Gefühle, Absichten)* verbergen, verhehlen; heucheln, vorgeben; ignorieren; *tech* ausea.nehmen; *itr* heucheln; sich verstellen; **~er** [-ə] Heuchler *m*.
disseminat|e [di'semineit] *tr fig* ausstreuen, verbreiten, unter die Leute bringen; **~ion** [-'neiʃən] Ausstreuen *n*, Verbreitung *f*.
dissen|sion [di'senʃən] Meinungsverschiedenheit; Uneinigkeit *f*; Zwist(igkeit *f*), Streit *m*; **~t** [di'sent] *itr* anderer Ansicht, Meinung sein, e-e abweichende Auffassung haben (*from* als); nicht zustimmen (*from s.th.* etw); nicht der Landeskirche *(in England der Hochkirche)* angehören; *s* andere, abweichende Ansicht, Meinung; von dem der Landeskirche abweichende(r) Glauben *m*; **~ter** [-tə] Andersdenkende(r); *rel* Dissenter *m*; **~tient** [di'senʃ(i)ənt] *a* andersdenkend; e-e eigene Meinung habend *od* vertretend; abweichend, nicht übereinstimmend; *s* Andersdenkende(r) *m*; *with one ~~ voice* mit e-r Gegenstimme.
dissertation [disə(:)'teiʃən] Abhandlung; Dissertation *f* (*on* über).
disservice ['dis'sə:vis] Benachteiligung *f* (*to* für); schlechte(r) Dienst *m* (*to* an); *to do s.o. a ~* jdm e-n schlechten Dienst erweisen.
dissever [dis'sevə] *tr* (ab)trennen, abschneiden (*from* von); teilen, zerteilen, zerlegen (*into* in); *itr* sich (ab-) trennen; ausea.gehen; **~ance** [rəns] Trennung; Zerlegung *f*.
dissiden|ce ['disidəns] Uneinigkeit; eigene, abweichende Meinung *f*; **~t** [-t] *a* andersdenkend; abweichend (*from* von); *s* Andersdenkende(r); Dissident *m*.
dissimil|ar ['di'similə] unähnlich, ungleich (*to* dat); verschieden (*to* von); anders (*to* als); **~arity** [disimi'læriti], **~itude** [disi'militju:d] Unähnlichkeit, Verschiedenartigkeit, Ungleichheit *f*.
dissimulat|e [di'simjuleit] *tr (Gefühle, Absichten)* verbergen; *itr* sich verstellen, heucheln; **~ion** [disimju'leiʃən] Verstellung; Heuchelei *f*.
dissipat|e ['disipeit] *tr* zerstreuen; vertreiben, auflösen; verschwenden, vergeuden; *fig* ablenken; *tech* verbrauchen; verwandeln (*into heat* in Wärme); *itr* sich zerstreuen, sich auflösen; *(Kräfte)* sich zersplittern; ein lockeres Leben führen; *(Nebel)* sich verflüchtigen; **~ed** [-id] *a* leichtlebig, vergnügungssüchtig, ausschweifend; liederlich; vertan; zerstreut; *to have a ~~ look* verlebt aussehen; **~ion** [-'peiʃən] Zerstreuung, Auflösung; Verflüchtigung; Verschwendung, Vergeudung, Verzettelung; Leichtlebigkeit, Ausschweifung; Liederlichkeit; *tech* Ableitung, Abgabe; *(Kräfte)* Zersplitterung *f*.
dissoci|able [di'souʃjəbl] spaltbar, trennbar; unterscheidbar; nicht zs.-passend; [di'souʃəbl] ungesellig; unsozial; **~ate** [di'souʃieit] *tr* trennen, ab-, loslösen, (ab)spalten (*from* von); ausea.halten, unterscheiden; *chem* spalten, zersetzen, dissoziieren; *itr* sich trennen; *chem* sich spalten, sich zersetzen; *to ~~ o.s. from* sich lossagen, sich trennen von; **~ation** [disousi'eiʃən] Trennung; *chem* Spaltung, Zersetzung, Dissoziation *f*, Zerfall *m*; *psychol* Bewußtseinsspaltung *f*; *~~ product* Spalt-, Zerfallsprodukt *n*.
dissolub|ility [disɔlju'biliti] *chem* Löslichkeit; *allg* Auflösbarkeit, Trennbarkeit *f*; **~le** [di'sɔljubl] löslich; auflösbar, trennbar.
dissolut|e ['disəlu:t] ausschweifend, zügellos, liederlich; **~ion** [-'lu:ʃən] Auflösung *(in e-r Flüssigkeit u. allg, a. jur)*; Beendigung *f*, Ende *n*, Tod *m*; Liquidierung; *Am* Entflechtung; Annullierung; Vertagung *f*.
dissolv|able [di'zɔlvəbl] löslich, auflösbar; trennbar; **~e** [di'zɔlv] *tr* verflüssigen, auflösen *a. fig*; trennen; liquidieren; *(Versammlung)* aufheben; *(Sitzung)* schließen; beenden; verschwinden lassen; *film* ein-, überblenden; *itr* sich (auf)lösen, zergehen, schmelzen; *allg* sich auflösen, zerfallen; aufhören, zu Ende gehen; verschwinden; *~ed in tears* in Tränen aufgelöst; **~ent** [di'zɔlvənt] *a* lösend; *fig* zersetzend; *s* Lösungsmittel *n*.
disson|ance ['disənəns] Mißklang *m*, Dissonanz; mangelnde Übereinstimmung, Unstimmigkeit, Mißhelligkeit, Disharmonie *f*; **~ant** ['-ənt] un-, disharmonisch; entgegengesetzt, gegensätzlich; unvereinbar (*from, to* mit); nicht zs.passend.
dissua|de [di'sweid] *tr* abraten (*s.o. from s.th.* jdm von e-r S), ausreden, (*s.o. from s.th.* jdm etw); abbringen (*from doing s.th.* etw zu tun); **~sion** [di'sweiʒən] Ausreden, Abbringen, Abraten *n*; **~sive** [-siv] abratend.
dis(s)yllab|ic ['disi'læbik] zweisilbig; **~le** [di'siləbl] zweisilbige(s) Wort *n*.
distaff ['distɑ:f] Spinnrocken *m*; *on the ~ side* in der Familie der Frau.
distan|ce ['distəns] *s* Abstand *m*, Entfernung, Ferne *f*; Zwischenraum *m*, Strecke *f*; Zeitraum *m*; *sport* Distanz; *fig* Zurückhaltung, Reserve, Distanz *f*; *mus* Intervall *n*; *mil* Tiefenabstand *m*; *tr* hinter sich lassen *a. fig, (beim Rennen)* abhängen; *fig* übertreffen, überragen, überholen; *fig* Abstand halten, sich distanzieren von; *(Kunst)* den Hintergrund herausbringen *gen*, Tiefe geben *dat*; *at, from a ~~* in, aus e-r gewissen Entfernung; von fern, von weitem; *at some ~~* in einiger Entfernung; *at this ~~ of time* in diesem zeitlichen Abstand; *in the ~~* in der Ferne, weit weg; *no ~~ at all* gar nicht weit; *within easy ~~ of* nicht weit von... (weg); nahe bei; *(with)in walking ~~* noch zu Fuß zu erreichen(d) (*of* von); *to cover a ~~* e-e Strecke zurücklegen; *to keep o.'s ~~* Abstand halten *od* wahren; kühl, zurückhaltend sein; *to keep s.o. at a ~~* sich mit jdm nicht näher einlassen; jdn fernhalten; *it is a great ~~ off, quite a ~~ from here* es ist sehr weit weg (von hier); *it is no ~~ at all* es ist ein Katzensprung; *keep your ~~* bleib mir vom Leibe! *what is the ~~ to* wie weit ist es nach; *the ~~ covered* die zurückgelegte Strecke; **~t** ['-t] (ent-) fern(t) *a. fig*, weit weg (*from* von); *fig*

weit zurückliegend; *(Vetter)* weitläufig; zurückhaltend, kühl; ~~ *(air) reconnaissance* strategische Luftaufklärung, Fernaufklärung *f*; **~tly** [-tli] *adv*: ~~ *related* entfernt, weitläufig verwandt.

distaste ['dis'teist] Abneigung *f*, Widerwille (*for* gegen), Ekel *m* (*for* vor); **~ful** [-ful] widerwärtig, ekelhaft, eklig; zuwider, unangenehm *m*; **~fulness** [-fulnis] Widerlichkeit *f*.

distemper [dis'tempə] **1.** Unpäßlichkeit, Störung, Krankheit; Staupe *(Hundekrankheit)*; Druse *f (Pferdekrankheit)*; *pol* Unruhen *f pl*; **2.** *s* Temperatechnik, -malerei, -farbe *f*; *tr (Farbe)* mit e-m Bindemittel vermischen; in Temperatechnik malen.

disten|d [dis'tend] *tr itr* (sich) ausdehnen, (sich) (aus)strecken; (sich) blähen; *itr* (an)schwellen; **~sible** [-'tensəbl] dehnbar; **~sion,** *Am* **~tion** [dis'tenʃən] (Aus-)Dehnung, Schwellung, Blähung *f*.

distich ['distik] Distichon, Verspaar *n*.

distil(l) [dis'til] *itr* (herab-, herunter-) tropfen, tröpfeln, sickern, rieseln; destillieren; *tr* (ab)tropfen lassen; destillieren (*from* aus); *(Schnaps)* brennen; läutern, reinigen; **~late** ['distilit, -leit] Destillat *n*; **~lation** [-'leiʃən] Destillation *f*; Destillat *n*; **~ler** [-'tilə] Destillateur, Branntweinbrenner; Destillierapparat *m*; **~lery** [-'tiləri] Branntweinbrennerei *f*; **~ling** Destillier-; ~~ *flask, vessel* Destillierkolben *m*, -gefäß *n*.

distinct [dis'tiŋkt] verschieden, ungleich (*from* von); ander, besonder, abgesondert, getrennt, einzeln, eigen; deutlich, klar, scharf; fest umrissen, ausgeprägt; genau (ausgedrückt), unmißverständlich, entschieden; *to keep* ~ ausea.halten, nicht verwechseln; **~ion** [-'tiŋkʃən] Unterscheidung *f*; Unterschied *m*; Besonderheit, Eigenart; Qualität; Vornehmheit *f*; Wert *m*, Würde *f*, Rang, Ruf *m*; Auszeichnung *f*, Ehrenzeichen *n*; *of* ~~ ausgezeichnet, von Rang; *without* ~~ ohne Unterschied, unterschiedslos; ohne Ansehung der Person; *to confer a* ~~ *on s.o.* jdm e-e Auszeichnung verleihen, jdn auszeichnen; *to draw a* ~~ *between* e-n Unterschied machen zwischen; *to gain* ~~ sich auszeichnen; *to make* ~~*s* Unterschiede machen, unterscheiden; *a* ~~ *without a difference* e-e spitzfindige Unterscheidung; *class* ~~ Klassenunterschied *m*; ~~ *of rank* Rangunterschied *m*; **~ive** [-iv] unterscheidend, kennzeichnend, charakteristisch, spezifisch (*of* für); Unterscheidungs-, Kenn-; ~~ *badge* Abzeichen *n*; ~~ *feature, mark* Unterscheidungsmerkmal, Kennzeichen *n*, -marke, Kennung *f*; ~~ *number* Kennummer *f*; **~ness** [-nis] Verschiedenheit; Besonderheit, Eigenart; Deutlichkeit, Klarheit, Genauigkeit *f*.

distinguish [dis'tiŋgwiʃ] *tr* unterscheiden (*from* von); erkennen, wahrnehmen, bemerken; unterscheiden, ausea.halten; einteilen (*into* in); *itr* unterscheiden *(between, among* zwischen); *to* ~ *o.s.* sich auszeichnen, sich hervortun; **~able** [-əbl] zu unterscheiden(d), unterscheidbar, erkennbar; **~ed** [-t] *a* ausgezeichnet, vorzüglich; bemerkenswert (*for* wegen); bedeutend, hervorragend, berühmt; verdient; vornehm (aussehend); ~~ *by* kenntlich an.

distort [dis'tɔ:t] *tr* verdrehen *a. fig*, verrenken, verformen, verzerren *a. fig*; *fig* entstellen, verzerrt darstellen; **~ion** [-'tɔ:ʃən] Verrenkung, Verzerrung *a. fig*, Verformung, Verwindung; Entstellung *a. fig*, (Wort-)Verdrehung; *fig* verzerrte Darstellung *f*; **~ionist** [-ʃənist] Schlangenmensch; Karikaturist *m*.

distract [dis'trækt] *tr (geistig)* ablenken (*from* von), zerstreuen; verwirren, durchea.bringen (*from* bei); geistig zerrütten; **~ed** [-id] *a* (ver)wirr(t), konfus, durcheinander; aus dem Häuschen, außer sich (*with* vor); wahnsinnig; *to drive* ~~ verwirrt *od* ärgerlich *od* verrückt machen; **~ion** [-kʃən] Ablenkung *a. pej*, Zerstreuung, Unterhaltung; Zerstreutheit, mangelnde Aufmerksamkeit; Verwirrung, Konfusion *f*; Wahnsinn *m*; *to* ~~ bis zur Raserei, aufs äußerste; *to drive to* ~~ = *to drive* ~*ed*; *to love to* ~~ bis zum Wahnsinn lieben.

distrain [dis'trein] *tr u. itr*: *to* ~ *upon* pfänden, zwangsvollstrecken, beschlagnahmen (*for* wegen); **~able** [-əbl] pfändbar; **~ee** [-'ni:] Gepfändete(r), Pfandschuldner *m*; **~er, ~or** [-ə, *a.* -'nɔ:] Pfandgläubiger *m*; **~t** [-t] Pfändung, Beschlagnahme *f*.

distraught [dis'trɔ:t] *a* bestürzt, verwirrt.

distress [dis'tres] *s* Kummer, Jammer *m*, Verzweiflung; völlige Erschöpfung *f*; Sorgen *f pl*; Trübsal, Bedrängnis, Not *f*, Elend *n*, Not-, verzweifelte Lage *f*, Notstand; Schmerz *m*; *jur* Pfändung, Beschlagnahme *f*, Zwangsvollstreckung *f*; Pfandsachen *f pl*; *mar* Seenot *f*; *tr* Leid zufügen (*s.o.* jdm), betrüben, unglücklich machen; Kummer, Sorgen bereiten (*s.o.* jdm); in Not bringen, ins Elend stürzen; *jur* pfänden, beschlagnahmen; *to* ~ *o.s.* sich sorgen; *in* ~ *(Schiff)* in Not; *under* ~ gepfändet; *to be in great* ~ sich in großer Not(lage) befinden; *to levy a* ~ *on s.th.* etw pfänden; **~ed** [-t] *a* in Sorgen, in Not, im Elend; ~~ *area* Notstandsgebiet *n*; **~ful** [-ful] leid-, qual-, kummer-, sorgenvoll; jämmerlich, elend; erschöpft; **~ing** [-iŋ] betrüblich, schmerzlich; ~ **rocket, signal** *mar* Notsignal *n*; ~ **sale** Zwangsversteigerung *f*; ~ **warrant** Vollstreckungsbefehl *m*.

distribut|able [dis'tribjutəbl] verteilbar; **~e** [dis'tribju(:)t, '-u:t] *tr* ver-, auf-, aus-, zuteilen; ausbreiten; *(Dividende)* ausschütten (*among* unter; *to* an); *com* vertreiben, absetzen; einteilen, klassifizieren (*into* in); *typ (Satz)* ablegen; *mil* gliedern; **~ing** [-iŋ] Verteilungs-; ~~ *agent* Großhandelsvertreter *m*; ~~ *box* Verteilerdose *f*, -kasten *m*; ~~ *network, system* Verteilungsnetz *n*; ~~ *pillar* Verteilersäule *f*; ~~ *point* Verteilerpunkt *m*; *mil* Verteiler-, Ausgabestelle *f*; ~~ *station* Verteilerbahnhof *m*; ~~ *trade* Verteilergewerbe *n*; **~ion** [distri'bju:ʃən] Ver-, Auf-, Aus-, Zuteilung; Ausgabe; *fin* Ausschüttung *f*; Anteil *m*; Verbreitung *f*; *film* Verleih; *com* Vertrieb, Absatz *m*; *(Statistik, auf Schriftstücken)* Verteiler(schlüssel) *m*; *(Schriftsatz)* Ablegen *n*; *mil* Gliederung, Aufstellung *f*; ~~ *area (com)* Absatzgebiet *n*; ~~ *board, box (el)* Verteilerschalttafel, -dose *f*; ~~ *cost, expense* Vertriebs-, Absatzkosten *pl*; ~~ *main (el)* Verteilungssammelschiene; *(Wasser)* Hauptleitung *f*; ~~ *office* Wirtschaftsamt *n*; ~~ *panel* Schalttafel *f*; ~~ *point (mil)* Verteilungs-, Kraftstoffausgabestelle *f*; ~~ *of power, of prices, of profits, of wealth* Macht-, Preis-, Gewinn-, Güterverteilung *f*; ~~ *switchboard* Verteilerschrank *m*; ~~ *warehouse* Auslieferungslager *n*; **~ive** [dis'tribjutiv] *a* verteilend; einzeln; ausgleichend; *s* Distributivzahl *f*; ~~ *justice* ausgleichende Gerechtigkeit *f*; ~~ *facilities (pl com)* Verteilerapparat *m*; **~or** [dis'tribjutə] Verteiler *a. tech*; Vertriebs-, Verkaufsagent, Konzessionär *m*; Konzessionsfirma *f*; Filmverleiher *m*; ~~ *arm (mot)* Verteilerfinger *m*; ~~ *box (el)* Abzweigdose *f*; ~~ *discount* Händlerrabatt *m*; ~~ *duct* Kabelkanal *m*.

district ['distrikt] *s* Gebiet, Land(strich *m*) *n*, Gau *m*, Gegend *f*; (Stadt-)Viertel *n*; (Verwaltungs-)Bezirk, Kreis; *mar* Abschnitt *m*; *tr* in Bezirke einteilen; *business* ~ Geschäftsbereich *m* od *n*; *customs* ~ Zollbezirk *m*; *electoral, polling* ~ Wahlbezirk *m*; *postal* ~ Post-, Zustellbezirk *m*; *rural* ~ Landbezirk *m*; ~ **attorney** *Am* Amts-, Staatsanwalt *m*; ~ **court** *Am* Bezirksgericht *n*; ~ **heating** Fernheizung *f*; ~ **manager** Bezirksdirektor *m*; ~ **representative** Bezirksvertreter *m*.

distrust [dis'trʌst] *s* Mißtrauen *n*, Verdacht *m* (*of, towards* gegen); Zweifel *m pl* (*of* an); *tr* mißtrauen (*s.o.* jdm); verdächtigen, an-, bezweifeln; **~ful** [-ful] mißtrauisch, argwöhnisch (*of* gegenüber); zweifelnd (*of* an).

disturb [dis'tə:b] *tr* stören; unterbrechen; beeinträchtigen; aufrühren, durchea.wirbeln; durchea.-, in Unordnung bringen; beunruhigen, verwirren; *(Pläne)* durchkreuzen; vernichten, zerstören; *to be* ~*ed at, by s.th.* über etw beunruhigt sein; *don't* ~ *yourself* lassen Sie sich nicht stören; **~ance** [-əns] Störung; *jur* Behinderung; Unordnung *f*, Durcheinander *n*; Aufregung, Erregung *f*; *pl pol* Unruhen *f pl*; *to cause a* ~~ die öffentliche Ordnung stören; ~~ *of the peace* öffentliche Ruhestörung *f*; **~ing** [-iŋ] störend (*to* für).

disuni|on ['dis'ju:njən], **~ty** [-'juniti] Trennung, Spaltung; Uneinigkeit; Unstimmigkeit, Mißhelligkeit *f*; **~te** ['disju:'nait] *tr* trennen, spalten, entzweien; *itr* sich trennen, ausea.-, getrennte Wege gehen.

disuse ['dis'ju:z] *tr (meist Passiv)* nicht mehr gebrauchen *od* benutzen; aufgeben; *s* ['-'ju:s] Nichtgebrauch *m*, -benutzung; Ungebräuchlichkeit *f*; *to fall, to go into* ~ außer Gebrauch kommen; **~d** ['-zd] *a* außer Gebrauch (gekommen), veraltet.

disyllabic ['disi'læbik] *s. dissyllabic.*

ditch [ditʃ] *s* (Wasser-, Abzugs-)Graben; Wasserlauf *m*; *aero sl* Meer *n*, Bach *m*; *the D~ (sl)* die Nordsee, der Kanal; *tr* e-n (Abzugs-)Graben ziehen durch; in den Graben werfen *od* fahren; *Am rail* zum Entgleisen bringen; *sl* im Stich lassen, wegwerfen; *itr* Gräben ziehen *od* ausbessern; *aero* notwassern; notlanden; *to be in a dry* ~ *(fig)* im warmen Nest sitzen; **~er** ['-ə] Deicharbeiter; Tieflöffelbagger *m*; **~ing** ['-iŋ] *aero* Notwasserung *f*; ~ **water** stehende(s) Wasser *n*; *clear as* ~~ klar wie Kloßbrühe; *dull as* ~~ dumm wie Bohnenstroh; stinklangweilig.

dither ['diðə] *itr* zittern, beben (*with* vor); *fam* zaudern, schwanken; *s* Zittern *n*; *to be all of a* ~, *to have the* ~*s (fam)* ganz verdattert sein.

dithyramb ['diθiræm(b)] *lit* Dithyrambus *m*; **~ic** [-'ræmbik] dithyrambisch; begeistert, enthusiastisch.

ditto ['ditou] *pl -os fam* Kopie *f*, Duplikat *n*; Wiederholung *f*; *(~ mark)* Wiederholungszeichen *n*; *adv* desgleichen, ebenso, ebenfalls, dito; *tr* wieder-

holen; abschreiben; *to say ~ to (fam)* ins gleiche Horn tuten, einer Meinung sein.
ditty ['diti] Liedchen *n*; **~-bag, box** *mar* Beutel *m*, Kästchen *n* für persönliche Gebrauchsgegenstände.
diure|sis [daijuə'ri:sis] Diurese *f*; **~tic** [-'retik] *a u. s* harntreibend(es Mittel*n*).
diurnal [dai'ə:nl] täglich; Tag(es)-; *zoo* e-n Tag lebend.
diva ['di:və] Primadonna *f*.
divagat|e ['daivəgeit] *itr* umherstreifen; *fig* abschweifen; **~ion** [-'geiʃən] Umherstreifen *n*; *fig* Abschweifung *f*.
divan [di'væn, dai'v-, 'daivæn] Diwan *m*; *(~-bed)* Liege *f*; Rauchzimmer *n*; (Hotel-)Halle *f*; Café *n*; Tabakladen *m*.
divaricat|e [dai'værikeit] *itr* sich gabeln; abzweigen; *tr* weit ausbreiten; *a* [-kit] gegabelt; **~ion** [-'keiʃən] Gabelung; *fig* Meinungsverschiedenheit *f*.
div|e [daiv] *Am irr dove, dove itr* (unter-)tauchen (*into* in; *for* nach); e-n Kopfsprung machen; *aero* e-n Sturzflug machen, stürzen; *fam* sich ducken; *(plötzlich)* verschwinden (*into* in); rasch hineingehen, hineingreifen (*into* in); *fig* sich vergraben, sich vertiefen, sich versenken (*into* in); *s* Tauchen *n*; Kopfsprung *m*; plötzliche(s) Verschwinden, Versinken *n*; *aero* Sturzflug; *Br* Keller(lokal *n*) *m*; *Am fam* Spelunke, Spielhölle *f*; *to make a ~~* schnappen, haschen (*at* nach); herumwühlen (*into* in); *to ~ into o.'s pockets* die Hände in die Tasche stecken; **~er** ['-ə] Taucher *a. orn*; *Br sl* Taschendieb *m*; **~ing** ['-iŋ] Tauchen; Kunstspringen *n*; *~~-bell* Taucherglocke *f*; *~~-board* Sprungbrett *n*; *~~-depth* Tauchtiefe *f*; *~~-dress, -suit* Taucheranzug *m*; *~~ flipper, -goggles (pl)* Tauchflosse, -brille *f*; *~~-helmet* Taucherhelm *m*; *~~-pool* Sprungbecken *n*; *~~-tower* Sprungturm *m*.
diverg|e [dai'və:dʒ] *itr* ausea.gehen, -laufen, sich trennen; divergieren; (vonea.) abweichen (*from* von); *~~ing junction (rail)* Streckenabzweigung *f*; **~ence, -cy** [-əns(i)] Divergieren *n*, Trennung; Abweichung; Divergenz *f*, Öffnungswinkel *m*; Verschiedenheit; *mete* Divergenz *f*; **~ent** [-ənt] ausea.gehend, divergierend; abweichend, verschieden; kritisch.
divers ['daivə(:)z] *lit* etliche, mancherlei; **~e** [dai'və:s, 'dai-] verschieden(artig); mannigfaltig, abwechslungsreich, wechselnd; **~ification** [daivə:sifi'keiʃən] Veränderung, Umgestaltung; *(Risiko)* Verteilung; Streuung; Abwechslung, Mannigfaltigkeit *f*; *broad ~~* breite(s) Produktionsprogramm *n*; **~ify** [dai'və:sifai] *tr* verschieden(artig), abwechslungsreich gestalten; Abwechslung bringen in; variieren, beleben; **~ion** [dai'və:ʃən, di'v-] Ableitung, Ablenkung; Verteilung; *Br* (Verkehrs-)Umleitung; *fig* Ablenkung, Zerstreuung *f*; *mil* Ablenkungsangriff *m*, Täuschungsmanöver *n*; **~ionary** [-'və:ʃnəri] *a mil* Ablenkungs-; **~ity** [dai'və:siti] Verschiedenheit, Verschiedenartigkeit, Mannigfaltigkeit, Vielfalt *f*; *~~ of interest* Interessenkonflikt *m*; *~~ of opinion* Meinungsverschiedenheit *f*.
divert [dai'və:t, di'v-] *tr* ableiten, -lenken (*from* von); *Br (den Verkehr)* umleiten; *(Geld)* abzweigen; *fig* ablenken; zerstreuen, unterhalten; **~ing** [-iŋ] unterhaltsam, amüsant; *~~ attack* Entlastungsangriff *m*.
divest [dai'vest, di'v-] *tr* entkleiden; (ab)nehmen, widerrechtlich entziehen (*s.o. of s.th.* jdm etw); berauben (*s.o. of s.th.* jdn e-r S); *to ~ o.s. of* sich trennen von, sich entäußern *gen*; verzichten auf; *(Kleidungsstück)* ablegen; *(von e-m Amt)* zurücktreten; **~(it)ure** [-'vest(it)ʃə], **~ment** [-mənt] Entkleidung; Besitzentziehung, Beraubung; *Am* Entflechtung *f*.
divid|e [di'vaid] *tr* teilen, zerschneiden, (auf-)spalten, trennen; *math* dividieren, teilen (*by* durch; 2 *into* 6 6 durch 2); auf-, verteilen (*among* unter), austeilen; *(Dividende)* ausschütten; gliedern, einteilen (*into* in), klassifizieren, (an)ordnen; (ab)sondern, scheiden, trennen (*from* von); *(Haar)* scheiteln; entzweien, ausea.-bringen; *parl* durch Hammelsprung abstimmen lassen; *itr* sich teilen, sich trennen, sich auflösen (*into* in); verschiedener Meinung sein; *parl* (durch Hammelsprung) abstimmen; *s* Trennung; Wasserscheide *f*; **~ed** [-id] *a* getrennt; geteilt; *(Dividende)* ausgeschüttet; *to be ~~ on a question* in e-r Frage geteilter Meinung sein; **~end** ['dividend, -ənd] *fin* Dividende *f*, Gewinnanteil *m*; *fin* Ausschüttung *f*; *math* Dividend *m*; *(Versicherung)* Jahresrückzahlung; *(Konkurs)* Quote *f*; *to pass the ~* keine Dividende ausschütten; *to pay, to distribute a ~* e-e Dividende ausschütten; *~~-bill, -coupon, -warrant* (Gewinn-)Anteilschein *m*; **~er** [-ə] (Ver-)Teiler; *pl* Stechzirkel *m*; **~ing** [-iŋ] *a* Teilungs-, Trenn(ungs)-; *~~ line* Trenn(ungs)-linie *f*; *~~ wall* Trennwand *f*.
divin|ation [divi'neiʃən] Ahnung; Weissagung, Prophezeiung *f*; **~e** [di'vain] *tr* ahnen; weissagen, prophezeien; vermuten, erraten; *itr* wahrsagen; *a* göttlich; göttergleich, erhaben; *fam* herrlich, prächtig; *s* Theologe; *fam* Geistliche(r) *m*; *~~ service* Gottesdienst *m*; **~er** [-'vainə] Wahrsager, Prophet; Rutengänger *m*; **~ing** [-'vainiŋ]: *~~ rod* Wünschelrute *f*; **~ity** [di'viniti] Göttlichkeit; Gottheit *f*; göttliche(s) Wesen *n*; Theologie *f*.
divisib|ility [divizi'biliti] Teilbarkeit *f*; **~le** [di'vizəbl] teilbar *a. math* (*by* durch); *6 is ~~ by 2* 2 geht in 6 auf.
division [di'viʒən] (Ein-, Ver-)Teilung; *(Wertpapiere)* Stückelung; Klassifizierung, Klassifikation; *math* Division *f*, Dividieren, Teilen *n*; Teil *m*; Gruppe, Abteilung *f*, Abschnitt, Zweig *m*, Branche; *(Gericht)* Kammer; Stufe; Klasse; *mil* Division; *rail* Strecke *f*; Bezirk; Trennungsstrich *m*, Trennlinie, Grenze; *parl* Abstimmung durch Hammelsprung; *fig* Uneinigkeit, Spaltung *f*; *to come to, to take a ~ (parl)* zur Abstimmung schreiten; *to insist on a ~* (namentliche) Abstimmung verlangen; *~ into degrees* Gradeinteilung *f*; *~ of labo(u)r* Arbeitsteilung *f*; *~ into shares* Stückelung *f*; **~al** [-l] *a* Abteilungs-; *mil* Divisions-; divisionseigen; *~~ sector* Divisionsabschnitt *m*; **~ artillery** Divisionsartillerie *f*; **~ bell** Abstimmungsglocke *f*; **~ commander** Divisionskommandeur *m*; **~ command post** Divisionsgefechtsstand *m*; **~ engineer** Pionierführer *m*; **~ manager** Abteilungsleiter *m*.
divisor [di'vaizə] *math* Divisor *m*.
divorc|e [di'vɔ:s] *s* (Ehe-)Scheidung; *allg* Trennung *f* (*between ... and* von ... und; *from* von); *tr* scheiden; sich scheiden lassen von; *allg* trennen (*from* von); *to apply, to sue, to petition for a ~~* die Scheidungsklage einreichen; *to grant a ~~* die Scheidung aussprechen; *to have been ~ed* geschieden sein; *to obtain a ~~* geschieden werden; *cause of, ground for ~~* Scheidungsgrund *m*; *~~ action, petition* Scheidungsklage *f*; *~~ case, suit* Scheidungsprozeß *m*; **~ee** [divɔ:'si:] Geschiedene(r *m*) *f*; **~ement** [-mənt] *s. ~e*.
divot ['divət] Rasenstück *n*, Sode *f*; *(Golf)* (losgeschlagener) Rasenklumpen *m*.
divulg|ation [daivʌl'geiʃən], **~ence** [di'vʌldʒəns], **~ement** [di'vʌldʒmənt] Bekanntmachung, Veröffentlichung, Verbreitung; Enthüllung, Aufdeckung *f*; **~e** [dai'vʌldʒ] *tr* bekanntmachen, veröffentlichen, ausplaudern.
divvy ['divi] *sl tr itr (to ~ up) (den Gewinn)* teilen; *s* (Gewinn-)Anteil *m*.
Dixie ['diksi], **~-Land** die Südstaaten *pl (der US)*; **~land** [lænd] Dixieland *m (Jazzart)*.
dixy, dixie ['diksi] *obs mil* (Feld-)Kessel *m*, Kochgeschirr *n*.
dizz|iness ['dizinis] Schwindel(anfall) *m*; **~y** ['dizi] *a* schwind(e)lig; benommen; schwindelerregend; verwirrt, aufgeregt; *fam* dämlich, dumm; *tr* schwindlig machen; *fig* verwirren, verwirrt machen, durchea.bringen.

*

do [du:] **1.** *irr did, done tr* tun, machen, herstellen, anfertigen; verrichten, zustande, zuwege bringen, bewirken, aus-, durchführen; vollführen, -bringen; schaffen; *(Pflicht)* erfüllen; ausrichten; bereiten, herrichten; zurechtmachen; in Ordnung bringen, aufräumen, putzen; beenden, vollenden, fertigmachen, zum Abschluß bringen; *(Aufgabe, Problem)* lösen, *(Frage)* erledigen; antun, widerfahren lassen, erweisen; passen, recht sein (*s.o.* jdm); *(Stück)* aufführen, spielen, auf die Bühne bringen; *(Rolle)* spielen, darstellen; übersetzen, übertragen; *(Strecke, Entfernung)* zurücklegen; *fam (Land, Stadt, Museum)* besichtigen, *(Perfekt)* gesehen haben; *(Essen)* zubereiten, fertigmachen, kochen *od* braten *od* backen; *fam* behandeln, bedienen, freihalten; *fam* reinlegen, anführen, betrügen, übers Ohr hauen, prellen; *fam* erledigen, ruinieren, den Rest geben (*s.o.* jdm), zugrunde richten; **2.** *itr* tätig sein, handeln, arbeiten; *(Wagen)* fahren; sich verhalten, sich benehmen, sich aufführen; *(Perfekt)* fertig sein (*with* mit); sich befinden; aus-, zurechtkommen; genügen, ausreichen (*s.o.* jdm); passen, recht, dem Zweck entsprechend sein; fort-, weiterkommen, es weiter bringen; **3.** *aux*: *(bleibt in Frage u. Verneinung, bei Inversion u. als Ersatz für ein anderes Verbum unübersetzt:) ~ you go?* gehen Sie? *I ~ not, don't go* ich gehe nicht; *you play better than I ~* Sie spielen besser als ich; *so ~ I* ich auch; *nor ~ I (either), neither ~ I* ich auch nicht; *(als Verstärkung adverbial übersetzt:) I ~ wish I could* ich wünsche so sehr, ich könnte es, ich würde es so gern können; *I ~ feel better* ich fühle mich wirklich, tatsächlich besser; *~ come!* kommen Sie doch! **4.** *s pl fam* Vergnügen *n*, Fest(lichkeit *f*) *n*, Feier *f* (*there is a ~ on* da ist was los); *sl* Schwindel, Betrug, Nepp *m*; *mil* Unternehmen *n*, Angriff *m*; *pl fam* Anteile *m pl*; *fair ~'s!* nicht schummeln! **5.** *to get s.th. done* etw machen lassen; *to have to ~ with* zu tun haben mit; *to have done with* fertig sein mit; *to ~ badly* schlechte Geschäfte machen; übel dran sein; *to ~ the beds, the dishes* die Betten machen; das Geschirr spülen; *to ~ o.'s best, the best* od *all one can, o.'s utmost, everything in* *o.'s power* sein bestes, sein möglichstes, das menschenmögliche, alles, was man kann, tun; *to ~ o.'s bit* s-e Pflicht tun; *(Geflügel)* gut zubereiten; *to ~ business with s.o.* mit jdm Geschäfte machen; *to ~ credit to s.o.* jdm Ehre machen; *to ~ o.'s damnedest (fam)* sich gewaltig am Riemen reißen; *to ~ the downy (sl)* im Bett bleiben; *to ~ o.'s duty* s-e Pflicht tun; *to ~ duty as* dienen, gebraucht werden als; *to ~ evil* Böses tun; *to ~ good* Gutes tun; gut tun, nützen; *to ~ any* od *some, no good* etwas, nichts nützen; *to ~ o.'s hair* sich kämmen, sich frisieren; *to ~ harm* schaden; *to ~ hono(u)r to s.o.* jdm Ehre erweisen; *to ~ justice to* gerecht werden *dat*; *to ~ the laundry* Wäsche waschen; *to ~ like for like* Gleiches mit Gleichem vergelten; *to ~ o.'s nails* sich die Nägel reinigen; *to ~ proud* sehr splendid sein; *s.o.* jdn fürstlich bewirten; *to ~ to a turn (Fleisch)* hervorragend zubereiten; *to ~ well* s-e Sache gut machen; *(Getreide)* gut stehen; *to ~ s.o. well* jdm guttun; *to ~ o.s. well* sein Ziel erreichen; *to ~ well by s.o.* jdm großzügig helfen; **6.** *I could ~ with the money* ich könnte das Geld gut gebrauchen; *I have done writing* ich bin fertig mit Schreiben; *I have done with him* er ist für mich erledigt; *I am doing well* es geht mir gut; *have done!* hör auf! *how ~ you ~?* wie geht es Ihnen? wie geht's? guten Tag! *(beim Vorstellen)* sehr angenehm! *that will ~* das genügt; *that won't ~!* das geht nicht! *what can I ~ for you?* womit kann ich Ihnen dienen? *what's to be done with it?* was soll damit geschehen? *easier said than done* das ist leichter gesagt als getan; *no sooner said than done* gesagt, getan; *well begun is half done (prov)* frisch gewagt ist halb gewonnen; **7.** *to ~* **again**, *to ~ over again* noch (ein)mal tun *od* machen, wiederholen; *to ~* **away** *with* abschaffen; beseitigen, weg-, beiseite, auf die Seite schaffen; *(Menschen)* aus dem Wege räumen, erledigen; *o.s.* sich das Leben nehmen; *to ~* **by** behandeln; sich verhalten, sich aufführen, sich benehmen gegenüber; *to ~* **down** *fam* übers Ohr hauen, reinlegen; *to ~* **for** *Br* sich kümmern um, haushalten (*s.o.* jdm); e-n Ersatz darstellen; *fam* kaputt machen, ruinieren, den Rest geben (*s.o.* jdm); *sl* um die Ecke bringen, umbringen; *to ~ for o.s.* Selbstmord verüben; die Hausarbeiten selbst erledigen; *to be done for* hinüber *od* erledigt sein; *to ~* **in** *sl* um die Ecke bringen, erledigen, umlegen, killen; *fam* reinreißen, reinlegen; *to ~* **into** übersetzen; *to ~* **on** *(Kleidung)* anziehen, anlegen; *to ~* **out** leer machen, leeren, aus-, aufräumen, ausfegen, -wischen, reinigen, putzen; *(Licht)* ausmachen; *to ~ out of* abschwindeln, abnehmen; hinauswerfen; *to ~* **over** neu be-, überziehen, (neu) (an)streichen; wiederholen; *to ~* **up** überholen, erneuern, auffrischen, instand setzen; *(Wäsche)* waschen; einwickeln, -pakken; zumachen, -knöpfen, -haken, -schnüren, -binden; *(die Haare)* auf-, hochstecken; *nur pp* erschöpft, erledigt, fertig; *to ~ up brown (Am)* gründlich, großzügig erledigen; *to ~* **with** auskommen, fertigwerden mit; *I can ~ with* ich bin zufrieden mit; ich könnte gebrauchen, hätte nötig; *to ~* **without** auskommen, fertigwerden ohne, nicht brauchen, nicht nötig haben; **~able** ausführbar; **~-all** Faktotum *n*; **~-it-yourself** *s* Eigenbau *m*; *a* Bastel-.

doat [dout] *s. dote.*

doc [dɔk] *fam* Doktor *m.*

docil|e ['dousail, *Am* 'dɔsəl] gelehrig; lenk-, folg-, fügsam; **~ity** [do(u)'siliti] Gelehrigkeit; Folg-, Fügsamkeit *f.*

dock [dɔk] **1.** *bot* Ampfer *m*; *sour ~* Sauerampfer *m*; **2.** *s* Schwanzrübe *f*; Stutzschwanz *m*; *tr (bes. Schwanz)* stutzen; *fig (bes. Lohn)* kürzen; *to ~ s.o. for s.th.* jdm etw abziehen; beschneiden, vermindern, verringern; **3.** *jur* Anklagebank *f*; *in the ~* auf der Anklagebank; **4.** *s mar* Dock *n*; Laderampe *f*; *Am* Kai *m*, Mole *f*, Pier *m* od *f*; Hafenbahnhof *m*; *rail* Abstellgeleise *n*; *pl* Hafenbecken *n pl*, -anlagen *f pl*; *aero* Luftschiff-, Flugzeughalle *f (für die Inspektion)*; *tr itr* docken, ins Dock bringen, im Dock liegen; *Am* anlegen; *(Luftschiff)* in die Halle bringen; *(Flugzeug)* zur Reparatur *od* Überprüfung bringen; *loc rail* abstellen; *naval ~s (pl)* Marinewerft *f* **~age** ['-idʒ] **1.** *(~ dues)* Dockgebühren; Dockanlagen *f pl*; Docken *n*; **2.** Kürzung *f*, Abzug *m*; **~er** ['-ə], **~ labo(u)rer** Schauermann, Dockarbeiter *m*; **~ gate** Dock-, Schleusentor *n*; **~ yard** ['-jɑːd] (Schiffs-)Werft *f*; *~~ crane* Werftkran *m.*

docket ['dɔkit] *jur* Prozeß-, Urteilsregister *n*; Gerichts-, *allg* Terminkalender *m*; *jur* Aktenregister; *allg* (Inhalts-)Verzeichnis, Register *n*, Liste *f*, Auszug *m*; Etikett *n*, Anhänger; Aktenschwanz; *com* Bestell-, Lieferschein *m*; Zollquittung *f*; *tr* registrieren, e-n Auszug machen von; etikettieren; *wages ~~* Lohnliste *f.*

doctor ['dɔktə] *(D~)* Doktor *(als akad. Grad)*; Doktor, Arzt; *hist* Kirchenlehrer; *sl mar* Schiffskoch *m*; Abstreichmesser *n*; *(~ knife)* Rakel; künstliche Fliege *f (zum Angeln)*; *tr (to ~ up) fam (Kranken)* verarzten, *(Krankheit)* zurechtdoktern, behandeln; ausbessern; *fam* manipulieren, verfälschen, zurechtbiegen; *(Bilanz)* frisieren; *itr fam* praktizieren; *to take o.'s ~'s degree* promovieren, den Doktorgrad erwerben; *factory ~* Werk(s)arzt *m*; *lady, woman ~* Ärztin *f*; *panel ~* Kassenarzt *m*; *ship's ~* Schiffsarzt *m*; *~'s certificate* ärztliche(s) Attest *n*; **~ate** [-rit] Doktorgrad *m*, -würde *f.*

doctrin|aire [dɔktri'nɛə] *s* Ideologe, Prinzipienreiter *m*; *a* doktrinär; lebensfremd; **~al** [dɔk'trainl, 'dɔktrinl] lehrhaft; **~e** ['dɔktrin] Lehre, Doktrin *f*, Dogma *n*, Grundsatz *m.*

document ['dɔkjumənt] *s* Urkunde *f*, Dokument *n*, Akte *f*; Beleg *m*; Schriftstück *n*; *pl* Papiere *n pl*, Unterlagen *f pl*; *tr* ['-ment] e-e Urkunde ausstellen (*s.o.* jdm); mit Unterlagen versehen; urkundlich nachweisen *od* belegen; Belege beifügen; *to draw up a ~* e-e Urkunde abfassen; *to have a ~ authenticated* e-e Urkunde beglaubigen lassen; *to produce, to present a ~* e-e Urkunde vorlegen, e-n Beleg beibringen; *to support by ~s* urkundlich belegen; *commercial ~s (pl)* Geschäftspapiere *n pl*; *execution, issue of a ~* Ausstellung *f* e-s Dokuments; *forging, falsification of ~s* Urkundenfälschung *f*; *human ~* Lebenszeugnisse *n pl*; *negotiable ~* Wertpapier *n*; *secret ~* Geheimdokument *n*; *shipping ~s (pl)* Verladepapiere *n pl*; **~ary** [-'mentəri] *a* urkundlich, dokumentarisch; *s (~~ film)* Kultur-, Lehrfilm *m*; *~~ bill, credit* Dokumentenwechsel, -kredit *m*; *~~ evidence* Urkundenbeweis *m*; **~ation** [dɔkjumen'teiʃən] urkundliche(r) Beleg, Nachweis, Quellennachweis *m*, Dokumentation *f*; *~~ centre* Dokumentenzentrale, Literatursammelstelle *f.*

dodder ['dɔdə] **1.** *itr* zittern, schwanken, torkeln; schlurfen; *fam* tattern, e-n Tatterich haben; **~er** ['-rə] *sl* Zittergreis *m*; **~y** ['-ri] zitterig; verwirrt; vertrottelt; **2.** *s bot* Seide, Klebe *f.*

dodge [dɔdʒ] *tr* schnell (nach der Seite) ausweichen (*s.th.* e-r S), beiseite springen, schnell verschwinden vor; *fig* umgehen, vermeiden; sich drücken (*s.th.* um etw); überspielen, hinters Licht, an der Nase herumführen, spielen mit; kreuz u. quer fragen; *itr* ausweichen; Ausflüchte machen; Kniffe anwenden; *s* Sprung *m* zur Seite; List *f*, Kunstgriff, Kniff, Trick *m*; Ausrede *f*, Ausflüchte *f pl*; *to ~ the issue (Am)* den Folgen aus dem Wege gehen; **~r** ['-ə] geriebene(r), gerissene(r) Kerl, *fam* Schlaumeier; Drückeberger *m*; *Am* (Mais-)Brot *n*, Fladen; *Am* Anschlag-, Handzettel *m*; *mar* Schanzkleid *n*; *work ~~* Arbeitsscheuer *m.*

dodo ['doudou] *pl -o(e)s orn* Dronte; *dead as a ~* völlig veraltet.

doe [dou] Reh *n*, Ricke; Hirschkuh, Hindin; Häsin *f*; Weibchen *n*; *John, Jane D~ (jur)* unbekannt; **~skin** ['-skin] Wildleder *n*; *Art (feiner, weicher)* Wollstoff *m.*

doer ['duːə] Täter; Vollzieher; energische(r) Mensch *m*; *a good ~* eine gut gedeihende Pflanze *a. Tier.*

doff [dɔf] *tr (Kleider)* ausziehen, ablegen; *(Hut)* abnehmen; *fig* von sich tun, aufgeben, ablegen.

dog [dɔg] **1.** *s* Hund *m*; Männchen *n*; *fam* Bursche, Kerl; Versager, Tagedieb *m*; *Am sl* häßliche, langweilige Frau *f*; *tech* Klaue *f*, Sperrzahn *m*, Klammer (-haken *m*) *f*; *tech* Mitnehmer; *tech* Anschlag; (Feuer-, Säge-) Bock *m*; *Am sl* alte(s) Auto *n*; *mete* Nebensonne *f*; *min* Hund, Förderwagen *m*; *(D~) astr* Hundsstern, Sirius *m*; *pl mil sl* Füße *m pl*; *pl fam* Windhundrennen *n*; **2.** *tr* auf dem Fuß, auf Schritt u. Tritt folgen, nachspüren (*s.o.* jdm); *fig* stehenden Fußes folgen (*s.o.* jdm); **3.** *itr Am sl*: *to ~ it* sich drücken; abhauen; sich aufgedonnert anziehen; *adv (in Zssgen)* völlig, sehr; hunde-; **4.** *to die a ~'s death* im Elend sterben; *to give, to throw to the ~s* vor die Hunde, wegwerfen; *to go to the ~s (fam)* vor die Hunde gehen, ruiniert sein; *not to have a ~'s chance* nicht die geringsten Aussichten haben; *to lead a ~'s life* ein Hundeleben führen; *to live a cat and ~ life* wie Hund und Katze leben; *to put on the ~ (Am fam)* sich aufspielen, groß tun; *to ~ the (foot) steps of s.o.* jdm auf Schritt u. Tritt folgen; **5.** *it is raining cats and ~s* es regnet junge Hunde, gießt in Strömen; *every ~ has his day (prov)* es kommt jedem sein Tag; *let sleeping ~s lie (prov)* man soll schlafende Hunde nicht wecken; **6.** *hot ~* warme(s) Würstchen *n*; *a sly old ~* ein alter Fuchs, Schlaukopf *m*; *a ~ in the manger* Neidhammel *m*; **~-berry** *bot* Hundsbeere *f*; **~-biscuit** Hundekuchen; *mil sl* Zwieback *m*; **~-bowl** Freßnapf *m*; **~-box** *rail* Hundeabteil *n*; **~-cart** (leichter) Jagdwagen *m*; **~-collar** Hundehalsband *n*, Halsung *f*; **~-days** *pl* Hundstage *m pl*; **~-eared** *a (Buch)* mit Eselsohren; **~fight** Handgemenge *n*; *mil* Nahkampf; **~fish** Hundshai *m*; **~ged** ['dɔgid] *a* verbissen, hartnäckig; widerborstig, störrisch; **~gedness** ['-idnis] Hartnäckigkeit, Verbissenheit *f*; Starrsinn *m*, Widerborstigkeit *f*, störrische(s)

Wesen *n*; **~gish** ['-iʃ] hündisch; mürrisch; *Am fam* aufgedonnert; **~go** ['-gou] *fam* verborgen; *to lie ~~ (sl)* sich nicht rühren; **~-gone** *a* verdammt, verflixt; **~gy** ['-i] *s* Hündchen *n*; *a fam* aufgemacht; **~-house** *Am* Hundehütte *f*; *Am* Versuchstheater *n*; *in the ~~ (fam)* in Ungnade; **~-kennel** Hundehütte *f*; **~ Latin** Mönchs-, Küchenlatein *n*; **~ lead** Hundeleine *f*, *(Jagd)* Schweißriemen *m*; **~-rose** Hunds-, Heckenrose *f*; **~sled** ['-sled], **~sledge** ['-sledʒ] Hundeschlitten *m*; **~-sleep** leichte(r), leise(r) Schlaf *m*; **~ tag** *mil sl* Erkennungsmarke *f*; **~'s age** *Am fam* Ewigkeit, lange Zeit *f*; **~'s dinner** *sl* Überbleibsel *n pl*; *fig* aufgedonnerte Kleidung *f*; **~'s ear** Eselsohr *n (im Buch)*; **~'s tail** Rute *f*, Hundeschwanz *m*; **~'s trick** gemeine(r), hinterhältige(r) Streich *m*; **~ tick** *zoo* Holzbock *m*; Milbe; Zecke *f*; **~-tired, -weary** hundemüde; **~-tooth** *arch* Zahnfries *m*; **~-watch** *mar* Hundswache *f*; **~-whip** Hundepeitsche *f*; **~-wood** *bot* Hartriegel *m*.

doge [doudʒ] *hist* Doge *m*.

dogg(e)rel ['dɔg(ə)rəl] *(~ rhyme)* Knüttelvers *m*.

dogma ['dɔgmə] Dogma *n*, Glaubens-, Lehrsatz *m*, Doktrin *f*; Glaubens-, Lehrsystem *n*, Lehre *f*; Grundsatz *m*; unerschütterliche Meinung *f*; **~tic(al)** [dɔg'mætik(əl)] dogmatisch; keinen Widerspruch duldend, rechthaberisch, anmaßend, arrogant; bestimmt; *~tic theology*, **~tics** *pl mit sing* Dogmatik *f*; **~tism** ['dɔgmətizm] Dogmatismus; anmaßende(r) Ton *m*, Arroganz, Dreistigkeit *f*; **~tist** ['-ist] Dogmatiker; anmaßende(r), arrogante(r) Mensch *m*; **~tize** ['dɔgmətaiz] *itr* sich anmaßend äußern (*on* über); *tr* mit Bestimmtheit behaupten.

doily ['dɔili] (Tisch-, Zier-)Deckchen *n*.

doing ['du(:)iŋ] *p pr* tuend; *s pl* Taten, Handlungen *f pl*; Ereignisse, Geschehnisse, Vorkommnisse *n pl*, Begebenheiten *f pl*; Verhalten, Betragen, Benehmen *n*; *sl* Prügel *m pl*, Anschnauzer *m*; *that's his ~* das ist sein Werk; *nothing ~* nichts los; *fam* geht nicht! nichts zu machen! *fine ~s!* schöne Geschichten!

*

doldrums ['dɔldrəmz] *pl* Niedergeschlagenheit *f*; *mar* Kalmen(gürtel *m*) *f pl*; *in the ~* niedergeschlagen; in e-r Flaute; *mar* ohne Wind.

dole [doul] *s* Spende, milde Gabe *f*, Almosen *n*; Arbeits-, Erwerbslosenunterstützung *f*; *tr (to ~ out)* spenden, austeilen; sparsam ausgeben; *to be, to go on the ~* arbeits-, erwerbslos sein, *fam* stempeln (gehen); **~ful** ['-ful] kummer-, leidvoll, schmerzlich, traurig, trübselig; **~fulness** ['-fulnis] Kummer *m*, Leid *n*, Traurigkeit, Betrübtheit *f*.

doll [dɔl] *s* Puppe *f*; *fig* Püppchen *n*; *tr sl (to ~ up)* herausputzen, herausstaffieren, auftakeln; *itr* sich in Schale schmeißen; **~'s face** Puppengesicht *n*; **~'s house,** *Am* **~ house** Puppenhaus *n*, -stube *f a. fig*; **~s pram, ~ carriage** Puppenwagen *m*; **~ stroller** Puppensportwagen *m*.

dollar ['dɔlə] Dollar *m*; *Br sl* 5 Schilling.

dollop ['dɔləp] *fam* Klumpen, Brocken, Happen *m*.

dolly ['dɔli] *s (Kindersprache)* Püppchen *n*; *fam* Schlampe *f*; *tech* Gegenhalter, Nietkloben; Preßstempel; Stampfer; Transport-, Montagewagen; *film video* Kamera-, Mikrowagen *m*; *itr* den Kamerawagen bewegen; *to ~ in, out (film video)* den Kamerawagen näher heran-, weiter wegfahren; **~ shot** *film* Fahraufnahme *f*; **~-tub** *min* Rühr-, Schlämmfaß *n*.

dolomite ['dɔləmait] *geol* Dolomit *m*.

dol|orous ['dɔlərəs] schmerz-, kummervoll; **~o(u)r** ['doulə] *poet hum* Schmerz, Kummer *m*.

dolphin ['dɔlfin] *zoo* Delphin, Tümmler *m*; *mar* Ankerboje, Dalbe *f*.

dolt [doult] Tölpel, Tolpatsch *m*; **~ish** ['-iʃ] schwerfällig, tölpelhaft, tolpatschig.

domain [də'mein, do(u)'m-] Domäne *f*, (Staats-)Gut *n*; Herrschaftsbereich *m*, -gebiet; *fig* Gebiet *n*, Bereich *m* od *n*; *to fall into public ~* den Urheberrechtsschutz verlieren; *economic ~* Wirtschaftsraum *m*; *public ~* Staatseigentum; Gemeingut *n*.

dome [doum] *arch* Kuppel *a. fig*; (Berg-)Kuppe *f*; Gewölbe *n*; *poet* Palast *m*; *Am sl* Birne *f*, Kopf *m*.

domestic [də'mestik] *a* häuslich, hauswirtschaftlich; Haus-; familiär, Familien-; privat, Privat-; einheimisch, inländisch; Inland-, Binnen-; inner, Innen-; *(Tier)* zahm, Haus-; *s (~ servant)* Hausangestellte(r *m*) *f*; *pl* inländische Waren *f pl*, Güter *n pl*; *Am* Baumwollzeug *n*; **~ animal** Haustier *n*; **~ appliance** Haushaltgerät *n*; **~ate** [də'mestikeit, do(u)'m-] *tr* ans Haus gewöhnen; häuslich machen; *(Tiere)* zähmen, *scient* domestizieren; heimisch machen; **~ation** [-'keiʃən] Eingewöhnung (*with* bei); Zähmung, *scient* Domestikation *f*; **~ coal** Hausbrand *m*; **~ commerce** Binnenhandel *m*; **~ demand** Inlands-, Haushaltsbedarf *m*; **~ industry** Heimarbeit; heimische Industrie *f*; **~ity** [doumes'tisiti, dom-] häusliche(s), Familienleben *n*; Häuslichkeit *f*, häusliche(s) Wesen *n*; *pl* häusliche Angelegenheiten *od* Pflichten *f pl*; **~ market** Binnenmarkt *m*; **~ policy** Innenpolitik *f*; **~ price** Inlandspreis *m*; **~ production** Inlandsproduktion *f*; **~ sales** *pl* Inlandsabsatz *m*; **~ trade** Binnenhandel *m*.

domicil|e ['dɔmisail] *s* Wohnort; (fester) Wohnsitz; Aufenthalt(sort); *fin* Zahlungsort *m*; *tr* ansässig machen; *(Wechsel)* domizilieren; *to ~~ o.s.* sich niederlassen, s-n Wohnsitz nehmen; **~ed** ['-d] *a* wohnhaft, ansässig; *~~ bill* Domizilwechsel *m*; **~iary** [dɔmi'siljəri] *a* Haus-; Wohnungs-; *~~ search, visit* Haussuchung *f*; **~iate** [dɔmi'silieit] *tr com* domizilieren.

domin|ance, -cy ['dɔminəns(i)] Vorherrschaft *f*; Übergewicht *n*, Einfluß *m*; **~ant** ['-ənt] *a* (vor-, be)herrschend, bestimmend, entscheidend; überragend; *biol mus* dominant; *s biol* dominante Eigenschaft; *mus* Dominante *f*; **~ate** [-eit] *tr u. itr*: *to ~~ over* beherrschen *a. fig*; **~ation** [-'neiʃən] Beherrschung, Herrschaft *f*; **~eer** [dɔmi'niə] *itr* den Ton angeben; *to ~~ over* beherrschen, tyrannisieren; **~eering** [dɔmi'niəriŋ] *a* tonangebend, herrisch, beherrschend, tyrannisch; anmaßend.

dominic|al [də'minikəl] *a rel* des Herrn (Jesus); sonntäglich; *~~ prayer* Vaterunser *n*; **D~an** [-ən] *a rel geog* dominikanisch; *s* Dominikaner *m*.

dominie ['dɔmini] *Scot* (Volksschul-)Lehrer; *Am fam* Pfarrer *m*.

domini|on [də'minjən] Herrschaft, Souveränität, Oberhoheit *f* (*over* über); Herrschaftsgebiet *n*, -bereich *m*; *D~~* Dominion *n*.

domino ['dɔminou] *pl -oes* Domino *(Maskenkostüm u. Träger)*; Dominostein *m*; *pl mit sing* Domino(spiel) *n*; *Am sl* Zähne, Würfel *m pl*.

don [dɔn] **1.** *s* Respektsperson; *fam* Kanone *f*, Kenner (*at* in); Direktor, (Studien-)Leiter *m*; **2.** *tr (Kleider)* anziehen; *(Hut)* aufsetzen; **~nish** ['-iʃ] pedantisch.

donat|e [do(u)'neit] *tr* schenken, geben, spenden, stiften; **~ion** [-'neiʃən] Schenkung, Zuwendung, Stiftung; Spende, Gabe *f*; *deed of ~~* Schenkungsurkunde *f*; *~~ in kind* Sachspende *f*; **~ive** ['-ətiv] Schenkung, Stiftung; Gabe *f*.

done [dʌn] *pp von do* getan; erledigt; abgemacht; *jur* ausgefertigt; *a* fertig; gar; *fam* erschöpft, kaputt; *half-~* halbgar; *well -~* gut (gar); gut durchgebraten; *well ~!* bravo! **~ for** *fam* erledigt, verloren; geliefert, kaputt, hin; **~ in, up** *fam* kaputt, fertig, völlig erschöpft (*from doing s.th.* von der Arbeit); **~ with** fertig.

donee [do(u)'ni:] *jur* Beschenkte(r), Schenkungsempfänger *m*.

donjon ['dɔndʒən] Bergfried *m*.

donkey ['dɔŋki] Esel *a. fig*; *fig* Dummkopf; *tech* Traktor *m*, Zugmaschine; *(Kran)* Laufkatze *f*; **~-engine** Hilfsmaschine; kleine Lokomotive; Zugmaschine *f*; **~'s years** *fam* Ewigkeit *f*; **~ work** Routinearbeit *f*.

donor ['dounə] *jur* Schenkende(r), Stifter; *med* Blutspender *m*.

don't [dount, doun, dən] = *do not*; *Imperativ*: laß (das, doch)! *s hum* Verbot *n*.

*

do(o)dad ['du:dæd] *Am fam* Dingsda *n*; Kleinigkeit, Spielerei *f*, Tand *m*.

doodle ['du:dl] *itr (geistesabwesend* od *nebenbei)* herumkritzeln, Männchen malen; *Scot* dudeln, Dudelsack spielen; *s* Gekritzel *n*; *fam* Dussel, Depp *m*; **~bug** ['-bʌg] *Am zoo* Larve *f* des Ameisenlöwen; *Am fam* Wünschelrute *f*; *Am sl rail* Dieseltriebwagen *m*; *sl mil* Rakete; V-Waffe *f*.

doom [du:m] Verhängnis, Geschick, Schicksal *n*; Verderb(en *n*), Untergang *m*; Jüngste(s) Gericht *n*; *tr* verurteilen (*to death* zum Tode); verdammen; **~sday** ['du:mzdei] das Jüngste Gericht; *from now till ~~* bis zum Jüngsten Tag, für immer.

door [dɔ:, dɔə] Tür *f*, Tor *n a. fig*; Pforte; Luke *f*; *fig* Weg *m* (*to* zu); *at death's ~* an der Schwelle des Todes; *from ~ to ~* von Haus zu Haus; *next ~* nebenan, im Neben-, Nachbarhaus; *to* neben; *fig* beinahe, fast; *out of ~s* draußen, im Freien; *two ~s off* zwei Häuser weiter, im übernächsten Haus; *within ~s* drinnen, im Hause; *to close the ~ upon s.th.* etw den Weg versperren dat, unmöglich machen; *to lay s.th. at s.o.'s ~* jdm etw vorhalten, zum Vorwurf machen; *to lie at s.o.'s ~* jds Schuld sein; *to show s.o. the ~* jdn vor die Tür setzen; *back ~* Hintertür *f*; *front ~* Haustür *f*; **~-bell** Türklingel *f*; *~~ pusher* Hausierer *m*; **~-case, -frame** Türrahmen *m*; **~-jamb, -post** Türpfosten *m*; **~-keeper,** *Am* **~man** Pförtner, Portier *m*; **~-knob** (Tür-)Knopf *m*; **~-mat** Türvorleger; *fig* Schwächling *m*; **~-money** Eintrittsgeld *n*; **~-nail**: *dead as a ~~* mausetot; **~-plate** Türschild *n*; **~-sill** Türschwelle *f*; **~-step** Türstufe *f*; **~-stop** Türpuffer *m*; **~-to-~**: *~~ salesman* Hausierer *m*; *~~ selling* Hausieren *n*; *~~ transport* Beförderung *f* von Tür zu Tür; **~-way** Eingang; Torweg *fig*; Zugang *m*; **~-yard** *Am* Vorhof *m*.

dop|e [doup] *s* Schmiere *f*, Schmiermittel; *mot* Additiv; Einreibmittel *n*; (halbfester) Überzug; Firnis; Lack; *aero* Spann-, Flieglack; *phot* Entwickler *m*; Reizmittel; *sl* Rauschgift, Narkotikum *n*; *sl* Tip *m*, geheime, vertrauliche Information *f*; *Am sl* Coca-Cola; *Am sl* Rauschgiftsüchtige(r), Morphinist; *sl* Depp, Trottel *m*; *tr (Rennpferd)* dopen; verdrogen, Drogen eingeben (*s.o.* jdm); Alkohol zusetzen; *fig* beruhigen; hintergehen; *mot* mit Zusätzen versehen; *Am sl (to ~~ out)* rauskriegen, ausfindig machen; *to ~ off (Am sl)* tief u. lange schlafen; sich dumm benehmen; *to give s.o. all the ~~* jdm alle Einzelheiten mitteilen; *~~ addict, fiend (sl)* Rauschgiftsüchtige(r), Morphinist *m*; *~~ den* Opiumhöhle *f*; *~~ pedlar (sl)* Rauschgifthändler, -schieber *m*; *~ed petrol* Bleibenzin *n*; **~ester** ['-stə] *Am sl* jem, der geheime, vertrauliche Informationen liefert; **~(e)y** ['-i] *Am sl* narkotisiert, benommen; schlafmützig, dämlich, dusselig.

Doric ['dɔrik] *arch* dorisch; *~* **order** dorische Säulenordnung *f*.

dorm [dɔ:m] *fam* Studentenwohnheim *n*; **~ancy** ['-ənsi] Schlaf-, Ruhezustand *m*; **~ant** ['-ənt] schlafend; ruhend, ruhig, still; untätig, unwirksam, ungenutzt, tot; *zoo* im Winterschlaf; *bot* in der Winterruhe; *to lie ~~* den Winterschlaf halten; *com* sich nicht verzinsen; *jur* den Termin versäumen; *~~ partner* stille(r) Teilhaber *m*; **~er** ['-ə] *(~~ window)* Dachfenster *n*, Gaube, Gaupe; Mansarde *f*; **~itory** ['-itri] Schlafsaal *m*; *Am* (Studenten-) Wohnheim *n*; *~~ town* Schlafstadt *f*.

dormouse ['dɔ:maus] *pl -mice* Haselmaus *f*; *fig* Schlafmütze *f*.

dor(r) [dɔ:] Mist-, Mai- *od* Rosenkäfer *m*.

dorsal ['dɔ:səl] *anat zoo bot* Rücken-; *~* **fin** *(Fisch)* Rückenflosse *f*; *~* **shell, shield** *(Schildkröte)* Rückenschild *m*.

dory ['dɔ:ri] *Art* (flaches) Fischerboot *n*; *zoo* Heringskönig, Petersfisch *m*.

dose [dous] *s pharm* Dosis *a. fig*; *fig* Portion, Menge; *sl* Ansteckung *f*; *(bes. Wein)* Zusatz *m*; *tr* e-e Dosis Arznei geben (*s.o.* jdm); *(Arznei)* dosieren; *(Bestandteil)* zusetzen; vermischen (*with* mit); *(Wein)* fälschen.

doss [dɔs] *s sl* Falle, Kiste *f*, Bett *n*; billige Unterkunft *f*; *itr* pennen; **~-house** Übernachtungsheim *n*.

dossier ['dɔsiei] Akten(bündel *n*) *f pl*, Dossier, Vorgang *m*.

*

dot [dɔt] **1.** Mitgift *f*; **2.** *s* Punkt *m*; Pünktchen *n*, Tüpfel(chen *n*); I-Punkt; Knirps *m*; kleine(s) Ding *n (Mädchen)*; *tr* mit Punkten versehen; tüpfeln; übersäen (*with* mit); *off o.'s ~ (sl)* plemplem; *on the ~ (fam)* auf die Sekunde, ganz pünktlich *adv*; *to ~ o.'s i's and cross o.'s t's* es ganz genau nehmen; *he ~ted him one (fam)* er langte, versetzte ihm eine; **~ted** ['-id] *a* be-, übersät (*with* mit); *~~ line* punktierte Linie *f*; *to sign on the ~~ line (fig)* bedingungslos zustimmen; **~ty** ['-i] getüpfelt, gesprenkelt; *fam* schwach, unsicher, zitt(e)rig, schwankend; *fam* verrückt.

dot|age ['doutidʒ] Senilität, Greisenhaftigkeit *f*, Kindischwerden *n*; Affenliebe *f*; *to be in o.'s ~~* kindisch sein *od* werden; **~ard** ['doutəd] kindische(r) Greis *m*; **~e** [dout] *itr (Greis)* kindisch sein, faseln, durchea.reden; *to ~~ (up)on* vernarrt sein in, abgöttisch lieben; **~ing** ['-iŋ] (alt u.) kindisch; vernarrt, heftig verliebt (*on* in).

double ['dʌbl] **1.** *a* doppelt, zweifach, zwiefach; Doppel-; gepaart, paarig; zweischichtig, gefaltet, überea.gelegt; *(Blume)* gefüllt; *fig* zweideutig; doppelzüngig, falsch, scheinheilig; **2.** *adv* doppelt, noch einmal so(viel); zweimal; **3.** *s das* Doppelte, *das* Zweifache; Doppel *n*, Zweitschrift, -ausfertigung *f*, Duplikat; Ebenbild *n*, Doppelgänger *m*; *theat film* Double *n*; *mil* Laufschritt *m*; Falte, Schlinge; *(Fluß)* Schleife; starke Biegung, scharfe Wendung; Kehrtwendung *f*; plötzliche(r) Richtungswechsel; Winkelzug, Trick *m*; *pl (Tennis)* Doppel(spiel) *n*; **4.** *tr* verdoppeln; umbiegen, -legen, -schlagen, falten; *(die Faust)* ballen; *(Garn)* zwirnen; wiederholen; abschreiben; *theat film* das Double sein (*s.o.* jds); *mar* umsegeln, umschiffen, umfahren; *(Kartenspiel)* kontrieren; **5.** *itr* sich verdoppeln; *mil* die Geschwindigkeit verdoppeln; sich zurückbiegen; sich umwenden, umkehren; scharf umbiegen, e-n Haken schlagen; *film* ein Double sein; e-n doppelten Zweck erfüllen; auch noch arbeiten (*as* als); zwei Rollen spielen; *at the ~ (mil)* im Geschwindschritt; *on the ~ (Am fam)* im Nu, fix; **6.** *to ~ back (tr)* umschlagen, falten; *itr* umkehren, auf dem gleichen Wege zurückkehren; *to ~ up (itr)* sich zs.legen, zs.klappen; sich zs.krümmen; die Faust ballen; sich *(vor Lachen)* biegen, sich *(vor Schmerz)* krümmen; *tr (Zimmer)* teilen, zu zweit, zs. bewohnen; *to ~ upon (mil)* zwischen zwei Feuer nehmen; **7.** *to have a ~ meaning* zweideutig sein; *to wear a ~ face* falsch, hinterhältig sein; *men's, ladies' ~s (pl) (Tennis)* Herren-, Damendoppel *n*; **~-acting** doppelt wirksam; **~-barrelled** *a (Schußwaffe)* doppelläufig; *fig* zweideutig; *gram* doppelglied(e)rig; **~-bass** *s* Baß *m (Musikinstrument)*; *a mus* Kontrabaß-; *~* **bed** Doppelbett *n*; *~-~ded room* Zweibettzimmer *n*; **~-breasted** *a (Jacke, Mantel)* zweireihig; *~* **chin** Doppelkinn *n*; **~-cross** *sl tr* anführen, betrügen, hintergehen; *s* Betrug *m*; **~-crosser** *sl* Betrüger *m*; **~-dealer** falsche(r) Mensch; Betrüger *m*; *~* **dealing** Falschheit *f*; Betrug *m*; *to engage in ~~* falsch sein, betrügen; **~-decker** zweigeschossige(s, r) Schiff *n*, Autobus *m*; doppelte(s) Sandwich *n*; **~-Dutch** *fam* Kauderwelsch, Chinesisch *n*; **~-dyed** *a* Erz-; durchtrieben, gerieben, raffiniert; eingefleischt; **~-eagle** *(Heraldik)* Doppeladler *m (mit zwei Köpfen)*; **~-edged** *a* zweischneidig *a. fig*; **~-entry** doppelte Buchführung *f*; **~-faced** *a* falsch, unaufrichtig, heuchlerisch; *~* **feature** Filmvorführung *f* mit zwei Hauptfilmen; **~ganger** ['-gæŋə] Doppelgänger *m*; **~-lock** *tr* zweimal verschließen; *~* **meaning** *a* zweideutig; *s* Zweideutigkeit *f*; **~-minded** *a* unentschieden, schwankend; **~ness** ['-nis] *das* Doppelte; Zweideutigkeit; Falschheit *f*, Verrat *m*; **~-O** *tr Am sl* prüfend anblicken; *s* genaue Prüfung *f*; **~-park** *itr* neben e-m geparkten Fahrzeug parken; **~quick** ['-kwik] *a adv* sehr schnell; *s* Geschwindschritt *m*; *tr itr* im Geschwindschritt marschieren (lassen); **~-saw(buck)** *Am* 20-Dollar-Note *f*; *~* **seated** *a* zweisitzig; *~* **shuffle** *Am fam* kalte Schulter; Enttäuschung; kurze Abfertigung *f*; *~* **standard** *fin* Doppelwährung *f*; **~t** ['dʌblit] *hist* Wams *n*; Doppelform, Dublette *f*; paarige(r) Gegenstand *m*; Paar *n*; *tech* Dipol; *pl (Würfelspiel)* Pasch *m*; **~-take** *fig fam* Spätzündung *f*; *~-* **talk** zweideutige Reden *f pl*; *~* **taxation** Doppelbesteuerung *f*; **~-threaded** *a*: *~~ screw* Doppelschraube *f*; *~* **time** Lauf-, Sturmschritt *m*; **~-tongued** *a* doppelzüngig; **~-tooth** Backenzahn *m*; *~* **track**: *with a ~~ (rail)* zweispurig; *~* **window** Doppelfenster *n*.

doubl|ing ['dʌbliŋ] Verdoppelung; Falte, zweite Lage *od* Schicht *f*, Futter *n*; Umsegelung *f*; Seitensprung; Winkelzug *m*; **~y** ['dʌbli] *adv* doppelt.

doubt [daut] *itr* zweifeln, Zweifel hegen (*whether, if* ob); nicht sicher sein; schwanken, zögern; *tr* be-, anzweifeln, in Frage ziehen; mißtrauen (*s.th.* e-r S); *s* Zweifel *m* (*of, about* an); Ungewißheit, Unsicherheit *f*; Bedenken *n*; unerledigte Sache, Schwierigkeit *f*; *beyond (all) ~* ohne (jeden) Zweifel, ganz sicher, ganz gewiß; *in ~* im Zweifel (*about* über); zweifelhaft, unentschieden; unschlüssig; *in case of ~* im Zweifelsfall; *no ~* zweifellos, ohne Zweifel; *fam* sicher, höchstwahrscheinlich; *without (a) ~* ohne Zweifel, ganz bestimmt; *to be in ~ about s.th.* über etw im Zweifel sein; *to give s.o. the benefit of the ~* jdn wegen Mangels an Beweisen freisprechen; *to have no ~* keinen Zweifel haben (*of* an; *that* daran, daß); **~er** ['-ə] Zweifler *m*; **~ful** ['-ful] zweifelnd, im Zweifel, skeptisch; unsicher; unschlüssig, schwankend; zweifelhaft, ungewiß; fraglich, fragwürdig; *(Forderungen)* dubios; dunkel, zweideutig, verdächtig, anrüchig; *to be ~~* im Zweifel sein (*about* über); zweifelhaft, fraglich sein; **~fulness** ['-fulnis] Unsicherheit, Ungewißheit; Unschlüssigkeit; Fragwürdigkeit, Zweideutigkeit *f*; **~less** ['-lis] *adv* ohne Zweifel, zweifellos; *fam* zweifelsohne, sicher(lich).

douche [du:ʃ] *s* Dusche *f*; Brausebad *n*; Spülung *f*; Spülapparat *m*; *tr* (ab-) duschen; spülen; *itr* sich duschen.

dough [dou] Teig *m*; *sl* Moos *n*, Zaster *m*, Moneten *pl*; **~boy** ['-bɔi] Kloß, Knödel; *Am sl* Fußlatscher, Infanterist; Landser *m*; **~face** *Am sl pol* Extremist, Fortschrittler *m*; **~nut** ['-nʌt] Berliner (Pfannkuchen); *Am mot sl* Reifen *m*; **~y** ['-i] teigig, pappig; *fam* käsig, bleich; weich.

doughty ['dauti] *obs hum* tapfer, beherzt, wacker, tüchtig.

dour ['duə] *Scot* hart, starr(sinnig); herb, streng, ernst; finster, düster.

douse [daus] *tr* eintauchen; löschen; *fam (Licht)* auslöschen; *fam (Kleider)* ausziehen; *(Hut)* abnehmen; *(Segel)* schnell herunterlassen.

dove [dʌv] Taube *f*; *fig* (sanftes) Lamm; Unschuldslamm; Täubchen, Liebchen *n*; Friedenstaube *f*, -bote *m*; **~-colo(u)red** *a* taubengrau; **~-cot(e)** ['dʌvkɔt, -kout] Taubenschlag *m*, -haus *n*; *to flutter the ~~s* friedliche Bürger erschrecken; **~-eyed** *a* mit sanften Augen; **~'s-foot** *bot* Storchschnabel *m*; **~tail** ['-teil] *s tech* Schwalbenschwanz(verzapfung *f*) *m*; *tr tech* (ver)zinken, verschwalben; *fig* zs.stükken, -setzen, (zu e-m Ganzen) verbinden; eingliedern (*into* in); *itr* zs.-passen, ein Ganzes bilden; passen (*into* zu); übereinstimmen (*with* mit).

dowager ['dauədʒə, -idʒə] Witwe von Stande; *fam* Matrone *f*.

dowd|iness ['daudinis] Schäbigkeit, Schlampigkeit *f*; **~y** ['daudi] *a* schäbig, schlampig, schlecht, nachlässig gekleidet; unmodern; *s* Schlampe *f*.

dowel ['dauəl] *s* Dübel, Holzpflock *m*; *tr* verdübeln.

dower ['dauə] *s* Witwenteil *m*, Leibgedinge, *obs* Wittum *n*; Mitgift; (natürliche) Gabe *f*, Talent *n*, Begabung *f*; *tr* e-e Mitgift geben (*s.o.* jdm); begaben (*with* mit).

dowlas ['dauləs] Daulas *n*.

down [daun] **1.** baumlose(r) Höhenzug, -rücken *m*; Düne *f*; **2.** Daunen *f pl*, Flaum(federn *f pl*, -haare *n pl*) *m*; ~ **quilt** Daunendecke *f*; **3.** *adv* her-, hinunter, her-, hinab, nieder *a. fig*; seewärts; von der (größeren) Stadt weg (*to the country* auf das Land); von der Universität; unten, am Boden; *fig* in gedrückter Lage *od* Stimmung; im Bett (*with a cold* mit e-r Erkältung); *(Sonne)* untergegangen; *(Ware)* billiger (geworden); *(Preis)* gefallen, gesunken; (in) bar; *mot (Reifen)* platt; *up and ~* hin und her; auf u. ab; *upside ~* das Oberste zuunterst; auf dem Kopf; *~ in the country* draußen auf dem Lande; *~ at heel (fam)* abgebrannt; *(Absatz)* abgelaufen; *~ on o.'s luck* in unglücklicher Lage, im Unglück; *~ in the mouth (fam)* niedergedrückt, -geschlagen *fig*; *~ and out (fam)* erledigt, hin, ruiniert; auf den Hund gekommen; *~ to* bis hinunter (zu); *~ to the present time* bis heute; bis in unsere Tage; *~ under* auf der andern Seite der Erde; *~ upon* über ... her; *to be ~ on s.o. (fig)* auf jdm herumtrampeln; auf jdn wütend sein; *it's right ~ my alley (Am sl)* das hat glänzend in meinen Kram gepaßt; *~!* hinlegen! *~ with him!* nieder mit ihm! **4.** *prp* her-, hinunter, her-, hinab *(nachgestellt)*; *(zeitlich)* durch, *(nachgestellt)* hindurch; *~ (the) wind* mit dem Winde; **5.** *s*: *to have a ~ on s.o. (fam)* jdn nicht mögen, nicht leiden können; etwas gegen jdn haben; *the ups and ~s of life* das Auf und Ab, die Wechselfälle des Lebens; **6.** *v fam tr* nieder-, zu Boden legen, auf den Boden legen *od* setzen *od* stellen; *aero* herunterholen, abschießen; niederschlagen, -strecken; *fig* ducken, demütigen; *itr* hinuntergehen, herunterkommen; *to ~ a glass of beer* ein Glas Bier 'runterkippen.

down|cast ['daunkɑ:st] *a* niedergeschlagen, (nieder)gedrückt, entmutigt; *(Augen)* gesenkt; *s min* Wetterschacht *m*; **~-draught** *aero* Abwind *m*; **~fall** Sturz *a. fig* Zs.-bruch; *fig* Ruin, Verderb(en *n*), Untergang *m*; *(~~ of rain)* Regenschauer, -guß, Platzregen *m*; *(~~ of snow)* Schneeschauer *m*; **~grade** *s* Neigung *f*, Hang *m*, Gefälle *n (bes. e-r Straße)*; *adv a* bergab, abwärts(führend); *tr* ['-'-] *(beruflich)* niedriger einstufen; heruntersetzen; *on the ~~ (fig)* auf der schiefen Ebene, auf dem absteigenden Ast; **~hearted** ['-'-] *a* niedergeschlagen, gedrückt, mut-, hoffnungslos; **~hill** ['-'-] *adv* bergab, abwärts; *a* abwärts geneigt; abschüssig; *he is going ~~ (fig)* es geht mit ihm bergab; *~~ race (Schi)* Abfahrt(slauf *m*) *f*; **~land** Hügelland *n*; **~light** Deckenbeleuchtung *f*; **~most** unterste(r, s); **~ payment** Bar-, *Am* Anzahlung *f*; **~pour** Platzregen, Wolkenbruch, heftige(r) (Regen-)Guß *m*; **~right** *a (Mensch)* aufrecht, gerade, offen, freimütig; völlig, vollständig; *adv* völlig, vollständig, gänzlich, ganz u. gar, durch u. durch; durchaus, höchst; *a ~~ lie* e-e glatte Lüge; **~rightness** Offenheit *f*, Freimut *m*; **~rush** (Ab-)Sturz *m*; **~stairs** ['-'-] *adv* treppab, die Treppe hinunter; (weiter) unten *(im Haus)*; *aero* niedrig; *a* ['-] in e-m tieferen Stockwerk (befindlich); *to go ~~* die Treppe hinuntergehen; **~-stream** ['-'-] *adv* stromabwärts; **~stroke** *(Schrift)* Grundstrich *m*; *tech* Abwärtsbewegung *f*, Niedergang *m (des Kolbens)*; **~town** ['-'-] *Am adv* zum *od* im tiefer gelegenen Teil e-r Stadt, zum *od* im Geschäftsviertel; ['--] *a* im unteren Stadtteil *od* im Geschäftsviertel gelegen; *s (~ town)* Geschäftsviertel, -zentrum *n*; *to go ~~* in die Stadt gehen; **~ train** von der Hauptstation, *bes.* von London abgehende(r) Zug *m*; **~trodden** *a* niedergetrampelt, -getreten; *fig* unterworfen, unterdrückt; **~ward** *a* abwärts führend, geneigt; *fig* absteigend; *(Börse)* fallend; später; *adv a.* **~wards** abwärts, bergab; bis in unsere Zeit; nach unten; **~wash** *aero* Abwind *m*; **~ wind** Rückenwind *m*.

downy ['dauni] **1.** flaumig, mit Flaum (-federn, -haaren) bedeckt; weich wie Flaum; *sl* auf Draht, helle, (auf)geweckt; gerissen; **2.** hügelig u. baumlos.

dowry ['dauəri] Aussteuer, Mitgift; (natürliche) Gabe *f*, Talent *n*; Begabung *f*.

dows|e [daus] **1.** *s. douse*; **2.** [dauz] *tr* mit der Wünschelrute suchen; **~er** ['-zə] Rutengänger *m*; **~ing** ['-ziŋ]: *~~-rod* Wünschelrute *f*.

doxology [dɔk'sɔlədʒi] *rel* Lobpreisung *f*.

doxy ['dɔksi] **1.** *sl* Nutte *f*; **2.** *fam rel* Lehrmeinung, Lehre *f*.

doyen ['dɔiən] Alterspräsident, Doyen *m*.

doze [douz] *itr* (vor sich hin)dösen; *tr (to ~ away, out) (Zeit)* verdösen; *s* Halbschlaf *m*; Nickerchen *n*; *to ~ off* eindösen, -nicken.

dozen ['dʌzn] Dutzend *n*; *by the ~* dutzendweise; *to do o.'s daily ~ (fam)* Frühsport treiben; *to talk nineteen to a ~* unaufhörlich reden.

*

drab [dræb] **1.** *s* khakifarbene(r) Stoff *m*; Erd-, Lehmfarbe *f*, Khaki *n*; *a* gelb-, graubraun, erd-, lehm-, khakifarben; *fig* trüb(e), düster, grau; eintönig; **2.** Schlampe, Dirne *f*.

drabble ['dræbl] *tr* beschmutzen.

drachm [dræm], **~a** ['drækmə] Drachme *f*.

Dracon|ian [drei'kounjən, drə-], **~ic** [-'kɔnik] *(Maßnahme, Gesetz)* drakonisch, rigoros, streng.

draff [dræf] Bodensatz *m*; Treber *pl*; Rückstand, Abfall *m*; *fig* wertlose(s) Zeug *n*; **~y** ['-i] voller Rückstände; *fig* wertlos.

draft [drɑ:ft] *s* Skizze *f*, Entwurf *m*; Konzept; Projekt *n*, Plan; *fin* Wechsel *m*, Tratte *f*, Akzept *n*; Abruf *m*; Abhebung; *fig* starke Inanspruchnahme (*on* gen), Belastung (*on* für); *mil* Abkommandierung *f*; Kommando; Kontingent *n*; Verstärkung; *Am mil (~ call)* Rekrutierung, Aushebung, Einberufung *f*, Einziehen *n*; Rekruten *m pl*; *Am* Luftzug *m*, Zugluft *f*, Zug *m*, Luftklappe *f*; *s. draught*; *tr* skizzieren, entwerfen; zeichnen; *(Brief)* aufsetzen, abfassen; *mil* aussuchen, -wählen, abkommandieren; *Am* rekrutieren, ausheben, einziehen, einberufen; *to give a ~ due protection* e-n Wechsel einlösen; *to have a quick ~* reißend abgehen; *to make a ~ on s.th.* etw stark in Anspruch nehmen; *on s.o.* e-e Tratte auf jdn ziehen; *on ~* vom Faß; **~ board** *Am* (zivile) Rekrutierungsbehörde *f*; **~ bracket** *Am* wehrpflichtige(r) Jahrgang *m*; **~ dodger** *Am* Drückeberger *m*; **~ee** [-'ti:] *Am* Rekrut, Einberufene(r), Wehrpflichtige(r) *m*; **~er** ['-ə] *tele* Aufgeber *m*; **~ing** ['-iŋ] (Ausarbeitung *f* e-s) Entwurf(s) *m*, Abfassung; *mil* Aushebung *f*; *~~ committee* Redaktionsausschuß *m*; **~sman** ['-smən] Planer; (Text-)Redakteur; Konstruktions-, technische(r) Zeichner *m*; **~ term** *Am* (Militär-)Dienstzeit *f*; **~y** ['-i] *Am* zugig.

drag [dræg] *tr* (hinter sich her) ziehen, schleppen, schleifen, zerren; *(den Grund e-s Gewässers)* absuchen (*for* nach); *(Anker)* lichten; ausbaggern; eggen; *mus (Tempo)* verlangsamen; *Am sl* rauchen, langweilen, zu e-m Tanz begleiten; *fig (to ~ on)* hin-, in die Länge ziehen; *fig (to ~ in, to ~ in by the head and shoulders)* an den Haaren herbeiziehen; hineinziehen (*into a quarrel* in e-n Streit); *itr* (auf dem Boden) schleppen; nicht recht (vorwärts) wollen, nicht mehr (so recht) können; *(to ~ out)* den Grund *(e-s Gewässers)* absuchen (*for* nach); *fig (to ~ on)* sich (endlos) in die Länge ziehen, sich dahinschleppen, sich hinziehen (*towards* bis zu); *(Zeit)* schleichen; *com* flaugehen; *fig* nachhinken (*behind* hinter); hinterherkommen; *mus* schleppen, nachklappen; *Am sl* in Begleitung zum Tanz gehen; *to ~ o.s.* sich schleppen (*to work* an die Arbeit); *s (~-net)* Schlepp-, Baggernetz *n*; Enterhaken *m*; schwere Egge *f*; schwere(r) Schlitten *m*, schwere Kutsche *f*; Schlepper *m*; Bremse *f a. fig*; *fig* Hemmschuh, Klotz *m* am Bein, Hemmnis, Hindernis *n* (*on* für); Belastung *f*; *aero* Luftwiderstand *m*; schleppende, langsame Bewegung; *(Jagd)* Geruchsspur *f*; *sl* Einfluß *m*; *Am sl* Attraktion, Anziehungskraft; *Am sl* Straße *f* (in e-r Stadt); *Am sl* Begleiterin, Freundin; *Am sl* langweilige Person *od* Angelegenheit *f*; *sl* Zug *m (beim Rauchen)*, Zigarette *f*; *Am sl* Schwof, Tanz *m*; *to ~ down* herunterziehen *a. fig*; *to ~ from* entreißen; *to ~ in* hereinziehen; in die Debatte werfen; *to ~ up (fam) (Kind)* (irgendwie) aufziehen; *(Bäume)* herausreißen; *fig* aufs Tapet bringen; *to ~ o.'s feet* schlurfen, *fam* latschen; *sl* absichtlich langsam arbeiten; *to ~ out a meeting* e-e Sitzung in die Länge ziehen; *business ~s* das Geschäft geht schlecht, ist schleppend, flau; **~ anchor** Treibanker *m*; **~-chain** Bremskette *f*; *fig* Hemmschuh *m*; **~ging** ['-iŋ] *fig* schleppend, lähmend; **~gy** ['-i] *Am fam* langweilig; unbefriedigend; **~hound** *(Jagd)* Spürhund *m*; **~line, ~rope** Schleppseil *n*; **~shoe** Hemmschuh *m*; **~ster** ['-ə] *Am* Rennfahrer *m*; **~ strip** *Am* Rennbahn *f*.

draggle ['drægl] *tr* durch den Schmutz ziehen, beschmutzen; *itr* durch den Schmutz schleppen, nachziehen; *fig* nachhinken; **~-tail** ['-teil] Schlampe *f*.

dragoman ['drægo(u)mən, -mæn] *pl a.* *-men* Dolmetscher, Fremdenführer *m*.

dragon ['drægən] *(Mythologie)* Drache *a. fig*; *zoo* Flug(eid)echse; *bot* Drachenwurz *f*, Schlangenkraut *n*; **~-fly** Libelle, Wasserjungfer *f*; **~head** *bot* Drachenkopf *m*; **~'s teeth** *mil* Höckerhindernis *n*.

dragoon [drə'gu:n] *s mil* Dragoner; *fig* brutale(r) Mensch, Rohling *m*; *tr* zwingen (*into doing* zu tun).

drain [drein] *tr* dränieren *a. med*, entwässern, trockenlegen; *(to ~ off)* abziehen; *(to ~ away) (Wasser)* ableiten (*from* aus); (aus)trinken; *(Becken)* ablassen; *(Geld)* abziehen; *(Glas)* leeren; *fig* allmählich erschöpfen, aufbrauchen, verzehren; berauben, entblößen (*of* von); verbluten lassen; entziehen (*s.o. of s.th.* jdm etw); filtern, filtrieren; *itr (Land)* s-n Abfluß haben (*into* in); *(to ~ away) (Wasser)* ablaufen (*into* in), abtropfen; sickern (*into* in; *through* durch); *fig* sich verzehren, sich verbrauchen; *to ~ off* ablaufen, abfließen; *s* Abzugsgraben, Abfluß(rinne *f*, -rohr *n*), Drän *a. med*; *fig* Abfluß *m*, starke, übermäßige Inanspruchnahme, Belastung, Erschöpfung *f* (*on s.th.* e-r S); Kräfteverschleiß; *fam* Mundvoll, Schluck *m*, Schlückchen *n*; *pl* Kanalisation, Kanalisierung, Kanalanlage *f*; *to ~ dry (to the dregs)* bis zur Neige leeren; *s.o.* jdn zugrunde richten; *to go down the ~ (fam)* den Weg alles Fleisches gehen; *foreign ~ (fin)* Kapitalabwanderung *f (ins Ausland)*; *~ of capital, of money* Geld-, Kapitalabfluß *m*; **~age** ['-idʒ] Entwässerung(sanlage *f*, -ssystem *n*), Dränage *f a. med*; Abfluß *m*; Entleerung *f*; Abwässer *n pl*; *(~~ basin, (Am) area) geog* Flußgebiet *n*; *~~ tube (med)* Kanüle *f*; **~-cock** Abflußhahn *m*; **~er** ['-ə] Kanalarbeiter *m*; **~ing** ['-iŋ] Dränage *f*; *~~ board, rack* Abtropfbrett, -gestell *n*; **~pipe** ['-paip] Abfluß-, Kanalisationsrohr *n*.

drake [dreik] Enterich, Erpel *m*; *(~ fly)* Gemeine Eintagsfliege *f*.

dram [dræm] Quent(chen) *n (= $^1/_{16}$ Unze (1,77 g), als Apothekergewicht $^1/_8$ Unze (3,54 g))*; Schluck *m* Schnaps; *a ~* ein bißchen, ein wenig.

drama ['drɑːmə] Drama, Schauspiel *n*; Dramatik; spannende Handlung *f*; **~tic(al)** [drə'mætik(əl)] dramatisch *a. allg*; *allg* lebhaft, spannungsreich; **~tics** *s pl mit sing* Dramatik *f*, Theater; Laienspiel *n (als Einrichtung)*; **~tis personae** ['dræmətis-pəː'souniː, 'drɑː-, -nai] Personen(verzeichnis *n*) *f pl*; **~tist** ['dræmətist] Dramatiker, Schauspieldichter *m*; **~tization** [dræmətai'zeiʃən] Dramatisierung, Bühnen-, Filmbearbeitung *f*; **~tize** ['dræmətaiz] *tr* dramatisieren; für die Bühne, den Film bearbeiten; **~turge** ['dræmətəːdʒ] Dramaturg *m*; **~turgic** [-'təːdʒik] dramaturgisch; **~turgy** ['-təːdʒi] Dramaturgie *f*.

drap|e [dreip] *tr* drapieren, (mit Stoff) behängen, verkleiden, (aus)schmücken; in Falten legen, raffen; *itr (Stoff, Kleidung)* lose fallen, (lose) hängen; *s (Kleidung)* Sitz, (Zu-)Schnitt *m*; *pl* Draperie, (Stoff-)Verkleidung *f*, Vorhang *m*; *Am sl* modische Kleidung *f*; **~er** ['-ə] Tuch-, Manufakturwarenhändler *m*; **~ery** ['-əri] Tuch *n*, (modische(r) Stoff *m*; Tuchfabrikation *f*, -handel *m*; Draperie *f*; Faltenwurf *m*; *pl* Vorhänge *m pl*; *~~ goods (pl)* Modewaren *f pl*.

drastic ['dræstik] drastisch, stark, kräftig, derb, streng, durchgreifend.

drat [dræt] *interj fam* zum Teufel mit...!

draught [drɑːft] Ziehen *n*, Zug; (Luft-) Zug *m*, Zugluft *f*, Luftstrom; Schornsteinzug; Luftregler; Atemzug; Schluck, Zug *m*; (Ab-)Zapfen *n (e-r Flüssigkeit)*; *mar* Tiefgang; (Fisch-) Fang; Fang *m* (Fische); *(Netz)* Einholen *n*; *pl Br* Damespiel *n*; *to drink at a, one ~* in einem Zug, auf einmal austrinken; *beer on ~* Bier vom Faß, Faßbier *n*; **~-animal, -horse** Zugtier, -pferd *n*; **~beer** Faßbier *n*; **~-board** *Br* Damebrett *n*; **~sman** ['-smæn] Damestein; ['-smən] Zeichner, Entwerfer *m*; **~y** ['-i] zugig; undicht.

draw [drɔː] *irr drew* [druː], *drawn* [drɔːn] **1.** *tr* (an-, an sich, auf-, aus-, ein-, herab-, heran-, heraus-, herunter-, hinab-, zu)ziehen (*from* aus); hineinziehen (*into s.th.* in etw); *(Segel)* heißen, hissen; *(Jalousie)* herab-, herunterlassen; *(Vorhang)* zuziehen; *(Bogen)* spannen; *mar (Wasser)* verdrängen; e-n Tiefgang haben (*ten feet* von zehn Fuß); einatmen, inhalieren; anziehen, Anziehungskraft ausüben auf, reizen, (ver)locken, bewegen; hervorrufen, -bringen, bewirken, zur Folge haben (*on s.o.* für jdn); *(Zinsen)* tragen, bringen; *(Gehalt)* beziehen; ausreißen, entfernen; *(Zahn, Kork, Schwert)* ziehen; *(Flüssigkeit)* abziehen(lassen), (ab)zapfen, (ab)schöpfen, laufen lassen; *tech* einsaugen; *(Strom)* entnehmen (*from* aus); *(Tee)* ziehen lassen; *(Tier)* ausnehmen, -weiden; erhalten, bekommen, *fam* kriegen; *mil (Rationen)* empfangen, beziehen; *(Essen)* fassen; *(Geld von e-m Konto)* abheben; *(Ware)* beziehen; *(Scheck, Wechsel)* ausstellen; *(in der Lotterie)* gewinnen; *(Karte im Spiel)* nehmen, bekommen; *(aus dem Gegner)* herausziehen; ausfragen; entlocken (*from s.o.* jdm); *(Schluß)* ziehen, folgern, ableiten; in die Länge ziehen, strecken, dehnen, spannen, *tech* treiben; *(Draht)* ziehen; verzerren; zeichnen; *(Linie)* ziehen; beschreiben, schildern; abfassen; *(Tabelle)* aufstellen; *(Vergleich)* ziehen; **2.** *itr* ziehen; gehen, sich wenden, sich bewegen; sich nähern, näher heranrücken (*to* an); sich zs.-ziehen; *(Ofen, Kamin, Tee)* ziehen; *(Wagen)* sich ziehen lassen; *rail (Zug)* einfahren (*into the station* in den Bahnhof); *(Jagd)* das Wild verfolgen; losen; trainieren; unentschieden spielen; **3.** *s* Zug *m*; *(Lotterie)* Ziehung; Verlosung; Anziehung(skraft), Zugkraft *f*, -artikel *m*, -nummer *f*, Schlager *m*; starke Inanspruchnahme *f* (*on s.th.* e-r S); Unentschieden *n*; *Am* bewegliche(r) Teil *m (e-r Zugbrücke)*; *Am* Binnengewässer *n*; **4.** *to end in a ~* unentschieden ausgehen; *to ~ a blank* leer ausgehen; *to ~ blood* Blut vergießen; *fig* auf die Palme bringen; *to ~ the long bow* übertreiben; *to ~ a deep breath* tief Atem holen; *to ~ o.'s first breath* das Licht der Welt erblicken; *to ~ o.'s last breath* den letzten Atemzug tun; *to ~ a comparison* e-n Vergleich ziehen; *to ~ to a close* dem Ende zugehen, sich dem Ende nähern; *to ~ a distinction* e-n Unterschied machen (*between* zwischen); *to ~ the line (fig)* e-e Grenze ziehen; *to ~ lots* das Los ziehen, entscheiden lassen; *to ~ it mild (fam)* die Kirche im Dorf lassen; *to ~ a parallel* e-e Parallele ziehen (*between* zwischen); *to ~ the sword* das Schwert ziehen; *fig* den Fehdehandschuh hinwerfen; *to ~ a sigh* seufzen; *to ~ the winner* Glück haben; *~ it mild! (fam)* nun mal langsam! sachte! **5.** *to ~* **along** fort-, wegschleppen; *to ~* **aside** zur Seite ziehen; beiseite nehmen; *to ~* **away** *tr* wegziehen; entwenden; entführen; *(Kunden)* abspenstig machen; *itr* sich entfernen; *to ~* **back** *tr itr* (sich) zurückziehen; *to ~* **down** herunterziehen; *on o.s.* sich zuziehen; *to ~ down the curtain* den Vorhang fallen lassen; Schluß machen, aufhören; *to ~* **forth** herausholen, entlocken; hervor-, wachrufen, erwecken, ins Leben rufen; *to ~* **in** *tr* einziehen, -holen; *(Wechsel)* einlösen; *(Ausgaben)* einschränken, verringern, kürzen; *(Anleihe)* zurückfordern; *itr* kürzer werden; *to ~ in o.'s horns* vorsichtiger sein; *to ~* **near** (heran)nahen, sich nähern; *to ~* **off** *tr* weg-, ab-, ausziehen; ableiten; herausziehen, -holen; herausdestillieren; *itr* sich zurückziehen; Druckbogen abziehen; *to ~* **on** *tr* anziehen, überstreifen; heranziehen; anziehen, -locken; herbeiführen, zur Folge haben; *(Kapital)* angreifen, -brechen, zehren, leben von; in Anspruch nehmen; bekommen von; Bezug nehmen auf; *(Wechsel)* ziehen auf; *itr* sich nähern, (heran-) nahen; *to ~* **out** *tr* herausziehen; aus-, in die Länge ziehen, verlängern *(a. zeitlich)*; entwerfen, skizzieren; zum Sprechen bringen *od* bewegen, aushorchen; *(Geheimnis)* entlocken; *(Geld)* abheben; *(Plan)* ausarbeiten, entwerfen; *itr* länger werden; sich in die Länge ziehen; *sport* vorgehen; *of (rail)* abfahren aus, losfahren; *to ~* **round** näherrücken, -kommen; *to ~* **together** sich ea. nähern; *to ~* **up** *tr* (her)aufziehen; aufstellen; *mil* aufmarschieren lassen; ausfertigen, ausstellen, abfassen, aufsetzen; *(Plan)* entwerfen, ausarbeiten; *(Heer)* aufstellen; *itr* aufsteigen; verfahren, vorgehen; *sport* aufholen; *(Auto)* vorfahren; *mil* aufziehen; *with* einholen, erreichen; *to ~ o.s. up* sich aufrichten.

draw|back ['drɔːbæk] Nachteil, Haken *m*; Kehr-, Schattenseite *f*; Hindernis, Hemmnis *n (to* für); Last, Unbequemlichkeit *f*; wunde(r) *od* dunkle(r) Punkt, dunkle(r) Schatten *m*; ärgerliche Sache; *(bes.* Zoll-)Rückerstattung, Rückvergütung *f*; **~bridge** Zugbrücke *f*; **~ee** [-'iː] *fin* Bezogene(r), Trassant; Akzeptant *m*; **~er** ['drɔ(ː)ə] Zeichner; Büfettier, Zapfer; *fin* Trassant, Aussteller *m (e-s Wechsels, a. e-r Urkunde)*; [drɔː] Schublade *f*, -fach *n*; *pl* Unterhose; *(chest of ~~s)* Kommode *f*; **~-well** Ziehbrunnen *m*.

drawing ['drɔːiŋ] Ziehen; Zeichnen *n*; Zeichnung, Skizze; *fin* Rücknahme; *(Wechsel)* Ausstellung, Trassierung, Ziehung (*on s.o.* auf jdn); *(Lotterie)* Ziehung; Aus-, Verlosung *f*; *out of ~* verzeichnet, falsch gezeichnet; *mechanical ~* Bau-, Konstruktionszeichnung *f*; *rough, working ~* (Arbeits-) Skizze *f*; **~-account** Girokonto *n*; **~-block** Zeichenblock *m*; *tech* Zieheisen *n*; **~-board** Reißbrett *n*; **~-card** *Am fig* Zugnummer, Attraktion *f*; **~-ink** Tusche *f*; **~-list** *(Lotterie)* Gewinnliste *f*; **~-office** Konstruktions-, Zeichenbüro *n*; **~-paper** Zeichenpapier *n*; **~-pen** Reiß-, Zeichenfeder *f*; **~-pin** *Br* Reißbrettstift *m*, Heftzwecke *f*; **~-room** Wohn-, Empfangszimmer *n*, Salon; (großer) Empfang; Besuch *m*, Gäste *m pl*; *Am rail* Privatabteil *n*.

drawl [drɔːl] *tr itr* langsam sprechen, (die Worte) (beim Sprechen) dehnen; *s* langsame(s), gedehnte(s) Sprechen *n*.

drawn [drɔːn] *a (Spiel)* unentschieden; *(Nummer)* gezogen; *(Tier)* ausgenommen; *(Gesicht)* eingefallen; verzerrt (*with* vor); *tech* gezogen, gestreckt; *~ by lot* ausgelost; *~* **butter** ausgelassene Butter, Buttersoße *f*; *~* **threadwork** Hohlsaum(arbeit *f*) *m*.

dray [drei] Rollwagen *m*; **~age** ['-idʒ] Rollfuhre *f*; **~-horse** (schweres) Zugpferd *n*; **~man** ['-mən] Roll-, Bierkutscher *m*.

dread [dred] *tr* (be)fürchten, Angst haben vor (*doing s.th.* etw zu tun); *itr* sich fürchten, Angst haben; *s* Furcht, Scheu, (große) Angst *f*, Grauen *n* (*of* vor); *a (~ed)* gefürchtet, furchterregend, furchtbar; **~ful** ['-ful] furchterregend, schaurig; *(a. fam übertreibend)* furchtbar, fürchterlich, schrecklich, entsetzlich; *penny ~~* Schauerroman *m*; **~nought, ~naught** ['-nɔ:t] Draufgänger; Loden(mantel) *m*; Schlacht-, Großkampfschiff *n*.

dream [dri:m] *s* Traum *m*; Träumerei *f*, Tagtraum; Wunsch(bild *n*); Traum (-gedicht *n*) *m*, Wunder, Märchen *n*; *v irr ~ed* od *~t* [dremt] *itr* träumen (*of* von); sich vorstellen, sich denken (*of s.th.* etw); *tr* erträumen, träumen von, ersehnen, sich wünschen; *(to ~ away, to ~ out)* verträumen; sich ausdenken, sich ausmalen, sich vorstellen; *to ~ up* (sich) erträumen; erfinden; *I wouldn't ~ of doing it* es fiele mir nicht im Traume ein, das zu tun; **~er** ['-ə] Träumer, Phantast *m*; **~iness** ['-inis] Verträumtheit, Verspieltheit *f*; **~-land, -world** Traumland *n*, -welt *f*; **~less** ['-lis] traumlos; **~like** traumartig; **~y** ['-i] träumerisch, verträumt, verspielt; *sl* reizend, süß.

drear|iness ['driərinis] Düsterkeit, Traurigkeit; Trübseligkeit; Freudlosigkeit, Einsamkeit, Öde *f*; **~y** ['driəri] trüb(e), düster, niederdrükkend, traurig; freudlos, trübselig; unfreundlich; einsam, öde, langweilig.

dredge [dredʒ] **1.** *s (Fischerei)* Schleppnetz *n*; Bagger(maschine *f*) *m*; *tr (to ~ for)* mit dem Schleppnetz fischen; ausbaggern; **~r** ['-ə] *(bes.* Austern-) Fischer *m*; Fischerboot *n*; (Naß-)Bagger *m*; **2.** *tr (Küche)* streuen (*over* über); panieren, bestreuen (*with* mit); **~r** ['-ə] Streubüchse; *(Zucker)* Streudose *f*.

dregs [dregs] *pl* Bodensatz *m*; *fig* Hefe *f*, Abschaum *m*; *sing* Rest *m*, Überbleibsel *n*; *to drink, to drain to the ~* bis zur Neige leeren; *not a dreg* (auch) nicht das geringste; *the ~ of humanity* der Abschaum der Menschheit.

drench [dren(t)ʃ] *tr* e-n Trank eingeben (*a horse* e-m Pferde); durchnässen; einweichen, eintauchen; *s vet* (Arznei-)Trank; Regenguß *m*; Einweichbrühe *f*; **~er** ['-ə] *fam* Regenguß *m*.

dress [dres] *tr* (an-, be)kleiden, anziehen; kleiden, mit Kleidung versorgen; schmücken, (heraus)putzen, dekorieren *(a. Schaufenster)*; *(die Haare)* kämmen, machen, ordnen, aufstecken; *(Wunde)* verbinden, behandeln; ein-, her-, zurichten, vorbereiten; *(Salat)* anmachen; *(Geflügel)* putzen, rupfen u. ausnehmen; *(Pferd)* striegeln; *(Pflanzen)* anbinden, beschneiden; *(Feld)* bestellen; düngen; *tech* (aus-, zu)richten; *(Erz)* aufbereiten; *(Textilien)* appretieren; polieren, glätten; *(Leder)* gerben; *(Flachs)* hecheln; *(Tuch)* rauhen; *(Stein)* behauen, bossieren; *mil (Front)* ausrichten; *mar* beflaggen; *itr* sich anziehen, -kleiden, sich fertigmachen; sich salonfähig, sich fein machen; *s* Kleidung *f*, Kleider *n pl*, Anzug *m*, Aufmachung *f*; (Damen-) Kleid *n*; Gesellschaftskleidung *f*; *a* Bekleidungs-; Gesellschafts-; *to ~ down (fam) tr* abkanzeln, heruntermachen, e-e Zigarre verpassen (*s.o.* jdm); vertobaken, verprügeln; *(Pferd)* striegeln; *itr* sich unauffällig anziehen; *to ~ up* Gesellschaftskleidung anziehen; sich salonfähig, sich fein machen; *mil* antreten; *in full ~* in Gala; **~-circle** *theat Br* erste(r) Rang *m*; **~-clothes** *pl* Gesellschaftskleidung *f*; **~-coat** Frack *m*; **~ designer** Modezeichner *m*; **~er** ['-ə] Kammerdiener *m*; Zofe; *theat* Ankleidefrau *f*; *med* Assistent; Dekorateur *m*; Friseuse *f*; Zurichter, Aufbereiter *m*; Anrichte *f*, (Küchen-)Büfett *n*; *Am* Frisiertisch *m*, -kommode *f*; **~-form** Schneiderfigur *f*; **~maker** Schneiderin *f*; **~making** Damenschneiderei *f*; **~ parade** Modenschau; *mil* Parade *f*; **~-rehearsal** *theat* Generalprobe *f*; **~-shield, -preserver** Schweißblatt *n*; **~-shirt** Frackhemd *n*; **~-suit** Gesellschaftsanzug *m*; **~ uniform** große(r) Dienstanzug *m*; **~y** ['-i] putzsüchtig, geschniegelt; *(Kleidung)* fein, elegant, modisch, chic.

dressing ['dresiŋ] Ankleiden; Verbinden *n*, Verband *m*, Binde *f*; Putzen; Zurichten *n*, Vorbereitung; *agr* Bestellung; Düngung; (Be-)Kleidung *f*; Verband(szeug *n*) *m*; *(Textil)* Füllung, Appretur; *(Salat-)* Soße; *(Geflügel)* Füllung *f*; *fam* Prügel *pl*; **~-bag** Kulturbeutel *m*; **~-case** (Reise-)Necessaire *n*; Verbandskasten *m*; **~-down** *fam* Rüffel, Anschnauzer *m*, Zigarre, Strafpredigt; *fam* Tracht *f* Prügel; **~-glass** (großer) Drehspiegel *m*; **~-gown** Morgenrock *m*; **~-jacket** *Br*, **-sack** *Am* Frisiermantel *m*; **~ material** Verbandszeug *n*; **~-room** Ankleidezimmer *n*; *theat* Garderobe *f (e-s Schauspielers)*; **~-station** *mil* Verbandsplatz *m*; **~-table** Toilettentisch, Frisiertisch *m*, -kommode *f*.

dribble ['dribl] *tr itr* tröpfeln, rinnen (lassen); *itr* sabbern, geifern; *sport tr itr* dribbeln, (den Ball) vor sich hertreiben; *s* Tröpfchen; Gerinnsel, Rinnsal; *sport* Dribbeln *n*; *fam* Nieselregen *m*.

driblet ['driblit]: *a ~* ein bißchen, ein wenig, etwas; *in ~s* nach und nach; *to pay off by ~s* in kleinen Beträgen abbezahlen.

dried [draid] *a* getrocknet; Trocken-, Dörr-; **~ egg** Eipulver *n*; **~ fruit** Dörr-, Backobst *n*; **~ vegetables** *pl* Dörrgemüse *n*.

drier, dryer ['draiə] *meist in Zssgen* Trockner *m*, Trockengerät *n*, -apparat *m*; Trockenmittel *n*; *hair-~* Fön *m*.

drift [drift] *s* Strömung *f*; Luftstrom *m*; Meeresströmung; Fahrt-, Flugrichtung; Kurs-, Flugbahnabweichung, Abtrift; Richtung *f*, Zug *m*, Tendenz, Neigung *f*; *(Ereignisse)* Gang *m*; *(Gedanke)* Tragweite, Bedeutung *f*, Zweck *m*, Absicht *f*; Sichtreibenlassen *n*; (Schnee-)Verwehung *f*; *geol* Geschiebe, Geröll *n*, Treibsand *m*, Schwemmland *n*; Regenschauer *m*, Schneetreiben *n*; *min* Strecke *f*; *tech* Ramme *f*, Rammbock *m*; *itr* getrieben, verweht werden; treiben (*in the open sea* auf die offene See); *aero* abtreiben, vom Kurs abweichen; *fig* sich treiben lassen; *(to ~ along)* plan-, ziellos umherwandern, herumbummeln; *to ~ apart (fig)* sich ausea.leben; *tr* (zs.)treiben; aufhäufen; *to ~ in* im Vorbeigehen besuchen, *fam* hereinschneien; *to ~ off (fam)* sich verkrümeln; *(to sleep)* einschlafen; *to let things ~* die Dinge laufenlassen; *~ from the land* Landflucht *f*; *~ of snow* Schneeverwehung *f*; **~ anchor** Warp-, Stromanker *m*; **~er** ['-ə] kleine(r) Schleppdampfer, Logger; Treibnetzfischer; *Am sl* Vagabund *m*; **~-ice** Treibeis *n*; **~ pin** *tech* Durchschlag *m*; **~ sand** Treibsand *m*; **~-wood** Treibholz *n*.

drill [dril] **1.** *s* Drillbohrer *m*; *tr* (aus-, durch)bohren; **~er** ['-ə], **~ing machine** Bohrmaschine *f*; **~ hole** Bohrloch *n*; **~ings** *pl* Bohrspäne *m pl*; **2.** *s* strenge Schulung *f*, Training *n*; *mil* Drill *m*, Exerzieren *n*, formale, Grundausbildung *f*; *tr* eintrainieren; einpauken, einexerzieren, drillen; *itr* trainieren, üben; exerzieren, militärisch ausgebildet werden; **~-ground** Exerzierplatz *m*; **~master** *Am*, **~instructor** *mil* Ausbilder *m*; **~-sergeant** Rekrutenfeldwebel *m*; **3.** *s agr* Furche, Rille; Reihe (Pflanzen); *(~ machine, plough)* Drillmaschine *f*; *tr* drillen, in Rillen säen; in Reihen (be)pflanzen; **4.** *(a. ~ing) (Textil)* Drillich, Drell *m*.

drink [driŋk] *irr drank, drunk tr* trinken; *(Tier)* saufen; *(to ~ off)* austrinken, leeren; auf-, einsaugen, absorbieren; *(Feuchtigkeit)* anziehen; *(to ~ away) (Geld)* vertrinken, versaufen; *itr* (gewohnheitsmäßig) *(Alkohol)* trinken, saufen; *to ~ to s.o.* jdm zutrinken, *fam* zuprosten, auf jds Gesundheit trinken; *to s.th.* auf etw trinken; *s* Trunk; *(Wasser)* Schluck *m*; Getränk *n*; *(Gläschen)* Schnaps *m*; (Gewohnheits- *od* unmäßiges) Trinken *n*; *sl Am* der große Teich *(Ozean)*; *to ~ down, off, up* austrinken; *to ~ in (fig)* begierig aufnehmen; *to have a ~* ein Gläschen trinken; *to take to ~* sich dem Trunk, *fam* Suff ergeben; *to ~ s.o.'s health* auf jds Gesundheit trinken; **~able** ['-əbl] *a* trinkbar; *s pl* Getränke *n pl*; **~er** ['-ə] Trinker, (Gewohnheits-) Säufer *m*.

drinking ['driŋkiŋ] Trinken, Saufen *n*; **~-bout** Trink-, Saufgelage *n*, Zecherei *f*, *fam* Besäufnis *n*; **~-fountain** (öffentlicher) Trinkwasserspender, -brunnen *m*; **~-song** Trinklied *n*; **~-straw** Trinkhalm *m*; **~-water** Trinkwasser *n*; *~~ supply* Trinkwasserversorgung *f*.

drip [drip] *itr* tropfen, tröpfeln (*from* von); triefen, rinnen (*with* von); *tr: to ~ sweat* von Schweiß triefen; *s* Tropfen, Tröpfeln, Triefen, Rinnen; *tech* Lecken; Tropfgeräusch, -wasser *n*; (Dach-)Traufe *f*; *sl* miese(r), unangenehme(r) Kerl *m*; **~-dry** bügelfrei, no iron; **~olator** ['-əleitə] *Am* Filter(kaffee)kanne *f*; **~ping** ['-iŋ] *a (~~ wet)* triefend, patschnaß; *s pl* Bratenfett *n*; *das* Abgetropfte; *~(~) pan* Bratpfanne *f*; **~stone** *arch* Traufstein; *geol* Tropfstein *m*.

drive [draiv] *irr drove, driven* **1.** *tr* (an-, be)treiben *a. fig*; (vor-, vorwärts) stoßen, jagen, hetzen; *(Regen)* peitschen; *(Wolken)* jagen; *(Pfahl)* einrammen; *(Stollen)* vortreiben; *fig* drängen, an-, aufstacheln, aufhetzen; zwingen, veranlassen (*to do* zu tun); hinein-, hindurchtreiben, -schlagen (*into* in); bohren; *(Arbeiter)* antreiben; *(Fahrzeug)* fahren, lenken; kutschieren; *(Person od Sache in e-m Fahrzeug)* fahren, bringen; *(als Motor)* (be)treiben, in Betrieb setzen *od* halten; *(Schraube)* anziehen; *el* steuern; *(Sache)* energisch betreiben, durchsetzen, -führen, zum Abschluß bringen; aufschieben, hinziehen, -halten; **2.** *itr* eilen, stürmen, jagen, hetzen, brausen; *(im Winde, (sport) den Ball)* treiben; *(Fahrzeug, Fahrer, Fahrgast)* fahren; schwer arbeiten (*at* an); **3.** *s* Fahren *n*; (Aus-, Spazier-) Fahrt; Fahrstraße *f*, -weg *m*; Autostraße; Auf-, Ausfahrt *f*; *mot tech* Antrieb *m*, Triebwerk *n*; *sport* heftige(r) Schlag, Stoß *m*; Schlagart, -weise; Trieb-, Stoßkraft *f*; *psychol* Trieb; Antrieb, Schwung, Unternehmungsgeist *m*, Energie, Tatkraft *f*; Unternehmen *n* (*against* gegen); Kampagne *f*, (Werbe-, Propaganda-)Feldzug, Vorstoß *m* (*against* gegen); *Am* (besondere) Anstrengung; eilige, dringende Sache *f*;

Druck *m*; Treibjagd *f*; *(Vieh)* Auftrieb *m*; Floß *n*; **4.** *to go for, to have, to take a* ~ aus-, spazierenfahren; *to lack* ~ es an Energie fehlen lassen; *to let* ~ zielen, schlagen, schießen (*at* nach); *to* ~ *a bargain* hart sein (bei Verhandlungen); den niedrigsten Preis zahlen; das Höchstmögliche verlangen; *to* ~ *into a corner (fig)* in die Enge treiben; *to* ~ *home (itr)* nach Hause, heimfahren; *fig* nahelegen, zu Gemüte führen; *tr (Nagel)* einschlagen; *to* ~ *o.'s point home* s-n Standpunkt überzeugend darlegen; *to* ~ *crazy, mad, insane* verrückt machen; *to* ~ *a well* e-n Brunnen bohren; **5.** *to* ~ **at** *fam* (hin)zielen auf; beabsichtigen; sagen wollen, meinen; *what are you driving at?* worauf wollen Sie denn hinaus? *to* ~ **away** wegtreiben, -jagen; vertreiben; fort-, verjagen; schwer, eifrig arbeiten (*at* an); *to* ~ **back** zurücktreiben, -jagen; *to* ~ **in** *tr (Nagel)* einschlagen; *itr* (hin)einfahren; *to* ~ **off** wegfahren; *mar* abtreiben; *to* ~ **on** vorankommen; ~~*!* vorwärts! los! marsch! *to* ~ **out** hinausfahren (*into the country* aufs Land); herausfahren (*to* zu, nach); ~ **past** vorbeifahren; *to* ~ **up** *tr* hinauf-, in die Höhe treiben; *itr* vorfahren (*to* bei, vor); **6.** *sales* ~ Absatzsteigerung *f*; **~-in** *s Am mot* Restaurant *n*, Laden *m*, Bank *f* mit Bedienung am Auto; ~~ *cinema (mot)* Autokino *n*; **~r** ['-ə] Fuhrmann, Kutscher; Fahrer, Chauffeur, (Wagen-)Führer; (Vieh-)Treiber; *rail (car* ~~*)* Triebwagenführer; Antreiber; *tech* Mitnehmer *m*, Ramme *f*; Treibrad *n*; *(Radar)* Steuerstufe *f*; *(Golf)* Schläger *m*; ~~*'s cab* Führerstand *m*, -haus *n*; ~~*'s license, permit (Am)* Führerschein *m*; ~~*'s seat* Führersitz; *(Wagen)* Bock *m*; ~ **shaft** Antriebswelle *f*; **~way** *Am* Zufahrt *f*; **~-yourself service** Wagenvermietung *f (für Selbstfahrer)*.

drivel ['drivl] *itr* sabbern, geifern; faseln, Unsinn reden; *s* Geschwätz, Gerede *n*, Unsinn *m*.

driving ['draiviŋ] *a tech* treibend, Treib-; heftig, stark; *s* Treiben; Fahren *n*; ~ **ban** Führerscheinentzug *m*; **~-belt** Treibriemen *m*; ~ **force** Trieb-, treibende Kraft *f*; **~-gear** Getriebe, Triebwerk *n*; ~ **instructor** Fahrlehrer *m*; ~ **lessons** *pl* Fahrunterricht *m*; **~-licence** Führerschein *m*; **~-mirror** *mot* Rückspiegel *m*; ~ **moment** Antriebsmoment *n*; **~-power** Antriebs-, Steuerleistung *f*; ~ **school** Fahrschule *f*; **~-shaft** Antriebswelle *f*; ~ **test** Fahrprüfung *f*; **~-wheel** Treibrad *n*.

drizzl|e ['drizl] *itr* nieseln, misseln; *s* Sprühregen *m*; **~y** ['-i] feucht u. neblig.

droll [droul] *a* drollig, ulkig, spaßig, komisch; *s* ulkige(r) Mensch, Spaßvogel *m*; *itr* Witze, Ulk, Spaß machen; **~ery** ['-əri] ulkige Sache *f*; Spaß, Ulk *m*; Drolligkeit, Ulkigkeit *f*.

drome [droum] *fam* Flugplatz *m*.

dromedary ['drʌmədəri, 'drɔm-] Dromedar, einhöckrige(s) Kamel *n*.

drone [droun] *s zoo* Drohn(e *f*) *m*; *fig* Drohne *f*, Faulenzer, Schmarotzer *m*; Summen, Brummen, Gebrumm; ferngelenkte(s) Flugzeug *n*; *itr* summen, brummen; monoton reden; faulenzen; *tr* (her)leiern; *to* ~ *away o.'s life* sein Leben verbummeln.

drool [dru:l] *s. drivel*.

droop [dru:p] *itr* herabsinken, sich senken; herunterhängen (*over* über); schlaff, matt, kraftlos, welk werden, welken; *(Preise)* fallen; *fig* den Kopf hängen lassen, den Mut verlieren; *tr* senken, hängen lassen; *s* Herunterhängen *n*; **~ing, ~y** ['-iŋ, '-i] schlaff, matt, kraftlos; mutlos; *(Schulter)* abfallend.

drop [drɔp] **1.** *s* Tropfen *m a. allg*; ein bißchen, ein wenig, etwas; Sinken, Fallen *n*; Fall, (Ab-)Sturz; Abwurf *m*; Senkung *f*; *com* Rückgang *m*, Baisse *f*; Höhenunterschied *m*; *tele* Klappe; Falltür *f*; *Am* Briefeinwurf; *el* Abfall; *(Fallschirm)* Abwurf, Absprung; *(~ curtain)* (Theater-)Vorhang; *(~ hammer, press)* Gesenkhammer *m*; *pl pharm* Tropfen *m pl*; Drops *pl*, saure, Fruchtbonbons *m pl*; **2.** *itr* (herab)tropfen, tröpfeln, laufen; (herab-, herunter)fallen (*out of the window* aus dem Fenster); sich fallen lassen; hineingeraten *(into)*, stoßen (*into* auf); hin-, umfallen, zs.brechen, tot umfallen (*from exhaustion* vor Erschöpfung); schwächer werden, nachlassen; *(Wind)* abflauen; *fig* keine Bedeutung mehr haben, keine Rolle mehr spielen, zu Ende gehen, aufhören; (herab-)sinken; *(Temperatur)* fallen, sinken; *(Stimme)* sich senken; *(Tiere)* geworfen werden; *Am sl* auf frischer Tat ertappt werden; **3.** *tr* tropfen (lassen), tröpfeln; besprengen, bespritzen; fallen lassen *a. fig*; (hin-)werfen; *(Arbeit)* niederlegen; *(Lot)* fällen; *(Bomben)* abwerfen; *(Geld)* verlieren; herunterlassen; *(Knicks)* machen; *(Fahrgäste)* absetzen, aussteigen lassen; niederstrecken, -werfen, zu Boden strecken; abschießen; *(Äußerung, Vermutung)* fallenlassen; *(Thema)* fallen, auf sich beruhen lassen; verzichten, aufgeben; *(Briefwechsel)* einstellen; *(Gewohnheit)* aufgeben; *(Buchstaben, Wort)* auslassen; *(Buchstaben)* nicht (aus)sprechen; *(Brief)* schreiben, schicken; einwerfen (*in the letter-box* in den Briefkasten); *Am* entlassen; ausschließen (*from a club* aus e-m Klub); *(Ei)* aufgeschlagen kochen; *(Junge)* werfen; *Am fam* stehen-, sitzen-, liegenlassen, entlassen; *Am sl* verlieren (*money* Geld); *s.o.* jdn niederschlagen; **4.** *at the* ~ *of a hat* auf ein Zeichen; im Nu; ohne zu zögern; *in* ~*s* tropfenweise; *to the last* ~ bis auf den letzten Tropfen; *to get the* ~ *on* schneller sein (*s.o.* als jem); *to let* ~ fallenlassen, aufgeben; *to* ~ *anchor* den Anker werfen; *to* ~ *a brick (fam)* e-e Dummheit machen; *to* ~ *a hint* e-e Andeutung fallenlassen; *to* ~ *a line* ein paar Zeilen schreiben; ~ *it!* laß das! **5.** *ear-~s (pl)* Ohrringe *m pl*; *tear* ~ Tränentropfen *m*; ~ *of blood* Blutstropfen *m*; *a* ~ *in the bucket, in the ocean* ein Tropfen auf den heißen Stein; ~ *in prices* Preissturz, -rückgang *m*, Sinken *n* der Preise; ~ *of rain* Regentropfen *m*; ~ *of potential (el)* Spannungsabfall *m*; ~ *in the temperature* Temperatursturz *m*; **6.** *to* ~ **across** *fam* treffen; begegnen, in die Arme laufen (*s.o.* jdm); *to* ~ **away** *s.* ~ *off*; *to* ~ **behind** abfallen (gegenüber), zurückbleiben (hinter); *to* ~ **down** niedersinken; sich niederwerfen; herunterfallen; *(Schiff)* hinunterfahren; *to* ~ **in** *at, on, upon s.o.* bei jdm unerwartet vorsprechen, *fam* hereingeschneit kommen, auf e-n Sprung vorbeikommen; *(Aufträge)* bei jdm eingehen; *to* ~ **off** sich zurückziehen, (allmählich, einer nach dem andern) weg-, ausbleiben; abnehmen, nachlassen, zurückgehen; *s.th.* etw abgeben (*at* bei); *(to* ~ *off to sleep) fam* einnicken, -schlafen; das Zeitliche segnen; *to* ~ **on** fallen auf; sich niederlassen (*o.'s knees* auf die Knie); *s.o.* jdn herunterputzen; *to* ~ **out** sich zurückziehen (*of* von), aufgeben (*of s.th.* etw), nicht mehr teilnehmen (*of* an); ausfallen; ausscheiden; *to* ~ **through** *fig* ins Wasser, unter den Tisch fallen; ~ **altitude** *aero* Abwurf-, Absprunghöhe *f*; ~ **container** *aero* Abwurfbehälter *m*; **~-forge** *tr* gesenkschmieden; **~-kick** *sport* Prellstoß *m*; **~let** ['-lit] Tröpfchen *n*; ~ **letter** *Am* Ortsbrief *m*; **~per** ['-ə] Tropfglas *n*; **~ping** ['-iŋ] Fall(en *n*) *m*; *das* (Hin-, Herunter-)Gefallene; *pl* Dung, Dünger, Mist *m*; ~~ *area, zone* Absprungraum *m*; **~-scene** *theat* Vorhang *m*; *fig* Schlußszene *f*.

drops|ical ['drɔpsikəl] wassersüchtig; **~y** ['drɔpsi] Wassersucht *f*.

dross [drɔs] (Metall-)Schlacken *f pl*; *allg* Abfall *m*; *fig* wertlose(s) Zeug; *fam* Geld *n*; **~y** ['-i] schlackenartig, -haltig.

drought [draut], *bes. Am* **drouth** [drauθ] Trockenheit; Dürre(periode, -zeit) *f*; **~y, drouthy** ['-ti, '-θi] trocken, dürr; ausgetrocknet.

drove [drouv] Auftrieb *m (Vieh)*; Herde; Menschenmenge, Masse *f*; *arch* Scharnier-, Breiteisen *n*; **~r** ['-ə] Viehtreiber, -händler *m*.

drown [draun] *tr* ertränken, ersäufen; überfluten, überschwemmen; einweichen; verdünnen; *fig* übertönen, ersticken *(a. in Tränen)*; *(Kummer)* betäuben; *to be ~ed u. itr* ertrinken; *to* ~ *out (Stimme)* übertönen.

drows|e [drauz] *s* Schläfrigkeit *f*; *itr* schläfrig, am Einschlafen sein; dösen; *tr* müde, schläfrig machen; *(Zeit)* verdösen; *to* ~ *off* eindösen; **~iness** ['-inis] Schläfrigkeit; Apathie *f*; **~y** ['-i] schläfrig; einschläfernd; *fig* schlafmützig, langsam, träge.

drub [drʌb] *tr* (ver)prügeln, verdreschen; *sport* haushoch schlagen; *s* (Stock-)Schlag; Puff *m*; **~bing** ['-iŋ] Tracht Prügel, Dresche; *sport* gewaltige Niederlage *f*.

drudg|e [drʌdʒ] *s fig* Packesel *m*, Aschenbrödel *n*; *itr* sich placken, sich (ab)schinden; **~ery** ['-əri] Plackerei, Fron-, Sklavenarbeit *f*.

drug [drʌg] *s* Droge; Arznei(mittel *n*) *f*, Präparat; Narkotikum, Rauschgift *n*; *tr (Speise, Getränk)* etwas zusetzen (*s.th.* e-r S); verfälschen; betäuben, narkotisieren; vergiften; anekeln; *to* ~ *o.s.* Rauschgift nehmen; ~ *in, on the market* Ladenhüter *m*; ~ **addict** Rauschgiftsüchtige(r); Morphinist; Kokainist *m*; **~gist** ['-ist] Drogist; *Am* Apotheker *m*; ~~*'s shop* Drogerie *f*; **~store** ['-stɔ:] *Am* Apotheke (u. Drogerie) *f*, die auch Papier, Tabak u. leichte Mahlzeiten verkauft; ~ **traffic** Rauschgifthandel *m*.

drugget ['drʌgit] Bodenbelag *m* aus grobem Wollstoff.

Druid ['dru(:)id] *rel hist* Druide *m*.

drum [drʌm] *s* Trommel *f*, -schlag *m*; *tech* Trommel *f*, Zylinder *m*; Spule *f*; (metallenes) Faß *n*; *arch* Trommel *f*; Unterbau *m (e-r Kuppel)*; *anat (ear-~)* Mittelohr, Trommelfell *n*; *itr tr* trommeln (*s.th., on s.th.* auf etw); *tr (to* ~ *up)* zs.trommeln; einhämmern (*s.th. into s.o.* jdm etw); hinauswerfen (*out of* aus); *sl* (als Reisender) verkaufen, absetzen; *itr* die Werbetrommel rühren; *to beat the* ~ die Trommel rühren; **~beat** Trommeln, Getrommel *n*; **~fire** Trommelfeuer *n*; **~head** Trommelfell *n a. anat*; ~~ *court-martial (mil)* Standgericht *n*; **~-major** Tambourmajor *m*; **~mer** ['-ə]

Trommler; *Am fam* Geschäftsreisende(r), Vertreter *m*; ~ **roll** Trommelwirbel *m*; ~**stick** Trommelstock; *(Geflügel)* Schlegel *m*.

drunk [drʌŋk] *a* betrunken; *fig* trunken, selig (*with* vor); *s* Betrunkene(r) *m*; *to be (out) on a* ~ e-e Sauftour machen; *to get* ~ e-n Schwips kriegen; sich betrinken; ~ *as a lord* sternhagelvoll; ~**ard** ['-əd] Trinker, Trunkenbold *m*; ~**en** ['-ən] *a* betrunken; trunksüchtig; ~**enness** ['-ənnis] (Be-)Trunkenheit *f*, Rausch *m a. fig*; Trunksucht *f*.

drupe [dru:p] *bot* Steinfrucht *f*.

dry [drai] *a* trocken; *(Holz)* dürr; ausgetrocknet; *fig* trocken, langweilig, uninteressant; ergebnis-, nutzlos; *(Wein)* herb, trocken; durstig(machend); unter Alkoholverbot; *tr* (ab-)trocknen; dörren; *itr* trocknen, trocken werden; *to run* ~ trocken werden; *mot* kein Benzin mehr haben; *to* ~ *up (tr itr)* austrocknen, -dörren *a. fig*; *theat* steckenbleiben; *keep* ~! vor Feuchtigkeit zu schützen; ~ *up! (sl)* halt die Schnauze! halt's Maul! ~ **battery** *el* Trockenbatterie *f*; ~ **cell** *el* Trockenelement *n*; ~-**clean** *tr* chemisch reinigen; ~-**cleaner('s)** chemische Reinigungsanstalt *f*; ~ **cleaning** chemische Reinigung *f*; ~ **dock** *mar* Trockendock *n*; ~**er** ['-ə] *s. drier*; ~ **farming** Ackerbau *m* in fast regenlosem und unbewässertem Gebiet; ~ **goods** *pl Am* Manufakturwaren *f pl od* Textilien *pl*, Kurzwaren *f pl*; ~ **ice** Trockeneis *n*; ~**ing** ['-iŋ] trocknend; ~~ *chamber* Trockenkammer *f*; ~ **kiln** Trockenofen *m*, Darre *f*; ~ **land** feste(r) Boden *m*; ~ **measure** Trocken(hohl)maß *n*; ~**ness** ['-nis] Trockenheit *f*; ~ **nurse** Kinderfrau *f*, -mädchen *n*; ~ **pile** Trockenbatterie *f*; ~ **point** *(Kunst)* Kaltnadelradierung *f*; ~-**rot** *bot* Trockenfäule *f (a. des Holzes)*; *fig* Verfall *m*, Entartung *f*; ~ **run** *Am mil* Schießen *n* mit Exerzierpatronen; *allg* Probe; *aero* Leerlaufprüfung *f (des Motors)*; Übungsluftangriff *m*; ~-**salt** *tr* (ein)pökeln u. dörren; ~**salter** Drogist *m*; ~**saltery** Drogerie *f*; ~-**shod** *a* trockenen Fußes; ~ **wash** Trockenwäsche *f*.

dryad ['draiəd] Dryade *f*.

dual ['dju(:)əl] zwei-, zwiefach, doppelt; Zwei-, Doppel-; ~ **carriage-way** doppelte Fahrbahn *f*; ~ **control** *aero* Doppelsteuerung *f*; ~**ism** ['-izm] Dualismus *m*; ~**ist** ['-ist] Dualist *m*; ~**istic** [-'listik] dualistisch; ~**ity** [dju(:)'æliti] Zweiheit *f*; ~ **personality** *psychol* Persönlichkeitsspaltung *f*.

dub [dʌb] *tr* zum Ritter schlagen; e-n Spitznamen geben (*s.o.* jdm); *tech* zurichten; *(Leder)* einfetten; *sl (to* ~ *up)* blechen; *film* synchronisieren, einblenden; *s Am fam* dumme(r) Kerl; *sport* schlechte(r) Spieler *m*; ~**bing** ['-iŋ] Lederfett *n*; *film* Synchronisation *f*.

dubious ['dju:biəs] zweifelhaft, fraglich; mißverständlich, zwei-, mehrdeutig; verdächtig; *(Zukunft, Ergebnis)* ungewiß; unsicher, im Zweifel (*of, about* über); skeptisch, schwankend, zögernd; *to be* ~ zweifeln (*of* an); ~**ness** ['-nis], **dubiety** [dju(:)'baiəti] Zweifelhaftigkeit; Ungewißheit; Unsicherheit *f*.

ducal ['dju:kəl] herzoglich.

ducat ['dʌkət] Dukaten *m (Goldmünze)*; *Am sl* (Eintritts-, Zulassungs-) Karte *f*; *Am sl* Dollar *m*.

duch|ess ['dʌtʃis] Herzogin *f*; ~**y** ['dʌtʃi] Herzogtum *n*.

duck [dʌk] **1.** *s* (weibliche) Ente; Ente(nfleisch *n*) *f*; *fam* Täubchen *n*, Liebling; *Am sl* Kerl *m*; *fig (lame* ~*)* lahme Ente *f*, kranke(s) Huhn *n*; *sport (*~*'s egg)* Null *f*; *Am sl* nichtwiedergewählte(r) Kongreßabgeordnete(r *m*); *Am sl* Kippe *f*; *s.* ~*ing*; *itr* sich ducken, sich schnell bücken; (kurz) untertauchen; *tr (den Kopf)* schnell *od* plötzlich einziehen; ins Wasser tauchen; *Am sl* aus dem Wege gehen (*s.o.* jdm; *s.th.* e-r S); *like a* ~ *takes to water (fig)* natürlich, mit der größten Selbstverständlichkeit; *like a dying* ~ *in a thunderstorm* gottverlassen, hilflos; *like water off a* ~*'s back* wirkungs-, eindruckslos *adv*; *to play* ~*s and drakes* e-n Stein über e-e Wasseroberfläche hüpfen lassen; *with o.'s money* sein Geld aus dem Fenster werfen; ~**bill** *zoo* Schnabeltier *n*; ~**boards** *pl* Lattenrost *m*; ~**er** ['-ə] Taucher; Entenjäger *m*; *orn* Tauchentchen *n*, Taucher *m*; ~**ing** ['-iŋ] (Unter-)Tauchen *n*; *to get a* ~~ völlig durchnäßt werden; ~~-*stool* Wippe *f*; ~**ling** ['-liŋ] Entchen *n*; ~**pins** *pl Art Am* Kegelspiel *n*; ~**pond** Ententeich *m*; ~**('s) egg** Entenei *n*; *sport* Null *f*; ~ **soup** *Am sl* Gimpel *m*; leichte Arbeit *f*; ~**weed** ['-wi:d] *bot* Entengrütze, Wasserlinse *f*; ~**y** ['-i] *fam a* süß, reizend, lieb, nett; *s* Herz(blätt)chen *n*, Liebling *m*; **2.** Segeltuch *n*; *pl* weiße Leinenhose *f*; **3.** *fam mil* Schwimmkampfwagen *m*.

duct [dʌkt] Rohr(leitung *f*) *n*; Kanal *m*; *anat* Gang, Duktus *m*; *bile-, milk-, tear-*~ Gallen-, Milch-, Tränengang *m*; *spermatic* ~ *(anat)* Samenleiter *m*; ~**ile** ['-ail, *Am* -il] *tech* streckbar, dehnbar, biegsam, geschmeidig; formbar, bildsam, plastisch; *fig* lenksam, umgänglich; ~**ility** [dʌk'tiliti] Dehnbarkeit, Biegsamkeit; Plastizität *f*.

dud [dʌd] *s (*~*man)* Vogelscheuche *f*; *sl* Blindgänger *(a. Mensch)*; Versager *m*; *pl* Klamotten *pl*, Lumpen *m pl*; alte(s) Zeug *n*, Plunder; *Am sl* ungedeckte(r) Scheck *m*; *a* nachgemacht, falsch; unnütz, unbrauchbar, wertlos.

dud|e [dju:d] *Am* Stutzer; *Am (Westen) sl* Sommerfrischler; Tourist *m*; ~~-*ranch (Am)* für Sommerfrischler unterhaltene Farm *f*.

dudgeon ['dʌdʒən] Groll, Ärger, Grimm, Zorn *m*; *in high* ~ voller Zorn.

due [dju:] *a* geschuldet, Schuld-; zahlbar, zu zahlen(d); *(Zahlung, Arbeit)* fällig; *(Verkehrsmittel)* planmäßig ankommend, fällig (*at noon* um 12 Uhr mittags); gebührend, gehörig, schuldig, angebracht, passend; nötig, erforderlich, ausreichend, genügend; zu verdanken(d), zuzuschreiben(d) (*to* dat); *Am* die Folge, infolge (*to* gen); zurückzuführend (*to* auf); *adv mar (vor e-r Himmelsrichtung)* genau; *s ohne pl* Geschuldete(s); Zustehende(s) *n*; Anspruch, (gerechter) Lohn *m*; *pl* Abgaben, Gebühren *f pl*; Zoll (-gebühren *f pl*); (Mitglieds-)Beitrag *m*; *after* ~ *consideration* nach reiflicher Überlegung; *for a full* ~ vollständig, völlig, ganz *adv*; *in* ~ *course* im rechten Augenblick, im gegebenen Moment; *in* ~ *form* ordnungsgemäß; *in* ~ *time* zur festgesetzten, zur rechten Zeit; *when* ~ *(fin)* bei Fälligkeit, bei Verfall; *with all* ~ *respect to* bei aller Achtung vor; ~ *east (mar)* genau Ost; *to be* ~ *to* sollen, müssen; *Am* im Begriff sein zu; *s.o.* jdm zustehen, gebühren; *s.th.* auf etw beruhen; *to become, to fall* ~ fällig werden; *to give the devil his* ~ Gnade vor Recht ergehen lassen; *he is* ~ *to do it* es ist seine Sache *od* Angelegenheit, es zu tun; *the train is* ~ *at* ... die planmäßige Ankunft(szeit) des Zuges ist ...; *the plane is already* ~ das Flugzeug müßte schon da sein; *amount, sum* ~ Schuldbetrag *m*, -summe *f*; *club* ~*s (pl)* Vereinsbeitrag *m*; *harbo(u)r* ~*s (pl)* Hafengebühren *f pl*; ~ **date** Fälligkeitstermin *m*.

duel ['dju(:)əl] *s* Duell *n*, Zweikampf; *allg fig* Kampf, Streit *m*; *itr* sich duellieren; ~**(l)ist** ['-ist] Duellant *m*.

duenna [dju(:)'enə] Anstandsdame *f*.

duet(t) [dju(:)'et] *mus* Duett; Duo *n*.

duffel, duffle ['dʌfl] Düffel *m (Wollstoff)*; Waldarbeiter-, Jagd-, Wander-, Campingkleidung, -ausrüstung *f*; ~ **bag** *bes. mil* Kleidersack *m*.

duffer ['dʌfə] Dummkopf *m*.

dug [dʌg] Zitze *f*; Euter *n*.

dugong ['du:gɔŋ, 'dju-] *zoo* Seekuh *f*.

dug-out ['dʌg'aut] Einbaum *(Boot)*; *bes. mil* Unterstand *m*; Erdloch *n*; *sl* reaktivierte(r) Offizier *m*.

duke [dju:k] Herzog *m*; *pl sl* Hände, Fäuste *f pl*; ~**dom** ['-dəm] Herzogtum *n*; Herzogswürde *f*.

dulci|fy ['dʌlsifai] *tr* versüßen; *fig* milde stimmen, besänftigen; ~**mer** ['-simə] *mus* Hackbrett *n*.

dull [dʌl] *a* schwerfällig, dumm; abgestumpft, gefühllos, unempfindlich; geistlos; langweilig, uninteressant, öde, fade; langsam, träge; lustlos; schwer verkäuflich; *(Geschäft)* flau, lustlos; *(Messer)* stumpf; *(Schmerz)* dumpf; *(Farbe)* trüb(e), matt, düster; *mar* windstill; *tr* stumpf, unempfindlich machen; abstumpfen; abschwächen, mildern, lindern; *itr* stumpf, schwächer, unempfindlich werden; *as* ~ *as ditch-water* sterbenslangweilig; ~**ard** ['dʌləd] Dummkopf; Nachtwächter *m fig*; ~**ish** ['dʌliʃ] ziemlich langweilig; ~**ness, dulness** ['dʌlnis] Schwerfälligkeit, Dummheit; Geistlosigkeit *f*, Stumpfsinn *m*; Stumpfheit; Trübe, Trübheit, Düsterkeit; *(Farbe)* Mattheit; Flau(t)e, Flauheit, Lustlosigkeit *f*; ~~ *of hearing* Schwerhörigkeit *f*; ~ **season** *com* tote Jahreszeit *f*.

duly ['dju:li] *adv* gebührend, gehörig, passend, richtig, ordnungsgemäß; genügend; zur gegebenen, zur rechten Zeit, rechtzeitig.

dumb [dʌm] stumm; schweigend, sprachlos (*with* vor); *Am fam* doof, dumm; *to strike* ~ zum Verstummen bringen, die Sprache verschlagen (*s.o.* jdm); *to be struck* ~ sprachlos sein; *deaf and* ~ taubstumm; ~**bell** *sport* Hantel *f*; *sl* Esel *m*, Kamel *n*, Hornochse *m*; ~ **bunny,** ~-**head,** ~**o** *Am sl* Dummkopf *m*; ~**found, dumfound** ['-faund] *tr* die Sprache verschlagen (*s.o.* jdm), verblüffen; ~**founded** *a* völlig sprachlos, wie vom Donner gerührt, wie vom Schlag getroffen; *fam* perplex, platt; ~**ness** ['-nis] Stummheit *f*; ~ **show** Pantomime *f*; ~-**waiter** stumme(r) Diener, Servierwagen, (drehbarer) Serviertisch; *Am* (Speisen-)Aufzug *m*.

dumdum ['dʌmdʌm] *(*~ *bullet)* Dumdumgeschoß *n*.

dummy ['dʌmi] *s fig* Statist; Strohmann *m*, Werkzeug *n*, Puppe; Schneiderpuppe *f*; Schnuller *m*; Attrappe; Nachahmung *f*; *typ* Blindband, Entwurf *m*; *a* nachgeahmt, fingiert, vorgeschoben, blind; ~ **cartridge** Exerzierpatrone *f*; ~ **editor** Sitzredakteur *m*; ~ **pack** Schaupackung *f*; ~ **works** *pl mil* Scheinanlage *f*.

dump [dʌmp] *tr* (mit Gewalt, mit Wucht) (hin)werfen, (hin)schütten, fallen lassen, umkippen, -stürzen; *(in Massen)* ausladen, auskippen; wegwerfen; *(im Freien)* stapeln, lagern; (in Massen u. billig) *(im Ausland)* auf den Markt werfen; den Markt überschwemmen mit; *s* Fall, Sturz, Plumps, (dumpfer) Aufschlag; Müll-, Schutthaufen, -abladeplatz *m*; Lager(platz *m*) *n*, Ablade-, Stapelplatz *m*; *mil* (Nachschub-)Lager, Munitions-, Kleiderdepot; Verpflegungslager *n*; *pl* trübe Stimmung *f*; *Am sl* Dreckloch *n*, Bruchbude; *Am sl* Stelle *f*, Platz *m*; *in the ~s (fam)* in schlechter Laune; **~er** ['-ə] Kipper *m*; **~ing** ['-iŋ] Unterbieten *n* der Preise *(im Ausland)*; Schleuderverkauf *m (im Ausland)*, Dumping *n*; *~(~) cart* Kippkarren *m*; *~~ ground* Schuttabladeplatz *m*; **~-truck** *mot* Kippwagen, Kipper *m*; **~y** ['-i] kurz und dick, gedrungen, plump, stämmig, untersetzt.

dumpling ['dʌmpliŋ] Kloß; *(apple ~)* Apfel im Schlafrock; *fam* Dickerchen *n*, Wonneproppen *m*.

dun [dʌn] **1.** *a* graubraun; *s* graubraune(s) Pferd *n*; **2.** *tr (e-n Schuldner)* mahnen, drängen, treten; *s* drängende(r) Gläubiger *m*; Mahnung, Zahlungsaufforderung *f*; *~ning letter* Mahnbrief *m*.

dunce [dʌns] Dummkopf *m*.

dunderhead ['dʌndəhed] Dummkopf; bornierte(r) Mensch *m*.

dune [dju:n] Düne *f*.

dung [dʌŋ] *s* Mist, Dung, Dünger; *fig* Schmutz *m*, Gemeinheit *f*; *tr itr* düngen; **~-beetle** Mistkäfer *m*; **~-cart** Mistwagen *m*; **~-fork** Mistgabel, Forke *f*; **~hill** Misthaufen *m*.

dungaree [dʌŋgə'ri:] grobe(r) Baumwollstoff *m*; *pl* Arbeitshose *f*.

dungeon ['dʌndʒən] *s* (Burg-)Verlies *n*.

dunk [dʌŋk] *tr* (ein)tunken, stippen.

dunlin ['dʌnlin] *orn* Meerlerche *f*.

dunnage ['dʌnidʒ] *mar* Stauholz *n*, Unterlegebohle *f*; *Am* Gepäck *n*, Sachen *f pl*, Kleider *n pl*.

duo ['dju(:)ou] *pl -os mus* Duo; Duett *n*; **~decimal** [-'desiməl] *a* Duodezimal-; **~decimo** [-'desimou] *typ* Duodezformat *n*, -band *m*; **~denum** [-'di:nəm] Zwölffingerdarm *m*; **~logue** ['djuəlɔg] *bes. theat* Zwiegespräch *n*.

dup|e [dju:p] *s* Gimpel, Dumme(r); Betrogene(r) *m*; *tr* betrügen, anführen.

duplex ['dju:pleks] *a* doppelt, zwei-, zwiefach; Doppel-; *tech tele* Duplex-; *s rail* private(s) Doppelabteil *n*; *(~ apartment)* Wohnung *f* in zwei Stockwerken; *(~ house) Am* Zweifamilien-, Doppelhaus *n*; *tr* duplex schalten.

duplic|able ['dju:plikəbl] zu verdoppeln(d); **~ate** ['-it] *a* doppelt; völlig gleich, genau übereinstimmend, gleichlautend; *s* Duplikat *n*, Zweitschrift, gleichlautende Abschrift; Kopie; doppelte Ausfertigung; *fin* Wechselsekunda; Nachahmung, -bildung *f*; *tr* ['-eit] verdoppeln; abschreiben, kopieren; vervielfältigen; nachahmen, -machen; noch einmal tun; *in ~~* in doppelter Ausfertigung; **~ation** [-'keiʃən] Verdoppelung; Vervielfältigung, Reproduktion, Wiedergabe; Nachbildung; *com* doppelte Buchung *f*; **~ator** ['dju:plikeitə] Vervielfältigungsapparat *m*; **~ity** [dju(:)'plisiti] Falschheit *f*.

dur|ability [djuərə'biliti] Dauerhaftigkeit, Haltbarkeit; Beständigkeit; lange Lebensdauer *f*; **|~able** ['djuərəbl] *a* dauerhaft, haltbar; beständig; *s pl (~~ goods)* Gebrauchsgüter *n pl*; **~ance** ['djuərəns] *(bes.* lange) Haft *f*; **~ation** [djuə'reiʃən] Fortdauer *f*, -bestand *m*; Dauer *f*; *for ~~* für lange Zeit; bis Kriegsende.

duralumin [djuə'ræljumin] Duralumin *n*.

duress(e) [djuə'res, 'dju-] Zwang, Druck *m*, Nötigung *f*, Drohungen *f pl*.

during [djuəriŋ] *prp* während.

dusk [dʌsk] *a poet* dunkel(farben), düster; *s* (Abend-)Dämmerung *f*; *at ~* bei Einbruch der Dunkelheit; **~y** ['-i] schwärzlich; dämmerig, düster *a. fig*.

dust [dʌst] *s* Staub(wolke *f*) *m*; Erde *f*; Blüten-, Goldstaub *m*; *sl* Moos *n*, Moneten *pl*, Geld *n*; Müll *m*, Kehricht *m* od *n*; Plunder *m*, wertlose(s) Zeug *n*; *fig* Asche *f*, sterbliche Überreste *m pl*; *tr* pudern; ausbürsten, abstauben; *aero* abblasen; *itr* staubig werden; *to ~ off (Am sl)* verprügeln; schlagen; *to bite the ~* ins Gras beißen müssen; *to throw ~ in s.o.'s eyes (fig)* jdm Sand in die Augen streuen; *to ~ s.o.'s jacket* jdm das Fell versohlen *od* gerben; *cloud of ~* Staubwolke *f*; **~bin** Mülleimer, -kasten *m*; **~ bowl** Sandsturmgebiet *n (in den US)*; **~-cover, -jacket** *(Buch)* Schutzumschlag *m*; **~er** ['-ə] Staubtuch *n*, -lappen, -wedel *m*; Streudose *f*; *Am* Staubmantel *m*; **~iness** ['-inis] Staubigkeit *f*; **~less** ['-lis] staubfrei; **~man** Müllfuhrmann; Sandmann *m* (der Kinder); **~proof** staubdicht; **~ storm** Sandsturm *m*; **~up** *fam* Aufregung *m*, Durcheinander *n*, Krawall *m*; **~y** ['-i] staubig; verstaubt; grau, fahl; *fig* langweilig, uninteressant; *not so ~~ (sl)* (gar) nicht (so) übel.

Dutch [dʌtʃ] *a* holländisch, niederländisch; *Am sl* deutsch; *s* Holländisch *n*; *the ~* die Holländer, *Am sl* die Deutschen; *in ~ (Am sl)* (dr)unter durch, in Ungnade; in der Patsche, im Druck; *to go ~ (fam)* getrennt bezahlen; *to talk to s.o. like a ~ uncle (fam)* jdn ernstlich ermahnen; *double ~* Kauderwelsch *n*; **~ auction** Auktion *f*, die mit e-m hohen Gebot beginnt u. dann heruntergeht; **~ courage** *fam* angetrunkene(r) Mut *m*; **~ lunch** kalte(s) Büfett *n*; **~man** ['-mən] Holländer *m*; holländische(s) Schiff *n*; *the Flying ~~* der Fliegende Holländer; **~ tile** (Ofen-)Kachel *f*; **~ treat** *Am fam* Beisammensein *n* bei getrennter Kasse; **~woman** ['-wumən] Holländerin *f*.

duteous ['dju:tjəs] = *dutiful*.

dutiable ['dju:tjəbl] abgaben-, zoll-, steuerpflichtig.

dutiful ['dju:tiful] pflichtgetreu, -bewußt, -schuldig, -gemäß; gehorsam; respektvoll; ehrerbietig.

duty ['dju:ti] Pflicht, Verpflichtung (*to* gegenüber); Schuldigkeit; Aufgabe, Obliegenheit *f*, Dienst *m*; Gebühr, Abgabe, Steuer *f*, Zoll *m*; *tech* Arbeits-, Nutzleistung, Betriebsart *f (e-r Maschine)*; *as in ~ bound* pflichtgemäß; *free from ~* gebühren-, zoll-, abgabenfrei; *off ~* außer Dienst; dienstfrei; *on ~* im Dienst; *to do ~* Dienst tun *od* haben; *for s.o.* jdn vertreten, ersetzen; *sense of ~* Pflichtbewußtsein *n*; *~ of maintenance* Unterhaltspflicht *f*; **~ call** Pflichtbesuch *m*; **~ car** Dienstwagen *m*; **~ copy** Pflichtexemplar *n*; **~-free** abgaben-, steuer-, zollfrei; **~ officer** Offizier *m* vom Dienst; **~-paid** *a* verzollt; **~ roster** Dienstplan *m*.

dwarf [dwɔ:f] *s* Zwerg *m a. allg*; *a* zwergenhaft, winzig, klein; Zwerg-; *tr* verkümmern lassen; verkleinern, herabdrücken, herabsetzen; **~ish** ['-iʃ] zwergenhaft, winzig.

dwell [dwel] *itr irr dwelt, dwelt* wohnen; *to ~ (up)on (in Gedanken)* bleiben bei, sich aufhalten, sich abgeben mit; verweilen bei; beharren, bestehen auf; **~er** ['-ə] Be-, Einwohner *m*; **~ing** ['-iŋ] *s* Wohnung *f*; *(~~ place)* Wohnort, -sitz, Aufenthalt(sort) *m*, Bleibe *f*.

dwindl|e ['dwindl] *itr* abnehmen; *(to ~~ down)* (zs.)schrumpfen (*to* zu); *(Preis)* fallen, sinken; *to ~~ away* dahinschwinden; **~ing** ['-iŋ] *s* Abnahme *f*; *(Preis)* Fallen *n*; *a*: *~~ production* Produktionsabnahme *f*.

*

dye [dai] *s* Farbe; Färbung *f*; Farbstoff *m*; *tr* färben; e-e Färbung, Farbe geben (*s.th.* e-r S); *itr* sich färben (lassen); *to ~ in the grain, in the wool* in der Wolle färben; **~d-in-the-wool** *a* in der Wolle gefärbt; *fig* (wasch-) echt; **~ing** ['-iŋ] *s* Färben; Färbereigewerbe *n*; **~r** ['-ə] Färber *m*; **~-stuff** Farbstoff *m*, Farbe *f*; **~weed** *bot* (Färber-)Wau *m*.

dying ['daiiŋ] *a* sterbend; (dahin-) schwindend; Sterbe-; schmachtend; *s* Sterben *n*; **~ bed** Sterbebett *n*; **~ day** Sterbetag *m*.

dynam|ic(al) [dai'næmik, di'n-] dynamisch *a. fig*; *fig* energisch, kraftvoll; **~ics** [-ks] *pl mit sing* Dynamik *a. fig*; *fig* Bewegkraft *f*; **~ite** ['dainəmait] *s* Dynamit *n*; *tr* (mit D.) sprengen; **~o** ['dainəmou] *pl -os* Dynamo(maschine *f*) *m*.

dynast ['dinəst] Herrscher, Monarch *m*; **~ic(al)** [di'næstik(əl), dai'n-] dynastisch; **~y** ['dinəsti] Dynastie *f*

dyne [dain] *phys* Dyn *n*.

dysenter|ic [disn'terik] *a* Ruhr-; **~y** ['disntri] *med* Ruhr *f*.

dyspep|sia [dis'pepsiə] Verdauungsstörung *f*; **~tic** [-tik] *a* magenkrank; *fig* mißgestimmt; *s* Magenkranke(r) *m*.

E

E, e [i:] *pl* **~'s** [i:z] E, e; *mus* E *n*; *Am (Schule)* mangelhaft; **~ flat** Es *n*; **~ minor** e-moll *n*; **~ sharp** Eis *n*.

each [i:tʃ] *a prn* jede(r, s) (einzelne); *adv* je; *~ and every one* jede(r, s) einzelne; **~ other** einander, sich (gegenseitig); *with ~~* miteinander.

eager ['i:gə] eifrig, besorgt, ungeduldig; Feuer und Flamme; begierig (*about, after, for* auf, nach); versessen, erpicht (*about, after, for* auf); *to be ~* begierig sein; darauf brennen (*to do* zu tun); **~ beaver** *Am sl* Streber *m*; **~ness** ['-nis] Eifer *m*; Ungeduld; Begierde *f*, heftige(s) Verlangen *n*.

eagle ['i:gl] Adler *m*; *hist* (goldenes) Zehndollarstück *(der US)*; **~-eyed** *a* scharfsichtig; **~-owl** Uhu *m*; **~t** ['-it] junge(r) Adler *m*.

eagre ['eigə, 'i:gə] Sprungwelle *f*.

*

ear [iə] **1.** Ohr; Gehör; *fig* feine(s) Gehör *n* (*for* für); Schlaufe *f*, Öhr *n*; Henkel *m*; *in (at) one ~ and out (at) the other* zu einem Ohr hinein und zum andern hinaus; *over head and ~s, up to o.'s ~s (fig)* bis über die Ohren (*in debt* in Schulden); *to be all ~s* ganz Ohr sein; *to fall on deaf ~s* tauben Ohren predigen; *to give, to lend ~ to* hören, achten auf; *to give o.'s ~s* sein Letztes (her)geben, kein Opfer scheuen; *to have, to win s.o.'s ~* bei jdm Gehör finden; *to have, to keep an ~ to the ground* Augen u. Ohren offenhalten; *to pin back s.o.'s ~s (Am sl)* jdn in die Pfanne hauen; *to play by ~ (mus)* nach Gehör, ohne Noten spielen; *to set s.o. by the ~s* zwischen jdm Streit säen; jdn aufhetzen; *to turn a deaf ~ to s.th.* etw in den Wind schlagen; *I would give my ~s* koste es, was es wolle! *I pricked up my ~s* ich spitzte die Ohren; *I'm all ~s* ich bin ganz Ohr; *middle ~* Mittelohr *n*; *musical ~, ~ for music* musikalische(s) Gehör *n*; *quick ~* scharfe(s) Gehör *n*; **~-ache** ['-reik] Ohrenschmerzen *m pl*; **~-deafening** ohrenbetäubend; **~-drop** Ohrgehänge *n pl*; *pharm* Ohrentropfen *m pl*; **~-drum** Mittelohr; Trommelfell *n*; **~-duster** *Am sl* Schwätzer *m*; intime(s) Gerede *n*; **~-flap** Ohrenklappe *f (e-r Mütze)*; **~ful**: *an ~~ (fam)* die Ohren voll (*of* von); Tadel *m*, Abreibung *f*; *to hear an ~~* mehr als genug hören; **~-lap, ~lobe** Ohrläppchen *n*; **~mark** *s* Eigentumszeichen am Ohr *(e-s Haustieres)*; *fig* Kennzeichen, Charakteristikum *n*; *tr (Vieh am Ohr)* (kenn)zeichnen; *allg* kennzeichnen; identifizieren; vormerken, -sehen, reservieren, zurücklegen, bereitstellen, zweckbestimmen (*for* für); *(Scheck)* sperren; **~-minded** *a* auditiv; **~-muffs** *pl Am* Ohrenschützer *m pl*; **~-phones** *pl tele radio* Kopfhörer *m pl*; **~piece** *tele* Hörer *m*, Hörmuschel *f*; **~-piercing** schrill; **~-plug** Ohropax *n (Schutzmarke)*; **-shot**: *within, out of ~~* in, außer Hörweite; **~-ring** Ohrring *m*; **~-splitting** ohrenbetäubend; **~-trumpet** Hörrohr *n*; **~-wax** Ohrenschmalz *n*; **~-wig** *zoo* Ohrwurm *m*; **~witness** Ohrenzeuge *m*; **2.** Ähre *f*; *~ of corn* Kornähre *f*, *Am* Maiskolben *m*.

earl [ə:l] (englischer) Graf *m*; **~dom** ['-dəm] Grafenwürde *f* **E~ Marshal** Hofmarschall, Oberzeremonienmeister *m*.

earl|iness ['ə:linis] Frühzeitigkeit, Frühe *f*; **~y** ['-i] *a adv* früh(zeitig); (vor)zeitig; Früh-, Anfangs-; *a* baldig; *adv* bald; *as ~~ as* schon; *at an ~~ date* zu e-m früheren Zeitpunkt; *at your earliest convenience (com)* umgehend; bei erster Gelegenheit; *in ~~ summer* zu Beginn des Sommers; *~~ in life* in jungen Jahren; *~~ bird, riser* Frühaufsteher *m*; *it's the ~~ bird that catches the worm* Morgenstund' hat Gold im Mund'; *~~ closing day* frühzeitige(r) Arbeits-, Ladenschluß *m*; *~~ vegetables (pl)* Frühgemüse *n*; *~~ warning* Vorwarnung *f*.

earn [ə:n] *tr itr* (sich) verdienen, (sich) erwerben *a. fig*; eintragen, einbringen, verschaffen, abwerfen; *(Zinsen)* bringen; **~ed** [-d] *a* verdient; angefallen; Arbeits-, Betriebs-; *~~ income* Arbeits-, Lohneinkommen *n*; **~er** ['-ə] Verdiener *m*; *salary, wage ~~* Gehalts-, Lohnempfänger *m*; **~ing** ['-iŋ]: *~~ capacity* od *power* Erwerbs-, Ertragsfähigkeit *f*; **~ings** ['-iŋz] *pl* Verdienst *m*, Einkommen *n*; Lohn *m*, Gehalt *n*; Einkünfte *pl*, Einnahme(n *pl*) *f*, Ertrag, Gewinn *m*.

earnest ['ə:nist] **1.** *a* ernst(haft); aufrichtig, ehrlich; gewissenhaft; eifrig; ernst gemeint; dringend; *s* Ernst *m*; *in ~* im Ernst; *in dead ~* in vollem Ernst; *are you in ~* ist das Ihr Ernst? **~ly** ['-li] *adv* ernstlich, -haft; inständig; **~ness** ['-nis] Ernsthaftigkeit *f*; **2.** *(~-money)* An-, Handgeld *n*, Anzahlung *f* (*of* auf); (Unter-)Pfand *n*, Beweis *m*, Zeichen *n*; *fig* Hinweis *m* (*of* auf), Andeutung *f*, Vorgeschmack *m* (*of* von).

earth [ə:θ] *s* Erde *f*; Erdreich *n*, Welt *f*; Irdische(s), Diesseits; (festes) Land *n*; (Erd-)Boden *m*, Erde *f*; (Fuchs-, Dachs-)Bau *m*; *chem* Erde; *el radio* Erde, Erdung *f*, Erdschluß *m*, Masse *f*; *tr el radio* erden; *(to ~ up)* mit Erde bedecken; *(Kartoffeln)* häufeln; *(Fuchs)* in den Bau treiben; *itr* sich (im Bau) verkriechen; sich einscharren; *on ~* auf der Erde; auf Erden; auf der Welt; *(in Fragen)* auch immer, denn nur; *to (the) ~* auf die Erde, zu Boden; *to be down to ~* mit beiden Beinen in der Welt stehen; *to come back, to come down to ~* auf den Boden der Wirklichkeit zurückkehren; *to move heaven and ~* Himmel u. Hölle, alle Hebel in Bewegung setzen; *to run to ~ (tr) (Jagd u. fig)* aufstöbern; *to run, to go to ~ (itr) (Fuchs)* sich im Bau verkriechen; *down to ~* praktisch, einfach, mit beiden Füßen auf der Erde stehend; **~-born** *a* irdisch; menschlich, sterblich; **~-bound** *a* erdgebunden; **~-connection** Erdleitung *f*; **~en** ['-ən] irden; **~enware** ['-ənwεə] *s* irdene(s) Geschirr; Steingut *n*; Ton *m*; *a* irden; **~ing** ['-iŋ] *el radio* Erdung *f*, Erdschluß *m*; *~~ lead (mot el)* Massekabel *n*; **~liness** ['-linis] irdische(s) Wesen, Weltlichkeit, Diesseitigkeit *f*; **~ly** ['-li] irdisch, weltlich, auf Erden, diesseitig; *fam* vernünftig, denkbar; *not an ~~ … (fam)* nicht den, die, das geringste(n), kleinste(n) …; *no ~~ use* völlig unnütz; **~moving** Erdbewegung *f*; **~nut** Erdnuß *f*; **~quake** ['-kweik] Erdbeben *n*; **~ward** ['-wəd] *a* irdisch; **~ward(s)** *adv* erdwärts; **~work** Erdarbeit; Aufschüttung *f*; Damm-, Deichbau *m*; **~worm** ['-wə:m] Regenwurm; *fig* Kriecher *m*; **~y** ['ə:θi] erdig; irdisch, diesseitig, weltlich; grob(sinnlich).

ease [i:z] *s* Wohlbefinden, -gefühl *n*; Behaglichkeit, Bequemlichkeit; Ruhe, Muße, Entspannung *f*, Behagen *n*; Zwanglosigkeit, Leichtigkeit, Mühelosigkeit, Gewandtheit; Weite *f*, Spielraum *m*; *(~ of money)* (Geld-)Flüssigkeit *f*; *tr* entlasten, befreien (*of* von); beruhigen; *(Schmerz)* lindern, mildern; erleichtern; ermäßigen, herabsetzen; *(to ~ down)* verlangsamen; vorsichtig, behutsam bewegen *od* befördern; lavieren; *(Saum)* auslassen; *to ~ away, down, off, up (tr)* entspannen, lockern, leichter machen; *(Fahrt)* vermindern; *mar (Tau)* abfieren; *(itr)* nachlassen; leichter werden; *(Preise)* fallen, sinken; *itr* nachgeben, nachlassen, geringer werden; *(Lage)* sich entspannen; *at ~* frei, ungezwungen; behaglich; *with ~* mit Leichtigkeit, ohne Mühe, mühelos; *to be (ill) at ~* sich (nicht) wohlfühlen, (nicht) in s-m Element sein; *to live at ~* in angenehmen Verhältnissen leben; *to take o.'s ~* es sich bequem machen; *to ~ off the throttle (aero)* Gas wegnehmen; *(stand) at ~! (mil)* rührt euch! *at ~, march!* ohne Tritt, marsch! **~ment** ['-mənt] *jur* Grunddienstbarkeit *f*.

easel ['i:zl] Staffelei *f*; Gestell *n*.

easi|ly ['i:zili] *adv* leicht, mühelos; fraglos, ohne Frage; zweifellos; bestimmt, bei weitem; wahrscheinlich; **~ness** ['i:zinis] Leichtigkeit; Unbeschwertheit, Unbekümmertheit; Ungezwungenheit; Umgänglichkeit *f*.

east [i:st] *s* Ost(en); *(~ wind)* Ostwind *m*; *the E~* der Osten, der Orient; *Am* der Osten *(der US)*; *a* östlich; Ost-; *adv* ostwärts, in östlicher Richtung; nach Osten; *to the ~* im Osten, östlich (*of* von); *the Far E~* der Ferne Osten, Ostasien *n (China, Japan)*; *the Middle E~ (Br)* der Vordere Orient, der Nahe Osten; *Am* Vorder- (Süd- u. Mittel-) Asien *n*; **~-bound** *a* nach Osten verlaufend *od* gehend, fahrend; **~erly** ['-əli] *a* östlich; Ost-; *adv* nach, von Osten; **~ern** ['-ən] *a* östlich; Ost-; *(E~~)* orientalisch; *s* Orientale *m*, Orientalin *f*; **~erner** ['-ənə] Orientale *m*, Orientalin *f*; *(E~~) (Am)* Bewohner (-in *f*) *m* der Oststaaten *(der US)*; **~ernmost** ['-nmoust] östlichst; **E~ India, the E~ Indies** *pl* (Ost-)Indien *n*; **~ing** ['-iŋ] *mar* zurückgelegte(r) östliche(r) Kurs *m*; X-Koordinate *f*; **~ward** ['-wəd] *a* östlich; **~ward(s)** *adv* ostwärts, in östlicher Richtung.

Easter ['i:stə] Ostern *n od f pl*; *at ~* an, zu Ostern; **~ Day, Sunday** Ostersonntag *m*; **~ egg** Osterei *n*; **~ holidays** *pl* Osterferien *pl*; **~tide** Osterzeit *f*; **~-week** Osterwoche *f*.

easy ['i:zi] *a* leicht *(zu tun)*, nicht schwer, nicht schwierig; frei von Schmerzen; sorgenfrei, sorglos, unbekümmert, unbeschwert; bequem, angenehm, behaglich; *(Kleidung)* lose, locker, bequem; zwanglos, ungezwungen, lässig; nachgiebig, -sichtig, großzügig, tolerant; umgänglich, gefällig; ruhig, bescheiden, mäßig; *(Ware)* wenig gefragt; *(Geschäft)* lustlos, flau; *(Geld)* flüssig, billig; *(Börse)* freundlich; *adv fam = easily*; *s mil* Zigarettenpause *f*; *in ~ circumstances, (Am) on ~ street* in angenehmen Verhältnissen; *on ~ terms (com)* zu günstigen Bedingungen; auf Ab-, Teilzahlung; *~ on the eye (sl)* hübsch, knusperig; *to go, to take it ~* sich kein Bein ausreißen, *sl* e-e ruhige Kugel schieben; *it's ~ for you to talk* Sie haben gut reden! *stand ~! (mil)* rührt euch! *take it ~!* ruhig Blut! nur (immer) mit der Ruhe! *~ all!* (an-)halt(en)! *as ~ as falling, rolling off a log (Am)* kinderleicht, ein Kinderspiel; *~ does it!* nimm dir Zeit! **~-chair** Lehnstuhl, (Lehn-)Sessel *m*; **~-going** *fig* leichtlebig; bequem, lässig; großzügig.

eat [i:t] *irr ate* [et, eit] od *eat* [et], *eaten* ['i:tn] *tr* essen; *(to ~ up)* aufessen, verzehren; (auf)fressen; *(to ~ into)* zerfressen, zersetzen, ätzen; sich hineinfressen in; *(to ~ away, to ~ up)* aufessen; verbrauchen; zerstören, vernichten; vertun; *(Feuer)* verzehren; *(Wasser)* wegreißen, fortspülen; *(Kilometer)* verschlingen, fressen; *itr* essen; speisen; *s pl fam* Essen, Futter *n*; Eßwaren *f pl*; *to ~ out* auswärts, außer Haus essen; zum Essen ausgehen; *s.o. (Am sl)* jdn heruntermachen; *to ~ dirt (fam)* e-e Beleidigung, Ärger hinunterschlucken; *to ~ humble pie, (Am) crow* klein beigeben müssen; *to ~ o.'s heart out* sich in Kummer verzehren; *to ~ o.'s words* das Gesagte, s-e Aussage zurücknehmen, widerrufen; *what's ~ing you? (fam)* was kommt dich an? **~able** ['-əbl] *a* eß-, genießbar; *s meist pl* Essen *n*, Speise, Nahrung(smittel *n*) *f*; **~er** ['-ə] Esser *m*; Tafelobst *n*; *a big* od *good, a poor ~~* ein starker *od* guter, ein schwacher Esser *m*; **~ery** ['-əri] *Am hum* Freßlokal *n*; **~ing** ['-iŋ] Essen *n*; Speise *f*; *~~ apron (Am)* Lätzchen *n*; *~~ hall (Am)* Eßraum *m*; *~~-house* Speisehaus, Restaurant *n*.

eaves [i:vz] *pl* (überstehender) Dachrand *m*, Dachrinne, Traufe *f*; **~drop** *itr* horchen, lauschen; **~dropper** Horcher(in *f*), Lauscher(in *f*) *m*.

*

ebb [eb] *s (~-tide)* Ebbe *f*; *fig* Tiefstand *m*; Abnahme *f*, Nachlassen *n*, Verfall *m*; *itr* zurückfluten *(from* von); verebben *a. fig*; *fig (to ~ away)* nachlassen, abnehmen, zurückgehen; *at a low ~* (sehr) heruntergekommen; *(Preis)* gedrückt; auf e-m Tiefstand.

ebon ['ebən] *a* aus Ebenholz; tief-, pechschwarz; **~ite** ['-ait] Hartgummi *m* od *n*, Ebonit *n*; **~ize** ['-aiz] *tr* schwärzen, schwarz beizen; **~y** ['-i] *s* Ebenholz *n*; *a s. ebon.*

ebulli|ence, -cy [i(:)'bʌljəns(i)] Enthusiasmus *m*, Überschwenglichkeit *f*; **~ent** [-ənt] *fig* übersprudelnd *(with* von); (hoch)begeistert, enthusiastisch, überschwenglich; **~tion** [ebə'liʃən, -bu'l-] Sprudeln, Wallen *n*; *fig* Aufwallung *f*, (Gefühls-)Ausbruch *m*.

eccentric [ik'sentrik] *a math* exzentrisch *a. fig*; *fig* ungewöhnlich, ausgefallen, unkonventionell, aus dem Rahmen fallend, absonderlich, eigenartig; überspannt, verstiegen; *s* Sonderling; *tech* Exzenter *m*; **~ity** [eksen'trisiti] *math tech* Exzentrizität; *fig* Überspanntheit, Verstiegenheit *f*.

Ecclesiast|es [ikli:zi'æsti:z] Prediger *m* Salomo *(Buch des Alten Testamentes)*; **e~ic** [-ik] *s* Geistliche(r) *m*; **e~ical** [-ikəl] kirchlich; geistlich; *~~ law* Kirchenrecht *n*; *~~ year* Kirchenjahr *n*; **~icus** [-ikəs] *(Bibel)* Ekklesiastikus *m*.

echelon ['eʃələn] *s mil* Gliederung, *mil aero* Staffelung; *aero* Staffel *f (Formation)*; *mil* (Befehls-)Bereich *m*, Stufe, Ebene; (Angriffs-)Welle *f*; *tr* staffeln, gliedern.

echin|ite ['ekinait] versteinerte(r) Seeigel *m*; **~oderm** [i'kainədə:m] *zoo* Stachelhäuter *m*; **~us** [e'kainəs] *pl* *-ni* [-nai] *zoo* Seeigel; *arch* (Säulen-)Wulst *m*.

echo ['ekou] *pl -oes* Echo *n a. fig*; *fig* Wiederholung, Nachahmung *f*; Nachsprecher, -ahmer *m*; *itr* echoen, widerhallen *(with* von); *tr (Schall)* zurückwerfen; *fig* nachsprechen, wiederholen; *pej* nachbeten; **~-sounder** *mar* Echolot *n*; **~-sounding** Echolotung *f*.

éclat ['eikla:, ekla] glänzende(r) Erfolg, große(r) Beifall *m*, Aufsehen *n*; Berühmtheit *f*, Ruhm; Glanz *m*.

eclectic [ek'lektik] *a* auswählend; eklektisch; zs.getragen, zs.gesetzt; *s* Eklektiker *m*; **~ism** [-tisizm] Eklektizismus *m*.

eclip|se [i'klips] *s bes. astr* Finsternis, Verfinsterung; *fig* Verdunkelung, Verringerung, Abnahme *f*, Nachlassen, (Ver-)Schwinden *n*; Schatten *m (of* auf); *tr* verfinstern; *fig* e-n Schatten werfen auf; in den Schatten stellen, überstrahlen; **~tic** [i'kliptik] (scheinbare) Sonnenbahn *f*.

eclogue ['eklɔg] Hirtenlied *n*.

ecolog|ic(al) [ikə'lɔdʒik(əl)] ökologisch; **~y** [i'kɔlədʒi] Ökologie *f*.

economic [i:kə'nɔmik, e-] ökonomisch, (volks)wirtschaftlich; Wirtschafts-; *~~ agreement* Handels-, Wirtschaftsabkommen *n*; *~~ boom* Konjunkturaufschwung *m*; *~~ commission* Wirtschaftskommission *f*; *~~ conditions (pl), situation* Wirtschaftslage *f*; *~~ conference* Wirtschaftskonferenz *f*; *~~ council* Wirtschaftsrat *m*; *(world) ~~ crisis* (Welt-)Wirtschaftskrise *f*; *~~ cycle* Konjunkturzyklus *m*; *~~ development* wirtschaftliche Entwicklung *f*; *~~ geography* Wirtschaftsgeographie *f*; *~~ goods (pl)* Wirtschaftsgüter *n pl*; *~~ plan* Wirtschaftsplan *m*; *~~ planning* gesamtwirtschaftliche Planung *f*; *~~ policy* Wirtschaftspolitik *f*; *~~ profit* Grenzkostenergebnis *n*; *~~ recovery* Wirtschaftsbelebung *f*; *~~ structure* Wirtschaftsstruktur *f*; *~~ union* Wirtschaftsunion *f*; **~ical** [-əl] haushälterisch, wirtschaftlich, sparsam *(of* mit); **~ics** [-iks] *pl mit sing* Wirtschaftswissenschaften *f pl*, Volkswirtschaft(slehre), Nationalökonomie *f*; **~ist** [i(:)'kɔnəmist] gute(r) Haushälter, sparsame(r) Mensch; Volkswirt(schaftler) *m*; **~ize** [i(:)'kɔnəmaiz] *itr* sparsam sein, sparen, gut wirtschaften *(in, on* mit); *tr* sparsam umgehen mit, haushalten *(s.th.* mit etw); **~izer** [-'kɔnəmaizə] *tech* Vorwärmer *m*; **~y** [i(:)'kɔnəmi] Wirtschaft *f*, Haushalt *m*; Wirtschaftssystem *n*; Wirtschaftlichkeit, Sparsamkeit; Sparmaßnahme, Einsparung, Ersparnis; Einrichtung, Organisation, (An-)Ordnung *f*, Bau *m*; *competitive ~~* Wettbewerbswirtschaft *f*; *controlled, planned ~~* Planwirtschaft *f*; *home, internal ~~* Binnenwirtschaft *f*; *political ~~ s. ~ics*; *private ~~* Privatwirtschaft *f*; *uncontrolled ~~* freie Wirtschaft *f*; *world ~~* Weltwirtschaft *f*; *~~ drive* Sparaktion *f*.

ecsta|sy ['ekstəsi] Verzückung, Ekstase *a. rel*; Hingerissenheit *f*, -sein *n*, Begeisterung(staumel *m*) *f*, Enthusiasmus *m*; *to be thrown, to go into ~sies* in Verzückung geraten *(over* wegen), hingerissen werden *(over* von); **~tic** [ek'stætik] *a* ekstatisch; begeistert, verzückt, hingerissen.

ecumenic(al) *s. oecumenic(al).*

eczema ['eksimə] *med* Ausschlag *m*, Flechte *f*, Ekzem *n*.

*

edacious [i'deiʃəs] gefräßig, gierig.

eddy ['edi] *s* Wirbel, Strudel *m*; *itr* wirbeln, strudeln; *~~ of dust* Staubwirbel *m*; *~* **current** Wirbelstrom *m*.

edelweiss ['eidlvais] *bot* Edelweiß *n*.

Eden ['i:dn] *rel* das Paradies *a. fig*.

edentate [i(:)'denteit] *a* zahnlos; *s pl* Zahnarme *m pl (Säugetierordnung)*.

edge [edʒ] *s (Klinge)* Schneide; Schärfe *(e-r Schneide, a. fig)*; *fig* Stärke, Kraft, Heftigkeit *(e-s Gefühls)*; (scharfe) Kante *f*; Rand, Saum *m*; Ufer *n*; (Berg-)Kamm, Grat; *(Buch)* Schnitt; *fam* Vorteil *m (on* vor); *tr* (um)säumen, einfassen, bördeln; *(to put an ~ on)* mit e-r Schneide versehen, schärfen; schieben, rücken; *itr* sich e-n Weg bahnen; vorsichtig gehen, schleichen; sich schieben, vorrücken; *at the ~ of* am Rande *gen*; *on ~* hochkant; *fig* nervös, reizbar; ungeduldig, begierig; *on the very ~ of doing* gerade im Begriff zu tun; *to give s.o. the ~ of o.'s tongue* jdn herunterputzen, ausschimpfen; *to have the ~ on s.o. (Am fam)* jdm gegenüber ein Plus haben, im Vorteil sein; *to have an ~ on (Am fam)* angetrunken sein, einen sitzen haben; *to set s.o.'s teeth on ~* jdn nervös machen, reizen, aufbringen; *to take the ~ off* abschwächen; die Schärfe nehmen; *to ~ o.'s way through* sich schlagen, zwängen durch; *to ~* **away** sich davonmachen, sich wegschleichen; *to ~* **forward** sich vorschieben, vorrücken; *to ~* **in(to)** hineinschieben, -schmuggeln; *(Wort)* einwerfen; *to ~ o.s. into a conversation* sich in ein Gespräch einmischen; *to ~* **off** ab-, wegrücken; *to ~* **out** *tr itr* (sich) hinausschieben, -drängen; *s.o.* jdn mit geringem Vorsprung besiegen; **~-tool** Schneidwerkzeug *n*; **~ways, ~wise** seitwärts, von der Seite; hochkant; *to get a word in ~ways* zu Worte kommen.

edg|ed [edʒd] *a* mit e-r Schneide, e-m Rand versehen; scharf; gesäumt; **~ing** ['-iŋ] Vorstoß, Rand, Saum *m*, Einfassung; Borte *f*, Besatz *m*, Litze, Paspel *f*; **~y** ['-i] gesäumt; scharf; *fig* nervös, gereizt, kratzbürstig; *(Kunst)* mit zu scharfen Konturen.

edib|ility [edi'biliti] Eß-, Genießbarkeit *f*; **~le** ['edibl] *a* eß-, genießbar; Nahrungs-; *s pl* Lebensmittel *n pl*; *~~ fat, oil* Speisefett, -öl *n*.

edict ['i:dikt] Erlaß *m*, Edikt *n*.

edif|ication [edifi'keiʃən] *fig* Erbauung *f*; **~ice** ['edifis] Bauwerk, Gebäude *n a. fig*; **~y** ['edifai] *tr* (geistig) erbauen, stärken; *~~ing* erbaulich.

edit ['edit] *tr (Buch)* herausgeben; *(Zeitung)* redigieren; *film* zs.stellen; **~ion** [i'diʃən] *(Buch)* Ausgabe; Auflage *f*; *cheap, popular ~~* Volksausgabe *f*; *first ~~* Erstausgabe *f*; *morning, evening ~~* Morgen-, Abendausgabe *f*; *pocket ~~* Taschenausgabe *f*; **~or** ['-ə] Herausgeber; Redakteur, Schriftleiter *m*; *chief ~~, ~~ in chief* Hauptschriftleiter *m*; *letter to the ~~* Leserbrief *m*, Eingesandt *n*; **~orial** [edi'tɔ:riəl] *a* redaktionell; Redaktions-; *s (Zeitung)* Leitartikel *m*; *~~ department* Redaktion, Schriftleitung *f*; *~~ office* Redaktion *f (Raum)*; *~~ staff* Redaktionsstab, Mitarbeiterstab *m (e-r Zeitung)*; *~~ writer* Leitartikler *m*; **~orialize** [edi'tɔ:riəlaiz] *Am itr* e-n Leitartikel schreiben *(on* über); **~orship** ['-əʃip]

Amt *n*, Tätigkeit, Eigenschaft *f* als Schriftleiter; Schriftleitung *f*.

educat|e ['edju(:)keit] *tr* auf-, erziehen, (aus-, heran)bilden, unterrichten, lehren; **~ion** [edju(:)'keiʃən] Erziehung, (Aus-, Heran-)Bildung *f*; Unterricht(ssystem *n*) *m*, Schulwesen *n*; Pädagogik *f*; *adult ~~* Erwachsenenbildung *f*; *Board of E~~, E~~ Department* Erziehungs-, Unterrichtsministerium *n*; *compulsory ~~* Schulzwang *m*, -pflicht *f*; *general ~~* Allgemeinbildung *f*; **~ional** [-'keiʃənl] erzieherisch; Erziehungs-, Bildungs-, Unterrichts-; *~~ background* Vorbildung *f*; *~~ establishment, institute, institution* Bildungsanstalt *f*; *~~ film* Lehrfilm *m*; **~ion(al)ist** [edju(:)'keiʃn(əl)ist] Schulmann, Pädagoge *m*; **~ive** ['edju(:)kətiv, -dʒu(:)-, -keit-] erzieherisch, bildend; **~or** ['edju(:)keitə] Erzieher *m*.

educ|e [i(:)'dju:s] *tr* herausziehen, hervorholen, -locken; entwickeln, -falten; darstellen; ableiten (*from* von); *chem* frei machen; **~tion** [i(:)'dʌkʃən] Entwick(e)lung, -faltung; Darstellung; Ableitung *f*.

eel [i:l] Aal *m*; *as slippery as an ~* aalglatt; **~-buck, -pot** Aalreuse *f*; **-pout** Aalraute, (Aal-)Quappe *f*.

e'en [i:n] **1.** *adv poet = even*; **2.** *s poet = even(ing)*.

e'er [ɛə] *poet = ever*.

eer|ie, ~y ['iəri] schaurig, gespenstisch.

efface [i'feis] *tr* ausradieren, auslöschen, streichen, tilgen *a. fig*; *fig* in den Schatten stellen; *to ~ o.s.* sich zurück-, sich im Hintergrund halten, im H. bleiben *fig*; **~able** [-əbl] tilgbar; **~ment** [-mənt] Löschung, Tilgung *f*.

effect [i'fekt] *s* Wirkung (*on* auf), Folge *f*, Ergebnis, Resultat *n*, Konsequenz (*of* gen); Aus-, Nachwirkung *f*; Eindruck, Effekt *m*; Wirksamkeit; *jur* Gültigkeit *f*; *tech* (Nutz-)Effekt *m*, Leistung *f*; *pl* Gegenstände *n pl*, Sachen *f pl*; Besitz *m*, (bewegliches) Eigentum *n*, Habe *f*, Vermögen; Guthaben *n*; Effekten *pl*, Wertpapiere *n pl*; *tr* bewirken, zur Folge haben; zustande bringen; aus-, durchführen, erstellen; *(Zweck)* erfüllen; *(Buchung, Verhaftung)* vornehmen; *(Zahlung)* leisten; *(Vertrag, Versicherung)* abschließen; *for ~* der Wirkung halber, wegen; *in ~* in der Tat, wirklich, in Wirklichkeit; im wesentlichen; *(Gesetz, Bestimmung)* gültig, in Kraft; *of no ~* wirkungslos; vergeblich; *to the ~* des Inhalts; *to this ~* zu dem Zweck; *to bring to, to carry into ~* wirksam werden lassen; bewerkstelligen, *fam* zuwege bringen; *to come, to go into ~* in Kraft treten; *to give ~ to* in die Praxis umsetzen, Wirklichkeit werden lassen; wirksam machen, Nachdruck verleihen (*s.th.* e-r S); *to have an ~* wirken (*on* auf); *to put into ~* in Kraft setzen; *to take ~* wirksam werden, die gewünschte Wirkung, den gewünschten Erfolg haben; in Kraft treten; *to ~ a settlement* zu e-r Einigung kommen; *coming into ~* Inkrafttreten *n*; *final ~* Endergebnis *n*; *legal ~* Rechtskraft *f*; *sound ~s (film pl)* Geräuschkulisse *f*; **~ive** [-iv] *a* wirksam; wirkungs-, eindrucksvoll; tatsächlich, wirklich, effektiv; *tech* nutzbar; *mil* einsatzbereit; dienst-, kampffähig; *s pl mil* Ist-Stärke *f*, Effektivbestand *m*; *~~ immediately* mit sofortiger Wirkung; *to be ~~* gelten; *to become ~~* Gültigkeit erlangen; *~~ area* Nutzfläche *f*; *~~ capital* Betriebskapital *n*; *~~ date* Zeitpunkt *m* des Inkrafttretens; *~~ power* Effektivleistung *f*; *~~ pressure* Arbeitsdruck *m*; *~~ range* Wirkungsbereich; *el* Nutzmeßbereich *m*; *mil* Schußfeld *n*; *~~ strength (mil)* Iststärke *f*; **~iveness** [-ivnis] Wirksamkeit *f*; **~ual** [i'fektjuəl] wirksam; gültig, in Kraft; *to be ~~* die gewünschte Wirkung haben; **~uate** [-jueit] *tr* bewirken, bewerkstelligen, zustande bringen; aus-, durchführen.

effemina|cy [i'feminəsi] Verweichlichung *f*; **~te** [-it] verweichlicht.

effervesc|e [efə'ves] *itr* perlen, sprudeln, moussieren; aufbrausen, -wallen; *fig* überschäumen; **~ence** [-əns] Sprudeln, Aufwallen *n*; *fig* Munterkeit, Lebhaftigkeit *f*; **~ent** [-ənt] sprudelnd, aufbrausend; *fig* überschäumend; *~~ powder* Brausepulver *n*.

effete [e'fi:t] abgenutzt, erschöpft, verbraucht, unproduktiv, steril.

efficac|ious [efi'keiʃəs] wirksam; **~y** ['efikəsi] Wirksamkeit, Wirkungskraft *f*.

efficien|cy [i'fiʃəns(i)] Leistungsfähigkeit, Ergiebigkeit; Tüchtigkeit *f*; *tech* Wirkungsgrad *m*, Nutzleistung *f*, -effekt *m*, (tatsächliche) Leistung *f*, Ausstoß *m*; *commercial ~~* Wirtschaftlichkeit *f*; *productive ~~* Produktionsfähigkeit *f*; *~~ engineer* Rationalisierungsfachmann *m*; *~~ expert (Am)* Wirtschaftsberater *m*; *~~ rating (Am)* Leistungsbewertung *f*; *~~ report* Leistungsbericht *m*; **~t** [-t] wirksam, wirkungsvoll; rationell, wirtschaftlich; leistungsfähig, ergiebig; *(Mensch)* tüchtig, fähig.

effigy ['efidʒi] Bild(nis), Abbild, Porträt(figur *f*) *n*; *to burn, to hang in ~* in effigie verbrennen, hängen.

effloresc|e [eflɔ:'res] *itr* (auf-, er-) blühen; *chem min* ausblühen, verwittern; *med* e-n Ausschlag bekommen; **~ence** [-ns] Blüte(zeit) *f a. fig*; *fig* Höhepunkt; *chem min* Beschlag *m*, Ausblühen *n*, Aus-, Verwitterung *f*; *med* Ausschlag *m*; **~ent** [-nt] (auf)blühend; *chem min* ausblühend, verwitternd.

efflu|ence ['efluəns] Ausströmen *n*; Ausfluß *m*; Ausstrahlung *f*; **~ent** ['-t] *a* aus-, entströmend; *s* Aus-, Abfluß *m*; **~vium** [e'flu:vjəm] *pl -via* [-iə] Ausstrahlung, Aura; Ausdünstung *f*, Dunst *m*; **~x** ['eflʌks] Aus-, Entströmen *n*; Ausfluß *m*; Ausstrahlung *f*.

effort ['efət] Anstrengung, Mühe *f*; Kraftaufwand *m*; Bemühung *f*; *fam* Werk *n*, Tat, Leistung *f*; *without ~* mühelos; *to be worth the ~* der Mühe wert sein; *to make every ~* sich alle Mühe geben; *to spare no ~* keine Mühe scheuen; *~ of will* Willensanstrengung *f*; **~less** ['-lis] mühelos.

effrontery [e'frʌntəri] Unverschämtheit, Schamlosigkeit, Frechheit, Unverfrorenheit, Anmaßung *f*.

effulg|ence [e'fʌldʒəns] Glanz, Schimmer *m*; Pracht *f*; **~ent** [-ənt] schimmernd, glänzend, strahlend.

effus|e [e'fju:z, i'f-] *tr* aus-, vergießen; aus-, verbreiten; *itr* ausströmen; *a* [-s] *bot* ausgebreitet; *zoo* klaffend; **~ion** [i'fju:ʒən] Ausgießen *n*, *fig* Ausgießung *f*; *med* Erguß *m a. fig*; **~ive** [i'fju:siv] sich ergießend, überfließend; *fig* überschwenglich; aufdringlich.

eft [eft] *zoo* Kammolch *m*.

egalitarianism [igæli'tɛəriənizm] (Lehre *f* von der) Gleichheit *f* aller.

egg [eg] **1.** *s* (*bes.* Hühner-)Ei; *biol* Ei(zelle *f*) *n*; *sl* Handgranate *f*, Torpedo *m*, Bombe *f*; *sl* Kopf *m*; *sl* Null; *sl* Niete *f*; **2.** *tr*: *to ~ on* reizen; antreiben, aufstacheln, -hetzen; *as full as an ~* gerammelt voll; *Am sl* volltrunken; *as sure as ~s are ~s* todsicher; *in the ~ (fig)* in den Kinderschuhen, in den Anfängen; *to lay an ~* ein Ei legen; *Am sl fig* e-e völlige Niete, ein völliger Reinfall, Versager sein; *to put, to have all o.'s ~s in one basket (fig)* alles auf eine Karte setzen; *to teach o.'s grandmother to suck ~s* das Ei will klüger sein als die Henne; *a bad ~ (sl)* ein Strolch, ein Taugenichts; ein Dreck; *battered* od *scrambled, boiled, fried ~s (pl)* Rührei *n*, gekochte, Spiegeleier *n pl*; *hen's ~* Hühnerei *n*; **~-beater, -whisk** *(Küche)* Schneebesen *m*; **~-beater** *sl* Hubschrauber *m*; *sl* Luftschraube, Latte; Windstoßfrisur *f*; **~ cell** *biol* Eizelle *f*; **~-cosy** Eierwärmer *m*; **~-cup** Eierbecher *m*; **~-dance** Eiertanz *m a. fig*; **~-flip, -nog** Eierflip *m*; **~-head** *sl* Intellektuelle(r) *m*; **~-laying** *zoo* eierlegend; **~-plant** *bot* Aubergine *f*; **~-shell** Eierschale *f*.

eglantine ['egləntain] Heckenrose *f*.

ego ['egou, *Am* 'i:gou] *pl -os* Ich *n*; *fam* Ichsucht *f*; **~centric** [-'sentrik] egozentrisch, alles auf sich beziehend; **~ism** ['-izm] Egoismus *m*, Selbstsucht *f*; **~ist** ['-ist] Egoist, selbstsüchtige(r) Mensch *m*; **~istic(al)** [ego(u)'istik(l)] egoistisch, selbstsüchtig; **~mania** [-'meinjə] Ichsucht *f*; **~tism** ['-tizm] ständige(s) Sich-in-den-Vordergrund-Stellen; Geltungsbedürfnis *n*; Überheblichkeit *f*, Dünkel *m*; **~tist** ['-tist] sich ständig in den Vordergrund stellende(r), überhebliche(r) Mensch *m*; **~tistic(al)** [-'tistik(l)] selbstgefällig; geltungsbedürftig; überheblich, dünkelhaft.

egregious [i'gri:dʒəs] *pej* unerhört, unglaublich, haarsträubend; *(Esel)* ausgemacht; *(Fehler)* kraß.

egress ['i:gres] (Recht *n* auf) freie(n) Ausgang; *astr* Austritt; *fig* Ausweg *m*; **~ion** [i(:)'greʃən] Aus-, Fortgang *m*.

egret ['i:gret] *orn* Silberreiher *m*; Reiherfeder *f*; Federbusch *m*; *bot* Federkrone *f* (der Korbblütler).

Egypt ['i:dʒipt] Ägypten *n*; **~ian** [i'dʒipʃən] *a* ägyptisch; *s* Ägypter(in *f*) *m*; **~ologist** [-'tɔlədʒist] Ägyptologe *m*; **~ology** [-'tɔlədʒi] Ägyptologie *f*.

*

eh [ei] *interj* nanu? hm! *(unhöflich)* was? nicht wahr?

eider ['aidə] *(~ duck)* Eiderente *f*; **~-down** Eiderdaune; Daunendecke *f*, -kissen *n*.

eight [eit] *a* acht; *s* Acht *f (Ziffer, Zahl, Figur)*; Achter(boot *n*) *m*; *to have one over the ~ (sl)* einen sitzen haben; **~een** ['ei'ti:n] achtzehn; **~eenth** ['ei'ti:nθ] *a* achtzehnte(r, s); *s* Achtzehntel *n*; **~fold** ['eitfould] *a adv* achtfach; **~h** ['eitθ] *a* achte(r, s); *s* Achtel *n*; *mus* Oktave *f*; *~~ note* Achtelnote *f*; **~hly** ['eitθli] *adv* achtens; **~-hour day** Achtstundentag *m*; **~ieth** ['eitiiθ] *a* achtzigste(r, s); *s* Achtzigstel *n*; **~y** ['eiti] *a* achtzig; *s* Achtzig *f*; *pl* die achtziger Jahre *(e-s Jahrhunderts)*; die Achtzigerjahre *pl (e-s Menschenlebens)*.

Eire ['ɛərə] (Republik) Irland *n*.

either ['aiðə, *Am* 'i:ðə] *prn a u. ~ one(s)* ein(er, e, s), jede(r, s) von beiden, beide(s); *not ... ~* kein(er, e, s) von beiden; *adv*: *(mit Verneinung)* auch nicht; *I shall not go ~* ich gehe auch nicht; *conj*: *~ ... or* entweder ... oder.

ejaculat|e [i'dʒækjuleit] *tr* ausspritzen, -stoßen; *(Worte)* ausstoßen; **~ion** [idʒækju'leiʃən] *physiol* Samenerguß *m*; Ausruf, (Auf-)Schrei *m*; Stoßgebet *n*;

~ory [i'dʒækjulətəri] hastig; Stoß-; *med* Ejakulations-.
eject [i(:)'dʒekt] *tr (Menschen)* hinauswerfen (*from* aus); ausstoßen, vertreiben; *jur* exmittieren; entlassen, absetzen, s-s Amtes entheben; **~ion** [i(:)'dʒekʃən] Vertreibung, Absetzung, Entlassung, Amtsenthebung *f*; Auswurf, -stoß *m*; **~ment** [-mənt] Vertreibung; *jur* Klage *f* auf Wiederherstellung des Besitzstandes; Räumungsklage *f*; **~or** [i(:)'dʒektə] Vertreibende(r); *tech* Auswerfer *m (a. am Gewehr)*; *~~ seat (aero)* Schleudersitz *m*.
eke [i:k]: *to ~ out (tr)* verlängern, erweitern, ergänzen, vervollständigen, abrunden (*with, by* durch); *tech* ansetzen, anstücken; *(Vorrat)* strecken; *to ~ out a living* sich mühsam durchschlagen.
el [el] **1.** *arch* Seitenflügel *m*; **2.** *Am fam (= elevated railway)* Hochbahn *f*.
elaborat|e [i'læbərit] *a* sorgfältig, genau ausgearbeitet, aus-, durchgeführt, durchdacht; ausführlich; vielgestaltig; hochentwickelt; *tr* [-eit] sorgfältig, genau aus-, durcharbeiten; ersinnen, erfinden; genauere Einzelheiten (an)geben (*on, upon* über); näher ausführen (*on, upon s.th.* etw); **~eness** [i'læbəritnis] sorgfältige, genaue Ausarbeitung *od* Durchführung; Ausfeilung; Kompliziertheit *f*; **~ion** [ilæbə'reiʃən] = *~eness*; genauere Angaben *f pl*; Einzelheit *f*.
elapse [i'læps] *itr (Zeit)* vergehen, verfließen, verstreichen, enteilen.
elastic [i'læstik] *a* biegsam, dehnbar, elastisch *a. fig*; Gummi-; *s* Gummiband *n*; **~ity** [i(:)læs'tisiti, e-] Biegsamkeit, Dehnbarkeit, Elastizität; *fig* Spannkraft, Anpassungsfähigkeit *f*.
elat|e [i'leit] *tr* die Stimmung heben (*s.o.* jds); anregen, begeistern; froh, glücklich, stolz machen; *a obs poet* = *~ed*; **~ed** [-id] *a* in gehobener Stimmung; heiter, froh, glücklich, stolz; angeregt, begeistert (*at, with* von); **~ion** [i'leiʃən] gehobene Stimmung, Begeisterung, Freude *f*, Stolz *m*.
elbow ['elbou] *s anat* Ellbogen *(a. Teil des Ärmels)*; *tech* Winkel *m*, Biegung *f*, Krümmer *m*, Knie(stück) *n (bes. e-s Ofenrohrs)*; *tr* sich bahnen (*o.'s way through* e-n Weg durch); *itr (to ~ o.s. forward)* sich e-n, s-n Weg bahnen; *at o.'s ~* bei der Hand, dicht dabei; *out at (the) ~s (Kleidung)* schäbig; *(Person)* heruntergekommen; *to be up to the ~s in work* alle Händevoll zu tun haben; *to rub ~s with s.o.* mit jdm in nähere Berührung kommen; *to ~ s.o. out of the way* jdn zur Seite drängen, verdrängen; **~-grease** *fam* Armschmalz *n*; Schufterei, Anstrengung *f*; **~-room** Bewegungsfreiheit *f*, Spielraum *m*.
elder ['eldə] **1.** *a nur attr (unter Verwandten)* älter; dienstälter, (rang-)höher; früher, ehemalig; *s* Ältere(r *m*) *f*; Vorfahr; (*bes.* Kirchen-)Älteste(r)*m*; *my ~s* ältere Leute als ich; **~ly** ['-li] *a* ältlich, ältere(r); **2.** *bot* Holunder *m*; **~berry** Holunderstrauch *m*, -beere *f*.
eldest ['eldist] *a nur attr (unter Verwandten)* älteste(r).
elect [i'lekt] *a* ausgewählt, erwählt; *(nachgestellt)* designiert, zukünftig; *rel* auserwählt; *s rel* Auserwählte(r) *m*; *the ~* die Elite; *rel* die Auserwählten *pl*; *tr* (aus)wählen (*president* zum Präsidenten); vorziehen, bevorzugen; *rel* erwählen; *itr* wählen; sich entschließen; *bride-~* Verlobte *f*.
election [i'lekʃən] Wahl *bes. pol*; *rel* Gnadenwahl, Prädestination *f*; *to hold an ~* e-e Wahl durchführen; *by-~, (Am) special ~* Nachwahl *f*; *~* **address, speech** Wahlrede *f*; *~* **booth** Wahlzelle *f*; *~* **campaign** Wahlkampf *m*; *~* **commission, committee** Wahlausschuß *m*, -komitee *n*; *~* **day** Wahltag *m*; *~* **district** Wahlbezirk *m*; **~eer** [ilekʃə'niə] *itr* Wahlpropaganda treiben; *s* Wahlredner *m*; **~eering** [ilekʃə'niəriŋ] Wahlpropaganda *f*, -kampf *m*; *~* **manifesto** Wahlmanifest *n*; *~* **meeting** Wahlversammlung *f*; *~* **platform, program(me)** Wahlprogramm *n*; *~* **poster** Wahlplakat *n*; *~* **propaganda** Wahlpropaganda *f*; *~* **results, returns** *pl* Wahlergebnis *n*.
elective [i'lektiv] *a* wahlfähig; gewählt; *(Schule) Am* wahlfrei; Wahl-; *s (Schule) Am* Wahlfach *n*; **~ly** [-li] *adv* durch Wahl; wahlweise.
elector [i'lektə] *Br* Wähler; *Am* Wahlmann; *hist* Kurfürst *m*; **~al** [-rəl] *a* Wahl-, Wähler-; kurfürstlich; *~~ ballot* Wahl-, Abstimmungsergebnis *n*; *~~ campaign* Wahlkampf *m*; *~~ coalition* Wahlbündnis *n*; *~~ college* Wahlkollegium *n*; *Am* Wahlmänner *m pl*; *~~ commission, committee* Wahlausschuß *m*, -komitee *n*; *~~ district* Wahlbezirk *m*; *~~ list, register, roll* Wählerliste *f*; *~~ rally* Wahlversammlung *f*; *~~ reform* Wahlreform *f*; *~~ system* Wahlsystem *n*; *~~ victory* Wahlsieg *m*; *~~ vote* Wahlstimme *f*; **~ate** [-rit] Wähler(schaft *f*) *m pl*; *hist* Kurwürde *f*; Kurfürstentum *n*.
electri|c [i'lektrik] *a* elektrisch; *~~ arc* Lichtbogen *m*; *~~ blanket* Heizdecke *f*; *~~ bulb* Glühbirne *f*; *~~ chair* elektrische(r) Stuhl *m*; *~~ circuit* Stromkreis *m*; elektrische Leitung *f*; *~~ cooker* Elektroherd *m*; *~~ cushion, pad* Heizkissen *n*; *~~ discharge* Elektrizitätsentladung *f*; *~~ eel* Zitteraal *m*; *~~ eye* Photozelle *f*; *~~ fan* Ventilator *m*; *~~ fire* Heizsonne *f*; *~~ furnace* Elektroofen *m*; *~~ generator* Lichtmaschine *f*; *~~ industry* Elektroindustrie *f*; *~~ load* Strombelastung *f*; *~~ meter* (Elektrizitäts-)Zähler *m*; *~~ motor* Elektromotor *m*; *~~ needle (med)* elektrische(s) Messer *n*; *~~ plant* Elektrizitätswerk *n*; *~~ razor* elektrische(r) Rasierapparat *m*; *~~ saw* Motorsäge *f*; *~~ sign* Lichtreklame *f*; *~~ source* Stromquelle *f*; *~~ starter* Elektroanlasser *m*; *~~ steel* Elektrostahl *m*; *~~ supply* Stromversorgung *f*; *~~ torch* Taschenlampe *f*; *~~ welding* Elektroschweißung *f*; *~~ wire* Leitungsdraht *m*; **~cal** [-əl] elektrisch; *~~ appliances (pl)* Elektrogeräte *n pl*; *~~ engineer* Elektroingenieur *m*; *~~ engineering* Elektrotechnik *f*; *~~ recording* elektrische Registrierung *f*; *~~ shop* Elektrowerkstatt *f*; *~~ transcription* (Übertragung *f* von) Rundfunkschallplatte(n) *f*; **~cian** [-'triʃən] Elektriker *m*; **~city** [-'trisiti] Elektrizität *f*; *~~ cut* Stromsperre *f*; *~~ meter* Stromzähler *m*; *~~ rates (pl)* Stromtarif *m*; *~~ supply* Stromversorgung *f*; *~~ works* Elektrizitätswerk *n*.
electrif|iable [ilektri'faiəbl] elektrifizierbar; **~ication** [-fi'keiʃən] Elektrifizierung; Elektrisierung *f*; **~y** [i'lektrifai], **electrize** [i'lektraiz] *tr* elektrisieren *a. fig*; elektrifizieren; *fig* anfeuern, begeistern.
electro|analysis [i'lektro(u)ə'næləsis] Elektrolyse *f*; **~cardiogram** Elektrokardiogramm, EKG *n*; **~cardiograph** Elektrokardiograph *m*; **~-chemistry** Elektrochemie *f*; **~cute** [i'lektrəkju:t] *tr* auf dem elektrischen Stuhl hinrichten; durch elektrischen Strom töten; **~cution** [ilektrə'kju:ʃən] Hinrichtung *f*, Tod *m* durch elektrischen Strom; **~de** [i'lektroud] Elektrode *f*; **~-deposition** Galvanisierung *f*; **~dynamic** [-dai'næmik] *a* elektrodynamisch; *s pl mit sing* Elektrodynamik *f*; **~lysis** [ilek'trəlisis] Elektrolyse *f*; **~lyte** [i'lektro(u)lait] Elektrolyt *m*; **~lytic** [ilektro(u)'litik] elektrolytisch; *~~ copper* Elektrolytkupfer *n*; *~~ oxidation* Eloxierung *f*; **~magnet** Elektromagnet *m*; **~magnetic** elektromagnetisch; **~meter** Stromzähler *m*, Elektrometer *n*; **~motive** elektromotorisch; *~~ force* elektromotorische Kraft *f*; *~~ intensity* Feldstärke *f*; **~motor** Elektromotor *m*; **~n** [i'lektrən] Elektron *n*; *~~ beam* Elektronenstrahl *m*; *~~ camera* Ikonoskop *n*; *~~ emission* Elektronenemission *f*; *~~ gun* Elektronenquelle *f*; *~~ microscope* Elektronenmikroskop *n*; *~~ tube, valve* Elektronenröhre *f*; **~nic** [ilek'trənik] *a* elektronisch; Elektronen-; *s pl mit sing* Elektronik *f*; *~~ brain* Elektronengehirn *n*; *~~ engineering* (technische) Elektronik *f*; *~~ microscope* Elektronenmikroskop *n*; *~~ rectifier* Röhrengleichrichter *m*; **~plate** [i'lektro(u)pleit] *tr* galvanisieren; *s* versilberte(s) Besteck *n*; **~scope** [i'lektrəskoup] Elektroskop *n*; **~-static** *a* elektrostatisch; *s pl mit sing* Elektrostatik *f*; **~therapy** [ilektro(u)'θerəpi] Elektrotherapie *f*; **~type** [i'lektro(u)taip] *itr* Galvanos herstellen; *tr* galvanoplastisch vervielfältigen; *s* Galvano *n*.
electuary [i'lektjuəri] *pharm* Latwerge *f*.
eleemosynary [elii:'məzinəri] *a* Wohltätigkeits-; von Almosen, von der Wohltätigkeit lebend; gespendet.
elegan|ce, -cy ['eligəns(i)] Eleganz, Feinheit, Zierlichkeit, Gewähltheit, Vornehmheit *f*, Geschmack *m*, Gefälligkeit, Anmut, Gewandtheit *f*; **~t** ['eligənt] elegant, fein, zierlich, gewählt, vornehm, geschmackvoll, gefällig, anmutig, gewandt; *fam* tadellos, prachtvoll, prächtig, prima.
eleg|iac [eli'dʒaiək] *a lit* elegisch; *s* Elegie *f*; **~y** ['elidʒi] Elegie *f*, Klagelied *n*, Trauergesang *m*.
element ['elimənt] Element *n a. math chem el*; Grundstoff; (Grund-)Bestandteil *m*, Grundtatsache *f*, Prinzip *n*; Faktor, Umstand *m*; *jur* Tatbestandsmerkmal *n*; Umgebung, Sphäre *f*, Milieu *n*; *mil* Truppenteil *m*; *aero* Rotte *f*; *tech* Bauelement *n*, -teil *m*; *the ~s (pl)* die Elemente, Anfangsgründe, Grundlagen, Grundzüge *(e-r Wissenschaft)*; die Elemente *pl*, die Natur(gewalten *pl*), die Unbilden *pl* des Wetters; *rel* Brot u. Wein *(beim Abendmahl)*; *in, out of o.'s ~* in s-m, nicht in s-m Element; *~~ of surprise* Überraschungsmoment *n*; **~al** [eli'mentl] elementar; natürlich, Natur-; urgewaltig; einfach, Anfangs-, Grund-; prinzipiell; wesentlich; **~ary** [eli'mentəri] elementar, Elementar-, einführend, Einführungs-, Anfangs-, Grund-; unentwickelt; *chem* einfach, Elementar-; *~~ particle* Elementarteilchen *n*; *~~ school* Volks-, Grundschule *f*; *~~ training* Grundausbildung *f*.
elephant ['elifənt] Elefant *m*; *(~ paper)* Zeichenpapier im Format 71×58 cm; *a white ~* kostspielige(r), unrentable(r) u. unveräußerliche(r) Besitz *m*; **~iasis** [elifən'taiəsis] *med* Elefantiasis *f*; **~ine** [eli'fæntain] *a* Elefanten-; plump; *fig* schwerfällig, ungeschickt; **~'s ear** *bot* Begonie *f*.
elevat|e ['eliveit] *tr* (hoch)heben; *(die Stimme)* heben; *(Person)* erheben, er-

höhen, befördern (*to* zu); auf e-e höhere geistige *od* sittliche Stufe heben; die Stimmung heben (*s.o.* jds), auf-, erheitern; *tech* hochheben, -schwenken; **~ed** [-id] *a* gehoben, erhöht, hoch; hochgestellt, erhaben, würdevoll, würdig; eingebildet (*with* auf); gut gelaunt, in froher Stimmung; *s Am fam u.* **~~** *railway* Hochbahn *f*; **~ion** [eli'veiʃən] Erhöhung, Erhebung; erhöhte Lage, Höhe, Höhenlage; Anhöhe; Erhabenheit, Hoheit, Würde *f*; Hochmut *m*; *geog* (Meeres-)Höhe; *astr* Höhe *f (über dem Horizont)*; *tech arch* Aufriß *m*; Ansicht *f*; *sectional* **~~** Längsschnitt *m*; **~~** *angle* Höhen-, Ansatzwinkel *m*; **~or** ['eliveitə] Heber, Hebel; *(~~ muscle)* Hebemuskel *m*; *aero* Höhenruder; *tech* Becherwerk *n*, Elevator; *Am* Aufzug, Fahrstuhl; *Am* (Getreide-)Silo *m*; *freight* **~~** *(Am)* Hebezeug *n*, Warenaufzug *m*; **~~** *boy (Am)* Fahrstuhlführer, Liftboy *m*; **~~** *control (aero)* Höhenleitwerk *n*.

eleven [i'levn] *a* elf; *s sport* Elf *f*; **~ses** [-ziz] *Br fam* zweite(s) Frühstück *n*; **~th** [-θ] *a* elfte; *s* Elftel *n*; *at the* **~~** *hour* in letzter Minute, im letzten Augenblick.

elf [elf] *pl elves* Elf(e *f*), Kobold *m*; *fig* Giftnudel *f*; **~in** ['elfin] elfen-, koboldhaft; **~ish** ['elfiʃ] = **~***in*; mißgünstig, gehässig; **~lock** Weichselzopf *m*; **~-struck** *a* verhext.

elicit [i'lisit] *tr* ent-, hervorlocken, herausholen (*from* aus); entlocken.

elide [i'laid] *tr gram* elidieren.

eligib|ility [elidʒə'biliti] Wählbarkeit *f*, passive(s) Wahlrecht *n*; Befähigung, Eignung, Qualifikation *f*; Vorzug *m*; wünschenswerte Eigenschaft *f*; **~le** ['elidʒəbl] wählbar; befähigt (*for* zu), qualifiziert (*for* für); geeignet, passend; berechtigt; wünschenswert; vorzuziehen(d); *fam* heiratsfähig; *Am* bank-, diskontfähig; *to be* **~~** in Frage kommen.

eliminat|e [i'limineit] *tr* weg-, fortschaffen, entfernen; ausscheiden, -schalten, -lassen, beseitigen (*from* aus); ausmerzen; *(Konto)* auflösen; außer acht, unberücksichtigt lassen; *math* eliminieren; *physiol* ausscheiden; **~ion** [ilimi'neiʃən] Auslassung, Ausschaltung; Ausmerzung, Beseitigung; Streichung; Nichtberücksichtigung; *med sport chem* Ausscheidung; *(Konto)* Auflösung *f*; **~~** *contest* Ausscheidungswettbewerb *m*; **~or** [ilimi'neitə] *sport* Ausscheidungskampf *m*; *el* Sperre *f*, Sieb *n*.

elision [i'liʒən] *gram* Elision *f*.

elite [ei'li:t, el-] Elite, Auslese *f*.

elixir [i'liksə] Elixier *n*, Heiltrank *m*; Allheil-, Wundermittel *n*; **~** *of life* Lebenselixier *n*.

Elizabeth [i'lizəbəθ] Elisabeth *f*; **~an** [ilizə'bi:θən] elisabethanisch.

elk [elk] Elch *m*, Elen(tier); *Am* Wapiti *n*.

ell [el] **1.** Elle *f (= 45 inches = 114,2 cm)*; **2.** *Am* L-förmiger Gegenstand; *arch* Seitenflügel *m*; Knie(stück) *n (Rohr)*.

ellip|se [i'lips] *math* Ellipse *f*; **~sis** [i'lipsis] *pl -ses* [-i:z] *gram* Ellipse, Auslassung *f*; **~soid** [-ɔid] *math* Ellipsoid *n*; **~tic(al)** [i'liptik(əl)] elliptisch.

elm [elm] *(~ tree)* Ulme, Rüster *f*.

elocution [elə'kju:ʃən] Vortragskunst, -weise *f*; **~ary** [-ʃnəri] Vortrags-; *(Ausdrucksweise)* gekünstelt, deklamatorisch; **~ist** [-ʃnist] Vortragskünstler, Rezitator; Sprecherzieher *m*.

elongat|e ['i:ləŋgeit, *Am* i'lɔŋgeit] *tr* verlängern, dehnen, strecken; *itr* länger werden, sich dehnen, sich strecken; *a* verlängert, gedehnt, gestreckt; länglich; *bot* langgestreckt; **~ion** [i:lɔŋ'geiʃən] Dehnung, Streckung; Verlängerung; *astr* Elongation *f*.

elope [i'loup] *itr* entlaufen, ausreißen, -rücken; durchgehen, -brennen, auf u. davon gehen *(bes. mit e-m Liebhaber)*; **~ment** [-mənt] Entlaufen *n*.

eloquen|ce ['eləkwəns] Beredsamkeit; beredte Sprache *f*; **~t** ['-t] beredsam; beredt, redegewandt; ausdrucksvoll.

else [els] *adv* sonst, weiter, außerdem, noch; anders; *anybody* **~?** sonst noch jemand? *anything* **~?** sonst noch etwas? *everybody* **~** alle andern; *everything* **~** alles andere; *nothing* **~** nichts weiter; *or* **~** sonst, andernfalls; *somebody* **~** jemand anders; *what* **~?** was noch? was sonst? was weiter? **~where** ['els'wɛə] *adv* anders-, sonstwo, woanders; anderswohin.

elucidat|e [i'lu:sideit] *tr* auf-, erhellen, erklären, erläutern; **~ion** [ilu:si'deiʃən] Auf-, Erhellung, Auf-, Erklärung, Erläuterung *f*; **~ory** [i'lu:sideitəri] erhellend, erklärend, erläuternd.

elude [i'l(j)u:d] *tr* (geschickt) umgehen, vermeiden; sich fernhalten (*s.th.* etw); ausweichen, entgehen, sich entziehen (*s.th.* e-r S).

elus|ion [i'lu:ʒən] (geschickte) Umgehung, Vermeidung; Ausflucht *f*; **~ive** [i'lu:siv] ausweichend; flüchtig; schwer zu begreifen(d), zu (er)fassen(d), zu behalten(d); **~ory** [i'lu:səri] verschwimmend, täuschend, trügerisch.

elvish ['elviʃ] *s. elfish.*

Elysi|an [i'liziən] elys(ä)isch; paradiesisch; **~um** [-əm] Elysium *n a. fig.*

*

em [em] *typ (Maß)* Einheit *f*; **~(quad)** Geviert *n*.

emaciat|e [i'meiʃieit] *tr* abmagern lassen, mager machen; **~ed** [-id] *a* abgemagert; **~ion** [imeisi'eiʃən] Auszehrung, Abmagerung *f*.

emanat|e ['eməneit] *itr* ausfließen, -strömen, -strahlen, emanieren (*from* von); *fig* ausgehen, herkommen, herrühren, herstammen (*from* von); **~ion** [-'neiʃən] Ausstrahlung *f*; Ausfluß *m*; *philos phys* Emanation *f*.

emancipat|e [i'mænsipeit] *tr (Sklaven)* freilassen; für volljährig erklären; *allg* befreien, frei machen, emanzipieren; **~ed** [-id] *a* emanzipiert, ungebunden, frei; vorurteilslos; **~ion** [-'peiʃən] Freilassung; Volljährigkeitserklärung; *allg* Befreiung, Emanzipation, Gleichstellung *f (bes. der Frau)*.

emasculat|e [i'mæskjuleit] *tr* entmannen, kastrieren; *fig* abschwächen; *a* [-lit] verweichlicht, effeminiert, weibisch; **~ion** [-'leiʃən] Entmannung; Abschwächung; Verweichlichung *f*.

embalm [im'bɑ:m] *tr (Leichnam)* (ein-)balsamieren; parfümieren, mit Duft erfüllen; *fig* (das Andenken) bewahren *od* erhalten (*s.o.* jds, an jdn); **~ment** [-mənt] Einbalsamierung *f*.

embank [im'bæŋk] *tr* die Ufer befestigen (*a river* e-s Flusses); eindämmen; **~ment** [-mənt] Uferbefestigung; Ufermauer *f*, Kai, Damm *m*; Uferstraße; Aufschüttung *f*, (Straßen-, Eisenbahn-)Damm *m*.

embargo [em'bɑ:gou] *s pl -es* Embargo *n*; Hafen-, Handelssperre; Beschlagnahme; *allg* Behinderung, Unterdrückung *f*, Verbot *n*; *tr* sperren; beschlagnahmen; *under an* **~** gesperrt; mit Beschlag belegt; *to lay, to put an* **~** *on* mit Beschlag belegen, beschlagnahmen; *to lift, to raise, to take off the* **~** die Beschlagnahme aufheben; *arms* **~** Waffenausfuhrverbot, -embargo *n*; *export, import* **~** Aus-, Einfuhrsperre *f*.

embark [im'bɑ:k] *tr* einschiffen, verladen (*for* nach); an Bord nehmen; *(Geld)* anlegen, investieren (*in* in); *itr* sich einschiffen (*for* nach), an Bord gehen; abreisen, -fahren (*for* nach); sich einlassen (*in* in; *on* auf), *fam* einsteigen (*in, on* in); sich widmen (*on s.th.* gen); **~ation** [embɑ:'keiʃən] Ein-, Verschiffung, Verladung *f*.

embarrass [im'bærəs] *tr* in Verlegenheit, aus der Fassung bringen; (be)hindern, hinderlich, lästig sein (*s.o.* jdm); in Schulden stürzen; in finanzielle Schwierigkeiten bringen; **~ed** [-t] *a* in Verlegenheit; in Schulden, in (finanziellen) Schwierigkeiten; verwickelt, kompliziert; *to be* **~~** verlegen sein, sich genieren; **~ing** [-iŋ] peinlich, unangenehm; ungelegen, unpassend; **~ment** [-mənt] (Geld-)Verlegenheit; Störung *f*; Hindernis *n*; Verwirrung *f*.

embassy ['embəsi] *pol* Botschaft(sgebäude, -personal *n*); Botschafterstelle *f*; Sonderauftrag *m*, Mission *f*.

embattle [im'bætl] *tr* mit Schießscharten versehen; befestigen; in Schlachtordnung aufstellen.

embed [im'bed] *tr* einpflanzen; einbetten, einlagern; *to be* **~ded** eingebettet, *fig* fest verankert sein (*in* in); *to* **~** *in concrete* einbetonieren.

embellish [im'beliʃ] *tr* verschönern, verzieren, ausschmücken; ausgestalten, -staffieren; **~ment** [-mənt] Verschönerung, Ausschmückung *(a. e-r Erzählung)*; Verzierung *f*, Schmuck, Dekor(ation *f*) *m*, Staffage *f*.

ember ['embə] **1.** verglühende(s) Stück *n* Holz *od* Kohle; *fig*: *life's last* **~s** der letzte Lebensfunke; **2.** *(~ days)* Quatember *m*; **3.** *(~ goose, diver) orn* Eistaucher *m*.

embezzle [im'bezl] *tr* entwenden, veruntreuen, unterschlagen; **~ment** [-mənt] Entwendung, Veruntreuung, Unterschlagung *f*; **~r** [-ə] Veruntreuer *m*.

embitter [im'bitə] *tr* verbittern, vergrämen; verschlimmern.

emblazon [im'bleizən] *tr* heraldisch aus-, bemalen (*with* mit); (aus-)schmücken, verzieren; farbenreich, prächtig ausgestalten; verherrlichen, feiern, preisen, den Ruhm verkünden (*s.o.* jds); **~ment** [-mənt] (heraldische) Ausmalung, Ausschmückung *f*.

emblem ['embləm] Sinnbild, Symbol, Emblem *n*; **~atic(al)** [embli'mætik(əl)] sinnbildlich, symbolisch (*of* für).

embod|iment [im'bɔdimənt] Verkörperung; Einfügung; Verwirklichung *f*; **~y** [im'bɔdi] *tr* verkörpern; konkretisieren, feste Form, Gestalt geben (*s.th.* e-r S); verwirklichen; einfügen, aufnehmen, einverleiben, eingliedern (*in s.th.* e-r S); verankern, einschließen, niederlegen (*in* in).

embolden [im'bouldən] *tr* ermutigen (*to* zu).

embolism ['embəlizm] *med* Embolie *f*.

embosom [im'buzəm] *tr* ins Herz schließen; *meist Passiv*: *to be* **~ed** eingeschlossen, eingehüllt, schützend umgeben sein (*in, with* von).

emboss [im'bɔs] *tr (Verzierung)* erhaben arbeiten; *(dünnes Metall)* treiben, bossieren, prägen; **~ed** [-t] *a* erhaben (gearbeitet), getrieben; **~~** *map* Reliefkarte *f*; **~~** *printing* Blindenschrift *f*; **~~** *sheet* Prägefolie *f*.

embowel [im'bauəl] *tr* ausweiden; *fig* ausschlachten.

embrace [im'breis] *tr* umarmen, in die Arme nehmen *od* schließen; *(Gelegen-*

heit, Beruf) ergreifen; *(Glauben, Beruf, Angebot)* annehmen; *(Hoffnung)* hegen; umgeben, einschließen *a. fig*; *fig* enthalten, umfassen; (geistig) erfassen; *itr* sich umarmen; *s* Umarmung *f*.

embrasure [im'breiʒə] Leibung; Schießscharte *f*.

embrocat|e ['embro(u)keit] *tr med* einreiben; **~ion** [-'keiʃən] Einreibung *f*; Mittel *n* zum Einreiben.

embroider [im'brɔidə] *tr* besticken; *fig (Erzählung)* ausschmücken; übertreiben; *itr* sticken; **~y** [-ri] Stickerei; *fig* Ausschmückung *f*; *~~ frame* Stickrahmen *m*.

embroil [im'brɔil] *tr* verwirren, durchea.bringen; *(in e-e Affäre)* verwickeln; hineinziehen (*in* in); **~ment** [-mənt] Verwirrung, Verwick(e)lung *f*.

embryo ['embriou] *pl -os* Embryo; Fruchtkeim *m*; *in ~ (fig)* in den Anfängen; **~nic** [embri'ɔnik] *physiol* embryonal; *fig* (noch) unentwickelt.

embus [im'bʌs] *mil tr* auf Lastkraftwagen verladen; *itr* aufsitzen.

emcee ['em'si:] *s Am sl theat radio* Conferencier, Ansager *m (bes. beim Werbefunk)*; *tr Am sl* die Ansage machen für; einleiten, einführen.

emend [i(:)'mend] *tr (bes. e-n Text)* verbessern, berichtigen; **~ation** [i:men'deiʃən, em-] Verbesserung, Berichtigung *f*; **~ator** ['i:mendeitə] Korrektor, Verbesserer *m*; **~atory** [i(:)'mendətəri] verbessernd, berichtigend.

emerald ['emərəld] *s* Smaragd; *typ* Schriftgrad *m* von 6½ Punkten; *a* smaragdgrün; Smaragd-; *the E~ Isle* die Grüne Insel *(Irland)*.

emerg|e [i'mə:dʒ] *itr (aus dem Wasser)* auftauchen, an die Oberfläche, emporsteigen, hochkommen, hervorbrechen, -treten, entstehen (*from, out of* aus); *fig* auftauchen, in Erscheinung treten, sich ergeben, sichtbar, deutlich, klar, bekanntwerden; **~ence** [-əns] Auftauchen *a. geol*; Sichergeben, Sichtbarwerden; Hervorkommen *n*; **~ency** [-ənsi] Dringlichkeits-, Notfall *m*; kritische Situation *f*; *sport* Ersatzspieler *m*; *attr* Not-, (Aus-)Hilfs-, Behelfs-, Ersatz-; *in an ~~, in case of ~~* im Not-, im Ernstfall; *to meet an ~~* e-m Notstand abhelfen; *to provide for ~encies* gegen Notfälle Vorsorge treffen; *to rise to the ~~* der Lage gewachsen sein; *it'll do in an ~~* zur Not wird's gehen; *state of ~~* Ausnahmezustand *m*; *~~ aid* Soforthilfe *f*; *~~ brake* Notbremse *f*; *~~ bridge* Behelfsbrücke *f*; *~~ call* Notruf *m*; *~~ committee* Hilfskomitee *n*; *~~ decree* Notverordnung *f*; *~~ door, exit* Notausgang *m*; *~~ dressing* Notverband *m*; *~~ fund* Reserve, Rücklage *f* für den Notfall; *~~ hatch* Notausstieg *m*; *~~ home* Behelfsheim *n*; *~~ landing (aero)* Notlandung *f*; *~~ landing-field* Notlandeplatz *m*; *~~ law* Ausnahmegesetz *n*; *~~ light* Notlicht *n*; *~~ man* Aushilfe, Aushilfskraft *f*; *sport* Ersatzspieler *m*; *~~ measure* Notmaßnahme *f*; *~~ money* Notgeld *n*; *~~ powers (pl)* Sondervollmachten *f pl*; *~~-powers act* Notstandsgesetz *n*; *~~ ration* eiserne Ration *f*; *~~ release (aero mil)* Notabwurf *m*; *~~ seat* Notsitz *m*; *~~ service* Bereitschaftsdienst *m*; *~~ solution* Notlösung *f*; *~~ steps (pl)* Notmaßnahmen *f pl*; *~~ tank* Reservetank *m*; *~~ train* Hilfszug *m*; *~~ valve* Sicherheitsventil *n*; **~ent** [-ənt] *a* auftauchend, sich ergebend, in Erscheinung tretend; plötzlich, dringend; *s scient* Endergebnis *n*, Folge *f*.

emersion [i(:)'mə:ʃən] *s. emergence.*

emery ['eməri] *min* Schmirgel *m*; *to rub with ~* abschmirgeln; *~* **cloth** Schmirgelleinwand *f*; *~* **paper** Schmirgelpapier *n*; *~* **wheel, disc** Schmirgelscheibe *f*.

emetic [i'metik] *a pharm* Brech-; *s* Brechmittel *n*.

emigrant ['emigrənt] *a* auswandernd; *s* Auswanderer *m*; *returning ~* Rückwanderer *m*; **~ate** ['emigreit] *itr* auswandern, emigrieren (*from* aus; *to* nach); **~ation** [emi'greiʃən] Auswanderung *f*, Auswanderer *m pl*.

eminen|ce ['eminəns] (An-)Höhe *f*; hohe *od* höhere Stellung; Besonderheit *f*; hervorragende Fähigkeiten, Leistungen *f pl*; Ansehen *n*, Größe, Berühmtheit; *E~ (rel)* Eminenz *f (Titel e-s Kardinals)*; **~t** ['-t] erhaben, hoch, (auf)ragend; hervorragend, außerordentlich, bemerkenswert, bedeutend, ausgezeichnet (*in* in; *for* durch); *(power, right of) ~~ domain* Enteignungsrecht *n*; **~tly** ['-tli] *adv* in hohem Maße, ganz besonders.

emiss|ary ['emisəri] (Geheim-)Bote; Geheimagent, Kundschafter, Emissär *m*; **~ion** [i'miʃən] *fin* Ausgabe, Emission; *phys* Emission, Ausstrahlung *f*; Ausströmen *n*, Ausfluß, Austritt; *(bes.* Samen-)Erguß *m*; **~ive** [i'misiv] emittierend; **~ivity** [emi'siviti] Ausstrahlungsvermögen *n*.

emit [i'mit] *tr* von sich geben; auswerfen, -speien, ausströmen, ausfließen lassen; *(Gebrüll)* ausstoßen; *(Meinung)* von sich geben; *fin* in Umlauf setzen; *tech* ausstrahlen.

*

emollient [i'mɔliənt] *a pharm* erweichend; *s* erweichende(s) Mittel *n*.

emolument [i'mɔljumənt] Gehalt *n*, Lohn; Gewinn *m*; *pl* (Neben-)Einkünfte, (Dienst-)Bezüge *pl*.

emote [i'mout] *itr Am fam, oft hum* Theater machen, sich verrückt, affektiert benehmen.

emotion [i'mouʃən] (Gefühls-)Erregung, (innere) Bewegung, Erregtheit *f*; (starkes) Gefühl *n*; Rührung *f*; **~al** [-ʃənl] *a* Gefühls-; gefühlsmäßig, gefühlsbetont; bewegt, erregt; (leicht) erregbar; *(Person u. Sache)* gefühlvoll, sentimental; **~alism** [i'mouʃnəlizm] Gefühlsbetontheit, Empfindsamkeit, Sentimentalität; leichte Erregbarkeit; Rührseligkeit, Affektiertheit *f*; **~alist** [-ʃnəlist] gefühlvolle(r), sentimentale(r) Mensch; an das Gefühl appellierende(r) Redner *m*; **~ality** [imouʃə'næliti] Empfindsamkeit, Sentimentalität *f*; **~less** [-lis] gefühllos, unbewegt, kalt.

emotive [i'moutiv] gefühlserregend.

empanel [im'pænl] *tr (Schöffen)* in die Geschworenenliste eintragen; *to ~ the jury* die Geschworenenbank zs.stellen.

empathy ['empəθi] Einfühlung(svermögen *n*) *f*.

empennage [im'penidʒ] *aero* Leitwerk *n*.

emperor ['empərə] Kaiser *m*.

empha|sis ['emfəsis] *pl -ses* [-si:z] Nachdruck *m*, Betonung *f* (*on* auf); *to put, to lay ~ on s.th* großes Gewicht auf etw legen; **~size** ['emfəsaiz] *tr* Nachdruck legen auf, besonders betonen, hervorheben, unterstreichen, herausstellen; **~tic** [im'fætik] emphatisch; nachdrücklich, betont; *(in der Rede)* stark betonend; bedeutend, eindeutig, entscheidend, auffallend.

empire ['empaiə] (Ober-)Herrschaft, (Ober-)Gewalt, Beherrschung; kaiserliche Gewalt *f*; Kaisertum; (Kaiser-)Reich *n*; *the E~* das (Britische) Empire.

empiric [em'pirik] *s* Mann *m* der Praxis; Quacksalber, Scharlatan *m*; **~(al)** *a* empirisch; auf Erfahrung beruhend; *(Heilmittel)* (in der Praxis) erprobt; *~~ rule* Erfahrungssatz *m*; **~ism** [-sizm] Empirismus *m*; Quacksalberei *f*; **~ist** [-sist] Empiriker *m*.

emplacement [im'pleismənt] Aufstellung; Einweisung *f*; *mil* (Geschütz-, Werfer-, MG-)Stand *m*, Bettung *f*.

emplane [im'plein] *itr* das Flugzeug besteigen; *tr* in ein Flugzeug verladen.

employ [im'plɔi] *tr* gebrauchen, benutzen, an-, verwenden (*in doing s.th.* beim Tun); beschäftigen (*in* mit); *(Arbeitskraft)* an-, einstellen; einsetzen; *(Geld)* anlegen; *to ~ o.s. with s.th.* sich mit etw beschäftigen; *out of ~* arbeits-, stellungslos; **~able** [-əbl] brauchbar; verwendbar, verwendungsfähig; **~ed** [-d] *a* beschäftigt, angestellt (*in a bank* bei e-r Bank); **~é(e** *f*) *m* [ɔm'plɔiei], **~e(e)** [emplɔi'i:] Arbeitnehmer(in *f*) *m*, Angestellte(r *m*) *f*; *pl* Belegschaft *f*; *~~s' representatives (pl)* Arbeitnehmervertreter *m pl*; **~er** [-ə] Unternehmer, Arbeitgeber *m*; *pl* Arbeitgeberschaft *f*; *~~s' association, federation* Arbeitgeberverband *m*; **~ment** [-mənt] Beschäftigung, Verwendung; Arbeit(sverhältnis *n*) *f*, Dienst *m*, Geschäft, Amt *n*, Beruf *m*; *out of ~~* arbeits-, stellungslos; *to enter an ~~* e-e Arbeit annehmen, e-e Stellung antreten; *casual ~~* Gelegenheitsarbeit *f*; *full ~~* Vollbeschäftigung *f*; *permanent ~~* Dauerbeschäftigung; feste(s) Anstellung(sverhältnis *n*) *f*; *~~ agency, bureau, exchange* Stellenvermittlung *f*, Arbeitsnachweis *m*; *~~ manager* Personalchef *m*; *~~ market* Arbeitsmarkt *m*; *~~ office* Arbeitsamt; Einstellungsbüro *n*; *~~ procedure* Einstellungsverfahren *n*; *~~ records (pl)* Arbeitspapiere *n pl*.

emporium [em'pɔ:riəm] Handelsplatz *m*, -zentrum *n*, Markt *m*; Warenhaus *n*, Laden *m*, Geschäft *n*.

empower [im'pauə] *tr* berechtigen, ermächtigen, autorisieren (*to do* zu tun); *allg* befähigen, in den Stand setzen (*to* zu); erlauben (*s.o. to* jdm zu); *~ed to* ermächtigt, befugt zu.

empress ['empris] Kaiserin *f*.

empt|iness ['emptinis] Leere; *fig* Nichtigkeit, Bedeutungslosigkeit *f*; **~y** ['-i] *a* leer(stehend); ohne Ladung; *fig* inhaltslos, leer, nichtssagend, unbefriedigend, bedeutungslos; unaufrichtig; sinnlos; *(Magen)* nüchtern, leer; *fam* hungrig; *(Drohungen)* leer; *s pl* Leergut *n*; *mil* abgeschossene Hülsen *f pl*; *tr (to ~~ out)* (aus-, ent)leeren; *itr* sich leeren; *(Fluß)* sich ergießen, münden (*into* in); *returned ~~* leer zurück; *~~-handed (a)* mit leeren Händen; *~~-headed (a)* hohlköpfig; *~~ weight* Eigen-, Leergewicht *n*.

emu ['i:mju:] *orn* Emu *m*.

emul|ate ['emjuleit] *tr* nacheifern (*s.o.* jdm); wetteifern (*s.o.* mit jdm), gleichzukommen (*s.o.* jdm), zu übertreffen suchen; **~ation** [-'leiʃən] Nacheiferung *f*; Wetteifer *m*; **~ous** ['emjuləs] voller Wetteifer; nacheifernd (*of* dat); begierig (*of* auf, nach).

emuls|ify [i'mʌlsifai] *tr* emulgieren, in Emulsion verwandeln; **~ion** [-ʃən] Emulsion *f*.

*

enable [i'neibl] *tr* in den Stand setzen, befähigen (*to do* zu tun); ermöglichen, die Möglichkeit geben, möglich machen (*s.o. to* jdm zu); berechtigen, ermächtigen (*to* zu); *to be ~d to* in der Lage sein zu.

enact [i'nækt] *tr* verfügen, verordnen, erlassen; Gesetzeskraft geben *od* verleihen (*s.th.* e-r S); *theat* spielen, darstellen; *to be ~ed* stattfinden; sich abspielen; **~ion** [-kʃən] Verfügung *f*, Erlaß *m (e-s Gesetzes)*; **~ment** [-mənt] *s.* *~ion*; gesetzliche Bestimmung *f*; *(~~ of a law)* Annahme *f* e-s Gesetzes; *theat* Spiel *n*, Darstellung *f*.

enamel [i'næməl] *s* Emaille *f*, Lack *m*; (*a.* Zahn-)Schmelz *m*; Glasur *f*; Schmelz-, Nagellack *m*; *tr* emaillieren; (*bes.* farbig) glasieren; farbig verzieren; **~ paint** Isolierlack *m*.

enamour [i'næmə] *tr* verliebt machen; *to be, to become ~ed of* verliebt sein, sich verlieben in; versessen sein auf.

*

encage [in'keidʒ] *tr* (in e-n Käfig) einsperren.

encamp [in'kæmp] *tr* in e-m Lager unterbringen; unterbringen (*in tents* in Zelten); *itr* ein Lager aufschlagen; lagern; **~ment** [-mənt] (Feld-, Zelt-) Lager; Lagern *n*.

encase [in'keis] *tr* einschließen; einschachteln; verkleiden, umschließen, umhüllen; *arch* verschalen; *tech* einbauen; **~ment** [-mənt] Gehäuse *n*; Hülle *f*; Verschlag *m*; Verschalung *f*.

encash [in'kæʃ] *tr* einkassieren, einziehen; *(Wertpapier)* einlösen; **~ment** [-mənt] Einkassierung *f*, Inkasso *n*.

encaustic [en'kɔːstik] *a (Ton)* gebrannt; *s* Brandmalerei *f*.

encephal|ic [enke'fælik, -s-] *a* Gehirn-; **~itis** [enkefə'laitis] Gehirnentzündung *f*.

enchain [in'tʃein] *tr* in Ketten legen, anketten, fesseln *a. fig*; *fig* bannen; ganz in Anspruch nehmen.

enchant [in'tʃɑːnt] *tr* verzaubern, verhexen; bezaubern, entzücken; **~er** [-ə] Zauberer *m*; **~ing** [-iŋ] faszinierend; bezaubernd, entzückend; **~ment** [-mənt] Verzauberung *f*; Zauber *m*; (Gegenstand *m* des) Entzücken(s) *n*; **~ress** [-ris] Zauberin; bezaubernde Frau *f*.

enchase [in'tʃeis] *tr (Edelstein)* fassen; ziselieren; *(Zeichnung)* eingravieren.

encipher [in'saifə] *tr* verschlüsseln, chiffrieren.

encircle [in'səːkl] *tr* ein-, umschließen; umgeben, umstehen; einkreisen; umkreisen; *mil* einkesseln, umzingeln, umfassen; **~ment** [-mənt] Einschließung, Einkesselung; Einkreisung *f*; *policy of ~~* Einkreisungspolitik *f*.

enclave ['enkleiv] Enklave *f*.

enclos|e [in'klouz] *tr* umgeben, einschließen (*in* in); einfassen; einzäunen, ummauern; (hin)einstecken; *(e-m Brief)* beilegen, -fügen; enthalten; *tech* abschirmen; **~ed** [-d] *a* beigefügt, beigeschlossen, in der Anlage, anbei; *tech* geschlossen, gekapselt; *please find ~~* in der Anlage erhalten Sie; *~~ area* umbaute(r) Raum *m*; *~~ porch* Glasveranda *f*; **~ure** [in'klouʒə] Einfassung, Einzäunung, Umfassungsmauer *f*; eingehegte(s) Grundstück *n*; *(Brief)* Anlage *f*.

encode [in'koud] *tr* (nach e-m Kode) verschlüsseln.

encomi|ast [en'koumiæst] Lobredner *m*; **~um** [en'koumiəm] Lobrede *f*.

encompass [in'kʌmpəs] *tr* umgeben; ein-, umschließen, einkreisen; umzingeln; enthalten.

encore [ɔŋ'kɔː] *interj* noch einmal! *s* Dakaporuf *m*; Dakapo *n*, Wiederholung; Zugabe *f*; *tr (Stück* od *Künstler)* noch einmal hören wollen.

encounter [in'kauntə] *tr* (unerwartet) treffen, begegnen (*s.o.* jdm); zs.stoßen mit, (feindlich) entgegentreten (*s.o.* jdm); *(Widerstand)* finden; stoßen auf *(Schwierigkeiten)*; ins Auge fassen, auf sich nehmen; *(Abenteuer)* bestehen; *s* Begegnung *f*; Zs.prallen *n*, -stoß *m*; Treffen, Gefecht *n*.

encourag|e [in'kʌridʒ] *tr* ermutigen, Mut machen (*s.o.* jdm), er-, aufmuntern, zuversichtlich machen; bestärken in; unterstützen, helfen (*s.o.* jdm), begünstigen, fördern; *(Handel)* beleben; **~ement** [-mənt] Ermutigung, Aufmunterung; Unterstützung, Förderung *f*; Ansporn *m* (*to* für).

encroach [in'froutʃ] *itr* (unberechtigt) übergreifen (*on, upon* auf); eingreifen (*on, upon* in); beeinträchtigen, verletzen (*on, upon s.th.* etw); sich anmaßen, mißbrauchen (*on, upon s.th.* etw); über Gebühr, übermäßig in Anspruch nehmen (*on, upon s.th.* etw); **~ment** [-mənt] Über-, Eingriff *m*; Beeinträchtigung; Anmaßung; übermäßige Inanspruchnahme *f*.

encrust [in'krʌst] *tr* mit e-r Kruste überziehen *od* inkrustieren; verzieren; *itr* e-e Kruste bilden; verkrusten.

encumb|er [in'kʌmbə] *tr* (be)hindern, belasten, überladen; versperren, vollstopfen, anfüllen; *fig (mit Arbeit, Schulden)* überlasten; *(Grundstück mit e-r Hypothek)* belasten; verschulden; **~rance** [-rəns] Hindernis *n*; (Schulden-)Last; Belastung, Hypothek *f*; *without ~~* ohne Anhang, kinderlos; **~rancer** [-brənsə] Pfand-, Hypothekengläubiger *m*.

encyclop(a)edi|a [ensaiklo(u)'piːdjə] Enzyklopädie *f*, Konversationslexikon *n*; **~c** [-'piːdik] enzyklopädisch.

encyst [en'sist] *tr* einkapseln; *itr* sich verkapseln; **~ment** [-mənt] Verkapselung *f*.

end [end] *s* Ende *n*; Schluß; Zweck *m*, Ziel *n*, Absicht *f*; Ergebnis, Resultat *n*, Folge, Konsequenz *f*; *sl* Hinterteil *n*; *Am fam* Anteil *m*; *tr* beend(ig)en, abschließen; aufhören, Schluß machen, zu Ende kommen mit, schließen; beschließen, den Beschluß bilden *gen*; *itr* enden, aufhören, ausgehen, ein Ende machen *od* finden; zu Ende sein, aus sein; enden, sein Leben beschließen; *to ~ up (itr)* enden; schließlich werden zu; landen (*in* in); *to ~ up with* beenden; abschließen mit; *at the ~* am Ende, schließlich; *a few loose ~s* einige Kleinigkeiten; *for this ~* zu diesem Zweck; *~ for ~* umgedreht, umgekehrt; *in the ~* schließlich, am Ende; auf die Dauer; *no ~ (adv fam)* mächtig, gewaltig, sehr; *no ~ of* unendlich viel(e); sehr groß; endlos; *on ~* aufrecht, aufgerichtet; *(Kiste)* hochkant; hinterea., ohne Unterbrechung; einer nach dem andern; *~ on* mit dem Ende voran; *to an ~* zu e-m Zweck; *to the ~ that* zu dem Zweck, daß; damit; *to no ~* vergeblich; *~ to ~* mit den Enden anea., sich mit den Enden berührend; *without ~* endlos; *to be at an ~* zu Ende kommen; *to be at a loose ~ (fam)* gerade nichts (Besonderes) zu tun *od* vorhaben; sich verloren vorkommen; *to be at the ~ of o.'s patience* am Ende s-r Geduld sein; *to be at the ~ of o.'s tether* am Ende s-r Kraft sein; *to be at o.'s wits'* od *wit's ~* am Ende s-r Kunst sein; *to come to an ~* zu Ende gehen; *to come to a bad ~* ein schlimmes Ende finden; *to gain o.'s ~s* sein Ziel erreichen; *to go off the deep ~* sich unnötig aufregen; *to have s.th. at o.'s fingers' ~s* etwas parat haben; *to keep o.'s ~ up* seinen Mann stehen; *to make an ~ of, to put an ~ to* ein Ende, Schluß machen mit; *to make (both) ~s meet* gerade (mit s-m Gelde) auskommen; *to stand on ~* zu Berge stehen, sich sträuben; *to turn ~ for ~* umdrehen; *to ~ in smoke (fig)* wie das Hornberger Schießen ausgehen; *I have no ~ of it* es will bei mir nicht abreißen; *he gave us no ~ of trouble* wir hatten unsere liebe Not mit ihm; *there is no ~ of it* es nimmt kein Ende; *there's an ~ of it!* Schluß (damit)! fertig! abgemacht! basta! *the ~ justifies the means* der Zweck heiligt die Mittel; *all's well that ~s well* Ende gut, alles gut; *odds and ~s* alles mögliche, Kleinkram *m*; **~-all** Schluß *m* vom Ganzen; **~ elevation** Seitenriß *m*; **~ing** ['-iŋ] Ende *n*, Schluß; Tod *m*; *gram* Endung *f*; **~less** ['-lis] endlos, ohne Ende *a. pej tech*; unendlich; ewig; *~~ band, ribbon* Transport-, Förderband *n*; *~~ chain* Eimerkette *f*, Paternosterwerk *n*; *~~ cloth* Rundtuch *n*; *~~ cordrope* Förderseil *n*; **~lessness** ['-lisnis] Endlosigkeit, Unendlichkeit *f*; **~ man** letzte(r) Mann *m* (e-r Reihe); **~-moraine** *geol* Endmoräne *f*; **~ paper, leaf** *(Buch)* Vorsatzpapier, -blatt *n*; **~ product** Endergebnis; *chem* Endprodukt *n*; **~ways, ~wise** ['-weiz, '-waiz] *adv* mit dem Ende voran; aufrecht, aufgerichtet; der Länge nach.

endanger [in'deindʒə] *tr* gefährden, e-r Gefahr aussetzen, in Gefahr bringen.

endear [in'diə] *tr* sympathisch, wert, teuer machen; *to ~ o.s.* sich beliebt machen (*to* bei); **~ing** [-riŋ] gewinnend, einnehmend; reizend; zärtlich; **~ment** [-mənt] Zuneigung; Zärtlichkeit; Liebkosung *f*; *(term of ~~)* Kosewort *n*.

endeavo(u)r [in'devə] *itr* sich bemühen, sich Mühe geben, sich anstrengen, sich (eifrig) bestreben (*to do* zu tun); *s* Bemühung, Anstrengung *f* (*to do, at doing* etw zu tun); Streben *n* (*after* nach); Eifer *m*.

endemic(al) [en'demik(əl)] *bot zoo* einheimisch, endemisch; national, regional, lokal; **~ disease** *med* Endemie *f*.

endive ['endiv, *Am a.* -aiv] *bot Br* Endivie; *Am* Zichorie *f*.

endocarp ['endoukɑːp] *bot* Endokarp *n*.

endocrin|e ['endo(u)krain] *a physiol* endokrin; *~~ gland* endokrine Drüse *f*.

endogenous [en'dɔdʒinəs] *biol* endogen, innen entstehend.

endors|e [in'dɔːs] *tr* auf die Rückseite schreiben, (auf der Rückseite) unterschreiben; indossieren, durch Indossament übertragen, girieren; billigen, gutheißen; zustimmen, beipflichten (*s.th.* e-r S), sanktionieren; unterstützen, sich anschließen (*s.th.* an etw); **~ee** [endɔː'siː] *fin* Indossat; Girat(ar) *m*; **~ement** [-mənt] *fin* (Übertragung *f* durch) Indossament; Giro *n*; rückseitige(r) Vermerk *m*; Bestätigung, Billigung, Zustimmung, Sanktion; Unterstützung *f*; *(Versicherung)* Nachtrag *m*; *~~ of a bill* Wechselbürgschaft *f*; **~er** [-ə] Indossant; Girant, Überweiser; Wechselbürge *m*.

endosperm ['endo(u)spəːm] *bot* Endosperm, Nährgewebe *n (des Samens)*.

endow [in'dau] *tr* ausstatten, dotieren; aussteuern, beschenken; stiften; *fig* begaben; **~ment** [-mənt] Ausstattung, Dotierung; Stiftung; *pl* Begabung *f*, Talent *n*, Anlage *f*; *~~ fund* Stiftungsvermögen; *~~ insurance* Versicherung *f* auf den Erlebensfall.

endue [in'dju:] *tr* ausrüsten, bekleiden; begaben; *(mit Eigenschaften)* ausstatten; *pp* begabt (*with* mit).

endur|able [in'djuərəbl] erträglich, auszuhalten(d); **~ance** [-rəns] Dauer; Dauerhaftigkeit; Ausdauer, Beständigkeit, Geduld; (Stand-)Festigkeit; *(Kleidung)* Haltbarkeit, Strapazierfähigkeit; Lebensdauer; Schmerz-, Leidensfähigkeit; Mühsal, Härte; *aero* Flugdauer *f*; *past, beyond ~~* nicht auszuhalten(d), unerträglich; *~~ flight (aero)* Dauerflug *m*; *~~ limit* Ermüdungsgrenze *f*; *~~ run (sport)* Dauerlauf *m*; *~~ test (Material)* Dauerprüfung; Geduldsprobe *f*; **~e** [in'djuə] *tr* ertragen, aushalten, durchmachen, erdulden, erleiden (*to do, doing* zu tun); *(verneint)* ausstehen; *itr* Bestand haben; währen; aus-, durchhalten; **~ing** [-riŋ] beständig; dauerhaft; lange leidend, duldend.

enema ['enimə] *med* Einlauf *m*, Klistier *n*; Klistierspritze *f*.

enemy ['enimi] Feind *m*; *the ~ (mit pl)* der Feind; die Feindstreitkräfte *pl*; *a mil* feindlich; Feind-; *how goes the E~? (fam)* wie spät ist es? **~ action, activity** Feindtätigkeit, -einwirkung *f*; **~ alien** feindliche(r) Ausländer *m*; **~ contact** Feindberührung *f*; **~ fire** Feindbeschuß *m*; **~-occupied** *a* feindbesetzt; **~ property** Feindvermögen *n*; **~ resistance** Feindwiderstand *m*; **~ situation** Feindlage *f*; **~ territory** Feindgebiet *n*; **~ waters** *pl* Feindgewässer *n pl*.

energ|etic [enə'dʒetik] energisch, tatkräftig, energiegeladen, voller Energie; **~ize** ['enədʒaiz] *tr* Energie, Tatkraft geben *od* verleihen (*s.o.* jdm); anspornen; *el* Energie liefern an, speisen; unter Strom setzen; *itr* energisch, tatkräftig sein; **~umen** [enə:'gju:mən] Besessene(r); Fanatiker, Enthusiast *m*; **~y** ['enədʒi] Arbeitskraft, Tatkraft, Energie; Ausdruckskraft *f*, Nachdruck *m*; Wirksamkeit; *phys* Kraft, Energie, Arbeit(swert *m*) *f*; *pl* (persönliche) Kraft *f*, Kräfte *pl*; *~~ drop* Energieabfall *m*; *~~ expenditure* Energieaufwand *m*; *~~ supply* Energielieferung *f*; *~~ unit* Energieeinheit *f*.

enervat|e ['enə(:)veit] *tr* kraftlos machen, die (Lebens-)Kraft nehmen, rauben (*s.o.* jdm); entnerven, schwächen; ermüden *a. fig*; **~ion** [enə(:)'veiʃən] Entkräftung, Schwächung, Entnervung; Kraftlosigkeit, Schwäche, Lebensuntüchtigkeit *f*.

enfeeble [in'fi:bl] *tr* schwächen, entkräften.

enfeoff [in'fef] *tr* belehnen (*with* mit); **~ment** [-mənt] Belehnung *f*; Lehnsbrief *m*; Lehen *n*; Lehnsbesitz *m*.

enfilad|e [enfi'leid] *mil* Längsbestreichung *f*; Flankenfeuer *n*; Linie *f* (von Anlagen *od* Menschen); *tr* bestreichen.

enfold [in'fould] *tr* (zs.)falten; einwickeln, -packen, -hüllen (*in, with* in); umarmen, -fassen, -schließen.

enforce [in'fɔ:s] *tr* bekräftigen, stützen; (be)zwingen; zum Gehorsam zwingen; erzwingen (*upon s.o.* von jdm); (mit Gewalt) durchsetzen, durchdrücken, durchführen; auferlegen (*upon s.o.* jdm); zur Anerkennung bringen, Anerkennung verschaffen (*s.th.* e-r S), zur Geltung bringen; geltend machen; einklagen; vollstrecken; wirksam, rechtskräftig machen; **~able** [-əbl] vollstreckbar, erzwingbar, klagbar; **~ment** [-mənt] Bekräftigung; Erzwingung; (gewaltsame) Durchsetzung; *(Urteil)* Vollstreckung; *(Gesetz)* Anwendung; *(Forderung)* Geltendmachung *f*; *~~ officer* Vollstreckungs-, Überwachungsbeamte(r) *m*; *~~ order* Vollstreckungsbefehl *m*.

enfranchise [in'fræntʃaiz] *tr (Sklaven)* freilassen; befreien *a. fig*; für frei erklären; das Bürgerrecht gewähren, das Wahlrecht zuerkennen (*s.o.* jdm); *(Gemeinde)* zur Stadt erheben; **~ment** [-izmənt] Freilassung; Gewährung *f* des Bürger-, Zuerkennung *f* des Wahlrechts; Einbürgerung *f*.

engag|e [in'geidʒ] *tr* verpflichten; *(sein Wort)* verpfänden; an-, einstellen, engagieren; *(als Rechtsanwalt)* nehmen; *mar* (an)heuern; *(Zimmer)* mieten, belegen, reservieren; *(Platz)* bestellen, belegen; *(Kapital)* investieren; *(in e-e S)* verwickeln, hineinziehen, -bringen; dazu bringen; anziehen, einnehmen, reizen; in Anspruch nehmen; *(die Aufmerksamkeit)* fesseln; *mil* zum Kampf stellen, ins Gefecht verwickeln, angreifen; *(Truppen)* einsetzen; *arch* im Verband mauern; *tech* einrücken, kuppeln; *itr* sich verpflichten, sich festlegen, sein Wort (daraufl) geben (*to do* zu tun); Versprechungen machen; sich einlassen (*in* auf), sich abgeben (*with* mit); auf sich nehmen (*in s.th.* etw); sich beschäftigen, sich befassen (*with* mit); sich betätigen; sich werfen (*in* auf); *mil* ins Gefecht kommen; *tech* inea.greifen; eingreifen, einrasten; *to ~~ o.s.* sich verpflichten; sich verloben (*to* mit); *to ~~ for* garantieren, verbürgen; bürgen, die Verantwortung übernehmen für; **~ed** [-d] *a* verpflichtet; verlobt; beschäftigt, nicht abkömmlich, nicht zu sprechen(d); in Anspruch genommen; *(Platz)* belegt, besetzt; *tele* besetzt; *mil* im Gefecht; *arch* verbunden; *tech* gekuppelt; *to be ~~* beschäftigt sein (*in doing s.th.* mit etw); *to become ~~ to s.o.* sich mit jdm verloben; *~~ couple* Brautpaar *n*; *~~ signal (tele)* Besetztzeichen *n*; **~ement** [-mənt] Verpflichtung, Verbindlichkeit, Versprechung *f*; Verlöbnis *n*, Verlobung (*to* mit); Abmachung, Verabredung, Vereinbarung; Beschäftigung, (An-)Stellung, Stelle *f*, Engagement; *tech* Einkuppeln, Einrücken; *mil* Gefecht *n*, Kampf(handlung *f*); Einsatz *m*; *meist pl fin com* (finanzielle) Verpflichtungen, Verbindlichkeiten *f pl*; *without ~~* unverbindlich, freibleibend, ohne Gewähr; *to meet, to carry out o.'s ~~s* s-n Verpflichtungen nachkommen; *I have a previous ~~* ich bin schon verabredet; *~~ book* Terminkalender *m*; *~~ ring* Verlobungsring *m*; **~ing** [-iŋ] anziehend, einnehmend, gewinnend, gefällig, reizend, reizvoll.

engender [in'dʒendə] *tr* hervorrufen, verursachen, veranlassen, zustande bringen, ins Leben rufen, hervorbringen, erzeugen, wecken.

engin|e ['endʒin] (Kraft-)Maschine *f*; (Benzin-)Motor *m*; Triebwerk *n*; *rail* Lokomotive *f*; *fig* Mittel, Werkzeug *n*; *to start, to shut off the ~~* den Motor anlassen, abstellen; *fire ~~* Feuerlöschwagen *m*; *internal combustion ~~* Verbrennungsmotor *m*; *steam-~~* Dampfmaschine *f*; *~~ block* Motorblock *m*; *~~ bonnet, (Am) hood* Motorhaube *f*; *~~ brake* Motorbremse *f*; *~~ cowling (aero)* Triebwerksgehäuse *n*; *~~ crankshaft* Motorwelle *f*; *~~ damage, failure* Motorschaden *m*; *~~-driven (a)* motorgetrieben; *~~ driver* Maschinist; *Br* Lok(omotiv)führer *m*; *~~ fitter* Maschinenschlosser *m*; *~~-house* Lok(omotiv)schuppen *m*; Maschinenhalle *f*; *~~ number* Motornummer *f*; *~~ oil* Motorenöl *n*; *~~ operator* Maschinist *m*; *~~ power, performance, output* Motorleistung *f*; *~~ room* Maschinenraum *m*; *~~ speed, r.p.m.* Motordrehzahl *f*; *~~ test bench* Motorprüfstand *m*; *~~ trouble* Motorstörung *f*; **~eer** [endʒi'niə] *s* Ingenieur, Techniker; Maschinist; *mil* Pionier; Bauoffizier; *Am* Lok(omotiv)führer *m*; *tr* (als Ingenieur) planen, konstruieren, bauen, leiten; *fig fam* geschickt einfädeln, deichseln, durchsetzen, organisieren, in Gang setzen; *itr* als Ingenieur arbeiten; *chief ~~* Oberingenieur *m*; *electrical ~~* Elektrotechniker *m*; *ship's, naval ~~* Schiffsingenieur *m*; *~~ battalion* Pionierbataillon *n*; **~eering** [endʒi'niəriŋ] *s* Ingenieurwesen *n*, Technik *f*; *(mechanical ~~)* Maschinenbau *m*; *a* technisch; *automotive ~~* Kraftfahrzeugtechnik *f*; *civil ~~* Tiefbau *m*; *electrical ~~* Elektrotechnik *f*; *marine ~~* Schiffsbau *m*; *~~ college* Technikum *n*, Ingenieurschule *f*; *~~ department* technische Abteilung *f*; *~~ industry* Maschinenindustrie *f*; *~~ manager* technische(r) Direktor *m*; *~~ staff* technische(r) Stab *m*; *~~ steel* Baustahl *m*; *~~ works (pl a. mit sing)* Maschinenfabrik *f*.

engird [in'gə:d] *tr* (um)gürten, umgeben, einschließen, einfassen.

England ['iŋglənd] England *n*.

English ['iŋgliʃ] *a* englisch; *s (das)* Englisch(e), *die* englische Sprache; *typ* Mittel *f (14 Punkte)*; *the ~ (pl)* die Engländer; *in plain ~* schlicht u. einfach *(ausdrücken)*; *fig* unverblümt; *he's ~* er ist Engländer; **~man** ['-mən] *pl* **~men** Engländer *m*; **~woman** ['-wumən] *pl ~women* ['-wimin] Engländerin *f*.

engorge [in'gɔ:dʒ] *tr* (gierig) verschlingen; *med* verstopfen.

engraft [in'gra:ft] *tr (Schößling)* pfropfen (*into, upon* auf); *fig* einpflanzen, fest verankern, einprägen (*in* in); einverleiben (*into* in).

engrain [in'grein] *tr* in der Faser färben; *meist fig* fest einprägen (*in s.o.* jdm); **~ed** [-d] *a* fest verwurzelt, eingefleischt; unverbesserlich.

engrav|e [in'greiv] *tr* (ein)gravieren, (ein)ritzen (*on* in); stechen, radieren, (in Holz) schneiden; *fig* fest einprägen (*on, upon* in); **~er** [-ə] Graveur, (Kupfer-, Stahl-)Stecher, Radierer, (Holz-)Schneider *m*; **~ing** [-iŋ] Gravieren, Stechen, Radieren, Schneiden *n*; bearbeitete Platte *f*; (Kupfer-, Stahl-)Stich *m*, Radierung *f*; *(wood ~~)* Holzschnitt, -stich *m*; *~~ needle* Radiernadel *f*.

engross [in'grous] *tr* ins reine, in Reinschrift schreiben; in gesetz-, vorschriftsmäßiger, vorgeschriebener Form abfassen *od* ausdrücken; ganz in Anspruch nehmen; ausschließlich beschäftigen; an sich reißen; *com* monopolisieren; *to be ~ed* ganz vertieft sein (*in* in); ausschließlich beschäftigt sein (*in* mit), gefesselt sein (*in* von); **~er** [-ə] Schreiber, Kanzlist *m*; **~ing** [-iŋ] stark in Anspruch nehmend, fesselnd, sehr interessant; *~~-hand* Kanzleischrift *f*; **~ment** [-mənt] Ausfertigung, Reinschrift (e-r Urkunde); (völlige) Inanspruchnahme *f*.

engulf [in'gʌlf] *tr* (wie) in e-n Abgrund stürzen; verschlingen; *fig* überwältigen.

enhance [in'ha:ns] *tr* steigern; erhöhen, vergrößern, vermehren, verstärken, verbessern, verschönern, wertvoller machen.

enigma [i'nigmə] Rätsel *n fig*; **~tic(al)** [enig'mætik(əl)] rätselhaft, *(anscheinend)* unerklärlich, mysteriös, dunkel, geheimnisvoll.
enjoin [in'dʒɔin] *tr* (an)befehlen, anordnen, auferlegen (*on s.o.* jdm); einschärfen (*on s.o. to do* jdm zu tun); *Am* verbieten (*s.o. from doing* jdm, etw zu tun); gerichtlich untersagen.
enjoy [in'dʒɔi] *tr* genießen; sich erfreuen (*s.th.* an etw, e-r S); sich freuen (*seeing* zu sehen); *to ~ o.s.* sich gut unterhalten, sich amüsieren; *to ~ credit, s.o.'s confidence* Kredit, jds Vertrauen genießen; *to ~ good health* sich e-r guten Gesundheit erfreuen; *how are you ~ing London?* wie gefällt es Ihnen in London? **~able** [-əbl] angenehm, unterhaltsam, genußreich; **~ment** [-mənt] Freude *f*, Spaß; Genuß *m*; angenehme Unterhaltung *f*; *jur* Genuß, Besitz *m*; *to be in the ~~ of good health, great wealth* im Genuß e-r guten Gesundheit, e-s großen Reichtums sein; *to take ~~ in* Freude, Spaß haben an.

*

enkindle [in'kindl] *tr fig (Leidenschaft)* entzünden, entflammen.
enlace [in'leis] *tr* umschlingen, -strikken; inea. verschlingen; verflechten.
enlarge [in'lɑːdʒ] *tr itr* (sich) vergrößern, (sich) verbreitern, (sich) erweitern, (sich) (aus)dehnen; ausweiten, erhöhen; *tr phot* vergrößern; *Am* freilassen, befreien; *to ~ (up)on* sich *(in Rede* od *Schrift)* verbreiten über, näher eingehen auf, sich auslassen über; **~ment** [-mənt] Vergrößerung *bes. phot*; Verbreiterung, Erweiterung, Ausdehnung *f*; Zusatz *m*, Erweiterung *f*; *arch* Anbau *m*; *Am* Entlassung *f*; **~r** [-ə] *phot* Vergrößerungsapparat *m*.
enlighten [in'laitn] *tr fig* erleuchten, aufklären, belehren (*on, as to* über); **~ed** [-d] *a* aufgeklärt, vorurteilsfrei, -los; **~ing** [-niŋ] aufschlußreich; **~ment** [-mənt] Aufklärung *f*; *the E~* die Aufklärung.
enlist [in'list] *tr* (in e-e Liste) eintragen; *mil* anwerben; *(Truppen)* ausheben; an-, einstellen; *mar* anmustern; werben, gewinnen (*in* für); *(Hilfe)* in Anspruch nehmen; interessieren (*for* an); *itr* sich anwerben lassen, Soldat werden; sich freiwillig melden (*in the navy* zur Marine); sich einsetzen, eintreten (*in* für), unterstützen (*in s.th.* etw); *to ~ s.o.'s services* jds Dienste in Anspruch nehmen; *~ed man (Am)* Soldat *m*; *pl* Unteroffiziere *m pl* u. Mannschaften *f pl*; **~ment** [-mənt] Anwerbung, Einstellung; (Militär-)Dienstzeit *f*.
enliven [in'laivn] *tr* beleben, aufmuntern, anfeuern; *fig* er-, aufheitern.
enmesh [in'meʃ] *tr fig* verstricken, umgarnen; in e-m Netz fangen.
enmity ['enmiti] Feindschaft, Feindseligkeit *f*, Haß *m* (*of, against* gegen); *at ~ with* in Feindschaft mit.
ennoble [i'noubl] *tr* adeln, in den Adelsstand erheben, den Adel verleihen (*s.o.* jdm); *fig* adeln; **~ment** [-mənt] Erhebung *f* in den Adelsstand; *fig* Veredelung *f*.
enorm|ity [i'nɔːmiti] Ungeheuerlichkeit *f*; Greuel *m*; Gemeinheit *f*; **~ous** [i'nɔːməs] riesig, enorm, gewaltig, ungeheuer.
enough [i'nʌf] *adv* genug, genügend, zur Genüge; *a* aus-, hinreichend, hinlänglich, genügend; *s* Genüge *f*; *good ~!* sehr gut! *likely ~* sehr, höchstwahrscheinlich; *more than ~* mehr als genug, wirklich genug; *quite ~* wahrhaft genug; *true ~* nur zu wahr; *sure ~* freilich, gewiß, allerdings; *surprisingly ~* überraschenderweise; *well ~* ziemlich *od* ganz gut, ganz ordentlich, nicht schlecht; sehr, recht gut; *~ and to spare* vollauf, übergenug, reichlich; *to be ~* genug sein, genügen, langen; *be kind ~ to come* sei so gut und komm! *I had ~ to do* ich hatte genug, alle Händevoll zu tun; *that's quite ~* mir langt's jetzt; *he's good ~ in his way* er ist nicht übel; *the best is just good ~* das Beste ist gerade gut genug.
enplane [in'plein] *itr* das Flugzeug besteigen.
enquir|e, ~y *s. inquire.*
enrage [in'reidʒ] *tr* wütend, rasend machen; **~d** [-d] *a* wütend, aufgebracht, entrüstet (*at, by, with* über).
enrapt [in'ræpt] *a* hingerissen, entzückt; **~ure** [-tʃə] *tr* hinreißen, bezaubern, entzücken.
enrich [in'ritʃ] *tr* reicher machen *a. fig*; veredeln; *fig* bereichern, befruchten, steigern, erhöhen, wertvoller, schöner machen, verschönen; verschönern, (aus)schmücken, verzieren, ausstatten; *(den Boden)* düngen; *(mit Vitaminen, Mineralien)* anreichern; **~ment** [-mənt] Bereicherung, Steigerung; Befruchtung; Verschönerung, Ausschmückung; Düngung; Anreicherung *f*.
enrol(l) [in'roul] *tr (in e-e Stammrolle, e-e Liste, ein Register)* eintragen, registrieren; verzeichnen (*in* in); *mil (a. Arbeitskräfte)* anwerben; *mar* anmustern; *itr Am* sich registrieren, sich einschreiben, sich immatrikulieren lassen; Mitglied werden; *mil* sich verpflichten; *to ~ o.s.* sich anwerben lassen; **~ment** [-mənt] Registrierung *f*; Register *n*, Listen *f pl*; Beitrittserklärung; Anwerbung, Einstellung; *mil* Meldung, Verpflichtung *f*.
en route [ɑ̃ːn 'ruːt] auf dem Wege (*to, for* nach).
ensconce [in'skɔns] *tr* verstecken, verbergen, (be)schirmen, decken; *to ~ o.s.* sich bequem, behaglich niederlassen.
ensemble [ɑ̃ːn'sɑ̃ːmbl] *das* Ganze, *die* Gesamtheit; *der* Gesamteindruck; *mus* Zs.spiel; *theat* Ensemble; Komplet *n (Kleid mit Mantel* od *Jacke)*.
enshrine [in'ʃrain] *tr* in e-n Schrein einschließen; sicher verwahren; wie s-n Augapfel hüten; in sich tragen.
enshroud [in'ʃraud] *tr* ein-, verhüllen (*in* in); *fig* verschleiern.
ensign ['ensain, *mar* 'ensn] (Rang-) Abzeichen *n*; Fahne, Flagge *f*; *Br hist* Fähnrich, Kornett *m*; ['ensn] *Am* Leutnant *m* zur See; *white, red ~* Flagge *f* der britischen Kriegs-, Handelsmarine.
ensil|age ['ensilidʒ] *s* Silospeicherung *f*; Grün-, Süßpreß-, Gärfutter *n*; *tr u.* **~e** [in'sail] *tr* in e-m Silo einlagern; zu Süßpreßfutter verarbeiten.
enslave [in'sleiv] *tr* in die Sklaverei verkaufen; versklaven; knechten, unterjochen, unterdrücken, beherrschen; *fig* fesseln, binden, verstricken; **~ment** [-mənt] Versklavung; Knechtung; Knechtschaft, Unterjochung; sklavische Bindung *f* (*to* an); **~r** [-ə] Unterdrücker, Beherrscher(in *f*) *m*.
ensnare [in'snɛə] *tr* (in e-r Schlinge) fangen; *fig* verstricken, umgarnen, betören, verleiten, verführen.
ensue [in'sjuː] *itr* (unmittelbar) folgen, nachfolgen; folgen, sich ergeben (*from* aus); die Folge, das Ergebnis sein (*from* von); **~ing** [-iŋ] (darauf) folgend; Folge-; nächst; *~~ age(s pl)* Nachwelt *f*.
ensure [in'ʃuə] *tr* (ver)sichern, sicherstellen (*against, from* gegen); gewährleisten, garantieren (*s.th.* etwas); schützen (*against* gegen); *fin* versichern (*against, from* gegen).
entabl|ature [en'tæblətʃə] (von Säulen getragenes) Gebälk *n*; **~ement** [in'teiblmənt] Gebälk *n*; Deckplatte *f*.
entail [in'teil] *tr* nach sich ziehen, erfordern, zur Folge haben, mit sich bringen (*on* für); aufbürden (*on s.o.* jdm); *jur* als Fideikommiß vererben (*on s.o.* jdm); *s* festgelegte Erbfolge *f*; *(~ed inheritance)* Fideikommiß, Majorat; *fig* unveräußerliche(s) Erbe *n*.
entangle [in'tæŋgl] *tr* verwickeln; *fig* verwirren, verwirrt machen, in Verlegenheit bringen; hineinziehen (*in* in); verstricken (*in* in); *to ~ o.s., to get ~d* sich verwickeln, sich verwirren, sich verfangen (*in* in); **~ment** [-mənt] Verwick(e)lung; *fig* Verwirrung, Verlegenheit; Liebesaffäre *f*; *pl mil* Verhau *m* od *n*; Sperre *f*; *(barbed) wire ~~* (Stachel-)Drahtverhau *m* od *n*.
enter ['entə] *tr* betreten; *(Wagen)* besteigen, einsteigen in; einziehen in; einfahren in; eindringen in, durchbohren; hineinstellen, -setzen, -legen, einfügen; einschreiben, -tragen, auf die Liste setzen *gen*, zu Protokoll geben; *com* buchen; anmelden (*for* für); *(in die Schule)* führen; *(Wörter)* aufführen; eintreten in, Mitglied werden *gen od* in, aufgenommen werden in; aufnehmen, zulassen, Eintritt verschaffen (*s.o.* jdm); anfangen, beginnen, in Angriff nehmen; *(Stelle)* antreten; *(Beruf)* einschlagen, ergreifen; *(e-e Praxis)* anfangen; abrichten, dressieren, *(Pferd)* einreiten; (zur Verzollung) deklarieren; *jur (Prozeß)* anstrengen, anhängig machen; *(Klage)* einreichen (*against* gegen); *itr* eintreten, hereinkommen; einsteigen; eindringen; *(Schiff)* einlaufen; sich anmelden (*for* für); sich melden (*for* zu); *to ~ the army* Soldat werden; *to ~ the Church* in den geistlichen Stand treten; *to ~ into details* auf Einzelheiten eingehen; *to ~ for an examination* sich e-r Prüfung unterziehen, sich zur Prüfung melden; *to ~ a judg(e)ment (jur)* ein Urteil fällen; *to ~ the lists* in die Schranken treten (*for* für; *against* gegen); *to ~ o.'s name* sich eintragen, -schreiben (lassen); *to ~ a protest* Einspruch, Protest erheben, Verwahrung einlegen; *it never ~ed my head* das ist mir nie in den Sinn gekommen, eingefallen; *to ~* **into** *itr* sich einlassen in, auf; eingehen auf; teilnehmen an; hineinkommen in; e-n Teil bilden *gen*, e-e Rolle spielen bei, Einfluß haben auf; Anteil nehmen an; *(Abkommen, Vereinbarung)* treffen; *(Vertrag, Geschäft)* (ab)schließen; *(Vergleich)* eingehen; *(e-m Bündnis)* beitreten; *to ~ into correspondence with* in Briefwechsel treten mit; *to ~ into an engagement* e-e Verpflichtung übernehmen; *to ~ into relations with* in Beziehungen treten, Beziehungen anknüpfen zu; *to ~* **up** *tr* vollständig verbuchen; *to ~* **(up)on** *tr* anfangen, beginnen, in Angriff nehmen; *(Laufbahn)* einschlagen; *(Besitz, Erbe)* antreten; eingehen auf; *(Thema)* anschneiden; *he ~ed (upon) his 8th year* ist gerade 8 Jahre alt (geworden); **~ing** ['-riŋ] *s* Eintritt *m*; Auftreten, Erscheinen *n*; Antritt *m* (e-r Stelle); Verbuchung; Eintragung, -schrei-

bung; Zulassung; *(Universität)* Immatrikulation *f*; *attr* Eintritts-, Eingangs-; ~~ *clerk* Buchhalter *m*.

enter|ic [en'terik] *a* Eingeweide-; Darm-; *s (~~ fever)* Typhus *m*; **~itis** [entə'raitis] (*bes.* Dünn-)Darmentzündung *f*; Darmkatarrh *m*.

enterpris|e ['entəpraiz] Unternehmen, Vorhaben *n*, Pläne *m pl*, Versuch *m*; Unternehmen *n*, Unternehmung *f*, Geschäft *n*, Betrieb *m*; *(spirit of ~~)* Unternehmungsgeist, Wagemut *m*; *insurance* ~~ Versicherungsgesellschaft *f*; *manufacturing* ~~ Fabrikationsbetrieb *m*; *private* ~~ Privatunternehmen *n*, -betrieb *m*; Privatwirtschaft *f*; freie(s) Unternehmertum *n*; ~~ *value* Unternehmenswert *m*; **~ing** ['-iŋ] unternehmend, unternehmungslustig, wagemutig.

entertain [entə'tein] *tr* unterhalten, (geistig) beschäftigen, belustigen; bewirten; einladen (*at dinner* zum Essen); sich *(geistig)* befassen mit; *(Angebot)* in Betracht ziehen; *(Besprechungen)* halten; *(Gedanken, Pläne, Verdacht)* hegen; *(Ansicht)* haben, vertreten; *(Vorschlag)* in Erwägung ziehen; *(Risiko)* tragen, übernehmen; *itr* Gäste haben, Gesellschaften geben; *they ~ a great deal* sie haben sehr oft Gäste; **~er** [-ə] Vortragende(r); Vortragskünstler; Gastgeber *m*; **~ing** [-iŋ] unterhaltend, unterhaltsam; **~ment** [-mənt] Unterhaltung, Belustigung *f*, Vergnügen *n*, Spaß *m*; Bewirtung, Aufnahme (e-s Gastes); Einladung, Gesellschaft; Repräsentation; *mus* Darbietung; *theat* Aufführung *f*; ~~ *allowance* Aufwandsentschädigung *f*; ~~ *expenses (pl)* Bewirtungsspesen *pl*; ~~ *tax* Vergnügungssteuer *f*.

enthral(l) [in'θrɔ:l] *tr fig* fesseln, (für sich) einnehmen, bezaubern; **~ment** [-mənt] *fig* Bezauberung *f*.

enthron|e [in'θroun] *tr* auf den Thron setzen; *rel* inthronisieren; *fig* hochschätzen, verehren; **~ement** [-mənt] Inthronisation; *fig* hohe Verehrung *f*.

enthus|e [in'θju:z] *itr fam* begeistert, voller Begeisterung sein; schwärmen (*about* für, von); **~iasm** [in'θju:ziæzm] Begeisterung *f*, Enthusiasmus *m*; (helles) Entzücken *n*; **~iast** [-iæst] Schwärmer, Enthusiast; begeisterte(r) Anhänger, große(r) Verehrer, Bewunderer *m* (*about* gen); **~iastic** [inθju:si'æstik] begeistert, leidenschaftlich eingenommen (*at, about* für).

entic|e [in'tais] *tr* (an-, ver)locken, verführen, verleiten (*into s.th.* zu etw; *to do, into doing* zu tun); *to ~~ away* weglocken, abspenstig machen (*from* von); *com* abwerben; **~ement** [-mənt] Verlockung, Verführung, Verleitung *f*; Reiz *m*; Lockmittel *n*; **~ing** [-iŋ] verlockend, verführerisch, reizend.

entire [in'taiə] *a* ganz, vollständig, völlig, gesamt, total; aus einem Stück, ungeteilt, fortlaufend; unversehrt, unbeeinträchtigt; unverschnitten; *(Zustimmung)* uneingeschränkt, rückhaltlos; *(Vertrauen)* voll; *s das* Ganze; Ganzheit *f*; Hengst *m*; **~ly** [-li] *adv* gänzlich, durchaus, völlig, vollkommen; entschieden; ~~ *different* grundverschieden; **~ty** [-ti] Ganzheit, Vollständigkeit, Gesamtheit *f*; *das* Ganze; *jur* Alleinbesitz *m*; *in its ~~* in s-r Gesamtheit, in vollem Umfang.

entitl|e [in'taitl] *tr* betiteln, nennen; berechtigen (*to* zu); e-n Anspruch, ein Anrecht geben (*to* auf); das Recht geben (*to do* zu tun); **~ed** [-d] *a* berechtigt; *to be ~~ to* Anspruch, ein Anrecht haben auf, berechtigt sein zu; ~~ *to dispose, to inherit, to a pension, to sign, to vote* verfügungs-, erb-, pensions-, zeichnungs-, stimmberechtigt.

entity ['entiti] (Da-)Sein *n*, Existenz, Wirklichkeit, Ding-, Wesenhaftigkeit *f*; *das* Seiende, Ding an sich, Wesen *n*; Einheit *f*; *legal ~* juristische Person *f*.

entomb [in'tu:m] *tr* begraben, beerdigen, bestatten; ein Grab sein für; **~ment** [-mənt] Begräbnis *n*, Beerdigung, Bestattung *f*.

entomolog|ic(al) [entəmə'lɔdʒik(əl)] entomologisch, insektenkundlich; **~ist** [entə'mɔlədʒist] Entomologe *m*; **~y** [entə'mɔlədʒi] Insektenkunde *f*.

entr'acte ['ɔntrækt] Zwischenakt(smusik *f*) *m*, (Tanz-)Einlage *f*.

entrails ['entreilz] *pl* Eingeweide *n (pl)*; *fig das* Innere.

entrain [in'train] *tr (Truppen)* ein-, verladen; *itr* ein-, in den Zug steigen; **~ing** [-iŋ] *mil* Verladen *n*, Verladung *f*; ~~ *point* Verladeplatz *m*; ~~ *station* Verladebahnhof *m*; ~~ *table* Verladeplan *m*; **~ment** = *~ing*.

entrance 1. ['entrəns] Eintritt; *theat* Auftritt; Zugang (*into* zu); Eingang(stür *f*) *m*; Einfahrt *f*, Tor *n*; (Amts-)Antritt *m* (*into, upon* gen); Aufnahme (*to* in); Zulassung *f*; Eintritt(sgeld *n*) *m*; Eintragung, -schreibung; Meldung *f*; *on ~ into office* beim Dienstantritt; *to make o.'s ~* eintreten; *no ~!* keine Einfahrt! *main ~* Haupteingang *m*; *~* **duty** Einfuhrzoll *m*; *~* **examination** Aufnahmeprüfung *f*; *~* **fee** Eintrittsgeld *n*; Aufnahme-, Einschreibgebühr *f*; *~* **form** Anmeldeformular *n*; *~* **hall** Vorhalle *f*; Hausflur *m*; *~* **money** Eintrittsgeld *n*; **2.** [in'trɑ:ns] *tr* fort-, hin-, mitreißen, überwältigen (*with* vor); bezaubern, entzücken.

entrant ['entrənt] Eintretende(r) *m*; neue(s) Mitglied *n*; (Berufs-)Anfänger, Neuling; *(Wettkampf)* Teilnehmer, Bewerber *m*.

entrap [in'træp] *tr* (in e-r Falle) fangen; *fig* überlisten, hereinlegen; verführen (*to s.th.* zu etw; *into doing* zu tun).

entreat [in'tri:t] *tr (a. itr: to ~ of)* ernstlich, dringend bitten, anflehen, ersuchen (*for* um); *(Sache)* erbitten, erflehen; **~y** [-i] ernste, dringende Bitte *f*, Ersuchen, Flehen *n*; *at his ~~* auf s-e Bitte (hin).

entrée ['ɔntrei] Zulassung *f*; Zugang *m* (*of* zu); Eintrittsgeld; Zwischen-, *Am* Hauptgericht *n (außer Braten)*.

entremets ['ɔntrəmei] *(Küche)* Zwischengericht *n*.

entrench [in'trentʃ] *tr* mit e-m (Schützen-)Graben umgeben; verschanzen; *(Lager)* befestigen; *fig*: *to be ~ed* (fest) verankert, eingewurzelt sein (*in* in); *itr* übergreifen, eingreifen (*upon* in); *to ~ o.s.* sich eingraben; *fig* sich festsetzen; **~ment** [-mənt] Verschanzung *f*, Schanzwerk *n*; *pl* Schützengräben *m pl*.

entrepôt ['ɔntrəpou] Lagerhaus *n*, Stapelplatz *m*, Transitlager *n*; Niederlage *f*.

entrepreneur [ɔntrəprə'nə:] Unternehmer; Veranstalter *m*.

entresol ['ɔntrəsɔl] Zwischengeschoß *n*.

entrust [in'trʌst] *tr* betrauen (*s.o. with s.th.* jdn mit e-r S); anvertrauen (*s.th. to s.o.* jdm etw).

entry ['entri] Eintritt *m*, Einfahrt *f*; (feierlicher) Einzug; Einmarsch; *bes. Am* Eingang(stür *f*) *m*; *(~way)* Einfahrt; Eingangshalle *f*, Flur; *theat* Auftritt; Durchgang; *Am* Anfang, Beginn *m*; Mündung *f* (e-s Flusses); Vermerk, Eintrag(ung *f*) *m*; Buchung(sposten *m*) *f*, Posten *m*; *(Lexikon)* Stichwort *n*; Anmeldung; Zollerklärung, -deklaration; *jur* Besitzergreifung, Inbesitznahme *f* (*upon s.th.* e-r S); Eindringen *n*; *Am* Antritt *m*; Namensliste; Liste *f* der Bewerber; Bewerber *m (bei e-m Wettkampf)*; *as per ~* laut Eintrag; *upon ~* nach Eingang; *to make an ~ of s.th.* etw buchen; *to make an ~ in* eintragen in; *no ~* kein Zugang! *credit, debit ~* Gut-, Lastschrift *f*; *unlawful ~* Hausfriedensbruch *m*; *~* **fee** Eintritts-, *sport* Nenngeld *n*; *~* **form** Anmelde-, Nennungs- *(sport)*, Antragsformular *n*; *~* **permit** Einreiseerlaubnis *f*; *~* **regulations** *pl* Einreisebestimmungen *f pl*; *~* **test** Zulassungsprüfung *f*; *~* **visa** Einreisevisum *n*.

entwine [in'twain] *tr* ver-, durchweben (*with* mit); umschlingen, umwinden (*with* mit); winden (*about, around* um).

enucleat|e [i'nju:klieit] *tr (Nuß, Mandel)* schälen; *(Geschwür)* ausschälen; *fig* klarmachen, erklären, erläutern.

enumerat|e [i'nju:məreit] *tr* (auf-) zählen; einzeln aufführen; genau durchgehen; **~ion** [-'reiʃən] (Auf-) Zählung; (genaue) Liste *f*.

enunciat|e [i'nʌnsieit, -ʃi-] *tr* endgültig formulieren, abschließend aussagen; ankündigen, verkünd(ig)en, aussprechen; *(Behauptung)* aufstellen; *itr* deutlich sprechen; **~ion** [-'eiʃən] Aussage, Formulierung; Erklärung, Ankündigung, Verkündung; Aussprache *f*.

envelop [in'veləp] *tr* einwickeln, -hüllen; einschließen, umfassen, umklammern *a. mil*; verstecken, verbergen, verhüllen; **~e** ['enviloup] Decke, Hülle; *bot* Haut, Hülse, Schale *f*; (Brief-)Umschlag *m*; *aero* Ballonhülle *f*; *mil* Geschoßmantel *m*; Feldschanze; *(~~ curve)* Mantelkurve *f*; *to put in an ~~* in e-n Briefumschlag stecken; *pay ~~* Lohntüte *f*; *window ~~* Fenster(brief)umschlag *m*; ~~ *opener* Brieföffner *m*; **~ing** [-iŋ] einhüllend; umfassend; ~~ *movement (mil)* Umfassungsbewegung *f*; **~ment** [in'veləpmənt] Einwickeln *n*; Hülle; *mil* Umfassung, Umklammerung *f*.

envenom [in'venəm] *tr* vergiften *a. fig*; *fig* verbittern.

envi|able ['enviəbl] beneidens-, begehrenswert; **~er** ['enviə] Neider, Neidhammel *m*; **~ous** ['enviəs] mißgünstig, neidisch (*of* auf).

environ [in'vaiərən] *tr* umgeben, umfassen; einschließen (*with* mit); umringen, umzingeln; **~ment** [-mənt] Umgebung; *biol* Umwelt *f*; *psychol* Milieu *n*; **~mental** [-'mentəl] *a* Umwelt-, Milieu-; ~~ *conditions, factors (pl biol)* Umweltbedingungen *f pl*, -faktoren *m pl*; ~~ *influences (pl)* Umwelteinflüsse *m pl*; **~s** ['envirənz, in'vaiərənz] *s pl* Umgebung *(e-r Stadt usw)*, Umgegend *f*, Vororte *m pl*.

envisage [in'vizidʒ] *tr* ins Auge schauen *a. fig (e-r Gefahr)* (*s.o., s.th.* jdm, e-r S); *fig* ins Auge fassen; im Geiste sehen, sich vorstellen; *philos* durch Intuition wahrnehmen.

envision [in'viʒən] *tr Am* sich vorstellen, sich ausmalen.

envoy ['envɔi] **1.** Bote, Vertreter, Agent; *pol* Gesandte(r) *m*; **2.** Schlußstrophe *f*; Nachwort *n*.

envy ['envi] *s* Neid *m* (*at, of s.o., s.th.* auf jdn, über etw), Mißgunst *f*; *tr* beneiden (*s.o. s.th.* jdn um etw); mißgönnen (*s.o. s.th.* jdm etw); *out of ~* aus Neid; *to be eaten up with ~* vor

Neid platzen; *to be the ~ of s.o.* jds Neid erregen; *to be green with ~* grün sein vor Neid.
enwrap [in'ræp] *tr* einwickeln, einhüllen (*in* in).
enzym|e ['enzaim] *chem* Enzym, Ferment *n*.
eo|cene ['i(:)o(u)si:n] *a geol* eozän; *s (~~ epoch)* Eozän *n*; **~lith** ['io(u)liθ] Eolith *m*; **~lithic** [-'liθik] eolithisch; **~zoic** [-'zouik]: *~~ era* Eozoikum *n*.
epaul|ement [e'pɔ:lmənt] *mil* Schulterwehr *f*; **~et(te)** ['epo(u)let, -pɔ:-, -pə-] *mil* Schulterstück *n*.
epergne [i'pə:n] Tafelaufsatz *m*.
ephemer|a, ~id [i'femərə, -id] *zoo* Eintagsfliege *f a. fig*; **~al** [-əl] eintägig; kurzlebig, ephemer.
epic ['epik] *s* Epos, Heldengedicht *n*; *a* episch; heldenhaft; Helden-; *art, literary ~* Kunstepos *n*.
epicur|e ['epikjuə] Feinschmecker; Genießer, Lebemann *m*; **~ean** [epikjuə'ri(:)ən] *a* genießerisch; *s* Genießer *m*; *E~~ (philos) a* epikureisch; *s* Epikureer *m*.
epicycl|e ['episaikl] *math* Auf-, Rollkreis *m*; **~ic gear** Planetengetriebe *n*.
epidem|ic(al) [epi'demik(əl)] *a* epidemisch, seuchenartig; *fig* sich rasch verbreitend; weitverbreitet; *s u. ~ic disease* Epidemie, Seuche *f*; **~iology** [epidemi'ɔlədʒi, -di:-] Seuchenlehre *f*.
epiderm|al, ~ic, ~oid [epi'də:məl, -ik, -ɔid] *a* Epidermis-; **~is** [-is] *anat* Oberhaut, Epidermis *f*.
epidiascope [epi'daiəskoup] Epidiaskop *n*.
epigastrium [epi'gæstriəm] *anat* Magengrube *f*, Epigastrium *n*.
epiglottis [epi'glɔtis] *anat* Kehldeckel *m*.
epigram ['epigræm] Epigramm *n*; **~matic(al)** [epigrə'mætik(əl)] epigrammatisch; **~matist** [epi'græmətist] Epigrammatiker *m*.
epigraph ['epigrɑ:f] Inschrift *f*; Motto *n*; **~y** [e'pigrəfi] Inschriftenkunde, Epigraphik *f*.
epilep|sy ['epilepsi] Epilepsie, Fallsucht *f*, Krämpfe *m pl*; **~tic** [epi'leptik] *a* epileptisch; *s* Epileptiker *m*.
epilog(ue) ['epilɔg] Epilog *m*, Nachwort *n*.
Epiphany [i'pifəni] *rel* Epiphanias-, Erscheinungs-, Dreikönigsfest *n*.
episcop|acy [i'piskəpəsi] bischöfliche Verfassung; Bischofswürde *f*, -amt *n*; Episkopat *m* od *n*; **~al** [i'piskəpəl] bischöflich; **E~alian** [ipiskə'peiljən] Anhänger *m* der Episkopalkirche; **~ate** [i'piskəpit] Bischofswürde *f*, -amt *n*; Bischofssitz *m*; Gesamtheit *f* der Bischöfe, Episkopat *m* od *n*.
episod|e ['episoud] Episode, Einschaltung, Neben-, Zwischenhandlung *f*; **~ic(al)** [epi'sɔdik(əl)] episodisch, eingeschaltet; gelegentlich; Zwischen-.
epist|le [i'pisl] *rel* Epistel *f*; *~~ to the Romans* Römerbrief *m*; **~olary** [i'pistələri] *a* Brief-.
epistyle ['epistail] *arch* Architrav *m*.
epitaph ['epitɑ:f] Grabschrift *f*.
epithalamium [epiθə'leimjəm] *pl a. -ia* [-iə] Hochzeitsgedicht *n*.
epithelium [epi'θi:ljəm] *anat* Epithel(ium) *n*.
epithet ['epiθet] Beiwort, Epitheton *n*; Beiname *m*.
epitom|e [i'pitəmi] Auszug, Abriß *m*, Zs.fassung, Inhaltsangabe; charakteristische, typische Einzelheit *f*; **~ize** [-aiz] *tr* e-n Auszug, Abriß machen von, zs.fassen.
epoch ['i:pɔk, *Am* 'epɔk] Epoche *f*, Zeitabschnitt *m*; Beginn *m* e-r neuen Epoche, Wendepunkt *m*; **~al** ['epɔkəl] epochal, (hoch)bedeutend, aufsehenerregend; **~-making** aufsehenerregend, umwälzend, bahnbrechend.
Epsom salt ['epsəm sɔ:lt] Magnesiumsulfat *n*.
equab|ility [ekwə'biliti] Gleichmäßigkeit, Gleichförmigkeit; *fig* (innere) Ausgeglichenheit, Abgewogenheit, Abgeklärtheit *f*, Gleichmut *m*, (innere) Ruhe *f*; **~le** ['ekwəbl, 'i:k-] gleichmäßig, gleichförmig; *fig* (innerlich) ausgeglichen, abgewogen, abgeklärt, gleichmütig, ruhig.
equal ['i:kwəl] *a* gleich(artig, -wertig), angemessen; gleichgestellt; ebenbürtig (*to* dat); gleich(förmig), gleichmäßig; ruhig, gleichmütig; *pol* gleichberechtigt (*to, with s.o.* jdm); gewachsen (*to s.th.* e-r S); in der Lage, fähig, imstande (*to doing* zu tun); *s* Gleichgestellte(r) *m*; *to be the ~ of s.th., s.o.'s ~* e-r S, jdm gleich sein; *my ~s* meinesgleichen; *tr* gleichen, gleich sein (*s.o., s.th.* jdm, e-r S); *(Leistung)* erreichen; gleichkommen (*s.o.* jdm); *sport* gleichziehen (*s.th.* mit etw); *math* ergeben; *not to be ~led* nicht seinesgleichen haben; *in ~ parts* zu gleichen Teilen; *on ~ terms* auf gleichem Fuß, zu gleichen Bedingungen; *to be ~ to the occasion* der Lage gewachsen sein; *to fight on ~ terms (fig)* mit gleichen Waffen kämpfen; *he has no ~* er hat nicht seinesgleichen; **~ity** [i(:)'kwɔliti] Gleichheit; Gleichsetzung; *pol* Gleichberechtigung *f*; *on an ~~, on a footing of ~~ with* auf gleichem Fuß mit; *~~ of votes* Stimmengleichheit *f*; **~ization** [i:kwəlai'zeiʃən] Angleichung *f*, Ausgleich *m*; Gleichschaltung, -stellung; Glättung; *tele* Entzerrung *f*; *~~ fund* Ausgleichsfond *m*; **~ize** ['i:kwəlaiz] *tr* gleichmachen, -schalten, an-, ausgleichen; *tele phot* entzerren; **~izer** [-ə] *tech* Ausgleich, Stabilisator; *tele* Entzerrer *m*; *sport* Ausgleichstor *n*; **~ly** ['-li] *adv* gleich, ebenso, genauso; **~ mark, sign** *math* Gleichheitszeichen (=).
equanimity [i:kwə'nimiti] Gleichmut *m*; Ausgeglichenheit *f*.
equat|e [i'kweit] *tr* gleichsetzen *a. math*, -stellen (*to, with* mit); als gleich ansehen *od* betrachten; **~ion** [i'kweiʃən] *math chem* Gleichung; *allg* Gleichsetzung, -stellung *f*; Ausgleich(ung *f*) *m*; **~or** [i'kweitə] Äquator *m*; **~orial** [ekwə'tɔ:riəl] äquatorial; Äquatorial-; *~~ region* Äquatorialzone *f*.
equerry [i'kweri] königliche(r) Hofbeamte(r); *hist* Stallmeister *m*.
equestrian [i'kwestriən] *a* Reit-, Reiter-; *s* (Kunst-)Reiter *m*; **~ statue** Reiterstandbild *n*.
equi|angular [i:kwi'æŋgjulə] *math* gleichwinklig; **~distant** ['i:kwi'distənt] *a* in gleichen Abständen, gleichweit entfernt; **~lateral** ['i:kwi'lætərəl] *a s math* gleichseitig(e Figur *f*).
equilibr|ate [i:kwi'laibreit] *tr* ins Gleichgewicht bringen, ausbalancieren; **~ation** [-lai'breiʃən] Gleichgewicht *n* (*to* zu; *with* mit); **~ist** [i(:)'kwilibrist] Gleichgewichtskünstler, Äquilibrist, *bes.* Seiltänzer *m*; **~ium** [i:kwi'libriəm] *pl a. -ia* [-iə] Gleichgewicht *n a. fig*; *in ~~* im Gleichgewicht; *to come into ~~* ins Gleichgewicht kommen; *price ~~* Preisausgleich *m*; *~~ of forces* Kräfteausgleich *m*; *~~ of payments* Zahlungsausgleich *m*.
equine ['i:kwain] *a* Pferde-.
equino|ctial [i:kwi'nɔkʃəl] *a* Äquinoktial-; Äquatorial-; *s (~~ circle, line)* Himmelsäquator; *(~~ gale)* Äquinoktialsturm *m*; **~x** ['i:kwinɔks] Tagundnachtgleiche *f*, Äquinoktium *n*; *astr (~ctial point)* Äquinoktial-(Frühlings- *od* Herbst-)Punkt *m*.
equip [i'kwip] *tr* ausrüsten, -statten, versehen (*with* mit); **~age** ['ekwipidʒ] Ausrüstung; Equipage *f*; Luxus-, Staatswagen *m*; *obs* Gefolge *n (e-s Fürsten)*; **~ment** [i'kwipmənt] Ausstattung, Ausrüstung, Einrichtung; Bestückung; *(a. pl)* Ausrüstung(sgegenstände *m pl*) *f*, Gerät(schaften *f pl*) *n*; Apparatur; Anlage *f*; *rail* rollende(s) Material *n*; *camping ~~* Campingausrüstung *f*; *office ~~* Büroeinrichtung *f*; *~~ box* Gerätekasten *m*; *~~ record* Liste *f* der Einrichtungsgegenstände.
equipoise ['ekwipɔiz] Gleichgewicht; Gegengewicht *n a. fig*.
equit|able ['ekwitəbl] billig, gerecht, unparteiisch, unvoreingenommen; *pred* recht u. billig; **~y** ['-ti] Billigkeit, Gerechtigkeit, Unvoreingenommenheit *f*; *jur* Billigkeitsrecht *n*; gerechte(r) Anspruch *m*; *com* Eigenkapital *n*, Nettowert *m*; *pl* Dividendenpapiere *n pl*; *~~ and good faith* Treu u. Glauben.
equivalen|ce, -cy [i'kwivələns(i)] Gleichwertigkeit, Äquivalenz *f a. chem*; **~t** [-t] *a* gleichwertig, äquivalent *a. chem*; gleichbedeutend (*to* mit); *s* Gegenwert *m*; Äquivalent *a. chem el*; Gegenstück *n* (*of, to* zu).
equivoc|al [i'kwivəkəl] zwei-, mehrdeutig; fragwürdig; unsicher; irreführend, zweifelhaft *a. pej*; **~alness** [-əlnis] Zwei-, Mehrdeutigkeit *f*; **~ate** [i'kwivəkeit] *itr* zweideutig reden; **~ation** [ikwivə'keiʃən] Zwei-, Mehrdeutigkeit *f*; zweideutige(r) Ausdruck *m*.
era ['iərə] Zeitrechnung; Ära *f*, Zeitalter *n a. geol*; Zeitabschnitt *m*.
eradic|able [i'rædikəbl] ausrottbar; **~ate** [-eit] *tr* ausrotten, vertilgen, völlig vernichten, unterdrücken; **~ation** [-'keiʃən] Ausrottung; völlige Vernichtung *f*.
eras|able [i'reizəbl] tilgbar, zu entfernen(d); **~e** [i'reiz, *Am* -s] *tr* ausradieren, -kratzen, -wischen; *(Tafel)* ab-, auswischen; vertilgen, entfernen; *fig* auslöschen (*from* aus); *(Tonband)* löschen; **~er** [-ə] Radiermesser *n*; *Am* Radiergum; *Am* Tafelwischer *m*; **~ion** [i'reiʒən] Rasur, Streichung; *med* Auskratzung *f*; **~ure** [i'reiʒə] Radieren *n*; Rasur, radierte Stelle; Streichung *f*.
ere [ɛə] *prp obs poet (zeitlich)* vor; *conj obs poet* ehe, bevor; *~ long* (schon) bald; *~ now, this* schon früher.
erect [i'rekt] *a* aufrecht, senkrecht, aufgerichtet; *(Haare)* gesträubt; *tr (Gebäude)* errichten; aufrichten, senkrecht stellen; *(die Ohren)* spitzen; *(Haare)* sträuben; *(Ofen, Maschine)* aufstellen, montieren; *fig (Schranken)* aufrichten; *fig* erheben (*into* zu); gründen, schaffen; *(Regierung)* bilden; *math (Senkrechte)* errichten; *(Lot)* fällen; *to stand ~ (Haare)* zu Berge stehen; **~ile** [-ail] *physiol* erektil, erigibel; *~~ tissue (anat)* Schwellkörper *m pl*; **~ing** [-iŋ] Aufrichten *n*; Aufbau *m*, Montierung, Montage *f*; *~~ crane* Montagekran *m*; **~ion** [i'rekʃən] Errichtung *f*, (Auf-)Bau *m*; Aufrichtung, -stellung, Montage *f*; Bau(werk *n*) *m*, Gebäude *n*; *physiol* Erektion *f*; **~ness** [-nis] Geradheit; gerade, aufrechte Haltung; senkrechte Stellung *f*; **~or** [-ə] Erbauer; *anat* Aufrichter *m*.
eremit|e ['erimait] Eremit, Klausner *m*.

erg [əːg] *phys* Erg *n (Arbeitseinheit).*
ergot ['əːgət] *bot* Mutterkorn *n.*
Erin ['iərin] *poet* Irland *n.*
ermin|e ['əːmin] *zoo* Hermelin *n*; Hermelin *m (Pelz)*; *fig* Richteramt *n*, -würde *f.*
erne [əːn] See-, Fischadler, Steingeier *m.*
ero|de [i'roud] *tr* zerfressen, -nagen, ätzen; *geol* auswaschen, abtragen, erodieren; fressen (*in* in); *tech* auskolken; **~se** [i'rous] *a* zerfressen; (aus-)gezackt, gekerbt; **~sion** [i'rouʒən] *geol* Auswaschung, Abtragung, Erosion; *med* Abschürfung *f*; *tech* Verschleiß *m*; *soil* ~~ Bodenerosion *f*, Erdabtragungen *f pl*; **~sive** [i'rousiv] ätzend; erodierend.
erot|ic [i'rɔtik, e'r-] *a* erotisch; Liebes-; *s* Erotiker *m*; Liebesgedicht *n*; **~(ic)ism** [e'rɔtisizm, 'erɔtizm] Erotik *f.*
err [əː] *itr* (sich) irren (*in* in); e-m Irrtum verfallen; *rel* fehlen, sich vergehen; *(Angabe)* falsch sein.
errand ['erənd] Botengang *m*, Besorgung *f*; (kleiner) Auftrag *m*; *to go on ~s, to run ~s* Botengänge, (kleine) Besorgungen machen; *a fool's ~* Metzgersgang *m*; **~-boy** Laufbursche *m.*
errant ['erənt] umherstreifend; sündig; *knight-~* fahrende(r) Ritter *m*; **~ry** ['-ri] Irrfahrt *f* (e-s Ritters); Rittertum *n*; ritterliche Taten *f pl.*
erratic [i'rætik] *(adv ~ally) a* regel-, wahllos; umherirrend, schweifend; *(Denken)* sprunghaft; abweichend; unbeständig, unberechenbar; absonderlich; verschroben; *geol* erratisch; **~ boulder, rock** erratische(r) Block, Findling *m*; **~ fever** Wechselfieber *n.*
errat|um [e'rɑːtəm, i'r-, -'reit-] Schreib-, Druckfehler *m*; *pl -ta* [-tə] Druckfehler(verzeichnis *n*) *m pl.*
erroneous [i'rounjəs] irrig, falsch, unrichtig; irrtümlich; **~ judg(e)ment** Fehlurteil *n.*
error ['erə] Irrtum, Fehler *m*, Versehen; Vergehen *n*, Fehltritt; Irrtum *m*, falsche Annahme, falsche Ansicht, verkehrte Auffassung *f*, Irrglaube; *jur* Form-, *tech* Ablesefehler *m*; *astr tech* Abweichung *f*; *by way of trial and ~* durch Ausprobieren; *in ~, through an ~* aus Versehen, versehentlich, irrtümlich; *to be in ~* im Irrtum sein, sich im Irrtum befinden, (sich) irren; fehlerhaft sein (*by* um); *to make, to commit an ~* e-n Fehler machen *od* begehen; *to see the ~s of o.'s ways* s-e Fehler einsehen; *~s excepted* Irrtümer vorbehalten; *free from ~* fehlerfrei, -los; *~ of construction* Konstruktionsfehler *m*; *~ of fact* Tatsachenirrtum *m*; *~ of judg(e)ment* Fehlurteil *n*; *~ of law* Rechtsirrtum *m*; *~ of omission* Unterlassungssünde *f*; **~-proof** fehlersicher.
erstwhile ['əːstwail] *a adv* ehemalig, früher.
eruct [i'rʌkt] *itr* aufstoßen, rülpsen; *tr (Vulkan)* ausstoßen; **~ation** [-'teiʃən] Aufstoßen, Rülpsen *n*; *(Vulkan)* Ausbruch; Auswurf *m.*
erudit|e ['eru(:)dait] gelehrt *(a. Sache)*, belesen; **~ion** [-'diʃən] Gelehrsamkeit, Gelehrtheit, Belesenheit *f.*
erupt [i'rʌpt] *itr* hervorbrechen; *(Vulkan)* ausbrechen; *(Zahn)* durchbrechen, kommen; *(Haut)* e-n Ausschlag bekommen; **~ion** [i'rʌpʃən] (Vulkan-)Ausbruch; (Haut-)Ausschlag; *fig* (Gefühls-)Ausbruch *m*; **~ive** [-iv] *a* ausbrechend; *geol* Eruptiv-; *med* Ausschlag hervorrufend.
erysipelas [eri'sipiləs] *med* Rotlauf *m*, Wundrose *f.*
escal|ade [eskə'leid] *s mil* Ersteigung *f*, Sturm *m* mit Leitern; *tr* mit Leitern ersteigen, erklettern, stürmen, eskalieren; **~ation** [-'leiʃən] *mil* Steigerung *f* des Einsatzes; **~ator** ['eskəleitə] Rolltreppe *f*; *com* Indexlohn *m*; *~~ clause* Indexklausel, gleitende Lohnskala *f.*
escapade [eskə'peid] Seitensprung; tolle(r), dumme(r) Streich *m.*
escap|e [is'keip] *itr* (ent)fliehen, flüchten, entweichen, entkommen, ausbrechen, *fam* ausrücken, entwischen (*from* aus); sich retten; entgehen (*from s.th.* e-r S), davonkommen (*with* mit); *(Flüssigkeit, Gas)* entweichen, ausströmen, auslaufen (*from* aus); entschlüpfen, entschwinden (*from* dat); *tr* entfliehen (*s.th.* e-r S); ausweichen (*s.th.* e-r S), umgehen, vermeiden; entgehen (*s.th.* e-r S), sich entziehen (*s.th.* dat); *(Schrei)* entfahren (*s.o.* jdm); *(Name)* entfallen (*s.o.* jdm); *(Fehler)* entgehen; *s* Flucht *f*, Entweichen; Entkommen *n*; Fluchtfall *m*; Rettung *f* (*from* von); Fluchtweg *m*, Möglichkeit zu entkommen; *tech* undichte Stelle; Flucht aus der Wirklichkeit; *bot* verwilderte Gartenpflanze *f*; *attr* Auslaß-, Abfluß-; *to have a narrow ~~* mit knapper Not davonkommen; *fire-~~* Feuerleiter *f*; *~~ clause* Rücktrittsklausel *f*; *~~ hatch (aero)* Notausstieg *m*, Bodenluke, Falltür *f*; *~~ literature* Unterhaltungsliteratur *f*; *~~-pipe (tech)* Abfluß-, Dampfausströmungsrohr *n*; *~~-shaft* Notschacht *m*; *~~-valve* Auslaß-, Sicherheitsventil *n*; **~ee** [eskə'piː] Ausreißer *m*; **~ement** [-mənt] *(Uhr)* Hemmung *f*; **~ism** [-izm] *psych* (dauernde) Flucht *f* aus der Wirklichkeit; **~ist** [-ist] *s* Wirklichkeitsflüchtige(r) *m*; *a* Unterhaltungs-.
escarp [is'kɑːp] *tr* abdachen, -schrägen; *s u.* **~ment** [-mənt] Steilabhang *m*; Klippe; Böschung, Abdachung *f.*
eschalot ['eʃəlɔt] *s. shallot.*
eschar ['eskɑː] *med* (Brand-)Schorf *m.*
eschatolog|ical [eskətə'lɔdʒikəl] *rel* eschatologisch; **~y** [eskə'tɔlədʒi] Eschatologie *f.*
escheat [is'tʃiːt] Heimfall *m (an den Lehnsherrn, die Krone, den Staat)*; heimgefallene(s) Gut *n*; = *~age*; *tr* konfiszieren; *itr* heimfallen; **~age** [-idʒ] Heimfallsrecht *n.*
eschew [is'tʃuː] *tr* (ver)meiden, ausweichen (*s.th.* e-r S); umgehen, unterlassen; scheuen; sich enthalten (*s.th.* e-r S).
escort ['eskɔːt] Begleiter *m*, Begleit-, Schutzmannschaft *f*; (Ehren-)Geleit, Gefolge *n*; *mil* Bedeckung *f*; *mar* Geleitschiff *n*; *aero* Begleitschutz *m*; *tr* [is'kɔːt] begleiten, geleiten, decken, eskortieren; **~ fighter** *aero* Begleitjäger *m.*
escritoire [eskri(:)'twɑː] Sekretär, Schreibtisch *m*, -pult *n.*
esculent ['eskjulənt] *a* eßbar, genießbar; *s* Nahrungsmittel *n.*
escutcheon [is'kʌtʃən] Wappen (-schild), (Namens-)Schild *n*; *to have a blot on o.'s ~ (fig)* keine reine Weste haben.
Eskimo ['eskimou] *pl -o(e)s* Eskimo *m.*
esophagus *s. oesophagus.*
esoteric [eso(u)'terik] esoterisch, geheim, Geheim-; vertraulich, privat.
espalier [is'pæljə] *s* Spalier *n.*
especial [is'peʃəl] *a* besonder; un-, außergewöhnlich, hervorragend, ausgezeichnet, vorzüglich; **~ly** [-li] *adv* (ganz) besonders, insbesondere, vor allem, namentlich.
espi|al [is'paiəl] Spionieren, Auskundschaften *n*; **~onage** [espiə'nɑːʒ, *Am* 'espiənidʒ, -pai-] Spionieren *n*, Spionage *f*; *industrial ~~* Werkspionage *f.*
esplanade [esplə'neid] Esplanade *f*; freie(r) Platz *m*; (Ufer-)Promenade *f.*
espous|al [is'pauzəl] Parteiergreifung, -nahme (*of* für); *meist pl obs* Verlobung; Trauung *f*; **~e** [is'pauz] *tr* Partei ergreifen, eintreten für, unterstützen; sich annehmen (*s.th.* e-r S); übertreten (*a new religion* zu e-m anderen Glauben); *(Mann) obs* heiraten.
espresso [es'presou] Espresso *m (Getränk)*; **~ bar, café** Espresso *n.*
espy [is'pai] *tr* erblicken, erspähen; auskundschaften, ausspionieren.
Esquimau ['eskimou] *pl ~x s. Eskimo.*
esquire [is'kwaiə] *obs* Edle(r); Landadlige(r) *m*; *(als Esq. nach e-m Namen in der Anschrift)* hochwohlgeboren.
essay [e'sei] *tr* versuchen; erproben; *s* ['esei] Versuch *m* (*at s.th.* an e-r S; *at doing s.th.* etw zu tun), Probe *f*; *lit* Essay, Aufsatz *m*, Betrachtung *f*; **~ist** ['eseiist] Essayist *m.*
essen|ce ['esns] (inneres) Wesen *n*, Kern *m*, Natur *f*, Geist *m (e-r Sache)*; *das* Wesentliche; Auszug, Extrakt *m*; ätherische(s) Öl *n*; Essenz *f*; Duft *m*; *in ~~* (im) wesentlich(en); *meat ~~* Fleischextrakt *m*; **~tial** [i'senʃəl] *a* wesentlich (*to* für); unentbehrlich; (lebens)notwendig, unerläßlich, lebenswichtig (*to* für); wichtig, Haupt-; *s das* Wesentliche, Wichtigste, Notwendigste, Hauptsache *f*; wesentliche Umstände *m pl*; *~~s of life* Lebensbedürfnisse *n pl*; *~~ oil* ätherische(s) Öl *n*; *~~ user* Bedarfsträger *m*; **~tiality** [isenʃi'æliti] Notwendigkeit, Unerläßlichkeit, (Lebens-)Wichtigkeit *f*; **~tially** [i'senʃəli] *adv* (im) wesentlich(en), im besonderen, in der Hauptsache; *~~ necessary* unerläßlich notwendig.

*

establish [is'tæbliʃ] *tr* aufstellen, er-, einrichten, gründen; *(Wohnung)* einrichten; *(Geschäft)* eröffnen; *(Konto)* ein-, errichten, eröffnen; festsetzen, bestimmen; *(Gesetz)* erlassen; *(Gesetz fig, Regel, Theorie)* aufstellen; *(Ordnung)* herstellen; *(Regierung)* bilden; *(Beziehungen)* anknüpfen, aufnehmen; *(Verbindungen)* herstellen; *(Beamten)* einsetzen; *(Rekord)* aufstellen; versorgen; (einwandfrei) feststellen, darlegen; be-, nachweisen, begründen; klarstellen; zur Geltung bringen, Geltung verschaffen (*s.th.* e-r S), durchsetzen; verbürgen; *(Kirche)* als staatlich erklären; *to ~ o.s.* sich niederlassen, sich selbständig machen (*as a grocer* als Kolonialwarenhändler); ein Geschäft gründen; **~ed** [-t] *a* feststehend, verankert, eingewurzelt; eingeführt; fundiert; begründet, erwiesen; *com* zugelassen; *(Beamter)* planmäßig; *(Recht)* geltend; *~~ church* Staatskirche *f*; *the E~~ Church* die Kirche von England; *~~ place (Br com)* Sitz *m* (e-r Gesellschaft); **~ment** [-mənt] Aufstellung, Er-, Einrichtung, Gründung, Eröffnung; *(Regierung)* Bildung; *(Beziehungen)* Aufnahme, Festsetzung, Bestimmung; *(Steuer)* Erhebung; Einsetzung; Versorgung; Lebensstellung; Fest-, Klarstellung, Begründung *f*, Beweis *m*; Haus(halt *m*) *n*, Wohnung *f*; Geschäft(shaus) *n*, Firma *f*, Unternehmen *n*, Betrieb *m*, Werk *n*, Fabrik, Anlage, Niederlassung *f*, Etablissement *n*; Anstalt *f*, Institut *n*; Dienststelle, Organisation *f*, (Verwaltungs-, Beamten-)Apparat, Personalbestand *m*; Heeresorganisation; *mil Br* Sollstärke *f*; *to break up o.'s ~~* s-n Haushalt auflösen; *to keep up a large ~~* ein großes Haus führen; *branch* ~~ Zweigniederlassung, Filiale *f*; *educational* ~~ Lehranstalt *f*; *industrial* ~~ Industrieunternehmung *f*; *peace* ~~ *(mil)* Friedensstärke *f*; *penitentiary* ~~ Strafanstalt *f*; *principal* ~~ Stammhaus *n*; Hauptbetrieb *m*; *subsidiary* ~~ Nebenbetrieb *m*; ~~ *charges (pl)* allgemeine Unkosten *pl*.

estate [is'teit] (Lebens-)Alter *n*; Stand *m*, Klasse *f*; Besitz *m*, Eigentum, Vermögen; Anrecht; Kapital *n*; Grund-, Landbesitz *m*, (Land-)Gut *n*, Besitzung *f*; Besitzrecht *n*; Nutznießung *f*; Gelände, Grundstück *n*; Nachlaß *m*, Hinterlassenschaft, Erbmasse; *(bankrupt's ~)* Konkursmasse *f*; *to come to, to reach man's ~* in die Mannesjahre, ins Mannesalter kommen; *crown ~s (pl)* Krongüter *n pl*, -land *n*; *entailed ~* Fideikommiß *n*; *family ~* Familienbesitz *m*; *the fourth ~ (hum)* die Presse; *housing ~* Wohnsiedlung *f*; *leasehold ~* Pachtgrundstück *n*; *life ~* lebenslängliche Nutznießung *f*; *personal ~* bewegliche Habe *f*; *private ~* Privatbesitz *m*, -eigentum *n*; *real ~* Grundbesitz, Grund u. Boden *m*, Liegenschaften, Immobilien *pl*; ~ **agent** Grundstücksmakler *m*; ~ **car** Kombiwagen *m*; ~ **duty,** *Am* **tax** Erbschaftssteuer *f*; ~ **owner** Grundstückseigentümer *m*.

esteem [is'ti:m] *tr* hoch-, sehr schätzen, (sehr) achten; ansehen, betrachten, erachten als, halten für; *s* (Hoch-)Achtung (*for, of* vor); Wertschätzung *f* (*for, of* gen); Ansehen *n*; *to hold in ~* hochachten, wertschätzen.

ester ['estə] *chem* Ester *m*.

Est(h)onia [es'tounjə] Estland *n*; **~n** [-n] *a* estnisch; *s* Este *m*; Estin *f*; (das) Estnisch(e).

estimable ['estiməbl] schätzbar, errechenbar; schätzens-, achtenswert.

estimat|e ['estimeit] *tr* (ab-, ein)schätzen, taxieren, bewerten; annähernd berechnen, veranschlagen (*at* auf); beurteilen; *itr* e-n Kostenvoranschlag machen (*for* für); *s* [-mit] (Ab-)Schätzung, Bewertung *f*; Überschlag; Kosten-, Vor-, Kostenvoranschlag *m*; Berechnung; *(Lage)* Beurteilung *f*; *the E~~s (pl)* der Haushaltsplan, der Haushaltsvoranschlag, der Etat, das Budget; *at, on a rough ~~* grob überschlagen; *in accordance with the E~~s* etatmäßig; *to make up the E~~s* den Etat aufstellen; *building ~~* Baukostenanschlag *m*; *conservative ~~* vorsichtige Schätzung *f*; *rough ~~* Überschlag *m*; *~~ of damages* Schadensberechnung *f*; **~ed** [-id] *a* geschätzt; voraussichtlich; *~~ cost* Sollkosten *pl*; *~~ value* Taxwert *m*; **~ion** [-'meiʃən] (Ein-)Schätzung, Bewertung *f*; Ab-, Einschätzen *n*; Würdigung, Beurteilung *f*; Urteil *n*, Ansicht, Meinung; Hochschätzung, Achtung *f*, Respekt *m*; *pl* Budget *n*; *in my ~~* meines Erachtens; *to hold in (high) ~~* (sehr) hochschätzen.

estop [is'tɔp] *tr* hindern, hemmen (*from* an) *a. jur*; **~pel** [-əl] prozeßhindernde Einrede *f*.

estrange [is'treindʒ] *tr* entfernen (*from* von, aus), fernhalten (*from* dat); entfremden, abspenstig machen (*from s.o.* jdm); **~ment** [-mənt] Entfremdung *f*.

estuary ['estjuəri] (Meeres-)Bucht *f*; Mündungsbecken *n*, (weite) Gezeitenflußmündung *f*.

et cetera [it'setrə] *(etc)* und so weiter, und so fort (usw.); **etceteras** *s pl* Drum und Dran *n*; alles mögliche, Sammelsurium *n*.

etch [etʃ] *tr itr (Kunst)* radieren; ätzen (*on* auf); **~er** ['-ə] Radierer *m*; **~ing** ['-iŋ] (Maler-)Radierung *f*; *~~-needle* Radiernadel *f*.

etern|al [i'tə:nl] *a* ewig, immerwährend; zeitlos; immer gleich, unveränderlich; *fam* fortwährend, ununterbrochen; *s*: *the E~~* Gott *m*; *the ~~ life* das ewige Leben; **~alize** [i(:)'tə:nəlaiz], **~ize** [i:'tə:naiz] *tr* verewigen, unsterblich machen; **~ally** [-əli] *adv* für alle Zeit(en), für immer, für ewig(e Zeiten); immer, stets, ewig; *fam* ununterbrochen, fortwährend; **~ity** [i(:)'tə:niti] Ewigkeit *a. fam fig*; Unsterblichkeit *f*, ewige(s) Leben *n*.

ether ['i:θə] *chem phys hist poet* Äther *m*; **~eal** [i(:)'θiəriəl] *chem fig* ätherisch; *fig* leicht, zart, schwebend; himmlisch; *poet* Äther-; **~ize** ['i:θəraiz] *tr* mit Äther betäuben.

ethic|al ['eθikəl] sittlich, moralisch, ethisch; **~s** ['eθiks] *pl, a. mit sing* Ethik, Sittenlehre, Moral *f*; Sittenkodex *m*, *(bestimmte)* Moral *f*.

Ethiopia [i:θi'oupjə] Äthiopien *n*; **~n** [-n] *a* äthiopisch; *s* Äthiopier(in *f*) *m*.

ethn|ic(al) ['eθnik(əl)] heidnisch; *scient* ethnisch, völkisch; **~ographer** [eθ'nɔgrəfə] Ethnograph *m*; **~ographic(al)** [eθnə'græfik(əl)] ethnographisch; **~ography** [eθ'nɔgrəfi] Ethnographie, beschreibende Völkerkunde *f*; **~ological)** [eθnə'lɔdʒik(əl)] völkerkundlich; **~ologist** [eθ'nɔlədʒist] Völkerkundler *m*; **~ology** [eθ'nɔlədʒi] Völkerkunde, Ethnologie *f*.

ethos ['i:θɔs] Ethos *n*, Gesinnung *f*.

ethyl ['eθil, 'i:θail] *chem* Äthyl *n*; ~ **alcohol** Äthylalkohol *m*; **~ene** ['eθili:n] Äthylen *n (Gas)*.

etiolate ['i:tio(u)leit] *tr bot* (durch Entzug des Sonnenlichtes) bleichen.

etiquette [eti'ket, *Am* 'etəket] Etikette *f*, Umgangsformen *f pl*; feine(s) Benehmen *n*, gute(r) Ton *m*; ungeschriebene Gesetze *n pl*, Pflichten *f pl*.

Eton ['i:tn]: ~ **collar** breite(r), steife(r) Leinenkragen *m*; ~ **crop** Herrenschnitt *m*; ~ **jacket** kurze Jacke *f*.

Etru|ria [i'truəriə] *hist* Etrurien *n*; **~scan** [i'trʌskən] *a* etruskisch; *s pl* die Etrusker *m pl*.

etymolog|ical [etimə'lɔdʒik(əl)] etymologisch; **~y** [eti'mɔlədʒi] Etymologie *f*.

eucalyptus [ju:kə'liptəs] *bot pharm* Eukalyptus *m*; ~ **oil** Eukalyptusöl *n*.

Eucharist ['jukərist] das heilige Abendmahl; **~ic(al)** [ju:kə'ristik(əl)] *a* Abendmahls-.

euchre ['ju:kə] *tr Am fam* reinlegen.

eugenic [ju:'dʒenik] *a* eugenisch, rassenhygienisch; *s pl mit sing* Eugenik, Erbgesundheitslehre *f*.

eulog|ist ['ju:lədʒist] Lobredner *m*; **~istic** [ju:lə'dʒistik] lobrednerisch, lobend; **~ize** ['ju:lədʒaiz] *tr* übermäßig loben, (lob)preisen; **~y** ['ju:lədʒi] Lobrede, -preisung *f*, hohe(s) Lob *n*.

eunuch ['ju:nək] Eunuch *m*.

euphem|ism ['ju:fimizm] Euphemismus, beschönigende(r) Ausdruck *m*; **~istic(al)** [ju:fi'mistik(əl)] euphemistisch, beschönigend.

euphon|ic(al) [ju:'fɔnik(əl)], **~ious** [ju:'founjəs] wohlklingend; *gram* euphonisch; **~y** ['ju:fəni] Wohlklang, -laut *m*.

euphorbia [ju:'fɔ:biə] *bot* Wolfsmilch *f*.

euphor|ia [ju:'fɔ:riə] Wohlbefinden *n*; *med* Euphorie *f*; **~ic** [ju:'fɔrik] *med* euphorisch.

euphuism ['ju:fju(:)izm] gezierte Ausdrucks-, Rede-, Schreibweise *f*.

Eurasia [juə'reiʒə] Eurasien *n*; **~n** [juə'reiʒjən] *a* eurasisch; *s* Eurasier *m*.

eurhythmics [ju:'riθmiks] *pl mit sing* Eurhythmie *f*.

Europe ['juərəp] Europa *n*; *the Council of ~* der Europarat; **~an** [juərə'pi(:)ən] *a* europäisch; *s* Europäer(in *f*) *m*; *~~ Community* Europäische Gemeinschaft *f*; *~~ Coal and Steel Community* Montanunion *f*; *~~ Economic Community* Europäische Wirtschaftsgemeinschaft *f*; *~~ Monetary Agreement* Europäische(s) Währungsabkommen *n*; *~~ Payments Union* Europäische Zahlungsunion *f*; *~~ plan (Am)* Hotelpreis *m* nur für die Übernachtung (ohne Mahlzeiten); *~~ Recovery Program (Am)* Marshall-Plan *m*; **~anize** [juərə'pi(:)ənaiz] *tr* europäisieren.

Eurovision [juərə'viʒən] europäische(s) Fernsehsendernetz *n*.

Eustachian [ju:s'teiʃjən]: ~ **tube** *anat* Eustachische Röhre, Ohrtrompete *f*.

euthanasia [ju:θə'neizjə] Euthanasie *f*.

*

evacu|ant [i'vækjuənt] *a* abführend, abtreibend; Brechen erregend; *s* Abführ-, Brechmittel *n*; **~ate** [-eit] *tr* (aus)leeren; (aus)räumen; fortschaffen; freimachen; *(Darm)* entleeren; *(Blase)* leeren; *pharm* abführen, purgieren; *mil* räumen; *(Ort od Gebiet, Bevölkerung)* evakuieren, abtransportieren, abbefördern; verlagern; *tech* leerpumpen; **~ation** [-'eiʃən] Leerung, Räumung *f a. mil*; Abtransport, Abschub *m*; Evakuierung; Verlagerung; (Darm-)Entleerung *f*, Stuhlgang *m*; **~ee** [-ju(:)'i:] Evakuierte(r *m*) *f*, Um-, Aussiedler *m*.

evade [i'veid] *tr* aus dem Wege gehen, ausweichen (*s.th.* e-r S); sich entziehen (*s.th.* gen); sich fernhalten von; umgehen, vermeiden (*doing s.th.* etw zu tun); entgehen (*s.th.* e-r S); *(Zoll)* hinterziehen.

evaluat|e [i'væljueit] *tr* (ab)schätzen, bewerten, taxieren; auswerten, berechnen; *math* errechnen; **~ion** [-'eiʃən] Abschätzung, Taxierung; Wertberechnung, -bestimmung, Bewertung *f*.

evanesc|e [i:və'nes, *bes. Am* ev-] *itr* (dahin-, ent-, ver)schwinden, vergehen; **~ence** [-ns] (Dahin-)Schwinden, Vergehen *n*; Vergänglichkeit, Flüchtigkeit *f*; **~ent** [-nt] (ver)schwindend; flüchtig, vorübergehend, kurzlebig, vergänglich.

evangel|ic(al) [i:væn'dʒelik(əl)] *a* evangelisch; **~icalism** [i:væn'dʒelikəlizm] Protestantismus *m*; **~ist** [i'vændʒilist] Evangelist; Wanderprediger *m*; **~ize** [i'vændʒilaiz] *tr* das Evangelium predigen (*s.o.* jdm); (zum Christentum) bekehren.

evaporat|e [i'væpəreit] *tr* verdampfen lassen; trocknen; *(Milch)* kondensieren; *itr* verdampfen, verdunsten; eintrocknen; sich verflüchtigen; *fig* (dahin)schwinden, vergehen, sich in Nichts auflösen, verfliegen; *~ed milk* kondensierte, Büchsen-, Dosenmilch *f*; **~ion** [-'reiʃən] Verdampfung, Verdunstung *f*; Einkochen, Kondensieren *n*; **~or** [-ə] Verdampfer *m*.

evas|ion [i'veiʒən] Ausweichen; Umgehen, Vermeiden (*of* gen); Sichentziehen *n*; Ausflucht, Ausrede *f*; *(Steuer)* Hinterziehung *f*; **~ive** [-siv] ausweichend; schwer verständlich.

Eve [i:v] Eva *f*; *daughter of ~* Evastochter *f*.

eve [iːv] Vorabend, -tag; *poet* Abend *m*; *on the ~ of* am Vorabend *gen*, (unmittelbar) vor.

even ['iːvən] **1.** *a* eben, flach, glatt; in gleicher Höhe *od* Linie (befindlich); eben-, gleichmäßig, gleichförmig, -bleibend, regelmäßig; *(Mensch)* ausgeglichen, abgeklärt, gesetzt, ruhig; *(Handlung)* gerecht, fair, billig, redlich; *pred* quitt; gleich (groß); *(Zahl)* gerade; *(Zahlen-, Maßangabe)* genau; *to be, to get ~ with s.o.* jdm nichts mehr schulden; mit jdm abrechnen; *to break ~ (fam)* das Spiel unentschieden abbrechen; auf s-e Kosten kommen; *to get ~* abrechnen (*with s.o.* mit jdm); heimzahlen (*with s.o.* jdm); *to make ~ with the ground* dem Erdboden gleichmachen; *I'm ~ with you* wir sind quitt; *odd or ~* gerade oder ungerade; *of ~ date* gleichen Datums; *~ odds* gleiche Aussichten für und wider; **2.** *tr* einebnen, gleichmachen, gleichstellen; *itr* eben, in gleicher Ebene, gleich sein; *to ~ up* ausgleichen; **~-handed** *a* unparteiisch, unvoreingenommen, gerecht, sachlich; **~ly** ['-li] *adv* gleichmäßig; **~-minded** *a* ausgeglichen, ruhig, bedächtig; **~ness** ['-nis] Ebenheit; Gleich-, Regelmäßigkeit; Gleichheit; (innere) Ausgeglichenheit, (Seelen-)Ruhe *f*, Gleichmut *m*; Geradheit, Redlichkeit, Gerechtigkeit *f*; **~-tempered** *a* gelassen, gleichmütig, ruhig, harmonisch; nicht aus der Ruhe zu bringen(d); **3.** *adv* sogar, selbst; gerade, genau, in dem Augenblick; noch, sogar *(mit Komparativ)*; nämlich; gleich *(gut, schnell usw)*; *never ~* nie ... auch nur; *not ~* nicht einmal; selbst ... nicht; *~ if, though* selbst, wenn; wenn ... auch; obwohl, obgleich; *~ now* sogar jetzt, selbst jetzt, auch jetzt; *~ so* trotzdem; **3.** *poet* Abend *m*; **~song** Abendandacht *f*.

evening ['iːvniŋ] Abend; *Am a.* Spätnachmittag; Abend(veranstaltung, -gesellschaft *f*) *m*, Soiree *f*; *fig* Ende *n*; *in the ~* am Abend; *on Sunday ~* Sonntag abend; *one ~* eines Abends; *this, yesterday, tomorrow ~* heute, gestern, morgen abend; *musical ~* Musikabend *m*; *~ of life* Lebensabend *m*; **~ class, school** Abendschule *f*; **~ clothes** *pl*, **~ dress** Gesellschafts-, Abendanzug *m*; Abendkleid *n*; **~ gown** Abendkleid *n*; **~ paper** Abendzeitung *f*; **~ party** Abendgesellschaft *f*; **~ performance** Abendvorstellung *f*; **~ prayer** Abendgebet *n*, -andacht *f*; **~ shift** Abendschicht *f*; **~ star** Abendstern *m*.

event [i'vent] Ereignis, Geschehnis *n*, Begebenheit *f*; Ergebnis *n*, Folge *f*, Resultat *n*; *sport* Programmnummer *f*, -punkt *m*; (sportliche) Übung, Sportart *f*; *at all ~s, in any ~* auf alle Fälle, jedenfalls, sowieso; *in the ~ of* im Falle *gen od* daß; *in either ~* in dem einen oder andern Falle; *in that ~* in d(ies)em Fall; *athletic ~s (pl)* Leichtathletikkämpfe *m pl*; *table of ~s* Veranstaltungsprogramm *n*; **~ful** [-ful] ereignis-, ergebnisreich.

eventual [i'ventjuəl] *a attr* etwaig, eventuell, möglich; schließlich; **~ity** [-'æliti] Möglichkeit *f*; **~ly** [-li] *adv* schließlich, endlich, am Ende.

eventuate [i'ventjueit] *itr* ausgehen, -fallen; enden (*in* in); zur Folge haben (*in s.th.* etw); *Am* geschehen, eintreten, sich ereignen, stattfinden.

ever ['evə] *adv* je(mals); *(in bestimmten Ausdrücken u. vor comp, sonst obs)* immer, stets, beständig, dauernd; irgend, (auch) immer, noch (irgend); *fam* in aller Welt, zum Kuckuck, in Gottes Namen; *as ~* wie (auch) immer; *for ~ (and ~)* für alle Zeiten; für immer; *for ~ and a day* allezeit; *hardly, scarcely ~* kaum je; fast nie; *not ... ~* noch nie; *~ after, since* seitdem (immer); seit ... ständig; die ganze Zeit danach; *~ and again* immer wieder; *~ before* von jeher; stets zuvor; *~ so (much) (fam)* sehr; *~ such a (fam)* ein mächtig, tüchtig, sehr, schwer- *adv*; **~glade** *Am* Sumpf *m*, Moor *n*; **~green** *a u. s bot* immergrün(e Pflanze *f*); *s mus* Evergreen *m*; **~lasting** *a* ewig, beständig, fortwährend, dauernd; unverwüstlich; *s* Ewigkeit; *(~~ flower)* Strohblume, Immortelle *f*; dauerhafte(r) Wollstoff *m*; *the E~~* Gott *m*; **~more** ['-'-] *adv* immer, stets, ständig; *for ~~* für immer; **~-ready case** *phot* Bereitschaftstasche *f*.

evert [i'vəːt] *tr* nach außen kehren.

every ['evri] jede(r, s) (mögliche) *nur attr*; *(mit nachfolgendem Zahlwort)* alle; *each and ~ one* jede(r, s) einzelne; *~ bit* alles; ganz; *~ bit of ...* das ganze ...; *~ man* jeder(mann); *~ minute* jeden Augenblick; *~ now and then, now and again, once in a while, (fam) so often* ab und zu, von Zeit zu Zeit, hin u. wieder, manchmal, bisweilen, dann u. wann; *~ one of them* alle ohne Ausnahme; *~ other* jede(r, s) zweite; *~ other day* jeden zweiten, einen um den andern Tag; *~ other week* alle zwei Wochen, alle vierzehn Tage; *my ~ thought* alle meine Gedanken; *~ time (fam)* jedesmal; *~ way* in jeder Hinsicht *od* Beziehung; *~ which way (Am fam)* in allen Richtungen, völlig durchea.; *with ~ good wish* mit allen guten Wünschen; **~body, ~one, ~ one** *prn* jeder, alle; jedermann; *~body else* jeder, alle andere(n), alle übrigen; **~day** *a attr* täglich, Alltags-; alltäglich, gewöhnlich; **~thing** *prn* alles; *s* die Hauptsache; **~where** *adv* überall; wo(hin) auch immer.

evict [i(ː)'vikt] *tr (Person)* exmittieren, hinaussetzen; *(Sache)* gerichtlich räumen lassen; **~ion** [i(ː)'vikʃən] Vertreibung *f* aus dem Besitz; Exmittierung, (Besitz-)Entsetzung; Wiederinbesitznahme *f*; *to sue for ~~* auf Räumung klagen, Räumungsklage erheben; *~~ decree, notice, order* Räumungsbefehl *m*.

evidence ['evidəns] *s* Offenkundigkeit, Klarheit *f*, Augenschein *m*; (An-)Zeichen *n*, Anhaltspunkt, Hin-, Nachweis; Beweis(grund *m*, -material, -stück *n*) *m*, Beweise *pl*, Tatsachen *f pl*, Unterlagen *f pl*; *jur* Zeugenaussage *f*, Zeugnis *n*; Zeuge(n *pl*); *com* Nachweis, Titel *m*; *tr* klarmachen, deutlich, dartun, klarstellen; bezeugen; *for lack of ~* wegen Mangels an Beweisen; *in ~* deutlich sichtbar, offenkundig; *fig* im Vordergrund; *jur* als Beweis; *to be in ~* auffallen; zu sehen, zu finden sein; klar zutage liegen; *jur* als Beweis gelten; *to call s.o. in ~* jdn als Zeugen benennen; *to furnish ~* den Beweis erbringen (*of* für); *to give ~* e-e (Zeugen-)Aussage machen (*for* für; *against* gegen); *to give, to bear ~ of* Zeugnis ablegen, Beweise geben für; deutliche Anzeichen zeigen von; *to hear ~* Zeugen vernehmen; *to offer, to tender ~* den Beweis antreten; *to produce ~* Beweise erbringen; *circumstantial ~* Indizienbeweis *m*; *conclusive ~* schlüssige(r) Beweis *m*; *hearing, taking of ~* Beweisaufnahme *f*; *King's, Queen's, (Am) state's ~* Belastungsmaterial *n*; *to turn King's ~* gegen s-e Mitangeklagten aussagen; *a piece of ~* ein Beweis; *refusal to give ~* Aussageverweigerung *f*; *~ for the defence, for the prosecution* entlastende(s), belastende(s) Beweismaterial *n*; Entlastungs-, Belastungszeuge *m*; *~ to the contrary* Gegenbeweis, Beweis *m* des Gegenteils.

evident ['evidənt] offenkundig, -sichtlich, augenscheinlich; einleuchtend, deutlich, klar; *to make ~* an den Tag legen; deutlich machen, klarstellen; **~ial** [-'denʃəl] beweiskräftig; **~ially** [-'denʃəli] *adv* erwiesenermaßen.

evil ['iːvl, 'iːvil] *a* schlecht, böse, sündig; übel, schlimm, verheerend, unglücklich; *adv* schlecht, übel; *s* Übel *n*, Schlechtigkeit, Sünde *f*; Leid(en) *n*, Schmerz *m*, Krankheit *f*; Unheil, Unglück, Übel(stand *m*) *n*; *to wish s.o. ~* jdm Böses wünschen; *deliver us from ~* erlöse uns vom Übel; *the lesser ~* das kleinere Übel; *the ~ eye (Magie)* der böse Blick; *the E~ One* der Böse, der Teufel, Satan *m*; **~ day** Unglückstag *m*; **~-disposed** *a* boshaft, bösartig; **~-doer** Übeltäter *m*; **~-minded** *a* übelgesinnt, boshaft; *(Bemerkung)* hämisch; **~-speaking** *a* verleumderisch; *s* üble Nachrede *f*.

evince [i'vins] *tr* (offen, deutlich) zeigen, an den Tag legen; sehen, merken lassen, zur Schau tragen.

eviscerate [i'visəreit] *tr* ausweiden; *fig* entkräften, schwächen; der Substanz berauben.

evoc|ation [evo(u)'keiʃən] (Geister-)Beschwörung *f*; Wach-, Zurück-, Hervorrufen *n*; **~ative** [i'vɔkətiv] beschwörend; wachrufend.

evoke [i'vouk] *tr (Geister)* beschwören *a. fig*; in die Erinnerung zurück-, wachrufen; hervorrufen, verursachen.

evolut|e ['iːvəluːt] *math* Evolute *f*; **~ion** [iːvə'luːʃən, *Am* evə'l-] Entwick(e)lung *a. phys chem*; Entfaltung, Evolution; *(Gas)* Abgabe *f*; *math* Wurzelziehen, Radizieren *n*; *mil mar* Formationsänderung; *(Tänzer)* Bewegung *f*, Tanzschritt *m*; *theory of ~~ (biol)* Entwicklungstheorie *f*, Evolutionismus *m*; **~ionary** [-'luːʃnəri] *a biol* Entwicklungs-, Evolutions-.

evolve [i'vɔlv] *tr itr* (sich) entwickeln, (sich) entfalten (*into* zu); *tr (Plan)* ausarbeiten, ausdenken; *(Hitze)* abgeben; hervorbringen; *chem* ausscheiden; *itr* entstehen (*from* aus).

ewe [juː] (Mutter-)Schaf *n*.

ewer ['juə] Wasserkrug *m*, -kanne *f*.

*

ex [eks] **1.** *prp fin com* ohne, ausschließlich; frei von, -frei; ab; *price ~ works* Preis ab Werk; *~ dividend, interest* ohne Dividende, ohne Zinsen; **2.** *pref* ehemalige(r, s), frühere(r, s), Ex-.

exacerbat|e [eks'æsə(ː)beit, *Am* ig'zæsəbeit, ik'sæ-] *tr* verschärfen, verschlimmern; verbittern, verärgern, reizen; **~ion** [-'beiʃən] Verschlimmerung; Verbitterung, Verärgerung *f*.

exact [ig'zækt] *a* genau, exakt; pünktlich, gewissenhaft; richtig, korrekt; strikt, streng, scharf, rigoros; *tr (Forderung)* eintreiben, erzwingen; *(Geld)* erpressen (*from, of* von); erfordern, erforderlich machen; fordern, verlangen; **~ing** [-iŋ] anspruchsvoll, streng; anstrengend; *to be ~~* es sehr genau nehmen; viel verlangen; *~~ penalty* Ordnungsstrafe *f*; **~ion** [ig'zækʃən] Eintreibung, Erpressung; (unbillige) Forderung; erpreßte Abgabe; hohe Anforderung *f*; **~itude** [ig'zæktitjuːd], **~ness** [-nis] Genauigkeit, Exaktheit; Pünktlichkeit, Gewissenhaftigkeit;

Richtigkeit, Korrektheit *f*; **~ly** [-li] *adv (als Antwort)* so ist es, allerdings, freilich; genau, ganz; gerade; *(vor Fragewörtern)* eigentlich.

exaggerat|e [ig'zædʒəreit] *tr itr* verstärken; übertreiben; überbewerten; **~ed** [-id] *a* übertrieben hoch; *com* übersetzt *(Preis)*; **~ion** [-'reiʃən] Übertreibung *f*; **~~** *of value* Überbewertung *f*.

exalt [ig'zɔ:lt] *tr fig* erhöhen; *(in e-n Stand)* erheben; verstärken; preisen, rühmen, verherrlichen; (in der Wirkung) verstärken; *to ~ to the skies* in den Himmel heben; **~ation** [egzɔ:l'teiʃən] Erhebung, Erhöhung, Höhe *f*; Jubel; unbändige(r) Stolz *m*; Verzükkung *f*; **~ed** [ig'zɔ:ltid] *a* hoch, erhaben; jubelnd, voller Stolz; begeistert, verzückt, exaltiert.

exam [ig'zæm] *fam* = *examination.*

examin|ation [igzæmi'neiʃən] Prüfung *f*, Examen *n* (*in* in); Untersuchung(smethode), Überprüfung; Durchsicht, Besichtigung, Kontrolle, Inspektion, Revision; Erhebung; *mil* Musterung; *jur* Vernehmung *f*, Verhör *n*; *(Zoll-)*Revision *f*; *(up)on ~~* bei näherer, eingehender Prüfung; *to admit to an ~~* zu e-r Prüfung zulassen; *to be under ~~* geprüft, vernommen werden; untersucht werden; *to enter, to sit for, to take an ~~* sich e-r Prüfung unterziehen; *to fail in an ~~* bei e-r Prüfung durchfallen, e-e P. nicht bestehen; *to make an ~~ of* (genau) prüfen, durchsehen, besichtigen; *to pass an ~~* e-e Prüfung bestehen; *to undergo an ~~ (med)* sich e-r Untersuchung unterziehen; *competitive ~~* Wettbewerb *m*; *intermediate ~~* Zwischenprüfung *f*; *leaving, terminal ~~* Abschlußprüfung *f*; *medical ~~* ärztliche Untersuchung *f*; *oral, written ~~* mündliche, schriftliche Prüfung *f*; *qualifying ~~* Eignungsprüfung *f*; *random ~~* Stichprobe *f*; *state ~~* Staatsprüfung *f*; *~~ of accounts* Rechnungsprüfung *f*; *~~ of the books* Bücherrevision *f*; *~~ paper* (schriftliche) Prüfungsarbeit *f*; *~~ question* Prüfungsfrage *f*; *~~ of witnesses* Zeugenverhör *n*; **~e** [ig'zæmin] *tr* prüfen, e-r Prüfung unterziehen; untersuchen, (über)prüfen, durchsehen, e-r (genauen) Durchsicht unterziehen; besichtigen, inspizieren; verhören, vernehmen; *itr* prüfen, untersuchen (*into s.th.* etw); sich e-e Meinung bilden (*into* von); *to ~~ o.'s conscience* sein Gewissen erforschen; **~ee** [igzæmi'ni:] Prüfling, Kandidat *m*; **~er** [ig'zæminə] Prüfende(r), Examinator; Revisor; Untersuchende(r); Zollbeamte(r); *jur* Vernehmer *m*; **~ing** [-iŋ]: *~~ body* Prüfungsausschuß *m*, -kommission *f*; *~~ magistrate* Untersuchungsrichter *m*.

example [ig'zɑ:mpl] Beispiel; Muster (-beispiel) (*of* für); Vorbild *n*; Warnung *f*, warnende(s) Beispiel *n*; *math* Aufgabe *f*, *obs* Exempel *n*; *beyond, without ~* beispiellos; *for ~* zum Beispiel; *to be an ~ to s.o.* für jdn ein Beispiel sein; *to follow s.o.'s ~* jds Beispiel folgen; *to give, to set an ~, a good ~* ein Beispiel geben, mit dem guten Beispiel vorangehen; *to make an ~ of* an jdm ein Exempel statuieren an.

exasperat|e [ig'zɑ:spəreit] *tr* erbittern; ärgerlich machen, (ver)ärgern; (auf)reizen; verschärfen, verstärken, verschlimmern; **~ion** [-'reiʃən] Erbitterung *f*, Ärger *m*; *in ~~* aus Wut.

excavat|e ['ekskəveit] *tr* ausheben, -baggern, -schachten, -graben; **~ion** [-'veiʃən] Aushöhlung, -hebung, -schachtung, -baggerung; Höhlung, Höhle; Ausgrabung *(a. Gegenstand)*; Erdarbeit *f*; Aushub *m*; **~or** ['ekskəveitə] Erdarbeiter; Trockenbagger *m*.

exceed [ik'si:d] *tr* überschreiten, übersteigen, hinausgehen über, größer sein (*by* als); übertreffen (*s.o.'s expectations* jds Erwartungen); übersteigen; *(Rechte)* mißbrauchen; *itr* sich auszeichnen, sich hervortun (*in* in); **~ing** [-iŋ] hervorragend, gewaltig, un-, außergewöhnlich, außerordentlich; *(Betrag)* überschießend; *an amount not ~~* ein Betrag von nicht über; **~ingly** [-iŋli] *adv* äußerst, (ganz) besonders, in hohem Maße, außerordentlich.

excel [ik'sel] *tr* übertreffen, überragen (*in* in); *itr* sich auszeichnen, sich hervortun (*at* bei; *in* in; *as* als); hervorragend sein; **~lence** ['eksələns] Vortrefflichkeit, Vorzüglichkeit; (besondere) Güte, Fähigkeit; hervorragende Leistung *f* (*at, in* in); Vorzug *m*, Stärke *f*; **E~lency** Exzellenz *f (Titel)*; **~lent** ['eksələnt] ausgezeichnet, hervorragend, vortrefflich, vorzüglich; vollendet; **~sior** [ek'selsiɔ:] *a* höher, größer; *s* [ik'selsiə] *Am* Holzwolle; *typ* Brillant *f (Schriftgrad)*.

except [ik'sept] *tr* (her)ausnehmen, auslassen, ausschließen (*from* aus); e-e Ausnahme machen mit; *itr* widersprechen, Widerspruch erheben, Einwendungen machen (*against* gegen); *prp* außer, ausgenommen; *~ for* bis auf; mit Ausnahme *gen*; *present company ~ed* Anwesende ausgenommen; **~ing** [-iŋ] *prp (nach: not, without, nothing u. always)* außer, ausgenommen; **~ion** [-pʃən] Ausnahme *f* (*to* von); Einwand *m*, Einwendung; Beanstandung; *jur* Einrede; *(Zeuge)* Ablehnung *f*; *as an ~, by way of an ~* als Ausnahme; ausnahmsweise; *with the ~ of, that* mit Ausnahme *gen*, mit der Ausnahme, daß; *with certain ~s* mit bestimmten, gewissen Ausnahmen; *without ~* ohne Ausnahme, ausnahmslos; *to be an ~~ to s.th.* e-e Ausnahme von etw bilden; *to make an ~~ to s.th.* von etw e-e Ausnahme machen; *to take ~* Anstoß nehmen (*to* an); beanstanden (*to s.th.* etw); Einwendungen machen (*to* gegen); widersprechen (*to s.th.* etw); ablehnen (*to s.o.* jdn); *the ~ proves the rule* Ausnahmen bestätigen die Regel; **~ionable** [-pʃnəbl] auszunehmen(d); anfechtbar; **~ional** [-pʃənl] un-, außergewöhnlich; *~~ case, law, price, provisions (pl)* Ausnahmefall *m*, -gesetz *n*, -preis *m*, -vorschriften *f pl*; **~ionally** [-pʃnəli] *adv* außergewöhnlich, ungewöhnlich, ganz besonders.

excerpt [ek'sə:pt] *tr* ausziehen, e-n Auszug machen (*from* aus); *s* ['eksə:pt] Auszug *m*, Exzerpt; Zitat *n*.

excess [ik'ses] *s* Übermaß *n* (*of* an); Überschuß *m*; Mehr *n*; (Fahrpreis-) Zuschlag *m*; *pl* Ausschweifungen *f pl*, übermäßige(r) Genuß *m*, Unmäßigkeit, Maßlosigkeit *f*; Ausschreitungen *f pl*; *a* [ik'ses, 'ekses] Mehr-, Über-; überschüssig; *in ~ of* mehr als, über ... hinaus; *to ~* im Übermaß; *to be in ~ of* hinausgehen über, überschreiten, -steigen; *to carry to ~* übertreiben; über das Ziel hinausschießen (*s.th.* mit etw); *~ of exports* Ausfuhrüberschuß *m*; *~ of money* Geldüberhang *m*; *~ of population* Bevölkerungsüberschuß *m*; *~ of purchasing power* Kaufkraftüberhang *m*; **~ amount** Mehrbetrag, Überschuß *m*; **~ consumption** Mehrverbrauch *m*; **~ expenditure** Mehrausgaben *f pl*; **~ fare** *rail* Zuschlag *m*; **~ freight, luggage,** *Am* **baggage** Überfracht *f*; *Am fig* Ballast *m*; **~ive** [-iv] übermäßig, übertrieben, Über-; unmäßig, maßlos; **~iveness** [-ivnis] Übermäßigkeit, Übertriebenheit; Maßlosigkeit *f*; **~ postage** Strafporto *n*, Nachgebühr *f*; **~ pressure** Überdruck *m*; **~ price** Überpreis *m*; **~ production** Produktionsüberschuß *m*; **~ profits** *pl* Mehrgewinn *m*; *~~ tax (Am), (Br) duty* Mehrgewinnsteuer *f*; **~ stock** Mehrbestand *m*; **~ value** Mehrwert *m*; **~ weight** Übergewicht *n*.

exchange [iks'tʃeindʒ] *tr* (aus-, ein-, um)tauschen (*with* mit); (aus-, ein-, um)wechseln (*for* gegen); vertauschen (*for* mit); *itr* wert sein; *mil* sich versetzen lassen; übergehen (*from* von; *into* zu); *s* (Aus-, Um-)Tausch *m*; Aus-, Ein-, Umwechs(e)lung *f*; (Geld-)Wechseln *n*; Wechsel-, Umrechnungskurs *m*; *(foreign ~)* Valuta *f*, Devisen *pl*, ausländische Zahlungsmittel *n pl*; Wechsel *m*, Tratte *f*, Akzept *n*; Umrechnung *f*; Umsatz *m*; Börse *f*, Markt *m*; (Arbeits-, Fernsprech-, Fernschreib-)Vermitt(e)lung *f*, Amt *n*; *Am mil* Kantine, Marketenderei *f*; *pl Am* Verrechnungsschecks *m pl*; *at the ~ of* zum Kurs von; *by way of ~* im Tausch, auf dem Tauschwege; *in ~* dafür; als Ersatz; *in ~ for* im Tausch gegen, für; als Entschädigung für; *to give in ~* in Tausch geben, einwechseln; *to make an ~* e-n Tausch machen; *to obtain, to receive in ~ for s.th.* im Tausch gegen etw erhalten; *to take in ~* in Tausch nehmen; *account of ~* Wechselkonto *n*; *bill of ~* Wechsel *m*, Tratte *f*; *corn, cotton ~* Getreide-, Baumwollmarkt *m*, -börse *f*; *difference of ~* Kursunterschied *m*; *labo(u)r ~* Arbeitsamt *n*, Arbeits-, Stellenvermitt(e)lung *f*; *produce ~* Produktenbörse *f*; *rate of ~* Wechsel-, Verrechnungskurs *m*; *stock ~* Börse *f*; *telephone ~* Fernsprechamt *n*, Fernsprechvermitt(e)lung *f*; *~ of goods* Güter-, Warenaustausch *m*; *~ of letters* Briefwechsel *m*; *~ of notes (pol)* Notenwechsel *m*; *~ of prisoners* Gefangenenaustausch *m*; *~ of territories* Gebietsaustausch *m*; *~ of views* Meinungsaustausch *m*; **~able** [-əbl] austauschbar (*for* gegen); **~ advice** Kursbericht *m*; **~ arbitration** Wechselarbitrage *f*; **~ bank** Wechselbank *f*; **~ broker** Börsenmakler, Wechselagent *m*; **~ brokerage** Wechselprovision *f*; **~ business** Wechsel-, Börsengeschäft *n*; **~ control** Devisenbewirtschaftung *f*; *~~ office* Devisenstelle *f*; **~ fluctuations** *pl* Kursschwankungen *f pl*; **~ list** Kurszettel *m*, -notierung *f*; **~ office** Wechselstube *f*; **~ quotation** Börsennotierung *f*; **~ rate** Umrechnungs-, Wechselkurs *m*; **~ regulations** *pl* Devisenbestimmungen *f pl*, Wechselordnung *f*; **~ report** Börsen-, Kursbericht *m*; **~ restrictions** *pl* Devisenbeschränkungen *f pl*; **~ stability** Währungsstabilität *f*; **~ student, teacher** Austauschstudent, -lehrer *m*; **~ transactions** *pl* Börsen-, Devisenumsatz *m*; **~ usages** *pl* Börsenusancen *f pl*; **~ value** Tausch-, Gegenwert *m*.

exchequer [iks'tʃekə] Staatskasse *f*, -schatz, Fiskus *m*, Finanzverwaltung *f*; *fam* Geldmittel *n pl*, Finanzen *f pl*; *the E~ (Großbritannien)* das Schatzamt, das Finanzministerium; *the Chancellor of the E~* der Schatzkanzler, der Finanzminister; **~ bond** Schatzanweisung *f*.

excis|e [ek'saiz, ik-] **1.** *s (~~ tax)* indirekte, Verbrauchssteuer *f*; *tr* besteuern, mit e-r Verbrauchssteuer belegen; *~~ licence (Am)* Schankkonzession *f*; *~-man, officer* Steuereinnehmer *m*; **2.** *tr* (her)ausschneiden; *med* operativ entfernen; *bot zoo* einkerben; **~ion** [ek'siʒən] Ausschneiden *n*; *med* Entfernung *f*; Ausschluß *m*.

excit|ability [iksaitə'biliti] Erregbarkeit, Reizbarkeit; *biol* Reaktion *f* auf Reize; **~able** [ik'saitəbl] erregbar, reizbar, nervös; **~ant** ['eksitənt] *med* Reizmittel *n*; **~ation** [eksi'teiʃən] Erregung, Reizung; *fig* Auf-, Ermunterung, Anregung *f*; Stimulus *m*; *phys* Erregung, Speisung *f*; **~e** [ik'sait] *tr* anregen, (an)reizen (*to* zu); hervorrufen, erwecken, erregen; in Erregung versetzen, aufregen, nervös machen; *phys* erregen; *(Schwingungen)* erzeugen, hervorrufen; *physiol* e-e Reaktion hervorrufen in; **~ed** [-id] *a* erregt, aufgeregt, nervös; *to get ~~* sich aufregen (*over* über); **~ement** [-mənt] Erregung, Aufregung, Nervosität; Aufregung *f*, Reiz *m*; **~er** [-ə] *phys* Erreger *m*; **~ing** [-iŋ] auf-, erregend; hochinteressant, spannend, erstaunlich, fesselnd; *el* Erreger-; *~~ current* Erregerstrom *m*; *~~ voltage* Erreger-, Gitterspannung *f*.

*

exclaim [iks'kleim] *tr* (aus)rufen, ausstoßen; *tr itr* (auf)schreien (*from pain* vor Schmerz); *to ~ against s.o.* jdn anschreien, -brüllen; *to ~ at* s-e Überraschung äußern über.

exclamation [eksklə'meiʃən] Ausruf, (Auf-)Schrei; *gram* Ausrufesatz *m*, -wort *n*; *note of ~~, ~~ mark, point* Ausrufezeichen *n*; **~ory** [eks'klæmətəri] Ausrufe-; *~~ sentence* Ausrufesatz *m*.

exclude [iks'klu:d] *tr* aussperren, entfernen, ausschließen (*from* aus); *(Wettbewerb)* ausschalten; *to ~ all possibility of doubt* jeden Zweifel ausschließen; *to be ~d* nicht zugelassen, ausgeschlossen sein (*from* von).

exclus|ion [iks'klu:ʒən] Ausschluß *m*; Zurückweisung, Ablehnung; Ausschaltung, Ausscheidung *f*; *tech* Abschluß *m*; *to the ~~ of* unter Ausschluß *gen*; **~ive** [-siv] ausschließend, -schließlich; alleinig, Allein-; sich abschließend, exklusiv; abweisend, reserviert, dünkelhaft; ausgewählt, vornehm, elegant; *fam (Laden)* teuer; *film* mit alleinigem Vorführungsrecht; *~~ of* ausschließlich *gen*, ohne, abgesehen von; *to be mutually ~~* sich gegenseitig ausschließen; *~~ agent* Alleinvertreter *m*; *~~ report* Sonderbericht *m*; *~~ right* ausschließliche(s), Alleinrecht, Monopol *n* (*to* auf); *~~ sale* Alleinverkauf(srecht *n*) *m*; **~iveness** [-sivnis] Exklusivität *f*.

excogitat|e [eks'kɔdʒiteit] *tr* ausdenken, ersinnen, *fam* austüfteln, *pej* aushecken; erfinden; **~ion** [-'teiʃən] Überlegung *f*; Gedanke *m*, Idee; Erfindung *f*.

excommunicat|e [ekskə'mju:nikeit] *tr* mit dem Kirchenbann belegen, exkommunizieren; **~ion** ['-keiʃən] Kirchenbann *m*, Exkommunikation *f*.

excoriat|e [eks'kɔ:rieit] *tr (Haut)* abschürfen, wund reiben *od* scheuern; *(Rinde)* abschälen; *Am* heruntermachen; scharf, vernichtend kritisieren; *s.o.* keinen guten Faden an jdm lassen; **~ion** [-'eiʃən] Schinden; Wundreiben *n*; wunde Stelle *f*.

excrement ['ekskrimənt] Kot *m*, Ausscheidung *f*, Exkrement *n*; *pl* Fäkalien *pl*.

excrescen|ce [iks'kresəns] Auswuchs *m a.fig*; *med* Wucherung *f*, Gewächs *n*; **~t** [-t] e-n Auswuchs bildend; *med* wuchernd; *fig* überflüssig.

excret|a [eks'kri:tə] *pl med* Ausscheidungsstoffe *m pl*; **~e** [eks'kri:t] *tr physiol* ausscheiden, absondern; **~ion** [-'kri:ʃən] Ausscheidung, Absonderung *f*.

excruciat|e [iks'kru:ʃieit] *tr* martern, peinigen, quälen *a. fig*; **~ing** [-iŋ] qualvoll, schmerzhaft; *fig* schmerzlich, quälend.

exculpat|e ['ekskʌlpeit] *tr* entschuldigen, freisprechen (*from* von); entlasten, rechtfertigen, reinwaschen (*from* von); **~ion** [-'peiʃən] Rechtfertigung; Entlastung, Freisprechung; Entschuldigung(sgrund *m*) *f*.

excursion [iks'kə:ʃən] Ausflug *m*; Rundfahrt, -reise; *(~ trip)* Gesellschaftsfahrt; *Am* Reisegesellschaft; Abschweifung *f*; *mil* Ausfall *m*; *to go on, to make an ~* e-n Ausflug machen; *alarms and ~~s (fig)* Aufregung *f*; **~ist** [-'kə:ʃnist] Ausflügler, Tourist *m*; **~ ticket** Ausflugskarte *f*; **~ train** Gesellschafts-, Sonderzug *m*.

excursive [eks'kə:siv] umherschweifend; *(Lektüre)* kursorisch; sprunghaft; abschweifend.

excus|able [iks'kju:zəbl] entschuldbar, verzeihlich; **~e** [iks'kju:z] *tr* entschuldigen (*for* wegen; *for being late* für das Zuspätkommen); verzeihen (*s.o.* jdm); Nachsicht üben gegen, in Schutz nehmen; rechtfertigen, verteidigen; erlassen (*s.o. from s.th.* jdm etw); befreien, entbinden, entheben (*from* von); *to ~~ o.s.* sich entschuldigen (*from* wegen, für); *~~ me* entschuldigen Sie! erlauben Sie mal! *you may be ~ed now* Sie können jetzt gehen; *s* [-'kju:s] Entschuldigung; Rechtfertigung; Ausrede, Ausflucht *f*, Vorwand *m*; Befreiung *f* (*from* von); *fam* Ersatz *m*; *in ~~ of* als, zur Entschuldigung *gen*; *without ~~* unentschuldigt; *to admit of no ~~* unentschuldbar sein; *to make, to offer an ~~* sich entschuldigen (*to* bei); *to make ~~s for s.o.* jdn entschuldigen; *to make s.th. o.'s ~~* etw zur Entschuldigung vorbringen.

exeat ['eksiæt] *(Schule)* Ausgeherlaubnis *f*.

execr|able ['eksikrəbl] abscheulich, scheußlich, gräßlich; *Am* minderwertig; **~ate** ['eksikreit] *tr* verfluchen, fluchen (*s.o.* jdm), verwünschen; verabscheuen, hassen, sich ekeln vor; *I ~~ it* mir *od* mich schaudert davor; **~ation** [-'kreiʃən] Fluch *m*, Verwünschung *f*; Abscheu, Ekel, Schauder *m*.

execute ['eksikju:t] *tr (Arbeit, Befehl, Auftrag)* ausführen; *(Auftrag)* durchführen, erledigen; *(Verkauf)* tätigen; *(Gesetz)* anwenden, zur Anwendung bringen; *(Amt)* ausüben, verwalten; *(Erklärung)* abgeben; *(Urteil)* vollstrecken; *(Strafe)* vollziehen; hinrichten; unterzeichnen, ausfertigen, rechtsgültig, -kräftig machen; *(Kunst)* ausführen; *mus* vortragen; *theat* darstellen, spielen, aufführen.

execution [eksi'kju:ʃən] Aus-, Durchführung, Erledigung; Anwendung, Handhabung; Vollziehung *f*, Vollzug *m*; Vollstreckung; Pfändung; Hinrichtung; Unterzeichnung, Siegelung, Ausfertigung *f*; (schriftliches) Urteil *n*; *(Kunst)* Ausführung, Technik *f*, Vortrag *m*, Darstellung *f*, Spiel *n*; (vernichtende) Wirkung; *tech* Bauweise *f*; *of ~* tatkräftig; *to carry into ~, to put in(to) ~* vollenden, aus-, durchführen, bewerkstelligen; *to do great ~* e-e verheerende Wirkung haben; vernichtend wirken; *to take out an ~ against s.o.* jdn (aus)pfänden lassen; *compulsory ~* Zwangsvollstreckung *f*; *mass ~* Massenhinrichtung *f*; *writ of ~* Vollstreckungsbefehl *m*; *~ of a sentence* Strafvollstreckung *f*; **~er** [-ʃnə] Scharfrichter, Henker *m*; **~ proceedings** *pl s* Zwangsvollstreckungsverfahren *n*; **~ sales** *pl Am* Zwangsverkauf *m*, -versteigerung *f*.

executive [ig'zekjutiv] *a pol* ausführend, vollziehend; *(Stellung)* leitend; Exekutiv-; *s pol* vollziehende Gewalt; *(~ branch)* Exekutive; Direktion, Geschäftsleitung, -führung *f*; leitende(r) Angestellter *m*; Leiter, Direktor, Geschäftsführer; *Am* Beamte(r) *m*; Staatsführung *f*; *top ~* Spitzenkraft *f*; **~ board, committee, council** Exekutivausschuß *m*, -komitee *n*, -rat; geschäftsführende(r) Vorstand *m*; **~ functions** *pl* Führungsaufgaben *f pl*; **~ order** *Am* Durchführungsverordnung *f*; **~ power** vollziehende Gewalt *f*; **~ secretary** Geschäftsführer *m*; **~ staff** leitende Angestellte *m pl*.

execut|or [ig'zekjutə] *m*, **~rix** [-triks] *f* Ausführende(r *m*) *f*; Testamentsvollstrecker *m*; **~ory** [-əri] *pol* vollziehend, ausübend; *jur* noch zu vollziehen(d).

exegesis [eksi'dʒi:sis] *rel* Exegese *f*.

exemplar [ig'zemplə] Vorbild, Muster, Modell, (Muster-)Beispiel; Exemplar, Stück *n*; **~iness** [-rinis] Mustergültigkeit *f*; **~y** [-ri] musterhaft, -gültig, vorbildlich; abschreckend, exemplarisch.

exemplif|ication [igzemplifi'keiʃən] (Erläuterung *f* durch ein) Beispiel *n*; *jur* beglaubigte Abschrift *f*; **~y** [ig'zemplifai] *tr* durch ein Beispiel erläutern, beispielhaft zeigen; als Beispiel dienen für, erläutern; e-e beglaubigte Abschrift anfertigen von.

exempt [ig'zempt] *tr* befreien, freistellen, dispensieren (*from* von); erlassen (*s.o. from s.th.* jdm etw); *a* befreit, frei, ausgenommen (*from* von), bevorrechtet; *s* Befreite(r), Bevorrechtete(r) *m*; *~ from charges* spesen-, kostenfrei; *~ from duty* gebühren-, abgaben-, zollfrei; *~ from military service* vom Wehrdienst befreit; *~ from postage* portofrei; *~ from taxation* steuerfrei; **~ion** [ig'zempʃən] Befreiung, Freistellung, Dispensierung *f*, Freisein *n* (*from* von), Ausnahme *f*; Ausschluß *m*, Ausschließung; *com* Lastenfreiheit *f*, Steuerfreibetrag *m*; *~~ from duty* Gebühren-, Abgabenfreiheit *f*; *~~ from liability* Haftungsausschluß *m*; *~~ from military service* Befreiung *f* vom Wehrdienst; Freistellung *f*; *~~ from taxation* Steuerfreiheit *f*.

exercise ['eksəsaiz] *s* Übung; (Schul-)Aufgabe; Übersetzung; Tätigkeit, Betätigung, Anwendung *f*, Gebrauch *m*, Ausübung, Praxis; Bewegung; *rel* heilige Handlung; *mus* Etüde *f*; *meist pl (bes.* Leibes-)Übungen *f pl*, *mil* Exerzieren *n*, Drill *m*; *pl Am* Feier(lichkeiten *f pl*) *f*; *tr* üben, anwenden; praktizieren, ausüben, gebrauchen; *(Geduld)* aufbringen; *(Pflichten)* erfüllen; üben lassen, *bes. mil* drillen, ausbilden, einexerzieren; *nur im Passiv*: *to be ~d* sich aufregen; aufgeregt, verärgert sein; sich Gedanken machen (*about* über); *itr u. to ~ o.s.* üben (*in s.th.* etw), sich üben (*in* in); sich Bewegung verschaffen; *mil* exerzieren; *to take ~* sich Bewegung machen; *to ~ care* aufpassen, achtgeben (*in doing s.th.* wenn man etw tut); *deep-breathing ~s (pl)* Atemübungen *f pl*; *finger ~s (pl mus)* Fingerübungen *f pl*; *gymnastic ~s (pl)* Leibesübungen *f pl*; *opening ~s (pl) (Am)* Eröffnungsfeierlichkeiten *f pl*; *physical ~(s) (pl)* Leibesübungen *f pl*; *~s for the piano, for the violin* Klavier-, Geigenübung *f*; ~ **area** Übungsgelände *n*; **~-book** Schul-, Schreibheft *n*.

exert [ig'zə:t] *tr* gebrauchen, anwenden, einsetzen; *(Druck)* ausüben; *(Einfluß)* aufbieten; anspannen, anstrengen; zur Geltung bringen; *to ~ o.s.* sich anstrengen, sich bemühen, sich Mühe geben (*for* um, wegen); **~ion** [ig'zə:ʃən] Gebrauch *m*, Anwendung, Ausübung *f*; Einsatz *m*; Anspannung; Anstrengung *f*.

exeunt ['eksiʌnt] (sie gehen) ab *(Bühnenanweisung)*; ~ **omnes** alle ab.

exfoliat|e [eks'foulieit] *itr* abblättern; **~ion** [-'eiʃən] Abblätterung *f*.

exhal|ation [ekshə'leiʃən, egzə'l-] Ausatmung *f*, -atmen *n*; Atem, Hauch *m*, Ausdünstung, Gas-, Dampfabgabe *f*; Dunst, Dampf, Geruch; *fig* Ausbruch *m*; **~e** [eks'heil, eg'z-] *itr* ausatmen, verdunsten, verdampfen; ausströmen (*from* vom); *fig* verschwinden; *tr* ausatmen, -hauchen; *(Dampf)* ausstoßen; ausdünsten (*from, out of* aus); *(e-m Gefühl)* Luft machen.

exhaust [ig'zə:st] *tr* erschöpfen, völlig aufbrauchen; (aus)leeren, aussaugen, auspumpen; trockenlegen; *(Thema)* erschöpfen(d behandeln); *itr* ausströmen, entweichen; *s tech* Exhaustor; Auslaß; *mot* Auspuff(rohr *n*) *m*; Auspuff-, Abgas *n*; Abdampf *m*; **~ed** [-id] *a* ver-, aufgebraucht; *tech* ausgebraucht; erschöpft; ermüdet, ermattet; *(Buch)* vergriffen; *(Frist)* abgelaufen; *min* abgebaut; *to be ~~* erschöpft, völlig ausgepumpt sein; **~er** [-ə] Sauglüfter, Exhaustor *m*; ~ **fan** Absaugventilator *m*; ~ **gas** Ab-, Auspuffgas *n*; **~ing** [-iŋ] mühsam, -selig, anstrengend, ermüdend; **~ion** [ig'zə:stʃən] Auf-, Verbrauchen *n*; Erschöpfung, Ermüdung, Ermattung *f*; Verbraucht-, Vergriffensein *n*; *min* Abbau *m*; *(Dampf)* Ausströmen *n*; **~ive** [-iv] erschöpfend, eingehend, vollständig, völlig; **~-pipe** Auspuffrohr *n*; **~-steam** Abdampf *m*.

exhibit [ig'zibit] *tr* zeigen, sehen lassen, an den Tag legen, zur Schau stellen; *(im Schaufenster, auf Ausstellungen)* ausstellen; *(Ware)* auslegen; vorführen *a. film*; *(Papiere)* vorzeigen, -weisen, -legen; einreichen; *jur (Klage)* ein-, vorbringen; *med (Arznei)* verordnen, applizieren; *s* Ausstellung; Darbietung; Schaustellung *f*; Ausstellungsstück *n*, -gegenstand *m*; *jur* Beweisstück *n*, Beleg *m*; Anlage; Eingabe *f*; *pl film* Reklamephotos *n pl*; **~ion** [eksi'biʃən] Ausstellung, Schau; Zurschaustellung, Darlegung; Vorlage, Vorzeigung, Einreichung; Vorführung *f*; *Br* Stipendium *n*; *to make an ~~ of o.s.* sich lächerlich machen; *to put on an ~~* e-e Ausstellung veranstalten; *art ~~* Kunstausstellung *f*; *industrial ~~* Gewerbeschau *f*; *motor ~~* Automobilausstellung *f*; *universal ~~* Weltausstellung *f*; *~~ hall* Ausstellungshalle *f*; *~~ of pictures* Gemäldeausstellung *f*; *~~ room* Ausstellungsraum *m*; **~ioner** [eksi'biʃnə] *Br* Stipendiat *m*; **~ionism** [eksi'biʃnizm] Exhibitionismus *m*; **~ionist** [eksi'biʃnist] Exhibitionist *m*; **~or** [-ə] Aussteller; Kinobesitzer *m*.

exhilarat|e [ig'zilәreit] *tr* auf-, erheitern; ermuntern, anregen; **~ion** [-'reiʃən] Auf-, Erheiterung; Ermunterung *f*; Frohsinn *m*, Heiterkeit *f*.

exhort [ig'zə:t] *tr* ermahnen, mahnen (*s.o.* jdm); **~ation** [egzə:'teiʃən] (Er-)Mahnung *f*.

exhum|ation[ekshju:'meiʃən]Exhumierung *f*; **~e** [eks'hju:m] *tr (Toten)* wiederausgraben; *fig* ausgraben, enthüllen, ans Licht bringen.

exig|ence, -cy ['eksidʒəns(i)] Dringlichkeit; Notwendigkeit, Notlage *f*; dringende(s) Bedürfnis, Erfordernis *n*; dringende(r) Fall *m*; **~ent** ['-ənt] dringend, eilig, ernst; anspruchsvoll; *to be ~~ of s.th.* etw dringend erfordern.

exigu|ity [eksi'gju(:)iti] Winzigkeit, Kleinheit, Dürftigkeit, Unerheblichkeit *f*; **~ous** [eg'zigjuəs] klein, winzig, dürftig, schwach; unerheblich.

exile ['eksail, 'egz-] *s* Verbannung *f*, Exil *n*; *fig* lange Abwesenheit *f*; Verbannte(r) *m*; *tr* verbannen, in die Verbannung schicken (*from* aus); *to go into ~* in die Verbannung gehen; *to live in ~* im Exil leben.

exist [ig'zist] *itr* bestehen, existieren, (wirklich, Wirklichkeit) sein; leben (*on* von); auskommen (*on* mit); vorkommen, vorhanden sein; *fam* vegetieren; *does that ~?* gibt es das? **~ence** [-əns] Dasein, Bestehen *n*, Existenz *f*; Leben(sweise *f*) *n*; Dauer *f*; *in ~~* bestehend, vorhanden; *to be in ~~* bestehen; *to bring, to call into ~~* ins Leben rufen; *to come, to spring into ~~* (plötzlich) auftreten, dasein; *conditions of ~~* Lebens-, Existenzbedingungen *f pl*; **~ent** [-ənt] bestehend, wirklich; vorhanden, gegenwärtig; **~ential** [egzis'tenʃəl] existentiell; **~entialism** [egzis'tenʃəlizm] Existentialismus *m*; **~ing** [-iŋ] bestehend, vorhanden; *under ~~ circumstances* unter den gegenwärtigen Umständen.

exit ['eksit] *s theat* Abgang *m*; Ausreise *f*; *fam* Tod; Ausgang *(aus e-m Gebäude)*; *tech* Abzug *m*; *itr*: (er, sie geht) ab *(Bühnenanweisung)*; *she made a hasty ~* sie empfahl sich schleunigst; ~ **permit** Ausreisegenehmigung *f*.

ex libris [eks'laibris] Exlibris *n*.

exodus ['eksədəs] Aufbruch, Auszug *m*, Aus-, Abwanderung *f*; *the E~* der Exodus, das 2. Buch Mosis; *mass ~* Massenabwanderung *f*; *rural ~* Landflucht *f*; *~ of capital* Kapitalabwanderung *f*.

ex officio [eksə'fiʃiou] *a adv* von Amts wegen, dienstlich.

exogenous [ek'sədʒinəs] von außen verursacht, exogen.

exonerat|e [ig'zənəreit] *tr* rechtfertigen; *jur* entlasten; *(von e-r Verbindlichkeit)* befreien, entbinden (*from* von); **~ion** [-'reiʃən] Rechtfertigung; Entlastung; Befreiung *f* (*from* von).

exorbitan|ce, -cy [ig'zə:bitəns(i)] Übermaß *n*; Übertreibung, Maßlosigkeit *f*; **~t** [-t] übertrieben, maßlos; *~~ price* Wucherpreis *m*.

exorc|ism ['eksə:sizm] Geisterbeschwörung *f*; **~ist** ['-ist] Geisterbeschwörer *m*; **~ize, ~ise** ['-aiz] *tr (e-n bösen Geist)* beschwören, bannen, austreiben (*from, out of* aus).

exoteric [ekso(u)'terik] exoterisch, für e-n weiteren Kreis bestimmt, allgemein(verständlich); *fig* volkstümlich.

exotic [eg'zətik] ausländisch; fremdartig, exotisch.

expan|d [iks'pænd] *tr* ausstrecken, -spannen, ausbreiten; (aus)dehnen, weiten; vergrößern; erweitern (*into* zu) *a. math*; *math* ausmultiplizieren, entwickeln; *fig* eingehend erörtern, behandeln; *itr* sich ausstrecken, sich entfalten; sich dehnen (*with heat* durch Hitze); sich (aus)weiten; sich erweitern, sich verbreitern; gesprächig werden; **~der** [-də] *sport* Expander *(Gerät)*; *mot* Spreizring *m*; **~se** [iks'pæns] (große) Ausdehnung; weite(r) Raum *m*; **~sion** [iks'pænʃən] Ausdehnung, Erweiterung *a. math*, Ausweitung; Vervollkommnung; *pol* Expansion, Ausbreitung *f*; weite(r) Raum *m*, Weite *f*, Umfang; Zuwachs *m*; *tech* Dehnung *f*; **~sionism** [-'pænʃənizm] Expansionspolitik *f*; **~sive** [-'pænsiv] sich ausdehnend, dehnbar, expansiv; ausgedehnt, weit, umfassend, umfangreich; verständnisvoll, sich einfühlend; frei, offen, mitteilsam; gefühlvoll; überschwenglich; *psychol* größenwahnsinnig; **~siveness** [-'pænsivnis] Expansivkraft; Weite *f*; Verständnis, Einfühlungsvermögen *n*, Offenheit, Mitteilsamkeit; Überschwenglichkeit *f*; *psychol* Größenwahn *m*.

expatiat|e [eks'peiʃieit] *itr* sich verbreiten, sich auslassen, sich äußern (*on, upon* über); **~ion** [-'eiʃən] Auslassung; eingehende, breite Darstellung *f*.

expatriat|e [eks'pætrieit, *Am* -pei-] *tr* ausbürgern; *itr u. to ~~ o.s.* auswandern; auf s-e Staatsangehörigkeit verzichten; [-iit] *a* heimatlos; *s* Heimatlose(r) *m*; **~ion** [-'eiʃən] Vertreibung, Verbannung; Auswanderung; Ausbürgerung; Aufgabe *f* der Staatsangehörigkeit.

expect [iks'pekt] *tr* erwarten, rechnen mit; zumuten (*from s.o.* jdm); *fam* annehmen, meinen, vermuten; *to be ~ing (fam) (Frau)* in andern Umständen sein; *I ~ed as much* das habe ich erwartet; *I can't be ~ed* man kann nicht von mir erwarten; **~ance, -cy** [-əns(i)] Erwartung; Anwartschaft *f*; *life ~ancy* (statistisch errechnete) Lebenserwartung *f*; **~ant** [-ənt] *a* (er)wartend; erwartungsvoll; *s* Anwärter *m* (*of* auf); *~~ heir* Erbschaftsanwärter *m*; *~~ mother* werdende Mutter *f*; **~ation** [ekspek'teiʃən] *oft pl* Erwartung(en *pl*), Hoffnung(en *pl*), Aussicht(en *pl*); Anwartschaft *f* (*of* auf); Erbaussicht (*from* bei); *according to ~~(s)* erwartungsgemäß; *against, contrary to ~~(s)* wider Erwarten; *beyond ~~(s)* über Erwarten; *in ~~ of* in Erwartung *gen*; *to answer, to come up to, to meet s.o.'s ~~s* jds Erwartungen entsprechen; *to fall short of, not to come up to s.o.'s ~~s* jds Erwartungen nicht entsprechen; *to have great ~~s of s.th.* in etw große Erwartungen setzen; *~~ of life* Lebenserwartung *f*.

expectorat|e [eks'pektəreit] *tr* aushusten, ausspeien; *itr* speien; **~ion** [-'reiʃən] Auswurf; Schleim *m*.

exped|ience, -cy [iks'pi:djəns(i)] Brauchbarkeit, Zweckmäßigkeit, -dienlichkeit; Tunlichkeit, Ratsamkeit *f*; Vorteil(haftigkeit *f*) *m*; eigene(s) Interesse *n*; *on grounds of ~~* aus Zweckmäßigkeitsgründen; **~ient** [-djənt] *a* brauchbar, passend, angebracht, zweckmäßig, -dienlich, vorteilhaft, nützlich (*to* für); tunlich, dienlich, ratsam; im eigenen Interesse liegend; *s* Mittel *n* (zum Zweck); Kniff, Ausweg; (Not-)Behelf *m*; *to resort to ~~s* zu Notbehelfen s-e Zuflucht nehmen; **~ite** ['ekspidait] *tr* beschleunigen; erleichtern, fördern; (schnell) erledigen; absenden, abfertigen; **~ition** [ekspi'diʃən] *(exploring ~~)* (Forschungs-)Reise, Expedition *f a. mil*; *mil* Feldzug *m*; Eile, Geschwindigkeit *f*; **~ionary** [ekspi'diʃnəri] *a* Expeditions-; *~~ force (mil)* Expeditionskorps *n*; **~itious**

[ekspi'diʃəs] schleunig, eilig, prompt; schnell, flink.

expel [iks'pel] *tr* ausweisen, abschieben, des Landes verweisen; hinauswerfen, ausstoßen, ausschließen (*from* aus); *(von der Universität)* relegieren; *tech* hinausdrücken, -treiben, -schleudern; **~lee** [ekspe'li:] *Am* Ausgewiesene(r),Vertriebene(r),Flüchtling*m*.

expend [iks'pend] *tr (Geld)* ausgeben, verausgaben; verbrauchen; *(Mittel)* einsetzen, erschöpfen; *(Munition)* verschießen; *(Zeit, Arbeit, Mühe)* auf-, verwenden (*on, in* auf); *(Sorgfalt)* anwenden; **~able** [-əbl] *a mil* für den Verbrauch *od* Verzehr (bestimmt); zu ersetzen(d); entbehrlich; *s pl* Himmelfahrtskommando *n (die Männer)*; *Am* Verbrauchsmaterial *n*; **~iture** [-itʃə] (Geld-)Ausgabe; Verausgabung, Aufwendung *f*; Verbrauch, Aufwand *m* (*of* an); *administrative* ~~ Verwaltungsunkosten *pl*; *capital* ~~ Kapitalanlage *f*; *cash* ~~ Geld-, Barausgabe *f*; *estimate of* ~~ Kostenanschlag *m*; *excess* ~~ Mehrausgaben *f pl*; *government, national, state* ~~ Staatsausgaben *f pl*; *initial* ~~ Anlagekosten *pl*; *operating* ~~ Betriebsausgaben; *permanent* ~~ laufende Ausgaben *f pl*; *social* ~~ Soziallasten *f pl*; ~~ *authorization* Beschaffungsgenehmigung *f*.

expense [iks'pens] (Geld-)Ausgabe *f*, Auslagen *f pl*, Aufwendungen *f pl*; Aufwand; Verbrauch; Verlust *m*, Opfer *n*; *a. pl* (Un-)Kosten, Lasten *pl*; *pl* Auslagen, Spesen *pl*; *after deducting ~s* nach Abzug der Kosten; *at s.o.'s* ~ auf jds Kosten *a. fig*; zu jds Lasten; *at any* ~ um jeden Preis; *at great, little* ~ mit großen, geringen Kosten; *dividing the ~(s), at joint* ~ auf gemeinsame Kosten; *free of* ~ kosten-, spesenfrei; *regardless of* ~ ohne Rücksicht auf die Kosten; *to allow s.o. his ~(s)* jdm die Auslagen, Kosten ersetzen; *to bear, to defray, to meet, to pay the ~(s)* die Kosten tragen, bestreiten, bezahlen; *to cut down the ~(s)* die Kosten verringern; *to go to great* ~ sich in Unkosten stürzen; *to incur ~s* es sich etw kosten lassen; *to involve* ~ mit Kosten verbunden sein, Kosten verursachen; *to make o.'s ~(s)* auf s-e Kosten kommen; *to put s.o. to* ~ jdm Kosten verursachen; *to spare no ~(s)* keine Kosten scheuen; ~ **account** Spesenkonto *n*; ~ **advanced** Kosten-, Spesenvorschuß *m*; ~ **allowance** Aufwandsentschädigung *f*; ~ **budget** Gemeinkostenbudget *n*; ~ **factor** Kostenfaktor *m*; ~ **voucher** Kosten-, Spesenaufstellung *f*.

expensive [iks'pensiv] kostspielig, mit hohen Kosten verbunden, aufwendig.

experience [iks'piəriəns] *s* Erfahrung (*in, of* in); Praxis, Sachkenntnis, Beschlagenheit, Bewandertheit *f*; Erleben, Erlebnis *n*; *com* Kenntnisse, praktische Fertigkeiten *f pl*; *tr* erfahren; erleben; begegnen; mit-, durchmachen; *(Verluste)* erleiden; *(auf Schwierigkeiten)* stoßen; *from* ~ aus Erfahrung; *to gain* ~ Erfahrungen sammeln; *to have a wide* ~ über umfangreiche Erfahrungen verfügen; *to learn by* ~ aus der Erfahrung lernen; *business* ~ Geschäftserfahrung *f*; *driving* ~ Fahrpraxis *f*; *professional* ~ Berufserfahrung *f*; ~ *in life* Lebenserfahrung *f*; **~d** [-t] *a* erfahren, bewandert, sachkundig, *com* versiert.

experiment [iks'perimənt] *s* Versuch *m*, Experiment *n*, Probe *f*; *itr* [-ment] Versuche anstellen; Experimente machen, experimentieren (*on* an; *with* mit); erproben (*with s.th.* etw); **~al** [eksperi'mentl] versuchsweise, experimentell; Versuchs-; ~~ *animal* Versuchstier *n*; ~~ *department* Versuchsabteilung *f*; ~~ *farm* Versuchsfarm *f*; ~~ *field* Versuchsgelände *n*; ~~ *run (mot)* Probelauf *m*; ~~ *stage* Versuchsstadium *n*; ~~ *station* Versuchsanstalt *f*; **~alist** [eksperi'mentəlist], **~er** [eks'perimentə] Experimentator *m*; **~ation** [eksperimen'teiʃən] Experimentieren *n*.

expert ['ekspə:t] *a* [*pred a.* iks'pə:t] erfahren, sachkundig, -verständig; geübt, geschickt (*in, at* in; *with* an); Kenner-, Sachverständigen-, Experten-; *s* (Sach-)Kenner, Sachverständige(r), Experte, Fachmann, Spezialist (*in a field* auf e-m Gebiet); Gutachter *m*; *the ~s* die Fachwelt; *to be ~ at driving* ein ausgezeichneter Fahrer sein; *financial* ~ Finanzsachverständige(r) *m*; ~ **advice** fachmännische(r) Rat *m*; ~ **appraiser** amtliche(r) Schätzer *m*; ~ **evidence**: *according to* ~~ nach Ansicht der Sachverständigen; ~ **inquiry** Sachverständigenuntersuchung *f*; **~ise** [ekspə:'ti:z] Sachverständigengutachten *n*, Expertise *f*; ~ **knowledge** Sachkenntnis *f*, Fachwissen *n*; **~ness** [-nis] fachliche Qualifikation; Erfahrenheit; Geschicklichkeit *f*; ~ **opinion** Sachverständigengutachten *n*; ~ **witness** *jur* Sachverständige(r) *m*; ~ **worker** Facharbeiter, Spezialist *m*.

expi|able ['ekspiəbl] sühnbar; **~ate** ['ekspieit] *tr* sühnen, büßen (für), abbüßen, Buße tun für; **~ation** [-'eiʃən] Sühne, Buße *f*; **~atory** ['ekspieitəri, -piət-] sühnend, büßend; Sühn-, Buß-.

expir|ation [ekspaiə'reiʃən, -pi-] Ausatmen *n*, -atmung *f*; Tod *m*, (Lebens-) Ende; Ende *n*, Ablauf *m*, Erlöschen *n*; *fin* Verfall *m*; *at the ~~ of* nach Ablauf *gen*; *at the time of* ~~ zur Verfallzeit; bei Verfall; *upon* ~~ bei Verfall; *date of* ~~ Ablaufzeit *f*; Verfalltag *m*; **~atory** [iks'paiərətəri] *a* Ausatmungs-; **~e** [iks'paiə] *itr* ausatmen; *lit* in den letzten Zügen liegen, sterben; aufhören, enden; erlöschen, ablaufen, verfallen, die Gültigkeit verlieren; **~y** [iks'paiəri] Verfall, Ablauf *m*.

explain [iks'plein] *tr* erklären, ausea.setzen, verständlich machen; erläutern; deuten, auslegen; begründen, e-n Grund angeben für, rechtfertigen; *itr* e-e Erklärung geben; *to ~ o.s.* sich verständlich machen; s-e Gründe angeben, sich rechtfertigen; *to ~ away* wegerklären, vertuschen.

explanat|ion [eksplə'neiʃən] Erklärung, Erläuterung; Begründung *f*, Grund *m* (*of* für); Auslegung, Deutung; Ausea.setzung; Verständigung *f*; *in ~~ of* zur Erklärung *gen*; *to come to an ~~ with s.o. about s.th.* sich mit jdm über etw verständigen; *to make some* ~~ e-e Erklärung abgeben; **~ory** [iks'plænətəri] erklärend, erläuternd.

expletive [eks'pli:tiv, iks-] *a* (aus-) füllend; überflüssig; Füll-; *s* Flick-, Füllwort *n*; Lückenbüßer; Fluch *m*.

explic|able ['eksplikəbl] erklärbar; deutbar; **~ate** ['-keit] *tr* erklären, deutlich machen; **~ation** [-'keiʃən] Erklärung, Erläuterung, Darlegung, Auslegung, Deutung *f*.

explicit [iks'plisit] eindeutig, deutlich, klar; formell, bestimmt, ausdrücklich; offen, freimütig; *to be ~ about s.th.* detaillierte Angaben über etw machen.

explode [iks'ploud] *itr* explodieren, in die Luft fliegen, (zer)platzen, zerspringen; *(Granate)* krepieren, detonieren; ausbrechen (*with laughter* in ein Gelächter); *(Mensch)* bersten (*with* vor); *tr* explodieren lassen, in die Luft jagen, sprengen; *fig* zerstören; (gründlich) widerlegen, aufräumen mit, ad adsurdum führen; *(Plan)* über den Haufen werfen; **~d** [-id] *a* erledigt, veraltet; ~~ *view* Ansicht *f* der Einzelteile.

exploit ['eksplɔit] *s* Heldentat; Groß-, große Tat *f*; *tr* [iks'plɔit] aus-, benutzen; verwerten; in Betrieb nehmen; *min* abbauen; *pej* ausbeuten, mißbrauchen; **~able** [eks'plɔitəbl] benutzbar, verwertbar; **~ation** [-'teiʃən] Nutzung; Inbetriebnahme, Bewirtschaftung; Verwertung *f*; Betrieb; *min* Abbau *m*; Ausnutzung, Ausbeutung *f*; **~er** [eks'plɔitə] Ausbeuter *m*.

explor|ation [eksplɔ:'reiʃən] Erforschung; Forschungsreise; Untersuchung *a. med*, Erhebung *f*; *tech* Schürfen *n*; **~ative** [eks'plɔ:rətiv], **~atory** [eks'plɔ:rətəri] Forschungs-, Untersuchungs-; *~atory flight* Erkundungsflug *m*; **~e** [iks'plɔ:] *tr* er-, durchforschen; auskundschaften; untersuchen *a. med*; *to ~~ every possibility* jede Möglichkeit genau prüfen; **~er** [iks'plɔ:rə] Forscher, Forschungsreisende(r) *m*; *med* Sonde *f*.

explos|ion [iks'plouʒən] Explosion; Sprengung; Detonation *f*, Knall; *fig* Ausbruch *m*; *bomb* ~~ Bombenexplosion *f*; ~~ *of laughter* Lachanfall *m*; ~~ *pressure* Explosionsdruck *m*; ~~ *of wrath* Zornesausbruch *m*; **~ive** [-'plousiv] *a* explosiv *a. fig*; *fig* jähzornig; aufbrausend; *s (~~ substance)* Sprengstoff, -körper; *gram (~~ consonant)* Verschlußlaut *m*; ~~ *charge* Sprengladung *f*; ~~ *cotton* Schießbaumwolle *f*; ~~ *flame* Stichflamme *f*; ~~ *force, power* Sprengkraft, Brisanz *f*.

exponent [eks'pounənt] *a* erklärend; *s* Erklärer; Vertreter *m*, Beispiel, Muster *n*; *math* Exponent *m*.

export [eks'pɔ:t, iks-] *tr* ausführen, exportieren; *s* ['ekspɔ:t] Ausfuhr *f*, Export; *(~ article)* Ausfuhrartikel *m*; *pl* Ausfuhrgüter *n pl*, (Gesamt-)Ausfuhr *f*; *to be engaged in* ~ im Außenhandel tätig sein; *to go for* ~ für den Export bestimmt sein; *capital* ~ Kapitalausfuhr *f*; **~able** [eks'pɔ:təbl] zur Ausfuhr geeignet, exportfähig; **~ation** [-'teiʃən] Ausfuhr *f*, Export *m* (*from* aus; *of* von); ~ **bounty, subsidy** Ausfuhrprämie *f*; ~ **business** Ausfuhrhandel *m*; Exportfirma *f*; ~ **certificate, licence, permit** Ausfuhrlizenz *f*; ~ **country** Ausfuhrland *n*; ~ **department** Exportabteilung *f*; ~ **drive** (planmäßige) Exportförderung *f*; ~ **duty** Ausfuhrzoll *m*; **~er** [eks'pɔ:tə] Exporteur *m*; ~ **firm, house** Exportfirma *f*; ~ **goods** *pl* Exportwaren *f pl*; **~-import balance** Handelsbilanz *f*; ~ **increase** Ausfuhrsteigerung *f*; ~ **manager** Leiter *m* der Exportabteilung *f*; ~ **merchant** Exportkaufmann *m*; ~ **order** Exportauftrag *m*; ~ **prohibition** Ausfuhrverbot *n*, -sperre *f*, Embargo *n*; ~ **promotion** Exportförderung *f*; ~ **regulations** *pl* Ausfuhrbestimmungen *f pl*; ~ **surplus** Exportüberschuß *m*; ~ **trade** Exporthandel *m*.

expos|e [iks'pouz] *tr (Kind)* aussetzen *a. fig* (*to a danger* e-r Gefahr); *fig* überlassen; entblößen; enthüllen, aufdecken, bloßlegen; *(Person)* bloßstellen, entlarven (*as* als); *phot* belichten; *(Tonband)* besprechen; *com allg* ausstellen, -legen, feilbieten; *to be ~ed for sale* zum Verkauf ausliegen; *to ~~ to ridicule* der Lächerlichkeit preisgeben; **~é** [eks'pouzei] Darlegung, -stellung, Denkschrift; Enthüllung, Bloßstellung *f*; **~ed** [-d] *a* ausgesetzt, offen, ungedeckt, ungeschützt, exponiert, gefährdet; *mil (Gelände)* eingesehen; *phot* belichtet; **~ition** [ekspə'ziʃən] Darlegung, -stellung, genaue Ausführung, eingehende Erklärung; *lit mus* Exposition; *com allg bes. Am* Ausstellung, Schau *f*.

ex post facto [eks poust 'fæktou] *a* nachträglich; rückwirkend.

expostulat|e [iks'pɔstjuleit] *itr* zur Rede stellen (*with s.o.* jdn); Vorhaltungen machen (*with s.o.* jdm); zurechtweisen (*with s.o.* jdn; *about, for, on s.th.* wegen e-r S); **~ion** [-'leiʃən] Zurechtweisung *f*, Vorhaltungen *f pl*, Vorwürfe *m pl*.

exposure [iks'pouʒə] (Kindes-)Aussetzung *f*; Ausgesetztsein *n* (*to the rain* dem Regen); Aus-, Zurschaustellung; Entblößung; Bloßlegung, Enthüllung, Aufdeckung; Bloßstellung, Entlarvung; Lage *f (e-s Gebäudes)*; Erfrieren *n*, Erschöpfung; *phot* Belichtung(szeit), Aufnahme *f*; *to die of ~* erfrieren; *conditions of ~* Belichtungsbedingungen *f pl*; *southern ~* Südlage *f*; *time ~ (phot)* Zeitaufnahme *f*; **~-meter** *phot* Belichtungsmesser *m*; **~-table** Belichtungstabelle *f*.

expound [iks'paund] *tr* genau darlegen; eingehend, ausführlich erörtern; erklären, erläutern.

*

express [iks'pres] *tr* ausdrücken, aussprechen, in Worte kleiden, bekunden, zum Ausdruck bringen, äußern; *(Zeichen)* bedeuten; durch Eilboten, als Eilgut schicken; *Am* durch e-e Speditionsfirma befördern lassen; *to ~ o.s.* sich ausdrücken, sich verständlich machen; *a* ausdrücklich; klar, deutlich, bestimmt, genau, unmißverständlich; Eil-, Schnell-, Expreß-; *adv (by ~)* durch Eilboten; als Eilgut; *s* Eilbote *m*; eilige Nachricht *f*; *(~ train)* Schnell-, D-Zug; *(~ wagon)* Expreßgutwagen *m*; *(~ bus)* durchfahrende(r) Bus *m*; *(~ delivery) Br* Eilgutzustellung, -beförderung; *Am* Zustellung *f* durch e-e Spedition; *(~ company) Am* Speditionsgesellschaft *f*; **~age** [-idʒ] *Am* Eilgutfracht; Eilgutbeförderung(sgebühr) *f*; **~ agency** *Am* Rollfuhrdienst *m*; **~ goods** *pl* Eilgut *n*; **~ highway** *Am* Autobahn *f*; **~ion** [iks'preʃn] Redewendung *f*, Ausdrucksweise *f*; Ausdruck *m*; Äußerung; *math* Formel *f*; *beyond, past ~~* unaussprechlich, unbeschreiblich *adv*; *to find ~~ in* zum Ausdruck kommen in; *to give ~~ to* zum Ausdruck bringen, Ausdruck verleihen *dat*; *~~ (on o.'s face)* Gesichtsausdruck *m*; **~ionism** [iks'preʃnizm] Expressionismus *m*; **~ionist** [iks'preʃnist] Expressionist *m*; **~ionless** [iks'preʃənlis] ausdruckslos; **~ive** [iks'presiv] ausdrucksvoll; ausdrückend (*of s.th.* etw); nachdrücklich, bedeutungsvoll; **~ letter** *Br* Eilbrief *m*; **~man** *Am* Angestellte(r) *m* e-r Speditionsgesellschaft; **~ messenger** Eilbote *m*; **~ service** Eilzustelldienst, Eilgutverkehr *m*; **~ package** Eilpaket *n*; **~way** *Am* Schnellverkehrsstraße, Autobahn *f*.

expropriat|e [eks'prouprieit] *tr* enteignen (*s.o. from his estate* jds Grundstück); **~ion** [-'eiʃən] Enteignung *f*.

expuls|ion [iks'pʌlʃən] Vertreibung; Ausweisung, Landesverweisung *f*; Ausschluß *m (from)*; *tech* Hinauspressen *n*; **~ive** [-'pʌlsiv] *a* Ausweisungs-, Ausschluß-.

expunge [eks'pʌndʒ] *tr* (aus)streichen, ausradieren, auslöschen, tilgen *a. fig.*

expurgat|e ['ekspə:geit] *tr (Buch)* reinigen, säubern (*from* von); **~ion** [-'geiʃən] *(Buch)* Säuberung, Reinigung *f*.

exquisite ['ekskwizit, iks'kw-] *a* fein (-gearbeitet), gediegen; vorzüglich, ausgesucht; ausgezeichnet, herrlich; feinfühlig, empfindlich; *(Sinn)* scharf; *(Gefühl)* stark; *(Freude)* groß; *(Schmerz)* stechend.

ex-serviceman ['eks'sə:vismən] Veteran, ehemalige(r) Soldat *m*.

extant [eks'tænt, iks't-, 'ekstənt] *(bes. Bücher, Papiere)* noch vorhanden.

extempor|aneous [ekstempə'reinjəs] **~ary** [iks'tempərəri], **~e** [eks'tempəri] *a adv* unvorbereitet, aus dem Stegreif; improvisiert; **~ize** [iks'tempəraiz] *itr* aus dem Stegreif sprechen *od* reden; *tr* aus dem Stegreif dichten *od* komponieren; improvisieren; **~izer** [iks'tempəraizə] Stegreifredner, -dichter *m*.

extend [iks'tend] *tr* (aus)dehnen, -strecken, in die Länge ziehen, verlängern *(a. zeitlich)*; *(räumlich u. fig)* weiten, erweitern, verbreitern, ausbreiten; *(Geschäft)* ausbauen; ausstrecken, hinhalten; (an)bieten; *(Sympathie)* zeigen; *(Freundlichkeit)* erweisen; *(Geduld)* üben; *(Hilfe)* gewähren; *(Glückwünsche, Einladung)* aussprechen; die Zahlungsfrist verlängern, Aufschub gewähren für; *sport* zur Höchstleistung anspornen; *(Protest)* erheben; *(Saldo)* vor-, übertragen; *(Stenogramm)* umschreiben, in Langschrift übertragen; *jur* pfänden; *(Urkunde)* ausfertigen; *(Küche)* verlängern, strecken; *(Truppen)* ausea.-ziehen; *(Fahrgestell) aero* ausfahren; *itr* sich erstrecken, (hinaus)reichen (*beyond* über; *to* bis); *to ~ a line* e-e Linie ziehen; **~ed** [-id] *a* verlängert, *com* prolongiert; zusätzlich; umfangreich; *(Diskussion, Reise)* länger; *~~ formation* ausea.gezogene Formation *f*; *~~ period* längere Zeit *f*.

extens|ibility [ikstensə'biliti] Dehnbarkeit *f*; **~ible** [iks'tensəbl] dehnbar, streckbar; *(Tisch)* ausziehbar.

extension [iks'tenʃən] (Aus-)Dehnung, Streckung *f*; Ausstrecken *n*; Verlängerung *(a. zeitlich)*; (Aus-)Weitung, Erweiterung, Verbreiterung *f*; Zusatz; Umfang; Bedeutungsumfang *m (e-s Wortes)*; *med* Streckung; *(Wechsel)* Prolongation; Fristverlängerung *f*, Zahlungsaufschub; *(Saldo)* Vor-, Übertrag; *tele* (Neben-)Anschluß *m*, -stelle *f*, Apparat *m*, *(Öst.)* Klappe *f*; An-, Erweiterungsbau *m*; *(Truppen)* Ausea.ziehen; *aero (Fahrgestell)* Ausfahren *n*; *University E~ (Br)* Volkshochschule *f*; *~ of business* Geschäftserweiterung, -ausweitung *f*; *~ of credit* Kreditverlängerung *f*; *~ of leave* Nachurlaub *m*; *~ of time (limit), of a term* Fristverlängerung *f*; *~ of time for payment* Zahlungsaufschub *m*; *~ of validity* Verlängerung *f* der Gültigkeitsdauer; *~ of working hours (pl)* Arbeitszeitverlängerung *f*; **~ apparatus** *med* Streckverband *m*; **~ board** *el* (Telefon-, Haus-)Zentrale *f*; **~ cord, flex** *Br el* Verlängerungsschnur *f*; **~ course** *Br* Volkshochschulkurs; *Am* Fernlehrgang *m*; **~ ladder** Ausziehleiter *f*; **~ line, station** *tele* Nebenanschluß *m*; **~ loudspeaker** zweite(r) Lautsprecher *m*; **~ piece** Verlängerungs-, Ansatzstück *n*; **~ table** Ausziehtisch *m*.

extens|ity [iks'tensiti] Ausdehnung *f (als Eigenschaft)*; *psychol* Raum-Zeit-Empfinden *n*; **~ive** [-iv] ausgedehnt, umfangreich; *fig* umfassend, weitreichend; beträchtlich; Ausdehnungs-; *agr* extensiv; **~iveness** [-ivnis] Ausgedehntheit *f*, (großer) Umfang *m*, Weite *f*; **~or** [-ə] *anat* Streckmuskel *m*.

extent [iks'tent] Ausdehnung, Größe *f*, Umfang *m*, Weite; Breite; Länge *f*; Bereich; Betrag, Grad *m*, Ausmaß *n*, Umfang *m*; *(Anleihe)* Höhe; *fig* Fassungskraft *f*, Umfang *m*, Weite *f*; *to any ~* in beliebiger Höhe; *to a certain ~* bis zu e-m gewissen Grade; gewissermaßen; *to the full ~* in vollem Umfang; *to a great ~* in hohem Maße; *to some ~* bis zu e-m gewissen Grade; einigermaßen; *to what ~* in welchem Maße *od* Umfang? *to the ~ of* bis zum Betrage von.

extenuat|e [eks'tenjueit] *tr* abschwächen, mildern, beschönigen; *~ing circumstances (jur)* mildernde Umstände *m pl*; **~ion** [-'eiʃən] Abschwächung, Milderung, Beschönigung *f*; *in ~~ of* zur Entschuldigung *gen.*

exterior [eks'tiəriə] *a* äußer, Außen-; außerhalb (*to s.th.* e-r S); auswärtig, fremd; ausländisch, Auslands-; *s das* Äußere, Außenseite; Außenansicht *f*; (äußerer) Schein *m*; *film* Außenaufnahme *f*; **~ angle** *math* Außenwinkel *m*.

exterminat|e [eks'tə:mineit] *tr* vertilgen, ausmerzen, ausrotten; **~ion** [-'neiʃən] Vertilgung, Ausrottung *f*; **~or** [-ə] Kammerjäger *m*; Insektenvertilgungsmittel *n*.

external [eks'tə:nl] *a* äußer; *bes. pharm* äußerlich; oberflächlich; körperlich; *com* außerbetrieblich; auswärtig, fremd; Auslands-; *s das* Äußere, *die* Außenseite; *pl* Äußerlichkeiten, Nebensächlichkeiten *f pl*; *to judge by ~s* nach dem Äußeren urteilen; **~ aerial** Außenantenne *f*; **~ affairs** *pl pol* auswärtige Angelegenheiten *f pl*; **~ economy** Außenwirtschaft *f*; **~ize** [-nəlaiz] *tr* verkörpern; als körperlich, materiell ansehen; **~ line** *tele* Amtsleitung; Außenleitung *f*; **~ loan** Auslandsanleihe *f*; **~ pressure** Außendruck *m*; **~ relations** *pl* Auslandsbeziehungen *f pl*; **~ resistance** Außenwiderstand *m*; **~ trade** Außenhandel *m*; **~ treatment** *med* äußere Behandlung *f*; **~ world** *psychol* Außenwelt *f*.

exterritorial ['eksteri'tɔ:riəl] *pol* exterritorial.

extinct [iks'tiŋkt] *(Vulkan)* erloschen *a. fig*; *(Tier)* ausgestorben; *fig* aufgehoben, abgeschafft; gestrichen, gelöscht; **~ion** [-kʃən] (Er-)Löschen; *el* Abschalten; *fig* Erlöschen, Aussterben *n*; Vernichtung *f*; Untergang *m*.

extinguish [iks'tiŋgwiʃ] *tr (Feuer)* (aus)löschen, ersticken; *el* abschalten; *allg* auslöschen, vernichten, austilgen, ausmerzen; in den Schatten stellen, an die Wand drücken; *jur* aufheben, abschaffen; *(Schuld)* tilgen; **~er** [-ə] *(fire ~~)* Feuerlöscher *m*, Feuerlöschgerät *n*.

extirpat|e ['ekstə:peit] *tr* ausrotten, ausmerzen, völlig vernichten; *med* (operativ) entfernen; **~ion** [-'peiʃən] Ausrottung, Vernichtung, Ausmerzung; *med* Entfernung *f*.

extol(l) [iks'tɔl] *tr* preisen, rühmen; *to ~ to the skies* in den Himmel heben.

extort [iks'tɔ:t] *tr* er-, abpressen (*from* von); abnötigen; **~ion** [iks'tɔ:ʃən] Erpressung *f*; **~ionate** [iks'tɔ:ʃnit] erpresserisch, wucherisch; Wucher-; *~~ price*

Wucherpreis *m*; **~ioner** [iks'tɔ:ʃnə] Erpresser, Wucherer *m*.

extra ['ekstrə] *a* besonder, zusätzlich, nachträglich; Sonder-, Extra-, Zusatz-, Nach-; außer-; *adv* besonders; zusätzlich; übrig, extra; *s* Zuschlag *m*, Sonderleistung, zusätzliche Arbeitskraft *od* Belastung *f*; Extrablatt *n*, Sondernummer *f*; *film* Statist *m*; *oft pl* Mehr-, Nebenausgaben, Nebenkosten *pl*; *to be charged for ~* gesondert berechnet werden; **~ allowance** Sondervergütung *f*; **~-budgetary** außeretatmäßig; **~ charge** Nebenkosten *pl*; Aufschlag; *rail* Zuschlag *m*; **~-curricular** ['-kə'rikjulə] außerhalb des Lehrplans; *~~ activity* Arbeitsgemeinschaft *f*; **~ duty** *mil* Strafdienst; Zollaufschlag *m*; **~ equipment** Sonderausstattung *f*; **~ hour** Überstunde *f*; **~ income** Nebeneinkommen *n*; **~ pay** Zulage *f (zum Lohn)*; **~ postage** Nachporto *n*; **~ train** Vor-, Nach-, Entlastungszug *m*; **~ weight** Übergewicht *n*; **~ work** Überstunden *f pl*.

extract [iks'trækt] *tr* (her)ausziehen, herauslösen; *(Zahn)*, *math (Wurzel)* ziehen; *(Flüssigkeit, Saft)* abziehen; *el (Spannung)* abnehmen; *chem* auslaugen (*from* aus); herausbekommen (*from s.o.* aus jdm); *(Geständnis)* erpressen, entlocken; erhalten (*from* von); her-, ableiten (*from* von); *(Stelle, Zitat)* entnehmen (*from a book* e-m Buch); e-n Auszug machen (*from* aus); *s* ['ekstrækt] *(Küche, pharm)* Extrakt; *(Buch)* Auszug *m*; *~ of account* Konto-, Rechnungsauszug *m*; *~ of beef* Fleischextrakt *m*; **~ion** [iks'trækʃən] Ausziehen *n*; Auszug, Extrakt *m*; Ab-, Herkunft, Abstammung; *chem* Entziehung; *tech* Gewinnung *f*; *(Mehl)* Ausmahlen *n*; **~or** [-ə] *tech* Extraktionsapparat; *(Gewehr)* Auszieher *m*; *med* Zange *f*.

extradit|able ['ekstrədaitəbl] auslieferungspflichtig; **~e** ['ekstrədait] *tr (Verbrecher)* ausliefern; **~ion** [-'diʃən] Auslieferung *f*.

extrados [eks'treidɔs] *arch* Bogen-, Gewölberücken *m*.

extramarital ['ekstrə'mæritl] außerehelich.

extramural ['ekstrə'mjuərəl] außerhalb der Mauern, der Grenzen *(e-r Stadt)*, des Bereichs *(e-r Universität)*; Volkshochschul-.

extraneous [eks'treinjəs] fremd; nicht gehörig (*to* zu).

extraordinary [iks'trɔ:dnri] außerordentlich, außer-, ungewöhnlich, bemerkenswert, merkwürdig, seltsam, sonderbar; Ausnahme-; *a.* [ekstrə-'ɔ:dinəri] außerordentlich, außerplanmäßig, Sonder-; *ambassador, envoy ~* Sonderbotschafter, -gesandte(r) *m*.

extraterritorial ['ekstrəteri'tɔ:riəl] *pol* exterritorial; **~ity** [-'æliti] Exterritorialität *f*.

extravagan|ce, -cy [iks'trævigəns(i)] Übertriebenheit, Überspanntheit, Maß-, Zügellosigkeit, Extravaganz; Verschwendung(ssucht) *f*; **~t** [-ənt] übertrieben, übermäßig; überspannt, maßlos, zügellos, extravagant; verschwenderisch; **~za** [ekstrævə'gænzə] Ausstattungsstück *n*.

extrem|e [iks'tri:m] *a* äußerst; letzt; frühest; höchst, größt; übertrieben, extrem, radikal; gewagt, ausgefallen; sehr streng, drastisch; *s* Extrem *n*; höchste(r) Grad *m*; *das* Äußerste; *der* äußerste Fall; *at the ~~ end* am äußersten Ende (*of* gen); *in the ~~* im Höchstfall, allerhöchstens; im höchsten Grade; *in ~~ old age* im höchsten Alter; *in ~~ youth* in frühester Jugend; *to go to ~~s* bis zum äußersten gehen; *to resort to ~~ measures* zu den äußersten Maßnahmen greifen; *the ~~ left (pol)* die äußerste Linke; *~~ penalty* Todesstrafe *f*; *the ~~ unction (rel)* die Letzte Ölung; **~ely** [-li] *adv* äußerst, höchst, aufs äußerste *od* höchste; überaus; **~ism** [iks'tri:mizm] Extremismus *m*; **~ist** [-ist] Extremist, Radikale(r) *m*; **~ity** [iks'tremiti] äußerste(s) Ende *n*; höchste(r) Grad *m*; höchste Not, äußerste(r) Not(fall *m*) *f*; (Lebens-) Ende *n*; *meist pl* äußerste Maßnahmen *f pl*; *pl* Extremitäten *f pl (Hände u. Füße)*; *to be in ~~* in höchster Not sein; *to be forced to the ~~ of doing s.th.* etw als äußerste Maßnahme tun müssen; *to be reduced to ~ities* völlig heruntergekommen sein, aus dem letzten Loch pfeifen; *to drive to ~ities* auf die Spitze, zum äußersten treiben; *to go to, to proceed to ~ities* aufs Äußerste, aufs Ganze gehen.

extricat|e ['ekstrikeit] *tr* befreien (*from* aus, von); los-, freimachen; *chem (Gas, Hitze)* sich entwickeln lassen; **~ion** [-'keiʃən] Befreiung; *chem* (Gas-, Hitze-)Entwick(e)lung *f*.

extrinsic(al) [eks'trinsik(əl)] äußerlich; fremd, nicht zugehörig (*to* zu).

extrovert ['ekstro(u)və:t] *psychol* extravertiert.

extru|de [eks'tru:d] *tr* (her)austreiben, ausstoßen, herauspressen, -drücken (*from* aus); *tech* strangpressen; **~sion** [-'tru:ʒən] Austreiben, Ausstoßen, Herausdrücken; *tech* Strangpressen *n*.

exuberan|ce, -cy [ig'zju:bərəns(i)] Üppigkeit, Überfülle *f*, Überfluß *m*; Übermaß *n*; Überschwang *m*, Überschwenglichkeit *f*; **~t** [-rənt] üppig, reich; überfließend, verschwenderisch, übersprudelnd, überschwenglich *a. fig.*

exud|ation [eksju:'deiʃən] Ausschwitzen *n*; Ausschwitzung *f*; **~e** [ig'zju:d] *itr* (*tr* aus)schwitzen; austreten (*from* aus); *tr* absondern, von sich geben; *fig* ausstrahlen, -strömen.

exult [ig'zʌlt] *itr* frohlocken, jubeln (*at, over, in* über); **~ant** [-ənt] frohlockend, jubelnd, triumphierend; **~ation** [egzʌl'teiʃən] Frohlocken *n*, Jubel, Triumph *m*.

eye [ai] *s* Auge *n*; Gesichtssinn *m*; Augenmaß; Auge *n (an e-r Kartoffel)*; Knospe *f*; Pfauenauge *(auf der Feder)*; Zentrum *(der Schießscheibe)*; Loch *n*, (runde) Öffnung *f*, Öhr *n*, Öse, Schlinge *f*; *zoo* Pigment-, Augenfleck *m*; photoelektrische Zelle *f*; *Am sl* Privatdetektiv *m*; *tr* (scharf) ins Auge fassen; anschauen, mustern; schielen nach; mit Ösen versehen; *an ~ for an ~* Auge um Auge; *in s.o.'s ~s* in jds Augen, nach jds Ansicht, Meinung, Dafürhalten, Urteil; *in the ~ of the law* vom Standpunkt des Gesetzes aus; *under the very ~s of s.o.* direkt unter jds Augen; *up to the ~s, the ~brows* bis über die Ohren, bis an den Hals; *with an ~ to* mit e-m Auge, mit Rücksicht auf; in der Hoffnung auf; in der Absicht zu; *with the naked ~* mit bloßem Auge; *to be all ~s* aufpassen wie ein Luchs; große Augen machen; *to be in the public ~* im Brennpunkt des öffentlichen Interesses stehen; *to catch s.o.'s ~* jds Blick auf sich ziehen; jds Aufmerksamkeit auf sich lenken; *to catch the Speaker's ~ (parl)* das Wort erhalten; *to clap, to lay, to set ~s on s.o.* jdn anblicken, anschauen; jdn zu Gesicht bekommen; *to close, to shut o.'s ~ to* nicht sehen wollen; *to do s.o. in the ~ (fig)* jdn übers Ohr hauen; *to feast o.'s ~s on s.th.* sich am Anblick e-r S erfreuen; *to have an ~ for* ein Auge, Sinn haben für; *to have an ~ on s.th.* auf etw ein (wachsames) Auge haben; beabsichtigen; *to have an ~ to* achten, aufpassen auf; *to have a cast in o.'s ~* schielen; *to keep an ~ on (fig)* im Auge behalten; aufpassen, achtgeben auf; *to keep o.'s ~s open* od *peeled* od *skinned* die Augen offen haben, aufpassen; *to lose an ~* ein Auge verlieren, auf einem Auge blind werden; *to make ~s at s.o.* jdm verliebte Blicke zuwerfen, jdm schöne Augen machen; *to make s.o. open his ~s, to open s.o.'s ~s (fig)* jdm die Augen öffnen; *to run o.'s ~s over s.th. (fig)* etw überfliegen; *to see ~ to ~ with s.o.* mit jdm Hand in Hand gehen, völlig übereinstimmen, einer Meinung sein; *to see s.th. in o.'s mind's ~* sich etw vorstellen können; *to take o.'s ~ off* wegblicken; das Auge wegwenden von; *to turn a blind ~ to s.th.* etw ignorieren, nicht sehen wollen; *mind your ~!* aufgepaßt! *my ~(s)!* nanu! du meine Güte! das ist ja allerhand! *all my ~! (sl)* Quatsch! Unsinn! Blödsinn! *black ~* blaue(s) Auge; *~s left (mil)* die Augen links! *~s right (mil)* Augen rechts! *his ~s are bigger than his belly* s-e Augen sind größer als sein Magen; **~ball** Augapfel *m*; **~-bath, -cup** *med* Augenschale *f*; **~beam** kurze(r) Blick *m*; **~bright** *bot* Augentrost *m*; **~brow** ['-brau] Augenbraue(nwulst *m*) *f*; **~-catcher, stopper** Blickfang *m*; **~d** [-d] *a in Zssgen* -äugig; *blue-~d* blauäugig; **~ful** ['-ful] *Am sl*: *to get an ~~* etw Hübsches sehen; *I had an ~~* ich hatte genug gesehen; **~-glass** *opt* Linse *f*; Augenglas; Monokel; Okular *n*; Augenschale *f*; *pl* Augengläser *n pl*, Kneifer *m*; Brille *f*; **~hole** Augenhöhle *f*; **~lash** Wimper *f*; **~less** ['-lis] augenlos, blind; **~let** ['-lit] *s* Öhr *n*, Öse *f*; Guckloch; kleine(s) Loch, Auge *n*; *itr* mit Ösen, Löchern versehen; **~leteer** [ailə'tiə] Pfriem *m*; **~lid** ['-lid] Augenlid *n*; *it hangs on by the ~~s* es hängt an e-m Faden; **~-opener** *fam* Überraschung, (große) Neuigkeit, Entdeckung *f* (*to* für); *Am fam* Schnäpschen *n (bes. am Morgen)*; **~piece** Okular *n*; **~ protection** Augenschutz *m*; **~shot**: *within ~~* in Sehweite; **~sight** Sehkraft, -schärfe *f*; Gesichtssinn *m*, Augen *f pl*; *bad ~~* schlechte Augen *n pl*, Sehfehler *m*; **~-socket** Augenhöhle *f*; **~some** *Am sl* hübsch; **~sore** Schandfleck, Dorn *m* im Auge; *med* Gerstenkorn *n*; *it's an ~~* das tut den Augen weh; **~-splice** Tauöhr *n*; **~strain** Ermüdung *f* der Augen, schlechte Augen *n pl*; **~-tooth** Augen-, Eckzahn *m*; *to have cut o.'s ~-teeth* kein Kind mehr sein; **~-wash** *s pharm* Augenwasser *n*; *sl* Quatsch, Blödsinn *m*; schöne Worte *n pl*, Speichelleckerei *f*; faule(r) Zauber, Bluff, Schwindel *m*; **~-water** Tränen (-flüssigkeit *f*) *f pl*; *pharm* Augenwasser *n*; **~-witness** Augenzeuge *m*; *~-account* Augenzeugenbericht *m*.

eyr|ie, ~y ['aiəri, 'ɛəri] *s. aerie.*

F

F [ef] *pl* **~'s** F, f *n a. mus; (Schule) Am* ungenügend; **~ flat** Fes *n*; **~ sharp** Fis *n*.
Fabian ['feibjən] *a* zögernd.
fable ['feibl] *s* (Tier-)Fabel *f*; Märchen *n*; *(kollektiv)* Sage, Legende *f*; (dummes) Geschwätz *n*, Lüge, Unwahrheit *f*; **~d** ['-d] *a* sagenhaft; *fig* erdichtet.
fabric ['fæbrik] Bau *m*, Gebäude *n*, Konstruktion *f*; (Bau-)Plan *m*, Struktur, Anlage *f*, Gefüge *n*, Aufbau *m*; *(textile ~)* Gewebe *n*, Stoff *m*; *pl* Textilien *pl*; Fabrikat *n*; *dress, silk ~s (pl)* Kleider-, Seidenstoffe *m pl*; **~ate** ['-eit] *tr* machen, an-, verfertigen, zs.setzen, errichten, bauen; (fabrik-, serienmäßig) herstellen, fabrizieren; *fig* erdichten, -finden; fälschen; **~ation** [-'keiʃən] Herstellung; *fig* Fälschung, Erfindung, Lüge *f*.
fabul|ist ['fæbjulist] Fabeldichter; Märchenerzähler; Lügner *m*; **~ous** ['-ləs] erdichtet, Phantasie-, Fabel-; sagenhaft, legendär; *fig fam* phantastisch.
face [feis] **1.** *s* Gesicht, *lit poet* Antlitz *n*, (Gesichts-)Züge *m pl*; Miene *f*, (Gesichts-)Ausdruck *m*; (Ober-)Fläche, Vorder-, Stirnseite; obere, rechte Seite *f*; Zifferblatt *n*; *com* genaue(r) Betrag *m*; *das* Äußere, *die* Erscheinung; Würde *f*, Gesicht, Ansehen *n*; *fam* Grimasse, Fratze; *fam* Frechheit, Dreistigkeit, Unverfrorenheit *f*; **2.** *tr* das Gesicht zuwenden (*s.o.* jdm); ansehen, ins Gesicht sehen (*s.o.* jdm); sich mit dem Gesicht drehen (*s.th.* zu etw); gegenüberstehen, -liegen (*s.th.* e-r S); nach ..., auf ... liegen; nach ... gehen; *fig* mutig gegenübertreten, trotzen, Trotz bieten (*s.o.* jdm, *a. e-r Gefahr*); *(e-r Gefahr)* ins Auge sehen; hinnehmen, anerkennen; *tech* abflächen, planarbeiten; *arch* verblenden; besetzen, einfassen, verkleiden (*with* mit); glätten; *(Flicken)* aufsetzen; ein falsches Aussehen geben (*s.th.* e-r S); *(Spielkarte)* aufdecken; *mil* e-e Kehrtwendung ausführen lassen; **3.** *itr* hin-, hersehen; sehen, blikken (*to, towards* nach); *mil* e-e Kehrtwendung machen; *to ~ down* einschüchtern; *to ~ on* gehen auf, nach; liegen nach; *to ~ it out* durchhalten, nicht nachgeben; *to ~ round* sich umdrehen; *to ~ up to* es aufnehmen mit; mutig herangehen an; **4.** *in (the) ~ of* angesichts *gen* trotz *gen*; *in s.o.'s ~* jdm ins Gesicht *a. fig*; vor jds Augen, offen vor jdm; *on the ~ of it* anscheinend, dem Schein nach; augenscheinlich; *to s.o.'s ~ (fig)* jdm (offen) ins Gesicht; *~ to ~ (with)* Auge in Auge (mit); *tech* aufea.gelegt; *to be unable to look s.o. in the ~* jdm nicht in die Augen sehen können; *to be ~d with s.th.* etw gegenüberstehen, sich etw gegenübersehen; vor etw stehen; *to fly in s.o.'s ~ (fig)* jdm ins Gesicht springen, jdn auffressen wollen; *to have the ~* die Frechheit besitzen; *to look s.o. in the ~* jdm ins Gesicht, jdn fest ansehen; *to lose (o.'s) ~* das Gesicht verlieren; *to make, to pull a ~, ~s* ein Gesicht, Grimassen schneiden (*at s.o.* jdm); *to make, to pull, to wear a long ~* ein langes Gesicht machen; *to put on a bold ~* keine Angst haben vor; *to put a new ~ on s.th. (fig)* e-r S ein ganz anderes Aussehen, e-e neue Wendung geben; *to save o.'s ~* das Gesicht, den Schein wahren; *to set o.'s ~ against* mißbilligen, entgegentreten, sich widersetzen *dat*; *to show o.'s ~* sich blicken, sich sehen lassen; sich zeigen; *to ~ the music (fam)* dafür geradestehen, die Suppe auslöffeln; *about ~! (mil)* ganze Abteilung — kehrt! *left, right ~!* links —, rechts — um! *he slammed the door in my ~* er schlug mir die Tür vor der Nase zu; *full ~* Vorderansicht *f*; *half ~* Profil *n*; **~-ache** Neuralgie *f*, Nerven-, Gesichtsschmerz *m*; **~ amount** Nominalbetrag *m*; **~-card** *(Kartenspiel)* Bild *n*, Figur *f*; **~-cloth, -flannel** Waschlappen *m*; **~-cream** Gesichtskrem *f*; **~-lift(ing)** Gesichtsstraffung; *fig* Schönheitsreparatur *f*; **~-lotion** Gesichtswasser *n*; **~-pack** Gesichtspackung *f*; **~-powder** (Gesichts-)Puder *m*; **~r** ['-ə] Schlag *m* ins Gesicht, Ohrfeige; *fig* ernstliche Schwierigkeit *f*, Rückschlag *m*; **~-value** *fin* Nennwert *m*; *to take at ~~* wörtlich, für bare Münze nehmen.
facet ['fæsit] *s* Facette; *fig* Seite *f*, Aspekt *m*; *tr* facettieren.
facetious [fə'si:ʃəs] scherzend, scherz-, spaßhaft, spaßig, ulkig, drollig; **~ness** [-nis] Scherzhaftigkeit *f*; Humor *m*.
facia ['feiʃə] Ladenschild *n*; *(~ board, panel) mot* Armaturenbrett *n*.
facial ['feiʃəl] *a scient* Gesichts-; *s fam (~ treatment)* Gesichtspflege, -behandlung; *(~ massage)* Gesichtsmassage *f*; **~ angle** *(Rassenkunde)* Gesichtswinkel *m*; **~ hair** Barthaare *n pl*; **~ muscle, nerve** Gesichtsmuskel, -nerv *m*; **~ neuralgia, paralysis** Gesichtsneuralgie, -lähmung *f*.
facil|e ['fæsail] leicht, mühelos; gewandt, geschickt, behende; *(Stil)* fließend; leicht beeinflußbar, leicht zu überzeugen(d), zu überreden(d), nachgiebig; zu-, umgänglich; **~itate** [fə'siliteit] *tr (Arbeit)* erleichtern, fördern, unterstützen; **~itation** [-'teiʃən] Erleichterung; *psychol* Hemmungslosigkeit *f*; **~ity** [fə'siliti] Leichtigkeit, Mühelosigkeit; Gewandtheit, Geschicklichkeit, Geschicktheit; Nachgiebigkeit, Um-, Zugänglichkeit *f*; *pl* Erleichterungen *f pl*, Möglichkeit(en *pl*), Gelegenheit *f* (*for* für); Vor-, Einrichtungen, Anlagen *f pl*; Vorteile *m pl*; Hilfsmittel *n pl*.
facing ['feisiŋ] Besatz(stoff); (Ärmel-)Aufschlag; *arch* Verputz, Bewurf *m*; Verblendung; Verschalung; *tech* Auflage *f*; *pl* (Rock-)Aufschläge *m pl bes. mil*; *mil* Wendungen *f pl*; *to go through o.'s ~s* erprobt werden; *to put s.o. through his ~s* jdn auf die Probe stellen; **~ brick** Verblendstein *m*; **~ lathe** Plandrehbank *f*; **~ sand** Modellsand *m*.
facsimile [fæk'simili] Faksimile *n*, genaue Nachbildung, Reproduktion *f*; **~ broadcast(ing)** Bildfunk *m*, -telegraphie *f*; **~ equipment** Bildfunkgerät *n*; **~ signature, stamp** Unterschriftstempel *m*; **~ transceiver** Bild-Sender-Empfänger *m*; **~ transmission** Bildübertragung *f*.
fact [fækt] Tatsache; Wirklichkeit, Realität, Wahrheit *f*; *jur* Tatbestand *m*; *pl jur* Tatumstände *m pl*; *after, before the ~* nach, vor der Tat; *apart from the ~ that* abgesehen davon, daß; *as a matter of ~, in (point of) ~* in Wirklichkeit, tatsächlich; *the ~ of its being ...* die Tatsache, daß es ... ist; *it's a ~* das ist Tatsache; *stick to the ~s* bleiben Sie sachlich; *founded on ~* auf Wirklichkeit, auf Tatsachen beruhend; *the hard ~s* die nackten Tatsachen *pl*; *~s of the case* Sachverhalt *m*; **~ finding** Tatsachenfeststellung *f*; *~~ committee* Untersuchungsausschuß *m*; *~~ tour* Informationsreise *f*; **~ual** ['-juəl] *a* Tatsachen-; tatsächlich, wirklich, real.
faction ['fækʃən] Gruppe (Unzufriedener), Clique, Partei; Uneinigkeit *f*, Ausea.setzungen *f pl*, Aufruhr *m*.
factious ['fækʃəs] streit-, zanksüchtig; aufrührerisch; Partei-; **~ness** ['-nis], **~ spirit** Parteigeist *m*.
factitious [fæk'tiʃəs] gezwungen, künstlich, unnatürlich, unecht, falsch.
factitive ['fæktitiv] *gram* faktitiv.
factor ['fæktə] *com* Agent, Kommissionär, Vertreter, Faktor; Treuhänder; Geschäftsführer; *Scot* (Guts-)Verwalter; Umstand, Faktor; Grund (*behind* für); *biol* Erbfaktor; *math* Faktor *m*; *production, safety ~* Produktions-, Sicherheitsfaktor *m*; **~age** ['-ridʒ] Kommissionshandel *m*, -geschäft *n*; Kommission(sgebühr) *f*; **~y** ['fæktəri] Fabrik(anlage); Betriebsanlage *f*, Werk *n*; Handelsniederlassung, Faktorei *f*; *owner, proprietor of a ~~* Fabrikbesitzer *m*; *~~ accounting* Betriebsbuchhaltung *f*; *~~ area* Fabrikgelände *n*; *~~ building* Fabrikgebäude *n*; *~~ committee, council* Betriebsrat, -ausschuß *m*; *~~ cost* Herstellungskosten *pl*; *~~ overheads (pl)* Fertigungsgemeinkosten *pl*; *~~ equipment* Betriebseinrichtung *f*; *~~ fitting* Werkstattleuchte *f*; *~~ hand, worker* Fabrikarbeiter *m*; *~~ inspection* Gewerbepolizei *f*; *~~ management* Fabrikdirektor, Werkleiter *m*; *~~ manager* Betriebsleiter *m*; *~~ number* Fabriknummer *f*; *~~ owner* Fabrikbesitzer *m*; *~~ plant* Fabrikanlage *f*; *~~ premises (pl)* Fabrikgebäude *n pl*; *~~ price* Fabrikpreis *m*; *~~ product* Fabrikat *n*; gewerbliche(s) Erzeugnis *n*; *~~ site* Fabrikgelände *n*; *~~ town* Fabrikstadt *f*; *~~ woman, girl* Fabrikarbeiterin *f*; *~~ work* Fabrikarbeit *f*.
factotum [fæk'toutəm] Faktotum, Mädchen *n* für alles.
facult|ative ['fækəltətiv, -teitiv] wahlfrei, fakultativ, beliebig; möglich, zufällig; *biol* anpassungsfähig; **~y** ['fækəlti] Fähigkeit; Befähigung, Gabe, Fertigkeit (*for* für); Kraft, Geschicklichkeit, Gewandtheit, Kunst; *(Universität)* Fakultät *f*; *Am (Schule)* Lehrkörper *m*; Lehrerkollegium *n*; Berufsgruppe *f*, -stand *m*; Fachwelt; *jur* Befähigung, Berechtigung, Vollmacht *f*; *rel* Dispens *m*; *~~ meeting* Fakultätssitzung; *Am a.* Sitzung *f* des Lehrkörpers.

*

fad [fæd] Laune, Schrulle, Mode(laune, -torheit, -narrheit) *f*; Hobby, Steckenpferd *n*, Liebbaberei *f*; *latest ~* letzte(r) Schrei *m*; **~dish, ~dy** ['-iʃ, '-i] launisch, launen-, grillenhaft, schrullig, versponnen; **~dist** ['-ist] Grillenfänger, Sonderling, Eigenbrötler *m*.
fade [feid] *itr* schwinden, nachlassen; vergehen, (ver)welken; schwächer, matter werden; *(Farbe)* an Frische verlieren, trüber werden, verblassen, verbleichen, verschießen; *(Ton) (to ~*

away, out) leiser werden, verklingen; *tr* abblenden; bleichen; verblassen lassen; *s*: *cross* ~ *(film video)* Überblendung *f*; *to* ~ *into silence* allmählich verstummen; *to do a* ~*-out (fam)* französischen Abschied nehmen; *to* ~ **down,** *to* ~ **up** *film radio video* ab-, aufblenden; *to* ~ **in,** *to* ~ **out** *film radio video* sich ein-, sich ausblenden; **fading** ['-iŋ] *radio* (Ton-)Schwund *m*; *tech* Abnutzung *f*.

f(a)eces ['fi:si:z] Kot *m*, Exkremente *n pl*.

faery, -ie ['fɛəri] *obs* Feen-, Märchen-, Traumland *n*.

fag [fæg] *itr (to* ~ *away)* schuften, sich abrackern, sich ab-, müde arbeiten (*with* mit); *(Schüler)* Burschendienste für e-n älteren Schüler tun; *tr* schuften lassen; (durch Arbeit) ermüden, auspumpen; fertigmachen; *(Schüler)* als Burschen haben; *s* Schufterei, Plackerei; Ermüdung, Erschöpfung *f*; *Br (Schule)* Fuchs; *sl* Glimmstengel, Sargnagel *m*, Zigarette *f*; ~**ged** [d] *a* ab-, müde gearbeitet, erschöpft, *fam* kaputt; ~**-end** *(Textil)* Salband; ausgefranste(s) Tauende *n*; *fig* schäbige(r) Rest *m*; *sl* Kippe *f*, Zigarettenstummel *m*.

fag(g)ot ['fægət] Reisigbündel *n*; Faschine *f*; Bündel *n* Stahlstangen; *tech* Schweißpaket *n*; ~**ing** ['-iŋ] Kreuzstich *m*; *tech* Paketierung *f*.

fail [feil] *itr* fehlen, mangeln (*of* an), nicht genügen, nicht ausreichen; versagen (*of* in), s-n Zweck nicht erfüllen, fehlschlagen, scheitern, mißlingen; versäumen (*to do s.th.* etw zu tun); schwächer werden, nachlassen, abnehmen, versiegen, ins Stocken geraten, stocken; *(Ernte)* schlecht ausfallen; *(Mensch)* s-e Pflicht nicht erfüllen, den Erwartungen nicht entsprechen, versagen (*in* in); sein Ziel nicht erreichen, scheitern; *(im Examen)* durchfallen; in Konkurs gehen, Bankrott, *fam* Pleite machen; *tr* nicht dienlich sein, nicht(s) nützen (*s.o.* jdm), nicht passen zu, keinen Zweck haben für, enttäuschen; verlassen, im Stich lassen; unterlassen (*to do* zu tun); *(im Examen)* durchfallen lassen; durchfallen, versagen in *(e-m Fach)*; *s nur in*: *without* ~ ganz bestimmt, ganz gewiß, auf jeden Fall, unbedingt; *never* ~ *to do s.th.* immer etw tun müssen; *I cannot* ~ *to* ich muß; *my heart* ~*ed* ich getraute mich nicht, ich wagte es nicht; *if all else* ~*s* wenn alle Stricke reißen, *fam* wenn alles schiefgeht; *to* ~ *to appear* nicht erscheinen; *to* ~ *to answer an invitation* e-e Einladung nicht annehmen; ~**ed** [-d] *a* zahlungsunfähig; ~**ing** ['-iŋ] *s* Fehlen *n*, Mangel *m*; Versagen, Fehlschlagen, Scheitern *n*; Schwäche *f*, (kleiner) Fehler *m*; *prp* in Ermangelung *gen*, ohne, mangels; ~~ *proof to the contrary* bis zum Beweis des Gegenteils; ~**ure** ['feiljə] Fehlen *n*, Mangel *m*, Ausbleiben; Schwächerwerden, Nachlassen *n*, Abnahme *f*; Versäumnis, Ausbleiben *n*, Unterlassung *f*; Versagen, Fehlschlagen, Scheitern, Mißlingen *n*; Fehlschlag, Mißerfolg *m*; *(Schule)* Durchfallen *n*; schlechte, ungenügende Zensur *f*; *tech* Ausfall *m*; *mot* Panne; *com* Zahlungsunfähigkeit, -einstellung *f*, Konkurs, Bankrott *m*, *fam* Pleite *f*; Zs.bruch; *(Mensch)* Versager *m*, Niete *f*; *to end in* ~~ mit e-m Mißerfolg enden; *he is a* ~~ er taugt nicht viel; ~~ *to appear* Nichterscheinen *n*; ~~ *to deliver, of performance* Nichterfüllung *f*.

fain [fein] *a pred obs poet* genötigt, bereit (*to* zu); *adv nur mit would*: gern(e); *I would* ~ *do it* ich würde es gern tun.

faint [feint] *a* schwach (*with* vor); matt, kraftlos; mutlos, ängstlich, schüchtern; feige; *(Farbe)* matt, blaß; *(Ton)* schwach, leise; *(Linie)* dünn; *s* Ohnmacht *f*; *itr (to* ~ *away)* schwächer werden, sich verlieren; e-n Schwächeanfall haben, ohnmächtig werden (*from, with hunger* vor Hunger; *because of the heat* infolge der Hitze); *to become, to grow* ~ schwächer werden, nachlassen; *I haven't the* ~*est idea* ich habe keine Ahnung, keinen blassen Schimmer; *I lay in a dead* ~ ich lag in e-r tiefen Ohnmacht; ~**-hearted** *a* ängstlich, mutlos, verzagt, kleinmütig; ~**-heartedness** Mutlosigkeit, Verzagtheit *f*, Kleinmut *m*; ~**ness** ['-nis] Schwäche; Mattigkeit; Ängstlichkeit *f*.

fair [fɛə] **1.** *a* tadellos, untadelig, einwandfrei, rein, sauber; *(Ruf)* gut; frisch, neu; hell, licht; blond; *(Wetter)* schön, hell, klar, heiter, sonnig; offen, unbe-, ungehindert, g(e)rade; gerecht, ehrlich, billig, redlich, anständig; unparteiisch, unvoreingenommen, vorurteilslos, -frei; *(Spiel)* den Regeln entsprechend, fair, einwandfrei; *(Preis)* angemessen; günstig, vorteilhaft, annehmbar, aussichtsreich, vielversprechend, verheißungsvoll; angenehm, gefällig, entgegenkommend, höflich; ziemlich, einigermaßen groß; mittelmäßig, (ganz) leidlich, ordentlich, einigermaßen gut; lesbar, leserlich; *obs poet* schön, hübsch, lieblich, anmutig; *adv* den Regeln entsprechend, einwandfrei, anständig; gerade(swegs), mitten (*in* in); *by* ~ *means* (auf) anständig(e Weise); *to be in a* ~ *way to* auf dem besten Wege sein zu; *to bid, to promise* ~ verheißungsvoll sein, gute Aussichten bieten; *to copy* ~ *(Urkunde)* ins reine schreiben; *to play* ~ sich anständig verhalten, anständig handeln (*with s.o.* gegenüber jdm); *that's only* ~ das ist nicht mehr als recht und billig; *the* ~ *sex* das schöne Geschlecht, die Frauen *pl*; ~ *and just* recht u. billig; ~ *and square* offen und ehrlich; ~ **catch** *Am (Fußball)* Freifang *m*; ~ **copy** Reinschrift *f (e-r Urkunde)*; ~ **dealing** Redlichkeit, Anständigkeit *f*; ~**-~** *(a)* ehrlich, unparteiisch; ~ **game** jagdbare(s) Wild *n*; ~**-haired** *a* blond; ~**ish** ['-riʃ] leidlich, einigermaßen gut *od* groß; ~**ly** ['-li] *adv* gerecht, redlich, anständig; einigermaßen, leidlich, erträglich, ziemlich; klar, deutlich; völlig, vollständig, ganz, gänzlich; wirklich, tatsächlich; ~**-minded** *a* gerecht, ehrlich, redlich; unparteiisch, unvoreingenommen; ~**ness** ['-nis] Gerechtigkeit, Redlichkeit, Billigkeit, Ehrlichkeit, Anständigkeit; Unparteilichkeit, Unvoreingenommenheit, Vorurteilslosigkeit; Freundlichkeit; Schönheit; Blondheit *f*; *in* ~~ *to s.o.* um jdm Gerechtigkeit widerfahren zu lassen; ~ **play** ehrliche(s) Spiel *n*; ~**-spoken** *a* höflich, gefällig, nett, freundlich; einleuchtend; ~**way** ['fɛəwei] *mar* Fahrtrinne *f*, Fahrwasser *n*; *(Golf)* Spielfläche *f*; ~**-weather** *a* Schönwetter-; ~~ *friends (pl)* unzuverlässige Freunde *m pl*; **2.** *s (bes. Jahr-)*Markt *m*; Messe *f*; *(fancy* ~*)* Wohltätigkeitsbasar *m*; *to be at a* ~ auf e-r Messe sein; *autumn, spring* ~ Herbst-, Frühjahrsmesse *f*; *world* ~ Weltausstellung *f*; ~**goer** Messebesucher *m*; ~**-ground, site** Messegelände *n*; ~**ing** ['-riŋ] **1.** Jahrmarktsgeschenk *n*.

fairing ['fɛəriŋ] **2.** *mar aero* Verschalung, Verkleidung, Profilierung *f*.

fairy ['fɛəri] *s* Fee *f*, Elf(e *f*); *sl* Homosexuelle(r) *m*; *a* Feen-; feenhaft, zart, anmutig, graziös; ~**-dance** Elfenreigen *m*; ~**-lamps, -lights** *pl* Illumination, feenhafte Beleuchtung *f (bes. in Gärten)*; ~**land** Feen-, Elfenreich; Märchen-, Traum-, Wunderland, Zauberreich *n*; ~**-like** feenhaft, anmutig, zierlich, zart; ~**-tale** Märchen *n*.

faith [feiθ] Glaube(n) *m* (*in* an); Religion *f*; Vertrauen *n* (*in* zu); Treue; Zuverlässigkeit; Ehrlichkeit, Ehrenhaftigkeit, Redlichkeit *f*; Wort, Versprechen *n*, Zusage *f*; *in* ~ wirklich, tatsächlich; *in good* ~ in gutem Glauben, gutgläubig; *in bad* ~ unaufrichtig, unehrlich *adv*; *on the* ~ *of* im Vertrauen auf; *to break, to keep (o.'s)* ~ sein Versprechen nicht halten, halten (*with s.o.* jdm); *to lose* ~ *in s.o.* das Vertrauen zu jdm verlieren; *to put o.'s* ~ *in* sein Vertrauen setzen auf; *breach of* ~ Vertrauensbruch, -mißbrauch; Wortbruch *m*; ~**-cure, -healing** Gesundbeten *n*; ~**-curer, -healer** Gesundbeter *m*; ~**ful** ['-ful] treu, ergeben (*to s.o.* jdm); zuverlässig, gewissenhaft, sorgfältig; ehrlich, redlich; *(Abschrift)* genau, getreu, korrekt; *the* ~~ *(pl)* die Gläubigen *pl (bes. Mohammedaner)*; ~**fully** ['-fuli] *adv* ergeben; *Yours* ~~ *(am Briefende)* Ihr (sehr) ergebener, hochachtungsvoll; ~**fulness** ['-fulnis] Treue, Ergebenheit, Redlichkeit *f*; ~**less** ['-lis] treulos (*to* gegenüber); unehrlich, unredlich; unzuverlässig; *rel* ungläubig; ~**lessness** ['-lisnis] Treulosigkeit *f*.

*

fake [feik] *tr (to* ~ *up)* fälschen; *(in betrügerischer Absicht)* zurechtmachen, herrichten; *(Bilanz)* verschleiern; *fam* (auf)frisieren, aufmachen; heucheln, schwindeln, vortäuschen, erfinden; *mus* improvisieren; *s* Fälschung *f*, Schwindel, Betrug *m*; *attr* gefälscht, falsch, unecht; *a.* ~**r** ['-ə] Fälscher, Schwindler, Betrüger *m*.

fakir ['fɑ:kiə, fə'kiə, *Am* 'feikə] *rel* Fakir *m*.

falchion ['fɔ:ltʃən] Pallasch, Krummsäbel *m*; *poet* Schwert *n*.

falcon ['fɔ(:)lkən, 'fɔ:k-] *orn* Falke *m*; ~**er** ['-nə] Falkner *m*; ~**ry** ['-nri] Falknerei; Falkenbeize, -jagd *f*.

fall [fɔ:l] *irr fell, fallen* **1.** *itr* (herab-, herunter-, hinab-, hinunter)fallen, -stürzen; einstürzen, zs.brechen; *(im Kampf)* fallen; (herab-, nieder)sinken; niedergehen; sich senken *(a. Stimme)*, abfallen; (herab)fließen; *(Fluß)* sich ergießen, münden (*into* in); *(Wind)* nachlassen, sich legen, abflauen; *(Temperatur, Preise)* sinken, fallen; *(Regierung)* gestürzt werden; an Achtung, Ansehen verlieren; entgleisen, sündigen; *(Mädchen)* fallen; *(Stadt)* fallen, erobert werden; fallen (*on s.o.* auf jdn), zufallen (*on s.o.* jdm); *(auf e-n Tag)* fallen (*on* auf); *(Preis, Gewinn)* fallen (*to s.o.* auf jdn, *(Erbschaft)* an jdn); *(Akzent)* fallen (*on* auf); (zufällig) stoßen (*on* auf); herfallen (*on* über); verfallen (*on* auf); zerfallen, eingeteilt sein (*into* in); *(Tier)* geworfen werden; *Am sl* ins Kittchen kommen; **2.** *s* Fall; Sturz *m*; (Herab-)Hängen *n*, (Ab-)Hang *m*; Sinken, Fallen *n (der Preise)*, *com* Baisse; *tech* Senkung *f*, Abfall; Verfall, Sturz *fig*, Untergang *m*, Niederlage *f*; *sport* Schultersieg; Fehltritt *m*, Entgleisung *f*, (sittlicher) Fall; *(Tiere)* Wurf *m*; *das* Ab-, Heruntergefallene; Gefälle *n*; *Am* Herbst *m*; *das* Herabhängende, lose(s) Ende; *(Flaschenzug)* Seil *n*; offene(r), Schillerkragen *m*; *Am sl* Verhaftung, Verurteilung *f*; *meist pl* Wasserfall *m*, Kaskade *f*; **3.** *to ride for a* ~ s-m Verderben entgegengehen; *to* ~ *into disuse* außer Gebrauch kommen; *to* ~ *on o.'s feet (fig)* auf die Füße, Beine fallen; *to* ~ *to ground (fig)* ins Wasser fallen; *to* ~ *into bad habits* schlechte Gewohnheiten annehmen; *to* ~ *ill, sick* krank werden; *to* ~ *into line (mil)* antreten; *with* übereinstimmen, einer Meinung sein mit; *to* ~ *in love with* sich verlieben in; *to* ~ *over o.s.* über die eigenen Füße fallen; *to* ~ *to pieces* ausea.-, zer-, verfallen; *to* ~ *under suspicion* in Verdacht geraten; *his countenance, his face fell* er machte ein langes Gesicht; *I had a bad* ~ ich habe e-n bösen Sturz getan; **4.** ~ *in the birthrate* Geburtenrückgang *m*; ~ *from a horse* Sturz *m* vom Pferd; *the F~ (of Man)* der Sündenfall; ~ *in output* Leistungsrückgang *m*; ~ *in prices* Fallen, Sinken *n* der Preise, Preisrückgang *m*; ~ *in potential* Spannungsabfall *m*; ~ *of rain, of snow* Regen-, Schneefall *m*; ~ *in value* Wertminderung *f*, -verlust *m*; **5.** *to* ~ **among** unter ... fallen; *to* ~ **apart** ausea.-, zs.-, zerfallen; aus dem Leim gehen; *to* ~ **asleep** einschlafen; *to* ~ **away** abfallen (*from* von); abnehmen; abmagern; verlassen (*from s.o.* jdn); *to* ~ **back** zurückgehen, -weichen, sich zurückziehen, nachgeben; *(up)on s.th.* sich auf etw zurückziehen; auf etw zurückgreifen; zu e-r S s-e Zuflucht nehmen; sich mit etw begnügen; *to* ~ **behind** zurückbleiben, *fam* hinterherhinken; *(mit Zahlungen)* im Rückstand bleiben (*with* mit); in Verzug, ins Hintertreffen geraten; *to* ~ **down** (auf die Knie) niederfallen; einstürzen; herunterfallen (*the stairs* die Treppe); zu Bruch gehen; *on (sl)* Pech haben, reinfallen mit; *on the job* versagen; *dead* tot umfallen; *to* ~ **due** fällig werden; *to* ~ **flat** keinen Eindruck machen, keine Wirkung haben, wirkungslos verpuffen, nicht einschlagen; scheitern; *to* ~ **for** *sl* sich verknallen, sich vergaffen in; reinfallen auf; schwärmen für; *to* ~ **foul** *(Schiff)* zs.stoßen (*of* mit); sich in die Haare geraten, in Streit geraten (*of* mit); *to* ~ **in** einfallen, -stürzen, zs.brechen; zustimmen, ja sagen; *mil* (in Linie) antreten, sich formieren, sich aufstellen; *with s.o.* jdn zufällig treffen, jdm zufällig begegnen; jdm zustimmen, beipflichten; *to* ~ **into** verfallen in; *(Unterhaltung)* beginnen; *to* ~ **off** herab-, herunterfallen; nachlassen, zurückgehen, geringer, schwächer werden; *fam* magerer werden; sich verschlimmern, verfallen; *mar* sich leewärts legen; *aero* abrutschen, -kippen; *to* ~ **on** fallen auf; herfallen über; *the expense will* ~ *on me* ich werde die Kosten zu tragen haben; *to* ~ **out** sich streiten, sich zanken, in Streit geraten, sich überwerfen (*with* mit); *(Haar)* ausgehen, -fallen; *mil* wegtreten; *Am fam* hemmungslos tun, überwältigt sein von; *imp* geschehen, sich ereignen; ausfallen; *out of step* außer Tritt fallen; *to* ~ **over** *o.s. fig* sich die Beine ausreißen; *to* ~ **short** knapp werden, nicht (aus)reichen; *of* zurückbleiben hinter, nicht erreichen; *we fell short of provisions* die Vorräte gingen uns aus; *to* ~ **through** scheitern, fehlschlagen, ins Wasser fallen; *to* ~ **to** beginnen, anfangen, sich machen an, in Angriff nehmen (*doing s.th.* etw zu tun); herfallen über *(a. Essen)*; zugreifen, *fam* 'reinhauen; *to* ~ **under** *(s.o.'s influence)* unter *(jds Einfluß)* geraten; **6.** ~ **fashions** *pl Am* Herbstmoden *f pl*; ~ **guy** *sl* Sündenbock; Hereingefallene(r) *m*; **~-out** Ausfall *m*; radioaktive Niederschläge *m pl*; **~-wind** Fallwind *m*.

fallac|ious [fə'leiʃəs] trügerisch, verfänglich; irreführend; *philos* Trug-, Fang-; **~y** ['fæləsi] Trugschluß; Irrtum *m*, Täuschung; Verfänglichkeit *f*.

fallen ['fɔːlən] *pp a* gefallen *a. fig*; zu Boden gestreckt, am Boden (liegend); niedergeworfen, unterworfen, besiegt; vernichtet, zerstört; gefallen, tot; *the* ~ die Gefallenen *(Soldaten)*; ~ **arches** *pl* Senkfüße *m pl*.

fallib|ility [fæli'biliti] Fallibilität *f*; **~le** ['fæləbl] fallibel, fehlbar.

falling ['fɔːliŋ] *a* fallend, sinkend, abnehmend, rückgängig; *(Haar)* ausgehend; *s* Fallen *n*; *to have a* ~ *out* Streit haben; ~ *(of the) birthrate* Geburtenrückgang *m*; ~ *of the womb (med)* Gebärmuttervorfall *m*; ~ **due** *fin* Fälligkeit *f*, Verfall *m*; **~-off** Verminderung, Verringerung, Abnahme *f*; Nieder-, Rückgang *m*; **~-star** Sternschnuppe *f*, Meteor *m* od *n*.

fallow ['fælou] **1.** *a agr* brach *a. fig*; *fig* vernachlässigt; untätig; *s* Brache *f*, Brachfeld *n*; **2.** falb, fahl, gelbbraun; **~-deer** Damhirsch *m*, -wild *n*.

false [fɔːls] *a* falsch; unrichtig, unwahr, irrtümlich; unaufrichtig, lügnerisch, lügenhaft, unehrlich; treulos (*to* gegen); trügerisch, irreführend; unecht; gefälscht, nachgemacht, künstlich; unrichtig, fehlerhaft; *adv nur in*: *to play s.o.* ~ jdn hintergehen, betrügen; *to be in a* ~ *position* sich in e-r schiefen Lage befinden; *to be* ~ *to o.'s promises* s-e Versprechungen nicht halten; *to take a* ~ *step* danebentreten; ~ **alarm** blinde(r) Alarm *m*; ~ **bottom** doppelte(r) Boden *m*; ~ **coiner** Falschmünzer *m*; ~ **coining** Falschmünzerei *f*; **~-hearted** *a* unaufrichtig; unehrlich; **~hood** ['-hud] Unwahrheit; Lüge *f*, Lügen *n*; irrtümliche Meinung *od* Auffassung *f*; ~ **imprisonment** Freiheitsberaubung *f*; ~ **judg(e)ment, verdict** Fehlurteil *n*; ~ **key** Nachschlüssel *m*; **~ness** ['-nis] Falschheit, Unaufrichtigkeit, Hinterhältigkeit; Treulosigkeit *f*, Verrat *m*; ~ **news, report** Falschmeldung *f*; ~ **oath** Meineid *m*; ~ **pretences** *pl* Vorspiegelung *f* falscher Tatsachen; *by, on, under* ~~ unter Vorspiegelung falscher Tatsachen; ~ **reasoning** Fehlschluß *m*; ~ **ribs** *pl anat* falsche Rippen *f pl*; ~ **start** Fehlstart *m*; ~ **step** Fehltritt *a. fig*; *fig* Mißgriff *m*; ~ **take-off** *aero* Fehlstart *m*; ~ **teeth** falsche Zähne *m pl*, (künstliches) Gebiß *n*.

falsetto [fɔːl'setou] *pl -os* Fistel-, Kopfstimme *f*, Falsett *n*.

falsif|ication [fɔːlsifi'keiʃən] (Ver-) Fälschung *f*; **~ier** ['fɔːlsifaiə] Fälscher *m*; **~y** ['fɔːlsifai] *tr* (ver)fälschen; falsch darstellen *od* berichten; willkürlich abändern, -wandeln; als falsch nachweisen, widerlegen; vereiteln, durchkreuzen; *to be* ~*ied* sich als *(Hoffnung)* trügerisch, *(Befürchtung)* grundlos erweisen; widerlegt werden.

falsity ['fɔːlsiti] Falschheit; Unrichtigkeit *f*, trügerische(r) Irrtum *m*; Unaufrichtigkeit, Unehrlichkeit, Lügenhaftigkeit *f*.

faltboat ['fʌltbout] *Am* Faltboot *n*.

falter ['fɔːltə] *itr* (sch)wanken; torkeln, stolpern, straucheln; stottern, stammeln; zögern, zaudern; *tr (to* ~ *out)* stammeln; **~ing** ['-riŋ] stockend; unsicher, schwach; wankend.

fame [feim] (*bes.* guter) Ruf *m*; Berühmtheit *f*, Ruhm *m*; **~d** [-d] *a* bekannt (*as, for* als); berühmt (*for* wegen, durch); *ill-*~~ berüchtigt.

familiar [fə'miljə] *a* vertraut (*to s.o.* jdm); gut bekannt (*with, to* mit); vertraulich, zwanglos, intim; (zu) frei; aufdringlich; wohlbekannt; *(Freunde)* eng, nahestehend; gewohnt, alltäglich, (nicht un)gewöhnlich; *(Tier)* zahm; *s* Vertraute(r), vertraute(r) Freund; *hist* Hausgeist *m*; *to be* ~ *with s.th.* sich in etw auskennen; *to make o.s.* ~ *with s.th.* sich mit etw vertraut machen; **~ity** [fəmili'æriti] Vertrautheit; Vertraulichkeit, Intimität, Zwanglosigkeit; Aufdringlichkeit; Bekanntheit, Vertrautheit (*with* mit); *meist pl* Vertraulichkeiten *f pl*; **~ization** [fəmiliərai'zeiʃən] Gewöhnung (*with* an); **~ize** [fə'miljəraiz] *tr* bekannt machen, verbreiten; vertraut machen (*with* mit), gewöhnen (*with* an); *to* ~~ *o.s. with s.th.* sich mit etw vertraut machen.

family ['fæmili] Familie *f*; Kinder *n pl (e-r Familie)*; Verwandtschaft *f*; Haus(gemeinschaft *f*); Haus, Geschlecht *n*, Stamm *m*; Abstammung, (gute) Herkunft; (Sprach-, Tier-, Pflanzen-)Familie; *math* Schar *f*; *in a* ~ *way* ungezwungen, ungeniert, zwanglos *adv*; *in the* ~ *way (fam) (Frau)* in andern Umständen; *of (good)* ~ aus gutem Hause; *of no* ~ von niedriger Herkunft; ~ **allowance** Familienbeihilfe, Kinderzulage *f*; ~ **circle** Familienkreis *m*; ~ **council** Familienrat *m*; ~ **doctor** Hausarzt *m*; ~ **estate** Stammgut *n*; ~ **hotel** Familienpension *f*; ~ **life** Familienleben *n*; ~ **likeness** Familienähnlichkeit *f*; ~ **man** Familienvater; häusliche(r) Mensch *m*; ~ **name** Familienname *m*; ~ **partnership** Familienunternehmen *n*; ~ **status** Familienstand *m*; ~ **tree** Stammbaum *m*; ~ **welfare** Familienfürsorge *f*.

fam|ine ['fæmin] Hungersnot *f*; (akuter) Mangel *m*, Knappheit *f*; Hunger *m*; *coal, water* ~~ Kohlen-, Wassermangel *m*; ~~ *price* Mangelpreis *m*; **~ish** ['fæmiʃ] *tr* (ver)hungern lassen; *itr* Hunger leiden; verhungern; darben; *I'm* ~~*ing (fam)* ich bin am Verhungern; *half-*~~*ed* halbverhungert.

famous ['feiməs] berühmt (*for* durch, wegen); *fam* prima, erstklassig.

fan [fæn] **1.** *s* Fächer; Ventilator; (Schiffsschrauben-, Propeller-)Flügel *m*; *agr* Schwinge *f*; *tr* (an)fächeln; *(Feuer, Leidenschaft)* an-, entfachen (*into* zu); fächerförmig ausbreiten *od* aufstellen; *agr* worfeln, schwingen; *Am fam* durchsuchen; *itr (to* ~ *out) mil* sich fächerförmig entfalten, ausschwärmen; *(Straßen)* fächerförmig ausea.gehen; *Am sl* plaudern; ~ **belt** Ventilatorriemen *m*; ~ **blade** Ventilatorflügel *m*; **~-cooled** *a* fremdgekühlt; ~ **palm** Fächerpalme *f*; **~-shaped** *a* fächerförmig; **~-tail** ['-teil] *orn* Pfauentaube *f*; Schleierschwanz *m (Fisch)*; ~ **vaulting** *arch* Fächer-, Trichtergewölbe *n*; **~wise** ['-waiz] *adv* fächerartig; **2.** *fam* begeisterte(r) Anhänger *(e-s Sportes)*, Fan(atiker), Verehrer *m*; *film (od Am) movie, radio ~* Film-, Radionarr *m*; ~ **mag(azine)** *Am fam* Filmzeitschrift *f*; ~ **mail** Verehrerbriefe *m pl*.

fanatic(al) [fəˈnætik(əl)] *a* fanatisch; *s (fanatic)* Fanatiker, Eiferer, (religiöser) Schwärmer *m*; **~ism** [-sizm] Fanatismus *m*.

fanci|ed [ˈfænsid] *a* vorgestellt, eingebildet; **~er** [ˈ-ə] Liebhaber, Freund, Kenner; (Tier-, Pflanzen-)Züchter *m (aus Liebhaberei)*; *dog ~~* Hundeliebhaber *m*; **~ful** [ˈ-ful] phantasiebegabt, einfallsreich; verspielt, launenhaft; unwirklich, phantastisch; wunderlich, sonderbar, seltsam, eigenartig.

fancy [ˈfænsi] *s* Einbildungskraft, Phantasie; ˈLaunenhaftigkeit, Verspieltheit; Einbildung, Vorstellung *f*, vage(r) Gedanke; Einfall *m*, Laune, Schrulle *f*, Spleen; Hang *m*, Neigung, Vorliebe (*for* für); Liebhaberei *f*, Steckenpferd *n*; (Kunst-)Geschmack *m*; *a* Phantasie-; phantastisch, einfallsreich, verspielt, launenhaft, wunderlich; bunt, lebhaft gemustert; modisch, elegant; ausgefallen, ungewöhnlich, extravagant; Luxus-; Kunst-; *Am* ausgesucht, erstklassig, teuer; *(Preis)* übertrieben, Phantasie-, Liebhaber-; *(Tier)* Zucht-, Rasse-; *tr* sich vorstellen, sich einbilden; gern haben, (gern) mögen, lieben, Gefallen haben an; sich denken, meinen; *(Tiere aus Liebhaberei)* züchten; *to have a ~ for s.th.* den Wunsch nach, Appetit auf etw haben; etw gern haben; *to take a ~ for, to* Gefallen, Geschmack finden an, liebgewinnen; *to take, to catch s.o.'s ~* jdm gefallen, jdn anziehen, jdn begeistern; *~ that (now)! just ~!* denken Sie mal, nur! sehen Sie (mal)! *I ~* ich kann mir schon vorstellen; *I have a ~* mir scheint so; ich habe so e-e Idee; *a passing ~* e-e vorübergehende Laune (*with s.o.* jds); **~-articles, -goods** *pl* Luxus-, Geschenkartikel *m pl*; **~-ball** Maskenball *m*, Maskerade *f*; ~ **bazaar, fair** Wohltätigkeitsbasar *m*; ~ **bread** Feinbrot *n*; ~ **cakes** *pl* Feingebäck *n*, Konditoreiwaren *f pl*; ~ **dog** Rassehund *m*; ~ **dress** Maskenkostüm *n*; **~-free** ungebunden, frei, ledig; sorgenfrei, sorglos; ~ **man** Zuhälter *m*; ~ **package** Luxuspakkung *f*; ~ **price** Phantasie-, Liebhaber-, Luxuspreis *m*; **~-work** Stickerei *od* Häkelarbeit *f*.

fandango [fænˈdæŋgou] *pl -oes* Fandango *m*.

fane [fein] *poet lit* Tempel *m*, Kirche *f*.

fanfar|e [ˈfænfɛə] Fanfare *f*; Tusch, Trompetenstoß; geräuschvolle(r) *od* prächtige(r) Aufzug *m*; **~onade** [fænfærəˈnɑːd] Großsprecherei, -tuerei *f*.

fang [fæŋ] Fangzahn *(der Raubtiere)*; Giftzahn *(der Schlangen)*; *(Eber)* Hauer *m*; (Zahn-)Wurzel; *allg* Spitze *f*, Dorn *m*, Klaue *f*.

fanner [ˈfænə] *tech* Gebläse *n*.

fantas|ia [fænˈteizjə, fæntəˈziə] *mus* Fantasia *f*; **~tic(al)** [fænˈtæstik(əl)] eingebildet, unwirklich; phantastisch, wunderlich, seltsam, bizarr, grotesk; überspannt, launenhaft, (aus)schweifend; **~y** [ˈfæntəsi] Phantasie; Vorstellung, Einbildung, Illusion; Laune, Schrulle *f*, Hirngespinst *n*; Träumerei; *mus* Fantasia *f*.

far [fɑː] *a* weit, entfernt, fern *(a. zeitl.)*; ganz andere(r, s), völlig andersartig; vorgerückt; *a ~ cry* weit weg; *few and ~ between* selten; *the F~ East* der Ferne Osten *(Ostasien)*; *adv* weit (weg, entfernt), in weiter Ferne; weither; weitweg; *(zeitl.)* lange hin, lange her; bei weitem, beträchtlich, (sehr) viel; *as, so ~ as* bis (zu); *as ~ as, (in) so ~ as* soweit; soviel; *by ~* bei weitem; weitaus; *from ~* von weitem; von weit her; *in so ~ as* insofern; *in the ~ future* in der fernen Zukunft; *on the ~ side* auf der anderen Seite; *so ~, thus ~* so weit, bis dahin, bis hierher; bis jetzt; *so ~ as* so weit, wie; soviel; *so ~ so good* kurz und gut; *~ afield* weit ab; *to get ~~ from a subject* von e-m Gegenstand weit abschweifen; *~ and away (fig)* bei weitem; zweifellos; *~ and near* überall; nah u. fern; *~ and wide* weit und breit; *~ from* alles andere als; lange nicht, keineswegs; *~ from it* weit davon entfernt, nicht im geringsten; *~ into the night* bis spät in die Nacht hinein; *~ on in the day* spät am Tage; *to be a ~ cry from ... to* ein himmelweiter Unterschied sein zwischen ... und; *to be few and ~ between (fig)* dünn gesät sein; *to go ~* es weit bringen, viel erreichen; *towards* viel beitragen zu; *I am ~ from doing it* ich denke nicht daran, es zu tun; *he's ~ gone* es steht schlecht um ihn; *~ be it from me* das sei fern von mir! *I wouldn't carry things too ~* ich würde die Sache nicht auf die Spitze treiben; **~-away** *a* weit entfernt; längst vergangen; verträumt, (geistes) abwesend; **~-between** *a* vereinzelt; **~-famed** *a* weithin bekannt; **~-fetched** *a* weit hergeholt *fig*, gesucht, gezwungen; übertrieben, phantastisch; **~-flung** *a* weit ausgedehnt; **~-gone** *a* vorgeschritten; heruntergekommen, abgewirtschaftet; stark betrunken; **~-off** *a* (weit) entfernt; *(zeitlich)* fernliegend; **~-reaching** weitreichend; wirkungsvoll; einflußreich; **~-seeing** vorausschauend, weitblickend; weit im voraus planend; **~-sighted** *a* weitsichtig; *fig* weitblickend, vorausschauend; **~-sightedness** Weitsichtigkeit; *fig* weise Vorausschau *f*, Scharfblick *m*.

farc|e [fɑːs] Posse(nhaftigkeit) *f*; Schwank *m*; **~ical** [ˈfɑːsikəl] possenhaft; ulkig, komisch; lächerlich.

fare [ˈfɛə] *itr* sich befinden, voran-, vorwärtskommen; ergehen; *poet* wandern, ziehen, reisen, fahren; *s* Fahrgeld *n*, -preis *m*, Reisegeld *n*; Fahrgast *m*; Kost, Verpflegung *f*, Essen *n*, Speise(n *pl*) *f*; *~s, please!* noch jem zugestiegen? *have your ~s ready* Fahrgeld bereithalten! *how did you ~? how did it ~ with you?* wie ist es dir ergangen? *he is faring well in his business* sein Geschäft geht gut; *he ~d alike* es erging ihm nicht anders; *what's the ~?* was kostet die Fahrt? *bill of ~* Speisekarte *f*; *full ~* Fahrkarte *f* zum vollen Preis; **~-stage** Teilstrecken-, Zahlgrenze *f*; **~well** *s* Abschied(sworte *n pl*) *m*, Lebewohl *n*; *a* Abschieds-; *interj* lebe(n Sie) wohl! *to bid s.o. ~~* jdm Lebewohl sagen; *~~ to ...* Schluß mit ...!

farin|a [fəˈrainə, fəˈriːnə] Stärke(mehl *n*) *f*; *Am* Gries; Puder; *bot* Blütenstaub *m*; *chem* Stärke *f*; **~aceous** [færiˈneiʃəs] mehlhaltig; Mehl-; mehlig; stärkeartig; *~~ food* Nährmittel *n pl*.

farm [fɑːm] *s* (Bauern-)Gut *n*; Bauern-, Gutshof *m*; *(~-house)* Bauern-, Gutshaus; *(leased ~)* Pachtgut *n*, -hof; landwirtschaftliche(r) Betrieb *m*; Farm; Züchterei *f*; *tr (Land)* bestellen, bebauen, bewirtschaften; *(to ~ out)* verpachten; *(Arbeitskraft)* zur Verfügung stellen; *(Menschen)* in Pflege geben *od* nehmen; *itr* in der Landwirtschaft arbeiten; Landwirtschaft betreiben; *to ~ out (Arbeit)* vergeben; *Am (Aufträge)* weitergeben; *baby ~* Kinderbewahranstalt *f*, -hort *m*; *chicken-~* Hühnerfarm *f*; *experimental ~* Versuchsfarm *f*; *oyster ~* Austernzucht *f*; ~ **buildings** *pl* landwirtschaftliche Gebäude *n pl*; **~er** [ˈ-ə] Bauer, Landwirt, Farmer; Pächter *m*; *the ~~s* die Bauernschaft; *baby ~~* Kindergärtnerin *f*; *poultry ~~* Geflügelzüchter *m*; *~~s' association* landwirtschaftliche Genossenschaft *f*; *~~s' bank* Landwirtschaftsbank *f*; *~~'s wife* Bäuerin, Bauersfrau *f*; **~erette** [-ˈret] *Am fam* Landarbeiterin *f*; **~-hand, -labo(u)rer, -worker** Landarbeiter *m*; **~-house** Bauernhaus *n*; *~~ bread* Bauernbrot *n*; **~(ing) implements** *pl* landwirtschaftliche, Acker-Geräte *n pl*; **~ing** [ˈ-iŋ] *s* Landwirtschaft *f*, Ackerbau *m*; *a* landwirtschaftlich, Landwirtschafts-; *baby ~~* Kinderbetreuung *f*; *chicken-~~* Hühnerzucht *f*; *fur ~~* Pelztierzucht *f*; *poultry ~~* Geflügelzucht *f*; *stock ~~* Viehzucht *f*; *~~ and breeding* Ackerbau u. Viehzucht; *~~ lease* Pachtvertrag *m*; ~ **land** Ackerland *n*; **~stead** [ˈ-sted] Bauernhof *m (mit dem Land)*; ~ **work** Landarbeit *f*; **~yard** Wirtschaftshof *m*; *~~ buildings (pl)* Wirtschaftsgebäude *n pl*.

faro [ˈfɛərou] Phar(a)o *n (Kartenglücksspiel)*.

farrago [fəˈrɑːgou, -ˈreig-] *pl -o(e)s* Mischmasch *m*, Durcheinander *n*.

farrier [ˈfæriə] Hufschmied *m*.

farrow [ˈfærou] *s* Wurf *m* Ferkel; *tr (Ferkel)* werfen; *itr* ferkeln; *in, with ~* trächtig *(Sau)*.

fart [fɑːt] *s vulg* Furz *m*; *itr* furzen.

farther [ˈfɑːðə] *(Komparativ von far) a* weiter entfernt, entfernter; zusätzlich; weiter; *adv* weiter (weg); außerdem; noch; überdies; in höherem Maße; *nothing is ~ from my mind* nichts liegt mir ferner; **~ermost** *a = ~est (a)*; **~est** [ˈ-ist] *(Superlativ von far) a* entferntest, weitest; ausgedehntest, längst; *adv* am weitesten weg; *(at (the) ~~)* höchstens; spätestens.

farthing [ˈfɑːðiŋ] Viertelpenny *m*; *not to care a ~* sich nicht das geringste machen aus; *not to matter a ~* nicht das geringste, gar nichts ausmachen; *not worth a (brass) ~* keinen Pfifferling wert.

fasci|a [ˈfeiʃə, *anat* ˈfæʃiə] *pl -ae* [-iː], *arch -as* Band *n*, Streifen *m*, *med* Binde *f*; *arch* Gesimsstreifen *m*, -band; Firmenschild; Armaturenbrett *n*; *zoo bot* (Farb-)Streifen *m*; *anat* Bindegewebe *n*; **~ate(d)** [ˈfæʃieit(id)] *a bot* bandartig verbreitert u. abgeflacht; gebündelt; *zoo* gestreift.

fascic|le [ˈfæsikl], **~ule** [ˈ-kjuːl] Bündel; Faszikel *n*; *(Buch)* Lieferung *f (Teil)*; **~ular** [fəˈsikjulə], **~ulate** [-lit], **-ulated** [-leitid] *a* gebündelt, Bündel bildend.

fascinat|e [ˈfæsineit] *tr* fesseln, bezaubern, faszinieren; hypnotisieren; **~ing** [ˈ-iŋ] spannend, fesselnd; **~ion** [-ˈneiʃən] Bezauberung, Faszination *f*; Zauber, hohe(r) Reiz *m*.

fascine [fæˈsiːn] Faschine *f*, Reisiggeflecht, -bündel *n*.

fasc|ism, F~ [ˈfæʃizm] Faschismus *m*; **~ist** [ˈfæʃist] *s* Faschist *m*; *a* faschistisch.

fashion [ˈfæʃən] *s* Form, Gestalt *f*, (Zu-)Schnitt *m*; Fasson; Mode; Art, Weise, Art u. Weise *f*; gute(s) Benehmen *n*, Lebensart, gute Sitte *f*; *tr* formen, gestalten; machen, anfertigen; zustande, zuwege bringen, bewerkstelligen; Gestalt geben (*s.th.* e-r S); anpassen (*to* an); *after, in a ~* in gewisser Weise, in s-r Art; so gut es geht;

gewisser-, einigermaßen; *after the ~ of* nach Art *gen*; *in ~* in Mode, modern; *out of ~* aus der Mode, unmodern; *to be all the ~* die große Mode sein; *to come into ~* Mode werden; *to go out of ~* unmodern werden; *to set the ~* den Ton angeben; *it is the ~ to do* es ist üblich, man pflegt zu tun; **~able** ['fæʃnəbl] *a* modern, modisch, Mode-; elegant, schick, fein; üblich; beliebt; *s* elegante(r) Mann *m*, Frau *f*; **~ableness** ['-əblnis] Schick *m*, Eleganz; Beliebtheit *f*; **~-designer** Modezeichner *m*; **~ house** Modesalon *m*; **~ magazine** Modejournal *n*, -zeitschrift *f*; **~-monger** Modenarr *m*; **~-parade, -show** Modeschau *f*; **~-plate** Modebild *n*, -zeichnung *f*; Modenarr *m*, -püppchen *n*.

fast [fɑ:st] **1.** *a* fest; dicht; festsitzend; *(Schlaf)* fest, tief; *(Farben)* (licht- u. wasch)echt; *(Freund(schaft))* fest, treu, beständig; schnell; kurz (dauernd); *(Uhr)* vorgehend; flott, frei, locker, ausschweifend, unsolide; *(Bakterien)* resistent; *phot* lichtstark; *adv* fest, dicht; schnell; *(regnen)* stark, heftig; *to be (an hour) ~ (Uhr)* (eine Stunde) vorgehen; *to lead a ~ life, to live ~* ausschweifend leben, e-n lockeren Lebenswandel haben; *to make ~* festmachen, befestigen; *(Tür)* zumachen; *to play ~ and loose* ein doppeltes Spiel treiben (*with* mit); *to rain ~* stark regnen; *to stand ~* feststehen; sich nicht rühren; nicht wanken; *to stick ~* nicht vorwärts-, vorankommen; festsitzen; *to take (a) ~ hold of s.th.* etw festhalten; *hard and ~* streng; starr; unumstößlich; *~ to light* lichtecht; **~ asleep** in tiefem Schlaf; **~ buck** *Am sl* leichtverdiente(s) Geld *n*; **~ freight** *Am* Eilgut *n*; **~ highway** *Am* Schnellstraße *f*; **~train** Schnellzug *m*; **2.** *itr* fasten, nüchtern bleiben; *s* Fasten *n*, Fasttag *m*, Fastenzeit *f*; *to break o.'s ~* frühstücken; *to keep the ~* das Fasten einhalten; **~-day** *a.* **~ing-day** *rel* Fasttag *m*.

fasten ['fɑ:sn] *tr* befestigen, festmachen, anbinden, anheften (*to* an); zumachen, (ver)schließen; (*o.'s eyes* den Blick) heften, richten (*on* auf); in Verbindung bringen (*on* mit), beimessen (*on s.o.* jdm), anhängen, andichten (*on s.o.* jdm); *itr* sich anheften; haften, festhalten; zugehen; zugemacht werden; sich konzentrieren (*on* auf); sich halten (*upon* an); *to ~ off* ver-, zuknoten; *to ~ up* zumachen; *to ~ (up)on* ergreifen, herausgreifen, (her)aussuchen; aufs Korn nehmen; *to ~ the blame on s.o.* die Schuld jdm zuschieben; **~er** ['-ə] Befestiger; Verschluß *m*; Sperre *f*, Riegel *m*; Musterklammer *f*; Druckknopf; *(zip, slide ~~)* Reißverschluß *m*; **~ing** ['-iŋ] Befestigung; Schließe *f*, Halter, Haken, Riegel *m*, Schloß *n*, Klammer *f*, Knopf *m*, Band *n*; *~~ pin* Heftbolzen *m*.

fastidious [fæs'tidiəs] mäk(e)lig, wählerisch, anspruchsvoll; **~ness** [-nis] Mäkelei *f*, anspruchsvolle(s) Wesen *n*.

fastness ['fɑ:stnis] Festigkeit; *(Farbe)* Haltbarkeit, Lichtechtheit; Schnelligkeit; Kürze (der Zeit); Leichtlebigkeit; Feste *f*, Bollwerk *n*; *med* Widerstandskraft *f* (*to* gegen).

*

fat [fæt] *a* fett; fettig; fett(leibig, -wanstig), dick(bäuchig); dick, stark, umfangreich, breit; reichlich, im Überfluß vorhanden; fruchtbar, (ertrag)reich, ergiebig, einträglich, gewinnbringend; *fam* dumm; *s* Fett *n a. chem*; Fettigkeit; Fettheit, Fettleibigkeit *f*; *das* Beste (*an e-r S)*; *theat sl* gute Rolle *f*; *tr* mästen; *to chew the ~ (sl)* die Köpfe zs.stecken; *to get ~* fett, dick werden; *to have a ~ chance (sl)* geringe Aussichten haben (*of getting* zu bekommen); *to kill the ~ted calf for s.o. (fig)* jdm e-n großartigen Empfang bereiten; *to live on the ~ of the land* wie Gott in Frankreich leben; *to run to ~* Fett ansetzen; *the ~ is in the fire* jetzt ist der Teufel los; *a ~ lot you care (sl)* Sie kümmern sich e-n Dreck drum; *a ~ book* ein dicker Wälzer; *a ~ purse* ein dickes Portemonnaie; **~ cat** *Am sl* Arrivierte(r); *pol* Geldgeber *m*; **~ content** Fettgehalt *m*; **~-guts** *sing* Fettwanst, Dickbauch *m (Person)*; **~-head** Dummkopf *m*; **~-headed, -witted** *a* dumm, blöd(e); **~ling** ['fætliŋ] Stück *n* junges Mastvieh; **~ness** [-nis] Fettheit, Fettigkeit; Fettleibigkeit; Fruchtbarkeit, Ergiebigkeit *f*; **~ requirement** Fettbedarf *m*; **~so** ['fætsou] *Am sl* Fettmops *m*; **~-soluble** fettlöslich; **~ stock** Mastvieh *n*; **~ten** ['fætn] *tr* fett, dick machen, mästen; düngen; bereichern, füllen; *itr* fett, dick werden; *to ~~ up* dicker werden *od* machen; **~tish** ['-iʃ] ein bißchen fett; **~ty** ['fæti] *a* fett(ig), ölig; *s fam* Dickerchen *n*; *~~ acid* Fettsäure *f*; *~~ degeneration (med)* Verfettung *f*; *~~ heart* Herzverfettung *f*; *~~ tissue* Fettgewebe *n*; **~ type** Fettdruck *m*.

fatal ['feitl] schicksalhaft; verhängnisvoll, fatal (*to* für); verderblich, vernichtend (*to* für); tödlich; Schicksals-; **~ accident** tödliche(r) Unfall *m*; **~ism** ['feitəlizm] Fatalismus *m*, Schicksalsgläubigkeit *f*; **~ist** ['-list] Fatalist *m*; **~istic** [feitə'listik] fatalistisch, schicksalsgläubig; **~ity** [fə'tæliti] Schicksal, Geschick, Verhängnis; Mißgeschick, Unglück(sfall *m*) *n*, Tod(esfall) *m*; verhängnisvolle Wirkung *f*; **~ly injured** tödlich verletzt, verwundet (*in an accident* bei e-m Unfall); **~ sisters** *pl* Parzen *f pl*; **~ thread** Lebensfaden *m*.

fate [feit] Schicksal, Geschick, Los, Fatum; Verhängnis, Verderben *n*, Untergang, Tod *m*; *the F~s (pl)* die Parzen *f pl*; *as sure as ~* todsicher; *to meet o.'s ~* sein Ende finden; vom Schicksal ereilt werden; **~d** [-id] *a* vom Schicksal bestimmt; dem Untergang geweiht; **~ful** ['-ful] schicksalhaft, verhängnisvoll; entscheidend.

father ['fɑ:ðə] *s* Vater *a. fig*; (Be-)Gründer, Urheber, Erfinder, geistige(r) Vater; Pater; *F~* Vater, Gott *m*; *pl* (Vor-)Väter, Vorfahren; Stadtväter *m pl*; *tr* der Vater sein *gen*; (er)zeugen; die Vaterschaft übernehmen für; Vaterstelle vertreten bei; (be)gründen, (er-)schaffen, erfinden, ins Leben rufen; die Verantwortung übernehmen für; die Vater-, Urheberschaft zuschreiben (*on s.o.* jdm); *the child is ~ to the man* die Kinderjahre sind entscheidend; *like ~ like son* der Apfel fällt nicht weit vom Stamm; *the wish is ~ to the thought* der Wunsch ist der Vater des Gedankens; *the Holy F~* der Heilige Vater, der Papst; *Reverend F~* Ehrwürdiger Vater *(Anrede e-s Geistlichen)*; *the F~s of the Church* die Kirchenväter *pl*; **F~ Christmas** Weihnachtsmann; Nikolaus *m*; **~ confessor** Beichtvater *m*; **F~'s Day** *Am* Vatertag *m*; **~ figure** *psychol* Leitbild *n*; **~hood** ['-hud] Vaterschaft *f*; **~-in-law** ['-rinlɔ:] Schwiegervater *m*; **~land** ['-lænd] Vaterland *n*; **~less** ['-lis] vaterlos; **~liness** ['-linis] Väterlichkeit *f*; **~ly** ['-li] väterlich.

fathom ['fæðəm] *s* Faden *(Längenmaß = 6 Fuß = 1,83 m)*; Klafter *m (= 216 cubic feet = 6,12 cbm)*; *tr (die Wassertiefe)* ausmessen, sondieren, loten; *fig* ergründen, ermessen, erfassen; **~less** ['-lis] unergründlich; unermeßlich.

fatigue [fə'ti:g] *s* Abspannung, Ermüdung, Erschöpfung; Strapaze, Anstrengung *f*; *(~ duty) mil* Arbeitsdienst *m*; *med* (Organ-), *tech* (Material-)Abnutzung; *(Metall)* Ermüdung *f*; *pl (~ clothes, dress, uniform) mil* Drillich-, Arbeitsanzug *m*; *tr* ermüden, strapazieren; erschöpfen, übermüden; *itr tech* ermüden, altern; **~-cap** *mil* Feldmütze *f*, *fam* Krätzchen *n*; **~-party, detail** Arbeitskommando *n*; **~-strength** *tech* Dauerfestigkeit *f*; **~ test** Dauerprüfung *f*.

fatu|ity [fə'tju(:)iti] Albernheit *f*; **~ous** ['fætjuəs] töricht, albern, närrisch.

fauc|al ['fɔ:kəl] *a* Rachen-, tiefe(r) Kehl-; **~es** ['fɔ:si:z] *pl* Rachen, Schlund *m*; Rachenenge *f*.

faucet ['fɔ:sit] *bes. Am* (Wasser-)Hahn, (Faß-)Zapfen *m*.

faugh [fɔ:] *interj* pfui!

fault [fɔ:lt] Fehler; Mangel; Defekt *m*; Versehen *n*; Irrtum *m*; Schuld *f*; Verschulden *n*; *tech* Störung *f*; *el* Erdfehler *m*; *geol* Verwerfung(sspalte), Sprungkluft *f*; *at ~ (Hund)* auf falscher Fährte *a. fig*; in Verlegenheit; im Irrtum; fehlerhaft; *tech* defekt; *in ~* im Irrtum; schuld; *to a ~* im Übermaß, zu (sehr); *without o.'s ~* ohne Verschulden; *to find ~* etw auszusetzen haben, herumnörgeln (*with* an); Fehler finden (*in* an); *the ~ lies with* der Fehler liegt bei; *it's not my ~* es ist nicht meine Schuld; **~-finder** Krittler *m*; **~-finding** *s* Tadelsucht, Nörgelei, Meckerei *f*; *a* tadelsüchtig, nörg(e)lig; **~iness** ['fɔ:ltinis] Fehler-, Mangelhaftigkeit *f*; **~less** ['-lis] fehlerfrei, untadelig, tadellos; **~sman** *tele* Störungssucher *m*; **~y** ['fɔ:lti] fehler-, mangelhaft; schadhaft, defekt; ungenau, unvollkommen; falsch; *(Besitz)* widerrechtlich; *~~ design* Konstruktionsfehler *m*; *~~ drafting* Formfehler *m*.

faun [fɔ:n] Faun *m*; **~a** ['fɔ:nə] Fauna, Tierwelt *f*.

favo(u)r ['feivə] *s* Gunst *f*, Wohlwollen *n*, Gefallen *m*; Vergünstigung; Nachsicht *f*, Einvernehmen, Einverständnis *n*, Erlaubnis; Begünstigung *f*, Schutz *m*, Obhut, Hilfe; Gunstbezeigung, Gefälligkeit *f*; Andenken; Abzeichen *n*; Schleife, Knopflochblume; *pl* Hingabe *f (e-r Frau)*; *tr* Wohlwollen entgegenbringen *od* zeigen (*s.o.* jdm); Gefallen finden (*s.o.* an jdm); bevorzugen, begünstigen; Nachsicht üben (*s.o.* jdm gegenüber); befürworten, sprechen für; unterstützen, helfen (*s.o.* jdm), decken; ermutigen; e-n Gefallen tun (*s.o.* jdm); schonen; *fam* ähnlich sehen (*s.o.* jdm); *as a ~* aus Gefälligkeit; *by ~ of (Brief)* durch Vermittlung *gen*; *by, with your ~* mit Ihrer Erlaubnis; *in ~ of* wohlwollend gegenüber; für, zugunsten; *fin* zahlbar an; *in s.o.'s ~* zu jds Gunsten *od* Vorteil; für; *out of ~* nicht beliebt (*with* bei); aus der Mode; *under ~* mit Verlaub (zu sagen), wenn ich so sagen darf; *under ~ of darkness, night* im Schutz der Dunkelheit; *with ~* wohlgefällig; zustimmend; günstig; *to ask a ~ of s.o.* jdn um e-n Gefallen bitten; *to be in (great) ~* (sehr) in Gunst stehen, (sehr) beliebt, gefragt sein; *to be in ~ of s.th.* für etw sein; *of doing s.th.* dafür sein, etw zu tun; *to do s.o.*

a ~ jdm e-n Gefallen erweisen; *to find* ~ *in s.o.'s eyes* jds Zustimmung, Gefallen finden; *to speak in s.o.'s* ~ für jdn eintreten; *to withdraw o.'s* ~ *from s.o.* jdm s-e Gunst entziehen; *fortune* ~*s the bold* od *the brave* dem Mutigen gehört die Welt; *who is in* ~*?* wer ist dafür? *your* ~ Ihr wertes Schreiben; **~able** ['-rəbl] günstig, vorteilhaft (*to* für); *(Antwort)* positiv; *(Handelsbilanz)* aktiv; *on* ~~ *terms* zu günstigen Bedingungen; **~ed** ['-d] *a* begünstigt, bevorzugt; *ill-*~~ unansehnlich, häßlich; **~ite** ['-rit] *s* Günstling; *sport* Favorit *m*; *a* Lieblings-; *to be a general* ~~ allgemein beliebt sein; ~~ *book, colo(u)r, pastime, son* Lieblingsbuch *n*, -farbe, -beschäftigung *f*, -sohn *m*; **~itism** ['feivəritizm] Vettern-, Günstlingswirtschaft *f*.

fawn [fɔ:n] **1.** *s* Rehkitz, junge(s) Reh; Hirschkalb *n*; Rehfarbe *f*; *a* rehfarben, -braun; *tr itr (Reh, Hirschkuh)* (Junge) setzen; **2.** *itr (Hund)* s-e Freude zeigen; mit dem Schwanz wedeln; *(Mensch)* schmeicheln (*on, upon s.o.* jdm), kriechen (*on, upon s.o.* vor jdm); **~ing** *fig* kriecherisch.

fay [fei] Fee *f*.

faze [feiz] *tr Am fam* auf die Palme, aus der Fassung, in Verlegenheit bringen.

fealty ['fi:əlti] Lehnspflicht, -treue *f*.

fear [fiə] *s* Angst, Furcht(samkeit); Befürchtung, Besorgnis *f*; Schreck *m*; Scheu, Ehrfurcht *f*; Grund *m* zu Befürchtungen; *tr* (be)fürchten, (sich) scheuen (vor); (Ehr-)Furcht haben vor; *itr* sich fürchten, Angst haben (*for* um); bange sein; *for* ~ *of* aus Angst vor (*of doing s.th.* etw zu tun); *for* ~ *that, lest* damit nicht; *never* ~*!* (nur) keine Angst! *without* ~ *or favo(u)r* unparteiisch, gerecht; *to be in* ~ *of* sich fürchten vor; bangen um; *to stand in great* ~ *of* große Angst haben vor; **~ful** ['-ful] furchtbar, schrecklich, entsetzlich *a. fam*; furchtsam, ängstlich, bange, besorgt; *to be* ~~ *of* Angst haben vor; *of doing s.th.* zögern, etw zu tun; **~fulness** ['-fulnis] Furchtbarkeit; Furchtsamkeit, Ängstlichkeit *f*; **~less** ['-lis] furchtlos (*of* vor); **~lessness** ['lisnis] Furchtlosigkeit *f*; **~some** ['-səm] fürchterlich.

feasib|ility [fi:zə'biliti] Aus-, Durchführbarkeit, Möglichkeit *f*; **~le** ['fi:zəbl] tunlich, aus-, durchführbar; anwendbar; *(Material)* brauchbar; vernünftig; *(Weg)* gangbar, befahrbar.

feast [fi:st] *s (~-day)* Fest *n bes. rel*, Feier, Festlichkeit *f*; Festmahl, -essen, Bankett *n*; *fig* Hochgenuß *m*; *tr* ein Fest(essen) geben (*s.o.* jdm, für jdn); festlich bewirten; erfreuen; *(Nacht)* durchfeiern; *itr* (ein Fest) feiern, tafeln; sich ergötzen (*on* an); *to* ~ *o.'s eyes on* s-e Augen weiden an.

feat [fi:t] Heldentat *f*; Kunststück *n*; große Leistung *f*.

feather ['feðə] *s* Feder; *(Pfeil)* Fiederung *f*; Federbusch *m*; *(a. pl)* Gefieder; Stück *n* Federvieh *od* Geflügel; Bagatelle; Schaumkrone *f*; *tr* mit Federn versehen *od* schmücken; *(Ruder)* flach werfen; *aero* auf Segelstellung fahren; *as light as a* ~ federleicht; *in* ~ gefiedert; *in fine, full, good, high* ~ in (froher) Stimmung, guter Dinge; gesund und munter; in guter Form, auf der Höhe; *to show the white* ~ Angst verraten; kneifen; *to* ~ *o.'s nest* sein Schäfchen ins trockene bringen; die Gelegenheiten nutzen; *fig* sich warm betten; *birds of a* ~ *flock together* gleich u. gleich gesellt sich gern; *fur and* ~ Haar- u. Federwild *n*; *a* ~ *in o.'s cap* Leistung *f*, auf die man stolz sein kann; **~-bed** *s* Federbett *n*; *Am sl* leichte Arbeit *f*; *tr* verwöhnen; *(Arbeit)* strecken; **~-bedding** *Am sl* (gewerkschaftlicher Zwang *m* zur) Einstellung *f* nicht benötigter Arbeitskräfte; **~-brained, -headed** *a* dumm; albern; leichtsinnig; **~-broom, -duster** Staubwedel *m*; **~ed** ['-d] *a* gefiedert; **~-edge** ['-redʒ] scharfe Kante *f*; **~few** = *feverfew*; **~ing** ['-riŋ] Gefieder *n*; *(Pfeil)* Fiederung; *aero (*~~ *position)* Segelstellung *f* der Luftschraube; **~-stitch** *(Stickerei)* Fischgrätenstich *m*; **~-weight** *(Boxen)* Federgewicht *n*; **~y** ['-ri] gefiedert; federleicht, weich.

feature ['fi:tʃə] *s* Gestalt, Form, Erscheinung(sform) *f*; Aussehen; angenehme(s) Äußere(s) *n*; Gesichtsteil *m*, *pl* Gesichtsbildung *f*, (Gesichts-)Züge *m pl*, Gesicht *n*; *allg* Charakterzug *m*, Charakteristikum, hervorragende(s) Kennzeichen, Merkmal *n*; typische(r), wesentliche(r) Bestandteil *m*; *(chief, leading* ~*)* Grund-, Hauptzug, Hauptbestandteil *m*, -eigenschaft *f*; Anziehungspunkt *m*, Attraktion *f*; *(*~ *film, picture)* Spiel-, Hauptfilm; *(Radio)* Tatsachenbericht *m*, Reportage, Hörfolge *f*; *(Zeitung)* Sonderbericht; aktuelle(r) Artikel *m*; *tr* kennzeichnen, charakterisieren, darstellen; ein Bild sein *gen*, verkörpern; *fam* sich vorstellen, verstehen, kapieren; wiedergeben, abbilden, gestalten; *(Rolle)* spielen, darstellen; *bes. Am* (groß) heraus-, zur Schau stellen; groß aufmachen, -ziehen; besonders behandeln, bringen; *to make a special* ~ *of s.th.* sich auf etw spezialisieren; *with X.* ~*d, featuring X. (film)* mit X. in der Hauptrolle; *distinctive, main* ~ Unterscheidungs-, Hauptmerkmal *n*; **~d** ['-d] *a* geformt, gestaltet, geprägt; (besonders) herausgestellt, hervorgehoben; **~-length** ['-leŋθ] *a film* programmfüllend, Haupt-; **~less** ['-lis] nichtssagend, ohne eigenes Gepräge; uninteressant; *(Markt)* lustlos; **~-program(me)** *radio* Hörbericht *m*, -folge *f*; **~tte** ['-rɛt] *Am* kurze(r) Spielfilm *m*; **~-writer** *(Zeitung)* Sonderberichterstatter *m*.

febri|fuge ['febrifju:dʒ] Fiebermittel *n*; **~le** ['fi:brail, 'fi:brəl, 'febril] fieberhaft, fiebernd; *fig* erregt.

February ['februəri] Februar *m*.

feces *s. faeces.*

feckless ['feklis] schwach, kraftlos; unwirksam; untüchtig, unfähig.

feculen|ce ['fekjuləns] kotige, faulige Beschaffenheit *f*; Bodensatz *m*, Hefe *f*; Schmutz *m*; **~t** ['-t] kotig; faulig, schlammig; schmutzig.

fecund ['fi:kənd, 'fek-, -kʌnd] fruchtbar; ertragreich; **~ate** ['-eit] *tr* fruchtbar machen; befruchten; **~ation** [-'deiʃən] Fruchtbarmachung, Befruchtung *f a. biol*; **~ity** [fi'kʌnditi] Fruchtbarkeit; Zeugungsfähigkeit; *bot* Keimfähigkeit *f*.

fed [fed] *(pret u.) pp von feed*: *to be* ~ *up with s.o., s.th. (sl)* jdn, etw satt haben; *I'm* ~ *up with it (sl)* das hängt mir zum Halse 'raus; *poorly* ~ unterernährt; *well* ~ wohlgenährt.

feder|al ['fedərəl] *a* bundesstaatlich; *(F*~~*)* Bundes-; *s (F*~~*) Am* Föderalist *m*; ~~ *aid (Am)* Bundeshilfe *f*; ~~ *army* Bundesheer *n*; ~~ *authority* Bundesbehörden *f pl*; *F*~ *Bureau of Investigation* Bundeskriminalamt *n*; ~~ *council* Bundesrat *m*; ~~ *diet, parliament* Bundestag *m*; ~~ *government* Bundesregierung *f*; *F*~~ *Income Tax (Am)* Bundeseinkommensteuer *f*; ~~ *judge* Bundesrichter *m*; ~~ *law* Bundesgesetz *n*; ~~ *legislation* Bundesgesetzgebung *f*; *F*~~ *Register (Am)* Bundesanzeiger *m*; *F*~~ *Republic* Bundesrepublik *f*; ~~ *state* Bundesstaat *m*, -land *n*; ~~ *territory* Bundesgebiet *n*; ~~ *union* Staatenbund, Bundesstaat *m*; **~alism** ['fedərəlizm] Föderalismus *m*; **~alist** ['-rəlist] Föderalist *m*; **~alize** ['fedərəlaiz] *tr s. ~ate*; **~ate** ['fedərit] *a* bundesstaatlich; Bundes-; verbündet; *tr itr* ['federeit] (sich) zu e-m Bundesstaat *od* Staatenbund zs.schließen, vereinigen; **~ation** [fedə'reiʃən] Zs.schluß *m*; Vereinigung, Verbindung *f*, Bündnis *n*, Bund; *com* Verband *m*, Syndikat *n*; *economic* ~~ Wirtschaftsverband *m*; *employers'* ~~ Arbeitgeberverband *m*; *American F*~~ *of Labor (AFL)* amerikanische(r) Gewerkschaftsverband *m*; **~ative** ['fedərətiv] bundesmäßig, föderativ.

fee [fi:] *s a. pl* Gebühr(en *pl*), Sportel, Taxe *f*, Honorar *n*; Tantieme *f*; Trinkgeld; Geldgeschenk *n*; Bezahlung *f*; Schulgeld; *jur* Eigentumsrecht; *hist* Lehensgut *n*; *tr* e-e Gebühr entrichten an, ein Honorar bezahlen *dat*; *for a small* ~ gegen e-e geringe Gebühr; *to charge, to collect a* ~ e-e Gebühr erheben; *to hold in* ~ besitzen; *basic* ~ Grundgebühr *f*; *booking* ~ Eintragungs-, Platzgebühr *f*; *scale of* ~*s* Gebührentarif *m*; **~ simple** *jur* Eigengut, uneingeschränkte(s) Eigentum *n*: **~ tail** *jur* (Grund-)Eigentum *n* mit Erbbeschränkung.

feeble ['fi:bl] schwach, kraftlos, matt; wirkungslos, unwirksam; zart, zerbrechlich; leicht beeinflußbar; **~-minded** *a* schwachsinnig; willenlos, unentschlossen; *s* Schwachsinnige(r *m*) *f*; **~-mindedness** Schwachsinn *m*; **~ness** ['-nis] Schwäche *f*.

feed [fi:d] *irr fed, fed tr* füttern (*on* mit; *Am s.th. to*); mit Futter versorgen; speisen; verpflegen, verköstigen (*at a restaurant* in e-m Restaurant); (ver-)füttern, (als Futter) geben; mästen; ernähren *a. physiol*, versorgen; Nahrung geben *dat a. fig*; *(Hoffnung)* nähren; *(Zorn)* schüren; *(Eitelkeit)* befriedigen; Brenn-, Betriebsstoff, Material zuführen (*the stove* dem Ofen, *a machine* e-r Maschine); das Wasser zuführen (*a lake* e-m See); *agr* weiden lassen; *itr* (fr)essen *a. fam hum (von Menschen)*; sich ernähren, leben (*on, upon* von); *agr* weiden; *s* Füttern *n*, Fütterung; Mahlzeit *f*, Essen; (Vieh-)Futter *n*; Futtermenge; *tech* Zuführung, Zufuhr, Beschickung, Ladung, Speisung *f*; Vorschub; Brenn-, Betriebsstoff *m*, Material *n*; Zubringevorrichtung, Zuführung, Speiseleitung *f*; *to* ~ *up* herausfüttern, mästen; *to be fed up with s.th.* etw satt haben; *to be off o.'s* ~ keinen Appetit haben; **~-back** Rückkopp(e)lung *f*; **~-bag** Futtersack *m*; *to put on the* ~~ *(Am sl)* sich ans Essen machen; **~-cock** Einfüllstutzen *m*; **~er** ['-ə] Fütterer; Viehmäster; Futterverbraucher, -verwerter; Esser *m*; Mastvieh *n*; (Saug-)Flasche *f*; (Kinder-)Lätzchen *n*, (Brust-)Schurz; Wasser-, Bewässerungsgraben; Nebenfluß *m*; *tech* Zuführung(svorrichtung), Aufgabevorrichtung, Speiseleitung *f*; *(Verkehr)* Zubringer *m*; *(*~~ *line)* Zubringerlinie, -strecke *f*; ~~ *cable* Leitungskabel *n*; ~~ *line aircraft* Zubringerflugzeug *n*; ~~ *road* Zubringerstraße *f*; ~~ *service* Zubringerdienst *m*; **~ing** ['-iŋ] *s* Fütterung, Mästung, Weide *f*; Essen *n*; Ernährung; Speisung; Zuführung, Zufuhr, Beschickung *f*; *attr* Futter-;

a zunehmend; *sl* ärgerlich; *high* ~~ Wohlleben *n*; ~~*-bottle* (Saug-)Flasche *f*; ~~ *cup* Schnabeltasse *f*; ~~*-tank* Wasserbehälter *m*; ~~ *turnip* Futterrübe *f*; **~-pipe** *tech* Speiserohr *n*; **~-pump** *tech* Speise-, *mot* Benzinpumpe *f*; **~-screw** Förderschnecke *f*; **~-water** *tech* Speisewasser *n*.

feel [fi:l] *irr felt, felt tr* (be)fühlen, betasten; spüren, empfinden *a. fig*; ein Gefühl, ein Empfinden, Sinn haben für; ahnen; einsehen, erkennen, begreifen; glauben, meinen, halten für; *itr* sich fühlen; sich anfühlen; sich (vor-, vorwärts)tasten (*after, for* nach); mitfühlen (*for s.o.* mit jdm); *s* Fühlen, Gefühl *n*, Gefühlssinn *m*; Fingerspitzengefühl *n*; Gefühlseindruck *m*; Empfinden *n*; *to ~ about* denken über; *to ~ for s.o.* mit jdm fühlen; mit jdm Mitgefühl haben; *to ~ out (Menschen)* ergründen; auf den Zahn fühlen; *to ~ up* in der Lage sein; sich in der Lage, sich gewachsen fühlen (*to* zu); *by the ~* dem Gefühl nach; *to get (used to) the ~ of s.th.* sich an etw gewöhnen; *to ~ cheap (sl)* sich elend fühlen; niedergeschlagen sein; *to ~ cold, hungry, tired* frieren, hungrig, müde sein; *to ~ compelled* sich genötigt sehen; *to ~ like doing s.th.* Lust haben, etw zu tun; gern etw tun; *to ~ (quite) o.s.* (gesundheitlich) auf der Höhe, *fam* auf dem Posten sein; *to ~ sure, certain* sicher sein; *to ~ o.'s way* sich vorwärtstasten *a. fig*; *to* sich tasten zu; *he ~s like a fool* er kommt sich wie ein Narr vor; *I ~ as if* mir ist, als ob; ich komme mir vor, als ob; *I'm ~ing much better* ich fühle mich viel wohler, es geht mir viel besser; *I know just how you ~* ich kann es Ihnen nachfühlen; *it has a soft ~* es fühlt sich weich an; **~er** ['-ə] *zoo* Fühler *m*; *(Schnecke)* Fühlhorn *n*; Tasthaare *n pl*; *fig* Versuchsballon; Kundschafter *m*; *tech* Stichmaß *n*; *to put, to throw out a ~~ (fig)* e-n Fühler ausstrecken, die Lage sondieren, *fam* peilen; **~ing** ['-iŋ] *a* gefühlvoll; mitfühlend, teilnahmsvoll; *s* Gefühl(ssinn *m*) *n*; Gefühl *n* (*of* gen), Sinn *m* (*of* für); Empfindung *f*; Fein-, Zartgefühl; Herz, Mitgefühl *n*; Ahnung *f*; Verständnis *n*, Sinn *m* (*for* für); Auffassung, Meinung, Haltung, Überzeugung; Luft, Atmosphäre *f fig*; *pl* Gefühle *n pl*, Gefühlsleben *n*; *good ~~* Freundlichkeit *f*; *ill ~~* abweisende Haltung *f*; *I have a ~~ that* ich habe das Gefühl, daß ...; *~~ for nature, of pain* Natur-, Schmerzgefühl *n*.

feign [fein] *tr* sich einbilden; (er)heucheln, simulieren, vorgeben, vortäuschen, fingieren; *itr* sich verstellen; **~ed** [-d] *a* verstellt, geheuchelt, simuliert, fingiert; *(Name)* angenommen, falsch; Schein-.

feint [feint] *s* Heuchelei, Verstellung, Finte *f*; *(~ attack)* Scheinangriff *m*; *itr* e-n Scheinangriff machen (*at, upon* auf); *to make a ~ of doing* so tun, als ob man tut.

fel(d)spar ['fel(d)spa:r] *min* Feldspat *m*.

felicitat|e [fi'lisiteit] *tr* beglückwünschen (*on, upon* zu); Glück wünschen (*s.o.* jdm; *on* zu); **~ion** ['-teiʃən] Glückwunsch *m*, -wünsche *m pl*.

felicit|ous [fi'lisitəs] *(Ausdruck)* gut gewählt, treffend; **~y** [-ti] Glückseligkeit *f*, Glück *n*; glückliche(r) Umstand; glückliche(r), passende(r) Ausdruck *m*; *to phrase s.th. with ~~* etw sehr geschickt ausdrücken.

feline ['fi:lain] Katzen-; katzenartig; gewandt; schlau; verstohlen.

fell [fel] **1.** *pret* von *fall*; **2.** *tr (to ~ to the ground)* nieder-, zu Boden werfen; *(Baum)* fällen, schlagen, umhauen; *(Stoff)* (ein)säumen; *s* (Holz-)Schlag; *(Stoff)* Saum *m*; **~er** ['-ə] (Holz-)Fäller; Saatstreifen *m*; *sl dial* = *fellow*; **3.** *poet* grausam, grimmig, schreckenerregend, schrecklich, wild; **4.** (Tier-) Fell *n*, Haut *f*; *(Mensch)* (Haar-) Schopf *m*; **~monger** ['-mʌŋgə] Fellhändler *m*; **5.** kahle (An-)Höhe; Heide *f*, Ödland *n*.

fellah ['felə] Fellache *m*.

felloe ['felou], **felly** ['feli] Felge *f*, Radkranz *m*.

fellow ['felou] Gefährte, Genosse, Kamerad, Kollege *m*; *F~* (vollberechtigtes) Mitglied *n* der Körperschaft e-r Universität, e-s College *od* e-r gelehrten Gesellschaft; *(Universität)* Absolvent *m* mit Stipendium; *fam* Bursche, Junge, Kerl; *Am fam* Liebhaber, Galan *m*; Gegenstück *n (bei e-m Paar)*, der, die, das andere; *attr* Mit-; -gefährte, -kamerad *m*; *a ~* man, einer; *to be ~s* immer zs.sein, zs.gehören; *to be hail ~ well met (with)* gut befreundet sein (mit); *not to have o.'s ~* nicht seinesgleichen haben; *my dear, my good ~! (fam)* mein lieber Mann! *old ~! (fam)* alter Bursche! alter Junge! *poor ~! (fam)* armer Junge! *school-~* Schulkamerad *m*; **~-citizen** Mitbürger *m*; **~-countryman** Landsmann *m*; **~-creature** Mitmensch *m*; **~-debtor** Mitschuldner *m*; **~-delinquent** Mitschuldige(r), Mitangeklagte(r) *m*; **~-feeling** Sympathie *f*; Gefühl *n* der Zs.gehörigkeit, Harmonie *f* (zwischen Menschen); **~-heir** Miterbe *m*; **~-member**: *to be a ~~* auch zum Klub gehören; **~-men,** *(seltener)* **-beings** *pl* Mitmenschen *m pl*; **~-passenger** Mitreisender *m*; **~-prisoner** Mitgefangene(r) *m*; **~ship** ['-ʃip] *(oft: good ~~)* Kameradschaft, Gemeinschaft(lichkeit) *f*, kameradschaftliche(s), freundschaftliche(s) Verhältnis *n*, Gemeinsamkeit; Gesellschaft *f*, (Kameraden-, Freundes-) Kreis *m*; Stellung, Würde *f* e-s Fellow *(s. F~)*; (Forschungs-)Stipendium; *Am* (privates) Stipendium *n*; **~-sufferer** Leidensgenosse, -gefährte *m*; **~-traveller** Reisegefährte; *pol* Mitläufer, Sympathisierende(r) *m*; **~-worker** Arbeitskamerad; Mitarbeiter *m*.

felon ['felən] *s* (Schwer-)Verbrecher *m*; *med* Nagelgeschwür *n*; *a poet* grausam, böse, mörderisch; **~ious** [fi'lounjəs] verbrecherisch; **~y** ['feləni] schwere(s), Kapitalverbrechen *n*.

felt [felt] **1.** *pret* u. *pp von feel*; *a ~ want* ein Bedürfnis *n*; ein Mangel *m*; **2.** *s* Filz *m*; *attr* Filz-; *tr* zu Filz verarbeiten; mit Filz überziehen; *roofing-~* Dach-, Teerpappe *f*; **~ boot** Filzstiefel *m*; **~ cloth** Filztuch *n*; **~ hat** Filzhut *m*; **~ing** ['-iŋ] (Material *n* zur) Filzherstellung *f*; Filztuch *n*; **~ joint, packing** Filzdichtung *f*; **~ ring, washer** Filzring *m*; **~ slipper** Filzpantoffel *m*; **~ sole** Filzsohle *f*; **~y** ['-i] filzartig.

*

female ['fi:meil] *a* weiblich; Frauen-; *s zoo* Weibchen *a. pej*; **~ labo(u)r** Frauenarbeit *f*; **~ operatives** *pl* weibliche Arbeitskräfte *f pl*; **~ screw** Schraubenmutter *f*; *the* **~ sex** das weibliche Geschlecht; **~ suffrage** Frauenstimmrecht *n*; **~ thread** Innengewinde *n*.

feme [fi:m] *jur* Frau *f*; **~ covert** Ehefrau *f*; **~ sole** unverheiratete Frau; Witwe; geschiedene Frau *f*; **~-sole merchant** *od* **trader** selbständige Geschäftsfrau *f*.

femin|ine ['feminin] *a* weiblich *a. gram*; fraulich, mädchenhaft; *(Mann)* weibisch; *s gram* Femininum *n*; **~inity** [femi'niniti] Weiblichkeit; Fraulichkeit *f*; **~ism** ['-izm] Frauenbewegung *f*; **~ist** ['-ist] Frauenrechtler(in *f*) *m*.

fem|oral ['femərəl] *a* Oberschenkelknochen-; **~ur** ['fi:mə] *pl a.* **~ora** *(scient)* Oberschenkelknochen, Femur *m*.

fen [fen] *Br* Moor, Fenn *n*, Bruch *m*, Sumpfland *n*; Marsch(boden *m*) *f*; **~-berry** Moosbeere *f*; **~-fire** Irrlicht *n*; **~-goose** *orn* Graugans *f*; **~-land** Marschland *n*; **~ny** ['-i] sumpfig, moorig, bruchig; Sumpf-, Moor-.

fence [fens] *s* (Garten-, *a.* Draht-) Zaun *m*; *allg* Umfried(ig)ung; Hecke; *Am* Mauer; Schutzwehr, -verkleidung *f*; *(iron-~)* Gitter *n*; Fechtkunst *f*; *sport* Hindernis *n*, Hürde; *fig* Debattierkunst *f*; *sl* Hehlernest *n*; Hehler *m*; *tr (to ~ about, in, round, up)* ein-, umzäunen, umfried(ig)en; befestigen; verkleiden, vergittern; (ab-, be-) schirmen, (be)schützen, verteidigen (*from, against* gegen); *itr* fechten; parieren; ausweichen (*with a question* e-r Frage); Ausflüchte machen; *sl* Hehlerei treiben; *sport* e-e Hürde nehmen; *to ~ off* abwehren, sich entziehen *dat*; (durch ein Gitter) absperren; *to come down on the right side of the ~* sich *(in e-m Konflikt)* auf die richtige Seite schlagen; *to sit on the ~* neutral bleiben, (e-e) abwarten(de Haltung einnehmen); **~-month, -season, -time** *(Jagd)* Schonzeit *f*; **~r** ['-ə] Fechter; Hürdenläufer *m*; **~-rider, -sitter, -man** *Am* Neutrale(r), Parteilose(r), Abwartende(r); Zaungast, (unerwünschter) Zuschauer *m*; **~-riding** *Am* Neutralität, Parteilosigkeit, abwartende Haltung *f*.

fencing ['fensiŋ] Fechtkunst *f*; Debattieren, Wortgefecht; Material *n* zum Einfriedigen; Umzäunung; Einfriedigung(ssystem *n*); *sl* Hehlerei *f*; **~ foil** *sport* Rapier *n*; **~-glove** Fechthandschuh *m*; **~-instructor, -master** Fechtlehrer, -meister *m*; **~-room** Fechtboden *m*; **~-school** Fechtschule *f*.

fend [fend] *itr* sorgen (*for o.s.* für sich selbst); *tr*: *to ~ off* abwehren; **~er** ['-ə] Kamingitter *n*; *mot* Stoßstange *f*; *rail* Schienenräumer; *mar* (Schiffs-, Boots-) Fender *m*; *Am mot* Kotflügel *m*.

fennel ['fenl] *bot* Fenchel *m*.

feoff [fef] *s s. fief*; *tr* belehnen; **~ee** [fe'fi:] Lehnsträger *m*; **~or, ~er** ['fefə] Lehnsherr *m*.

feral ['fiərəl] **1.** wild, ungezähmt; roh, brutal; **2.** tödlich, verhängnisvoll.

ferment ['fə:mənt] *s* Ferment *n*, Gärungsstoff *m*; Hefe; Gärung *a. fig*, Fermentierung; *fig* Unruhe, Bewegung, Erregung *f*; *v* [fə(:)'ment] *tr* gären lassen, vergären; *fig* in Bewegung, in Erregung bringen, erregen; *itr* gären *a. fig*; **~ation** [fə:men'teiʃən] Gärung *a. fig*; *fig* Erregung, Unruhe, Bewegung *f*.

fern [fə:n] Farn(kraut *n*) *m*.

feroci|ous [fə'rouʃəs] wild, grausam; *fam (übertreibend)* unbändig; **~ty** [fə'rɔsiti] Wildheit, Grausamkeit *f*.

ferreous ['feriəs] *chem* eisenhaltig.

ferret ['ferit] *s zoo* Frettchen *n*; *fig* Detektiv, Spion *m*, Spürnase *f*; *tr itr* frettieren, mit dem Frettchen jagen; *tr* durchsuchen, -stöbern, -wühlen; *itr (to ~ about)* herumsuchen, -stöbern, -wühlen (*among* zwischen, in); *to ~ out* aufstöbern; auskundschaften.

ferr|i ['feri] *in Zssgen chem* Ferri-, Eisen-; **~ic** ['ferik] *a* Eisen-; *chem* Ferri-, Eisen; *~~ chloride* Eisenchlorid *n*; *~~ oxide* Eisenoxyd *n*; **~iferous** [fe'rifərəs] eisenhaltig; **~ite** ['ferait] Ferrit *n*; **~o** ['ferə(u)] *in Zssgen* Eisen-; *chem* Ferro-, Eisen-; *~~-alloy* Ferrolegierung *f*; *~~-concrete* Eisen-, Stahlbeton *m*; *~~nickel* Ferronickel *n*; **~ous** ['ferəs] *chem* Ferro-, Eisen-; *~~ chloride* Eisenchlorür *n*; *~~ oxide* Eisenoxydul *n*; *~~ sulphate* Ferrosulphat *n*; **~uginous** [fe'ru:dʒinəs] Eisen-; eisenartig, -haltig; rostfarben, -braun.

ferrule ['feru:l] *s* Zwinge *f*; Metallring *m*; *tr* mit e-r Zwinge versehen.

ferry ['feri] *s (~boat)* Fähre *f*; *aero* Überführung *f*; *tr (über ein Gewässer)* übersetzen; *aero* überführen; **~-bridge** Fährschiff *n*; **~ cable** Fährseil *n*; **~ fare** Fährgeld *n*; **~ing** ['-iŋ]: *~~ point* Übersetzstelle *f*; *~~ service (aero)* Zubringer-, Überführungsdienst; Fährbetrieb *m*; **~man** ['-mən] Fährmann *m*; **~ pilot** *aero* Überführungspilot *m*.

fertil|e ['fə:tail] fruchtbar, ergiebig, ertragreich; reich (*of, in* an); einfallsreich, erfinderisch; *(Phantasie, Einbildungskraft)* lebhaft, rege; *(Ei)* befruchtet; **~ity** [fə:'tiliti] Fruchtbarkeit, Ergiebigkeit *f*, Reichtum *m* (*of* an); **~ization** [fə:tilai'zeiʃən, -li-] Fruchtbarmachung; Düngung; Befruchtung *f a. biol*; **~ize** ['fə:tilaiz] *tr* düngen; *biol* befruchten; **~izer** ['fə:tilaizə] Kunstdünger *m*.

ferule ['feru:l] *s* flache(s) Lineal *n (zur Züchtigung)*.

ferv|ency ['fə:vənsi] Inbrunst, Glut, Hingabe *f*, Eifer *m*; **~ent** ['-ənt] heiß, brennend, glühend; inbrünstig, hingebungsvoll, innig, voller Eifer; **~id** ['-id] leidenschaftlich, voller Hingabe, hingebungsvoll; **~o(u)r** ['fə:və] Glut, Hitze; Inbrunst, Hingabe *f*, Eifer *m*.

fess(e) [fes] *(Heraldik)* Balken *m*.

festal ['festl] festlich; Fest(es)-; heiter.

fester ['festə] *itr* eitern, schwären; *fig (Ärger)* fressen, nagen (*in* in); (ver)faulen, verderben; *tr* eitern lassen; *fig* verbittern; fressen, nagen an; *s* Geschwür *n*, Schwäre *f*; **~ing sore** Eiterbeule *f a. fig*.

festiv|al ['festəvəl] *s* Fest *n*; Feier *f*; *mus theat* Festspiele *n pl*; Festlichkeit, Lustbarkeit *f*; *a* festlich, feierlich; *music ~~* Musikfestspiele *n pl*; *~~ day* Festtag *m*; **~e** ['festiv] festlich; lustig, fröhlich, froh, heiter; **~ity** [fes'tiviti] Lustbarkeit; Festesfreude, Fröhlichkeit, Heiterkeit *f*; Fest *n*, Feier *f*; *pl* Festlichkeiten, Feierlichkeiten *f pl*.

festoon [fes'tu:n] *s* Girlande *f*, (Blumen-, Laub-)Gewinde *n (a. arch u. an Möbeln)*; *tr* mit Girlanden verzieren; **~ cloud** Schäfchenwolke *f*.

fet|al, ~us *s. foetal*.

fetch [fetʃ] *tr* (her-, herbei-, hervor-)holen, (her-, herbei)bringen; *(Hund)* apportieren; kommen lassen; hervorlocken; vorlegen; *(Atem)* holen, schöpfen; *(Seufzer)* ausstoßen; *(Tränen)* vergießen; *(Preis)* holen, gewinnen, erzielen; *(Geld)* einbringen; erreichen; *fam* anziehen, -locken, reizen, bezaubern, fesseln, einnehmen; *fam (Schlag)* versetzen, *(Schläge)* austeilen; *itr* apportieren; *mar* Kurs nehmen *od* halten; *(Tau)* fieren; *s lit fig* (Herbei-)Holen; Gespenst *n*; *fam* Kniff, Trick *m*; *mar* Linie, Strecke *f*; *to ~ a breath* Atem, Luft holen; *to ~ and carry* alle Arbeiten verrichten, Mädchen für alles sein (*for s.o.* für jdn); *to ~ delight* Vergnügen machen; *to ~ a sigh* seufzen; *to* **~ along** mitnehmen; *fig* auf die Höhe bringen, *fam* aufmöbeln; *to* **~ away** wegholen; *to* **~ back** *to mind* sich erinnern; *to* **~ down** herunterholen, abschießen; *to* **~ in** hereinholen, -bringen; *to* **~ out** herausholen, -bringen; *to* **~ up** *tr* einholen, erreichen; aus-, erbrechen; *(Preis)* erzielen; herbeiholen; *itr* stehenbleiben, anhalten; scheitern; *Am* enden; **~ing** ['-iŋ] *fam* bezaubernd, reizend, entzückend, süß.

fête, *Am meist* **fete** [feit] *s* (*bes.* Garten-)Fest *n*; *tr* feiern; ein Fest geben (*s.o.* jdm); **~-day** Namenstag *m*.

fetid ['fetid, 'fi:tid] übelriechend, stinkend.

fetish ['fi:tiʃ, 'fetiʃ] *rel psychol* Fetisch *m*; **~ism** ['-izm] Fetischismus *m*.

fetlock ['fetlɔk] *(Pferd)* Kötenschopf *m*; Köten-, Fesselgelenk *n*.

fetter ['fetə] *s meist pl* (Fuß-)Fesseln *f pl a. fig*; *fig* Zwang *m*, Hemmung *f*; *tr* fesseln; *fig* in Schranken halten, unterdrücken, unterbinden.

fettle ['fetl] Zustand *m*, Verfassung, Beschaffenheit *f*; *in fine, in good ~* in guter Verfassung, *fam* in Form.

feud [fju:d] **1.** *s* Fehde *f*; Streit *m*; *itr* sich befehden; *at ~* im Streit; **~al** ['-l] *a* Fehde-; **2.** Lehen *n*; **~al** *a* Lehns-, Feudal-; *~~ law* Lehnsrecht *n*; *~~ system*, **~alism** ['-əlizm] Feudalsystem, Lehnswesen *n*; **~ality** [fju:'dæliti] Lehnsverhältnis *n*; Feudalherrschaft *f*, -system; Lehen *n*; **~atory** ['fju:dətəri] *s* Lehnsmann, Vasall *m*; Lehen *n*; *a* Lehns-; lehnspflichtig (*to* dat).

fever ['fi:və] Fieber *n*; *fig* innere Unruhe, Erregung *f*; *to be in a ~ of excitement* in fieberhafter Aufregung sein; *to have, to run a ~* Fieber haben; **~ed** ['-d] *a* fiebernd, fieberkrank; *fig* fieberhaft; erregt, unruhig; **~ heat** Fieberhitze *f*; **~ish** ['-riʃ] fiebernd; *fig* fieberhaft; *to work ~~ly on s.th.* fieberhaft an etw arbeiten; **~ishness** ['-riʃnis] Fieberhaftigkeit *f*.

few [fju:] *prn a u. s pl* wenig(e); nicht zahlreich; *a ~* einige, ein paar, *lit* etliche; *the ~* die wenigsten, e-e kleine Minderheit; *every ~ minutes, hours, days* alle paar Minuten, Stunden, Tage; *a good ~, quite a ~, not a ~ (of)* nicht wenige, ziemlich viele; e-e ganze Menge; *~ and far between* dünn gesät; *a ~ times* ein paar Mal; einige Male; *no ~er than* nicht weniger als; mindestens; *some ~* schon einige; **~ness** ['-nis] geringe Anzahl *f*.

fiancé [fi'ɑ̃:sei] Verlobte(r) *m*; **~e** Verlobte *f*.

fiasco [fi'æskou] *pl -os, Am -oes* Mißerfolg *m*; Fiasko *n*, Reinfall *m*, Pleite *f*.

fiat ['faiæt] Befehl *m*, Anordnung, Verfügung *f*, Erlaß *m*, Dekret *n*; Ermächtigung, Vollmacht *f*; **~ money** *Am* (ungedecktes) Papiergeld *n*.

fib [fib] **1.** *s fam* Flunkerei, kleine Lüge, Schwindelei *f*; *itr (to tell a ~)* flunkern, schwindeln; **~ber** ['-ə] Flunkerer *m*; **2.** *s (Boxen)* Schlag *m*; *tr* verprügeln.

fibr|e, *Am meist* **fiber** ['faibə] *anat zoo bot* Faser, Fiber; *bot* Faserwurzel; *(Textil)* Spinnfaser, Faserung, Struktur *f*; *fig* Charakter *m*, Wesen *n*, Natur *f*; *artificial ~~* Kunstfaser *f*; *cotton ~~* Baumwollfaser *f*; *~~ slab* Faserplatte *f*; *~~ structure* Faserstruktur *f*; *a man of coarse, fine ~~* ein grobschlächtiger, ein zartbesaiteter Mensch *m*; **~eboard** Hartfaserplatte *f (Baustoff)*; **~ed** = *~ous*; **~eglas** Glaswolle *f*; **~eless** ['-əlis] faserlos; *fig* (innerlich) haltlos; **~iform** ['faibrifɔ:m] faserförmig; **~il** ['faibril] *anat* Einzelfaser, Fibrille; *bot* Wurzelfaser *f*; **~in** ['faibrin] Fibrin *n (Faserstoff des Blutes, a. bot)*; **~oid** ['faibrɔid] *a* gefasert; *s med* Fasergeschwulst *f*; **~osis** [fai'brousis] *med* Fibrose *f*; **~ous** ['faibrəs] faserig; *~~ material* Spinnstoff *m*; *~~ tissue* Fasergewebe *n*.

fibul|a ['fibjulə] *pl -ae* ['-li:] *anat* Wadenbein *n*; *hist* Fibel, Gewandnadel *f*; **~ar** ['-] *a* Wadenbein-.

fickle ['fikl] wechselhaft, unbeständig, unsicher; schwankend; wankelmütig, launenhaft, launisch; **~ness** ['-nis] Wechselhaftigkeit, Unbeständigkeit *f*.

fictile ['fiktail] formbar, plastisch; tönern, Ton-; irden; keramisch; **~ ware** Steingut *n*.

fiction ['fikʃən] Fiktion *f a. jur*; (Prosa-)Dichtung(en *pl*) *f*, *bes.* Romane *m pl*, Erzählungen *f pl*; Dichtkunst *f*; *work of ~* Roman *m*, Erzählung *f*; **~al** ['fikʃənl] erfunden, erdacht, erdichtet; *~~ literature* Unterhaltungsliteratur *f*.

fict|itious [fik'tiʃəs] eingebildet, unwirklich; erdichtet, erdacht, erfunden; vorgetäuscht, fingiert, gespielt, *fam* markiert; falsch, unecht; Schein-; *(Name)* angenommen; *~~ bargain* Scheingeschäft *n*; *~~ bill (Br)* Kellerwechsel *m*; *~~ person* juristische Person *f*; *~~ sale* Scheinverkauf *m*.

*

fiddle ['fidl] *s* Fiedel, Geige *f*, Streichinstrument *n meist hum od pej*; *sl* Schiebung *f*; *tr itr fam* fiedeln; *tr (to ~ away) (Zeit)* vertrödeln, verplempern; *itr (fam)* fiedeln; *(to ~ about)* nervöse Bewegungen machen; nervös spielen (*with* mit), herumspielen (*with* an); *tr sl* beschwindeln, begaunern; *to be fit as a ~* gesund u. munter sein, sich wie ein Fisch im Wasser fühlen; *to hang up o.'s ~* keinen Ton mehr sagen; *to play first, second ~ (fig)* die erste, die zweite Geige spielen; *a face as long as a ~* ein langes *od* trauriges Gesicht; **~-bow** Geigenbogen *m*; **~-bridge** Geigensteg *m*; **~-case** Geigenkasten *m*; **~deedee, ~-dedee** ['-didi:] *s, meist interj* Quatsch! Unsinn! **~-faddle** ['fidlfædl] *s* Unsinn, Nonsens *m*; Lappalie *f*; *itr* die Zeit vertrödeln; **~r** ['-ə] Geiger; *sl* Gauner; Sixpence *m*; **~stick** Geigen-, Fiedelbogen *m*; *~~s! (interj)* Unsinn! Quatsch! **~-string** Geigensaite *f*.

fiddling *fam* läppisch; geringfügig.

fidelity [fi'deliti] Treue, Gewissenhaftigkeit *f*, Pflichtbewußtsein *n* (*to* gegenüber); Genauigkeit *f*; *high ~* einwandfreie Tonwiedergabe *f*.

fidget ['fidʒit] *s* Unruhe, Ungeduld, Nervosität *f*; nervöse(r) Mensch, unruhige(r) Geist, *fam* Zappelphilipp *m*, Nervenbündel *n*; *itr (to ~ about)* unruhig, nervös, zappelig sein; nervös spielen (*with* mit); *tr u. to give (s.o.) the ~s* (jdn) nervös machen; *to have the ~s* kein Sitzfleisch haben; ganz nervös sein; **~iness** ['-inis] Zappeligkeit, Nervosität *f*; **~y** ['-i] unruhig, zappelig, nervös.

fiduci|al [fi'dju:ʃjəl] *a* Glaubens-, Vertrauens-; *scient* Vergleichs-; **~ary** [-əri] *a* treuhänderisch; *com* ungedeckt; *s* Treuhänder *m*.

fie [fai] *interj* pfui!

fief [fi:f] Lehen *n*.

field [fi:ld] *s* Feld *n*, Acker *m*; *bes. in Zssgen* (große) Fläche *f*, Feld; *bes. in Zssgen* (Spiel-)Feld *n*, (Sport-, Flug-, Lande-)Platz *m*; (Schlacht-)Feld, (Kampf-)Gelände, Gebiet; *fig* (Fach-)Gebiet, Fach *n*, Bereich, Sektor *m*; *com* Außendienst *m*; Praxis *f*; *(~ of vision)* Gesichtsfeld *n*; Hinter-, Untergrund *m*; *(Wappen)* Feld; *phys (~ of force)* Kraftfeld *n*; *sport die* Wettkampfteilnehmer, *die* Mannschaften *pl*, *die* Besetzung; *die* an e-m Rennen teilnehmenden Pferde *pl*; *pl* Gelände, Land(strich *m*) *n*; *tr (Kricket, Baseball) (den Ball)* halten *od* auffangen u. zurückwerfen; *(Spieler)* als Fänger im Ausfeld einsetzen; *itr* als Fänger, im Ausfeld spielen; *in the ~ (mil)* im Felde; im Kampf, im Gefecht, im Einsatz; *allg* im Wettbewerb; *in this ~* auf diesem Gebiet; *to hold, to keep the ~ (mil allg)* das Feld behaupten; *to lose the ~* verlieren, geschlagen werden; *to play the ~ (Am)* in voller Breite vorgehen, sich nicht auf ein Ziel beschränken; *to take the ~ (mil)* die Feindseligkeiten, *sport* das Spiel eröffnen; *to win the ~* gewinnen; den Sieg davontragen; *~ of activity* Tätigkeits-, Wirkungsbereich *m*; Arbeitsgebiet *n*; *~ of application* Anwendungsbereich *m*; *~ of battle* Schlachtfeld *n*; *~ of operations (mil)* Operationsgebiet *n*; *~ of view* Gesichts-, Blickfeld *n*; **~-allowance** Frontzulage *f*; **~-ambulance** *Br* Sanitätsbataillon *n*; Krankenkraftwagen, Sanka *m*; **~-artillery** Feldartillerie *f*; **~-bag** Brotbeutel *m*; **~ damage** Flurschaden *m*; **~-day** *mil* Geländedienstübung *f*; *fig* große(r) Tag *m*; *Am* Sportfest *n*; **~ dressing** Notverband *m*; Verbandpäckchen *n*; **~er** ['-ə], **~sman** ['-zmən] *(Baseball, Kricket)* Fänger, Spieler *m* im Ausfeld; **~-events** *pl* Hoch-u. Weitsprung *m*, Stoßen u. Werfen *n*; **~fare** ['-fɛə] Krammetsvogel *m*, Wacholderdrossel *f*; **~-glass(es** *pl*) Feldstecher *m*; **~-gun, -piece** Feldgeschütz *n*; **~-hand** *Am* Landarbeiter *m*; **~-hospital** Feldlazarett *n*; **~ing side** *(Krikket)* Fangpartei *f*; **~ intensity** *phys* Feldstärke *f*; **~ investigator** Marktforscher *m*; **~-jacket** Windjacke; *mil* Feldbluse *f*; **~-kitchen** Feldküche *f*; **~-manual** *mil* Dienstvorschrift *f*; **F-Marshal** Feldmarschall *m*; **~-mouse** Feldmaus *f*; **~-music** *Am* Pfeifer u. Trommler *m pl*; **~-officer** *(Heer)* Stabsoffizier *m*; **~-service** Außendienst *m*; *~-~ regulations pl* Felddienstordnung *f*; **~-sports** *pl* Leichtathletik *f* (außer Laufen); Jagd u. Fischfang; **~ strength** Feldstärke *f*; **~-telephone** Feldfernsprecher *m*; **~-training** Geländeausbildung *f*; **~-trip** *(Schule) Am* Exkursion *f*, Ausflug *m*; **~-work** Feldbefestigung; *scient* Feldforschung, Außenarbeit *f*; **~-worker** *scient* Außenarbeiter; Befrager *m*.

fiend [fi:nd] Unhold, Dämon; Satan; *fam in Zssgen* Begeisterte(r), Fanatiker, Besessene(r), Narr; Süchtige(r) *m*; *fam* As *n*, Kanone *f*; *the F~* der Böse (Feind), der Teufel, Satan *m*; *bridge ~* begeisterte(r) Bridgespieler *m*; *cigarette ~* Kettenraucher *m*; *fresh-air, jazz ~* Frischluft-, Jazzfanatiker *m*; *morphia ~* Morphinist *m*; *movie ~* Filmbegeisterte(r), eifrige(r) Kinobesucher *m*; **~ish** ['-iʃ] teuflisch, satanisch.

fierce [fiəs] wild, unbändig, ungebärdig, ungezügelt, zügellos; *(Hund)* scharf; heftig, wütend, grimmig, tobend, tosend; *(Konkurrenz)* erbittert; *(Bremse) mot* scharf; ungestüm, übermächtig, -groß, berserkerhaft; *sl* (übertreibend) scheußlich, gräßlich, eklig, ekelhaft; *to give s.o. a ~ look* jdn wütend ansehen; **~ness** ['-nis] Wildheit; Schärfe; Heftigkeit, Wut *f*, Grimm *m*; Ungestüm *n*.

fier|iness ['faiərinis] Feuer *n*, Hitze, Glut *f a. fig*; **~y** ['faiəri] feurig, brennend, glühend, heiß *a. fig*; *fig* erregt, aufwühlend, mitreißend; feuergefährlich; *med* entzündet.

fife [faif] *s mus* Querpfeife *f*; *tr itr* auf der (Quer-)Pfeife spielen; **~r** ['-ə] Pfeifer *m*.

fifteen ['fif'ti:n] *a* fünfzehn; *s* Fünfzehn; *fam* Rugbymannschaft *f*; **~th** [-θ] *a* fünfzehnt; *s* Fünfzehntel *n*.

fifth [fifθ] *a* fünft; *s* Fünftel *n*; *mus* Quinte *f*; **~ column** *pol* Fünfte Kolonne *f*; **~ly** ['-li] *adv* fünftens; **~ wheel** *fig* fünfte(s) Rad *n* am Wagen.

fift|ieth ['fiftjəθ, -iiθ] *a* fünfzigst; *s* Fünfzigstel *n*; **~y** ['fifti] fünfzig; *s pl*: *the ~ies* die Fünfziger Jahre *(e-s Jahrhunderts)*; die Fünfzigerjahre *(e-s Menschenlebens)*; *to go ~-~ with s.o.* mit jdm halbpart machen; mit jdm teilen (*on s.th.* etw).

fig [fig] **1.** Feige *f*; *(~-tree)* Feigenbaum *m*; *med* Feigwarze *f*; *under o.'s vine and ~-tree (fig)* in s-n vier Wänden; *not to care a ~ for s.th. (fig)* sich einen Dreck aus etw machen; *(I don't care) a ~ for it!* das ist mir ganz egal, (völlig) schnuppe; **~-leaf** Feigenblatt *n*; **~-wort** *bot* Knotenwurz *f*, Feigwarzenkraut *n*; **2.** *fam tr (to ~ out, to ~ up)* aufputzen, ausstaffieren; *s* Aufmachung *f*, Staat, Putz; Zustand *m*; *in full ~* in vollem Wichs, gut in Schale; *in good ~* (gut) in Form.

fight [fait] *irr fought, fought itr* fechten, kämpfen *(against, with* gegen; *on the side of, with* auf Seiten *gen*); streiten, sich raufen; sich schlagen, sich duellieren; *tr* sich schlagen mit, kämpfen gegen; bekämpfen *(a. mit geistigen Waffen)*; *(Prozeß)* durchkämpfen; *(Krieg)* führen; *(Konflikt)* austragen; *(Weg)* erkämpfen; *sport* kämpfen lassen; *s* Gefecht *n*, Kampf (*for* um); Streit *a. fig*; Boxkampf *m*; Schlägerei; Kampfkraft, -bereitschaft *f*, -geist *m*, Streitlust *f*; *to ~ down* niederkämpfen; *(Fehler)* wiedergutmachen, ausbügeln; *to ~ off* abwehren, zurückschlagen; *to ~ on* weiterkämpfen; *to give, to make a ~* e-n Kampf führen; kämpfen (*for* um); *to make a ~ of it* sich in die Schanze schlagen, sein Bestes geben; *to put up a good, a bad ~* sich wacker schlagen, schlecht kämpfen; *to show ~* sich zur Wehr setzen, Widerstand leisten; *to ~ through a campaign* e-n Feldzug mitmachen; *to ~ to a finish, to ~ it out* bis zur Entscheidung kämpfen, es ausfechten; *to ~ shy of s.o., s.th.* jdm, e-r S aus dem Wege gehen; *to ~ o.'s way in life, in the world* s-n Weg machen, sich durchsetzen, sich durchschlagen; *it is a ~ to the finish* es ist ein Kampf bis aufs Messer; *prize-~* Boxwettkampf *m*; *running ~* Verfolgungskampf *m*; *sham ~* Scheingefecht *n*; *stand-up ~* offene(r), regelrechte(r) Kampf *m*; *valiant in ~* kampftüchtig; **~er** ['-ə] Kämpfer, Fechter, Streiter; *(prize-~~)* Berufsboxer; *aero* Jäger *m*, Jagdflugzeug *n*; *~~ base* Jagdfliegerhorst *m*; *~~-bomber* Jagdbomber *m*; *~~ command (Am)* Jagdfliegerkommando *n*; *~~ cover* Jagdschutz *m*; *~~ defence* Jagdabwehr *f*; *~~ escort* Jagd(begleit)schutz *m*; *~~ formation* Jagdverband *m*; *~~ group (Am)* Jagdgruppe *f*; *Br* Jagdgeschwader *n*; *~~ interceptor* Abfangjäger *m*; *~~ pilot* Jagdflieger *m*; *~~ reconnaissance* Jagdaufklärung *f*; *~~ screen* Jagdsperre *f*; *~~ squadron* Jagdstaffel *f*; *~~ wing (Am)* Jagdgeschwader *n*; *Br* Jagdgruppe *f*; **~ing** ['-iŋ] Gefecht *n*, Kampf *m*; Kampfführung *f*; *attr* Kampf-; *prize-~~* Berufsboxen *n*; *~~ capacity* Kampfkraft *f*; *~~ chance* Aussicht *f* auf Erfolg bei Einsatz aller Kräfte; *~~-cock* Kampfhahn *m a. fig*; *to feel like a ~~-cock* in bester Form sein; *the ~~ forces, services (pl)* die Kampf-, Fronttruppen *f pl*; *the ~~ men* die (Front-)Soldaten *m pl*; *~~-plane* Jäger *m*, Jagdflugzeug *n*; *~~-power, -quality, -spirit* Kampfkraft *f*, -wert, -geist *m*; *~~ unit* Kampfeinheit *f*; *~~ value* Kampfwert *m*; *~~-zone* Kampfgebiet *n*.

figment ['figmənt] Fiktion, (freie) Erfindung; erfundene Geschichte *f*.

figurant *m*, **~e** *f* ['figjurənt, figju'rɑ̃nt *od* figju'rænti] (Ballett-)Tänzer(in *f*) *m*; *theat* Nebenperson *f*, Statist(in *f*) *m*.

figurat|ion [figju'reiʃən] Gestaltung, Formung; Gestalt, Form, Figur; symbolische Darstellung *f*; Bilderreichtum *m*; **~ive** ['figjurətiv] bildlich, plastisch, metaphorisch, übertragen; **~ively** *adv* in übertragener Bedeutung.

figure ['figə, *Am* 'figj(u)ə] *s* Figur, Form, *(äußere, a. menschliche)* Gestalt; Persönlichkeit *f*, Mensch *m*; Abbildung, Darstellung *f*, Bild *n*; *(Buch)* Zeichnung, Illustration *f*; Muster *n (auf Stoffen)*; Zahl(zeichen *n*), Ziffer; (Geld-)Summe *f*; *(Tanz, math, Logik, Rhetorik, mus)* Figur *f*; *pl* Rechnen *n*; *tr* formen, gestalten; (figürlich) darstellen; *s.th. to, for o.s.* sich etw vorstellen, sich etw denken, ausdenken; *(Stoff)* mustern; aus-, berechnen; skizzieren; *fam* glauben, meinen, ansehen als, voraus-, vorhersagen; *itr* figurieren, e-e Rolle spielen; in Erscheinung treten, erscheinen, aussehen; sich darstellen, sich zeigen (*as* als); teilnehmen (*at* an); rechnen; *fam* (hin u. her) überlegen; *Am* meinen, glauben; *at a low, high ~* billig, teuer; *to add up a column of ~s* e-e Zahlenreihe zs.zählen; *to be good at ~s* gut im Rechnen, ein guter Rechner sein; *to be a ~ of distress* ein Bild des Elends sein; *to cut a fine, poor ~* e-e gute, schlechte Figur machen *od* abgeben; *to have no head for ~s* kein Verständnis für Zahlen haben; *to keep o.'s ~* s-e Figur behalten, schlank bleiben; *to ~ on a list* auf e-r Liste stehen; *this didn't ~ in my plans* das hatte ich nicht beabsichtigt; *a fine ~ of a man* ein Bild von e-m Mann, ein schöner Mann; *~ of speech* Redefigur *f*; *to* **~ on** *Am* ins Auge fassen, einkalkulieren (*doing s.th.* etw zu tun); rechnen mit, sich verlassen auf; *to* **~ out** *tr* aus-, berechnen, lösen; verstehen, ausdenken, *fam* -knobeln; sich vorstellen; ausfindig machen; *itr* sich belaufen (*at* auf); veranschlagt werden (*at* auf); *to* **~ up** *tr* zs.zählen, -rechnen; be-, ausrechnen; *itr* kommen, sich belaufen (*to* auf); **~d** ['-d] *a* geformt, gestaltet; dargestellt, abgebildet; *(Stoff)* gemustert; **~-head** ['-hed] Bugfigur; *arch* Konsol-, Kragsteinfigur; *fig* Puppe *f*, Strohmann *m*, *fam* Repräsentations-, Dekorationsstück *n*; **~-skating** Eiskunstlauf *m*.

filament ['filəmənt] (dünner) Faden, (feiner) Draht *m*, (feine) Faser *f*; *el* Glüh-, Heizfaden; *bot* Staubfaden *m*; *~ of carbon (el)* Kohlenfaden *m*; **~ous** [filə'mentəs] Faden-; dünn, fein; **~ battery** *radio* Heizbatterie *f*; **~ current** Heizstrom *m*; **~ lamp** Glühlampe *f*; **~ voltage** *radio* Heizspannung *f*.

filbert ['filbə(:)t] Haselnuß(strauch *m*) *f*.

filch [filtʃ] *tr* mausen, stibitzen.

fil|e [fail] **1.** *s* Feile *f*; *sl (old, deep ~~)* alter Fuchs, Schlaumeier *m*; *tr* feilen *a.fig*; *to bite, to gnaw a ~~ (fig)* sich die Zähne ausbeißen, sich vergebens abmühen; *to ~~ away* abfeilen; *to ~~ smooth* glattfeilen; *to ~~ in two* durchfeilen; *~~ cutter, maker* Feilenhauer *m*; **2.** *s* Aktenschrank; (Brief-)Ordner *m*; Aktenbündel *n*, Stoß *m* Akten *od* Papiere, Briefbündel *n*; *die* Akten *pl*; *(card index ~~)* Kartei *f*; Register *n*, Rolle, Liste *f*; Archiv *n*, Registratur, Kartothek; Reihe, *fam* Schlange; *mil* Rotte *f*; *tr (Briefe, Papiere, Akten)* ordnen, bündeln; abheften, einordnen; *(to ~~ away)* ab-, zu den Akten legen; *Am (Zeitungsartikel)* telegraphisch durchgeben; *jur* vorlegen; *(Antrag)* einreichen (*with* bei); *(Anspruch)* anmelden; *itr* hinterea., im Gänsemarsch gehen; vorbeimarschieren, defilieren; *in the ~~* in der Registratur; *in single, in Indian ~~ (mil)* in Reihe, *allg* im Gänsemarsch; *on ~~ (Akte)* abgelegt; bei, in den Akten; *to line up in single-~* sich in einer Reihe aufstellen; *to take o.'s place in the ~~* sich anstellen; *to ~~ an action, a charge (jur)* Klage erheben; *to ~~ a petition for divorce* die Scheidung(sklage) einreichen; *to ~~ o.'s petition* Konkurs anmelden; *the rank and ~~ (mil)* die Mannschaften *pl*; *fig* die große Masse; *~~ clerk (Am)* Registrator *m*; *~~ copy* Archivexemplar *n*; *~~ mark* Eingangsvermerk *m*; *~~ number* Aktenzeichen *n*; *~~ punch* Locher *m*; **~ing** ['-iŋ] Ablegen *n*, Ablage; Vorlage, Einreichung; *(Meldung)* Aufgabe *f*; *pl* Feilspäne *m pl*; *~~ cabinet* Aktenschrank, Karteikasten *m*, Kartothek, Registratur *f*; *~~ card* Karteikarte *f*; *~~ fee* Anmeldegebühr *f*.

fili|al ['filjəl] kindlich, Kindes-; *biol (Generation)* (nach)folgend; **~ation** [fili'eiʃən] Kindschaft; Nachkommenschaft, Abstammung; Abzweigung; Tochtergesellschaft, -firma; *jur* Feststellung *f* der Vaterschaft.

filibuster ['filibʌstə] *s* Freibeuter, Seeräuber; *Am parl* Obstruktionist, Dauerredner *m*; Obstruktion *f*; *itr Am parl* Obstruktion treiben.

filigree ['filigri:] Filigran(arbeit *f*) *n*.

Filipino [fili'pi:nou] *pl -os* Filipino *m*.

fill [fil] *tr* (an-, auf-, aus)füllen; vollstopfen, -pfropfen (*with* mit); *(Zahn)* füllen, plombieren; *(Pfeife)* stopfen; *(Loch)* zustopfen; *(Raum)* ein-, in Anspruch nehmen; *(Segel)* blähen; *(Stellung)* einnehmen; *(Amt)* bekleiden, versehen; *(in ein Amt)* einsetzen; *(Anforderungen)* genügen; *(Stelle)* besetzen; *tech* beschicken (*with* mit); *(Fugen)* ausgießen; *Am (Befehl)* ausführen; *(Auftrag)* erledigen; *(Rezept)* anfertigen; *itr* voll werden, sich füllen; *s* Füllung; Aufschüttung *f*; Genüge *n*; *to eat, to drink o.'s ~* sich satt essen, trinken (*of* an); *to have o.'s ~ of* sein Teil, sein gerüttelt Maß ... haben; *to ~ the bill* seinen Platz ausfüllen, seinen Mann stehen; *to ~ the chair* den Vorsitz führen; *not to be able to ~ s.o.'s shoes* kein Ersatz für jdn sein; *I have had my ~ of it* ich habe es satt; *to ~* **in** *tr (Hohlraum)* (aus)füllen; vervollständigen, ergänzen; *(Graben)* zuschütten; *(Formular)* ausfüllen; *(in e-n Vordruck)* eintragen; *(Namen)* einsetzen; ausführen; *s.o. on s.th. (Am fam)* jdm über etw nähere Mitteilungen machen; *itr* aushilfsweise tätig sein, aushelfen; *to ~* **out** *tr itr* (sich) weiten, (sich) erweitern, (sich) (aus)dehnen, (sich) abrunden, (sich) aufblähen; *itr* sich runden, (an)schwellen; *tr Am (Formular)* ausfüllen; *(Daten)* eintragen; *to ~* **up** *tr* (aus-, auf)füllen, voll machen; auf-, zuschütten; *mot* auftanken; *fig* vervollständigen; *itr* sich (an)füllen, voll werden; **~ed** [-d] *a* gefüllt, voll; *(Stelle)* besetzt; *fig* erfüllt (*with* von); *~~ to capacity* bis auf den letzten Platz, voll besetzt; **~er** ['-ə] Füller; *(Malerei)* Spachtel; Trichter; Ersatzblock *m*; Füllmaterial *n*, Füllung *f*, Zuschlag; Ersatzmann *m*; *Am* Einlage *f*, Füller, Lückenbüßer *m*; Flickwort *n*; *pl mil* Ersatz(mannschaften *f pl*) *m*; *(Zigarre)* Einlage *f*; *~~ cap* Einfüllstutzen *m*; **~-in** Vertreter, Ersatzmann; (zeitweiliger) Ersatz *m*; **~ing** ['-iŋ] (An-, Auf-, Aus-) Füllen *n*; Füllung; Aufschüttung *f*; *pej* Füllsel *n*; *(Zahn-)* Plombe, Füllung *f*; *(Weberei)* Einschuß, -schlag; *(Brot)* Belag *m*; *~~-in* Ergänzung, Vervollständigung; *(Auftrag)* Erledigung; *(Stelle)* Besetzung; Ausfüllung; Eintragung *f*; *~~ material* Kabelmasse *f*; *~~ sleeve* Füllstutzen *m*; *~~ station (Am)* Tankstelle *f*; *~~-up* Auffüllung *f*; Zuschütten; Füllmaterial; *mot* Auftanken *n*.

fillet ['filit] *s* Stirnband; Band *n*, (schmaler) Streifen *m*; *arch* Leiste *f*; *(Bucheinband)* Filet *n*, Goldverzierung *f*; *(Küche) (a. Fisch-)* Filet, Lendenstück *n*; *tr* mit e-m Band, e-m Streifen, e-r Leiste verzieren; *(Fleisch, Fisch)* ablösen u. in Streifen schneiden.

fillip ['filip] *s* Schnippchen *n*; (sanfter) Klaps *m*; *fig* Auf-, Ermunterung *f*; Anreiz *m*, Anregung *f* (*to* für); *tr* e-n Klaps geben (*s.o.* jdm); *fig* aufmuntern, anreizen, anregen; *itr* ein Schnippchen schlagen; *not worth a ~* nicht der Rede wert.

filly ['fili] Stutfohlen; *fig* ausgelassene(s) Mädchen *n*.

film [film] *s* Häutchen *n*; Membran(e) *f*, Überzug, (feiner) Belag; Reif *(auf Früchten)*; Schleier *m (über den Augen)*, Trübung *(der Augen)*; Dunsthaube, -schicht *f*; dünne(r), feine(r) Faden *od* Draht; *phot* Film(streifen), Rollfilm; *film* Bildstreifen, Film *m*; *attr* Film-; *tr* (ver)filmen; *itr* sich mit e-m Häutchen, e-m Schleier überziehen; verfilmt werden; sich verfilmen lassen; *to act for the ~s* beim Film tätig sein; *to dub a ~* e-n Film synchronisieren; *to have a ~ over the eyes* nicht gut sehen können; *to make, to shoot, to take a ~* e-n Film drehen; *colo(u)r ~* Farbfilm *m*; *documentary ~* Kulturfilm *m*; *educational ~* Lehrfilm *m*; *full-length ~* Hauptfilm *m*; *narrow ~* Schmalfilm *m*; *news, topical ~* Wochenschau *f*; *roll, (Am) spool of ~* Filmrolle *f*; *silent, sound ~* Stumm-, Tonfilm *m*; *supplementary, supporting ~* Beifilm *m*; *talking ~* Sprechfilm *m*; *~* **advertisement** Filmwerbung *f*; *~* **archives** *pl* Filmarchiv *n*; *~* **camera** Filmkamera *f*; *~* **cartoon(ist)** Trickfilm(zeichner) *m*; *~* **company** Filmgesellschaft; *~* **emulsion** Filmschicht *f*; *~* **fan** begeisterte(r) Kinobesucher *m*; *~* **formation** *tech* Hautbildung *f*; *~* **industry** Filmwirtschaft *f*; *~* **library** Filmarchiv *n*; *~* **pack** Filmpack *m*; *~* **producer** Filmproduzent *m*; *~* **production** Filmherstellung *f*; *~* **projectionist** Filmvorführer *m*; *~* **projector** Filmprojektor *m*; *~* **reel** Filmrolle *f*; *~* **release** Filmverleih *m*; *~* **spool** Filmspule *f*; *~* **star** Filmstar *m*; *~* **strip** Filmband *n*; Stehfilm *m*; *~* **studio** Filmatelier *n*; *~* **track** Filmkanal *m*; *~* **transmission** Filmübertragung *f* im Fernsehen; *~* **version** Verfilmung *f*; **~y** ['-i] trüb(e), verschleiert; zart, dünn; *(Frucht)* bereift.

filter ['filtə] *s* Filter; Seiher *m*, Seihtuch *n*; *el tele radio* Siebkette, -schaltung *f*; *tr* filtern, filtrieren, abklären; glätten; sieben, (durch)seihen; *el* als Siebkette dienen für; *itr* durch-, einsickern; *air-~* Luftfilter *m*; *sewage-~* Klärbassin *n*, -anlage *f*; *to ~* **in** sich (im Verkehr) einreihen, einfädeln; einsickern; *to ~* **into** (ein)dringen in *a. fig*; *to ~* **through** durchsikkern *a. fig*; *fig* sich herumsprechen; *~* **circuit** *radio* Sperrkreis *m*; **~ing** ['-riŋ] *a* filtrierend; Filtrier-; *s* Filterung, Filtration *f*; *aero* Sammeln *n*, Auswertung u. Weitergabe *f* der Flugmeldungen; **~paper** Filterpapier *n*; **~-tip** Filtermundstück *n*; *~~ cigarette* Filterzigarette *f*.

filth [filθ] (häßlicher) Schmutz, (schmieriger) Dreck, Kot *m*, widerliche(s) Zeug(s) *n*, Unflat; *fig* Sumpf *m*, Verkommenheit; Unanständigkeit; Zote *f*; **~iness** ['-inis] Unflätigkeit, Unanständigkeit *f*; Unflat *m*; **~y** ['-i] schmutzig, dreckig; scheußlich; unflätig, unanständig, zotig.

filtrat|e ['filtreit] *tr* filtern, filtrieren, (durch)seihen; *s* ['-it, '-eit] Filtrat *n*; **~ion** [-'treiʃən] Filterung, Filtration *f*; *~~ plant* Klär-, Filtrieranlage *f*.

fin [fin] Flosse *a. sl (= Hand)*; *aero* Kiel-, Seitenflosse, Leitfläche; *(Heizkörper)* Rippe; *(Flugzeugmotor)* Kühlrippe *f*; *(Bombe)* Steuerschwanz *m*.

finagle [fi'neigl] *fam itr* mogeln; gerissen sein; *tr* betrügen; ergaunern.

final ['fainl] *a* letzt, End-, Schluß-; endlich, schließlich; abschließend, entscheidend, endgültig, unabänderlich; *jur* rechtskräftig; absichtlich; *gram* final, Absichts-; *s a. pl* (Ab-)Schlußprüfung *f*, -examen *n*; *sport* Endspiel *n*, End-, Schlußrunde *f*, Finale *n*; Spätausgabe *f*; *to become ~* rechtskräftig werden; *to take o.'s ~s* s-e Abschlußprüfung machen; *to take it as ~* es sich gesagt sein lassen; *~* **account** Schlußabrechnung *f*; *~* **address** Schlußansprache *f*, -vortrag *m*; *~* **aim, objective** Endziel *n*; *~* **amplifier** Endverstärker *m*; *~* **assembly** *mil* Bereitstellung; *tech* End-, Fertigmontage *f*; *~* **chapter** Schlußkapitel *n*; *~* **clause** Schlußbestimmung *f*; *gram* Finalsatz *m*; *~* **conclusion** Schlußfolgerung *f*; *~* **conference, discussion** Schlußbesprechung *f*; *~* **decision** endgültige Entscheidung *f*; *~~,* *~* **judg(e)ment** Endurteil *n*; *~* **dividend** Abschlußdividende *f*; **~e** [fi'nɑ:li] *mus theat* Finale *n*; *~* **hearing** *jur* Schlußverhandlung *f*; **~ist** ['-əlist] *sport* Teilnehmer *m* an der Schlußrunde; **~ity** [fai'næliti] Endgültigkeit, Unabänderlich-, Unwiderruflichkeit *f*; **~ize** ['fainəlaiz] *tr* abschließen, endgültig machen, erledigen, festlegen; *~* **lecture** Schlußvorlesung *f*; **~ly** ['-i] *adv* am Ende, zuletzt; endlich, schließlich; endgültig, unwiderruflich; *~* **plea** *jur* Schlußantrag *m*; *~* **point** Endpunkt *m*; *~* **product** Endprodukt *n*; *~* **protocol** *pol* Schlußprotokoll *n*; *~* **remark** Schlußbemerkung *f*; *~* **report** (Ab-)Schlußbericht *m*; *~* **result** Endergebnis *n*; *~* **speed, velocity** Endgeschwindigkeit *f*; *~* **stage** Endstufe *f*; *~* **state** Endzustand *m*; *~* **term** letzte(r) Termin *m*; Schlußsemester *n*; *~* **test** *tech* Schlußprüfung, Endabnahme *f*; *~* **value** Endwert *m*; *~* **vote** Schlußabstimmung *f*.

finan|ce [fai'næns, *Am a.* 'fai-, *Br a.* fi'n-] *s* Geld-, Finanzwesen *n*, Finanz (-gebaren *n*) *f*; Finanzen *f pl*; Finanzwissenschaft *f*; *pl* Einkommen *n*, Finanzen *f pl*, Vermögen(slage *f*) *n*;

Staatseinkünfte *pl*, -wirtschaft *f*; *tr* finanzieren; die (Geld-)Mittel zur Verfügung stellen für; *aristocracy of* ~~ Finanzaristokratie *f*; *(the world of) high* ~~ Hochfinanz *f*; *minister, ministry of* ~~ Finanzminister(ium *n*) *m (außerhalb Englands)*; *F~~ Act (Br)* Finanzgesetz *n*; ~~ *administration* Finanzverwaltung *f*; *F~~ Bill (Br)* Finanzvorlage *f*; ~~ *committee* Finanzausschuß *m*; ~~ *department* Finanzbehörde *f*, -amt *n*; **~cial** [fai'nænʃəl, fi'n-] finanziell, geldlich, pekuniär; Geld-, Finanz-; ~~ *affairs (pl)* Geldangelegenheiten, -sachen *f pl*; ~~ *aid* Kredithilfe *f*; ~~ *background* finanzielle(r) Rückhalt *m*, Rückendeckung *f*; ~~ *backing* Finanzhilfe *f*; *the* ~~ *circumstances* die finanziellen Verhältnisse, die Vermögensumstände *pl*; ~~ *committee* Finanzausschuß *m*; ~~ *control* Finanzkontrolle *f*; ~~ *crisis* Finanzkrise *f*; ~~ *expense* Finanzierungskosten *pl*; ~~ *law* Finanzgesetz *n*; ~~ *paper* Börsenblatt *n*; ~~ *participation* finanzielle Beteiligung *f*; ~~ *plan* Finanzierungsplan *m*; ~~ *policy* Finanzpolitik *f*; ~~ *program(me), scheme* Finanzierungsplan *m*; ~~ *rehabilitation* Sanierung *f* der Finanzen; ~~ *requirements (pl)* Geldbedarf *m*; ~~ *resource* Geldquelle *f*; *pl* Hilfs-, Steuerquellen *f pl*; ~~ *settlement* Kapitalabfindung *f*; ~~ *situation, standing* Finanzlage *f*; ~~ *statement* Bilanz *f*; ~~ *support* finanzielle Unterstützung *f*; ~~ *syndicate* Finanzkonsortium *n*; ~~ *year* Wirtschafts-, Haushalts-, Finanzjahr *n*; **~cially** *adv*: ~~ *strong* kapitalkräftig; ~~ *weak* kapitalschwach; **~cier** [fai'nænsiə, fi'n-, *Am* -'siə] Finanz-, Geldmann; Geldgeber *m*.

finch [fintʃ] *orn* Fink *m*.

find [faind] *irr found, found* [faund] **1.** *tr* (zufällig) finden, entdecken, stoßen auf, begegnen (*s.o.* jdm), (an)treffen; treffen auf, erreichen; *(~ out)* (heraus-)finden, ausfindig machen, herausbekommen, *fam* rauskriegen, dahinterkommen; feststellen; ansichtig werden (*s.th.* e-r S), bemerken, gewahr werden, erfahren; wiederfinden; zurück-, wiedererlangen; suchen, holen; (her)bekommen; finden, befinden für, halten für, ansehen als; *(Schlag, Wurf)* treffen (auf); *jur* erkennen als, erklären, befinden für (*guilty* schuldig); liefern, (zur Verfügung) stellen, beschaffen; *(Geld)* geben; versorgen, versehen (*in* mit); **2.** *itr jur* das Urteil finden (*for s.o.* für jdn); *to ~ o.s.* sich sehen, sich finden; s-n Weg finden; sich selbst erkennen; **3.** *s* Fund *m*; *fig* Goldkorn *n*; *to ~ against s.o.* gegen jdn entscheiden; *to ~ for s.o.* zugunsten jds entscheiden; *to ~ out* herausfinden, in Erfahrung bringen, ermitteln; ertappen; durchschauen *fig*; *all found* alles einbegriffen, alles inklusive, (in) freie(r) Station; *not to be able to ~ it in o.'s heart to* es nicht übers Herz bringen können zu; *to be well found in* gut versehen, versorgt sein mit; *to ~ amusement, enjoyment in* Vergnügen finden an; *to ~ fault with* etw auszusetzen haben an; *to ~ favo(u)r with s.o.* jds Gunst erwerben; *to ~ o.'s feet* Selbstvertrauen erwerben; sich auf eigene Beine stellen; sich durchsetzen; *to ~ a market* Absatz finden; *to ~ o.'s voice, tongue* die Sprache wiederfinden; *to ~ o.'s way* s-n Weg finden; *in, out, back, home* hinein-, hinaus-, zurück-, heimfinden; *(Am)* around sich zurechtfinden; **~er** ['-ə] Finder; *phot* Sucher *m*; Richtfernrohr *n*; **~ing** ['-iŋ] Fund *m*, Entdeckung *f*; Ergebnis *n*, Befund *m*; Feststellung; Beschaffung *f*; *jur* Untersuchungsergebnis *n*; (Wahr-)Spruch *m*, Urteil *n*; *pl Am* Handwerkszeug *n*, Bedarf *m (e-s Handwerkers)*; ~~ *of capital* Kapitalbeschaffung *f*.

fine [fain] **1.** *a* fein, schön *(a. Wetter)*, gut, nett; *(Klima)* gesund; ausgezeichnet, hervorragend; tadel-, makellos, rein, lauter; anständig; *(Metall)* Fein-; fein, zart, dünn, spitz, scharf; *fig* fein, genau, scharfsinnig, spitzfindig, schlau, klug; hübsch, schön, gutaussehend; stattlich, prächtig, auffällig, auffallend; *adv fam* sehr gut, prima; *tr* verfeinern, reinigen, läutern, (ab)klären; *metal* frischen; *itr* feiner werden, sich verfeinern; sich (ab)klären, klar werden; *s pl* Feinkies *m*; *to ~ away, down, off (tr itr)* feiner, dünner machen, werden; (sich) verfeinern; *one ~ day, one of these ~ days* eines schönen Tages; *to call by ~ names* beschönigen; *to cut, to run it, things (rather) ~* es haarscharf, haargenau hinkriegen; *com* scharf kalkulieren; *that's ~!* das ist prima! *that's all very ~, but ...* das ist alles ganz gut und schön, aber ...; *that will suit me ~* das paßt mir gut; *these are ~ doings! (iro)* das sind mir (ja) schöne Geschichten! *I'm feeling ~* mir geht's bestens; *you're looking very ~ to-day* du siehst heute gut aus; *~ feathers make ~ birds (prov)* Kleider machen Leute; *a ~ thing* e-e gefundene Sache; *the ~ arts* die Schönen, *bes.* die Bildenden Künste *f pl*; **~ adjustment** Feineinstellung *f*; **~-cut** Feinschnitt *m (Tabak)*; **~-draw** *irr tr* kunststopfen; fein ausspinnen *a. fig*; *~~n (fig)* feingesponnen; **~-fit** *tech* Feinpassung *f*; **~ gold** Feingold *n*; **~-grained** *a* feinkörnig; **~-looking** gut aussehend; **~-meshed** *a* fein-, engmaschig; **~ness** ['-nis] Feinheit; Schönheit; Reinheit; Zartheit; Schärfe; Genauigkeit; Schlauheit; Eleganz *f*; *(Edelmetall)* Feingehalt *m*; **~ry** ['fainəri] Pracht *f*; Putz, Staat; *tech* Frischofen *m*; **~ sight** *mil* Feinkorn *n*; **~spun** ['-spʌn] *a* feingesponnen; zart; *fig* überspitzt; überspannt; **~ tuning** *radio* Feineinstellung *f*; **2.** *s* Geldstrafe, (Geld-)Buße *f*; *tr* mit e-r Geldstrafe belegen (*£ 1* von 1 Pfund); **3.** *s*: *in ~* schließlich, endlich, am Ende; in Kürze.

finesse [fi'nes] *s* Geschicklichkeit, Gewandtheit; Schlauheit *f*; *(Karten)* Schneiden *n*.

finger ['fiŋgə] *s* Finger *m (a. des Handschuhs)*; Fingerbreite, -länge *f*; *Am sl* Polizist *m*; *Am sl* Bodendeckevoll *f*; *tr* befühlen, berühren, bearbeiten; betasten; *fam* (weg)nehmen, entwenden, stehlen; *mus* spielen; mit dem Fingersatz bezeichnen; *Am sl* ausbaldowern; *with a wet ~ (fig)* mit Leichtigkeit, spielend; *to cut o.'s ~* sich in den Finger schneiden; *to burn o.'s ~s (fig)* sich die Finger verbrennen; *to have s.th. at o.'s ~s ends* etw aus dem ff beherrschen; *to have a ~ in the pie* die Hand im Spiel haben; *to lay, to put o.'s ~ on (fig)* den Finger legen auf; auffinden; identifizieren; *to let s.th. slip through o.'s ~s (fig)* sich etw entgehen lassen; *to look through o.'s ~s at (fig)* ein Auge zudrücken vor; *not to stir a ~* keinen Finger rühren; *to turn, to twist s.o. around o.'s (little) ~* jdn um den kleinen Finger wickeln; *my ~s itch (fig)* mich juckt die Hand; *his ~s are all thumbs (fig)* er hat zwei linke Hände; *keep your ~s crossed!* halten Sie mir den Daumen! **~-alphabet, -language** Finger-, Taubstummensprache *f*; **~-board** *(Geige)* Steg *m*; *(Klavier)* Tastatur *f*, Griffbrett *n*; **~-bowl** Fingerschale *f*; **~-breadth** Fingerbreite *f*; **~ed** ['-d] *a in Zssgen* -fingerig; **~ing** ['-riŋ] **1.** Berührung *od* Bearbeitung *f* mit den Fingern; *mus* Fingersatz *m*; **2.** Strickwolle *f*; **~-mark** Fingerspur *f*; **~-nail** Fingernagel *m*; *to the ~~s* vollständig; **~-plate** Türschoner *m*; **~-post** Wegweiser *m*; **~-print** *s* Fingerabdruck *m*; *tr* e-n Fingerabdruck nehmen von; **~ push switch** Druckknopfschalter *m*; **~-stall** Fingerling *m*; **~-tip** Fingerspitze *f*; *to o.'s ~~s* voll u. ganz; *to have s.th. at o.'s ~~s* etw zur Hand haben; etw wie am Schnürchen können.

fin|ical ['finikəl], **~icking** ['finikiŋ], **~icky** ['finiki], **~ikin** ['finikin] wählerisch, genau, anspruchsvoll, verwöhnt (*about* in); affektiert; knifflig.

fining ['fainiŋ] Reinigen, Klären; *metal* Frischen; *pl* Klärmittel *n*.

finish ['finiʃ] *tr* beenden, aufhören mit (*doing s.th.* etw zu tun); erledigen, vollenden; ver-, aufbrauchen, verzehren; aufessen; austrinken; ausreden; fertigstellen, die letzte Vollendung, den letzten Schliff geben (*s.th.* e-r S); polieren; appretieren; glätten; schlichten; lackieren; *fam* fertigmachen, erledigen, um die Ecke, umbringen; *fam* kaputt machen; *itr* enden (*first* als erster); zu Ende kommen, aufhören (*with* mit); *s* Ende *n*, Schluß; *sport* Endkampf *m*, Entscheidung *f*; Abschluß *m*, Vollendung *f*; *die* letzte Hand, *der* letzte Schliff; *die* letzten Feinheiten *pl*; Polieren *n*; Politur; Appretur *f*; Lack *m*; Lackierung; Oberfläche(nbehandlung) *f*; Anstrich *m*; gute(s) Benehmen, tadellose(s) Auftreten *n*, hohe Bildung *f*; *arch* Innenausbau *m*; Furnierholz *n*; *to ~ off, to ~ up* völlig, restlos aufessen; *(Arbeit)* völlig erledigen; *fam* erledigen, zur Strecke bringen; *to ~ up with* den Beschluß, Schluß machen mit; *to be in at the ~* den Schluß miterleben; *sport* in die Endrunde kommen *a. fig*; *to fight to the ~* bis zum letzten durchhalten; *from start to ~* von Anfang bis zum Ende; **~ed** ['-t] *a* beendet; vollendet, vervollkommnet; hervorragend; poliert; erledigt, kaputt; ~~ *article, product* Fertigware *f*, -produkt *n*; ~~ *goods (pl)* Fertigerzeugnisse *n pl*; **~er** ['-ə] *tech* Fertiggesenk *n*; Polierer; Appretierer *m*; Polierwalze *f*; *fam* K.o.-Schlag; Knalleffekt *m*; **~ing** ['-iŋ] *a* letzt, abschließend, Schluß-; *s* Fertigstellung, Vollendung; Ausrüstung *f*; Schlichten *n*; letzte(r) Schliff; Anstrich *m*; Lackierung; *(Neubau)* Installation *f*; *to give the ~~ touch, to put the ~~ hand to s.th.* die letzte Hand an etw legen; ~~ *coat* Deckanstrich *m*; ~~ *industry* Veredelungsindustrie *f*; ~~ *line (sport)* Ziellinie *f*; ~~ *school* Mädchenpensionat *n*; ~~ *sprint* Endspurt *m*; ~~ *stroke* Gnadenstoß *m*.

fin|ite ['fainait] *a* begrenzt, abgegrenzt; endlich *a. math*; *s* endliche Größe *f*; ~~ *verb (gram)* Verbum *n* finitum.

fink [fiŋk] *s Am sl* Spitzel; Streikbrecher; Verräter *m*; *tr* im Stich lassen.

Fin|land ['finlənd] Finnland *n*; **~n** [fin] Finne *m*, Finnin *f*; **~nish** ['-iʃ] *a* finnisch; **~nish** *s* (das) Finnisch(e).

finny ['fini] Flossen-.

fiord [fjɔ:d, fi'ɔ:d], **fjord** [fjɔ:d] *geog* Fjord *m*.

fir [fə:] *(~-tree)* Nadelbaum *m*, Konifere *f*; Tanne(nholz *n*), Kiefer(nholz *n*) *f*; **~-cone** Tannen-, Fichten- *od* Kiefernzapfen *m*; **~-needle** Tannennadel *f*; **~-wood** Tannenwald *m*; Nadelholz *n*.

fire ['faiə] **1.** *s* Feuer *n (a. fig u. mil)*, Brand *m*; Feuersbrunst *f*, Schadenfeuer n; Glut, Hitze f, helle(r) Glanz m; Fieberhitze f; (Feuer-, innere) Qualen f pl; (heftige) innere Erregung, Leidenschaft, Feurigkeit f; mil Feuer n, Beschuß m; **2.** tr anzünden, an-, in Brand stecken; (Feuer) unter-, in Gang halten; (be)heizen; (Ziegel, Ton) brennen; trocknen, dörren; (Ofen) beschicken; med ausbrennen; fig anfeuern, entflammen, entfachen, erregen; (Feuerwaffe, Geschoß) abfeuern; fam schleudern a. fig (Fragen); fam 'rausfeuern, -werfen, auf die Straße setzen,'rausschmeißen, entlassen; **3.** itr (Feuer) anbrennen; sich entzünden; brennen; das Feuer unterhalten, in Gang halten; sich auf-, sich erregen; schießen, feuern; (Feuerwaffe) in Tätigkeit sein; between two ~s zwischen zwei Feuern, von beiden Seiten angegriffen a. fig; on ~ in Brand, brennend; under ~ unter Beschuß; to be on ~ in Flammen stehen; to be under ~ heftig angegriffen a. fig, fig heftig kritisiert werden; mil unter Feuer liegen; to build a ~ ein Feuer machen; to catch ~ sich entzünden; Feuer fangen, in Brand geraten; to cease ~ (mil) das Feuer einstellen; to go through ~ and water for s.o. für jdn durchs Feuer gehen; to hang ~ (Feuerwaffe) nicht losgehen (wollen); fig nicht in Gang, nicht vorwärtskommen; to have s.th. on the ~ (Am fam) etw in Vorbereitung haben; an etw arbeiten; to lay a ~ ein Feuer anlegen; to light a ~ den Ofen anstecken; ein Feuer anmachen od anzünden; to make a ~ Feuer (an)machen; einheizen; to miss ~ with s.o. (Am fam) bei jdm nicht ankommen; to open ~ (mil) das Feuer eröffnen; fig anfangen; to play with ~ mit dem Feuer spielen; to set ~ to, (Am) to set a ~ anzünden, in Brand stecken; to set on ~ an-, in Brand stecken; anzünden; fig: s.o. jdn in Aufregung versetzen, jds Leidenschaft erwecken; to strike ~ Feuer schlagen; to take ~ Feuer fangen a. fig; fig in Erregung geraten, leidenschaftlich werden; he won't set the Thames on ~ er hat das Pulver nicht erfunden; danger of ~ Feuers-, Brandgefahr f; running ~ Schnellfeuer n; fig Sturm m von Fragen; sure-~ (Am fam) todsicher; to ~ **away** tr abschießen; (dauernd) beschießen; (Munition) verschießen; itr fam losschießen, -legen (mit Reden); to ~ **off** abfeuern, -schießen (at, on, upon auf); to ~ **up** Feuer machen; fig auffahren, in Erregung geraten (at über); **~-alarm** Feueralarm m; ~~(box) Feuermelder m; **~-arms** pl Feuer-, bes. Schußwaffen f pl; **~ball** Feuerkugel, Bolide f (Meteor); Kugelblitz; (Atom) Feuerball; Am sl rasche(r) Arbeiter m; **~-boat** Feuerlöschboot n; **~-box** tech rail Feuerraum m; **~-brand** brennende(s) Holzscheit n; fig Unruhestifter, Aufwiegler, Hetzer m; **~-break** Am Feuerschneise f (im Wald od in der Prärie); **~-brick** Schamottestein m; **~-brigade** Br Feuerwehr f; **~bug** ['-bʌg] Am fam Brandstifter m; **~-clay** Schamotte f; **~ company** Br Feuerversicherung(sgesellschaft); Am Feuerwehr f; **~-control** mil Feuerleitung, -überwachung; Feuer-, Artillerieleitstelle f; **~-cracker** (Feuerwerk) Schwärmer m; **~-curtain** theat eiserne(r), Asbestvorhang m; **~-damage** Brandschaden m; **~-damp** min Grubengas n, schlagende Wetter n pl; ~~ indicator Schlagwetteranzeiger m; **~ department** Am Feuerwehr; Br (Versicherung) Feuerschadensabteilung f; **~-detector** automatische(r) Feuermelder m; **~ direction** mil Feuerleitung f; **~-dog** Feuerbock m; **~ door** feuersichere Tür f; **~-drill** Feuerwehrübung f; **~ duel** mil Feuergefecht n; **~-eater** Feuerfresser; fig Hitzkopf, Raufbold, Streithahn m; **~-engine** Feuerspritze f; Feuerwehrauto n; **~-escape** Nottreppe; Feuerleiter f; Sprungtuch n; **~ exit** Notausgang m; **~-extinguisher** Feuerlöschgerät n, -löscher m; Am sl (Schule) Anstandswauwau m; **~-fighter** Am Feuerwehrmann m; **~-fighting** Brandschutz m; Brandbekämpfung f; Feuerlöschwesen n; **~-fly** Leuchtkäfer m, Glühwürmchen n; **~-guard, -screen** Ofenschirm m; **~ hazard, risk** Feuersgefahr f; **~-hose** Feuerwehr-, Spritzenschlauch m; **~-house, station** Spritzenhaus n, Feuerwache f; **~-insurance** Feuerversicherung f; **~-irons** pl Ofengerät n; Schüreisen n, Feuerzange u. Kohlenschaufel f; **~less cooker** Kochkiste f; **~-light** Schein m des Kaminfeuers; **~-lighter** Feueranzünder m; **~lock** hist Steinschloßgewehr n; **~man** Feuerwehrmann; Heizer m a. rail; **~-office** Brandkasse, Feuerversicherungsanstalt f; **~ order** Feuerbefehl m; pl Br Feuerlöschordnung f; **~place** Kamin; (offener) Herd m; **~-plug** Hydrant m; **~ point** Brandwache f; Zündpunkt m; **~-policy** Feuerversicherungspolice f; **~ pond** Feuerlöschteich m; **~-power** mil Feuerkraft f; **~ prevention** Feuerverhütung f; **~-proof** feuerfest, -sicher, unverbrennbar; ~~ curtain (theat) eiserne(r), Asbestvorhang m; ~~ wall Brandschott n; **~-protection** Brandschutz m; **~-raiser** Brandstifter m; **~-raising** Brandstiftung f; **~-resistant** feuerbeständig; **~side** ['-said] Platz m vor dem od um den Kamin; fig Häuslichkeit f, Familienleben n; attr häuslich; by the ~~ am Kamin; ~~ chat Plauderei f am Kamin; ~~ comfort häusliche Bequemlichkeit f; **~stone** min Feuerstein m; **~ support** Feuerunterstützung f; **~-teaser** Schüreisen n; **~-tongs** pl Feuerzange f; **~-wall** Brandmauer f; **~-ward(en)** Am Branddirektor m; **~-watcher** Brandwache f; **~-water** fam Feuerwasser n; **~wood** Brennholz n; **~work** Feuerwerkskörper m; meist pl Feuerwerk n a. fig; pl Am plötzliche Wertpapierhausse; fig Erregung f; ~~(s) display Feuerwerk n; **~-worshipper** Feueranbeter m.

firing ['faiəriŋ] Heizen; Brennen (von Ziegeln, Ton); mil Feuern, Schießen n; Feuerkampf m; Brenn-, Heizmaterial n, Feuerung; mot Zündung f; **~-line** Feuer-, vorderste Linie, Front; Feuerkette; Schützenstandlinie f; **~-party, -squad** mil Exekutionskommando; Kommando n zum Abfeuern e-r Ehrensalve; **~-pin** (Gewehr) Schlagbolzen m; **~ range** Schießplatz, -stand m; Schußweite f.

firkin ['fə:kin] Fäßchen n (40,9 l).

firm 1. a (a. adv) fest; hart; fest(stehend); beständig, dauernd, unaufhörlich; standhaft, entschlossen, unerschütterlich; unabänderlich, endgültig; (Bestellung, Vertrag) fest; on ~ account auf feste Rechnung; to be a ~ believer in s.th. fest an etw glauben; to buy ~ fest, auf feste Rechnung kaufen; to hold ~ to festhalten an; to stand ~ s-r Sache treu bleiben; sich nicht erschüttern lassen; **~ament** ['fə:məmənt] poet Firmament, Himmelszelt, -gewölbe n; **~ness** ['-nis] Festigkeit; Beständigkeit; Standhaftigkeit; Entschlossenheit f; **2.** Firma, Handelsgesellschaft f, (Handels-)Haus, Geschäft, Unternehmen n; Firmenname m, -bezeichnung f; affiliated ~ Schwesterfirma f; associated ~ Zweiggeschäft n, -niederlassung f; commercial, trading ~ Handelshaus n.

first [fə:st] a erst; vorderst; frühest; oberst, höchst, Haupt-; best; (Zeugnis) vorzüglich; adv erstens; zuerst, am Anfang, anfangs, erstlich, zunächst; zum erstenmal; das erstemal; zuerst, als erste(r,s), vorher; fam eher, lieber; s der, die, das Erste; (the F~) der Erste (Tag e-s Monats); Anfang, Beginn m; rail erste Klasse; sport erste(r) Platz; mot erste(r) Gang; mus erste (höchste) Stimme; pl (Ware) erste Qualität f; at ~ (zu)erst, am Anfang, zunächst; at ~ hand aus erster Hand; at ~ sight, view, blush auf den ersten Blick; for the ~ time zum erstenmal, das erstemal; from the ~ von Anfang an; from ~ to last von Anfang bis zu Ende; head ~ kopfüber; in the ~ instance in erster Linie; in the ~ place an erster Stelle; zuerst (einmal), zunächst, zuerst; erstens; of the ~ water reinsten Wassers; ~ of all, ~ and foremost zuallererst, erstens, vor allem, vor allen Dingen; zunächst, (zu)erst; ~ and last alles in allem, aufs Ganze gesehen; ~, last, and all the time (Am) ein für allemal; ~ thing off the bat (Am fam) sofort, auf der Stelle; to come in ~ das Rennen gewinnen; to do s.th. (the) ~ thing etw als erstes, zuerst tun; not to get to ~ base (Am fam) keinerlei Erfolg haben; to give s.th. ~ consideration etw in erster Linie berücksichtigen; to go ~ vorangehen; to obey s.o. at his ~ word jdm aufs Wort gehorchen; ~ come ~ served (prov) wer zuerst kommt, mahlt zuerst; the ~ comer der erste beste; ~ of exchange Primawechsel m; the ~ of the month, year der Monats-, Jahresanfang; not the ~ thing überhaupt nichts; **~ aid** med Erste Hilfe f; **~-aid** attr: ~~ bandage Notverband m; ~~ box Verbandskasten m; ~~ dog Sanitätshund m; ~~ dressing Notverband m; ~~ kit, outfit Verbandszeug n; Reiseapotheke f; ~~ man Laienhelfer; Am Krankenträger m; ~~ packet Verbandspäckchen n; ~~ post, station Unfallstation f; **~-born** a erstgeboren; s Erstgeborene(r), Älteste(r) m; **~-chop** s (Ware) beste Qualität f, das Beste; a erstklassig; **~-class** a erste(r) Klasse gen (Attribut), erstklassig, ausgesucht, vorzüglich, hervorragend, auserlesen, fam prima; adv erste(r) Klasse gen (adverb. Bestimmung); ~~ mail (Am) Briefpost f; ~~ ticket Fahrkarte f erster Klasse; **~ coat** (Farb-)Grund, Grundanstrich m; **~ cost** Gestehungskosten pl, Selbstkosten-, Einkaufspreis m; **~ cousin** Vetter m, Kusine f 1. Grades; pl Geschwisterkinder n pl; **~ draft** Konzept n; **~ edition** (Buch) Erstausgabe f; **~ feature** Am Hauptfilm m; **~ finger** Zeigefinger m; **~ floor** 1. Stock m, 1. Etage f; Am Erdgeschoß, Parterre n; **~ form** unterste (Schul-)Klasse f; **~ fruits** pl Erstlinge m pl (als Opfergabe); die ersten Früchte a. fig; fig erste Ergebnisse n pl; **~ gear** 1. Gang m; **~ grade** Am a erstklassig; s erste Klasse f; **~-hand** a direkt, unmittelbar; adv aus erster Hand; **F~ Lady** Am Gemahlin f des Präsidenten der US; **~ lieutenant** Am Oberleutnant m; **~ling** ['-liŋ] Erstling(swerk n) m; erste Zucht f; **~ly** ['-li] adv erstens; **~ mate** Obersteuermann, 1. Offizier m; **~ name** Vorname m; **~-name** tr Am mit Vornamen anreden; **~ night**

theat Erstaufführung *f*; **~-nighter** Premierenbesucher *m*; **~-offender** *jur* Nichtvorbestrafte(r) *m*; **~ papers** *pl Am* erste Ausweise *m pl* für zukünftige Neubürger; **~-rate** ['-'reit] *a* erstrangig, -klassig; *fam* prima, großartig, herrlich, prächtig, Klasse; *adv* [-'reit] *fam* prima, großartig, erstklassig; **F~ Sealord** Chef *m* des britischen Admiralstabs; **~ sergeant** *Am* Hauptfeldwebel, -wachtmeister, *sl* Spieß *m*.

firth [fə:θ] Meeresarm *m*, Förde *f*.

fiscal ['fiskəl] fiskalisch; Steuer-; Finanz-; **~ administration** Steuer-, Finanzverwaltung *f*; **~ authorities** *pl* Fiskus *m*; **~ policy** Steuer-, Finanzpolitik *f*; **~ year** Rechnungs-, Haushalt(s)-, Geschäftsjahr *n*.

fish 1. *s (pl ~ u. ~es)* Fisch; *fig fam* Kerl; Tropf; *Am sl* Neuling; *Am sl* Dollar *m*; *F~(es) pl astr* Fische *pl*; *itr* fischen; angeln *a. fig* (*for* nach); *tr* fischen, angeln in; *(Fisch)* fangen; *(to ~ out, to ~ up)* aus dem Wasser, *allg* hervorholen; herausfischen, hervorziehen; suchen, herumwühlen (*through o.'s pockets* in den Taschen); *fig* forschen nach; *to ~ out (Teich)* ausfischen; *to drink like a ~* wie ein Bürstenbinder saufen; *to feed the ~* seekrank sein; untergehen, ertrinken; *to feel like a ~ out of water* sich fehl am Platze vorkommen; *to have other ~ to fry* andere, wichtigere Dinge zu tun haben; *to ~ for compliments* Komplimente haben wollen; *to ~ in troubled waters (fig)* im Trüben fischen; *all's ~ that comes to his net* er nimmt alles, was er kriegen kann; *that's neither ~, flesh, nor fowl* od *nor good red herring (fig)* das ist weder Fisch noch Fleisch; *there's as good ~ in the sea as ever came out of it* es ist alles reichlich vorhanden; *drunk as a ~* sternhagelvoll; *a pretty kettle of ~ (iro)* eine schöne Bescherung; *mute as a ~* stumm wie ein Fisch; *~ and chips* gebackene(s) Fischfilet *n* mit Pommes frites; **~-ball, -cake** Fischfrikadelle *f*; **~-basket** Fischkorb *m*; **~-bone** (Fisch-)Gräte *f*; Fischbein *n*; **~-bowl, -globe** (Gold-)Fischglas *n*; **~-carver, -slice** Fischvorlegemesser *n*; **~-dealer** *Am* Fischhändler *m*; **~er** ['-ə] *obs* Fischer; *zoo* Fischermarder, Pekan *m*; Fischerboot *n*; **~erman** ['-əmən] Fischer; Angler; Fischdampfer *m*; **~ery** ['-əri] Fischerei *f*, Fischfang *m*; Fischgründe, Fischteiche *m pl*; Fischrecht *n*; *inshore, deep-sea ~~* Küsten-, Hochseefischerei *f*; **~ farming** Fischzucht *f*; **~-flour, -meal** Fischmehl *n (Dünger)*; **~-glue** Fischleim *m*; **~-hawk** Fischadler *m*; **~-hook** Angelhaken; *Am sl* Finger *m*; **~iness** ['-inis] *fam* Verdächtigkeit, Anrüchigkeit *f*; **~ing** ['-iŋ] Fischen *n*, Fischerei *f*, Fischfang *m*; Angeln *n*; *~~-banks, -grounds (pl)* Fischgründe *m pl*, Fischereigebiet *n*; *~~-boots (pl)* Wasserstiefel *m pl*; *~~-fleet* Fischereiflotte *f*; *~~-fly* künstliche Fliege *f*; *~~-licence* Angelschein *m*; *~~-line* Angelschnur *f*; *~~-port* Fischereihafen *m*; *~~-rod* Angelrute *f*; *~~-smack* Fischkutter *m*; *~~-tackle* Angelgerät *n*; *~~ village* Fischerdorf *n*; **~-knife** Fischmesser *n*; **~-ladder** Fischleiter *f*; **~-line** Angelschnur *f*; **~-market** Fischmarkt *m*; **~monger** *Br* Fischhändler *m*; *~~'s shop* Fischgeschäft *n*; **~-oil** (Fisch-)Tran *m*; **~-pole** *Am* Angelrute *f*; **~-pond** Fischteich *m*; **~-sound** Fischblase *f*; **~ story** *Am fam* Jägerlatein *n*; **~-tail** *s* Fischschwanz *m*; *aero* Abbremsen *n*; *tr aero* abbremsen; *mot* hin u. her schleudern; *~~ burner (tech)* Flachbrenner *m*; **~-warden** Fischereiaufseher *m*; **~wife** Fischfrau *f*; **~ worm** *Am* Köder *m*; **~y** ['fiʃi] fischreich; fischartig; *(Augen, Blick)* trübe, verschwommen, ausdruckslos; *fam* verdächtig, zweifelhaft, nicht (ganz) astrein, mulmig, faul; **2.** *s* Spielmarke *f*; **3.** *s mar* Schale, Backe; *rail (~-plate)* (Schienen-)Lasche *f*; *tr rail* verlaschen.

fissil|e ['fisail] spaltbar; **~ity** [fi'siliti] Spaltbarkeit *f*.

fission ['fiʃən] Spaltung, Zersplitterung; *biol* (Zell-)Teilung; *phys* (Kern-) Spaltung *f*; *nuclear ~* Kernspaltung *f*; **~able** ['fiʃnəbl] *(bes. Kernphysik)* spaltbar; **~ product** *phys* Spaltprodukt *n*.

fissure ['fiʃə, -ʃuə] *s* Spalt(e *f*) *m*, Ritze *f*, Riß, Sprung *m*; *anat* (Gehirn-)Furche *f*.

fist [fist] *s* Faust; *fam* Pranke, Flosse, Hand *f*; Griff *m*; *fam* Klaue, (Hand-) Schrift *f*; *tr* mit der Faust schlagen, boxen; *mar* (er)greifen, handhaben; *to shake o.'s ~ at s.o.* jdm mit der Faust drohen; **~ed** ['-id] *a* mit ... Fäusten; *tight-~~* geizig; **~ic** ['fistik] *a fam* Box-; **~icuffs** ['fistikʌfs] *pl* Faustschläge *m pl*; Faust-, Boxkampf; Boxsport *m*.

fistul|a ['fistjulə] *med* Fistel *f*.

fit [fit] **1.** *s med* Anfall *a. fig*; *(plötzlichen) Ausbruch m (e-r seelischen Regung, Leidenschaft)*; Anwandlung, Laune, Stimmung *f*; plötzliche(r), kurze(r) Eifer, Auftrieb, (innerer) Ruck, Stoß, Einfall *m*, vorübergehende (starke) Steigerung; Ohnmacht *f*; *by ~s (and starts)* ruck-, stoßweise, mit Unterbrechungen, nur zeitweise; *to beat, to knock s.o. into ~s (fam)* jdn völlig fertigmachen; *to fall down in a ~, to go into ~s* in Ohnmacht *od* Krämpfe fallen; *to give s.o. a ~, ~s (fam)* jdn auf die Palme bringen, umhauen *fig*; jdm e-n Schrecken einjagen; *to have, to throw a ~ (fig)* e-n Wutanfall haben *od* kriegen; e-e Überraschung erleben; *(just) as the ~ takes one* wie einen gerade die Laune anwandelt; *~ of anger* Wutausbruch *m*; *~ of apoplexy* Schlaganfall *m*; *~ of coughing* Hustenanfall *m*; *~ of despair* Anfall *m* von Verzweiflung; *~ of energy* Kraftausbruch *m*; *~ of hysteria* hysterische(r) Anfall *m*; *~ of jealousy* Anwandlung *f* von Eifersucht; *~ of laughter* Lachkrampf *m*; *~ of passion* Ausbruch *m* der Leidenschaft; **~ful** ['-ful] unterbrochen; unberechenbar, unregelmäßig, ungleichmäßig; von Launen abhängig; krampfhaft; **~fulness** ['-fulnis] Unregelmäßigkeit, Ungleichmäßigkeit, Launenhaftigkeit *f*; **2.** *a* tauglich, geeignet, passend, ratsam, angebracht, gut, (wie) geschaffen, gut genug (*for* für; *to* zu); richtig, (gerade) recht; fähig (*for* zu), gewachsen (*for s.th.* e-r S); vorbereitet (*to* auf), bereit (*to* zu), fertig (*to* für); schicklich, angemessen, angebracht; gesund (und munter), (gesundheitlich) auf der Höhe, *fam* auf dem Damm, auf dem Posten; *sport* (gut) in Form; *mil* wehrtauglich; *fam* drauf und dran, im Begriff zu; *tr* passen zu, in Übereinstimmung sein *od* sich befinden, harmonisieren mit; geeignet sein für, passen für, in; *(bes. Kleidung)* passen, gut sitzen (*s.o.* jdm), (gut) kleiden; passend machen (*for, to* dat), anpassen (*for, to* dat); anprobieren; tauglich, geeignet machen (*for, to* für); her-, einrichten, ausrüsten, ausstatten, versehen (*with* mit); montieren, anbringen, einbauen, -passen, -fügen; *itr* passen, *(bes. Kleidung)* sitzen; sich eignen, taugen, sich schicken, ratsam, angebracht sein; *to ~ o.s.* sich vorbereiten (*for* auf); *s* Passen *n*; *(Kleidung)* Paßform *f*; (guter) Sitz *m*; *more than is ~* mehr als ratsam, über Gebühr; *to be ~* sich schicken; geeignet, tauglich sein, taugen; *not to be ~ to hold a candle for s.o.* jdm das Wasser nicht reichen können; *to be ~ to be tied (Am sl)* Gift u. Galle spucken; *to feel (quite) ~* sich (ganz) auf der Höhe fühlen; *to keep ~* gesund, in Form bleiben; *to think, to see ~* für recht, richtig halten; *to ~ like a glove* wie angegossen sitzen; *he was crying, laughing ~ to burst* er schrie wie am Spieß, platzte vor Lachen; *~ to eat* genießbar, zu essen(d); *~ to drink* trinkbar; *~ for duty* dienstfähig; *~ as a fiddle* munter wie ein Fisch im Wasser; *~ for a position* für e-e Stelle geeignet; *~ for active service (mil)* kriegsverwendungsfähig; *~ to travel* reisefähig; *~ for work* arbeitsfähig; *to ~* **in** *tr* einfügen, an die rechte Stelle bringen, *fam* 'reinkriegen, ein-, dazwischenschieben; *tech* einbauen, einführen, einmontieren; *itr* passen (*with* zu), in Einklang, in Übereinstimmung sein (*with* mit); *to ~* **on** anpassen, -probieren; verpassen; an-, an s-e Stelle bringen, aufsetzen; befestigen (*to* an); *fam (Deckel)* 'raufkriegen; *to ~* **out** ausrüsten, ausstatten, ausstaffieren, einrichten (*for* für); *to ~* **together** zs.passen, -setzen; *to ~* **up** *(bes. Haus)* einrichten, ausstatten, möblieren; ausrüsten (*with* mit); *(Maschine)* aufstellen, montieren; **~ment** ['-mənt] Einrichtungsgegenstand *m*, -stück, Möbel(stück) *n*; *pl* (Wohnungs-)Einrichtung, Ausstattung *f*; *tech* Paßteile *m pl*; **~ness** ['-nis] Tauglichkeit, Geeignetheit; Fähigkeit; Ratsamkeit, Angebrachtheit; Angemessenheit, Schicklichkeit; Gesundheit *f*; *~~ for military service* Wehrtauglichkeit *f*; *~~ test* Eignungsprüfung *f*; **~-out** *fam* Ausstattung, Einrichtung *f*; **~ted** ['-id] *a* passend, geeignet; *(~~ up)* eingerichtet, ausgestattet; aufgestellt, montiert; *(Kleid)* anliegend; **~ten** ['-ən] *Am sl* fähig; **~ter** ['-ə] Anprobierer; Einrichter, Ausstatter; *(engine-~~)* Monteur, Schlosser; *(gas-~~)* Installateur *m*; **~ting** ['-iŋ] *a* passend, recht, gut, angebracht, angemessen; am Platze; *s (Kleider)* Änderung; Anprobe; *(~~-up)* Einrichtung, Aufstellung, Montage *f*, Einbau *m*; *pl* Einrichtung(sgegenstände *m pl*) *f*, Zubehör(teile *n pl*) *n*, Armatur(en *pl*) *f*; Beschläge *m pl*; Leuchten *f pl*, Beleuchtungskörper *m pl*; *to be ready for a ~~* zur Anprobe fertig sein; *~~-shop* Montagehalle, -werkstatt *f*; *~~ stand* Montagebock *m*; *~~-work* Paßarbeit *f*; **~-up** *theat* Bühneneinrichtung *f*.

fitchew ['fitʃu:] *zoo* Iltis *m*.

five [faiv] *a* fünf; *s die* Fünf; *fam* Fünfpfund-, Fünfdollarschein *m*; *pl Art* Handball(spiel *n*) *m*; *~-day week* Fünftagewoche *f*; *~-o'clock tea* Fünfuhrtee *m*; *~-year plan* Fünfjahresplan *m*; **~fold** ['-fould] fünffach; **~r** ['-ə] *fam* Fünfpfund-, Fünfdollarschein *m*.

fix [fiks] **1.** *tr* festmachen, befestigen (*to* an; *in* in), (an)heften (*to* an); *(Bild)* aufhängen; *(Seitengewehr)* aufpflanzen; sich einprägen (*in o.'s mind* im Gedächtnis); heften, richten (*the eyes* den Blick; *on, upon* auf); den Blick heften, richten auf, starren auf, anstarren, fixieren; *(Hoffnung)* setzen (*on* auf); fest werden, erstarren lassen, härten, dauerhaft machen; *(Preis)* festsetzen, festlegen (*at* auf); *(Aufmerksamkeit)* fesseln; regeln; vereinbaren, abmachen; *(Besprechung)* ansetzen, anberaumen; *(Etat)* aufstellen; mit Sicherheit angeben, festlegen; *chem phot* fixieren; *fam (Alkohol)* zu Kopf steigen (*s.o.* jdm); *(to ~ up)* machen, zubereiten, (her)richten, unterhalten; (wieder) in Ordnung bringen, richten, reparieren, instand setzen; *Am fam* drehen, schieben, manipulieren, frisieren; durch Kunstgriffe, Bestechung beeinflussen; sich rächen an (*s.o.* jdm); in Schwierigkeiten bringen, erledigen (*s.o.* jdn); *fam* es heimzahlen, es zurückgeben (*s.o.* jdm); *(Katze)* kastrieren; *(Rauschgift)* verkaufen; **2.** *itr* fest, hart, steif werden; sich festlegen (*on, upon* auf), sich entschließen (*on, upon* zu); wählen (*upon s.th.* etw); *(a. to ~ o.s.)* sich festsetzen, sich niederlassen, s-n Wohnsitz nehmen *od* aufschlagen; *aero* den Standort bestimmen; *Am fam* vorhaben, sich fertigmachen (*to do* um zu tun); *to ~ over (Kleider)* abändern; *to ~ up* Anordnungen treffen für, (an-)ordnen, arrangieren, regeln, einrichten, besorgen; ausrüsten (*with* mit); *(Menschen)* unterbringen (*for the night* für die Nacht); verschaffen (*s.o. with a job* jdm e-e Stelle); machen, herrichten, in Ordnung bringen; **3.** *s fam* Klemme, Patsche, Verlegenheit; *Am sl* manipulierbare Sache *f*; bestechliche(r) Mensch; feste(r) Polizeiposten *m*; (Heroin-)Spritze; Dose *f* Heroin; *mar aero* Standortbestimmung; (Funk-)Peilung *f*; **4.** *in a ~* in e-r Klemme; *to ~ up a quarrel* e-n Streit beilegen; *to ~ the bed* das Bett machen; *to ~ the blame on s.o.* jdm die Schuld geben *od* zuschieben; *to ~ up o.'s face (sl)* sich schminken; *to ~ the fire* das Feuer unterhalten, in Gang halten; *to ~ o.'s hair* sich die Haare machen *od* ordnen, sich kämmen; *to ~ the meal* das Essen fertigmachen *od* zubereiten; *to ~ a position* den Standort bestimmen; sich orientieren; *to ~ the table* den Tisch decken; *to ~ a tyre* e-n Reifen montieren; *to ~ s.o.'s wagon (Am sl)* jdn umbringen; jdn scheitern lassen; *~ bayonets!* Seitengewehr pflanzt auf! *everybody is well ~ed (Am)* alle haben, was sie brauchen; *I'll ~ him! (Am)* ich werde es ihm schon geben! **~ate** [fik'seit] *tr psychol (Triebrichtung)* fixieren; **~ation** [fik'seiʃən] Festsetzung, -legung, Bestimmung, Regelung; *scient* Fixierung, Bindung *f*; **~ative** ['fiksətiv] *a* Fixier-; *s* Fixativ, Fixiermittel *n*; **~ature** ['fiksətʃə] (Haar-)Fixativ *n*, Frisiercreme *f*; **~ed** [fikst] *a* fest(sitzend, -stehend, -liegend), unbeweglich, starr; *(Motor)* ortsfest; festgesetzt, -gelegt, geregelt, abgemacht; ständig; *(Ausgaben)* laufend; *Am* manipuliert, arrangiert; *chem* (luft-, feuer)beständig; *well ~~ (Am)* wohlhabend; *~~ allowance* Fixum *n*; *~~ assets (pl)* Sachanlagevermögen *n*; *~~ capital* Anlagevermögen, -kapital *n*; *~~ charges, expenses (pl)* allgemeine, feste Unkosten *pl*; *~~ date, day* festgesetzte(r) Zeitpunkt, Tag; Termin *m*; *~~ idea* fixe Idee *f*; *~~ income* feste(s) Einkommen *n*; *~~ period* vorgeschriebene Frist *f*; *~~ plant* Betriebsanlage *f*; *~~ price* Festpreis *m*; *pl* feste Preise *m pl*; *~~ rule* feste Regel *f*; *~~ salary* feste(s) Gehalt *n*; *~~ star* Fixstern *m*; **~edly** ['-idli] *adv* unverwandt, starr *(blicken)*; bestimmt; **~er** ['fiksə] Fixierer *m*; *phot* Fixierbad *n*; *Am* Bastler; *Am sl* Winkeladvokat, Mittelsmann, Rauschgifthändler *m*; **~ing** ['-iŋ] Befestigen, Festmachen *n*; Festsetzung, Bestimmung *f*; *phot* Fixieren *n*; *pl fam* Drum und Dran *n*, Zubehör *n*; Klamotten, Sachen *f pl*, Zeug *n*; *(Küche)* Gemüsebeilagen *f pl*; *~~ bath* Fixierbad *n*; **F~it**: *Mr. ~~ (Am fam)* Tausendkünstler *m*; **~ity** ['fiksiti] Festigkeit, Stabilität, Beständigkeit, Dauerhaftigkeit *f*; *~~ of purpose* Zielstrebigkeit *f*; **~ture** ['fikstʃə] feste(r) Gegenstand *m*, feste Anlage; feste Verabredung, Abmachung; *sport* feste Veranstaltung *f*; festgesetzte(r) Zeitpunkt, (fester) Termin *m*; kurzfristige(s) Darlehen; *fig fam* alte(s) Inventarstück *n*; *meist pl (Haus)* feste Einrichtung, Installation *f*; Spanner *m*; Zubehör *n*; *pl sport* Spielplan *m*.

fizz [fiz] *itr* zischen; gluckern; sprudeln, moussieren; *s* Zischen, Glukkern *n*; *fam* Sprudel; Schampus, Sekt *m*; **~er** ['-ə] *fam* Pfundssache *f*; **~le** ['fizl] *itr* zischen(d sprühen); *fam (to ~~ out, to ~~ through)* steckenbleiben, nicht (mehr) weiterkommen, absacken, schließlich (doch) versagen; ohne Ergebnis enden; *s* Zischen *n*; *fam* Reinfall *m*, Fiasko *n*, Schlappe *f*; *to be in a ~~* (wie) auf heißen Kohlen sitzen; **~y** ['fizi] zischend, sprühend, sprudelnd.

fjord *s. fiord.*

flabbergast ['flæbəgɑːst] *tr fam* verblüffen; *to be ~ed* platt sein.

flabb|iness ['flæbinis] Schlaffheit, Schlappheit; Schwäche *f*; **~y** ['flæbi] schlaff, schlapp; *fig* saft- u. kraftlos.

flaccid ['flæksid] lose hängend; schlaff; *fig* kraftlos; **~ity** [-'siditi] Schlaffheit; *fig* Schwäche *f*.

flag [flæg] **1.** *s* Flagge, Fahne *f*; *tr* beflaggen; mit Fahnen abstecken; *(to ~ down)* das Haltesignal geben (*a train* e-m Zuge); anhalten; *(Nachricht, Befehl)* signalisieren; *to dip, to lower, to strike a, o.'s ~* salutieren; die Fahne streichen, sich ergeben; *to drop the ~ (sport)* das Zeichen zum Start geben; *to keep the ~ flying* die Fahne hochhalten; *black ~* Seeräuberflagge *f*; *small ~* Fähnchen *n*; *~ of truce* Parlamentärsfahne *f*; *bearer of a ~ of truce* Parlamentär, Unterhändler *m*; **~-day** Opfertag; *Am (F~ Day)* Tag *m* der „Stars and Stripes" *(14. Juni)*; **~man** *sport* Starter; *mil* Winker *m*; **~-officer** *mar* Flaggoffizier *m*; **~-pole, ~staff** Fahnenstange *f*, -mast *m*; **~ship** Flaggschiff *n*; **~-signal** Flaggensignal *n*; **~-wagging** Winken, Signalisieren *n*; **~-waver** Chauvinist *m*; **2.** *(~stone)* *s* Steinplatte *f*; *tr (Hof, Weg)* mit Steinplatten belegen; **3.** Schwertlilie *f*; *a. pl* Riedgras *n*; Blattscheide *f*; **4.** *orn* Schwungfeder *f*; **5.** *itr* schlaff werden, erschlaffen; *fig* ermatten, erlahmen, nachlassen; gleichgültig werden.

flagell|ant ['flædʒilənt] *hist rel* Geißler, Flagellant *m*; **~ate** ['flædʒeleit] *tr* geißeln; *a biol* mit Geißeln versehen; geißelförmig; *s* Geißeltierchen *n*; **~ation** [flædʒe'leiʃən] Geißelung *f*.

flagitious [flə'dʒiʃəs] schändlich, schandbar; abscheulich, häßlich.

flagon ['flægən] bauchige Kanne *od* Flasche *f*.

flagran|cy ['fleigrənsi] Schändlichkeit, öffentliche(s) Ärgernis *n*; **~t** ['-t] himmelschreiend, empörend, skandalös, ärgerniserregend, schamlos.

flail [fleil] *s* Dreschflegel *m*; *tr* dreschen.

flair [flɛə] Spürsinn *m*, Witterung, feine Nase *f*, Fingerspitzengefühl *n*, *fam* Riecher *m*, Ahnung *f*; *to have a ~ for* e-e Nase, *fam* e-n Riecher für etw haben.

flak|e [fleik] *s* Flocke *f*; Schnitzel *n* od *m*, Span, Schnipfel *m*; *(Eis)* Scholle; *(Rost)* Schuppe *f*; *tr* zerschnipfeln, -schneiden; *(to ~~ off)* abschiefern, abblättern, abschuppen; *itr* Flocken bilden; sich schuppen; **~y** ['-i] flockig, schuppig; *~~ pastry* Blätterteig *m*.

flam [flæm] *s* Schwindel *m*; *itr* schwindeln; *tr* beschwindeln.

flamb|eau ['flæmbou] *pl -s, -x* [-z] (brennende) Fackel; große Zierkerze *f*; **~oyance, -cy** [-'bɔiəns(i)] Pracht *f*, Prunk *m*; **~oyant** [-'bɔiənt] *arch* spätgotisch; reichverziert, prunkvoll, (farben)prächtig; überladen.

flam|e [fleim] *s* Flamme *f*; (helles, loderndes) Feuer *n*; Glanz; *tech* Lichtbogen *m*; *(Edelstein)* Feuer *n*; *fig* (Gefühls-)Wallung, Erregung; heftige Leidenschaft; *fam* Angebetete, Geliebte, Flamme *f*; *itr* flammen, lodern; glänzen; entflammen, auflodern; heiß, rot werden, sich röten; *fig* entflammen, (ent)brennen; kochen, schäumen *(vor Wut)*; auffahren, in Zorn geraten; *to ~~ up, to ~~ out* auflodern, auf-, entflammen *a. fig*; erröten; *fig* aufwallen, auffahren, in Wut geraten; *(to be) in ~~s* in Flammen (stehen); *to burst into ~~s* in Flammen aufgehen; *to commit to the ~~s* den Flammen übergeben, verbrennen; *to fan the ~ (fig)* Öl ins Feuer gießen; *~~ cutter* Schneidbrenner *m*; *~~-projector, -thrower* Flammenwerfer *m*; *~~-proof* schlagwettersicher; **~ing** ['-iŋ] flammend, lodernd; brennend; *fig* feurig, glühend, heiß, leidenschaftlich; *fam* verflixt; **~mable** [flæməbl] *Am* leicht brennbar.

flamingo [flə'miŋgou] *pl -o(e)s orn* Flamingo *m*.

flan [flæn] (Obst-)Torte, Pastete *f*.

Flanders ['flɑːndəz] Flandern *n*.

flange [flændʒ] *s* Flansche *f*, Bördelrand; Spur-, Radkranz *m*; *tr* flanschen, umbördeln, umkrempeln.

flank [flæŋk] *s anat zoo* Flanke, Weiche *f*; *(Rind)* Querlierenstück *n*; *allg* Seite, Flanke; *mil* Flanke *f*; *a* Seiten-; *tr allg mil* flankieren; *mil* seitlich bestreichen; in die Flanke fallen; umgehen; *itr* angrenzen *(on, upon* an); *to turn the ~* die Flanke aufrollen; **~ attack** Flankenangriff *m*; **~ers** *pl*, **~ guard** *mil* Flankendekkung, -sicherung *f*; **~ing** ['-iŋ]: *~~ fire* Flankenfeuer *m*; **~ man** Flügelmann *m*; **~ protection** Flankenschutz *m*.

flannel ['flænl] *s* Flanell; Flanell-, Wasch-, Wisch-, Putzlappen *m*; *pl* Flanellhose; *fam* warme wollene Unterwäsche *f*; *fig* Schmeicheleien *f pl*; *tr* in Flanell kleiden; mit Flanell abreiben; **~-suit** Flanellanzug *m*; **~et(te)** [flæn'let] Baumwollflanell *m*; **~mouth** ['-mauθ] *Am* Wels *m (Fisch)*; **~mouthed** ['-mauðd] *a Am fam* schüchtern, still; *not to be ~~* nicht auf den Mund gefallen sein.

flap [flæp] Klappe; *(Hut)* Krempe *f*; (Kiemen-)Deckel; (Haut-)Lappen *m*; (Ohr-)Läppchen *n*; Klapptür *f*; Klaps, leichte(r) Schlag *m*, Schlagen *n*; Flügelschlag *m*; *aero* Landeklappe *f*; *pl hum* Ohren *n pl*; *sl mil* Schiß *m*, Angst *f*; *Am fam* Fliegeralarm, Luftangriff *m*; *sl* Aufregung, Ausea.setzung *f*, Streit *m*, Verwirrung *f*, Mißgriff *m*; lärmende Party *f*; *tr* leicht schlagen; (auf und nieder) schlagen, klappen; *itr* mit den Flügeln schlagen; flattern; lose herabhängen, baumeln; *to get into a ~* es mit der Angst zu tun kriegen; *to ~ o.'s chops, lip (Am sl)* gedankenlos daherreden; **~doodle** ['-du:dl] *fam* Blödsinn, Quatsch, Quack *m*, Blech *n*; **~-eared** *a* mit Schlappohren; **~-hat** Schlapphut *m*; **~jack** *s Am dial* Pfannkuchen *m*; Puderdose *f*; *Am* Luftsprung *m*; *itr* (im Freien) kampieren; **~jaw** ['-dʒɔ:] *Am sl* Gespräch *n*; Schwätzer(in *f*) *m*; **~per** ['-ə] (Fliegen-)Klappe, Fliegenklatsche; Flosse; junge Wildente; *sl* Flosse *f*; *fam* Backfisch, Teenager *m*; **~-seat** Klappsitz *m*; **~-table** Klapptisch *m*; **~ valve** Klappenventil *n*.

flar|e [flɛə] *itr* (auf)flackern, (auf)lodern; flackernd brennen; *fig* aufbrausen, in Wut geraten; Leuchtsignale geben; e-e Ausbuchtung bilden; sich (trichterförmig) erweitern; *tr* (auf-)flackern lassen; durch Leuchtsignale übermitteln, mitteilen; *s* (kurzes) Aufleuchten; Aufflackern *n*; flackernde(r) Brand *m*; Fackel; Leuchtkugel, Leuchtrakete *f*, *fam* Christbaum *m*; Signallicht; Leuchtsignal *n*; *fig* Ausbruch *m*, Aufbrausen *n*; Prahlerei *f*, Protzentum *n*, *fam* Angabe; trichterförmige Erweiterung, Auskragung, Ausbuchtung; Wölbung *f*; *to ~~ up, to ~~ out* aufflackern; *fig* aufbrausen, auffahren; *~~ bomb* Leuchtbombe *f*; *~~ cartridge* Leuchtpatrone *f*; *(aero)* Leuchtpfad *m*; *~~ pistol* Leuchtpistole *f*; *~~ signal* Leuchtsignal *n*; *~~-up* Aufflackern *n*; *fig* (Zornes-)Ausbruch *m*; Aufbrausen *n*; kurze glanzvolle Laufbahn *f*, kometenhafte(s) Auftreten; Leuchtsignal *n*; **~ing** ['-riŋ] *a* flackernd; (kurz) aufleuchtend; blendend; protzig, übertrieben; gewölbt, ausladend; glocken-, trichterförmig.

flash [flæʃ] **1.** *itr* (auf)blitzen, blinken, glühen, flammen, funkeln *a. fig* (*with anger* vor Zorn); *phot* blitzen, e-e Blitzlichtaufnahme machen; *fig* (plötzlich) auftauchen; ausbrechen, schießen, sausen, flitzen, fahren; *tech (Funke)* überspringen; **2.** *tr* aufblitzen, aufleuchten lassen (*on* auf); *(Blick)* zuwerfen; *(Signal)* blinken; *(Mitteilung)* signalisieren; *(Nachricht)* durchgeben, drahten, funken, schnell verbreiten; *Am fam* scheinbar unabsichtlich sehen lassen (um damit anzugeben); *to ~ by* vorbeisausen; *to ~ on* aufleuchten, aufflammen; *to ~ over (el)* überschlagen; **3.** *s* Blitz-, plötzliche(r) Lichtstrahl, Lichtschein *m*; Stichflamme *f*; *mil* Mündungsfeuer *n*; *photo* Blitzlichtaufnahme *f*; Augenblick, Moment *m*, Sekunde *f*; Aufblitzen *(e-s Gedankens, des Verständnisses)*, plötzliche(s) Auflodern *n (e-s Gefühls)*, plötzliche(r) Ausbruch *m*; Szenen *f pl* aus e-m Film; *Am* kurze(r) Blick *m*; *Am fam fig* Strohfeuer; kurze(s) Telegramm *n*, Funkspruch *m*, *mil* Blitzmeldung *f*; auffällige Pracht *f*, Pomp; *Am com* Blickfang *m*; Gaunersprache *f*; Durchschleusen *n*; Schleusenanlage; Zuckercouleur *f*; *tech* plötzliche(r) Stoß *m*; **4.** *a* = *~y*; Gauner-; *(Scheck)* ungedeckt; gefälscht; **5.** *in a ~* im Nu, blitzschnell, im Handumdrehen; *to ~ a light* mit e-m Licht leuchten (*in s.o.'s face* in jds Gesicht); *his eyes ~ed fire* s-e Augen sprühten Blitze; *the idea ~ed into, across, through my mind* es fuhr mir durch den Sinn; *~ of the eyes* Blitzen, Aufleuchten *n* der Augen; *~ of fire* Feuergarbe *f*; *~ of hope* Hoffnungsstrahl *m*; *~ of lightning* Blitzstrahl *m*; *~ in the pan (Feuerwaffe)* Fehlzündung *f a. fig*, Versager *m (a. Person)*; *fig* Strohfeuer *n*; **~-back** Zurückschlagen *n* der Flamme; *film* Rückblendung *f*; **~-bulb** *phot* Blitzlicht(lampe *f*) *n*; **~ burn** *med* Verbrennung *f* durch Hitzestrahlung *(bes. bei Atomexplosion)*; **~er** ['-ə] Blinkeinrichtung *f*; **~iness** ['-inis] Prunk-, Pomphaftigkeit; Geschmacklosigkeit, Unechtheit *f*; **~ing** ['-iŋ] *a* aufblitzend, -leuchtend; *s* Aufblitzen, Glühen; Rundfeuer; Steigen des Wassers in e-m Kanal; Abdeck-, Kehlblech *n (Regenschutz in Dachkehlen)*; *~~ period* Brenndauer *f*; **~-lamp** Taschenlampe *f*; *mil* Blinkgerät *n*; **~-light** *mar aero* Blinklicht *n*; Scheinwerfer *m*, Suchlicht *n*; *Am* Taschenlampe *f*; *phot* Blitzlicht *n*; *electronic ~~* Elektronenblitz *m*; *~~ battery* Taschenlampenbatterie *f*; *~~ (photograph)* Blitzlichtaufnahme *f*; **~-over** *el* Überschlag *m*; **~-point** Flammpunkt *m*; **~y** ['-i] auffallend, blendend; überladen, geschmacklos, unecht.

flask [flɑ:sk] *hist* Pulverhorn *n*; Feldflasche *f*; Flakon *m*; *tech* Formkasten; *chem* Glaskolben *m*; *thermos ~* Thermosflasche *f*.

flat [flæt] *a* flach, platt *(a. Reifen e-s Fahrzeugs)*; *(Absage, Weigerung)* glatt, klar, deutlich, offen, kategorisch; *com* einheitlich, gleichbleibend, pauschal; *com* matt, flau, lustlos; schwer zu verkaufen; *(Getränk)* fade, schal, geschmacklos; eintönig, monoton, langweilig, uninteressant; *el* breitbandig; *(Kunst)* unplastisch, ohne Perspektive, matt, glanzlos; *mus* erniedrigt; *Am* ohne (Berechnung aufgelaufener) Zinsen; *Am sl* pleite; *adv* flach *(hinfallen)*, platt, der Länge nach, ausgestreckt *(daliegen)*; glatt, offen, frei-, rundheraus *(sagen)*; zu niedrig *(singen)*; *s* Fläche; glatte Oberfläche, flache *od* breite, Breitseite *f (e-s Gegenstandes)*; flache(s) Land *n*; (*bes.* Tief-)Ebene; (sumpfige) Niederung; Sandbank *f*; Flur *m*; Stockwerk *n*, Etage, (Etagen-)Wohnung; flache Schale *f*, flache(r) Korb *od* Kasten *m*; flache(s) Boot *n*; *theat* (Landschafts-)Kulisse *f*; *Am* = *~car*; *Am* Reifenpanne *f*, platte(r) Reifen, *fam* Plattfuß *m*; *mus* Erniedrigungszeichen, B *n*; *fig* Hohlkopf, Depp; *Am sl* Mulus, angehende(r) Student *m*; *pl* Mietshaus *n*; *pl* Schuhe *m pl* mit flachen Absätzen; *Am sl* Füße *m pl*; *tr* flach machen, abflachen; *to ~ out (Am)* zs.brechen, scheitern, ins Wasser fallen *fig*; *mot* Vollgas geben; *to fall ~* wirkungslos verpuffen, nicht einschlagen; *to go ~ out (fam)* sich mächtig anstrengen; *to knock ~* zu Boden strecken, niederschlagen; *a ~ denial, refusal* e-e glatte Absage, e-e strikte Weigerung; *the ~ of the hand* die Handfläche; **~-bar** Flacheisen *n*; **~-bed:** *~~ trailer* Tiefladeanhänger *m*; **~-boat** (flacher) Lastkahn *m*; **~-bottomed** *a (Boot, Kahn)* flach; **~car** *Am rail* Flach-, Plattform(güter)wagen, Rungenwagen *m*; **~ coat** Mattanstrich *m*; **~-fish** Plattfisch *m*; **~-foot** Plattfuß; *Am sl* Schupo, Polizist *m*; **~-footed** *a* plattfüßig; *fam* schwerfällig; *Am fam* entschlossen; rundweg, energisch, stur, (ganz) offen; *to catch ~~ (Am fam)* (überraschend) schnappen, erwischen; auf frischer Tat ertappen; **~-head** Flachkopf; *Am* Dummkopf *m*; **~-iron** Plätt-, Bügeleisen *n*; **~let** ['-let] kleine, Kleinwohnung *f*; **~ness** ['-nis] Flachheit, Plattheit; Fadheit; Offenheit; Entschiedenheit; *com* Flaute, Lustlosigkeit; *mil* Rasanz *f*; **~nose pliers** *pl* Flachzange *f*; **~ price** Einheitspreis *m*; **~ race** Flachrennen *n*; **~ rate** Einheits-, Pauschalsatz *m*; Pauschale *f*; *~~ method* lineare Abschreibung *f*; **~ roof** Flachdach *n*; **~ silver** *Am* Tafelsilber *n*; **~ sum** Pauschalbetrag *m*; **~ten** ['-n] *tr* planieren, einebnen; abflachen, niederschlagen, -strecken; flachdrücken, -hämmern; mattieren; abstumpfen; *mus* erniedrigen, dämpfen; *fig* be-, niederdrücken; *itr* flach(er) werden; schal, matt werden; *to ~~ out (tr)* ausbreiten, strekken; *aero (Maschine)* abfangen; *itr aero* ausschweben; **~ third** *mus* kleine Terz *f*; **~tie** ['-i] *Am sl* Polizist, Polyp *m*; **~ tire** *Am* Reifenpanne *f*; *fig* langweilige(r) Mensch *m*; Pleite *f*; **~ting** ['-iŋ] Abflachen; *metal* Ausrollen; Mattieren *n*; *~~ varnish* Schleiflack *m*; **~-top** *Am sl* Flugzeugträger; *(Kurve)* flache(r) Kopf *m*; **~ tuning** Grobabstimmung *f*; **~ware** ['-wɛə] *Am* Besteck *n*; **~work** glatte Wäschestücke *n pl (die gemangelt werden können)*; **~worm** ['-wə:m] Plattwurm *m*.

flatter ['flætə] *tr* schmeicheln (*s.o.* jdm); sich einschmeicheln, *fam* sich lieb Kind machen (*s.o.* bei jdm); (*bes.* falsche) Hoffnung machen (*s.o.* jdm), (trügerische) Hoffnungen erwecken (*s.o.* in jdm); angenehm sein, wohltun (*the eye* dem Auge); *to ~ o.s.* sich einbilden (*that* daß), sich der trügerischen Hoffnung hingeben (*that* daß); *to feel ~ed* sich geschmeichelt fühlen; **~er** ['-rə] Schmeichler *m*; **~ing** ['-riŋ] schmeichelhaft; **~y** ['-ri] Schmeichelei *f*.

flatulen|ce, -cy ['flætjuləns(i)] *physiol* Blähung; *fig* Aufgeblasenheit *f*, Schwulst *m*; **~t** ['-t] aufgebläht; blähend; Bläh(ungs)-; *fig* aufgeblasen, schwülstig, (innerlich) leer, hohl.

flaunt [flɔ:nt] *itr* prunken, paradieren, prahlen; *(Fahne)* frei, stolz flattern, wehen; *tr* zur Schau stellen *od* tragen, prahlen, großtun mit.

flavo(u)r ['fleivə] *s* (Wohl-)Geschmack; (Wohl-)Geruch, Duft; besondere(r), charakteristische(r) Geschmack, Duft *m*; Aroma *n*, Würze; *(Wein)* Blume *f*; *fig* Reiz *(der Neuheit)*; *fig* Beigeschmack *m*; *tr* würzen *a. fig*; **~ed** ['-d] *a* gewürzt; **~ing** ['-riŋ] Würze *f*, Aroma *n (als Stoff)*; **~less** ['-lis] geschmacklos, fade.

flaw [flɔ:] **1.** *s* Sprung, Riß *m*; Blase *f (im Guß)*; *(Edelstein)* Fleck *m*; *allg* fehlerhafte, beschädigte Stelle *f*; (Material-)Fehler, Defekt; Mangel; *fig* (Form-)Fehler *a. jur*, Irrtum *m*, Versehen *n*; **~less** ['-lis] fehlerlos, -frei, makellos, untadelig; **2.** Windstoß *m*, (Regen-)Bö *f*.

flax [flæks] Flachs, Lein *m*; **~en** ['-ən] flächse(r)n; strohgelb; *~~ hair* Flachshaar *n*; **~-seed** Leinsaat *f*, -samen *m*; **~y** ['-i] flachsartig; Flachs-.

flay [flei] *tr* schinden; die Haut abziehen (*s.o.* jdm); *fig* herunterreißen, -machen, -putzen, keinen guten Faden lassen an; *fig* das Fell über die Ohren ziehen (*s.o.* jdm); *sl* aus-, berauben, (aus)plündern.

flea [fli:] Floh *m*; *to go away with a ~ in o.'s ear* wie ein begossener Pudel abziehen; **~bag** *sl* Schlafsack *m*; billige(s) Hotel, armselige(s) Lokal *n*; **~-bane** Flohkraut *n*; **~-bite** Flohbiß; *fig* Mückenstich *m*, Bagatelle *f*; **~-bitten** *a* von Flöhen zerstochen; *(Pferd)* rotbraun getupft; *fam* schäbig; **~-pit** *sl* armselige(s) Kino *n*; Bude *f*.

fleck [flek] *s* Fleck(en), Tupfen *m*; Teilchen *n*; *pl (~s of sunlight)* Sommersprossen *f pl*; *tr* sprenkeln, tupfen; *~ of* *colo(u)r, of dust* Farbfleck *m*; Stäubchen *n*; **~less** ['-lis] fleckenlos.

flection *s. flexion.*

fledg|e [fledʒ] *itr* flügge werden; *tr* mit Federn versehen *od* bedecken; **~ed** [-d] *a* flügge; **~(e)ling** ['-liŋ] eben flügge gewordene(r) Vogel; *fig* Gelb-, Grünschnabel *m*.

flee [fli:] *irr fled, fled* [fled] *itr* (ent-)fliehen, flüchten (*from* vor; *to* zu, auf); entweichen; verschwinden; sich fernhalten; *tr* fliehen vor, aus; meiden, ausweichen (*s.o.* jdm).

fleec|e [fli:s] *s* Vlies; Vliesgewicht *n*, Rohschurertrag *m*; (Schnee-)Decke; Schäfchenwolke; Haarmähne *f*; *tr (Schaf)* scheren; *fig* rupfen, übers Ohr hauen, berauben, beschwindeln, schröpfen (*of* um); **~y** ['-i] wollig, flockig, weich; Schäfchen-; *~~ clouds (pl)* Schäfchenwolken *f pl*.

fleer ['fliə] *itr* höhnen, spotten (*at* über); *s* Hohn, Spott *m*.

fleet [fli:t] *s* Flotte *f*; Geschwader *n*; Marine; Luftflotte *f*, -geschwader *n*; Wagenkolonne *f*; *a lit poet* schnell, flink, eilig; flüchtig; *~ of cars* Wagenpark *m*; **F~ Air Arm** Marineluftwaffe *f*; **~-base** Flottenstützpunkt *m*; **~ commander** Flottenchef *m*; **~-fighter** Bordjäger *m*; **~ing** ['-iŋ] flüchtig, dahinschwindend, vergänglich; **~ness** ['-nis] Flüchtigkeit, Vergänglichkeit *f*; **F~ Street** die (Londoner) Presse.

Flem|ing ['flemiŋ] Flame *m*, Flamin *od* Flämin *f*; **~ish** ['-iʃ] *a* flämisch, flandrisch; *s* (das) Flämisch(e).

flesh [fleʃ] *s* (*bes.* Muskel-)Fleisch; (Frucht-)Fleisch *n*; (menschlicher) Leib, Körper(fülle *f*) *m*; Fett *n*; menschliche Natur, *bes.* Sinnlichkeit, Fleischlichkeit, Fleischeslust; *poet* Menschheit *f*; *(Kunst)* Fleisch *n*; Fleischfarbe *f*; *tr* mit Fleisch füttern; zur Jagd abrichten; scharf machen; *fig* e-n Vorgeschmack geben; *(Waffe)* in Blut tauchen; ausfleischen; mästen; *(Leidenschaft)* befriedigen; *itr fam* Fleisch ansetzen, dick(er) werden; *in ~* (wohl)beleibt, dick, fett; *in the ~* lebend(ig); leibhaftig; in Person, in natura; *to go the way of all ~* den Weg allen Fleisches gehen, sterben; *to have o.'s pound of ~* alles auf Heller und Pfennig bekommen; *to make s.o.'s ~ creep* jdm kalte Schauer über den Rükken jagen; *to put on, to lose ~* dicker, dünner werden; zu-, abnehmen; *proud ~* wilde(s) Fleisch *n*; *~ and blood* die menschliche Natur *od* Schwäche; *o.'s (own) ~ and blood* sein (eigenes) Fleisch u. Blut, nahe Verwandte *pl*; **~-brush, -glove** Frottierbürste *f*, -handschuh *m*; **~-colo(u)red** *a* fleischfarben; **~-diet, -meat** Fleischkost *f*; **~-eater** Fleischesser, -fresser *m*; **~-eating** *s* Fleischgenuß *m*; *a* fleischfressend; **~er** ['-ə] *Scot* Fleischer *m*; **~-fly** Schmeißfliege *f*; **~iness** ['-inis] Fleischigkeit *f*; **~ings** ['-iŋz], **~(-coloured) tights** *pl* fleischfarbene(s) Trikot *n*; **~ly** ['-li] leiblich; fleischlich, sinnlich; **~pots** *pl fig* Fleischtöpfe *m pl* Ägyptens, Wohlleben *n*, -stand *m*; **~ tints** *pl (Malerei)* Karnation, Fleischdarstellung *f*; **~-wound** Fleischwunde *f*; **~y** [-i] fleischig; fett; dick; *(Frucht)* fest.

flews [flu:z] *pl (Hund)* Lefzen *f pl*.

flex [fleks] *tr* biegen, beugen; *(Muskel)* zs.ziehen, kontrahieren; *s el* (Anschluß-, Leitungs-)Schnur, Litze, *fam* Strippe *f*; **~ibility** [fleksə'biliti] Elastizität, Biegsamkeit; Anpassungsfähigkeit; Beweglichkeit *f*; **~ible** ['fleksəbl] biegsam, elastisch, dehnbar, geschmeidig; anpassungsfähig; federnd; nachgiebig; *(Schallplatte)* unzerbrechlich; *(Auto)* wendig; *fig* leicht zu beeinflussen(d), lenksam; abänderungsfähig, modifizierbar; *~~ axle* Schwingachse *f*; *~~ cable, cord* Anschlußschnur *f*; **~ile** ['fleksil] biegsam; beweglich; wendig; **~ion** ['flekʃən] Biegung, Beugung, Krümmung; Kurve *f*, Knie *n*; *gram* Flexion *f*; **~or** ['fleksə] Beugemuskel *m*; **~ure** ['flekʃə] Krümmung, Biegung; *geol* Falte *f*.

*

flibbertigibbet ['flibəti'dʒibit] Klatschbase *f*, Schwätzer; *fig* Windhund *m*.

flick [flik] *s* Schnippen, Schnipsen; Knipsen *n*; (Peitschen-)Knall; leichte(r) Schlag; *sl* Film, *pl* Kintopp *m*; *tr (Staub, Fliege)* wegschnippen; wegklopfen; knallen mit *(e-r Peitsche.)*

flicker ['flikə] *itr* flattern; zappeln, zittern; züngeln; flackern; flimmern; zucken; *s* Flackern, Flimmern, Zucken *n*; *fig* Funke, Schimmer; *Am* Specht *m*; *~ of hope* Hoffnungsschimmer *m*.

flier *s. flyer.*

flight [flait] **1.** Flug *m*, Fliegen *n*; (Vogel-)Zug *m*; Fliegerei, Luftfahrt; Flugstrecke *f*, -weg *m*; Schar *f*, Schwarm *(Vögel, Insekten)*; *(Pfeile)* Hagel; *aero* Schwarm *m (Einheit)*; Kette *(Flugformation)*; *mil* Flugbahn *f*; *fig* (Gedanken-)Flug, Aufschwung *m*; *(~ of stairs)* Treppenflucht *f*; *in ~* im Fluge; *in the first, highest ~* an der Spitze, *fam* Tete; **~ allowance** Fliegerzulage *f*; **~ altitude** Flughöhe *f*; **~ characteristics** *pl* Flugeigenschaften *f pl*; **~ crew** fliegende Besatzung *f*; **~ deck** Flugdeck *n*; **~ engineer** Bordmechaniker *m*; **~-feather** Schwungfeder *f*; **~ formation** Flugformation *f*; **~iness** ['-inis] Launenhaftigkeit; Unausgeglichenheit *f*; **~ instructor** Fluglehrer *m*; **~ lane** Flugschneise *f*; **~less** ['-lis] *(Vogel)* flugunfähig; **~lessness** ['-lisnis] Flugunfähigkeit *f*; **~ lieutenant** Hauptmann *m* d. L.; **~ log** Bordbuch *n*; **~ manifest** Ladeliste *f*; **~ mechanic** Bordwart *m*; **~ path** Flugbahn *f*; **~ security** Flugsicherung *f*; **~ sergeant** Oberfeldwebel *m*; **~-time** Flugzeit *f a. zoo*; **~y** ['-i] launenhaft, launisch; unausgeglichen, labil, unbeständig, unberechenbar; **2.** Flucht *f*; *to put to ~* in die Flucht schlagen; *to seek safety in ~* sein Heil in der Flucht suchen; *to take (to) ~* fliehen, weglaufen, sich davonmachen; *~ of capital* Kapitalflucht *f*.

flim-flam ['flim-flæm] *s fam* Unsinn *m*, dumme(s) Zeug, Gewäsch *n*.

flims|iness ['flimzinis] Empfindlichkeit; Unzulänglichkeit, Fadenscheinigkeit; Oberflächlichkeit *f*; **~y** ['flimzi] *a* dünn, zerbrechlich, empfindlich; *fig* schwach, unzulänglich, fadenscheinig; nicht überzeugend; *s* dünne(s), Durchschlagpapier *n*; Durchschlag *m (e-s Berichtes)*, Duplikat *n*; *sl* Geldschein, Lappen *m*; *sl* Telegramm *n*; *pl fam* Reizwäsche *f*.

flinch [flintʃ] *itr* (zurück)weichen, nachgeben; sich zurückziehen, abstehen, sich drücken (*from* von); zurückfahren, -zucken, -schrecken (*from* vor); *s Am* Patience *f (Kartenspiel)*; *without ~ing* ohne e-e Miene zu verziehen.

fling [fliŋ] *irr flung, flung tr* schleudern, werfen, *fam* schmeißen; *(Angel)* auswerfen; umwerfen, umstoßen; schlingen (*o.'s arms about s.o.* die Arme um jdn); *itr* stürzen, jagen, fahren, eilen; drauflosreden; *s* Wurf *m*, Schleudern *n*; Schlag, Hieb *m*; schnelle, hastige Bewegung *f*; *(Pferd)* Ausschlagen *n*; *fig* Versuch, Anlauf; Ausfall *m*, bissige, spöttische Bemerkung, Stichelei *f*; Rappel *m*, Laune *f*; Sichaustoben *n*, Zügellosigkeit, volle Freiheit *f*; *Art* lebhafter (*bes.* schottischer *(Highland ~)*) Tanz *m*; *in full ~* in vollem Gange; *to have a ~ at* sich versuchen an, verspotten (*at s.o.* jdn); *to have o.'s ~* sich austoben; *to ~ s.th. at s.o.* jdm etw nach, an den Kopf werfen; *to ~ o.s. into s.th. (fig)* sich in etw stürzen; *to ~ into prison* ins Gefängnis werfen; *to ~ s.th. in s.o.'s teeth* jdm etw ins Gesicht schleudern; *to ~ to the winds* in den Wind schlagen, außer acht lassen; *that's a ~ at you* das gilt dir, das ist auf dich gemünzt; *to ~* **about** um sich werfen; zerstreuen; *to ~* **aside** zur Seite werfen *od* schleudern; weg-, von sich werfen; *to ~* **away** wegwerfen, -schleudern; *to ~* **back** heftig erwidern; *to ~* **off** *itr* davon-, hinausstürzen; *tr (Verfolger)* abschütteln; wegschleudern; *to ~* **on** *(Kleider)* schnell überwerfen; *to ~* **open** *(Tür)* aufreißen; *to ~* **out** *tr* hinauswerfen; *(Arme)* weit öffnen, ausbreiten; *(Drohung)* ausstoßen (*at s.o.* gegen jdn); *itr* (hinten) ausschlagen; hinausstürzen (*of the house* aus dem Hause); *he flung out* ihm platzte der Kragen; *to ~* **up** in die Luft werfen; *(Studium)* aufgeben; *to ~* **(up)on** werfen, schleudern auf, über; *o.s.* sich anheimgeben.

flint [flint] Feuerstein, Flint; (Feuerstein-)Kiesel *m*; *to set o.'s face like a ~* keine Miene verziehen, fest bleiben; *to skin a ~* alles zs.kratzen, sehr geizig sein; *to wring water from a ~* zaubern, Wunder tun; **~glass** Flintglas *n*; **~lock (gun)** Steinschloß(gewehr) *n*; **~y** ['-i] *a* aus Feuerstein; steinhart; *fig* hart(herzig), unnachgiebig.

flip [flip] *tr* wegschnippen, -schnipsen; schnellen; *Am sl (auf e-n fahrenden Zug)* aufspringen; in gute Stimmung bringen; beeindrucken; *itr* schnippen; *Am sl* sich kaputtlachen; völlig perplex, ganz begeistert sein; hin u. her tanzen; *to ~ back (Zweig)* zurückschnellen; *a sl* schnippisch; *s* Schnippen, Knipsen *n*; Klaps; Ruck *m*; (kleine) Spritztour *f*; *Am sl* Spaß, Clou; *aero sl* kurze(r) Rund-, Probeflug; *Art* (Eier-)Punsch *m*; *to ~ o.'s lid (Am sl)* rasend werden; sich totlachen wollen; **~-flap** Klippklapp *n*; Purzelbaum; Schwärmer *m (Feuerwerkskörper)*; **~-flop** *Am sl* starke(s) Auf u. Ab *n*; schneller Umschwung *m*; **~pancy** ['-ənsi] Respektlosigkeit *f*, vorlaute(s) Benehmen *n*, Keckheit *f*; **~pant** ['-ənt] vorlaut, respektlos, leichtfertig; **~per** ['-ə] *zoo tech* Flosse; *sl* Flosse, Hand *f*; *aero sl* Höhenruder, -steuer *n*; **~ side** *sl (Schallplatte)* Rückseite *f*.

flirt [flə:t] *tr* schnell hin- u. herwerfen, -bewegen, wippen mit; schnellen; *itr* hin u. her tanzen, wippen; flattern, springen; *fig* kokettieren, flirten, poussieren; liebäugeln, spielen (*with an idea of doing s.th.* mit e-m Gedanken, etw zu tun); *s* schnelle Bewegung *f*, Ruck *m*; Wippen, Flattern *n*; schnelle(r) Wurf; Poussierstengel *m*; Kokette *f*; **~ation** [flə:'teiʃən] Koketterie *f*, Flirten *n*; Flirt *m*, Liebelei *f*; **~atious** [flə:'teiʃəs] gefallsüchtig, locker, kokett; flirtend, tändelnd.

flit [flit] *itr* wandern, ziehen; (heimlich) weg-, umziehen; *(Vögel)* fortfliegen; flattern, huschen, flitzen; *fig fam* sich aus dem Staub machen; *to ~ about* umherflattern, -huschen; lautlos hin- u. hergehen; *to ~ by* vorbeihuschen, -flitzen; *(Zeit)* rasch vergehen; *to ~ to and fro* hin u. her huschen; *to ~ through o.'s mind* im Kopf herumgehen.

flitch [flitʃ] Speckseite; (Holz-)Schwarte *f*; Heilbuttschnitte *f*.

flitter ['flitə] *itr* flattern; zittern; *(Herz)* pochen; **~-mouse** Fledermaus *f*.

flivver ['flivə] *s Am sl* Kiste *f*, Klapperkasten *m*, Plunder; Versager *m*; *itr Am sl* schiefgehen, mißlingen.

float [flout] *s tech* Schwimmer *m*; Fischblase *f*; Rettungsring *m*; Floß *n*; schwimmende Masse *f*; *aero* Schwimmwerk *n*; Karren; Plattform-, Rollwagen; Festzugswagen *m*; Reibebrett *n (der Maurer)*; *Am (Schule)* Spring-, Hohlstunde *f*; *a. pl theat* Rampenlicht *n*; *itr* (obenauf) schwimmen; hochsteigen; (dahin)treiben *(a. im Winde)*; sich treiben lassen; sich sacht bewegen; schweben, gleiten; *fig (durch den Kopf)* ziehen; *com* im Umlauf sein; *el* auf freiem Potential liegen; *tr* flottmachen, über Wasser halten; flößen; überfluten, überschwemmen; *(mit Zement)* bestreichen; in Umlauf bringen; *(Gerücht)* verbreiten; auf den Markt bringen, umsetzen; *(Obligation)* ausgeben; *(Anleihe)* auflegen, begeben; *(Handelsgesellschaft)* gründen; *to ~ out* hinaustreiben (*to sea* auf das Meer; *upon the lake* auf den See); **~able** ['-əbl] schwimmfähig; *(Wasserlauf)* flößbar; **~age, flotage** ['-idʒ] Schwimmen *n*; Schwimmfähigkeit *f*; Schwimmende(s); Treibgut *n*; **~ation, flotation** [-'teiʃən] Schwimmen; Flottmachen *n*; Ausgabe *(von Obligationen)*; *(Anleihe)* Auflage; *com* Gründung *f*; **~ chamber** *mot* Schwimmergehäuse *n*; **~er** ['-ə] *mot* Schwimmer; Gründer *m (e-r Handelsgesellschaft)*; erstklassige(s) Wertpapier *n*; Pauschalversicherung *f*; *sl fig* Fehler, Mißgriff; *Am* Parteilose(r) *m*; jem, der häufig die Wohnung *od* den Arbeitsplatz wechselt; **~ file** Umlaufmappe *f*; **~ing** ['-iŋ] *a* schwimmend, treibend, schwebend; beweglich, schwankend, Veränderungen unterworfen; *(Bevölkerung)* fluktuierend; *tech* federnd gelagert; *el* ohne definiertes Potential; *com* im Umlauf befindlich, zirkulierend; Umlaufs-; *(Schuld)* schwebend; *(Verbindlichkeiten)* laufend; *(Kapital)* flüssig; Betriebs-; *s* Finanzierung *f*; *to be ~~ on air (Am fam)* im siebenten Himmel sein; *~~ anchor* Treibanker *m*; *~~ assets (pl), capital, fund* Umlaufs-, Betriebskapital *n*; *~~ bridge* Schiffs-, Floßbrücke *f*; *~~ crane* Schwimmkran *m*; *~~ dock* Schwimmdock *n*; *~~ ice* Treibeis *n*; *~~ island* Eierkrem *f* mit Schneeklößchen; *~~ kidney (med)* Wanderniere *f*; *~~ light* Leuchtschiff *n*; *~~ mine* Treibmine *f*; *~~ rates (pl)* Seefrachtsätze *m pl*; *~~ ribs (anat) pl* fliegende Rippen *f pl*; *~~ supply (com)* laufende(s) Angebot *n*; *~~ vote* Mitläufer *m pl*; **~ needle** *mot* Schwimmernadel *f*; **~-plane** Schwimmerflugzeug *n*; **~ valve** Schwimmerventil *n*.

floccul|e ['flɔkju:l] Staubflocke *f*; Flöckchen *n*; **~ent** ['flɔkjulənt] wollig, flauschig; *(Insekt)* bepelzt.

flock [flɔk] **1.** *s* Herde *f (von Kleinvieh)*; *(Vögel)* Schwarm, Zug; Flug *m (Wildgänse)*; Menge *(Menschen* od *Dinge)*, Schar *f*, Haufen *m*; *die* Gläubigen *pl (e-r Kirche)*; Kinderschar *f (in einer Familie)*; *itr (to ~ together)* zs.kommen, sich sammeln, sich zs.-scharen; sich scharen (*round s.o.* um jdn); strömen (*into* in); in Gruppen wandern *od* reisen; *in ~s* in (hellen) Scharen; *to ~ out of* herausströmen; *to ~ to* strömen, sich drängen nach; **2.** flockige(r) Niederschlag; Woll- *od* Baumwollabfall *m*, Polsterflocke *f*; *tr* mit Wolle *od* Baumwolle ausstopfen; *(Glas)* aufrauhen; **~ mattress** Wollmatratze *f*; **~ silk** Flockseide *f*; **~y** ['-i] flockig.

floe [flou] Treibeis *n*; Eisscholle *f*.

flog [flɔg] *tr* (aus)peitschen, verprügeln, verdreschen; *sl* verschachern; klauen; *to ~ a dead horse* offene Türen einrennen; **~ging** ['-iŋ] Prügel *m pl*; Auspeitschen *n*; Prügelstrafe *f*.

flood [flʌd] *s* Flut *f*, Hochwasser *n*, Überschwemmung; *mar (~-tide)* Flut; *fig* Flut *f*, (Wort-)Schwall *m*; *(Menschen)* Menge *f*; Strom; *fam* Scheinwerfer(licht *n*) *m*; *the F~* die Sintflut; *tr* überschwemmen, überfluten *a. fig*; *mar* fluten; *fig* überschütten (*with* mit); *tech* anstrahlen; *itr (Wasser)* steigen; strömen; sich ergießen, sich stürzen; überlaufen; *(Fluß)* über die Ufer treten; *at the ~ (fig)* im günstigsten Augenblick; *to ~ in* hereinstürmen; hineinströmen; *to ~ out (itr)* herausströmen; *tr* durch Hochwasser aus der Wohnung vertreiben; *to ~ over* überspülen; *~s of rain* Regenfluten *f pl*; **~ control** Schutzmaßnahmen *f pl* gegen Überschwemmung; **~ disaster** Hochwasserkatastrophe *f*; **~-gate** Schleusentor *n*; *fig* Riegel *m*, Schleuse *f*; **~-lamp** Fotolampe *f*, Strahler *m*; **~-level** Hochwasserspiegel *m*; **~light** *s* Scheinwerfer(licht *n*) *m*, Flutleuchte; *(~~ system)* Anstrahlung *f*; *tr* anstrahlen, beleuchten; *~~ projector* Scheinwerfer *m*; **~lit** ['-lit] *a* angestrahlt, angeleuchtet; **~-mark** Hochwassermarke *f*; **~-plain** Schwemmland *n*.

floor [flɔ:, flɔə] *s* Fußboden; Flur *m*, Diele *f*; Stockwerk *n*, Etage, *f*, Geschoß *n*; *allg (z.B. Meeres-)* Boden, Grund *m*; *tech* Brückenfahrbahn *f*; *fig die* Anwesenden, *parl* Abgeordneten *m pl*; Sitzungssaal *m*; Mindestgrenze, unterste Grenze *f*; *(~ price)* Mindestpreis; Börsensaal *m*, Parkett *n*; *tr (Haus)* dielen; zu Boden strecken, niederschlagen; *fam (Menschen)* erledigen, fertigmachen; *fam* den Mund stopfen (*s.o.* jdm) *sl (Examensfrage)* mühelos beantworten; *Am sl* mit Vollgas fahren; *to give the ~ (Am)* das Wort erteilen; *to take the ~* tanzen; *Am* das Wort ergreifen; *may I have the ~ (Am)* ich bitte ums Wort; **~-cloth** Bodenbelag *m*; Scheuertuch *n*; **~er** ['-rə] harte(r), schwere(r) Schlag *m a. fig*; *fig fam* harte Nuß, Fang-, schwere Frage *f*; *fig* Schlag *m* ins Gesicht; **~ing** ['-riŋ] Fußboden *m*, -böden *pl*; Fußbodenmaterial *n*, -belag *m*; **~-lamp, standard** Stehlampe *f*; **~ leader** *Am parl* Fraktionsvorsitzende(r) *m*; **~ mat** Bodenmatte *f*; **~-plan** Stockwerkgrundriß *m*; **~-show** Nachtklubprogramm *n*; **~ space** Bodenfläche *f*; **~ switch** Stockwerkschalter *m*; **~ tile** Fliese *f*; **~-walker** *Am* Abteilungsleiter *m (in e-m Warenhaus)*; **~-wax, ~ polish** Bohnerwachs *n*.

flop [flɔp] *itr* (herum)flattern, (herum-)hopsen; plumpsen, sacken; *(to ~ down)* sich *(in e-n Sessel)* fallen lassen; sich werfen; *fam* zs.sacken; schiefgehen; *theat* durchfallen; *sl* einpennen; *Am (zur andern Partei)* übergehen, umschwenken; *Am sl* sich zum Schlafen hinlegen; *Am sl (in e-m Examen)* durchfallen; *tr* (hin)knallen, (hin)schmeißen; durchfallen lassen; *s* Schwupp, Wupp, Plumps *m*; *Am fam* Umschwenken *n*; *fam* Reinfall *m*, Fiasko *n*, Mißerfolg *m*; Niete *f*, Versager *m (Mensch)*; *sl* Falle *f (Schlafstelle)*; **~house** *Am sl* Übernachtungsheim *n*, Penne *f*; **~per** ['-ə] *Am fam fig* Windfahne *f*; **~(p)eroo** ['-əru:] *Am sl* Reinfall *m*; **~py** ['-i] schlaff; schlapp *a. fig*; schluderig.

flor|a ['flɔ:rə] *pl -as* u. *-ae* [-i:] Flora, Pflanzenwelt *f*; **~al** ['flɔ:rəl] *a* Blumen-, Blüten-; *~~ design* Blumenmuster *n*; **~et** ['flɔ:rit] kleine Blüte *f (bes. der Korbblütler)*; **~iculture** ['flɔ:rikʌltʃə] Blumenzucht *f*; **~id** ['flɔrid] *(Aussehen, Gesichtsfarbe)* blühend, gesund, rosig, frisch; *(Kunst)* (zu) reich verziert, überladen; blumig; **~idity** [-'riditi], **~idness** ['-idnis] gesunde Farbe *f*, blühende(s) Aussehen *n*; Überladenheit *f*, blumige(r) Stil *m*; **~ist** ['flɔrist] Blumenhändler, -züchter, -liebhaber *m*; *~~'s shop* Blumenladen *m*.

Floren|ce ['flɔrəns] Florenz *n*; **~tine** ['-tain] *a* florentinisch; *s* Florentiner(in *f*) *m*.

florin ['flɔrin] Gulden *m*; Zweischillingstück *n*.

floss [flɔs] Rohseide; Flockseide; *(-silk)* Florett-, Galettseide, Schappe, Filoselle *f*; *bot* Samenflaum *m*; **~y** ['-i] *a* flaumig, (seiden)weich; *Am sl* aufgedonnert; elegant; modisch; *s Am sl* Mädchen *n*, Frau *f*.

flotage, ~ation *s. floatage, floatation.*

flotilla [flo(u)'tilə] Flotille *f*.

flotsam ['flɔtsəm] Seetrift *f*; *~ and jetsam* Strandgut *n a. fig.*

flounce [flauns] **1.** *itr (to ~ up) (gereizt)* auf-, in die Höhe fahren (*out of a chair* aus e-m Stuhl); *(to ~ down)* sich verärgert, erregt hinsetzen; (sich) stürzen, losstürzen; *to ~ out* verärgert hinausstürzen (*of a room* aus e-m Zimmer); *s* (plötzlicher) Ruck *m (des Körpers)*; ärgerliche Bewegung *f*; **2.** *s* Besatz, Volant *m*, Falbel *f*; *tr* fälbeln.

flounder ['flaundə] **1.** *itr* sich vergeblich abmühen; sich zu befreien, los-, vorwärtszukommen suchen; herumpflatschen, -waten (*about the water* im Wasser); hilflos, (*fam* sich tot)zappeln; sich abquälen (*through s.th.* mit etw); umhertappen, -taumeln, -stolpern; *fam* Murks machen; sich verheddern; **2.** Flunder *f*, Butt *m (Fisch)*.

flour ['flauə] *s* (*bes.* Weizen-, Weiß-) Mehl; *allg* Mehl, Pulver *n*, Puder *m*; *tr Am* zu Mehl mahlen; *(Küche)* mit Mehl bestreuen; pudern; **~-mill** Getreidemühle *f*; **~y** ['-ri] mehlig.

flourish ['flʌriʃ] *itr* sich gut entwickeln, gedeihen, blühen, (gut) vorankommen; prahlen; Schnörkel, Floskeln machen; geziert schreiben *od* sprechen; *mus* präludieren; e-n Tusch ausbringen; *tr* verschnörkeln; verzieren, schmücken; *(Waffe)* schwingen; *(Fahne)* schwenken; *(Tusch)* blasen, ausbringen; *s* Schnörkel *m*, Floskel *a. fig*; Zierleiste; *mus* Verzierung *f*; Tusch *m*, Fanfare *f*; Schwenken, Schwingen *n*; große Geste *f*; **~ing** ['-iŋ] blühend.

flout [flaut] *tr* verspotten, verhöhnen, verlachen; mißachten; *(Befehl)* verweigern; *itr* spotten, höhnen (*at* über); *s* Spott, Hohn *m*.

flow [flou] *itr* fließen, strömen *a. fig*; *(Blut)* zirkulieren; münden (*into the lake* in den See); rinnen, gleiten; überfließen *a. fig* (*with* von); *(Flut)* steigen; herrühren, -kommen, -stammen (*from* von); *(Menschen)* strömen (*out of the theatre* aus dem Theater); *tr* überfluten; *to ~ down (Haar)* herunterhängen; fallen; *to ~ in* hereinströmen; *s* Fließen, Strömen, Rinnen *n*; Fluß, Strom *m*, Gerinnsel, Rinnsal *n*; Strömung *f*; Zu-, Ab-, Überfluß; Zustrom *m*; *com* Menge *f*, Verkehr; *(~ of words)* (Wort-)Schwall *m*; *(~ing tide)* Flut *f*; *the river ~ed over its banks* der Fluß trat über die Ufer; *~ of business* Geschäftsgang *m*; *~ of commodities* Warenverkehr *m*; *~ of currency* Geldumlauf *m*; *~ of traffic* Verkehrsstrom *m*; **~ing** ['-iŋ] fließend, strömend, gleitend; überströmend, -schäumend; wallend; *fig* flüssig, lebhaft; *~~ well* artesische(r) Brunnen *m*.

flower ['flauə] *s* Blume, Blüte *a. fig*; *fig* Zier(de) *f*, Schmuck *m*; *das* Beste, *die* Auslese; Blütezeit *f*, Höhepunkt *m*; *fam* Blutung; *pl chem* Blüte *f*; *itr* blühen *a. fig*; *fig* den Höhepunkt erreicht haben; *(to be) in ~* in Blüte (stehen); *say it with ~s* laßt Blumen sprechen; *in the ~ of o.'s age, strength* in der Blüte der Jahre; *cut ~s (pl)* Schnittblumen *f pl*; *~s of sulphur (chem)* Schwefelblüte *f*; **~age** ['-ridʒ] Blumenflor *m*; Blüte(zeit) *f*; **~-bed** Blumenbeet *n*; **~ cup** Blütenkelch *m*; **~-de-luce** [flauədə'lju:s] *Am* Lilie; Schwertlilie *f*; **~ed** ['-d] *a* mit Blumen geschmückt; geblümt; **~-garden** Blumengarten *m*; **~-girl** Blumenverkäuferin *f*; **~iness** ['-rinis] Blüten-, Blumen-, Bilderreichtum *m*; **~ing** ['-riŋ] (lebhaft) blühend; **~ petal** Blumenblatt *n*; **~pot** ['-pɔt] Blumentopf *m*; **~ shop** Blumengeschäft *n*, -laden *m*; **~-show** Blumenschau *f*, -korso *m*; **~y** ['-ri] blumenreich, blumig; *(Stil)* bilderreich, überladen.

*

flu [flu:] *(influenza) fam* Grippe *f*.

flub [flʌb] *Am fam tr* verkorksen; *s* Doofling; Schnitzer, Versager *m*; **~dub** ['-dʌb] *Am sl* Gequatsche, Gefasel *n*; Ungeschicklichkeit *f*.

fluctuat|e ['flʌktjueit] *itr* schwanken *a. fig*, fluktuieren, steigen u. fallen; sich ändern; **~ion** [flʌktju'eiʃən] Schwanken *n*, Schwankung *f*; *seasonal ~~s (pl)* Saisonschwankungen *f pl*; *~~ of costs* Kostenbewegung *f*; *~~ of power* Leistungsschwankung *f*; *~~s of prices, of temperature* Preis-, Temperaturschwankungen *f pl*.

flue [flu:] **1.** *s* Rauchfang, -schacht, -abzug; Ofen-, Feuerzug *m*, Heizröhre *f*, Heizungsrohr *n*; Kernspalt, *(~-pipe)* Lippenpfeife *f*; **~ boiler** Flammrohrkessel *m*; **~ dust, ash** Flugasche *f*; **~ gas** Rauchgas *n*; **2.** *s* Flocke *f*; **3.** *s* Schleppnetz *n*; **4.** *tr (Fenster)* ausschrägen; *itr* geweitet, ausgeschrägt sein.

fluen|cy ['flu(:)ənsi] (Rede-)Fluß *m*; Geläufigkeit, (Rede-)Gewandtheit *f*; **~t** ['-t] *(Rede)* fließend; *(Redner)* gewandt; *(Stil)* flüssig; *to speak ~~ English* fließend Englisch sprechen.

fluff [flʌf] *s* Flaumfeder; (Feder-, Haar-, Woll-, Staub-)Flocke *f*; Flaum; Bartflaum *m*; *Am* junge(s) Volk; *(bit of ~) sl* Mädel *n*; *theat* schlecht gelernte Rolle *f*; *theat radio* Sprechfehler *m*, Versprechen *n*; *Am sl* Entlassung; *Am sl* leichte Arbeit *f*; *tr (to ~ out)* aufplustern; *theat radio* falsch sagen, falsch lesen; *(Auftritt) sl* verpfuschen, versauen; *to ~ off (Am sl)* herunterputzen; *itr* Flocken bilden; *to give s.o. the ~ (Am sl)* jdn abkanzeln, 'rauswerfen; **~-off** *Am sl* Drückeberger; ungeschickte(r) Mensch *m*; **~y** ['-i] (feder)weich, flaumig; aufgeplustert; *theat sl* stümperhaft; *sl* torkelnd, schwankend; besoffen.

fluid ['flu(:)id] *a* flüssig; gasförmig; *fig* veränderlich, beweglich; *s chem* Flüssigkeit *f*, Gas *n*; **~ drive** hydraulische(s) Getriebe *n*; **~ity** [flu(:)'iditi] Dünnflüssigkeit *f*.

fluk|e [flu:k] **1.** *s* Ankerpflug, -flügel *m*, -hand; *(Pfeil)* Fiederung *f*; Schwanzflosse des Wales; Flunder; Scholle *f*, Plattfisch; *med* Plattwurm *m*; **2.** *s* glückliche(r) Zufall, *sl* Dusel *m*; **~ey, ~y** ['-i] *sl* wechsel-, launenhaft, ungewiß; Zufalls-.

flume [flu:m] (künstlicher) Wassergraben, Kanal *m*; *Am* Klamm *f*.

flummery ['flʌməri] Hafer-, Mehlbrei; Flammeri *m*; *fig* bloße Schmeichelei *f*; dumme(s) Gerede *n*.

flummox ['flʌməks] *tr sl* durchea.-bringen, verrückt machen.

flunk [flʌŋk] *Am fam tr* durchfallen in *(e-r Prüfung)*; durchfallen lassen; zum Scheitern bringen; *itr* versagen, *(in e-r Prüfung)* durchfallen; sich drücken, sich verdünnisieren; die Flinte ins Korn werfen; aufgeben; *s* Versagen, Durchfallen *n*; Reinfall *m*; schlechte Note *f*; Durchgefallene(r) *m*; *to ~ out (fam) tr* aus der Schule entfernen; *itr* ausscheiden.

flunkey, *Am* **flunky** ['flʌŋki] Lakai *m meist pej*; Bedientenseele *f*, Speichellecker *m*; **~ism** ['-izm] Herumscharwenzeln *n*; Speichelleckerei *f*.

fluor [flu(:)ɔ:] *min* Flußspat *m*; **~esce** [fluə'res] *itr phys* fluoreszieren; **~escence** [fluə'resns] Fluoreszenz *f*; **~escent** [fluə'resnt] fluoreszierend; *~~ lamp* Leuchtstofflampe *f*; *~~ lighting* Neonbeleuchtung *f*; *~~ screen* Leuchtschirm *m*; *~~ tube* Leuchtstoffröhre *f*; **~ide** ['fluəraid] *chem* Fluorid *n*; **~ine** ['fluəri:n] *chem* Fluor *n*; **~ite** ['fluərait], **~spar** ['fluə-spa:] *min* Flußspat *m*.

flurry ['flʌri] *s (~ of wind)* Windstoß; Regen-, Hagelschauer *m*, Schneegestöber; *fig* plötzliche(s) Durcheinander *n*, Verwirrung, Aufregung *f*; *tr* durchea.bringen; konfus, verwirrt machen, aufregen; *in a ~ (of alarm, of excitement)* in (großer) Aufregung.

flush [flʌʃ] *itr* strömen, sich ergießen; *(Blut)* schießen; rot werden *(with anger* vor Wut); erröten, erglühen; begeistert sein *(with* über); (aus)gespült werden; *(Vogel)* auffliegen; *tr* (aus-, durch)spülen; überfluten, überschwemmen; erröten lassen; in Stimmung bringen, aufheitern, aufmuntern, ermutigen, stolz machen; an-, erregen; *(Vögel)* aufjagen, -scheuchen; *(Mauer)* verstreichen; *s* (Wasser-)Guß *m*, Spülung *f*; (Auf-, Empor-)Schießen; kräftige(s) Wachstum, Auf-, Erblühen *n*, Blüte, Frische, Kraft, Fülle; Aufheiterung, (frohe) Erregung *f*, Aufwallen; Erröten, Erglühen *n*; Fieberanfall, -schauer *m*; *(Karten)* Sequenz *f*; Vogelschwarm *m*; *a* reichlich *(bes. mit Geld)* versehen, versorgt *(of* mit); im Überfluß vorhanden, üppig, reichlich; verschwenderisch, großzügig, freigebig *(with* mit); kräftig, frisch, blühend; von frischer Farbe; glühend; eben, platt, flach, in gleicher Ebene, bündig *(with* mit); *typ* ohne Einzug; *tech* versenkbar, versenkt; *adv* gerade; direkt; *to be ~* gut bei Kasse, reichlich versorgt sein *(of* mit); **~ing** ['-iŋ] Spülung *f*; *~~ box* Spülkasten *m*.

fluster ['flʌstə] *tr* verwirrt, nervös, aufgeregt machen; *s* Verwirrung, Nervosität *f*; *all in a ~* ganz verwirrt.

flut|e [flu:t] *s* Flöte; Stange *f* (Brot); Sektglas *n*; *(Kleidung)* (Zier-)Falte, Rüsche; *arch* Rinne, Kehle *f*; *tr* auf der Flöte spielen; flöten; kräuseln, fälteln, plissieren; *arch* auskehlen, riefe(l)n; *itr* Flöte spielen; **~ed** ['-id] *a (Säule)* kanneliert; flötenartig; **~ing** ['-iŋ] Flötenspiel; Flöten *n*; Fältelung *f*, Plissee *n*; Riefelung; *arch* Kannelierung *f*; *~~-iron* Plissiereisen *n*; **~ist** ['-ist] Flötenspieler, Flötist *m*.

flutter ['flʌtə] *itr (Vogel)* flattern *(a. Fahne im Wind)*; sich ziellos hin u. her bewegen; nervös umhergehen; zittern; erregt, unruhig, nervös sein; *(Herz)* schnell schlagen; *(Puls)* jagen; *tr* (schnell) hin u. her bewegen; in Unruhe, Aufregung versetzen; *s* Geflatter; Zittern *n*; Erregung, innere Unruhe, Aufregung; Herzbeschleunigung; *sl* Spekulation *f*; *to be, to put in a ~* in Unruhe, Aufregung sein, versetzen; *to cause, to make a ~ (fig)* Wind machen; *to have a ~ (sl)* spekulieren.

fluvi|al ['flu:viəl] *a* Fluß-.

flux [flʌks] *s* Fluß *m*, Fließen, Strömen; Steigen *n* der Flut; ständige Bewegung *f*, dauernde(r) Wechsel *m*, Veränderung *f*; *med* Fluß *m*; *tech* Löt-, Schweißpaste *f*, Zuschlag *m*: *tr (Metall)* schmelzen; *med* purgieren; **~ion** ['flʌkʃən] Fluß *a. med*, beständige(r) Wechsel; (Aus-)Fluß *m*; *math* Differential *n*; *method of ~~s* Differential- u. Integralrechnung *f*; **~ionary** ['-kʃnəri] fließend, wechselnd; veränderlich.

*

fly [flai] *irr flew, flown* [flu:, floun] **1.** *itr (Vogel, Insekt, Flugzeug, Pilot, Fluggast)* fliegen; fliegen, schweben, wehen, flattern; fliegen, sausen, schlagen; herbeieilen, -stürzen *(to the rescue* zur Rettung); jagen, sich stürzen, (ent)fliehen, (ent)eilen; *(Zeit)* vergehen, verfliegen; *(Geld)* dahinschwinden; *(Glas)* e-n Sprung bekommen; **2.** *tr* fliegen lassen; *(Drachen)* steigen lassen; *(Flugzeug, Fluggast, Fracht)* fliegen; im Flugzeug befördern; fliegen über, überfliegen; befliegen; fliehen, meiden, aus dem Wege gehen *(s.o., s.th.* jdm, e-r S); **3.** *s* Fliegen *n*, Flug *m*; Flugstrecke; *(bes.* Stuben-)Fliege; *(künstliche)* Angelfliege; Klappe *f*; (Hosen-)Schlitz *m*; Zelttür *f*, Überzelt *n*; *typ* Greifer *m*; *(Uhr)* Unruhe; *Br* Droschke; Freitreppe *f*; Flugblatt *n*; *pl theat* Soffitten *f pl*; **4.** *a sl* fix, flink, geschickt; gewieft, gerissen, auf Draht; **5.** *a ~ in the ointment* ein Haar in der Suppe; *on the ~* im Fluge; *sl* in Eile; *there are no flies on him* er ist auf Draht; **6.** *to let ~ (at)* angreifen; *to make the dust* od *feathers ~ (fig)* Staub aufwirbeln; *to make the money ~ (fig)* das Geld zum Fenster hinauswerfen, unter die Leute bringen; *to ~ blind, on instruments* blindfliegen; *to ~ the coop (Am fam)* sich aus dem Staub machen; *to ~ in s.o.'s face (fig)* jdm ins Gesicht fahren *od* springen; jdn herausfordern; *to ~ a flag* e-e Fahne hissen, *(Schiff)* führen; unter e-r Flagge fahren; *to ~ (at) high (game)* hochfliegende Pläne, *fam* große Rosinen im Kopf haben; *to ~ a kite* e-n Versuchsballon steigen lassen; *com* auf Gefälligkeitswechsel borgen; *to ~ in pieces* in Stücke springen; *to ~ into a rage, temper, passion* wütend werden, in Wut geraten; *to ~ off the handle (fig)* außer sich geraten; *to ~ right (Am fam)* ein ordentlicher Mensch sein; *I told him to go ~ a kite (Am sl)* ich sagte ihm, er solle sich zum Teufel scheren; *to ~* **about** herumfliegen; *(Nachrichten)* sich verbreiten; *to ~* **abroad** sich verbreiten; *to ~* **apart** ausea.fliegen; sich abstoßen; *to ~* **at,** *to ~* **upon** sich stürzen auf, herfallen über; *to ~* **in** *aero* einfliegen; *to* ~ **into** geraten in; *to* ~ **off** wegfliegen; *(Knopf)* abgehen; abdampfen, abhauen; *to* ~ **out** ausfällig werden (*at s.o.* gegen jdn); *aero* ausfliegen; herausstürzen (*of the room* aus dem Zimmer); außer sich geraten; *to* ~ **over** überfliegen; *to* ~ **past** vorbeirasen; *to* ~ **up** hinauffliegen (*to* zu); ~**able** ['-əbl]: ~~ *weather* Flugwetter *n*; ~ **agaric** Fliegenpilz *m*; ~**away** *a* flatternd, wehend; flüchtig, unbeständig; *s* Ausreißer; wetterwendische(r) Mensch *m*; ~**-blow** *s meist pl* (Schmeiß-)Fliegeneier *n pl*; *tr* beschmeißen *(Fleisch)*; *fig* beschmutzen, verderben; ~**-blown** *a* verschmutzt, verdorben, schlecht; anrüchig, verrufen; *sl* besoffen; *sl* schäbig; ~**-by-night** *s* Nachtbummler; flüchtige(r) Schuldner *m*; *a* unzuverlässig; zweifelhaft; (finanziell) schwach; ~**catcher** *orn* Fliegenschnäpper *m*; fleischfressende Pflanze *f*; Fliegenfänger *m*; ~**-fisher** Fischer *m*, der mit e-r künstlichen Fliege fischt; ~**-leaf** *(Buch)* Vorsatzblatt *n*; ~**-mug, -dick, -bob** *Am sl* Polizist *m*; ~**-over** überschneidungsfreie Kreuzung *f*; ~**-paper** Fliegenfänger *m*; ~**-past, -by** Flugparade *f*, Vorbeiflug *m*; ~**-sheet** Flugblatt *n*; ~**-speck** Fliegenschmutz *m*; ~**-trap** Fliegenfalle; fleischfressende Pflanze *f*; *Venus's* ~~ *(bot)* Venusfliegenfalle *f*; ~**way** Flugweg *m (der Zugvögel)*; ~**-weight** *(Boxen)* Fliegengewicht *n*; ~**-wheel** ['-wi:l] *tech* Schwungrad *n*.

flyer, flier ['flaiə] Flieger, Flugzeugführer; Expreß, Blitz(zug); Flüchtling *m*; Rennpferd *n*; *Am sport* Sprung *m* mit Anlauf; *Am* Handzettel *m*, Flugblatt *n*; (Treppen-)Stufe *f*; *tech* (Spindel-)Flügel, Fleier *m*; *Am fam* gewagte (Börsen-)Spekulation *f*; *Am* (Spezial-)Versandkatalog *m*; *pl* Freitreppe *f*.

flying ['flaiiŋ] *a* fliegend, flugfähig; fliegend, wehend; schnell; eilig, kurz; *bes. aero* Flug-; *s* Fliegen; Flugwesen *n*, Luftfahrt *f*; *in* ~ *condition* flug-, startbereit; *with flags* ~, *(bes. fig) with* ~ *colo(u)rs* mit fliegenden Fahnen; ~ **accident** Flugzeugunglück *n*; ~ **allowance** Fliegerzulage *f*; ~ **badge** Fliegerabzeichen *n*; ~ **boat** Flugboot *n*; ~ **bomb** V-Waffe *f*; ~ **boot** Fliegerstiefel *m*; ~ **boxcar** *Am* fliegende(r) Güterwagen *m*; ~ **buttress** *arch* Strebebogen *m*; ~ **clothing** Fliegerkleidung *f*; ~ **control** *Br* Flugleitung *f*; ~ **crew** Flugzeugbesatzung *f*; ~ **deck** Landedeck *n (Flugzeugträger)*; ~ **distance** Flugstrecke *f*; **F**~ **Dutchman** Fliegende(r) Holländer *m*; ~ **exhibition** Wanderausstellung *f*; ~ **experience** Flugerfahrung *f*; ~ **field** Flugplatz *m*; ~**-fish** fliegende(r) Fisch *m*; ~ **formation** fliegende(r) Verband *m*; ~ **hour** Flugstunde *f*; ~ **instructor** Fluglehrer *m*; ~ **jump** Sprung *m* mit Anlauf; ~ **lane** Flugschneise *f*; ~ **man** Flieger *m*; **F**~ **Officer** Oberleutnant *m*; ~ **pay** Fliegerzulage *f*; ~ **personnel** fliegende(s) Personal *n*; ~ **pupil, student** Flugschüler *m*; ~ **range** Aktionsradius *m*; ~ **safety** Flugsicherheit *f*; ~**-saucer** fliegende Untertasse *f*; ~ **speed** Fluggeschwindigkeit *f*; ~ **squad** *Br* Überfallkommando *n*; *(Arbeitseinsatz)* fliegende Gruppe *f*; ~ **squadron** Fliegerstaffel *f*; ~ **suit** Kombination *f*; ~ **time** Flugzeit *f*; ~ **unit** fliegende(r) Verband *m*; ~ **visit** Stippvisite *f*; ~ **weather** Flugwetter *n*; ~ **wing** Nurflügelflugzeug *n*.

foal [foul] *s* Fohlen, Füllen *n*; *itr* fohlen; *tr (ein Fohlen)* werfen; *in, with* ~ *(Stute)* trächtig.

foam [foum] *s* Schaum; Gischt *m*; *itr* schäumen (*with rage* vor Wut); *to* ~ *at the mouth* vor Wut schäumen; ~**ing** ['-iŋ] schäumend; ~ **extinguisher** Schaumfeuerlöscher *m*; ~ **rubber** Schaumgummi *m* od *n*; ~**y** ['-i] schaumig; schaumbedeckt.

fob [fɔb] **1.** Uhrtasche (in der Kleidung); *Am* Uhrkette(nanhänger *m*) *f*; **2.** *tr* foppen, prellen, anführen, betrügen; *to* ~ *off* aufschwatzen, andrehen (*s.th. on s.o.* jdm etw); loskriegen; *to* ~ *s.o. off with empty promises* jdn mit leeren Versprechungen abspeisen; **3.** *Abk. für* free on board.

foc|al ['foukəl] *opt* fokal, Brenn(punkt-); ~~ *distance, length* Brennweite *f*; ~~ *point* Brennpunkt *m*; ~~ *plane shutter* Schlitzverschluß *m*; ~~ *view* Blickfeld *n*; ~**us** ['foukəs] *pl -es* od *-ci* ['fousai] *s math opt* Brennpunkt *m*, -weite; Bildschärfe *f*; *med* Krankheitsherd; *(Erdbeben)* Herd; *fig* Brennpunkt, Herd *m*, Zentrum *n*; *tr opt* im Brennpunkt vereinigen; *opt phot (to bring into* ~~*)* richtig, scharf einstellen; sammeln, bündeln; *fig* richten, konzentrieren (*on* auf); *in (out of)* ~~ *(opt phot)* (un)scharf eingestellt; ~**us(s)ing** ['-əsiŋ] Scharfeinstellung *f*; ~~ *lamp* Projektionslampe *f*; ~~ *magnifier* Einstellupe *f*; ~~ *point* Brennpunkt *m*; ~~ *screen* Mattscheibe *f*.

fodder ['fɔdə] *s* Trockenfutter *n*, Heu u. Stroh; *tr* füttern.

foe [fou] *poet* Feind, Widersacher *m* (*to* gen).

f(o)et|al ['fi:tl] *a scient* fötal; ~**us** ['fi:təs] Fötus *m*, Leibesfrucht *f*.

fog [fɔg] *s* (dicker) Nebel *m*; Rauch-, Staubdecke *(in der Atmosphäre)*; *fig* Umneb(e)lung, Verwirrung *f*; *phot film* (Grau-)Schleier *m*; *tr* vernebeln; *fig* umnebeln, trüben, verdunkeln; *phot* verschleiern; *itr* sich in Nebel hüllen; sich trüben, sich verdunkeln, sich beschlagen; ~**-bank** dichte Nebelschicht, -hülle, -bank *f*; ~**bound** *a mar aero* durch Nebel behindert; in Nebel gehüllt; ~**giness** ['-inis] Nebel *m*; Dunstigkeit, Nebligkeit; Um-, Verneb(e)lung *f*; ~**gy** ['-i] neb(e)lig; *fig* trüb(e), umwölkt, undeutlich, verwirrt; *phot* verschleiert; ~**horn** *mar* Nebelhorn *n*; ~**-lamp, light** *mot* Nebellampe *f*, -scheinwerfer *m*; ~**-layer** Nebelschicht *f*; ~**-signal** Nebelsignal *n*.

fog(e)y ['fougi] *meist: old* ~ altmodische(r), rückständige(r) Mensch *m*.

foible ['fɔibl] schwache Seite, Schwäche *f* (des Charakters).

foil [fɔil] **1.** *tr* e-n Strich durch die Rechnung machen (*s.o. in s.th.* jdm bei e-r S); *(Plan)* durchkreuzen; *(Versuch)* vereiteln, zuschanden machen; *s (Jagd)* (Duft-)Spur *f*; (Fechten mit) stumpfe(m) Rapier; Florett *n*; **2.** (Metall-)Folie; Goldfolie *f*, Goldgrund; Spiegelbelag; *fig* Hintergrund *m* (*to* für); *arch* Blattverzierung *f*.

foist [fɔist] *tr* (heimlich) einfügen, -schieben, -schmuggeln; unterschieben, unterstellen, anhängen, -drehen (*s.th. on, upon s.o.* jdm etw).

fold [fould] **1.** *tr* (zs.)falten, falzen, zs.-legen, -klappen; *(die Arme)* kreuzen, verschränken; *(die Hände)* falten; *(die Flügel)* anlegen; *(to* ~ *in o.'s arms)* in die Arme schließen, umarmen; einhüllen, -wickeln, -schlagen; *itr* sich zs.legen, zs.gelegt werden; gefaltet sein; *s* Falten *n*, Faltung; Falte *f*, Falz, Kniff, Knick, Bruch *m (im Papier)*; *(als Lesezeichen)* umgeschlagene Ecke *f*, Eselsohr *n*; Falte, Windung; *geol* Bodenfalte *f*; *in Zssgen* -fach; *to* ~ **back** zurückschlagen; umklappen; *(Ärmel)* umkrempeln; *to* ~ **down** *(Blatt Papier)* umschlagen, -knicken; *to* ~ **in,** *to* ~ **over,** *to* ~ **together** ein-, über-, zs.schlagen; *to* ~ **up** *tr* zs.legen; *(Geschäft)* schließen; *itr sl (Spiel)* verlieren, aufgeben (müssen); *(Zeitung)* eingehen; *allg* aufhören (müssen); *(Mensch)* zs.klappen; ~**er** ['-ə] Falzer *m*; Falzbein *n*; Schnellhefter, Aktendeckel *m*; Mappe *f*; Faltplan, -prospekt *m*; gefaltete Broschüre *f*; Merkblatt *n*; *pl* (zs.klappbarer) Kneifer, Klemmer *m*; ~**ing** ['-iŋ] *a* zs.leg-, zs.klappbar; Falt-; *s* Faltung *f*; Kniff *m*; *Am fam* Papiergeld *n*; ~~ *bed* Feldbett *n*; ~~ *boat* Faltboot *n*; ~~ *camera* Klappkamera *f*; ~~ *chair* Klappstuhl *m*; ~~ *deck* Klappverdeck *n*; ~~ *door* Falttür; *pl* Flügeltür *f*; ~~ *hat* Klappzylinder *m*; ~~ *money (Am fam)* Papiergeld *n*; ~ *roof (mot)* Klappverdeck *n*; ~~ *screen* spanische Wand *f*; ~~ *seat* Klappsitz *m*; ~~ *table* Klapptisch *m*; **2.** *s* Schafhürde *f*, Pferch *m*; Schafherde; *fig* Herde; (Gläubige *m pl* e-r) Kirche *f*; ((Mit-)Glieder *n pl* e-r) kirchliche(n) Organisation, weltanschauliche(n) *od* Interessengemeinschaft *f*; *tr (Schafe)* einpferchen; *to return to the* ~ *(fig)* reumütig zurückkehren.

foli|age ['fouliidʒ] *die* Blätter *pl (e-r Pflanze)*; Laub; Blatt-, Laubwerk *n (als Verzierung)*; ~~ *plant* Blattpflanze *f*; ~**ate** ['-eit] *tr* in dünne Schichten, Folien aufspalten; *(Gold)* zu Folie schlagen; *(Glas)* mit e-r Folie unterlegen, foliieren; mit Blattwerk verzieren; *(Buch)* foliieren, mit Blattzahlen versehen; *itr bot* Blätter treiben; *a* ['-it, '-eit] belaubt; Blatt-; ~**ation** [fouli'eiʃən] *bot* Blattbildung; Belaubung *f*; *metal* (Blatt-)Schlagen; *(Glas)* Unterlegen *n*, Foliierung; *min* Schieferung; *arch* Blattverzierung; *(Buch)* Foliierung, Blattzählung *f*; ~**o** ['fouliou] *pl -os s* Folio *n*, Halbbogen(größe *f*); Foliant *m*; *(Buch)* Blatt, *com* Folio *n*, Kontobuchseite; Seitenzahl *f*; *jur (US)* 100, *(England)* 72 *od* 90 Wörter *n pl*; *in* ~~ in Folio, im Folioformat; *first* ~~ Erstausgabe *f*.

folk [fouk] *pl* Volk *n*, Leute *pl*; *fam (o.'s* ~*s)* Familie *f*, Angehörige, Verwandte *m pl*; *the old* ~*s at home* die alten Herrschaften *f pl*; *just* ~*s (fam)* (nette) einfache Leute *pl*; ~**-dance** Volkstanz *m*; ~**lore** ['-lɔ:] Volkskunde *f*; ~**lorist** ['-lɔ:rist] Volkskundler, Folklorist *m*; ~**-music** Volksmusik *f*; ~**-song** *a Am fam* einfach, schlicht; gesellig; *s* Volkslied *n*; ~**sy** *fam* gesellig; volkstümlich; ~**-tale** Volkssage *f*.

follic|le ['fɔlikl] *anat* Follikel, (Haar-)Balg; *zoo* Kokon; *bot* Fruchtbalg *m*.

follow ['fɔlou] *tr* folgen, nachgehen, nachkommen (*s.o.* jdm); folgen auf; sich anschließen (*s.o.* jdm); begleiten; Gesellschaft leisten, zu Diensten sein (*s.o.* jdm); verfolgen *(a. e-n Weg, ein Ziel)*; *(zeitl., im Amt)* folgen (*s.o.* jdm), folgen auf; *(Beruf)* ausüben; *(Geschäft)* (be)treiben; *(Laufbahn)* einschlagen; nachfolgen, -eifern (*s.o.* jdm); nachahmen, zum Vorbild nehmen, sich richten nach; einverstanden sein mit; gehorchen (*s.o.* jdm); *(Regel)* beachten, befolgen; *(e-m Gedankengang)* sich anschließen; folgen (*s.o.'s ideas* jds Gedankengängen); mitkommen mit; *(Gespräch, Geschehen, die*

Politik) (mit Interesse) verfolgen; sich kümmern um; *itr* (er)folgen, sich ergeben (*from* aus); zunächst kommen; sich später ereignen; *s* Folgen *n*; *(Billard)* Nachläufer *m*; *(Gaststätte)* Nachbestellung *f*; *to ~ one another* aufea.folgen; *to ~ close* auf dem Fuße folgen; *to ~ the fashion* sich nach der Mode richten, die M. mitmachen; *to ~ suit (Kartenspiel)* bedienen; *allg* es genauso machen; *as ~s* wie folgt; folgendermaßen; *it ~s that* daraus folgt, es ergibt sich, daß; *do you ~ my argument?* können Sie mir *(geistig)* folgen? *to ~* **in** nachfolgen; *to ~* **on** später folgen; weitermachen; *to ~* **out** *(Plan)* aus-, durchführen; *(Anweisung)* genau befolgen; *to ~* **through** *tr* zu Ende führen; nachdrücklich verfolgen; *itr* bis ans Ende gehen; *sport* durchziehen; *to ~* **up** (ständig, eifrig) verfolgen, *(e-r S)* nachgehen; zu Ende führen; *com* nachfassen; *(Bericht)* ergänzen; *(Vorteil, Sieg)* weiterverfolgen, auswerten, (aus)nutzen, auskosten; *mil* nachdrängen, -stoßen; *to ~ s.th. up with s.th.* e-r S etw folgen lassen; **~er** ['-ə] Nach-, Verfolger; Nacheiferer; Anhänger, Jünger, *pej* Mitläufer; Gefolgsmann; Diener, Bedienstete(r); *fam obs* Verehrer, Schatz (e-s Hausmädchens); *tech* Führungsstift, Stößel, Zubringer *m*; *pl* Anhängerschaft *f*, *pej* Anhang *m*, Gefolge *n*; **~ing** ['-iŋ] *a* folgend, weiter, im Anschluß an, nächst; nachstehend; *prp* nach; *s* Anhängerschaft *f*, Gefolge *n*; Anhang *m*; Gefolgschaft *f*; *the ~~* der, die, das Folgende, *pl* die Folgenden *pl*; *~~ wind* Rückenwind *m*; **~-on** *sport* sofortige(s) Wiederauftreten *n*; **~-through** *sport* Durchziehen *n*; **~-up** *s* Weiterverfolgen, Ausnutzen *n*; *mil* Nachstoß *m*; *(Erfolg)* Auswertung; Folge (-erscheinung); Mahnung *f*; *a*: *~~ file* Wiedervorlagemappe *f*; *~~ letter* Nachfaß-, Erinnerungsschreiben *n*; Mahnbrief *m*; *~~ report* Ergänzungsmeldung *f*; *~~ system* Wiedervorlageverfahren *n*; *~~ visit (com)* nachfassende(r) Besuch *m*; *~~ wave (mil)* nachdrängende Welle *f*.

folly ['fɔli] Torheit, Narrheit, Verrücktheit *f*, *fam* Wahnsinn *m*; *pl Am* Revue *f*; törichte(s) Unternehmen *n*.

foment [fo(u)'ment] *tr* bähen, mit warmen Umschlägen behandeln, warm baden; *fig* erregen, aufrühren, schüren; **~ation** [-'teiʃən] Bähung *f*, warme(r) Umschlag *m*, Packung; *fig* Aufreizung, Aufstachelung, Aufhetzung *f*; **~er** [fou'mentə] Aufwiegler, Hetzer *m*.

fond [fɔnd] zärtlich, liebevoll; vernarrt (*of* in); zu nachsichtig; *to be ~ of* gernhaben, mögen; lieben; *of doing s.th.* etw gern tun; *to become ~ of s.o.* jdn lieb gewinnen; *a ~ hope* e-e Illusion; *my ~est wish* mein sehnlichster, höchster Wunsch *m*; **~le** ['-l] *tr* (zärtlich, liebevoll) streicheln, hätscheln; **~ly** ['-li] *adv* naiv, in aller Harmlosigkeit; zärtlich; **~ness** ['-nis] Zärtlichkeit; Vorliebe *f* (*for* für); Hang *m* (*for* zu).

fondant ['fɔndənt] Fondant *m (Zukkerwerk)*, *bes.* (Bonbon-)Füllung *f*.

font [fɔnt], **fount** [faunt] **1.** Taufstein *m*, -becken; Weihwasserbecken *n*; *tech* Ölbehälter; *poet* Brunnen *m*; *fig* Quelle *f*, Ursprung *m*; **2.** *s. fount 2.*; **~anel** [fɔntə'nel] *anat* Fontanelle *f*.

food [fu:d] Nahrung *f*; *bot* Nährstoffe *m pl*; Essen *n*; Kost, Speise *f*; Nahrungsmittel *n*, Verpflegung *f*; *(Tiere)* Futter *n*; *fig* (geistige) Nahrung, Anregung, Beschäftigung *f*; *a. pl* Lebensmittel *n pl*; *concentrated ~* hochwertige Lebensmittel *n pl*; Kraftnahrung *f*; *~ for thought* Stoff *m* zum Nachdenken; **~-chemist** Nahrungsmittelchemiker *m*; **~ container** Essenbehälter *m*; **~-cuts** *pl* Lebensmittelkürzungen *f pl*; **~-hoarder** (Lebensmittel-)Hamsterer *m*; **~ import** Lebensmittelimport *m*, -einfuhr *f*; **~less** ['-lis] ohne Essen; *to go ~~* nichts gegessen haben; **~ office** Ernährungsamt *n*; **~ package** Lebensmittelpaket *n*; **~-pipe** *anat* Speiseröhre *f*; **~-processing industry** Nahrungsmittelindustrie *f*; **~-ration**: *~-~ card* Lebensmittelkarte *f*; *~-~ ticket* Lebensmittelmarke *f*; **~-shortage** Lebensmittelverknappung, -knappheit *f*; **~stuff** ['-stʌf] Nahrungsmittel *n*; *pl* Nahrungs-, Lebensmittel *n pl*; **~-supply** Lebensmittelversorgung, -zufuhr *f*, -vorrat *m*; **~ value** Nährwert *m*.

fool [fu:l] *s* Dummkopf, Esel, Tor, Narr; *hist* (Hof-)Narr; Spaßmacher, Possenreißer, Hanswurst, dumme(r) August *m*; *a attr fam* dumm, töricht; närrisch; *itr* dumm, närrisch sein; sich dumm anstellen; herumspielen (*with* mit); Spaß machen; *tr* zum Narren haben *od* halten; s-n Spaß haben mit; anführen, hereinlegen, betrügen, prellen (*s.o. out of s.th.* jdn um etw); *to ~ about, to ~ around* herumtrödeln, die Zeit totschlagen; herumalbern, -spielen, -lungern, sich herumtreiben; *to ~ away (fam)* vergeuden, verschwenden; *(Zeit)* vertrödeln; *to be a ~ for o.'s pains* sich umsonst geplagt haben; *(to live in) a ~'s paradise* Luftschlösser *n pl* (bauen); *to make a ~ of o.s.* sich lächerlich machen; sich blamieren; *to make a ~ of s.o.* jdn zum Narren, zum besten haben; *to play the ~* Dummheiten machen; Ulk, Spaß machen; *he's nobody's ~* man kann ihm kein X für ein U vormachen; *you can't ~ me* Sie können mir nichts vormachen; *stop your ~ing!* laß den Blödsinn! *there is no ~ like an old ~ (prov)* Alter schützt vor Torheit nicht; *All F~s' Day* der 1. April; *April ~* in den April Geschickte(r) *m*; **~ery** ['-əri] Dummheit, Torheit *f*; **~hardiness** Tollkühnheit *f*; **~hardy** tollkühn; **~ing** ['-iŋ] Ulk *m*, Späße *m pl*; **~ish** ['-iʃ] dumm, töricht, unklug; albern, lächerlich; närrisch; **~ishness** ['-iʃnis] Dummheit, Torheit; Albernheit, Lächerlichkeit *f*; Unsinn *m*; **~proof** einfach, leicht zu handhaben; betriebs-, narrensicher; **~'s(-)cap** Narrenkappe *f*; **~scap** ['-skæp] Akten-, Kanzleipapier *n*; **~'s errand** vergebliche(r) Gang *m*; *to send, to go on a ~~* in den April schicken, geschickt werden; **2.** Kompott *n* mit Schlagsahne; Fruchtkrem *f*.

*

foot [fut] *s pl feet* [fi:t] Fuß; untere(r) Teil *m*, Ende *n*; Basis; *(Tier)* Tatze, Pfote *f*; *(Bett, Grab)* Fußende *n*; *(Strumpf)* Füßling; *(Zirkel)* Schenkel; Fuß *m (= 12 Zoll = 30,5 cm)*; Fußsoldaten *m pl*, -truppe, Infanterie *f*; Versfuß; *(pl ~s)* (Boden-)Satz, Niederschlag *m (in e-r Flüssigkeit)*; *itr* tanzen; *(to ~ it)* (zu Fuß) gehen; *tr* (hinweg)tanzen, -schreiten über; betreten; *(Strumpf)* anfußen, anstrikken; zs.zählen, -rechnen; *fam* bezahlen, begleichen; *to ~ up (tr)* zs.rechnen, addieren; *itr* sich belaufen (*to* auf); *at a ~'s pace* zu Fuß; *at the ~ of* am Fußende *gen*; *at the ~ of the page* unten auf der Seite; *on ~* zu Fuß; auf den Beinen; *fig* im Gange; *on o.'s feet* stehend; (wieder) auf den Beinen; *under ~* unter den Füßen; auf dem Boden; *to be on o.'s feet (nach e-r Krankheit)* wieder auf den Beinen, auf dem Posten, auf der Höhe sein; *(finanziell)* auf eigenen Füßen stehen; *to carry s.o. off his feet* jdn umreißen; jdn begeistern, erregen; *to fall on o.'s feet (fig)* auf die Füße *od* Beine fallen; Glück haben; *to have one ~ in the grave (fig)* mit einem Fuß *od* Bein im Grabe stehen; *to keep o.'s feet* nicht hinfallen; *to know the length of s.o.'s ~* jdn ganz genau kennen; *to measure another's ~ by o.'s own last* von sich auf andere schließen; *to put o.'s ~ down (fig)* fest auftreten; energisch werden; Einspruch erheben; *to put o.'s best ~ forward* sich ins rechte Licht setzen; sein Bestes tun; so schnell gehen, wie man kann; *to put o.'s ~ in(to) it (fam)* ins Fettnäpfchen treten, was Dummes machen; *to set on ~ (fig)* auf die Beine stellen; in Gang bringen *od* setzen; *to set s.o. on his feet* jdn finanziell unabhängig machen; *to ~ the bill (fam)* blechen, alles bezahlen; für die Rechnung aufkommen; *my ~! (sl)* Quatsch! **~age** ['-idʒ] Länge *f (bes. e-s (Spiel-)Filmes)* (in Fuß); **~-and-mouth disease** Maul- u. Klauenseuche *f*; **~ball** Fußball *m*; *(association ~~, soccer)* Fußballspiel *n*, -sport *m*; *~~ ground* Fußballplatz *m*; **~baller** Fußball(spiel)er *m*; **~-bath** Fußbad *n*; **~board** *bes. mot* Trittbrett *n*; **~boy** Page *m*; **~-brake** *mot* Fußbremse *f*; **~-bridge** Fußgängerbrücke, -überführung *f*; Steg *m*; **~ control** *mot* Fußschaltung *f*; **~ed** ['-id] *a* in Zssgen: -füßig; *four-~~* vierfüßig; **~er** ['-ə] *sl* Kick *m*; **~fall** ['-fɔ:l] Schritt; Tritt *m (als Geräusch)*; **~-gear** Fußbekleidung *f*; **F~-Guards** *pl mil* Gardeinfanterie *f*; **~-hills** *pl* Vorberge *m pl*; **~hold** Halt *a. fig*; *fig* feste(r) Stand *m*; *to have a ~~ (fig)* eingewurzelt sein; **~less** ['-lis] ohne Füße; *Am fig* in der Luft hängend, nutzlos; *fam* schwerfällig; hilflos, unfähig; **~lights** *pl theat* Rampenlicht *n*; *fig die* Bretter *pl*; **~ling** ['-liŋ] *fam* läppisch; kleinlich; **~-loose** ungebunden, frei; ziellos; **~man** ['-mən] Lakai, Diener, Bediente(r); Fußsoldat, Infanterist *m*; **~mark** (Fuß-)Spur *f*; **~-note** *s* Fußnote, Anmerkung *f*; *tr* mit Anmerkungen versehen; **~pace** (langsamer) Schritt *m*; **~pad** ['-pæd] *obs* Straßenräuber *m*; **~-passenger** Fußgänger *m*; **~path** Fuß-, Gehweg *m*; **~print** Fußstapfe(n *m*), -spur *f*; **~-race** Wettlauf *m*, -rennen *n*; **~-rest** Fußstütze *f*; **~-rule** Zollstock *m*; **~-scraper** Fußabstreicher *m*, Kratzeisen *n*; **~-slog** *mil sl tr* latschen; **~-slogger** *sl* Fußlatscher *m*; **~-soldier** Infanterist *m*; **~sore** ['-sɔ:] fußkrank; **~stalk** ['-stɔ:k] *bot* Stengel, Stiel *m*; **~step** Schritt, Tritt *m*; Fußstapfe, Spur *f*; *to follow in s.o.'s ~~s* sich jdn zum Vorbild nehmen; **~-stone** *arch* Grundstein *m*; **~stool** ['-stu:l] Fußbank *f*, -schemel *m*; **~ switch** Fußschalter *m*; **~way** Fuß-, Gehweg *m*; **~wear** ['-wɛə] *com* Fußbekleidung *f*; **~work** ['-wə:k] *sport* Beinarbeit; *Am sl* Lauferei *f*.

footing ['futiŋ] Standort, -punkt, Halt *m*; Stufe; Grundlage, Basis *f*, Fundament *n*; Beziehungen *f pl*; *(Strumpf)* Anfußen, Anstricken; Zs.-zählen, -rechnen *n*; (End-, Gesamt-) Summe *f*; Einstand(ssumme *f*) *m*;

arch (vorspringende) Basis *f*; *on a peace, war* ~ im Frieden, im Krieg(szustand); *to be on a friendly* ~ *with s.o.* mit jdm auf freundschaftlichem Fuß stehen; *to be on the same* ~ *with s.o.* mit jdm auf gleichem Fuß stehen; *to gain, to get a* ~ (festen) Fuß fassen (*in* in); *to lose o.'s* ~ den Halt verlieren; *to pay (for) o.'s* ~ (s-n) Einstand zahlen.

footl|e ['fu:tl] *itr sl* herumalbern; *s sl* Albernheit, Kinderei *f*, Quatsch *m*.

foozle ['fu:zl] *sl tr* verkorksen, -pfuschen; *itr* schlampern, (herum)pfuschen, -stümpern; *s* Pfuscherei, Stümperei, Schlamperei *f*; Murks *m*.

fop [fɔp] Geck, Stutzer, Fatzke *m*; **~pery** ['-əri] Affigkeit *f*; **~pish** ['-iʃ] gecken-, stutzerhaft; geziert; eitel.

*

for [fɔ:, fə] *prp (Grundbedeutung)* für; **1.** *(bei Zeitangaben: die Vergangenheit betreffend)* seit, ... lang *od bleibt unübersetzt*; *I haven't been there* ~ *three years* ich bin seit drei Jahren, drei Jahre (lang) nicht dort gewesen; *(die Zukunft betreffend)* für, auf; ~ *three weeks* für, auf drei Wochen; *(bei Ortsangaben)* ... weit; ~ *2 miles* 2 Meilen weit; ~ *ever (and ever)* für (immer u.) ewig; *Mary* ~ *ever!* Mary soll leben! ~ *good* für immer; ~ *life* fürs Leben; lebenslänglich *adv*; ~ *once* (für) diesmal; ~ *the present* im Augenblick, zur Zeit; **2.** *(Ursache, Grund)* für, wegen, infolge, durch; aus, vor, zu; ~ *joy* vor Freude; ~ *fear* aus Furcht; ~ *want, lack* aus Mangel (*of* an); *(just)* ~ *fun* (nur) zum Spaß; *but* ~ ohne; *(all, none) the better, worse* ~ (nicht) besser, schlechter durch; *to be out* ~ aus sein auf; **3.** *(konzessiv)* ~ *all his wealth* bei all s-m Reichtum, trotz s-s Reichtums; ~ *all that* trotz allem, trotzdem; ~ *all I know* soviel ich weiß; ~ *all I care* was mich betrifft; ~ *all the world (like)* ganz genau(so); **4.** *(Absicht, Zweck)* für, zu, nach, um; *to dress, to come* ~ *dinner* sich zum Essen anziehen, zum Essen kommen; *the struggle* ~ *existence* der Kampf ums Dasein; *it's difficult* ~ *me* es ist schwer für mich; *what* ~? zu welchem Zweck? wofür? weshalb? **5.** *(Wunsch, Erwartung)* auf, um, nach; *to hope, to wait* ~ hoffen, warten auf; *eager* ~ versessen, erpicht auf; *appetite* ~ Appetit auf; Verlangen nach; *oh,* ~ ...*!* wenn ... doch ... ! **6.** *(Richtung)* nach; *to leave* ~ *Paris* nach Paris abreisen, -fahren; **7.** *(Bestimmung)* als; ~ *a joke* (nur) zum Spaß; *he is in* ~ *it* er ist dran, fällig; **8.** *(Austausch, Ersatz)* für, um, gegen; (an)statt, anstelle; ~ *£10* für, um 10 Pfund; ~ *how much* wieviel? wie teuer? *word* ~ *word* Wort für Wort, wörtlich; *once* ~ *all* ein für allemal; *to take* ~ halten für; **9.** *(Beziehung, Verhältnis)* ~ *o.s.* selbst, allein, ohne Hilfe; *fit* ~ *consumption* zum Verzehr geeignet, eß-, genießbar; ~ *my part, as* ~ *me, I* ~ *one* ich für meinen Teil, was mich betrifft; *it is* ~ *me to speak* es ist meine Sache, es ist an mir zu reden; ~ *the most part* größtenteils; ~ *example, instance* zum Beispiel; **10.** *conj* denn.

forage ['fɔridʒ] *bes. mil* Futter *n*; *itr* Futter suchen; umherstöbern, suchen (*for, about* nach); *tr fig* ausplündern; mit Futter versorgen; aufstöbern; ~ **cap** Feldmütze *f*, *sl* Schiffchen *n*.

forasmuch [fərəz'mʌtʃ]: ~ *as (conj jur)* insofern, insoweit (als).

foray ['fɔrei] *tr* räuberisch überfallen, plündern; *s* räuberische(r) Überfall, Raubzug *m*; Plünderung *f*.

forbear [fɔ:'bɛə] **1.** *irr forbore* [-'bɔ:], *forborne* [-'bɔ:n] *tr* sich enthalten (*s.th.* e-r S), unterlassen, vermeiden (*to do, doing* zu tun); *itr* ablassen (*from* von); sich beherrschen, sich im Zaum halten; sich gedulden (*with* mit); **~ance** [-rəns] Enthaltung, Unterlassung, Vermeidung, Abstandnahme; Enthaltsamkeit, (Selbst-)Beherrschung, Geduld *f*; *jur fin* (Zahlungs-) Aufschub *m*, Stundung *f*; **2.** ['fɔ:bɛə] *s meist pl die* Vorfahren, *die* Ahnen *m pl*.

forbid [fə'bid] *irr forbad(e)* [-'beid, -'bæd], *forbidden* [-'bidn] *tr* verbieten; ausschließen; verhindern, verhüten; *God* ~*!* Gott bewahre! Gott behüte! **~den** [-n] *a* verboten; **~ding** [-iŋ] drohend, abschreckend, -stoßend; widerwärtig; unfreundlich.

force [fɔ:s] *s* Stärke, Kraft, Energie; Wucht; Gewalt *f*; Zwang, Druck *m*; Macht *f*, Einfluß *m*, Wirksamkeit; innere Stärke, sittliche Kraft; Überzeugungskraft *f*; genaue(r) Sinn *m*; beherrschende Kraft *f*, Machtfaktor *m*; *(armed* ~*s)* Streitmacht, -kraft *f*, Heer *n*; *(police* ~*) die* Polizeitruppen *f pl*; *Am* Mannschaft, Kolonne, Belegschaft *f*; Arbeitskräfte *f pl*; Gruppe, Gesellschaft; *jur* Gültigkeit *f*; *tr (to* ~ *the hand of)* zwingen; Zwang antun (*s.o.* jdm); erzwingen, mit Gewalt verschaffen; überwältigen; *(to* ~ *open)* auf-, erbrechen; sprengen; *(Frau)* vergewaltigen, notzüchtigen; entreißen (*from* dat); aufzwingen, -drängen, -nötigen (*on s.o.* jdm); sich zwingen zu; überfordern, -anstrengen; erkünsteln; forcieren, beschleunigen, vorantreiben; *(Pflanzen)* zu beschleunigtem Wachstum anregen; *(Preise)* in die Höhe treiben; *phot* überentwickeln; *by* ~ mit Gewalt, gewaltsam, zwangsweise; *by* ~ *of* kraft *gen*, mit Hilfe *gen*; *by main* ~ mit roher Gewalt; *by* ~ *of arms* mit Waffengewalt; *in* ~ in voller Stärke *od* Zahl; in Kraft; rechtsgültig; bindend; in großer Zahl; *in full* ~ in voller Stärke; vollzählig; *of no* ~ nicht bindend, ungültig; *to be in* ~ in Kraft, rechtskräftig, gültig sein; *to come into* ~ in Kraft treten; rechtskräftig werden; *to join* ~*s with* sich vereinigen, sich zs.tun mit; *to lose* ~ außer Kraft treten; ungültig werden; *to put into* ~ in Kraft setzen; rechtskräftig werden lassen; *to resort to, to use* ~ Gewalt anwenden *od* gebrauchen; *to* ~ *the issue* die Entscheidung erzwingen, es aufs Äußerste ankommen lassen; *to* ~ *the pace* den Schritt beschleunigen; *you can't* ~ *things* das kann man nicht übers Knie brechen; *use of* ~ Gewaltanwendung *f*; ~ *of character* Charakterstärke *f*; ~ *of gravity* Schwerkraft *f*; *the* ~ *of habit* die Macht der Gewohnheit; ~ *of law* Gesetzeskraft *f*; *the* ~*s of nature* die Naturkräfte *pl*; ~ *of numbers* zahlenmäßige Überlegenheit *f*; *to* ~ **along** vorwärtstreiben, weg-, fort-, mitreißen (*with* mit); *to* ~ **away** wegtreiben; *to* ~ **back** zurücktreiben, -drängen; *to* ~ **down** hinab-, hinunterdrücken; *(Preise)* drücken; *aero* zum Landen zwingen; *to* ~ **into** hineindrücken, -pressen; sich hineindrängeln; *to* ~ **off** *com* losschlagen, verschleudern; *to* ~ **on** antreiben; *to* ~ **out** hinausdrängen; *to* ~ **through** hindurchtreiben; *to* ~ **up** hinauftreiben, in die Höhe treiben; *to* ~ **upon** *s.o.* jdm aufzwingen; **~d** [-t] *a* erzwungen, Zwangs-; erzwungen, erkünstelt; *(Lächeln)* gezwungen; **~~** *agreement* Zwangsvergleich *m*; **~~** *labo(u)r* Zwangsarbeit *f*; **~~** *landing* Notlandung *f*; *to make a* **~~** *landing* notlanden; **~~** *loan* Zwangsanleihe *f*; **~~** *march* Gewaltmarsch *m*; **~~** *sale* Zwangsverkauf *m*, -versteigerung *f*; **~dly** ['-idli] *adv* zwangsweise; **~-feed lubrication** Druckschmierung *f*; **~ful** ['-ful] kraftvoll, energisch, stark; wirkungsvoll, eindringlich; gewaltsam; **~fulness** ['-fulnis] Energie *f*, Schwung *m*; Eindringlichkeit *f*; **~-meat** (zum Füllen bestimmtes) Hackfleisch *n*; **~-pump** Druckpumpe *f*.

forceps ['fɔ:seps] *pl u. sing med* (*bes.* Zahn-)Zange; Pinzette; *zoo* Zange *f*; ~ **delivery** Zangengeburt *f*.

forcibl|e ['fɔ:səbl] gewaltsam, erzwungen, Zwangs-; stark, kräftig; kraftvoll, eindringlich, überzeugend; **~y** ['-i] *adv* zwangsweise, gewaltsam.

forcing ['fɔ:siŋ] Zwingen *n*; **~-bed, ~frame** Mistbeet(kasten *m*) *n*; **~-house** Treibhaus *n*; **~-pump** Druckpumpe *f*.

ford [fɔ:d] *s* Furt *f*; *tr* durchwaten; **~able** ['-əbl] durchwatbar, passierbar; flach, seicht.

fore [fɔ:] *adv (nur noch mar)* vorn; *a* vordere(r, s); *interj (Golf)* Achtung! *s* Vorder-, vordere(r) Teil *m*; *als Vorsilbe*: Vor(der)-; *to the* ~ nach vorn, *fig* ans Licht, an die Öffentlichkeit; zur Hand, zur Verfügung; (noch) am Leben; ~ *and aft (mar)* längsschiffs; *to come to the* ~ zum Vorschein kommen; in den Vordergrund treten; ans Ruder kommen; berühmt werden.

fore|arm ['fɔ:rɑ:m] *s* Unterarm *m*; *tr* [-r'ɑ:m] im voraus, vorher bewaffnen; auf e-n Kampf, e-e Schwierigkeit vorbereiten; **~bear** *s. forbear 2.*; **~bode** [-'boud] *tr (Unheil)* voraus-, vorhersagen, prophezeien, verkünden; ahnen, im Gefühl haben; ein Zeichen sein für; **~boding** [-'boudiŋ] Prophezeiung, Vorhersage; schlimme Ahnung *f*; **~cast** [-'kɑ:st, '--], *irr u. Am*: **~~** *(ed)*, **~~***(ed) tr* planen, vorher überlegen; vorhersehen; vorhersagen, prophezeien; ein Vorzeichen sein für; *s* ['-kɑ:st] Vorhersage, Vorherbestimmung *f*; *(weather-~~)* (Wetter-)Voraus-, Vorhersage *f*; **~caster** (beratender) Meteorologe *m*; **~castle** ['fouksl] *mar* Vorschiff, Vorderdeck *n*; Back *f*; **~close** [fɔ:'klouz] *tr jur* ausschließen (*from* von); *fin* für verfallen erklären; **~closure** [-'klouʒə] *jur* Ausschluß *m*; Verfallserklärung *f*; **~court** ['-kɔ:t] Vorhof *m*; *sport* Vorfeld *n*; **~date** [-'deit] *tr* vordatieren; **~dated** *a* vordatiert; **~doom** [-'du:m] *tr* vorher verurteilen; vorherbestimmen (*to* zu, für); *s* ['-du:m] vorherige Verurteilung; Vorsehung *f*; **~father** Ahnherr, Vorfahr *m*; **~finger** Zeigefinger *m*; **~foot** *pl* **~feet** Vorderfuß *m*, -pfote *f*; *mar* vordere(s) Kielende *n*; **~front** Vorderseite *f*; *fig* vorderste Reihe *f*; *to be in the* **~~** im Vordergrund stehen; **~go** [-'gou] *irr -went, -gone* **1.** *itr tr* voran-, -auf-, -ausgehen (*s.th.* e-r S); **2.** *s. forgo*; **~going** *a* vorhergehend; obig, oben gesagt, erwähnt; *s the* **~~** die Genannten *m pl*; das Vorhergehende, oben Gesagte, Erwähnte; **~gone** [-'gɔn, *attr* '--] *a* vorherig, früher; vorher bekannt; im voraus angenommen; vorweggenommen; vorherbestimmt, vorher, im voraus festgelegt; *(Meinung)* vorgefaßt; unvermeidlich, unausweichlich; **~~** *conclusion* von vornherein feststehende Sache; **~ground** Vordergrund *m a. fig; in the ~~* im Vordergrund; **~hand** *a* vorder, Vorder-; *(Tennis)* Vorhand-; *s* Vorhand *f*, Vorteil *m*; *(Pferd, Tennis)* Vorhand *f*; **~handed** *a Am* vorausschauend, vorsorgend, sparsam; vorsorglich; reich, wohlhabend; vorher erledigt, früh-, rechtzeitig; **~head** ['fɔrid, -red] Stirn *a. fig; fig* Vorderseite *f*; **~hold** Vorderteil *m* des Schiffsraumes.

foreign ['fɔrin] fremd, nicht (da)zugehörig; auswärtig, ausländisch; **~ affairs** *pl pol* auswärtige Angelegenheiten *f pl*; *Secretary of State, Minister for F~ Affairs* Außenminister *m*; **~ aid** Auslandshilfe *f*; **~ assets** *pl* Auslandsvermögen *n*; Fremdwerte *m pl*; **~ body** Fremdkörper *m a. fig*; **~-born** *a* im Ausland geboren; **~ business** Auslandsgeschäft *n*; **~ commerce** Auslandshandel *m*; **~ correspondent** *(com u. Zeitung)* Auslandskorrespondent *m*; **~ currency** Devisen *f pl*; *~-currency control-office* Devisenstelle *f*; **~ debt** Auslandsschuld(en *pl*) *f*; **~ department** Auslandsabteilung *f*; **~er** ['-ə] Ausländer(in *f*) *m*; Fremde(r *m*) *f*; **~ exchange** Auslandswechsel *m*; *pl (Am sing)* ausländische Zahlungsmittel *n pl*, Devisen *f pl*; *~-exchange control, department, market, shortage* Devisenbewirtschaftung, -stelle *f*, -markt *m*, -knappheit *f*; **~ labo(u)r** Gast-, Fremdarbeiter *m pl*; **~ language** Fremdsprache *f*; **~ legion** Fremdenlegion *f*; **~ liabilities** *pl* Auslandsverbindlichkeiten *f pl*; **~ mission** *rel* Äußere Mission; *pol* Auslandsdelegation *f*; **~ness** ['-nis] Fremdheit, Fremdartigkeit *f*; **~ news** *pl mit sing* Auslandsnachrichten *f pl*; *the* **F~ Office** *Br* das Außenministerium, d. Ministerium für Auswärtige Angelegenheiten; **~ policy** Außenpolitik *f*; *the* **F~ Secretary** der Außenminister; **~ service** auswärtige(r), *bes.* diplomatische(r) Dienst *m*; **~ trade** Außenhandel *m*; *~~ policy* Außenhandelspolitik *f*; **~ transaction** Auslandsgeschäft *n*; **~ word** Fremdwort *n*.

fore|judge [fɔ:'dʒʌdʒ] **1.** *tr* im voraus, voreilig beurteilen *od* entscheiden; **2.** *s. forjudge*; **~know** *irr -knew, -known tr* vorherwissen; **~knowledge** ['fɔ:'nɔlidʒ] Vorherwissen *n*; **~land** ['-lænd, '-lənd] Vorgebirge, Kap; Vorgelände, -feld *n*; **~leg** ['-leg] Vorderbein *n*; **~lock** ['-lɔk] Stirnlocke *f*; *tech* Splint *m*; *to take time by the ~~* die Gelegenheit beim Schopf ergreifen; **~man** ['-mən] *pl -men* ['-mən] Obmann, Sprecher; Vorarbeiter, Werkmeister, Polier, Aufseher; *min* Steiger *m*; **~mast** ['-mɑ:st] *mar* Fock-, Vor(der)mast *m*; **~-mentioned** [-'menʃnd] *a* vorerwähnt, -genannt; **~most** ['-moust] *a* vorderst, erst, führend; *adv* zuerst; *first and ~~* in erster Linie, vor allem, zuallererst; **~name** ['--] *Am* Vorname *m*; **~-named** *a* vorgenannt, -erwähnt; **~noon** ['-nu:n] *s* Vormittag *m*; *a* Vormittags-; *in the ~~* am Vormittag.

forensic [fə'rensik] gerichtlich, forensisch; Gerichts-; **~ medicine** Gerichtsmedizin *f*.

fore|ordain ['fɔ:rɔ:'dein] *tr* vorher anordnen *od* festlegen; vorherbestimmen *(to* zu); **~ordination** [-ɔ:di'neiʃən] *rel* Vorherbestimmung, Prädestination *f*; **~part** ['-pɑ:t] Vorderteil *n*; erste(r) Teil, Anfang *m*; **~paw** ['-pɔ:] Vorderpfote *f*; **~quarter** ['-kwɔ:tə] *(Schlachtvieh)* Vorderviertel *n*; **~reach** [-'ri:tʃ] *tr* überholen *a. fig; itr* aufholen *a. fig*; **~runner** ['-rʌnə, *a.* -'-] Vorläufer, Herold; Vorbote *m*, -zeichen *n*; Vorgänger; Vorfahr *m*; **~sail** ['-seil, *mar* 'fɔ:sl] Focksegel *n*; **~see** [-'si:] *irr -saw, -seen tr* vorhersehen; vorher wissen; **~seeable** [-'si:əbl] vorhersehbar, absehbar; *(Zukunft)* überschaubar; **~shadow** [fɔ:'ʃædou] *tr* Schatten vorauswerfen auf, ahnen lassen, ankünden, vorher andeuten; **~shore** ['-ʃɔ:] Watt(enmeer) *n*; **~shorten** [-'ʃɔ:tn] *tr (Deckenmalerei)* in Verkürzung darstellen; **~show** [-'ʃou] *irr -showed, -shown tr* ankündigen; ahnen lassen; **~sight** ['-sait] Vorhersehen *n*; Sehergabe *f*; Voraussicht, -schau; Vorsorge *f*; *mil* Korn *n (des Visiers)*; *~~ stud* (Korn-)Warze *f*; **~sighted** ['-saitid, *a.* -'-] *a* vorausblickend, -schauend; vorsorgend; vorsorglich; **~skin** ['-skin] *anat* Vorhaut *f*.

forest ['fɔrist] *s* Wald, Forst *m*; Jagdgebiet *n*; *tr* aufforsten; **~ clearing** Waldlichtung *f*; **~ edge** Waldrand *m*; **~er** ['-ə] Förster; Waldbewohner *m*; im Wald lebende(s) Tier *n*; hochstämmige(r) Baum *m*; **~ fire** Waldbrand *m*; *~-firefighting* Waldbrandbekämpfung *f*; **~ry** ['-ri] Forstwirtschaft, -wissenschaft; Waldkultur *f*.

fore|stall [fɔ:'stɔ:l] *tr* vorwegnehmen; zuvorkommen *(s.o., s.th.* jdm, e-r S); aufkaufen; **~stay** ['-stei] *mar* Fockstag *m*; **~taste** ['-teist] Vorgeschmack *m*; Vorwegnahme *f*; **~tell** [-'tel] *irr -told, -told tr* vorhersagen, prophezeien; schließen lassen auf; im voraus anzeigen; **~thought** ['-θɔ:t] Voraussicht *f*, Vorbedacht *m*, Vorsorge *f*; **~top** ['-tɔp, *a.* -'-] *mar* Fockmars *m*; **~warn** [-'wɔ:n] *tr* vorher warnen *(of* vor); warnend vorhersagen; **~woman** ['-wumən] Vorarbeiterin; Direktrice, (Abteilungs-)Vorsteherin *f*; **~word** ['-wə:d] *(Buch)* Vorwort *n*.

forever [fə'revə] *Am* = *Br for ever* für immer, ewig; immer wieder.

forfeit ['fɔ:fit] *s* verwirkte(s) Pfand *n*; Verlust; *fig* Preis *m*; Strafe, Buße; *com* Vertragsstrafe; Verwirkung *f*; (Verlust durch) Verfall *m*; *pl* Pfänderspiel *n*; *a* verwirkt, verfallen; verloren, verscherzt; *tr* verwirken, verfallen lassen; verlieren, einbüßen, verlustig gehen; *to play ~s* ein Pfänderspiel machen; *to ~ o.'s driving licence* s-n Führerschein entzogen bekommen; **~ money** Abstandssumme *f*; **~ure** ['-ʃə] Verwirkung *f*; Entzug; Verlust *m* (durch Verfall); (Geld-)Strafe, (Vermögens-)Einziehung *f*.

forfend [fɔ:'fend] *tr obs* verbieten, verhindern, verhüten.

forgather [fɔ:'gæðə] *itr* sich begegnen, sich treffen, verkehren *(with* mit).

forg|e [fɔ:dʒ] **1.** *s* Schmiedefeuer *n*, -herd *m*, -esse; Schmiede; *tech* Hütte *f*; Eisen-, Hüttenwerk *n*; *tr* schmieden; formen, gestalten, herstellen; nachahmen, nachmachen, fälschen; (frei) erfinden; *to ~~ coin* falschmünzen; *~~ pig* Puddelroheisen *n*; **~ed** [-d] *a* falsch, gefälscht, nachgemacht; *~~ money* Falschgeld *n*; **~er** ['-ə] Schmied; Fälscher; Falschmünzer; Aufschneider, Lügner *m*; *~~ of banknotes* Banknotenfälscher *m*; **~ery** ['-əri] Fälschung; Nachahmung; Falschmünzerei *f*; Betrug *m*; falsche Unterschrift; *lit* dichterische Erfindung *f*; *~~ of banknotes* Banknotenfälschung *f*; *~~ of documents* Urkundenfälschung *f*; **2.** *itr (to ~~ ahead)* sich vorarbeiten; *sport* in Führung gehen.

forget [fə'get] *irr forgot, forgotten; tr* vergessen (haben) *(to do, about doing s.th.* etw zu tun); *(unabsichtlich)* unterlassen; übersehen; *(absichtlich)* übergehen, außer acht lassen, vernachlässigen; *itr* vergeßlich sein; sich nicht mehr entsinnen; *to ~ o.s.* (immer) nur an andere denken; sich vergessen, aus der Rolle fallen; *~ about it!* denk nicht mehr dran! **~ful** [-ful] vergeßlich; achtlos; nachlässig; **~fulness** [-fulnis] Vergeßlichkeit; Vergessenheit *f*; **~-me-not** [-minɔt] *bot* Vergißmeinnicht *n*.

forgiv|e [fə'giv] *irr forgave, forgiven; tr* vergeben, verzeihen *(s.o. s.th.* jdm etw); *(Schuld)* erlassen; *itr (to ~ easily)* nicht nachtragend sein; **~eness** [-nis] Vergebung (der Sünden), Verzeihung; Versöhnlichkeit, Nachsicht *f*; *to ask s.o.'s ~~* jdn um Verzeihung bitten; **~ing** [-iŋ] nachsichtig; versöhnlich; großmütig.

forgo [fɔ:'gou] *irr -went, -gone tr* sich enthalten *(s.th.* e-r S); verzichten auf.

fork [fɔ:k] *s* Gabel; Gabelung, Abzweigung *f*; *Am* Nebenfluß *m*; *pl sl* Finger *m pl*; *itr* sich gabeln; *tr* gabeln, spalten; aufgabeln; mit e-r Gabel aufladen; *to ~ in (Am fam)* 'runterschlingen; *to ~ over, out, up (fam)* aushändigen, übergeben; (aus)zahlen, blechen; **~ed** [-t] *a* gabelförmig, gegabelt, gespalten; *(Blitz)* verästelt; -zinkig; **~-lift truck** Gabelstapler *m*.

forlorn [fə'lɔ:n] *a* verlassen, verloren; hilflos, elend; hoffnungslos, verzweifelt; beraubt *(of* gen); **~ hope** *mil* Himmelfahrtskommando *n*, verlorene(r) Haufen *m*; *allg* aussichtslose(s) Unternehmen *n*.

form [fɔ:m] Form, Gestalt, Figur *f*, Bau, Umriß *m*; (Guß-)Form *f*; (Aggregat-)Zustand *m*; *fig* Form, Gestalt *f*, Charakter *m*, Wesenszüge *m pl*; (An-)Ordnung *f*, Ordnungsprinzip, Schema, Muster, Modell *n*; Art (u. Weise); Formalität, Zeremonie, Sitte *f*, Brauch, Ritus *m*; Förmlichkeit *f*, Anstand *m*; Form *f (e-s Schreibens* od *Schriftstücks)*; *(~ letter)* Formbrief *m*; Formblatt, Formular *n*, Vordruck *m*; *sport* Form, (körperliche) Verfassung *f*; Lager *n (e-s wilden Tieres)*; *Br* Bank (ohne Lehne), Schulbank; *Br* (Schul-)Klasse; *gram* (Wort-)Form; *typ* (Druck-)Form *f*; *tr* formen, bilden, gestalten, entwickeln; formieren; erwerben; *tech* formpressen, profildrehen; bilden, unterrichten, erziehen; aus-, erdenken, ersinnen, entwerfen, entwickeln, gestalten; auffassen; bilden, konstituieren, organisieren, zs.-stellen, zs.schließen, vereinigen *(into* zu); *(Gesellschaft)* gründen; *(Regierung)* bilden; *gram (Wort, Satz)* bilden; *itr* sich bilden, sich entwickeln; (feste) Gestalt annehmen; *mil* sich formieren; *to ~ up (tr itr)* antreten, aufmarschieren (lassen), (sich) aufstellen; *in due ~* vorschriftsmäßig, in gültiger Form; *without ~* formlos; *to be in good ~* in guter Verfassung, gut in Form sein; *to be out of ~* nicht in Form sein; *to fill out (Am), up, in a ~* ein Formular ausfüllen; *to ~ an alliance* e-n Bund, ein Bündnis schließen; *to ~ a conclusion* zu e-m Schluß kommen; *to ~ an idea, a plan* e-n Gedanken, e-n Plan fassen; *to ~ a judg(e)ment, an opinion* sich ein Urteil, e-e Meinung bilden; *application ~* Antragsformular *n*; *bad, good ~* schlechte(s), gute(s) Benehmen *n*; *that is bad, good ~* das gehört sich nicht; *a (mere) matter of ~* e-e (bloße) Formsache *f*; *~ of government* Regierungsform *f*; **~al** ['-əl] *a* formal, formell, äußerlich; künstlich, gezwungen; scheinbar, Schein-, nur zum Schein; steif, förmlich, zeremoniell, feierlich; offiziell; ausdrücklich; korrekt, tadellos, gehörig, ordnungsgemäß; wesensmäßig, wesentlich; *s Am fam* Tanz *m* mit vorgeschriebener Gesellschaftskleidung; Abendkleid *n*; *to go ~~ (fam)* Gesellschaftskleidung anhaben; *to make a ~~ apology* sich in aller Form entschuldigen; *~~ call* Höflichkeitsbesuch *m*; *~~ defect* Formfehler *m*; *~~ dress* Abendanzug *m*, -kleid *n*; *~~ requirements (pl)* Formvorschriften *f pl*; **~alism** ['fɔ:məlizm] Formalismus *m*; **~alist** ['-əlist] Pedant *m*; **~ality** [fɔ:'mæliti] Förmlichkeit, Steifheit, förmliche(s) Wesen *n*; Formalität, Formsache *f*; *as a ~~* der (bloßen) Form wegen; *without ~~* ohne Umstände; **~alize** ['-əlaiz] *tr* s-e endgültige Gestalt geben (*s.th.* e-r S); zur Formsache machen; **~at** ['fɔ:mæt] *(Buch)* Format *n*; äußere Aufmachung *f*; **~ation** [fɔ:'meiʃən] Bildung; Herstellung, Gestalt(ung); Struktur, (An-)Ordnung, Gliederung *f*, Aufbau *m*; *(Gesellschaft)* Gründung; *(Truppen)* Aufstellung; *geol mil* Formation *f*; *~~ flying* Fliegen *n* im Verband; *~~ of terrain* Geländegestaltung *f*; **~ative** ['fɔ:mətiv] *a* bildend, gestaltend; plastisch; Entwick(e)lungs-; *s* Wortbildungselement *n*; *~~ years (pl)* Entwicklungsjahre *n pl*; *~* **cutter** Profilfräser *m*; **~er** ['-ə] **1.** Bildner, Gestalter, Formgeber; *aero* Spant *m*; *tech* Schablone, Vorlage *f*, Rahmen, Wickelkörper *m*; **~less** ['-lis] formlos; *~* **letter** *Am* Rundschreiben *n*; *~* **master, mistress** Klassenlehrer(in *f*) *m*.

formal|dehyde [fɔ:'mældihaid] *chem* Formaldehyd *m*; **~in** ['fɔ:məlin] *chem* Formalin, Formol *n*.

former ['fɔ:mə] **2.** *a* früher, vorhergehend, vergangen, ehemalig; *the ~* der ersterwähnte, erste; erstere(r, s), jene(r, s); *in ~ times* in früheren Zeiten, einst; **~ly** ['-li] *adv* früher, ehemals.

formic ['fɔ:mik] *a* Ameisen-; *~~ acid* Ameisensäure *f*.

formidable ['fɔ:midəbl] furchtbar, fürchterlich, grauenvoll, -erregend, schrecklich, entsetzlich; schwierig; *fam* gewaltig, riesig.

formul|a ['fɔ:mjulə] *pl -s u. scient -ae* ['-i:] Formel; stehende Redensart; *rel* (Tauf-)Formel *f*; Glaubensbekenntnis; *pharm* Rezept *n*; *Am* Säuglingsnahrung *f*; **~ary** ['-əri] Formelsammlung *f*, -buch *n*; Formel *f*; *pharm* Rezeptliste *f*; **~ate** ['-leit] *tr* auf e-e Formel bringen; formulieren, ausdrücken; **~ation** [-'leiʃən] Formulierung *f*.

fornicat|e ['fɔ:nikeit] *itr* Unzucht treiben, huren; **~ion** [-'keiʃən] Unzucht, Hurerei *f*; **~or** ['-keitə] unzüchtige(r) Mensch *m*.

forrader ['fɔrədə] *adv fam* weiter voran; *to get no ~* nicht vorwärtskommen.

forsake [fə'seik] *irr -sook, -saken tr* aufgeben, sich lossagen, sich trennen von, verzichten auf; verlassen, im Stich lassen, sitzenlassen.

forsooth [fə'su:θ] *obs* fürwahr.

for|swear [fɔ:'swɛə] *irr -swore, -sworn tr* abschwören; *itr* meineidig werden; *to ~ o.s.* e-n Meineid schwören.

forsythia [fɔ:'saiθjə] *bot* Forsythie *f*.

fort [fɔ:t] *mil* Fort *n*, Schanze *f*.

forte 1. [fɔ:t] Stärke, starke Seite *f*; **2.** ['fɔ:ti] *mus a adv* forte; *s* Forte *n*.

forth [fɔ:θ] *adv (räumlich)* vorwärts, weiter; *(zeitlich)* weiter; *(graduell)* vorwärts, voran, weiter; heraus, hervor, ans Licht; *and so ~* und so fort, und so weiter; *back and ~* vor und zurück, hin und her; *from this day ~* von heute an; **~coming** [fɔ:θ'kʌmiŋ, *attr a.* '-] (unmittelbar) bevorstehend; *(Buch)* im Erscheinen begriffen, herauskommend; bereit, zur Hand, zur Verfügung (stehend); *fig* hilfsbereit, liebenswürdig, zuvorkommend, nett; *to be ~~* bevorstehen; zum Vorschein kommen; *(Buch)* im Erscheinen begriffen sein; *~~ attractions (pl)* Filmvorschau *f*; *~~ books (pl)* Neuerscheinungen *f pl*; *~~ events (pl)* Veranstaltungskalender *m*; **~right** ['fɔ:θrait] *a* frei, offen, aufrichtig; *adv* [-'rait] geradeaus; *fig* gerade heraus; **~with** ['fɔ:θ'wiθ] *adv* sofort, (so)gleich.

fortieth ['fɔ:tiiθ] *a* vierzigst; *s* Vierzigstel *n*.

fortif|ication [fɔ:tifi'keiʃən] Befestigung *f*; Festungsbau *m*, -wesen *n*; Festung(swerk *n*, -anlage) *f*; **~ier** ['fɔ:tifaiə] Stärkungsmittel *n*; **~y** ['fɔ:tifai] *tr* stärken, kräftigen, festigen; *fig* bestärken, bekräftigen, (unter)stützen; *mil* befestigen; *(alkohol. Getränk)* verstärken; *(Nahrungsmittel)* anreichern; *to ~~ o.s.* sich stärken *od* wappnen (*against* gegen).

fortitude ['fɔ:titju:d] Standhaftigkeit, Unerschütterlichkeit; (innere) Ausgeglichenheit *f*, Gleichmut *m*.

fortnight ['fɔ:tnait] *s* 14 Tage *m pl*; *for a ~* für, auf 14 Tage; *this ~* (seit) 14 Tage(n); *this day* od *today, tomorrow, next Monday ~, a ~ today, tomorrow, next Monday* heute, morgen, Montag in 14 Tagen; **~ly** ['-li] *a* vierzehntägig; halbmonatlich; *adv* alle 14 Tage; *s (~~ review)* Halbmonatsschrift *f*.

fortress ['fɔ:tris] *s* Festung *f a. fig*.

fortuit|ous [fɔ:'tju(:)itəs] zufällig; Zufalls-; **~ousness** [-təsnis], **~y** [fɔ:'tju(:)iti] Zufälligkeit *f*; Zufall *m*.

fortunate ['fɔ:tʃnit] glücklich; glückbringend, -verheißend, günstig; *to be ~ in s.th.* bei etw Glück haben; **~ly** ['-li] *adv* glücklicherweise.

fortune ['fɔ:tʃən] Geschick, Schicksal; Glück *n*, Erfolg *m*, Gedeihen *n*; Wohlstand, Reichtum *m*, Vermögen *n*, (großer) Besitz *m*; *by ~* zufällig *adv*; *to have good (bad) ~* (kein) Glück haben; *to have ~ on o.'s side* das Glück auf s-r Seite haben; *to have o.'s ~ told* sich die Zukunft sagen lassen; *to make a ~* ein Vermögen verdienen (*out of s.th.* mit etw); *to try o.'s ~* sein Glück versuchen; *bad ~* Unglück *n*; *good ~* Glück *n*; *a man of ~* ein reicher Mann; *soldier of ~* Glücksritter *m*; *~ of wa* Kriegsglück *n*; **~-hunter** Mitgiftjäger *m*; **~-teller** Wahrsager(in *f*) *m*; **~-telling** Wahrsagen *n*.

forty ['fɔ:ti] *a* vierzig; *s pl*: *the forties* die vierziger Jahre *(e-s Jahrhunderts)*; *~* **winks** *pl* Nickerchen *n*.

forum ['fɔ:rəm] *allg fig* Forum; Gericht(shof, -sort *m*) *n*.

forward ['fɔ:wəd] *a* vorder, Vorder-; vorderseitig; vorgerückt; früh, früh-, vorzeitig; frühreif; vor-, fortgeschritten; fortschreitend; fortschrittlich; schnell, eilig, bereit(willig), eifrig; voreilig, draufgängerisch, anmaßend, unbescheiden, keck; *com* kommend, künftig, später, auf Ziel; Termin-; *mil* vorgeschoben; *adv* [*mar* 'fɔrəd] vorwärts, nach vorn; in die Zukunft; hervor, ans Licht; *s sport (bes. Fußball)* Stürmer *m*; *tr* voran-, weiterbringen; fördern, unterstützen; befördern, schicken, (über-, zu)senden; nachschicken, -senden; weiterleiten, -befördern; *from that, this time ~* seitdem; nunmehr; *to bring ~* vorbringen, -tragen, -legen; *to buy ~* auf Termin kaufen; *to carry ~ (com)* übertragen; *(Saldo)* vortragen; *to look ~* an die Zukunft denken; sich freuen (*to s.th.* auf etw; *to doing s.th.* etw zu tun); *to put, to set o.s. ~* sich vor-, nach vorn drängen; *to take a step ~* e-n Schritt nach vorwärts tun; *~! (mil)* vorwärts! *please ~!, (Am) to be ~ed, ~ mail* bitte nachsenden! *balance carried ~* Saldovortrag *m*; *sum brought ~* Übertrag *m*; *~* **area** Frontgebiet *n*; *~* **contract** Liefer-, Terminabschluß *m*; *~* **deal, transaction** Termingeschäft *n*; **~er** ['-ə] Spediteur *m*; **~ing** ['-iŋ] Beförderung; Absendung, Verschickung *f*; Versand *m*, Spedition; Nachsendung *f*; *~~ advice* Versandanzeige *f*; *~~-agency, -business, -house* Fuhrunternehmen, -geschäft *n*, Speditionsfirma *f*; *~~-agent* Spediteur, Fuhrunternehmer *m*; *~~-company, -agency* Speditionsgesellschaft *f*, -geschäft *n*; *~~ department* Versandabteilung *f*; *~~-expenses (pl)* Versandkosten *pl*; *~~ of goods* Güterverkehr *m*; *~~-note* Frachtbrief *m*; *~~-office* Versandbüro *n*; Güterabfertigung *f*; *~* **motion** Vorwärtsbewegung *f*; **~ness** ['-nis] Frühreife *f*; Fortgeschrittenheit, Fortschrittlichkeit; Bereitschaft, Bereitwilligkeit *f*, Eifer *m*; Anmaßung, Unbescheidenheit, Keckheit *f*; *~* **order** Terminauftrag *m*; *~* **pass** *Am sport* Vorlage *f*; **~s** [-z] *s. forward adv*; *~* **sale** Terminverkauf *m*; *~* **speed** Vorwärtsgang *m*.

foss|a ['fɔsə] *pl -ae* ['-i:] *anat* Grube, Rinne, Höhle *f*; **~(e)** [fɔs] (*bes.* Festungs-)Graben *n*; *anat* Grube *f*; **~ick** ['-ik] *itr fam* herumstöbern; **~il** ['fɔsl, -sil] *s geol* Versteinerung *f*, Fossil *n*; *fam* verkalkte(r) Mensch *m*; *a* versteinert; *fig* veraltet, antiquiert; **~ilization** [fɔsilai'zeiʃən] Versteinerung *f*; **~ilize** ['-ilaiz] *tr* versteinern; *fig* verknöchern.

foster ['fɔstə] *tr* ernähren; *(Kind)* aufziehen; fördern, begünstigen; anregen, ermutigen; förderlich, günstig sein (*s.th.* e-r S); *(Hoffnung)* hegen; *attr* Pflege-; *to ~ hopes* sich der Hoffnung hingeben (*of obtaining* zu erhalten); **~-brother** Pflegebruder *m*; **~-child** Pflegekind *n*; **~er** ['-rə] Pflegevater; Förderer, Beschützer *m*; **~-father** Pflegevater *m*; **~ling** Pflegekind *n*, Pflegling; Schützling *m*; **~-mother** Pflegemutter *f*; Brutapparat *m*; **~-parents** *pl* Pflegeeltern *pl*; **~-sister** Pflegeschwester *f*; **~-son** Pflegesohn *m*.

foul [faul] *a* widerlich, ekelhaft, -erregend; übelriechend, stinkend, faulig; *(Luft)* verbraucht; dreckig, schmutzig, verschmutzt, schmutzstarrend; *(Rohr)* verstopft; *(Seil)* verheddert; *(Wetter)* schlecht; *(Wind)* ungünstig, widrig; *(Nahrungsmittel)* faul, verdorben; modrig; *(Druck)* unsauber; unzüchtig, zotig, obszön, lasziv; *(Sprache)* gewöhnlich, anstößig; gemein, schlecht, übel, häßlich, abscheulich, scheußlich, schändlich, verrucht, ruchlos, böse; unredlich, unehrlich; *sport* unfair, regelwidrig, falsch; *typ* voller Druckfehler; *fam* unangenehm, häßlich; mies, mau; *s* Zs.stoß, -prall; *bes. sport* ungültige(r) Versuch *m*, Foul *n*; *tr* dreckig, schmutzig machen; verschmutzen, verstopfen; anfüllen; verwickeln, fangen; zs.stoßen mit, auffahren auf; beschädigen; *sport* verstoßen gegen; *itr* dreckig, trübe, schmutzig werden; verschmutzen; sich verstopfen; sich verwickeln, sich fangen; zs.stoßen; *sport* gegen die Regeln verstoßen; *to ~ up (Am fam)* durchea.bringen; *by fair means or ~* im Guten oder im Bösen, so oder so; *through fair and ~* durch dick und dünn; *to fall, to go, to run ~ of (mar)* zs.stoßen mit, auffahren auf; sich verwickeln in; in Konflikt geraten mit; *to play ~* unfair handeln (*s.o.* jdm gegenüber); *to ~ o.'s own nest (fig)* das eigene Nest beschmutzen; **~ ball** *(Baseball)* über die Grenzlinie fallende(r) Ball *m*; **~ line** *sport* Grenzlinie *f*; **~-mouthed** *a* schmutzige, lose Reden führend; **~ness** ['-nis] Schmutz(igkeit *f*) *m*; Gemeinheit, Schlechtigkeit, Schändlichkeit, Ruchlosigkeit *f*; unfaire(s) Verhalten *n*; **~ page** *typ* Schmutzseite *f*; **~ play** unfaire(s) Spiel *n*, Verstoß *m* gegen die Regeln; Verbrechen *n*; **~ tongue** belegte Zunge *f*; *fig* lose(r) Mund *m*.

found [faund] **1.** *tr* gründen (*on* auf), begründen (*on* mit); *(Gebäude, Einrichtung)* gründen, stiften, errichten; *to ~ o.s. on* sich stützen auf *(fig)*; *to ~ a family* e-e Familie gründen; **2.** *tr metal* (schmelzen u.) gießen.

foundation [faun'deiʃən] (Be-)Gründung; Errichtung; Schenkung, Stiftung; Grundmauer *f*, Fundament *n*, Unterlage *f*, Unterbau; Baugrund *m*; *fig* Grundlage, Basis; Stütze; *mil* Bettung *f*; *to be completely without ~* jeder Grundlage entbehren; völlig unbegründet sein; *to lay the ~s of s.th.* für etw den Grund legen; **~-cream** Puderunterlage, Tageskrem *f*; **~er** [-ʃnə] *Br* Stipendiat *m*; **~-garment** Korsett *n*, Hüfthalter *m*; **~-member** Mitbegründer *m*; **~-muslin** Steifgaze *f*; **~-school** Stiftsschule *f*; **~ scholar** Stipendiat *m*; **~-stone** Grundstein; Eckstein *m*; *to lay the ~~* den Grundstein legen; **~ wall** Grundmauer *f*.

founder ['faundə] **1.** *s* (Be-)Gründer, Stifter *m*; **2.** *s metal* Gießer *m*; **3.** *itr (Pferd)* lahmen, e-n entzündeten Huf haben; *(Schiff)* sinken, untergehen; *allg* zs.brechen, scheitern.

foundling ['faundliŋ] Findling *m*; **~ hospital** Findelhaus *n*.

foundry ['faundri] Gießerei *f*.

fount [faunt] **1.** *poet* Quell, Born *m*; **2.** *(Am: font) typ* Guß *m*; **~-case** Setzkasten *m*.

fountain ['fauntin] Quelle *f a. fig*; *fig* Ursprung; Springquell, -brunnen; *(drinking ~)* Trinkwasserspender; Behälter *m*, Reservoir *n (für Flüssigkeiten)*; *(soda ~) bes. Am* Mineralwasserausschank *m*; Erfrischungshalle *f*; *~ of youth* Jungbrunnen *m*; **~-head** Quelle (e-s Flusses); *fig* (Ur-, Haupt-)Quelle *f*; **~-pen** Füll(federhalt)er *m*.

four [fɔ:] *a* vier; *s sport* Vierer *m*; *to go on all ~s* auf allen Vieren gehen; **~-cornered** *a* viereckig; **~-digit** vierstellig; **~-door sedan** *Am* viertürige Limousine *f*; **~-flush** *tr Am sl* bluffen, verblüffen, täuschen; **~-flusher** ['-flʌʃə] *Am sl* Bluffer, Blender *m*; **~fold** ['-fould] *a adv* vierfach, -fältig; **~-footed** *a* vierfüßig; **~-handed** *a* vierhändig *a. mus*; **F~-H club** *Am* Organisation *f* zur Förderung u. Fortbildung der Landjugend; **~-in-hand** ['fɔ:rin'hænd] Vierspänner *m (Wagen)*; **~-leaf clover** vierblättrige(s) Kleeblatt *n*; **~-letter word** unanständige(s) Wort *n*; **~-O** *Am sl* prima, erstklassig; **~-oar** Viererboot *n*; **~pence** ['-pəns] vier Pence; **~poster** ['-'poustə] Himmelbett *n*; **~score** ['fɔ:'skɔ:] *obs poet* achtzig; **~-seater** Viersitzer *m*; **~-sided** *a* vierseitig; **~some** ['-səm] *(Golf)* Viererspiel *n*; **~square** ['-'skwɛə] *a* viereckig; wuchtig, solide; fest, entschlossen, unnachgiebig; gerade, offen; *s* Viereck *n*; **~ star** *a Am fam* hervorragend, unübertrefflich; **~-stroke** *mot* Viertakt-; **~teen** ['fɔ:'ti:n] vierzehn; **~teenth** ['fɔ:'ti:nθ] *a* vierzehnt; *s* Vierzehntel *n*; **~th** [fɔ:θ] *a* viert; *s* Viertel *n*; *the F~~ of July* der amerikanische Nationalfeiertag; **~thly** ['fɔ:θli] *adv* viertens; **~-wheel**: *~~ brake* Vierradbremse *f*; *~~ drive* Vierradantrieb *m*; **~-wheeled** *a* vierrädrig.

fowl [faul] *s* Stück Geflügel; Huhn; Geflügel *(Fleisch)*; *a. pl* Geflügel *(Tiere)*, Federvieh *n*; *obs* Vogel *m*; *itr* Vögel schießen *od* jagen; Vogelfang, -stellerei betreiben; **~er** ['-ə] Vogeljäger, -fänger, -steller *m*; **~ing** ['-iŋ] Vogeljagd *f*, -fang *m*, -stellerei *f*; *~~-piece* Vogelflinte *f*; **~pest** Hühnerpest *f*; **~-run** Hühnerhof *m*.

*

fox [fɔks] *s* Fuchs; *(~-fur)* Fuchspelz; *fig* schlaue(r) Fuchs *m (Mensch)*; *tr* überlisten, anführen, hereinlegen; täuschen; berauschen; *(Schuhe)* ausbessern; *itr (Papier)* Stockflecken bekommen; *~ and geese* Gänsespiel *n (Brettspiel)*; **~-brush** Fuchsschwanz *m*; **~-earth** Fuchsbau *m*; **~ed** [-t] *a* stockfleckig; modrig; verstockt; *sl* besoffen; **~glove** *bot* Fingerhut *m*; **~hole** *mil* Schützenloch *n*; **~hound** Jagdhund *m*; **~hunt** Fuchsjagd *f*; **~tail** ['-teil] Fuchsschwanz *m bes. bot*; *~~-saw* Fuchsschwanz *m (Säge)*; **~terrier** ['-teriə] Foxterrier *m (Hunderasse)*; *wire-haired ~~* Drahthaarterrier *m*; **~-trap** Fuchsfalle *f*; **~trot** ['-trɔt] *s* Foxtrott *m (Tanz)*; *itr* Foxtrott tanzen; **~y** ['-i] fuchsartig; schlau, listig; fuchsig *(gelbrot)*; stockfleckig.

foyer ['fɔiei] *bes. theat* Foyer *n*, Wandelhalle *f*.

frabjous ['fræbʒəs] *fam* hervorragend.

fracas ['frækɑ:, *Am* 'freikəs] *pl Br ~* ['-z] *Am -es* Lärm, Krach *m*, Geschrei *n*; Streit, Tumult *m*.

fraction ['frækʃən] *rel* Brechen *(des Brotes)*; Bruchstück *n*, -teil, Fetzen, Splitter; *chem math* Bruch *m*; *by a ~ of an inch (fig)* um ein Haar; *not a ~* nicht ein bißchen; **~al** ['-l] gebrochen, Bruch-; *chem* fraktioniert; *fam* winzig; *~~ amount* Teilbetrag *m*; **~ate** ['-eit] *tr chem* fraktionieren; **~ize** ['-aiz] *tr* zerlegen; **~ line** Bruchstrich *m*.

fractious ['frækʃəs] aufsässig, aufrührerisch, rebellisch; zänkisch, bissig, reizbar, launisch.

fracture ['fræktʃə] *s (bes.* Knochen-) Bruch *m*; Bruchstelle; *(~ plane)* Bruchfläche; *gram* Brechung *f*; *tr itr* (zer)brechen; *~ of the skull* Schädelbruch *m*; **~d** ['-d] *a Am sl* besoffen.

fragil|e ['frædʒail] zerbrechlich, empfindlich; *tech* brüchig; *med* anfällig, schwach; **~ity** [frə'dʒiliti] Zerbrechlichkeit, Empfindlichkeit, Zartheit; *tech* Brüchigkeit *f*.

fragment ['frægmənt] Bruchstück *n*, -teil *m*; *lit* Fragment; *mil* Sprengstück *n*, Splitter *m*; **~ary** ['-əri] bruchstückhaft, fragmentarisch, in Bruchstücken; unvollständig; unzs.hängend, zs.hanglos; **~ation** [-'teiʃən] Ausea.-, Zerbrechen, Zersplittern *n*; *mil (~~ effect)* Splitterwirkung *f*; *~~ bomb* Splitterbombe *f*.

fragran|ce ['freigrəns] Duft, Wohlgeruch *m*; **~t** ['-t] duftend, wohlriechend; *fig* angenehm.

frail [freil] **1.** *a* zerbrechlich; empfindlich, zart, schwach *a. med*; gebrechlich, schwächlich; (innerlich) haltlos, schwankend; sündig; *s Am sl* Püppchen *n*; **~ty** ['-ti] Hinfälligkeit; Schwäche, Schwachheit, (innere) Haltlosigkeit *f*; Fehltritt *m*, Verfehlung *f*; **2.** Binsenkorb *m* (für Trockenfrüchte).

fraise [freiz] **1.** *hist* Halskrause; Palisade *f*; **2.** *tech* Fräser *m (Gerät)*.

frame [freim] *tr* gestalten, bilden, formen, schaffen; entwerfen, ausarbeiten, auf-, zs.stellen; zs.setzen, (auf)bauen, errichten; in Worte fassen *od* kleiden; Ausdruck geben *od* verleihen (*s.th.* e-r S), ausdrücken; abverfassen; *(Rede)* aufsetzen; aus-, erdenken, ersinnen, planen; einfassen, (ein)rahmen; *(to ~ up) fam* fälschlich bezichtigen; aushecken; *itr* sich entwickeln, sich anlassen, *fam* sich machen; versprechen; *s* Bau *m*, Konstruktion *f*; Gerüst, Gestell, Gebälk; Gerippe, Rahmenwerk, Gehäuse *n*; Fassung *f*; *mar aero* Spant; *(Tür-, Fenster-, Bilder-)* Rahmen; Türstock *m*, Zarge *f*; Knochengerüst, Skelett *n*; Körperbau *m*, Figur, Gestalt *f*; Gefüge *n*, (Auf-)Bau *m*, Konstruktion, Anordnung, Gestaltung; *(~ of mind)* Veranlagung, (geistige) Verfassung, Geistes-, Sinnesart *f*, Temperament *n*; Ordnung, Verfassung *f*, (*bes.* Regierungs-)System *n*; *(Gärtnerei)* Treibkasten *m*; *sport* Feld *n*; *phot film* (Einzel-)Aufnahme *f (auf e-m Filmstreifen)*; *video* Rasterfeld, Bild *n*; *mot* Rahmen *m*, Chassis *n*; *(Statistik)* Erhebungsgrundlage *f*; *picture ~* Bilderrahmen *m*; **~ aerial** Rahmenantenne *f*; **~-house** Holzhaus *n*; **~r** ['-ə] Former, Bildner, Gestalter, Planer, Erfinder; Rahmenmacher *m*; **~-saw** Spannsäge *f*; **~-up** *fam* Anschlag *m*, Komplott, abgekartete(s) Spiel *n*, Machenschaften *f pl*; **~work** Gestell, Gerüst, Gebälk, Gerippe; Fachwerk *n*; Rahmenkonstruktion *f*; Traggerüst *n*; *mar* Spanten *m pl*; *fig* Gefüge *n*, Bau *m*, Struktur *f*, Rahmen *m*, System *n*; *to come within the ~~ of s.th.* in den Rahmen e-r S fallen; *~~ of society* Gesellschaftsaufbau *m*.

France [frɑ:ns] Frankreich *n*.

Franc|es ['frɑ:nsis] Franziska *f*; **~is** [-] Franz(iskus) *m*.

franchise ['fræntʃaiz] *die* bürgerlichen Rechte *pl*, Wahlrecht; *bes. Am* Privileg, Alleinverkaufsrecht *n*, Konzession, Lizenz *f*.

Franciscan [fræn'siskən] *a rel* franziskanisch; *s* Franziskaner(in *f*) *m*.

Franconia [fræŋ'kounjə] Franken *n*; **~n** [-n] *a* fränkisch; *s* Franke *m*, Fränkin *f*.

frangib|ility [frændʒi'biliti] Zerbrechlichkeit, Empfindlichkeit *f*; **~le** ['frændʒibl] zerbrechlich; empfindlich.

Frank [fræŋk] *hist* Franke *m*.

frank [fræŋk] **1.** frei(mütig), offen (-herzig); ehrlich, aufrichtig, unverstellt; unverhohlen; *to be ~* aufrichtig gesagt, offen gestanden; **~ly** ['-li] *adv* aufrichtig, offen, ehrlich; ehrlich gesagt; **~ness** ['-nis] Freimütigkeit, Offenheit *f*; **2.** *tr* portofrei senden; frankieren, freimachen; befreien (*from* von); freien Eintritt gewähren (*s.o.* jdm); *s* Portofreiheit *f*; Frankovermerk *m*; portofreie Sendung *f*; **~ing machine** Frankiermaschine *f*; **3.** *Am sl* Frankfurter *f (Würstchen)*.

frankfurt(er), frankfort(er) ['fræŋkfət(ə)] Frankfurter *od* Wiener (Würstchen *n*) *f*.

frankincense ['fræŋkinsens] Weihrauch *m*.

franklin ['fræŋklin] *hist Br* freie(r) Bauer, Freisasse *m*.
frantic ['fræntik] *adv* **~ally** ['-əli] rasend, wütend (*with* vor); *(Anstrengung)* krampfhaft; *obs* irr(e); *to be ~* außer sich sein, toben; *with pain* vor Schmerz wahnsinnig werden; *to drive ~* auf die Palme bringen.
frap [fræp] *tr mar* (fest)zurren.
frappé ['fræpei] *a (Getränk)* eisgekühlt; *s* Eisgetränk; Halbgefrorene(s) *n*; gefrorene(r) u. gesüßte(r) Obstsaft *m*.
frat [fræt] *Am sl* (studentische) Verbindung *f*.
fratern|al [frə'tə:nl] brüderlich; Bruderschafts-, Brüder-; *~~ twins (pl)* zweieiige Zwillinge *m pl*; **~ity** [-iti] Brüderschaft; Brüderlichkeit; *rel* Bruderschaft; *allg* Genossenschaft; *Am* (studentische) Verbindung *f*; **~ization** [frætənai'zeiʃən, -ni-] Verbrüderung *f*; **~ize** ['frætənaiz] *itr* sich verbrüdern.
fratricid|al [freitri'saidl] brudermörderisch; *~~ war* Bruderkrieg *m*; **~e** ['freitrisaid] Brudermord; Brudermörder *m*.
fraud [frɔ:d] Betrug *m*, arglistige Täuschung (*on* gegenüber); Unterschlagung *f*; Schwindel *m*; *jur* Arglist *f*; *fam* Schwindler; Hochstapler *m*; **~ulence, -cy** ['-juləns(i)] Betrügerei, Untreue *f*; **~ulent** ['-julənt] betrügerisch; arglistig; böswillig; *with ~~ intent(ion)* in betrügerischer Absicht; *~~ conversion* Unterschlagung *f*; *~~ representation* Vorspiegelung *f* falscher Tatsachen; *~~ transaction* Schwindelgeschäft *n*.
fraught [frɔ:t] beladen, voll (*with* mit); *fig* geladen (*with* mit); *~ with* voller.
fray [frei] **1.** *s* Schlägerei *f*, Streit *m*; *eager for the ~ (lit)* streitsüchtig; **2.** *tr itr* (sich) verschleißen, (sich) abnutzen, (sich) abtragen; ausfransen; sich durchscheuern; *fig* erbittern.
frazil ['freizil] *Am* Grundeis *n*.
frazzle ['fræzl] *Am fam tr* verschleißen, abtragen, abnutzen; ermüden, erschöpfen; *s* Lumpen, Fetzen *m*; *to a ~* bis zur Erschöpfung; *to beat to a ~* windelweich schlagen.
freak [fri:k] Laune *f*, Einfall *m*, Spielerei; Launenhaftigkeit, Verspieltheit *f*; *(~ of nature)* Spiel *n* der Natur, Mißbildung *f*, Monstrum *n*; *fam* verrückte(r) Kerl *m*; **~ish** ['-iʃ] launisch, launenhaft, verspielt; abnorm.
freckle ['frekl] *s* Sommersprosse *f*; *tr itr* sommersprossig machen, werden; **~d** ['-d] *a* sommersprossig.
free [fri:] **1.** *a* frei (*from, of* von); freiwillig; freiheitlich; unabhängig; frei beweglich, lose, locker; unbehindert, ungehindert, uneingeschränkt; zwanglos, ungebunden; unvoreingenommen, vorurteilsfrei; nicht verpflichtet; zur Verfügung stehend; *(Platz, Zimmer)* frei, nicht besetzt, unbesetzt, nicht reserviert; *(Bewegung)* ungezwungen, leicht, spielerisch, anmutig; freigebig, großzügig, *fam hum* spendabel (*with* mit); verschwenderisch, reichlich, massenhaft, im Überfluß (vorhanden); freimütig, offen(herzig), aufrichtig, gerade, unverhohlen, unversteckt; wenig zurückhaltend, rücksichtslos, dreist, keck, ungezügelt, ungebührlich; unziemlich, ungesittet, unanständig; gratis, kostenlos, unentgeltlich, umsonst; öffentlich, allgemein zugänglich; *chem* frei; *~ from ...* -los; ohne; befreit von; **2.** *adv* gratis; frei, ungehindert, uneingeschränkt; **3.** *tr* frei machen, befreien; freilassen; (ab-, los)lösen; *(Straße)* (wieder) frei machen; entlasten; reinigen, befreien (*from* von); *with a ~ hand* großzügig, verschwenderisch *adv*; *to do s.th. of o.'s own ~ will* etw aus freien Stücken tun; *to give, to have a ~ hand* freie Hand geben *od* lassen, haben; *to make, to set ~* freilassen; *to make, to be ~ with s.th.* mit e-r S schalten u. walten; *with o.'s money* sein Geld verschwenden; *with s.o.* sich jdm gegenüber Freiheiten erlauben; *to run ~ (tech)* leer laufen; *I am ~ to* es steht mir frei zu; *~ alongside ship* frei Schiff; *~ and easy (a)* zwanglos, ungeniert; *~ from acid* säurefrei; *~ on board* frei Schiff; *~ from care* sorgenfrei; *~ of carriage, of freight* frachtfrei; *~ of charge(s)* kostenlos, -frei, spesenfrei; *~ of debt* schuldenfrei, ohne Schulden; *~ of duty* gebühren-, abgabenfrei; zollfrei; *~ from error, from defect* fehlerfrei; *~ of interest* zinsfrei, -los; *~ of postage* portofrei; *~ on rail* frei Eisenbahn; *~ of responsibility* frei von Verantwortung; *~ on sale* frei verkäuflich; *~ of (all) tax(es)* steuer-, abgabenfrei; **~-board** *mar* Freibord *m*; **~booter** ['-bu:tə] Freibeuter *m*; **~-born** *a* freigeboren; **~by, ~bie** *Am sl* etw Geschenktes *n*; **F~ Church** Freikirche *f*; **~ delivery** kostenfreie Zustellung, Zustellung *f* frei Haus; **~dman** ['-dmæn] Freigelassene(r) *m*; **~dom** ['-dəm] Freiheit *f*, Freisein *n*, Befreiung (*from* von); Unabhängigkeit, Ungebundenheit, Ungezwungenheit; Offenheit, Aufrichtigkeit, Geradheit; Auf-, Zudringlichkeit; freie Benutzung *f*; freie(r) Zutritt *m* (*of* zu); Vorrecht, Privileg *n*; *to give s.o. the ~ of the house* jdm Hausrecht gewähren; *to take, to use ~s with s.o.* sich jdm gegenüber zuviel herausnehmen; *~~ of action* Handlungsfreiheit *f*; *~~ of association* Vereinsrecht *n*; *~~ of the city* (Ehren-)Bürgerrecht *n*; *~~ of the company* Meisterrecht *n*; *~~ of conscience* Gewissensfreiheit *f*; *~~ of faith, of religion* Glaubens-, Religionsfreiheit *f*; *~~ of movement* Bewegungsfreiheit; Freizügigkeit *f*; *~~ of opinion* Meinungsfreiheit *f*; *~~ of the press* Pressefreiheit *f*; *the ~~ of the seas* die Freiheit der Meere; *~~ of speech* Redefreiheit *f*; *~~ to strike* Streikrecht *n*; *~~ of the will* Willensfreiheit *f*; **~ enterprise** freie Marktwirtschaft *f*; **~ entry** ungehinderte Einreise; zollfreie Einfuhr *f*; **~-fight, -for-all** *Am* freie(r) Wettbewerb *m*; allgemeine Schlägerei *f*; **~hand** ['-hænd] freihändig; *~~ drawing* Freihandzeichnen *n*; **~-handed** *a* freigebig, großzügig; **~ headroom** lichte Höhe *f*; **~-hearted** *a* freimütig, offenherzig; **~hold** freie(r) Grundbesitz *m*; *~~ flat* Eigentumswohnung *f*; **~holder** Grundeigentümer; *hist* Freisasse *m*; **~ kick** *sport* Freistoß *m*; **~ labo(u)r** nicht gewerkschaftlich organisierte Arbeitskräfte *f pl*; **~ lance** *s hist* Landsknecht; Freiberufliche(r), Freischaffende(r); *pol* Unabhängige(r), Parteilose(r) *m*; *~-~ (a)* freiberuflich; *itr* freiberuflich tätig sein; **~-list** (Zoll-)Freiliste *f*; **~ liver** Schlemmer *m*; **~-living** schlemmerisch; *biol* freilebend, nicht parasitisch; **~-load** *Am fam itr* auf Kosten anderer leben; *s* Freibier *n*, freie Mahlzeit *f*; **~ love** freie Liebe *f*; **~ly** ['-li] frei; offen; reichlich; umsonst, gratis; **~man** ['-mæn] Freie(r); ['-mən] (Voll-, Ehren-) Bürger *m*; **~mason** ['-meisn] Freimaurer *m*; *~~s' lodge* Freimaurerloge *f*; **~ moving** freibeweglich; **~ pass** Frei-, Einlaß-, Durchlaß-, *rail* Netzkarte *f*; **~ place** *(Schule)* Freistelle *f*; **~ play** *tech* Spielraum *m*; **~ port** Freihafen *m*; **~ speech** Redefreiheit *f*; **~-spoken** *a* freimütig, offen; **~-thinker** Freidenker, -geist *m*; **~-thinking** *a* freidenkerisch, -geistig; *s u.* **~-thought** Freidenkerei, -geisterei, Gedankenfreiheit *f*; **~ ticket** Freikarte *f*, -billett *n*; **~ time** Freizeit *f*; *com* freie Liegezeit, Abladefrist *f*; **~ trade** Freihandel *m*; *~~ area* Freihandelszone *f*; **~way** *Am Art* Autobahn *f*; **~-wheel** *(Fahrrad)* Freilauf *m*; *~~ hub* Freilaufnabe *f*; **~-wheeling** *Am sl* freigebig; hemmungs-, rücksichtslos; ohne Zurückhaltung; **~ will** *s* Willensfreiheit *f*; freie(r) Wille *m*; Freiwilligkeit *f*; **~-~ (a)** freiwillig; *of o.'s own ~~* freiwillig *adv*.
freesia ['fri:zjə] *bot* Freesie *f*.
freez|e [fri:z] *irr froze, frozen itr* (ge-)frieren; zu-, anfrieren (*to* an); *(Wasserleitung)* einfrieren; (vor Kälte) erstarren; *(Mensch)* eiskalt werden, frieren; *(~~ to death)* erfrieren; steif, *fig* starr werden (*with* vor); *fam* sich (völlig) ruhig verhalten, sich nicht rühren; förmlich, abweisend, kühl, unfreundlich werden; *(Flüssigkeit)* (durch Überhitzung) dick, steif werden; *tr* gefrieren, erstarren lassen; mit Eis überziehen; stark abkühlen lassen; *(Lebensmittel)* tiefkühlen; anfrieren lassen; *(Menschen od Körperteil)* erfrieren lassen; steif (werden) lassen; *fig* mutlos machen, entmutigen, lähmen; *Am fam* blockieren, sperren, kaltstellen; *(Kapital)* einfrieren; *(Löhne, Preise)* stoppen; *s* Frost(periode *f*) *m*; *to ~~ in* einfrieren; *to ~~ off* abfrieren; *to ~~ (on) to (fam)* anwachsen an; sich anklammern an; festhalten; *to ~~ out (fam)* 'rausekeln; sich vom Leibe halten; überstimmen; ausschalten, an die Wand drücken; *to ~~ over (itr)* zu-, überfrieren; *tr* mit Eis bedecken; *to ~~ together* zs.-, anea.frieren; *to ~~ up (aero)* vereisen; *to be frozen* gefrieren; eiskalt werden; *to make s.o.'s blood ~~, to ~~ s.o.'s blood (fig)* jdm das Blut in den Adern erstarren lassen; *to put the ~~ on s.o. (Am sl)* jdm die kalte Schulter zeigen; *I'm ~ing* ich friere, mich friert; *~~ box* Kühlraum *m*; *~~-up* Frostperiode *f*; **~er** ['-ə] Kühlschrank *m*; *(ice-cream ~~)* Eismaschine *f*; *rail* Kühlwagen *m*; **~ing** ['-iŋ] *a* eisig, eiskalt; *s* Frost *m*, Frieren; Einfrieren *n*; Erstarrung *f*; *below ~~* unter dem Gefrierpunkt; *~~-machine* Eismaschine *f*; *~~-mixture* Kältemischung *f*; *~~-point* Gefrierpunkt *m*; *~~ of prices* Preisstopp *m*.

*

freight [freit] *s* Fracht(beförderung), Ladung *(Br mar, Am a. rail)*; Fracht(-gut *n*) *f*; Frachtkosten *pl*; Lade-, Frachtraum *m*; Schiffsladung, -miete *f*; *(~ train) Am* Güterzug *m*; *tr (Br nur Schiff, Am allg)* beladen; verfrachten, befördern; *by ~ (Am)* als Frachtgut; *to take in ~* Ladung einnehmen (*for* nach); *~ by air (Am)* Luftfracht *f*; **~age** ['-idʒ] Fracht(gut *n*, -beförderung *f*, -geld *n*) *f*; **~ bill** *Am* Frachtbrief *m*; **~-car** *Am* Güterwagen *m*; **~ depot** *Am* Güterbahnhof *m*; **~-carrying glider** *aero* Lastensegler *m*; **~ elevator** *Am* Güteraufzug *m*; **~ engine** *Am* Güterzuglokomotive *f*; **~er** ['-ə] Befrachter; Reeder, Transportunternehmer *m*; Frachtschiff *n*, -dampfer, Frachter *m*; Transportflugzeug *n*; **~ house** *Am* Güterschuppen *m*; **~ing** ['-iŋ] Befrachtung *f*; **~ insurance** Gütertransportversicherung *f*; **~-list** Fracht(güter)liste *f*; **~-rate, -tariff** Frachtsatz *m*; **~-reduction** Frachtermäßigung *f*; **~-service, -traffic** *Am* Güterverkehr *m*; **~ station** *Am* Güterbahnhof *m*; **~-steamer** Frachtdampfer *m*; **~ train** *Am* Güterzug *m*; **~ truck** *Am* Fernlaster *m*; **~ warrant** Frachtbrief *m*; **~-yard** *Am* Güterbahnhof *m*.

French [frentʃ] *a* französisch; *s* (das) Französisch(e); *the ~ (pl)* die Franzosen *pl*; *to take ~ leave* heimlich, ohne sich zu verabschieden, (weg)gehen; **~ beans** *pl* grüne Bohnen *f pl*; **~ chalk** Schlämm-, Schneiderkreide *f*; **~ dressing** Salattunke *f*; **~ fried potatoes,** *Am fam* **~ fries** *pl* Pommes frites *f pl*; **~ heel** hohe(r) (Damen-)Absatz *m*; **~ horn** Waldhorn *n*; **~ ice-cream** Sahneeis *n*; **~ letter** Kondom *m*; **~man** ['-mən] *pl* **~men** Franzose *m*; **~ roof** Mansardendach *n*; **~ seam** überwendige Naht *f*; **~ toast** *(Küche)* Arme Ritter *m pl*; **~ window** *(tiefreichendes)* Flügelfenster *n*, Balkontür *f*; **~woman** ['-wumən] *pl* **~women** ['-wimən] Französin *f*; **~y** ['-i] *Am a* französisch; *s fam* Franzose *m*.

frenetic(al) [frə'netik(əl)] tobend, rasend, toll; wild, stürmisch, begeistert, frenetisch.

frenz|ied ['frenzid] *a* tobend, rasend, toll; wahnsinnig; **~y** ['-i] Raserei *f*; Wahnsinn; *fig* Anfall *m*, Ekstase *f*; *in a ~~ of despair* in wilder Verzweiflung; *to rouse to ~~* in Raserei, in e-n Taumel der Begeisterung versetzen.

frequen|ce, -cy ['fri:kwəns(i)] häufige(s) Vorkommen *n*, Häufigkeit *f a. math*; *phys, bes. el* Frequenz, Schwingungszahl *f*; *~cy of accidents* Unfallhäufigkeit *f*; *~cy band* Frequenzband *n*; *~cy range, coverage* Frequenzbereich *m*; *~cy selection (radio)* Grobeinstellung *f*; **~t** ['fri:kwənt] *a* häufig, sich schnell wiederholend; (be)ständig; gewohnt; regelmäßig; *(Puls)* hoch, frequent; *tr* [fri'kwent] häufig, oft, ständig besuchen; häufig vorkommen in; **~tation** [fri:kwen'teiʃən] häufige(r), ständige(r) Besuch *m*; **~er** [fri'kwentə] häufige(r), ständige(r) Besucher; Kunde; Stammgast *m*.

fresco ['freskou] *pl -(e)s* Freskomalerei; *(painting in ~)* Freske *f*, Fresko *n*; *to paint in ~, to ~ (tr)* in Fresko malen.

fresh [freʃ] **1.** *a* frisch; *bes. a.* (noch) ungesalzen, (noch) nicht konserviert; *(Hering)* grün; (noch) nicht abgestanden *od* abgelagert, (noch) gut, unverdorben, (noch) nicht welk; (noch) munter, (noch) nicht müde, (noch) auf der Höhe, kräftig, stark; jung u. gesund aussehend; neu; zusätzlich, weiter; (noch) unerfahren; ungewohnt; fremd; ursprünglich, anregend, lebhaft; kühl, (er)frisch(end), belebend; *(Wind)* frisch, rein, kräftig, mäßig stark; *(Wasser)* frisch, nicht salzhaltig; *fam* beschwipst; *Am sl* unverschämt; frech, dreist; *s* (Morgen-)Frühe *f*; Jahresbeginn, -anfang *m*; Frische, Kühle; Welle, Flut *f*; *to break ~ ground (fig)* Neuland gewinnen *od* erschließen; *~ paint* frisch gestrichen! **~ air** Frischluft *f*; *~~ duct* Frischluftkanal *m*; **~en** ['-n] *tr* frischmachen, auffrischen; erfrischen; waschen; stärken, kräftigen; *itr* frisch werden; *(Wind)* auffrischen, zunehmen; **~et** ['-it] kleine(r) Wasserlauf; Süßwasserzufluß, Küstenfluß *m*; Hochwasser *n*, Überschwemmung *f*; **~man** ['-mən] Anfänger, Neuling; *(Univ., Am a. Schule)* Fuchs *m*; **~ness** ['-nis] Frische, Kühle; Neuheit; Unerfahrenheit; Fremdheit *f*; **~water** *a* Süßwasser-; *fig fam* unerfahren, ahnungslos; *Am* Binnen-; provinziell, hinterwäldlerisch; *~~fish* Süßwasserfisch *m*.

fret [fret] **1.** *tr* zerfressen, -setzen, -nagen, -reiben; aufscheuern; *(Wasser)* kräuseln; *fig* aufreiben, ermüden, quälen, ärgern, reizen; *itr* fressen, nagen *(into, on, upon* an); *(Wasser)* sich kräuseln; *fig* gereizt sein, schlechte Laune haben; sich ärgern, querulieren, (herum)nörgeln, quengeln; sich grämen, sich sorgen *(about* über); *s* Abnutzung; abgenutzte Stelle; *fig* Aufregung, Gereiztheit *f*; Ärger; Verdruß *m*; *to ~ away* abnutzen; *fig* ruinieren; *to ~ away, to ~ out o.'s life, to ~ to death* sich totärgern; *to be in a ~* beunruhigt, besorgt sein; **~ful** ['-ful] gereizt, reizbar, knurrig, verdrießlich, unzufrieden; **~fulness** ['-fulnis] schlechte Laune, Reizbarkeit, Verdrießlichkeit *f*, Unmut *m*, Unzufriedenheit *f*; **2.** *s* Gitterleiste; Mäanderlinie *f*; *tr* mit e-r Gitterleiste, e-m durchbrochenen Muster verzieren; **~-saw** Laubsäge *f*; **~work** Gitterwerk *n*; Laubsägearbeit *f*; **3.** *(Saiteninstrument)* Bund, Griff(leiste *f*) *m*.

friab|ility [fraiə'biliti], **~leness** ['fraiəblnis] Mürbheit, Bröck(e)ligkeit *f*; **~le** ['fraiəbl] mürbe, krüm(e)lig.

friar ['fraiə] *(bes.* Bettel-)Mönch *m*; *Augustinian, Black, Grey ~s (pl)* Augustiner; Dominikaner; Franziskaner *m pl*; **~y** ['fraiəri] Mönchskloster *n*, -orden *m*.

fribble ['fribl] *s* Trödler, alberne(r) Mensch *m*; Albernheit, alberne Idee *f*; *itr* die Zeit verplempern *od* vertrödeln.

fricassee [frikə'si:] *s (Küche)* Frikassee *n*; *tr (Fleisch)* frikassieren.

fricative ['frikətiv] *a gram* Reibe-; *s* Reibelaut *m*.

friction ['frikʃən] Reibung *f a. tech*; Frottieren *n*, Abreibung *f*; *fig* Reibungen, Spannungen, Differenzen, Schwierigkeiten *f pl*; *attr tech* Friktions-, Reibungs-; **~al** ['-l] *a* Reibungs-; **~ disk** Bremsscheibe *f*; **~-surface** Reib(ungs)fläche *f*.

Friday ['fraidi, -dei] Freitag *m*; *on ~s* freitags; *Good ~* Karfreitag *m*.

fri(d)ge [fridʒ] *Br fam* Kühlschrank *m*.

fried [fraid] *a* gebraten; Brat-; *Am sl* besoffen; **~cake** *Am* Berliner (Pfannkuchen) *m*; **~ chicken** gebratene(s) Hühnchen *n*; **~ egg** Spiegel-, Setzei *n*.

friend [frend] Freund(in *f*); (guter) Bekannte(r), Kollege, Kamerad; (Partei-)Freund; Anhänger; *F~* Quäker *m*; *to be ~s with* befreundet sein mit; *to be great ~s* eng mitea. befreundet, *fam* dicke Freunde sein; *to make ~s with* Freundschaft schließen, sich anfreunden mit; *to make ~s again* sich wieder vertragen, sich (wieder) versöhnen; *business ~* Geschäftsfreund *m*; *a ~ at court* ein einflußreicher Freund, *fam* Vetter *m*; *the Society of F~s* die Quäker *pl*; **~less** ['-lis] ohne Freund; **~liness** ['-linis] Freundlichkeit *f*; **~ly** ['-li] *a* freundschaftlich; befreundet *(to, with* mit); freundlich, zuvor-, entgegenkommend, hilfsbereit, hilfreich, *fam* nett; günstig, förderlich *(to* für); *to be on ~~ terms with s.o.* mit jdm auf freundschaftlichem Fuß stehen; *~~ letter (Am)* Privatbrief *m*; *~~ society* Versicherungsverein *m* auf Gegenseitigkeit; **~ship** ['-ʃip] Freundschaft *f (between* zwischen; *with* mit); *that's in ~~* das bleibt unter uns.

frieze [fri:z] **1.** Zierstreifen, *arch* Fries *m*; **2.** Fries *m (schwerer Wollstoff)*.

frigate ['frigit] *mar* Fregatte *f*; *(~-bird)* Fregattvogel *m*.

fright [frait] Schreck(en); *fam* Kinderschreck *m*, Vogelscheuche *f (Mensch)*; Ungetüm, Schreckgespenst, Monstrum *n (Sache)*; *to get off with a bad ~* mit dem Schrecken davonkommen; *to look a ~* völlig verstört aussehen; *to take ~* erschrecken *(at* über); **~en** ['-n] *tr itr* erschrecken; *tr* verängstigen; abschrecken, einschüchtern; *to ~~ away* vergraulen; *to ~~ s.o. into doing s.th.* jdn dazu treiben, daß er etw tut; *to ~~ out, off* hinausgraulen; **~ened** ['-nd] *a* erschrocken, entsetzt *(at* über); *fam* bange *(of* vor); *to be, to get ~~* erschrecken; **~ful** ['-ful] schrecklich, fürchterlich *a. fam*; schreckenerregend; anstößig, anstoßerregend; **~fully** ['-fuli] *adv* schrecklich; *fam* sehr; **~fulness** ['-fulnis] Schrecklichkeit *f*; Terror(maßnahme *f*) *m*.

frigid ['fridʒid] (sehr, eisig, eis)kalt; *fig* frostig, eisig, kühl; *med (Frau)* frigid(e), nicht hingabefähig; *the ~ zone (geog)* die kalte Zone; **~aire** ['-ɛə] *Am* Kühlschrank *m (Warenzeichen)*; **~ity** [fri'dʒiditi] *(bes.* Gefühls-)Kälte *f*; frostige(s) Wesen *n*.

frigo ['frigou] *Am fam* Gefrierfleisch *n*; **~rific** [frigə'rifik] kälteerzeugend; Gefrier-; Kühl-.

frill [fril] *s zoo* (Hals-)Krause; Rüsche *f*; *lit* Schnörkel *m a. fig*; *pl* Spitzen *f pl*, Besatz *m*; *pl* Getue *n*, Affektiertheit *f*, Sums *m*, Trara *n*; *tr* kraus machen, kräuseln; fälteln; *to put on ~s* sich aufspielen; **~ies** ['-i:z] *pl fam* Reizwäsche *f*; **~ing** ['-iŋ] Rüschen *f pl*.

fringe [frindʒ] *s* Franse; *allg* Kante *f*, Saum; *bes. fig* Rand *m*; *opt* (Spektral-)Linie *f*; *pl* Pony(frisur *f*) *m*; *attr* Rand-; *tr* mit Fransen besetzen; ausfransen; *allg* säumen, einfassen; **~ area** Randgebiet *n*; **~ benefits** *pl* zusätzliche Sozialaufwendungen *f pl*; **~less** ['-lis] randlos; **~ parking** Parken *n* am Stadtrand.

frippery ['fripəri] Plunder, Firlefanz, Flitterkram, Tand *m*.

Frisian ['friziən] *a* friesisch; *s* (das) Friesisch(e); Friese *m*, Friesin *f*.

frisk [frisk] *s* Luftsprung *m*; *itr* tanzen und springen, hüpfen, herumtollen; *tr* hin und her hüpfen lassen; *sl* durchsuchen; *sl* filzen, beklauen; das Geld aus der Tasche ziehen *(s.o.* jdm); **~iness** ['-inis] Fröhlichkeit, Ausgelassenheit, Munterkeit *f*; **~y** ['-i] ausgelassen, lustig, munter, lebhaft.

frit [frit] *tr tech* fritten, zs.backen, verglasen; *s* Fritte *f*; **~ kiln** Frittenofen *m*.

frith [friθ] **1.** Meeresarm *m*, Förde; (weite Fluß-)Mündung *f*; **2.** Wald (-land, -gebiet *n*); Busch(wald) *m*, Unterholz *n*; Hecke, Hürde *f*.

fritillary [fri'tiləri] *bot bes. (Common F~)* Schachbrettblume *f*; *zoo* Perlmutterfalter *m*.

fritter ['fritə] **1.** *tr (to ~ away)* vergeuden, vertrödeln; *(Geld)* verschwenden; *tech* abbröckeln; **2.** Eier-, Pfannkuchen *m* mit Obstfüllung; *tech* Fritte *f*.

frivol ['frivəl] *tr (itr* die Zeit) vertrödeln; **~ity** [fri'vɔliti] Unwichtigkeit, Nebensächlichkeit, Nichtigkeit; Leichtfertigkeit *f*, Leichtsinn *m*, Oberflächlichkeit *f*; **~ous** ['frivələs] unbedeutend, unwichtig, nebensächlich; wertlos; *(Mensch)* leichtfertig, -sinnig.

frizz [friz] *itr tr (beim Braten)* brutzeln, brotzeln (lassen).

friz(z) [friz] *tr itr* (sich) kräuseln; *s* Kraushaar *n*.

frizz|le ['frizl] **1.** *tr itr* (sich) kräuseln; *s* kleine Locke *f*, Löckchen *n*; **~(l)y** ['friz(l)i] kraus, gekräuselt; **2.** *tr itr* brotzeln (lassen); knusprig braten.

fro [frou] *adv nur in: to and ~* ['tu(:)ən 'frou] vor u. zurück, hin u. her, auf u. ab.

frock [frɔk] *s* (Mönchs-)Kutte *f*; *fig* Priesteramt *n*; Robe *f*, Kittel *m*; Kinderröckchen, -kleid *n*; (*a.* Seemanns-)Bluse *f*; (Frauen-)Rock *m*, (Damen-)Kleid *n*; Waffenrock; *(~-coat)* Gehrock *m*; *tr* in die Kutte stecken; zum Priester machen.

frog [frɔg] Frosch; *vet* Knollenhuf; Schnürverschluß, -besatz; Säbel-, Seitengewehrhalter *m*; *rail* (Schienen-)Herzstück *n*; *(~-eater) hum pej* Franzose; *Am sl* Bizeps *m*; *to have a ~ in the throat* e-n Frosch im Halse haben, heiser sein; **~-hopper** *zoo* Schaumzirpe, -zikade *f*; **~man** Froschmann, Kampfschwimmer *m*; **~'s legs** *pl* Froschschenkel *m pl*; **~-spawn** Froschlaich *m*.

frolic ['frɔlik] *s* Scherz, Spaß, lustige(r) Streich *m*; Lustbarkeit *f*; Vergnügen *n*, (gute) Stimmung, Ausgelassenheit *f*; *itr (~king, ~ked)* lustig, ausgelassen sein, Spaß machen, scherzen; spielen; **~some** ['-səm] lustig, ausgelassen; verspielt.

from [frɔm, frəm] *prp* von (... ab, an); aus; von (... her); *(zeitlich)* seit; *(away ~)* weg, entfernt, in Entfernung von; aus, von (e-r Anzahl von); von ... ab *(halten)*; *(schützen)* vor; *(entlassen)* aus; *(unterschieden sein)* von; wegen, infolge, vor, aus *(Furcht usw)*; *apart ~* abgesehen von; *~ the beginning* von Anfang an; *~ a child* von Kindheit an, von klein auf; *~ experience* aus Erfahrung; *~ first to last* von Anfang bis zu Ende, von A bis Z; *~ morning to night* von früh bis spät; *~ nature, life (Kunst)* nach der Natur, nach dem Leben; *~ time to time* von Zeit zu Zeit, ab und zu; *~ year's end to year's end* jahraus, jahrein; *to go ~ bad to worse* immer schlimmer werden; *to judge ~ appearances* nach dem Äußeren urteilen; *not to know s.o. ~ Adam* jdn überhaupt nicht kennen; *to pass ~ mouth to mouth* von Mund zu Mund gehen; *where are you ~* wo sind Sie her? *~ what I know* meines Wissens; **~ above** von oben (herab, herunter); **~ afar** von fern, aus der Ferne; **~ amidst** mitten aus; **~ among** von, aus (... heraus); **~ before** aus der Zeit vor; **~ behind** hinter ... her; von hinten; **~ below, beneath** unter ... her; von unten; **~ between** aus, zwischen ... hervor; **~ beyond** von jenseits *prp* od *adv*; **~ now on** von jetzt ab; **~ on high** von oben, aus der Höhe, vom Himmel; **~ out** aus ... heraus; **~ over** über ... weg; *~ ~ o.'s glasses* über den Brillenrand; **~ under** unter ... hervor; **~ within** von innen; **~ without** von außen.

frond [frɔnd] (Farn-, Palm-)Wedel *m*; *poet* Palme *f*, Palmzweig *m*; **~age** ['-idʒ] Laub, Laub-, Blattwerk *n*.

front [frʌnt] *s* Stirn *a. fig*; *fig* Frechheit, Dreistigkeit, Unverschämtheit; Stirn-, Vorderseite, Vorderfront *f a. arch*; *fig* äußere(r) Eindruck *m*; Vorhemd *n*; Einsatz *m (am Kleid)*; *(Buch)* Titelbild *n*; Uferstreifen *m*, -promenade; *mil pol* Front *f*; *Am* Strohmann *m*, -männer *pl*; (falscher) Schein *m*; *meteor* (Kalt-, Warmluft-)Front *f*; *gram* Vorderzunge *f*, vordere(r) Teil *m* der Mundhöhle; *theat* Publikum *n*; *attr* Vor(der)-; *tr* gegenüberstehen, sich gegenüberbefinden (*s.th.* e-r S); gegenübertreten (*s.o.* jdm); herausfordern; *itr* mit der Front liegen (*upon, towards* nach); *Am sl* als Strohmann tätig sein; *to ~ on* s-e Vorderseite haben nach; blicken, schauen auf; grenzen an; *at, to the ~ (mil)* an der, an die Front; *in ~* vorn, davor, gegenüber *adv*; *in ~ of* vor, gegenüber *prp*; *in the ~* vorne *(im Buch)*; *to come to the ~ (fig)* hervortreten, bekanntwerden; *to have the ~ to* die Stirn haben zu; *to put a bold ~ on s.th.* e-r S mutig ins Auge sehen; *to put up a bold ~* Eindruck machen wollen; *to show, to present a bold ~* Mut zeigen; *(Börse)* feste Haltung zeigen; *eyes ~! (mil)* Augen gerade-aus! **~age** ['-idʒ] *arch* Vorderfront, Frontseite; Straßenfront *f*; Frontstreifen *m*, -linie; *mil* Frontbreite *f*, -abschnitt *m*; *~~ line* Baufluchtlinie *f*; **~al** ['-l] *a* Stirn-; Vorder-, Frontal-; *s anat* Stirnbein; Stirnband; *rel* Antependium *n (des Altars)*; Fassade *f*; *~~ area* Vorderfläche *f*; *mil* Frontgebiet *n*; *~~ attack* Frontalangriff *m*; *to make a ~~ attack against s.o.* jdn frontal angreifen; **~ bench** *parl* Regierungsbank *f*; **~ box** *theat* Orchesterloge *f*; **~ door** Haustür *f*; Haupteingang *m*; **~ elevation** Aufriß *m*; **~ garden** Vorgarten *m*; **~ier** ['-jə, *Am* frʌn'tiə] Grenze *a. fig*; *hist* (Siedlungs-)Grenze *f*; *state ~~* Staats-, Landesgrenze *f*; *the ~~s of knowledge* die Grenzen *pl* der Erkenntnis; *~~ dispute* Grenzstreitigkeiten *f pl*; *~~ district* Grenzgebiet *n*, -bezirk *m*; *~~ incident* Grenzzwischenfall *m*; *~~ police* Grenzpolizei *f*; *~~sman* Grenzbewohner; *Am* Siedler, Pionier *m*; *~~ station* Grenzbahnhof *m*; *~~ traffic* Grenzverkehr *m*; **~ispiece** ['-ispi:s] *(Buch)* Titelbild *n*; *arch* Hauptfassade *f*; **~let** ['-lit] Stirnband *n*; *zoo* Stirn *f*; **~line** *mil* Front *f*; *~~ baptism* Feuertaufe *f*; *~~ fighter* Frontkämpfer, -soldat *m*; *~~ officer* Frontoffizier *m*; *~~ pay* Frontzulage *f*; *~~ service* Frontdienst *m*; *~~ unit* Gefechtsverband *m*; **~ name** *Am* Vorname *m*; **~ office** *Am fam* Verwaltung *f*; *die* maßgebenden Herrn; **~ page** *s (Zeitung)* Titel-, Vorderseite *f*; *~-page (a)* sensationell; hochaktuell; *tr Am (in der Zeitung)* groß herausstellen; **~ rank** *mil* vordere(s) Glied *n*; *to be in the ~~ (fig)* im Vordergrund stehen, bekannt sein; **~ runner** Spitzenkandidat *m*; **~ seat** Vordersitz *m*; **~ sector** Frontabschnitt *m*; **~ sight** *(Gewehr)* Korn *n*; **~ soaring** *aero* Frontensegeln *n*, Gewitterflug *m*; **~view** Vorderansicht *f*; **~wheel** Vorderrad *n*; *~~ drive* Vorderradantrieb *m*; **~ yard** *Am* Vorgarten *m*.

frosh [frɔʃ] *Am fam* (Schul-)Anfänger, Neuling; Fuchs *m*.

frost [frɔst] *s* Frost *m*, Kälte *f*; Reif *m*; Eisblumen *f pl (am Fenster)*; *fig* Kälte, Lauheit *f*; *fam* Reinfall, Versager *m*; *tr* erfrieren lassen; mit Reif *od* Eisblumen überziehen; glasieren, mit Zuckerguß überziehen; *(Glas)* undurchsichtig machen, mattieren; *black ~* Frost *m* ohne Reif; *glazed ~* Glatteis *n*; *hoar, white ~* Rauhreif *m*; *Jack F~* der *(personifizierte)* Frost, der Winter; **~bite** *tr* erfrieren lassen; *s* Erfrierung; Frostbeule *f*; **~bitten** *a* erfroren; **~ed** *a* erfroren; bereift, überfroren, vereist; glasiert, mit Zuckerguß; *~~ glass* Matt-, Milchglas *n*; **~iness** ['-inis] Frost *m*, Kälte; *fig* Frostigkeit *f*; **~ing** ['-iŋ] Zuckerguß *m*; Glasur; Mattierung *f*; **~-line** *geog* Frostgrenze *f*; **~-proof** frostbeständig; **~work** Eisblumen *f pl (am Fenster)*; **~y** ['-i] kalt; frostig, eisig *a. fig*; *fig* ergraut, greisenhaft; *~~ weather* Frostwetter *n*.

froth [frɔθ] *s* Schaum; Geifer *m*; *fig* Schaumschlägerei *f*, dumme Gedanken *m pl*, leere(s) Gerede *n*; *tr* zum Schäumen bringen; *itr* schäumen, geifern; **~iness** ['-inis] schaumige(r) Zustand *m*; *fig* Leere *f*; **~y** ['-i] schaumig, schäumend; schaumbedeckt; *fig* dumm, albern, leer.

frou-frou ['fru:-fru:] Rauschen *n* (der Seide); *fam* Aufgedonnertheit *f*.

froward ['frouəd] eigenwillig, -sinnig, störrisch, halsstarrig, widerspenstig.

frown [fraun] *itr* die Stirn runzeln *od* in Falten legen; mißbilligen, mit Mißfallen betrachten (*on, upon s.th.* etw); böse anschauen (*at s.o.* jdn); *tr (to ~ down)* (durch finstere Blicke) einschüchtern; *s* Stirnrunzeln *n*; finstere(r) Blick *m*; **~ing** ['-iŋ] stirnrunzelnd; *(Blick)* drohend; *(Gesicht)* verärgert.

frowst [fraust] *s fam* Mief *m*; *itr* in schlecht gelüfteten Räumen leben; herumlungern.

frowziness ['frauzinis] muffige(r), mod(e)rige(r) Geruch; Schmutz *m*; **~y** ['frauzi] übelriechend; muffig, mod(e)rig; ranzig; schmutzig, schlampig.

frozen ['frouzn] *pp freeze a (~ up)* (zu-) gefroren; *(~ to death)* erfroren; eisig, sehr kalt; Gefrier-; *Am fig* starr (*with terror* vor Schreck); frostig, kalt, kühl; *fin* eingefroren, blockiert, gesperrt; festliegend; *fig* gefühllos; **~ food** tiefgekühlte Lebensmittel *pl*; **~ meat** Gefrierfleisch *n*.

fruct|iferous [frʌk'tifərəs] fruchttragend; **~ification** [frʌktifi'keiʃən] *bot* Befruchtung *f*; **~ify** ['frʌktifai] *tr* befruchten; *itr* Früchte tragen *a. fig*; **~ose** ['frʌktous] Fruchtzucker *m*.

frugal ['fru:gəl] sparsam, haushälterisch, wirtschaftlich (*of* mit); genügsam; einfach, schlicht; bescheiden, dürftig; **~ity** [fru(:)'gæliti] Sparsamkeit, Wirtschaftlichkeit; Einfachheit *f*.

fruit [fru:t] *s* Frucht *f*; Früchte *pl*, Obst *n*; *a. pl fig* Ergebnis, Resultat *n*, Folge *f*; Erfolg, Ertrag, Gewinn, Nutzen *m*; *pl* (verschiedene) Früchte, Obstsorten *f pl*; *tr* befruchten; *itr u. to bear ~ (a. fig)* Früchte tragen; *the ~s of the earth* die Früchte des Feldes, die Bodenfrüchte *pl*; *dried ~* Backobst *n*; *wall-~* Spalierobst *n*; **~age** ['-idʒ] Fruchtbarkeit; Obsternte *f*; Obst; Ergebnis *n*, Folge *f*, Ertrag *m*; **~arian** [fru:'tεəriən] Obstesser; Rohköstler *m*; **~ beverage** Fruchtsaftgetränk *n*; **~-cake** *Art* Früchtebrot *n*, Stollen *m*; **~ cup** Früchtebecher *m (Nachtisch)*; Fruchtsaftgetränk *n*; **~er** ['fru:tə] Obstzüchter; Obstbaum; Fruchtdampfer *m*; **~erer** ['-ərə] Obsthändler; Fruchtdampfer *m*; **~ful** ['-ful] fruchtbar *a. fig*; *fig* ertragreich, ergiebig, gewinnbringend, erfolgreich, vorteilhaft; **~iness** ['-inis] Würze *f*; **~ion** [fru(:)'iʃən] Genuß *m*; Fruchttragen *n*; Verwirklichung *f*; Ergebnis *n*, Erfolg *m*; **~ jar** *Am* Konservenglas *n*; **~ juice** Obstsaft *m*; **~ knife** Obstmesser *n*; **~less** ['-lis] unfruchtbar; *fig* frucht-, ergebnis-, erfolglos, vergeblich; **~lessness** ['-lisnis] Unfruchtbarkeit; *fig* Frucht-, Ergebnis-, Erfolglosigkeit *f*; **~-salad** Obstsalat *m*; *fig* Lametta *n*; **~-seller** Obstverkäufer *m*; **~ stand** Obststand; kleine(r) Obstladen *m*; **~ store** *Am* Obstgeschäft *n*; **~-sugar** Fruchtzucker *m*; **~-tree** Obstbaum *m*; **~ vinegar** Fruchtessig *m*; **~y** ['-i] aromatisch, würzig; *(Wein)* vollmundig, ausgereift, *fam* süffig; *fam fig* saftig.

frump [frʌmp] *fig* alte Schachtel *f*; **~ish** ['-iʃ], **~y** ['-i] altmodisch (u. wunderlich).
frustrat|e [frʌs'treit] *tr* zunichte machen, vereiteln, zum Scheitern bringen, durchkreuzen; *s.o.* jdn an der Durchführung s-r Absichten, Pläne hindern; enttäuschen; *psychol* hemmen; **~ion** [-ʃən] Vereitelung, Durchkreuzung, Verhinderung, Hemmung; Enttäuschung *f*; Minderwertigkeitsgefühl; Hindernis, Hemmnis *n*.
frustum ['frʌstəm] *pl a. -ta math* Kegel-, Pyramidenstumpf *m*.
fry [frai] **1.** *tr itr* braten, backen; *s Br* Gekröse; Bratfleisch *n*, -fisch, Braten *m*; *tele* Brutzeln *n*; *fried eggs (pl)* Spiegeleier *n pl*; *fried potatoes (pl)* Bratkartoffeln *f pl*; **~ing-pan** ['-iŋpæn] Bratpfanne *f*; *out of the ~~ into the fire (fig)* vom Regen in die Traufe; **2.** Fischbrut *f*; kleine Fische *m pl*; *allg* Brut *f*; Kinder(schar *f*) *n pl*; *small ~ (pej)* Gören *n pl*; kleine Leute *pl*; Kleinzeug *n*, -kram *m*, *fam* kleine Fische *m pl (Belanglosigkeiten)*.

*

fubsy ['fʌbsi] pumm(e)lig, rundlich.
fuchs|ia ['fju:ʃə] *bot* Fuchsie *f*; **~ine** ['fu:ksi:n] Fuchsin *n (Farbstoff)*.
fudd|le ['fʌdl] *tr* betrunken machen; berauschen; *itr* sich betrinken; *s* Trunkenheit *f*, Rausch *m*; **~y-duddy** ['-idʌdi] *sl* altmodische(r) Kauz; Umstandskrämer; Weichling *m*.
fudge [fʌdʒ] *s* Schwindel *m*; Gewäsch *n*; Unsinn, Blödsinn, Quatsch *m*; *(Zeitung)* (Raum *m* für) letzte Nachrichten *f pl*; Praline *f*, (weicher) Bonbon *m*; Flickwerk *n*; *interj* Unsinn! *tr* zs.stoppeln, hinpfuschen; fälschen; *itr* pfuschen, schlampern.
fuel [fjuəl] *s* Heiz-, Brennmaterial *n*; Brenn-, Betriebs-, Treib-, Kraftstoff *m*; Benzin *n*; *fig* Nahrung *f*; *tr* mit Brenn-, Kraftstoff versorgen; *fig* nähren; *itr* Kraftstoff einnehmen, tanken; *mar* bunkern; *to add ~ to the flames (fig)* Öl ins Feuer gießen, das Feuer schüren; *to be ~ to s.o.'s hatred* den Haß schüren; *aviation ~* Flugkraftstoff *m*; **~ cock** Brennstoffhahnen *m*; **~ consumption** Kraftstoffverbrauch *m*; **~ drum** Kraftstoffbehälter *m*; **~ dump, depot** Kraftstofflager *n*; **~ feed** Kraftstoffzuführung *f*; **~ gas** Treib-, Heizgas *n*; **~ ga(u)ge** Benzinstandsmesser *m*, Benzinuhr *f*; **~ injection** Kraftstoffeinspritzung *f*; **~(l)er** ['-ə] *Am* Heizer *m*; **~ling** Auftanken *n*; *~~ station* Tankstelle *f*; **~ mixture** Kraftstoffgemisch *n*; **~ nozzle** Kraftstoffdüse *f*; **~ oil** Heizöl *n*; **~ pipe** Kraftstoffleitung *f*; **~ pump** Kraftstoffpumpe *f*; **~-saving** kraftstoffsparend; **~ storage** Brennstofflagerung *f*; *~~ tank* Benzintank *m*; **~ supply** Brenn-, Kraftstoffversorgung *f*; **~ tank** *aero* Kraftstoffbehälter *m*.
fug [fʌg] *a* muffig; *s* Staubflocke *f*; Mief *m*; *itr* ein Stubenhocker sein; *to have a good ~* sich weich betten; **~gy** ['-i] muffig (riechend).
fugac|ious [fju(:)'geiʃəs] flüchtig, vergänglich, kurz(lebig); **~ity** [-'gæsiti] Flüchtigkeit, Vergänglichkeit *f*.
fugitive ['fju:dʒitiv] *a* flüchtig, entwichen, entflohen; flüchtig, vergänglich; *lit* Gelegenheits-; *s* Flüchtling *m*.
fugle ['fju:gl] *itr* Flügelmann, Vorbild sein; führen; **~man** [-mæn] *pl ~men mil* Flügelmann *m*; *fig* Vorbild *n*.
fugue [fju:g] *mus* Fuge *f*.
fulcrum ['fʌlkrəm] *pl a. -cra (Hebel)* Dreh-, Stützpunkt; *fig* Angriffspunkt *m*.
fulfil(l) [ful'fil] *tr (Wunsch, Bedingung)* erfüllen; entsprechen, nachkommen *(a request* e-r Bitte); *(Versprechen)* einlösen; ausführen; vollbringen; *(e-m Befehl)* gehorchen; *(Verpflichtung)* einhalten; *to ~ o.s.* s-e Erfüllung finden; *to ~ o.'s purpose* s-n Zweck erfüllen; **~ment** [-mənt] Erfüllung; Ausführung *f*.
fulgent ['fʌldʒənt] *poet* strahlend.
fulgur|ate ['fʌlgjuəreit] *itr* blitzen *a. fig*; **~ous** ['fʌlgjuərəs] blitzend *a. fig*.
fuliginous [fju:'lidʒinəs] rauchig, rußig.
full [ful] **1.** *a* voll, (voll)gefüllt; satt; angefüllt *(of* mit); voller; (voll)besetzt; reichlich; wimmelnd *(of* von); voll (-zählig, -ständig), völlig, voll, höchst *(Geschwindigkeit)*; unbe-, uneingeschränkt; rund(lich), voll (ausgefüllt), pausbäckig, drall; *(Stoff, Kleid)* füllig, weit, lose, locker, Falten werfend; *fig* innerlich, tief erfüllt; voller Gedanken; *adv* voll(kommen), völlig, genau, direkt; sehr, ganz; *s* volle Zahl, Größe, Ausdehnung *f*; volle(r) Betrag *m*; *the ~ (of it)* das Ganze, alles; *tr (Kleid)* raffen, fälteln, plissieren; beschweren; *at the ~* in der Fülle; *in ~* voll, ganz *adv*, in voller Höhe, in vollem Umfang, ungekürzt; voll ausgeschrieben, unabgekürzt; *in ~ blossom* in voller Blüte; *in ~ career* in vollem Lauf; *to the ~* völlig, voll u. ganz, durchaus; *(sl) ~ of beans, hops, (Am fam) prunes* lebhaft, tüchtig; *~ blast* auf vollen Touren; *~ nigh* fast, beinahe; *~ ride (Am fam)* einschließlich aller Unkosten; *~ sail* mit vollen Segeln *a. fig*; *~ steam ahead* Volldampf voraus; *~ to overflowing* bis zum Überlaufen voll; *~ up* vollbesetzt; dem Weinen nahe; *fig* satt; *~ well* sehr wohl, sehr gut *adv*; *to be in ~ swing* in vollem Gange sein; *to come to a ~ stop* plötzlich stehenbleiben; *to pay in ~* voll bezahlen; *to write in ~* ausschreiben; *half ~* halbvoll; *a ~ house (theat)* ein volles Haus; **~ age** Volljährigkeit *f*; **~-back** *(Fußball)* Verteidiger *m*; **~-blood** Vollbürtigkeit *f*; Vollblut *n*; **~-blooded** *a* vollblütig *a. fig*, (rasse-)rein; *fig* lebhaft, temperamentvoll; kräftig; leidenschaftlich; **~-blown** *a bot* voll aufgeblüht; *fig* voll erblüht; **~-bodied** *a (Wein)* würzig, stark, schwer; **~ details** *pl* genaue Einzelheiten *f pl*; **~ dress** Gesellschaftsanzug *m*, -kleid(ung *f*) *n*; Galauniform *f*; *in ~~* in Gala; **~-dress** *attr* Gala-; *~~ rehearsal (theat)* Generalprobe *f*; **~ employment** Vollbeschäftigung *f*; **~-faced** *a* pausbäckig; voll zugewandt; **~-fledged** *a* flügge; *fig* voll entwickelt; selbständig; *fig* richtig (-gehend); **~-grown** *a* voll ausgewachsen; **~-hearted** *a* zuversichtlich, vertrauensvoll; **~-length** *a* in voller Größe; *(Mensch)* in Lebensgröße; ungekürzt; **~ moon** Vollmond *m*; **~-mouthed** *a* in voller Lautstärke; **~ness** ['-nis] Fülle *f*, Reichtum *m*; Vollständigkeit, Vollzähligkeit *f*; *in the ~~ of time* zur rechten Zeit; **~-page** *a* ganzseitig; **~ pay** volle(r) (Arbeits-)Lohn *m*; **~ power** Volllastleistung *f*; Vollgas *n*; **~ professor** ordentliche(r) Professor *m*; **~-rigged** *a mar* voll betakelt; *allg* voll ausgerüstet, bestückt; **~-scale, -size** in voller, in Lebensgröße; Voll-; **~ speed** *s* Volldampf *m*; *a* mit voller Kraft, mit Höchstgeschwindigkeit; **~ stop** Punkt *m*; **~ swing**: *in ~~* in vollem Gang; **~ text** volle(r) Wortlaut *m*; **~-time** ganztägig; hauptamtlich, vollberuflich; **~ turn** Kehrtwendung *f*; **~-track vehicle** Gleiskettenfahrzeug *n*; **~y** *adv* reichlich; ausführlich; völlig, ganz, vollständig, durchaus; genau; *(bei Zahlangabe)* gut, mindestens, mehr als; *to be ~~ booked* ausverkauft sein; *~~-fashioned (Strumpf)* formgerecht; *~~ resolved* fest entschlossen; **2.** *tr* walken; **~er** ['-ə] Walker *m*; *~~'s earth* Bleich-, Fullererde *f*; *~~'s herb* gemeine(s) Seifenkraut *n*; **~ing-mill** ['-iŋ 'mil] Walkmühle *f*.
fulmar ['fulmə] Eissturmvogel *m*.
fulminat|e ['fʌlmineit] *itr fig* donnern, wettern *(against* gegen); *tr* explodieren lassen; donnern, wettern gegen; *(Bann)* schleudern; *s chem* Knallverbindung *f*; *~~ of mercury* Knallquecksilber *n*; **~ing** ['-iŋ] *a* Knall-; donnernd; *~~ cotton* Schießbaumwolle *f*; *~~ powder* Knallpulver *n*; **~ion** [-'neiʃən] Donnern, Krachen *n*; Explosion *f*, Knall *m*; *fig* laute(s) Fluchen; Wettern *n*.
fulsome ['fulsəm] *(Lob, Schmeichelei)* übertrieben, widerlich.
fumbl|e ['fʌmbl] *itr (to ~~ about)* (herum)fummeln, -tasten, -suchen *(for* nach; *at* an); ungeschickt sein mit; *tr* tasten nach; linkisch handhaben, ungeschickt umgehen *(s.th.* mit etw); verpatzen; *(bes. Ball)* fallen lassen, vermasseln; **~er** ['-ə] Tolpatsch, ungeschickte(r) Mensch *m*; **~ing** ['-iŋ] unbeholfen, täppisch, linkisch.
fum|e [fju:m] *s meist pl (bes. unangenehmer, lästiger)* Rauch, Dampf, Dunst, Schwaden *m*, Gas *n*; *sing* Aufregung *f*, Ärger *m*; *itr* rauchen, dampfen, verdampfen, verdunsten; *fig* sich aufregen, sich ärgern; aufgebracht, wütend sein, toben *(about, over* über); *tr (Eichenholz)* räuchern; **~igate** ['fju:migeit] *tr* ausräuchern; entwanzen, entlausen; **~igation** [fju:mi'geiʃən] Ausräucherung; Entwanzung, Entlausung *f*; **~ing** ['-iŋ] erregt, aufgebracht, ärgerlich; *~~ with rage* vor Wut schäumend.
fun [fʌn] Vergnügen *n*, Belustigung *f*; Spaß, Scherz *m*; *(only) for, in ~* (nur) zum Spaß; *for the ~ of it* spaßeshalber; *to be (great) ~* (viel) Spaß machen; *to have ~ with s.th.* Spaß an etw haben; *to make ~ of s.o., to poke ~ at s.o.* jdn auslachen, lächerlich machen, zum besten halten; *like ~ (Am sl)* denkste! *he's ~* er ist ein netter Kerl.
function ['fʌŋkʃən] *s* Funktion, Tätigkeit, Verrichtung, Wirksamkeit *f*; Zweck *m*; Arbeitsweise; Beschäftigung, Dienstleistung, -stellung *f*, Beruf *m*; Tätigkeit; *math* Funktion *f*; Amt *n*, Obliegenheit, Aufgabe, Pflicht, Verpflichtung; öffentliche Veranstaltung, Feier(lichkeiten *f pl*) *f*; *pl* Aufgaben *f pl*; *itr* funktionieren, laufen; in Betrieb, in Ordnung sein, *fam* klappen; arbeiten, tätig sein *(as* als); **~al** ['-l] *physiol* funktionell; funktional; zweckmäßig, praktisch; offiziell, amtlich; *~~ building* Zweckbau *m*; *~~ disorder (med)* Funktionsstörung *f*; **~ary** ['-əri] Beamte(r); *pol* Funktionär *m*.
fund [fʌnd] *s* Vorrat, Schatz; *fin* Fonds *m*, Kapital *n*, Kasse *f*; *pl* (zur Verfügung stehende) Gelder, Geldmittel *n pl*, Kapital *n*; Staatspapiere *n pl*, -anleihen *f pl*, -schuld *f*; *tr (Geld)* anlegen, investieren; kapitalisieren; *(Anleihe, Staatsschuld)* konsolidieren, fundieren; *out of ~s* mittellos; *without ~s in hand* ohne Deckung; *to be out of ~s* schlecht bei Kasse sein; *to raise ~s* Gelder, Mittel aufbringen *od* beschaffen; *insufficient ~s (pl)* ungenügende Deckung *f*; *operating ~* Betriebsmittel *n pl*; *original ~s (pl)* Stammkapital *n*; *trading, working ~* Betriebskapital *n*; *~ of a company* Gesellschaftskapital *n*.

fundament ['fʌndəmənt] Gesäß *n*; **~al** [fʌndə'mentl] grundlegend, fundamental, Grund-; wesentlich (*to* für); hauptsächlich; Wesens-, Haupt-; *phys mus* Grund-; *s meist pl* Grundlage, Basis *f*; Grundzüge *m pl*; Hauptsachen *f pl*; *sing phys mus* Grundton *m*; *~~ bass (mus)* Grundbaß *m*; *~~ note* Grundton *m*; **~alism** [fʌndə'mentəlizm] *rel* Fundamentalismus *m*, Orthodoxie *f*.

funeral ['fju:nərəl] *a* Beerdigungs-, Begräbnis-, Leichen-, Trauer-; *s* Beerdigung *f*, Begräbnis *n*, Beisetzung *f*; *(~ procession, cortege)* Leichenbegängnis *n*, Leichen-, Totenfeier *f*; *(~ procession)* Leichenzug *m*, Trauergefolge *n*; ~ **expenses** *pl* Begräbniskosten *pl*; ~ **march** Trauermarsch *m*; ~ **pile, pyre** Scheiterhaufen *m*.

funereal [fju(:)'niəriəl] *a* Leichen-, Trauer-; traurig, düster, unheilvoll.

fungible ['fʌndʒibl] *a jur* ersetzbar, vertretbar; *s* ersetzbare Sache *f*.

fung|icide ['fʌndʒisaid] Schwamm-, Pilzvernichtungsmittel *n*; **~oid** ['fʌŋgɔid] pilzartig; **~ous** ['fʌŋgəs] pilz-, schwammartig; *med* fungös; Pilz-, Schwamm-; *fig* pilzartig; *~~ flesh* wilde(s) Fleisch *n*; **~us** ['fʌŋgəs] *pl* *-i* ['fʌŋgai, -dʒi, -dʒai] *u.* *-es*; Pilz, Schwamm; *med* Schwamm(gewächs *n*) *m*, Krebsgeschwulst *f*.

funicular [fju(:)'nikjulə] seilartig; Seil-; *~~ railway* Seilbahn *f*.

funk [fʌŋk] *s sl* Schiß *m*, Mordsangst *f* (*of* vor); Angsthase, Hasenfuß *m*, Memme *f*, Feigling; Drückeberger *m*; *tr sl* Schiß haben, sich drücken vor, sich vorbeidrücken an; bange machen; *itr sl u.* *to be in a ~* Schiß, Angst haben, sich drücken; *he is in a ~* ihm schlottern die Knie; *he got into a ~* ihm fiel das Herz in die Hose(n); *a blue ~* ein Mordsschiß; **~-hole** Heldenkeller, Unterstand; Druckposten *m*; **~y** ['-i] feige.

funnel ['fʌnl] Trichter; *mar rail* Schornstein; Rauchfang, -abzug; Licht-, Luftschacht *m*.

funny ['fʌni] *a* lustig, spaßig, ulkig, drollig, amüsant; unwohl; unerwartet; *(Geschäft)* unehrlich, faul; *fam* komisch, sonderbar; *Am sl* verrückt (*for* nach, auf); *s fam* komische Bemerkung *f*, Witz *m*; *s pl Am (Zeitung)* Witzecke *f*, *bes.* Comic Strips *pl*; **~-bone** *anat* Musikantenknochen *m*; ~ **paper** *Am* Witzblatt *n*.

*

fur [fə:] *s* Fell *n*; Pelz *m*; Pelztiere *n pl*; Belag (auf der Zunge); Kessel-, Weinstein; *(in e-r Flasche)* Satz *m*; *pl* Pelz-, Rauchwerk *n*, -waren *f pl*; *tr* mit Pelz füttern; verbrämen; *itr* sich (mit e-m Belag) überziehen; Kesselstein bilden; *to make the ~ fly (fig)* Staub aufwirbeln; Streit anfangen; ~ **coat** Pelzmantel *m*; **~-lined** *a* pelzgefüttert; **~red** [-d] *a* pelzgefüttert, -besetzt; *(Zunge)* belegt; mit Kessel- *od* Weinstein überzogen.

furbelow ['fə:bilou] *s* Falbel *f*; *pl pej* Flitterkram, Putz *m*; *tr* fälbeln.

furbish ['fə:biʃ] *tr* blank putzen, polieren; *(to ~ up)* aufpolieren *a. fig*; auffrischen; **~er** ['-ə] Polierer *m*.

furcat|e ['fə:keit] *itr* sich gabeln; *a* [*a.* -kit] gegabelt; **~ion** [fə:'keiʃən] Gabelung *f*.

furious ['fjuəriəs] wütend; heftig, wild; *fast and ~* wild, toll, ausgelassen.

furl [fə:l] *tr (Flagge)* auf-, zs.rollen u. festmachen; *(Segel)* raffen; *(Vorhang)* aufziehen; *(Schirm)* zumachen; zs.-klappen, falten.

furlong ['fə:lɔŋ] Achtelmeile *f (201 m)*.

furlough ['fə:lou] *s* Urlaub *m*; *tr Am u.* *to grant ~ to* Urlaub bewilligen *dat*; *on ~* auf Urlaub; *men on ~* Urlauber *m pl*.

furnace ['fə:nis] Heizraum; Brenn-, Schmelz-, Hochofen; Heizkessel, Ofen; *fig* Backofen *m*; *fig* Feuerprobe *f*; *tried in the ~* auf Herz und Nieren geprüft; *blast ~* Hochofen *m*; ~ **coke** Zechenkoks *m*; ~ **throat, top** *tech* Gicht *f*.

furnish ['fə:niʃ] *tr* versehen, versorgen, beliefern, ausrüsten, ausstatten (*with* mit); einrichten, möblieren; liefern, beschaffen; *to ~ proof* den Beweis erbringen; den Nachweis führen; *to ~ security* Sicherheit leisten; **~er** ['-ə] Lieferant *m*; *~~ and upholsterer* Dekorateur *m*; **~ing** ['-iŋ] Lieferung; Einrichtung, Ausstattung, Möblierung *f*; *pl* Einrichtung(sgegenstände *m pl*), Inneneinrichtung (e-s Hauses), Ausstattung *f*; Mobiliar *n*, Möbel *pl*; *Am* Installation; Kleidung(sstücke *n pl*) *f*; *~~ fabrics (pl)* Möbelstoffe *m pl*.

furniture ['fə:nitʃə] Möbel *n pl*, Mobiliar *n*, Hausrat *m*; *tech* Ausrüstung *f*, Beschläge; *typ* (Format-)Stege *m pl*; *a piece of ~* ein Möbelstück *n*; *a set of ~* e-e Möbelgarnitur *f*; *~ and fixtures* Einrichtungsgegenstände *m pl*; *office ~* Büromöbel *n pl*; ~ **dealer** Möbelhändler *m*; ~ **polish** Möbelpolitur *f*; ~ **van** Möbelwagen *m*.

furr|ier ['fʌriə] Kürschner; Pelzhändler *m*; **~iery** ['-əri] Kürschnerei *f*; Pelzhandel *m*; Pelz-, Rauchwerk *n*, -waren *f pl*; **~ing** ['fə:riŋ] Pelzwerk *n*, Pelze *m pl*; *tech* Kesselstein *m*; Krustenbildung *f*; *med* Belag *m (e-r Zunge)*; *mar* Bekleidung (e-s Schiffes); *arch* Füllung, Einlage *f*.

furrow ['fʌrou] *s* (Acker-)Furche; (Wagen-, Rad-)Spur, Rinne; Furche *(im Gesicht)*, Runzel *f*; *poet* Acker *m*; Querrinne *(auf der Straße)*; *geog* Bodenfalte; *tech* Rille, Riefe, Nut; *arch* Hohlkehle *f*; *tr* (zer)furchen; auskehlen, riefeln; *(das Meer)* durchfurchen; *(Acker)* pflügen; *itr* sich runzeln, Runzeln bekommen.

furry ['fə:ri] *a* Pelz-; pelzbedeckt, e-n Pelz tragend; pelzbesetzt; pelzartig.

further ['fə:ðə] *a* weiter (entfernt), entfernter; weiter, ferner, zusätzlich; *adv* weiter, ferner (weg); ferner, weiterhin, des weiteren, darüber hinaus; überdies, noch dazu; mehr, in höherem Maße; *tr* (be)fördern, unterstützen; vorwärts-, weiterbringen; *till ~ notice* bis auf weiteres; *I'll see you ~ first (fam)* das kommt nie in Frage; **~ance** ['-rəns] Förderung, Unterstützung; Hilfe *f*; **~more** ['-'mɔ:] *adv* überdies, darüber hinaus, des weiteren, ferner; **~most** ['-moust] *a* entferntest, weitest; ~ **particulars** *pl* nähere Einzelheiten *f pl*.

furthest ['fə:ðist] *a* fernst, entferntest, weitest; spätest; *adv* am weitesten weg *od* entfernt; am meisten.

furtive ['fə:tiv] verstohlen, heimlich; diebisch; **~ness** ['-nis] Heimlichkeit *f*.

furunc|le ['fjuərʌŋkl] *med* Furunkel *m*; **~ulosis** [fjurʌŋkju'lousis] Furunkulose *f*.

fury ['fjuəri] Wut, Raserei *f*; Wutanfall, -ausbruch *m*; Heftigkeit, Wildheit *f*; Jähzornige(r) *m*, Furie *f*; *to be in a ~* wütend sein; *to fly into a ~* in Wut geraten; *like ~* wie wild.

furz|e [fə:z] *bot* (Stech-)Ginster *m*.

fuse [fju:z] **1.** *tr itr* schmelzen; *fig* (sich) verschmelzen; *pol Am* e-e Koalition eingehen; *tr fig* fusionieren; *itr el (Sicherung)* durchbrennen; *s el* Sicherung *f*; *the ~ has blown out* die Sicherung ist durchgebrannt; **~-box** Sicherungskasten *m*; **2.** *s tech chem mil* Zünder *m*, Zündschnur *f*.

fusee [fju:'zi:] Windstreichholz; (Sturm-)Feuerzeug *n*; *rail* Signallaterne; Schnecke *f* (in alten Uhren).

fuselage ['fju:zilidʒ] *aero* Rumpf *m*.

fusel oil ['fju:zl'ɔil] *chem* Fuselöl *n*.

fusib|ility [fju:zə'biliti] (leichte) Schmelzbarkeit *f*; **~le** ['fju:zəbl] (leicht) schmelzbar; *~~ wire* Schmelzdraht *m*.

fusilier [fju:zi'liə] *mil* Füsilier *m*.

fusillade [fju:zi'leid] *s* Gewehrfeuer *n*; Salve; standrechtliche Erschießung *f*; *fig* Hagel *m (von Fragen)*; *tr* niederschießen; standrechtlich erschießen.

fusion ['fju:ʒən] Schmelzen *n*; Verschmelzung *a. fig*, Legierung *f*; *(Sicherung) el* Durchbrennen *n*; *fig* Vereinigung; *com* Fusion; *pol* Koalition *f*; ~ **bomb** Wasserstoffbombe *f*; ~ **point** Schmelzpunkt *m*; **~welding** Schmelzschweißen *n*.

fuss [fʌs] *s* Aufregung, Nervosität *f*; Getue, Wesen *n*; (sinnlose) Geschäftigkeit *f*; Nervenbündel *n* (Person); *itr* sich aufregen (*about, over* über); sich viele Umstände machen; Lärm, Aufhebens machen; *tr fam* nervös, verrückt machen; *to ~ around* herumwirtschaften; *to ~ with s.th.* nervös an etw herummachen; *to make a (great) ~* (viel) Wind, Theater, Aufhebens machen (*about s.th.* um etw); *of s.o.* viel Wesens um jdn machen; *don't make so much ~* mach kein Theater! *stop ~ing!* sei nicht so nervös! **~-budget** *Am fam* ewig unzufriedene(r) Mensch; G(e)schaftlhuber *m*; **~ed-up** *a Am fam* aus der Fassung, in Verlegenheit; aufgedonnert; **~iness** ['-inis] Betriebsamkeit *f*; **~-pot** Umstandskrämer *m*; **~y** ['-i] aufgeregt, nervös; geschäftig; schwer zufriedenzustellen(d); umständlich; *(Kleider)* aufgedonnert; *to be ~~ about s.th.* mit etw heikel, wählerisch sein.

fustian ['fʌstiən, *Am* 'fʌstʃən] *s* Barchent; *fig* Schwulst *m*; *a* aus Barchent; *fig* schwülstig.

fustigate ['fʌstigeit] *tr* (ver)prügeln.

fust|iness ['fʌstinis] Modergeruch *m*, Muffigkeit *f*; **~y** ['fʌsti] mod(e)rig, muffig; schal; *fig* veraltet.

*

futil|e ['fju:tail] nutzlos, vergeblich, unnütz; unerheblich, unwichtig, nebensächlich; oberflächlich; **~ity** [fju(:)'tiliti] Nutz-, Wert-, Wirkungslosigkeit; Oberflächlichkeit; Kleinigkeit *f*.

futur|e ['fju:tʃə] *a* (zu)künftig, kommend, bevorstehend; *s* Zukunft *f*; Aussichten *f pl*; *gram (~~ tense)* Futur(um) *n*; *pl* Termingeschäfte *n pl*; *for the ~~, in (the) ~~* in Zukunft; *in the near ~~* in naher Zukunft; *~~ life (rel)* Leben *n* nach dem Tode; *~~ market* Terminmarkt *m*; **~ism** ['-rizm] *(Kunst)* Futurismus *m*; **~ity** [fju(:)'tjuəriti] Zukunft *f*; *das* Zukünftige.

fuzz [fʌz] *s* (Feder-, Woll-)Flocken *f pl*; Flaum; *Am sl* Polizist *m*; *tr itr* (sich) mit Flaum bedecken; zer-, ausfasern; **~y** ['-i] *a* flockig, flaumig; flaumbedeckt; kraus; unklar.

G

G [dʒiː] *pl* ~'*s* G, g *n a. mus*; *Am sl* tausend Dollar *m pl*; *Am (Schule)* Gut *n*; ~ **flat** Ges *n*; ~ **major** G-Dur *n*; ~**-man** *Am* Geheimpolizist *m*; ~ **minor** g-Moll *n*; ~ **sharp** Gis *n*.

gab [gæb] *itr fam* plappern, schwatzen, plaudern, schnattern; babbeln; *s fam* Geschnatter; Gebabbel *n*; *to have the gift of (the)* ~ *(fam)* ein gutes Mundwerk haben; ~**ble** ['gæbl] *itr* schnattern, plappern, durchea.reden; *tr* (schnell) daherreden; *s* Geschnatter, Geplapper *n*; ~**bler** ['gæblə] Schwätzer *m*; ~**by** ['-i] *Am fam* geschwätzig, schwatzhaft.

gabardine ['gæbədiːn] Gabardine *m*.

gabion ['geibjən] *mil* Schanzkorb *m*.

gable ['geibl] Giebel *m*; *(~-end)* Giebelwand *f*; ~ **roof** Giebeldach *n*.

gaby ['geibi] *fam* Trottel, Tropf *m*.

gad [gæd] *itr (meist: to* ~ *about)* planziellos umherwandern, herumstreichen; umherschweifen, herumlungern; auf Abenteuer ausgehen; *on the* ~ *(Vieh)* unruhig; *fig* immer in Bewegung; *interj: by* ~ bei Gott! ~**about** ['-əbaut] *s fam* Nichtstuer *m*.

gadfly ['gædflai] Viehbremse *f*; *fig* Störenfried, Quäl-, Plaggeist *m*.

gadget ['gædʒit] *fam* Vorrichtung, sinnreiche Einrichtung *f*; Teilchen *n*; Trick, Kniff *n*, Ding *n* mit 'nem Pfiff; Ding(s) *n*; *pl* Krimskrams *m*.

Gael [geil] Gäle *m*; ~**ic** ['-ik] *a* gälisch; *s* (das) Gälisch(e).

gaff [gæf] **1.** *s* Fischhaken *m*; Harpune; *mar* Gaffel *f*; **2.** *sl s* Rummelplatz; *(penny* ~*)* Tingeltangel *m u. n*; Trick *m*; *tr* beschwindeln, 'reinlegen, anführen; **3.** *sl* Quatsch, Blödsinn *m*; *to blow the* ~ *(sl)* die Sache verpfeifen; *to stand the* ~ *(Am sl)* sich nicht unterkriegen lassen; ~**er** ['-ə] Gevatter; *fam* (Zirkus-)Direktor; *film* Chefbeleuchter; Vorarbeiter *m*.

gag [gæg] *s* Knebel *m*; *(~-bit)* Kandare *f*; *fig* Maulkorb; *parl* Schluß *m* der Debatte; *theat* Einschiebsel *n*, Improvisation, witzige Zwischenbemerkung *f (e-s Schauspielers)*; witzige(r) Einfall; *sl* Schwindel *m*; *tr* würgen; knebeln; den Mund stopfen (*s.o.* jdm), mundtot machen; *parl* das Wort entziehen (*s.o.* jdm); *tech* verstopfen, verschließen; *sl* beschwindeln; *itr theat* e-e witzige Zwischenbemerkung, *allg* e-n Witz, Spaß machen, ulken; improvisieren; ersticken, würgen (*on s.th.* an etw); *sl* schwindeln; ~**(s)man** *theat film* Verfasser *m* witziger Zwischenbemerkungen.

gaga ['gægaː] *a sl* plemplem, meschugge; *to go* ~ *over s.o.* in jdn vernarrt sein.

gage [geidʒ] **1.** *s* Pfand *n*, Bürgschaft, Sicherheit *f*; Fehdehandschuh *m*; Herausforderung *f*; *tr* verpfänden; *to* ~ *up (Am sl)* wütend werden; *to throw down the* ~ *to s.o.* jdm den Fehdehandschuh hinwerfen; **2.** *s. gauge*; ~**rs** ['-əz] *pl Am sl* Gucker *pl*.

gaggle ['gægl] *itr (Gans)* schnattern.

gai|ety ['geiəti] Heiterkeit, Fröhlichkeit, Freude *f*; *meist pl* Festlichkeiten *f pl*; Pracht *f*, Putz *m*; ~**ly** *adv s. gay.*

gain [gein] *s* Gewinn, Zuwachs *m*; Verbesserung *f*, Fortschritt; Vorteil, größere(r) Nutzen, Profit; Erwerb, Verdienst *m*, Einkommen *n*; *pl* Einkünfte *pl*; *radio* Verstärkung *f*; *(Uhr)* Vorgehen *n*; *tr* gewinnen, (sich) erwerben, verdienen; erreichen; erlangen; *(Geld)* einbringen; *itr (Kräfte, an Gewicht)* zunehmen; vorankommen, Fortschritte machen; sich (ver)bessern; näherkommen, herankommen (*on, upon* an); e-n Vorteil erlangen (*on* über); Vorsprung gewinnen (*on, upon* vor); sich ausbreiten auf Kosten (*on* von); *(See)* vorrücken (*on the land* gegenüber dem Land); *(Uhr)* vorgehen; *mot* aufholen; *to* ~ *over (Menschen)* für sich gewinnen, auf s-e Seite ziehen; *for* ~ zu Erwerbszwecken; aus Gewinnsucht; *to* ~ *a footing* festen Fuß fassen; *to* ~ *ground (fig)* Boden gewinnen, Fortschritte machen; sich durchsetzen; *to* ~ *the upper hand* die Oberhand gewinnen, siegen; *to* ~ *speed* schneller werden; Fahrt aufnehmen; *to* ~ *time* Zeit gewinnen; *to* ~ *weight* (an Gewicht) zunehmen; *clear* ~ Reingewinn *m*; *love of* ~ Gewinnsucht *f*; ~ *in weight* (Gewichts-)Zunahme *f*; ~**er** ['-ə] Gewinner; *Am (Schwimmen)* Auerbachsprung *m*; *to be the* ~~ gewinnen; ~**ful** ['-ful] einträglich, gewinnbringend; *Am* bezahlt; ~~ *occupation (Am)* Erwerbstätigkeit *f*; ~**ings** ['-iŋz] *pl* Gewinn(e *pl*) *m*, Ertrag *m*.

gainsay [gein'sai] *a. irr -said, -said tr arch lit* (ab)leugnen, abstreiten; widersprechen (*s.o.* jdm).

gait [geit] Gang *m*; Haltung; *bes. Am (Pferd)* Gangart *f*.

gaiter ['geitə] Gamasche *f*.

gal [gæl] *Am sl* Mädchen *n*, Kleine *f*.

gala ['gɑːlə, 'geilə] *s* Fest(lichkeit *f*) *n*, Feier *f*; *attr* festlich; Gala-.

galact|ic [gə'læktik] *a scient* Milch-; *astr* galaktisch, Milchstraßen-; ~**ometer** [gælæk'təmitə] Milchmesser *m*, -waage *f*.

galantine ['gælentiːn] gewickelte(s) Kalbfleisch *od* Huhn *n* in Gelee.

galaxy ['gæləksi] *astr* Milchstraße *f*; *fig* glänzende Gesellschaft; erlesene Schar *f*.

gale [geil] **1.** steife Brise *f*, steife(r) *od* stürmische(r) Wind; Sturm; *poet* frische(r) Wind; *fig* Ausbruch, Sturm *m*; *Am fam* Erregung; allgemeine Heiterkeit *f*; *it is blowing a* ~ es stürmt; ~ *of laughter* schallende(s) Gelächter *n*; ~ **warning** Sturmwarnung *f*; **2.** *jur* Pacht-, Zinszahlung *f*; **3.** *bot* Heidemyrthe *f*.

galena [gə'liːnə] *min* Bleiglanz *m*.

galipot ['gælipət] Fichtenharz *n*.

gall [gɔːl] **1.** *s physiol* Galle; Galle(nblase) *f*; Bittere(s) *n*; (Gefühl *n* der) Bitterkeit *f*, Groll; Haß *m*; *Am fam* Unverschämtheit, Frechheit *f*; ~**-bladder** Gallenblase *f*; ~**-stone** Gallenstein *m*; **2.** *s* wund(gerieben)e Stelle *f*, Wolf; *fig* Ärger *m*, Qual; *fig* schwache(r) Stelle *f od* Punkt *m*; *tr* wundreiben; *fig* reizen, ärgern, quälen; **3.** *(~-nut)* Gallapfel *m*; ~**-fly** *zoo* Gallwespe *f*.

gallant ['gælənt] *a* prächtig; stattlich; tapfer; [selten: gə'lænt] galant; Liebes-; *s* [selten: gə'lænt] Held; Galan; Liebhaber; Geliebte(r) *m*; ~**ry** ['-ri] Tapferkeit; Ritterlichkeit, Galanterie; Liebesaffäre *f*.

galleon ['gæliən] *mar hist* Galeone *f*.

gallery ['gæləri] *arch theat (Kunst)* Galerie *f*; *theat* 3. Rang *m*; Tribüne, Empore; Kolonnade, Säulenhalle *f*, -gang; Korridor, (Lauf-)Gang; *zoo* Gang; *mil* Schießstand; *mil min* Stollen; Tunnel *m*; *sport* Zuschauer *m pl*; *Am* Veranda *f*; *to play to the* ~ *(theat)* Effekthascherei treiben.

galley ['gæli] *mar hist* Galeere; Kombüse, Schiffsküche *f*; (großes) Ruderboot; *typ* (Setz-)Schiff *n*; ~**-proof** *typ* Fahnenabzug *m*; ~**-slave** *hist* Galeerensklave *m*; *fig* Packesel *m*.

Gallic ['gælik] *hist* gallisch; französisch; *g* ~ *(chem)* gallensauer; *g*~ *acid* Gallensäure *f*; **g**~**ism** ['gælisizm] Gallizismus *m*.

gallipot ['gælipət] **1.** *pharm* Salbentopf *m*; **2.** *s. galipot.*

gallivant [gæli'vænt] *itr* (herum)flirten, auf Abenteuer ausgehen.

gallon ['gælən] Gallone *f (Hohlmaß; 4,54, Am 3,78 l)*.

galloon [gə'luːn] Borte; Tresse *f*.

gallop ['gæləp] *s (Pferd)* Galopp *m a. fam allg*; *itr* u. *to ride at a* ~ galoppieren; *allg* fliegen, sausen; *tr* galoppieren lassen; *at a* ~ im Galopp; *to break into a* ~ in e-n Galopp fallen.

gallows ['gælouz] *pl meist mit sing* Galgen *m*; Erhängen *n*; ~**-bird** Galgenvogel *m*.

galluses ['gæləsiz] *pl Am fam* Hosenträger *m*.

galore [gə'lɔː] *adv* in Hülle und Fülle.

galosh [gə'lɔʃ] Gummi-, Überschuh *m*.

galumph [gə'lʌmf] *itr fam* einherstolzieren.

galvan|ic [gæl'vænik] *el* galvanisch; ~**ism** ['gælvənizm] Galvanismus *m*; ~**ization** [gælvənai'zeiʃən] Galvanisierung *f*; ~**ize** ['gælvənaiz] *tr* galvanisieren, verzinken; *med* elektrisieren; *fig* aufschrecken; ~**ometer** [gælvə'nɔmitə] Strom(stärke)messer *m*; ~**oplastic** [gælvano(u)'plæstik] *a* galvanoplastisch; *s pl* Galvanoplastik *f*; ~**oscope** [gæl'vænəskoup, '-] Galvanoskop *n*.

gambit ['gæmbit] *(Schach)* Gambit *n*; *fig* Schachzug *m*, Eröffnungsmanöver *n*.

gambl|e ['gæmbl] *itr* (um Geld) spielen (*for high stakes* um hohe Einsätze); *fig* ein Risiko auf sich nehmen, etw riskieren, wagen; spekulieren; *to* ~~ *with s.th.* etw aufs Spiel setzen; *tr (to* ~ *away)* verspielen; (ver)wetten; *s* gewagte(s) Spiel, Risiko *n*; Wette *f*; Glücksspiel *n*; Spekulation *f*; *to* ~~ *on a fall, on a rise* auf Baisse, Hausse spekulieren; ~**er** ['-ə] Spieler; Spekulant *m*; ~**ing** ['-iŋ] *s* Spielen; gewagte(s) Spiel; Spekulieren *n*; ~~ *debts (pl)* Spielschulden *f pl*; ~~*-den, -hell* Spielhölle *f*; ~~*-house* Spielsaal *m*.

gamboge [gæm'buːʒ] Gummigutt *n*.

gambol ['gæmbəl] *s* Luftsprung *m*; *meist pl* Umhertollen *n*; *itr* umherspringen, -tollen.

game [geim] **1.** *s* Spiel *n*, Belustigung, Unterhaltung *f*, Zeitvertreib *m*; *sport* Spiel *n*; Runde, Partie *f*; (für den) Sieg (nötige Punktzahl *f*); Spielstand *m*; (für ein) Spiel (notwendige Ausrüstung *f*); *fig* Spiel *n*, Machenschaften *f pl*; Wild(bret); *fam* Opfer *n* (das man sich sucht); Kniff, Schlich *m*; *sl* Risiko *n*; *fig Am* Schneid; *pl (Schule)* Sport *m*; *a* Wild-; *fam* tapfer, wacker, nicht bange; *fam* aufgelegt, bereit, zu gebrauchen(d) (*for* zu; *to do* zu tun); *itr* spielen; *tr* verspielen; *to be* ~ *for anything* zu allem zu gebrauchen, für alles zu haben sein; bei allem mitmachen; *to be on (off) o.'s* ~

(nicht) in Form sein; *to give the ~ away (fam)* die Stellung verraten; *to have the ~ in o.'s hands* den Sieg in der Tasche haben; *to make ~ of s.o.* jdn zum besten haben; sich über jdn lustig machen; *to play a losing ~* für e-e verlorene Sache eintreten; *to play the ~* sich an die Regeln halten, fair spielen; *to play a winning (losing) ~* (keine) Aussichten haben; *to put up a ~ fight (sport)* tapfer kämpfen; *the ~ is up (fig)* das Spiel ist aus; *the ~ is not worth the candle* die Sache ist nicht der Mühe wert; *big ~* Großwild; *fam* hohe(s) Spiel *n*; *fair ~* jagdbare(s) Wild; *fam (Mensch)* passende(s) Opfer *n*; *the Olympic G~s* die Olympischen Spiele *n pl*; *~ of chance, of skill* Glücks-, Geschicklichkeitsspiel *n*; *a ~ of chess* e-e Partie Schach; **~-bag** Jagdtasche *f*; **~-cock** Kampfhahn *m*; **~keeper** Wildhüter *m*; **~-laws** *pl* Jagdrecht *n*; **~-licence** Jagdschein *m*; **~ness** ['-nis] Tapferkeit *f*; **~-preserve** Wildpark *m*; **~s-master, -mistress** Sportlehrer (-in *f*) *m*; **~some** ['-səm] spielerisch; sportlich; lustig; **~ster** ['-stə] Spieler *m*; **~-warden** *Am* Jagdaufseher *m*; **2.** *a (bes. Bein)* lahm; verkrüppelt.

gaming ['geimiŋ] (Glücks-)Spiel, Spielen *n (um Geld)*; **~-house** Spielhölle, -bank *f*; **~-table** Spieltisch *m*.

gammer ['gæmə] alte(s) Mütterchen *n*.

gammon ['gæmən] **1.** *s* gesalzene(r) *od* geräucherte(r) Schinken *m*; Speckseite *f*; *tr* räuchern; (ein)salzen; **2.** *s* Doppelsieg *m* im Puffspiel *(back~)*; *mar* Bugspriet(befestigung *f*) *m*; *tr* e-n Doppelsieg im Puffspiel erringen gegen; **3.** *s fam* Blödsinn *m*, Flunkerei *f*; *itr* dumm quatschen, flunkern; *tr* etw vorflunkern, -machen (*s.o.* jdm); beschwindeln, foppen.

gamp ['gæmp] *Br fam* Musspritze *f*, (*bes.* großer) Regenschirm *m*.

gamut ['gæmət] Tonleiter; *fig* Skala *f*.

*

gander ['gændə] *s* Ganter, Gänserich; *fig* Dussel, Depp; *Am sl* Blick *m*; *itr Am sl* blicken (*at* nach); *to take a ~ (sl)* e-n Blick werfen (*at* auf).

gang [gæŋ] *s (Menschen)* Gruppe, Abteilung; Gesellschaft; Clique; *(Arbeiter)* Rotte, Kolonne *f*; *(Gefangene)* Trupp *m*; *(Verbrecher)* Bande *f*; *(Werkzeug)* Satz *m*; *itr (to ~ up)* e-e Gruppe, Rotte, Bande bilden (*on* gegen); *tr radio* abgleichen; *interj (~way)* Platz, bitte! **~-board, -plank** Laufplanke *f*, -steg *m*; **~er** ['-ə] Rottenführer, Vorarbeiter *m*; **~ster** ['-stə] (Angehöriger e-r) Verbrecher(bande) *m*; **~way** ['-wei] Gang *(zwischen Sitzreihen)*; Korridor *m*; *min* Strecke; *mar* Laufplanke *f*, -steg; *aero* Durchgang *m*; *to clear the ~~* Platz machen; **~-work** Serienfabrikation *f*.

ganglion ['gæŋgliən] *pl a. ganglia* [-ə] *anat* Nervenknoten *m*, Ganglion; *med* Überbein, Ganglion; *fig* Kräftezentrum *n*, Knotenpunkt *m*.

gangren|e ['gæŋgri:n] *s med* Gangrän(e *f*) *n*, Brand *m*; *tr itr* brandig machen, werden; **~ous** ['-inəs] *med* brandig.

gannet ['gænit] *zoo* Tölpel *m*.

gantry ['gæntri] *tech* Gerüst *n*, Bock *m*; *rail* Signalbrücke *f*.

gaol [dʒeil] *s. jail*.

gap [gæp] *s* Lücke *f*, Spalt(e *f*) *m*, Loch *n*, Bresche, Öffnung *f*; Abstand *m*; (Gebirgs-)Schlucht, Klamm *f*, Paß *m*; *(Minenfeld)* Gasse; Lücke, Unterbrechung; *(Versicherung)* Wartezeit *f*; Ausea.gehen, -klaffen *n (der Ansichten, Meinungen)*; Verschiedenheit *(der Naturen)*; *tech* Aussparung, Fuge, Maulweite; *math* Nullstelle *f*; *tr* e-e Bresche schlagen, e-e Lücke reißen in; *to bridge a ~* e-e Lücke überbrücken; *to close, to fill, to stop, to supply a ~* e-e Lücke füllen, schließen.

gape [geip] *itr* gaffen; Mund u. Ohren aufsperren; klaffen, gähnen; anstarren (*at s.o.* jdn); *s* Gaffen; Gähnen; Staunen *n*; klaffende, große Lücke *f*; *the ~s (pl)* der Pips *(Geflügelkrankheit)*; *hum* Gähnanfall *m*.

garage ['gærɑ:ʒ, '-ridʒ, *Am* gə'rɑ:ʒ] *s* Garage; Großgarage *f*, Autoreparaturwerkstatt; Tankstelle *f*; Schuppen *m*; *tr (Wagen)* in die Garage stellen.

garb [gɑ:b] *s* Tracht, Kleidung *f*; *tr* kleiden (*in* in).

garbage ['gɑ:bidʒ] (Küchen-, Markt-) Abfall *m*, Abfälle *pl*, Müll *m*; *fig* Ausschuß, Schund *m*; **~ can, pail** *Am* Mülleimer *m*, -tonne *f*; **~ disposer** *Am* Müllschlucker *m*; **~ man** *Am* Müllfuhrmann *m*.

garble ['gɑ:bl] *tr (Geschichte, Bericht)* durchea.bringen, entstellen.

garden ['gɑ:dn] *s* Garten *m a. fig*; *pl a.* Anlagen *f pl*, Park *m*; *itr* im Garten arbeiten; *a* Garten-; gewöhnlich, alltäglich; *to lead s.o. up the ~ (fam)* jdn hereinlegen; *flower ~* Blumengarten *m*; *kitchen ~* Küchen-, Gemüsegarten *m*; *market ~* Handelsgärtnerei *f*; *vegetable ~* Gemüsegarten *m*; **~-bed** Gartenbeet *n*; **~ city, suburb** Gartenstadt *f*; **~-cress** Gartenkresse *f*; **~er** ['-ə] Gärtner *m*; **~-frame** Mistbeet *n*; **~-glass** Glasglocke; Gartenkugel *f*; **~ hose** Gartenschlauch *m*; **~ing** ['-iŋ] Gartenarbeit *f*, -bau *m*; Gärtnerei *f*; **~-mo(u)ld** Gartenerde *f*; **~-party** Gartenfest *n*; **~-plot** Gartengrundstück *n*; **~ produce** Gemüse *n*; **~-seat** Gartenstuhl *m*, -bank *f*; **~-stuff** Obst u. Gemüse *n*; **~ tools** *pl* Gartenwerkzeuge *n pl*; **~-wall** Gartenmauer *f*; **~-warbler** *orn* Gartengrasmücke *f*; **~white** *zoo* Kohlweißling *m*.

gardenia [gɑ:'di:njə] *bot* Gardenia *f*.

gargantuan [gɑ:'gæntjuən] riesig, gewaltig.

gargle ['gɑ:gl] *tr itr* gurgeln; *s* Mundwasser *n*.

gargoyle ['gɑ:gɔil] *arch* Wasserspeier *m*.

garish ['gɛəriʃ] *(Farbe)* grell, schreiend.

garland ['gɑ:lənd] *s* Kranz *m*; Girlande *f*; *tr* bekränzen.

garlic ['gɑ:lik] *bot* Knoblauch *m*.

garment ['gɑ:mənt] *s* Kleidungsstück *n*; Hülle *a. fig*; *pl* Kleidung *f*; *tr* kleiden.

garner ['gɑ:nə] *s* Kornspeicher *m*, -haus *n*; *allg* Vorrat *m*; *fig* Sammlung *f*; *tr* (auf)speichern, sammeln *a. fig*.

garnet ['gɑ:nit] *min* Granat *m*.

garnish ['gɑ:niʃ] *tr (Küche)* garnieren; *allg* verzieren, schmücken, verschönern; *jur* pfänden; *s* Verzierung; *(Küche)* Garnierung *f*; **~ment** ['-mənt] Garnierung; Verzierung *f*, Schmuck *m*; *~ment of wages* Lohnpfändung *f*.

garniture ['gɑ:nitʃə] Verzierung *f*; *(Küche)* Garnierung; Ausstattung *f*, Zubehör(teile *n pl*) *n*, *a. m.*

garret ['gærət] Dachkammer *f*, -boden *m*; *to be wrong in the ~* nicht ganz klar im Oberstübchen sein.

garrison ['gærisn] *s mil* Garnison *f*, Standort *m*; *(~ town)* Garnison(stadt) *f*; *tr (Stadt, Festung)* mit e-r Garnison belegen; *(Truppe, Soldaten)* in Garnison legen, stationieren; **~ area** Standortbereich *m*; **~ cap** Feldmütze *f*; **~ commander** Standortkommandant *m*; **~ headquarters** *pl oft mit sing* Standortkommandantur *f*.

garrul|ity [gæ'ru:liti] Schwatzhaftigkeit, Redseligkeit *f*; **~ous** ['gæruləs] schwatzhaft; *(Bach)* plätschernd.

garter ['gɑ:tə] Strumpfband *n*; *Am* Sockenhalter *m*; *(the Order of) the G~* der Hosenbandorden; **~-belt** *Am* Strumpfgürtel *m*; **~ girdle** Hüfthalter *m*.

gas [gæs] *s* Gas *n*, gasförmige(r) Körper *m*; *(coal-~)* (Leucht-)Gas; *mil* (Gift-)Gas *n*; *min* Schlagwetter *n pl*; *Am fam* Benzin; *fig sl* leere(s) Gerede *n*; *tr* mit Gas versorgen; mit Gas vergiften, vergasen; *sl* faseln; *Am sl* beeindrucken, gefangennehmen; *mil* mit Gas angreifen; *to ~ up (Am sl)* aufmöbeln; *mot* auftanken; *to be ~sed* e-e Gasvergiftung haben; *itr sl (to ~ away)* angeben, dämlich quatschen; plaudern; *to cook by ~* auf Gas kochen; *to step on the ~ (Am fam) mot* Gas geben *a. fig*; *to turn on, off the ~* den Gashahn auf-, zudrehen; *laughing ~* Lachgas *n*; *mixture of ~* Gasgemisch *n*; **~-a-teria** *Am* Benzinautomat *m*; **~ attack** *mil* Gasangriff *m*; **~-bag** (Gas-)Zelle *f*; *fig pej* Schwätzer *m*; **~-bracket** Gasarm *m*; **~-burner, -jet, -ring** (Gas-)Brenner *m*; **~conduit** Gasrohr *n*, -leitung *f*; **~-cooker** Gaskocher *m*; **~ detector** Gasspürgerät *n*; **~-engine** Gasmotor; *Am* Benzinmotor *m*; Verbrennungsmaschine *f*; **~eous** ['geizjəs, *bes. Am* 'gæsiəs], **~iform** ['-ifɔ:m] gasförmig; **~ explosion** Gasexplosion *f*; **~-fire** Gasofen *m*; **~-fitter** Installateur, Rohrleger *m*; **~-fittings** *pl* Gasanlage *f*; **~-fixture** Gasschlauch *m*; **~-flame** Gasflamme *f*; **~ formation** Gasentwicklung *f*; **~ heating** Gasheizung *f*; **~ification** [gæsifi'keiʃən] *chem* Vergasung *f*; **~ify** ['gæsifai] *tr chem* vergasen; in den gasförmigen Zustand überführen; **~ lever** Gashebel *m*; **~light** Gaslicht *n*, -beleuchtung *f*; **~-lighter** Gasanzünder *m*; **~-main** Hauptgasrohr *n*; **~man** Gasmann *m (Kassierer)*; **~-mantle** (Gas-)Glühstrumpf *m*; **~-mask** Gasmaske *f*; *~~ canister* Filterbüchse *f*; *~~ drum* Filtereinsatz *m*; **~meter** ['gæsmi:tə] Gasuhr *f*; **~ oil** Gas-, Treiböl *n*; **~oline,** *Am* **~olene** ['gæs(ə)li:n, -'li:n] *Am* Benzin *n*; *~~ gauge* Benzinuhr *f*; *~~ tank* Benzintank *m*; **~ometer** [gæ'sɔmitə] *Br* Gasbehälter, Gasometer *m*; **~ pedal** *Am* Gashebel *m*, -pedal *n*; **~ pipe** Gasrohr *n*; Benzinleitung *f*; **~ pressure** Gasdruck *m*; **~-proof, -tight** gassicher; **~-range, -stove** Gasherd *m*; **~ser** ['-ə] *Am sl s* tolle(r) Witz; Aufschneider; Pfundskerl *m*, -sache *f*; *a* zum Totlachen; enorm, phänomenal; **~-shell** *mil* Gasgranate *f*; **~ station** *Am* Tankstelle *f*; *~ operator* Tankwart *m*; **~sy** ['-i] Gas enthaltend; gasartig; *fam* angeberisch; geschwätzig; **~ tank** *Am* Gasbehälter, Gasometer; Benzinbehälter *m*; **~ tap** Gashahn *m*; **~-tar** Steinkohlenteer *m*; **~ trap** Gasschleuse *f*; **~-turbine** Gasturbine *f*; *attr* Turbo-; **~ warning, alarm** Gasalarm *m*; **~-welding** autogene(s) Schweißen *n*; **~-works** *pl mit sing, Am* **plant** Gasanstalt *f*, Gaswerke *n pl*.

gash [gæʃ] *s* lange, klaffende Wunde *f*, Schmiß; Hieb, Schnitt *m*; *tr* (auf-)schlitzen; e-e tiefe Wunde beibringen.

gasket ['gæskit] *tech* (Flanschen-) Dichtung; *mar* Zeising, Seising *f*.

gasp [gɑ:sp] *itr* keuchen, mühsam atmen; *tr (to ~ out) (Worte)* hervorbringen; hervorkeuchen; *s* Keuchen, schwere(s) Atmen *n*; *at o.'s, at* *the last* ~ in den letzten Zügen; im letzten Augenblick; *to* ~ *for breath* nach Luft schnappen; *to* ~ *o.'s life away, out* sein Leben aushauchen, s-n Geist aufgeben; **~er** ['-ə] *sl* schlechte, billige Zigarette *f*, Sargnagel *m*; **~ing** ['-iŋ] keuchend; krampfhaft.

gastr|ic ['gæstrik] *scient* gastrisch, Magen-; *~~ acid* Magensäure *f*; *~~ juice (physiol)* Magensaft *m*; *~~ lavage* Magenspülung *f*; *~~ ulcer* Magengeschwür *n*; **~itis** [gæs'traitis] Magenschleimhautentzündung *f*.

gastro|enteritis ['gæstro(u)entə'raitis] Magen-Darm-Katarrh *m*; **~intestinal** [-in'testinəl] *a* Magen-Darm-.

gastronom|e ['gæstrənoum], **~er** [gæs'trɔnəmə], **~ist** [gæs'trɔnəmist] Feinschmecker *m*; **~ic(al)** [gæstrə'nɔmik(əl)] gastronomisch; **~y** [gæs'trɔnəmi] Gastronomie, feinere Kochkunst *f*.

gate [geit] *s* (Garten-, Stadt-)Tor *n*; (Garten-)Pforte *f*; *fig* Tor *n*, Zugang *m* (*to* zu); (enge) Durchfahrt *f*, Durchlaß; (Eng-)Paß *m*, Schlucht *f*; *tech* Eingußtrichter, Einlauf *m*; (Tor-, Bahn-)Schranke *f*; Schlagbaum *m*; (Straßen-)Sperre *f*; *phot* Filmfenster; Wehr *(in e-m Wasserlauf)*; Schleusentor *n*; Besucherzahl, Gesamteinnahme *f*; *Am sl* Entlassung *f*, Laufpaß *m*; *itr aero* mit Höchstgeschwindigkeit fliegen; *to give the* ~ *to s.o. (Am fam)* jdn an die Luft setzen; **~-crash** *itr tr* eindringen, ungebeten erscheinen (*in* bei); **~-crasher** Eindringling, ungebetene(r) Gast *m*; **~house** Tor, Pförtnerhaus *n*; **~-keeper** Torwärter, Pförtner; Schranken-, Bahnwärter *m*; **~-latch** Türriegel *m*; **~-leg(ged) table** Klapptisch *m*; **~-man** *Am rail* Schaffner *m* an der Sperre; **~-money** Eintrittsgeld *n*; **~-post** Torpfosten *m*; *between you and me and the ~~* in strengstem Vertrauen; **~way** Torweg *m*, Einfahrt *f*; *fig* Weg *m* (*to* zu).

gather ['gæðə] *tr* versammeln; zs.bringen, sammeln, anhäufen; *(Ernte)* einbringen; pflücken; *(Rost)* ansetzen; *(Geld)* einziehen, kassieren; *(Eindruck)* gewinnen; schließen (*from* aus), den Schluß ziehen (*that* daß); entnehmen (*from* aus); zunehmen an *(Kraft, Umfang)*; fälteln, kräuseln; *(die Stirn)* in Falten legen, runzeln; *itr* sich versammeln, zs.kommen; *(Wolken)* sich zs.-ziehen; *(Wunde)* eitern; *(Eiter)* sich zs.ziehen, e-n Kopf bilden; zunehmen, (an)wachsen; *(Stirn)* sich in Falten legen; *s* Falte *f*; *to* ~ *o.s. together* sich sammeln, sich konzentrieren, sich innerlich vorbereiten, sich gefaßt machen; *to* ~ *together* zs.lesen; *to* ~ *up* zs.lesen, -ziehen; *to* ~ *a bunch of flowers* e-n Blumenstrauß pflücken; *to* ~ *information* Erkundigung einziehen; *to* ~ *speed, way* an Geschwindigkeit zunehmen; schneller werden; **~ing** ['-riŋ] Sammeln *n*; Versammlung, (versammelte) Menge; Zs.kunft; (Geld-)Sammlung *(für wohltätige Zwecke)*; Eiterbeule *f*, Abszeß *m*; *pl* (Kräusel-)Falten *f pl*; *family ~~* Familientreffen *n*.

gaud [gɔ:d] Flitter *m*; **~iness** ['-inis] geschmacklose(r) Prunk *m*; **~y** ['-i] *a* auffällig, geschmacklos, protzig; *s* (jährliches) Festessen *n (College)*.

ga(u)ge [geidʒ] *s* Eichmaß *n*, Haupt-, Kontroll-, Gebrauchsnormale *f*; *tech* Maß *n*, Meßkörper *m*, -uhr *f*, -gefäß *n*; Lehre; *(Draht, Blech)* Dicke, Stärke *f*; Manometer *n*; Zollstock *m*; *mar* Wasserverdrängung *f*, Tiefgang *m*, Tonnage *f*; Pegel *m*; Luv-, Windseite; *rail* Spurweite *f*; *mil* Kaliber; *typ* Kolumnenmaß *n*; *(Strumpf)* gg-Zahl *f*; *fig* Maß(stab *m*) *n*; *tr* eichen; lehren; kalibrieren; genau, exakt (aus)messen; *(to take the* ~ *of s.o.)* jdn beurteilen, (ab)schätzen (*by* nach); *narrow* ~ Schmalspur *f*; *standard* ~ Normalspur *f*; **~r** ['-ə] Eichmeister *m*.

Gaul [gɔ:l] *hist* Gallien *n*; Gallier; Franzose *m*; **~ish** ['-iʃ] gallisch.

gaunt [gɔ:nt] hager, hohlwangig, -äugig; finster, abweisend, trostlos.

gauntlet ['gɔ:ntlit] *hist* Fehdehandschuh; Stulpenhandschuh *m*; (Handschuh-)Stulpe *f*; *to fling, to throw down the* ~ herausfordern (*to s.o.* jdn); *to pick, to take up the* ~ die Herausforderung annehmen; *to run the* ~ Spießruten laufen *a. fig.*

gauz|e [gɔ:z] *s* Gaze *f*, Flor *m*; feine(s) Drahtgeflecht *n*; (leichter) Dunst *m (in der Luft)*; *surgical ~~* Verbandmull *m*; **~iness** ['-inis] Zartheit *f (e-s Gewebes)*; **~y** ['-i] gazeartig; hauchdünn, -zart, durchscheinend.

gavel ['gævl] (kleiner) Hammer *m*.

gavotte [gə'vɔt] Gavotte *f (Tanz)*.

gawk [gɔ:k] *s* Tölpel, Dämlack, Depp *m*; *tr Am* blöde anstarren; **~iness** ['-inis] Tölpelhaftig-, Tolpatschigkeit *f*; **~y** ['-i] ungeschickt, linkisch.

gay [gei] lustig, vergnügt, fröhlich, munter, lebhaft; gesellig, vergnügungssüchtig, ausschweifend, zügellos; hell, glänzend, farbenfroh, bunt; *to get* ~ *(Am sl)* frech werden, sich Frechheiten erlauben (*with s.o.* gegenüber jdm).

gaze [geiz] *itr* starren, glotzen (*at, on, upon* auf); anstarren, -glotzen; *s* starre(r) Blick *m*; *to stand at* ~ Glotzaugen machen, *fam* in die Gegend starren.

gazebo [gə'zi:bou] Aussichtsturm *m*; Sommerhaus *n* mit weiter Sicht.

gazelle [gə'zel] *zoo* Gazelle *f*.

gazett|e [gə'zet] *s (meist in Titeln)* Zeitung *f*; Staatsanzeiger *m*; *tr* amtlich bekanntgeben, -machen; **~er** [gæzi'tiə] geographische(s) Namensverzeichnis *n*.

gear [giə] *s* Handwerks-, Werkzeug; (Pferde-)Geschirr; Gerät *n*, Ausrüstung *f*; *tech* (Gang-)Getriebe *n*, Antrieb *m*, Triebwerk *n*; *mot* Gang *m*; *(Fahrrad)* Übersetzung *f*; *tr* ausrüsten; *(Pferd)* anschirren; *(Betrieb)* abstellen (*to* auf); *tech* mit e-m Getriebe verbinden *od* versehen; in Betrieb setzen; einkuppeln; eng verbinden (*to* mit); *itr* durch ein Getriebe verbunden sein; inea.greifen; eingreifen (*into* in); zs.arbeiten (*with* mit); *in* ~ in Betrieb, in Gang; eingekuppelt; *fig* in Ordnung; *out of* ~ außer Betrieb; ausgekuppelt; *fig* nicht in Ordnung; *to go, to shift into low* ~ den ersten Gang einschalten; *to put, to throw into* ~ einschalten; auf Touren bringen *a. fig*; *to shift, to change* ~ umschalten (*on a car* bei e-m Wagen); *to throw out of* ~ *(tech)* ausrücken; *fig* aus dem Gleichgewicht bringen; *to* ~ *the car down, up (mot)* e-n niedrigeren, höheren Gang einschalten; 'runter-, 'raufschalten; *to* ~ *up (fig)* auf höhere Touren bringen; steigern; *low, second, top, reverse* ~ *(mot)* erste(r), zweite(r), dritte(r), Rückwärtsgang *m*; **~-box, -case** *mot* Getriebekasten *m*; **~-change** *mot* Gangschaltung *f*; **~ed** [-d] *a* Getriebe-; eingestellt (*to* auf); gerüstet (*to* für); *~~ turbine* Getriebeturbine *f*; **~ing** ['-riŋ] Trieb-, Räderwerk; Getriebe *n*; Verzahnung *f*; Vorgelege *n*; *(Fahrrad)* Übersetzung *f*; **~-lever,** *Am* **-shift** Schalthebel *m*; **~ oil** Getriebeöl *n*; **~ rim** Zahnkranz *m*; **~-wheel** Zahn-, Getrieberad *n*.

gee [dʒi:] **1.** *interj (~ up)* hott! *s (~-~)* Hottehü, Hotto, Pferdchen *n*; *Am sl* Bursche *m*; **2.** *interj (~ whiz) Am* du lieber Himmel! du meine Güte!

geezer ['gi:zə] *sl* Mummelgreis *m*; alte Oma *f*; *Am sl* Schluck *m* Schnaps.

Geiger counter ['gaigə'kauntə] *el* Geigerzähler *m*.

geisha ['geiʃə] Geisha *f*.

gelatin(e) [dʒelə'ti:n] *(tierische)* Gallerte; *(pflanzliche)* Gelatine; Gallertmasse *f*; **~ate, ~ize** [dʒi'lætineit, -naiz] *itr tr* gelieren(lassen); **~ous** [dʒi'lætinəs] gallert(art)ig.

geld [geld] *a. irr gelt, gelt tr* kastrieren; verschneiden; *fig* verstümmeln; **~ing** ['-iŋ] Wallach *m*; Kastrieren *n*.

gelid ['dʒelid] eisig, eiskalt.

gem [dʒem] *s* (geschliffener) Edelstein *m*; *Am* Brötchen *n*; *fig* Perle *f*, Prachtstück *n*; *tr* mit Edelsteinen besetzen.

gemin|ate ['dʒemineit] *a scient* paarig; *tr* paarig anordnen; verdoppeln; **~ation** [dʒemi'neiʃən] paarige Anordnung *f*; **G~i** ['dʒeminai] *astr* Zwillinge *m pl*.

gemm|a ['dʒemə] *pl -ae* [-i:] Knospe *a. zoo*; *bot* Spore *f*; **~ate** ['dʒemeit] *itr zoo* sich durch Knospung fortpflanzen; *a* knospig; **~ation** [dʒe'meiʃən] Knospung; *biol* Fortpflanzung *f* durch Knospen.

gen [dʒen] *sl* Wahrheit *f*.

gender ['dʒendə] *gram* Geschlecht *n*.

gene [dʒi:n] *biol* Gen *n*.

genealog|ical [dʒi:njə'lɔdʒikəl] genealogisch; Abstammungs-; *~~ table* Ahnentafel *f*; *~~ tree* Stammbaum *m*; **~ist** [dʒi:ni'ælədʒist] Genealoge *m*; **~y** [dʒi:ni'ælədʒi] Genealogie *f*.

general ['dʒenərəl] *a* allgemein; üblich, gewöhnlich, normal; *(Bemerkungen)* andeutend, unbestimmt, allgemein gehalten; Haupt-, General-; *s mil* (*rel* Ordens-)General; Stratege *m*; *fam* Mädchen *n* für alles; *as a* ~ *rule, in* ~ im allgemeinen; ~ *quarters! (mar)* Klarschiff zum Gefecht! *brigadier* ~ Brigadegeneral *m*; *consul(ate)* ~ Generalkonsul(at *n*) *m*; *full* ~ *(Am)* General *m* (der Infanterie *usw*); *lieutenant* ~ Generalleutnant *m*; *major* ~ Generalmajor *m*; *secretary* ~ Generalsekretär *m*; *G~ of the Army (Am)* Oberbefehlshaber des Heeres; **~ agency** Generalvertretung *f*; **~ agent** Generalvertreter *m*; **~ assembly** Voll-, Generalversammlung *f*; **~ bookseller** Sortimentsbuchhändler *m*; **~ dealer** Gemischtwarenhändler *m*; **~ delivery** postlagernd; **~ director, manager** Generaldirektor *m*; **~ editor** Hauptschriftleiter *m*; **~ headquarters** *pl oft mit sing mil* Große(s) Hauptquartier *n*; **~ holiday** öffentliche(r) Feiertag *m*; **~issimo** [dʒenərə'lisimou] *pl -s* Oberbefehlshaber *m*; **~ity** [dʒenə'ræliti] Allgemeinheit; allgemeine Redensart *od* Bemerkung; Grundregel; Allgemeingültigkeit *f*; *mit pl* große Masse, Mehrheit, Mehrzahl *f*; **~ization** [dʒenərəlai'zeiʃən] Verallgemeinerung *f*; **~ize** ['-aiz] *tr* verallgemeinern; allgemein verbreiten; **~ly** ['-i] *adv* (im) allgemein(en), gemeinhin, gewöhnlich, meist; weithin; ganz allgemein, andeutungsweise; **~ management** Geschäftsleitung *f*; **~ map** Übersichtskarte *f*; **~ officer** Offizier *m* im Generalsrang; *~~ commanding-in-chief* Oberbefehlshaber *m*; **~ pardon** Amnestie *f*; Gnadenerlaß *m*; **~ post office** Hauptpost *f*; **~ practitioner** praktische(r) Arzt *m*; **~ public** Allgemeinheit, Öffentlichkeit *f*; **~-purpose vehicle** Mehrzweckfahrzeug *n*; **~ reader** Durchschnittsleser *m*; **~ servant** Mädchen *n* für alles; **~ship** ['-ʃip] Generalsrang *m*; (Kunst der) Kriegführung; Führereigenschaft; *fig* geschickte Leitung *f*; ~ **staff** *mil* Generalstab *m*; ~ **store** *Am* Warenhaus *n*; ~ **strike** Generalstreik *m*; ~ **view** Gesamtbild *n*, -ansicht *f*, Überblick *m*.

generat|e ['dʒenəreit] *tr biol* (er)zeugen; *allg* erzeugen, hervorbringen, -rufen; *(Linie)* ziehen; *(Figur)* zeichnen; *fig* verursachen; *~ing station, plant (el)* Kraftwerk *n*; **~ion** [dʒenə'reiʃən] *biol* Zeugung; *allg* Erzeugung; Generation *f*; Menschenalter *n*; **~ive** ['dʒenərətiv] zeugungsfähig, fruchtbar; Zeugungs-; **~or** ['dʒenəreitə] Erzeuger; *tech* Generator; Gas-, Stromerzeuger; Dynamo (-maschine *f*) *m*, Lichtmaschine *f*; Dampfkessel; *chem* Entwickler; *mus* Grundton *m*; *~~ gas* Generatorgas *n*.

generic [dʒi'nerik] allgemein; *biol* Gattungs-; ~ **term** Gattungsbegriff *m*.

gener|osity [dʒenə'rɔsiti] Edelmut *m*, Großmut; Großzügigkeit, Freigebigkeit *f*; **~ous** ['dʒenərəs] edel, großmütig (*to* gegenüber); großzügig, freigebig (*of, with* mit); selbstlos; *(Boden)* ergiebig, fruchtbar; reichlich, groß; *(Wein)* vollmundig u. schwer.

genesis ['dʒenisis] Ursprung *m*, Werden *n*, Entstehung, Genese, Genesis *f*; *G~* 1. Buch *n* Mosis, Genesis; Schöpfungsgeschichte *f*.

genet ['dʒenit] *zoo* Ginsterkatze *f*.

genetic [dʒi'netik] *a* genetisch; Entstehungs-, Ursprungs-; *s pl mit sing* Genetik *f*; **~ist** [-sist] Genetiker *m*.

geneva [dʒi'ni:və] Genever, Wacholder, Steinhäger *m*; **G~** Genf *n*.

genial ['dʒi:njəl] anregend, belebend; angenehm, heiter, froh; liebenswürdig, freundlich, herzlich; *(Klima)* mild, warm; **~ity** [dʒi:ni'æliti] Heiterkeit *f*, Frohsinn *m*; Wärme, Liebenswürdigkeit, Freundlichkeit, Herzlichkeit; *(Wetter)* Milde *f*.

genital ['dʒenitl] *a* Zeugungs-, Geschlechts-; *s pl* Geschlechtsteile *n pl*, Genitalien *pl*.

genitive ['dʒenitiv] *gram* Genitiv *m*.

genius ['dʒi:niəs] *pl genii* ['-niai] Schutzgeist, Genius, (guter *od* böser) Geist, Dämon *m*; *pl ~es* ['-njəsiz] Geist *m*, Eigentümlichkeit, Besonderheit; Eigenart *f*, Wesen *n*, Charakter *m*, Natur, Anlage; Fähigkeit *f* (*for, to* zu); geniale(r) Mensch *m*.

genocide ['dʒeno(u)said] Gruppen-, Völkermord *m*.

genotype ['dʒeno(u)taip] *biol* Genotyp *m*, Erbbild *n*.

genre [ʒɑ:ŋr] *lit (Kunst)* Genre *n*, Gattung *f*; ~ **painting** Genremalerei *f*.

gent [dʒent] *fam* feine(r) Mann, Gent *m*; **~eel** [-'ti:l] *obs* vornehm, fein, wohlerzogen; elegant, modisch; vornehmtuend, affektiert; **~ility** [-'tiliti] *meist iro* Vornehmheit, Wohlerzogenheit, Eleganz *f*.

gentian ['dʒenʃiən] *bot* Enzian *m*.

gentile ['dʒentail] *a* nichtjüdisch; *s* Nichtjude *m*.

gentle ['dʒentl] *adv gently* vornehm, fein; wohlerzogen, gebildet, höflich; hochgesinnt; wohlmeinend; leutselig, umgänglich; gutmütig, geduldig; sanft; mild, lind, zart; leise; *(Tier)* zahm; *(Abhang)* sanft ansteigend; *(Brise)* leicht; *(Wärme)* mäßig; *the ~ art, craft* das Angeln; *the ~ reader* der geneigte Leser; *the ~ sex* das schöne Geschlecht; **~folk(s)** ['-fouk(s)] *pl* vornehme, feine Leute *pl*; **~man** [-mən] *pl ~men* [-mən] vornehme(r), feine(r), gebildete(r) Mann, Ehrenmann *m*; *(Ladies and) G~men* meine (Damen und) Herren! *~~'s, ~men's agreement* stillschweigende(s) Abkommen *n*; *~~ driver* Herrenfahrer *m*; *~~-farmer* Gutsbesitzer *m*; *~~ of fortune* Glücksritter, Abenteurer *m*; *~~ in waiting* Kammerherr *m*; **~manlike** ['-mənlaik], **~manly** ['-mənli] *a* vornehm, fein, gebildet, von guten Umgangsformen; **~ness** [-nis] Sanftmut, Milde, Gutmütigkeit; Güte; Zartheit *f*; **~woman** ['-wumən] *pl ~women* ['-wimən] (vornehme, feine, gebildete) Dame; *hist* Kammerfrau *f*.

gentry ['dʒentri] niedere(r) Adel *m*; vornehme Welt *f*, feine Leute; *hum pej (bestimmte)* Leute *pl*.

genufle|ct ['dʒenju(:)flekt] *itr* die Knie beugen; **~ction, ~xion** [-'flekʃən] Kniefall *m*, -beuge *f*.

genuine ['dʒenjuin] wirklich, wahr (-haftig), echt; unverfälscht; authentisch; aufrichtig, ehrlich, offen; *(Käufer)* ernsthaft; *zoo* reinrassig; **~ness** ['-nis] Echtheit *f*.

genus ['dʒi:nəs] *pl genera* ['dʒenərə] *zoo bot* Gattung; *allg* Art *f*; *(Logik)* Oberbegriff *m*.

geocentric(al) [dʒi(:)o(u)'sentrik(əl)] geozentrisch.

geode|sy [dʒi(:)'ɔdisi] Erdvermessung, Geodäsie *f*; **~tic** [dʒio(u)'detik] geodätisch; *~~ mapping* Landesaufnahme *f*.

geograph|er [dʒi'ɔgrəfə] Geograph *m*; **~ic(al)** [dʒiə'græfik(əl)] geographisch; **~y** [dʒi'ɔgrəfi] Erdkunde, Geographie *f*; *economic ~~* Wirtschaftsgeographie *f*.

geolog|ic(al) [dʒiə'lɔdʒik(əl)] geologisch; **~ist** [dʒi'ɔlədʒist] Geologe *m*; **~y** [dʒi'ɔlədʒi] Geologie *f*.

geomagnetic [dʒio(u)mæg'netik] geomagnetisch.

geomet|ric(al) [dʒiə'metrik(əl)] geometrisch; **~ry** [dʒi'ɔmitri] Geometrie *f*.

geophysic|al [dʒio(u)'fizikəl] geophysikalisch; **~s** [-ks] *pl mit sing* Geophysik *f*.

geopolitics [dʒio(u)'pɔlitiks] *pl mit sing* Geopolitik *f*.

Georg|e [dʒɔ:dʒ] *s* Georg *m*; *Br sl aero* automatische Steuerung; Pfundssache *f*; *a Am sl* pfundig, erstklassig; *by ~!* Donnerwetter! **~ia** ['dʒɔ:dʒjə] **1.** Georgia *(USA)*; **2.** Georgien *n (UdSSR)*; **~ian** ['-ən] **1.** *(Kunst)* georgisch; **2.** *s* Georgier(in *f*) *m*.

georgette [dʒɔ:'dʒet] Georgette *f*.

geranium [dʒi'reinjəm] *bot* Storchschnabel *m*; Geranie *f*, Geranium *n*.

geriatric|ian [dʒeriə'triʃən] Facharzt *m* für Alterskrankheiten; **~s** [dʒeri'ætriks] *pl mit sing* Geriatrie *f*.

germ [dʒə:m] *s biol med fig* Keim; *(~ of disease)* Krankheitskeim *m*; *itr fig* keimen; *in ~ (fig)* im Keim; *free from ~s* keimfrei; **~-carrier** *med* Keimträger *m*; **~-cell** *biol* Keimzelle *f*; **~-free** keimfrei; **~icidal** [-i'saidl] keimtötend, antiseptisch; **~icide** ['dʒə:misaid] Desinfektionsmittel *n*; **~inal** ['-inl] *a* Keim-; *fig* im Anfangsstadium; *~~ disk, vesicle (biol)* Keimscheibe *f*, -bläschen *n*; **~inate** ['-ineit] *itr tr* keimen (lassen); **~inating** ['-ineitiŋ] keimend; *~~ power* Keimfähigkeit *f*; **~ination** [dʒə:mi'neiʃən] Keimen *n*; *~~ test* Keimversuch *m*; **~-plasm** *biol* Protoplasma *n*; ~ **warfare** Bakterienkrieg *m*, biologische Kriegführung *f*.

German ['dʒə:mən] *a* deutsch; *s* (das) Deutsch(e); Deutsche(r *m*) *f*; ~ **clock** Kuckucksuhr *f*; **~ic** [dʒə:'mænik] germanisch; **~ism** ['dʒə:mənizm] Germanismus *m*, deutsche (Sprach-)Eigentümlichkeit *f*; **~ist** ['-ist] Germanist *m*; **~ity** [dʒə:'mæniti] Deutschtum *n*; **~ization** [dʒə:mənai'zeiʃən] Germanisierung *f*; **~ize** ['dʒə:mənaiz] *tr* germanisieren; verdeutschen; *itr* deutsche Sitten annehmen; ~ **measles** *pl med* Röteln *pl*; ~ **Ocean** Nordsee *f*; **~ophil(e)** [dʒə:'mæno(u)fil] *s* Deutschenfreund *m*; *a* deutschfreundlich; **~ophobe** [-'mæno(u)foub] *s* Deutschenhasser *m*; *a* deutschfeindlich; ~ **sausage** Bier-, Jagdwurst *f*; ~ **shepherd dog** *Am* Deutsche(r) Schäferhund *m*; ~ **silver** Neusilber *n*; ~ **steel** gefrischte(r) Stahl *m*; ~ **text, type** *typ* Fraktur *f*; **~y** ['dʒə:məni] Deutschland *n*.

german ['dʒə:mən] eng, nah verwandt (*to* mit); *brother-~* leibliche(r) Bruder *m*; *cousin-~* Vetter *m* 1. Grades.

germane [dʒə:'mein] zugehörig; entsprechend; geeignet (*to* für); passend (*to* zu); eng, nah verwandt (*to* mit).

gerontolog|ist [dʒerən'tɔlədʒist] *s. geriatrician*; **~y** [-'tɔlədʒi] *s. geriatrics*.

gerrymander ['gerimændə, 'dʒ-] *tr (Wahlbezirk)* (zugunsten e-r Partei) neu einteilen; *allg* manipulieren, fälschen; *itr* sich unlauterer Mittel bedienen; *s* Wahlschiebung *f*.

gerund ['dʒerənd] *gram* Gerundium *n*.

gestation [dʒes'teiʃən] Trächtigkeit; Schwangerschaft *f*.

gesticulat|e [dʒes'tikjuleit] *itr* Gebärden machen, gestikulieren; **~ion** [dʒestikju'leiʃən] Gestikulieren; Mienenspiel *n*; Gesten *f pl*, Gebärde *f*; **~ive, ~ory** [dʒes'tikjulətiv, -leitəri, -lət-] gestikulierend; Gebärden-.

gesture ['dʒestʃə] Gebärde, Miene; Geste *f*.

get [get] *irr got, got* od *(obs u. Am) gotten* **1.** *tr* bekommen, erhalten, empfangen; verdienen, gewinnen, erreichen, erwerben, *fam* kriegen; holen, besorgen, beschaffen, verschaffen (*him* sich), bringen; (zu) fassen (kriegen), schnappen, kriegen; verstehen, begreifen, *fam* mitkriegen; lernen, sich merken, sich einprägen; veranlassen, überreden, (dazu) bewegen; dahin *fam* dahin-, soweit kriegen; machen; bringen (*to* zu); *(Essen)* (fertig-) machen; *fam* treffen, schlagen; *fam* fertigmachen, umhauen, totschlagen; *fam* nicht loslassen, nicht aus dem Sinn gehen (*s.o.* jdm); *fam* Spaß machen (*s.o.* jdm); *fam (Strafe)* (aufgebrummt) kriegen; *fam* ärgern, verwirren; *fam* mitkriegen, sehen; *to have got (fam)* haben, besitzen; *fam* müssen (*to do* tun); *(Kleine)* kriegen; *(Junge)* werfen; **2.** *itr* kommen (*from* von; *at* zu; *to* nach); gelangen (*to* nach); erreichen (*to* acc); herankönnen (*at* an); *(in e-e Lage)* kommen, versetzt werden, gelangen, geraten; *(beim Passiv verstärkend)* werden; *fam* anfangen (*doing* zu tun); **3.** *to ~ s.o.'s back up* jdn auf die Palme bringen; *to ~ the better of s.o.* jdn klein kriegen, auf die Knie zwingen, überwinden; *to ~ the boot (fam)* entlassen werden, 'rausfliegen; *to ~ to the bottom* auf den Grund gehen; *to ~ cheated on s.th.* mit etw hereinfallen; *to ~ done with* fertigwerden mit; *to ~ even with s.o.* mit jdm abrechnen; *to ~ a glimpse, a sight of* flüchtig sehen, zu Gesicht bekommen; *to ~ s.o.'s goat* jdn auf die Palme bringen; *to ~ going* in Gang setzen; *to ~ to grips with s.th.* sich mit etw energisch befassen; *to ~ o.'s hair cut* sich die Haare schneiden lassen; *to ~ o.'s hand in* sich angewöhnen; *to ~ the hang of s.th. (sl)* von etw den Dreh herauskriegen; *to ~ into* *s.o.'s head* jdm zu Kopf steigen; *to ~ it into o.'s head* sich in etw festbeißen, verrennen; *to ~ hold of* zu fassen kriegen; *fam* aufgabeln, auftreiben; *to ~ home* heim-, nach Hause kommen; *fig* zum springenden Punkt kommen; *to ~ it hot (sl)* eine hineingewürgt bekommen; *to ~ to know* in Erfahrung bringen; *to ~ married* sich verheiraten; *to ~ rid of s.th.* etw loswerden; *to ~ shut (Tür) fam* zukriegen; *to ~ into o.'s stride* sich anpassen; *to ~ there (fam)* sein Ziel erreichen, Erfolg haben; *ahead of s.o.* jdm zuvorkommen; *to ~ in touch with* in Berührung kommen mit, in Beziehungen treten zu; *to ~ o.'s own way* zum Ziele kommen; *to ~ o.'s second wind (Am)* wieder zu Kräften kommen; *to ~ to work on s.th.* sich an etw machen; *to ~ the worst of it* am schlechtesten wegkommen; *to ~ s.o. wrong (Am)* jdn falsch verstehen; *it's ~ting warmer* es wird wärmer; *I ~ it* ich begreife schon; *I've got it* ich hab's! *I got my foot broken* ich habe mir den Fuß gebrochen; *~ going* mach, daß du weiterkommst! *~ you gone! (fam)* hau ab! *~ along* od *away with you* sei so gut! *to ~* **about** (viel) herum-, unter die Leute kommen; *(a. to ~ abroad) (Nachricht)* sich verbreiten, bekanntwerden; *to ~* **above** *o.s.* sich etwas einbilden; *to ~* **across** *tr itr* klar-, verständlich machen, sein; *to ~* **ahead** vorwärts-, vorankommen; *of* überholen, -treffen, -runden; *t ~* **along** weiter-, voran-, vorwärtskommen (*with* mit); durch-, auskommen, fertigwerden, sich vertragen (*with s.o.* mit jdm); *how are you ~ting along?* wie geht's Ihnen? *~~ with you!* das mach anderen weis! *to ~~ in years* älter werden; *to ~* **around** *tr* herumkriegen, gewinnen; *s.o.* um jdn herumkommen; *to doing* dazu kommen, etw zu tun; *itr* herum-, unter die Leute kommen; sich herumsprechen; *to ~* **at** *s.o. (sl)* jdn erreichen; jdn beeinflussen, auf s-e Seite ziehen; *s.th.* an etw herankommen; etw herausfinden; *to ~* **away** *tr* wegkriegen, entfernen; wegbringen; *itr* sich fort-, sich aus dem Staube machen; wegkommen, sich freimachen; *from s.o.* jdn loswerden; *with s.th.* mit e-r S fertigwerden; ungestraft davonkommen; durchkommen; *to ~* **back** *tr* zurückbekommen, -kriegen; wiederhaben; *itr* zurückkehren, -kommen, wiederkommen, sich wieder erholen; *to ~ o.'s own back on s.o., to ~ back at s.o. (fam)* mit jdm abrechnen; es heimzahlen; *to ~* **behind** *Am* unterstützen; *(in der Arbeit)* zurückkommen; *to ~* **by** vorbeigehen, -kommen an; *fam* durchkommen, es schaffen, es hinkriegen; *(mit Geld)* auskommen; es überstehen; *Am* den Anforderungen entsprechen; *to ~* **down** *tr* hinunterbringen; schlucken; 'runterkriegen; *fig* verkraften; entmutigen; *itr* hinuntersteigen (*from* von); *to* sich wieder machen an; sich konzentrieren auf; *to ~ down to brass tacks* zur Sache kommen; *to ~ s.o. down* jdn deprimieren, niederdrücken; *to ~* **in** *tr* hinein-, *(Ernte)* einbringen; hereinholen; hereinbekommen; *itr* herein-, hineinkommen, -gelangen; *(Zug)* ankommen, einfahren; sich einlassen (*with* mit); *parl* gewählt werden (*for* in); *to ~ in on s.th.* bei etw einsteigen; *he doesn't let you ~ a word in edgewise* er läßt einen überhaupt nicht zu Wort kommen; *to ~* **off** *tr* ab-, weg-, herunter-, los-, herauskriegen; verlassen, aussteigen aus, herunterkommen von; davonkommen; *(vor der Strafe)* retten; *(Brief)* abschicken; *(Witz)* machen; *itr* herunter-, ab-, aussteigen; weggehen, *fam* abhauen; davonkommen; Erfolg haben; *aero* vom Boden frei-, loskommen, aufsteigen, starten; *to ~* **on** *tr (Kleidung)* anziehen; *itr* aufsitzen, auf-, einsteigen; fortfahren (*with* mit); weiterführen (*with s.th.* etw); vorwärts-, voran-, weiterkommen, Erfolg haben; älter werden; einverstanden sein, übereinstimmen; es gut verstehen (*with* mit); mitea. auskommen; *to s.th. (Am)* etw verstehen; *to ~ on the ball* sich zs.nehmen; *to ~ on o.'s nerves* auf die Nerven fallen; *to ~* **out** *tr* herausbringen, -bekommen, -holen; (*s.th. out of s.o.* etw aus jdm; *a few words* ein paar Worte); vorbereiten, ausarbeiten; herausbringen, -geben, veröffentlichen; herausbekommen, -kriegen, -schaffen (*out of s.th.* aus etw); *itr* aussteigen, weggehen; her-, hinauskommen, -gelangen; entkommen, entgehen *(of s.th.* e-r S); *(Geheimnis)* herauskommen, bekanntwerden, an die Öffentlichkeit kommen; *~ that out of your head* schlagen Sie sich das aus dem Kopf; *to ~* **over** *tr* hinwegkommen über, hinter sich bringen, überstehen, fertigwerden mit, ver-, überwinden, sich trösten über; übersehen, auslassen; *sl* überzeugen; klarmachen, anbringen; *itr* durchkommen; *to ~* **round** *tr (Sache)* umgehen; *(Person)* herumkriegen, umstimmen; *to ~* **straight** *tr* in Ordnung bringen; *itr* sich im klaren sein über; *to ~* **through** *tr* durchkriegen, -bringen; *(Geld)* ausgeben; *itr* durchkommen; *tele* Anschluß bekommen; *to ~* **together** *tr* zs.bringen; *itr* zs.-kommen, sich treffen; einig werden (*on* über); *to ~* **under** unter Kontrolle bekommen; *to ~* **up** *tr* auf die Beine, zustande, zuwege bringen; herrichten, zurechtmachen, aufputzen; inszenieren; steigen, verstärken, erhöhen (*speed* die Geschwindigkeit); durcharbeiten; *itr* aufstehen, sich erheben; (hinauf)steigen; vorwärtskommen, Fortschritte machen; *(Wind)* auffrischen; *(bei der Lektüre)* kommen (*to* bis); stärker werden; *to ~ o.s. up* sich herausputzen, sich kostümieren; *to ~ up to* gelangen bis; **~-at-able** ['-ætəbl] (leicht) erreichbar, zugänglich; **~-away** Entkommen; *mot* Anfahren *n*, Start *m*; *aero* Abheben *n*; *to make o.'s ~~* entkommen, -wischen; **~-off** *s aero* Start, Abflug *m*; **~-rich-quick** *com* faul, unreell; *(Plan)* phantastisch; **~table** ['-əbl] erhältlich, zu bekommen(d); **~ter** ['-ə] Erzeuger; *min* Häuer *m*; *der* Erhaltende, Erlangende; *~~up (fam)* Organisator *m*; **~-together** (zwangloses) Treffen *n*, Zs.kunft *f*; **~-up** Aufmachung, Ausstattung *f*; *(Kleidung)* Aufzug *m*; Einrichtung, Inszenierung *f*; *Am* Unternehmungsgeist *m*.

gewgaw ['gju:gɔ:] Plunder, Flitter, Tand *m*, Spielerei *f*, Kinkerlitzchen *n*.

geyser ['gaizə] Geysir, Geiser *m*, (zeitweilig springende) heiße Quelle *f*; *Am sl* Quatschkopf *m*; *Br* ['gi:zə] Durchlauferhitzer, Boiler, Gasbadeofen *m*.

ghastl|iness ['gɑ:stlinis] gespenstische(s) Aussehen *n*; Totenblässe *f*; **~y** ['gɑ:stli] *a* geisterhaft, gespenstisch; totenblaß; grausig, entsetzlich, schrecklich; *adv* gräßlich.

gherkin ['gə:kin] Essig-, Gewürzgurke; Angurie *f*.

ghetto ['getou] *pl -s* Getto *n a. fig.*

ghost [goust] *s* Geist *m (e-s Verstorbenen)*, Gespenst *n a. fig*; *fig* Schatten *m*, Spur *f*; *tech* Trugbild *n*; *theat* Schatzmeister *m*; *itr Am fam* für e-n andern Reden aufsetzen, Artikel schreiben; *tr (Artikel)* für e-n andern schreiben; *to give up the ~* den Geist aufgeben, sterben; *the Holy G~* der Heilige Geist; *not a ~ of a chance* nicht die geringsten Aussichten *pl* (*with s.o.* bei jdm); **~like** ['-laik] geisterhaft, gespenstisch; **~liness** ['-linis] Gespensterhaftigkeit *f*; **~ly** ['-li] geistlich; *s. ~like*; **~ speaker** *film* akustische(s) Double *n*; **~-story** Geistergeschichte *f*; **~ writer** Neger, ungenannte(r) eigentliche(r) Verfasser *m*.

ghoul [gu:l] leichenschänderische(r) Geist; Leichenfledderer; grauenhafte(r), brutale(r) Kerl *m*.

GI, G.I. ['dʒi:'ai] *(government issue)* *a Am mil* heereseigen; *fam* kommißmäßig, Kommiß-; *s fam (~ Joe)* amerikanische(r) Soldat *m*.

giant ['dʒaiənt] *s* Riese; *(Mythologie)* Gigant *m*; *a (~like)* riesenhaft, riesig, Riesen-; **~ess** ['-is] Riesin *f*; **~('s) stride** *sport* Rundlauf *m*.

gib 1. [gib, dʒib] *s tech* Bolzen, Stift, Keil *m*; *tr* verbolzen, verkeilen; **2.** [gib] Katze *f*, *bes.* Kater *m*.

gibber ['dʒibə] *itr* kauderwelschen, quatschen; *s u.* **~ish** ['gibəriʃ, *Am a.* dʒ-] Kauderwelsch; Geschnatter *n*.

gibbet ['dʒibit] *s* Galgen; *tech* Kranbalken *m*; *tr* auf-, erhängen; *fig* anprangern; lächerlich machen.

gibbon ['gibən] Gibbon *m (Affe)*.

gibb|osity [gi'bɔsiti] Wölbung, Ausbuchtung *f*; Höcker, Buckel *m*; **~ous** ['gibəs] vorspringend; bucklig; *(Mond)* im 3. Viertel, fast voll.

gibe [dʒaib] *tr u. itr* (*at s.o.* jdn) verspotten, ver-, auslachen, *fam* auf-, durch den Kakao ziehen; *s* Spott *m*, Hohngelächter *n*; Stichelei *f*.

giblets ['dʒiblits] *pl* Gänseklein *n*.

gidd|iness ['gidinis] Schwindel(gefühl *n*); Wankelmut; Leichtsinn *m*; **~y** ['gidi] *a* schwind(e)lig (*with* von, vor); *(Höhe)* schwindelerregend; wirbelnd; schwankend, wankelmütig; leichtfertig, leichtsinnig, unbesonnen.

gift [gift] Gabe *f*, Geschenk *n*; *fig* Gabe, Veranlagung, Anlage *f*, Talent *n* (*for* zu); *jur* Schenkung *f*; *jur* Verfügungsrecht *n*; *com* Zugabe *f*; *by ~* als Geschenk; *that is my ~* darüber kann ich verfügen; *I wouldn't take that as a ~* das möchte ich nicht geschenkt haben; *never look a ~ horse in the mouth (prov)* e-m geschenkten Gaul schaut man nicht ins Maul; *the ~ of the gab* ein gutes Mundwerk; **~ed** ['-id] *a* begabt, talentiert, gut veranlagt; **~ shop** Geschenkartikelladen *m*; **~ tax** Schenkungssteuer *f*; **~-wrap** *tr* als Geschenk verpacken.

gig [gig] **1.** Gig *n*, leichte(r) Einspänner *m*, Sportruder- *od* leichte(s) Beiboot *n*; **2.** Harpune *f*; **3.** *(~-mill)* Tuchrauhmaschine *f*; **4.** *Am fam* Spielzeug *n*; *sl* Party *f*; *mot sl* alte(r) Kasten; *mil sl* Tadel *m*.

gigantic [dʒai'gæntik] riesenhaft, riesig; ungeheuer, gewaltig, riesengroß.

giggle ['gigl] *itr* kichern; *s* Kichern, Gekicher *n*; **~ water** *Am sl* alkoholische(s) Getränk *n*.

gigolo ['ʒigəlou] *pl -s* Eintänzer; *pop* Zuhälter *m*.

gild [gild] **1.** *a. irr gilt, gilt tr* vergolden; *fig* Glanz geben *od* verleihen (*s.th.* e-r S); wertvoller erscheinen lassen; *to ~ the pill (fig)* die bittere Pille versüßen;

~ed youth Jeunesse dorée *f*; **~er** ['-ə] Vergolder *m*; **~ing** ['-iŋ] Vergoldung; *fig* Tünche *f*; *hot ~~* Feuervergoldung *f*; **2.** *s. guild.*

gill 1. [gil] *s zoo* Kieme *f*; *(Huhn)* Kehllappen *m*; *(Mensch)* Doppelkinn *n*; *pl (Pilz)* Lamellen *f pl*; *pl fam* Mund *m*; *tr (Fisch)* ausnehmen; **2.** [gil] *Br* Schlucht *f*; (Gebirgs-)Bach *m*; **3.** [dʒil] Viertelpinte *f (Flüssigkeitsmaß: 0,14, Am 0,12 l)*; **4.** [dʒil] Mädchen *n*, Frau; Liebste *f*, Liebchen *n*.

gillie ['gili] *Scot* Jagdgehilfe; *Am allg* Diener; *Am sl* (Zirkus-)Wagen *m*.

gillyflower ['dʒiliflauə] Levkoje, Gartennelke *f*.

gilt [gilt] *a* vergoldet; *s* Vergoldung *f*; *fig* Reiz *m*; **~-edged** *a (Buch)* mit Goldschnitt; *(Papier)* mit Goldrand; *fig fin* mündelsicher; erstklassig, prima; todsicher, unfehlbar.

gimcrack ['dʒimkræk] *s* Tand, Kram *m*, Kinkerlitzchen *n*; billige Sachen *f pl*; *a* billig, wertlos, unbrauchbar; protzig, überladen.

gimlet ['gimlit] (Hand-, Vor-)Bohrer *m*; **~-eyed** *a* mit stechenden Augen.

gimmick ['gimik] *sl* Trick *m*, Tour; Sensationswerbung *f*, Knüller *m*; Dings(da) *n*; persönliche Eigenheit *f*.

gimp [gimp] Besatz(schnur *f*) *m*, Kordel *f*; Nonnenschleier; *Am sl* Krüppel *m*; **~er** ['-ə] *Am mil aero sl* Pfundskerl *m*; **~ stick** *Am sl* Krücke *f*.

gin [dʒin] **1.** Wacholderschnaps, Gin *m*; **~ mill** *Am sl* Kneipe *f*; **2.** *s* Schlinge *f*, Netz *n*, Falle *f*; Hebezeug *n*, Winde *f*, Kran *m*; *(cotton ~)* Egrenier-, Entkörnmaschine *f*; *tr (Rohbaumwolle)* entkörnen, egrenieren, fangen.

ginger ['dʒindʒə] *s* Ingwer *m*; rötliche Farbe *f*, Rotblond *n*; *fam* Lebhaftigkeit, Lebendigkeit *f*, Schwung, Mumm, Schneid *m*; *tr (meist: to ~ up)* aufmöbeln, aufrütteln, in Schwung bringen; *a* rötlich; *fam* lebhaft, schneidig; **~-ale, -beer, -pop** *s (alkoholfreies)* Ingwerbier *n*; **~-bread** *s* Pfefferkuchen *m*, *a arch* verschnörkelt, Zuckerguß-; *fig* aufgedonnert, auffallend; *to take the gilt off the ~~* die Illusion rauben; der Sache den Reiz nehmen; **~ly** ['-li] *a u. adv* vorsichtig, zimperlich, behutsam, ängstlich; **~-nut,** *Am* **-snap** Ingwerkeks *m*, Pfeffernuß *f*.

gingham ['giŋəm] Gingan *(gestreifter Baumwollstoff)*; *fam* Regenschirm *m*.

gingiv|al [dʒin'dʒaivəl] *a scient* Zahnfleisch-; **~itis** [dʒindʒi'vaitis] Zahnfleischentzündung *f*.

gink [giŋk] *Am sl* Bursche, Kerl, (komischer) Kauz *m*.

ginkgo *Am*, **gingko** ['giŋkou] *pl -oes* Ginkgo(baum) *m*.

gipsy, gypsy ['dʒipsi] *s* Zigeuner(in *f*) *m*; *a* zigeunerhaft; Zigeuner-; *itr* wie ein Zigeuner leben; **~ caravan** Zigeunerwagen *m*; **~ girl** Zigeunermädchen *n*; **~ orchestra** Zigeunerkapelle *f*.

giraffe [dʒi'rɑ:f] *zoo* Giraffe *f*.

gird [gə:d] **1.** *irr girt, girt; a. regelmäßig tr (Person)* gürten; *allg* umgeben, einfassen; *mil* einschließen; bekleiden, ausrüsten, versehen (*with* mit); *to ~ on (Sache)* umgürten, -schnallen, -tun; *to ~ up* auf-, hochbinden; *to ~ o.s.* sich fertigmachen (*for* zu); *sea-girt (poet)* meerumschlungen; **~er** ['-ə] Tragbalken, Träger, Binder *m*; **~le** ['-l] *s* Gurt, Gürtel *a. fig*; Hüftgürtel *m*; *fig* Umgebung *f*; *tr (to ~~ about, in, round)* umgürten, umgeben, einfassen; **2.** *itr* sticheln; spotten (*at* über); *tr* verspotten; *s* Spott *m*, Stichelei *f*.

girl [gə:l] (kleines, junges) Mädchen *n*; Tochter; Hausgehilfin *f*; *fam (best ~)* Liebchen *n*, Liebste *f*; **~ friend** Freundin, Geliebte *f*; **~ guide** *Br*, **~ scout** *Am* Pfadfinderin *f*; **~hood** ['-hud] Mädchenzeit *f*, -jahre *n pl*; **~ish** ['-iʃ] mädchenhaft; **~ishness** ['-iʃnis] Mädchenhaftigkeit *f*; **~'s name** Mädchenname *m*; **~s' school** Mädchenschule *f*.

girt [gə:t] **1.** *s. gird*; **2.** *tr (Person)* gürten; *(Sache)* umgürten; die Gürtelweite, den Umfang *(e-s Baumes)* messen (*s.o.* jds) *a. itr.*

girth [gə:θ] *s* Sattelgurt; Umfang *m (e-s Baumes)*; Gürtel-, Taillenweite *f*; Gürtel *m*; *tr (Sache)* umgürten; mit e-m Gurt befestigen; *(Pferd)* gürten; *itr* den Umfang, die Taillenweite messen; *of ample ~* korpulent.

gist [dʒist] *jur* Rechtsgrund; Haupt-, Kernpunkt, des Pudels Kern *m*; *the ~ of the matter* der Kern der Sache.

give [giv] *irr gave, given* **1.** *tr* (ab-, über-) geben, übermitteln, zukommen lassen; *iro* beglücken; schenken; widmen; verleihen, übertragen; bewilligen; spenden, hervorbringen, liefern; veranlassen, verursachen; einräumen, ein-, zugestehen; vorbringen; *(Vorschlag)* machen; *(Grund)* angeben; *(Schulaufgabe)* aufgeben; hervorbringen, äußern; *(Antwort)* geben; *(Blick)* zuwerfen; *theat mus* geben, aufführen, zur Aufführung bringen; *med* anstecken; *lit (Kunst)* darstellen, zeigen; zufügen; *(Strafe)* auferlegen, verhängen; **2.** *itr* (gern) geben, Geschenke machen; *(e-m Druck)* nachgeben, elastisch sein; nachlassen; sich dehnen; *(Fenster)* gehen (*on, upon* auf); **3.** *s* Nachgeben *n*; Elastizität *f*; **4.** *to ~ o.s. airs* sich aufspielen; *to ~ s.o. the air (Am)* jdn an die Luft setzen; *to ~ birth to* das Leben schenken *dat*; *to ~ credit* Glauben schenken *od* beimessen (*to* dat); zugute halten (*for s.th.* etw); *to ~ ear* Gehör schenken (*to* dat); *to ~ evidence of s.th.* etw zeigen, sehen lassen; *to ~ an example to s.o.* jdm ein Beispiel geben; *to ~ s.o. the gate* jdm den Laufpaß geben; *to ~ s.o. the go by* jdn schneiden, nicht beachten; *to ~ ground* weichen, sich zurückziehen *a. mil*; *to ~ it the gun (Am mot)* Vollgas geben; *to ~ s.o. a hand* jdm helfen; *Am* jdm applaudieren; *to ~ it to s.o.* es jdm (aber) geben, jdm gehörig die Meinung sagen, den Marsch blasen; *to ~ s.o. a lift (mot)* jdn mitnehmen; *to ~ notice* ankündigen, anzeigen; *to ~ offence* Anstoß erregen (*to* bei); *to ~ place* Platz machen (*to* für); das Feld überlassen (*to* an); Ursache sein (*to* für); *to ~ a report* e-n Bericht erstatten; *to ~ rise to* veranlassen, wecken; erzeugen, hervorbringen; *to ~ s.o. trouble* jdm Unannehmlichkeiten bereiten; jdm Ärger, jdm zu schaffen machen; *to ~ to understand* zu verstehen geben; *to ~ voice* Ausdruck verleihen (*to* dat); *to ~ way* nicht halten, reißen; einstürzen, zs.brechen; weichen; nachgeben; sich hingeben, sich überlassen; *(Preis)* fallen; *~ her my regards* bestellen Sie ihr Grüße von mir; *I don't ~ a damn* ich scher' mich den Teufel darum; *nobody's going to ~ a hoot about that* kein Hahn wird danach krähen; *to ~* **away** *tr* weggeben, verschenken, opfern; *(Gelegenheit)* verpassen, versäumen, vorbei-, vorübergehen lassen; preisgeben, verraten, enthüllen, an den Tag bringen; verteilen; *to ~ o.s. away* sich verraten; *to ~ away o.'s daughter* die Hand s-r Tochter geben (*to s.o.* jdm); *to ~* **back** *tr* zurück-, wiedergeben; rückerstatten; *to ~* **forth** *tr* ankündigen, bekanntgeben, -machen; hergeben, liefern; *to ~* **in** *tr* einreichen; *(Name)* eintragen; *itr* nachgeben; weichen, das Feld räumen; *to ~* **off** *tr* von sich geben; *(Licht)* ausstrahlen; *(Geruch)* ausströmen; *(Tag)* freigeben; *to ~* **out** *tr* ab-, ausgeben, verteilen; bekanntgeben, -machen, veröffentlichen; von sich geben, ausströmen; *itr* aus-, zu Ende gehen; sich erschöpfen, nachlassen, ermatten; müde, erschöpft sein; *to ~ o.s. out for, as, to be* sich ausgeben für, als; ausgeben zu sein; *to ~* **over** *tr* übergeben, aushändigen, abliefern; aufgeben, s-m Schicksal überlassen, verlassen; *itr* aufhören; nachlassen; es aufgeben (*doing s.th.* etw zu tun); *to ~* **up** *tr* auf-, über-, hingeben; abtreten; opfern; *(Zeitung)* abbestellen; *(Kranken, Hoffnung)* aufgeben; *(Wärme)* abgeben; ansehen als; *itr* aufgeben; aufhören; sich abgewöhnen (*doing s.th.* etw zu tun); *to ~ o.s. up* sich stellen; *I don't ~ up that easily* so leicht werfe ich die Flinte nicht ins Korn; **~ and take** ['-ən'teik] (Aus-) Tausch; Meinungsaustausch *m*; gegenseitige(s) Entgegenkommen *n*; Kompromiß(bereitschaft *f*) *m od n*; **~-away** unbeabsichtigte Preisgabe *f*, Verplappern *n*; *com* Gratisprobe *f*; Reklameartikel *m*; *~~ price* Reklame-, Schleuderpreis *m*; *~~ show (radio video)* Preisrätselsendung *f*; **~n** ['-n] *pp a* gegeben (*at* zu), datiert; abgemacht, festgesetzt, bestimmt; *math* angenommen; *(dem Trunk)* ergeben; geneigt, veranlagt (*to* zu); *~~ that* unter der Voraussetzung, unter der Annahme, vorausgesetzt, angenommen, daß; *she is ~~ that way (fam)* so ist sie eben; *~~ name (Am)* Vorname *m*; **~r** ['-ə] Geber; Aussteller *m (e-s Wechsels usw)*.

gizzard ['gizəd] *orn* Kaumagen *m*; *to stick in o.'s ~ (fig)* jdm schwer auf dem Magen liegen.

glabrous ['gleibrəs] glatt, unbehaart.

glacé ['glæsei] poliert; glasiert; kandiert; *(Leder)* Glanz-.

glac|ial ['gleisjəl, 'glæs-, *Am* 'gleiʃəl] *a scient* Eis-, Gletscher-; glazial; eiszeitlich; *allg* eisig *a. fig*; eiskalt; steinhart; **~ epoch, era, period** Eiszeit *f*; **~iated** ['glæsjeitid] *a* vereist; **~iation** [glæsi'eiʃən] Vereisung *f*; **~ier** ['glæsjə, *Am* 'gleiʃə] Gletscher *m*; *~~ snow* Firnschnee *m*; *~~ table* Gletschertisch *m*; **~is** ['glæsis, 'gleisis] *pl* ~ ['-iz] (Ab-)Hang *m*; *mil* Glacis *n*.

glad [glæd] froh, fröhlich; glücklich (*about, at, of* über; *to hear* zu hören; *that* daß); freudig, erfreulich, angenehm; erfreut; gern bereit (*to do* zu tun); glänzend, prächtig; *to be ~* sich freuen; *to give s.o. the ~ eye (sl)* jdm verliebte Blicke zuwerfen; *~ to meet you* sehr angenehm! **~den** ['glædn] *tr* froh machen, erfreuen; *itr* sich freuen; **~ly** ['-li] *adv* gern(e); mit Freuden; **~ness** ['-nis] Freude; frohe, freudige Stimmung, Fröhlichkeit *f*; **~ rags** *pl fam* Abendkleidung *f*; **~some** ['-səm] *lit* erfreulich, freudig, froh, fröhlich.

glade [gleid] Lichtung *f*; *Am* Sumpfland *n*, -niederung *f*.

gladiator ['glædieitə] *hist* Gladiator; *allg* Streiter *m*.

gladiolus [glædi'ouləs] *pl -li* [-ai] u. *~es* [-əsiz] *bot* Gladiole *f*.

glair [glεə] *s* (rohes) Eiweiß *n*; klebrige Masse *f*; *tr* mit Eiweiß bestreichen.

glam|orize ['glæməraiz] *tr* (durch Reklame) verherrlichen; **~orous** ['-ərəs] zauberhaft, bezaubernd (schön), blendend; **~o(u)r** ['-ə] *s* Zauber(glanz), (hoher) Reiz *m*, hinreißende Schönheit *f*; *tr* bezaubern; *to cast a ~~ over s.th.* etw verzaubern, in s-n Bann schlagen; *~~ girl* Reklameschönheit *f*.

glance [glɑ:ns] **1.** *itr (to ~ aside, off)* abgleiten; *(im Gespräch)* (flüchtig) streifen, berühren (*over s.th.* etw), anspielen (*at* auf); abkommen (*off, from the subject* vom Thema); blitzen, glänzen, schimmern; e-n flüchtigen Blick werfen (*at* auf); *s* Abgleiten; Aufblitzen *n*, kurze(r) Schimmer; flüchtige(r) Blick *m*; *at a ~* auf e-n Blick, mit e-m Blick; *to ~ o.'s eye over s.th.* etw flüchtig durchsehen; **2.** *min* Glanz *m*; **~ coal** Glanzkohle *f*, Anthrazit *m*.

gland [glænd] *anat* Drüse; *tech* Stopfbuchse *f*; **~ered** ['glændəd], **~erous** ['-ərəs] *a vet* rotzig; Rotz-; **~ers** ['glændəz] *pl vet* Rotz(krankheit *f*) *m (der Pferde)*; **~ular** ['glændjulə], **~ulous** ['-ləs] *a* Drüsen-; *~~ body, secretion, tissue* Drüsenkörper *m*, -sekretion *f*, -gewebe *n*.

glar|e [glεə] *itr* hell glänzen, leuchten, ein blendendes Licht verbreiten; auffallen, in die Augen springen; (an)starren (*at s.o.* jdn); wütend, böse anblikken (*at s.o.* jdn); *s* helle(r), blendende(r) Glanz, Schimmer *m*; auffällige Aufmachung *f*; wütende(r), böse(r), starre(r), durchdringende(r) Blick; *fig* Mittelpunkt *m*; *Am* spiegelglatte, glänzende Fläche *f*; *a Am* spiegelglatt, glänzend; **~ing** ['-riŋ] blendend hell, grell; glänzend, strahlend; schreiend, aufdringlich, auffällig, auffallend.

glass [glɑ:s] *s* Glas *n*; Glaswaren *f pl*; (Trink-)Glas *n*; *(pane of ~)* (Fenster-)Scheibe *f*; *(looking-~)* Spiegel *m*; (Vergrößerungs-, Fern-)Glas; Fernrohr; Wetterglas, Barometer *n*; *pl (eye-~es)* Augengläser *n pl*, Brille *f*; *a* gläsern, Glas-; *tr* verglasen; *piece of ~* Glasscherbe *f*; **~-bead** Glasperle *f*; **~-blower** Glasbläser *m*; **~-blowing** Glasbläserei *f*; **~ cloth** Gläser-, Poliertuch *n*; **~-cutter** Glasschneider, -schleifer *m*; **~ eye** Glasauge *n*; **~ful** ['-ful] Glasvoll *n*; **~-house** Treib-, Gewächshaus; Atelier *n*; *mil sl* Bau *m*; *aero sl* (Vollsicht-, Führer-)Kanzel *f*; *to sit in a ~~* im Glashaus sitzen; **~iness** ['-inis] glasartige Beschaffenheit *f*; **~maker** Glasmacher *m*; **~ paper** Schleif-, Glaspapier *n*; **~-ware** Glaswaren *f pl*; **~ wool** Glaswolle *f*; **~-works** *pl*, **~ factory** Glashütte *f*; **~y** ['-i] glasartig, gläsern; *(Augen)* glasig; *(Wasser)* klar.

Glauber('s) salt(s *pl)* ['glɔ:bəz, 'glau-, sɔ:lt] *chem* Glaubersalz *n*.

glauc|oma [glɔ:'koumə] *med* grüne(r) Star *m*; **~ous** ['glɔ:kəs] blaugrün; *bot* bereift.

glaz|e [gleiz] *tr* verglasen; unter Glas legen; glasieren; polieren; mit Zuckerguß bestreichen; *(die Augen)* trüben; *(Papier)* satinieren; *itr* glasig, trübe werden; *s* Glasur; Politur; Satinierung *f*; Häutchen *n*; *~ed frost* Glatteis *n*; *~ed paper* Glanzpapier *n*; *~ed tile* Kachel, Fliese *f*; **~ier** ['-jə] Glaser; Glasierer *m*; *~~'s putty* Glaserkitt *m*.

gleam [gli:m] *s* Lichtstrahl *m*; schwache(s) Licht *n*; Lichtschein, Schimmer *m*; *fig (~ of hope)* schwache Hoffnung *f*, Hoffnungsschimmer *m*; *itr* strahlen, leuchten, schimmern, funkeln; blinken, aufleuchten.

glean [gli:n] *itr* Ähren lesen; Nachlese halten; *tr (Ähren)* lesen; *allg* sammeln; *fig* entnehmen, erfahren (*from* von); **~er** ['-ə] Ährenleser(in *f*); *fig* Sammler *m*; **~ings** ['-iŋz] *pl* Nachlese *f*; Gesammelte(s) *n*.

glebe [gli:b] *poet* Scholle, Erde *f*, Boden *m*; Kirchen-, Pfarrland *n*.

glee [gli:] Fröhlichkeit, (frohe) Stimmung *f*; Rundgesang *m*; **~ club** Gesangverein *m*; **~ful** ['-ful], **~some** ['-səm] fröhlich, froh.

glen [glen] enge(s) Tal *n*, Klamm *f*; **~garry** [-'gæri] *(~~ bonnet, cap)* schottische Mütze *f*.

glib [glib] glatt, flüssig, (rede)gewandt; leichtfertig, unaufrichtig, oberflächlich, wenig überzeugend; **~ness** ['-nis] (Rede-)Gewandtheit *f*.

glid|e [glaid] *itr* gleiten, schweben, dahinfließen, -ziehen; vorübergleiten, -ziehen; *(Zeit)* verfließen, vergehen; *aero* im Gleitflug niedergehen; *aero* segeln; *to ~~ out* sich hinausschleichen; *s* Gleiten, Schweben *n*, Gleitbewegung *f*; Gleit-, Segelflug; Gleitlaut *m*; **~er** ['-ə] Gleit-, Segelflugzeug *n*; *~~ pilot* Segelflieger *m*; *~~ tow (aero)* Schleppseil *n*; *~~ towing* Schleppflug *m*; *~~ tug* Schleppflugzeug *n*; **~ing** ['-iŋ] Gleit-, Segelflug *m*; Segelfliegen *n*, -fliegerei *f*; *~~ site* Segelfluggelände *n*.

glim [glim] *sl* Licht *n*, Kerze, Lampe *f*; Auge; *Am sl* Streichholz, Feuer *n*.

glimmer ['glimə] *itr* flimmern; schimmern; *s* Flimmern *n*; Schimmer *m a. fig*; *pl Am sl* Augen *n pl*, *mot* Scheinwerfer *m pl*, Brille *f*.

glimpse [glimps] *s* kurze(s) Aufleuchten *n*; flüchtige Erscheinung, schwache Spur *f*; kurze(r), flüchtige(r) Blick *m*; *tr* im Vorübergehen sehen; *itr* flüchtig blicken (*at* auf); *poet* (schwach) dämmern; *to catch a ~ of s.th.* etw flüchtig zu sehen bekommen.

glint [glint] *itr* glänzen; glitzern, funkeln; strahlen; *tech* flackern; *s* Schimmer; Lichtstrahl; Glanz *m*.

glissade [gli'sɑ:d] *s* Gleiten *n*; Abfahrt *f*, Abrutsch *(im Schnee)*; *(Tanz)* Schleifschritt *m*; *itr (im Gebirge)* rutschen, gleiten; *(Tanz)* Schleifschritte machen.

glisten ['glisn] *itr* gleißen, glänzen, schimmern, funkeln.

glitter ['glitə] *itr* glitzern, funkeln, strahlen; erstrahlen; *s* Schimmer, Glanz *m*, Funkeln *n*; *fig* Pracht *f*; **~ing** ['-riŋ] glänzend; *fig* verlockend.

gloaming ['gloumiŋ] Abenddämmerung *f*.

gloat [glout] *itr* sich hämisch freuen, sich weiden (*on, upon, over* an); mit den Augen verschlingen (*over s.th.* etw); **~ing** ['-iŋ] hämisch.

glob|al ['gloubəl] weltweit, -umspannend, Welt-; umfassend, global, Gesamt-; **~e** [gloub] Kugel *f*, Ball; Erd-, Sonnenball *m*; *(terrestrial ~~)* Weltkugel *f*, (Erd-)Globus *m*; *(celestial ~~)* Himmelskugel *f*; Kugelglas *n*; Glaskugel *f*; (runder) Lampenschirm *m*; (Glüh-)Birne *f*; Reichsapfel; Augapfel *m*; *~~ joint* Kugelgelenk *n*; *~~ lightning* Kugelblitz *m*; *~~-trotter* Weltbummler *m*; **~ose** ['gloubous], **~ular** ['glɔbjulə] kugelförmig; **~osity** [glo(u)'bɔsiti] Kugelgestalt *f*; **~ule** ['glɔbju:l] Kügelchen, Tröpfchen *n*.

glomer|ate ['glɔmərit] zs.geballt; **~ation** [-'reiʃən] Zs.ballung *f*.

gloom [glu:m] *s (a. ~iness* ['glu:minis]) Dunkel(heit *f*), Düster *n*; *fig* Traurigkeit, Schwermut, Melancholie, düstere Stimmung *f*; *itr* dunkel, trübe werden; traurig sein, trübselig aussehen; *tr* verdunkeln, verdüstern, trübe machen; **~y** ['-i] dunkel, düster, trüb(e); verdrießlich, trübselig, -sinnig, traurig, schwermütig, bedrückt, melancholisch; niederdrückend.

glor|ification [glɔ:rifi'keiʃən] Verherrlichung; *rel* Lobpreisung *f*; *Am fam* Fest(lichkeit *f*) *n*, Feier *f*; **~ify** ['glɔ:rifai] *tr* rühmen, preisen, verherrlichen; herausstreichen, -putzen; **~ious** ['glɔ:riəs] ruhmreich, -voll, glorreich; prächtig, majestätisch; *fam* prachtvoll, großartig, herrlich, pfundig, Pfunds-; *~~ fun* ein Bomben-, ein Mordsspaß *m*; **~y** ['glɔ:ri] *s* Ruhm *m*; Verherrlichung; Herrlichkeit *f*, Glanz; *fig* Glanzpunkt *m*; strahlende(s) Glück *n*; Pracht, Majestät; *rel* Verklärung *f*; Heiligenschein *m*; *itr* sehr stolz sein; frohlocken (*in* über); sich rühmen (*in* gen); *to be in o.'s ~* im siebenten Himmel sein; *to send to ~~ (fam)* ins Jenseits befördern, töten; *the Old G~* das Sternenbanner; *~~-hole (sl)* Rumpelkammer *f*.

gloss [glɔs] **1.** *s* Glanz, Schimmer, Schein; *fig* äußere(r) Schein, Firnis *m*, Tünche *f*, Anstrich *m*; *tr* polieren, auf Hochglanz bringen; glanzpressen; *fig (to ~ over)* beschönigen, bemänteln, vertuschen; *high-~ painting* Schleiflack *m*; **~iness** ['-inis] Glanz *m*, Politur, Glätte *f*; **~y** ['-i] *a* glänzend, spiegelblank; *fig* einleuchtend; scheinbar, Schein-; salbungsvoll; *s fam* Illustrierte *f*; **2.** *s* Glosse, Randbemerkung, Fußnote; falsche Auslegung *f*; *tr* erklären, glossieren, kommentieren; *(to ~ over) fig* falsch auslegen; **~ary** ['-əri] Wörterverzeichnis, Glossar *n*.

glott|al ['glɔtl]: **~ stop** Knacklaut *m*; **~is** ['glɔtis] *anat* Stimmritze *f*.

glove [glʌv] *s* Handschuh *m*; *tr* e-n Handschuh ziehen über; die Handschuhe anziehen (*s.o.* jdm); *to fit like a ~* haargenau passen; wie angegossen sitzen; *to handle with (kid) ~s (fig)* mit seidenen Handschuhen anfassen; *to take up the ~* die Herausforderung annehmen; *to throw down the ~ to s.o.* jdm den Fehdehandschuh hinwerfen; *he is hand in ~ with him* sie sind unzertrennlich, ein Herz und eine Seele; *boxing ~* Boxhandschuh *m*; *rubber ~* Gummihandschuh *m*; **~ factory** Handschuhfabrik *f*; **~ leather** Handschuhleder *n*; **~r** ['-ə], **~ maker** Handschuhmacher *m*.

glow [glou] *itr* glühen; leuchten *(a. Farben)*; *fig (Wangen; vor Erregung, Eifer)* glühen, *(Augen)* leuchten (*with* vor); rot werden, erröten; *s* Glut *f*; helle(s) Licht *n*; *(Farben)* Lebhaftigkeit, Frische; *(Haut)* Röte; wohlige Wärme *f*, Wohlgefühl *n*; *fig* Glut, Heftigkeit *f (des Gefühls)*; *tech* Glimmen, Glühen *n*; **~ lamp** Glimmlampe *f*; **~ tube** Glüh-, Neonröhre *f*; **~-worm** Glühwürmchen *n*.

glower ['glauə] *itr* stieren; *at s.o., s.th.* jdn, etw anstarren; jdn, etw finster, wütend anblicken.

gloxinia [glɔk'sinjə] *bot* Gloxinie *f*.

gloze [glouz] *tr (to ~ over)* beschönigen, bemänteln, abschwächen, mildern.

glucose ['glu:kous] Glukose, Dextrose *f*, Traubenzucker *m*.

glue [glu:] *s* Leim; Kleister, Klebstoff *m*; *tr* leimen; kleben (*on* auf; *to* an); *fig* heften (*to* auf); *to ~ on* anleimen; *to ~ together* zs.leimen; *to be ~d to s.o., to stick to s.o. like ~* jdm nicht von den Fersen gehen; *she stood as if ~d to the spot* sie stand wie angewurzelt da; **~-factory** Leimsiederei *f*; **~-pot** Leimtopf *m*; **~y** ['-i] leimig; klebrig; leimbeschmiert.

glum [glʌm] finster, verdrießlich, mürrisch; niedergedrückt; **~ness** ['-nis] Verdrießlichkeit *f*.

glut [glʌt] *tr* (über)sättigen, überfüttern, vollstopfen; *fig (den Markt)* überschwemmen; *s* Übersättigung,

-fütterung; Fülle; *com* Schwemme *f*, Überangebot *n*.

glut|en ['glu:tən] Gluten *n*, Kleber *m*; **~inous** ['glu:tinəs] klebrig.

glutton ['glʌtn] starke(r) Esser, *fam* Fresser, Freßsack; unersättliche(r) Mensch; *zoo* Vielfraß *m*; *to be a ~ for s.th.* von e-r S nicht genug kriegen können; **~ous** ['-əs] gefräßig, *fam* verfressen; gierig (*of* nach); **~y** ['-i] Gefräßigkeit *f*.

glyc|erin(e), ~erol [glisə'ri(:)n, 'glisəroul] Glyzerin*n*; **~ogene** ['gliko(u)dʒen] Glykogen *n*, tierische Stärke *f*; **~ol** ['gl(a)ikɔl] Glykol *n*.

G-man ['dʒi:mæn] *Am* FBI-Agent, Bundeskriminalbeamte(r) *m*.

gnarl [nɑ:l] Knorren, Knoten *m*; **~ed** [-d], **~y** ['-i] *a* knorrig, knotig; *fig* rauh.

gnash [næʃ] *tr* knirschen (*o.'s teeth* mit den Zähnen); zerkauen, zermahlen.

gnat [næt] *Br* (Stech-)Mücke; *Am* Kriebel-, Zuckmücke *f*; *to strain at a ~* über e-e Lappalie nicht hinwegkommen; **~-bite** Mückenstich *m*.

gnaw [nɔ:] *tr* (zer)nagen; (zer)fressen; *fig* quälen, martern; *itr* nagen, fressen (*at, on* an).

gneiss [nais] *min* Gneis *m*.

gnome 1. [noum] Gnom, Zwerg, Erdgeist *m*; **2.** ['noumi:] Sinnspruch *m*.

gnomon ['noumɔn] Zeiger *m* der Sonnenuhr.

gnosis ['nousis] *rel philos* Gnosis *f*.

gnostic ['nɔstik] *a rel philos* gnostisch; *s* Gnostiker *m*; **G~ism** ['nɔstisizm] Gnostik, Gnosis *f*.

gnu [nu:, nju:] *zoo* Gnu *n*.

go [gou] *irr went* [went], *gone* [gɔn], *he goes* [gouz]; **1.** *itr* gehen; *(to ~ on horseback)* reiten; fahren (*by train* mit dem Zuge, mit der Bahn); *(to ~ by air)* fliegen; reisen; *(Maschine)* gehen, arbeiten, in Tätigkeit, in Betrieb sein; funktionieren; sich erstrecken, reichen (*to* bis zu); *(Weg)* führen (*to* nach); darauf hinausgehen, -laufen (*to* zu); übergehen (*to* auf); zuteil werden (*to s.o.* jdm); *(Preis)* zufallen, gehen (*to* an), zugeteilt werden; ab-, verlaufen, s-n Verlauf nehmen, ausgehen; *(Zeit)* ver-, weitergehen, verstreichen; (um)laufen, kursieren, bekannt sein, gelten; Erfolg haben; *(örtlich)* kommen, gehören (*into* in); werden; sein; *(Worte)* lauten; sich befinden; leben (*in fear* in dauernder Furcht); sich richten (*by, upon* nach); weggehen, aufbrechen, abreisen, -fahren, -fliegen; zu Ende gehen, ein Ende nehmen, aufhören; verschwinden; abbrechen, weggerissen werden; nachlassen, schwächer werden; fallen, verschwinden; sterben; *Am* zs.brechen, nachgeben; *(mit a)* werden; **2.** *tr* wetten; *fam* in Angriff, in die Hand nehmen; *(Bewegung* od *Geräusch)* machen; *Am sl* aushalten, dulden, ertragen; **3.** *s* (*pl goes* [gouz] Gehen *n*, Gang; Erfolg; *fam* Schwung, Schneid *m*, Tatkraft, Energie; *fam* Sache *f*, Umstand *m*; dumme Sache *od* Geschichte; *fam* Portion *f*, Schlag *m* (Essen), Glas *n* *(zu trinken)*; *the ~ (fam)* die Mode; *a ~* ein Geschäft *n*; ein Versuch *m*; *pred* abgemacht; *from the word ~ (fam)* von Anfang bis zu Ende, völlig; **4.** *to be on the ~ (fam)* im Gange, beschäftigt, tätig, in Bewegung, auf den Beinen, unterwegs sein; dem Ende zugehen; *to have a ~ at (fam)* versuchen; *to let ~* laufenlassen; aufgeben; *to let o.s. ~* sich gehenlassen; *s.o.* jdn laufenlassen; **5.** *to ~ on the air (radio)* senden *itr*; *to ~ bad (Speise, Getränk)* schlecht werden, verderben; *to ~ from bad to worse* immer schlechter werden; *to ~ to bat for s.o. (Am)* für jdn eintreten; *to ~ to the country (pol)* das Volk befragen; *to ~ crazy* verrückt werden; *to ~ for a drive* ausfahren; *to ~ into effect* in Kraft treten; *to ~ to expense* sich in Unkosten stürzen; *to ~ so far as to say* so weit gehen zu sagen; *to ~ s.o. against the grain* jdm gegen den Strich gehen; *to ~ halves, shares* ehrlich teilen; *to ~ hard with s.o.* schwierig sein für; *to ~ off o.'s head* den Verstand verlieren *to ~ to o.'s head* in den Kopf steigen; *to ~ the whole hog (Am fam)* etw gründlich tun; *to ~ hungry* hungern, Hunger leiden; *to ~ hunting* auf die Jagd gehen; *to ~ to law* den Rechtsweg beschreiten; *to ~ mad* verrückt werden; *to ~ to pieces* in Stücke gehen, zerbrechen; *to ~ to pot (Am fam)* auf den Hund kommen; *to ~ into production* in Produktion gehen; *to ~ for a ride* ausreiten; *to ~ to sea* zur See gehen, Seemann werden; *to ~ to see* besuchen; *to ~ to seed (bot)* Früchte ansetzen; *to ~ shopping* einkaufen gehen; *to ~ to show (Am)* ein Beweis sein für; *to ~ sick (mil)* sich krank melden; *to ~ to sleep* einschlafen; *to ~ for a song* für ein Butterbrot weggehen *od* verkauft werden; *to ~ it strong* energisch, forsch auftreten; angeben; *to ~ for a swim* schwimmen gehen; *to ~ with the time, tide* mit der Zeit gehen; *to ~ to trouble* sich Mühe, Umstände machen; sich bemühen; *to ~ unnoticed* unbemerkt bleiben; *to ~ unpunished* ungestraft davonkommen; *to ~ on a visit* e-n Besuch machen; *to ~ for a walk* spazierengehen; ausgehen; *to ~ to waste* in den Abfall kommen; *to ~ the way of all flesh* den Weg alles Fleisches gehen, sterben; *to ~ west (sl)* abkratzen, sterben; *to ~ wrong* schiefgehen; auf dem Holzweg sein, fehlgehen, sich irren; auf Abwege geraten; **6.** *as things ~* wie die Dinge nun einmal liegen; *as people ~* wie die Leute nun mal sind; *as the story ~es* wie man sich erzählt; *as times ~* wie die Zeiten nun (ein)mal sind; *so, as far as it ~es* soweit *adv*; *it's all, quite the ~ (fam)* das ist die große Mode; *it was a near ~ (fam)* es war dicht dran; *it is a queer, a rum ~ (fam)* das ist e-e komische, eigenartige Geschichte; *it's no ~ (fam)* da ist nichts zu machen, da kann man nichts machen; es ist sinn-, zwecklos; *is it a ~? (fam)* abgemacht? *here's a ~, what a ~! (fam)* das ist e-e dumme Sache, böse Geschichte; *let me have a ~ (fam)* laß mich mal ('ran)! *I'll ~ you* ich nehme die Wette an; *don't ~ and make a fool of yourself* mach dich doch nicht zum Narren! *we'll let it ~ at that* wir wollen es dabei belassen; *just ~ and try!* versuchen Sie es doch einmal! *let ~!* laß los! *let it ~!* laß sein! laß laufen! *~ it! (fam)* los! 'ran! *~ easy!* übernimm dich nicht! *where do you want it to ~?* wo soll es hin (-gestellt werden)? *here ~es!* nun los! *who ~es there?* wer da? *how far did he ~? (fig)* wie weit ist er gegangen? *things have gone badly with him* es ist ihm schlecht er-, gegangen; *one, two, three — ~! (sport)* Achtung — fertig — los! *to ~* **about** *itr* (umher)gehen; sich umwenden; die Richtung ändern; *(Gerücht)* im Umlauf sein, umgehen; sich abgeben, sich befassen mit; *tr* anfassen, behandeln; *to ~* **abroad** *itr (Gerücht)* umgehen, sich verbreiten; *to ~* **after** *s.o. (fam)* jdm nachsteigen; *to ~* **ahead** *itr* losgehen, anfangen; vorangehen; voran-, vorwärtskommen, Fortschritte machen; weitermachen; *~~!* vorwärts! los! *to ~* **along** *itr* weitermachen, -kommen, vorwärtskommen; Fortschritte machen; *with s.o.* mit jdm mitkommen, jdn begleiten; *~~ with you! (fam)* mach doch keine Witze! *to ~* **around** *itr* herumgehen; hinkommen, (für jeden) (aus)reichen; *there's enough bread to ~ around* es ist genug Brot für alle da; *to ~* **astray** *itr* sich verirren, abirren, e-n Fehltritt begehen; verlorengehen; *to ~* **at** *s.o.* auf jdn losgehen; *s.th.* an etw herangehen, etw anpacken; über etw herfallen; *to ~* **away** *itr* weggehen; abreisen; *to ~* **back** *itr* zurückkehren; zurückgehen, nachlassen, schwächer werden; *(zeitlich)* zurückgehen, sich zurückführen lassen (*to* auf); *(up)on (sein Wort)* brechen; *on s.o.* jdn betrügen, hintergehen, im Stich lassen; *to ~* **before** *itr* voraus-, voraufgehen; *to ~* **behind** *itr* hinterhergehen, folgen; *s.th.* e-r S auf den Grund gehen; *to ~* **between** *itr* in der Mitte gehen; vermitteln; *to ~* **beyond** *itr* darüber hinausgehen; hinausgehen über; *to ~* **by** *itr* vorüber-, vorbeigehen *(a. Zeit)*; *(Zeit)* vergehen, verstreichen, verrinnen; sich richten nach; *(Namen)* führen; *math* sich lösen lassen nach; *to ~* **down** *itr* hinab-, hinuntergehen, -steigen; *med* sich hinlegen (*with flu* mit Grippe); *(Schiff)* untergehen, sinken; *(Sonne)* untergehen; verlieren, unterliegen (*before s.o.* jdm); an Qualität verlieren, einbüßen; schlechter werden; *(Wind, Preise)* nachlassen; *(Universität)* abgehen; Glauben, Beifall finden (*with* bei); zurückgehen, sich zurückführen lassen (*to* bis auf); *to ~~ in history* in die Geschichte eingehen; *to ~~ on o.'s knees* auf die Knie gehen; *that won't ~~ with me* das lasse ich mir nicht gefallen; *to ~* **far** *itr* weit gehen; es weit, zu etwas bringen; *towards* viel dazu beitragen; *to ~* **for** *s.th.* nach etw gehen, etw holen; *sl* sich interessieren, eintreten für; angesehen, betrachtet werden als; hinauslaufen auf; *s.o. (sl)* auf jdn losgehen; *to ~ for a drive* ausfahren; *to ~ for nothing* nichts gelten; *how much did it ~ for?* für wieviel wurde es verkauft? *to ~* **forth** *itr (Buch)* erscheinen; *(Erlaß)* ergehen; *to ~* **forward** *itr* weiterkommen, Fortschritte machen; *fig* vorangehen; *to ~* **in** *itr* hineingehen; hineinpassen; *(Sonne hinter Wolken)* verschwinden; *for* sich interessieren für, Spaß haben an, sich widmen *dat*; teilnehmen an *(e-r Prüfung)*; *with* teilen mit, sich beteiligen an; *to ~* **into** *itr* enthalten sein in; untersuchen (*s.th.* etw); eingehen auf; einsteigen in; *to ~* **off** *itr* weg-, hinausgehen; ausrücken; stattfinden, sich ereignen, verlaufen, sich abwickeln; einschlafen; das Bewußtsein verlieren; *(Veranstaltung)* zu Ende gehen, aus sein; *(Ware)* weg-, abgehen, Absatz finden; *(Zug)* (ab)gehen; *(Feuerwaffe)* losgehen, sich entladen; explodieren; *to ~ off well (badly)* (keinen) Beifall, Anklang finden, nicht gefallen; nachlassen, schlechter werden; *to ~ off into a fit of laughter* laut loslachen; *~es off (theat)* ab; *to ~* **on** *itr* weitermachen, fortfahren (*with* mit); *(Zeit)* vorrücken, weitergehen; fortfahren (*talking* zu reden); vor sich gehen, vorgehen, geschehen, stattfinden, sich ereignen; *fam* meckern; sich aufführen, sich benehmen; *theat* auftreten; *(Kleidungsstück)* passen; *(wirtschaftlich)* getragen werden von; *(Jahre)* gehen auf; sich stützen auf; *to ~ on to do* als nächstes tun; *to ~ on the road (com)* auf die Reise, *theat* auf Tournee gehen; *to be ~ing on for fifty* auf die Fünfzig gehen; *this can't ~ on any longer* das kann nicht mehr so weitergehen; *~ on! interj* ach was! *to ~* **out** *itr* hinausgehen; auswandern (*to* nach); *(zum Vergnügen)* ausgehen; *pol (to ~ out of office)* zurücktreten; *(on strike)* streiken; *(Feuer, Licht)* ausgehen; *(to ~ out of fashion)* aus der Mode kommen; *(Jahr)* zu Ende, ausgehen, ausklingen; *Am* zs.brechen; *(Herz)* sich hängen (*to* an); sich bemühen (*for* um), wollen (*for s.th.* etw); *to ~ out of o.'s way* sich besonders anstrengen; *to ~* **over** *tr* durchgehen, -sehen, (über)prüfen, untersuchen; überlesen; *itr* übergehen (*to the other party* zur andern Partei); hinübergehen (*to* zu); *fam* Erfolg haben; *(Theaterstück)* einschlagen; *to ~ over the figures* nachrechnen; *to ~* **through** *tr itr* durchgehen, -sehen; durchführen; *(Gesuch)* durchgehen, angenommen werden; durchmachen, erleiden, erdulden; *(Geld)* ausgeben, *fam* unter die Leute bringen; *(Verkehrszeichen)* überfahren; *with* zu Ende führen, vollenden; *to ~ through ten editions (Buch)* zehn Auflagen erleben; *to ~* **together** *itr* zs.passen; sich (gut) vertragen; *fam (Verliebte)* zs.gehen; *to ~* **under** *itr* untergehen, sinken; zugrunde, eingehen; *(Namen)* führen; *to ~* **up** *itr* hinaufgehen, -steigen; *(im Preis)* steigen; *(Häuser)* emporwachsen, gebaut werden; in die Luft fliegen, explodieren; die Universität beziehen; *to ~~ in the air (fig)* wütend werden; *to ~~ in flames, in smoke* in Flammen, in Rauch aufgehen; *to ~* **with** *s.o.* mit jdm e-r Meinung sein; zu jdm passen; mit jdm gehen *(fam a. von Verliebten)*; *s.th.* zu etw passen; *to ~* **without** *itr* auskommen, fertigwerden, sich behelfen müssen ohne, entbehren müssen; *that ~es without saying* das versteht sich von selbst, das ist selbstverständlich; **~-ahead** *s (Signal)* freie Bahn *f*; *a* fortschreitend; unternehmungslustig, forsch, schneidig, draufgängerisch; **~-aheadativeness** [gouə'hedətivnis] *Am fam* Unternehmungsgeist *m*; **~-as-you-please** *a* zwanglos, ungebunden, ungeregelt, planlos, beliebig; **~-between** Vermittler, Mittelsmann; Zwischenträger *m*; **~-by** *fam* Vorüber-, Vorbeigehen *n*; *to give the ~~ to* schneiden, links liegenlassen, ignorieren; *to get the ~~* geschnitten werden; **~-cart** Laufställchen *n*; zs.klappbare(r) Sportwagen *m (Kinderwagen)*; Sänfte *f*; Handwagen; Go-Cart *m*; **~-getter** *Am sl* Draufgänger *m*; **~-off**: *at the first ~~* ganz am Anfang; **~-slow strike** Bummelstreik *m*; **~-to-meeting** *a (Kleidung)* Ausgeh-, Sonntags-.

goad [goud] *s* Stachelstock *(zum Viehtreiben)*; *fig* Stachel, Ansporn, Antrieb *m*; *tr (Vieh)* antreiben *a. fig*; *fig* aufstacheln (*into doing s.th.* etw zu tun).

goal [goul] *sport* Ziel, Mal; Tor(schuß *m*); *fig* Ziel *n*; *to score a ~* ein Tor schießen; *to set o.s. a high ~* sich ein hohes Ziel stecken; *to win by three ~s to one* 3:1 gewinnen; **~ie** ['-i] *fam*, **~-keeper** Torwart *m*; **~-line** Torlinie *f*; **~-post** Torpfosten *m*.

goat [gout] Ziege, Geiß *f*; *(he-~)* (Ziegen-, Geiß-)Bock; *fig* geile(r) Bock; *(scape~)* Sündenbock *m*; *the G~ (astr)* der Steinbock; *to get s.o.'s ~ (sl)* jdn auf die Palme bringen; jdn aufziehen; *to play the giddy ~ (fig)* sich albern benehmen; *to separate the sheep from the ~s (fig)* die Schafe von den Böcken sondern; **~ee** [-'ti:] Ziegen-, Spitzbart *m*; **~herd** Ziegen-, Geißhirt *m*; **~ish** ['-iʃ] ziegen(bocks)artig; geil; **~skin** Ziegenleder(flasche *f*) *n*; **~sucker** *orn* Ziegenmelker *m*; **~'s wool** *fig* Mückenfett *n*.

gob [gɔb] **1.** *vulg* Auswurf *m*, Spucke *f*, Rotz; *sl* Mund *m*; *fig* (große) Menge, Masse *f*; *itr* spucken; **2.** *min* Alte(r) Mann *m*; taube(s) Gestein *n*; **3.** *Am sl* Blaujacke *f*, Matrose *m*.

gobble ['gɔbl] **1.** *itr (Puter)* kollern; *s* Kollern *n*; **~r** ['-ə] Puter, Truthahn *m*; **2.** *tr* hinunter-, verschlingen; *itr* gierig essen, fressen; **~r** ['-ə] Fresser *m*.

gobbledygook ['gɔbldi'guk] *Am sl* Geschwafel, Amtsdeutsch *n*.

gobelin ['goubəlin] Gobelin *m*.

goblet ['gɔblit] Kelch(glas *n*) *m*.

goblin ['gɔblin] Kobold *m*.

god [gɔd] (heidnischer) Gott *m*, Gottheit *f*; *fig* Abgott, Götze *m*; *G~* Gott *m*; *to make a ~ of s.o., s.th.* jdn, etw zu s-m (Ab-)Gott machen, vergötzen; *for G~'s sake!* um Gottes willen! *thank G~!* Gott sei Dank! **~child** Patenkind *n*; **~dess** ['gɔdis] Göttin *f*; **~father** Pate *m*; *to stand ~~* Pate stehen (*to* bei); **~fearing** gottesfürchtig; **~forsaken** *a* gottverlassen; **~head** ['-hed] Gottheit *f*; göttliche Natur *f*; **~less** ['-lis] gottlos; **~lessness** ['-lisnis] Gottlosigkeit *f*; **~like** göttlich; erhaben; **~liness** ['-linis] Frömmigkeit *f*; **~ly** ['-li] fromm, gottselig; **~mother** Patin *f*; **~parent** Pate *m*; **~send** Retter *m* in der Not; unerwartete(s) Glück *n*; Gottesgabe *f*; **~son** ['-sʌn] Patensohn *m*, -kind *n*; **~-speed** ['-'-]: *to bid, to wish s.o. ~~* jdm Lebewohl sagen, e-e glückliche Reise, alles Gute wünschen; **~ward** ['-wəd] *a* Gott zugewandt; *adv u.* **~wards** *adv* zu Gott; **~wit** ['-wit] *zoo* Uferschnepfe *f*.

goer ['gouə] Gänger, Gehende(r), Läufer; *sl* Fachmann *m*.

gof(f)er ['gɔfə] *tr* kräuseln; fälteln, plissieren; *s* Plissiereisen *n*.

goggle ['gɔgl] *itr* glotzen, starren; mit den Augen rollen; *tr (die Augen)* rollen; *s pl* Schutzbrille; *fam* (runde) Brille *f*; **~-eyed** *a* glotzäugig.

going ['gouiŋ] *ppr von go*; *a* gehend, laufend, im Gang; arbeitend, funktionierend, in Tätigkeit, in Betrieb; fertig, bereit, vorhanden, erhältlich, zu haben(d); *s* Ab-, Weggang; Aufbruch *m*, Abreise, -fahrt *f*; Gang(art *f*) *m*, Geschwindigkeit; Bodenbeschaffenheit *f*, Straßenzustand *m*; Fortbewegung *f*, Weiterkommen *n*; *to be ~ to* im Begriff sein zu, werden; gerade wollen, die Absicht, vorhaben zu; *to get ~ (fam)* in Gang kommen; *to set (a-)~* in Gang bringen; *~! ~! gone! (Versteigerung)* zum ersten! zum zweiten! zum dritten! *a ~ concern* ein gutgehendes Geschäft; **~s-on** *meist in: such ~~* ein solches Benehmen *n*; **~-over** *fam* Berichtigung; *Am sl* Dresche *f*, Prügel *m pl*; Anschnauzer *m*.

goitre, *Am* **goiter** ['gɔitə] *med* Kropf *m*.

gold [gould] *s* Gold *a. fig*; Gold(geld) *n*; Reichtum *m*; Gold(farbe *f*) *n*; *a* golden; gold(farb)en; Gold-; *on ~ (com)* auf Goldbasis; *to be pure ~* Gold wert sein; *all that glisters* od *glitters is not ~ (prov)* es ist nicht alles Gold, was glänzt; **~-beater** Goldschläger *m*; *~~'s skin* Goldschlägerhaut *f*, -häutchen *n*; **~-brick** *fam* Tinnef, Schwindel; *Am sl mil* Drückeberger *m*; *to sell a ~~ to s.o. (sl Am)* jdn anschmieren, 'reinlegen, anführen; **~ bullion** Goldbarren *m*; **~ coin** Goldmünze *f*; **~ content** Goldgehalt *m*; **~-digger** Goldsucher; *sl* Vamp *m*; **~-dust** Goldstaub *m*; **~en** ['-ən] golden; gold(farb)en, goldgelb; kostbar; blühend; *(Gelegenheit)* günstig; *(Stunden)* glücklich; *the ~~ age* das Goldene Zeitalter; *the ~~ calf* das Goldene Kalb; *the ~~ mean* die goldene Mitte; *~~ pheasant* Goldfasan *m*; *the ~ rule* die goldene Regel; *~~ wedding* goldene Hochzeit *f*; **~ fever** Goldrausch *m*; **~-field** Goldfeld *n*; **~finch** Stieglitz, Distelfink *m*; *sl* Goldstück *n*; **~fish** Goldfisch *m*; **~-foil, -leaf** Blattgold *n*; **~ilocks** ['-ilɔks] *bot* Hahnenfuß *m*; *fig* Mädchen *n* mit goldfarbigem Haar; **~-ingot** Goldbarren *m*; **~-mine** Goldgrube *f a. fam fig*; **~-nugget** Goldklumpen *m*; **~ plate** Goldgeschirr *n*; **~ plating** Vergoldung *f*; **~ reserve** *fin* Goldreserve *f*; **~ rush** Goldrausch *m*; **~smith** Goldschmied *m*; **~ standard** Goldwährung *f*.

golf [gɔlf] *s* Golf(spiel) *n*; *itr* Golf spielen; **~-club** Golfschläger, -klub *m*; **~-course, -links** *pl mit sing* Golfplatz *m*; **~er** ['-ə] Golf(spiel)er *m*.

Goliath [gə'laiəθ] *fig* Riese, Goliath *m*.

golliwog(g) ['gɔliwɔg] groteske Puppe; Vogelscheuche *f*, häßliche(r) Mensch *m*.

golly ['gɔli] *interj (by ~)* Donnerwetter!

goloptious [gə'lɔpʃəs] *Br fam* herrlich, köstlich.

golosh [gə'lɔʃ] *s. galosh.*

gonad ['gɔnæd] *biol* Keimdrüse *f*.

gondol|a ['gɔndələ] Gondel *f a. aero*; *Am* flache(s) Flußboot *n*, Barke *f*; *Am rail (~~ car)* Niederbordwagen *m*; **~ier** [gɔndə'liə] Gondoliere *m*.

gone [gɔn] *pp von go*; *a* vergangen, gewesen, dahin, vorbei; geistig abwesend, ekstatisch; *fam* hin, erledigt; weg, fort, *fam* futsch; *to be ~ on s.o. (sl)* in jdn verknallt, verschossen, sterblich verliebt sein; *he is ~* er ist fort; *he is a ~ man, case, coon (sl)* er ist erledigt, es ist aus, vorbei mit ihm; *be ~! get you ~!* hau ab! scher dich weg! pack dich! zieh ab! *far ~* weit vorgerückt, tief verwickelt; sehr müde; *past and ~, dead and ~* vorüber und vorbei, ein für allemal dahin; **~r** ['-ə] *sl* erschossene(r), erledigte(r), ruinierte(r) Mann *m*.

gonfalon ['gɔnfələn] Banner *n*.

gong [gɔŋ] *s* Gong *m*; Alarmglocke; *sl* Medaille *f*; *tr (Polizei) mot* stoppen.

goniometry [gouni'ɔmitri] Goniometrie, Winkelmessung, -rechnung *f*.

gono|coccus [gɔnə'kɔkəs] *pl* -*ci* [-ksai] *med* Gonokokkus *m*; **~rrh(o)ea** [gɔnə'ri:ə] *med* Tripper *m*, Gonorrhöe *f*.

goo [gu:] *Am sl* Klebstoff *m*; verlogene Schmeichelei; übertriebene Sentimentalität *f*; **~ber** ['-bə] *Am* Erdnuß *f*. **~ey** ['-i] *Am sl* klebrig; sentimental.

good [gud] **1.** *a* gut, ausgezeichnet, vorteilhaft; geeignet, passend, angebracht (*for* für); ausreichend, genügend, zufriedenstellend; *(Nahrungsmittel)* frisch, vollwertig, genießbar, zuträglich, bekömmlich; *physiol* gesund, normal, kräftig, stark; tüchtig, geschickt, gewandt; ordentlich; brauchbar, zuverlässig; pflichtbewußt; tugendhaft, fromm; schicklich; artig, wohlerzogen; höflich; gütig, wohlwollend, freundlich; erfreulich, angenehm, glücklich; ehrenhaft, -voll, würdig; echt; *(Geld)* gangbar, gängig; *(Kaufmann)* sicher, kredit-, zahlungsfähig; **2.** *s das* Gute; Gut *n allg; das* Wohl, *das* Beste; *the ~* die Guten; *pl* Sachen *f pl,* bewegliche Habe *f*; *com* Güter *n pl,* Waren *f pl*; *rail* Fracht *f*; *Am* Gewebe *n,* Stoff *m*; *~s (Am sl)* das, worauf es ankommt; Beweis; anständige(r) Kerl *m*; *der* Richtige; Diebesgut *n*; **3.** *a ~ deal* ziemlich viel, *fam* eine Menge; *a ~ few* schon einige, nicht wenige; *a ~ many* ziemlich viele, *fam* eine Menge; *all in ~ time* alles zu s-r Zeit; *as ~ as* so gut wie; *for ~* für immer; endgültig; *for ~ and all* ein für allemal; *for a ~ while* e-e ganze Weile, längere Zeit; *in ~ earnest* in vollem Ernst; *in ~ faith* in gutem Glauben, gutgläubig *adv*; *no ~* nichts wert, nicht zu (ge)brauchen, unbrauchbar; *on ~ authority* aus guter Quelle; *to the ~* zum Guten; zum Vorteil; *com* Kreditsaldo, Nettogewinn *m*; *~ and (fam)* mächtig, sehr; recht, (voll und) ganz; **4.** *to be ~* gelten, gültig sein; *to be a ~ boy, girl* artig sein; *to be ~ enough to* so gut sein und; *to be ~ at figures* gut im Rechnen sein; *to deliver the ~s (sl)* s-e Pflicht tun; *to do it ~* es gut haben; *to have ~ looks* gut aussehen; *to have a ~ night* gut schlafen; *to have a ~ time* sich gut unterhalten, sich gut amüsieren; *to have, to get the ~s on s.o.* etw Nachteiliges über jdn erfahren; am stärkeren Hebelarm sitzen; *to make ~* es schaffen; durchführen, bewerkstelligen; wiedergutmachen; bestätigen, bekräftigen; *(Versprechen)* erfüllen; Erfolg haben; sich durchsetzen; aufkommen für, gutmachen; *to say a ~ word for s.o.* ein gutes Wort für jdn einlegen; *to stand ~* gültig bleiben; bürgen, haften (*for* für); **5.** *he will come to no ~* es wird mit ihm kein gutes Ende nehmen; *~ for you!* gut so! bravo! *~ gracious!* ach du meine Güte! ach du lieber Gott! *my ~ man, my ~ sir! (iro)* mein lieber Mann! *~ morning! ~ afternoon! ~ evening! ~ night!* guten Morgen! guten Tag! guten Abend! gute Nacht! *is it any ~ trying? what ~ is it?* hat es Sinn, Zweck? *that's all to the ~* um so besser! *the common ~* das allgemeine Wohl; das öffentliche Interesse; *dry ~s (Am) pl* Schnitt-, Kurzwaren *f pl*; *fancy ~s (pl)* Luxusartikel *m pl,* Neuheiten *f pl*; *~s and chattels (pl)* bewegliche Habe *f*; *a ~ half* die gute Hälfte; *a ~ hour* e-e gute, reichlich eine Stunde; *a ~ turn* ein gutes Werk; **~-bye,** *Am* **by** [-'-] *s* Lebewohl *n*; *interj* ['-'-] auf Wiedersehen! *to bid, to say ~~ to s.o.* jdm Lebewohl sagen; sich von jdm verabschieden; **~-conduct certificate** Führungs-, Leumundszeugnis *n*; **~-for-nothing** *a* wert-, zwecklos; *s* Taugenichts *m*; **G~ Friday** Karfreitag *m*; **~-hearted** *a* gutherzig, -mütig; **~ humo(u)r** gute Laune *f*; **~-humo(u)red** *a* gutgelaunt, aufgeräumt; gutmütig, freundlich; **~ish** ['-iʃ] einigermaßen, ziemlich gut; beträchtlich; **~liness** ['-linis] hübsche(s), nette(s) Aussehen *n*; **~-looking** gutaussehend, hübsch; **~ looks** *pl* gute(s) Aussehen *n*; **~ly** ['-li] hübsch, nett, gefällig, angenehm; ziemlich, beträchtlich; *a ~~ number* viele; **~-natured** *a* gutmütig, gütig, freundlich, nett, entgegenkommend; **~ness** ['-nis] Güte *f*; Kern *m* der Sache; *das* Beste; *interj (~~ gracious!)* (ach) du meine Güte! *for ~~' sake* um Gottes, um Himmels willen! **~-sized** *a* ziemlich groß; **~s station** *Br* Güterbahnhof *m*; **~s traffic** *Br* Güterverkehr *m*; **~s train** *Br* Güterzug *m*; **~-tempered** *a* heiter, froh; umgänglich; freundlich; **~ turn** Gefallen *m*; *one ~~ deserves another* e-e Hand wäscht die andere; **~will** gute(r) Wille *m,* Bereitwilligkeit *f*; Wohlwollen *n,* Freundlichkeit; Kundschaft *f*; Firmenwert *m*; *~~ mission* Mission *f* des guten Willens; **~y** ['-i] *a* scheinheilig, frömmelnd, zimperlich; *s (~~-~~)* Frömmler(in *f*) *m*; gute Frau, Gevatterin *f*; *meist pl* Süßigkeiten, Leckereien *f pl*; *interj* prima! pfundig!

goof [gu:f] *s sl (a.* **~er***)* Dämlack, Depp *m*; *Am* Dummheit *f,* Schnitzer *m*; *itr* sich verhauen, Mist machen; in Gedanken versunken sein; *tr* necken; **~ ball** *Am* Narkotikum *n*; Beruhigungspille *f*; **~iness** ['-inis] Dämlichkeit *f*; **~y** ['-i] doof, dämlich; vernarrt (*about* in).

gook [gu:k] *Am sl mil pej* Ostasiate; Schmutz, Dreck *m.*

goon [gu:n] *fam* komische(r) Kauz; Schläger; Streikbrecher *m*; **~k** [-k] *Am sl* schmierige Flüssigkeit; widerliche Sache *f.*

goop [gu:p] *Am sl* Tölpel; Schwindel *m.*

goose [gu:s] *pl geese s* Gans *f*; Gänsefleisch *n*; dumme Person *f*; *pl ~s:* Schneiderbügeleisen *n*; *Am sl* Stoß *m* in den Rücken; *tr Am sl* in den Rücken stoßen; *to be unable to say "bo" to a ~* ein Angsthase sein; *to cook o.'s ~ (fam)* sich die Chancen, Aussichten verderben; *to kill the ~ that lays the golden eggs* die Zukunft opfern; *all his geese are swans* er ist ein großer Optimist; *the ~ hangs high (Am)* alles ist in bester Ordnung; die Zukunft ist glänzend; *sauce for the ~ is sauce for the gander (prov)* was dem einen recht ist, ist dem andern billig; **~berry** ['guzbəri] Stachelbeere *f*; Stachelbeerstrauch; *mil* Drahtigel; *fam* unbequeme(r) Dritte(r), Anstandswauwau *m*; Zeitungsente *f*; **~-egg** Gänseei *n*; *Am (Schule)* ganz ungenügend; **~-flesh, -skin, -pimples** *pl* Gänsehaut *f (beim Menschen)*; **~-grease** Gänseschmalz *n*; **~herd** Gänsejunge *m,* -magd *f*; **~-neck** *tech* Schwanenhals *m,* Anschlußstück *n*; **~-quill** Gänsekiel *m,* -feder *f (zum Schreiben)*; **~-step** Stechschritt *m*; **~y, goosy** ['gu:si] *a* dumm, blöd(e); *Am sl* wild, nervös, aufgeregt; *s fam* Gänschen *n.*

*

gopher ['goufə] *(nordamerik.)* Taschenratte *f*; Backen-, Erdhörnchen *n*; *Am sl* Taugenichts, Einbrecher *m.*

gorcock ['gɔ:kɔk] Birkhahn *m.*

Gordian ['gɔ:djən] *a*: *to cut the ~ knot* den gordischen Knoten durchhauen.

gore [gɔ:] **1.** *s (bes.* geronnenes) Blut *n*; **2.** *s* Zwickel, (eingesetzter) Keil *m*; *tr* e-n Keil, Zwickel einsetzen in; **3.** *tr* durchbohren, aufspießen.

gorge [gɔ:dʒ] *s* Schlucht, Klamm; Sperre; *Arch* Hohlkehle *f*; *itr* schlingen, gierig essen; *tr* vollstopfen; hinunter-, verschlingen; *my ~ rises* mir wird übel (*at* bei).

gorgeous ['gɔ:dʒəs] prächtig, prachtvoll, glänzend, herrlich; *fam* fabelhaft, großartig; **~ ness** ['-nis] Pracht, Herrlichkeit *f.*

gorget ['gɔ:dʒit] *hist* Halsberge *f*; (Ring-)Kragen *m (a. der Vögel)*; **~ patch** *mil* (Kragen-)Spiegel *m.*

Gorgon ['gɔ:gən] Gorgo; *fig* schreckliche Frau *f.*

gorilla [gə'rilə] *zoo* Gorilla *m.*

gormand ['gɔ:mənd] Schlemmer; Vielfraß *m*; **~ize** ['-aiz] *itr* prassen, schlemmen; fressen.

gorse [gɔ:s] *bot* (Stech-)Ginster *m.*

gory ['gɔ:ri] blutig.

gosh [gɔʃ] *interj (by ~!)* bei Gott! alle Wetter! Donnerwetter!

goshawk ['gɔshɔ:k] *zoo* Hühnerhabicht *m.*

gosling ['gɔzliŋ] Gänschen *n a. fig.*

gospel ['gɔspəl] Evangelium *n a. fig*; *the G~ according to St. John* das Johannesevangelium; **~ truth** unumstößliche Wahrheit *f.*

gossamer ['gɔsəmə] *s* Altweibersommer *m*; sehr feine Gaze; Regenhaut *f*; *a u.* **~y** ['-ri] leicht, zart, (hauch)dünn.

gossip ['gɔsip] *s* Schwätzer *m,* Klatschbase *f*; Klatsch *m*; Geschwätz, Gerede *n*; *itr* schwatzen; klatschen; **~ column** Klatschspalte *f*; **~y** ['-i] geschwätzig, klatschhaft.

Goth [gɔθ] *hist* Gote; *fig* Barbar, Vandale *m*; **~ic** ['-ik] *a hist (Kunst)* gotisch; *s* (das) Gotisch(e); Gotik *f*; *typ* Fraktur, *Am* Grotesk *f*; *~~ arch* Spitzbogen *m.*

gouache [gu'ɑ:ʃ] Guasch-, Deckfarben *f pl*; Guasch(malerei) *f.*

gouge [gaudʒ] *s* Hohlmeißel *m,* -eisen; *Am fam* Betrugsmanöver *n,* Schwindel *m*; *tr* mit dem Hohlmeißel bearbeiten, aushöhlen; *Am fam* anschmieren.

goulash ['gu:læʃ] Gulasch *n.*

gourd [guəd] Kürbis *m*; *(bottle ~)* Flaschenkürbis *m*; Kürbisflasche *f.*

gourm|and ['guəmənd] *s. gormand*; **~et** ['-mei] Feinschmecker *m.*

gout [gaut] Gicht *f,* Podagra *n*; Tropfen, Spritzer *m*; *articular ~* Gelenkrheumatismus *m*; **~iness** ['-inis] Anlage *f* zur Gicht; **~y** ['-i] gichtisch.

govern ['gʌvən] *tr* regieren; verwalten; leiten, lenken; bestimmen, beeinflussen; *fig* beherrschen, zügeln, im Zaum halten; *gram* regieren; *tech* regeln, steuern; *itr* die Regierung(sgewalt) ausüben, regieren; *to be ~ed by* sich richten nach; sich leiten lassen von; **~able** ['-əbl] lenksam; **~ance** ['-əns] Regierung(sführung) *f*; **~ess** ['-is] Erzieherin, Gouvernante *f*; **~ing** ['-iŋ] regierend, Regierungs-; geschäftsführend; führend, leitend, (be)herrschend; *~~ body* Verwaltungsrat *m*; Führungsgremium *n*; *~~ commission* Regierungskommission *f,* -ausschuß *m*; *the ~~ idea* der Leitgedanke; **~ment** ['-mənt] Regierung *f,* Kabinett, Ministerium *n*; Regierung(sgewalt); Regierungs-, Staatsform; Verwaltung(srat *m*); (Geschäfts-)Führung, Leitung *f*; Gouvernement *n,* Verwaltungsbezirk *m*; *to form a ~~* e-e Regierung bilden; *to overthrow a ~~* e-e Regierung stürzen; *the ~~ has resigned* die Regierung ist zurückgetreten; *coalition ~~* Koalitionsregierung *f*; *federal ~~* Bundesregierung *f*; *local ~~* Gemeindeverwaltung *f*; *military ~~* Militärregierung *f*; *self-~~* Autonomie *f*; *~~ bank* Staats-, Nationalbank *f*; *~~ bill* Regierungsvorlage *f*; *~~ bonds (pl)* Staatspapiere *n pl*; *~~ commission* Regierungskommission *f,* -ausschuß *m*; *~~ commissioner* Regierungskommissar *m*; *~~ contract* Staatsauftrag *m*; *~~ control* Staatsaufsicht *f*; *~~-controlled (a)* unter staatlicher Aufsicht; *~~ department* Ministerium *n*; *~~ expenditure* Staatsausgaben *f pl*; *~~ grant* Staatszuschuß *m*; *~~-in-exile* Exilregierung *f*; *~~ loan* Staatsanleihe *f*; *~~ monopoly* Staatsmonopol *n*; *~~ officer, official* Staatsbeamte(r) *m*; *~~ party* Regierungspartei *f*; *~~ property* Staatseigentum *n*; *~~ revenue* Staatseinkünfte, -einnahmen *f pl*; *~~ securities (pl Br)* Staatsanleihe *f*; *~~ spokesman* Regierungssprecher *m*; **~mental** [gʌvən'mentl] *a* Regierungs-, Staats-; behördlich; **~or** ['gʌvənə] Regierungsbeamte(r); Statthalter, Gouverneur; Leiter, Direktor, Präsident; Erzieher, Hofmeister; *fam* Chef, Prinzipal;

Alte(r) Herr; *tech* Regulator, Regler *m*; *~~-general* Generalgouverneur *m*; **~orship** ['-ʃip] Statthalterschaft *f*; Amtszeit *f* e-s Gouverneurs.

gow [gau] *Am sl* Opium *n*; *(Werbung)* Blickfang *m*; **~k** [-k] *fam* Depp *m*.

gown [gaun] *s* (Damen-)Kleid *n*; *(dressing-~)* Morgenrock *m*; *(night-~)* Nachthemd *n*; Robe *f*, Talar; Lehrkörper *m (e-r Universität)*; *tr* ein Kleid, e-n Talar anziehen; **~sman** ['-zmən] akademische(r) Würdenträger *m*.

grab [græb] *tr* ergreifen, packen, schnappen, *fam* grapschen; an sich reißen, sich (gewaltsam *od* unrechtmäßig) aneignen; *itr* die Hand legen (*at* auf); greifen (*at* nach); *s* schnelle(r) (Zu-)Griff *m*; *das* Ergriffene; *tech* Greifer *m*; *to have the ~ on s.th.* sich den Löwenanteil sichern; *to ~ a bite* e-e Kleinigkeit essen; **~ bag** *Am* Glückstopf *m*; **~ber** ['-ə] habgierige(r) Mensch *m*; **~bing** ['-iŋ] gewaltsame Zugriffe *m pl*; unsaubere Geschäfte *n pl*; **~ble** ['græbl] *itr* (herum)grabbeln, -fummeln; tasten, (auf allen vieren) suchen (*for* nach); **~ dredger** Greifbagger *m*.

grace [greis] *s* Anmut, Grazie; Zierlichkeit *f*; Charme, Reiz; Anstand *m*; Gefälligkeit *f*, Entgegenkommen *n*, Bereitwilligkeit *f*, Wohlwollen *n*, Nachsicht; *rel* Gnade *f*; Tischgebet *n*; *mus* Verzierung *f*; *fin* Aufschub *m*; *pl* gefällige(s) Äußere(s) *od* Wesen *n*; Gunst *f*; *the G~s* die Grazien *f pl*; *tr* verschönen, zieren, schmücken, heben, auszeichnen; ehren; *mus* verzieren; *with (a) good, bad ~* bereit-, widerwillig *adv*; *to add ~ to* verschönen, zieren; *to be in s.o.'s good (bad) ~s* bei jdm (nicht) in Gunst stehen, *fam* gut (schlecht) angeschrieben sein; *to give s.o. a day's ~* jdm e-n Tag Aufschub gewähren; *to say ~* das Tischgebet sprechen; *days of ~ (fin)* Nachfrist *f*; Respekttage *m pl*; *petition of ~* Gnadengesuch *n*; *Your G~* Euer Gnaden; **~ful** ['-ful] anmutig, graziös, zierlich, reizend, reizvoll; **~fulness** ['-fulnis] Anmut, Grazie, Zierlichkeit *f*; **~less** ['-lis] schwerfällig, plump, ungeschickt; reizlos; unverschämt, unpassend, unangebracht.

gracious ['greiʃəs] gütig, wohlwollend, gefällig; gnädig; leutselig; *good ~! ~ goodness! ~ me!* ach du meine Güte, ach du lieber Himmel! **~ness** ['-nis] Güte *f*, Wohlwollen *n*; Gnade *f*.

grad|ate [grə'deit] *tr* abstufen, schattieren; **~ation** [-'deiʃən] Stufenfolge; Abstufung *f*; (allmählicher) Übergang *m*; Schattierung, Tönung; Stufe; *geol* Abtragung *f*; *gram* Ablaut *m*; **~e** [greid] *s* Stufe *f*, Schritt; Grad; Rang *m*; (Rang-, Güte-)Klasse, Sorte, Qualität; *Am* (Schul-)Klasse; *Am (Schule)* Zensur; *Am (Straße, Bahnlinie)* Steigung, Neigung *f*, Gefälle *n*; *Am mil* Dienstgrad *m*; *the ~s (Am)* die Volksschule; *tr* ab-, einstufen, sortieren; bewerten; einteilen, klassifizieren; *agr (to ~~ up)* (auf)kreuzen; *Am (Schule)* bewerten, zensieren; *Am* abflachen, (ein)ebnen; *mil (Dokument)* mit e-r Geheimhaltungsstufe versehen; *to ~ up* verbessern; in e-e höhere Gruppe einstufen; *at ~~* auf gleicher Höhe; *down ~~* abfallend; sich verschlimmernd; *on the up, down ~~ (Am)* steigend, fallend; *up ~~* ansteigend; sich bessernd; *up to ~~ (fig)* auf der Höhe; dem Standard entsprechend; *to make the ~~ (Am)* die Steigung, *fig* die Schwierigkeiten überwinden; es schaffen; *~~ crossing (Am)* schienengleiche(r) Bahnübergang *m*; *~~ label(l)ing (com)* Güteklassebezeichnung *f*; *~~ school (Am)* Grundschule *f*; *~~ teacher (Am)* Grundschullehrer *m*; **~er** ['greidə] Sortierer; *tech* Straßenhobel *m*, Planiermaschine; Sortiermaschine *f*; *first~~ (Am)* Erstkläßler *m*; **~ient** ['greidjənt] *a* ansteigend; abfallend; *s* (Ab-)Hang *m*; Steigung, Neigung *f*, Gefälle *n*; *phys* Anstieg *m*, Zunahme *f*; **~ing** ['greidiŋ] Einstufung, Eingruppierung, Klassi(fizi)erung; *com* Güteklasseneinteilung *f*; *~~ rule* Klassifizierungsvorschrift *f*.

gradual ['grædjuəl] *a* graduell, stufen-, schrittweise erfolgend *od* sich vollziehend, allmählich; **~ly** ['-i] *adv* stufen-, schrittweise, Schritt für Schritt, nach und nach, allmählich.

graduat|e ['grædjuit] *s (Universität, USa. Schule)* Absolvent; Graduierte(r); Meßzylinder *m*; *a Am* (staatlich) geprüft; ['-djeit] *itr* e-n Grad erlangen, graduieren, promovieren; *Am* ein Abschlußzeugnis erhalten; absolvieren (*from high school* die höhere Schule); *tr Am* graduieren, promovieren, e-n Grad, ein Abschlußzeugnis erteilen (*s.o.* jdm); *(Meßgerät)* einteilen; mit e-r Skala versehen; abstufen; **~ion** [grædju'eiʃən] Promotion *f*; *Am* Schul-, Lehrgangsabschluß *m*; (Grad-)Einteilung; *tech* Grad-, Skaleneinteilung; Abstufung *f*; *(~~ mark)* Teilstrich *m*.

Gr(a)ec|ism ['gri:sizm] Gräzismus *m*, griechische (Sprach-)Eigentümlichkeit *f*; **~ize** ['-saiz] *tr* gräzisieren; **~o-** ['grikou] *pref* griechisch-.

graft [grɑ:ft] **1.** *s* Pfropfreis; *(~ing, ~age)* Pfropfen; *med* Transplantat *n*; *tr* (auf-, ein)pfropfen (*in* in; *on* auf); okulieren; *med* verpflanzen; *itr* gepfropft, verpflanzt werden; **2.** *s Am* Bestechung, Schiebung, Korruption *f*; Bestechungs-, Schmiergelder *n pl*, Korruptionsgewinn *m*; *sl* Schufterei *f*; *tr (Bestechungsgelder)* erhalten, annehmen; *itr* sich bestechen lassen, schieben; **~er** ['-ə] *Am fam* bestechliche(r), korrupte(r) Beamte(r); Schieber *m*.

Grail [greil] : *the Holy G~* der Heilige Gral.

grain [grein] *s* (Samen-, *bes.* Getreide-) Korn; Getreide, Korn; *allg (Sand-, Salz-)* Korn, Körnchen *n*; *fig* Anlage, Neigung *f*, Wesen; Gran *n (0,065 g)*; *(Leder, Holz, Marmor)* Struktur, Faser, Maserung; *(Fleisch)* Faser *f*; *(Fell)* Strich *m*; *(Leder)* Narbe; Musterung *f (e-r Oberfläche)*; *tr* marmorieren; narben, körnen; *(Fell)* enthaaren; *a ~ of* ein (kleines) bißchen; e-e Spur *gen*; *against the ~* gegen den Strich; *in ~* im Grunde, an und für sich; *to be without a ~ of sense* nicht ein Fünkchen Vernunft haben; *to dye in the ~* in der Wolle färben; *it is, goes against my ~* das geht mir gegen den Strich; *a cargo of ~* e-e Getreideladung; *a ~ of truth* ein Körnchen *n* Wahrheit; **~ elevator** Getreidesilo *m*; **~ export** Getreideausfuhr *f*; **~field** *Am* Getreide-, Kornfeld *n*; **~ market** Getreidemarkt *m*; **~ weevil** Kornkäfer *m*; **~y** ['-i] körnig, faserig.

gramineous [grei'miniəs] grasartig.

grammalogue ['græmələg] *(Stenographie)* Kürzel, Sigel *n*.

gramm|ar ['græmə] Grammatik *f*; *~~ school* Gymnasium *n*; **~arian** [grə'meəriən] Grammatiker *m*; **~atical** [grə'mætikəl] grammati(kali)sch.

gram(me) [græm] *(Masse)* Gramm; *(Kraft)* Pond *n*; **~ calory** *phys* kleine Kalorie *f*.

gramophone ['græməfoun] Grammophon *n*, Plattenspieler *m*; **~-record** Schallplatte *f*.

grampus ['græmpəs] *zoo* Schwertwal, Butzkopf *m*; *to blow like a ~ (fam)* wie ein Walroß schnauben.

granary ['grænəri] Getreide-, Kornspeicher *m*; *fig* Kornkammer *f*.

grand [grænd] *a* groß, hoch, erhaben; vornehm, bedeutend, berühmt; würdevoll, würdig; stattlich, prächtig, prachtvoll; anspruchsvoll, hochmütig; *fam* großartig, phantastisch, prima, Klasse; vollständig, endgültig; Haupt-; *s (~ piano)* Flügel *m*; *Am sl* tausend Dollar *m pl*; *baby ~ (mus)* Stutzflügel *m*; *to live in ~ style* auf großem Fuße leben; **~-aunt** Großtante *f*; **~child** Enkelkind *n*; **~ council** *pol* Großrat *m*; **~(d)ad** ['-æd] Opa *m*; **~daughter** Enkelin *f*; **~ duchess** Großherzogin,- fürstin *f*; **~ duchy** Großherzogtum *n*; **~ duke** Großherzog, -fürst *m*; **~ee** [græn'di:] Grande; Große(r) *m*; **~eur** ['grændʒə] Größe, Hoheit, Erhabenheit, Vornehmheit, Würde *f*; (Seelen-) Adel *m*; Bedeutung, Berühmtheit; Stattlichkeit, Pracht *f*; **~father** Großvater; Ahn(herr) *m*; *~~('s) clock* Standuhr *f*; **~fatherly** *a* großväterlich; gütig, nachsichtig; **~iloquence** [græn'diləkwəns] Schwulst, Bombast *m*; Prahlerei *f*; **~iloquent** [-'diləkwənt] schwülstig, aufgebauscht, hochtrabend, bombastisch; prahlerisch; **~iose** ['grændious] großartig, eindrucksvoll; bombastisch, hochtrabend; **~iosity** [grændi'ɔsiti] Großartigkeit *f*; **~ma** ['grænmɑ:], **~mam(m)a** ['grænməmɑ:] Oma *f*; **~ master** Großmeister *m*; **~mother** Großmutter *f*; **~motherly** *a* großmütterlich; gütig, nachsichtig; **~-nephew** Großneffe *m*; **~ness** ['-nis] = *~eur*; **~-niece** Großnichte *f*; **~pa** ['grænpɑ:], **~papa** ['-pəpɑ:] Opa *m*; **~parents** ['grænpεərənts] *pl* Großeltern *pl*; **~ piano** *mus* Flügel *m*; **~sire** ['grænsaiə] *obs* Großvater; Ahnherr *m*; **~son** ['grænsʌn] Enkel *m*; **~stand** *s* überdachte Tribüne *f*; *itr Am* für die Galerie spielen; **~ total** Gesamt-, Endsumme *f*; **~-uncle** Großonkel *m*.

grange [greindʒ] Bauernhof *m*, -haus *n*.

granit|e ['grænit] *min* Granit *m*; *to bite on ~~ (fig)* auf Granit beißen; **~ic** [grə'nitik] granitartig; Granit-.

granivorous [grə'nivərəs] körnerfressend.

granny, grannie ['græni] *fam* Oma; *allg* alte Oma *f*.

grant [grɑ:nt] *tr* bewilligen, gewähren, stattgeben (*s.th.* e-r S); zusprechen, erteilen; *(Bescheinigung)* ausstellen; *(Eigentum)* übertragen; *(e-m Gesuch)* entsprechen; zugeben, einräumen, zugestehen; *s* Bewilligung, Gewährung, Erteilung; Verleihung; Übertragung; Konzession *f*; zuerkannte(s) Recht *n*; bewilligte *od* zugewiesene Gelder *n pl*; Zuschuß *m*; Stipendium; zugewiesene(s) Land *n*; *to take for ~ed* (fest) annehmen, für sicher, für ausgemacht halten; als selbstverständlich voraussetzen; *~ed!* zugegeben! **~ee** [grɑ:n'ti:] Berechtigte(r); Konzessionsinhaber, Konzessionär *m*; **~-in-aid** staatliche Beihilfe *f*, Zuschuß *m*, Subvention *f*; **~ing** ['-iŋ] angenommen, zugegeben (*that* daß); **~or** ['-ə, -'tɔ:] Übertragende(r) *m*.

granul|ar ['grænjulə] körnig, gekörnt, graupig, granulös; **~ate** ['grænjuleit] *tr* körnen, granulieren; *tr itr* körnig machen, werden; **~ated** *a* gekörnt, granuliert; *~~ carbon* Kohlegrieß *m*; *~~ sugar* Kristallzucker *m*; **~ation** [grænju'leiʃən] Körnung; *pl med* Granulation *f*, wilde(s) Fleisch *n*; **~e** ['-ju:l] Körnchen *n*; **~oma** [-'loumə] *med* Granulom *n*; **~ous** ['grænjuləs] körnig.

grape [greip] Weinbeere *f*; Wein *m*; Weinrot *n*; *pl* Weintrauben *f pl*; *vet* Mauke *(der Pferde)*; Rindertuberkulose *f*; **~-brandy** Weinbrand *m*; **~-cure** Traubenkur *f*; **~fruit** ['-fru:t] Pampelmuse *f*; **~juice** Traubensaft *m*; **~ry** ['-əri] Treibhaus *n* für Weintrauben; **~-shot** *mil* Kartätsche *f*; **~-stone** Traubenkern *m*; **~-sugar** Traubenzucker *m*; **~-vine** Weinstock *m*; *fig (~~ telegraph)* Flüsterpropaganda *f*; Gerücht; Hörensagen *n*.

graph [græf] *s* graphische Darstellung *f*, Schaubild, Diagramm *n*; Kurve *f*; *tr* graphisch darstellen; **~er** ['-ə] Registriergerät *n*; **~ic(al)** ['græfik(əl)] graphisch; (hand)schriftlich; geschrieben; Schrift-, Schreib-; anschaulich, lebendig, lebensnah, -wahr; *~~ artist* Gebrauchsgraphiker *m*; *~~ arts (pl)* die bildenden Künste *f pl*; Graphik *f*; **~ite** ['græfait] *min* Graphit *m*; *~~ crucible* Graphittiegel *m*; **~ological** [græfə'lɔdʒik(əl)] graphologisch; **~ologist** [græ'fɔlədʒist] Graphologe *m*; **~ology** [græ'fɔlədʒi] Graphologie, Handschriftendeutung *f*; **~ paper** Millimeterpapier *n*.

grapnel ['græpnəl] Dregganker, Draggen; Enterhaken *m*.

grappl|e ['græpl] *s* Enterhaken; *tech* Greifer; feste(r) (Zu-)Griff *m*; Ringen; Handgemenge *n*; *tr* ergreifen, packen; entern; *itr* e-n Enterhaken benutzen; ringen; sich herumschlagen (*with* mit); **~ing** ['-iŋ], *~~-iron, -hook* Enterhaken *m*.

grasp [grɑ:sp] *tr* (er)greifen, fassen, packen; *fig* begreifen, verstehen, (er)fassen; *itr* greifen, trachten, streben (*at* nach); schnappen (*at* nach); *s* (Zu-)Griff *m*; *fig* Reichweite, Gewalt *f*; Begriffsvermögen *n*, Fassungskraft *f*; Verständnis *n*; *within s.o.'s ~* in jds Gewalt; in jds Reichweite; *to have a good ~ of s.th.* etw sehr gut beherrschen; *to lose o.'s ~* loslassen; **~ing** ['-iŋ] habgierig.

grass [grɑ:s] *s* Gras *n*; Rasen *m*; Weide(land *n*) *f*; *sl* Polizist, V-Mann *m*; *tr* mit Gras einsäen; auf Rasen bleichen; *sl* niederschlagen; *sl* verpfeifen; *out at ~* auf der Weide; *fig* in Ferien; *to go to ~* weiden (gehen); *fig* sich ausruhen; in die Ferien gehen; *Am fam* in die Binsen gehen; *to hear the ~ grow (fig)* das Gras wachsen hören; *not to let the ~ grow under o.'s feet* nicht müßig sein; *keep off the ~* Betreten des Rasens verboten! **~cutter** *Am* Rasenmäher *m*; **~hopper** Grashüpfer *m*, Heuschrecke *f*; *aero* Leicht-, Verbindungsflugzeug *n*; **~land** Gras-, Weideland *n*; **~-plot** Rasenstück *n*, -platz *m*; **~roots** *s pl Am* Erdboden *m*, oberste Erdschicht *f*; *a (~~) Am fam* erdverbunden, bodenständig, urwüchsig; volksnah, -verbunden, -tümlich; *to get down to ~~* ganz von vorn beginnen; **~-snake** Ringelnatter *f*; **~ widow(er)** Strohwitwe(r *m*); *Am a.* geschiedene *od* getrennt lebende Frau *f*; **~-work** Arbeit *f* über Tage; **~y** ['-i] grasbewachsen, -bedeckt; grasartig; *(~~-green)* grasgrün.

grat|e [greit] **1.** *tr* (zer)kratzen, (zer-)reiben, schaben, raspeln; knirschen (*o.'s teeth* mit den Zähnen); reizen, ärgern; *itr* kratzen, kreischen; reizen, aufregen (*on s.o.* jdn); *to ~~ on s.o.'s nerves* an jds Nerven zerren; **~er** ['-ə] Reiber, Schaber *m (Person* od *Sache)*; Reibeisen *n*; **~ing** ['-iŋ] *a* kratzend, kreischend; aufreizend, -regend; **2.** *s* (Fenster-, Tür-)Gitter *n*; (Feuer-)Rost *m*, Heizgitter *n*; Kamin *m*; *tr* vergittern; mit e-m Gitter, Rost versehen; **~icule** ['grætikju:l] Strichgitter, Gradnetz, Fadenkreuz *n*; **~ing** ['-iŋ] *s* Gitter *n*; *mar* Gräting *f*.

grat|eful ['greitful] dankbar (*to s.o.* jdm); *obs* willkommen, angenehm, erfreulich, wohltuend; **~efulness** ['-fulnis] Dankbarkeit; *obs* Annehmlichkeit *f*; **~ification** [grætifi'keiʃən] Genugtuung, Befriedigung *f* (*at* über); Genuß *m*, Freude; *obs* Belohnung *f*; **~ify** ['grætifai] *tr* erfreuen, befriedigen; *(Wunsch)* erfüllen; freien Lauf lassen (*s.th.* e-r S); *to be ~ified* sich freuen; **~ifying** erfreulich, angenehm (*to* für); **~is** ['greitis] *adv* gratis, umsonst; *a* kostenlos, unentgeltlich, Gratis-; *~~ copy* Freiexemplar *n*; **~itude** ['grætitju:d] Dankbarkeit *f* (*to* gegenüber; *for* für); *in ~~ for* aus Dankbarkeit für; **~uitous** [grə'tju(:)itəs] kostenlos, unentgeltlich, umsonst; freiwillig; unverdient, grundlos, unbegründet, haltlos; *~~ article (com)* Zugabe *f*; **~uity** [grə'tju(:)iti] Trinkgeld, Geldgeschenk *n*; Zuwendung, Vergütung, Gratifikation; Abfindung *f*; *no ~uities* kein Trinkgeld!

gravamen [grə'veimən] *jur* Beschwerde *f*; Klagegrund *m*.

grave [greiv] **1.** *a* ernst(haft), schwer; besorgniserregend; wichtig, bedeutend; schwerwiegend; feierlich; *(Mann)* gesetzt; dunkel, düster; *(Ton)* tief; *s* [grɑ:v] *u.* **~ accent** *gram* Gravis *m (Akzent)*; **2.** *s* Grab *n a. fig*; Grabhügel *m*, -mal *n*; *fig* Tod *m*, Ende *n*; *tr obs* schnitzen, (ein)gravieren; *fig* tief beeindrucken; endgültig festlegen; *to have one foot in the ~ (fig)* mit einem Fuß im Grabe stehen; **~-clothes** *pl* Leichentuch *n*; **~-digger** Totengräber *m*; **~stone** Grabstein *m*; **~yard** Friedhof *m*; **3.** *tr mar* kalfatern; **graving** ['-iŋ] Kalfatern *n*; *~~-dock* Trockendock *n*.

gravel ['grævəl] *s* Kies; *med* Harngrieß *m*; *tr* mit Kies bestreuen; *fig* in Verlegenheit bringen; **~-pit** Kiesgrube *f*; **~-stone** Kieselstein *m*.

Graves disease [greivz] Basedowsche Krankheit *f*.

gravid ['grævid] schwanger; **~ity** [græ'viditi] Schwangerschaft *f*.

gravit|ate ['græviteit] *itr phys* gravitieren; *chem* sich absetzen, sich niederschlagen; *fig* tendieren, neigen, streben (*to, towards* zu); **~ation** [grævi'teiʃən] Schwerkraft, Gravitation; Neigung *f*, Zug; *chem* Niederschlag *m*; **~ational** [-ʃnəl] Schwere-; *~~ field* Schwerefeld *n*; **~y** ['græviti] Schwere *f*, Ernst *m*; Gemessenheit; Bedeutung; *mus* Tiefe; *phys* Schwere *f*, Gewicht *n*; *(force of ~~)* Anziehungs-, Schwerkraft *f* der Erde; Erdbeschleunigung *f*; *~~ fault (geol)* Verwerfung *f*; *~~ tank, wind* Fallbehälter, -wind *m*.

gravy ['greivi] Fleischsaft *m*; Bratenfett *n*; (Braten-)Soße *f*; *Am sl* gefundene(s) Fressen *n*; **~ beef** Saftbraten *m*; **~-boat** Soßenschüssel, Sauciere *f*; **~ train** *Am* leichte Arbeit *f*.

gray *s. grey.*

graz|e [greiz] **1.** *tr (Vieh)* weiden lassen; *(Gras, Weide)* abweiden (lassen); *(Vieh)* hüten; *itr* weiden, grasen; *to ~~ down* abgrasen, -weiden; **~ier** ['-jə] *Br* Viehzüchter *m*; **~ing (-land)** (Vieh-)Weide *f*; **2.** *tr* streifen; *med* (ab)schürfen; *s* Streifen *n*; Streifschuß *m*; Schramme *f*.

*

greas|e [gri:s] *s* zerlassenes tierische(s) Fett; Schmierfett *n*, Schmiere *f*; Wollschweiß *m*; ungereinigte(s) Fell; *fam* Schmiergeld *n*; *fam* Schmeichelei; *vet* Mauke *f*; *tr* [gri:z, gri:s] *tr* (ab-, ein)schmieren, (ein)fetten; ölen; *fig* bestechen (*s.o., s.o.'s hand, palm* jdn); *axle ~~* Wagenschmiere *f*; *~~ box, cup (tech)* Schmierbuchse *f*; *~~-cutting* fettlösend; *~~ gun* Fettpresse *f*; *~~ monkey (Am sl)* Auto-, Flugzeugmechaniker *m*; *~~-paint* Schminke *f*; *~~-proof paper* Butterbrotpapier *n*; *~~ spot* Fettfleck *m*; **~er** ['-ə] (Ein-)Schmierer, Öler; *Am sl pej* Mexikaner *od* Lateinamerikaner, Schmierfink *m*; **~iness** ['gri:zinis] Fettigkeit; Schlüpfrigkeit, *fig* Glätte *f*; **~y** ['gri:zi] fett, fettig, ölig; schmierig; glitschig, schlüpfrig; *fig* aalglatt; *~~ lustre* Speckglanz *m*.

great [greit] *a* groß; beträchtlich, ausgedehnt; *(Zeit)* lange, langdauernd; zahlreich; stark, mächtig, gewaltig; überlegen, hervorragend, bedeutend, berühmt; eindrucksvoll, imposant; *(Freund)* eng, intim; *fam* (ganz) groß (*in* in); geschickt (*at* bei, in), beschlagen (*at* in); Feuer und Flamme (*on* für), interessiert (*on* an); *fam* großartig, prima, Klasse; *adv fam* prima, glänzend; *(bei a)* gewaltig, herrlich, mächtig; *s pl fam (Universität) (~ go)* Abschlußprüfung *f*; *the ~* die Großen, die Vornehmen *m pl*; *a ~ age* ein hohes Alter; *a ~ deal* e-e (ganze) Menge, viel; *a ~ many* sehr viele; eine Menge; *no ~* kein(e) besondere(r, s); *no ~ matter* nichts von Bedeutung; *that's ~!* das ist (ja) prima! *the* **G~ Bear** *astr* der Große Bär; **G~ Britain** Großbritannien *n*; **~coat** Paletot, (Winter-)Mantel *m*; **~grandchild, ~granddaughter, ~grandfather, ~grandmother, ~grandparents, ~grandson** Urenkel(in *f*) *m*, -enkelin *f*, -großvater *m*, -großmutter *f*, -großeltern *pl*, -enkel *m*; **~~~grandfather** Ururgroßvater *m*; **~-hearted** *a* mutig, tapfer; großmütig, selbstlos; **G~er London** Groß-London *n*; **~ly** ['-li] *adv* sehr, höchst; in hohem Grade; **~ness** ['-nis] Größe, Stärke, Bedeutung *f*; *the* **G~ War** der (erste) Weltkrieg.

greaves [gri:vs] *pl* **1.** Fett-, Speckgrieben *f pl*; **2.** Beinschienen *f pl*.

grebe [gri:b] *orn* Taucher *m*.

Grecian ['gri:ʃən] *a u. s* = *Greek.*

Greece [gri:s] Griechenland *n*.

greed [gri:d], **~iness** ['-inis] Gier (*for* nach); Habsucht *f*; **~y** ['-i] habsüchtig, gierig (*for* nach); gefräßig, *fam* verfressen; begierig (*of* auf).

Greek [gri:k] *a* griechisch; *s* Grieche *m*, Griechin *f*; (das) Griechisch(e); *it's ~ to me* das sind mir böhmische Dörfer.

green [gri:n] *a* grün (*with* vor); frisch, lebendig; neu; *(Fleisch)* roh, ungesalzen; unreif; unerfahren, ungeübt (*at* in); *fam* eifersüchtig, neidisch; *fig* voller Leben, lebenskräftig; *tech* neu, jung; *s* Grün *n*, grüne Farbe; Grünfläche *f*, Rasen *m*, Laub *n*; Golfplatz *m*; *pl Am* Grün *n (zur Dekoration)*; Grünkram *m*, -zeug *n*; *fig* Lebenskraft *f*; *to give the ~ light* freie Fahrt geben *a. fig*; *he was ~ with envy* er platzte vor Neid; **~back** *Am* Geldschein *m*; **~ belt** Grüngürtel *m (e-r Stadt)*; **~-blue** blaugrün; **~ crop** Grünfutter *n*; **~ery** ['-əri] *das* Grün *(in der Natur)*; **~-eyed** *a* grünäugig; *fig* eifersüchtig; **~finch** Grünfink *m*; **~ fingers** *pl* gärtnerische(s) Geschick *n*; **~fly** grüne Blattlaus *f*; **~gage** Reineclaude *f*; **~goods** *pl Am sl* falsche Geldscheine *m pl*; **~grocer**

(Obst- u.) Gemüsehändler *m*; **~grocery** Obst- u. Gemüsehandlung *f*; **~horn** Grünschnabel; Anfänger *m*; **~house** Gewächshaus *n*; **~ish** ['-iʃ] grünlich; **~ manure** Gründünger *m*; **~ness** ['-nis] grüne Farbe; *fig* Frische; Unreife, Unerfahrenheit *f*; **~ pasture** Grünfutter *n*; **~ proof** *sl* nicht korrigierte(r) Bürstenabzug *m*; **~room** *theat* Künstlerzimmer *n*; **~ run** Einlaufen *n (e-r neuen Maschine)*; **~sickness** Bleichsucht *f*; **~ soap** Schmierseife *f*; **~sward** ['-swɔ:d] Grünfläche *f*, Rasen *m*; **~ thumb**: *to have a ~~ (Am)* e-e geschickte Hand beim Ziehen von Pflanzen haben; **~ vegetables** *pl* Grüngemüse *n*; **~ vitriol** *chem* Eisenvitriol *n*; **~wood** Laubwald *m*.

Greenland ['gri:nlənd] Grönland *n*; **~er** ['-ə] Grönländer(in *f*) *m*; **~ic** [gri:n'lændik] grönländisch; **~man** ['-mən] Grönlandfahrer *m*.

Greenwich ['grinidʒ] *(Vorort von London)*; **~ time** Weltzeit *f*.

greet [gri:t] *tr* (be)grüßen (*on behalf of* im Namen *gen*); entgegen-, in Empfang nehmen; empfangen, entgegenkommen (*s.o.* jdm); sich darbieten (*her eyes* ihren Augen); **~ing** ['-iŋ] Begrüßung *f*; Gruß *m*; *~~-card* Glückwunschkarte *f*; *~~-telegram* Glückwunschtelegramm *n*.

gregarious [gri'gɛəriəs, gre-] *zoo* in Herden lebend; *(Mensch)* gesellig; *bot* in Trauben, Büscheln wachsend; **~ness** [-nis] Geselligkeit *f*; Herdenleben *n*.

Gregorian [gre'gɔ:riən]: *the* **~calendar** der Gregorianische Kalender; *the* **~ chant** *rel* der Gregorianische Gesang.

gremlin ['gremlin] *aero hum* Kobold *m*, der an allem schuld ist.

grenad|e [gri'neid] (Hand-)Granate *f*; **~ier** [grenə'diə] Grenadier *m*; **~ine** [grenə'di:n] Granatapfelsaft; Grenadin *m (durchbrochener Stoff)*.

grey, *Am meist* **gray** [grei] *a* grau; trüb(e), düster *a. fig*; grau(haarig), ergraut, alt; *s* Grau *n*, graue Farbe *f*; Grauschimmel *m (Pferd)*; *tr itr* grau machen, werden; *to turn ~* grau werden; **~-back** Grauwal *m*; *a.* = **~crow** Nebelkrähe *f*; **~beard** Graubart, alte(r) Mann *m*; **~ friar** Franziskaner *m*; **~-headed** *a* grauköpfig; **~hound** Windhund *m*; *(ocean ~~)* Schnelldampfer *m*; *~~ race, ~cing (fam)* Windhundrennen *n*; **~ish** ['-iʃ] gräulich; **~lag** Wildgans *f*; **~ matter** *anat* graue Hirnsubstanz *f*; *fam* Verstand, Grips *m*; **~wacke** ['-weik] *min* Grauwacke *f*.

grid [grid] *s* (Schutz-)Gitter; *el radio* Gitter(netz); *el* Stromnetz; Leitungs-, Ferngasnetz; *(Karte)* Gitter *n*; *mot* Gepäckträger *m*; *a Am sl* Fußball-; **~ battery** Gitterbatterie *f*; **~ bias** Gittervorspann *m*; **~ circuit** Gitterkreis *m*; **~ current** Gitterstrom *m*; **~der** ['-ə] *Am sl* Fußballer *m*; **~ gas** Ferngas *n*; **~iron** (Brat-)Rost, Grill *m*; *(Schiffswerft)* Kielbank *f*; *theat* Soffitten *f pl*, Schnürboden *m*; *rail* Schienennetz; *Am (Fußball)* Spielfeld *n*; **~-plate** *el* Gitterplatte *f*; **~ rectifier** Gittergleichrichter *m*; **~ square** Planquadrat *n*; **~-valve** *radio* Gitterröhre *f*; **~ voltage** Gitterspannung *f*.

griddle ['gridl] (rundes) Kuchenblech *n*, (flache) Bratpfanne *f*; *tech* Drahtblech *n*; **~cake** Pfannkuchen *m*.

grief [gri:f] Kummer, Gram *m*, Leid(en) *n*; *to bring to ~* Nachteil bringen, Schaden verursachen, Schwierigkeiten machen (*s.o.* jdm); *to come to ~* Schaden erleiden; scheitern.

griev|ance ['gri:vəns] Übelstand *m*; Beschwerde(grund *m*) *f*; Groll *m*; *to have a ~~ against s.o.* gegen jdn e-n Groll haben; **~e** [gri:v] *tr* bekümmern, betrüben; traurig machen *od* stimmen; *itr* bekümmert sein; sich grämen, Schmerz empfinden (*at, for, over* bei *od* über); trauern (*at, for, over* um); *it ~~s me* es fällt mir schwer; **~ous** ['-əs] schwer (zu ertragen(d)), heftig; schmerzlich, gram-, kummervoll, bekümmert; bedauerlich; *(Fehler)* schwer; furchtbar, abscheulich, scheußlich, grausig; *~~ bodily harm (jur)* schwere Körperverletzung *f*.

griff(e) [grif] Dreiviertelneger *m*.

griffin ['grifin], **griffon, gryphon** ['-fən] Greif *m (Fabeltier)*.

griffon ['grifən] *(Hund)* Griffon; Weißköpfige(r) Geier *m*.

grift [grift] *Am sl* erschwindelte(s) Geld *n*; Schwindelei *f*; **~er** ['-ə] Schwindler; Vagabund *m*.

grig [grig] kleine(r) Aal; Grashüpfer *m*, Grille *f*; *(Mensch)* Quecksilber *n*; *merry, lively as a ~* quicklebendig.

grill [gril] *s* Bratrost, Grill *m*; gegrillte(s) Fleisch *n*; Rostbraten *m*; *(~room)* Bratstube *f*, Grillroom *m*; *tr* rösten, grillen; *sl* (hochnot)peinlich, *Am fig* streng verhören; *itr (Fleisch)* rösten; schmoren; *(Mensch in der Sonne)* rösten, braun braten; **~e** [-] Gitter *n*.

grim [grim] grimmig, grausam, wild, erbarmungslos; hart, streng, unnachgiebig, verbissen; finster, abschreckend, abstoßend; grausig, grauenhaft, -voll; **~ness** ['-nis] Grimmigkeit, Härte; Grauenhaftigkeit *f*.

grimace [gri'meis] *s* Grimasse *f*; *itr* Grimassen schneiden.

grimalkin [gri'mælkin] alte Katze; *fig* alte Hexe *f*.

grim|e [graim] *s* (eingefressener) Schmutz *m*; *tr* schmutzig machen, verschmutzen; **~y** ['-i] schmutzig, verschmutzt; rußig.

grin [grin] *itr* grinsen; gezwungen lächeln; *(Hund)* die Zähne zeigen; *to ~ at s.o.* jdn angrinsen; *tr* durch Grinsen zum Ausdruck bringen; *s* Grinsen; gezwungene(s) Lächeln *n*; *to ~ from ear to ear* über das ganze Gesicht grinsen; *I had to ~ and bear it* ich mußte gute Miene zum bösen Spiel machen.

grind [graind] *irr ground, ground* [graund] *tr* (zer)mahlen, zerstoßen, zerreiben; schleifen, wetzen; *(Linse)* schleifen; reiben, bohren; *(Absatz)* bohren (*into the earth* in die Erde); *(Kaffeemühle, Leierkasten)* drehen; *fig* eintrichtern (*s.th. into s.o.'s head* jdm etw); *fig* quälen, bedrücken, plagen; *to ~ down* unterdrücken; *itr* sich mahlen lassen; *(Boot)* knirschend auffahren; *fam* pauken, büffeln, ochsen; sich abplagen; *s* Mahlen *n*; *sl* Gesundheitsspaziergang *m*; Hindernisrennen *n*; *fam* Schinderei, Plackerei; Schufterei, Paukerei, Büffelei *f*; *Am fam* Büffler *m*; *to ~ out* mühsam hervorbringen; fabrizieren; *to ~ o.'s teeth (together)* mit den Zähnen knirschen (*in anger* vor Wut); **~er** ['-ə] *(bes. in Zssgen)* Schleifer *(a. Gerät)*, Dreher; Mahlstein *m*; Mühle *f*; Bakkenzahn; (Orgel-)Dreher; *fam* Einpauker; Marktschreier *m*; Bauchtänzerin *f*; *Am* belegte(s) Brot *n*; Pauker *m*; *pl fam* Zähne *m pl*; **~ing** ['-iŋ] *s* Mahlen; Schleifen *n*; *a* quälend; *(Arbeit)* mühsam; **~stone** Schleifstein *m*; *to keep, to put o.'s nose to the ~~* schuften; pauken, büffeln.

gringo ['griŋgou] *pl -os pej* (Nord-)Amerikaner, Engländer *m*.

grip [grip] *s* (fester, Zu-)Griff *m*; Greifen, Packen, Halten *n*; Halt *m*; Fassungskraft *f*, Verständnis *n*; Herrschaft *f* (*of, on* über); *tech* Greifer; (Hand-)Griff *m*; Klammer, Schelle; *mot* Griffigkeit; *Am* Reisetasche *f*; plötzliche(r), heftige(r) Schmerz *m*; Grippe *f*; *tr* (er)greifen, packen, fassen, festhalten; einspannen, umfassen; *(die Aufmerksamkeit)* fesseln; *to come to ~s* handgemein werden; anea.geraten; *with (fig)* sich ausea.setzen mit; *to have a ~ on s.o.* jds Aufmerksamkeit fesseln; *to let go o.'s ~ on s.th.* etw loslassen; *to take a ~ on s.th.* etw ergreifen, fassen; **~per** ['-ə] Greifer *m (Person od Sache)*; **~ping** ['-iŋ] *a (Buch)* spannend, fesselnd; **~sack** *Am* Reisetasche *f*.

gripe [graip] *tr* Leibschneiden verursachen (*s.o.* bei jdm); *mar (Boot)* festmachen; *itr* Leibschneiden haben; *Am fam* meckern; *s Am fam* Mekkerei, Beschwerde *f*; Meckerer *m*; *pl fam* Leibschneiden *n*; **~r** ['-ə] Greifer; *Am sl* Meckerer *m*.

grippe [grip] *med* Grippe *f*.

grisly ['grisli] gräßlich, schrecklich.

grist [grist] Mahlgut; Mehl *n*; *Am fam* e-e Menge; *to bring ~ to the mill* Nutzen abwerfen, Gewinn bringen; von Vorteil sein; *all is ~ (that comes) to his mill* ihm ist alles recht; er kann alles brauchen.

gristl|e ['grisl] Knorpel *m*; **~y** ['-i] knorp(e)lig.

grit [grit] *s* (grober) Sand, (feiner) Kies *m*; Schlacke, (Flug-)Asche *f*; Korn *n*, Struktur *f (e-s Gesteins)*; *(~stone)* (grober) Sandstein; *fam* Mumm, Schneid *m*, Zackigkeit; *pl* Hafergrütze *f*; *tr* mit Sand, Kies bestreuen; *itr* knirschen; *to ~ o.'s teeth* die Zähne zs.beißen; **~ty** ['-i] sandig, kiesig; *fam* schneidig.

grizzl|e ['grizl] **1.** *s* graue(s) (meliert) Haar; Grau *n*; **~ed** ['-d] *a* grau(meliert); grauhaarig, ergraut; **~y** ['-i] *a* grau(lich); *s (~~ bear)* Grisly-, Graubär *m*; **2.** *itr fam (Kind)* flennen, quengeln.

groan [groun] *itr* seufzen, stöhnen, ächzen (*with* vor); brummen, murren; (zu) leiden (haben), seufzen (*davon* unter); sich sehnen (*for* nach); *tr (to ~ out)* seufzend, stöhnend hervorbringen, erzählen; *s* Seufzen, Ächzen; Murren *n*; *to ~ down (Redner)* durch Gemurmel nicht zu Wort kommen lassen; *to ~ for* jammern nach.

groat [grout] **1.** *hist* Groschen *m*; **2.** *pl* (Hafer-)Grütze *f*.

grocer ['grousə] Kolonial-, Materialwaren-, Spezereihändler; *fam* Kaufmann *m*; **~'s shop** Kolonialwaren-, Spezereihandlung *f*; **~y** ['-ri] *Am* Kolonialwarenhandel *m*, *(~~ store)* -handlung *f*; Lebensmittelgeschäft *n*; *pl* Lebensmittel *n pl*, Kolonialwaren *f pl*.

groceteria [grousi'tiəriə] *Am* Selbstbedienungsgeschäft *n*.

grog [grɔg] Grog; Schnaps *m*; **~gery** ['-əri] *Am* = *~shop*; **~giness** ['-inis] Schwips *m*; Benommenheit; Schwäche *f*; **~gy** ['-i] benommen, schwindlig, (sch)wankend, schwach; *sport* groggy; **~-shop** Gastwirtschaft, *fam* Kneipe *f*.

groin [grɔin] *s anat* Leiste(ngegend) *f*; *arch* Grat *m*; Gewölberippe *f*; *tr (Gewölbe)* mit Rippen versehen; *~ed vault* Kreuzgewölbe *n*.

groom [gru:m] *s* Stallbursche, Reitknecht; Hofbeamte(r); Bräutigam; Jungverheiratete(r) *m*; *tr (Pferd)* besorgen, pflegen; *(Menschen, Frisur, Kleidung)* pflegen; vorbereiten, schulen, heranziehen (*for* für); *well, badly ~ed* gut, schlecht gepflegt; **~sman** ['-zmən] Brautführer *m*.

groov|e [gru:v] *s* Furche, Rille *(a. der Schallplatte)*, Nut, Rinne; Tonspur *f*;

fig eingefahrene(s) Geleise, Schema F *n*, Schablone, Routine, Gewohnheit *f*; *pl (Gewehrlauf)* Züge *m pl*; *tr* auskehlen, mit Rillen versehen, riefeln, nuten; kannelieren; *in the ~~* glatt, mühelos; wie am Schnürchen; vernünftig; in Höchstform; *to get into a ~~ (fig)* in e-e Gewohnheit verfallen; **~y** ['-i] engstirnig; *Am sl* ausgezeichnet.

grope [group] *itr (to ~ about)* (herum-) tappen; suchen *a. fig* (*for* nach); *itr tr* (s-n Weg) tasten; *to ~ in the dark* im Dunkeln tappen *a. fig*; *to ~ o.'s way* tastend den Weg suchen.

grosbeak ['grousbi:k] *orn* Kernbeißer *m*.

gross [grous] *a* dick, fett, massig, korpulent; dicht, dick; schwer(fällig), plump; *(Sinne)* stumpf; grob, rauh, roh, unfein, unzart; gewöhnlich, vulgär, gemein, anstößig, unanständig; *(Fehler)* schwer, grob; *(Essen)* unappetitlich, unsauber, fettig; *(Pflanzenwuchs)* üppig; *com* vollständig, gesamt, Gesamt-; brutto, Brutto-; *s pl* ~ Gros *n*, 12 Dutzend; *s pl ~es* Masse, Gesamtmenge *f*, -betrag *m*; *in (the) ~* im ganzen, im großen, in Bausch u. Bogen, brutto; **~ amount** Gesamtbetrag *m*; **~ earnings** *pl*, **income, receipts** *pl* Bruttoverdienst *m*, -einkommen *n*, -einnahme *f*; **~ feeder** unappetitliche(r) Esser *m*; **~ly** ['-li] *adv* sehr, stark, schwer; **~ness** ['-nis] Korpulenz; Dichte; Plumpheit; Grobheit, Roheit; Gemeinheit, Unanständigkeit *f*; **~ price** Bruttopreis *m*; **~ proceeds, produce** Rohertrag *m*; **~ ton** Bruttoregistertonne *f* (= *2240 pounds)*; **~ weight** Bruttogewicht *n*.

grot [grɔ:t] *poet* Grotte *f*.

grotesque [gro(u)'tesk] *a* grotesk, bizarr, phantastisch; komisch, lächerlich; *s das* Groteske; Groteske *f a. typ*; **~ness** [-nis] *das* Groteske.

grotto ['grɔtou] *pl -o(e)s* Grotte *f*.

grouch [grautʃ] *itr fam* meckern, nörgeln, brummen, murren; *s Am* Mekkerer, Nörgler *m*; Brummigkeit *f*, mürrische(s) Wesen *n*; **~y** ['-i] *fam* meckerig, brummig, mürrisch.

ground [graund] **1.** *s* Grund, Boden; Meeresboden *m*; Erdoberfläche *f*, (Erd-) Boden *m*, Erde *f*, Land *n*; Grund und Boden; Platz *m*; (Jagd-)Gebiet *n*; (Fisch-)Gründe *m pl*; Gebiet *a. fig*; *fig* Thema *n a. mus*; *(Kunst)* Untergrund *m*, Grundierung *f*; Hinter-, Untergrund *m*; *fig* Grundlage, Basis *f*; (Beweg-)Grund *m* (*for* für, zu), Motiv *n*, Ursache, Veranlassung *f*, Anlaß *m*; *el* Erdung *f*; *pl* Grundstück; Gelände *n* um ein Haus, Anlagen *f pl*, Gärten *m pl*; *chem* Niederschlag, (Boden-)Satz; (Rechts-)Grund *m*; Begründung; Grundlage *f*; Anfangsgründe *m pl*; **2.** *a* Grund-, Boden-; **3.** *tr* auf den Boden legen, setzen, stellen; den Boden berühren lassen; *(Schiff)* auf Grund auflaufen lassen; *aero* am Aufsteigen hindern; *(Pilot)* sperren; *el* erden; *(Kunst)* unterlegen, grundieren; *fig* begründen; gründen, basieren (*on* auf); den Anfangsunterricht erteilen, die Grundlagen beibringen (*s.o.* jdm; *in* in); **4.** *itr* zu Boden, auf den Boden, hinfallen; *(Schiff)* auflaufen; **5.** *above ~* am Leben; *below ~* unter der Erde, tot; *down to the ~ (fam)* voll und ganz, durchaus, in jeder Weise; *from the ~ up* von Grund auf, durch und durch; vollständig, -kommen *adv*; *on the ~ of* auf Grund *gen*, wegen; *on o.'s own ~* daheim, zu Hause *a. fig*, in gewohnter Umgebung; *on firm ~ (fig)* auf festem Boden; *under ~ (min)* unter Tag; **6.** *to be on common ~ (fig)* auf gleichem Boden stehen; *to be forbidden ~ (fig)* tabu sein; *to be well ~ed in* gute Vorkenntnisse haben in; *to break ~* den Boden bearbeiten; *arch* mit dem Bau beginnen; *fig* den Anfang machen; *to break fresh ~* Neuland gewinnen *a. fig*; *to cover (much) ~* sich (weit) erstrecken; e-e (große) Strecke zurücklegen: (gut) vorankommen, (gute) Fortschritte machen; viel umfassen, weitreichend sein; *to cut the ~ from under s.o.'s feet (fig)* jdm den Boden unter den Füßen wegziehen; *to fall to the ~ (fig)* versagen, scheitern; *allg* hinfallen; *to gain ~* Boden gewinnen; sich verbreiten, um sich greifen; *to give ~* nachgeben, weichen; *to hold, to keep, to stand o.'s ~* s-n Platz, sich behaupten; s-n Mann stellen; *to lose ~* an Boden verlieren; *to run into the ~ (Am fam)* übertreiben *itr*; *on what ~s?* aus welchen Gründen? **7.** *coffee-~s (pl)* Kaffeesatz *m*; *fishing-~s (pl)* Fischgründe *m pl*; *~ for divorce* Scheidungsgrund *m*; *~ for suspicion* Verdachtsmoment *m*; **~ attack** *aero* Tiefangriff *m*; *~ ~ aircraft* Schlachtflugzeug *n*; **~ bass** *mus* Grundbaß *m*; **~-colo(u)r** Grundfarbe *f*, -anstrich *m*; **~-connexion** *radio* Erdung *f*; **~ cover** Bodenwuchs *m*, -bedeckung *f*; **~ crew** *Am*, **~ staff** *Br aero* Bodenpersonal *n*; **~ defence** Bodenabwehr *f*; **~ elevation** Bodenerhebung *f*; **~ floor** Erdgeschoß *n*; *to get in on the ~~ (fig fam)* gleich zu Beginn einsteigen; **~ fog** Bodennebel *m*; **~ frost** Bodenfrost *m*; **~ glass** Milchglas *n*; Mattscheibe *f*; **~ hog** amerik. Waldmurmeltier *n*; *G~~ day (Am)* Lichtmeß *n*; **~-ice** Grundeis *n*; **~ing** ['-iŋ] Grundkenntnisse *f pl*; *el* Erden *n*; Unterbau *m*, Fundament *n*; **~ ivy** *bot* Gundermann *m*; **~ keeper** *Am sport* Platzwart *m*; **~ landlord** Grundeigentümer *m*; **~less** ['-lis] grundlos, unbegründet, ungerechtfertigt; **~lessness** ['-lisnis] Grundlosigkeit *f*; **~ level(l)ing** Planierung *f*; **~-line** *math* Grundlinie *f*; *pl (fig)* Grundlinien *f pl*; **~ling** ['-liŋ] Gründling *m (Fisch)*; geschmacklose Person *f*; **~ marking** *aero* Bodenmarkierung *f*; **~-nut, -pea** Erdnuß *f*; **~ panel** Fliegertuch *n*; **~ pine** *bot* Bärlapp *m*; **~-plan** Grundriß; *fig* Grundplan, Entwurf *m*; **~-rent** *fin* Grundrente *f*; **~sel** ['graunsl] *bot* Kreuzkraut, *bes. (common ~~)* Gold-, Grindkraut *n*; (Boden-)Schwelle *f*; **~(s)man** ['-(z)mən] (Sportplatz-)Wärter *m*; **~-squirrel** *zoo* Erdhörnchen *n*; **~-station** *aero* Bodenstation *f*; **~ strafing** *aero* Tiefangriff *m*; **~ survey** Geländevermessung *f*; **~-swell** Dünung; *fig* große Erregung *f*; **~ visibility** Bodensicht *f*; **~-water** Grundwasser *n*; *~~ level* Grundwasserspiegel *m*; **~ wave** *tele* Bodenwelle *f*; **~ wind** Bodenwind *m*; **~-wire** *el radio* Erdleitung *f*, -kabel *n*; **~work** Fundament *n a. fig*; Untergrund; *rail* Unterbau *m*; *fig* Grundlage, Basis *f*.

group [gru:p] *s* Gruppe *f a. zoo bot chem*; *aero Br* Geschwader *n*, *Am* Gruppe *f*; *com* Konsortium *n*; *parl* Fraktion *f*; *tr itr* (sich) gruppieren; *to divide into ~s* in Gruppen einteilen; **~-captain** *Br* Oberst *m* der Luftwaffe; **~-commander** *Am* Gruppenkommandeur *m*; **~ing** ['-iŋ] (Ein-)Gruppierung, (An-) Ordnung *f*.

grouse [graus] **1.** *s pl ~ (Red G~)* Birk-, Moorhuhn *n*; *Great G~*, *Wood G~* Auerhahn *m*; *White G~* Schneehuhn *n*; **2.** *itr sl* meckern (*about* über), nörgeln, murren; *s pl ~s* Meckerei, Nörgelei *f*; **~r** ['-ə] Meckerer, Nörgler *m*.

grout [graut] **1.** *s* dünne(r) Mörtel *(zum Verstreichen)*; (Ver-)Putz *m*; Vergußmasse *f*; *tr* verstreichen; verputzen; **2.** *itr (Schwein)* in der Erde wühlen; *tr (die Erde)* aufwühlen; **3.** *pl* Hefe *f*; Schrot *m*.

grove [grouv] Wäldchen, Gehölz *n*.

grovel ['grɔvl] *itr* liegen (*at s.o.'s feet* jdm zu Füßen; *before s.o.* vor jdm); kriechen *a. fig* (*in the dirt, dust* im Staube); **~ler** ['-ə] Kriecher *m*; **~ling** ['-iŋ] *a* kriechend; *fig* kriecherisch.

grow [grou] *irr grew* [gru:], *grown* [groun] *itr* wachsen *a. fig*; *fig* zunehmen, sich entwickeln, sich ausdehnen; sich vergrößern; sich vermehren; werden (*into* zu); dahin kommen (*to do* zu tun); erwachsen (*from* aus); *tr* züchten, (an)bauen; *(Bart)* sich wachsen lassen; entwickeln; *to ~ into fashion* Mode werden, in Mode kommen; *to ~ into a habit* zur Gewohnheit werden; *to ~ on s.o.* jdm ans Herz wachsen; jdm vertraut werden; bei jdm immer mehr Einfluß gewinnen, Eindruck machen; *to ~ out of s.th.* aus etw *(Kleidung)* herauswachsen; *fig* aus etw entstehen; von etw herrühren; *to ~ out of fashion, use* aus der Mode, aus dem Gebrauch kommen; *to ~* **down(wards)** zurückgehen, abnehmen; *to ~* **together** zs.wachsen; *to ~* **up** auf-, heranwachsen; *fig* sich entwickeln; *to ~* **worse** sich verschlimmern; **~er** ['-ə] *meist in Zssgen* Züchter; Bauer; Erzeuger *m*; **~ing** ['-iŋ] *a* (heran)wachsend; *s* Züchten, Anbauen *n*; *~~ pains (pl)* Wachstumsschwierigkeiten *f pl*; *fig* Kinderkrankheiten *f pl*.

growl [graul] *s* Brummen; *(Hund)* Knurren; *(Donner)* Rollen *n*; *Am sl* Spickzettel *m*; *itr* knurren; brummen, murren; *(Donner)* grollen; *fam* mekkern; *tr (to ~ out)* murren über; hervorstoßen; *to ~ at s.o. (Hund)* jdn anknurren; **~er** ['-ə] knurrige(r) Hund; *(Mensch)* Brummbär; *Am* Bierkrug *m*, -kanne *f*; *Am* (Bier-)Fäßchen, -tönnchen *n*; *Br obs* Droscke *f*: *~~ rushing (Am sl)* Trinkgelage *n*.

grown [groun] *a* herangewachsen, voll entwickelt, reif; bewachsen (*with* mit); *full-~* voll ausgewachsen; **~-up** *a* erwachsen; *s* Erwachsene(r *m*) *f*.

growth [grouθ] Wachstum; Heranwachsen *n*; Entwicklung *a. fig*; Züchtung, Erzeugung; Ernte; *fig* Zunahme *f*, Zuwachs (*in* an); Wuchs *m*; Ausdehnung *f*; *med* Tumor *m*, Gewächs *n*; *(Wein)* Sorte *f*, Gewächs *n*; *~ of o.'s own* selbstgezogen; *~ of grass* Graswuchs *m*.

groyne, *Am* **groin** [grɔin] *mar* Buhne *f*.

grub [grʌb] *itr* graben; (herum)wühlen, stöbern; sich plagen, *fam* sich abrackern, schuften; *tr* ausgraben, -roden; *(Gelände)* roden; *(Feld)* jäten; *sl* futtern, fressen; *s* Larve, Made *f*, *fam* Wurm; (schwer) Schuftende(r); *sl* Fraß *m*, Futter; *sl fig* Ferkel *n*; *to ~ about* herumwühlen; *to ~ out, up* ausgraben; **~ber** ['-ə] Grabende(r) *m*; Scharegge, Jätehacke *f*; **~by** ['-i] voller Maden; schmutzig, dreckig; unsauber, schlampig.

grudg|e [grʌdʒ] *tr* neiden, mißgönnen (*s.o. s.th.* jdm etw), beneiden (*s.o. s.th.* jdn um etw); nur ungern, mit Widerwillen geben; *s* Groll; Neid; böse(r) Wille *m*; *not to ~~ s.o. s.th.* jdm etw gönnen; *to bear, to owe s.o. a ~~, to hold, to have a ~~ against s.o.* etw gegen jdn haben; jdm etw nachtragen; *to ~~ the time* sich die Zeit nicht gönnen; **~er** ['-ə] Neidhammel *m*; **~ingly** ['-iŋli] *adv* (nur) ungern, widerwillig.

gruel ['gruəl] Haferschleim *m*, Schleim-, Mehlsuppe; *sl* Tracht *f* Prügel; *to* *have, to get o.'s ~ (fam)* sein Fett, s-e Strafe (weg)haben; eins aufs Dach kriegen; **~ling** ['-iŋ] *a* zermürbend, aufreibend; entnervend, erschöpfend; *s* Qual; *sl* Tracht *f* Prügel.

gruesome ['gru:səm] grausig, schauerlich, schaurig.

gruff [grʌf] bärbeißig, unfreundlich, schroff; grob, barsch; *(Stimme)* rauh; **~ness** ['-nis] Bärbeißigkeit; Grobheit *f*.

grumbl|e ['grʌmbl] *itr* brummen; nörgeln, murren (*at, about, over* über); *(Donner)* (g)rollen; *tr* murrend sagen; *s* Murren; Grollen; Nörgeln *n*; **~er** ['-ə] Nörgler; Brummbär *m*; **~y** ['-i] brummend; brummig, mürrisch.

grump|iness ['grʌmpinis] mürrische(s) Wesen *n*, Reizbarkeit *f*; **~y** ['-i] verdrießlich, mürrisch, reizbar.

grunt [grʌnt] *itr (Schwein)* grunzen; *(Mensch)* stöhnen; *tr (to ~ out)* brummend sagen; *s* Grunzen; Stöhnen *n*; *zoo* Knurrhahn *m*; *Am sl* Rechnung, Unterhaltung *f*, Sport, Ringkampf; *Am rail* Lokführer; *Am tele mil* Helfer *m* beim Verlegen von Leitungen; **~er** ['-ə] Schwein *n*; *fig* Brummbär; *sport* Ringkämpfer *m*.

gryphon ['grifən] *s. griffin.*

guarant|ee [gærən'ti:] *s* Garantie; Bürgschaft; Sicherheit, Gewähr(leistung) *f*; *allg* Beweis *m*, Sicherheit, *fam* Garantie *f*; Garant; Bürge; Gewährsmann *m*; *tr* garantieren, gewährleisten, bürgen, Bürgschaft leisten für, ein-, *fam* g(e)radestehen für; dafür bürgen (*that* daß); *he can't ~~ that* dafür kann er nicht garantieren; *conditional ~~* Ausfallbürgschaft *f*; *joint ~~* Mitgarant, -bürge *m*; *~~ of a bill of exchange* Wechselbürgschaft *f*, -bürge *m*; **~eed** [-d] *a* garantiert; gesichert; **~or** [-'tɔ:] Garant; Bürge *m*; *to stand as ~~ for s.o.* für jdn Bürgschaft leisten; **~y** ['gærənti] *jur* Garantie; Kaution, Bürgschaft; Gewähr, Sicherheit *f*.

guard [gɑ:d] *tr* wachen über, bewahren, behüten, beschützen (*from, against* vor); *(Gefangene)* bewachen; im Zaum halten; überwachen, kontrollieren; *tech* schützen; *itr* Wache halten; Vorsichtsmaßnahmen treffen (*against* gegen); auf der Hut sein; sich hüten (*against* vor); Vorkehrungen treffen, sich absichern, sich vorsehen (*against* gegen); *s* Wache, *obs poet* Wacht; Wachsamkeit, Vorsicht; Abwehrbereitschaft, Verteidigungsstellung; Schutzvorrichtung; Wache, Wachmannschaft *f*; Wachmann, Posten; (Gefangenen-)Wärter, *bes. Am*; *rail* Schaffner, Zugführer, *Am* Bahnwärter *m*; *sport* Auslage, Parade *f*; *(Gewehr)* Abzugsbügel *m*; *the G~s (pl)* das Wachregiment, die Garde *f*; *to be on (off) o.'s ~* (nicht) auf der Hut sein; *to keep under close ~* scharf bewachen; *to lower o.'s ~* in der Wachsamkeit nachlassen; *fig* sich e-e Blöße geben; *to mount, to go on ~* auf Wache ziehen; *to relieve ~* die Wache ablösen; *to stand ~* Posten stehen; **~ commander** Wachhabende(r) *m*; **~ed** ['-id] *a* beschützt, behütet; be-, überwacht; *(Antwort)* vorsichtig; **~-house** Wache *f (Gebäude)*; Arrestlokal *n*; **~-rail** Geländer *n*; Schutzwehr; Sicherheits-, Leitschiene *f*; **~-room** Wachraum *m*, -stube *f*; **~-ship** Wachschiff *n*; **~sman** ['-zmən] Wärter; (National-)Gardist *m*.

guardian ['gɑ:djən] Wächter, Wärter; Vormund; Pfleger *m*; *a* Schutz-; *~ of the poor* Armenpfleger *m*; **~ angel** Schutzengel *m*; **~ship** ['-ʃip] Vormundschaft; Kuratel; Pflegschaft *f*; *fig* Schutz *m*; *to be, to place under ~~* unter Vormundschaft stehen, stellen; *court of ~~* Vormundschaftsgericht *n*.

gubernatorial [gju:bənə'tɔ:riəl] *a* Gouverneurs-.

gudgeon ['gʌdʒən] **1.** *s* Gründling *(Fisch)*; *fig* Gimpel *m*; **2.** *tech* Zapfen, Bolzen *m*.

guerdon ['gə:dən] *poet* Lohn *m*.

guernsey ['gə:nsi] Wolljacke *f*.

guer(r)illa [gə'rilə] *s* Partisan; Heckenschütze *m*; *a* Partisanen-; **~ war (-fare)** Partisanen-, Kleinkrieg *m*.

guess [ges] *tr* (er)raten, vermuten, ahnen; schätzen; *Am fam* annehmen, glauben, meinen, der Ansicht sein, denken; *itr* raten; schätzen (*at s.th.* etw); *s* Vermutung, Mutmaßung *f*; *at a ~, by ~* aufs Geratewohl; schätzungsweise; *to make a ~ at s.th.* über etw Vermutungen äußern; *I ~ (Am fam)* ich glaube; *I ~ so* vermutlich! *have a ~!* rate mal! *I'll give you three ~es (Am)* dreimal darfst du raten; **~-work** Vermutung, Mutmaßung *f*.

guest [gest] *s* Gast; *zoo* Parasit *m*; *a* Gast-, Gäste-; *itr* als Gast mitwirken; *paying ~* Pensionsgast *m*; **~-appearance** Gastspiel *n*; **~-chamber, -room** Gäste-, Fremdenzimmer *n*; **~-house** (Privat-)Pension *f*; **~-night** Gästeabend *m*; **~ rope** *mar* Schleppseil *n*, -trosse *f*.

guff [gʌf] *Am sl* Quatsch, Unsinn *m*.

guffaw [gʌ'fɔ:] *s* schallende(s) Gelächter, *fam* Gewieher *n*; *itr* schallend lachen, *fam* wiehern.

guggle ['gʌgl] *itr* glucksen, gurgeln.

guid|able ['gaidəbl] lenkbar, -sam; **~ance** ['-əns] Lenkung, Leitung, Führung; Anleitung, Richtschnur; Studienberatung; *tech* Führungsschiene *f*; *for s.o.'s ~~* zu jds Orientierung; *under s.o.'s ~~* unter jds Leitung; *vocational ~~* Berufsberatung *f*.

guide [gaid] *s* (Fremden-)Führer; *mil* Flügelmann; *allg* Ratgeber *m*; Vorbild *n*; *(~-book)* Reiseführer *m (Buch)*; Einführung *f*, Leitfaden *(Buch)*; Hinweis; *(~-post)* Wegweiser *m*; *(Lochkarte)* Leitkarte; *tech* Führung *f*; *G~ (Br)* Pfadfinderin *f*; *tr* führen, leiten, lenken; beraten; instruieren, Anweisungen geben (*s.o.* jdm); *tech* (fern)steuern; *epistolary ~* Briefsteller *m*; *railway, (Am) railroad ~* Kursbuch *n*; **~ bar** Führungsschiene *f*; **~d** ['-id] *a tech* geführt, (fern)gelenkt, gesteuert, gerichtet; *to be ~~ by* sich leiten lassen von; *~~ missile* ferngelenkte(s) Geschoß *n*; *~~ tour* Gesellschaftsfahrt, -reise *f*; **~pin** Führungsstift *m*; **~-rail, -way** Lauf-, Führungsschiene *f*; **~-rope** Schlepptau; Leitseil *n*.

guidon ['gaidən] *hist* Fähnlein *n*, Wimpel *m*; Standarte; *Am* Regiments-, Kompaniefahne *f*; *Am* Fahnenträger *m*.

g(u)ild [gild] Gilde, Zunft, Innung *f*; **~hall** Zunft-, Gilde-, Innungshaus; Rathaus *n*; *the G~~* das (Londoner) Rathaus; **~sman** Innungsmitglied *n*.

guilder ['gildə] Gulden *m*.

guile [gail] Arg-, Hinterlist *f*; **~ful** ['-ful] arg-, hinterlistig; **~less** ['-lis] arglos, (frei und) offen; ohne Falsch.

guillotine ['gilətiːn, -'ti:n] *s* Fallbeil *n*, Guillotine; Papierschneidemaschine; Kurbel-, Blechtafelschere; *parl* Befristung *f* der Debatten; *tr* [-'ti:n] mit dem Fallbeil hinrichten; *parl* Debatten abkürzen.

guilt [gilt] Schuld *f*; Verschulden *n*; *to admit o.'s ~* s-e Schuld eingestehen, sich schuldig bekennen, ein Geständnis ablegen; **~iness** ['-inis] Schuld(-haftigkeit) *f*; **~less** ['-lis] schuldlos, unschuldig (*of* an); unerfahren (*of* in); *~~ of* ohne; **~y** ['-i] schuldig, schuldhaft; schuldbeladen; *(Blick)* schuldbewußt; *to plead ~~* sich schuldig bekennen; *to pronounce s.o. ~~ of s.th.* jdn e-r S schuldig sprechen; *the ~~ person* der, die Schuldige.

guinea ['gini] Guinee *f (21 Schilling)*; *Am sl* Italiener *m*; **~-fowl** Perlhuhn *n*; **~-pig** Meerschweinchen; *fig* Versuchskaninchen *n*.

guise [gaiz] Äußere(s), Aussehen *n*; *fig* Deckmantel *m*, Maske *f*, Vorwand *m*; *under, in the ~ of* unter dem Vorwand.

guitar [gi'tɑ:] Gitarre *f*; **~ist** [-rist] Gitarrist, Gitarrespieler *m*.

gulch [gʌlʃ] *Am* Schlucht, Klamm *f*.

gulf [gʌlf] *s* Meerbusen, Golf *m*; Kluft *f*, Abgrund *m a. fig*; *fig* Trennwand *f*; Strudel *m (im Wasser)*; *tr* verschlingen; *the G~ Stream* der Golfstrom.

gull [gʌl] **1.** *(sea-~)* Möwe *f*; **2.** *s fig* Gimpel *m*; *tr* hereinlegen, anführen, betrügen; verleiten (*into* zu); **~ibility** [-i'biliti] Leichtgläubigkeit *f*; **~ible** ['-əbl] leichtgläubig.

gullet ['gʌlit] *anat* Speiseröhre *f*; Schlund *m*, Kehle *f*, Hals *m*; *obs u. Am* Wasserrinne *f*, Kanal *m*.

gully ['gʌli] (tiefe) (Wasser-)Rinne, Schlucht *f*; Wasser-, Abzugsgraben; (Abzugs-)Kanal *m*; **~-drain** Abzugs-, Kanalrohr *n*; **~-hole** Sink-, Abflußloch *n*.

gulp [gʌlp] *tr (to ~ down)* hinunter-, verschlingen; *(Seufzer)* unterdrücken; *(Getränk)* hinunterstürzen; hinunterschlucken; *itr* würgen; *s* Schlingen *n*; (großer) Schluck *m*; *to empty at one ~* in einem Zug leeren.

*

gum [gʌm] **1.** *s* Harz *n*; Kautschuk; Gummibaum *m*; Gummi(lösung *f*), Klebstoff; *Am* Radiergummi; *Am* Kaugummi *m*; *pl Am* Gummi-, Überschuhe *m pl*; *itr* Harz ausscheiden *od* absondern; dick *od* klebrig werden; verharzen; zukleben; *Am sl* schwätzen; *tr* gummieren; mit Gummilösung kleben; ankleben (*to* an); *Am sl* betrügen, ruinieren, verderben; *to ~ down, together, up* an- *od* fest-, zs.-, aufkleben; *to ~ up the works (fam)* das Spiel, den Spaß, die Arbeit vermasseln; *by ~! (vulg)* verflixt! *chewing ~* Kaugummi *m*; **~ arabic** Gummiarabikum *n*; **~-beater** *Am* Schwätzer *m*; **~drop** *Am* Geleebonbon *m* od *n*; **~ elastic** Kautschuk *m*, Gummi *m* od *n*; **~mer** ['-ə] *Am sl* alte(r), gebrechliche(r) Mann *m*; **~mous** ['-əs] gummiartig; **~my** ['-i] gummiartig; klebrig; gummiert; kautschuk-, harzhaltig; *sl* zahnlos; *Am sl* minderwertig, widerlich, sentimental; **~shoe** ['-ʃu:] *s* Gummi-, Überschuh; *Am* Turnschuh; *Am sl (a. ~-foot)* Kriminalbeamte(r); Detektiv; Schleicher *m*; *attr* Geheim-; *itr Am sl* (herum)schleichen; **~-tree** Gummibaum *m*; *to be up a ~~ (sl)* in der Patsche sitzen, in der Klemme sein; **2.** Zahnfleisch *n*; **~boil** ['-bɔil] Zahngeschwür *n*.

gumbo ['gʌmbou] *Am bot* Rosenpappel *f*; Okragemüse *n (die unreifen Samenkapseln)*; *(dicke)* Okrasuppe *f*; *Am* Lehmboden; *Am* französische(r) Dialekt *m* von Louisiana u. Westindien.

gumption ['gʌmpʃən] *fam* Pfiffigkeit *f*, Grips, Unternehmungsgeist *m*.

gun [gʌn] *s* Kanone *f*, Geschütz; Maschinengewehr; Gewehr *n*, Flinte, Büchse; *Am fam* Pistole *f*, Revolver; *Am mot sl* Gashebel; *Am sl* Dieb;

Am sl scharfer Blick; Signal-, Salutschuß; Schütze *m*; *aero* Drosselklappe *f*; *itr* auf die Jagd gehen; *mot* Gas geben; *tr Am fam* abknallen; *Am sl tech* auf Hochtour bringen; scharf blicken nach; *(e-e Aufnahme)* machen; *to blow great ~s* stürmen; *to give s.th. the ~ (Am sl)* etw in Schwung, auf Hochtour bringen; *to go great ~s (Am sl)* mit Hochdruck arbeiten; *to beat, to jump the ~* voreilig sein; *to spike s.o.'s ~s (fig)* jdn mattsetzen; *to stand, to stick to o.'s ~s* nicht nachgeben, durchhalten; bei der Stange bleiben; *he's ~ning for you* er hat dich auf dem Korn; *great, big ~ (sl)* hohe(s) Tier *n*; *son of a ~ (pej)* Strolch *m*; *sure as a ~* bombensicher; **~-barrel** Gewehrlauf *m*; Geschützrohr *n*; **~boat** Kanonenboot *n*; **~-carriage** Lafette *f*; **~-cotton** Schießbaumwolle *f*; **~ dog** Jagdhund *m*; **~fight** *Am* (Revolver-)Schießerei *f*; **~-fire** Geschütz-, Artilleriefeuer *n*; **~-flash** Mündungsfeuer *n*; **~-layer** Richtkanonier *m*; **~-licence** Waffenschein *m*; **~-lock** (Gewehr-)Schloß *n*; **~man** ['-mən] *Am* bewaffnete(r) Bandit *m*; **~nage** ['-idʒ] Bestückung *f*; **~ner** ['-ə] Kanonier; *Am* Geschützführer; *aero* Bordschütze *m*; *~~'s cockpit (aero)* MG-Kanzel *f*; **~nery** ['-əri] Geschütze *n pl*; Fabrikation u. Bedienung *f* der Geschütze; *attr* Geschütz-; **~ pointer** Richtkanonier *m*; **~powder** Schießpulver *n*; **~-room** *Br mar* Fähnrichsmesse *f*; **~-runner** Waffenschmuggler *m*; **~-running** Waffenschmuggel *m*; **~shot** Schuß(weite *f*) *m*; *(~~ wound)* Schußwunde *f*; *within, out of ~~* in, außer Schußweite; **~smith** Büchsenmacher *m*; **~stock** (Gewehr-)Schaft *m*; **~-turret** Geschützturm *m*; **~wale** ['-weil] *mar* Schandeckel *m*, Dollbord *n*.

*

gunk [gʌŋk] *Am sl* Schmutz *m*, ölige Flüssigkeit; Schminke *f*.

gunsel, gonsel ['gʌnsl] *Am sl* unerfahrene(r) junge(r) Mann *m*.

gup [gʌp] *fam* Geschwätz *n*; Unsinn *m*.

gurgitation [gə:dʒi'teiʃən] Sprudeln *n*.

gurgle ['gə:gl] *itr* glucksen, gurgeln, murmeln; *tr* hervorsprudeln.

gush [gʌʃ] *itr* herausspritzen, -sprudeln, sich ergießen (*from* aus); überfließen (*with* von); *fig* schwärmen (*over* von); *s* Guß; *fig* Erguß *m*, Schwärmerei *f*; **~er** ['-ə] (sprudelnde) Ölquelle *f*; *fig* Schwärmer *m*; **~ing** ['-iŋ] sprudelnd; *fig* schwärmerisch; überspannt, überschwenglich; **~y** ['-i] schwärmerisch.

gusset ['gʌsit] Zwickel *m*; Eckblech *n*, -beschlag *m*; Versteifungsplatte *f*.

gust [gʌst] Windstoß *m*, Bö *f*; Schauer, Schwall *m*; *(Rauch)* Wolke *f*; Ausbruch *m*; **~y** ['-i] stürmisch.

gustat|ion [gʌs'teiʃən] Geschmack(ssinn) *m*; **~ory** ['-təri] *a physiol* Geschmacks-.

gusto ['gʌstou] *fig* Geschmack; Genuß *m*; besondere Vorliebe *f* (*for* für); Vergnügen *n*; *with ~* mit Schwung.

*

gut [gʌt] *s* Darm *m*; Darmsaite *f*; Catgut; enge(r) Durchlaß, -gang; *Am sl* Magen *m*; *Am (Schule)* leichte Übung *f*; *pl fam* Gedärm, Eingeweide *n*; *pl mit sing* Mumm, Mut *m*, Ausdauer, Purre, Kraft *f*, Mark *n*; *mit pl* Mumm *m*; Bestandteile *m pl* im Innern e-r Maschine; *tr* ausweiden, -nehmen; ausplündern; exzerpieren; im Innern völlig zerstören; *to be ~ted by fire* ausgebrannt sein; *it has no ~s in it* das hat weder Saft noch Kraft; *blind ~* Blinddarm *m*; **~sy** ['-si] *Am sl* mutig.

gutta-percha ['gʌtə'pə:tʃə] Guttapercha *f* od *n*.

gutter ['gʌtə] *s* Dachrinne *f*; Rinnstein *m*, Gosse *f* a. *fig*; *fig* Elend *n*, Armut; *allg* Rinne, Rille *f*; *typ* Bundsteg *m*; *tr* mit (Dach-)Rinnen *od* Gossen versehen; *tech* riefen; *itr* rinnen; triefen; *(Kerze)* tropfen; *of the ~* vulgär, ordinär; *to rise from the ~* von nichts herkommen; *to take out of the ~ (fig)* aus der Gosse auflesen; **~-child, -snipe** Straßenjunge *m*; **~-man** Straßenverkäufer *m*; **~ press** Skandalpresse *f*; **~ tile** Hohlziegel *m*.

guttural ['gʌtərəl] *a* guttural, Kehl-; *s* Kehllaut, Guttural *m*.

guy [gai] **1.** *mar* Backstag *m*; Geitau *n*; Ankerkette *f*; *(~-rope)* Haltetau *n*, Halterung; Zeltleine *f*; **~-wire** *aero* Spanndraht *m*; **2.** *s* Vogelscheuche *f fig*; *Am fam* Kerl, Bursche *m*; *tr fam* lächerlich machen, necken, foppen, frotzeln; *to do a ~ (sl)* verduften, abhauen.

guzzle ['gʌzl] *itr tr* saufen; fressen; *tr (to ~ away)* verprassen; *s Am sl* Kehle *f*; **~-shop** *Am sl* (Bier-)Lokal *n*.

gym [dʒim] *fam (= gymnasium)* Turnhalle *f*; *(= gymnastics)* Turnen *n*, Turnstunde *f*; **~ shoes** *pl* Turnschuhe *m pl*; **~ shorts** *pl* Turnhose *f*

gymkhana [dʒim'kɑ:nə] Sportplatz *m*, Kampfbahn *f*, Stadion *n*; Sportveranstaltung *f*, -wettkampf *m*.

gymn|asium [dʒim'neizjəm] *pl a. -ia* [-jə] Turnhalle *f*; Sportplatz *m*; Arena *f*; **~ast** ['dʒimnæst] Turner; (Leicht-)Athlet *m*; **~astic(al)** [dʒim'næstik(əl)] *a* turnerisch, (leicht)athletisch, gymnastisch; Turn-; **~astics** *pl meist mit sing* Turnen *n*, Leibesübungen *f pl*.

gymnospermous [dʒimnə'spə:məs] *bot* nacktsamig.

gyn(a)ecolog|ic(al) [gainikə'lədʒik(əl), *Am a.* dʒai-] gynäkologisch; **~ist** [gaini'kələdʒist] Gynäkologe, Frauenarzt (u. Geburtshelfer) *m*; **~y** [gaini'kələdʒi] Frauenheilkunde, Gynäkologie *f*.

gyp [dʒip] **1.** *(in Cambridge u. Durham)* Studentendiener *m*; **2.** *s Am sl* Schwindel *m*, Gaunerei *f*; Schwindler, Gauner, Ganove; *Br fam* heftige(r) Schmerz *m*; *tr Am sl* beschwindeln, anführen, begaunern, beganeffen, abstauben; *itr* schwindeln; **~-joint** *Am sl* üble(s) Lokal *n*, Kaschemme *f*; **~o** *Am sl* Gelegenheitsarbeiter *m*; **3.**: *to give s.o. ~ (sl)* jdm Saures geben, jdn fertigmachen.

gyps|eous ['dʒipsiəs] gipsartig, -haltig, Gips-; **~um** ['dʒipsəm] Gips *m*.

gypsy *s. gipsy*.

gyrat|e [dʒaiə'reit] *itr* rotieren, kreise(l)n, sich drehen, wirbeln (*round* um); *a* ['-rit] spiralig, Ringe bildend; **~ion** [-'reiʃən] Rotation, Kreisbewegung *f*; Wirbel *m*; **~ory** ['dʒaiərətəri] rotierend, sich im Kreise drehend, kreiselnd, wirbelnd; Kreis-, Dreh-; *~~ system (of traffic)* Kreisverkehr.

gyro ['dʒaiərou] *pl -s* Kreisel *m*; *fam (= autogiro) aero* Tragschrauber *m*, Drehflügelflugzeug *n*; = *~compass*; = *~scope*; **~compass** ['-rəkʌmpəs] Kreiselkompaß *m*; **~graph** ['-grɑ:f] *tech* Umdrehungszähler *m*; **~pilot** ['-rəpailət] *aero* Selbststeuergerät *n*; **~plane** ['-rəplein] *aero* Tragschrauber *m*; **~scope** ['-rəskoup, 'gai-] Gyroskop *n*; **~(scopic) stabilizer** [-'skɔpik] *mar aero* Lagekreisel *m*; **~stat** ['-rəstæt] Gyrostat, Kreisel(vorrichtung *f*) *m*; **~-wheel** *sport* Rhönrad *n*.

gyve [dʒaiv] *s meist pl obs poet* Hand-, Fußfesseln *f pl*; *tr* die Hände *od* Füße fesseln (*s.o.* jdm).

H

H, h [eitʃ] *pl ~'s* ['-iz] H, h *n*; *to drop o.'s ~s* das H (im Anlaut) nicht sprechen; *fig* ungebildet sein; **~-bomb** Wasserstoffbombe *f*.

ha [hɑ:] *interj* ha! ah! *(zweifelnd)* wie?

habeas corpus ['heibjəs'kɔ:pəs] *(writ of ~) jur* Vorführungsbefehl *m*.

haberdasher ['hæbədæʃə] Kurzwarenhändler; *Am* Inhaber *m* e-s Herrenartikelgeschäfts; **~y** ['-ri] Kurzwaren(-handlung *f*) *f pl*; *Am* Herrenartikel (-geschäft *n*) *m pl*.

habiliments [hə'bilimənts] *pl* (Fest-, Amts-)Kleidung *f*.

habit ['hæbit] *s* (körperliche *od* geistige) Beschaffenheit *f*, Habitus *a. bot*; Zustand *m*, Anlage, Veranlagung, Disposition; Lebensweise *f a. zoo*, Verhalten(sweise *f*) *n*; Angewohnheit, Gewohnheit(ssache), Gewöhnung *f*; Kleid, Gewand, Kostüm *n*; (kirchliche) Tracht *f*; *tr* (an)kleiden; *from, out of ~* aus Gewohnheit; *to be in the ~* die Gewohnheit haben, pflegen (*of doing s.th.* etw zu tun); *to fall, to get into the ~* die Gewohnheit annehmen; sich angewöhnen (*of doing s.th.* etw zu tun); *to break o.s. of a ~* sich etwas abgewöhnen; *~ of mind* geistige Verfassung *f*; **~able** ['-əbl] *(Haus)* bewohnbar; **~ant** ['-ənt] Be-, Einwohner *m*; *a.* [abitɑ̃] *(Louisiana u. Kanada)* Farmer *m* französischer Abstammung; **~at** ['hæbitæt] *biol* Standort *m*, Vorkommen, Verbreitungsgebiet *n*; *fig* Heimat *f*; **~ation** [hæbi'teiʃən] (Be-)Wohnen *n*; Wohnung, Wohnstätte *f*; *fit for ~~* bewohnbar; **~ual** [hə'bitjuəl] gewohnt, gewöhnlich, üblich; Gewohnheits-; *~~ criminal, drunkard* Gewohnheitsverbrecher; -trinker *m*; **~ually** *adv* gewöhnlich, gewohnheitsmäßig; **~uate** [hə'bitjueit] *tr* gewöhnen (*to* an; *to do; doing* daran, zu tun); *Am fam* häufig besuchen; **~ude** ['hæbitju:d] Neigung, Gewohnheit *f*; Brauch *m*; **~ué** [hə'bitjuei] Stammgast *m*.

hachures [hæ'ʃjuə] *pl* Schraffierung *f*.

hacienda [hæsi'endə] große(s) (Bauern-)Gut *n*, Farm *f*.

hack [hæk] **1.** *tr* (zer)hacken (*to pieces* in Stücke); einkerben; *agr* hacken; *(Fußball)* vors Schienbein treten (*s.o.* jdm); *itr* hacken (*at* nach); trocken husten; *s* Hacke; Kerbe *f*, Hieb (-wunde *f*); Tritt *m* vors Schienbein; *~ing cough* trockene(r) Husten *m*; **~saw** Metallsäge *f*; **2.** *s* Miet-, Arbeitspferd *n*; Schindmähre *f*; Gelegenheitsarbeiter; *(~ writer)* Lohnschreiber, Skribent, Schreiberling; *Am* Mietwagen *m*, -kutsche, Droschke *f*; Taxi *n*; *Am (~man)* Droschkenkutscher *m*; *a* Miet-; abgedroschen, abgenutzt; *itr* über Land reiten; als Lohnschreiber arbeiten; *Am* ein Taxi fahren; **~er** ['-ə] *Am* Taxifahrer *m*.

hackle ['hækl] **1.** *s* (Flachs-)Hechel; Nackenfeder *(des Haushahns u. anderer Vögel)*; *(~ fly)* künstliche Fliege *f (zum Angeln)*; *tr (Flachs)* hecheln; *with his ~s up* mit gesträubten Federn *od* Haaren; *fig* wütend, kampfbereit; *to get s.o.'s ~s up* jdn verärgern; **2.** *tr* zerhacken, zerstückeln.

hackney ['hækni] *s* Reit-, Kutschpferd *n*; Mietwagen; Tagelöhner *m*; *tr* endlos wiederholen, wiederkäuen; **~-carriage, -coach** Mietwagen *m*, -kutsche *f*; **~ed** ['-d] *a* abgedroschen.

haddock ['hædək] *pl ~* Schellfisch *m*.

h(a)em|al ['hi:məl] *a* Blut-; **~atite** ['hemətait] *min* Roteisenstein *m*, -erz *n*; **~oglobin** [hi:mo(u)'gloubin] Hämoglobin *n*, rote(r) Blutfarbstoff *m*; **~ophilia** [hi:mo(u)'filiə] Bluterkrankheit *f*; **~orrhage** ['hemərid͡ʒ] *s* (schwere) Blutung *f*; Blutsturz *m*; *itr* stark bluten; **~orrhoids** ['hemərɔidz] *pl med* Hämorrhoiden *f pl*.

haft [hɑ:ft] Griff *m*, Heft *n*, Stiel *m*.

hag [hæg] Hexe *f*; häßliche(s), böse(s) alte(s) Weib *n*; **~-ridden** *a* verängstigt; an Alpdrücken leidend.

haggard ['hægəd] verstört; übernächtigt; verhärmt; hohläugig, -wangig; hager; *(Falke)* ungezähmt.

haggle ['hægl] *itr* sich ausea.setzen, streiten; feilschen (*about, for, over* über, um); *tr* (zer)hacken, zerstückeln.

hagi|ography [hægi'ɔgrəfi] Heiligengeschichte *f*; **~ology** [hægi'ɔləd͡ʒi] Heiligenliteratur *f*.

ha-ha ['hɑ(:)hɑ:] versenkte(r) Grenzzaun *m*; verdeckte(r) Graben *m*.

hail [heil] **1.** *s* Hagel *m a. fig* (*of* von); *itr* hageln; *tr fig (to ~ down)* hageln, niederprasseln, -gehen (lassen) (*on, upon* auf); **~-insurance** Hagelversicherung *f*; **~ stone** Hagelkorn *n*; **~ storm** Hagelschauer *m*, -wetter *n*; **2.** *tr* zujubeln (*s.o.* jdm); begrüßen (*as winner* als Sieger); zurufen (*s.o.* jdm), anrufen; loben, preisen; *itr mar* ein Signal geben; *(Schiff, fam a. Mensch)* kommen, (her)stammen (*from* aus, von); *s* Gruß, An-, Zuruf *m*; *interj lit poet* Heil! *within ~* in Rufweite; *to be ~ fellow (wellmet) (with everybody)* mit jedem gut Freund sein.

hair [hɛə] *s* (einzelnes) Haar *n a. bot*; *das* (Kopf-)Haar, *die* Haare *pl*; *against the ~* gegen den Strich; *by a ~* um ein Haar, beinahe; *by a ~'s breadth* um Haaresbreite; *to a ~* ganz genau *adv*; *to do o.'s ~* sich frisieren; *to get s.o. by the short ~s (fam)* jdn um den kleinen Finger wickeln; *to have o.'s ~ cut* sich die Haare schneiden lassen; *to let o.'s ~ down* sich die Haare losmachen; *fig* sich gehenlassen; vertraulich werden; *to lose o.'s ~* die Haare verlieren; *fam* den Kopf verlieren; *to put up, to turn up o.'s ~* das Haar auf-, hochstecken; *to split ~s* Haarspalterei treiben; *not to turn a ~* nicht mit der Wimper zucken; *his ~ stood on end* die Haare standen ihm zu Berge; *keep your ~ on (fam)* reg dich doch nicht so auf! *it turned on a ~* es hing an e-m Faden; **~-breadth** *s = ~'s breadth* Haaresbreite *f*; *a* haarscharf; knapp; **~-brush** Haarbürste *f*; **~-cut** Haarschnitt *m*; *to have a ~~* sich die Haare schneiden lassen; **~-do** *pl -dos* Frisur *f*; **~dresser** Friseur *m*; Friseuse *f*; **~dressing** Frisieren *n*; *~~ saloon (Am)* Frisiersalon *m*; **~-dryer** Fön *m (Warenzeichen)*; **~-dye** Haarfärbemittel *n*; **~ed** [-d] *a* behaart; *in Zssgen* -haarig; **~ felt** Haarfilz *m*; **~iness** ['-rinis] Behaartheit *f*; **~less** ['-lis] kahl; **~line** Haarstrich; Beginn *m* des Haaransatzes; *tech* Strichmarke *f*; **~-net** Haarnetz *n*; **~-oil** Haaröl *n*; **~pin** Haarnadel *f*; *~~ bend* Haarnadelkurve *f*; **~-raiser** *fam* schreckliche Geschichte *f*; **~-raising** haarsträubend; **~-restorer** Haarwuchsmittel *n*; **~-shirt** Büßerhemd *n*; **~-splitter** Wortklauber *m*; **~-splitting** Haarspalterei, Wortklauberei *f*; **~-spring** Uhrfeder *f*; **~-stroke** *(Schrift)* Haarstrich *m*; **~ tonic** Haarwasser *n*; **~-trigger** *s (Gewehr)* Stecher *m*; *a fam* sehr empfindlich; **~-wash** Haarwasser *n*; **~y** ['-ri] behaart; haarig; *Am fam (Witz)* abgestanden.

hake [heik] *pl ~* Hechtdorsch; Meer-, Seehecht *m*.

halation [hə'leiʃən] *phot* Lichthof *m*; *no ~ (auf Fotomaterial)* lichthoffrei.

halberd, halbert ['hælbə(:)d, -t] *hist* Hellebarde *f*.

halcyon ['hælsiən] *poet* Eisvogel; *zoo* Königsfischer *m*; *~* **days** *pl* stille, ruhige, friedliche, glückliche Tage *m pl*.

hale [heil] rüstig, gesund; *~ and hearty* gesund und munter.

half [hɑ:f] *pl halves s* Hälfte *f*; *(Schule)* Halbjahr *n*; *sport* Spielhälfte; Halbzeit *f*; *(~-back)* Läufer *m*; *mus* halbe Note *f*; *a* halb; die Hälfte *gen*; *in Zssgen* Halb-; *adv* halb; zur Hälfte; *fam* ziemlich; *~ the book* das halbe Buch; *~ an hour* e-e halbe Stunde; *at ~ the price, for ~ price* zum halben Preis; *by ~* außerordentlich, erstaunlich, mehr als (erwartet), über Erwarten, zu (...um wahr zu sein); *too good by ~* viel zu gut; *in ~, into halves* in zwei gleiche Teile *(teilen)*; *not ~* längst, durchaus nicht; nicht annähernd; alles andere als; *fam* durchaus nicht; *sl* ganz gehörig; *not ~ bad (fam)* gar nicht (mal) so schlecht *od* übel; *~ and ~* halb und halb; *~ as much again* noch mal soviel; *~ asleep* halb im Schlaf; *~ dead* halbtot; *~ past three, ~ after three* halb vier (Uhr); *~ (of) his time* die Hälfte s-r Zeit; *to cut in ~, in(to) halves* halbieren; *to do s.th. by halves* etw nur halb tun; *to go halves* halbpart machen (*with s.o. in s.th.* mit jdm in e-r S); *to have ~ a mind to do s.th.* halb entschlossen sein, etw zu tun; *my better ~ (hum)* meine bessere Hälfte, meine Frau; **~-and-~** Halbundhalb, Gemischte(s) (Bier) *n*; *Am* halb Milch, halb Sahne; **~-back** *(Fußball)* Läufer *m*; **~-baked** *a* halbgar; *fam* noch nicht ausgereift, unfertig; unerfahren; **~ binding** Halbfranz-, -leder(-band *m*) *n*; **~-blood, -breed, -caste** Halbblut *n*, Mischling *m*; **~-bound** *a* in Halbleder gebunden; **~-brother** Halb-, Stiefbruder *m*; **~-cloth** Halbleinen (-band *m*) *n*; **~-cock**: *to go off ~~, to go off at ~ cock (Schußwaffe)* zu früh losgehen; *fam* es zu eilig haben; unüberlegt, überstürzt handeln; **~-crown** *(silbernes)* Zweieinhalbschillingstück *n*; **~-day** *adv* halbtags *(arbeiten)*; **~-fare** halbe(r) Fahrpreis *m*; *~~ ticket* Fahrkarte *f* zum halben Preis; **~-finished** *a* halb-, unfertig; *~~ goods (pl)* Halbfertigwaren *f pl*; **~-hearted** *a* lau, wenig interessiert, nur halb bei der Sache; unentschlossen; ohne Schwung; **~-holiday** freie(r) Nachmittag *m*; **~-hose** Socken *f pl*; Kniestrümpfe *m pl*; **~-hour** *s* halbe Stunde *f*; *a* halbstündig, -stündlich; **~-hourly** *a adv* halbstündlich; *adv* alle halben Stunden; **~-length** *(~~ portrait)* Brustbild *n*; **~-mast,** *Am a.* **~-staff**: *at ~~ (Flagge)* auf Halbmast; **~-monthly** *a adv* halbmonatlich; **~-moon** Halbmond *m*; **~-mourning** Halbtrauer *f*; **~ note** *mus* halbe Note *f*; **~ pay** Wartegehalt, -geld *n*; *to be on ~~* Wartegeld beziehen; **~penny** ['heipni] *pl ~pennies* Halbpennystück *n*; *~~ (pl a. ~pence* ['heipəns]) *u.* *~~worth* ['heipniwə:θ, 'heipəθ] (Wert e-s) halbe(n) Penny *m*; **~-seas-over** *fam* halbbesoffen, stark angeheitert; **~-shot** *a Am sl* angesäuselt, betrunken; haltlos; **~-sister** Halb-, Stiefschwester *f*; **~-sovereign** *(goldenes)* Zehnschillingstück *n*; **~-timbered** *a* Fachwerk-; **~-time** *s sport* Halbzeit; Halbtagsarbeit *f*; *adv* halbtags *(arbeiten)*; *at ~~ (sport)* bei Halbzeit; **~-title** *(Buch)* Schmutztitel *m*; **~-tone** *mus* halbe(r) Ton; *(Kunst)* Halbschatten *m*; *typ* Autotypie, photomechanische Reproduktion *f*; *~~ process (typ)* Rasterverfahren *n*; **~-track** Halbraupenfahrzeug *n*, -schlepper; *Am mil* Schützenpanzerwagen *m*; *~~ motorcycle* Kettenkrad *n*; **~-truth** halbe, Halbwahrheit *f*; **~-way** *a* auf halbem Wege liegend; *fig* unvollständig, halb; *adv* halbwegs *a. fig*; *fig* (nur) halb, *fam* (auch nur) einigermaßen; *to meet ~~ (fig)* entgegenkommen (*s.o.* jdm); *~~ house* Rasthaus *n*; Zwischenstation *f*; *fig* Kompromiß *m od n*; **~-weekly** *a adv* halbwöchentlich; **~-wit** Einfaltspinsel *m*; **~-witted** *a* dumm, einfältig; **~-yearly** *a adv* halbjährlich.

halibut ['hælibət] *pl ~* Heilbutt *m*.

halitosis [hæli'tousis] unreine(r) Atem, üble(r) Mundgeruch *m*.

hall [hɔ:l] Halle *f*, Saal; *(in e-m College)* Speisesaal, Eßraum *m*; gemeinsame(s) Mahl *od* Mittagessen *n*; Diele, (Eingangs-)Halle *f*, Vestibül *n*; Flur, Korridor; Fürsten-, Herrensitz *m*; Herren-, Gutshaus; College(gebäude); Zunft-, Gildehaus *n*; *Am (H~)* öffentliche(s) Gebäude; Verwaltungsgebäude; wissenschaftliche(s) Institut *n*; *Am (meeting ~)* (öffentlicher *od* halböffentlicher) Versammlungs-, Sitzungs-, Fest-, *(banqueting ~)* Speise-, *(dance ~)* Tanzsaal *m*; *H~ of Fame* Ruhmeshalle *f (in New York City)*; *~ of residence (Universität)* Wohngebäude, -heim *n*; *booking ~* Schalterhalle *f*; *city ~* Rathaus *n*; *music ~* Varieté *n*; *Am* Konzertsaal *m*; **~mark** *s (Edelmetall)* (Feingehalts-)Stempel *m*; *fig* (untrügliches) Kennzeichen *n*; *tr* stempeln; kennzeichnen; **~-stand,** *Am* **~ tree** Flurgarderobe *f*, Garderobenständer *m*; **~way** *Am* Eingang(shalle *f*) *m*, Diele *f*, Vestibül *n*; Flur, Gang *m*.

hallelujah, halleluiah [hæli'lu:jə] *interj* halleluja! *s* Halleluja *n*.

halliard *s. halyard.*

hallo(a) [hə'lou] *interj* hallo! *s* Hallo (-ruf *m*) *n*; *itr tr* hallo schreien, (zu)rufen (*s.o.* jdm).

halloo [hə'lu:] *interj* hallo! *s* Hallo *n*; *tr (Hund)* durch den Ruf hallo antreiben; *itr* hallo rufen.

hallow ['hælou] *tr* heiligen, weihen; (als heilig) verehren; **H~e'en** ['hælo(u)'i:n] Abend *m* vor Allerheiligen *(31. Okt.)*; **H~mas** ['hælo(u)mæs, -məs] *obs* Allerheiligen(fest) *n (1. Nov.)*.
hallucination [həlu:si'neiʃən] Halluzination, Sinnestäuschung, Wahnvorstellung *f*, -gebilde *n*.
halm *s. haulm.*
halo ['heilou] *pl -(e)s astr* Hof; Heiligenschein *a. fig*; *phot* Lichthof *m*.
halt [hɔ:lt] **1.** *s mil* (Marsch-)Pause, kurze Rast; Haltestelle, *rail* Haltepunkt *m*; *itr* (an)halten; *tr* halten lassen, stoppen; Einhalt gebieten (*s.o.* jdm); *to call a ~* halten lassen *itr*; *to come to a ~* (an)halten, stehenbleiben, zum Stillstand kommen; *to make (a) ~* haltmachen; **2.** *itr* schwanken, unsicher sein, zögern; *fig (Vers, Beweis)* hinken; **~ing** ['-iŋ] *a* hinkend; stotternd; *fig* unsicher; schwankend.
halter ['hɔ:ltə] Halfter *f*; Strick *m (zum Erhängen)*; (Tod *m* durch) Erhängen *n*; *Am* Oberteil *m* od *n* (e-s zweiteiligen Strand- *od* Badeanzuges).
halve [hɑ:v] *tr* halbieren; *(Zeit)* um die Hälfte verkürzen; teilen (*with* mit).
halyard, halliard ['hæljəd] *mar* Fall, Ziehtau *n*.

*

ham [hæm] *s* (Hinter-)Schenkel; Schinken *m*; *fam* Hinterteil *n*; *sl* schlechte(r), übertreibend spielende(r) Schauspieler; *sl* Funkamateur *m*; *tr itr sl (Rolle)* übertreibend spielen; *slice of ~* Scheibe *f* Schinken; *~ and eggs* Schinken *m* mit Ei; *~ on rye (Am)* Schinkenbrot *n*; **~-fisted, -handed** *a* tappig, täppisch, ungeschickt; **~-roll** Schinkenbrötchen *n*; **~-sandwich** Schinkenbrot *n*; **~string** *s anat* Kniesehne *f*; *tr* verkrüppeln; *fig* lähmen, hemmen.
hamburger ['hæmbə:gə] *Am* Rindergehackte(s); *(~ steak, Hamburg steak)* deutsche(s) Beefsteak *n*, Frikadelle *f* von Rindergehacktem; Brot, Brötchen *n* mit Deutschem Beefsteak; **~ with, without** *Am* Deutsche(s) Beefsteak *n* mit, ohne Zwiebeln.
hames [heimz] *pl* Kum(me)t *n*.
Hamit|e ['hæmait] Hamit *m*; **~ic** [hæ'mitik] hamitisch.
hamlet ['hæmlit] Weiler *m*, Dörfchen *n (ohne Kirche)*.
hammer ['hæmə] *s* Hammer *a. sport anat mus*; *(Gewehr)* Hahn *m*; *tr* hämmern (auf), schlagen; *(Sichel)* dengeln; *(to ~ down)* festhämmern; *fig (s.th. into s.o.* jdm etw) einhämmern, -bleuen; für zahlungsunfähig erklären; *fig* besiegen, schlagen; *itr* hämmern (*at the door* gegen die Tür); *(to ~ away)* angestrengt, unermüdlich arbeiten (*at* an), ununterbrochen reden (*at* über); *to ~ in (Nagel)* einschlagen; *to ~ out* aushämmern; flachhämmern; *fig* (her)ausarbeiten, klären, klarstellen; *(Schwierigkeiten)* beilegen; ausdenken, ersinnen; *~ and tongs (adv)* mit aller Kraft, Gewalt, Macht; gewaltig, mächtig; *to bring under the ~* unter den Hammer, zur Versteigerung bringen; *to come under the ~, to be put to the ~* unter den Hammer, zur Versteigerung kommen; *throwing the ~ (sport)* Hammerwerfen *n*; *~ and sickle (pol)* Hammer u. Sichel; **~-blow** Hammerschlag *m*; **~-head** *tech* Hammerkopf *m a. orn*; *zoo* Hammerhai *m*; **~ing** ['-riŋ] *s* Hämmern *n*; wiederholte Bombenangriffe *m pl*; *to give s.o. a ~~ (fig)* jdn bombardieren, bearbeiten *(a. beim Boxen)*; es jdm tüchtig geben; *a: ~~ fire (mil)* Trommelfeuer *n*; **~-lock** *(Ringen)* Hammergriff *m*.
hammock ['hæmək] Hängematte *f*; **~ chair** Liegestuhl *m*.
hamper ['hæmpə] **1.** (großer) Deckelkorb; Geschenkkorb *m*; **2.** *tr* (in der Bewegung) hindern; *fig* behindern, einengen, hemmen, hinderlich sein (*s.o.* jdm).
hamster ['hæmstə] *zoo* Hamster *m*.
hand [hænd] **1.** *s* Hand *(a. einiger Tiere)*; Handbreit *(Maß für die Schulterhöhe der Pferde = 4 Zoll)*; Seite; Richtung; Arbeit, Tätigkeit, Verrichtung, Handreichung, Hilfeleistung; Handfertigkeit *f*, Geschick *n*, Fähigkeit *f*, Können *n*; Anteil *m*, Hand *f* im Spiele, Einfluß *m*; Macht, Gewalt; Aufsicht, Obhut *f*; Besitz *m*, Eigentum *n*; (Hand-, Fabrik-, Land-)Arbeiter *m*, Arbeitskraft *f*, Mann *m (bes. e-r Mannschaft*; *pl* Leute); *(Schiff)* Besatzungsmitglied *n*; Mensch; Experte, Kenner *m*, *fam* Kapazität; Handschrift; Unterschrift *f*; *fam theat* (Hände-)Klatschen *n*, Beifall, Applaus *m*; *(Kartenspiel)* Hand *f*, Karten *f pl (e-s Spielers)*; Spieler *m*; *(einzelnes)* Spiel; Bündel *n*, Hand *f (Bananen)*; (Uhr-)Zeiger *m*; *attr* Hand-; **2.** *tr* aus-, einhändigen, übergeben, -reichen; ausliefern; übertragen; geleiten (*to* zu), helfen (*s.o. into, out of s.th.* jdm in, aus e-r S); *(Segel)* festmachen; *Am sl* zutrauen (*s.o. s.th.* jdm etw); **3.** *at ~* zur Hand, greifbar, in Reichweite; in der Nähe; *(zeitlich)* in greifbarer Nähe; bereit; *at o.'s right, left ~* rechter Hand, rechts; linker Hand, links; *at first, second ~* aus erster, zweiter Hand *od* Quelle; *at the ~s of* von seiten *gen*; *at s.o.'s ~s* von jdm; *by ~* mit der Hand; von Hand; durch *(persönlichen)* Boten; *com* frei *adv*; *by s.o.'s ~* mit jds Hilfe; *for o.'s own ~* auf eigene Rechnung; *in ~* in der Hand, zur Verfügung; in Arbeit; im Gange; unter Kontrolle; *in s.o.'s ~s* in jds Händen; *in good ~s (fig)* in guten Händen; *~ in ~* Hand in Hand; *off ~* aus dem Stegreif; *on ~* in Händen; in Reichweite, nahe; auf Lager, vorrätig; sofort, sogleich; *(Geld)* bar gezahlt; *Am* anwesend; *on the one ~ ... on the other ~* einerseits ... andererseits; *on either ~* auf beiden Seiten, beiderseits; *on all ~s* auf allen Seiten, in allen Richtungen; *out of ~* selbständig, eigenwillig, außer Rand u. Band, unbeherrscht; erledigt; sofort; *~ over ~ od fist* Stück für Stück, Zug um Zug; schnell, rasch; *(ready) to o.'s ~* zur Hand, greifbar, in Reichweite; *under s.o.'s ~s* mit jds Unterschrift; *with a bold, high ~* anmaßend; willkürlich; selbstherrlich *adv*; *with clean ~s (fig)* mit weißer Weste; *with a heavy ~* schwerfällig; streng, ernst *adv*; *with an iron ~ (fig)* mit eiserner Faust; *with a light ~* leicht, mühelos *adv*; **4.** *to be a poor ~* ungeschickt sein (*at* bei, in); *to bear, to lend s.o. a ~* jdm helfen, behilflich sein (*in, with* bei); *to bind s.o. ~ and foot* jdm Hände und Füße binden *a. fig*; *to bite the ~ that feeds one* Gutes mit Bösem vergelten; *to bring up by ~* mit der Flasche aufziehen; *to change ~s* den Besitzer wechseln; in andere Hände übergehen; *not to do a ~'s turn, not to lift a ~* keinen Handschlag tun, keinen Finger rühren; *to eat, to feed out of s.o.'s ~ (fig)* jdm aus der Hand fressen; *to force s.o.'s ~ (fig)* jdn zwingen, mit offenen Karten zu spielen; jdn zu etw zwingen; *to get s.th. off o.'s ~s* sich etw vom Halse schaffen; etw loswerden; *to get the upper ~ of* die Oberhand gewinnen über; *to give s.o. a ~* jdm Beifall spenden; jdm behilflich sein, mit Hand anlegen (*with* bei); *to give s.o. o.'s ~ on s.th.* jdm die Hand auf etw geben; *to go ~ in ~ with s.o.* mit jdm Schritt halten *a. fig*; *to have o.'s ~s full* viel zu tun haben; *to have o.'s ~ out* aus der Übung sein; *to have in ~* in der Hand haben; *to have a ~ in s.th.* bei e-r S die Hand im Spiel haben; *to have s.th. on o.'s ~s (fig)* etw auf dem Halse haben; *to hold ~s* sich (in Liebe) bei den Händen halten; *to join ~s* sich zs.tun, -schließen, sich vereinigen; sich heiraten; *to keep o.'s ~ in* in der Übung bleiben; *to keep o.'s ~s, a firm ~ on (fig)* fest in Händen haben; *to lay ~s on s.th.* die Hand auf etw legen; verhaften; *rel* die Hand auflegen, segnen; jdm zu Leibe gehen; *to let s.o. have a ~* jdn ans Spiel lassen; *to lift, to raise o.'s ~s to, against* die Hände erheben gegen; *to live from ~ to mouth* von der Hand in den Mund leben; *to pass through many ~s (fig)* durch viele Hände gehen; *to play a good ~* gut spielen, ein guter Spieler sein; *to play for o.'s own ~ (fig)* in s-e eigene Tasche arbeiten; *to play into s.o.'s ~s* jdm in die Hände spielen; *to put, to set o.'s ~ to s.th.* etw in Angriff nehmen; etw anpacken; *to shake s.o.'s ~, to shake ~s with s.o.* jdm die Hand drükken; sich die Hand geben; *to show o.'s ~ (fig)* s-e Karten aufdecken; *to take a ~* ein Spiel gewinnen (*at* bei); *to take a ~ in* mitarbeiten, -schaffen, -wirken an, bei; *to take in ~* in die Hand, in Angriff nehmen; versuchen; unter Kontrolle bringen; *to wait on, to serve s.o. ~ and foot* alles für jdn tun; *to wash o.'s ~ of* nichts wissen wollen von; s-e Hände in Unschuld waschen; *to win ~s down* leichtes Spiel haben; **5.** *I have to ~ it to you* ich muß Sie loben; ich muß Ihnen recht geben; *I'm in his ~s* er hat mich in s-r Gewalt; *he is ~ and glove, ~ in glove with him* sie sind unzertrennlich, ein Herz und eine Seele; *he can turn his ~ to anything* er ist in allen Sätteln gerecht; *he has won her ~* sie hat ihm ihr Jawort gegeben; *the matter is out of his ~s* er kann in der Sache nichts mehr tun; *keep your ~s off that!* laß die Finger davon! *~s off!* Hände weg! *~s up!* Hände hoch! **6.** *all ~s* die ganze, gesamte Mannschaft; *child brought up by ~* Flaschenkind *n*; *a cool ~ (fig)* ein kühler Kopf, ein bedächtiger Mensch *m*; *the elder ~ (Kartenspiel)* die Vorhand; *extra ~* zusätzliche Arbeits-, Hilfskraft *f*; *the fourth ~* der vierte Mann *(zum Kartenspiel)*; *a good ~* ein guter Arbeiter *m*; gute Karten *f pl (im Spiel)*; *heart and ~* sehr herzlich; *hour ~* Stundenzeiger *m*; *made by ~* handgearbeitet, -gefertigt; *minute ~* Minutenzeiger *m*; *second ~* ['sekənd-] *s* Sekundenzeiger *m*; *a* ['sekənd] alt, gebraucht, *(Buch)* antiquarisch; *the upper ~* die Oberhand; *to ~* **about** herumreichen; *to ~* **down** her-, hinunterreichen (*from* von); *fig* überliefern; *jur* vermachen, hinterlassen; *(Urteil)* fällen; *to ~* **in** einliefern; vorlegen; *(Gesuch)* einreichen; hineinhelfen (*s.o.* jdm); *to ~* **on** weiterreichen, -geben; übergeben; *to ~* **out** ausgeben, verteilen; hinaushelfen (*s.o.* jdm); *to ~* **over** heraus-, abgeben, aus-, abliefern; aushändigen, übergeben, -lassen; herüberreichen; *to ~* **round** herumreichen; *to ~* **up** her-, hinaufreichen; **~bag** Handtasche *f*; **~ball** Handball(spiel *n*) *m*; *Am* Hal-

len-Faustball *n*; **~-barrow** Trage, Bahre; Schubkarre(n *m*) *f*; **~bell** Tischglocke *f*; **~bill** Reklamezettel *m*; Flugblatt *n*; *com* trockene(r) Wechsel *m*; **~book** Handbuch *n*, Reiseführer *m* (*to* für); *Am* Wettliste *f*; **~-brake** Handbremse *f*; **~breadth** Handbreite *f*; **~cart** Handwagen *m*; **~clasp** *Am* Händedruck *m (als Gruß)*; **~cuff** ['-kʌf] *s meist pl* Handschellen *f pl*; *tr* Handschellen anlegen (*s.o.* jdm); **~ed** ['-id] *a in Zssgen* -händig; *four-~~* vierhändig; **~ful** ['-ful] *s*: *a ~~ of* e-e Handvoll; ein paar *(Leute)*; *fam* Unruhegeist *m*; unangenehme(s) Problem *n*; **~gear** *tech* Hebel *m*; **~glass** Lupe *f*; Handspiegel *m*; *(Gärtnerei)* Glasglocke *f*; **~-grenade** Handgranate *f*; **~grip** Handgriff; Händedruck *m*; *to come to ~~s (Am)* handgreiflich werden; **~ guard** *tech* Handschutz *m*; **~hold** (fester) Halt *m* (für die Hände); **~icap** ['-ikæp] *s sport* Vorgabe *f*, Ausgleich *m*, Benachteiligung *f*, Handikap *n*; Ausgleich-, Vorgaberennen, -spiel *n*; *fig* Belastung *f*, Hindernis, Hemmnis *n* (*to* für); *tr sport* (zum Ausgleich) benachteiligen *a. fig*; *fig* beeinträchtigen, behindern, hemmen, *fam* handikapen; **~icraft** ['-ikrɑ:ft] Geschicklichkeit *f*; Handwerk *n*; **~icraftsman** ['-ikrɑ:ftsmən] Handwerker *m*; **~iness** ['-inis] Handlichkeit, leichte Handhabung; Geschicklichkeit *f*; **~iwork** ['-iwə:k] Handarbeit; eigene Arbeit *f*; *this is my ~~ (fig)* das ist mein Werk; **~kerchief** ['hæŋkətʃif] Taschen-, Ziertuch; Hals-, Kopftuch *n*; **~-loom** Handwebstuhl *m*; **~-luggage** Handgepäck *n*; **~-made** *a* handgearbeitet; Hand-; **~maid** *obs* Magd, Dienerin, Zofe *f*; **~-me-down** *a Am fam* von der Stange, Konfektions-; billig; getragen; *s* getragene(s) Kleidungsstück *n*; **~-operated** *a* handbetätigt; **~-organ** Drehorgel *f*; **~-out** *(Kartenspiel)* Geben *n*; *Am* milde Gabe *f*, Almosen *n*; Verlautbarung, Pressenotiz *f*; Handzettel *m*; **~-picked** *a* handgepflückt; erlesen, ausgesucht; **~-rail** Geländer(stange *f*) *n*; **~saw** Handsäge *f*; **~set** *tele* Hörer; Handapparat *m*; **~shake** Händedruck *m*; **~spike** Brechstange *f*, *bes. mar* Hebebaum *m*; *tech* Tastspitze *f*; **~spring** Radschlagen *n*; *to turn ~~s* radschlagen; **~stand** Handstand *m*; *to do a ~~* e-n Handstand machen; **~-to-~** *a adv*: *~~ fighting, struggle* Nahkampf *m*; **~-to-mouth** *a adv* unsicher; von der Hand in den Mund, verschwenderisch; **~-wheel** Handrad *n*; **~work** Handarbeit *f*; **~writing** Handschrift *f*; Stil *m*; **~y** ['-i] greifbar, zur Hand; handlich; leicht zu handhaben *od* zu regieren; geschickt; *to come in ~~* sich als nützlich erweisen; gerade gut passen; *~~-dandy* Raten *n*, in welcher Hand ein Gegenstand ist; *~~ man* Handlanger; Gelegenheitsarbeiter; *fam* Seemann *m*.

handl|e ['hændl] *s* Henkel, Stiel, (Hand-)Griff *m*, Klinke, Kurbel; *fig* Handhabe (*against* gegen); (gute) Gelegenheit *f*; *fam (~~ to the name)* Titel *m*; *tr* anfassen, in die Hand nehmen; handhaben *a. fig*, manipulieren, bedienen; verarbeiten; auf-, abladen; *fig* in die Hand nehmen, erledigen; leiten, führen; *(Sache)* behandeln, sich befassen, sich abgeben mit; verwalten; *(Geschäft)* erledigen; abfertigen; *(Thema)* abhandeln, schreiben *od* sprechen über, handeln von; *(Verkehr)* abwickeln; *com* handeln mit; *(Waren)* führen; *(Menschen)* behandeln, umgehen mit, fertigwerden mit; *itr* sich handhaben lassen; *to fly off the ~~ (fam)* aufbrausen, wütend werden; *to give a ~~ to s.o.* jdm e-e Handhabe bieten, die Möglichkeit geben (*to* zu); als Vorwand dienen können (*to* für); *glass! ~~ with care!* Vorsicht! Glas! *~~-bar (Fahrrad)* Lenkstange *f*; **~er** ['-ə] Handhabende(r); *(Boxen)* Trainer, Manager *m*; **~ing** ['-iŋ] Handhabung, Bedienung; Leitung; *(Geld)* Verwaltung *f*.

han(d)sel ['hænsəl] *s* Neujahrsgeschenk; Geschenk zur Geschäftseröffnung, zum Einstand; An-, Handgeld *n*; erste Einnahme; *fig* erste Erfahrung *f*; *fig* Vorgeschmack *m*; *tr obs* ein Handgeld geben (*s.o.* jdm); die Eröffnung feiern (*s.th.* e-r S), einweihen; zum erstenmal benutzen.

handsome ['hænsəm] hübsch; stattlich, gutaussehend; gefällig, angenehm; großzügig; ansehnlich, beträchtlich, bedeutend; *to come down ~ (fig fam)* großzügig sein; **~ness** ['-nis] Stattlichkeit, Ansehnlichkeit; Großzügigkeit *f*.

hang [hæŋ] *irr hung, hung* [hʌŋ] *tr* (auf-)hängen (*by* an); *(Tür)* einhängen (*on* in); *(den Kopf)* hängen lassen; *(frisch geschlachtetes Tier)* abhängen lassen; *(Wand)* behängen (*with* mit); *(to ~ with paper)* tapezieren; *(Tapete)* ankleben; *a. (hanged, hanged)* er-, *fam* aufhängen, henken; *Am* an e-r Entscheidung hindern; *itr* hängen, hangen, aufgehängt sein, *fam* baumeln; schwingen; schweben; herabhängen, sich neigen; *(Stoff, weites Kleidungsstück)* fallen; *(Gefahr)* schweben (*over s.o.* über jds Haupt); *fig* unentschlossen sein, zögern, schwanken; *to ~ o.s.* sich er-, *fam* sich aufhängen; *s* (Ab-)Hang *m*, Neigung *f a. fig*, Gefälle *n*; Sitz *m (e-s Kleidungsstückes)*; kurze Unterbrechung *f*; *fam das* Wieso und Warum; *fig fam* Sinn *m*, Bedeutung *f*; *not to care a ~ about s.th., to let s.th. go ~ (fam)* sich den Dreck um etw kümmern; *to get the ~ of s.th. (fam)* etw herauskriegen; *to ~ in the balance (fig)* in der Schwebe sein; *to ~ fire (Feuerwaffe)* nicht losgehen; *fig* nicht recht in Gang kommen wollen; *to ~ by a hair, by a single thread (fig)* an e-m (seidenen) Faden hängen; *to ~ out o.'s shingle (Am pop)* e-n Laden eröffnen, e-n Betrieb aufmachen; *~ it!* zum Henker! verdammt noch mal! *to ~* **about**, *Am a. to ~* **around** sich herumtreiben, sich herumdrücken, herumlungern; *fig* in der Luft liegen; *s.o.* jdm nicht von den Fersen gehen, jdm am Schürzenzipfel hängen; *to ~* **back** zögern, sich zurückhalten; zurück sein; *to ~* **down** herab-, herunterhängen; *to ~* **on** *(to)* (fest)hängen (an); sich hängen, sich (fest)halten, sich klammern (an), sich stützen (auf); abhängen (von), beruhen auf; durchhalten; *tele* am Apparat, in der Leitung bleiben; *to s.o. (fig)* an jds Lippen hängen; *to s.th.* etw halten; etw behalten; etw aufbewahren; *to ~* **out** hinaus-, heraushängen (*of* aus); hinauslehnen; *sl* wohnen; *for s.th.* hinauszögern wegen etw; *to ~* **over** überhängen, übriggeblieben sein; sich beugen über; drohen, bevorstehen; *to ~* **together** zs.hängen, ein Ganzes bilden, zs.passen; *(Menschen)* zs.halten; *to ~* **up** aufhängen; zurückhalten; hinauszögern; *tele* (den Hörer) auflegen, einhängen; unterbrechen, aufschieben; *on s.o. (tele)* auf-, einhängen; **~-dog** Galgenvogel, -strick *m*; **~er** ['-ə] *meist in Zssgen* Aufhänger *(Person u. Sache, a. Zeitung)*; Haken *m*; Seitengewehr *n*, Hirschfänger; Waldhang; *Am* Aushang; Kleiderbügel *m*; *~~-on* [hæŋər'ən] *pl -s-on* Nachläufer; Schmarotzer, Parasit *m (Mensch)*; **~ing** ['-iŋ] *a* hängend; überhängend; *fig* schwebend; niedergeschlagen; zur Hinrichtung führend; *s* (Auf-)Hängen; Erhängen *n*, Hinrichtung; *pl* Wandbekleidung, Tapete *f*; *~~ bridge* Hängebrücke *f*; *~~ lamp* Hängelampe *f*; *~~ wall (min)* Hangende(s) *n*; **~man** ['-mən] Henker, Scharfrichter *m*; **~nail** ['-neil] Niednagel *m*; **~-out** *sl* Treffpunkt *m*, Stammkneipe *f*, -lokal *n*; Wohnung *f*; **~-over** *Am* Überbleibsel *n*, Rest *m*; *sl* Kater, Katzenjammer *m*.

hangar ['hæŋə, -ŋgə, -ŋgɑ:] (Flugzeug-)Halle *f*; *allg* Schuppen *m*.

hank [hæŋk] *(Garn)* Strähne *f*, Bund *n*, Docke *f*, Wickel *m*; *allg* Schlinge *f*, Ring *m a. mar*, *mar* Segel *n*.

hanker ['hæŋkə] *itr* sich sehnen, Verlangen tragen (*after, for* nach); **~ing** ['-riŋ] Sehnsucht *f*, Verlangen *n* (*after, for* nach).

hanky ['hæŋki] *fam* Taschentuch *n*.

hanky-panky ['hæŋki'pæŋki] *s fam* Hokuspokus *m*, Taschenspielerkünste *f pl*, Trick, Bluff, Schwindel *m*.

Hansard ['hænsəd] Sitzungsbericht *m* des britischen Parlaments.

hansom ['hænsəm] (bespanntes) Kabriolett *n*.

hap [hæp] *s obs* glückliche(r) Zufall *m*, Glück(sfall *m*) *n*; *itr obs* zufällig geschehen; **~hazard** ['-'hæzəd] *s* (bloßer) Zufall *m*; *a, adv (a. at, by ~~)* ganz zufällig; **~less** ['-lis] unglücklich.

ha'p'orth ['heipəθ] *fam* (Wert e-s) halbe(n) Penny *m*.

happen ['hæpən] *itr* sich ereignen, geschehen, stattfinden, vorfallen, vorkommen, *fam* passieren; auftreten; *to ~ to s.o.* jdm zustoßen, *fam* passieren; *to ~ to do* zufällig tun; *to ~ (up)on s.o., s.th.* zufällig auf jdn, etw stoßen, jdn zufällig treffen; *to ~ along, in (Am fam)* hereingeschneit kommen; **~ing** ['hæpniŋ] Ereignis, Geschehnis *n*, Vorfall *m*; **~stance** ['hæpən'stɑ:ns] *Am fam* Zufall *m*.

happ|ily ['hæpili] *adv* glücklicherweise; glücklich, passend, geschickt *(ausgedrückt, formuliert)*; **~iness** ['hæpinis] Glück *n*; Freude, Zufriedenheit; Angebrachtheit, Geschicktheit *f*; **~y** ['hæpi] glücklich; voller Freude, (über)glücklich, (innerlich) zufrieden (*about* mit); (wohl)gelungen, glücklich(gewählt), angemessen, angebracht, passend, treffend, geschickt; *fam* (ange)heiter(t), beschwipst; *to feel ~~ about s.th.* über etw erfreut sein; *as ~~ as the day is long, as ~~ as a king* überglücklich, glücklich wie noch nie; *~~ birthday!* herzlichen Glückwunsch zum Geburtstag! *~~ landing! (vor e-r Seefahrt od e-m Flug) fam* komm gut hin! *~~ dispatch* Harakiri *n*; *~~-go-lucky (a)* sorglos, unbekümmert, unbeschwert, frei und leicht; *to go through life in a ~~-go-lucky fashion* in den Tag hinein leben.

*

harangue [hə'ræŋ] *s* Ansprache; (lange, geschwollene *od* heftige) Rede *f*; *itr* e-e Ansprache halten; (lang, geschwollen *od* heftig) reden; *tr* e-e Ansprache halten an, ins Gewissen reden (*s.o.* jdm).

harass ['hærəs] *tr* stören, beunruhigen, besorgt machen, aufreiben, *fam* mitnehmen, quälen; *mil* stören, nicht zur

Ruhe kommen lassen; **~ing** ['-iŋ] *a mil* Stör-; *~~ action, fire, raid* Störaktion *f*, -feuer *n*, -angriff *m*.

harbinger ['hɑ:bindʒə] *s* Herold; *fig* Künder, Vorbote *(a. Sache)*; *hist* Quartiermacher *m*; *tr* (an)melden, ankündigen.

harbo(u)r ['hɑ:bə] *s* Hafen *m*; *fig* geschützte Stelle *f*, sichere(r) Ort, Unterschlupf *m*; *mil* (getarnte) Bereitschaftsstellung *f*, (*bes.* Panzer-)Depot *n*; *tr* beherbergen, schützen; Unterschlupf gewähren, Versteck, Deckung bieten (*s.o.* jdm); verbergen; *fig* sich tragen mit *(e-m Gedanken)*; *(Groll)* hegen; *itr* vor Anker gehen, ankern; Schutz, Zuflucht suchen; *to enter, to leave ~* ein-, auslaufen; **~age** ['-ridʒ] Ankerplatz; Unterschlupf *m*, Unterkunft *f*; **~ captain** Hafenkommandant *m*; **~ charges, dues** *pl* Anker-, Hafengebühren *f pl*; **~ commissioner, master** Hafenmeister *m*; **~ craft** Hafenfahrzeug *n*; **~ entrance** Hafeneinfahrt *f*; **~ police** Hafenpolizei *f*; **~ station** Hafenbahnhof *m*.

hard [hɑ:d] **1.** *a* hart, fest, starr, widerstandsfähig, unnachgiebig; *(Geld)* Hart-, Metall-; muskulös, kräftig, stark, robust; *(Schlag, Stoß)* stark, heftig, kräftig, kraftvoll, gewaltig, tüchtig; anstrengend, ermüdend, mühsam, (be-)schwer(lich); schwer (zu bewältigen), schwierig, knifflig, verzwickt; wenig umgänglich, schwer zu behandeln(d) *od* zu lenken(d); hart, schwer (zu ertragen); *(Winter)* streng; *(Zeiten)* schlecht, schlimm; hart(herzig), gefühllos, streng, unerbittlich; *(Worte)* hart, grob; zäh, verbissen, unermüdlich, energisch, tüchtig, fleißig, gründlich; hart, scharf, grell, beißend; *(Wasser durch Mineralgehalt)* hart; *Am fam (alkoholisches Getränk)* stark, schwer, zu Kopf steigend, berauschend, hochprozentig; *com* fest, beständig; *(Phonetik)* stimmlos, hart; **2.** *adv* heftig, kräftig, mit Gewalt; mit Mühe, mühsam, -selig, *bes. in Zssgen*: schwer(-); unverdrossen, unermüdlich, unentwegt, eifrig, verbissen, zäh; stark *(frieren)*; dicht *(dabei)*; sehr, (zu)viel; **3.** *s* Steilufer *n*, -küste; (befestigte) Uferstraße *f*, Kai *m*; *sl* Zuchthaus(strafe *f*) *n*; **4.** *~ by* dicht dabei, ganz in der Nähe; *~ up* in arger Bedrängnis, in großer Not, schlimm, übel dran; *~ upon* dicht auf den Fersen; **5.** *to be ~ put to s.th.* mit etw s-e Schwierigkeiten, s-e Last haben; *to be ~ up* sehr knapp sein *(for* an); *to be ~ (up)on s.o.* jdm schwer zusetzen; mit jdm streng sein; *to die ~* ein zähes Leben haben; *to run s.o. ~* jdm dicht auf den Fersen sein; *to try ~* sich große Mühe geben; *to work ~* schwer, tüchtig arbeiten; *he is ~ to deal with* mit ihm ist schlecht Kirschen essen; *~ to believe* kaum zu glauben(d); *it will go ~* es wird Schwierigkeiten geben; **6.** *a ~ drinker* ein Säufer *m*; *the ~ facts (pl)* die rauhe Wirklichkeit; *~ and fast (Brauch)* streng; *(Regel)* starr, unumstößlich; *a ~ fight* ein schwerer Kampf *m*; *~ of hearing* schwerhörig; *~ hit* schwer betroffen; *~ luck* kein Glück; Pech *n*; *a ~ nut to crack (fig)* e-e harte Nuß, ein schweres Problem *n*; *~ to please* schwer zu befriedigen(d); **~ aluminium** Duralumin *n (Warenzeichen)*; **~-beset** *a* hart bedrängt, in schwerer Bedrängnis; **~-bitten** *a* hartnäckig, zäh; **~board** Hartfaserplatte *f*; **~-boiled** *a (Ei)* hartgekocht; *fig fam* hartgesotten, unsentimental, nüchtern, kaltberechnend, geschäftsmäßig; steif; **~ cash, money** Bar-, Hart-, Metallgeld *n*; **~ cider** *Am* Apfelwein, Most *m*; **~coal** Anthrazit *m*; **~-earned** *a* schwer verdient, sauer erworben; **~en** ['-ən] *tr (Stahl)* härten; *(Zement)* abbinden; hart machen; abhärten, stählen; *fig* stärken, festigen; hart, streng, unerbittlich machen; *(das Herz)* verhärten; *itr* hart, fest, starr werden *a. fig*; *fig* sich versteifen; streng, unerbittlich werden; *(Preise)* anziehen; *to ~~ off (Pflanzen)* abhärten; **~ener** ['-nə] Härter *m*; Härtemittel *n*, -zusatz *m*; **~ening** ['-niŋ] *tech* Härten *n*, Härtung *f*; Härtemittel *n*; **~-favo(u)red, -featured** *a* mit harten (Gesichts-)Zügen, hartem Gesichtsausdruck; **~-fisted** *a* eigen-, selbstsüchtig; geizig, knauserig, knickerig; **~-handed** *a* mit schwieligen Händen; *(Herrscher, Regierung)* streng, tyrannisch; **~-headed** *a* nüchtern, praktisch; eigensinnig, stur; **~-hearted** *a* hartherzig, mitleidlos; **~ihood** ['-ihud] Kühnheit, Verwegenheit *f*, Wagemut *m*; Dreistigkeit, Frechheit *f*; **~iness** ['-inis] Stärke, Kraft, Energie, Ausdauer, Zähigkeit, Festigkeit; Unerschrockenheit, Kühnheit; Dreistigkeit *f*; **~ labour** Zwangsarbeit *f*, Zuchthaus (-strafe *f*) *n*; **~ lines** *pl* Unglück *n*; **~ly** ['-li] *adv* (nur) mit Mühe, mit Anstrengung, mühsam, angestrengt; streng, barsch; schwerlich, kaum, fast nicht, nicht recht, eigentlich nicht; *~~ any* fast kein; *~~ ever* kaum je(mals), fast nie, so gut wie nie; **~-mouthed** *a (Pferd)* hartmäulig; *fig* eigensinnig; widerspenstig; **~ness** ['-nis] Härte; Kraft, Stärke; Heftigkeit; Beschwerlichkeit, Schwierigkeit; Not; Schwere, Strenge, Schärfe; Hartherzigkeit, Unerbittlichkeit *f*; *~~ degree* Härtegrad *m*; *~~ reduction* Enthärtung *f*; **~pan** ['-pæn] *Am* feste(r) Untergrund; harte(r), unbearbeitete(r) Boden *m*; *fig* feste Grundlage; harte Wirklichkeit *f*; Tiefstand, niedrigste(r) Stand *m*; *prices have reached ~~* die Preise haben e-n Tiefstand erreicht; **~ rubber** Hartgummi *m od n*; **~ sauce** *Am* süße Buttersoße *f*; **~-set** *a* in Bedrängnis, in Schwierigkeiten; starr, fest, hart; unbeugsam, unnachgiebig, hartnäckig; **~-shell** *a* mit harter Schale; *fig* starr, unnachgiebig, zu keinem Kompromiß bereit; *Am* streng, orthodox, konservativ; **~ship** ['-ʃip] Mühsal, Plage, Härte; Not(lage), Bedrängnis, schwierige Lage *f*; *pl* schwierige Umstände *m pl od* Verhältnisse *n pl*; *to relieve ~~* Härten lindern; **~ soap** Kernseife *f*; **~-tack** Schiffszwieback *m*; **~top** *mot* Limousine *f*; **~ware** ['-wɛə] Eisen-, Stahlwaren *f pl*; harte Güter *n pl*; **~wood** Hartholz *n*; **~-working** arbeitsam, emsig, fleißig; **~y** ['-i] kühn, verwegen, unerschrocken, wagemutig; waghalsig, unbedacht, voreilig; ausdauernd, zäh, unempfindlich, abgehärtet; *bot* nicht frostempfindlich, winterfest.

*

hare [hɛə] Hase *m*; *to be mad as a (March) ~ (fam)* total verrückt sein; *to run with the ~ and hunt with the hounds* es mit beiden Parteien halten, ein doppeltes Spiel spielen; *~ and hounds* Schnitzeljagd *f*; **~bell** Glockenblume *f*; **~-brained** *a* gedankenlos, flüchtig; flatterhaft, unbesonnen; rücksichtslos; **~lip** *med* Hasenscharte *f*.

harem ['hɛərəm] Harem *m*.

haricot ['hærikou] *(~-mutton)* (Hammel-)Ragout *n*; *(~ bean)* grüne Bohne *f*.

hark [hɑ:k] *itr*, meist *~!* horch! *to ~ back (Hund)* umkehren, um die Fährte wiederzufinden; *fig* zurückdenken, -gehen *(to* auf); *(in der Rede)* auf das Gesagte zurückkommen.

Harlequin ['hɑ:likwin] *s* Harlekin *m*; *h~* Spaßmacher *m*; *a* vielfarbig; bunt; **h~ade** [hɑ:likwi'neid] Possenspiel *n*.

harlot ['hɑ:lət] Hure, Dirne *f*; **~ry** ['-ri] Hurerei, Unzucht; Prostitution *f*.

harm [hɑ:m] *s* Schaden, Nachteil *m*; Unrecht, Böse(s) *n*; *tr* verletzen; ein Leid zufügen, wehtun (*s.o.* jdm); Schaden zufügen (*s.o.* jdm), schädigen; Unrecht tun (*s.o.* jdm); *out of ~'s way* in Sicherheit; *to do ~* Schaden anrichten; *to s.o.* jdm schaden; *to mean no ~* nichts Böses im Schilde führen; *no ~ done!* kein (großes) Unglück! **~ful** ['-ful] schädlich, nachteilig; böswillig; **~fulness** ['-fulnis] Schädlichkeit; Böswilligkeit *f*; **~less** ['-lis] harmlos, unschädlich; unschuldig, unbeteiligt, arglos; **~lessness** ['-lisnis] Harmlosigkeit, Unschädlichkeit; Unschuld, Arglosigkeit *f*.

harmon|ic [hɑ:'mənik] *a* harmonisch *a. mus*, harmonierend, übereinstimmend; *math (Reihe)* arithmetisch; *s phys mus* Oberschwingung *f*, Oberton *m*; *mus* Flageolett *n*; *pl oft mit sing mus* Harmonielehre *f*; **~ica** [-ikə], Glas-, *Am* Mundharmonika *f*; **~ious** [hɑ:'mounjəs] harmonisch; gleichgestimmt, mit gleichen Anschauungen *od* Interessen; **~ist** ['-mənist] Musiker; Komponist *m*; **~ium** [-'mouniəm] Harmonium *n*; **~ize** ['hɑ:mənaiz] *tr* harmonisieren; in Einklang, *fig* auf einen Nenner bringen; *itr* in Einklang sein, harmonieren; in Einklang stehen, übereinstimmen; **~y** ['hɑ:məni] Harmonie *f a. mus*, Einklang *m*; Übereinstimmung; (Evangelien-)Harmonie *f*; *to be in ~~* im Einklang stehen, übereinstimmen (*with* mit).

harness ['hɑ:nis] *s* (Pferde-, *tech* Web-) Geschirr; Gurtzeug *n (des Fallschirms)*; Kopfhörerbügel; *hist* Harnisch *m*, Rüstung *f*; *tr (Pferd)* anschirren; anspannen; *(Naturkraft)* nutzbar machen; *in ~* in der Routine, in der gewohnten Arbeit; *to die in ~* in den Sielen sterben; *to work, to run in double ~* e-n Partner haben; verheiratet sein.

harp [hɑ:p] *s* Harfe *f*; *the H~ (astr)* die Leier; *itr* Harfe spielen; *fig* herumreiten *(on, upon* auf); **~er** ['-ə], **~ist** ['-ist] Harfner, Harfenist *m*.

harpoon [hɑ:'pu:n] *s* Harpune *f*; *tr* harpunieren.

Harpy ['hɑ:pi] *(Mythologie)* Harpyie *f*; *h~* (hab)gierige, unersättliche Person *f*.

harridan ['hæridən] alte Vettel *f*.

harrier ['hæriə] **1.** Plünderer; *orn* Feldweih *m*; **2.** Hasenhund; *sport* Geländeläufer *m*; *pl* Jäger und Hunde *pl*.

harrow ['hærou] *s* Egge *f*; *tr* eggen; *(fig)* verwunden, verletzen; *fig* martern, quälen, plagen; *under the ~ (fig)* in großer Not; **~ing** ['-iŋ] *a* quälend, qualvoll, *fam* schrecklich, herzzerreißend.

Harry ['hæri] Heinrich, Heinz *m*.

harry ['hæri] *tr* stürmen; plündern; verwüsten, zerstören; *(Nest)* ausnehmen; belästigen, quälen, martern.

harsh [hɑ:ʃ] scharf, rauh; grell; schrill; herb; roh; streng, hart; barsch; **~ness** ['-nis] Schärfe, Rauheit; Herbheit; Strenge, Härte *f*.

hart [hɑ:t] Hirsch *m*; *~ of ten* Zehnender *m*; **~(e)beest** ['hɑ:t(i)bi(:)st] *zoo* Hartebeest *n*, Kama *f*; **~shorn** ['-ʃɔ:n] Hirschhorn *n*; *salt of ~~* Hirschhornsalz *n*; **~'s-tongue** *bot* Hirschzunge *f*.

harum-scarum ['hɛərəm'skɛərəm] *a* wild, unbändig, lebhaft; hastig, eilig; leichtsinnig, verantwortungs-, rücksichtslos; *adv* in (aller) Eile, Hals über Kopf; *s* Wildfang; Luftikus *m*.

harvest ['hɑːvist] *s* Ernte(zeit); Ernte *f*, (Ernte-)Ertrag *m*; *fig* Früchte, Folgen *f pl*; *tr* ernten, einbringen; *(Feld)* abernten; *itr* ernten, Ernte halten; *bad* ~ Mißernte *f*; ~**-bug, -louse, -mite, -tick** Ernte-, Grasmilbe *f*; ~**er** ['-ə] Erntearbeiter; Mäher, Schnitter *m*; Mähmaschine *f*, *(combined* ~~*)* -drescher *m*; ~ **festival** Erntedankfest *n*; ~**-home** Erntelied, -fest *n*; ~**man** Schnitter; *zoo* Weberknecht *m*; ~**-moon** Vollmond *m* um die Zeit der Herbst-Tagundnachtgleiche; ~**-mouse** Zwergmaus *f*; ~ **prospects** *pl* Ernteaussichten *f pl*; ~**-time** Erntezeit *f*.

has [hæz, həz, əz, z, s] *s. have*; ~**-been** *fam* Größe *f* von gestern; Gewesene(s) *n*; ~**n't** ['hæznt] = *has not*.

hash [hæʃ] *tr (Fleisch)* hacken, haschieren; *(Gemüse)* wiegen; *fam* verman(t)schen, durchea.bringen, vermasseln; *(to* ~ *over) Am sl* des langen u. breiten bereden; *(e-e Geschichte)* wieder aufwärmen; *s* Haschee, Ragout *n*; *Am sl* Mahlzeit; *fam fig* aufgewärmte Geschichte *f*; Kuddelmuddel *m*, Durcheinander *n*; *to make (a)* ~ *of* vermurksen, verwursteln, verhunzen, vermasseln; *to settle s.o.'s* ~ jdn kleinkriegen; mit jdm e-e Rechnung begleichen; ~**er** ['-ə], ~ **slinger** *Am sl* Kellner *m*; ~**ery** ['-əri] *Am sl* kleine(s) Eßlokal *n*; ~ **house** *Am sl* billige(s) Eßlokal *n*.

hashish, hasheesh ['hæʃiːʃ] Haschisch *n (Rauschgift)*.

haslets ['heizlits] *pl* Innereien *pl*.

hasp [hɑːsp] *s* Haspe, Krampe *f*; Überfall *m (an e-r Tür, Kiste)*; *(Garn)* Strähne, Docke *f*, Strang *m*; *tr* mit e-r Haspe, e-m Überfall versehen.

hassock ['hæsək] Grasbüschel; Knie-, Fuß-, Sitzkissen *n*.

hast|e [heist] Hast, Eile, Geschwindigkeit, *fam* Fixigkeit *f*; *in* ~~ in (aller) Eile, auf dem schnellsten Wege; *to make* ~~ sich beeilen, ~~ *makes waste (prov)* Eile mit Weile! blinder Eifer schadet nur; ~**en** ['heisn] *tr* beschleunigen; antreiben, Beine machen *(s.o.* jdm); *itr* (sich be)eilen; ~**ily** ['-ili] *adv* eilig, hastig; ~**iness** ['heistinis] Hastigkeit, Überstürztheit, Übereiltheit, Voreiligkeit; Heftigkeit *f*, Jähzorn *m*; ~**y** ['heisti] eilig, schnell; hastig, überhastet, überstürzt, übereilt, voreilig; *(Arbeit)* flüchtig; stürmisch, heftig, hitzig, jäh(zornig); ~~ *bridge* Behelfsbrücke *f*; ~~ *pudding (Am* Mais-)Mehlpudding, Flammeri *m*.

*

hat [hæt] *s* Hut; *(cardinal's, red* ~*) rel* Kardinalshut *m*; Kardinalswürde *f*; *tr* e-n Hut aufsetzen *(s.o.* jdm); mit e-m Hut versehen; *as black as my* ~ kohlrabenschwarz; *under o.'s* ~ *(fam)* heimlich, (ins)geheim; ~ *in hand* unterwürfig; *to be high* ~ hochmütig sein; *to hang up o.'s* ~ sich häuslich niederlassen *(with s.o.* bei jdm); *to keep s.th. under o.'s* ~ etw für sich behalten; *to pass, to send round o.'s* ~ Geld (ein)sammeln *(for* für); *to take o.'s* ~ *off* den Hut abnehmen *(to* vor); *to talk out of, (Am) through o.'s* ~ *(fam)* ins Blaue, drauflos reden, faseln, aufschneiden, angeben, kohlen, schwindeln; *to throw o.'s* ~ *into the ring* als (Mit-)Bewerber auftreten; *my* ~*! (sl) a bad* ~ ein Taugenichts; ~**band** Hutband *n*; *black* ~~ Trauerflor *m* (um den Hut); ~**-block** Hutform *f*; ~**-box** Hutschachtel *f*; ~**-check girl** *Am* Garderobenfrau *f*; ~**-peg** Garderoben-, Kleiderhaken *m*; ~**-pin** Hutnadel *f*; ~**-rack** Kleiderrechen *m*; *Am sl* Klappergestell *n*; ~**-shop** Hutladen *m*; ~**-stand,** *Am* **-tree** Garderobenständer *m*; ~**ter** ['-ə] Hutmacher; Inhaber *m* e-s Hutgeschäfts; *as mad as a* ~~ rabiat, fuchsteufelswild; übergeschnappt.

hatch [hætʃ] **1.** *tr* ausbrüten *a. fig*; *fig* ausdenken, ersinnen; *fam pej* aushekken; *itr* brüten; *(Ei)* ausgebrütet werden; *(aus dem Ei)* ausschlüpfen; *s* Brüten *n*; Brut, Hecke; *fig* Folge *f*, Ergebnis *n*; *sl* Plan *m*; ~*es, matches and despatches* od *snatches* Familiennachrichten *f pl (bes. in der Times)*; ~**ery** ['-əri] Brutanstalt; Fischzuchtanstalt *f*; **2.** untere Halbtür; Klapp-, Falltür *f a. mar*; *(Flugzeug, Panzer)* Einstieg *m*; Luke; Durchreiche *f*, Servierfenster *n*; Schütz(e *f*) *n*; *under* ~*es (mar)* (in Arrest) unter Deck; *fig* außer Sicht; hin(über), erledigt, unter der Erde, tot; ~ **list** Ladeliste *f*; ~**way** Klappe; (Lade-) Luke *f*; **3.** *tr* schraffieren, schummern; *s* schraffierte Linie *f*; ~**ing** ['-iŋ] Schraffur *f*.

hatchet ['hætʃit] Beil *n*; *to bury the* ~ das Kriegsbeil begraben, Frieden machen; *to dig up, to take up the* ~ Streit, Krieg anfangen; ~**-face** scharf geschnittene(s) Gesicht *n*.

hat|e [heit] *tr* hassen, verabscheuen, sich ekeln vor; nicht mögen; *to* ~ *to do, doing s.th.* etw nicht gern, ungern tun; etw mit Bedauern tun; einem sehr peinlich sein, etw zu tun; *itr* Haß empfinden; *s lit poet* Haß *m*; ~**eful** ['-ful] verhaßt, hassenswert, verabscheuungswürdig, ekelhaft; ~**er** ['-ə] Hasser, Feind *m*; ~**red** ['heitrid] Haß *m*, (starke) Abneigung *f*, Groll *(of, for* gegen); Abscheu, Ekel *m (of* vor).

haught|iness ['hɔːtinis] Stolz, Hochmut *m*, Arroganz, Geringschätzigkeit *f*; ~**y** ['-i] stolz, hochmütig, *fam* -näsig, arrogant, anmaßend.

haul [hɔːl] *tr* ziehen, zerren *(at, upon* an); (ab-, weg)schleppen; (be)fördern, transportieren, fahren; *min* fördern; *mar* den Kurs ändern *(a ship* e-s Schiffes); *Am fam* herausholen *(out of bed* aus dem Bett); *itr* ziehen, zerren *(at, upon* an); *(Wind)* umschlagen, -springen; *fig* s-e Meinung, sein Verhalten ändern; *mar* den Kurs wechseln; *s* Ziehen, Zerren *n*; Fisch-, Beutezug; Fang *m*, Beute *f*, Gewinn; Transportweg; Schlepptransport *m*; (Beförderungs-)Last *f*; *to make a good* ~ reiche Beute machen; *to* ~ *over the coals* = *to* ~ *up*; *to* ~ *on, to the wind (mar)* an den Wind segeln; *to* ~ **down** *(Flagge)* einziehen, niederholen; *to* ~~ *o.'s flag, colo(u)rs (fig)* die Segel streichen, nach-, *fam* klein beigeben; *to* ~ **off** *mar* abdrehen *itr*; sich zurückziehen; *fam* zurückzucken; *Am* ausholen; *on s.o. (Am sl)* jdn mit den Fäusten bearbeiten; *to* ~ **up** zurechtweisen, tadeln, abkanzeln; ~**age** ['-idʒ] Schleppen *n*; Beförderung *f*, Transport *m*; *min* Förderung; Zugkraft *f*; Beförderungs-, Transportkosten *pl*; Rollgeld *n*; ~~ *contractor* Transportunternehmer *m*; ~~ *installation* Förderanlage *f*; ~~ *speed* Förder-, Transportgeschwindigkeit *f*; ~**er** ['-ə], ~**ier** ['-jə] Schleppende(r); Transportarbeiter Spediteur *m*.

haulm [hɔːm], **halm** [hɑːm] *(bes.* trokkener) (Getreide-)Halm, (Erbsen-, Bohnen-)Stengel *m*; (Dach-)Stroh *n*.

haunch [hɔːntʃ] Hüftpartie *f* und Hinterviertel, Gesäß *n*; Lendenstück *n*, Keule *f*; ~**-bone** Hüftbein *n*.

haunt [hɔːnt] *tr* häufig besuchen; (dauernd) verfolgen, belästigen, plagen, quälen- *(Erinnerung)* haften an; *(Vorstellung)* verbunden sein mit; *(Geist, Gespenst)* umgehen in; *s* häufig besuchte(r) Ort *m*; (Wirkungs-) Stätte *f*; gewöhnliche(r) Aufenthalt(sort); Schlupfwinkel *m*; Räuberhöhle *f*; *a* ~*ed house* ein Haus, in dem es spukt; ~**ing** ['-iŋ] *a*: *a* ~~ *idea* ein Gedanke, der e-n nicht losläßt.

hautboy ['(h)oubɔi] *mus* Oboe *f*.

Havana [hə'vænə] Havanna(zigarre) *f*.

have [hæv] *irr had, had* **1.** *tr allg* haben *(about one* bei sich, *on one* bei, an sich); haben, wissen *(from* von); (in Händen, zur Verfügung) haben, besitzen; wissen, können, verstehen; wollen, besagen, versichern, behaupten, glauben, verstehen; bekommen, erhalten, *fam* kriegen; lassen; zulassen, erlauben, gestatten; *fam* haben *(I* ~ *him* ich habe ihn, er kann mir nicht mehr entwischen); *fam* ('reingelegt) haben; *(als Hilfszeitwort in zs.-gesetzten Zeiten)* haben, sein; müssen *(to do* tun); **2.** *s fam* Dreh *m*, List *f*; Besitzende(r), Wohlhabende(r) *m*; **3.** *to* ~ *a bath* ein Bad nehmen; *to* ~ *it on the ball (Am sl)* intelligent sein, etw auf dem Kasten haben; *to* ~ *a cigarette* e-e Zigarette rauchen; *to* ~ *a cold* erkältet sein; *to* ~ *a dance* tanzen (gehen); *to* ~ *to do with s.o., s.th.* mit jdm, e-r S zu tun haben; *to* ~ *done* fertig, durch sein; *to* ~ *no doubt* nicht (be)zweifeln; *to* ~ *a game* ein Spiel machen; *to* ~ *the goods on s.o. (Am sl)* gegen jdn Beweise in den Händen haben; *to* ~ *got (fam)* haben; *to* ~ *it* (beim Spiel) gewonnen haben; *to* ~ *it in for s.o.* sich an jdm rächen wollen; jdn auf dem Strich haben; *to* ~ *it out with s.o.* sich mit jdm ausea.setzen, streiten; etw mit jdm ausfechten; *to* ~ *in keeping* in Aufbewahrung, in Verwahrung haben; *to* ~ *kittens, puppies, young (Tier)* Kleine, Junge kriegen *od* werfen; *to* ~ *o.'s leg broken* sich das Bein gebrochen haben; *to* ~ *a look* mal sehen, schauen, gucken; *to* ~ *in mind* im Sinn haben; *to* ~ *a smoke* rauchen; *to* ~ *a swim* schwimmen, baden; *to* ~ *tea* Tee trinken; *to* ~ *a try* e-n Versuch machen; *to* ~ *a walk* spazierengehen; *to* ~ *o.'s way* s-n Willen durchsetzen; *to* ~ *much work* viel zu tun haben; **4.** *you had better* es wäre besser, wenn du; *you had best* das beste, am besten wäre es, wenn du; *I wouldn't* ~ *you do that* das dürfen Sie nicht tun! *what would you* ~ *me do?* was soll ich machen? *will you* ~, *please* ~ *the goodness, kindness* haben Sie die Güte, seien Sie so gut! *I* ~ *it at heart* es liegt mir am Herzen; *you* ~ *it* Sie haben's getroffen; so ist's; *let him* ~ *it! (fam)* gib ihm (Saures)! *he's had it* er ist erledigt, er hat sein Sach! *I would* ~ *you know* Sie müssen wissen; *you* ~ *me, have you?* Sie haben mich verstanden, nicht wahr? *I had rather ... than* ich möchte lieber ... als; ~ *you the time on you?* können Sie mir sagen, wie spät es ist? ~ *it your own way!* mach, was du willst! *I had as well* ich könnte ebensogut; *to* ~ **at** *obs* losgehen auf, angreifen; schlagen, prügeln; *to* ~ **away** wegkriegen, entfernen; *to* ~ **back** zurückbekommen, -kriegen; sich zurückgeben lassen; *to* ~ **in** hereinholen; einladen; *to* ~ **off** wegbringen, -schaffen; *to* ~ **on** *(Kleidung)* anhaben; *sl* beschummeln; *to* ~ *s.th. on s.o. (Am fam)* etw vor jdm voraushaben; *to* ~ **out** hinausschaffen; *to* ~ **up** heraufholen, heraufkommen lassen; *to be*

had up vor den Richter kommen (*for* wegen); **~-not** *fam* Habenichts *m.*
haven ['heivn] Hafen; *fig* geschützte(r) Platz *m*, Zufluchtsort *m.*
haven't ['hævn(t)] = *have not.*
haversack ['hævəsæk] Brotbeutel *m.*
having ['hæviŋ] *s (häufig pl)* Habe *f.*
havoc ['hævək] *s* Verwüstung, Verheerung, Zerstörung *f*; *to make ~ of, to play ~ with, among* verwüsten; *bes. fig* vernichten, zugrunde richten.
haw [hɔ:] **1.** Hagebutte *f*; **2.** *itr (meist hum and ~)* stammeln, stottern; *s* (Verlegenheits-)Räuspern *n*; *interj* hm! **3.** *interj* hü! **4.** *zoo* Nickhaut *f.*
hawfinch ['hɔ:fintʃ] *orn* Kirschkernbeißer *m.*
haw-haw ['hɔ:'hɔ] *interj* haha! *s* schallende(s) Gelächter *n.*
hawk [hɔ:k] **1.** Habicht *m*; *pl* Falken *m pl (Familie)*; *sing fig* habgierige(r) Mensch; Gauner, Schwindler *m*; *itr* Falkenjagd treiben (*at* auf); **~er** ['-ə] Falkner *m*; **~-eyed** *a* mit scharfen Augen; scharfsichtig; **~ing** ['-iŋ] Falkenjagd, -beize, Falknerei *f*; **~-nosed** *a* mit e-r Adlernase; **~-weed** *bot* Habichtskraut *n*; **2.** *itr tr* hausieren (mit); *tr (Nachricht) (to ~ about)* verbreiten, ausposaunen; **~er** ['-ə] Straßenhändler; Hausierer *m*; **3.** *itr* sich räuspern; *s* Räuspern *n.*
hawse [hɔ:z] *mar* Klüsenwand; *(~-hole)* Klüse *f*; **~r** ['-ə] *mar* (Anker-)Tau, Kabel *n*, Trosse *f.*
hawthorn ['hɔ:θɔ:n] *bot* Weiß-, Hagedorn *m.*
hay [hei] *s* Heu; *Am sl* Bett *n*, Falle *f*; *itr (to make ~)* Heu machen; *between ~ and grass (Am fam)* für das eine zu früh und fürs andere zu spät; *to hit the ~ (Am sl)* sich in die Falle hauen, zu Bett gehen; *to look for a needle in a bottle of ~* etw Unmögliches versuchen; *to make ~ of s.th.* etw durchea.bringen; *to make ~ while the sun shines* das Eisen schmieden, solange es heiß ist; *that isn't ~ (Am sl)* das ist kein Pappenstiel, keine Kleinigkeit; **~-box** Kochkiste *f*; **~-cart** Heuwagen *m*; **~cock, ~rick, ~stack** Heuhaufen *m*; **~-fever** Heuschnupfen *m*; **~-fork** Heugabel *f*; **~-loft** Heuboden *m*; **~maker** Heu(mach)er *m*; *Am sl* K.o.-Schlag *m*, bissige Bemerkung *f*, beste(s) Stück *n*; **~seed** Grassamen *m*; Heuabfälle *m pl*; *Am sl* Bauer(ntölpel) *m*; **~wire** *a Am sl* durcheinander, in Unordnung; verkehrt; verpfuscht, kaputt; verrückt, übergeschnappt; *to go ~~* verrückt, wahnsinnig werden; kaputtgehen; durcheinandergeraten.
hazard ['hæzəd] *s* Zufall *m*; Wagnis, Risiko *n*, Gefahr; *tech* Gefahrenquelle *f*; *jur* Versicherungsrisiko; Hasardspiel *n*; *tr* aufs Spiel setzen (*s.th. on* etw für); wagen, *fam* riskieren; sich aussetzen (*s.th.* dat); *at all ~s* auf alle Gefahren hin; unter allen Umständen; **~ous** ['-əs] zufallsbedingt; gewagt, gefährlich, *fam* riskant.
haz|e [heiz] **1.** Dunst, leichte(r) Nebel; Höhenrauch *m*; *fig* geistige Trübung, Unklarheit *f*; *tr* diesig, dunstig machen; **~iness** ['-inis] Verschwommenheit, Unklarheit *f*; **~y** ['-i] dunstig, diesig; verschwommen, vage, unklar, getrübt; **2.** *tr Am* schikanieren, schlauchen, bimsen; hochnehmen.
hazel ['heizl] *s* Hasel(strauch *m*) *f*; Haselstock *m*, -holz; Nußbraun *n*; *a* Hasel-; nußbraun; **~-nut** Haselnuß *f.*
he [hi:] *prn* er; *~ who* derjenige, welcher; *s*: *a ~* ein Er *m*; *he who laughs last laughs best (prov)* wer zuletzt lacht, lacht am besten; *~- (pref) (von Tieren)* männlich; **~-goat** Ziegenbock *m*; **~-man** *Am* starke(r) Mann, Kraftmensch, *fam* Muskelprotz *m*; **~-togs** *pl Am sl* Männerkleider *m pl.*
head [hed] **1.** *s* Kopf *m*, *poet* Haupt *n*; *fig* Geist *m*, Vernunft *f*, Verstand *m*; Überlegung, Phantasie *f*, Wille *m*, Gedächtnis *n*, Fähigkeit *f*; *(mit Zahlwort)* Mann, Mensch *m*, Person *f*; *(pl ~) (Vieh)* Stück *n*; Kopf-, *lit* Haupteslänge *f*; Haupt *n*, Häuptling *m*, (An-)Führer, Leiter, Chef, Vorsteher, Direktor *m*; Führung, Leitung, führende Stellung, Spitze *f (e-r Organisation)*; ober(st)e(r) Teil *m*, obere(s) Ende *n*, Spitze *f*, Gipfel; (Baum-)Wipfel *m*, Krone *f*; Geweih *n*; Schaum(krone *f*) *m (auf dem Bier)*; Sahne *f*, Rahm *m*; (Kohl-, Salat-)Kopf; (Stecknadel-)Knopf; *(Nagel)* Kopf; Eiterpfropfen *m*; vordere(s) Ende *n*, Spitze *f (a. e-r marschierenden Kolonne, e-s Schiffes)*; *(Schiff)* Bug *m*; *(Bett)* Kopfende *n*; Landspitze *f*, Kap, Vorgebirge *n*; Quelle *f*; Mühlteich; (Wasser-, Dampf-)Druck; Wasserstand *m*; Gefälle *n*; *typ* Kolumnentitel *m*; Schlagzeile; (Kapitel-)Überschrift; Rubrik, Kategorie *f*; Abschnitt *m*, Kapitel *n*, Hauptteil *m*; Thema *n*, (Haupt-)Punkt; (Rechnungs-)Posten; Höhe-, Wendepunkt *m*, Krisis *f*; *sport* Kopfball; *Am sl* Mund *m*; hübsche(s) Mädchen *n*; *Am mil sl* Toilette *f*; **2.** *a* hauptsächlich, Haupt-, Ober-; Spitzen-; **3.** *tr* (an)führen, leiten; an der Spitze stehen *od* gehen (*s.th.* e-r S); vorstehen (*s.th.* e-r S); mit e-m Kopf *od* e-r Überschrift versehen; *(Baum)* köpfen, abwipfeln; *sport (Ball)* köpfen; *(in e-e bestimmte Richtung)* stellen; **4.** *itr (Pflanze)* e-n Kopf ansetzen *od* bilden; sich *(in e-r bestimmten Richtung)* bewegen, fahren (*for* in Richtung auf); *(Fluß)* entspringen; als erster stehen (*a list* auf e-r Liste); der Erste sein (*a class* in e-r Klasse); *to ~ off* ableiten, -lenken; in e-e andere Richtung bringen; verhindern, verhüten; abbiegen; *to ~ up (Pflanze)* e-n Kopf ansetzen; *fig* den Höhepunkt erreichen; kritisch werden; **5.** *a ~* pro Kopf; *at the ~ of* an der Spitze *gen*; oben, am oberen Ende; *by a ~ (Pferderennen)* um e-e Kopflänge; *by a short ~* um e-e Nasenlänge; *by the ~ and ears, shoulders* mit Gewalt; *from ~ to foot* von Kopf bis Fuß; *off, out of o.'s ~* verrückt; *on s.o.'s ~ (fig) (Schuld)* auf jds Haupt; auf jds Verantwortung; *on this ~* zu diesem Punkt; *out of o.'s own ~* aus sich selbst (heraus); *under the same ~* unter der gleichen Rubrik; *~ first, foremost* kopfüber; *~ over heels* kopfüber; *fig* bis über die Ohren *(verliebt)*; bis an den Hals *(in Schulden)*; Hals über Kopf; völlig, gründlich; **6.** *to ~ for ruin* in sein Verderben stürzen; *to be ~ing for* auf dem Wege sein nach; zusteuern, Kurs nehmen auf; *aero* anfliegen (*for s.th.* etw); *to be off, out of o.'s ~* aus dem Häuschen sein; den Verstand verloren haben; *to be weak in the ~* e-e weiche Birne haben; *to be ~ and shoulders above s.o. (fig)* weit, *fam* haushoch über jdm stehen; *to beat s.o.~ off* jdn übertrumpfen; *to bringt to a ~* zur Entscheidung bringen; *to come to a ~ (Geschwür)* reif werden; *fig* sich zuspitzen; zum Krach kommen; *to eat s.o.'s ~ off (fig)* essen wie ein Scheunendrescher; *to gather ~* Kräfte sammeln; an Kraft gewinnen; überhandnehmen; *to give s.o. his ~* jdm freien Lauf lassen; *to go to the ~ (Getränk)* zu Kopf steigen *a. fig*; *to go over s.o.'s ~* über jds Kopf hinweg handeln; *to hang, to hide o.'s ~* die Augen *(vor Scham)* niederschlagen; *to have a ~* begabt sein (*for* für); *Am sl* e-n Kater haben; *to have a poor ~ for* nicht viel loshaben in; keine Begabung haben für; *to hit the nail on the ~* den Nagel auf den Kopf treffen; *to keep o.'s ~* die Ruhe bewahren, (ganz) ruhig bleiben; *to keep o.'s ~ over water* sich *(wirtschaftlich)* über Wasser halten; *to lay, to put ~s together (fig)* die Köpfe zs.stecken; gemeinsam beraten; sich zs.setzen; *to lose o.'s ~ (fig)* den Kopf verlieren; *to make ~* vorwärtsdrängen; Fortschritte machen; *against s.o.* jdm die Spitze bieten; *to be unable to make ~ or tail of* nicht schlau werden aus; *to put s.th. into s.o.'s ~* jdm etw in den Kopf setzen; *to put s.th. out of o.'s, s.o.'s ~* sich etw aus dem Kopf schlagen; jdn von etw abbringen; *to reckon in o.'s ~* im Kopf rechnen; *to shake o.'s ~* den Kopf schütteln (*at* zu); *to take the ~* die Führung übernehmen; *to take it into o.'s ~* sich etw in den Kopf setzen, sich auf etw versteifen; beabsichtigen, planen; *to talk s.o.'s ~ off* jdn dumm u. dämlich reden; *to talk over s.o.'s ~, over the ~s of o.'s audience* über jdn, über die Köpfe der Zuhörer hinwegreden; *to turn s.o.'s ~* jdn schwindlig machen; *fig* jdm den Kopf verdrehen; **7.** *that's over his ~* das geht über s-n Verstand; *my ~ is spinning* mir dreht sich alles im Kopf herum; *where are you ~ed?* wo wollen Sie hin? *two ~s are better than one* zwei sehen mehr als einer; *~s up!* aufpassen! *~(s) or tail(s)?* Kopf oder Wappen *(e-r Münze)*? **8.** *back of the ~* Hinterkopf *m*; *old ~ on young shoulders* geistige Reife *f*; *spread ~* ganzseitige Überschrift *f*; *top of the ~* Scheitel *m*; *~ of a charge* Anklagepunkt *m*; *~ of the department* Abteilungsleiter *m*; *~ of the family* Familienoberhaupt *n*; *~ of the government* Regierungschef *m*; *~ of hair* (Haar-)Schopf *m*; *~ of a letter* Briefkopf *m*; *~ of negotiation* Verhandlungspunkt *m*; **~ache** ['-eik] Kopfweh *n*, -schmerzen *m pl a. fam fig*; *fam* Sorgen *f pl*; *to have a bad ~~* schlimme Kopfschmerzen haben; *to suffer from ~~* an Kopfschmerzen leiden; *~~ pill, powder* Kopfwehtablette *f*, -pulver *n*; **~achy** ['-eiki] *a* mit Kopfschmerzen behaftet sein; Kopfschmerzen hervorrufend; **~band** Stirnband *n*; *typ* Kopfleiste *f*; *(Einband)* Kapitäl *n*; **~board** Kopfbrett *n*; **~cheese** *Am (Küche)* Kopfsülze *f*, *a.* Eisbein *n* in Gelee; **~-clerk** Bürovorsteher *m*; **~-dress** Kopfputz *m*; Frisur *f*; **~ed** ['-id] *a (Kohl)* e-n Kopf bildend, Kopf-; mit e-r Überschrift (versehen); *in Zssgen* -köpfig; **~er** ['-ə] Kopfball *m (Fußball)*; Stecknadelwippe, Knopfspindel *f*; *Am* Ährenköpfer *m (Maschine)*; Verbindungsrohr, -stück *n*; *mot* Falltank; *arch* Binder, Tragstein *m*, Bodenplatte *f*; Kopfstück *n*, Scheinbinder; *fam* Kopfsprung *(ins Wasser)*; *sl* Versuch, Mißgriff *m*; *to take a ~~* e-n Kopfsprung machen; **~gear** ['-giə] Kopfbedeckung *f*; *(Pferd)* Zaumzeug; *tech* Fördergerüst *n*; **~-hunter** Kopfjäger *m*; **~iness** ['-inis] Halsstarrigkeit *f*, Eigensinn *m*; Unüberlegtheit *f*, Ungestüm *n*; *(Getränk)* berauschende Wirkung *f*; **~ing** ['-iŋ] *typ* Titel *m*, Überschrift *f*, Kopf; *com* Posten *m*, Rubrik, Position; *(Zeitung)* Schlagzeile

f; Thema *n*, Punkt; *sport* Kopfball; *mar aero* Steuerkurs *m*; **~land** Landzunge *f*, Vorgebirge, Kap *n*; *agr* Rain *m*; **~less** ['-lis] kopf-, *fig* führerlos; **~light** Scheinwerfer(licht *n*) *m*; *mar aero* Buglicht *n*; *to turn the ~~s on* aufblenden; **~-line** *typ* Titel(zeile *f*) *m (bes. Zeitung)*, Schlagzeile *f*; *pl tele* das Wichtigste in Schlagzeilen; *to hit the ~~ s (sl fig)* Schlagzeilen liefern; **~liner** *Am theat* Zugkraft *f*, Hauptdarsteller(in *f*) *m*; **~long** *adv* kopfüber; *a. a* überstürzt, übereilt, voreilig, unüberlegt, rasch, stürmisch, ungestüm; *a (Sturz)* mit dem Kopf nach unten; **~man** ['-mæn] Häuptling; Chef, (An-)Führer, Leiter, Vorsteher; ['-'-] Vorarbeiter *m*; **~master** *(Schule)* (Di-)Rektor *m*; **~mistress** *(Schule)* (Di-)Rektorin, Schulvorsteherin *f*; **~-money** Kopfsteuer *f*; Kopfgeld *n*, -prämie *f*; **~-office** Hauptbüro *n*; **~-on** *a* u. *adv* mit der (den) Vorderseite(n); frontal; *adv* direkt aufgegenea.; *~~ attack* Frontalangriff *m*; *~~ collision* Auf-, Zs.prall, Frontalzs.stoß *m*; **~-phones** *pl tele radio* Kopfhörer *m pl*; **~piece** *obs* Helm *m*; Kopfbedeckung *f*, -stück *n*, *radio* -hörer *m*; Kopf *(a. Person)*, Verstand *m*; *typ* Kopfleiste *f*; *arch* Sturz *m*; **~quarters** *pl oft mit sing* Hauptquartier *n*; Befehls-, Gefechtsstand; Stab *m*; Oberkommando *n*; *com* Hauptsitz *m*, Zentrale *f*, Stammhaus *n*; Hauptgeschäftsstelle *f*; *police ~~* Polizeidirektion *f*; **~-rest** Kopfstütze *f*; **~room** lichte Höhe *f*; **~-sail** *mar* Vorstengestagsegel *n*; **~-set** *radio* Kopfstück *n*, -hörer *m*; **~ship** ['-ʃip] Führerschaft, Führung, Leitung, führende, leitende Stellung *f*; **~sman** ['-zmən] Henker, Scharfrichter *m*; **~spring** (Haupt-)Quelle *f a. fig*; *fig* Ursprung *m*; **~ start** *Am fam* Vorsprung *m*; **~stock** ['-stɔk] Spindelstock *m*; **~stone** Grabstein; Grund-, Eckstein *m a. fig*; **~stream** Quellfluß *m*; **~strong** eigenwillig, -sinnig, starrköpfig, verbissen; **~-voice** Kopfstimme *f*; **~-waiter** Oberkellner *m*; **~waters** *pl* Quellen *f pl*, Quellflüsse *m pl*; **~way** Vorwärtsbewegung, *bes. mar* Fahrt *f*; *fig* Fortschritte *m pl*, Erfolg; Vorsprung *m*; *arch* lichte Höhe *f*; *rail* Zugabstand *m*, -folge *f*; *to make ~~* vorwärts-, vorankommen *a. fig*; *fig* Fortschritte machen; **~wind** Gegenwind *m*; **~-word** Stich-, Leitwort *n*; **~-work** Kopf-, geistige Arbeit *f*; **~-worker** Kopf-, Geistesarbeiter *m*; **~y** ['-i] eigenwillig, -sinnig, halsstarrig, dickköpfig; unüberlegt, voreilig; *(Getränk)* berauschend.

heal [hi:l] *tr* heilen; befreien *(von Kummer, Ärger)*; *(Streit)* schlichten, beilegen; *(Streitende)* versöhnen; *itr (Kranker)* wieder gesund werden; *to ~ up, over* zuheilen; *time ~s all sorrows* die Zeit heilt Wunden; **~-all** Allheilmittel *n*; **~er** ['-ə] Heilkundige(r), -praktiker; Gesundbeter *m*; Heilmittel *n*; **~ing** ['-iŋ] *a* heilend; Heil-; *s* Heilung *f*.

health [helθ] Gesundheit(szustand *m*) *f*; *to be in poor ~* kränklich sein; *to drink a ~ to s.o.* auf jds Gesundheit trinken; *board of ~* Gesundheitsamt *n*, -behörde *f*; *ministry of ~* Gesundheitsministerium *n*; *public ~* öffentliche Gesundheitspflege *f*, -wesen *n*; **~ certificate** Gesundheitspaß *m*; **~-food store** Reformhaus *n*; **~ful** ['-ful] gesund, zuträglich (*to* für); **~iness** ['-inis] Gesundheit, Zuträglichkeit *f*; **~ insurance** Krankenversicherung *f*; *National H~ I~* Staatliche Krankenversicherung *f*; **~-resort** Kurort *m*; **~y** ['-i] gesund; zuträglich; *fam* mächtig, tüchtig.

heap [hi:p] *s* Haufen *m*; *Am sl* alte(s) Vehikel *n*; *~s (fam)* ein Haufen, e-e Menge, e-e Masse (*of money* Geld); *tr (to ~ up, together)* an-, auf-, zs.häufen; voll bepacken, be-, überladen (*with* mit); *fig* überhäufen (*with favo(u)rs* mit Gunstbezeigungen); *in ~s* in Haufen, haufenweise; *~s of times (fam)* mächtig oft; *to be struck, to be knocked all of a ~ (fam)* (völlig) platt, ganz verblüfft sein.

hear [hiːə] *irr heard, heard* [hə:d] *tr* hören (*of* von; *doing, do* tun); anhören; zuhören (*s.th.* e-r S); achten, aufmerken, -passen, achtgeben auf; zur Notiz, zur Kenntnis nehmen; erfahren; *(Lektion)* abhören; *jur* verhandeln; *(Zeugen)* vernehmen; verhören; *itr* (zu)hören; erfahren (*of, about* von); Nachricht erhalten, Bescheid bekommen (*from* von); *to ~ out* bis zu Ende anhören; *~! ~! (parl)* hört! hört! ausgezeichnet! bravo! *he won't ~ of it* er will davon nichts wissen; *let me ~ from you* lassen Sie von sich hören; **~er** ['-rə] (Zu-)Hörer *m*; **~ing** ['-riŋ] Hören; Gehör(ssinn *m*) *n*; Audienz *f*; *jur* Verhör *n*, Vernehmung, Verhandlung; Hörweite *f*; *within, out of ~~* in, außer Hörweite *f*; *hard of ~~* schwerhörig; *his ~~ is poor* er hört schlecht; *~~-aid* Hörgerät *n*; **~say** ['-sei] Gerede, Geschwätz, Gerücht *n*; *by, from ~~* vom Hörensagen; gerüchtweise.

hearken ['hɑ:kən] *itr* zuhören (*to s.o.* jdm); hinhören (*to* auf); horchen.

hearse [hə:s] Leichenwagen *m*.

heart [hɑ:t] Herz *n a. fig*; *fig* Brust *f*, Busen *m*; Innere(s) *n*, tiefste Gefühle *n pl*, Gedanken *m pl*, Bewußtsein *n*; Charakter *m*, Wesen *n*, Natur; Anlage; Seele *f*; Geist; Mut *m*, Energie, Kraft, Entschlossenheit *f*; Herzchen *n*, Liebling, Schatz *m*; Innerste(s), Zentrum *n*, Mittelpunkt *m*, Hauptsache *f*; *das* Wesentliche, *der* Kern; *pl (Kartenspiel)* Herz *n*; *after o.'s own ~* nach Herzenslust; *at ~* im Herzen, im Innersten; wirklich; im Grunde genommen; *by ~* auswendig *(können)*; *for my ~* um mein Leben gern; *from (the bottom of) o.'s ~* aus (tiefstem) Herzensgrund; aufrichtig; *in o.'s ~ of ~s (fig)* im Innersten; *in good ~ (agr)* e-n guten Ertrag abwerfend; *out of ~* niedergeschlagen; *to o.'s ~'s content* nach Herzenslust; *with all o.'s ~* von ganzem Herzen; *with half a ~* nur halb bei der Sache; *~ and soul* von ganzem Herzen; mit Leib u. Seele; *to be near to s.o.'s ~* jdm am Herzen liegen; *to break s.o.'s ~* jdm das Herz brechen; *to cry o.'s ~ out* sich die Seele aus dem Leibe weinen; *to eat o.'s ~ out* vor Kummer *od* Sehnsucht vergehen; *to get* od *to learn, to know by ~* auswendig lernen, wissen; *to get to the ~ of s.th.* etw auf den Grund kommen; *to have a ~ (fig)* ein Herz haben; Verständnis haben; *to have o.'s ~ in the right place* das Herz am rechten Fleck haben; *not to have the ~ to* es nicht übers Herz bringen, zu; *to lay to ~* beherzigen, sich angelegen sein lassen; *to lose o.'s ~ to* sich verlieben in; *to set o.'s ~ at rest* sich zufrieden geben; *to set o.'s ~ on* sein Herz hängen an; *to take ~* sich ein Herz fassen; *to take to ~* sich zu Herzen nehmen; *to wear o.'s ~ on o.'s sleeve* das Herz auf der Zunge haben; *I have it at ~, I have my ~ in it* das liegt mir sehr am Herzen; *I have a heavy ~* das Herz ist mir schwer; *he has his ~ in his mouth, boots* das Herz fiel ihm in die Hose(n); *don't lose ~* verlier den Mut nicht! *change of ~* Gefühlsumschwung *m*; *~-to-~ talk* offene Aussprache *f*; **~ache** Herzeleid *n*, Kummer *m*; **~-attack** *med* Herzanfall *m*; **~-beat** *physiol* Puls, Herzschlag *m*; **~ break** Herzeleid *n*; **~-breaking** herzzerbrechend; **~-broken** *a* mit gebrochenem Herzen, in tiefem Schmerz; **~-burn** Sodbrennen *n*; *fig* Eifersucht *f*, Neid *m*; **~-burning** Unzufriedenheit *f*, Neid *m*, Eifersucht *f*, Groll *m*; **~-disease** Herzleiden *n*; **~en** ['-n] *tr* auf-, ermuntern, ermutigen, stärken; **~ failure** *med* Herzschlag *m*; **~felt** *a* aufrichtig; tief empfunden; **~ily** ['-ili] *adv* herzhaft, tüchtig; herzlich; **~iness** ['-inis] Herzlichkeit, Innigkeit; Aufrichtigkeit *f*; **~land** Kernland *n*; **~less** ['-lis] herzlos, ohne Erbarmen; mutlos, verzagt, kleinmütig; kühl, ohne Begeisterung, schwunglos; **~lessness** ['-lisnis] Herzlosigkeit; Verzagtheit; Schwunglosigkeit *f*; **~-rending** herzzerreißend; **~-searching** *a* schmerzlich; *s* Gewissenserforschung *f*; **~sease, ~'s ease** *bot* wilde(s) Stiefmütterchen *n*; **~-shaped** *a* herzförmig; **~sick** gemütsleidend; sehr unglücklich, niedergeschlagen, trübsinnig; **~sore** bekümmert, bedrückt; **~-strings** *pl* stärkste Gefühle *n pl*; tiefste Zuneigung *f*; *to pull at s.o.'s ~~* jdn zutiefst erregen; **~-throb** *fam* Schwarm *m*; Angebetete(r *m*) *f*; **~-whole** frei, innerlich nicht gebunden; aufrichtig, offen(herzig); unerschrokken, tapfer; **~-wood** Kernholz *n*; **~y** ['-i] *a* herzlich, innig; aufrichtig; stark, kräftig; tüchtig, gesund; *(Essen)* nahrhaft, herzhaft; ausreichend; reichlich; *(Esser)* tüchtig; *(Boden)* fruchtbar; *s sl* Sportler *m*; *pl sl* Kameraden, Jung(en)s *m pl*; *hale and ~~* gesund u. munter; *he is not ~~ in it* das ist nicht sein Ernst.

hearth [hɑ:θ] *fig* (häuslicher) Herd *m*; (trautes) Heim *n*, Familienkreis; Feuerrost; Schmiedeofen ; *(Hochofen)* Herd, Eisenkasten *m*; **~-rug** Kaminvorleger *m*; **~-stone** Kaminplatte *f*; *fig* (häuslicher) Herd *m*.

heat [hi:t] *s* Hitze, *phys* Wärme *f*; Wärmegrad *m*; Wärmeempfindung *f*; heiße(s) Wetter *od* Klima *n*; Heizung *f*; Brennen *(scharfer Speisen* od *Getränke)*; Fieber(hitze *f*) *n*; Glut *a. fig*; *fig* Erregung *f*, Zorn, Eifer *m*, Leidenschaft; Brunst, *(weidmännisch)* Brunft; *(Hund)* Läufigkeit; *sport* Anstrengung *f*; Lauf, Gang *m*, (*bes.* Vor-)Runde, Vorentscheidung *f*; *sl* (Hoch-)Druck; Zwang *m*; *attr* Hitze-, Wärme-, Heiz-; *tr* erhitzen *a. fig*, heiß machen, heizen, entzünden; auf-, erregen, in Auf-, Erregung versetzen; *itr* sich erhitzen, heiß werden; sich entzünden; sich aufregen, in Erregung geraten; *to ~ up* erhitzen; *(Speise)* heiß machen, aufwärmen; *at, in, on ~* brünstig, läufig; *in the ~ of the debate* in der Hitze, im Eifer des Gefechts; *to turn on the ~ (Am sl)* erpressen; unter Druck setzen; *dead ~* unentschiedene(s) Rennen *n*; *final ~ (sport)* Ausscheidungskampf *m*; **~-apoplexy, -stroke** Hitzschlag *m*; **~ barrier** Hitzemauer *f*; **~edly** ['-idli] *adv* in Erregung; **~er** ['-ə] Heizer; Heizkörper, -apparat *m*, -element *n*, -sonne; *Am sl* Pistole *f*; *gas-~~* Gasbadeofen *m*; *~~ current, voltage* Heizstrom *m*, -spannung *f*; **~ flash** Hitzestrahlung *f*; **~ing** ['-iŋ] Heizung; Erwärmung *f*; *central ~~* Zentralheizung *f*; *~~ coil* Heizspule *f*; *~~ cushion, pad*

Heizkissen *n*; ~~ *filament* Heizfaden *m*; ~~ *plate* Heizplatte *f*; ~~ *power* Heizkraft *f*; ~~ *surface* Heizfläche *f*; ~ **insulation** Wärmeisolierung *f*; ~ **lightning** *Am* Wetterleuchten *n*; ~ **production** Wärmeentwicklung *f*; **~-proof** hitzebeständig, wärmefest; ~ **radiation** Wärmestrahlung *f*; **~-resistant** wärmebeständig; **~-treat** *tr* pasteurisieren; wärmebehandeln; **~-treatment** Wärmebehandlung *f*; **~-unit** Wärmeeinheit *f*; **~-value** Heizwert *m*; **~-wave** *mete* Hitzewelle *f*.

heath [hi:θ] Heide *f*, Ödland *n*; *bot* Erika, Heide(kraut *n*) *f*; **~-cock** Birkhahn *m*; **~y** ['-i] heidebestanden; Heide-.

heathen ['hi:ðən] *s* Heide; Barbar *m*; *the* ~ die Heiden; *a* heidnisch; **~dom** ['-dəm] Heidentum *n*; die Heiden *pl*; **~ish** ['-iʃ] heidnisch; barbarisch; **~ism** ['-izm] Heidentum *n*; Götzendienst *m*, Abgötterei; Barbarei *f*.

heather ['heðə] *s* Heide(kraut *n*), Erika *f*; **~-bell** Heideblüte *f*; **~y** ['-ri] mit Heide bestanden; Heide-.

heave [hi:v] *mar irr hove, hove* [houv] *tr* (an-, hoch)heben; *mar* hieven; *(den Anker)* lichten; (an)schwellen lassen; *(Brust)* dehnen, weiten; *(Seufzer)* ausstoßen; *(Stein)* werfen; *geol* verwerfen; *itr* sich heben und senken, wogen; (an)schwellen; *physiol* brechen, sich übergeben wollen; keuchen, schwer atmen; *mar* ziehen (*at, on* an); *s* Heben; Wogen, Anschwellen *n*; *geol* Verschiebung *f*; *to ~ in sight (Schiff)* in Sicht kommen; *to ~ down (mar)* kielholen; *to ~ out* auswerfen; *to ~ to (mar)* beidrehen; *~ ho!* hau ruck! **~r** ['-ə] *mar* Trimmer *m*; Hebebaum, -bock *m*; Brechstange *f*.

heaven ['hevn] *rel* Himmel; *fig* (Freuden-)Himmel *m*; *H~* der Himmel, die Vorsehung, Gott *m*; *meist pl, bes. lit poet* (sichtbarer) Himmel *m*, Firmament *n*; *to move ~ and earth* Himmel und Erde in Bewegung setzen, das menschenmögliche tun; *for ~'s sake, good ~s!* du lieber Himmel! du meine Güte! *thank ~!* Gott sei Dank! *~ forbid!* Gott bewahre! **~ly** ['-li] *rel* himmlisch *a. fig*; Himmels-; *~~ bodies (pl)* Himmelskörper *m pl*; **~ward** ['-wəd] *a* himmelwärts gerichtet; *adv* u. **~wards** ['-wədz] himmelwärts; *obs poet* gen Himmel.

heaviness ['hevinis] Schwere *f*, Druck *m*, Gewichtigkeit, Heftigkeit; Stärke *f*, große(r) Umfang *m*; Lästigkeit; Niedergedrücktheit, Bekümmertheit *f*; Ernst; *(Straße)* schlechte(r) Zustand *m*.

heavy ['hevi] *a* schwer *(von Gewicht)*; (spezifisch) schwer; gewichtig, stark, fest; heftig, laut; grob, dick, massiv; überdurchschnittlich; anhaltend; umfangreich; hoch; ernst(haft, -lich); schwer (zu ertragen), drückend, lästig, unangenehm, unerfreulich, schlimm, schlecht; schwer (zu tun), anstrengend; niedergedrückt, (tief) bekümmert; müde, schläfrig; *(Speise)* schwer, fett, teigig; *(Geruch)* durchdringend, penetrant; *(Himmel)* bedeckt; *(Regen)* stark, heftig; *(Boden)* schwer, lehmig; *(Straße)* schlammig, schmutzig, schwer passierbar; *(Verkehr)* stark; trüb(e); *(Abhang)* steil; *(Strich)* dick; schwerfällig, ungelenk, ungeschickt; *com (Absatz)* schlecht; *(Geldstrafe)* hoch; *(Börse)* lustlos; *mil* schwerbewaffnet; *theat* düster, tragisch; ernst, feierlich; *Am sl (Verabredung)* wichtig; *adv bes. in Zssgen* schwer; *s theat* Bösewicht; *sport* Schwergewichtler *m*; *with a ~ heart* schweren Herzens; *to lie ~ (fig)* schwer liegen, lasten (*on* auf); *time hangs ~* die Zeit schleicht dahin, will nicht weitergehen; *a ~ sea* e-e schwere See; **~-armed** *a* schwerbewaffnet; *~* **beer** Starkbier *n*; *~* **buyer** Großeinkäufer *m*; *~* **current** Starkstrom *m*; **~-duty** Hochleistungs-, Hochdruck-; *~* **gymnastics** *pl* Geräteturnen *n*; **~-handed** *a* unbeholfen, ungeschickt; bedrückend, hart; **~-hearted** *a* traurig, (nieder)gedrückt; *~* **industry** Schwerindustrie *f*; **~-laden** *a* schwerbeladen; *fig* kummervoll; *~* **oil** Schweröl *n*; *~* **print** Fettdruck *m*; *~* **water** *chem* schwere(s) Wasser *n*; **~-weight** *s sport a. allg* Schwergewichtler *m*; *fam* Kanone *f*; *a sport* Schwergewichts-; schwer *a. fig*; *~* **worker** Schwerarbeiter *m*.

hebdomadal [heb'dɔmədl] wöchentlich.

Hebr|aic [hi(:)'breiik] *a* hebräisch; *s* (das) Hebräisch(e); **~ew** ['hi:bru:] *s* Hebräer, Jude *m*; *a* hebräisch, jüdisch.

hecatomb ['hekətoum] *hist* Hekatombe *f a. fig*; Gemetzel *n*.

heck [hek] *interj fam* verflixt! *s fam* Hölle *f*; *a ~ of a row* ein Höllenlärm.

heckl|e ['hekl] *tr (Flachs)* hecheln; *fig (e-m Redner)* Fangfragen stellen (*s.o.* jdm); belästigen, verwirren, durchea.bringen; in die Enge treiben; **~er** ['-ə] lästige(r) Frager; Zwischenrufer *m*.

hectic ['hektik] *a* schwindsüchtig; *med fig* hektisch, fieberhaft; *(Wangen)* fieberheiß, -rot; *fam* aufregend; *s (~ fever)* Schwindsucht; *to have a ~ time* keinen Augenblick Ruhe haben.

hectograph ['hekto(u)gra:f] *s* Hektograph *m*; *tr* hektographieren.

hector ['hektə] *s* Prahlhans, Bramarbas, *fam* Angeber *m*; *tr* von oben herab behandeln; einschüchtern; necken, reizen; *itr* prahlen, *fam* angeben.

he'd [hi:d] = *he had; he would.*

heddle ['hedl] (Webe-, Schaft-)Litze *f*.

hedge [hedʒ] *s* Hecke *f*; *(dead ~)* Zaun *m*, Umzäunung; *fig* Schranke *f*; *fin* Deckungsgeschäft *n*; *attr* Hecken-; *pej* Winkel-; *tr* mit e-r Hecke umgeben *od* säumen; *(~ in, round)* einhegen, -friedigen, *fig (e-n Menschen in s-m Handeln)* einengen, behindern; *itr* e-e Hecke pflanzen *od* beschneiden; sich verschanzen *a. fig* (*behind* hinter); sich Ausweichmöglichkeiten freihalten, Vorbehalte machen; sich sichern, sich den Rücken decken, sich rückversichern; *to ~ about, on* zu umgehen versuchen; *to ~ in (mil)* einschließen; *to ~ off (tr)* abtrennen; *itr Am sl* unentschieden sein; *~* **buying** Vorratseinkäufe *m pl*; *~* **clause** Schutzklausel *f*; **~-garlic** *bot* Rauke *f*, Rautensenf *m*; **~hog** ['-hɔg] Igel *m*; *Am* Stachelschwein *n*; *fig* widerborstige(r) Mensch; *mil* Wasserbombenwerfer *m*; *~~ defence, position (mil)* Igelstellung *f*; **~-hop** *itr aero* tief fliegen; **~-hopper** *aero* Tiefflieger, Heckenspringer *m*, Kleinflugzeug *n*; **~r** ['-ə] Heckenpflanzer, -beschneider, -stutzer; *fig* Drückeberger *m*; **~row** ['-rou] Hecke *f*; **~-sparrow** *orn* Braunelle *f*, Graukehlchen *n*.

hedon|ic [hi:'dɔnik] *scient* hedonisch; Lust-; **~ism** ['hi:dənizm] *psychol* Hedonismus *m*.

heed [hi:d] *tr (to give, to pay ~ to, to take ~ of)* achten, aufmerken, aufpassen auf, beachten; *itr* (gut) aufpassen, Obacht geben; *s* Aufmerksamkeit *f*; *to take no ~ of s.th.* etw nicht beachten; *to take ~ of s.o.* sich vor jdm in acht nehmen; **~ful** ['-ful] aufmerksam, sorgfältig, behutsam; **~fulness** ['-fulnis] Aufmerksamkeit, Behutsamkeit, Sorgfalt *f*; **~less** ['-lis] unaufmerksam; sorglos, leichtsinnig; **~lessly** ['-lisli] *adv* achtlos; **~lessness** ['-lisnis] Unachtsamkeit; Sorglosigkeit *f*.

hee-haw ['hi:'hɔ:] *s* Iah *(des Esels)*; wiehernde(s), schallende(s) Gelächter *n*; *itr (Esel)* iahen; schallend lachen.

heel [hi:l] **1.** *s* Ferse *f (a. des Strumpfes)*; *(Schuh)* Absatz, *fam* Hacken; *allg* unterste(r) Teil *m*, hinterste(s) Ende *n*; Rest; *(Brot)* Anschnitt; *Am sl* Schuft *m*; *pl zoo* Hinterfüße *m pl*; *tr* mit Absätzen versehen; *(den Boden)* mit den Fersen, Absätzen berühren; auf den Fersen folgen (*s.o.* jdm); *Am sl* versehen mit *(bes. Geld)*; *itr* die Fersen *(beim Tanzen)* rhythmisch bewegen; *at, (up)on s.o.'s ~s* jdm auf den Fersen; *down at (the) ~* mit schief(gelaufen)en Absätzen; abgerissen, schäbig, heruntergekommen; *out at ~(s), out at the ~* mit Löchern in den Strümpfen; heruntergekommen, ärmlich; *to ~ (Hund)* bei Fuß; *under s.o.'s ~s (fig)* unter jds Füßen, Stiefel; *head over ~s, ~s over head* kopfüber; Hals über Kopf; *to bring to ~* zum Gehorsam bringen, *fam* kleinkriegen; *to come on the ~s* dicht folgen (*of* auf); *to come to ~* klein beigeben; *to cool, to kick o.'s ~s (fam)* sich die Beine in den Leib stehen; warten müssen; *to kick up o.'s ~s* vor Freude tanzen; *to lay by the ~s* fesseln; einsperren; unterkriegen; *to show o.'s ~s, a clean pair of ~s, to take to o.'s ~s* das Weite suchen, Fersengeld zahlen, *to turn on o.'s ~(s)* sich auf dem Absatz umdrehen; **~ed** [-d] *a Am sl* gut fundiert, wohlhabend; bewaffnet; **~er** ['-ə] Schuhflicker; *Am sl pol* Mitläufer, *allg* Anhänger *m*; **~less** ['-lis] *a* ohne Absätze; **~-piece** Absatz; (Absatz-)Fleck *m*, Ecke *f*; **~-plate** Stoßplatte *f (am Absatz)*; **~-tap** Absatzfleck; Schnaps-, Likörrest *m (im Glas)*; *no ~~s!* ausgetrunken! ex! **2.** *(to ~ over) itr* sich auf die Seite legen; *mar* Schlagseite haben, krängen; *tr (Schiff)* auf die Seite legen; *s mar* Krängung; Schlagseite *f*.

heft [heft] *s Am fam* Gewicht *n*, Schwere *a. fig*; *Am fam* Bedeutung *f*, Einfluß; *Am* Hauptteil; schwere(r) Mann *m*; *dial* (An-)Heben *n*, Stoß *m*; *tr* anheben, um das Gewicht zu schätzen; *itr Am fam* wiegen; **~y** ['-i] schwer (zu heben); stämmig, stramm; *fig* gewichtig; *(Rechnung)* hoch.

hegemony [hi(:)'geməni, -dʒ-] Führung, Vorherrschaft, Hegemonie *f*.

heifer ['hefə] Färse *f*; *Am fam* hübsche(s) Mädchen *n*.

heigh [hei, hai] *interj* he! nun! **~-ho** ['hei'hou] *interj* ach! aha! so!

height [hait] Höhe *a. geog astr*; (Körper-)Größe *f*; Höhepunkt, höchste(r) Grad *m*, oberste Grenze *f*; *das* Höchste, *das* Äußerste; (An-)Höhe, Erhebung *f*; *at its ~* auf s-m, ihrem Höhepunkt; *he is six feet in ~* er ist 6 Fuß groß; *~ of drop, fall* Fallhöhe *f*; *~ of fashion* neueste Mode *f*; *the ~ of folly* der Gipfel der Torheit; *~* **difference** Höhenunterschied *m*; **~en** ['-n] *tr meist fig* erhöhen, verstärken; *~* **indicator** Höhenmesser *m*.

heinous ['heinəs] hassenswert, abscheulich; verrucht, schändlich; **~ness** ['-nis] Abscheulichkeit, Verruchtheit, Schändlichkeit *f*.

heir [ɛə] Erbe *m* (*to, of s.o.* jds) *a. fig*; *to appoint as o.'s ~* als Erben einsetzen; *to be ~ to s.th.* Erbe *m* e-r S sein; *to become s.o.'s ~* jdn beerben; *sole, universal ~* Alleinerbe *m*; *~*

apparent zukünftige(r) Erbe; Thronfolger *m*; **~-at-law** gesetzmäßige(r) Erbe *m*; **~dom** ['ɛədəm] Erbrecht *n*; Erbschaft *f*; **~ess** ['ɛəris] Erbin *f*; **~less** ['ɛəlis] *a* ohne Erben; **~loom** ['ɛəlu:m] Erbstück *n*; **~ presumptive** *pl* mutmaßliche(r) Erbe *m*.

heist [haist] *s Am sl* bewaffnete(r) Raubüberfall *m*; *tr* rauben; **~er** ['-ə] Räuber *m*.

helic|al ['helikl], **~oid(al)** [heli'kɔid(l)] spiralig, schraubenförmig.

helicopter ['helikɔptə], *fam* **helic** ['helik] *s aero* Hubschrauber *m*; **~ air-station, terminal** Hubschrauberlandeplatz, -Flughafen *m*; **~ist** [heli'kɔptərist] Hubschrauberpilot *m*.

helidrome ['helidroum], **heliport** ['helipɔ:t] = *helicopter air-station*.

helio|centric [hi:lio(u)'sentrik] heliozentrisch; **~chrome, ~chromy** ['hi:lio(u)kroum(i)] Farb(en)photographie *f*; **~graph** ['hi:lio(u)grɑ:f] *s* Heliograph, -stat, Spiegeltelegraph *m*; *tr* heliographieren; **~graphic** [hi:lio(u)'græfik] heliographisch; **~~** *print* Lichtpause *f*; **~graphy** [hi:li'ɔgrəfi] Heliographie *f*; Lichtdruckverfahren *n*; **~gravure** ['hi:lio(u)grə'vjuə] Lichtdruck *m*, Heliogravüre *f*; **~therapy** [hi:lio(u)'θerəpi] *med* Lichtbehandlung *f*; **~trope** ['heljətroup] *bot min* Heliotrop *m*; Heliotropfarbe *f*, Purpurrot *n*; **~tropism** ['heljo(u)trəpizm] *biol* Lichtwendigkeit *f*; **~type** ['hi:lio(u)taip] Lichtdruck *m*; **~typy** ['hi:lio(u)taipi] Lichtdruckverfahren *n*.

helium ['hi:ljəm] *chem* Helium *n*.

helix ['hi:liks] *pl a. helices* ['helisi:z] Spirale; Schraubenlinie; *anat* Helix, Ohrleiste; *arch* Volute, Schnecke *f*.

hell [hel] *rel* u. *fig* Hölle *f*; *interj* verdammt (noch mal)! *like ~* verdammt, sehr; nicht im mindesten; *~ for leather* wie ein Wilder *od* Verrückter; *to be ~ on s.o. (Am sl)* die Hölle für jdn sein; *to catch, to get ~ (Am sl)* e-n tüchtigen Anschnauzer, e-e Strafe aufgebrummt kriegen; *to give s.o. ~* jdm die Hölle heiß machen; *to make s.o.'s life a ~* jdm das Leben zur Hölle machen; *to play ~ with s.o. (sl)* jdm übel mitspielen; *to raise ~ (sl)* Klamauk machen, Unruhe stiften; *he suffers ~ on earth* ihm ist das Leben zur Hölle geworden; *oh, ~!* verdammte Schweinerei! *go to ~!* scher dich zum Teufel! *what the ~ are you doing here?* was zum Teufel machen Sie denn hier? *gambling ~* Spielhölle *f*; *a ~ of a noise* ein Höllenlärm, ein Heidenspektakel *m*; **~bender** Riesensalamander *m*; *Am sl* Saufgelage *n*; Säufer, Randalierer *m*; **~bent** *a Am sl* versessen, erpicht (*on, for* auf); verrückt (*on, for* nach); *to go ~~ for* sich stürzen auf; **~-cat** Zankteufel *m*, böse(s) Weib *n*; Draufgängerin *f*; **~fire** Höllen-, höllische(s) Feuer *n*; **~hound** Höllenhund *a. fig*; *fig* ekelhafte(r) Kerl *m*; **~ish** ['-iʃ] höllisch, teuflisch; *fam* entsetzlich; **~kite** Unmensch *m*.

he'll [hi:l] = *he will*.

hellebore ['helibɔ:] *bot* Nieswurz *f*.

Hellen|e ['heli:n] *hist* Hellene, Grieche *m*; **~ic** [he'li:nik] hellenisch, griechisch; **~ism** ['helinizm] Hellenismus *m*; **~ist** ['-ist] Hellenist *m*; **~istic(al)** [heli'nistik(əl)] hellenistisch; **~ize** ['helinaiz] *tr* hellenisieren.

hello ['helou] *interj bes. Am für hallo*; **~-girl** *Am fam tele* Fräulein *n* vom Amt.

helm [helm] Steuer(rad, -ruder) *a. fig*; *fig* Ruder *n*; **~sman** ['-zmən] Steuermann *m*.

helmet ['helmit] Helm *m a. fig*; Maske *f (beim Fechten)*; *crash ~* Sturzhelm *m*; **~ed** ['-id] *a* behelmt; helmförmig.

help [help] *tr* helfen, behilflich sein (*s.o.* jdm); unterstützen; verhelfen (*to* zu); dienlich, zuträglich, förderlich sein (*s.th.* e-r S); fördern; bedienen; *itr* helfen, behilflich, dienlich, nützlich sein; *(Kellner)* bedienen; *s* Hilfe, Unterstützung; Abhilfe, Erleichterung; Bedienung *f*; (Halbtags-)Hilfe *f* im Haushalt; Arbeiter *m*; Personal *n*; *to ~ out* aushelfen (*s.o.* jdm); *to ~ s.o. on, off with o.'s coat* jdm in den, aus dem Mantel helfen; *I can't ~ it* ich kann nichts dafür; ich kann nichts daran ändern; *can I ~ you?* womit kann ich Ihnen dienen? was wünschen Sie? *I can't ~ smiling* ich muß lächeln; *that can't be ~ed* das läßt sich nicht ändern; es geht nicht anders; *~ yourself!* bedienen Sie sich! langen Sie zu! *so ~ me God!* so wahr mir Gott helfe! *~ wanted (Zeitung)* Stellenangebot *n*; **~er** ['-ə] Helfer *m (Person)*; Hilfe *f (Sache)*; **~ful** ['-ful] behilflich, hilfreich; dienlich, nützlich; **~fulness** ['-fulnis] Behilflichkeit; Dienlichkeit *f*; **~ing** ['-iŋ] *a* hilfreich; *s* Hilfe(leistung), Unterstützung; Portion *f*, *fam* Schlag *m (Essen)*; **~less** ['-lis] hilflos; auf sich selbst angewiesen *od* gestellt; von keinem Nutzen; **~lessness** ['-lisnis] Hilflosigkeit *f*; **~mate, ~meet** Gehilfe *m*, Gehilfin *f*; Gatte *m*, Gattin *f*; **~-yourself** *a* Selbstbedienungs-.

helter-skelter ['heltə'skeltə] *adv* holterdiepolter, durcheinander; Hals über Kopf; *a* stürmisch; wirr; *s* (wüstes) Durcheinander *n*.

helve [helv] Griff, Stiel *m (bes. e-r Axt)*; *to throw the ~ after the hatchet* alles dransetzen; das Kind mit dem Bad ausschütten.

Helvet|ian [hel'vi:ʃjən] *a* schweizerisch; *s* Schweizer(in *f*) *m*; **~ic** [hel'vetik] schweizerisch.

hem 1. [hem] *s* Saum *a. allg*; *allg* Rand *m*; *tech* Stoßkante *f*; *tr* säumen; umgeben; *to ~ in, (a)round, about* einschließen, einengen; einzwängen; **~-line** *(Damen-)*Rocklänge *f*; **~stitch** *s* Hohlsaum *m*; *tr* mit einem Hohlsaum versehen; **2.** [mm, hm] *interj* hm! *itr* sich räuspern; *(beim Sprechen)* e-e Pause machen, zögern; *to ~ and haw* stottern.

hem|al, ~atite, ~oglobin, ~ophilia, ~orrhage, ~orrhoids, ~ostatic *s. haem.*

hemi|cycle ['hemisaikl] Halbkreis *m*; **~sphere** ['hemisfiə] (*bes.* Erd-, Himmels-)Halbkugel, Hemisphäre; *anat* Gehirnhemisphäre *f*; *fig* Fach, Gebiet *n*; **~spheric(al)** [hemi'sferik(əl)] halbkugelförmig.

hemlock ['hemlɔk] *bot* Schierling *m*; Schierlingsgift *n*, *lit* -becher *m*; Schierlings-, Kanadische Hemlocktanne *f*.

hemp [hemp] Hanf; *fig* Strand *m*; **~en** ['-ən] hanfen, hänfen, aus Hanf, Hanf-.

hen [hen] *s* Henne *f*, Huhn; *(bes. Vogel-)* Weibchen *n*; *itr Am sl* klatschen; *like a ~ with one chicken* überbesorgt; **~bane** Bilsenkraut(gift) *n*; **~-coop** Hühnerkäfig, kleine(r) Hühnerstall *m*; *Am sl* Studentinnenheim *n*; **~-harrier** *orn* Kornweih *m*; **~-house** Hühnerstall *m*; **~nery** ['-əri] Hühnerstall, -hof *m*; **~-party** *fam* Damengesellschaft *f*, Kaffeekränzchen *n*, *pej* -klatsch *m*; **~peck** *tr (Frau ihren Mann)* unter dem Pantoffel haben; *to be ~~ed* unter dem Pantoffel stehen; *a ~~ed husband* ein Pantoffelheld *m*; **~-roost** Hühnerstange *f*, -wiemen *m*.

hence [hens] *adv obs* von hier, weg, fort; von jetzt, nun an, *poet* hinfort; hieraus; folglich, deshalb; *a year ~* übers Jahr, in einem Jahr; **~forth** ['-'fɔ:θ], **~forward** ['-'fɔ:wəd] *adv* hinfort, nunmehr, in Zukunft.

henchman ['hen(t)ʃmən] *hist* Knappe, Page; *pol* Gefolgsmann, Anhänger, Helfershelfer *m*.

henna ['henə] *bot* Hennastrauch *m*; Henna *f (Haarfärbemittel)*.

hep [hep] **1.** *interj mil* links *(zur Schrittmarkierung)*; **2.** *a Am sl*: *to be ~ to* im Bilde sein, Bescheid wissen über; **~-cat, ~ster** ['-stə] Jazzkenner, -begeisterter; junge(r) Mann *m* auf Draht.

hepat|ic [hi'pætik] *a scient* Leber-; **~ica** [-ə] *bot* Leberblümchen *n*; **~itis** [hepə'taitis] Leberentzündung *f*.

hepta|chord ['heptəkɔ:d] *mus* große Septime *f*, Heptachord *m* od *n*; **~gon** ['heptəgən] Siebeneck *n*; **~gonal** [hep'tægənl] siebeneckig; **~hedral** ['heptə'hedrəl] siebenflächig; **~hedron** ['heptə'hedrən] Heptaeder *n*.

her [hə:] *prn* sie *acc sing*; ihr *dat*, ihr(e).

herald ['herəld] *s* Herold; *fig* (Vor-) Bote *m*; *tr* ankündigen, verkünden; *to ~ in* einführen; *a ~ of spring* ein Frühlingsbote *m*; **~ic** [he'rældik] heraldisch, Wappen-; **~ry** ['herəldri] Heraldik, Wappenkunde *f*.

herb [hə:b] (einjährige) Pflanze *f*; (Heil-, wohlriechendes) Kraut *n*; **~aceous** [hə:'beiʃəs] Kräuter-, Pflanzen-; bepflanzt; **~age** ['hə:bidʒ] Kräuter *n pl*, Grün *n*; Weide(recht *n*) *f*; **~al** ['hə:bəl] *a* Pflanzen-, Kräuter-; *s* Kräuterbuch *n*; **~alist** ['hə:bəlist] Botaniker; Pflanzensammler; Kräuterhändler *m*; **~arium** [hə:'bɛəriəm] Herbarium *n*; **~ivorous** [hə:'bivərəs] *zoo* pflanzenfressend; **~y** ['-i] grasig.

Herculean [hə:kju'li:ən, *Am* -'kju:ljən] herkulisch, riesenstark; ungeheuer; *(Arbeit)* schwer zu vollbringen(d).

herd [hə:d] *s* (Vieh-, Elefanten-)Herde *f*, Rudel *n*; Hirte *m*; *fig pej* (Menschen-) Herde, breite Masse, Menge *f*, Haufen *m*; *tr (Vieh)* hüten, weiden; (hinein-) treiben (*into* in); *itr bes. fig* e-e Herde bilden, in e-m Haufen gehen; *to ~ together* sich zs.rotten; sich zs.tun (*with* mit); *the common, vulgar ~* die große Masse; **~-book** *agr* Herdenzuchtliste *f*; **~ instinct** *psychol* Herdentrieb *m*; **~sman** ['hə:dzmən] Hirt *m*.

here [hiə] *adv* hier(her); her; *(zeitl.)* an dieser Stelle, jetzt, nun; *interj* hier! *s das* Hier, *das* Jetzt; *dieses* Leben; *~ below* hienieden; *~ and there* hier(hin) und dort(hin); hie u. da; *~, there and everywhere* vielerorts; *neither ~ nor there* nebensächlich, unwichtig, unbedeutend; *come ~!* komm her! *look ~!* sieh, schau mal (her)! hör zu! *~ he comes!* da kommt er (ja)! *~ you are!* da haben Sie es! *~ goes!* auf! *~'s to...!* auf das Wohl *gen!* **~about(s)** ['hiərəbaut(s)] *adv* hier herum; **~after** [hiər'ɑ:ftə] *adv* h(i)ernach, von jetzt an, nachher, später, in Zukunft; *s die* Zukunft; *das* künftige Leben; **~ below** auf Erden; **~by** ['hiə'bai] *adv* hierdurch; -mit; *obs* dicht dabei; **~in** ['hiər'in] *adv* hierin; **~inafter, ~inbefore** ['hiərin'ɑ:ftə, -bi'fɔ:] *adv* vor-, nachstehend; **~of** [hiər'ɔv] *adv* hiervon; **~on** = *~upon*; **~to** [hiə'tu:] *adv obs* hierzu; **~tofore** ['hiətu'fɔ:] *adv* zuvor, bisher; **~under** [hiər'ʌndə] *adv* weiter unten *(im Buch)*; **~unto** ['hiərʌn'tu:] *adv* hierzu; **~upon** ['hiərə'pɔn] *adv* hierauf; **~with** ['hiə'wið] *adv* hiermit.

heredit|ariness [hi'reditərinis] Erblichkeit *f*; **~ary** [-əri] (ver)erblich;

Erb-; *fig* überkommen; ~~ *aristocracy* Erbadel *m*; ~~ *disease* Erbkrankheit *f*; ~~ *lease* Erbpacht *f*; ~~ *monarchy* Erbmonarchie *f*; ~**y** [hi'rediti] Erblichkeit *f a. biol*; Erbgut *n*, -masse *f*.

here|sy ['herəsi] *rel* Ketzerei, Irrlehre, Häresie *f*; ~**tic** ['herətik] Ketzer, Häretiker *m*; ~**tic(al)** [hi'retik(əl)] ketzerisch, häretisch.

herit|able ['heritəbl] erblich; erbfähig; ~**age** ['heritidʒ] Erbschaft *f*, -gut, Erbe; Erbrecht *n*.

hermaphrodit|e [hə:'mæfrədait] Zwitter *m a. bot.*

hermetic(al) [hə:'metik(əl)] hermetisch (abgeschlossen); luftdicht.

hermit ['hə:mit] Einsiedler, Klausner, Eremit *m*; ~**age** ['-idʒ] Einsiedelei, Klause *f*; ~ **crab** Einsiedlerkrebs *m*.

herni|a ['hə:njə] (Eingeweide-)Bruch *m*; ~**al** ['-l] *a* Bruch-; ~**otomy** [hə:ni'ɔtəmi] Bruchoperation *f*.

hero ['hiərou] *pl -es* Held *(a. e-r Dichtung)*; *(Mythologie)* Heros, Heroe *m*; ~**ic(al)** [hi'ro(u)ik(əl)] *a* heldisch, heroisch; heldenhaft, -mütig; hochtrabend; *s pl* große Worte *n pl*, hohle(s) Pathos *n*; ~*ic age* Heldenzeitalter *n*; ~*ic couplet* heroische(s) Reimpaar *n*; ~*ic tenor* Heldentenor *m*; ~**in** ['hero(u)in] *med* Heroin *n*; ~**ine** ['hero(u)in] Heldin *f (a. e-r Dichtung)*; ~**ism** ['hero(u)izm] Heldenhaftigkeit *f*, -mut, Heroismus *m*; Heldentat *f*; ~-**worship** Heldenverehrung *f*.

heron ['herən] *orn* Reiher *m*; ~**ry** ['-ri] Reiherstand *m*, -kolonie *f*.

herpes ['hə:pi:z] *med* (Bläschen-) Flechte *f*.

herring ['heriŋ] *pl* ~*(s)* Hering *m*; *packed as close as* ~*s* wie eingepfercht; *kippered* ~ Stockfisch *m*; *red* ~ Bückling *m*; *fig* Ablenkungsmanöver *n*; *neither fish, nor flesh, nor good red* ~ *(fig)* weder Fisch noch Fleisch; ~-**bone** *(*~~ *pattern)* Fischgrätenmuster *n*; *(*~~ *stitch) (Stickerei)* Grätenstich *m*; *arch* Zickzackband *n*; *the* ~-**pond** *hum* der große Teich, der (Nord-)Atlantik.

hers [hə:z] der, die, das ihre, ihrige; *a friend of* ~ e-r ihrer Freunde, ein Freund von ihr; *the book is* ~ das Buch gehört ihr.

herself [hə:'self] *prn* sie *sing* (...)selbst, ihr selbst; *(sie)* sich (selbst); *(all) by* ~ allein; ohne Hilfe; *she's not* ~ *today* sie ist heute nicht wie sonst.

hesit|ance, -cy ['hezitəns(i)] Zögern, Schwanken *n*, Unentschlossenheit, Unschlüssigkeit *f*; ~**ant** ['-ənt] zögernd, schwankend, unentschlossen, unschlüssig; ~**ate** ['heziteit] *itr* stocken, zaudern, zögern *(about doing, to do* zu tun); schwanken; unsicher, unentschlossen, unschlüssig sein; Bedenken tragen *od* haben *(about, over* wegen); stammeln, stottern; ~**atingly** ['-eitiŋli] *adv* (nur) zögernd; unschlüssig; ~**ation** [hezi'teiʃən] Unschlüssigkeit, Unentschlossenheit, Unsicherheit *f*; Schwanken, Zögern; Bedenken *n*; Zurückhaltung *f*; Stocken; Stammeln *n*; *without a moment's* ~~ ohne e-n Augenblick zu zögern; *to have no* ~~ keine Bedenken tragen *(in* bei).

Hess|e ['hesi] Hessen *n*; ~**ian** ['-iən] *a* hessisch; *s* Hesse *m*, Hessin *f*; ~~ *boots (pl)* Schaftstiefel *m pl*.

hetero|clite ['hetəro(u)klait] *a* (von der Norm) abweichend, anomal; *s gram* unregelmäßige(s) Hauptwort *n*; ~**clitical** [hetəro(u)'klitikəl] abweichend; ~**dox** ['hetərədɔks] *rel* andersgläubig; ketzerisch; ~**doxy** ['hetərədɔksi] *rel* Irrglaube *m*, Ketzerei *f*; ~**dyne** ['hetərədain] *a radio* Überlagerungs-; *tr* überlagern *(between* mit); ~**geneity** [hetəro(u)dʒi'ni:iti] Anders-, Ungleichartigkeit; Verschiedenartigkeit *f*; ~**geneous** ['hetəro(u)'dʒi:njəs] anders-, ungleich-, fremdartig; uneinheitlich, heterogen.

het-up ['hetʌp] *a fam* aufge-, erregt; überarbeitet.

hew [hju:] *pp a. hewn tr* zerhauen, -hacken, -schneiden; hauen, schlagen; *(to* ~ *out)* behauen; *(to* ~ *down) (Baum)* fällen; *to* ~ *asunder, to pieces* in Stücke schlagen; *to* ~ *away, to* ~ *off* abhauen, -hacken; *to* ~ *up* spalten; *to* ~ *o.'s way* sich e-n Weg bahnen; ~**er** ['-ə] (Holz-) Hauer; *min* Häuer *m*.

hex [heks] *s Am sl* Hexe *f*, Zauberer *m*; *fam* Unglücksmensch *m*, -ding *n*; *tr* be-, verhexen; Unglück bringen *(s.o.* jdm).

hexa|chord ['heksəkɔ:d] *mus* große Sexte *f*, Hexachord *m*; ~**gon** ['heksəgən] Sechseck *n*; ~**gonal** [hek'sægənl] sechseckig; ~**gram** ['heksəgræm] Hexagramm *n*, Davidstern *m*; ~**hedral** ['heksə'hedrəl] sechsflächig; ~**hedron** ['heksə'hedrən] Sechsflach *n*; ~**meter** [hek'sæmitə] Hexameter *m*.

hey [hei] *interj* he! hei! hallo!

heyday ['heidei] *s (zeitl.)* Höhepunkt, Gipfel *m*, Glanzzeit, Jugendkraft *f*; *in his* ~ in der Blüte s-s Lebens; *in the* ~ *of youth* in der Vollkraft der Jugend.

hi [hai] *interj fam* hallo! (guten) Tag! wie geht's? he(da)!

hiatus [hai'eitəs] Lücke *f*, Zwischenraum; *gram* Hiatus *m*.

hibern|al [hai'bə:nl] *a* Winter-; ~**ate** ['haibə:neit] *itr* überwintern; Winterschlaf halten; *fig* e-e Pause einlegen *od* machen; faulenzen; ~**ation** [haibə:'neiʃən] Überwinterung *f*; Winterschlaf *m*.

hibiscus [hi'biskəs] *bot* Eibisch *m*.

hiccup, hiccough ['hikʌp] *s* Schluckauf *m*, Schlucken *n*; *itr* den Schluckauf haben.

hick [hik] *s Am sl pej* (Bauern-)Tölpel, Simpel, Tolpatsch *m*; *a* tölpelhaft; ~ **town** Provinzstadt *f*, *fam* Nest *n*.

hickey ['hiki] *Am* Kniff, Pfiff; *el* Lampenträger *m*, -fassung *f*; *sl* Pickel *m*.

hickory ['hikəri] Hickory(holz *n*) *m (Baum)*; *(*~*-nut)* Hickorynuß *f*.

hide [haid] **1.** *irr hid* [hid], *hidden* ['hidn] *od hid tr* verstecken, verbergen *(from* vor); verhüllen, verdecken; verheimlichen, geheimhalten *(from* vor); beiseite schaffen; *itr* verborgen, unsichtbar sein; sich verbergen, sich verstecken; *s* Versteck *n (des Jägers)*; ~-**and-(go-)seek** Versteckspiel *n*; *to play at* ~~ Versteck spielen; ~-**away** *Am fam* Unterschlupf *m*; Kleinstadt *f*; kleine(s) Lokal *n*; ~-**out** *s fam* Versteck *n*, Schlupfwinkel, Unterschlupf *m*; **hiding** ['-iŋ] Verstecken *n*; Verborgenheit *f*; *(*~*-place)* Versteck *n*, Schlupfwinkel *m*; *to be in* ~~ sich versteckt halten; **2.** *s* Haut *f*, Fell; *hum pej* Fell *(e-s Menschen)*; *Am sl* Rennpferd *n*; *pl Am sl* (Jazz-)Trommel *f*; *tr* häuten, das Fell abziehen *(a cow* e-r Kuh); *(to tan the* ~ *of) fam* verdreschen, verwalken, durchbleuen; *neither* ~ *nor hair* gar nichts; *to have a thick* ~ *(fig fam)* ein dickes Fell haben; ~-**bound** *a* mit straffer Haut; *(Baum)* mit praller Rinde; *fig* stockkonservativ, engstirnig, engherzig, stur; **hiding** ['-iŋ] *s fam* Dresche, Wichse, Tracht *f* Prügel; **3.** Hufe *f*.

hideous ['hidiəs] scheußlich, gräßlich; abstoßend, abscheulich, widerlich.

hie [hai] *p pr* ~*ing u. hying itr poet* eilen, *hum* schnell machen.

hierarch ['haiəra:k] Hohe(r)priester; Erzbischof *m*; ~**ic(al)** [haiə'ra:kik(əl)] hierarchisch; ~**y** ['haiəra:ki] Hierarchie; Priesterherrschaft *f*, Kirchenregiment *n*; Klerus *m*; Rangordnung *f*.

hieroglyph ['haiərəglif] Hieroglyphe *f*; ~**ic** [-'glifik] *a* Hieroglyphen-; *s* Hieroglyphe *f a. fig.*

hi-fi ['hai'fai] Hifi-; Plattenspieler *m* mit tongetreuer Wiedergabe.

higgle ['higl] *itr* feilschen *(over* um, über).

higgledy-piggledy ['higldi'pigldi] *adv* drunter und drüber, durcheinander; *a* verwirrt, kunterbunt; *s* Durcheinander *n*, Verwirrung, Konfusion *f*.

high [hai] *a* hoch; *fig* hoch, erhaben *(above* über); *(Ton)* hoch, schrill, scharf; *fig* hochgestellt, -stehend; hervor-, überragend; überlegen; ausgezeichnet, bedeutend; vornehm, edel; groß, mächtig, gewaltig; intensiv; *(Wind)* stark; *(Worte)* heftig; *pol* extrem; *(Fleisch)* leicht angegangen; kostspielig, teuer; luxuriös, üppig, extravagant; hochfahrend, anmaßend, stolz; unbeugsam, unnachgiebig; ärgerlich, wütend; schwer, ernst; hochgestimmt, froh(gemut), heiter; *(Gesichtsfarbe)* rot, frisch; *sl* (ange)heiter(t), schicker, blau, besoffen, duhn; *adv* hoch, stark, sehr; in hohem Maße; *s* Höhe *f*, Hoch-, Höchststand *m*; Höchstziffer *f*, Maximum *n*, Rekord(höhe *f*) *m*; *mete* Hoch (-druckgebiet) *n*; *mot* größte(r) Gang *m*; *from (on)* ~ vom Himmel; *in* ~ *favo(u)r* in hoher Gunst; *in* ~ *spirits* in guter Laune, gutgelaunt; *on* ~ hoch oben; im Himmel; *on the* ~ *ropes (fam)* in Stimmung; in Fahrt; *with a* ~ *hand* hochfahrend, anmaßend, überheblich; ~ *and dry (mar)* gestrandet; auf dem Trockenen; *fig* hilflos, sich selbst überlassen; ~ *and low* überall; weit u. breit; *to fly* ~ hochfliegende Pläne haben; *to play* ~ um e-n hohen Einsatz spielen; *to ride the* ~ *horse, to be on o.'s* ~ *horse (fig)* auf dem hohen Roß sitzen; *to run* ~ *(mar)* hochgehen; *it is* ~ *time* es ist hohe Zeit; *the Most H*~ der Allerhöchste, Gott *m*; ~ *and mighty (fam)* hochnäsig, übermütig; ~ **altar** Hochaltar *m*; ~-**altitude**: ~~ *nausea* Höhenkrankheit *f*; ~**ball** *s Am* Schnellzug; *fam* Whisky *m* (mit) Soda; *itr sl* aufdrehen, Gas geben, rasch fahren; ~**binder** *Am sl* Rowdy, Gangster, Ganove *m*; ~-**blown** *a* aufgeblasen; ~-**born** *a* von hoher Geburt, von hohem Stande; ~**boy** *Am* Aufsatzkommode *f*; ~-**bred** *a* von hoher Herkunft; vornehm erzogen; ~**brow** ['-brau] *s sl* Intellektuelle(r), Bildungsprotz *m*; *a* intellektuell, voller Bildungsdünkel; **H**~ **Chancellor** Großkanzler *m*; **H**~ **Church** (anglikanische) Hochkirche *f*; **H**~-**Church** *a* hochkirchlich; ~-**class** erstklassig, hervorragend; ~-**colo(u)red** *a* von leuchtender Farbe, in lebhaften Farben; gerötet; blühend; lebhaft; übertrieben, gefärbt; ~ **comedy** *theat* Konversationsstück *n*; **H**~ **Command** *mil* Oberkommando *n*; **H**~ **Court (of Justice)** Hohe(r) Gerichtshof *m*; ~**day** Feier-, Fest-, Freudentag *m*; ~-**diving** *sport* Turmspringen *n*; ~-**duty** Hochleistungs-, Qualitäts-; ~**er**: ~~ *education* Hochschulbildung *f*; ~~ *mathematics* höhere Mathematik *f*; ~~-*up (Am fam)* Höhergestellte(r) *m*; ~-**explosive** hochexplosiv, brisant; ~ **falutin,** *Am a.* ~~*g* [fə'lu:tin, -ŋ] *fam* geschwollen, bombastisch, hochtrabend; ~-**fed** *a* wohlgenährt; ~-**fidelity** *attr radio (Wiedergabe)* von höchster Tontreue; ~-**finished** *a* in vollendeter Bearbeitung; ~-**flavo(u)red**

a stark gewürzt, von feinem Geschmack; **~-flown** *a* hochfliegend, -trabend, überschwenglich; **~-flyer** ehrgeizige(r) Mensch *m*; **~-flying** hochfliegend, ehrgeizig; **~-frequency** *el* Hochfrequenz *f*; **H~German** Hoch-, Schriftdeutsch *n*; **~ gloss** Hochglanz *m*; **~-grade** *a* hochwertig, erstklassig; *tr Am sl* klauen; **~ hand** Willkür (-maßnahmen *f pl*) *f*; **~-handed** *a* anmaßend; willkürlich, gewaltsam; **~ hat** Zylinder; *Am sl* Snob, eingebildete(r) Mensch *m*; **~-hat** *a Am sl* elegant; stutzer-, geckenhaft; snobistisch; *s* Geck, Snob *m*; *tr* von oben herab behandeln; **~ jinks** *pl sl* Ausgelassenheit *f*; **~-jump** *sport* Hochsprung *m*; **~land** Hochland *n*; *the H~~s* das Schottische Hochland; **~lander** ['-ləndə] Hochlandbewohner *m*; *H~~ (schottischer)* Hochländer *m*; **~-level**: *~~ bombing (aero)* Bombardierung *f* aus großer Höhe; *~~ railway* Hochbahn *f*; **~ life** (Leben *n*, Lebensart der) vornehme(n) Welt, höhere(n) Gesellschaft *f*; **~ light** hellste Stelle *f*, Glanzlicht *n*; *fig* Glanz-, Höhepunkt *m*; **~light** *tr* Glanzlichter aufsetzen (*s.th.* e-r S); *fig* (stark) hervorheben, herausstellen, krönen; **~ly** ['-li] *adv* in hohem Maße, stark, sehr, äußerst; hoch *(im Rang)*; ehrenhaft; günstig; hoch, teuer; *to speak ~~ of s.o.* von jdm in den höchsten Tönen reden; *to think ~~ of s.o.* große Stücke auf jdn halten; **H~ Mass** *rel* Hochamt *n*; **~-minded** *a* ideal (gesinnt), edel, hochherzig; **~-mindedness** ideale Gesinnung *f*, Edelmut *m*, Hochherzigkeit *f*; **~ muck-a-muck** *Am fam* wichtige, hochstehende Persönlichkeit *f*; **~-necked** *a (Kleid)* hochgeschlossen; **~ness** ['-nis] Höhe, Erhabenheit; Vornehmheit; Größe; Stärke *f*; *H~~* Hoheit *f (Anrede)*; **~-pitched** *a (Ton)* hoch, schrill; *(Dach)* steil; *fig* erhaben, gehoben, exaltiert; **~-power** Hochleistungs-; *~~ station* Großkraftwerk *n*; *~~ radio-station* Großfunkstation *f*; **~-powered** *a* sehr mächtig; **~ pressure** Hochdruck *m*; **~-pressure** *tr fig* bearbeiten (*s.o.* jdn); *a* energisch, selbstbewußt, willensstark, konzentriert, zielbewußt; gezielt; *~~ aera* Hochdruckgebiet *n*; *~~ tire* Hochdruckreifen *m*; **~-priced** *a* teuer, kostspielig; **~ priest** Hohe(r)-priester *m*; **~-proof** *Am* stark alkoholisch; **~ relief** *(Kunst)* Hochrelief *n*; **~ road** Hauptverkehrsstraße *f*; *fig* sicherste(r) Weg *m*; **~ roller** *Am sl* Verschwender, Spieler *m*; **~ school** *Am* höhere Schule *f*; **~ seas** *pl* hohe See *f*; *attr* Hochsee-; *~~ fleet* Hochseeflotte *f*; **~-seasoned** *a* scharf gewürzt; *fig (Witz)* gesalzen; **~-sounding** hochtönend, -trabend, überheblich; **~-speed** von hoher, großer Geschwindigkeit; schnell(laufend); **~-spirited** *a* edel; stolz; (wage)mutig; **~ spirits** *pl* gehobene Stimmung *f*; **~ spot** *Am* Hauptpunkt *m*, -sache *f*; *to hit, to touch the ~~s (rail)* nur auf den Hauptstationen halten; *fig (in der Rede)* nur die Hauptpunkte berühren; **~-stepping** hochtrabend; **~-strung** *a* überempfindlich, nervös, reizbar; **~-tail** *Am sl itr* sich schleunigst aus dem Staub machen; *tr mot* dicht fahren hinter; **~ tea** (Fünfuhr-)Tee *m* mit Imbiß; **~ tension** *el* Hochspannung *f*; *~~ circuit, current* Hochspannungsleitung *f*, Starkstrom *m*; **~-test** *a* streng geprüft; **~ tide** Fluthöhe, -eintrittszeit; Flut *f*; *fig* Höhe-, Wendepunkt *m*; **~ time** hohe, höchste Zeit; schöne, herrliche Zeit *f*; *to have a ~~* sich glänzend unterhalten (*at* bei); **~-toned** *a mus* hoch; *fig* hochstehend, erhaben, würdig; *Am fam* schick, elegant, modisch; *Am fam* prächtig, großartig; **~ treason** Hochverrat *m*; **~-up** hoch(gestellt); **~ voltage** *el* Hochspannung *f*; *~~ line* Hochspannungsleitung *f*; **~ water** Hochwasser *n*; *~~ mark* Hochwasserstand; *fig* Höchststand *m*; **~way** Landstraße; Haupt(durchgangs)straße *f*; *fig* direkte(r) Weg *m*; *~~ code* Straßenverkehrsordnung *f*; *~~s department* Straßenbauamt *n*; *~~man* Straßenräuber *m*; *~~ robbery* Straßenraub *m*; *~~ surveyor* Wegemeister *m*.

hijack, a. highjack ['haidʒæk] *Am tr (Transportgut, bes. geschmuggelte Güter)* rauben; *(bes. Schmuggler)* berauben; **~er** ['-ə] (bewaffneter) Straßenräuber *m*.

hik|e [haik] *s fam* Fußtour, Wanderung *f*; *itr* wandern, e-e (Fuß-)Tour machen; *(Preise) Am* steigen; *tr fam* (hoch)ziehen; **~er** ['-ə] Wanderer *m*; **~ing** ['-iŋ] Wandern *n*.

hilari|ous [hi'lɛəriəs] fröhlich, lustig, vergnügt, heiter; **~ty** [hi'læriti] Lustigkeit, Fröhlichkeit, Vergnügtheit *f*.

Hilary term ['hiləri'tə:m] *jur* im Januar beginnende(r) Termin; *(Schule)* zweite Hälfte *f* des Wintersemesters.

hill [hil] *s* Hügel, Berg *m*, (An-)Höhe *f*; Haufen *m*; *tr* mit Erde umgeben; *agr (Kartoffeln)* häufeln; *up ~ and down dale* über Berg u. Tal; *ant-, mole-, dung-~* Ameisen-, Maulwurfs-, Misthaufen *m*; **~billy** ['-bili] *s Am fam* Hinterwäldler *m*; *a* hinterwäldlerisch; rückständig; **~-climbing**: *~~ ability* Steigfähigkeit, Bergfreudigkeit *f*; *~~ contest (mot)* Bergrennen *n*; **~iness** ['-inis] Hüg(e)ligkeit *f*; **~ock** ['-ək] (kleiner) Hügel *m*; **~side** (Berg-, Ab-) Hang *m*; *~~ up-current* Hangwind *m*; **~ top** Berggipfel *m*, -spitze *f*; **~y** ['-i] hüg(e)lig, bergig.

hilt [hilt] Griff *m*, Heft *n (e-r Hieb- u. Stichwaffe)*; *(up) to the ~* bis an den Hals, (voll und) ganz, völlig, durch und durch.

him [him] *prn* ihn, ihm; dem(-), denjenigen (*who* welcher); sich; *that's ~ (fam)* das ist er; **~self** [-'self] (er) selbst; sich (selbst); *(all) by ~~* (ganz) allein, ohne (fremde) Hilfe; *of ~~* von selbst; *he is quite beside ~* er ist ganz außer sich.

hind [haind] **1.** Hindin, Hirschkuh *f*; **2.** *(Nordengland u. Schottland)* Landarbeiter; Kleinbauer *m*; **3.** *a* hinter; Hinter-; **~brain** *anat* Kleinhirn *n*; **~-leg** Hinterbein *n*; **~most** ['-moust] hinterst, letzt; **~-quarters** *pl* Hinterviertel, -teil, Gesäß *n*; *(Pferd)* Hinterhand *f*; **~sight** späte Einsicht *f*; *mil* Visier *n*; *foresight is better than ~~* Vorsicht ist besser als Nachsicht; **~-wheel** Hinterrad *n*.

hinder ['hində] *tr* verhindern, verhüten; hemmen, aufhalten; hindern (*from* an); *itr* im Wege sein.

Hind|i ['hin'di:] Hindi *n (Sprache)*; **~u, ~oo** ['-'du:] *s* Hindu; Inder *m*; *a* hinduistisch; indisch; **~uism** ['hindu(:)izm] *rel* Hinduismus *m*; **~ustani** [hindu'stɑ:ni] Hindustani *n*.

hindrance ['hindrəns] Behinderung *f*; Hemmnis, Hindernis *n* (*to* für).

hinge [hindʒ] *s* (Tür-)Angel *f*; Scharnier; Gelenk *n*; *fig* Angelpunkt *m*; Hauptsache *f*; *tr* mit e-m Scharnier versehen *od* befestigen; drehbar aufhängen; *itr* schwingen an; *fig* abhängen (*on, upon* von); sich drehen (*on, upon* um), abhängen (*on* von); *off the ~s (fig)* aus den Fugen; aus dem Häuschen; **~d** [-d] *a* drehbar; umlegbar; *~~ lid* Klappdeckel *m*; **~ joint** Scharnier(gelenk) *n*.

hinny ['hini] **1.** *s* Maulesel *m*; **2.** *itr* wiehern.

hint [hint] *s* Hinweis, Wink, Fingerzeig *m*; Andeutung, Anspielung *f* (*at* auf); *tr* andeuten, anspielen auf, zu verstehen geben; *itr* Andeutungen, Anspielungen machen (*at* auf); *to drop a ~* e-e Bemerkung fallenlassen; *to take a ~* es sich gesagt sein lassen; *a broad ~* ein Wink mit dem Zaunpfahl.

hinterland ['hintəlænd] Hinterland *n*.

hip [hip] **1.** *anat* Hüfte *f*; Gratabfall *m (des Walmdaches)*; *(up)on the ~* in ungünstiger Lage, im Nachteil; *~ and thigh* erbarmungslos; **~-bath** Sitzbad *n*; **~-bone** Hüftbein *n*; **~-disease** Hüftgelenksentzündung *f*; **~-joint** Hüftgelenk *n*; **~-pocket** Gesäßtasche *f*; **~-roof** Walmdach *n*; **~-shot** *a* hüft-, *fig* lendenlahm; *s* Hüftverrenkung *f*; **2.** Hagebutte *f*; **3.** *s* Schwermut *f*, Trübsinn *m*, Melancholie *f*; *tr* trübsinnig machen; *to be ~* dagegen sein; den Ohne-mich-Standpunkt vertreten; **~ped** [-t] *a* schwermütig, trübsinnig, melancholisch; beleidigt; *Am sl* versessen (*on* auf), verrückt (*on* nach); **~pish** ['-iʃ] etwas schwermütig; **~py** ['-i] *Am sl* Beatnik *m*; **~ster** ['-ə] krasse(r) Individualist *m*; **4.** *interj*: *~, ~, hurrah!* hipp, hipp, hurra!

hippo|drome ['hipədroum] Hippodrom *n*; **~griff, ~gryph** ['hipəgrif] Pegasus *m*; **~potamus** [hipə'pɔtəməs] *pl a.* -*mi* [-ai] Fluß-, Nilpferd *n*.

hircine ['hə:sain] bocksartig; (wie ein Bock) stinkend.

hire ['haiə] *s* Miete *f*, Mietpreis; (Arbeits-)Lohn *m*; *mar* Heuer *f*; Mieten *n*; *tr* mieten; (gegen Gebühr) leihen; engagieren, ein-, anstellen; *mar* heuern; *Am (Geld)* leihen; *to ~ out* vermieten; *o.s.* sich verdingen; *for ~* zu vermieten; *(Taxi)* frei; *for, on ~* zu vermieten(d); mietweise; *to let on ~* vermieten; *to take on ~* mieten; **~ling** ['-liŋ] *s* Mietling *m*; *a* feil; gedungen; **~-purchase** Ratenkauf *m*, Abzahlungsgeschäft *n*; *by ~~* auf Raten, auf Abzahlung; *~~ agreement, price* Mietkaufvertrag, -preis *m*; *~~ system* Raten-, Abzahlungssystem *n*.

hirsute ['hə:sju:t] zott(el)ig, struwwelig, struppig, haarig, rauh.

his [hiz] *prn* sein(e, r); der, die, das seine, seinige; *a friend of ~* e-r s-r Freunde, ein Freund von ihm; *the book is ~* das Buch gehört ihm.

hispid ['hispid] *zoo bot* borstig, struppig, rauh.

hiss [his] *itr* zischen; *tr (to ~ away, down, off)* auszischen, -pfeifen; *s* Zischen, Gezisch *n*; *gram* Zischlaut *m*; **~ing** ['-iŋ] Zischen *n*.

hist [s:t, hist] *interj* pst! st! still! Ruhe!

histology [his'tɔlədʒi] *anat* Gewebelehre, Histologie *f*.

histor|ian [his'tɔ:riən] Historiker, Geschichtsforscher, -schreiber *m*; **~ic(al)** [his'tɔrik(əl)] geschichtlich, historisch; **~icity** [histə'risiti] Geschichtlichkeit *f*; **~iographer** [histɔ:ri'ɔgrəfə] Geschichtsschreiber *m*; **~iography** [histɔ:ri'ɔgrəfi] Geschichtsschreibung *f*; **~y** ['histəri] *s* Geschichte *f*, Werden *n*, Entwicklung; Lebensgeschichte *f*, Werdegang *m*; Geschichte, Erzählung; Geschichte, Geschichtswissenschaft; *med* Anamnese, Vorgeschichte *f*; *attr* Geschichts-; *ancient, medi(a)eval, modern ~~* Alte, Mittlere, Neuere Geschichte *f*;

natural ~ Naturgeschichte *f*; *universal* ~~ Weltgeschichte *f*; ~~ *of art* Kunstgeschichte *f*; ~~ *of the (Christian) Church* Kirchengeschichte *f*; ~~ *of life* Lebensgeschichte *f*; ~~ *of literature* Literaturgeschichte *f*; ~~ *of religion* Religionsgeschichte *f*; ~~ *sheet* Personalbogen *m*; ~~ *of war* Kriegsgeschichte *f*.

histrionic [histri'ɔnik] *a* schauspielerisch; theatralisch; übertrieben, gemacht, gekünstelt, affektiert; *s pl mit sing* Schauspielkunst *f*; Theaterwesen *n*; Dramatik; *fig* Übertriebenheit, Affektiertheit *f*.

hit [hit] *irr hit, hit* **1.** *tr* treffen, stoßen an, auf; aufschlagen auf; schlagen, e-n Schlag versetzen (*s.o.* jdm); *(mit e-m Geschoß)* treffen; *(etw)* stoßen, mit *(etw)* schlagen (*on, against* an, gegen); *fig (Ziel)* erreichen; *Am (in e-r Stadt)* ankommen; *(Schicksalsschlag)* treffen, in Mitleidenschaft ziehen, *fam* mitnehmen; *(das Richtige)* treffen, finden, stoßen auf; *Am sl (Examen)* gut bestehen, *(e-r Versammlung)* beiwohnen, teilnehmen an; *(jds Geschmack)* treffen, *(e-m Wunsch)* genau entsprechen; *s.o.* auf jdn Eindruck machen; verwirren; e-n Vorschlag machen; anpumpen; **2.** *itr* schlagen, stoßen, treffen (*against* gegen); geraten, kommen, stoßen, treffen, verfallen (*upon* auf); *(to ~ out)* ausholen, schlagen (*at* nach); *Am sl* e-e starke Wirkung haben; sich aufmachen (*for* nach); **3.** *a* sehr erfolgreich, vom Glück begünstigt; **4.** *s* Treffer; Auf-, Zs.stoß, -prall *m*; treffende Bemerkung *f*; Glückstreffer, glückliche(r) Zufall; (Erfolgs-)Treffer, (Bomben-)Erfolg *m*, ausgezeichnete Idee *f*; treffende(r) Ausdruck, Knüller; *bes. mus* Schlager *m*; **5.** *to make a ~ (fig fam)* Erfolg haben; Eindruck schinden (*with* bei); *to ~ off (tr)* nachmachen, -ahmen; abschlagen; kurz und treffend beschreiben; *itr* sich treffen (*well* gut); *to ~ it off* gut mitea. auskommen (*with s.o.* mit jdm); *to ~ (it) up (Am mot sl)* Gas geben; *to ~ s.o. below the belt (Boxen)* jdm e-n Tiefschlag versetzen; *fig* sich jdm gegenüber unfair verhalten; *to ~ s.o. a blow* jdm e-n Schlag versetzen; *to ~ the ceiling* aus der Haut fahren; *to ~ s.o.'s fancy* jdm gefallen; *to ~ the hay (sl)* in die Falle, ins Bett gehen; *to ~ home (mit e-r Bemerkung)* ins Schwarze treffen; *to ~ the jackpot (Am sl) (beim Spiel)* die Bank sprengen; *to ~ the spot* genau das richtige sein; Erfolg haben; *he ~ the (right) nail on the head* er hat den Nagel auf den Kopf getroffen; *that was a ~ at me* das galt mir; *they ~ the town (Am sl)* sie kamen an; *hard ~* schwer ge-, betroffen; *direct ~* Volltreffer *m*; *stage ~* Bühnenerfolg *m*; *~ or miss* auf gut Glück; **~-and-run** *a* der Fahrerflucht schuldig; ~~ *driver* der Fahrerflucht Schuldige(r) *m*; ~~ *driving* Fahrerflucht *f*; ~ **parade** Schlagerparade *f*; ~ **song** Schlager (-lied *n*) *m*.

hitch [hitʃ] *itr* rücken, sich ruckweise (vorwärts)bewegen; humpeln, hinken; hängenbleiben, sich (ver)fangen (*to* an); *Am fam* ein Herz und eine Seele, einer Meinung sein; *Am sl* = *~hike*; *tr* rücken; ruck-, stoßweise (fort)bewegen; ruckweise ziehen, zerren; stoßweise schieben; an-, festhaken, -binden, befestigen (*to* an; *round* um); *(Pferd)* anspannen (*to* an); *to be ~ed (Am fam)* verheiratet sein; *to ~ up (Am)* anschirren; *(Ärmel)* aufkrempeln; *s* Ruck, Stoß *m*, Ziehen; Humpeln, Hinken; Hindernis, Hemmnis; Hängenbleiben *n*; Befestigung *f*, Haken, einfache(r) Knoten *m*; Schwierigkeit; *Am sl* Fahrt per Anhalter; Strecke; *Am sl mil* (aktive) Dienstzeit *f*; *without a ~* ohne Störung, reibungslos, glatt; *to ~ a ride to (Am sl)* per Anhalter fahren nach; *that won't ~ (Am sl)* das klappt nicht, haut nicht hin; *that's where the ~ comes in* da liegt der Hase im Pfeffer; *technical ~* technische(s) Versagen *n*; **~-hike** ['-haik] *Am sl itr* per Anhalter fahren; Autostop machen; trampen; **~-hiker** ['-haikə] *fam* Anhalter *m*.

hither ['hiðə] *adv* hierher, -hin; *~ and thither* hierhin und dorthin; hin u. her; *a* näher; **~to** ['-'tu:] *adv* bisher, bis jetzt.

hive [haiv] *s (bee~)* Bienenstock, -korb *m*, -volk *n*, -schwarm *m*; *fig* (Menschen-)Menge, belebte Gegend *f*; *tr (Bienen)* einfangen; *(Honig im Stock)* speichern; *allg* e-n Vorrat anlegen von; *itr (Bienen)* e-n Stock beziehen; in e-m Bienenstock leben; *fig* eng zs.leben, -wohnen (*with* mit); *to ~ off* ausschwärmen; *com* verlagern.

hives [haivz] *pl* Nesselsucht *f*, -fieber *n*; Windpocken *pl*; (Hals-)Bräune *f*.

ho [hou] *interj* oh! oha! he! holla! heda! *westward ~!* auf nach Westen!

hoar [hɔ:] weiß(lich), eisgrau; bereift; altersgrau, grau-, weißhaarig; **~frost** (Rauh-)Reif *m*; **~iness** ['-rinis] weiß(grau)e, graue Farbe; Grau-, Weißhaarigkeit *f*; **~y** ['-ri] weiß, grau (-weiß), eisgrau; grau-, weißhaarig; altersgrau, uralt; ehrwürdig.

hoard [hɔ:d] *s* (stille) Reserve *f*, Vorrat; Schatz, Hort *m*; *tr (to ~ up)* sammeln, anhäufen, e-n Vorrat anlegen von, hamstern, horten; *fig* heimlich lieben; *itr* hamstern, horten; **~er** ['-ə] Hamsterer *m*; **~ing** ['-iŋ] **1.** Hamstern, Horten *n*; Reserve *f*, Vorrat *m*; *pl* Ersparnisse *f pl*; **2.** Bau-, Bretterzaun *m*; Reklametafel, -fläche *f*.

hoarse [hɔ:s] rauh; heiser; **~n** ['-n] *tr itr* rauh, heiser machen, werden; **~ness** ['-nis] Rauheit; Heiserkeit *f*.

hoax [houks] *s* Scherz, Ulk; Streich, Schabernack *m*; (Zeitungs-)Ente *f*; *tr* zum Narren, zum besten haben, foppen, e-n Possen spielen (*s.o.* jdm).

hob [hɔb] **1.** *s* Kamineinsatz, -leiste *(zum Warmhalten)*; (Schlitten-)Kufe; *tech* Schraube *f*; *(Wurfspiel)* Zielpflock *m*; Wurfspiel *n* mit Zielpflöcken; *tr* wälzfräsen; **~nail** Schuhnagel *m*; **2.** (Bauern-)Tölpel; Kobold *m*; *(Am) to play, to raise ~* Unheil anrichten, Verwirrung stiften; **~goblin** ['-gɔblin] Kobold *m*; *fig* Gespenst *n*.

hobble ['hɔbl] *itr* humpeln, *fig* untüchtig sein; *tr* e-e Fußfessel anlegen (*a horse* e-m Pferd); *fig* (be)hindern; *s* Humpeln *n*; Fußfessel *f (für Pferde)*; *fig (selten)* Verlegenheit, Schwierigkeit *f*; **~dehoy** ['-di'hɔi] Tolpatsch *m*.

hobby ['hɔbi] Steckenpferd *n meist fig*, Liebhaberei *f*; *to ride a ~ (fig)* ein Steckenpferd haben; **~-horse** Stekken-, Schaukel-, *(hölzernes)* Karussellpferd *n*; *fig* Lieblingsthema *n*.

hobnob ['hɔbnɔb] *itr* zs. zechen, kneipen; auf freundschaftlichem Fuß, auf du und du stehen (*with* mit); *s sl* Geplauder *n*.

hobo ['houbou] *pl -(e)s Am* Wanderarbeiter; *pej* Landstreicher, Stromer *m*.

hock [hɔk] **1.** *s (Pferd, Rind)* Sprunggelenk *n (am Hinterbein)*; *tr* die Sehnen des Sprunggelenks zerschneiden (*a horse* e-m Pferd); lähmen; **2.** (weißer) Rheinwein *m*; **3.** *s Am* Pfand; Kittchen *n*; *tr Am sl (to put in ~)* verpfänden, versetzen; *in ~* verpfändet; verschuldet; eingesperrt; **~(shop)** *Am sl* Pfandleihe *f*.

hockey ['hɔki] *sport* Hockey *n*; *Am* = *ice ~* Eishockey *n*; ~ **ball, stick** Hockeyball, -schläger *m*.

hocus ['houkəs] *tr* betrügen, beschwindeln; berauschen, betäuben; *(Getränk)* mischen; *(Wein)* verschneiden; **~-pocus** ['-'poukəs] *s* Hokuspokus, Schwindel *m*, Gaunerei *f*; Trick *m*, Kunststück(chen) *n*.

hod [hɔd] Trage *f* (für Steine); Mörteltrog; Kohlenfüller *m*; **~-bearer, -carrier, ~man** ['-mən] Handlanger *m*.

hodge-podge *s. hotch-potch.*

hoe [hou] *s agr* Hacke *f*; *tr itr* hacken; *garden-~* Gartenhacke *f*; **~cake** *Am* (dünnes) Maisbrot *n*; **~down** *Am sl* (Volks-)Tanz *m*; Streiterei *f*.

hog [hɔg] *s (bes.* Mast-)Schwein *n*, Sau *f a. fig*; kastrierte(r) Eber; *fig* schmutzige(r), selbstsüchtige(r), gierige(r), gefräßige(r), gemeine(r) Kerl; *mar* (Schiffs-)Besen *m*; *tr (Rücken, Schiff)* wölben; *(Pferdemähne)* stutzen; *(Schiffsboden)* kehren, fegen; *fam* alles *od* das meiste an sich reißen *od* bringen; sich aneignen (*s.th.* e-r S); *itr* e-n Buckel machen, sich wölben; *mot* rücksichtslos fahren; *to go the whole ~ (sl)* alles mitmachen; aufs Ganze gehen; *to ~ it (sl)* im Schmutz leben; pennen; ~ **age** *Am* Flegeljahre *n pl*; **~back, ~'s back** Bergrücken *m* (mit schmalem Grat); **~ged** [-d] *a* gewölbt; *(Pferdemähne)* gestutzt; **~get** ['-it] einjährige(s) Schaf *od dial* Fohlen *n*; **~gish** ['-iʃ] *fig* schweinisch, säuisch, dreckig, schmutzig, gierig, gemein; **~manay** ['hɔgmənei] *Scot* Silvester (-abend *m*) *n*; Silvestergabe *f*; ~ **mane** *(Pferd)* gestutzte Mähne *f*; **~-pen** *Am* Schweinestall *m*; **~-raiser** *Am* Schweinezüchter *m*; **~shead** ['-zhed] große(s) Faß; Oxhoft *n (Flüssigkeitsmaß, 238* od *245 l)*; **~-skin** Schweinsleder *n*; **~sty** Schweinestall *m*; **~tie** *Am tr* an allen vier Füßen, an Händen und Füßen fesseln; *I'm ~~d (fig)* mir sind Hände und Füße gebunden; ich kann nichts machen; **~wash** ['-wɔʃ] Spül-, Abwaschwasser *n*; Abfälle *m pl*; *fig* Gewäsch, (dummes) Gerede; Geschreibsel *n*; **~-wild** *Am sl* erregt.

hoi(c)k [hɔik] *tr itr* (das Flugzeug) plötzlich hochreißen.

hoick(s) [hɔik(s)] *interj* hallo! *(Jagdruf an die Hunde)*.

hoist [hɔist] *tr (bes. mit Winde* od *Kran)* auf-, hochziehen, -winden; *mar* hissen; *min* fördern; *s* Auf-, Hochziehen *n*; Aufzug(svorrichtung *f*) *m*, Winde *f*, Flaschenzug; (Lade-)Kran *m*, Hebewerk *n*; *mar* Segel- *od* Flaggenhöhe *f*; *to ~ with o.'s own petard* sich in der eigenen Schlinge fangen; **~ing** ['-iŋ] Aufziehen, Heben, *mar* Hissen *n*; *~~-apparatus* Hebevorrichtung *f*, -werk, -zeug *n*; *~~ cable* Zugseil *n*; *~~-cage, -rope, -shaft (min)* Förderkorb *m*, -seil *n*, -schacht *m*; *~~ winch* Seilwinde *f*; **~way** Fahr(stuhl)schacht *m*.

hoity-toity ['hɔiti'tɔiti] *a* leicht(sinnig), flüchtig, launenhaft; übermütig, anmaßend, arrogant; eingeschnappt; herablassend; *interj* pah! bah!

hok(e)y-pok(e)y ['houki 'pouki] billige(s) Speiseeis *n*.

hokum ['houkəm] *Am fam lit theat film* Schnulze *f*; Kitsch *m*; (bloße) Aufmachung *f*; Bluff *m*, Angabe *f*, (dummes) Geschwätz *n*.

hold [hould] *irr held, held* **1.** *tr (mit den Händen* od *indirekt)* (fest)halten; zurückhalten, nicht gehen *od* fahren lassen; *(Körper, Körperteil in e-r bestimmten Lage, Richtung)* halten; festhalten, nicht fallen lassen, tragen *a. arch*; besitzen, innehaben, einnehmen, bekleiden; *(Funktion, Amt)* ausüben, versehen, bekleiden, innehaben; *(Versammlung, Gericht)* abhalten; *(Gespräch)* führen; *(Ansicht)* vertreten; *mil (Stellung)* halten, behaupten; enthalten; *(Raum, Gefäß)* fassen; *fig* im Sinne haben; ansehen, betrachten als, halten für, der Ansicht sein, daß; meinen, glauben; *(Ansicht, Meinung)* vertreten; behaupten; *(Zuhörer)* fesseln, packen; *jur* entscheiden; vertraglich verpflichten; *mus (Ton)* halten; **2.** *itr* festhalten, sich halten (*by, to* an); halten, nicht reißen, nicht brechen; *(Preise, Wetter)* sich halten; *fig* Geltung haben, gelten, in Geltung, in Kraft sein; übereinstimmen (*with* mit), billigen (*with s.th.* etw); *(meist im Imperativ:)* halt! **3.** *s* Ergreifen *n*, Griff *m*, (Fest-)Halten *n*; Halt; Behälter *m*; *fig* Gewalt, Macht *f*, starke(r) Einfluß *m* (*on* auf); Gewahrsam, Gefängnis *n*; *obs* Festung; *mus* Pause *f (Zeichen)*; *mar* Laderaum *m*; **4.** *to catch, to get, to lay, to seize, to take ~ of s.th.* etw fassen, pakken, ergreifen, *fam* erwischen; von etw Besitz ergreifen, etw in s-e Gewalt bringen; *to have ~ of s.th.* etw halten; *to keep ~ of s.th.* etw festhalten; *to let go o.'s ~, to lose ~ of s.th.* etw los-, fahrenlassen, sich etw entgleiten lassen; *to miss o.'s ~* daneben-, fehlgreifen; *to ~ s.o.'s attention* jds Aufmerksamkeit fesseln; *to ~ the baby, (Am) the bag* für den Schaden einstehen, aufkommen müssen; *to ~ at bay* in der Schwebe halten; *to ~ o.'s breath* den Atem anhalten; *to ~ cheap* geringachten; keinen Wert legen auf; *to ~ in contempt* verachten; *to ~ dear* werthalten; *to ~ in esteem* hochschätzen, achten; *to ~ good, true* zutreffen, gelten, sich bewähren; *to ~ o.'s ground, to ~ o.'s own* sich behaupten; die Stellung halten; *to ~ under a lease* gepachtet haben; *to ~ the line, the wire (tele)* am Apparat bleiben; *to ~ in mind* im Gedächtnis behalten; *to ~ office (Partei)* an der Macht, im Amt sein; *to ~ o.'s peace, tongue* still sein, den Mund halten; *to ~ s.o. to his promise* jdm zur Einlösung s-s Versprechens zwingen; *to ~ the road well (mot)* e-gute Straßenlage haben; *to ~ o.'s sides with laughter* sich den Bauch halten vor Lachen; *to ~ a wager* wetten; *to ~ water* wasserdicht, *fig* stichhaltig sein; *to ~ on o.'s way* weitergehen; **5.** *there's no ~ing him* er ist nicht zu halten; *~ it!* halt! *~ hard! ~ on! ~ up! (fam)* einen Moment! nicht so eilig! wart (doch), halt mal! *~ the line, please!* einen Augenblick, bitte! *to ~* **against** nachtragen, verübeln (*s.o.* jdm); *to ~* **aloof** sich abseits halten; *to ~* **back** *tr* zurück-, geheimhalten; *itr* sich zurückhalten (*from* von), zögern; *to ~* **by** sich richten nach; *to ~* **down** nieder-, unter Kontrolle, zurückhalten; *Am fam (Stelle, Stellung)* halten; behalten; *to ~* **fast** *to* festhalten an *a. fig*; *to ~* **forth** *itr* offen, öffentlich, in der Öffentlichkeit reden (*from* von), sprechen, *fam* loslegen (*from* über); *tr* anbieten, vorschlagen; *to ~* **in** zügeln; *to ~ o.s. in* sich zurückhalten, sich in der Gewalt haben, sich beherrschen; *to ~* **off** *tr* ab-, fernhalten; abwehren; *(Flugzeug)* abfangen; *itr* sich abseits-, sich fernhalten; *to ~* **on** (sich) festhalten; sich halten, bleiben; durchhalten, ausdauern; fortfahren; warten; *tele* am Apparat bleiben; *to* sich festhalten an; behalten; aushalten; *to ~* **out** *itr* Bestand haben, sich halten, ausdauern, bleiben; aushalten, -harren, standhalten, sich behaupten (*against* gegen); abwarten (*for s.th.* etw); *tr* ausstrecken, (dar-, an)bieten; *(Angebot, Hoffnung)* machen; *Am sl* zurück-, vorenthalten; *to ~ s.th. out on s.o. (fam)* jdm etw verschweigen; *to ~* **over** *tr* auf-, verschieben; reservieren, in Reserve halten; *(Waren)* zurücklegen; verlängern; *(Wechsel)* prolongieren; *itr Am* (für e-e weitere Periode) im Amt (ver-)bleiben; *to ~* **together** *tr itr* zs.halten; *to ~* **up** *tr* (hoch-, aufrecht)halten, stützen; zeigen, preisgeben (*to* dat, *to ridicule* der Lächerlichkeit); *Am* als Kandidaten aufstellen; *fam* auf-, zurückhalten; (gewaltsam) festhalten; *Am* überfallen (und ausrauben); *itr (Wetter)* sich halten; *(Waren)* dauerhaft sein, halten; sich (aufrecht)halten, nicht fallen, nicht umkippen; sich halten, bleiben, andauern *(a. Wetter)*; *to be held up* aufgehalten werden; *to ~* **with** es halten mit, übereinstimmen mit, billigen; **~-all** Reisetasche *f*; **~-back** Hindernis *n*; **~er** ['-ə] *in Zssgen* -halter; Halterung, Fassung *f*; Halter; Inhaber, Besitzer, Pächter *m*; *~~ of shares* Aktionär *m*; *~~ for value* gutgläubige(r) Erwerber *m*; **~fast** ['-fɑːst] Festhalten *n*; Halter, Haken, Nagel *m*, Krampe, Zwinge; *bot* Haftscheibe *f*; **~ file** Wiedervorlage(mappe) *f*; **~ing** ['-iŋ] (Fest-)Halten; Abhalten *n*; Meinung *f*; Pachtgut *n*, -hof *m*; *meist pl* (Grund-)Besitz, Grundstück *n*; Besitz *m*, Guthaben *n*, (Kapital-)Einlage, (Aktien-)Beteiligung, Teilhaberschaft *f*; Vorrat *m*, Lager *n*, Bestand *m*; *small ~~* Kleinbesitz *m (an Grund u. Boden* od *Aktien)*; kleine Spareinlage *f*, Sparguthaben *n*, -groschen *m*; *~~-attack* Fesselungsangriff *m*; *~~ capacity* Fassungsvermögen *n*; *~~-company* Dach-, Holdinggesellschaft *f*, Trust *m*; *~~ of the court* Gerichtsentscheidung *f*; *~~ device* Haltevorrichtung *f*; *~~ power* Durchstehvermögen *n*; *~~ wire* Prüfdraht *m*; **~over** ['-ouvə] *Am fam* Verbleibende(r) *m*, Verbleibende(s), Überbleibsel *n*; *(Schule)* Wiederholer, Repetent *m*; **~-up** Behinderung, Störung; *(traffic ~~)* Verkehrsstörung, -stockung *f*; (bewaffneter) Raubüberfall *m*; *Am sl* Gehaltsforderung *f*.

hole [houl] *s* Loch *n*, Lücke; Öffnung; kleine Bucht; Aushöhlung; Höhle *f*; Bau *m*, Nest *(wilder Tiere)*; (elendes) Loch, Elendsquartier; Gefängnis, *fam* Loch *n*; Fehler, Makel, Defekt *m*, Versehen *n*, Lücke *(in e-m Argument)*; *fam* Patsche, Klemme, schwierige Lage *od* Situation *f*; *tr* durchlöchern, (aus)höhlen; durchbohren; *(to ~ out) (Ball)* in ein Loch spielen; *itr* ein Loch bekommen; *zoo* in den Bau gehen; *to ~ up* sich ein-, vergraben; *in the ~* in der Patsche, Klemme; *to be like a rat in a ~* gefangen sein, keinen Ausweg (mehr) haben; *to make a ~ in s. th* ein (großes) Loch in e-e S reißen; *to pick ~s in s.th.* an etw herumkritisieren; *to put in a ~* in Verlegenheit bringen; *to wear into ~s (Kleidung)* völlig auftragen; *mouse's ~* Mauseloch *n*; *a square peg in a round ~* ein s-r Stellung nicht gewachsener Mensch; *~ in the wall (sl)* Kleinstbetrieb *m*; **~-and-corner** *a attr fam* heimlich, geheim, versteckt, unter der Hand; **~ proof** unzerreißbar; **~y** ['-i] *fam* voller Löcher.

holiday ['hɔlidei] *s (rel* od *gesetzlicher)* Feiertag, arbeitsfreie(r) Tag, Ruhetag; Gedenktag *m*; *oft pl* Ferien *pl*, Urlaub *m*; *a* Ferien-, Urlaubs-; froh, heiter; *on ~* in Urlaub; *to take a ~* Urlaub, frei nehmen; in Urlaub gehen; *bank ~* Bankfeiertag *m*; *a month's ~* ein Monat Urlaub; *~s with pay* bezahlte(r) Urlaub *m*; **~ camp** Ferienlager *n*; **~ clothes** *pl* Freizeitkleidung *f*; **~ course** Ferienkurs *m*; **~ing** ['-iŋ] Ferienmachen, Urlaubnehmen *n*; Sommerfrische *f*; **~-maker** Feriengast, Sommerfrischler *m*; **~ mood** Ferienstimmung *f*; **~ resort** Sommerfrische *f*.

holiness ['houlinis] Heiligkeit *f*; *Your, His H~* Euere, S-e Heiligkeit *f*.

holla ['hɔlɑː], **hollo** ['hɔlou, hə'lou] *interj* hallo! guten Tag! *tr* hallo zurufen *(s.o.* jdm); *itr* hallo rufen.

Holland ['hɔlənd] Holland *n*; *(brown) h~* (ungebleichte) Leinwand, Baumwolle *f*; **H~er** ['-ə] Holländer(in *f*) *m*; **~s, ~ gin** Genever, Wacholder *m*.

holler ['hɔlə] *Am fam s* einfache(s), traurige(s) Liedchen *n*; *itr tr* schreien, brüllen; *sl* (bei der Polizei) auspacken; *tr* anschreien, anbrüllen; zurufen (*s.o. s.th.* jdm etw).

hollow ['hɔlou] *a* hohl; eingefallen, eingesunken; *fig* leer, hohl, nichtig, wertlos, nichtssagend, unwirklich, falsch, unaufrichtig; *fam* hungrig, mit leerem Magen; hohl(tönend); *adv* völlig, durch u. durch; *s* (Aus-)Höhlung, Vertiefung *f*; Loch *n*, Grube; Niederung *f*, Tal *n*; *tr (to ~ out)* aushöhlen; vertiefen; *itr* hohl werden; *to beat all ~ (fam)* windelweich schlagen; **~ brick** Hohlziegel *m*; **~ charge** Hafthohlladung *f*; **~-eyed** *a* hohläugig; **~-hearted** *a* unaufrichtig; **~ness** ['-nis] Hohlheit, Nichtigkeit, Falschheit *f*; **~ punch** Locheisen *n*; **~-ware** (tiefes) Küchengeschirr *n*.

holly ['hɔli] Stechpalme *f*.

hollyhock ['hɔlihɔk] *bot* Pappelrose, Rosenmalve *f*.

holm [houm] Werder *m*, kleine (*bes.* Fluß-)Insel *f*; Überschwemmungsgebiet *n*; **~-oak** Steineiche *f*.

holocaust ['hɔləkɔːst] Brandopfer *n*; Brandkatastrophe *f*, Großbrand *m*; Massenvernichtung *f*, -mord *m*.

holograph ['hɔləgrɑːf] eigenhändig geschrieben(e Urkunde *f*).

hols [hɔlz] *fam* = *holidays*.

holster ['houlstə] Pistolentasche *f*.

holy ['houli] *a* heilig; geweiht; gottgefällig; rein, sündenlos; verehrungswürdig; *s* Heiligtum *n*; *a ~ terror* ein entsetzlicher Mensch, ein schreckliches Kind; *a ~ war* ein Kreuzzug *fig*; *the (Most)* **H~ Father** der Heilige Vater *(der Papst)*; the **H~ Ghost,** *the* **H~ Spirit** der Heilige Geist; *the* **H~ of Holies** das Allerheiligste; *the* **H~ Land** das Heilige Land *(Palästina)*; **H~ Rood** Kreuz *n* Christi; **H~ Saturday** Karsamstag *m*; *the* **H~ Scripture,** *the* **H~ Writ** die Heilige Schrift, die Bibel; *the* **H~ See** der Heilige Stuhl; **H~ Thursday** Himmelfahrt *f od* Gründonnerstag *m*; **~ water** Weihwasser *n*; *the* **H~ Week** die Karwoche.

homage ['hɔmidʒ] *hist allg* Huldigung *f*; *to do, to pay ~* huldigen (*to s.o.* jdm).

home [houm] *s* Heim, Zuhause *n*, Wohnung; Heimat, Heimstätte, Freistatt *f*; *Am* Bungalow *m*, Eigenheim, Haus *n*; Familie *f*, Haushalt *m*; *(Alters-, Blinden-usw)* Heim, (Waisen-, Armen-)Haus *n*; *zoo bot* Standort *m*; Zentrum; *sport* Mal *n*; *a* einheimisch, inländisch; häuslich; Inlands-, Binnen-; Familien-; *adv* heim, nach Hause; *itr* heimgehen; *tr* unterbringen; *(to) (Rakete)* automatisch ins Ziel steuern; *at ~* daheim, zu Hause; *at ~ in* wie zu Hause, bewandert in; *not at ~* nicht zu Hause (*to* für); *at ~ and abroad* im In- u. Ausland; *to be, to feel o.s. at ~ (fig)* zu Hause sein, sich zu Hause fühlen; *to bring ~ to s.o.* jdn beeindrucken; *s.th. to s.o.* jdm etw klarmachen; jdm etw zur Last legen, beweisen; jdn überführen; *to come ~* heimkehren, nach Hause kommen; nahegehen (*to s.o.* jdm), empfindlich treffen (*to s.o.* jdn); *(Anker)* nicht halten; *to drive ~ (Nagel)* einschlagen; *(Beweis)* durchpauken; *s.th. to s.o.* jdm etw beibringen; *to go ~* nach Hause, heimgehen; *to s.o.* jdn empfindlich treffen; *fig* sitzen; *to hit, to strike ~* den Nagel auf den Kopf treffen; *to make o.s. at home* es sich bequem machen; sich niederlassen; *to see s.o. ~* jdn nach Hause begleiten; *to send ~* heim-, nach Hause schicken; *it has come ~ to me* ich bin mir darüber im klaren; *that comes ~ to you* das gilt Ihnen; das müssen Sie büßen; *there is no place like ~* zu Hause ist es am schönsten; *nothing to write ~ about* nichts Besonderes; **~-address** Heimatanschrift *f*; **~-affairs** *pl pol* innere Angelegenheiten *f pl*; **~-baked** *a* selbstgebacken; **~-base** Heimatflughafen *m*; **~body** *Am* häuslich; **~-born** *a* eingeboren; einheimisch; **~-bred** *a* daheim aufgewachsen; *fig* hausbacken; **~-brew(ed)** *a (Bier)* selbstgebraut; **~-coming** Heimkehr *f*; *Am (Schule)* Beginn *m* des neuen Schuljahrs; **~-consumption** Inlandsverbrauch *m*; *the* **H~ Counties** *pl* die Grafschaften um London; **~-country** Heimatstaat *m*, Muster-, Herkunftsland *n*; **~ economics** *pl mit sing Am* Hauswirtschaftslehre *f*; **~ economy** Binnenwirtschaft *f*; **~ free** *Am sl* todsicher erfolgreich; **~-grown** *a*: *~~ produce (agr)* einheimische(s) Erzeugnis *n*; **H~-Guard** Heimatwehr *f*; **~-keeping** *(Mensch)* häuslich; **~land** ['-lænd] Heimat(land *n*) *f*; **~less** ['-lis] obdachlos; heimatlos; **~like** ['-laik] heimelig, behaglich, wie zu Hause; **~liness** ['-linis] Häuslichkeit; Einfachheit, Schlichtheit *f*; **~lot** *Am* Wohngrundstück *n*; **~ly** ['-li] häuslich, heimisch; einfach, schlicht, alltäglich, anspruchslos; *Am* hausbacken, unansehnlich; *~~ fare* bürgerliche Küche *f*; **~-made** *a* selbstgemacht, -gebacken; Hausmacher-; **~maker** *Am* Hausfrau *f*; **~making** *Am* Hausarbeit, Haushaltführung *f*; **~ market** Inlandsmarkt *m*; **H~ Office** Innenministerium *n*; **~ plate** *(Baseball)* Schlagmal *n*; **~r** ['-ə] Brieftaube *f*; *aero* Peilanfluggerät *n*; *Am fam* = *~ run*; **~ rule** Selbstverwaltung *f*; **~ run** *s (Baseball)* Vier-Mal-Lauf *m*; *a Am sl* erstklassig; **H~ Secretary** Minister des Innern, Innenminister *m*; **~sick** an Heimweh leidend; *to be ~~* Heimweh haben; **~sickness** Heimweh *n*; **~ signal** Einfahrtssignal *n*; **~spun** ['-spʌn] *a (Textil)* heimischen Ursprungs; *fig* einfach, schlicht; rauh, grob; *s* rauhe(r) Wollstoff *m*; **~ state** Heimatstaat *m*; **~stead** ['-sted] Heimstätte *f*; *Am* Wohn-, Eigenheim, Siedlungshaus, -grundstück; *Am* zugewiesene(s) Freiland *n (160 acres)*; **~steader** ['-stedə] *Am* Siedler; Eigenheimbesitzer *m*; **~stretch** *sport* Endspurt *m*; letzte Arbeiten *f pl*; **~ study** Fernunterricht *m*; **~thrust** ['-θrʌst] entscheidende(r) Schlag *m a. fig*; **~town** *Am* Geburts-, Heimatstadt *f*; **~-trade** Binnenhandel *m*; **~-truth** bittere Wahrheit *f*; **~ward** ['-wəd] *a* Heim-, Nachhause-, Rück-; *adv* u. **~wards** *adv* heim, nach Hause, zurück; *~~ bound (mar)* auf der Rückfahrt; **~work** Heimarbeit *f*; *(Schule)* Hausaufgaben *f pl*; **~y** ['-i] *fam* anheimelnd, behaglich, heimelig.

homicide ['hɔmisaid] Tötung *f*; Totschlag; Mord; Totschläger; Mörder *m*; **~ squad** Mordkommission *f*.

homily ['hɔmili] *rel* Predigt; *allg* Moralpredigt *f*.

homing ['houmiŋ] *a* heimkehrend; heimwärts gerichtet; *mil* zielsuchend; *s* Heimkehr *f*, Nachhausegehen *n*; *aero* Anflugpeilung *f*; **~ instinct** Heimatsinn *m*, Ortsgedächtnis *n*; **~ pigeon** Brieftaube *f*.

hominy ['hɔmini] *Am* Bruchmais *m*; grobe(s) Maismehl *n*; Maisbrei *m*.

hom(o)eopath ['houmjəpæθ] Homöopath, homöopathische(r) Arzt *m*; **~ic** [houmiə'pæθik] homöopathisch; **~ist** [houmi'ɔpəθist] = *~*; **~y** [houmi'ɔpəθi] Homöopathie *f*.

homo|geneity [hɔmo(u)dʒe'ni:iti] *scient* Gleichartigkeit *f*; **~geneous** [hɔmə'dʒi:njəs] gleichartig, homogen; **~logize** [hɔ'mɔlədʒaiz] *tr itr scient* in Übereinstimmung bringen *od* sein; **~logous** [hɔ'mɔləgəs] übereinstimmend; **~logy** [hɔ'mɔlədʒi] Übereinstimmung *f*; **~nym** ['hɔmənim] Homonym, gleichlautende(s) Wort *n*; **~nymous** [hɔ'mɔniməs] homonym, mehrdeutig; **~sexual** ['houmo(u)'seksjuəl] homosexuell, gleichgeschlechtlich empfindend; **~sexuality** ['houmo(u)seksju'æliti] Homosexualität *f*.

hone [houn] *s* Wetzstein *m*; *tr (Messer)* abziehen; *tech* ziehschleifen.

honest ['ɔnist] ehrlich, aufrichtig, zuverlässig, vertrauenswürdig; (frei und) offen, ehrlich, g(e)rade; anständig; ehrenhaft; *to earn an ~ penny* sein Geld ehrlich verdienen; *an ~ man is as good as his word* ein Mann, ein Wort; **~ly** ['-li] *adv* auf ehrliche Weise; wirklich, tatsächlich; *to tell you ~~* offengestanden; **~y** ['-i] Ehrenhaftigkeit; Ehrlichkeit, Aufrichtigkeit; Zuverlässigkeit *f*.

honey ['hʌni] *s* Honig *m*; Süßigkeit *f*; *fig* Goldkind, Schätzchen *n*, Liebling *m*; *Am* Pfundssache *f*; *a* honigartig, -süß; *fig* süß, (ge)lieb(t); *tr* mit Honig süßen; herzen, liebtun mit; Honig ums Maul schmieren, schmeicheln (*s.o.* jdm); *itr* schäkern; zärtlich sein, schmeicheln; **~-bee** Honigbiene *f*; **~-buzzard** Wespenbussard, Bienen-, Honigfalk *m*; **~comb** ['-koum] *s* Honigwabe *f*; *tech* Waben-; *~~ decoration, pattern* Wabenmuster *n*; *~~ed* ['-d] *a* durchbohrt, durchlöchert, löcherig; *fig* durchsetzt (*with* von); untergraben; **~-dew** Honigtau, Blatthonig *m*; süße Melone *f*; süße(r) Tabak *m*; **~ed** ['-d] *a* voller Honig; mit Honig gesüßt; *fig* honigsüß; **~-locust** *bot* Christusakazie *f*; **~moon** ['-mu:n] *s* Flitterwochen *f pl*; *itr* Flitterwochen verbringen; **~suckle** ['-sʌkl] *bot* Geißblatt *n*.

honied *s. honeyed.*

honk [hɔŋk] *s* Schrei *m* der Wildgans; *mot* Hupen, Hupsignal *n*; *itr (Wildgans)* schreien; *mot* hupen.

honky-tonk ['hɔŋkitɔŋk] *Am sl* Spelunke, Kaschemme *f*, Bumslokal *n*.

honorar|ium [ɔnə'rɛəriəm] *pl a. ~ia* Honorar *n*; **~y** ['ɔnərəri] *a* Ehren-; ehrenamtlich, unbesoldet, ehrenhalber *(nachgestellt)*; *~~ appointment, function, office* Ehrenamt *n*; *~~ citizen* Ehrenbürger *m*; *~~ debt* Ehrenschuld *f*; *~~ degree* Ehrendoktor *m*; *~~ member* Ehrenmitglied *n*.

hono(u)r ['ɔnə] *s* Ehre, Würde, Auszeichnung; (Hoch-)Achtung *f*; Ruhm, Ruf *m*; Ehrenhaftigkeit, Unbescholtenheit; *(Frau, Mädchen)* Ehre, Unberührtheit, Reinheit, Keuschheit *f*; Ehrenzeichen *n*, -gabe *f*; *pl* öffentliche Ehrungen *f pl*; *(Schule)* Auszeichnung *f*; *your H~* Euer Gnaden *(Anrede für e-n Richter)*; *tr* ehren, (hoch)achten, hochschätzen; verehren; e-e Ehrung zuteil werden lassen (*s.o.* jdm); *fin* honorieren; einlösen; *in s.o.'s ~* zu jds Ehre; *with all due ~, with full ~s* mit allen Ehren; *to do s.o. the ~ of* jdm die Ehre erweisen, jdn beehren, zu; *to do the ~s* die Honneurs machen; *to give o.'s word of ~, to pledge o.'s ~* sein Ehrenwort geben; *to have the ~* die Ehre haben (*of, to* zu); *to put s.o. on his ~* jdn an s-r Ehre packen; jdn moralisch verpflichten; *to take ~s in (Universität)* sich spezialisieren in; *(up)on my ~* auf (meine) Ehre! *~ bright* stehen Sie dafür ein? auf mein Wort! *bound in ~* moralisch verpflichtet; *code of ~* Ehrenkodex *m*; *of ~* Ehrenschuld *f*; *guard of ~* Ehrenwache *f*; *guest of ~* Ehrengast *m*; *the last, funeral ~s (pl)* die letzten Ehren *f pl*; *maid of ~* Ehrendame *f*; *seat of ~* Ehrenplatz *m*; *sense of ~* Ehrgefühl *n*; *word of ~* Ehrenwort *n*; **~able** ['-rəbl] ehrenhaft, -voll, -wert; Ehren-; *Right H~~* ... Sehr Ehrenwerter...; *with ~~ intentions* in ehrlicher Absicht; *my H~~ friend the member for...* *(Br parl)* der Abgeordnete für....

hood [hud] *s* Kapuze *f*; Talarüberwurf *m*; *tech* Haube, Kappe *f*, Aufsatz *m*; Wagenplane *f*; *mot* Verdeck *n*; *Am mot* Kühlerhaube *f*; *orn* Kamm *m*, Haube *f*; *Am sl* Dieb, Bandit *m*; *tr* zudecken, ein-, verhüllen; **~ed** ['-id] *a* mit e-r Kappe, Haube versehen; haubenförmig; *fig* verhüllt; **~ie, ~y** ['-i] *(~ed-crow)* Nebelkrähe *f*; **~lum** ['hu:dləm] *Am sl* Rowdy, Gangster *m*; **~wink** ['-wiŋk] *tr* die Augen verbinden, *fig* Sand in die Augen streuen (*s.o.* jdm); täuschen; betrügen.

hoodoo ['hu:du:] *s* Unheilbringer *m*; Pech, Unglück *n*; *tr* Unglück bringen (*s.o.* jdm); ver-, behexen.

hooey ['hui] *s interj Am sl* Quatsch *m*.

hoof [hu:f] *pl a. hooves s* Huf *m*; Klaue *f*; *fam hum* Fuß *m (des Menschen)*; *tr* treten; *itr* trampeln; *(to ~ it) fam* tippeln, trampen, *sl* schwofen, tanzen; *to ~ out (sl)* rausschmeißen; *on the ~ (Vieh)* lebend; **~ed** [-t] *a* Huf-; **~er** ['-ə] *sl* Berufstänzer *m*.

hoo-ha ['hu:hə] *fam* Krach; Streit *m*.

hook [huk] *s* Haken; Kleider-, Angelhaken; *mar sl* Anker *m*; Sichel *f*; gekrümmte Landspitze, -zunge; Biegung *(e-s Wasserlaufs)*; Klammer, Schlinge; *fig* Falle *f*; *(Boxen)* Haken; *(Werbung)* Blickfang *m*, Lockmittel *n*; *mus* Notenschwanz *m*; *tr* an-, fest-, zuhaken; mit e-m Haken festhalten (*to* an); fangen; angeln *a. fig*; *(Wagen)* anhängen (*on to* an); *fam* schnappen, stehlen; betrügen, beschwindeln; *(Bulle, Bock)* mit den Hörnern stoßen, aufspießen; hakenförmig biegen; *sport (Ball)* e-n Haken schlagen lassen; *(Boxen)* e-n Haken versetzen (*s.o.* jdm); *itr* (hakenförmig) gekrümmt sein; mit (e-m) Haken befestigt sein, gefangen werden; *to ~ on* an e-n Haken hängen; sitzen bleiben (*to s.o.* bei jdm); *to ~ up* mit (e-m) Haken festmachen, verbinden, herausziehen; zs.setzen, -bauen, verbinden; *el* anschließen; *sl* heiraten; *by ~ or by crook* ganz gleich, einerlei, gleichgültig, wie; mit allen Mitteln; mit aller Gewalt; *off the ~ (Am sl)* aus Schwierigkeiten heraus; *on o.'s own ~ (fam)* ganz allein, ohne (fremde) Hilfe; auf eigene Faust; *~, line, and sinker (fam)* vollkommen, -ständig *adv*; mit allem Drum u. Dran; *to drop off the ~s (sl)* abkratzen, sterben; *to get o.'s ~s on to s.o.* jdn mit Beschlag belegen; *to get ~ ed on* süchtig werden; *to get the ~ (fam)* 'rausgeschmissen, entlassen werden; *to take the ~* auf den Leim gehen; anbeißen; *to ~ it, to sling o.'s. ~ (sl)* abhauen, türmen, stiftengehen; *reaping-~* Sichel *f*; *~ and eye* Haken u. Öse; *~ and ladder (Am)* Feuerwehrleiter *f*; *~-and--ladder truck (Am)* Feuerwehrauto *n*; **~ed** [-t] *a* hakenförmig (gebogen), krumm; mit Haken versehen; *Am sl* rauschgiftsüchtig; **~er** ['-ə] Fischerboot *n*, alte Kiste *f (Schiff)*; *Am* Werkspionwerber *m*; *Am sl* Prostituierte *f*; *Am sl* (Glas *n*) Whisky *m*; **~-nose** Hakennase *f*; **~-up** Zs.setzung, Verbindung; *radio* Schaltung *f*, Schaltplan *m*, Schema *n*; *radio* Sendergruppe, Ringsendung *f*; Übereinkommen *(zwischen Firmen)*; *pol* Bündnis *n*; **~-worm** Hakenwurm *m*; **~y** ['-i] hakenförmig, gekrümmt; *to play ~~ (Am fam)* die Schule schwänzen.

hooka(h) ['hukə] Wasserpfeife *f*.

hooligan ['hu:ligən] Rowdy *m*.

hoop [hu:p] *s* Reif(en); Bügel, Ring *m*; *sport* (Krocket-)Tor *n*; rauche(r) Schrei; *Am fam* Fingerring *m*; *tr* die Reifen auftreiben *(a barrel* auf ein Faß); *a Am* Korbball-; *to go trough the ~ (fam)* e-e schwere Zeit durchmachen; **~er** ['-ə] Böttcher, Küfer *m*; *~~-doo(per) (Am sl) a* lärmend; *s* lärmende Angelegenheit *f*; große(s) Tier *n*; **~-iron** Bandeisen *n*; **~-la** ['-lɑ:] Ringwerfen *n*; *Am sl* lärmende Propaganda *f*; **~-man** *Am* Korbballspieler *m*; **~-skirt** Reifrock *m*.

hooping-cough ['hu:piŋkɔ(:)f] Keuchhusten *m*.

hoopoe ['hu:pu:] *orn* Wiedehopf *m*.

hoos(e)gow ['hu:sgau] *n Am sl* Kittchen *n*; öffentliche Bedürfnisanstalt *f*.

hoot [hu:t] *itr* schreien; pfeifen; ertönen; hupen; verhöhnen *(at s.o.* jdn); *tr (s-e Wut)* herausschreien; *(Menschen)* anschreien; *to ~ (at) s.o., to ~ s.o. away, off, out* jdn auspfeifen, -zischen; *to ~ down* niederschreien; *s* Geschrei *(bes. der Eule)*; Wutgeschrei, -geheul; *tech* Hupen *n*; *not to give a ~ for s.th.* keinen Pfifferling für etw geben; **~er** ['-ə] *tech* Sirene; *mot* Hupe *f*; **~-owl** *orn* Waldkauz *m*.

hoover ['hu:və] *tr* staubsaugen.

hop [hɔp] **1.** *itr* hüpfen; springen; *fam* das Tanzbein schwingen; *sl* gehen; *tr* springen über; *Am* springen auf *(ein Fahrzeug)*; *fam (im Flugzeug)* überfliegen; *(Auto)* frisieren; *s* Hupf; Sprung *m*; *fam* Tänzchen *n*; *aero fam* kurze(r) Flug, Rutsch *m*; Etappe *f*; *Am sl* Rauschgift *n*; Verwirrung *f*; Unsinn *m*; *to ~ about, (Am) around* umherhüpfen, -springen; *to ~ off (aero fam)* starten; *to ~ over to s.o.* zu jdm e-n Sprung machen; *to ~ up (Am sl)* doppen; *mot* frisieren; *~ it!* hau ab! *to ~ the twig (sl)* ins Gras beißen; *on the ~* unruhig; unvorbereitet; *~, step, and jump (sport)* Dreisprung *m*; **~-o'-my-thumb** ['hɔpəmi'θʌm] Knirps *m (Mensch)*; **~per** ['-ə] *s* Hüpfende(r) *m*, Hüpfende(s); hüpfende(s) Insekt *n*, Heuschrecke *f*, Floh *m*, Käsemade *f*; *tech* Mahl-, Fülltrichter *m*; *~~ waggon, (Am) car (rail)* Trichterwagen *m*; **~scotch** ['-skɔtʃ] Himmel u. Hölle *(Kinderspiel)*; **2.** *s* Hopfen *m (Kletterpflanze)*; *pl* Hopfen *m (Bierzusatz)*; *tr* hopfen, mit Hopfen versehen; *itr* Hopfen tragen *od* zupfen; **~-bind, ~-bine** Hopfenranke *f*; **~-garden** Hopfengarten *m*; **~-picker** Hopfenpflücker *m*; **~-pole** Hopfenstange *f*.

hope [houp] *s a. pl* Hoffnung *f (of* auf); Vertrauen *n (in* zu); Zuversicht *f*; *tr* hoffen auf, erhoffen, ersehnen; *itr* hoffen *(for* auf), erhoffen *(for s.th.* etw); vertrauen *(in* auf); *past, beyond ~* hoffnungslos; *to hold out a ~* Hoffnung haben; *to live in ~s of s.th.* auf etw hoffen; *I ~ so* hoffentlich! *I ~ not* hoffentlich nicht! *~ against ~* verzweifelte Hoffnung *f*; **~ chest** *Am* Aussteuertruhe *f*; **~ful** ['-ful] *a* hoffnungsvoll; vielversprechend; ermutigend; *s: a young ~~* ein hoffnungsvoller Sprößling; **~fulness** ['-fulnis] Hoffnungsfreudigkeit, Zuversicht *f*; Optimismus *m*; **~less** ['-lis] hoffnungslos; aussichtslos; unverbesserlich; **~lessness** ['-lisnis] Hoffnungslosigkeit; Vergeblichkeit *f*.

horde [hɔ:d] *s* Horde; Menge *f*, Schwarm *m*; *itr* e-e Horde bilden; in Horden zs.leben.

horizon [hə'raizn] Horizont *m a. fig*; **~tal** [hɔri'zɔntl] Horizont-; dicht am Horizont; horizontal, waagerecht; eben, flach; *~~ bar (sport)* Reck *n*.

hormone ['hɔ:moun] Hormon *n*.

horn [hɔ:n] *s zoo* Horn *n*; *zoo* Fühler *m*; Hornsubstanz *f*; (Pulver-, Trink-) Horn; Füllhorn; *mus* Horn, Blasinstrument *n*; Horn-, Schalltrichter *m*; *mot* Hupe *f*; *allg* Vorsprung *m*, Spitze; Bergspitze; Spitze *f* der (Mond-)Sichel; *Am sl* Nase *f*; *pl* Geweih, Gehörn *n*; *tr* mit den Hörnern stoßen; *to ~ in (Am sl)* hereinplatzen, -schneien *(on* bei); sich einmischen; *to be on the ~s of a dilemma* in e-r Zwickmühle sitzen; *to blow o.'s own ~ (fam)* ins eigene Horn stoßen, sein eigenes Lob singen; *to blow, to honk the ~ (mot)* hupen; *to draw, to haul, to pull in o.'s ~s (fig)* gelindere Saiten aufziehen; *to take the bull by the ~s (fig)* der Gefahr ins Auge sehen; *to take a ~ (Am fam)* sich einen *(e-n Schnaps)* genehmigen; *~ of plenty* Füllhorn *n*; **~beam, ~beech** Hain-, Weißbuche, Heister *f*; **~bill** Nashornvogel *m*; **~blende** ['-blend] *min* Hornblende *f*; **~ed** [-d] *a* gehörnt; Horn-; *~~ viper* Hornviper *f*; **~et** ['-it] Hornisse *f*; *to stir up a nest of ~~s, to bring a ~~s' nest about o.'s ears (fig)* ins Wespennest stechen; **~less** ['-lis] hornlos; **~-owl** Ohreule *f*; **~pipe** *mus hist* Hornpfeife *f*; *hist* Seemannstanz *m*; **~rimmed** *a*: *~~ spectacles (pl)* Hornbrille *f*; **~swoggle** ['-swɔgl] *tr Am sl* beschwindeln; 'reinlegen; **~y** ['-i] horn(art)ig; gehörnt; schwielig; *Am sl* fleischlich, leicht erregt; *~~-handed (a)* mit schwieligen Händen.

horolog|e ['hɔrələdʒ] Zeitmesser *m (Gerät)*; **~er** [hɔ'rɔlədʒə] Uhrmacher *m*; **~y** [hɔ'rɔlədʒi] Zeitmessung *f*.

horoscope ['hɔrəskoup] Horoskop *n*; *to cast a ~* ein Horoskop stellen.

horr|ible ['hɔribl] schrecklich, furchtbar, entsetzlich; gräßlich, fürchterlich; **~ibleness** ['-nis] Furchtbarkeit, Entsetzlichkeit *f*; **~id** ['-id] schrecklich, furchtbar, entsetzlich, gräßlich, greulich, abscheulich, ekelhaft, abstoßend; **~ify** ['hɔrifai] *tr* entsetzen; Schrecken einjagen *(s.o.* jdm); *fam* schockieren; **~or** ['hɔrə] Schrecken *m*, Entsetzen, Grauen *n*; Abscheu, Ekel *m (of* vor); *fam* scheußliche Sache *f*; *pl* Grausen *n*; *it gives me the ~~s* es läuft mir kalt über den Rücken; *~~-stricken, -struck (a)* von Entsetzen, von Grauen gepackt.

horse [hɔ:s] *s* Pferd, Roß *n*, Gaul; Hengst *m*; *fam* od *hum* od *pej* Kerl; Bock *a. sport*, Ständer *m*, Gestell; *sport* Pferd *n*; Sägebock *m*; *fam (Schach)* Pferd *n*, Springer; *Am sl (Schule)* Schlauch *m*; *mil (pl ~)* Kavallerie, Reiterei *f*; *itr Am sl (to ~ around)* herumalbern; *out of the ~'s mouth* direkt von der Quelle; *to back the wrong ~ (fig)* aufs falsche Pferd setzen; *to be on, to mount, to ride o.'s high ~ (fig)* auf dem hohen Roß sitzen; *to eat like a ~* fressen wie ein Scheunendrescher; *to flog a dead ~ (fig)* s-e Zeit verlieren; *to put the cart before the ~ (fig)* das Pferd beim Schwanz aufzäumen; *to take ~* aufsitzen; *to work like a ~* arbeiten wie ein Pferd; *that's a ~ of another, of a different colo(u)r* das ist etwas ganz anderes; *to ~! (mil)* aufgesessen! *never look a gift ~ in the mouth! (prov)* einem geschenkten Gaul schaut man nicht ins Maul; *hold your ~s (fam)* immer mit der Ruhe! *a dark ~ (fig)* ein unbeschriebenes Blatt; *sport* Außenseiter *m*; **~-and--buggy** *Am* Pferdekutsche *f*; **~-artillery** berittene Artillerie *f*; **~back** *s* Pferderücken; Bergrücken *m*; *a Am sl* schnell erledigt; *adv u. on ~~* zu Pferde; *to be, to go on ~~* reiten; *to get on ~~* aufsitzen; **~-bean** Saubohne *f*; **~-box** *rail* Pferdetransportwagen *m*; **~-breaker** Bereiter *m*; **~-butchery** Pferdemetzgerei, -schlächterei *f*; **~-chestnut** Roßkastanie *f*; **~-cloth** Pferdedecke *f*; **~-collar** Kum(me)t *n*; **~-dealer** Pferdehändler *m*; **~-drawn** *a* (pferde)bespannt; **~-flesh** Pferdefleisch *n*; Pferde *n pl*; **~-fly** Pferdebremse *f*; *the* **H~-Guards** das Garde-Kavallerie-Regiment *n*; **~-hair** Roßhaar *n*; **~-latitudes** *pl geog* Roßbreiten *f pl*; **~-laugh** Gewieher, wiehernde(s) Gelächter *n*; **~-leech** *zoo* Pferdeegel; *fig* Nimmersatt *m*; **~man** ['-mən] Reiter *m*; **~manship** Reitkunst *f*; **~-marines** *pl hum* reitende Gebirgsmarine *f*; *tell that to the ~~* machen Sie das einem andern weis; **~-nail** = *~shoe-nail*; **~ opera** *Am sl* Wildwestfilm *m*; **~-play** grobe(r) Unfug *m*; **~-pond** Pferdeschwemme *f*; **~-power** *phys tech* Pferdestärke *f (= 550 ft. lbs./sec. = 1,014 PS = 0,75 kW)*; **~-race** Pferderennen *n*; **~-radish** Meerrettich *m*; **~ sense** *fam* gesunde(r) Menschenverstand *m*; **~shoe** ['-ʃʃu:, -sʃ-] Hufeisen *n*; *~~ bend* Schleife *f (Straße)*; *~~-nail* Hufeisen *n*; *~~-pitching (Am sport)* Hufeisenwerfen *n*; **~-tail** Pferdeschwanz *m*; **~ trade** *Am fig* Kuhhandel *m*; **~-whip** *s* Reitpeitsche *f*; *tr* durchprügeln; **~woman** ['-wumən] Reiterin *f*.

hors|iness ['hɔ:sinis] Stallgeruch *m*; Pferdeliebhaberei *f*; **~y** ['hɔ:si] pferdeartig; Pferde-; pferdeliebend; Renn-.

hortat|ive ['hɔ:tətiv], **~ory** ['-əri] (er)mahnend; Mahn-.

horticultur|al [hɔ:ti'kʌltʃərəl] *a* Gartenbau-; *~~ exhibition* Gartenschau, -bauausstellung *f*; **~e** ['-kʌltʃə] Gartenbau *m*; **~ist** [-'kʌltʃərist] Handelsgärtner; Gartengestalter *m*.

hosanna [ho(u)'zænə] *s* Hosianna *n*; *interj* hosianna!

hos|e [houz] *tr* mit e-m Schlauch bespritzen; *s hist* (Knie-)Hose *f*; (langer) Damenstrumpf; (Gummi-)Schlauch *m*; *pl ~~* Strümpfe *m pl*; *rubber ~~* Gummischlauch *m*; **~ier** ['houʒə] Strumpfwaren-, Trikotagenhändler, -fabrikant *m*; **~iery** ['houʒəri] Strumpf-, Wirkwaren, Trikotagen *pl*; *(~~ mill)* Wirkerei, Strumpffabrik *f*.

hospice ['hɔspis] Hospiz *n*.
hospitable ['hɔspitəbl] gastfrei, -lich, -freundlich; *fig* aufgeschlossen (*to* für); **~ness** ['-nis] Gastlichkeit *f*.
hospital ['hɔspitl] Klinik *f*, Krankenhaus, Hospital; *mil* Lazarett *n*; *mental, (Am) insane* ~ Irrenhaus *n*; ~ **fever** Flecktyphus *m*; **~ity** [hɔspi'tæliti] Gastlichkeit; Gastfreundschaft *f*; **~ization** [hɔspitəlai'zeiʃən, -li-] Einlieferung in ein, Unterbringung *f* in e-m Krankenhaus; **~ize** ['hɔspitəlaiz] *tr* in ein Krankenhaus einliefern *od* überweisen; **~(l)er** ['hɔspitlə] *hist* Hospitalbruder, Hospitaliter *m*; **~-nurse** Krankenschwester *f*; **~-orderlies** *pl* Sanitätsmannschaften *f pl*; **~-ship** Lazarettschiff *n*; **~-train** Lazarettzug *m*; ~ **treatment** Lazarettbehandlung *f*.
host [houst] **1.** Gastgeber, Wirt; Hausherr; (Gast-)Wirt; *biol* Wirt(stier *n*) *m* (*e-s Schmarotzers*); *to reckon without o.'s* ~ *(fig)* die Rechnung ohne den Wirt machen; **~ess** ['-is] Gastgeberin, Wirtin, Dame *f* des Hauses; (Gast-) Wirtin; Empfangsdame; Geschäftsführerin; *mar aero* Stewardeß *f*; Taxigirl *n*; ~~ *gown* Morgenrock *m*; **2.** *lit obs* Heer *n*; *pl rel* Heerscharen *f pl*; *a* ~ *of*, ~*s of* e-e Unzahl, e-e (ganze) Reihe, Menge *f*, Schwarm *m*; sehr viel(e); *the Lord of H~s* der Herr der Heerscharen; **3.** *rel* Hostie *f*.
hostage ['hɔstidʒ] Geisel *f*; *fig* Pfand *n*; *to give ~s to fortune* sich Gefahren aussetzen.
hostel ['hɔstəl] Herberge *f*, Hospiz, Übernachtungsheim; Wohnheim *n*; **~(l)er** ['-ə] Jugendwanderer; im Wohnheim untergebrachte(r) Student; **~ry** ['-ri] *obs* Gasthaus *n*, -hof *m*.
hostil|e ['hɔstail] feindlich; feindselig (*to* gegen); ~~ *territory* Feindesland *n*; **~ity** [hɔs'tiliti] Feindseligkeit *f* (*to, towards, against* gegen); *pl* Feindseligkeiten *f pl* Krieg(szustand *m*, -shandlungen *f pl*) *m*.
hostler ['ɔslə] *s. ostler.*

*

hot [hɔt] *a* heiß, sehr warm; brennend, beißend; scharf, stark gewürzt; *fig* heiß(blütig), feurig, hitzig, leicht erregbar, aufgeregt; erregt; heftig; eifrig; (hell) begeistert, leidenschaftlich, glühend; verliebt; *fam* erpicht, scharf (*on, for* auf); *sl* geil, lüstern; wollüstig; *(Kampf, Ringen)* heiß, heftig; heißgelaufen; *el* unter Spannung; eingeschaltet; radioaktiv; *mus* heiß; *sport* Favorit-; erfolgreich; *fam* noch warm, (noch) frisch; *sl* geklaut, gestohlen; geschmuggelt, Schmuggel-; *sl* prima, Klasse; wunderbar, hübsch, anziehend; gefährlich, bedenklich; *adv* heftig, eifrig; *in* ~ *haste* in größter Eile, überstürzt; ~ *and* ~ frisch vom Feuer, aus dem Ofen; ~ *with fever* fieberheiß; *not so* ~ *(fam)* ergebnislos; wirkungslos; *to blow* ~ *and cold* nicht wissen, was man will; *to get* ~ *(sl)* in Fahrt kommen; *to get into* ~ *water* in die Patsche geraten; *to get* ~ *over s.th.* sich wegen etw erhitzen; *to make it* ~ *for s.o.* jdm die Hölle heiß machen; *I'm* ~ *on his trail* od *track* ich bin ihm dicht auf der Spur; *I don't feel so* ~ *(Am sl)* ich fühle mich nicht besonders; *give it him* ~*! (fam)* gib ihm Saures! ~ **air** Heißluft *f*; *Am sl* dumme(s) Zeug *n*, Flausen *pl*, blaue(r) Dunst *m*; Angeberei *f*; **~bed** Mistbeet *n*; *fig* Brutstätte *f*; **~-blast** *attr tech* Heißwind-; **~-blooded** *a* heißblütig, feurig, hitzig; **~box** *Am tech* heißgelaufene(s) Lager *n*; **~-brained, -headed** *a* leicht erregbar, aufbrausend, heftig, ungestüm; ~ **cake** Pfannkuchen *m*; *to sell like ~~s* ab-, weggehen wie warme Semmeln; ~ **corner** *Am fam* gefährliche Gegend *f*; ~ **dog** *s Am fam* warme(s), heiße(s) Würstchen *n* (mit Brötchen); *interj* prima! hervorragend! *~-dog stand (Am fam)* Würstchenstand *m*, -bude *f*; **~foot** *adv fam* auf dem schnellsten Wege, in aller Eile; *itr fam* schnell machen, sich beeilen; *tr* beschleunigen; **~head** Hitz-, Brausekopf *m*; **~headed** ['-id] *a* hitzköpfig; **~house** Treibhaus *n*; **~pad** Heizkissen *n*; ~ **plate** Heiz-, Kochplatte *f*; **~-poo** *Am sl das* Neueste, letzte Neuigkeit *f*; **~-pot** Eintopf *m* von Fleisch und Kartoffeln; ~ **potato** *fig fam* schwierige(s) Problem *n*; **~-press** *tr (Gewebe)* dekatieren, dämpfen; *s* Dekatiermaschine *f*; ~ **rod** *Am sl mot* alte Kiste *f* mit überverdichtetem Motor; Rennwagen *m*; **~-rodder** *Am sl* Rennfahrer *m*, -sau *f*; **~-rolled** *a* warmgewalzt; **~-short** *(Eisen)* rotbrüchig; ~ **shot** *Am sl* tolle(r) Kerl *m*; neueste Nachricht *f*; ~ **spot** *Am sl* Nachtlokal *n*; **~spur** ['-spə:] Heißsporn *m*; ~ **stuff** *sl iro* tolle(r) Bursche *m*; was ganz Besonderes; Diebesgut *n*; **~-tempered** *a* heißblütig, feurig, leicht erregt, heftig; ~ **tip** todsichere(r) Tip *m*; ~ **war** heiße(r) Krieg *m*; ~ **waste** radioaktive(r) Abfall *m*; ~ **water** heiße(s) Wasser; Heißwasser *n*; *in ~~ (fam)* in der Tinte; *~-water bottle* Wärm-, Bettflasche *f*; *~-water heater* Warmwasserbehälter *m*; *~-water tank* Heißwasserbehälter *m*; ~ **wire** *fam* (gute) Nachricht *f*; *tech* Hitzdraht *m*.
hotchpotch ['hɔtʃpɔtʃ] (dicke) Gemüsesuppe *f*, Eintopf *m*; gemeinsame(s) Vermögen *n*; *fig* Mischmasch *m*.
hotel [ho(u)'tel, ou't-, ə't-] Hotel, Gasthaus *n*, -hof *m*; ~ **accommodation** Unterbringung *f* im Hotel; ~ **bill** Hotelrechnung *f*; ~ **keeper, proprietor** Hotelbesitzer *m*; ~ **register** Fremdenbuch *n*; *the* ~ **trade** das Beherbergungsgewerbe.
hough [hɔk] *s. hock* 1.
hound [haund] *s* Jagdhund; Hund *a. fig pej*; *fig* Schurke; *(Spiel)* Verfolger *m*; *tr (mit Hunden)* jagen, hetzen; (beständig) verfolgen; hetzen (*at, on* auf); *to follow the ~s, to ride to ~s* mit der Meute jagen.
hour ['auə] Stunde; Zeit *f*; Zeitpunkt *m*; (Unterrichts-)Stunde; Stunde Weg, Fahrt; Uhr(zeit) *f*; *rel* Stundengebet *n*; *the H~s (Mythologie)* die Horen *f pl*; *rel (Kunst)* Stundenbuch *n*; *after ~s* nach Feierabend; nach Geschäftsschluß; ~ *after* ~, ~ *by* ~ Stunde für Stunde; *at all ~s* jederzeit, zu jeder Stunde; *at the eleventh* ~ in letzter Minute; *for ~s* stundenlang; *in a good, evil* ~ zu rechter, zu unpassender Zeit; im rechten, im falschen Augenblick; *to keep early, late ~s* früh aufstehen; spät zu Bett gehen *od* lange aufbleiben; *to keep regular ~s* ein geregeltes Leben führen; *the rush* ~ die Hauptgeschäfts-, -verkehrszeit *f*; *the small ~s* die frühen Morgenstunden *f pl*; *working ~s (pl)* Arbeitszeit *f*; Dienststunden *f pl*; ~ *of operation* Betriebsstunde *f*; ~ *of service* Betriebs-, Brennstunde *f*; **~-circle** *astr* Stundenkreis *m*; ~ **flown** *aero* Flugstunde *f*; **~-glass** Sanduhr *f*, Stundenglas *n*; **~-hand** Stundenzeiger *m*; **~ly** ['-li] *a* stündlich; beständig, dauernd; *adv* stündlich, alle Stunde; von Stunde zu Stunde; oft, häufig, beständig; ~~ *wage* Stundenlohn *m*.
house [haus] *pl -s* ['hauziz] (*bes.* Wohn-)Haus *n*; Hausgemeinschaft *f*, -halt *m*; Familie *f*, Geschlecht, *(bes. adliges od fürstl.)* Haus; Geschäft(shaus) *n*, Firma *f*; Gasthaus *n*, -hof *m*; *theat* Vorstellung *f*, Publikum, Theater, Haus *n*; Börse *f*; *(Univ.)* College; Wohngebäude *(e-s Internats)*; Ordenshaus; Gotteshaus; (Abgeordneten-) Haus, Parlament; (Schnecken-)Haus; (Vogel-, Raubtier-, Affen-)Haus *n*; Schuppen *m*, (Wagen-)Remise *f*; *v* [hauz] *tr* unterbringen; unter Dach und Fach bringen; verstauen; *itr* unterkommen; wohnen; *on the* ~ auf Kosten der Firma; *to bring down the* ~ *(theat)* großen Beifall ernten; *to clean* ~ das Haus putzen, reinemachen; *fig* ausmisten; *to keep* ~ haushalten (*for s.o.* jdm); e-n Haushalt haben; zs.leben (*with* mit); *to keep the* ~ das Haus hüten; *to make H~ (parl)* beschlußfähig sein; *to put, to set o.'s* ~ *in order* reinen Tisch machen; sein Haus bestellen; *apartment-~* Mietshaus *n*; *boarding-~* Pension *f*; *dwelling-~* Wohnhaus *n*; *hen-~* Hühnerhaus *n*; ~ *of cards (fig)* Kartenhaus *n*; *the H~ of Commons (parl)* das Unterhaus; ~ *of correction* Besserungsanstalt *f*; ~ *of detention* Untersuchungsgefängnis *n*; *the H~ of Lords (parl)* das Oberhaus; *the H~ of Parliament* das Parlamentsgebäude; *the H~s of Parliament* die Kammern *f pl*; *the H~ of Representatives (Am)* das Repräsentantenhaus; **~-agent** Grundstücksmakler *m*; **~-boat** Hausboot *n*; **~breaker** Einbrecher; Abbrucharbeiter, -unternehmer *m*; **~breaking** Einbruch; Abbruch *m*; **~broken, ~trained** *a (Tier)* stubenrein; ~ **check** *Am* Haussuchung *f*; ~ **coal** Hausbrand *m*; ~ **coat** ['-kout] *Am* Morgenrock *m*; **~-dog** Hofhund *m*; **~dress** Hauskleid *n*; **~-flag** Reedereiflagge *f*; **~fly** ['-flai] Stubenfliege *f*; **~hold** *s* Haushalt *m*; Hofhaltung *f*; *a* Haushalt(s)-, Hof-; ~~ *arts (pl)* Hauswirtschaft u. Heimgestaltung *f*; ~~ *goods (pl)* Haushaltswaren *f pl*, -gegenstände *m pl*; ~~ *jam* billige Marmelade *f*; ~~ *money* Wirtschaftsgeld *n*; ~~ *soap* Kernseife *f*; ~~ *word* alltägliche(r) Ausdruck *m*; *it's a* ~~ *word* das ist ein Begriff; **~holder** Haushaltungsvorstand; Wohnungsinhaber, Hauptmieter *m*; ~ **hunting** Wohnungssuche *f*; **~keeper** Haushälterin *f*; Hausmeister *m*; **~keeping** Haushalten *n*, Führung *f* e-s Haushalts; ~~ *money* Wirtschaftsgeld *n*; **~maid** Hausmädchen *n*, -angestellte, -tochter *f*; *~~'s knee* Schleimbeutelentzündung *f*; ~ **mark** Hausmarke *f*; **~master** *(Schule)* Hausmeister *m*; **~-number** Hausnummer *f*; ~ **organ** Hauszeitschrift *f (e-r Firma)*; ~ **painter** Anstreicher *m*; **~-physician** Anstaltsarzt *m*; ~ **plant** Zimmerpflanze *f*; **~-rent** Miete *f*, Hauszins *m*; **~-room** Wohnraum *m*; *to give ~~ to s.o.* jdn aufnehmen; *I would not give it ~~* das möchte ich nicht geschenkt haben; **~-servants** *pl* (Haus-)Personal *n*, Dienerschaft *f*; **~-surgeon** Krankenhauschirurg *m*; ~ **tent** Hauszelt *n*; **~-to-~ collection** Haussammlung *f*; **~-to-~ distribution** Postwurfsendung *f*; **~-top** Dach *n*; *(meist in:) to publish s.th. from the ~~s* etw ausposaunen; **~-wares** *pl com* Haushaltsartikel *m pl*; **~-warming** Einzugsfest *n*; **~wife** ['-waif] Hausfrau; Haushälterin, Wirtschafterin *f*; ['hʌzif] Nähkasten,

-beutel *m*; **~wifely** ['-waifli] *a adv* haushälterisch, wirtschaftlich, sparsam; **~wifery** ['-wifəri] Haushalten *n*, -wirtschaft *f*, -wesen *n*; **~work** Hausarbeit *f*; **~wrecker** ['-rekə] *Am* Abbrucharbeiter *m*.

housing ['hauziŋ] **1.** Unterbringung, Aufnahme, Unterkunft, Wohnung *f*; vorhandene(r) Wohnraum *m*; Wohnungsbeschaffung *f*, -wesen; *(Waren)* (Ein-)Lagern *n*, (Ein-)Lagerung *f*; Lagergeld *n*; *tech* Hülse *f*, Gehäuse, Gerüst *n*; *mar* Hüsing *f*; *public ~* öffentliche(r) Wohnungsbau *m*; **~ area** Wohngebiet *n*; **H~ Board** Wohnungsamt *n*; **~ conditions** *pl* Wohnverhältnisse *n pl*; **~ estate** Wohnbezirk *m*, Siedlung *f*; **~ market** Wohnungsmarkt *m*; **~ problem** Wohnungsproblem *n*; **~ program(me)** Wohnungsbauprogramm *n*; **~ requirements** *pl* Wohnraumbedarf *m*; **~ shortage** Wohnungsnot *f*, Wohnraummangel *m*; **2.** Pferdedecke *f*.

hovel ['hɔvəl] *s* Schuppen, Stall *m*; Hütte; *pej* Bruchbude *f*, Loch *n*.

hover ['hɔvə] *itr* schweben; (in der Luft) kreisen, flattern (*about, over* über); herumlungern, sich herumtreiben (*about, near* in der Nähe *gen*); warten (*about, near* bei); *fig* unsicher sein, schwanken (*between* zwischen); *fig* schweben (*between life and death* zwischen Leben u. Tod); *s* Schweben *n*; *fig* Ungewißheit *f*; **~craft** ['-kra:ft] *mot* Luftkissenfahrzeug *n*; **~ing** ['-riŋ] schwebend *(a. Akzent)*; schwankend, zögernd.

how [hau] *adv* wie; wieso; zu welchem Preis, wie teuer? *fam* was? *s das* Wie; *and ~! (Am sl)* und wie! *~ about ...?* wie steht es mit ...? *~ come ...? (Am sl), ~ is it?* wie kommt es, daß ...? wieso? *~ ever? ~ on earth? ~ the goodness? ~ the deuce? ~ the devil, ~ the dickens?* wie nur, bloß? wie in aller Welt? wie zum Teufel? *~ many?* wie viele? *~ much?* wieviel? *~ now?* nun? was ist, bedeutet das? *~ so?* wieso? warum? *~ then?* wie denn nun? wie sonst? was heißt das? *~ are you? ~ do you do?* wie geht's? Guten Tag! *(bei e-r Vorstellung)* sehr erfreut! **~-d'ye-do, ~dy-do** ['haudi'du:] *fam* fatale, dumme Geschichte *f*; **~ever** [hau'evə] *adv* wie auch immer; wie groß auch; *conj* indessen; jedoch, aber; trotzdem; **~soever** [ha(u)sou'evə] wie auch immer; wie sehr auch.

howitzer ['hauitsə] *mil* Haubitze *f*.

howl [haul] *itr (bes. Wolf, Hund, Wind)* heulen; *(vor Schmerz, Wut, Angst)* brüllen, schreien; *radio* pfeifen; *tr* schreien, brüllen; *s* Geheul, Gebrüll, Gelächter; *radio* Pfeifen *n*; *Am sl* Witz *m*; *to ~ down* niederbrüllen, -schreien; *to ~ with laughter* vor Lachen brüllen; *he's a ~* er ist zum Brüllen; **~er** ['-ə] Brüllaffe; *fam* Bock, Schnitzer, dumme(r) Fehler *m*; **~ing** ['-iŋ] heulend; *sl* gewaltig, phantastisch, ungeheuer; *(Ungerechtigkeit)* schreiend; *(Erfolg)* toll; *(Bildnis)* trostlos; *~~ monkey* Brüllaffe *m*.

hoy [hɔi] **1.** schwere Barke *f*; **2.** *interj* he!

hoyden ['hɔidn] *s* Range *f*, Wildfang *m*, jungenhafte(s) Mädchen *n*.

*

hub [hʌb] **1.** *(Rad)* Nabe *f*; *fig* Mittelpunkt *m*, Zentrum *n*, Schwerpunkt *m*; *the H~ (Am)* Boston *n*; **~-cap, -cover, -plate** Radkappe *f*; **~-remover** *mot* Radabzieher *m*; **2.** *a.* **~by** ['-i] *fam* Gatte(rich) *m*.

hubble-bubble ['hʌblbʌbl] (einfache) Wasserpfeife *f*; Gurgeln, Murmeln, Plätschern *(e-r Flüssigkeit)*; Stimmengewirr *n*, Aufruhr *m*.

hubbub ['hʌbʌb] Stimmengewirr *n*, Lärm; Wirrwarr *m*, Durcheinander *n*; Tumult, Aufruhr *m*.

hubris ['hu:bris] Hybris *f*.

huckaback ['hʌkəbæk] *(Textil)* Drillich, Drell *m*; Gerstenkornleinen *n*.

huckle ['hʌkl] *(selten)* Hüfte *f*; **~-bone** *anat* Hüftknochen; Fußknöchel *m*.

huckleberry ['hʌklbəri] *Am Art* Heidelbeere *f*.

huckst|er ['hʌkstə] *(a.* *~~er* ['-rə]) *s* (*bes.* Gemüse-, Obst-)Höker, (Straßen-)Händler, Krämer *m*; *fig* Krämerseele *f*; *Am fam* Reklamefritze *m*; *tr* hökern, handeln mit; feilschen um.

huddle ['hʌdl] *itr* sich drängen, sich drücken; sich schmiegen (*to* an); *(to ~ o.s.)* sich hocken, sich kauern; *(Fußball)* sich gruppieren; *tr* zs.drängen, -drükken; durchea.werfen; *(to ~ over)* pfuschen, sudeln; *s* Wirrwarr *m*, Durcheinander *n*, Verwirrung; *(Fußball)* Gruppe; *Am sl* intime Zs.kunft, Geheimbesprechung *f*; *to ~ on (Kleider)* rasch überwerfen; *to ~ together, up* (sich) zs.-, (sich) anea.drängen, -drükken; *to be, to go into a ~ (Am sl)* die Köpfe zs.stecken.

hue [hju:] **1.** Farbe; Färbung *f*; Farbton *m*, Schattierung *f*; **2.** *s*: *~ and cry* ['-ənkrai] laute(s) Geschrei, Zetergeschrei *n*; *fig* Hetze *f*; *to raise a ~ and cry against s.o. (fig)* gegen jdn heftig protestieren.

huff [hʌf] *tr* anfahren (*s.o.* jdn); unverschämt, frech werden (*s.o.* gegenüber jdm), einschüchtern; ärgerlich machen, aufbringen; beleidigen; *(Damestein)* pusten, wegnehmen; *itr* blasen, pusten; ärgerlich werden, sich beleidigt fühlen; *s* Ärger, Groll *m*, üble Laune *f*; *to take the ~* beleidigt sein; **~iness** ['-inis] Empfindlichkeit *f*; Ärger *m*; Eingeschnapptheit *f*; **~ish** ['-iʃ] mürrisch, verdrießlich; launisch, launenhaft; übelnehmerisch; **~ishness** ['-iʃnis] mürrische(s) Wesen *n*; Launenhaftigkeit *f*; **~y** ['-i] leicht beleidigt, empfindlich, *fam* eingeschnappt.

*

hug [hʌg] *tr* umarmen, in die Arme nehmen *od* schließen; sich dicht halten (*the shore* am Ufer); *mot* sich legen (*the curb* in die Kurve); *fig* hängen an, (großen) Wert legen auf, festhalten an; *to ~ o.s.* sich schmeicheln, stolz sein (*over* auf); *s* Umarmung *f*; *sport* Griff *m*.

huge [hju:dʒ] sehr, gewaltig, ungeheuer; **~ness** ['-nis] gewaltige Größe *f*.

hugger-mugger ['hʌgəmʌgə] *s* Durcheinander *n*, Verwirrung *f*; Geheimnis *n*; *a* unordentlich, in Unordnung, durcheinander, (ver)wirr(t); *adv* durcheinander; insgeheim; **~y** ['-ri] *Am sl* Enttäuschung *f*.

Huguenot ['hju:gənɔt] Hugenotte *m*.

hulk [hʌlk] *s* schwerfällige(r) Mensch, Klotz, Trampel *m*; unförmige Masse *f*; *mar* abgetakelte(s) Schiff *n*; **~ing** ['-iŋ] umfangreich, unförmig; plump.

hull [hʌl] *s bot* Hülse, Schale; Schote; *allg* Hülle *f*, Schiffs-, Flugzeugrumpf *m*; *tr* enthülsen, schälen; *(Schiff)* torpedieren; *(Schiffswand)* mit e-m Geschoß durchbohren; *~ down (Schiff)* dem Blick entschwunden; **~ insurance** Flugzeug-, Schiffsversicherung *f*.

hullabaloo [hʌləbə'lu:] Lärm *m*, Verwirrung *f*, Wirrwarr, Tumult *m*.

hullo ['hʌ'lou] *interj* hallo! *(Überraschung)* nanu!

hum [hʌm] **1.** *itr* summen, brummen; (er)dröhnen (*with* von); *fam* geschäftig, betriebsam sein; *sl* unangenehm riechen; *tr (Melodie)* summen (*to o.s.* vor sich hin); *s* Summen, Brummen *n*; *to ~ to sleep* in den Schlaf summen; *to make things ~ (fig) fam* den Laden in Schwung bringen; **~mer** ['-ə] Summer *m*, Schnarre *f*; *fam* Geschaftlhuber *m*; **~ming** ['-iŋ] summend, brummend; *fam* geschäftig, eifrig; gewaltig, mächtig, stark, kräftig; *things are always ~~* es ist immer Betrieb; *~~-bird* Kolibri *m*; *~~-top* Brummkreisel *m*; **2.** *interj* hm! *itr* hm machen; (*meist: to ~ and ha, (Am) haw* [hɑ:]) sich räuspern; zögern, Ausflüchte machen; **3.** *(= humbug)* Schwindel *m*; *it's all ~* das ist (ja) alles Schwindel.

human ['hju:mən] *a* menschlich; Menschen-; *s (~ being)* Mensch *m*, menschliche(s) Wesen *n*; *to err is ~* Irren ist menschlich; *I'm only ~* ich bin auch nur ein Mensch; *the ~ nature* die menschliche Natur, das Wesen des Menschen; **~e** [hju(:)'mein] menschlich, wohlwollend, gütig, human, besonnen, vernünftig, weise; verfeinernd, bildend; *~~ learning* humanistische Bildung *f*; **~ism** ['hju:mənizm] klassische Bildung *f*; Humanismus *m*; **~istic** [hju:mə'nistik] humanistisch; **~itarian** [hju(:)mæni'tɛəriən] *s* Menschenfeund, Philanthrop *m*; *a* menschenfreundlich; **~itarianism** [hjumæni'tɛəriənizm] Menschenfreundlichkeit *f*; **~ity** [hju(:)'mæniti] das Menschengeschlecht, die Menschheit, die Menschen *pl*; Menschennatur *f*; Menschlichkeit, Güte, Menschenliebe *f*; *the ~ities (pl)* die klassische Philologie; die Geisteswissenschaften *pl*; **~ization** [hju:mənai'zeiʃən] Vermenschlichung; Gesittung, Bildung, geistige, sittliche Hebung *f*; **~ize** ['hju:mənaiz] *tr* vermenschlichen; menschlich, gesittet machen, bilden, geistig, sittlich heben; *itr* menschlich, gesittet werden, sich bilden; **~kind** ['hju:mən'kaind] das Menschengeschlecht, die Menschheit; **~ly** ['hju:mənli] *adv* menschlich; *~~ possible* menschenmöglich; *~~ speaking* nach menschlichem Ermessen.

humble ['hʌmbl] *a* demütig, unterwürfig, bescheiden, anspruchslos; niedrig, gering, einfach, schlicht, unbedeutend; *tr* demütigen, herabwürdigen; erniedrigen, herabsetzen; *to eat ~ pie* sich demütigen; s-e Schuld eingestehen; Abbitte tun; *my ~ self* meine Wenigkeit; **~-bee** Hummel *f*; **~ness** ['-nis] Demut; Bescheidenheit, Anspruchslosigkeit, Niedrigkeit *f*.

humbug ['hʌmbʌg] *s* Schwindel, Humbug *m*; dumme(s) Gerede *n*, Blödsinn, Quatsch; Schwindler, Hochstapler *m*; Pfefferminzbonbon *n*; *tr* beschwindeln (*out of* um); 'reinlegen, anführen, *fam* -schmieren, prellen; verleiten (*into* zu).

humdinger [hʌm'diŋə] *Am sl* prima Kerl *m*; phantastische Sache *f*.

humdrum ['hʌmdrʌm] *a* eintönig, monoton, öde, fade, langweilig; *s* Eintönigkeit, Langweiligkeit *f*.

humer|al ['hju:mərəl] *a* Oberarmbein-; Schulter-; **~us** ['hju:mərəs] *pl -i* ['-ai] *anat* Oberarmknochen *m*.

humid ['hju:mid] feucht; dampfgesättigt; **~ification** [hju(:)midifi'keiʃən] Verdunstung *f*; **~ifier** [hju(:)'midifaiə] Verdunster *m*; **~ify** [hju(:)'midifai] *tr* an-, befeuchten; feucht machen *od* halten; **~ity** [hju(:)'miditi] Feuchtigkeit *f*; *mete* Feuchtigkeitsgehalt *m*.

humili|ate [hju(:)'milieit] *tr* demütigen, herabwürdigen, erniedrigen; **~ation** [hju(:)mili'eiʃən] Demütigung, Erniedrigung *f*; **~ty** [hju(:)'militi] Demut; Bescheidenheit, Niedrigkeit *f*.

hummock ['hʌmək] (kleiner) (Erd- *od* Eis-)Hügel, Höcker, Buckel *m*; flache Anhöhe *f*; Landrücken *m*.
humor|al ['hju:mərəl] *a med* Humoral-, die Körpersäfte betreffend; **~esque** [hju:mə'resk] *mus* Capriccio *n*; **~ist** ['hju:mərist] humorvolle(r) Mensch; Humorist *m*; **~istic** [hju:mə'ristik] humorvoll; humoristisch; **~ous** ['hju:mərəs] launisch; humorvoll, launig, lustig, spaßig, amüsant, drollig, komisch; *~~ paper* Witzzeitschrift *f*.
humo(u)r ['hju:mə] *s (sense of)* ~ Humor; lustige(r) Einfall, Spaß, Scherz *m*; Laune, Stimmung *f*; Temperament *n*; *tr* willfahren (*s.o.* jdm); nachgeben (*s.o.* jdm gegenüber), den Willen lassen (*s.o.* jdm); sich anpassen (*s.o.* jdm); *to be in a good, bad ~* gute, schlechte Laune haben; gut, schlecht aufgelegt sein; *to be out of ~* nicht in Stimmung, schlecht aufgelegt sein; *sense of ~* Sinn *m* für Humor.
hump [hʌmp] *s (Kamel)* Höcker; *(Mensch)* Buckel; Buckel, (kleiner) Hügel; *min rail* Ablaufberg *m*; *Am sl aero* Flug-, Luftfahrthindernis *n*; *allg* kritische(r) Augenblick *m*; schlechte, üble Laune *f*, Ärger, Verdruß *m*; *tr* krumm machen, krümmen; *(Australien)* schultern, auf die Schulter nehmen; *fam* aus dem Häuschen bringen; *to ~ o.s. (Am sl)* sich am Riemen reißen, sich (große) Mühe geben; *to ~ up* die Schultern hochziehen; *to be over the ~ (fig)* über den Berg sein; *to give s.o. the ~* jdm die Laune verderben; *the cat ~ed her back* die Katze machte e-n Buckel; **~back** ['-bæk] Buckel; Bucklige(r); *zoo* Buckelwal *m*; **~backed** *a* bucklig.
humph [mm(m), hʌmf] *interj* hm!
humpty-dumpty ['hʌmpti'dʌmpti] Dickmops *m*, Dickerchen *n*.
humus ['hju:məs] Humus *m*.
Hun [hʌn] *hist* Hunne; *pej* Barbar *m*.
hunch [hʌn(t)ʃ] *tr* wölben, biegen, krümmen; *itr* nach vorn rücken, stoßen, schieben, drücken; schubsen, puffen; *to ~ o.'s back* e-n Buckel machen; *s* Höcker, Buckel *m*; (dickes) Stück *n* *(Brot)*; *Am sl* (Vor-)Ahnung *f*, (Vor-)Gefühl *n*; *to ~ out, to ~ up* nach außen, nach oben wölben *od* biegen; *to be ~ed up* zs.gekauert sein; *to have a ~ (Am sl)* e-n Riecher haben; *with ~ed shoulders* mit hochgezogenen Schultern; **~back** Buckel; Bucklige(r) *m*; *to be a ~~* bucklig sein.
hundred ['hʌndrəd] *a* hundert; *s das* Hundert; Hundertschaft *f*; *hist* Amt(sbezirk *m*) *n*; *a ~* hundert; *one ~* einhundert; *~s of* Hunderte von; **~fold** ['-fould] *a adv* hundertfach, -fältig; **~th** ['-θ] *a* hundertst; *s* Hundertstel *n*; **~weight** ['-weit] Zentner *m* *(in England = 112 Pfund bzw 50,8 kg, in den US = 100 Pfund bzw 45,36 kg)*.
hung [hʌŋ] *pp von hang*: *~ up (Am sl)* altmodisch; rückständig; gequält; verspätet.
Hungar|ian [hʌŋ'gɛəriən] *a* ungarisch; *s* (das) Ungarisch(e); Ungar(in *f*) *m*; **~y** ['hʌŋgəri] Ungarn *n*.
hung|er ['hʌŋgə] *s* Hunger(gefühl *n*) *m*; *fig* (heftiges) Verlangen *n* (*for, after* nach); *itr* hungern, hungrig sein; sich sehnen, (heftig) verlangen (*for, after* nach); *to die of ~~* verhungern; *~~ strike* Hungerstreik *m*; **~ry** ['hʌŋgri] hungrig, hungernd; verlangend, (be)gierig (*for* nach); *(Boden)* mager; *to be ~~* Hunger haben, hungrig sein.
hunk [hʌŋk] *fam* dicke(s) Stück *n*, Ranken *m (bes. Brot)*; **~er** *fam* Hinterteil *n*; *on o.'s ~~s (Br sl)* niedergekauert.
hunk|s [hʌŋks] *fam* alte(r) Knacker, Knauser *m*; **~y** ['-i] *Am sl* genügend.
hunt [hʌnt] *tr* jagen, hetzen, *Am* jagen, schießen; treiben, verfolgen; eifrig, intensiv suchen; durchjagen, -streifen; *itr* auf die Jagd gehen, jagen; zur Fuchsjagd benutzen; suchen, forschen (*for* nach); *tech* pendeln; *s Br* Parforcejagd; Fuchsjagd; Jagd(gesellschaft *f*, -revier *n*); *fig* Jagd, Suche *f* (*for* nach); *to ~ down* erjagen, zur Strecke bringen; *to ~ out* ausfindig machen, auffinden; *to ~ up* aufstöbern, -spüren, -treiben; *to go ~ing* auf die Jagd gehen; *the ~ is up* die Jagd ist eröffnet; **~er** ['-ə] (Großwild-)Jäger, *Am allg* Jäger *m*; Jagdpferd *n*; Taschenuhr *f* mit Sprungdeckel; *~~'s moon* Vollmond *m* im Herbst; **~ing** ['-iŋ] (Fuchs-)Jagen *n*, Jagd; Verfolgung; Suche; *el* Regelschwankung *f*; *tech* Pendeln *n*; *attr* Jagd-; *fox-~~* Fuchsjagd *f*; *~~-ground* Jagdgründe *m pl*, -revier *n a. fig*; *~~-horn* Jagdhorn *n*; *~~-knife* Hirschfänger *m*; *~~-licence* Jagdschein *m*; *~~-lodge* Jagd-, Hochsitz *m*; *~~-party* Jagdgesellschaft *f*; *~~-season* Jagdzeit *f*; *~~-watch* Sprungdeckeluhr *f*; **~ress** ['-ris] Jägerin *f*; **~sman** ['-smən] Jäger, Weidmann *m*; Pikör, Aufseher *m* der Jagdhunde; **~smanship** ['-ʃip] Jägerei *f*.
hurdle ['hə:dl] *s agr sport* Hürde; *mil* Faschine *f*; *fig* Hindernis *n*, Schwierigkeit *f*; *pl u.* **~-race** Hürdenlauf *m*, Hindernisrennen *n*; *tr* überspringen; mit Hürden umgeben; *fig (Hindernis)* überwinden; *itr* über ein Hindernis setzen; *hundred meters (Am with) ~s* 100 m Hürden(lauf); **~r** ['-ə] Hürdenläufer *m*.
hurdy-gurdy ['hə:digə:di] Drehorgel *f*, Leierkasten *m*.
hurl [hə:l] *tr* schleudern; um-, über den Haufen werfen; hinausbrüllen, -schreien; *(Worte)* ausstoßen (*at* gegen); *itr* schleudern (*at* auf, gegen); *to ~ o.s. on* sich stürzen auf; *s* Schleudern, Stoßen *n*.
hurly-burly ['hə:libə:li] Wirrwarr *m*, Verwirrung *f*; Lärm, Tumult, Aufruhr *m*.
hurrah [hu'rɑ:], **hurray** [hu'rei] *interj* hurra! *s* Hurra(ruf *m*) *n*; *itr* hurra schreien; *tr* mit Hurrarufen umjubeln.
hurricane ['hʌrikən, *bes. Am* -kein] Wirbelsturm, Orkan *m a. fig*; **~-deck** *mar* Sturmdeck *n*; **~-lamp, -lantern** Sturmlaterne *f*; **~ warnings** *pl* Sturmwarnung *f*.
hurried ['hʌrid] *a* hastig, eilig, gehetzt; übereilt, schnell.
hurry ['hʌri] *tr (to ~ up)* erledigen *od* schicken; beschleunigen; hetzen, jagen, antreiben; schnell überstürzen; *itr* sich beeilen, sich abhetzen; *s* (große) Eile, Hast, Übereilung, Überstürzung, Übereile *f*; Drängen *n*, (innere) Unruhe, Ungeduld; *tech* Rutsche *f*; *a Am* rasch, überstürzt, beschleunigt; *in a ~* in (großer) Eile, in Hast, (zu) schnell, überstürzt; ungeduldig; *not ... in a ~ (fam)* nicht ... so leicht, bald; nicht von sich aus, nicht ohne Not, nicht freiwillig; *in the ~ of business* im Drang der Geschäfte; *to be in a ~* es sehr eilig haben; darauf brennen (*to do s.th.* etw zu tun); *to be in too big (too much of) a ~* sich übereilen; *there is no ~* damit hat's keine Eile, das hat (noch) Zeit; *why (all) this ~? is there a ~?* ist das so eilig? *don't ~* nur, immer mit der Ruhe! *to ~* **away** *tr* (schnell) wegschaffen, *fam* auf die Seite bringen; *itr* davoneilen, sich eiligst davonmachen, *fam* schnell abhauen; *to ~* **back** *tr* zurückjagen, -treiben, -schicken; *itr* zurückeilen; *to ~* **in** schnell hineinbringen, -schaffen, -tun; *to ~* **off** *itr* wegeilen; *tr* wegschicken; *to ~* **on** beschleunigen, an-, zu größerer Eile treiben; *to ~* **over** schnell erledigen, abtun; überstürzen; schnell weggehen über; *to ~* **through** *(Gesetzesvorlage)* durchpeitschen; *to ~* **up** *tr* an-, zu größerer Eile treiben; *itr* eilen, sich beeilen, sich beschleunigen; schnell machen; *~ up!* schnell, schnell! los! **~-scurry** ['-'skʌri] *s* Hast, Übereilung, Überstürzung *f*, Hin und Her, Durcheinander *n*, Wirbel *m*; *a adv* hastig, übereilt, überstürzt; durcheinander, in Verwirrung, verwirrt.
hurt [hə:t] *irr hurt, hurt tr* wehtun (*s.o.* jdm); verletzen, verwunden; schaden, schädigen, Schaden zufügen (*s.o.* jdm); *fig* verletzen, kränken, beleidigen, wehtun (*s.o.* jdm); *itr (Körperteil)* wehtun; *s* Schmerz *m*; Verletzung, Verwundung *f*; Schaden *m*, Schädigung *f*, Nachteil *m* (*to* für); *to be, to feel ~* sich verletzt, beleidigt, gekränkt fühlen; *to ~ s.o.'s feelings* jdn kränken, verletzen; *that won't ~* das schadet nichts; **~er** ['-ə] Stoßdämpfer *m*, -platte *f*, -balken *m*; Stoß-, Achsring *m*; **~ful** ['-ful] schädlich, nachteilig (*to* für).
hurtle ['hə:tl] *itr* stoßen, zs.prallen, krachen, poltern, (p)rasseln, sausen (*against* auf, gegen; *together* zusammen); *tr* schleudern, werfen, schießen.
husband ['hʌzbənd] *s* (Ehe-)Mann, Gatte, Gemahl *m*; *tr* haushälterisch, sparsam umgehen mit; *ship's ~* Korrespondentreeder *m*; *~ and wife* Eheleute *pl*; **~man** ['-mən] Bauer, Landwirt; Landarbeiter *m*; **~ry** ['-ri] Landwirtschaft *f*; Ackerbau *m*; sparsame(s) Wirtschaften *n*; Wirtschaftsführung *f*; *animal ~~* Viehzucht *f*.
hush [hʌʃ] *tr* zum Schweigen bringen, *fam* den Mund stopfen (*s.o.* jdm); beruhigen; einlullen; *itr* verstummen, schweigen; still, ruhig werden; *s* Stille, Ruhe *f*; *interj* still! Ruhe (da)! *to ~ up (itr)* sich still, ruhig verhalten; *tr* vertuschen, verheimlichen; **~aby** ['-əbai] *interj* psch! **~-hush** ['hʌʃ'hʌʃ] *a* streng (vertraulich und) geheim; Geheim-; **~-money** Schweigegeld *n*.
husk [hʌsk] *s bot* Hülse, Schote; *allg* Hülle, Schale *f*; *tr* enthülsen, schälen; **~iness** ['-inis] Heiserkeit *f*; *Am* kräftige(r) Wuchs *m*, Stämmigkeit *f*; **~y** ['-i] *a* voller Hülsen; hülsenartig; trokken, rauh, heiser; *(Stimme)* belegt; *Am fam* kräftig, stämmig, stark, robust; *s fam* starke(r) Mann *m*.
Husky ['hʌski] Eskimo *m*; Eskimosprache *f*; *h~* Eskimohund *m*.
hussar [hu'zɑ:] Husar *m*.
hussy ['hʌsi] Schlampe *f*; freche(s) Ding *n*, Range *f*, Gör *n*.
hustings ['hʌstiŋz] *pl meist mit sing* Wahlversammlungslokal *n*; Wahlkampf *m*; Rednertribüne *f*.
hustle ['hʌsl] *tr* (herum)stoßen, -schieben, -treiben; drängen (*into* zu); *Am fam* übereilen, überstürzen; *(Kunden)* fangen; schnell erledigen; *itr* sich durchschlagen, sich (vor)drängen, sich beeilen, eilen; sich e-n Weg bahnen (*through* durch); *Am fam* wie ein Wilder, wie ein Verrückter, wie toll schuften; *Am sl* betteln, stehlen; *s* Herumstoßen, -schieben *n*; *Am fam* Schufterei, Betriebsamkeit *f*; Drängen *n*; (Hoch-)Betrieb *m*; **~r** ['-ə] tatkräftige(r) Mensch *m*.
hut [hʌt] *s* Hütte; Baracke *f*; *tr* in Baracken unterbringen; *itr* in e-r Hütte, Baracke wohnen; **~ment**

['-mənt] Unterbringung *f* in Baracken; *(~ted camp)* Barackenlager *n*.

hutch [hʌtʃ] Kasten *m*, Kiste *f*; Käfig (*bes.* Kaninchen-)Stall *m*; Hütte; (Back-)Mulde *f*; *min* Trog; Hund *m*.

huzza [hu'zɑ:] *interj obs* heißa! hussa!

hyacinth ['haiəsinθ] *bot* Hyazinthe *f*; *min* Hyazinth *m*.

hyaena [hai'i:nə] *s. hyena.*

hyal|ine ['haiəlin] glasartig, -klar, durchsichtig, hyalin; **~ite** ['-ait] *min* Hyalit, Glasopal *m*.

hybrid ['haibrid] *s bot* Hybride, Bastardpflanze *f*; *zoo* Bastard; *allg* Zwitter(bildung *f*) *m*; hybride Wortbildung *f*; *a* hybrid(isch), von zweierlei Herkunft, Bastard-; **~ism** ['-izm] *biol* Kreuzung, Bastardierung; *allg* Zwitterbildung *f*; **~ity** [hai'briditi] Zwitterbildung *f*; **~ization** [haibridai'zeiʃən] Bastardierung, Kreuzung *f*; **~ize** ['haibridaiz] *tr* bastardieren, kreuzen; *itr* sich kreuzen (lassen).

hydra ['haidrə] *zoo* Hydra *f a. fig*; **~ngea** [-'dreindʒə] *bot* Hortensie *f*.

hydr|ant ['haidrənt] Hydrant *m*; **~ate** ['-eit] *s chem* Hydrat *n*; *tr* hydratisieren; hydrieren; **~ation** [hai'dreiʃən] *chem* Hydrierung *f*; **~aulic** [hai'drɔ:lik] *a* hydraulisch; *s pl mit sing* Hydraulik *f*; *~~ brake* Öldruckbremse *f*; *~~ engineering* Wasserbau *m*; *~~ pressure* Flüssigkeitsdruck *m*.

hydro|(aero)plane [haidro(u)'ɛərəplein] Wasserflugzeug; Gleitboot *n*; **~carbon** ['haidro(u)'kɑ:bən] Kohlenwasserstoff *m*; *~~ compound* Kohlenwasserstoffverbindung *f*; **~cephalus** ['haidro(u)'sefələs] *med* Wasserkopf *m*; **~chloric** ['haidrə'klɔrik] *a*: *~~ acid* Salzsäure *f*; **~chloride** ['haidrə'klɔ:raid] Chlorhydrat *n*; **~cyanic** ['haidro(u)sai'ænik] *a*: *~~ acid* Blausäure *f*; **~dynamic(al)** ['haidro(u)dainæmik(əl)] hydrodynamisch; **~dynamics** [-dai'næmiks] *pl mit sing* Hydrodynamik *f*; **~electric** ['haidro(u)i'lektrik] *a*: *~~ power-station* Wasserkraftwerk *n*; **~fluoric** ['haidro(u)flu'ɔrik] *a*: *~~ acid* Flußsäure *f*; **~gen** ['haidridʒən] Wasserstoff *m*; *~~ bomb* Wasserstoffbombe *f*; *~~ peroxide* Wasserstoffsuperoxyd *n*; *~~ sulphide* Schwefelwasserstoff *m*; **~genate** [hai'drɔdʒineit] *tr chem* hydrieren; **~genation** ['haidrədʒə'neiʃən] Hydrierung; *(Öl)* Härtung *f*; *~~ plant* Hydrieranlage *f*; **~genize** [hai'drɔdʒinaiz] = *~genate*; **~genous** [hai'drɔdʒinəs] wasserstoffhaltig; **~graphic** [haidro(u)'græfik] hydrographisch; **~graphy** [hai'drɔgrəfi] Gewässerkunde, Hydrographie *f*; **~logy** [hai'drɔlədʒi] Hydrologie *f*; **~lysis** [hai'drɔlisis] *chem* Hydrolyse *f*; **~meter** [hai'drɔmitə] Senkwaage *f*; **~pathy** [hai'drɔpəθi] Wasserheilkunde, Hydropathie, Wasserkur *f*; **~phobia** [haidrə'foubjə] Wasserscheu; *med* Tollwut *f*; **~phobic** [haidrə'foubik] wasserscheu; **~phone** ['haidrəfoun] Unterwasser-Horchgerät *n*; **~pic** [hai'drɔpik] *med* wassersüchtig; **~ponics** [haidrə'pɔniks] *pl mit sing* Hydroponik, Wasserkultur *f*; **~static** [haidro(u)'stætik] *a* hydrostatisch; *s pl mit sing* Hydrostatik *f*; *~~ pressure (phys)* Wasserdruck *m*; **~therapeutic** ['haidroθerə'pju:tik *a* hydrotherapeutisch; *s pl u.* **~therapy** [-'θerəpi] Wasserheilkunde, Hydrotherapie *f*; **~us** ['haidrəs] *scient* wasserhaltig; wässerig; **~xide** [hai'drɔksaid] *chem* Hydroxyd *n*; *~~ of sodium* Ätznatron *n*.

hyena [hai'i:nə] Hyäne *f*.

hygien|e ['haidʒi:n] Gesundheitspflege, Hygiene *f*; *personal ~~* Körperpflege *f*; **~ic(al)** [hai'dʒi:nik(əl), *Am* -dʒi'enik] hygienisch; **~ics** [hai'dʒi:niks] *pl mit sing* Gesundheitslehre, -pflege, Hygiene *f*; **~ist** [hai'dʒi:nist] Hygieniker *m*.

hygro|meter [hai'grɔmitə] Hygrometer, Feuchtigkeitsmesser *m*; **~scope** ['haigrəskoup] Hygroskop *n*, Feuchtigkeitsanzeiger *m*; **~scopic** [-grə'skɔpik] hygroskopisch.

Hymen ['haimen] Hymen *m*, der Hochzeitsgott; *h~ (poet)* Hochzeit *f*; Hochzeitsgesang *m*, -lied *n*; Jungfernhäutchen, Hymen *n*; **h~eal** [haime'ni(:)əl] *a* hochzeitlich, Hochzeit(s)-; *s* Hochzeitsgesang *m*, -lied *n*.

hymn [him] *s* Hymne *f*; Loblied *n*, -gesang; Kirchengesang *m*, -lied *n*, Choral *m*; *itr tr* Loblieder singen (auf); **~al** ['himnəl] *s* Gesangbuch *n*; *a* hymnisch; **~-book** Gesangbuch *n*; **~ic** ['himnik] hymnisch.

hyper|(a)emia [haipər'i:miə] Hyperämie, Blutüberfüllung *f* (in e-m Körperteil); **~(a)esthesia** [haipəres'θi:siə] Überempfindlichkeit, nervöse Reizbarkeit *f*; **~bola** [hai'pə:bələ] *math* Hyperbel *f*; **~bole** [hai'pə:bəli] *(stilistische)* Übertreibung, Hyperbel *f*; **~bolic(al)** [haipə(:)'bɔlik(əl)] *(Stil)* übertreibend; *math* Hyperbel-; **~borean** [haipə(:)bɔ:'ri(:)ən] im hohen Norden (gelegen, wohnend), Nord-; **~critic(al)** ['haipə(:)'kritik(əl)] überstreng urteilend; schwer zu befriedigen(d); **~sensitive** ['haipə(:)'sensitiv] überempfindlich; **~tension** ['haipə(:)'tenʃən] (zu) hohe(r) Blutdruck *m*; **~tonia** [haipə(:)'touniə] Hypertonie, Überspannung *f*; **~trophic** [haipə(:)'trɔfik] hypertrophisch; **~trophy** [hai'pə:trəfi] *s* übermäßige(s) Vergrößerung *f od* Wachstum *n*; *itr* sich übermäßig vergrößern.

hyphen ['haifən] *s* Bindestrich; Trennstrich *m*, *typ* Divis *n*; *tr* = *~ate*; **~ate** ['-eit] *tr* mit e-m Bindestrich versehen *od* schreiben; *(Silben)* trennen.

hypno|sis [hip'nousis] *pl -ses* [-i:z] Hypnose *f*, Zwangsschlaf *m*; **~tic** [hip'nɔtik] *a* einschläfernd; hypnotisch; *s* Schlafmittel, Hypnotikum *n*; **~tism** ['hipnətizm] Hypnotismus *m*; **~tist** ['hipnətist] Hypnotiseur *m*; **~tize** ['hipnətaiz] *tr* hypnotisieren; *fam fig* mitreißen, begeistern, faszinieren.

hypo ['haipou] *pl -os phot* Fixiersalz *n*; *fam med* Spritze *f*; *sl* Hypochonder *m*; **~chondria** [haipo(u)'kɔndriə] Hypochondrie *f*, Krankheitswahn *m*, Schwermut *f*; **~chondriac** [haipo(u)'kɔndriæk] *a* hypochondrisch; *s* Hypochonder *m*; **~chondriacal** [haipo(u)kɔn'draiəkəl] hypochondrisch; **~crisy** [hi'pɔkrəsi] Heuchelei *f*; Schwindel *m*; **~crite** ['hipəkrit] Heuchler, Scheinheilige(r); Schwindler *m*; **~critical** [hipə'kritikəl] heuchlerisch, scheinheilig, unaufrichtig; **~dermic** [haipə'də:mik] *a* unter der Haut befindlich, subkutan, hypodermatisch; *s (~~ injection)* Einspritzung unter die Haut, subkutane Injektion; *(~~ syringe) med* Injektionsspritze, -nadel *f*; **~gastric** [haipə'gæstrik] *a* Unterleibs-; **~gastrium** [haipə'gæstriəm] Unterleib *m*; **~physis** [hai'pɔfisis] *anat* Hypophyse *f*, Hirnanhang *m*; **~stasis** [hai'pɔstəsis] *pl -ses* [-i:z] *philos* Grundlage, Substanz *f*, Prinzip, Wesen *n*, Natur *f*; *rel* (göttliche) Person; *med* Hypostase *f*; **~tension** [haipə'tenʃən] niedrige(r) Blutdruck *m*; **~tenuse** [hai'pɔtinju:z] *math* Hypotenuse *f*; **~thecary** [hai'pɔθikəri] pfandrechtlich, hypothekarisch; **~thecate** [hai'pɔθikeit] *tr* verpfänden, lombardieren; hypothekarisch, mit e-r Hypothek belasten; **~thesis** [hai'pɔθisis] *pl -ses* [-i:z] Hypothese *f*; **~thetic(al)** [haipo(u)'θetik(əl)] hypothetisch.

hypsomet|er [hip'sɔmitə] Höhenmesser *m*, Hypsometer *n*; **~ry** [-ri] Höhenmessung *f*.

hyssop ['hisəp] *bot* Ysop; *rel* Weihwedel *m*.

hyster|ectomy [histə'rektəmi] Hysterektomie *f*; **~ia** [his'tiəriə] Hysterie *f*; **~ic** [his'terik] *a* hysterisch; *s* Hysteriker(in *f*) *m*; *to go into ~~s, to have a fit of ~~s* e-n hysterischen Anfall, hysterische Zustände bekommen, haben; **~ical** [-'terikəl] hysterisch; **~otomy** [histə'rɔtəmi] *med* Kaiserschnitt *m*, Gebärmutteroperation *f*.

I

I [ai] *pl* **~'s** I, i *n*; *prn* ich; *s*: *the* ~ das Ich. **iamb** ['aiæmb], **~us** [ai'æmbəs] *pl a.* *-i* [-ai] Jambus *m*; **~ic** [ai'æmbik] *a* jambisch, Jamben-; *s* Jambus *m.*
Iberia [ai'biəriə] *hist* Iberien *n*; *geog* die Iberische Halbinsel; **~n** [-n] *a* iberisch; *s hist* Iberer *m.*
ibex ['aibeks] *pl a. ibices* ['aibisi:z] *zoo* Steinbock *m.*
ibidem [i'baidem] *adv lit* ebenda.
ibis ['aibis] *pl -es* ['-i:z] u. ~ *orn* Ibis *m.*
ice [ais] *s* Eis; Speiseeis, Gefrorene(s) *n*; Zuckerguß *m*, Glasur *f*; *Am sl* Diamant *m*, Bestechungsgeld *n*; *tr* gefrieren lassen, in Eis verwandeln; mit Eis bedecken; in, auf Eis packen, mit Eis kühlen; mit Zuckerguß überziehen, glasieren; *itr (to ~ up, to ~ ove)* gefrieren, zufrieren, vereisen *a. aero*; *on thin ~* in einer gefährlichen *od* schwierigen Lage *od* Situation; *to break the ~ (fig)* das Eis brechen, die anfänglichen Schwierigkeiten überwinden; den ersten Schritt tun; *to cut no ~* keine Wirkung haben, keinen Eindruck machen; nicht von Belang sein; *to put on ~ (fig)* auf Eis legen, aufschieben; *dry ~* Trockeneis *n*; **~-age, -period** Eiszeit *f*; **~-axe, -pick** Eispickel *m*; **~-bag** *med* Eisbeutel *m*; **~berg** ['aisbə:g] *(schwimmender)* Eisberg *m a. fig*; **~blink** *mete* Eisblink *m*; **~-boat** Eisjacht *f*; **~bound** ['-baund] *a* (ein-, zu)gefroren; **~-box, -chest** Eisschrank; *Am* Kühlschrank *m*; **~-breaker, -fender** Eisbrecher *m*; **-bucket** Sektkübel *m*; **~cap** *geog* Eiskappe *f*; **~ coating** Eisschicht *f*; **~-cream** Sahneeis *n*, Eiskrem *f*; *a dish of ~~* e-e Portion Eis; *~~ cone* Tüte *f* Eis; *~~ parlo(u)r* Eisdiele *f*; **~ crystal** Eiskristall *m*; **~ cube** Eiswürfel *m*; **~d** [-t] *a* eisgekühlt; glasiert; *~~ coffee* Eiskaffee *m*; *~~ fruits (pl)* kandierte Früchte *f pl*; **~(-)eliminating (system)** *aero* Enteisung(sanlage) *f*; **~fall** Eissturz *m*; **~-ferns** *pl* Eisblumen *f pl*; **~-field** *geog* Eisfeld *n*; **~-floe** Treibeisscholle *f*; **~-foot** (Küsten-)Eisgürtel *m*; **~-formation** Eisbildung *f*; **~-free** *(Hafen)* eisfrei; **~-hockey** Eishockey *n*; **~-house** Eiskeller *m*; **~-indicator** *aero* Vereisungsanzeiger *m*; **~-layer** Eisschicht *f*; **~man** *Am* Eismann, -verkäufer, -händler *m*; **~-needle** *mete* Eisnadel *f*; **~-pack** *geog* Packeis *n*; *med* Eisbeutel *m*; **~pantomime, ~show** Eisrevue *f*; **~-rink** Eisbahn *f*; **~-run** Rodelbahn *f*; **~-water** Schmelzwasser; *Am* Eiswasser *n (Getränk)*.
Iceland ['aislənd] Island *n*; **~er** ['-ə] Isländer(in *f*) *m*; **~ic** [ais'lændik] isländisch; **~ moss** Isländische(s) Moos *n.*
ichneumon [ik'nju:mən] *zoo* Ichneumon *n*; Schlupfwespe *f.*
ichor ['aikɔ:] *med* Jauche Wundsekret *n*, Absonderung *f.*
ichthyo|logist [ikθi'ɔlədʒist] Ichthyologe *m*; **~logy** [-i] Fischkunde, Ichthyologie *f*; **~saur(us)** [ikθiə'sɔ:r(əs)] *pl -ri* [-rai] *zoo* Ichthyosaurus *m.*
ic|icle ['aisikl] Eiszapfen *m*; **~iness** ['aisinis] Eisglätte; eisige Kälte; *fig* Frostigkeit, Unfreundlichkeit *f*; **~ing** ['-iŋ] Zuckerguß *m*, Glasur; *aero* Vereisung *f*; *~~ sugar* Puderzucker *m*; **~y** ['-i] eisbedeckt; Eis-; *(Straße)* vereist; (glatt) wie Eis; eisig, eiskalt; *fig* eisig.
icky ['iki] *Am sl* altmodisch, gefühlsduselig.
icon ['aikɔn, -ən] Bild(werk) *n*; *rel* Ikone *f*; **~oclasm** [ai'kɔnəklæzm] *rel* Bilderstürmerei *f a. fig*; **~oclast** [-'kɔnəklæst] Bilderstürmer *m a. fig.*

*

I'd [aid] *fam* = *I had*; *I should*; *I would.*
idea [ai'diə] Gedanke *m*, Idee *f*; Begriff *m*; Vorstellung, Auffassung, Annahme, Meinung *f*; Plan *m*, Projekt, Vorhaben *n (of doing s.th.* etw zu tun); Absicht *f*, Ziel *n*; Eindruck *m*, vage Vorstellung *f*, Einfall *m*; *to form an ~* sich e-e Vorstellung machen (*of* von); *to get ~s into o.'s head* sich trügerischen Hoffnungen hingeben; *I have an ~ (that)* mir ist (so), als ob; *I have no ~* da komme ich nicht drauf, das kann ich mir nicht denken; *I had no ~ of it* davon hatte ich keine Ahnung; *that's the ~* darum dreht es sich, darauf kommt es an; so ist's richtig; *the ~ of such a thing! what an ~!* das ist doch nicht möglich! man stelle sich so was vor! *what's the big ~? (fam)* was hast du schon wieder für Rosinen im Kopf? *what gives you that ~* wie kommen Sie darauf?
ideal [ai'diəl] *a* ideal, vorbildlich, vollendet, vollkommen; ideell, (nur) gedacht, (nur) vorgestellt, eingebildet, unwirklich; *s* Ideal *n*; **~ism** [-lizm] Idealismus *m*; **~ist** [-list] Idealist *m*; **~istic(al)** [aidiə'listik(əl)] idealistisch; **~ization** [aidiəlai'zeiʃən] Idealisierung *f*; **~ize** [ai'diəlaiz] *tr* idealisieren.
ident|ic(al) [ai'dentik(əl)] identisch (*with* mit); der-, die-, dasselbe, gleich; übereinstimmend; *pol (Schreiben)* gleichlautend; *to be ~~(al)* übereinstimmen (*in* mit); *~~al twins (pl)* eineiige Zwillinge *m pl*; **~ifiable** [ai'dentifaiəbl] identifizierbar; **~ification** [aidentifi'keiʃən] Identifikation; Identifizierung; Legitimation *f*, Ausweis *m*; *~~-card* Personalausweis *m*, Kennkarte *f*; *~~-disk, (Am) -tag* Erkennungsmarke *f*; *~~-mark* Kenn-, Erkennungszeichen *n*; *~~-papers (pl)* Ausweispapiere *n pl*; **~ify** [ai'dentifai] *tr* identifizieren; *(Gegenstand)* wiedererkennen; kennzeichnen; machen (*with* zu); gleichsetzen, eng verbinden (*with* mit); *s.o.* jdn ausweisen (*as* als); *to become ~ified* zu einem Begriff werden, mitea. verschmelzen; *to ~~ o.s. with s.o.* sich mit jdm solidarisch erklären; **~ity** [ai'dentiti] Identität; (völlige) Gleichheit; Persönlichkeit, Individualität *f*; *to establish, to prove o.'s ~~* sich ausweisen; *mistaken ~~* Personenverwechslung *f*; *~~-card, -certificate* (Personal-)Ausweis *m*, Kennkarte *f.*
ideolog|ic(al) [aidiə'lɔdʒik(əl)] ideologisch, weltanschaulich; **~ist** [aidi'ɔlədʒist] Ideologe, Theoretiker *m*; **~y** [aidi'ɔlədʒi] Ideologie, Theorie; Weltanschauung; Denkweise; *philos* Begriffs-, Ideenlehre; *pej* Schwärmerei *f.*
idiocy ['idiəsi] *med* Schwachsinn *m*; Idiotie, (große) Dummheit *f*, Unsinn *m.*
idiom ['idiəm] Sprache *f*, Dialekt *m*, Sprech-, Ausdrucksweise, Spracheigentümlichkeit *f*, Stil *m*; (idiomatische) Redewendung *f*, Ausdruck *m*; **~atic(al)** [idiə'mætik(əl)] idiomatisch.
idiosyncrasy [idiə'siŋkrəsi] geistige Eigenart; individuelle Besonderheit; (individuelle) körperliche Beschaffenheit; *med* Überempfindlichkeit *f.*
idiot ['idiət] *med* Schwachsinnige(r); *(übertreibend)* Idiot, blöde(r) Kerl *m*; **~ic** [idi'ɔtik] *med* schwachsinnig; blöd(sinnig), idiotisch.
idle ['aidl] *a* wert-, nutzlos, unbrauchbar; unwirksam, wirkungslos; vergeblich, zwecklos, nichtig; leer, eitel, hohl; unbegründet; unbeschäftigt, untätig, müßig; faul, arbeitsscheu; unbenutzt, brachliegend, unproduktiv; unbeschäftigt; *(Wohnung)* leerstehend; *tech* nicht in Betrieb; leerlaufend; *itr (to ~ about)* (umher-) bummeln, müßiggehen, faulenzen; unbeschäftigt, untätig sein; *tech* leerlaufen; *tr (to ~ away) (Zeit)* vertun, vergeuden, verschwenden, vertrödeln; *to lie ~* brachliegen; *(Fabrik)* stilliegen; *(Geld)* nicht arbeiten; *to run ~ (tech)* leer laufen; *to stand ~* stillstehen, außer Betrieb sein; **~ capacity** ungenützte Kapazität *f*; **~ capital** tote(s) Kapital *n*; **~ current** Blindstrom *m*; **~ hours** *pl* Mußestunden *f pl*; **~ motion** Leerlauf; *mot* Leergang *m*; **~ness** ['-nis] Nutzlosigkeit, Wirkungslosigkeit; Nichtigkeit; Untätigkeit, Muße; Trägheit, Faulheit *f*; **~ pretext** bloße(r) Vorwand *m*; **~ pulley, wheel** *tech* Leerscheibe *f*; leerlaufende(s) Rad *n*; **~r** ['-ə] Müßiggänger, Trödler, Faulpelz *m*; *tech* leerlaufende(s) Rad *n*, Leerlaufrolle *f*; **idling** ['-iŋ] *a* unbeschäftigt, untätig; müßig; *tech* leerlaufend; *s tech* Leerlauf *m*; *to be ~~* leerlaufen; *~~ speed* Leerlauf, -gang *m.*
idol ['aidl] Götter-, Götzenbild *n*; Abgott *m*; Idol *n a. fig*; **~ater** [ai'dɔlətə] Götzendiener; *allg* leidenschaftliche(r) Verehrer *m*; **~atress** [-'dɔlətris] Götzendienerin; *allg* leidenschaftliche Verehrerin *f*; **~atrize** [ai'dɔlətraiz] *tr* vergöttern; leidenschaftlich, abgöttisch verehren; *itr* Götzen verehren; **~atrous** [-'dɔlətrəs] Götzen verehrend, Abgötterei treibend; leidenschaftlich ergeben; **~atry** [ai'dɔlətri] Götzendienst *m*, Abgötterei; *allg* leidenschaftliche Verehrung *f*; **~ization** [aidəlai'zeiʃən] Vergötterung, Vergötzung *f*; **~ize** ['aidəlaiz] = *~atrize.*
idyl|(l) ['idil, 'aid-] *lit mus* Idylle *f*; Idyll *n*; **~lic** [ai'dilik, i'd-] idyllisch.
if [if] *conj* wenn, falls; wenn auch; wenn schon; ob; *as ~* als ob, als wenn; *and ~ ...!* und ob ...! *even ~* auch wenn; *~ only!* wenn ... nur ...! *s das* Wenn; Annahme, Voraussetzung *f*; *without ~s or ans* ohne Wenn und Aber; *as ~ ~s and ans were pots and pans!* als wenn das so einfach wäre!
igloo ['iglu:] Iglu *m* od *n.*
ign|eous ['igniəs] feurig, glühend; *geol* vulkanisch; *~~ rocks (pl)* Eruptivgestein *n*; **~is fatuus** ['ignis 'fætjuəs] *pl -es fatui* [-i:z -uai] Irrlicht *n*; *fig* Illusion *f*; **~ite** [ig'nait] *tr* entzünden, in Brand setzen; erhitzen, glühend machen; *fig* in Erregung versetzen; *itr* sich entzünden, in Brand geraten, Feuer fangen, anbrennen; **~ition** [ig'niʃən] Entzündung *f*, Anzünden *n*, Erhitzung *f*; *mot* Zündung *f*; *~~ cable, coil* Zündkabel *n*, -spule

f; ~~ *charge (Am)* Zündladung *f*; ~~ *failure* Fehlzündung *f*; ~~*-key* Zündschlüssel *m*; ~~*-spark* Zündfunke *m*.

ignoble [ig'noubl] unedel, niedrig, gemein, unehrenhaft, schändlich; **~ness** [-nis] Niedrigkeit, Gemeinheit, Schändlichkeit *f*.

ignomin|ious [ignə'miniəs] schändlich, unehrenhaft, schmachvoll; verächtlich; herabwürdigend; **~y** ['ignəmini] Schande, Schmach; Schandtat, Schändlichkeit *f*.

ignor|amus [ignə'reiməs] *pl -ses* Unwissende(r), Ignorant *m*; **~ance** ['ignərəns] Unwissenheit, Ignoranz, Unkenntnis; **~ant** ['ignərənt] unwissend, unerfahren, ungebildet; nicht informiert (*in* über); *to be* ~~ *of* nicht bemerken, nicht beachten; nicht wissen, nicht kennen; **~e** [ig'nɔ:] *tr* keine Beachtung schenken (*s.th.* e-r S); hinweggehen über; *(Verbot)* übertreten; *jur* abweisen, verwerfen.

iguan|a [i'gwɑ:nə] *zoo* Leguan *m*; **~odon** [i'gwɑ:nədɔn] *zoo* Iguanodon *n*.

ike [aik] *s tele sl* Ikonoskop *n*, Fernseh-Senderöhre *f*; *tr Am sl* herunterhandeln, betrügen.

il|eum ['iliəm] *anat* Krummdarm *m*; **~eus** ['iliəs] *med* Darmverschluß *m*; Kotbrechen *n*; **~ium** ['iliəm] *pl -ia* [-iə] *anat* Darmbein *n*; Hüfte *f*.

ilex ['aileks] Stechpalme; Stein-, Stech-, Immergrüne Eiche *f*.

ilk [ilk] *fam* Familie; Sorte, Klasse *f*; *of that* ~ desselben Namens, Ortes.

ill [il] *a* schlecht, übel, schlimm, böse; unfreundlich, hart, grausam; ungünstig, unglücklich, mißlich; Miß-; krank (*with* an); falsch, fehlerhaft, unvollkommen, unvollständig, ungenau; *adv* schlecht; hart, grausam, unfreundlich; falsch, unvollkommen, ungenau; mit Mühe; kaum, schwerlich; *s* Übel, Böse(s); Unglück, Mißgeschick *n*; Krankheit *f*; *to be* ~ *at ease* sich in s-r Haut nicht wohlfühlen; *to be taken* ~, *to fall* ~ krank werden; *to speak* ~ *of s.o.* schlecht von jdm, über jdn sprechen; *to take* ~ abgestoßen werden; Anstoß nehmen (*s.th.* an etw); **~-advised** *a* schlecht beraten; unbesonnen, unklug, unvernünftig; **~-affected** *a* schlecht aufgelegt, übelgelaunt; übelgesinnt (*to* dat); **~-arranged** *a* schlecht eingerichtet; **~-bred** *a* schlecht erzogen; ungezogen, unhöflich, ungesittet, ungebildet; **~-breeding** schlechte Erziehung; Ungezogenheit; Unhöflichkeit *f*; **~-conditioned** *a* schlecht angelegt; in üblem Zustand; **~-disposed** *a* bösartig, übelgesinnt; unfreundlich (*towards* gegen); nicht günstig (gesinnt) (*towards* dat); **~-fated** *a* unglücklich; unheilvoll; **~-favo(u)red** *a* unschön, häßlich; ungefällig, abweisend; **~-gotten** *a* unrechtmäßig erworben; **~-humoured** *a* schlecht-, übelgelaunt; **~-judged** *a* mißverstanden; unüberlegt, unklug; zur Unzeit; **~-mannered** *a* schlecht erzogen; mit schlechten Umgangsformen; unhöflich; **~-matched** *a* schlecht zs.passend; **~-natured** *a (Mensch)* unangenehm, ungenießbar; bösartig; launisch; mürrisch, verdrießlich; **~ness** ['-nis] Krankheit *f*; **~-omened** *a* von schlechten Vorzeichen begleitet; **~-spent** *a* schlecht angelegt; verschwendet; **~-starred** *a* unter e-m ungünstigen Stern geboren; unglücklich; **~-suited** *a* unpassend; **~-tempered** *a* launisch, launenhaft; mürrisch, verdrießlich; querköpfig, zänkisch, reizbar; **~-timed** *a* zur Unzeit; ungelegen, unpassend, unangebracht; **~-treat, -use** *tr* schlecht behandeln, mißhandeln; mißbrauchen; **~-treatment, ~-usage** schlechte Behandlung, Mißhandlung *f*; Mißbrauch *m*; ~ **will** Übelwollen *n*, Feindseligkeit, Feindschaft *f*, Haß *m*.

I'll [ail] *fam* = *I will; I shall.*

illegal [i'li:gəl] ungesetzlich, unrechtmäßig, illegal; rechtswidrig, widerrechtlich; *(Streik)* wild; *to declare, to make* ~ für ungesetzlich erklären; **~ity** [ili(:)'gæliti] Ungesetzlichkeit, Illegalität *f*; ~ **trade, traffic** Schleich-, Schwarzhandel *m*.

illegib|ility [iledʒi'biliti] Unleserlichkeit; Unlesbarkeit *f*; **~le** [i'ledʒəbl] unleserlich; unlesbar.

illegitim|acy [ili'dʒitiməsi] Unehelichkeit; Unrechtmäßigkeit; Ungültigkeit, Ungesetzlichkeit *f*; **~ate** [ili'dʒitimit] unehelich, illegitim; unrechtmäßig, ungesetzlich.

illiberal [i'libərəl] unduldsam, intolerant, engstirnig, -herzig; geizig, knauserig; ungebildet; **~ility** [ilibə'ræliti] Unduldsamkeit, Engherzigkeit *f*; Geiz *m*, Knauserei; Unbildung *f*.

illicit [i'lisit] unerlaubt, verboten; ungesetzlich, gesetz-, rechtswidrig; sittenwidrig; unüblich; ~ **trade, trading** Schleich-, Schwarzhandel *m*; ~ **work** Schwarzarbeit *f*.

illimitable [i'limitəbl] grenzenlos, unbegrenzt, unbeschränkt; unermeßlich.

*

illiquid [i'likwid] *Am* zahlungsunfähig; nicht flüssig; *(Anspruch)* unbewiesen; **~ity** [ili'kwiditi] *Am* Zahlungsunfähigkeit *f*.

illiter|acy [i'litərəsi] Unwissenheit, mangelnde Bildung *f*; Analphabetentum *n*; *Am* Schreib-, Sprechfehler *m*; **~ate** [i'litərit] *a* unwissend, ungebildet; des Schreibens und Lesens unkundig; *s* Analphabet, Ungebildete(r) *m*.

illogical [i'lɔdʒikəl] unlogisch; unsinnig.

illum|e [i'lju:m] *tr poet* erleuchten, erhellen *a. fig*; **~inant** [-inənt] *a* (er)leuchtend; erklärend, belehrend; *s* Lichtquelle *f*; **~inate** [i'lju:mineit] *tr* be-, erleuchten, erhellen; *fig* erklären, erläutern, verständlich machen; aufklären, belehren, informieren; berühmt machen; illuminieren, festlich beleuchten; illuminieren, bunt ausmalen, kolorieren; künstlerisch ausführen; ~~*d advertising* Lichtreklame *f*; **~ination** [ilju:mi'neiʃən] Beleuchtung; *fig* Erläuterung, Erklärung; Belehrung, Unterrichtung, Aufklärung; Festbeleuchtung; Illumination; Ausmalung *f*; Buchschmuck *m*; *opt phot* Bildhelligkeit *f*; **~inative** [i'lju:minətiv] *a* Leucht-, Beleuchtungs-; *fig* belehrend, aufklärend; **~inator** [-ineitə] Beleuchtungskörper; Beleuchter *(Person)* Illuminator, Buchmaler *m*; **~ine** [i'lju:min] *tr* beleuchten, erhellen *a. fig*; *(Licht)* anstecken, -machen.

illus|ion [i'lu:ʒən] Illusion, irrtümliche Annahme, falsche Vorstellung *f*; Trugbild *n*, trügerische Erscheinung; (Sinnes-)Täuschung *f*, Wahn *m*; **~ionist** [-ist] Zauberkünstler *m*; **~ive** [i'lu:siv], **~ory** [-səri] unwirklich, täuschend, trügerisch.

illustrat|e ['iləstreit] *tr* erklären, (*bes.* durch Beispiele) erläutern, veranschaulichen; *(Buch)* illustrieren, bebildern; **~ion** [iləs'treiʃən] Erklärung, Erläuterung, Veranschaulichung *f*; Beispiel *n*, Abbildung, Illustration *f*; **~ive** ['iləstreitiv, i'lʌstrətiv] erklärend, erläuternd; anschaulich; ~~ *material, data* Anschauungsmaterial *n*; **~or** ['iləstreitə] Illustrator, Buchkünstler *m*.

illustrious [i'lʌstriəs] bedeutend, berühmt, gefeiert; **~ness** [-nis] Bedeutung, Berühmtheit *f*.

I'm [aim] *fam* = *I am.*

image ['imidʒ] *s* Bild; Bildwerk, Standbild *n*, Statue, Figur; Abbildung, Darstellung *f*; Abbild; Götzenbild; Gegenstück *n*; Eindruck *m*, Vorstellung, Auffassung, Idee; Verkörperung, Versinnbildlichung *f*, Sinnbild *n*; Inbegriff *m*; *psychol* Leit-, Urbild *n*; Metapher, Redefigur *f*; *tr* abbilden, *(bildlich)* darstellen; reflektieren, spiegeln; sich vor-, vor Augen stellen; ein Inbegriff sein *gen*; *(mit Worten)* lebendig darstellen; **~ry** ['-əri] Bildwerke, *bes.* Standbilder *n pl*; *fig* Vorstellungen *f pl*; Metaphorik *f*, bildhafte Redewendungen *f pl*.

imagin|able [i'mædʒinəbl] vorstellbar; denkbar; erdenklich; *to try everything* ~~ alles Erdenkliche versuchen; **~ary** [-əri] eingebildet, unwirklich, imaginär *a. math*; **~ation** [imædʒi'neiʃən] Einbildungs-, Bildkraft; Phantasie(begabtheit); Einbildung, Phantasie *f*; **~ative** [i'mædʒinətiv] reich an Einbildungskraft, phantasiebegabt, -voll, schöpferisch, einfallsreich; dichterisch, Dicht-; **~e** [i'mædʒin] *tr itr* sich vorstellen, sich ausdenken, ersinnen, geistig erschaffen; sich denken, annehmen, glauben; *just* ~~*!* denken Sie nur (mal)! *I* ~~ *so* ich glaube schon.

imag|o [i'meigou] *pl a. -ines* [i'meidʒini:z] fertige(s) Insekt *n*, Imago *f*.

imbecil|e ['imbisi:l, -ail, *Am* -il] *a* schwachsinnig, geistesschwach; sehr dumm, stupide; *s* Schwachsinnige(r); Idiot, Einfaltspinsel *m*; **~ity** [imbi'siliti] Schwachsinn *m*, Geistesschwäche *f*.

imbed *s. embed.*

imbibe [im'baib] *tr* auf-, einsaugen; *fam* trinken; *fig (geistig)* aufnehmen.

imbricat|e ['imbrikeit] *tr* dachziegelartig überea.legen, *itr* -liegen; [*a.* -it] *a* dachziegelartig angeordnet.

imbroglio [im'brouliou] *pl* **~s** Verwirrung *f*, Durcheinander *n*, verwickelte, komplizierte Lage *f*; Mißverständnis *n*, Meinungsverschiedenheit *f*.

imbrue [im'bru:] *tr* (*bes.* mit Blut) beflecken, benetzen (*with* mit).

imbue [im'bju:] *tr* durchtränken, durchfeuchten, (durch)färben; *fig* durchdringen, erfüllen, inspirieren (*with* mit).

imit|able ['imitəbl] nachahmbar; **~ate** ['imiteit] *tr* nachahmen, -machen; kopieren; nacheifern (*s.o.* jdm); ähnlich sehen, ähneln, sich anpassen (*s.o., s.th.* jdm, e-r S); **~ation** [imi'teiʃən] *s* Nachahmung, -bildung; Fälschung; *(Schmuck)* Imitation; *biol* Mimikry *f*; *attr* Kunst-; falsch, unecht; *in* ~~ *of* nach dem Muster, dem Vorbild *gen*, in Anlehnung an; *beware of* ~~*s* vor Nachahmungen wird gewarnt; ~~ *jewellery* unechte(r), falsche(r) Schmuck *m*; ~~ *leather* Kunstleder *n*; **~ative** ['imitətiv, -tə-] nachgeahmt, -macht; unecht, falsch; (schall-, klang)nachahmend; ~~ *word* lautmalende(s) Wort *n*; **~ator** ['imiteitə] Nachahmer, Imitator *m*.

immaculate [i'mækjulit] fleckenlos, rein; fehlerlos, untadelig; unschuldig, von Sünden rein, unbefleckt.

immanen|ce ['imənəns] *philos* Immanenz *f*; **~t** ['-t] immanent.

immaterial [imə'tiəriəl] immateriell, unkörperlich, geistig; unwesentlich, unerheblich, unwichtig, nebensächlich.

immatur|e [imə'tjuə] unreif; unentwickelt, unfertig; unvollständig; **~ity** [imə'tjuəriti] Unreife *f*.

immeasurable [i'meʒərəbl] unermeßlich, unmeßbar, grenzenlos.

immedi|acy [i'mi:djəsi] Unmittelbarkeit, Unvermitteltheit *f*; **~ate** [-ət] unmittelbar, unvermittelt, direkt; *(zeitlich* od *räumlich)* (unmittelbar) folgend, anschließend; nächst; sofortig, unverzüglich; **~ately** [-li] *adv* direkt; unverzüglich, sofort, gleich, ohne Aufschub; *conj* sobald, sowie.

immemorial [imi'mɔ:riəl] unvordenklich; uralt; *from time ~* seit unvordenklichen Zeiten.

immens|e [i'mens] ungeheuer (groß), gewaltig; *sl* prachtvoll, prächtig, prima, Klasse; **~ity** [-iti] Grenzenlosigkeit, Unermeßlichkeit *f*.

immers|e [i'mə:s] *tr* ein-, untertauchen, versenken; *fig* verstricken (*in* in); **~ed** [-t] *a fig*: *~~ in a book* in ein Buch vertieft; *to be ~~ in debt(s)* voller Schulden stecken; *to be ~~ in difficulties* vor Schwierigkeiten weder ein noch aus wissen; *to be ~~ in o.'s work* in der Arbeit aufgehen; *~~ in thought* in Gedanken versunken; **~ion** [i'mə:ʃən] Ein-, Untertauchen *n*, Versenkung; *fig* Versunkenheit *f*; *~~ heater* Tauchsieder *m*.

immigr|ant ['imigrənt] Einwanderer *m*; **~ate** ['-eit] *itr* einwandern (*into* in, nach); *tr (Arbeitskräfte)* einführen; **~ation** [-'greiʃən] Einwanderung *f*; *~~ country* Einwanderungsland *n*; *~~ papers (pl)* Einwanderungspapiere *n pl*; *~~ restrictions (pl)* Einwanderungsbeschränkungen *f pl*.

imminen|ce, -cy ['iminəns(i)] unmittelbare Drohung; drohende Gefahr *f*; **~t** ['-t] *(Gefahr)* drohend; *(Unglück)* nahe bevorstehend.

immiscible [i'misəbl] unvermischbar.

immitigable [i'mitigəbl] nicht zu mildern(d), nicht zu mäßigen(d), nicht zu besänftigen(d); unerbittlich.

immobil|e [i'moubail] unbeweglich, fest; unveränderlich; reglos; **~ity** [imo(u)'biliti] Unbeweglichkeit, Unveränderlichkeit *f*; **~ization** [imoubilai'zeiʃən] *fin* Immobilisierung, Festlegung; *(Geld)* Einziehung *f*; **~ize** [i'moubilaiz] *tr* unbeweglich, festmachen; *fin* immobilisieren, festlegen; *(Geld)* aus dem Umlauf ziehen; *mil* bewegungsunfähig machen, fesseln; *med* ruhigstellen.

immoderat|e [i'mɔdərit] unmäßig, maßlos, übertrieben, unvernünftig; **~ion** [imɔdə'reiʃən] Unmäßigkeit, Maßlosigkeit, Übertriebenheit *f*.

immodest [i'mɔdist] unbescheiden; dreist, vorlaut, frech, unverschämt; unanständig; **~y** [-i] Unbescheidenheit; Dreistigkeit, Frechheit, Unverschämtheit; Unanständigkeit *f*.

immolat|e ['imo(u)leit] *tr rel* opfern; **~ion** [imo(u)'leiʃən] Opfer(ung *f*) *n*.

immoral [i'mɔrəl] unrecht, unmoralisch; sittenwidrig, unsittlich, unzüchtig; **~ity** [imə'ræliti] Unrecht *n*; Verderbtheit; Unsittlichkeit; Unzucht *f*; Laster *n*.

immort|al [i'mɔ:tl] *a* unsterblich; unvergänglich, ewig; göttlich, himmlisch; *s* Unsterbliche(r) *m*; **~ality** [imɔ:'tæliti] Unsterblichkeit *f*; unvergängliche(r) Ruhm *m*; **~alize** [i'mɔ:təlaiz] *tr* unsterblich machen *bes. fig*; **~elle** [imɔ:'tel] *bot* Immortelle, Strohblume *f*.

immovable [i'mu:vəbl] *a* unbeweglich, fest(sitzend), unveränderlich, beständig; *fig* unerschütterlich; *jur* unabänderlich; *(Eigentum)* unbeweglich; gefühllos; *s pl* Immobilien *pl*, Liegenschaften *f pl*, Grundbesitz *m*.

immun|e [i'mju:n] *med* immun, geschützt (*against, to* gegen); unempfänglich (*against, to* für); *jur* unverletzlich; befreit (*from* von); **~ity** [-iti] *med* Immunität, Unempfänglichkeit (*from* für); *jur* Immunität, Unverletzlichkeit, Straffreiheit; Freiheit, Befreiung *f* (*from* von); Privileg *n*; *(~~ from taxation, from taxes)* Abgaben-, Steuerfreiheit *f*; **~ization** [imju(:)nai'zeiʃən] *med* Immunisierung *f* (*against* gegen); **~ize** ['imju(:)naiz] *tr* unempfänglich machen, immunisieren (*against* gegen); **~ology** [-'nɔlədʒi] Serologie *f*.

immure [i'mjuə] *tr* einsperren, einschließen, einkerkern; *to ~ o.s.* sich abschließen, sich vergraben (*in* in).

immutab|ility [imju:tə'biliti] Unveränderlichkeit *f*; **~le** [i'mju:təbl] unveränderlich, unwandelbar.

*

imp [imp] Wechselbalg, Kobold *m*, Teufelchen *n*; *hum* (kleiner) Schelm, Racker, Spitzbube *m*; **~ish** ['-iʃ] koboldhaft; *hum* schelmisch, spitzbübisch.

impact ['impækt] *s* (heftiger) Stoß; Zs.stoß, -prall; Aufschlag, -prall; (Geschoß-)Einschlag *m*; *fig* (Aus-)Wirkung *f*, Einfluß *m*; Wucht, Stoßkraft *f*; [im'pækt] *tr* zs.pressen, -drücken, -drängen; einpferchen, einkeilen, einzwängen (*into* in); *itr* stoßen (*against, with* gegen); **~ fuse** Aufschlagzünder *m*; **~ strength** Stoßfestigkeit *f*.

impair [im'pɛə] *tr* verschlechtern, verschlimmern; beschädigen; beeinträchtigen, vermindern, verringern, abschwächen; entkräften; **~ment** [-mənt] Verschlechterung; Beeinträchtigung, Verminderung, Abschwächung *f*; Nachteil, Schaden *m*.

impale [im'peil] *tr* durchbohren; *(zur Strafe)* pfählen; *fig* erstarren lassen, lähmen, hilflos machen; quälen.

impalpable [im'pælpəbl] unfühlbar, dem Tastsinn verborgen; *fig* unbegreiflich, unverständlich, unfaßbar.

impanel *s. empanel.*

impart [im'pɑ:t] *tr* geben, verleihen; übermitteln, mitteilen, Mitteilung machen von (*to s.o.* jdm).

impartial [im'pɑ:ʃəl] unparteiisch, objektiv; unvoreingenommen, vorurteilslos, -frei; gerecht; **~ity** ['impɑ:ʃi'æliti] Unparteilichkeit, Objektivität; Gerechtigkeit; Unvoreingenommenheit, Vorurteilslosigkeit *f*.

impassab|ility ['impɑ:sə'biliti] Unwegsamkeit *f*; **~le** [im'pɑ:səbl] unwegsam; unüberschreitbar, unpassierbar.

impasse [im'pɑ:s, æm-] Sackgasse *bes. fig*; *fig* ausweglose Situation *od* Lage *f*.

impassib|ility ['impæsi'biliti] Unempfindlichkeit *f*; **~le** [im'pæsəbl] unempfindlich (*to* für); unverletzbar; gefühl-, teilnahmslos.

impassioned [im'pæʃənd] *a* leidenschaftlich, erregt, aufgewühlt.

impassiv|e [im'pæsiv] unempfindlich, gefühllos; unverwundbar; leidenschaftslos; gefühllos; ruhig, still.

impaste [im'peist] *tr* pastos malen.

impatien|ce [im'peiʃəns] Ungeduld *f*; Übereifer *m*; Aufgeregtheit, *fam* Zappeligkeit; Abgeneigtheit; Unduldsamkeit *f* (*of* gegen); **~t** [-t] ungeduldig; übereifrig, begierig (*for* auf, nach; *to do* zu tun); aufgeregt, *fam* zappelig; unduldsam (*of* gegen); *to be ~~ of* abgeneigt sein, *fam* etwas haben gegen; *for s.th.* etw nicht erwarten können.

impeach [im'pi:tʃ] *tr* anklagen, bezichtigen, zur Rechenschaft, zur Verantwortung ziehen (*of, for, with* wegen); sich beklagen über, etwas auszusetzen haben an; in Zweifel ziehen, verdächtigen, die Glaubwürdigkeit bestreiten (*a witness* e-s Zeugen); **~able** [-əbl] anfechtbar; angreifbar; **~ment** [im'pi:tʃmənt] (Stellung unter) Anklage; Anfechtung, Bestreitung; Ablehnung *f*; Tadel *m*; Verdächtigung *f*.

impeccab|ility [impekə'biliti] Sündlosigkeit; Unfehlbarkeit *f*; **~le** [im'pekəbl] sündlos; untadelig; unfehlbar.

impecunious [impi'kju:njəs] mittellos, unbemittelt, arm; ohne Geld.

impedance [im'pi:dəns] Wechselstrom-, Scheinwiderstand *m*.

imped|e [im'pi:d] *tr* verhindern, vereiteln; behindern, hemmen, erschweren; verzögern; **~iment** [im'pedimənt] Behinderung, Erschwerung *f*; Hindernis, Hemmnis *n* (*to* für); Sprachfehler; *jur* Hinderungsgrund *m*; Ehehindernis *n*; *~~ to traffic* Verkehrshindernis *n*; **~imenta** [impedi'mentə] *pl* Gepäck *n*; *mil* Troß *m*; *fig* Belastung *f*.

impel [im'pel] *tr* (an)treiben; zwingen, nötigen; veranlassen; **~lent** [-ənt] *a* treibend; Treib-, Trieb-, Antriebs-; *s* (An-)Trieb *m*; treibende Kraft *f*; Grund *m*; **~ler** [-ə] Schaufel-, Lauf-, Antriebsrad *n*.

impend [im'pend] *itr* hängen (*over* über); *fig* schweben (*over* über); drohen, nahe bevorstehen; **~ing** [-iŋ] (nahe) bevorstehend; drohend; *(Felsen)* überhängend.

impenetrab|ility [impenitrə'biliti] Undurchdringlichkeit; Unzugänglichkeit; Unergründlichkeit; Unempfänglichkeit *f*; **~le** [im'penitrəbl] undurchdringlich; unwegsam, unzugänglich; *fig* unerforschlich, unergründlich; unverständlich; unlösbar; unempfänglich (*to, by* für); *(Einflüssen)* unzugänglich.

impeniten|ce, -cy [im'penitəns(i)] Unbußfertigkeit, Verstocktheit *f*; **~t** [-t] unbußfertig, verstockt; ohne Reue.

imperative [im'perətiv] *a* befehlend, gebieterisch; zwingend, dringend, unerläßlich, absolut erforderlich, notwendig; *s* Befehl *m*, Gebot *n*; *(~ mood)* Befehlsform *f*, Imperativ *m*.

imperceptible [impə'septəbl] nicht wahrnehmbar, unmerklich, verschwindend klein, äußerst fein, geringfügig.

imperfect [im'pə:fikt] *a* unvollständig, unvollkommen, unvollendet; nicht fehlerfrei, fehlerhaft, mangelhaft; *(Wettbewerb)* ungleich; *(Verpflichtung)* einseitig; *(Reim)* unrein; *s (~ tense) gram* Imperfekt *n*, erste Vergangenheit *f*; **~ion** [impə'fekʃən] Unvollständigkeit, Unvollkommenheit *f*; Mangel, Fehler *m*, Schwäche *f*.

imperforat|e [im'pə:fərit] *(Briefmarke)* ungezahnt, ungezähnt, nicht perforiert; *anat* ohne Öffnung.

imperial [im'piəriəl] *a* kaiserlich; Reichs-; Hoheits-; souverän; majestätisch, hoheitsvoll; *Br* gesetzlich; *s hist* Kaiserliche(r) *m*; Imperial(papier) *n (im Format 56 × 76 od 81, Am 58 × 79 cm)*; Knebelbart *m*; **~ism** [-izm] Imperialismus *m*, Weltmacht-, Großmachtpolitik *f*; **~ist** [-ist] *hist* Kaiserliche(r); Imperialist *m*; **~istic** [impiəriə'listik] imperialistisch.

imperil [im'peril] *tr* in Gefahr bringen, gefährden, aufs Spiel setzen.

imperious [im'piəriəs] anmaßend; gebieterisch, herrschsüchtig, beherrschend; dringend, notwendig, unabweisbar; **~ness** [-nis] gebieterische(s) Wesen *n*, Herrschsucht; Dringlichkeit, Unabweisbarkeit *f*.

imperishable [im'periʃəbl] unvergänglich, unzerstörbar; widerstandsfähig.

impermanent [im'pə:mənənt] unbeständig, vorübergehend; vergänglich.

impermeab|ility [impə:mjə'biliti] Undurchlässigkeit *f*; **~le** [im'pə:mjəbl] undurchlässig; *(~~ to water)* wasserdicht; undurchdringlich,undurchlässig(*to* für).

impersonal [im'pə:snl] unpersönlich *a. gram*; sachlich; Sach-; **~ity** [impə:sə'næliti] Unpersönlichkeit *f*.

imperson|ate [im'pə:səneit] *tr* personifizieren; verkörpern; *theat* darstellen, spielen; *(zur Unterhaltung)* nachahmen, -machen; *a* personifiziert, leibhaftig; **~ation** [impə:sə'neiʃən] Personifizierung; Verkörperung; *theat* Darstellung; Nachahmung *f*; **~ator** [im'pə:səneitə] Verkörperer; Darsteller; Imitator *m*.

impertinen|ce, -cy [im'pə:tinəns(i)] Unangebrachtheit, Ungehörigkeit; Frechheit, Unverschämtheit; Unsachlichkeit; Belanglosigkeit *f*; **~t** [-t] unpassend, unangebracht, ungehörig; frech, unverschämt; *jur* nicht zur Sache gehörig; unerheblich.

imperturbab|ility ['impə(:)tə:bə'biliti] Unerschütterlichkeit *f*; Gleichmut *m*; **~le** [impə(:)'tə:bəbl] unerschütterlich.

impervious [im'pə:viəs] undurchdringlich, unwegsam, undurchlässig (*to* für); *fig (Mensch)* unzugänglich (*to* für), taub (*to* gegen); **~ness** [-nis] Undurchdringlichkeit; Undurchlässigkeit; *fig* Unzugänglichkeit *f*.

impetigo [impi'taigou] *med* Impetigo, Eiterpustel *f*; Eitergrind *m*.

impet|uosity [impetju'ɔsiti] Ungestüm *n*, Heftigkeit *f*; **~uous** [im'petjuəs] ungestüm, wild, heftig, wuchtig; rasch, übereilt, unüberlegt, der ersten Eingebung folgend, impulsiv; **~us** ['impitəs] Wucht *f*; Schwung, Anstoß, Auf-, Antrieb *m*, Stoßkraft, treibende Kraft *f*, Impuls *m*; *to give a fresh ~~ to s.th.* e-r S neuen Auftrieb geben.

impiety [im'paiəti] Gottlosigkeit; Ehrfurchtslosigkeit, Pietätlosigkeit; Respektlosigkeit *f*.

impinge [im'pindʒ] *itr* stoßen, schlagen (*on, upon* auf; *against* gegen); verstoßen (*on, upon* gegen); übergreifen (*on, upon* auf); verletzen (*on, upon s.th.* etw); **~ment** [-mənt] Zs.stoß *m* (*against* mit); Verletzung *f*, Verstoß, Übergriff *m*; Einwirkung *f* (*on* auf).

impious ['impiəs] gottlos; pietätlos; respektlos, unehrerbietig.

implacab|ility [implækə'biliti, -pleik-] Unversöhnlichkeit; Unerbittlichkeit *f*; **~le** [im'plækəbl, -'pleik-] unversöhnlich, unnachgiebig, unerbittlich.

implant [im'plɑ:nt] *tr* einpflanzen; *med* verpflanzen, übertragen; *fig* einpflanzen, einimpfen, einprägen.

implausible [im'plɔ:zəbl] unglaubhaft, -würdig, unwahrscheinlich.

implement ['implimənt] *s* Gerät, Werkzeug *n*; *pl* Gerätschaften *pl*, Geräte *n pl*, Utensilien *f pl*, Maschinen *f pl*; *tr* ['-ment] aus-, durchführen, vollenden; *(Abkommen, Vertrag)* erfüllen, nachkommen (*an obligation* e-r Verpflichtung); **~ation** [-'teiʃən], **~ing** ['-iŋ] Aus-, Durchführung; Erfüllung *(e-s Vertrages)*; *tech* Inbetriebnahme *f*; *~ing provision* Durchführungsbestimmung *f*.

implicat|e ['implikeit] *tr* zs.falten, -flechten; (mitea.) verflechten; verwickeln, (mit) hineinziehen, *lit* verstricken (*in* in); bloßstellen; zur Folge haben; in Zs.hang bringen (*in* mit); *med* beteiligen, in Mitleidenschaft ziehen; **~ion** [impli'keiʃən] Verwick(e)lung; Einbeziehung *f* (*in* in); Anzeichen *n*, Hinweis *m*; Bedeutung, selbstverständliche Folgerung; *pl* Tragweite *f*; *by ~~* stillschweigend, ohne weiteres, selbstverständlich.

implicit [im'plisit] stillschweigend (zu verstehen gegeben), unausgesprochen; einbegriffen, mit enthalten, zugehörig; selbstverständlich; *(Vertrauen, Gehorsam)* unbedingt, blind.

implied [im'plaid] *a* stillschweigend, selbstverständlich; indirekt.

implore [im'plɔ:] *tr* anflehen, ernstlich, dringend bitten (*for* um).

imply [im'plai] *tr* enthalten, einschließen, bedeuten; (stillschweigend) voraussetzen; nach sich ziehen, zur Folge haben; andeuten, durchblicken lassen, schließen lassen auf.

impolite [impə'lait] unhöflich, schlecht erzogen, grob; **~ness** [-nis] Unhöflichkeit, Grobheit *f*.

impolitic [im'pɔlitik] unpolitisch, undiplomatisch, unklug, unvorsichtig.

imponderable [im'pɔndərəbl] *a* unwägbar, unmeßbar; nicht abzuschätzen; *s* etw Unwägbares *n*; *pl* Imponderabilien *pl*.

import [im'pɔ:t] *tr com* einführen, importieren; bedeuten, besagen; angehen, betreffen; wichtig, von Bedeutung sein für; *s* ['impɔ:t] Einfuhr *f*, Import; Einfuhr-, Importartikel; Inhalt *m*, Bedeutung *f*, Sinn *m*; Wichtigkeit *f*; **~ance** [im'pɔ:təns] Wichtigkeit, Bedeutung *f*, Gewicht *n fig*, Einfluß *m*, Wirkung *f*; *of ~~* von Bedeutung, von Belang; *of no ~~* ohne Bedeutung, bedeutungs-, belanglos, unwichtig; *to attach ~~ to s.th.* e-r S Bedeutung beimessen; **~ant** [-ənt] (ge)wichtig, bedeutend, erheblich (*to* für); folge-, einflußreich; überheblich, wichtigtuerisch; **~ation** [impɔ:'teiʃən] Einfuhr *f*, Import; Einfuhr-, Importartikel *m*; **~ certificate, licence, permit** Einfuhrerlaubnis, -bewilligung *f*; **~ dealer, ~er** [im'pɔ:tə] Einfuhrhändler, Importeur *m*; **~ duty, tariff** Einfuhrzoll *m*; **~ entry** Einfuhrdeklaration *f*; **~ figure** Einfuhrziffer *f*; **~ firm, house** Importgeschäft, -haus *n*, -firma *f*; **~ goods** *pl*, Einfuhrwaren *f pl*; **~ing** [im'pɔ:tiŋ]: *~~ country* Einfuhrland *n*; *~~ firm* Importfirma *f*; **~ list** Einfuhrliste *f*; **~premium** Einfuhrprämie *f*; **~ quota** Einfuhrkontingent *n*; **~ regulations** *pl* Einfuhrbestimmungen *f pl*; **~ restrictions** *pl* Einfuhrbeschränkungen *f pl*; **~ surplus** Einfuhrüberschuß *m*; **~ taxes** *pl* Einfuhrabgaben *f pl*; **~ trade** Einfuhr-, Import-, Passivhandel *m*.

importun|ate [im'pɔ:tjunit] auf-, zudringlich, lästig; **~e** [im'pɔ:tju:n, *Am* -'tju:n] *tr* mit Bitten belästigen; bestürmen; **~ity** [impɔ:'tjuniti] Auf-, Zudringlichkeit *f*; *pl* zudringliche, stürmische Bitten *f pl*.

impos|e [im'pouz] *tr (Last, Steuer, Strafe)* auferlegen (*on, upon s.o.* jdm); *(Last)* aufbürden; *(Hände)* auflegen; *(Strafe)* verhängen; *(Grenze)* setzen; aufzwingen, aufdrängen (*on, upon s.o.* jdm); *typ* ausschießen; *itr* Eindruck machen (*on, upon* auf); sich Freiheiten erlauben, sich etwas herausnehmen (*on, upon s.o.* jdm gegenüber); ausnützen, täuschen, betrügen, hintergehen (*on, upon s.o.* jdn); *to ~~ o.s. on, upon s.o.* sich jdm aufdrängen; **~ing** [-iŋ] eindrucksvoll, imponierend, imposant; **~ition** [impə'ziʃən] Auferlegung, Verhängung; Auf-, Zudringlichkeit; Zumutung, Ausnutzung; Bürde; Last; Abgabe, Steuer(last); Strafe, Strafarbeit; Täuschung *f*, Betrug *m*; *typ* Ausschießen *n*, Umbruch *m*; *~~ of taxes* Besteuerung *f*.

impossib|ility [impɔsi'biliti] (Ding *n* der) Unmöglichkeit *f*; **~le** [im'pɔsibl] unmöglich *a. fam. übertreibend*; *fam* unausstehlich, unerträglich, unglaublich.

impost ['impoust] Steuer, Abgabe *f*; Einfuhrzoll; *arch* Kämpfer *m*.

impost|or [im'pɔstə] Betrüger, Schwindler, Hochstapler *m*; **~ure** [-tʃə] Betrug, Schwindel *m*, Hochstapelei *f*.

impoten|ce, -cy ['impətəns(i)] Unfähigkeit, Schwäche *f*; Unvermögen *n*, Hilflosigkeit; *med* Impotenz *f*; **~t** ['-t] schwach, unfähig; hilflos; unwirksam; *med* impotent.

impound [im'paund] *tr (Vieh)* einpferchen; einsperren, -schließen; *(Wasser)* fassen; beschlagnahmen, in Verwahrung nehmen.

impoverish [im'pɔvəriʃ] *tr* arm machen; schwächen; aussaugen; abnutzen; *agr (Boden)* erschöpfen, auslaugen; *to be ~ed* verarmen.

impractic|ability [impræktikə'biliti] Unaus-, Undurchführbarkeit; Unbenutzbarkeit; Unlenksamkeit *f*; etwas Undurchführbares *n*; *(Straße)* Unpassierbarkeit *f*; **~able** [im'præktikəbl] unaus-, undurchführbar; unbrauchbar; unbenutzbar, ungangbar, unwegsam; *(Mensch)* unlenksam, störrisch, widerspenstig, schwierig (im Umgang); **~al** [-'præktikəl] unpraktisch.

imprecat|e ['imprikeit] *tr (Böses)* herabwünschen (*on, upon* auf); **~ion** [impri'keiʃən] Verwünschung, Verfluchung *f*, Fluch *m*; **~ory** ['imprikeitəri] verwünschend; Verwünschungs-.

impregnab|ility [impregnə'biliti] Uneinnehmbarkeit; Unerschütterlichkeit *f*; **~le** [im'pregnəbl] uneinnehmbar; unerschütterlich, unnachgiebig, fest (*to* gegenüber); unwiderlegbar.

impregnat|e ['impregneit, -'preg-] *tr (Ei)* befruchten; schwängern; *agr (Boden)* düngen, fruchtbar machen; durchtränken; *(mit Flüssigkeit)* sättigen; imprägnieren (*with* mit); *fig* erfüllen; *a* [im'pregnit] befruchtet; geschwängert; durchtränkt, gesättigt, imprägniert (*with* mit); voll (*with* von); **~ion** [impreg'neiʃən] Befruchtung *a. fig*; Schwängerung; Durchtränkung, Sättigung, Imprägnierung *f*.

impresario [impre'sɑ:riou] *pl -os* Impresario *m*.

imprescriptible [impris'kriptəbl] unverjährbar; unverlierbar; unverletzlich.

impress [im'pres] *tr* (ein)drücken, (ein)prägen (*with* mit; *on* auf); (ab-)stempeln; (auf-, ein-, hinein)drücken (*in* in); verleihen, mitteilen (*on, upon* dat); erfüllen, durchdringen (*with* mit); übertragen (*on, upon* auf); imponieren (*s.o.* jdm), beeindrucken, Eindruck machen auf, (stark) wirken auf; *(Worte)* einprägen (*in o.'s memory* im Gedächtnis), einschärfen, *fam* einbleuen (*on s.o.* jdm); *(Meinung)* aufzwingen (*on s.o.* jdm); *mil, bes. mar* pressen, gewaltsam (an)werben; requirieren, beschlagnahmen; einführen, Gebrauch machen von; *s* ['impres] Abdruck, Stempel *m*; Beeindruckung *f*, Eindruck; *fig* Einfluß *m*; Merkmal *n*; **~ed** [im'prest] *a* beeindruckt; durchdrungen, beseelt (*with* von); **~ion** [im'preʃən] Eindrücken *n*; Prägung, (Ab-)Stempelung *f*; Stempel; *fig* Eindruck *m*; Ahnung *f*, unbestimmte(s) Gefühl *n*; (Wachs-, Gips-) Abdruck; *typ* Druck; Abzug *m*; (Gesamt-)Auflage *f*; *to give the ~~* den Eindruck erwecken *od* machen (*of being s.th.* etw zu sein); **~ionability** [impreʃnə'biliti] Eindrucksfähigkeit, Empfänglichkeit *f*; **~ionable** [im'preʃnəbl] eindrucksfähig, empfänglich; leicht zu beeindrucken; **~ionism** [im'preʃnizm] Impressionismus *m*; **~ionist** [-'preʃnist] Impressionist *m*; **~ionistic** [impreʃə-

'nistik] impressionistisch; **~ive** [im'presiv] eindrucksvoll; ergreifend; **~ment** [im'presmənt] *mil mar* Pressen *n*, gewaltsame Anwerbung *f*.

imprimis [im'praimis] *adv* zuerst, zunächst, vorab.

imprint [im'print] *tr* (auf)drücken auf (*a letter with a postmark* e-e Briefmarke auf e-n Brief); (ab)stempeln; drücken (*on* auf); (ab)drucken; einprägen (*on s.o.'s memory* in jds Gedächtnis); *s* ['imprint] Druckstelle *f*; *(Fuß)* Abdruck *m*; sichtbare, deutliche Folge *f*, Stempel *fig*, Eindruck *m*; *typ* Impressum *n*, Druckvermerk *m*.

imprison [im'prizn] *tr* einsperren, ins Gefängnis stecken, einkerkern; gefangenhalten; *allg* einschränken, einengen, begrenzen; **~ment** [-mənt] Einkerkerung, Inhaftierung; Haft *f*, Gefängnis *n*; *false, illegal ~~* Freiheitsberaubung *f*; *~~ for life* lebenslängliche Haft *f*; *~~ on remand* Untersuchungshaft *f*.

improbab|ility [imprɔbə'biliti] Unwahrscheinlichkeit *f*; **~le** [im'prɔbəbl] unwahrscheinlich; unglaubhaft.

improbity [im'proubiti] Unredlichkeit; Unehrlichkeit *f*.

impromptu [im'prɔmptju:] *a* Stegreif-; *a adv* aus dem Stegreif; *s* Improvisation *f*; *theat* Stegreifstück *n*.

improp|er [im'prɔpə] unpassend, unangebracht, untauglich (*to* für); unrichtig, inkorrekt, falsch, ungenau; unzulässig; ungehörig, unziemlich, ungebührlich, unschicklich, unanständig; **~riety** [imprə'praiəti] Unangebrachtheit, Untauglichkeit; Unrichtigkeit, Ungenauigkeit; Ungehörigkeit, Unschicklichkeit, Ungebühr(lichkeit), Unanständigkeit *f*; Versehen *n*, Irrtum *m*; ungehörige(s) Benehmen *n*.

improv|able [im'pru:vəbl] (ver)besserungsfähig; *(Land)* ameliorierbar; **~e** [im'pru:v] *tr* aus-, benutzen, gebrauchen; (ver)bessern, (an)heben, auf e-e höhere Stufe stellen; wertvoller machen, im Wert, wertmäßig steigern, veredeln; *(Beziehungen)* ausbauen; *(Wert)* erhöhen; *agr (Land)* ameliorieren; *itr* besser werden; *(Gesundheit)* sich bessern; sich verbessern; *(Markt)* sich erholen; steigen (*in value* im Wert); *to ~~ (up)on* es besser machen als, übertreffen, überbieten; *to ~~ on acquaintance* bei näherer Bekanntschaft gewinnen; *to ~~ an occasion* e-e Gelegenheit wahrnehmen; **~ement** [-mənt] Verbesserung, Veredelung, Steigerung, Anhebung, Vervollkommnung; Errungenschaft; *(Gehalt)* Aufbesserung *f*; *(Preise)* Anziehen *n*; Fortschritt *m* (*on, over* gegenüber); *(Land)* Amelioration *f*; *mil (Stellung)* Ausbau *m*; *to be an ~~ on s.th.* etw übertreffen; *~~ industry* Veredelungsindustrie *f*; **~er** [-ə] Mittel *n* zur Verbesserung; Verbesserer; Volontär *m*.

improviden|ce [im'prɔvidəns] mangelnde Vorsorge, mangelnde Voraussicht *f*; **~t** [-t] leichtsinnig, sorglos.

improvis|ation [imprəvai'zeiʃən, -əvi-] Improvisation *f*; Behelf *m*; improvisierte Aufführung *f*, Stegreifvortrag *m*; **~e** ['imprəvaiz] *tr* improvisieren, extemporieren; unvorbereitet, aus dem Stegreif tun; **~ed** ['imprəvaizd] *a* improvisiert; behelfsmäßig, Behelfs-; aus dem Stegreif, Stegreif-.

impruden|ce [im'pru:dəns] Unüberlegtheit, Unklugheit, Unvorsichtigkeit *f*; unkluge(s) Verhalten *n*; **~t** [-t] unklug, unvorsichtig, unüberlegt.

impuden|ce ['impjudəns] Unverschämtheit, Frechheit *f*; **~t** [-t] unverschämt, frech; schamlos.

impugn [im'pju:n] *tr* bestreiten, in Frage stellen, bezweifeln; anfechten; **~able** [-əbl] fraglich; anfechtbar; **~ment** [im'pju:nmənt] Bestreitung; Anfechtung, Widerlegung *f*, Einwand *m*.

impuls|e ['impʌls] Anstoß, Antrieb, Impuls *a. phys physiol*; *psychol* Trieb, Drang *m*; Regung, Anwandlung *f*; Anreiz *m*, Anregung *f*; *to act on ~~* impulsiv handeln; **~ion** [im'pʌlʃən] Antrieb, Anstoß *m*; Triebkraft *f*; Stoß; Trieb, Drang *m*; Regung *f*; Anreiz *m*; **~ive** [im'pʌlsiv] (an)treibend; (leicht) erregbar, impulsiv, lebhaft; spontan, rasch; **~iveness** [-'pʌlsivnis] (leichte) Erregbarkeit, Lebhaftigkeit *f*.

impunity [im'pju:niti] Straflosigkeit, Straffreiheit *f*; *with ~* straffrei.

impur|e [im'pjuə] unrein *a. rel*, unsauber; unsittlich, unzüchtig, unkeusch; mit fremdem Zusatz, verfälscht; **~ity** [-riti] Unreinheit; Unanständigkeit; *tech* Verunreinigung *f*.

imput|able [im'pju:təbl] zuzuschreiben(d), anzurechnen(d); **~ation** [impju(:)'teiʃən] Unterstellung, Be-, Anschuldigung (*on* gegen); Beimessung, Anrechnung *f*; **~e** [im'pju:t] *tr* zuschreiben, zur Last legen, beimessen; zu-, anrechnen.

imshi ['imʃi] *interj mil sl* hau ab!

*

in [in] **1.** *prp (räumlich)* in; *~ the house* im Hause; ins Haus; *~ the envelope* im Umschlag; *~ the book* im Buch *a. fig*; *~ black* in Schwarz *(gekleidet)*; **2.** *(zeitlich)* an, im Verlauf *gen*, innerhalb *gen*; in, nach Ablauf *gen*; in, mit Bezug auf, in Hinsicht auf; **3.** *~ the affirmative* positiv; mit Ja *(antworten)*; *~ amazement* vor Verwunderung; *~ appearance* dem Anschein nach, anscheinend; *~ the circumstances* unter diesen Umständen; *~ my defence* zu meiner Verteidigung; *~ difficulties* in Schwierigkeiten; *~ this direction* in dieser Richtung; *~ the distance* in der Entfernung; *~ doubt* im Zweifel; *~ English* auf englisch; *~ fact* in der Tat; *~ his hand* in der Hand; *~ him* in, an, bei ihm; *~ a good humo(u)r* bei, in guter Laune; *~ ink* mit Tinte *(schreiben)*; *~ all my life* in meinem ganzen Leben; *~ the morning* am Morgen; morgens; *~ the night* in der Nacht; bei Nacht, nachts; *~ oil* in Öl *(gemalt)*; *~ my opinion* meiner Meinung nach, meines Erachtens; *~ pain* vor Schmerz(en); *~ particular* im besonderen; *~ prison* im Gefängnis; *~ a rage* in Wut; *~ the rain* im Regen; *~ reading* beim Lesen; *~ search for* auf der Suche nach; *~ sight* in Sicht; *~ size* in der Größe; *~ the sky* am Himmel; *~ a storm* bei Sturm; *~ the sun* in der Sonne, im Sonnenschein; *~ wood* in, aus Holz *(gearbeitet)*; **4.** *to be wanting ~* es fehlen lassen an; *to believe ~* glauben an; *to have a hand ~ s.th.* bei e-r S die Hand im Spiel haben, an e-r S beteiligt sein; *belief ~ God* Glauben an Gott; Gottesglauben *m*; *trust ~ God* Vertrauen auf Gott; Gottvertrauen *n*; **5.** *adv* hin-, herein; (dr)innen; daheim, zu Hause; da; dabei; vorhanden, erhältlich; an der Regierung; **6.** *to be ~ for s.th.* etw zu erwarten, zu befürchten haben; *for an examination* vor e-r Prüfung stehen; *to be ~ (good) with s.o.* mit jdm auf gutem Fuß stehen; *to breed ~ and ~* Inzucht treiben; *to have it ~ for s.o. (fam)* etw gegen jdn haben; *now you are ~ for it* jetzt geht's dir aber schlecht; *are you ~ on it, too?* sind Sie auch dabei? *she has it ~ for you* sie hat dich auf dem Strich; *summer is ~* der Sommer ist da; *~ with it!* hinein damit! **7.** *a* innen befindlich, Innen-; *(Tür)* nach innen gehend; hereinkommend; herkommend, -fahrend; intern *(ganz in e-r Anstalt lebend)*; an der Regierung befindlich; **8.** *s fam* Zugang *a. fig*; *fam* Einfluß *m*; *pl pol die* Regierungspartei; *sport die* am Spiel befindliche Partei; *the ~s and outs* alle Winkel und Ecken *pl*; alle Schliche *m pl*; *fig* alle Einzelheiten *f pl*; die Regierungspartei u. die Opposition; **9.** *tr dial (Ernte)* einbringen; *dial* einschließen; **~-and-~ breeding** Inzucht *f*; **~ so far as** *conj* soweit; **~ that** *conj* da; weil.

inability [inə'biliti] Unfähigkeit *f*, Unvermögen *n*; Mittel-, Machtlosigkeit *f*; *~ to pay* Zahlungsunfähigkeit *f*.

inaccessib|ility ['inæksesə'biliti] Unzugänglichkeit; Unnahbarkeit; Unerreichbarkeit *f*; **~le** [inæk'sesəbl] unzugänglich *a. fig* (*to* für); unbetretbar, unbefahrbar; *fig* unnahbar; unerreichbar.

inaccur|acy [in'ækjurəsi] Nachlässigkeit; Unrichtigkeit, Ungenauigkeit *f*; **~ate** [-rit] nachlässig; unrichtig, ungenau; fehlerhaft, falsch.

inact|ion [in'ækʃən] Untätigkeit *f*, Nichtstun *n*, Muße; Ruhe *f*; **~ive** [-tiv] untätig, müßig; in Ruhe befindlich, stilliegend; träge, faul; *med* unwirksam; *com* flau, geschäftslos; *(Kapital)* brachliegend; *(Markt)* lustlos; **~ivity** [inæk'tiviti] Untätigkeit, Muße *f*; Stilliegen *n*; Unwirksamkeit; Trägheit, Faulheit; *com* Lustlosigkeit, Stille, Flaute *f*.

inadequ|acy [in'ædikwəsi] Unangemessenheit; Unzulänglichkeit *f*; **~ate** [-kwit] unangemessen; unzulänglich; unzureichend, ungenügend.

inadmissib|ility ['inədmisi'biliti] Unzulässigkeit *f*; **~ble** [inəd'misibl] unzulässig; unstatthaft.

inadverten|ce, -cy [inəd'və:təns(i)] Unachtsamkeit; Nachlässigkeit, Fahrlässigkeit *f*; Versehen *n*, Irrtum *m*; **~t** [inəd'və:tənt] unaufmerksam, unachtsam; nachlässig, gleichgültig, fahrlässig (*to* gegenüber); unabsichtlich, unbedacht.

inadvisable [inəd'vaisəbl] nicht ratsam, nicht zu empfehlen(d), nicht empfehlenswert; unklug.

inalienab|ility [ineiljənə'biliti] Unveräußerlichkeit, Unübertragbarkeit *f*; **~le** [in'eiljənəbl] unveräußerlich; nicht übertragbar, unübertragbar.

inalterable [in'ɔ:ltərəbl] unveränderlich.

inamorat|a [inæmə'rɑ:tə] Geliebte *f*; **~o** [-tou] *pl -os* Liebhaber *m*.

inan|e [i'nein] leer, hohl, nichtig; inhalt-, bedeutungs-, sinnlos; dumm; **~ition** [inə'niʃən] Leere; *physiol* Entkräftung *f*; **~ity** [i'næniti] Leere, Hohlheit, Nichtigkeit; Inhalt-, Bedeutungs-, Sinnlosigkeit; Dummheit *f*.

inanimate [in'ænimit] unbeseelt, leblos, tot; dumpf, seelen-, geistlos.

inappeasable [inə'pi:zəbl] nicht zu besänftigen(d), unstillbar.

inapplicab|ility ['inæplikə'biliti] Unanwendbarkeit; Ungeeignetheit *f*; **~le** [in'æplikəbl] unanwendbar (*to* auf); ungeeignet, unpassend (*to* für); nicht zutreffend (*to* für).

inapposite [in'æpəzit] ungeeignet, unpassend; unerheblich, belanglos.

inappreciable [inə'pri:ʃəbl] nicht wahrnehmbar, unmerklich; unerheblich.

inapproachable [inə'proutʃəbl] unnahbar, unzugänglich; konkurrenzlos.

inappropriate [inə'proupriit] unangemessen, unangebracht; unpassend, un-

geeignet; **~ness** [-nis] Unangemessenheit; Ungeeignetheit *f*.
inapt [in'æpt] unpassend, ungeeignet, untauglich; ungeschickt, linkisch; **~itude** [-itju:d], **~ness** [-nis] Ungeeignetheit, Untauglichkeit; Ungeschicktheit *f*.
inarch [in'ɑ:tʃ] *tr (Gartenbau)* ablaktieren, ab-, ansäugen.
inarticulate [inɑ:'tikjulit] undeutlich, inartikuliert; sprechunfähig, stumm; unfähig, deutlich zu sprechen; *zoo* ungegliedert; **~ness** [-nis] Undeutlichkeit (der Sprache); Sprechunfähigkeit; *zoo* Ungegliedertheit *f*.
inart|ificial [inɑ:ti'fiʃəl] natürlich; kunstlos; einfach, schlicht; **~istic** [inɑ:'tistik] unkünstlerisch.
inasmuch [inəz'mʌtʃ] *conj*: *~as* da, weil.
inattent|ion [inə'tenʃən] Unaufmerksamkeit; Unachtsamkeit, Nachlässigkeit *f (to* gegenüber); **~ive** [-tiv] unaufmerksam, unachtsam, nachlässig (*to* gegenüber *dat*).
inaudib|ility [inɔ:də'biliti] Unhörbarkeit *f*; **~le** [in'ɔ:dəbl] unhörbar.
inaugur|al [i'nɔ:gjurəl] *a* Eröffnungs-, Einweihungs-, Antritts-; *s* Antrittsrede, -vorlesung *f*; **~ate** [-reit] *tr* (feierlich) (ins Amt) einsetzen; (feierlich) eröffnen, einweihen; (feierlich) beginnen; einführen; **~ation** [inɔ:gju'reiʃən] Amtseinsetzung; (feierliche) Eröffnung; Einweihung *f*; Beginn *m*, Einleitung *f*; *I~~ Day* Tag *m* der Amtseinsetzung des Präsidenten der USA *(20. Januar)*.
inauspicious [inɔ:s'piʃəs] ungünstig, unglücklich; von schlechter Vorbedeutung, unheilvoll.
inboard ['inbɔ:d] *adv mar* (b)innenbords; *a mar* Innenbord-; *tech* Innen-; *s mar* Innenbordmotor *m*.
inborn ['in'bɔ:n] *a* angeboren.
in-bound ['inbaund] *aero* im Anflug; *mar* auf der Heimfahrt (befindlich).
inbred ['in'bred] *a* angeboren; aus Inzucht hervorgegangen.
inbreeding ['in'bri:diŋ] Inzucht *f*.
incalculab|ility [inkælkjulə'biliti] Unberechenbarkeit; Unzuverlässigkeit *f*; **~le** [in'kælkjuləbl] unberechenbar, unabsehbar; unzuverlässig, unsicher.
incandesc|ence, -cy [inkæn'desns(i)] Weißglut *f*; **~ent** [-ənt] weißglühend; (hell)glänzend; *fig* leuchtend; *~~ bulb* Glühbirne *f*; *~~ lamp, light* Glühlampe *f*, -licht *n*.
incantation [inkæn'teiʃən] Beschwörung *f*; Zauber; Zauberspruch *m*.
incapab|ility [inkeipə'biliti] Unfähigkeit; Untauglichkeit, Ungeeignetheit *f*; **~le** [in'keipəbl] unfähig, nicht imstande, nicht in der Lage (*of doing* zu tun); untauglich, ungeeignet (*of* für); *jur* nicht berechtigt, unfähig; *(legally ~~)* geschäftsunfähig; *~~ of proof* unbeweisbar; *~~ of work* arbeitsunfähig.
incapac|itate [inkə'pæsiteit] *tr* unfähig machen (*for, from* für, zu); disqualifizieren; entmündigen; **~itated** [-id] *a* arbeits-, geschäftsunfähig; **~itation** ['inkəpæsi'teiʃən] Disqualifizierung; Entmündigung *f*; *~~ for work* Arbeitsunfähigkeit *f*; **~ity** [inkə'pæsiti] Untüchtigkeit, Unfähigkeit (*for* zu); *(legal ~~)* Geschäftsunfähigkeit *f*.
incarcerat|e [in'kɑ:səreit] *tr* einsperren, gefangen setzen; *med* einklemmen; **~ion** [in'kɑ:sə'reiʃən] Gefangensetzung; *med (Bruch)* Einklemmung *f*.
incarn|ate [in'kɑ:nit] *a* Fleisch, Mensch geworden; verkörpert, personifiziert, leibhaftig; fleischfarben, rosig, rot; *tr* ['inkɑ:neit] verkörpern, darstellen; verwirklichen; **~ation** [inkɑ:'neiʃən] Fleisch-, Menschwerdung *(Christi)*; *allg* Verkörperung *f*, Inbegriff, Typ *m*.
incase [in'keis] *s. encase.*
incautious [in'kɔ:ʃəs] unvorsichtig; sorglos; unklug; unbedacht, übereilt; **~ness** [-nis] Unvorsichtigkeit; Sorglosigkeit; Unbedachtheit *f*.
incendiar|ism [in'sendjərizm] Brandstiftung; *fig* Aufwiegelung, Verhetzung *f*; **~y** [-i] *a* Brandstiftungs-; Brand-; aufrührerisch, Hetz-; *s* Brandstifter; *fig* Aufwiegler, Aufrührer, Hetzer *m*; *~~ bomb* Brandbombe *f*; *~~ speech* Brandrede *f*.
incense 1. [in'sens] *tr* wütend, zornig machen, in Wut bringen, erzürnen (*against* gegen; *with, at, by* mit); **2.** ['insens] *s* Weihrauch; *allg* Wohlgeruch *m*; *fig* Beweihräucherung, Schmeichelei *f*; *tr* mit Weihrauchduft, mit Wohlgeruch erfüllen; Weihrauch streuen (*s.o.* jdm); be(weih)räuchern.
incentive [in'sentiv] *a* anregend, anspornend; *s* Antrieb *m*, Ermutigung; Anregung *f*, Anreiz *m (to* zu); **~ pay, wage** Leistungslohn *m*.
incept|ion [in'sepʃən] Anfang, Beginn *m*; **~ive** [in'septiv] *a* anfangend, beginnend; Anfangs-; *gram* inchoativ; *s (~~ verb) gram* Inchoativ(um) *n*.
incertitude [in'sə:titjud] Ungewißheit; Unsicherheit *f*.
incessant [in'sesnt] unablässig, unaufhörlich, beständig, ununterbrochen.
incest ['insest] Blutschande *f*; **~uous** [in'sestjuəs] blutschänderisch.
inch [intʃ] Zoll *m* ($^{1}/_{12}$ *Fuß = 2,54 cm)*; Kleinigkeit *f*, ein bißchen, (ein) wenig; *tr* (langsam) schieben; *itr* sich (langsam, schrittweise) bewegen; *to ~ along* dahinschleichen; *to ~ forward (tr)* langsam vorschieben; *itr* vorrücken; *to ~ out* hinausschieben, -drängen; (sparsam) zumessen; *at an ~* um Haaresbreite, um ein Haar; *by ~es, ~ by ~* nach und nach, Schritt für Schritt, (ganz) allmählich; *every ~* jeder Zoll, von Kopf bis Fuß, durch und durch; *within an ~ of* ganz dicht an, bei; *(mit Dauerform)* beinahe, fast; *not to yield an ~* keinen Fußbreit nachgeben; *give him an ~ and he'll take an ell* wenn man ihm den kleinen Finger gibt, nimmt er die ganze Hand; **~ed** [intʃt] *a in Zssgen* -zöllig; **~meal**: *(by ~~)* Schritt für Schritt, nach und nach, langsam, allmählich; **~ rule** Zollstock *m*.
inchoat|e ['inko(u)eit] *a* noch in den Anfängen steckend; **~ive** ['inko(u)eitiv] *a selten = ~e (a)*; *gram* inchoativ; *s* Inchoativ(um) *n*.
inciden|ce ['insidəns] Einfall; Einfluß; Umfang *m*, Vorkommen *n*, Verbreitung, Häufigkeit *f*; *phys* Einfall(srichtung *f*) *m*, Auftreffen, Einfallen *n*; *angle of ~~ (phys)* Einfallswinkel; *aero* Anstellwinkel *m*; **~t** ['insidənt] *a* einfallend; zufällig; vorkommend (*to* bei); verbunden (*to* mit); gehörend (*to* zu); *jur* gebunden (*to* an), abhängig (*to* von); *s* Zufall; Zwischenfall; Vorfall *m*, Vorkommnis, Ereignis, Geschehen *n*; Nebenumstand *m*; *lit* Zwischenhandlung, Episode *f*; **~tal** [insi'dentl] *a* zufällig, beiläufig; Neben-; gehörend (*to* zu); *mus* Begleit-; *s* Nebensache *f*, Anhängsel *n*; *pl* Vermischte(s), Diverse(s) *n*, diverse Ausgaben *f pl*, Nebenspesen *pl*; *to be ~~ to* gehören zu; *~~ expenses (pl)* Nebenausgaben *f pl*; *~~ income* Nebeneinkommen *n*; *~~ intention* Nebenabsicht *f*; *~~ly (adv)* so nebenbei, nebenbei gesagt, übrigens; *~~ music* Hintergrundsmusik *f*; *~~ plea (jur)* Einwand *m*, Einrede *f*; *~~ question* Neben-, Zwischenfrage *f*.
incinerat|e [in'sinəreit] *tr* einäschern, verbrennen; *tech* veraschen; **~ion** [insinə'reiʃən] Einäscherung, Verbrennung; *tech* Veraschung *f*; **~or** [in'sinəreitə] Verbrennungsofen *m*.
incipien|ce, -cy [in'sipiəns(i)] Beginn, Anfang(sstadium *n*) *m*; **~t** [-t] beginnend; Anfangs-.
incis|e [in'saiz] *tr* (ein)schneiden in; einkerben; *(Figuren, Inschrift)* einschneiden, einritzen; **~ion** [in'siʒən] Einschnitt *a. med*; Schnitt *m*, Kerbe; Markierung *f*; **~ive** [in'saisiv] (ein-)schneidend; scharf; beißend; durchdringend; **~or** [-ə] Schneidezahn *m*.
incit|ation [insai'teiʃən] Ansporn *m*, Anregung; Aufreizung *f*; **~e** [in'sait] *tr* anregen, auf-, anreizen, anstacheln, aufwiegeln, aufhetzen (*to* zu); **~ement** [-mənt] Anregung *f*; Anreiz, Antrieb *m*, Triebfeder (*to* für); Aufwiegelung, Aufhetzung *f*.
incivility [insi'viliti] Unhöflichkeit, Grobheit *f*.
incivism ['insivizm] Mangel *m* an staatsbürgerlicher Gesinnung.
inclemen|cy [in'klemənsi] Ungunst; Rauheit, Strenge, Härte; Unfreundlichkeit *f*; **~t** [-t] ungünstig; rauh, streng, hart; barsch, unfreundlich.
inclin|ation [inkli'neiʃən] Neigung *f*, Hang *m a. fig*; *fig* Vorliebe *f* (*for* für); *tech* Neigungswinkel *m*; *(Kompaß)* Inklination *f*; **~e** [in'klain] *s* (Ab-)Hang *m*, Steigung, geneigte Fläche *f*; *itr (Fläche)* sich neigen, sich senken (*to* zu); *(Mensch)* sich neigen, sich beugen; dazu neigen (*to, toward* zu; *to do* zu tun); e-n Hang, e-e Neigung, e-e Vorliebe haben; *tr (Fläche)* abschrägen; e-e Neigung geben (*s.th.* e-r S); *fig* geneigt machen, veranlassen; **~ed** [in'klaind] *a* geneigt *a. fig*; schräg, schief; *~~ plane (phys)* schiefe Ebene *f*; **~ometer** [inkli'nɔmitə] Neigungsmesser *m*.
inclos|e [in'klouz] *tr* einschließen; umgeben; *(e-m Brief)* beifügen; enthalten; *please find ~ed* in der Anlage erhalten Sie; **~ure** [in'klouʒə] Einschließung; Umfassung(smauer) *f*, Zaun; abgeschlossene(r) Platz *m*; *(Brief)* Anlage *f*.
includ|e [in'klu:d] *tr* einschließen, umfassen; enthalten; einbeziehen, einbegreifen; mit aufnehmen (*in* in); *tech* mit einbauen; *to ~~ in a bill* auf e-e Rechnung setzen; **~ed** [-id] *a* einbegriffen, enthalten, eingeschlossen, einschließlich, inklusiv; **~ing** [-iŋ] einschließlich (*s.th.* e-r S).
inclus|ion [in'klu:ʒən] Einschließung *f*; Einschluß *m a. min*; **~ive** [in'klu:siv] eingerechnet, einschließlich (*of* gen); umfassend, gesamt; *to be ~ of* einschließen; *all ~~* alles (e)inbegriffen; *~~ terms (pl)* Pauschalpreis *m*.
incog [in'kɔg] *a adv fam* inkognito.
incogn|ito [in'kɔgnitou] *a adv* inkognito; unerkannt; unter fremdem Namen; *s pl -os* Inkognito *n*.
incoheren|ce, -cy ['inko(u)'hiərəns(i)] Zs.hanglosigkeit *f*; Widerspruch *m*; unzs.hängende Rede *f*, Gedanken *m pl*; **~t** [-t] zs.hanglos; lose (anea.gereiht), (logisch) unverbunden, unzs.hängend, widerspruchsvoll.
incombustib|ility [inkəmbʌstə'biliti] Unverbrennbarkeit *f*; **~le** [inkəm'bʌstəbl] *a* unverbrennbar; feuersicher; *s* unverbrennbare(s) Material *n*.
income ['inkəm] Einkommen *n*, Einkünfte *pl* (*from* aus); Ertrag *m*; *to draw an ~* ein Einkommen beziehen (*from* aus); *to exceed, to outrun o.'s ~* über s-e Verhältnisse leben; *to live up to o.'s ~* sein (ganzes) Geld ausgeben *od* verbrauchen; *to live within o.'s ~* mit s-m

Gelde auskommen; *additional, casual, extra* ~ Nebeneinkommen *n*, -einkünfte *pl*; *earned* ~ Arbeitseinkommen *n*; Einkünfte *pl* aus selbständiger Arbeit; *national* ~ National-, Volkseinkommen *n*; Staatseinkünfte *pl*; *net* ~ Nettoeinkommen *n*; Reinertrag, -erlös *m*; *unearned* ~ Kapitaleinkommen *n*; **~-bracket** Einkommensgruppe, -stufe *f*; **~r** ['-ə] Hereinkommende(r), Eintretende(r), Ankömmling; Zugezogene(r); Nachfolger *m*; **~-tax** Einkommensteuer *f*; *corporation* ~~ Körperschaft(s)steuer *f*; ~~ *computation* Einkommensteuerberechnung *f*; ~~ *law* Einkommensteuergesetz *n*; ~~ *rate* Einkommensteuersatz *m*; ~~ *return* Einkommensteuererklärung *f*.

incoming ['inkʌmiŋ] *a* (her)einkommend, eingehend, -laufend; zurückkommend; neu eingehend, neu ein-, antretend; *(Jahr)* beginnend; *tech* ankommend; *s* Eintritt *m*; *(Zug)* Einlaufen *n*; *(Waren)* Zugang *m*; *pl* (Zahlungs-)Eingänge *m pl*; ~ **orders** *pl* Auftragseingänge *m pl*.

incommensur|ability ['inkəmenʃərə'biliti] Unvergleichbarkeit; inkommensurable Eigenschaft *f*; **~able** [inkə'menʃərəbl] nicht (mit gleichem Maßstab) meßbar; nicht vergleichbar, unvereinbar (*with* mit); *math* inkommensurabel; **~ate** [inkə'menʃərit] ungleich; nicht gewachsen (*to, with* dat); nicht vergleichbar.

incommod|e [inkə'moud] *tr* belästigen, zur Last fallen (*s.o.* jdm); **~ious** [-iəs] lästig, unbequem, mühevoll; (räumlich) beengt.

incommunic|able [inkə'mju:nikəbl] nicht mittelbar; **~ado** [inkəmjuni'kɑ:dou] *a Am* von der Außenwelt abgeschnitten; *jur* in Einzelhaft; **~ative** [inkə'mjunikətiv] nicht mitteilsam, zurückhaltend, reserviert, schweigsam.

incomparable [in'kɔmpərəbl] nicht vergleichbar (*to, with* mit); unvergleichlich.

incompatib|ility ['inkəmpætə'biliti] Unvereinbarkeit; Unverträglichkeit *f*; **~le** [inkəm'pætəbl] unvereinbar (*with* mit); nicht zs.passend; *(Mensch)* unverträglich; *to be* ~~ *with* nicht passen zu, sich nicht vereinbaren.

incompeten|ce, -cy [in'kɔmpitəns(i)] Unfähigkeit, Unzulänglichkeit; Unzuständigkeit, Inkompetenz; *Am jur* Geschäftsunfähigkeit *f*; **~t** [-t] unfähig, unbrauchbar, unzulänglich; unbefugt, unzuständig, inkompetent (*to* für); *Am jur* nicht geschäftsfähig; ~~ *to act* handlungsunfähig.

incomplet|e [inkəm'pli:t] unvollständig *a. chem*, unfertig, unvollkommen, mangelhaft.

incomprehensib|ility [inkɔmprihensə'biliti] Unbegreiflichkeit *f*; **~le** [inkɔmpri'hensəbl] unverständlich, unbegreiflich.

incompressible [inkəm'presəbl] nicht zs.drückbar, unelastisch.

incomputable [inkəm'pju:təbl] unberechenbar.

inconceivab|ility ['inkənsi:və'biliti], Unbegreiflichkeit, Unfaßbarkeit *f*; **~le** [inkən'si:vəbl] unbegreiflich, unfaßbar, -lich, undenkbar.

inconclusive [inkən'klu:siv] nicht überzeugend, nicht beweiskräftig, nicht schlüssig; nicht endgültig; wirkungs-, ergebnis-, erfolglos; **~ness** [-nis] Mangel *m* an Beweiskraft.

incongru|ity [inkɔŋ'gru(:)iti] Unvereinbarkeit; Unausgeglichenheit *f*; Mißverhältnis *n*; Ungereimtheit; Ungeeignetheit; *math* Inkongruenz *f*; **~ous** [in'kɔŋgruəs] nicht zs.passend, unvereinbar; disharmonisch, unausgeglichen; widerspruchsvoll; unrecht; unvernünftig, widersinnig, ungereimt; unpassend, ungeeignet; *math* inkongruent.

inconsequen|ce [in'kɔnsikwəns] Widersinn *m*; Inkonsequenz; Belanglosigkeit *f*; **~t** [-t] folgewidrig; inkonsequent; belanglos; **~tial** [inkɔnsi'kwenʃəl] inkonsequent, unlogisch, widersinnig, sprunghaft; belanglos, unwichtig.

inconsider|able [inkən'sidərəbl] bedeutungslos, unbedeutend, unwichtig, belanglos; **~ate** [inkən'sidərit] unüberlegt, unbesonnen, gedankenlos; achtlos; rücksichtslos (*towards* gegen); **~ateness** [-ritnis] Unüberlegtheit; Gedankenlosigkeit; Rücksichtslosigkeit *f*.

inconsisten|ce, -cy [inkən'sistəns(i)] Unvereinbarkeit *f*; Widerspruch *m*; Unbeständigkeit *f*; **~t** [-t] unvereinbar (*with* mit); widersprechend, widerspruchsvoll; uneinheitlich; inkonsequent; unbeständig, wechselnd.

inconsolable [inkən'souləbl] untröstlich; mit gebrochenem Herzen.

inconspicuous [inkən'spikjuəs] unauffällig, kaum bemerkbar, unmerklich, unscheinbar.

inconstan|cy [in'kɔnstənsi] Unbeständigkeit; Wechselhaftigkeit, Wandelbarkeit; Ungleichheit, Ungleichmäßigkeit, Unregelmäßigkeit *f*; **~t** [-t] unbeständig, unstet, schwankend, inkonstant; wechselhaft, wandelbar; ungleich(mäßig), verschieden(artig).

incontestab|ility [inkəntestə'biliti] Unbestreitbarkeit *f*; **~le** [inkən'testəbl] unbestreitbar, unstreitig, unanfechtbar; *(Beweis)* unwiderlegbar.

incontinen|ce [in'kɔntinəns] mangelnde Enthaltsamkeit; Unkeuschheit *f*; ~~ *of urine* Harnfluß *m*; **~t** [-t] *a* unenthaltsam, unkeusch, ausschweifend; *(~~ of information)* geschwätzig; *med* unfähig, das Wasser zu halten; *adv* unterbrochen; **~t(ly)** [-li] *adv lit* sofort, unverzüglich, alsbald.

incontrovertible [inkɔntrə'və:təbl] unbestreitbar, unwiderlegbar, unleugbar.

inconvenien|ce [inkən'vi:njəns] *s* Unbequemlichkeit; Lästigkeit, Mühe, Schwierigkeit *f*, Umstände *m pl*; Ungehörigkeit *f*; *tr* belästigen, bemühen; Umstände, Mühe, Schwierigkeiten machen (*s.o.* jdm); *to put s.o. to great* ~~ jdm große Ungelegenheiten bereiten; **~t** [-t] unbequem, unbehaglich, lästig, mühevoll, mühselig, umständlich.

inconvertib|ility [inkənvə:tə'biliti] *fin* Unkonvertierbarkeit; Nichteinlösbarkeit; *(Waren)* Nichtumsetzbarkeit *f*; **~le** [inkən'və:təbl] *(Papiergeld)* nicht konvertierbar, nicht einlösbar; *(Waren)* nicht umsetzbar.

inconvincible [inkən'vinsəbl] nicht zu überzeugen(d).

incorporat|e [in'kɔ:pəreit] *tr* (sich) einverleiben, (sich) angliedern, eingliedern, (in sich) aufnehmen; einarbeiten, einbauen, einsetzen; *(als Mitglied)* aufnehmen (*in* in); (zu e-r Körperschaft, zu e-m Verein) zs.schließen; *Am* als Aktiengesellschaft eintragen; gestalten, Gestalt geben, verleihen (*s.th.* e-r S); (amtlich) eintragen, registrieren, inkorporieren; *itr* sich zs.schließen (*with* mit); e-e Körperschaft gründen; e-n Verein bilden; innewohnen; *a* [-rit] vereinigt, (mitea.) verbunden, zs.geschlossen; einverleibt, eingegliedert, aufgenommen; **~ed** [-id] *a* einverleibt; zs.geschlossen, vereinigt; *(Verein)* eingetragen; *Am* als Aktiengesellschaft eingetragen; *to be* ~~ *in* zugehören zu; ~~ *accountant* Wirtschaftsprüfer *m*; ~~ *company (Am)* Aktiengesellschaft *f*; ~~ *town (Am)* Stadtgemeinde *f*; **~ion** [inkɔ:pə'reiʃən] Einverleibung; Registrierung; Verbindung *f*, Zs.schluß *m*; Eingemeindung; Gründung *f* e-r juristischen Person; *articles (pl) of* ~~ Satzung *f*; **~or** [-ə] *Am com* Gründungsmitglied *n*.

incorpore|al [inkɔ:'pɔ:riəl] unkörperlich, immateriell, geistig.

incorrect [inkə'rekt] unrichtig, unwahr; falsch; fehlerhaft, ungenau; ungehörig.

incorrigible [in'kɔridʒəbl] *a* unverbesserlich; nicht korrigierbar; *s* unverbesserliche(r) Mensch *m*.

incorrupt|ibility [inkərʌptə'biliti] Unbestechlichkeit; Unverderblichkeit *f*; **~ible** [inkə'rʌptəbl] unbestechlich; unverderblich, unzerstörbar.

*

increase [in'kri:s] *itr* (an)wachsen, (an-)steigen, zunehmen (*a. zahlenmäßig*); sich vergrößern, sich vermehren, sich erhöhen; *tr* vergrößern, erhöhen; vermehren; steigern; *(Preis)* heraufsetzen; *s* ['inkri:s] Wachstum *n*, Vergrößerung; Erhöhung, Steigerung (*on* gegenüber); Zulage; Vermehrung, Zunahme *f*; Aufschlag; Zuwachs; Fortschritt *m*; *(Strafe)* Verschärfung *f*; *on the* ~ im Zunehmen, im Steigen, (an-)steigend; im Wachsen; *to* ~ *in size* an Größe zunehmen; ~ *of capital* Kapitalerhöhung *f*; ~ *in consumption* Verbrauchssteigerung *f*; ~ *in costs* Kostensteigerung *f*; ~ *in demand* steigende Nachfrage *f*; ~ *in efficiency* Leistungssteigerung *f*; ~ *of exports, imports* Aus-, Einfuhrsteigerung *f*; ~ *in pay* Gehalts-, *mil* Solderhöhung *f*; ~ *in population* Bevölkerungszunahme *f*, -zuwachs *m*; ~ *in power* Machtzunahme *f*; ~ *in prices* Preiserhöhung *f*, -aufschlag *m*; ~ *of production* Produktionssteigerung *f*; ~ *in the discount rate* Diskonterhöhung *f*; ~ *of rent* Mieterhöhung *f*; ~ *in salary* Gehaltserhöhung, -aufbesserung, -zulage *f*; ~ *in taxes* Steuererhöhung *f*; ~ *of trade* Aufschwung *m* des Handels; ~ *in turnover* Umsatzsteigerung *f*; ~ *in, of value* Wertsteigerung *f*, -zuwachs *m*; ~ *in velocity* Geschwindigkeitszunahme *f*; ~ *of wages* Lohnerhöhung *f*; ~ *in weight* Gewichtszunahme *f*.

incredib|ility [inkredi'biliti] Unglaubhaftigkeit *f*; **~le** [in'kredəbl] unglaubhaft, -würdig, -lich.

incredul|ity [inkri'dju:liti] Ungläubigkeit *f*; **~ous** [in'kredjuləs] ungläubig, zweifelnd, skeptisch.

increment ['inkrimənt] Wachstum *n*, Zuwachs *m*, Zunahme (*of* an); Erhöhung, Steigerung *f a. math*; Vermögenszuwachs; *(unearned ~)* Wertzuwachs *m*, -steigerung *f*, Mehrwert; Gewinn *m*.

incriminat|e [in'krimineit] *tr* an-, beschuldigen; e-s Verbrechens, e-s Vergehens anklagen; belasten; **~ing** [-iŋ], **~ory** [in'kriminətəri] belastend; Belastungs-; **~ion** [inkrimi'neiʃən] An-, Beschuldigung; Belastung *f*.

incrust [in'krʌst] *tr* mit e-r Kruste überziehen, überkrusten; *arch (Kunstgewerbe)* inkrustieren; **~ation** [inkrʌs'teiʃən] Krusten-, Schlacken-, Kesselsteinbildung; Überkrustung; *tech* Sinterung *f*, Kesselstein *m*; *arch (Kunstgewerbe)* Bekleidung *f*, Einlegen *n*, Verschalung, Inkrustation *f*.

incub|ate ['inkjubeit] *tr* be-, ausbrüten; in e-r Nährlösung züchten; *fig* aushecken; *itr* ausgebrütet werden; **~ation** [inkju'beiʃən] (Aus-, Be-)Brüten *n*; *med* Inkubation(sstadium *n*) *f*; **~ator** [-ə] Brutapparat, -ofen, *med*

-kasten *m*; **~us** ['iŋkjubəs] Alp(drükken *n*) *m*; *fig* Last, Bürde *f*.

inculcat|e ['inkʌlkeit, *Am* in'k-] *tr* einschärfen, einprägen, *fam* einbleuen (*on, upon* dat); **~ion** [inkʌl'keiʃən] Einprägung, Einschärfung *f*.

inculpat|e ['inkʌlpeit, *Am* in'k-] *tr* an-, beschuldigen; belasten; anklagen; tadeln; **~ion** [inkʌl'peiʃən] Beschuldigung; Belastung *f*; Tadel *m*.

incumben|cy [in'kʌmbənsi] (drückende) Last; Obliegenheit, Pflicht *f*; Amt *n*, Pfründe; Amtsdauer, -zeit *f*; **~t** [-t] *a* aufliegend; drückend; obliegend; *poet* drohend; *s* Pfründeninhaber; Pfarrer; *Am* Amtsinhaber *m*; *to be ~~ (up)on s.o.* jdm obliegen; *it is ~~ on him* er ist dazu verpflichtet.

incunabul|um [inkju(:)'næbjuləm] *pl -a* [-ə] Wiegendruck *m*, Inkunabel *f*; *pl a. allg* Anfangsstadium *n*.

incur [in'kə:] *tr* sich *(etw Unerwünschtes)* zuziehen, auf sich laden, auf sich nehmen; herbeiführen; *to ~ a danger* sich e-r Gefahr aussetzen; *to ~ debts* Schulden machen; *to ~ heavy expenses* sich in große Unkosten stürzen; *to ~ a liability* e-e Verpflichtung eingehen; *to ~ the loss of s.th.* e-r S verlustig gehen; etw verwirken; *to ~ a loss* e-n Verlust erleiden; *to ~ a risk* ein Risiko eingehen *od* übernehmen.

incurab|ility [inkjuərə'biliti] Unheilbarkeit *f*; **~le** [in'kjuərəbl] *a* unheilbar; *s* unheilbare(r) Kranke(r) *m*.

incuri|ous [in'kjuəriəs] nicht neugierig, gleichgültig, uninteressiert.

incursion [in'kə:ʃən] (feindlicher) Einfall, plötzliche(r) Angriff; Einbruch *m*, Invasion *f*; Streifzug *m*; *(Wasser)* Hereinströmen, -fluten *n*.

incurve [in'kə:v] *tr itr* (sich) einwärts biegen, krümmen, beugen.

incuse [iŋ'kju:z] *s* Prägung *f*; *a*, **~d** [-d] *a* geprägt.

*

indebted [in'detid] *a* verschuldet (*to* bei); in Schulden; (zu Dank) verpflichtet; *to be ~ to s.o. for s.th.* jdm etw zu verdanken haben; **~ness** [-nis] Verbindlichkeit, Verpflichtung; Schuldenlast, Verschuldung *f*; Schuldbetrag *m*; Gesamtschuld *f*.

indecenc|y [in'di:snsi] Ungehörigkeit; Unanständigkeit *f*; **~t** [-t] unpassend, ungebührlich; unanständig, anstößig, obszön; *~~ assault* Sittlichkeitsvergehen *n*.

indecipherable [indi'saifərəbl] unentzifferbar; unleserlich.

indecis|ion [indi'siʒən] Unentschlossenheit; Wankelmütigkeit *f*, Wankelmut *m*; Zögern, Schwanken *n*; **~ive** [indi'saisiv] nicht entscheidend, nicht endgültig, unentschieden; unentschlossen, wankelmütig, zögernd.

indeclinable [indi'klainəbl] *gram* undeklinierbar, ohne Kasusendungen.

indecomposable ['indi:kəm'pouzəbl] nicht ausea.nehmbar; unzersetzlich, unzerlegbar (*into* in).

indec|orous [in'dekərəs] unziemlich, unschicklich; **~orum** [indi'kɔ:rəm] Unziemlichkeit, Unschicklichkeit *f*.

indeed [in'di:d] *adv* in der Tat, natürlich, allerdings, gewiß, sicher; *interj* wirklich? so? allerdings! das ist ja allerhand! nicht möglich! *thank you very much ~* vielen herzlichen Dank!

indefatigable [indi'fætigəbl] unermüdlich.

indefeasible [indi'fi:zəbl] unantastbar; unveräußerlich.

indefectible [indi'fektibl] haltbar; fehlerfrei.

indefensib|ility [indifensi'biliti] Unhaltbarkeit *f*; **~le** [-əbl] *mil* nicht zu verteidigen(d), unhaltbar *a. fig*.

indefinable [indi'fainəbl] unbestimmbar, undefinierbar.

indefinite [in'definit] unbegrenzt; undeutlich, verschwommen; unsicher, ungewiß, unbestimmt; unbeschränkt; *bot* variabel, veränderlich *(in der Zahl)*; *gram* unbestimmt; **~ness** [-nis] Unbegrenztheit; Undeutlichkeit; Unbestimmtheit *f*.

indelib|ility [indeli'biliti] Unvergänglichkeit, Unauslöschlichkeit *f*; **~le** [in'delibl] *(Schrift, Farbe)* nicht zu entfernen(d), dauerhaft; *fig* unauslöschlich, unvergänglich; *~~ ink* Wäschetinte *f*; *~~ pencil* Tintenstift *m*.

indelic|acy [in'delikəsi] Unfeinheit, Grobheit; Taktlosigkeit *f*, Mangel *m* an Feingefühl; Unanständigkeit *f*; **~ate** [in'delikit] unzart, unfein, grob, roh, rauh; unziemlich, ungebührlich, taktlos; gemein, unanständig.

indemn|ification [indemnifi'keiʃən] Entschädigung, Schadloshaltung, Ersatzleistung; Abfindung, Entschädigung(ssumme) *f*, Schadenersatz *m*; *claim of ~~* Schadenersatzanspruch *m*; *~~ in cash* Geldentschädigung *f*; **~ify** [in'demnifai] *tr* entschädigen, schadlos halten, Schadenersatz leisten (*for* für); sicherstellen (*against, from* gegen); *jur* Straflosigkeit zusichern (*s.o.* jdm); **~ity** [in'demniti] Schadenersatz *m*, Entschädigung; Abfindung; Sicherstellung, Versicherung; Amnestie, Straflosigkeit *f*; *to pay full ~~ to s.o.* jdn den Schaden in voller Höhe ersetzen; *~~ bond* Garantieschein *m*, -erklärung; Ausfallbürgschaft *f*.

indent [in'dent] *tr* (ein)kerben, auszacken, einschneiden, zähnen; ausbuchten; *(Zeile)* einrücken; *(Urkunde)* doppelt ausfertigen; *(Vertrag)* (ab-)schließen; *(Waren)* bestellen; *itr* (ein-)gekerbt, ausgezackt, gezähnt sein; Einkerbungen, Zacken haben; einrücken, e-n Absatz machen; e-e doppelte Ausfertigung machen; e-n Vertrag (ab)schließen; *to ~ on s.o. for s.th.* etw bei jdm anfordern; jdn für etw in Anspruch nehmen; *s* ['indent] Kerbe *f*, Einschnitt *m*; Einrückung *f*, Absatz; (schriftlicher) Vertrag *m*; Warenbestellung *f*, Auftrag *m*; Anforderung *f*; **~ation** [inden'teiʃən] Einkerbung, Auszackung *f*, Einschnitt *m*; Ausbuchtung; *typ* Einrückung *f*, Absatz *m*; **~ed** [in'dentid] *a* gekerbt, gezackt, gezahnt; ausgebuchtet; vertraglich; (durch Lehrvertrag) gebunden; **~ion** [in'denʃən] *s. ~ation*; **~ure** [in'dentʃə] *s* (schriftlicher, in mehreren Ausfertigungen vorliegender) Vertrag, Kontrakt *m*; Liste, Aufstellung *f*, Inventar *n*; *meist pl* Arbeits-, Lehrvertrag *m*; *tr* vertraglich binden, verpflichten, in die Lehre geben; *to take up o.'s ~~s, to be out of ~~s* ausgelernt haben.

independen|ce, -cy [indi'pendəns(i)] Unabhängigkeit, Selbständigkeit, Autonomie *f*; reichliche(s) Auskommen *n*; *I~~ Day (Am)* Unabhängigkeitstag *(4. Juli 1776)*; **~t** [-t] *a* unabhängig (*of* von); selbständig; autonom; *pol* parteilos, wild; finanziell unabhängig; *s pol* Unabhängige(r), Parteilose(r); *rel* Kongregationalist, Independente(r), Sektierer *m*; *to be ~~* vom (eigenen) Gelde leben können; auf eigenen Füßen stehen; *~~ fire, firing (mil)* Einzel-, Schützenfeuer *n*; *~~ suspension (mot)* Einzelaufhängung *f*.

indescribable [indis'kraibəbl] unbeschreiblich.

indestructib|ility ['indistrʌktə'biliti] Unzerstörbarkeit *f*; **~le** [indis'trʌktəbl] unzerstörbar.

indetermin|able [indi'tə:minəbl] unbestimmbar; unentscheidbar; **~ate** [-it] unbestimmt; unsicher; ungenau, vage; unentschieden; unentschlossen; **~ation** ['inditə:mi'neiʃən] Unbestimmtheit; Unentschiedenheit; Unentschlossenheit *f*; **~ism** [indi'tə:minizm] *philos* Indeterminismus *m*.

index ['indeks] *pl -es* [-iz], *math indices* ['indisi:z] *s (~-finger)* Zeigefinger; *(Uhr-)*Zeiger *m*; (Kompaß-)Nadel *f*; Zünglein *n (an der Waage)*; Wegweiser *m*; *typ* Hinweiszeichen *n*; *fig* Fingerzeig, Hinweis *m* (*to* auf); (Kenn-)Zeichen *n* (*of* für, von); *(Buch) (alphabetisches)* (Namens-, Sach-)Register; (Stichwort-)Verzeichnis *n*, Liste *f*, Katalog *m*, Kartei *f*; *eccl com* Index *m*, Verbotsliste *f*; *math* Exponent *m*, Hochzahl *f*; *(~-number)* Index *m*, Meßzahl; Kennziffer *f*; *tr (Buch)* mit e-m Register versehen, ein Register machen zu; registrieren, katalogisieren; *tech* indexieren, (um)schalten; zeigen, hinweisen auf; *to be an ~ of s.th.* ein Gradmesser für etw sein; *to be, to put on the ~* auf dem Index stehen, auf den I. setzen; *business ~* Handelsregister *n*; *card ~* Kartei, Kartothek *f*; *cost-of-living ~* Lebenshaltungsindex *m*; *price ~* Preisindex *m*; *wholesale-price ~* Großhandelsindex *m*; *~ of intelligence* Intelligenz-(meß)zahl *f*; *~ of names* Namensverzeichnis *n*; **~-card** Karteikarte *f*; **~ed** ['-t] *a* mit e-m Register versehen; katalogisiert; **~er** ['-ə] Bearbeiter *m* e-s Registers, e-s Katalogs; **~ error** Ablesefehler *m*; **~ing** ['indeksiŋ] Registrierung, Katalogisierung, Anlage *f* e-r Kartei; **~-mark** (Katalog-)Nummernschild *n*; Kennmarke *f*; **~ number** Index-Meßziffer *f*; *~~ wages (pl)* an den Lebenshaltungsindex gebundene Löhne *m pl*.

India ['indjə] (Vorder-)Indien *n*; *Further ~* Hinterindien *n*; **~ ink** *Am* chinesische, Ausziehtusche *f*; **~-paper** Chinapapier *n*; **~ proof** *typ* Dünndruck *m*; **~-rubber** Kautschuk *m*, Radiergummi *m*; *~~ ball* Gummiball *m*.

Indian ['indjən] *a* indisch; indianisch, Indianer-; *Am* Mais-; *s* Inder(in *f*); Indianer(in *f*) *m*; Indianersprache *f*; **~ bread** *Am* Maisbrot *n*; **~ club** *sport* Keule *f*; **~ corn** *Am* Mais *m*; **~ file**: *in ~~* im Gänsemarsch; **~ ink** *s. India ink*; **~ meal** Maismehl *n*; **~ millet** *bot* Sorgho *m*, Sorghum *n*; **~ pudding** *Am* Pudding *m* aus Maismehl, Milch u. Sirup; **~ summer** Altweiber-, Nachsommer *m*.

indicat|e ['indikeit] *tr* hinweisen, zeigen (auf), deuten auf; anzeigen, an-, bedeuten; markieren; angezeigt, ratsam, nützlich erscheinen lassen; *med* indizieren, anzeigen, erforderlich machen; kurz *od* allgemein andeuten; *as ~ed* wie angegeben; **~ion** [indi'keiʃən] Hinweis *m*, Andeutung *f*; An-, Kennzeichen, Merkmal *n*; Anhaltspunkt *m*; *med* Indikation, Anzeige *f* (*of* für); *~~ of origin* Ursprungsbezeichnung *f*; **~ive** [in'dikətiv] *a* andeutend, hinweisend (*of* auf); anzeigend (*of s. th.* etw); *s u. ~~ mood (gram)* Indikativ *m*; *to be ~~ of* ein Hinweis sein für; **~or** ['indikeitə] (An-)Zeiger; Zähler; Registrierapparat *m*; Schauwerk *n*; Indikator *a. chem*; *mot* Winker *m*; Nullinstrument *n*; *flashing ~~ (mot)* Blinker *m*; **~ory** [in'dikətəri, 'indikeitəri] anzeigend (*of s.th.* etw), hinweisend (*of s.th.* auf etw).

indict [in'dait] *tr jur* Anklage erheben

gegen, anklagen (*for* wegen); **~able** [-əbl] *(Person)* anklagbar; *(Vergehen)* strafwürdig; **~ed** [-id] *a* unter Anklage (stehend); **~ment** [-mənt] *jur* Anklage; Anklageschrift *f*.

indifferen|ce [in'difrəns] Gleichgültigkeit (*to, towards* gegen); Interesselosigkeit, Apathie; Bedeutungslosigkeit *f*; **~t** [-t] gleichgültig (*to, towards* gegenüber); nebensächlich, unwichtig (*to* für); uninteressiert, interesselos, apathisch; uninteressant, gewöhnlich; mittelmäßig, leidlich; *el chem* neutral; *very* ~~ ziemlich, recht schlecht, *fam* nicht besonders.

indigenc|e ['indidʒəns] Bedürftigkeit, Armut *f*; **~t** [-t] bedürftig, arm.

indigen|e ['indidʒi:n] *a obs* = *~ous*; *s* einheimische Pflanze *f od* Tier *n*; **~ous** [in'didʒinəs] *bot zoo* eingeboren; einheimisch (*to* in); angeboren (*to* dat).

indigest|ed [indi'dʒestid] *a* undurchdacht, ungestaltet, gestalt-, formlos, ungeordnet, wirr, konfus; unverdaut; **~ible** [-əbl] unverdaulich *a. fig*; **~ion** [indi'dʒestʃən] Verdauungsstörung, Magenverstimmung *f*; **~ive** [-iv] schwer verdaulich.

indign|ant [in'dignənt] aufgebracht, entrüstet, empört (*at s.th.* über etw; *with s.o.* über jdn); **~ation** [indig'neiʃən] Entrüstung, Empörung *f* (*at* über); *~~-meeting* Protestversammlung *f*; **~ity** [in'digniti] Beleidigung, Herabsetzung, -würdigung *f*, Schimpf *m*; schimpfliche Behandlung *f*.

indigo ['indigou] *pl -os* Indigo *m* *(blauer Farbstoff)*; Indigopflanze *f*; Indigoblau *n*; **~-blue** *s* Indigoblau *n*.

indirect [indi'rekt] indirekt, nicht gerade, auf Umwegen; mittelbar, Neben-; *fig* nicht frei und offen, unredlich; **~ cost** Fertigungsgemeinkosten *pl*; **~ discourse, speech** *gram* indirekte Rede *f*; **~ion** [indi'rekʃən] Umschweife *pl*, Umwege *m pl*; Unaufrichtigkeit, Unredlichkeit *f*; **~ labo(u)r** Gemeinkostenlohn *m*; **~ taxes** *pl* indirekte Steuern *f pl*.

indiscernible [indi'sə:nəbl] nicht wahrnehmbar, unmerklich.

indiscr|eet [indis'kri:t] unvorsichtig, unbesonnen, unklug; taktlos, unüberlegt, achtlos; **~ete** [-] ungetrennt, zs.-hängend; **~etion** [-'kreʃən] Unvorsichtigkeit, Unbesonnenheit; Unklugheit; Taktlosigkeit, Indiskretion *f*.

indiscriminat|e [indis'kriminit] unterschiedslos; wahllos, blind; unkritisch, kritiklos; **~eness** [-nis], **~ion** [indiskrimi'neiʃən] Unterschiedslosigkeit; unkritische Haltung, Kritiklosigkeit *f*.

indispensab|ility [indispensə'biliti] Unerläßlichkeit, unbedingte Notwendigkeit *f*; **~le** [indis'pensəbl] unbedingt notwendig, erforderlich; unerläßlich, unentbehrlich (*for, to* für); *mil* unabkömmlich.

indispos|e [indis'pouz] *tr* unfähig, untauglich machen (*to, for* für); unpäßlich machen; abgeneigt machen (*to* zu); abraten (*to do* zu tun); **~ed** [-d] *a* unpäßlich, *fam* (gesundheitlich) nicht auf der Höhe, nicht auf dem Posten; abgeneigt (*to* dat); *~~ to (fam)* nicht für; **~ition** [indispə'ziʃən] Unpäßlichkeit *f*, Unwohlsein *n*; Widerwille *m*, Abgeneigtheit, Abneigung *f* (*to, towards* gegen).

indisputab|ility ['indispju:tə'biliti] Unbestreitbarkeit, Fraglosigkeit *f*; **~le** [indis'pju:təbl] unbestreitbar, unstreitig, fraglos.

indissolub|ility [indisəlju'biliti] Unauflösbarkeit, Unzerstörbarkeit; Festigkeit, Dauerhaftigkeit *f*; **~le** [indi'səljubl, in'dis-] unauflösbar, unlöslich, unzersetzbar, unzerstörbar; unauflöslich, fest, beständig, dauerhaft.

indistinct [indis'tiŋkt] undeutlich, unscharf, schwach, trübe, dunkel; *fig* unklar, verworren; **~ive** [-iv] uncharakteristisch; keinen Unterschied machend; **~ness** [-nis] Undeutlichkeit, Unschärfe; *fig* Unklarheit, Verschwommenheit; Verworrenheit *f*.

indistinguishable [indis'tiŋgwiʃəbl] nicht zu unterscheiden(d), nicht ausea.zuhalten(d); unmerklich.

indite [in'dait] *tr* niederschreiben; ab-, verfassen; *(Rede)* aufsetzen.

individual [indi'vidjuəl] *a* einzeln, getrennt, besondere; Einzel-; persönlich, individuell, eigen; *s* Individuum *n*, Einzelne(r), Einzelmensch *m*, (Einzel-)Person *f*; **~ case** Einzelfall *m*; **~ credit** Personalkredit *m*; **~ fighter** Einzelkämpfer *m*; **~ income** Privateinkommen *n*; **~ism** [-izm] Individualismus; Egoismus *m*; **~ist** [-ist] *s* Individualist *m*; *a. u.* **~istic** [-'listik] individualistisch; **~ity** [individju'æliti] Individualität, Persönlichkeit *f*; Einzelwesen *n*, -mensch *m*, Individuum *n*; *pl* individuelle Neigungen *f pl*; **~ization** [individjuəlai'zeiʃən] gesonderte Betrachtung *f*; **~ize** [indi'vidjuəlaiz], **individuate** [indi'vidjueit] *tr* e-e persönliche Note geben (*s.o.* jdm); individualisieren, kennzeichnen; einzeln, gesondert betrachten; **~ member** Einzelmitglied *n*; **~ part** Einzelteil *m*; **~ performance** Einzelleistung *f*; **~ property** Privatvermögen *n*; **~ purchaser** Einzelkäufer *m*; **~ rights** *pl* Privatrechte *n pl*; **~ training** Einzelausbildung *f*.

indivisib|ility ['indivizi'biliti] Unteilbarkeit *f*; **~le** [indi'vizəbl] unteilbar; *~~ number (math)* Primzahl *f*.

Indo- ['indo(u)]: **~-European** *a* indogermanisch; *s* die indogermanischen Sprachen *f pl*; die indogermanische Ursprache.

indocil|e [in'dousail] ungelehrig; undisziplinierbar; **~ity** [indo(u)'siliti] Ungelehrigkeit; Undisziplinierbarkeit *f*.

indoctrinat|e [in'dɔktrineit] *tr* schulen; unterweisen, unterrichten, belehren; **~ion** [-'neiʃən] Schulung, Unterweisung, Belehrung *f*, Unterricht *m*; *~~ film* Schulungs-, Propagandafilm *m*.

indolen|ce ['indələns] Lässigkeit, Trägheit, Faulheit *f*; **~t** [-t] lässig, träge, arbeitsscheu, faul; *med* nicht schmerzend.

indomitable [in'dɔmitəbl] unbezähmbar, unbesiegbar, nicht unterzukriegen(d); unnachgiebig.

Indonesia [indo(u)'ni:zjə] Indonesien *n*; **~n** *a* indonesisch; *s* Indonesier(in *f*) *m*.

indoor ['indɔ:] *a* Innen-, Haus-, Zimmer-; *sport* Hallen-; **~ aerial** Zimmerantenne *f*; **~ games** *pl* Spiele *n pl* in der Turnhalle, im Zimmer; **~ relief** Krankenhausbehandlung *f*; **~s** ['in'dɔ:z] *adv* innen, drin(nen); hinein; *to stay* ~~ zu Hause bleiben.

indorse [in'dɔ:s] *s. endorse etc.*

indraught, *Am* **indraft** ['indrɑ:ft] Hereinziehen; Einströmen *n a. fig*.

indubitabl|e [in'dju:bitəbl] unzweifelhaft, fest(stehend); **~y** [-i] *adv* fraglos, (ganz) bestimmt.

induc|e [in'dju:s] *tr* veranlassen, bewegen, dazu bringen, überreden, verleiten, verführen (*to do* zu tun); herbeiführen, bewirken, hervorrufen, verursachen; schließen, die Folgerung ziehen (*from* von, aus); *phys el* induzieren; erzeugen; *~ed consumption* Verbrauchssteigerung *f*; *~ed current* Induktionsstrom *m*; **~ment** [-mənt] Veranlassung; Überredung; Verleitung, Verführung, Verlockung; Herbeiführung *f*; *com* Anreiz; Anlaß, (Beweg-)Grund (*to* zu); Schluß *m*, Folgerung *f*; *to hold out an ~~ to s.o.* jdm etw als Anreiz bieten.

induct [in'dʌkt] *tr* hineinbringen, einführen; *(in ein Amt)* einsetzen, (feierlich) einführen; *(in e-e Organisation, e-n Verein)* aufnehmen; *(in e-e Gesellschaft)* einführen (*into* in); einweihen (*in* in); *Am mil* einziehen, einberufen (*into* zu); *phys* induzieren; **~ance** [-əns] *el* Induktivität *f*; **~ee** [-'ti:] *Am* Rekrut *m*; **~ion** [in'dʌkʃən] (Amts-)Einsetzung, Einführung; Aufnahme *(in e-e Organisation)*; *Am mil* Einberufung, Einziehung; (Schluß-)Folgerung *f*, Schluß *m*, Verallgemeinerung; Veranlassung, Herbeiführung *f*; *~~ coil (el)* Induktionsspule *f*, Induktor *m*; *~~ current* Induktionsstrom *m*; *~~ order (Am mil)* Gestellungsbefehl *m*; *~~ station* Gestellungsort *m*; *~~ valve* Einlaßventil *n*; **~ive** [in'dʌktiv] führend (*to* zu); anziehend, überzeugend; *(Logik)* induktiv, folgernd; *phys* Induktions-; *physiol* wirksam; Einführungs-; **~ivity** [indʌk'tiviti] *phys* Induktivität *f*; **~or** [-ə] Einführende(r); *el* Induktor *m*; *~~ current* Erregerstrom *m*.

indue [in'dju:] *s. endue*.

indulg|e [in'dʌldʒ] *tr* willfahren, nachgeben, frönen (*a desire* e-m Verlangen); befriedigen (*s.o.* jdn; *s.th., in s.th.* etw); nachsichtig sein; Nachsicht üben (*s.o.* jdm gegenüber); nachsehen; verwöhnen (*in s.th.* in e-r S); verzeihen; *rel* e-n Dispens erteilen (*s.o.* jdm); *fin* Aufschub gewähren (*s.o.* jdm); *itr u. to ~ o.s.* frönen (*in s.th.* e-r S), *fam* sich genehmigen, sich bewilligen, sich gestatten (*in s.th.* etw); sich gütlich tun (*in* an); *itr* (zu viel) *(Alkohol)* trinken; sich (den Luxus) erlauben (*in* zu); **~ence** [-əns] Nachgeben *n*, Nachsicht, Nachgiebigkeit, Duldung, Befriedigung; Hingabe (*in* an); Schwäche *f (gegenüber sich selbst)*; Genuß *m*; Gunst *f*; Vorrecht, Privileg *n*; *fin* Aufschub *m*, Stundung *f*; *rel* Ablaß *m*; **~ent** [-ənt] nachsichtig; nachgiebig (*to* gegen); gutmütig, schwach.

indurat|e ['indjuəreit] *tr* härten, hart machen; *fig* abstumpfen, unempfindlich machen (*against, to* gegen); *itr* hart werden, sich verhärten; *a* verhärtet, hart; *fig* stumpf, unempfindlich; **~ion** [indju'reiʃən] Verhärtung; *fig* Abstumpfung *f*.

industr|ial [in'dʌstriəl] *a* gewerblich, industriell; Gewerbe-, Industrie-; gewerbetreibend; *s* Gewerbetreibende(r), Industrielle(r) *m*; *pl* Industriepapiere *n pl*; *~~ accident* Betriebsunfall *m*; *~~ area, district* Industriegebiet *n*; *~~ arts (pl)* Kunstgewerbe *n*; *~~ bank* Gewerbebank *f*; *~~ branch* Arbeitszweig *m*; *~~ buildings (pl)* Fabrikgebäude *n pl*; *~~ centre* Industriezentrum *n*; *~~ code* Gewerbeordnung *f*; *~~ concern, enterprise* Industrie-, Gewerbebetrieb *m*; *~~ conflict* Arbeitskonflikt *m*; *~~ country* Industrieland *n*; *~~ court* Gewerbegericht *n*; *~~ design* Gebrauchsmuster *n*; *~~ disease* Berufskrankheit *f*; *~~ district* Industriebezirk *m*, -gegend *f*; *~~ engineer* Wirtschaftsingenieur *m*; *~~ exhibition* Gewerbeausstellung *f*; *~~ goods (pl)* Produktions-, Investitionsgüter *n pl*; *~~ law* Gewerberecht *n*;

~~ *leader* Wirtschaftsführer *m*; ~~ *life* Wirtschaftsleben *n*; ~~ *management* Betriebsführung *f*; ~~ *output* Industrieproduktion *f*; ~~ *partnership* Gewinnbeteiligung *f* der Arbeiter; ~~ *peace* Arbeitsfrieden *m*; ~~ *plant* Industrie-, Fabrikanlage *f*; ~~ *product* Industrieprodukt *n*; ~~ *school* Gewerbeschule; Besserungs-, Erziehungsanstalt *f*; ~~ *show* Gewerbeausstellung *f*; ~~ *town* Industriestadt *f*; ~~ *union* Betriebsgewerkschaft *f*; ~~ *wages (pl)* Industriearbeiterlöhne *m pl*; ~~ *worker* Fabrikarbeiter *m*; **~ialism** [-izm] Industrialismus *m*; **~ialist** [-ist] Industrielle(r) *m*; **~ialization** [indʌstriəlai'zeiʃən] Industrialisierung *f*; **~ialize** [in'dʌstriəlaiz] *tr* industrialisieren; **~ious** [in'dʌstriəs] arbeitsam, betriebsam, fleißig, rege, regsam; **~y** ['indəstri] Arbeitsamkeit, Betriebsamkeit, Regsamkeit *f*, Fleiß; Beruf *m*, Beschäftigung *f*; Gewerbefleiß *m*; Gewerbe *n*; Industrie(zweig *m*) *f*; *automobile* ~~ Kraftfahrzeugindustrie *f*; *basic* ~~ Grundstoffindustrie *f*; *chamber of* ~~ *and commerce* Industrie- u. Handelskammer *f*; *cloathing* ~~ Bekleidungsindustrie *f*; *coal-mining* ~~ Kohlenbergbau *m*; *construction* ~~ Bauindustrie *f*; *electricity* ~~ Energiewirtschaft *f*; *extractive* ~~ Industrie *f* der Steine u. Erden; *finishing* ~~ Veredelungsindustrie *f*; *garment*-~~ Bekleidungsindustrie *f*; *heavy* ~~ Schwerindustrie *f*; *home-, domestic* ~~ Heimindustrie *f*; *iron*-~~ Eisenindustrie *f*; *key*-~~ Schlüsselindustrie *f*; *manufacturing, transforming* ~~ verarbeitende Industrie *f*; *metal*-~~ Metallindustrie *f*; *mining*-~~ Montanindustrie *f*; Bergbau *m*; *motion-picture* ~~ Filmindustrie *f*; *oil*-~~ Erdölindustrie *f*; *power* ~~ Energiewirtschaft *f*; *primary* ~~ Grundstoffindustrie *f*; *processing* ~~ Veredelungsindustrie *f*; *textile* ~~ Textilindustrie *f*; *tourist* ~~ Fremdenverkehr *m*; ~~ *management* führende Wirtschaftskreise *m pl*.

indwell ['indwel] *itr irr* wohnen (*in* in); *tr* bewohnen; **~ing** [-iŋ] innewohnend.

inebriat|e [i'ni:brieit] *tr* betrunken machen, berauschen *a. fig*; *fig* anregen, erheitern; [in'i:briit] *a* betrunken; *s* Betrunkene(r); Trunkenbold *m*; **~ed** [-id] *a* betrunken; **~ion** [ini:bri'eiʃən], **inebriety** [ini(:)'braiəti] Trunkenheit *f*, Rausch *m*.

inedib|ility [inedi'biliti] Ungenießbarkeit *f*; **~le** [in'edibl] ungenießbar.

inedited [in'editid] *a* unveröffentlicht; unverändert herausgegeben.

ineffab|ility [inefə'biliti] Unaussprechlichkeit *f*; **~le** [in'efəbl] unaussprechlich.

ineffaceable [ini'feisəbl] *(Schrift)* untilgbar; *fig* unauslöschlich.

ineffect|ive [ini'fektiv], **~ual** [ini'fektjuəl] unwirksam, wirkungslos; unbrauchbar, untauglich, unnütz; dienst-, arbeitsunfähig; *jur* außer Kraft; **~iveness** [-ivnis] Unwirksamkeit; Unbrauchbarkeit; Dienst-, Arbeitsunfähigkeit *f*.

inefficac|ious [inefi'keiʃəs] *med* unwirksam, wirkungslos; erfolglos; **~y** [in'efikəsi] Unwirksamkeit *f*.

inefficien|cy [ini'fiʃənsi] Unwirksamkeit; Unbrauchbarkeit; Unfähigkeit, Untüchtigkeit; Unwirtschaftlichkeit *f*; Leerlauf *m*; **~t** [-t] unwirksam, wirkungslos; unrentabel, unwirtschaftlich; unfähig, untüchtig, ungeschickt; nicht leistungsfähig; *(Betrieb)* unrationell.

inelastic [ini'læstik] unelastisch, unbiegsam, steif; *fig* nicht anpassungsfähig; **~ity** [inilæs'tisiti] mangelnde Elastizität, Steifheit *f*.

inelegan|ce, -cy [in'eligəns(i)] mangelnde Eleganz, Unfeinheit, Geschmacklosigkeit *f*; **~t** [-t] wenig elegant, unfein, geschmacklos.

ineligib|ility [inelidʒə'biliti] mangelnde Wählbarkeit, Wahlunwürdigkeit; Ungeeignetheit; *mil* (Dienst-) Untauglichkeit *f*; **~le** [in'elidʒəbl] nicht wählbar; *(für ein Amt)* ungeeignet, nicht geeignet, nicht qualifiziert; *mil* (dienst)untauglich; *to be* ~~ nicht in Frage kommen.

ineluctable [ini'lʌktəbl] unvermeidbar, -lich, unentrinnbar, unausweichlich.

inept [i'nept] untauglich, unbrauchbar, ungeeignet, unfähig, untüchtig; unangebracht; ungeschickt, unbeholfen; unvernünftig, unsinnig, absurd, albern, abgeschmackt; **~itude** [-itju:d], **~ness** [-nis] Ungeeignetheit, Unfähigkeit (*for* zu); Ungeschicktheit; Albernheit, Unvernunft *f*, Unsinn *m*.

inequality [ini(:)'kwɔliti] Ungleichheit *a. math*; Unebenheit; ungleich(mäßig)e Verteilung *f*.

inequit|able [in'ekwitəbl] unbillig, un(ge)recht; **~y** [-i] Unbilligkeit, Ungerechtigkeit *f*, Unrecht *n*.

ineradicable [ini'rædikəbl] unausrottbar, zu fest verhaftet.

inerrab|le [in'ə:rəbl] unfehlbar.

inert [i'nə:t] träge *a. phys*, schwerfällig, langsam; *chem* inaktiv, unwirksam; **~ia** [i'nə:ʃjə] Beharrungsvermögen *n*; *bes. phys* Trägheit *f*; ~~ *factor* Trägheitsmoment *n*; **~ness** [i'nə:tnis] Trägheit, Schwerfälligkeit, Langsamkeit *f*; Mangel *m* an Reaktionsfähigkeit.

inescapable [inis'keipəbl] unentrinnbar, unvermeidbar, -lich.

inessential ['ini'senʃəl] *a* unwesentlich; nicht erforderlich, nicht unbedingt notwendig; *s etwas* Unwesentliches *n*.

inestimable [in'estiməbl] unschätzbar.

inevitab|ility [inevitə'biliti], **~leness** [in'evitəblnis] Unvermeidbar-, -lichkeit *f*; **~le** [in'evitəbl] unvermeidbar, -lich, unausweichlich, unumgänglich.

inexact [inig'zækt] ungenau, inexakt; **~itude** [-itju:d], **~ness** [-nis] Ungenauigkeit *f*.

inexcusable [iniks'kju:zəbl] unentschuldbar, unverzeihlich, nicht zu rechtfertigen(d), unverantwortlich.

inexhaust|ibility ['inigzɔ:stə'biliti] Unerschöpflichkeit; Unermüdlichkeit *f*; **~le** [inig'zɔ:stəbl] unerschöpflich; unermüdlich.

inexorab|ility [ineksərə'biliti] Unerbittlichkeit *f*; **~le** [in'eksərəbl] unerbittlich; *fig* unzugänglich.

inexpedien|ce, -cy [iniks'pi:djəns(i)] Unangebrachtheit, Unzweckmäßigkeit; Unklugheit *f*; **~t** [-t] unangebracht, unzweckmäßig, unpassend, ungeeignet; unklug.

inexpensive [iniks'pensiv] billig, preiswert, wohlfeil.

inexperience [iniks'piəriəns] Unerfahrenheit *f*; **~d** [-t] *a* unerfahren.

inexpert [ineks'pə:t] unerfahren, ungeübt; unfachmännisch, laienhaft.

inexpiable [in'ekspiəbl] unsühnbar, nicht wieder gutzumachen(d).

inexplicable [in'eksplikəbl] unerklärlich, unverständlich, unfaßlich.

inexplicit [iniks'plisit] nicht genau, undeutlich ausgedrückt; undeutlich, unklar, vage; allgemein.

inexpress|ible [iniks'presəbl] *a* unaussprechlich; unbeschreiblich; *pred* nicht zu sagen; *s pl hum* Hose *f*; **~ive** [-'presiv] ausdruckslos, leer.

inexpugnable [iniks'pʌgnəbl] unüberwindlich, unschlagbar.

inextensible [iniks'tensəbl] nicht ausdehnbar.

inextinguishable [iniks'tiŋgwiʃəbl] unauslöschlich.

inextricable [in'ekstrikəbl] unentwirrbar; unlösbar.

infallib|ility [infælə'biliti] Unfehlbarkeit *f*; **~le** [in'fæləbl] unfehlbar.

infam|ous ['infəməs] berüchtigt, ehrlos, stadtbekannt; schändlich, schimpflich, unehrenhaft, niederträchtig; **~y** ['infəmi] schlechte(r) Ruf *m*, Ehrlosigkeit; Schande; Schändlichkeit, Niedertracht, Niederträchtigkeit *f*.

infancy ['infənsi] (frühe) Kindheit *f*; Säuglingsalter *n*; *jur* Minderjährigkeit, Unmündigkeit *f*; *fig* Anfänge *m pl*, Frühzeit *f*; *flying was still in its* ~ die Fliegerei steckte noch in den Kinderschuhen.

infant ['infənt] *s* (Klein-)Kind *n (unter 7 Jahren)*; Säugling *m*; *jur* Minderjährige(r), Unmündige(r) *m*; *a* kindlich; Kinder-; *jur* minderjährig; *fig* noch in den Anfängen *od* Kinderschuhen steckend; **~a** [in'fæntə] *hist* Infantin *f*; **~e** [in'fænti] *hist* Infant *m*; **~icide** [in'fæntisaid] Kindesmord; Kindesmörder(in *f*) *m*; **~icipate** [-'tisipeit] *itr Am hum (Frau)* in anderen Umständen sein; **~ile** ['infəntail] kindlich, kindisch, Kinder-; infantil, (noch) unentwickelt, zurückgeblieben; (noch) in den Anfängen, Kinderschuhen steckend, Anfangs-; ~~ *disease* Kinderkrankheit *f*; ~~ *paralysis* Kinderlähmung *f*; **~ilism** [in'fæntilizm] Infantilismus *m*; **~ industry** (noch) unterentwickelte Industrie *f*; **~ mortality, death-rate** Kinder-, Säuglingssterblichkeit *f*; **~ school** Kindergarten *m*; **~ welfare** Kinder-, Säuglingsfürsorge *f*.

infantry ['infəntri] Infanterie, Fußtruppe *f*; **~ attack** Infanterieangriff *m*; **~ battalion** Infanterie-, Schützenbataillon *n*; **~ brigade** Infanterieregiment *n (als taktische Einheit)*; **~ carrier** Mannschaftswagen *m*; **~ division** Infanteriedivision *f*; **~ gun** Infanteriegeschütz *n*; **~man** ['-mən] Infant(e)rist *m*; **~ point** Infanteriespitze *f*; **~ regiment** Infanterieregiment *n*; **~ scout, spotter** Nahaufklärer *m*; **~ screen** Schützenschleier *m*; **~ section** Schützengruppe *f*; *Am* Halbzug *m*; **~ training** infant(e)ristische Grundausbildung *f*.

infarct [in'fɑ:kt] *med* Infarkt *m*; *cardiac* ~ Herzinfarkt *m*.

infatuat|e [in'fætjueit] *tr* närrisch, *fam* verrückt machen, den Verstand rauben (*s.o.* jdm); betören, verblenden (*with* durch); **~ed** [-id] *a* närrisch, von Sinnen, *fam* verrückt, (ganz) aus dem Häuschen; verblendet; vernarrt (*with* in); *to be* ~~ *(fig)* ein Brett vor dem Kopf haben; *to become* ~~ *with s.o.* sich in jdn unsterblich verlieben; **~ion** [infætju'eiʃən] Verblendung, Verblendetheit, Vernarrtheit (*for, about* in); sinnlose Leidenschaft *f*.

infect [in'fekt] *tr med* infizieren; anstecken (*with* mit); verseuchen; *(bes. im schlechten Sinne)* beeinflussen; ausstrahlen (*s.o.* auf jdn), mitreißen; *fam* anstecken, verderben (*with* durch); *to become, to get* ~*ed* sich anstecken, angesteckt werden (*by* von); **~ion** [in'fekʃən] Ansteckung, Infektion;

Verseuchung *f*; *fig* schlechte(r) Einfluß *m*; *to catch an ~~* sich anstecken, angesteckt werden; *risk of ~~* Ansteckungsgefahr *f*; **~ious** [in'fekʃəs] ansteckend *a. fig*, infektiös; Infektions-; *~~ carrier* Bazillenträger *m*; *~~ disease* ansteckende, Infektionskrankheit *f*; **~iousness** [-'fekʃəsnis] ansteckende Wirkung *f*.

infelicit|ous [infi'lisitəs] unglücklich; ungeeignet, unpassend; **~y** [-i] Unglück, Elend *n*; Ungeeignetheit *f*; Ungeschicktheit, unpassende Bemerkung *f*.

infer [in'fə:] *tr* folgern, den Schluß ziehen, schließen, ableiten, entnehmen (*from* aus); zu der Annahme führen, darauf schließen lassen; nahelegen, andeuten; **~able** [-rəbl] ableitbar, herzuleiten(d), zu folgern(d); naheliegend; **~ence** ['infərəns] Folgerung, Ableitung *f*, Schluß *m*; *to draw an ~~ from* e-n Schluß, e-e Folgerung ziehen aus; **~ential** [infə'renʃəl] *a* Folgerungs-, Schluß-; abgeleitet, gefolgert; *~~ proof* Indizienbeweis *m*; **~entially** [-'renʃəli] *adv* durch Schlußfolgerung.

inferior [in'fiəriə] *a (räumlich)* niedriger, unter; Unter-; (rang-)niedriger, untergeordnet, untergeben (*to* dat); gering(wertig)er, weniger wert (*to* als); minderwertig, unterdurchschnittlich, sehr mäßig; *typ* tiefgestellt; *rail* nicht vorfahrtberechtigt; *s* tiefer Stehende(r), Untergebene(r) *m*; *das* weniger Wertvolle; *to be ~ to s.o.* hinter jdm zurückstehen; **~ity** [infiəri'əriti] niedrigere(r) Rang *od* Stand *m*; Untergeordnetheit *f*; geringere(r) Grad *od* Wert *m*; *~~ complex* Minderwertigkeitskomplex *m*.

infernal [in'fə:nl] Unterwelt-, Höllen-; höllisch; *fig* teuflisch, infernalisch, diabolisch, unmenschlich; *fam (übertreibend)* gemein, schuftig; scheußlich, gräßlich; *~* **machine** Höllenmaschine *f*; *the ~* **regions** *pl* die Unterwelt.

infertil|e [in'fə:tail] unfruchtbar; *(Ei)* unbefruchtet; **~ity** [infə:'tiliti] Unfruchtbarkeit *f*.

infest [in'fest] *tr* in Massen, in Schwärmen überfallen, herfallen über, überschwemmen *fig*; verseuchen; umherschwärmen, sein Wesen treiben in, unsicher machen, heimsuchen; **~ed** [-id] *a* voller (*with* gen); *med u. fig* verseucht (*with* mit); *to be ~~ with* wimmeln von; **~ation** [infes'teiʃən] Heimsuchung, Plage, Seuche *f*.

infidel ['infidəl] *a rel* ungläubig; glaubenslos; *s* Ungläubige(r); Glaubenslose(r) *m*; **~ity** [infi'deliti] Unglaube *m*; Untreue *f* (*to* gegen).

infield ['infi:ld] Ackerland (in der Nähe des Hofes); *(Br Kricket, Am Baseball)* innere(s) Spielfeld *n*; Spieler *m pl* des inneren Spielfeldes.

infighting ['infaitiŋ] *(Boxen)* Nahkampf *m*.

infiltr|ate ['infiltreit, in'f-] *tr* durch-, einsickern lassen, infiltrieren (*through* durch; *into* in) *a. mil*; *fig (Ideen)* einsickern, eindringen lassen (*into* in); durchdrängen (*with* mit); *pol* unterwandern; *itr* durch-, einsickern *a. mil*, eindringen *a. fig* (*into* in); **~ated** ['-id] *a* durchtränkt, *fig* durchdrungen (*with* von); **~ation** [-'treiʃən] Durch-, Einsickern, Eindringen *n a. fig*; Infiltration *a. mil*; *pol* Unterwanderung *f*; **~ee** [-'tri:] *mil* Eindringling *m*.

infinit|e ['infinit] *a* unendlich *a. math*, unbegrenzt; endlos, unermeßlich; zahllos, unzählig; unerschöpflich; *s math* unendliche Größe *f*; *the I~~* Gott *m*; **~esimal** [infini'tesiməl] infinitesimal, unendlich klein; *~~ calculus* Infinitesimalrechnung *f*; **~ive** [in'finitiv] *s gram* Infinitiv *m*; *a* Infinitiv-; **~ude** [in'finitju:d], **~y** [-'finiti] Unendlichkeit; unendliche Größe *od* Zahl *f*; *math* Unendlich *n*; *to ~y* endlos, unermeßlich.

infirm [in'fə:m] schwach, kraftlos, gebrechlich; altersschwach; unsicher, schwankend; *jur* anfechtbar; **~ary** [-əri] Krankenhaus *n*, Krankenstube *f (in e-r Schule)*; *mil* Revier *n*; **~ity** [-iti]Schwäche,Kraftlosigkeit,Gebrechlichkeit *f*, Gebrechen *n*, Körperfehler; (Charakter-)Fehler *m*, Schwäche *f*.

infix [in'fiks] *tr* hineintreiben; *fig* einprägen, beibringen, *fam* eintrichtern; *gram* einfügen; *s* ['infiks] *gram* Infix *n*, Einfügung *f*.

inflame [in'fleim] *tr* anzünden; *fig (Leidenschaft)* entflammen; *(Zorn)* erregen; *med* entzünden; *itr* Feuer fangen; *fig* entflammen, entbrennen (*with* vor); in Wut geraten; *med* sich entzünden.

inflamm|ability[inflæmə'biliti]leichte Entzündbarkeit, Brennbarkeit; *fig* Erregbarkeit, Reizbarkeit *f*; **~able** [in'flæməbl] *a* leicht entzündbar, leicht brennbar, feuergefährlich; *Am* nicht brennbar; *fig* leicht erregt, erregbar, reizbar; *s* feuergefährliche(s) Material *n*; **~ation** [inflə'meiʃən] Entflammen *n*; *med* Entzündung; *fig* Auf-,Erregung *f*; **~atory** [in'flæmətəri] *fig* aufreizend, aufrührerisch, Hetz-; *med* entzündlich.

inflat|e [in'fleit] *tr* aufblasen, -blähen; *(Gummireifen)* aufpumpen; *fig* aufgeblasen, stolz, hochmütig machen; *allg* aufblähen; *(Geld-, Notenumlauf)* steigern; *(Preise)* hochtreiben; **~ed** [-id] *a* aufgebläht; geschwollen, schwülstig, aufgeblasen, bombastisch, pompös; *(Preis)* überhöht; *~~ with pride* vor Stolz geschwellt; **~ion** [in'fleiʃən] Aufblähung; *fig* Aufgeblasenheit; *(Stil)* Schwülstigkeit; *fin* Inflation *f*; **~ionary** [-'fleiʃnəri] *a* Inflations-; **~ionist** [-'fleiʃnist] inflationistisch, inflatorisch.

inflect [in'flekt] *tr* (einwärts) biegen; *(die Stimme)* modulieren; *gram* flektieren, beugen; **~ion** *bes. Am* = *inflexion*.

inflex|ibility [infleksə'biliti] Steifheit, Starre; Halsstarrigkeit, Unnachgiebigkeit; Unveränderlichkeit *f*; **~ible** [-əbl] steif, starr; halsstarrig, unnachgiebig, unerschütterlich; unveränderlich, starr; **~ion** [-kʃən] Biegung, Beugung, Krümmung; *(Stimme)* Modulation; *gram* Flexion, Beugung *f*.

inflict [in'flikt] *tr (Schmerz, Wunden)* zufügen; *(Schlag)* versetzen; *(Niederlage)* beibringen; *(Strafe)* auferlegen (*on, upon s.o.* jdm), verhängen (*on, upon* über); *to ~ o.s. on s.o.* sich jdm aufdrängen; **~ion** [in'flikʃən] Zufügung; Auferlegung, Verhängung; (verhängte) Strafe; Heimsuchung, Plage *f*.

inflorescence [inflə'resns] Blühen *n*, Blüte *f*; Blüten *f pl*; Blüte(nstand *m*) *f*.

influen|ce ['influəns] *s* Einfluß *m*, Wirkung (*on, over*; *with* auf); einflußreiche Persönlichkeit; wirkende Kraft *f*; *tr* beeinflussen, Einfluß haben *od* ausüben; (ein)wirken auf; *to be a good ~~* von gutem Einfluß sein; *to bring o.'s ~~ to bear on s.o.* s-n Einfluß bei jdm geltend machen; *to use o.'s ~~ with s.o.* s-n Einfluß bei jdm geltend machen; **~t** ['-t] *a* hineinfließend, mündend; *s* Nebenfluß *m*; **~tial** [influ'enʃəl] von Einfluß (*on* auf; *in* in); einflußreich; maßgebend, maßgeblich; wirksam, wirkungsvoll, entscheidend.

influenz|a [influ'enzə] Grippe *f*.

influx ['inflʌks] (Hin-)Einfließen, Einströmen *n*; Zufluß, Zustrom *m*; *(Fluß)* Mündung *f*.

inform [in'fɔ:m] *tr* benachrichtigen, verständigen, unterrichten, wissen lassen (*of* von); informieren (*about* über); in Kenntnis setzen (*of* von), Nachricht, Bescheid geben, Mitteilung machen (*s.o. of s.th.* jdm von e-r S); *(selten)* erfüllen (*with* mit), beseelen, inspirieren; *itr* anzeigen, denunzieren (*against s.o., s.th.* jdn, etw); zur Anzeige bringen (*against s.th.* etw); Anzeige erstatten (*against s.o.* gegen jdn); *to keep s.o. ~ed* jdn auf dem laufenden halten; **~al** [-l] form-, regelwidrig; informell; form-, zwanglos, ungezwungen, *fam* leger; gewöhnlich, Alltags-, Umgangs-; *jur* formlos; **~ality** [infɔ:'mæliti] Formwidrigkeit *f*, Formfehler *m*, Regelwidrigkeit; Form-, Zwanglosigkeit, Ungezwungenheit *f*; **~ant** [in'fɔ:mənt] Anzeige-, Berichterstatter, Auskunftgeber; Einsender; Gewährsmann *m*; **~ation** [infə'meiʃən] Nachricht, Auskunft *f*, Bescheid *m*, Information; Benachrichtigung; Mitteilung; Anzeige; Belehrung, Unterweisung; Unterrichtung, Orientierung; Kenntnis *f*, Wissen *n*, Bildung; Auskunftsperson *f*, -büro *n*, -stelle; *jur* Anklage *f*; *a piece of ~~* e-e Auskunft; *for ~~* zur Kenntnisnahme; *to file, to lay, to prefer an ~~ against s.o.* gegen jdn Anzeige erstatten; *to gather ~~ upon* Erkundigungen einziehen, Auskünfte einholen über; *to give ~~* Auskunft erteilen (*on, about* über); *so far as my ~~ goes* soweit ich unterrichtet bin, soviel ich weiß; *for your ~~* zu Ihrer Information *od* Kenntnisnahme; *~~ bureau (Am), office* Auskunftei *f*, Auskunftsbüro *n*, -stelle *f*; *~~ department* Auskunftsabteilung *f*; *~~ desk* Auskunft(sstelle) *f*; *~~ window* Auskunftsschalter *m*; **~ative** [in'fɔ:mətiv] belehrend, unterrichtend, bildend; **~ed** [-d] *a* unterrichtet, gebildet; **~er** [-ə] Anzeigeerstatter; Denunziant; Spitzel *m*.

infra ['infrə] *adv* (weiter) unten *(in e-m Buch, Text)*; **~costal** ['-kɔstəl] *a* unter den Rippen (befindlich); *~* **dignitatem** [-digni'teitəm], *fam ~* **dig** ['-'dig] unter jds Würde; **~-red** *a phys* infrarot; *s* Infrarot *n*; **~structure** Unterbau *m*, Grundlage, Basis; *mil* Infrastruktur *f*.

infract [in'frækt] *tr Am (Recht)* brechen, verletzen; *(Gesetz)* übertreten, verstoßen gegen; **~ion** [in'frækʃən] *jur* Übertretung, Verletzung *f*, Verstoß; *med* (Knick-)Bruch *m*.

infrangible [in'frændʒibl] unzerbrechlich; *fig* unverletzlich.

infrequen|ce, -cy [in'fri:kwəns(i)] Seltenheit *f*; **~t** [-t] nicht häufig, selten, gelegentlich, ungewöhnlich.

infringe [in'frindʒ] *tr (Gesetz)* übertreten, verletzen, zuwiderhandeln (*s.th.* e-r S); *to ~ (upon)* ein-, übergreifen in, verletzen (*s.o.'s rights* jds Rechte); **~ment** [-mənt] Übertretung, Verletzung *f*, Zuwiderhandeln *n*, Verstoß *m* (*of* gegen); *~~ of duty* Pflichtverletzung *f*; *~~ of a treaty* Vertragsbruch *m*.

infructuous [in'frʌktjuəs] unfruchtbar; *fig* fruchtlos, vergeblich.

infuriate [in'fjuərieit] *tr* wütend, rasend machen, aufbringen, *fam* auf die Palme bringen.

infus|e [in'fju:z] *tr* ein-, aufgießen; auslaugen; *(Tee)* aufgießen, -brühen; einweichen (*in* in); *fig* einflößen (*into s.o.* jdm); erfüllen, inspirieren (*with* mit); **~ible** [-əbl] unschmelzbar; **~ion** [in'fju:ʒən] Einweichen *n*; Auslaugung *f*; Aufguß *m*; Lauge *f*; **~oria** [infju:'zɔ:riə] *pl zoo* Aufgußtierchen *n pl*, Infusorien *f pl*; **~orial** [-'zɔ:riəl] *a zoo* Infusorien-; *~~ earth* Infusorienerde, Kieselgur *f*.

ingather [in'gæðə] *tr itr lit fig* ernten; **~ing** ['ingæðəriŋ] Einsammeln *n*, Ernte *f*.

ingen|ious [in'dʒi:njəs] scharfsinnig, klug; geschickt, erfinderisch; geistreich; *(Sache)* sinnreich, originell; **~uity** [indʒi'nju(:)iti] Scharfsinn *m*, Klugheit, Geschicktheit, Erfindergabe; Genialität *f*, Einfallsreichtum *m*; Originalität *f*; **~uous** [in'dʒenjuəs] frei, offen, aufrichtig, gerade; einfach, schlicht, naiv, unschuldig.

ingest [in'dʒest] *tr (Nahrung)* zu sich nehmen; *(Arznei)* einnehmen.

ingle ['iŋgl] Kamin-, Herdfeuer *n*; Feuerstelle *f*; **~-nook** Kaminecke *f*; *in the ~~* am Kamin.

inglorious [in'glɔ:riəs] ruhmlos, schändlich, schimpflich, unehrenhaft; kaum bekannt, dunkel.

ingoing ['ingo(u)iŋ] *a* hineingehend; *(Amt)* antretend; *(Post)* eingehend.

ingot ['iŋgət] (Metall-)Barren; Gußblock *m*; *~ of gold* Goldbarren *m*; **~-mo(u)ld** Blockform, Kokille *f*; **~-steel** Block-, Flußstahl *m*.

ingraft [in'grɑ:ft] *s. engraft.*

ingrain ['in'grein] *tr* in der Wolle färben; *pred a* [-'-] in der Wolle gefärbt; *fig = ~ed*; *s* (noch unverarbeitete) gefärbte Wolle *f*; **~ed** [-'greind] *a fig* (fest) eingewurzelt, in Fleisch und Blut übergegangen; eingefleischt.

ingratiate [in'greiʃieit]: *to ~ o.s.* sich beliebt machen, sich einschmeicheln (*with* bei).

ingratitude [in'grætitju:d] Undank (-barkeit *f*) *m*.

ingredient [in'gri:djənt] Bestandteil *m*; *pl (Küche)* Zutaten *f pl*.

ingress ['ingres] Eintritt (*into* in); Zugang *m* (*into* zu).

ingrown ['ingroun] *a (Zehennagel)* eingewachsen; angeboren; eingeboren.

inguinal ['iŋgwinl] *anat* Leisten-.

ingurgitate [in'gə:dʒiteit] *tr* hinunter-, verschlingen.

inhabit [in'hæbit] *tr* bewohnen, wohnen, leben in; **~able** [in'hæbitəbl] bewohnbar; **~ancy** [-ənsi] Bewohnen; Bewohntsein *n*; Wohnung *f*; **~ant** [-ənt] Be-, Einwohner *m*.

inhal|ation [inhə'leiʃən] *med* Inhalieren; Inhaliermittel *n*; **~e** [in'heil] *tr itr* inhalieren; *itr* auf Lunge rauchen, e-n Lungenzug machen; **~er** [-ə] Inhalierende(r); Luftreiniger, Rauchverzehrer *(Apparat)*; *med* Inhalator *m*.

inharmonious [inhɑ:'mounjəs] un-, disharmonisch; *fig* uneinig.

inher|e [in'hiə] *itr* inhärieren, inhärent sein (*in s.o.* in jdm); innewohnen, anhaften (*s.o.* jdm); angeboren sein (*in s.o.* jdm); **~ence, -cy** [-rəns(i)] Inhärenz *f*, Innewohnen, Anhaften *n*; **~ent** [-rənt] inhärent, innewohnend, anhaftend; angeboren.

inherit [in'herit] *tr itr* erben (*s.th. from s.o.* etw von jdm); *tr biol (Eigenschaft, Merkmal)* geerbt haben; **~able** [in'heritəbl] *jur biol* erblich, vererbbar; **~ance** [-əns] Nachlaß *m*, Hinterlassenschaft, Erbschaft *f*, Erbe, Erbteil *n*; Erbfolge; *biol* Vererbung *f*; *to come into an ~~* e-e Erbschaft machen *od* antreten; *to disclaim an ~~* e-e Erbschaft ausschlagen; *law of ~~* Erbrecht *n*; *~~ tax (Am)* Erbschaft(s)steuer *f*; **~ed** [-id] *a* ge-, ererbt; **~or** [-ə] Erbe *m*; **~ress** [-ris], **~rix** [-riks] Erbin *f*.

inhibit [in'hibit] *tr* verbieten, untersagen (*s.o. from s.th.* jdm etw); unterdrücken, -binden, verhindern; *psychol* hemmen; **~ion** [inhi'biʃən] Verbot *n*; Unterdrückung, Verhinderung; *chem psychol* Hemmung *f*; **~ive** [-iv], **~ory** [-əri] verbietend; hindernd, hemmend; **~or** [-ə] Verbietende(r), Hemmende(r); *chem* Hemmungskörper *m*; Sparbeize *f*.

inhospit|able [in'hɔspitəbl] ungastlich; *(Gegend)* unwirtlich; **~ality** ['inhɔspi'tæliti] Ungastlichkeit; ungastliche Aufnahme; Unwirtlichkeit *f*.

inhuman [in'hju:mən] unmenschlich, gefühllos, hartherzig, mitleidlos, grausam; **~e** [inhju(:)'mein] inhuman, schonungslos, hart, brutal; **~ity** [inhju(:)'mæniti] Unmenschlichkeit; Gefühllosigkeit, Hartherzigkeit; Brutalität; Grausamkeit *f*.

inhum|ation [inhju(:)'meiʃən] Beerdigung, Bestattung, Beisetzung *f*; **~e** [in'hju:m] *tr* beerdigen, bestatten, beisetzen, begraben.

inimical [i'nimik(ə)l] feindlich, feindselig; nachteilig, ungünstig, schädlich, abträglich (*to* für).

inimitable [i'nimitəbl] unnachahmlich, unerreichbar; einzigartig.

iniquit|ous [i'nikwitəs] unbillig, un(ge)recht, boshaft; frevelhaft; niederträchtig; **~y** [-i] Unbilligkeit, Unredlichkeit, Schlechtigkeit, Niederträchtigkeit, Bosheit *f*, Unrecht *n*; Frevel *m*, Schandtat *f*.

initi|al [i'niʃəl] *a* Anfangs-, erst; ursprünglich; *s* (großer) Anfangsbuchstabe *m*, Initiale *f*; *pl* Monogramm *n*, Anfangsbuchstaben *m pl (des Namens)*; *tr* abzeichnen; mit s-n *od* s-m Anfangsbuchstaben (unter)zeichnen; *(Vertrag)* paraphieren; *~~ cost* Anschaffungspreis *m*; *~~ letter* Anfangsbuchstabe *m*; *~~ meeting* Eröffnungssitzung *f*; *~~ point* Abgangspunkt *m*; *~~ salary* Anfangsgehalt *n*; *~~ stage* Anfangsstadium *n*; *~~ velocity* Anfangsgeschwindigkeit *f*; **~ate** [i'niʃieit] *tr (in e-e Tätigkeit)* einweihen, -führen (*into* in); die Anfangsgründe beibringen (*s.o.* jdm; *into s.th.* e-r S); *(in e-e Bruderschaft)* (feierlich) aufnehmen; anfangen, beginnen, einleiten, eröffnen, *fam* starten; *(e-n Prozeß)* anstrengen; *pol* als Initiativantrag stellen; *a* [-ʃiit] eingeweiht, eingeführt; Anfangs-; *s* [-ʃiit] Eingeweihte(r), Neuling, Anfänger *m*; **~ation** [iniʃi'eiʃən] Einführung, Einweihung *f*; *~~ fee (Am)* Aufnahmegebühr *f*, Einstand *m*; **~ative** [i'niʃiətiv] *a* einleitend, -führend, eröffnend; Einleitungs-, -führungs-, Eröffnungs-, Einweihungs-; *s* erste(r) Schritt *m*, Initiative, Anregung, Veranlassung; geistige Selbständigkeit *f*, Unternehmungsgeist *m*; Gesetzesinitiative *f*; *of, on o.'s own ~~* aus eigenem Antrieb; *to take the ~~* die Initiative ergreifen (*in* bei); *private ~~* Privatinitiative *f*; **~ator** [i'niʃieitə] Anreger, Initiator, geistige(r) Vater, Urheber *m*; **~atory** [i'niʃiətəri] *a* Anfangs-, Einführungs-, Eröffnungs-; einleitend, einführend; Einweihungs-.

*

inject [in'dʒekt] *tr med* einspritzen, injizieren; *tech* einführen, anlegen; *bes. Am (Bemerkung)* ein-, dazwischenwerfen, fallenlassen; *fig* einflößen; **~ion** [-kʃən] Einspritzung, Injektion, *fam* Spritze; *tech* Ein-, Zuführung *f*; *~~ cock, engine* Einspritzhahn, -motor *m*; **~or** [-ə] Einspritz-, Strahlpumpe *f*.

injudicious [indʒu(:)'diʃəs] unverständig, ohne Verstand, unklug; unüberlegt, unsinnig, dumm.

injunction [in'dʒʌŋkʃən] Ersuchen, Gebot *n*; (richterlicher) Befehl *m*; Anweisung, (gerichtliche) Anordnung, Verfügung *f*; *to allow* od *to grant, to lift an ~* e-e Verfügung erlassen, aufheben.

injur|e ['indʒə] *tr* beschädigen, verletzen; ungerecht behandeln, kränken, Unrecht tun (*s.o.* jdm); beeinträchtigen, Abbruch tun (*s.o.* jdm); **~ed** [-d] *a* beschädigt; verletzt; beleidigt; *the ~~ party* der Geschädigte; **~ious** [in'dʒuəriəs] schädlich, nachteilig (*to* für); beleidigend, Schmäh-; unrecht; **~y** ['indʒəri] Beschädigung, Verletzung *f* (*to* an); Schaden, Nachteil *m*, Schädigung *f*; Kränkung *f*, Unrecht *n*, Ungerechtigkeit *f*; *to the ~~ of s.o.* zu jds Nachteil; *bodily, personal ~~* Körperverletzung *f*; *~~ to property* Sachbeschädigung *f*.

injustice [in'dʒʌstis] Ungerechtigkeit *f*; Unrecht *n*; *to do s.o. an ~* jdm Unrecht tun.

ink [iŋk] *s* Tinte; Tusche; Stempelfarbe; *(printer's ~)* Druckerschwärze; Sepia *f*; *tr* mit Tinte bespritzen; e-n Tintenfleck machen auf; mit Tinte (be)zeichnen; (ein)schwärzen; *in ~* mit Tinte; **~-bag** *zoo* Tintenbeutel *m*; **~-blot, -stain** Tintenklecks, -fleck *m*; **~-bottle** Tintenflasche *f*, -fläschchen *n*; **~er** ['-ə] *typ* Einschwärzer *m*; **~-eraser** Tintengummi *m*; **~ing** ['-iŋ] *typ* Einschwärzen *n*; *~~-roller (typ)* Auftragwalze *f*; **~-pad** Stempelkissen *n*; **~-pencil** Tintenstift *m*; **~-pot** Tintenfaß *n*; **~-stand** Schreibzeug; Tintenfaß *n*; **~-well** (in den Tisch) versenkte(s) Tintenfaß *n*; **~y** ['-i] tintenartig; (tief)schwarz; verkleckst.

inkling ['iŋkliŋ] Wink *m*, (leise) Andeutung; Ahnung *f*, Vorgefühl *n*, vage Vermutung *f*; *to have no ~ of s.th.* von etw keine Ahnung.

inlaid ['in'leid] *a* eingelegt, getäfelt; **~ floor** Parkett(fuß)boden *m*; **~ work** Einlegearbeit *f*.

inland ['inlənd] *a* inländisch, Inlands-; Binnen-; einheimisch; *s* Inland; Binnenland *n*; *adv* [in'lænd] landeinwärts; **~ bill** Inlandswechsel *m*; **~ duty** Binnenzoll *m*; **~er** [-ə] Binnenländer *m*, *hum* Landratte *f*; **~ manufacture, produce** Inlandserzeugnis *n*; *pl* Landesprodukte *n pl*; **~ market** Binnenmarkt *m*; **~ navigation** Binnen-, Flußschiffahrt *f*; **~ postage** Inlandsporto *n*; **~ revenue** Steuereinnahmen *f pl*; Finanzverwaltung *f*, Fiskus *m*; **~ sea** Binnenmeer *n*; **~ trade** Binnenhandel *m*; **~ traffic** Binnenverkehr *m*; **~ waters** *pl* Binnengewässer *n pl*; **~ waterway** Binnenwasserstraße *f*.

in-laws ['inlɔ:z] *pl fam* Verschwägerte *m pl*.

inlay ['in'lei] *irr inlaid, inlaid tr (als Verzierung in e-e Fläche)* einlegen; furnieren, täfeln, auslegen (*with* mit); *s* ['--] eingelegte Arbeit, Täfelung *f*; Furnier *n*; Plombe *f (im Zahn)*.

inlet ['inlet] Meeres-, Flußarm *m*; (kleine) Bucht, Ausbuchtung *f*; Einlaß *m*, Öffnung; Einlage *f*, Einschiebsel *n*, Einsatz *m*; **~-valve** Einlaßventil *n*.

in-line engine ['inlain'endʒin] *aero* Reihenmotor *m*.

inly ['inli] *adv poet* im Innern, im Herzen, innerlich, zutiefst.

inmate ['inmeit] Hausgenosse, Mitbewohner, (Anstalts-)Insasse; Bewohner *m a. fig.*

inmost ['inmoust] innerst; *fig* geheimst.

inn [in] Gast-, Wirtshaus *n*; *I~s of Court* (vier Londoner) Rechtsschulen *f pl*; **~keeper** Gast-, Schankwirt *m*; **~-sign** Wirtshausschild *n*.

innards ['inədz] *sl* Magen *m*.

innate ['i'neit, '--] angeboren (*in s.o.* jdm); natürlich, wesensmäßig.

inner ['inə] *a* inner, inwendig; seelisch, geistig; Seelen-, Geistes-; geheim, verborgen; *com (Reserven)* still; **~ harbo(u)r** Binnenhafen *m*; *the* **~ man** *hum* der Magen; der Gaumen; Seele *f*, Geist *m*; **I~ Mongolia** die Innere Mongolei; **~most** innerst, geheimst; **~ tube** *mot* Schlauch *m*; **~width** lichte Weite *f*.

innerv|ate ['inə:veit] *tr* anregen, beleben, innervieren *a. physiol*; **~ation** [inə:'veiʃən] *physiol* Innervation *f*.

innings ['iniŋz] *sing od pl sport* Dran-, Am-Spiel-Sein *n*; *pol* Am-Ruder-Sein *n*; Amtszeit; Regierung; Gelegenheit *f*, Glück *n*; *to have o.'s ~ (sport)* dran, am Spiel sein, *pol* am Ruder, an der Macht, an der Regierung sein; *a good ~* e-e gute Gelegenheit.

innocen|ce, -cy ['inəsns(i)] Unschuld (*of* an); Schuldlosigkeit; Naivität, Einfachheit, Schlichtheit; Einfalt; Harmlosigkeit *f*; **~t** [-t] *a* unschuldig (*of* an); schuldlos; rein; harmlos; unschädlich; *(Geschwulst)* gutartig; schlicht, einfach, naiv, *fam* ahnungslos; dumm, einfältig; *fam* frei (*of* von); *jur* gutgläubig; *s* Unschuldige(r) *m*, *fam* Unschuldslamm *n*; Simpel, Einfaltspinsel *m*; *the massacre of the I~~s* der Bethlehemitische Kindermord.

innocuous [i'nɔkjuəs] harmlos, unschädlich.

innominate [i'nɔminit] unbenannt, namenlos; **~ bone** Hüftbein *n*.

innovat|e ['ino(u)veit, -nə-] *itr* Neuerungen einführen, Veränderungen vornehmen; **~ion** [ino(u)'veiʃən] Neuerung *f*; **~or** ['ino(u)veitə] Neuerer *m*.

innoxious [i'nɔkʃəs] unschädlich.

innuendo [inju(:)'endou] *pl -es* [-z] (versteckte) Andeutung, Anspielung *f*, Wink *m*, Geste; *jur* Unterstellung; Anzüglichkeit *f*.

innumer|able [i'nju:mərəbl] unzählig, zahllos; **~ous** [-rəs] *poet* ungezählt.

inobservan|ce [inəb'zə:vəns] Nichtbe(ob)achtung (*of* gen); Unachtsamkeit, Unaufmerksamkeit *f* (*of* gegenüber); **~t** [-t] unaufmerksam.

inoccupation ['inɔkju'peiʃən] Beschäftigungslosigkeit, Untätigkeit *f*.

inoculat|e [i'nɔkjuleit] *tr med (Menschen)* impfen (*into, on* in; *for* gegen); *(Serum)* einimpfen; *fig* einimpfen, einpflanzen (*s.o. with s.th.* jdm etw); *bot* okulieren; **~ion** [-'leiʃən] *med* Impfung; *bot* Okulierung *f*; *preventive ~~* Schutzimpfung *f*; *~~ lymph* Impfflüssigkeit *f*.

inodorous [in'oudərəs] geruchlos.

inoffensive [inə'fensiv] harmlos, ungefährlich, unschädlich; einwandfrei; **~ness** [-nis] Harmlosigkeit *f*.

inoffici|al [inə'fiʃəl] nichtamtlich, inoffiziell; **~ous** [-əs] funktionslos, ohne Amt; *jur* pflichtwidrig, gegen die gute Sitte verstoßend, unwirksam.

inoperative [in'ɔpərətiv] nicht in Betrieb (befindlich); nicht betriebsfähig; stillgelegt; unwirksam.

inopportune [in'ɔpətju:n] ungelegen, unzeitig; unangebracht, unpassend.

inordinate [i'nɔ:dinit] ungeordnet, ungeregelt; regellos; unmäßig, ausschweifend; maßlos.

inorgan|ic [inɔ:'gænik] *chem* anorganisch; *allg* unorganisch.

inosculate [i'nɔskjuleit] *tr* umea.-schlingen, -winden; *fig* eng mitea. verbinden, vereinigen; *itr* verschlungen, inea.geschlungen sein; *fig* eng mitea. verbunden, vereinigt sein.

in-patient ['inpeiʃənt] Anstaltskranke(r), klinische(r) Patient *m*; **~ treatment** stationäre Behandlung *f*.

input ['input] *tech* Eingangsleistung, (Energie-, *bes.* Strom-)Zufuhr *f*; Energie-,Kraft-,Strombedarf,-verbrauch *m*.

inquest ['inkwest] gerichtliche Untersuchung *f*; *coroner's ~* Leichenschau *f*.

inquietude [in'kwaiitju:d] Unruhe *f*.

inquir|e [in'kwaiə] *itr* sich erkundigen, fragen (*about, after* nach; *of* bei), Auskunft suchen, Erkundigung einziehen, (*about, after* über); fragen (*for an article in a shop* in e-m Laden nach e-r Ware; *for s.o.* nach jdm); untersuchen (*into s.th.* etw); *tr* fragen, sich erkundigen nach; **~er** [-rə] Fragende(r), Untersuchende(r) *m*; **~y** [-ri] An-, Nachfrage; Nachforschung; Untersuchung *a. jur*, Erhebung *f*; *upon ~~* auf Anfrage; *to make ~ies* Erkundigungen einziehen (*about* über; *of s.o.* bei jdm); *~~ form* Fragebogen *m*, Antragsformular *n*; *~~ office* Auskunftsbüro *n*, -stelle *f*, -schalter *m*; Auskunftei *f*.

inquisit|ion [inkwi'ziʃən] (strenge) Untersuchung *f a. jur*; *I~~ (rel)* Inquisition *f*, Ketzergericht *n*; **~ional** [-(ə)l] *a* Untersuchungs-, Inquisitions-; **~ive** [in'kwizitiv] wißbegierig, wissensdurstig, neugierig (*about* auf); **~iveness** [-'kwizitivnis] Wißbegierde *f*, Wissensdrang, -durst *m*; Neugier(de) *f*; **~or** [-'kwizitə] Untersuchungsrichter; Ermitt(e)lungsbeamte(r); *rel* Inquisitor *m*; **~orial** [inkwizi'tɔ:riəl] *a* Untersuchungs-, Inquisitions-; wißbegierig; (zu) neugierig.

inroad ['inroud] (feindlicher) Ein-, Überfall *m* (*into* in); *allg* Übergriff (*on* auf), Eingriff *m* (*on* in); *to make ~s upon s.o.'s savings* ein Loch in jds Ersparnisse reißen.

inrush ['inrʌʃ] Zustrom *m*.

insalubr|ious [insə'lu:briəs] ungesund; *(Klima)* unzuträglich; **~ity** [-iti] Gesundheitsschädlichkeit *f*.

insan|e [in'sein] *a* geisteskrank, irr(e); wahn-, unsinnig, sinnlos; Irren-; *s pl* Geisteskranke *m pl*; *~~ asylum* Irren-, Heilanstalt *f*; **~itary** [in'sænitəri] ungesund, gesundheitsschädlich; **~ity** [in'sæniti] Geisteskrankheit, geistige Umnachtung *f*.

insati|ability [inseiʃiə'biliti] Unersättlichkeit, (Hab-)Gier *f*; **~able** [in'seiʃjəbl] unersättlich, (hab)gierig; gierig (*of* auf, nach).

inscribe [in'skraib] *tr* einritzen, -meißeln, gravieren (*on* auf); mit e-r Gravierung versehen; *(Namen)* einschreiben, -zeichnen, -tragen; *(Buch)* widmen; *fig* einprägen, eingraben (*on s.o.'s memory* in jds Gedächtnis); *math* einbeschreiben; *~d stock* Namensaktien *f pl*.

inscription [in'skripʃən] Einschreibung, -zeichnung, -tragung; Auf-, Überschrift; (alte) Inschrift; Widmung *f*; **~ form** Anmeldeformular *n*.

inscrutab|ility [inskru:tə'biliti] Unerforschlichkeit, Unverständlichkeit *f*; **~le** [-'skru:təbl] unerforschlich, unergründlich, unerklärlich, unverständlich, rätselhaft.

insect ['insekt] Insekt, Kerbtier *n*; *fig pej* Wurm *m (Mensch)*; **~arium** [insek'tɛəriəm] Insektarium *n*; **~icide** [in'sektisaid] Insektenpulver *n*; **~ivora** [insek'tivərə] *zoo* Insektenfresser *m pl*; **~ivorous** [-'tivərəs] *zoo* insektenfressend; Insektenfresser-; **~ology** [-'tɔlədʒi] Insektenkunde, Entomologie *f*; **~ powder** Insektenpulver *n*.

insecur|e [insi'kjuə] unsicher, gefährdet; *(Kredit)* ungedeckt; schwankend, ängstlich; trügerisch, ungewiß, unzuverlässig; *(Gebäude)* baufällig; **~ity** [-riti] Unsicherheit; Ungewißheit, Unzuverlässigkeit *f*.

inseminat|e [in'semineit] *tr* (die) Saat legen in; befruchten, schwängern; *fig* einpflanzen in; **~ion** [-'neiʃən] Saat *(Tätigkeit)*; Befruchtung *f*; *artificial ~~* künstliche Befruchtung *f*.

insens|ate [in'senseit] gefühl-, empfindungslos, leblos, (wie) tot; unsinnig, unvernünftig, dumm; gefühlskalt; **~ibility** [insensi'biliti] Empfindungslosigkeit, Unempfindlichkeit (*to* für); Bewußtlosigkeit, Ohnmacht; Gleichgültigkeit, Stumpfheit *f*; **~ible** [in'sensəbl] *physiol* empfindungs-, wahrnehmungslos; bewußtlos, ohne Bewußtsein, ohnmächtig; gleichgültig (*to, of* gegen); achtlos (*of s.th.* gegen etw); winzig (klein), unmerklich, ganz allmählich; **~itive** [-itiv] gefühllos, unempfindlich (*to* gegen); unempfänglich (*to* für); **insentient** [in'senʃiənt] empfindungs-, bewußt-, leblos.

inseparab|ility [insepərə'biliti] Untrennbarkeit; Unzertrennlichkeit *f*; **~le** [in'sepərəbl] untrennbar; unzertrennlich.

insert [in'sə:t] *tr* einsetzen, -fügen, -passen, -schalten; einrücken, aufgeben, setzen lassen (*an advertisement in a newspaper* e-e Anzeige in die Zeitung); setzen (*in brackets* in Klammern); *s* ['insə:t] Einsatz *m*, -fügung, -schaltung *f*; *Am (Buch)* Bei-, Einlage, (Zeitungs-)Beilage *f*; Einlege-, Beilageblatt *n*; *(Zeitung)* Zusatz *m*, Einschaltung *f*; *tech* Einsatzstück *n*; **~ion** [in'sə:ʃən] Einfügung, -schaltung *f*; Zusatz; Einsatz *(a. in e-m Kleid)*; *tech* Einbau *m*; Inserat *n*, Anzeige, Annonce *f*; *(Münze)* Einwurf *m*; Beilage *f*.

inset ['in'set] *tr* einsetzen, -legen, -fügen, -schalten; *s* ['inset] Einsatz *m*, Bei-, Einlage, Einfügung *f*; Nebenbild *n*, -karte *f (e-r Landkarte)*; Bild *n* im Text; *(Kleid)* Einsatz *m*; *attr* Einsatz-, Einlage-.

inshore ['in'ʃɔ:] *adv a* in der Nähe der Küste (befindlich); *a* Küsten-.

*

inside ['in'said] *s* Innen-, innere Seite *f*; *das* Innere; der Fahrbahn abgewendete Seite *f* des Gehweges; Fahrgast *m* im Wagen; *a. pl fam* Eingeweide *pl*; *a* inner, inwendig, innerlich; Innen-; Haus-, Heim-; privat, geheim, vertraulich; *adv* innen, im Innern; auf der Innenseite; drin(nen); *prp* auf der Innenseite, im Innern *gen*; *(a. zeitlich)* innerhalb *gen*; *~ of (fam)*: *~ of a week* innerhalb e-r Woche; mitten in der Woche; *to come, to go ~* hereinkommen; hineingehen; *to know ~ out* in- u. auswendig, *fam* aus dem ff kennen; *(turned) ~ out* das Innere nach außen, das Oberste zuunterst (gekehrt, gestülpt); *(Kleidungsstück)* verkehrt an; **~ diameter** lichte Weite *f*; **~ door** Innentür *f*; **~ left** *sport* Halblinke(r) *m*; **~r** ['-ə] Eingeweihte(r) *m*; *pl* eingeweihte Kreise *m pl*; **~ track** *sport* Innenbahn; *fig* günstigere Lage *f*, Vorteil *m*; *to have an* ~~ günstig dran, im Vorteil sein (*to doing s.th.* etw zu tun); ~ **wall** Innenwand *f*.

insidious [in'sidjəs] verräterisch, hinterhältig, -listig, heimtückisch; *(Krankheit)* schleichend.

insight ['insait] Einsicht *f*, Einblick *m* (*into* in), Verständnis *n* (*into* für); Lebenserfahrung *f*.

insignia [in'signiə] *pl*, *Am a. sing* Insignien *pl*, Hoheitszeichen *n pl*; ~ *of rank* Rangabzeichen *n pl*.

insignifican|ce, -cy [insig'nifikəns(i)] Bedeutungslosigkeit, Belanglosigkeit, Nebensächlichkeit, Geringfügigkeit *f*; **~t** [-t] bedeutungslos; unbedeutend, nebensächlich, belanglos, unerheblich, geringfügig; nichtssagend, unscheinbar; verächtlich.

insincer|e [insin'siə] unaufrichtig, unehrlich, lügenhaft, heuchlerisch, falsch; **~ity** [insin'seriti] Unaufrichtigkeit, Unehrlichkeit, Lügenhaftigkeit, Heuchelei, Falschheit *f*.

insinuat|e [in'sinjueit] *tr* langsam, auf Umwegen, geschickt hineinbringen, hineinmanövrieren; hineinschmuggeln (*into* in); zu verstehen geben, andeuten, anspielen auf; einflüstern; beibringen; *to* ~~ *o.s. into s.o.'s favo(u)r* jds Gunst erschleichen; **~ing** [-iŋ] einschmeichelnd; **~ion** [insinju'eiʃən] (versteckte) Andeutung, Anspielung *f*; leise(r) Wink *m*; Schmeichelei *f*.

insipid [in'sipid] abgeschmackt, geschmacklos; fade, schal; *fig* langweilig, uninteressant, unlebendig; **~ity** [-'piditi] Fadheit, Schalheit; Abgeschmacktheit, Uninteressantheit *f*.

insist [in'sist] *itr* bestehen, beharren, immer wieder zurückkommen, großes Gewicht, (sehr) großen Wert legen (*on, upon* auf); nachdrücklich betonen (*on s.th.* etw); *tr* bestehen auf; *to* ~ *on doing s.th.* immer wieder tun; **~ence, -cy** [-əns(i)] Bestehen (*on* auf); Beharren *n*, Nachdruck *m*; Beharrlichkeit, Hartnäckigkeit; Eindringlichkeit *f*; **~ent** [-ənt] darauf bestehend, beharrend; beharrlich, standhaft, hartnäckig; eindringlich, eindrucksvoll; *to be* ~~ bestehen (*on* auf); darauf bestehen (*that* daß).

insnare *s. ensnare.*

insobriety [inso(u)'braiəti] Unmäßigkeit *f*, Ausschweifungen *f pl*; Trunksucht *f*.

insolat|e ['inso(u)leit] *tr* in die Sonne legen; **~ion** [inso(u)'leiʃən] Sonnenbad *n*; *med* Sonnenstich *m*; *mete* Sonneneinstrahlung *f*.

insole ['insoul] Brand-, Einlegesohle *f*.

insolen|ce ['insələns] Unverschämtheit, Frechheit; Anmaßung *f* (*in doing s.th.* etw zu tun); **~t** ['-t] unverschämt, anmaßend, frech.

insolub|ility [insəlju'biliti] Unauflöslichkeit; Unlösbarkeit *f*; **~le** [in'səljubl] un(auf)löslich; unlösbar.

insolven|cy [in'səlvənsi] Zahlungsunfähigkeit, Insolvenz; Zahlungseinstellung *f*, Konkurs, Bank(e)rott *m*; **~t** [in'səlvənt] *a* zahlungsunfähig, insolvent; bank(e)rott, in Konkurs; *(Konto)* dubios; *s* zahlungsunfähige(r) Schuldner *m*; *to become* ~~ die Zahlungen einstellen; in Konkurs gehen; *to declare o.s.* ~~ Konkurs anmelden; ~~ *debtor* Gemeinschuldner *m*; ~~ *estate* Konkursmasse *f*.

insomni|a [in'səmniə] Schlaflosigkeit *f*; **~ous** [-əs] an Schlaflosigkeit leidend.

insomuch [insou'mʌtʃ] *adv* dermaßen, dergestalt (*as to, that* daß); ~ *as* (in)sofern, soweit.

insoucian|ce [in'su:sjəns] Sorglosigkeit, Unbekümmertheit *f*; **~t** [-t] sorglos, unbekümmert, gleichgültig.

inspect [in'spekt] *tr* genau ansehen, besichtigen, (kritisch) prüfen, genau untersuchen; *com (Bücher)* revidieren; nach-, überprüfen; *(amtlich)* besichtigen, inspizieren; beaufsichtigen, überwachen, kontrollieren; **~ion** [in'spekʃən] genaue Durchsicht, (kritische) Prüfung, genaue Untersuchung; Nachschau, Nach-, Überprüfung; Einsichtnahme; *(amtliche)* Besichtigung, Inspektion *f*; *mil* Appell *m*; Aufsicht, Kontrolle; Revision *f*; *for your* ~~ zur Ansicht; *to allow, to grant, to permit* ~~ Einsicht gewähren (*of s.th.* in etw); *to conduct an* ~~ e-e Überprüfung durchführen; *to be open to public* ~~ öffentlich zur Einsichtnahme ausliegen; *to send on* ~~ zur Ansicht zusenden; *to submit for* ~~ zur Einsichtnahme vorlegen; *committee of* ~~ Untersuchungs-, Gläubigerausschuß *m*; *customs* ~~ Zollrevision, -kontrolle *f*; *free* ~~ Besichtigung *f* ohne Kaufzwang; *judicial* ~~ gerichtliche(r), richterliche(r) Augenschein *m*; *medical* ~~ ärztliche Untersuchung *f*; ~~ *lamp* Hand-, Ableuchtlampe *f*; ~~ *pit* Montagegrube *f*; ~~ *room* Prüf-, Kontrollraum *m*; **~or** [-ə] Kontrolleur, Prüfungs-, Aufsichtsbeamte(r), Inspektor; Aufseher *m*; *customs* ~~ Zollinspektor *m*; *police* ~~ Polizeiinspektor *m*; *road* ~~ Straßenaufseher *m*; *school* ~~ Schulrat *m*; *ticket* ~~ Fahrkartenkontrolleur *m*; ~~ *of taxes* Steuerinspektor *m*; ~~ *of weights and measures* Eichmeister *m*; ~~ *of works* Bauaufseher *m*; **~oral** [-ərəl], **~orial** [-'tɔ:riəl] *a* Kontroll-, Aufsichts-; **~orate** [-ərit] Inspektorenamt *n*; Kontrollbezirk, -abschnitt *m*; Abnahmestelle *f*; **~orship** [-əʃip] Inspektorenstelle *f*.

inspir|ation [inspə'reiʃən] Eingebung, Begeisterung, Inspiration *a. rel*; Erleuchtung *f*; Einatmen *n*; **~ational** [-'reiʃnəl] begeisternd; begeistert; **~ator** ['inspəreitə] Inhalierapparat *m*; **~atory** [in'spaiərətəri] *a* Einatmungs-, Inhalier-; **~e** [in'spaiə] *tr* einatmen; inhalieren; einhauchen; begeistern, inspirieren *a. rel*; *(Gefühl, Gedanken)* wecken; hervorrufen; einflößen (*into s.o.* jdm); *(mit e-m Gefühl, Gedanken)* erfüllen; eingeben, veranlassen; *to* ~~ *s.o. with fear* jdn mit Schrecken erfüllen; **~it** [in'spirit] *tr* beleben, anfeuern, aufmuntern, ermutigen, begeistern (*to* zu).

inspissate [in'spiseit] *tr* eindicken, -dampfen; *itr* dick, fest werden.

instab|ility [instə'biliti] Unbeständigkeit; Labilität *a. tech*; Unsicherheit; Haltlosigkeit; Unentschlossenheit *f*; **~le** [in'steibl] *s. unstable.*

install [in'stɔ:l] *tr (in ein Amt)* einsetzen, bestallen; (feierlich) einführen; einrichten, anbringen; *tech* installieren, einbauen; *(Maschine)* aufstellen; *(Draht)* verlegen; *to* ~ *o.s.* sich einrichten, sich niederlassen; **~ation** [instɔ:'leiʃən, -stə-] (Amts-)Einsetzung, Bestallung, (Amts-)Einführung; Einrichtung, Installation *f*; Werk *n*, Anlage *f*; Auf-, Einbau *m*; *(Maschine)* Aufstellung *f*; ~~ *plan* Einbauzeichnung *f*.

instal(l)ment [in'stɔ:lmənt] Rate, Abschlags-, Ab-, Teilzahlung; Teillieferung; *(Veröffentlichung)* Fortsetzung *f*; *by, in* ~*s* in Raten, ratenweise, auf Teilzahlung, *fam* auf Stottern; *to appear in* ~*s* in Fortsetzungen erscheinen; *first* ~ Anzahlung, erste Rate *f*; *final* ~ letzte, Schlußrate, Abschlußzahlung *f*; *monthly* ~ Monatsrate *f*; *payment by* ~*s* Raten-, Teil-, Abzahlung *f*; ~ **business** Raten-, Abzahlungsgeschäft *n*; ~ **plan, system** Ab-, Teilzahlungsgeschäft *n*, Ratenplan *m*; ~ **sale** Teil-, Abzahlungsverkauf *m*.

instan|ce ['instəns] *s* (dringende) Bitte *f*, Er-, Nachsuchen *n*, Vorschlag *m*, Veranlassung *f*, Betreiben; Beispiel *n*, Fall, Beleg *m*; *jur* Instanz *f*; *tr* (als Beispiel) anführen, nennen, zitieren; *at s.o.'s* ~~ auf jds Veranlassung, Ersuchen, Bitte; *for* ~~ zum Beispiel; *in this* ~~ in diesem Fall; *in the first* ~~ in erster Linie, vor allem, zunächst; *in the last* ~~ in letzter Instanz, endgültig; *through all* ~~*s* durch alle Instanzen; *appeal* ~~ *(jur)* Berufungsinstanz *f*; **~cy** ['-i] Dringlichkeit *f*; **~t** ['-t] *a* dringend, eilig; sofortig, unmittelbar, augenblicklich; (unmittelbar) bevorstehend, drohend; dieses, des laufenden Monats; *s* Augenblick, Moment *m*; *at this* ~~ in diesem Augenblick; *in an* ~~ im Augenblick; im Nu; *on the* ~~, *this* ~~ sofort, gleich, im Augenblick; *on the 5th* ~~ *(meist: inst.)* am 5. des laufenden Monats; *the* ~~ *(that)* sobald (als); ~~ *coffee* lösliche(r) Kaffee *m*; **~taneous** [-'teinjəs] augenblicklich, momentan, sofortig, unmittelbar, unverzüglich; Augenblicks-; ~~ *exposure, photograph* Momentaufnahme *f*; **~taneously** *adv* unverzüglich, sofort; **~ter** [in'stæntə] *adv* sofort, sogleich, unverzüglich; **~tly** ['-tli] *adv* sofort, augenblicklich, im Augenblick.

instate [in'steit] *tr (in e-n Rang)* erheben; *(in e-e Stellung)* einsetzen.

instead [in'sted] *adv* statt dessen, dafür; ~ *of (prp)* (an)statt *gen*, an Stelle *gen*, an ... Stelle; ~ *of doing* statt zu tun; *to be* ~ *of s.o.* jdn vertreten, an jds Stelle treten.

instep ['instep] *anat* Spann, Rist *m*; *(Pferd)* Röhre *f*, Mittelfuß *m*; *to be high in the* ~ *(fam)* die Nase hoch tragen; *to break o.'s* ~ sich den Fuß brechen; ~ **raiser** Senkfußeinlage *f*.

instigat|e ['instigeit] *tr* (auf)reizen, aufstacheln, anspornen, aufhetzen (*to* zu); anstiften (*to a crime* zu e-m Verbrechen); *(Aufruhr)* anzetteln; veranlassen; **~ion** [-'geiʃən] Aufreizung, Aufhetzung, Anstiftung *f*; *at, on his* ~~ auf sein Betreiben; **~or** [-ə] Hetzer, Anstifter, Verführer *m*.

instil(l) [in'stil] *tr* einträufeln (*into* in); *fig (Gedanken)* allmählich nahebringen, beibringen; *(Gefühl)* langsam erwecken; *(Angst)* einflößen; **~lation** [insti'leiʃən], **~(l)ment** [in'stilmənt] Einträufeln; *fig* Nahebringen, Erwecken, Einflößen *n*.

instinct ['instiŋkt] *s* Instinkt, (Natur-) Trieb *m*; Gabe *f*, Talent *n*, Fähigkeit *f* (*for* für); *by, on, from* ~ instinktiv; *pred a* [in'stiŋkt] erfüllt (*with* von); voller (*with* gen); belebt (*with* von); **~ive** [in'stiŋktiv] instinktiv, triebhaft, angeboren; unwillkürlich.

institut|e ['institju:t] *tr* aufstellen, einrichten, (be)gründen, stiften; anordnen, ein-, in die Wege leiten, einführen; *(Untersuchung)* einleiten; *(in ein Amt)* einsetzen; *(zum Erben)* bestimmen; *(Klage)* einreichen; *s* Einrichtung *f*; Institut *n*; *pl jur* Institutionen *f pl*; *to* ~~ *legal proceedings against s.o.* Klage erheben gegen; **~ion** [insti'tju:ʃən] Errichtung, (Be-) Gründung, Stiftung; Einleitung, -führung; Einrichtung, Anordnung; Praxis *f*, Regeln, Bestimmungen, Anweisungen *f pl*; Gesetz; Organ *n*; (wissenschaftliche) Gesellschaft *f*, Institut *n*, Anstalt; *rel* Einsetzung; *fam* altbekannte Person *od* Sache *f*; *charitable* ~~ Wohlfahrtseinrichtung *f*; *credit* ~~ Kreditanstalt *f*; *educational* ~~ Lehranstalt *f*; *financial* ~~ Geldinstitut *n*; *penal, penitentiary* ~~ Strafanstalt *f*; **~ional** [insti'tju:ʃənl] *a* Instituts-, Anstalts-; institutionell; ~~ *advertising (Am)* Firmenwerbung *f*; ~~ *buyer* Kapitalsammelstelle *f*; ~~ *care* Anstaltsfürsorge *f*; ~ **ionalize** [-'tju:ʃnəlaiz] *tr* institutionalisieren; *fam (Person)* in e-e Anstalt stecken.

instruct [in'strʌkt] *tr* unterrichten, belehren, anleiten, unterweisen, ausbilden, erziehen; ein-, anweisen; die Anweisung geben (*s.o.* jdm); auftragen (*s.o.* jdm); unterrichten, informieren (*of s.th.* von e-r S); **~ion** [in'strʌkʃən] Unterricht *m*, Erziehung; Schulung; Ein-, Unterweisung, Belehrung, Ausbildung *f*; Lehrberuf *m*; Anleitung; Anordnung, Anweisung, Vorschrift; Instruktion *f*, Auftrag *m a. mil*; (~~*s for use*) Gebrauchsanweisung *f*; *pl* Verhaltensmaßregeln *f pl*; *jur* Instruktionen, Weisungen, Richtlinien *f pl*; *according to* ~~*s* auftrags-, weisungsgemäß; *to ask for* ~~*s* Weisungen einholen; *to comply with* ~~*s received* sich nach den empfangenen Weisungen richten; *to give* ~~*s* Anweisungen erteilen, Weisungen geben, Anordnungen treffen; *private* ~~ Privatunterricht *m*; *self-*~~ Selbstunterricht *m*; *service* ~~ Dienstanweisung *f*; *visual* ~~ Anschauungsunterricht *m*; *working* ~~ Betriebsordnung *f*; ~~ *book* Bedienungs-, Gebrauchsanweisung *f*; ~~ *slip* Kennblatt *n*; **~ional** [in'strʌkʃənl] Unterrichts-, Lehr-, Erziehungs-; erzieherisch; ~~ *film* Kultur-, Lehrfilm *m*; ~~ *school* Fortbildungsschule *f*; ~~ *trip* Informationsreise *f*; **~ive** [-iv] belehrend; lehrreich, instruktiv; **~or** [-ə] Lehrer *m*, Lehrperson *f*, Erzieher *m*; Lehrbuch *n*; *mil* Ausbilder, Instrukteur *m*; *pl* Lehrpersonal *n*; *Am* (Universitäts-)Dozent *m*; **~ress** [-ris] Lehrerin, Erzieherin *f*.

instrument ['instrumənt] Werkzeug, *(bes. feines)* Instrument; Gerät; (Musik-)Instrument; *fig* Mittel, Werkzeug *n (Person)*; *jur* Urkunde *f*, Dokument, Papier, Instrument; *pl med* Besteck *n*; *of acceptance* Annahmeurkunde *f*; ~ *of debt* Schuldbrief *m*; **~al** [instru'məntl] Instrumenten-; als Werkzeug dienend; nützlich, brauchbar, förderlich; behilflich; *mus* instrumental; *s* Instrumental(is) *m*; *to be* ~~ *in s.th.*, *to s.th.* bei, zu e-r S behilflich sein; zu e-r S beitragen; ~~ *music* Instrumentalmusik *f*; **~ality** [instrumen'tæliti] Brauchbarkeit, Nützlichkeit, Zweckhaftigkeit *f*; Mittel *n*; Mitwirkung, Vermitt(e)lung *f*; *through, by the* ~~ *of* durch Vermittlung *gen*; ~ **board, panel** *mot aero* Armaturenbrett *n*; ~ **flight, flying** Instrumenten-, Blindflug *m*.

insubordinat|e [insə'bɔ:dnit] ungehorsam, widersetzlich; **~ion** ['insəbɔ:di'neiʃən] Ungehorsam *m*, Widersetzlichkeit, Auflehnung; *mil* Gehorsamsverweigerung *f*.

insubstantial [insəb'stænʃ(ə)l] unwirklich, eingebildet, imaginär; dünn, schwach; gehaltlos, dürftig; **~ity** [insʌbstænʃi'æliti] Unwirklichkeit; Gehaltlosigkeit *f*.

insufferable [in'sʌfərəbl] unerträglich; unausstehlich, unleidlich.

insufficien|cy [insə'fiʃənsi] Mangel *m*; Unzulänglichkeit; *med* Insuffizienz *f*; *cardiac* ~~ Herzinsuffizienz *f*; **~t** [-t] ungenügend, unzureichend, unzulänglich; untauglich, mangelhaft.

insul|ar ['insjulə] *a* Insel-, insular; abgesondert, isoliert; engstirnig, stur, voller Vorurteile; *med* insulär; **~arity** [insju'læriti] insulare Lage *f*; *fig* Abgeschlossenheit; *fig* Engstirnigkeit, Sturheit, Beschränktheit *f*; **~ate** ['insjuleit] *tr* isolieren, absondern; *el* isolieren; **~ating** ['-leitiŋ] *el* isolierend, Isolier-; nichtleitend; ~~ *cardboard* Isolierpappe *f*; ~~ *layer* Isolierschicht *f*; ~~ *material (el)* Isoliermaterial *n*; ~~ *switch* Trennschalter *m*; ~~ *tape* Isolierband *n*, -streifen *m*; **~ation** [insju'leiʃən] Absonderung, Isolierung *f a. el*; *el* Isoliermaterial *n*; **~ator** ['insjuleitə] *el* Nichtleiter; Isolator *m*; **~in** ['insjulin] *pharm* Insulin *n (Warenzeichen)*.

insult ['insʌlt] *s* Beleidigung, Beschimpfung, Schmähung, Verunglimpfung *f* (*to s.o.* jds); *tr* [in'sʌlt] beleidigen, beschimpfen, schmähen, verunglimpfen; **~ing** [-'sʌltiŋ] beleidigend, verletzend; ~~ *language, words (pl)* beleidigende Äußerungen *f pl*.

insuperab|ility [insjupərə'biliti] Unüberwindlichkeit *f*; **~le** [in'sju:pərəbl] unüberwindlich, unschlagbar.

insupportable [insə'pɔ:təbl] unerträglich, unausstehlich.

insur|ance [in'ʃuərəns] Versicherung; (Versicherungs-)Prämie *f*; *to effect, to take out an* ~~ e-e Versicherung abschließen; *accident-*~~ Unfallversicherung *f*; *disability-, disablement-, invalidity-*~~ Invalidenversicherung *f*; *fire-*~~ Feuerversicherung *f*; *hail-*~~ Hagelversicherung *f*; *health* ~~ Krankenversicherung *f*; *liability-*~~ Haftpflichtversicherung *f*; *life-*~~ Lebensversicherung *f*; *luggage-*~~ Reisegepäckversicherung *f*; *motor-car* ~~ Kfz.-Versicherung *f*; *old-age* ~~ Altersversicherung *f*; *period, term of* ~~ Versicherungsdauer *f*; *sick(ness)-*~~ Krankenversicherung *f*; *social* ~~ Sozialversicherung *f*; *transportation-*~~ Transportversicherung *f*; *unemployment-*~~ Arbeitslosenversicherung *f*; ~~ *act* Versicherungsgesetz *n*; ~~ *agent* Versicherungsvertreter *m*; ~~ *agreement, contract* Versicherungsvertrag *m*; ~~ *benefit* Versicherungsleistung *f*; ~~ *against burglary* Einbruchversicherung *f*; ~~ *claim* Versicherungsanspruch *m*; ~~ *company* Versicherungsgesellschaft *f*; ~~ *conditions (pl)* Versicherungsbedingungen *f pl*; ~~ *coverage* Versicherungsschutz *m*, -deckung *f*; ~~ *fee* Versicherungsgebühr *f*; ~~ *fraud* Versicherungsbetrug *m*; ~~ *matters (pl)* das Versicherungswesen; ~~ *officer* Versicherungsbeamte(r) *m*; ~~ *policy* Versicherungsschein *m*, Police *f*; *to effect, to take out an* ~~ *policy* e-e Versicherung abschließen; ~~ *rate* Prämiensatz *m*; ~~ *regulations (pl)* Versicherungsbestimmungen *f pl*; ~~ *sum* Versicherungssumme *f*; ~~ *swindler* Versicherungsbetrüger *m*; ~~ *value* Versicherungswert *m*; **~ant** [in'ʃuərənt] *Am* Versicherte(r), Versicherungsnehmer *m*; **~e** [in'ʃuə] *tr* bestätigen; garantieren, verbürgen, gewährleisten; sichern, sicherstellen; schützen (*against* gegen); versichern; **~ed** [-d] *a* versichert; *s* Versicherte(r), Versicherungsnehmer *m*; ~~ *letter, parcel, package* Wertbrief *m*, -päckchen, -paket *n*; ~~ *value* Versicherungswert *m*; **~er** [-rə] Versicherer *m*; *pl* Versicherungsgesellschaft *f*.

insurgen|ce, -cy [in'sə:dʒəns(i)] Aufruhr, Aufstand *m*, Erhebung, Rebellion *f*; **~t** [-t] *a* aufrührerisch, aufständisch; *s* Aufrührer, Aufständische(r), Rebell *m*.

insurmountable [insə:'mauntəbl] unübersteigbar, unüberwindlich.

insurrection [insə'rekʃən] Aufruhr, Aufstand *m*, Empörung, Rebellion, Revolte *f*; **~al** [-l], **~ary** [-əri] aufrührerisch, aufständisch, rebellierend; **~ist** [-ʃnist] Aufrührer, Empörer, Rebell *m*.

insusceptib|ility ['insəseptə'biliti] Unempfindlichkeit; Unempfänglichkeit *f*; **~le** [insə'septəbl] unempfindlich, gefühllos; unempfänglich (*of, to* für).

*

intact [in'tækt] unberührt, unbeschädigt, unverletzt, intakt, ganz.

intaglio [in'tɑ:liou] *pl -os* Intaglio *n*, Gemme *f*.

intake ['inteik] Aufnahme *f*; Einlaß *m*, Öffnung; Verengung *f*; *mot* Ansaugrohr *n*, -öffnung *f*; *min* Luftschacht *m*; aufgenommene Energiemenge; Ein-, Annahme *f*; trockengelegte(s) Land *n*; ~ **valve** Einlaßventil *n*.

intangib|ility [intændʒə'biliti] Unberührbarkeit, Unwirklichkeit; Unklarheit, Ungreifbarkeit *f*; **~le** [in'tændʒəbl] unberührbar, unwirklich, schemenhaft; ungreifbar, unklar, nebelhaft, vage; *(Werte)* immateriell.

integ|er ['intidʒə] Ganze(s) *n*, Einheit; *math* ganze Zahl *f*; **~ral** ['intigrəl] *a (Bestandteil)* wesentlich; vollständig, ganz; *math* ganzzahlig; Integral-; *s* Ganze(s); *math* Integral *n*; ~~ *calculus* Integralrechnung *f*; **~rality** [inti'græliti] Ganzheit, Integrität *f*; **~rant** ['intigrənt] *a* wesentlich, integrierend; *s* wesentliche(r), integrale(r), konstituierende(r) Bestandteil *m*; **~rate** ['-greit] *tr* ergänzen, vervollständigen; vereinigen; zs.fassen; zs.zählen, -rechnen, -fügen; integrieren, eingliedern; die Rassenschranken beseitigen gegenüber; *math* integrieren; *el* zählen; ~~*d school* Einheitsschule *f*; ~~*d store* Filialbetrieb *m*; ~~*d trust* vertikale(r) Konzern *m*; **~ration** [inti'greiʃən] Ergänzung, Vervollständigung, Vereinigung, Summierung; Integrierung *f*; Zs.schluß *m*; *math* Integration; *Am* Aufhebung *f* der Rassenschranken; **~rity** [in'tegriti] Vollständigkeit, Ganzheit, Integrität; Unverletztheit, Unversehrtheit; *fig* Geradheit, Aufrichtigkeit, Ehrlichkeit, Lauterkeit, Offenheit, Rechtschaffenheit *f*.

integument [in'tegjumənt] *bot zoo* Bedeckung, Decke, Hülle *f*.

intellect ['intilekt] Verstand *m*, Urteilskraft *f*, Intellekt *m*; *a. pl* Intellektuelle *m pl*; Intelligenz *f*; **~ion** [inti'lekʃən] Denken, Erkennen, Verstehen *n*; **~ual** [inti'lektjuəl] *a* verstandesmäßig, Verstandes-; intellektuell, geistig; vernünftig; verständig; Geistes-; *s* Intellektuelle(r); Geistes-, Kopfarbeiter *m*; **~uality** ['intilektju'æliti] Intelligenz *f*, hohe(r) Verstand *m*; **~ualize** [inti'lektjuəlaiz] *tr* vergeistigen; *itr* urteilen, denken.

intelligen|ce [in'telidʒəns] Intelligenz, Auffassungsgabe *f*, -vermögen *n*, geistige Wendigkeit; *(bei Tieren)* Klugheit; Mitteilung, Nachricht, Information, Auskunft; Spionage *f*; Nachrichten-, Geheimdienst *m*; *mil* Spionageabwehr, (Abteilung) Abwehr *f*; ~~ *bureau, department, office* Nachrichtenbüro *n*; ~~ *with the enemy* (verräterische) Beziehungen *f pl* zum Feinde; ~~ *quotient (psychol)* Intelligenz-Quotient *m*; ~~*-service* Nachrichten-, Geheimdienst *m*; ~~ *test* Intelligenzprüfung *f*; **~cer** [-sə] Spion *m*; **~t** [-t] intelligent, geistig wendig; geistig hochstehend, (hoch)gebildet, kenntnisreich; sehr bewandert (*of* in); **~tsia** [inteli'dʒentsiə, -'ge-] Intelligenz *f*, Intellektuellen(schicht) *m pl*, gebildete Oberschicht *f*.

intelligib|ility [intelidʒə'biliti] Verständlichkeit *f*; **~le** [in'telidʒəbl] verständlich, begreiflich, klar (*to s.o.* jdm); *philos* (nur) verstandesmäßig faßbar.

intemper|ance [in'tempərəns] Unmäßigkeit; Trunksucht *f*; **~ate** [-it] unmäßig, maß-, zügellos; trunksüchtig; heftig, streng; *(Klima)* rauh.

intend [in'tend] *tr* beabsichtigen, planen, vorhaben (*to do, doing* zu tun); meinen, sagen wollen; bestimmen (*for* für, zu); bedeuten, darstellen; *jur* den Vorsatz haben; *this is ~ed for me* das ist auf mich gemünzt; *is this ~ed to be me?* soll ich das sein? **~ed** [-id] *a* beabsichtigt, geplant; kommend, zukünftig, in spe; *s fam* Bräutigam, Verlobte(r) *m*; Braut, Verlobte *f*.

intens|e [in'tens] sehr stark, heftig, groß, hochgradig; gespannt, angestrengt, intensiv; *(Farbe)* lebhaft, kräftig; *(Licht)* hell; überspannt; **~eness** [-nis] Stärke, Heftigkeit, Intensität; Angespanntheit, Angestrengtheit *f*; **~ification** [intensifi'keiʃən] Verstärkung, Steigerung, Intensivierung; *tech* Helltastung *f*; **~ifier** [in'tensifaiə] Verstärker *m*; **~ify** [in'tensifai] *tr* verstärken, steigern, intensivieren, vermehren; *itr* stärker werden, sich steigern, zunehmen; *tech* helltasten; **~ion** [in'tenʃən] Stärke, Intensität *f*, hohe(r) Grad *m*; Verstärkung; Gespanntheit, Entschlossenheit *f*; **~ity** [in'tensiti] hohe(r) Grad *m*, Intensität; Stärke, Kraft, Heftigkeit *f*; ~~ *of heat* Hitzegrad *m*; ~~ *of light, sound, electric current* Licht-, Ton-, Stromstärke *f*; **~ive** [-iv] verstärkend, steigernd; stark, gründlich, intensiv; *med* stark wirkend.

intent [in'tent] *a* fest gerichtet (*on* auf); (an)gespannt; eifrig bedacht (*on* auf); fest entschlossen (*on* zu); *s* Absicht *f*, Zweck *m*; Bedeutung *f*, Sinn *m*; *to this ~* in dieser Absicht; *to the ~ that* in der Absicht, daß; *to all ~s and purposes* in jeder Hinsicht; im Grunde, in Wirklichkeit; *with ~* absichtlich, mit Absicht; *with ~ to do* in der Absicht zu tun; **~ion** [in'tenʃən] Absicht *f*, Vorhaben *n*; Zweck *m*; Bedeutung *f*, Sinn *m*; *the road to hell is paved with good ~~s (prov)* der Weg zur Hölle ist mit guten Vorsätzen gepflastert; **~ional** [-'tenʃənl] absichtlich; **~ioned** [-d] *a*: *well-~~* wohlgesinnt; **~ness** [in'tentnis] (gespannte) Aufmerksamkeit *f*; Eifer *m*; (feste) Entschlossenheit *f*.

inter [in'tə:] *tr* begraben, beerdigen, bestatten.

interact ['intərækt] **1.** *s* Zwischenakt *m*, -spiel *n*; **2.** [intər'ækt] *itr* aufea. wirken, ea., sich gegenseitig beeinflussen; **~ion** [intər'ækʃən] gegenseitige Beeinflussung, Wechselwirkung; *tech* Überlagerung *f*; **~ive** [intər'æktiv] sich gegenseitig beeinflussend.

interbreed [intə(:)'bri:d] *irr -bred, -bred tr itr biol* (sich) kreuzen.

intercal|ary [in'tə:kələri] eingeschaltet; interpoliert; Schalt-; ~~ *day, year* Schalttag *m*, -jahr *n*; **~ate** [-leit] *tr* einschalten, einschieben; interpolieren; **~ation** [intə:kə'leiʃən] Einschaltung; Interpolation *f*.

interced|e [intə(:)'si:d] *itr* sich verwenden, sich einsetzen, Fürsprache einlegen (*with* bei; *for* für); vermitteln; **~er** [-ə] Fürsprecher; Vermittler *m*.

intercept [intə(:)'sept] *tr* auf-, abfangen, abstellen; *(Wasser, Licht)* sperren; unterbrechen; verhindern, verhüten, unterbinden, unmöglich machen; *(Rückzug)* abschneiden; die Verbindung abschneiden (*s.o.* mit jdm); *tele radio* abhören, -horchen; *aero* abschneiden, -fangen; *s* ['intə(:)sept] aufgefangene Meldung *f*; **~ion** [-'sepʃən] Abfangen, Abschneiden; Abhören, Abhorchen *n*; Unterbindung, Verhinderung, Verhütung *f*; ~~ *flight (aero)* Sperrflug *m*; ~~ *service* Abhördienst *m*; **~or** [-'septə] Abfangende(r); Abhörende(r); *aero* Abfang-, Verteidigungsjäger *m*; *tele* Unterbrecherklappe *f*.

intercess|ion [intə'seʃən] Fürsprache; Vermittlung; *rel* Fürbitte *f*; **~ional** [-ʃənl] *a* Vermitt(e)lungs-; **~or** [-'sesə] Fürsprecher; Vermittler *m* (*with* bei); **~ory** [-'sesəri] vermittelnd.

interchange [intə(:)'tʃeindʒ] *tr* austauschen; auswechseln; abwechseln lassen; *itr* e-n Austausch vornehmen; abwechseln (*with* mit); *s* ['intə(:)'tʃeindʒ] Austausch *m*; Abwechs(e)lung; *(Verkehr)* kreuzungsfreie Überfahrt; *(Autobahn)* Auffahrt *f*; **~ability** ['intə(:)tʃeindʒə'biliti] Auswechselbarkeit *f*; **~able** [intə(:)'tʃeindʒəbl] austauschbar, auswechselbar.

intercom ['intə(:)kɔm] *aero sl (= ~munication)* Bordverständigung, -sprechanlage *f*; **~municate** [intə(:)kə'mju:nikeit] *itr* mitea. in Verbindung stehen; **~munication** ['intə(:)kəmju:ni'keiʃən] gegenseitige Verbindung *f*, gegenseitige(r) Verkehr *m*; **~munion** [intə(:)kə'mju:njən] innere(r) Austausch *m*; Beziehung(en *pl*) *f*; **~munity** [intə(:)kə'mju:niti] Gemeinsamkeit *f*.

intercompany [intə'kʌmpəni] zwischenbetrieblich; Konzern-.

interconnect ['intə(:)kə'nekt] *tr* mitea. verbinden; *itr* mitea. in Verbindung stehen; *~ed system* Verbundsystem *n*; **~ion** ['-'nekʃən] gegenseitige Verbindung; *el* Kupplungsleitung *f*.

intercontinental ['intə(:)kɔnti'nentl] interkontinental.

intercourse ['intə(:)kɔ:s] Verkehr, Umgang (*with* mit); (Gedanken-, Kultur-, Waren-)Austausch *m*; *business, commercial ~* Geschäftsverkehr *m*, geschäftliche Beziehungen *f pl*; *sexual ~* Geschlechtsverkehr *m*.

intercross [intə(:)'krɔs] *tr itr biol* (sich) kreuzen; *s* ['intə(:)krɔs] Kreuzung *f*; Bastard *m*.

intercurrent [intə(:)'kʌrənt] dazwischenlaufend, -tretend; *med* hinzutretend.

interdepend [intə(:)di'pend] *itr* vonea. abhängen, vonea. abhängig sein; **~ence, -cy** [-əns(i)] gegenseitige Abhängigkeit *f*; **~ent** [-ənt] gegenseitig, vonea. abhängig; inea.greifend; *to be ~~* vonea. abhängen.

interdict [intə(:)'dikt] *tr* (von Amts wegen) verbieten; untersagen (*from doing* zu tun); mit dem Kirchenbann belegen; *mil* sperren, abschnüren, abriegeln; *s* ['intə(:)dikt] *u.* **~ion** [-'dikʃən] (offizielles) Verbot *n*; Kirchenbann *m*; *mil* Abriegelung; *jur* Entmündigung *f*; ~~ *fire (mil)* Feuerriegel *m*.

interest ['intrist] *s* Anspruch *m*, Recht (*in* auf); Anrecht *n*, Anteil *m*, Beteiligung *f*, Interesse *n*, (innere) Anteilnahme (*in* an); Anziehungskraft *f*, Reiz; Anziehungspunkt *m*; Bedeutung, Wichtigkeit *f*, Belang; Einfluß *m*, Macht (*with* bei); Interessengemeinschaft *f*, Interessenten *m pl*; Zins(en *pl*) *a. fig*; Zinssatz, -fuß; *a. pl* Gewinn, Nutzen, Vorteil *m*; *pl* Belange *m pl*, Interessen *n pl*; *tr* interessieren (*in* an); anziehen, fesseln; Teilnahme erregen *od* erwecken (*s.o.* jds); betreffen, angehen; *at, (up)on ~* gegen Zinsen; *in the ~(s) of* im Interesse, im Sinne *gen*; *of general ~* von allgemeinem Interesse; *with ~ (fig)* mit Zinsen; *to bear, to bring, to carry ~* Zinsen tragen, bringen, abwerfen; sich verzinsen; *to have an ~ in* beteiligt sein, Anteil haben an; *to lend, to place, to put out money at ~* Geld gegen Zinsen anlegen; *to pay ~ for s.th.* etw verzinsen, Zinsen für etw zahlen; *to protect, to safeguard s.o.'s ~s* jds Interessen, Belange wahren; *to return, to yield ~* Zinsen tragen *od* bringen *od* abwerfen; *to take an ~ in* Anteil nehmen an, sich interessieren für; *to use o.'s ~* s-n Einfluß geltend machen; *this is of no ~ to me* das interessiert mich nicht; *arrears (pl) of ~* Zinsrückstände *m pl*; *calculation of ~* Zinsrechnung *f*; *compound ~* Zinseszinsen *m pl*; *outstanding, payable ~* fällige Zinsen *m pl*; *overdue ~* rückständige Zinsen *m pl*; *penal ~* Verzugszinsen *m pl*; *private ~s (pl)* Privatinteressen *n pl*; *rate of ~* Zinsfuß *m*; *sphere of ~* Interessengebiet *n*, -sphäre *f*; *usurious ~* Wucherzinsen *m pl*; *~* **burden** Zinslast *f*; **~ed** ['-id] *a* interessiert; betroffen; beteiligt; eigennützig; *to be ~~ in* sich interessieren für, interessiert sein an; *~* **income** Zinsertrag *m*; **~ing** ['-iŋ] interessant, anziehend, reizvoll, fesselnd; *~* **table** Zinstabelle *f*.

interfer|e [intə'fiə] *itr* zs.stoßen, -prallen; dazwischenkommen; in Widerstreit geraten, sich im Widerstreit befinden (*with* mit); sich dazwischenstecken, s-e Nase hineinstecken; sich einschalten, sich einmischen, eingreifen, intervenieren (*with, in* in); aufhalten, im Wege sein, stören, beeinträchtigen (*with s.th.* etw); *phys* sich überlagern; **~ence** [-rəns] Zs.stoß, -prall; Widerstreit; Eingriff *m*; Einmischung, Intervention; Störung, Beeinträchtigung *f* (*with* gen); *jur* Patenteinspruch *m*; *phys* Interferenz; *radio* Störung *f* (*from* durch); Störgeräusch *n*; ~~ *elimination (radio)* Entstörung *f*; **~ential** [intəfə(:)'renʃəl] *a phys* Interferenz-.

interfus|e [intə(:)'fju:z] *tr* hineingießen; vermischen; durchdringen; *itr* sich (ver)mischen; **~ion** [-'fju:ʒən] (Ver-)Mischung; Durchdringung *f*.

interim ['intərim] *s* Zwischenzeit *f*; *a* Interims-, Zwischen-; vorläufig, einstweilig; *ad ~* vorläufig; *in the ~* in der Zwischenzeit; *~* **aid** Übergangs-, Überbrückungshilfe *f*; *~* **bill** Interimswechsel *m*; *~* **credit** Zwischenkredit *m*; *~* **report** Zwischenbericht *m*; *~* **solution** Zwischenlösung *f*.

interior [in'tiəriə] *a* inner, inwendig, Innen-; binnenländisch, Binnen-; *pol* Innen-; privat, eigen; *s das* Innere; Binnenland; *(Kunst)* Interieur *n*; *phot* Innenaufnahme *f*; *the I~ (pol)* das Innere; *the (Department of the) I~ (Am)* das Innenministerium; *~* **decoration** Innendekoration *f*; *~* **duty** Innendienst *m*; *~* **lighting** Innenbeleuchtung *f*; *~* **market** Binnenmarkt *m*; *~* **view** Innenansicht *f*.

interjacent [intə(:)'dʒeisənt] dazwischenliegend.
interject [intə(:)'dʒekt] *tr (Frage)* ein-, dazwischenwerfen; **~ion** [-'dʒekʃən] Einwurf; Ausruf *m*; *gram* Interjektion *f*; **~ional** [-ʃənl], **~ory** [-əri] dazwischen-, eingeworfen.
interlace [intə(:)'leis] *tr* (mitea.) verflechten, verweben, verschlingen; eng mitea. verbinden; *itr* sich verflechten, sich eng (mitea.) verbinden.
interlard [intə(:)'lɑ:d] *tr* spicken *a. fig*, vermischen (*with* mit); *fig* ausstaffieren (*with* mit).
interlea|f ['intəli:f] *(Buch)* Durchschuß *m*; **~ve** [intə(:)'li:v] *tr (Buch)* durchschießen.
interlin|e [intə(:)'lain] *tr* zwischen die Zeilen schreiben *od* drucken; **~eal** [-'liniəl], **~ear** [-'liniə] *a* interlinear, zwischenzeilig, Interlinear-.
interlink [intə(:)'liŋk] *tr* (mitea.) verketten; kuppeln; *s* ['intə(:)liŋk] Zwischenglied *n*.
interlock [intə(:)'lɔk] *tr* mitea. verbinden, verknüpfen; verschachteln; *tech* blockieren; *itr* eng inea.greifen; *s* ['--] Verriegelung *f*.
interlocut|ion [intə(:)lo(u)'kju:ʃən] Unterredung, Besprechung *f*, Gespräch *n*; **~or** [intə(:)'lɔkjutə] Gesprächspartner, -teilnehmer *m*; **~ory** [-'lɔkjutəri] *a* Gesprächs-; *jur* Zwischen-; vorläufig, einstweilen; *~~ decision, decree, judg(e)ment (jur)* Zwischenentscheid *m*.
interlope [intə(:)'loup] *itr* sich in fremde Angelegenheiten mischen; *com* wilden Handel treiben; **~r** ['intə(:)loupə] Eindringling; wilde(r) Händler *m*.
interlude ['intə(:)l(j)u:d] *theat mus* Zwischenspiel; Intermezzo *n*; Pause; Unterbrechung *f* (*of* durch).
intermarr|iage [intə(:)'mæridʒ] Misch-, Verwandtenehe *f*; **~y** ['intə(:)'mæri] *itr (soziale Gruppen)* unterea. heiraten; *(nahe Verwandte)* sich heiraten.
intermeddle [intə(:)'medl] *itr* sich einmischen (*with, in* in).
intermedi|ary [intə(:)'mi:diəri] *a* vermittelnd; dazwischenliegend; Zwischen-; *s* Vermittler; Mittelsmann *m*, -person *f*, Zwischenträger, -händler *m*; Zwischen-, Übergangsform *f*; Zwischenprodukt, -glied *n*; **~ate** [-djət] *a* dazwischen-, in der Mitte liegend; Zwischen-, Mittel-; *s* Zwischenglied, *fam* -ding *n*; Übergang(serscheinung *f*); Vermittler, Mittelsmann *m*; *~~ cable* Zwischenkabel *n*; *~~ (examination)* Zwischenprüfung *f*; *~~ landing* Zwischenlandung *f*; *~~ trade* Zwischen-, Transithandel *m*.
interment [in'tə:mənt] Begräbnis *n*, Beerdigung, Bestattung *f*.
intermezzo [intə(:)'medsou] *pl -s theat mus* Intermezzo *n*.
interminable [in'tə:minəbl] endlos; unaufhörlich; **~ness** [-nis] Endlosigkeit *f*.
intermingle [intə(:)'miŋgl] *itr tr* (sich) (ver)mischen (*with* mit).
intermiss|ion [intə(:)'miʃən] Unterbrechung, Pause *f*; *without ~~* pausenlos, ununterbrochen.
intermit [intə:'mit] *tr* unterbrechen; *itr* (zeitweilig) aussetzen; **~tence, -cy** [-əns(i)] Periodizität *f*; **~tent** [-ənt] zeitweilig aussetzend, *scient* periodisch; *med* intermittierend; *~~ fever* Wechselfieber *n*; *~~ fire (mil)* Störfeuer *n*; *~~ light* Blinklicht *n*.
intermix [intə(:)'miks] *tr itr* (sich) vermischen; **~ture** [-tʃə] (Ver-)Mischung; Beimischung *f*.
intern [in'tə:n] *tr* internieren; *s* ['intə:n] *(a. ~e) Am med* Assistenzarzt; Internierte(r) *m*; **~al** [-l] inner, inwendig, innerlich, intern; Innen-; inländisch, (ein)heimisch; innerbetrieblich; *~~ affairs (pl) (pol)* innere Angelegenheiten *f pl*; *~~ arrangements (pl)* interne Abmachungen *od* Vereinbarungen *f pl*; *~~-combustion engine* Verbrennungsmotor *m*; *~~ market* Inlandsmarkt *m*; *~~ medicine* innere Medizin *f*; *~~ navigation* Binnenschiffahrt *f*; *~~ policy* Innenpolitik *f*; *~~ revenue* Staatseinkommen; Steueraufkommen *n*; *~~ specialist, specialist for ~~ diseases* = *~ist*; *~~ trade* Binnenhandel *m*; *~~ troubles (pl) (pol)* innere Unruhen *f pl*; *~~ waters (pl)* Binnengewässer *n pl*; **~ee** [intə:'ni] Internierte(r) *m*; **~ist** [-ist] Internist, Facharzt *m* für innere Krankheiten; **~ment** [-mənt] Internierung *f*; *~~ camp* Internierungslager *n*.
international [intə(:)'næʃənl] *a* international, zwischenstaatlich; *s sport* internationale(r) Spieler *m*; *the I~(e)* [-'nɑ:l] *(pol)* die Internationale; **~ exhibition** Weltausstellung *f*; **I~ Monetary Fund** Internationale(r) Währungsfonds *m*; **~ity** [-næʃə'næliti] internationale(r) Charakter *m*; **~ization** [-næʃnəlai'zeiʃən] Internationalisierung *f*; **~ize** [-'næʃnəlaiz] *tr* internationalisieren; unter internationale Kontrolle stellen; **~ law** Völkerrecht *n*; **I~ Labo(u)r Office** Internationale(s) Arbeitsamt *n*; **~ reply coupon** internationale(r) Postantwortschein *m*; **~ trade** Welthandel *m*.
internecine [intə(:)'ni:sain] tödlich, verderblich, mörderisch.

*

interoffice ['intərɔfis] Haus-; innerbetrieblich; **~ communication** Haustelephon *n*; **~ slip, tag** Laufzettel *m*.
interpellat|e [in'tə:peleit] *itr parl* interpellieren; **~ion** [intə:pe'leiʃən] *parl* Interpellation, Anfrage *f*.
interpenetrat|e [intə(:)'penitreit] *tr* völlig durchdringen; *itr* sich gegenseitig durchdringen; **~ion** [-'treiʃən] völlige, gegenseitige Durchdringung *f*.
interphone ['intə(:)foun] *tele mil aero* Eigenverständigungsanlage *f*; Haustelephon *n*.
interplanetary [intə:'plænitəri] interplanetarisch; **~ aviation, travel, flight** Raumfahrt *f*, -flug *m*.
interplay ['intə:'plei] *s* Wechselspiel *n*, -wirkung *f*; Inea.greifen *n*; *itr* aufea. (ein)wirken.
interpolat|e [in'tə:po(u)leit] *tr (Text)* erweitern, ändern, verfälschen; *(Textteile)* einschieben, -schalten; interpolieren *a. math*; **~ion** [intə:po(u)'leiʃən] Einschaltung, -schiebung, Erweiterung, Änderung, Verfälschung; Interpolation *a. math*; *med* Gewebeverpflanzung *f*.
interpos|al [intə(:)'pouzl] = *~ition*; **~e** [-'pouz] *tr* dazwischensetzen, -stellen, -legen; einschalten; einwenden; *(Bemerkung)* einwerfen; *itr* dazwischentreten; intervenieren; vermitteln; e-e Unterbrechung verursachen; **~ition** [-pə'ziʃən] Einschaltung *f*; Einwand *m*; Intervention; Unterbrechung *f*.
interpret [in'tə:prit] *tr* erklären, darlegen, interpretieren; dolmetschen; deuten, auslegen; *theat* darstellen, wiedergeben; **~able** [-əbl] erklärbar, deutbar; **~ation** [-'teiʃən] Erklärung, Darlegung; Interpretation; Deutung, Auslegung; Darstellung *f*; Dolmetschen *n*; *consecutive, simultaneous ~~* Konsekutiv-, Simultanübertragung *f*; **~er** [-ə] Dolmetscher; Erklärer, Deuter, Ausleger; Darsteller *m*.
interrelation ['intə(:)ri'leiʃən] Wechselbeziehung *f*.
interrogat|e [in'terəgeit] *tr* aus-, befragen; verhören, vernehmen; **~ion** [interə'geiʃən] Befragung *f*; Verhör *n*, Vernehmung; Frage *f*; Fragezeichen *n*; *mark, note, point of ~~*, *~~ mark, (Am) point* Fragezeichen *n*; *~~ officer* Vernehmungsoffizier *m*; **~ive** [intə'rɔgətiv] *a* fragend; Frage-; *s gram (~~ word)* Frage(für)wort *n*; **~or** [in'terəgeitə] Frag(end)er *m*; Abfragegerät *n*; **~ory** [intə'rɔgətəri] *a* Frage-; *s* Befragung *f*; Verhör *n*.
interrupt [intə'rʌpt] *tr* unterbrechen; stören; be-, verhindern; ins Wort fallen (*s.o.* jdm); *itr* stören; *tech* ab-, ausschalten; *tele* trennen; **~ed** [-id] *a* unterbrochen; **~edly** [-idli] *adv* mit Unterbrechungen; **~er** [intə'rʌptə] *el* Unterbrecher, Schalter *m*; **~ion** [intə'rʌpʃən] Unterbrechung; Störung *f*; *el* Abreißen *n*; *tele* Trennung; *tech* Betriebsstörung *f*; *without ~~* ununterbrochen.
intersect [intə(:)'sekt] *tr* durchschneiden, (in zwei Teile) teilen, zerlegen; *math* anschneiden; *itr* sich (über-)schneiden, sich kreuzen; **~ion** [-'sekʃən] Teilung, Zerlegung *f*; Durchschnitt; Schnitt(punkt) *m a. math*; *(Straße, rail)* Kreuzung; *arch* Vierung *f*; *~~ line* Schnittlinie *f*; **~ional** [-'sekʃənl] *a* Schnitt-, Kreuzungs-.
interspace ['intə(:)'speis] *s* Zwischenraum *m*; *tr* Zwischenräume lassen *od* ausfüllen zwischen.
interspers|e [intə(:)'spə:s] *tr* einstreuen (*between, among* unter); bestreuen; durchsetzen (*with* mit); fein verteilen.
interstate ['intə(:)steit] *Am (von Bundesstaaten)* zwischenstaatlich.
interstellar ['intə(:)'stelə] *a* zwischen den Sternen (befindlich); Weltraum-; *~~ aviation* Raumfahrt *f*; *~~ craft* Raumschiff *n*; *~~ space* Weltraum *m*.
intersti|ce [in'tə:stis] Hohl-, Zwischenraum *m*; Lücke *f*, Spalt(e *f*) *m*; **~tial** [intə(:)'stiʃəl] Zwischenräume bildend; *med* interstitiell.
inter|twine [intə(:)'twain], **~twist** [-'twist] *tr* (mitea.) verflechten, verdrillen; zs.drehen, verknoten, verschlingen.
interurban [intə(:)r'ə:bən] *s Am rail* Städtebahn *f*, -zug *m*; *a* Vorort-; **~ bus** Überland(omni)bus *m*.
interval ['intəvəl] Zwischenraum, Abstand *m*, Lücke *f*; Zeitabstand *m*, Zwischenzeit, Zeitspanne; Pause *f a. theat*; Unterschied *m*; *mus* Intervall *n*; *after a week's ~* eine Woche später; *at ~s* ab und zu, dann und wann, hin und wieder; hier und da, hier und dort; in Abständen; **~ signal** *radio* Pausenzeichen *n*.
interven|e [intə(:)'vi:n] *itr* dazwischentreten, -kommen, -liegen; eingreifen, einschreiten; sich einmischen, intervenieren; vermitteln; *(Ereignis)* eintreten, vorfallen, sich ereignen; *jur* als dritter in e-n (bestehenden) Vertrag eintreten; **~tion** [-'venʃən] Dazwischentreten, -liegen, -kommen *n*; *bes. pol* Einmischung, Intervention *f*; *non-~~* Nichteinmischung *f*; *treaty of non-~~* Nichteinmischungspakt *m*; *policy of (non-)~~* (Nicht-)Einmischungspolitik *f*.
interview ['intəvju:] *s* Unterredung, Besprechung *f*; Interview *n*, Befragung *f*; *tr* interviewen, befragen; *to*

give an ~ ein Interview geben; **~ee** [intəvju'i:] Befragte(r) *m*; **~er** ['intəvju:ə] Befragende(r), Interviewer *m*.
interweave [intə(:)'wi:v] *irr -wove, -woven tr* inea.weben; durchwirken (*with* mit); *fig* verweben, vermischen; verflechten.
interzonal [intə(:)'zounl] interzonal.
intest|acy [in'testəsi] Fehlen *n* e-s Testaments; Intestaterbfolge *f*; **~ate** [in'testit] *a* ohne ein Testament zu hinterlassen *(verstorben)*; nicht testamentarisch geregelt; *s* ohne Testament verstorbene(r) Erblasser *m*; **~~** *heir* Intestaterbe *m*.
intestin|al [in'testinl] *a* Eingeweide-, Darm-; **~e** [-tin] *a* inner, einheimisch; *s meist pl* Eingeweide *pl*, Gedärme *pl*; *large, small* **~~** Dick-, Dünndarm *m*; **~~** *war* Bürgerkrieg *m*.
inthral(l) *s. enthral(l)*.
intim|acy ['intiməsi] Vertraulichkeit; Intimität; Vertrautheit *f*; **~ate** ['-mit] *a* innerst; eigentlich, wesentlich; ureigenst, ganz persönlich; vertraut, intim, innig, eng; *s* gute(r) Freund, Vertraute(r), Busenfreund, Intimus *m*; *tr* ['-meit] bekanntmachen, verkünden; ankündigen, andeuten, zu verstehen geben, nahelegen; **~ation** [inti'meiʃən] Bekanntmachung, Verkündung, Benachrichtigung, Erklärung; Ankündigung; Andeutung *f*, Wink *m*.
intimidat|e [in'timideit] *tr* ängstlich, bange machen; einschüchtern (*into doing s.th.* etw zu tun); **~ion** [-'deiʃən] Einschüchterung *f*.
into ['intu, 'intə] *prp (räumlich)* in *acc*, in ... hinein; *(zeitlich)* bis in (... hinein); *(verwandeln)* in *acc*.
intoler|able [in'tɔlərəbl] unerträglich, nicht auszuhalten(d); **~ableness** [-nis] Unverträglichkeit *f*; **~ance** [-rəns] Unduldsamkeit, Intoleranz *f a. med* (*for, of* gegenüber); **~ant** [-rənt] unduldsam, intolerant (*of* gegenüber).
inton|ate ['into(u)neit] = **~e**; **~ation** [-'neiʃən] Tonfall *m*; Stimmlage; Betonung *f*; *mus* Anstimmen *n*; **~e** [in'toun] *tr* singen(d sprechen); anstimmen, intonieren; *itr* singen(d) sprechen; heulen, jaulen.
intoxic|ant [in'tɔksikənt] *a* berauschend, zu Kopf steigend; *s* Rauschgift; berauschende(s) Getränk *n*; **~ate** [-keit] *tr* berauschen *a. fig*, zu Kopf steigen (*s.o.* jdm); *fig* begeistern; *med* vergiften; **~ated** [-keitid] *a* berauscht (*with* von); **~ation** [-'keiʃən] Trunkenheit *f*, Rausch *m*; *fig* Begeisterung; *med* Vergiftung *f*.
intractab|ility [intræktə'biliti] Eigensinn *m*, Halsstarrigkeit, Widerspenstigkeit *f*; **~le** [in'træktəbl] *(Mensch)* schwer zu behandeln(d), eigenwillig, -sinnig, halsstarrig, dickköpfig, widerspenstig.
intrados [in'treidɔs] *arch* Laibung *f*.
intramural ['intrə'mjuərəl] *a* innerhalb der Mauern, der Grenzen *(e-r Stadt, e-r Universität)*; *anat med* intramural.
intransigen|ce, -cy [in'trænsidʒəns(i)] mangelnde Kompromißbereitschaft, Unnachgiebigkeit, Unversöhnlichkeit *f*; **~t** [-t] starr, unnachgiebig, unversöhnlich.
intransitive [in'trænsitiv] *a gram* intransitiv; *s (~ verb)* intransitive(s) Verbum *n*.
intrant ['intrənt] Neuein-, -antretende(r) *m*.
intrepid [in'trepid] unerschrocken, furchtlos; **~ity** [intri'piditi] Unerschrockenheit *f*; Mut *m*.
intric|acy ['intrikəsi] Kompliziertheit, Verwickeltheit, Schwierigkeit *f*; **~ate** [-kit] kompliziert, verwickelt, schwierig.
intrigu|e [in'tri:g] *itr* intrigieren; ein Verhältnis haben (*with* mit); *tr* durch Intrige (zu) erreichen (suchen); neugierig machen, fesseln; verblüffen; *s* Intrige *f*, Ränke(spiel *n*) *pl*; Liebesaffäre *f*, -handel *m*; **~ing** [-iŋ] sehr spannend, höchst interessant; verblüffend.
intrinsic [in'trinsik] inner, wesentlich, eigentlich, wahr, wirklich.
introduc|e [intrə'dju:s] *tr* hereinführen, -bringen; ein-, dazwischenschalten; hinzufügen, -tun; einflechten; *(neue Sitte, Ware, Menschen in e-e Gesellschaft)* einführen; *(Menschen)* vorstellen (*to s.o.* jdm); bekannt machen (*to s.o.* mit jdm); vertraut machen mit; zur Sprache bringen; *(Thema)* anschneiden; einleiten, beginnen, eröffnen; *Am parl (Vorlage)* einbringen (*into* in); *tech* einführen, einfügen, hineinstecken; *to* **~~** *into the market* auf den Markt bringen; **~tion** [intrə'dʌkʃən] Einführung, Einleitung *f (a. e-s Buches)*; Vorwort *n*; Leitfaden *m*; *mus* Introduktion; Vorstellung *(e-s Menschen)*; *parl* Einbringung *f*; **~tory** [-'dʌktəri] einführend, -leitend; Einführungs-, Einleitungs-.
intromission [intro(u)'miʃən] Einschaltung *f*; Einlaß *m*.
introspect [intro(u)'spekt] *itr* sich selbst beobachten *od* prüfen; **~ion** [-kʃən] Innenschau, Selbstbeobachtung *f*; **~ive** [-ktiv] einwärts, nach innen gerichtet; Selbstbeobachtungs-.
introver|sion [intro(u)'və:ʃən] *psychol* Introversion *f*; **~t** [-'və:t] *tr* nach innen richten, einwärts kehren; *s* ['intro(u)-və:t] Introvertierte(r), nach innen gerichtete(r) Mensch *m*.
intru|de [in'tru:d] *tr* hineinstoßen, -schieben; *itr u. to* **~~** *o.s.* sich eindrängen; eindringen (*into* in); *to* **~~** *upon s.o.* jdn stören, jdm lästig fallen; *to* **~~** *s.th. upon s.o.* jdm etw aufdrängen; *to* **~~** *upon s.o.'s time* jds Zeit in Anspruch nehmen; **~der** [-ə] Eindringling; Störenfried *m*; *aero* Störflugzeug *n*; **~sion** [in'tru:ʒən] Eindringen; (Sich-)Aufdrängen *n*; Zudringlichkeit *f*; Übergriff *m*; *jur* Besitzstörung; *geol* Intrusion *f*; *mil aero* Einflug *m*; **~sive** [-siv] auf-, zudringlich; *geol* intrusiv; **~siveness** [-sivnis] Aufdringlichkeit, Zudringlichkeit *f*.
intrust *s. entrust*.
intuit|ion [intju(:)'iʃən] Intuition, unmittelbare Erkenntnis *od* Erfahrung *f*; **~ive** [-'tju(:)itiv] intuitiv.
intumesc|e [intju(:)'mes] *itr* (an-)schwellen; **~ence** [-əns] *med* (An-)Schwellung; Geschwulst *f*; **~ent** [-ənt] *med* (an)schwellend; geschwollen.
intwine, intwist *Am s. entwine* ...
inund|ate ['inʌndeit] *tr* überschwemmen, -fluten *a. fig*; **~ation** [-'deiʃən] Überschwemmung, -flutung, Flut *f a. fig*.
inure [i'njuə] *tr* gewöhnen (*to* an), abhärten (*to* gegen); *itr* in Gebrauch kommen; *jur* in Kraft treten, wirksam werden.
inutility [inju(:)'tiliti] Nutzlosigkeit, Unbrauchbarkeit *f*; nutzlose(r) Gegenstand *m*.
invade [in'veid] *tr* einfallen, -dringen in; überfallen; stürmen; *(Krankheit)* befallen; heimsuchen; *(Rechte)* antasten, verletzen, übergreifen; **~r** [-ə] Eindringling, Angreifer *m*.
invalid ['invəli:d] *a* schwächlich, kränklich, gebrechlich; kriegsbeschädigt, -versehrt; nicht mehr (dienst)tauglich, -verwendungsfähig; *s* Invalide *m*; *tr* [invə'li:d] schwächen; krank, (dienst)untauglich machen; dienstuntauglich, dienstunfähig sprechen *od* schreiben; *a* [in'vælid] ungültig; **~ate** [in'vælideit] *tr* ungültig machen, für ungültig, nichtig erklären, annullieren; *(Urteil)* aufheben; *(Gesetz)* außer Kraft setzen; **~ation** [invæli'deiʃən] Ungültigkeitserklärung, Annullierung, Aufhebung *f*; **~ity** [invə'liditi] *Am* Arbeits-, Erwerbsunfähigkeit, Invalidität; Ungültigkeit, Nichtigkeit *f*; **~~** *insurance, pension* Invalidenversicherung, -rente *f*.
invaluable [in'væljuəbl] unschätzbar.
invariab|ility [invɛəriə'biliti] Unveränderlichkeit *f*; **~le** [in'vɛəriəbl] unveränderlich, gleichbleibend; fest.
invas|ion [in'veiʒən] Invasion *f*, (feindlicher) Einfall, Einbruch (*of* in); *jur* Über-, Eingriff *m* (*of* in); Störung *f*; *med* Anfall *m*; **~ive** [in'veisiv] *a* angreifend; Angriffs-.
invective [in'vektiv] Schmähung, Beschimpfung *f*; *oft pl* Schimpfrede, *fam* Schimpferei *f*; *volley of* **~s** Flut von Schmähungen, Schimpfkanonade *f*.
inveigh [in'vei] *itr* schimpfen (*against* auf), *fam* herziehen (*against* über).
inveigle [in'vi:gl] *tr* verführen, -leiten, -locken (*into doing* etw zu tun); *to* ~ *s.o. out of s.th.* jdm etw abschwatzen; **~ment** [-mənt] Verführung, Verleitung *f*.
invent [in'vent] *tr* erfinden; ersinnen, erdichten; (sich) ausdenken, sich zurechtlegen; **~ion** [-ʃən] Erfindung(sgabe) *f*, Erdichten, Ausdenken *n*; reine Erfindung, Lüge, Unwahrheit *f*; **~ive** [-tiv] erfinderisch; Erfindungs-; **~~** *powers, talent, spirit*, **~iveness** [-ivnis] Erfindungsgabe *f*, Erfindergeist *m*; **~or** [-ə] Erfinder *m*; **~ory** ['invəntri] *s* Bestandsverzeichnis *n*, -liste *f*, -nachweis; (Waren-)Bestand *m*, Inventar *n*; *tr* inventarisieren; *to draw up, to make, to take up an* **~~** den Bestand aufnehmen, Inventur machen; **~~** *book* Inventarbuch *n*; **~~** *of fixtures* Zubehörliste *f*; **~~** *cutting* Lagerabbau *m*; **~~** *holdings (pl)* Lagerbestände *m pl*; **~~** *loan* Warenkredit *m*; **~~** *sale* Inventurausverkauf *m*; **~~** *taking* Inventur, Bestandsaufnahme *f*; **~~** *valuation* Bestandsbewertung *f*; **~~** *verification* Inventurprüfung *f*.
invers|e ['in'və:s] *a* umgekehrt *a. math*, entgegengesetzt; *s* Gegenteil *n*, Gegensatz *m*, Umkehrung *f*; **~~** *flow* Gegenstrom *m*; **~~ly** *proportional* umgekehrt proportional; **~ion** [in'və:ʃən] Umkehrung *a. math chem*; *med psychol gram* Inversion, *gram* Umstellung *f*.
invert [in'və:t] *tr* auf den Kopf stellen; umkehren; *chem* invertieren; *gram* umstellen; *el* wechselrichten; *s* ['invə:t] Invertierte(r), Homosexuelle(r) *m*; Lesbierin; *tech* Sohle *f*; **~ed** *commas (pl)* Anführungszeichen, *fam* Gänsefüßchen *n pl*; **~ed** *flying (aero)* Rückenflug *m*; **~ed** *rectifier* Wechselrichter *m*; **~ed** *valve* Hängeventil *n*.
invertebrate [in'və:tibrit] *a zoo* wirbellos; *fig* rückgratlos, (innerlich) haltlos; *s* wirbellose(s) Tier *n*; *fig* rückgrat-, haltlose(r) Mensch *m*.
invest [in'vest] *tr* (ein)hüllen, umgeben; *(feierlich)* ins Amt einführen; ausstatten, versehen, belehnen (*with* mit); *(Geld)* anlegen, investieren, *fam* ausgeben (*in* für); *(Geld, Zeit)* aufbringen, verwenden; *(Arbeit, Mühe)*

sich machen; *mil* einschließen, belagern; *itr* Geld anlegen; *fam* sich kaufen (*in s.th.* etw); *~ed capital* Anlagekapital *n*; **~iture** [-itʃə] Belehnung; Investitur; *fig* Ausstattung *f*; **~ment** [-mənt] (Amts-)Einführung; Belehnung; *com* (Geld-, Kapital-)Anlage, Investition, Einlage; Beteiligung; *mil* Einschließung, Belagerung, Blockade *f*; *pl* Wertpapiere *n pl*; *~~ bill, paper (fin)* Anlagepapier *n*; *~~ company, trust* Investmentgesellschaft *f*; *~~ funds (pl)* Anlagekapital *n*; Investmentfonds *m*; *~~ house (Am)* Emissionsbank *f*, -haus *n*; *~~ securities, shares, stocks (pl)* Anlagewerte *m pl*, -papiere *n pl*; **~or** [-ə] Geld-, Kapitalanlegende(r) *m*.

investigat|e [in'vestigeit] *tr* erforschen, untersuchen, forschen nach; *itr* forschen, Forschungen anstellen (*into* nach); **~ion** [investi'geiʃən] Erforschung, Untersuchung, Prüfung; *jur* Ermitt(e)lung *f*; *criminal ~~* Strafuntersuchung *f*; *preliminary ~~* Voruntersuchung *f*; **~or** [-ə] Forscher; Untersuchende(r); Ermittlungsbeamte(r) *m*.

inveter|acy [in'vetərəsi] Eingewurzeltheit; *med* Hartnäckigkeit; (schlechte) Gewohnheit *f*; **~ate** [-rit] eingewurzelt; zur Gewohnheit geworden; eingefleischt; *med* hartnäckig.

invidious [in'vidiəs] neid-, haß-, ärgerniserregend; anstößig; böswillig, ungerecht, gehässig; **~ness** [-nis] Anstößigkeit; Böswilligkeit *f*.

invigilate [in'vidʒileit] *Br itr* Prüflinge beaufsichtigen.

invigorat|e [in'vigəreit] *tr* stärken, kräftigen, beleben, auffrischen; **~ion** [invigə'reiʃən] Stärkung, Kräftigung, Belebung, Auffrischung *f*.

invincib|ility [invinsi'biliti] Unbesiegbarkeit, Unüberwindlichkeit *f*; **~le** [in'vinsəbl] unbesiegbar, unschlagbar, unüberwindlich.

inviol|ability [invaiələ'biliti] Unverletzlichkeit *f*; **~able** [in'vaiələbl] unverletzlich, unverbrüchlich; unzerstörbar; heilig; **~ate** [-it] unverletzt, unversehrt.

invisib|ility [invizi'biliti] Unsichtbarkeit *f*; **~le** [in'vizəbl] unsichtbar, nicht wahrnehmbar (*to* für); *to be ~~* sich nicht sehen lassen; *~~ ink* Geheimtinte *f*.

invit|ation [invi'teiʃən] Einladung(sschreiben *n*) (*to* an; zu); Verlockung *f*; *~~ card* Einladungskarte *f*; *~~ to tender* Ausschreibung *f*; **~e** [in'vait] *tr* einladen; bitten, ersuchen um; auffordern, ermuntern zu; führen, Gelegenheit geben zu; (ver)locken, versuchen; *(Kritik)* herausfordern; *to ~~ applications for a position* e-e Stelle ausschreiben; **~ing** [-'vaitiŋ] (ver)lockend, einladend.

invocation [invo(u)'keiʃən] Anrufung *f*; *rel* Bittgebet *n*.

invoice ['invɔis] *s* (Waren-)Rechnung, Faktur(a) *f*; *tr* fakturieren, *(Waren)* berechnen, in Rechnung stellen; *as per ~* laut Rechnung; *to make out an ~* e-e Rechnung ausstellen; *~* **amount** Rechnungsbetrag *m*; *~* **book** Rechnungs-, Einkaufsbuch *n*; *~* **clerk** Fakturist *m*; *~* **machine** Fakturiermaschine *f*; *~* **number** Rechnungsnummer *f*.

invoke [in'vouk] *tr rel* anrufen; *(Geist)* beschwören; erflehen, herabflehen (*on* auf).

involucre ['invəlu:kə] *anat bot* Hülle *f*.

involuntar|iness [in'vɔləntərinis] Unfreiwilligkeit; Unabsichtlichkeit *f*; **~y** [-ri] unfreiwillig; unabsichtlich, zufällig; *physiol* unwillkürlich.

involut|e ['invəlu:t] *a zoo* mit engen Windungen; *bot* nach innen gerollt; *fig* verwickelt, kompliziert; *s* Evolvente *f*; **~ion** [invə'lu:ʃən] *bot* Einrollen; Einbegriffene(s) *n*; *fig* Verwickeltheit, Kompliziertheit; Verflechtung *f*; *gram* Schachtelsatz *m*; *math* Potenzieren *n*; *(Geometrie)* Involution; *physiol med* Rückbildung; *biol* Entartung *f*.

involve [in'vɔlv] *tr* aufrollen; einwickeln; einhüllen, umgeben *a. fig*; aufrollen, aufwickeln; enthalten, einschließen, erfassen, einbeziehen, berühren; mit sich bringen, bedingen, zur Folge haben, nach sich ziehen; hineinziehen (*in* in); in sich begreifen, enthalten, verbunden sein mit; hineinverwickeln, in Schwierigkeiten *od* in Gefahr bringen; beschäftigt sein (*in working* mit Arbeit); anregen (*in doing* zu tun); *math* potenzieren; *to ~ much expense* große Unkosten verursachen; **~d** [-d] *a* verwickelt (*in* in); kompliziert, schwierig; *to be ~~* auf dem Spiele stehen; *the person ~~* der Betroffene; *~~ sentence* Schachtelsatz *m*.

invulnerab|ility [invʌlnərə'biliti] Unverwundbarkeit; *fig* Unangreifbarkeit, Unanfechtbarkeit *f*; **~le** [in'vʌlnərəbl] unverwundbar; *fig* unangreifbar, unantastbar, unanfechtbar.

inward ['inwəd] *a* inner; Innen-; innerlich; nach innen gerichtet; binnenländisch, Inner-; dazugehörig; *s das* Innere; *fam pl* ['inədz] Eingeweide *n pl*; Einfuhrartikel *m pl*, -zoll *m*; *adv* einwärts, nach innen; zu Gemüte, zu Herzen; *~* **bill**: *~~ of lading* Importkonnossement *n*; *~* **duty** Eingangszoll *m*; *~* **flight** *aero* Einflug *m*; **~ly** ['-li] *adv* innerlich; im Herzen; **~ness** ['-nis] innere Natur *f*, Wesen *n*; Innerlichkeit; Gefühls-, Gedankentiefe *f*; *~* **passage** Rückfahrt *f*; *~* **trade** Binnenhandel *m*; **~s** [-z] *adv* = *~ adv*.

inweave ['in'wi:v] *irr -wove, -woven tr* einweben (*in, into* in); *fig* verflechten, eng verbinden (*with* mit).

*

inwrought ['in'rɔ:t] *(Muster)* eingewebt, eingewirkt, hineingearbeitet (*into* in); *(Gewebe)* mit eingearbeitetem Muster; *fig* (eng) verflochten, verwoben (*with* mit).

iod|ate ['aiədeit] *tr chem* jodieren; *s* Jodat, jodsaure(s) Salz *n*; **~ation** [-'deiʃən] Jodierung *f*; **~ic** [ai'ɔdik] *a* Jod-; *~~ acid* Jodsäure *f*; **~ide** ['aiədaid] Jodid *n*, Jodverbindung *f*; **~ine** ['aiədi:n, *bes. Am* -ain] Jod *n*; *fam* = *tincture of ~~ (pharm)* Jodtinktur *f*; *~~ poisoning*, **~ism** ['aiədizm] Jodvergiftung *f*; **~ize** ['-aiz] *tr* jodieren; **~oform** [ai'ɔdəfɔ:m] *pharm* Jodoform *n*.

ion ['aiən, 'aiɔn] *phys* Ion *n*; *~* **beam** Ionenstrahl *m*; *~* **counter** Ionenzähler *m*; **~ic** [ai'ɔnik] *a* Ionen-; *~~ cleavage* Ionenspaltung *f*; *~~ ray* Ionenstrahl *m*; *~~ theory* Ionentheorie *f*; **~ium** [ai'ouniəm] *chem* Ionium *n*; **~izable** ['aiənaizəbl] ionisierbar; **~ization** [aiənai'zeiʃən] Ionisierung *f*; *~~ chamber* Ionisationskammer *f*; **~ize** ['aiənaiz] *tr* ionisieren; *tr itr* (sich) in Ionen spalten; **~osphere** [ai'ɔnəsfiə] Ionosphäre *f*.

Ion|ia [ai'ounjə] Ionien *n*; **~ian** [-ən] *a geog hist* ionisch; *s* Ionier *m*; *the ~~ Islands* die Ionischen Inseln *f pl*; *the ~~ Sea* das Ionische Meer; **~ic** [ai'ɔnik] *geog hist arch* ionisch; *~~ order* ionische Säulenordnung *f*.

iota [ai'outə] Jota; I-Tüpfelchen *n*; *not an ~* nicht das geringste.

IOU ['aio(u)'ju:] Schuldschein *m*.

ipecac['ipikæk], **~uanha**[ipikækju'ænə] *bot* Brechwurz(el) *f*.

Irak, Iraq [i'rɑ:k] der Irak; **~i, Iraqi** [-i] *a* irakisch; *s* Iraker *m*.

Iran [i'rɑ:n] Iran *m*; Persien *n*; **~ian** [i'reinjən] *a* iranisch, persisch; *s* Iran(i)er, Perser *m*.

irascib|ility [iræsi'biliti] Reizbarkeit *f*, Jähzorn *m*; **~le** [i'ræsibl] reizbar, aufbrausend, jähzornig.

ir|ate [ai'reit] wütend, erzürnt, zornig.

ire ['aiə] *poet* Zorn, Grimm *m*; **~ful** ['-ful] zornig, ergrimmt.

Ireland ['aiələnd] Irland *n*.

irid|escent [iri'desnt] schillernd, irisierend; **~ium** [ai'ridiəm] Iridium *n*.

iris ['aiəris] *anat* Regenbogenhaut *(des Auges)*; Schwertlilie *f*; *~* **diaphragm** *phot* (Iris-)Blende *f*.

Irish ['aiəriʃ] *a* irisch; *s* (das) Irisch(e); *the ~ (pl)* die Iren *m pl*; **~man** [-mən] *pl ~men* Ire *m*; *~* **moss** *bot* Irische(s) Moos *n*, Karrag(h)een *pl*; *the ~* **Sea** die Irische See; *~* **stew** Irish-Stew *n (Eintopf aus Weißkohl, Kartoffeln u. Hammelfleisch)*; **~woman** [-wumən] *pl ~women* Irin *f*.

irk [ə:k] *tr* ärgern; langweilen; *bes. in: it ~s me* es verdrießt, es ärgert mich, es ist mir unangenehm; **~some** ['ə:ksəm] ärgerlich, unangenehm; beschwerlich, verdrießlich, lästig.

iron ['aiən] *s* Eisen; Werkzeug, Gerät *n*, Waffe *f (aus Eisen)*; *(flat ~)* Bügeleisen *n*; *sl* Schießprügel *m*, Flinte *f*; (Golf-)Schläger *m*; *pharm* eisenhaltige(s) Präparat *n*; *fig* Stärke, Kraft, Macht, Gewalt *f*; *pl* Ketten, Fesseln *f pl*; *a* eisern, Eisen-; *fig* eisern, stark, fest, unerschütterlich, unnachgiebig; hart, erbarmungs-, mitleidlos, grausam; *tr* (mit Eisen) beschlagen; anketten, in Ketten *od* Fesseln legen, fesseln; bügeln, plätten; *to ~ out (fig)* ausbügeln; *(Fehler)* beseitigen, ausgleichen; ins reine, in Ordnung bringen; *as hard as ~* stahlhart; *in ~s* in Ketten, in Fesseln; *to have (too many) ~ sin the fire* (zu viele) Eisen im Feuer haben; *to put in ~s* in Ketten legen; *to rule with a rod of ~, with an ~ hand (fig)* mit eiserner Faust, streng regieren; *to strike while the ~ is hot* das Eisen schmieden, solange es heiß ist; *cast ~* Gußeisen *n*; *wrought ~* Schmiedeeisen *n*; *~* **age** *hist* Eisenzeit *f*; **~-bar** Eisenstange *f*; **~-bound** *a* eisenbeschlagen; felsig; Fels(en)-; hart, steif; unbeugsam, unnachgiebig; *~~ coast* Steilküste *f*; **~-casting(s)** Eisenguß *m*; **~-clad** *a* gepanzert; eingekapselt; *fig* hart, streng; *s* Panzerschiff *n*; *~* **concrete** Eisenbeton *m*; *~* **core** Eisenkern *m*; *the* **I~ Cross** das Eiserne Kreuz *(Auszeichnung)*; *the ~* **curtain** *pol* der Eiserne Vorhang; *~* **dust** Eisenpulver *n*; **~er** [-ə] Bügler(in *f*) *m*, Plätterin *f*; *~* **filings** *pl* Eisenfeilspäne *m pl*; **~-fisted** *a* geizig; **~-fittings** *pl* Eisenbeschläge *m pl*; **~-foundry** Eisengießerei *f*; *~* **grating** Eisenrost *m*; **~-grey** stahlgrau; *~* **hand** *fig* eiserne Faust *f*; **~-handed** *a fig* hart, streng; **~-hearted** *a* hartherzig, kalt; **~ing** ['-niŋ] Bügeln, Plätten *n*; *~~ board* Bügel-, Plättbrett *n*; *~* **lung** *med* eiserne Lunge *f*; **~master** Hüttenmeister, -besitzer *m*; **~-mine** Eisenbergwerk *n*; **~monger** ['-mʌŋgə] *Br* Eisenhändler *m*; **~mongery** ['-mʌŋgəri] Eisenhandel *m*, -handlung *f*, -waren *f pl*; **~-mould** Rost-, Tintenfleck *m*; **~-ore** Eisenerz *n*; **~-plate** Eisenblech *n*; **~ pyrites** *pl* Eisenkies, Pyrit *m*; **~ ration** *mil* eiserne Ration *f*; **~ scrap** Eisenschrott *m*; **~-stone** Eisenstein *m*; **~ trade** Eisenhandel *m*; **~ware** Eisenwaren *f pl*; **~-wire** Eisendraht *m*; **~wood** Eisenholz *n*; **~work** Eisenarbeit, -konstruktion *f*, -beschläge *m pl*, -waren *f pl*; **~worker** Eisenarbeiter *m*; **~-works** *pl mit sing* (Eisen-)Hütte *f*, Hüttenwerk *n*.

iron|ic(al) [ai'rɔnik(əl)] ironisch, spöttisch; (etwas) bissig; **~y** ['aiərəni] Ironie *f*, Spott, beißende(r) Humor *m*.

irradi|ance, -cy [i'reidiəns(i)] (Aus-)Strahlen *n*; strahlende(r) Glanz *m*; *tech* Beleuchtungsdichte *f*; **~ant** [-t] strahlend *a. fig* (*with* vor); glänzend, hell leuchtend; **~ate** [-eit] *tr* anstrahlen, erleuchten; *fig* erhellen, Licht werfen auf, aufklären; *(Gesicht)* aufheitern; ein-, ausstrahlen; beleuchten; *med* bestrahlen; elektrisch heizen; **~ation** [ireidi'eiʃən] An-, Aus-, Ein-, Bestrahlung; *fig* Erleuchtung, Aufklärung; *opt* Irradiation *f a. med.*

irrational [i'ræʃənl] *a* vernunftlos; unvernünftig, vernunftwidrig, widersinnig, unsinnig, absurd; *math* irrational; *s u.* **~ number** Irrationalzahl, irrationale Zahl *od* Größe *f*; **~ity** [iræʃə'næliti] Unvernunft, Vernunftwidrigkeit *f*; Widersinn, Unsinn *m*, Absurdität; Irrationalität *f*.

irreclaimable [iri'kleiməbl] unverbesserlich; *(Ödland)* nicht kultivierbar, nicht anbaufähig.

irrecognizable [i'rekəgnaizəbl] nicht wiederzuerkennen(d).

irreconcilable [i'rekənsailəbl] unversöhnlich; unvereinbar (*to, with* mit).

irrecoverable [iri'kʌvərəbl] nicht wiederzuerlangen(d); endgültig, für immer, unwiderruflich verloren; *jur* nicht eintreibbar, uneinbringlich; nicht abzustellen(d), unheilbar.

irredeemable [iri'di:məbl] nicht rückkaufbar, nicht tilgbar; unablösbar; nicht einlösbar; *(Verlust)* uneinbringlich; unabänderlich; unverbesserlich; unrettbar verloren; nicht wiedergutzumachen(d).

irreducible [iri'dju:səbl] nicht reduzierbar; nicht zurückführbar (*to* auf).

irrefragab|ility [irefrəgə'biliti] Unwiderlegbarkeit, Unumstößlichkeit *f*; **~le** [i'refrəgəbl] unbestreitbar, unwiderlegbar, unumstößlich.

irrefutab|ility [irefjutə'biliti] Unwiderlegbarkeit *f*; **~le** [i'refjutəbl] unwiderlegbar.

irregular [i'regjulə] *a* ungebräuchlich, abweichend; unvorschriftsmäßig; ungesetzlich, unmoralisch, unsittlich, liederlich; unregelmäßig, regellos, regelwidrig; ungleich(förmig); nicht einheitlich; ungewöhnlich; *mil* irregulär; *gram* unregelmäßig; *s pl* irreguläre Truppen *f pl*; **~ity** [iregju'læriti] Unregelmäßigkeit, Regellosigkeit; Unordnung; Uneinheitlichkeit; Liederlichkeit; unerlaubte Handlung; Ausschweifung *f*; *jur* Formfehler *m*; *pl* liederliche(r) Lebenswandel *m*.

irrelative [i'relətiv] beziehungslos; vereinzelt; unerheblich, belanglos.

irrelevan|ce, -cy [i'relivəns(i)] Belanglosigkeit, Unerheblichkeit; Unanwendbarkeit *f* (*to* auf); **~t** [-t] unerheblich, belanglos, unbedeutend, unwichtig; nicht zur Sache gehörig, nicht anwendbar (*to* auf).

irrelig|ion [iri'lidʒən] Religionslosigkeit, -feindlichkeit; weltliche Gesinnung, Gottlosigkeit *f*; **~ious** [iri'lidʒəs] irreligiös, religionslos, -feindlich; weltlich gesinnt, gottlos.

irremediable [iri'mi:djəbl] unheilbar; nicht wiedergutzumachen(d).

irremissible [iri'misəbl] unverzeihlich, unentschuldbar; unerläßlich.

irremovable [iri'mu:vəbl] nicht zu entfernen(d); unabsetzbar.

irreparable [i'repərəbl] nicht wiedergutzumachen(d); unersetzlich.

irreplaceable [iri'pleisəbl] unersetzlich.

irrepressible [iri'presəbl] nicht zurückzuhalten(d), nicht einzudämmen(d); unbezähmbar.

irreproachable [iri'proutʃəbl] untadelig, tadellos, fehlerfrei, einwandfrei.

irresistib|ility ['irizistə'biliti] Unwiderstehlichkeit *f*; **~le** [iri'zistəbl] unwiderstehlich, überwältigend.

irresolut|e [i'rezəlu:t] unentschlossen, unschlüssig, zögernd, schwankend; **~eness** [-nis], **~ion** [irezə'lu:ʃən] Unentschlossenheit, Unschlüssigkeit *f*.

irresolvable [iri'zɔlvəbl] un(auf)löslich; unauflösbar; nicht unterteilbar.

irrespective [iris'pektiv] *a*: **~~** *of (a. adv)* ohne Rücksicht auf; unabhängig von.

irrespons|ibility ['irispɔnsə'biliti] Unverantwortlichkeit; Verantwortungslosigkeit; Unzurechnungsfähigkeit; Zahlungsunfähigkeit *f*; **~ible** [iris'pɔnsəbl] unverantwortlich; verantwortungslos; *(legally ~~)* unzurechnungsfähig; zahlungsunfähig; **~ive** [-'pɔnsiv] uninteressiert; verständnis-, teilnahmslos (*to* gegenüber); unempfänglich (*to* für); *to be ~~* nicht reagieren (*to* auf).

irretentive [iri'tentiv] nicht (be)haltend; *(Gedächtnis)* schwach; gedächtnisschwach.

irretrievable [iri'tri:vəbl] nicht wiederzuerlangen(d), unwiederbringlich; unersetzbar, -lich.

irreveren|ce [i'revərəns] Unehrerbietigkeit, Respektlosigkeit *f*; **~t** [-t] unehrerbietig, respektlos.

irreversib|ility ['irivə:sə'biliti] Nichtumkehrbarkeit; Unwiderruflichkeit *f*; **~le** [iri'və:səbl] nicht umkehrbar; unabänderlich, unwiderruflich.

irrevocab|ility [irevəkə'biliti] Unwiderruflichkeit, Unumstößlichkeit *f*; **~le** [i'revəkəbl] unwiderruflich, unumstößlich.

irrig|able ['irigəbl] *a* zu bewässern(d); **~ate** ['-geit] *tr* bewässern; berieseln; *med* ausspülen; **~ation** [iri'geiʃən] Bewässerung; Berieselung; *med* Spülung *f*; **~~** *plant, tower* Bewässerungsanlage *f*; Rieselturm *m*; **~ator** ['irigeitə] *med* Irrigator, Spülapparat *m*.

irrit|ability [iritə'biliti] Reizbarkeit; *med* Erregbarkeit *f*; **~able** ['iritəbl] reizbar, leicht erregt, gereizt, ungeduldig; *med* erregbar, empfindlich, leicht entzündlich; **~ancy** ['iritənsi] Ärgernis *n*; *jur* Annullierung *f*; **~ant** ['iritənt] *a med* reizerregend; *s* Reizmittel *n*, -stoff *m*; **~~** *clause (jur)* Nichtigkeitsklausel *f*; **~ate** ['iriteit] *tr* reizen, ärgern, aufregen, erzürnen, hoch-, aufbringen; irritieren, nervös machen; *med* reizen, wundscheuern, entzünden; *(Haut)* angreifen; **~ated** ['-eitid] *a* verärgert, entrüstet (*at, by, with, against* über); **~ation** [iri'teiʃən] Erbitterung, Verärgerung, Entrüstung *f* (*at, against* über); *med* Reiz *m*, Entzündung *f*.

irrupt|ion [i'rʌpʃən] Einbruch, -fall; Überfall *m*; **~ive** [-ptiv] (her)einbrechend, eindringend.

ischium ['iskiəm] *pl -ia* [-iə] *anat* Sitzbein *n*.

isinglass ['aiziŋgla:s] Fischleim *m*, Hausenblase *f*; Glimmer *m*.

Islam ['izla:m] Islam *m*; **~ic** [iz'læmik] islamisch.

island ['ailənd] *s* Insel *a. fig*; Verkehrsinsel *f*; *tr* zur Insel machen; isolieren; durchsetzen (*with* mit); *the I~s of the Blessed* die Inseln *pl* der Seligen; *~ of resistance* Widerstandsnest *n*; **~er** ['-ə] Insulaner, Inselbewohner *m*.

isle [ail] *poet* (kleine) Insel *f*; **~t** ['-it] Inselchen *n*.

ism ['izəm] *meist pej* Ismus *m*, bloße Theorie, Doktrin *f*, abstrakte(s) System *n*, reine Lehre *f*.

isn't ['izn(t)] = *is not.*

iso- ['aiso(u)] *(in Zssgen)* iso-, gleich-; **~bar** ['-ba:] *mete* Isobare *f*; *phys* Isobar *n*; **~baric** [-'bærik] *a* gleichen Luftdrucks; **~chromatic** [aiso(u)kro(u)'mætik] einfarbig; farbtonrichtig; **~clinal** [aiso(u)'klainəl] *phys geog* Isokline *f*; **~~** *chart* Isoklinenkarte *f*; **~~** *fold (geol)* Isoklinalfalte *f*; **~meric** [-'merik] *a chem* isomer; **~metric** [-'metrik] *a* isometrisch; **~sceles** [ai'sɔsili:z] *math* gleichschenklig; **~therm** ['-θə:m] *mete* Isotherme *f*; **~thermal** [-'θə:məl] *a* isothermisch; **~tope** ['-toup] *chem* Isotop *n*.

isol|ate ['aisəleit] *tr* aus-, absondern, trennen (*from* von); isolieren *a. tech*; *tech* abdichten; rein darstellen; *mil* abschneiden; **~ated** ['-eitid] *a* isoliert; abgesondert; freistehend; vereinzelt; **~~** *case* Einzelfall *m*; **~ating** ['-eitiŋ] isolierend, trennend; Isolier-, Trenn-; **~ation** [aisə'leiʃən] Absonderung, Isolierung *f*; *mil* Abschneiden *n*; **~~** *ward* Isolierstation *f*; **~ationism** [-'leiʃnizm] Isolationismus *m*, Neutralitätspolitik *f*; **~ationist** [-'leiʃnist] Isolationist *m*.

Israel ['izreiəl] (das Volk) Israel *n* *(Staat)*; **~i** [iz'reili] *a* israelisch; *s* Israeli *m*; **~ite** ['izriəlait] *s* Israelit *m*; *a* israelitisch.

issu|able ['isju(:)əbl] *fin* ausgabe-, emissionsfähig, emittierbar; *(Termin)* anstehend; **~ance** ['-əns] Ausgabe, Ausfertigung, Erteilung *f*, Erlaß *m*; *(Scheck)* Ausstellung *f*.

issue ['isju:, 'iʃ(j)u:] **1.** *s* Ausgang; Ab-, Ausfluß(stelle *f*); *med* Blut-, Eiterfluß; *med* Einschnitt *m*; Folge *f*, Ergebnis, Resultat, Ende *n*, Ausgang *m*, Konsequenz *f*; *jur* Kind(er *pl*) *n*, Nachkomme(n *pl*) *m*, Nachkommenschaft *f*; Punkt *m*, Angelegenheit, Sache *f*, Fall *m*, Problem *n*, (Streit-)Frage *f*, Kern-, Angelpunkt *m*; Einkünfte *pl*, Einnahmen *f pl*; Erlaß *m*, Erteilung, Herausgabe, Emission; Ausgabe, Lieferung, Verteilung; *(Zeitung, Zeitschrift)* Ausgabe, Nummer; Auflage *f*; Vorzeigen *n (e-s Ausweises)*; **2.** *itr* herausgehen, -kommen; hervorkommen, -dringen; (her)ausfließen, -strömen (*from* aus); herkommen, (her-, ab-)stammen; sich ableiten, folgen, resultieren; enden (*in* in); *(Gelder)* hereinkommen, eingehen; *(Druckwerk)* erscheinen; **3.** *tr* her-, hinauslassen; ablassen; verabfolgen; ausgeben, -stellen, erteilen, erlassen; *(Dokument)* ausfertigen; *(Ausweis)* vorzeigen; herausgeben, in Umlauf setzen, veröffentlichen; *bes. mil* ausstatten, versehen mit; *(Anleihe)* auflegen, begeben; emittieren; *at ~* zur Debatte stehend; strittig; *to be the ~* sich handeln um; gehen um; *to die without ~* kinderlos, ohne Nachkommen sterben; *to force an ~* e-e Entscheidung erzwingen; *to leave ~* Kinder, Nachkommen hinterlassen; *to take, to join* ~ nicht übereinstimmen, ausea.gehen, differieren (*on* über); *just* ~*d* soeben erschienen; Neuerscheinung *f*; *date of* ~ Ausgabetag *m*, -datum *n*, -termin *m*; *(im)material* ~ (un)wesentliche(r) Einwand *m*; *place, year of* ~ *(Buch)* Erscheinungsort *m*, -jahr *n*; ~ *of fact (jur)* Tatfrage *f*; ~ *of law* Rechtsfrage *f*; ~ *of orders* Befehlsausgabe *f*; ~ *of tickets* Fahrkartenausgabe *f*; ~**d** ['-d] *a* ausgestellt, lautend (*to* auf); ~**er** ['-ə] Ausgeber, Emittent; Aussteller; Vorzeiger *m*; ~**less** ['-lis] kinderlos, ohne Nachkommen; ~ **market, price** *fin* Emissionsmarkt, -preis, -kurs *m*; ~ **slip** Ausgabezettel *m*; ~ **voucher** Ausgabebeleg *m*.

isthmus ['isməs] *pl -es* Landenge *f*, Isthmus *m a. anat.*

it [it] *pron pers* es; er, sie; ihm, ihr, ihn; *(mit prp)* da*(bei, -für, -mit usw)*, dar*(an, -über, -unter)*; *s fam* italienische(r) Wermut *m*; *Am sl* das gewisse Etwas; *for* ~ dafür, deshalb, deswegen; *to carry* ~ *off* sich darüber hinwegsetzen; *to lord* ~ sich aufspielen, angeben; *to swim* ~ schwimmen; *he is* ~ *(Am fam)* er ist ganz groß, der Mann, e-e Kanone; *it is* ~ *(Am fam)* das ist die Sache, das größte, was drin ist; *she has, looks* ~ *(Am fam)* sie hat Sex-Appeal; *that's* ~*!* das ist es ja! *go* ~*!* nur zu! los!

Ital|ian [i'tæljən] *a* italienisch; *s* Italiener(in *f*) *m*; (das) Italienisch(e); ~~ *handwriting* lateinische (Schreib-) Schrift *f*; ~~ *warehouse* Kolonialwarenhandlung *f*; ~~ *warehouseman* Kolonialwarenhändler *m*; ~**ianate** [-eit] italienisch aussehend; italienisch gekleidet; ~**ianism** [-izm] italienische (Sprach-)Eigentümlichkeit *f*; ~**ianize** [-aiz] *tr* italianisieren, italienisch machen; *itr* italienisch werden; ~**ic** [i'tælik] *a hist* italisch; *i*~~ *(typ)* kursiv; *i*~~*(s) (pl) (typ)* Kursive *f*; **i**~**icize** [i'tælisaiz] *tr* kursiv drucken; *(im Druckmanuskript)* auszeichnen; ~**y** ['itəli] Italien *n*.

itch [itʃ] *itr* jucken; *fig* sich sehnen (*for* nach); darauf brennen (*to do s.th.* etw zu tun); *s* Jucken *n*, Juckreiz *m*; *med* Krätze *f*; Gelüst *n* (*for* nach); *I* ~ es juckt mich; *I have an* ~, *I* ~ *for it, I am* ~*ing to get it* es gelüstet mich danach; ~**iness** ['-inis] Juckreiz *m*; ~**ing** ['-iŋ] *s* Jucken; Gelüst *n*; ~**y** ['-i] juckend; krätzig; Juck-.

item ['aitəm] *s* Ein(zel)heit *f*; Gegenstand, Artikel; Posten *m*, Position *f*, Punkt *m (e-r Aufzählung)*; Notiz; *com* Buchung *f*, Posten *m*; *(einzelne)* Nachricht, Mitteilung, Information *f*; Zeitungsartikel *m*; *(in e-m Vertrag)* Ziffer *f*, Abschnitt; *tech* Bauteil *m*; *tr* (einzeln) aufführen, aufzählen; in die Liste setzen, anführen; *adv* desgleichen, ferner; ~**ize** ['-aiz] *tr Am* einzeln aufführen, genau angeben, spezifizieren, detaillieren.

iterat|e ['itəreit] *tr* wiederholen, nochmal tun; immer wieder sagen *od* tun; wiederholt vorbringen; ~**ion** [itə'reiʃən] (dauernde) Wiederholung *f*; ~**ive** ['itərətiv] *a* Wiederholungs-; (sich) wiederholend; wiederholt; *gram* iterativ.

itiner|a(n)cy [i'tinərə(n)si] Umherziehen, -reisen, -wandern *n*; Rundreise, Tournee *f*; ~**ant** [-ənt] *a* wandernd, umherziehend, auf der Rundfahrt, -reise; Wander-; *s* Wanderer, Reisende(r) *m*; ~~ *trade* Hausierhandel *m*; ~**ary** [i'tinərəri, ai't-] Route *f*, Reiseweg *m*, Fahrtstrecke *f*; Reise-, Fahrtenplan; Reiseführer *m*; Reisebuch *n*, -beschreibung *f*, -erinnerungen *f pl*; *attr* Reise-, Straßen-; ~**ate** [i'tinəreit, ai't-] *itr* wandern, herumziehen, (herum)reisen; e-e Rundfahrt, Rundreise machen.

it'll [itl] = *it will*; *it shall*.

its [its] *prn* sein, ihr; dessen, deren.

it's [its] = *it is*.

itself [it'self] (es) selbst; sich (selbst) *(all) by* ~ (ganz) allein *adv*; *in* ~ an sich, für sich; *of* ~ von selbst.

I've [aiv] = *I have*.

ivied ['aivid] *a* efeube-, überwachsen, efeuumrankt.

ivory ['aivəri] Elfenbein; *allg* Zahnbein, Dentin *n*; elfenbeinartige Substanz; Elfenbeinfarbe *f*; Stoßzahn *m*; *pl sl* Zähne, Würfel *m pl*, Billardkugeln, *(Klavier-)*Tasten *f pl*; **I**~ **Coast** Elfenbeinküste *f*; ~ **tower** *fig* Elfenbeinturm *m*; Wirklichkeitsferne *f*; ~**-white** elfenbein-, kremfarben.

ivy ['aivi] *(English* ~*)* Efeu *m*.

izard ['izəd] *zoo* Bergsteinbock *m*.

J

J, j [dʒei] *pl* ~*'s*, ~*s* J, j *n*.

jab [dʒæb] *tr* (hinein)stechen, stecken, stoßen (*into* in); *itr* stoßen (*with* mit); *s* Stich, (kurzer) Stoß *m*; *(Boxen)* linke Gerade; *fam* Spritze *f*.

jabber ['dʒæbə] *itr tr* daherreden, faseln; schwätzen, plappern, tratschen, quasseln; *s* Gefasel; Geplapper *n*.

*

Jack [dʒæk] *fam* Hans, Johann(es); Jakob *m*; ~ *is as good as his master (prov)* jeder ist seines Lohnes wert; *Cheap* ~ billige(r) Jakob, fliegende(r) Händler *m*; *the Union* ~ die britische Nationalflagge; *Yellow* ~ das gelbe Fieber; ~*-a-dandy* Stutzer, Dandy *m*; ~ *Frost* der Reif, der Winter; ~ *and Gill, Jill* Hans und Grete; ~ *in office* übereifrige(r) Beamte(r), Bürokrat *m*; ~ *Robinson*: *before you could say* ~~ im Nu, im Handumdrehen, ehe man sich's versah; ~ *on, of, o' both sides* Opportunist *m*; ~ *of all trades* Hans Dampf in allen Gassen; ~ *of all work* Faktotum *n*; ~**ie** ['-i] Hänschen *n*, Hansel, Hansi *m*.

jack [dʒæk] *s* Kerl, Bursche, Geselle; (Gelegenheits-)Arbeiter, Taglöhner; *Am (lumber*~*)* Holzfäller *m*; *(bes. in Zssgen)* Männchen, männliche(s) Tier *n*; *Am (*~*ass)* Esel; Kaninchenbock *m*; *(*~*daw)* Dohle *f*; männliche(r) Lachs; *(boot-*~*)* Stiefelknecht; (Säge-)Bock *m*; Gestell, Gerüst *n*; *(kitchen-*~*)* Bratenwender; *(lifting-*~*)* Wagenheber *m*, Winde *f*, Hebebock *m*; *tele* Klinke; *el* Buchse, Steckdose *f*; *(Kartenspiel)* Bube; *(Spiel)* Stein *m*; *sl* Moos *n*, Zaster *m*, Geld *n*; *mar* Gösch *f*; Matrose *m*; *tr* (an)heben, (hoch)winden; *to* ~ *up (mot)* aufbocken; *Am fam (Preise, Löhne)* in die Höhe treiben, hinaufschrauben; *fam* in Trab bringen, antreiben, anfeuern (*s.o.* jdn); *(Versuch)* aufgeben; *itr* die Flinte ins Korn werfen; *every man* ~ jeder (einzelne); ~**anapes** ['-əneips] Geck, Affe, hochnäsige(r), eingebildete(r) Kerl; Naseweis; Schelm *m*; ~**ass** ['-æs] Esel *a. fig*; *meist* ['-ɑ:s] *fig* blöde(r) Kerl, Dummkopf *m*; ~**boot** hohe(r) Wasserstiefel *m*; ~**daw** ['-dɔ:] Dohle *f*; *fig* Nörgler *m*; ~ **easy** *fam* gleichgültig; ~**-hare** Rammler, (männl.) Hase *m*; ~**ie** ['-i] *fam* Matrose *m*; ~**-in-the-box** Springteufel *m (Spielzeug)*; ~**-knife** (großes) Taschenmesser *n*; *(*~~ *dive)* Hechtsprung *m*; ~**-o'-lantern** Irrlicht *n a. fig*; Elmsfeuer *n*; *fig* Irrwisch *m*; ~**-plane** Schrupphobel *m*; ~**pot** *Am (Spiel)* Einsatz; (Haupt-)Treffer, Hauptgewinn *m*; *to hit the* ~~ *(Am sl)* den Gewinn einstreichen; *fig* das Rennen machen; das Große Los gewinnen; ~**-rabbit** *Am* Eselhase *m*; ~**roll** *tr Am sl* ausplündern; ~ **screw** Wagenheber *m*; ~**-snipe** Zwergschnepfe *f*; ~**-staff** *mar* Göschstock *m*; ~**-stay** *mar* Stag *n*; Gaffel *f*; ~**stone** *Am* Marmel *f*; *pl mit sing* Marmelspiel *n*; ~**straw** Strohmann *m*, Puppe *f a. fig*; ~**-tar** *fam* Teerjacke *f*, Matrose, Seemann *m*; ~**-towel** Rollhandtuch *n*.

jackal ['dʒækɔ:l] *zoo* Schakal; *pej* Handlanger; gemeine(r) Betrüger *m*.

jacket ['dʒækit] *s* Jacke *f*, Jackett *n*, Joppe; *allg* Hülle; *(Kartoffel)* Pelle, Schale *f*; *(Tier)* Fell *n*; *tech* Mantel *m*; Gehäuse *n*; *(Buch)* Schutzumschlag; Aktendeckel *m*; *tr* einhüllen, -wikkeln; *tech* verschalen, ummanteln; *s.o., to dust s.o.'s* ~ *(fam)* jdn verdreschen, verprügeln; *potatoes in the* ~ Pellkartoffeln *f pl*.

Jacob ['dʒeikəb] Jakob *m*; ~*'s ladder* Jakobsleiter; Schiffsleiter *f*; *bot* Sperrkraut *n*, Jakobs-, Himmelsleiter *f*; ~**ean** [dʒækə'bi(:)ən] aus der Zeit Jakobs I. *(1603—25)*; ~**in** ['dʒækəbin] *rel hist* Jakobiner *m*.

jade [dʒeid] **1.** *s* Schindmähre *f*; Weibsbild, -stück, Frauenzimmer *n*; ~**d** ['-id] *a* abgehetzt, abgearbeitet; erschöpft; **2.** *min* Jade; Nephrit *m*.

jag [dʒæg] **1.** *s* Zacke(n *m*); Kerbe *f*, Riß; *(Kleid)* Schlitz *m*; *tr* kerben, einreißen; ~**ged** ['-id], ~**gy** ['-i] *a* zackig; gezahnt, gekerbt, eingerissen; zerklüftet; schartig; **2.** *sl* Suff, Schwips *m*; Besäufnis, Sauferei *f*; ~**ged** ['-id] *a sl* besoffen, betrunken.

jaguar ['dʒægjuə, *Am* '-wɑ:] *zoo* Jaguar *m*.

jail *(Am nur so)*, **gaol** [dʒeil] *s* (Untersuchungs-)Gefängnis *n*; Haftanstalt *f*; *tr (to send to* ~*)* einsperren, ins Gefängnis einliefern *od* stecken; *to break* ~ (aus dem Gefängnis) ausbrechen; ~**-bird** (Straf-)Gefangene(r); Gefängnisinsasse; Zuchthäusler; Gewohnheitsverbrecher *m*; **~-book** Gefangenenliste *f*; **~-breaker** Ausbrecher *m*; **~-delivery** *Br jur* Aburteilung *f* der (Untersuchungs-)Gefangenen; (gewaltsame) Gefangenenbefreiung *f*; **~er, ~or, gaoler** ['-ə] Gefangenenwärter, -aufseher *m*; **~-fever** (Fleck-)Typhus *m*.

jake [dʒeik] **1.** *s Am fam* Bauernlümmel, -flegel *m*; **2.** *s Am sl (ginger ~)* Ingwerschnaps *m*; **3.** *a Am sl* prima, Klasse, gewaltig; ehrlich, anständig.

jalop(p)y [dʒə'lɔpi] *Am sl mot* Kiste *f*, Klapperkasten *m*; *aero* alte Mühle *f*.

jam [dʒæm] **1.** *tr* ein-, festklemmen, einkeilen; hinein-, durchzwängen; quetschen, drücken, pressen (*against* gegen); stoßen, schieben, (zs.)drängen; *(Straße)* versperren, verstopfen; *tech* verklemmen; blockieren; *radio (durch Störsender)* stören; *Am pol (Gesetzesvorlage)* durchpeitschen; *itr* sich ein-, festklemmen; sich festfressen; *tech* nicht mehr gehen, nicht mehr arbeiten, nicht mehr funktionieren; sich drücken, sich drängen; sich hineinquetschen; *sl (Jazz)* improvisieren; *mil* Ladehemmung haben; *s* Einklemmen, Einkeilen; Quetschen, Drücken, Stoßen, Schieben; Gewühl, Gedränge *n*; Verstopfung, Verkehrsstockung, -störung; *tech* Verklemmung, Stokkung; *mil* Ladehemmung; *radio* Störung *(durch Störsender)*; *fam* Klemme, Patsche, schwierige Lage *f*; *to be ~med* gestopft voll sein; verklemmt sein; *to ~ the brakes on* mit aller Kraft bremsen; **~-full** *Am fam* knallvoll; **~mer** ['-ə] Störsender *m*; **~ming** ['-iŋ] *s radio* Störsendung; *tech* Hemmung *f*; *~~ station, transmitter* Störsender *m*; **~packed** *a Am fam* gestopft voll, proppenvoll; *~* **session** *Am* improvisierte(s) Zs.spiel *n* von Jazzmusikern; **2.** Marmelade, Konfitüre *f*; *real ~ (Br sl)* Mordsspaß *m*; *~* **jar, pot** Marmeladeglas *n*, -topf *m*; *~*(**ming**) **sugar** Einmachzucker *m*; **~my** ['-i] mit Marmelade verschmiert, klebrig; *sl* prima.

Jamaica [dʒə'meikə]: *~ rum* Jamaika-Rum *m*.

jamb [dʒæm] *(Tür)* Pfosten *m*; *(Tür, Fenster, Kamin)* Gewände *n*.

jamboree [dʒæmbə'ri:] Pfadfindertreffen *n*; *sl* Remmidemmi *n*, (Fest-)Trubel *m*; Saufgelage *n*.

James [dʒeimz] Jakob *m*.

Jane [dʒein] Johanna *f*; *j~ (sl)* Weibsstück, Mädchen *n*; **~t** ['dʒænit] Hanna *f*, Hannchen *n*.

jangl|e ['dʒæŋgl] *itr* schrill ertönen; (sich) zanken, keifen; *tr* schrill ertönen lassen; mißtönend hervor-, herausbringen; krächzen; *s* Mißklang, schrille(r) Ton *m*, Geschrei, Gekreisch; Gezänk *n*, Streit *m*; **~ing** ['-iŋ] mißtönend, schrill, kreischend.

janit|or ['dʒænitə] Pförtner, Portier; *Am* Hausmeister *m*; **~ress** ['-tris] Portiers-, Hausmeistersfrau *f*.

janizary ['dʒænizəri] *hist* Janitschar *m*.

January ['dʒænjuəri] Januar *m*.

Jap [dʒæp] *fam* Japaner *m*; **~an** [dʒə'pæn] *s* Japan *n*; *j~~* japanische(r) Lack *m*; japanische Lackarbeit, -malerei *f*; *tr* mit japanischem Lack überziehen *od* lackieren; **~anese** [dʒæpə'ni:z] *a* japanisch; *s* (das) Japanisch(e); Japaner(in *f*) *m*; *the ~~ (pl)* die Japaner *m pl*; **j~anner** [-'pænə] Lackarbeiter *m*.

jape [dʒeip] *itr* Spaß, Ulk machen; *tr* verulken, verspotten; e-n Streich spielen (*s.o.* jdm), 'reinlegen; *s* Spaß, Ulk; Streich *m*.

jar [dʒɑ:] **1.** *itr* knarren, quietschen; *fig* unangenehm berühren (*on s.o.* jdn); Mißbehagen erregen (*on s.o.* jds); auf die Nerven gehen (*on s.o.* jdm); in Mißklang stehen (*against, with* zu); nicht harmonieren; sich widersprechen; (er)zittern, schwanken; aufea.stoßen, -prallen, in Streit geraten, (sich) streiten, zanken; *tr* zum Knarren, Quietschen bringen; rütteln an, erzittern lassen; erschüttern; *s* Knarren, Quietschen *n*; Mißton *m*; Erschütterung *f*, Zittern, Schwanken *n*; Stoß, Schlag; Schock, Schreck; Zs.stoß, -prall, Streit, Zank *m*; *to ~ on s.o.'s nerves* jdm auf die Nerven gehen; **~ring** ['-riŋ] mißtönend; unangenehm; quietschend; (nerven-)aufreibend; **2.** Krug; Steintopf *m*; Einmachglas *n*; **3.** *s*: *on (the) ~ (Tür)* halboffen, angelehnt.

jardinière [ʒɑ:di'njɛə] Blumentisch, -ständer *m*, -schale *f*.

jargon ['dʒɑ:gən] Kauderwelsch *n*; Mischsprache *f*, -dialekt *m*; Zunft-, Standessprache *f*; Jargon *m*.

jasmin(e) ['dʒæsmin], **jessamin(e)** ['dʒesəmin] *bot* Jasmin *m*.

jasper ['dʒæspə] *min* Jaspis *m*.

jaundice ['dʒɔ:ndis, 'dʒɑ:n-] Gelbsucht *f*; *fig* gallige(s) Wesen *n*; Voreingenommenheit, Bitterkeit, Gehässigkeit *f*; Neid *m*, Eifersucht *f*; **~d** ['-t] *a* gelbsüchtig; *fig* gallig, verbittert, gehässig; neidisch, eifersüchtig; krankhaft.

jaunt [dʒɔ:nt] *itr* e-e Wanderung, e-n Ausflug, e-e Tour machen; bummeln; *s* Wanderung *f*, Ausflug *m*, (Spritz-)Tour *f*; **~iness** ['-inis] Lebhaftigkeit, Munterkeit *f*, Frohsinn *m*; Sorglosigkeit; Flottheit, Eleganz *f*; **~ing-car** (irischer) zweirädrige(r) Wagen *m*; **~y** ['-i] schick, elegant; lebhaft; munter; übermütig; sorgenfrei.

Java ['dʒɑ:və] Java *n*; Java(kaffee); *(j~) Am fam* Kaffee *m*; **~nese** [dʒɑ:və'ni:z] *a* javanisch; *s* Javaner(in *f*) *m*; *the ~~ (pl)* die Javaner *m pl*.

javelin ['dʒævlin] Wurfspieß; *sport* Speer *m*; *throwing the ~* Speerwerfen *n*.

jaw [dʒɔ:] *s anat* Kiefer, Kinnbacken *m*; Kinn; *fig fam* Gerede *n*, Salbaderei *f*, langweilige(s) Geschwätz *n*; Moralpauke; *tech* (Klemm-, Brech-)Backe, Klaue *f*; *pl* Mund *m*, Maul *n*, Rachen *m*; Mündung, Öffnung *f*; Ein-, Ausgang *m*; *itr sl* quasseln, schwatzen; *tr sl* anschnauzen, ausschimpfen; *into, out of the ~s of death* in, aus den Klauen des Todes; *lower, upper ~* Unter-, Oberkiefer *m*; *stop your ~ (fam)* halt's Maul! **~-bone** *s* Kieferknochen; *Am sl* Kredit *m*; *itr Am sl* vernünftig reden; **~-breaker** Zungenbrecher *(Wort)*; *tech* Backenbrecher *m*; **~-breaking** schwer auszusprechen(d); **~-clutch, -coupling** *tech* Klauenkupp(e)lung *f*.

jay [dʒei] *orn* (Eichel-)Häher; *sl* Dämlack *m*; Quasselstrippe *f*; **~walk** *itr Am fam* verkehrswidrig auf der Straße herumlaufen; dösen, träumen; **~-walker** *fam* unachtsame(r) Fußgänger; Träumer *m*.

jazz [dʒæz] *s* Jazz *m*; *(~-music)* Jazzmusik; (billige) Tanzmusik; *fig* Lebhaftigkeit *f*; Schwung; *Am sl* Schwindel, Unsinn *m*; *a* wild, ausgelassen, stürmisch, turbulent, laut; aufreizend; schreiend, grell, bunt; *tr* als Jazz spielen *od* arrangieren; *Am sl* beschleunigen, übertreiben; *itr* Jazz spielen *od* tanzen; *Am sl* auf die Tube drücken; *meist*: *to ~ up (sl)* aufmöbeln; Leben, Schwung bringen in; *~* **band** Jazzkapelle *f*; **~er** ['-ə] Jazzmusiker, -spieler *m*; **~-fiend** Jazzfanatiker *m*; **~y** ['-i] = *~ (a)*.

jealous ['dʒeləs] eifersüchtig, neidisch; besorgt (*of* um); eifrig bedacht (*of* auf); **~y** ['-i] Eifersucht *f* (*of* auf); Neid (*of* auf); Achtsamkeit (*of* auf).

jean [dʒein, *bes. Am* dʒi:n] Baumwollköper *m*; *pl* Arbeitshose *f*, -anzug *m*; *blue ~s (pl)* Niethose *f*.

jeep [dʒi:p] *s Am mil* Kübelwagen, Jeep; *Am sl* Rekrut *m*; *Am sl* kleine(s) Nahaufklärungsflugzeug *n*.

jeer [dʒiə] *tr* verhöhnen, verspotten; *itr* spotten, sich lustig machen (*at* über); *s* Spott, Hohn *m*; höhnische, spöttische Bemerkung *f*; **~ingly** ['-riŋli] *adv* spöttisch, höhnisch.

Jehovah [dʒi'houvə] Jehova *m*, *(Luther:)* der Herr; *~'s Witnesses* die Zeugen *m pl* Jehovas.

jejun|e [dʒi'dʒu:n] dürftig, mager, dürr; *(Land)* unfruchtbar; *fig* nüchtern, unbefriedigend; fade, uninteressant, langweilig; **~eness** [-nis] *fig* Dürftigkeit; Fadheit, Nüchternheit *f*; **~um** [-əm] *anat* Leerdarm *m*.

jell [dʒel] *itr (Küche)* gelieren; *(Flüssigkeit)* fest werden; *fig fam* feste Form, Gestalt annehmen; sich herauskristallisieren; klappen; *tr* gelieren lassen; *fig* Gestalt geben (*s.th.* e-r S); verdichten; *s fam* = *~y*; **~ied** ['-id] *a (Küche)* geliert, eingedickt; in Gelee; **~y** ['-i] *s* Gallerte, Sülze *f*; Gelee *n*; *tr* gelieren lassen; in Sülze legen; *itr* gelieren; **~-fish** Qualle *f*; *fig fam* Schlappschwanz, Waschlappen *m*.

jemmy ['dʒemi] Brecheisen *n*.

Jenny ['dʒini, 'dʒeni] Hanna *f*, Hannchen *n*; *j~* Weibchen *n (bestimmtes Tier)*; *pref* -weibchen; *(spinning-~)* Jenny-, Spinnmaschine *f*; Laufkran *m*; **j~-ass** Eselin *f*; **j-wren** weibliche(r) Zaunkönig *m*.

jeopard ['dʒepəd], **~ize** ['-aiz] *tr* gefährden, in Gefahr bringen, aufs Spiel setzen (*with* mit); **~y** ['-i] Gefahr *f*, Risiko *n*; *to be in ~~ of o.'s life* in Lebensgefahr schweben.

jeremiade [dʒeri'maiəd] Klagelied *n*, Jeremiade *f*.

Jericho ['dʒerikou] Jericho *n*; *go to ~! (sl)* scher dich zum Teufel!

jerk [dʒə:k] **1.** *tr* (heftig) ziehen (an), reißen, stoßen, schnellen, werfen; *Am (Mineralwasser)* ausschenken; *itr* auf-, hochfahren; anrücken; sich ruckweise (fort)bewegen, ruckweise fahren; rucken, zucken; *sport* stemmen; *s* Ruck, Stoß, Sprung, Satz *m*; Zs.fahren, -zucken *n*; *med* Zuckung *f*, (Muskel-)Krampf; *Am sl* Trottel, Narr *m*; *to ~ off (Am sl)* Unfug anstellen; *to ~ out (Worte)* hervorstoßen, -sprudeln; *by ~s* ruck-, stoßweise; *with a ~* mit e-m Ruck, plötzlich; *put a ~ in it! (fam)* los, los! dalli, dalli! nun mal zu! *physical ~s (pl fam)* Leibesübungen *f pl*, Sport *m*; **~in** ['-in] Wams *n*; **~iness** ['-inis] Sprunghaftigkeit *f*; **~water** *s Am (~~ train)* Kleinbahn; *(~~ line)* Nebenlinie *f*; *a Am fam* gottverlassen; *~(~) town* (abgelegenes) Nest *n*; **~y** ['-i] sprunghaft; *med* krampfhaft; **2.** *tr (Fleisch)* in Streifen schneiden u. dörren; *s* u. **~y** ['-i] Dörrfleisch, *bes.* gedörrte(s) Rindfleisch *n (in Streifen)*.

jerry ['dʒeri] *sl* Nachttopf *m*; *J~ (sl mil)* deutsche(r) Soldat, Deutsche(r) *m*; **~-builder** Bauschwindler *m*; **~-building** schlechte(r) Bau(weise *f*) *m*; **~-built** *a* schlecht, nicht solide (genug), billig gebaut; *~~ house (fam)* Bruchbude *f*; **~can** *sl* Benzinkanister *m*.

jersey ['dʒə:zi] Turnhemd *n*, Unterjacke; (enganliegende) Wolljacke *f*, Pullover *m*.

jessamin(e) *s. jasmin.*

jest [dʒest] *s* Spott *m*, Stichelei *f*; Scherz, Witz, Spaß, Ulk *m*; Zielscheibe *f* des Spottes; *itr* spotten, sticheln; scherzen; Witze, Spaß, Ulk machen (*about* über); spaßen; *in* ~ im, zum Spaß, im Scherz; *a standing* ~ e-e Witzfigur; **~er** ['-ə] Witzbold; *hist* Spaßmacher, Hofnarr *m*; **~ing** ['-iŋ] lustig; scherzhaft; **~ingly** ['-iŋli] *adv* im Scherz *od* Spaß; zum Spaß.

Jesu|it ['dʒez(j)uit] *rel* Jesuit *m*; **~ic(al)** [dʒez(j)u'itik(əl)] jesuitisch, Jesuiten-; **~s** ['dʒi:zəs] Jesus *m*; *the Society of* ~ die Gesellschaft Jesu, der Jesuitenorden.

jet [dʒet] **1.** *tr* ausstoßen, -werfen, -speien; aus-, entströmen lassen; *itr* hervor-, heraussprudeln, aus-, entströmen (*from, out of* aus); mit e-m Düsenflugzeug fliegen; *s (Flüssigkeit, Gas)* Strahl *m*; Strahlrohr *n*; Mündung, Öffnung; *mot aero* Düse *f*; *aero* Düsenantrieb, Strahlmotor *m*, -triebwerk; Düsen-, Strahlflugzeug *n*; ~ *of steam* Dampfstrahl *m*; **~-airliner** Düsenverkehrsflugzeug *n*; **~-bomber** Düsen-, Strahlbomber *m*; **~-carburet(t)or** Düsenvergaser *m*; **~-engine** Strahl-, Rückstoßmotor *m*; **~-fighter** Düsenjäger *m*; ~~ *pilot* Düsenjägerpilot *m*; **~-helicopter** Düsenhubschrauber *m*; **~-interceptor** Abfangdüsenjäger *m*; **~-liner** = *~-airliner*; ~ **night-fighter** Düsennachtjäger *m*; **~-pilot** = *~-fighter pilot*; **~-plane** Düsenflugzeug *n*; **~-propelled** *a* strahl(an)getrieben; **~-propulsion** Düsen-, Strahl-, Rückstoßantrieb *m*; ~ **turbine-engine**, ~ **turbine-unit** Turbinenluftstrahltriebwerk *n*; **~-unit** Strahl-, Düsentriebwerk *n*; **2.** *s* Gagat *m*, Pechkohle *f (Schmuckstein)*; glänzende(s) Schwarz *n*; *a* aus Gagat; glänzend schwarz; **~-black** pechschwarz.

jetsam ['dʒetsəm] *mar* über Bord geworfene(s) Gut; *allg* Gerümpel; *fig* Wrack *n*, haltlose(r) Mensch *m*; *flotsam and* ~ Strandgut *n a. fig.*

jettison ['dʒetisən] *s* Seewurf; *aero* Notwurf *m*; Strandgut *n*; *tr mar* über Bord werfen *a. fig*; *aero* abwerfen *(bes. Bomben im Notwurf)*; **~able** [-əbl] abwerfbar; ~~ *fuel-tank* abwerfbare(r) Benzintank, -kanister *m*; ~~ *seat* Schleudersitz *m*.

jetty ['dʒeti] Hafendamm *m*, Mole *f*; Pier *m*, Landungsbrücke *f*.

Jew [dʒu:] *s* Jude *m*, Jüdin *f*; *a pej* Juden-; *tr fam* prellen, *(fam)* übers Ohr hauen, schachern (*s.o.* mit jdm); *to j~ down* herunterhandeln (*to* auf); *an unbelieving* ~ ein ungläubiger Thomas; *the Wandering* ~ der Ewige Jude; **~-baiting** Judenverfolgung *f*; **~ess** ['dʒu(:)is] Jüdin *f*; **~ish** ['dʒu(:)iʃ] jüdisch; **~ry** ['dʒuəri] Judenviertel, Getto *n*; Judenschaft *f*; **j~'s ear** *bot* Judas-, Judenohr *n*, Ohrpilz *m*; **j~'s harp** *mus* Maultrommel *f*; **~'s thorn** Christusdorn *m*.

jewel ['dʒu:əl] *s* Juwel *a. fig*; *lit poet* Kleinod *n*; Edelstein; *(Uhr)* Stein *m*; *tr* mit Edelsteinen besetzen *od* schmücken; **~-box, -case** Schmuckkasten *m*; **~(l)er** ['-ə] Juwelier *m*; **~(le)ry** ['dʒu:əlri] Juwelen *n pl*, Schmuck (-sachen, -waren *f pl*) *m*.

jib [dʒib] **1.** Kranbalken, Ladebaum, Ausleger; *mar* Klüver *m*; *itr tr (die Segel)* umlegen; *s* Klüver *m (Vorsegel)*; *the cut of o.'s* ~ *(fam)* die äußere Erscheinung *f*; **~-boom** *mar* Klüverbaum *m*; ~ **crane** Auslegerkran *m*; **~-door** Tapetentür *f*; **2.** *itr* störrisch sein, bocken, scheuen (*at* vor); *fig* abgeneigt sein (*at* dat); *s (~bing)* Bokken, Scheuen *n*; *(~ber)* störrische(r) Esel *m*, bockige(s) Pferd *n*.

jibe [dʒaib] *itr (Segel)* sich wenden; den Kurs des Schiffes ändern; *Am fam* konform gehen, sich decken, übereinstimmen; *tr (die Segel)* durchkaien; *s* Drehen *n* der Segel; *mar* Kurswechsel *m*.

jiff(y) ['dʒif(i)] *fam* Augenblick, Moment *m*; *in a* ~ im Nu; gleich, sofort; ~ **bag** *Am* Henkeltüte *f*.

jig [dʒig] *s* Gigue *f (Tanz)*; *tech* Montagegestell *n*, -bock *m*, Bauvorrichtung *f*; *min* Setzkasten *m*; Bohrfutter *n*, -lehre, -schablone *f*; *Am sl pej* Neger *m*, *Am sl* Tanzveranstaltung *f*; *itr* Gigue tanzen; hin u. her hüpfen, -springen; *tech* mit e-r Schablone, *(min)* e-m Setzkasten arbeiten; *tr (e-e Gigue)* tanzen; *tech* einspannen; mit e-r Schablone herstellen; *min* setzen, scheiden; *the* ~ *is up (Am sl)* es ist alles aus; wir können einpacken; **~ger** ['-ə] **1.** Giguetänzer; *tech* Maschinenformer *m*; *min* Setzmaschine *f*; *mar* Handtalje *f*; Besan *m (Segel)*; Töpferscheibe *f*; *Am* Meßbecher; *Am fam* Schluck; *radio* Jigger *m*; *fam* Dingsbums *n*; **2.** Sandfloh *m*; **~gered** ['-əd] *a* verdammt, *fam* baff; **~saw** Wippsäge *f*; ~~ *puzzle* Zs.setzspiel *n*.

jiggle ['dʒigl] *tr* rütteln, schütteln.

jilt [dʒilt] *s* Kokette *f*; *tr (den Liebhaber)* sitzenlassen.

Jim Crow ['dʒim'krou] *Am fam* Diskriminierung *f* der Neger; *Am sl* Nigger, Neger *m*; **Jim-Crow** *attr Am* Neger-; ~~ *car (rail)* Negerwagen *m*; ~~ *section (Straßenbahn)* Negerabteil *n*.

jim-dandy ['dʒimdændi] *s Am fam* Prachtkerl *m*; *a* famos, prima, prächtig.

jimjams ['dʒimdʒæmz] *pl sl* Säuferwahn *m*, Delirium *n* tremens; Bammel *m*, Angst(zustände *m pl*) *f*.

jimmy ['dʒimi] *s. jemmy.*

jingle ['dʒiŋgl] *itr* (leise) klingeln, klirren, klimpern; *(Kette)* rasseln; *fig (Verse, Musik)* sanft plätschern, gleichmäßig fallen; sich reimen; *tr* klirren lassen; klimpern mit; *s* Klirren, Geklirr; Wortgeklingel *n*.

jingo ['dʒiŋgou] *pl -es s* Chauvinist, Hurrapatriot *m*; *a* = *~istic*; *by ~!* weiß Gott! alle Wetter! **~ism** ['-izm] Chauvinismus *m*; **~ist** ['-ist] = ~ *(s)*; **~istic** [dʒiŋgo(u)'istik] chauvinistisch.

jink [dʒiŋk]: *high ~s (pl)* Ausgelassenheit *f*, Übermut, tolle(r) Spaß *m*.

jinx [dʒiŋks] *s sl* Unglücksrabe *m*, -ding *n*; *tr* Pech bringen (*s.o.* jdm); *to be ~ed* vom Pech verfolgt sein.

jitney ['dʒitni] *Am sl* Fünfcentstück; *Am sl* billige(s) Verkehrsmittel *n*.

jitter ['dʒitə] *itr Am sl* nervös, aufgeregt sein; den Tatterich haben; Swing tanzen; *s pl Am sl* Nervosität, Aufgeregtheit *f*; Schiß, Bammel *m*, Angst *f*; *to give s.o. the ~s* jdn nervös machen, aufregen; *to have the ~s* die Hosen voll haben; wahnsinnig nervös sein; **~bug** ['-bʌg] Swingenthusiast, -tänzer; Swing *m (Tanz)*; *fig* Nervenbündel *n*; **~y** ['-ri] *Am sl* nervös, aufgeregt, durchgedreht; verdattert, ängstlich.

jiu-jitsu *s. ju-jitsu.*

jive [dʒaiv] *sl* Jazz-, Swingjargon; Jazz, Swing *m*; *fig* dumme(s) Geschwätz *n*.

Joan [dʒoun] Johanna, Hanna *f*.

Job [dʒoub] Hiob *m*; *(the Book of ~)* das Buch Hiob; *~'s news* Hiobsbotschaft, schlechte Nachricht *f*; *patience of* ~ Engelsgeduld *f*.

job [dʒɔb] **1.** *s* (Stück *n*) Arbeit; Arbeit(sleistung) *f*; Werkstück *n*; Stück-, Akkordarbeit; *typ* Akzidenzarbeit; Verrichtung, Aufgabe, Pflicht; *fam* schwierige Sache *f*; (faules) Geschäft *n*, Schiebung, Spekulation *f*; *Am fam* Ding *n*, Straftat *f*, Verbrechen *n*, *fam* krumme Sache; *Am fam* Arbeit, Stelle *f*, Arbeitsplatz, Posten *m*, Pöstchen *n*; Stellung *f*, Beruf *m*, Handwerk *n*; *Am fam* Sache, Angelegenheit *f*, Fahrzeug *n*; Person *f*; *attr* Stück-, Lohn-, Miet-; *itr* Gelegenheitsarbeit verrichten; im Stücklohn, im Akkord arbeiten; Zwischenhandel treiben; Maklergeschäfte machen; schieben, spekulieren; sein Amt mißbrauchen; *tr* Großhandel treiben mit, vermitteln; verschieben; unterschlagen; *(Arbeit)* vergeben, vermitteln; vermieten; mieten; *by the* ~ im Stücklohn, im Akkord; *on the* ~ *(fam)* bei der Arbeit; *sl* auf Draht, bei der Sache; *to be out of (a)* ~ keine Arbeit haben, arbeits-, stellungslos sein; *to do a good, bad* ~ s-e Sache gut, schlecht machen; *to do odd ~s* Gelegenheitsarbeiten verrichten; *to lie down on the* ~ s-e Pflicht nicht erfüllen; *to make a good, bad* ~ *of s.th.* etw gut, schlecht erledigen; *that's a good, bad* ~ das ist gut, dumm; *odd ~s (pl)* Gelegenheitsarbeit *f*; *odd-~ man* Gelegenheitsarbeiter *n*; *permanent* ~ Dauerstellung *f*; *put-up* ~ abgekartete Sache *f*; ~ **analysis** Arbeitsanalyse *f*; **~ber** ['-ə] Gelegenheits-, Stücklohn-, Akkordarbeiter; Handlanger; Zwischenhändler, Makler; Effektenhändler, *fam* Börsenjobber; Schieber, Spekulant *m*; **~bery** ['-əri] Schiebung; Durchstecherei; Spekulation *f*; **~bing** ['-iŋ] *s* Akkordarbeit *f*; Zwischenhandel; Effektenhandel *m*, Börsengeschäfte *n pl*; Spekulation; Schiebung; *(~~ in bills)* Wechselreiterei *f*; *attr* Gelegenheits-; ~~ *man* Gelegenheitsarbeiter *m*; ~ **counsellor** *Am* Berufsberater *m*; ~ **description** Tätigkeitsbeschreibung *f*; ~ **evaluation** Arbeitsplatzbewertung *f*; ~ **goods** *pl*, **lot** Partiewaren *f pl*, Ramsch(ware *f*) *m*; **~holder** *Am*: *to be a* ~~ e-e Lebensstellung haben; **~-horse** Mietpferd *n*; ~ **hunter** Stellenjäger *m*; **~master** Pferde-, Wagenvermieter *m*; ~ **order** Arbeitsauftrag *m*; ~~ *number* Fabrikationsauftragsnummer *f*; ~ **printer** Akzidenzdrucker *m*; ~ **printing, -work** *typ* Akzidenzdruck *m*, -arbeit *f*; ~ **rate** Akkordlohnsatz *m*; ~ **rotation** Arbeitsplatzwechsel *m*; ~ **time** Stückzeit *f*; **~-work** Akkordarbeit *f*; **2.** *tr* (leicht) stechen, stoßen, schlagen; *itr* stoßen, schlagen (*at* nach); *s* Stich, (leichter) Stoß, Schlag *m*.

*

jockey ['dʒɔki] *s* Jockei; *Br* Handlanger; *Am sl* (Auto-)Fahrer *m*; *tr itr (Pferd)* im Rennen reiten; *tr* betrügen, beschwindeln (*out of* um); *fam* einseifen, übers Ohr hauen; zuwege, fertig, dazu bringen (*into doing* zu tun); davon abhalten (*out of doing* zu tun); *to* ~ *away, in, out* weg-, hinein-, hinausbugsieren; **~-cap** Jockeymütze *f*.

jocos|e [dʒə'kous] scherzhaft, spaßig, lustig, drollig, humorvoll; **~eness** [-nis], **~ity** [dʒo(u)'kɔsiti] Lustigkeit;

Scherzhaftigkeit, Drolligkeit *f*; Humor; Spaß *m*.

jocular ['dʒɔkjulə] scherzhaft, spaßig, witzig, humorvoll; lustig; **~ity** [dʒɔkju'læriti] Scherzhaftigkeit *f*, Humor; Spaß, Scherz, Witz *m*.

jocund ['dʒɔkənd, 'dʒou-] froh, fröhlich, lustig, munter, heiter; **~ity** [dʒo(u)'kʌnditi] Fröhlichkeit, Munterkeit *f*; Scherz *m*.

Joe [dʒou] *fam* Sepp, Jupp; amerikanische(r) Landser *m*.

jog [dʒɔg] **1.** *tr* hin- u. herschieben, leicht rütteln, schütteln; (leise) anstoßen, antippen; schaukeln; *(das Gedächtnis)* auffrischen; *fig* e-n Stoß geben; *itr* dahinschlendern, -trotten; aufbrechen; *s* leichte(s) Schütteln, Rütteln *n*; (An-)Stoß *m*, Antippen; *(~-trot)* Trotten *n*; *fig (~-trot)* Trott, Schlendrian *m*; *to ~ along, to ~ on* sich fortschleppen; *fig* fort-, weiterwursteln; **2.** *s Am* Ausbuchtung *f*, Vorsprung *m*; Einbuchtung, Kerbe *f*; Einschnitt *m*; *itr Am* e-e Aus-, Einbuchtung haben.

joggle ['dʒɔgl] **1.** *tr itr* (sich) leicht, etwas schütteln; rütteln; vorwärtsstolpern; *s* leichte(s) Schütteln, Rütteln *n*; **2.** Verschränkung, Verzahnung, Vernutung; Nut, Fuge *f*, Falz *m*; *tr* vernuten, verschränken, verzapfen, verzahnen.

John [dʒɔn] Johann(es), Hans *m*; *~ the Baptist* Johannes der Täufer; *~ Bull* England *n*; Engländer *m*; *~ Doe* [-'dou] *jur* Partei *f* X; *~ Hancock (Am fam)* Friedrich Wilhelm *m*, Unterschrift *f*; **~ny, ~nie** ['-i] Hänschen *n*; *j~~* Kerl, Bursche *m*; *~~-cake (Am)* Maisbrot; *(Australien)* Weizenbrot *n*; *~~-come-lately (Am fam)* Neuling *m*; *~~-jump-up (Am)* Veilchen; wilde(s) Stiefmütterchen *n*; *~~ on the spot (Am fam)* Hansdampf *m*.

join [dʒɔin] **1.** *tr* zs.bringen, -stellen, kombinieren; verbinden *a. math*, vereinigen (*to, on to* mit); einholen; stoßen, kommen, sich gesellen (*s.o.* zu jdm); sich anschließen (*s.o.* an jdn); eintreten in *(e-n Verein)*; sich vereinigen, sich verbinden mit, aufgehen in, verschmelzen mit; münden in; *mil* aufschließen; *fam* grenzen an; **2.** *itr* sich begegnen, sich treffen, zs.-kommen; anstoßen, angrenzen (*to* an); *(Wege)* zs.laufen; sich zs.tun, sich verbinden, sich vereinigen (*with, to* mit); mitmachen, sich beteiligen, teilnehmen (*in* an); einstimmen (*in* in); **3.** *s* Verbindung, Vereinigung *f*; Berührungspunkt *m*, Verbindungsstelle, Fuge, Naht; *math* Verbindungslinie *f*; *Am* Vereinsmeier *m*; *to ~ up (fam), to ~ the army* Soldat werden, einrücken; *to ~ battle* den Kampf aufnehmen; *to ~ company with s.o.* sich an jdn anschließen, sich zu jdm gesellen; *to ~ forces with s.o.* sich mit jdm zs.schließen *od* verbünden; mit jdm zs.arbeiten; *to ~ hands with s.o.* jdm die Hand geben *od* drücken; *fig* mit jdm gemeinsame Sache machen; *to ~ issue with s.o. on s.th.* sich mit jdm über etw ausea.setzen; *to ~ in series* in Reihe schalten; *everybody ~ in the chorus* alles im Chor; **~der** ['-də] *bes. jur* Verbindung, Vereinigung *f*; Beitritt *m (zu e-m Prozeß)*; **~er** ['-ə] *(bes.* Bau-)Tischler, -Schreiner *m*; *~~'s bench* Hobelbank *f*; **~ery** ['-əri] Tischlerei, Schreinerei; Tischler-, Schreinerarbeit *f*.

joint [dʒɔint] *s* Berührungspunkt *m*, Verbindungsstelle; *(Kabel)* Lötstelle; Naht, Fuge *f*; *rail* Schienenstoß *m*; Scharnier; *anat* Gelenk; *(Küche)* Stück Fleisch, Bratenfleisch *n* mit Knochen; *bot* Vegetationspunkt, Gelenkknoten *m*; *geol* Spalt; *Am sl* Kasten *m*, Gebäude, Haus; *Am sl* Freßlokal *n*, Kneipe *f*, Bumslokal *n*, Spelunke, Spielhölle *f*; *a* gemeinschaftlich, gemeinsam; Mit-; *tr* durch ein Gelenk *od* Gelenke mitea. verbinden; *(Fleisch)* in (Braten-)Stücke schneiden; *tech* (ver)fugen, verzapfen; an den Kanten glatthobeln; *during their ~ lives* zu ihren Lebzeiten; *out of ~* ver-, ausgerenkt; *fig* aus den Fugen; *~ and several* gesamtschuldnerisch; *to put, to throw out of ~* aus-, verrenken; *to put s.o.'s nose out of ~ (fig)* jdn ausstechen; *to take ~ action* gemeinsam vorgehen; *universal ~* Kardan-, Kreuzgelenk *n*; *~* **account** gemeinschaftliche(s) (Bank-)Konto *n*; *on ~* auf gemeinsame Rechnung; *~* **capital** Gesellschaftskapital, -vermögen *n*; *~* **committee** gemischte(r) Ausschuß *m*; *~* **costs** *pl* Schlüsselkosten *pl*; *~* **debtor** Mitschuldner *m*; **~ed** ['-id] *a* gegliedert; **~er** ['-ə] Löter *m (Person)*; Fügemaschine *f*; Langhobel *m*; *arch* Eisenklammer *f*; *~* **guardian** Mit-, Gegenvormund *m*; *~* **heir** Miterbe *m*; *~* **liability** Gesamthaftung *f*; **~ly** ['-li] *adv* gemeinsam, zusammen; *~* **owner, ownership** Miteigentümer *m*, Miteigentum *n*; *~* **partner** Mitinhaber, Teilhaber, (Geschäfts-)Partner *m*; *~* **plaintiff** Mitkläger *m*; *~* **property** Gütergemeinschaft *f*; *~* **proprietor** Miteigentümer *m*; *~* **resolution** *pol* gemeinsame Entschließung *f*; *~* **stock** Aktienkapital *n*; *~~ company* Aktiengesellschaft; *Am* Offene Handelsgesellschaft *f* auf Aktien; *~* **tenant** Mitmieter, -pächter *m*; **~ure** ['-ʃə] *jur* Witwenleibgedinge, *obs* Wittum *n*.

joist [dʒɔist] *s* Trag-, Querbalken *m*; *pl* Gebälk *n*; *tr* mit Querbalken versehen.

jok|e [dʒouk] *s* Ulk, Spaß, Scherz, Witz; Gegenstand *m* des Gelächters; *itr* Spaß, Witze machen; *tr* verulken, sich lustig machen über, hänseln, necken; *in ~~* (nur) zum Spaß, im Scherz; *to carry the ~~ too far* den Scherz zu weit treiben; *to crack a ~~* e-n Witz machen, *fam* reißen; *to make a ~~ of s.th.* etw ins Lächerliche ziehen; *to play a ~~ on s.o.* jdm e-e Streich, e-n Schabernack spielen; *to turn s.th. into a ~~* sich über etw lustig machen, *fam* etw durch den Kakao ziehen; *he cannot see* od *take a ~~* er versteht keinen Spaß; *it is no ~~* das ist kein Spaß; das ist Ernst; *the best of the ~~* die Pointe *f*; *a practical ~~* ein Streich, Schabernack *m*; *the ~~ of the town* das Gelächter der ganzen Stadt; **~er** ['-ə] Spaßvogel, Witzbold; *sl* Kerl, Bursche; *(Kartenspiel)* Joker *m*; *Am (Gesetz, Urkunde) fig* Hintertüre, versteckte, zweideutige Klausel *f*; **~ing** ['-iŋ] Spaßen, Scherzen *n*; *~~ apart!* Scherz beiseite! **~ingly** ['-iŋli] im Scherz, im Spaß.

joll|ification [dʒɔlifi'keiʃən] *fam* Remmidemmi *n*, (Jubel u.) Trubel *m*, Festlichkeit, Lustbarkeit *f*; **~ify** ['dʒɔlifai] *fam tr* in Stimmung bringen; *itr* in Stimmung, lustig, ausgelassen sein; **~iness** ['dʒɔlinis], **~ity** ['-iti] Lustigkeit, Fröhlichkeit, Ausgelassenheit, Stimmung; Lustbarkeit, Festlichkeit *f*; **~y** ['dʒɔli] *a* fröhlich, lustig, heiter, in Stimmung, ausgelassen; angeheitert; *Br fam* prächtig, prachtvoll, famos, tadellos, gut, angenehm; *iro* schön; *adv Br fam* riesig, mächtig, sehr; *tr fam (to ~ along)* gut zureden, schmeicheln (*s.o.* jdm); aufmuntern, aufheitern; aufziehen, zum besten haben.

jolly(-boat) ['dʒɔlibout] Jolle *f*.

jolt [dʒoult] *tr* (auf-, durch)rütteln, -schütteln; *itr* dahinschlendern; *s* plötzliche(r) Stoß *od* Schlag *m*; Rütteln *n*; Schock *m*, Überraschung *f*.

Jonathan ['dʒɔnəθən] Jonathan *m*; *(Brother ~)* Amerika *n (US)*, Amerikaner *m*.

jonquil ['dʒɔŋkwil] Jonquille *f (Narzissenart)*.

jorum ['dʒɔːrəm] Humpen *m*; Bowle *f*.

josh [dʒɔʃ] *Am sl tr* zum besten haben, verulken; *s* Spaß, Scherz, Ulk *m*.

joss [dʒɔs] chinesische(r, s) Götze(nbild *n*) *m*; **~-house** chinesische(r) Tempel *m*; **~-stick** Räucherstäbchen *n*.

josser ['dʒɔsə] *sl* Depp, (blöder) Kerl *m*.

jostle ['dʒɔsl] *tr* stoßen (*against* gegen); schubsen, anrempeln; schieben, drängen; *itr* kämpfen (*with s.o. for s.th.* mit jdm um etw); zs.stoßen (*with* mit); *s* Stoß, Schubs, Puff *m*; *to ~ away* wegschubsen, -schieben.

jot [dʒɔt] *s*: *not a ~* nicht das geringste, nicht im geringsten; kein Jota; *tr (to ~ down)* (sich) (kurz) notieren, vermerken; **~ter** ['-ə] Notizbuch *n*; **~tings** ['-iŋz] *s pl* Notiz *f*, Vermerk *m*.

joule [dʒuːl, dʒaul] *el* Joule *n*.

jounce [dʒauns] *tr* (durch)schütteln, -rütteln; *itr* durchgeschüttelt, durchgerüttelt werden; *s* Stoß, Ruck, Schubs *m*.

journal ['dʒəːnl] Tagebuch *n*, Aufzeichnungen *f pl*; *com* Journal; *mar* Logbuch *n*; (Tages-)Zeitung, Zeitschrift *f*, Magazin *n*; *tech* (Wellen-)Zapfen, Achsschenkel *m*; *~* **box** Achslager *n*; **~ese** ['dʒəːnə'liːz] Zeitungsstil *m*; **~ism** ['-lizm] Zeitungswesen *n*, -schriftstellerei; die Presse *f*; **~ist** ['-ist] Journalist, Zeitungsschreiber, Tagesschriftsteller *m*; **~istic** [dʒəːnə'listik] journalistisch; **~ize** ['-əlaiz] *tr com* in das Journal eintragen; *itr* ein Tagebuch führen; Journalist sein.

journey ['dʒəːni] *s* Reise *f*; *itr* reisen, e-e Reise machen; *to go on a ~* verreisen; *a day's ~* e-e Tagesreise; **~man** ['-mən] Geselle, gelernte(r), Facharbeiter *m*; *~~ baker* Bäckergeselle *m*; **~-work** Gesellenarbeit; *fig* Tag(e)löhnerarbeit *f*.

j(o)ust [dʒaust, dʒuːst] *s hist* Lanzenstechen *n*, Tjost *f*; *itr* turnieren.

Jove [dʒouv] *poet* Jupiter *m*; *by ~!* Donnerwetter! Himmel!

jovial ['dʒouvjəl] heiter, fröhlich, jovial; **~ity** [dʒouvi'æliti] Heiterkeit, Fröhlichkeit *f*, Frohsinn *m*.

jowl [dʒaul] Kinnbacken *m*; Backe; Kehle *f*; *zoo* Kehllappen *m*, Wamme *f*; *(gewisse Fische)* Kopf *m*; *cheek by ~* (ganz) dicht beiea.

joy [dʒɔi] *s* Freude *f* (*in, of* an; *at* über), Vergnügen (*at* an); Entzücken *n*, (Glück-)Seligkeit *f*; *itr poet* sich freuen (*in* über); *for, with ~* vor Freude; *in ~ and sorrow* in Freud und Leid; *to the ~ of s.o.* zu jds Freude, Vergnügen; *with ~* mit Vergnügen, mit Freude, erfreut *adv*; *tears (pl) of ~* Freudentränen *f pl*; **~-bells** *pl* Freudenglocken *f pl*; **~ful** ['-ful] voller Freude; freudig, froh, glücklich; **~fulness** ['-fulnis] Freudigkeit, Fröhlichkeit *f*; **~less** ['-lis] freudlos, traurig, trüb(e); **~lessness** ['-lisnis] Freudlosigkeit, Traurigkeit *f*; **~ous** ['-əs] freudig, froh, glücklich; **~ousness** ['-əsnis] Freude, Fröhlichkeit *f*;

~-ride *s fam* Auto-, Spritztour, Vergnügungs-, Spazierfahrt; Schwarzfahrt *f*; *itr fam* e-e Spritztour, e-e Schwarzfahrt machen; **~-rider** Schwarzfahrer *m*; **~-stick** *aero sl* Steuerknüppel *m*.

*

jubil|ant ['dʒu:bilənt] frohlockend, triumphierend; **~ate** ['-leit] *itr* jubeln, jubilieren; **~ation** [dʒu:bi'leiʃən] Jubel, Freudentaumel *m*; Freudenfest *n*; **~ee** ['dʒubili:] *rel* Jubeljahr; (50jähr.) Jubiläum; Freudenfest *n*; *silver, diamond ~~* 25-, 60jährige(s) Jubiläum *n*.

Jud|(a)ea, ~ea [dʒu:'diə] Judäa *n*; **~aic** [dʒu(:)'deiik] jüdisch; **~aism** ['dʒu:deiizm] Judentum *n*; **~aize** ['dʒu:deiaiz] *itr* Jude werden; *tr* jüdisch machen.

Judas ['dʒu:dəs] Judas; *j~* Verräter *m*; Guckloch *n*, Spion *m*; **~-colo(u)red** *a (Haare)* rot; **~ kiss** Judaskuß *m*; **~-tree** *bot* Judasbaum *m*.

judge [dʒʌdʒ] *s* Richter (*of* über) *a. rel hist*; Schieds-, Preisrichter; Kenner, Sachverständige(r) *m* (*of* in); *tr* richten, aburteilen; *(Streit)* schlichten; *(Wettbewerb)* die Entscheidung treffen in; entscheiden; sich ein Urteil bilden über; beurteilen, urteilen über; halten für, ansehen als; *itr* Recht sprechen, richten; das Urteil fällen; entscheiden; urteilen (*of* über; *by, from* nach); vermuten, annehmen; *rel hist* das Richteramt innehaben; *to be a (no) ~ of s.th.* sich in etw (nicht) auskennen, sich auf etw (nicht) verstehen; *as God is my ~!* so wahr mir Gott helfe! *~ of human nature* Menschenkenner *m*; *associate ~* Beisitzer *m*; *chief ~* Gerichtspräsident *m*; *election ~* Wahlprüfer *m*; *federal ~* Bundesrichter *m*; *lay ~* Laienrichter, Schöffe *m*; *police-court ~* Polizei-, Schnellrichter *m*; *presiding ~* Gerichtsvorsitzende(r) *m*; *professional ~* Berufsrichter *m*; *~ in lunacy* Entmündigungs-, Vormundschaftsrichter *m*; **~-advocate** Kriegsgerichtsrat *m*; *~~ general* Vorsitzende(r) *m* des Obersten Kriegsgerichts; **~-made law** Richterrecht *n*; **~ship** ['-ʃip] Richteramt *n*

judg(e)ment ['dʒʌdʒmənt] Urteil *n* (*on* über); Urteils-, Richterspruch *m*, Gerichtsurteil *n*, gerichtliche Entscheidung; *fin (~ debt)* ausgeklagte, Urteilsforderung *f*; *fig* Strafgericht *n*, Strafe; Meinung, Ansicht *f*, Urteil; Urteilsvermögen *n*, Scharfsinn *m*, Einsicht *f*, Verständnis *n*, gesunde(r) Menschenverstand *m*; *according to my ~* nach meinem Dafürhalten, meiner Meinung nach; *against o.'s better ~* gegen die eigene Überzeugung; *in my ~* meines Erachtens; meiner Ansicht nach; *to the best of my ~* soweit ich das beurteilen kann; *to bring to ~* vor Gericht bringen; *to give, to pass ~* ein Urteil fällen, entscheiden, erkennen (*on* über); *to give ~ for, (against) s.o.* zu jds (Un-)Gunsten entscheiden; *to pass ~ on s.o.* jdn verurteilen; *to pronounce a ~* ein Urteil verkünden; *to quash, to reverse, to set aside a ~* ein Urteil aufheben; *to show ~* Urteilsvermögen besitzen; *to sit in ~* zu Gericht sitzen (*on* über); *to suspend a ~* ein Urteil aussetzen; *it is a ~ for it* das ist die Strafe dafür; *the Day of J~* der Jüngste Tag, das Jüngste Gericht; *declaratory ~* Feststellungsurteil *n*; *default ~* Versäumnisurteil *n*; *error of ~* Fehlurteil *n*; *interlocutory, provisional ~* vorläufige(s), Zwischenurteil *n*; **(J)~-day** = *the Day of J~*; **~-proof** unpfändbar; **~-seat** Richterstuhl *m*.

judicature ['dʒu:dikətʃə] Gerichtsverwaltung, Rechtspflege *f*, -wesen *n*; Rechtsprechung *f*; Richteramt *n*, richterliche Gewalt *f*; Gerichtsbezirk *m*, Jurisdiktion *f*; Gericht(shof *m*) *n*; Richter *m pl*.

judici|al [dʒu(:)'diʃəl] rechtlich, richterlich; Rechts-, Justiz-; gerichtlich, Gerichts-; richterlich; gerecht, unparteiisch, sachlich; kritisch; *~~ act* Rechtshandlung *f*; *~~ assembly* Gerichtshof *m*; *~~ bench* Richterbank *f*; *~~ code* Prozeßordnung *f*; *~~ court* Gerichtshof *m*; *~~ decision* Gerichtsentscheid *m*; *~~ error* Justizirrtum *m*; *~~ finding* Richterspruch *m*; *~~ murder* Justizmord *m*; *~~ order* richterliche Verfügung *f*; *~~ power* richterliche Gewalt *f*; *~~ proceedings (pl)* Gerichtsverfahren *n*; *~~ reform* Rechtsreform *f*; *~~ sale* gerichtliche Versteigerung *f*; *~~ separation* Trennung *f* von Tisch u. Bett, Aufhebung *f* der ehelichen Gemeinschaft; *~~ system* Justizverfassung *f*, Rechtswesen *n*; **~ary** [dʒu(:)'diʃiəri] *a* Rechts-, Gerichts-, Justiz-; gerichtlich, richterlich; *s* Gerichtsverwaltung, Rechtspflege *f*, Rechtswesen *n*, Richterschaft *f*; **~ous** [dʒu(:)'diʃəs] urteilsfähig, verständig, einsichtig, klug, weise; **~ousness** [-'diʃəsnis] Einsicht *f*, Verstand *m*, Klugheit, Weisheit *f*.

judy ['dʒu:di] *sl* Frau, Göre *f*; *fig* lächerliche(s) Stück *n*; *to make a ~ of o.s. (fam)* sich blamieren.

jug [dʒʌg] *s* Krug *m*, Kanne *f*; *sl* Knast *m*, Kittchen *n*; *tr* in e-n Krug, e-e Kanne füllen; schmoren, dämpfen; *sl* einlochen; *~ged hare* Hasenpfeffer *m*; **~ful** ['-ful] Krug- *m*, Kannevoll *f*; *not by a ~~ (Am)* nicht im geringsten, nicht entfernt, auf keinen Fall.

juggernaut ['dʒʌgənɔ:t] *(J~ car)* Moloch *m*.

juggins ['dʒʌginz] *sl* Trottel *m*.

juggl|e ['dʒʌgl] *tr* Kunststücke machen mit; fälschen; betrügen (*out of* um); verzaubern; *itr* jonglieren; verfälschen (*with s.th.* etw); *s* Kunststück *n*; Schwindelei *f*, Trick, Betrug *m*; **~er** ['-ə] Taschenspieler, Gaukler; Betrüger, Schwindler *m*; **~ery** ['-əri] Taschenspielerei *f*; Schwindel, Betrug *m*.

Jugoslav ['ju:go(u)'slɑ:v] *s* Jugoslawe *m*, Jugoslawin *f*; *a* jugoslawisch; **~ia** [-jə] Jugoslawien *n*.

jugul|ar ['dʒʌgjulə] *a* Kehl-, Hals-; *s u. ~~ vein (anat)* Drosselader *f*; **~ate** ['-eit] *tr* die Kehle durchschneiden (*s.o.* jdm); erdrosseln, erwürgen; *bes. fig* abdrosseln, unterbinden, -drücken; *med* kupieren.

*

juic|e [dʒu:s] Saft *a. bot zoo anat*; *fig* Gehalt *m*, Wesen; *sl* Benzin, Öl *n*, Treibstoff; *sl el* Strom *m*; *to stew in o.'s own ~~ (fig)* im eigenen Saft schmoren; *gastric ~~ (physiol)* Magensaft *m*; **~eless** ['-lis] saftlos, trocken; **~er** ['-ə] *film sl* Beleuchter *m*; **~iness** ['-inis] Saftigkeit; *fam* Nässe *f*; **~y** ['-i] saftig; *(Wetter)* naß, feucht; *fam* interessant, spannend, pikant, gepfeffert.

ju-jitsu, jiu-jitsu [dʒu:'dʒitsu] *sport* Jiu-Jitsu *n*.

jujube ['dʒu:dʒu(:)b] Brustbeere *f*; Brustbeerenbaum, Judendorn *m*; Brustbeerbonbon, -gelee *m*.

juke|box ['dʒu:kbɔks] *Am fam* Musikautomat *m*; **~ joint** *Am fam* Kneipe, Kaschemme *f*, Bumslokal *n*.

julep ['dʒu:lep] Heiltrank; *Am* Kühltrank; *(mint ~)* Pfefferminzlikör *m*.

July [dʒu(:)'lai] Juli *m*; *in ~* im Juli.

jumble ['dʒʌmbl] *tr* (ver)mischen, (ver)mengen; *fig* durchea.bringen, *fam* -würfeln; *itr (to ~ up)* durchea.-geraten; *s* Mischmasch *m*; Durcheinander *n*, Wirrwarr *m*; **~-sale** Wohltätigkeitsbasar *m*; **~-shop** Kramladen *m*.

jumbo ['dʒʌmbou] *pl -os s* Koloß *m (Mensch, Tier od Sache)*; *sl fig* Kanone *f*; *a Am com* Riesen-; riesig.

jump [dʒʌmp] **1.** *itr* springen; auf-, hochfahren; *rail* entgleisen; *aero (mit dem Fallschirm)* abspringen; *fig (Preise)* in die Höhe schnellen; *(von e-m Thema zum andern)* springen; sich stürzen (*at* auf); schnell, eilig, eifrig ergreifen, annehmen (*at s.th.* etw); *(Entschluß)* fassen (*to s.th.* etw); anfahren, angreifen (*on, upon s.o.* jdn); übereinstimmen, sich decken (*with* mit); **2.** *tr* (hinweg)springen über; springen lassen; *(Küche)* schwenken; *fig (Preise)* in die Höhe schnellen lassen; *(Angebot)* überbieten; *(Buchseite)* überspringen; *fam* sich stürzen auf; *fam* Hals über Kopf verlassen, *Am sl* aufscheuchen, unrechtmäßig in Besitz nehmen, (be)rauben; **3.** *s* Sprung *a. sport*, *fam* Satz *m*; Auffahren *n*, Zuckung *f*; *aero* (Fallschirm-)Absprung *m*; plötzliche(s) Ansteigen *n (der Preise)*; (Gedanken-)Sprung *m*; *the ~s (pl sl)* der Veitstanz; der Tatterich; *on the ~ (fam)* eifrig im Gange, sehr beschäftigt; zerfahren, nervös; *to be on the ~* auf den Beinen sein; *to get, to have the ~ on s.o. (sl)* vor jdm e-n Vorsprung haben; jdm zuvorkommen; *to ~ bail, bonds* s-e Kaution aufgeben; *to ~ a claim* sich über e-n fremden Anspruch hinwegsetzen; *to ~ to conclusions* voreilige Schlüsse ziehen; *to ~ the gun (Am sl sport)* vor dem Signal starten; *allg* die Zeit nicht abwarten können, vorher anfangen; *to ~ the queue* sich vordrängeln; s-e Sachen hinten herum kriegen; *to ~ the rails, (Am) the track* entgleisen; *to ~ out of o.'s skin (fig)* aus der Haut fahren; *broad* od *long, high, pole ~ (sport)* Weit-, Hoch-, Stabhochsprung *m*; *to* **~ down** hinab-, hinunter-, herunterspringen (*from* von); *to* **~ in, out** hinein-, hinausspringen; *to ~ s.o. into* jdn verleiten zu; *to* **~ off** herabspringen; *sl mil* losschlagen; *to* **~ on** aufspringen (*to* auf); *to* **~ together** zs.fallen, übereinstimmen; *to* **~ up** auf-, hochspringen; **~ area** *mil* Sprunggebiet *n*; **~ed-up** *a fam* mangelhaft vorbereitet, improvisiert; hochnäsig; **~er** ['-ə] Springer; Floh *m*; Made *f*; *tech* Stauchhammer; Stoßbohrer *m*; Rauhbank *f*; *radio* Schalt-, Überbrückungsdraht *m*, Anschlußstrippe *f*; Woll-, Überjacke *f*, Jumper; *fam* (Fahrkarten-)Schaffner *m*; *high ~~* Hochspringer *m*; **~iness** ['-inis] Sprunghaftigkeit *f*; **~ing** ['-iŋ]: *~~-bean* Springbohne *f*; *~~ board* Sprungbrett *n*; *~~-hare, -louse, -mouse* Springhase *m*, -laus, -maus *f*; *~~-jack* Hampelmann *m*; *~~-off (mil)* Ausgang; *aero* Absprung *m (mit dem Fallschirm)*; *~~-off place* Endstation *f*; *fig* Ende *n* (der Welt); *~~-off position, ground (mil)* Ausgangsstellung *f*; *~~-pole* Sprungstange *f*; **~-master** *(Fallschirmtruppe)* Absetzer *m*; **~-off** *aero* Absprung *m (mit dem Fallschirm)*; *~~-base (Am aero)* Absprungplatz *m*; **~y** ['-i] sprunghaft; *fam* nervös, aufgeregt.

junct|ion ['dʒʌŋkʃən] Verbindung, Vereinigung *f*; Schnittpunkt *m*; *(road ~~)* (Straßen-)Kreuzung *f*, (Verkehrs-)Knotenpunkt; Treffpunkt; *rail* Umsteigebahnhof, Eisenbahnknoten(punkt) *m*; *tech* Stoß-, Lötstelle *f*; *~~ box (el)* Abzweigdose *f*; *~~ line (rail)* Zweig-, Verbindungslinie; *tele* Amtsleitung *f*; **~ure** ['dʒʌŋktʃə] Verbindung, Vereinigung *f*; Berührungspunkt *m*, Verbindungsstelle *f*, -stück *n*, Fuge, Naht *f*; Gelenk *n*; Zeitpunkt; kritische(r) Augenblick *m*, Krise *f*; Stand *m* der Dinge.

June [dʒu:n] Juni *m*; *in ~* im Juni; **~-berry** *bot* Trauben-, Felsenbirne *f*; **~-bug, -beetle** *Am* Juni-, Maikäfer *m*.

jungle ['dʒʌŋgl] Dschungel *m*, *f* od *n*; Dickicht *n*; *Am sl* Landstreicherlager *n*, gefährliche(r) Stadtteil *m*; **~-fever** Sumpffieber *n*.

junior ['dʒu:njə] *a* jünger; von geringerem Dienstalter *od* niedrigerem Rang; später; *(nach e-m Namen)* junior, der Jüngere, Sohn; *sport* Junioren-; *s* Jüngere(r); Rangniedrigere(r); jüngere(r) Schüler *od* Student; *Am* Schüler *od* Student *m* im 3. Schul- *bzw.* Studienjahr; *to be s.o.'s ~* jünger als jem sein (*by two years* zwei Jahre); *~* **clerk** zweite(r) Buchhalter *m*; *~* **college** *Am* College *n* nur für die beiden ersten Studienjahre; *~* **counsel** (Anwalts-)Assessor *m*; *~* **high school** *Am* Schule *f*, die das 8. u. 9. Schuljahr umfaßt; **~ity** [dʒu:ni'ɔriti] geringere(s) Alter *n*; niedrigere(r) Rang *m*; *~* **partner** jüngere(r) Teilhaber *m*; *the* **J~ Service** das (brit.) Heer; *~* **school** *Br* Grundschule *f*.

juniper ['dʒu:nipə] *bot* Wacholder *m*.

junk [dʒʌŋk] **1.** *s* alte(s) Tauwerk; Altmaterial *n*, -waren *f pl*, Schrott *m*; dicke(s) Stück *n*; *fam* Abfall, Trödel *m*, Gerümpel *n*; Schund *m*; *mar* Pökelfleisch *n*; *zoo* Walrat *m* od *n*; *Am sl* Rauschgift *n*; *tr fam* ausrangieren, wegwerfen, zum alten Eisen werfen; **~-dealer** *Am*, *fam* **~man** ['-mən] Altwarenhändler, Trödler, Lumpensammler *m*; **~pile, ~yard** *Am* Schuttabladeplatz; Autofriedhof *m*; **~-shop** Marine-Verpflegungslager *n*; *Am* Altwarenhandlung *f*, Trödelladen *m*; **~y** ['-i] *Am sl* Rauschgiftsüchtige(r) *m*; **2.** Dschunke *f*.

junket ['dʒʌŋkit] *s* Sahne-, Rahmquark *m*; süße Dickmilch *f*; Schmaus *m*, Bankett, Fest; *Am* Picknick *n*, Fahrt *f* ins Grüne, Spritztour, Vergnügungsfahrt *f*, Ausflug *m*, Exkursion *f (auf Staatskosten)*; *tr* bewirten; *itr* schmausen; feiern; *Am* e-e Spritztour machen *(auf Staatskosten)*.

junt|a ['dʒʌntə] *pol* Junta *f*; *a.* **~o** ['-ou] *pl -os (pol)* Junta *f*; Geheimbund *f*, Verschwörerclique *f*, Komplott *n*.

juridic|(al) [dʒuə'ridik(əl)] gerichtlich, Gerichts-; Rechts-; juristisch; *~al days (pl)* Gerichtstage *m pl*; *~al insecurity* Rechtsunsicherheit *f*; *~al person* juristische Person.

jurisdiction [dʒu(ə)ris'dikʃən] Rechtshoheit, -pflege *f*, -wesen *n*, Rechtsprechung, Gerichtsbarkeit *f*, -bezirk *m*; Zuständigkeit(sbereich *m* od *n*) *f*; Gerichtsstand *m*; *to come under the ~* unter die Zuständigkeit fallen (*of* von); *to have ~ over* zuständig sein für.

jurispruden|ce [dʒu(ə)ris'pru:dəns, 'dʒu-] Rechtswissenschaft, Jurisprudenz; Rechtsphilosophie *f*, -system *n*; *medical ~* gerichtliche, Gerichtsmedizin *f*; **~t** [-t] *s* Rechtsgelehrte(r), Jurist *m*; *a* rechtskundig; **~tial** [-'denʃəl] rechtswissenschaftlich, juristisch.

jurist ['dʒu(ə)rist] Jurist; *Am* Anwalt; *Br* Student *m* der Rechte.

juror ['dʒu(ə)rə] Geschworene(r), Schöffe; Preisrichter *m*.

jury ['dʒu(ə)ri] Geschworenen-, Schwur-, Schöffengericht *n*; *die* Geschworenen, *die* Schöffen *m pl*; Preisgericht, -richterkollegium *n*; Jury *f*; Sachverständigenausschuß *m*; *gentlemen of the ~!* meine Herren Geschworenen! *common, petty ~* Urteilsjury *f*; *foreman of the ~* Geschworenenobmann *m*; *grand ~* Anklagejury *f*; *trial by ~* Schwurgerichtsverhandlung *f*; *verdict of the ~* (Wahr-)Spruch *m* der Geschworenen; **~-box** Geschworenen-, Schöffenbank *f*; **~-list, -panel** Geschworenen-, Schöffenliste *f*; **~man** ['-mən] Geschworene(r) *m*.

jury-mast ['dʒu(ə)rima:st] *mar* Notmast *m*.

just [dʒʌst] **1.** *a* gerecht, unparteiisch, fair; ehrlich, gerade, aufrecht; verdient; *pred* recht u. billig; gesetzlich, rechtlich, in aller Form rechtens; recht, richtig; berechtigt, begründet; genau, korrekt; *adv* genau, gerade; (so) etwa; nur, nicht mehr als; gerade noch, mit knapper Not, mit Müh und Not; gerade, (so) eben; nur (so), bloß; mal; *Am fam* ganz, recht, einfach, wirklich, eigentlich; *but ~, ~ now* eben erst, im Augenblick; *only ~* gerade noch; *~ as* ebenso, geradeso; *~ as well* ebensogut; *~ then* gerade in dem Augenblick; *to receive o.'s ~ deserts* s-n gerechten Lohn empfangen; *that's ~ it!* ganz recht (so)! *~ the same (fam)* macht nichts! *~ a moment!* einen Augenblick, bitte! *~ let me see!* laß doch bitte mal sehen; *~ so* ganz richtig; genau so; *~ shut the door!* mach doch, bitte, die Tür zu! *~ tell me!* sag doch mal! *~ for that* nun gerade; **~ly** ['-li] *adv* richtig; mit Recht; verdientermaßen; **~ness** ['-nis] Gerechtigkeit, Billigkeit; Ehrlichkeit, Geradheit *f*; **2.** *s. joust.*

justice ['dʒʌstis] Gerechtigkeit; Rechtmäßigkeit, Richtigkeit, Korrektheit *f* (*to* gegenüber); Recht(swesen *n*, -pflege *f*) *n*, Gerichtsbarkeit *f*; Richter *m*; *in ~ to s.o.* um jdm Gerechtigkeit widerfahren zu lassen, um jdm gerecht zu werden; *to administer, to dispense ~* Recht sprechen; *to bring to ~* vor Gericht bringen; *to do s.o. ~* jdm Gerechtigkeit widerfahren lassen, jdm gerecht werden; *to do o.s. ~* sein Licht nicht unter den Scheffel stellen, mit s-n Pfunden wuchern; *to evade ~* sich der Strafverfolgung, Bestrafung entziehen; *chief ~* Oberrichter *m*; *court of ~* Gericht(shof *m*) *n*; *equal ~ under the law* Gleichheit *f* vor dem Gesetz; *lay ~* Laienrichter *m*; *minister of ~* Justizminister *m*; *ministry of ~* Justizministerium *n*; *~ of the peace* Friedensrichter *m*; **~ship** ['-ʃip] Richteramt *n*; **justiciable** [dʒʌs'tiʃiəbl] der Gerichtsbarkeit unterworfen.

justif|iability [dʒʌstifaiə'biliti] Berechtigung, Rechtmäßigkeit *f*; **~iable** ['dʒʌstifaiəbl] zu rechtfertigen(d), gerechtfertigt, berechtigt; *~~ defence* Notwehr *f*; **~ication** [dʒʌstifi'keiʃən] Rechtfertigung; *tech* Justierung *f*; *~~ by faith* Rechtfertigung *f* durch den Glauben; **~icative, ~icatory** ['dʒʌstifikeitiv, -əri] rechtfertigend, Rechtfertigungs-; Berechtigungs-; **~ier** ['-faiə] Rechtfertiger *m*; **~y** ['-fai] *tr* begründen; rechtfertigen *a. rel* (*to* vor); *typ* justieren; *to be ~ied* recht haben (*in doing s.th.* etw zu tun).

*

jut [dʒʌt] *itr (to ~ out, forth)* vorspringen, hervorstehen, -ragen; *s* Vorsprung *m*.

Jut|e [dʒu:t] Jüte *m*, Jütin *f*; **~ish** ['-iʃ] jütisch; **~land** ['dʒʌtlənd] Jütland *n*.

jute [dʒu:t] Jute *f*.

juven|escence [dʒu:vi'nesəns] Heranreifen; Jugendalter *n*; *well of ~~* Jungbrunnen *m*; **~escent** [-t] heranwachsend; **~ile** ['dʒu:vinail] *a* jugendlich, jung; unreif; Jugend-; *s* Jugendliche(r) *m*; *(~~ book)* Jugendbuch *n*; *~~ court* Jugendgericht *n*; *~~ delinquency* Jugendkriminalität *f*; *~~ security* Jugendschutz *m*; **~ility** [-'niliti] Jugend(lichkeit) *f*; jugendliche(r) Leichtsinn *m*; *pl* Jugendstreiche *m pl*.

juxtapos|e ['dʒʌkstəpouz] *tr* nebenea.stellen; **~ition** [dʒʌkstəpə'ziʃən] Nebenea.stellung *f*.

K

K, k [kei] *pl* ~'s K, k *n.*

Kaf(f)ir ['kæfə] *s pej* Kaffer *m*; Kaffernsprache *f*; *pl* Bergwerksaktien *f pl* der Südafrikanischen Union.

kale, kail [keil] Grün-, Krauskohl *m*; *(~ seed) Am sl* Moos, Geld *n*; **~-yard** *Scot* Gemüse-, Küchengarten *m.*

kaleidoscop|e [kə'laidəskoup] Kaleidoskop *n a. fig*; **~ic** [kəlaidə'skɔpik] kaleidoskopisch, ständig wechselnd.

kali ['kɑ:li, 'keili] *bot* Salzkraut *n.*

kangaroo [kæŋgə'ru:] *pl -os* Känguruh *n*; *parl (~ closure)* Abkürzung *f* e-r Diskussion durch Behandlung einzelner Punkte; **~ court** *Am fam* inoffizielle(s), Scheingericht *n*; **~ landing** *aero sl* Bumslandung *f*; **~-rat** *zoo* Känguruh-, Beutelratte *f.*

kaolin ['keiəlin] Porzellanerde *f*, Kaolin *n* od *m.*

kapok ['keipɔk, 'kɑ:-] Kapok *m.*

katabatic [kætə'bætik] *(Wind)* fallend; **~ wind** Fallwind *m.*

Kate [keit] Käthe *f.*

katydid ['keitidid] *Am zoo* Laubheuschrecke *f.*

kayak ['kaiæk] Kajak *m* od *n.*

kayo ['kei'ou] *tr sl* k.o. schlagen; *s sl* K.o., Knockout *m.*

keck [kek] *itr* Würgen, Brechreiz haben; *fig* sich ekeln, sich schütteln (*at* vor); **~le** ['-l] *itr* kichern.

kedge [kedʒ] *s (~ anchor)* Warp-, Stromanker *m*; *tr mar* verholen, warpen; *itr (Schiff)* verholt werden.

keel [ki:l] *s mar aero bot* Kiel *m*; *bot* Längsrippe *f*; *poet* Schiff *n*; *mar* Schute *f*; *tr* mit e-m Kiel versehen; *(Schiff)* auf die Seite legen; *itr (Schiff)* sich auf die Seite legen; *to ~ over (tr) (fam)* auf den Kopf stellen *od* stülpen; *mar* kentern lassen; *itr* (um)kippen; kentern; *on an even ~* gerade *adv*, ohne zu schwanken; *fig* gleichmäßig, glatt, ruhig *adv*; *to lay down a ~* ein Schiff auf Kiel legen; **~haul** ['-hɔ:l] *tr mar* kielholen; *fig* anschnauzen.

keen [ki:n] **1.** *(Messer, Senf, Augen, Verstand)* scharf; *(Ironie)* beißend; *(Wind)* scharf, schneidend; *(Kälte)* schneidend, durchdringend, streng; *(Ton)* schrill, ohrenbetäubend; *(Schmerz)* stechend, brennend, heftig, stark; *(Appetit)* stark, groß; *(Interesse)* lebhaft, stark; *(Bemühen, Ringen)* heiß; *(Wettstreit)* heftig; *(Mensch)* stark interessiert (*on* an); eifrig (*on* in); begierig, versessen, erpicht, *fam* scharf (*on* auf; *to do, (fam) on doing* darauf, zu tun); begeistert (*about* von); *Am sl* prächtig; *(as) ~ as mustard (fam)* ganz wild, (ganz) verrückt (*on* nach); *she is ~ on riding* sie ist e-e leidenschaftliche Reiterin; **~-edged** *a* scharf(geschliffen); **~ness** ['-nis] Schärfe, Heftigkeit, Strenge; Lebhaftigkeit, Stärke; Verstandesschärfe *f*, Scharfsinn *m*; **~-witted** *a* scharfsinnig; **2.** *s (Irland)* Totenklage *f*; *tr itr (e-n Toten)* beweinen.

keep [ki:p] *irr kept, kept* **1.** *tr* (be)halten, haben; einhalten, beobachten, befolgen, festhalten an; bewahren, bewachen, beschützen; überwachen; aufbewahren, aufheben; für sich behalten; in Ordnung halten, er-, unterhalten, versorgen, sorgen für; in Verpflegung, in Pension haben; ernähren, beköstigen; *(Vieh)* halten; *(Personal)* beschäftigen; buchführen über; *(Waren, Tagebuch)* führen; *(Fest)* feiern; *(Hotel)* betreiben; *(Zeitung)* halten; handhaben; *(waiting* warten) lassen; aufheben; vorrätig haben; auf-, zurück-, festhalten; hindern, abhalten (*from* von); *Am (Versammlung)* abhalten, veranstalten; verbergen, verheimlichen, verschweigen (*from s.o.* jdm); **2.** *itr* bleiben; fortfahren, weitermachen; festhalten (*at s.th.* etw); bleiben (*at s.th.* bei e-r S); sich halten (*to s.o.* an jdn); sich enthalten (*from s.th.* e-r S); *(Lebensmittel)* sich halten, gut bleiben; *fam* dauern; sich befinden; *Am fam* sich aufhalten, wohnen, leben; *to ~ (o.s.) to o.s. (Mensch)* sehr reserviert sein; *to ~ doing s.th.* immer wieder etw tun; **3.** *s* (Lebens-)Unterhalt *m*; Unterhaltskosten *pl*; *(Vieh)* Versorgtsein *n*; *hist* Bergfried, Festungsturm *m*; *for ~s (fam)* für immer; *to ~ o.'s bed* das Bett hüten; *to ~ a close check on s.th.* etw scharf überwachen; *to ~ company* Gesellschaft leisten (*s.o.* jdm); *with s.o.* jdm den Hof machen; *to ~ under control* in Schranken halten; *to ~ cool* e-n kühlen Kopf bewahren; *tech* kühl aufbewahren; *to ~ o.'s end up (Am)* s-e Aufgabe erfüllen; *to ~ o.'s eye, hand in s.th.* sich in e-r S auf dem laufenden halten; *to ~ goal (sport)* Torwart sein; *to ~ going (fig)* nicht einschlafen lassen; *to ~ o.'s ground* s-e Stellung behaupten; *to ~ o.'s head* die Ruhe bewahren; *to ~ hold of s.th.* etw festhalten; *to ~ early* od *good, late* od *bad hours* früh (zu Bett) gehen, lange (auf)bleiben; *to ~ house* haushalten; *to ~ left (right)* sich links (rechts) halten; links (rechts) gehen *od* fahren; *to ~ a stiff upper lip* die Ohren steif halten; *to ~ in mind* im Auge behalten; sich merken; *to ~ posted (Am)* auf dem laufenden halten; *to ~ a promise* ein Versprechen halten; *to ~ quiet* still sein; *to ~ in (good) repair* in gutem Zustand (er)halten; *to ~ o.'s seat* sitzen bleiben; *to ~ a shop* e-n Laden führen *od* haben; *to ~ silence* Stillschweigen bewahren; *to ~ in suspense* in der Schwebe, im ungewissen lassen; *to ~ tabs on s.o. (Am)* jdn scharf beobachten; *to ~ o.'s temper* ruhig bleiben; sich beherrschen können; *to ~ time* richtiggehen; Takt, Schritt halten; pünktlich sein; *to ~ in touch* in Fühlung bleiben (*with* mit); *to ~ track of s.th.* sich etw merken; *to ~ in view (fig)* im Auge behalten; *to ~ watch* aufpassen; *to ~ to o.'s word* zu s-m Wort stehen, sein Wort halten; *~ smiling!* Kopf hoch! *~ your seat* bleiben Sie doch sitzen; *to ~* **about** sich noch immer aufhalten; s-e Pflicht tun; *to ~* **alive** *tr* am Leben erhalten; *itr fam* auf Draht sein; *to ~* **away** *itr* fernhalten; *itr* wegbleiben; *to ~* **back** *itr* zurückbleiben, sich entfernthalten; *tr* abhalten; zurückhalten; *(Geld)* zurückbehalten; *fig* verschweigen; *to ~* **down** *tr* niedrighalten; unterdrücken; bezähmen; *itr* sich nicht aufrichten, nicht aufstehen; *to ~* **in** *tr* zurückhalten, am Ausgehen hindern; *(Feuer)* nicht ausgehen lassen; *(Schüler)* nachsitzen lassen; *itr* zu Hause, daheim bleiben, nicht aus-, weggehen; *fam* auf gutem Fuß stehen (*with* mit); *(Kunden)* pflegen; *to ~* **off** *itr* weg-, fernbleiben; *~~ the grass!* Betreten (des Rasens) verboten! *to ~* **on** *tr (Hut)* aufbehalten; *allg* behalten; *itr* dabeibleiben, weitermachen; fortfahren (*doing* zu tun); *at s.o.* jdn nicht in Ruhe lassen; sich ernähren von; *to ~ on talking* weiterreden; *to ~* **out** *tr* nicht durch-, hereinlassen; *itr* draußen bleiben; sich fernhalten (*of* von); *~ out!* Eintritt verboten! *~ out of her way* geh ihr aus dem Weg! *to ~* **over** behalten; *com* übertragen; *to ~* **together** zs.bleiben, -halten; *to ~* **under** unter Kontrolle behalten; *to ~* **up** *tr* fortfahren mit, weitermachen; aufrechterhalten, in Ordnung halten; *(Geschäft)* fortführen; *itr* sich hochhalten; aufbleiben; andauern; *(Wetter)* schön bleiben; *(Preise)* sich behaupten; ausharren; auf dem laufenden halten; *with* auf dem laufenden bleiben, mitkommen, Schritt halten mit; *to ~~ appearances* den Schein wahren; *to ~~ with the Jones's* hinter den Nachbarn nicht zurückbleiben; *to ~ it up* so weitermachen; *~ it up!* nur so weiter! nicht nachgeben; **~er** ['-ə] Inhaber, Besitzer; (Tier-) Halter; Aufbewahrer; *(park-~~)* (Park-)Wächter; (Gefangenen-, Tier-) Wärter; Pfleger; Beschützer; *com* Buchhalter; Haken *m*, Klammer, Schlaufe *f*, Verschluß *m*; haltbare Ware *f*; *game-~~* Wildhüter *m*; *goal-~~* Torwart *m*; *lighthouse-~~* Leuchtturmwärter *m*; *shop~~* Ladeninhaber *m*; **~ing** ['-iŋ] Einhalten, Befolgen *n*; Aufbewahrung; Verwahrung, Obhut, Pflege *f*; (Lebens-)Unterhalt *m*; Einbehaltung *f*, Gewahrsam *m*; *in ~~ with* in Übereinstimmung, in Einklang mit; *~~ room (Am)* Wohnzimmer *n*; **~sake** ['-seik] *s* Andenken *n*, Erinnerung *f* *(an den Geber)*; *a* kitschig; *as, for a ~~* als Andenken, zur Erinnerung.

keg [keg] Fäßchen *n.*

kelp [kelp] (See-)Tang *m*; Seetangasche *f.*

Kelt *s. Celt.*

ken [ken] *tr itr Scot* kennen, wissen (*of, about s.th.* etw); *s* (Er-)Kenntnis *f*, Wissen *n*; Gesichtskreis *m.*

kennel ['kenl] **1.** *s* Hundehütte *f*, *(a. pl)* -stall, -zwinger *m*; Koppel *f* Hunde; *fig* armselige Behausung *f*, Loch *n*; *tr itr* in e-r Hundehütte unterbringen *od* untergebracht sein; *fig* in e-m Loch hausen; **2.** Gosse *f*, Rinnstein *m.*

kerb [kə:b] *(a. curb)* Bordkante *f*; **~ drill** Verkehrserziehung *f*; **~ market** schwarze Börse; Nachbörse *f*; **~stone** Bord-, Gossenstein *m.*

kerchief ['kə:tʃif] Hals-, Kopftuch *n.*

kerf [kə:f] Kerbe *f*, Einschnitt *m*; *(Säge)* Schnittbreite; Schnitte *f*,

kermes ['kə:mi(:)z] Kermes *m (Farbstoff).*

kermis, kermess ['kə:mis] Kirmes, Kirchweih *f*; *Am* Wohltätigkeitsbasar *m.*

kernel ['kə:nl] Korn *n*; Kern *a. fig*; *fig* Kernpunkt *m*, Hauptsache *f.*

kerosene ['kerəsi:n] Kerosin, *bes. Am* Petroleum *n.*

kestrel ['kestrəl] *orn* Turmfalke *m.*

ketch [ketʃ] *mar* Ketsch *f.*

ketchup ['ketʃəp] Ketchup *m* od *n.*

kettle ['ketl] Kessel *a. geog*; *(tea-~)* Teekessel *m*; *(~-hole) geol* Gletschermühle *f*; *the pot should not call the ~ black (prov)* wer im Glashaus sitzt, soll nicht mit Steinen werfen; *a (pretty) ~ of fish* e-e dumme Geschichte; e-e schöne Bescherung; **~drum** *mus* Kesselpauke *f*; **~-holder** Topflappen *m*.

key [ki:] *s* Schlüssel *m a. allg fig*; *fig* Lösung *f* (*to* für); *tech* Keil, Splint; Schraubenschlüssel; *tele* Manipulator *m*, Taste(r *m*); *mus (a. Schreibmaschine)* Taste; *(Blasinstrument)* Klappe *f*; *mus* Schlüssel *m*; Tonart; Stimmlage, -höhe; Ausdrucksweise *f*, Stil; Grundgedanke, Ausgangspunkt *m*; Zeichenerklärung *f*, Schlüssel *m*; Schlüsselkraft *(Person)*; *(~ number)* Kennziffer *f*; *tr* festkeilen, -klemmen; mit e-m Keil, *arch* e-m Schlußstein versehen; e-e Zeichenerklärung, e-n Schlüssel geben zu; mit e-r Kennziffer versehen; *mus* stimmen; *fig* aufea. abstimmen; *to ~ up* in e-e höhere Stimmlage bringen; *(Angebot)* erhöhen; *fig* gespannt, aufgeregt, nervös machen; *in ~ with* in Übereinstimmung mit; *in a minor ~ (fig)* gedrückt, mißmutig; *all in the same ~ (fig)* monoton, ohne Abwechslung, ausdruckslos; alles dasselbe; *under lock and ~* unter Verschluß; hinter Schloß und Riegel; *skeleton-~* Haupt-, Nachschlüssel, Dietrich *m*; **~-bit** Schlüsselbart *m*; **~-board** Klaviatur, Tastatur, Tastenplatte *f*, Tasten-, Griffbrett; *(Orgel)* Manual *n*; **~-bugle** *mus* Klappen-, Kenthorn *n*; **~ed** [-d] *a* mit Tasten, Klappen (versehen); mit e-m Keil befestigt *od* verstärkt; festgekeilt; chiffriert; *~~ up* angeregt, in Stimmung; *~~ down* beniedergedrückt; **~-game** *sport* Entscheidungsspiel *n*; **~hole** Schlüsselloch *n*; **~ industry** Schlüsselindustrie *f*; **~ man** Schlüsselkraft, -figur *f*; **~ map** Übersichtskarte *f*; **~ money** Wohnungsprovision *f*; **~-note** *s mus* Grundton; *fig* Grundgedanke *m*; *tr* das Programm festlegen für; *~~ speech (pol)* programmatische Rede *f*; **~-noter** *pol* Programmatiker *m*; **~-novel** Schlüsselroman *m*; **~ position** Schlüsselstellung *f*; **~-punch** Tastenlocher *m*; **~-ring** Schlüsselring, -bund *m*; **~ signature** *mus* Vorzeichen *n*; **~-station** *radio* Hauptsender *m*; **~stone** *arch* Schlußstein *m*; *fig* Grundlage *f*, -gedanke *m*; **~way** Keilnut *f*; **~ word** Schlüsselwort *n*.

khaki ['kɑ:ki] *a* khakifarben, erdgrau; *s* Khaki, Erdgrau *n*; Khaki, gelbbraune(r) Stoff *m*; Khakiuniform *f*.

kibe [kaib] aufgesprungene *od* vereiterte Frostbeule *f*.

kibitz ['ki:bits] *itr Am fam fig* kiebitzen; **~er** ['-ə] *fam fig* Kiebitz; Besserwisser *m*.

kibosch ['kaibɔʃ] *sl* Quatsch, Unsinn *m*; *to put the ~ on* Schluß machen mit.

kick [kik] *tr* mit dem Fuß, mit den Füßen stoßen *od* treten; *(Fußball)* kicken; *(Tor)* schießen; *itr (mit den Füßen)* strampeln; *(Pferd)* ausschlagen; *(Feuerwaffe)* zurückschlagen; *(Ball)* hochfliegen; *fam* die Zähne zeigen, sich wehren; nörgeln, meckern (*against, at, about* über); *s* (Fuß-)Tritt, Stoß; *(Fußball)* Schuß; *(Feuerwaffe)* Rückstoß *m*; *fam* Widerrede, Meckerei *f*; *fam (bes. alkohol. Getränk)* Feuer, Spritzige(s) *n*; *fam* Mumm, Schwung, Spaß *m*, Laune *f*, Fez, Übermut *m*, Begeisterung; *fam* Widerstandskraft *f*; *sl* Sixpence(stück *n*) *pl*; *the ~ (sl)* der letzte Schrei *(der Mode)*; *to get the ~ (sl)* 'rausfliegen, -geschmissen werden; *to get a big ~ out of s.th.* viel Spaß an etw haben; *to have no ~ left (fam)* keinen Mumm mehr haben, nicht mehr können; *to ~ the bucket (sl)* ins Gras beißen, abkratzen; *to ~ o.'s heels* sich die Beine in den Bauch stehen, lange warten (müssen); *to ~ against the pricks* wider den Stachel löcken; *I could ~ myself* ich könnte mich ohrfeigen; *to ~* **about,** *to ~* **around** *tr fam* herumstoßen, schlecht behandeln; denken an, reden über; beschwatzen; herumbummeln, sich herumdrücken; *to ~* **back** *itr fam* zurückschlagen; zurückprallen; *tr sl (Gestohlenes)* 'rausrücken; *(Geld)* wieder 'rausrücken, 'rausrücken mit; bestechen; *to ~* **downstairs** die Treppe hinunterwerfen; *to ~* **in** *tr* einstoßen, -treten; *itr Am sl* sein Teil, s-n Anteil beitragen, -steuern; *Am sl* abkratzen, sterben; *to ~* **off** *tr* wegschleudern, -stoßen; *(Fußball)* anspielen; *itr Am sl* abkratzen, ins Gras beißen; *Am fam* beginnen; *to ~* **out** *tr fam* 'rauswerfen, -schmeißen; *(Fußball)* ins Aus schießen; *itr* sich wehren; *to ~* **over** umwerfen; *to ~~ the traces* über die Stränge schlagen; *to ~* **up** *tr* hochstoßen, -schleudern; *sl (Verwirrung)* stiften; *to ~~ a dust, a fuss, a row (fig)* Staub aufwirbeln, auf die Pauke hauen, Krach schlagen; *to ~~ o.'s heels* über die Stränge schlagen; *to ~* **upstairs** *tr* (durch Beförderung) kaltstellen; **~back** *fam* Ausschlagen *n*; *fig* scharfe Antwort *f*; *sl* Wiederherausrücken *n (von Gestohlenem)*; Schmiergelder *n pl*; **~er** ['-ə] Fußballspieler, Kicker; Schläger *(Pferd)*; *tech* Stößel; *Am fam* Meckerer; Unruhestifter *m*; *Am sl* Quelle *f* des Vergnügens; **~-off** ['-'ɔ:f] *(Fußball)* Anstoß *m a. fig*, Anspiel *n*; *fig* Anlaß; *Am fam* Anfang *m*; **~shaw** ['-ʃɔ:] Leckerei *f*, Leckerbissen *m*, Schlekkerei, Delikatesse; Spielerei *f*, Flitter (-kram), Tand *m*, Nippsache *f*; **~-starter** *mot* Tretanlasser; Anlaßhebel *m*; **~up** ['-'ʌp] *fam* Wirbel, Wirrwarr *m*, Theater *n*, Spektakel, Krach *m*.

kid [kid] *s* Zicklein, (Ziegen-)Lamm, Lammfleisch; *(~skin)* Ziegenleder *n*; *(~glove)* Glacéhandschuh *m*; *fam* Kind, Küken *n*; *sl* Schwindel, Bluff *m*; *itr (Ziege)* Junge werfen; albern, schwindeln; *tr sl* 'reinlegen, anführen, bluffen, beschwindeln, foppen, an der Nase herumführen; zum besten haben, verulken, aufziehen; **~der** ['-ə] Schwindler *m*; **~dy** ['-i] *fam* Kind *n*, Kleine(r *m*) *f*; **~ glove** Glacéhandschuh *m*; *to handle with ~~s (fig)* mit Glacéhandschuhen anfassen; **~-glove** *a* sanft; wählerisch; **~nap** *tr (Kind)* entführen; **~nap(p)er** Kidnapper, Kindes-, Menschenräuber *m*.

kidney ['kidni] *anat* Niere; *fig* Veranlagung, Natur, Art *f*; *of the right ~* vom rechten Schlag; **~-bean** (Vits-, Schmink-)Bohne *f*; **~-shaped** *a* nierenförmig; **~-stone** *med* Nierenstein; *min* Nephrit *m*.

kike [kaik] *Am sl pej* Jude *m*.

kill [kil] **1.** *tr* töten, totschlagen, umbringen, erschlagen; schlachten; erlegen; vernichten, zerstören, ruinieren; *mil* versenken; abschießen; vereiteln; widerrufen, für ungültig erklären; unterdrücken, *fam* unter den Tisch fallen lassen; *(Gesetzesvorlage)* zu Fall bringen; *(Motor)* abwürgen; *(Maschine)* anhalten, zum Stehen bringen; *el* ausschalten; *(Fußball)* stoppen; überwältigen, erdrücken; wirkungslos machen, um s-e Wirkung bringen; *(Tennisball)* (ab)töten; *(Farben)* unwirksam machen; *Am typ* streichen; *fam* auslachen, in Verlegenheit bringen; *Am sl* austrinken, *(Zigarette)* ausdrücken; *itr* den Tod herbeiführen; *fam* e-n tollen Eindruck machen; *s* Tötung *f*, Totschlag *m*; Todesursache; (Jagd-)Beute; *mil* Versenkung *f*; Abschuß; *Am sl* Mord *m*; *sport* Abstoppen *n*; *to ~ off* beseitigen, vernichten; *to be in at the ~ (fig)* am Schluß dabeisein; *to be ~ed in action (mil)* fallen; *to ~ two birds with one stone* zwei Fliegen mit einer Klappe schlagen; *to ~ with kindness* vor Liebe umbringen (wollen); *to ~ time* die Zeit totschlagen *od* vertreiben; *thou shalt not ~* du sollst nicht töten; **~er** ['-ə] Totschläger; *(~~-whale) zoo* Schwertwal, Butzkopf; *Am sl* Frauenheld, gutaussehende(r) Mann *m*, tolle Frau *f*; **~ing** ['-iŋ] *a* tödlich, mörderisch, zerstörerisch; ermüdend; *fam* ulkig, zum Totlachen; *fam* ganz reizend, unwiderstehlich; *s* Tötung *f*, Totschlag; *Am fam* unverhoffte(r) Gewinn *od* Erfolg *m*; **~-joy** Spaß-, Spielverderber, Störenfried *m*; **~-time** Zeitvertreib *m*; **2.** *Am* Bach *m*.

kiln [kil(n)] *s tech* (Brenn-, Röst-, Darr-)Ofen *m*, Darre *f*; *tr* brennen, rösten, darren; **~-dry** *tr* darren.

kilo ['ki(:)lou] Kilo(gramm); Kilometer *n* u. *m*; **~calorie** ['kiləkæləri] *phys* große Kalorie *f*; **~cycle** ['kilo(u)saikl] Kilohertz *n*; **~gram(me)** ['kiləgræm] Kilogramm *n*; **~litre, ~liter** ['kilo(u)li:tə] Kiloliter *n* u. *m*; **~metre, ~meter** ['kiləmi:tə] Kilometer *n*; **~watt** ['kiləwɔt] Kilowatt *n*; *~~-hour* Kilowattstunde *f*.

kilt [kilt] *tr* (auf)schürzen; fälteln; *s* Schottenröckchen *n*.

kilter ['kiltə] *s Am fam*: *in ~* heil, in Ordnung; *out of ~* kaputt, nicht in Ordnung; *to be in (out of) ~* (nicht) gehen, funktionieren.

kimono [ki'mounou] *pl -os* Kimono *m*.

kin [kin] *s die* Verwandten *pl*, Verwandtschaft, Sippe, Familie; (Bluts-) Verwandtschaft; *fig* Art, Natur *f*; *a* verwandt (*to* mit); *of ~* (bluts)verwandt; *near of ~* nahe, eng verwandt; *the next of ~* die nächsten Angehörigen *pl*; **~sfolk** ['-zfouk] *die* Verwandtschaft *f*, *die* (Bluts-)Verwandten *pl*; **~ship** ['-ʃip] Verwandtschaft *f a. fig*; **~sman** ['-zmən] Verwandte(r) *m*; **~swoman** ['-zwumən] Verwandte *f*.

kin|(a)esthesia [k(a)ini(:)s'θi:ziə] **~(a)esthesis** [-'θi:sis] *physiol* Bewegungswahrnehmung, Kinästhesie *f*; **~(a)esthetic** [-i(:)s'θetik] kinästhetisch; **~ematic(al)** [k(a)ini'mætik(əl)] kinematisch; **~ematics** [-i(:)'mætiks] *pl mit sing* Getriebelehre, Kinematik *f*; **~ematograph** [-i(:)'mætəgrɑ:f] *s. cin* ...; **~escope** ['k(a)iniskoup] Fernsehempfangsröhre *f*; *med* Kineskop *n*; **~etic** [k(a)i'netik] *a phys* kinetisch; *s pl mit sing* Kinetik *f*; *~~ energy* kinetische, Bewegungsenergie *f*.

kind [kaind] *s* Geschlecht *n*, Rasse, Art, Gattung *f*; Wesen *n*, Natur; (Spiel-)Art, Sorte, Klasse; Art (und Weise) *f*; *a* gütig, gutmütig, freundlich, herzlich, liebenswürdig, nett, entgegenkommend, großzügig (*to s.o.* gegenüber jdm); *a ~ of* e-e Art (von); *all ~s of* allerlei, alle möglichen; *~ of (fam)* irgendwie, ziemlich, schon, fast, beinahe, ungefähr; gewissermaßen, sozusagen; *of a ~* gleich(artig, -wertig); *of the ~* dergleichen; *in ~* in gleicher, auf gleiche Weise; *com* in Waren, in Naturalien, in natura;

payment in ~ Natural-, Sachleistung *f*; *what* ~ *of?* was für ein? *something, nothing of the* ~ etwas, nichts Derartiges; *with* ~ *regards* mit freundlichen Grüßen; **~a** ['-ə] *Am fam* = ~ *of*; **~-hearted** *a* gutmütig, gütig; **~liness** ['-linis] Güte, Freundlichkeit, Liebenswürdigkeit *f*; **~ly** ['-li] *a* gütig, freundlich, gefällig, entgegenkommend, nett, liebenswürdig; angenehm; *adv* freundlicher-, liebenswürdigerweise, in entgegenkommender Weise; gefälligst; bitte, seien Sie so freundlich und; *to take* ~~ *to s.o.* jdn ins Herz schließen, liebgewinnen; **~ness** ['-nis] Güte, Gutmütigkeit, Freundlichkeit, Herzlichkeit, Liebenswürdigkeit; Gefälligkeit *f*, Entgegenkommen *n*.

kindergart|en ['kindəgɑ:tn] Kindergarten *m*; **~(e)ner** ['-nə] Kindergärtnerin *f*; Kindergartenkind *n*.

kindl|e ['kindl] *tr* in Brand stecken; anstecken, anzünden; entfachen *a. fig*; *fig* erwecken, erregen; *itr* Feuer fangen, sich entzünden; erglühen, aufleuchten (*with* vor); *fig* wach werden, sich regen, sich begeistern (*at* an); erregt werden (*at* über); **~er** ['-ə] Brandstifter; *fig* Aufwiegler, Aufrührer; *tech* Feueranzünder *m*; **~ing** ['-iŋ] Anmach(e)holz; Anzünden *n*.

kindred ['kindrid] *s* (Bluts-)Verwandtschaft *f*; Verwandte *pl*, Familie, Sippe *f*, Stamm *m*; Ähnlichkeit *f*; *a* (bluts-)verwandt; *fig* verwandt, ähnlich.

king [kiŋ] *s* König *m (a. fig; Kartenspiel, Schach)*; *(Damespiel)* Dame *f*; *itr: to* ~ *it* als König auftreten; **~bird** Königsparadiesvogel, *Am* -würger, -tyrann *m*; **~bolt** *tech* Königs-, Drehzapfen; Achsschenkelbolzen *m*; **~-crab** *zoo* Molukkenkrebs *m*; Meerspinne *f*; **~craft** Kunst *f* des Herrschens; **~cup** *bot* Hahnenfuß *m*, Butterblume; (Sumpf-)Dotterblume *f*; **~dom** ['-dəm] (König-)Reich *n a. fig*; *gone to* ~~*-come (fam)* tot; *the animal, vegetable, mineral* ~~ das Tier-, das Pflanzen-, das Mineralreich *n*; *the United K*~~ das Vereinigte Königreich *(Großbritannien und Nordirland)*; *the* ~~ *of heaven* das Himmelreich; **~fish** Königsmakrele *f*, -dorsch; *Am fam* Oberbonze, Boß *m*; **~fisher** Eisvogel *m*; **~let** ['-lit] kleine(r) König, Schattenkönig *m*; *orn* Goldhähnchen *n*; **~like** ['-laik] königlich; **~liness** ['-linis] königliche Haltung *od* Art *f*; **~ly** ['-li] *a adv* königlich; edel, vornehm, stattlich; **~pin** *tech* = ~*bolt*; *(Kegeln)* König *m*; *fam* Hauptperson, -sache *f*; **~post** *(Dachstuhl)* Stuhl(säule *f*) *m*; **K~'s Bench** *Br jur* Erste Kammer *f* des High Court; **~'s evil** *med* Skrofulose *f*; **~ship** Königtum *n*; **~ size** *a Am fam* besonders groß *od* lang.

kink [kiŋk] *s* Knoten *m*, Schleife *f*; (Muskel-)Krampf *m*; Kräuselung; *fig* Schrulle, Verrücktheit *f*, Spleen; Kniff *m*; *tr itr* verknoten; *to have a* ~ e-n Sparren zuviel, e-n Vogel, e-n Klaps haben; **~y** ['-i] *(Haar)* filzig; *(Tau)* verdreht; *fam* überspannt; *Am sl* unredlich.

kiosk [ki'ɔsk, 'ki:-] Pavillon; Kiosk *m*; *(telephone* ~*)* Telefonzelle *f*.

kip [kip] **1.** noch ungegerbte Haut *f* e-s jungen *od* kleinen Tieres; **2.** *s fam* Loch *n*, Gasthof *m*; Übernachtung; Falle *f*, Bett *n*; *itr* pennen, schlafen; **3.** *Am sport* Kippe *f*.

kipper ['kipə] Räucherlachs, -hering; männliche(r) Lachs *(in u. kurz nach der Laichzeit)*; *sl* Kerl *m*; *tr (Hering, Lachs)* einsalzen u. räuchern.

kirk [kə:k] *Scot* Kirche *f*.

kiss [kis] *tr itr* (sich) küssen; (sich) leicht berühren; *s* Kuß *m*; leichte Berührung *f*; Bonbon *m* od *n*; Baiser *n*, Meringe *f*; *to* ~ *the dust, the ground* den Staub küssen, sich demütigen; umkommen; *to* ~ *and be friends, to* ~ *and make up* sich den Versöhnungskuß geben; *to* ~ *s.o.'s hand* jdm die Hand küssen; *to* ~ *the rod* alles über sich ergehen lassen; **~aroo** [kisə'ru:] *Am sl* Kuß *m*; **~er** ['-ə] *sl* Mund *m*, Gesicht *n*, Fresse *f*; **~ing-crust** weiche Stelle *f* in der Brotkruste, an der das Brot beim Backen ein anderes berührt hat; **~-me-quick, ~-curl** Schmachtlocke *f*; **~-off** *Am sl* Herauswurf *m*, Entlassung *f*; **~-proof** kußecht, -fest.

kit [kit] **1.** *s* Eimer, Kübel *m*, Bütte *f*, Fäßchen; Gepäck *n*; Ausrüstung, Werkzeugtasche *f*, -kasten, -schrank *m*; Handwerkszeug *n*; *fam* Satz *m*, Kollektion; *fam* Blase, Sippschaft *f*; *tr (to* ~ *up)* ausrüsten, ausstaffieren; *itr* ausgerüstet werden; *the whole* ~ *and caboodle (fam)* der ganze Kram, *m*; **~-bag** *mil mar* (Kleider-)Sack, Tornister *m*; Reisetasche *f*; **~ inspection** *mil* Sachenappell *m*; **2.** Kätzchen *n*, Miez(e) *f*.

kitchen ['kitʃin] Küche *f*; *field* ~ *(mil)* Feldküche *f*; *unit* ~ Einbauküche *f*; **~-chair** Küchenstuhl *m*; **~-clock** Küchenuhr *f*; **~-cupboard** Küchenschrank *m*; **~-dresser** (Küchen-)Anrichte *f*; **~er** ['-ə] Küchenmeister *(im Kloster)*; (Küchen-)Herd *m*; **~et(te)** [-'net] kleine Küche; Kochnische *f*; **~-garden** Küchen-, Gemüsegarten *m*; **~-implements** *pl*, **-ware** Küchengeräte *n pl*; **~-maid** Küchenmädchen *n*; **~ midden** *hist* Kökkenmöddinger *pl*; **~ police** *mil Am* Küchendienst *m*; **~-range** Küchen-, Kochherd *m*; **~-sink** *s* Schüttstein, Ausguß *m*; *a* Schmutz-; *everything but the* ~~ *(hum)* alles und noch mehr, die unmöglichsten Dinge; **~-stuff** Eßwaren *f pl*, Lebensmittel *n pl*; Küchenabfälle *m pl*; **~-table** Küchentisch *m*; **~-unit** Universalküchenschrank *m*.

kite [kait] *s orn* Gabelweih, Rote(r) Milan; *fig* Geizhals, Knicker, Gauner; (Papier-)Drachen *m*; *aero sl* (alte) Kiste, Mühle *f*; *fin* Kellerwechsel *m*; *pl* Toppsegel *n pl*; *itr* durch die Luft, dahingleiten; *fin (to fly a* ~*)* Wechselreiterei treiben; *tr* aufsteigen lassen; *(ungedeckten Wechsel)* ausstellen; *to fly a* ~ e-n Drachen, *fig* e-n Versuchsballon steigen lassen; *com* e-n Gefälligkeitswechsel ziehen; **~-balloon** Drachen-, Sperrballon *m*; **~-flying** Steigenlassen e-s Drachens; *fig* Sondieren *n*; *fin* Wechselreiterei *f*.

kith [kiθ] *s*: ~ *and kin* Freunde und Verwandte *pl*; die ganze Familie.

kitten ['kitn] *s* Kätzchen *n a. fig*; *tr itr (Katze)* (Junge) werfen; *to have* ~*s* aufgeregt *od* erschrocken sein; **~ish** ['-iʃ] *a* verspielt, spielerisch; kokett.

kittiwake ['kitiweik] Stummel-, *bes.* Dreizehenmöwe *f*.

Kitty ['kiti] Käthchen *n*, Käthe *f*.

kitty ['kiti] **1.** Kätzchen *n*; **2.** *(Kartenspiel)* gemeinsame Kasse *f*.

kiwi ['ki:wi(:)] *orn* Kiwi; *fam* Neuseeländer *m*; *sl aero* Angehörige(r) *m* des Bodenpersonals.

klaxon ['klæksn] *mot* Hupe *f*; Signalhorn *n*.

kleptomania [klepto(u)'meinjə] Kleptomanie *f*; **~c** [-niæk] Kleptomane *m*.

klieg(light) ['kli:g(lait)] *s Am film* (starker) Scheinwerfer, Aufheller *m*; *tr film* anstrahlen.

knack [næk] Kniff, Trick, Kunstgriff *m*; Geschicklichkeit, Fertigkeit (*at, of* in); Gewohnheit *f*; *to have the* ~ *of it* den Bogen 'raushaben; *there's a* ~ *in it* man muß den Dreh kennen.

knacker ['nækə] Abdecker; Abbruchunternehmer *m*.

knag [næg] Knorren, Ast *m (im Holz)*.

knap [næp] *tr (Steine)* klopfen; *sl* klauen.

knapsack ['næpsæk] Tornister, Rucksack, Ranzen *m*.

knar [nɑ:] Knorren *m*.

knav|e [neiv] Kerl, Bursche; Schuft, Lump, Schelm, Bube *m (a. Kartenspiel)*; **~ery** ['-əri] Lumperei, Schuftigkeit *f*; Schurken-, Buben-, Schelmenstreich *m*; **~ish** ['-iʃ] schurkenhaft, schuftig; **~ishness** ['-iʃnis] Schurkenhaftigkeit, Schuftigkeit *f*.

knead [ni:d] *tr* kneten; massieren; *(durch Kneten)* formen, bilden *a. fig*; **~er** ['-ə] Knetmaschine *f*; **~ing-trough** Backmulde *f*.

knee [ni:] Knie; Kniestück, -rohr *n*; *bot* Knoten *m*; *zoo* (Vorder-)Fußwurzelgelenk *n*; *tr* mit dem Knie berühren; *itr (Hose)* ausgebeult sein; *to bring s.o. on his* ~*s* jdn auf die Knie zwingen; *to go on o.'s* ~*s* niederknien; kniefällig bitten; **~ bending** Kniebeuge *f*; **~-breeches** *pl* Kniehose *f*; **~-cap** *anat* Kniescheibe *f*; Knieschützer *m*, -leder *n*; **~-deep, -high** knietief; **~-joint** Kniegelenk *n*; **~-pad** Knieschützer *m*; **~-pan** *anat* Kniescheibe *f*; **~ pine** *bot* Legföhre *f*; **~-timber** Knieholz *n*.

kneel [ni:l] *irr knelt, knelt itr (to* ~ *down)* (nieder)knien (*to* vor).

knell [nel] Totenglocke *f*; *fig* böse(s) Vorzeichen *n*, Vorbote *m*.

knicker|(bocker)s ['nikə(bɔkə)z] *pl* Knickerbocker *pl*; **~s** *pl* (Damen-)Schlüpfer *m*.

(k)nick-(k)nack ['niknæk] Kleinigkeit *f*; Tand *m*, Zierstück *n*, Nippsache *f*; Geschenkartikel *m*.

knife [naif] *pl knives s* Messer *n a. tech*; *tr* (mit e-m Messer) schneiden, stechen; erstechen, erdolchen; *(Pflanzen)* ausputzen; *Am fam* hinterrücks überfallen, hintergehen, abschießen; *under the* ~ *(med fam)* unter dem Messer; *to get o.'s* ~ *into s.o. (fig)* jdn nicht ausstehen können; *to play a good* ~ *and fork (beim Essen)* tüchtig zulangen, *fam* 'reinhauen; *before you can say* ~ im Nu, im Handumdrehen; *carving-*~ Schnitzmesser *n*; *kitchen-*~ Küchenmesser *n*; *pocket-*~ Taschenmesser *n*; *table-*~ Tischmesser *n*; *war to the* ~ Krieg *m* bis aufs Messer; **~-battle** Messerstecherei *f*; **~-edge** (Messer-)Schneide *f a. tech*; **~-grinder** Scherenschleifer *m*; **~-handle** Messergriff *m*; **~-rest** Messerbänkchen *n*; **~-switch** Hebelschalter *m*; **~-tray** Messerkorb *m*.

knight [nait] *s* Ritter *a. fig*; *(Schach)* Springer *m*; *tr* zum Ritter schlagen; in den Ritterstand erheben; **~age** ['-idʒ] Ritterschaft *f*; **~-errant** fahrende(r) Ritter *m*; **~hood** ['-hud] Ritterwürde *f*, -stand *m*; Rittertum *n*; Ritterschaft *f*; **~liness** ['-linis] Ritterlichkeit *f*; **~ly** ['-li] ritterlich.

knit [nit] *irr knit, knit* od **~ted, ~ted** *tr* stricken; *fig* (mitea.) verknüpfen, verbinden, zs.fügen; *(Brauen)* zs.-ziehen; *itr* stricken; zs.wachsen; *(Stirn)* sich in Falten legen; *to* ~ *together* (mitea.) verbinden; *to* ~ *up* anstricken; *fig* eng verbinden; *to* ~ *the brows* die Stirn runzeln *od* in Falten legen; **~goods** *pl*, **~wear** Wirk-,

Strickwaren *f pl*; Strickkleidung *f*; **~ter** ['-ə] Stricker(in *f*) *m*; Wirk-, Strickmaschine *f*; **~ing** ['-iŋ] Stricken *n*; Strickarbeit, -ware *f*, -zeug *n*; *~~-machine* Strickmaschine *f*; *~~-needle* Stricknadel *f*; *~~-yarn* Strickgarn *n*.

knob [nɔb] runde(r) Vorsprung, Auswuchs, Knorren *m*; Schwellung, Beule *f*; (Griff-)Knopf *m*; Bergkuppe *f*; runde(s) Stück *n*; *sl* Kopf *m*, Birne *f*; *with ~s on (sl)* allerdings! **~by, ~ly** ['-(l)i] knorrig; knopfartig, rund.

knock [nɔk] *itr* schlagen, stoßen, prallen (*on, against* gegen); klopfen, pochen (*at* an); krachen, knallen; *tech mot* klopfen, flattern; *fig* sich unterwerfen (*under s.o.* jdm); *Am fam* meckern, nörgeln, etw auszusetzen haben; diskutieren; *tr* schlagen, stoßen, treffen; umstoßen, nieder-, zu Boden werfen; *fam* umhauen, überraschen, stark beeindrucken; *Am fam* meckern über, heruntermachen; *s* Schlag, Stoß *m*; (An-)Klopfen, Pochen; *tech mot* Klopfen *n*; *Am fam* Meckerei; Unannehmlichkeit *f*; *to take a ~ (sl)* e-n schweren finanziellen Verlust erleiden; *that ~s you sideways (fam)* das haut dich um; *to ~* **about,** *to ~* **around** *itr* sich herumtreiben; *tr* herumstoßen, böse mitnehmen; *to ~* **against** stoßen auf; kollidieren mit; *to ~* **back** *Am sl (Glasvoll)* hinunterstürzen; *to ~* **down** niederschlagen; umstoßen, -werfen, zu Boden werfen *od* schleudern; umfahren; einschlagen; *(Gebäude)* abbrechen; *(für den Transport)* ausea.-nehmen, zerlegen; *(Auktion)* zuschlagen (*to s.o.* jdm); *(im Preis)* herabsetzen; *Br fam* auffordern; *to ~* **in** *(bes. Nagel)* einschlagen; *to ~* **off** *itr fam* abhauen; Schluß, Feierabend machen (*with o.'s work* mit der Arbeit); *tr* weg-, abschlagen; *(Staub)* herunterklopfen; *(Arbeit)* einstellen, *fam* hinhauen, rasch erledigen; *(von e-m Preis)* ab-, herunterlassen; abziehen; *sl* stehlen, organisieren; *sl Am (Menschen)* erledigen; *to ~ s.o.'s head off (fig)* jdn mühelos übertreffen; *to ~* **out** *(Pfeife)* ausklopfen; *(Boxen)* k.o. schlagen, kampfunfähig machen; das Bewußtsein nehmen (*s.o.* jdm), *fam* fertigmachen, mitnehmen; auf-, erregen; besiegen; *Am fam* schnell machen; *to ~* **over** umwerfen; *Am sl* berauben; *to ~* **together** *itr* anea.-stoßen; *tr* zu-, anea.schlagen; *Am fam* zubereiten; *(Arbeit)* schnell zs.hauen; *to ~* **under** nachgeben, klein beigeben; *to ~* **up** *itr* hochgestoßen, hochgeschlagen werden; zs.stoßen (*against* mit); *tr* hochstoßen, -schlagen; *(durch Klopfen an die Tür)* wecken; improvisieren; *fam* fertigmachen, ermüden, erschöpfen; *Am sl* ein Kind anhängen (*a woman* e-r Frau); **~about** *a (Kleidung)* strapazierfähig; umherschweifend, -streifend, unstet; laut, lärmend; derb, rauh; *s (~~ performance)* Radaustück *n*; *Am* kleine einmastige Jacht *f*; **~-down** *a (Schlag)* niederstreckend; *fig* niederschmetternd, überwältigend; *(Möbelstück)* ausea.nehmbar; *(Preis)* äußerst (niedrig); *tech* zerlegbar; *s* Niederstrecken *n*, gewaltige(r) Schlag *m*; Rauferei *f*; **~er** ['-ə] Schläger, Türklopfer; *Am fam* Meckerer, Nörgler, Miesmacher *m*; **~-kneed** *a* X-beinig; *fig* feige; **~-knees** *pl* X-Beine *n pl*; **~-out** *a (Schlag)* niederstreckend; *s (Boxen)* K.o.-Schlag *m*; *fig* vernichtende Niederlage *f*; *sl* Pfundskerl *m*, -weib *n*; Ausscheidung(srunde) *f*; *up to the ~~* einwandfrei, tadellos; *~~ blow* Vernichtungsschlag *m*; *~~ price* Schleuderpreis *m*; **~proof** ['-pru:f] *mot* klopffest; **~up** ['-ʌp] *sport* Trainingsspiel *n*.

knoll [noul] (Erd-)Hügel *m*.

knot [nɔt] *s* Knoten *m*; Schleife; Kokarde *f*, Schulterstück *n*; Gruppe *f*, Grüppchen; einigende(s) Band *n*; *fig* Verwirrung, Schwierigkeit *f*; Klumpen, Knorren, Ast *(im Holz)*; *bot* Knoten *(im Pflanzenstengel)*; *mar* Knoten *m (1,853 km/h)*; *tr* (e-n) Knoten machen in; verknoten, verschnüren; *(Franse)* machen; *fig* mitea. verknüpfen, eng mitea. verbinden; *itr* e-n Knoten bilden, sich verknoten; sich verwirren; Fransen machen; *to cut the ~ (fig)* den Knoten durchhauen; *to stand about in ~s* in Gruppen herumstehen; *to tie o.s. (up) in(to) ~s, to get into ~s* in Schwierigkeiten geraten; **~-grass** *bot* Knöterich *m*; **~-hole** Astloch *n (im Brett)*; **~ted** ['-id] *a* verknotet, verschnürt; *fig* verwirrt, kompliziert; knotig; *(Holz)* voller Äste; **~ty** ['-i] knotig, knorrig, voller Äste; *fig* verwickelt, schwierig.

know [nou] *irr knew* [nju:], *known* [noun] *tr* wissen, kennen; wissen von; sich auskennen in, vertraut sein mit; verstehen (*how to do* zu tun); können; erkennen; erfahren; kennenlernen; unterscheiden (*from* von); *(biblisch u. jur)* erkennen, beiwohnen *dat*; *itr* wissen (*about, of s.th.* über, von etw); verstehen (*about* von); *s*: *to be in the ~ (fam)* im Bilde sein; *to ~ again* wieder(er)kennen; *to be ~n* bekannt sein (*to s.o.* jdm; *as* als); *to come to ~* in Erfahrung bringen, erfahren; *to come to be ~n* bekannt werden; *to let s.o. ~* jdn wissen lassen, jdm mitteilen, jdm Bescheid geben; *to make o.s. ~n* sich bekannt machen, sich vorstellen; *to ~ better* (sehr) wohl wissen, *than* klug genug sein, nicht zu ...; *to ~ o.'s own business, (sl) to ~ o.'s onions, (fam) to ~ the ropes, to ~ a thing or two, to ~ what's what* Bescheid wissen, sich auskennen, auf der Höhe sein; *to ~ how to* können; *to ~ o.'s way around (Am)* sich auskennen; *not that I ~ of* nicht, daß ich wüßte; *he wouldn't ~* er ist dafür nicht zuständig; **~ability** [nouə'biliti], **~ableness** ['-əblnis] Erkennbarkeit *f*; **~able** ['-əbl] erkennbar, erfahrbar; **~-all** *s* Besserwisser *m*; **~-how** *s fam* Erfahrung *f*, (Fach-)Wissen, Können *n*; **~ing** ['-iŋ] informiert, unterrichtet; wissend, (welt-)weise, klug, einsichtig; schlau; *(a. Blick)* verständnisvoll; absichtlich; *there's no ~~* man kann nie wissen; **~ingly** ['-iŋli] *adv* mit Bewußtsein, bewußt; absichtlich; wissentlich; **~-it-all** *a fam* allwissend; *s fam* Vielwisser *m*; **~ledge** ['nɔlidʒ] Kenntnis, Kunde (*of* von), Bekanntschaft, Vertrautheit (*of* mit); Verständnis; Wissen *n* (*of* von), Kenntnisse *f pl*; Bildung *f*, Wissensschatz *m*; *to (the best of) my ~~* soviel ich weiß, soweit ich orientiert bin; *to the best of my ~~ and belief* nach bestem Wissen und Gewissen; *to my certain ~~* wie ich mit Sicherheit weiß; *without my ~~* ohne mein Wissen; *working ~~* praktisch verwertbare Grundkenntnisse *f pl*; **~ledgeable** ['nɔlidʒəbl] *fam* gebildet, intelligent; **~-nothing** Nichtswisser, Dummkopf; Agnostiker *m*.

knout [naut] *s* Knute *f*; *tr* auspeitschen.

knuckle ['nʌkl] *s* Knöchel *m*; *(Schlachtvieh)* Kniestück *n*, Haxe *f*; *(~ of ham)* Eisbein; *allg* Gelenk *n a. tech*; *pl* Schlagring *m*; *itr*: *to ~ down, to ~ under* nachgeben, sich fügen (*to s.o.* jdm); *to ~ down (to work)* sich eifrig an die Arbeit machen; *to rap s.o.'s ~s, to give s.o. a rap on, over the ~s* jdm auf die Finger klopfen; *near the ~* an der Grenze des Anständigen; **~-deep** knöcheltief; *fig* eindringlich; **~-duster** Schlagring *m*; **~-joint** *anat tech* (Finger-)Gelenk; Kardangelenk *n*.

knurl [nə:l] *s* Knoten, Knopf, Knorren *m*; *(Münze)* Riefelung *f*; *tr tech* kordieren, rändeln; *(Münze)* riefeln.

knur(r) [nə:] *bot* Knorren *m*.

koala [kou'a:lə] *zoo* Koala *m*.

*

kodak, Kodak ['koudæk] *s Am* Kodak *f od m (Warenzeichen)*; *allg* Kleinbildkamera.

kohlrabi ['koul'ra:bi] Kohlrabi *m*.

Koran [kɔ'ra:n] *rel* Koran *m*.

Korea [kə'riə] Korea *n*; **~n** [-n] *a* koreanisch; *s* (das) Koreanisch(e); Koreaner(in *f*) *m*.

kosher ['kouʃə] *a rel* koscher, rein; *Am sl* in Ordnung, klar; *s* koschere(s, r) Essen *n od* Laden *m*.

ko(w)tow ['kau'tau, 'kou-] Kotau *m*; *itr* e-n Kotau machen; *fig* kriechen (*to s.o.* vor jdm).

*

kraal [kra:l, *(Südafrika)* krɔ:l] Kral *m*.

kraft [kra:ft, kræft] *(~ paper) Am* (starkes, braunes) Packpapier *n*.

Kremlin ['kremlin] Kreml *m*.

kris [kri:s] *s. creese*.

Kriss Kringle ['kris 'kriŋl] *Am* Nikolaus *m*, „Christkind" *n*.

kudos ['kju:dɔs] *fam* Renommee *n*, gute(r) Ruf *m*, Ansehen *n*.

Ku-Klux(-Klan) ['kju:klʌks(klæn)] *Am* Ku-Klux-Klan *m*.

kumquat ['kʌmkwɔt] Japanische Orange *f*.

L

L, l [el] *pl* ~'s L, *n.*

la [lɑ:] *mus* la *n.*

lab [læb] *fam* Labor(atorium) *n.*

label ['leibl] *s* Etikett(e *f*), Schildchen *n (mit Aufschrift)*; (Paket-)Zettel *m*; Beschriftung, Aufschrift; Kennzeichnung *f*; *jur* Kodizill *n*; *(Buch)* Signatur; *fig* Bezeichnung, Benennung, Klassifikation, Klassifizierung *f*; *arch* Sims *m* od *n*, Rand-, Zierleiste *f*; *tr* etikettieren, mit e-m Etikett, Schildchen, Zettel, e-r Aufschrift versehen; beschriften, kennzeichnen; *fig* bezeichnen, benennen, klassifizieren; (ab)stempeln (*as* als).

labi|al ['leibjəl] *a* Lippen-, labial; *s* Lippenlaut, Labial *m*; **~ate** ['-biit] *a* lippenförmig, -artig; *bot* lippenblütig; *s bot* Lippenblütler *m*; **~odental** ['-o(u)'dentl] labiodental.

labil|e ['leibil] *phys chem* labil, unbeständig.

laboratory [lə'bɔrətəri, 'læbərə-; *Am* 'læbrətɔ:ri] *s* Labor(atorium) *n*, Versuchsraum *m*; Untersuchungsanstalt, Forschungsstätte *f*; Filmlabor *n*; *(Töpferofen)* Brennraum *m*; *fig* Werkstätte *f*; *a* Laboratoriums-; **~ assistant, helper, technician** Laborant(in *f*) *m*; **~ stage** Versuchsstadium *n*; **~ test** Labor(atoriums)versuch *m.*

laborious [lə'bɔ:riəs] *(Arbeit)* schwer, schwierig, anstrengend, mühsam, mühselig; *(Mensch)* arbeitsam, fleißig; *(Stil)* schwerfällig, schleppend; **~ness** [-nis] Mühseligkeit; Arbeitsamkeit; Schwerfälligkeit *f.*

labo(u)r ['leibə] *s* Arbeit, Anstrengung, Mühe, Mühsal *f*, Beschwerden *f pl*; Stück Arbeit, Werk *n*, Aufgabe *f*; Arbeiter(schaft *f*), Lohnarbeiter *m pl*; Arbeitskraft *f*, -kräfte *f pl*; *(direct ~)* Fertigungslohn *m*; *med* Wehen *f pl*, Geburt *f*; *mar* Schlingern, Stampfen *n*; *attr* Arbeits-, Arbeiter-; *itr* arbeiten (*at* an); schaffen, sich anstrengen, sich (ab)mühen (*for* um); *fam* sich abrackern, schuften; *(to ~ along)* sich mühsam (vorwärts)bewegen, kriechen, schleichen, fahren; *(Schiff)* stampfen, schlingern; *med* in den Wehen liegen; leiden, kranken (*under* an); zu kämpfen haben (*under* mit); *tr* zuviel Arbeit verwenden auf; zu genau, zu sorgfältig ausarbeiten; genau ausführen, ausführlich eingehen auf; *to be in ~* in den Wehen liegen; *casual ~* Gelegenheitsarbeit *f*; *hard ~* Zuchthaus *n*, Zwangsarbeit *f*; *manual ~* Handarbeit *f*; *Ministry (Br), (Am) Department of L~* Arbeitsministerium *n*; *skilled ~* Facharbeit *f*; gelernte, Facharbeiter *m pl*; Facharbeiterschaft *f*; *unskilled ~* ungelernte Arbeiter *m pl*; *~ of love* gern *od* umsonst getane Arbeit *f*; **~ bureau** Arbeitsamt *n*; **~ camp** Arbeitslager *n*; **~ charter** Arbeitsordnung *f*; **~ colony** Arbeitersiedlung *f*; **~ contract** Tarif-, Arbeitsvertrag *m*; **~ convention** Arbeitsabkommen *n*; **~ council** Betriebsrat *m*; **~ court** *Am* Arbeitsgericht *n*; **~-creation (programme)** Arbeitsbeschaffung(sprogramm *n*) *f*; **L~ Day** *Am* Tag *m* der Arbeit *(in den meisten Staaten 1. Montag im September)*; **~ disputes** *pl* Arbeitskämpfe *m pl*; **~ed** ['-d] *a* mit großer Mühe, unter Mühen, mühsam; schwerfällig, schleppend; **~er** ['-rə] Arbeiter *m*; *casual ~~* Gelegenheitsarbeiter *m*; *day-~~* Tag(e)löhner *m*; *farm-, agricultural ~~* Landarbeiter *m*; *industrial ~~* Industriearbeiter *m*; *(un)skilled ~~* (un)gelernte(r) Arbeiter *m*; **~ exchange** Arbeitsamt *n*, -nachweis *m*; **~ing** ['-riŋ] *a* arbeitend; *fig* mühsam; *s* (körperliche, ungelernte) Arbeit *f*; *the ~~ class* die Arbeiterklasse *f*; **~ite** ['-rait] Anhänger *m*, Mitglied *n*, Abgeordnete(r *m*) *f* der (engl.) Arbeiterpartei; **~ law** Arbeitsrecht *n*; **~ leader** Arbeiter-, Gewerkschaftsführer *m*; **~ market** Arbeitsmarkt *m*; **~ movement** Arbeiterbewegung *f*; **~ office** Arbeitsamt *n*; **~ paper** Arbeiterzeitung *f*; **L~ Party** (engl.) Arbeiterpartei *f*; **~ permit** Arbeitserlaubnis, -bewilligung *f*; **~ question** Arbeiterfrage *f*; **~ rate** Lohnstundensatz *m*; **~-saving** arbeitssparend; **~ shortage** Mangel *m* an Arbeitskräften; **~ troubles** *pl* Arbeiterunruhen *f pl*; **~ turnover** Arbeitsplatzwechsel *m*; **~ union** *Am* Gewerkschaft *f.*

laburnum [lə'bə:nəm] *bot* Goldregen *m.*

labyrinth ['læbərinθ] Irrgarten *m*, Labyrinth *a. anat*; *anat* innere(s) Ohr; *fig* Gewirr, Durcheinander *n*, Wirrwarr *m*, verwickelte Verhältnisse *n pl*; **~ine** [læbə'rinθain] labyrinthisch, verwickelt, wirr, verworren.

lac [læk] **1.** *(gum-~)* Gummilack *m*; **2.** *s* 100000 (*bes.*: *of rupies* Rupien); sehr viele.

lace [leis] *s* Schnur *f*; (Schnür-, Schuh-)Senkel *m*; Tresse, Litze, Borte; *(Textil)* Spitze *f*; Schuß *m (Alkohol)*; *tr (to ~ up) (Schuhe, Kleidungsstück)* (zu-)schnüren; *(die Taille)* schnüren; (ver-)flechten; *(to ~ through)* durchflechten, -ziehen; mit Borten *od* Spitzen besetzen; mit Streifen versehen; e-n Schuß *(Alkohol)* zugeben in *(ein Getränk)*; verdreschen, verprügeln; *itr fam* herfallen (*into s.o.* über jdn); *fam* heruntermachen (*into s.o.* jdn), e-e Zigarre verpassen (*into s.o.* jdm); **~-bobbin** Spitzenklöppel *m*; **~d** [leist] *a* geschnürt; bunt gestreift; *~(~) boots (pl)* Schnürstiefel *m pl*; *~~ coffee* Kaffee *m* mit e-m Schuß Branntwein; **~-glass** Venezianische(s) (Faden-)Glas *n*; **~-pillow** Klöppelkissen *n*; **~-ups** *pl fam* Schnürschuhe, -stiefel *m pl*; **~-wings** *pl ent* Netzflügler *m pl*; **~-work** Spitze(narbeit), Petmetware *f*; *fig* Filigran *n.*

lacerat|e ['læsəreit] *tr* zerreißen; zerhacken, zerhauen, zerfleischen; *fig (Gefühle)* verletzen; quälen, foltern; *a* [*a.* '-rit] zerrissen, zerfetzt; *(Blatt)* gezackt, gefranst; **~ion** [læsə'reiʃən] Zerreißen; Zerfleischen *n*; Riß *m*; *med* Fleischwunde; *fig* Verletzung *f.*

laches ['leitʃiz, 'læt-] *jur* (schuldhafte) Unterlassung *f*, Verzug *m.*

lachrym|al ['lækriməl] *a* Tränen-; Wein-; *s pl* Tränendrüsen *f pl*; Weinkrampf *m*; *~~ bone, duct, gland, sac* Tränenbein *n*, -gang *m*, -drüse *f*, -sack *m*; **~ator** ['-eitə] Tränengas *n*; **~atory** ['-ətəri] zum Weinen reizend; *~~ gas* Tränengas *n*; **~ose** ['lækrimous] weinerlich; tränenreich; (tief)traurig.

lacing ['leisiŋ] (Zu-)Schnüren *n*; Schnur *f*, (Schnür-, Schuh-)Senkel *m*; (Gold-, Silber-)Tresse, Litze; *fam* Tracht *f* Prügel; *tech* Versteifung *f.*

lack [læk] *s* Mangel *m* (*of* an); Fehlen *n*; dringend benötigte Sache *f*; *itr* fehlen, nicht (in genügendem Maße) vorhanden sein; Mangel haben *od* leiden (*of, in* an); es fehlen lassen an; *tr* nicht *od* nicht genug haben; brauchen, benötigen; *for ~ of* aus Mangel an; in Ermangelung; **~ing** ['-iŋ] fehlend; *fam* dumm; *to be ~~* fehlen; **~-lustre** glanzlos, trübe.

lackadaisical [lækə'deizikəl] interesse-, lustlos, gelangweilt, langweilig; sentimental, schmachtend; geziert.

lackey ['læki] *s* Lakai *a. fig*; *fig* Speichellecker; Nassauer *m*; *itr* Lakaiendienste verrichten; *tr* herumscharwenzeln um.

laconic [lə'kɔnik] *adv ~ally (Worte)* lakonisch, kurz; *(Mensch)* wortkarg.

lacquer ['lækə] *s* (Farb-)Lack, Firnis *m*; (ostasiatische) Lackarbeit(en *pl*) *f*; *tr* lackieren.

lact|ate ['lækteit] *itr* Milch absondern *od* geben; Junge säugen; stillen; *s* Laktat, milchsaure(s) Salz *n*; **~ation** [læk'teiʃən] Milchabsonderung *f*; Säugen, Stillen *n*; Säuge-, Stillzeit *f*; **~eal** ['læktiəl] milchig; milchartig; *scient* Milch-; Lymph-; Milchsaft *m*, Chylus enthaltend; *s anat* Lymphgefäß *n*; *~~ gland* Milchdrüse *f*; **~ic** ['læktik] *a scient* Milch-; *~~ acid* Milchsäure *f*; **~oflavin** [lækto(u)'fleivin] Vitamin *n* B_2; **~ometer** [læk'tɔmitə] Milchwaage *f*, Laktometer *n*; **~ose** ['læktous] Milchzucker *m*, Laktose *f.*

lacun|a [lə'kju:nə] *pl a. -ae* [-i:] Lücke *f*, Zwischenraum; *biol* Hohlraum *m*; **~ar** [-ə] *arch* Kassettendecke *f.*

lad [læd] Junge; Bursche; *fam* Kerl *m.*

ladder ['lædə] Leiter; Laufmasche *(im Strumpf)*; *fig* Stufenleiter *f*, Weg *m*; *to kick down the ~ (fig)* undankbar sein; *rope ~* Strickleiter *f*; *the ~ of success* der Weg zum Erfolg; **~-proof** *(Strumpf)* maschenfest; **~-rope** *mar* Fallreep *n*; **~-rung** Leitersprosse *f*; **~ truck** *Am (Feuerwehr)* Drehleiterwagen *m*; **~-way** *min* Fahrschacht *m.*

lad|e [leid] *irr laded, laden* od *laded tr (Fahrzeug)* beladen; *(Last)* (auf-, ver)laden, verfrachten; *(Wasser)* ausschöpfen; **~en** ['leidn] *a* beladen (*with* mit); *fig* bedrückt; **~ing** ['-iŋ] Be-, Verladen *n*; Ladung *f*; *bill of ~~* Seefrachtbrief *m*, Konnossement *n.*

ladida ['lɑ:di'dɑ:] *a fam* affektiert, geziert; *s* Fatzke, Geck *m.*

ladle ['leidl] *s* Schöpflöffel *m*, Kelle; Gießkelle; Rad-, Baggerschaufel *f*; *tr (to ~ out)* (aus)schöpfen, auslöffeln; *fig* austeilen, großzügig verteilen.

lady ['leidi] *s allg* Dame; Frau; *obs* Gemahlin; Herrin; *fam* Liebste, Geliebte, Freundin *f*; *L~ (Adelsprädikat)*; *a* weiblich; *Ladies and Gentlemen* meine Damen und Herren! *ladies room* Damentoilette *f*; *Our L~ (rel)* Unsere Liebe Frau; *L~ of the Bedchamber* königliche Kammerfrau *f*; *the ~ of the house* die Dame, die Frau des Hauses; **L~-altar** Marienaltar *m*; **~-bird,** *Am* **~bug** Marienkäfer *m*; **~-chair** zu e-m Sitz verschränkte Hände *f pl*; **L~-chapel** Marienkapelle *f*; **L~ Day** Mariä Verkündigung *f (25. März)*; **~ doctor** Ärztin *f*; **~-finger** *Am* Löffelbiskuit *m*; **~ help** Stütze *f* (im Haushalt); **~-in-waiting** Hofdame *f*; **~-killer** *fam* Herzensbrecher, Schürzenjäger, Don Juan *m*; **~like** damenhaft; fein; fraulich; **~-love** Geliebte, Angebetete, Freundin *f*; **~'s man, ladies' man** Frauenliebhaber *m*; **~ship**: *your, her* ~~ Ihre Ladyschaft; **~-slipper, ~'s slipper** *bot* Frauenschuh *m*, Kalzeolarie *f*; **~-smock, ~'s smock** *bot* Wiesenschaumkraut *n*.

lag [læg] **1.** *itr* sich (nur) langsam vorwärtsbewegen, bummeln, zögern, zaudern; *(to ~ behind)* zurückbleiben; *s (time ~)* Verzögerung *f*, Aufschub *m*; *el* Nacheilung *f*; **~an** ['lægən], **~-end** *mar* (versenktes) Wrackgut *n*, Seewurf *m*; **~gard** ['-əd] *s* Nachzügler, Bummler, *fam* Bummelant *m*; *a u.* **~ging** ['-iŋ] langsam, *lit* saumselig, *fam* bumm(e)lig, zögernd, zaudernd, zurückbleibend; **2.** *s* (Faß-)Daube *f*; *tr tech* verschalen; **~ging** Verschalung, Verkleidung *f*; **3.** *tr sl* einbuchten, -lochen, -sperren; *s sl* schwere(r) Junge; Knast *m*, Kittchen *n*.

lager (beer) ['lɑːgə(biə)] Lagerbier *n*.

lagoon [lə'guːn] Lagune *f*.

laic ['leiik] *a* weltlich; Laien-; *s* Laie *m*; **~ize** ['leiisaiz] *tr* verweltlichen, säkularisieren.

laid [leid] *pp von lay*: **~ off** vorübergehend arbeitslos, ohne Arbeit; **~ out** geschmackvoll, mit Geschmack ein-, hergerichtet *od* angelegt; *(Geld)* gut angelegt; **~ paper** gerippte(s) Papier *n*; **~-up** weg-, zurückgelegt; abgelegt, ausrangiert; *fam* bettlägerig (*with* an, mit).

lair [lɛə] *s* Lager *n (bes. e-s wilden Tieres)*; Lagerstatt *f*; *fig* Zufluchtsort *m*.

laird [lɛəd] *Scot* Gutsbesitzer *m*.

laity ['leiiti] *rel u. allg die* Laien *m pl*.

lake [leik] **1.** See *m*; **~-dweller** Pfahlbaubewohner *m*; **~-dwellings** *pl* Pfahlbauten *m pl*; *the* **Lakeland(s)** das Seengebiet *(in Nordwestengland)*; **2.** rote Pigmentfarbe *f*.

lam [læm] **1.** *tr sl* verdreschen, verprügeln; **2.** *s Am sl* eilige Flucht *f*; *itr Am sl (to take it on the ~)* türmen, stiftengehen, verduften; *on the ~* in eiliger Flucht.

lama ['lɑːmə] *rel* Lama *m*; **~ism** ['-izm] Lamaismus *m*.

lamb [læm] *s* (Schaf-)Lamm; Lammfleisch, -fell; *fig* Unschuldslamm, Schäfchen *n*; Hereingefallene(r) *m*; *itr (Schaf)* lammen; *L~ of God* Lamm *n* Gottes *(Jesus)*; **~kin** ['-kin] Lämmchen *n a. fig*; **~like** ['-laik] (lamm-)fromm, unschuldig, sanft; **~skin** ['-skin] Lammfell *n*; *a wolf in ~~* ein Wolf im Schafspelz; **~'s wool** Lammwolle *f*.

lambaste [læm'beist] *tr sl* vermöbeln, verdreschen, verprügeln; den Kopf waschen (*s.o.* jdm), 'runterputzen.

lambent ['læmbənt] *(Flamme)* züngelnd, flackernd; (sanft) strahlend; *(Augen)* leuchtend; funkelnd, blitzend *a. fig*.

lame [leim] *a* lahm (*of, in* auf) *a. fig*; *fig* schwach, nicht überzeugend, unbefriedigend, unwirksam; *(Ausrede)* faul; *tr* lähmen; *itr* lahm werden; lahmen; *to walk ~* hinken; **~ duck** *fig* kranke(s) Huhn *n*, Niete, lahme Ente *f*, Pechvogel, Unglücksmensch; ruinierte(r) (Börsen-)Spekulant; *Am* nicht wieder gewählte(r) Abgeordnete(r) *m*; **~ness** ['-nis] Lähmung, Lahmheit *a. fig*; *fig* Schwäche, mangelnde Überzeugungskraft *f*.

lamell|a [lə'melə] *pl a. -ae* [-liː] Plättchen *n*, Lamelle *f a. zoo bot*; **~ar** [-ə], **~ate** ['læməleit] lamellar, schichtig.

lament [lə'ment] *itr* trauern, klagen (*for s.o.* um jdn); beklagen (*over s.o.'s death* jds Tod); *tr* betrauern, beklagen; sehr, zutiefst bedauern; *s* Wehklage *f*; Klagelied *n*; **~able** ['læməntəbl] beklagens-, bejammerns-, bedauernswert; trauernd, traurig; erbärmlich; **~ation** [læmen'teiʃən] Klagen *n*; Wehklage *f*, Jammer *m*.

lamin|a ['læminə] *pl a. -ae* [-iː] (dünne) Platte, Scheibe *f*, Plättchen *n*; Überzug *m*, Schicht; *bot* Blattfläche *f*; **~able** ['-əbl] *tech* streckbar; **~al** ['-l], **~ar** ['-ə], **~ate** ['-it] laminar, gewalzt; geblättert; **~ate** ['-eit] *tr* (aus-) walzen, strecken; blechen; lamellieren; *s* ['-it] Kunststoffolie *f*; **~ated** ['-eitid] *a* laminar, lamellenförmig, geschichtet, blätterförmig; *~~ contact* Bürstenkontakt *m*; *~~ glass* Verbundglas *n*; *~~ paper* Hartpapier *n*; **~ation** [-'neiʃən] Schichtung, Lamellierung *f*.

lammer|geyer, ~geier ['læməgaiə] *orn* Lämmer-, Bartgeier *m*.

lamp [læmp] Lampe; *fig (Mensch)* Leuchte *f*; *poet* Himmelslicht *n*; *pl sl* Augen *f pl*; *desk ~* Schreibtischlampe *f*; *oil ~* Öl-, Petroleumlampe *f*; **~-black** Lampenruß *m*; **~light** Lampenlicht *n*; **~-post** Laternenpfahl *m*; *between you and me and the ~~ (fam)* unter uns (gesagt); **~-shade** Lampenschirm *m*.

lampoon [læm'puːn] *s* Schmäh-, Spottschrift *f*; *tr* (mit e-r Schmähschrift) verspotten, schmähen; **~er** [-ə], **~ist** [-ist] Schmähschriftenschreiber *m*.

lamprey ['læmpri] *zoo* Neunauge *n*, Lamprete *f*.

*

lance [lɑːns] *s* Lanze *f*, Speer *m*; *tr* mit e-r Lanze angreifen *od* durchbohren; *med* aufschneiden, aufstechen, öffnen; *to break a ~ for s.o. (fig)* für jdn e-e Lanze brechen; *with s.o.* mit jdm streiten; **~-corporal** Ober-, Hauptgefreite(r) *m*; **~r** ['-ə] *mil hist* Ulan *m*; *pl* Lanciers *pl*; **~-sergeant** *Br* Stabsunteroffizier *m*; **~t** ['lɑːnsit] *med* Lanzette *f*; *~~-arch (arch)* Spitzbogen *m*; *~~-window* Spitzbogenfenster *n*.

land [lænd] *s* (Fest-)Land; Land *n*, Staat *m*, Reich, Volk *n*, Nation *f*; Bereich *m od n*, Gebiet *n*, Region *f*, Bezirk *m*, Landschaft *f*, Gelände *n*; *(Acker-, Wald-)*Land *n*; Grund u. Boden *m*; Ländereien *f pl*; Land-, Grundbesitz *m*, (Land-)Gut *n*; *tr* an(s) Land bringen, ausladen, löschen; *(Fische)* ins Boot, auf den Dampfer, an Land ziehen, fangen; *(Flugzeug)* landen, (an)wassern; *(Fallschirmtruppen)* absetzen; *allg fig* bringen (*in, at* nach, in, zu); absetzen (*in, on* in, auf); *fam* einheimsen, -stecken; *(Sache)* durchdrücken; *(Preis)* erringen; nach Hause bringen, in Nummer Sicher haben; *fam* erreichen; *fam (Schlag)* verpassen, versetzen; *itr (Schiff)* landen, anlegen; an Land gehen; *aero* landen; *allg* ankommen, ans Ziel gelangen; *sport* durchs Ziel gehen; *fam* landen; *to ~ o.s. in* hineingeraten in; *by ~* zu Lande; auf dem Landwege; per Achse; *on the ~* auf dem Lande; *over ~ and sea* über Land und Meer; *to come to ~* an Land kommen; *to make ~* Land sichten, die Küste erreichen; *to ~ on instruments (aero)* e-e Blindlandung machen; *how the ~ lies* wie die Dinge liegen; *forest ~* Wald(land *n*) *m*; *grass, meadow ~* Wiesen(land *n*) *f pl*; *pasture ~* Weideland *n*; *waste ~* Brach-, Ödland *n*; *the L~ of Promise* das Gelobte Land *(Palästina)*; **~-agent** Gutsverwalter; Gütermakler *m*; **~ annuity** Grundrente *f*; **~-bank** Bodenkreditanstalt, Hypothekenbank; *Am* Landwirtschaftsbank *f*; **~-breeze, -wind** *mar* Landwind *m*; **~ carriage, conveyance, freight, transport** Landtransport *m*, Beförderung *f* auf dem Landwege; **~ charge** Grundschuld *f*; **~ credit** Bodenkredit *m*; **~ development** Geländeerschließung *f*; **~fall** Sichten *n* von Land; gesichtete(s) Land *n*; Landung *f a. aero*; *to make ~~* landen; **~ fighting, operations** *pl* Erdkampf *m*; **~-force(s)** *(pl)* Landmacht *f*, -streitkräfte *f pl*; **~-frontier** Landgrenze *f*; **~-girl** Landhelferin *f*; **~-grabber** jem, der sich auf unfaire Weise *od* unrechtmäßig in Besitz von Land bringt; **~-grant** *Am* Übereignung *f* von staatlichem Grund und Boden; **~holder** Gutsbesitzer, *bes.* -pächter *m*; **~-hunger** Landhunger *m*; **~-jobber** Bodenspekulant *m*; **~lady** ['lænleidi] (Haus-, Gast-)Wirtin *f*; **~less** ['-lis] unbegütert; **~-locked** *a* von Land eingeschlossen; ohne Zugang zum Meer, vom Meer abgeschnitten; **~loper** Landstreicher, Vagabund *m*; **~lord** ['lænlɔːd] (Haus-, Gast-)Wirt, Gutseigentümer, -herr *m*; **~lubber** ['-lʌbə] *mar pej* Landratte *f*; **~mark** Grenzstein; *mil* Geländepunkt *m*; *mar* Seezeichen *n*; *fig* Markstein, Wendepunkt *m*; **~mine** *mil* Landmine *f*; **~ office** *Am* Grundbuchamt *n*; **~-owner** Grund-, Gutsbesitzer *m*; *big ~~* Großgrundbesitzer *m*; **~-owning** Landbesitz *m*; **~-reform(er)** Bodenreform(er *m*) *f*; **~-register** Grundbuch *n*; **~-registration** Grundbucheintragung *f*; **~-rover** *agr mot* (geländegängiger) Kraftwagen *m*; **~scape** ['lænskeip] Landschaft *f*; *~~ architect* Landschaftsarchitekt *m*; *~~ architecture* Landschaftsgestaltung *f*; *~~ gardener* Landschaftsgärtner *m*; *~~ gardening* Landschaftsgärtnerei *f*; *~~ painter*, **~scapist** ['lænskeipist] Landschaftsmaler *m*; **~-shark** *mar* Halsabschneider *m*; **~slide** *Am* Erdrutsch *a. fig pol*; überwältigende(r) (Wahl-)Sieg; Umschwung *m*; **~slip** Erdrutsch, Bergsturz *m*; **~sman** ['-zmən] Landbewohner *m*, -ratte *f*; **~ speculation** Bodenspekulation *f*; **~-survey(ing)** Landvermessung, Landesaufnahme *f*; **~-surveyor** Land-, Feldmesser *m*; **~-swell** *mar* Dünung *f*; **~-tax** Grundsteuer *f*; **~ value** Grundwert *m*; **~ward** *a* land(ein)wärts gerichtet; **~ward(s)** *adv* land(ein)wärts.

landed ['lændid] *a* landbesitzend, begütert; Land-, Grund-; *fam* in der Tinte; **~ estate** Landgut *n*; **~ gentry** Landadel *m*; **~ interests** *pl* Interessen *n pl* des Grundbesitzes; **~ price** Endpreis *m*; **~ property** Land-, Grundbesitz *m*, Liegenschaften, Ländereien *f pl*; *speculation in ~~* Bodenspekulation *f*; **~ proprietor** Grund-, Gutsbesitzer *m*; *big ~~* Großgrundbesitzer *m*.

landing ['lændiŋ] *s mar aero* Landen *n*, Landung; Lande-, Anlegestelle *f*, Landeplatz *m a. aero*; *(Fracht)* Löschen *n*; Treppenabsatz; Flur, Korridor; *min* Füllort *m*; *attr* Landungs-, Lande-; *to make a safe ~* glücklich landen; *crash ~* Bruchlandung *f*; *emergency, forced ~* Notlandung *f*; **~ area** (Start- u.) Landebereich *m od n*, -zone, -fläche *f*; *(Fallschirm)* Absetzgelände *n*; **~ barge, craft** *mil* Landungs-, Sturmboot *n*; **~ beacon** Ansteuerungsfeuer *n*; **~ beam** *radio* Gleit-, Landestrahl *m*; **~ charges** *pl*, **fee** Landegebühren *f pl*; **~ crew** *(Segelflug)* Haltemannschaft *f*; **~ cross, ~ T** Landekreuz *n*; **~ deck** *(Flugzeug-*

träger) Flug-, Landedeck *n*; ~ **direction** Landerichtung *f*; ~~ *indicator* Landeweiser *m*; ~~ *light* Landerichtungsfeuer *n*; ~ **facilities** *pl* Landeeinrichtungen *f pl*; ~ **field, ground, place, site** Landefläche *f*, Flugplatz *m*; ~ **flap** *aero* Landeklappe *f*; ~ **flare** Landelicht *n*, -scheinwerfer *m*, *pl* Landebahnbefeuerung *f*; ~ **force** *mil* Landekorps *n*; ~ **gear** *aero* Fahrgestell, -werk *n*; ~ **impact** Landestoß *m*; ~ **light** Lande-, Bordscheinwerfer *m*; ~ **load** Landebeanspruchung *f (des Fahrgestells)*; ~ **mat** *Am aero* Landematte *f*; ~ **net** Ke(t)scher *m*, *(beim Angeln verwendetes)* Beutelnetz *n*; ~**-party** *mar mil* Landeabteilung *f*; ~ **path** Lande-, Gleitweg *m*; ~ **point** *mil* Landestelle *f*; ~ **run** Auslauf *m*, -rollen *n*; Ausroll-, Landestrecke *f*; ~ **runway** Landebahn *f*; ~ **searchlight** Landescheinwerfer *m*; ~ **sequence** Landefolge *f*; ~ **ship** Landungsschiff *n*; ~ **signal** Landesignal *n*; ~ **ski** Gleitkufe *f*; ~ **speed** Landegeschwindigkeit *f*; ~**-stage** *mar* Landungssteg *m*, -brücke *f*; ~ **strip** Landebahn *f*, Rollfeld *n*; ~ **surface** Landefläche *f*; ~ **wheel** Laufrad *n (des Fahrgestells)*; ~ **zone** *aero* Landezone *f*, Rollfeld; *(Fallschirmtruppe)* Absetzgebiet, -gelände *n*.

lane [lein] Gasse *f*; Pfad *m*, schmale Landstraße; *sport* (Renn-)Bahn; Gasse, Schneise *f*, Weg *m (durch e-e Menschenmasse)*; *mar* Fahrrinne, Route; *mot* Fahrbahn; *mil* Minensperrlücke *f*; *air, flying* ~ *(aero)* (An-, Ab-)Flugschneise *f*; ~ *of approach (aero)* Einflugschneise *f*.

langsyne ['læŋ'sain] *adv Scot* seit, vor langer Zeit; *s Scot* längstvergangene Zeit *f*.

language ['læŋgwidʒ] Sprache *f a. fig*; Sprachvermögen *n*, Sprechfähigkeit; Ausdrucks-, Sprech-, Rede-, Schreibweise; Spracheigentümlichkeit; Sprachwissenschaft *f*; *bad* ~ gemeine Ausdrücke *m pl*; *command of* ~ Sprach-, Redegewalt *f*; *finger* ~ Finger-, Zeichensprache *f*; *foreign* ~ Fremdsprache *f*; *strong* ~ Kraftausdrücke *m pl*; *technical* ~ Fachsprache *f*; ~ *of flowers* Blumensprache *f*.

langu|id ['læŋgwid] kraftlos, matt, schwach; *(Markt)* flau; *fig* lust-, interesselos, gleichgültig; ~**idness** ['-nis] Kraftlosigkeit, Mattheit, Flauheit; Interesselosigkeit, Gleichgültigkeit *f*; ~**ish** ['læŋgwiʃ] *itr* ermatten, schwach werden, Kraft verlieren; dahinsiechen; (dahin)vegetieren; sich sehnen, schmachten (*for* nach); ~**ishing** ['-iʃiŋ] interesselos; nachlassend; flau; schmachtend, sehnsüchtig; ~**or** ['læŋgə] Kraftlosigkeit, Mattigkeit; Interesselosigkeit, Gleichgültigkeit; Stumpfheit; Sehnsucht; Gedrücktheit; Stille; Schwüle *f*; ~**orous** ['-gərəs] kraftlos, matt; gleichgültig, stumpf; sehnsüchtig; gedrückt; dumpf, schwül, drückend.

lank [læŋk] schlank, dünn, mager; *(Haar)* glatt, schlicht, straff; ~**iness** ['-inis] Schmächtigkeit *f*; ~**y** ['-i] hager, schmächtig, schlaksig.

lanolin ['lænəli:n] Lanolin *n*.

lantern ['læntən] Laterne, Lampe *f*; Lampion *m*; *(magic* ~*)* Laterna magica *f*; *(Leuchtturm)* Scheinwerferraum *m*; *arch* Laterne *f*; *dark* ~ Blendlaterne *f*; ~**-jawed** *a* hohlwangig; ~ **light** Oberlichtfenster *n*; ~**-slide** Dia(positiv), Lichtbild *n*; ~*(~) lecture* Lichtbildervortrag *m*.

lanyard ['lænjəd] *mar* Schnur *f*; kurze(s) Tau, Taljereep *n*; *mil* Traggurt *f*.

lap [læp] **1.** *s* Schoß *m (des Körpers, der Kleidung)*; *allg* Senke *f*, (Tal-)Grund; *fig* Schoß *m*, Geborgenheit *f*; Vorsprung *m*, vorspringende Kante; *tech* Überlappung *f*, Wickel *m*, Windung; Polierscheibe *f*; *(Buchbinderei)* Falz *m*; Schlaufe, Schleife; *sport* Runde *f*; *tr* falten (*on* auf; *over* über); umschlagen, -legen, überea.-legen; einschlagen, einwickeln (*in* in); *fig (meist im pp)* (ein)hüllen, betten (*in* in); sich überlappend legen über, überstehen lassen; überstehen, hinausragen über; *sport* überrunden; *(Strecke)* zurücklegen; *tech* polieren; *itr* gefaltet werden; überlappen; vor-, überstehen, hervorragen; *(räumlich* od *zeitlich)* hinausragen (*over* über); übergreifen; *in, on o.'s* ~ im, auf dem Schoß; auf den Knien; *in Fortune's* ~ in glücklichen Umständen *od* Verhältnissen; *in the* ~ *of luxury* wie Gott in Frankreich; ~**-dog** Schoßhund *m*; **2.** *tr itr (Hund)* saufen; schlecken; *itr* plätschern (*at, against* an; *on* gegen, auf); *s* Saufen; Schlecken, Lecken; Plätschern, Geplätscher; dünne(s) Futter, Gesöff *n*; *to* ~ *up* auflecken, -schlecken; *fam* 'runterkippen; *fig fam* fressen; *fam* an sich reißen.

lapel [lə'pel] (Rock-)Aufschlag *m*.

lapid|ary ['læpidəri] *s* Steinschneider *m*; *a* Steinschneide-; in Stein geschnitten; *fig (Stil)* lapidar, wuchtig, kurz und bündig; ~**ate** ['-eit] *tr* steinigen; ~**ation** [læpi'deiʃən] Steinigung *f*.

Lapland ['læplænd] Lappland *n*; ~**er** ['-ə], **Lapp** [læp] Lappe *m*, Lappin *f*.

lappet ['læpit] (Rock-)Zipfel *m*; (Hut-)Band *n*; *anat zoo* Lappen, Fetzen *m*.

lapse [læps] *s* Versehen *n*, Irrtum, Fehler, Fehltritt *m*, (sittliche) Verfehlung, Entgleisung *f*; Versäumnis; Absinken, Abgleiten *n*, Verfall *m*; Dahingleiten, *(bes. Zeit)* Vergehen, Verstreichen *n*, Ablauf, Verlauf *m*; *(~ of time)* Zeitspanne *f*, -raum *m*; *jur* Erlöschen *n*, Verfall; Heimfall; Abfall *m* (*from* von); *itr* ausgleiten, fallen; fehlen, e-n Fehltritt tun; entgleisen, absinken, abgleiten (*into* in); *(bes. Zeit)* dahin-, vergehen, verstreichen, ablaufen; *jur* verfallen, erlöschen, hinfällig werden, ablaufen, außer Kraft treten, verjähren; heimfallen (*to* an); *to* ~ *into unconsciousness* das Bewußtsein verlieren.

lapwing ['læpwiŋ] *orn* Kiebitz *m*.

larcen|er ['lɑ:snə], ~**ist** ['-ist] Dieb *m*; ~**y** ['-i] Diebstahl *m*, Entwendung *f*; *grand, compound* ~~ schwere(r) Diebstahl *m*; *petty* ~~ Bagatelldiebstahl *m*.

larch [lɑ:tʃ] *bot* Lärche *f*.

lard [lɑ:d] *s* (Schweine-)Schmalz *n*; *tr* einfetten, schmieren; spicken *a. fig*; *fig* ausschmücken (*with* mit); ~**er** ['lɑ:də] Speisekammer *f*; (Lebensmittel-)Vorräte *m pl*; ~**ing** ['-iŋ]: ~~*-needle, -pin* Spicknadel *f*; ~ **oil** Schmalzöl *n*; ~**on** ['lɑ:dən], ~**oon** [lɑ:'du:n] Speckstreifen *m*; ~**y** ['lɑ:di] schmalzig; schmalzartig.

large [lɑ:dʒ] *a* groß, weit, geräumig, umfangreich, ausgedehnt, umfassend, weitreichend; dick, stark; gewaltig, bedeutend, nennenswert; verständnisvoll, einsichtig, weitherzig, großzügig; *mar (Wind)* günstig; *adv* prahlerisch; *Am fam* ereignisreich, populär; *s*: *at* ~ auf freiem Fuß; ausführlich, in allen Einzelheiten; im allgemeinen, im großen und ganzen; planlos, ziellos; *by and* ~ im großen und ganzen; *in* ~, *on a* ~ *scale* in großem Umfang; *to talk* ~ großspurig reden; *to talk at* ~ ins Blaue hineinreden; *the world at* ~ die ganze (weite) Welt; ~**-hearted** *a* weitherzig, großzügig, gutmütig; ~ **intestine** Dickdarm *m*; ~**ly** ['-li] *adv* allgemein; größtenteils, hauptsächlich; in hohem Maße; reichlich; ~**-minded** *a* frei in s-n Ansichten, tolerant, großherzig; ~**-mindedness** Großzügigkeit *f*; ~**ness** ['-nis] Größe, Weite, Geräumigkeit; Stärke, Gewalt, Bedeutung; Großzügigkeit *f*; ~**-scale** *a* in großem Maßstab; im großen, ausgedehnt, umfangreich, Groß-; ~~ *attack* Großangriff *m*; ~~ *production* Großfertigung *f*; ~**-sized** *a* großformatig.

largess(e) ['lɑ:dʒes] Freigebigkeit; Gabe *f*, großzügige(s) Geschenk *n*.

largish ['lɑ:dʒiʃ] *adv* ziemlich groß.

larg|hetto [lɑ:'getou] *mus* Larghetto *n*; ~**o** ['lɑ:gou] *mus* Largo *n*.

lariat ['læriət] Strick *m*; Lasso *m* od *n*.

lark [lɑ:k] **1.** *orn* Lerche *f*; ~**spur** *bot* Rittersporn *m*; **2.** *fam s* Spaß, Ulk, Scherz *m*, Vergnügen *n*; *itr* sich vergnügen, lustig sein; *(to* ~ *about)* herumtollen; *for a* ~ zum Spaß, Vergnügen; *what a* ~*!* wie lustig! zum Schießen! ~**spur** *bot* Rittersporn *m*; ~**y** ['-i] zum Spaßen, zu Späßen aufgelegt.

larrikin ['lærikin] Halbstarker, Rowdy *m*.

larrup ['lærəp] *tr fam* verdreschen.

larv|a ['lɑ:və] *pl* ~*ae* ['-i:] *ent* Larve *f*; ~**al** ['-əl] larvenartig, Larven-.

laryn|gal [lə'riŋgəl], ~**geal** [lærin-'dʒi(:)əl] *a* Kehlkopf-; ~**gitis** [lærin'dʒaitis] Kehlkopfentzündung *f*; ~**goscope** [lə'riŋgəskoup] Kehlkopfspiegel *m*; ~**x** ['læriŋks] *pl a. larynges* [lə'rindʒi:z] Kehlkopf m.

lascivious [lə'siviəs] geil, wollüstig, unzüchtig; ~**ness** [-nis] Geilheit, Lüsternheit *f*.

laser ['leisə] Laser *m*.

lash [læʃ] *s* Peitsche(nschnur) *f*; Peitschen *n*; Peitschenhieb *m*; *the* ~ die Prügelstrafe *f*; *fig* (Seiten-)Hieb *m*, bissige Bemerkung *f*, scharfe(r) Tadel *m*; *(eye~)* Wimper *f*; *tr* (aus)peitschen; (heftig) schlagen; *fig* heruntermachen, heftig tadeln; aufstacheln, (an)treiben (*into* zu); binden (*on, to* an); *mar* (fest)zurren; *itr* schlagen, peitschen, prasseln (*at* gegen); *(Tränen)* strömen; *to* ~ **down** *tr* anbinden (*to, on* an); *itr (Regen)* niederprasseln; *to* ~ **out** *itr (Pferd)* ausschlagen; *fig* ausfällig werden (*at* gegen); *to* ~ **together** *tr* zs.binden; ~**ing** ['-iŋ] Schlagen, Peitschen; *fig* Schimpfen *n*; *mar* Laschung *f*; *pl fam* e-e Menge *od* Masse; ~**-up** Improvisation *f*.

lass [læs], ~**ie** ['-i] Mädchen, Mädel; Liebchen *n*, Geliebte, Freundin *f*.

lassitude ['læsitju:d] Müdigkeit, Mattigkeit *f*.

lasso ['læsou] *pl -os s* Lasso *m* od *n*; *tr* mit dem Lasso (ein)fangen.

last [lɑ:st] **1.** *a* letzt, hinterst; spätest, jüngst; neuest; vorig, vergangen, äußerst, höchst; geringst, niedrigst; *adv* zuletzt, zum Schluß, am Ende; zum letzten Mal; *s der, die, das* Letzte, Jüngste, Neueste, Modernste; Schluß *m*, Ende *n*; *at* ~ schließlich, endlich, zuletzt, am Ende; *at long* ~ zu guter Letzt; *for the* ~ *time* zum letzten Mal; *next to the* ~ vorletzt(e, r); *to the* ~ bis zum Letzten *od* Äußersten; bis zum Ende, bis zum letzten Atemzug; ~ *of all* zuallerletzt; ~ *not least* nicht zum wenigsten; ~ *night* gestern abend; heute nacht; ~ *week* in der letzten, vorigen Woche; ~ *but one* vorletzte(r, s); *the week before* ~ vorletzte Woche *f*; *to breathe o.'s* ~ den letzten Atemzug, *fam* Schnaufer tun; den Geist aufgeben; *never to hear the* ~ *of s.th.* nichts mehr hören wollen; *to see the* ~ *of s.th.* etw nicht mehr wiedersehen; *I've said my* ~ *word on the matter* ich habe nichts mehr hinzuzufügen; *that's the* ~ *thing I should do* das wäre das letzte, was ich täte; *the L~ Judg(e)ment (rel)* das Jüngste Gericht; *the* ~ *meal* die Henkersmahlzeit; ~ *quarter (Mond)* letzte(s) Viertel *n*; *the L~ Supper (rel)* das Abendmahl; *the* ~ *word* das letzte Wort; das Beste s-r Art; *fam* der letzte Schrei; das Neueste; **~ly** ['-li] *adv* zuletzt, schließlich; **2.** *itr* (an)dauern, (an)halten, bleiben; ausdauern, aushalten; sich (gut) halten; langen, (aus)reichen (*for* für); **~ing** ['-iŋ] *a* dauernd, bleibend; dauerhaft, beständig; *s (Textil)* Lasting *m*; **~ingness** ['-iŋnis] Dauerhaftigkeit, Beständigkeit *f*; **3.** (Schuh-)Leisten *m*; *to stick to o.'s* ~ *(fig)* bei s-m Leisten bleiben; **4.** Last *f (Gewichtseinheit, meist = 4000 (engl.) Pfund)*.

latch [lætʃ] *s* (Tür-)Drücker *m*, Sperrklinke *f*, Schnappschloß *n*; (Fenster-) Riegel *m*; *Art* Sicherheitsschloß *n*; *tr* zudrücken, einschnappen lassen; *itr (Tür)* schließen; *to* ~ *on to s.th. (sl)* etw (spitz) kriegen; *on the* ~ *(Tür)* eingeklinkt, zugeschnappt; ~ **key** Haus-, Sperrklinkenschlüssel *m*; ~~ *kid* Schlüsselkind *n*.

late [leit] *a* spät, verspätet, vorgerückt, Spät-; jüngst, (jüngst)vergangen, bisherig; (jüngst)verstorben; *adv* spät; *as* ~ *as* erst, noch; *at a* ~ *hour* zu später Stunde; *of* ~ (erst) kürzlich, neulich (noch), vor noch nicht langer Zeit; *of* ~ *years* in den letzten Jahren; *to keep* ~ *hours* lange auf- *od* fortbleiben; ~ **afternoon** Spätnachmittag *m*; **~-comer** Spätkommende(r); Spätling *m*; **~ly** ['-li] *adv* neulich, kürzlich, vor kurzem; in der letzten Zeit; **~ness** ['-nis] Verspätung *f*, Zuspätkommen *n*; vorgerückte Stunde, *od* (Jahres-)Zeit; Neuheit *f*; **~r** ['-ə] *a* später; *one day* ~~ einen Tag darauf; ~~ *on* später *adv*; *in* ~*-on life* im späteren Leben; *sooner or* ~~ früher oder später; *see you* ~~, *till* ~~ *on* bis später! bis bald! auf Wiedersehen! **~st** ['-əst] *a* spätest; neuest; *adv* zuletzt; *s the* ~~ das Allerneueste; *at the* ~~ spätestens.

laten|cy ['leitənsi] Verborgenheit, Unentwickeltheit, *scient* Latenz *f*; **~t** ['-t] verborgen, unentwickelt, *scient* latent; *phys (Wärme)* gebunden; ~~ *period (med)* Inkubationszeit *f*.

lateral ['lætərəl] *a* seitlich; Seiten-, Neben- *a. fig*; *s* Seitenteil *n*; ~ **branch** Seiten-, Nebenlinie *f (e-r Familie)*; ~ **(gallery)** Querstollen *m*; ~ **pressure** Seitendruck *m*; ~ **thrust** Querschub *m*; ~ **view** Seitenansicht *f*; ~ **wind** Seitenwind *m*.

latex ['leiteks] *bot* Milchsaft *m*.

lath [lɑ:θ] *pl -s* [-θs, -ðz] Latte; Leiste *f*; Lattenwerk *n*; Putzträger *m*.

lathe [leið] *(turning* ~*)* Drehbank; Lade *f*, Schlag *m (am Webstuhl)*; ~ **hand, operator** Dreher *m*; ~ **spindle** Drehbankspindel *f*; ~ **tool** Drehstahl *m*, -werkzeug *n*.

lather ['læðə, -ɑ:-] *s* (Seifen-)Schaum *m*; *tr* einseifen; *fam* verdreschen; *itr* schäumen; **~y** ['-ri] schaumig.

Latin ['lætin] *a* lateinisch, Latein-; romanisch; *rel* römisch-katholisch; *s* (das) Latein(ische); Romane *m*; *Old* ~ klassische(s) Latein *n*; *Medi(a)eval* ~ Mittellatein *n*; *Vulgar* ~ Vulgärlatein *n*; ~ **America** Lateinamerika *n*; ~ **American** *s* Lateinamerikaner(in *f*) *m*; ~~ *(a)* lateinamerikanisch; **~ism** ['-izm] Latinismus *m*, lateinische Spracheigentümlichkeit *f*; **~ist** ['-ist] Latinist *m*; **~ity** [lə'tiniti] Latinität *f*; **~ize** ['lætinaiz] *tr* latinisieren; ins Lateinische übersetzen.

latish ['leitiʃ] *a adv* etwas, ziemlich, reichlich spät.

latitud|e ['lætitju:d] *meist fig* Breite, Weite *f*, Umfang; Spielraum *m a. phot*, Bewegungsfreiheit; geistige, Religionsfreiheit; *geog* Breite; *astr* Deklination *f*; *pl* Breiten, Gegenden, Regionen *f pl*; *of* ~~ *north, south of the equator* nördlicher, südlicher Breite; *degree of* ~~, ~~ *circle* Breitengrad *m*; **~inal** [læti'tju:dinl] *a* Breiten-; **~inarian** ['lætitju:di'nɛəriən] *a* freiheitlich, liberal, freisinnig, tolerant, duldsam; *s* Freidenker, tolerante(r) Mensch; *rel hist* Latitudinarier *m*.

latrine [lə'tri:n] Latrine *f*; *Am* Waschraum *m*; ~ **news, rumour, gossip** *mil sl* Latrinengerücht *n*, -parole *f*.

latter ['lætə] *a* später, neuer; letzter; *s der, die, das* letztere; *in these* ~ *days* in der jüngsten Zeit; **~-day** *a* neuest, modern, aus neuester, jüngster Zeit; *L~~ Saint (rel)* Mormone *m*; ~ **end** Ende *n*, Tod *m*; ~ **grass** Grum(me)t *n*; ~ **half** zweite Hälfte *f (des Jahres, Jahrhunderts)*; **~ly** ['-li] *adv* neuerlich, neuerdings, kürzlich; am Ende; **~most** *a* letzt, hinterst.

lattice ['lætis] *s* Gitter(werk) *n*; *tr* gitter-, rautenförmig anordnen; *(to* ~ *up, to* ~ *over)* vergittern; ~ **bridge** Gitterbrücke *f*; ~ **door** Gittertür *f*; ~ **frame** Gitterrahmen *m*; ~ **gate** Gittertor *n*; ~ **girder** Gitterträger *m*; ~ **pylon, tower** Gittermast *m*; ~ **window** Gitterfenster *n*; ~ **work** Gitterwerk *n*, -konstruktion *f*.

Latvia ['lætviə] Lettland *n*; **~n** ['-n] *a* lettisch; *s* Lette *m*, Lettin *f*; (das) Lettisch(e).

*

laud [lɔ:d] *s* Lob(lied) *n*, Lobeshymne *f*; *tr* loben, preisen; **~ability** [-ə'biliti] Löblichkeit *f*; **~able** ['lɔ:dəbl] löblich, lobenswert; **~ation** [lɔ:'deiʃən] Lob *n*, Preis *m*; **~ative** ['lɔ:dətiv], **~atory** ['-ətəri] lobend, Lob(es)-.

laudanum ['lɔdnəm] Opiumpräparat *n*, -tinktur *f*.

laugh [lɑ:f] *itr* lachen (*at* über; *over* bei) *a. fig*; auslachen (*at s.o.* jdn); *tr* lachend sagen; durch Lachen zum Ausdruck bringen; durch Lachen bringen (*into* zu); *s* Lachen, Gelächter *n*; Spaß *m*; *for* ~*s (Am sl)* zum Spaß; *to break into a* ~ in ein Gelächter ausbrechen; *to get, to have s.o.'s* ~, *to have the* ~ *on o.'s side* die Lacher auf seiner Seite haben; *to raise a* ~ ein Gelächter verursachen, alle zum Lachen bringen; *to* ~ *in s.o.'s face* jdm ins Gesicht lachen; *to* ~ *out of, on the other, the wrong side of o.'s mouth* das Gesicht verziehen; enttäuscht sein; *to* ~ *in o.'s sleeve* sich ins Fäustchen lachen; *he* ~*s best who* ~*s last (prov)* wer zuletzt lacht, lacht am besten; *to* ~ **away,** *to* ~ **off** sich lachend hinwegsetzen über; mit e-m Lachen abtun; *to* ~ **down** durch Lachen zum Schweigen bringen; *to* ~ *s.o.* **out** *of s.th.* jdn durch Lachen von etw abbringen; **~able** ['-əbl] lächerlich; **~ing** ['-iŋ] lachend; *it's no* ~~ *matter* das ist nicht zum Lachen; ~~*-gas* Lachgas *n*; *to make a* ~~*-stock of o.s.* sich lächerlich machen; **~ter** ['-tə] Gelächter *n*; *to shake with* ~~ sich vor Lachen schütteln.

launch [lɔ:ntʃ] **1.** *tr* schleudern, werfen (*at, against* gegen); *(Schlag)* versetzen; in Gang setzen; *(Schiff)* vom Stapel lassen; *(Boot)* aussetzen; in Angriff nehmen, beginnen, starten; *(Rakete)* abschießen; *aero* katapultieren; *(Menschen)* lancieren, starten; *com (Anleihe)* auflegen; *(Geschäft)* gründen; *(Gesetz)* erlassen; *(Rede)* vom Stapel lassen; *itr (to* ~ *out, forth)* vom Stapel laufen; hinausfahren; beginnen, loslegen; sich in Bewegung setzen; sich an die Arbeit machen; sich stürzen, einsteigen (*into* in); *s* Stapellauf; Abschuß; Start *m*; Barkasse *f*; **~ing** ['-iŋ] Starten *n*; Abschuß; *mar* Stapellauf *m*; ~~*-pad, -platform, ramp* Abschußrampe *f*; ~~ *rope* Startseil *n*; ~~ *site* Abschußbasis *f*; ~~*-tube* Torpedorohr *n*; ~~*-way (mar)* Helling *f*.

laund|er ['lɔ:ndə] *tr* waschen (u. bügeln); *itr* sich waschen lassen; **~erette** [-ə'ret] Waschsalon *m*; **~ress** ['lɔ:ndris] Wäscherin *f*; **~ry** ['lɔ:ndri] *s* Waschen *n*; Wäsche; Waschküche; Wäscherei, Waschanstalt *f*; *itr Am fam* waschen; ~~*man* ['-mən] Wäschereiangestellter *m*; ~~*-owner* Wäschereibesitzer *m*; ~~*-soap* Waschseife *f*; ~~*woman* Wäscherin *f*.

laureate ['lɔ:riit] *a* lorbeerbekränzt; *s (poet* ~*)* Hofdichter *m*.

laurel ['lɔrəl, *Am* 'lɔ:-] Lorbeer(baum *m*); *pl* Lorbeer(en *pl*) *m*, Ehre *f*, Sieg *m*; *to rest on o.'s* ~*s* auf s-n Lorbeeren ausruhen; **~(l)ed** ['-d] *a* lorbeerbekränzt; preisgekrönt.

lava ['lɑ:və] *geol* Lava *f*.

lav|ation [lə'veiʃən] *lit* Waschung *f*; **~atory** ['lævətəri] Waschschüssel *f*, -becken *n*; Waschraum *m*; Toilette *f*, (Spül-)Klosett *n*; *(public* ~~*)* Bedürfnisanstalt *f*; **~e** [leiv] *poet itr tr* (sich) waschen.

lavender ['lævində] *bot* Lavendel *m*.

lavish ['læviʃ] *a* verschwenderisch (*of* mit; *in doing*); reich, üppig; *tr* verschwenden (*on* für); **~ness** ['-nis] Verschwendungssucht; verschwenderische, üppige Fülle *f*.

law [lɔ:] **1.** Gesetz, Statut *n*, Bestimmung; Vorschrift *f*; Recht *n*; Rechtszustand *m*, -ordnung *f*; Rechtswissenschaft, Jurisprudenz *f*; Gericht *n*; Juristenberuf; Richterstand *m*; Rechtskenntnis *f*; (Natur-)Gesetz *n*; *math gram* (Spiel-)Regel *f*; *rel* Gebot(e *pl*) *n*; *sport* Vorgabe *f*; *Am fam* Polizist *m*; **2.** *according to* ~ nach dem Gesetz, gesetz-, rechtmäßig *adv*, von Rechts wegen; *at* ~ vor Gericht; *by* ~ von Rechts wegen; *contrary to* ~ rechtswidrig; *under the* ~ nach dem Gesetz; **3.** *to abide by the* ~, *to act within the* ~ sich ans Gesetz halten, das Gesetz befolgen; *to administer the* ~ Recht sprechen; *to be at* ~ *with s.o.* mit jdm prozessieren; *to be in the* ~ Jurist sein; *to become* ~ Gesetzeskraft erlangen; *to break the* ~ das Gesetz brechen *od* verletzen *od* übertreten; *to circumvent, to dodge, to elude, to evade the* ~ das Gesetz umgehen; *to give o.s. up to the* ~ sich dem Gericht stellen; *to go to* ~ den Rechtsweg beschreiten; *with s.o.* jdn verklagen; *to infringe, to violate a* ~ gegen ein Gesetz verstoßen, ein G. übertreten; *to keep within the* ~ sich im Rahmen der gesetzlichen Vorschriften halten; *to lay down the* ~ Recht setzen; gebieterisch auftreten; *to s.o.* jdm Vorschriften machen; *to observe the* ~ das Gesetz befolgen; *to practice* ~ e-e Rechtsanwaltspraxis haben; *to proceed at, by* ~ den Rechtsweg beschreiten, e-n Prozeß anstrengen; *to read, to go in for* ~ Rechtswissenschaft studieren; *to resort to* ~ sich ans Gericht wenden; *necessity knows no* ~ *(prov)* Not kennt kein Gebot; **4.** *contrary to the* ~ gesetzwidrig; *game* ~*s (pl)* Jagdrecht *n*; *international* ~ Völkerrecht *n*; *labo(u)r* ~*(s) (pl)* Arbeitsrecht *n*; *Lynch* ~ Lynchjustiz *f*; *maritime, naval, sea* ~ Seerecht *n*; *martial* ~ Kriegsrecht *n*; *matter, question of* ~ Rechtsfrage *f*; *natural* ~ Naturrecht *n*; *poor-*~ Armen-, Fürsorgerecht *n*; *principle of* ~ Rechtsgrundsatz *m*; *private* ~ Privatrecht *n*; *public* ~ öffentliche(s) Recht *n*; *statute, statutory* ~ gesetzte(s) Recht *n*; *tribal* ~ Stammesrecht *n*; *unwritten* ~ ungeschriebene(s), Gewohnheitsrecht *n*; *written* ~ geschriebene(s), Gesetzesrecht *n*; **5.** ~ *and order* Recht und Ordnung; *maintenance of* ~ *and order* Aufrechterhaltung *f* der öffentlichen Sicherheit; ~ *of causality* Kausalgesetz *n*; ~ *of health* Gesundheitsregel *f*; ~ *of inheritance, of succession, (Am) of descent* Erbrecht *n*; ~ *of nations* Völkerrecht *n*; ~ *of nature* Naturgesetz *n*; ~ *of supply and demand* Gesetz *n* von Angebot und Nachfrage; **~-abiding** fried-, ordnungsliebend; **~-action** *jur* Klage *f*, gerichtliche(s) Vorgehen *n*; Zivilprozeß *m*; **~-adviser** Rechtsberater *m*; **~-affair** Rechtssache *f*; **~-book** Gesetzbuch; juristische(s) Werk *n*; **~-breaker** Rechtsbrecher *m*; **~-breaking** Rechtsbruch *m*; **~-case** Rechtsfall *m*; ~ **charges, costs, expenses** *pl* Gerichts-, Prozeßkosten *pl*; **~-court** Gerichtshof *m*; *pl* Justizgebäude *n*; ~ **faculty** juristische Fakultät *f*; **~ful** ['-ful] gesetz-, rechtmäßig; legitim; ehelich (geboren); gültig; erlaubt; berechtigt; ~~ *age* Volljährigkeit *f*; *to reach* ~~ *age* mündig werden; **~fulness** ['-fulnis] Recht-, Gesetzmäßigkeit; Legitimität; Ehelichkeit; Gültigkeit; Erlaubtheit; Berechtigung *f*; ~ **gazette** Gesetzblatt *n*; **~giver, ~maker** Gesetzgeber *m*; **~giving, ~making** Gesetzgebung *f*; ~ **language** Rechtssprache *f*; **~less** ['-lis] gesetzlos, -widrig, ungesetzlich; unrechtmäßig; unberechtigt; unerlaubt; friedlos; zügellos; **~lessness** ['-lisnis] Gesetzlosigkeit; Ungesetzlichkeit, Unrechtmäßigkeit; Unerlaubtheit; Fried-,Zügellosigkeit *f*; **~-office** Anwaltsbüro *n*; **~-practice** Rechts-, Gerichtspraxis *f*; **~-school** juristische Fakultät *f*; **~-student** Student *m* der Rechte; **~-studies** *pl* Rechts-, juristische(s) Studium *n*; **~suit** ['-sju:t] Rechtsstreit, -handel, (Zivil-)Prozeß *m*; Klage *f*; *to be involved, entangled in a* ~~ in e-n Prozeß verwickelt sein; *to carry on a* ~~ e-n P. führen; *to commence, to enter a* ~~ e-n P. anstrengen (*against* gegen); *to lose, to settle, to win a* ~~ e-n P. verlieren, beilegen, gewinnen; ~ **term** juristische(r) Fachausdruck *m*; Sitzungsperiode *f*; **~yer** ['-jə] Jurist, Rechtsgelehrte(r); Rechtsbeistand, -anwalt, Anwalt; *(Bibel)* Schriftgelehrte(r) *m*; *criminal* ~~ Kriminalist *m*; *patent* ~~ Patentanwalt *m*.

lawn [lɔ:n] **1.** Rasen; Rasen(sport)-platz *m*; **~-fete** ['-feit] *Am* Gartenfest *n*; **~-mower** Rasenmäher *m*; **~-sprinkler** Rasensprenger *m*; **~-tennis** (Rasen-)Tennis(spiel) *n*; **2.** Batist; *fig* Episkopat *m*.

lax [læks] lose, locker, schlaff; *(Stuhlgang)* geregelt; *fig* lax, (nach)lässig, ungenau; **~ative** ['læksətiv] Abführmittel *n*; **~ity** ['læksiti], **~ness** ['læksnis] Lockerheit, Schlaffheit; (Nach-)Lässigkeit, Ungenauigkeit *f*; weiche(r) Stuhlgang *m*.

lay [lei] **1.** *irr laid, laid tr* (hin-, nieder-, um)legen (*on* auf; *in* in); setzen, stellen; *(Linoleum, Ziegel, Kabel, Eier)* legen; *fig (Wert, den Nachdruck)* legen (*on* auf); *(Wette)* abschließen; wetten; *(den Schauplatz)* (ver)legen (*in* nach); *(Staub)* sich legen, sich setzen lassen; *(Falte)* glätten; *fig* mäßigen, erleichtern, lindern, stillen, beruhigen, befriedigen, löschen; unterdrücken, überwinden; *(Geist)* bannen; setzen, wetten; *(Steuer, Strafe)* belegen mit; *(Steuer)* legen auf; (zur Ansicht) vorlegen (*s.th. before s.o.* jdm etw); beilegen, -messen, zuschreiben (*s.th. to s.o.* jdm etw); belasten (*s.o. with s.th.* jdn mit e-r S); festlegen, -setzen (*at* auf); niederlegen, ausarbeiten; *(Feuer)* anlegen; *(Geschütz)* richten; *(den Tisch)* decken; (die Litzen e-s Seil(s) zs.drehen; *fam* auflauern (*for s.o.* jdm); *Am sl* (Geschlechts-)Verkehr haben mit; *itr* (Eier) legen; wetten; *fam* liegen; sich intensiv befassen (*to* mit); *s* Lage, Situation *f*; (Gewinn-)Anteil *m*; *sl* Geschäft *n*, Beschäftigung *f*, Job *m*, Branche; *fam* Wette *f*; *Am* Preis *m*; Richtung, Windung *f (der Litzen e-s Seils)*; *to* ~ *bare* bloßlegen, enthüllen, zeigen; *o.'s heart* sein Herz ausschütten; *to* ~ *the blame on s.o.* jdm die Schuld zuschieben; *to* ~ *claim to* Anspruch erheben auf, beanspruchen; *to* ~ *a complaint* Beschwerde führen; *to* ~ *under contribution* Zahlungen auferlegen (*s.o.* jdm); *to* ~ *s.th. to, at s.o.'s door, charge* jdm etw zur Last legen, in die Schuhe schieben; *to* ~ *eyes on* erblicken, sehen; *to* ~ *o.'s finger on* s-n Finger legen auf; *to* ~ *a finger on* anrühren; *to* ~ *hands on* in s-n Besitz bringen, festhalten; packen; finden; *rel* die Hände auflegen (*s.o.* jdm); *to* ~ *violent hands on o.s.* Hand an sich legen; *to* ~ *heads together* die Köpfe zs.stecken; *to* ~ *to heart* ins Auge fassen; im Auge behalten; *to* ~ *(fast) by the heels* festnehmen, einsperren; *fig* bewegungs-, handlungsunfähig machen; *to* ~ *hold of* ergreifen; bekommen; *to* ~ *o.'s hopes on* s-e Hoffnung setzen auf; *to* ~ *an information against* zur Anzeige bringen, anzeigen; *to* ~ *low* niederstrecken, *fam* flachlegen; ans Bett fesseln; *to* ~ *under a necessity* zwingen; *to* ~ *under an obligation* verpflichten; *to* ~ *open* aufdecken, enthüllen; freilegen; *to* ~ *o.'s chin open* sich das Kinn aufschlagen, -stoßen; *to* ~ *o.s. open to s.th.* sich e-r S aussetzen; *to* ~ *siege to* belagern; *to* ~ *a snare, trap, an ambush* e-e Falle stellen (*for s.o.* jdm); *to* ~ *great, little store upon* großen *od* viel, wenig Wert legen auf; *to* ~ *stress, emphasis on* betonen, herausstellen; *to* ~ *the table* den Tisch decken; *to* ~ *a tax on* mit e-r Steuer belegen, besteuern; *to* ~ *waste* verwüsten; *to* ~ *weight on* Gewicht legen auf; *to* ~ **about** *(one)* um sich schlagen; tüchtig loslegen; *to* ~ **aside,** *to* ~ **away** auf die Seite legen, aufheben, sparen; ab-, weglegen; *to* ~ **back** zurücklegen, -lehnen; *to* ~ **by** aufheben, sparen; *to* ~ **down** hin-, niederlegen; (ein)lagern, einkellern; her-, aufgeben, opfern; (be)zahlen; wetten; niederlegen, entwerfen, planen, festlegen; formulieren; *(Grundsatz)* aufstellen; erklären, behaupten; *agr* anbauen (*with, to* mit); *to* ~ **in** sammeln, e-n Vorrat anlegen von, einkellern, stapeln; *to* ~ **into** *fam* verdreschen; fertig-, 'runtermachen; *to* ~ **off** *tr* weg-, ablegen; *Am* (vorübergehend) entlassen, abbauen; abgrenzen; *mar* wegsteuern; *itr Am sl* aufhören; den Mund, die Schnauze halten; *to* ~ **on** *tr* auflegen; *tech* einrichten, installieren, verlegen; *(Schläge)* verpassen, austeilen; *itr* los-, zuschlagen; *to* ~ *it on thick, with a trowel (fam)* übertreiben, aufschneiden; dick auftragen; schmeicheln, Komplimente machen; *to* ~ **out** zurechtlegen; auslegen, -breiten, zur Schau stellen; aufbahren; entwerfen, planen, trassieren; anlegen, -ordnen; gruppieren; *(Geld)* ausgeben, auslegen, aufwenden; *typ* umbrechen; *sl (Menschen)* fertigmachen, umlegen; *to* ~ *o.s. out* sich Mühe geben, sich bemühen; *to* ~ **to** *tr (Schiff)* beidrehen; *itr (Schiff)* fest-, stilliegen; *to* ~ **up** aufheben, -bewahren, sammeln, horten; lagern; sparen; *(Land)* brachliegen lassen; *(Schiff)* auflegen; *to be laid up* das Bett hüten (müssen) (*with* wegen); *I'll* ~ *three to one* ich wette drei zu eins; **~-by** *mar* Liegeplatz; *mot* Rastplatz *m*; ~ **days** *pl mar* Liegetage *m pl*, -zeit *f*; **~er** ['-ə] *s* Leger(in *f*) *m*; Legehenne *f*, -huhn *n*; [*a.* lɛə] Schicht, Lage, Hülle *f*, Überzug; *bot* Ableger; *agr* Setzling *m*; *itr bot* Ableger treiben; *tr agr* durch Setzlinge ziehen; *~~-cake* (Schicht-)Torte *f*; **~erage** ['lei-, 'lɛəridʒ], **~ering** ['lei-, 'lɛəriŋ] Ziehen *n* von Setzlingen; **~ette** [lei'et] Babyausstattung *f*; ~ **figure** Gliederpuppe; *fig* Puppe *f*, Strohmann *m*; **~ing** ['-iŋ] Legen *n*; *(Hühner)* Legezeit *f*; Gelege *n*; *arch* Bewurf, Putz *m*; Verputzen *n*; *~~-down* Entwurf *m*, Planung; Formulierung, Aufstellung *f*; *~~-off (Am)* (vorübergehende) Entlassung *f*; *~~-out* Auslage, Zurschaustellung *f*; Entwurf, Plan *m*, Anlage; Trassierung, Linienführung *f (e-r Bahnstrecke)*; *~~-up (Schiff)* Außerdienststellung *f*; **~-off** (zeitweilige) Arbeitsunterbrechung, -pause; (vorübergehende) Entlassung *f*; **~out** Anlage, Einrichtung *f*, Plan *m*, Anordnung, Ausgestaltung *f*; Grundriß *m*; *Am typ* Layout *n*; Auslage; Aufmachung, Ausstattung *f*; Satz *m (Werkzeuge)*; ~~ *of rooms* Raumverteilung *f*; **~over** Aufenthalt *m*, Fahrtunterbrechung *f*; **~shaft** *tech* Vorlege-, Zwischenwelle *f*; **2.** *rel* weltlich, Laien-; *allg* laienhaft, Laien-; ~ **brother** Laienbruder *m*; **~man** ['-mən] *rel allg* Laie *m*; Laien(-welt *f*) *m pl*; **3.** (gesungene) Ballade *f*, Gesang *m*, Lied *n*.

lazaret(to) [læzə'ret(ou)] *pl -os* Leprakrankenhaus, Spital *n*; Quarantänestation, -anstalt *f*.

laz|e [leiz] *itr* faulenzen, bummeln; *tr (to* ~~ *away)* verbummeln, vertrödeln; **~iness** ['-inis] Faulheit, Trägheit; Langsamkeit *f*; **~y** ['-i] faul, träge; langsam, schwerfällig; *~~-bones fam* Faulpelz, Faulenzer *m*.

lea [li:] **1.** *poet* Aue, Trift, Flur *f*; **2.** Gebinde *n (Garnmaß 80—300 yards)*.

leach [li:tʃ] *tr* auslaugen; durchsickern lassen.

lead 1. [li:d] *irr led, led tr* (an)führen, leiten; vorangehen (*s.o.* jdm); *(den Weg)* zeigen; *(Wasser)* leiten; *(Schüler)* anleiten; veranlassen (*to* zu); *mil* anführen; an der Spitze stehen (*of* gen); *mus* dirigieren; *(ein Leben)* führen; eröffnen; *(Kartenspiel)* ausspielen; *itr* an der Spitze, vorangehen, (an)führen; sich führen, leiten lassen; (hin)führen (*to* zu); herbeiführen (*to* *s.th.* etw); führend sein, die erste Stelle einnehmen, an der Spitze stehen, der Anführer sein; *sport* in Führung gehen; angreifen; anfangen; *(Kartenspiel)* ausspielen, die Vorhand haben; *s* Führung, Leitung *f*; Beispiel *n*; Hinweis, Fingerzeig *m*; erste(r) Stelle *f od* Platz *m*; leitende Idee *f*, Leitbild *n*; *theat* tragende, Hauptrolle *f*; Hauptdarsteller *m*; *(Kartenspiel)* Vorhand *f*; *sport* Vorsprung *m*; *Am* einleitende, zs.fassende Worte *n pl (e-s Zeitungsartikels)*, *die* wichtigste(n) Meldungen *f pl*; *Am* (Erz-)Ader; (Hunde-)Leine *f*; *mar* Tau(führung *f*), Kabel *n*; Mühlgraben, Kanal *m*; Rinne *f (in e-m Eisfeld)*; *(Schießen)* Vorhalt *m*; *tech* Ganghöhe; *el* Leitung(sdraht *m*) *f*, Kabel *n*; *pl* Richtlinien *f pl*; *on the* ~ an der Leine; *to be in the* ~ e-n Vorsprung haben (*by* von); *to give s.o. a* ~ jdm mit gutem Beispiel vorangehen; jdn ermutigen; *to have the* ~ die Führung haben; den Ton angeben; *to take the* ~ die Führung übernehmen; *to* ~ *s.o. a (fine, pretty) dance, a chase, a dog's life* jdm (viel) zu schaffen machen; *to* ~ *by the nose* an der Nase herumführen; an der Kandare haben; *to* ~ *nowhere* zu nichts führen, keinen Sinn, Zweck haben; *to* ~ *the way* den Weg weisen *od* zeigen; voraus-, vorangehen; *fig* die ersten Schritte tun; *to* ~ **astray** *fig* auf Abwege, in die Irre führen; *to* ~ **off** *tr* beginnen, anfangen; *itr* den Anfang machen; *sport* anspielen; *to* ~ **on** weiterführen; vorantreiben; verlocken; täuschen; *to* ~ **out** beginnen, anfangen; zum Tanz führen; *to* ~ **up** *to* vorbereiten auf; hinführen, überleiten zu; lenken auf; hinauswollen auf; **~-in** *radio* Zuleitung(sdraht *m*) *f*; *radio* Einführung; Ansage *f*; *attr* Zuleitungs-; **~-off** Anfang, Beginn *m*; *sport* Anspielen *n*, Anstoß, Anschlag *m*; **~-out** *radio* Absage *f*; **~ story** *Am* (aktuelle) Spitzennachricht *f*, -artikel *m*; **~ time** *tech mil* Anlauf-, Entwicklungszeit *f*; **2.** [led] *s* Blei; Lot *n*; *typ* Durchschuß *m*; Blei(kugeln *f pl*); *(black* ~*)* Blei(mine *f*) *n*; Graphit *m*; *pl* Bleifassung *f (von Fensterscheiben)*; *(Dach)* Bleiplatten *f pl*; *a* Blei-; *tr* verbleien; plombieren; *(Töpferei)* glasieren; *(to* ~ *out) typ* durchschießen; *to cast, to heave the* ~ loten; *to have* ~ *in o.'s pants (Am fam)* e-e lange Leitung haben; *to swing the* ~ *(sl)* sich *(von der Arbeit)* drücken; *red* ~ Mennige *f*; *white* ~ Bleiweiß *n*; **~-accumulator** *el* Bleisammler *m*; **~ casing** Bleifassung *f*; **~-coat** *tr* verbleien; **~-coating, -plating** Verbleiung *f*; **~ cut-out** *el* Bleisicherung *f*; **~-doped petrol** Bleibenzin *n*; **~en** ['-n] bleiern; bleifarben; drükkend, schwül; *fig* schwerfällig; Blei-; **~ glance** Bleiglanz *m*; **~ing** ['-iŋ] Bleiüberzug *m*; Bleistreifen *m pl*, -platten *f pl*; **~-lining** Bleiauskleidung *f*; **~ monoxide** Bleiglätte *f*; **~-pencil** Bleistift *m*; **~ pipe** Bleirohr *n*; **~ plate** Bleiplatte *f*; **~-poisoning** Bleivergiftung *f*; **~-solder** Lötblei *n*.

leader ['li:də] (An-)Führer, Leiter *m*; Leitpferd *n*; Leitung(srohr *n*) *f*; *bot* Haupttrieb *m*; *anat* Sehne; *Am (Angel)* Leitschnur; *typ* Auspunktierung *f*; *(Zeitung)* Leit-, Hauptartikel; *tech* Vorlauf; *film* Vorspann; *mus* Dirigent; erste(r) Geiger, Chorführer; *com* Schlager, zugkräftigste(r) Artikel *m*; Suggestivfrage *f*; *industrial, labo(u)r, party* ~ Wirtschafts-, Arbeiter-, Parteiführer *m*; **~ette** [li:də'ret] kurze(r) Leitartikel *m*; **~ship** ['-ʃip] Führerschaft, Führung, Leitung *f*; Führereigenschaften *f pl*; **~-writer** Leitartikler *m*.

leading ['li:diŋ] *a* führend, leitend; Haupt-; *s* Führung, Leitung, Direktion *f*; *men of light and* ~ einsichtige und einflußreiche Männer *m pl*; **~ aircraft** Führungsflugzeug *n (e-s Verbandes)*; **~ aircraftman** Luftwaffenobergefreite(r) *m*; **~ article** Leit-, Hauptartikel; *com* Zugartikel *m*; **~ case** *jur* Präzedenzfall *m*; **~ dimensions** *pl* Hauptabmessungen *f pl*; **~ edge** *aero (Flügel, Luftschraubenblatt)* Vorderkante; *(Rotor)* Blattnase *f*; **~ element** Vorausabteilung *f*; **~ feature** Grundzug *m*, Hauptmerkmal *n*; **~ idea** Grundgedanke *m*; **~-in** (**wire**) *el* Leitungseinführung *f*; **~ man, lady** *theat* Hauptdarsteller(in *f*) *m*; **~ motive** Leitmotiv *n*; **~ principle** oberste(r) Grundsatz *m*; **~ question** Suggestivfrage *f*; **~-strings** *pl* Gängelband *n a. pl*; *to conduct in* ~~ am Gängelband führen; **~ vehicle** Spitzenfahrzeug *n*; **~ wheel** Vorderrad *n*.

leaf [li:f] *s pl leaves*; *bot* Blatt; Blumenblatt *n*; Blätter *n pl*; *(Buch)* Blatt; (Metall-)Blättchen *n*, Lamelle *f*; Blattmetall; (Feder-)Blatt *n*; Tischklappe *f*; Türflügel; *mil sl* Urlaub *m*; *tr Am (to* ~ *through)* durchblättern; *in* ~ im Laub; *to be in* ~ *(Bäume, Sträucher)* grün sein; *to come into* ~ *(bot)* ausschlagen; *to take a* ~ *out of s.o.'s book* jdm etw nachmachen, jds Beispiel folgen; *to turn over a new* ~ e-n neuen Anfang machen; *gold-*~ Blattgold *n*; *tobacco* ~ Tabakblätter *n pl*; **~age** ['-idʒ] Laub(werk) *n*; **~-bud** Blattknospe *f*; **~less** ['-lis] blattlos; **~let** ['-lit] Blättchen *n*; Drucksache *f*, Prospekt *m*, Broschüre *f*; Flug-, Merk-, Faltblatt *n*, Reklamezettel *m*; **~~ bomb** Flugblattbombe *f*; **~ mo(u)ld** Kompost *m*; **~ sight** Klappvisier *n*; **~-spring** *tech* Flach-, Blattfeder *f*; **~-table** Klapptisch *m*; **~y** ['-i] (dicht)belaubt; breitblättrig.

league [li:g] **1.** *s* Bund *m*, Bündnis *n*; Vereinigung, Union, *bes. sport* Liga *f*; *tr itr* (sich) verbünden; *in* ~ verbündet (*with* mit); *the L~ of Nations* der Völkerbund *m*; **~r** ['-ə] Verbündete(r), Bündnispartner *m*; **2.** Meile, Wegstunde *f (= 4,8 km)*.

leak [li:k] *itr* leck, undicht sein; *(Wasserhahn)* tropfen, laufen; *(to* ~ *in, out)* durchsickern *a. fig*; auslaufen; *fig* bekannt, *fam* publik, *lit* ruchbar werden; *s* Leck *n*, undichte Stelle *f*, Loch *n*; *el* Ableitung *f*; *to spring a* ~ ein Leck bekommen, undicht werden; **~age** ['-idʒ] Leck(sein) *n*; durchsikkernde Flüssigkeit; Leckage *f*, Gewichtsverlust *(bei Flüssigkeiten)*; *el* Isolationsfehler *m*; unerklärliche(s) Verschwinden *n (von Geld)*; Schwund *m*; *fig* Durchsickern, Bekanntwerden *n*; **~y** ['-i] leck, undicht; *fam (Mensch)* nicht dicht.

lean [li:n] **1.** *a. irr leant, leant* [lent] *itr* sich neigen; sich beugen, sich (an-)lehnen (*against* gegen, an; *on* auf); *fig* sich anlehnen (*on, upon* an); sich stützen (*on, upon* auf); neigen (*toward* zu); e-e Vorliebe haben (*to* für); *tr (to* ~ *over)* schrägstellen, (zur Seite) biegen; lehnen (*against* an); *s* Neigung, (*to* nach); Schrägstellung *f*; *to* ~ *over backward(s) (fig fam)* sich mächtig anstrengen; **~ing** ['-iŋ] *s* Neigung *f a. fig*; *fig* Hang *m* (*towards* zu); *a*: *the L~~ Tower of Pisa* der Schiefe Turm von Pisa; **~-to** *arch (~~ roof)* Pultdach *n*; Anbau *m (mit P.)*; **2.** *a* mager *(a. Fleisch)*; hager, dürr; **~ness** ['- nis] Magerkeit *a. fig*, Hagerkeit *f*.

leap [li:p] *a. irr leapt, leapt* [lept] *itr* springen, hüpfen; schnellen; sich stürzen (*at* auf); *tr* springen über; springen lassen; überspringen; *s* Sprung(weite *f*); *fig* Sprung, unvermittelte(r) Übergang *m*; *by* ~*s and bounds* mit Windeseile; in großen Sätzen; *fig* sprunghaft; *to* ~ *at an opportunity* e-e Gelegenheit (beim Schopf) ergreifen; *look before you* ~ erst wäg's, dann wag's; *a* ~ *in the dark (fig)* ein Sprung ins Ungewisse; **~-day** Schalttag *m (29. Februar)*; **~er** ['-ə] Springer *m*; **~-frog** *s* Bockspringen *n*; *itr mil* im überschlagenden Einsatz vorgehen; **~-year** Schaltjahr *n*.

learn [lə:n] *a. irr learnt, learnt* [-t] *tr* (er)lernen; erfahren, hören, *lit* vernehmen (*from* von); ersehen, entnehmen (*from* aus); *itr* lernen, erfahren (*of* von); *to* ~ *by heart* auswendig lernen; *to* ~ *to write* schreiben lernen; **~ed** ['-id] *a* (hoch)gebildet, gelehrt; fachkundig; wissenschaftlich; **~er** ['-ə] Lernende(r), Schüler, Anfänger; *mot* Fahrschüler *m*; **~ing** ['-iŋ] Lernen *n*; Bildung *f*, Wissen *n*, Gelehrsamkeit *f*; Fachwissen *n*, -kenntnisse *f pl*.

lease [li:s] *s* Pacht, Miete; Verpachtung, Vermietung *f* (*to* an); Pacht-, Mietverhältnis *n*; Pacht-, Mietvertrag *m*; Pacht-, Mietdauer, -zeit; Frist *f*; *tr (to* ~ *out)* verpachten, vermieten (*to* an); pachten, mieten; *on* ~, *by way of* ~ pacht-, mietweise; in Pacht *od* Miete; *to give, to let (out) on* ~ verpachten, in Pacht geben, vermieten; *to take on* ~, *to take a* ~ *of* in Pacht nehmen, pachten, mieten; *a new* ~ *of life* neue Hoffnungen, neue Lebenschancen *f pl*; **~hold** *s* Pacht(ung) *f*, Pachtvertrag *m*; Erbpacht *f*, -baurecht; Pachtgut, -grundstück *n*; *a* gepachtet; Pacht-; **~holder** Pächter; Erbpächter, -bauberechtigte(r) *m*; **leasing** ['-iŋ] Verpachtung, Vermietung; Pacht, Miete *f*.

leash [li:ʃ] *s* (Hunde-)Leine; Koppel *f*; *tr* an die Leine nehmen; *fig u. to hold in* ~ *(fig)* an der Kandare, an der Leine haben; *to keep on the* ~ an der Leine führen; *to strain at the* ~ *(fig)* an der Leine zerren; vor Ungeduld platzen.

least [li:st] *a* kleinst, geringst, wenigst; *adv* am wenigsten; *s der, die, das* Kleinste, Geringste; *das* wenigste, mindeste; *at (the)* ~ wenigstens, mindestens, zumindest; auf jeden Fall; *not in the* ~ nicht im geringsten *od* mindesten; durchaus nicht; ~ *of all* am allerwenigsten; *to say the* ~ *of it* milde ausgedrückt *od* gesagt; ohne zu übertreiben.

leather ['leðə] *s* Leder; Lederzeug; Streichleder *n*; (Leder-)Ball *m*; *pl* Lederhose *f*; Boxhandschuhe *m pl*; *fam* Fell *n (des Menschen)*; *a* Leder-; *tr* mit Leder überziehen; *fam* verdreschen; **~-bound** *a* ledergebunden; **~et(te)** [leðə'ret] Kunstleder *n*; **~ glove** Lederhandschuh *m*; **~-jacket** *zoo* Schweinsfisch *m*, Schnakenlarve; Lederjacke *f*; **~n** ['-n] ledern, lederig; **~neck** *Am fam* Marineinfanterist *m*; **~oid** ['-rɔid] Kunstleder *n*; **~y** ['-ri] ledern; zäh.

leave [li:v] **1.** *irr left, left* [left] *tr* (ver-, zurück-, übrig-, hinter)lassen; da-, liegen-, stehenlassen; im Stich lassen; überlassen, -geben, abgeben, aushändigen, anvertrauen; verlassen, herausgehen aus; *fig* überlassen, anheimstellen; *Am sl* lassen *mit inf*; *itr* fort-, weggehen, -fahren; abgehen, -fahren, -reisen (*for* nach); kündigen, gehen, (die Stelle, das Amt) aufgeben; austreten; abgehen (*school* von der Schule); *to be left* übrigbleiben; *to be left back (Schule)* sitzenbleiben; *to be left out in the cold* das Nachsehen haben; *to be, to get (nicely) left* reinfallen, 'reingelegt werden; *to be better left unsaid* besser ungesagt bleiben; *to ~ alone* in Ruhe, in Frieden, liegenlassen; sich nicht kümmern um; auf sich beruhen, bleiben lassen; *to ~ to chance* dem Zufall überlassen; *to ~ go* los-, fahrenlassen (*of s.th.* etw); *to ~ s.o. on the left* jdn links liegenlassen; *to ~ it at that* es dabei bewenden, sein Bewenden haben lassen; *to ~ lying about, (Am) around* herumliegen lassen; *to ~ much to be desired* viel zu wünschen übriglassen; *to ~ open, shut* auf-, offen, zu-, geschlossen lassen; *to ~ nothing undone* nichts unversucht lassen; *to ~ word* Bescheid hinterlassen; ausrichten lassen; *three minus one ~s two* drei weniger eins ist zwei; *~ it to me* überlassen Sie es mir; *where does that ~ me?* und was ist mit mir? *to be left till called for* postlagernd; *to ~* **about** herumliegen lassen; *to ~* **behind** zurück-, hinter sich lassen; hinterlassen, vermachen; *to ~* **off** aufhören; Schluß, ein Ende machen; *(Tätigkeit)* aufhören mit, beenden, aufgeben; *(Kleidungsstück)* ablegen; *to ~* **on** *(Mantel)* anbehalten; *to ~* **out** aus-, fort-, weg-, unterlassen; übersehen, überschlagen, -gehen; *to ~ s.o. out of the picture (fig)* jdn ausschalten; *to ~* **over** übriglassen; unentschieden lassen; **leavings** *pl* Überbleibsel *n pl*, Reste *m pl*; **2.** *s* Erlaubnis *f*; *bes. mil* Urlaub; Abschied *m*; *on ~* auf Urlaub; *to ask for ~* Urlaub einreichen, um U. nachsuchen; *to beg ~* um Erlaubnis bitten; *to go on ~* in Urlaub gehen, Urlaub nehmen; *to take o.'s ~* Abschied nehmen; aufbrechen, abreisen; *to take ~ of s.o.* sich von jdm verabschieden; *to take ~ of o.'s senses* den Verstand verlieren; *to take French ~* sich französisch empfehlen; *by, with your ~* Sie gestatten! *absent on ~* beurlaubt; *man on ~* Urlauber *m*; *~ of absence (mil)* Urlaub *m*; *~* **certificate** *Am, Br* **pass** Urlaubsschein *m*; **~-taking** Abschied *m (von jdm)*; **~-train** Urlauberzug *m*.

leaved [li:vd] *a in Zssgen* -blättrig; *(Tür)* mit ... Flügeln.

leaven ['levn] *s* Hefe *f*; Sauerteig *a. fig*; *fig* Gärungs-, Zersetzungsstoff *m*, schleichende(s) Gift *n*; zersetzende, umgestaltende Wirkung *f*; *tr* säuern; treiben; durchdringen (*with* mit); *fig* durch-, zersetzen (*with* mit); stark beeinflussen.

*

Leban|ese [lebə'ni:z] *a* libanesisch; *s* Libanese *m*, Libanesin *f*; **~on** ['lebənən] Libanon *m (Land)*; *~~ Mountains (pl)* Libanon *m (Gebirge)*.

lecher ['letʃə] Wüstling, Lüstling *m*; **~ous** ['-rəs] geil; wollüstig; **~y** ['-ri] Geilheit; Wollust; Unzucht *f*.

lect|ern ['lektə(:)n] *rel* Lesepult *n*; **~ure** ['lektʃə] *s (Univ.)* Vorlesung *f* (*on* über; *to* vor); *allg* Vortrag *m* (*on* über); Strafpredigt *f*; *itr (Univ.)* lesen, e-e Vorlesung halten (*on* über; *to s.o.* vor jdm); e-n Vortrag, Vorträge halten; *tr* e-e Strafpredigt halten (*s.o.* jdm); schulmeistern, abkanzeln (*s.o.* jdn); *to give, to read a ~* e-n Vortrag halten; *to s.o.* jdm e-e Strafpredigt halten; jdn abkanzeln; *to shirk, to cut a ~~* e-e Vorlesung schwänzen; *course of ~~s* Vortragsreihe *f*; *~~ room* Vortrags-, Hörsaal *m*; *~~ tour* Vortragsreise *f*; **~urer** ['-rə] *(engl. Hochkirche)* Hilfsprediger; Vortragende(r), Redner; *(Univ.)* Dozent *m*; **~ureship** ['lektʃəʃip] Hilfspredigeramt *n*; Dozentur *f*.

ledge [ledʒ] Leiste, vorspringende Kante *f*, Saum, Sims *m*; (Felsen-)Riff; *min* Lager *n*, Ader *f*.

ledger ['ledʒə] *com (general ~)* Hauptbuch *n*; *arch* Querbalken *m*; Grabplatte *f*; *(~ bait)* Köder *m* an e-r ruhenden Angel; *~* **clerk** Buchhalter *m*; *~* **folio** Buchfolio *n*; *~* **line** *mus* Hilfslinie *f*; *~* **sheet** Kontoblatt *n*.

lee [li:] *s* (Wind-)Schutz *m*; (wind)geschützte Stelle; *mar* Lee(seite) *f*; *aero* Windschatten *m*; *a* leeseitig, -wärtig; *~* **shore** Leeküste *f*; **~ward** ['-wəd] *a* leeseitig, -wärtig, unter dem Wind; *s* Leeseite *f*; *adv* leewärts; in Lee; *to drive to ~~* abtreiben; **~way** *mar aero* Abdrift *f*; *fig* Zurückbleiben *n*, Rückständigkeit *f*; *fig* Spielraum *m*, Bewegungs-, Aktionsfreiheit *f*; *to make ~~* abdriften; *fig* zurückbleiben; *to (have to) make up ~~ (Versäumtes)* auf(zu)holen (haben).

leech [li:tʃ] *s zoo* Blutegel; *fig* Blutsauger; *med* Schnäpper *m*; *tr* zur Ader lassen (*s.o.* jdm); *to stick like a ~ to s.o.* wie e-e Klette an jdm hängen.

leek [li:k] Lauch, Porree *m*.

leer [liə] **1.** *s* Seiten-, scheele(r) Blick *m*; *itr* lüstern, scheel blicken (*at* auf); schielen (*at* nach); **~y** ['-ri] *fam* im Bilde; gerissen, gerieben; mißtrauisch; **2.** *tech* Glasglühofen *m*.

lees [li:z] *pl* Bodensatz *m*, Hefe *f*; *to drink, to drain to the ~ (fig)* bis zur Neige leeren.

left [left] **1.** *a* link *a. pol*; *s* linke Seite *f*; *(Boxen)* (Schlag *m* mit der) Linke(n) *f*; *the (L)~ (pol)* die Linke; *adv* (nach) links; *on the ~* links, zur Linken; *to the ~* nach links; links (*of* von); **~-hand** *a* link; **~-handed** *a* linkshändig; linkisch, ungeschickt; unaufrichtig, zweifelhaft; *(Ehe)* morganatisch, linker Hand; *tech* linksgängig; gegen den Uhrzeigersinn; **~-hander** Linkshänder *m*; **~ist** ['-ist] *s pol* Anhänger *m* der Linken; *a pol* linksgerichtet, Links-; *~* **wing** *pol sport* linke(r) Flügel *m*; *~~ (a pol)* Links-; dem linken Flügel angehörend; **~y** ['-i] *Am fam* Linkshänder; linke(r) Handschuh; *pol* links Gerichtete(r) *m*. **2.** *pret u. pp von leave* 1.: *to get ~ (sl)* abgehängt werden *fig*; **~-luggage**: *~~ office (rail)* Gepäckaufbewahrung *f*; *~~ ticket* Gepäckschein *m*; **~-off** abgelegt; **~over** *s* Überrest *m*, -bleibsel *n pl*; *a* übrig(geblieben).

leg [leg] *s* Bein *n*; *(Küche)* Keule *f*, Schinken *m*; Strumpf-, Hosenbein *n*; (Stiefel-)Schaft *m*; Tisch-, Stuhlbein *n*; Stütze *f*; Schenkel *m a. math*; *bes. aero* Strecke, Etappe *f*; *itr fam*: *to ~ it* sich beeilen; *on o.'s (hum: hind) ~s* auf den Beinen; stehend; *to be all ~s (Mensch)* hoch aufgeschossen sein; *to be on o.'s last ~s (fam)* aus dem letzten Loch pfeifen; *to feel, to find o.'s ~s (Kind)* stehen, laufen können; *to give s.o. a ~ up* jdm hochhelfen *a. fig*; *fig* jdm unter die Arme greifen; *not to have a ~ to stand on* keine Ursache, keinen Grund, keine Ausrede haben; *to pull s.o.'s ~ (fam)* jdn zum besten haben; jdn aufziehen; frotzeln; *to run s.o. off his ~s* jdn nicht zur Besinnung kommen lassen; *to set s.o. on his ~s* jdn wieder auf die Beine bringen; *to shake a ~ (fam)* das Tanzbein schwingen; sich sputen; *to stand on o.'s own ~s* auf eigenen Füßen stehen; *to stretch o.'s ~s* sich die Beine vertreten, e-n kleinen Spaziergang machen; *to take to o.'s ~s* das Weite suchen; Fersengeld geben; *to walk s.o. off his ~s* jdn sich müde laufen lassen; **~-bail**: *to give ~~* Fersengeld geben; **~ged** [-d] *a in Zssgen.* -beinig: **~gings** ['-iŋz] *pl* (lange) Gamaschen *f pl*; **~-guard** *sport* Beinschiene *f*; **~gy** ['-i] langbeinig; **~less** ['-lis] *a* ohne Beine; **~-of-mutton** *a* keulenförmig, Keulen-; *~~ sleeve* Schinkenärmel *m*; **~-pull** *fam* Versuch *m*, jdn 'reinzulegen; **~-up** *fam* tatkräftige Unterstützung *f*; **~work** *fam* Lauferei *f*.

legacy ['legəsi] Vermächtnis *a. fig*, Legat; Erbe *n a. fig*, Erbschaft *f*; *to come into a ~* e-e Erbschaft machen; **~-hunter** Erbschleicher *m*; **~-hunting** Erbschleicherei *f*.

legal ['li:gəl] gesetzlich, gesetz-, rechtmäßig, legal; rechtlich, juristisch, Rechts-; *rel* Gesetzes-; Werk-; *to take ~ measures* den Rechtsweg beschreiten; *to take ~ steps against s.o.* gerichtlich gegen jdn vorgehen; *~* **act** Rechtshandlung *f*; *~* **advice** Rechtsberatung *f*; *~* **adviser** Rechtsberater, -beistand *m*; *~* **aid, assistance** Rechtshilfe *f*, -schutz *m*; *~* **basis** Rechtsgrundlage *f*; *~* **capacity** Geschäftsfähigkeit *f*; *~* **case** Rechtsfall *m*; *~* **charges, costs, fees** *pl* Gerichtskosten *pl*, Prozeßgebühren *f pl*; *~* **claim** Rechtsanspruch *m*; *~* **concept** Rechtsauffassung *f*; *~* **currency, coin, tender** gesetzliche(s) Zahlungsmittel *n*; *~* **decision** richterliche Entscheidung *f*, Richterspruch *m*, Gerichtsurteil *n*; *~* **department** Rechtsabteilung *f*; *~* **effect** Rechtswirksamkeit *f*; *~* **entity** juristische Person *f*; *~* **expert** Gerichtssachverständige(r) *m*; *~* **force** Gesetzeskraft; Rechtswirksamkeit *f*; *~* **holiday** gesetzliche(r) Feiertag *m*; *~* **incapacity** mangelnde Rechtsfähigkeit, Geschäftsunfähigkeit *f*; **~ity** [li(:)'gæliti] Gesetz-, Rechtmäßigkeit, Legalität *f*; **~ization** [li:gəlai'zeiʃən] gerichtliche Bestätigung, Beglaubigung, Legalisierung *f*; **~ize** ['li:gəlaiz] *tr* rechtskräftig machen, gerichtlich bestätigen, legalisieren, autorisieren, beglaubigen; *~* **language** Rechts-, Gerichtssprache *f*; *~* **maxim** Rechtsgrundsatz *m*; *~* **offence** Rechtsbruch *m*; *~* **opinion** Rechtsgutachten *n*; *~* **opponent** Prozeßgegner *m*; *~* **plea** Einrede *f*; *~* **procedure, proceedings** *pl* Gerichtsverfahren *n*, Prozeß, Rechtsstreit *m*; *to take, to institute, to initiate ~ proceedings against s.o.* gerichtlich gegen jdn vorgehen, e-n Prozeß gegen jdn anstrengen; *~* **protection** Rechtsschutz *m*; *~* **regulation, rule** Rechtsvorschrift, Gesetzesbestimmung *f*; *~* **relation** Rechtsverhältnis *n*; *~* **remedy** Rechtsmittel *n*; *~* **representative** gesetzliche(r) Vertreter *m*; *~* **status** rechtliche Stellung; Rechtsfähigkeit *f*; *~* **successor** Rechtsnachfolger *m*; *~* **title** Rechtsanspruch *m*; *~* **validity** Rechtsgültigkeit *f*; *~* **year** Kalenderjahr *n*.

legat|e ['legit] *s hist rel* Legat *m*; *tr* [li'geit] *(testamentarisch)* vermachen; **~ee** [legə'ti:] Vermächtnisnehmer, Legatar, Erbe *m*; **~ion** [li'geiʃən] Gesandtschaft, Legation *f*; **~or** [li'geitə] Erblasser *m*.

legend ['ledʒənd] Legende; Sage; *(Münze)* Aufschrift; Bilderklärung *f*,

-text *m*; **~ary** ['-əri] *a* legendär, sagenhaft; Sagen-; *s* Legendensammlung *f*.
legerdemain ['ledʒədə'mein] (Taschenspieler-)Kunststück *n*; Trick, Schwindel *m*.
Leghorn ['legho:n] Livorno *n*; *l*~ [le'gɔ:n] Leghorn *n (Hühnerrasse)*; ['--] Strohgeflecht *n*; (breitrandiger) Strohhut *m*.
legib|ility [ledʒi'biliti] Lesbarkeit; Leserlichkeit *f*; **~le** ['ledʒəbl] lesbar; leserlich, deutlich.
legion ['li:dʒən] Legion *f*; **~ary** ['-əri] *a* Legions-; *s* Legionär *m*.
legislat|e ['ledʒisleit] *itr* Gesetze erlassen; **~ion** [ledʒis'leiʃən] Gesetzgebung *f*; **~ive** ['ledʒisleitiv, -lət-] gesetzgebend; *~~ power* gesetzgebende Gewalt *f*; **~or** ['-ə] Gesetzgeber *m*; **~ure** ['-ʃə] gesetzgebende Körperschaft *od* Versammlung; Legislaturperiode *f*.
legitim|acy [li'dʒitiməsi] Gesetz-, Rechtmäßigkeit, Legitimität; Echtheit; Ehelichkeit, eheliche Geburt *f*; **~ate** [-mit] *a* recht-, gesetzmäßig, gesetzlich; legitim; ehelich; berechtigt, einwandfrei; *~~ portion* Pflichtteil *m* od *n*; *tr* [-eit] *u.* **~ize** [-maiz] *tr* legitimieren, für ehelich erklären; rechtfertigen; berechtigen, autorisieren; **~ation** [lidʒiti'meiʃən] Ehelicherklärung, Legitimierung; Legitimation *f*, Ausweis *m*; Berechtigung *f*.
legum|e ['legju:m] Hülse(nfrucht) *f*; *pl* Hülsenfrüchte *f pl*, Gemüse *n*; **~inous** [le'gju:minəs] *a* Hülsen-(frucht).
leister ['li:stə] Fisch-, *bes.* Lachsspeer *m*.
leisure ['leʒə, *Am* 'li:ʒə] *s (~ time)* Muße, freie Zeit, Freizeit *f* (*for* zu); *a* Muße-; frei; müßig, ohne ernsthafte Beschäftigung; *at ~* müßig, frei; in (aller) Ruhe, ohne Hast; *at o.'s ~* wenn man Zeit hat; wenn es einem paßt; *the ~(ed) class* die Wohlhabenden; **~d** ['-d] *a* müßig; gemächlich; *~* **hours** *pl* Mußestunden *f pl*; **~liness** ['-linis] Ruhe, Gemächlichkeit *f*; **~ly** ['-li] *a* gemächlich, ruhig; *adv* ohne Eile; in (aller) Ruhe.
Leman ['lemən]: *the Lake ~* der Genfer See.
lemme ['lemi] *fam (= let me)* laß mich!
lemon ['lemən] *s* Zitrone *f*; Zitronenbaum *m*, -gelb *n*; *sl* üble(r) Dreh *m*; *sl* häßliche(s) Entchen *n*, *fig* Niete *f*; *a* zitronengelb; Zitronen-; **~ade** [lemə'neid] Zitronenwasser *n*; *~* **drop** Zitronenbonbon *m*, *pl* -drops *pl*; *~* **juice** Zitronensaft *m*; **~-peel, -rind** Zitronenschale *f*; **~-squash** Sodawasser *n* mit Zitrone; **~-squeezer** Zitronenpresse *f*.
lend [lend] *irr lent, lent* [lent] *tr* (aus-, ver)leihen, borgen, *fam* pumpen (*at interest* auf Zinsen); zur Verfügung stellen, hergeben; gewähren; *(Eigenschaft)* geben, verleihen; beitragen (*to* zu); *itr* Geld verleihen; *to ~ o.s. to s.th.* sich zu etw hergeben, etw mitmachen; *to ~ itself to* sich eignen zu, für; *to ~ a (helping) hand* behilflich sein, mit Hand anlegen; **~er** ['-ə] Aus-, Verleiher *m*; *money-~~* Geldgeber *m*; **~ing** ['-iŋ] (Aus-, Ver-)Leihen; Darlehen *n*; *~~-library* Leihbibliothek, -bücherei *f*; **~-lease** Pacht-Leihe *f*.
length [leŋθ] Länge; Strecke; Dauer *f*; Stück *n (Stoff)*; *sport* (Pferde-, Boots-) Länge; *(Phonetik)* Länge *f*; *at ~* schließlich, endlich; ausführlich; ungekürzt; *at (full, great) ~* sehr ausführlich *adv*; *at full ~* in voller Länge, ganz ausgestreckt; *at some ~* in einiger Entfernung; *fig* ziemlich ausführlich; *by a ~ (sport)* um e-e Länge (*from* von); *full ~* der Länge nach; *three feet in ~* drei Fuß lang; *to go (to) all ~s* bis zum äußersten gehen; *to go any ~* vor nichts zurückschrecken; *for s.o.* alles für jdn tun; *to go (to) great ~s (fig)* sehr weit gehen; alles Erdenkliche tun; *to keep s.o. at arm's ~* Abstand zu jdm wahren; **~en** ['-ən] *tr* verlängern, längen; (aus)dehnen; *(Wein)* verdünnen; *itr* länger werden; *(to ~~ out)* sich (aus)dehnen; **~iness** ['-inis] Länge, Weitschweifigkeit, Langatmigkeit *f*; **~ways, ~wise** *a* langseitig; *adv* der Länge nach; **~y** ['-i] weitschweifig, langatmig, -weilig, -wierig; *Am fam (Mensch)* lang, groß.
len|ience, -cy ['li:njəns(i)], **~ity** ['leniti] Milde, Nachsicht *f*; **~ient** ['li:njənt] mild(e), sanft, gelind(e), nachsichtig (*towards* gegen); **~itive** ['lenitiv] *a u. s* mildernd(es), lindernd(es), schmerzstillend(es) (Mittel *n*).
lens [lens] *opt phot anat* Linse *f*; (Brillen-)Glas *n*; *anat* Kristallkörper *m*; *phot* Objektiv *n*; **~-cap, -cover** Objektivdeckel *m*; **~-hood, -shade, -screen** Sonnen-, Gegenlichtblende *f*; **~-mount** Linsen-, Objektivfassung *f*; **~-opening** Blende *f*; **~-shaped** *a* linsenförmig; *~* **system** Optik *f*.
Lent [lent] Fastenzeit *f*; **~en** ['-ən] *a* Fasten-; fleischlos; *~* **lily** Narzisse *f*.
lent|icular [len'tikjulə], **~iculated** [-leited], **~oid** ['lentɔid] *a* linsenförmig; *phys* bikonvex; **~il** ['lentil] *bot* Linse *f*.
leonine ['li(:)ənain] *a* Löwen-.
leopard ['lepəd] *zoo* Leopard *m*.
lep|er ['lepə] Aussätzige(r), Leprakranke(r) *m*; **~rosarium** [leprə'zæriəm] Leprakrankenhaus, -asyl *n*; **~rosy** ['leprəsi] Aussatz *m*, Lepra *f*; **~rous** ['leprəs] aussätzig, leprös.
lese-majesty ['li:z'mædʒisti] Majestätsbeleidigung *f*; Hochverrat *m*.
lesion ['li:ʒən] *med jur* Verletzung, Schädigung *f*.
less [les] *a* kleiner, geringer, weniger, minder; *adv* weniger, in geringerem Maße; *s* der, die, das Kleinere, Geringere, Wenigere; kleinere(r) Betrag *m*; *prp* abzüglich *gen*, weniger; *for ~* für weniger, billiger; *much ~* geschweige denn; *no ~*, *nothing ~* nicht weniger (*than* als); *no ~ than* ebensogut wie; kein Geringerer als; *none the ~* nichtsdestoweniger; **~en** ['lesn] *tr* vermindern, schmälern; herabsetzen, verkleinern; *itr* weniger werden, abnehmen, nachlassen; **~er** ['-ə] *nur attr* kleiner, geringer, unbedeutender; *the L~~ Bear (astr)* der Kleine Bär.
lessee [le'si:] Pächter; Mieter *m*.
lesson ['lesn] *(Schule, Lehrbuch)* Übung, Aufgabe, Lektion; Schularbeit; Lehr-, Unterrichtsstunde; Lehre *f*, Denkzettel *m*; *rel* Lektion *f*; *pl* Kurs(us); Unterricht *m*; Stunden *f pl*; *tr* unterrichten; e-n Verweis geben (*s.o.* jdm), tadeln; *to give s.o. a ~* jdm e-e Lehre erteilen; *to give ~s* Unterricht geben *od* erteilen; *to take ~s from s.o.* bei jdm Unterricht nehmen; *let this be a ~ to you* laß dir das e-e Lehre sein! *an English ~, a ~ in music* e-e Englisch-, e-e Musikstunde.
lessor [le'sɔ:] Vermieter; Verpächter *m*.
lest [lest] *conj* aus Furcht, daß; damit, daß nicht; im Fall, daß, falls; *(nach e-m Ausdruck des Fürchtens)* daß.
let [let] **1.** *irr let, let tr* lassen; *mit inf* zulassen, daß; erlauben, zu, daß; einweihen (*into a secret* in ein Geheimnis); vermieten, verpachten (*to* an); *itr* vermietet werden, zu mieten sein (*at, for* für); sich vermieten lassen; *s fam* Vermietung *f*; *to get a ~ (fam)* e-n Mieter finden (*for* für); *to ~ alone* in Ruhe, gewähren lassen; *fam* links liegenlassen; *~ alone* geschweige denn, gar nicht zu reden von; *to ~ be* in Ruhe lassen; *to ~ drive* losschlagen (*at* auf); *to ~ drop od fall* fallen lassen; *to ~ fly (tr)* werfen, feuern; schleudern; *fig* vom Stapel lassen; *itr* loswettern; *to ~ go* gehen lassen; los-, frei-, fortlassen; hingehen lassen; bleiben lassen; loslassen (*of s.th.* etw); loslegen; *to ~ o.s. go* sich gehen lassen; *to ~ have* geben; *to ~ know* wissen lassen, Bescheid geben; *to ~ loose* los-, freilassen; *to ~ pass* übersehen, nicht beachten; durchlassen; *to ~ things slide* die Dinge laufenlassen; *to ~ slip* loslassen; *(Gelegenheit)* sich entgehen lassen, verpassen; *~ bygones be bygones* lassen wir das Vergangene ruhen! *~ us go* wir wollen gehen; *~ me know it* laß es mich wissen! *to ~* **by** vorbeilassen; *to ~* **down** herunterlassen; im Stich lassen; enttäuschen; *(in der Arbeit)* nachlassen; *~~ easily, gently* nicht vor den Kopf stoßen (*s.o.* jdn); *to ~* **in** hinein-, hereinlassen; 'reinlegen; einweihen (*on* in), aufklären (*on* über); *to be ~~* reinfallen; *to ~ o.s. in* sich Eingang verschaffen; *for s.th.* sich etw einbrocken; *to ~* **into** einsetzen; *to ~* **off** *(Wasser, Dampf)* ablassen; *(Gewehr)* abdrücken, abfeuern; aus-, absteigen lassen, absetzen (*s.o.* jdn); davonkommen, entwischen lassen; *to ~* **on** *fam* so tun als ob; durchblicken lassen; *not to ~~* sich nichts (an)merken lassen; *to ~* **out** *tr* heraus-, hinauslassen; *(Flüssigkeit)* ablassen, auslaufen lassen; *(Kleidungsstück, Saum)* auslassen; ausplaudern, verraten; vermieten, verpachten; *(Arbeit)* vergeben; *fam* entlasten; *Am fam* hinauswerfen; entlassen; *itr Am fam (aus der Schule)* fliegen; herausgeworfen werden; *to ~ out at* losgehen auf; beschimpfen; *to ~* **up** *tr* hinauf-, herauflassen; *itr fam* nachlassen; aufhören; *Am* ablassen (*on* von); **~-alone principle** Laissez-faire *n*, Grundsatz *m* der freien Wirtschaft; **~-down** Nachlassen *n*, Verlangsamung; *fam* Enttäuschung *f*; Reinfall *m*; Demütigung *f*; **~-off** *tech* Ablassen *n*; *fam* Remmidemmi *n*; **~-up** Nachlassen *n*; Stillstand *m*, Unterbrechung, Pause *f*; **2.** *tr obs* hindern; *s* Hindernis *n*; *(Tennis)* Netzball *m*; *without ~ or hindrance* ohne Hindernis, ungehindert.
lethal ['li:θəl] tödlich; *~* **chamber** Todeszelle *f*.
letharg|ic(al) [le'θɑ:dʒik(əl)] schlafsüchtig; energielos, träge, schlaff; stumpf, dumpf, teilnahms-, interesselos; **~y** ['leθədʒi] Schlafsucht; Energielosigkeit; Stumpfheit, Teilnahms-, Interesselosigkeit *f*.
Lethe ['li:θi(:)] *(Mythologie)* Lethe; Vergessenheit *f*.
Lett [let] Lette *m*, Lettin *f*; (das) Lettisch(e); **~ic** ['-ik] *a* lettisch (u. litauisch); *s* (das) Lettisch(e); **~ish** ['-iʃ] *a* lettisch; *s* (das) Lettisch(e).
letter ['letə] *s* Buchstabe *m*; *typ* Letter, Type; Schrift(gattung) *f*; Brief *m*, Schreiben *n*, Zuschrift (*to* an); *pl* Urkunde *f*; *pl* Literatur *f*, Schrifttum *n*; (*bes.* Literatur-)Wissenschaft; Schriftstellerei *f*; *tr* mit Buchstaben versehen *od* (be)zeichnen; *(mit der Hand)* bedrucken; *itr (mit der Hand)* drucken

(*on* auf); *by* ~ brieflich; schriftlich; *to the* ~ wörtlich, buchstäblich, genau; *to post, (Am) to mail a* ~ e-n Brief aufgeben; *airgraph* ~ Radiogramm *n*; *airmail* ~ Luftpostbrief *m*; *business, commercial* ~ Geschäftsbrief *m*; *capital* ~ große(r) Anfangsbuchstabe *m*; *chain* ~ Kettenbrief *m*; *circular* ~ Rundschreiben *n*; *covering* ~ Begleitschreiben *n*, -brief *m*; *delivery of* ~*s* Briefzustellung *f*; *express* ~ Eilbrief *m*; *follow-up* ~ Mahnschreiben *n*; *German* ~ Fraktur *f*; *Italic* ~ Kursive *f*; *man of* ~*s* Literat, Schriftsteller *m*; *money* ~ Wertbrief *m*; *the profession of* ~*s* Schriftstellerberuf *m*; *rectifying* ~ Berichtigungsschreiben *n*; *registered* ~ eingeschriebene(r) Brief *m*; *Roman* ~ Antiqua *f*; *secrecy of* ~*s* Briefgeheimnis *n*; *small* ~ Kleinbuchstabe *m*; *spaced* ~*s (pl)* Sperrdruck *m*; *turned* ~ *(typ)* verkehrt stehende(r) Buchstabe *m*; *violation of the secrecy of* ~*s* Verletzung *f* des Briefgeheimnisses; ~ *of acknowledgement, of confirmation* Bestätigungsschreiben *n*; ~ *of apology* Entschuldigungsschreiben *n*; ~ *of application* Bewerbungsschreiben *n*; ~ *of attorney* Vollmacht *f*; ~ *of authority* Ermächtigungsschreiben *n*; ~ *of condolence* Beileidsbrief *m*; ~ *of congratulation* Glückwunschschreiben *n*; ~ *of consignment* Hinterlegungsschein; (~ *of conveyance)* Frachtbrief *m*; ~ *of credence* Beglaubigungsschreiben *n*; ~ *of credit* Kreditbrief *m*; *traveller's* ~~ Reisekreditbrief *m*; ~*s to the editor* Eingesandt *n*; ~ *of instruction* Weisung *f*; ~ *of introduction* Empfehlungsschreiben *n*; ~ *of mortgage* Hypothekenbrief *m*; ~ *of naturalization* Einbürgerungsurkunde *f*; ~ *of notification* amtliche Mitteilung *f*; ~ *of protection* Schutzbrief *m*; ~ *of recommendation* Empfehlungsschreiben *n*; ~ *of reminder* Mahnbrief *m*; ~ *of thanks* Dankschreiben *n*; **~-bag** Briefbeutel *m*; **~-balance** Briefwaage *f*; **~-binder, -file** Briefordner *m*; **~-book** Briefordner *m (für Kopien)*; **~-box** Briefkasten *m*; **~-card** Briefkarte *f*, Kartenbrief *m*; **~ carrier** *Am* Briefträger; *Br* Briefsortierer *m*; **~-case** Brieftasche *f*; *typ* Setzksten *m*; **~-chute** *Am* Briefeinwurf *m*; **~-cover** Briefumschlag *m*; **~-drop** *Am* Briefkastenschlitz *m*; **~ed** ['-d] *a* mit Buchstaben bezeichnet *od* versehen; des Schreibens u. Lesens kundig; belesen, (akademisch) gebildet, gelehrt; **~-founder** Schriftgießer *m*; **~gram** ['-græm] *Am* Brieftelegramm *n*; **~-head** Briefkopf *m*; **~ing** ['-riŋ] Beschriftung *f*; **~-mail** Briefpost *f*; **~-opener** Brieföffner *m*; **~-order** schriftliche(r) Befehl *m*; **~-pad** Briefblock *m*; **~-paper** Briefpapier *n*; **~-perfect** buchstabengetreu; *theat* sicher in s-r, ihrer Rolle; **~-postage** Briefporto *n*; **~press** *(Buch)* Gedruckte(s) *n*, Text; Satz; Hochdruck *m*; ~~ *printing* Typendruck *m*; **~-press** Vervielfältigungsapparat *m*; Kopierpresse *f*; **~s patent** Ernennungsurkunde *f*; Patent *n*; ~~ *of nobility* Adelsbrief *m*; **~-telegram** Brieftelegramm *n*; **~-weight** Briefbeschwerer *m*; **~-writer** Briefschreiber; Briefsteller *m (Buch)*.

lettuce ['letis] *bot* Lattich; Kopfsalat *m*; *sl* Lappen, (Geld-)Scheine *m pl*; *cabbage, (Am) head* ~ Kopfsalat *m*.

leuco- ['lju:ko(u)-, 'ljukə-] *in Zssgen* Leuko-, Weiß-; **~cyte** ['lju:kəsait] weiße(s) Blutkörperchen *n*; **~ma** [lju:'koumə] *med* weiße(r) Hornhautfleck *m*; **~rrh(o)ea** [lju:kə'riə] *med* Weißfluß *m*; **leuk(a)emia** [lju:'ki:miə] *med* Leukämie *f*.

Levant, *the* [li'vænt] die Levante, das östliche Mittelmeergebiet; **~ine** ['levəntain, li'v] Levantiner(in *f*) *m*.

levant [li'vænt] *itr Br (mit Schulden)* durchbrennen, ausreißen; **~er** [-ə] *Br* Ausreißer *m*.

levee ['levi] **1.** *Am s* Uferdamm, Kai *m*, Landestelle *f (an e-m Fluß)*; *tr (Fluß)* eindämmen, in Dämme fassen; **2.** Lever *n*; Empfang *m*.

level ['levl] **1.** *s* Ebene *a. fig*; gleiche Höhe; Kote, Höhenlinie *f*; Pegel *m*; (Meeres-)Höhe; Fläche *f*, Spiegel *m*; Niveau *n a. fig*, Stand *m*; Libelle, Wasserwaage *f*; *fig* Platz, Stand *m*, Stufe *f*; **2.** *a* eben, flach; waagerecht; gleich hoch; *(Löffelvoll)* gestrichen; *fig* von gleicher Bedeutung, von gleichem Rang; gleich weit (entwickelt), gleich(wertig); ruhig, vernünftig, ausgeglichen; **3.** *adv* auf gleicher Ebene *od* Höhe (*with* wie); **4.** *tr* planieren, ebnen, eben machen; *(to* ~ *off)* einebnen, nivellieren; gleichmachen, aufea. abstimmen; *aero* abfangen; sich einpendeln, sich normalisieren lassen; *(fig) to* ~ *down, to* ~ *up* angleichen, ea. anpassen; niederstrecken, um-, flachlegen; *(Gewehr)* anlegen, in Anschlag bringen (*at* auf); *fig (Anklage, Blick)* richten (*at, against* gegen); **5.** *on a* ~ *with* auf gleicher Höhe, *fig* Stufe mit, wie; *on the* ~ *(fam)* offen und ehrlich, gerade; *on a high, low* ~ auf hohem, niedrigem Niveau; *to be* ~ *with s.th.* so hoch sein wie etw; *to do o.'s* ~ *best* sein möglichstes tun; *to find o.'s* ~ den rechten Platz finden; *to have a* ~ *head* ausgeglichen sein; *to* ~ *with* od *to the ground* dem Erdboden gleichmachen; *he keeps a* ~ *head* er behält e-n klaren Kopf; **6.** *dead* ~ Gleichförmigkeit, Eintönigkeit *f*; *peak* ~ Höhepunkt *m*; Preisspitze *f*; *pre-war* ~ Vorkriegsstand *m*; *price* ~ Preisniveau *n*; *lowest price* ~ Preisspiegel *m*; *salary* ~ Gehaltsstufe *f*; *sea* ~ Meeresspiegel *m*; *subsistence* ~ Existenzminimum *n*; *wage* ~ Lohnniveau *n*; ~ *of employment* Beschäftigungsstand *m*; ~ *of living* Lebensstandard *m*; ~ *of performance* Leistungsniveau *n*; ~ *of production* Produktionsstand *m*; *to* ~ **down** erniedrigen; herabdrücken, herabsetzen; nach unten ausgleichen; *to* ~ **off** einebnen; planieren; *aero* abfangen; *to* ~ **up** erhöhen; nach oben ausgleichen; ~ **crossing** *Br* ebenerdige(r), schienengleiche(r) Bahnübergang *m*; **~-headed** *a (Mensch)* ausgeglichen; verständig; **~(l)er** ['-ə] Nivellierer; *fig* Gleichmacher *m*; **~(l)ing** ['-iŋ] *a* Nivellier-; *s* Planieren *n*; ~~ *screw* Stellschraube *f*; ~ **stress** *(Phonetik)* schwebende(r) Ton *m*.

lever ['li:və, *Am a.* 'levə] *s* Brechstange *f*, Hebebaum, Hebel *a. fig*; *(Uhr)* Anker *m*; *tr* mit e-r Brechstange heben *od* fortbewegen; als Hebel benutzen; *itr* e-n Hebel benutzen; **~age** ['-ridʒ] Hebelansatz *m*, -wirkung, -kraft, -übersetzung; *fig* Macht *f*, Einfluß *m*; **~-arm** Hebelarm *m*; **~-watch** Ankeruhr *f*.

leveret ['levərit] Häschen *n*; Junghase *m*.

lev|iable ['leviəbl] besteuerbar; pfändbar; **~y** ['levi] *s* Umlage, Erhebung, Abgabe; Steuer; *(~~ of execution)* Pfändung, Zwangsvollstreckung; *mil* Aushebung, Rekrutierung *f*; *a. pl* ausgehobene Truppen *f pl*; *tr (Steuer)* erheben, legen auf; *(Pfändung)* betreiben, vornehmen; *mil* ausheben, rekrutieren; *(Krieg)* beginnen (*on* gegen); *to* ~~ *blackmail* erpressen; *capital* ~~ Vermögensabgabe *f*.

leviathan [li'vaiəθən] Seeungeheuer *n*, Leviathan *m*; *allg* Monstrum *n*, Riese *m*.

levigate ['levigeit] *tr* glätten; zerreiben; verreiben, pulverisieren.

levitat|e ['leviteit] *itr* (frei) schweben; *tr* zum Schweben bringen; **~ion** [levi'teiʃən] Schweben *n*.

Levit|e ['li:vait] *rel* Levit *m*; **~icus** [li'vitikəs] 3. Buch *n* Mosis.

levity ['leviti] Leichtigkeit *bes. fig*; Beschwingtheit; Wendigkeit *f*; Leichtsinn *m*, Unbeständigkeit *f*.

lewd [lu:d, lju:d] unkeusch, unzüchtig, geil; liederlich; **~ness** ['-nis] Unkeuschheit, Lüsternheit *f*.

Lewis ['lu(:)is, 'lju:-] Ludwig *m*.

lexicograph|er [leksi'kɔgrəfə] Lexikograph *m*; **~y** [-i] Lexikographie *f*.

liab|ility [laiə'biliti] Verbindlichkeit, Haftbarkeit, Haftpflicht, Verpflichtung; Neigung *f* (*to* zu), Hang *m*, Empfänglichkeit *f* (*to* für); *pl* Verbindlichkeiten, Verpflichtungen; (Gesamtheit *f* der) Schulden *f pl*, Passiva *n pl*; *without* ~~ unverbindlich; *to contract, to undertake, to incur a* ~~ e-e Verpflichtung eingehen *od* übernehmen; *to discharge a* ~~ e-e Verpflichtung erfüllen, e-r V. nachkommen; *to fulfil(l), to meet o.'s* ~*ilities* s-e Verpflichtungen erfüllen, s-n V. nachkommen; *assets and* ~*ilities (pl)* Aktiva u. Passiva *pl*; Forderungen u. Verbindlichkeiten *f pl*; *joint* ~~ gemeinsame Verbindlichkeit *f*; *joint and several* ~~ Gesamthaftung, -schuld *f*; ~~ *to compensation, to pay damages* (Schadens-)Ersatzpflicht *f*; ~~ *for defects* Mängelhaftung *f*; ~~ *insurance* Haftpflichtversicherung *f*; ~~ *for maintenance* Unterhaltspflicht *f*; ~~ *for military service* Wehrpflicht *f*; **~le** ['laiəbl] verpflichtet (*for* zu); verantwortlich; haftpflichtig, haftbar (*for* für); ausgesetzt, unterworfen (*to s.th.* e-r S); neigend (*to* zu); *to be* ~~ *for* haften für; *to be* ~~ *to* verpflichtet sein zu, müssen; imstande sein, können; sich aussetzen *dat*; leiden an; *to do* leicht tun (können); *s.th.* empfänglich sein für; ~~ *to duty, service, tax* zoll-, dienst-, steuerpflichtig; ~~ *to prosecution, to punishment* unter Strafe gestellt; straffällig; ~~ *to recourse* regreßpflichtig.

liaise [li'eiz] *itr sl mil* Verbindung aufnehmen, in V. stehen (*with* mit); Verbindungsoffizier sein (*with* zu).

liaison [li(:)'eizən] *mil* Verbindung *f*; (Liebes-)Verhältnis *n*; *gram* Bindung *f*; *(Küche)* Binden, Dicken *n*; ~ **officer** Verbindungsoffizier *m*.

liana, -ne [li'ɑ:n(ə)] *bot* Liane *f*.

liar ['laiə] Lügner(in *f*) *m*.

Lias ['laiəs] *geol* Lias *m od f*.

libation [lai'beiʃən] Trankopfer *n hum* Zecherei *f*.

libel ['laibəl] *s* Schmähschrift; (öffentliche) Verleumdung; Beleidigung (*upon* gen); Klageschrift *f (wegen e-r Beleidigung)*; *tr* e-e Schmähschrift richten gegen; (öffentlich) verleumden; *fam* beleidigen, verunglimpfen; e-e (Privat-)Klage erheben gegen; *action for* ~ Verleumdungsklage *f*; **~(l)ant** ['-ənt] *jur* Kläger *m (in e-r Beleidigungsklage)*; **~(l)ee** [laibə'li:] Beklagte(r) *m (in e-r Beleidigungsklage)*; **~(l)ous** ['-bləs] Schmäh-; verleumderisch, beleidigend, ehrenrührig.

liberal ['libərəl] *a* freigebig, großzügig (*of* mit); frei(sinnig), aufgeschlossen, offen, duldsam, tolerant; freiheitlich, liberal, fortschrittlich; *s* Freisinnige(r), Liberale(r) *m*; *the* ~ **arts** *pl* die Geisteswissenschaften *f pl*; ~ **education** Unterricht *m* in den allgemeinbildenden Fächern; **~ism** ['-izm] Liberalismus *m*; **~ity** [libə'ræliti] Freigebigkeit, Großzügigkeit *f*; Freisinn *m*, Aufgeschlossenheit *f*; **~ization** [-ai-'zeiʃən] *com* Liberalisierung *f*; **~ize** ['-aiz] *tr com* liberalisieren; ~ **profession** freie(r) Beruf *m*.

liberat|e ['libəreit] *tr* freilassen, befreien (*from* von); *chem* frei machen; *Am sl mil* organisieren, klauen; **~ion** [libə'reiʃən] Befreiung, Freilassung *f*; *chem* Freimachen *n* (*from* aus); **~or** ['libəreitə] Befreier *m*.

Liberia [lai'biəriə] Liberia *n*; **~n** [-n] *a* liberisch; *s* Liberier(in *f*) *m*.

libert|arian [libə'tεəriən] *philos* Indeterminist *m*; **~ine** ['libə(:)tain, -ti(:)n] Wüstling *m*; **~inism, ~inage** ['libətinizm, -idʒ] Liederlichkeit, liederliche(s), wüste(s) Leben *n*.

liberty ['libəti] Freiheit; Erlaubnis *f*; *mar* Landurlaub *m*; *oft pl* (Vor-)Recht(e *pl*) *n*, Freiheiten *f pl*; *at* ~ frei; unbenützt; *to be at* ~ frei sein; nicht benützt werden; *to do* tun dürfen; freie Hand haben zu tun; *to set at* ~ freilassen; *to take the* ~ *of doing, to do* sich herausnehmen zu tun; *to take liberties* sich Freiheiten herausnehmen (*with s.o.* gegen jdn); *civil liberties (pl)* die bürgerlichen (Ehren-)Rechte *n pl*; ~ *of action* Handlungsfreiheit *f*; ~ *of conscience* Gewissensfreiheit *f*; ~ *of movement* Bewegungsfreiheit *f*; ~ *of the press* Pressefreiheit *f*; ~ *of speech* Redefreiheit *f*; ~ *of thought* Gedankenfreiheit *f*; ~ *of trade* Gewerbefreiheit *f*.

libid|inous [li'bidinəs] wollüstig, geil; unzüchtig, lasziv, obszön; **~o** [li'bi:dou] *scient* Geschlechtstrieb *m*.

librar|ian [lai'brεəriən] Bibliothekar(in *f*) *m*; **~y** ['laibrəri] Bibliothek, Bücherei *f*; *circulating, lending* ~~ Leihbücherei *f*; *the L~~ of Congress* die Kongreßbibliothek *(in Washington)*; *public, free* ~~ Volksbücherei *f*; *reference* ~~ Präsenzbibliothek *f*; ~~ *edition (Buch)* Vorzugsausgabe *f*.

librett|ist [li'bretist] *mus* Librettist *m*; **~o** [li'bretou] *pl -os mus* Text(buch *n*) *m*.

licen|ce, -se ['laisəns] *s* Erlaubnis, Bewilligung, Genehmigung, Lizenz, Konzession *f*, Gewerbeschein; Erlaubnisschein *m*; Freiheit; Zügellosigkeit *f*; *tr (meist: ~se)* erlauben, gestatten, bewilligen, genehmigen, zulassen, ermächtigen; e-e Lizenz, e-e Konzession erteilen (*s.o.* jdm), konzessionieren, privilegieren; *theat* zensieren; *under* ~~ *from* mit Erlaubnis, Genehmigung *gen*; *to cancel, to revoke, to withdraw a* ~~ e-e Lizenz zurückziehen; *to give, to grant a* ~~ e-e Lizenz, e-e Konzession erteilen; *to take out a* ~~ sich e-e Lizenz, Konzession erteilen lassen; *requiring a* ~~, *subject to a* ~~ genehmigungs-, konzessionspflichtig; *shooting-*~~ Jagdschein *m*; *special* ~~ Sondergenehmigung *f*; *trading-*~~ Handelserlaubnis; Gewerbekonzession *f*; Gewerbeschein *m*; *wireless-*~~ Rundfunkgenehmigung *f*; ~~ *fee* Lizenzgebühr *f*; ~~ *number (mot)* Zulassungsnummer *f*; ~~ *plate (mot)* Nummernschild *n*; **~sed** ['-t] *a* konzessioniert; privilegiert, zugelassen; *fully* ~~ mit voller Konzession *od* Schankerlaubnis; ~~ *victualler* Inhaber *m* e-r Schankkonzession; **~see** [laisən'si:] Lizenznehmer, Konzessionsinhaber *m*; **~ser** ['-ə] Lizenz-, Konzessionsgeber; *theat* Zensor *m*; **~sing** ['-iŋ] Lizenz-, Konzessionserteilung *f*.

licenciate [lai'senʃiit] Lizentiat *m*.

licentious [lai'senʃəs] zügellos, liederlich; unanständig, obszön; **~ness** [-nis] Zügellosigkeit, Liederlichkeit; Unanständigkeit *f*.

lich [litʃ] *Scot dial* Leiche *f*; **~-gate** (überdachtes) Friedhofstor *n*; **~-house** Leichenhalle *f*.

lichen ['laikən] *bot med* Flechte *f*; **~ous** ['-inəs] *bot* mit Flechten bewachsen; *med* lichenös.

lick [lik] *tr* (auf-, ab-, be)lecken; *fam* verdreschen, vermöbeln; *fam (Menschen)* fertigmachen, erledigen, überwinden, schlagen; *itr (Flamme)* tanzen, züngeln; *sl* rasen, eilen; *s* Lecken *n*; *ein* bißchen; Schuß, Spritzer *m*; *(salt-~)* Salzlecke *f*; *fam* deftige(r) Schlag; *fam* Anfall *m* von Arbeitswut; *fam* Eiltempo *n*; *mus (Jazz)* eingeschobene Improvisation *f*; *oft pl fam* Chance *f*; *to* ~ *up, to* ~ *off* ab-, blanklecken; *at full* ~ *(sl)* mit Höchstgeschwindigkeit; *to* ~ *the dust* ins Gras beißen, sterben; *to* ~ *o.'s lips (fig)* sich die Lippen lecken; *to* ~ *into shape (fam)* auf Hochglanz, auf Fasson, in Form bringen; *to* ~ *s.o.'s shoes (fig)* vor jdm kriechen; *that* ~*s creation (fam)* das setzt allem die Krone auf, das haut dem Faß den Boden aus; *a* ~ *and a promise* e-e Katzenwäsche; **~er** ['-ə] Leckende(r); *sl* Schläger; *tech* (Tropf-)Öler *m*; ~~*-in (tech)* Vorreißer *m*; **~ing** ['-iŋ] (Ab-)Lecken *n*; Niederlage; *fam* Dresche *f*; **~spit(tle)** ['-spit(l)] Speichellecker *m*.

lickety-split ['likəti 'split] *adv Am sl* mit affenartiger Geschwindigkeit.

licorice *s. liquorice.*

lid [lid] Deckel *m*, Klappe *f*; (Augen-)Lid *n*; *sl* Deckel, Hut *m*; *Am fam* Beschränkung *f*; *with the* ~ *off* unverhüllt, ohne Beschönigung; *to put the* ~ *on (fam)* aufräumen, Schluß machen mit; *that puts the* ~ *on! (fam)* das schlägt dem Faß den Boden aus, das setzt der Sache die Krone auf.

lido ['li:dou] Freibad *n*.

lie [lai] **1.** *irr lay, lain itr* liegen *(a. Schiff, Truppen, geog u. fig)*; *(Straße)* führen, verlaufen; (begraben) liegen, ruhen; schlafen (*with s.o.* mit jdm); obliegen (*on s.o.* jdm); *fig* beruhen (*in* auf); bestehen (*in* in); sich verhalten; *jur* zulässig sein; *mar* vor Anker liegen; *s* Lage *f*; *(Tier)* Lager *n*; *to* ~ *in ambush* auf der Lauer liegen; *to* ~ *at anchor* vor Anker liegen; *to* ~ *in bed* im Bett liegen; *to* ~ *on the bed one has made* die Folgen tragen, die Sache ausbaden; *to* ~ *under the charge of* unter der Anklage stehen *gen*; *to* ~ *heavy on s.o.'s conscience* jds Gewissen belasten; *to* ~ *doggo (sl)* (ganz) still(da-)liegen, sich nicht mucksen; *to* ~ *in the dust, in ruins* in Trümmern liegen; *to* ~ *at s.o.'s feet* vor jds Füßen, jdm zu Füßen liegen; *to* ~ *idle* müßig sein, nichts tun; stilliegen, nicht gebraucht, nicht benützt werden; *to* ~ *low* am Boden, darniederliegen; *fam* keinen Ton sagen, sich nicht mucksen; *sl* nichts verlauten lassen; *to* ~ *open to s.th.* e-r S ausgesetzt sein; *to* ~ *in s.o.'s power* in jds Macht liegen; *to* ~ *heavy on s.o.'s stomach* jdm schwer im Magen liegen; *to* ~ *under the suspicion* unter dem Verdacht stehen; *as far as in me* ~*s* was in meinen Kräften steht; *how the land* ~*s* wie die Dinge liegen, wie die Sache steht; *the blame* ~*s at your door* das ist deine Schuld; *life still* ~*s in front of you* das Leben liegt noch vor dir; *let sleeping dogs* ~*!* rühr nicht an die Sache! laß das auf sich beruhen! *to* ~ **back** sich zurücklehnen; *to* ~ **by** nicht benutzt werden, brachliegen; sich zurückhalten; rasten; *to* ~ **down** sich hinlegen; ~~ *under* widerspruchslos hinnehmen; *to* ~~ *on the job (Am fam)* sich kein Bein ausreißen, e-e ruhige Kugel schieben; *to* ~ **in** im Wochenbett liegen; *to* ~ **off** *mar* in einiger Entfernung liegen; Pause machen; *to* ~ **over** überfällig, aufgeschoben sein; *to let* ~~ aufschieben, liegenlassen; *to* ~ **to** *mar* beiliegen; *s.th.* alle Kraft an etw setzen; *to* ~ **under** unterstehen; ~~ *an obligation* e-e Verpflichtung haben; *to* ~ **up** sich zurückziehen, sich zur Ruhe begeben (haben); das Zimmer hüten (müssen); **~-abed** Langschläfer *m*; **~-down** Ruhe *f*; **~-in** Bettruhe *f* bis tief in den Morgen hinein; **2.** *itr* lügen; e-n falschen Eindruck erwecken, täuschen; *to* ~ *o.s. out of* sich herauslügen aus; *to* ~ *to s.o.* jdn anlügen; *s* Lüge, Unwahrheit *f*; *to act a* ~ *to s.o.* jdm etw vormachen, falsche Vorstellungen in jdm erwecken; *to give s.o. the* ~ jdn Lügen strafen; *to give s.th. the* ~ etw widerlegen, als falsch nachweisen; behaupten, daß etw falsch ist; *to tell a* ~ lügen; *to* ~ *in o.'s throat, to* ~ *like truth* das Blaue vom Himmel, wie gedruckt lügen; lügen, daß sich die Balken biegen; *white* ~ Notlüge *f*; **~-detector** Lügendetektor *m*.

lief [li:f] *adv*: *I would, had as* ~ ich würde ebenso gern.

liege [li:dʒ] *a attr* Lehns-; *s (~ lord)* Lehnsherr; *(~man)* Lehnsmann *m*.

lien [li(:)ən] Pfandrecht *n* (*on* an); *under a* ~ auf Grund e-s Pfandrechts.

lieu [lju:]: *in* ~ *of* anstatt, an Stelle *gen*.

lieutenan|cy [lef'tenənsi, *in der brit. Marine*: le't-, *Am*: lu:'t-] Leutnantsrang *m*, -stelle; Statthalterschaft *f*; *die* Leutnante; **~t** [-t] *Am* Oberleutnant; *mar Br* Kapitänleutnant *m*; *first* ~~ *(Br)* Oberleutnant *m*; *flight* ~~ *(aero Br)* Hauptmann *m*; *second* ~~ *(Br)* Leutnant *m*; ~~*-colonel* Oberstleutnant *m*; ~~*-commander* Korvettenkapitän *m*; ~~*-general* Generalleutnant *m*; ~~ *governor (US)* stellvertretende(r) Gouverneur *m*; ~~ *junior grade (Am)* Oberleutnant zur See; ~~ *R.N. (Br)* Kapitänleutnant *m*; ~~ *senior grade (Am)* Kapitänleutnant *m*.

life [laif] *pl lives* [laivz] Leben *n*; Lebenszeit *f*; Menschenleben *n*; Lebensgeschichte, -beschreibung, Biographie; Lebensweise, -führung; Lebensdauer *f a. tech*; Dasein *n*; Schwung *m*, Lebenskraft; Seele *f*, Inbegriff *m*, Wesen *n*; *jur* Geltungsdauer *f*; *as large* od *big as* ~ in Lebensgröße; *fam hum* in Person; wie er *usw* leibt u. lebt; *at great sacrifice of* ~ unter hohen Verlusten an Menschenleben; *during* ~ zu Lebzeiten; *for* ~ auf Lebenszeit, fürs (ganze) Leben; lebenslänglich; *for dear* ~ um sein Leben *(laufen)*; *not for the* ~ *of me* beim besten Willen nicht; *from the* ~ *(Kunst)* nach dem Leben; nach der Natur; *in* ~ lebend; im Leben; *early, late in* ~ früh, spät; *late in* ~ in vorgerücktem Alter; *in the prime of o.'s* ~ im besten Alter; *not on your* ~ *(fam)* auf keinen Fall; *to the* ~ lebenswahr, -echt *adv*; *with all the pleasure in* ~ mit dem größten Vergnügen; *to bring to* ~ ins Leben rufen; beleben, *fam* Schwung bringen in; *to bring back to* ~ wieder zum Bewußtsein bringen; *to come to* ~ ins Leben treten; in

Schwung kommen; wieder zu sich kommen; *to have nine lives* ein zähes Leben haben; *to seek s.o.'s ~* jdm nach dem Leben trachten; *to take s.o.'s, o.'s own ~* jdm, sich das Leben nehmen; *he has the time of his ~* es geht ihm gut; *community, social ~* Gemeinschaftsleben *n*; *concept of ~* Lebensauffassung *f*; *conditions (pl) of ~* Lebensbedingungen *f pl*; *conjugal, marriage ~* Eheleben *n*; *danger of ~* Lebensgefahr *f*; *(mean) duration of ~* (mittlere) Lebensdauer *f*; *economic ~* Nutzungsdauer *f*; *eternal ~* das ewige Leben; *expectation of ~* Lebenserwartung *f*; *experience in ~* Lebenserfahrung *f*; *family ~* Familienleben *n*; *manner, mode of ~* Lebensart *f*, -stil *m*; *married ~* Ehestand *m*; *a matter of ~ and death* e-e lebenswichtige Frage; *military ~* Soldatenleben *n*; *professional ~* Berufsleben *n*; *standard of ~* Lebensstandard *m*; *station in ~* soziale Stellung *f*; *struggle for ~* Kampf *m* ums Dasein, Existenzkampf *m*; *true to ~* lebenswahr; **~-annuity** Leibrente *f*; **~-belt** Rettungsgürtel *m*; **~-blood** *poet* Herzblut *n*; *fig* Kraftquell *m*; **~-boat** Rettungsboot *n*; **~-buoy** Rettungsboje *f*; **~-company** Lebensversicherungsgesellschaft *f*; **~-ex-pectancy** Lebenserwartung *f*; **~-giving** lebenspendend; kraftspendend, belebend, anregend; **~-guard** Leibwache *f*; Rettungsschwimmer *m*; **~hold** Nießbrauch *m*; **~-insurance, -assurance** Lebensversicherung *f*; **~-interest** lebenslängliche(r) Nießbrauch *m*; **~-jacket** Schwimmweste *f*; **~less** ['-lis] leblos; unbelebt; *fig* matt, flau, trüb(e); **~lessness** ['-lisnis] Leblosigkeit; Unbelebtheit, Mattheit; *com* Flaute *f*; **~like** lebenswahr; **~-line** *mar* Rettungsleine; Lebenslinie *(in der Hand)*; lebenswichtige Versorgungs-, Verbindungslinie *f*; **~long** *a* lebenslänglich, auf Lebenszeit; *he was a ~~ defender of liberty* er hat zeitlebens, zeit s-s Lebens die Freiheit verteidigt; **~-net** *(Feuerwehr)* Sprungtuch *n*; **~-pension** lebenslängliche Rente *f*; **~-preserver** Rettungsring, Schwimmgürtel *m*, -weste *f*; Totschläger *m (Stock)*; **~r** ['-ə] *sl* Lebenslängliche(r) *m*; **~-saver** Lebensretter; Rettungsschwimmer *m*; *he is my ~~ (fam)* ich kann ohne ihn nicht leben; **~-saving** *s* Lebensrettung *f*; *a* Lebensrettungs-; *~~ apparatus* Tauchretter *m*; **~-sentence** Verurteilung *f* zu lebenslänglicher Haft; **~-size(d)** *a* lebensgroß, in Lebensgröße; **~-stock** lebende(s) Inventar *n*; **~-strings** *pl fig* Lebensfaden *m*; **~-subscription** einmalige(r) Beitrag *m*; **~-table** Sterblichkeitstabelle *f*; **~time** Lebenszeit *f*; *in, during s.o.'s ~~* zu jds Lebzeiten; **~-work** Lebenswerk *n*.

lift [lift] *tr* (auf-, er-, hoch-, in die Höhe) heben; hoch-, in die Höhe halten; *fig* befördern, erhöhen *(a. Preis)*; heben, auf e-e höhere Stufe stellen *od* bringen; weiterbringen; die Laune heben (*s.o.* jdm), froher stimmen; Mut machen, Lebenskraft geben (*s.o.* jdm); *(Gesicht)* straffen; *(junge Pflanzen)* ziehen; *(Kartoffeln)* ernten, roden; *(Lager)* abbrechen; *mil (Sperrfeuer)* vorverlegen; *min* fördern; *Am (Beschlagnahmung, Sperre)* aufheben; *fam* abschreiben, plagiieren; *sl* klauen, stibitzen, mausen, mopsen, *mil* organisieren; *(Zoll)* erhöhen, hinaufschrauben; *itr* sich erheben, steigen; *aero* aufsteigen; *(Nebel, Wolken)* sich auflösen, sich heben, steigen; *s* Hochheben; (Auf-)Steigen *n*; Auftrieb *a. aero*; *tech* Hub; Hebebaum; Aufzug, Fahrstuhl *m*; *fig* Hebung *f*, Auftrieb *m*; Hilfe *f*, Beistand *m*; Mitnahme *f (im Auto)*; *to give s.o. a ~* jdn mitnehmen, mitfahren lassen; jdm e-n Gefallen tun, jdm helfen; *fam* jdn aufmöbeln; *not to ~ a finger* keinen Finger rühren; *to ~ o.'s hand* die Hand (zum Schwur) erheben; *against s.o.* die Hand gegen jdn erheben; *to ~ up a cry, o.'s voice* aufschreien; *to ~ up o.'s eyes* die Augen aufschlagen; *to ~ up o.'s head (fig)* sich wieder erheben, wieder hochkommen; *to ~ up o.'s horn* von oben herabsehen, hochnäsig sein; ehrgeizig sein; *passenger ~* Personenaufzug *m*; **~boy, ~man** Fahrstuhlführer *m*; **~er** ['-ə] *tech* Stößel, Stempel, Nocken, Hebedaumen; *typ* Aufleger; *sport* (Gewicht-)Heber; *sl* Langfinger, Dieb *m*; *aero* Auftriebskraft *f*; **~ing** ['-iŋ] *s* Heben *n*; *a* Hebe-, Aufzug-, Förder-; *aero* Auftrieb(s)-; *~~-jack* Hebebock *m*, -winde *f*; Wagenheber *m*; *~~-stage* Hebebühne *f*; **~-up seat** Klappsitz *m*.

lig|ament ['ligəmənt] *anat* Band *n*; **~ature** ['ligətʃuə] *s* Binden; Band *n*; *med* Bindung; *typ mus* Ligatur *f*; *tr* (ab-, ver)binden.

light [lait] **1.** *s* Licht *n a. fig*; Beleuchtung, Helligkeit; Lichtquelle *f*, -schein; Tag(eslicht *n*) *m*; *aero* Positionslicht *n*; *(flood-~)* Scheinwerfer *m*; Feuer(zeug), Streichholz; Feuer *n (im Blick)*; Gesichtssinn *m*, *poet* Augenlicht; *fig* Licht, Wissen *n*, Kenntnis *f*; Licht *n*, Beleuchtung *f*, Aspekt *m*; Hinsicht *f*, Gesichtspunkt *m*; *pl* Geistesgaben, Fähigkeiten *f pl*; *pl* Erkenntnisse *f pl*, Einsicht *f*; *pl sl* Augen *n pl*; *(Kunst)* Licht *n*; *a* licht, hell, leuchtend; hell(häutig, -haarig), blond; *in Zssgen* hell-; *tr a. irr lit, lit* [lit] *(Feuer, Licht)* anzünden, -machen; *(Licht)* anstecken; *(mit Scheinwerfern)* anstrahlen; be-, erleuchten; *(Flugplatz)* befeuern; leuchten (*s.o.* jdm); aufheitern; erhellen, beleben; *to ~ up (tr)* auf-, erhellen; aufheitern; *fam (Zigarette)* sich anstecken; *itr* aufleuchten, -strahlen, sich erheitern; *according to his ~s* s-n Fähigkeiten entsprechend; nach bester Einsicht; *by the ~ of nature* aus eigener Vernunft; *in the ~ of* im Licht *gen*, angesichts *gen*, im Hinblick auf; *in a favo(u)rable ~* in günstigem Licht; *in a good ~* deutlich (sichtbar); *to bring to ~* an den Tag, ans Licht bringen; *to come to ~* an den Tag kommen; *to put a ~ to s.th.* etw anzünden; *to put in a false ~* in ein falsches Licht stellen; *to see the ~ (of day)* das Licht (der Welt) erblicken; bekannt werden; verstehen, begreifen; *to shed, to throw (a) ~ on (fig)* ein Licht werfen auf; *to stand in s.o.'s ~* jdm im Licht, *fig* im Wege stehen; *to stand in o.'s own ~* sich selbst im Licht stehen; *fig* sich selbst schaden; *to strike a ~* Feuer anzünden *od* machen; *may I trouble you for a ~?* darf ich Sie um Feuer bitten? *that throws a different ~ on the matter* die Sache bekommt dadurch ein anderes Gesicht; *green ~* grüne(s) Licht; freie Fahrt; *fig* freie Hand; *~ and shade (fig)* Licht u. Schatten; **~-ball** Leuchtkugel *f*; **~-bath** Lichtbad *n*; **~ beacon** Leuchtfeuer *n*, -bake *f*; **~ beam** Lichtstrahl *f*; **~-cartridge** Leuchtpatrone *f*; **~ cone** Lichtkegel *m*; **~-dynamo** Lichtmaschine *f*; **~en** ['-n] *tr* erleuchten, erhellen; *fig* aufhellen, aufklären; *(to ~~ out, forth)* blitzen lassen; *itr* sich erhellen, aufleuchten; glänzen, strahlen; blitzen; **~er** ['-ə] Anzünder *m*; (Taschen-) Feuerzeug *n*; **~-fitting** Beleuchtungskörper *m*; **~house** Leuchtturm *m*; *~~ keeper* Leuchtturmwärter *m*; **~ing** ['-iŋ] *s* Anzünden *n*; Beleuchtung; *aero* Befeuerung *f*; *emergency ~~* Notbeleuchtung *f*; *~~-circuit* Lichtleitung *f*; *~~-equipment, installation, -plant* Lichtanlage *f*; *~~-fixture* Beleuchtungskörper *m*; *~~ gas* Leuchtgas *n*; *~~-line* Lichtnetz *n*; *~~-point(el)* Brennstelle *f*; *~~ up (mot)* Aufblenden *n*; **~-intensity** Lichtstärke *f*; **~less** ['-lis] lichtlos; **~-lock, -trap** Lichtschleuse *f*; **~meter** Photometer *n*, Lichtmesser *m*; **~ness** ['-nis] Helligkeit *f*; **~ quantum** *phys* Photon *n*; **~ ray** Lichtstrahl *m*; **~-resisting** lichtecht; **~ screen** Lichtschirm *m*; **~-sensitive** lichtempfindlich; **~ sheaf** Lichtgarbe *f*; **~ship** Feuerschiff *n*; **~-signal** Lichtsignal *n*; **~ source** Lichtquelle *f*; **~some** ['-səm] leuchtend; hell; **~ switch** Lichtschalter *m*; **~ velocity** Lichtgeschwindigkeit *f*; **~ wave** Lichtwelle *f*; **~-wood** *Am* Kienholz *n*; **~-year** Lichtjahr *n*; **2.** *a* leicht; (spezifisch) leicht; zu leicht; geringfügig, schwach; fein, zart; sanft; flink; seicht, oberflächlich; unbedeutend; leicht(lebig, -sinnig); sorglos; flatterhaft; unterhaltsam; leicht (-verdaulich); *(Erde)* locker; *(Wein)* leicht, schwach; unbeschwert; (leicht-) bewaffnet; nicht beladen; *(Phonetik)* unbetont; *adv* leicht; *s pl* Lunge *f (von Tieren)*; *itr obs (aus der Luft)* herabkommen, -stoßen; sich niederlassen, sich setzen (*on* auf); fallen, stoßen (*on* auf); *fig* (zufällig) stoßen (*on* auf); *Am sl* herfallen (*into* über); fertigmachen, herunterputzen (*into s.o.* jdn); *to ~ out (Am sl)* ausreißen, -kneifen, türmen, abhauen; *to make ~ of* nicht ernst, auf die leichte Schulter nehmen; *~ in the head* schwindlig; simpel, doof, dumm; **~ alloy, metal** Leichtmetall *n*; **~-armed** *a* leichtbewaffnet; **~ athletics** *pl mit sing* Leichtathletik *f*; **~ car** Kleinwagen *m*; **~ comedian** Komiker *m*; **~ comedy** Unterhaltungsstück *n*; Schwank *m*; **~ current** Schwachstrom *m*; **~en** ['-n] *tr* leichter machen; entlasten, erleichtern; *fig* aufheitern; *mar* löschen, leichtern; **~ engineering** Feinmechanik *f*; **~er** ['-ə] *s mar* Leichter *m*; *tr itr (Güter)* auf e-m Leichter befördern; **~erage** ['-əridʒ] Be-, Ausladen *n*; Leichterkosten *pl*; **~-fingered** *a* langfingerig, diebisch; *allg* fingerfertig; **~-footed** *a* leichtfüßig, behende; **~-handed** *a* geschickt, behutsam; unbeschwert; **~-headed** *a* schwindlig, benommen, wirr (im Kopf); gedankenlos, vergeßlich; **~-hearted** *a* sorglos, unbeschwert, heiter, fröhlich; **~ heavy-weight** *(Boxen)* Halbschwergewicht (-ler *m*) *n*; **~-heeled** *a* = *~-footed*; **~ horse** leichte Kavallerie *f*; **~ literature** Unterhaltungsliteratur *f*; **~ly** ['-li] *adv* leicht; sacht, sanft; gewandt, flink; froh; gleichgültig, uninteressiert; unvernünftig, unbesonnen; liederlich, schamlos; *~~ come, ~~ gone* wie gewonnen, so zerronnen; **~ metal** Leichtmetall *n*; **~-minded** *a* flüchtig, gedankenlos, leichtsinnig; **~mindedness** Gedankenlosigkeit *f*, Leichtsinn *m*; **~ music** leichte, Unterhaltungsmusik *f*; **~ness** ['-nis] Leichtheit, Leichtigkeit Zartheit, Sanftheit; Heiterkeit *f*, Frohsinn; Leichtsinn *m*, Leichtfertigkeit, Gedankenlosigkeit; Beweglichkeit, Gewandtheit *f*; ~ **oil** Leichtöl *n*; ~**-o'-love** leichte(s) Mädchen *n*; ~ **opera** Operette *f*; ~**some** ['-səm] behende, anmutig, lebhaft; unbeschwert, heiter, fröhlich; leichtfertig; ~**weight** *s (Boxen)* Leichtgewicht(ler *m*) *n*; *Am fam* Niete *f*; *a* leicht *(im Gewicht)*; Leichtgewichts-.

lightning ['laitniŋ] Blitz *m*; *like* ~, *as quick as* ~, *with* ~ *speed* wie der Blitz, blitzschnell; *like greased* ~ *(fam)* wie ein geölter Blitz, wie geschmiert; *ball, globular* ~ Kugelblitz *m*; *heet, summer* ~ Wetterleuchten *n*; *sheet* ~ Flächenblitz *m*; *struck by* ~ vom Blitz getroffen; ~**-arrester, -discharger** *radio* Blitzschutz *m*, -sicherung *f*; ~ **artist** Schnellzeichner *m*; ~**-bug** *Am* Glühwürmchen *n*, Leuchtkäfer *m*; ~**-conductor, -rod** Blitzableiter *m*; ~**-discharge** Blitzschlag *m*; ~ **strike** Blitzstreik *m*.

lign|eous ['ligniəs] holzig; hölzern; ~**ify** ['-fai] *tr itr* holzig machen, werden; ~**ite** ['-ait] Braunkohle *f*; Lignit *m*; ~~ *deposit* Braunkohlenlager *n*; ~**itic** [lig'nitik] *a* Braunkohlen-.

lik|able ['laikəbl] liebenswert, gefällig, angenehm; ~**e** [laik] *tr* gern haben, (gern) mögen, lieben; gern ... (*doing, to do s.th.* etw tun); gern essen *od* trinken; *itr* wollen; *I* ~ es gefällt, paßt, beliebt mir; *s*: ~~*s and dislikes (pl)* Zu- u. Abneigungen *f pl*; *as you* ~ wie Sie wollen; ~**ing** ['-iŋ] Gefallen *n* (*for* an); Zuneigung, Vorliebe *f*, Geschmack *m*; *to s.o.'s* ~~ nach jds Geschmack; *to have, to take a* ~~ *for* Geschmack, Gefallen haben, finden an.

like [laik] *a* gleich, ähnlich; *adv* wie, gleichsam, gewissermaßen; *fam (~ enough)* wahrscheinlich; *conj fam* wie; als ob; *s* Gleiche(r) *m*; *the ~ of him* seinesgleichen; *something* ~ so ungefähr, so gegen, so etwa; ~ *mad* wie verrückt *adv*, wie ein Verrückter; ~ *that* so, auf diese Weise; *they are very ~ each other* sie sehen sich sehr ähnlich; *they are as ~ as two peas* sie sehen sich ähnlich wie ein Ei dem andern; *it is just ~ him* das sieht ihm ähnlich; *there is nothing* ~ es geht nichts über; *I don't feel ~ work(ing) to-day* ich bin heute nicht zum Arbeiten aufgelegt, ich habe heute keine Lust zur Arbeit; *the rain looks ~ lasting* es sieht so aus, als wolle es sich einregnen; *it looks ~ snow* es sieht nach Schnee aus; es sieht aus, als ob es schneien wolle; *he is ~ to come* er wird wohl, sicher kommen; es sieht so aus, als ob er kommen würde; *what is he ~?* wie ist er? wie sieht er aus? ~ *father ~ son (prov)* der Apfel fällt nicht weit vom Stamm; ~ *master ~ man (prov)* wie der Herr, so's Gescherr; *people ~ that* solche Leute; *such* ~ dergleichen, so (et)was; *the ~s of you (fam)* Leute wie Sie, ihresgleichen; *and the* ~ und was dergleichen mehr ist, usw.; ~**lihood** ['-lihud] Wahrscheinlichkeit *f*; *in all* ~~ aller Voraussicht nach, höchstwahrscheinlich; ~**liness** ['-linis] = ~*lihood*; ~**ly** ['-li] *a* wahrscheinlich; glaubwürdig; aussichtsreich, (viel)versprechend; passend, geeignet; *adv* wahrscheinlich; *as ~~ as not* nicht unwahrscheinlich; *not* ~~ schwerlich, kaum; *very, most* ~~ höchst-, sehr wahrscheinlich; *to be ~~ to do* wahrscheinlich tun; *that's more* ~~ das ist eher möglich; ~**-minded** *a* gleichgesinnt; ~**n** ['laikən] *tr* vergleichen (*to* mit); ~**ness** ['-nis] Ähnlichkeit *f*; Aussehen *n*, Gestalt *f*; (Ab-)Bild *n*; *in the ~~ of* in Gestalt *gen*; *to have o.'s ~~ taken* sich photographieren, sich malen lassen; ~**wise** *adv conj* ebenso; gleicherweise, ebenfalls, auch.

lilac ['lailək] *s* Spanische(r) Flieder (-strauch) *m*; Lila *n*; *a* fliederfarben, lila.

lilt [lilt] *tr itr* trällern; klimpern; *s* lustige(s) Lied *n*, beschwingte(r) Melodie *f od* Rhythmus *m*.

lily ['lili] Lilie *f*; *water* ~ Wasserlilie *f*; ~ *of the valley* Maiglöckchen *n*; ~**-livered** *a* hasenfüßig, feige.

limb [lim] **1.** (Körper-)Glied *n*; Ast; *(Gebirge)* Ausläufer *m*; (Mit-)Glied *n*, Angehörige(r) *m*; Glied *n*, Teil *m*; *fam* Range *f*, Racker *m*, ungezogene(s) Balg *n*; *pl* Gliedmaßen *pl*; *Am sl* (Frauen-)Beine *n pl*; *a ~ of the law* das Auge des Gesetzes; *out on a ~ (Am fam)* gefährdet, in einer prekären Lage; *to escape with life and* ~ mit e-m blauen Auge davonkommen; ~**ed** [-d] *a in Zssgen* -gliedrig; **2.** Blütenrand; *astr* Rand; Teilkreis *m (e-s Quadranten)*.

limber ['limbə] **1.** *a* biegsam; geschmeidig, gelenkig; *tr* geschmeidig machen; *itr (to ~ up)* geschmeidig werden; **2.** *s mil* Protze *f*; *tr itr (to ~ up)* aufprotzen.

limbo ['limbou] *pl -os* Vorhölle *f*; Gefängnis *n*; Gefangenschaft; Rumpelkammer; Vernachlässigung, Vergessenheit *f*; *to cast into ~ (fig)* zum alten Eisen tun *od* werfen.

lime [laim] **1.** *s (burnt, caustic ~)* (gebrannter) Kalk *(meist: bird-~)* Vogelleim *m*; *tr* mit Kalk düngen; mit (Vogel-)Leim bestreichen; *(Vögel)* mit Leim fangen; *med* mit Kalkwasser waschen; (ver)zementieren *(bes. fig)*; *fig* umgarnen; *quick-~* ungelöschte(r) Kalk *m*; *slaked* ~ gelöschte(r) Kalk *m*; ~**-burner** Kalkbrenner *m*; ~**-cast** *arch* Kalkbewurf, (Ver-)Putz *m*; ~ **deposit** Kalkablagerung *f*; ~ **dust** Kalkstaub *m*; ~**-kiln** Kalkofen *m*; ~**light** *s* Kalklicht; *theat u. fig* Rampen-, Scheinwerferlicht *n*; *the ~~ (fig)* das Licht der Öffentlichkeit; *tr (mit e-m Scheinwerfer)* anstrahlen; *in the* ~~ im Mittelpunkt des öffentlichen Interesses; *to bring into the ~~ (fig)* ins Licht rücken, ans Licht der Öffentlichkeit bringen; *to disappear from the ~~ (fig)* von der Bildfläche verschwinden; ~**-milk** Kalkmilch *f*; ~**-pit** Kalkgrube *f*; ~**-rod, -twig** Leimrute *f*; ~**stone** Kalkstein, ungebrannte(r) Kalk *m*; ~**-wash** *s* (Kalk-)Tünche *f*; *tr* kalken, weißen, tünchen; ~**-water** *med* Kalkwasser *n*, -lösung *f*; **2.** *s* Zitronelle *f*; Zitronellen-, Limonellenbaum *m*; *a* Zitronellen-; ~**-juice** Zitronensaft *m*; ~**-juicer** *Am sl mar* brit. Matrose *m*; **3.** *(~-tree)* Linde(nbaum *m*) *f*.

limerick ['limərik] fünfzeilige(s) Scherzgedicht *n* ohne Sinn.

lim(e)y ['laimi] *Am sl mar s. lime-juicer*; Tommy *m*.

limit ['limit] *s* Grenze, Schranke *f*; Endpunkt *m*; Höchstgrenze, -zahl *f*; *math* Grenzwert *m*; *com* Limit *n*, Preisgrenze *f*, Höchstpreis *m*; Gültigkeitsdauer *f*; *tech* zulässige(r) Spielraum *m*; *pl* Schranken *f pl*; *tr* begrenzen, be-, einschränken (*to* auf); *(Preis)* limitieren; *within ~s* in Grenzen; *without* ~ beliebig, unbegrenzt, unbeschränkt; *to exceed the* ~ die Grenze überschreiten; *to go to the ~ (Am fam)* bis zum Äußersten gehen; *to set a ~ to* e-e Grenze setzen *dat*; *that's the ~ (fam)* das ist doch die Höhe! da hört doch alles auf! *off ~s! (Am)* Zutritt verboten! (*to* für); *there is a ~ to everything* es hat alles seine Grenzen; ~**ation** [limi'teiʃən] Begrenzung; Be-, Einschränkung; *jur* Verjährung *f*; *to know o.'s ~~s* s-e Grenzen kennen; ~~ *of armaments* Rüstungsbeschränkung *f*; ~~ *of liability* Haftungsbeschränkung *f*; ~ **case** Grenzfall *m*; ~**ed** ['-id] *a* begrenzt; beschränkt (*to* auf); *com* limitiert; *(Markt)* begrenzt aufnahmefähig; *s Am* Schnellzug, -bus *m (mit Platzkarten)*; *in a ~~ sense* in gewissem Sinne; ~~ *liability company (Ltd)* Gesellschaft *f* mit beschränkter Haftung (GmbH); ~~ *monarchy* konstitutionelle Monarchie *f*; ~~ *partnership* Kommanditgesellschaft *f*; ~**less** [-lis] grenzenlos, weit (-räumig), unendlich.

limn [lim] *tr poet* malen; zeichnen; *fig* beschreiben; ~**er** ['-nə] Maler *m*.

limousine ['limu(:)zi:n] *mot* Limousine *f*.

limp [limp] **1.** *itr* hinken; *s* Hinken *n*; *to walk with a* ~ hinken, humpeln; **2.** schlaff, weich; *fig* schwach, haltlos; ~**ness** Schlaffheit *f*.

limpet ['limpit] *zoo* Napfschnecke; *fig fam* Klette *f*; ~ **mine** *mar* Haftmine *f*.

limpid ['limpid] hell, klar, durchsichtig, ungetrübt; ~**ity** [lim'piditi], ~**ness** ['limpidnis] Klarheit, Durchsichtigkeit *f*.

limy ['laimi] kalkig; Kalk-; mit (Vogel-)Leim bestrichen; klebrig.

linage ['lainidʒ] Absteckung; Zeilenzahl *f*; Zeilenhonorar *n*.

linchpin ['lin(t)ʃpin] Splint *m*, Lünse *f*, Achsnagel; *fig* lebenswichtige(r) Teil *m*.

linden ['lindən] *(~-tree)* Linde(nbaum *m*) *f*.

line [lain] **1.** *s* Leine; (Angel-)Schnur *f*; Zügel; Telephon-, Telegraphendraht *m*, -leitung, -linie; Leitung(sdraht *m*, -rohr *n*); Linie *f a. sport*, Strich *m*; *mus* Notenlinie *f*; Riß *m*; Handlinie; Falte, Runzel, Furche; Grenzlinie, Grenze; Demarkationslinie; Verkehrs-, Eisenbahn-, Straßenbahn-, Bus-, Dampferlinie; Bahn-, Flugstrecke; Fahrbahn *f*; Schienenstrang *m*, Gleis *n*; (Menschen-)Schlange; Reihe; Bauflucht, Häuserzeile; Zeile *f*; Vers *m*; kurze Nachricht *f*, Brief *m*; Aufea.folge; Ahnenreihe *f*; Zweig *m* (der Familie), Familie *f*, Geschlecht *n*; Richtung *f*, Verlauf, Weg; (Gedanken-)Gang *m*; Vorgehen *n*, Handlungsweise; Beschäftigung *f*, Beruf *m*, Fach; Geschäft(szweig *m*) *n*, Branche *f*; (Fach-, Interessen-)Gebiet *n*, Fachrichtung *f*; *com* Artikel *m*, Ware *f*, Posten *m*; Kollektion; Marke; Linie *f (Längenmaß = $^1/_{12}$ Zoll od 2,1 mm)*; *geog* Meridian, Breitenkreis; *L~* Äquator *m*; *mil* Linie; Front *f*; *meist pl* Zügel *m pl*; *pl* Zeilen *f pl*, (kurzes) Schreiben *n*; Linienführung *f*, Konturen *f pl*; *(Schule)* Strafarbeit *f*; *theat* (Text *m* e-r) Rolle *f*; (Trau-)Schein; Entwurf, Plan *m*; Richtlinien *f pl*, Grundsätze *m pl*; Geschick, Schicksal, Los *n*; *tr* lin(i)ieren, mit Linien versehen; zeichnen; *(to ~ up)* in Linie aufstellen *od* anordnen; *fig* auf Linie bringen; *(e-n Weg mit Bäumen)* säumen; *itr (to ~ up)* antreten; sich aufstellen; e-e Reihe, Spalier bilden; grenzen (*with* an); *all along the* ~ auf der ganzen Linie; *in* ~ in Reih und Glied; in Linie; *fig* in Einklang; bereit; *in ~ of duty (mil)* im Dienst; *on a ~ with* auf gleicher Ebene wie; *on this* ~ auf diese Weise; *out of* ~ nicht ausgerichtet; nicht in Einklang; in Unordnung; *to bring into ~ (Menschen)* auf Linie bringen; zum Mitmachen bewegen; *to come into ~, to fall in ~* sich anschließen, sich einfügen (*with* in); *fam* mitmachen (*with* mit); *fam* nicht aus der Reihe tanzen; *to draw the ~ (fig)* e-e Grenze ziehen (*at* bei); *to draw up in ~* antreten lassen; *to drop s.o. a ~* jdm kurz, ein paar Zeilen schreiben; *to form a ~* sich in e-r Reihe aufstellen; *to get a ~ on s.th. (fam)* etw herausklamüsern, -finden; *to get off the ~* entgleisen; *to give s.o. a ~ on* jdm Mitteilung machen über; *to go down the ~ (fam)* auf den Bummel gehen; *to have a smooth ~* schöne Worte machen; *to hit the ~ (Fußball)* versuchen durchzustoßen; *fig* aufs Ganze gehen; *to hold the ~* die Stellung halten *a. fig*; *tele* am Apparat bleiben; *to keep in ~* in Reih und Glied, *fam* bei der Stange bleiben; im Zaum halten; *to read between the ~s* zwischen den Zeilen lesen; *to stand in ~* sich anstellen, anstehen, Schlange stehen (*for* um); *to take, to keep to o.'s ~* (s-e) eigene(n) Wege gehen; *to take a strong ~* entschlossen vorgehen; *to toe the ~* bei der Stange bleiben; *that's not in my ~* das schlägt nicht in mein Fach; *~ engaged! (Am) ~ busy! (tele)* besetzt! *bus ~* Buslinie *f*; *catch ~* Schlagzeile *f*; *date ~* Datumsgrenze *f*; *demarcation ~* Demarkationslinie *f*; *direction of the ~* Linienführung *f*; *feeder ~* Zubringerlinie *f*; *hard ~s (pl fam)* Pech *n*; *life ~* lebenswichtige Verbindung *f*; *local ~* Nebenlinie *f*; *main ~* Hauptverkehrslinie *f*; *tele* Hauptanschluß *m*; *marriage ~s (pl)* Trauschein *m*; *party ~ (pol)* Programm *n*; gemeinsame(r) Anschluß *m*; *shipping ~* Schiffahrtslinie *f*; *steamship ~* Dampferlinie; Dampfschiffahrtsgesellschaft *f*; *telegraph, telephone ~* Telegraphen-, Telephonverbindung *f*; *tram(way) ~* Straßenbahnlinie *f*; *trunk ~* Hauptverkehrslinie; *tele* direkte Fernverbindung *f*; *~ of action* Handlungsweise *f*, Vorgehen *n*; *tech* Angriffslinie *f*; *~ of administration* Verwaltungszweig *m*; *~ of approach* Anflugschneise *f*; *~ of argument* Beweisführung *f*; *~ of battle* Schlachtreihe *f*; *~ of buildings* Häuserreihe *f*; *~ of business* Geschäftszweig *m*; *~ of communication (mil)* Verbindungslinie *f*; *~~'s area* Etappe *f*; *~ of conduct* Verhalten *n*, Lebensführung, -weise *f*; *~ of fire* Schußlinie *f*; *~ of force (phys)* Kraftlinie *f*; *~ of industry* Industriezweig *m*; *~ of march* Marschroute *f*; *~ of policy* politische Richtung *od* Linie *f*; *~ of production* Produktionszweig *m*; *main ~ of resistance (mil)* Hauptkampflinie *f* (HKL); *~ of sight (mil)* Visier-, Ziellinie *f*; *~ of thought* Gedankengang *m*, Denkweise *f*; *to ~* **in** einzeichnen; *to ~* **off** abgrenzen; *to ~* **out** skizzieren, entwerfen, planen; *to ~* **through** aus-, durchstreichen; *to ~* **up** *tr mil* aufstellen; *tech* ausrichten, abgleichen; *itr mil* antreten; sich aufstellen; *Am* an-, Schlange stehen; Stellung beziehen (*against* gegen); sich zs.tun (*with* mit); *to be ~d up* anstehen (*in front of* vor); *~* **abreast** *mar* Dwarslinie *f*; **~-assembly work** Fließarbeit *f*; *~* **astern** *mar* Kiellinie *f*; *~* **chart** Linienschaubild *n*; *~* **current** Netzstrom *m*; *~* **finder** Vorwähler *m*; *~* **graph** Liniendiagramm *n*; **~-keeper** Bahnwärter *m*; **~man** ['-mən] Telephon-, Telegraphen(bau)-arbeiter; *rail* Streckenwärter *m*; **~-shooter** *sl* Angeber, Großkotz, Prahlhans *m*; **~sman** ['-zmən] Frontsoldat; Telephon-, Telegraphenarbeiter; *rail* Streckenwärter; *sport* Linienrichter *m*; **~-up** Linie, Reihe, Aufstellung *f a. sport*; Tip *m*; *tele* Netz *n*; *fig* Schlange *f*; **2.** *tr (Kleidungsstück)* füttern; das Futter bilden (*s.th.* e-r S); *tech* auskleiden, -füttern, -mauern; *to ~ o.'s purse, pocket* Geld einstecken.

line|age ['liniidʒ] **1.** Abstammung *f*; Vorfahren *m pl*, Geschlecht *n*, Stamm *m*; **2.** = *linage*; **~al** ['liniəl] *a (Nachkomme)* in direkter Linie; erblich; = *~ar*; **~ament** ['liniəmənt] Gesichts-, *fig* Charakterzug *m*; **~ar** ['liniə] *a* Linien-; Strich-; linear; *~~ measure* Längenmaß *n*.

linen ['linin] *s* Leinwand *f*, Leinen, Linnen; Leinengarn, -zeug *n*; Wäsche *f*; *(~ paper)* gute(s) Schreib-, Briefpapier *n*; *a* leinen, linnen; *to wash o.'s dirty ~ at home, in public (fig)* s-e schmutzige Wäsche daheim *od* zu Hause, in der Öffentlichkeit waschen; *bed-~* Bettwäsche *f*; *table-~* Tischwäsche *f*; **~-bag** Wäschesack *m*; **~-draper** *Br* Weißwarenhändler, Inhaber *m* e-s Wäschegeschäftes; **~-goods** *pl* Weißwaren *f pl*, Wäsche *f*; **~-press, closet** Wäscheschrank *m*; **~-weaver** Leinweber *m*.

liner ['lainə] **1.** *mar* Personen-, Passagierdampfer *m*; *(air-~)* Verkehrsflugzeug *n*, -maschine *f*; *(penny-a-~)* Zeilenschinder *m*; **2.** Ausfütterer; Einsatz *m*, Ausfütterung *f*; *mil* Einstecklauf *m*.

ling [liŋ] **1.** Leng(fisch) *m*; *Am* (Aal-) Quappe *f*; Seehecht *m*; **2.** Heide (-kraut *n*) *f*.

linger ['liŋgə] *itr* zögern; sich nicht trennen, sich nicht losreißen können; *(to ~ about)* sich (noch) herumdrücken an, bei; *(to ~ on)* sich lange halten; sich hinschleppen; zurückbleiben; lange bleiben, verweilen (*on, upon, over* an, bei); sich sehnen (*after* nach); *to ~ away* vertrödeln, verbummeln; *to ~ out* hin-, in die Länge ziehen; **~ing** ['-riŋ] *a* schleppend; langsam, langwierig; widerwillig, abweisend; *(Krankheit)* schleichend; nachwirkend; *(Ton)* nachklingend; *(Blick)* sehnsüchtig.

lingerie ['lɛ̃:nʒəri:, 'lænʒ-] Damenunterwäsche *f*.

lingo ['liŋgou] *pl -oes hum pej* Jargon *m*, Kauderwelsch *n*.

lingu|al ['liŋgwəl] *a* Zungen- *(a. Phonetik)*; *s* Zungenlaut *m*; **~ist** ['-gwist] Sprachkundige(r); Sprachwissenschaftler *m*; **~istic** [liŋ'gwistik] *a* sprachlich; sprachwissenschaftlich; *s pl mit sing* Sprachwissenschaft *f*.

liniment ['linimənt] Liniment, Mittel *n* zum Einreiben.

lining ['lainiŋ] Ausfütterung *f*; Futter *n*; Auskleidung *f*; (Brems-)Belag; *fig* Inhalt *m*; *every cloud has a silver ~ (prov)* auf Regen folgt Sonnenschein; *a silver ~ on the horizon* ein Silberstreifen am Horizont.

link [liŋk] **1.** *s* (Ketten-)Glied *n*; Ring *m*; Lasche *f*, Verbindungsstück *n*; *(cuff-, sleeve-~)* Manschettenknopf *m*; Schlinge *f*; *fig* (Binde-)Glied, Band *n*, Verbindung; Kettenlänge *f (= 7,92 Zoll* od *20,12 cm)*; *tr (to ~ together)* (als Kettenglied) verbinden; anschließen (*to* an); *itr (to ~ up)* verbunden sein; sich anschließen (*to, with* an); *to ~ o.'s arm in, through s.o.'s arm* jdn einhaken; **~age** ['-idʒ] Verbindung(ssystem *n*); *tech* Kupplung *f*; Gestänge *n*; **2.** (Pech-) Fackel *f*; **~boy, ~man** ['-mən] Fackelträger *m*.

links [liŋks] *pl Scot* sandige(s) Gelände *n*, Dünen *f pl*; Golfplatz *m*.

linnet ['linit] *orn* Hänfling *m*.

lino ['lainou] **1.** = *linoleum*; **2.** = *linotype*; **~cut** Linolschnitt *m*.

linoleum [li'nouljəm] Linoleum *n*.

linotype ['laino(u)taip] Linotype *f*.

linseed ['linsi:d] Leinsamen *m*; **~-cake** Lein-, Ölkuchen *m*; **~-oil** Leinöl *n*.

linsey(-woolsey) ['linzi'wulzi] Halbwolle(ntuch *n*) *f*; billige(s) Zeug *n*.

lint [lint] Scharpie; Baumwollfaser *f*.

lintel ['lintl] *arch* Sturz *m*, Oberschwelle *f*.

lion ['laiən] Löwe; *fig* Herkules; Draufgänger; Held *m* des Tages, Prominenz *f*; *L~ (astr)* Löwe *m*; *pl* Sehenswürdigkeiten *f pl*; *to go into the ~'s den* sich in die Höhle des Löwen wagen; **~ess** ['-is] Löwin *f*; **~et** ['-it] junge(r) Löwe *m*; **~-hearted** *a* beherzt, tapfer, heldenhaft; **~-hunter** Löwen-, *fig* Prominentenjäger *m*; **~ize** ['-aiz] *tr* (als Helden des Tages) feiern; anhimmeln; *tr itr* die Sehenswürdigkeiten zeigen *od* ansehen (*a city* e-r Stadt); **~'s share** Löwenanteil *m*.

lip [lip] *s* Lippe *f a. bot*; Wundrand; (umgebogener) Rand *m*, Schnauze *(e-s Gefäßes)*; *tech* Schneidkante, Schnittfläche; *sl* Frechheit, Unverschämtheit *f*; *a* Lippen-; oberflächlich, unecht; *to bite o.'s ~* sich auf die Lippen beißen, s-n Ärger 'runterwürgen; *to curl o.'s ~s* verächtlich den Mund verziehen; *to hang on s.o.'s ~s* an jds Lippen hängen; *to keep a stiff upper ~ (fig fam)* den Kopf hochhalten; *to lick, to smack o.'s ~s* sich die Lippen ablecken, *fig* (die) Vorfreude genießen; *none of your ~!* sei nicht unverschämt! *lower, under ~* Unterlippe *f*; *upper ~* Oberlippe; *stiff upper ~ (fam)* Mumm; Mut *m*; Bockbeinigkeit, Hartnäckigkeit *f*; **~ped** [-t] *a* mit Lippen versehen; mit ... Lippen; gerandet; **~-reading** Lippenlesen *n*; **~salve** Lippensalbe; *fig* Schmeichelei *f*; **~-service** Lippendienst *m*; **~stick** Lippenstift *m*.

liquat|e ['laikweit] *tr (Metall)* (aus-) schmelzen, seigern; **~ion** ['laikweiʃən] Schmelzen *n*, (Aus-)Seigerung *f*.

lique|faction [likwi'fækʃən] Schmelzen *n*; *(Gas)* Verflüssigung *f*; **~fiable** ['likwifaiəbl] schmelzbar; **~fy** ['-fai] *tr itr* schmelzen; *(Gas)* verflüssigen; *itr* sich verflüssigen; **~scent** [-'kwesənt] schmelzend; flüssig werdend.

liqueur [li'kjuə, *Am* li'kə:] Likör *m*.

liquid ['likwid] *a* flüssig *a. fin*; *(bes. Luft)* klar; *(Augen)* hell u. glänzend; *fin* liquid; *(Meinung) (Sprache)* sanft fließend, melodisch; unbeständig; *s* Flüssigkeit; *gram* Liquida *f*; *~* **air** flüssige Luft *f*; **~ate** ['likwideit] *tr fin* liquidieren; *(Geschäft)* auflösen, abwickeln; *(Schuld)* ablösen, tilgen, begleichen, bezahlen; *(Geld)* flüssig machen; *pol (mißliebigen Menschen)* liquidieren, beseitigen; **~ation** [likwi'deiʃən] Liquidation, Auflösung, Abwick(e)lung, Abrechnung; Ablösung, Tilgung, Begleichung, Bezahlung; Flüssigmachung; Ausea.setzung, (Vermögens-)Teilung; *(Mensch)* Beseitigung *f*; *in ~~* in Liquidation; *to go into ~~* in L. gehen, liquidieren; *compulsory, voluntary ~~* Zwangs-, freiwillige L.; *proceeds (pl) of ~~* Liquidationserlös *m*; *~~ by order of the court* gerichtliche L.; **~ator** ['likwideitə] Liquidator, Abwickler, Masseverwalter *m*; **~ity** [li'kwiditi] flüssige(r) Zustand *m*; Klarheit; *fin* Liquidität *f*; **~measure** Flüssigkeitsmaß *n*.

liquor ['likə] *s* Flüssigkeit *f*; Saft *m*; alkoholische(s) Getränk *n*, *bes.* Schnaps; Alkohol *m*; *pharm a.* ['laikwɔ:] Lösung *f*; *pl* Spirituosen *pl*; *tr* einweichen, -schmieren; *(to ~ up) sl* besoffen machen; *itr (to ~ up) sl* sich besaufen; *in ~, the worse for ~* betrunken; *under the influence of ~* unter Alkoholeinfluß.

liquorice, *Am* licorice ['likəris] Süßholz *n*; Lakritze *f*.

lisp [lisp] *itr tr* lispeln; mit der Zunge anstoßen; stammeln; *s* Lispeln *n*.

lissom(e) ['lisəm] biegsam, geschmeidig, gelenk(ig), beweglich; behende, gewandt, flink, *fam* fix; **~ness** ['-nis] Biegsamkeit, Gelenkigkeit; Behendigkeit, Gewandtheit *f*.

list [list] **1.** *s* Streifen, Rand, Saum *m*, Leiste, (Webe-)Kante; (Holz-)Leiste *f*; Erdstreifen *m*; Liste *f*, Verzeichnis, Register *n*, Aufstellung *f*; Katalog *m*; (Stamm-)Rolle; *fin* Kursliste; *mil* Rangliste *f*; *tr* säumen; streifenartig einteilen; *(in e-e Liste)* eintragen, -schreiben; verzeichnen; registrieren; katalogisieren; *(Posten)* aufführen; *to be on a ~* auf e-r Liste stehen; *to draw up, to make out a ~* e-e L. aufstellen; *to enter in a ~* in e-e Liste eintragen; *to put on a ~* auf e-e L. setzen; *to strike off (from) a ~* von e-r L. streichen; *cause ~* Terminliste *f*; *hono(u)r ~* Ehrentafel *f*; *price ~* Preisliste *f*; Kurszettel; Tarif *m*; *voter's ~* Wählerliste *f*; *wine ~* Weinkarte *f*; *~ of charges* Kostenrechnung *f*; (Gebühren-)Tarif *m*; *~ of customers* Kundenliste *f*; *~ of members* Mitgliederverzeichnis *n*; *~ of questions* Fragebogen *m*; **~ broker** Adressenbüro *n*; **~er** ['-ə] Häufelpflug *m*; **~ing** ['-iŋ] Anfertigung e-r Liste, Aufstellung e-s Verzeichnisses; Katalogisierung *f*; **~ price** Listenpreis *m*; **2.** *itr obs* gefallen (*to s.o.* jdm); (gern) wollen; **3.** *itr obs* lauschen (*to* dat); **4.** *s mar* Schlagseite *f*; *itr* Schlagseite haben.

listen ['lisn] *itr* horchen, lauschen, hören (*to* auf); aufpassen, achten (*for* auf); zuhören, (geistig) folgen (*to s.o.* jdm); anhören (*to s.th.* etw); gehorchen (*to s.o.* jdm); *to ~ in (tele)* mithören (*to a conversation* ein Gespräch); Radio hören; *to ~ in to a program, to a speech, to London (radio)* ein Programm, e-e Rede, London hören; **~er** ['-ə] Horcher, Lauscher; Zuhörer; *radio* Hörer *m*; *not to be a good ~~* nicht zuhören können, immer selbst reden wollen; *~~ research (radio)* Umfrage unter den Hörern; Hörermeinungsforschung *f*; **~ing** ['-iŋ] *a* (Ab-)Hör-, Horch-; *~~ post (mil)* Horchposten *m*; *~~ public (radio)* Hörerschaft *f*, -kreis *m*.

listless ['listlis] abgestumpft, gleichgültig, uninteressiert, teilnahmslos.

lists [lists] *pl* Schranken *f pl*; Turnier-, *fig* Kampfplatz *m*; *to enter the ~* in die Schranken treten (*against* gegen).

lit [lit] *pret u. pp von light* 1.; **~-up** *sl* benebelt, blau.

litany ['litəni] *rel* Litanei *f*.

liter|acy ['litərəsi] Kenntnis *f* des Lesens u. Schreibens; **~al** ['-əl] *a* Buchstaben-; wörtlich, wortgetreu; wörtlich, ursprünglich; sachlich; wirklich, unverfälscht, echt, rein; genau, pedantisch; *(Wahrheit)* ungeschminkt; *(Sinn)* eigentlich; Buchstaben-; **~ally** ['-əli] *adv* wörtlich, wortgetreu, Wort für Wort; *fam* buchstäblich; **~ary** ['-əri] literarisch (gebildet); *~~ property* geistige(s) Eigentum *n*; **~ate** ['-it] *a* des Lesens u. Schreibens kundig; (literarisch) gebildet; gelehrt; *s* Gebildete(r), Gelehrte(r), Literat *m*; **~ati** [litə'rɑ:ti:] *pl* Gelehrten, Literaten *m pl*; **~ature** ['litəritʃə, -rətʃə, -tjuə] Literatur *f*, Schrifttum *n* (*of* über); literarische Produktion *f*; *fam* Drucksachen *f pl*.

lith(a)emia [li'θi:miə] *med* Urämie, Harnvergiftung *f*.

litharge ['liθɑ:dʒ] *chem* (Blei-)Glätte *f*.

lithe|(some) ['laið(səm)] biegsam, geschmeidig, gelenkig; **~ness** ['-nis] Biegsamkeit; Gelenkigkeit *f*.

litho|graph ['liθəgrɑ:f] *s* Lithographie *f*, Steindruck *m*, -zeichnung *f*; *tr itr* lithographieren; **~grapher** [li'θɔgrəfə] Lithograph *m*; **~graphic(al)** [liθə'græfik(əl)] lithographisch; **~graphy** [li'θɔgrəfi] *(Kunst der)* Lithographie *f*; **~logy** [li'θɔlədʒi] Gesteinskunde *f*.

Lithuania [liθju(:)'einjə] Litauen *n*; **~n** [-n] *a* litauisch; *s* (das) Litauisch(e); Litauer(in *f*) *m*.

litig|ant ['litigənt] *a* prozessierend, prozeßführend; *s pl u. the ~~ parties (pl jur)* die streitenden Parteien *f pl*; **~ate** ['-eit] *itr (tr)* prozessieren (gegen); streiten (um); *(Forderung)* einklagen; **~ation** [liti'geiʃən] Prozessieren *n*; Prozeß, Rechtsstreit *m*; **~ious** [li'tidʒəs] prozeßsüchtig; zänkisch; strittig, umstritten; Prozeß-, Streit-.

litmus ['litməs] *chem* Lackmus *m* od *n*; **~ paper** Lackmuspapier *n*.

litre, *Am* liter ['li:tə] Liter *n* od *m*.

litter ['litə] *s* Sänfte, Trage, (Trag-)Bahre; Streu *f*; *(bes. Hunde u. Schweine)* Wurf *m*; herumliegende Sachen *f pl*, Kram, Plunder *m*; Unordnung; Streudecke *f (auf dem Waldboden)*; *tr* mit e-r Streu versehen *od* bedecken; *(Junge)* werfen; *(to ~ up)* verunreinigen; verstreuen, umherwerfen, in Unordnung bringen; *itr* Junge werfen; *to ~ down (Boden)* Streu aufschütten für; Streu geben (*a horse* e-m Pferd); **~-bearer** Krankenträger *m*; **~-bin, -basket** Abfallkorb *m*; **~-case** Schwerverwundete(r) *m*.

little ['litl] *a* klein; niedlich, nett; *(Zahl)* niedrig, gering; kurz; schwach; wenig; belanglos, unwichtig, nebensächlich; eng(stirnig); gemein; *adv* wenig; nicht viel, kaum, schwerlich; *s*: *a ~* ein (klein) wenig, ein bißchen, etwas, e-e Kleinigkeit; *the ~ ones* die Kleinen; *the ~* das wenige; *for a ~* für e-n Augenblick; auf kurze Zeit; *in ~* im kleinen; *in a ~ while* in kurzer Zeit, bald; *~ by ~, by ~ and ~* nach u. nach, allmählich; *~ or nothing* wenig oder gar nichts; *not a ~* nicht wenig; *too ~* zu wenig, nicht genug; *to make ~ of* wenig halten von; *I think ~ of it* davon halte ich nicht viel; das macht mir nicht viel, nichts aus; *the* **L~ Bear** *astr* der Kleine Bär *od* Wagen; **~-ease** Stehzelle *f*; **~ Mary** *fam* Magen *m*; **~ness** ['-nis] Kleinheit; Geringfügigkeit; Kleinlichkeit *f*; **L~ Red Ridinghood** Rotkäppchen *n*.

littoral ['litərəl] *a* Küsten-; *s* Küstengegend *f*, -land *n*.

liturg|ic(al) [li'tə:dʒik(əl)] *a rel* liturgisch; **~y** ['litə(:)dʒi] Liturgie *f*.

livable ['livəbl] *(Leben)* auszuhalten(d), zu ertragen(d); *(Mensch)* umgänglich; *(Raum)* wohnlich.

live [liv] **1.** *itr* leben; am Leben bleiben, über-, weiterleben; bleiben, andauern, bestehen, aushalten; leben, sein Leben führen; sein Auskommen haben, sich nähren, leben (*on* von); auskommen (*on* mit); wohnen (*with* bei; *at* in); *tr (ein Leben)* leben, führen; vorleben, in die Tat umsetzen; *to ~ high* im Überfluß leben; *to ~ and learn* dazulernen; *to ~ and let ~* leben und leben lassen; *to ~ to see* erleben; *to ~ well* gut leben; *to have barely enough to ~ on* kaum genug zum Leben haben; *to ~* **down** wiedergutmachen; *to ~* **in** im Hause schlafen; *to ~* **off** zehren von; *to ~* **on** weiterleben; *to ~* **out** *itr* außer dem Haus schlafen; *tr* (das Ende *gen*) erleben; durchmachen; *to ~* **through** er-, überleben; *to ~* **to** *o.s.* für sich leben; *to ~* **up** *to* in Einklang leben mit; *s.th.* etw gemäß *od* entsprechend leben; *(Erwartungen)* erfüllen; **2.** [laiv] *a attr* lebend(ig), am Leben; lebendig, lebhaft, voller Leben; lebensprühend; *(Luft)* frisch, rein; *(Kohlen)* glühend *a. fig*; *(Diskussion)* lebhaft; *(Streichholz)* (noch) ungebraucht; *(Geschoß)* scharf; *el* geladen, unter Strom, stromführend; *tech* treibend; *typ* gesetzt, druckfertig; *radio* unmittelbar übertragen; *Am* modern, aktuell; *s (~ broadcast)* Live(sendung) *f*; **~ rail** Stromschiene *f*; **~-stock** lebende(s) Inventar *n*; **~-weight** Lebendgewicht *n*; **~ wire** Draht *m* unter Strom; *fam* unternehmungslustige(r) Mensch *m*.

lived [livd] *a in Zssgen* -lebig.

livelihood ['laivlihud] Lebensunterhalt *m*, Auskommen *n*; *to earn, to make, to gain a ~* s-n Lebensunterhalt verdienen.

live|liness ['laivlinis] Lebendigkeit, Lebhaftigkeit; Tatkraft *f*; **~ly** ['laivli] (quick)lebendig, lebhaft, voller Leben, lebensprühend, frisch, tatkräftig, aktiv, energisch, kraftvoll; angeregt, lebhaft, belebt, heftig, hitzig, sprudelnd; froh, fröhlich, heiter, lustig, anregend; aufregend; flink, schnell, lebhaft; stark; *(Farbe)* lebhaft; *(Ball)* elastisch; *to make things ~~ for s.o.* jdm die Hölle heiß machen.

livelong ['livlɔŋ] *a*: *the ~ day* den lieben langen Tag.

liven ['laivən] *(to ~ up) tr* aufmuntern, -heitern; in Schwung, in Stimmung bringen; *itr* lebhaft, munter werden, in Stimmung kommen.

liver ['livə] **1.** Lebende(r) *m*; *evil ~* Bösewicht; *fast, loose ~* Lebemann *m*; *plain ~* einfache(r) Mensch *m*; **2.** Leber *f*; **~-colo(u)red** *a* schokoladenbraun; **~ complaint** Leberleiden *n*; **~ish** ['-riʃ] *fam* leberkrank, -leidend; verdrießlich, mürrisch; **~-sausage, *Am* -wurst** ['-wə:st] Leberwurst *f*; **~ spot** Leberfleck *m*; **~wort** ['-wə:t] *bot* Leberblümchen *n*.

livery ['livəri] Livree; (Amts-)Tracht; Mitgliedschaft *f* in e-r Innung *od* Zunft; Unterbringen *f* u. Füttern *n* von Pferden; Halten *n* von Mietpferden, -wagen; *jur* Einweisung, Besitzübertragung *f*; *in ~* in Livree; *out of ~* in gewöhnlicher Kleidung; **~man** ['-mən] Zunftmitglied *n*; **~ stable** Mietstall *m*.

livid ['livid] bleifarben, aschgrau, fahl, verfärbt, leichenblaß; *Br fam* wütend; **~ity** [li'viditi], **~ness** ['lividnis] aschgraue, fahle Farbe, Leichenblässe *f*.

living ['liviŋ] *a* lebend, lebendig *a. fig*; fließend; leibhaftig; belebend; zum Leben ausreichend; Lebens-; *(Fels)* gewachsen; *s* Leben *n*; (Lebens-)Unterhalt *m*, Auskommen *n*, Existenz *f*; Lebensstandard *m*, -weise *f*; *rel* Pfründe, Pfarrstelle *f*; *the ~* die Lebenden *pl*; *within ~ memory* seit Menschengedenken; *to make a ~* sein Auskommen haben (*as* als; *out of* durch); ~ **conditions** *pl* Lebensbedingungen *f pl*; ~ **costs** *pl* Lebenshaltungskosten *pl*; ~ **habits** *pl* Lebensgewohnheiten *f pl*; ~ **image** genaue(s) Ebenbild *n*; *to be the* ~~ *of s.o.* jdm aus dem Gesicht geschnitten sein; ~ **picture** lebende(s) Bild *n* *(gestellte Gruppe)*; ~ **quarters** *pl* Wohnviertel *n pl*; ~ **room** Wohnzimmer *n*; ~ **space** Lebensraum *m*; ~ **wage** auskömmliche(r) Lohn *m*, Existenzminimum *n*.

Livonia [li'vounjə] Livland *n*; ~**n** [-n] *a* livländisch; *s* Livländer(in *f*) *m*.

lizard ['lizəd] Eidechse *f*.

Lizzie ['lizi] *Am mot sl (tin* ~*)* alte Kiste *f*; Auto *n*.

llama ['lɑ:mə] Lama *n*.

lo [lou] *interj* siehe!

loach [loutʃ] *zoo* Schmerle *f*.

load [loud] *s* (Trag-)Last, Ladung, Fuhre; Fracht; Last *(englische Gewichts-, Mengeneinheit)*; (schwere) Last, Belastung *a. fig*; *fig* Bürde; Tragfähigkeit, -kraft; Arbeitsleistung, Belastung, Beanspruchung; Arbeitsleistung; *(Feuerwaffe)* Ladung *f*; *oft pl*: ~*s of* e-e Menge *od* Masse; *itr* Ladung übernehmen; *(Börse)* stark kaufen; *tr (Transportmittel)* (be)laden; *(Ladung)* auf-, ein-, verladen; überhäufen, überladen, überlasten, zu sehr belasten *a. fig*; beschweren; *fig* überbürden, mit Arbeit überhäufen, überlasten; *(Feuerwaffe)* laden; *(Photoapparat)* e-n Film einlegen in; *(Kabel)* pupinisieren; *(Würfel)* fälschen; *(Ofen)* beschicken; *(Getränk)* verfälschen; *(Frage)* die Antwort in den Mund legen; *to* ~ *down* beladen; *to get a* ~ *of s.th. (Am sl)* etw prüfen, sehen; *that's a* ~ *off my mind* mir ist (damit) ein Stein vom Herzen gefallen; *breaking* ~ Bruchfestigkeit *f*; *live, pay-, useful, working* ~ Nutzlast *f*; *maximum* ~ Höchstbelastung *f*; *peak* ~ Spitzenbelastung *f*; *safe* ~ zulässige Belastung *f*; *ship*~, *ship's* ~ Schiffsladung *f*; *total* ~ *(aero)* Fluggewicht *n*; ~**ed** ['-id] *a* beladen; belastet; geladen; *(Wein)* verfälscht, *fam* gepan(t)scht; *(Zunge)* belegt; ~~ *up with (com)* mit e-m reichlichen Vorrat versehen sein an; ~~ *dice* falsche Würfel *m pl*; *(total)* ~~ *weight* Fluggewicht *n*; ~**er** ['-ə] Ladearbeiter *m*; Verladevorrichtung *f*; ~ **factor** *el* Belastungsfaktor *m*; ~**ing** ['-iŋ] *s* Be-, Verladung; Verfrachtung, Fracht; Belastung; Zusatzprämie *f*; *fin* Zuschlag *m*; *el* Pupinisierung *f*; *attr* Lade-, Verladungs-; ~~ *area* Ladefläche *f*; ~~ *bridge* Verladebrücke *f*; ~~-*capacity* Ladefähigkeit; Belastbarkeit *f*; ~~-*charges (pl)* Ladegebühren *f pl*; ~~-*days (pl)* Ladetage *m pl*, -frist *f*; ~~ *jib* Ladebaum *m*; ~~-*place* Ladeplatz *m*, -station *f*; ~~-*platform, -ramp* Laderampe *f*; ~~ *road* Verladestrecke *f*; ~-**limit** Belastungsgrenze *f*; ~-**line** *mar* Lade-, *tech* Belastungskennlinie *f*; ~ **peak** Belastungsspitze *f*; ~-**shedding** *el* Stromverteilung *f (durch Abschalten)*; ~**space** Laderaum *m*; ~**star** *s. lodestar*; ~**stone** *min* Magneteisenstein *m*; ~-**test** Belastungsprobe *f*.

loaf [louf] **1.** *s pl loaves (bes. Brot)* Laib; *(meat*~*)* Hackbraten; *(sugar-*~*)* (Zucker-)Hut *m*; *sl* Birne *f*; *half a* ~ *is better than no bread (prov)* besser wenig als gar nichts; ~-**cake** *Am* Königskuchen, Stollen *m*; ~-**sugar** Hut-, Würfelzucker *m*; **2.** *itr* herumbummeln, -lungern, umherschlendern, sich herumtreiben; *(bei der Arbeit)* bummeln; *tr (to* ~ *away) (Zeit)* vertrödeln; *to be on the* ~ faulenzen; ~**er** ['-ə] Bummler, Herumtreiber, Landstreicher, Vagabund *m*.

loam [loum] Lehm(boden) *m*; ~-**pit** Lehmgrube *f*; ~**y** ['-i] lehmig.

loan [loun] *s* (Aus-, Ver-)Leihen; Darlehen *n (to* an, für); Anleihe; Leihgabe *f*; *com* Vorschuß, Kredit *m*; *tr* (aus-, ver)leihen; als Darlehen geben *(to* an); *itr* leihen; *as a* ~ als Leihgabe; *on* ~ leihweise; geliehen, geborgt; *to contract a* ~ e-e Anleihe aufnehmen; *to grant a* ~ ein Darlehen geben *od* gewähren *(to s.o.* jdm); *to have the* ~ *of s.th.* etw ausleihen; *to put to* ~ aus-, verleihen; *to subscribe to a* ~ e-e Anleihe zeichnen; *domestic, foreign* ~ In-, Auslandsanleihe *f*; *forced* ~ Zwangsanleihe *f*; *government* ~ Staatsanleihe *f*; *victory, war* ~ Kriegsanleihe *f*; ~**bank** Kredit-, Darlehensbank *f*; ~-**collection** *(Kunst)* Ausstellung *f* von Leihgaben; ~ **interest** Darlehenszinsen *m pl*; ~ **office** Darlehnskasse; Pfandleihe *f*; ~ **society** *Br* Kredit-, Darlehnsverein *m*; ~-**word** Lehnwort *n*.

loath, loth [louθ] *a pred, meist mit inf*: *to be* ~ *to do* nur mit Widerwillen tun; *nothing* ~ ganz gern; ~**e** [louð] *tr* sich ekeln vor, verabscheuen, hassen; ~**ing** ['louðiŋ] Ekel, Abscheu *(at* vor); Haß *m*; ~**some** ['louðsəm] ekelhaft, abscheuerregend, abscheulich, verabscheuenswert.

lob [lɔb] *itr (to* ~ *along)* herumstapfen, -staksen; *itr tr sport* lobben; *s sport* Hochball *m*.

lobby ['lɔbi] *s* Vorraum *m*, (Vor-)Halle, Wandelhalle *f*, Foyer *n*; *pol* Interessengruppe *f*; *tr (to* ~ *through)* durch Beeinflussung der Kongreß-, der Parlamentsmitglieder durch(zu)setzen (suchen); *itr pol* intrigieren; ~**ist** ['-ist] *Am* Lobbyist *m*.

lobe [loub] *anat bot* Lappen; *el* Zipfel *m*, Schleife *f*; ~ *of the brain* Gehirnlappen *m*; ~ *of the ear* Ohrläppchen *n*; ~ *of the lung* Lungenflügel *m*.

lobelia [lo(u)'bi:ljə] *bot* Lobelie *f*.

loblolly ['lɔblɔli] *(*~ *pine)* Sumpfkiefer *f*; *fam* Sumpf-, Dreckloch *n*.

lobo ['loubou] *pl -os Am* Steppenwolf *m*.

lobster ['lɔbstə] Hummer; *Am fam* Tölpel, Stümper *m*; ~ **pot** Hummerreuse *f*.

local ['loukəl] *a* örtlich; Orts-, Lokal-; ortsansässig; *med* örtlich; hiesig; beschränkt, eng(stirnig), Kirchturms-; *s* Ortsansässige(r) *m*; *(*~ *train)* Kleinbahn, Nebenlinie *f*, Vorortzug *m*; *(Zeitung)* Lokalnotiz *f*, -nachrichten *f pl*, -teil *m*, -blatt *n*; *Am* Ortsgruppe *f*; *Br fam* Gasthaus *n* am Ort; ~ **administration, government** Gemeindeverwaltung *f*; ~ **authorities** *pl* Ortsbehörden *f pl*; ~ **bill** *fin* Platzwechsel *m*; ~ **branch** Ortsgruppe *f*; ~ **call** *tele* Ortsgespräch *n*; ~ **charge** *tele* Ortsgebühr *f*; ~ **colo(u)r** *lit* Lokalkolorit *n*; ~**e** [lou'kɑ:l] Ort *m*, Örtlichkeit *f*, Schauplatz *m*; ~ **elections** *pl* Gemeindewahlen *f pl*; ~**ism** ['loukəlizm] lokale Eigenheit *f*; Lokalpatriotismus; Provinzialismus *m*; ~**ity** [lo(u)'kæliti] Örtlichkeit, Lokalität; Lage *f*; Standort; *min* Fundort *m*; *sense, (fam) good bump of* ~~ Ortssinn *m*; ~**ization** [loukəlai'zeiʃən] Lokalisierung *f*; ~**ize** ['loukəlaiz] *tr* örtlich beschränken; dezentralisieren; lokalisieren *(to* auf); konzentrieren *(upon* auf); ~ **knowledge** Ortskenntnis *f*; ~ **news** *pl mit sing* Lokalnachrichten *f pl*; ~ **press** Lokalpresse *f*; ~ **rate** Gemeindesteuer *f*; Ortstarif *m*; ~ **road** Gemeindeweg *m*; ~ **service** Nahverkehr *m*; ~ **(mean) time** (mittlere) Ortszeit *f*; ~ **traffic** Ortsverkehr *m*; ~ **train** Personenzug; Zug *m* im Nahverkehr.

locat|e [lou'keit] *tr* (örtlich) festlegen, abstecken, abgrenzen, die Grenzen abstecken *(s.th.* e-r S); ausfindig machen, feststellen; die Lage bestimmen *(s.th.* e-r S); *radio* einpeilen, orten; *(auf der Karte)* zeigen; *(in e-e Arbeit, ein Amt)* einweisen; *Am* er-, einrichten; *to be* ~*ed* liegen, sich befinden; *itr Am fam* sich niederlassen, sich ansiedeln; ~**ion** [-ʃən] Absteckung, Abgrenzung; Lage; Stelle; Orts-, Lagebestimmung; Ortsangabe *f*; Platz *m (for* für); Grundstück *n*, Bauplatz *m*; Niederlassung, Ansiedlung *f*; Standort *m*; *film* (Platz *m*, Gelände *n* für) Außenaufnahmen *f pl*; *Am* Errichtung; *jur* Vermietung *f*; *on* ~~ *(film)* auf Außenaufnahme.

loch [lɔx] *Scot* See, Meeresarm *m*.

lock [lɔk] **1.** (Tür-)Schloß *n*; Verschluß *m (a. e-r Feuerwaffe)*; Sperre; Bremse *f tech*; Hindernis *n*; (Verkehrs-)Stokkung, Stauung; *(Ringen)* Fesselung; *fig* Sackgasse; *mar* Schleuse, Staustufe; (Gas-)Schleuse *f*; *mot* Einschlag *m*; *tr (to* ~ *up)* ver-, zuschließen, -sperren; einschließen, ein-, absperren *(in, into* in); *(die Arme)* verschränken; fest umschlingen, -fassen, -spannen; bremsen; versperren, abriegeln, blokkieren; mit e-r Schleuse, mit Schleusen versehen; durchschleusen; *itr (Schloß)* zuschnappen; verschließbar sein; sich inea.schlingen, inea.greifen; sich fest schließen, klemmen; *under* ~ *and key* hinter Schloß u. Riegel; ~, *stock, and barrel* alles zusammen, *fam* der ganze Kram; *to* ~ **away** wegschließen; *to* ~ **in** einschließen, -sperren; *to* ~ **out** aussperren *(a. Arbeiter)*; *to* ~ **up** zu-, verschließen, -sperren; einschließen, -sperren; *(Geld)* wegschließen; *(Kapital)* fest anlegen; ~**age** ['-idʒ] Durchschleusung *f*; Schleusengeld *n*; Schleusenanlage, -bedienung; Schleusendifferenz *f*; ~-**chamber** Schleusenkammer *f*; ~**er** ['-ə] (verschließbarer) Kasten, Schrank *m*; Bank-, Schließfach *n*; *mar* verschließbare Kabine *f*; *to be in, to go to Davy Jones's* ~~ im feuchten Grab liegen, im Meer ertrinken; *not a shot in the* ~~ keinen Pfennig Geld in der Tasche; ~~ *room* Umkleideraum *m*; ~**et** ['-it] Medaillon *n*; ~-**gate** Schleusentor *n*; ~-**jaw** *med* Mund-, Kiefersperre *f*; ~-**keeper** Schleusenwärter *m*; ~-**nut** *tech* Gegenmutter *f*; Klemmring *m*; ~-**out** Aussperrung *f (von Arbeitern)*; ~**smith** Schlosser *m*; ~~*'s shop* Schlosserei, Schlosserwerkstatt *f*; ~**stitch** Ketten-, Steppstich *m*; ~-**up** *s* Ver-, Zuschließen *n*; Torschluß *m*; Einsperren; (Polizei-)Gewahrsam *n*; Haft(anstalt) *f*, Gefängnis *n*; feste Anlage *(e-s Kapitals)*; *mot* Einzelgarage *f*; *a attr* verschließbar; ~ **washer** Sicherungsring *m*; **2.** (Haar-)Locke *f*; Büschel *n*, Strähne *f*; *pl* Haare *n pl*.

loco ['loukou] *a sl* verrückt; *s* Lok *f*.

locomot|ion [loukə'mouʃən] (Fort-)Bewegung, Ortsveränderung *f*, Platzwechsel *m*; Fähigkeit *f*, sich von der Stelle zu bewegen; ~**ive** [-tiv] *a* beweglich; sich selbst fortbewegend; *fam* fahrend, reisend; *s* Lokomotive *f*.

loc|um tenens ['loukəm 'ti:nenz] (Stell-)Vertreter *m*; ~**us** ['loukəs] *pl* ~*i* ['lousai] Ort *m*, Stelle *f*; *math* geometrische(r) Ort *m*; ~~ *in quo* [-in'kwou] *jur* Tatort *m*.

locust ['loukəst] (Wander-)Heuschrecke; Zikade *f*; *(~-tree)* Johannisbrotbaum *m*; Robinie *f*; *migratory ~* Wanderheuschrecke *f*.
locution [lo(u)'kju:ʃən] Rede-, Sprechweise; Redensart *f*, Ausdruck *m*.
ode [loud] Abzugsgraben *m*; *min* Erzader *f*, Flöz *n*; **~star** Leit-, *bes.* Polarstern; *fig* Leitstern *m*, Vorbild *n*; **~-stone** *s. load-stone.*
lodge [lɔdʒ] *s* kleine(s) Haus, Häuschen; (Tor-, Pförtner-, Gärtner-, Jagd-) Haus *n*; Pförtner-, Portiersloge; (Freimaurer-)Loge *f*; Lager *n (e-s wilden Tieres), bes.* Biberbau *m*, -burg *f*; Indianerhütte *f*, Wigwam *m*; *tr* unterbringen, einquartieren; beherbergen; e-n Raum, e-e Wohnung vermieten an; als Untermieter, als Pensionsgast aufnehmen; als Wohnung dienen für; *(Geld, Wertsachen)* zur Aufbewahrung übergeben (*with s.o.* jdm); hinterlegen, deponieren (*with s.o.* bei jdm); *jur (Forderung)* erheben, anmelden; *(Anspruch)* erheben, geltend machen; *(Berufung, Beschwerde)* einlegen, einreichen; *fam (Einwand)* machen, erheben; *(Vollmacht)* übertragen (*in, with, in the hands of s.o.* jdm); bringen, treiben, stoßen, stecken (*in* in); *(Kugel)* jagen (*in* in); *(Getreide)* umlegen; *(Schlag)* versetzen; *itr* wohnen (*with* bei); *(Pfeil, Kugel)* steckenbleiben (*in* in); *(Getreide)* sich umlegen; *to ~ a complaint* Beschwerde einlegen, Klage erheben *od* führen (*with* bei; *at* über; *against* gegen); *to ~ an information* Anzeige erstatten (*against* gegen); *to ~ a protest* Protest einlegen *od* erheben; protestieren (*with* bei; *against* gegen); *caretaker's ~* Hausmeisterwohnung *f*; *grand ~ (Freimaurerei)* Großloge *f*; *hunting, shooting ~* Jagdhütte *f*, -haus *n*; **~r** ['-ə] Untermieter; Pensionsgast; Schlafgänger *m*.
lodg(e)ment ['lɔdʒmənt] Unterbringung; Wohnung; *(meist lästige)* Ansammlung, Anhäufung, Ablagerung; *mil* (eroberte) Stellung *f*; *fig* feste(r) Halt, Ausgangspunkt *m*; Festsetzen *n*; *(Geld)* Hinterlegung *f*, Deponieren *n*; *jur (Klage)* Einreichung, *(Berufung)* Einlegung *f*; *to make, to effect a ~ (mil)* (festen) Fuß fassen.
lodging ['lɔdʒiŋ] Unterbringung, Beherbergung *f*; Wohnen, Logieren *n*; Wohnung, Unterkunft *f*, Logis; *jur (Berufung)* Einlegen; *pl* möblierte(s) Zimmer *n*, möblierte Wohnung *f*; *board and ~* Unterkunft und Verpflegung; Kost und Logis; *free board and ~* freie Station *f*; *a night's ~* ein Nachtquartier, -lager *n*; **~ allowance** Wohnungsgeld *n*; **~-house** Pension *f*, Fremdenheim *n*.
loess ['lo(u)is] *geol* Löß *m*.
loft [lɔft] *s* (Dach-)Boden, Speicher, Bodenraum *m*; Taubenhaus *n*, -schlag; (Orgel-)Chor *m*; *Am* Obergeschoß, obere(s) Stockwerk *n (in e-m Warenhaus* od *e-r Fabrik)*; *arch* Empore, Galerie *f*; *tr* auf dem Boden einlagern, speichern; e-n Boden einbauen in; *(Golfball)* hochschlagen; *(Golfschläger)* schräg nach hinten halten; **~iness** ['-inis] Höhe; Erhabenheit, Vornehmheit *f*; Hochmut *m*, Arroganz *f*; **~y** ['-i] hoch(ragend); erhaben, stattlich, groß, edel, vornehm, stolz; hochmütig, eingebildet, arrogant.
log [lɔg] *s* (Holz-)Klotz, Block *m*; *mar* Log *n*; *(~-book)* Log-, Schiffstagebuch, -journal; *mot* Fahrtenbuch; *aero* Bordbuch, Flug(tage)buch *n*; *tech (~sheet)* (Zustands-)Bericht *m*, Betriebsprotokoll *n*; *math* Logarithmus *m*; *tr (Baumstamm)* (in Blöcke) zersägen; abholzen; *mar* loggen *(e-e Entfernung)* zurücklegen, ins Logbuch eintragen; *itr* Holz fällen und abtransportieren; *in the ~ (Holz)* unbearbeitet; *like a (bump on a) ~* unbeholfen, ungeschickt; wie ein Klotz, leblos; *to sleep like a ~* wie ein Murmeltier schlafen; *roll my ~ and I'll roll yours (fig)* e-e Hand wäscht die andere; **~-cabin, -house, -hut** Blockhaus *n*; **~-chip** *mar* Logbrett *n*; **~ger** ['-ə] Holzfäller *m*; Blockwinde *f*; **~gerhead** ['-əhed] *obs* Dummkopf *m*; *I was at ~~s with him* wir lagen uns in den Haaren; **~ging** ['-iŋ] Holzfällen *n*; **~-line** *mar* Logleine *f*; **~-reel** *mar* Logtrommel *f*; **~roll** *itr Am parl* e-e Politik gegenseitiger Unterstützung betreiben; *tr (Anträge)* durch gegenseitige Unterstützung durchbringen; **~rolling** Nachbarschaftshilfe; *parl* gegenseitige Unterstützung *f* (der Parteien); *pej* politische(r) Schacher, Kuhhandel *m*; **~wood** Kampesche-, Blau-, Blutholz *n*.
loganberry ['lougənbəri] Kreuzung *f* von Himbeere und Brombeere.
logarithm ['lɔgəriθəm] *math* Logarithmus *m*; **~ic** [lɔgə'riθmik] logarithmisch.
logic ['lɔdʒik] Logik *f*; **~al** ['-əl] logisch; folgerichtig, natürlich; **~ian** [lo(u)-'dʒiʃən] Logiker *m*.
logistic(al) [lo(u)'dʒistik(əl)] *a mil* Nachschub-, Versorgungs-; *pl -ics mil* Logistik *f*.
logy ['lougi] *Am fam* (abge)stumpf(t), müde, schwerfällig, träge, wie vor den Kopf geschlagen; *(Nahrung)* stopfend.
loin [lɔin] *(Rind)* Blume *f*; *(Kalb, Hammel)* Nierenstück; *(Schwein)* Rippenstück *n*; *meist pl* Lenden *f pl (des Menschen)*; *to gird up o.'s ~s (lit)* sich rüsten, sich anschicken; *roast ~* Lenden-, Nierenbraten *m*; *(roast) ~ of veal* Kalbsnierenbraten *m*; **~cloth** Lendentuch *n*.
loiter ['lɔitə] *itr (to ~ about)* herumbummeln, herumlungern; zaudern, zögern; bummeln, trödeln, *fam* langsam machen; *tr (to ~ away) (Zeit)* vertrödeln, verbummeln; **~er** ['-rə] Zauderer; Bummler, *fam* Bummelant *m*.
loll [lɔl] *itr* sich (bequem) ausstrecken, sich rekeln; sich zurück-, sich anlehnen; *tr (Kopf, Rücken)* anlehnen; *to ~ (out) tr itr* (die Zunge) herausstrecken.
loll|apalooza, ~apaloosa [lɔləpə-'luzə], **~ypalooza, ~ypaloosa** [lɔli-] *Am sl* Mordsding *n*.
lollipop ['lɔlipɔp] *fam* Bonbon *m* od *n* (*Am*: am Stiel); *pl* Süßigkeiten *f pl*.
lollop ['lɔləp] *itr fam (beim Gehen)* hin-u. herschlenkern, watscheln, torkeln.
Lombard ['lɔmbəd] *s hist* Langobarde; Lombarde *m*; *a* langobardisch; lombardisch; **~ic** [lɔm'bɑ:dik] *(bes. Kunst)* lombardisch; **~Street** die Londoner Großfinanz; **~y** ['lɔmbədi] die Lombardei.
lone [loun] *attr* alleinig, *pred* allein; einsam; isoliert; *hum* alleinstehend; **~ hand** *(Kartenspiel)* Solo(spieler *m*) *n*; *to play a ~~ (fig)* etw im Alleingang tun; **~liness** ['-linis] Einsamkeit *f*; **~ly** ['-li] verlassen, einsam; vereinsamt; sich einsam fühlend; *to live a ~~ life* ein einsames Leben führen; **~some** ['-səm] einsam; verlassen, öde; *to be ~~ for s.o.* sich nach jdm sehnen.
long [lɔŋ] **1.** *a* lang; *(Weg)* weit; Längen-; langsam, -weilig; groß; *(Schätzung)* unsicher; *fin* langfristig; *(Preis)* hoch; *com* eingedeckt (*of* mit); *adv* lange; *(all day) ~* (den ganzen Tag) lang; *s* lange Zeit; *(Phonetik, Prosodie)* Länge *f*; *fam* große Ferien *pl*; *as, so ~ as* solange; vorausgesetzt, unter der Bedingung, daß; wenn nur; *Am* da(ja); wenn; *at (the) ~est* höchstens; längstens; *before, (lit) ere ~* in kurzem, bald; *in the ~ run* auf die Dauer, am Ende; *no ~er* nicht mehr; *not ... any ~er* nicht länger, nicht weiter, nicht mehr; *not ... for ~* nicht lange, nur kurz(e Zeit); *of ~ standing* alt, langjährig; *~ after, before* lange nachher, viel später; lange vorher, viel früher; *~ ago, since* vor langem, vor langer Zeit; schon lange; *to be ~ (in) doing s.th.* viel Zeit brauchen, um etw zu tun; *not to be ~ for ...* nicht lange dauern bis ...; *to have the ~ arm* die größere Macht haben, *fam* am Drükker sitzen; *to have a ~ head (fig)* e-n klugen Kopf haben; vorausschauend sein; *to have a ~ tongue* ein gutes Mundwerk haben, viel reden; *to have a ~ wind* e-n langen Atem haben; *to take a ~ time* viel Zeit brauchen; *to take ~ views* auf lange Sicht planen; *don't be ~!* mach schnell! beeil dich! *so ~! (fam)* bis später! auf Wiedersehn! *a ~ dozen* dreizehn; *a ~ face* ein langes, betrübtes Gesicht; *the ~ and the short of it* der langen Rede kurzer Sinn, kurz (gesagt); *a ~ way round* ein großer Umweg; **~-boat** *mar* große(s) Beiboot *n*, Pinasse *f*; **~bow** ['-bou] *hist* (englischer) Langbogen *m (Waffe)*; *to draw, to pull the ~~ (fam)* übertreiben, aufschneiden, angeben; **~ clothes** *pl* Babytragkleid *n*; **~-dated** *a fin* langfristig; **~ distance** *Am* Fernamt; Ferngespräch *n*; **~-distance** *a* Langstrecken-; Dauer-; *Am tele* Fern-; *(Wettervorhersage)* langfristig; *~~ call (Am tele)* Ferngespräch *n*; *~~ central station (el)* Überlandzentrale *f*; *~~ flight* Langstreckenflug *m*; *~~ reconnaissance (aero)* Fernaufklärung *f*; **~-drawn(-out)** *a* lang-, in die Länge gezogen, ausgedehnt; *fig* langatmig; **~ drink** *Am* mit Wasser verdünnte(s) alkoholische(s) Getränk *n*; **~-eared** *a* langohrig; **~-faced** *a* mit langem Gesicht *a. fig*; **~ finger** Mittelfinger *m*; **~ firm** Schwindelfirma *f*; **~ green** *Am sl* Geldschein, Lappen *m*; **~hair** *a Am fam* intellektuell; theoretisch; klassische Musik bevorzugend; *s* Intellektuelle(r); konservative(r) Musiker *m*; **~hand** Langschrift *f*; **~ haul** *Am aero* Langstrecken-, Nonstopflug *m*; **~-headed** *a* langschädelig; *fig* klug, schlau; vorausschauend; **~horn** langhörnige(s) Rind *n*; *Am fam* Alteingesessene(r) *m*; **~ hundredweight** *Am* englische(r) Zentner (*= 112 engl. Pfund* od *50,8 kg)*; **~ish** ['-iʃ] etwas lang; **~ jump** *sport* Weitsprung *m*; **~-legged** *a* langbeinig; **~-lived** *a* langlebig; **~ measure** Längenmaß *n*; **~ neck** *orn* Rohrdommel *f*; **~-playing record** Langspielplatte *f*; **~ primer** Korpus, Garmond *f (Schriftgröße von 10 Punkten)*; **~ range** *s* Tragweite *f*; **~-range** *a* weitreichend; weit vorausschauend; *~~ artillery* Fernkampfartillerie *f*; *~~ bomber* Langstrecken-, Fernbomber *m*; *~~ fighter (aero)* Langstreckenjäger, Zerstörer *m*; *~~ (air-)navigation (system), loran (aero)* Funkfernnavigation(ssystem *n*) *f*, Funkfernpeilung *f*; **~shoreman** Hafenarbeiter *m*; **~ shot** *film* Fernaufnahme *f*; *fam* schwache Vermutung; riskante Wette *f*; *not by a ~~ (fam)*

nicht im Traum; **~-sighted** *a med* weitsichtig; *fig* vorausschauend; **~-sightedness** Weitsichtigkeit *f*; **~-spun** *a* lang, weit ausgesponnen; langatmig, -wierig, -weilig; **~-standing** langwährend, langdauernd, anhaltend; **~-suffering** *a* geduldig, langmütig; *s* Geduld, Langmut *f*; **~-tailed** *a* langschwänzig; *that's a ~~ bear!* so ein Schwindel! **~-term** *fin* langfristig; **~ ton** (engl.) Tonne *f* *(= 2240 Pfund od 1017 kg)*; **~-tongued** *a* mit e-r langen Zunge (versehen); *fig* redselig, geschwätzig, schwatzhaft; **~ vacation,** *(fam)* **vac** große Ferien *pl*; **~ wave** *s radio* Langwelle *f*; **~-wave** *a radio* Langwellen-; *~~ band* Langwellenbereich *m*; *~~ transmitter* Langwellensender *m*; **~ways, ~wise** *adv* lang, der Länge nach; **~-winded** *a* langatmig *a. fig*; *fig* von ermüdender Länge, langweilig; **2.** *itr* sich sehnen (*for* nach); *I ~ for (lit)* es verlangt mich nach; **~ing** ['-iŋ] *a* sich sehnend, *lit* verlangend, voll Verlangen (*for* nach); *s* Sehnsucht *f*, Verlangen *n* (*for* nach).

longeron ['lɔndʒərən] *aero* Rumpf-, Längsholm *m*.

longevity [lɔn'dʒeviti] lange(s) Leben *n*, Langlebigkeit *f*.

longitud|e ['lɔndʒitju:d] (geographische) Länge *f*; **~inal** [lɔndʒi'tju:dinl] *a* längslaufend, Längs-; *geog* Längen-.

loo [lu:] *fam* Toilette *f*.

look [luk] *itr* sehen, schauen, blicken (*at, on, upon* auf, nach); ansehen, -schauen (*at, on s.o., s.th.* jdn, etw); achtgeben, aufpassen (*to* auf); zusehen (*to s.o., s.th.* jdm, e-r S); s-n Blick richten (*towards* auf); suchen, erwarten (*for s.o., s.th.* jdn, etw); warten (*for s.o., s.th.* auf jdn, etw); prüfen(d ansehen), abschätzen, erwägen, beurteilen (*at s.th.* etw); genau ansehen, prüfen, mustern, zu erforschen suchen (*into s.th.* etw); sich kümmern (*after* um), aufpassen (*after* auf); überwachen (*after s.o., s.th.* jdn, etw); *(mit: a, like* od *as if)* aussehen, scheinen; *tr* sehen (*s.o. in the face* jdm ins Gesicht); zum Ausdruck bringen, Ausdruck geben (*s.th.* e-r S); aussehen wie; *s* Blick *m* (*at* auf, nach); *a. pl* Aussehen *n*, Anblick *m*, Erscheinung *f*; *to cast, to throw a ~* e-n Blick werfen (*at* auf); *to give s.o. a ~* jdm e-n Blick zuwerfen; *to have, to take a ~ at s.th.* etw mal ansehen, -schauen; *to ~ o.s. again (nach e-r Krankheit)* wieder besser aussehen; *to ~ ahead* geradeaus sehen; *fig* an die Zukunft denken; *to ~ daggers at s.o.* jdn wütend anschauen; *to ~ high and low for s.th. (Am fam)* etw sorgfältig suchen; *to ~ down o.'s nose at* (geringschätzig) herabsehen auf; *I don't like its ~* das gefällt mir nicht, das sieht mir nicht gut aus; *he ~s his age* man sieht ihm sein Alter an; *it ~s like rain* es sieht nach Regen aus; *~ alive! ~ sharp!* mach zu! schnell! los, los! *to ~* **about** sich umsehen, sich umschauen (*for* nach); *one* sich Zeit lassen; *to ~* **back** zurückschauen, -blicken (*on, upon* auf); unsicher werden; *to ~* **down** *on* hochmütig herabsehen auf, verachten; sich für mehr halten als; *to ~* **down**(**wards**) die Augen niederschlagen; *to ~* **forward** *to* sich freuen auf; *to ~* **in** hereinschauen (*on s.o.* bei jdm), e-n kurzen Besuch abstatten (*on s.o.* jdm); *to ~* **into** untersuchen, nachgehen (*s.th.* e-r S); *to ~* **out** *itr* aufpassen, achtgeben (*for* auf); hinaussehen, -gehen (*on* auf); *tr* sich aussuchen; *~ out!* aufpassen! Achtung! Vorsicht! *to ~* **over** mustern; prüfen, durchsehen; hinwegsehen über; *to ~* **round** *fig* sich alles, die Sache gut überlegen; sich umsehen; *to ~* **through** durchsehen; *fig* durchschauen; *to ~* **to** abzielen auf; *to ~* **up** *itr* aufblicken, -schauen, -sehen (*at* auf); *(Preise)* steigen, aufschlagen, *fam* klettern; *to s.o.* zu jdm aufsehen, jdn hochschätzen, bewundern; *tr (Wort im Wörterbuch)* nachschlagen; *fam* besuchen; *things are (he is) ~ing up* es geht (ihm) besser; *to ~* **up and down** überall suchen; genau untersuchen; **~er** ['-ə] Betrachter, Beschauer; *fam (~~-in)* Fernseher *(Mensch)*; *fam* hübsche(r) Kerl *m*, *bes.* hübsche(s) Ding *n*; **~er-on** [lukə'rɔn] *pl -ers-on* Zuschauer *m* (*at* bei); **~-in** kurze(r), schnelle(r), flüchtige(r) Blick; kurze(r) Besuch *m*, *fam* Stippvisite *f*; *to have a ~~ (fam, bes. sport)* Aussichten, Chancen haben; **~ing** ['-iŋ] *s* Schauen *n*; *a in Zssgen* aussehend; *good-~~* gut aussehend, ansehnlich, stattlich, hübsch; *~~-glass* Spiegel *m*; **~-out** Ausschau *f*, Ausblick *m*; Wache *f*; Ausguck, *mar* Mastkorb, Wachtposten *m*; *fam* Angelegenheit *f*; Aussicht(en *pl*) *f*; *to be on the ~~* Ausschau halten, auf der Lauer liegen (*for* nach); *to keep a good ~~* ein wachsames Auge haben; *that is his ~~ (fam)* das ist seine Sache; *that is not my ~~* das geht mich nichts an, das ist nicht meine Sache; *~~-hole* Sehschlitz *m*; *~~-post (Jagd)* Hochsitz *m*; **~-over** Überprüfung *f*; *to give s.th. a ~~* etw in Augenschein nehmen; **~-see** *sl* flüchtige(r), kurze(r) Blick *m*; Inaugenscheinnahme *f*; *aero sl* Aufklärungsflug *m*, Luftaufklärung *f*; *to have a ~~ (sl)* sich umsehen.

loom [lu:m] **1.** *s* Webstuhl *m*; **2.** *itr (to ~ up)* allmählich, undeutlich sichtbar werden; drohend aufragen; *to ~ large* unheimlich vor Augen treten.

loon [lu:n] **1.** *orn* Haubensteißfuß, -taucher; Eis-, Riesentaucher *m*; **2.** Tolpatsch, Tölpel, Dussel, Depp *m*.

loony ['lu:ni] *a sl* verrückt; *s* Verrückte(r) *m*; **~ bin** *sl* Irrenhaus *n*.

loop [lu:p] *s* Schlinge, Schleife; Windung; Öse *f*, Öhr *n*, Ring *m*; *aero* Looping *m* od *n*, Überschlag *m*; *el* Leitungsschleife; *radio* Rahmenantenne *f*; *(direction-finding ~)* Peilrahmen; *phys* Gegenknoten *m*; *tr* in Schlingen, Schleifen legen; schlingen, winden (*around* um); *el* zu e-r Leitungsschleife verbinden; *(Weberei)* ketteln; *itr* Schlingen, Schleifen bilden; *aero (to ~ the ~)* e-n Looping drehen, sich überschlagen; *(Spannerraupe)* spannen; *to ~ up (Masche)* aufnehmen; *(Haar)* aufstecken; **~-antenna, -aerial** Rahmenantenne *f*, Peilrahmen *m*; **~er** ['-ə] *zoo* Spannerraupe *f*; **~hole** *s* Luft-, Guckloch *n*, Sehschlitz *m*; Schießscharte *f*; *fig* Ausweg *m*; *tr* mit Schießscharten versehen; *a ~~ in the law* e-e Gesetzeslücke; **~-line** *rail* Überholgeleise *n*, Schleife; *el* Nebenleitung, Schleife *f*; *Am aero* Looping *m* od *n*; **~-stitch** Kettenstich *m*; **~-tip terminal** *el* Kabelschuh *m*; **~-way** Umweg *m*; Umleitung *f*; **~y** ['-i] *sl* verrückt.

loose [lu:s] *a* frei, ungebunden; lose, unverpackt; offen, unverschlossen; lose, locker, wack(e)lig, ungenau; *(Kleidung)* weit; *com* frei verfügbar; locker, aufgelockert; *chem* frei; *fig* unzs.-hängend, zwanglos; *(Übersetzung)* frei; *(Lebenswandel)* locker, ausschweifend; *adv* frei, ungebunden, ungezwungen; lose, locker; *tr* los-, freilassen; lockern; auflockern; lösen; freimachen, befreien, lossprechen (*from* von); abdrücken, -schießen; *itr* sich lockern, locker, lose werden; *at a ~ end* ohne feste Beschäftigung; *in ~ order (mil)* in geöffneter Marschordnung; *on the ~* frei, ungebunden, ohne Bindungen; übermütig, losgelassen; *to be on the ~ (sl)* sich amüsieren; *to break ~* ausbrechen; sich frei machen; *to cast ~ (tr)* freisetzen; *itr* frei werden; *to come ~ (Band, Knoten)* aufgehen; *(Knopf)* abgehen; *to cut ~ (tr itr)* (sich) losreißen; *itr* sich befreien; sich ungeniert amüsieren; außer Rand u. Band geraten; *to have a ~ tongue* ein loses Mundwerk haben; *to let, to set, to turn ~* befreien; *to play fast and ~* ein falsches Spiel treiben; *to ride a ~ rein* die Zügel locker lassen *a. fig*; *to work ~ (Schraube)* sich lockern, locker werden; *there is a screw ~ somewhere* es ist was nicht in Ordnung; es ist mulmig, es riecht sauer; **~ bowels** *pl med* offene(r) Leib *m*; **~ contact** *el* Wackelkontakt *m*; **~-jointed, -limbed** *a* gelenkig, beweglich, gewandt; **~-leaf notebook** Loseblattbuch *n*; **~ money** Klein-, Wechselgeld *n*; **~n** ['lu:sn] *tr* freilassen, frei machen, lösen, (auf)lockern, mildern; *itr* frei werden, sich lösen, sich lockern; schwächer, milder werden; **~ness** ['-nis] Lockerheit; Ungebundenheit, Zwanglosigkeit, Freiheit; Ungenauigkeit; Schlüpfrigkeit *f*; *med* Durchfall *m*; **~strife** *bot* (Gelb-)Weiderich *m*.

loot [lu:t] *s* Beute *f*, Raub *m*; *tr* plündern; erbeuten; **~er** ['-ə] Plünderer *m*; **~ing** ['-iŋ] Plünderung *f*.

lop [lɔp] **1.** *tr (Baum)* beschneiden, stutzen; *(to ~ off)* abschneiden, -sägen, entfernen; **2.** *itr tr* lose, locker, schlaff herab-, herunterhängen (lassen); **~-ears** *pl* Hängeohren *n pl*; **~sided** *a* (nach einer Seite) hängend, unsymmetrisch, schief; *mar* mit Schlagseite.

lope [loup] *itr* galoppieren, traben; (in leichten Sprüngen) rennen; *s* Galopp, Trab *m*; *at a ~* im Galopp.

loquac|ious [lo(u)'kweiʃəs] schwatzhaft, geschwätzig; **~iousness** [-nis], **~ity** ['-kwæsiti] Schwatzhaftigkeit, Geschwätzigkeit *f*.

loran ['lɔ:rən, 'lou-] *s. long-range navigation.*

lord [lɔ:d] *s* Herr(scher) (*of* über); Adlige(r); Lord; *hist* Lehnsherr; *hum* (Götter-)Gatte *m*; *the L~* der Herr(gott), Gott; *(Our) L~* der Herr (Jesus); *tr* zum Lord machen; *itr* herrschen (*over* über); *to ~ it, to act the ~* den Herrn spielen, als Herr auftreten; *as drunk as a ~* blau wie e-e Strandhaubitze; *the House of L~s* das (Brit.) Oberhaus; *my L~* [mi'l-] gnädiger Herr! *the L~'s day* der Tag des Herrn, Sonntag; *the L~ of hosts* der Herr der Heerscharen; *the L~'s Prayer* das Vaterunser; *the L~'s Supper* das heilige Abendmahl; **~liness** ['-linis] Würde, Hoheit *f*, Adel *fig*; Hochmut, Stolz *m*; **~(l)ing** ['-(l)iŋ] *pej* Herrchen *n*, Krautjunker *m*; **~ly** ['-li] würdig, würde-, hoheitsvoll, adlig *fig*; hochmütig, stolz, gebieterisch; **~ship** ['-ʃip] Lord-, Herrschaft *f*; *Your, His L~~* Eure, Seine Lordschaft; Euer, Seine Gnaden; **~s spiritual, ~s temporal,** geistliche, weltliche Herren *m pl (im Brit. Oberhaus)*.

lore [lɔ:] Wissen *n*, Lehre, Kunde, Überlieferung *f*.

loric|a ['lɔrikə] *pl -ae* [-si:] *zoo* Panzer *m*; **~ate(d)** ['-eit(id)] *zoo* gepanzert.
Lorraine [lɔ'rein] Lothringen *n*.
lorry ['lɔri] *(motor-~) Br* Last(kraft)-wagen *m*, -auto *n*; *rail* Lore *f*; *min* Hund *m*; *convoy of lorries* Lastwagenkolonne *f*; **~-borne** *a* verlastet; **~-hop** *itr sl* per Anhalter fahren *od* reisen.
lose [lu:z] *irr lost, lost tr* verlieren, verlustig gehen (*s.th.* e-r S); einbüßen, *fam* loswerden, kommen um; sich entgehen, *fam* sich aus der Nase gehen lassen, nicht mitbekommen; vergessen; *(Gelegenheit)* versäumen; *(a. Zug)* verpassen; verschwenden, vergeuden; *sport* abhängen; bringen (*s.o. s.th.* jdn um etw), kosten (*s.o. s.th.* jdn etw); *itr* e-n Verlust, Verluste erleiden (*on* bei; *by* durch); *(Am: to ~ out) (im Spiel, Kampf)* verlieren, unterliegen, *fam* den kürzeren ziehen (*to* gegen); *(Uhr)* nachgehen; *to be lost* verlorengehen; *to ~ o.s.* sich verirren; verwirrt, verlegen werden; sich verlieren (*in* in); (in Träumerei) versinken; *to ~ ground* den Boden unter den Füßen, den Halt verlieren; *with s.o.* bei jdm an Einfluß verlieren; *to ~ o.'s head (fig)* den Kopf verlieren; *to ~ interest* uninteressant werden; *to ~ o.'s life* ums Leben kommen; *to ~ o.'s place* nicht mehr wissen, wo man *(bei der Lektüre)* stehengeblieben ist; *to ~ reason, senses* den Verstand verlieren *(a. übertreibend)*; sich mächtig aufregen; *to ~ sight of* aus den Augen verlieren; sich nicht mehr kümmern um, vernachlässigen; *to ~ o.'s strength* von Kräften kommen; *to ~ o.'s temper* die Geduld verlieren, aus der Fassung geraten; heftig werden; *to ~ track of* jede Spur *gen*, aus den Augen verlieren; *to ~ o.'s way* den Weg verlieren, sich verirren, sich verlaufen; *I ~ my hair* die Haare gehen mir aus; **~r** ['-ə] Verlierer *m*; *to be a ~~ by s.th.* durch e-e S Verluste erleiden; *to come off a ~~* den kürzeren ziehen; **~ing** ['-iŋ] *a* verlierend, geschlagen; verloren; aussichtslos; *com* verlustbringend; *s* Verlust *m*; *pl* Spielverluste *m pl*; *~~ business* Verlustgeschäft *n*; *~~ game* aussichtslose(s) Spiel *n*.
loss [lɔs] Verlust *m*; Einbuße *f*, Nachteil, Schaden, Ausfall *m* (*in* an); *com* Wertminderung *f*; *at a ~* in Verlegenheit (*for* um); *com* mit Verlust; *to be at a ~ to do s.th.* etw nicht fertigbringen; *how to do s.th.* nicht wissen, wie man etw anfangen soll; *for s.th.* verlegen sein um; *to sell at a ~* mit Verlust verkaufen; *to suffer heavy ~es* schwere Verluste erleiden; *he is no great ~* an ihm ist nicht viel verloren; *dead ~* vollständige(r) Verlust *m*; *partial, total ~* Teil-, Gesamtschaden *m*; *~ of altitude* Höhenverlust *m*; *~ of appetite* Appetitlosigkeit *f*; *~ of blood* Blutverlust *m*; *~ by fire* Brandschaden *m*; *~ of life* Verluste *m pl* an Menschenleben; *~ of money* Geldverlust *m*; *~ of power* Leistungsabfall *m*; *~ of prestige* Prestigeverlust *m*; *~ of production* Produktionsausfall *m*; *~ of civic rights* Aberkennung *f* der bürgerlichen Ehrenrechte; *~ of time* Zeitverlust *m*; *~ of tonnage* Tonnageverlust *m*; *~ of wages* Lohnausfall *m*; *~ in weight* Gewichtsverlust *m*; *~* **leader** *Am* Reklameschlager *m*.
lost [lɔ(:)st] *pret u. pp von lose*; *a* verloren; vergessen; verirrt; abhanden gekommen; verschwunden; *to be ~ upon s.o.* auf jdn keinen Eindruck machen; *to be ~ to hono(u)r, to shame* kein Ehrgefühl mehr haben, keine Scham mehr empfinden; *to be ~ in thought* in Gedanken versunken sein; *a ~ cause* e-e aussichtslose Sache; *~* **motion** *tech* tote(r) Gang; Leerlauf *m*; **~-property office** Fundbüro *n*.
lot [lɔt] *s* Los *a. fig*; *fig* Schicksal, Geschick *n*; (Gewinn-, Steuer-)Anteil *m*; Parzelle *f*; (Begräbnis-)Platz *m*; *Am* Filmgelände *n*; Gruppe; *com* Partie *f*, Posten *m*; *the (whole) ~ (fam)* der ganze Kram *od* Krempel; *a ~, ~s(of) (fam)* e-e Menge *od* Masse, ein Haufen; viel; beträchtlich; *tr* parzellieren; zuteilen; *itr (to draw, to cast ~s)* losen, das Los entscheiden lassen; (*for* um) *to ~ out* auslosen; *by ~* durch das Los; *to cast, to throw in o.'s ~ with s.o.* jds Schicksal teilen; *a ~ you care! (iro)* das interessiert dich ja doch nicht! *the ~ decides* das Los entscheidet; *a bad ~ (fam)* ein schlechter Kerl, e-e miese Person; *broken ~* Partieware *f*.
lotion ['louʃən] *pharm* Tinktur *f*, Wasser *n*; *hair, shaving ~* Haar-, Rasierwasser *n*.
lottery ['lɔtəri] Lotterie, Verlosung *f*; *fig* Glücksspiel *n*, *fam* -sache *f*; *charity ~* Tombola *f*; *class-, serial ~* Klassenlotterie *f*; **~-collector** Lotterieeinnehmer *m*; *~* **list** Ziehungsliste *f*; **~-loan** Prämienanleihe *f*; **~-number** Losnummer *f*; **~-prize** Lotteriegewinn *m*; **~-tax** Lotteriesteuer *f*; **~-ticket** Lotterielos *n*; *~* **wheel** Lostrommel *f*, Glücksrad *n*.
lotto ['lɔtou] Lotto *n*.
lotus ['loutəs] Lotos(blume *f*); Honigklee; *(Mythologie)* Lotos *m*; **~-eater** *(Mythologie)* Lotosesser; *fig* stille(r) Genießer, Träumer *m*.
loud [laud] *a* laut; geräuschvoll, lärmend; *fig* lebhaft, eifrig; schreiend, grell; auffallend; auffällig, unfein; *Am* stark riechend; *adv* laut; **~ness** ['-nis] Lautstärke *f a. radio*, Lärm *m*; *fig* Lebhaftigkeit; Auffälligkeit *f*; **~-speaker, -hailer** Lautsprecher *m*; Megaphon *n*.
lounge [laundʒ] *itr* herumliegen, -sitzen, -stehen, -bummeln, -lungern, -trödeln; sich rekeln; (herum)faulenzen; *s* Herumbummeln *n*; (Hotel-)Halle, Diele; Eingangshalle *f*, Foyer *n*; Gesellschafts-, Unterhaltungsraum *m*; Chaiselongue *f* od *n*, Couch *f*, (Liege-) Sofa *n*; *to ~ away (Zeit)* vertrödeln, verbummeln; **~-chair** Klubsessel *m*; **~-coat** Sakko *m*; **~-lizard** *sl* Salonlöwe; Gigolo *m*; **~r** ['-ə] Bummler, Faulenzer *m*; **~-seat** kleine(s) Sofa *n*; **~-suit** *Br* Straßenanzug *m*.
lour, lower ['lauə] *itr* finster, drohend blicken (*on, upon, at* auf); die Stirn runzeln; *(Himmel)* finster, schwarz, drohend aussehen; sich verfinstern; *s* finstere(r), drohende(r) Blick *m*; Düsterkeit *f*; **~ing** ['-riŋ] finster blickend; düster, trüb(e), finster.
lous|e [laus] *pl lice* [lais] *s* Laus *f*; *sl* gemeine(r) Kerl *m*, gemeine Person *f*; *tr* [lauz] (ab)lausen; *to ~~ up (sl)* versauen; **~ewort** ['lauswə:t] *bot* Stinkende Nieswurz *f*; **~y** ['lauzi] verlaust; *sl* lausig, gemein, ekelhaft; *~~ with (sl)* voll von, übersät mit.
lout [laut] Tölpel, Lümmel, Flegel *m*; **~ish** ['-iʃ] tölpel-, lümmelhaft.
louver ['lu:və] *arch* Laterne *f*, Dachreiter *m*; Jalousiefenster *n*, -wand *f*; Lüftungsschlitz *m*.
lovable ['lʌvəbl] liebenswert, anziehend.
love [lʌv] *s* Liebe, Zuneigung (*of, for, to, towards s.o.* zu jdm); Liebe, Neigung *f*, Hang *m* (*of, for s.th.* zu e-r S); Vorliebe *f* (*of, for s.th.* für etw); Liebe(slust, -erfüllung *f*, -erlebnis *n*); Liebe *(Person)*, Geliebte(r *m*), Liebste(r *m*) *f*, Liebchen *n*, Liebling; Liebhaber *m*; *fam* etw Reizendes; *sport (bes. Tennis)* Null *f*, nichts; *tr* lieben, lieb-, gern haben; (gern) mögen *(a. Speisen)*; *to ~ to do* gern tun; *itr* lieben, verliebt sein; *for ~* aus, zum Spaß *od* Vergnügen; *for the ~ of* aus Liebe zu, *dat* zuliebe, um ... willen; *not for ~ or money* nicht für Geld und gute Worte; *in ~* verliebt; *to be in ~ with s.o.* in jdn verliebt sein, jdn lieben; *to fall in ~ with s.o.* sich in jdn verlieben; *to give o.'s ~ to s.o.* jdn herzlich grüßen; *to make ~ (sl)* poussieren; sich mitea. amüsieren, geschlechtlich mitea. verkehren; *to s.o.* jdm den Hof machen; *to send o.'s ~ to s.o.* jdn grüßen lassen; *there's no ~ lost between them* sie können sich nicht ausstehen, *fam* riechen; *fam* sie sind sich nicht grün; **~-affair** Liebesgeschichte *f*, -handel *m*; **~-bird** *orn* Edelsittich, Unzertrennliche(r) *m*; **~-child** Kind *n* der Liebe; **~-drink, -philtre, -potion** Liebestrank *m*; **~-feast** *rel* Liebesmahl *n*, Agape *f*; **~-game, -set** Nullpartie *f*; **~-in--idleness** (wildes) Stiefmütterchen *n*; **~-knot** Liebesschleife *f*; **~less** ['-lis] lieblos; **~-letter** Liebesbrief *m*; **~-lies--(a-)bleeding** *bot* Fuchsschwanz *m*; **~liness** ['-linis] Lieblichkeit *f*, Liebreiz *m*; *fam* Köstlichkeit *f*; **~-lock** Schmachtlocke *f*; **~-longing** Liebessehnen *n*; **~lorn** ['-lɔ:n]: *to be ~~* Liebeskummer haben; **~ly** ['-li] lieblich, liebreizend; schön, hübsch; *fam* herrlich, großartig; **~-making** Liebeswerben *n*; *sl* Poussage *f*; Geschlechtsverkehr *m*; **~-match** Liebesheirat *f*; **~r** ['-ə] Liebhaber *a. allg*, Freund, Geliebte(r) *m*; *pl (pair of ~~s)* Liebespaar *n*, *die* Liebende(n) *pl*; *~~ of horses* Pferdeliebhaber *m*; *a ~~ of good music* ein Freund guter Musik; *to be a ~~ of good wine* e-n guten Tropfen lieben; **~-scene** *theat lit* Liebesszene *f*; **~-sick** liebeskrank; **~-song** Liebeslied *n*; **~-story** Liebesgeschichte *f*; *~* **token** Liebespfand *n*; **~y** ['-i] *sl* Schätzchen *n*.
loving ['lʌviŋ] *a* liebend; liebevoll, zärtlich; Liebes-; *your ~ (Brief)* Dein(e) Dich liebende(r); **~-cup** Pokal *m (a. als Sportpreis)*; **~-kindness** Herzensgüte *f*.

*

low [lou] **1.** *a* niedrig, nieder; tief, tief(er) gelegen, tief(er)liegend; *(Gewässer)* flach, seicht; *(~ in the sky) (Gestirn)* tief am Himmel (stehend), tief(stehend); *geog (Breite)* äquatornah, südlicher; *(~-necked) (Kleid, Bluse)* tief ausgeschnitten; *(Verbeugung)* tief; versteckt, verborgen; *fig* schwach, kraft-, energielos; *(Stimmung)* gedrückt, trüb(e), melancholisch; niedergedrückt, -geschlagen; klein, gering(fügig, -wertig); mäßig, bescheiden, einfach, schlicht, niedrig, nieder *(a. Herkunft, Stand, Rang)*; gewöhnlich; *(Gesellschaft)* schlecht; *(Gesinnung, Verhalten, Ausdrucksweise)* niedrig, niederträchtig, gemein, roh, pöbelhaft, unwürdig, schamlos; *(Meinung)* ungünstig, gering, schlecht; *(Preis, Kosten, Kurs, Lohn, Gehalt, Temperatur)* niedrig; *(Luftdruck, Puls)* schwach; *(Vorrat, Bestand)* erschöpft, verbraucht, zs.geschmolzen, (zs.)geschrumpft; nicht gut versehen (*on* mit); *fam* knapp bei Kasse; *(Verpflegung)* knapp, dürftig, kümmerlich, mager, einfach; *(Kost)* schmal; *(Gesundheit)* schwach, schlecht; *(biol, Kultur)* niedrig, primitiv, unentwickelt; *(Zeit)* noch nicht weit zurückliegend; *(Datum)* neuere(s), jüngere(s); *(Stimme, Laut)* schwach, leise; tief; *mot (Gang)* niedrigst; *rel* niederkirchlich, auf die Low Church bezüglich; *adv* niedrig, tief; nach unten; *fig* auf niedriger Stufe; einfach, bescheiden; gemein, roh; schlecht, ungünstig; schwach; leise *(sprechen, singen)*; tief *(singen)*; billig *(kaufen, verkaufen)*; *s das* Niedrige; *mot der* niedrigste, *der* erste Gang; *(Kartenspiel)* niedrigste(r) Trumpf; *sport* (Spieler *m*, Mannschaft *f* mit der) niedrigste(n) Punktzahl *f*; *fam* Tiefstand, tiefe(r) Stand *m*; *Am mete* Tief(druckgebiet) *n*; *pl geog* Niederung *f*; *as ~ as* so niedrig, so tief wie; hinab, hinunter bis zu; *to be ~ (Sonne, Barometer, Preise, Kurse)* niedrig stehen; *to bring ~* zu Fall bringen; erniedrigen, demütigen; *to fall ~* tief fallen *a. fig*; *fig* tief sinken; *to feel ~* sich krank, elend fühlen; niedergeschlagen, deprimiert sein; *to fly ~* tief fliegen; *to get ~ (mit der Stimme)* heruntergehen; *to have a ~ opinion of s.o.* von jdm nicht viel halten; *to lay ~* umstoßen, -werfen, über den Haufen werfen; umlegen, -bringen, töten; *to be laid ~* ans Bett gefesselt sein; *to lie ~* flach, lang, ausgestreckt liegen; sich versteckt halten, sich nicht sehen lassen, sich nicht zeigen; *to live ~* sehr bescheiden leben, ein kümmerliches Dasein fristen; *to play ~* (mit) niedrig(em Einsatz) spielen; *to run ~ (Vorrat)* erschöpft sein, zu Ende gehen; *the sands are running ~* es ist nicht mehr viel Zeit, die Zeit drängt; das Leben geht zu Ende, *lit* neigt sich; **~ altitude, level** *aero* geringe Höhe *f*; *~ altitude flight* Tiefflug *m*; **~-born** *a* von niederer Herkunft; **~-boy** *Am* Kommode *f*; **~-bred** *a* von niederer Herkunft, aus niederem Stand; ungesittet, ungebildet, gewöhnlich, roh; **~-brow** *a s fam* geistig *od* künstlerisch anspruchslos(er Mensch *m*); *s* Banause, Philister, Spießer *m*; **~-browed** *a* mit niedriger, fliehender Stirn; *(Raum)* düster; **~-budget** billig; *the* **L~ Church** die niederkirchliche, pietistische Bewegung der anglikanischen Kirche; **~ comedy** Schwank *m*, Posse, Farce, Burleske *f*; **~-cost** *a* billig; *the* **L~ Countries** *pl* die Niederlande *pl (einschließlich Belgiens u. Luxemburgs)*; **~-down** *a fam* niedrig, gemein, verkommen; *s sl* ungeschminkte Wahrheit *f*, bloße Tatsachen *f pl*, rauhe Wirklichkeit *f*; Geheimnachrichten *f pl*; **~-flung** *a Am* gemein, niederträchtig; **~ flying** *aero* Tiefflug *m*; *~-~ attack (aero)* Tiefangriff *m*; **~ frequency** *el* Niederfrequenz *f*; **~ gear** *Am mot* 1. Gang *m*; **L~ German** Nieder-, Plattdeutsch *n*; **~-grade** *a* minderwertig; **~land** ['-lənd] *meist pl (bes. das schottische)* Tief-, Unterland *n*; **~-level**: *~-~ attack (aero)* Tiefangriff *m*; *~-~ flight (aero)* Tiefflug *m*; **~ life** das Leben des Volkes; **~liness** ['-linis] Schlichtheit; Demut, Bescheidenheit; Gemeinheit *f*; **~ly** ['-li] *a adv* einfach, schlicht; demütig, bescheiden; sanft; gemein, niederträchtig; **~-lying** flach; *~-~ coast* Flachküste *f*; **L~ Mass** *rel* stille Messe *f*; **~-minded** *a* niedriggesinnt, gemein, gewöhnlich; **~ neck** (Kleider-)Ausschnitt *m*; **~-necked** *a (Kleid)* (tief, weit) ausgeschnitten; **~ness** ['-nis] Niedrigkeit *(a. d. Geburt, d. Gesinnung, e-s Preises)*; Tiefe *(a. d. Stimme, e-s Tones)*; Flachheit; Schwäche; Gedrücktheit; Gemeinheit *f*; *~~ of spirits* Niedergeschlagenheit *f*; **~-pitched** *a (Stimme)* tief; *(Dach)* mit geringer Neigung; **~-powered** *a* mit geringer Leistung; **~ pressure** *mete* Tiefdruck *m*; *~-~ area* Tiefdruckgebiet *n*; *~-~ chamber* Unterdruckkammer *f*; **~-priced, -rated** *a* billig; **~ relief** *(Kunst)* Basrelief *n*; **~ shoes** *pl* Halbschuhe *m pl*; **~-spirited** *a* niedergeschlagen, (nieder)gedrückt, traurig, melancholisch; **L~ Sunday** *der* Weiße Sonntag, *der* 1. S. nach Ostern; **~ tension** *el* Niederspannung *f*; **~ tide** Ebbe *f*; *fig* Tiefstand *m*; **~ water** Niedrigwasser *n*; Ebbe *f*; *fam* Geldmangel *m*; *to be in ~~* knapp bei Kasse sein, auf dem Trockenen sitzen; *~-~ mark* Tiefpunkt, tiefste(r) Punkt *m*; *the* **L~ Week** die Woche nach Ostern; **2.** *itr (Kuh)* muhen, brüllen; *s* Muhen, Brüllen *n (der Kuh)*.

lower ['louə] **1.** *Komparativ von low* tiefer, niedriger, niederer; tiefer gelegen, tiefer liegend, tiefer befindlich; tiefer stehend; *(in Zssgen meist)* Unter-, *geog a.* Nieder-; **L~ Austria** Niederösterreich *n*; **~ berth** *rail* untere(s) Bett *n*; **~ case** *typ* Kleinbuchstaben *m pl*; **~-case** *a* Kleinbuchstaben-; *tr* in Kleinbuchstaben (um)setzen; **L~ Chamber, L~ House** *parl* Unter-, Abgeordnetenhaus *n*, 2. Kammer *f*; *the* **~ classes** *pl* die unteren Gesellschaftsschichten, Klassen *f pl (Am a. Schule)*; **~ deck** *mar* Unter-, Zwischendeck *n*; Unteroffiziere u. Mannschaften *pl*; **~ form** *(Schule)* Unterklasse *f*; **~most** ['-moust] *a* niedrigst, niederst, tiefst, unterst; *adv* am niedrigsten, zuunterst; *the* **~ school** die Mittel- und Unterstufe, die unteren Klassen *f pl*; **2.** *tr* hinunter-, herunterlassen, senken; *(die Augen)* niederschlagen; *(Flagge)* niederholen, streichen; (ab)schwächen; *(die Stimme)* senken; *(Tonumfang)* verringern; *(Preis)* senken, drücken; herabsetzen, ermäßigen; *(Stellung, Rang)* herabsetzen; erniedrigen, demütigen, herabwürdigen; *(Boot)* fieren; *aero (Fahrgestell)* ausfahren; *itr* sich senken; *(Preise)* sinken, fallen, heruntergehen; abnehmen, nachlassen, schwächer werden; sich mäßigen, sich vermindern; *(Boden)* sich neigen, abfallen; *to ~ o.s.* sich erniedrigen, sich demütigen, sich herablassen; **~ing** ['louəriŋ] *s* Senkung *f*, Sinken *n*; *a* Senk-; **3.** ['lauə] *s. lour*.

loyal ['lɔiəl] loyal, (pflichtge)treu, zuverlässig, anständig, aufrecht; **~ist** ['-ist] Regierungstreue(r), Treugesinnte(r) *m*; **~ty** ['-ti] Loyalität, Treue *(to* zu, gegen); Zuverlässigkeit *f*.

lozenge ['lɔzindʒ] *math* Rhombus *m*, Raute; *pharm* Pastille, Tablette *f*, Bonbon *m od n*.

lubber ['lʌbə] Tolpatsch, Tölpel; *m*; *pej* Landratte *f*; **~ly** ['-li] *a adv* tolpatschig, tölpelhaft.

lube ['l(j)u:b] *(~ oil) Am = lubricant.*

lubric|ant ['lu:brikənt] *(Am a.: ~)* Schmiermittel *n*; **~ate** ['-eit] *tr* (ein-, ab)schmieren, (ein)fetten, (ein)ölen; *fig* erleichtern, schmieren; **~ation** [lu:bri'keiʃən] (Ab-, Ein-)Schmieren, (Ein-)Fetten, (Ein-)Ölen *n*, Schmierung *f*; *fig* Schmieren *n*; *~~ diagram* Schmierplan *m*; **~ator** ['lu:brikeitə] Ab-, Einschmierer *m*; Schmierbüchse *f*, -nippel *m*, -mittel *n*; **~ity** [lu:'brisiti] Schlüpfrigkeit *a. fig*; *fig* Laszivität, Geilheit; Durchtriebenheit *f*.

luce [lju:s] (ausgewachsener) Hecht *m*.

lucen|cy ['lu:snsi] Leuchtfähigkeit, -kraft; Transparenz *f*; **~t** ['-t] leuchtend; durchscheinend, transparent.

Lucern|e [lu'sə:n] Luzern *n*; *the Lake of ~~* der Vierwaldstätter See; **l~(e)** [lu:'sə:n] *bot* Luzerne *f*.

lucid ['lu:sid] klar, verständlich, einleuchtend; scharf(sichtig); *(Stern)* sichtbar; (geistig) normal, bei (vollem) Verstand; *poet* leuchtend, hell; **~ity** [lu:'siditi] Klarheit; Verständlichkeit; (Verstandes-)Schärfe; Helle *f*; **~ intervals** *pl* lichte Momente *m pl*.

Lucifer ['lu:sifə] Luzifer *m*, der Teufel; *astr* der Morgenstern.

luck [lʌk] Glücksumstände *m pl*, Zufall *m*, Schicksal, Geschick; Glück(sfall *m*) *n*; *for ~* als Glückbringer; *in ~* glücklich; *out of ~* unglücklich; *worse ~* unglücklicherweise, leider; *to be down on o.'s ~ (fam)* Pech haben, ein Pechvogel sein; *to have no ~* kein Glück haben; *to have a streak of ~* e-e Glückssträhne haben; *to try o.'s ~* sein Glück versuchen; *just my ~! (Am) tough ~! (fam)* so'n Pech! Pech gehabt! Pech wie immer! *bad ~ to him!* der Teufel soll ihn holen! *as ~ would have it* wie es der Zufall wollte; *good, bad ~* Glück, Unglück *n*; **~ily** ['-ili] glücklicherweise; **~iness** ['-inis] Glück(haftigkeit *f*) *n*; **~less** ['-lis] unglücklich; **~y** ['-i] glücklich; glückbringend, günstig; erfolgreich; *to be ~~* Glück haben; *~~-bag, -dip, -tub* Glückstopf *m*; *~~ day, penny, stone* Glückstag, -pfennig, -stein *m*; *~~ guess, hit, shot* Glückstreffer *m*.

lucr|ative ['lu:krətiv] einträglich, gewinnbringend, lukrativ, lohnend; **~e** ['lu:kə] *meist hum pej (filthy ~~)* schmutzige(s) Geschäft *n*; Profitgier *f*; *hum* Mammon *m*, Geld *n*.

lucubrat|e ['lu:kju(:)breit] *itr* fleißig, *bes.* bei Nacht arbeiten *od* studieren; gelehrt, trocken schreiben; **~ion** [lu:kju(:)'breiʃən] fleißige, Nachtarbeit; gelehrte Tätigkeit *f*; *a. (bes. pl) hum* hochwissenschaftliche(s) Werk *n*, gelehrte Abhandlung *f*.

ludicrous ['lu:dikrəs] possierlich, drollig, spaßig, ulkig, *fam* komisch.

ludo ['lu:dou] Mensch, ärgere dich nicht *n*.

luff [lʌf] *s mar* Luv(seite) *f*; *itr tr (to ~ up)* anluven.

lug [lʌg] *tr* schleppen, (hinter sich her)ziehen, zerren *(at* an); *fig (Thema, Argument)* an den Haaren herbeiziehen *(in, into a conversation* bei e-m Gespräch); *s Scot* Ohr; Öhr *n*; Henkel, Griff *m*; Ziehen, Zerren *n*, Ruck; *Am sl* Dämlack, Depp *m*; *to put the ~ on* Geld ziehen aus.

luge [lu:ʒ] *s* Rodel(schlitten) *m*; *itr* rodeln.

luggage ['lʌgidʒ] *s Br* (Reise-)Gepäck; *Am* Rotbraun *n*, Lohfarbe *f*; *a Am* rotbraun, lohfarben; *to have o.'s ~ registered* sein Gepäck aufgeben; *article, piece of ~* Gepäckstück *n*; *free ~* Freigepäck *n*; *passenger's ~* Reisegepäck *n*; *personal ~* Handgepäck *n*; **~boot** *mot* Kofferraum *m*; **~-carrier** Gepäckträger *m (am Fahrrad)*; **~-check, -ticket, -receipt** Gepäckschein *m*; **~-dispatch** Gepäckabfertigung *f*; **~-insurance** Gepäckversicherung *f*; **~ label** Gepäckadresse *f*; **~ locker** Gepäckschließfach *n*; **~-office** Gepäckaufgabe, Gepäckaufbewahrung *f*; **~-rack** Gepäcknetz *n*; **~-rail** Gepäckträger, Kuli *m*; **~-room, -space** *mot* Koffer-

raum *m*; **~-tag** Gepäckanhänger *m (Zettel)*; **~-van** *rail* Packwagen *m*.
lugger ['lʌgə] *mar* Logger, Lugger *m*.
lugubrious [lu:'g(j)u:briəs] tieftraurig, unheilvoll, (äußerst) schmerzlich.
lukewarm ['lu:kwɔ:m] *(Flüssigkeit)* lauwarm; *fig* lau, gleichgültig, ohne Eifer; **~ness** ['-nis] *fig* Lauheit, Gleichgültigkeit *f*.
lull [lʌl] *tr* einlullen, beruhigen; beschwichtigen, besänftigen; mildern, abschwächen; *itr* sich beruhigen *(a. die See)*; *(Sturm, Wind)* sich legen; *s* Windstille; (kurze) Ruhe(pause); (kurze) Unterbrechung *f*, Stillstand *m*; einschläfernde(s) Geräusch *n*; *com* Flaute *f*; *to ~ to sleep* in den Schlaf wiegen; *a ~ in conversation* e-e Gesprächspause; **~aby** ['lʌləbai] Wiegenlied *n*.
lulu ['lu:lu:] *Am sl* etwas Pfundiges; Zulage *f* (zum Gehalt).
lumb|ago [lʌm'beigou] *med* Lumbago *f*, Hexenschuß *m*; **~ar** ['lʌmbə] *anat* Lenden-.
lumber ['lʌmbə] **1.** *s* Gerümpel; (gesägtes) Bau-, Nutzholz *n*; *tr (mit Gerümpel)* vollstopfen, -pfropfen; auf e-n Haufen werfen; *(Bäume)* fällen, schlagen, zu Nutzholz sägen (u. abtransportieren); **~er** ['-rə], **~man** ['-mən]Holzfäller, -arbeiter; *sl* Schwindler *m*; **~ing** ['-riŋ] Holzfällen *n*, -bearbeitung *f*; **~jack** = *~man*; Lumberjack *m*; *to eat like a ~~ (fam)* fressen wie ein Scheunendrescher; **~mill** Sägemühle *f*, -werk *n*; **~-room** Rumpelkammer *f*; **~-trade** Holzhandel *m*; **~-yard** Holzlager *n*; **2.** *itr* rumpeln, poltern; *s* Rumpeln, Gerumpel *n*; *to ~ along* dahinrumpeln; *to ~ by, to ~ past* vorüberrumpeln; **~ing** ['-riŋ] rumpelnd.
lumin|ary ['lu:minəri] Leuchtkörper *m*, Licht(quelle *f*) *n*; *fig* Leuchte *f*; **~esce** [lu:mi'nes] *itr* lumineszieren, nachleuchten; **~escence** [-'nesns] Lumineszenz *f*; **~escent** [-'nesnt] lumineszierend, nachleuchtend; **~osity** [lu:mi'nɔsiti] Helligkeit, Leuchtkraft; Lichtstärke *f*; **~ous** ['lu:minəs] leuchtend, lichtausstrahlend; Leucht-, Licht-; hell (erleuchtet); *fig* einleuchtend, verständlich, klar; glänzend, hervorragend; *~~ dial* Leuchtzifferblatt *n*; *~~ energy (phys)* strahlende Energie *f*; *~~ intensity* Lichtstärke *f*; *~~ paint* Leuchtfarbe *f*; *~~ ray* Lichtstrahl *m*; *~~ screen* Leuchtschirm *m*.
lummox ['lʌməks] *fam* Tolpatsch, Tölpel; Pfuscher *m*.
lump [lʌmp] *s* (kleinerer) Klumpen *m*, Stück *n (Zucker)*; *fig* Haufen *m*, Masse, Menge; *med* Beule *f (on the forehead* auf der Stirne); *fam* Klotz, Tolpatsch *m*; *tech* Luppe *f*; *com* Pauschal-; *tr (to ~ together)* e-n Klumpen bilden, e-n Haufen machen aus; auf e-n Haufen werfen, zs.werfen, -tun; zs.-fassen (*under a title* unter e-r Überschrift); *(to ~ in)* in e-n Topf werfen (*with* mit); *fam* bleibenlassen; *to ~ it (sl)* sich damit abfinden; *itr* Klumpen bilden; *(to ~ along)* sich weiterschleppen; *in the ~* im ganzen; *com* pauschal; in Bausch u. Bogen; *to have a ~ in o.'s throat* vor Erregung nicht sprechen können; e-n Kloß im Hals haben; *a ~ of gold* ein Klumpen Gold; *a ~ of sugar, a sugar ~* ein Stück Zucker; **~-coal** Stückkohle *f*; **~ing** ['-iŋ] *a fam* völlig, reichlich; voll; massig, schwer; **~ish** ['-iʃ] klumpig, massig, schwer; schwerfällig, dumm; **~-sugar** Würfelzucker *m*; **~ sum** runde Summe *f*; Pauschalbetrag *m*; *attr* Pauschal-; *~~ allowance* Pauschalvergütung *f*; *~~ charge* Pauschalgebühr *f*; **~y** ['-i] klumpig; holprig; *(Wasser)* bewegt, unruhig; *fig* schwerfällig, tolpatschig.
lun|acy ['lu:nəsi] Geisteskrankheit; Verrücktheit *f*, Wahn-, Irr-, Blödsinn *m*; **~ar** ['lu:nə] *a* Mond-; *~~ caustic* Höllenstein *m*; *~~ month, year* Mondmonat *m*, -jahr *n*; **~atic** ['lu:nətik] *a* geisteskrank, irr(e); wahn-, blödsinnig, verrückt; *s* Wahnsinnige(r) *m*; *~~ asylum* Irrenhaus *n*, Heil- (u. Pflege-)Anstalt *f*; *~~ fringe (Am pol)* radikale(r) Flügel *m*.
lunch [lʌntʃ] *s* Gabelfrühstück; (2.) Frühstück *n*; *itr* (zu) Mittag essen; **~ counter** Theke *f*; **~eon** ['-ən] (offizielles) (Gabel-)Frühstück *n*; **~eonette** [lʌntʃə'net] Imbiß *m*; Schnellgaststätte, Frühstücksstube, Imbißhalle *f*; **~ stand** *Am* (kleine) Imbißhalle *f*; **~ time, hour** Mittag(szeit *f*) *m*.
lunette [lu:'net] *arch* Lünette *f*, Bogenfeld *n*; Unterwasserbrille; *mil* Schlepp-, Zug-, Protzöse; *(Pferd)* Scheuklappe *f*.
lung [lʌŋ] Lungenflügel *m*; *pl* Lunge; *fig* Grünfläche, Lunge *f* e-r Großstadt; *at the top of his ~s* so laut er konnte; *to have good ~s* ein lautes Organ haben; *iron ~ (med)* eiserne Lunge *f*; **~er** ['-ə] *sl* Lungenkranke(r); Schwindsüchtige(r) *m*; **~-power** Stimmkraft *f*; **~wort** ['-wə:t] *bot* Lungenkraut *n*.
lunge [lʌndʒ] *s (Fechten)* Ausfall; plötzliche(r) Stoß *od* Sprung *m* (nach vorn); Longe, Laufleine *f (für Pferde)*; *itr* e-n Ausfall machen, (vorwärts-)stoßen; losstürzen, -rasen (*at* auf).
lupin|e ['l(j)u:pin] *bot* Lupine *f*; **~e** ['l(j)u:pain] wölfisch, gefräßig.
lupus ['lu:pəs] Hauttuberkulose *f*.
lurch [lə:tʃ] **1.** *s* Zurseiterollen, Seitwärtskippen; Taumeln; *mar* Überholen *n*; *itr* zur Seite rollen, seitwärts kippen; taumeln, torkeln; *mar* überholen; **2.** *s*: *to leave in the ~* im Stich lassen, *fam* sitzenlassen, versetzen; **~er** ['-ə] (kleiner) Dieb; Spion; *Art* Spürhund *m*.
lure [ljuə] *s* Köder *a. fig*; *fig* Zauber, Reiz *m*; *tr (to ~ on)* ködern *a. fig*; *fig* anlocken, -ziehen; verlocken (*into* zu).
lurid ['ljuərid] (toten)bleich, (asch-)fahl; gespenstisch rot; aufregend, (nerven)aufpeitschend; grausig, grauenhaft, unheimlich.
lurk [lə:k] *itr* auf der Lauer, im Hinterhalt liegen; warten; ein verborgenes Dasein führen, unbekannt sein; herumschleichen; *s*: *on the ~* auf der Lauer; **~ing-place** Schlupfwinkel *m*, Versteck *n*.
luscious ['lʌʃəs] wohlschmeckend; duftend; köstlich *a. allg*; widerlich süß; *fig* überladen; **~ness** ['-nis] Wohlgeschmack, Duft *m*; Köstlichkeit; (widerliche) Süße *f*.
lush [lʌʃ] **1.** saftig, weich; üppig; luxuriös; *fig* reich (verziert), extravagant; **2.** *sl* Schnaps; Besoffene(r) *m*; *itr tr* saufen, picheln; *a* besoffen.
lust [lʌst] *s* Gelüst, Verlangen *n*, Drang *m*, Gier; *(bes. geschlechtliche)* Begierde *f* (*for* nach); *itr* verlangen, gierig sein (*after, for* nach); *fam* scharf sein (*after, for* auf); *~s of the flesh (Bibel)* Fleischeslust *f*; **~ful** ['-ful] gierig, begehrlich; lüstern, geil.
lust|iness ['lʌstinis] Energie, Kraft, Stärke, Jugendfrische *f*; **~y** ['lʌsti] kraftvoll, kräftig, stark; jugendfrisch; lebhaft.
lustr|e, *Am* **luster** ['lʌstə] Glanz, Schimmer *m*; strahlende Schönheit *f*; Ruhm *m*; Kristallgehänge *n*; Kronleuchter, Lüster *m*; Poliermittel *n*, Politur *f*; Lüster *m (Glanzgewebe)*; *min* Glanzfläche *f*; *(Töpferei)* metallische(r) Glanz *m*; *to add ~ to, to throw ~ on* mit neuem Glanz erfüllen, in neuem Glanz erstrahlen lassen; **~ous** ['lʌstrəs] glänzend, schimmernd; strahlend, hell; *fig* erstklassig.
lut|anist, ~ist ['lu:t(ən)ist] Lautenspieler *m*; **~e** [lu:t] **1.** Laute *f*; **2.** Kitt; Gummiring *m*; *tr* (ver)kitten (*with* mit).
Lutheran ['lu:θərən] *a* lutherisch; *s* Lutheraner *m*; **~ism** ['-izm] Luthertum *n*.
lux [lʌks] *pl. a. luces* ['l(j)usi:z] Lux *n (Einheit der Beleuchtungsstärke)*.
luxat|e ['lʌkseit] *tr* aus-, verrenken; **~ion** [lʌk'seiʃən] Aus-, Verrenkung *f*.
luxur|iance, -cy [lʌg'zjuəriəns(i)] Üppigkeit *f*, Reichtum *m*; Fülle *f* (*of* an); **~iant** [-t] üppig, reich; wuchernd; *fig* überschwenglich; *~~ imagination* reiche, blühende Phantasie *f*; **~iate** [-eit] *itr* üppig wachsen, *pej* wuchern; prassen; schwelgen (*in* in); **~ious** [lʌg'zjuəriəs] schwelgerisch; üppig; luxuriös; **~y** ['lʌkʃəri] Wohlleben *n*, Verschwendung(ssucht) *f*; Luxus(gegenstand) *m*; Extravaganz *f*.

*

lyceum [lai'siəm] Vortragssaal *m*; literarische Vereinigung, *Am* Volkshochschule *f*.
lych-gate *s. lich-gate*.
lye [lai] *chem* Lauge *f*.
lying [laiiŋ] **1.** *ppr von lie* 1. liegend; horizontal; **~-in** Wochenbett *n*; *~~ hospital* Entbindungsanstalt *f*, -heim *n*; *~~ woman* Wöchnerin *f*; **2.** *ppr von lie* 2.; *a* lügnerisch, unaufrichtig, -ehrlich, falsch; *s* Lügen *n*.
lymph [limf] *anat med* Lymphe; *poet obs* Quelle *f*; **~atic** [-'fætik] *a anat* lymphatisch, Lymph-; *fig* kraftlos; *s anat* Lymphgefäß *n*; **~(atic) gland** Lymphdrüse *f*.
lynch [lintʃ] *tr* lynchen; **~ law** Lynchjustiz *f*.
lynx [liŋks] *zoo* Luchs *m*; **~-eyed** *a*: *to be ~~* Luchsaugen haben.
lyre ['laiə] Leier, Lyra *f*.
lyric ['lirik] *a* lyrisch *a. mus*; *s* lyrische(s) Gedicht *n*; *pl* Lyrik *f*; Text *m (e-s Liedes)*; **~al** ['-əl] lyrisch; *fam* begeistert; *to become ~~ over s.th.* in Begeisterung für etw geraten; **~ drama, ~ stage** Oper *f*; **~ism** ['lirisizm] Lyrik *f*; Gefühlsüberschwang *m*; **~ist** ['-sist] Schlagerdichter *m*.
lyr|ism ['lirizm] **1.** Lyrik *f*; **2.** Leierspiel *n*; **~ist** ['-ist] Lyriker *m*.
lysol ['laisəl] *pharm* Lysol *n*.

M

M, m [em] *pl* **~'s** M, m *n*.
ma [mɑ:] *fam* Mama, Mutti *f*.
ma'am [mæm, məm] *fam* gnä(dige) Frau; [mæm, ma:m] Majestät *f*.
mac [mæk] *fam* = *mackintosh*.
macabre [mə'kɑ:br] grauenhaft, -voll, schauerlich.
macadam [mə'kædəm] *s* Schotter *m*; *(~ road)* Schotterstraße *f*; *a* beschottert; Schotter-; **~ize** [-aiz] *tr* beschottern, makadamisieren.
macaroni [mækə'rouni] Makkaroni *pl*.
macaroon [mækə'ru:n] Makrone *f*.
mace [meis] **1.** Streitkolben; (Amts-) Stab; *(~-bearer)* Amtsträger *m*; **2.** Muskatblüte *f*.
macerat|e ['mæsəreit] *tr* auf-, einweichen, mazerieren; *(aufgenommene Nahrung)* in Speisebrei verwandeln; ausmergeln, kasteien; quälen.
Mach [mɑ:k] *(~ number) phys* Machsche Zahl *f*.
machinat|e ['mækineit] *itr* Ränke schmieden; *tr* aushecken; **~ion** [mæki'neiʃən] *oft pl* Intrige *f*, Ränke *pl*, Machenschaften *f pl*.
machine [mə'ʃi:n] *s* Maschine *a. fig*; Lokomotive *f*, Fahrrad, Motorrad, Auto, Flugzeug; Triebwerk, Getriebe *n*; Apparat, Mechanismus; *fig* Roboter *m*; (gut funktionierende) Organisation; *Am* politische Gruppe, Partei (-organisation) *f*; *a* Maschinen-; *tr* maschinell herstellen, bearbeiten, *bes.* säen, drucken; (zer)spanen; *itr* maschinell arbeiten; *to operate a ~* e-e Maschine bedienen *od* handhaben; *political ~* Staatsmaschine *f*; *party ~* Parteiapparat *m*; **~ age** Maschinenzeitalter *n*; **~-composition** *typ* Maschinensatz *m*; **~d** [-d] *a* (maschinell) bearbeitet; **~ factory** Maschinenfabrik *f*; **~ fitter** Maschinenschlosser *m*; **~-gun** *s* Maschinengewehr, MG *n*; *tr* unter Maschinengewehrfeuer nehmen; *~~ belt* MG-Gurt *m*; **~-made** *a* maschinell hergestellt, maschinengefertigt, Maschinen-; *fig* genormt; **~ry** [mə'ʃi:nəri] Maschinerie *f*, Mechanismus *m*, Getriebe *n*; Maschinenpark *m*; *fig* Maschine *f*, Räderwerk *n*; **~-shop** Maschinenwerkstatt, *Am* -fabrik; Reparaturwerkstatt; Dreherei *f*; **~-tool** Werkzeugmaschine *f*; **~-unit** Maschinensatz *m*, -anlage *f*; **machinist** [mə'ʃi:nist] Maschinist; Maschinenbauer, -ingenieur; Maschinenschlosser, -wärter *m*; *(sewing-~~)* Maschinennäherin *f*.
mackerel ['mækrəl] *pl ~* Makrele[2] *(Fisch)*; **~-sky** (Himmel *m* mit) Schäfchenwolken *f pl*.
mackinaw ['mækinɔ:] *Am (M~ blanket)* schwere Wolldecke *f*; *(M~ coat)* kurze(r), schwere(r) Wintermantel *m*.
mackintosh ['mækintɔʃ] Gummi-, Regenmantel *m*.
macro|- ['mækrə, -ou] *pref* Makro- *(Groß-)*; **~cephalic** [mækrousi'fælik] großköpfig; **~cosm** ['mækrəkɔzm] Makrokosmos *m*.
macul|a ['mækjulə] *pl -ae* [-i:] *(bes.* Haut-)Fleck; Sonnenfleck *m*; **~ar** ['-ə] *a* Fleck-; gefleckt; **~ate** ['-eit] *tr* fleckig machen; *fig* beflecken; *a* ['-lit] fleckig; *fig* befleckt.
mad [mæd] irr(e), geisteskrank; verrückt, wahnsinnig, toll *(with* vor); sinnlos, unvernünftig, töricht, dumm; verknallt, vernarrt *(about, after, at, for* in); versessen *(about, after, at, for* auf); närrisch vor Freude, *fam* ganz aus dem Häuschen; tollwütig *(Hund)*; *fam* wütend *(at, about* über; *with s.o.* auf jdn); *as ~ as a March hare* od *as a hatter* fuchsteufelswild; *like ~* wie verrückt *adv*; *to be raving ~* vor Wut kochen; *to drive, to send ~* verrücktmachen; *to go ~* verrückt werden; *to have a ~ time* sich toll amüsieren; **~cap** *s* verrückte(r) Kerl; Wildfang *m*, wilde Hummel *f (Mädchen)*; *a* übermütig, toll, wild, rasend, rücksichtslos; **~den** ['-n] *tr* verrückt, rasend, toll machen; **~-doctor** Irrenarzt *m*; **~house** Irrenhaus; *fam* Tollhaus *n*; **~man, ~woman** Irre(r *m*), Wahnsinnige(r *m*), Verrückte(r *m*) *f*; *to talk like a ~man* wie irr reden; faseln; **~ness** ['-nis] Geisteskrankheit *f*, Irresein *n*; Verrücktheit *f*; Blödsinn *m*; Besessenheit, Aufgeregtheit; *Am* Wut *f*, Ärger *m (at* über).
madam ['mædəm] gnädige Frau *f*, gnädiges Fräulein *n (Anrede)*.
madder ['mædə] *bot* Krapp *m*.
made [meid] *pret u. pp von make*; *a (mit adv)* gebaut, gestaltet, geformt; angefertigt *(of* aus); künstlich; *fig* erfunden, ausgedacht; *ready-~* fertig; Konfektions-; *a ~ man* ein gemachter Mann; **~-to-order** *a* auf Bestellung, nach Wunsch, nach Maß angefertigt; Maß-; **~-up** *a* zs.gestellt, angeordnet; *com* Fabrik-, Konfektions-; *fig* erfunden, ersonnen, ausgedacht; falsch, unwahr; geschminkt.
Madonna [mə'dɔnə] Muttergottesbild *n*, Madonna *f*.
Madeira [mə'diərə] Madeira *m (Süßwein)*; **~ cake** Sandtorte *f*.
madrigal ['mædrigəl] *mus* Madrigal *n*.
Maecenas [mi(:)'si:næs] Mäzen *m*.
maelstrom ['meilstroum] Strudel *(im Wasser u. fig)*; *fig* Wirbel, Sog *m*.
Mae West ['mei'west] *aero sl* Schwimmweste *f*.
maffick ['mæfik] *itr fam* (laut) jubeln, lärmend feiern.
magazine [mægə'zi:n, 'mæg-] Lager (-haus), Magazin; Vorrats-, Munitionslager; *(Gewehr)* Magazin; Magazin *n*, Zeitschrift *f*; *illustrated ~* Illustrierte *f*; **~-rifle** Mehrlader *m*.
Maggie ['mægi] Gretchen *n*.
maggot ['mægət] *ent* Made; *fig* Grille, Laune *f*; **~y** ['-i] madig, voller Maden; *fig* launisch, launenhaft.
Magi, *the* ['meidʒai] *pl rel hist* die Magier; *(Bibel)* die Weisen aus dem Morgenland(e).
magic ['mædʒik] *s* Magie, Zauberei *f*; Zauber *m a. fig*; Zauberkunst *f*; *a* u. **~al** ['-əl] magisch, zauberhaft; Zauber-; **~ carpet** fliegende(r) Teppich *m*; **~ eye** magische(s) Auge *n*; **~ian** [mə'dʒiʃən] Zauberer; Zauberkünstler *m*.
magist|erial [mædʒis'tiəriəl] obrigkeitlich, behördlich; Herrschafts-; gebieterisch, autoritativ; feierlich, pomphaft, pompös; **~racy** ['mædʒistrəsi] (Friedens-, Polizei-)Richteramt *n*; **~rate** ['mædʒistrit] (höherer richterlicher) Beamte(r); Polizei-, Friedensrichter *m*.
Magna C(h)arta ['mægnə'kɑ:tə] Magna Charta *f (englisches Grundgesetz von 1215)*; *allg* (Staats-)Grundgesetz *n*.
magnanim|ity [mægnə'nimiti] Großmut; großmütige Tat *f*; **~ous** [mæg'næniməs] großmütig.
magnate ['mægneit] Magnat *m*; *financial ~* Finanzgewaltige(r), -magnat *m*; *industrial ~* Großindustrielle(r), Industriemagnat *m*; *territorial ~* Großgrundbesitzer, Großagrarier *m*.
magnes|ia [mæg'ni:ʃə] *chem* Magnesia *f*; **~ium** [mæg'ni:ziəm, -ʃiəm] *chem* Magnesium *n*.
magnet ['mægnit] Magnet *m a. fig*; **~ coil** Magnetspule *f*; **~ core** Magnetkern *m*; **~ic** [mæg'netik] *a* magnetisch; Magnet-; *med* magnetisierbar; *fig* faszinierend; *s pl mit sing phys* Lehre *f* vom Magnetismus; *~~ declination* Mißweisung *f*; *~~ field* Magnetfeld *n*; *~~ needle* Magnetnadel *f*; *~~ pole* Magnetpol *m*; *~~ tape* Tonband *n*; **~ism** ['-izm] Magnetismus *m*; *fig* Faszination *f*; *animal ~~* tierische(r) Magnetismus, Mesmerismus *m*; *terrestrial ~~* Erdmagnetismus *m*; **~ization** [mægnitai'zeiʃən] Magnetisierung *f*; **~ize** ['mægnitaiz] *tr* magnetisieren; *fig* faszinieren, in Bann schlagen; **~o** [mæg'ni:tou] *pl -os s mot* Magnetzünder *m*; *~~ board* Klappenschrank *m*; *~~-electric* magnetoelektrisch; *~~-generator* Kurbelinduktor *m*; *~~-ignition* Magnetzündung *f*; **~ron** ['mægnitrɔn] Magnetron *n*.
magni|fication [mægnifi'keiʃən] *opt phot* Vergrößerung; *el* Verstärkung; *fig* Übertreibung; Verherrlichung *f*; **~ficence** [mæg'nifisns] Pracht *f*, Prunk, Pomp *m*; **~ficent** [mæg'nifisənt] herrlich, stattlich, prächtig, prunkvoll; großartig; glänzend *a. fig*; **~fier** ['mægnifaiə] Vergrößerungsglas *n*, Lupe *f*; Mikroskop *n*; *el* Verstärker; *fig* Lobredner *m*; **~fy** ['mægnifai] *tr opt phot* vergrößern; *el* verstärken; *fig* übertreiben; *~~ing glass* Vergrößerungsglas *n*.
magniloquen|ce [mæg'niləkwəns] Bombast, Schwulst *m*; Prahlerei *f*; **~t** [-t] hochtrabend, bombastisch, schwülstig; großsprecherisch.
magnitude ['mægnitju:d] Größe; Ausdehnung *f*, Umfang *m*; Bedeutung, Wichtigkeit; *math astr* Größe *f*; *of the first ~ (Stern)* 1. Größe; *fig* von größter Bedeutung *od* äußerster Wichtigkeit.
magnolia [mæg'nouljə] *bot* Magnolie *f*.
magnum ['mægnəm] große Wein- *od* Likörflasche; große Flaschevoll *f*.
magpie ['mægpai] *orn* Elster *f*; *fig* Schwätzer *m*, Klatschbase *f*; Dieb *m*.
Magyar ['mægjɑ:] *s* Madjar, Ungar *m*; (das) Madjarisch(e), Ungarisch(e); *a* madjarisch, ungarisch.

mahara|ja(h) [mɑ:hə'rɑ:dʒə] Maharadscha *m*; **~nee,** *Am* **~ni** [-ni:] Maharani *f*.
mahlstick *s. maulstick.*
mahogany [mə'hɔgəni] *s* Mahagoni (-holz) *n*; Mahagonibaum *m*; Mahagoni *n (Farbe)*; *a* mahagonifarben.
Mahomet [mə'hɔmit] Mohammed *m*; **~an** [-ən] mohammedanisch; **~anism** [-ənizm] Islam *m*.
maid [meid] *lit* Mädchen; Hausmädchen *n*, -angestellte *f*; *bar~* Bardame *f*; *house-~* Hausmädchen *n*; *lady's-~* Zofe, Kammerfrau *f*; *nurse-~* Kindermädchen *n*; *old ~* alte Jungfer *f*; *~ of hono(u)r* Hofdame; *Am* Brautjungfer *f*; *the M~ (of Orleans)* die Jungfrau von Orleans; *~ in waiting* Hofdame *f*; **~-of-all-work** Mädchen

n für alles; **~-servant** (weibliche) Hausangestellte *f*.
maiden ['meidn] *s* Mädchen *n*; Jungfrau *f*; *a attr* Mädchen-; unverheiratet; jungfräulich; erst, Erstlings-; *fig* neu, ungebraucht, unerprobt, unerfahren; **~hair** *(~~ fern) bot* Frauenhaar *n*; *(~~ tree)* Ginkgo *m (Schmuckbaum)*; **~head** ['-hed] Jungfräulichkeit *f*; **~hood** ['-hud] Mädchenjahre *n pl*, Jungmädchenzeit; Jungfräulichkeit *f*; **~ish** ['-iʃ], **~like** ['-laik], **~ly** ['-li] mädchenhaft; **~liness** ['-linis] Mädchenhaftigkeit *f*; **~ name** Mädchenname *m*; **~ speech** Jungfernrede *f*; **~ voyage** Jungfernfahrt *f*.
mail [meil] *s* Postsack *m*, -sendung, -beförderung; *(ein- u. ausgehende)* Post; Post(dienst *m*) *f*; *attr* Post-; *tr* mit der Post (ver)senden; abschicken, aufgeben; *Am* in den (Brief-)Kasten stecken, zur Post geben; *by, via air ~* mit Luftpost; *by (the) return(ing) (of) ~* postwendend; *to do the ~* die Post erledigen; *incoming* od *in-going, outgoing ~* ein-, ausgehende Post *f*; **~ability** [meilə'biliti] *Am* (Post-)Versandfähigkeit *f*; **~able** ['meiləbl] *Am* (post)versandfähig; **~-bag,** *Am* **~ pouch** Postsack *m*; **~-boat** Post-, Paketschiff *n*; **~-box** Post-, *Am* Briefkasten *m*; **~ carrier, ~man** ['-mən] *Am* Briefträger *m*; **~-carrier aircraft, ~plane** Postflugzeug *n*; **~-cart** Postwagen *m*; **~-charges** *pl* Postgebühren *f pl*, Porto *n*; **~-coach** Postwagen *m*, *hist* -kutsche *f*; **~-delivery** (Post-)Zustellung *f*; **~-depredation** Postraub *m*; **~er** ['-ə] *Am* Adressier-, Frankiermaschine *f*; **~ing** ['-iŋ] Postbeförderung; *~~ list* Postversandliste *f*; *~~-machine* Adressiermaschine, Adrema *f*; **~ order** Bestellung *f* durch die Post; **~-order business house** *Am* Versandgeschäft *n*; **~-order catalog(ue)** Katalog *m* e-s Versandgeschäfts; **~ stamp** *Am* Poststempel *m*; **~-van,** *Am* **~-car** *rail* Postwagen *m*; **2.** *s hist* (Ketten-)Panzer *m*, (Ritter-)Rüstung *f*; *zoo* Panzer *m*; *tr* panzern; *coat of ~* Panzerhemd *n*; **~-clad, ~ed** [-d] *a* gepanzert.
maim [meim] *tr* verstümmeln *a. fig*, zum Krüppel machen.
main [mein] *a attr* hauptsächlich, größt, bedeutendst, wichtigst, erst; Haupt-; *s* Hauptsache; Hauptleitung *f*, -rohr *n*, -kanal *m*, -linie, -strecke *f*; *the ~ (poet)* die (hohe) See, das (Welt-)Meer, der Ozean; *pl* Leitungs-, *el* Stromnetz *n*; *by ~ force* mit voller Kraft *od* Wucht; *in the ~* im ganzen, im wesentlichen, in der Hauptsache, hauptsächlich *adv*; *with might and ~* mit aller Kraft *od* Gewalt; *to have an eye to the ~ chance* s-n eigenen Vorteil im Auge haben; *operating on the ~s* mit Netzanschluß; **~ action** *jur* Hauptklage *f*; **~ business** Hauptgeschäft *n*; **~ clause** *gram* Hauptsatz *m*; **~ condition** Grund-, Hauptbedingung *f*; **~ constituent** Hauptbestandteil *m*; **~ creditor** Hauptgläubiger *m*; **~-deck** *mar* Oberdeck *n*; **~ feature** Grundzug *m*; **~ film** Hauptfilm *m*; **~ idea** Grundgedanke *m*; **~land** Festland *n*, Landmasse *f*; **~ line** Haupt(verkehrs-, -bahn)linie; *Am sl* Prominenz *f*; *~~ of resistance* Hauptkampflinie *f*; **~ly** ['-li] *adv* hauptsächlich, im wesentlichen, größtenteils; **~mast** *mar* Großmast *m*; **~ office** Hauptbüro *n*, Zentrale *f*; **~ point** Haupt-, springende(r) Punkt *m*; **~ profession** Hauptberuf *m*; **~ question** Haupt-, wichtigste, entscheidende Frage *f*; **~sail** Großsegel *n*; **~sheet** *mar* Großschot *f*; **~ spring** *fig* Haupttriebfeder; Uhrfeder *f*; **~s receiving-set** Netzempfänger *m*; **~stay** *mar* Großstag *m*; *fig* Hauptstütze *f*; **~s transformer** Netztransformator *m*; **~ street,** *sl* **drag, stem** Hauptstraße *f*; **~s voltage** Netzspannung *f*; **~ switch** Hauptschalter *m*; **~ tenant** Hauptmieter *m*; **~top** *mar* Großmars *m*.
maintain [mein'tein] *tr* aufrechterhalten; fortsetzen; in gutem Zustand (er)halten, instand halten, pflegen, warten; *(Straße, Familie, Beziehungen)* unterhalten; versorgen; *(Stellung)* halten, behaupten; *(Haltung)* einnehmen; *(mit Worten)* behaupten, stützen, verteidigen; *(Bücher)* führen; *to ~ o.'s ground* sich behaupten, sich halten; **~able** [-əbl] zu halten(d); **~er** [-ə] Versorger *(e-r Familie)*; Verteidiger *m*.
maintenance ['meintinəns] Aufrechterhaltung, Wahrung; Fortsetzung; Erhaltung, Instandhaltung, Wartung *f*; (Lebens-)Unterhalt *m*; Behauptung; Verteidigung, Unterstützung *f a. jur*; *to provide ~ to s.o.* jdm Unterhalt gewähren; *claim for ~* Unterhaltsanspruch *m*; *cost of ~* Instandhaltungskosten *pl*; *entitled to ~* unterhaltsberechtigt; *grant of ~* Unterhaltsgewährung *f*; *obligation of ~* Unterhaltspflicht *f*; *~ and repair* Unterhaltung u. Instandsetzung *f*; *~ of the poor* Fürsorge, Wohlfahrt *f*; **~ man** Monteur *m*.
maiso(n)nette [meizə'net] Häuschen *n*; vermietete(r) Hausteil *m*.
maize [meiz] *s* Mais *m*; Maisgelb *n*.
majest|ic(al) [mə'dʒestik(əl)] majestätisch, stattlich, vornehm, erhaben; **~y** ['mædʒisti] Majestät; Hoheit; *fig* Würde, Erhabenheit, Vornehmheit, Stattlichkeit *f*.
major ['meidʒə] *a* größer; höher; Groß-, Haupt-; mündig, volljährig; *(hinter Familiennamen)* der Ältere; *Am (Studienfach)* Haupt-; *mus (nachgestellt)* Dur; *(Intervall)* groß; *(Straße)* bevorrechtet; *s* Höhere(r); Major; Mündige(r), Volljährige(r) *m*; *Am (Univ.)* Hauptfach *n*; *(Logik)* Obersatz, -begriff *m*; *mus* Dur *n*; *itr Am (Univ.)* im Hauptfach studieren (*in s.th.* etw), sich spezialisieren (*in* in); *tr* als Hauptfach studieren; *a ~ repair* e-e größere Reparatur; *the ~ part of s.th.* der größte Teil von etw; **~-domo** [-'doumou] *pl -os* Haushofmeister *m*; **~ette** [meidʒə'ret] *Am* Tambourmajorin *f*; **~-general** Generalmajor *m*; **~ity** [mə'dʒɔriti] Mehrheit; *parl* Stimmenmehrheit; Mehrheitspartei(en *pl*), Parlamentsmehrheit; Volljährigkeit, Mündigkeit *f*; Majorsrang *m*, -stelle *f*; *to attain, to reach o.'s ~~* mündig werden; *to join the ~~* das Zeitliche segnen, sterben; *parl* sich der Mehrheit anschließen; *absolute, crushing, government, great, narrow, overwhelming, parliamentary, qualified, relative, required, simple, two-thirds ~~* absolute, erdrückende, Regierungs-, große, knappe, überwältigende, Parlaments-, qualifizierte, relative, erforderliche, einfache, Zweidrittelmehrheit *f*; *(by) ~~ of votes* (mit) Stimmenmehrheit *f*, *~~-vote (parl)* Mehrheitsbeschluß *m*; **~ event** *sport* Großveranstaltung *f*; **~ league** *Am sport* Oberliga *f*; **~ mode** Durtonart *f*; **~ offender** Hauptschuldige(r) *m*; **~ premise** *(Logik)* Obersatz *m*; **~ scale** *mus* Durtonleiter *f*; **~ term** *(Logik)* Oberbegriff *m*; **~ third** *mus* große Terz *f*; **~ unit** *mil* Verband *m*.
make [meik] *irr made, made* [meid] **1.** *tr* machen (*from, of* aus; *into* zu); herstellen, anfertigen, fabrizieren, (zu)bereiten, fertigmachen, ausführen; hervorbringen, (er)schaffen, bilden; konstruieren, zs.stellen; ausdenken, formulieren; *(Schriftstück)* aufsetzen; *(Urkunde)* ausfertigen; ab-, verfassen; *mus* komponieren; herbeiführen, bewirken, veranlassen, bewerkstelligen, zustande bringen; lassen, veranlassen, daß; machen zu, ernennen zu; machen, erscheinen lassen; *(Mensch etw)* vorstellen, sich erweisen als; (aus)machen, sich belaufen auf, abgeben; machen (*of* aus), halten (*of* von), einschätzen als (*of s.o., of s.th.* jdn, etw), schätzen auf; erwerben, verdienen; *(Gewinn)* einstreichen, einstecken; *(Verlust)* erleiden; *(Schule) (Zensur)* erhalten, bekommen; *(Menschen)* gewinnen als; *(den Zug, die Bahn)* noch kriegen, erreichen; zum Erfolg verhelfen (*s.o.* jdm); *(Arbeit)* erledigen; *(Entfernung)* zurücklegen; *(e-e bestimmte Geschwindigkeit)* fahren; *(Mahlzeit)* haben; *(Spiel)* gewinnen; *(Kartenspiel; die Karten)* mischen; *(Trumpf, Gebot, Stich)* machen; den Stich nehmen mit; *el (Kreis)* schließen; *(Kontakt)* herstellen; *fam* sich Eingang verschaffen in, kommen in; *sl* verführen; **2.** *itr* sich daranmachen, sich anschicken (*to do* zu tun); sich bewegen, gehen (*for* auf – zu), zugehen (*for* auf), sich wenden (*for* zu), sich begeben (*for* nach); folgen (*after s.o.* jdm), verfolgen (*after s.o.* jdn); *(mit nachfolgendem a)* sich benehmen, auftreten; so tun, sich stellen (*as if* als ob); *like s.o. (sl)* jdn nachmachen, nachäffen; zunehmen, sich vermehren, sich ansammeln, sich anhäufen; *(Flut)* steigen; zielen (*for* auf); beitragen (*for* zu); mithelfen, mitwirken (*for* bei); wirken (*for* auf); **3.** *s* Herstellung, (An-)Fertigung, Produktion *f*; Ertrag *m*; Erzeugnis, Fabrikat *n*; (Mach-)Art, Fasson, Form *f*, (Zu-)Schnitt, Bau(art, -weise *f*) *m*, Marke, Type; Art, Anlage, Veranlagung, Natur *f*, Wesen *n*, Charakter *m*; **4.** *to be on the ~ (fam)* auf Gewinn aus sein; *sl* auf Eroberungen, Liebesabenteuer ausgehen; *to ~ much ado about s.th.* viel Lärm, Aufhebens, Wesens machen um; *to ~ the bed* das Bett machen; *to ~ believe* weismachen, den Glauben, die Vorstellung erwecken, so tun als ob; vorgeben, vortäuschen; *to ~ the best, most of s.th.* aus e-r S herausholen, was man kann; *to ~ bold* sich erkühnen, sich erdreisten; *to ~ no bones about* kein Blatt vor den Mund nehmen; *to ~ a bow* e-e Verbeugung machen; *to ~ or break, to ~ or mar* auf biegen od brechen ankommen lassen; *to ~ certain, sure* sich vergewissern *od* versichern (*of s.th.* e-r S; *that* daß); *to ~ a choice* e-e Wahl treffen; *to ~ clear* erklären; *to ~ o.s. comfortable* es sich gemütlich machen; *to ~ a confession* ein Geständnis ablegen; *to ~ default* sich ein Versäumnis zuschulden kommen lassen; *to ~ a difference* e-n Unterschied, etwas ausmachen; *to ~ eyes at s.o.* mit jdm flirten; *to ~ fire* Feuer (an)machen; *to ~ a fool of s.o.* jdn zum Narren, zum besten halten; *of o.s.* sich lächerlich machen; *to ~ free with s.th.* sich e-r S ungehemmt bedienen; *to ~ friends* Freunde gewinnen; *to ~ fun of* sich

lustig machen über, lächerlich machen (*s.o.* jdn); *to ~ a go of s.th.* mit etw Erfolg haben; *to ~ good (tr)* wiedergutmachen; aufkommen für; bestätigen, bekräftigen; wahrmachen; *(Versprechen)* halten; glücklich durchführen, vollenden; *itr fam* Glück, Schwein haben; es zu etwas bringen; *to ~ haste* sich beeilen, *fam* schnell machen; *to ~ hay of s.th.* etw in Unordnung bringen; *to ~ hay while the sun shines* das Eisen schmieden, solange es heiß ist; *to ~ head or tail of s.th.* aus etw klug werden; *to ~ headway* vorwärts-, vorankommen; *to ~ a hit* viel Erfolg haben (*with* bei); *to ~ o.s. at home* sich wie zu Hause fühlen; *to ~ it (fam)* es schaffen; *to ~ a killing (Am fam)* plötzlich viel Geld verdienen; *to ~ land (mar)* Land sehen; *to ~ a living* sich sein Brot verdienen; *to ~ o.'s mark in the world* berühmt werden; *to ~ a match* e-e Verlobung *od* Heirat zustande bringen; *to ~ a meal on, of s.th.* aus etw e-e Mahlzeit machen; *to ~ mention of s.th.* etw erwähnen; *to ~ merry* sich e-n Spaß machen; lustig u. vergnügt sein; *to ~ mouths at s.o.* jdm Gesichter schneiden; *to ~ a movement* e-e Bewegung machen; *to ~ much, little of s.th.* (sich) viel, wenig aus e-r S machen; viel, wenig aus e-r S machen *od* herausholen; *to ~ a night of it* sich die Nacht um die Ohren schlagen; *to ~ an oath* e-n Eid ablegen; *to ~ one of s.th.* sich an e-r S beteiligen, bei e-r S mitmachen; *to ~ peace* Frieden schließen; *to ~ place, room, way for* Platz machen für; *to ~ a point of s.th.* Wert legen auf etw; *to ~ port (Schiff)* den Hafen erreichen; *to ~ s.o. a present* jdm ein Geschenk machen; *to ~ provision* sorgen, Vorkehrungen treffen (*for* für); *to ~ ready* fertigmachen, vorbereiten; *to ~ a remark* e-e Bemerkung machen (*on, upon* über); *to ~ room for s.o.* für jdn Platz schaffen; *to ~ it a rule* es sich zur Regel machen; *to ~ sail* die Segel aufziehen; *to ~ shift* sich behelfen; *to ~ a speech* e-e Rede halten; *to ~ a stay* sich aufhalten; *to ~ things hum* die Sache in Schwung bringen; *to ~ time* Zeit gewinnen; *to ~ the train* den Zug erreichen; *to ~ o.s. useful* sich nützlich machen; *to ~ war* Krieg führen (*on, upon* gegen); *to ~ way* Platz machen; *fig* vorwärts-, vorankommen; *to ~ o.'s way in the world* s-n Weg gehen, Erfolg haben, erfolgreich sein; **5.** *I'll never ~ it* ich werde es nie schaffen; *don't ~ such a fuss* mach kein solches Theater; *he ~s good (fam)* es geht gut mit ihm; *I don't know what ~s him tick* ich weiß nicht, worauf er reagiert; *he made her his wife* er nahm sie zur Frau; *what do you ~ with it? (sl)* was machst du damit? *one swallow does not ~ a summer (prov)* e-e Schwalbe macht (noch) keinen Sommer; *does this ~ sense to you?* werden Sie daraus klug? *~ it snappy!* beeile dich; *own ~* eigene Herstellung *f*; **6.** *to ~* **after** *obs tr* verfolgen; *to ~* **against** *tr* ungünstig sein für; *to ~* **away** *itr* sich aus dem Staube machen, *sl* sich wegmachen; *with* durchbringen, verprassen; loswerden; verputzen, verdrücken, essen; klauen, stibitzen; über die Seite, um die Ecke, umbringen; *to ~* **for** *tr* losgehen auf; gut sein für; *to ~* **off** *itr* abhauen, durchbrennen (*with* mit); sich aus dem Staub machen; *to ~* **on** *itr* weitergehen, -eilen; *to ~* **out** *tr* ausfindig machen, herausbekommen, -kriegen, entziffern; *sl* 'rausknobeln; erkennen; begreifen, verstehen; (zu) beweisen (suchen); ausschreiben, -fertigen, -stellen; *(Liste)* aufstellen; *(Formular)* ausfüllen; *Am* zs.bringen, vervollständigen; *itr* weiter-, vorwärtskommen *a. fig*, Erfolg haben; abschneiden; *to ~* **over** *tr* um-, überarbeiten; erneuern, aufarbeiten, auffrischen; *(Eigentum)* übertragen, -schreiben; *fam* sich auslassen über, eingehen auf; *to ~* **up** *tr* zs.stellen, -legen, -setzen, -nähen; erfinden, erschaffen, ins Leben rufen, auf die Beine bringen; ausdenken, *fam* austüfteln, ausklamüsern; vollenden, vervollständigen, ab-, beschließen; bilden, ausmachen; zurechtmachen, herrichten, ausstaffieren; *theat* frisieren u. schminken; *typ* umbrechen; *(Satz)* bilden; *(Streit)* beilegen; *(Unrecht)* wiedergutmachen; *(Schaden)* ersetzen; *(Schulden)* bezahlen; *(Rechnung)* begleichen; *(Prüfung)* noch mal machen, wiederholen; *(Liste)* zs.-stellen; *itr* sich zurechtmachen, sich schminken, sich pudern, Puder auflegen; sich wieder aus-, versöhnen (*with* mit); wiedergutmachen, ersetzen; *(verlorene Zeit)* wieder aufholen (*for s.th.* etw); *(e-e Stunde)* nachholen; schöntun, flattieren (*to s.o.* jdn), herumsein, -scharwenzeln (*to s.o.* um jdn); *to ~~ o.'s mind* sich entschließen; **~-believe** *s* Vorwand *m*; Verstellung, Heuchelei *f*; Heuchler, Schwindler *m*; *a* angeblich; verstellt, geheuchelt; falsch; **~r** ['-ə] Hersteller, Verfertiger, Fabrikant; *(Urkunde)* Aussteller *m*; *the M~~* der Schöpfer, Gott *m*; *~~'s number* Fabriknummer *f*; *~~-up (typ)* Metteur *m*; **~shift** *s* (zeitweiliger) Ersatz, Notbehelf *m*, Aushilfe *f*; *attr* behelfsmäßig; Behelfs-, Aushilfs-, Not-; **~-up** Machart *f*, (Auf-)Bau *m*, Struktur, Gestaltung, Anlage; Ausstattung, Aufmachung; Verpackung *f*; Make-up *n*; Kosmetika *pl*; *fig* erfundene Geschichte, Erfindung *f*; *typ* Umbruch *m*; *to have ~~ on* geschminkt sein; *to put ~~ on* sich schminken, sich herrichten; *~~ man (film)* Maskenbildner *m*; **~weight** das Gewicht vollmachende Menge *f*; Zusatz; *fig* Lückenbüßer *m*.

making ['meikiŋ] Herstellung, Fertigung, Fabrikation, Produktion; Anlage, Bildung *f*, (Auf-)Bau *m*, Konstruktion, Entwick(e)lung; Schulung; Dar-, Vorstellung *f*; Werk; Produkt *n*, Ertrag, Gewinn *m*; Sprungbrett *n fig*, Chance *f*; *oft pl* Fähigkeiten *f pl*, Talent *n*, Anlage(n *pl*), Veranlagung *f*; *pl* Verdienst *m*, Einnahmen *f pl*; *pl Am fam* Tabak *m* u. Papier *n* zum Zigarettendrehen; *to be the ~ of s.o.* das Glück für jdn sein; *to be in the ~* in der Entwicklung, in der Herstellung sein; *to have the ~s of* das Zeug haben zu.

malachite ['mæləkait] *min* Malachit *m*.

maladjust|ed ['mælə'dʒʌstid] *a* schlecht eingerichtet *od* angeordnet *od* eingestellt *od* angepaßt; *psych* nicht eingegliedert; **~ment** ['mælə'dʒʌstmənt] schlechte Anordnung *od* Anpassung *f*; Mißverhältnis *n*.

maladminist|er ['mæləd'ministə] *tr* schlecht verwalten; **~ration** ['mælədminis'treiʃən] Mißwirtschaft *f*.

maladroit ['mælə'drɔit] ungeschickt, unbeholfen, linkisch.

malady ['mælədi] Krankheit *f a. fig*; Gebrechen, Übel *n*.

malaise [mæ'leiz] Unbehagen; Unwohlsein *n*.

malaprop|ism ['mæləprɔpizm] (komische) Wortverwechs(e)lung *f*; **~os** ['mæl'æprəpou, mæləprə'pou] *a* unangebracht, -passend; *adv* in unpassender Weise; zur Unzeit.

malar ['meilə] *a* Backen-; *s* Wangen-, Jochbein *n*, *fam* Backenknochen *m*.

malaria [mə'lɛəriə] Malaria *f*, Sumpffieber *n*.

malark(e)y [mə'lɑ:ki] *Am sl* Quatsch, Unsinn *m*.

Malay|(an) [mə'lei(ən)] *s* Malaie *m*, Malaiin *f*; (das) Malaiisch(e); *a* malaiisch; **~a** [~ə] Malaya *n*.

malcontent ['mælkəntent] *a* unzufrieden, mißvergnügt; *pol* aufsässig; *s* Mißvergnügte(r); Rebell *m*.

male [meil] *a* männlich; stark, kraftvoll; *s* Mann *m*; *zoo* Männchen *n*; männliche Pflanze *f*; **~ child** *jur* Kind *n* männlichen Geschlechts; **~ choir** Männerchor *m*; **~ screw** Schraube(nspindel) *f*.

malediction [mæli'dikʃən] Verwünschung *f*, Fluch *m*; Verleumdung *f*.

malefact|ion [mæli'fækʃən] Übeltat *f*, Verbrechen *n*; **~or** ['mælifæktə] Übeltäter, Verbrecher *m*.

malefic [mə'lefik], **~ent** [-snt] böse, bösartig, übel; schädlich (*to* für).

malevolen|ce [mə'levələns] Böswilligkeit *f*, böse(r) Wille *m*, Boshaftigkeit *f*; **~t** [-t] boshaft; feindselig, böswillig (*to* gegen).

malfeasance [mæl'fi:zəns] strafbare Handlung *f*, gesetzwidrige(s) Verhalten *n*; *~ in office* Amtsvergehen *n*, -unterschlagung *f*.

malform|ation ['mælfɔ:'meiʃən] (körperliche) Mißbildung *f*; **~ed** [mæl'fɔ:md] *a* mißgestalt, -gebildet.

malic|e ['mælis] Bosheit, Boshaftigkeit; Böswilligkeit *f*, böse(r) Wille *m*; Arglist *f*; *with ~~ aforethought, prepense* in böser Absicht, arglistig *adv*; mit Vorbedacht, vorsätzlich *adv*; *to bear s.o. no ~~* jdm nicht grollen; **~ious** [mə'liʃəs] boshaft, böswillig; arglistig; **~iousness** [-'liʃəsnis] Bosheit, Boshaftigkeit *f*.

malign [mə'lain] *tr* verleumden; *a* boshaft, böswillig; unheilvoll, übel, böse; hämisch; **~ance, ~ancy** [mə'lignəns(i)] Böswilligkeit, Bosheit; Gefährlichkeit; Bösartigkeit *f a. med*; **~ant** [-'lignənt] böswillig, übelgesinnt; bösartig, boshaft; tückisch; unheilvoll, ungünstig, widrig; sehr nachteilig; gefährlich; *(Geschwulst)* bösartig; **~ity** [mə'ligniti] Böswilligkeit, Boshaftigkeit, Bosheit; schlechte Gesinnung; Gefährlichkeit *f*; schlechte(r) Streich *m*; üble, böse Geschichte *f fig*.

malinger [mə'liŋgə] *itr* sich krank stellen, simulieren; sich drücken; **~er** [-rə] Simulant; Drückeberger *m*.

mall [mɔ:l] **1.** *s* (Schläger *m* für das) Pall-Mall-Spiel *n*; [*a.* mæl] schattige Promenade, Allee *f*; **2.** *tr s. maul*; **3.** *orn* Sturmmöwe *f*.

mallard ['mæləd] *orn* Stockente *f*.

malleab|ility [mæliə'biliti] Hämmerbarkeit, Dehnbarkeit; *fig* Geschmeidigkeit, Anpassungsfähigkeit *f*; **~le** ['mæliəbl] *(Metall)* hämmerbar, dehnbar; verformbar; *fig* nachgiebig, anpassungsfähig, geschmeidig; *~~ cast iron* Temperguß *m*; *~~ iron* Schmiedeeisen *n*.

mallet ['mælit] Holzhammer, Schlegel; (Krocket-, Polo-)Schläger *m*.

mallow ['mælou] *bot* Malve *f*.

malmsey ['mɑ:mzi] Malvasier(wein) *m*.

malnutrition ['mælnju(:)'triʃən] Unterernährung, falsche Ernährung *f*.

malod|orant [mæ'loudərənt], **~orous** [-rəs] übelriechend.

malposition [mælpə'ziʃən] *med* Lageanomalie *f*.

malpractice ['mæl'præktis] *med* falsche Behandlung *f*; *jur* Amtsmißbrauch *m*, Übeltat *f*.

malt [mɔ:lt] *s* Malz *n*; *tr itr* malzen; *itr* zu Malz werden; Malz herstellen; ~ **extract** Malzextrakt *m*; ~ **house** Mälzerei *f*; ~**ing** ['-iŋ] Malzen *n*, Mälzerei *f*; ~ **kiln** Malzdarre *f*; ~ **liquor** Gerstensaft *m*, (Malz-)Bier *n*; ~**ose** ['mɔ:ltous], ~ **sugar** Malzzucker *m*, Maltose *f*; ~**ster** ['-stə] Mälzer *m*; ~**y** ['-i] malzhaltig, -artig; *to be* ~~ gern Bier trinken.

Malt|a ['mɔ:ltə] Malta *n*; ~**ese** ['mɔ:l-'ti:z] *a* maltesisch; *s pl* ~~ Malteser(in *f*) *m*; *M~~ Cross* Malteserkreuz *n*.

maltreat [mæl'tri:t] *tr* schlecht behandeln; mißhandeln; ~**ment** [-mənt] schlechte Behandlung; Mißhandlung *f*.

malversation [mælvə:'seiʃən] Unterschlagung *f* öffentlicher Gelder; Amtsmißbrauch *m*; Veruntreuung *f*.

mama, mamma [mə'mɑ:] *(Kindersprache)* Mama, Mutti *f*.

mamm|a ['mæmə] *pl -ae* [-i:] *anat* Brust(drüse) *f*; *zoo* Euter *n*; ~**al** ['-l] Säugetier *n*; ~**illa, mamilla** [mə'milə] *anat* Brustwarze *f*.

mammon ['mæmən] Mammon *m*.

mammoth ['mæməθ] *s zoo* Mammut *n*; *a* Mammut-; *fam* gewaltig, ungeheuer (groß).

mammy ['mæmi] *(Kindersprache)* Mama(chen *n*), Mutti *f*; *Am (bes. in den Südstaaten)* Negeramme *f*; *to do a ~ act (Am sl)* e-e rührselige Szene machen.

man [mæn] *pl men* [men] *s* Mensch; *(ohne Artikel)* der Mensch, die Menschen *pl*, die Menschheit; Mann; (Ehe-)Mann; Liebhaber; (Gefolgs-) Mann, Untergebene(r), Bedienstete(r), Diener, Arbeiter; *mil* Mann; *hist* Lehnsmann, Vasall; *sport* Spieler *m*; *(Schach)* Figur *f*; *(Damespiel)* Stein *m*; *in Zssgen* Schiff *n*; *pl mil* Mannschaften *f pl*, Mannschaftsdienstgrade *m pl*; *attr* männlich; *tr* bemannen; *(Stellung)* besetzen; *(wildes Tier, bes. Falken)* an den Menschen gewöhnen; *to ~ o.s.* sich ermannen, Mut fassen; *a ~* jemand; *not a ~* niemand; *as a, one ~* wie ein Mann; *to a ~* bis auf den letzten Mann; *to the last ~* (alle) ohne Ausnahme; *~ and boy* von klein auf; *to be o.'s own ~* sein eigener Herr sein; im Vollbesitz s-r Kräfte sein; *I'm your ~* ich bin Ihr Mann, ich mache die Sache; *~!* Mann! Mensch(enskind)! *key ~* Mann *m* in Schlüsselstellung; *~ of business* Geschäftsmann; Vertreter *m*; *~ of God* Gottesmann *m*; *the ~ in the moon* der Mann im Monde; *M~ of Sorrows* Schmerzensmann *m (Jesus)*; *~ of straw* Strohmann *m*; *the ~ in the street* der Mann auf der Straße, der gewöhnliche Mensch; *~ about town* reicher Nichtstuer *m*; *~ of the world* Mann von Welt, Weltmann *m*; ~**-ape** Menschenaffe *m*; ~**-at-arms** Soldat, *bes. hist* Ritter *m*; ~**-child** Kind *n* männlichen Geschlechts, Knabe *m*; ~**-eater** Menschenfresser, Kannibale; menschenfressende(r) Löwe, Tiger, Hai *m*; ~ **Friday** Freitag *m (im „Robinson")*; *fig* treue(r) Anhänger *od* Diener *m*; ~**ful** ['ful] mannhaft, tapfer, entschlossen; ~**fulness** ['-fulnis] Mannhaftigkeit *f*; ~**handle** *tr tech* nur mit Menschenkraft betreiben; *fam* rauh, derb anpacken, schlecht behandeln, mißhandeln; ~**-hater** Menschenfeind *m*; ~**-hole** Einsteigloch *n*, Kanalschacht *m*; ~**hood** ['-hud] Mannesalter *n*, -jahre *n pl*; Männlichkeit, Mannhaftigkeit, Tapferkeit *f*, Mut *m*, Entschlossenheit *f*; Männer(welt *f*) *m pl*; ~**-hour** ['-'-] Arbeitsstunde *f*; ~**-hunt** Menschen-, Verbrecherjagd *f*; ~**kind** [-'kaind] die Menschheit, das Menschengeschlecht; ['--] das männliche Geschlecht, die Männerwelt; ~**like** ['-laik] menschlich; männlich; ~**liness** ['-linis] Mannhaftigkeit; Männlichkeit *f*; ~**ly** ['-li] mannhaft, beherzt, tapfer, entschlossen, ehrenhaft; männlich, Männer-; ~**-made** *a* künstlich; ~**nish** ['-iʃ] männlich, wie ein Mann; ~**-of-war** Kriegsschiff *n*; ~~ *bird (orn)* Fregattenvogel *m*; ~**-power** menschliche Arbeitskraft *f*; Arbeitspotential, Menschenmaterial *n*; **men's-room** Herrentoilette *f*; ~**-servant** Diener, männliche(r) Hausangestellte(r) *m*; ~**-sized** *a fam* von menschlicher Statur, groß; ~**-slaughter** ['mænslɔ:tə] Totschlag *m*, fahrlässige Tötung *f*; ~**-slayer** Totschläger *m (Person)*; ~**-trap** Fußangel *f*.

manacle ['mænəkl] *meist pl* Handschellen *f pl*; *sing fig* Fessel, Einengung *f*, Hindernis *n*; *tr* Handschellen anlegen (*s.o.* jdm), fesseln; *fig* einengen, (be)hindern.

manage ['mænidʒ] *tr* handhaben; gebrauchen, benutzen; *(Fahrzeug)* fahren, führen; *(Haushalt, Geschäft, Staat)* leiten; verwalten, dirigieren, führen; *(Menschen)* bearbeiten, beeinflussen; (für s-e Zwecke) geneigt machen, *fam* 'rumkriegen; *(Sache)* in die Wege leiten, zustande bringen, einrichten, regeln, *fam* hinkriegen, *sl* drehen, deichseln, schaukeln; *iro* fertigbringen; *(Tier)* bändigen; *obs (Pferd)* zureiten; *itr* die Geschäfte führen; es schaffen, es zuwege bringen; wirtschaften, auskommen (*with, on* mit); ~**able** ['mænidʒəbl] handlich, leicht zu handhaben(d); leicht zu führen; überschaubar, kontrollierbar; beeinflußbar; einzurichten(d); ~**ment** [-mənt] Handhabung *f*; Gebrauch *m*, Benutzung; (Geschäfts-)Führung; Leitung *f*, Betrieb *m*; Verwaltung, Direktion *(a. d. Personen)*; Bewirtschaftung; Bearbeitung, Beeinflussung; Einrichtung, Regelung; geschickte Handhabung, Behandlung; Betriebs- u. Menschenführung; Geschicklichkeit, Wendigkeit *f*; *factory ~~* Werk(s)leitung *f*; *~~ consultant* Industrieberater *m*; *~~ department* Verwaltungsabteilung *f*; *~~ group* Führungsgruppe *f*; ~**r** ['-ə] Führer, (Betriebs-)Leiter, Prokurist, Verwalter, Direktor; Bewirtschafter; gute(r) Verwalter, Haushälter, haushälterisch veranlagte(r) Mensch; *theat* Intendant, Regisseur *m*; *bank ~~* Bankdirektor *m*; *branch ~~* Filialleiter *m*; *business ~~* Geschäftsführer *m*; *commercial ~~* kaufmännische(r) Direktor *m*; *department ~~* Abteilungsleiter *m*; *district ~~* Bezirksleiter *m*; *factory, works ~~* Fabrikdirektor, Werk(s)leiter *m*; *general ~~* Generaldirektor; Betriebsführer *m*; *office ~~* Büroleiter *m*; *production ~~* Produktionsleiter *m*; *sales ~~* Verkaufsleiter *m*; *stage ~~* Bühnenleiter, Regisseur *m*; *traffic ~~* Fahrdienstleiter *m*; ~**ress** ['mænidʒəres] Vorsteherin, Leiterin, Geschäftsführerin, Betriebsleiterin, Directrice *f*; ~**rial** [mænə'dʒiəriəl] führend, leitend; Direktions-, Verwaltungs-; *in ~~ capacity* in leitender Stellung.

managing ['mænidʒiŋ] *a* führend, leitend, geschäftsführend; haushälterisch, sparsam; beherrschend; ~ **agent** Geschäftsführer *m*; ~ **clerk** Büro-, Kanzleivorsteher; Prokurist *m*; ~ **director** geschäftsführende(s) Vorstandsmitglied *n*; ~ **engineer** leitende(r) Chefingenieur, technische(r) Leiter *od* Direktor *m*.

Manchu [mæn'tʃu:] Mandschu *m*; Mandschu *n (Sprache)*; ~**ria** [mæn-'tʃuəriə] Mandschurei *f*; ~**rian** [-n] mandschurisch.

mandamus [mæn'deiməs] *(order of ~)* schriftliche Anweisung *f* e-s höheren Gerichts.

mandarin ['mændərin] Mandarin *m*; *fig* hohe(s) Tier *n*; ~**(e)** ['-ri:n] *bot* Mandarine *f*.

mandat|ary ['mændətəri] = ~*ory*; ~**e** ['mændeit] *s* (schriftliche) Verfügung, Anordnung, Anweisung; Vollmacht *f*, Mandat *n*; *s. mandamus*; *tr (Land)* als Mandat unterstellen; *territory under ~~* Mandatsgebiet *n*; *~~ government* Mandatsregierung *f*; *~~ power* Mandatarmacht *f*; ~**or** [mæn-'deitə] Auftraggeber, Mandant *m*; ~**ory** ['mændətəri, *Am* -təri] *a* zwingend, verbindlich, obligatorisch; zwangsweise; Mandatar-, Mandats-; *s* Beauftragte(r), (Prozeß-)Bevollmächtigte(r); Mandatar(staat) *m*.

mandible ['mændibl] Kinnlade *f*, -backen, Unterkiefer *m*; *ent* Mandibel *f*; *zoo* Vorderkiefer *m*.

mandolin(e) [mændə'li(:)n, 'mæn-] Mandoline *f*.

mandrake ['mændreik] *bot* Alraun(e *f*) *m*.

mandrel, mandril ['mændrəl] *tech* (Richt-, Steck-)Dorn *m*; Docke *f*.

mandrill ['mændril] Mandrill *m (Affe)*.

mane [mein] Mähne *f (a. beim Menschen)*.

manes ['mɑ:neiz, 'meini:z] *rel hist* Manen *pl*.

*

mangan|ese [mæŋgə'ni:z] *chem* Mangan *n*; *~~ ore* Braunstein *m*; *~~ steel* Manganstahl *m*; ~**ic** [mæŋ'gænik] *a* Mangan-.

mang|e [meindʒ] Räude *f*; ~**iness** ['-inis] Schäbigkeit; Gemeinheit *f*; ~**y** ['-i] räudig; *fig* schmutzig, schäbig; niedrig, gemein.

mangel(-wurzel) ['mæŋgl'wə:zl] *bot* Mangold *m*.

manger ['meindʒə] Krippe *f*, Futtertrog *m*; *to leave all at rack and ~* alles stehen und liegen lassen; *dog in the ~* Neidhammel, Spaßverderber *m*.

mangle ['mæŋgl] **1.** *tr* zerfetzen, zerstückeln, zerfleischen, verstümmeln, entstellen (*beyond recognition* bis zur Unkenntlichkeit); *fig (Text)* verstümmeln, verderben; *(Wort)* falsch aussprechen; *mus* falsch singen *od* spielen; ~**r** ['-ə] (Fleisch-)Wolf *m*; (Fleisch-) Hackmaschine *f*; *fig* Verstümmler *m*; **2.** *s* Wäscherolle, (Wäsche-)Mangel *f*; *tr (Wäsche)* rollen, mangeln; ~**r** ['-ə] Wäschemangler(in *f*) *m*; *tech* Mangel *f*.

mango ['mæŋgou] *pl -(e)s* Mangobaum *m*; Mangopflaume *f*.

mangold *s. mangel(-wurzel)*.

mangrove ['mæŋgrouv] *bot* Mangrove *f*, Mangrove(n)baum *m*.

man|ia ['meiniə] *med* Manie *f*, manische(r) Zustand *m*; *allg* Manie, Sucht, Besessenheit *f* (*for* nach); *to have a ~~ for* verrückt sein auf; ~**iac** ['meiniæk] *s* Irre(r), Geisteskranke(r) *m*; *a* u. ~**iacal** [mə'naiəkəl] manisch, irre; wahnsinnig, verrückt, toll, besessen;

~ic-depressive ['meinik-] *med* manisch-depressiv.

manicur|e ['mænikjuə] *s* Maniküre, Hand-(*u. bes.* Nagel-)Pflege *f*; *selten* = *~ist*; *tr* maniküren; **~ist** ['-rist] Maniküre *f*.

manifest ['mænifest] *a* offen (zutage liegend), (offen)sichtlich, offenbar, -kundig, augenscheinlich, nicht zu leugnen(d); *tr* offenbaren, enthüllen, offenkundig machen, kundtun, (öffentlich) bekanntmachen; beweisen, bestätigen, darlegen, -tun, klarstellen; *mar* in die Frachtliste eintragen; *itr* sich zeigen, (offen) zutage treten, bekannt-, offenkundig werden; *pol* e-e Kundgebung veranstalten, öffentlich auftreten; *(Geist)* erscheinen; *s mar* Ladungsverzeichnis *n*, Fracht(güter)-liste *f*; **~ation** [mænifes'teiʃən] Offenbarung, Enthüllung, Kund-, Bekanntmachung *f*; Symptom *n*; *pol* Kundgebung, Demonstration *f*; *(Geist)* Erscheinen *n*; **~o** [mæni'festou] *pl -o(e)s* öffentliche Erklärung *f*, Manifest *n*; Kundgebung *f*; *election ~~* Wahlmanifest *n*, -aufruf *m*.

manifold ['mænifould] *a* mannigfaltig, -fach, verschiedenartig; Mehrzweck-; *s* Mannigfaltigkeit, Verschiedenartigkeit *f*; Durchschlag, Abzug *m*, Kopie *f*; *(~ pipe)* Sammelrohr *n*, -leitung *f*; Auslaßverteiler *m*; *tr* vervielfältigen; **~er** ['-ə], **~ writer** Vervielfältiger *m*, Vervielfältigungsgerät *n*, -apparat *m*; **~ paper** Vervielfältigungspapier *n*; **~ plug** Vielfachstecker *m*; **~ writer** Vervielfältigungsapparat *m*.

manikin ['mænikin] Männchen, -lein *n*, Zwerg *m*; anatomische(s) Modell, Phantom *n*; Gliederpuppe *(für Künstler)*; Schneiderpuppe *f*.

manipulat|e [mə'nipjuleit] *tr* handhaben; *(Schaltbrett)* bedienen; (in unfairer *od* unerlaubter Weise) beeinflussen; manipulieren, *fam* deichseln, frisieren, *(bes. com: die Bücher)* fälschen; **~ion** [mənipju'leiʃən] geschickte Handhabung, Manipulation; geschickte Behandlung *f*, kunstvolle(s) Verfahren *n*; (unfaire, unerlaubte) Beeinflussung *f*, Manöver *n*, Kunstgriff *m*, Schiebung; Manipulation; Fälschung *f*; **~ive** [-leitiv], **~ory** [-əri] (geschickt) gehandhabt; manipulierend; gefälscht; **~or** [-ə] Handhaber; *fig* Drahtzieher; *tech* Wender *m*.

mannequin ['mænikin] Glieder-, Schneiderpuppe; Vorführdame *f*, Mannequin *n*; **~ parade** Mode(n)schau *f*.

manner ['mænə] Art, Weise, Art u. Weise, Methode *f*, Vorgehen *n*; Verhalten(sweise *f*), Benehmen *n*; Manieren *f pl*, Lebensart *f*, gute(s), feine(s) Benehmen *n*; *(Kunst)* Manier *f*, Stil *m*; *obs lit* Art, Sorte; *pl* Sitte *f*; Gepflogenheiten *f pl*; gute(s) Benehmen *n*, gute(r) Ton *m*; *all ~ of (lit)* aller Art, alle Arten, Sorten (von); *no ~ of* nicht der geringste, gar kein; *by all ~ of means* selbstverständlich, auf jeden Fall; *by no ~ of means* auf keinen Fall; *in a ~* gewissermaßen; bis zu e-m gewissen Grade; *in a ~ of speaking* sozusagen; *in such a ~ that* derart, daß; *in this ~* auf diese Weise; *to the ~ born* von klein auf gewohnt, daran gewöhnt; wie geschaffen dafür; *comedy of ~s* Sittenkomödie *f*; *good, bad ~s (pl)* gute(s), schlechte(s) Benehmen *n*; *it's bad ~s* es schickt sich nicht; **~ed** ['-d] *a* affektiert; *(Kunst)* manieriert; *ill-~~* ungesittet; *well-~~* wohlgesittet; **~ism** ['-rizm] Manieriertheit, Affektiertheit; Eigenwilligkeit *f*; **~ist** ['-rist] affektierte(r) Mensch; Künstler, Schriftsteller *m* mit eigenwilligem Stil; **~less** ['-lis] ungesittet, ungezogen; **~liness** ['-linis] Anstand *m*, gute(s) Benehmen, (gute) Lebensart *f*; **~ly** ['-li] *a* (wohl)gesittet, (wohl)anständig, von gutem Benehmen.

manœuvr|ability, *Am meist* **maneuverability** [mənu:vrə'biliti] Lenkbarkeit, Manövrierbarkeit *f*; **~able** [mə'nu:vrəbl] manövrierbar; **~e** [mə'nu:və] *s mil mar* Manöver *n*, (Truppen-)Bewegung *f*; *allg* Kunstgriff, Trick *m*, List *f*; *pl* Manöver *n*, Truppen-, Gefechtsübungen *f pl*; *itr tr* manövrieren (lassen); *tr* geschickt einrichten, vorbereiten, einfädeln, *fam* deichseln, drehen, verleiten (*into* zu); *to ~~ o.s. out of s.th. (fig)* sich aus e-r S herausmanövrieren; **~er** [mə'nu:vərə] pfiffige(r) Kopf, Intrigant *m*.

manometer [mə'nɔmitə] Manometer *n*, Druckmesser *m*.

manor ['mænə] *hist* Herrschafts-, Gutsbezirk *m*; Rittergut *n*; *lord of the ~* Gutsherr, Rittergutsbesitzer *m*; **~-house** Herrenhaus, (kleines) Landschloß *n*; **~ial** [mə'nɔ:riəl] herrschaftlich.

mansard ['mænsəd] Mansarde, Dachkammer *f*; Dachgeschoß *n*; *(~-roof)* Mansardendach *n*.

manse [mæns] *Scot* Pfarrhaus *n*.

mansion ['mænʃən] (stattlicher) Bau *m*, Palais; *hist* Herrenhaus; *(Astrologie)* Haus *n*; *pl* Wohn-, Häuserblock *m*; *Br* Mietshaus *n*; *the M~-house* Amtssitz *m* des Lord Mayor von London.

mantel ['mæntl] Kaminmantel *m*; *a.* **~-board, -piece, -shelf** Kaminsims *m*, -platte *f*.

mant(e)let ['mæntlit] kurze(r) Mantel, Überwurf, Umhang *m*, Cape *n*; *mil* Schutzwehr *f*.

mantic ['mæntik] prophetisch.

mantilla [mæn'tilə] Mantille *f*, Schleiertuch *n*; Umhang *m*, Cape *n*.

mantis ['mæntis] *pl a. -tes* ['-iz] *ent (praying ~)* Gottesanbeterin *f*.

mantle ['mæntl] *s* Umhang, ärmellose(r) Mantel *m*, Cape *n*; *allg* Mantel *m*, Hülle *f*; (Glüh-)Strumpf *m*; (Guß-)Form; *arch* Decklage *f*; *(Hochofen)* Rauhgemäuer *n*; *geol* (Erd-)Boden *m*; *anat* (Gehirn-)Rinde *f*; *fig* (Deck-)Mantel *m*; *tr* ver-, einhüllen, bedecken, überziehen (*with* mit); *itr* sich bedecken, sich überziehen (*with* mit); *(Wangen)* angehaucht werden (*with blushes* rot); *blushes ~d on her cheecks* Röte überzog ihre Wangen.

manual ['mænjuəl] *a* Hand-, manuell; handbuchartig; *jur* tatsächlich; *s* Handbuch *n*, Leitfaden *m*; *(Orgel)* Manual *n*; *mil (~ of arms)* Dienstvorschrift *f*; *sign ~* eigenhändige Unterschrift *f*; **~ aid** Handreichung *f*; **~ exercises** *pl* (Gewehr-)Griffe *m pl*, *sl* Griffekloppen *n*; **~ labo(u)r, work** Handarbeit *f*; **~ operation** Handbedienung *f*; **~ training** Werkunterricht *m*.

manufactur|e [mænju'fæktʃə] *s* Herstellung, Fabrikation, (Ver-)Fertigung, Produktion *f*; Erzeugnis, Produkt, Fabrikat *n*; *tr* herstellen, fabrizieren, (ver)fertigen, produzieren; verarbeiten (*into* zu); *pej (Kunst-, Literaturwerk)* fabrizieren; *(Ausrede, Entschuldigung)* finden; **~ed** [-d] *a*: *~~ articles, goods (pl)* Fabrikerzeugnisse *n pl*, -waren *f pl*; *~~ goods (pl)* Fertigwaren *f pl*; *~~ ice* Kunsteis *n*; **~er** [-rə] Hersteller, Erzeuger, Verfertiger; Fabrikant, Fabrikbesitzer *m*; *~~'s mark* Fabrikmarke *f*, Warenzeichen *n*; *~~'s number* Fabrikationsnummer *f*; *~~'s price* Hersteller-, Fabrik-, Gestehungspreis *m*; *~~'s sign* Fabrikzeichen *n*; **~ing** [-riŋ] *s* Fabrikation, (fabrikmäßige) Herstellung *f*; *a* Herstellungs-, Fabrikations-, Industrie-, Gewerbe-; *~~ branch* Industriezweig *m*; *~~ capacity* Produktionskapazität *f*; *~~ centre, district* Industriegebiet *n*; *~~ company* Produktionsgesellschaft *f*; *~~ country* Industriestaat *m*; *~~ efficiency* Produktionsleistung *f*; *~~ engineer* Betriebsingenieur *m*; *~~ expenses (pl)* Gestehungskosten *pl*; *~~ industry* verarbeitende, Fertigungsindustrie *f*; *~~ licence* Herstellungserlaubnis, -lizenz *f*; *~~ plant* Fabrik-, Werkanlage; Produktionsstätte *f*; *~~ population* Arbeiterbevölkerung *f*; *~~ price* Selbstkostenpreis *m*; *~~ process* Fabrikationsverfahren *n*; *~~ program(me)* Fabrikationsprogramm *n*; *~~ town* Industriestadt *f*.

manure [mə'njuə] *s* Dünger *m*; *tr* düngen.

manuscript ['mænjuskript] *(bes. alte)* Handschrift *f*; *typ* Manuskript *n*, Satzvorlage *f*; *a u. in ~* handschriftlich; *still in ~* (noch) ungedruckt.

Manx [mæŋks] *a* (von) der Insel Man; *s* Bewohner(in *f*) *m* der Insel Man.

many ['meni] *prn* viel(e); *the ~* die Vielen, die große Menge *od* Masse; *~ a* manche(r, s), manch ein(e); *~ a man* manch einer; *~ a time* manchesmal, nicht selten; *a good ~ times* ziemlich oft; *a great ~ times* sehr oft; *as ~* ebenso viele; *as ~ again* noch mal so viele; *a good ~, a great ~* sehr viele; *one too ~* einer zuviel; *to be one too ~ for s.o. (fig)* jdn in den Schatten stellen, in die Ecke drücken; **~-sided** *a* vielseitig; **~-sidedness** Vielseitigkeit *f*.

*

map [mæp] *s (Land-, See-, Stern-)* Karte *f*; *(Stadt-)*Plan *m*; *sl* Fresse *f*, Gesicht *n*; *tr* kartographisch darstellen *od* aufnehmen; *(to ~ out)* genau festlegen, einteilen; planen, entwerfen, ausarbeiten; *off the ~ (fam)* ohne Interesse; nicht mehr aktuell; abgelegen; *on the ~ (fam)* von (allgemeinem) Interesse, (hoch)aktuell; *to put on the ~ (fam)* ausposaunen; *road ~* Straßenkarte *f*; *motor road-~* Autokarte *f*; *~ of the city* Stadtplan *m*; **~ case** Kartentasche *f*; **~ grid** Kartengitter *n*; **~ reading** Kartenlesen *n*; **~ room** *mil* Kartenraum *m*; **~ sheet** Kartenblatt *n*; **~ table** Kartentisch *m*.

maple ['meipl] *bot* Ahorn *m*, -holz *n*; **~-sirup** *Am* Ahornsirup *m*; **~-sugar** *Am* Ahornzucker *m*.

mar [mɑ:] *tr* beschädigen, beeinträchtigen; verderben, entstellen.

marabou ['mærəbu:] *orn* Marabu *m*.

maraschino [mærəs'ki:nou] Maraschino *m (Likör)*.

marasmus [mə'ræzməs] *med* Abzehrung, Entkräftung *f*, Kräfteverfall *m*.

marathon ['mærəθən] *sport* Marathonlauf; *allg* Dauerwettbewerb *m*.

maraud [mə'rɔ:d] *itr* marodieren, plündern; *tr* (aus)plündern; **~er** [-ə] Marodeur, Plünderer *m*.

marble ['mɑ:bl] *s* Marmor *m*; Marmorbild(werk) *n*; Marmel, Murmel; Marmorierung *f*; *a* marmorartig, marmoriert; Marmor-; *fig* gefühllos; *tr* marmorieren, sprenkeln.

marcel [mɑ:'sel] *tr (Haar)* ondulieren.
March [mɑ:tʃ] März *m*; *in* ~ im März; ~ **hare** Märzhase *m a. fig*; *as mad as a* ~~ *(fam)* total verrückt.
march [mɑ:tʃ] **1.** *itr* marschieren; fortschreiten; vorrücken, weitergehen; *tr* marschieren lassen; wegschicken, -jagen; *s* Marsch *a. mus*; Schritt; weite(r) Weg; *mil* Vormarsch (*on* auf); (Ver-)Lauf, Gang *(der Ereignisse)*; *fig* Fortschritt *m*; *on the* ~ auf dem Marsch; *to steal a* ~ *on s.o.* jdm den Rang ablaufen, jdn abhängen; jdm zuvorkommen; ~ *at ease!* ohne Tritt (marsch)! *dead, forced* ~ Trauer-, Gewaltmarsch *m*; *line of* ~ Marschrichtung *f*; *the* ~ *of events* der Gang der Ereignisse; *the* ~ *of time* der Lauf der Zeit; *to* ~ **away,** *to* ~ **off** *itr tr* abmarschieren (lassen), abrücken; *tr* abführen; *to* ~ **forth,** *to* ~ **on** *itr tr* weitermarschieren (lassen); *to* ~ **in,** *to* ~ **out** *itr tr* ein-, ausmarschieren (lassen); *to* ~ **past** *itr tr* vorbeimarschieren (lassen); ~**ing** ['-iŋ] *a* Marsch-; ~~ *order* Marschordnung, -ausrüstung *f*; *pl* Marschbefehl *m*; ~~ *song* Marschlied *n*; ~ **order** *Am* Marschbefehl *m*; ~ **past** Vorbeimarsch *m*; ~ **security** Marschsicherung *f*; **2.** *s meist pl* Grenze *f*; Grenzland *n*, Mark *f*; *itr* grenzen (*upon* an); e-e gemeinsame Grenze haben (*with* mit); ~**land** Grenzland *n*.
marchioness ['mɑ:ʃənis] *(englische)* Marquise, Markgräfin *f*.
marchpane ['mɑ:tʃpein] Marzipan *n*.
Margaret ['mɑ:gərit] Margarete *f*.
mare [mɛə] Stute *f*; ~**'s nest** Scherz, Jux, Schwindel *m*; (Zeitungs-)Ente *f*; Reinfall *m*; ~**'s tail** Seegras *n*, Tang *m*; Streifenwolken *f pl*.
margarine [mɑ:dʒə'ri:n, *Am* '-] Margarine *f*.
marge [mɑ:dʒ] **1.** *poet* Rand, Saum *m*; **2.** *fam* Margarine *f*.
margin ['mɑ:dʒin] *s* Rand *m*, Kante *f*; *(Schriftstück, Buch)* (weißer, freibleibender) Rand *m*; Grenze *f*; Spielraum *m*, Spanne; *com (profit* ~*)* Gewinnspanne *f*, Überschuß *m*; *tech* Toleranzgrenze; *fin* Deckung, Anschaffung *f*; *sport* Vorsprung *m*; *tr* mit e-m Rand versehen; einfassen, begrenzen; auf den Rand schreiben, am Rande vermerken, notieren; *fin (to put up a* ~ *for)* Deckung anschaffen für; *to* ~ *up* zusätzliche Deckung anschaffen für; *by a narrow* ~ mit knapper (Müh und) Not; *in the* ~ auf den Rand; *on the* ~ am Rande; *to allow, to reserve a* ~ Spielraum lassen; *to have (enough)* ~ (genügend) Spielraum haben; *to leave a* ~ Spielraum lassen; Gewinn abwerfen, einträglich sein; *they won by a narrow* ~ sie haben knapp gewonnen; ~ *of income* Einkommensgrenze *f*; ~ *of power* Kraftreserve *f*; ~ *of profit* Gewinn-, Verdienstspanne *f*; ~ *of safety* Sicherheitsfaktor, -abstand *m*; ~**al** ['-əl] e-n Rand, e-e Grenze bildend; begrenzend; Rand-, Grenz-; *(Land)* weniger rentabel; *com* zum Selbstkostenpreis; ~~ *case* Grenzfall *m*; ~~ *cost* Grenzkosten *pl*; ~~ *note* Randbemerkung, -notiz *f*; ~~ *price* äußerste(r) Preis *m*; ~~ *utility* Grenznutzen *m*; ~**alia** [mɑ:dʒi'neiljə] *pl* Randbemerkungen *f pl*, Marginalien *pl*.
marguerite [mɑ:gə'ri:t] *bot* Margerite *f*; Gänseblümchen *n*.
marigold ['mærigould] Ringel-, *bes.* Gold-, Totenblume *f*.
marijuana, marihuana [mɑ:ri'(h)wɑ:nə] Marihuana *n (Rauschgift)*.
marin|ade [mæri'neid] *s* Marinade *f*; *tr, a.* ~**ate** [-eit] *tr* marinieren.
marine [mə'ri:n] *a* See-, Meer(es)-; Marine-; *s* Matrose *m*; (Kriegs-, Handels-)Marine *f*; Marineinfant(e)rist *m*; Marineministerium; *(Kunst)* Seestück *n*; *tell that to the* ~*s* das mach andern weis! *mercantile, merchant* ~ Handelsmarine *f*; ~ **adventure, peril, risk** Seegefahr *f*, -risiko *n*; ~ **affairs** *pl* Seewesen *n*, Schiffahrt *f*; ~ **belt** Hoheitsgewässer *n pl*; **M**~ **Corps** *Am* Marineinfanterie *f*; ~ **engineering** Schiffsmaschinenbau *m*; ~ **insurance** Seetransportversicherung *f*; ~ **plant** Meerespflanze *f*; ~**r** ['mærinə] Seemann, Matrose *m*; *master* ~~ Kapitän *m*; ~ **stores** *pl* Schiffsproviant(amt *n*), -bedarf(smagazin *n*) *m*.
marionette [mæriə'net] Marionette, Puppe *f a. fig*.
marital [mə'raitl, 'mæritl] ehe(männ)lich, Ehe-; ~ **partners** *pl* Ehegatten *m pl*; ~ **rights** *pl* eheliche Rechte *n pl*; ~ **status** Familienstand *m*.
maritime ['mæritaim] *a* See-; Küsten-; Seefahrt treibend; Schiffahrt(s)-; seemännisch; ~ **assurance, insurance** Seetransportversicherung, Versicherung *f* gegen Seegefahr; ~ **code, law** Seerecht *n*; ~ **commerce, trade** (Über-)Seehandel *m*; ~ **court** See-, Marineamt *n*; ~ **forces** *pl* Seestreitkräfte *f pl*; ~ **loan** Bodmerei(darlehen *n*) *f*; ~ **navigation** (Hoch-) Seeschiffahrt *f*; ~ **power** Seemacht *f*; ~ **route** Seeweg *m*; ~ **traffic** Seeverkehr *m*; ~ **transport(ation)** Seetransport *m*, Beförderung *f* auf dem Seewege; ~ **warfare** Seekrieg(führung *f*) *m*.
marjoram ['mɑ:dʒərəm] *(sweet* ~*)* Majoran, Meiran *m (Gewürz(pflanze))*.
Mark [mɑ:k] Markus *m*.
mark [mɑ:k] **1.** *s* Spur *f*, Mal *n*, Narbe *f*; Brandmal *n*; Fleck *m*; (Kenn-) Zeichen *n*; Stempel *m*, Siegel, Etikett *n*, (Preis-)Zettel *m*, Aufschrift, Auszeichnung; (Fabrik-)Marke, Sorte *f*; *mil* Modell; *fig* (An-, Kenn-)Zeichen (*of* von), Merkmal *n*; Marke *f*, Strich; Einschnitt; *(Bewertungs-)* Punkt *m*, Note, Zensur *f*; Durchschnitt(smaß *n*), Standard *m*; Abzeichen *n*; (hohe) Auszeichnung *f*, Rang *m*; (große) Bedeutung *f*; Eindruck, Einfluß *m*; Beachtung; Markierung(szeichen *n*); *sport* Startlinie; *(Boxen)* Magengrube *f*; Mal, Ziel(punkt *m*) *n a. fig*; *Am sl* Gimpel, leichtgläubige(r) Mensch *m*; *tr* (be-, kenn-, aus)zeichnen, markieren *a. mil*; notieren, anstreichen; (auf)zeigen, herausstellen, zu erkennen, zu verstehen geben; charakterisieren; heraus-, hervorheben, auszeichnen; bewerten, zensieren; *(Ware mit Preis)* auszeichnen; auf-, verzeichnen, (schriftlich) niederlegen; beachten; achten, achtgeben, aufpassen auf; *itr* (ein) Zeichen machen; *(bei Spielen die Punkte)* anschreiben; aufpassen, achtgeben; sich merken; *beside the* ~, *wide of the* ~ am Ziel vorbei, vorbeigeschossen; nicht zur Sache gehörig; *to be below the* ~ unter dem Durchschnitt bleiben *od* sein; *to be up to the* ~ auf der Höhe sein *(a. gesundheitlich)*; den Erwartungen entsprechen; *to get off the* ~ *(sport)* starten; *to hit, to miss the* ~ das Ziel, ins Schwarze treffen; das Ziel verfehlen, *fam* danebenhauen; *to make o.'s* ~ sich e-n Namen machen, berühmt werden; sich durchsetzen; es zu etwas bringen; *to* ~ *time (mil)* auf der Stelle treten; *fig* nicht weiter-, nicht vom Fleck kommen; den Takt schlagen; ~*!* gib acht! paß auf! Achtung! ~ *me!* höre mich an! *save the* ~*!* alle Achtung! *birth-*~ Muttermal *n*; *book-*~ Lesezeichen *n*; *coiner's, mint-*~ Münzzeichen *n*; *ear-*~ Erkennungs-, Kennzeichen *n*; *finger-*~ Fingerabdruck *m*; *foot-*~ Fußspur *f*; *hall-*~ Feingehaltstempel *m*; *identity-*~ Erkennungsmarke *f*; *land* ~ Grenzstein; *fig* Höhe-, Wendepunkt *m*; *a man of* ~ ein bedeutender Mann; *post-*~ Poststempel *m*; *price-*~ *(com)* Preisbezeichnung *f*, -schildchen *n*; *proof-correction* ~ *(typ)* Korrekturzeichen *n*; *punctuation* ~ Satzzeichen *n*; *reference-*~ Verweisungszeichen *n*; *trade-*~ Firmenzeichen *n*, Fabrik-, Haus-, Schutzmarke *f*; *water-*~ Wasserstandsanzeiger *m*; *(Papier)* Wasserzeichen *n*; ~ *of identification* Merkmal *n*; *to* ~ **down** *tr* auf-, niederschreiben, notieren, aufzeichnen; vormerken; bezeichnen; im Preis herabsetzen; *to* ~ **off** *tr* abgrenzen *a. fig*; trennen; *to* ~ **out** *tr* abgrenzen, -stecken; aussuchen, -wählen, bestimmen, vormerken (*for* für); durchstreichen; *to* ~ **up** *tr* mit Zeichen versehen; im Preis heraufsetzen; ~**down** Preisnachlaß, -abschlag *m*, Herabsetzung *f* des Preises; ~**ed** [-t] *a* bezeichnet, gekennzeichnet; verdächtig(t); merklich, auffällig, in die Augen fallend, hervorstechend; ~~*-down (im Preis)* herabgesetzt; ~**er** ['-ə] *(Spiel)* (An-)Schreiber; *(Schießstand)* Anzeiger; Flügelmann; *(Billard)* Markör *m (Vorrichtung)*; Lesezeichen *n*; *mil aero* Markierungs-, Leuchtzeichen *n*; *(*~~ *aircraft)* Beleuchter; Meilen-, Kilometerstein *m*; *Am* Verkehrsschild *n*; *Am* Gedenktafel *f*, Grabstein *m*; ~**ing** ['-iŋ] Be-, Kennzeichnung, Markierung; *zoo bot* Zeichnung, Färbung; *com* Notierung, Kursnotiz *f*; ~~*-ink* Wäschetinte *f*; ~~*-iron* Brenneisen *n*; ~**sman** ['-smən] gute(r) Schütze; *sport* Torschütze *m*; ~**smanship** ['-smənʃip] gute(s) Schießen *n*; ~**-up** Preiserhöhung *f*; **2.** Mark *f (Währungseinheit)*.
market ['mɑ:kit] *s* Markt; Marktplatz *m*, -halle *f*; *Am* große(s) Lebensmittelgeschäft *n*; Markt *m*, Börse *f*, Absatz (-gebiet *n*), Umsatz; Handel(sverkehr); Marktpreis, -wert *m*, -lage *f*; Vorteil, Gewinn; Kurs *m*; *attr* Markt-; *tr* auf den Markt bringen; an-, zum Verkauf, feilbieten; verkaufen, absetzen; *itr* auf dem Markt Geschäfte machen; handeln; einkaufen; *at the* ~ zum Marktpreis; auf dem Markt; *Am* bestens; *in the* ~ am Markt; zum Verkauf angeboten; *on the* ~ auf dem Markt; *to be in the* ~ *for s.th.* Bedarf haben an; für etw Abnehmer sein; *to be off the* ~ nicht mehr im Handel zu haben sein; *to be on the* ~ zum Verkauf stehen, an-, feilgeboten werden; *to bring o.'s eggs, hogs to a bad, to the wrong* ~ an die falsche Adresse geraten; *to corner the* ~ den Markt aufkaufen; *to find a, to meet with a ready* ~ guten Absatz finden, sich gut verkaufen, gut weggehen; *to put on the* ~ auf den Markt bringen; *black* ~ Schwarzmarkt *m*; *bond* ~ Pfandbrief-, Effektenmarkt *m*; *buyer's* ~ Baisse *f*; Käufermarkt *m*; *capital, money, credit* ~ Kapitalmarkt *m*; *cattle* ~ Viehmarkt *m*; *Common M*~ Gemeinsame(r) Markt *m*; *domestic, home, internal* ~ Binnen-, Inlands-

markt *m*; *easy, firm* ~ freundliche, feste Börse *f*; *employment, labo(u)r* ~ Stellen-, Arbeitsmarkt *m*; *grain* ~ Getreidemarkt *m*, -börse *f*; *official* ~ amtliche Notierung *f*; *position, situation, state of the* ~ Marktlage, Konjunktur *f*; *property, real estate* ~ Grundstücks-, Immobilienmarkt *m*; *security, share, stock* ~ Effekten-, Aktienmarkt *m*; *spot* ~ Barverkehr *m*; *world* ~ Weltmarkt *m*; ~ *of consumption* Verbrauchermarkt *m*; **~ability** [ma:kitə'biliti] Marktfähigkeit; Absatzmöglichkeit *f*; **~able** ['ma:kitəbl] marktfähig, gangbar, gängig, gut verkäuflich, absatzfähig; börsenfähig; ~ **analysis, study** Marktforschung, -analyse *f*; ~ **analyst** Marktbeobachter *m*; **~-condition** Marktlage *f*; Absatzbedingungen *f pl*; ~ **coverage** Marktanteil *m*; **~-day** Markttag *m*; **~-dues** *pl* Marktgebühren *pl*, Standgeld *n*; **~-fluctuations** *pl* Markt-, Preisschwankungen *f pl*; **~-garden** *Br* Handelsgärtnerei *f*; **~ing** ['-iŋ] Marketing *n*; Vertriebslehre *f*; (Waren-) Absatz *m*; *to do* ~~ Einkäufe machen, einkaufen, einholen; ~~ *area* Absatzgebiet *n*, -bereich *m* od *n*; ~~ *company* Vertriebsgesellschaft *f*; ~~ *co-operative* Absatzgenossenschaft *f*; ~~ *costs (pl)* Vertriebskosten *pl*; ~~ *organisation, system* Absatzorganisation *f*; ~ **inquiry** Marktanalyse *f*; ~ **jobbery** Börsenterminhandel *m*; **~-news,** *Am* **-letters** *pl* Markt-, Börsenbericht *m*; **~-place** Markt(platz) *m*; ~ **price** Markt-, Handelspreis; Börsenpreis, -kurs, Kurs(wert) *m*; ~~ *list* Marktbericht *m*; ~ **quotation** Kursbericht *m*; ~ **rate** (amtlicher) Diskontsatz; Tageskurs *m*; ~ **regulations** *pl* Marktordnung *f*; ~ **research** Absatz-, Marktforschung *f*; ~ **rigging** Kurstreiberei *f*; ~ **risk** Markt-, Konjunkturrisiko *n*; **~-swing** Konjunktur(umschwung *m*) *f*; **~-town** Markt (-flecken) *m*; ~ **transactions** *pl* Börsengeschäfte *n pl*, -transaktionen *f pl*; ~ **value** Marktwert *m*; Notierung *f*.

marl [ma:l] *s geol* Mergel *m*; *tr* mit Mergel düngen; ~ **pit** Mergelgrube *f*.

marm [ma:m] *Am s. ma'am*.

marmalade ['ma:məleid] (*bes.* Orangen-)Konfitüre, Marmelade *f*.

marmore|al, ~an [ma:'mɔ:riəl, -ən] marmorn *a. fig*, Marmor-.

marmose ['ma:mous] Äneasratte *f* *(Beutelratte)*; **~t** ['-məzet] Krallenaffe *m*.

marmot ['ma:mət] Murmeltier *n*.

maroon [mə'ru:n] **1.** *a* kastanienbraun; *s* Kastanienbraun *n*; **2.** *s* entlaufene(r), flüchtige(r) Negersklave *m*; *tr (in e-r einsamen Gegend)* aussetzen; *fig* aufgeben, sich selbst überlassen; *itr* herumbummeln; *Am (Südstaaten)* einzeln zelten.

marplot ['ma:plɔt] Spiel-, Spaßverderber *m*.

marque [ma:k]: *letter(s pl) of* ~ *(and reprisal)* Kaperbrief *m*.

marquee [ma:'ki:] *Br* (großes) *(an den Seiten)* offene(s) Zelt; *Am* Schutzdach *n (vor e-m Theater, Hotel)*.

marquet(e)ry ['ma:kitri] Einlegearbeit, Intarsia *f*.

marqu|is, ~ess ['ma:kwis] Marquis *m*.

marriage ['mæridʒ] Ehe; Heirat, Hochzeit, Trauung, Eheschließung, Verehelichung *f (to* mit); Ehestand *m*; Trauungszeremoniell *n*, Hochzeitsfeierlichkeiten *f pl*; *fig* enge Verbindung, Vereinigung *f*; *by* ~ angeheiratet; *in, of the first* ~ in, aus erster Ehe; *to contract a* ~ e-e Ehe eingehen; *to give in* ~ *(Tochter)* verheiraten; *to propose* ~ e-n Antrag machen, e-n Heiratsantrag stellen; *civil, common law* ~, ~ *before the registrar* standesamtliche, Ziviltrauung *f*; *to perform civil* ~ standesamtlich trauen; *impediment to* ~ Ehehindernis *n*; *mixed* ~ Mischehe *f*; *morganatic* ~ Ehe *f* zur linken Hand; *offer of* ~ (Heirats-)Antrag *m*; *procurement of* ~ Ehevermitt(e)lung, -anbahnung *f*; *promise of* ~ Eheversprechen *n*; *related by* ~ verschwägert; ~ *of convenience, of propriety* Vernunftehe *f*; ~ *for money* Geldheirat *f*; ~ *by proxy* Ferntrauung *f*; **~able** ['mæridʒəbl] heiratsfähig; ~~ *age* Ehemündigkeit *f*; *of* ~~ *age* im heiratsfähigen Alter; **~-articles** *pl*, **contract, settlement** Ehevertrag *m*; ~ **bed** Ehebett *n*; **~-brokage** Heiratsvermitt(e)lung *f*; **~-broker** Heiratsvermittler(in *f*) *m*; **~-ceremony** Trauung *f*; **~-certificate,** *fam* **-lines** *pl* Heiratsurkunde *f*, Trauschein *m*; **~-law** Eherecht *n*; **~-licence** Heiratserlaubnis, -urkunde *f*; **~-portion** Mitgift *f*, Heiratsgut *n*; **~-register** Heiratsregister *n*; **~-ring** Trau-, Ehering *m*; **~-rites** *pl* Hochzeitsbräuche *m pl*; ~ **vow** Ehegelöbnis *n*.

married ['mærid] *a* verheiratet (*to* mit); ehelich; Ehe-; *fig* (eng) verbunden; *to be* ~ *in church* kirchlich getraut werden; *to get* ~ (sich ver)heiraten; ~ **couple** Ehepaar *n*; *newly* ~~ junge(s) Ehepaar *n*; ~ **life** Eheleben *n*; ~ **man** Ehemann *m*; ~ **people** Eheleute *pl*; ~ **state** Ehestand *m*; ~ **woman** Ehefrau *f*.

marrow ['mærou] (Knochen-)Mark; *fig* Mark *n*, Seele *f*, *das* Innerste, *der* Kern; Lebenskraft, Vitalität *f*; *to the* ~ bis aufs Mark; *spinal* ~ Rückenmark *n*; *vegetable* ~ Markkürbis *m*; **~bone** Markknochen *m*; *pl fam* Knie *n pl*; **~y** ['-i] markig.

marry ['mæri] *tr* trauen, vermählen (*to s.o.* mit jdm); heiraten (*s.o.* jdn); *fig* (eng) verbinden (*to* mit); *(to* ~ *off)* verheiraten (*to* an, mit); *itr* heiraten, sich verheiraten; *fig* sich eng verbinden, sich vereinigen.

marsh [ma:ʃ] Marsch(land *n*) *f*, Sumpf, Morast *m*, Moor *n*; **~-fever** Sumpffieber *n*, Malaria *f*; **~-fire** Irrlicht *n*; **~-gas** Sumpfgas *n*; **~iness** ['-inis] Sumpfigkeit *f*; **~land** Marschland, Sumpfgebiet *n*; **~-mallow** *bot* Eibisch *m*; *Art* Konfekt *n*; **~-marigold** (Sumpf-)Dotter-, Kuh-, Butterblume *f*; **~y** ['-i] sumpfig, morastig, moorig; Sumpf-, Moor-.

marshal ['ma:ʃəl] *s hist* Hofmarschall, Zeremonienmeister; *mil* Marschall; Gerichtsmarschall *(Begleiter e-s hohen Richters)*; *Am jur* Vollstreckungsbeamte(r); *Am* Polizeidirektor, -präsident *m*; *tr (Truppen)* aufstellen; *(Einheit)* zs.stellen; *(Zeremonie, Feier)* leiten; *allg fig* (an)ordnen, arrangieren, disponieren; *aero* einwinken; *field* ~ Feldmarschall *m*; **~(l)ing yard** Verschiebebahnhof *m*.

marsupi|al [ma:'sju:pjəl] *a* Beutel-(tier-); *s* Beuteltier *n*; **~um** [-əm] Beutel *m (der Beuteltiere)*.

mart [ma:t] Markt, Handelsplatz *m*; Auktionshalle *f*; *obs poet* Markt (-platz); Handel und Wandel *m*.

marten ['ma:tin] Marder(fell *n*) *m*; *beech-, stone-~* Stein-, Hausmarder *m*; *pine, fir* ~ Edel-, Baummarder *m*.

martial ['ma:ʃəl] *a* Kriegs-; kriegerisch, soldatisch, tapfer; *court* ~ Kriegs-, Militärgericht *n*; ~ **law** Kriegs-, Standrecht *n*; *under* ~~ standrechtlich; *to declare* ~~ das Standrecht verhängen; den Ausnahme-, Belagerungszustand erklären; *to try by* ~~ vor ein Kriegsgericht stellen; ~ **music** Militärmusik *f*.

Martian ['ma:ʃjən] *a (Mythologie) astr* Mars-; *s* Marsbewohner *m*.

Martin ['ma:tin]: *St.* ~*'s summer* Altweibersommer *m*; *St.* ~*'s day*, **~mas** ['-məs] Martinstag *m*, Martini *n* *(11. November)*.

martin ['ma:tin] *(house-~)* Mauerschwalbe *f*; *bank-, sand-~* Uferschwalbe *f*; *bee-~* Königsvogel, Tyrann *m*; *purple-~* Purpurschwalbe *f*.

martinet [ma:ti'net] strenge(r), pedantische(r) Vorgesetzte(r) *m*.

martini [ma:'ti:ni] Martini *m (Cocktail)*.

martyr ['ma:tə] *s* Märtyrer, Blutzeuge; *allg* Märtyrer *m*, Opfer *n*; *tr* martern; foltern; verfolgen; *to make a* ~ *of o.s.* sich opfern (*for* für); *a* ~ *to gout* ein Gichtleidender; **~dom** ['-dəm] Märtyrertum; Martyrium *n a. allg*; Tortur *f*, Leiden *n pl*; **~ize** ['-raiz] *tr* zum Märtyrer machen; quälen, foltern.

marvel ['ma:vəl] *s* Wunder; Muster *n*; *itr* sich wundern, erstaunt sein (*at* über); sich fragen (*why* warum); *to work ~s* Wunder wirken; **~(l)ous** ['-əs] wunderbar; unfaßbar, unglaublich; erstaunlich, außerordentlich; *fam* wunderbar, prachtvoll, prächtig, herrlich; **~(l)ousness** ['-əsnis] *das* Wunderbare, Unfaßbare, Erstaunliche.

Marx|ian ['ma:ksjən], **~ist** ['-ist] *a* marxistisch; *s* Marxist *m*; **~(ian)ism** ['-(jən)izm] Marxismus *m*.

marzipan [ma:zi'pæn] Marzipan *n*.

mascara [mæs'ka:rə] Wimpern-, Augenbrauentusche *f*.

mascot(te) ['mæskət] Maskottchen *n*, Talisman, Glücksbringer, Anhänger *m*; *radiator* ~ Kühlerfigur *f*.

masculin|e ['ma:skjulin, mæs-] *a* männlich *a gram*; mannhaft; typisch, betont männlich; Männer-, Herren-; *s gram* Maskulinum *n*; ~~ *woman* Mannweib *n*; **~ity** [mæskju'liniti] Männlichkeit; Mannhaftigkeit *f*.

mash [mæʃ] *s (Brauerei)* Maische *f*; *agr* Mengfutter; *allg* breiige(s) Gemisch *n*, Brei *m*, Mus *n*; *Br sl* Kartoffelbrei *m*; *fig* Durcheinander *n*; *tr* maischen; (zer)mahlen, zerstoßen, zu Brei schlagen, verrühren; *~ed potatoes (pl)* Kartoffelbrei *m*, -püree *n*; **~er** ['-ə] Maischer; Maischapparat *m*; **~ing tub** Maischbottich *m*.

mask [ma:sk] *s* Maske *(a. arch)*; Schablone; *fig* Hülle *f*, Schleier; Vorwand *m*; Maskenspiel *n*; Verkleidung, Maskerade; *mil* Tarnung *f*; *tr* maskieren; verdecken; *fig* verhüllen, verschleiern, verheimlichen; *mil* tarnen; *(to* ~ *out)* korrigieren, retuschieren; *itr* sich maskieren; sich verstellen; *to throw off o.'s* ~ *(fig)* sein wahres Gesicht zeigen; *death-, gas-, oxygen* ~ Toten-, Gas-, Sauerstoffmaske *f*; **~ed** [-t] *a* maskiert; *mil* getarnt; *fig* verhüllt, verborgen, versteckt; ~~ *ball* Maskenball *m*; **~er** ['-ə] Maske *f* *(Person)*.

mason ['meisn] *s* Maurer; Steinmetz; *(free-~)* Freimaurer *m*; *tr* mauern; **~ic** [mə'sɔnik] freimaurerisch; **~ry** ['meisnri] Maurerhandwerk *n*, -arbeit *f*; Mauerwerk *n*; Freimaurerei *f*.

masque [ma:sk] Maskenspiel *n*; Maskerade *f*, Maskenball *m*; **~rade** [mæskə'reid] *s* Maskenball *m*, Maskerade *f*; Maskenkostüm *n*; *fig* Maskerade *f*, Theater *n*, Vorspiegelung falscher Tatsachen; Maske, Verkleidung *f*; *itr* e-n Maskenball mitmachen; sich verkleiden; *fig* sich verstellen, sich ausgeben (*as* als).

mass [mæs] **1.** *s* Masse *a. phys*, Menge; (Knet-)Masse *f*; *(Blut)* Klumpen; Umfang *m*, Größe; Mehrheit; *mil* Massierung *f*; *the ~es (pl)* das gewöhnliche Volk; *attr* Massen-; *tr* massieren, zs.ziehen, anhäufen, konzentrieren; *itr* sich ansammeln, sich anhäufen; *(Wolken)* sich zs.ballen; *in the ~* im ganzen; *the great ~* die große Masse; **~ action** Massenwirkung *f*; **~ arrests** *pl* Massenverhaftungen *f pl*; **~ distribution** *com* Massenabsatz *m*; **~ flight** Massenflucht *f*; **~ jump** *aero* Massenabsprung *m*; **~ meeting** Massenversammlung *f*; **~ murder** Massenmord *m*; **~ murderer** Massenmörder *m*; **~ number** Massenzahl *f*; **~-produce** *tr* serienmäßig herstellen; **~ production** Massenproduktion, -herstellung *f*; **~ survey** Reihenuntersuchung *f*; **~y** ['-i] massig, massiv, kompakt, schwer, umfangreich; **2.** *(a. M~)* [*a.* mɑːs] *rel mus* Messe *f*; *to attend, to go to ~* die Messe besuchen; *to hear ~* die Messe hören; *to say ~* Messe lesen; *high ~* Hochamt *n*; *low ~* stille Messe *f*.

massacre ['mæsəkə] *s* Blutbad, Gemetzel, Massaker *n*; *Am sl (bes. sport)* gewaltige Niederlage *f*; *tr* niedermetzeln, massakrieren; *Am sl* haushoch schlagen.

mass|age ['mæsɑːʒ, *Am* mə'sɑːʒ] *s* Massage *f*; *tr* massieren; *thorough ~~* Vollmassage *f*; **~ager** [mæ'sɑːʒə], **~agist** [-'sɑːʒist], **~eur** [mæ'səː] Masseur *m*; **~ageuse** [mæsə'ʒəːz], **~euse** [mæ'səːz] Masseuse *f*; **~otherapy** [mæso'θerəpi] *med* Massagebehandlung *f*.

massif ['mæsiːf] (Gebirgs-)Massiv *n*.

massive ['mæsiv] massiv, massig, schwer, solide, fest, umfangreich; massiv, gediegen; *fig* gewichtig, bedeutend; **~ness** ['-nis] Massigkeit, Schwere, Festigkeit; *fig* Wucht, Gewichtigkeit *f*.

mast [mɑːst] **1.** *s bes. mar* Mast; *tech* Kranbaum *m*; *tr* bemasten; *to sail before the ~* einfacher Matrose sein; **~er** ['-ə] *in Zssgen mar* -master *m*; *three-~~* Dreimaster *m*; **~head** (Mast-)Topp *m*; *Am (Zeitung)* Impressum *n*; **2.** *s agr* Baum-, Obermast *f*.

master ['mɑːstə] *s* Herr (u. Meister); Hausherr, Haushaltungsvorstand; Besitzer, Eigentümer; Vorsteher, Leiter, Direktor; Kapitän *(e-s Handelsschiffes)*; Arbeitgeber, Chef; (Handwerks-)Meister, Dienst-, Lehrherr; *Br* Lehrer; *(bei einzelnen Colleges)* Rektor; Magister *(akad. Grad)*; Meister *m*; *M~ (Anrede)* (junger) Herr; *our M~* unser Herr (Jesus); *attr* Haupt-; *tr* unter s-e Gewalt bringen, unterwerfen; übertreffen, schlagen; *(Tier)* zähmen; *(Wissensgebiet, Stoff, Aufgabe)* bewältigen; beherrschen *(a. ein Fach, Gebiet, e-e Sprache)*; *to be ~ of* Herr sein *gen*, über; beherrschen (*s.th.* etw); *to be o.'s own ~* sein eigener Herr sein; *to be ~ in o.'s own house* Herr im eigenen Hause sein; *to make o.s. (the) ~ of a language* es zur völligen Beherrschung e-r Sprache bringen; *ballet ~* Ballettmeister *m*; *dancing ~* Tanzlehrer *m*; *English ~* Englischlehrer *m*; *fencing ~* Fechtmeister *m*; *geography, history, mathematics ~* Erdkunde-, Geschichts-, Mathematiklehrer *m*; *music ~* Musiklehrer *m*; *sports ~* Sportlehrer *m*; *M~ of Arts* Magister *m* der freien Künste; *~ of ceremonies* Zeremonienmeister; *Am* Conférencier *m*; *~ of the lodge (Freimaurerei)* Meister *m* vom Stuhl; **~-at-arms** *mar* Polizeioffizier *m*; **~-builder** Baumeister *m*; **~-carpenter, -locksmith, -mechanic** Zimmer-, Schlosser-, Mechanikermeister *m*; **~ clock** Kontrolluhr *f*; **~-copy** *film* Originalkopie *f*; Handexemplar *n*; **~ful** ['-ful] herrisch, gebieterisch; meisterhaft, kundig, erfahren, geschickt; **~hand** Meister *m* (s-s Faches); Meisterschaft *f*, große(s) Können *n*; **~-key** Hauptschlüssel *m*; **~less** ['-lis] herrenlos, umherschweifend; **~liness** ['-linis] Erfahrenheit, Geschicktheit; Vorzüglichkeit *f*; **~ly** ['-li] meisterhaft; erfahren, kundig, geschickt; hervorragend, ausgezeichnet, vorzüglich, meisterlich; **~-mind** *s* führende(r) Kopf *m*, Kapazität *f*; *tr Am* geschickt lenken; **~piece, work** Meisterstück, -werk *n*; **~-sergeant** *Am* Stabsfeldwebel *m*; **~ship** ['-ʃip] (Vor-)Herrschaft, Macht (*over* über); Direktion, Leitung *f*; Vorsteher-, Lehramt *n*; Magistergrad *m*; Meisterschaft *f*, (überragendes) Können *n*; **~singer** *hist mus* Meistersinger *m*; **~-stroke** gelungene(r) Schlag *m*, Glanz-, Meisterstück *n*; **~ switch** Hauptschalter *m*; **~ tooth** Eckzahn *m*; **~ touch** Meisterschaft *f*; letzte(r) Schliff *m a. fig*; **~-watch** Hauptuhr *f*; **~-workman** Meister *m* s-s Faches; Vorarbeiter, Werkmeister *m*; **~y** ['-ri] (Vor-)Herrschaft, Macht, Vormacht(stellung) *f*, Vorrang; Sieg *m* (*of, over* über); Meisterschaft *f*, meisterliche(s) Können *n*, Beherrschung *f* (*of* gen); *to gain the ~~* die Oberhand gewinnen, den Sieg davontragen; es zur Meisterschaft bringen (*in* in).

mastic ['mæstik] Mastix; Kitt *m*.

masticat|e ['mæstikeit] *tr* (zer)kauen; *allg* zerkleinern, -mahlen, -reiben; **~ion** [mæsti'keiʃən] (Zer-)Kauen; Zerkleinern *n*; **~or** ['-ə] Kauende(r) *m*; *anat zoo* Kauwerkzeug *n*; *tech* Mahl-, Knetmaschine *f*; **~ory** ['-əri] *a* Kau-; *s* Kaumasse *f*.

mastiff ['mæstif, 'mɑːs-] Mastiff, Bullenbeißer *m*.

masturbat|e ['mæstəbeit] *itr* onanieren; **~ion** [-'beiʃən] Onanie *f*.

*

mat [mæt] **1.** *s* Matte *f a. sport*; *(door ~)* Türvorleger, Schuhabtreter; Untersetzer *m*, Unterlage *f (für ein Gefäß)*; *allg* Geflecht, feste(s) Gewebe *n*; Verfilzung *f*; *tr* mit e-r Matte belegen; verflechten, verfilzen; *itr* sich (eng) verflechten, verfilzen; **~ted** ['-id] *a* mit Matten belegt; dicht bewachsen; *(Haar)* verfilzt; **~ting** ['-iŋ] Mattenflechten *n*; Mattenbelag *m*; Matten *f pl*; **2.** *a* matt, glanzlos, stumpf; *s* matte Fläche *f*; Passepartout *n*; *tr* mattieren; **~ted** ['-id] *a* mattiert; **~ting** ['-iŋ] Mattieren *n*.

match [mætʃ] **1.** *s* Gleich(wertig)e(r, s), Ebenbürtige(r, s); dazu Passende(r, s) *m f n*; Gegenstück, Pendant; Paar, Ganze(s) *n*, Einheit; Partie, Heirat *f*; (passender) (Ehe-)Partner *m*; (Wett-)Spiel *n*, Wettkampf *m*, Partie *f*; Turnier *n*; *tr* gleichkommen, gleich(wertig), ebenbürtig sein, passen zu, entsprechen (*s.o.* jdm); etw Passendes finden für, passend machen für, abstimmen auf; *tech* anpassen; vergleichen; *(im Wettstreit)* messen (*with, against* mit); e-n (passenden) (Ehe-)Partner finden, beschaffen für; *(Paar)* zs.bringen; es aufnehmen (können) mit, sich messen können mit, gewachsen sein, die Spitze bieten (*s.o.* jdm); *itr* zs.passen, zuea. passen; passen (*with* zu); *nur pl* (sich) heiraten; *to be a ~ for s.o.* zu jdm passen; jdm ebenbürtig, gewachsen sein; es aufnehmen, sich messen können mit; *to be a good, bad ~* gut, schlecht zs.passen; *(Farben)* sich vertragen, sich beißen; *to be a good ~ (Mädchen, Frau)* e-e gute Partie sein; *to be more than a ~ for s.o.* jdm überlegen sein; *to find, to meet o.'s ~* s-n Mann finden; *to make a ~ (of it)* ein Paar zs.bringen, e-e Heirat vermitteln; *a dress with a hat and gloves to ~* ein Kleid mit (dazu) passendem Hut u. passenden Handschuhen; *boxing ~* Boxkampf *m*; *football ~* Fußballspiel *n*; *love ~* Liebesheirat *f*; *wrestling ~* Ringkampf *m*; **~ed** [-t] *a*: *well-, ill-~~* gut, schlecht zs.passend; **~less** ['-lis] unerreicht, unübertroffen; unvergleichlich; *to be ~~* nicht seinesgleichen haben; **~-maker** Ehestifter(in *f*), Heiratsvermittler(in *f*) *m*; **~-making** Heiratsvermittlung *f*; **2.** Streich-, Zündholz *n*; *hist mil* Zündschnur, Lunte *f*; **~-box** Streich-, Zündholzschachtel *f*; **~ book** Streichholzbrief *m*; **~lock** *hist* Muskete *f*; **~-wood** Holz *n* für Streichhölzer; (Holz-)Splitter *m pl*; *to make ~~ of, to reduce to ~~, to break into ~~* kurz u. klein schlagen, *fam* Kleinholz machen aus.

mate [meit] **1.** *s* Kamerad, Genosse; (Ehe-)Partner; Gatte *m*, Gattin *f*, Mann *m*, Frau *f*; *(Tiere)* Männchen, Weibchen *n*; *mar* Begleitoffizier; *mar* Maat, Gehilfe *m*; *tr itr* (sich) vereinigen, sich verbinden; (sich) paaren; (sich) verheiraten; **~y** ['-i] *a* kameradschaftlich, familiär (*with* mit); **2.** *s (Schach)* Matt *n*; *tr* mattsetzen.

material [mə'ti(ə)riəl] *a* materiell, physisch, gegenständlich; körperlich, sinnlich; materiell eingestellt, materialistisch; zur Sache gehörend; wesentlich (*to* für); *jur* erheblich; *s* Material *n*, Stoff *m* (*for* für); Bestandteile *m pl*; Stoff *m*, Gewebe *n*; *pl* (Arbeits-)Material, Gerät, Werkzeug; *pl* Unterlagen *f pl*; *building ~* Baumaterial *n*; *direct, raw ~* Rohmaterial *n*, -stoff *m*; *war ~* Kriegsmaterial *n*; *writing ~s (pl)* Schreibmaterial *n*; **~ budget** Materialkostenplan *m*; **~ damage** Sachschaden *m*; **~ goods** *pl* Sachgüter *pl*; **~ism** [-izm] Materialismus *m*; **~ist** [-ist] *s* Materialist *m*; *a u.* **~istic** [mətiəriə'listik] materialistisch; **~ization** [mətiəriəlai'zeiʃən] Verkörperung, Materialisierung *f*; **~ize** [mə'tiəriəlaiz] *tr* (körperliche) Gestalt geben (*s.th.* e-r S); verkörpern, materialisieren; *(Geist)* erscheinen lassen; *itr* (feste) Gestalt annehmen, Tatsache, Wirklichkeit werden, sich verwirklichen; *(Geist)* erscheinen; **~ requirement** Materialbedarf *m*; **~ shortage** Materialknappheit *f*; **~ witness** Hauptzeuge *m*.

materia medica [mə'tiəriə 'medikə] Arzneimittel *n pl*, Drogen *f pl*; Arzneimittellehre *f*.

matériel, materiel [mətiəri'el] (Arbeits-)Material, Werkzeug *n*, *bes. mil* Ausrüstung *f*; Versorgungsgüter *n pl*.

matern|al [mə'təːnl] mütterlich; *(Verwandter)* mütterlicherseits; *~~ mortality* Müttersterblichkeit *f*; **~ity** [-iti] *s* Mutterschaft *f*; *a* für werdende Mütter; Schwangerschafts-; *~~ dress,* *wear* Umstandskleid *n*, -kleidung *f*; *~~ hospital, home* Entbindungsanstalt *f*, -heim *n*; *~~ nurse* Hebamme *f*; *~~ ward* Wöchnerinnenstation *f*.

mathematic|(al) [mæθi'mætik(əl)] mathematisch; **~ian** [mæθimə'tiʃən] Mathematiker *m*; **~s** [mæθi'mætiks] *pl mit sing* Mathematik *f*.

matinée, *Am a.* **matinee** ['mætinei] Matinee, Nachmittagsvorstellung, -veranstaltung *f*; *Am* Morgenrock *m*.

matins ['mætinz] *s pl (kath.)* Frühmette *f*; *(anglikan.)* kirchliche(s) Morgengebet *n*.

matri ['meitri] *in Zssgen* Mutter-; **~archal, ~archic** [meitri'ɑ:kl, -ik] matriarchalisch; **~archate, ~archy** ['-ɑ:kit, -i] Matriarchat *n*; **~cidal** ['-'saidl] muttermörderisch; **~cide** ['-said] Muttermord; Muttermörder *m*; **~monial** [mætri'mounjəl] *a* Ehe-, Heirats-; *~~ agency* Heiratsvermittlung(sbüro *n*) *f*; **~mony** ['mætriməni, *Am* 'mætrəmouni] Ehe(stand *m*, -leben *n*); Heirat, Trauung *f*.

matriculat|e [mə'trikjuleit] *tr itr* (sich) immatrikulieren (lassen); *s* Immatrikulierte(r) *m*; **~ion** [mətrikju'leiʃən] Immatrikulation *f*, -sexamen *n*.

matrix ['meitriks, 'mæt-] *pl a.* -ces [-si:z], *anat* Gebärmutter; *geol* Gesteinshülle; *tech* Gußform; *typ* Matrize *f*; *bot* Nährboden *m*; *math* Matrix *f*.

matron ['meitrən] Matrone; Hausdame, -mutter; (Anstalts-)Leiterin, Vorsteherin, Oberin *f*; **~ize** ['-aiz] *tr* bemuttern; *itr* e-e Matrone werden; **~ly** ['-li] matronenhaft, gesetzt, würdig.

matter ['mætə] Stoff *m*, Material *n*; *phys* Materie, Substanz *f*, Stoff; Gegenstand, Inhalt *m (e-r Rede, e-s Schriftstückes)*; Sache, Angelegenheit; Entfernung *f*, Zeitraum *m*, -spanne *f*; Betrag (*of* von); Anlaß, Grund *m*, Ursache *f*; *med* Eiter; *typ* (Schrift-)Satz *m*; Manuskript *n*; *pl* Dinge *n pl*, Umstände *m pl*; *itr* von Belang, von Bedeutung, von Wichtigkeit sein (*to* für); *med* eitern; *for that ~, for the ~ of that* was das betrifft; *to make ~s worse* die Sache noch schlimmer machen; was die Sache noch schlimmer macht; *not to mince ~s* kein Blatt vor den Mund nehmen; *to take ~s easy* alles auf die leichte Schulter nehmen; *what does it ~?* was kommt darauf an? was macht das (schon)? *he'll look into the ~* er geht der Sache nach; *it doesn't ~* das spielt keine Rolle, das macht nichts; *it is* od *makes no ~* das macht nichts, darauf kommt es nicht an; *no ~ what he does* ganz gleich, einerlei, was er tut; *no ~!* macht nichts! *what's the ~* was ist (denn) los? worum geht's, dreht es sich? *it's no laughing ~* das ist nicht zum Lachen; *it's a ~ of life and death* es geht um Leben u. Tod; *first-class ~ (Am)* Briefpost *f*; *postal ~* Post (-sachen *f pl*) *f*; *printed ~* Drucksache *f*; *a ~ of consequence* e-e wichtige Angelegenheit; *a ~ of course* e-e Selbstverständlichkeit; *~-of-course* ['-tərəv'k-] *a* selbstverständlich; *~-of-fact* ['-tərəv'f-] *a* tatsächlich, den Tatsachen entsprechend; praktisch, nüchtern, realistisch, prosaisch; *as a ~ of fact* in Wirklichkeit, tatsächlich; eigentlich; *a ~ of form* e-e Formsache *f*; *a ~ of hono(u)r* e-e Ehrensache; *a ~ of law* e-e Rechtsfrage; *a ~ of life and death* e-e Lebensfrage; *a ~ of opinion* Ansichtssache *f*; *a ~ of taste* Geschmackssache *f*; *a ~ of time* e-e Frage der Zeit.

mattock ['mætək] Hacke, Haue *f*; *cutter, pick ~* Breit-, Spitzhacke *f*.

mattress ['mætris] Matratze *f*; *air-, spring-~* Luft-, Sprungfedermatratze *f*.

matur|ate ['mætjuəreit] *tr* eitern; reifen; **~ation** [mætjuə'reiʃən] Eiterung; Reifung *f*; **~e** [mə'tjuə] *a* reif *a. fig*; *fig* ausgereift; durchdacht; *fin* fällig; *tr* zur Reife bringen; reifen lassen; *itr* reifen, reif werden; *fin* fällig werden; **~ity** [mə'tjuəriti] Reife *a. fig*; *fig* Vollkommenheit, Vollendetheit *f*; *fin* Fälligkeit(stermin *m*), Verfallzeit *f*; *at, on ~~* bei Verfall, bei Fälligkeit; *~~ date* Fälligkeitstag *m*; *~~ index, (Am) tickler* Verfallbuch *n*.

matutinal [mætju(:)'tainl, mə'tju:tinl] morgendlich, Morgen-; früh.

maudlin ['mɔ:dlin] *a* rührselig, weinerlich; weinselig; *s* Rührseligkeit; Weinseligkeit *f*.

maul [mɔ:l] *s* Vorschlag-, Holzhammer, Schlegel *m*; *tr* beschädigen, verletzen; verprügeln; *(to ~ about)* ungeschickt, grob umgehen mit; *fig* heftig kritisieren; *(mit Hammer u. Keil)* spalten.

maulstick ['mɔ:lstik] *(Kunst)* Malstock *m*.

maunder ['mɔ:ndə] *itr* herumträumen, -dösen; plan-, ziellos herumschlendern; drauflos reden, faseln.

Maundy Thursday ['mɔ:ndi'θə:zdi] Gründonnerstag *m*.

mausoleum [mɔ:sə'li:əm] Mausoleum *n*.

mauve [mouv] *s* Malvenfarbe *f*; *a* malvenfarben.

maverick ['mævərik] *Am s* Rind *n* ohne Brandmal, *bes.* verlorene(s) Kalb *n*; *fig fam* Einzelgänger; Parteilose(r) *m*; *itr* ziellos umherstreifen; *fam* sich absondern.

mavis ['meivis] *poet* Singdrossel *f*.

maw [mɔ:] (Tier-)Magen; *(Wiederkäuer)* Drüsen-, Fett-, Labmagen; *(Vogel)* Kropf *m*; *(Fisch)* Luftblase *f*; *fig* Rachen *m*; **~worm** Eingeweidewurm *m*.

mawkish ['mɔ:kiʃ] widerlich, ekelhaft, -erregend; weichlich, süßlich; **~ness** ['-nis] Widerlichkeit; Süßlichkeit *f*.

mawseed ['mɔ:si:d] Mohnsamen *m*.

maxilla [mæk'silə] *pl -ae* [-i:] Kiefer (-knochen), *bes.* Oberkiefer *m*; *(Gliedertiere)* Maxille *f*, Unterkiefer *m*; **~ry** [-ri] *a* (Ober-)Kiefer-; *s* = ~.

maxim ['mæksim] Grundsatz *m*, Maxime *f*; **~al** ['-əl] größtmöglich; höchst, maximal; **~ize** ['-aiz] *tr* bis aufs äußerste steigern; **~um** [-əm] *pl a.* -a [-ə] *s* Maximum *n*, Höchstmenge *f*, -maß *n*, -zahl *f*, -wert; Höhepunkt *m*; *a* höchst, größt; Höchst-; maximal; *~~ amount* Höchstbetrag *m*; *~~ duration* Höchstdauer *f*; *~~ effect (tech)* Maximal-, Höchstleistung *f*; *~~ limit* Höchstgrenze *f*; *~~ load* Höchstbelastung *f*; *~~ output (tech)* Höchstleistung *f*; *~~ penalty, punishment* Höchststrafe *f*; *~~ performance* Spitzenleistung *f*; *~~ price* Höchstpreis *m*; *~~ safety stress* zulässige Beanspruchung *f*; *~~ salary* Höchstgehalt *n*; *~~ speed* Höchstgeschwindigkeit *f*; *~~ tariff* Höchsttarif *m*; *~~ value* Höchstwert *m*; *~~ wages (pl)* Höchst-, Spitzenlohn *m*; *~~ weight* Höchstgewicht *n*.

May [mei] **1.** Mai *m*; Maifeier *f*; Frühling(szeit *f*), Lenz *m*; *m~ (m~-bush)* blühende(r) Weißdornzweig *m*; *attr* Mai-; *in ~* im Mai; **m~-beetle, -bug** Maikäfer *m*; **m~-bush, -thorn, -tree** Weißdorn *m*; **~ Day** 1. Mai *m*; Maifeier *f*; *vgl. Mayday*; **m~flower** Maiblume *f*; *Am* Primelstrauch *m*; **m~-fly** Eintagsfliege *f*; **~ing** [-iŋ] Maifeier *f*; **m~pole** Maibaum *m*; **~ Queen** Maienkönigin *f*; **~tide, time** Maienzeit *f*; **2.** Mariechen; Gretchen *n*.

may [mei] **1.** *aux (pret: might)* mögen, können; dürfen; *~ I?* darf ich? *yes, you ~* ja, bitte! *be that as it ~* wie dem auch sei; *it ~ be too late* es ist vielleicht zu spät; **~be** ['meibi:], *obs* **~hap** ['meihæp] *adv* vielleicht; **2.** *obs poet* Maid *f*.

Mayday ['meidei] *mar aero internationaler Notruf.*

mayhem ['mei(h)əm] *jur* schwere Körperverletzung *f*.

mayonnaise [meiə'neiz] *(Küche)* Mayonnaise *f*.

mayor [mɛə] Bürgermeister *m*; **~alty** ['mɛərəlti] Bürgermeisteramt *n*; Amtszeit *f* e-s Bürgermeisters; **~ess** ['mɛəris] Bürgermeistersfrau; Bürgermeisterin *f*.

mazarine [mæzə'ri:n] *s* tiefe(s) Blau *n*; *a* tiefblau.

maz|e [meiz] Irrgarten *m*, Labyrinth *n*; Verwirrung, Bestürzung, Ratlosigkeit, Verlegenheit *f*; *to be in a ~~* bestürzt, ratlos, verlegen sein; **~y** ['-i] labyrinthisch, wirr, verzwickt; verwirrend.

McCoy [mə'kɔi]: *the (real) ~ (Am sl)* der wahre Jakob.

*

me [mi:, mi] mich; mir; *fam* ich; *that's ~ (fam)* ich bin's.

mead [mi:d] *hist* Met *m*; *poet* Au(e) *f*.

meadow ['medou] Wiese; Aue *f*; **~ bird** *Am* Boblink, Sperlingsvogel *m*; **~-grass** *(bes.* Wiesen-)Rispengras *n*; **~ lark** *orn* Wiesenpieper *m*; *Am orn* Atzel *f*; **~-ore** Raseneisenerz *n*, -stein *m*; **~-saffron, -crocus** *bot* Herbstzeitlose *f*; **~y** ['-i] wiesenartig; Wiesen-.

meagre, *Am* **meager** ['mi:gə] mager, dünn, dürr; *fig* arm, ärmlich, dürftig; **~ness** ['-nis] Magerkeit; Dürftigkeit *f*.

meal [mi:l] **1.** Mahl(zeit *f*) *n*; *to make a ~ of s.th.* etw verzehren; *to take o.'s ~s* zu speisen pflegen; **~ ticket** Eßmarke *f*; *Am sl* Brötchengeber *m*, nahrhafte(s) Etwas *n*; **~ time** Essenszeit *f*; **2.** grobe(s) Mehl; Pulver *n*; *whole ~* Vollkornmehl *n*; **~ie** ['-i] *(Südafrika)* Maiskolben; *meist pl* Mais *m*; **~iness** ['-inis] Mehligkeit *f*; **~y** ['-i] mehlig, pulverförmig; mehlhaltig, Mehl-; bestäubt, gesprenkelt, fleckig; bleich, blaß; = *~~-mouthed (Sprache)* versteckt, gewunden, zögernd, kleinlaut, schüchtern, leisetretend.

mean [mi:n] **1.** *irr meant, meant tr* meinen, denken; sich mit dem Gedanken tragen, vorhaben, beabsichtigen (*to do* zu tun); wollen; aussuchen, -wählen, bestimmen (*for* für, zu); (*to be ~t for* gedacht, bestimmt sein für); sagen wollen (*by* mit); *(Wort)* bedeuten; soviel sein wie, bedeuten, heißen; *itr* gesonnen, gesinnt sein; *(hauptsächlich: to ~ well)* wohlgesinnt sein (*by, to s.o.* jdm), es gut meinen (*by, to s.o.* mit jdm); *to ~ little, much* wenig, viel bedeuten (*to s.o.* jdm); *to ~ business, to ~ what one says* es ernst meinen, nicht spaßen, nicht scherzen; *to ~ s.o. no harm* jdm nichts tun wollen; *to ~ mischief* Böses im Schilde führen; *I did not ~ to hurt you* ich wollte Sie nicht verletzen; *he didn't ~ any harm* er hat sich nichts Böses gedacht; *what did you ~ by that?* was wollten Sie damit sagen? *you don't really ~ that?* das ist doch nicht Ihr Ernst? *this ~s war* das bedeutet Krieg; *it ~s a lot to me to meet him* mir liegt viel daran, ihn zu treffen; **2.** *a* gemein, niedrig, gewöhnlich; bescheiden; unerheblich, unbedeutend, belanglos; unscheinbar; dürftig, schäbig, armselig, ärmlich; minderwertig; gemein, niedriggesinnt, kleinlich; *fam* selbstsüchtig, eigenwillig, unwirsch, übelgelaunt, unangenehm, schlecht, böse, boshaft; kleinlaut, verschämt; (gesundheitlich) nicht auf dem Posten, nicht auf dem Damme, nicht auf der Höhe; *sl Am* verdammt schwer, toll; aufregend; *sl Am* auf Draht; *no* ~ kein(e) schlechte(r, s), *fam* nicht von Pappe; *to feel* ~ *(fam)* sich genieren, sich schämen; *Am* sich nicht wohl fühlen; **~ness** ['-nis] Gemeinheit, Niedrigkeit; Belanglosigkeit; Dürftigkeit, Armseligkeit; niedrige Gesinnung; *Am fam* Bösartigkeit *f*; ~ **trick** Gemeinheit *f*; **3.** *a* mittler; mittelmäßig, durchschnittlich; Mittel-, Durchschnitts-; *s* Mitte(lpunkt *m*) *f*; Durchschnitt, Mittelwert *m*, -maß; *math* Mittel *n*; *(Logik)* Mittelbegriff *m*; *pl a. mit sing* Mittel *n (zu e-m Zweck)*, Weg *m*; *pl* (Hilfs-, Geld-)Mittel *n pl*; Vermögen *n*, Reichtum *m*; *by ~s of* (ver)mittels, mit Hilfe *gen*, durch; *by all (manner of) ~s* auf alle Fälle, auf jeden Fall, jedenfalls, unter allen Umständen; selbstverständlich, gewiß; *by any ~s* auf alle mögliche Weise; irgendwie; etwa; überhaupt; *by fair ~s or foul* ganz gleich wie, im guten oder im bösen; *by lawful, legal ~s* auf dem Rechtswege; *by no (manner of) ~s* auf keinen Fall, keinesfalls, -wegs; *by some ~s or other* auf die eine oder andere Weise; *by this ~s* auf diese Weise, hierdurch; *to find the ~s* Mittel und Wege finden; *he lives beyond his ~s* er lebt über seine Verhältnisse; *the end justifies the ~s* der Zweck heiligt die Mittel; *the golden, happy* ~ die goldene Mitte; der goldene Mittelweg; *~s of communication* Verkehrsmittel *n pl*; *~s to an end* Mittel *n pl* zum Zweck; *~s of payment* Zahlungsmittel *n pl*; *~s of production* Produktionsmittel *n pl*; *~s of proving* Beweismittel *n pl*; *~s of redress* Rechtsmittel *n pl*; *~s of transportation* Transportmittel *n pl*; ~ **latitude** *geog* mittlere Breite *f*; ~ **number** *math* Mittelwert *m*; ~ **(solar) time** mittlere (Sonnen-) Zeit *f*; *Greenwich M~ Time* Westeuropäische Zeit, Weltzeit *f*; **~time** *s* Zwischenzeit *f*; *(adv u.) in the ~~*, **~while** inzwischen, unterdessen, mittlerweile.

meander [mi'ændə] *itr* sich winden, sich schlängeln; umherirren, -streifen; *tr* mit Mäanderlinien versehen; *s* gewundene(r) Lauf; Irrweg; *(Kunst)* Mäander *m*.

meaning ['mi:niŋ] *s* Absicht *f*, Zweck; Sinn *m*, Bedeutung *f*; *a* sinn-, bedeutungs-, ausdrucksvoll; beabsichtigt, absichtlich; *well-~* wohlmeinend, -gesinnt; **~ful** ['-ful] bedeutungs-, sinnvoll; absichtlich; **~less** ['-lis] bedeutungs-, sinnlos; unabsichtlich.

measl|ed ['mi:zld] *a vet* finnig; **~es** ['mi:zlz] *pl mit sing med* Masern *pl*; *vet* Finne *f (Krankheit)*; Finnen *pl*; *German ~~ (med)* Röteln *pl*; **~y** ['mi:zli] *a* an den Masern erkrankt; *vet* finnig; *fig fam* lumpig, kümmerlich, schäbig.

measurab|ility [meʒərə'biliti], **~leness** ['meʒərəblnis] Meßbarkeit *f*; **~le** ['meʒərəbl] meßbar; mäßig; *within ~~ distance of* nicht (mehr) fern *dat*, nicht (mehr) weit entfernt von; **~ly** ['-li] *adv Am* bis zu einem gewissen Grade.

measure ['meʒə] *s* Maß *n*; Messung; Maßeinheit *f*, -system *n*; *fig* Maßstab *m (of* für); Maß(band, -gefäß); Maß *n*, abgemessene Menge *f*; Maß *n*, (vernünftige) Grenze *f*; Ausmaß *n*, Grad, Umfang *m*; Maßnahme, -regel *f*, Schritt(e *pl*) *m*; (gesetzliche) Bestimmung *f*, Gesetz; Silben-, Versmaß *n*, Versfuß; Rhythmus; *mus* Takt; *math* Teiler; (Tanz-)Schritt *m*; *typ* Spalten-, Satzbreite *f*; *pl geol* Flöz *n*; *tr* messen; *(to ~ off, to ~ out)* ab-, aus-, vermessen; Maß nehmen (*s.o.* jdm); *fig* abwägen, ermessen; einstellen, abstufen (*by* nach); durchmessen; *itr* e-e Messung vornehmen; sich messen lassen, meßbar sein; *to ~ o.s.* sich messen (*against* mit); *to ~ up to (Erwartungen)* entsprechen *dat*; *(Forderungen)* erfüllen; *(vorgeschriebenes Maß)* erreichen; *beyond ~* übermäßig *adv*; *lit* über die, *poet* über alle Maßen; *in a great, large ~* in weitem Umfang, großenteils; *in a, some ~* gewissermaßen, in gewissem Sinne; *to ~* nach Maß; *made to ~ (Anzug)* Maß-; *to give the ~ of* (richtig) ermessen lassen; *to give full, short ~* gut, schlecht messen; *to remain within ~s* sich in (gewissen) Grenzen halten; *to set ~s* Grenzen setzen (*to* dat); *to take ~s against* Maßnahmen ergreifen gegen; *to take s.o.'s ~ (Schneider)* jdm Maß nehmen; *fig* jdn abschätzen, -wägen; *to ~ s.o. with o.'s eye* jdn mit dem Blick messen, von oben bis unten ansehen, prüfend betrachten; *to ~ o.'s length* der Länge nach hinfallen; *to ~ o.'s strength with s.o.* s-e Kräfte mit jdm messen; *to ~ swords with s.o.* mit jdm die Klingen kreuzen; *coercive, decisive, drastic, harsh, inefficient, legal, preventive, protective, punitive, restrictive, secondary, thorough ~s (pl)* Zwangs-, entscheidende, drastische, einschneidende *od* strenge, ungenügende, gesetzliche, vorbeugende, Schutz- *od* Sicherheits-, Straf-, einschränkende, Hilfs-, durchgreifende Maßnahmen *f pl*; *counter-~* Gegenmaßnahme; Repressalie *f*; *dry, linear, liquid ~* Hohl-, Längen-, Flüssigkeitsmaß *n*; *waist ~* Taillenweite *f*; *tape-~* Bandmaß *n*; *~ of capacity, of length* Hohl-, Längenmaß *n*; *~s of coercion* Zwangsmaßnahmen *f pl*; *~ of economy, of retaliation* Spar-, Vergeltungsmaßnahme *f*; **~d** ['-d] *a* (ab)gemessen; geregelt, regelmäßig; gleichmäßig, einheitlich; *fig* gemessen, bedächtig, wohlüberlegt; gebunden, metrisch, rhythmisch; **~less** ['-lis] unermeßlich, grenzenlos; **~ment** ['-mənt] Messung; Größe *f*, Umfang *m*; *(Schiff)* Tonnage *f*; *meist pl* Maße *n pl*, Abmessungen *f pl*; *min* Markscheidung *f*; *(system of ~~)* Maßsystem *n*.

measuring ['meʒəriŋ] *s* Messen *n*, Messung *f*; Meß-, Maß-; ~ **container, glass** Meßgefäß, -glas *n*; ~ **range** Meßbereich *m*; ~ **tape** Bandmaß *n*; ~ **worm** *ent* Spannerraupe *f*.

meat [mi:t] Fleisch *(als Nahrung)*; *Am* (Frucht-)Fleisch *n*; Fleischspeise *f*; *fig* Inhalt, Gehalt, Kern *m* (der Sache), Quintessenz *f*; *Am sl* Hobby, Steckenpferd, Vergnügen *n*; *canned, preserved ~* Büchsenfleisch *n*, Fleischkonserve *f*; *cold ~* kalte Platte *f*; *cooked, salted, smoked ~* gekochte(s), Salz-, Rauchfleisch *n*; *fresh ~* frische(s) Fleisch *n*; *fresh-killed ~* Frischfleisch *n*; *frozen ~* Gefrierfleisch *n*; *mince-~ (Art)* Gebäckfüllung *f*; *minced ~* Gehackte(s), Mett *n*; *roast ~* Braten *m*; *strong ~ (fig)* scharfe(r) Tobak *m*; *~ and drink* Speise und Trank; *to be ~~ to s.o.* jdm viel Spaß machen, ein großes Vergnügen für jdn sein; ~ **ball** Fleischklößchen *n*; **~-broth** Fleischbrühe *f*; **~-chopper** Hackmesser *n*, -maschine *f*; **~-eater** Fleischesser *m*; **~-extract** Fleischextrakt *m*; **~-flour** Fleischmehl *n*; **~-fly** Schmeißfliege *f*; **~-grinder** Fleischwolf *m*; **~head** *Am sl* Dummkopf *m*; **~-hook** Fleischhaken *m*; **~-inspection** Fleischbeschau *f*; **~-jelly** Sülze *f*; **~less** ['-lis] fleischlos; **~man** ['-mən] *Am* Fleischer, Schlachter, Metzger *m*; **~-packing plant** *Am* Großschlächterei *f*; **~-pie** Fleischpastete *m*; **~-safe** Speise-, Fliegenschrank *m*; **~-tea** Nachmittagstee *m* mit kalter Küche; **~-wagon** *Am sl* Sanitätswagen *m*; **~-waste** Fleischabfälle *m pl*; **~y** ['-i] fleischig; fleischartig; kräftig; *fig* gehaltvoll, inhaltreich, markig, lapidar.

mechanic [mi'kænik] Mechaniker, Autoschlosser, Maschinist, Monteur *m*; *pl mit sing phys tech* Mechanik; *fig* Technik *f*; **~al** [-əl] mechanisch, maschinell, Maschinen-; automatisch; *fig* mechanisch, automatisch; gewohnheitsmäßig, unbewußt; *~~ engineering* Maschinenbau *m*; *~~ plant* maschinelle Einrichtung *f*; *~~ press (typ)* Schnellpresse *f*; *~~ transport* Kraftfahrwesen *n*; *~~ troops (pl)* Kraftfahrtruppen *f pl*; *~~ woodpulp* Holzschliff *m*; *~~ workshop* mechanische Werkstatt *f*; **~alness** [-əlnis] das Mechanische, Automatische; *fig* Gedankenlosigkeit *f*; **~ian** [mekə'niʃən] = ~.

mechan|ism ['mekənizm] Mechanismus *m a. fig*; Schaltwerk *n*, Einrichtung, Technik *f*; *fig* Funktionssystem *n*, Apparat *m*; *philos* Mechanismus *m*, mechanistische Weltanschauung *f*; **~istic** [mekə'nistik] *philos* mechanistisch; **~ization** [mekənai'zeiʃən] Mechanisierung *f*; **~ize** ['mekənaiz] *tr* mechanisieren, auf Maschinenbetrieb umstellen; *mil* motorisieren; *~~d division* Panzergrenadierdivision *f*.

meconium [mi'kouniəm] *physiol* Kindspech *n*.

medal ['medl] *s* Medaille, Denk-, Schaumünze; Plakette *f*; Orden *m*; **~lion** [mi'dæljən] große Denkmünze *f*; Medaillon *n a. arch*; **~(l)ist** ['medlist] Stempelschneider; Ordensinhaber; Medaillengewinner *m*; ~ **ribbon** Ordensband *n*.

meddle ['medl] *itr* sich einmischen (*with, in* in); sich abgeben (*with* mit); **~r** ['-ə] Unberufene(r); Schnüffler; G(e)schaftlhuber *m*; **~some** ['-səm] aufdringlich; neugierig; geschäftig.

medi(a)eval [medi'i:vəl] mittelalterlich; **~ism** [-izm] Geist *m* des Mittelalters; **~ist** [-ist] Spezialist *m* für das Mittelalter; **M~ Latin** Mittellatein *n*.

medial ['mi:djəl] mittler; durchschnittlich, Durchschnitts-; gewöhnlich; *gram* medial; **~ly** ['-i] *adv* in der Mitte, in Mittellage; *gram* im Inlaut.

median ['mi:djən] *a* mittler, Mittel- *bes. math*; *s math* Mittelwert, -punkt *m*; *(~ line)* Mittellinie, Seitenhalbierende *f*.

mediat|e ['mi:diit] *a* in der Mitte liegend, Mittel-; vermittelnd, Vermitt(e)lungs-; mittelbar, indirekt; *tr* ['-eit] durch Vermitt(e)lung beilegen, durch Intervention regeln; vermitteln (*between* zwischen); **~ion** [mi:di'eiʃən] Vermitt(e)lung; *math* Interpolation; *rel* Fürsprache *f*; *offer of ~~* Vermitt(e)lungsangebot *n*; **~or** ['mi:dieitə] (Ver-)Mittler, Mittelsmann *m*; **~orial** [mi:diə'tɔ:riəl], **~ory** ['mi:diətəri] vermittelnd; Vermitt(e)lungs-.

medic ['medik] *fam* Doktor, Arzt; *Am* Medizinstudent; *mil fam* Sani (-täter) *m*; **~al** ['medikəl] *a* medizinisch, ärztlich, Heil-; *s fam* Medizinstudent *m*; *~~ advice* ärztliche(r) Rat *m*; *~~ adviser* beratende(r) Arzt *m*; *~~ board* Gesundheitsamt *n*; *~~ certificate* ärztliche(s) Attest *n*; *M~~ Corps (mil)* Sanitätstruppe *f*; *~~ department* Gesundheitswesen *n*; *~~ examination, inspection* ärztliche Untersuchung *f*; *~~ expert* medizinische(r) Sachverständige(r) *m*; *M~~ Faculty* medizinische Fakultät *f*; *~~ history* Krankengeschichte *f*; *~~ jurisprudence* Gerichtsmedizin *f*; *~~ man (fam)* Doktor, Arzt *m*; *~~ officer* Amtsarzt; *mil* Sanitätsoffizier *m*; *~~ opinion* ärztliche(s) Gutachten *n*; *~~ plant* Arzneipflanze *f*; *~~ practitioner* praktische(r) Arzt *m*; *the ~~ profession* der Arztberuf; die Ärzteschaft; *~~ services (pl)* ärztliche Bemühungen *f pl*; *~~ specialist* Facharzt *m*; *~~ student* Medizinstudent *m*; *~~ ward* innere Abteilung *f (e-r Klinik)*; **~ament** [me'dikəmənt] Medikament, Heilmittel *n*, Arznei, *fam* Medizin *f*; **~ate** ['medikeit] *tr* medikamentös behandeln; *(Verbandstoff)* mit e-m Heilmittel imprägnieren; **~ation** [medi'keiʃən] medikamentöse Behandlung; Imprägnierung *f* mit e-m Heilmittel; Behandlung, Verordnung; Arznei *f*; **~ative** ['medikətiv] medikamentös; heilkräftig; **~inal** [me'disinl] medizinisch, medikamentös; heilkräftig, heilend, Heil-; *~~ spring* Heilquelle *f*; **~ine** ['medsin, *Am* 'medisin] Medizin, Heilkunde; Arzneimittellehre, Pharmakologie; Arznei *f*, Heilmittel *n*, *fam* Medizin *f*; *to practice ~~* den Arztberuf ausüben; *to take o.'s ~~* s-e Medizin einnehmen; *(fig)* in den sauren Apfel beißen; *forensic, legal ~~* Gerichtsmedizin *f*; *~~-ball* Medizinball *m*; *~~ bottle* Arzneiflasche *f*; *~~-chest* Hausapotheke *f*; *~~-man* Medizinmann *m*; **~o** ['-ou] *pl -os (fam)* Arzt *m*; **~o-legal** gerichtsmedizinisch.

mediocr|e ['mi:dioukə] (mittel)mäßig, durchschnittlich, gewöhnlich, alltäglich; **~ity** [mi:di'ɔkriti] Mittelmäßigkeit; Alltäglichkeit *f*; Durchschnittsmensch *m*.

meditat|e ['mediteit] *tr* nachdenken über, betrachten; sinnen auf, vorhaben, planen; *itr* nachdenken, sinnen, grübeln (*on, upon* über); **~ion** [medi'teiʃən] Nachdenken, Grübeln *n*; Betrachtung; *rel* Meditation *f*; **~ive** ['meditətiv, -teit-] nachdenklich; grüblerisch.

Mediterranean [meditə'reinjən] *a (m~)* mittelländisch; Mittelmeer-; *scient* mediterran; *s (~ Sea)* Mittelländische(s), Mittelmeer *n*; *(Anthropologie)* mediterrane(r) Mensch *m*.

medium ['mi:djəm] *pl a. -ia* ['-ə] *s* Mittel, Werkzeug; *(Kunst)* Ausdrucksmittel *n*; *das* Vermittelnde, Mittelweg *m*; Mittelsperson *f*, -mann, (Ver-)Mittler *m*; *(Spiritismus)* Medium *n*; *phys* Träger *m*; tragende(s), umgebende(s) Element *n*, Umgebung *f*, Milieu *n*; *(culture ~)* Nährflüssigkeit, -lösung *f*, -boden *m*; *(Farbe)* Bindemittel *(Öl)*; *(advertising ~)* Werbemittel *n*; Mitte *(zwischen Extremen)*, mittlere Qualität *f*, mittlere(r) Grad *m*; *typ* Medianpapier *n*; *a* mittler, Mittel-; durchschnittlich, Durchschnitts-; mäßig; *by, through the ~ of* durch Vermitt(e)lung, vermittels, mit Hilfe *gen*; *the happy ~* die goldene Mitte, der goldene Mittelweg; *~ of circulation (fin)* Umlaufsmittel *n*; *~ of exchange* Tauschmittel *n*; *~* **faced** *a typ* halbfett; *~* **price** Durchschnittspreis *m*; *~* **size** mittlere Größe *f*; **~-sized** *a* mittelgroß; *~* **wave** *radio* Mittelwelle *f*; *~~ range* Mittelwellenbereich *m*; *~~ transmitter* Mittelwellensender *m*.

medlar ['medlə] Mispel *f*.

medley ['medli] Gemisch *n*, Mischmasch *m*, Durcheinander, Konglomerat; *mus* Potpourri *n*.

medulla [me'dʌlə] *anat* Knochen-, Rückenmark; *(Gehirn)* verlängerte(s) Mark; *bot* Mark *n*.

*

meed [mi:d] *poet* Lohn, Sold *m*.

meek [mi:k] sanft(mütig), weich (-herzig); freundlich; (zu) nachgiebig; haltlos; *as ~ as a lamb, as Moses* sanft wie ein Lamm; **~ness** ['-nis] Sanftmut, Weichherzigkeit; Nachgiebigkeit; Haltlosigkeit *f*.

meerschaum ['miəʃəm] Meerschaum (-pfeife *f*) *m*.

meet [mi:t] *irr met, met* [met] **1.** *tr* treffen, begegnen (*s.o.* jdm); stoßen auf; entgegenkommen; berühren, in Berührung kommen mit; zu sehen, zu hören bekommen; erfahren, erleben; in Verbindung treten zu; bekannt werden mit, kennenlernen; sich treffen mit; gegenüber-, entgegentreten (*s.o.* jdm); (feindlich) zs.stoßen, -prallen mit; (*s.o.* jdm); *(e-m Einwand)* begegnen, zurückweisen, -schlagen, fertig werden mit, widerlegen; *(Rechnung, Schuld)* bezahlen; *(e-r Verpflichtung)* nachkommen; *(Wunsch)* erfüllen; **2.** *itr* sich begegnen, sich treffen; mitea. in Berührung kommen, in Verbindung treten; sich kennenlernen; sich versammeln; sich vereinigen; sich feindlich gegenübertreten, mitea. streiten, kämpfen, sich schlagen; treffen, begegnen (*with s.o.* jdn); bekommen, erhalten (*with s.th.* etw); erfahren, erleben, erleiden (*with s.th.* etw); **3.** *s sport* (Teilnehmer *m pl*, Ort *m* e-s) Treffen(s) *n*; Jagdgesellschaft *f*; **4.** *a obs* richtig, passend, angebracht, geeignet, tauglich; *to be well met* (gut) zuea. passen, sich (gut) vertragen; *to come, to go to ~ s.o.* jdm entgegenkommen, -gehen; *to make both ends ~* (gerade) (mit s-m Gelde) auskommen; *to ~ with an accident* verunglücken; e-n Unfall erleiden; *to ~ with approval* Billigung finden; *to ~ the case* das Nötige, Erforderliche tun; *to ~ the deadline* den Termin einhalten; *to ~ o.'s death* den Tod finden; *to ~ demands* Ansprüche befriedigen; *to ~ s.o.'s ear* zu Ohren kommen; *to ~ expenses* Ausgaben bestreiten; *to ~ s.o.'s eye* jdm zu Gesicht kommen; mit jdm e-n Blick tauschen; *to ~ s.o. half-way* jdm auf halbem Wege entgegenkommen; *to ~ a loss* e-n Verlust erleiden; *to ~ an objection* e-m Einwand begegnen; *to ~ the train* zum Zug gehen; *will you ~ him at the train?* holen Sie ihn von der Bahn ab? *I want you to ~ Mr X* ich möchte Ihnen Herrn X. vorstellen; **~ing** ['-iŋ] Zs.-treffen *n*; Begegnung *f*; Treffen *n*, Zs.kunft, Versammlung, Sitzung, Tagung; *sport* Veranstaltung; Versammlung(steilnehmer *m pl*) *f*; Versammlungs-, Tagungsort, Treffpunkt; Zweikampf *m*, Duell; *(Fluß)* Zs.fließen *n*; *fig* Berührungspunkt *m*; *at a ~~* auf e-r Versammlung; *board, committee ~~* Vorstands-, Ausschußsitzung *f*; *~~-house* Versammlungshaus *n (der Quäker)*; *~~-place* Versammlungsort; Treffpunkt *m*; *~~-room* Versammlungsraum; Sitzungssaal *m*.

mega|(lo) ['megə(lou)] *pref* Mega(lo)-, Groß-, groß-; **~cycle** ['-saikl] *phys* Megahertz *n (1000 Kilohertz)*; **~lith** ['-liθ] Megalith *m*; **~lithic** [megə'liθik] megalithisch; Megalith-; **~locardia** [megəlo(u)'ka:diə] *med* Herzerweiterung *f*; **~lomania** ['megəlo(u)'meiniə] Größenwahn *m*; **~lomaniac** [megəlo(u)'meiniæk] größenwahnsinnig; **~phone** ['megəfoun] *s* Sprachrohr *n*, Schalltrichter *m*, Megaphon *n*; *tr* durch e-n Schalltrichter verstärken; *itr* in e-n Sch. sprechen; **~ton** ['-tʌn] Megatonne *f*.

megohm ['megoum] *el* Megohm *n*.

megrim ['mi:grim] Migräne *f*, halbseitige(r) Kopfschmerz *m*; Grille, Laune *f*; *pl* Trübsinn *m*, Schwermut *f*.

melanchol|ia [melən'kouljə] *med* Melancholie *f*; **~i(a)c** [-'kɔlik (-'kouljək)] *a med* melancholisch; *s med* Melancholiker *m*; **~y** ['melənkəli] *s* Melancholie *a. med*, Schwermut *f*, Trübsinn *m*; trübe Stimmung, Depression; Grübelei *f*; *a* melancholisch, schwermütig, trübsinnig; grüblerisch; düster, traurig, kläglich, jämmerlich.

meld [meld] *tr itr (Kartenspiel)* melden; *Am* mischen; *s* Melden *n*; Kombination *f*.

mêlée, *Am* **melee** ['melei] Handgemenge *n*.

meliorat|e ['mi:ljəreit] *tr itr* (sich) verbessern; **~ion** [mi:ljə'reiʃən] Verbesserung; *agr* Melioration *f*.

melli|ferous [me'lifərəs] *ent* honigerzeugend; **~fluence** [-fluəns] Honigfluß *m*; *fig* Sanftheit, Lieblichkeit *f*; **~fluent** [-fluənt], **~fluous** [-fluəs] sanft, angenehm, einschmeichelnd.

mellow ['melou] *a (Frucht)* reif, weich, mürbe, saftig, süß; *(Wein)* vollmundig, ausgereift, *fam* süffig; *(Farbe)* satt; *(Licht)* wohltuend; *(Ton)* voll, schmelzend; *(Stimme)* volltönend; *(Wetter)* heiter, angenehm; *(Boden)* fett, fruchtbar; leicht; *(Mensch)* (ge)reif(t), abgeklärt, verständnisvoll, einfühlend; *fam* gemütvoll; Gemüts-; *sl* angeheitert, beschwipst; *tr* zur Reife bringen; weich, süß machen; *(Boden)* auflockern; *fig* mildern; *itr* reifen; reif, weich, süß werden; *fig* sich abklären; **~ness** ['-nis] Reife; Ausgereiftheit; Sattheit; Fülle *f*; Schmelz *m*; Abgeklärtheit *f*; Verständnis, Einfühlungsvermögen *n*, -bereitschaft *f*.

melod|eon [mi'loudjən] *Art* Harmonium *od* Akkordeon; *Am* Varieté *n*; **~ic** [mi'lɔdik] *a* = *~ious*; *s pl mit sing* Melodik *f*; **~ious** [mi'loudjəs] melodisch, wohllautend, -klingend; **~iousness** [-'loudjəsnis] Wohllaut, -klang *m*; **~ist** ['melədist] Liederkomponist, -sänger *m*; **~ize** ['melədaiz] *tr* melodisch machen; vertonen; *itr* melodisch sein; Lieder komponieren; **~y** ['melədi] Melodie, (Sing-)Weise *f*.

melodrama ['melədra:mə] Melodrama *n*; **~tic** [melədrə'mætik] melodramatisch.

melon ['melən] Melone *f*; *sl* Rebbach, Gewinn, Profit *m*; *to cut a ~* e-n großen Gewinn ausschütten; *water ~* Wassermelone *f*.

melt [melt] *itr tr* schmelzen, auftauen; *el (Sicherung)* durchbrennen; *itr* sich auflösen, zergehen, verschwimmen, sich zersetzen; *(to ~ away)* dahinschwinden, vergehen; verschmelzen (*into* mit); übergehen (*into* in); *fig* erweichen, sanft werden, auftauen; sich besänftigen, sich legen; *tr (to ~ away)* auflösen, zersetzen; zum Schwinden bringen; übergehen lassen (*into* in); *fig* erweichen, besänftigen;

(Butter) zerlassen; *s* Schmelzen *n*; Schmelzung, geschmolzene Masse *f*, Schmelzgut *n*; *tech* Gicht *f*; *to ~ down* einschmelzen; *to ~ in the mouth* auf der Zunge zergehen; *to ~ into tears* in Tränen zerfließen; **~er** ['-ə] Glas-, Tiegelschmelzer; Schmelzofen *m*; **~ing** ['-iŋ] *a fig* gerührt; rührselig, sentimental, weich(herzig); Schmelz-; *(Hitze)* schwül; *s* Schmelzen *n*; *snow-~~* Schneeschmelze *f*; *~~ point* Schmelzpunkt *m*; *~~ pot* Schmelztiegel *m a. fig*; *to go into the ~~-pot* große Veränderungen erfahren, *fig* umgekrempelt werden.

*

member ['membə] (Körper-)Glied; Glied *n*, (Bestand-, Bau-)Teil *m*; Einteilungsglied *n*, Abteilung *f*; Angehörige(r) *m*, Mitglied *n*; *gram* Satzteil *m*; *M~ of Congress* Kongreßmitglied *n*, -abgeordnete(r) *m*; *M~ of Parliament* Parlamentsmitglied *n*, -abgeordnete(r) *m*; **~ country** Mitgliedsstaat *m*; **~ship** ['-ʃip] Mitgliedschaft *f*; Mitglieder *n pl*; Mitgliederzahl *f*, -stand *m*; *~~ card* Mitgliedskarte *f*; *~~ fee, dues (pl)* Mitgliedsbeitrag *m*; *~~ list* Mitgliederliste *f*; *~~ number* Mitgliedsnummer *f*.

membran|aceous [membrə'neiʃəs] = *membran(e)ous*; **~e** ['membrein] *phys anat zoo* Membran(e) *f*; Häutchen *n*; *drum ~~* Trommelfell *n*; **~(e)ous** [mem'brein(j)əs] membranartig; Membran-; häutig *a. med.*

memento [mi'mentou] *pl -o(e)s* Andenken *n*; Erinnerung *f* (*of* an); Denkzettel, Mahnruf *m*; *rel* Memento *n*.

memo ['memou] *fam* Notiz *f*.

memoir ['memwa:] Denkschrift; biographische Notiz *f*; *pl* Memoiren *pl*, Erinnerungen, Denkwürdigkeiten *f pl*; Tätigkeitsbericht *m*.

memorab|ilia [memərə'biliə] *pl* Denkwürdigkeiten *f pl*; **~le** ['memərəbl] denkwürdig, bemerkenswert.

memo(randum) [memə'rændəm] *pl a. -da* [-ə] Notiz *f*, Vermerk *m*, Aufzeichnung; kurze Mitteilung, Note; *com* (Waren-)Liste *f*, Verzeichnis *n*; Rechnung *f*; *pol* Memorandum *n*, Denkschrift; *jur* (Vertrags-)Urkunde *f*; *urgent ~* Dringlichkeitsvermerk *m*; **~-book, -pad** Notizbuch *n*, -block *m*; **~-goods** *pl* Kommissionsware *f*.

memorial [mi'mɔ:riəl] *a* Erinnerungs-, Gedächtnis-; *s* Denkmal *n*, Gedenkstätte *f*, -tag *m*; *pol* Denkschrift; Eingabe, Bittschrift *f*; *war ~* Gefallenen-, Kriegerdenkmal *n*; **M~ Day** *Am* Gefallenen-, Heldengedenktag *m (30. Mai)*; **~ist** [-ist] Bittsteller; Memoirenschreiber *m*; **~ize** [-aiz] *tr* gedenken (*s.o., s.th.* jds, e-r S), feiern; e-e Eingabe machen, e-e Bittschrift richten an; **~ plaque, slate, tablet** Gedenktafel *f*; **~ service** Gedächtnisgottesdienst *m*.

memorize ['meməraiz] *tr* auswendig lernen, memorieren, sich einprägen, sich merken; notieren, aufzeichnen, schriftlich festhalten.

memory ['meməri] Erinnerungsvermögen; Gedächtnis; Gedenken, Andenken *n*, Erinnerung *f* (*of* an); *from, by ~* auswendig; *in ~ of* zur Erinnerung an; *of blessed ~* seligen Angedenkens; *within living ~* seit Menschengedenken; *to call to ~* sich ins Gedächtnis zurückrufen; *to commit to ~* auswendig lernen; *to escape s.o.'s ~* jds Gedächtnis entfallen; *to keep alive the ~ of* die Erinnerung wachhalten an.

menace ['menəs] *s* (Be-)Drohung *f* (*to* gen); *tr* bedrohen; *itr* drohen.

ménage, *Am a.* **menage** ['mena:ʒ] Haushalt(führung *f*) *m*.

menagerie [mi'nædʒəri] Menagerie *f*.

mend [mend] *tr* ausbessern, reparieren, flicken; *(Strümpfe)* stopfen; verbessern, berichtigen, richtigstellen; *(Feuer)* wieder in Gang bringen, schüren; *itr* sich bessern; wieder gesund werden, genesen; *s* Ausbesserung, Reparatur; ausgebesserte Stelle *f*, Flicken *m*; *on the ~* auf dem Wege der Besserung; *to ~ o.'s pace* s-e Schritte beschleunigen, schneller gehen; *to ~ o.'s ways* sich bessern; *that won't ~ matters* das ändert auch nichts daran; *least said, soonest ~ed (prov)* je weniger man redet, desto schneller wird alles besser; *it is never too late to ~ (prov)* es ist nie zu spät, ein anderes Leben anzufangen; **~able** ['-əbl] (aus)besserungsfähig; **~er** ['-ə] Ausbesserer, Flicker *m*; **~ing** ['-iŋ] (Aus-)Bessern, Flicken *n*; *pl* Stopfgarn *n*; *invisible ~~* Kunststopfen *n*.

mendac|ious [men'deiʃəs] lügnerisch, verlogen, unaufrichtig, falsch; **~ity** [men'dæsiti] Lügenhaftigkeit, Verlogenheit, Unaufrichtigkeit, Falschheit *f*.

mendic|ancy ['mendikənsi] Bettelei; Bettelhaftigkeit *f*; **~ant** ['-kənt] *a* bettelnd; Bettel-; bettelhaft; *s* Bettler; *(~~ friar)* Bettelmönch *m*; **~ity** [men'disiti] Bettelei *f*; Bettelunwesen *n*; Bettelarmut *f*; *to reduce to ~~* an den Bettelstab bringen.

menfolk(s) ['menfouk(s)] *pl* die Mannsleute *pl*, *fam* -bilder *n pl*.

menhir ['menhiə] Menhir *m*.

menial ['mi:njəl] *a* Gesinde-; untertänig; niedrig, gewöhnlich; *s* Diener, Knecht; *fig* Lakai *m*.

meningitis [menin'dʒaitis] Hirnhautentzündung *f*.

miniscus [mi'niskəs] *pl -ci* [-sai] Mondsichel, konkav-konvexe Linse *f*; *anat phys* Meniskus *m*.

menopause ['menəpɔ:z] *physiol* Wechseljahre *f*, Klimakterium *n*.

mens|al ['mensl] monatlich; **~es** ['-si:z] = *menstruation*.

menstru|al ['menstruəl] *a physiol* Menstruations-; *astr* monatlich; **~ate** ['-eit] *itr* menstruieren, die Regel haben, unwohl sein; **~ation** [menstru'eiʃən] Menstruation, monatliche Blutung *f*, Monatsfluß *m*.

mensur|ability [menʃurə'biliti] Meßbarkeit *f*; **~able** ['menʃurəbl] meßbar; **~ation** [mensjuə'reiʃən, *Am* menʃə'r-] (Ab-, Aus-, Ver-)Messung; *math* Meßkunst *f*.

mental ['mentl] **1.** geistig; Geistes-, Verstandes-, Kopf-; *med* geisteskrank, Irren-; **~ age** geistige(s) Alter *n*; **~ arithmetic** Kopfrechnen *n*; **~ asylum, home, hospital** Irrenanstalt *f*, -haus *n*, Heil-(u. Pflege-)Anstalt *f*; **~ case** Fall *m* von Geisteskrankheit; **~ deficiency** Schwachsinn *m*; **~ disease** Geisteskrankheit *f*; **~ healing** *Am* Psychotherapie *f*; **~ity** [men'tæliti] Geistesverfassung, Mentalität *f*; = **~ powers** *pl* Geisteskräfte *f pl*; **~ reservation** geistige(r) Vorbehalt *m*; **~ specialist** Psychiater *m*; **~ test** Intelligenzprüfung *f*; **2.** *scient* Kinn-.

menthol ['menθɔl] *chem* Menthol *n*.

mention ['menʃən] *s* Erwähnung *f*; *tr* erwähnen; *not to ~, without ~ing* abgesehen von, ganz zu schweigen von; *to make ~ of* erwähnen; *don't ~ it!* keine Ursache (zu danken)! *that's not worth ~ing* das ist nicht der Rede wert; **~able** ['-əbl] erwähnens-, nennenswert.

mentor ['mentɔ:] Mentor, treue(r) Ratgeber *m*.

menu ['menju:] Speisekarte, -nfolge *f*, Menu *n*.

meou, meow [mi(:)'au] *Am s. mew* 2.

mephit|ic [me'fitik] verpestet, stickig; übelriechend; **~is** [-'faitis] Ausdünstung, Stickluft *f*; üble(r) Geruch *m*.

mercantil|e ['mə:kəntail, *Am* -til] kaufmännisch; Handels-; *~~ academy* Handelshochschule *f*; *~~ agency* Handelsvertretung; Kreditauskunftei *f*; *~~ agent* Handelsvertreter *m*; *~~ broker* Handelsmakler *m*; *~~ correspondence* Handelskorrespondenz *f*; *~~ enterprise* kaufmännische(s) Unternehmen *n*; *~~ law* Handelsrecht, -gesetz(buch) *n*; *~~ marine* Handelsmarine *f*; *~~ report* Marktbericht *m*; *~~ system (hist)* Merkantilsystem *n*; *~~ training* kaufmännische Ausbildung *f*; **~ism** ['mə:kəntailizm] *hist* Merkantilismus *m*.

mercenary ['mə:sinəri] *a (Person)* käuflich; gewinnsüchtig; bezahlt, gedungen; *s* Söldner; *obs* Mietling *m*.

mercer ['mə:sə] Schnittwaren-, Tuchhändler *m*; **~ize** ['-raiz] *tr (Textil)* merzerisieren; **~y** ['-ri] Schnittwaren *f pl*, Tuche *n pl*, (*bes.* Seiden-)Stoffe *m pl*; Schnittwaren-, Tuchhandel *m*, -handlung *f*.

merchandis|e ['mə:tʃəndaiz] *s* Ware(n *pl*) *f*; *itr tr Am* Handel treiben, handeln (mit); *an article of ~* e-e Ware; **~ing** ['-iŋ] Verkaufspolitik *f*.

merchant ['mə:tʃənt] *s* (Groß-)Kaufmann, Handelsherr, Geschäftsmann; *Am* Kleinhändler, Ladeninhaber, Kaufmann, Krämer; *sl* auf etw versessene(r) Kerl *m*; *a* kaufmännisch; Handels-; *speed ~ (sl)* rücksichtslose(r) Autofahrer *m*; **~able** ['-əbl] verkäuflich, gangbar; **~ bar** *tech* Stabeisen *n*; **~ flag** Handelsflagge *f*; **~man** ['-mən], **~ ship, vessel** Handelsschiff *n*; **~ marine** Handelsmarine, -flotte *f*; **~ prince** reiche(r) Kaufmann *m*, große(r) Handelsherr *m*; **~'s apprentice** Kaufmannslehrling *m*; **~'s clerk** Handlungsgehilfe *m*; **~-seaman** Matrose *m* der Handelsmarine; **~ service, shipping** Handelsschiffahrt *f*; **~-tailor** Inhaber *m* e-s Maßkleidungsgeschäftes.

merci|ful ['mə:siful] gnädig; barmherzig, mitleidig, mild, gütig (*to* zu); **~fulness** ['-fulnis] Barmherzigkeit, Milde, Güte *f*; **~less** ['-lis] unbarmherzig, erbarmungs-, mitleidlos; **~lessness** ['-lisnis] Unbarmherzigkeit, Mitleidlosigkeit *f*.

mercur|ial [mə:'kjuəriəl] *a* Quecksilber-; *fig* quecksilb(e)rig, lebhaft, lebendig; wechsel-, flatterhaft; **~ialism** [-izm] Quecksilbervergiftung *f*; **~ic** [mə:'kjuərik], **~ous** ['mə:kjurəs] *a* Quecksilber-; **~y** ['mə:kjuri] Quecksilber *n*; *astr* Merkur; *fig* Bote *m*.

mercy ['mə:si] Gnade *f*, Erbarmen *n*; Barmherzigkeit *f*, Mitleid *n*, Milde, Güte, Wohltat *f*, Liebesdienst; Segen *m*, Glück *n*; *at the ~ of* in der Gewalt, in den Händen *gen*; preisgegeben, ausgeliefert *dat*; *without ~* erbarmungs-, mitleidlos; *to beg, to plead for ~* um Gnade flehen; *to show s.o. little ~* wenig Mitleid mit jdm haben; *that's a ~!* das ist ein Segen *od* Glück! **~ killing** Euthanasie *f*.

mere [miə] **1.** *a attr* bloß, rein, lauter, nichts als; *a ~* bloß ein(e), nur ein(e), nichts als; *for the ~ purpose of* nur zu dem Zweck *gen*; **~ly** ['-li] *adv* bloß, nur; **2.** *obs poet* (kleiner) See *m*.

meretricious [meri'triʃəs] dirnenhaft; aufdringlich, übertrieben, überladen *(a. Stil)*; (innerlich) hohl, unecht, falsch; *fig* verführerisch.

merg|e [mə:dʒ] *itr* aufgehen, übergehen (*in* in); verschmelzen (*in* mit); *tr* aufgehen lassen (*into* in); eng verbinden (*into* mit); *com* zs.legen, fusionieren; **~ence** ['-əns], **~ing** ['-iŋ] Verschmelzung, Vereinigung *f* (*into* mit); **~er** ['-ə] Zs.legung *f*, -schluß *m*, Fusion *f*.

meridi|an [mə'ridiən] *s geog* Meridian, Längen-, Mittagskreis; *astr* Meridian; Kulminationspunkt; Mittag; *fig* Höhepunkt *m*; Blütezeit *f*; *a* Längen-, Meridian-; Kulminations-, Mittags-, mittäglich; *fig* höchst; **~onal** [mə'ridiənl] *a* südlich, südländisch; Meridian-; *s* Südländer, *bes.* Südfranzose *m*.

meringue [mə'ræŋ] Meringe *f*, Baiser *n (Gebäck)*.

merino [mə'ri:nou] *pl -os* Merinoschaf *n*, -wolle *f*.

merit ['merit] *a. pl* Verdienst *n*; Wert, Vorzug *m*, Besonderheit, Verdienstlichkeit; Auszeichnung *f*, Ehrenzeichen *n*; *pl* innere Berechtigung *f*; (wahrer, tatsächlicher) Sachverhalt *m*; *die* Sache selbst; *das* Wesentliche, *die* wesentlichen Punkte, Hauptpunkte; *tr* verdienen, wert sein, beanspruchen können; *according to o.'s ~s* nach Verdienst; *on the ~s of the case* nach Lage der Dinge, wie die Dinge nun einmal liegen; *to go, to inquire into the ~s of s.th.* e-r S auf den Grund gehen; *to make a ~ of s.th.* sich etw als Verdienst anrechnen; etw als verdienstvoll hinstellen; *a man of ~* ein verdienter Mann; **~ed** ['-id] *a* verdient; **~orious** [meri'tɔ:riəs] verdienstlich, anerkennens-, lobenswert; *to be ~~* Anerkennung verdienen.

merlin ['mə:lin] *orn* Merlin-, Zwerg-, Stein-, Blaufalke *m*.

mer|maid ['mə:meid] (Wasser-)Nixe; *fam* Badenixe *f*; **~man** ['-mən] Nix, Triton *m*; *fam* Wasserratte *f*.

merri|ment ['merimənt] Lustigkeit, Fröhlichkeit, Ausgelassenheit, Heiterkeit *f*.

merry ['meri] lustig, ausgelassen, fröhlich, froh, vergnügt, heiter, in Stimmung; *sl* beschwipst; *to make ~* ausgelassen, lustig, vergnügt sein, feiern; *over, of* sich lustig machen über; *~ as a lark* kreuzfidel; *a ~ Christmas* fröhliche Weihnachten *f pl*; *the ~ month (of May)* der Wonnemonat (Mai); **~-andrew** Spaßmacher *m*; **~-go--round** Karussell *n*; **~-making** Lustbarkeit *f*; **~thought** Gabelbein *n*, -knochen *m (e-s Huhnes)*.

mesa ['meisə] *Am* Tafelland *n*.

mesentery ['mesəntəri] *anat* Gekröse *n*.

mesh [meʃ] *s* Masche *f*; *pl* Geflecht, Netz(werk) *n*; *pl fig* Schlingen *f pl*, Falle *f*; Inea.greifen *n* der Zahnräder; *tr itr* (sich) *(in e-m Netz, a. fig)* fangen, verwickeln; *fig* (sich) verstricken, umgarnen (lassen); zs.passen; *tech* einrücken; *in ~ (Zahnräder)* inea.greifend; **~ connection** *el* Dreiecks-, Deltaschaltung *f*; **~ed** [-t] *a* maschig, netzartig; *close-, fine-~~* eng-, feinmaschig; **~work** Gewebe, Gespinst *n*, Maschen *f pl*, Netzwerk *n*.

mesmer|ic [mez'merik] hypnotisch; **~ism** ['mezmərizm] Lehre *f* vom tierischen Magnetismus; **~ist** ['-ist] Heilmagnetiseur, Hypnotiseur *m*; **~ize** [-aiz] *tr* hypnotisieren; *fig* e-n großen Einfluß haben auf, beherrschen.

mesne [mi:n] *a jur* Zwischen-; **~ process, profits** *pl* Zwischenprozeß *m*, -gewinne *m pl*.

meso ['meso(u)] *in Zssgen* Meso-, Zwischen-; mittler; **~carp** ['-kɑ:p] Mesokarp *n*; **~lithic** [-'liθik] *a hist* mesolithisch; *s u.*: *~~ era, period* mittlere Steinzeit *f*, Mesolithikum *n*; **~(tro)n** ['mesətrən, 'mi:zən] *phys* Meso(tro)n *n*; **~zoic** [-'zo(u)ik] *geol* mesozoisch; *s u.*: *~~ era, period* Erdmittelalter, Mesozoikum *n*.

mess [mes] *s mil* Kasino *n*; *mar* Back, Messe *f*; Offiziersheim; Essen *n*, Mahlzeit *f* im Kasino *od* in der Messe; (wüstes) Durcheinander *n*, wirrer Haufen; Schmutz, Dreck *m*, *fam* Schweinerei; schwierige, verzweifelte Lage, *fam* Patsche, Klemme *f*, Schlamassel *m* od *n*; *Am sl* Dummkopf *m*; *Am sl* aufregende Sache *f*; *tr* schmutzig, dreckig machen; *(to ~ up)* durchea., in Unordnung bringen; beschmutzen; *itr* gemeinsam essen (*with* mit); alles durchea., in Unordnung bringen; Verwirrung stiften; *a Am sl* ausgezeichnet, beachtlich; *Am sl* blöde, haltlos; *to ~ about, to ~ around* herumtrödeln, nichts Rechtes anfangen, *fam* herummurksen; *with s.o. (Am sl)* hänseln, beleidigen; *at ~* beim Essen, im Kasino, in der Messe; *to be in, to get into a ~* in der Klemme sein, in die K. geraten; schmutzig sein, werden; *to go to ~* zum Essen, ins Kasino gehen; *to make a ~ of* verpfuschen, verhunzen; durchea.bringen, auf den Kopf stellen; *o.s.* sich beschmutzen, sich beschmieren; *that's a fine ~* das ist e-e schöne Bescherung; *officers' ~* Offiziersmesse *f*; **~-allowance** Verpflegungsgeld *n*; **~-attendant** Ordonnanz *f (im Kasino)*; **~-jacket** im Kasino getragene Jacke *f*; **~-kit, -gear** Eßgeschirr *n*; **~mate** *bes. mar* Tischgenosse, -kamerad *m*; **~-room** Kasino *n*, Messe *f*; **~-sergeant** Küchenfeldwebel, -wachtmeister *m*; **~-tin** Kochgeschirr *n*; **~-up** Durcheinander *n*; Verwirrung *f*; Mißverständnis *n*; **~y** ['-i] unordentlich; unsauber, schmutzig, dreckig.

message ['mesidʒ] *s* Mitteilung, Nachricht, Benachrichtigung, Meldung *f*, Bericht *m*; Botschaft, Verkündung *f*; (Boten-)Auftrag, Botengang *m*; Bestellung *f*; *tr* mitteilen, melden, berichten; *to go on a ~* e-n Botengang machen, e-n Auftrag erledigen; *could you take a ~ for him?* könnten Sie ihm etwas ausrichten? *telegraph ~* Telegramm *n*; *telephone(d) ~* telephonische Benachrichtigung *f*; *wireless ~* Funkspruch *m*; *~ of congratulation (pol)* Glückwunschbotschaft *f*; **~ bag, card** *od* **form, pad** *mil* Meldetasche *f*, -blatt *od* -formular *n*, -block *m*; **~ centre** *mil* Meldesammelstelle *f*, -kopf *m*; **~ form** *tele* Spruchformular *n*.

messenger ['mesindʒə] Bote; Kurier; *mil* Melder; Überbringer; Ausläufer; Dienstmann; *(express, special ~)* Eilbote *m*; *(~ cable)* Tragdraht *m*, -seil, -kabel *n*; **~ boy** Laufbursche *m*; **~ dog** *mil* Meldehund *m*; **~ pigeon** (Heeres-)Brieftaube *f*; **~'s fee** Botenlohn *m*, Bestellgeld *n*; **~ vehicle** Meldefahrzeug *n*.

Messiah, *the* [mi'saiə] *rel* der Messias.

messuage ['meswidʒ] *jur* (Wohn-)Grundstück, Anwesen *n*.

mestiz|o [mes'ti:zou] *pl -os* Mestize *m*.

metabol|ic [metə'bɔlik] *a* Stoffwechsel-; *biol* sich verwandelnd; **~ism** [me'tæbəlizm] *physiol* Stoffwechsel; *biol* Metabolismus *m*; *constructive ~~* Aufbau *m*; *destructive ~~* Abbau *m*; **~ize** [me'tæbəlaiz] *tr* umwandeln.

metacarpus [metə'kɑ:pəs] *pl -pi* [-ai] *anat* Mittelhand *f*.

metage ['mi:tidʒ] amtliches Messen *od* Wiegen *n* (e-r Ladung); (amtliche) Meß- *od* Wiegegebühr *f*.

metal ['metl] *s* Metall; Gußmetall; *min* Korn *n*, Schieferton *m*; (flüssige) Glasmasse *f*; *(road-~)* Schotter *m*; *typ* Satzmaterial *n*; (druck)fertige(r) Satz *m*; *fig* Material *n*, Substanz *f*, Stoff *m*; *pl rail* Schienen *f pl*, Gleise *n pl*; *attr* Metall-; *tr* mit Metall verstärken *od* überziehen; *(Straße)* verschottern; *to leave, to run off the ~s (rail)* entgleisen; *coined ~* Metallgeld *n*; *heavy, light ~* Schwer-, Leichtmetall *n*; *precious ~* Edelmetall *n*; *white ~* Weißguß *m*, Neusilber *n*; **~ cutting** spanabhebende Bearbeitung *f*; **~ foil** Metallfolie *f*; **~ founder** Metallgießer *m*; **~lic** [mi'tælik] metallen; Metall-; *(Glanz)* metallisch; *~~ compound* Metallegierung *f*; *~~ currency* od *standard, money* Metallwährung *f*, -geld *n*; *~~ vein (min)* Erzader *f*; **~liferous** [metə'lifərəs] metall-, erzhaltig, -führend; **~line** ['metlain] metallisch, Metall-; metallhaltig, -führend; **~(l)ing** ['metliŋ] Beschotterung *f*; **~(l)ize** ['metlaiz] *tr* metallisieren; **~lography** [metə'lɔgrəfi] Metallographie, Metallkunde *f*; **~loid** ['metəlɔid] *s* Nichtmetall *n*; *a* metallartig; **~lurgic(al)** [metə'lə:dʒik(əl)] metallurgisch; **~lurgist** [me'tælə:dʒist] Metallurge *m*; **~lurgy** [me'tælə:dʒi, metə'lə:dʒi] Metallurgie, Hüttenkunde *f*; **~ plating** Plattierung *f*; **~ shears** *pl* Blech-, Drahtschere *f*; **~ strip** Metallstreifen *m*; **~worker** Metallarbeiter *m*; **~ working** Metallbearbeitung *f*.

metamorph|ic [metə'mɔ:fik] *geol* metamorphisch; *biol* gestaltverändernd; **~ose** [-fouz] *tr itr* (sich) um-, verwandeln (*to, into* in); **~osis** [-'mɔ:fəsis] *pl -ses* [-si:z] Um-, Verwandlung; *biol* Metamorphose *f*.

metaphor ['metəfə] Metapher *f*, bildliche(r) Ausdruck *m*; **~ic(al)** [metə'fɔrik(əl)] bildlich, übertragen.

metaphysic|al [metə'fizikəl] metaphysisch; **~ian** [-fi'ziʃən] Metaphysiker *m*; **~s** [-'fiziks] *pl mit sing* Metaphysik; *fam* reine Theorie *f*.

metastasis [mi'tæstəsis] *pl -ses* [-si:z] *med (Krebs)* Metastase *f*; *biol* Substanz-, Stoffwechsel; *(Rede)* unvermittelte(r) Übergang *m*.

metatarsus [metə'tɑ:səs] *pl -si* [-sai] *anat* Mittelfuß *m*.

metathesis [me'tæθəsis] *pl -ses* [-si:z] (Laut-)Umstellung, Metathese *f*.

metcast ['metkast] Wettervoraussage *f*.

mete [mi:t] **1.** *(to ~ out)* aus-, verteilen; zumessen, -teilen; *obs poet* messen; **2.** *meist pl* Grenze; Grenzlinie *f*, -stein *m*; *~s and bounds (fig)* Grenzen *f pl*.

meteor ['mi:tjə] Meteor *m* od *n a. fig*, Sternschnuppe *f*; **~ic** [mi:ti'ɔrik] atmosphärisch, Luft-; Meteoren-; *fig* meteorhaft; glanzvoll; schnell, kurz; *~~ iron* Meteoreisen *n*; *~~ shower* Sternschnuppenschwarm *m*; **~ite** ['mi:tjərait] Meteorit, Meteorstein *m*; **~ologic(al)** [mi:tjərə'lɔdʒik(əl)] meteorologisch, Wetter-, Klima-; atmosphärisch; *~~ office* Wetterwarte *f*; **~ologist** [mi:tjə'rɔlədʒist] Meteorologe, *fam* Wetterfrosch *m*; **~ology** [-ə'rɔlədʒi] Meteorologie, Wetter-, Klimakunde *f*.

meter ['mi:tə] **1.** Messer *m*, Meßinstrument *n*, (Meß-)Uhr *f*, Zähler *m*; *gas, water ~* Gas-, Wasseruhr *f*; **2.** *Am s. metre*; **~ board, panel** Zählertafel *f*.

methane ['meθein] *chem* Methan, Sumpf-, Grubengas *n*.

methinks [mi'θiŋks] *irr pret methought* [-'θɔ:t] mich dünkt, mich deucht.

method ['meθəd] Methode *f*, Verfahren(sweise *f*) *n*, Prozeß *m*; Denk-, Ausdrucksweise; Lehr-, Heilmethode *f*; (Denk-)Schema, System *n*; **~ic(al)** [mi'θɔdik(əl)] methodisch, planmäßig, systematisch; **~ism** ['-izm] (übertriebene) Systematik *f*; *(M) ~~ (rel)* Methodismus *m*; **(M)~ist** ['-ist] *rel* Methodist *m*; **~ize** ['meθədaiz] *tr* systematisieren, in ein System bringen; **~ology** [meθə'dɔlədʒi] Methodenlehre, Methodologie *f*.
Methuselah [mi'θju:zələ] Methusalem *m*; *as old as ~* ur-, steinalt.
methyl ['meθil, 'mi:θail] *chem* Methyl *n*; ~ **acetate** Methylazetat, essigsaure(s) Methyl *n*; ~ **alcohol** Methylalkohol, Holzgeist *m*, Methanol *n*; **~ate** ['meθileit] *tr* methylieren, denaturieren; **~ated** [-id] *a*: *~~ alcohol, spirit* denaturierte(r) Alkohol, Spiritus *m*; **~ene** ['-li:n] Methylen *n*.
meticul|osity [mitikju'lɔsiti] große Sorgfalt, Gewissenhaftigkeit *f*; **~ous** [mi'tikjuləs] über-, peinlich genau, sehr sorgfältig, (äußerst) gewissenhaft.
metonymy [mi'tɔnimi] Metonymie, übertragene Bedeutung *f (e-s Wortes)*.
me-too ['mi:tu:] *tr Am sl* nachmachen.
metr|e, *Am* **meter** ['mi:tə] Versmaß, Metrum *n*; *mus* Takt *m*; Meter *n* od *m*; **~ic(al)** ['metrik(əl)] *a* metrisch; Maß-; Vers-; *metric system* metrische(s) System *n*; **~ics** ['metriks] *s pl mit sing* Metrik, Verslehre *f*; *mus* Rhythmus *m*.
Metro, metro ['metrou] Untergrund-, U-Bahn *f*.
metronome ['metrənoum] Metronom *n*, Taktmesser *m*.
metropol|is [mi'trɔpəlis] Metropole *f*, Zentrum *n*; Hauptstadt *f*; Sitz *m* e-s Erzbischofs; **~itan** [metrə'pɔlitən] *a* hauptstädtisch; erzbischöflich; *s* Großstädter; Erzbischof; *(orthodoxe Kirche)* Metropolit *m*.
mettle ['metl] (Menschen-)Schlag *m*; Anlage, Veranlagung *f*, Temperament *n*; (hohe) Begabung *f*, Geist *m*, Feuer *n*, Mut *m*; *to try s.o.'s ~, to put s.o. on his ~* jdn auf die Probe stellen; *he was on his ~* alle s-e Kräfte waren angespannt; **~d** ['-d], **~some** ['-səm] begeistert; mutig; feurig.
mew [mju:] **1.** *s* (Mauser-)Käfig *m*; Mausern *n*; *pl mit sing* Marstall; Stallkomplex *m*; *tr (to ~ up)* einsperren; verstecken; **2.** *s* Miau *n*; *itr* miauen; **3.** (See-)Möwe *f*.
mewl, mule [mju:l] *itr* wimmern, (leise) vor sich hinweinen; miauen.
Mexic|an ['meksikən] *a* mexikanisch; *s* Mexikaner(in *f*) *m*; **~o** ['-kou] Mexiko *n*.
mezzanine ['mezəni:n] *arch* Zwischenstock *m*, Mezzanin *n*.
mezzo|relievo ['medzo(u)ri'li:vou] *(Kunst)* Halbrelief *n*; **~soprano** [-sə'prɑ:nou] *mus* Mezzosopran *m*; **~tint** ['-tint] *(Graphik)* Mezzotinto *n*, Schabkunst(blatt *n*) *f*.
miaow [mi(:)'au] *s. mew 2.*
miasm|a [mi'æzmə] *pl a.* *-ata* [-ətə] Miasma *n*, Gifthauch *m*.
mia(o)ul [mi'ɔ:l, mi'aul] *s. mew* 2.
mica ['maikə] *min* Glimmer *m*; **~ceous** [mai'keiʃəs] glimmerhaltig, -artig, Glimmer-; **~-schist, -slate** Glimmerschiefer *m*.
Michael ['maikl] Mich(a)el *m*; **~mas** ['mikləs] *(~~ Day)* Michaeli(s) *n*, Michaelstag *m (29. Sept.)*; *at ~~* auf, zu Michaeli(s); *~~ daisy (bot)* Strandaster *f*; *~~ term (jur)* Herbsttermin *m*; *(Univ.)* Herbsttrimester, -semester *n*.
Mick [mik] *(= Michael) Am pej* Ire *m*.
mickey ['miki] *Am aero sl* Radarmann *m*, -gerät *n*; *sl* Ire *m*; *to take the ~ out of s.o. (sl)* jdn aufziehen, beleidigen; ~ **finn** *Am sl* (Schnaps, Cocktail *m* mit starkem) Betäubungs- *od* Abführmittel *n*.
micro ['maikro(u)-] *in Zssgen*: Mikro-; Klein(st)-; **~be** ['maikroub] Mikrobe *f*; **~bial, ~bic** [mai'kroubiəl, -bik] *a* Mikroben-; **~cosm** ['-kɔzm] Mikrokosmos *m a. fig*; **~cosmic(al)** [-'kɔzmik(əl)] mikrokosmisch; **~film** ['-film] *s* Mikrofilm *m*; *tr* mikrofilmen; **~meter** [mai'krɔmitə] Mikrometer *n*; *~~ screw* Mikrometerschraube *f*; **~n** ['maikrɔn] Mikron, My *n*; **~organism** [-'ɔ:gənizm] Mikroorganismus *m*; **~phone** ['maikrəfoun] Mikrophon; *fam* Radio *n*; *at the ~~* am Mikrophon; **~photograph** ['maikrə'foutəgrɑ:f] Mikrophotogramm *n (Bild)*; **~photography** [-fə'tɔgrəfi] Mikrophotographie *f*; **~scope** ['maikrəskoup] Mikroskop *n*; **~scopic(al)** [maikrə'skɔpik(əl)] mikroskopisch; mikroskopisch klein; peinlich genau; **~scopy** [mai'krɔskəpi] Mikroskopie *f*; **~tome** ['-toum] Mikrotom *n*; **~wave** *el* Mikrowelle *f*.
mictur|ate ['miktjureit] *itr med* urinieren, Wasser lassen; **~ition** [miktju'riʃən] *med* Harndrang *m*; *fam* Wasserlassen *n*.

*

mid [mid] *a* mittler, in der Mitte befindlich; Mittel-; *in Zssgen: in ~(-)air* in der frischen Luft, frei schwebend; *in ~(-)Atlantic* mitten auf dem Atlantik; *from ~(-)May to ~(-)June* von Mitte Mai bis Mitte Juni; **~brain** *anat* Mittelhirn *n*; **~day** *s* Mittag *m*; *a* mittäglich; Mittags-; *~~ meal* Mittagsmahlzeit *f*; **~land** *s das* Landesinnere; *the M~~s (pl)* Mittelengland *n*; *a* binnenländisch; Binnen-; **M~-lent** Lätare, 4. Fastensonntag *m*, Mittfasten *pl*; **~most** *a* mittelst; *adv* genau in der Mitte; *prp* mitten in; **~night** *s* Mitternacht; tiefe Dunkelheit, Finsternis *f*; *a* mitternächtlich, Mitternachts-; finster; *at ~~* um Mitternacht; *to burn the ~~ oil* bis tief in die Nacht arbeiten; *~~ sun* Mitternachtssonne *f*; **~-off, ~on** *(Kricket)* Spieler *m* links, rechts vom Werfer; **~rib** *bot* Mittelrippe *f (e-s Blattes)*; **~riff** *anat* Zwerchfell *n*; mittlere Körpergegend; Obertaille *f*; **~ship** *s* Mitte *f* des Schiffes; Mittelschiff(s)-; **~shipman,** *sl* **~shipmite** Fähnrich *m* zur See; **~ships** *adv* mittschiffs; **~stream** die Mitte des Stromes; *into the ~~ of* mitten in ... hinein; **~summer** Mittsommer *m*; *~~ daisy* Margerite(nblume) *f*; *M~~ Day* Johannistag *m*, Johanni(s) *s. (24. Juni)*; *~~ madness* der Gipfel des Wahnsinns, helle(r) Wahnsinn *m*; **~term** *a s Am* (Prüfung *f*) mitten im Quartal *od* Semester; **~way** *s* Mitte des Weges, Hälfte *f* der Entfernung; Mittelweg *m*; *Am* Rummel-, Festplatz *n*; *a* ['-'-] in der Mitte (befindlich); *adv* ['-'-] halbwegs *(nur räumlich)*; **~week** *s* Wochenmitte, Mitte *f* der Woche; *a u.* **~weekly** *a adv* in der Mitte der Woche; **~wife** *pl* *-wives* Hebamme *f*; **~wifery** ['-wifəri, *Am* -waif-] Geburtshilfe; *fig* Mithilfe *f*; **~winter** Mittwinter *m*; **~year** *a u. s (oft pl) Am* (Prüfung *f*) in der Mitte des (Studien-)Jahres.
midden ['midn] *obs* Misthaufen *m*; *(kitchen ~)* K(j)ökkenmöddinger *pl*.
middle ['midl] *s* Mitte(lpunkt *m*, -stück, -teil *n*) *f*; Zwischenstück *n*; Zwischenzeit; Körpermitte, Taille *f*; *a* mittler; Mittel-, Zwischen-; *(gram, Phonetik)* medial; *in the ~ of* in der Mitte *gen*; *in the ~ of the night* mitten in der Nacht; *in the ~ of reading* gerade beim Lesen; ~ **age** *das* mittlere (Lebens-)Alter; *the M~ Ages* das Mittelalter; **~-aged** *a* mittleren Alters; **M~ America** Mittelamerika *n*; **~brow** *fam* geistige(r) Normalverbraucher *m*; **~-class** mittelständisch, bürgerlich; ~ **class(es** *pl*) Mittelstand *m*, Bürgertum *n*; ~ **course,** ~ **way** Mittelweg *m*, Kompromiß *m* od *n*; ~ **distance** Mittelgrund *m*; *sport* Mittelstrecke *f*; ~ **ear** Mittelohr *n*; *the* **M~ East** der Vordere Orient, der Nahe Osten; *Am* der Mittlere Osten; **M~ English, M~ High, Low German, M~ Latin** Mittelenglisch, -hoch-, -niederdeutsch, -latein *n*; **~finger** Mittelfinger *m*; **~man** Mittelsmann *m*, -person *f*, Vermittler; Zwischenhändler, Wiederverkäufer; *Br* Feuilletonist *m*; **~most** = *midmost*; **~-of-the-road** neutral; **~-rate** mittelmäßig; ~ **size** Mittelgröße *f*; **~-sized** *a* mittelgroß, von mittlerer Größe; **~-weight** *s sport* Mittelgewicht *n*; Mittelgewichtler *m*; *a* Mittelgewichts-; *the* **M~ West** der Mittelwesten.
middling ['midliŋ] *a* mittler, Mittel-; durchschnittlich, Durchschnitts-; (mittel)mäßig, gewöhnlich, leidlich, *adv fam* einigermaßen, leidlich; *s Am (Schweinefleisch)* Rücken *m*; Speckseite *f*; *pl com* Mittelsorte *f*; *Am* Tabak *m*, Baumwolle *f*, Nutzholz *n* mittlerer Qualität; Mittelmehl *n*.
middy ['midi] *fam* Fähnrich *m* (zur See); *Am (~ blouse)* Matrosenbluse *f*.
midg|e [midʒ] Mücke *f*; = *~et*; **~et** ['-it] *s* kleine(s), winzige(s) Ding *n*; Knirps, Zwerg *m*; Puppe *f*, Püppchen *n*; *a* zwergenhaft; Miniatur-, Klein(st)-; *~~ car* Kleinauto *n*; *~~ railway, (Am) railroad* Liliputbahn *f*; *~~ set* Zwergempfänger *m*; *~~ submarine* Kleinst-U-Boot *n*.
midst [midst] *s lit nur in: in(to) the ~ of* mitten in, mitten unter *dat (acc)*; *in our ~* in unserer Mitte, mitten unter uns; *out of, from the ~ of* mitten aus (... heraus), aus der Mitte *gen*; *prp poet* mitten in, mitten unter *dat*.
mien [mi:n] Miene *f*, (Gesichts-)Ausdruck *m*; Verhalten(sweise *f*) *n*.
miff [mif] *s fam* kleine Reiberei, Ausea.setzung *f*; (Anfall *m* von) schlechte(r) Laune *f*; *tr* beleidigen; *(to ~ off)* leicht welken.
might [mait] Macht, Gewalt, Stärke, Kraft *f*; *with all o.'s ~, with ~ and main* mit aller, mit voller Kraft; **~ily** ['-ili] *adv* gewaltig, kräftig; *fam (übertrieben)* mächtig, gewaltig, sehr; **~iness** ['-inis] Kraft, Stärke, Gewalt, Heftigkeit *f*; **~y** ['-i] *a* mächtig, gewaltig, stark, kräftig, heftig; gewaltig (groß), bedeutend; *fam* eingebildet; *adv* sehr, riesig, gewaltig.
mignonette [minjə'net] *bot* Reseda *f*.
migraine [mi:'grein] Migräne *f*.
migr|ant ['maigrənt] Auswanderer; Nomade; *zoo* Zugvogel *m*; **~ate** [mai'greit, *Am* 'mai-] *itr* umziehen; auswandern; *zoo* wandern; **~ation** [-'greiʃən] (Aus-, Ab-)Wanderung *f*; Fortziehen *n*; (Vogel-)Zug *m*; *internal ~~* Binnenwanderung *f*; *~~ of the peoples* Völkerwanderung *f*; **~atory** ['maigrətəri] (aus)wandernd; Wander(ungs)-; umherstreifend, nomadisch, wanderlustig; *~~ bird* Zugvogel *m*; *~~ worker* Wanderarbeiter *m*.
mike [maik] **1.** *s sl* Mikrophon; Radio *n*; **2.** *itr sl* herumlungern; **3.** *M~* Michael; *sl* Ire *m*.

milch [miltʃ] *a nur in:* ~ **cow** Milchkuh *f*.
mild [maild] mild, sanft, weich(herzig); leicht, schwach, mäßig; *(Wetter, Klima)* mild; *(Wetter)* gelinde; *(Klima)* gemäßigt; *(Nahrungs-, Genußmittel)* mild, leicht; *(Stahl)* elastisch, schmied-, hämmerbar; *to put it ~ly* gelinde gesagt *od* ausgedrückt; *draw it ~! (fam)* gib nicht so (schaurig) an! ~**ness** ['-nis] Milde; Sanftmut *f*.
mildew ['mildju:] *s* Mehltau(pilz); Schimmel *m*; Stockflecken *m pl*; *tr itr* (sich) mit Mehltau überziehen; schimm(e)lig werden (lassen); ~**y** ['-i] vom Mehltau befallen; schimm(e)lig.
mile [mail] Meile *f (1,61 km)*; *geographical, nautical, sea* ~ Seemeile *f (1,852 km)*; *~s apart* meilenweit ausea.; *fig* himmelweit entfernt; *to feel ~s better* sich erheblich besser fühlen; ~**age, milage** ['-idʒ] Entfernung, zurückgelegte Strecke *f (in Meilen)*; Kilometergeld *n*; Fahrt-, Frachttarif *m*; *~~ (book) (Am)* Fahrscheinheft *n*; *~~ indicator, recorder,* ~**ometer** [-'lɔmitə] Meilen-, Kilometerzähler *m*; ~ **post** Wegweiser *m* mit Entfernungsangabe; ~**r** *sport* Meilenläufer *m*; ~**stone** Meilenstein; *fig* Markstein *m*.
milfoil ['milfɔil] *bot* Schafgarbe *f*.
miliar|ia [mili'ɛəriə] *med* Frieseln *pl*; ~**y** ['miliəri] *a med* Miliar-.
milit|ancy ['militənsi] Kriegszustand *m*; Kriegsbereitschaft; Kampfeslust *f*, Kampfgeist *m*; ~**ant** ['-t] *a* kämpfend, Kampf-; kriegführend; kriegsbereit, -lustig, kriegerisch, militant; *s* Kämpfer, Streiter *m*; ~**arism** ['-ərizm] Militarismus *m*; ~**arist** ['-ərist] *pol* Militarist *m*; ~**aristic** [militə'ristik] kriegerisch; militaristisch; ~**arize** ['militəraiz] *tr* auf den Krieg vorbereiten; ~**ary** ['militəri] *a* militärisch, Militär-, Kriegs-; Heeres-; *s: the ~~ (mit pl)* das Militär, das Heer; die Soldaten *m pl*; *~~ academy, college* Militärakademie, Kriegsschule *f*; *~~ attaché* Militärattaché *m*; *~~ band* Militärkapelle *f*; *~~ cemetery* Soldatenfriedhof *m*; *~~ chest* Kriegskasse *f*; *~~ commander* Militärbefehlshaber *m*; *~~ court* Militär-, Kriegsgericht *n*; *~~ courtesy* militärische Formen *f pl*; *M~~ Cross* Kriegsverdienstkreuz *n*; *~~ fever* Unterleibstyphus *m*; *~~ forces (pl)* Streitkräfte *f pl*; *M~~ Government* Militärregierung *f*; *~~ history* Kriegsgeschichte *f*; *~~ intelligence* (Spionage-)Abwehr *f*; *~~ law* Militärgesetzgebung *f*; Kriegsrecht *n*; *~~ map* Generalstabskarte *f*; *~~-minded (a)* kriegerisch, soldatisch; *~~ music* Militärmusik *f*; *~~ personnel* Militärpersonal *n*; *~~ police* Militär-, Feldpolizei *f*; *~~ school* Kadettenanstalt *f*; *~~ science* Kriegswissenschaft *f*; *~~ service* Wehrdienst *m*; *universal compulsory ~~ service* allgemeine Wehrpflicht *f*; *~~ service book* Wehrpaß *m*; *~~ song* Soldatenlied *n*; *~~ training* Militärausbildung *f*; *~~ tribunal* Militärgericht *n*; ~**ate** ['-eit] *itr fig (Tatsache)* sprechen, entgegenwirken (*against* gegen); ~**ia** [mi'liʃə] Miliz, Bürgerwehr *f*; *~~man* Milizsoldat *m*.
milk [milk] *s (bes. Kuh-)*Milch; *bot* Milch(saft *m*); *(Kalk-)*Milch *f*; *tr* melken; anzapfen *(fam a. fig, bes. tele)*; *fig* schröpfen, ausnutzen; *(Nachricht)* abfangen; *itr* Milch geben; *to ~ well* viel Milch geben, e-e gute Milchkuh sein; *no use crying over spilt ~* man soll Verlorenem nicht nachtrauern; *butter~* Buttermilch *f*; *coconut ~* Kokosmilch *f*; *condensed ~* kondensierte, Kondens-, Büchsenmilch *f*; *cow's ~* Kuhmilch *f*; *full-cream, unskimmed ~* Vollmilch *f*; *skimmed ~* Magermilch *f*; *~ of almonds* Mandelmilch *f*; *~ for babes (fig)* etwas für Kinder; *~ and honey* Milch u. Honig, Überfluß *m*; *the ~ of human kindness* die Milch der frommen Denkungsart; *~ and water* dumme(s) Gerede *n*; Gefühlsduselei *f*; *~ and-water (a)* läppisch, albern; saft- u. kraftlos; ~-**bar** Milchbar *f*; ~-**bill, -can, chocolate, -crust, diet** Milchrechnung, -kanne, -schokolade *f*, -schorf *m*; -diät *f*; ~**er** ['-ə] Melker(in *f*), Schweizer *m*; Melkmaschine; *(meist mit a)* Milchkuh *f*; ~-**filter, -float** Milchsieb *n*, -wagen *m*; ~**iness** ['-inis] milchige Beschaffenheit *f*; *das* Weichliche; ~-**jug** Milchtopf *m*, -kännchen *n*; ~**maid** Milchmädchen *n*; ~**man** Milchmann *m*; ~-**powder** Milchpulver *n*; ~ **pudding** Reis-, Grießpudding *m*; ~ **run** *Am aero sl* Routineeinsatz *m*; ~-**shake** Milchmischgetränk *n*; ~**sop** ['-sɔp] Schwächling, Weichling *m*, Muttersöhnchen *n*; ~-**sugar** Milchzucker *m*; ~-**tooth** Milchzahn *m*; ~**weed** *bot* Wolfsmilch *f*; ~-**white** milchweiß; ~**wort** *bot* Kreuz-, Milchblume *f*; ~**y** ['-i] milchig *a. bot*; milchweiß; Milch-; *fig* sanft, weich(lich); *the M~~ Way (astr)* die Milchstraße.
mill [mil] **1.** Mühle; (Saft-)Presse; *(bes. Textil-)*Fabrik *f*, Werk *n*; *(spinning ~)* Spinnerei; Weberei *f*; Walzwerk *n*; Fräsmaschine *f*; *typ* Präg(e)werk *n*, Prägepresse; *sl* Boxkampf *m*, Schlägerei *f*; *tr (Korn)* mahlen; *tech* bearbeiten; prägen; *(Tuch)* walken; walzen, polieren; fräsen, rändeln, bördeln; maschinell hobeln; *(Küche)* quirlen, schlagen; *(Vieh)* im Kreis herumtreiben; *sl* verdreschen, verkloppen; *itr (to ~ around)* sich im Kreise bewegen; *sl* sich prügeln; *to go through the ~* e-e harte Schule durchmachen; *to put s.o. through the ~* jdn durch e-e harte Schule schicken; *that's grist to his ~* das ist Wasser auf seine Mühle; *coffee-~* Kaffeemühle *f*; *cotton-~* mechanische Weberei *f*; *hammer-, marble-, oil-~* Hammer-, Marmor-, Ölmühle *f*; *paper-~* Papierfabrik *f*; *pepper-~* Pfeffermühle *f*; *rolling ~* Walzwerk *n*; *saw-~* Sägemühle *f*, -werk *n*; *steam-~* Dampfmühle *f*; *textile ~* Textilfabrik *f*; *water-, wind-~* Wasser-, Windmühle *f*; ~ **board** Graupappe *f*; *~~ing* Faserplatte *f*; ~**cake** Ölkuchen *m*; ~-**dam** Mühlwehr *n*; ~**ed** [-d] *a* gemahlen; bearbeitet; geprägt; gefräst; gebördelt; ~**er** ['-ə] Müller *m*; Fräsmaschine; *zoo* Motte *f*; *~~'s thumb* Kaul-, Dickkopf *m (Fisch)*; ~-**hand** Spinnerei-, Fabrikarbeiter *m*; ~-**owner** Mühlen-, Fabrikbesitzer *m*; ~-**pond** Mühlteich *m*; ~-**race, -run, -stream** Mühlbach *m*; ~**stone** Mühlstein *m*; *fig* schwere Last *f*; *to see far into a ~~ (iro)* das Gras wachsen hören; ~-**wheel** Mühlrad *n*; ~**wright** Mühlenbauer; Maschinenschlosser *m*; **2.** Zehntelcent, Tausendsteldollar *m*.
mill|enarian [mili'nɛəriən], ~**ennial** [mi'leniəl] tausendjährig; ~**enary** ['milinəri, mi'len-] *a* tausendjährig; Tausendjahr-; *s* (Jahr-)Tausend *n*; Tausendjahrfeier *f*; ~**ennium** [mi'leniəm] *pl a. -nia* Jahrtausend *n*; *rel das* Tausendjährige Reich; *allg* Goldene(s) Zeitalter *n*; ~**eped(e)** ['milipi:d] *zoo* Tausendfuß, -füß(l)er *m*; ~**esimal** [mi'lesiməl] *a* tausendstel; tausendfach; *s* Tausendstel *n*; ~**iampere** [mili'æmpɛə] *el* Milliampere *n*; ~**iard** ['miljɑ:d] Milliarde *f*; ~**ibar** ['-ibɑ:] *mete* Millibar *n*; ~**igram(me)** ['-igræm] Milligramm *n* ($^1/_{1000}$ *g*); ~**imetre,** *Am* ~**imeter** ['-imi:tə] Millimeter *n*; ~**imicron** ['-imaikrɔn] Millimikron *n*; ~**ion** ['miljən] Million *f a. fin*; *two ~ men* 2 Millionen Menschen; ~**ionaire(ss)** [miljə'nɛə(res)] Millionär(in *f*) *m*; ~**fold** ['miljənfould] *a adv* millionenfach; ~**th** ['miljənθ] *a* millionst; millionstel; *s* Millionstel *n*.
millet ['milit] Hirse *f*.
milliner ['milinə] Putzmacherin, Modistin *f*; ~**y** ['-ri] Damenhüte *m pl*, Modewaren *f pl*, -geschäft *n*.
milling ['miliŋ] Mahlen *n*; Bearbeitung; Prägung *f*; Walken, Walzen, Fräsen; Rändeln, Bördeln *n*; Bördelung; Kreisbewegung; *sl* Prügelei *f*; ~ **cutter** Fräser *m*; ~ **machine** Fräsmaschine *f*; ~ **plant** Mahlwerk *n*; ~ **product** Walz-, Mahlprodukt *n*; ~ **shop** Fräserei *f*.
milt [milt] *s anat* Milz; *(Fisch)* Milch *f*; *tr (Fischeier)* befruchten; ~**er** ['-ə] *zoo* Milchner *m*.
mim|e [maim] *theat hist* Mimenspiel *n*; Burleske, Farce *f*; Mime; Komiker, Spaßmacher *m*; ~**eograph** ['mimiəgrɑ:f] *s* Vervielfältigungsgerät *n*; *tr* vervielfältigen; ~**esis** [mai'mi:sis, mi'm-] Nachahmung; *biol* Mimikry *f*; ~**etic** [mi'metik] nachahmend, sich verstellend; nachgeahmt, Schein-; mimisch; Mimikry-; ~**ic** ['mimik] *a* = *~etic*; *s* Nachahmer, Imitator *m*; *tr* nachahmen, -machen; kopieren; gleichen, ähneln (*s.o.* jdn); *s.o.* jds Aussehen haben *od* annehmen; ~**icry** ['-ri] Nachahmung; *biol* Mimikry *f*; ~**osa** [mi'mouzə] *bot* Mimose *f*.
minaret ['minəret, --'-] *arch* Minarett *n*.
minatory ['minətəri] drohend, bedrohlich.
minc|e [mins] *tr (Fleisch)* (zer)hacken, klein schneiden, zerkleinern; zerlegen, zerteilen; *fig* geziert, affektiert tun *od* ausdrücken *od* sagen; beschönigen, abschwächen; bemänteln; *itr fig* sich zieren, sich affektiert benehmen, affektiert, geziert tun *od* sprechen *od* gehen; Fleisch, Gemüse zerkleinern; *s* Hackfleisch *n*; *not to ~~ matters, o.'s words* kein Blatt vor den Mund nehmen; *~~meat* Pasteten-, Gebäckfüllung *f bes. aus Apfelstückchen, Rosinen, Korinthen, Sukkade, Zucker*; *to make ~~meat of* zerhacken, zerkleinern; *fig* heruntermachen, -reißen, -putzen; keinen guten Faden lassen an; *~~-pie* mit *~~meat* gefüllte Pastete *f*; ~**er** ['-ə], ~**ing machine** Fleischwolf *m*, Hackmaschine *f*; ~**ing** ['-iŋ] *a* Hack-; *fig* geziert, affektiert.
mind [maind] **1.** *s* Gedächtnis *n*, Erinnerung; Aufmerksamkeit, Achtsamkeit, Sorge *f*; Gedanke *m*; Meinung, Ansicht, Anschauung, Überzeugung; geistige Verfassung; Absicht *f*, Wille, Wunsch *m*, Neigung, Lust *f (zu etw)*; (bewußtes) Ich *n*; Intellekt, Verstand *m*, Vernunft *f*, Geist *m*; Seele *f*, Gemüt, Gefühl *n*, Sinn *m*, Herz *n*; Geist, Kopf, Mensch *m*; Denken *n*, Denkweise *f*, Geist *m (e-r Zeit, e-s Volkes)*; *philos* Bewußtsein *n*; *rel* Seelenmesse *f*; **2.** *tr* (be)merken, beachten; sich in acht nehmen vor; achten, aufmerken, -passen auf, s-e Aufmerksamkeit schenken (*s.th.* e-r S); gehorchen (*s.o.* jdm); denken an; sich abgeben, sich befassen mit, sich (be)kümmern um, sorgen für, (be)hüten; etw einzuwenden haben, *fam* etw haben gegen;

3. *itr* aufpassen, bei der Sache sein, sich Mühe geben; gehorchen; etw dagegen haben; widersprechen; es übelnehmen; **4.** *in my ~'s eye* vor meinem geistigen Auge; *time out of ~* vor undenklichen Zeiten; *to my ~* meines Erachtens, nach meiner Meinung; nach meinem Dafürhalten; **5.** *to be in, of two ~s* nicht wissen, was man will; schwanken, zögern; *to be of one ~* ein Herz und e-e Seele sein; *to be of s.o.'s ~* jds Meinung, Ansicht sein; *to be of the same ~* e-r *od* derselben Meinung sein; *to be out of o.'s (right) ~* den Verstand verloren haben; von Sinnen sein; ganz aus dem Häuschen sein (*with* vor); *to bear, to keep in ~* behalten haben, sich (noch) erinnern an; *to bring, to call to s.o.'s ~* jdn erinnern an; *to change o.'s ~* s-e Meinung *od* s-e Absicht ändern; sich (anders) besinnen *od* entschließen; *to give s.o. a piece, a bit of o.'s ~* jdm (gründlich) die Meinung sagen; *to go, to pass out of s.o.'s ~* bei jdm in Vergessenheit geraten; *to have a (good, great) ~ to* große Lust haben zu; *to have half a ~ to s.th.* e-r S nicht abgeneigt sein; halb entschlossen sein zu; *to have in ~* sich erinnern an; denken an; vorhaben; *to have s.th. on o.'s ~* an etw immer denken müssen; sich um etw Gedanken, Sorgen machen; *to keep in ~* denken an; *to keep o.'s ~ on* achten, aufpassen auf; *to keep an open ~* zu keinem Entschluß kommen, sich nicht entscheiden können; *to know o.'s ~* sich (selbst) kennen; *to know o.'s own ~* wissen, was man will; *to make up o.'s ~* zu e-m Entschluß kommen; sich klarwerden (*over* über); sich abfinden (*to* mit); *to put s.o. in ~ of s.th.* jdn an etw erinnern; *to set o.'s ~ on* sein Sinnen und Trachten richten auf; sich etw in den Kopf setzen; *to slip o.'s ~* entfallen; *to speak o.'s ~* offen s-e Meinung sagen; *to take o.'s ~ off* nicht mehr denken an, sich nicht mehr kümmern um; *to tell s.o. o.'s ~* jdm s-e Meinung sagen; *to ~ o.'s P's and Q's* sich in acht nehmen, vorsichtig sein; **6.** *~! ~ out!* gib acht! paß auf! *~ (you)* wohlgemerkt; *~ the dog!* Warnung vor dem Hund! *~ the step!* Achtung, Stufe! *~ your own business!* kümmern Sie sich um Ihre (eigenen) Sachen, *fam* um Ihren Dreck! *never ~!* macht nichts! schon gut! *I don't ~* ich habe nichts dagegen; meinetwegen! *I don't ~ the rain* der Regen macht mir nichts aus; *do you ~ if I smoke, my smoking?* stört es Sie, macht es Ihnen (et)was aus, wenn ich rauche? *what's on your ~* was haben Sie auf dem Herzen? *would you ~ opening the window?* würden Sie bitte, würden Sie so freundlich sein und das Fenster öffnen? *would you ~ holding your tongue!* willst du wohl still sein! *I shouldn't ~ a glass of beer now* ich hätte jetzt Lust auf ein Glas Bier; *he doesn't know his own ~* er weiß selbst nicht, was er will; *out of sight, out of ~ (prov)* aus den Augen, aus dem Sinn; **7.** *absence, presence of ~* Geistesabwesenheit, -gegenwart *f*; *frame, state of ~* Geistesverfassung *f*; *meeting of ~s* Übereinkunft *f*; **~ed** ['-id] *a* gesonnen, gewillt, geneigt (*to do* zu tun); *in Zssgen* gesinnt, gestimmt; -mütig, -herzig; -freudig, -bewußt; *air-~~* flugbegeistert; **~ful** ['-ful] eingedenk, bewußt (*of* gen); *to be ~~ of* im Auge haben, beachten, achten auf; **~less** ['-lis] unverständig, unvernünftig, dumm; verständnis-, rücksichtslos; unbekümmert (*of* um); nicht achtend (*of* gen); **~ reader** Gedankenleser *m*; **~ reading** Gedankenlesen *n*.

mine [main] **1.** *prn* der, die, das mei-n(ig)e; *~ is better* meine(r, s) ist besser; *this is ~* das gehört mir; *a friend of ~* e-r meiner Freunde, ein Freund von mir; *attr obs poet* mein; **2.** *s* Bergwerk *n*, *(Kohlen-)* Grube, Zeche *f*; *(Erz-, Kohlen-)* Lager, Vorkommen *n*; *fig* Quelle, Fundgrube (*of* an); *mil mar* Mine *f*; *itr* Bergbau treiben; graben (*for* nach); *mil* Stollen treiben; Minen legen; *fig* wühlen; *tr (Bodenschätze)* abbauen, schürfen; *(Kohle)* fördern; Stollen treiben in; *mil* unterminieren *a. fig*; verminen; (zu) sprengen (suchen), in die Luft jagen; *to run into a ~* auf e-e Mine laufen; *board of ~s* Bergamt *n*; *~ of information* Informationsquelle *f*; **~-barrier, -blockade** Minensperre *f*; **~ car** Förderwagen, Hund *m*; **~-chamber** Sprengkammer *f*; **~-clearance** Minenräumen *n*; **~-crater** Sprengtrichter *m*; **~d** [-d] *a* vermint; *~~ area = ~-field*; **~-detector** Minensuchgerät *n*; **~-field** Minenfeld *n*; **~ fire** Grubenbrand *m*; **~-gallery** Minengang *m*; **~ gas** Grubengas *n*; **~-layer** Minenleger *m*; **~r** ['-ə] Bergmann, -arbeiter, Kumpel; *mar* Minenleger *m*, -suchboot *n*; *~~'s association* Knappschaft *f*; *~~'s lamp* Grubenlampe *f*; *~~'s lung* Kohlen(staub)-lunge *f*; **~-shaft** Minenschacht *m*; **~ surveyor** Markscheider *m*; **~-sweeper** (Minen-)Räumboot *n*; **~-thrower** Minenwerfer *m*.

mineral ['minərəl] *s* Mineral *n*; *pl* Mineralwasser *n*; *a* mineralisch, Mineral-; **~ coal** Steinkohle *f*; **~ize** [-aiz] *tr (Metall)* vererzen; *(organischen Überrest)* versteinern; *(Wasser)* Mineralien zusetzen (*s.th.* e-r S); **~ogical** [minərə'lɔdʒikəl] mineralogisch; **~ogist** [minə'rælədʒist] Mineraloge *m*; **~ogy** [-'rælədʒi] Mineralogie, Gesteinskunde *f*; **~ oil, ore** Mineralöl *n*, -erz *n*; **~ pitch** Naturasphalt *m*; **~ spring** Mineralquelle *f*; **~ substance** anorganische Materie *f*; **~ tar** Kohlenteer *m*; **~ water** Mineralwasser *n*.

minever, miniver ['minivə] Hermelin *m (Pelz)*.

mingle ['miŋgl] *tr* (ver)mischen, mengen; *itr* sich (ver)mischen, sich (ver)mengen, verschmelzen; *fig* sich mischen (*in* in; *among, with* unter).

mingy ['mindʒi] *fam* knickerig.

miniature ['minjətʃə] Miniatur(bild, -gemälde *n*); Miniaturmalerei *f*; stark verkleinerte(s) Abbild, Modell *n*; *attr* Miniatur-, Klein-; *in ~* in Miniatur; im kleinen, in kleinem Maßstab; **~ camera** Kleinbildkamera *f*; **~ grand** *mus* Stutzflügel *m*; **~ railway** Spielzeug-, Modelleisenbahn *f*; **~-rifle** Kleinkalibergewehr *n*; **~-rifle shooting** Kleinkaliberschießen *n*.

mini|cab ['minikæb] Kleintaxi *n*; **~car** *mot* Kleinwagen *m*; **~fy** ['-fai] *tr* verkleinern; *fig* herabsetzen.

minikin ['minikin] *s fig* Knirps *m*; Püppchen, kleine(s) Ding *n (a. Sache)*; kleine Stecknadel *f*; *a* winzig; *fig* geziert, affektiert.

minim ['minim] *mus* halbe Note *f*; Grundstrich *m*; 1/60 Drachme *f (0,59 ccm)*; *(etwa ein)* Tropfen *m*; winzige Menge *f*; **~al** ['-əl] minimal, kleinst; **~ize** ['minimaiz] *tr* auf ein Minimum herabsetzen; *fig* verkleinern, herabsetzen, geringschätzen; **~um** ['-əm] *pl a.* -*a* ['-ə] *s* Minimum *n*, kleinste Menge *f*, kleinste(s) Maß *n*, Kleinstwert, Mindestbetrag *m*; *a* minimal; Minimal-, Mindest-; *to reduce to a ~~* auf ein Minimum reduzieren; *~~ of existence* Existenzminimum *n*; *~~ amount* Mindestbetrag *m*; *~~ number* Mindestzahl *f*; *~~ penalty* Mindeststrafe *f*; *~~ price* Mindestpreis *m*; *~~ value* Mindestwert *m*; *~~ wage* Mindestlohn *m*; *~~ weight* Mindestgewicht *n*.

mining ['mainiŋ] *s* Bergbau *m*; *mil* Minenlegen *n*; *attr* Bergbau-, Montan-; *open-cast ~* Tagebau *m*; **~ academy** Bergakademie *f*; **~ area** Grubenrevier *n*; **~ association** Knappschaft *f*; **~ board, office** Bergamt *n*; **~ disaster** Grubenunglück *n*; **~ district** Bergbaugebiet *n*; **~ engineer** Bergingenieur *m*; **~ industry** Montanindustrie *f*; **~ lamp** Grubenlampe *f*; **~ share** Kux *m*.

minion ['minjən] Günstling, Liebling; Schmeichler, Speichellecker *m*; *typ* Kolonel, Mignon *f (Schriftgrad)*.

minister ['ministər] *s* Minister; Gesandte(r); *(bes. nichtanglikanischer u. nichtkatholischer)* Geistliche(r), Pastor; *fig* Gehilfe, (Helfers-)Helfer, Handlanger *m*; *itr* dienen (*to s.o.* jdm); arbeiten (*to s.o.* für jdn); helfen, Hilfe leisten (*to s.o.* jdm), unterstützen; betreuen; *(Kranken)* pflegen (*to s.o.* jdn); mitwirken (*to* an); beitragen (*to* zu); *M~ of Commerce* Handelsminister *m*; *M~ of Defence* Verteidigungsminister *m*; *M~ of Finance* Finanzminister *m*; *~ plenipotentiary* Bevollmächtigte(r) *m*; *M~ without portfolio* Minister *m* ohne Geschäftsbereich; *M~ of State* Staatsminister *m*; **~ial** [minis'tiəriəl] dienend; ausführend, Ausführungs-; vollziehend, Vollzugs-; ministeriell, Regierungs-; amtlich; geistlich; *~~ crisis* Regierungskrise *f*; *~~ decree, decision* Kabinettsbeschluß *m*; **~ialist** [-'tiəriəlist] Regierungsanhänger *m*.

ministr|ant ['ministrənt] *a* dienend, helfend, unterstützend; *s* Diener, Gehilfe; *rel* Ministrant *m*; **~ation** [minis'treiʃən] Dienst *m* (*to* an) *a. rel*; Hilfe, Unterstützung *f*; **~y** ['ministri] Dienst *m*; Unterstützung *f*; geistliche(s), Priester-, kirchliche(s) Amt *n*; Geistlichkeit, Priesterschaft *f*; *Br* Ministerium *n*; *Br* Regierung *f*, Kabinett *n*; *Br* Amt *n* e-s Gesandten; *to enter the ~~* Geistlicher werden; *M~~ of Agriculture* Landwirtschaftsministerium *n*; *M~~ of Commerce* Handelsministerium *n*; *M~~ of Education* Erziehungs-, Unterrichtsministerium *n*; *M~~ of Finance* Finanzministerium *n*; *M~~ of Foreign, of Home Affairs* Außen-, Innenministerium *n*; *M~~ of Health* Gesundheitsministerium *n*; *M~~ of Labo(u)r* Arbeitsministerium *n*; *M~~ of Transport* Verkehrsministerium *n*.

minitape machine ['miniteip mə'ʃi:n] Bandaufnahmegerät *n*.

minium ['miniəm] Mennige *f*; Zinnober *m*.

miniver *s. minever*.

mink [miŋk] *zoo* Nerz *m (a. Pelz)*.

minnow ['minou] *zoo* Elritze, Pfrille *f*.

minor ['mainə] *a* kleiner, gering(fügig)er; *(Zahl, Betrag)* niedriger, weniger bedeutend; Unter-, Neben-; minderjährig, unmündig; *(hinter Familiennamen)* der Jüngere; *Am (Studienfach)* Neben-; *mus (nachgestellt)* Moll; *(Intervall)* klein; *s* Minderjährige(r), Unmündige(r) *m*; *Am (Univ.) (~ subject)* Nebenfach *n*; *(Logik)* Untersatz, -begriff *m*; *mus* Moll *n*; *itr Am (Univ.)* als Nebenfach wählen (*in s.th.* etw); *in a ~ key (fig)*

gedrückt, niedergeschlagen; *to be a* ~ minderjährig sein; **~ity** [mai'nɔriti, mi-] Minderheit; Minderjährigkeit, Unmündigkeit *f*; *to be in a* ~~ in der Minderheit sein; **~ league** *sport* Unterliga *f*; **~ matter** Nebensache *f*; **~ mode** Molltonart *f*; **~ point** Nebensache *f*; **~ premise** *(Logik)* Untersatz *m*.
minster ['minstə] Klosterkirche *f*; Münster *n*, Dom *m*, Kathedrale *f*.
minstrel ['minstrəl] *hist* (fahrender) Sänger, Spielmann, Minnesänger; *poet* Sänger, Dichter *m*; **~sy** ['-si] Minnesang *m*; Sängergruppe, -truppe; Lieder-, Balladensammlung *f*.
mint [mint] **1.** *s* Münz(stätt)e; *fig* unerschöpfliche Quelle, Fundgrube; *fam* gewaltige Menge *od* Masse *f*; *a* neu(wertig), tadellos, einwandfrei; *tr (Geld)* prägen, münzen, schlagen; *fig* erfinden; *(Wort)* prägen; *in* ~ *condition (Buch, Briefmarke)* in tadellosem Zustand; *a* ~ *of money* ein Haufen Geld; **~age** ['-idʒ] Münzen *n*; (Aus-)Prägung; Münzgebühr; *fig* Erfindung *f*; **~ed** ['-id] *a* gemünzt; **2.** *bot* Minze *f*; **~-sauce** Pfefferminzsoße *f*; **~-water** Pfefferminzlikör *m*.
minuet [minju'et] Menuett *n (Tanz)*.
minus ['mainəs] *prp* weniger, minus; *fam* mit ... weniger, ohne; *a* Minus-; negativ; *(Schule)* minus; *s (~ sign)* Minuszeichen; Minus *n*, Fehlbetrag, Verlust *m*; **~ quantity** *math* negative Größe *f*; *fam* völlig unbedeutende(r) Mensch *m*; **~cule** [mi'nʌskju:l, 'minə-] Minuskel *f (Schriftart)*; Kleinbuchstabe *m*.
minute ['minit] *s* Minute *f*; Augenblick; Entwurf *m*, Konzept *n*; Note, Denkschrift *f*; *pl* Protokoll *n*, Niederschrift *f*; *tr* entwerfen, aufsetzen; zu Protokoll nehmen, protokollieren, aufzeichnen; *a* [mai'njut] sehr klein, winzig; *fig* unbedeutend, geringfügig; genau, exakt, sorgfältig; *the* ~ *(that)* in dem Augenblick, als; *to the* ~ *(bei e-r Zeitangabe)* genau, pünktlich; *up to the* ~ nach der neuesten Mode; *to keep the* ~*s* das Protokoll führen; *to make a* ~ *of* schriftlich festhalten *od* fixieren; **~-book** Protokoll-, Geschäfts-, Urkundenbuch *n*; **~-hand** Minutenzeiger *m*; **~ly** ['minitli] *a* Minuten-; laufend; *adv* jede Minute, dauernd; [mai'nju:tli] ganz genau, in allen Einzelheiten; **~ness** [mai'nju:tnis] Kleinheit, Winzigkeit; Genauigkeit, Exaktheit, Sorgfalt *f*; **minutiae** [mai'nju:ʃii:] *pl* Einzelheiten *f pl*.
minx [miŋks] freche(s) Ding *n*, Range *f*.
miocene ['maiəsi:n] *geol* Miozän *n*.
mirac|le ['mirəkl] Wunder(tat *f*) *a. fam fig*; große(s) Ereignis; Muster (-beispiel); *(~ play) hist theat* Mirakelspiel *n*; *to a* ~~ wunderbar *adv*; *to work* ~~*s* Wunder wirken; **~~-man** Wundertäter, *fam* -mann *m*; **~ulous** [mi'rækjuləs] wunderbar, übernatürlich; *(übertreibend)* wunderbar, großartig.
mirage ['mirɑ:ʒ, -'-] Luftspiegelung, Fata Morgana; *fig* Illusion *f*.
mir|e ['maiə] *s* Sumpf; Schlamm, Dreck, Schmutz *m*; *fig* Verlegenheit *f*; *tr* in den Sumpf laufen lassen *od* fahren; mit Dreck bespritzen, beschmutzen, besudeln; *fig* in die Patsche bringen; *itr* im Sumpf, Dreck versinken *od* stecken; *to be in the* ~~ *(fig)* in der Patsche, in der Tinte sitzen; *to drag s.o. through the* ~~ *(fig)* jdn durch den Dreck ziehen; **~y** ['-ri] sumpfig, schlammig, schmutzig.
mirk(y) *s. murk(y)*.
mirror ['mirə] *s* Spiegel *m a. fig*; *fig* Spiegel-, Abbild *n*; *tr* (wider)spiegeln *a. fig*; **~ finish** Hochglanz *m*; **~ image, writing** Spiegelbild *n*, -schrift *f*.
mirth [mə:θ] Freude *f*, Frohsinn *m*, Fröhlichkeit, Heiterkeit *f*; **~ful** ['-ful] froh, fröhlich, heiter; freudig; **~fulness** ['-fulnis] Fröhlichkeit; Freudigkeit *f*; **~less** ['-lis] freudlos, trüb(e).
mis- [mis] *in Zssgen* miß-, Miß-; falsch, fälschlich, schlecht, übel.
misadventure ['misəd'ventʃə] Mißgeschick *n*, unglückliche(r) Zufall *m*, Unglück(sfall *m*) *n*.
misalliance ['misə'laiəns] Mißheirat *f*.
misanthrop|e ['mizənθroup], **~ist** [mi'zænθrəpist] Menschenfeind; Einsiedler; mißtrauische(r) Mensch *m*; **~ic(al)** [mizən'θrɔpik(əl)] menschenfeindlich, -scheu; **~y** [mi'zænθrəpi] Menschenhaß *m*, -scheu *f*.
misappl|ication ['misæpli'keiʃən] falsche Anwendung *f*, Mißbrauch *m*; schlechte Verwendung, Verschwendung *f*; **~y** ['misə'plai] *tr* falsch, schlecht anwenden, verschwenden; mißbrauchen.
misapprehen|d ['misæpri'hend] *tr* mißverstehen; **~sion** [-'henʃən] Mißverständnis *n*.
misappropriat|e ['misə'prouprieit] *tr* mißbrauchen, widerrechtlich verwenden; sich widerrechtlich aneignen, veruntreuen, unterschlagen; **~ion** ['misəproupri'eiʃən] Mißbrauch *m*, widerrechtliche Verwendung *od* Aneignung, Veruntreuung, Unterschlagung *f*.
misbecom|e ['misbi'kʌm] *irr -became, -become tr* sich nicht schicken *od* passen *od lit* geziemen für; **~ing** ['-iŋ] unschicklich, unpassend.
misbegot(ten) ['misbi'gɔt(n)] *a* unehelich; *fig* elend, erbärmlich.
misbehav|e ['misbi'heiv] *itr u. to* ~ *o.s.* sich schlecht, ungebührlich benehmen *od* betragen *od* aufführen, *fam* sich vorbeibenehmen; **~iour** [-jə] schlechte(s) Benehmen *od* Betragen *n*.
misbelie|f ['misbi'li:f] Irrglaube *m*; **~ver** ['-'li:və] Irrgläubige(r) *m*.
miscalculat|e ['mis'kælkjuleit] *tr* falsch (be)rechnen; *itr* sich verrechnen; sich irren; **~ion** ['-kælkju'leiʃən] Rechenfehler *m*; falsche (Be-)Rechnung *f*; Irrtum *m*.
miscall ['mis'kɔ:l] *tr* mit e-m falschen Namen rufen *od* nennen.
miscarr|iage [mis'kæridʒ] Versehen *n*, Fehler, Fehl-, Mißgriff *m*, Mißlingen *n*; *(Post)* Fehlleitung *f*; Fehlgeburt *f*; ~~ *of justice* Justizirrtum *m*; **~y** [-i] *itr* fehlschlagen, mißlingen; *(Post)* verlorengehen; *med* e-e Fehlgeburt haben.
miscasting [mis'kɑ:stiŋ] *theat* falsche *od* schlechte (Rollen-)Besetzung *f*.
miscegenation [misidʒi'neiʃən] Rassenmischung *f*.
miscellan|ea [misi'leiniə] = **~y** *(oft pl)*; **~eous** [-jəs] ge-, vermischt; mannigfaltig; vielseitig; **~eousness** [-jəsnis] Gemischtheit; Mannigfaltigkeit; Vielseitigkeit *f*; **~y** [mi'seləni, *Am* 'misəleini] Gemisch *n*; Sammlung *f*; *oft pl* Sammelband *m*, vermischte Schriften *f pl*.
mischance [mis'tʃɑ:ns] Mißgeschick, Unglück(sfall *m*) *n*, Unfall *m*; *by* ~ unglücklicherweise.
mischie|f ['mistʃif] Unheil *n*, Schaden, Nachteil *m*; Gefahr; Bosheit, Boshaftigkeit, Ungezogenheit *f*, Übermut; Lausejunge, Lausbub, Schelm, Frechdachs *m*, Range *f*; böse(r), üble(r) Streich *m*, Teufelei, Frechheit *f*; *up to* ~~ zu bösen Streichen aufgelegt; *where the* ~~? wo zum Teufel? *to do s.o. a* ~~ *(fam)* jdm schaden; jdn verletzen; *to make* ~~ böses Blut machen, Unfrieden stiften (*between* zwischen); *to play the* ~~ *with s.o.* jdm Schaden zufügen; *with s.th.* etw in Unordnung bringen; *to work* ~~ Unheil stiften *od* anrichten; *he's up to* ~~ er führt Böses im Schild; *the* ~~ *of it is that* das dumme an der Sache ist, daß; **~~-maker** Unruhestifter *m*; **~~-making** Unruhestiftung *f*; **~vous** ['-tʃivəs] unheilvoll, schädlich, nachteilig; boshaft, frech, mutwillig.
miscible ['misibl] mischbar.
misconce|ive ['miskən'si:v] *tr* falsch auffassen, mißverstehen, mißdeuten; **~ption** ['-'sepʃən] falsche Auffassung, falsche Deutung *f*, Mißverständnis *n*.
misconduct ['miskən'dʌkt] *tr (Geschäft)* schlecht führen, schlecht verwalten; *to* ~ *o.s.* sich schlecht benehmen *od* aufführen; Ehebruch begehen; *s* [-'kɔndəkt] mangelhafte, schlechte Geschäfts-, Amtsführung *f*; schlechte(s) Benehmen *n*; Ehebruch *m*.
misconstru|ction ['miskəns'trʌkʃən] falsche Über-, Auslegung, Mißdeutung *f*; **~e** ['-'stru:] *tr* falsch über-, auslegen, mißdeuten.
miscount ['mis'kaunt] *tr* falsch (be-)rechnen *od* zählen; *itr* sich verrechnen, sich verzählen; *s* Rechenfehler *m*; falsche Zählung *f*.
miscrean|cy ['miskriənsi] Schurkenhaftigkeit *f*; **~t** ['-t] *a* schurkenhaft, gemein, abscheulich, häßlich; *s* Schurke, Lump, gemeine(r) Verbrecher *m*.
miscreated ['miskri'eitid] *a* mißgestaltet; *pej* ungeheuerlich.
misdate ['mis'deit] *tr* falsch datieren; *s* falsche(s) Datum *n*.
misdeal ['mis'di:l] *irr -dealt, -dealt tr (Karten)* falsch geben; *itr* sich vergeben; *s* falsche(s) Geben *n*.
misdeed ['mis'di:d] Missetat *f*, Verbrechen *n*.
misdemean [misdi'mi:n] *(selten) itr u. to* ~ *o.s.* sich schlecht benehmen *od* aufführen; **~ant** [-ənt] Delinquent *m*; **~o(u)r** [-ə] Übertretung *f*, Vergehen *n*.
misdirect ['misdi'rekt] *tr* schlecht *od* falsch anbringen, verfehlen; *(Brief)* falsch adressieren; falsch unterrichten, irreleiten, -führen; **~ion** ['-'rekʃən] falsche Adresse; Irreführung *f*.
misdo|er ['mis'du:ə] Übel-, Missetäter *m*; **~ing** ['-iŋ] *meist pl* Übel-, Missetat *f*.
mise [mi:z, maiz] *hist* Vertrag *m*; *jur* Kosten *pl*; *sport* Einsatz *m*; ~ *en scène* ['mizɑ̃:n'sein] *theat* Inszenierung *f*; *fig* Hintergrund *m (e-s Ereignisses)*.
misemploy ['misim'plɔi] *tr* schlecht, falsch anwenden, mißbrauchen; **~ment** ['-mənt] schlechte, falsche Anwendung *f*, Mißbrauch *m*.
miser ['maizə] Geizhals, Knicker, Filz *m*; **~able** ['mizərəbl] *a* elend (*from* vor); unglücklich; erbärmlich, schauderhaft, (hunds)miserabel; jämmerlich; armselig; *s* elende(r) Mensch *m*; *to make life* ~~ *for s.o.* jdm das Leben sauer machen; **~liness** ['maizəlinis] Geiz *m*; **~ly** ['maizəli] geizig, knickerig, filzig; **~y** ['mizəri] Elend *n*; (große) Not *f*, Jammer; *fam* Jammerlappen *m*.
misfeasance [mis'fi:zəns] *jur* Übertretung, -schreitung *f*; Mißbrauch *m*.
misfire ['mis'faiə] *itr (Feuerwaffe)* versagen, nicht losgehen; wirkungslos sein; *mot* fehlzünden; *s mil* Versager *m*; *mot* Fehlzündung *f*.
misfit ['misfit] *itr tr* nicht passen (zu); zu groß, zu klein sein (für); *s (Kleidung)* schlechte(r) Sitz *m*; schlecht sitzende(s) Kleidungsstück; nicht passende(s) Stück *n*; Versager *m*.

misfortune [mis'fɔ:tʃən] Mißgeschick; Unglück *n*; unglückliche(r) Zufall *m*.
misgiv|e [mis'giv] *irr -gave, -given tr*: *my heart misgave me* ich ahnte Böses *od* Schlimmes; **~ing** [mis'giviŋ] Befürchtung; schlimme, böse Ahnung *f*.
misgovern ['mis'gʌvən] *tr* schlecht regieren *od* verwalten *od* leiten; **~ment** ['-mənt] schlechte Regierung *od* Verwaltung; Mißwirtschaft *f*.
misguid|ance ['mis'gaidəns] Irreführung; Verleitung, Verführung *f*; **~e** ['-'gaid] *tr* irreführen, fehlleiten; verleiten, verführen; **~ed** ['-id] *a* irregeführt; verleitet, verführt; verfehlt.
mishandle ['mis'hændl] *tr* schlecht, ungeschickt umgehen mit; falsch handhaben; mißhandeln.
mishap ['mishæp, -'hæp] Mißgeschick *n*, Unglücks-, Unfall *m*; *mot* Panne *f*.
mishear ['mis'hiə] *irr -heard, -heard tr* schlecht verstehen; *itr* sich verhören.
mishmash ['miʃmæʃ] Mischmasch *m*, Durcheinander *n*.
misinform ['misin'fɔ:m] *tr* falsch informieren; *itr* falsch berichten; **~ation** ['-fə'meiʃən] falsche, irreführende Auskunft *f*; falsche(r) Bericht *m*.
misinterpret ['misin'tə:prit] *tr* falsch auslegen *od* deuten; mißdeuten, -verstehen; **~ation** ['-tə:pri'teiʃən] falsche Auslegung, Mißdeutung *f*.
misjoin ['mis'dʒɔin] *tr jur* in unpassender Weise mitea. verbinden; **~der** [-də] *jur* unzulässige Klagehäufung *f*.
misjudg|e ['mis'dʒʌdʒ] *itr (tr)* falsch *od* ungerecht (be)urteilen; **~(e)ment** ['-mənt] Fehlurteil *n*.
mislay [mis'lei] *tr irr -laid, -laid tr* verlegen.
mislead [mis'li:d] *irr -led, -led* e-n falschen Weg führen; *fig* irreführen; verführen, verleiten (*into doing s.th.* etw zu tun); **~ing** [-iŋ] irreführend.
mismanage ['mis'mænidʒ] *tr* schlecht verwalten; *itr* schlecht wirtschaften; **~ment** ['-mənt] schlechte Verwaltung; Mißwirtschaft *f*.
misname ['mis'neim] *tr* mit e-m falschen Namen rufen; falsch benennen.
misnomer ['mis'noumə] falsche Benennung; falsche Bezeichnung *f*, falsche(r) Name *m*; *sport* Fehlbesetzung *f*.
miso|gamist [mi'sɔgəmist] ehescheue(r) Mensch *m*; **~gamy** [-gəmi] Ehescheu *f*; **~gynist** [mi-, mai-'sɔdʒinist] Weiberfeind *m*; **~gyny** [-dʒini] Weiberfeindschaft *f*.
misplace ['mis'pleis] *tr* an e-n falschen Platz legen; an die falsche Stelle setzen; *(Vertrauen, Zuneigung)* übel anbringen; *fam* verlegen.
misplay [mis'plei] *itr Am sport* falsch, schlecht spielen; *s* falsche(s), schlechte(s) Spiel *n*.
misprint ['mis'print] *s* Druckfehler *m*; *tr* ['-'-] verdrucken.
misprision [mis'priʒ(ə)n] *jur* (Pflicht-) Versäumnis *n*; pflichtwidrige Unterlassung *f* e-r Anzeige.
misprize [mis'praiz] *tr* verachten.
mispro|nounce ['misprə'nauns] *tr itr* falsch aussprechen; **~nunciation** ['misprənʌnsi'eiʃən] falsche Aussprache *f*.
misquot|ation ['miskwou'teiʃən] falsche(s) Zitat *n*; **~e** ['-'kwout] *tr* falsch zitieren *od* anführen.
misread ['mis'ri:d] *irr -read, -read* [-'red] *tr* falsch lesen; mißverstehen, -deuten.
misrepresent ['misrepri'zent] *tr* falsch darstellen, e-e falsche Vorstellung geben von; entstellen; **~ation** ['-zen'teiʃən] falsche Darstellung, Verdrehung *f* der Tatsachen; falsche(r) Bericht *m*, unrichtige Angaben *f pl*; *wilful ~~* Betrug *m*.
misrule ['mis'ru:l] *tr* schlecht regieren; *s* schlechte Regierung *f*; ungeordnete Verhältnisse *n pl*; Aufruhr *m*.
miss [mis] **1.** *tr (Ziel)* verfehlen; *(Gelegenheit, Zug)* verpassen; versäumen; übersehen, -hören; nicht verstehen, *fam* nicht mitkriegen; vermeiden; ausweichen, aus dem Wege gehen (*s.th.* e-r S); vermissen, (sehr) entbehren, nicht verschmerzen können; *itr* danebenschießen; das Ziel verfehlen, fehlgehen; keinen Erfolg haben, erfolg-, ergebnislos sein, mißglücken; *s* Fehlschuß, -schlag, *fam* Versager; Verlust *m*; *fam* Fehlgeburt *f*; *to ~ out* auslassen, übergehen; *on (Am)* verfehlen, verpassen; *to be ~ing* vermißt werden; fehlen; *to ~ doing s.th.* beinahe etw tun; *to ~ fire (Feuerwaffe)* versagen, nicht losgehen; *to ~ o.'s footing, o.'s step* ausgleiten, -rutschen; *to ~ o.'s mark* keinen Erfolg haben; nicht genügen, nicht gut genug sein; *to give it a ~* etw auslassen, vermeiden; *a ~ is as good as a mile* immerhin hat es noch gelangt; dicht daneben ist auch vorbei; *a lucky ~* glückliche(s) Entkommen *n*; *you ~ed the point* Sie haben das Wesentliche nicht begriffen; **2.** (junges) Mädchen, *bes. pej* junge(s) Ding, Mädel *n*; *M~ (in d. Anrede)* Fräulein *n*.
missal ['misəl] *rel* Meßbuch, Missale *n*; **~ sacrifice** Meßopfer *n*.
missel ['misəl] *(~-bird, -thrush) orn* Misteldrossel *f*.
misshapen ['mis'ʃeipən] mißgestalt(et), ungestalt, deformiert.
missile ['misail, *Am* 'misl] *s* (Wurf-)Geschoß *n*; Rakete *f*; *guided ~* ferngesteuerte Rakete *f*.
missing ['misiŋ] fehlend, nicht vorhanden, nicht da; verloren(gegangen); *mil (~ in action)* vermißt; *s*: *the ~* die Vermißten *m pl*; **~ link** fehlende(s) Zwischenglied *n*.
mission ['miʃən] Sendung, Mission *f*, Auftrag; Beruf *m*, (Lebens-)Aufgabe; *rel* Missionsgesellschaft *f*, -zentrum *n*, Gruppe *f* von Missionaren; Sendung; *pol* Gesandtschaft, Delegation, Vertretung *f*; *mil bes. aero* (Kampf-)Auftrag, (taktischer) Einsatz *m*; *pl* (Heiden-) Mission *f*; *on a secret ~* in geheimem Auftrag; *Foreign M~s, Home M~s* Äußere, Innere Mission *f*; *military ~* Militärmission *f*; *special ~* Sonderauftrag *m*; *trade ~* Handelsmission *f*; **~ary** ['-ʃnəri] *a* missionarisch; *s* Missionar; *fig* Bote *m*.
missis, missus ['misiz] *fam dial* Frau (des Hauses); bessere Hälfte *f*.
missive ['misiv] Sendschreiben *n*, Botschaft *f*.
misspell ['mis'spel] *a. irr -spelt, -spelt tr itr* falsch buchstabieren *od* schreiben; **~ing** ['-iŋ] falsche Schreibung *f*, Schreibfehler *m*.
misspend ['mis'spend] *irr -spent, -spent tr (Geld)* schlecht anwenden; verschwenden, vergeuden.
misstate ['mis'steit] *tr* falsch, unrichtig angeben; **~ment** ['-mənt] falsche, unrichtige Angabe; falsche, schiefe Darstellung *f*.
missy ['misi] *fam* Fräuleinchen *n*.
mist [mist] *s* (feiner) Nebel; Dunst *m*; *(Staub-, Rauch-)*Wolke *f*; Schleier (vor den Augen); *fig* Nebel, Schleier *m*; *(Glas)* Trübung *f*, Beschlag *m*; *tr* vernebeln; *fig* umnebeln, verdunkeln, verhüllen; *itr* nieseln; *fig* umnebelt, dunkel, verhüllt sein; *to be in a ~* ganz irre sein; **~iness** ['-inis] Nebel, Dunst *m*; *fig* Verschwommenheit; Undeutlichkeit *f*; **~y** ['-i] neblig; *fig* verschwommen; trüb(e); *fig* undeutlich, unklar.
mistak|able [mis'teikəbl] mißverständlich, nicht eindeutig, unklar; **~e** [mis'teik] *irr -took, -taken tr* mißverstehen, verkennen; irrtümlich, versehentlich, fälschlich halten (*for* für); verwechseln (*for* mit); sich irren in; *itr* sich versehen, sich irren, e-n Fehler machen; *s* Fehler *m*, Versehen *n*; Mißgriff; Irrtum *m*, Mißverständnis *n*; *by ~~* irrtümlich, versehentlich, aus Versehen; *to make a ~* e-n Fehler machen, sich versehen, sich irren; *and no ~! (fam)* da kannst du Gift drauf nehmen! *there's no ~ing* Irrtum ausgeschlossen! *spelling ~~* Rechtschreibungs-, orthographische(r) Fehler *m*; **~en** [-ən] *a* irrig, irrtümlich, versehentlich; falsch; *to be ~~* im Irrtum sein, sich irren; *about, in s.th.* sich über, in e-r S täuschen; *~~ idea* falsche Vorstellung *f*; *~~ identity* (Personen-)Verwechs(e)lung *f*; *~~ policy* falsche Politik *f*.
mister ['mistə] Herr *m (Mr)*; *(als Anrede) fam* Herr! Chef! Meister!
mistimed ['mis'taimd] *a* unzeitig, zur Unzeit; unpassend.
mistletoe ['misltou] *bot* Mistel *f*.
mistranslat|e ['mistræns'leit] *tr* falsch übersetzen; **~ion** ['-'leiʃən] falsche Übersetzung *f*; Übersetzungsfehler *m*.
mistress ['mistris] Herrin *a. fig*; Hausherrin; Lehrerin; Kennerin; Mätresse, Geliebte *f*; *M~ stets abgekürzt*: *Mrs* ['misiz] *(vor dem Familiennamen)* Frau ...; *music-~* Musiklehrerin *f*.
mistrial ['mis'traiəl] *jur* fehlerhafte(s) (Prozeß-)Verfahren *n*; Justizirrtum *m*.
mistrust ['mis'trʌst] *tr* mißtrauen (*s.o., s.th.* jdm, e-r S); kein Vertrauen haben (*s.o.* zu jdm); zweifeln (*s.th.* an e-r S); *itr* kein Vertrauen haben; *s* Mißtrauen *n*, Argwohn *m* (*of* gegen); **~ful** ['-ful] mißtrauisch (*of* gegen).
misunderstand ['misʌndə'stænd] *irr -understood, -understood tr* falsch, mißverstehen; **~ing** ['-iŋ] Mißverständnis *n*; Uneinigkeit *f*, Streit *m* (*over* über).
misus|age ['mis'ju:sidʒ] falsche Anwendung *f*, falsche(r) Gebrauch *m*; schlechte Behandlung *f*; **~use** ['-'ju:z] *tr* falsch anwenden *od* gebrauchen; mißbrauchen; schlecht behandeln; *s* ['-'ju:s] Mißbrauch; falsche(r) Gebrauch *m*.
mite [mait] **1.** Heller *m*, Scherflein *a. fig*; *fig* kleine(s) bißchen *n*; Knirps *m*; **2.** *zoo* Milbe *f*.
mitigat|e ['mitigeit] *tr* mildern, erleichtern, lindern; abschwächen, mäßigen; *(Zorn)* besänftigen; **~ion** [mit'igeiʃən] Milderung, Erleichterung, Linderung; Abschwächung, Mäßigung *f*; *reason for ~~ (jur)* Milderungsgrund *m*; *~~ of penalty* Strafmilderung *f*; *in ~~ of penalty* strafmildernd *adv*; **~ive** ['mitigeitiv], **~ory** ['-geitəri, *Am* '-gətɔri] mildernd, mäßigend.
mitre, *Am* miter ['maitə] *s* Mitra, Inful, Bischofsmütze; Bischofswürde *f*, -amt; Bistum *n*; Kaminaufsatz *m*; *(~ joint) tech* Gehrung *f*; *tr rel* infulieren; *tech* auf Gehrung verbinden; **~-block, -box** Gehrlade *f*; **~-square** Gehrdreieck *n*; **~-wheel** Kegelrad *n*.
mitt|(en) ['mit(n)] Fausthandschuh; lange(r) Handschuh *m* ohne Finger; *(~) Am* Baseballhandschuh *m*; *meist pl sl* Boxhandschuhe *m pl*; *Am sl* Flosse, Hand *f*; *to get, to give the ~~ (fig)* e-n Korb bekommen, geben

(*to s.o.* jdm); *to hand s.o. the frozen* ~~ jdm die kalte Schulter zeigen.
mittimus ['mitiməs] *jur* richterliche(r) Befehl *m* zur Aufnahme e-s Häftlings; *fam* Laufpaß *m*, Entlassung *f*; *to get o.'s* ~ s-n Laufpaß erhalten, auf die Straße gesetzt werden.
mix [miks] *tr* (ver)mischen, (ver)mengen (*with* mit); zs.rühren; mixen; *(Kuchen)* anrühren; (mitea.) verbinden, kombinieren; *(Menschen)* zs.bringen; *(Tiere)* kreuzen; *itr* sich (ver)mischen (lassen); *fig* (mitea.) verkehren, (mitea.) Umgang haben (*with* mit); zs.passen; sich vertragen; *s* Vermischung, Vermengung *f*; Durcheinander *n*, Kuddelmuddel *m od n*; Mischung *f*, Gemisch *n*; *Am* vorgekochte Speise *f*; *to* ~ *in* sich einmischen; *to* ~ *up* (völlig) vermischen; durchea.-bringen; verwirren, *fam* konfus machen; verwechseln (*with* mit); hineinbringen, -ziehen, verwickeln (*in, with* in); **~ed** [-t] *a* gemischt; Misch-; (bunt) durchea.gewürfelt; durchea.gebracht, (ver)wirr(t); *to be* ~~ *up (fig)* verwickelt sein (*in, with* in); ~~ *bathing* Familienbad *n*; ~~ *breed* Halbblut *n*; ~~ *cargo* Stückgutladung *f*; ~~ *doubles (pl) (Tennis)* gemischte(s) Doppel *n*; ~~ *feelings (pl)* gemischte Gefühle *n pl*; ~~ *forest* Mischwald *m*; ~~ *marriage* Mischehe *f*; ~~ *number (math)* gemischte Zahl *f*; ~~ *pickles (pl)* Mixed Pickles, Mixpickles *pl (Mischgemüse in Essig)*; ~~ *school* Koedukationsschule *f*; **~er** ['-ə] Mischer *m*; Mischgerät *n*; (Bar-)Mixer *m*; (Beton-) Mischmaschine; Mischflüssigkeit *f (für Whisky)*; *radio* Toningenieur *m*; Tonmischgerät, Mischpult *n*; *(good, bad)* ~~ (gute(r) *od* angenehme(r), schlechte(r) Gesellschafter *m*; *Am sl* gesellschaftliche Veranstaltung *f* zum Zweck gegenseitigen Sich-Kennenlernens; **~ing** ['-iŋ] *s* Mischen *n*; *a* Misch-; *~~-desk (film) (fahrbare)* Abhörbox *f (für Tonaufnahmen)*; *~~-table (radio)* Misch-, Regiepult *n*; **~ture** ['-tʃə] (Ver-)Mischen *n*; Mischung *f*, Gemisch, Gemenge *n*; *pharm* Mixtur; *biol* Kreuzung *f*; **~-up** Durcheinander, Gewirr(e) *n*; *fam* Schlägerei *f*.
miz(z)en ['mizn] *mar* Besan *m (Segel)*; *(~mast)* Besanmast *m*.
mizzle ['mizl] *itr* nieseln, leise regnen; *sl* abhauen; *s* Nieselregen *m*.
mnemo|nic [ni(:)'mɔnik] *a* Gedächtnis-; mnemotechnisch; *s pl mit sing* Gedächtniskunst, Mnemotechnik *f*; Gedächtnisstützen *f pl*, Merkverse *m pl*; **~technу** [ni(:)mo(u)'tekni] Mnemotechnik, Gedächtniskunst *f*.

*

mo [mou] *fam* Moment *m*; *half a* ~! e-e Sekunde!
moan [moun] *s* Stöhnen, Ächzen *n (a. d. Windes)*; *itr* stöhnen, ächzen; *tr* stöhnend sagen; beklagen, bejammern; *fam* meckern.
moat [mout] *s* Burg-, Wallgraben *m*; *tr* mit e-m Graben umgeben *od* befestigen.
mob [mɔb] *s* (Menschen-)Ansammlung *f*; Menschen-, Volksmassen *f pl*, Pöbelhaufen; Auflauf *m*, Zs.rottung *f*; Pöbel, Mob *m*, *das* (gemeine) Volk, *die* Massen *f pl*; *sl* Gesindel *n*, Diebes-, Räuberbande *f*; *tr* sich zs.rotten u. herfallen über; sich (lärmend) drängen um; anpöbeln; **~bish** ['-iʃ] pöbelhaft; **~-law** das Gesetz der Straße; Lynch-, Volksjustiz *f*; **~ocracy** [mɔ'bɔkrəsi] Pöbelherrschaft *f*; **~sman** Hochstapler *m*; **~ster** ['-stə] *Am sl* Gangster *m*.
mobcap ['mɔbkæp] *hist (im Haus getragene)* (Frauen-)Haube *f*.
mobil|e ['moubail, -bi(:)l] beweglich; leicht, sehr beweglich, wendig; lebhaft; *(Charakter)* wetterwendisch; dünnflüssig; *mil* beweglich, elastisch; fliegend, schnell; motorisiert; ~~ *library* Autobücherei *f*; ~~ *warfare* Bewegungskrieg *m*; **~ity** [mo(u)'biliti] Beweglichkeit; Lebhaftigkeit; Erregtheit; *tech* Leichtflüssigkeit *f*; **~ization** [mo(u)bilai'zeiʃən] Mobilisierung *f*; Aufgebot *n*; Mobilmachung; *com* Flüssigmachung *f*; ~~ *order* Mobilmachungsbefehl *m*; **~ize** ['moubilaiz] *tr* beweglich machen; mobilisieren, einsatzbereit machen, heranziehen, *fam* auf die Beine bringen; *mil* mobil machen; *(Truppen)* aufbieten; *(Kapital)* flüssig machen.
mocassin ['mɔkəsin] Mokassin(slipper) *m*; Mokassinschlange *f*; ~ **flower** *Am bot* Frauenschuh *m*.
mocha ['moukə, 'mɔkə] *s* Mokka; *fam* Kaffee *m*; *a* Mokka-.
mock [mɔk] *tr* verspotten, verhöhnen, verulken, lächerlich machen, sich lustig machen über, *fam* durch den Kakao ziehen, verhohnepipeln; nachmachen, -äffen; irreführen, täuschen, *fam* an der Nase herumführen; standhalten, widerstehen, trotzen (*s.o.* jdm); *to* ~ *up (fam)* improvisieren; *itr* spotten, höhnen, ulken; sich lustig machen (*at* über); *s* Spott, Hohn *m*; Gespött *n*, Zielscheibe des Spottes; Nachahmung; Fälschung *f*; *a* nachgemacht, imitiert; Schein-, Schwindel-; falsch; *to make a* ~ *of* sich lustig machen über; ~ **attack** Scheinangriff *m*; ~ **battle, fight** Scheingefecht *n*; ~ **duck, goose** falsche Ente *od* Gans *f (Schweinebraten mit Zwiebel- u. Salbeifüllung)*; **~er** ['-ə] Spötter; Betrüger *m*; **~ery** ['-əri] Spott, Hohn *m*; Spöttelei *f*; Gespött *n* (der Menschen); Spottfigur *f*, Ulk *m* (*of* auf); verlorene Mühe vergebliche Bemühung *f*; Blendwerk *n*; Farce *f*; **~-heroic** komisch-heroisch; **~ing** ['-iŋ] Hohn, Spott *m*, Gespött *n*, Spöttelei *f*; *~~-bird* Spottdrossel *f*; **~ingly** ['-iŋli] *adv* spottend, spöttisch, zum Spott; ~ **king** Schattenkönig *m*; ~ **purchase** Scheinkauf *m*; ~ **trial** Schauprozeß *m*; **~-turtle soup** Mockturtlesuppe *f*; **~-up** (Lehr-)Modell *n* (in voller Größe); Attrappe *f a. mil.*
mod|al ['moudl] *a gram philos* modal; Modal-; **~ity** [mo(u)'dæliti] Modalität, Art u. Weise *f*; *pl* Bedingungen *f pl*; **~e** [moud] Modus *m*, Art u. Weise, Methode *f*, Verfahren *n*; Sitte *f*, Brauch *m*; Mode *f*; *gram* Modus *m*, Aussageweise; *mus* Tonart *f*; *(Statistik)* häufigste Zahl *od* Größe *f od* Wert *m*; *major, minor* ~~ Dur-, Molltonart *f*; ~~ *of life, of operation* Lebens-, Arbeitsweise *f*.
model ['mɔdl] *s* Modell, Muster (*for* für); Modell(kleid) *n*; *mot* Type; Vorlage *f*, Vorbild, Beispiel; *(Kunst, Photo)* Modell *n (Person)*; Vorführdame *f*, Mannequin *n*; *a* muster-, beispielhaft, vorbildlich; Muster-; *tr* ein Modell anfertigen *gen*; modellieren; gestalten, formen; einrichten, zu(recht)stutzen (*after, on, upon* nach); *Am (Kleid)* vorführen; *itr* modellieren (*in clay* in Ton); als Vorführdame arbeiten; Modell stehen; *(Kunst)* plastisch wirken; **~(l)er** [-ə] Modellierer *m*; ~ **farm** Mustergut *n*; ~ **husband** Mustergatte *m*; **~(l)ing** ['-iŋ] Modellieren *n*; Form, Gestalt *f*; Modellstehen *n*; *(Kunst)* plastische Wirkung *f*; ~ **number** Typennummer *f*; ~ **plant** Versuchsanlage *f*; ~ **test** Modellversuch *m*.
moderat|e ['mɔdərit] *a* (ge)mäßig(t); mild, sanft, ruhig; (mittel)mäßig; *(Forderung)* maßvoll; *s pol* Gemäßigte(r) *m*; ['-reit] *tr* mäßigen, mildern, abschwächen; den Vorsitz führen über; *itr* nachlassen, schwächer werden, sich legen; den Vorsitz führen; ~~ *gale* steife Brise *f*; **~eness** ['mɔdəritnis] Mäßigkeit; Mittelmäßigkeit; Billigkeit *f*; **~ion** [mɔdə'reiʃən] Mäßigung, Milderung, Abschwächung; Mäßigkeit; Sanftheit; Ruhe *f*; *pl (Oxford)* erste öffentliche Universitätsprüfung *f*; *in* ~~ in Maßen, ohne Übertreibungen; **~or** ['mɔdəreitə] Beschwichtigende(r), Vermittelnde(r); Diskussionsleiter; Vorsitzende(r); Schiedsrichter; *(Oxford)* Prüfungsvorsitzende(r); *phys* Moderator *m*, Bremssubstanz *f*.
modern ['mɔdən] *a* modern, neuzeitlich; Neu-; *s* moderne(r) Mensch *m*; **M~ English, Latin, Greek, Hebrew** Neuenglisch, Neulatein; Neugriechisch, Neuhebräisch *n*; ~ **history** Neuere Geschichte *f*; **~ism** ['mɔdə(:)nizm] moderne Richtung *f*, heutige(r) Geschmack; *rel* Modernismus *m*; **~ity** [mɔ'də:niti] Modernität; Modesache, -erscheinung *f*; **~ization** [mɔdə(:)nai'zeiʃən] Modernisierung *f*; **~ize** ['mɔdənaiz] *tr* modernisieren; **~ness** ['mɔdənnis] Modernität *f*; ~ **times** *pl* die Neuzeit.
modest ['mɔdist] bescheiden, anspruchslos; zurückhaltend, reserviert; sittsam, anständig; mäßig; einfach, unauffällig; **~y** ['-i] Bescheidenheit; Zurückhaltung; Sittsamkeit; Mäßigkeit; Einfachheit *f*.
modicum ['mɔdikəm] Kleinigkeit *f*, ein bißchen, ein wenig.
modi|fiable ['mɔdifaiəbl] modifizierbar, abänderungsfähig; **~fication** [mɔdifi'keiʃən] Modifikation, Modifizierung, Veränderung, Abänderung, -wandlung; Einschränkung, Abschwächung; Abart; *(Bedeutung)* nähere Bestimmung; *gram* Umlautung *f*; **~fy** ['mɔdifai] *tr* abändern, modifizieren; einschränken, abschwächen, mildern; *(Bedeutung)* näher bestimmen; *tr itr gram* umlauten.
mod|ish ['moudiʃ] modisch, modern; **~iste** [mo(u)'di:st] Modistin *f*.
mods [mɔdz] *pl* (gutgekleidete) Halbstarke *m pl*.
modulat|e ['mɔdjuleit] *tr* regulieren, einstellen, abmessen, anpassen (*to* an); *tr itr mus* modulieren, in e-e andere Tonart übergehen (lassen); *radio* abstimmen; **~ion** [mɔdju'leiʃən] Regulierung, Einstellung, Anpassung; *radio mus* Modulation; Abstimmung *f*; **~or** ['mɔdjuleitə] Regulierende(r), Regulator; *radio* Modulator *m*; Mischstufe *f*.
Mogul [mo(u)'gʌl]: *Great, Grand* ~ *(hist)* Großmogul *m a. fig.*
mohair ['mouhɛə] Angorawolle *f*, Mohair *m*.
Mohammed [mo(u)'hæmed] Mohammed *m*; **~an** [-idən] *a* mohammedanisch; *s* Mohammedaner *m*; **~anism** [-idənizm] Islam *m*.

*

moiety ['mɔiəti] Hälfte *f*; (An-)Teil *m*.
moil [mɔil] *itr (to toil and* ~*)* sich abrackern, schuften.
moire [mwɑ:] Moiré *m od n*.
moist [mɔist] feucht, naß; regnerisch; *med* nässend; **~en** ['mɔisn] *tr* feucht machen; an-, befeuchten; *itr* feucht

werden; ~**ness** ['-nis], ~**ure** ['-ʃə] Feuchtigkeit *f*; ~*ure proof* feuchtigkeitsfest.
moke [mouk] *sl* Esel *m a. fig.*
molar ['moulə] **1.** *a*: ~ *tooth u. s* Back(en)zahn *m*; **2.** *a chem* molar; *phys* Massen-; **3.** *a med* Molen-.
molasses [mə'læsiz] *pl mit sing* Melasse *f*, Sirup *m*; ~ **cake** *Am Art* Honigkuchen *m (mit Sirup)*; ~ **candy, taffy** *Am* Sirupbonbon *m* od *n*; ~ **gingerbread** *Am* Pfefferkuchen *m*.
mold *s. mould.*
mole [moul] **1.** Muttermal *n*, Leberfleck *m*; **2.** Maulwurf *m*; *blind as a* ~ stockblind; ~-**catcher** Maulwurfsfänger *m*; ~-**cricket** *ent* Maulwurfsgrille, Werre *f*; ~-**hill** Maulwurfshügel, -haufen *m*; *fig* Kleinigkeit *f*; *to make a mountain out of a* ~~ aus e-r Mücke e-n Elefanten machen; ~**skin** Maulwurf(sfell *n*) *m*; Moleskin *m* od *n*, Englischleder *n (Stoff)*; *pl* Moleskinhose *f*; **3.** *med* Mondkalb, Windei *n*, Mole *f*; **4.** Mole *f*, Hafendamm *m*; Mausoleum *n*.
molecul|ar [mo(u)'lekjulə] *a chem* molekular; Molekular-; ~~ *weight* Molekulargewicht *n*; ~**e** ['mɔlikju:l] Molekül *n*, Molekel *f*, *a. n.*
molest [mo(u)'lest] *tr* belästigen; ~**ation** [moules'teiʃən] Belästigung *f*.
Moll [mɔl], ~**y** ['-i] Mariechen *n*; *m*~ Gangsterliebchen *n*; Schickse, Landstreicherin; Nutte *f*.
molli|fication [mɔlifi'keiʃən] Besänftigung; Milderung *f*; ~**fy** ['mɔlifai] *tr* besänftigen, beschwichtigen; mildern, lindern, abschwächen.
mollusc, mollusk ['mɔləsk] Weichtier *n*, Molluske *f*; ~**an** [mɔ'lʌskən] *a* Mollusken-; ~**ous** [-'lʌskəs] *a* Mollusken-; *fig* weich, schwammig.
molly-coddle ['mɔlikɔdl] *s* Muttersöhnchen *n*, Weichling *m*; *tr* verhätscheln, verzärteln, verwöhnen.
Moloch ['moulɔk] *rel hist* Moloch *a. fig*; *fig* Götze *m*; *m*~ *(zoo)* Stachelechse *f*, Moloch *m*.
molt *s. moult.*
molten ['moultən] *a* geschmolzen, flüssig (gemacht); gegossen.
molybdenum [mɔ'libdinəm] *chem* Molybdän *n*.
mom [mɔm] *Am fam* Mama(chen *n*) *f*.
moment ['moumənt] Augenblick, Moment; Zeitpunkt *m*; *fig* Tragweite, Bedeutung, Wichtigkeit *f (to* für); *phys philos* Moment *n*; *at the* ~ im Augenblick, (gerade) jetzt, zur Zeit; *at this* ~ in diesem Augenblick, zu jenem Zeitpunkt; *at any* ~ jederzeit; *at a* ~*'s notice* jeden Augenblick; *in a* ~, *this (very)* ~ gleich, sofort, auf der Stelle; *in a few* ~*s* in wenigen Augenblicken, im Nu; *of (great)* ~ von Belang; *of no (great)* ~ ohne Belang, belanglos; *not for a* ~ keinen Augenblick; nie; *the* ~ *(that)* sowie, sobald; *to the* ~ auf die Minute *od* Sekunde, pünktlich; *please wait a* ~ warten Sie, bitte, e-n Augenblick! *(just) a* ~, *please!* e-n Augenblick, bitte! *the man of the* ~ der rechte Mann zur rechten Zeit; ~ *of inertia, of resistance (phys)* Trägheits-, Widerstandsmoment *n*; ~**arily** [-ərili] *adv* für den *od* im Augenblick, momentan; vorübergehend; ~**ary** ['mouməntəri] vorübergehend, flüchtig, von kurzer Dauer, kurzlebig; ~**ly** ['-li] *adv* jeden Augenblick; auf der Stelle; für e-n Augenblick; ~**ous** [mo(u)'mentəs] sehr wichtig, bedeutsam, bedeutungsvoll, folgenschwer; von großer Tragweite; ~**um** [-'mentəm] *pl a. -ta* ['-tə] *phys* Impuls *m*, Moment *n*, Trieb-, Schwungkraft *f*; *fig* Schwung *m*, Wucht *f*.
monad ['mɔnæd] *philos* Monade *f*; *biol* Einzeller *m*; *chem* einwertige(s) Element *n*.
monarch ['mɔnək] Monarch, (Allein-) Herrscher *m*; ~**(i)al** [mɔ'nɑ:k(i)əl] königlich, Herrscher-; ~**ic(al)** [-'nɑ:kik(əl)] monarchisch; ~**ism** ['mɔnəkizm] Monarchismus *m*; ~**ist** ['-ist] Monarchist *m*; ~**istic** [mɔnə'kistik] monarchistisch; ~**y** ['mɔ:əki] Monarchie *f*.
monast|erial [mɔnəs'tiəriəl] klösterlich, Kloster-; mönchisch, Mönchs-; ~**ery** ['mɔnəstəri] Kloster *n*; ~**ic(al)** [mə'næstik(əl)] klösterlich, Kloster-; mönchisch, Mönchs-; asketisch; ~**icism** [mə'næstisizm] Mönchswesen, Klosterleben *n*.
Monday ['mʌndi] Montag *m*; *on* ~ **am** Montag; *Black* ~ *(sl) (Schule)* erste(r) Schultag *m* nach den Ferien; *St.* ~, *(Am) Blue* ~ Blaue(r) Montag *m*.
monetary ['mʌnitəri] *a* Geld-, Münz-, Währungs-; ~ **agreement, convention** Währungsabkommen *n*; ~ **crisis** Währungskrise *f*; ~ **gold** Münzgold *n*; ~ **policy** Währungspolitik *f*; ~ **question** Geldfrage, -sache *f*; ~ **reform** Währungsreform *f*; ~ **standard** Münzfuß *m*; ~ **unit** Währungs-, Münzeinheit *f*; ~ **value** Geld(es)wert *m*.
monetiz|ation [mʌnitai'zeiʃən] Ausmünzung *f*; ~**e** ['mʌnitaiz] *tr* ausmünzen; zum gesetzlichen Zahlungsmittel machen.
money ['mʌni] Geld *n*; Münze *f*; Papiergeld; Zahlungsmittel *n*; Reichtum *m*, Geld *n*; *pl* Gelder *n pl*; *to be in the* ~ *(Am)*, *to be made of* ~ steinreich sein; *to be short of* ~ knapp bei Kasse sein; *to be worth* ~ Geld wert sein; *to coin* ~ im Gelde schwimmen; Geld scheffeln; *to draw* ~ Geld abheben; *to get o.'s* ~*'s worth* auf s-e Kosten kommen; *to lend* ~ *on interest* Geld auf Zinsen ausleihen; *to make* ~ Geld machen, reich werden (*by* bei, an); *to pay* ~ *down* bar (be)zahlen; *to put* ~ *into* Geld stecken in; *to put* ~ *on (bei e-r Wette)* Geld setzen auf; *time is* ~ *(prov)* Zeit ist Geld; *he has* ~ *to burn* er hat Geld wie Heu; *blood*~ Blutgeld *n*; *call* ~ Geld *n* auf Abruf; Tagesgeld *n*; *counterfeit, forged* ~ Falschgeld *n*; *foreign* ~ ausländische Zahlungsmittel *n pl*; *paper, soft, fiduciary* ~ Papiergeld *n*; *ready* ~ Bargeld *n*; *small* ~ Klein-, Wechselgeld *n*; *smart* ~ Reu-, Schmerzensgeld *n*; *sum of* ~ Geldsumme *f*, -betrag *m*; ~ *in hand* Bargeld *n*; ~ *or* ~*'s worth* Geld oder Geldeswert; ~ **affairs, matters** *pl* Geldangelegenheiten *f pl*; ~-**bag** Geldbeutel *m*; *pl fam* Reichtümer *m pl*; *mit sing* Geldsack, reiche(r) Knopf *m*; ~ **bill** Finanzvorlage *f*, -gesetz *n*; Haushaltplan *m*; ~-**box** Sparbüchse *f*; ~-**broker** Geldmakler *m*; ~-**changer** (Geld-)Wechsler *m*; ~-**circulation** Geldumlauf *m*; ~ **claims** *pl* Geldforderungen *f pl*; ~ **due** ausstehende(s) Geld *n*; ~**ed** ['-d] *a* vermögend, wohlhabend, reich, finanzkräftig; geldlich, pekuniär, finanziell; Geld-, Finanz-; ~~ *assistance* finanzielle Unterstützung *f*; ~~ *capital* Barvermögen *n*; *the* ~~ *classes (pl)* die besitzenden Klassen *f pl*; *the* ~~ *interest* die Finanzwelt, die Hochfinanz; ~~ *man* Geldmann, Kapitalist; Reiche(r) *m*; ~-**grubber** geldgierige(r) Mensch, *fam* Raffke *m*; ~-**lender** Geldverleiher, -geber *m*; ~ **letter** Geld-, Wertbrief *m*; ~-**maker** erfolgreiche(r) Geschäftsmann *m*; Goldgrube *f fig*; ~-**making** *s* Gelderwerb *m*, -verdienen *n*; *a* einträglich, gewinnbringend; geschäftstüchtig; ~ **market** Geld-, Kapitalmarkt *m*; *in the* ~~ an der Börse; ~~ *intelligence* Börsennachrichten *f pl*; ~~ *report* Börsen-, Kursbericht *m*; ~-**office** Kasse *f (Abteilung)*; ~-**order** Postanweisung *f*; ~~ *telegram* telegraphische Postanweisung *f*; ~-**payment** Barzahlung *f*; ~-**sale** Kassageschäft *n*; ~ **supply** Geldbedarf *m*; ~-**squeeze** Geldklemme *f*; ~-**token** Wertmarke *f*; ~-**transactions** *pl* Geldgeschäfte *n pl*, -verkehr *m*; ~-**value** Geldwert *m*; ~-**vault** *Am* Geld-, Kassenschrank *m*; ~**wort** *bot* Pfennigkraut *n*.
monger ['mʌŋgə] *bes. in Zssgen.* Händler *m*; *coster*~ Höker(in *f*) *m*; *fish-, iron*-~ Fisch-, Eisenhändler *m*; *news*~ Neuigkeitenkrämer *m*; *scandal*-~ *(fig pej)* Klatschmaul *n*; *war*~ Kriegshetzer *m*.
Mongol ['mɔŋgɔl] *s* Mongole *m*, Mongolin *f*; *a* mongolisch; Mongolen-; ~**ia** [mɔŋ'gouljə] die Mongolei; *Inner* ~~ die Innere Mongolei; ~**ian** [-'gouljən] *a* mongolisch; *s* Mongole *m*, Mongolin *f*; ~**oid** ['mɔŋgɔlɔid] mongol(o)id.
mongoose ['mɔŋgu:s] *zoo* Mungo *m*.
mongrel ['mʌŋgrəl] *s zoo* Bastard *m*; *fam* Promenadenmischung; *zoo bot* Kreuzung *f*; *a oft pej* Bastard-.
moni(c)ker ['mɔnikə] *Am sl* Zinke *f*, Gaunerzeichen *n*; (Spitz-)Name *m*.
mon|ism ['mɔnizm] *philos* Monismus *m*; ~**ist** ['mɔnist] Monist *m*; ~**istic(al)** [mɔ'nistik(əl)] monistisch.
monit|ion [mo(u)'niʃən] (Er-)Mahnung; (Ver-)Warnung *f*, Verweis *m*; *jur* Vorladung *f*; ~**or** ['mɔnitə] *s (Schule)* Klassensprecher, -ordner *m*; Erinnerung, Warnung *f*; *zoo* Waran; *mar* Monitor; *radio video* Kontrollempfänger, -lautsprecher; Abhörer *m*; *tr itr* abhören, -horchen *a. radio*; überwachen, steuern, kontrollieren; ~**orial** [mɔni'tɔriəl] *a* Repetitoren-; = ~*ory a*; ~**oring** ['mɔnitəriŋ] Mithören, Überwachen *n*; ~~ *service* Abhördienst *m*; ~**ory** ['mɔnitəri] *a* mahnend, warnend; Mahn-, Warn-; *s* Mahnschreiben *n*, -brief *m*.
monk [mʌŋk] Mönch *m*; ~**ery** ['-əri] Mönchswesen, Mönchtum *n*, *pej* Möncherei *f*; Kloster *n*; ~**'s hood** *bot* Eisenhut *m*.
monkey ['mʌŋki] *s* Affe *a. fig*; *tech* Rammblock *m*; *sl* 500 £; *tr* nachäffen; *itr Am fam* spielen, herumalbern (*with, around with* mit); herumfummeln (*with, around with* an); *to get o.'s* ~ *up (sl)* aus der Haut fahren; *to put s.o.'s* ~ *up (sl)* jdn auf die Palme bringen; *to suck, to sup the* ~ *(fam)* aus der Flasche trinken; *my* ~*'s up (sl)* ich bin auf 90, ich könnte aus der Haut fahren; ~ **bread** (Frucht *f* des) Affenbrotbaum(es) *m*; ~ **business** *Am sl* Blödsinn, Quatsch, Schwindel, Unfug *m*; ~-**engine** Rammaschine *f*; ~**ish** ['-iʃ] äffisch, wie ein Affe; ~-**jacket** *fam* (enge) Matrosenjacke *f*; ~**shines** *pl Am sl* dumme Streiche *m pl*, Albernheiten *f pl*; ~ **suit** *Am sl* Uniform *f*; ~-**wrench** Engländer, Universalschraubenschlüssel *m*.
mono ['mɔno(u)] *pref* Mono-, Einzel-, Ein-; ~**acid(ic)** [-'æsid, -ə'sidik] *chem* einsäurig; ~**atomic** [-ə'tɔmik] *(Molekül)* einatomig; ~**basic** [-'beisik] *chem* einbasig; ~**chromatic** ['mɔnəkro(u)-

'mætik] *a* einfarbig; *s video* Einfarbenbild *n*, -sendung *f*; **~chrome** ['-əkroum] einfarbige(s) Gemälde *n*; **~chromic(al)** [-ə'krɔmik(əl)] *a* einfarbig; **~cle** ['mɔnɔkl] Monokel *n*; **~cular** [mɔ'nɔkjulə] einäugig; für ein Auge (bestimmt); **~culture** ['mono(u)-'kʌltʃə] *agr* Monokultur *f*; **~gamous** [mɔ'nɔgəməs] *a* monogam; **~gamy** [-'nɔgəmi] Einehe, Monogamie *f*; **~gram** ['mɔnəgræm] Monogramm *n*; **~graph** ['-grɑ:f] Monographie *f (Buch)*; **~graphic** [mɔnə'græfik] monographisch; **~lith** ['mɔno(u)liθ] *scient* Monolith *m*; **~logize** [mɔ'nɔlədʒaiz] *itr* ein Selbstgespräch führen; **~logue** ['mɔnəlɔg] Selbstgespräch *n*, Monolog *m*; **~mania** ['mɔno(u)'meinjə] fixe Idee *f*; **~maniac** mit e-r fixen Idee behaftet, monoman; **~phthong** ['mɔnəfθɔŋ] Monophthong *m*; **~plane** ['-plein] *aero* Eindecker *m*; **~polist** [mə'nɔpəlist] Monopolist *m*; **~polize** [-'nɔpəlaiz] *tr* monopolisieren *a. fig*; *fig* an sich reißen; **~poly** [-'nɔpəli] Alleinverkauf(srecht *n*) *m*; Monopol *a. fig*; Alleinrecht *n*; **~rail** ['mɔno(u)reil] Einschienenbahn *f*; **~syllabic** ['mɔnəsi-'læbik] *(Wort)* einsilbig; **~syllable** [-'siləbl] einsilbige(s) Wort *n*; **~theism** ['mɔno(u)θi:izm] Monotheismus *m*; **~theist** ['-θiist] Monotheist *m*; **~theistic(al)** [mɔnəθi'istik(əl)] monotheistisch; **~tone** ['mɔnətoun] Geleier *n*; Einförmigkeit *f*; gleiche(r) Ton *m*; **~tonous** [mə'nɔt(ə)nəs] eintönig, -förmig, monoton; **~tony** [-'nɔt(ə)ni] Eintönigkeit, Einförmigkeit, Monotonie *f*.

monsoon [mɔn'su:n] Monsun *m*.

monster ['mɔnstə] *s* Mißgeburt *f*; Ungeheuer, Monstrum; Scheusal *n*; *a* ungeheuer (groß), riesig, gewaltig, enorm; Riesen-; ~ **film** Monsterfilm *m*; ~ **meeting** Massenversammlung *f*.

monstrance ['mɔnstrəns] *rel* Monstranz *f*.

monstr|osity [mɔns'trɔsiti] Absonderlichkeit, Abnormität, Ungeheuerlichkeit; Scheußlichkeit, Gräßlichkeit *f*; **~ous** ['mɔnstrəs] ungeheuer (groß), gewaltig, riesenhaft; abnorm, absonderlich, ungeheuerlich; scheußlich, gräßlich; schrecklich, furchtbar.

montage [mɔn'tɑ:ʒ] (Photo-)Montage; *film radio* Montage *f*.

month [mʌnθ] Monat *m*; *at the end of the* ~ am Monatsende; *by the* ~ monatlich; *every two* ~*s* alle zwei Monate; *every three* ~*s* jedes Vierteljahr, vierteljährlich *adv*; *once, twice a* ~ einmal, zweimal im Monat *od* monatlich; *this day* ~ heute in einem Monat; *within a* ~ in Monatsfrist; ~ *after* ~, ~ *by* ~, ~ *in*, ~ *out, every, each* ~ jeden Monat; *calendar* ~ Kalendermonat *m*; *current* ~ laufende(r) Monat *m*; *one* ~*'s bill* Monatswechsel *m*; *one* ~*'s notice* monatliche Kündigung *f*; **~ly** ['-li] *a* monatlich; Monats-; *adv* monatlich, einmal im Monat, jeden Monat; *s* Monatsschrift; *pl* monatliche Blutung *f*; ~~ *balance* Monatsbilanz *f*; ~~ *instalment* Monatsrate *f*; ~~ *production* Monatsproduktion *f*; ~~ *report* Monatsbericht *m*; ~~ *return* Monatsabschluß, -ausweis *m*; ~~ *salary* Monatsgehalt *n*; ~~ *ticket* Monatskarte *f*.

monument ['mɔnjumənt] (Bau-)Denkmal, Monument; *fig* Denkmal *n*; **~al** [mɔnju'mentl] monumental; überlebensgroß; *fig* riesig, gewaltig; ~~ *mason* Steinbildhauer *m*.

moo [mu:] *s (Kuh)* Muh(en) *n*; *itr* muhen, muh machen.

mooch, mouch [mu:tʃ] *itr sl (to* ~ *about, along)* herumlungern, -schleichen, -bummeln; *tr sl* mausen, mopsen, stibitzen; schnorren, zs.betteln; **~er** ['-ə] *sl* Bummler; Schnorrer *m*.

mood [mu:d] **1.** Stimmung, Laune *f*; *pl* (Anfall *m* von) schlechte(r) Laune *f*; *to be in the* ~ aufgelegt sein (*for* zu); *to be in a good* ~ gutgelaunt sein; **~iness** ['-inis] launische(s), mürrische(s) Wesen *n*; Niedergedrücktheit; Schwermut *f*; **~y** ['-i] launisch, wetterwendisch; schlechtgelaunt, mürrisch, niedergedrückt; düster, trüb(selig), traurig, schwermütig; **2.** *gram* Modus *m*, Aussageweise; *mus* Tonart *f*.

moola(h) ['mu:lə] *Am sl* Geld *n*.

moon [mu:n] *s* Mond *a. poet*; Mondschein *m*, -licht *n*; *astr* Mond, Satellit *m*; *itr (to* ~ *about, around)* herumtrödeln; *tr (to* ~ *away) (Zeit)* vertrödeln; *once in a blue* ~ alle Jubeljahre (einmal); *to cry for the* ~ *(fig)* nach den Sternen greifen; *there is a* ~ *to-night* heute nacht scheint der Mond; *age of the* ~ Mondphase *f*; *full* ~ Vollmond *m*; *half-*~ Halbmond *m*; *new* ~ Neumond *m*; *old, waning* ~ abnehmende(r) Mond *m*; **~beam** Mondstrahl *m*; **~calf** Tölpel, Idiot *m*; **~ed** [-d] *a* kreisrund, halbmond- *od* sichelförmig; mit Mondsicheln verziert; **~-faced** *a* mit e-m Vollmondgesicht; **~fish** Mondfisch *m*; **~light** *s* Mondschein *m*, -licht *n*; *a* mondhell, -beschienen; Mondschein-; nächtlich; ~~ *flit(ting)* heimliche(r) Auszug *m (bei Nacht und Nebel)*; ~~ *night* Mondnacht *f*; **~lit** *a* mondbeschienen, -hell; **~rise** Mondaufgang *m*; **~set** Monduntergang *m*; **~shine** *s* Mondschein *m*; *fig* dumme Reden *f pl*; Unsinn, Blödsinn, Quatsch; *sl* schwarz gebrannte(r) *od* geschmuggelte(r) Alkohol *m*; *a fig* eitel, nichtig; *all* ~~*!* Blödsinn! Quatsch! **~shiner** *Am sl* Schwarzbrenner; Alkoholschmuggler *m*; **~stone** *min* Mondstein *m*; **~stricken, ~struck** *a* mondsüchtig; **~y** ['-i] *a* Mond-; kreisrund, halbmond- *od* sichelförmig; mondhell, -beschienen; träumerisch, verträumt, geistesabwesend; *sl* beschwipst, besoffen.

Moor [muə] Maure *m*; **~ish** [-riʃ] *bes arch* maurisch.

moor [muə] **1.** Heide(land *n*) *f*, Ödland; Moor, Sumpfland; Jagdgebiet, -gelände *n*; **~-fowl** Schottische(s) Moorhuhn *n*; **~land** Heide *f*; Moor *n*; **2.** *tr (Schiff)* vertäuen, festmachen, verankern; *allg* festmachen, sichern; **~age** ['-ridʒ] Verankern *n*; Liege-, Ankerplatz *m*; Ankergebühr *f*; **~ing** ['-riŋ] Vertäuen, Festmachen, Verankern *n a. aero*; *oft pl* Haltetaue *n pl*; *pl* Ankerplatz *m*; ~~*-mast, -tower (aero)* Ankermast *m*; ~~*-rope* Haltetau *n*.

moose [mu:s] *inv zoo* Amerikanische(r) Elch *m*.

moot [mu:t] *s hist* Volksversammlung *f*; *jur* Streitfall, strittige(r) Punkt *m*, Streitfrage *f*; *a* strittig, umstritten; *tr* erörtern, diskutieren; debattieren über; zur Debatte stellen; *jur (als Anwalt)* vertreten.

mop [mɔp] **1.** *s* Scheuerwisch, Mop, *fig* Wuschel(kopf) *m*; *tr (to* ~ *up)* (feucht) aufwischen; *(Gesicht)* abwischen; *fam (Speise, Getränk)* hinunterstürzen; erledigen, zu Ende bringen; *mil* säubern, durchkämmen; *to* ~ *o.'s brow* sich den Schweiß von der Stirn wischen; *to* ~ *the floor with s.o. (sl)* jdn fertigmachen, erledigen; **~board** Scheuerleiste *f*; **~head** *fam* Wuschelkopf *m*; **~ping-up operations** *pl mil* Säuberungsaktion *f*; **2.** *s* Grimasse, Fratze *f*; *itr (to* ~ *and mow)* Grimassen schneiden, e-e Fratze machen; ~*s and mows* Grimassen *f pl*.

mop|e [moup] *itr* (dumpf) vor sich hinbrüten; teilnahmslos, apathisch sein; den Kopf hängen lassen, Trübsal blasen; *s* apathische(r), teilnahmslose(r) Mensch *m*; *fam* Häufchen *n* Elend; *pl* Teilnahmslosigkeit *f*, Trübsinn *m*, *fam* heulende(s) Elend; **~ed** [-t] *a* niedergeschlagen, entmutigt; **~ing** ['-iŋ], **~ish** ['-iʃ] teilnahmslos, apathisch; mutlos; bedrückt, trübsinnig; hoffnungs-, aussichtslos; *(Stimmung)* gedrückt.

moped ['mouped] Moped *n*.

moppet ['mɔpit] Püppchen *n a. fig*.

moraine [mɔ'rein] *geol* Moräne *f*; *lateral, terminal* ~ Seiten-, Endmoräne *f*.

moral ['mɔrəl] *a* sittlich, moralisch, ethisch; (sittlich) gut, rechtschaffen; sittenrein; pflichtbewußt; geistig; *s* Lehre, Nutzanwendung, Moral *f (e-r Geschichte)*; Grundsatz *m*, Maxime *f*; *pl* sittliche(s) Verhalten *n*, Sittlichkeit, Sittenlehre, Moral, Ethik *f*; ~ **certainty** innere Gewißheit *f*; **~e** [mɔ'rɑ:l] geistige Verfassung, Stimmung *bes. mil*; innere, geistige Zucht *f*; ~ **insanity** (innere) Haltlosigkeit *f*; **~ist** ['-ist] *(Literatur)* Moralist; Sittenlehrer *m*; **~ity** [mə'ræliti] Sittlichkeit; Sittenreinheit *f*; Sittenkodex *m*, -gesetz *n*; Sittenlehre, Ethik; Lehre *f*; *theat hist (*~~ *play)* Moralität *f*; **~ize** ['mɔrəlaiz] *itr* moralisieren, moralische Betrachtungen anstellen; *tr* vom moralischen Standpunkt betrachten; e-e Lehre ziehen aus; sittlich heben.

morass [mə'ræs] Morast, Sumpf *m*; *fig* verfahrene Lage, Klemme *f*; Schwierigkeiten *f pl*.

morator|ium [mɔrə'tɔ:riəm] Moratorium *n*, Zahlungsaufschub *m*, Stundung *f*; **~y** ['mɔrətəri] aufschiebend; Stundungs-.

morb|id ['mɔ:bid] krank(haft); kränklich; ungesund; pathologisch; *fig* greulich, grauenhaft, furchtbar, schrecklich, entsetzlich; ~~ *anatomy* pathologische Anatomie *f*; **~idity** [mɔ:'biditi], **~idness** ['-bidnis] Krankhaftigkeit; Kränklichkeit; Ungesundheit; Krankheitshäufigkeit, -ziffer *f*.

mordant ['mɔ:dənt] *a* ätzend; beißend *a. fig*; *(Schmerz)* brennend; *s* Beize *f*, Beizmittel *n*; ätzende Flüssigkeit *f*.

more [mɔ:] **1.** *a u. adv* mehr; noch (mehr); weitere(s); *any, some* ~ noch (mehr); *a few* ~ noch einige; noch ein paar; *a little* ~ etwas mehr; noch etwas; *many, much* ~ viel mehr; *no* ~ kein(e) ... mehr; *three* ~ noch drei; drei weitere; *what* ~*?* was noch? *what's* ~ außerdem; **2.** *adv* mehr, in höherem Maße; ausgiebiger, eher; **3.** *s* Mehr *n (of* an); *once* ~ noch einmal; *any od no, never* ~ nicht, nie mehr; ~ *or less* mehr oder weniger; ~ *and* ~ immer mehr; immer weiter; ~ *and* ~ *exciting* immer spannender; *so much the* ~ um so mehr (*as, because* als, da); *the* ~ *... the* ~ je mehr ... desto mehr; *to be no* ~ nicht mehr (am Leben) sein; *and what is* ~ und was wichtiger, entscheidender ist; *I don't care any* ~ es liegt mir nichts mehr dran; **~over** [mɔ:'rouvə] überdies, des weiteren, ferner.

morel [mɔ'rel] **1.** *bot* Schwarze(r) Nachtschatten *m*; **2.** *bot* Speisemorchel *f*.

morello [mə'relou], ~ **cherry** Weichselkirsche *f*.

Moresque [mɔ'resk] *(Kunst)* maurisch.
morganatic [mɔ:gə'nætik] *(Ehe)* morganatisch, zur linken Hand.
morgue [mɔ:g] Leichenschauhaus; *Am* Archiv *n (e-r Redaktion).*
moribund ['mɔribʌnd] sterbend, im Sterben, in den letzten Zügen (liegend); *fig* dem Ende entgegengehend.
Mormon ['mɔ:mən] *rel* Mormone *m*; *a* mormonisch; ~ **Church** Kirche *f* Jesu Christi der Heiligen der letzten Tage; ~**ism** ['-izm] Mormonentum *n*; *the* ~ **State** der Mormonenstaat, Utah *n (US).*
morn [mɔ:n] *poet* Morgen *m.*
morning ['mɔ:niŋ] *s* Morgen; Vormittag; Tagesanbruch *m*; Morgengrauen *n*; *fam* (Nach-)Mittag; *fig* Anfang *m*, erste Zeit *f*; *a* Morgen-, morgendlich; *(Kleidung)* Tages-; *from* ~ *till night* von früh bis spät; *in the* ~ am Morgen, morgens; *on Sunday* ~ am Sonntagmorgen; *this* ~ heute morgen; *to-morrow* ~ morgen früh; *yesterday* ~ gestern morgen; *good* ~*!* guten Morgen! ~ **call** Nachmittagsbesuch *m*; ~**-coat** Cut(away) *m*; ~**-dress** Haus-, Tageskleid *n*; Besuchsanzug *m*; ~**-gift** *hist* Morgengabe *f*; ~**-glory** *bot* Garten-, Trichterwinde *f*; ~**gown** Morgenrock *m*; ~ **paper** Morgenzeitung *f*; ~ **performance** Matinee, Nachmittagsvorstellung, -veranstaltung *f*; ~ **prayer** (anglikanische) Morgenandacht *f*; Morgengebet *n*; ~**-star** Morgenstern *m*; ~**-watch** *mar* Morgenwache *f (von 4 bis 8 Uhr).*
Morocc|an [mə'rɔkən] *a* marokkanisch; *s* Marokkaner(in *f*) *m*; ~**o** [-ou] Marokko *n*; *m*~~ *(leather)* Saffian, Maroquin *m.*
moron ['mɔ:rɔn] Schwachsinnige(r *m*) *f*, *fam* Trottel, Dämlack *m.*
morose [mə'rous] mürrisch, verdrießlich, griesgrämig, grämlich; ~**ness** [-nis] mürrische(s) Wesen *n*; Griesgrämigkeit *f.*
morph|ia ['mɔ:fjə], ~**in(e)** ['-i(:)n] Morphium *n*; ~**inism** ['-inizm] Morphinismus *m*; ~**inist** ['-inist] Morphinist *m.*
morpholog|ic(al) [mɔ:fə'lɔdʒik(əl)] morphologisch; ~**y** [mɔ:'fɔlədʒi] Morphologie *f.*
morrow ['mɔrou] *obs lit poet* Morgen; folgende(r) Tag *m*; *on the* ~ *of* bald, kurz nach.
Morse [mɔ:s] *a tele* Morse-; ~ **alphabet, code** Morsealphabet *n*; ~ **sign** Morsezeichen *n.*
morse [mɔ:s] **1.** *zoo* Walroß *n*; **2.** Agraffe, Gewandspange, Fibel *f.*
morsel ['mɔ:səl] *s* Bissen *m*; bißchen, Stückchen *n*; *tr* in kleine Teile teilen; in kleinen Portionen verteilen.
mortal ['mɔ:tl] *a* sterblich; irdisch; menschlich; Todes-; tödlich, verderbenbringend, unheilvoll (*to* für); schrecklich, entsetzlich; *fam* gewaltig, ungeheuer; endlos (lang); entsetzlich langweilig; *fam* menschenmöglich; *s* Sterbliche(r); *fam* Mensch *m*; ~ **agony** Todeskampf *m*; ~ **combat** Kampf *m* um Leben und Tod; ~ **enemy** Todfeind *m*; ~ **hour** Todesstunde *f*; ~**ity** [mɔ:'tæliti] Sterblichkeit(sziffer); Menschheit *f*; ~~ *table* Sterblichkeitstafel *f*; ~ **sin** Todsünde *f.*
mortar ['mɔ:tə] *s* Mörser *m*, Reibschale *f*; *mil* Mörser, Granatwerfer; Mörtel, Speis *m*; *tr* mit Granatwerferfeuer belegen; *(Steine beim Bau)* binden, verstreichen; ~**-board** *arch* Streichbrett; *(Universität)* quadratische(s) Barett *n.*
mortgage ['mɔ:gidʒ] *s* Verpfändung *f*; *(~ deed)* Pfandbrief *m*, Hypothek *f*; Pfandrecht *n*; *tr* verpfänden (*to* an); *(mit e-r Hypothek)* belasten; *to give in* ~ verpfänden; *to have a* ~ *on* e-e Hypothek haben auf; *to pay off, to redeem a* ~ e-e Hypothek tilgen; *to raise a* ~ e-e Hypothek aufnehmen (*on* auf); *to register a* ~ e-e Hypothek eintragen; *claim, debt on* ~ Hypothekenforderung, -schuld *f*; *first* ~ erste Hypothek *f*; *free of* ~*s* hypotheken-, schuldenfrei; *redemption of* ~ Tilgung *f* e-r Hypothek; *satisfaction of* ~ Erlöschen *n* e-r Hypothek; *secured by* ~ hypothekarisch gesichert; ~ *of goods* Sicherungsübereignung *f*; ~ **claim** Hypothekenforderung *f*; ~ **debt** Hypothekenschuld *f*; ~**e** [mɔ:gə'dʒi:] Hypothekengläubiger *m*; ~**r, mortgagor** ['mɔ:gidʒə, -gə'dʒɔ:] Hypothekenschuldner *m*; ~ **register** Hypotheken-, Grundbuch *n.*
mortice *s. mortise.*
mortician [mɔ:'tiʃən] *Am* Leichenbestatter *m.*
mortif|ication [mɔ:tifi'keiʃən] Abtötung, Kasteiung; Demütigung, Kränkung, Beschämung, Schande *f*; Verlust *m* der Selbstachtung; *med* kalte(r) Brand *m*; ~**y** ['mɔ:tifai] *tr* kasteien; abtöten; demütigen, beschämen, kränken; *s.o.* jdn verletzen; *med* brandig machen; *itr* sich kasteien; *med* brandig werden.
mortise, mortice ['mɔ:tis] *s* Zapfenloch *n*; Falz *m*, Fuge; (Keil-)Nut; *fig* Stütze *f*; *tr* mit e-m Zapfenloch, e-r Nut versehen; *(to* ~ *together)* verzapfen, mit e-m Zapfen verbinden; einzapfen, -lassen (*into* in); ~ **chisel** Lochbeitel *m.*
mortmain ['mɔ:tmein] *jur* (Recht *n* der) Tote(n) Hand *f*; *in* ~ unveräußerlich.
mortuary ['mɔ:tjuəri] *s* Leichenhalle *f*, -haus *n*; *a* Sterbe-, Toten-, Leichen-, Trauer-, Begräbnis-; ~ **rites** *pl* Beisetzungsfeierlichkeiten *f pl.*
Mosaic [mə'zeiik] *rel* mosaisch.
mosaic [mə'zeiik] *s* Mosaik(arbeit *f*) *n*; *fig* Mosaik-, *phot* Reihenluftbild *n*; *a*: ~ **gold** Musiv-, Mosaikgold *n.*
Moselle, *the* [mə'zel] die Mosel; *m*~ Mosel(wein) *m.*
mosey ['mouzi] *itr Am sl* dahinschlendern; abhauen, stiftengehen.
Moslem ['mɔzlem] Moslem, Mohammedaner *m.*
mosque [mɔsk] *rel* Moschee *f.*
mosquito [məs'ki:tou] *pl -oes* Stechmücke *f*, Moskito *m*; ~ **boat** Schnellboot *n*; ~ **net** Moskitonetz *n.*
moss [mɔs] Moos(polster) *n*; ~**back** *Am fam* bemooste(s) Haupt *n*; altmodische(r), rückständige(r) Mensch, Spießer *m*; ~**-grown** *a* moosbewachsen, bemoost; altmodisch, veraltet; ~**iness** ['-inis] moosige Beschaffenheit *f*; ~**y** ['-i] bemoost, moosig, moosbedeckt.
most [moust] *a* meist; größt; höchst; *adv* am meisten; höchst, überaus, äußerst; *s das* meiste; *das* Höchste, Äußerste; *at (the)* ~ höchstens; *for the* ~ *part* meist(ens); meisten-, größtenteils, in der überwiegenden Mehrheit; ~ *of all* am allermeisten; ~ *people* die meisten Leute; ~ *of the time* die meiste Zeit, meist; *to make the* ~ *of* alles herausholen aus, voll ausnutzen; ins rechte Licht setzen (*s.o.* jdn); ~**-favo(u)red-nation clause** *pol* Meistbegünstigungsklausel *f*; ~**ly** ['-li] meist(ens); in der Hauptsache, im wesentlichen.
mote [mout] Stäubchen, Körnchen *n*; *the* ~ *in another's eye (fig)* der Splitter im Auge des andern.
motel [mou'tel] *Am* Motel.
motet [mo(u)'tet] *mus* Motette *f.*
moth [mɔθ] Motte *f*; Nachtfalter *m*; *clothes-*~ Kleidermotte *f*; ~**-ball** *s* Mottenkugel *f*; Schutzüberzug *m*; *tr Am mil (Waffen)* einlagern, einmotten; ~**-eaten** *a* mottenzerfressen; *fig* abgenutzt, verbraucht; veraltet; ~**y** ['-i] vermottet; mottenzerfressen.
mother ['mʌðə] *s* Mutter *a. fig*; *rel (~ superior)* Oberin, Äbtissin; *fig* Ursache, Veranlassung *f*; *tr* bemuttern; zur Welt, *fig* hervorbringen; die Urheberschaft zugeben *od* anerkennen (*s.th.* an e-r S); *necessity is the* ~ *of invention (prov)* Not macht erfinderisch; *M*~ *of God* Mutter *f* Gottes; **M**~**-Church** Mutterkirche *f*; ~ **country,** ~**land** Mutterland *n*; ~ **earth** Mutter *f*, Erde; ~**hood** ['-hud] Mutterschaft; Mütterlichkeit *f*; die Mütter *pl*; ~**-in-law** *pl* ~*s-in-law* Schwiegermutter *f*; ~**less** ['-lis] mutterlos; ~**liness** ['-linis] Mütterlichkeit *f*; ~ **liquor** *chem* Mutterlauge *f*; ~ **lodge** *(Freimaurerei)* Mutterloge *f*; ~**ly** ['-li] *a* mütterlich; *adv* wie e-e Mutter; ~**-of-pearl** *s* Perlmutter *f*; *a* perlmuttern; ~**-rock** *geol* Urgestein *n*; **M**~**'s Day** Muttertag *m*; ~ **tongue** Muttersprache *f*; ~ **wit** Mutterwitz *m*; ~**y** ['-ri] *(Flüssigkeit)* trüb(e), getrübt, hefig.
motif [mo(u)'ti:f] *(Kunst) lit mus* Motiv; *fig* Leitmotiv *n*, -gedanke *m.*
motil|e ['moutail, '-il] *a biol* bewegungsfähig; *s* motorische(r) Mensch *m*; ~**ity** [mo(u)'tiliti] Bewegungsfähigkeit *f.*
motion ['mouʃən] *s* Bewegung; Körperbewegung; Hand-, Kopfbewegung, Geste *f*, Wink *m*, Zeichen *n*; *psychol* Antrieb; Vorschlag *m*; Anregung *f*; *parl* Antrag (*for, of, to* auf); *tech* Mechanismus *m*, Triebwerk *n*; *physiol* Stuhlgang *m*; *pl* Schritte *m pl*; *itr* e-e (bedeutungsvolle) Hand-, Kopfbewegung machen; winken (*with* mit; *to* dat); *tr* mit e-r Geste zu verstehen, ein Zeichen geben (*s.o.* jdm); *to* ~ *away* abwinken (*s.o.* jdm); *to* ~ *in* hereinwinken (*s.o.* jdm); *in* ~ in Bewegung, in Gang; *of o.'s own* ~ aus eigenem Antrieb; *to adopt a* ~ e-n Antrag annehmen; *to bring forward, to file, to make, to put a* ~ e-n Antrag einbringen, *od* stellen; *to carry a* ~ e-n Antrag durchbringen; *to defeat, to reject a* ~ e-n Antrag ablehnen; *to hear a* ~ über e-n Antrag verhandeln; *to put, to set in* ~ in Bewegung setzen, in Gang bringen; *to sustain a* ~ e-m Antrag stattgeben; *to withdraw a* ~ e-n Antrag zurücknehmen, -ziehen; *counter-*~ Gegenantrag *m*; *free* ~ Bewegungsfreiheit *f*, Spielraum *m*; *idle* ~ Leerlauf *m*; *slow-*~ *(a)* langsam; *film* Zeitlupen-; ~~ *picture* Zeitlupenaufnahme *f*; ~ *to adjourn,* ~ *for adjournment* Antrag *m* auf Vertagung; ~ *to amend* Ergänzungs-, Abänderungsantrag *m*; ~ *of censure* Tadelsantrag *m*; ~ *of 'no confidence'* Mißtrauensantrag *m*; ~**less** ['-lis] bewegungs-, reglos; bewegungsunfähig; ~ **picture** *Am* Film *m*; ~**-picture** *a Am* Film-; ~~ *actor, actress* Filmschauspieler(in *f*) *m*; ~~ *camera* Filmkamera *f*; ~~ *projector* Filmvorführapparat *m*; ~~ *theatre* Film-, Lichtspieltheater, Kino *n*; ~ **study** Zeitstudie *f.*
motiv|ate ['moutiveit] *tr* begründen, motivieren; anregen; ~**ation** [mouti'veiʃən] Begründung, Motivierung; Anregung *f*; ~**e** ['moutiv] *s* Beweg-

grund *m* (*for* zu); Absicht *f*, Zweck *m*, Ziel; *(Kunst) lit mus* Motiv *n*; *a* bewegend, treibend *a. fig*; *tr* motivieren, begründen; *~~ power* Triebkraft *f a. fig.*

motley ['mɔtli] *a* scheckig, bunt; buntgekleidet; gemischt; *s* Narrenkleid *n*; *fig* Mischmasch *m*; *to wear the ~* den Narren spielen.

motor ['moutə] *s* Motor *m*; treibende Kraft *f a. fig*; Kraftfahrzeug, *bes.* Auto(mobil) *n*; (Kraft-)Wagen; *(~ nerve)* motorische(r) Nerv *m*; *a* bewegend, (an)treibend; Motor(en)-, Kraft-; Auto-; *physiol* motorisch; *itr* Auto fahren; *tr* mit e-m Kraftfahrzeug befördern; **~-accident** Autounfall *m*; **~-ambulance** Krankenwagen *m*; **~-assisted bicycle** Fahrrad *n* mit Einbaumotor; **~-bicycle** = *~-cycle*; **~-bike** *fam* Motorrad *n*; **~-boat** Motorboot *n*; **~-bus** Autobus *m*; **~-cab** Taxe *f*; **~cade** ['-keid] *Am* Auto-, Wagenkolonne *f*; **~-car** Auto(mobil) *n*, Kraftwagen *m*; *~~ industry* Automobilindustrie *f*; **~-coach** *rail* Triebwagen; *Am* Bus *m*; **~ court, park** *Am* Rasthaus *n*, -stätte *f*, Motel *n*; Campingplatz *m*; **~-cycle** *s* Motor-, Kraftrad *n*; *itr* Motorrad fahren; *~~ dispatch-rider (mil)* Kradmelder *m*; *~~ tractor* Kettenkrad *n*; **~-cyclist** Motorradfahrer *m*; **~-drive** Motorantrieb *m*; **~-driven** *a* mit Motorantrieb; *~~ railway-car* Triebwagen *m*; **~drome** ['-droum] Auto-, Motorradrennbahn *f*; **~ed** ['-d] *a* mit e-m Motor, mit Motoren ausgestattet; *bes. in Zssgen*: -motorig; **~-engine** Kraftmaschine *f*; **~ fire-engine** Motorspritze *f*; **~-fitter, -mechanic** Autoschlosser *m*; **~-generator** Motorgenerator, -umformer *m*; **~-goggles** *pl* Motorrad-Schutzbrille *f*; **~ing** ['moutəriŋ] Kraftfahrwesen *n*; Motorsport *m*; **~ist** ['moutərist] Kraft-, Autofahrer *m*; **~ization** [moutərai'zeiʃən] Motorisierung *f*; **~ize** ['moutəraiz] *tr* motorisieren; **~-launch** Motorbarkasse *f*; **~less** ['-lis] motorlos; *~~ flight* Segelflug *m*; **~-lorry** *Br* Last(kraft)wagen *m*, -auto *n*; **~man** ['-mən] *el* Wagenführer *m*; **~ mimicry** *psychol* Einfühlung *f*; **~ noise** Motorenlärm *m*; **~-oil** Treiböl *n*; **~-pool** Fahrbereitschaft *f*; **~-road** Autobahn, Kraftverkehrsstraße *f*; **~ scooter** Motorroller *m*; **~-ship** Motorschiff *n*; **~-show** Automobilausstellung *f*; **~ sled, sleigh** Motorschlitten *m*; **~ spirit** Kraftstoff(gemisch *n*) *m*; **~ taxi** Kraftdroschke, Taxe *f*; **~ torpedo-boat** Schnellboot *n*; **~-tractor** Traktor, Trecker, Motorschlepper *m*; **~ transport** Kraftwagentransport *m*; **~ trip** Autotour *f*; **~-trouble** Motorschaden *m*, Panne *f*; **~ truck** *Am* Last(kraft)wagen *m*, -auto *n*; *el* Elektrokarren *m*; **~-van** Lieferwagen *m*; **~ vehicle** Kraftfahrzeug *n*; *~-vehicle repair-shop* Kraftfahrzeug-Reparaturwerkstatt *f*; **~way** *Br* Autostraße *f*; **~y** ['-ri] *physiol* motorisch; *allg* treibend.

mottl|e ['mɔtl] *tr* bunt machen; sprenkeln; marmorieren; **~ed** [-d] *a* buntscheckig; gesprenkelt; marmoriert; *(Roheisen)* meliert.

motto ['mɔtou] *pl -o(e)s* Motto *n*; Leitsatz; Wahlspruch *m*.

mo(u)ld [mould] **1.** *s* (Guß-)Form *f*; Formholz, -brett *n*; Schablone *f*, Modell, Muster, Vorbild *n*; Abguß, -klatsch *m*, -bild *n*; *typ* Matrize, Mater; Form, Gestalt, Struktur *f*, Bau *m*, Beschaffenheit, Natur, Art *f*; *tr* formen, pressen, gießen, bilden (*upon* nach); *(Gießerei)* abformen; *(Holz)* profilieren; **~er** ['-ə] Former, Gießer; *fig* Bildner *m*; *typ* Galvano *n*; **~ing** ['-iŋ] Formen, Pressen, Gießen, Bilden, Modellieren *n*; Preßling *m*; Gesims, Karnies *n*, Fries *m*; *~~ board* Formbrett *n*; *~~ box* Form-, Gießkasten *m*; *~~ material, sand* Formsand *m*; *~~ press* Formpresse *f*; *~~ shop* Gießerei, Presserei, Formerei *f*; *~~-wax* Modellierwachs *n*; **2.** *s* Moder; Schimmel; Schimmelpilz *m*; *itr tr* (ver)modern, (ver)faulen, (ver-)schimmeln (lassen); **~iness** ['-inis] mod(e)rige(r), schimm(e)lige(r) Zustand *m*; **~y** ['-i] mod(e)rig, schimm(e)lig; **3.** Humus(boden *m*, -schicht *f*); Kompost *m*, Gartenerde *f*; (Erd-)Boden *m*; Material *n*, Materie *f*; *tr* mit Gartenerde bedecken; **~er** ['-ə] *itr* vermodern; *(to ~~ away)* verfallen, vergehen; *tr* vermodern, verfallen lassen.

mo(u)lt [moult] *itr* sich mausern; sich häuten; *tr (das Federkleid)* wechseln; *(die Haut)* abwerfen; *s* Mauser(ung) *f*.

mound [maund] **1.** *s* Erdhügel, -wall *m*; Bodenerhebung *f*; *burial ~* Grabhügel *m*; **2.** *s* Reichsapfel *m*.

mount [maunt] **1.** *poet u. in Namen* Berg *m*; **2.** *itr (to ~ up)* (empor-, auf-, hinauf)steigen; (hinauf)klettern, (hinauf)fahren; aufs Pferd steigen, das Pferd besteigen; *fig* (an)steigen, sich vermehren, zunehmen, (an)wachsen; *tr* hinaufsteigen; klettern auf; *(Pferd)* besteigen, steigen auf; setzen auf; beritten machen; *(Tier)* decken; stellen (*on* auf); *tech* einbauen, montieren; zs.stellen; *(Edelstein)* fassen; *(Bild)* aufziehen, -kleben; *zoo bot* präparieren; *(Landkarte)* aufziehen; *theat* einrichten, inszenieren, auf die Bühne bringen; *(Kleidungsstück)* anziehen, zur Schau tragen, paradieren mit; *(Geschütz)* in Stellung bringen; *(Schiff mit Geschützen)* bewaffnet sein mit; *mil (Posten)* aufstellen; *(Stellung)* beziehen; *s* Besteigen *(e-s Pferdes)*, Aufsitzen; Montieren *n*; Reittier, Pferd; Fahrrad *n*; Fassung *f*, Rahmen *m*, Gestell *n*; *(Mikroskop)* Objektträger *m*; *to ~ up to* sich belaufen auf, betragen; *to ~ guard* auf Wache ziehen; **~ed** ['-id] *a* beritten; aufgezogen; *(Geschütz)* in Stellung gebracht; *(Truppe)* ausgerüstet; **~ing** ['-iŋ] Montage; Fassung, Halterung, Aufhängung *f*; Rahmen, Karton *m*; *el* Installation *f*; *pl* Beschläge *m pl*, Armaturen *f pl*.

mountain ['mauntin] *s* (hoher) Berg; *fig* (großer) Haufen, Berg *m*; *pl* Gebirge *n*; *a* Berg-, Gebirgs-; gewaltig, riesig, riesenhaft; *to make a ~ out of a molehill* aus e-r Mücke e-n Elefanten machen; *a ~ of debts* ein Haufen Schulden; **~-air** Gebirgsluft *f*; **~ artillery** Gebirgsartillerie *f*; **~ ash** Eberesche *f*, Vogelbeerbaum *m*; **~ cat, lion** *Am zoo* Puma; Kuguar *m*; **~ chain, range** Bergkette *f*; **~ cock** *zoo* Auerhahn *m*; **~ crest** Bergkamm *m*; **~ crystal** Bergkristall *m*; **~ cure** Höhenkur *f*; **~eer** [maunti'niə] *s* Bergbewohner; Bergsteiger *m*; *itr* Bergsport treiben; **~eering** [-'niəriŋ] Bergsteigen *n*; **~-high** haushoch; **~ous** ['mountinəs] bergig, gebirgig; *fig* riesenhaft, ungeheuer; **~ pass** Gebirgspaß *m*; **~ pasture** Alm *f*; **~ plant** Gebirgspflanze *f*; **~ railway** Bergbahn *f*; **~ range** Gebirgskette *f*; **~ resort** Höhenkurort *m*, -station *f*; **~ sickness** Bergkrankheit *f*; **~-side** (Berg-, Ab-)Hang *m*, Berglehne *f*; **~ slide** Bergrutsch *m*; **~-sun** Höhensonne *f*; **~ top** Bergspitze *f*; **~ track, trail** Saumpfad *m*; **~ troops** *pl* Gebirgstruppen *f pl*.

mountebank ['mauntibæŋk] Marktschreier, Quacksalber; Scharlatan *m*.

mourn [mɔ:n] *itr* trauern (*for, over* um); klagen, jammern (*at, over* über); in Trauer sein, Trauer tragen; *tr* bedauern, beklagen; betrauern; jammernd sagen; **~er** ['-ə] Leidtragende(r) *m*; *pl* Trauergäste *m pl*, -gemeinde *f*; **~ful** ['-ful] *a* Trauer-; traurig, kummervoll, bekümmert; schmerzlich; **~ing** ['-iŋ] *s* Trauer(kleidung, -zeit) *f*; *a* Trauer-; *in (deep) ~~* in (tiefer) Trauer; *to go into (out of) ~~* Trauer an-, ablegen; *~~-band* Trauerflor *m*; *~~-boarder, -edge* Trauerrand *m*.

mouse [maus] *pl mice s* Maus *f*; *fig* Angsthase *m*; *sl* blaue(s) Auge *n*; *itr* [mauz] mausen, Mäuse fangen; *fig* eifrig, heimlich suchen; *~ and man* mit Mann und Maus; *house-, field-~* Haus-, Feldmaus *f*; **~-colo(u)r** *s* Mausgrau *n*; *a* mausgrau; **~-deer** *zoo* Moschustier *n*; **~-ear** *bot* Vergißmeinnicht; Habichtskraut *n*; **~-hole** Mauseloch *n*; **~r** ['mauzə] *(Katze, Hund)* Mausefänger *m*; **~-trap** Mausefalle *f*; ungenießbare(r) Käse *m*; **~y** ['-i] *a* voller Mäuse; *fig* ängstlich, furchtsam; *fig* trübe.

mo(u)stache [məs'tɑ:ʃ] Schnurrbart *m*.

mouth [mauθ] *pl -s* [-ðz] *s* Mund *a. fig*; *fig* Esser, Mensch *m*; Maul *n*, Schnauze; Grimasse *f*; *fig* lose(s) Maul *n*, Frechheit; Öffnung; *(Gewehrlauf, Fluß)* Mündung *f*; Ein-, Ausgang *m*; *(Blasinstrument)* Mundstück *n*; *v* [mauð] *tr* affektiert sprechen; in den Mund nehmen; *(mit dem Mund)* berühren; *(Pferd)* ans Gebiß gewöhnen; *itr* affektiert sprechen; Grimassen schneiden; *by word of ~* mündlich; *down in the ~ (fam)* niedergeschlagen, gedrückt, traurig, betrübt; *to be down in the ~* den Kopf hängen lassen; *to give ~* anschlagen, bellen, Laut geben; *to keep o.'s ~ shut* den Mund halten; *to have a big ~ (Am sl)* das große Wort führen; *to laugh on the wrong side of o.'s ~, to make a wry ~* das Gesicht verziehen; jammern; *to put s.th. into s.o.'s ~ (fig)* jdm etw in den Mund legen; *to shoot off o.'s ~* aus der Schule plaudern; *to take the words out of s.o.'s ~ (fig)* jdm das Wort aus dem Munde nehmen; **~ful** ['-ful] Mundvoll, Bissen *m*; ein bißchen, etwas; *fam* Zungenbrecher *m (Wort)*; *to say a ~~ (sl)* den Mund vollnehmen *fig*; *Am* etwas Wichtiges sagen; **~-organ** Mundharmonika; Panflöte *f*; *zoo* Freßwerkzeug *n*; **~piece** *(Blasinstrument)* Mundstück; *fig* Sprachrohr *n*, Wortführer *m*.

movable ['mu:vəbl] *a* beweglich *a. jur (Habe)*; *s pl* Mobilien *pl*, Mobiliar *n*, bewegliche Habe *f*; **~ holidays** *pl* bewegliche Feiertage *m pl*; **~ kidney** Wanderniere *f*.

move [mu:v] *tr* bewegen; in Bewegung bringen *od* setzen *od* halten; veranlassen; wegbringen, -nehmen; *fig* erregen, bewegen, rühren, ergreifen, aus der Ruhe bringen; anregen, vorschlagen; beantragen; *(Antrag)* stellen; *com* verkaufen; *(den Darm)* entleeren; *Am sl* stehlen; *itr* sich bewegen *a. fig*, in Bewegung sein; gehen (*to* zu, nach); *(Maschine)* laufen; umziehen (*to* nach); die Wohnung wechseln; *fig* verkehren, sich bewegen; *(Brettspiel)* ziehen, e-n Zug machen; voran-, vorwärtskommen; fortschreiten; *com* verkauft werden; e-n Antrag stellen (*for* auf); *(Darm)* sich entleeren; *fam (to ~ on)* abhauen, losziehen, weggehen; *s* Bewegung *f*; Schritt *fig (zu e-m Ziel)*; Umzug; *(Brettspiel)* Zug *m*; *to ~ along, to ~ on* weitergehen; in Bewegung kommen; *to ~ away (itr)* wegziehen; *tr* wegschieben, -rücken; *to ~ in, out* ein-, ausziehen; *to ~ off* sich davonmachen; *to ~ up (tr)* versetzen (*s.o.* jdn); *itr (Preise)* anziehen; *on the ~ (fam)* in Bewegung; *to be ~d to tears* zu Tränen gerührt sein; *to get a ~ on (Am sl)* sich auf die Socken machen; *to make a ~* aufbrechen; *fig* Schritte unternehmen; *to ~ heaven and earth* Himmel und Erde in Bewegung setzen; alles (Erdenkliche) tun; *to ~ house* umziehen; *to ~ a motion* e-n Antrag stellen; *~ on!* weitergehen! *it's your ~* Sie sind am Zug; **~ment** ['-mənt] (Fort-)Bewegung; Tätigkeit, Handlung; Entwicklung; *mil* Truppenbewegung; *pol rel* (Massen-)Bewegung *f*, Bestrebungen *f pl*; Tendenz; Preis-, Kursbewegung *f*; (Waren-)Verkehr, Umsatz; *tech* Mechanismus *m*, (Uhr-)Werk; *mus* Tempo *n*, Rhythmus; *mus* Satz *m*; Darmentleerung *f*, Stuhlgang *m*; *pl* Maßnahmen *f pl*, Schritte *m pl*; *without ~~* bewegungs-, reg(ungs)los; *downward, upward ~~* Fallen; Steigen *n*; *underground ~~ (pol)* Untergrundbewegung *f*; *~~ by air* Lufttransport *m*; *~~ area (aero)* Rollfeld *n*; *~~ order (mil)* Marschbefehl *m*; *~~ of population* Bevölkerungsverschiebung *f*; **~r** ['-ə] *Am* Möbeltransporteur; *parl* Antragsteller; *tech* Motor *m*; *fig* Ursache *f*, Urheber *m*; *prime ~~* Haupttriebfeder *f*.

movie ['mu:vi] *Am fam* Film *m*; Kino *n*; *pl fam* Film *m (kollektiv)*; Kino(vorstellung *f*) *n*; Filmindustrie *f*; *to go to the ~s* ins Kino gehen; **~-goer** *Am fam* Kinobesucher(in *f*) *m*; **~ projector** Kinoprojektor *m*; **~ song** Filmschlager *m*.

moving ['mu:viŋ] beweglich; in Bewegung (befindlich); bewegend; *com* gut verkäuflich; *fig* (an)treibend, anregend, -reizend, aufstachelnd; rührend; hinreißend, packend; **~ band** Fließband *n*; **~-car, -van** Möbelwagen *m*; **~ coil** *el* Drehspule *f*; **~ force, power** treibende, Triebkraft *f*; **~-man** ['-mən] Möbeltransporteur *m*; **~ picture** Film; *pl* Film *m*, Kino, Lichtspieltheater *n*; *~~ advertising* Filmwerbung *f*; **~ spring** Antriebsfeder *f*; **~ stair (-case)** Rolltreppe *f*; **~ van** *Am* Möbelwagen *m*.

mow [mou] **1.** *irr mowed, mowed* od *mown tr* (ab)mähen; *itr* mähen, heuen, Heu machen; *to ~ down (den Feind)* niedermachen, -mähen; **~er** ['-ə] Mäher, Schnitter *m*; Mähmaschine *f*; **~ing** ['-iŋ] Mähen *n*; Mahd *f*; das geschnittene Gras *od* Korn; *~~-machine* Mähmaschine *f*; **2.** *meist dial Am* Heu-, Kornhaufen *m*; *(hay~, hayloft)* Heuboden; (Korn-)Speicher *m*.

much [mʌtʃ] *a* viel; *s* viel(es); Menge *f*; *adv* sehr; viel; oft; (so) ziemlich, beinahe, fast, ungefähr; *as ~* ebensoviel (*as* wie); ungefähr, etwa; so sehr; *as ~ again, more* noch (ein)mal soviel; *how ~?* wieviel? *so ~* soviel (*as* wie); nichts als; so sehr; *not ~ (fam)* sehr unwahrscheinlich; *not so ~ as* nicht einmal; *so ~ the more* um so mehr; *that, this ~* soviel; *very ~* sehr; *~ less* viel weniger; geschweige denn; *~ ado about nothing* viel Lärm um nichts! *~ of a size* ungefähr von der gleichen Größe; *to be not ~ of a* kein(e) gute(r) ... sein; nichts Besonderes leisten in; *to make ~ of* viel Aufhebens machen mit *od* von; *he is too ~ for me* ich komme mit ihm nicht mit; *I thought as ~* das dachte ich mir schon; **~ness** ['-nis] nur in: *~ of a ~~* so ziemlich dasselbe, ungefähr das gleiche; *that is ~ of a ~~* das läuft auf eins raus.

mucilag|e ['mju:silidʒ] (Pflanzen-)Schleim *m*; *Am* Gummilösung *f*; **~inous** [mjusi'lædʒinəs] schleimig, klebrig; schleimabsondernd.

muck [mʌk] *s* Dung *m*, Jauche *f*; Kompost(erde *f*); Dreck, Schmutz, Unrat, Kot; *min* Kohlengrus; *fam* Unsinn, Quatsch *m*; *tr* düngen; *fam* dreckig, schmutzig machen; *(to ~ out)* ausmisten; *fig sl (to ~ up)* versauen, zur Sau machen; verkorksen; *to make a ~ of* verschmieren; verpfuschen; *to ~ about (sl)* herumtrödeln, -bummeln; **~er** ['-ə] *sl* Sturz; Reinfall; *sl* Prolet, Scheißkerl *m*; *to come, to go a ~~ (sl)* stürzen; *fig* reinfallen; **~-heap, -hill** Misthaufen *m*; **~-rake** *s* Mistgabel *f*; *itr Am fig* im Dreck wühlen, *bes. pol* Korruptionsfälle aufspüren und Kapital daraus schlagen; **~raker** *Am* Sensationsmacher *m*; **~worm** *fig* Geizhals *m*; **~y** ['-i] schmutzig, dreckig.

muc|osity [mju'kɔsiti] schleimige Beschaffenheit *f*; **~ous** ['mju:kəs] *physiol* schleimig; Schleim-; *~~ membrane (anat)* Schleimhaut *f*; **~us** ['mju:kəs] *physiol* Schleim *m*.

mud [mʌd] *s* Schlamm, Kot, *(nasser)* Dreck, Schmutz; *fig* Dreck, Mist (-dreck), Plunder *m*, wertlose(s) Zeug *n*; Verleumdung, üble Nachrede *f*; *Am sl* Kaffee *m*, Schokolade *f*; *tr* mit Schmutz bespritzen; beschmutzen, schmutzig machen; *to drag in the ~ (fig)* in den Schmutz ziehen; *to fling, to throw ~ at (fig)* mit Dreck bewerfen, verleumden; *to stick in the ~* im Dreck stecken(geblieben sein); *here's ~ in your eye* zum Wohl! **~-bath** Schlamm-, Moorbad *n*; **~diness** ['-inis] Verschlammung; Trübung; *fig* Unklarheit, Verwirrung *f*; **~dy** ['-i] *a* schlammig, verschlammt, kotig, schmutzig, dreckig; *(Flüssigkeit)* trübe; dunkel; *(Farbe)* verschwommen; *fig* unklar, trüb(e), (ver)wirr(t); *tr itr* schmutzig machen, werden; *fig* verwirren; **~guard** *(Auto)* Kotflügel *m*; *(Fahrrad)* Schutzblech *n*; **~lark** Schmutzfink, Dreckspatz *m*; **~ rock** *geol* Schieferton *m*; **~-slinger** *fam* Verleumder *m*; **~-slinging** *fam* Verleumdung, üble Nachrede *f*.

muddle ['mʌdl] *tr* durchea.-, in Unordnung bringen; verwirren, über den Haufen werfen; verpfuschen; *Am (Flüssigkeiten)* mischen; umrühren; aufwühlen, trübe machen, trüben; *fig* verwirrt, konfus machen, durchea.bringen; benebeln; *itr* herumwursteln; pfuschen; *s* Durcheinander *n*, Unordnung, Verwirrung; *fig* Verwirrtheit, Unklarheit *f*; *to make a ~ of s.th. (fam)* etw verhunzen, vermasseln; *to ~ on, to ~ along* weiterwursteln; *to ~ through* sich durchwursteln; **~-headed** *a* durcheinander, geistig nicht auf der Höhe, wirr im Kopf; **~r** ['-ə] Wirrkopf; *Am* Rührlöffel *m*.

muff [mʌf] **1.** *tech* Muff, Stutzen *m*; *foot-~* Fußwärmer *m*; **~etee** [-ə'ti:] Pulswärmer *m*; **2.** *s sport* Niete *f*, Versager; *fam* Dummkopf, Tölpel *m*; *(Ball)* ungeschickte(s) Auffangen *n*; *tr* verderben, verpfuschen, *fam* verbocken, versieben, *sl* vermasseln; *(Ball)* verfehlen.

muffin ['mʌfin] *Art* kleine(s) flache(s) (Tee-)Gebäckstück *n*; **~eer** [mʌfi'niə] Salz-, Zuckerstreuer *m*.

muffle ['mʌfl] *tr (to ~ up)* einmumme(l)n; verhüllen; *(zwecks Schalldämpfung)* umwickeln, bedecken; *(Schall)* dämpfen; *s* gedämpfte(r) Ton; *zoo* Muffel *m*, *tech f*; *tech* Schalldämpfer, Auspufftopf; *min* Schmelztiegel *m*; **~ furnace** Muffelofen *m*; **~r** ['-ə] dicke(r) Wollschal; Faust-, Boxhandschuh; *mus* Dämpfer; Schalldämpfer, Auspufftopf *m*.

mufti ['mʌfti] Mufti *m*; *mil* Zivil (-anzug *m*) *n*; *in ~* in Zivil.

mug [mʌg] *s* Krug *m*, Kanne *f*; Humpen, Becher *m*; *sl* Schnauze; Fresse; Fratze; Grimasse *f*; *sl* Dussel, Dämlack, *Am sl* Kerl; *Am sl* Ganove; *Br sl* Büffler, Streber *m*; *itr sl* Gesichter, Grimassen schneiden; *that* dicht auftragen; *sl* büffeln, ochsen, pauken; *tr Am sl* fürs Verbrecheralbum knipsen; *Am sl* von hinten überfallen; *to ~ up (sl)* sich anmalen, sich schminken; büffeln, ochsen; **~ger** ['-ə] Gangster; schlechte(r) Schauspieler *m*; **~gins** ['-inz] *sl* Tölpel, Simpel, Dussel *m*.

mugg|iness ['mʌginis] Schwüle *f*; **~y** ['-i] schwül, dumpf; muffig.

mug|weed ['mʌgwi:d], **~wort** ['-wə:t] *bot* Beifuß *m*, Mutterkraut *n*.

mugwump ['mʌgwʌmp] *Am fam* Einzelgänger; *pol* Unabhängige(r), Parteilose(r) *m*; unzuverlässige(s) Parteimitglied; *fam* hohe(s) Tier *n*.

*

mulatto [mju:'lætou] *pl -oes s* Mulatte *m*, Mulattin *f*; *a* hellbraun.

mulberry ['mʌlbəri] Maulbeere *f*; Maulbeerbaum *m*.

mulch [mʌltʃ] *s (Gärtnerei)* Streu, Strohdecke *f*; *tr* mit e-r Streu, mit Stroh, Laub abdecken.

mulct [mʌlkt] *tr* mit e-r Geldstrafe belegen; betrügen (*of* um); *s* Geldstrafe *f*.

mule [mju:l] **1.** Maulesel *m*, *bes.* Maultier *n*; *biol (bes.* unfruchtbare) Kreuzung *f*, Bastard *m*, Hybride *f*; *fam* Dickkopf, eigensinnige(r) Mensch; *tech* Traktor *m*; *(Spinnerei)* Mule-, Jennymaschine *f*; **~-driver, ~teer** [mju:li'tiə], *Am* **~-skinner** Maultiertreiber *m*; **~-track, trail** Saumpfad *m*; **2.** Pantoffel *m*; **3.** *s. mewl*.

mulish ['mju:liʃ] *a* Maultier-; *fig* dick-, starrköpfig, bockig, eigensinnig.

mull [mʌl] **1.** Mull *m*; **2.** *s* Kuddelmuddel *m od n*, Wirrwarr *m*, Durcheinander *n*; Torfmull *m*; *tr (to make a ~ of)* durchea.bringen; verkorksen, verpfuschen; *itr Am* nachdenken, -sinnen, grübeln (*over* über); **3.** *tr (alkohol. Getränk)* erhitzen, süßen u. würzen; *~ed ale, beer* Warmbier *n*; *~ed wine* Glühwein *m*; **4.** *Scot* Vorgebirge, Kap *n*.

mullein, *Am a.* **mullen** ['mʌlin] *bot* Königskerze *f*.

mullet ['mʌlit] See-, Meerbarbe *(Fisch)*; Meeräsche *f (Fisch)*.

mulligan ['mʌligən] *(~ stew) Am* Eintopf *m*.

mulligatawny [mʌligə'tɔ:ni] *(indische)* Fleischsuppe *f* mit Curry.

mulligrubs ['mʌligrʌbz] *pl* schlechte Laune *f*; Rappel, Koller *m*; *hum* Bauchweh *n*, Kolik *f*.

mullion ['mʌliən] *s* Mittel-, Fensterpfosten *m*; *tr* mit Fensterpfosten versehen; abteilen.

mullock ['mʌlək] *(Australien) min* taube(s) Gestein *n*; *dial* Schutt *m*.

multeity [mʌl'ti:iti] Vielheit *f*.

multi [mʌlti] *pref* viel-, mehr-; **~cellular** [-'seljulə] *biol* vielzellig; **~colo(u)r** [-'kʌlə] viel-, mehrfarbig;

~~ *print* Mehrfarbendruck *m*; **~farious** [-'fɛəriəs] vielfältig, mannigfaltig, -fach; **~form** ['mʌltifɔ:m] vielgestaltig; **~formity** [mʌlti'fɔ:miti] Vielgestaltigkeit *f*; **~lateral** ['mʌlti'lætərəl] vielseitig; *biol* allseitwendig; *pol* multilateral; **~lingual** ['mʌlti'liŋgwəl] mehrsprachig; **~millionaire** ['mʌltimiljə'nɛə] Multi-, mehrfache(r) Millionär *m*; **~motored** ['mʌlti'moutəd] *a* mehrmotorig; **~ple** ['mʌltipl] *a* viel-, mehrfach *a. el*; mannigfaltig; *med* multipel; Vielfach-, Mehrfach-; *s (~~ switch)* Mehrfachschalter *m*; *math* Vielfache(s) *n*; *in ~~* parallel geschaltet; *~~-disk clutch* Mehrscheibenkupplung *f*; *~~ firm, shop, store (com)* Filialgroßbetrieb *m*; *~~ plug* Mehrfachstecker *m*; *~~ production* Serienherstellung *f*; *~~-road crossing* Straßenspinne *f*; *~~ sclerosis (med)* multiple Sklerose *f*; *~~ star* Sternhaufen *m*; **~plex** ['-pleks] viel-, mannigfach, -fältig; *~~ telephony* Mehrfachfernsprechen *n*; **~pliable** ['-plaiəbl], **~plicable** ['-plikəbl] *math* multiplizierbar; **~plicand** [mʌltipli'kænd] *math* Multiplikand *m*; **~plicate** ['mʌltiplikeit] viel-, mannigfach; **~plication** [mʌltipli'keiʃən] Vervielfachung; Vermehrung; *tech* Übersetzung; *bes. math* Multiplikation *f*; *~~ process (math)* Vervielfältigungsvorgang; *biol* Fortpflanzungsprozeß *m*; *~~ table* Einmaleins *n*; **~plicity** [mʌlti'plisiti] Vielfalt, -fältigkeit; (große) Menge *f*; **~plier** ['mʌltiplaiə] Vermehrer; *math* Multiplikator; *phys* Verstärker; *el* Vorwiderstand *m*; *tech* Übersetzung; *bot* Brutzwiebel *f*; **~ply** ['-plai] *tr itr* (sich) vervielfältigen, (sich) vermehren, (sich) vergrößern, (sich) erweitern, (sich) verstärken; *math* multiplizieren, malnehmen (*by* mit); *~~ing glass* Vergrößerungsglas *n*; **~polar** [-'poulə] mehrpolig; **~purpose** ['-pə:pəs] Mehrzweck-; **~stage** ['-steidʒ] mehrstufen-; **~stor(e)y** ['-stɔri] Hochhaus-; mehrgeschossig; *~~ car park* Parkhaus *n*; **~tude** ['-tju:d] Vielheit, große Zahl; Menge, Masse *f* (Menschen); *the ~~* die große Masse, der große Haufen, das gewöhnliche Volk; **~tudinous** [-'tju:dinəs] (sehr) zahlreich; mannigfach, vielfältig; **~way plug** Vielfachstecker *m*.

mum [mʌm] **1.** *a* still; *interj*: *~! u.*: *~'s the word* pst! still! Mund halten! **2.** Mama *f*; **3.** *tr itr* mimen.

mumble ['mʌmbl] *tr itr* murmeln; mummeln; *s* Gemurmel *n*.

mumbo jumbo ['mʌmbou 'dʒʌmbou] Medizinmann; Popanz, Götze *m*, Idol *n*; Fetisch *m*; Schreckgespenst; Wortgeklingel; Kauderwelsch *n*.

mummer ['mʌmə] Vermummte(r); Possenreißer; *hum* Mime, Schauspieler *m*; **~y** ['-ri] Mummenschanz; *pej* Firlefanz, Hokospokus *m*.

mumm|ification [mʌmifi'keiʃən] *med* trockene Gangrän; Mumifizierung; Einbalsamierung *f*; **~ify** ['mʌmifai] *tr* mumifizieren; einbalsamieren; *itr* austrocknen, einschrumpfen; **~y** ['mʌmi] **1.** Mumie *f a. fig*; *~~ case* Mumiensarg *m*; **2.** Mama *f*.

mumps [mʌmps] *pl mit sing med* Ziegenpeter, Mumps *m*.

munch [mʌntʃ] *itr* schmatzen.

mundane ['mʌndein] irdisch, weltlich; Welt-.

municipal [mju(:)'nisipəl] städtisch, kommunal; Stadt-, Gemeinde-; *pol* Landes-; **~ administration, government** Stadt-, Gemeindeverwaltung *f*; **~ borough** Stadtbezirk *m*; **~ budget** Gemeindehaushalt *m*; **~ building** öffentliche(s) Gebäude *n*; **~ council** Stadt-, Gemeinderat *m (Körperschaft)*; **~ council(l)or** Stadtrat, -verordnete(r) *m*; **~ elections** *pl* Gemeindewahlen *f pl*; **~ity** [mju(:)nisi'pæliti] Stadt-, Gemeindeverwaltung *f*, Magistrat *m*; (Stadt-)Gemeinde *f*; **~ loan** Kommunalanleihe *f*; **~ rates, taxes** *pl* Gemeindesteuern *f pl*; **~ undertakings** *pl* Stadtwerke *n pl*, Kommunalbetriebe *m pl*.

munificen|ce [mju:'nifis(ə)ns] Freigebigkeit *f*; **~t** [-t] freigebig; großzügig.

muniment ['mju:nimənt] *meist pl* (Besitz-)Urkunde *f*, Rechtstitel *m*; Archiv *n*.

munition [mju:'niʃən] *tr* mit Kriegsmaterial *od* Munition versorgen; *s pl* Kriegsmaterial *n*; Nachschub *m*; **~ plant** Rüstungsfabrik *f*.

mural ['mjuərəl] *a* Mauer-, Wand-; *s (~ painting)* Wandgemälde *n*, -malerei *f*.

murder ['mə:də] *s* Mord *m* (*of* an); Ermordung *f*; *tr* (er)morden, umbringen; *fig* verhunzen, verderben; *(Zeit)* totschlagen; *Am sl* besiegen, schlagen; *itr* morden; e-n Mord begehen; *a Am sl* schwierig; *(Mensch)* eigensinnig; *to commit (a) ~* e-n Mord begehen; *to cry blue ~ (fam)* zetermordio schreien; *to get away with ~ (Am sl)* sich aus der Affäre ziehen; *~ will out* die Sonne bringt es an den Tag; *accused of, charged with ~* unter Mordanklage; *attempted ~, attempt at ~* Mordversuch *m*; *~ in the first degree* vorsätzliche(r) Mord *m*; *~ in the second degree* Totschlag *m*; *~ by poisoning* Giftmord *m*; *~ with robbery* Raubmord *m*; **~er** ['-rə] Mörder *m*; *mass ~~* Massenmörder *m*; **~ess** ['-ris] Mörderin *f*; **~ous** ['-rəs] mörderisch *a. fig*; blutig; Mord-; *~~ weapon* Mordwaffe *f*.

muriat|e ['mjuəriit] *chem* Hydro-, Kaliumchlorid *n*; **~ic** [-'ætik]: *acid (com)* Salzsäure *f*.

murky ['mə:ki] dunkel, finster, trüb(e); *(Finsternis)* tief; *fam* schändlich.

murmur ['mə:mə] *s* Murmeln; Murren; *(Wasser)* Rauschen; *(Bienen)* Summen; *med* Rasseln, Geräusch *n*; *itr* murmeln; murren (*at, against* gegen); *tr* (vor sich hin) murmeln; **~ous** ['-rəs] murmelnd; murrend.

murrain ['mʌrin, *Am* 'mə:-] Vieh-, *bes.* Maul- u. Klauenseuche *f*.

musc|adel [mʌskə'del], **~at** ['mʌskət] **~atel** [mʌskə'tel] Muskateller(traube *f*) *m*.

musc|le ['mʌsl] *s* Muskel(gewebe *n*, -kraft *f*); *Am sl* Muskelprotz *m*; *itr*: *to ~ in (Am fam)* sich s-n Weg bahnen, sich ein-, vordrängen (*on* bei); *not to move a ~~* keine Miene verziehen; sich nicht rühren; *to be ~~-bound* e-n Muskelkater haben; **~ular** ['mʌskjulə] *a* Muskel-; muskulös, kräftig, stark; *~~ spasm* Muskelkrampf *m*; *~~ strength, tissue* Muskelkraft *f*, -gewebe *n*.

Muscovite ['mʌskəvait] *s* Moskowiter, Russe *m*; *a* moskowitisch, russisch.

Muse [mju:z] Muse *f a. fig*.

muse [mju:z] *itr tr* (nach)denken, -sinnen, -grübeln (*on, over* über); **~ful** ['-ful] grüblerisch; in Gedanken versunken; **~r** ['-ə] Grübler *m*.

museum [mju(:)'ziəm] Museum *n*; Sammlung(en *pl*) *f*; *fit for a ~ (a. pej)* museumsreif; **~ piece** Museumsstück *n a. fig*.

mush [mʌʃ] **1.** *Am* (Mais-)Mehlbrei; *allg* Brei *m*; *Am sl* Geschwätz *n*, Mund *m*, Gesicht; *Am sl* Süßholzraspeln; *radio* Knistern *n*; **~y** ['-i] breiig; *fig* rührselig, weinerlich; sentimental; **2.** *itr u. s Am (u. Kanada)* (mit e-m Hundeschlitten) (e-n) Fußmarsch *m* über Schneefelder (machen); durch den Schnee stapfen; **3.** *sl (~-room)* Musspritze *f*, (Regen-)Schirm *m*.

mushroom ['mʌʃrum] *s* (*bes.* eßbarer) Pilz; *fam (breitrandiger)* (Damen-)Strohhut *m*; *fig* Eintagsfliege, kurzlebige Erscheinung *f*; Emporkömmling, Neureich; *sl* Regenschirm *m*; *a* pilzartig, -förmig; *fig* wie Pilze aus dem Boden geschossen, Eintags-; rasch; *itr* Pilze sammeln; *(Gewehrkugel)* sich abplatten; *Am (Feuer)* sich ausbreiten; *to ~ up (Am)* wie Pilze aus dem Boden schießen.

music ['mju:zik] Musik; Tonkunst *f*; Musikstück; Orchester *n*, Musikkapelle *f*; Noten *f pl*, Musikalien *pl*; Klang, Wohllaut; Gesang *m*; *to face the ~ (fam)* keine Angst haben; für seine Sache gradestehen; *to play from ~* vom Blatt spielen; *to set to ~ (Gedicht)* in Musik setzen, vertonen; *background ~* musikalische Untermalung *f*; **~al** ['-əl] *a* musikalisch, Musik- *a. theat*; wohlklingend, melodisch; musikalisch, musikbegabt; *s (~ film)* Filmoperette *f*; *Am (~ comedy)* musikalische Komödie *f*; *~~ box (Br)* Spieldose *f*; *~~ clock* Spieluhr *f*; *~~ instrument* Musikinstrument *n*; *~~ piece* Musikstück *n*; **~ale** [mju:zi'kɑ:l, *Am* -'kæl] *Am (fam ~al)* Musik-, musikalische(r) Abend *m*; **~ality** [-'kæliti], **~alness** ['mju:zikəlnis] Musikalität *f*; Wohlklang *m*; **~-book** Notenheft *n*; **~-box** *Am* Spieldose *f*; **~ festival** Musikfestspiele *n pl*; **~-hall** Varieté(theater), Kabarett *n*, *fam pej* Tingeltangel *m* u. *n*; *Am theat mus* Zuhörerschaft *f*; **~ian** [mju(:)'ziʃən] Musiker; Musikant *m*; *to be a good ~~* sehr musikalisch sein; gut spielen; **~-paper** Notenpapier *n*; **~-rack, -stand** Notenständer *m*; **~-stool** Klavierhocker *m*.

musk [mʌsk] Moschus, Bisam *m*; Moschusparfüm; *(~-deer)* Moschustier *n*; *(~-mallow)* Moschusmalve *f*; **~-bag** Moschusbeutel *m*; **~-deer** Moschustier *n*; **~-ox** Moschus-, Bisamochse *m*; **~-rat** Bisamratte *f*; Bisam *m (Pelz)*; **~-shrew** Bisam-, Moschusspitzmaus *f*; **~y** ['-i] *a* Moschus-; nach Moschus riechend; moschusartig.

musket ['mʌskit] *hist mil* Muskete *f*; **~eer** [mʌski'tiə] Musketier *m*; **~ry** ['mʌskitri] Musketiere *m pl*; Musketen *f pl*; Musketenfeuer *n*; Schießkunst *f*, -unterricht *m*; *~~ manual* Schießvorschrift *f*.

muslin ['mʌzlin] Musselin *m*.

musquash ['mʌskwɔʃ] Bisamratte *f*; Bisam *m (Pelz)*.

muss [mʌs] *s Am fam* Durcheinander *n*, Unordnung *f*, Wirrwarr *m*; *tr Am fam (to ~ up)* durchea.-, in Unordnung bringen; vermasseln, verpfuschen; zerknittern; beschmutzen; **~y** ['-i] *Am fam* schmutzig; zerknittert, verwühlt; unordentlich.

mussel ['mʌsl] (Mies-, Fluß-)Muschel *f*.

Mussulman ['mʌslmən] *pl -s*; *s* Moslem, Mohammedaner *m*; *a* islamisch, mohammedanisch.

must [mʌst] **1.** *aux pret*: *must* muß, müssen; *I must (fam)* ich muß mal (austreten); *~ I?* darf ich? *you ~ not* du darfst nicht; *a* notwendig, erforderlich; unbedingt wichtig, wesentlich; *s* Notwendigkeit *f*, Muß, Erfordernis *n*; *this book is a ~* dieses Buch muß man gelesen haben; **2.** Most; neue(r) Wein *m*; **3.** Moder(geruch) *m*.

mustach|e [məs'tɑ:ʃ], **~io** [-ou] *Am* Schnurrbart *m.*

mustang ['mʌstæŋ] Mustang *m.*

mustard ['mʌstəd] Senf *a. bot,* Mostrich *m*; Senffarbe *f*; *Am mil sl* schneidige(r) Kerl *m*; **~-gas** Senfgas, Gelbkreuz *n*; **~-oil, plaster, poultice, pot, seed** Senföl *n*, -pflaster *n*, -packung *f*, -topf *m*, -same *m.*

muster ['mʌstə] *tr mil* antreten lassen; mustern; *(to ~ up)* sammeln, zs.-, aufbringen; *itr mil* antreten, sich sammeln; *s mil* Antreten *n*, Appell *m*, Parade; Musterung; angetretene Mannschaft *f*, vorgezeigte Sachen *f pl*; Stärkemeldung; Musterrolle *f*; *to ~ in, out (Am mil)* einziehen; entlassen; *to pass ~* die Bedingungen erfüllen; Zustimmung finden *(with* bei); *to ~ (up) courage, strength* allen Mut, s-e ganze Kraft zs.nehmen; **~~ roll** *mar mil* Muster-, Stammrolle *f.*

must|iness ['mʌstinis] Dumpfigkeit; Dumpfheit; *fig* Antiquiertheit *f*; **~y** ['-i] dumpfig, muffig, mod(e)rig; *fig* abgestanden; abgenutzt; antiquiert.

mutab|ility [mju:tə'biliti] Veränderlichkeit; *fig* Unbeständigkeit; *biol* Mutationsfähigkeit *f*; **~le** ['mju:təbl] veränderlich; unbeständig; wankelmütig; *biol* mutationsfähig.

mutation [mju:'teiʃən] (Ver-)Änderung; Wandlung *f*; Wandel *m*; *mus biol* Mutation; *tech* Umformung *f*; *gram* Umlaut *m.*

mute [mju:t] *a* stumm *(a. Buchstabe)*; schweigend; *s* (Taub-)Stumme(r); *theat* Statist; *gram* stumme(r) Buchstabe; *(~ consonant)* Verschlußlaut; *mus* (Schall-)Dämpfer *m*; *tr mus* dämpfen; *to stand ~ (jur)* die Antwort verweigern; sprachlos dastehen; **~ness** ['-nis] Stummheit *f.*

mutilat|e ['mju:tileit] *tr* verstümmeln *a. fig*; **~ion** [mju:ti'leiʃən] Verstümmelung *f.*

mutin|eer [mju:ti'niə] Meuterer *m*; **~ous** ['mju:tinəs] meuternd; meuterisch, aufrührerisch; **~y** ['-i] *s* Meuterei *f*; *itr* meutern.

mut(t) [mʌt] *sl* Schafskopf, Esel, Dussel; *sl* Köter *m.*

mutter ['mʌtə] *itr* (vor sich hin)murmeln; murren *(at* über); *(Donner)* rollen; *tr* brummen, murmeln; murren; *s* Gemurmel; Murren *n.*

mutton ['mʌtn] Hammelfleisch *n*; *to eat o.'s ~ with* zu Mittag essen mit; *dead as ~* mausetot; *leg of ~* Hammelkeule *f*; **~-chop** Hammelkotelett *n*; *pl* Koteletten *pl (Bart)*; **~-head** *fam* Schafs-, Dummkopf *m.*

mutual ['mju:tjuəl, *Am* -tʃu-] gegen-, wechselseitig; gemeinsam; *by ~ agreement, consent* in gegenseitigem Einverständnis; *for ~ benefit* zu beiderseitigem Nutzen; *on ~ terms* auf (der Grundlage der) Gegenseitigkeit; **~-aid society** Hilfs-, Unterstützungsverein *m* (auf Gegenseitigkeit); **~-aid treaty** *pol* Beistandspakt *m*; **~ association** Genossenschaft *f*; **~ assurance, insurance** Versicherung *f* auf Gegenseitigkeit; **~ building association** Baugenossenschaft *f*; **~ relations** *pl* Wechselbeziehungen *f pl*; **~ savings-bank** Genossenschaftsbank *f*; **~ity** [mju:tju'æliti] Gegen-, Wechselseitigkeit *f.*

*

muzzle ['mʌzl] *s* (vorspringende) Schnauze *f*, Maul *n*; Maulkorb *m*; *tech* Mündung *f*; *tr* e-n Maulkorb anlegen *(an animal* e-m Tier); *fig* den Mund, *sl* das Maul stopfen *(s.o.* jdm); *(Menschen; Presse)* knebeln; mundtot machen; *Am sl* küssen; *itr* herumschnüffeln, (herum)schnuppern; **~-loader, -loading gun** Vorderlader *m (Gewehr)*; **~-velocity** Anfangsgeschwindigkeit *f (e-s Geschosses).*

muzzy ['mʌzi] *fam* verwirrt, durcheinander, kopflos; benebelt, duselig.

my [mai] *prn attr* mein(e); *interj (oh, ~!)* ach, du Schreck!

myalgia [mai'ældʒiə] Muskelschmerz *m.*

myc|ology [mai'kɔlədʒi] Mykologie, Pilzkunde *f*; **~osis** [-'kousis] Pilzkrankheit *f.*

myelitis [maiə'laitis] Rücken-, Knochenmarkentzündung *f.*

myocardi|ogram [maio(u)'kɑ:diəgræm] *med* Elektrokardiogramm *n*; **~ograph** [-grɑ:f] EKG-Apparat *m*; **~tis** [-'daitis] Herzmuskelentzündung *f*; **~um** [-diəm] Herzmuskel *m.*

my|ology [mai'ɔlədʒi] Myologie, Muskellehre *f*; **~oma** [-'oumə] *pl a. -ta* Myom *n*, Muskelgeschwulst *f.*

myop|e ['maioup] Kurzsichtige(r) *m*; **~ia** [mai'oupjə], **~y** ['maioupi] Kurzsichtigkeit *f*; **~ic** [mai'ɔpik] kurzsichtig.

myriad ['miriəd] *s* große Zahl, Myriade *f*; *a ~* zehntausend; *a* zahllos.

myriapod ['miriəpɔd] *zoo* Tausendfuß, -füß(l)er *m.*

myrmidon ['mə:midən] blind gläubige(r) Anhänger *m*; willenlose(s) Werkzeug *n*; Scherge *m.*

myrrh [mə:] Myrrhe(nharz *n*) *f.*

myrtle ['mə:tl] Myrte *f*; *Am* Immer-, Singrün *n.*

*

myself [mai'self] *prn* ich (selbst); *(reflexiv)* mich, mir; *(my ... self)* mein eigenes Ich; *I'm not ~ today* ich bin heute nicht ganz bei mir.

myster|ious [mis'tiəriəs] geheimnisvoll, -umwoben, rätselhaft, mysteriös; **~iousness** [-nis] Rätselhaftigkeit *f*, *das* Geheimnisvolle, Mysteriöse, Dunkle; **~y** ['mistəri] Geheimnis, Rätsel *(to* für, dat); Dunkel; Mysterium *a. rel*; *(~~ play) theat hist* Mysterienspiel; *theat* Kriminalstück *n*; *pl rel hist* Mysterien *n pl*; **~~***(novel)* Kriminalroman *m*; *~~ station (radio)* Geheimsender *m*; *~~ tour* Fahrt *f* ins Blaue.

mystic ['mistik] *a* mystisch; geheim, okkult; rätselhaft, mysteriös; unklar; *s* Mystiker; *rel hist* Myste *m*; **~al** ['-əl] allegorisch, sinnbildlich, symbolisch; geheim; rätselhaft; **~ism** ['mistisizm] Mystizismus *m*; Mystik *f.*

mystif|ication [mistifi'keiʃən] Irreführung, Täuschung; Fopperei *f*; **~y** ['mistifai] *tr* stutzig, perplex machen; an der Nase herum-, anführen, foppen, narren; mit Geheimnissen umgeben, in Dunkel hüllen.

myth [miθ] Mythos, Mythus *m*, Mythe; Mythologie; *fig* Fabel, erfundene Geschichte; Fiktion, Erfindung *f*; **~ic(al)** ['miθik(əl)] mythisch; *fig* fiktiv, erfunden; **~ologic(al)** [miθə'lɔdʒik(əl), mai-] mythologisch; **~ology** [mi'θɔlədʒi, mai-] Mythologie, Götterlehre; Mythenforschung *f.*

myx|oedema [miksi'di:mə] *med* Myxödem *n*; **~omatosis** [miksəmə'tousis] *med* Myxomatose *f*; **~omycete** [miksoumai'si:t] Schleimpilz *m.*

N

N, n [en] *pl* '~s N, n *n.*

nab [næb] *tr fam* schnappen; erwischen; klauen; *s fam* Polizist *m.*

nabob ['neibɔb] *hist* Nabob *m a. fig.*

nacelle [nə'sel] *aero* (Flugzeug-)Rumpf *m*; (Motor-)Gondel *f*; Ballonkorb *m.*

nacr|e ['neikə] Perlmuschel, -mutter *f*; **~(e)ous** ['neikr(i)əs] Perlmutter-; perlmutterartig.

nadir ['neidiə] *astr* Nadir; *fig* Tiefpunkt *m*; *at the ~* auf dem Nullpunkt.

n(a)evus ['ni:vəs] *pl n(a)evi* ['-ai] Muttermal *n.*

nag [næg] **1.** *tr* (dauernd) herumnörgeln an, schimpfen mit; *itr* schimpfen, meckern, keifen *(at* mit); **2.** kleine(s) Pferd; Pony *n*; *pej* Klepper; *mot* Klapperkasten *m*; **~ger** ['-ə] Nörgler *m*; **~ging** ['-iŋ] nörgelnd; *(Schmerz)* bohrend.

naiad ['naiæd] Najade, Quellnymphe; *fig* Wassernixe *f.*

nail [neil] *s* (Finger-, Zehen-)Nagel *m*; *zoo* Kralle, Klaue *f*; Nagel *(zum Befestigen)*; *sl* Glimmstengel *m*, Zigarette *f*; *tr* nageln *(on* auf; *to* an); fest-, zs.-, an-, zunageln; befestigen; *(Pflock)* einschlagen; *(den Blick)* heften, *(s-e Aufmerksamkeit)* richten *(on* auf); *(Handel)* abschließen; bloßstellen; *fam* herauskriegen, entdecken; *fam* schnappen, festhalten, verhaften; *to ~ down (fig)* festnageln, -legen; *to ~ up* an-, zunageln; *on the ~* auf der Stelle; zur rechten Zeit; am rechten Ort; *to hit the ~ on the head (fig)* den Nagel auf den Kopf treffen; *to ~ o.'s colo(u)rs to the mast* Farbe bekennen; keinen Schritt nachgeben; *to ~ a lie to the counter* e-e Lüge festnageln; *coffin ~ (sl)* Sargnagel *m*, Zigarette *f*; *right as ~s* goldrichtig; *as hard as ~s* von eiserner Gesundheit; *fig* steinhart; **~-brush** Nagelbürste *f*; **~-claw, puller** Nagelzieher *m*; **~er** ['-ə] *hist* Nagelschmied *m*; *sl* Prachtding *n*, -kerl *m*; *sl* Kanone *f*, As *n*; **~-file** Nagelfeile *f*; **~-head** Nagelkopf *m*; **~ing** ['-iŋ] *a sl* prima, Klasse, famos; *s* Zu-, Vernageln; *(Schuh)* Nageln *n*; **~-scissors** *pl* Nagelschere *f*; **~-varnish** Nagellack *m.*

naïve, naive [nɑ:'i:v] naiv, unbefangen, kindlich; **naïveté** [nɑ:'i:vtei], **naïvety, naivety** [nɑ:'i:vti] Naivität, Unbefangenheit, Kindlichkeit *f.*

naked ['neikid] nackt, bloß, unbedeckt, unverhüllt; kahl, dürr; leer; offen; ungeschützt, schutzlos; mittellos, unbemittelt; *(Draht)* blank; *with* *the ~ eye* mit bloßem Auge; *with ~ fists* mit bloßen Fäusten; *the ~ fact, truth* die nackte Tatsache, reine Wahrheit; *N~ Lady (bot)* Herbstzeitlose *f*; **~ness** ['-nis] Nacktheit, Blöße, Unverhülltheit *a. fig*; Ungeschütztheit; Mittellosigkeit; Kahlheit; Leere *f*.

*

namby-pamby ['næmbi'pæmbi] *a* weichlich, süßlich, seicht; saft- u. kraftlos, abgeschmackt, albern; *s* alberne(r) Mensch *m*; dumme(s) Gerede *n*.

name [neim] *s* Name; (guter) Ruf *m*; Berühmtheit; Familie *f*; *a Am* bekannt, berühmt; *tr* (be)nennen (*after, from, (Am) for* nach); bezeichnen (als); erwähnen, auf-, anführen; festsetzen, bestimmen; *bes. Am* ernennen (*for, to* für, zu); *by ~* mit Namen, namentlich; dem Namen nach; *in ~ only* nur dem Namen nach; *in the ~ of* im Namen *gen*; *of the ~ of* mit Namen, namens; *to s.o.'s ~* jdm gehörig; *under the ~ of* unter dem Namen; *not to have a penny to o.'s ~* keinen Pfennig besitzen; *to call (bad) ~s* beschimpfen; *to give o.'s ~* s-n Namen nennen; *to give it a ~ (fam)* s-e Wünsche äußern; *to have a ~ for* bekannt sein für; *to know only by ~* nur dem Namen nach kennen; *to make a ~ for o.s.* sich e-n Namen machen; *to put o.'s ~ down for* kandidieren für; *to take o.'s ~ off the books* (aus e-m Verein) austreten; *to win o.s. a ~* berühmt werden; *to ~ o.'s price* den Preis sagen; *Christian ~, (Am) first, given ~* Vorname *m*; *family ~, (Am) last ~* Familien-, Nachname *m*; *full ~* Vor- u. Zuname *m*; **~-day** Namenstag *m*; **~less** ['-lis] namenlos, ohne Namen; unbe-, -genannt; unbekannt, obskur; unsagbar, unaussprechlich; unbeschreiblich, nicht wiederzugeben(d); *in ~~ dread* in namenloser Angst; **~ly** ['-li] *adv* nämlich; **~-part** *theat* Titelrolle *f*; **~-plate** Namens-, Firmen-, Türschild *n*; **~sake** Namensvetter *m*.

nam(e)able ['neim(i)əbl] nennbar; erwähnens-, bemerkenswert.

nancy ['nænsi] *sl* Muttersöhnchen *n*.

nankeen, nankin [næn'kin] Nanking *m (Stoff)*; *pl* Nankinghosen *f pl*.

nanny ['næni] *(Kindersprache)* Kindermädchen *n*; **~-goat** *fam* Ziege, Geiß *f*.

*

nap [næp] **1.** *itr* schlummern; *fam* ein Schläfchen machen; *s* Schlummer *m*, Schläfchen, *fam* Nickerchen *n*; *to catch s.o. ~ping* jdn überraschen, überrumpeln; *to take a ~* ein Nickerchen machen; **2.** *s* Flor *m*; Noppe *f*; *tr (Tuch)* (auf)rauhen; **~ fabric** Noppenstoff *m*; **~less** ['-lis] *(Tuch)* glatt; abgetragen, -genutzt, fadenscheinig; **3.** *(Kartenspiel)* Napoleon *m*; *to go ~ (fig)* aufs Ganze gehen.

napalm ['neipɑ:m] Napalm *n*; **~ bomb** Napalm-, Brandbombe *f*.

nape [neip] Genick *n*, Nacken *m*.

napery ['neipəri] *obs Scot Am* Haushalts-, *bes.* Tischwäsche *f*.

naphtha ['næfθə] Naphtha *n* od *f*, Roherdöl; *Am* Petroleum *n*; **~lene** ['-li:n] Naphthalin *n*.

napkin ['næpkin] Serviette *f*, Mundtuch; kleine(s) Handtuch *n*; *bes. Br* Windel; *Am (sanitary ~)* Monatsbinde *f*; **~-ring** Serviettenring *m*.

napoleon [nə'pouljən] *Am* Blätterteig *m*; **N~ic** [nəpouli'ɔnik] napoleonisch.

nap|oo [nə'pu:] *a sl* nichtsnutzig; erledigt; **~py** ['næpi] *a (Bier)* stark; *s* Windel *f*.

narciss|ism [nɑ:'sisizm] *psychol* Narzißmus *m*; **~us** [-'sisəs] *pl a. -cissi* [-ai] *bot* Narzisse *f*.

narc|osis [nɑ:'kousis] *pl a. -ses (med)* Narkose, Betäubung *f*; **~otic** [nɑ:'kɔtik] *a* narkotisch, betäubend; *s* Narkotikum; Betäubungsmittel; Rauschgift(süchtiger *m*) *n*; **~otism** ['nɑ:kətizm] Rauschgiftsucht *f*; **~otize** ['nɑ:kətaiz] *tr* narkotisieren, betäuben.

nard [nɑ:d] *bot* Narde(nöl *n*) *f*.

narghile ['nɑ:gili] Wasserpfeife *f*.

nark [nɑ:k] *s fam* Lockvogel, Spitzel *m*; *tr fam* bespitzeln; ärgern; *~ it!* hör auf.

narrat|e [næ'reit] *tr* erzählen; berichten; **~ion** [-ʃən] Erzählung *f*; Bericht *m*; erzählende Prosa *f*; *(Buchung)* Wortlaut *m*; **~ive** ['nærətiv] *a* erzählend; mitteilsam; *s* Erzählung, Geschichte *f*; Bericht *m*, Darstellung; Erzählkunst *f*; **~or,** *Am a.* **~er** [næ'reitə] Erzähler; Berichtende(r); *theat radio* Sprecher *m* (des Zwischentextes); **~ress** [-ris] Erzählerin *f*.

narrow ['nærou] *a* eng, schmal, eingeengt; *fig* begrenzt, beschränkt; knapp; *(Verhältnisse)* dürftig, ärmlich, eng; engherzig. -stirnig; genau, gründlich, sorgfältig; *s* Enge, enge Stelle; Straßenenge; *pl* Land-, Meerenge *f*; *itr* sich verengen (*into* zu); enger, schmäler werden; Maschen abnehmen; *tr* enger machen, einengen; begrenzen, beschränken; in die Enge treiben; *tech* bündeln; *to ~ down to* hinauslaufen auf; *by a ~ margin* knapp; gerade, noch; *in a ~ circle of friends* im engsten Freundeskreis; *in ~ circumstances* in dürftigen Verhältnissen; *in the ~est sense* im engsten Sinne des Wortes, ganz wörtlich; *with a ~ majority* mit knapper Mehrheit; *to have a ~ escape, (fam) squeak* mit knapper Not davonkommen; *to look ~ly into s.th.* etw genau untersuchen; *a ~ victory* ein knapper Sieg *m*; **~ gauge** *s* Schmalspur *f*; **~-gauge** *a* schmalspurig, Schmalspur-; *fam fig* verbohrt, engstirnig; *~~ railway* Schmalspurbahn *m*; **~ market** geringe(r) Umsatz, flaue(r) Markt *m*; **~-minded** *a* engstirnig, -herzig, voller Vorurteile; **~-mindedness** Kleinlichkeit; Engstirnigkeit *f*; **~ness** ['-nis] Enge; Begrenztheit, Beschränktheit, Knappheit; Genauigkeit; Engstirnigkeit *f*.

nasal ['neizəl] *a* Nasen-; *(Phonetik)* nasal, Nasal-; nasalierend, näselnd; *s (~ sound)* Nasallaut *m*; **~ bone** *anat* Nasenbein *n*; **~ cavity** *anat* Nasenhöhle *f*; **~ity** [nei'zæliti] nasale Beschaffenheit *f*; **~ization** [neizəlai'zeiʃən] Nasalierung *f*; **~ize** ['neizəlaiz] *tr* nasalieren; **~ partition, septum** Nasenscheidewand *f*; **~ twang** Näseln *n*.

nascent ['næsnt] werdend, entstehend, aufkeimend; *chem* freiwerdend.

nast|iness ['nɑ:stinis] Schmutz *m*; Häßlichkeit; Widerlichkeit; Anstößigkeit; Gemeinheit *f (a. Handlung)*; gemeine Reden *f pl*; *(Wetter)* Abscheulichkeit *f*; **~y** ['-i] schmutzig, dreckig; garstig, häßlich, scheußlich, sehr unangenehm; *(Wetter)* abscheulich, greulich; widerlich, eklig, ekelerregend; *fig* unflätig, anstößig, obszön; gemein, niedrig, tückisch, boshaft, bösartig; garstig, ekelhaft (*to* gegen); *(Krankheit)* schwer, ernst, gefährlich; *(See)* sehr bewegt.

nasturtium [nəs'tə:ʃəm] *bot* (*bes.* Brunnen-, Kapuziner-)Kresse *f*.

natal ['neitl] *a* Geburts-; **~ hour** Geburtsstunde *f*; **~ity** [nei'tæliti] Geburtenziffer *f*.

nat|ant ['neitənt] schwimmend; **~ation** [nei'teiʃən] Schwimmen *n*, Schwimmsport *m*; **~atorial** [neitə'tɔ:riəl], **~atory** ['neitətəri] *a* Schwimm-; **~atorium** [neitə'tɔ:riəm] *pl a. -ria* [-riə] *Am* (*bes.* Hallen-)Schwimmbad, -becken *n*.

nation ['neiʃən] Volk *n*, Nation *f*; *commonwealth of ~s* Staatengemeinschaft *f*; *creditor, debtor ~* Gläubiger-, Schuldnerstaat *m*; *law of ~s* Völkerrecht *n*; *the League of N~s* der Völkerbund; *member ~* Mitgliedsstaat *m*; **~al** ['næʃənl] *a* national; National-; Volks-; staatlich; Staats-; national (gesinnt), patriotisch; *s* Staatsangehörige(r), -bürger *m*; *~~ anthem* Nationalhymne *f*; *~~ assembly* Nationalversammlung *f*; *~~ bank* Staatsbank *f*; *N~~ Bureau of Economic Research (Am)* Statistische(s) Bundesamt *n*; *~~ character* Nationalcharakter *m*; *~~ church* Staatskirche *f*; *~~ costume* Volkstracht *f*; *~~ council* Nationalrat *m*; *~~ debt* Staatsschuld *f*; *~~ defence* Landesverteidigung *f*; *~~ economy* Volkswirtschaft *f*; *~~ flag* Nationalflagge *f*; *~~ government (Am)* Bundesregierung *f*; *~~ guard* Nationalgarde *f*; *~~ income* National-, Volkseinkommen *n*; *N~~ Industrial Conference Board (Am)* Arbeitgeberverband *m*; *~~ insurance* Sozialversicherung *f*; *~~ interest* Staatsinteresse *n*; *~~ language* Landessprache *f*; *~~ monument* (geschütztes) Natur-, Baudenkmal *m*; *~~ park* Nationalpark *m*; *~~ product* Sozialprodukt *n*; *~~ property* Volksvermögen; Staatseigentum *n*; *~~ security* Staatssicherheit *f*; *~~ status* Staatsangehörigkeit *f*; *~~ team (sport)* Ländermannschaft *f*; *~~ wealth* Volksvermögen *n*, -wohlstand *m*; **~alism** ['næʃnəlizm] Nationalismus *m*; **~alist** ['næʃnəlist] *s* Nationalist *m*; *a* u. **~alistic** [næʃnə'listik] nationalistisch; **~ality** [næʃə'næliti] Staatsangehörigkeit, Nationalität *f*; National-, Volkscharakter; *com* Ursprung *m*; *certificate of ~~* Staatsangehörigkeitsausweis *m*; **~alization** [næʃnəlai'zeiʃən] Verstaatlichung, Nationalisierung; Naturalisierung *f*; **~alize** ['næʃnəlaiz] *tr* verstaatlichen, nationalisieren; naturalisieren; **~-wide** national, Landes-; durch das ganze Land (gehend); allgemein.

nativ|e ['neitiv] *a* angeboren, natürlich; geboren, gebürtig (*of* aus); einheimisch, inländisch; Geburts-, Heimat-; naturrein, Natur-; *(Gold)* gediegen; Volks-; eingeboren, Eingeborenen-; *s* Landesprodukt *n*; einheimische(s) Gewächs *od* Tier *n*; Einheimische(r); Eingeborene(r); *(Astrologie)* Geborene(r) *m*; Zuchtauster *f*; *to go ~~* die Zivilisation abstreifen; *~~-born* einheimisch; *~~ country* Vaterland *n*; *~~ port* Heimathafen *m*; *~~ rock (geol)* gewachsene(r) Fels *m*; *~~ tongue* Muttersprache *f*; *~~ town* Vaterstadt *f*; **~ity** [nə'tiviti] Geburt(sumstände *m pl*) *f*; Horoskop *n*; *the N~~* Geburt *f* Christi *(a. Kunst)*; Weihnachten *n* u. *f pl*; *~~ play* Krippenspiel *n*.

natron ['neitrən] *chem* Natron; doppel(t)kohlensaure(s) Natrium *n*.

natter ['nætə] *itr fam* schwätzen; *s fam* Geschwätz; Gemecker *n*.

natty ['næti] schmuck, nett, sauber, adrett; elegant; gewandt, flink, fix.

natural ['nætʃrəl] *a* natürlich *a. math*; Natur-; ursprünglich, wild, primitiv, urtümlich, naturhaft; angeboren, naturgegeben; unbearbeitet; fleischfarben; *(Abbildung)* naturgetreu; lebenswahr, echt; ungekünstelt, ungezwungen, frei; selbstverständlich, natürlich; *(Kind)* unehelich; *mus* ohne Vorzeichen; *s* Idiot *m*; *Am fam* Kanone *f (Mensch)*, Treffer *m (Sache)*; Naturbegabung; *mus* weiße Taste; ganze Note *f*; *(~ sign)* Auflösungszeichen *n*; *during o.'s ~ life* auf Lebenszeit; *to come ~ to s.o.* jdm leichtfallen; *to die a ~ death* e-s natürlichen Todes sterben; **~-born** *a* gebürtig, von Geburt; **~-colo(u)red** *a* naturfarben; **~ fibre** Naturfaser *f*; **~ force** Naturerscheinung *f*; **~ frequency** Eigenfrequenz *f*; **~ gas** Erdgas *n*; **~ gift** Veranlagung, Anlage *f*; **~ history** Naturkunde, -geschichte, -beschreibung *f*; **~ism** ['-izm] Naturalismus *m*; Nackt-, Freikörperkultur *f*; **~ist** ['-ist] Naturwissenschaftler, -forscher; Tierhändler; Präparator; Naturalist; Anhänger *m* der Nackt-, Freikörperkultur; **~ization** [nætʃrəlai'zeiʃən] Naturalisierung, Einbürgerung *f*; **~ize** ['nætʃrəlaiz] *tr* naturalisieren, die Staatsangehörigkeit verleihen *(s.o.* jdm); einbürgern *a. fig (e-e Sitte, ein Wort)*; *(Tier, Pflanze)* akklimatisieren; heimisch machen; **~ philosophy** Physik; Naturphilosophie *f*; **~ product** Rohprodukt *n*; **~ resources** *pl* natürliche Hilfsquellen *f pl*; Bodenschätze *m pl*; **~ science** Naturwissenschaft *f*; **~ selection** *biol* natürliche Zuchtwahl *f*; **~ sign** *mus* Auflösungszeichen *n*; **~ silk** Naturseide *f*; **~ sponge** Naturschwamm *m*; **~ spring** Mineral-, Heilquelle *f*; **~ state** Naturzustand *m*; **~ vibration** Eigenschwingung *f*.

nature ['neitʃə] Natur *f*, Wesen *n*, Beschaffenheit, Art *f*, Charakter *m*, Naturell *n*, natürliche Anlage; Wirkungsweise *f*; die Natur; *against, contrary to ~* gegen die Natur(gesetze); *by ~* von Natur (aus); *from ~* nach der Natur; *in, of the ~ of* nach Art *gen*, in der Art *gen*; *in the course of ~* im Lauf der Dinge *od* der Entwick(e)lung; *to ease ~* sich erleichtern; *to pay the debt of ~, o.'s debt to ~* das Zeitliche segnen; sterben; *it's not in my ~* es liegt mir nicht; *~ of the ground* Bodenbeschaffenheit *f*; *good ~* Gutmütigkeit, Hilfsbereitschaft, Selbstlosigkeit *f*; *the human ~* die menschliche Natur; *true to ~* lebenswahr, -echt; **~ cure** Naturheilkunde *f*; *~-~ practitioner* Naturheilkundige(r) *m*; **~d** ['-d] *a in Zssgen.* geartet; *good-~~* gutmütig; *ill-~~* boshaft, bösartig; **~ lover** Naturfreund *m*.

naught, nought [nɔ:t] *s* Nichts *n*; Null *f*; *a* nichtig, wertlos, unnütz, unbrauchbar; *fam (Geschichte)* gesalzen; *all for ~* ganz umsonst; *to bring, to come to ~* zunichte machen, werden; *to care ~ for* sich nichts machen aus; *to set at ~* geringschätzen, verachten; **~inis** ['-inis] Ungezogenheit *f*; **~y** ['-i] unartig, ungezogen; nichtsnutzig; ungesittet; unanständig.

nause|a ['nɔ:siə, *Am* '-ʃ(i)ə] Übelkeit *f*; Brechgefühl *n*, -reiz; *fig* Ekel, Widerwille *m*; **~ate** ['-ieit] *tr* Übelkeit, Ekel erregen *(s.o.* jdm); *itr u. to be ~~d* sich ekeln, Ekel empfinden *(at* bei); ganz krank sein *(at* vor); **~ating** ['-eitiŋ], **~ous** ['nɔ:siəs] ekelerregend, ekelhaft.

nautical ['nɔ:tikəl] seemännisch; See-(manns-), Schiffs-; nautisch; **~ chart** Seekarte *f*; **~ mile** See-, nautische Meile *f (1,852 km)*.

naval ['neivəl] *a* Flotten-, Marine-, See-, Schiff-; **~ academy** Marineoffiziersschule *f*; **~ aerodrome** Marineflughafen *m*; **~ agreement** Flottenabkommen *n*; **~ airplane** Marineflugzeug *n*; **~ architect** Schiffbauingenieur *m*; **~ artillery** Schiffsartillerie *f*; **~ aviation** Seeflugwesen *n*, Seeflieger *m pl*; **~ base** Flottenstützpunkt *m*; **~ battle** Seeschlacht *f*; **~ construction** Schiffbau *m*; **~ forces** *pl* Seestreitkräfte *f pl*; **~ officer** Marineoffizier *m*; **~ pilot** Marineflieger *m*; **~ port** Kriegshafen *m*; **~ power** Seemacht *f*; **~ staff** Admiralstab *m*; **~ supremacy** Seeherrschaft *f*; **~ warfare** Seekrieg *m*.

nave [neiv] **1.** *(Kirche)* (Haupt-)Schiff *n*; **2.** (Rad-)Nabe *f*.

navel ['neivəl] (Bauch-)Nabel; *fig* Mittelpunkt *m*, Zentrum *n*; **~ orange** Navelorange *f*; **~-string, -cord** Nabelschnur *f*; **~-wort** *bot* Nabelkraut *n*.

navicert ['nævisə:t] *mar* Warendurchgangsbescheinigung *f*.

navicular [nə'vikjulə] *s* u. *a*: **~ bone** *anat* Kahnbein *n*.

navig|ability [nævigə'biliti] *(Fluß)* Schiffbarkeit; *aero* Lenkbarkeit *f*; **~able** ['nævigəbl] schiffbar; lenkbar; *~~ water* Fahrrinne *f*; **~ate** ['nævigeit] *itr* (mit dem Schiff) fahren; ein Schiff, Flugzeug steuern; *tr (Strecke)* befahren, befliegen; *(Schiff, Flugzeug)* steuern, segeln *(to* nach); den Kurs festlegen für, orten, navigieren; **~ation** [nævi'geiʃən] Schiffahrt(skunde); Navigation *f a. aero*; *coastal, high-sea, inland, river ~~* Küsten-, Hochsee-, Binnen-, Flußschiffahrt *f*; *~~ chart* Navigationskarte *f*; *~~ light (aero)* Positionslicht *n*; *~~ officer* Navigationsoffizier *m*; *~~ route* Schiffahrtsstraße *f*; *~~ school* Seemannsschule *f*; **~or** ['nævigeitə] Seefahrer; See-, Steuermann; *Am* Navigationsoffizier; *aero* Navigator; (Flugzeug-)Orter *m*; *~~'s compartment (aero)* Orterraum *m*.

navvy ['nævi] *(ungelernter)* Straßen-, Erd-, Kanalbau-, *rail* Streckenarbeiter; Löffelbagger, Exkavator *m*.

navy ['neivi] (Kriegs-)Marine *f*, Seestreitkräfte *f pl*; *Am* Marineministerium *n*; **~ bean** *Am* weiße Bohne *f*; **~ blue** marineblau; **N~ Department** *Am* Marineministerium *n*; **~ yard** Marinewerft *f*.

nay [nei] *adv* nein, ja (... sogar); *obs* nein; *s* Neinstimme *f*; Nein *n*; *to say ~* sich weigern, nein sagen.

naze [neiz] Landspitze *f*, Vorgebirge *n*.

neap [ni:p] *s u. a*: *~ tide* Nippflut, -tide *f*; *itr (Flut, Tide)* geringer, niedriger werden.

Neapolitan [niə'pɔlitən] *a* neapolitanisch; *s* Neapolitaner(in *f*) *m*; **~ ice-cream** Familieneis *n*.

near [niə] **1.** *a (räuml.* od *zeitl.)* nah(e) *(to the river* beim Fluß); nah(e) verwandt *(to* mit); eng befreundet, vertraut, intim, nahestehend; genau; *(Ähnlichkeit)* groß; *(Übersetzung)* wörtlich; sparsam; *(Tier, Fahrzeug)* link; *com* kurzfristig; Imitations-; Kunst-; *the ~ way* der kürzere Weg; *~est price* genaueste(r) Preis *m*; *to have a ~ escape, thing* mit knapper (Müh und) Not davonkommen; **2.** *adv (räuml.* od *zeitl.)* nah(e); eng, intim; *fam* sparsam; beinahe, fast; *far and ~* weit und breit; *those ~ and dear to me* die mir Nahestehenden; *~ at hand* bei der *od* zur Hand; kurz bevorstehend; *~ by* dicht dabei, (ganz) in der Nähe; *~ upon* kurz vor; *to come, to go ~ to do, doing* im Begriff sein, nahe daran sein etw zu tun; *to draw ~* nahen, vor der Tür stehen; *to live ~ to* in der Nähe wohnen von; *that's ~er the truth* das kommt der Wahrheit näher; **3.** *prp (räuml., zeitl., graduell)* nahe *dat*; **4.** *itr tr* sich nähern, näherkommen *(to s.th., s.th.* e-r S); **~ bear** Dünnbier *n*; **~by** *adv a* in der Nähe (befindlich); **~ly** ['-li] *adv* fast, beinahe; eng, intim; sparsam; *not ~~* (auch) nicht annähernd, durchaus nicht, auf keinen Fall; **~ miss** *mil* Nahkrepierer *m*; *fig* halbe(r) Erfolg *m*; **~ness** ['-nis] Nähe; nahe Verwandtschaft *(to* mit); Vertrautheit; Genauigkeit; (allzugroße) Sparsamkeit *f*; **~-sighted** *a* kurzsichtig; **~-sightedness** Kurzsichtigkeit *f*; **~ silk** Halbseide *f*.

neat [ni:t] **1.** rein, sauber; von angenehmem Äußeren, gut geformt, zierlich; gefällig, angenehm, nett; elegant; sauber, ordentlich, gepflegt; *(Äußerung)* kurz und bündig, treffend, gewählt, geschickt; *(Arbeit)* gelungen; *(Rede)* gewandt formuliert; *(alkohol. Getränk)* unvermischt, unverdünnt; **~ness** ['-nis] Sauberkeit *f*; gute(s) Aussehen *n*, Schönheit, Zierlichkeit; einfache Eleganz; Gefälligkeit; Gepflegtheit; Geschicklichkeit *f*; **2.** *fast obs* Rind(vieh) *n*; **~herd** Kuhhirte *m*; **~'s-foot oil** Klauenfett *n*; **~'s leather** Rindsleder *n*; **~'s tongue** Ochsenzunge *f*.

neb [neb] *zoo* Schnabel *m*; Schnauze *f*; Mund *m*, Nase *a. allg*; Spitze *f*.

nebul|a ['nebjulə] *pl -ae* [-i:] *astr* Nebelfleck, Sternnebel; *med* Hornhautfleck *m*; *(Harn)* leichte Trübung *f*; **~ar** ['-ə] *a astr* Nebel-; **~osity** [nebju'lɔsiti] Nebligkeit; *fig* Undurchsichtigkeit *f*; **~ous** ['nebjuləs] *astr* Nebel-; neblig, wolkig; verschwommen; *fig* nebelhaft, vag(e), unbestimmt, unklar.

necess|ary ['nesisəri] *a* notwendig, nötig, erforderlich, unerläßlich *(to, for* für); unvermeidlich, unumgänglich; ge-, erzwungen; *s* Bedürfnis *n*; *das* Notwendige; (notwendiger) Bedarfsartikel, Gebrauchsgegenstand *m*; *pl* unvermeidliche Ausgaben *f pl*; *no comment ~~* Kommentar überflüssig! *~aries of life* Lebensbedürfnisse *n pl*; *das* Nötigste; *if it is ~~* falls nötig; *it is ~~ to* man muß; **~itate** [ni'sesiteit] *tr* nötig, notwendig, erforderlich machen; (notwendigerweise) zur Folge haben; *to be ~~d* gezwungen sein *(to do* zu tun); **~itous** [ni'sesitəs] bedürftig, in Not; **~ity** [ni'sesiti] Notwendigkeit, Unabweislich-, Unerläßlich-, Unvermeidlich-, Unumgänglichkeit *f*; Zwang(släufigkeit *f*) *m*; logische Notwendigkeit; Not, Armut; Lebensnotwendigkeit *f*; *in case of ~~* im Notfall; *of ~~* notwendigerweise, zwangsläufig, notgedrungen, unvermeidlich; *to be in ~~* bittere Not leiden; *to bow to ~~* sich der Gewalt beugen; *to make a virtue of ~~* aus der Not e-e Tugend machen; *~~ is the mother of invention (prov)* Not macht erfinderisch; *~~ knows no law (prov)* Not kennt kein Gebot; *bare ~ities of life* Existenzminimum *n*.

neck [nek] *s* Hals *m a. tech*; Genick *n*; *(Kleidung)* (Hals-)Ausschnitt, Kragen; *tech* Einfüllstutzen *m*; Landenge *f*, Isthmus *m*; *fam* Unverschämtheit *f*; *tr* den Kopf abhacken *(a hen* e-m Huhn), schlachten; *tr itr Am sl* (sich) abknutschen, (sich) liebkosen; *to ~ down* verengen; *by a ~ (Pferderennen)* um e-e Halslänge; *allg* (mit) knapp(em Vorsprung); *~ and crop* von oben bis unten; völlig, ganz; *~ and ~* Seite an Seite, (genau) gleich, ohne Unterschied; *~ or nothing* auf Biegen oder Brechen; alles oder nichts; *to be up* *to o.'s ~ in work* bis über den Hals in Arbeit stecken; *to break o.'s ~* den Hals brechen; e-e übermenschliche Anstrengung machen (*doing s.th.* um etw zu tun); *to break the ~ of s.th.* das Schlimmste e-r S überstehen; *to fall upon s.o.'s ~* jdm um den Hals fallen; *to get it in the ~ (sl)* eins aufs Dach, den Laufpaß kriegen; *to give s.o. a pain in the ~* jdn anekeln, anwidern; *to have a ~* die Frechheit besitzen; *to risk o.'s ~, (fam) to stick o.'s ~ out* Kopf und Kragen riskieren; sich exponieren; *to save o.'s ~, to slip o.'s ~ out of the collar* den Hals aus der Schlinge ziehen, davonkommen; *I've a pain in my ~* mir tut der Hals weh; **~band** Halsband *n*; *(Kleidung)* Halsbund *m*; **~cloth** Halstuch *n*; Krawatte *f*; **~ed** [nekt] *a*: *stiff-~~* hartnäckig, halsstarrig; **~erchief** ['-ətʃif] Halstuch *n*, Schal *m*; **~ing** ['-iŋ] *arch* Säulenhals *m*; *Am sl* Abknutscherei *f*; **~lace** ['-lis] Halsband *n*, -kette *f*; *~~ microphone* Kehlkopfmikrophon *n*; **~let** ['-lit] (kleines) Halsband *n*; (Hals-)Pelzkragen *m*; **~line** *(Kleid)* Ausschnitt *m*, Dekolleté *n*; *with a low ~~* tief ausgeschnitten; tief dekolletiert; **~-strap** Umhängeriemen *m*; **~tie** ['-tai] Krawatte, Halsbinde *f*, Schlips *m*; *Am sl* Schlinge *f*; **~wear** ['-wɛə] Krawatten, Kragen und Halstücher *pl*.

necro|logist [ne'krɔlədʒist] Nachrufschreiber *m*; **~logy** [-lədʒi] Totenliste *f*; Nachruf *m*; Todesanzeige *f*; **~mancer** ['nekro(u)mænsə] Geisterbeschwörer, Nekromant *m*; **~mancy** Toten-, Geisterbeschwörung, Nekromantie *f*; **~polis** [ne'krɔpəlis] Totenstadt *f*; **~sis** [-'krousis] *med* Brand *m a. bot.*

nectar ['nektə, -ɑ:] *(Mythologie) bot fig* Nektar *m*.

née, nee [nei] *(vor dem Mädchennamen e-r Frau)* geborene.

need [ni:d] *s* Notwendigkeit *f*, Zwang(slage *f*) *m*; Bedürfnis *n*; Not(lage), Bedürftigkeit, Armut *f*; Mangel *m* (*of* an); *pl* Bedürfnisse *n pl*; *tr* nötig haben, brauchen; bedürfen, bedürftig sein (*s.th.* e-r S); müssen (*do, to do* tun); *itr* in Not sein; *v aux* brauchen, müssen, nötig sein; *in ~* in Not; *in ~ of repair* reparaturbedürftig; *in case of ~* im Notfall; *in times of ~* in schwierigen Zeiten; *more than ~s* mehr als nötig; *to be in ~, to have ~ of s.th.* etw brauchen, nötig haben; *to have ~ to do* etw tun müssen; *to supply the ~s of s.o.* für jds Bedürfnisse sorgen; *if ~ be, were* not-, nötigenfalls, wenn es die Umstände erfordern; *that's all we ~ed!* das hat uns gerade noch gefehlt; *this ~s no saying* das versteht sich von selbst; *he ~ not do it* er braucht es nicht zu tun; **~ful** ['-ful] *a* notwendig, nötig; erforderlich (*for, to* für); *s sl* Moneten *pl*, Geld *n*; *das* Notwendige; *to do the ~~* das Nötige tun; **~iness** ['-inis] Bedürftigkeit, Armut, Not *f*; **~less** ['-lis] unnötig, nicht notwendig, überflüssig; *~~ to say* es erübrigt sich zu sagen; **~lessness** ['-lisnis] Unnötigkeit, Überflüssigkeit *f*; **~s** [ni:dz] *adv (nur bei must)* notwendigerweise, unbedingt, durchaus; *~ must when the devil drives* da bleibt e-m nichts anderes übrig; **~y** ['-i] bedürftig, notleidend, in Not, arm.

needle ['ni:dl] *s* (Näh-)Nadel; Strick-, Häkelnadel; (Grammophon-)Nadel; Kompaßnadel *f*; Zeiger *m (e-s Meßgerätes)*; (Tannen-, Fichten-, Kiefern-)Nadel; Felsspitze; *tech* Graviernadel *f*, Schneidstift *m*; *allg* Nadel, Spitze *f*; Obelisk *m*; *med* Spritze; *fam* Aufregung, boshafte Bemerkung *f*; *tr* mit e-r Nadel durchbohren *od* stechen; *med* punktieren; *fam* auf-, anstacheln; *fam* sticheln, necken (*about* wegen); *sl* Alkohol beimischen *od* zusetzen (*s.th.* e-r S); *itr* nähen; stricken; häkeln; *(Kristallisation)* Nadeln bilden; *to get the ~(s)* Lampenfieber bekommen; *to look for a ~ in a bundle of hay* Unmögliches wollen; *to thread the ~* die Nadel einfädeln; *I'm on pins and ~s* ich sitze wie auf glühenden Kohlen; *darning-~* Stopfnadel *f*; *hypodermic ~* Injektionsnadel *f*; *packing-~* Packnadel *f*; *pins and ~s (physiol)* Prickeln *n*, eingeschlafene Füße *m pl*; *sewing-~* Nähnadel *f*; **~-book** Nadelheft *n*; **~-case** Nadelbüchse *f*; **~-gun** Zündnadelgewehr *n*; **~-lace** Klöppelspitzen *f pl*; **~-point** Nadelspitze *f (Handarbeit)*; **~'s eye** Nadelöhr *n*; **~-valve** Nadelventil *n*; **~woman** Näherin *f*; **~work** (weibliche) Handarbeit *f*; *~~ case* Nähkorb *m*.

ne'er [nɛə] *s. never*; **~-do-well** Tunichtgut *m*.

nefarious [ni'fɛəriəs] lasterhaft, ruchlos; **~ness** [-nis] Ruchlosigkeit *f*.

negat|e [ni'geit] *tr* verneinen, (ab-, ver)leugnen, ab-, bestreiten; ablehnen; verwerfen; **~ion** [-ʃən] Leugnung; Verneinung; Negation *f*; Nicht(vorhanden)sein *n*; Annullierung *f*; **~ive** ['negətiv] *a* ablehnend, verneinend; *(Antwort)* abschlägig; ergebnis-, erfolglos; unergiebig, unfruchtbar; *(Logik) math phys phot* negativ; negativ zu bewerten(d); *s* Verneinung; Ablehnung, Absage *f*; negative(r) Standpunkt *m*; Veto(recht) *n*; *math* negative Größe *f*; Minuszeichen; *el* negative(s) Element; *phot* Negativ *n*; *gram* Negation *f*; *tr* ablehnen, -weisen, verwerfen; leugnen, verneinen, widersprechen (*s.th.* e-r S); widerlegen; mißbilligen; entgegenwirken, zuwiderhandeln (*s.th.* e-r S); unwirksam machen, neutralisieren; *in the ~~* negativ; *to answer in the ~~* verneinen; *~~ lead (el)* Minusleitung *f*; *~~ sign* Minuszeichen *n*.

neglect [ni'glekt] *tr* vernachlässigen; versäumen, unterlassen (*to do, doing* zu tun); außer acht lassen; sich nicht kümmern um; geringschätzen, ignorieren; *jur* fahrlässig handeln; *s* Vernachlässigung; Nachlässigkeit *f*; Versäumnis *n*; Verwahrlosung; Fahrlässigkeit *f* (*of* gegenüber); *state of ~* verwahrloste(r) Zustand *m*; *~ of o.'s duties* Pflichtverletzung *f*; **~ful** [-ful] nachlässig; sorglos, unachtsam (*of* gegenüber); *jur* fahrlässig; **~fulness** [-fulnis] Nachlässigkeit, Unachtsamkeit *f*.

neglig|ence ['neglidʒəns] Nachlässigkeit, Unachtsamkeit, Gleichgültigkeit, Sorglosigkeit, Pflichtvergessenheit, Fahrlässigkeit *f*; Verschulden *n*; *contributory ~~* Mitverschulden *n*; *gross ~~* grobe Fahrlässigkeit *f*; *professional ~~* Verletzung *f* der beruflichen Sorgfaltspflicht; **~ent** ['-t] nachlässig, unachtsam, gleichgültig (*of* gegen); sorglos, pflichtvergessen; *jur* fahrlässig; *(Schuldner)* säumig; **~ible** ['neglidʒəbl] geringfügig, unerheblich, unbedeutend, unwichtig, belanglos, nebensächlich; *~~ quantity* Belanglosigkeit, Nebensache *f*.

negoti|ability [nigouʃjə'biliti] Übertrag-, Begebbarkeit; Börsen-, Bankfähigkeit; Verwertbarkeit, Verkäuflichkeit *f*; **~able** [ni'gouʃjəbl] diskutierbar; *com* verkäuflich, übertrag-, begebbar; börsen-, bankfähig; verwertbar; veräußerlich; *(Weg)* passierbar; *non-~~, not ~~* nicht übertragbar, nur zur Verrechnung; *~~ instrument, paper* Verkehrs-, Inhaberpapier *n*; **~ate** [ni'gouʃieit] *tr* verhandeln (über), aus-, unterhandeln; *(Vertrag)* zustande bringen; abschließen, tätigen; *(Wechsel)* begeben, in Verkehr setzen, unterbringen; *fam (Hindernis, Kurve)* nehmen, überwinden, bewältigen; *itr* ver-, unterhandeln (*with* mit; *for, about* um, wegen); **~ation** [nigouʃi'eiʃən] Unter-, Verhandlung; *fin* Begebung *f*; *fam* Nehmen *n (e-s Hindernisses, e-s Berges)*; *by way of ~~s* auf dem Verhandlungswege; *open to ~~* zu Verhandlungen bereit; *under ~~* in Verhandlung; *to be in ~~s with* in Verhandlungen stehen mit; *to enter into ~~s with* in Verhandlungen treten mit; **~ator** [ni'gouʃieitə] Unterhändler *m*.

negr|ess ['ni:gris] Negerin *f*; **N~o** ['ni:grou] *pl -oes* Neger *m*; *attr* Neger-; schwarz; *~~ question* Negerfrage *f*; **~oid** ['ni:grɔid] negroid.

Negus ['ni:gəs] Negus, Kaiser *m* von Abessinien; *n~* Glühwein *m*.

neigh [nei] *itr* wiehern; *s* Wiehern *n*.

neighbo(u)r ['neibə] *s* Nachbar(in *f*); Anwohner, Anlieger; Nächste(r) *m*; *tr itr* benachbart sein (*s.th.*; *upon, with s.th.* e-r S); angrenzen (*s.th.*; *upon, with s.th.* an); **~hood** ['-hud] Nachbarschaft; (Um-)Gegend *f*, Gebiet, Viertel *n*, Bezirk *m*; Nähe *f*; *in the ~~ of* in der Nähe von; *fam* (von) ungefähr, nahe an; in der Größenordnung von; *~~ unit* Wohngemeinschaft *f*; **~ing** ['-riŋ] benachbart, angrenzend; umliegend; *~~ community* Nachbargemeinde *f*; **~liness** ['-linis] gutnachbarliche Haltung *f od* Beziehungen *f pl*; **~ly** ['-li] *a* (gut)nachbarlich, freundschaftlich.

neither ['naiðə, *Am* 'ni:ðə] *prn* keine(r) (von beiden) (*of* gen); *adv conj* auch nicht; *~ ... nor* weder ... noch.

nelson ['nelsn] *sport* Nelson(griff) *m*.

nematode ['nemətoud] *zoo* Faden-, Rundwurm *m*.

nemesis ['nemesis] Nemesis *f a. fig.*

neo ['ni(:)o(u)] *in Zssgen* Neu-, Neo-, Jung-; **~lithic** [-'liθik] jungsteinzeitlich, neolithisch; **~logism** [ni(:)'ɔlədʒizm], **~logy** [-'ɔlədʒi] neue(s) Wort *n*, Neubildung *f*, Neologismus *m*, neue Bedeutung *f*; *(Theologie)* Rationalismus, Liberalismus *m*; **~phyte** ['ni(:)o(u)fait] Neubekehrte(r), Neophyt *m*.

neon ['ni:ən] *chem* Neon *n*; **~ lamp, light** Neonröhre *f*, -licht *n*; **~ sign** Neonreklame *f*.

nephew ['nevju(:), *Am* 'nefj-] Neffe *m*.

nephr|ite ['nefrait] *min* Nephrit *m*; **~itis** [ne'fraitis] Nierenentzündung *f*.

nepotism ['nepətizm] Vetternwirtschaft *f*; Nepotismus *m*.

nerv|e [nə:v] *s anat* Nerv *m*; *(Insektenflügel, Blatt)* Ader, Rippe; *arch* Gewölberippe; *fig* Selbstbeherrschung, Kaltblütigkeit *f*; Mut *m*; Stärke, (Tat-)Kraft, Energie; *fam* Unverschämtheit, Frechheit *f*; *pl* Nerven *m pl*; Kraft, Ausdauer, Zähigkeit, Beharrlichkeit *f*, Mut *m*; Nervosität, Reizbarkeit, Aufgeregtheit *f*; *tr* stärken, kräftigen, ermutigen; *to ~~ o.s.* Kräfte sammeln; sich zs.nehmen; *to get on s.o.'s ~~s (fam)* jdm auf die Nerven gehen; *to have the ~~ to do s.th.* den Mut haben, *fam* die Frechheit besitzen, etw zu tun; *not to know what ~~s are* nicht aus der Ruhe zu bringen sein; *to lose o.'s ~~* die Nerven verlieren;

to strain every ~~ alle Kraft anspannen; *bag of ~~s (fig)* Nervenbündel *n*; *fit of ~~s* Nervenkrise *f*; *~~-cell* Nervenzelle *f*; *~~-centre* Nervenzentrum *m*; *~~-fibre, cord* Nervenstrang *m*; *~~-knot* Nervenknoten *m*, Ganglion *n*; *~~-racking* nervenaufreibend; *~~-shattered (a)* innerlich zerrüttet, *fam* fertig mit den Nerven; *~~ specialist* Neurologe *m*; *~-strain (fig)* Belastung *f*; *~~-(w)racking* auf die Nerven gehend, aufregend; **~eless** ['-lis] kraft-, mutlos; *zoo bot* ungeädert; **~ine** ['-i:n] *a* Nerven-; *pharm* nervenstärkend, beruhigend; *s pharm* Beruhigungsmittel, Tonikum *n*; **~ous** ['-əs] *a* Nerven-; kräftig, stark; *(Stil)* markig; nervös, reizbar, erregbar; unruhig, aufgeregt; ängstlich, furchtsam, schüchtern; *~~ breakdown* Nervenzusammenbruch *m*; *~~ prostration* Nervenschwäche *f*; *~~ system* Nervensystem *n*; **~ousness** [-əsnis] Nervosität *f*; **~ure** ['-juə] *zoo bot* Ader, Rippe *f*; **~y** ['-i] *poet* sehnig, stark; *fam* draufgängerisch, unverschämt; *fam* nervös, aufgeregt; *sl* nervenzerfetzend.

nescien|ce ['nesiəns] Unwissenheit *f*; *philos* Agnostizismus *m*; **~t** ['-t] unwissend (*of* in); agnostisch.

ness [nes] Vorgebirge *n*, Landzunge *f*.

nest [nest] *s* (*bes.* Vogel-)Nest *n*; Wurf *m*, Brut *f*, Schwarm *m*, Volk; *fig* Nest, (trautes) Heim *n*, Ruheplatz *m*; *pej* (Räuber-)Höhle; Brutstätte; (Räuber-)Bande *f*; *tech* Bündel *n*; *(Kurven)* Schar *f*; Satz *m (Gegenstände)*; *itr* nisten; *(to go ~ing)* Nester ausnehmen; *tr* ein Nest machen für; *tech* einfügen, -passen; *to feather o.'s ~* sein Schäfchen ins trock(e)ne bringen; *to foul o.'s own ~ (fig)* das eigene Nest beschmutzen; *birds' ~* Vogelnest *n*; *wasps' ~* Wespennest *n*; *~ of drawers* Aktenschrank *m*; Aufsatzkommode *f*; *~ of pirates* Piratennest *n*; *~ of shelves* Regal *n*; *~ of tables* Satz *m* inea.geschobener Tische; *~ of vice* Lasterhöhle *f*; *~ of vipers (fig)* Otterngezücht *n*; **~-egg** Nestei *n*; *fig* Notpfennig, -groschen *m*; **~le** ['nesl] *itr* es sich bequem, gemütlich machen; sich anea.-schmiegen, versteckt liegen; sich anschmiegen (*to* an); *tr* an sich drücken; **~ling** ['-(t)liŋ] Nestling, -vogel *m*; *fig* Nesthäkchen *n*.

net [net] **1.** *s* Netz *n*; Schlinge, Falle *f*; Netzwerk; *(Textil)* lockere(s) Gewebe *n*, Tüll, Musselin, Batist; *(Tennis)* Netzball *m*; *tr* zu e-m Netz verarbeiten; mit e-m Netz bedecken *od* überziehen; *(Gewässer)* mit Netzen auslegen; mit dem Netz fangen; *(Tennisball)* ins Netz schlagen; *itr* Netze *od* Filetarbeiten machen; *a* Netz-; netzartig, durchbrochen; im Netz gefangen; *to fall into the ~* ins Garn gehen; *butterfly, fishing-~* Schmetterlings-, Fischnetz *n*; *hair-~* Haarnetz *n*; *mosquito-~* Moskitonetz *n*; *shopping ~* Einkaufsnetz *n*; *tennis-~* Tennisnetz *n*; **~ful** ['-ful] Netzvoll *n*; **~ting** ['-iŋ] Netzflechten; Fischen; *mil* Tarngeflecht *n*; Netze *n pl*, Netzwerk, Geflecht *n*, Filetarbeit *f*; *~~ wire* Maschendraht *m*; **~work** Netzwerk; (Straßen-, Autobahn-, Eisenbahn-, Kanal-, Flug-)Netz; *fig* Netz, (Filial-, Agenten-, Spionage-)Netz *n*; verzweigte Anlage *f*; *el* Stromnetz *n*; Schaltung *f*; *radio video* Sendenetz *n*, Sendergruppe *f*; *highway ~~* Straßennetz *n*; **2.** *a* netto, rein, ohne Abzug, kosten-, spesenfrei; *tr* netto einbringen *od* verdienen; Reingewinn erzielen; *~* **amount** Nettobetrag *m*; *~* **balance** Nettosaldo *m*; *~* **cost** Selbstkostenpreis *m*; *~* **earnings** *pl* Nettoverdienst *m*; *~* **gain, proceeds, profit** Reingewinn, -ertrag *m*; *~* **income, revenue** Reineinkommen *n*; *~* **load** Nutzlast *f*; *~* **national product** Nettosozialprodukt *n*; *~* **price** Nettopreis *m*; *~* **receipts** *pl* Reineinnahmen *f pl*; *~* **weight** Nettogewicht *n*; *~* **worth** Eigenkapital *n*; **~yield** Nettoertrag *m*.

nether ['neðə] *a* unter, nieder; Unter-; *~* **garments** *pl* Beinkleider *n pl*, Hose *f*; **~most** ['-moust] unterst; *~* **world** Unterwelt, Hölle *f*.

Netherland|er ['neðələndə] Niederländer(in *f*) *m*; **~s,** *the* ['-z] die Niederlande *pl*.

nettle ['netl] *s bot* Nessel *f*; *tr* mit e-r (Brenn-)Nessel stechen; *fig* reizen, (ver)ärgern, quälen; *to grasp the ~* schnell zufassen, entschlossen handeln; *stinging ~* Brennessel *f*; **~-rash** *med* Nesselsucht *f*.

neur|al ['njuərəl] *a* Nerven-; **~algia** [njuə'rældʒə] Neuralgie *f*, Nervenschmerz *m*; **~algic** [-'rældʒik] neuralgisch; **~asthenia** [njuərəs'θi:niə] Neurasthenie, Nervenschwäche *f*; **~asthenic** [-'θenik] neurasthenisch; **~itis** [-'raitis] Nervenentzündung, Neuritis *f*; **~ological** [njuərə'lɔdʒikəl] neurologisch; **~ologist** [njuə'rɔlədʒist] Neurologe, Nervenarzt *m*; **~ology** [-'rɔlədʒi] Neurologie *f*; **~on** ['-ɔn] *anat* Neuron *n*, Nervenzelle *f*; **~opath** ['-əpæθ] Neuropath *m*; **~opathic** [-rə'pæθik] neuropathisch; **~opathy** [-'rɔpəθi] Nervenleiden *n*, nervöse Veranlagung, Neuropathie *f*; **~osis** [-'rousis] *pl -ses* [-si:z] Neurose *f*; **~otic** [-'rɔtik] *a* neurotisch; Nerven-; *s pharm* Nervenmittel *n*; Neurotiker *m*.

neuter ['nju:tə] *a biol* geschlechtslos; *gram* sächlich; intransitiv; *s biol* geschlechtslose(s) Lebewesen; kastrierte(s) Tier; *gram* sächliche(s) Geschlecht *n*; *tr* kastrieren.

neutral ['nju:trəl] *a* neutral, unparteiisch, parteilos, unentschieden; *(zwischen zwei Dingen)* in der Mitte stehend, keins von beiden, unausgesprochen; uncharakteristisch, blaß, farblos, zurückhaltend; *(Farbe) chem* neutral; *tech* Ruhe-, Null-; *s* Neutrale(r); neutrale(r) Staat *m*; neutrale Farbe; *tech mot* Leerlaufstellung *f*; *to remain ~* neutral bleiben; *~* **conductor** *tech* Nulleiter *m*; *~* **gear** *mot* Leergang *m*; **~ity** [nju(:)'træliti] Neutralität; neutrale Haltung *f*; *armed, friendly ~~* bewaffnete, wohlwollende Neutralität *f*; *declaration of ~~* Neutralitätserklärung *f*; *policy of ~~* Neutralitätspolitik *f*; *violation of ~~* Neutralitätsverletzung *f*; **~ization** [nju:trəlai'zeiʃən] Neutralisierung; Nullung *f*; **~ize** ['nju:trəlaiz] *tr* neutralisieren *a. chem el*; nullen; kompensieren, aufheben; unwirksam machen, lähmen, behindern; *~* **line** *tech* Nullinie *f*; *~* **point** *tech* Nullpunkt *m*; *~* **position** *tech* Null-, Ruhestellung *f*.

neutron ['nju:trɔn] *phys* Neutron *n*.

never ['nevə], **ne'er** [nɛə] *adv* nie (-mals); durchaus nicht, ganz und gar nicht, keineswegs, auf keinen Fall, unter keinen Umständen; *interj* das glaube ich nicht! das ist unmöglich! nie! *~ so* (auch) noch so; *now or ~* jetzt oder nie; *on the ~~ (sl)* auf Abzahlung; *I should ~ have believed it* das hätte ich nie für möglich gehalten; *he ~ so much has smiled* er hat nicht einmal gelächelt; *~ again!* nie wieder! *I ~ (did)!* das ist mir noch nie begegnet, das ist mir ganz neu! nein, so was! *~ mind* das macht nichts; das hat nichts zu sagen; laß gut sein! *~~ country* Märchenland *n*; **~-ceasing, -ending** unaufhörlich; nicht enden wollend; **~-dying** unsterblich; **~-failing** unfehlbar; **~more** ['-mɔ:] *adv* nie wieder, nimmermehr; **~theless** [nevəðə'les] nichtsdestoweniger, trotzdem; **~-to-be-forgotten** unvergeßlich.

new [nju:] *a* neu (*from* aus); neu(entdeckt, -erschienen); ungewohnt, fremd(artig); noch nicht gewöhnt (*to* an); noch nicht vertraut (*to* mit); unerfahren; neu, ander; *(Brot)* frisch; *(Kartoffeln)* neu; neu(wertig); ungebraucht, noch unbenutzt; modern, modisch; weiter, zusätzlich; aufgefrischt, erholt; *I feel a ~ man* ich fühle mich wie neugeboren; *what's ~?* was gibt es Neues? **~born** *a* neu-, wiedergeboren; **~-build** *tr* wieder aufbauen; **~-building** Neubau *m*; **~-coined** *a* frisch geprägt; **~comer** (Neu-)Ankömmling; Neuling *m* (*to* in); **~fangled** ['nju:fæŋgld] *a* neu(modisch); neuerungssüchtig; *~* **formation** Neubildung *f*; *~* **high** *fam* neue(r) Höchststand *m*; **~-laid eggs** *pl* frische Eier *n pl*; **~ly** ['-li] *adv* neulich, unlängst, vor kurzem; aufs neue, von neuem; *~~-discovered (a)* neuentdeckt; *~~ married (a)* frisch verheiratet; *~~-weds (pl)* jungverheiratete(s) Paar *n*; *~* **moon** Neumond *m*; **~-mown** *a* frischgemäht, -geschnitten; **~ness** ['-nis] Neuheit; Ungewohntheit; Unerfahrenheit; Frische; Neuwertigkeit; Unbenutztheit *f*; *the* **N~ Testament** das Neue Testament; *the* **N~ World** die Neue Welt; **N~ Year,** *~~'s Day* Neujahr(stag *m*) *n*; *a happy ~~!* glückliches Neues Jahr! *~~'s Eve* Silvesterabend *m*.

newel ['nju:əl] Seele, (Treppen-)Spindel *f*; Treppen-, Geländerpfosten *m*.

Newfoundland [nju:fənd'lænd, nju(:)'faundlənd] Neufundland *n*; *~* **dog** [-'f-] Neufundländer *m*.

news [nju:z] *s pl mit sing* Neuigkeit(en *pl*); Nachricht(en *pl*) *a. radio*; Berichterstattung; Zeitung *f*; *to break the ~ to s.o.* jdm schlimme Nachricht beibringen; *what's the ~?* was gibt's Neues? *that's ~ to me* das ist mir neu, das habe ich (noch) nicht gewußt; *that's no ~ to me* das ist mir nicht neu; das wußte ich schon längst; *I've had no ~ from him for a long time* ich habe lange nichts von ihm gehört; *no ~ is good ~ (prov)* keine Nachricht ist gute Nachricht; *a piece of ~* e-e Neuigkeit, Nachricht *f*; **~-agency** Nachrichtenbüro *n*; **~-agent,** *Am* **-dealer** Zeitungshändler, -verkäufer *m*; **~-analyst** Nachrichten-, Rundfunkkommentator *m*; **~boy** Zeitungsjunge, -verkäufer, -austräger *m*; **~broadcast, ~cast** *radio* Nachrichten(sendung *f*) *f pl*; *~* **butcher** *Am* Zeitungs- u. Süßigkeitenverkäufer *m (im Zuge)*; **~caster** ['-ka:stə] *radio* Nachrichtensprecher *m*; *~* **cinema** Aktualitätenkino *n*; *~* **commentator** Rundfunkkommentator *m*; *~* **editor** Chef *m* vom Dienst; **~hawk** ['-hɔ:k] *Am sl* Nachrichtenjäger, Reporter *m*; *~* **item** Zeitungsnotiz *f*; **~let** ['-lit] Kurznachricht, kurze Meldung *f*; **~-letter** Rundschreiben *n*; **~-man** Zeitungsverkäufer; Journalist *m*; **~-monger** Neuigkeitskrämer *m*; **~paper** Zeitung *f*; *daily ~~* Tageszeitung *f*; *commercial ~~* Wirtschaftszeitung *f*; *~~ clipping, (Am) cutting* Zeitungsausschnitt *m*;

~~ *man* Zeitungsmann; Journalist *m*; ~~ *press* Nachrichtenpresse *f*; ~~ *reader* Zeitungsleser *m*; ~~ *report* Zeitungsbericht *m*; ~ **photographer** Bildbericht(erstatt)er, Pressephotograph *m*; ~**print** Zeitungspapier *n*; ~ **reader** Nachrichtensprecher *m*; ~~**reel, -picture** *film* Wochenschau *f*; ~ **reporter** Presseberichterstatter *m*; ~~**room** Zeitschriftenzimmer *n*, -raum, -saal *(e-r Bibliothek)*; *Am (Zeitung, radio)* Nachrichtenredaktion *f*; Zeitungskiosk *m*; ~ **service** Nachrichtendienst *m*; ~~**stall** *Br*, **-stand** *Am* Zeitungsstand, -kiosk *m*; ~ **summery** Nachrichten *f pl* in Kurzfassung; ~~**vendor** Zeitungsverkäufer *m*; ~**y** ['-i] *a fam* voller Neuigkeiten; *s Am* Zeitungsjunge *m*; *to be* ~~ voller Neuigkeiten stecken.

newt [nju:t] *zoo* Molch *m*.

next [nekst] *a* nächst, folgend; ~ *but one* übernächst; ~ *best* zweitbest; ~ *time* das nächste Mal; ~ *door* im Nachbarhaus, nebenan; *(to)* nebenan von; beinahe, fast; *in the* ~ *place* dann, darauf; *the* ~ *day* am nächsten Tag; tags darauf; *s der, die, das* Nächste, Folgende; ~ *of kin* nächste(r) Verwandte(r) *m*, nächste Verwandte, Angehörige *pl*; *in my* ~ im nächsten Brief; *who's* ~*?* wer ist dran? *adv* dann, darauf, nachher; das nächste Mal; zunächst; *what* ~*?* was nun, was noch? *to come* ~ folgen, der nächste sein; *prp (~ to)* (ganz) dicht bei; (ganz) in der Nähe *gen*; ~ *to (in der Reihenfolge)* nach; neben; bei; so gut wie, fast beinahe; ~ *to nothing* fast nichts; *to get* ~ *to s.o. (Am sl)* sich bei jdm lieb Kind machen; ~~**door** *a* im Nachbarhaus, in der unmittelbaren Nachbarschaft; ~~ *neighbo(u)r* unmittelbare(r) Nachbar *m*.

nexus ['neksəs] *pl* ~, *-es* Verbindung *f*, Band *n*; Zs.hang *m*.

nib [nib] Schnabel *m*; (Schreib-)Feder(spitze); *allg* Spitze *f*, Dorn; *pl sl* feine(r) Kerl *m*; *pl* gemahlene Kaffee- *od* Kakaobohnen *f pl*.

nibble ['nibl] *tr* knabbern; be-, anknabbern, -nagen, -beißen; *fig* nicht recht heranwollen an; *itr* (ein wenig) knabbern *(at* an); *fig* nicht recht anbeißen wollen; herumnörgeln, (herum-)kritteln *(at* an); *s* Knabbern *n*; *a* ~ ein bißchen.

niblick ['niblik] *Art* Golfschläger *m*.

nice [nais] hübsch, niedlich, zierlich; gefällig, angenehm; schön, geschmackvoll; gut, ausgezeichnet; nett, liebenswürdig, zuvorkommend, gütig, rücksichtsvoll *(to* gegen); bescheiden, zurückhaltend, (wohl)gesittet, anständig; umsichtig, bedacht; zart, fein, genau, gewissenhaft; sorgfältig, geschickt; fein, genau unterscheidend; alles genau nehmend, spitzfindig; wählerisch, schwierig, schwer zu befriedigen(d), heikel *(about* mit); schwer zu handhaben(d) *od* zu bewältigen(d), schwierig; *it's* ~ *and warm* es ist angenehm warm; *did you have a* ~ *time?* haben Sie sich gut unterhalten? ~ *and early* sehr früh; ~**ly** ['-li] *adv* angenehm, nett, liebenswürdig(erweise); hübsch, nett; prima, gut, schön; genau, gerade, richtig; zufriedenstellend; *he is doing* ~~ es geht ihm (ganz, recht) gut; ~**ness** ['-nis] Zierlichkeit; Schönheit; Liebenswürdigkeit, Güte; Bescheidenheit, Gesittetheit; Zartheit, Feinheit, Sorgfalt; Genauigkeit; Schwierigkeit *f*; ~**ty** ['-ti] Schüchternheit, Bescheidenheit; Gewissenhaftigkeit; Spitzfindigkeit; Genauigkeit, Sorgfalt; Feinheit *f*, hohe Anforderungen *f pl*; Bedeutung, Wichtigkeit; heikle, schwierige Sache *od* Angelegenheit *f*; *pl* unwichtige Einzelheiten, Kleinigkeiten *f pl*; *to a* ~~ aufs Haar, ganz genau, haargenau.

niche [nitʃ, ni:ʃ] *s* (Wand-)Nische; Auskehlung, Einbuchtung *f*; *fig* (rechter) Platz *m (for* für); *tr* in e-e Nische stellen.

Nick [nik] Klaus *m*; *Old* ~ der Teufel.

nick [nik] *s* Kerbe *f*, Einschnitt *m*; Auszackung; Scharte; *(Porzellan, Glas)* abgesplitterte Stelle *f*; *(Schraube)* Schlitz; *(Würfel)* Treffer *m*; *sl* Gefängnis *n*; *tr* (ein)kerben; ein-, durchschneiden; genau treffen *od* fassen; herausbekommen, (er)raten; gewinnen; *(Zug)* erwischen; *sl* schnappen, klauen; *sl* anschmieren, -führen, 'reinlegen; *Am sl* besteuern, fordern; *(Lohn)* zurückbehalten; *in the* ~ *of time* gerade im richtigen Augenblick.

nickel ['nikl] *s chem* Nickel; *(US, Kanada)* Fünfcentstück *n*; *tr* vernickeln; ~**odeon** [-'loudiən] *Am obs* Kintopp *n*; *Am* Musikautomat *m*; ~~**plate** *tr* vernickeln; ~ **plate** Vernickelung *f*; ~ **silver** Neusilber *n*; ~ **steel** Nickelstahl *m*.

nick-nack *s. knick-knack.*

nickname ['nikneim] *s* Spitzname; Kosename *m*; *tr* e-n Spitz-, Kosenamen geben *(s.o.* jdm); mit e-m Spitz-, Kosenamen rufen.

nicotin|e ['nikəti:n] Nikotin *n*; ~**ism** ['-izm] Nikotinvergiftung *f*.

niece [ni:s] Nichte *f*.

nifty ['nifti] *a Am sl* schick, fesch; prima, Klasse, Sache; riechend; *s Am sl* glänzende Bemerkung *f*, kluge(r) Einfall *m*; hübsche(s) Mädchen *n*; prima Sache *f*.

niggard ['nigəd] *s* Knicker, Knauser, Filz, Geizhals *m*; *a* knickerig, knauserig, filzig, geizig; ~**linis** ['-linis] Knickerigkeit, Knauserigkeit *f*, Geiz *m*; ~**ly** ['-li] *a* knauserig, geizig *(of* mit); klein, knapp, mäßig; schäbig.

nigger ['nigə] *s pej* Neger, Nigger *m*; *a (~-brown)* kaffeebraun; *to work like a* ~ wie ein Pferd arbeiten; *that's the* ~ *in the woodpile* da liegt der Hase im Pfeffer; das ist des Pudels Kern.

niggl|e ['nigl] *itr* sich in Einzelheiten verlieren; trödeln, bummeln; ~**ing** ['-iŋ] kleinlich, pusselig; unbedeutend; *(Handschrift)* verkrampft.

nigh [nai] *obs dial adv prp* nah(e).

night [nait] Nacht *f a. fig*; (später) Abend *m*; Dunkelheit, Finsternis *f*; *fig* geistige(r), sittliche(r) Tiefstand *m*; Bekümmernis, Trübsal *f*; Schatten *m pl* des Todes; *theat* Vorstellung, Aufführung *f*; *all* ~ *(long)* die ganze Nacht (über); *at* ~ abends; bei Nacht, nachts; *at the dead of* ~ mitten in der Nacht; in tiefer Nacht; *late at* ~ spät am Abend, spät abends; *at* ~*s* bei Nacht u. Nebel; *by* ~ bei Nacht, in der Nacht, nachts; *on the* ~ *of June 3rd* am Abend des 3. Juni; *last* ~ gestern abend; *the* ~ *before last* vorgestern abend; *o'* ~*s (fam)* bei Nacht, nachts; *the* ~ *after* übermorgen abend; ~ *and day* Tag und Nacht; immer, dauernd, ununterbrochen; ~ *after* ~ Nacht für Nacht, jede Nacht; *to have, to pass a good, bad* ~ gut, schlecht schlafen; *to have a* ~ *out, off* e-n freien Abend haben; ausgehen; *to make a* ~ *of it* durchfeiern, -zechen; *to stay the* ~ die Nacht verbringen *(at* in; *with* mit); *to turn* ~ *into day* die Nacht zum Tage machen; ~ *is falling* die Nacht bricht herein; *first* ~ Erstaufführung, Premiere, Eröffnungsvorstellung *f*; *the Arabian N~s* Tausendundeine Nacht; ~~**attack, -raid** *aero* Nachtangriff *m*; ~~**bell** Nachtglocke *f*; ~~**bird** Nachtvogel; *fig pej* Nachtschwärmer *m (Mensch)*; ~~**black** (kohl)rabenschwarz; ~~**blindness** Nachtblindheit *f*; ~~**bomber** Nachtbomber *m*; ~~**cap** Nachtmütze *f*; *fam* Schnäpschen *n* vor dem Schlafengehen; *sport* Schlußveranstaltung *f*; ~~**cellar** Kellerkneipe *f*; ~~**chair, -stool** Nachtstuhl *m*; ~~**clothes, -wear** Nachtgewand *n*; ~ **club** *Am*, **spot** *Am fam* Nachtlokal *n*; ~ **crawler** *Am fam* Nachtschwärmer *m (Mensch)*; ~ **current** Nachtstrom *m*; ~~**dress, ~gown, -robe** (Damen-)Nachthemd *n*; ~~**driver** *mot* Nachtfahrer *m*; ~**duty** Nachtdienst *m*; ~**ery** ['-əri] *Am fam* Nachtlokal *n*; ~ **exposure** *phot* Nachtaufnahme *f*; ~**fall** Dunkelwerden *n*, Einbruch *m* der Nacht; *at* ~~ beim Dunkelwerden; ~ **fighter, interceptor** *aero* Nachtjäger *m*; ~ **flight** *aero* Nachtflug *m*; ~~**haunt** Nachtlokal *n*; ~**ie** ['-i] *fam* Nachthemd *n*; ~**jar** ['-dʒɑ:] *orn* Ziegenmelker *m*; ~ **landing** *aero* Nachtlandung *f*; ~ **letter** *Am* Brieftelegramm *n*; ~~**light** Nachtlicht *n*; ~~**long** *a* die ganze Nacht dauernd; ~**ly** ['-li] *a* (all)nächtlich; abendlich; *adv* nachts; jede Nacht; ~ **march** Nachtmarsch *m*; ~**mare** ['-mεə] Alpdrücken *n*; *fig* Beklemmung *f*; ~**marish** ['-mεəriʃ] beklemmend, beängstigend; ~ **nurse** Nachtschwester *f*; ~ **nursery** Kinderschlafzimmer *n*; ~ **owl** Nachteule *f*; *fig* Nachtarbeiter, -schwärmer *m*; ~ **pass** *mil* Nachturlaub(schein) *m*; ~ **performance** Nachtvorstellung *f*; ~~**piece** *(Kunst)* Nachtstück *n*; ~~**porter** Nachtportier *m*; ~ **reconnaissance** *aero* Nachtaufklärung *f*; ~**s** ['-s] *fam dial, Am* nachts; ~~**school** Abendschule *f*; ~ **service** Nachtdienst *m*; ~ **session** Nachtsitzung *f*; ~**shade** *bot* Nachtschatten *m*; *deadly* ~~ Tollkirsche *f*; ~ **shelter** Nachtasyl *n*; ~**shift** Nachtschicht *f*; *to be on* ~~ Nachtschicht haben; ~~ *bonus* Nachtschichtvergütung *f*; ~**shirt** (Herren-)Nachthemd *n*; ~~**soil** Fäkalien *pl*; ~ **stick** *Am* Gummiknüppel *m (der Polizei)*; ~~**stop** *aero itr* über Nacht bleiben; *s* Übernachtung *f*; ~~**time** Nachtzeit *f*; *in the* ~~ bei Nacht, nachts; ~~**train** Nachtzug *m*; ~~**walker** Nacht-, Schlafwandler *m*; ~~**walking** Schlafwandeln *n*; ~~**watch** Nachtwache *f*; ~~**watchman** Nachtwächter *m*; ~~**work** Nachtarbeit *f*; ~**y** ['-i] *fam* Nachthemd *n*.

nightingale ['naitiŋgeil] Nachtigall *f*.

nihil|ism ['naiilizm] Nihilismus *m*; ~**ist** ['-ist] Nihilist *m*; ~**istic** [naii'listik] nihilistisch.

nil [nil] *s* Nichts *n*; Null *f*; *two (to)* ~ *(sport)* zwei zu null; ~ **return** Fehlanzeige *f*.

nimble ['nimbl] (geistig) gewandt, wendig, behende, hurtig, flink *(at*, *in* bei); *fam* fix, auf Draht; ~~**footed** *a* leichtfüßig; ~~**minded** *a* schlagfertig; ~**ness** ['-nis] Gewandtheit, Wendigkeit; Lebhaftigkeit *f*.

nimbus ['nimbəs] *pl a. -bi* [-ai] Nimbus *a. fig*; Strahlenkranz, Heiligenschein; Nimbus *m*, Regenwolke *f*.

niminy-piminy ['nimini'pimini] zimperlich, geziert, *fam* übergeschnappt.

nincompoop ['ninkəmpu:p] Einfaltspinsel, Simpel *m*.

nine [nain] *a* neun; *s* Neun *f (bes. Baseballmannschaft)*; *the N~* die (neun) Musen *f pl*; *dressed up to the ~s (fam)* geschniegelt und gebügelt; *~ days' wonder* Ereignis *n* des Tages; **~fold** ['-fould] *a adv* neunfach; *~* **months** *pl* Dreivierteljahr *n*; **~pins** ['-pinz] *pl mit sing* Kegel *m pl*; Kegelspiel, Kegeln *n*; *to play at ~~* kegeln; **~teen** ['nain'ti:n] neunzehn; **~teenth** ['-'ti:nθ] *a* neunzehnte; *s* Neunzehntel *n*; *a* **~tieth** ['naintiiθ] *a* neunzigst; *s* Neunzigstel *n*; Neunzigste(r) *m*; **~ty** ['nainti] *a* neunzig; *s* Neunzig *f*; *the ~ties* die neunziger Jahre *(e-s Jahrhunderts)*; die Neunzigerjahre *(e-s Menschenlebens)*.

ninny ['nini] Dummkopf, Tropf *m*.

ninth [nainθ] *a* neunt; *s* Neuntel *n*; Neunte(r *m*) *f*; *mus* None *f*.

*

nip [nip] **1.** *tr* kneifen; (ab)zwicken; (ein)klemmen; *(Pflanzentrieb)* abkneifen; erstarren lassen; *(Frost)* vernichten; Schaden zufügen (*s.th.* dat); *allg* unterdrücken, -binden, hemmen; *fam* schnappen, ergattern, mausen, stibitzen; sich unter den Nagel reißen; *itr (Kälte)* schneiden; *tech* klemmen; *fam* rasen, flitzen; *s* Kneifen, (Ein-)Klemmen *n*, Biß *m*; ein bißchen, Stück(chen); Schneiden *n (der Kälte)*; schneidende Kälte *f*; *agr* Frostbrand *m*; bissige Bemerkung *f*; *tech* Knick; *(Käse)* starke(r) Geruch *m*; *to ~ in the bud* im Keim ersticken; *~ and tuck* ganz knapp, haarscharf, gerade so eben; genau gleich, ohne Unterschied; *sport Am* Seite an Seite; *to ~* **along** *fam* dahinsausen; sich beeilen; *to ~* **away** *fam* abhauen, stiftengehen, türmen; *to ~* **in** *fam* dazwischenkommen, -fahren; hineinwitschen, sich hineindrängeln; *to ~* **off** *tr* abkneifen, abzwicken, abschneiden; *itr fam = to ~ away*; *to ~* **on ahead** *fam* nach vorn stürmen; *to ~* **out** herausschneiden; *fam* hinauswitschen (*of* aus); **~per** ['-ə] *(Pferd)* Schneidezahn *m*; *(Krebs)* Schere; *mar* Zeising *f*; *fam* Bengel, Bursche *m*; *pl* Drahtschere, (Kneif-)Zange, Pinzette *f*; *sl opt* Kneifer *m*; *sl* Handschellen, Fußfesseln *f pl*; *sl* Rindvieh *n*; **~ping** ['-iŋ] kneifend, schneidend, beißend; scharf; *fig* bissig, sarkastisch; **~py** ['-i] *a (Kälte)* schneidend; beißend, scharf; *fam* fix, flink, munter, lebhaft; *s fam* Kellnerin *f*; **2.** *s* Schlückchen *n*; *itr* nippen; *tr* nippen an, von; **3.** *N~ (Am pej)* Japaner *m*.

nipple ['nipl] Brustwarze; Zitze *f*; Schnuller; *tech* Nippel; (Rohr-)Stutzen *m*.

Nisei, nisei ['ni:'sei] (gebürtiger) Amerikaner *m* japanischer Abkunft.

Nissen hut ['nisn'hʌt] Nissenhütte, Wellblechbaracke *f*.

nit [nit] *ent* Nisse *f*; **~picker** *Am sl* Pedant *m*; **~wit** ['-wit] *fam* kleine(s) Licht *n*; Nichtskönner, Versager *m*.

nitr|ate ['naitreit] *s chem* Nitrat, salpetersaure(s) Salz *n*; *tr* nitrieren; **~e,** *Am* **niter** ['naitə] *chem* Salpeter *m*; **~ic** ['naitrik] salpetersauer; *~~ acid* Salpetersäure *f*; **~ide** ['naitraid] *tr* nitrierhärten; **~ification** [naitrifi'keiʃən] Nitrifikation *f*; **~ify** ['-ifai] *tr* nitrieren; **~ite** ['naitrait] Nitrit *n*; **~obacteria** [naitro(u)bæk'tiəriə] Nitro-, Salpeterbakterien *f pl*; **~o-cellulose** ['-o(u)'seljulous] Schießbaumwolle *f*; **~ogen** ['naitridʒən] Stickstoff *m*; *~~ fertilization* Stickstoffdüngung *f*; **~ogenous** [nai'trɔdʒinəs] *a* Stickstoff-; stickstoffhaltig; **~o-glycerin(e)** ['naitro(u)-glisə'ri:n] Nitroglyzerin *n*; **~ous** ['naitrəs] salpet(e)rig; *~~ acid* salpet(e)rige Säure *f*; *~~ oxide* Lachgas *n*.

nix [niks] **1.** Wassergeist, Nix *m*; (Wasser-)Nixe *f*; **~ie** ['-i] (Wasser-)Nixe *f*; **2.** *prn sl* nichts; niemand; *adv sl* nicht; *tr sl* ablehnen, zurückweisen; *to ~ out* abhauen; *interj sl* halt (mal)! das gibt's (aber) nicht! laß das! *~ on! (Am)* aus damit! *s Am* unbestellbare Postsendung *f*; *sl* Ablehnung *f*.

no [nou] **1.** *interj* nein; *~!* nein! nanu! was Sie nicht sagen! **2.** *s pl -es* Nein *n*; Absage; *parl* Neinstimme *f*; *the ~es have it* der Antrag ist abgelehnt; **3.** *adv (beim Komparativ)* nicht, um nichts; keineswegs; *no ... than* nicht ... als; *or ~* oder nicht; *whether or ~* in jedem Fall; ob ... oder nicht; *~ more* nicht mehr, kein(e, en) ... mehr; *~ sooner ... than* so schnell (wie); *~ sooner said than done* gesagt, getan; *~ such* kein solcher, keine solche; **4.** *a* kein(e); *~ one* keiner, niemand; *~ one man* nicht ein einziger; *by ~ means* auf keine Weise; *in ~ time* im Nu; *~ admittance* Zutritt verboten! *~ cards* statt Karten! *~ doubt* ohne Zweifel; *~ end of (fam)* e-e Menge *od* Masse; *~ go (fam)* zweck-, nutzlos; *~ great shakes (sl)* unbedeutend; *~ parking* Parkverbot *n*; *~ soap (Am sl)* ich weiß nicht! *~ smoking!* Rauchen verboten! *~ use* nutzlos, sinnlos; *~ thoroughfare* keine Durchfahrt; Durchfahrt verboten; *~ wonder* kein Wunder (*that* daß); *there's ~ getting away from the fact* man kommt nicht um die Tatsache (herum); es läßt sich nicht leugnen; **~-account** *Am sl* unbedeutend, unwichtig; **~-ball** *sport* ungültige(r) Ball *m*; **~-being** Nichtsein *n*; **~-confidence vote** *parl* Mißtrauensvotum *n*; **~-good** *s* Nichtsnutz *m*; *a* nichtsnutzig; **~-load** *tech* Leerlauf-; *~* **man's-land** Niemandsland *n*; *~* **show** *Am* Passagier *m*, der zum Abflug nicht erscheint.

nob [nɔb] **1.** Knopf *m*; *sl* Birne *f*, Kopf *m*; **2.** *sl* reiche(r) Kerl, feine(r) Knilch *m*; hohe(s) Tier *n*; *pl die* Reichen *m pl*; **~by** ['-i] *sl* schick, schmissig; pfundig, bombig, prima.

nobble ['nɔbl] *tr sl (Rennpferd)* untauglich machen; mit unreellen Mitteln gewinnen; beschwindeln, begaunern; *(Stimmen)* kaufen; klauen; **~r** ['-ə] *sl* Betrüger, Schwindler *m*.

Nobel prize ['noubel 'praiz] Nobelpreis *m*; **Nobel-prize winner** Nobelpreisträger *m*.

nobil|iary [no(u)'biliəri] *a* Adels-; **~ity** [no(u)'biliti] (hoher) Adel, Hochadel *m*; *die* Adligen; *fig* Vornehmheit *f*.

noble ['noubl] *a* adlig, hoch(geboren); *fig* edel, hochherzig; vornehm, würdig, würdevoll; stattlich, prächtig, prachtvoll; ausgezeichnet, vortrefflich; *(Metall)* edel, Edel-; *s* Adlige(r) *m*; *~* **gas** Edelgas *n*; **~man** ['-mən] Adlige(r), Edelmann *m*; *~* **metal** Edelmetall *n*; **~-minded** *a* edel, hochherzig; **~-mindedness** Edelmut *m*; **~ness** ['-nis] Adel *m*, Würde, Vornehmheit *f*.

nobody ['noubədi] *prn* niemand; *s fam* Null *f*, nichtssagende(r), unbedeutende(r) Mensch, Unbekannte(r) *m*.

nock [nɔk] *s (Bogen, Pfeil)* Kerbe *f*, Einschnitt *m*; *tr (Bogen, Pfeil)* kerben; *(Pfeil)* auflegen.

noctambul|ant [nɔk'tæmbjulənt], **~ist** [-ist] Schlafwandler *m*; **~ism** [-izm] Schlafwandeln *n*.

nocturn|al [nɔk'tə:nl] nächtlich; Nacht-; **~(e)** ['nɔktə:n] *(Kunst)* Nachtstück; *mus* Notturno *n*.

nocuous ['nɔkjuəs] schädlich, nachteilig.

nod [nɔd] *itr* (zu)nicken (*to s.o.* jdm); einnicken (*over* über); den Kopf (im Einschlafen) sinken lassen; schläfrig, müde, unaufmerksam, unachtsam sein; dösen; e-n Fehler machen; sich hin- und her-, auf und ab bewegen, schwanken; *tr* nicken (*o.'s head* mit dem Kopf); *(Einverständnis)* durch Zunicken zum Ausdruck bringen; *s* Nicken, Schwanken; Zunicken *n*; *sport* günstige Entscheidung *f*; *(land of) N~* Traumland *n*; *on the ~ (Am) fam* auf Pump; *to answer with a ~*, *to ~ assent* zustimmend nicken; *to get the ~ (sport)* ausgewählt werden (*over* vor); *to give s.o. a ~* jdm zunicken; *Homer sometimes ~s* hier irrt Goethe; *~ding acquaintance* oberflächliche Bekanntschaft *f*.

nod|al ['noudl] *a* Knoten-; *~~ point* Knotenpunkt *m*; **~e** [noud] Knoten *m a. anat bot astr phys math fig (e-r Erzählung, e-s Dramas)*; *med (gouty ~~)* (Gicht-)Knoten *m*; **~ose** ['no(u)dous] *bot* knotig; **~osity** [no(u)'dɔsiti] knotige Beschaffenheit *f*; **~ular** ['nɔdjulə] *a* Knoten-; knotenartig; **~ule** ['nɔdju:l] Knötchen *n*; *geol* Nest *n*, Niere *f*.

noddle ['nɔdl] *fam* Kürbis *m*, Birne *f*.

nog [nɔg] **1.** (Holz-)Pflock; Dübel; Aststumpf; kleine(r) Balken *m*; **~ging** ['-iŋ] Ausmauerung *f* e-r Riegelwand; **2.** *(egg~)* Eierflip *m*.

noggin ['nɔgin] Becher, Schoppen *m*; Viertelpinte *f (Großbrit.: 0,14 l; Am 0,12 l)*; *Am fam* Kürbis, Kopf *m*.

nohow ['nouhau] *adv fam* in kein(st)er Weise, nicht im geringsten; *sl (to feel) ~* nicht auf dem Damm (sein).

noil [nɔil] *sing u. pl* Kämmling *m*.

nois|e [nɔiz] *s* Geräusch *n*; Lärm *m*, Geschrei; *tele* Rauschen; *radio* Nebengeräusch *n*, Störung *f*; *tr (to ~ abroad) (Nachricht, Gerücht)* verbreiten; *to make a ~~* Krach machen (*about* wegen), *in the world* Aufsehen erregen; *big ~~ (fam)* hohe(s) Tier *n*; *~~ figure, level* Stör-, Geräuschpegel *m*; *~~ suppression (radio)* Entstörung *f*; **~eless** ['-lis] geräuschlos; ruhig, still; lärmfrei; leise; **~elessness** ['-lisnis] Geräuschlosigkeit; Ruhe, Stille *f*; **~emaker** Lärminstrument *n*; **~iness** ['nɔizinis] Lärm *m*, Geschrei *n*; Turbulenz *f*; **~y** ['nɔizi] geräuschvoll, laut, lärmend; *(Farbe)* schreiend, grell; lebhaft, turbulent; *(Stil)* geschwollen.

noisome ['nɔisəm] ungesund, schädlich; stinkend, eklig, widerlich.

nol-pros ['nɔl'prɔs] *tr Am jur (Anklage)* zurücknehmen; *(Verfahren)* niederschlagen.

nomad ['nɔməd, 'noumæd] *s* Nomade *m a. fig*; *a* u. **~ic** [no(u)'mædik, nɔ'm-] nomadisch; nomadenhaft; wandernd, unstet; **~ism** ['nɔmədizm] Nomadentum *n*; **~ize** [-aiz] *itr* nomadisieren.

nomenclature [no(u)'menklətʃə, 'noumenkleitʃə] Nomenklatur *f*, Namen-, Wörterverzeichnis *n*; Terminologie *f*, Fachausdrücke *m pl*, -sprache; Benennung, Bezeichnung *f*.

nomin|al ['nɔminl] *a* Namens-; namentlich; Nenn-; nominell, dem Namen nach; gering(fügig), klein; *gram* nominal; *~~ amount* Nennbetrag *m*; *~~ capital* Stammkapital *n*; *~~ exchange* Nominalkurs *m*; *~~ fine* Ordnungs-, Polizeistrafe *f*; *~~ load* Nennbelastung *f*; *~~ output* Nennleistung *f*; *~~ price* nominelle(r) Preis *m*; *~~ roll* Namensverzeichnis *n*; *~~ value* Nennwert *m*; *~~ wages (pl)* Nominallohn *m*; **~ally** ['-əli] *adv* namentlich, mit Namen; (nur) dem Namen nach; nominell; **~ate** ['-eit] *tr* ernennen (*to* zu); benennen, namhaft machen; zur Wahl vorschlagen, als Kandidaten aufstellen (*for* für); **~ation** [nɔmi'neiʃən] Ernennung (*to* zu); Namhaftmachung, Benennung *f*, Vorschlag *m*; Aufstellung *f* (*e-s Kandidaten*); (*right of ~~*) Vorschlagsrecht *n*; *to be in ~~ for* kandidieren für; **~ative** ['nɔminətiv] *a gram* Nominativ-; *s gram* Nominativ *m*; **~ator** ['-eitə] Benennende(r), Vorschlagende(r) *m*; **~ee** [nɔmi'ni:] (*vorgeschlagener*) Kandidat; (Renten-)Empfänger *m*.

non [nɔn] *pref* Nicht-, nicht-; **~-acceptance** Nichtannahme, Annahmeverweigerung; (*Wechsel*) Akzeptverweigerung *f*; **~-accomplishment** Nichtdurchführung *f*; **~-admission** Nichtzulassung *f*.

nonage ['nounidʒ, 'nɔn-] Minderjährigkeit, Unmündigkeit; *fig* Unreife *f*; Frühstadium *n*.

nonagenarian [nounədʒi'nɛəriən] *a* neunzigjährig; *s* Neunzigjährige(r) *m*.

non|-aggression pact ['nɔnə'greʃən-'pækt] *pol* Nichtangriffspakt *m*; **~-alcoholic** alkoholfrei; **~-appearance** Nichterscheinen, Ausbleiben *n*.

nonary ['nounəri] *a* Neuner-; *s* Neunergruppe *f*.

non|-attendance ['nɔnə'tendəns] Fernbleiben *n*; **~-automatic** nichtautomatisch; **~-available** unabkömmlich; **~-belligerent** nichtkriegführend; **~-burnable** nicht brennbar; **~-business day** Bankfeiertag *m*; **~-capitalistic** nichtkapitalistisch.

nonce [nɔns] *s*: *for the ~* im Augenblick, in diesem Fall; **~-word** Ad-hoc-Bildung *f* e-s Wortes.

nonchalan|ce ['nɔnʃələns] Gleichgültigkeit, Uninteressiertheit, (Nach-)Lässigkeit, Formlosigkeit *f*; **~t** ['-t] gleichgültig, uninteressiert, (nach-)lässig, saumselig; formlos.

non|-coagulating ['nɔnkou'ægjuleitiŋ] nicht gerinnend; **~-combatant** *s mil* Nichtkämpfer; Zivilist *m*; *a* nichtkämpfend; **~-commercial enterprise** nicht gewerbliche(s) Unternehmen *n*; **~-commissioned** *a* nicht bevollmächtigt; *~~ officer (N.C.O.)*, *fam* **noncom** Unteroffizier *m*; **~-committal** (sich) nicht verpflichtend; nicht bindend, unverbindlich; **~-compliance** Nichtbefolgung, Nichteinhaltung *f* (*with s.th.* e-r S); **~ compos mentis** *jur* unzurechnungsfähig; **~-conducting** *phys el* nichtleitend; **~-conductor** *phys el* Nichtleiter *m*.

nonconform|ist ['nɔnkən'fɔ:mist] Dissenter, Dissident *m*; **~ity** [-iti] Nichtübereinstimmung *f* (*with* mit); *rel* Dissentertum *n*; Nichtbefolgung *f* (*to s.th.* e-r S).

non|-contagious ['nɔnkən'teidʒəs] *med* nicht ansteckend; **~-contentious litigation** freiwillige Gerichtsbarkeit *f*; **~-contributory** beitragsfrei; **~-cooperation** passive(r) Widerstand *m*; **~-corroding, -corrosive** nichtrostend; **~-creasing** knitterfrei; **~-cutting** spanlos; **~-dazzle** *mot* blendfrei; **~-delivery** Nichtablieferung, -bestellung *f*.

nondescript ['nɔndiskript] *a* schwer zu beschreiben(d) *od* einzuordnen(d); unbestimmbar, unbestimmt; *s* schwer einzuordnende(r) Mensch *m od* Sache *f*; Arbeitsunfähige(r) *m*.

none [nʌn] *prn* kein; *mit pl* niemand, keine *pl*; nichts; *~ at all* kein einziger; *~ but* niemand, nichts außer; nur; *~ of that!* laß das! Schluß damit! *that's ~ of your business* das geht dich nichts an; *adv* (durchaus, gar) nicht; in keiner Weise; *~ too soon* gerade noch zur rechten Zeit; *~ the less* nichtsdestoweniger, trotzdem.

non|-edible ['nɔn'edibl] nicht genießbar; **~-effective** *a* unwirksam; *mil* (dienst)untauglich; *s mil* (Dienst-)Untaugliche(r) *m*; **~-ego** Nicht-Ich *n*; **~-enforceable** nicht vollstreckbar, nicht klagbar.

nonentity [nɔ'nentiti] Nichtvorhandensein; Phantasieprodukt; Unwirkliche(s) *n*; *fig* Null *f*.

non-essential ['nɔni'senʃəl] *a* unwesentlich, unbedeutend; unnötig, überflüssig, nicht lebenswichtig; *s* unbedeutende(r) Mensch *m*; Nebensache *f*; *pl* unwesentliche Bestandteile *m pl*, Nebensächlichkeiten *f pl*.

non(e)such ['nʌnsʌtʃ] Ausnahme (-mensch *m*) *f*; etwas Einmaliges; Vorbild *n*.

non|-existence Nichtvorhandensein, -bestehen *n*; Abwesenheit *f*; **~-existent** nicht vorhanden; **~-expendable supplies** *pl mil* Gebrauchsgüter *n pl*; **~-feasance** *jur* (pflichtwidrige) Unterlassung *f*; **~-ferrous metal** NE-Metall *n*; **~-fiction book** Sachbuch *n*; **~-flowering** nichtblühend; **~-freezing** kältebeständig; **~-fulfil(l)ment** Nichterfüllung *f*; **~-fusible** nicht schmelzbar; **~-graded** *a* nicht klassifiziert; **~-halation** *phot* lichthoffrei; **~-inductive** induktionsfrei; **~-intervention** *pol* Nichteinmischung *f*; *~~ policy* Nichteinmischungspolitik *f*; **~-linear** nichtlinear; **~-litigious** nicht streitig; **~-luminous** nichtleuchtend; **~-malignant** *med* gutartig; **~-member** Nichtmitglied *n*; *~~ state* Nichtmitgliedstaat *m*; **~-membership** Nichtmitgliedschaft *f*; **~-metal** *chem* Nichtmetall *n*; **~-military** nichtmilitärisch; **~-negotiable** nicht übertragbar; **~-observance** Nichtbeachtung, -befolgung, -einhaltung *f*; **~-official** nichtamtlich.

nonpareil ['nɔnpərəl, *Am* -'rel] *a* unvergleichlich; *s* Unvergleichliche(r *m*) *f*; etwas (völlig) Unvergleichliches; Muster *n*; *typ* Nonpareille *f* (*Schriftgrad*); *zoo* Papstfink *m*.

non|-participation ['nɔnpɑ:tisi'peiʃən] Nichtbeteiligung *f*; **~-partisan** unparteiisch; überparteilich; **~-party** nicht parteigebunden; **~-payment** Nicht(be)zahlung *f*; **~-performance** Nichtausführung, -erfüllung *f*.

nonplus ['nɔn'plʌs] *s* Verwirrung, völlige Ratlosigkeit *f*; *tr* verblüffen; verwirrt, ratlos, perplex machen; in größte Verlegenheit bringen.

non|-political ['nɔnpə'litikəl] unpolitisch; **~-productive** unproduktiv; **~-professional** nichtberuflich; **~-profit** gemeinnützig; **~-resident** *a* nicht (orts)ansässig, auswärtig; (*Geistlicher*) abwesend, nicht amtierend; *s* Auswärtige(r), Pendler; Devisenausländer; (*Schule*) Externe(r); Gelegenheitsgast *m*; **~-return valve** Rückschlagventil *n*; **~-rigid** unstarr; **~-scheduled** *a* außerplanmäßig.

nonsens|e ['nɔnsəns] *s* Unsinn *m*, dumme(s) Zeug *n* Blödsinn, Quatsch *m a. interj*; Albernheiten, Dummheiten *f pl*; *and no ~ about it!* keine falsche Vorstellung! **~ical** [nɔn'sensikəl] un-, blödsinnig, albern, dumm.

non|-shrinkable ['nɔn'ʃrinkəbl] nicht schrumpfend, nicht einlaufend; **~-skid** *a* Gleitschutz-; *~~ chain* Schneekette *f*; *~~ tyre* Gleitschutzreifen *m*; **~-smoker** Nichtraucher *m*; **~-smoking compartment** Nichtraucherabteil *n*; **~-stop** *a* Ohnehalt-; durchgehend; *~~ flight* Ohnehalt-, Nonstopflug *m*; *~~ journey* Reise *f* ohne Unterbrechung; *~~ performance* durchgehende Veranstaltung *f*; *~~ train* durchgehende(r) Zug *m*.

nonsuit ['nɔnsju:t] *s jur* Klagabweisung *f*; *tr* mit e-r Klage abweisen (*s.o.* jdn); (*Prozeß*) sistieren.

non|-support ['nɔnsə'pɔ:t] Vernachlässigung *f* der Unterhaltspflicht; **~-union** nicht (gewerkschaftlich) organisiert; *~~ shop* gewerkschaftsfreie(r) Betrieb *m*; **~-violence** Gewaltlosigkeit *f*; **~-voter** Nichtwähler *m*; **~-warranty clause** Haftungsausschlußklausel *f*.

noodle ['nu:dl] **1.** *fam* Dussel, Trottel, Depp *m*; *sl* Birne *f*, Kürbis, Kopf *m*; **2.** Nudel *f*; **~ soup** Nudelsuppe *f*.

nook [nuk] (Zimmer-)Ecke *f*; (Schlupf-)Winkel *m*; *breakfast ~* Eßecke *f*.

noon [nu:n] *s* Mittag *a. fig*; *fig* Höhepunkt *m*; *attr* Mittags-; *itr Am* Mittag machen; *at ~* mittags; um zwölf Uhr (mittags); **~day, ~tide, ~time** Mittag *m*; *at ~~* zu Mittag.

noose [nu:s] *s* Schlaufe, Schlinge *a. fig*; *fig* Einschnürung, Fessel *f*; *tr* in e-r Schlinge fangen; schlingen (*round* um); *to put o.'s head into the ~ (fig)* in die Falle gehen.

nope [noup] *Am sl* ne(e), nein.

nor [nɔ:] *adv* und (auch) nicht, noch; *neither ... ~* weder ... noch; *~ I* ich auch nicht.

Nordic ['nɔ:dik] nordisch.

norm [nɔ:m] Richtschnur, Norm; Regel *f*, Typ *m*, Muster *n*; Arbeitsnorm *f*; *biol* Typus *m*; **~al** ['-əl] *a* normal, durchschnittlich; Durchschnitts-, Normal-; regelrecht, normgerecht; gewöhnlich, natürlich; typisch; *math* senkrecht; *med* normal, ohne Befund (*o.B.*); *s das* Normale, *die* Norm, *die* Regel; normale Verhältnisse *n pl*; Normalwert, -stand *m*; *math* Senkrechte *f*; *~~ consumption* Normverbrauch *m*; *~~ output* Normalleistung *f*; *~~ school* Lehrerseminar *n*, pädagogische Akademie *f*; *~~ size* Normalgröße *f*; *~~ value* Durchschnittspreis *m*; *~~ velocity* Normalgeschwindigkeit *f*; **~alcy** ['-əlsi], **~ality** [nɔ:'mæliti] Normalzustand *m*, Vorschriftsmäßigkeit, Normalität *f*; **~alization** [nɔ:məlai'zeiʃən] Normalisierung *f*; **~alize** ['nɔ:məlaiz] *tr* normalisieren; standardisieren, normen; vereinheitlichen; **~ally** ['-əli] *adv* normalerweise, im Normalfall.

Norman ['nɔ:mən] *s* Normanne *m*; *a* normannisch; **~dy** ['-di] die Normandie.

normative ['nɔ:mətiv] normativ.

north [nɔ:θ] *s* Nord(en) *m* (*Richtung, Gegend*); *a* nördlich; Nord-; *adv* in nördlicher Richtung, nach Norden; *in the ~* im Norden; *to the ~ of* im Norden von; *to fly ~* nach Norden fliegen; **N~ America** Nordamerika *n*; **N~ American** nordamerikanisch; **N~ Atlantic Treaty Organization** NATO; **~-east** [nɔ:θ'i:st; *mar* nɔ:r-'i:st] *s* Nordost(en) *m*; *a* nordöstlich; *adv* (in) nordöstlich(er Richtung); **~-easter** Nordostwind *m*; **~-eastern** *a* nordöstlich; **~er** ['nɔ:ðə] *Am* Nordwind *m*; **~erly** ['-ðəli] *a* nördlich; Nord-; *adv* nach, von Norden; **~ern** ['nɔ:ðən] nördlich, nordisch; Nord-; *the N~~ Hemisphere* die Nordhalbkugel (*der Erde*); *N~~ Ireland* Nordirland *n*; *~~ lights (pl)* Nordlicht *n*; **~erner** Nordländer(in *f*); *(Am)* Nordstaatler *m*; **~ernmost** ['-moust] nördlichst; **N~ German** *s* Norddeutsche(r *m*) *f*; *a* norddeutsch; **~ing** ['nɔ:ðiŋ] *astr* nördliche Deklination *f*; *mar* Breitenunterschied *m* nach Norden; **N~man** ['-mən] Wikinger *m*; **N~ Pole** Nordpol *m*; **N~ Sea** Nordsee *f*; **N~ Star** Nord-, Polarstern *m*; **~ward** ['nɔ:θwəd] *a* nördlich (*of, from* von); *(~~s) adv* nach Norden; **~-west** [*mar* nɔ:'west] *s* Nordwest(en) *m*; *a* nordwestlich; *adv* (in) nordwestlich(er Richtung); **~-westerly** *a adv* nordwestlich; **~ wind** Nordwind *m*.

Norw|ay ['nɔ:wei] Norwegen *n*; **~egian** [nɔ:'wi:dʒən] *a* norwegisch; *s* Norweger(in *f*) *m*.

*

nose [nouz] *s* Nase; Schnauze *f*; Geruch(ssinn) *m*, Nase *f* (*for* für); Duft; *allg* Vorsprung *m*, Nase *f*; *tech* Vorderteil *n*; *mar* Bug *m*; *aero* Nase *f*, Bug *m*, Kanzel; *(Rohr)* Mündung *f*; *sl* Spion, Spitzel *m*; *tr* riechen, wittern; spüren; mit der Nase berühren *od* reiben; *mar* vorsichtig fahren; *itr* riechen, schnüffeln (*at* an; *for* nach; *into* in); *fig* herumschnüffeln (*after, for* nach); *sl* spionieren, Spitzeldienste leisten; *to ~ down (aero) tr* (an)drücken; *itr* im Steilflug niedergehen; *to ~ out* herausriechen; aufstöbern; ausspionieren; um e-e Nasenlänge schlagen; *to ~ over (aero)* sich *(beim Landen)* überschlagen; *to ~ up (aero)* hochziehen; *by a ~ (Pferderennen)* um e-e Nasenlänge; *fig* um Haaresbreite, ganz knapp; *on the ~ (sl)* haarscharf, -genau; *under s.o.'s (very) ~* vor, unter jds Augen; *to bite, to snap s.o.'s ~ off* jdn anfahren; *to blow o.'s ~* sich die Nase putzen; *to count, to tell ~s* die Köpfe, die Anwesenden zählen; *to cut off o.'s ~ to spite o.'s face (fig)* sich ins eigene Fleisch schneiden; *to follow o.'s ~* der Nase nach, geradeaus gehen; *to keep o.'s ~ to the grindstone* nicht von s-r Arbeit aufschauen; *to lead s.o. by the ~ (fig)* jdn um den Finger wickeln können; *to look down o.'s ~ at s.o.* jdn von oben herab, mit Verachtung ansehen; *to make a long ~ at s.o.* jdm e-e Nase drehen; *to pay through the ~* e-n zu hohen Preis bezahlen; *fam* bluten müssen; *to poke, to push, to thrust o.'s ~ into s.th. (fig)* s-e Nase in etw stecken; in e-r S herumschnüffeln; *to put s.o.'s ~ out of joint (fig)* jds Pläne vereiteln; jdn ausstechen; *to turn up o.'s ~ at* die Nase rümpfen über; nichts zu tun haben wollen mit; *to ~ o.'s way* sich (nach vorn) durcharbeiten, -schlagen; *as plain as the ~ on o.'s face* sonnenklar, *hum* klar wie dicke Tinte; *aquiline, crooked, pug, snub* Adler-, Haken-, Stumpf-, Stupsnase *f*; *tip of the nose* Nasenspitze *f*; **~-ape** Nasenaffe *m*; **~-bag** *(Pferd)* Futterbeutel *m*; **~-band** *(Pferd)* Nasenriemen; Eßkorb *m*; **~bleed(ing)** Nasenbluten *n*; **~d** [-d] *a in Zssgen* -nasig; **~-dive** *s aero* Sturzflug; *com fam* Preissturz *m*; *itr* e-n Sturzflug machen; *(Preise)* stürzen; **~gay** ['-gei] Blumenstrauß *m*; **~ gunner** Bugschütze *m*; **~heavy** *aero* kopflastig; **~-over** *aero* Kopfstand, Überschlag *m (beim Landen)*; **~-piece** Nasenschutz, -riemen *m*; Mündung, Öffnung *f*; Mundstück, Vorderteil *n*; *(Mikroskop)* Revolver; *(Brille)* Steg *m*; **~-ring** Nasenring *m*; **~-wheel** *aero* Bugrad *n*; **~y** *s. nosy.*

nosing ['nouziŋ] vorstehende Kante *f*; Schutzstreifen *m*.

nosology [nɔ'sɔlədʒi] Nosologie, Lehre *f* von den Krankheiten.

nostalgi|a [nɔs'tældʒiə] Heimweh *n*; **~c** [-k] heimwehkrank.

nostril ['nɔstril] Nasenloch *n*, Nüster *f*.

nostrum ['nɔstrəm] Haus-, Geheim-, Allheil-, Wundermittel *n a. fig.*

nosy ['nouzi] übelriechend, *fam* stinkig; duftend; *fam* neugierig; **~ parker** *fam* Topfgucker, Pottkieker *m*.

not [nɔt] *adv* nicht; *~ a* kein; *~ at all* durchaus, überhaupt, gar nicht; auf keinen Fall; keineswegs; *interj* keine Ursache! *~ but what, that* trotzdem; *~ a few* nicht wenige; *~ half (sl)* äußerst, tüchtig, mächtig; *~ in the least* nicht im geringsten; *~ to say* um nicht zu sagen; *~ seldom* nicht selten, oft; *~ so* nein; *~ to speak of* ganz zu schweigen von; *~ yet* noch nicht; *certainly ~* gewiß nicht; *as likely as ~* vielleicht; vielleicht auch nicht; *it's ~ to be thought of* daran ist nicht zu denken; das kommt nicht in Frage.

notab|ility [noutə'biliti] Auffälligkeit, Ungewöhnlichkeit; *(Hausfrau)* Tüchtigkeit *f*, Fleiß *m*; bemerkenswerte, bedeutende Persönlichkeit *f*; **~le** ['noutəbl] *a* bemerkenswert, angesehen, bedeutend, auffällig, in die Augen fallend; hervorragend, ungewöhnlich; *(Hausfrau)* tüchtig, fleißig, umsichtig; *s* Standesperson; bekannte Persönlichkeit *f*.

notar|ial [no(u)'tɛəriəl] notariell; Notariats-; *~~ act, deed, document* Notariatsurkunde *f*; *~~ fees (pl)* notarielle Gebühren *f pl*; *~~ verification* notarielle Beurkundung *f*; *~~ly certified* notariell beglaubigt; **~ize** ['noutəraiz] *tr* notariell beglaubigen; **~y** ['noutəri] *(~~ public)* (öffentlicher) Notar *m*; *before a ~~* vor e-m Notar; *by a ~~* durch e-n Notar; *office of a ~~* Notariat *n*.

notation [no(u)'teiʃən] Bezeichnung *f*, mathematische Zeichen *n pl*; *mus* Notenschrift; *Am* Notierung, Aufzeichnung, Anmerkung *f*.

notch [nɔtʃ] *s* Aussparung, Nute, Kerbe *f*, Einschnitt *m*; Scharte *f*; *tech* Zahn *m*; *Am* Schlucht *f*, Engpaß *m*; *Am fam* Nummer, Stufe *f*, Grad *m*; *tr* (ein)kerben, mit e-m Einschnitt versehen; *tech* nuten, zähneln, falzen; *fig* ankreiden, -schreiben.

note [nout] *s* (charakteristische) Note; *mus* Note; Taste *f*; *(Vogel)* Gesang *m*; (Satz-)Zeichen *n*; Zettel *m*, Notiz; Aufzeichnung, Anmerkung *f*; Kommentar *m*; Fußnote *f*; Vermerk; Brief *m*, kurze Mitteilung; (diplomatische) Note *f*; Memorandum *n*; Rechnung *f*; schriftliche(s) Zahlungsversprechen *n*; Banknote *f*; *fig* Ton, Klang; Ruf, Schrei *m*; (gegebenes) Zeichen; Ansehen *n*, Ruf *m*; *tr* bemerken, beachten, achten auf, beobachten; vermerken, vormerken, notieren, zu Notiz nehmen, aufzeichnen, schriftlich niederlegen, aufschreiben; besonders erwähnen; mit Anmerkungen, Fußnoten versehen; bezeichnen, bedeuten; *mus* in Noten festhalten *od* niederlegen, mit Noten versehen; *to ~ down* aufnotieren; *of ~* von Bedeutung *od* Rang; *to compare ~s* s-e Meinungen austauschen (*on* über); *to make a ~ of s.th.* sich etw aufschreiben; *fig* sich etw merken; *to strike the right, wrong ~ (fig)* den richtigen, falschen Ton treffen; *to take ~ of s.th.* etw Beachtung schenken; etw zur Kenntnis nehmen; *to take ~s* sich Notizen machen (*of* über); *bank ~* Banknote *f*; *biographical ~* biographische Notiz *f* *(in e-m Buch)*; *circular ~* Reisescheck, -kreditbrief *m*; *consignment ~* Versandanzeige *f*; *credit ~* Gutschriftanzeige *f*; *exchange of ~s (pol)* Notenwechsel *m*; *foot~* Fußnote *f*; *marginal ~* Randbemerkung, -notiz *f*; *promissory ~, ~ of hand* Schuldschein *m*; *~ of entry* Eintragungsvermerk *m*; *~ of sale* Verkaufsvertrag *m*; *~ of exclamation, interrogation* Ausrufe-, Fragezeichen *n*; **~book** Notizbuch; Heft *n*; **~ case** *Br* Geldscheintasche *f*; **~ circulation** Notenumlauf *m*; **~d** ['-id] *a* bedeutend, hervorragend; wohlbekannt, berühmt (*for* wegen); *~~ below* unten erwähnt; **~holder** Wertpapierinhaber *m*; **~ issue** Notenausgabe *f*, -umlauf *m*; **~pad** Schreibblock *m*; **~paper** Schreib-, Briefpapier *n*; **~ press** Banknotenpresse *f*; **~worthy** ['-wə:ði] bemerkens-, beachtenswert, beachtlich, bedeutend, hervorragend.

nothing ['nʌθiŋ] *s* Nichts *n*; *math fig* Null (*to* gegenüber); Kleinigkeit, Bagatelle *f*; *prn* nichts; *adv* durchaus nicht, keineswegs; *five feet ~* genau 5 Fuß; *for ~* für nichts und wieder nichts; um nichts; umsonst; *to say ~ of* ganz zu schweigen von; *~ but* nichts als; *~ less than* nichts weniger als; *~ much* nicht viel; *~ if not* äußerst, im höchsten Grade; *~ to write home about (fam)* völlig unbedeutend; *to come to ~* zunichte werden, sich zerschlagen; *to have ~ to do with* nichts zu tun haben mit; *to hear ~ of* nichts hören von; *to make ~ of* sich nichts machen aus, nichts halten von; nicht verstehen; nichts anfangen können mit; *to think ~ of* nichts halten von; *there is ~ like that* da kommt nichts mit; *~ came of it!* daraus wurde nichts! *~ doing!* nichts zu machen! *there is ~ for it but* es gibt keine andere Möglichkeit als; *good for ~* zu nichts zu gebrauchen; *good-for-~* Taugenichts *m*; *little or ~* wenig oder (gar) nichts; *next of* od *to ~* fast nichts; **~ness** ['-nis] Nicht(vorhanden)sein *n*; Nichtigkeit, Bedeutungslosigkeit; Lappalie *f*.

notice ['noutis] **1.** *s* Bemerkung, Be(ob)achtung, Kenntnis(nahme); Aufmerksamkeit, Rücksicht, Höflichkeit; Ankündigung, Mitteilung, Anzeige, Notiz, Nachricht, Benachrichtigung, Warnung; Bekanntmachung *f*, Anschlag *m* (*on the bulletin board* am Schwarzen Brett); Entlassung, Kündigung(sfrist); Frist; Vorschrift, Anordnung; *lit theat (Kunst)* Besprechung, Kritik, Rezension; *jur* Vorladung; *(Patent)* Anmeldung *f*; **2.** *tr* (be)merken, be(ob)achten, zur Kenntnis nehmen; beachten, achten auf, Aufmerksamkeit schenken (*s.th.* e-r S), aufpassen auf; Rücksicht nehmen auf, höflich sein gegen; erwähnen, Bezug nehmen auf; kommentieren; *(Buch, Theaterstück, Kunstwerk)* besprechen; kündigen; **3.** *at ~* gegen Kündigung; *at a moment's ~* sofort, unverzüglich, auf der Stelle, jeden Augenblick, jederzeit; *at short ~* kurzfristig; *at a week's ~* innerhalb e-r Woche; *till, until further ~* bis auf weiteres; *without ~* ohne Ankündigung; fristlos; **4.** *to bring s.th. to s.o.'s ~* jdn auf etw aufmerksam machen, jdm etw zur Kenntnis bringen; *to come under s.o.'s ~* jdm zur Kenntnis gelangen; *to escape ~* übersehen werden, unbeachtet bleiben; *o.'s ~* übersehen; *to give s.o. ~* jdm kündigen; *of s.th.* jdn von etw in Kenntnis setzen; *(e-n Schaden)* anmelden; *to put up a ~* e-e Bekanntmachung anschlagen; *to serve ~ on s.o.*

jdm etw ankündigen; *jur* jdn vorladen; *to take* ~ beobachten, aufpassen; *of s.th.* etw beachten, zur Kenntnis, von etw Notiz nehmen; *to take no* ~ *of* übersehen, -gehen, nicht beachten; ignorieren; **5.** *he sits up and takes* ~ *(hum)* es geht ihm wieder besser, das Essen schmeckt ihm (schon) wieder; *she gave us* ~ *to move* sie hat uns gekündigt; **6.** *advance* ~ Voranzeige *f*; *a month's* ~ monatliche Kündigung *f*; *obituary* ~ Nachruf *m*; *official* ~ amtliche Bekanntmachung *f*; Dienstvermerk *m*; *previous* ~ Voranzeige *f*; *public* ~ öffentliche Bekanntmachung *f*; *verbal* ~ mündliche(r) Bescheid *m*; ~ *of appeal (jur)* Berufung *f*; ~ *of assessment* Steuerbescheid *m*; ~ *of delivery, receipt* Empfangs-, Rückschein *m*; ~ *to pay* Zahlungsaufforderung *f*; ~ *to quit* Kündigung *f* e-s Mietverhältnisses; ~ *of trial (jur)* Ladung *f* zur mündlichen Verhandlung; **~able** ['-əbl] auffällig, nicht zu übersehen(d); bemerkenswert, beachtlich; **~-board** Anschlagbrett *n*, -tafel *f*, Schwarze(s) Brett *n*; (Warnungs-)Tafel *f*, Schild *n*; ~ **period** Kündigungsfrist *f*.

notif|iable ['noutifaiəbl] melde-, anzeigepflichtig; **~ication** [noutifi'keiʃən] Benachrichtigung, Mitteilung; Meldung, Anzeige; Bekanntmachung; *jur* Ladung *f*; ~~ *of birth, death* Geburts-, Todesanzeige *f*; ~~ *of loss* Schadensmeldung *f*; **~y** ['noutifai] *tr* benachrichtigen, anzeigen; informieren, (offiziell) unterrichten (*of* von); bekanntmachen, -geben; verkünden, melden, berichten; *(Anspruch)* anmelden; *(Behörde)* verständigen; *jur* vorladen; zustellen (*s.o. of a decision* jdm ein Urteil).

notion ['nouʃən] Begriff *m*, Vorstellung; Auffassung, Ansicht, Meinung; Neigung *f*, Hang, Wunsch *m*; Absicht; Laune *f*; *pl Am* Kurzwaren *f pl*; *to have no* ~ *of s.th.* von etw keine Ahnung haben; *I have a* ~ *that* ich denke mir, daß; **~al** ['-l] begrifflich, Begriffs-, Vorstellungs-; (nur) eingebildet; versonnen, versponnen.

notori|ety [noutə'raiəti] allgemeine Bekanntheit *f*; schlechte(r) Ruf *m*; bekannte Persönlichkeit *f*; **~ous** [no(u)-'tɔ:riəs] (all)bekannt, offenkundig, stadtbekannt; berüchtigt (*for* wegen).

notwithstanding [nɔtwiθ'stændiŋ] *prp* trotz, ungeachtet *gen*; *adv* trotzdem, dennoch, nichtsdestoweniger; *conj (~ that) obs* obgleich, obwohl.

nougat ['nu:gɑ:] Nugat *m* od *n*.

nought *s. naught.*

noun [naun] *gram* Hauptwort, Substantiv *n*.

nourish ['nʌriʃ] *tr* (er)nähren (*on, with* von); *fig* nähren, hegen, unterhalten, (unter)stützen, fördern, anregen, stärken; **~ing** ['-iŋ] *a* Nähr-; nahrhaft; förderlich, gesund; **~ment** ['-mənt] Ernährung *f*; Unterhalt *m*; Nahrung(smittel *n*) *f a. fig.*

nous [naus] Verstand; *fam* Mutterwitz *m*.

novel ['nɔvəl] *a* neu, ungewohnt, ungewöhnlich; überraschend; *s* Roman *m*; *jur* Novelle *f*, Gesetzesnachtrag *m*; **~ette** [nɔvə'let] Unterhaltungsroman *m*; **~ist** ['-ist] Romanschriftsteller *m*; **~istic** [nɔvə'listik] romanhaft; **~ty** ['nɔvəlti] Neuheit, Ungewohntheit, Neuartigkeit; Neuheit *f*, neue(r) Artikel *m*; *meist pl com* Neuheiten *f pl*; ~~ *item* Neuheit *f*, Schlager *m*.

November [no(u)'vembə] November *m*.

novic|e ['nɔvis] *rel* Novize; Neubekehrte(r); *allg* Anfänger, Neuling *m*; **~iate, novitiate** [no(u)'viʃiit] Noviziat *n (a. Räumlichkeiten)*; Novize *m*; *fam* Lehr-, Probezeit *f*.

now [nau] **1.** *s* Jetzt *n*, Gegenwart *f*; **2.** *adv* jetzt, nun; gleich, sofort; (so)eben; nun, da, dann; *before* ~ schon früher; *by* ~ jetzt, schon; *from* ~ *(on, onwards)* von nun, jetzt an; *in a week from* ~ heute in e-r Woche; *just* ~ gerade eben; im Augenblick; *up to, till, until* ~ bis jetzt; ~ ... ~ bald ... bald; ~ *then* nun also; *(every)* ~ *and again, (every* ~ *and then)* von Zeit zu Zeit, ab und zu, dann und wann, hin und wieder; ~ *or never* jetzt oder nie; **3.** *conj (~ that)* jetzt, wo; **~adays** ['-ədeiz] *adv* heutzutage, heutigentags.

no|way(s) ['nouwei(z)] *adv* auf keinen Fall, durchaus nicht, gar nicht, nicht im geringsten, keineswegs; **~where** ['-wɛə] *adv* nirgends, nirgendwo, -wohin; *sport* überrundet; ~~ *near (fam)* auch nicht annähernd; *to be, to get* ~~ zu nichts, auf keinen grünen Zweig kommen; *that will take you* ~~ das führt zu nichts; **~wise** ['-waiz] *adv* auf keine Weise, nicht im geringsten.

noxious ['nɔkʃəs] schädlich, verderblich, ungesund (*to* für); giftig; **~ness** ['-nis] Schädlichkeit *f*.

nozzle ['nɔzl] *tech* Düse, Spritze, Öffnung *f*; Ansatzrohr, Mundstück *n*, Stutzen; *sl* Zinken *m*, Nase *f*; Schnauze *f*.

*

nuance [nju(:)'ɑ:ns] Nuance, Schattierung *f*.

nub [nʌb] Knopf, Knoten *m*; Stück(-chen) *n*; *fam* Pointe *f*, Kern(punkt) *m*, *das* Wesentliche; **~bin** ['-in] *Am* Stückchen *n*; kleine(r) *od* unreife(r) Maiskolben *m*; unreife Frucht *f*; **~ble** ['-l] Knöpfchen, Knötchen; Stückchen *n*; **~bly** ['-li] knotig.

nubil|e ['nju:bil] *(Mädchen)* heiratsfähig; **~ity** [nju(:)'biliti] Heiratsfähigkeit *f*.

nucle|ar ['nju:kliə] *phys* Kern-; Atom-; ~~ *attack* Angriff *m* mit Atomwaffen; ~~ *attraction* Kernanziehung *f*; ~~ *bombardment* Kernbeschießung *f*; ~~ *chain reaction* Kern-Kettenreaktion *f*; ~~ *charge* Kernladung *f*; ~~ *chemistry* Kernchemie *f*; ~~ *disintegration* Kernzerfall *m*; ~~ *energy* Kernenergie, Atomkraft *f*; ~~ *energy plant, power station* Atomkraftwerk *n*; ~~ *fission* Kernspaltung *f*; ~~ *fuel* spaltbare(s) Material *n*; ~~ *fusion* Kernverschmelzung *f*; ~~ *mass* Kernmasse *f*; ~~ *particle* Kernteilchen *n*; ~~ *physicist* Kernphysiker *m*; ~~ *physics (pl mit sing)* Kernphysik *f*; ~~ *pile* Atommeiler *m*; ~~ *propulsion* Atomantrieb *m*; ~~ *reaction* Kernreaktion *f*; ~~ *reaction pile* Uranbrenner *m*; ~~ *reactor* Kernreaktor *m*, Zyklotron *n*; ~~ *research* Kernforschung *f*; ~~ *scientist* Kernforscher *m*; ~~ *test* Atom-, Kernwaffenversuch *m*; ~~ *theory* Kerntheorie *f*; ~~ *transformation* Kernumwandlung *f*; ~~ *warfare* Atomkrieg *m*; ~~ *warheads (pl)* Atomsprengköpfe *m pl*; ~~ *weapons (pl)* Atomwaffen *f pl*; **~ate** ['-eit] *tr* zu e-m Kern verdichten; um e-n Kern sammeln; *itr* e-n Kern bilden; **~ation** [nju:kli'eiʃən] Verdichtung zu e-m Kern; Kernbildung; künstliche Regenbildung *f*; **~ic** ['nju:kliik] *a chem*: ~~ *acid* Nukleinsäure *f*; **~in** ['-in] *chem* Nuklein *n*; **~on** ['-ɔn] *phys* Nukleon, Kernteilchen *n*; **~onics** [nju:kli'ɔniks] *pl mit sing* Kernphysik *f*; **~us** ['nju:kliəs] *pl -i* ['-ai] *fig* Kern, Mittelpunkt; Ausgangspunkt; *scient* (Kondensations-)Kern; Keim; *biol* Zellkern; *bot* Samenkern *m*; ~~ *of the atom* Atomkern *m*.

nud|e [nju:d] *a* nackt, bloß, unbekleidet, unbedeckt; *jur (Verpflichtung)* einseitig; *s* nackte(r) Körper *m*; *(Kunst)* nackte Figur *f*, Akt *m*; *from the* ~~ nach dem (lebenden) Modell; *in the* ~~ nackt; **~ism** ['-izm] Nackt-, Freikörperkultur *f*; **~ist** ['-ist] Anhänger *m* der Nackt-, Freikörperkultur; **~ity** ['-iti] *s* Nacktheit; Kahlheit; Aktfigur *f*.

nudge [nʌdʒ] *tr* (heimlich) *(mit dem Ellbogen)* anstoßen; *fam* e-n Schubs geben; *s* leise(s) Anstoßen *n*, *fam* Schubs *m*.

nugatory ['nju:gətəri] unwichtig nebensächlich, bedeutungslos, nichtig; wertlos; wirkungslos, *jur* unwirksam.

nugget ['nʌgit] (Gold-)Klumpen *m*; *pl sl* Moos *n*, Zaster *m*.

nuisance ['nju:sns] etwas Lästiges, Unangenehmes, Ärgerliches, Anstößiges, Häßliches, Widerliches; Ärgernis *n*; Plage; unangenehme, peinliche Lage *od* Situation *f*, Mißstand; unangenehme(r), lästige(r) Mensch *m*; *jur* Besitzstörung, Beeinträchtigung *f*; *commit no* ~ Verunreinigung, Schuttabladen verboten! *what a* ~*!* wie unangenehm! wie peinlich! *public* ~ öffentliche(s) Ärgernis *n*; ~ **raid** *aero mil* Störangriff, -flug *m*.

null [nʌl] *jur* ungültig, nicht bindend, ohne Rechtskraft, nichtig; ~ *and void* null und nichtig; **~ification** [-ifi-'keiʃən] Ungültigkeits-, Nichtigkeitserklärung, Annullierung *f*; *tech* Nullabgleich *m*; **~ify** ['nʌlifai] *tr* ungültig *od* nichtig machen, annullieren, für nichtig erklären; aufheben, auflösen; *tech* auf Null bringen; **~ity** ['nʌliti] Nichtigkeit, Ungültigkeit; *fig* Null *f*; ~~ *action, decree* Nichtigkeitsklage, -erklärung *f*; ~ **position** Nullstellung *f*.

numb [nʌm] *a* (er)starr(t), steif, gefühllos, unempfindlich, empfindungslos, benommen (*with* vor); *fig* betäubt; *tr* erstarren lassen; unempfindlich, gefühllos machen, betäuben; **~-fish** Zitterrochen *m*; **~ness** ['-nis] Erstarrung, Steifheit; Gefühllosigkeit, Benommenheit, Betäubung *f*.

number ['nʌmbə] *s* Zahl; (An-)Zahl; Nummer *(a. e-r Zeitschrift)*; Einzelnummer *f*, Heft *n*, Lieferung *f*; *gram* Numerus *m*, Zahl; Gruppe; *theat* (Programm-)Nummer; *fam* Nummer *f (Mensch)*; Ding *n*; *a large, great* ~ e-e große Zahl *od* Menge *f*, sehr viele (*of people* Leute); *pl (science of ~s)* Arithmetik *f*; *mus poet* Rhythmus *m*; Verse *m pl*; *N~s (pl)* Numeri *pl*, 4. Buch *n* Mosis; *tr* zählen; numerieren; einordnen, klassifizieren; zählen, rechnen (*among* zu); zs.zählen, -rechnen; sich belaufen auf; *beyond* ~ ohne Zahl, zahllos; *by (force of)* ~*s* durch zahlenmäßige Überlegenheit; *in* ~ an der Zahl; *in ~s* in Lieferungen; *in large ~s* in großen Mengen; *in equal ~s* in gleicher Stärke, gleichmäßig verteilt; paritätisch; *to the* ~ *of* in Höhe von; *without* ~ ohne Zahl, zahllos; *times without* ~ unzählige Male; *to dial a* ~ e-e Nummer wählen; *to get s.o.'s* ~ *(sl)* jdm auf die Schliche kommen; jdn durchschauen; *to look after, to take care of* ~ *one (fam)* für sich selbst sorgen; *he is not of our* ~ er gehört nicht zu uns; *my* ~ *is up (sl)* ich bin dran, am dransten; *his days are ~ed* s-e Tage sind gezählt; *back* ~ *(com)* Remittende *f*; *fig* Ladenhüter; Übriggebliebene(r) *m*; *(Zeitschrift)* alte Nummer *f*; *box* ~ Schließfachnummer *f*; *cardinal* ~ Grundzahl *f*; *collective* ~ Sammelnummer *f*; *decimal* ~ Dezimalbruch *m*; *even, odd* ~ gerade, ungerade Zahl *f*; *file* ~ Aktenzeichen *n*; *fraction* ~ Bruch(zahl *f*) *m*; *house* ~ Hausnummer *f*; *index* ~ Indexzahl *f*; *ordinal* ~ Ordnungszahl *f*; *serial* ~ Fabriknummer *f*; *telephone, call* ~ Fernsprechnummer *f*; ~ *of entry* Buchungsnummer *f*; ~ *one (fam)* das liebe Ich; große Klasse *f*; ~ *of votes recorded* abgegebene Stimme *f pl*; **~-card** *sport* Rückennummer *f*; **~ed** ['-d] *a* numeriert; **~less** ['-lis] zahllos, unzählig, ungezählt, ohne Zahl; nicht numeriert, ohne Nummer; **~-plate** *mot* Nummernschild *n*.

numer|able ['nju:mərəbl] zählbar; numerierbar; **~al** ['-əl] *a* Zahl-; *s* Zahl *f*; Zahlzeichen *n*, Ziffer *f*; *gram* Zahlwort *n*; *Arabic, Roman* **~~s** *(pl)* arabische, römische Ziffern *f pl*; **~ation** [nju:mə'reiʃən] Zählen; Rechnen *n*; Zählung, Numerierung *f*; **~ator** ['nju:məreitə] *(Bruch)* Zähler; Zählende(r) *m*; **~ic(al)** [nju(:)'merik(əl)] numerisch, zahlenmäßig; Zahl(en)-; ~~ *order* Reihen-, Zahlenfolge *f*; ~~ *value* Meßzahl *f*, Zahlenwert *m*; **~ous** ['nju:mərəs] zahlreich; groß, umfangreich, umfassend; **~ousness** ['-rəsnis] große Zahl *f*, große(r) Umfang *m*.

numismat|ic(al) [nju:miz'mætik(əl)] *a* Münz-, numismatisch; **~ics** [-iks] *pl mit sing* Münzkunde, Numismatik *f*; **~ist** [nju(:)'mizmətist] Numismatiker, Münzsammler *m*.

numskull ['nʌmskʌl] Dummkopf, Gimpel, Ignorant *m*.

nun [nʌn] *rel* Nonne; *orn* Blaumeise; Perücken-, Mähnentaube *f*; **~nery** ['-əri] Nonnenkloster *n*.

nuncio ['nʌnʃiou] *pl -os* Nuntius *m*.

nuptial ['nʌpʃəl] *a* Hochzeits-, Braut-; Ehe-; hochzeitlich; *s pl* Trauung, Hochzeit(sfeier *f*, -feierlichkeiten *f pl*), Vermählung *f*; ~ **day, rites** *pl* Hochzeitstag *m*, -bräuche *m pl*.

nurs|e [nə:s] *s (wet ~~)* Amme; Kinderfrau *f*, -mädchen *n*; *(dry ~~)* (Kranken-)Schwester; Pflege *f*; *allg* Ernährer, Pfleger, Beschützer *m*, Hüterin *f a. fig*; *ent* Amme; *zoo* Arbeiterin *f*; *tr* säugen, stillen, nähren, die Brust geben; Amme sein (*a child* e-s Kindes); *(Kind)* warten, betreuen, pflegen, großziehen; *(Kranke)* pflegen; *fig* nähren, Nahrung geben (*s.th.* e-r S), pfleglich behandeln; *(Krankheit)* behandeln, kurieren; *(Gefühl)* hegen, nähren; schonen, schonend behandeln, umgehen mit; *fig* sich eifrig kümmern um; hätscheln, liebkosen; *bot* pflegen, hegen; *itr* ein Kind stillen; als Amme dienen; *(Kind)* gestillt werden; *to put out to* ~~ in Pflege geben; *head* ~ Oberschwester *f*; *male* ~~ Krankenwärter *m*; *~~-child* Brustkind; Pflegekind *n*; *~~-maid* Kindermädchen *n*, -frau *f*; **~(e)ling** ['-liŋ] Brustkind *n*, Säugling *m*; Pflegekind *n*, Pflegling, Zögling *m*; **~ery** ['-ri] Kinderzimmer *n*; Kinderbetreuungsstelle; (Klein-)Kinderbewahranstalt *f*, Kinderhort *m*; *(~~-garden)* Pflanzenzuchtanstalt, Baumschule; *fig* Pflanzschule, Pflegestätte *f*; *day* ~~ Tageskinderheim; Spielzimmer *n*; *night* ~~ Kinderheim; Kinderschlafzimmer *n*; *~~-gardener* Baumschulenbesitzer *m*; *~~-governess* Kinderfräulein *n*; *~~-maid* Kindermädchen *n*; *~~-man* Baum-, Pflanzschulenbesitzer, -arbeiter *m*; ~~ *nurse* Kindergärtnerin *f*; *~~-rhyme* Kindervers *m*; *~~-school* Krippe, Kleinkinderbewahranstalt *f*; ~~ *slopes pl (Schi)* Anfänger-, *fam* Idiotenhügel *m pl*; *~~-tale* Ammenmärchen *n*; **~ing** ['-iŋ] Stillen *n*; Kinderbetreuung; Krankenpflege *f*; *~~-bottle* Säuglingsflasche *f*; *~~-home* Privatklinik *f*; (privates) Genesungsheim *n*; ~~ *mother* stillende Mutter; Pflegemutter *f*.

nurture ['nə:tʃə] *s* Nahrung; Ernährung; Erziehung, Aufzucht *f*; *(Soziologie)* Umweltfaktoren *m pl*; *tr* (er-)nähren; er-, aufziehen; hegen, fördern.

nut [nʌt] *s* Nuß; *fig (hard ~)* harte Nuß *f*, schwere(s) Problem *n*; (Schrauben-)Mutter *f*; *(Streichinstrument)* Saitenhalter; *(Geige)* Frosch *m*; *com Am* Betriebskosten *pl*; *sl* Birne *f*, Kürbis, Kopf; *sl* komische(r) Kerl, Knilch; *sl* Verrückte(r), Idiot *m*; *pl* Nußkohlen *f pl*; *pl sl* Hoden *f pl*; *itr* Nüsse suchen *od* pflücken; *to ~ out* ausknobeln; *not for ~s (sl)* nicht für Geld und gute Worte; *off o.'s ~ (sl)* nicht bei Trost; plemplem, verrückt; *to crack a ~* e-e Nuß knacken; *to do o.'s ~ (sl)* sich verrückt benehmen; *a hard ~ to crack* e-e harte Nuß, ein schweres Problem *n*; ein schwieriger Mensch; *chest~* Kastanie *f*; *earth-, pea-~* Erdnuß *f*; *hazel-~* Haselnuß *f*; *wal~* Walnuß *f*; **~-brown** nußbraun; **~-butter** Nußbutter *f*; **~cracker** *zoo* Tannenhäher; *pl* Nußknacker *m*; ~ **factory, house** *Am sl* Klapsmühle *f*, Irrenhaus *n*; **~-gall** ['-gɔ:l] *bot* Gallapfel *m*; **~hatch** *orn* Kleiber *m*, Spechtmeise *f*; **~-key** Schraubenschlüssel *m*; **~meg** ['-meg] Muskatnuß *f*; **~s** [-s] *a sl* verrückt, blöd(e); wirr, komisch; *interj sl* Quatsch! Blödsinn! Unsinn! *to be (dead) ~~ on, about, over* (ganz) verrückt sein nach, scharf sein auf; *to drive ~s (sl)* verrückt machen; *to go ~~ (sl)* verrückt werden; überschnappen; vor die Hunde gehen; *~~ to ...! (sl)* hau ab mit ...! geh weg mit ...! **~shell** Nußschale *f*; *in a ~~* kurz, mit wenigen Worten; *put it in a ~~!* machen Sie's, fassen Sie sich kurz! **~ting** ['-iŋ] Nüssesammeln *n*; **~-tree** Haselnußstrauch *m*; **~ty** ['-i] nußreich; nußartig; *sl* verrückt, blöd(e); *sl* verrückt, wild (*on, upon, about* nach), scharf (*on, upon* auf).

nut|ate [nju:'teit] *itr bot* den Kopf hängen lassen; **~ation** [-'teiʃən] Kopfnicken *n*; *astr bot* Nutation *f*.

nutria ['nju:triə] *zoo* Nutria *f (a. Pelz)*.

nutri|ent ['nju:triənt] *a* nahrhaft; *s (~~ medium)* Nährstoff *m*, -substanz, -flüssigkeit *f*; ~~ *solution* Nährlösung *f*; **~ment** [-mənt] Nahrung *f*; Aufbaustoff *m*; *mineral ~~* Nährsalz *n*; **~tion** [-'triʃən] Ernährung; Nahrungsaufnahme; Nahrung(smittel *n*) *f*; **~tional** [-l] *a* Ernährungs-; ernährungsmäßig; **~tionist** [-ist] Ernährungswissenschaftler *m*; **~tious** [nju(:)'triʃəs] nahrhaft; **~tive** ['-tritiv] *a* Ernährungs-, Nähr-; nahrhaft; *s* Nahrungsmittel *n*; *~~value* Nährwert *m*.

nux vomica ['nʌks'vɔmikə] Brechnuß *f*.

nuzzle ['nʌzl] *tr* mit der Nase *od* Schnauze stoßen *od* reiben an; mit der Schnauze wühlen in, aufwühlen; *(Kind)* liebkosen; *itr* mit der Nase, Schnauze stoßen (*against* an); mit der Schnauze fahren (*into* in), wühlen (*for* nach); *fam* sich kuscheln, sich schmiegen (*to* an).

*

nyctalopia [niktə'loupiə] Nachtblindheit *f*.

nylon ['nailən] *(Textil)* Nylon *n*; *pl (~ stockings)* Nylonstrümpfe *m pl*; *pl* Nylongarnitur, -wäsche *f*; ~ **bristle** Nylonborste *f*; **~-reinforced** nylonverstärkt; ~ **velvet** Nylonsamt *m*.

nymph [nimf] *(Mythologie)* Nymphe; hübsche junge Frau *f*; *ent* Larve, Puppe *f*; **~al** ['nimfəl] Nymphen-; *ent* Puppen-; **~omania** [nimfə'meiniə] Mannstollheit, Nymphomanie *f*; **~omaniac** [-ək] mannstoll.

O

O, o [ou] *pl ~'s* O, o *n*.

o, oh [ou] *interj* o ...! oh! ach! *s* O, o *n*; *tele* Null *f*; ~ *dear (me)!* ach Gott!

oaf [ouf] Tölpel *m*; **~ish** ['-iʃ] einfältig, blöd(e).

oak [ouk] *s* Eiche(nholz *n*) *f*; Eichenkranz *m*, -laub, -möbel *n*; *Br sl (Univ.)* (Eichen-)Tür *f*; *the O~s* Fohlenrennen in Epsom; *a* = *~en*; *to sport o.'s ~ (Br sl Univ.)* nicht gestört werden wollen, nicht zu sprechen sein; *the Hearts of O~* die (engl.) Marine; **~-apple, -gall** Gallapfel *m*; **~-bark** Eichenrinde *f*; **~en** ['-ən] eichen, aus Eiche(nholz); **~-leaves** *pl* Eichenlaub *n*; **~let** ['-lit], **~ling** ['-liŋ] junge Eiche *f*; **~-tree** Eichbaum *m*, Eiche *f*; **~-wood** Eichwald *m*, -enholz *n*.

oakum ['oukəm] Werg *n*.

oar [ɔ:] *s* Ruder *n*, Riemen; Ruderer *m*; *tr itr* rudern; *to have an ~ in every man's boat* überall s-e Hand im Spiel haben; *to pull a good ~* ein guter Ruderer sein; *to put o.'s ~ in* sich einmischen, *fam* s-n Senf dazu geben; *to rest on o.'s ~s* aufhören zu rudern; *fig* sich auf die faule Haut legen, auf s-n Lorbeeren ausruhen; *four-~* Vierer *m*; *pair-~* Zweier *m*; **~-blade** Ruderblatt *n*; **~ed** [-d] *a* mit Rudern ausgestattet; *in Zssgen* -rud(e)rig; **~-lock** Ruderklampe, -dolle *f*; **~sman** ['-zmən] Ruderer *m*; **~swoman** Rud(r)erin *f*.

oasis [o(u)'eisis] *pl oases* [-i:z] Oase *f a.fig.*

oast [oust] Hopfen-, Malz-, Tabakdarre *f*.

oat [out] *meist pl* Hafer; *pl mit sing* Haferbrei *m*; *to sow o.'s wild ~s (fig)* sich die Hörner abstoßen; *he feels his ~s (Am sl)* ihn sticht der Hafer; *rolled,* *crushed* ~*s* Haferflocken *f pl*; ~**-cake** (flacher, harter) Haferkuchen *m*; ~**en** ['outn] aus Hafer(stroh); Hafer-; ~**meal** Hafermehl *n*, -flocken *f pl*, -grütze *f*; *(~~ porridge)* Haferbrei *m*, -flockensuppe *f*, -schleim *m*; *~~ soup* Haferschleimsuppe *f*.

oath [ouθ, *pl* ouðz] Eid, Schwur *m*; Eidesformel *f*; Fluch *m*; *by, (up)on ~* auf Eid, eidlich; *in lieu of an ~* an Eides Statt, eidesstattlich; *under ~* unter Eid; *under the ~ of secrecy* unter dem Siegel der Verschwiegenheit; *to administer an ~ to s.o.* jdn unter Eid nehmen, vereidigen; *to be on ~, to be under ~* durch e-n Eid gebunden sein; *to bind by (an) ~* eidlich verpflichten; *to break an ~* e-n Eid brechen; meineidig werden; *to give s.o. the ~* jdm den Eid zuschieben; *to make, to swear, to take an ~* (e-n Eid) schwören; *to put s.o. (up)on his ~* jdn unter Eid nehmen, vereidigen; schwören lassen; *refusal to take an ~* Eidesverweigerung *f*; *~ of allegiance, of loyalty* Treu-, Fahneneid *m*; *~ of disclosure, of manifestation* Offenbarungseid *m*; ~**-breaker** Eidbrüchige(r), Meineidige(r) *m*; ~**-taking** Eidesleistung *f*.

obdur|acy ['ɔbdjurəsi] Verstocktheit; Halsstarrigkeit, Hartnäckigkeit *f*; ~**ate** [-it] verstockt; halsstarrig.

obedien|ce [ə'bi:djəns] Gehorsam *m* (*to* gegen); *in ~~ to* entsprechend, gemäß; *passive ~~* stillschweigende Duldung *f*; ~**t** [-t] gehorsam; folgsam; *Your ~~ servant (Briefschluß)* Ihr sehr ergebener.

obeisance [o(u)'beisəns] Ehrerbietung; Verbeugung *f*; *to do, to make, to pay ~ to s.o.* jdm huldigen.

obel|isk ['ɔbilisk] Obelisk *m*; *a.* ~**us** [-əs] *pl -i* [-ai] *typ* Kreuz *n*.

obes|e [o(u)'bi:s] dick, stark, korpulent, beleibt, fettleibig; ~**ity** [-iti] Beleibtheit, Korpulenz, Fettleibigkeit *f*.

obey [o(u)'bei, ə'b-] *tr* gehorchen, Folge leisten (*s.o.* jdm); *(Befehl)* ausführen, befolgen; hören auf, sich leiten lassen von; *itr* gehorchen, gehorsam sein (*to* dat).

obfuscat|e ['ɔbfʌskeit, *Am* -'fʌs-] *tr* verdunkeln; *fig* verwirren; scheu, stutzig machen; ~**ion** [ɔbfʌs'keiʃən] Verdunkelung; *fig* Verwirrung *f*.

obit ['ɔbit, 'oubit] Jahrgedächtnis *n*, Seelenmesse *f*; Todestag *m*, -anzeige *f*; ~**uary** [ə'bitjuəri] *s (~~ notice)* Todesanzeige *f*, Nachruf *m*; Totenregister *n*; *a* Todes-, Toten-.

object ['ɔbdʒikt] *s* Gegenstand *m*, Ding; Ziel *n*, Zweck *m*; *philos gram* Objekt *n*; *fam* lächerliche Person *f*, erbärmliche(r) Mensch *m*; *v* [əb'dʒekt] *tr* einwenden (*s.th. against s.o.* etw gegen jdn); beanstanden; *itr* e-n Einwand, Einwände, Einspruch erheben (*to* gegen); etw haben, protestieren (*to* gegen); *(Zeugen)* ablehnen (*to* acc); Anstoß nehmen (*to* an); *no ~ (in Anzeigen)* nicht entscheidend; Nebensache; *with this ~* in dieser Absicht; zu diesem Zweck; *there is no ~ in going* es nützt nichts zu gehen; *direct ~* Akkusativobjekt *n*; *indirect ~* Dativobjekt *n*; *~ of an action* Klaggegenstand *m*; *~ of exchange* Tauschobjekt *n*; ~ **ball** *(Billard)* Zielball *m*; ~**-finder** *phot* Sucher *m*; ~**-glass, -lens** *opt* Objektiv *n*; ~**ify** [əb'dʒektifai] *tr* vergegenständlichen, objektivieren; ~**ion** [əb'dʒəkʃən] Einwand, Einspruch *m*, Einwendung (*to* gegen), Beanstandung *f* (*to* gen); Hindernis *n*, Schwierigkeit *f*; Unwille *m*, Abneigung *f*, Widerwille *m* (*against* gegen); *(Zeuge)* Ablehnung *f*; *to have no ~~s* nichts einzuwenden haben; *to raise, to make an ~~* e-n Einwand erheben (*to* gegen); *to take ~~* s-n Unwillen äußern (*to* gegen); *if he has no ~~* wenn er nichts dagegen hat; *there is no ~~ to it* dagegen ist nichts einzuwenden; *are there any ~~s?* erhebt jemand Einspruch? ~**ionable** [-'dʒekʃnəbl] nicht einwandfrei, zu beanstanden(d); unzulässig; ungebührlich; unangenehm, anstößig (*to* für); ~**ive** [-'dʒektiv] *a* objektiv, sachlich, gegenständlich; wirklich, real; vorurteilsfrei, unvoreingenommen, unpersönlich; offensichtlich, augenscheinlich; Ziel-; *gram* Objekts-; *s* Ziel *n*; Zweck *m*; *gram (~~ case)* Objektsfall *m*; *opt* Objektiv *n*; *~~ point* Zielpunkt *m*; *~~ value* Schätzwert *m*; ~**iveness** [-ivnis], ~**ivity** [-'tiviti] Objektivität, Sachlichkeit; Wirklichkeit *f*; ~**less** ['ɔbdʒiktlis] gegenstands-, ziel-, zweck-, planlos; ~**-lesson** *fig* Denkzettel; Anschauungsunterricht *m*; ~**or** [əb'dʒektə] Gegner *m*; *conscientious ~~* Kriegsdienstverweigerer *m*; ~**-plate** *opt* Objektträger *m*.

objurgat|e ['ɔbdʒə:geit] *tr* heftig schelten, ausschimpfen, abkanzeln; ~**ion** [ɔbdʒə:'geiʃən] heftige(r) Tadel *m*; ~**ory** [ɔb'dʒə:gətəri] (heftig) scheltend; Schelt-.

oblat|e ['ɔbleit] *a rel (Mensch)* geweiht; abgeplattet; *s* Geweihte(r) *m*; ~**ion** [o(u)'bleiʃən] Opfer(gabe *f*) *n*.

obligat|e ['ɔbligeit] *tr* verpflichten, binden *meist pass*; ~**ion** [ɔbli'geiʃən] Verpflichtung, Bindung; Verbindlichkeit, Leistung; Dankesschuld *f*; Entgegenkommen *n*; Gefälligkeit; *jur* bindende Verpflichtung *f*; *com* Schuldschein *m*, -verschreibung *f*; *under an ~~* (zu Dank) verpflichtet (*to s.o. for s.th.* jdm für etw); *no, without ~~* unverbindlich; *to assume an ~~* e-e Verpflichtung übernehmen; sich verpflichten; *to contract, to incur, to undertake an ~~* e-e Verbindlichkeit eingehen; *to fulfil, to meet an ~~* e-r Verpflichtung nachkommen, e-e Verbindlichkeit erfüllen; *to impose an ~~* e-e Verpflichtung auferlegen; *~~ to buy* Kaufzwang *m*; *~~ to compensate* (Schadens-)Ersatzpflicht *f*; *~~ of guaranty* Bürgschaftsverpflichtung *f*; *~~ to give assistance* Beistands(ver-)pflicht(ung) *f*; *~~ of humanity* Gebot *n* der Menschlichkeit; *~~ of maintenance, to maintain, to support* Unterhaltspflicht *f*; *~~ to pay* Zahlungspflicht *f*; *~~ to vote* Wahlpflicht *f*; *~~ of warranty* Garantie(ver)pflicht(ung) *f*; ~**ory** ['ɔbligətəri, ɔ'bli-] verbindlich, bindend, verpflichtend, obligatorisch (*on, upon* für); *to be ~~* Pflicht, Vorschrift sein (*on* für); *to make it ~~ upon s.o.* jdm die Verpflichtung auferlegen; *~~ writing* Schuldschein *m*.

oblig|e [ə'blaidʒ] *tr* verpflichten; nötigen, zwingen; zu Dank verpflichten; e-e Gefälligkeit erweisen, gefällig sein, e-n Gefallen erweisen *od* tun, entgegenkommen (*s.o.* jdm); *s.o. with s.th.* jdm etw leihen; *(itr) to ~~ with s.th.* etw zum besten geben; *to ~~ o.s.* sich verpflichten, sich binden, sich festlegen (*to s.o.* gegenüber jdm); *please ~~ me by (... ing)* seien Sie so freundlich, liebenswürdig und ...; *to be ~ed to do* tun müssen; verpflichtet sein zu tun; *I'm much ~ed to you* ich bin Ihnen sehr verbunden, zu großem Dank verpflichtet (*for* für); *much ~ed!* verbindlichsten Dank! ~**ee** [ɔbli'dʒi:] (Obligations-)Gläubiger *m*; ~**ing** [ə'blaidʒiŋ] hilfsbereit, gefällig, zuvor-, entgegenkommend, liebenswürdig; ~**ingness** [-iŋnis] Gefälligkeit, Zuvorkommenheit *f*; ~**or** [ɔbli'gɔ:] Schuldner *m*.

obliqu|e [ə'bli:k] *a* schräg, geneigt, schief; gewunden, auf Umwegen, indirekt; ausweichend, nicht offen, versteckt, unaufrichtig, unehrlich, unredlich; *gram (Fall)* abhängig; *(Rede)* indirekt; *(Winkel)* schief; ~**eness** [-nis], ~**ity** [ə'blikwiti] schräge Richtung, Schiefe, Geneigtheit; *fig* Verstecktheit, Unaufrichtigkeit, Unredlichkeit *f*.

obliterat|e [ə'blitəreit] *tr* ausradieren, verwischen, unleserlich machen; ausstreichen; auslöschen, tilgen; *(die Erinnerung)* auslöschen; *(Briefmarke)* entwerten, abstempeln; ~**ion** [əblitə'reiʃən] Auslöschung, Tilgung; *fig* Vernichtung, Zerstörung; Entwertung *f*.

obliv|ion [ə'bliviən] Vergessen(heit *f*) *n*; Vergeßlichkeit; Nichtbeachtung; *(Act, Bill of ~~)* Amnestie *f*; *to fall, to sink into ~~* in Vergessenheit geraten; ~**ious** [-iəs] vergeßlich; uneingedenk (*of, to s.th.* e-r S); nichtachtend, nicht bemerkend; *to be ~~ of, to* vergessen (haben), nicht denken an; außer acht lassen; ~**iousness** [-iəsnis] Vergeßlichkeit *f*.

oblong ['ɔblɔŋ] *a* länglich; rechteckig; *s* Rechteck *n*.

obloquy ['ɔbləkwi] üble Nachrede, Schmähung, Verleumdung; Schande *f*, schlechte(r) Ruf *m*.

obnoxious [əb'nɔkʃəs] (sehr) unangenehm, widerwärtig, verhaßt, mißliebig, anstößig, herausfordernd (*to* für); *Am jur* verantwortlich (*to* für); *to be ~ to s.o.* jdm ein Dorn im Auge sein; ~**ness** [-nis] Verhaßtsein *n*, Mißliebigkeit, Anstößigkeit *f*.

obo|e ['oubou] *mus* Oboe *f*; ~**ist** ['-ist] Oboist *m*.

obscen|e [ɔb'si:n] unanständig, unzüchtig, schlüpfrig, obszön, lasziv; zotig; ~**ity** [-iti, -'sen-] Unanständigkeit, Schlüpfrigkeit, Obszönität; Zote *f*.

obscur|ant [ɔb'skjuərənt], ~**antist** [ɔbskjuə'ræntist] *s* Dunkelmann *m*; *a* bildungs-, fortschrittsfeindlich; ~**ism** [ɔbskjuə'ræntizm] Bildungs-, Fortschrittsfeindlichkeit *f*; ~**ation** [ɔbskjuə'reiʃən] Verdunkelung; *astr* Verfinsterung *f*; ~**e** [əb'skjuə] *a* dunkel, düster, finster; trüb(e), verschwommen, unklar, undeutlich; *fig* schwer verständlich, mehrdeutig, dunkel; *(Lage)* ungeklärt; verborgen, versteckt; unbekannt, obskur; *tr* verdunkeln, verfinstern; verdecken, verbergen; in den Hintergrund treten lassen, in den Schatten stellen; unklar(er) machen, verwirren; ~**ity** [-riti] Dunkelheit, Finsternis; *fig* Verschwommenheit, Unklarheit, Undeutlichkeit; Unverständlichkeit; Verborgenheit; Unbekanntheit *f*.

obsequies ['ɔbsikwiz] *pl* Leichenbegängnis *n*.

obsequious [əb'si:kwiəs] unterwürfig (*to* gegen); kriecherisch; ~**ness** [-nis] Unterwürfigkeit *f*.

observ|able [əb'zə:vəbl] bemerkbar, wahrnehmbar, sichtbar; bemerkenswert, beachtlich; einzuhalten(d), zu feiern(d); ~**ance** [-əns] Beachtung, Befolgung, Einhaltung, Be(ob)achtung *f*; Brauch *m*, herkömmliche Feier *f*, Ritus *m*, Zeremonie; *rel* Observanz, (Ordens-)Regel *f*; ~**ant** [-ənt] *a* einhaltend, beobachtend (*of s.th.* etw); (sehr) aufmerksam (*of* auf); beachtend (*of s.th.* etw); hellhörig; *s rel* Observant *m*; ~**ation** [ɔbzə(:)-

'veiʃən] Wahrnehmung, Beobachtung; Bemerkung; *mar* Standort-, Lagebestimmung *f*; *to keep s.o. under ~~* jdn beobachten lassen; *to take an ~~ (mar)* das Besteck aufnehmen; *final ~~* Schlußbemerkung *f*; *~~ aircraft* (Nah-)Aufklärungsflugzeug *n*; *~~ balloon* Fesselballon *m*; *~~ car (Am rail)* Aussichtswagen *m*; *~~ officer* Beobachtungsoffizier *m*; *~~ post* Beobachtungsstelle *f*, -stand; Gefechtsstand; Flugmeldeposten *m*; *~~ power* Beobachtungsgabe *f*; *~~ slit (mil)* Sehschlitz *m*; *~~ tower* Aussichtsturm *m*; *~~ ward (med)* Beobachtungsstation *f*; **~ational** [ɔbzə(:)'veiʃnəl] Beobachtungs-; *~~ data* Beobachtungsunterlagen *f pl*; **~atory** [əb'zə:vətri] Sternwarte *f*, Observatorium *n*; *meteorological ~~* Wetterwarte *f*; **~e** [əb'zə:v] *tr* be(ob)achten, befolgen, einhalten; *(Feier)* begehen; *(Feiertag)* halten; feiern; *(Stille)* bewahren; bemerken, beobachten, wahrnehmen, feststellen; einsehen; besonders beachten; *(Sorgfalt)* anwenden; (wissenschaftlich) beobachten; *itr* aufpassen, beobachten; äußern, bemerken, e-e Bemerkung machen (*on, upon* über, zu); **~er** [əb'zə:və] Beobachter *a. pol mil*; *aero* Orter *m*.

obsess [əb'ses] *tr* keine Ruhe lassen (*s.o.* jdm), verfolgen, quälen, plagen; *to be ~ed by, with* besessen sein von; **~ion** [əb'seʃən] *med* Zwangsvorstellung; Besessenheit; fixe Idee *f*.

obsol|escence [ɔbsə'lesns] Veralten *n*; **~escent** [-t] veraltend; **~ete** ['ɔbsəli:t] veraltet, altmodisch; *(Schrift)* verwischt; *(Ausweis)* verfallen, ungültig; verbraucht, abgenützt; *biol* unentwickelt, rudimentär.

obstacle ['ɔbstəkl] Hindernis *n* (*to* für); *to put ~s in the way of s.o.* jdm Hindernisse in den Weg legen; *~* **race** *sport* Hindernisrennen *n*.

obstetric|(al) [ɔb'stetrik(əl)] *a* Geburtshilfe-, Entbindungs-; **~ian** [ɔbste'triʃən] *med* Geburtshelfer *m*; **~s** [ɔb'stetriks] *pl mit sing* Geburtshilfe *f*.

obstin|acy ['ɔbstinəsi] Starr-, Eigensinn *m*, Hartnäckigkeit, Widerspenstigkeit, Verbohrtheit *f*; **~ate** ['-it] starr-, eigensinnig, widerspenstig.

obstreperous [əb'strepərəs] lärmend, schreiend; widerspenstig.

obstruct [əb'strʌkt] *tr* (ver)sperren, verstopfen; (be)hindern, hemmen; verdecken; *(die Sicht)* behindern, nehmen; *(Aussicht)* verbauen; **~ion** [əb'strʌkʃən] (Ver-)Sperrung, Verstopfung; Behinderung, Hemmung *f*; Hindernis *n* (*to* für); Störung; *parl* Obstruktion *f*; *to practice ~~* Obstruktionspolitik betreiben; **~ionism** [-ʃənizm] *parl* Obstruktionspolitik *f*; **~ionist** [-ʃənist] *parl* Obstruktionspolitiker *m*; **~ive** [-tiv] hinderlich, hindernd, hemmend (*of, to* für).

obtain [əb'tein] *tr* erhalten, erlangen, bekommen; *(Preis)* erzielen, erreichen; sich beschaffen; gewinnen; *chem* darstellen (*from* aus); *itr* bestehen, in Kraft, Geltung, Gebrauch sein; andauern, weiterbestehen; **~able** [-əbl] erhältlich, zu haben(d) (*at* bei); *to be ~~ (Börse)* gehandelt werden; **~ment** [-mənt] Erlangung *f*.

obtru|de [əb'tru:d] *tr* aufdrängen, aufnötigen, aufzuzwingen suchen (*on, upon s.o.* jdm); *itr* u. *to ~ o.s.* sich aufdrängen (*on, upon s.o.* jdm); **~sive** [-siv] zu-, aufdringlich; *(Geruch)* durchdringend; *(Irrtum)* sich aufdrängend.

obtuse [əb'tju:s] stumpf; abgestumpft, gefühllos; dumm; *(Gefühl)* dumpf; *~* **angle** stumpfe(r) Winkel *m*; **~ness** [-nis] Stumpfheit; Dummheit *f*.

obverse ['ɔbvə:s] *a* dem Betrachter zugekehrt; umgekehrt; gegenteilig; *s* Ober-, Vorder-, *(Münze)* Bildseite *f*; Gegenteil *n*; *(Logik)* Umkehrung *f*.

obviate ['ɔbvieit] *tr* ausschalten, beseitigen, entfernen; abhelfen (*s.th.* e-r S); verhindern; abwenden, verhüten; vorbeugen (*s.th.* e-r S); Vorsichtsmaßnahmen ergreifen (*s.th.* gegen etw); überflüssig machen.

obvious ['ɔbviəs] offenbar, -sichtlich, augenscheinlich; selbstverständlich, klar, deutlich; unverkennbar, offenkundig; durchsichtig; einleuchtend, naheliegend; *to be glaringly ~* in die Augen springen; *it's ~* das liegt auf der Hand; **~ness** ['-nis] Offensichtlichkeit, Augenscheinlichkeit; Deutlichkeit *f*.

*

occasion [ə'keiʒən] *s* (gute, passende) Gelegenheit *f* (*of* zu); Anlaß *m*, Veranlassung, Ursache *f*, Grund (*for* für); (Vor-)Fall *m*, Vorkommnis; Ereignis *n*; Notfall *m*; *tr* Anlaß, Veranlassung sein zu, ins Rollen bringen; *for the ~* für den Fall; *on ~* bei Gelegenheit, gelegentlich; wenn nötig; *on the ~ of* bei Gelegenheit, aus Anlaß, anläßlich *gen*; *to avoid all ~s of* jeden Anlaß vermeiden zu; *to give ~~ to* Anlaß geben zu; *to have no ~ for* keine Verwendung haben für; nicht brauchen; *to* keine Veranlassung haben zu; *to rise, to be equal to the ~* den Anforderungen gewachsen, Herr der Lage sein; die Situation meistern; *to take ~* die Gelegenheit benutzen, *by the forelock* die Gelegenheit beim Schopf ergreifen (*to do* zu tun); *there is no ~ to* es besteht kein Grund *od* Anlaß zu; *should the ~ arise* nötigenfalls; **~al** [-l] gelegentlich; Gelegenheits-; Gebrauchs-; zufällig; *~~ visit* Gelegenheitsbesuch *m*; **~ally** [-əli] *adv* gelegentlich, ab und zu.

Occident ['ɔksidənt] Westen *m*, Abendland *n*; *o~ (poet)* West(en) *m (Himmelsrichtung)*; **~al** [ɔksi'dentl] *a* westlich, abendländisch; *s* Abendländer *m*.

occip|ital [ɔk'sipitl] *a anat* Hinterhaupts-; *s* u. *~~ bone* Hinterhauptsbein *n*; **~ut** ['ɔksipʌt] Hinterhaupt *n*, -kopf *m*.

occlu|de [ɔ'klu:d] *tr* versperren, -schließen; ein-, ausschließen (*from* von); *chem* adsorbieren; **~sion** [-ʒən] Verschluß; Ein-, Ausschluß *m*; *(Wetter)* Okklusion *a. med*; *chem* Adsorption *f*.

occult [ɔ'kʌlt] *a* verborgen; geheim (-nisvoll); okkult; *tr itr (astr)* (sich) verfinstern, verdecken; **~ation** [ɔkəl'teiʃən] Verbergen; Verschwinden *n*; *astr* Verfinsterung, Verdeckung *f*; **~ism** ['ɔkəltizm] Okkultismus *m*; **~ist** ['ɔkəltist] Okkultist *m*.

occup|ancy ['ɔkjupənsi] Besitz *m*; Inbesitznahme, Besitzergreifung, Inanspruchnahme; Besitzdauer; *(Räume)* Belegung *f*; Einzug *m* (*of* in); *~~ expenses (pl)* Instandhaltungskosten *pl* für ein Haus; **~ant** ['-ənt] Besitzer, Inhaber; Bewohner; Besitzergreifende(r) *m*; **~ation** [ɔkju'peiʃən] Besetzung, Besitzergreifung, Inbesitznahme *f*; Besitz *m*; Inanspruchnahme; Beschäftigung, berufliche Tätigkeit *f*, Beruf *m*; Geschäft *n*; (militärische) Besetzung; Besatzung *f*; *by ~~* von Beruf; *in regular, secondary ~~* haupt-, nebenberuflich; *without ~~* ohne Arbeit, arbeitslos; *army of ~~* Besatzungsheer *n*; *clerical ~~* Bürotätigkeit *f*; *~~ census* Berufszählung *f*; *~~ troops (pl)* Besatzung(struppen *f pl*) *f*; **~ational** [ɔkju(:)'peiʃənl] beruflich, Berufs-, Arbeits-; Besatzungs-; *~~ description* Berufsbezeichnung *f*; *~~ disease* Berufskrankheit *f*; *~~ forces (pl)* Besatzungstruppen *f pl*; *~~ group* Berufs-, Fachgruppe *f*; *~~ injury, accident* Betriebsunfall *m*; *~~ power* Besatzungsmacht *f*; *~~ qualifications (pl)* berufliche Fähigkeiten *f pl*; *~~ therapy* Beschäftigungstherapie *f*; *~~ training* Fachausbildung *f*; **~ied** ['ɔkjupaid] *a* beschäftigt; *(Platz)* belegt, besetzt *a. mil*; *fully ~~* vollbeschäftigt; *~~ population* werktätige Bevölkerung *f*; **~ier** ['-aiə] Besitzer, Inhaber, Bewohner *m*; **~y** ['-ai] *tr* in Besitz nehmen, Besitz ergreifen von; besitzen, innehaben; bewohnen; *(Stellung)* ausfüllen, einnehmen, bekleiden; *(Zeit)* ausfüllen; *(Raum)* belegen; in Anspruch nehmen, beanspruchen, beschäftigen (*with* mit); (militärisch) besetzen; *to ~~ the chair* den Vorsitz führen; *to keep s.o. ~ied* jdn beschäftigen.

occur [ə'kə:] *itr* vorkommen, angetroffen werden; zustoßen, sich ereignen, geschehen; einfallen, in den Sinn kommen (*to s.o.* jdm); *it didn't ~ to me* darauf bin ich nicht gekommen (*to do* zu tun); **~rence** [ə'kʌrəns] Auftreten, Vorkommen Vorkommnis, Ereignis, Geschehen *n*, Vorfall *m*, Begebenheit *f*; *to be of frequent, rare ~~* häufig, selten vorkommen.

ocean ['ouʃən] Ozean *m*, (Welt-)Meer *n*, See *f*; *~s of (fam)* e-e Menge, e-e Masse ...; *by the ~* am Meer; *Arctic, Antarctic O~* Nördliche(s), Südliche(s) Eismeer *n*; *Atlantic, Indian, Pacific O~* Atlantische(r), Indische(r), Stille(r) *od* Große(r) Ozean *m*; *German O~* Nordsee *f*; *~* **freight** Seefracht *f*; **~-going** *a* Hochsee-; *~~ fleet* Hochseeflotte *f*; *~~ tug* Hochseeschlepper *m*; **O~ia** [ouʃi'einjə], **O~ica** [ouʃi'ænikə] Ozeanien *n*; **O~ian** [ouʃi'einjən] *a* ozeanisch; *s* Ozeanier(in *f*) *m*; **o~ic** [ouʃi'ænik] ozeanisch, Ozean-; *fig* (unendlich) weit; *~* **lane** Schiffahrtslinie *f*; *~* **liner** Ozeandampfer *m*; **~ographer** [ouʃjə'nɔgrəfə] Meereskundler, Ozeanograph *m*; **~ographic** [ouʃjəno(u)'græfik] meereskundlich, ozeanographisch; **~ography** [ouʃjə'nɔgrəfi] Meereskunde, Ozeanographie *f*; *~* **trade** Seehandel *m*; *~* **traffic** Seeverkehr *m*; *~* **tramp** Frachtdampfer *m*; *~* **voyage** Seereise *f*.

ocelot ['ousilət] *zoo* Ozelot *m*.

ochre, *Am* ocher ['oukə] *min* Ocker *m* od *n (a. Farbe)*; **~ous, *Am* ocherous** ['oukriəs, 'oukərəs] ockerartig, -haltig.

o'clock [ə'klɔk] ... Uhr.

oct|achord ['ɔktəkɔ:d] *mus* Oktachord *m*; **~agon** ['ɔktəgən] Achteck *n*; **~agonal** [ɔk'tægənl] achteckig; **~ahedron** ['ɔktə'hedrən] *math* Oktaeder *n*, Achtflächner *m*; **~ane** ['ɔktein] *chem* Oktan *n*; *high ~~ fuel* Superkraftstoff *m*; *~~ number, rating* Oktanzahl *f*; **~ant** ['ɔktənt] *mar* Oktant *m*; **~ave** [*mus* 'ɔktiv, *rel* 'ɔkteiv] *s* Oktave *f*; **~avo** [ɔk'teivou] *pl -os (Buch)* Oktav(format) *n*; Oktavband *m*; **O~ober** [ɔk'toubə] Oktober *m*; *in ~~* im Oktober; **~odecimo** ['ɔkto(u)'desimou] *pl -os (Buch)* Oktodez(format) *n*; Oktodezband *m*; **~ogenarian** [ɔkto(u)dʒi'nɛəriən] *a* achtzigjährig; *s* Achtzigjährige(r *m*) *f*; **~opus** ['ɔktəpəs] Polyp *m a. fig*, Krake *f*; **~osyllabic** ['ɔkto(u)si'læbik], **~osyllable** ['ɔkto(u)siləbl] *a* achtsilbig; *s* achtsilbige(r) Vers *m*.

ocul|ar ['ɔkjulə] *a* Augen-; *(Beweis)* unmittelbar; *s opt* Okular *n*; *~~ demonstration, proof* Beweis *m* ad oculos; *~~ inspection* Augenschein *m*; *~~ mirror* Augenspiegel *m*; **~ist** ['-ist] Augenarzt *m*.

odd [ɔd] *a* einzeln; *(Zahl)* ung(e)rade; *(Monat)* mit 31 Tagen; einige, u. etliche, u. darüber; überzählig, -schüssig; Extra-; nicht (mit)gezählt, -gerechnet; gelegentlich; Gelegenheits-; ungewöhnlich, ausgefallen, besonder, überspannt; *at ~ times* hin und wieder, dann und wann, ab und zu; **~-ball** *Am sl a* überspannt; unzuverlässig; *s* Sonderling *m*; **~ity** ['-iti] Ungewöhnlichkeit, Ausgefallenheit; Sonderbarkeit, Seltsamkeit *f*; sonderbare(r) Mensch *m*; eigenartige Sache *f*; **~job** Gelegenheitsarbeit; kleine Reparatur *f*; **~ lot** *com* Restpartie *f*; **~ly** ['-li] *adv* eigenartiger-, sonderbarerweise; *~~ enough* es klingt verwunderlich; seltsamerweise; **~ man** Gelegenheitsarbeiter; *com* Ersatzmann *m*; **~ment** ['-mənt] Rest *m*; Überbleibsel *n pl*; Abfall; Ramsch(waren *f pl*) *m*; *pl* Rest-, Einzelstücke *n pl*; *pl typ* Titelbogen, Vorspann *m*; **~ness** ['-nis] Ungewöhnlichkeit, Seltsamkeit, Sonderbarkeit *f*; **~ pair** Einzelpaar *n*; **~ size** *com* ausgefallene, wenig gefragte Größe *f*; **~ volume** Einzelband *m*.

odds [ɔdz] *s pl a. mit sing* Unterschied *m*, Ungleichheit *f*; ungleichmäßige, unregelmäßige, ungleiche Dinge *n pl*; Vorteil *m*, Überlegenheit *f*, *die* besseren Aussichten *od* Chancen *f pl*; Möglichkeit, größere Wahrscheinlichkeit *f*; Umstände *m pl*; *(Spiel, Wette)* Vorgabe *f*; Buchmacherkurs *m*; *at ~* uneins, uneinig, im Streit; *by (all, long) ~* bei weitem; mit großem Unterschied; *over the ~* zu viel; *to be at ~ with s.o.* sich mit jdm herumstreiten, -zanken, -schlagen; *to give, to lay ~ (Spiel, Wette)* vorgeben; *to take the ~* e-e ungleiche Wette eingehen; *the ~ are 2 to 1* die Chancen stehen 2 zu 1; *the ~ are that* es ist (sehr) wahrscheinlich, damit zu rechnen, daß; *the ~ are in his favour* der Vorteil ist auf s-r Seite; *it makes no ~* das ist einerlei, *fam* egal; *what's the ~?* was macht (denn) das? *~ and ends* Überbleibsel *n pl*; Reste *m pl*; dies und das, dies und jenes, alles mögliche, verschiedene(r) Kleinkram *m*; **~-on** *s* gute Chance *f*; *a* aussichtsreich.

ode [oud] Ode *f*.

odi|ous ['oudjəs] hassenswert, verhaßt; abstoßend, widerlich, ekelhaft, abscheulich, scheußlich; **~ousness** ['-jəsnis] Verhaßtheit; Widerlichkeit, Abscheulichkeit *f*; **~um** ['-jəm] Haß *m*, Gehässigkeit; Verhaßtheit, Mißliebigkeit *f*; Schimpf *m*, Schande *f*, Schandfleck *m*; *to cast ~~ upon s.o.* über jdn Schimpf u. Schande bringen.

odometer [o'dɔmitə] Kilometerzähler *m*.

odontology [ɔdɔn'tɔlədʒi] Zahnheilkunde *f*.

odor|iferous [oudə'rifərəs], *poet* **~ous** ['-rəs] wohlriechend, duftend.

odour ['oudə] Geruch *a. fig*; Wohlgeruch, Duft *m*, Aroma *n*; *fig* Geruch, Ruf *m* (*with* bei); *to be in bad, ill ~* in schlechtem Ruf stehen; *to be in good, bad od ill ~ with s.o.* bei jdm gut, schlecht angeschrieben sein; **~less** ['-lis] geruchlos.

oecumenical [i:kju(:)'menikəl] ökumenisch.

œdema [i(:)'di:mə] *pl -ta* [-tə] *med* Ödem *n*.

o'er ['ouə] *poet = over*.

oesophagus [i:'sɔfəgəs] *pl a. -gi* [-gai] *anat* Speiseröhre *f*.

of [ɔv, əv] *prp* **1.** *possessiv: the works ~ Shakespeare* Shakespeares Werke; *the Tower ~ London* der Londoner Tower; *the capital ~ France* die Hauptstadt Frankreichs, die französische Hauptstadt; *a friend ~ mine* ein Freund von mir; **2.** *attributiv: ~ great value* von großem Wert; *~ no importance* ohne Bedeutung, bedeutungslos; *~ ability* fähig; **3.** *bei Eigennamen: the City ~ Manchester* die Stadt M.; **4.** *it is kind ~ you* das ist nett von ihnen; *that is ~ his doing* das ist sein Werk; *to be quick ~ eye* alles gleich sehen; *to be robbed ~ o.'s money* s-s Geldes beraubt werden; *to get rid ~ a cold* e-e Erkältung los werden; *to make a fool ~ s.o.* jdn zum Narren halten; *to tell ~ s.th.* von e-r S erzählen, über e-e S berichten; *news ~ success* Erfolgsnachrichten *f pl*; *a story ~ adventure* e-e abenteuerliche Geschichte; *~ gold* von Gold, golden; *a piece ~ chalk* ein Stück Kreide; *a cup ~ tea* e-e Tasse Tee; *one ~ them* e-r von ihnen; *~ humble origin* von bescheidener Herkunft; *glad ~* froh über; *the fear ~* die Furcht vor; *~ fright* vor Angst; *the love ~ study* die Liebe zum Studium; *nimble ~ foot* flink auf den Beinen; *a quarter ~ ten (Am fam)* 3/410 (Uhr); **5.** *~ age* mündig, volljährig; *~ course* natürlich, selbstverständlich; *~ late* neulich, unlängst, jüngst; *~ necessity* notwendigerweise; *~ old, ~ yore* einst, ehemals, -dem; *~ rights* von Rechts wegen.

*

off [ɔ(:)f] **1.** *adv* weg, fort; ab, herunter, heraus; *el* aus; vorbei, aus; entfernt, weit (weg); *(zeitlich)* hin *it is still two weeks ~* das ist noch zwei Monate hin; *~ and on, on and ~* dann u. wann, ab u. zu, von Zeit zu Zeit; *far ~* lange hin; *to be ~* (weg)gehen, aufbrechen; verschwunden sein; *(Knopf)* ab sein, fehlen; entfernt sein; Ausgang haben; falsch sein; *to be well, badly ~* reich, arm sein; *to be ~ the market* nicht mehr im Handel zu haben sein; *to bite ~* abbeißen; *to cut ~* abschneiden; *tele* unterbrechen; *to drink ~* austrinken; *to drop, to fall ~* abnehmen, nachlassen; *to pass ~* vorüber-, vorbei-, vergehen; *to see ~* fortbegleiten; *to take ~ (Kleidungsstück)* ablegen, ausziehen; (sich) freinehmen; *aero* abfliegen; *to tear ~* abreißen; *to turn ~* aus-, abschalten, abstellen; *keep ~!* bleib weg! bleib mir vom Leibe!; *~ with you!* weg mit dir! *fam* hau ab! *sl* verdufte!; *he's a little ~* er ist nicht ganz richtig im Kopf; **2.** *prp* (herunter) von; *(leben)* von; abseits von; von ... abzweigend, ausgehend; frei von; weniger als; *mar* auf der Höhe von, gegenüber; **3.** *a* abgenommen, ausgezogen; abgetrennt, los; aus-, abgeschaltet; auf dem Wege (*to* zu); kleiner, geringer; schlechter; nicht anwesend, nicht da; abgelegen; weiter entfernt, entfernter *(Seite)*; recht; im Irrtum, *fam* auf dem Holzweg; *(gesundheitlich)* nicht auf der Höhe; *(Speise)* nicht mehr frisch, nicht mehr gut; **~ chance** geringe Aussicht *f*; *to go on the ~~ of doing s.th.* riskieren etw zu tun; **~-color** *a Am*: *to be ~~* e-e Fehlfarbe sein; *(Witz)* etwas gewagt sein; **~ colour** (gesundheitlich) nicht auf der Höhe; **~-day** Unglückstag *m*; **~ duty** dienstfrei; *to be ~~* dienstfrei haben; **~-face** *a* stirnfrei *(Damenhut)*; **~ o.'s feed** *sl* ohne Appetit; *to be ~~* keinen Appetit haben; **~ form** *fam* nicht in Form; **~-grade** *com* von geringerer Qualität; **~-hand** *adv* aus dem Stegreif, ohne Vorbereitung, sofort; *a* u. *~~ed* unvorbereitet, spontan, übers Knie gebrochen; unfreundlich; *~~ manner* ungezwungene Art *f*; **~ o.'s head** *sl* verrückt, plemplem; **~ key** *Am (Klavier)* verstimmt; **~-licence** *Br* Schankrecht *n* über die Straße; **~ limits** verboten (*to* für); **~ peak** abfallend; nicht auf der Höhe; **~-print** Sonderdruck *m*; **~ season** *com* Sauregurkenzeit *f*; **~ shade** Fehlfarbe *f*; **~-shore** *adv* von der Küste weg; in Küstennähe; *a* küstennah; **~-side** *a adv sport* abseits; **~ stage** *attr a* hinter den Kulissen; **~ street** *attr a* abseits der Straße; **~ the map** *fam* vorbei, passé; bei Hintertupfing; **~ the mark** am Ziel vorbei; *fig* nicht entscheidend, unerheblich; **~ the point**: *to wander ~~* vom Thema abkommen; **~-the-record** *attr* vertraulich, nicht zur Veröffentlichung bestimmt; **~ time** freie Zeit *f*; **~ year** schlechte(s) Jahr *n*.

offal ['ɔfəl] *mit sing od pl* Abfall *m*, Abfälle; Speisereste; Schlachtabfälle *m pl*, Innereien *pl*; *fig* Ausschuß, Schund *m*.

offbeat ['ɔ(:)fbi:t] *fam* ungewöhnlich.

offcast ['ɔ(:)fka:st] Ausschuß, -wurf; Verworfene(r), Verstoßene(r) *m*.

offence, *Am* **-se** [ə'fens] Verstoß *m*, Vergehen *n* (*against* gegen); Übertretung (*against* gen); strafbare Handlung, Straftat *f*, Delikt *n*; Sünde; Beleidigung, Kränkung, Verärgerung; Gekränktheit *f*, Ärger; Anstoß; *mil* Angriff; Angreifer *m*; *to cause, to give ~* Anstoß erregen (*to* bei); *to s.o.* jdn beleidigen, (ver)ärgern; *to commit an ~* sich vergehen (*against* gegen); *to take ~* sich beleidigt fühlen, sich ärgern; Anstoß nehmen (*at* an); übelnehmen (*at s.th.* etw); *I meant no ~* das habe ich nicht bös(e) gemeint; *no ~!* nichts für ungut! *petty ~* Übertretung *f*; *war, weapons of ~* Angriffskrieg *m*, -waffen *f pl*; *~ against common decency, propriety* Erregung *f* öffentlichen Ärgernisses; **~less** [-lis] harmlos.

offend [ə'fend] *itr* e-e Straftat, ein Verbrechen, e-e Sünde begehen; sich vergehen, verstoßen, zuwiderhandeln (*against* gegen); Anstoß, Ärgernis erregen; *tr* beleidigen, verletzen, (ver-)ärgern; mißfallen, unangenehm sein (*s.o.* jdm); *to be ~ed with s.o.* mit jdm beleidigt sein (*at s.th.* wegen etw); **~er** [-ə] Übertreter, Täter, Schuldige(r), Straffällige(r); Beleidiger *m*; *first ~~* nicht Vorbestrafte(r) *m*; *joint ~~* Mittäter *m*; *second, hardened ~~* Vorbestrafte(r), Rückfällige(r) *m*.

offens|e *s. offence*; **~ive** [ə'fensiv] *a* angreifend, offensiv; Angriffs-; unangenehm, widerlich; anstößig, Anstoß erregend; beleidigend, verletzend, kränkend; *s* Offensive *f*, Angriff(shaltung, -sstellung *f*) *m*; *to switch over to the ~~* zur Offensive übergehen; *to take the ~~, to act on the ~~* die Offensive ergreifen, angreifen; *~~ defence* offensive Verteidigung *f*; *~~ patrol* bewaffnete Aufklärung *f*; *~~ reconnaissance* gewaltsame Erkundigung *f*; *~~ spirit* Angriffsgeist *m*; *~~ sweep (aero)* Angriffsstreife *f*; *~~ war* Angriffskrieg *m*; *~~ weapon* Angriffswaffe *f*.

offer ['ɔfə] *tr rel (to ~ up) (Opfer)* darbringen, -bieten; opfern; (an)bieten, vorlegen; *com* offerieren; vorschlagen, unterbreiten; vorbringen; zeigen, ankündigen; versuchen, Miene machen (*to do* zu tun); *itr rel* ein Opfer bringen, opfern; sich an-, erbieten (*to* zu); *(Gelegenheit)* sich bieten, sich zeigen; *to ~ o.s.* sich bewerben (*for* um); *s* Darbringung, -bietung *f*; Angebot, Anerbieten *n*, Offerte *f*; (Heirats-)Antrag; Vorschlag *m*; *on ~* (zum Verkauf) angeboten; verkäuflich; *to submit ~s* Offerten vorlegen; *to ~ battle* sich zum Kampf stellen; *to ~ an excuse* sich entschuldigen (*for* wegen); *to ~ an explanation* e-e Erklärung geben; *to ~ guarantee* Bürgschaft leisten; *to ~ o.'s hand to s.o.* jdm die Hand bieten; jdm e-n (Heirats-)Antrag machen; *to ~ an opinion* e-e Meinung, Ansicht äußern; *to ~ a plan* e-n Plan vorlegen; *to ~ a price* ein Preisangebot machen; *to ~ a remark* e-e Bemerkung machen; *to ~ resistance* Widerstand leisten; *to ~ a reward* e-e Belohnung aussetzen; *to ~ violence to s.o.* jdm Gewalt antun; *counter-~* Gegen(an)gebot *n*; *firm ~* feste(s) Gebot *n*, Festofferte *f*; *free ~* freibleibende(s) Gebot *n*; *peace ~* Friedensangebot *n*; *sham ~* Scheinangebot *n*; *special ~* Sonder-, Vorzugsangebot *n*; *~ of compromise* Vergleichsvorschlag *m*; *~ and demand* Angebot u. Nachfrage; *~ of mediation* Vermittlungsvorschlag *m*; *~ by telegraph* Drahtofferte *f*; **~ee** ['-ri:] Empfänger *m* e-s Angebots; **~er** ['-rə] (An-)Biet(end)er *m*; *the highest ~~* der Meistbietende; *no ~~s (Auktion)* ohne Gebote; **~ing** ['-riŋ] Anerbieten; Angebot *n*; Vorschlag *m*; Darbringung; Gabe *f*, Opfer *n*; **~ price** *(Börse)* Briefkurs *m*; **~tory** ['-təri] *rel* Offertorium *n*; (Kirchen-)Kollekte *f*.

office ['ɔfis] Dienst *m*; Amt *n*, (Amts-)Pflicht, Aufgabe, Obliegenheit, Funktion; Stelle, Stellung *f*, Posten; Schalter *m*; Amt, Kontor, Büro *n*, (Geschäfts-, Dienst-)Stelle *f*; Ministerium; Büro *n* e-r Versicherungsgesellschaft *f*; Dienstraum *m*; Filiale, Zweigniederlassung *f*; Amts-, Büro-, Geschäftsgebäude *f*; Amts-, Büro-, Geschäftspersonal; *rel* Offizium *n*, Gottesdienst *m*, Abendmahlsfeier *f*; *(bestimmte)* Gebete *n pl*; *fam* Wink, Hinweis *m*; *pl* Geschäfts-, Wirtschaftsräume *m pl*; Wirtschafts-, Nebengebäude *n pl*; *in ~* im Amt; an der Macht, *fam* am Ruder; *out of ~* nicht an der Macht *od* an der Regierung; in der Opposition; *through s.o.'s good ~s* durch jds Vermittlung; *to accept, to come into, to enter upon, to take ~* ein Amt übernehmen *od* antreten; Minister werden; *to be called to ~* e-n Ministerposten erhalten; *to continue ~* im Amt bleiben; *to discharge, to fill, to hold, to perform an ~* ein Amt, e-e Stellung bekleiden; *to give the ~ (sl)* e-n Wink geben; *to leave ~, to resign, to surrender o.'s ~* sein Amt niederlegen; demissionieren; *to perform the last ~s to s.o.* jdm den letzten Dienst erweisen; **~ accommodations** *pl* Büroräume *m pl*; **~ appliances** *pl* Büroausstattung *f*; **~-bearer** Amtsträger, Beamte(r); Stelleninhaber *m*; **~-boy** Laufbursche, -junge *m*; **~ building** Bürohaus *n*; **~ car** Geschäftswagen *m*; **~-copy** beglaubigte, amtliche Abschrift *f*; **~ corrections** *pl typ* Hauskorrektur *f*; **~ day** Arbeitstag *m*; **~-employee** Büroangestellte(r) *m*; **~ equipment** Büroeinrichtung, -ausstattung *f*; **~ expenses** *pl* Bürounkosten *pl*; **~ furniture** Büromöbel *n pl*; **~-girl** Kontoristin, Bürohilfe *f*; **~-hands** *pl* Büropersonal *n*; **~-holder** Amts-, Stelleninhaber, Beamte(r) *m*; **~-hours** *pl* Dienst-, Büro-, Geschäftsstunden *f pl*; *in ~~* während der Geschäftszeit; **~-hunter, -seeker** *Am* Postenjäger *m*; **~-manager** Bürovorsteher *m*; **~ personnel** Büropersonal *n*; **~ politics** *pl Am* Stellen(besetzungs)politik *f*; **~-routine** Bürobetrieb *m*; **~-seal** Dienstsiegel *n*; **~ staff** Büropersonal *n*; **~-stamp** Firmenstempel *m*; **~ supply** Büromaterial *n*, -bedarf *m*; **~-tour** Dienstreise *f*, **~ work** Büroarbeit, -tätigkeit *f*, Innendienst *m*.

officer ['ɔfisə] *s* Beamte(r) *m*; Offizier; *(Verein)* Funktionär, Wart *m*, Vorstandsmitglied *n*; *pl* Vorstand *m*; *tr* mit Offizieren versehen; (an)führen, befehligen; leiten; *he was elected an ~ of our club* er wurde in den Vorstand unseres Vereins gewählt; *customs ~* Zollbeamte(r) *m*; *non-commissioned ~ (N.C.O.)* Unteroffizier *m*; *control ~* Kontrollbeamte(r) *m*; *police, reserve ~* Polizei-, Reserveoffizier *m*; *~ of the day* Offizier *m* vom Dienst (O.v.D.); *~ of the deck (mar)* Wachoffizier *m*; *~ of the guard* Offizier *m* vom Ortsdienst; *~ in the active list* aktive(r) Offizier *m*; *~ of state* Minister *m*; **~ cadet** Fähnrich *m*; **~ candidate** Offiziersanwärter *m*; **~s' carrier** Offizierslaufbahn *f*; **~s' club** Offiziersklub *m*; **~s' mess** Offizierskasino *n*; **~s' quarters** *pl* Offiziersunterkunft *f*; **~'s servant** (Offiziers-)Bursche *m*; **~s' training** Offiziersausbildung *f*.

offici|al [ə'fiʃəl] *a* amtlich; Amts-; Beamten-; offiziell; förmlich, zeremoniell; *s* Beamte(r) *m*; *administrative ~~* Verwaltungsbeamte(r) *m*; *bank ~~* Bankbeamte(r) *m*; *career ~~* Berufsbeamte(r) *m*; *court ~~* Justizbeamte(r) *m*; *customs ~~* Zollbeamte(r) *m*; *government ~~* Regierungsbeamte(r) *m*; *post-office ~~* Postbeamte(r) *m*; *railway ~~* Bahnbeamte(r) *m*; *semi-~~* halbamtlich; *state-~~* Staatsbeamte(r) *m*; *supervisory ~~* Aufsichtsbeamte(r) *m*; *top ~~s (pl)* Spitzenkräfte *f pl*; *~~ act* Amtshandlung *f*; *~~ advertisement, announcement* amtliche Bekanntmachung *f*; *~~ authority* Amtsgewalt *f*; *~~ business* Dienstsache *f*; *he's here on ~~ business* er ist dienstlich hier; *~~ call* Dienstgespräch *n*; *~~ channels (pl)* Dienstweg *m*; *through ~~ channels* auf dem Dienstweg; *~~ document* öffentliche Urkunde *f*; *~~ dress* Amtstracht *f*; *~~ duty* Amts-, Dienstpflicht *f*; *~~ function* Amtspflicht, -handlung *f*; *~~ gazette* Amtsblatt *n*, Staatsanzeiger *m*; *~~ hours (pl)* Dienststunden *f pl*; Geschäftszeit *f*; *~~ language* Amtssprache *f*; *~~ letter* amtliche(s) Schreiben *n*; *~~ mail* Dienstpost *f*; *~~ oath* Amtseid *m*; *~~ organ* Staats-, Regierungsorgan *n*; *~~ receiver* Konkursverwalter *m*; *~~ residence* Amtssitz *m*; *~~ seal* Dienstsiegel *n*; *~~ secret* Dienstgeheimnis *n*; *~~ stamp* Dienststempel *m*; *~~ statement* amtliche Verlautbarung *f*; *~~ title* Amtsbezeichnung *f*; *~~ tour* Dienstreise *f*; *~~ use* Dienstgebrauch *m*; *~~ year* Geschäftsjahr *n*; **~aldom** [-əldəm] Beamtentum *n*, -schaft *f*; **~alese** [-əli:z] Beamten-, Amtsjargon *m*; **~alism** [-əlizm] Beamtentum *n*, Bürokratie *f*; Bürokratismus, *fam* Amtsschimmel *m*; **~ate** [ə'fiʃieit] *itr* amtieren (*as* als); das Priester-, Predigeramt versehen; **~ous** [ə'fiʃəs] übereifrig, aufdringlich; halbamtlich, offiziös; **~ousness** [ə'fiʃəsnis] Übereifer *m*, Aufdringlichkeit *f*.

officinal [ɔfi'sainl] *med* offizinell; Arznei-, Heil-.

offing ['ɔfiŋ] hohe See; Entfernung *f od* Abstand *m* von der Küste; *in the ~* auf hoher See; *(zeitlich)* in (Aus-)Sicht.

offish ['ɔfiʃ] *fam* kühl, zurückhaltend.

offscourings ['ɔ(:)fskauriŋz] *pl*, **offscum** ['-skʌm] Kehricht *m od n*, Abfall, Schmutz *m*; *the ~ of humanity* der Abschaum der Menschheit.

offset ['ɔ(:)fset] *s bot* Ableger, Schößling *m*; Abzweigung *f*; *(Berg)* Ausläufer *m*; *el* Nebenleitung *f*; *arch* Mauerabsatz *m*, Kröpfung *f*; *tech* Knick *m*, Biegung, Krümmung *f (in e-m Rohr)*; *typ* Offsetdruck *m*; Abziehen *n*; *(Feldmessung)* Ordinate *f*; Höhenunterschied; Ausgleich *m*, Gegengewicht *n*; *com* Gegenposten *m*, -rechnung, Aufrechnung *f*, Ausgleich *m*; *tr irr -set, -set* abzweigen, -leiten; mit e-m Absatz versehen; knicken, biegen, krümmen; im Offsetverfahren drucken; ausgleichen, aufheben; *com* aufrechnen; *arch* kröpfen; *itr* sich abzweigen; *typ* abziehen; **~ account** Verrechnungskonto *n*; **~ printing** Offsetdruck *m*.

offshoot ['ɔ(:)fʃut] Sproß, Schößling, Ableger; Ausläufer *m*, Abzweigung; *fig* Nebenlinie *f*.

offspring ['ɔ(:)fspriŋ] *pl ~* Kind(er *pl*) *n*, Abkömmling(e *pl*) *m*, Nachkomme(n *pl*) *m*, Nachkommenschaft *f*; Sproß *m*; *fig* Ergebnis, Resultat *n*.

offstreet ['ɔ(:)fstri:t] Seiten-, Nebenstraße *f*.

offtake ['ɔ(:)fteik] Wegnahme *f*; Zurückziehen *n (bes. vom Markt)*; Abzug *m*.

oft [ɔ(:)ft] *poet* = **~en**; **~en** ['ɔ(:)fən], **~entimes** ['-taimz] *adv* oft(mals), häufig, wiederholt; *as ~en as not* sehr oft; *every so ~en* von Zeit zu Zeit.

ogee ['oudʒi:] Kehlleiste *f*, Karnies *n*; S-Kurve *f*; *(~ arch) arch* Eselsrücken *m*.

ogiv|al [o(u)'dʒaivəl] *arch* spitzbogig; Spitzbogen-; **~e** ['oudʒaiv] *arch* Gratrippe *f*; Spitzbogen *m*; *(Statistik)* Frequenzkurve *f*.

ogle ['ougl] *tr itr* liebäugeln (*at* mit); freche Blicke werfen (*at* auf).

ogr|e ['ougə] Menschenfresser *m (im Märchen)*; *allg* Scheusal *n*; **~(e)ish** ['ougriʃ] scheußlich; **~ess** ['ougris] Menschenfresserin *f*.

oh [ou] *interj* oh! ach!

oil [ɔil] *s* Öl *n*; Tran *m*; (Mineral-, Erd-)Öl, Petroleum *n*; Ölfarbe *f*, -gemälde, -bild *n*; *Am sl* Schmeichelei *f*, Schmiergeld *n*; *tr* (ein)ölen; *fig* bestechen; *Am sl* verprügeln; *itr* zu Öl, ölig werden; *mar* Öl aufnehmen; *to burn the midnight ~* bis spät in die Nacht (hinein) arbeiten *od* lernen; *to paint in ~s* in Öl malen; *to pour ~ on troubled waters* die Gemüter beruhigen; die Wogen zu glätten suchen; *to pour, to throw ~ on the flames (fig)* Öl aufs Feuer gießen; *to strike ~* auf Öl *(im Boden)* stoßen; *fig* sein Glück machen; *to ~ s.o.'s hand, palm, fist* jdn bestechen, jdn schmieren; *to ~ o.'s tongue* honigsüß reden, schmeicheln; *it is like ~ and vinegar* das paßt wie die Faust aufs Auge; *~ of almonds* Mandelöl *n*; *~ of turpentine* Terpentinöl *n*; *~ of vitriol* Schwefelsäure *f*; **~ bath** Ölbad *n*; **~-bearing** ölhaltig; **~-box** Schmierbüchse *f*; **~-brake** Öldruckbremse *f*; **~-burner** Ölbrenner *m*; *Am sl* alte Kiste *f*; **~-cake** Ölkuchen *m*; **~-can** Ölkanne *f*; **~-changing** *mot* Ölwechsel *m*; **~-circulation** Ölumlauf *m*; **~-cloth** Wachstuch *n*; **~-colo(u)r** Ölfarbe *f*; **~ consumption** Ölverbrauch *m*; **~-cup** *tech* Schmierbüchse *f*; **~ deposit** Ölvorkommen *n*; **~ duct** Ölleitung *f*;

~ **dumping** *mar* Lenzen *n*; ~-**engine** Diesel-, Ölmotor *m*; ~**ed** *a* geölt; *Am sl* betrunken; ~**er** ['-ə] Öler *m*; Ölkanne *f*; Tanker *m*; ~-**feed** *tech* Ölzufuhr *f*; ~-**field** (Erd-)Ölfeld *n*; ~ **film** Ölschicht *f*; ~ **filter** Ölfilter *n*; ~-**fuel** Heiz-, Treiböl *n*; ~ **ga(u)ge** Ölstandsanzeiger *m*; ~-**furnace** Ölfeuerung *f*; ~-**heater** Ölofen *m*; ~-**heating** Ölheizung *f*; ~ **industry** Erdölindustrie *f*; ~**iness** ['-inis] ölige Beschaffenheit *f*; *fig* salbungsvolle(s) Wesen *n*; ~-**level** *tech* Ölstand *m*; ~-**painting** Ölgemälde *n*, -malerei *f*; ~-**paper** Ölpapier *n*; ~-**pressure** *tech* Öldruck; ~~ *ga(u)ge* Öldruckanzeiger *m*; ~~ *lubrication* Öldruckschmierung *f*; ~ **pump** Ölpumpe *f*; ~ **refinery** Ölraffinerie *f*; ~ **residue** Ölrückstand *m*; ~ **shale** Ölschiefer *m*; ~-**silk** *(Textil)* Ölhaut *f*; ~-**skin** Öltuch; *pl* Ölzeug *n*; ~-**stone** geölte(r) Wetzstein *m*; ~-**strainer** Ölsieb *n*; ~-**sump**, *Am* ~ **pan** Ölwanne *f*; ~ **supply** Ölzufuhr *f*; ~ **tank** Öltank *m*; ~-**well** Ölquelle *f*; ~**y** ['-i] ölig; ölhaltig; fettig, schmierig; *fig* aalglatt; schlüpfrig; *fig* salbungsvoll.

ointment ['ɔintmənt] Salbe *f*; *there is a fly in the* ~ die Sache hat e-n Haken.

O. K., okay ['ou'kei] *a adv interj sl* (geht) in Ordnung; *tr* gutheißen, billigen; *s* Zustimmung, Billigung *f*.

old [ould] *a* alt; früher, ehemalig, vergangen; bejahrt, betagt; (lebens)erfahren; erprobt; geübt; ge-, verbraucht, abgenutzt, schäbig; altertümlich; weit zurückliegend, -reichend; *fam* alt(vertraut, -gewohnt), lieb(geworden); *sl* famos, prächtig, großartig; *s pl*: *the* ~ die Alten, die alten Leute; *as* ~ *as the hills* uralt; *of* ~ einst(ens), ehemals, -dem; *in times of* ~ in alten Zeiten; *to grow* ~ alt werden; altern; *he has an* ~ *head on his shoulders* er hat Verstand wie ein Alter; *young and* ~ alt u. jung; ~ **age** (hohes, Greisen-)Alter *n*; ~-~ *pension* Altersrente *f*; ~ **boy** *hum* alte(r) Knabe *od* Junge *m*, alte(s) Haus *n*; **O**~ **Catholic** altkatholisch; ~-**clothes shop** Trödelladen *m*; ~ **country** *Am* frühere Heimat *f*; ~**en** ['-ən] *poet* alt; **O**~ **English** (das) Altenglisch(e); ~-**fashioned** *a* altmodisch, unmodern; rückständig; ~ **fogy** alte(r) Kauz *m*; ~-**fog(e)yish** schrullenhaft, schrullig, kauzig; *the* **O**~ **Glory** *Am* das Sternenbanner; ~ **hand** erfahrene, geübte Kraft *f*; **O**~ **Harry, O**~ **Nick, O**~ **Scratch** der Teufel; ~ **hat** *Am fam* altmodisch; ~**ish** ['-iʃ] ältlich; *the* **O**~ **Lady** *fam* die Alte *(Frau)*, die alte Dame *(Mutter)*; ~-**line** alt(überliefert), traditionell; traditionsbewußt, konservativ; ~ **maid** alte(s), *hum* verspätete(s) Mädchen *n*, alte Jungfer; Zimperliese *f*; ~-**maidish** altjüngferlich; zimperlich; *the* **O**~ **Man** *fam* der Alte *(Ehemann, Chef)*; der alte Herr *(Vater)*; **O**~ **Man River** Mississippi *m*; ~ **master** *(Kunst)* alte(r) Meister *m*; ~ **moon** letzte(s) Viertel *n*; ~ **offender** alte(r) Sünder *m*; ~ **salt** alte(r) Seebär *m*; ~ **school**: *he is one of the* ~~, *he belongs to the* ~~ er ist noch von der alten Schule; ~-**standing** traditionell; alt renommiert; ~**ster** ['-stə] *fam* alte(r) Knabe *m*; ~ **style** *(Kalender)* alten Stils; **O**~ **Testament** Alte(s) Testament *n*; ~-**time** altmodisch; ~-**timer** *fam* e-r von der alten Garde; alte(r) Kunde; am Alten hängende(r) Mensch *m*; ~ **wives' tale** Altweibergeschichte *f*; ~-**womanish** altweiberhaft; ~-**world** unamerikanisch; vorsintflutlich; *the* **O**~**World** die Alte Welt.

oleaginous [ouli'ædʒinəs] ölig, fettig; ölhaltig; *fam* salbungsvoll.

oleander [ouli'ændə] *bot* Oleander *m*.

oleograph ['oulio(u)grɑ:f] Öldruck *m*.

olfact|ion [ɔl'fækʃən] *a* Geruchssinn *m*; ~**ory** [-təri] *a* Geruch-; ~~ *nerves (pl)* Geruchsnerven *m pl*; ~~ *organ* Geruchsorgan *n*.

olig|archic(al) [ɔli'gɑ:kik(əl)] oligarchisch; ~**archy** ['ɔligɑ:ki] Oligarchie *f*; ~**ocene** [ɔ'ligo(u)si:n, 'ɔ-] *geol* Oligozän *n*.

olio ['ouliou] *pl* -*os* Ragout *n*; *fig* Mischmasch *m*, (buntes) Durcheinander; *mus* Potpourri *n*.

oliv|aceous [ɔli'veiʃəs] *a* Oliven-; olivfarben; ~**e** ['ɔliv] *s* Olive *f*; Ölbaum, -zweig *m*; *(~~-green)* Olivgrün *n*; *a* Oliven-; olivgrün; *the Mount of O~~s (Bibel)* der Ölberg; *~~-branch* Ölzweig *m*; *~~-drab* olivgrün; *~~-grove* Olivenhain *m*; *~~-oil* Olivenöl *n*.

Olymp|iad [o(u)'limpiæd] Olympiade *f*; ~**ian** [-iən] *s* Olympier *m*; *a* olympisch; göttergleich; ~**ic** [-ik] *a* olympisch; *s pl*: *the* ~~*s*, *the* ~~ *Games* die Olympischen Spiele *n pl*; ~**us** [-əs], *Mount* ~~ der Olymp; der Himmel.

omelet(te) ['ɔmlit] Omelett(e *f*) *n*, Eierkuchen *m*.

om|en ['oumen] *s* Omen, Vorzeichen *n*, Vorbedeutung *f* (*for* für); *tr* ein Vorzeichen sein für; bedeuten, ankündigen; ~**inous** ['ɔminəs] unheilverkündend.

omiss|ible [o(u)'misibl] auslaßbar; ~**ion** [o(u)'miʃən] Aus-, Weglassung; Lücke; Unterlassung, Nichtbeachtung, Vernachlässigung, (Pflicht-)Versäumnis; *typ* Leiche *f*; *errors and* ~~*s excepted (com)* Irrtum vorbehalten; *sin of* ~~ Unterlassungssünde *f*.

omit [o(u)'mit] *tr* aus-, weglassen (*from* aus); übergehen; unterlassen, versäumen (*doing, to do* zu tun).

omnibus ['ɔmnibəs] *s* Omnibus, Autobus, Bus *m*; *a* um-, zs.fassend, Sammel-, Mantel-; *railway* ~ Schienenbus *m*; ~ **bill** Mantelgesetz *n*; ~ **(book), volume** Sammelband *m*; ~ **credit** Warenkredit *m*; ~ **driver** Omnibusfahrer *m*; ~ **edition** Gesamtausgabe *f* in e-m Band; ~ **order** Sammelbestellung *f*; ~-**route** Omnibuslinie *f*; ~ **train** Personenzug *m*.

omnifarious [ɔmni'fɛəriəs] mannigfaltig, abwechs(e)lungsreich, aller Art.

omnipoten|ce [ɔm'nipətəns] Allmacht *f*; ~**t** [-t] allmächtig.

omnipresen|ce ['ɔmni'prezəns] Allgegenwart *f*; ~**t** [-t] allgegenwärtig.

omniscien|ce [ɔm'nisiəns, *Am* -ʃəns] Allwissenheit *f*; ~**t** [-t] allwissend.

omnium ['ɔmniəm] *fin* Gesamtwert *m*; *fam* Habseligkeiten *f pl*; ~ **gatherum** ['-'gæðərəm] Sammelsurium *n*; bunt zs.gewürfelte Gesellschaft *f*.

omnivorous [ɔm'nivərəs] allesfressend; *fig (als Leser)* alles verschlingend.

omoplate ['oumo(u)pleit] *scient* Schulterblatt *n*.

omphal|o- ['ɔmfəlo(u)] *in Zssgen scient* Nabel-; ~**os** [-əs] *pl* -*i* [-ai] Nabel *m a. fig*; *fig* Mittelpunkt *m*.

on [ɔn] **1.** *prp (räumlich)* auf, an; ~ *the table* auf dem Tisch(e), auf den Tisch; ~ *the wall* auf der, die Mauer; an der, die Wand; ~ *the river* am, an den Fluß; *(zeitlich)* an, bei; ~ *that day* an dem Tage; ~ *Sunday* am Sonntag; ~ *entering* beim Eintritt; als ich *usw* eintrat; *(Art u. Weise)* ~ *the cheap* billig *adv*; *(verschiedene Umstände)* ~ *a trip* auf e-m Ausflug; ~ *a committee* in e-m Ausschuß; *to have* ~ *o.* bei sich haben; ~ *this occasion* bei dieser Gelegenheit; ~ *these conditions* unter diesen Bedingungen; *to draw a knife* ~ *s.o.* ein Messer gegen jdn ziehen; *a lecture* ~ *Shakespeare* ein Vortrag über Sh.; *to live* ~ *s.th.* von etw leben; *to have s.th.* ~ *s.o. (fam)* belastendes Material über jdn haben; *I got it* ~ *good authority* ich weiß es aus guter Quelle; *this is* ~ *me* das geht auf meine Kosten; *Ausdrücke*: ~ *no account* auf keinen Fall; ~ *authority* mit Vollmacht; ~ *an average* im Durchschnitt, im Mittel; ~ *board* an Bord; ~ *demand* auf Antrag; ~ *earth* auf der Welt; ~ *hand* zur Hand, zur Verfügung; auf Lager, vorrätig; ~ *the other hand* ander(er)seits; ~ *its own* für sich (selbst) *(betrachten)*; ~ *leave* auf, im Urlaub; ~ *my part* meinerseits; ~ *purpose* absichtlich; ~ *the spot* auf der Stelle; ~ *a sudden* plötzlich *adv*; ~ *time* pünktlich, auf die Minute; ~ *trial* zur Probe; nach Erprobung; ~ *the whole* im ganzen: **2.** *adv (in Verbindung mit e-m Verb)* an, auf; dran, an der Reihe; im Gange; fort, weiter; *to have nothing* ~ nichts an haben, nackt sein; *I had, put a hat* ~ ich hatte, setzte e-n Hut auf; *the light is* ~ das Licht ist an; *the radio is* ~ das Radio ist angestellt, spielt; *the water is* ~ das Wasser läuft; *the brakes are* ~ die Bremsen sind in Tätigkeit; *Hamlet is* ~ Hamlet wird gespielt; *he is* ~ *as Macbeth* er spielt M., tritt als M. auf; *the battle was still* ~ die Schlacht dauerte noch an, war noch im Gange; *he hurried* ~ er eilte weiter; *come* ~*!* mach weiter! *time is getting* ~ die Zeit rückt vor; *it's getting* ~ *for eight o'clock* es geht auf acht; *to be* ~ *(sl)* einen drauf haben, besoffen sein; *to s.th.* über etw im Bilde sein; ~ *to* auf (... hinauf) *mit acc*; *Ausdrücke*: *and so* ~ und so weiter, usw.; *later* ~ später; ~ *and off* mit Unterbrechungen, zeitweise, von Zeit zu Zeit; ~ *and* ~ in e-m fort, ununterbrochen, andauernd; **3.** *a sport (Seite)* link; *com* örtlich; *fam* gut; *Am sl* aufgeweckt, klug, bereitwillig; *(Licht)* eingeschaltet; **4.** *s Am sl* Eiskreme *f*; ~-**the-spot** [ɔnðə'spɔt] *a*: ~~ *decision* Sofortentscheid *m*; ~~ *observer, report* Augenzeuge(nbericht) *m*.

onanism ['ounənizm] Onanie *f*.

once [wʌns] *adv* einmal; früher einmal; je(mals); einmal, einst, ehemals; *conj* sobald; wenn ... einmal; *a* einstig, ehemalig, früher; *s*: *this* ~ dies e-e Mal, diesmal; *all at* ~ alle auf einmal, alle zugleich; *at* ~ sofort, sogleich, auf der Stelle; auf einmal, plötzlich; zu gleicher Zeit; *for (this)* ~ für diesmal; *more than* ~ mehr als einmal; mehrmals, -fach; öfter(s); *not* ~ nicht einmal, nie; ~ *a day* einmal am Tag; ~ *again*, ~ *more* noch (ein)mal; nochmals; ~ *and again*, ~ *in a way*, ~ *in a while* ab u. zu, von Zeit zu Zeit; dann u. wann, hin u. wieder; ~ *before* schon einmal, früher einmal; ~ *(and) for all* ein für allemal; ~ *in a blue moon* alle Jubeljahre einmal; ~ *or twice* das eine oder andere mal, nicht (gerade) oft; ~ *upon a time (there was)* (es war) einmal; ~ *doesn't count* einmal ist keinmal; ~-**over** *s fam* schnelle(r), prüfende(r) Blick *m*; *to give s.o. a* ~~ jdn von oben bis unten ansehen.

oncoming ['ɔnkʌmiŋ] *a* heran-, näherkommend, an-, vorrückend; *fig* entgegenkommend; *s* (Heran-)Nahen *n*; ~ **traffic** Gegenverkehr *m*.

one [wʌn] *a* ein(er, e, s); ein(e) einzige(r, s); ein(e) gewisse(r); *s* Eins *f*,

Einser *m*; eine(r, s); jemand, man; etwas; *a blue ribbon and a red* ~ ein blaues Band u. ein rotes; *the little ~s* die Kleinen; *another* ~ ein anderer; ~ *another* einander, sich gegenseitig; *every* ~ jeder; *no* ~ keiner, niemand; *such a* ~ so e-r; ein solcher; *that* ~ jener; *this* ~ dieser; *number* ~ man selbst; *all* ~ alle zs., einmütig; (ganz) egal, gleich(gültig), einerlei, eins, *fam* schnuppe, Wurst; *all in* ~ alles zs., zugleich, in e-m; *at* ~ e-r Meinung; in Übereinstimmung; *at* ~ *time* früher (einmal); *for* ~ zum Beispiel; jedenfalls; *for* ~ *thing* (erstens) einmal, zum ersten; ~ *after another* e-r nach dem andern; ~ *and all* alle (samt u. sonders); ~ *at a time*, ~ *by* ~ einzeln, jeder für sich; ~ *day* eines Tages; ~ *of these days* dieser Tage; *to be* ~ *with s.o.* mit jdm einig sein; *to give s.o.* ~ *in the eye* jdm e-e 'runterhauen; *to be given* ~ *in the eye* erledigt, fertig sein; *to make* ~ *(itr)* Mitglied sein, dazugehören; teilnehmen, dabei sein, sich anschließen (*of* an); *tr*: *to be made* ~ (sich ver)heiraten; *he's a* ~ *(pop)* der ist einmalig; **~-armed** *a* einarmig; **~-eyed** *a* einäugig; *sl* unbedeutend; **~-handed** *a* einhändig; **~-horse** *a* einspännig; *fam* bescheiden, mäßig, unbedeutend; **~-hour** einstündig; **~-legged** *a* einbeinig; *fig* einseitig; **~-line business** Fachgeschäft *n*; **~-man** *a* Einmann-; ~~ *operation* Einmannbedienung *f*; ~~ *rubber raft* Einmannschlauchboot *n*; ~~ *submarine* Kleinst-U-Boot *n*; ~~ *tent* Einmannzelt *n*; **~ness** ['-nis] Eins-, Alleinsein *n*; Einheit; Einmütigkeit, Einigkeit; Identität *f*; **~-night stand** *Am* einmalige Aufführung *od* Veranstaltung *f*; **~-piece** einteilig; **~-price shop** Einheitspreisgeschäft *n*; **~r** ['-ə] *sl* Pfundskerl; tolle(r) Schlag *m*; **~self** [-'self] *prn* man selbst; sich; *by* ~~, *for* ~~ *alone* (ganz) allein; ohne Begleitung; *to be* ~~ sein, wie man immer ist; sich geben, wie man ist; *to come to* ~~ wieder zu sich kommen; sich wieder fassen; *to take s.th. upon* ~~ etw auf sich nehmen; **~-shot** *s* einmalige(s) Ereignis *n*; *a* einmalig; **~-sided** *a* einseitig *a. fig*; *fig* voreingenommen, parteiisch, ungerecht; **~-sidedness** Einseitigkeit *a. fig*; *fig* Voreingenommenheit *f*; **~-step** Onestep *m (Tanz)*; **~-time** *a* einstig, ehemalig, früher; **~-track** *(Fahrbahn, Schienenweg)* einspurig; *fam (geistig)* beschränkt, einseitig; **~-way** *a (Verkehr)* Einbahn-; *tech* Einweg-; ~~ *street* Einbahnstraße *f*; ~~ *ticket (Am)* einfache Fahrkarte *f*; ~~ *traffic* Einbahnverkehr *m*.

onerous ['ɔnərəs] lästig, beschwerlich, drückend (*to* für); **~ness** ['-nis] Lästigkeit, Beschwerlichkeit *f*.

*

onion ['ʌnjən] Zwiebel *f*; *Am sl* Depp; *sport sl* Kürbis; *allg* Dollar *m*; *off o.'s* ~ *(sl)* ganz aus dem Häuschen; nicht ganz bei Trost; *to know o.'s ~s (sl)* sein Geschäft verstehen; **~skin** Zwiebelhaut *f*; Luftpost-, Durchschlagpapier *n*.

onlook|er ['ɔnlukə] Zuschauer; Gaffer *m* (*at* bei); **~ing** ['-iŋ] zuschauend.

only ['ounli] **1.** *a* alleinig, einzig, ausschließlich; von allen ... nur; *one and* ~ allereinzigst; **2.** *adv* nur, bloß, allein, erst; aber; gerade; *if* ~ wenn doch nur; *not* ~ ... *but also* nicht nur ... sondern auch; ~ *just*, ~ *yesterday* eben, gestern erst; ~ *too (mit a)* nur zu ...; **3.** *conj* nur daß, wenn nicht, wenn nur; ~ *that* nur, daß; außer, wenn.

onomatopoe(t)ic [ɔno(u)məto(u)'pi:ik, -po(u)'etik] *gram* lautmalend.

onrush ['ɔnrʌʃ] Anprall, Ansturm *m*.

onset ['ɔnset] Angriff, -sturm; *mil* Sturmangriff; Anfang, Beginn, Ansatz, Start; *med* Ausbruch, Anfall *m*; *at the* ~ am Anfang; *from the* ~ von Anfang an.

onslaught ['ɔnslɔ:t] heftige(r) Angriff; *med* Anfall *m*.

onto ['ɔntu, 'ɔntə] *prp* auf (... hinauf); *to be* ~ *s.th. (sl)* über etw im Bilde sein.

onto|genesis [ɔntə'dʒenəsis], **~geny** [ɔn'tɔdʒəni] *biol* Ontogenese *f*; **~logical** [ɔntə'lɔdʒikəl] *philos* ontologisch; **~logy** [ɔn'tɔlədʒi] Ontologie *f*.

onus ['ounəs] *nur sing* Last, Aufgabe, Verpflichtung, Verantwortung *f*; ~ *of proof (jur)* Beweislast *f*.

onward ['ɔnwəd] *adv* nach vorn, vorwärts, weiter; *a* nach vorn (gerichtet); vorwärtsgehend; fortschreitend; *from* ... ~ von ... an; **~s** [-z] *adv* = ~ *adv*.

onyx ['ɔniks] *min* Onyx *m a. med*.

oodles ['u:dlz] *pl sl* Unmassen, Unmengen *f pl* (*of* von); ein Haufen (*of money* Geld).

oof [u:f] *sl* Moos, Geld *n*; *sport* Stärke, Kraft *f*; **~-bird** *sl* reiche(r) Knopp *m*; **~y** ['-i] *sl* gut bestückt, schwerreich.

oomph [u:mf] *sl* Sex-Appeal; Charme *m*; Begeisterung *f*; Mumm *m*; Kraft *f*; Unternehmungsgeist *m*.

ooz|e [u:z] **1.** *s* Lohbrühe *f*; Sickern *n*; *itr* lecken, auslaufen, rinnen; *(Flüssigkeit)* (durch)sickern *(through, out of, into)*; *(Gefäß)* nicht dichthalten; *(to* ~~ *out, away)* vergehen, verschwinden; *fig* durchsickern, bekanntwerden; *tr (Gefäß)* ausschwitzen; ausstrahlen; *to* ~~ *with sweat* in Schweiß gebadet sein; **2.** Schlick, Schlamm; Sumpf *m*; **~y** ['-i] schlammig, schleimig.

opa|city [o(u)'pæsiti], **~queness** [ou'peiknis] Undurchsichtigkeit; Trübheit; *fig* Stumpfheit, Dunkelheit, Unverständlichkeit *f*; **~que** [o(u)'peik] undurchsichtig, milchig, trüb; nicht reflektierend, stumpf, dunkel; undurchlässig (*to* für); *fig* dunkel, unverständlich; stumpf, verständnislos.

opal ['oupəl] *min* Opal *m*; **~esce** [oupə'les] *itr* opalisieren, schillern; **~escence** [-'lesns] Opaleszenz *f*, Opalschiller *m*; **~escent** [-'lesnt] opalisierend, schillernd; **~ine** ['-li:n] *s* Opalglas *n*; *a* ['-lain] Opal-.

open ['oupən] **1.** *a* offen, unversperrt, unverschlossen, unbedeckt; frei; unverhüllt; ohne Verdeck, offen; ungeschützt; ausgesetzt (*to s.th.* etw); ausgebreitet; *(Buch)* aufgeschlagen, geöffnet, offen; *(Waren)* offen ausgelegt; aufgelockert, durch-, unterbrochen; *mil* geöffnet; *(Gewässer)* eis-, *(Wetter)* frost-, schneefrei, offen; *(Veranstaltung)* allgemein zugänglich, öffentlich, offen; allgemein bekannt, öffentlich; *(Frage)* unentschieden, unerledigt, (noch) offen; offen, aufgeschlossen (*to* für); weltoffen, freisinnig, -mütig; weitherzig, großzügig; (offen und) ehrlich, aufrichtig; zugänglich (*to s.o.* jdm); erhältlich (*to, for s.o.* für jdn); unterworfen (*to* dat); *(Stelle)* (noch) unbesetzt, frei; *(Konto)* offen, laufend; *(Phonetik)* offen; *(Gelände)* offen, unbe-, ungedeckt; *mar (Sicht)* (nebel)frei, klar; *Am* ohne Alkohol- *od* Spielverbot; **2.** *tr* öffnen, aufmachen; aufdecken, freimachen, -legen; beginnen, einleiten, eröffnen; erschließen; freigeben; auf-, einschneiden; (auf)lockern; *mil* öffnen; *(Buch)* aufschlagen, öffnen; *(Sitzung, Geschäft, Konto)* eröffnen; *(Voranschlag)* vorlegen; enthüllen, bekanntmachen, -geben; freigeben; aufgeschlossen, weltoffen machen; *Am sl* berauben; **3.** *itr* sich öffnen; offen sein *od* stehen; *(Fenster)* gehen (*on to* auf; *into* nach); sich entfalten, sich ausbreiten; bekannt-, offenkundig werden, auftauchen; in Sicht kommen; anfangen, beginnen; aufgeschlossen, weitherzig werden; *tech* zurückfedern; **4.** *s*: *the* ~ offene(s) Land *n*, offene See *f*; Öffentlichkeit *f*; *in the* ~ im Freien, draußen; *min* über Tag; *to* ~ *out (tr)* enthüllen; *tr itr* (sich) erweitern, ausdehnen; *itr* sich entwickeln; mitteilsam werden; *to* ~ *up (tr itr)* (sich) öffnen; (sich) erschließen; *itr* sich ausbreiten, sich entfalten; e-n Zugang haben (*into, on to* zu); anfangen, beginnen; *fam* sich aussprechen, reden, das Geheimnis preisgeben; ~ *day and night* Tag u. Nacht geöffnet; *in the* ~ *air* in der frischen Luft, unter freiem Himmel, im Freien; *in (the)* ~ *court* vor Gericht; *in* ~ *court (jur)* in öffentlicher Sitzung; *in the* ~ *market (com)* aus freier Hand, freihändig; *in the* ~ *sea* auf hoher See; *with* ~ *arms* mit offenen Armen, begeistert; *with* ~ *hands* mit offenen Händen, freigebig; *to be* ~ *and above board with s.o.* mit jdm offen u. ehrlich sein; *to come into the* ~ *(fig)* alle Karten auf den Tisch legen; *to have an* ~ *mind about s.th.* sich noch nicht auf etw festgelegt haben; *to keep* ~ *house* sehr gastfrei sein; *to lay o.s.* ~ *to s.th.* sich e-r S aussetzen; *to leave* ~ *(fig)* offen, unentschieden lassen; *to* ~ *a discussion* in e-e Diskussion eintreten; *to* ~ *o.'s eyes* große Augen machen; *to* ~ *s.o.'s eyes (fig)* jdm die Augen öffnen (*to* über); *to* ~ *fire (mil)* das Feuer eröffnen (*on, at* auf); *to* ~ *o.'s heart, mind to s.o.* jdm sein Herz, s-e Gedanken eröffnen; ~ *sesame* Sesam, öffne dich! *a. fig*; ~ *to bribery* bestechlich; **~-air** *a* Freiluft-, Freilicht-; im Freien, unter freiem Himmel; ~~ *storage* Lagerung *f* unter freiem Himmel; **~-and-shut** *Am fam*: ~~ *case* klare(r) Fall *m*; **~-cast mining, -pit mining, work(ings** *pl)* *min* Tagebau *m*; ~ **cheque** Barscheck *m*; **~-door policy** Politik *f* der offenen Tür; **~-eared** *a* hellhörig; **~er** ['-ə] *(bes. in Zssgen)* Öffner *m*; Eröffnungsspiel *n*; *bottle-*~~ Flaschenöffner *m*; *tin-, (Am) can-*~~ Büchsenöffner *m*; **~-eyed** *a* aufmerksam, mit offenen Augen; überrascht; **~-handed** *a* freigebig; **~-hearted** *a* offenherzig, frei; aufrichtig; großzügig; **~-hearth process** *tech* Siemens-Martin-Verfahren *n*; **~ing** ['-pniŋ] Öffnung; Lücke; *(Brücke)* Spannweite; *Am (Wald)* Lichtung; Errichtung, Eröffnung *f (a. Schach)*; Beginn, Anfang *m*; Inbetriebnahme, -setzung; (günstige) Gelegenheit, Aussicht; offene Stelle; Erschließung *f*; ~~ *balance sheet* Eröffnungsbilanz *f*; ~~ *bridge* Klappbrücke *f*; ~~ *speech* Eröffnungsrede *f*; **~-minded** *a* aufgeschlossen, nicht engstirnig; **~-mouthed** *a* mit offenem Mund, gaffend; gierig; laut; Schrei-; **~ness** ['-nis] Offenheit; Aufgeschlossenheit; Weitherzigkeit; Großzügigkeit; Aufrichtigkeit *f*; ~ **order** *mil* geöffnete Ordnung *f*; ~ **question** offene Frage *f*, strittige(r) Punkt *m*; ~ **season** Jagdzeit *f*; ~ **secret** offene(s) Geheimnis *n*; ~ **shop** *Am* Betrieb *m*, der auch nichtorganisierte Arbeiter einstellt; ~ **sight** *mil* Visierlinie *f*; ~ **war(fare)** Bewegungskrieg *m*; **~-wire circuit**

Freileitung *f*; **~-work** *a (Textil)* durchbrochen; *min* Tagebau-.

opera ['ɔpərə] Oper *f*; *(~ house)* Opernhaus *n*; *comic ~* komische Oper *f*; *grand ~* große Oper *f*; *light ~* Singspiel *n*, Operette *f*; **~-cloak** Abendmantel *m*; **~-dancer** Ballettänzer(in *f*) *m*; **~-glass(es** *pl*) Opernglas *n*; **~-hat** Klappzylinder *m*; **~tic** [ɔpə'rætik] opernhaft; Opern-.

oper|able ['ɔpərəbl] durchführbar, gangbar; *med* operierbar; *tech* betriebsfähig; **~ate** ['ɔpəreit] *itr* in Betrieb, im Gange sein, arbeiten (*on steam* mit Dampf); funktionieren, s-n Zweck erfüllen; wirken (*on* auf); tätig sein; in Kraft sein, gelten, gültig sein; handeln; *mil med* operieren (*against* gegen; *on s.o.* jdn); *com* spekulieren; *tr* bewerkstelligen, bewirken, herbeiführen; in Gang bringen, in Betrieb setzen, betätigen; in Gang, in Betrieb halten; handhaben, bedienen; *bes. Am* betreiben, leiten; *(Auto)* fahren; *(Geschäft)* führen, leiten; *to be ~d* betrieben werden; in Betrieb sein; **~ating** ['-reitiŋ] *s* Funktionieren *n*; Arbeitsgang *m*; *a attr*: *~~ cabin* Vorführraum *m*; *~~ characteristic* Betriebsmerkmal *n*; *~~ condition* Betriebsfähigkeit *f*; *pl* -bedingungen *f pl*; *~~ costs, expenses (pl)* Betriebskosten *pl*; *~~ crew* Bedienung(smannschaft) *f*; *~~ director, manager* Betriebsführer, Werkleiter, Direktor *m*; *~~ engineer* Betriebsingenieur *m*; *~~ hour* Betriebsstunde *f*; *~~ instructions (pl)* Bedienungsanweisung *f*; *~~ knob* Bedienungsknopf *m*; *~~ lever* Schalthebel *m*; *~~ panel* Bedienungstafel *f*; *~~ range* Arbeitsbereich *m*; *~~ receipts (pl)* Betriebseinnahmen *f pl*; *~~ room (tele)* Bedienungs-, *film* Vorführ-, *med* Operationsraum *m*; *~~ staff* Betriebspersonal *n*; *~~ table (med)* Operationstisch *m*; *~~ temperature* Betriebstemperatur *f*; *~~ theatre (med)* Operationssaal, -raum *m*; *~~ time* Betriebszeit, -dauer *f*; *~~ trouble* Betriebsstörung *f*; *~~ voltage* Betriebsspannung *f*; **~ation** [ɔpə'reiʃən] Arbeitsgang *m*, -weise *f*, Verfahren *n*, Vorgang; Betrieb, Gang *m*, Handhabung, Tätigkeit *f*, Funktionieren; Betreiben *n*; Führung, Leitung; Handlungsfähigkeit, Wirkung(skraft) (*on* auf); Wirksamkeit; Betätigung; Geltung; Arbeit; Operation *f allg mil med*; *med* Eingriff (*on s.o.* bei jdm; *for* wegen); *com* Geschäftsvorgang *m*, Transaktion; Spekulation *f*; *mil* Einsatz *m*, Kampfhandlung *f*; *aero* Feindflug *m*; *in ~~* in Betrieb; *out of ~~* außer Betrieb; *to be in, to come, to put into ~~* in Kraft sein, treten, setzen; in Betrieb sein, nehmen; *to undergo an ~~* sich e-r Operation unterziehen; *banking ~~* Banktransaktion *f*, -geschäft *n*; *financial ~~* Geldgeschäft *n*; *~~ analysis* Betriebsanalyse, Arbeitsstudie *f*; *~~ for appendicitis* Blinddarmoperation *f*; *~~s board* Lagekarte *f*; *~~ costs (pl)* Betriebskosten *pl*; *~~ of large formations (mil)* Führung *f* großer Verbände; *~~ lever* Bedienungshebel *m*; *~~ manual* Betriebshandbuch *n*; *~~ order (mil)* Operationsbefehl *m*; *~~ range (mil)* Operationsgebiet *n*; *aero* Aktionsradius *m*; *~~s section (mil)* Abteilung *f* Ia; *~~s staff (mil)* Führungsstab *m*; *~~ supervision* Betriebsüberwachung *f*; **~ational** [-'reiʃənl] *a* Betriebs-, Einsatz-; Führungs-; *mil* Operations-; taktisch; operativ; *tech* betrieblich; gebrauchs-, einsatzfähig; *~~ airfield* Einsatz-, Feldflugplatz *m*; *~~ base (mil)* Aufmarschgebiet *n*; *aero* Einsatzflugplatz *m*; *~~ chart (tech)* Schaubild *n*; *~~ difficulties (pl)* Betriebsschwierigkeiten *f pl*; *~~ flight* Feindflug *m*; *~~ funds (pl)* Betriebsmittel *n pl*; *~~ headquarters (pl)* Führungsstab; Gefechtsstand *m*; *~~ height* Einsatzflughöhe *f*; *~~ instructions (pl)* Bedienungsvorschrift *f*; *~~ order* Operationsbefehl *m*; *~~ plan (mil)* Aufmarschplan *m*; *~~ report* Gefechtsmeldung *f*; *~~ staff (mil)* Führungsstab *m*; **~ative** ['ɔpərətiv, 'ɔpəreitiv] *a* betriebs-, funktionsfähig; betriebsbereit, funktionierend, in Betrieb; wirksam, fähig; durchführbar, praktisch; *mil med* operativ; Operations-; *to become ~~* in Kraft treten; *s* (Industrie-, Fabrik-)Arbeiter; *Am* Detektiv *m*; **~ator** ['ɔpəreitə] Bedienende(r); Techniker; Maschinist; *med* Operateur; Kameramann; *(wireless ~~)* Funker; (Börsen-)Spekulant; *mot Am* Fahrer; *Am* Manager, Unternehmer, Betriebsleiter *m*; *fig* Triebkraft *f*; *Am sl* fabelhafte(r) Kerl *m*; *(telephone ~~)* Telephonistin *f*; *black-market ~~* Schwarzhändler *m*; *cinema ~~* Filmvorführer *m*.

opercul|ar [o(u)'pə:kjulə] deckelartig; Deckel-; **~um** [-əm] *pl -la bot zoo* Deckel *m*, Klappe *f*.

operetta [ɔpə'retə] Operette *f*.

ophthalm|ia [ɔf'θælmiə] Bindehautentzündung *f*; **~ic** [-ik] *a scient* Augen-; Ophthalmie-; *~~ dispenser (Am)* (Augen-)Optiker *m*; *~~ hospital* Augenklinik *f*; **~ologist** [ɔfθæl'mɔlədʒist] Augenarzt *m*; **~ology** [-'mɔlədʒi] Augenheilkunde *f*; **~oscope** [ɔf'θælməskoup] Augenspiegel *m*.

opiate ['oupiit] *s* Opiat; Schlaf-, Beruhigungsmittel *n*; *a* opiumhaltig; einschläfernd, beruhigend.

opine [o(u)'pain] *tr* meinen.

opinion [ə'pinjən] Meinung, Ansicht, Auffassung, Anschauung (*of* von); Stellungnahme *f*; Gutachten *n* (*on, upon* über); *jur* Urteil(sbegründung *f*) *n*; Schiedsspruch *m*; *pl* Anschauungen *f pl*, Überzeugung *f*; *by way of ~* gutachtlich; *in my ~* nach meiner Meinung; meiner Ansicht nach; meines Erachtens; *to act up to o.'s ~s* nach s-r Überzeugung handeln; *to be of (the) ~, to hold the ~ that* der Meinung *od* Ansicht sein, den Standpunkt vertreten, daß; *to form an ~* sich e-e Meinung bilden; *to have no ~ of* keine gute Meinung haben, nichts halten von; *to have the courage of o.'s ~s* sich zu s-r Überzeugung bekennen; *counsel's, legal ~* Rechtsgutachten *n*; *expert's ~* Sachverständigengutachten *n*; *a matter of ~* Ansichtssache *f*; *medical ~* ärztliche(s) Gutachten *n*; *press ~s (pl)* Pressestimmen *f pl*; **~ated** [-eitid] *a* starrsinnig, verbohrt; voreingenommen; **~ poll** Meinungsforschung *f*.

opium ['oupjəm] Opium *n*; **~-den** Opiumhöhle *f*; **~-eater** Opiumesser *m*; **~-smoker** Opiumraucher *m*.

opossum [ə'pɔsəm] *zoo* Opossum *n*.

opponen|cy [ə'pounənsi] Gegnerschaft, Opposition *f*, Widerstand *m*; **~t** [-t] *a* entgegengesetzt; gegnerisch, oppositionell (*to* dat); *s* Gegner, Opponent, Gegenspieler *m*.

opportun|e ['ɔpətju:n, *Am* ɔpə't(j)u:n] *(Zeit)* gelegen, günstig, passend, angebracht; rechtzeitig; **~ism** ['ɔpətju:nizm] Opportunismus *m*; **~ist** ['-ist, *Am* -'tju:nist] *s* Opportunist *m*; *a* opportunistisch; **~ity** [ɔpə'tju:niti] glückliche Umstände *m pl*; rechte, günstige Zeit; (gute) Gelegenheit, Chance *f* (*of doing, to do* zu tun; *for s.th.* zu etw); *at the first ~~* bei der ersten Gelegenheit; *to miss, to take* od *to seize an ~~* e-e Gelegenheit verpassen, ergreifen; *~~ for advancement* Aufstiegsmöglichkeit *f*.

oppos|e [ə'pouz] *tr* entgegen-, gegenüberstellen, entgegensetzen; entgegentreten, bekämpfen; einwenden, Einspruch erheben, sich widersetzen; *itr* Widerstand leisten, opponieren (*against* gegen); **~ed** [-d] *a* entgegengesetzt, gegenteilig; feindlich (*to* gegen); Gegen-; *to be ~~ to s.th* gegen etw sein; sich e-r S widersetzen; *~~ to common sense* vernunftwidrig; **~ing** [-iŋ] widerstrebend, -streitend, entgegengesetzt; **~ite** ['ɔpəzit] *a* gegenübergestellt, entgegengesetzt, feindlich (*to* dat); entgegengesetzt, völlig verschieden; *bot* gegenständig; *s* Gegenteil *n*, -satz *m*; *adv* im Gegensatz (*to* zu); *theat* in der Gegenrolle; *prp* gegenüber *dat*; *to take the ~~ view* die gegenteilige Auffassung vertreten; *~~ number* Gegenstück, Pendant *n*; Gegenspieler *m*; *~~ party* Gegenpartei *f*; *~~ side* gegenüberliegende Seite *f*; **~ition** [ɔpə'ziʃən] Gegenüberstellung *f*; Gegensatz (*to* zu); Widerstand, -spruch *m* (*to* gegen); Feindseligkeit; *pol astr* Opposition *f*; *jur* Einspruch *m*; *to be in ~~* in der Opposition sein; *to meet with ~~* auf Widerstand stoßen; *to offer ~~* Widerstand leisten; *~~ leader (parl)* Oppositionsführer *m*; *~~ meeting* Protestversammlung *f*.

oppress [ə'pres] *tr* be-, niederdrücken; (gewaltsam) unterdrücken; tyrannisieren; **~ed** [-t] *a* niedergedrückt (*with* von, durch); **~ion** [ə'preʃən] schwere(r) Druck *m*, Belastung; Be-, Unterdrückung; (schwere) Last; Niedergeschlagenheit, Verzweiflung *f*, Elend *n*, Not *f*; *jur* Mißbrauch *m* der Amtsgewalt; *feeling of ~~* Gefühl *n* der Beklemmung; **~ive** [ə'presiv] (be-, er)drückend, (schwer) lastend; tyrannisch; niederdrückend, beklemmend; *(Hitze)* drückend; **~iveness** [-'presivnis] Druck *m*, Belastung; Tyrannei *f*; *das* Niederdrückende, Beklemmende; **~or** [ə'presə] Unterdrücker, Tyrann *m*.

opprobr|ious [ə'proubriəs] schändlich, schimpflich, schmählich, infam; *~~ language* Schimpfworte *n pl*; **~ium** [-əm] Schande, Schmach *f* (*to* für).

oppugn [ɔ'pju:n] *tr (geistig)* bekämpfen, bestreiten.

opt [ɔpt] *itr* stimmen, optieren, sich entscheiden (*for* für); *to ~ out* sich heraushalten; **~ion** ['ɔpʃən] Wahl *f*; Abstimmung *f*, Entscheid *m*; Wahlrecht *n*, -möglichkeit, -freiheit; (freie) Wahl *(Sache) f*; *com* Termin-, Prämiengeschäft; *com* Option *f*, Vorkaufsrecht *n*; *at s.o.'s ~~* nach jds Wahl, Belieben; *to leave s.th. to s.o.'s ~~* jdm etw freistellen; etw in jds Belieben stellen; *to make o.'s ~~* s-e Wahl treffen; *I have the ~~ of doing* es steht mir frei zu tun; *I have no ~~ but to* es bleibt mir nichts anderes übrig als zu; *first ~~* Vorkaufsrecht *n*; *selling ~~* Verkaufsrecht *n*; *~~ of repurchase, redemption* Rückkaufsrecht *n*; *~~ market* Terminmarkt *m*; *~~ money* Prämie *f*; **~ional** ['ɔpʃənl] *a* wahlfrei, fakultativ; *s Am* Wahlfach *n*; *to be ~~* freistehen; *to leave ~~* freistellen; *~~ at extra cost* auf Wunsch gegen besondere Berechnung.

optic|(al) ['ɔptik(əl)] optisch; Seh-; *~al illusion* optische Täuschung *f*;

~*al range finder* optische(r) Entfernungsmesser *m*; ~*al refraction* Lichtbrechung *f*; ~*al view finder* Durchsichtssucher *m*; ~**ian** [ɔp'tiʃən] Optiker *m*; *dispensing* ~~ Brillenhändler *m*; ~ **nerve** *anat* Sehnerv *m*; ~**s** [-s] *pl mit sing* Optik *f*.

optim|ism ['ɔptimizm] Optimismus *m*; ~**ist** ['-ist] Optimist *m*; ~**istic(al)** [ɔpti'mistik(əl] optimistisch, hoffnungsfroh; ~**um** ['ɔptiməm] Optimum *n a. biol*, Bestwert *m*.

opulen|ce, -cy ['ɔpjuləns(i)] Reichtum, Wohlstand; Überfluß *m*; ~**t** ['-t] reich, wohlhabend; reichlich, üppig, luxuriös; *(Mahl)* opulent.

*

or [ɔ:, ə] *conj* oder; *either* ... ~ entweder ... oder; *whether* ... ~ ob ... oder; ~ *else* sonst, andernfalls; ~ *even* oder sogar; ~ *rather* oder vielmehr; ~ *so* oder so, etwa, ungefähr; ~ *somebody, something, somewhere* oder sonst jemand, etwas, -wo.

orac|le ['ɔrəkl] *rel hist* Orakel *n a. fig*; *fig* Prophet; Weisheitsspruch *m*; *to consult the* ~~ das Orakel befragen; *to work the* ~~ *(fig)* geheime Fäden spinnen; Geld beschaffen; ~**ular** [ɔ'rækjulə] orakelhaft, geheimnisvoll.

oral ['ɔ:rəl] *a* mündlich, gesprochen; *anat* Mund-; *s fam* mündliche Prüfung *f*; *in* ~ *contact (radio)* in Sprechverbindung; ~ **cavity** Mundhöhle *f*; ~ **evidence** Zeugenvernehmung *f*; ~ **examination, test** mündliche Prüfung; ~**ly** ['-i] *adv* mündlich; *med* oral.

orange ['ɔrindʒ] *s* Apfelsine, Orange *f*; *(~-tree)* Orangenbaum *m*; Orange(nfarbe *f*) *n*; *a* Apfelsinen-, Orangen-; orange(farben), kreß; *bitter, sour* ~ Pomeranze *f*; ~**ade** ['ɔrindʒ'eid] Orangeade *f*; ~ **peel** Orangenschale *f*.

orang|-outang, ~-utan ['ɔ:rəŋ'utæn(ŋ)] *zoo* Orang-Utan *m*.

orat|e [ɔ:'reit] *itr hum pej* große Reden schwingen; ~**ion** [ɔ:'reiʃən] (feierliche, Fest-)Rede; *funeral* ~~ Grabrede *f*; *(in)direct* ~~ *(gram)* (in)direkte Rede *f*; ~**or** ['ɔrətə] Redner; *jur Am* Kläger *m*; ~**orical** [ɔrə'tɔrikəl] rednerisch; Rede-; ~**orio** [ɔ:rə'tɔ:riou] *pl -os mus* Oratorium *n*; ~**ory** ['ɔrətəri] Redekunst, Rhetorik; *rel arch* (kleine) Kapelle *f*.

orb [ɔ:b] Kugel *f*; Himmelskörper; Reichsapfel; *poet* Augapfel *m*, Auge *n*; ~**ed** [-d] *a* gerundet, kreisförmig; umringt; ~**icular** [ɔ:'bikjulə] kugelig; kreisförmig; ~**it** ['ɔ:bit] *s med* Augenhöhle; *orn* Augenliderhaut; *phys astr* Kreis-, Umlauf-, Planetenbahn *f*; *fig* Erfahrungs-, Tätigkeits-, Wirkungs-, Lebensbereich *m*; *tr* auf e-e Bahn bringen um; *itr* kreisen; ~**ital** ['-itl] Kreis-, Bahn-; ~~ *cavity* Augenhöhle *f*.

orchard ['ɔ:tʃəd] Baumwiese *f*, (großer) Obstgarten *m*; ~**ing** ['-iŋ] Obstbau *m*.

orchestr|a ['ɔ:kistrə] Orchester *n*; *hist* Orchestra *f*; *(~~ pit) theat* Orchesterraum *m*; *(~~ stalls, (Am) ~~ chairs, seats) theat* Orchestersessel *m (Platz)*; *(Am: ~~ circle) theat* Parkett, Parterre *n*; ~**al** [ɔ:'kestrəl] orchestral; Orchester-; ~**ate** ['ɔ:kistreit] *tr mus* orchestrieren, instrumentieren; ~**ation** [ɔ:kes'treiʃən] Orchestrierung *f*.

orchid ['ɔ:kid] Orchidee *f*; ~**aceous** [ɔ:ki'deiʃəs] *bot* Orchideen-; *fig* prächtig, herrlich; ~ **grower** Orchideenzüchter *m*; **orchis** ['ɔ:kis] *pl -es* [-iz] Knabenkraut *n*; Orchidee *f*.

ordain [ɔ:'dein] *tr jur* an-, verordnen, verfügen, erlassen; *fig* bestimmen, festlegen; *rel* ordinieren, zum Priester weihen; ~**ing** [-iŋ] *rel* Ordination *f*.

ordeal [ɔ:'di:l] *hist* Gottesurteil *n*; *fig allg* Feuerprobe, Schicksals-, schwere Prüfung *f*, böse Erfahrungen *f pl*.

order ['ɔ:də] **1.** *s* (An-)Ordnung, (Reihen-)Folge *f*; Plan *m*, System *n*; Klasse, Gruppe; Art *f*; Stand, Rang *m*, gesellschaftliche Stellung *f*; Orden *m*, Bruderschaft *f*; Ordensabzeichen *n*; Ordnung *f*, geordnete(r) Zustand *m*, Verhältnisse *n pl*; ordentliche(s) Betragen; *mil* Kommando *n*, Befehl *m*; Anweisung, -ordnung, Verfügung *f*, Erlaß *m*; Vorschrift; Tages-, Geschäfts-, Festordnung *f*; *com* Auftrag *m*, Bestellung, Order (*for* auf); bestellte Ware; Portion *f*; Zahlungsauftrag *m*, (Geld-)Anweisung; *Br* Freikarte; *jur (vorläufige)* Verfügung *f*, Beschluß *m*; *mil (bestimmter)* Anzug *m*, Ausrüstung *f*; *arch* (Säulen-)Ordnung; *zoo bot* Ordnung; *med* Verordnung *f*; **2.** *tr* (an)ordnen, arrangieren; in Ordnung halten; befehlen, *mil* kommandieren; e-n Befehl, e-n Auftrag geben *od* erteilen (*s.o.* jdm), beauftragen, anweisen; verfügen, bestimmen; vorschreiben; in Auftrag geben, bestellen (*from* von); *rel* ordinieren; *med* verordnen; *to* ~ *about (tr)* herumkommandieren; **3.** *according to* ~ auftragsgemäß; *as per* ~ laut Bestellung; *by* ~ auf Befehl, im Auftrag (*of s.o.* jds); *com* auf Bestellung (*of* gen), laut Auftrag; *by* ~ *of the court* auf Gerichtsbeschluß; *in* ~ in Ordnung, der Reihe nach; passend, angebracht; *in* ~ *of* (geordnet) nach; *in* ~ *of size* der Größe nach geordnet; *in* ~ *to* um zu; *in* ~ *that* damit, daß; *in alphabetical* ~ in alphabetischer Ordnung, nach dem Alphabet; *in (good)* ~ in gutem Zustand; *in short* ~ *(Am)* in (aller) Eile, ohne weitere Umstände; *of the first* ~ erstklassig; *on* ~ bestellt; auf Bestellung; in Auftrag gegeben; *out of* ~ außer der Reihe *od* Ordnung; unpassend; in Unordnung; in schlechtem Zustand; nicht betriebsfähig; kaputt; *to* ~ auftragsgemäß; an Order; *under the* ~*s of (mil)* unter dem Befehl *gen*; **4.** *to be under* ~*s to* Befehl haben zu; *to call to* ~ zur Ordnung rufen; *Am (Versammlung)* eröffnen; für eröffnet erklären; *to call for* ~*s* Bestellungen einholen; *to execute an* ~ e-n Befehl, e-n Auftrag, e-e Bestellung ausführen; *to give an* ~ e-n Befehl, e-n Auftrag geben *od* erteilen *(com a.: to place an ~)*; *to keep in* ~ in Ordnung halten; *to make to* ~ auf Bestellung anfertigen; nach Maß machen; *to put in* ~ in Ordnung bringen; *to restore* ~ die Ordnung wiederherstellen; *to rise to* ~ zur Geschäftsordnung sprechen; *to take (holy)* ~*s* in den geistlichen Stand treten; ~*!* ~*!* zur Ordnung! ~ *arms!* Gewehr — ab! *you are out of* ~ Sie haben nicht das Wort! *I'm just following* ~*s* ich halte mich nur an die Anordnungen; **5.** *buying, purchasing* ~ Kaufauftrag *m*; *confirmation of an* ~ Auftragsbestätigung *f*; *counter-*~ Gegenbefehl *m*; Abbestellung *f*; *delivery* ~ Lieferschein *m*; *a large, tall* ~ *(fig)* keine leichte Sache; *law and* ~ öffentliche Ordnung *f*; *monastic* ~ Mönchsorden *m*; *money* ~ Zahlungsanweisung; Geldüberweisung *f*; *payable to* ~ zahlbar an Order; *peace and* ~ Ruhe u. Ordnung *f*; *postal* ~ Postanweisung *f*; *religious* ~ geistliche(r) Orden *m*; *rule of the* ~ *(rel)* Ordensregel *f*; *standing* ~ Geschäftsordnung *f*; *com* Dauerauftrag *m*; ~ *to arrest* Haftbefehl *m*; ~ *of battle* Schlachtordnung, Kampfgliederung *f*; ~ *of the court* Gerichtsbeschluß *m*; ~ *of the day* Tagesordnung *f*, -befehl *m*; *the O*~ *of the Garter* der Hosenbandorden; *the O*~ *of the Purple Heart* das (amerik.) Verwundetenabzeichen; ~ *of knighthood* Ritterorden *m*; ~ *to pay* Zahlungsbefehl *m*; ~ *of precedence* Rangordnung *f*; ~ *of, to release* Freilassungsbefehl *m*; ~ *to sell* Verkaufsauftrag *m*; ~-**bill** *com* Orderpapier *n*; ~ **blank, form** Auftragsformular *n*, Bestellschein, -zettel *m*; ~ **book** Auftragsbuch *n*; ~ **department** Auftragsabteilung *f*; ~**ed** ['-d] *a* bestellt; *as* ~~ laut Bestellung; *to be* ~~ *to pay costs* zu den Kosten verurteilt werden; ~**ing** ['-riŋ] Ordnen *n*, Regelung *f*; ~**less** ['-lis] ungeordnet, in Unordnung, unordentlich; ~**liness** ['-linis] (gute) Ordnung; Ordentlichkeit; Regelmäßigkeit; Disziplin *f*; ~**ly** ['-li] *a* ordentlich, geordnet, systematisch, regelrecht, -mäßig, sauber; gesetzlich, gesittet, friedlich, ruhig; *mil* Dienst-, Ordonnanz-; diensttuend; *s* Ordonnanz *f*; (Offiziers-)Bursche; Melder; *(hospital ~~)* (Kranken-)Wärter *m*; *street* ~~ Straßenkehrer *m*; ~~ *book* Dienstbuch *n*; ~~ *corporal* Unteroffizier *m* vom Dienst (U.v.D.); ~~ *officer* Offizier *m* vom Dienst (O.v.D.); Ordonnanzoffizier *m*; ~~ *room (mil)* Geschäftszimmer *n*, Schreibstube *f*; ~ **number** Bestell-, Auftragsnummer *f*; ~ **paper** Tagesordnung *f*; *Am* Orderpapier *n*; ~ **sheet** Bestellschein, -zettel *m*.

*

ordin|al ['ɔ:dinl] *a* Ordnungs-; *s (~~ number) gram* Ordnungszahl *f*; ~**ance** ['ɔ:dinəns] Anordnung, -weisung, Vorschrift; *Am* Verordnung *(e-r städtischen Behörde)*; Regel *f*, Brauch *m*, Sitte *f*; *rel* Ritus *m*, *bes.* Kommunion, Abendmahlsfeier *f*; ~**ary** ['ɔ:dnri] *a* gebräuchlich, üblich, alltäglich; regulär, normal, gewöhnlich; einfach, schlicht; vertraut; *s* ordentliche(r) Richter *od* Geistliche(r); Anstaltsgeistliche(r) *m*; *rel* Ordinarium; *Br* Tagesgericht; *Am* Wirtshaus; gewöhnliche(s) Leben *n*, Lauf *m* der Dinge; *hist* Hochrad *n*; *in* ~~ *(bei e-r Berufsbezeichnung)* ordentlich, aktiv; Leib-*(Arzt)*, Hof-*(Lieferant)*; *in the* ~~ *way* unter gewöhnlichen, normalen Umständen; *out of the* ~~ außerordentlich, außer-, ungewöhnlich, selten, Ausnahme-; *not out of the* ~~ nicht aus dem Rahmen fallend; ~~ *bill* Handelswechsel *m*; ~~ *court* ordentliche(s) Gericht *n*; ~~ *debt* Massenschuld *f*; *pl* Buchschulden *f pl*; ~~ *face* Alltagsgesicht *n*; ~~ *reader* Durchschnittsleser *m*; ~~ *seaman* Leichtmatrose *m*; ~~ *shares (pl) stock* Stammaktien *f pl*; ~**ate** ['ɔ:dnit] *math* Ordinate *f*; ~**ation** [ɔ:di'neiʃən] *rel* Priesterweihe *f*.

ordnance ['ɔ:dnəns] *s* Artillerie *f*, Geschützwesen *n*, Geschütze *n pl*; Waffen u. Geräte, Waffen u. Munition; *attr* Geschütz-, Waffen- u. Munitions-; *piece of* ~ Geschütz *n*; ~ **department** Waffenamt *n*, Feldzeugmeisterei *f*; ~ **depot** Artillerie-, Geschützdepot *n*; ~ **(field-)park** Gerätepark *m*; ~ **piece** Geschütz *n*; ~ **survey** Landesaufnahme *f*; Vermessungstrupp *m*; ~**(-survey) map** *Br* Generalstabskarte *f*, Meßtischblatt *n*; ~ **workshop company** Waffenausbesserungskompanie *f*; ~ **yard** Artillerieschießplatz *m*.

ordure ['ɔ:djuə] Schmutz, Kot; Dung *m*; *fig* schmutzige Rede *f*.

ore [ɔ:] *min* Erz *n*; ~**-bearing** erzhaltig; ~ **dressing** Erzaufbereitung *f*.

organ ['ɔ:gən] *biol* Organ *a. fig*; *fig* Werkzeug, Mittel *n*; Orgel; Stimm(stärk)e *f*; **~-builder** Orgelbauer *m*; **~-grinder** Leierkastenmann *m*; **~ic** [ɔ:'gænik] *physiol med chem fig* organisch; *mil* verbands-, einheitseigen; *~~ chemistry* organische Chemie *f*; *~~ disease* organische(s) Leiden *n*; *~~ law* Grundgesetz *n*, Verfassung *f*; *an ~~ unity* e-e organische Einheit; **~ism** ['ɔ:gənizm] *biol fig* Organismus *m*; *fig* Organisation *f*, Gefüge *n*; **~ist** ['-ist] *mus* Organist *m*; **~ization** [ɔ:gənai'zeiʃən] Organisation *f*; (Auf-)Bau *m*, Struktur, Bildung, Gliederung, Gestalt(ung); Gründung, Einrichtung *f*; *mil* Stellungsausbau *m*; Organisation, Gesellschaft, Vereinigung *f*, Verein, Verband *m*; Parteiorganisation, -leitung *f*, Funktionäre *m pl*; Dienststelle *f*; *charity ~~* Hilfswerk *n*; *marketing ~~* Absatzorganisation *f*; *youth ~~* Jugendorganisation *f*; *~~ chart* Organisationsplan *m*; **~ize** ['ɔ:gənaiz] *tr* organisieren, einrichten, aufbauen, gestalten, gliedern; ins Leben rufen, gründen; *(Arbeit)* einteilen; *Am (Arbeiter gewerkschaftlich)* organisieren; *itr* sich aufbauen, sich gliedern; *~~d labor (Am)* organisierte Arbeiterschaft *f*; **~izer** ['-aizə] Organisator; Gründer *m*; **~-loft** Orgelbühne *f*; **~-pipe** Orgelpfeife *f*; **~ recital** Orgelkonzert *n*; **~ stop** Orgelregister *n*.

organdie, organdy ['ɔgəndi] Organdy *m*.

orgasm ['ɔ:gæzm] *physiol* Orgasmus; *fig* Höhepunkt *m*.

org|iastic [ɔ:dʒi'æstik] orgiastisch; **~y** ['ɔ:dʒi] Orgie; Ausschweifung *f*.

oriel ['ɔ:riəl] Erker(fenster *n*) *m*.

*

orient ['ɔ:riənt] *s geog* Orient *m*; *obs poet* Morgenland *n*; *poet* Ost(en) *m (Himmelsrichtung)*; *a poet* östlich; *poet (Gestirn)* aufgehend; strahlend, glänzend; *v* ['ɔ:rient] *tr* orientieren *a. fig*, ausrichten (*to* nach); in Beziehung setzen; *(Karte)* einnorden; **~al** [ɔ:ri'entl] *a* östlich; *(O~~)* orientalisch, *obs* morgenländisch; *s* Orientale *m*, Orientalin *f*; *~~ carpet, rug* Orientteppich *m*; **~alist** [-'entəlist] Orientalist *m*; **~ate** ['ɔ:rienteit] *tr* orientieren *a. fig*; *itr* orientiert sein; sich anpassen; *to ~~ o.s. (fig)* sich orientieren; **~ation** [ɔ:rien'teiʃən] Orientierung *a. fig*; *fig* Informierung, Einweisung; Ortung; Anpassung *f*; Ortssinn *m*, Orientierungsgabe *f*; *(Karte)* Einnorden *n*; *~~ course* Schulungskurs *m*.

orifice ['ɔrifis] Öffnung, Mündung *f*.

origin ['ɔridʒin] *s* Ursprung, Anfang, Beginn *m*; Herkunft, Abstammung, Geburt; Quelle *f*; *tech* Nullpunkt *m*; *country of ~* Herkunftsland *n*; *place of ~* Herkunfts-, Aufgabe-, Geburtsort *m*; *proof of ~* Herkunftsnachweis *m*; **~al** [ə'ridʒənl] *a* ursprünglich, anfänglich; Anfangs-, Ausgangs-; Ur-; Original-; original; originell; selbständig, erfinderisch; *s* Ausgangsform *f*; *(Kunst, lit)* Original *n*; Erstausfertigung, Urschrift *f*, Urtext *m*; *(Kunst)* Modell *n*, Vorlage *f*; Original *n*, (komischer) Kauz *m*; *in the ~~* urschriftlich; *~~ capital* Anfangs-, Grundkapital *n*; *~~ cost* Anschaffungskosten *pl*; *~~ edition (Buch)* Originalausgabe *f*; *~~ firm* Stammhaus *n*; *~~ language* Ursprache *f*; *~~ price* Selbstkostenpreis *m*; *~~ share* Stammaktie *f*; *~~ sin* Erbsünde *f*; *~~ version* Urfassung *f*; **~ality** [əridʒi'næliti] Ursprünglichkeit; Selbständigkeit; Originalität; Echtheit *f*; **~ally** [ə'ridʒnəli] *adv* ursprünglich, anfänglich; hauptsächlich, in erster Linie; auf neue Weise; **~ate** [ə'ridʒineit] *tr* hervorbringen, erzeugen, (er)schaffen, ins Leben rufen; verursachen; begründen; erfinden; *itr* entstehen, entspringen (*from, in* aus; *with, from s.o.* bei, durch jdn); ins Leben treten, s-n Ausgang nehmen, anfangen, beginnen; **~ation** [əridʒi'neiʃən] Erzeugung, (Er-)Schaffung; Erfindung; Entstehung *f*, Ursprung, Beginn, Anfang *m*; **~ative** [ə'ridʒineitiv] schöpferisch; erfinderisch; **~ator** [ə'ridʒineitə] Erzeuger, Erschaffer, Urheber, Erfinder; Schöpfer, Begründer; Schreiber, Absender; Ausgangspunkt *m*, Motiv *n*; *~~'s number* Referenznummer *f*.

oriole ['ɔ:rioul] Pirol *m*.

ormolu ['ɔ:məlu:] Goldbronze *f*; unechte(s) Blattgold *n*.

ornament ['ɔ:nəmənt] *s* Schmuck *m*, Zier(de) (*to* für); Verzierung *f*, Dekor(ation *f*) *m* u. *n*; Zier-, Dekorationsstück *n*; *fig* Zierde *(Mensch)*; Ausschmückung, Verzierung *a. mus*, Verschönerung; Staffage *f*, äußere(r) Prunk *m*; *pl* kirchliche Geräte u. Kleidungsstücke *n pl*; *tr* ['-ent] ausschmücken, verzieren, dekorieren, verschönern; **~al** [ɔ:nə'mentl] ausschmückend, verschönernd, dekorativ; Schmuck-, Zier-; *~~ lantern* Schmuckleuchte *f*; *~~ painter* Dekorationsmaler *m*; *~~ shrub* Zierstrauch *m*; *~~ type* Zierschrift *f*; **~ation** [-men'teiʃən] Ausschmückung, Verschönerung *f*; Dekor(ation *f*), *m* u. *n* Schmuck *m*.

ornate [ɔ:'neit] *a* (mit Schmuck, Verzierungen) überladen *a. fig*; *(Stil)* geziert, gekünstelt.

ornitholog|ical [ɔ:niθə'lɔdʒikl] ornithologisch; **~ist** [ɔ:ni'θɔlədʒist] Ornithologe *m*; **~y** [-'θɔlədʒi] Ornithologie, Vogelkunde *f*.

oro|graphy [ɔ'rɔgrəfi] Orographie, Beschreibung *f* der Gebirgsformen; **~logy** [ɔ'rɔlədʒi] Gebirgskunde *f*.

orotund ['ɔro(u)tʌnd] *(Stimme)* (klang-)voll, kräftig, hell; *(Stil)* schwülstig, pomphaft, überladen.

orphan ['ɔ:fən] *s* Waise *f*; *a* verwaist *a. fig*; Waisen-; *tr* zu e-r Waise machen, der Eltern berauben; **~age** ['-idʒ] Verwaistheit *f*, -sein *n*; Waisen *f pl*; *(~-asylum, -home)* Waisenhaus *n*; **~-boy** Waisenknabe *m*; **~-child** Waisenkind *n*; **~ed** ['-d] *a* verwaist.

orrery ['ɔrəri] Planetarium *n*.

orris, *Am a.* orrice ['ɔris] **1.** Schwert-, *bes.* Himmelslilie; *(~root)* Gilgenwurzel *f*; **2.** Goldborte *f*.

ortho|- [ɔ:θə, 'ɔ:θə, 'ɔ:θo(u)] *in Zssgen* Recht-; **~chromatic** ['ɔ:θo(u)kro(u)'mætik] *photo* orthochromatisch; **~dox** ['ɔ:θədɔks] recht-, strenggläubig, orthodox; *the O~~ (Eastern) Church* die (Griechisch-)Orthodoxe Kirche *f*; **~doxy** ['-dɔksi] Recht-, Strenggläubigkeit, Orthodoxie *f*; **~graphic(al)** [ɔ:θə'græfik(əl)] orthographisch, Rechtschreib-; **~graphy** [ɔ:'θɔgrəfi] Rechtschreibung, Orthographie *f*; **~p(a)edic** [ɔ:θo(u)'pi:dik] *a* orthopädisch; *s pl* u. **~p(a)edy** ['ɔ:θo(u)pi:di] Orthopädie *f*; **~p(a)edist** [ɔ:θo(u)'pi:dist] Orthopäde *m*.

ortolan ['ɔ:tələn] *orn* Garten-, Fettammer *f*, Ortolan *m*.

Oscar ['ɔskə] Oskar; *Am sl* Zaster *m*.

oscill|ate ['ɔsileit] *itr* schwingen *a. el*; unentschieden, unentschlossen sein, schwanken; pendeln; **~ating** ['-eitiŋ] schwingend; Schwing-; *~~ circuit, period* Schwingkreis, -ungsdauer *f*; **~ation** [ɔsi'leiʃən] Schwingung *a. phys el*; Pendelbewegung *f*; Schwankungen *f pl*, Ungleichmäßigkeit *f*; *natural ~~* Eigenschwingung *f*; **~ator** ['ɔsileitə] *radio* Oszillator *m*; *~~ tube* Senderöhre *f*; **~atory** ['ɔsilətəri] schwingend; periodisch; **~ograph** [ɔ'siləgrɑ:f] *el* Oszillograph *m*; **~oscope** [ɔ'siləskoup] Braunsche Röhre *f*, Bildschirm *m*.

oscul|ant ['ɔskjulənt] sich berührend; *biol* Zwischen-, gemeinsam; *zoo* verwandt; **~ate** ['-eit] *tr itr* (sich) küssen; (sich) berühren; *math* (sich) schmiegen; *tr biol (Merkmale)* gemeinsam haben (*with* mit); **~ation** [ɔskju'leiʃən] *hum* Küssen *n*; Kuß *m*; enge Berührung *f*; *math* Schmiegungspunkt *m*.

osier ['ouʒə] Korbweide *f*; **~-bottle** Korbflasche *f*; **~-furniture** Korbmöbel *n pl*; **~-work** Korbwaren *f pl*.

osmo|sis [ɔz'mousis] *phys biol* Osmose *f*; **~tic** [ɔz'mɔtik] osmotisch.

osprey ['ɔspri] Fisch-, Flußadler *m*; Reiherfedern *f pl*.

oss|eous ['ɔsiəs] knöchern; Knochen-; knochig; *~~ system* Knochensystem *n*; **~icle** ['ɔsikl] Knöchelchen *n*; *auditory ~~ (anat)* Gehörknöchelchen *n*; **~ification** [ɔsifi'keiʃən] Verknöcherung *f*; **~ify** ['ɔsifai] *tr itr* verknöchern *a. fig*; verhärten (*into* zu); *itr fig* sich fixieren, sich einfressen, erstarren (*into* zu); **~uary** ['ɔsjuəri] Knochenurne *f*; Beinhaus *n*.

osten|sible [ɔs'tensəbl] vor-, angeblich, vorgetäuscht, scheinbar; **~tation** [ɔsten'teiʃən] Zurschautragen, Gepränge *n*, Prunk *m*; Protzen *n*; **~tatious** [-'teiʃəs] prahlerisch, prunkend, protzig, *fam* angeberisch.

osteo|logy [ɔsti'ɔlədʒi] Osteologie, Knochenlehre *f*; **~plasty** ['ɔstiəplæsti] Osteoplastik *f*, Knochenersatz *m*; **~tomy** [ɔsti'ɔtəmi] Osteotomie, Knochenresektion *f*.

ostler ['ɔslə] Stall-, Pferdeknecht *m*.

ostrac|ism ['ɔstrəsizm] *hist* Ostrazismus *m*, Scherbengericht *n*; *allg* (soziale) Ächtung *f*; **~ize** ['-aiz] *tr* verbannen; *fig* ächten.

ostrich ['ɔstritʃ] *orn* Strauß *m*; *to bury o.'s head ~-like in the sand (fig)* den Kopf in den Sand stecken; *to have the digestion of an ~* e-n guten Magen haben; **~ feather** Straußenfeder *f*.

*

other ['ʌðə] *a prn* ander; andersartig; weiter, zusätzlich; *s*: *the ~* der, die, das andere; *adv* anders, auf andere Weise; *among ~s* unter anderen; *among ~ things* unter anderem; *each ~, one another* einander, sich (gegenseitig); *every ~ day* einen Tag um den andern; jeden zweiten Tag; *none ~ than* kein anderer als; *of all ~s* von allen; *on the ~ hand* ander(er)seits; *one after the ~* e-r nach dem andern; *one from the ~* voneinander; *somehow or ~* irgendwie; *someone or ~* der eine oder andere; *some time, day or ~* (irgendwann) einmal, e-s (schönen) Tages; *some way or ~* auf irgendeine Weise; *the ~ day* neulich; *~ than* anders als; *~ things being equal* unter gleichen Umständen; *the ~ side of the coin (fig)* die Kehrseite *f* der Medaille; *the ~ world* das Jenseits; **~ness** ['-nis] Andersartigkeit, Verschiedenheit *f*; **~wise** ['-waiz] *adv* auf andere Weise; in anderer Hinsicht, sonst; im übrigen; unter andern Umständen; *a pred* anders; **~worldly** ['-'wə:ldli] *adv* aufs Jenseits gerichtet; weltfremd.

ot|ic ['outik, 'ɔtik] *a* Ohren-, Gehör-; **~itis** [o(u)'taitis] Ohrenentzündung *f*; *~~ media* [-'mediə] Mittelohrentzündung *f*; **~ologist** [o(u)'tɔlədʒist] Ohrenarzt *m*; **~ology** [o(u)'tɔlədʒi] Ohrenheilkunde *f*; **~o-rhino-laryngologist** ['outo(u)-'raino(u)læriŋ'gɔlədʒist] Facharzt *m* für Hals-, Nasen- u. Ohrenkrankheiten; **~o-rhino-laryngology** Hals-, Nasen- u. Ohrenheilkunde *f*; **~scope** ['outəskoup] *med* Ohrenspiegel *m*.

otiose ['ouʃious] müßig, unwirksam, unfruchtbar; unnütz, überflüssig.

otter ['ɔtə] *zoo* (Fisch-)Otter *(Marderart)*; Otterpelz *m*.

Ottoman ['ɔtəmən] *a* osmanisch, türkisch; *s* Osmane, (osmanischer) Türke *m*; *o~* Liegesofa *n*, Couch *f*.

ouch [autʃ] *interj* au! autsch!

ought [ɔ:t] **1.** *aux itr, nur pret* sollte, müßte; *you ~ to do it* du solltest es tun; *you ~ to have done it* du hättest es tun sollen; **2.** *s fam* Null *f*; **3.** *s aught*.

ounce [auns] **1.** Unze *f* *(Gewicht,* $= {}^{1}/_{16}$ *engl. Pfund* od *28,35 g)*; *ein* bißchen, etwas; *by the ~* dem Gewicht nach; **2.** *zoo* Luchs; Schneeleopard *m*.

our ['auə] *prn* unser(e); **~s** ['-z] der, die, das unsrige, uns(e)re; *pl* die unsrigen, uns(e)re; *that is ~~* das gehört uns; *a friend of ~~* ein Freund von uns; e-r unserer Freunde; **~selves** [-'selvz] *refl* uns (selbst); *(verstärkend) (wir ...)* selbst; *between, (all) by ~~* (ganz) unter uns, allein.

oust [aust] *tr* ver-, austreiben, hinauswerfen, verdrängen *(from* aus); enteignen; *(~ from office)* s-s Amtes entheben; *to ~ jurisdiction* den Rechtsweg ausschließen; **~er** ['-ə] *jur* Besitzstörung, (unrechtmäßige) Enteignung; Entfernung aus dem Amt; Amtsenthebung *f*.

*

out [aut] **1.** *adv* her-, hinaus, nach draußen; (von zu Haus) weg; draußen; aus dem Hause, nicht zu Hause, nicht daheim; außer Haus *(schlafen)*; in die Gesellschaft eingeführt; *(Buch)* erschienen; (bis) zu Ende, aus; *(Feuer, Licht)* aus; *(Gerät)* abgestellt; nicht in Tätigkeit, nicht bei der Arbeit, im Streik; nicht (mehr) im Amt, nicht (mehr) an der Regierung, entlassen; *(Buch)* verliehen; aus der Übung, aus der Mode, unmodern, veraltet; verschoben, verrutscht; im Irrtum; heraus, ans Licht (gekommen); *mit Verben*: aus, her-, hinaus-; *all ~ (fam mot)* mit Vollgas; *~ and about (nach e-r Krankheit)* wieder auf (dem Posten); *~ and away* bei weitem; *~ and ~ (adv)* durch u. durch, voll u. ganz, ganz u. gar; *~ from under (fam)* über den Berg *fig*; *to be ~* nicht zu Hause, ausgegangen sein; nicht mehr im Amt *od* am Ruder sein; aus der Mode sein; auf See, im Felde sein; zu Ende sein; streiken; *to be ~ after s.o.* hinter jdm her sein; *to be ~ at elbows* die Ärmel an den Ellbogen durchgestoßen haben; *fig* in schlechten Verhältnissen leben; *to be ~ for* aus sein auf, es abgesehen haben auf; *to be ~ of work* arbeitslos sein; *to break ~* ausbrechen; *to come ~* gesellschafts-, ballfähig werden; *to fill ~* ausfüllen; *to find ~* ausfindig machen; erfahren; *s.o.* jdn durchschauen; *to give ~* austeilen; zu Ende gehen; *to have it ~ with s.o.* sich mit jdm gründlich ausea.setzen; *to look ~* achtgeben, aufpassen; *(Fenster)* hinausgehen *(on* auf); *to read, speak ~* laut u. deutlich lesen, sprechen; *to stand ~* hervorragen; *to wash ~ (Fleck)* sich auswaschen; *to wear ~ (Kleidungsstück)* auftragen; *this isn't ~ of your way* das ist kein Umweg für Sie; *that's ~ of the question* das kommt nicht in Frage; **2.** *prp (meist: ~ of)* aus (... heraus); außer *dat*, nicht in, außerhalb *gen*; aus *(e-m Material)*, von; *(Grund)* aus, vor; *~ of bounds* verboten *(to* für); *~ of breath* außer Atem; *~ of curiosity* aus Neugierde; *~ of date* veraltet; *~ of doors* vor der, die Tür; im Freien; *~ of doubt* außer Zweifel, zweifellos; *~ of drawing* verzeichnet; *~ of fear* vor Angst; *~ of gold* aus Gold; *~-of-hand* sofort(ig); *~ of hearing* außer Hör-, Rufweite; *~ of it* nicht dabei; im Irrtum; *~ of joint* aus den Fugen; *~ of mind* nicht bei Verstand; *~ of money* nicht bei Kasse; *~ of number* ohne Zahl, zahllos, ungezählt; *~ of print (Buch)* vergriffen; *~ of sight* außer Sicht; *~ of step* nicht im Schritt; *~ of temper* aus der Fassung; *~ of town* auswärts, außerhalb; *~ of tune* verstimmt; *~ of the way* aus dem Wege; *~ of wedlock* unehelich; *~ of work* ohne Arbeit, arbeitslos; **3.** Außenstehende(r); Entlassene(r), *fam* Ausgebootete(r) *m*; ausgegebene Summe *f*; *sport* Aus *n*; Auslassung, *typ* Leiche; *fam* Ausrede, -flucht; *pl parl* Opposition *f*; *the ins and the ~s* die Regierung u. d. Opposition; alle Einzelheiten *f pl*; **4.** *itr* herauskommen, bekanntwerden; *tr fam* 'rauswerfen, an die Luft setzen; *(Boxen)* k.o. schlagen; besiegen; umbringen; **5.** *interj* hinaus *(with* mit)! **~-and-~** *a* völlig, vollständig, vollkommen; durch u. durch, ausgemacht; **~-and-~er** *sl* Pracht-, Pfundskerl *m*; Pfunds-, ganz große Sache *f*, tolle(s) Ding *n*; **~-of-date** *a* veraltet; unmodern, altmodisch; **~-of-door** *a* Außen-, Freiluft-, Freilicht-; **~-of-doors** *a* = *~-of-door*; *adv s* = *out-doors*; **~-of-fashion** altmodisch; **~-of-pocket**: *~~ expenses (pl)* Barauslagen *f pl*; **~-of-school** außerschulisch; **~-of-the-way** *a* abgelegen, einsam; ausgefallen, ungewöhnlich; abseitig; *(Preis)* übertrieben hoch; **~-of-work** *a* Arbeits-, Erwerbslosen-; *s* Arbeitslose(r) *m*.

out|age ['autidʒ] Aussetzen *n*, Unterbrechung, Pause *f*; **~balance** [-'bæləns] *tr* übertreffen, -steigen; **~bid** [-'bid] *irr (s. bid) tr* überbieten; **~bidder** [-'bidə] Mehrbietende(r) *m*; **~bidding** [-'bidiŋ] Mehrgebot; höhere(s) Gebot *n*; **~board** ['-bɔ:d] *a* Außenbord-; *~~ motor* Außenbordmotor *m*; **~bound** ['-baund] *a* für das Ausland bestimmt; ins A. fahrend; auf der Ausreise (begriffen); *aero* im Abflug; **~brave** [-'breiv] *tr* an Mut übertreffen, mutiger sein als; herausfordern, trotzen *(s.o.* jdm); **~break** ['-breik] Ausbruch *m (e-r Krankheit, e-s Aufstandes)*; *~~ of war* Kriegsausbruch *m*; **~breeding** ['-bri:diŋ] Exogamie, Heirat *f* außerhalb des Stammes; **~building** ['-bildiŋ] Nebengebäude *n*; **~burst** ['-bə:st] Ausbruch *m a. fig*; *an ~~ of anger* ein Zornausbruch *m*; **~cast** ['-kɑ:st] *s* Ausgestoßene(r); Auswurf *m*; *a* ausgestoßen, verbannt; *tr irr s. cast* ausstoßen, verbannen; **~caste** ['-kɑ:st] Kastenlose(r), Paria *m (in Indien)*; **~class** [-'klɑ:s] *tr* weit hinter sich lassen, weit übertreffen; **~come** ['-kʌm] Ausgang *m*, Ergebnis *n*, Folge *f*; **~crop** ['-krɔp] *s geol* Zutageliegende(s) *n*; *itr* [-'-] zutage liegen; *fig* hervortreten; **~cry** ['-krai] Aufschrei; *fig* Schrei *m* der Entrüstung.

out|dare [aut'dɛə] *tr* trotzen, Trotz bieten *(s.o.* jdm), herausfordern; mutiger sein als; **~dated** [-'deitid] *a* veraltet, überholt; unmodern, altmodisch; **~distance** [-'distəns] *tr sport allg* (weit) hinter sich lassen, überholen, *fam* abhängen; **~do** [-'du:] *irr s. do tr* übertreffen *(in* in), überbieten, ausstechen; *to ~~ o.s.* sich selbst übertreffen; alle Kräfte zs.nehmen; **~door** ['-dɔ:] *a* draußen, im Freien (befindlich); Straßen-; Freiluft-, Freilicht-; Außen-; *to lead an ~ life* viel im Freien, an der frischen Luft sein; *~~ advertising* Plakatwerbung, Straßenreklame *f*; *~~ relief* Fürsorgeunterstützung *f*; *~~ scenes (pl)* Außenaufnahmen *f pl*; **~doors** ['-'-z] *adv* draußen, im Freien, an der frischen Luft.

outer ['autə] *a* äußer; Außen-; *s* (Schuß auf den) Rand *m* (e-r Schießscheibe); *the ~ man* der äußere Mensch, die äußere Erscheinung; *the ~ regions (pl)* die Außenbezirke *m pl*; *the ~ world* die Außenwelt; **~ear** Ohrmuschel *f*; **~most** ['-moust] *a* äußerst; *adv* am weitesten weg; **~ skin** Außenhaut, Epidermis *f*; **~ wall** Außenwand *f*; **~wear** Überkleidung *f*.

out|face [aut'feis] *tr* mit e-m vernichtenden Blick messen; mit e-m Blick einschüchtern, aus der Fassung bringen; herausfordern, trotzen *(s.o.* jdm); **~fall** ['-fɔ:l] Ausfluß, Abfluß(röhre *f*, -kanal) *m*; Mündung *f*; **~field** ['-fi:ld] *sport* Außenfeld *n*; **~fit** ['-fit] *s* Einrichtung; Ausstattung, Ausrüstung *f*; *tech* Satz *m*; *Am* Arbeitsgruppe, Rotte, Mannschaft; Gesellschaft; *Am mil* Einheit *f*, Truppenteil *m*; *tr* ausstatten, ausrüsten, *fam* ausstaffieren *(with* mit); *a* ausgestattet, ausgerüstet; *bridal ~~* Aussteuer *f*; *camping ~~* Campingausrüstung *f*; *spring ~~* Frühlingsgarderobe *f*; **~fitter** ['-ə] (Herren-) Ausstatter; Lieferant *m*; *gentleman's ~~* Inhaber *m* e-s Herrenartikelgeschäftes; **~flank** [-'flæŋk] *tr mil* umfassen, überflügeln; *fig* umgarnen, überlisten; *~~ing movement (mil)* Umfassungsbewegung *f*; **~flow** ['-flou] Ausfluß; Ausstoß *m*.

out|general [aut'dʒenərəl] *tr* taktisch übertreffen; **~go** ['-gou] *s pl -es* Ausgang *m*; Ausgaben *f pl*; **~going** ['-gouiŋ] *a* aus-, weggehend; *(Post)* auslaufend; *(Beamter)* scheidend; *rail* abfahrend; gesellig; mitteilsam; *s* Aus-, Weggehen *n*; *pl* Ausgaben *f pl*; **~grow** [-'grou] *irr s. grow tr* schneller wachsen als, herauswachsen aus, entwachsen *(s.th.* e-r S) *a. fig*; *fig* ablegen; *to ~ o.'s strength* zu schnell wachsen; in die Höhe schießen; **~growth** ['-grouθ] Auswuchs *m*; Entwicklung *f*; Ergebnis, Resultat *n*, Folge *f*; **~guard** ['-gɑ:d] *mil* vorgeschobene(r) Posten *m*, Feldwache *f*; **~house** ['-haus] Nebengebäude *n*; *Am* Toilette *f* außer dem Haus; **~ing** ['-iŋ] *s* Ausflug; Spaziergang *m*; *a* Ausflugs-; *to go for an ~~* e-n Ausflug machen.

out|landish [aut'lændiʃ] fremdartig; eigenartig, sonderbar, merkwürdig, wunderlich; **~last** [-'lɑ:st] *itr* überdauern, überleben; **~law** ['-lɔ:] *s* Geächtete(r), Vogelfreie(r); Gewohnheitsverbrecher; Räuber *m*; *tr* ächten; für ungesetzlich, ungültig erklären; **~lawry** ['-lɔ:ri] Ächtung *f*; Geächtetsein; asoziale(s) Verhalten *n*; **~lay** ['-lei] *s* (Geld-)Ausgabe, Auslage *f*; Aufwand *m*; *capital, initial ~~* Anschaffungskosten *pl*; **~let** ['-let] Abfluß; Auslaß, -gang, -fluß, -zug *m*;

Öffnung *f*; *tech* Abzug *m*; *fig* Ventil, Ausdrucksmittel *n* (*for* für); *com* Absatzmarkt *m*, -gebiet *n*; Verkaufsstelle *f*; Abnehmer *m*; *el* Stromentnahmestelle, Steckdose *f*; *el* Verbraucher *m*; *Am radio* Sendestelle *f*; *to find an* ~~ sich Luft machen; sich austoben; ~~ *gutter* Ablaufrinne *f*; ~~ *pipe* Abflußrohr *n*; ~~ *valve* Ablaßventil *n*; **~lier** ['-laiə] Pendler; Außenstehende(r), -seiter *m*; **~line** ['-lain] *s* Umriß *m*, Kontur; Umrißzeichnung *f*; ungefähre(r) Plan *m*, Disposition; Zs.fassung, Übersicht *f*, -blick *m* (*of* über); Andeutung, Skizze *f*, Abriß *m*; *fig* Hauptzüge *m pl*; Sigel *n*; *tr* im Profil darstellen; in Umrißlinien zeichnen; *fig* umreißen, skizzieren; kurz zs.fassen, e-n Überblick geben über, in großen Zügen darstellen; *in* ~ im Umriß; *broad* ~~*s* Grundzüge *m pl*; ~~ *drawing* Umrißzeichnung *f*; ~~ *map* Umrißkarte *f* (*of* von); **~lined** ['-laind] *a* scharf umrissen, klar, deutlich; *to be* ~~ *against s.th.* sich gegen etw abheben; **~live** [-'liv] *tr* überleben, -dauern; **~look** ['-luk] Ausguck; Ausblick *m*, -sicht; Ausschau; *fig* Ansicht, Auffassung *f*, Standpunkt *m*, Anschauung; *fig* Aussicht, Erwartung *f*; *on the* ~~ auf der Suche (*for* nach); **~lying** ['-laiiŋ] *a* (weiter) abliegend, entfernt, abgelegen, entlegen; Außen-.

out|manoeuvre *Am meist* **outmaneuver** [autmə'nu:və] *tr mil* ausmanövrieren; *fig* überlisten; **~march** [-'mɑ:tʃ] *tr* (im Marschieren) überholen; **~match** [-'mætʃ] *tr* übertreffen, überlegen sein (*s.o.* jdm); **~moded** [-'moudid] *a* unmodern, aus der Mode, veraltet; **~most** ['-moust] *a* äußerst *a. fig*; **~number** [-'nʌmbə] *tr* an Zahl übertreffen, mehr sein als, zahlenmäßig überlegen sein (*s.o.* jdm).

out|pace [aut'peis] *tr* schneller gehen als, überholen; **~patient** ['-peiʃənt] Kranke(r) *m* in ambulanter Behandlung; ~~ *clinic* Poliklinik *f*; **~play** [-'plei] *tr* besser spielen als, schlagen; *fam* beherrschen; **~point** [-'pɔint] *tr sport* nach Punkten schlagen; **~post** ['autpoust] *mil* Vorposten *m a. fig*; ~~ *area (mil)* Vorfeld *n*; ~~ *engagement* Vorpostengefecht *n*; **~pouring** ['-pɔ:riŋ] Erguß *m bes. fig*; **~put** ['-put] Ausstoß, Ertrag *m*, Leistung; (Jahres-)Produktion *f*, Ausstoß *m*, Erzeugung; Ausbeute, Ausbringung; Produktionsmenge, -ziffer; *min* Förderung; *tech* Leistung; *radio* Sendeleistung *f*; *annual* ~~ Jahresertrag *m*, -produktion *f*; *capacity of* ~~ Produktionskraft, Leistungsfähigkeit *f*; *daily* ~~ Tagesproduktion *f*; *effective* ~~ Nutzleistung *f*; *maximum* ~~ Produktionsoptimum *n*; *world* ~~ Weltproduktion *f*; ~~ *boost* Leistungssteigerung *f*; ~~ *cost* Produktionskosten *pl*; ~~ *figure* Produktionsziffer *f*; ~~ *power (tech)* Nutzleistung *f*; ~~ *stage* Endstufe *f*; ~~ *target* Produktionsziel *n*; ~~ *valve (radio)* Endverstärkerröhre *f*; ~~ *voltage (el)* Ausgangsspannung *f*.

outrage ['autreidʒ, -ridʒ] *s* Greuel-, Gewalttat (*on* an); schwere Beleidigung, Beschimpfung, Herausforderung; Unverschämtheit *f*; (schwerer) Rechtsbruch *m*, (schwere) sittliche Verfehlung, schwere Ausschreitung *f*; Verbrechen *n* (*on* gegen); *tr* e-e Gewalttat begehen an; Gewalt antun (*s.o.* jdm), sich schwer vergehen gegen; vergewaltigen; gröblich beleidigen, beschimpfen, herausfordern; *(Recht, Gesetz)* brechen; *act of* ~ Gewalttat *f*; **~ous** [aut'reidʒəs] greulich, gräßlich, abscheulich; unverschämt, schändlich, schamlos, anstößig; empörend, unerhört; zügellos, heftig, unbändig; übermäßig.

out|range [aut'reindʒ] *tr* e-e größere Schuß-, Reich-, Tragweite haben als; *fig* übertreffen; **~rank** [-'ræŋk] *tr Am* e-n höheren Rang bekleiden als, den Vorrang haben vor; hinter sich lassen (*s.o.* jdn); **~reach** [-'ri:tʃ] *tr* weiter reichen als, hinausgehen über, übersteigen; *itr* sich erstrecken; **~ride** [-'raid] *irr s. ride tr* schneller reiten als; entkommen; **~rider** ['-raidə] Vorreiter *m*; **~rigger** ['-rigə] *mar* (Mast-) Ausleger, Luvbaum; *sport* Ausleger (-boot *n*); *arch tech* Ausleger *m*; **~right** ['-rait] *a* vorbehaltlos; aufrichtig; gerade; völlig, vollständig, gänzlich; *(Lüge)* glatt; *adv* [aut'rait] vorbehaltlos, offen, geradeheraus; ohne zu zögern, gleich, sofort; völlig, gänzlich; *to buy* ~~ auf feste Rechnung, per Kasse kaufen; *to refuse* ~~ glatt ablehnen; ~~ *expense* Gesamtausgaben *f pl*; ~~ *payment* vollständige Auszahlung *f*; **~rival** [-'raivəl] *tr (Rivalen)* ausstechen; überbieten, schlagen; **~run** [-'rʌn] *irr s. run tr* schneller laufen als; *fig* größer sein als, überschreiten; *(im Laufen)* überholen; entlaufen, entkommen (*s.o.* jdm); *to* ~~ *o.'s income* über s-e Verhältnisse leben; **~runner** ['-rʌnə] Vorläufer; Leithund *m*; Beipferd *n*.

out|sail [aut'seil] *tr mar (ein anderes Schiff)* überholen; **~sell** [-'sel] *irr s. sell tr* e-n größeren Umsatz haben als; e-n höheren Preis erzielen als, mehr einbringen als; teurer verkaufen; **~set** ['-set] Anfang, Beginn; *(Reise)* Aufbruch *m*; *at the* ~~ am Anfang, am Beginn (*of* gen); *from the* ~~ von Anfang an; **~shine** [-'ʃain] *irr s. shine tr* überstrahlen; *fig* übertreffen.

outside ['aut'said] *s*: *the* ~ die Außenseite, das Äußere; der äußere, sichtbare Teil; das Äußerliche; das Äußerste, die Grenze; *a* ['--] äußer, Außen-; von außen (kommend), äußerst, höchst, maximal; *adv* ['-'-] (dr)außen; außerhalb; nach (dr)außen; darüber hinaus; äußerlich; *prp* ['-'-] *(~ of)* außerhalb *gen*; aus (... hinaus); über ... hinaus, jenseits *gen*; *Am fam* außer *dat*, ausgenommen *acc*; *at the (very)* ~ (aller)höchstens; *from the* ~ von außen; *on the* ~ außerhalb; ~ **broadcast** *radio* Sendung *f* von außerhalb des Funkhauses; ~ **cabin** Außenkabine *f*; ~ **capital** Fremdkapital *n*; ~ **help** Hilfe *f* von außen; ~ **left, right** *(Fußball)* Links-, Rechtsaußen *m*; ~ **market** *com* Freiverkehr *m*; **~r** ['-ə] Außenstehende(r), Uneingeweihte(r) *m*; Nichtmitglied *n*; Außenseiter; *com* Freiverkehrsmakler *m*.

out|sit [aut'sit] *irr s. sit tr* länger sitzen als; **~size** ['-saiz] *s* Übergröße *f*; *a* übergroß; **~skirts** ['-skə:ts] *pl* Stadtrand *m*, Peripherie *f*; Weichbild *n*, Außenviertel, -gebiete *n pl*; (Wald-) Rand *m*; Grenze *f*; **~smart** [-'smɑ:t] *tr fam* einwickeln, überlisten, hereinlegen; **~spoken** [-'spoukən] *a* frei (-mütig), offen (ausgesprochen); unverblümt; **~spokenness** [-nis] Freimut *m*, ungeschminkte Offenheit *f*; **~standing** [-'stændiŋ] *a* vorstehend, -springend; *fig* hervorragend, prominent, (all)bekannt; *(Schulden)* (noch) ausstehend, rückständig, unerledigt, ungeregelt; *s pl* Außenstände *m pl*; Aktivschulden *f pl*; *to have money* ~~ Geld ausstehen haben; *to have work* ~~ Arbeitsrückstände haben; ~~ *event* Hauptereignis *n*; **~station** ['-steiʃən] Außenstelle; *tele* Gegenstation *f*; **~stay** [-'stei] *tr* länger bleiben als; über ... hinaus bleiben; *to* ~~ *o.'s welcome (fam)* Wurzeln schlagen; **~step** [-'step] *tr* überschreiten, hinausgehen über; **~stretch** [-'stretʃ] *tr* ausstrecken; sich über ... hinaus erstrecken; **~strip** [-'strip] *tr* schneller gehen als; überholen, überrunden *a. fig*; *fig* übertreffen; **~talk** [-'tɔ:k] *tr* lauter, eindringlicher sprechen als; im Reden übertreffen; **~vote** [-'vout] *tr* überstimmen; **~voter** ['-voutə] Wähler *m* mit Wahlschein.

outward ['autwəd] *a* äußer, äußerlich, Außen-; nach außen gekehrt; sichtbar; offen zutage, auf der Hand liegend; körperlich, physisch, materiell; äußerlich, oberflächlich; *adv*, *a.* **~s** ['-z] außen, auf der Außenseite, äußerlich; nach außen, nach auswärts; (ganz) offen, öffentlich; ~ **bound** *a (Schiff)* ausfahrend; ~ **freight** Hinfracht *f*; **~ly** ['-li] *adv* (nach) außen; in äußerer Hinsicht; ~ **room** nach außen gelegenes Zimmer *n*; ~ **voyage** Ausreise *f*.

out|wear [aut'wɛə] *irr s. wear tr* aufbrauchen, -tragen, abnutzen; länger halten als; überdauern, überleben; *fig* erschöpfen, ermüden; **~weigh** [aut'wei] *tr* an Gewicht übertreffen, mehr wiegen als; *fig* bedeutender, wertvoller sein als; übertreffen; **~wit** [aut'wit] *tr* überlisten; **~work** ['autwə:k] *mil* Vor-, Außenwerk; *fig* Bollwerk *n*; Heimarbeit *f*; **~worker** ['autwə:kə] Heimarbeiter *m*; **~worn** ['-wɔ:n, *pred* -'-] *a* abgenutzt; *fig* überholt, veraltet; erschöpft.

ouzel ['u:zl] Drossel, *bes.* Schwarzdrossel, Amsel *f*.

*

oval ['ouvəl] *a* oval, ei-, länglichrund; *s* Oval *n*.

ovar|ian [o(u)'vɛəriən] *a anat* Eierstock-; *bot* Fruchtknoten-; **~y** ['ouvəri] *anat* Eierstock; *bot* Fruchtknoten *m*.

ovation [o(u)'veiʃən] Ovation, Huldigung *f*.

oven ['ʌvn] Back-, Trockenofen *m*; *in a slow* ~ mit kleiner Flamme.

over ['ouvə] **1.** *adv* hin-, herüber; drüben; (vorn-, hinten-, kopf)über; vorüber, vorbei, aus, zu Ende; übrig, zurück; noch (ein)mal; *vor a*: über-, (all)zu, übermäßig; *in Verbindung mit v*: über-; *all* ~ über u. über; durch u. durch; überall; *it is all* ~ *with him* es ist mit ihm vorbei; *ten times* ~ zehnmal hintereinander; ~ *and above* obendrein, (noch) außerdem; ~ *again* noch (ein)mal; ~ *against* gegenüber *dat*, verglichen mit; ~ *all* von e-m Ende zum andern; ~ *and* ~ *(again)* immer wieder, (zu) wiederholt(en Malen); ~ *there* dort, da drüben; *to be all* ~ *s.o. (sl)* an jdm e-n Narren gefressen haben; *to boil* ~ überkochen; *to come* ~ herüberkommen; *to fall* ~ umfallen; *to get* ~ hinwegkommen über, sich trösten über; *to go* ~ hinübergehen; *(Rechnung)* durchgehen; *theat* einschlagen; *to make* ~ umarbeiten; *to think* ~ überdenken; *to turn* ~ (um)drehen; **2.** *prp* über; über (... hinüber); über, mehr als; *(zeitl.)* ... über; *all* ~ *the town* in der ganzen Stadt; ~ *and above* über ... hinaus; ~ *his newspaper* beim Zeitunglesen; ~ *a glass of wine* bei e-m Glas Wein; ~ *night* über Nacht; ~ *the way* gegenüber; *the lecture is* ~ *my head* der Vortrag ist mir zu hoch; **3.** *interj radio* Ende! bitte kommen! *(Buch)* bitte wenden! **4.** *s*

Überschuß; *mil* Weitschuß *m*; **5.** *a* überschüssig; Über-; ober, höher.

over|abundance ['ouvərə'bʌndəns] große(r) Überfluß *m*; **~act** ['-'rækt] *tr itr* übertreiben; *theat* chargieren, übertrieben spielen, an die Wand spielen; **~all** ['-rɔ:l] *a (a. ~-all)* durchgehend; umfassend; Gesamt-; *s* (Arbeits-)Kittel; Schutz-, Arbeitsanzug *m*; *pl* Arbeits-, Latzhose *f*; *~~ length* Gesamtlänge *f*; **~anxiety** ['-ræŋ'zaiəti] Überängstlichkeit *f*; **~anxious** ['-r'æŋkʃəs] überängstlich; **~arch** ['-r'ɑ:tʃ] *tr* überwölben; *itr* ein Gewölbe, e-e Laube bilden; **~arm** ['-rɑ:m] *a adv sport* Hand-über-Hand-; **~awe** [-r'ɔ:] *tr* verängstigen; einschüchtern.

over|balance [ouvə'bæləns] *tr* schwerer sein als; *fig* übertreffen; überwiegen; aus dem Gleichgewicht bringen; umkippen; *itr* das Gleichgewicht verlieren; umfallen, -kippen; *s* ['-] Übergewicht *n*; *com* Überschuß *m*; **~bear** [-'bɛə] *irr s. bear tr* niederdrücken; *fig* unterdrücken; überwältigen, gefügig machen; hinweggehen (*over s.o.'s wishes* über jds Wünsche); **~bearing** [-'bɛəriŋ] anmaßend, rücksichtslos; beherrschend; **~bid** [-'bid] *irr s. bid tr* überbieten, übersteigen; *(Bridge)* überreizen; **~blown** ['-'bloun] *a* verblüht; *(Sturm)* ausgetobt; *(Stahl)* übergar; **~board** ['-bɔ:d] *adv* über Bord; *fig* im Stich gelassen; *to throw s.th. ~~* über Bord werfen *a. fig*; etw völlig aufgeben; **~brim** ['-'brim] *itr tr* überfließen (über); **~build** ['-'bild] *irr s. build tr* überbauen; zu eng bebauen; **~burden** [-'bə:dn] *tr* überladen, überbelasten; *fig* überlasten; überbeanspruchen; **~busy** ['-'bizi] überbeschäftigt; **~buy** ['-'bai] *irr s. buy tr itr* zuviel, zu teuer kaufen.

over|call ['ouvə'kɔ:l] *tr (Bridge)* überbieten; **~capitalization** ['-kæpitəlai'zeiʃən] Überkapitalisierung *f*; **~capitalize** ['-'kæpitəlaiz] *tr* überkapitalisieren; **~cast** ['-'kɑ:st] *irr s. cast tr* überziehen, bedecken, verdunkeln, umwölken *a. fig*; säumen, einfassen; *(Geist)* verdüstern; *a* ['--] bedeckt, überzogen; bewölkt, dunkel, trübe; gesäumt, eingefaßt; überwendlich genäht; *s* ['--] Wolkendecke; *min* Stütze; überwendliche Naht *f*; **~charge** ['-'tʃɑ:dʒ] *tr* überladen; *fig* übertreiben; zu hoch berechnen, zu viel fordern, überteuern, -fordern; *s a.* ['--] zu große Last, Überlastung *f*; *tech el* Überdruck *m*; *com* zu hohe Forderung, Überteuerung *f*; *to make an ~~ on s.th.* etw zu teuer verkaufen; **~cloud** [-'klaud] *tr* mit Wolken bedecken; verdunkeln, trüben; *fig (das Gesicht)* verfinstern; *itr* sich verdunkeln, sich bewölken, sich verfinstern; **~coat** ['-kout] Überzieher, Mantel *m*; **~come** [-'kʌm] *irr s. come tr* besiegen, schlagen, siegen über; überwältigen; überwinden, meistern, Herr werden (*s.th.* e-r S), fertig werden mit *(e-r Aufgabe)*; *itr* siegen, siegreich sein; *to be ~~ (fig)* ergriffen, überwältigt sein; betäubt werden; *~~ with joy* vor Freude hingerissen; **~confidence** ['-'kɔnfidəns] zu große(s) (Selbst-)Vertrauen *n*; **~confident** ['-'kɔnfidənt] zu vertrauensvoll; **~credulous** ['-'kredjuləs] allzu leichtgläubig; **~crop** ['-'krɔp] *tr agr (Boden)* erschöpfen, auslaugen; **~crowded** [-'kraudid] *a (mit Menschen)* überfüllt; übervölkert; *com* übersetzt.

over|develop [əuvədi'veləp] *tr phot* überentwickeln; **~do** [-'du:] *irr s. do tr* übertreiben; (mit Arbeit) überlasten, -bürden; zu lange kochen *od* backen; *itr (to ~ it)* zuviel tun, sich überarbeiten, sich überanstrengen; (es) übertreiben; **~done** ['-'dʌn] *a* überbürdet, -lastet; überarbeitet, erschöpft; übertrieben; übergar; **~dose** ['-dous, '-'dous] *s* zu starke Dosis, Überdosierung *f*; *tr* ['-'dous] e-e zu starke Dosis geben (*s.o.* jdm); **~draft, ~draught** ['-drɑ:ft] *fin* (Konten-) Überziehung *f*; Debetsaldo *m*; **~draw** ['-'drɔ:] *irr s. draw tr* überspannen; übertreiben; verzeichnen; *(sein Konto)* überziehen; **~dress** ['-'dres] *tr itr* (sich) übertrieben kleiden; **~drive** ['-'draiv] *irr s. drive tr itr* (sich) überanstrengen; *itr* sich überarbeiten, sich abhetzen; *s* ['--] *mot* Schnellgang *m*; *~~ transmission* Schnellganggetriebe *n*; **~due** ['-'dju:] *fin* überfällig *a. allg*, rückständig, im Rückstand; *(Zug)* verspätet.

over|eat ['ouvər'i:t] *itr* sich überessen, *fam* -füttern, *sl* -fressen; **~emphasize** ['-r'emfəsaiz] *tr* zu starken Nachdruck legen auf; überbetonen; **~estimate** ['-r'estimeit] *tr* überschätzen; zu hoch bewerten; *s* [-mit] Überschätzung *f*; **~expansion** ['-riks'pænʃən] übermäßige Ausweitung *f*; **~expose** ['-riks'pouz] *tr phot* überbelichten; **~exposure** ['-iks'pouʒə] Überbelichtung *f*; **~extend** ['-iks'tend] *tr* übermäßig ausweiten; **~fatigue** ['-fə'ti:g] *tr* übermüden; *s* Übermüdung *f*; **~feed** ['-'fi:d] *irr s. feed tr* überfuttern; *itr* zuviel fressen; **~flow** [-'flou] *irr s. flow tr* überfluten *a. fig*; über *(die Ufer)* treten; *fig (Schranken)* durchbrechen; zum Überlaufen bringen; *itr* überfließen, -fluten; überlaufen (*into* in); über die Ufer treten; *fig* voll sein (*with* von); überfließen (*with* vor); im Überfluß vorhanden sein; *s* ['---] Überfließen *n*, -flutung, -schwemmung *f*; Überfluß, *fig* -schuß (*of* an); *tech (~~ pipe)* Überlauf *m*; *~~ meeting* Parallelversammlung *f*; **~freight** ['-'freit] *tr* überbefrachten; ['---] *s* Überfracht *f*.

overgrow ['ouvə'grou] *irr s. grow tr* überwachsen, -wuchern; hinauswachsen aus; *itr* zu schnell, zu stark, übermäßig wachsen; **~n** ['-'n] *a* überwachsen; übermäßig gewachsen; lang aufgeschossen; **~th** ['-grouθ] Überwucherung *f*; übermäßige(s) Wachstum *n*.

over|hand ['ouvəhænd] *a adv* von oben herab; *(Nähen)* überwendlich; *(Knoten)* einfach; *sport* überhand; *(Schwimmen)* Hand-über-Hand-; **~hang** ['-'hæŋ] *irr s. hang tr* hängen über; bedrohen, drohen (*s.o.* jdm); *itr* überhängen, -stehen; hinausragen über; überkragen; *s* ['---] Überhang *m*; **~happy** ['-'hæpi] überglücklich; **~hasty** ['-'heisti] übereilig; **~haul** ['-hɔ:l] *tr* durchsehen, genau überprüfen; abschreiben; *tech* überholen; instandsetzen; *mar* ein-, überholen; *s* ['---] *tech* Überholung *f*; **~head** ['-hed] *a* oberirdisch; *mot* obengesteuert; höher; allgemein; Gesamt-, General-; *s (~ charges, costs, expenses)* allgemeine Unkosten *pl*, Betriebskosten *pl*; *adv* ['-'hed] über dem Kopf, in der Luft; droben; *~~ line, wires (pl) el* Oberleitung *f*; *~~ price* Gesamtpreis *m*; *~~ railway, train* Hochbahn *f*; *~~ statement* Gesamtübersicht *f*; **~hear** [-'hiə] *irr s. hear tr* zufällig (mit)hören, abhören; erlauschen; **~heat** ['-'hi:t] *tr* überhitzen; *itr tech* zu heiß werden, heißlaufen; **~heated** ['-'hi:tid] *a* überhitzt, -heizt.

over|indulge ['ouvərin'dʌldʒ] *tr* verwöhnen; *itr* zuviel Vergnügen haben (*in* an); **~indulgence** ['-rin'dʌldʒəns] übermäßige(r) Genuß *m*; zu große Nachsicht *f*; **~indulgent** ['-rin'dʌldʒənt] zu nachsichtig; **~insure** ['-rin'ʃuə] *tr* überversichern; **~issue** ['-r'isju:, '-r'iʃju:] *tr* zuviel *(Papiergeld)* ausgeben; **~joyed** [-'dʒɔid] *a* voller Freude, überglücklich.

over|laden ['ouvə'leidn] *a* überbelastet, -beladen (*with* mit); **~land** [-'lænd] *adv* über Land; *a* ['ouvəlænd] Überland-; *~~ route* Überlandweg *m*; **~lap** [-'læp] *tr* hinüber-, hinausragen über; übergreifen auf; *itr* inea. übergreifen; sich überlappen, sich überlagern, sich überdecken, sich überschneiden; *s* ['ouvəlæp] Überschneidung, Überlappung *f*; Überhängende(s), -stehende(s) *n*; Überhang *m*; **~lapping** [ouvə'læpiŋ] *a* überhängend, -stehend; sich überschneidend; *s* Überschneidung *f*; **~lay** [-'lei] *irr s. lay tr* darauflegen, -breiten; auflegen; bedecken, überziehen; *tech* überlagern; *typ* zurichten; *s* ['---] Überzug *m*, Decke; Auflage *f*; *typ* Aufzug *m*, Zurichtung; Planpause *f*; **~leaf** ['-'li:f] *adv* umseitig; **~leap** [-'li:p] *irr s. leap tr* springen über; *fig* überspringen, auslassen; weiter springen als; ['--'-] *to ~~ o.s.* zu weit gehen *fig*, über das Ziel hinausschießen; **~lie** ['-'lai] *tr* liegen auf, über; *geol* überlagern; **~live** ['-'liv] *tr itr* überleben; **~load** ['-'loud] *tr* überladen, -belasten; *el* übersteuern; *s* ['-loud] zu große, schwere Last *f*; Übergewicht *n*, -belastung *f*; **~loading** ['ouvə'loudiŋ] Überlastung *f*; **~look** [-'luk] *tr* schauen über; überschauen; überragen, (hinaus)ragen über; *(Fehler)* übersehen, durchgehen lassen; nicht beachten, vernachlässigen; nachsehen, entschuldigen; durchsehen, prüfen; beaufsichtigen, leiten; **~lord** ['-lɔ:d] *hist* Ober(lehns)herr *m*; **~ly** ['-li] *adv bes. Am* (zu) sehr, übermäßig.

over|man ['ouvəmən] *s* Vorgesetzte(r), Führer, Leiter; Aufseher, Vorarbeiter; *min* Steiger; Schiedsrichter; ['-mæn] Übermensch *m*; *tr (Stelle)* überbesetzen; **~mantel** ['-mæntl] Kaminaufsatz *m*; **~master** [-'mɑ:stə] *tr* überwältigen, besiegen, unterwerfen; **~much** ['-'mʌtʃ] *a adv* zuviel; **~night** ['-'nait] *adv* über Nacht, die Nacht über *od* (hin)durch; letzte, vergangene Nacht; *a* ['---] Nacht-; *s* ['---] vergangene(r), letzte(r) Abend *m*; *to stay ~~* übernachten; *~~ bag, case* Stadtköfferchen *n*.

over|pass [ouvə'pɑ:s] *tr* überschreiten *a. fig*, -queren; kreuzen; überstehen; übertreffen, -ragen; übersehen, -gehen; *s* ['---] Überweg *m*; Überführung *f*; **~pay** ['-'pei] *irr s. pay itr* zuviel bezahlen; *tr* zu hoch, zu teuer bezahlen; **~peopled** ['-'pi:pld] *a* übervölkert; **~pitch** ['-'pitʃ] *tr sport* zu weit werfen; *fam* übertreiben; **~play** ['-'plei] *tr theat (Rolle)* übertreiben, übertrieben spielen; *to ~ o.'s hand (Kartenspiel)* zu hoch spielen; **~plus** ['-plʌs] Überschuß, Mehrbetrag *m*; **~populated** ['-'pɔpjuleitid] *a* übervölkert; **~power** [-'pauə] *tr* überwältigen *a. fig*; **~print** ['-'print] *tr typ* überdrucken; *phot* überkopieren; *s* ['---] Überdruck *m*; **~produc|e** ['-prə'dju:s] *tr itr* überproduzieren; **~production** ['-prə'dʌkʃən] Überproduktion *f*.

over|rate ['ouvə'reit] *tr* überschätzen, zu hoch einschätzen; zu hoch veranlagen; **~reach** [-'ri:tʃ] *tr* sich über ...

hinaus erstrecken *(a. zeitl.)*, hinausragen über; sich ausbreiten über, bedecken; hinausschießen über; überlisten, -vorteilen; *itr* zu weit reichen; betrügen; *to ~ o.s.* sich übernehmen; des Guten zuviel tun; **~rev** ['ouvə'rev] *tr tech* überdrehen; **~ride** [-'raid] *irr s. ride tr* hinwegreiten über; *fig* unterdrücken; unbeachtet lassen, sich hinwegsetzen über; *(Vollmacht)* überschreiten; außer Kraft setzen, aufheben; beiseite schieben; *~riding responsibility* Gesamtverantwortung *f*; **~rule** [-'ru:l] *tr* aufheben, annullieren, außer Kraft setzen, umstoßen; *(Urteil)* verwerfen; *(Anspruch)* nicht anerkennen; *(Einwand)* zurückweisen; Macht haben über, Einfluß haben auf; überstimmen (*s.o.* jdn); **~run** [-'rʌn] *irr s. run tr* überfluten, -schwemmen; überwachsen; herfallen über *(ein Land)*, besetzen, verwüsten, plündern; *rail (Signal)* überfahren; *fig* sich schnell verbreiten; überschreiten, hinausgehen über; *typ* umbrechen; *itr* überfließen; die Grenzen überschreiten; *s* ['---] *com* Überschuß *m*; *aero* Startbahnverlängerung *f*; *to be ~~ with* wimmeln von; überwuchert sein von.

over|sea ['ouvə'si:] *adv a.* **~~s** nach Übersee; ins Ausland; *a* Übersee-; Auslands-, ausländisch; *~~ market* Überseemarkt *m*; *~~ trade* Überseehandel *m*; **~see** ['-'si:] *irr s. see tr* überwachen, beaufsichtigen, leiten; **~seer** ['-siə] Aufseher; *(~~ of the poor)* Armenpfleger; Werkmeister, Polier; *typ* Faktor *m*; **~sell** ['-'sel] *tr* über den Bestand verkaufen; **~sensitive** ['-'sensitiv] überempfindlich; **~set** ['-'set] *irr s. set tr* überwinden, bezwingen; in Unruhe, Aufregung versetzen; umstürzen, über den Haufen werfen; **~sew** ['-'-sou] *irr s. sew tr* überwendlich nähen; **~shadow** [-'ʃædou] *tr* e-n Schatten werfen auf; überschatten, verdekken, verdunkeln *a. fig*; *fig* in den Schatten stellen; **~shoe** ['-ʃu:] Über-, Gummischuh *m*; **~shoot** ['-'ʃu:t] *irr s. shoot tr* hinausgehen über, überschreiten; *itr* zu weit schießen; *aero* durchstarten; *itr, to ~ o.s, to ~ the mark* übers Ziel (hinaus)schießen, zu weit gehen; **~shot** ['-ʃɔt] *a (Wasserrad)* oberschlächtig; **~sight** ['-sait] Aufsicht, Überwachung *f*; Übersehen *(e-s Fehlers)*; Versehen *n*; *through an ~~* aus Versehen; **~size** ['-saiz] *s* Übergröße *f*; *a* übergroß, zu groß; *~~ in tyres* Reifenübergröße *f*; **~slaugh** ['-slɔ:] *tr Am mil* bei e-r Beförderung übergehen; abkommandieren; **~sleep** ['-'sli:p] *irr s. sleep itr u. to ~ o.s* (sich) verschlafen, die Zeit verschlafen; **~specialized** ['-'speʃəlaizd] *a* überspezialisiert; **~speed** ['-'spi:d] *irr s. speed tr* zu schnell laufen lassen, überdrehen; **~spend** ['-'spend] *irr s. spend tr* mehr ausgeben als; *itr* zuviel ausgeben; *pp* erschöpft, überarbeitet; **~spill** ['-spil] (Bevölkerungs-)Überschuß *m*; **~spread** [-'spred] *irr s. spread tr* überziehen, bedecken (*with* mit); *itr* sich ausbreiten; **~staffed** ['-'sta:ft] *a* überbesetzt; *to be ~~* zuviel Personal haben; **~state** ['-'steit] *tr* besonders hervorheben, betonen; herausstreichen, übertreiben, zu stark auftragen; **~statement** ['-'steitmənt] Übertreibung *f*; **~stay** ['-'stei] *tr (Zeit, Urlaub)* überschreiten; *to ~ the market (Am)* die günstigste Zeit zum Kaufen *od* Verkaufen verpassen; **~step** ['-'step] *tr meist fig* überschreiten; **~stock** ['-'stɔk] *tr* überfüllen (*with goods, cattle* mit Waren, Vieh); übersättigen; *s* Überfüllung *f*, Überfluß *m*; *to ~~ the market* den Markt überschwemmen; **~strain** ['-'strein] *tr itr* (sich) überanstrengen, (sich) überarbeiten; *s* ['ouvəstrein] Überanstrengung, Überbürdung *f*; **~strung** ['-'strʌŋ] *a* überspannt; *(Nerven)* überreizt; **~subscribe** ['-səb'skraib] *tr fin* überzeichnen; **~subscription** ['-sʌb'skripʃən] Überzeichnung *f*; **~supply** ['-sə'plai] *tr (Ware)* reichlich anbieten; *s* Überangebot *n*.

overt ['ouvə:t] offen(kundig).

over|take [ouvə'teik] *irr s. take tr* einholen; überraschen, *(plötzlich)* überfallen, ertappen, *fam* erwischen; überwältigen; *mot* überholen; *to ~~ arrears of work* Rückstände aufarbeiten; **~task** ['-'ta:sk] *tr* überfordern (*s.o.* jdn); **~tax** ['-'tæks] *tr* zu hoch besteuern; überlasten, überbürden; zu sehr in Anspruch nehmen; *to ~~ o.'s strength* sich übernehmen; **~throw** ['-'θrou] *irr s. throw tr* umstürzen *a. fig*, über den Haufen werfen; überwältigen, besiegen; *s* ['ouvəθrou] (Um-)Sturz; Ruin *m*, Ende *n*; *mil* Niederlage *f*; **~thrust** ['-θrʌst] *geol* Überschiebung *f*; **~time** ['-taim] *s* Überstunden *f pl*; *sport* Verlängerung *f*; *a* Überstunden-; *tr phot* überbelichten; *to be on ~ u. adv: to work ~* Überstunden machen; *~~ pay* Überstundenbezahlung *f*; **~tire** ['-'taiə] *tr* übermüden; **~tone** ['-toun] *mus* Oberton *m*; *pl* Neben-, Hintergedanken *m pl*; **~top** ['-'tɔp] *tr* sich erheben über (... hinaus) überragen *a. fig*; *fig* übertreffen; **~train** ['-'trein] *itr tr sport* übertrainieren; **~trump** ['-'trʌmp] *tr* übertrumpfen *a. fig*.

overture ['ouvətjuə] Eröffnung *f*, Vorschlag *m*, Angebot *n*; *mus* Ouvertüre *f*, Vorspiel *n*; Einleitung *f (e-s Epos)*; *pl* Annäherungsversuche *m pl*.

over|turn [ouvə'tə:n] *tr* umwerfen, -stoßen, -stürzen; auf den Kopf stellen; *(Schraube)* überdrehen; niederwerfen; ruinieren; *itr* umkippen, -fallen; *mar* kentern; *aero* sich überschlagen; *s* ['ouvətə:n] Umsturz; Ruin *m*, Ende *n*; *Am* Umsatz *m*; **~valuation** ['-vælju'eiʃən] Überschätzung, Überbewertung *f*; **~value** ['-'vælju:] *tr* überschätzen, zu hoch einschätzen, überbewerten; *s* ['---] Mehrwert *m*; **~voltage** ['-voltidʒ] Überspannung *f*; **~weening** [-'wi:niŋ] eingebildet, arrogant, hochmütig, *fam* -näsig; **~weight** ['-weit] *s* Übergewicht *n a. fig*; *a* zu schwer; *~~ed* ['-weitid] *a* überlastet, überbeladen; **~whelm** [-'welm] *tr* bedecken (*with* mit); überschütten, überfluten; begraben, tauchen (*beneath* unter); niederdrücken, -werfen; überwältigen; besiegen; *~~ed with work* mit Arbeit überlastet; **~whelming** [-'welmiŋ] *a* erdrückend, überwältigend; *an ~~ majority* e-e erdrückende Mehrheit *f*; **~wind** ['-'waind] *irr s. wind tr (Uhr)* überdrehen; **~work** ['-'wə:k] *tr itr* (sich) überanstrengen; *tr* übertreiben; *to ~~ o.s.* sich überarbeiten; *tr* übertreiben; *s* Schwerarbeit; Überarbeitung *f*; ['ouvəwə:k] Überstunden *f pl*, Mehrarbeit *f*; **~wrought** ['-'rɔ:t] *a* überarbeitet, -müdet; überreizt, nervös; **~zealous** ['-'zeləs] übereifrig.

*

ov|iduct ['ouvidʌkt] *anat* Eileiter *m*; **~iform** ['-fɔ:m] eiförmig; **~iparous** [o(u)'vipərəs] *zoo* eierlegend, sich durch Eier fortpflanzend; **~ipositor** [ouvi'pɔzitə] *ent* Legeröhre *f*; **~oid** ['ouvɔid] = *~iform*; **~ular(y)** ['ouvjulə(ri)] *a* Ei-; **~ulation** [ouvju'leiʃən] *physiol* Eiaustritt, Follikelsprung *m*, Ovulation *f*; **~ule** ['ouvju:l] Ovulum, Ei *n*; *bot* Samenanlage *f*; **~um** ['ouvəm] *pl -a* ['-ə] *scient* Ei *n*.

ow|e [ou] *tr* schulden, schuldig sein *a. fig*; *fig* verpflichtet sein zu; verdanken; *(Gefühle)* hegen; *itr* Schulden haben; **~ing** ['-iŋ] *(Geld, Dank)* schuldig; geschuldet, (noch) unbezahlt; *(Betrag)* ausstehend; *~~ to* infolge, auf Grund *gen*; kraft, vermöge *gen*; dank *dat*; *to be ~~* noch offenstehen; *to* herrühren von, zu verdanken sein *dat*.

owl [aul] Eule *f*; *fig* Nachtvogel; *fam* Dummkopf *m*; *barn, screech ~* Schleiereule *f*; *brown ~* Waldkauz *m*; *horned ~* Ohreule *f*; **~ bus, car** *Am sl* letzte(r) Bus *m*; Nachtstraßenbahn *f*, Spätwagen, Lumpensammler *m*; **~ish** ['-iʃ] eulenartig, wie e-e Eule; **~ train** *Am sl* Nacht-, Spätzug *m*.

own [oun] *a* eigen; *s* Eigen *n*; *tr* (zu eigen) haben, besitzen, Eigentümer sein *gen*; zugeben, (sich) bekennen (zu), anerkennen; *itr* sich bekennen (*to* zu); *to ~ up to s.th.* etw bekennen, (ein)gestehen; *all o.'s ~* ganz besonder, eigentümlich; *at o.'s ~ risk* auf eigene Gefahr; *of o.'s ~* für sich allein; zu eigen, selbst; *of o.'s ~ accord* von sich aus; *on o.'s ~ account* auf eigene Rechnung; *on o.'s ~ (hook)* auf eigene Faust; *with o.'s ~ eyes* mit eigenen Augen; *to be s.o.'s ~* jdm gehören; *to be o.'s ~ man, master* sein eigener Herr sein; *to be (living) on o.'s ~ (fam)* auf eigenen Füßen stehen; selbständig sein; *to come into o.'s ~* zu s-m Recht kommen; Anerkennung finden; zu Geld kommen; *to get o.'s ~ back (fam)* es jdm heimzahlen; *to hold o.'s ~* sich behaupten, sich gut halten, durchhalten; *to make o.'s ~ dresses* s-e Kleider selbst nähen; *who ~s this house?* wem gehört dieses Haus? **~er** ['-ə] Eigentümer; *(Konto)* Inhaber; *mar* Reeder *m*; *policy ~~* Versicherungsnehmer *m*; *property ~~* Grundeigentümer *m*; *store ~~* Ladenbesitzer *m*; *~~-driver* Herrenfahrer *m*; *~~-operator (agr)* Eigenbetrieb *m*; *~~-pilot* Herrenflieger *m*; **~erless** ['-əlis] herrenlos; **~ership** ['-əʃip] Eigentum(srecht) *n*; Besitz *m*; *under new ~~* unter neuer Leitung; *co-, joint ~~* Miteigentum(srecht) *n*; *common, collective ~~* Kollektiv-, Gesamteigentum *n*; *public ~~* Eigentum *n* der öffentlichen Hand.

*

ox [ɔks] *pl -en* ['-n] Ochse *m*; Rind *n*; **~bow** Jochbogen *m*; *pl* Joch *n*; *Am* (Land *n* in e-r) Flußschleife *f*; **~-cart** Ochsenkarren *m*; **~eyed** *a* kuhäugig; **O~ford, ~~ shoe** Halbschuh *m*; *~~ blue* dunkelblau; **~hide** Rinderfell; Rindsleder *n*; **~lip** weiße Schlüsselblume *f*; **~tail**: *~~ soup* Ochsenschwanzsuppe *f*; **~-tongue salad** Ochsenmaulsalat *m*.

oxal|ate ['ɔksəleit] *chem* kleesaure(s) Salz *n*; **~ic** [ɔk'sælik] oxalsauer; *~~ acid* Oxalsäure *f*.

oxid|ate ['ɔksideit], **~ize** ['-daiz] *tr itr chem* oxydieren; **~ation** [ɔksi'deiʃən] Oxydierung, Oxydation *f*; **~e** ['ɔksaid] Oxyd *n*.

Oxonian [ɔk'sounjən] *a* Oxforder; *s* Oxforder(in *f*); (ehemaliger) Oxforder Student *m*.

oxy-acetylene ['ɔksiə'setili:n]: **~ welding** Autogenschweißen *n*.

oxygen ['ɔksidʒən] Sauerstoff *m*; **~ apparatus** Sauerstoffgerät *n*; **~ate** [ɔk'sidʒineit], **~ize** [-aiz] *tr (bes. Metalloide)* mit Sauerstoff anreichern;

~ation [ɔksidʒi'neiʃən] Anreicherung *f* mit Sauerstoff; **~ bottle, cylinder, flask** Sauerstoffflasche *f*; **~ compound** Sauerstoffverbindung *f*; **~ mask** Sauerstoffmaske *f*; **~ous** [ɔk'sidʒinəs] Sauerstoff-; **~ starvation** Sauerstoffmangel *m*; **~ tent** *med* Sauerstoffzelt *n*.
oxyhydrogen ['ɔksi'haidridʒən] Knallgas *n*; **~ blowpipe, torch** Knallgasgebläse *n*.
oyes, oyez [o(u)'jes] *interj* Achtung! Ruhe! *(Ruf der Gerichtsdiener)*; hört (zu)!
oyster ['ɔistə] Auster *f*; *as dumb as an ~* stumm wie ein Fisch; **~ bar** Austernbüfett *n*; **~-bed** Austernbank *f*; **~-catcher** *orn* Austernfischer *m*; **~-farm** Austernpark *m*; **~-knife** Austernmesser *n*; **~man** Austernsammler, -züchter, -händler, -verkäufer *m*; **~-shell** Austernschale *f*.
ozon|e ['ouzoun, o(u)'zoun] *chem* Ozon *n*; *sl* frische Luft *f*, Ozon *n*; *~~ cinema*, **~er** *Am sl* Freilichtkino *n*; **~ic** [o(u)-'zɔnik] *a* Ozon-; ozonhaltig; **~iferous** [ouzo(u)'nifərəs] ozonhaltig; **~ize** ['ouzo(u)naiz] *tr* ozonisieren.

P

P, p [pi:] *pl ~'s* P, p *n*; *to mind o.'s p's and q's* auf die gute Form achten.
pa [pɑ:] *fam* Papa, Vati *m*.
pabulum ['pæbjuləm] *oft fig* Nahrung, Speise *f*; *mental ~* Nahrung *f* des Geistes.
pace [peis] *s* Schritt; Gang(art *f*) *m*; (Marsch-)Tempo *n*; (Gleich-)Schritt; (Gehen *n* im) Schritt; *(Pferd)* Paßgang *m*; Stufe *f*, Podium *n*; *fig* Leistung *f*; *tr* durchschreiten; abschreiten, (ab)messen; *(Pferd)* einreiten; Schrittmacher sein, das Tempo angeben für; *itr* im Schritt gehen; (einher)schreiten; *(Pferd)* im Paßgang gehen; *at a quick ~* raschen Schrittes; *to ~ out, to ~ off* abschreiten, abmessen; *to ~ up and down* auf u. ab schreiten; *to go the ~* ein scharfes Tempo anschlagen; *fig* flott, leichtsinnig leben; *to go a good ~* e-n guten Schritt haben; flott gehen; *to keep ~* Schritt halten (*with* mit); *to put s.o. through his ~s* jdn auf die Probe stellen, jdn auf Herz u. Nieren prüfen; *to set the ~* das Tempo angeben; *fig* den Ton angeben; *double-time ~* Laufschritt *m*; **~d** [-t] *a* mit Schrittmacher; abgeschritten; *in Zssgen: fast-, slow-~~* mit schnellen, langsamen Schritten; *thorough-~~ (fig)* mit allen Hunden gehetzt, mit allen Wassern gewaschen; **~-maker** Schrittmacher *m*; **~-making** Schrittmachen *n*; **~r** ['-ə] Schreitende(r); Paßgänger *(Pferd)*; Schrittmacher *m*.
pachyderm ['pækidə:m] *zoo* Dickhäuter *m a. fig*.
paci|fic(al) [pə'sifik(əl)] *a* friedlich, friedfertig, -liebend; versöhnlich, beruhigend; *s*: *the P~fic (Ocean)* der Pazifik, der Pazifische, Stille *od* Große Ozean; **~fication** [pæsifi'keiʃən] Befriedung, Beruhigung, Beschwichtigung, Versöhnung *f*; **~fier** ['pæsifaiə] Friedensstifter, -vermittler; *Am* Schnuller *m*; **~fism, ~ficism** ['pæsifizm, '-fisizm] Pazifismus *m*; **~fist, ~ficist** ['pæsifist, '-fisist] Pazifist, Kriegsgegner *m*; **~fy** ['pæsifai] *tr* befrieden; beruhigen, besänftigen, veraussöhnen; *(Zorn)* beschwichtigen; *(Hunger, Durst)* stillen.
pack [pæk] *s* Pack, Ballen *m*, Bündel *n*, Stapel, Stoß *m*; (Trag-)Last; Rückentrage *f*; *mil* Gepäck(stück) *n*, Tornister; Haufen *m*, Menge, Anzahl, Gruppe *f*; *tech* Satz *m*; (Lumpen-)Pack *n*, Bande *f*; *(Tiere)* Rudel *n*; *(Hunde)* Koppel, Meute *f*; *(Rebhühner)* Volk *n*; *Am (Zigaretten, Bonbons, Gebäck)* Packung *f*; *(Karten)* Spiel *n*; Fallschirmsack *m*; *(~-ice)* Packeis *n*; *med* Packung *f*, Wickel; *(ice-~)* Eisbeutel *m*; *(Kosmetik)* Gesichtspackung *f*; *(Rugby)* Sturm *m*; *das* Eingemachte, in Konserven Verpackte; *a* Pack-; *tr* be-, ver-, einpakken; *(Koffer)* packen; *(Lebensmittel)* einmachen; eindosen; *(Menschen)* zs.drängen, einpferchen, vollstopfen, -pfropfen; fest ein-, umwickeln; *tech* abdichten; *med* e-e Packung geben (*s.o.* jdm), wickeln; feststampfen; *(Lasttier)* bepacken, beladen; *Am* (normalerweise, für gewöhnlich) tragen, mit sich führen, (bei sich) haben; *jur pol* parteiisch aufstellen *od* zs.setzen; *itr* (s-e Sachen) packen; *(to ~ easily)* sich (gut) (ver)packen lassen; sich (zs.)ballen; sich (zs.)drängen; *(to ~ (o.s.) off)* (schleunigst) abhauen, sich davonmachen; *to ~ in* einpacken; *fam* e-e große Menschenmenge anlocken; zs.pferchen; *to ~ it in (sl)* es aufgeben; *to ~ off, to send ~ing* wegjagen, Beine machen (*s.o.* jdm); *to ~ up* einpacken *a. fam*; *fam* es aufgeben; *(Motor)* stehenbleiben; *that's a ~ of lies* das sind lauter Lügen; **~age** ['-idʒ] *tr* eindosen, in Flaschen füllen; zs.stellen, konzentrieren, vorfabrizieren; bündeln; *s* Packen *n*; Pack, Ballen *m*, Bündel; *bes. Am* Paket *n*; Packung *f*, Päckchen *n*; Kiste *f*, Karton *m*, Schachtel; Emballage, Verpackung *f*, Packmaterial *n*; Packerlohn *m*; Vorteile *m pl* bei Tarifverhandlungen; Werbematerial *n* (für Händler); *Am sl* hübsche(s) Mädchen *n*, große Geldsumme *f*; *postal ~~* Postpaket *n*; *registered ~~* Einschreibpaket *n*; *~~ advertising* Versandwerbung *f*; *~~ deal* Koppelungsgeschäft *n*; *~~ freight* Stückgutfracht *f*; *~~ library* Wanderbücherei *f*; *~~ store (Am)* Wein- u. Likörhandlung *f*; *~~(d) tour* Pauschalreise *f*; **~ animal** Lasttier *n*; **~-cloth** Packleinwand *f*; **~ed** [-t] *a* ge-, verpackt; zs.gepfercht; *(Versammlung)* überfüllt; gestopft voll; **~er** ['-ə] Packer(in *f*) *m*; Packmaschine *f*; Eigentümer *m* e-r Konservenfabrik; **~et** ['-it] *s* (Post-)Paket, Päckchen *n*; *(Zigaretten)* Packung *f*; *(Briefe)* Stoß; *sl* Haufen *m* Geld; *sl* Schlag *m*, Strafe, *mil* Verwundung *f*; *(~~-boat)* Passagier-, Postdampfer *m*, Postschiff *n*; *tr* ein Paket, Päckchen machen aus; in e-n Karton packen; ein-, verpacken; **~horse** Pack-, Saumpferd *n*; **~ing** ['-iŋ] *s* (Ver-)Packen; Einmachen, -kochen *n*; *med* Packung, Wickelung; Tamponade; *tech* Dichtung, Liderung; Verpackung *f*, Packmaterial *n*; *attr* Pack-; *~~-box, -case* Kiste; Lattenkiste *f*, Verschlag *m*; *~~-cloth* Packleinen *n*; *~~ costs (pl)* Verpackungskosten *pl*; *~~ house, industry (Am)* Konservenfabrik, -industrie *f*; *~~ label* Packzettel *m*; *~~ list* Versandliste *f*; *~~-needle* Packnadel *f*; *~~-paper* Packpapier *n*; *~~ piece* Beilage *f*, Futter *n*; *~~-ring (tech)* Dichtungsring *m*; *~~-room* Packraum *m*; *~~-rubber* Dichtungsgummi *m* od *n*; *~~-sheet* Packleinwand *f*; *med* Umschlag *m*; *~~-washer (tech)* Dichtungsscheibe *f*; **~man** ['-mən] Hausierer *m*; **~-saddle** Packsattel *m*; **~thread** Bindfaden *m*, Schnur *f*; **~ train** *Am* Tragtierkolonne *f*.
pact [pækt] Vertrag *m*, Abkommen *n*, Pakt *m*; *to make a ~* e-n Vertrag schließen; *guarantee ~* Garantievertrag *m*; *secret ~* Geheimabkommen *n*, -vertrag *m*; *~ of mutual assistance* Beistandspakt *m*; *~ of non-aggression* Nichtangriffspakt *m*.
pad [pæd] **1.** *s* Kissen, Polster *n*; (Aus-)Polsterung, Wattierung; Füllung, Einlage; Unterlage *f*; *(writing-~)* Schreibblock *m*; *(stamp ~)* Stempelkissen *n*; *zoo* Ballen *m*; *(Kaninchen)* Pfote *f*; *sport* Beinschützer *m*; *(Rakete)* Abschußrampe *f*; *sl* Bett *n*, Opiumhöhle *f*; *tr* (aus)polstern, wattieren; ausstopfen, füllen; (mit Watte) füllen; *(Rede, Schrift)* aufbauschen; *(Verwaltung)* aufblähen; *warming ~* Heizkissen *n*; *to ~ out (fig)* in die Länge ziehen, Zeilen schinden; **~ded** ['-id] *a* gepolstert, wattiert; *~~ cell* Gummizelle *f*; **~ding** ['-iŋ] Polsterung, Wattierung *f*; Polstermaterial *n*; *fig* Füller *m*, (Zeilen-)Füllsel, Geschreibsel, (leeres) Gerede *n*; *tele* blinde Gruppe *f*; **2.** *itr* zu Fuß gehen, wandern, trampen; *s (~-nag) (Pferd)* Paßgänger *m*; *sl* Landstraße *f*; *to ~ it, to ~ the hoof (sl)* zu Fuß latschen, tippeln.
paddle ['pædl] *s* Paddel *n*; Radschaufel; Rührschaufel *f*, -holz *n*; Spachtel; *metal* Rührstange, Kratze *f*; Wäscheklopfer; *Am* Stock *m (zum Prügeln)*; *itr* paddeln; planschen; herumfummeln; (herum)torkeln; *tr* paddeln; (um)rühren; *Am* schlagen, (ver)prügeln; *to ~ o.'s own canoe (fig)* auf eigenen Füßen stehen; **~-box** Radkasten *m (e-s Raddampfers)*; **~r** ['-ə] Paddler *m*; **~-steamer** Raddampfer *m*; **~-wheel** Schaufelrad *n*.
paddock ['pædək] *s* Pferdekoppel *f*; *(Rennsport)* Sattelplatz *m*; *(Australien)* (eingefriedigtes) Gut *n*.
Paddy ['pædi] Ire *m (Spitzname)*.
paddy ['pædi] **1.** ungeschälte(r) Reis *m*; *(~-field)* Reisfeld *n*; **2.** *fam* Wut *f*, -anfall *m*; *to be in a ~* e-n Wutanfall haben; **~-wagon** *Am sl* Grüne Minna *f*.
padlock ['pædlɔk] *s* Vorhängeschloß *n*; *tr* mit e-m Vorhängeschloß verschließen.
padre ['pɑ:drei] *mil sl* (Feld-)Geistliche(r) *m*.

paean ['pi:ən] Päan *m*, Dankes-, Siegeslied *n*.
p(a)ederast ['pi:dəræst, 'ped-] Päderast *m*; **~y** ['-i] Päderastie *f*.
p(a)ediatr|ician [pi:diə'triʃən], **~ist** ['pi:diətrist] Kinderarzt *m*; **~ics** [pi:di-'ætriks] *pl mit sing* Kinderheilkunde *f*.
pagan ['peigən] *s* Heide *m*, Heidin *f*; *a* heidnisch; **~ism** ['-izm] Heidentum *n*.
page [peidʒ] **1.** *s (Buch)* Seite *f*, *a*. Blatt; *fig* Blatt *n*, Episode; *typ* Kolumne *f*; *tr* paginieren, mit Seitenzahlen versehen; *title* ~ Titelseite *f*; **~-one(r)** *Am sl* sensationelle Nachricht; Berühmtheit *f*; **~-number** Seitenzahl *f*; **~-proof** Umbruchkorrektur *f*, -abzug *m*; **2.** *s* Page, Edelknabe; (Hotel-)Page, Boy; *Am* Amts-, Gerichtsdiener *m*; *tr* durch e-n Pagen holen lassen; über den Lautsprecher rufen lassen.
pageant ['pædʒənt] Aufzug *m*, Prozession, Parade, Schau *f*; Festspiel *n*; leere(r) Pomp, bloße(r) Prunk *m*; **~ry** ['-ri] Aufzüge *m pl*, Paraden *f pl*; Prachtentfaltung; *fig* leere Pracht *f*.
pagination [pædʒi'neiʃən] *(Buch)* Seitenzählung, Paginierung *f*.
pagoda [pə'goudə] *rel arch* Pagode *f*.
pah [pɑ:] *interj* pah! pfui!
pail [peil] Eimer, Kübel *m*; *dinner-~ (Am)* Eßgeschirr *n*; **~ful** ['-ful] Eimervoll *m*.
paillasse, palliasse [pæl'jæs] Strohsack *m*.
pain [pein] *s* Schmerz(en *pl*) *m*; Weh, Leid(en) *n*, Qual *f*, Kummer *m*, Angst, Sorge, Not *f*, Elend *n*, Mühe *f*; *pl* (Geburts-)Wehen *f pl*; *pl* Mühe *f*; *tr itr* schmerzen, wehtun (*s.o.* jdm); Schmerz, Kummer bereiten (*s.o.* jdm); *under, (up)on ~ of* bei Strafe *gen*; *death* bei Todesstrafe; *to be at ~s of doing s.th.* Mühe haben, etw zu tun; *to be in ~* leiden; *to feel ~* Schmerz empfinden *od* spüren; *to give s.o. a ~ in the neck* jdn auf die Palme bringen; *to put to ~* quälen; *to spare no ~s* keine Mühe scheuen; *to take ~s* sich (große) Mühe geben *od* machen (*with* mit); *it ~s me to* es fällt mir schwer zu; *compensation for ~ and suffering* Schmerzensgeld *n*; *~s and penalties* Geld- u. Freiheitsstrafen *f pl*; *~ in the neck (Am sl)* widerliche(r) Kerl *m*; unangenehme Arbeit *f*; **~ed** [-d] *a* leidend; **~ful** ['-ful] schmerzhaft, schmerzend; schmerzlich, unangenehm, peinlich; mühsam, mühevoll, mühselig; **~fulness** ['-fulnis] Schmerzhaftigkeit; Peinlichkeit *f*; **~-killer** schmerzstillende(s) Mittel *n*; **~less** ['-lis] schmerzlos; **~lessness** ['-lisnis] Schmerzlosigkeit *f*; **~ sensation** Schmerzgefühl *n*; **~staking** ['-zteikiŋ] *a* arbeitsam; gewissenhaft, gründlich, sorgfältig; *s* Mühe(waltung); Gewissenhaftigkeit, Sorgfalt *f*.
paint [peint] *tr* (be)malen; anstreichen; schminken, *fam* anmalen; *med* auftragen; bepinseln; *fig* schildern, beschreiben; *itr* malen; sich schminken; *s* Farbe *f*; Anstrich; *mot* Lack *m*; Schminke *f*; *to ~ in* hineinmalen; *to ~ out* anmalen, -streichen; übermalen; *to ~ the town red (fig)* alles auf den Kopf stellen; *he is not so bad as he is ~ed* er ist besser als sein Ruf; *wet ~!* frisch gestrichen! *war ~* Kriegsbemalung *f*; **~-box** Malkasten *m*; **~brush** (Mal-)Pinsel *m*; **~ coat** Farbanstrich *m*; **~ed** ['-id] *a* ge-, bemalt; geschminkt; *bot zoo* bunt, scheckig; *fig* künstlich, gestellt; bunt, farbenprächtig; *P~~ Lady (ent)* Distelfalter *m*; *bot* Pinks-, Federnelke; Rote Wucherblume *f*; **~er** ['-ə] (Kunst- *od* Dekorations-)Maler; *mot* Lackierer; *(house ~~)* Anstreicher *m*; *mar* Vor-, Fangleine *f*; *zoo* Puma, Kuguar *m*; *to cut the ~~* sich aus dem Staube machen; sich loslösen; **~ing** ['-iŋ] Malen; Anstreichen; Spritzlackieren; Schminken *n*; Malerei *f*; Bild, Gemälde *n*; Schilderung *f*; **~ remover** Farbentferner *m*; **~ress** ['-ris] Malerin *f*; **~ spray gun** Farbspritzpistole *f*.
pair [pɛə] *s* Paar; Gespann *n*; Partner; *sport* Zweier *m*; *tr* paaren, ein Paar machen aus; *itr* sich paaren, ein Paar bilden; *to ~ off (itr)* sich paarweise absondern; ein Paar bilden; *fam* (sich) heiraten; *tr* verheiraten; ein Paar *od* Paare machen aus; paarweise ordnen; *in ~s* paarweise; *a ~ of gloves, shoes* ein Paar *n* Handschuhe, Schuhe; *a ~ of scissors, tongs, trousers* e-e Schere, Zange, Hose; *a ~ of stairs, steps* e-e Treppenflucht; *that's another ~ of shoes* das ist e-e andere Sache; **~ing** ['-riŋ] Paarung *f*; *~~-season, -time* Paarungszeit *f*.
pajamas *s. pyjamas.*
Pakistan [pɑ:ki'stɑ:n] Pakistan *n*; **~i** [-i] *a* pakistanisch; *s* Pakistaner(in *f*) *m*.
pal [pæl] *s sl* Kumpel, Genosse, Kamerad *m*; *itr (to ~ up) sl* dicke Freunde werden *od* sein; sich anfreunden (*with* mit); **~ly** ['-i] *adv sl* kameradschaftlich, freundschaftlich.
palace ['pælis] Palast *m*, Schloß *n*; **~-car** *rail* Salonwagen *m*; **~-yard** Schloßhof *m*.
pal(a)eo|grapher [pæli'ɔgrəfə] Paläograph *m*; **~graphic(al)** [pælio(u)-'græfik(əl)] paläographisch; **~graphy** [pæli'ɔgrəfi] Paläographie *f*; **~lithic** [pælio(u)'liθik] paläolithisch, altsteinzeitlich; **~logy** [pæli'ɔlədʒi] Paläologie, Altertumskunde *f*; **~ontologic(al)** ['pæliɔntə'lɔdʒik(əl)] paläontologisch; **~ontologist** [pæliɔn-'tɔlədʒist] Paläontologe *m*; **~ontology** [pæliɔn'tɔlədʒi] Paläontologie *f*.
palanquin, palankeen [pælən'ki:n, *Am* 'pæ-] Tragsessel *m*, Sänfte *f*.
palat|able ['pælətəbl] schmackhaft; *fig* angenehm; **~al** ['pælətl] *a* Gaumen-; *s* Gaumenlaut *m*; **~alization** [pælətəlai'zeiʃən] Palatalisierung *f*; **~e** ['pælit] Gaumen; Geschmack(ssinn); *fig* Geschmack *m (for* an), Vorliebe *f (for* für); *hard ~~* harte(r) Gaumen *m*; *soft ~~* weiche(r) Gaumen *m*, Gaumensegel *n*; **~ine** ['pælətain] **1.** *a* Gaumen-; *s (~~ bone)* Gaumenbein *n*.
palat|ial [pə'leiʃəl] palastartig; stattlich, prächtig; **~inate** [pə'lætinit] Pfalzgrafschaft; Pfalz *f*; *P~~* Pfälzer(in *f*) *m*; *the (Rhine) P~* die (Rhein-)Pfalz; **~ine** ['pælətain] **2.** *a* Palast-; Pfalz-; pfalzgräflich; *P~~* pfälzisch; *s* Pfalzgraf; *(Schulter-)* Pelz; *P~~* Pfälzer(in *f*) *m*.
palaver [pə'lɑ:və] *s* Palaver; (endloses) Gerede, Geschwätz *n*; Schmeichelei *f*, Schmus *m*; *itr* schwatzen, klatschen; schmeicheln.
pal|e [peil] **1.** *a* bleich, fahl; blaß; *(Licht)* schwach; *fig* schwach, matt, farblos; *itr* erbleichen, erblassen, die Farbe verlieren; *fig* verblassen (*before, beside* neben); *tr* bleich machen, erbleichen lassen; *to turn ~~* blaß, bleich werden, erbleichen; *~~ blue* blaßblau; *~~ face* Bleichgesicht *n*; *~~-faced* bleichgesichtig; **~eness** ['-nis] Blässe *f a. fig*; **2.** Pfahl; Pfosten; (Grenz-)Zaun *m*; *fig* Grenzen *f pl*; Gebiet *n*, Bezirk *m*; *inside* od *within, outside* od *beyond the ~ of* innerhalb, außerhalb der Grenzen *gen bes. fig*; im Schoße *gen*; **~ing** ['-iŋ] Einzäunung *f*; (Pfahl-)Zaun *m*.
paleo ... *s. palaeo-*.
Palestin|e ['pælistain] Palästina *n*; **~ian** [pæles'tiniən] *a* palästin(ens)isch.
paletot ['pæltou] Paletot, Überzieher; lose(r) (Damen-)Mantel *m*.
palette ['pælit] Palette *a. fig*; *fig* Farbskala *f*; **~-knife** Streichmesser *n*, Spa(ch)tel *m* od *f*.
palfrey ['pɔ:lfri] *obs* Zelter *m (Pferd)*.
palingenesis [pælin'dʒenisis] Wiedergeburt; *biol* Palingenese *f*.
palisade [pæli'seid] *s* Palisade(npfahl *m*) *f*; *pl Am* Flußklippen *f pl*; *tr* mit e-r Palisade umgeben; einzäunen; verschanzen.
pall [pɔ:l] **1.** *itr* zuviel, langweilig werden (*on, upon s.o.* jdm); überdrüssig werden (*with s.th.* e-r S); reizlos sein (*on* für); *it never ~s on you* man bekommt es nie satt; **2.** *s* Bahr-, Leichentuch *n*; Altar-, Kelchdecke *f*; *(Rauch)* Schleier; *obs* (Staats-)Mantel *m*; Pallium *n*; *fig* Decke, Hülle *f*; *tr* ein-, umhüllen; **~bearer** *Am* Leichenträger; *Br* Hauptleidtragende(r) *m*.
palladium [pə'leidjəm] *pl -dia* Palladium, Schutzheiligtum *n*; *fig* Schutz, Hort *m*; *chem* Palladium *n*.
pallet ['pælit] **1.** Töpferscheibe; Palette *f*; Vergoldestempel *m*; *(Uhr)* Radhemmung *f*; **2.** Strohsack *m*; Matratze *f*; Bettlager *n*.
palliasse *s. paillasse.*
palliat|e ['pælieit] *tr* lindern, erleichtern, beruhigen; *fig* beschönigen, bemänteln, entschuldigen; abschwächen; **~ion** [pæli'eiʃən] Linderung, Erleichterung; *fig* Beschönigung, Bemäntelung *f*; **~ive** ['pæliətiv] *a* lindernd, erleichternd; *fig* beschönigend; abschwächend; *s* Linderungsmittel *n*.
pall|id ['pælid] blaß, bleich; **~or** ['pælə] Blässe *f*.
palm [pɑ:m] *s* Handfläche *f*, -teller *m*; Handbreite, -länge *f*; flache(s) Ende *n*; (Anker-)Flügel *m*; Schaufel *(e-s Geweihs)*; Palme; Siegespalme *f*; Sieg, Triumph *m*; *tr* streicheln; durch e-e Handbewegung verschwinden lassen; in der Hand verbergen; *Am sl* klauen; *to ~ s.th. off on s.o.* jdm etw andrehen, an-, aufhängen; *to bear, to carry off the ~* den Sieg davontragen; *to give the ~* den Preis zuerkennen; *to grease, to oil s.o.'s ~* jdn bestechen; *to have an itching ~ (fam)* ein einnehmendes Wesen haben; *to have in the ~ of o.'s hands (fig)* fest in der Hand haben; *to know like the ~ of o.'s hand* wie s-e Hosentasche kennen; *to yield the ~ to s.o.* jds Überlegenheit anerkennen; **~ary** ['pælməri] ausgezeichnet, erstklassig, hervorragend; siegreich; **~ate** ['pælmit] handförmig; *bot (Blatt)* gefingert *od* handnervig; *zoo* mit Schwimmhäuten (versehen); **~ butter** Palmbutter *f*; **~er** ['-ə] Wallfahrer, Pilger; Taschenspieler, Schwindler *m*; *~~ worm (ent)* Prozessionsraupe *f*; **~ette** [pæl'met] Palmette *f (Ornament)*; **~etto** [pæl'metou] Zwergpalme *f*; **~-greasing** Bestechung *f*; **~house** Palmenhaus *n*; **~iped(e)** ['pælmiped, -pi:d] *zoo* mit Schwimmhäuten (versehen); **~ist** ['-ist] Handliniendeuter, -leser, Chiromant *m*; **~istry** ['-istri] Handliniendeuten *n*, Chiromantie *f*; **~-leaf** Palmzweig *m*; **~-nut oil** Palmkernöl *n*; **~-oil** Palmöl *n*; *hum* Bestechungsgelder *n pl*; **P~ Sunday** Palmsonntag *m*; **~-tree** Palmbaum *m*, Palme *f*; **~y** ['pɑ:mi]

palmenreich, -beschattet; Palmen-; *fig* glücklich, erfolgreich; *~~ days (pl)* Blüte-, Glanzzeit *f*.
palooka, paluka [pə'lu:kə] *Am sl* Versager *m*, Flasche *f*.
palp [pælp] *zoo* Fühler *m*, Tastorgan *n*; **~ability** [-ə'biliti] Fühlbarkeit; Wahrnehmbarkeit; Handgreiflichkeit *f*; **~able** ['-əbl] berührbar, fühlbar; *fig* handgreiflich, offenbar; **~ate** ['-eit] *tr med* palpieren, (untersuchend) ab-, betasten; *a* [-it] *zoo* mit Fühlern versehen; **~ation** [pæl'peiʃən] *med* Palpieren, Ab-, Betasten, Befühlen *n*; **~ebral** ['pælpəbrəl] *a scient* Augenlider-; **~itant** ['-itənt] pochend, zitternd; **~itate** ['-iteit] *itr (Herz)* klopfen, pochen, rasch schlagen; zittern, beben (*with* vor); **~itation** [pælpi'teiʃən] Herzklopfen, Zittern *n*.
palsy ['pɔ:lzi] *tr* lähmen; *s* Lähmung *a. fig*; Kraftlosigkeit *f*; Zittern *n*, Tremor *m*; *fig* lähmende(r) Einfluß *m*.
palter ['pɔ:ltə] *itr* unaufrichtig handeln (*with s.o.* an jdm); zweideutig reden (*with s.o.* mit jdm; *about s.th.* über etw); gleichgültig, leichtsinnig sein; leichtfertig umgehen (*with* mit); schachern, feilschen (*with s.o. about s.th.* mit jdm über etw).
paltr|iness ['pɔ:ltrinis] Belanglosigkeit, Wertlosigkeit, Erbärmlichkeit *f*; **~y** ['-i] belanglos, unwichtig, unbedeutend, nebensächlich, geringfügig; erbärmlich, jämmerlich; *~~ debts (pl)* Bagatellschulden *f pl*; *~~ excuses (pl)* fadenscheinige Ausreden *f pl*.
pampas ['pæmpəz] *pl* Pampas *f pl*.
pamper ['pæmpə] *tr* verwöhnen, verzärteln, verhätscheln; frönen.
pamphlet ['pæmflit] Broschüre *f*; Prospekt *m*, Werbe-, Flugschrift *f*; Pamphlet *n*; **~eer** [pæmfli'ti:ə] Pamphletist *m*.

*

pan [pæn] **1.** *s* Pfanne *a. allg min geog*; (flache) Schüssel, Schale; Zündpfanne *f (alter Feuerwaffen)*; *typ* Setzschiff *n*; Waagschale; *(kleine)* Eisscholle; *sl* Fresse *f*, Gesicht *n*; *Am sl* vernichtende Kritik *f*; *tr min (Kies, Sand in der Pfanne)* waschen; *(Kamera)* schwenken; *Am fam* bekommen; *Am fig* scharf kritisieren, verreißen; *itr min* Kies waschen; *(Kies)* Gold hergeben, liefern; *to ~ out (tr)* hergeben, liefern; *itr fam (to ~ out well)* klappen, glücken, hinhauen, einschlagen; *it was a flash in the ~* es war ein Strohfeuer; *bread-~* Brotschüssel *f*; *flushing-~* Klosettschale *f*; *frying-~* Bratpfanne *f*; *out of the ~~ into the fire* vom Regen in die Traufe; *meat-~* Fleischschüssel *f*; *sauce-~* Tiegel *m*, Schmorpfanne *f*; **~cake** *s* Eier-, Pfannkuchen *m*; *(~~ landing) aero* Bumslandung *f*; schwere(r) Fall *m*; *itr tr aero* durchsacken (lassen); *(fam) as flat as a ~~* flach wie ein Tisch; *to fall flat as a ~~ (sl)* ein großer Reinfall sein; schiefgehen; *P~~ Day* Fastnachtsdienstag *m*; **2.** *in Zssgen* Pan-, All-; **~handle** *s* Pfannenstiel; *Am* vorspringende(r) schmale(r) Gebietsstreifen *m*; *itr sl Am* fechten, betteln; **~handler** *Am sl* Bettler *m*; **~nikin** ['-ikin] Pfännchen *n*; (kleiner) Metallbecher *m*; *sl* Rübe *f*, Kopf *m*; **~tile** ['-tail] Dachpfanne *f*, Hohlziegel *m*.
Pan [pæn] **1.** *rel* Pan, Faun *m*; **2.** *geogr* Pan-, pan-; **~-American** panamerikanisch; **~-Europe** Paneuropa *n*; **~-Germanism** Pangermanismus *m*; **~-Islamic** panislamisch; **~-Slavism** Panslawismus *m*.
panacea [pænə'siə] Allheil-, Universalmittel *n*.
panache [pə'næʃ] Helm-, Federbusch; *fig* Prunk *m*, Pracht; Prahlerei *f*.
Panama [pænə'mɑ:, *in Zssgen*: 'pænəmɑ:] Panama *n*; **~ Canal** Panamakanal *m*; **~ hat** Panamahut *m*.
panchromatic [pænkro(u)'mætik] *phot* panchromatisch.
pancre|as ['pæŋkriəs] *anat* Pankreas *n*, Bauchspeicheldrüse *f*; **~atic** [pæŋkri'ætik] pankreatisch, Pankreas-; *~~ juice (physiol)* Bauchspeichel *m*.
panda ['pændə] *zoo* Panda *m*.
pandemic [pæn'demik] *(Krankheit)* allgemein verbreitet.
pandemonium [pændi'mounjəm] *fig* Inferno *n*; Tumult, Höllenlärm *m*.
pander ['pændə] *s* Kuppler(in *f*); (Ver-) Mittler *m*; *tr* (ver)kuppeln; *itr* Vorschub leisten (*to s.o., s.th.* jdm, e-r S).
pane [pein] (viereckige) Scheibe, Fläche *f*, (flaches) Fach *n*; Fensterscheibe; Tür-, Wandfüllung *f*.
panegyr|ic [pæni'dʒirik] Lobrede *f* (*on, upon* auf); **~ic(al)** [-ik(əl)] lobend, voller Lob; Lob-.
panel ['pænl] *s arch* Paneel *n*, Täfelung, Verkleidung; Tafel *f*, Feld *n*, (glatte, viereckige) Fläche; *(Wand, Tür)* Füllung; (Holz-)Platte; Fensterscheibe; *(Kleid)* Bahn *f*; *phot* Hochformat *n*; *(instrument ~)* Instrumententafel *f*; *mot* Armaturenbrett *n*; *el* Schalttafel *f*; *(Anzeige)* Kästchen; *aero* Signaltuch *n*; *min* Grubenabschnitt; Ausschuß *m*, Kommission; *jur* Geschworenenliste *f*, Geschworene, Schöffen *m pl*; Liste *f* der Kassenärzte; Diskussionsgruppe *f*, Forum *n*; *(Meinungsforschung)* Befragtengruppe *f*; *tr* täfeln (*with* mit); *(Fläche)* in Felder einteilen; *jur (Geschworenenliste)* aufstellen; *(Kleid)* mit Streifen verzieren; *on the ~ (Arzt)* zu allen Kassen zugelassen; krankenversichert; *advisory ~* beratende(r) Ausschuß *m*; *~ of experts* Sachverständigenausschuß *m*; **~ discussion** Podiumsgespräch *n*; **~ doctor** Kassenarzt *m*; **~ envelope** Fenster(brief)umschlag *m*; **~-house** *Am* Bordell *n*; **~ize** ['-aiz] *itr* an e-r Fernsehdiskussion teilnehmen; **~ist** ['-ist] Diskussionsteilnehmer *m*; **~(l)ing** ['-iŋ] Täfeln *n*; Täfelung *f*; **~ patient** Kassenpatient *m*; **~-work** *arch* Fachwerk *n*.
pang [pæŋ] stechende(r), plötzliche(r) heftige(r) Schmerz; Krampf *m*; *fig* plötzliche Angst, Beklemmung *f*; Weh *n*; *~ of conscience* Gewissensqual *f*; *~s of death* Todesangst *f*.
panic ['pænik] **1.** *(~ grass)* Hirse *f*; **2.** *a* panisch; *s* Panik *f*, panische(r) Schreck(en) *m*; plötzliche Panik *bes. fin*; *fig sl* Bombe *f*; *tr* in Schrecken versetzen, e-n Schreck einjagen (*s.o.* jdm); mit panischer Angst erfüllen; *Am sl* entzücken, begeistern, mitreißen; zum Lachen bringen, Beifall ernten von; *itr* von panischer Angst ergriffen sein; den Kopf verlieren; **~ky** ['-i] *fam* in panischem Schrecken; nervös, unruhig (*at* über); alarmierend; *~~ measures (pl)* Angstmaßnahmen *f pl*; **~ monger** Panikmacher *m*; **~ purchase, sale** Angstkauf, -verkauf *m*; **~-stricken** *a* in panischem Schrecken.
panicle ['pænikl] *bot* Rispe *f*.
panjandrum [pən'dʒændrəm] große(s) Tier *n*; *pej* Wichtigtuer, *fam* Angeber; Hochstapler *m*.
pannier ['pæniə] große(r) Korb; Rükkentragkorb *m*, Kiepe *f*; Reifrock *m*, Krinoline *f*; Petticoat *m*.
panocha [pə'noutʃə] *Am* Karamelbonbon *m* od *n*, (Sahne-)Karamelle *f*.
panoply ['pænəpli] vollständige Rüstung; *allg* Prachtausstattung *f*.
panoram|a [pænə'rɑ:mə] Panorama *n a. fig*, Rundblick *m* (*of* über); *fig* (gute) Übersicht *f* (*of* über); *~~ equipment* Rundsuchgerät *n*; **~ic** [-'ræmik] panoramaartig; *mot* Rundsicht-; *~~ sketch* Ansichtsskizze *f*; *~~ windscreen (mot)* Rundsichtverglasung *f*.
pansy ['pænzi] *s bot* Stiefmütterchen *n*; *sl* Weichling, Homosexuelle(r) *m*; *a sl* weibisch.
pant [pænt] *itr* keuchen; *(to ~ for breath)* nach Luft schnappen; *(Herz)* klopfen, pochen; verlangen, lechzen, *fam* wild sein (*for, after* nach); Dampf, Rauch ausstoßen; *tr (to ~ forth, to ~ out)* (keuchend) hervorstoßen; *s* keuchende(r) Atemzug *m*; Keuchen *n*; Schlag *m (des Herzens)*; *tech* Auspuffen *n*.
pantaloon [pæntə'lu:n] *hist* Hanswurst; dumme(r) August *m*; *Am pl* Hose *f*.
pantechnicon [pæn'teknikən] Lagerhaus *n*, (Möbel-)Speicher *m*; *(~ van)* Möbelwagen *m*.
panthe|ism ['pænθi(:)izm] Pantheismus *m*; **~ist** ['-ist] Pantheist *m*; **~istic(al)** [pænθi(:)'istik(əl)] pantheistisch.
panther ['pænθə] Panther; *Am* Puma *m*.
panties ['pæntiz] *pl* (Damen-)Schlüpfer *m*; Kinderhöschen *n pl*.
pantograph ['pæntəgrɑ:f] *tech* Storchschnabel *m*.
pantomim|e ['pæntəmaim] *theat* Pantomime *f*; *allg* Gebärdenspiel; *(in England)* Weihnachtsspiel *n*; **~ic** [pæntə'mimik] pantomimisch.
pantry ['pæntri] Vorrats-, Speisekammer *f*; *(butler's ~)* Anrichtezimmer *n*.
pants [pænts] *pl* (lange) Unterhose; *fam bes. Am* Hose *f*.
panty ['pænti]: **~ set** Garnitur *f* Unterwäsche; **~-waist** *Am pop* weibische(r) Mann *m*; Hemdhöschen *n*.
pap [pæp] **1.** *obs* Brustwarze; (Berg-) Kuppe *f*; **2.** (Kinder-)Brei *m*, Mus *n*, Papp; *allg* Brei *m*, Mark, (Frucht-) Fleisch *n*; *Am fam* Protektion *f*; **~py** ['-i] *a* breiig, musig; *fig* schwächlich; *s* Brei, Papp *m*.
papa [pə'pɑ:, *Am a.* 'pɑ:pə] *(Kindersprache)* Papa, Vati *m*.
pap|acy ['peipəsi] Pontifikat; Papsttum *n*; **~al** ['-əl] päpstlich; (römisch-) katholisch; *the P~ States (hist)* der Kirchenstaat; **~ist** ['-ist] *s pej* Papist *m*; *a u.* **~istic(al)** [pə'pistik(əl)] *pej* papistisch.
paper ['peipə] *s* Papier; Blatt *n*, Zettel *m*; Blatt Papier; Formblatt, Formular; Schriftstück *n*, Akte *f*, Dokument *n*, Urkunde *f*; Aufsatz *m*, Abhandlung *f*, Vortrag *m* (*on* über); *(examination ~)* Prüfungsarbeit *f*; Wertpapier *n*, Schuldtitel, Wechsel *m*; Banknote *f*; *(Börse)* Brief *m*; Zeitung *f*, Blatt *n*; *(wall ~)* Tapete *f*; *(Nadeln)* Brief *m*, Heft *n*; *theat* Freikarte *f*; *pl* (Ausweis-, Legitimations-)Papiere *n pl*; Akten *f pl*; Papiere *n pl*, Briefschaften, -sachen *f pl*; *a* papieren, aus Papier, Papier-; (hauch)dünn; nur auf dem Papier (stehend); *tr* zu Papier bringen, niederschreiben, aufzeichnen; einwickeln, verpacken; tapezieren; *fam (das Theater)* durch Verteilen von Freikarten füllen; *Am sl* Falschgeld verbreiten in; *on ~* auf dem Papier, geschrieben, gedruckt; *fig* in der

Theorie; *to commit to* ~, *to put down on* ~ zu Papier bringen, schriftlich niederlegen; *to move for* ~*s* die Vorlage der schriftlichen Unterlagen beantragen; *to read a* ~ e-n Vortrag halten (*on* über); *to send in o.'s* ~*s* s-n Abschied nehmen, abdanken, zurücktreten; *ballot(ing), voting* ~ Stimm-, Wahlzettel *m*; *bank*-~ Bankwechsel *m*, -akzept *n*; *blotting*-~ Löschblatt *n*; *brown* ~ Packpapier *n*; *call-up* ~*s (pl)* Einberufungsbefehl *m*; *carbon*-~ Kohle-, Durchschlag-, -schreibpapier *n*; *command*-~ Bestellzettel *m*; *commercial* ~ Waren-, Handelswechsel *m*; *daily, evening, sports* ~ Tages-, Abend-, Sportzeitung *f*; *fashion* ~ Modejournal *n*, -zeitung *f*; *illustrated* ~ Illustrierte *f*; *letter-, note*-~ Briefpapier *n*; *official* ~ Aktenpapier *n*; *parchment*-~ Pergament-, Butterbrotpapier *n*; *printing*-~ Druckpapier *n*; *sanitary, toilet*-~ Klosettpapier *n*; *sheet of* ~ Blatt *n* Papier; *stamped* ~ Stempelpapier *n*; *Sunday* ~ Sonntagsblatt *n*; *trade* ~ Fach-, Wirtschaftszeitschrift *f*; *typewriting*-~ Schreibmaschinenpapier *n*; *waste* ~ Altpapier *n*; *weekly* ~ Wochenblatt *n*; *wrapping* ~ Packpapier *n*; *writing*-~ Schreibpapier *n*; ~**back** Buch *n* in Pappband; ~-**bag** Tüte *f*; ~-**basket** Papierkorb *m*; ~-**board** Pappe *f*; ~**bound** *a* mit Pappeinband; ~-**boy** Zeitungsjunge *m*; ~-**carriage** Wagen *m* (e-r Schreibmaschine); ~-**chase** Schnitzeljagd *f*; ~ **circulation** *fin* Notenumlauf *m*; ~-**clip, -fastener** Büro-, Heft-, Musterklammer *f*; ~ **clipping** Zeitungsausschnitt *m*; ~-**credit** Wechselkredit *m*; ~ **currency** Papiergeld *n*; Notenumlauf *m*; ~-**cutter** Brieföffner *m*; Papierschneidemaschine *f*; ~-**folder** Falzbein *n*; ~-**hanger** Tapezierer; *Am sl* Wechselreiter, Banknotenfälscher *m*; ~-**hangings** *pl* Tapete *f*; *Am sl* Wechselreiterei, Banknotenfälschung *f*; ~-**industry** Papierindustrie *f*; ~-**knife** Brieföffner *m*; ~ **lantern** Lampion *m*; ~-**mill** Papierfabrik *f*; ~-**manufacture** Papierherstellung *f*; ~-**money** Papiergeld *n*; ~-**profits** *pl com* Buchgewinne *m pl*; ~-**pulp** Papierbrei *m*, -masse *f*; ~-**shavings** *pl* Papierschnitzel *m pl*; ~-**size** Kleister *m*; ~-**stainer** Tapetenmaler *m*; ~-**standard** Papierwährung *f*; ~-**war(fare)** Pressefehde *f*; Papierkrieg *m*; ~**weight** Briefbeschwerer *m*; ~-**work** Schreibarbeit *f*; ~**y** ['-ri] papierartig, blättrig, dünn.

papier mâché ['pæpjei'mɑ:ʃei, *Am* 'peipəmə'ʃei] Papier-, Pappmaché *n*.

papill|a [pə'pilə] *pl -ae* [-i:] Papille, Warze *f*; ~**ary** [-əri] warzenförmig, -artig, papillar.

papoose [pə'pu:s] (nordamerik.) Indianerkind *n*; *Am sl* nicht gewerkschaftlich organisierte(r) Arbeiter *m*.

paprika, *Am a.* **paprica** ['pæprikə] Paprika *m*.

papyrus [pə'paiərəs] *pl a. -ri* [-ai] Papyrus(staude *f*); Papyrus *m*.

par [pɑ:] *s fin* Pari *n*, Kurswert, Wechselkurs; *fam* Abschnitt, Zeitungsartikel *m*; *above* ~ über pari; *fig* überdurchschnittlich, überragend; *at* ~ al pari; zum Nennwert; *below* ~ unter pari; *fig* unterdurchschnittlich, nicht auf der Höhe; *on a* ~ *with* auf gleicher Stufe mit; ebenbürtig; *up to* ~ *(fig)* auf der Höhe; *to feel below* ~ sich nicht wohl fühlen; *issue* ~ Ausgabekurs *m*; *mint* ~ Münzparität *f*; ~ *of exchange* (Währungs-)Parität *f*, Parikurs *m*.

par(a) ['pær(ə)-] *pref scient* Para-.

Para ['pɑ:rə]: ~ **nut** Paranuß *f*.

parab|le ['pærəbl] Gleichnis(rede *f*) *n*, Parabel, Allegorie *f*; ~**ola** [pə'ræbələ] *math* Parabel *f*; ~**olic(al)** [pærə'bɔlik(əl)] gleichnishaft, allegorisch; ~*olic (math)* parabelartig, Parabel-; ~*olic mirror, reflector* Parabolspiegel *m*; ~**oloid** [pə'ræbəlɔid] *math* Paraboloid *n*.

parachut|e ['pærəʃu:t] *s* Fallschirm *m*; *zoo* Flughaut *f*; *tr* (mit dem Fallschirm) abwerfen, absetzen; *itr* abspringen; ~~ *bag, pack* Fallschirmsack *m*; ~~ *bomb* Fallschirmbombe *f*; ~~ *brake* Bremsschirm *m (e-s Flugzeuges)*; ~~ *canister, container* (Fallschirm-)Abwurfbehälter *m*; ~~ *cord* Fallschirm-, Fangleine *f*; ~~ *course* Fallschirmspringerlehrgang *m*; ~~ *descent* Fallschirmabsprung *m*; ~~ *drop* Fallschirmabwurf *m*; ~~ *equipment* Fallschirmausrüstung *f*; ~~ *flare* Leuchtfallschirm *m*; ~~ *harness* Fallschirmgurt *m*; ~~ *jump* Fallschirmabsprung *m*; ~~ *jumper* Fallschirmspringer *m*; ~~ *rigger* Fallschirmwart *m*; ~~ *rip-cord, rip-line* (Fallschirm-)Reißleine *f*; ~~ *tower* (Fallschirm-)Sprungturm *m*; ~~ *troops pl* Fallschirmtruppen *f pl*; ~**er** ['-ə] *Am* Fallschirmjäger *m*; ~**ist** ['-ist] Fallschirmspringer, *mil* -jäger *m*.

parade [pə'reid] *s* Prachtentfaltung *f*, Prunk, Pomp *m*, Gepränge *n*; (Truppen-)Parade, Truppen-, Heerschau *f*, Vorbeimarsch; *(~-ground)* Exerzier-, Paradeplatz; Appell; Auf-, Festzug *m*; Vorführung; *(fashion ~)* Modenschau, Modevorführung; *Br* Promenade *f (am Meer)*; Spaziergänger *m pl*; *tr* aufziehen, -marschieren, exerzieren lassen; festlich ziehen durch; prunken, protzen, *fam* angeben mit; *itr* paradieren; in e-m Festzug (mit)marschieren; herumstolzieren, großspurig auftreten, *fam* angeben; *mil* aufmarschieren, -ziehen; exerzieren; *to* ~ *over* nachexerzieren; *to be on* ~ aufmarschiert sein; exerzieren; *to make a* ~ *of s.th.* mit etw protzen; ~ *rest!* rührt Euch!

paradigm ['pærədaim, *Am* '-dim] Muster, (Muster-)Beispiel *n*; ~**atic** [pærədig'mætik] beispiel-, musterhaft, exemplarisch.

paradis|e ['pærədais] *(P)* ~ das Paradies, der Garten Eden; *in* ~~ im siebenten Himmel; *to live in a fool's* ~~ sich etw vormachen; ~**iac(al)** [pærə'disiæk, pærədi'saiəkəl] paradiesisch.

paradox ['pærədɔks] Paradox(on) *n*, Widersinn *m*, widersinnige Behauptung *f*; ~**ical** [pærə'dɔksikəl] paradox, widersinnig, sonderbar, seltsam.

paradrop ['pærədrɔp] *tr* (mit dem Fallschirm) abwerfen.

paraffin ['pærəfin], ~**e** [-fi:n] *chem* Paraffin; *(~ oil)* Paraffinöl *n*; ~ **candle** Paraffinkerze *f*.

paragon ['pærəgən] Vorbild, Muster *n*; *fam* Musterknabe; Paragon, (großer) Brillant *m*; *typ* Text *f (20 Punkte)*.

paragraph ['pærəgrɑ:f] *s typ* Absatz; Abschnitt *m*, Abteilung *f*, Paragraph; *(~ mark)* Paragraph; (kurzer) Zeitungsartikel *m*; *tr* in Absätze, Paragraphen einteilen; in e-m Zeitungsartikel behandeln; ~**er** ['pærəgræfə], ~ **writer** Artikelschreiber, Reporter, (Lokal-)Berichterstatter *m*.

Paraguay ['pærəgwai] Paraguay *n*; ~**an** [pærə'gwaiən] *a* paraguayisch; *s* Paraguayer(in *f*) *m*; ~ **tea** Matetee *m*.

parakeet ['pærəki:t], **paroquet** ['pærəket] Sittich *m*; *Australian grass* ~ Wellensittich *m*.

parall|actic [pærə'læktik] parallaktisch; ~**ax** ['pærəlæks] *astr* Parallaxe *f*.

parallel ['pærəlel] *a math* parallel (*with, to* mit); *fig* gleichlaufend, -gerichtet (*to, with* zu, mit); verwandt, ähnlich, entsprechend; *s math* Parallele *a. fig* (*to* zu); *fig* Entsprechung *f*, Gegenstück *n*, Parallelfall *m*; Parallelität *f*, Gleichlauf; *geog (~ of latitude)* Parallel-, Breitenkreis; *el* Mehrfachstromkreis *m*; *mil* Sperrlinie *f*; *typ* Parallel-, Hinweiszeichen *n* (||); *tr* parallel machen (*to* zu); parallel sein *od* (ver)laufen zu; vergleichen, ea. gegenüberstellen; ein Gegenstück bilden zu, passen zu, gleichkommen (*s.th.* e-r S); entsprechen (*s.th.* dat); *el* parallel schalten; *without* ~ unvergleichlich; *to be in* ~ *with* in Parallele stehen zu, vergleichbar sein mit; *to be without (a)* ~ einzig dastehen, keine Parallele haben; *to draw a* ~ *between* e-e Parallele ziehen zwischen, e-n Vergleich anstellen zwischen; ~ **bars** *pl sport* Barren *m*; ~ **connection** Parallelschaltung *f*; ~**epiped** [pærəle'lepiped] *math* Parallelepiped(on), Parallelflach *n*; ~**ism** ['pærəlelizm] Parallelismus *m*; ~**ogram** [pærə'leləgræm] Parallelogramm *n*; ~~ *of forces* Kräfteparallelogramm *n*.

paraly|se, *Am* ~**ze** ['pærəlaiz] *tr* lähmen *a. fig*; *(Verkehr)* lahmlegen; *fig* zum Erliegen, zum Stillstand bringen; unwirksam machen; ~~*d with fear* starr vor Schrecken; ~**sis** [pə'rælisis] *pl -ses* [-si:z] Lähmung *f a. fig*; *fig* Stillstand *m*, Unwirksamkeit *f*; ~**tic** [pærə'litik] *a* paralytisch; gelähmt; *s* Gelähmte(r), Paralytiker *m*.

paramilitary ['pærəmilitəri] halbmilitärisch, militärähnlich.

paramount [pærə'maunt] höherstehend (*to* als), überlegen (*to* dat); wichtigst, äußerst, höchst, größt, oberst, Haupt-; *to be* ~ an erster Stelle stehen.

paramour ['pærəmuə] Geliebte *f*; Liebhaber *m*.

paranoi|a [pærə'nɔiə] Geistesgestörtheit *f*; ~**ac** [-ək] *s* Paranoiker *m*; *a* geistesgestört, paranoisch; ~**d** [-ɔid] *a* paranoid.

parapet ['pærəpit, -pet] *mil* Brustwehr *f*; (Brücken-, Balkon-)Geländer *n*.

paraphernalia [pærəfə'neiljə] *pl* persönliche(s) Eigentum *n*; Gegenstände *m pl*, Dinge *n pl*; Zubehör *n*, Ausrüstung *f*.

paraphrase ['pærəfreiz] *s* Umschreibung *f*; *tr itr* umschreiben.

parapsychology ['pærəsai'kɔlədʒi] Parapsychologie *f*.

parasit|e ['pærəsait] *biol* Schmarotzer, Parasit *m a. fig*; ~**ic** [pærə'sitik] *biol* parasitisch; *med tech* parasitär; *fig* schmarotzerhaft; ~**ism** ['pærəsaitizm] *scient* Parasitismus *m*; *fig* Schmarotzertum *n*.

parasol [pærə'sɔl] Sonnenschirm *m*.

parasuit ['pærəsju:t] Fallschirmkombination *f*.

paratroop ['pærətru:p]: *attr* Fallschirmjäger-; Luftlande-; *s pl* Fallschirm-, Luftlandetruppen *f pl*; ~ **boots** *pl* Fallschirmjägerstiefel *m pl*; ~ **descent** Fallschirmjägerabsprung *m*; ~ **dropper** Absetzflugzeug *n*; ~**er** ['-ə] Fallschirmjäger *m*; ~~ *raid* Springerangriff *m*; ~ **operation** Luftlandeoperation *f*.

paratyphoid ['pærə'taifɔid] *(~ fever) med* Paratyphus *m*.

parboil ['pɑ:bɔil] *tr* ankochen; *(Raum)* überhitzen.

parcel ['pɑ:sl] *s* Paket, Päckchen *n*; *com* Partie *f*, Posten *m*, Los; Gepäckstück; *fig pej* (Lumpen-)Pack *n*; *(Land)* Parzelle *f*; *fam* Haufen *m*, Menge; *pl*

(Grundstücks-)Beschreibung *f*; *tr (to ~ up)* verpacken, ein Paket machen aus; *(to ~ out)* parzellieren, aufteilen; *mar* schmarten; *a* Teil-; *by ~s* stückweise; *part and ~* ein wesentlicher Bestandteil; *postal ~* Postpaket *n*; *~ of land* Landparzelle *f*; *~ of shares* Aktienpaket *n*; *~* **delivery** Paketzustellung *f*; *~* **lift** Warenaufzug *m*; *~* **office** Paketschalter *m*; *~* **post** Paketpost *f*; *to send by ~~* als Postpaket schicken; *~* **service** Paketzustelldienst *m*; *~* **sticker** Paketaufklebeadresse *f*; *~* **van** Gepäckwagen *m*.

parcenary ['pɑ:sinəri] Erbengemeinschaft *f*; gemeinschaftliche(s) Erbe *n*.

parch [pɑ:tʃ] *tr* dörren, rösten; austrocknen; durstig machen (*s.o.* jdn); *to be ~ed with thirst* vor Durst verschmachten *od* umkommen; **~ing** ['-iŋ] *(Hitze)* sengend; *(Durst)* brennend.

parchment ['pɑ:tʃmənt] Pergament (-handschrift, -urkunde *f*) *n*.

pard [pɑ:d] *Am sl* Partner, Kumpel *m*.

pardon ['pɑ:dn] *tr* begnadigen; vergeben, verzeihen (*s.o.* jdm); *s* Verzeihung, Vergebung; Begnadigung(sschreiben *n*) *f*; *rel* Ablaß *m*; *I beg your ~* ich bitte um Entschuldigung; Verzeihung! wie bitte? **~able** ['-əbl] verzeihlich, entschuldbar; *(Sünde)* läßlich; **~er** ['-ə] *hist rel* Ablaßprediger, *pej* -krämer *m*.

pare [pɛə] *tr* schälen; (ab)schälen; *(Nägel)* schneiden; *(Leder)* anschärfen; *fig* kürzen, reduzieren.

paregoric [pærə'gɔrik] *a* lindernd, schmerzstillend; *s* Linderungsmittel *n*.

parent ['pɛərənt] Elternteil, Vater *m*, Mutter *f*; Erzeuger *m*, Muttertier *n*, -pflanze *f*; Ursprung *m*, -sache, Quelle *f*; Ausgangs-, Grund-; *pl* Eltern *pl*; *attr* Vater-, Mutter-, Erzeuger-; *~s-in-law* Schwiegereltern *pl*; **~age** ['-idʒ] Abstammung, Ab-, Herkunft *f*, Ursprung *m*; Familie; Elternschaft *f*; **~al** [pə'rentl] elterlich; *fig* ursprünglich; *~* **company** Stammhaus *n*, Mutter-, Dachgesellschaft *f*; **~less** ['-lis] elternlos; *~* **metal** Grundmetall *n*; *~* **rock** Urgestein *n*; *~* **ship** Mutterschiff *n*; *~* **unit** Stammtruppenteil *m*.

parenthe|sis [pə'renθisis] *pl -ses* [-si:z] Einschaltung *(im Text)*, Parenthese; Zwischenbemerkung *f*; *pl* runde Klammern *f pl*; **~size** [-saiz] *tr* einschalten; in (runde) Klammern setzen; **~tic(al)** [pærən'θetik(əl)] eingeschaltet; eingeklammert; *fig* erläuternd; beiläufig.

parget ['pɑ:dʒit] *tr (Wand, Decke)* verputzen, gipsen; *s* Bewurf, Verputz; Stuck *m*.

pariah ['pæriə, *Am* pə'raiə] *rel* Paria *a. fig*; *fig* Ausgestoßene(r) *m*.

parietal [pə'raiitl] *anat bot* parietal; Parietal-, Wand-; *~* **bone** Scheitelbein *n*; *~* **lobe** Scheitellappen *m*.

paring ['pɛəriŋ] Abschneiden; Schälen *n*; *(abgetrennte)* Schale *f*, abgeschnittene(s) Stück *n*; *pl* Abschabsel *n pl*, Späne *m pl*, Abfall *m*, Schnitzel *m pl*; **~-knife** Schaber *m*; Schäl-, Schustermesser *n*; *~* **plough** Schälpflug *m*.

Paris ['pæris] Paris *n*; *attr* Pariser; **~ian** [pə'rizjən] *a* Pariser; aus Paris; *s* Pariser(in *f*) *m*.

parish ['pæriʃ] *s* Kirchspiel *n*; (Pfarr-, Kirchen-)Gemeinde; *(civil ~)* (Land-) Gemeinde *f*; *attr* Pfarr-, Gemeinde-; *to go on the ~* der Gemeinde zur Last fallen; *~* **church** Pfarrkirche *f*; *~* **clerk** Küster *m*; *~* **council** Gemeinderat *m*; **~ioner** [pə'riʃənə] Pfarrkind; Gemeindeglied *n*; *~* **meeting** Gemeindeversammlung *f*; **~(-pump) politics** Kirchturmpolitik *f*; *~* **priest** Ortspfarrer *m*; *~* **register** Kirchenbuch *n*; Einwohnerkartei *f*; *~* **relief** öffentliche Armenfürsorge, Fürsorgeunterstützung *f*; *~* **road** Gemeindeweg *m*; *~* **school** Gemeindeschule *f*.

parity ['pæriti] Gleichheit, Gleichberechtigung; Ähnlichkeit, Analogie; *fin* Parität *f*, Wechsel-Umrechnungskurs *m*; *to be at a ~* pari stehen; *~ of reasoning* Analogieschluß *m*; *~ of votes* Stimmengleichheit *f*.

park [pɑ:k] Park *m*, (Park-)Anlagen *f pl*; Grünfläche *f*; Naturpark *m*, -schutzgebiet *n*; *Am* weite Lichtung *f*, weite(s) Tal *n*; *mot* Parkplatz; *mil* Wagen-, Artilleriepark, Sammelplatz *m*, -stelle *f*; *tr (Gelände)* einfriedigen, einhegen; aufbewahren; abstellen; *mil* (auf e-r Sammelstelle) zs.bringen, sammeln; zs. auffahren; *mot* parken, abstellen; *itr mot* parken; *Am sl* sich ruhig hinsetzen; *to ~ out* in Pflege geben (*with* bei); *artillery ~* Artilleriepark *m*; *car ~ (Br)* Parkplatz; *national ~* Nationalpark *m*; *oyster ~* Austernpark *m*; *~ of tanks* Panzerpark *m*; *~* **guard** Parkwächter *m*; **~ing** ['-iŋ] Parken-; *attr* Park-; *problem of ~~* Parkproblem *n*; *~~ area, place* Abstell-, Parkplatz *m*; *~~ building* Parkhaus, -gebäude *n*; *~~ garage* Parkhaus *n*; *~~ light (mot)* Standlicht *n*; *~~ lot, space (Am)* Parkplatz *m*; *~~ meter* Parkuhr *f*; **~way** *Am* Allee *f*.

parka ['pɑ:kə] Anorak *m*; *mil* Schneehemd *n*.

parky ['pɑ:ki] *sl* eisig, kalt, frostig.

*

parlance ['pɑ:ləns] *obs u. Am* Rede-, Ausdrucks-, Sprechweise; Sprache *f*, Idiom *n*; *in common, ordinary ~* in der Alltags-, Umgangssprache; *in legal ~* in der Rechtssprache; *in vulgar ~* in vulgärer Ausdrucksweise.

parlay ['pɑ:li, -lei] *tr itr Am* (den ursprünglichen Einsatz mit Gewinn) wieder (ein)setzen; (e-n Vorteil) ausnutzen; vermehren.

parley ['pɑ:li] *itr* unter-, verhandeln; sich besprechen, konferieren (*with* mit); *hum* parlieren; *s* Unter-, Verhandlung, Unterredung, Konferenz *f*; *to hold a ~* unterhandeln (*with* mit); *peace ~s* Friedensverhandlungen *f pl*; **~voo** ['-vu:] *hum a* französisch; *s* Franzose *m*; *itr* französisch parlieren.

parliament ['pɑ:ləmənt] Parlament *n*, Volksvertretung *f*; *P~* das *(britische)* P.; *to convene, to summon P~* das Parlament einberufen; *to open P~* das P. eröffnen; *Member of P~* Parlamentsmitglied *n*; **~arian** [pɑ:ləmen'tɛəriən] *s* Parlamentarier *m*; *a* parlamentarisch; **~arism** [-'mentərizm] Parlamentarismus *m*; **~ary** [pɑ:lə'mentəri] parlamentarisch; höflich; Parlaments-; *~~ elections (pl)* Parlamentswahl *f*; *~~ majority* Parlamentsmehrheit *f*.

parlo(u)r ['pɑ:lə] *obs* Wohnzimmer; Empfangszimmer *n*, -raum, Salon *m*; *(bar ~)* kleine(s) Klubzimmer; *(Kloster)* Sprechzimmer *n*; *Am* Diele *f*, Salon *m*; *beauty ~ (Am)* Schönheitssalon *m*; *hair-dresser's, tonsorial ~ (Am)* Frisiersalon *m*; *ice-cream ~ (Am)* Eissalon *m*, -diele *f*; *ladies' ~ (Am)* Damenzimmer *n*; *refreshment ~ (Am)* Erfrischungsraum *m*; *shoe-shining ~ (Am)* Schuhputzsalon *m*; *~* **car** *Am* Salonwagen *m*; *~* **game** Gesellschaftsspiel *n*; *~* **lizard** *Am* Salonlöwe *m*; **~-maid** Stubenmädchen *n*; **~-organ** Harmonium *n*; *~* **pink, red** Salonbolschewist *m*; *~* **strategist** Bierbankpolitiker *m*.

parochial [pə'roukjəl] *a* Kirchspiel-, Pfarr-; *fig* beschränkt, eng(stirnig), provinzlerisch, provinziell; **~ism** [pə'roukjəlizm] *fig* Beschränktheit, Enge, Engstirnigkeit *f*; *~* **politics** Kirchturmpolitik *f*; *~* **school** *Am* Konfessionsschule *f*.

parod|ist ['pærədist] Parodist *m*; **~y** ['-i] *s* Parodie (*of* auf); schwache Nachahmung *f*, Abklatsch *m*; *tr* parodieren.

parol|e [pə'roul] *s bes. mil* Ehrenwort *n*; Entlassung, Freiheit auf Ehrenwort; *Am jur* bedingte Strafaussetzung *f*; *mil* Kennwort *n*, Parole *f*; *tr Am jur* bedingt entlassen; *on ~~* auf Ehrenwort; *to break o.'s ~~* sein Wort brechen; *~~ board (Am)* Kommission *f* zur Gewährung der bedingten Strafaussetzung; **~ee** [pərou'li:] *Am jur* bedingt Entlassene(r) *m*.

parot|ic [pə'rɔtik] *a anat* neben dem Ohr befindlich; **~id** [-id] *s (~~ gland)* Ohrspeicheldrüse *f*; **~itis** [pærə'taitis] *med* Ziegenpeter, Mumps *m*.

paroxysm ['pærəksizm] *med* plötzliche Verschlimmerung *f*, heftige(r) Anfall, Paroxysmus; Krampf; (plötzlicher) Ausbruch *m*; *fig* Krise *f*.

parquet ['pɑ:kei, -kit, *Am* -'kei] *s* Parkett *n*; Parkett-, getäfelte(r) Fußboden *m*; *Am theat* Orchestersessel, Sperrsitz *m*; Parterre *n*; *tr (Fußboden, Raum)* parkettieren, mit Parkett auslegen; *~* **circle** *Am theat* Parkett *n*; **~ry** ['pɑ:kitri] Parkett(fußboden *m*) *n*; Täfelung *f*.

parrakeet *s. parakeet.*

parricid|al [pæri'saidl] vater-, muttermörderisch; **~e** ['pærisaid] Vater-, Muttermörder; Vater-, Muttermord *m*.

parrot ['pærət] *s* Papagei; *fig* Nachplapperer, Schwätzer *m*; *tr* nachplappern; *~* **fever** Papageienkrankheit *f*.

parry ['pæri] *tr* abwehren, parieren; *(Frage)* ausweichen (*s.th.* e-r S) *a. fig*; *(Schwierigkeit)* umgehen; *s* Abwehr, Parade *f*.

parse [pɑ:z] *tr gram (Satz)* zerlegen, analysieren, (zer)gliedern, konstruieren; *(Wort)* grammatisch, im Satzzs.hang erklären.

parsimon|ious [pɑ:si'mounjəs] (übertrieben) sparsam, haushälterisch; geizig, knauserig (*of* mit); **~iousness** [-jəsnis], **~y** ['pɑ:simәni] (übertriebene) Sparsamkeit *f*; Geiz *m*, Knauserigkeit *f*.

parsley ['pɑ:sli] *bot* Petersilie *f*.

parsnip ['pɑ:snip] *bot* Pastinak(e *f*) *m*.

parson ['pɑ:sn] Pfarrer, Pastor; Geistliche(r) *m*; **~age** ['-idʒ] Pfarrhaus *n*, Pfarrei *f*; **~'s nose** *fam* Pfaffenschnittchen *n*, Bürzel *m*.

part [pɑ:t] *s* Teil *m u. n*; Bestandteil *m*; (Maschinen-, Bau-)Teil *n*; Stück *n (e-s Ganzen)*; Anteil; Abschnitt, Teil *m (a. e-s Buches)*; *(Buch)* Lieferung *f*; *math* aufgehende(r) Bruch *m*; Aufgabe, Pflicht *f*, Interesse *n*; Sache, Angelegenheit; *theat* Rolle; *mus* Stimme, Partie *f (a. d. Instrumente)*; *(Geschäft, Verhandlung, (Rechts-)Streit)* Partei *f*; *Am (Frisur)* Scheitel *m*; *pl* Fähigkeiten *f pl*, Talente *n pl*, Gaben *f pl*, Begabung *f*; Gegend *f*, Gebiet *n*, Bezirk *m*; Geschlechts-, Schamteile *pl*; *attr* Teil-; *adv* teilweise, teils, zum Teil; *tr* teilen; *(das Haar)* scheiteln; *(Menschen)* trennen, ausea.bringen (*from* von); *(Verbindung)* lösen; *chem* scheiden; *fig* unterscheiden; *mar* brechen, zerreißen; *itr* zerbrechen; zerreißen; sich teilen; aus-ea.gehen, sich trennen (*from, with* von); scheiden (*(as) friends* als Freunde) *a. chem*; aufgeben (*with s.th.* etw); gehen lassen, entlassen (*with s.o.* jdn); weggehen (*from* von); verlassen (*from s.o.* jdn); Platz machen; sterben; *the greater* ~ der größte Teil, die Mehrheit; *for the most* ~ meist(ens), größten-, meistenteils; *for my* ~ meinerseits, meinesteils, was mich betrifft; *in* ~ teilweise, teils, zum Teil; *in equal* ~*s* zu gleichen Teilen; *in foreign* ~*s* im Auslande; *in these* ~*s* hierzulande; *on the* ~ *of* von seiten, seitens; *to be* ~ *and parcel of s.th.* von etw wesentlicher Bestandteil sein; *to do o.'s* ~ s-e Pflicht *od* Schuldigkeit tun; *to have neither* ~ *nor lot in* nichts zu tun haben mit; *to pay in* ~ e-e Teilzahlung leisten; *to play, to act a* ~ e-e Rolle spielen, Anteil haben (*in* an); unaufrichtig sein; betrügen; *to take* ~ teilnehmen; sich beteiligen (*in* an); *to take s.o.'s* ~ für jdn, jds Partei ergreifen, für jdn eintreten, sich für jdn einsetzen; *to take s.th. in good* ~ etw nicht übelnehmen; etw gut aufnehmen; *to take s.th. in ill* ~ etw übel-, *fam* krummnehmen; *to take in* ~ *exchange* in Zahlung nehmen; *to* ~ *company* sich trennen (*with* von); anderer Ansicht, Meinung sein (*with* als); *with s.th.* etw aufgeben; *to* ~ *o.'s hair* e-n Scheitel haben; *it is not* ~ *of mine* das ist nicht meine Sache, das geht mich nichts an; *constituent* ~*s (pl)* Bestandteile *m pl*; *leading* ~ Hauptrolle *f*; *a man of* ~*s* ein begabter, talentierter Mensch; *name* ~ Titelrolle *f*; *spare* ~ Ersatzteil *n a. m*; ~ *of the body* Körperteil *m*; ~ *of the country* Gegend *f*; ~ *of speech (gram)* Wortart *f*; ~**ed** ['-id] *a* geteilt, getrennt, gespalten; ~ **damage** Teilschaden *m*; ~ **delivery** Teillieferung *f*; ~**ly** ['-li] *adv* teilweise, zum Teil, teils; ~ **owner** Miteigentümer *m*; ~ **ownership** Miteigentum *n*; ~ **payment** Raten-, Teilzahlung *f*; ~-~ *terms (pl)* Teilzahlungsbedingungen *f pl*; ~ **singing** mehrstimmige(r) Gesang *m*; ~-**time** *a* Kurz-, Neben-, Aushilfs-; *to be on* ~~ nicht ganztägig beschäftigt sein; ~~ *job* Nebenbeschäftigung *f*; ~~ *work* Kurz-, Halbtagsarbeit *f*; *to do* ~~ *work* e-r Halbtagsarbeit nachgehen; ~~ *worker* Kurz-, Aushilfsarbeiter *m*; ~-**timer** Kurzarbeiter *m*; Halbtagskraft *f*.

partak|e [pɑ:'teik] *irr s. take itr* teilnehmen, sich beteiligen (*of, in* an); mitessen (*of* von); *to* ~~ *of s.th.* etw (*e-e Eigenschaft*) an sich haben; von etw beeinflußt sein; *tr* teilhaben, Anteil haben an; ~**er** [-ə] Teilnehm(end)e(r *m*) *f* (*in, of* an).

parterre [pɑ:'tɛə] (regelmäßig angelegte) Blumenbeete *n pl*; *theat* (hinteres) Parkett, Parterre *n*.

partial ['pɑ:ʃəl] parteiisch, voreingenommen; eingenommen (*to* von, für); partiell, Teil-; *to be* ~ *to s.th.* für etw e-e Vorliebe, e-e Schwäche haben; etw bevorzugen; ~ **amount** Teilbetrag *m*; ~ **delivery** Teillieferung *f*; ~**ity** [pɑ:ʃi'æliti] Vorurteil *n*, Voreingenommenheit; Parteilichkeit; Vorliebe *f* (*for, to* für); ~ **loss** Teilschaden, -verlust *m*; ~**ly** ['-i] *adv* teilweise; ~ **payment** Abschlags-, Teilzahlung *f*; ~~ *plan* Abzahlungsplan *m*; ~ **sale** Partieverkauf *m*; ~ **success** Teilerfolg *m*.

particip|ance, -cy [pɑ:'tisipəns(i)] = ~*ation*; ~**ant** [-ənt] *a* teilnehmend; *s* Teilnehmer *m*; ~**ate** [-eit] *itr* teilnehmen, -haben, sich beteiligen (*in* an); gewinnbeteiligt sein; ~**ation** [pɑ:tisi'peiʃən] Mitwirkung, Teilnahme (*in* an); *com* Beteiligung *f*; *financial* ~~ Kapitalbeteiligung *f*; ~~ *in profits* Gewinnbeteiligung *f*; ~**ator** [pɑ:'tisipeitə] Teilnehmer, -haber *m* (*in* an); ~**ial** [pɑ:ti'sipiəl] *gram* partizipial, Partizipial-; ~**le** ['pɑ:t(i)sipl] *gram* Partizip, Mittelwort *n*.

particle ['pɑ:tikl] Teilchen *n a. phys*; *fig* Spur; *gram* Partikel *f*; *not a* ~ *of sense* kein Fünkchen Verstand.

parti-colo(u)red ['pɑ:tikʌləd] *a* bunt; verschiedenartig, mannigfach.

particular [pə'tikjulə] *a* besonder, einzeln, speziell, privat; Sonder-, Einzel-, Spezial-, Privat-; bestimmt; *(Freund)* vertraut; ungewöhnlich, ausgefallen, nicht alltäglich; ausgeprägt; in die Einzelheiten gehend, eingehend, ausführlich; anspruchsvoll, wählerisch, heikel, eigen (*about* in bezug auf); peinlich genau, korrekt, schwer zufriedenzustellen(d); *s* Einzelheit *f*, -fall; (einzelner) Punkt *m*; *pl* nähere Angaben *f pl*, Details *n pl*, Einzelheiten (*about, of* über); Personalangaben *f pl*, Personalien *pl*; *in* ~ insbesondere, im besonderen, besonders; *nothing* ~ nichts von Bedeutung; *without giving* ~*s, without entering* od *going into* ~*s* ohne nähere Angaben (zu machen), ohne auf Einzelheiten einzugehen; *to be* ~ es genau nehmen (*about* mit); *to enter, to go into* ~*s* auf Einzelheiten eingehen; ins einzelne gehen; *to take* ~ *pains* sich besonders bemühen; *for* ~*s apply to* ... (nähere) Auskünfte durch ...; *full* ~*s (pl)* genaue Angaben, alle Einzelheiten *pl*; ~ **case** Einzelfall *m*; ~ **interests** *pl* Privat-, Sonderinteressen *n pl*; ~**ism** [-ərizm] Sonderinteressen *n pl*, -bestrebungen *f pl*; *pol* Partikularismus *m*; ~**ity** [pətikju'læriti] Besonderheit, Seltsamkeit; Ausführlichkeit; Genauigkeit, Exaktheit, Korrektheit, Sorgfalt *f*; anspruchsvolle(s) Wesen *n*; Einzelheit *f*; ~**ization** [pətikjulərai'zeiʃən] Spezifizierung, Detaillierung *f*; ~**ize** [pə'tikjuləraiz] *tr* einzeln angeben *od* aufführen; ~**ly** [pə'tikjuləli] *adv* im einzelnen; im besonderen; insbesondere; ausdrücklich.

parting ['pɑ:tiŋ] *a* teilend; trennend; scheidend; sterbend; Abschieds-; *s* Teilung *f*; Riß, Bruch *m*, Trennung; *chem* Scheidung; Trenn-, Bruchstelle, Trennlinie *f*; Scheitel; Abschied (*with* von); Aufbruch; Tod *m*; *at* ~ beim Abschied; ~ *of the ways* Wegegabelung *f*; *fig* Scheideweg *m*; ~ **cup** Abschiedstrunk *m*; ~ **gift** Abschiedsgeschenk *n*; ~ **kiss** Abschiedskuß *m*; ~ **line** Trennlinie, -fuge *f*; ~ **strip** Trennstreifen *m*; ~ **visit** Abschiedsbesuch *m*; ~ **words** *pl* Abschiedsworte *n pl*.

partisan, partizan [pɑ:ti'zæn, *Am* 'pɑ:tizn] **1.** *s* Parteigänger, Anhänger; *mil* Partisan, Widerstandskämpfer *m*; *a* (blind) ergeben; Partisanen-, Widerstands-; ~**ship** [-ʃip, *Am* '-ʃip] Parteinahme, Parteigängerschaft; (blinde) Ergebenheit *f*; **2.** ['pɑ:tizn] Partisane *f*.

partit|e ['pɑ:tait] geteilt; *oft in Zssgen* -geteilt, -teilig; ~**ive** ['pɑ:titiv] *a* Teilungs-; *gram* partitiv; *s (gram)* Partitiv(um) *n*.

partition [pɑ:'tiʃən] *s* Teilung, Trennung; Ver-, Zer-, Aufteilung; Zerstückelung; Parzellierung; Trenn-, Zwischen-, Scheidewand *f*; Teil *m*, Abteilung *f*, Abschnitt *m*, Teilstück; Fach; Abteil *n*, Verschlag *m*; *tr* (auf-)teilen, zerstückeln; *(Land)* parzellieren; *to* ~ *off* abtrennen, -teilen; ~ **treaty** Teilungsvertrag *m*; ~ **wall** Zwischenwand; Brandmauer *f*.

partner ['pɑ:tnə] *s com* Partner, Teilhaber (*in* an), Gesellschafter, Kompagnon; (Ehe-, Tanz-, Spiel-)Partner; Teilnehmer *m* (*in, of* an); *tr* zs.schließen (*with* mit); *to be* ~*s* zs. spielen; *to become a* ~ *of, to enter, to join as* ~ als Teilhaber eintreten in; *to make s.o. a* ~ jdm zum Teilhaber machen; *active, working* ~ aktive(r), tätiger Teilhaber *m*; *contracting* ~ Vertragspartner *m*; *dormant, secret, silent, sleeping* ~ stille(r) Teilhaber *m*; *junior* ~ 2. Teilhaber; Juniorchef *m*; *limited* ~ Kommanditist *m*; *senior* ~ Haupt-, 1. Teilhaber *m*; ~ *in life* Lebensgefährte *m*; -gefährtin *f*; ~**ship** ['-ʃip] Partner-, Teilhaberschaft, Beteiligung; Mittäterschaft; offene (Handels-)Gesellschaft; Mitbeteiligung *f* (*in* an); *to enter, to go into* ~~ *with s.o.* sich mit jdm geschäftlich verbinden; *to take into* ~ als Gesellschafter aufnehmen; *industrial* ~~ Gewinnbeteiligung *f* der Arbeitnehmer; *limited* ~~ Kommanditgesellschaft *f*; ~~ *capital, deed, interest, property* Gesellschaftskapital *n*, -vertrag, -anteil *m*, -vermögen *n*.

partridge ['pɑ:tridʒ] Rebhuhn *n*.

parturl|ient [pɑ:'tjuəriənt] gebärend; kreißend, in den Wehen; Geburts-; *fig* ideenschwanger; ~**ition** [pɑ:tjuə'riʃən] Gebären *n*, Geburt *f*.

party ['pɑ:ti] (politische) Partei; (Arbeits-, Interessen-)Gruppe; *mil* Abteilung *f*, Kommando *n*; Einladung, Gesellschaft, Party, Veranstaltung *f*; Teilnehmer, Beteiligte(r) *m* (*to* an); *jur* Partei *f*; Teil; *com* Kontrahent, Teilhaber, Beteiligte(r); *fam hum* Kerl *m*, Person *f*; *mil fam* Unternehmen *n*, Einsatz *m*; *to be a* ~ *to s.th.* an e-r S beteiligt sein; sich hergeben zu etw; mitmachen bei etw; *to be of the* ~ mit dabei sein; mitmachen; *to become a* ~ *to s.th.* sich in e-e S einlassen; *to give a* ~ e-e Einladung geben, Gäste haben; *to go to a* ~ e-r Einladung folgen, eingeladen sein; *to join a* ~ in e-e Partei eintreten; *to make one of the* ~ sich anschließen; *adverse* ~ Prozeßgegner *m*; *coalition* ~ Koalitionspartei *f*; *dinner, tea* ~ Einladung *f* zum Essen, zum Tee; *evening* ~ Abendgesellschaft *f*; *firing* ~ Hinrichtungskommando *n*; *government* ~ Regierungspartei *f*; *Labour P*~ Arbeiterpartei *f*; *the opposing* ~ die Gegenpartei *f*; *opposition* ~ Oppositionspartei *f*; *splinter* ~ Splitterpartei *f*; *the surviving* ~ *(jur)* der überlebende Teil; *third* ~ Dritte(r), Unbeteiligte(r), Unparteiische(r) *m*; *working* ~ Arbeitsgruppe *f*; *the* ~ *concerned* der Beteiligte, der Betroffene; ~ *to a contract* Vertragspartei *f*; *the* ~ *opposed* die Gegenpartei *f*; *the* ~ *ordering* der Besteller; *the* ~ *receiving* der Empfänger; ~-**badge** Parteiabzeichen *n*; ~-**boss** Parteiführer, -bonze *m*; ~ **boy** *Am* Salonlöwe *m*; ~-**colo(u)red** *s. parti-colo(u)red*; ~-**-conference, -congress, -meeting, -rally** Parteiversammlung *f*, -kongreß, -tag *m*; ~ **discipline** Parteidisziplin *f*; ~-**leader** Parteiführer, -chef *m*; ~-**line** *jur* Eigentums-, Grundstücksgrenze *f*; *tele* Gemeinschaftsanschluß *m*; *Am* Parteilinie *f*; *pl Am* Parteidirektiven, -richtlinien *f pl*; *to follow the* ~~*s* Parteidisziplin halten, linientreu sein; ~-**liner** *Am* treue(r) Gefolgsmann *m*; **~-machinery** *Am* Parteimaschine, -organisation *f*; **~-man** (überzeugter) Parteimann *m*; **~-member** Parteimitglied *n*; **~-platform, -program(me)** Parteiprogramm *n*; **~ politics** *pl* Parteipolitik *f*; **~ pooper** *Am sl* Besucher *m*, der bei e-r Veranstaltung zuerst geht; **~ spirit** Parteigeist *m*; **~ status** Parteizugehörigkeit *f*; **~-ticket** Sammel-, Gesellschaftsfahrschein *m*; *pol* Parteiprogramm *n*, -wahlliste *f*; **~ truce** Burgfrieden *m* zwischen den Parteien; **~-wall** Brandmauer; Zwischenwand *f*.

parvenu ['pɑːvənjuː] Emporkömmling *m*.

parvis ['pɑːvis] *rel arch* Vorhof *m*.

paschal ['pɑːskəl] *a rel* Passah-; Oster-; **~ flower** *s. pasqueflower*; **~ lamb** *rel* Osterlamm *n*; *the P~ Lamb* das Lamm Gottes *(Jesus)*.

pasha, pacha ['pɑːʃə] Pascha *m*.

pasqueflower ['pæskflauə] *bot* Küchenschelle *f*.

pasqu|il ['pæskwil], **~inade** [pæskwi'neid] Schmähschrift *f*.

pass [pɑːs] **1.** *itr* sich (fort)bewegen, gehen, ziehen, fahren, fliegen, reisen; sich ziehen, sich erstrecken, führen; vorbei-, vorüber-, weitergehen, -ziehen, -fahren, -fliegen (*by* an); umgehen, zirkulieren; übergehen, -wechseln (*from ... to* von ... zu); *(Funke)* überspringen; *(Worte)* gesprochen, gewechselt werden; übergehen (*into* in; *to* auf); hinausgehen (*beyond* über); überschreiten (*beyond s.th.* etw); weg-, fortgehen, aufbrechen, abreisen; vorbei-, vorübergehen, aufhören, ein Ende haben; *(Zeit)* vergehen, verfließen, verstreichen; entschlafen, sterben; sich unterziehen (*under s.th.* e-r S); *parl* durchgehen, passieren, angenommen werden; (die Prüfung) bestehen; *(Schlimmes)* durchmachen (*through s.th.* etw); gelten, gehalten werden (*for* für); bekannt sein (*by the name of ...* unter dem Namen ...); stattfinden, geschehen, vorfallen, sich ereignen, vor sich gehen, *fam* passieren; *jur* zu Gericht sitzen, urteilen *(on, upon)* über; *(Urteil)* gefällt, gesprochen werden, ergehen; *(Kartenspiel)* passen; *sport* passen, den Ball weitergeben; **2.** *tr* vorbeigehen, -fahren an, hinausgehen über, hindurchgehen durch, passieren; hinter sich lassen; *mot* überholen; übergehen, -sehen, außer acht lassen, unterlassen, versäumen, auslassen; sich unterziehen (*s.th.* e-r S); *(Lehrgang)* mitmachen, absolvieren; *(Prüfung)* bestehen; *s.o.* jds Kräfte übersteigen; hinausgehen über, übertreffen, übersteigen; gehen, ziehen, reisen, passieren lassen; vorbei-, vorüber-, hindurchlassen; gleiten, fahren lassen; durchgehen lassen, genehmigen, billigen, sanktionieren; *(bei e-r Prüfung)* bestehen lassen; *(Zeit)* vergehen, verstreichen lassen *od* verbringen; *(Tuch)* ausbreiten (*over* über); *(Eintragung)* vornehmen; *o.'s hand* mit der Hand fahren (*over* über; *through* durch); legen, schieben, stecken (*around* um; *through* durch); (ab-) schicken, -senden, aufgeben, fortschaffen, in Umlauf setzen; reichen, weiterreichen, -geben, herumreichen; weiterleiten, befördern; abwälzen (*on* auf); *sport (den Ball)* weitergeben; *(Ansicht)* äußern; *(Meinung)* sich bilden; *jur (Urteil)* sprechen, fällen (*on* über); ergehen lassen; *parl (Entschließung, Antrag)* annehmen; durchbringen; genehmigen; *(Gesetz)* erlassen; verabschieden; *(Wort)* verpfänden; *(Eid)* schwören; **3.** *s* Gang, Zug *m*, Vorbei-, Vorübergehen *n*, Durchgang, -zug; Arbeitsgang *m*; Absolvieren *(e-s Kurses)*; Bestehen *(e-r Prüfung)*; Testat, Zeugnis; *(Univ.)* keine Berechtigung gebende(s) Zeugnis *n*; Passierschein, Ausweis(karte *f*); *mil* Urlaubsschein *m*; *(free ~) theat rail* Freikarte *f*; *(Kartenspiel)* Passen; *sport* Zuspielen *n (des Balles)*; (Taschenspieler-)Trick *m*; (Be-)Streichen *n (beim Magnetisieren* od *Hypnotisieren)*; *(Fechten)* Ausfall, Stoß; *sl* Annäherungsversuch *m (gegenüber e-r Frau)*; (*meist*: kritische, unangenehme, üble) Lage, Situation *f*, Umstände *m pl*, Verhältnisse *n pl*; *geog* Engpaß *m*, Gebirgsjoch *n*; Durchgang *m*, -fahrt *f*; **4.** *on ~ (mil)* auf Urlaub; **5.** *to bring to ~* zustande, fertigbringen; bewerkstelligen; *to come to ~* Wirklichkeit werden, sich ereignen, geschehen, sich zutragen, vorfallen; *to hold the ~* die Stellung halten; *to let ~* durchgehen, passieren lassen; *to make a ~ at* die Hand erheben, e-e drohende Haltung einnehmen gegen; *sl* zudringlich werden (gegenüber *e-r Frau)*; *to sell the ~ (fig)* die Katze aus dem Sack lassen; **6.** *to ~ to s.o.'s account* jdm in Rechnung stellen; *to ~ into the books* buchen, eintragen; *to ~ the baby, the buck (Am)* die Verantwortung abschieben; *to ~ a cheque* e-n Scheck einlösen; *to ~ current (Geld)* gültig sein, sich im Umlauf befinden; *(Gerücht)* umgehen; *to ~ over the details* über die Einzelheiten hinweggehen; *to ~ the dividend* keine Dividende zahlen; *to ~ the hat* e-e Sammlung veranstalten; *to ~ judg(e)ment* ein Urteil fällen; *to ~ into law* Gesetzeskraft annehmen, in Kraft treten; *to ~ s.o.'s lips* jdm über die Lippen kommen; *to ~ muster* annehmbar sein; dem Standard, den Anforderungen entsprechen; *to ~ a remark* e-e (unfreundliche) Bemerkung machen *od* fallenlassen; *to ~ a resolution* e-e Entschließung annehmen; *to ~ in review (mil)* vorbeimarschieren lassen; *to ~ a sentence (jur)* ein Urteil fällen, *od* sprechen; *to ~ in silence* mit Stillschweigen übergehen; *to ~ the time of day with s.o.* sich mit jdm grüßen; *to ~ unnoticed* unbemerkt durchschlüpfen; *to ~ a vote of confidence* das Vertrauen aussprechen; *to ~ o.'s word* sein Wort geben; *~ (me) the sugar, please* reichen Sie mir bitte den Zucker! darf ich um den Zucker bitten? **7.** *a pretty ~ (fam)* e-e Patsche, Klemme *f*; **8.** *to* **~ along** s-s Weges ziehen; weitergehen; *to* **~ around** *Am* herumreichen; *to* **~ away** *itr* zu Ende gehen, aufhören; dahinschwinden; vergehen, sterben; *tr (Zeit)* verbringen; *to* **~ back** zurückgeben, -reichen; *to* **~ by** *itr* vorübergehen, -fahren, -fließen; *tr* (stillschweigend) übergehen, unbeachtet lassen; vorübergehen an; übersehen, auslassen; *to* **~ down** hinuntergehen; *to* **~ for** gelten als; *to* **~ in** *itr* hineingehen; *tr (Gesuch)* einreichen; *to* **~ off** *itr* vorbei-, vorübergehen; ver-, dahinschwinden, aufhören; sich abspielen, stattfinden, vor sich gehen, verlaufen; *o.s. as* sich ausgeben als; *on s.o.* jdm andrehen; *tr* außer acht lassen, beiseite schieben; *to* **~ on** *itr* weitergehen; übergehen (*to* zu, an); *tr* weitergeben, -reichen, -sagen (*to s.o.* jdm); sterben; *to* **~ out** hinausgehen; *sl* das Bewußtsein verlieren; *sl* abkratzen, ins Gras beißen; *he ~ed out* die Sinne schwanden ihm; *to* **~ over** stillschweigend übergehen, nicht sehen (wollen), auslassen; überreichen, -tragen; *to* **~ round** *itr* herumgehen; *tr* herumreichen, -gehen lassen; *to* **~ through** *tr* durchgehen, -ziehen, -reisen, -stekken; *fig* erleben, durchmachen; *itr* durchkommen, -gehen; *to ~~ the regular channel* den Dienstweg gehen; *to* **~ up** *itr* hinaufgehen; *tr Am sl* in den Wind schlagen, sich aus der Nase gehen lassen; ablehnen; aus-, weglassen; *to* **~ upon** ein Urteil abgeben über; **~able** ['-əbl] passierbar, begehbar, befahrbar; *(Geld)* gangbar, gültig; *allg* ausreichend, genügend, leidlich; **~-book** Bankbuch *n*; **~-card** Ausweiskarte *f*; **~-check** Passierschein *m*; **~-degree** *(Univ.)* nicht mit e-m Titel *od* Berechtigungen verbundene(r) Grad *m*; **~ duty** Durchgangszoll *m*; **~-key** Hauptschlüssel *m*; **~-man** Inhaber *m* e-s *~-degree* (s. d.); **~-mark** Ausreichend *n (in der Prüfung)*; **~out** Verteilung *f*; *sl* Ohnmächtigwerden *n*; Betrunkene(r) *m*; **~port** (Reise-)Paß; Geleitbrief; *fig* Weg, Schlüssel *m* (*to* zu); *collective ~~* Sammelpaß *m*; *ship's ~~* Schiffs-, Seepaß *m*; *~~ application* Paßantrag *m*; *~~ inspection* Paßkontrolle *f*; *~~ office* Paßstelle *f*; **~word** *mil* Kennwort *n*, Parole, Losung(swort *n*) *f*.

passage ['pæsidʒ] Vorbei-, Vorübergehen, -ziehen, -fahren, Passieren *n*; Gang *m*, Fahrt *f*, Zug; Durchgang, -zug *m*, -fahrt, -reise; Überfahrt, Seefahrt, -reise, Passage *f*; Schiffsplatz *m*; *(~-money)* Überfahrtsgeld *n*; Flugreise *f*; (Durch-)Gang, Korridor *m*, Gasse *f*, Weg *m*; (Text-)Stelle *f*, Abschnitt, Passus; Austausch; Übergang *m fig*; Verabschiedung, Annahme *f (e-s Gesetzes)*; Durchgangs-, Durchfahrtsrecht *n*; *mus* Lauf *m*, Passage *f*; *med* Kanal, Gang; *(Stuhl)* Abgang *m*; *(Urin)* Ausscheiden *n*; *pl* Beziehungen *f pl*, Gedankenaustausch; Wortwechsel *m*, Ausea.-setzungen *f pl*; *to book o.'s ~* e-n Schiffsplatz belegen; *to take o.'s ~* sich einschiffen, an Bord gehen; *no ~* kein Durchgang; *bird of ~* Zugvogel *m*; *connecting ~* Verbindungsweg *m*; *~ of, at arms* Waffengang *m a. fig*; *~ into law* Inkrafttreten *n*; **~ back** *mar* Rückfahrt, -reise *f*; **~ money** Überfahrtsgeld *n*; **~ ticket** Schiffskarte *f*; **~ way** Reiseweg *m*, Route *f*; **~-way** Korridor; Durchgang *m*.

passenger ['pæsindʒə] Fahr-, Fluggast, Passagier, Reisende(r); *fam* Drückeberger *m*; *cabin ~* Kajütenpassagier *m*; *fellow ~* Mitreisende(r), Reisegefährte, -genosse *m*; *first-class ~* Passagier *m* der 1. Klasse; *foot-~* Fußgänger *m*; *tourist ~* Passagier *m* der Touristenklasse; **~-aircraft** Passagierflugzeug *n*; **~-boat, -ship** Passagierschiff *n*; **~ cabin** *aero* Fluggastraum *m*, -kabine *f*; **~-car** *mot*, *Am rail* Personenwagen *m*; *(Luftschiff)* Fahrgastgondel *f*; **~-carriage** *Br rail* Personenwagen *m*; **~-flight** Passagierflug *m*; **~-lift,** *Am* **-elevator** Personenaufzug *m*; **~ list** Passagierliste *f*; **~-pigeon** Wandertaube *f*; **~ plane** Verkehrsflugzeug *n*; **~-ramp** *aero* Flugsteig *m*; **~-rate, -tariff** Personentarif *m*; **~-service, -transport** Personenbeförderung *f*; **~-station,** *Am* **depot** Personenbahnhof *m*; **~-traffic** Personenverkehr *m*; **~-train** Personenzug *m*; *by ~~* als Eilgut.

passe-partout ['pæspɑ:tu:] Hauptschlüssel *m*; Passepartout *n*; *(~ frame)* Wechselrahmen *m*; ~ **reel** Klebstreifenrolle *f*.

passer-by ['pɑ:sə'bai] *pl passers-by* ['pɑ:səz'bai] Passant, Vorübergehende(r) *m*.

passim ['pæsim] *adv* an verschiedenen Stellen, verschiedentlich.

passing ['pɑ:siŋ] *a* vorübergehend *a. fig*; *fig* flüchtig, kurz, beiläufig; gelegentlich, zufällig; vorkommend; *tech* durchgehend; *adv obs* sehr, äußerst; *s* Vorbei-, Vorübergehen, Verstreichen *n*; Durchgang *m*, -fahrt *f*; *mot* Überholen; *(Prüfung)* Bestehen *n*; *(Gesetz)* Annahme, Verabschiedung; *fin* Ausgabe; *(Dividende)* Ausschüttung *f*; Ende; *poet* Hinscheiden, Ableben *n*; *in ~* beiläufig, bei Gelegenheit; nebenbei (bemerkt); *no ~!* Überholen verboten! *~ of judg(e)ment* Urteilsfällung *f*; *~ into law* Inkrafttreten *n*; **~-bell** Totenglocke *f*; ~ **events** *pl* Tagesereignisse *n pl*, Aktualitäten *f pl*; ~ **flight** Vorbeiflug *m*; **~-grade** *Am (Schule)* Ausreichend *n*; **~-on** Weitergabe *f*; **~-place** *rail* Weiche *f*; ~ **remark** flüchtige Bemerkung *f*.

passion ['pæʃən] Leidenschaft *f*; Zorn *m*, Wut, Raserei; Begeisterung *f*, Enthusiasmus *m*, Passion, Leidenschaft, Vorliebe (*for* für); heftige, starke Liebe, Zuneigung *f*; heftige(s) Verlangen *n* (*for* nach); heftige Begierde, Gier, Fleischeslust *f*; *(P~)* Leiden *n* Christi, Passion *a. fig*; Leidensgeschichte *f*; *in ~* in Wut; *to be in a ~* (vor Wut) rasen; *to conceive a ~* sich verlieben (*for* in); *to fly into a ~* aufbrausen; e-n Wutanfall bekommen; *smoking is a ~ with him* er ist ein leidenschaftlicher Raucher; *fit of ~* Wutanfall *m*; **~ate** ['-it] leidenschaftlich, heißblütig, feurig; hitzig, leicht erregt; jähzornig; hingebungsvoll, aufgewühlt; *(Gefühl)* heftig, stark; **~ateness** ['-itnis] Leidenschaftlichkeit; Erregtheit; Hingabe; Heftigkeit *f*; **~-flower** Passionsblume *f*; **~less** ['-lis] leidenschaftslos, ruhig, kühl; ~ **pit** *Am sl* Autokino *n*; **P~ play** *theat* Passionsspiel *n*; **P~ Sunday** (Sonntag) Judika *m (14 Tage vor Ostern)*; **P~ Week** Karwoche *f*.

passiv|e ['pæsiv] *a* passiv *a. gram fin chem*; widerstandslos, nachgebend, -giebig, geduldig; teilnahmslos, untätig; *fin* keine Zinsen tragend; *s (~ voice) gram* Passiv *n*; *to remain ~~* sich abwartend verhalten; *~~ resistance* passive(r) Widerstand *m*; *~~ trade* Einfuhrhandel *m*; **~eness** ['-nis]; **~ity** [pæ'siviti] Passivität, Untätigkeit; Teilnahmslosigkeit *f*.

Passover ['pɑ:souvə] *rel* Passah(fest) *n*.

past [pɑ:st] *a* beendet, zu Ende, vorüber, vorbei; vergangen, verflossen; einstig, ehemalig, früher; letzt, vergangen, abgelaufen; ehemalig; *gram* Vergangenheits-; *s* Vergangenheit *f a. gram*; *prp (zeitl.)* nach, später als; *(räuml.)* jenseits *gen*, weiter als; an vorbei; *(zeitl., räuml., graduell)* über(... hinaus); *adv (zeitl., räuml.)* vorbei, vorüber; *in the ~* früher, einst, ehemals; bisher; *for some time ~* seit einiger Zeit; *to be ~ s.th.* über etw hinausgehen, etw überschreiten, übersteigen; *to go ~* vorbei-, vorübergehen; *half ~ three (o'clock)* (um) halb vier (Uhr); ~ **bearing, endurance** unerträglich; ~ **belief** unglaublich; ~ **cure** unheilbar; ~ **due** *fin* überfällig; *~~ interest* Verzugszinsen *m pl*; ~ **hope** hoffnungslos, verzweifelt; **~-master** (Alt-)Meister, Experte *m* (*at, of, in* in); *to be a ~~ in s.th.* in etw unübertroffen sein; ~ **perfect** *gram* Plusquamperfekt *n*; ~ **praying for** (rettungslos) verloren; ~ **seventy** über 70 (Jahre alt); ~ **tense** Vergangenheit *f*, Imperfekt *n*; ~ **week** letzte, vergangene Woche *f*.

paste [peist] *s* (Kuchen-)Teig *m*; *Am* Teigwaren *f pl*; Paste, Krem *f*; Kleister, Klebstoff *m*; *tech* (Ton-, Glas-) Masse *f*; Glasstein *m*, Paste *f*; künstliche(r) Edelstein *m*; *tr* an-, fest-, über-, zukleben, -kleistern (*with* mit); kleben (*on* auf); *sl* verhauen, verdreschen, vertobaken; *Am sl sport* entscheidend schlagen; *Am sl* anklagen; *to ~ up* an-, aufkleben; *almond ~* Mandelpaste *f*; *anchovy ~* Sardellenpaste *f*; *shoe ~* Schuhkrem *f*; *short ~* Mürbeteig *m*; *starch ~* Stärkekleister *m*; *tooth-~* Zahnpasta *f*; *~ of lime, plaster* Kalk-, Gipsbrei *m*; **~board** *s* Pappe *f*, Karton *m*; *sl* Fahr-, Visiten-, Spielkarte *f*; *a* aus Pappe, Papp-; pappartig; *fig* schwach, dünn, fadenscheinig, gehaltlos; kitschig; *~~ articles (pl)* Kartonagen *f pl*; *~~ box* Pappschachtel *f*; **~-in** angeklebte(r) Zettel *m*; **~-pot** Kleistertopf *m*; **~-roller** Nudel-, Wellholz *n*; **~-up** Fotomontage *f*; **~-work** Papparbeit *f*.

pastel ['pæstel, -'tel] *s bot* Färberwaid *m*; Pastellfarbe *f*, -stift *m*, -bild *n*, -ton *m*; *lit* Skizze *f*; *a* ['pæstl] *(Farbe)* zart, matt; Pastell-; ~ **shades** *pl* Pastelltöne *m pl*.

pastern ['pæstə:n] *(Pferd)* Fessel *f*; **~-joint** Fesselgelenk *n*.

pasteuriz|ation [pæstərai'zeiʃən] Pasteurisierung *f*; **~e** ['pæstəraiz] *tr* pasteurisieren, keimfrei machen.

pastil(le) ['pæsti:l, -'-] *pharm* Pastille *f*; Räucherkerzchen *n*; Pastellstift *m*.

pastime ['pɑ:staim] Zeitvertreib *m*; Kurzweil, Unterhaltung, Zerstreuung, Belustigung, Erholung *f*; *as a ~, by way of ~* zum Zeitvertreib, zum (bloßen) Vergnügen.

pastiness ['peistinis] teigige Beschaffenheit; *fig* Blässe *f*.

pastor ['pɑ:stə] Pastor, Pfarrer, Seelsorger *m*; **~al** ['-rəl] *a* Hirten-; ländlich; Land-; Weide-; *poet* Schäfer-; einfach, geruhsam, friedlich; Pfarramts-, seelsorgerisch, seelsorgerlich; *s* Hirtengedicht; Schäferspiel *n*; Schäferpoesie; Hirten-, ländliche Szene; (Buch *n* über) Pastoraltheologie *f*; Hirtenbrief; *(~~ staff)* Krummstab *m*; *~~ land* Weideland *n*; *~~ tribe* Hirtenvolk *n*; **~ate** ['-rit], **~ship** ['-ʃip] Pfarramt *n*; Pfarrerschaft *f*; *Am* Pfarrhaus *n*.

pastry ['peistri] Pasteten-, Kuchenteig *m*; Pasteten *f pl*; Backwerk, Gebäck *n*, Konditor(ei)-, feine Backwaren *f pl*; **~-cook** Pastetenbäcker; Konditor, Kuchen-, Zuckerbäcker *m*; **~-mo(u)ld** Back-, Kuchenform *f*; **~-shop** *Am* Konditorei *f*.

pastur|age ['pɑ:stjuridʒ] Weiden; Weiderecht *n*; Weide *f*; **~e** ['pɑ:stʃə] *s* Grünfutter *n*; Weide *f*; *tr* weiden; abgrasen; *itr* grasen, weiden; *~~ land* Weideland *n*.

pasty ['peisti] *a* teigig, weich; *fig* bleich, blaß, milchig, käsig; *s* ['pæsti] *Br* (Fleisch-)Pastete *f*.

pat [pæt] **1.** *s* leichte(r) Schlag, Klaps *m*; Tapsen; Klümpchen, Stück(chen) *n*, *fam* Klacks *m (z. B. Butter)*; *tr* klopfen, e-n Klaps geben (*s.o.* jdm); streicheln, tätscheln; tapsen; *itr* klappen; klopfen (*on* auf); *to ~ s.o. on the back* jdm auf die Schulter klopfen; *fig* jdn beglückwünschen; **~-a-cake** backe, backe Kuchen; **2.** *a* passend, geeignet; *(Antwort)* treffend; *adv* (gerade) recht; zur Hand; *to have, to know s.th. ~ (fam)* etw in- u. auswendig wissen; *to stand ~ (fam)* bei der Stange *od* stur bleiben; *to answer ~* schlagfertig antworten.

Pat [pæt] *(Patrick)* Ire *m*.

patch [pætʃ] *s* Flicken, Fleck; Besatz (-stück *n*); Zwickel *m*; (Wund-)Pflaster *n*; (Augen-)Klappe, Binde *f*; Schönheitspflästerchen *n*; *(Schuhe)* Riester; (Farb-)Fleck *m*; Fleckchen *n* Erde, Stück *n* Land; Stück(chen) *n*, Rest; *mot* Flicken *m*; *tr* flicken; als Flicken dienen für; (ab)steppen; e-n Flecken setzen auf; *(Reifen)* flicken; *(to ~ up, to ~ together)* zs.flicken, -stücke(l)n, -stoppeln, -stümpern, notdürftig flikken; *fig* wieder in die Reihe bringen; *(Streit)* beilegen, schlichten; *(Freundschaft)* kitten; *not to be a ~ on (fam)* nicht tippen können an; *to strike a bad ~* e-e Pechsträhne haben; **~ed** [-t] *a* gestümpert, *fam* hingehauen; **~-pocket** *(Kleidung)* aufgesetzte Tasche *f*; **~-test** *med* Reizprobe *f*; **~work** Flickarbeit *f*; *fig* Stückwerk *n*; *(~~ quilt)* Flickendecke *f*; **~y** ['-i] zs.geflickt, -gestoppelt; bunt zs.gewürfelt; unregelmäßig.

patchouli ['pætʃuli, pə'tʃu:li] *bot* Patschuli *n (a. Parfüm)*.

pat|e [peit] *fam hum pej* Kürbis, Kopf; Schädel; *fig* Grips, Verstand *m*; **~ed** ['-id] *a in Zssgen*: -köpfig.

patell|a [pə'telə] *pl -ae* [-i:] *anat* Kniescheibe *f*; **~ar** [-] *a* Kniescheiben-; *~~ reflex (physiol)* Kniescheibenreflex *m*.

paten ['pætən] *rel* Patene *f*, Hostienteller *m*; Metallscheibe *f*.

patent ['peitənt, 'pæ-] *a* offen, öffentlich, allgemein zugänglich; offenkundig, -sichtlich, augenscheinlich; unge-, unbehindert; *jur* patentiert, gesetzlich geschützt; *fam* neu, patent, praktisch, brauchbar; vorzüglich; *(Mehl)* hochwertig, 1. Güte; *s (letters ~ ['pæ-])* Urkunde *f*, Brief *m*, Patent, Privileg; *bes.* Patent, Schutzrecht; *fig* Vorrecht *n*, Anspruch *m* (*on* auf); *tr* patentieren; sich patentieren lassen; *to apply for a ~* ein Patent anmelden; *to grant, to issue a ~* ein Patent erteilen; *to take out a ~ for s.th.* etw zum Patent anmelden; sich etw patentieren lassen; *it's ~ to me that* mir ist klar, daß; *~ applied for, ~ pending* (zum) Patent angemeldet; *application for a ~* Patentanmeldung *f*; *design, (Am) petty ~* Gebrauchsmuster *n*; *holder, owner of a ~* Patentinhaber *m*; *~ of gentility* Adelsbrief *m*; **~able** ['-əbl] patentierbar, patentfähig; **~-act** Patentgesetz *n*; **~-agent,** *Am* **-attorney** Patentanwalt *m*; **~-application** Patentanmeldung *f*; ~ **article** *com* Markenartikel *m*; ~ **coverage** Patentschutz *m*; ~ **department** Patentabteilung *f*; **~ed** ['-id] *a* patentiert, gesetzlich geschützt; **~ee** [peitən'ti:, *Am* pæ-] Patentinhaber *m*; **~-engineer** technische(r) Berater *m* in Patentsachen; ~ **fastener** Druckknopf *m*; ~ **goods** *pl* Markenartikel *m pl*; **~-holder** Patentinhaber *m*; ~ **infringement** Patentverletzung *f*; ~ **key** Sicherheitsschlüssel *m*; **~-law** Patentrecht *n*; ~ **leather** Lackleder *n*; *~(~) boot* Lackstiefel *m*; ~ **medicine** pharmazeutische(s) Präparat *n*; **P~-Office** ['pæ-] Patentamt *n*; **~-owner** Patentinhaber *m*; **~-register, -roll** Patentregister *n*; **~-right** Schutzrecht *n*;

pl gewerbliche(r) Rechtsschutz *m*; ~**-specification** Patentschrift *f*.

patern|al [pə'tə:nl] väterlich; *on the* ~ *side* väterlicherseits; ~~ *authority, power* väterliche, elterliche Gewalt *f*; ~**ity** [-iti] Vater-, Urheberschaft *f*; ~~ *case* Vaterschaftsprozeß *m*, -klage *f*.

paternoster ['pætə'nɔstə] *(P~)* Vaterunser *n*; Rosenkranz *m*.

path [pɑ:θ] *pl -s* [pɑ:ðz] Pfad; *(Fluß)* Lauf; *(foot~)* (Fuß-)Weg *m*; *astr sport* Bahn *f*; *fig* Weg *m*; (Verhaltens-) Weise; (Mach-, Herstellungs-)Art *f*; *cinder-~* Aschenbahn *f*; ~**finder** Pfadfinder; *fig* Pionier; *aero* Zielbeleuchter *m*; ~**less** ['-lis] unwegsam, pfad-, weglos; unbegangen, -betreten; ~**way** Pfad, Weg *m*.

path|etic(al) [pə'θetik(əl)] mitleiderweckend, ergreifend, erschütternd, rührend, sympathieerregend, mitreißend, gefühlsmäßig, Gefühls-; ~*etic fallacy (lit)* Vermenschlichung *f* der unbelebten Natur; ~**ologic(al)** [pæθə'lɔdʒik(əl)] pathologisch; krankheitsbedingt; Krankheits-; ~**ologist** [pə'θɔlədʒist] Pathologe *m*; ~**ology** [-'θɔlədʒi] *med* Pathologie *f*; *Am* Krankheitsbild *n*; ~**os** ['peiθɔs] *das* Ergreifende, Erschütternde; *(lit, Kunst)* Pathos *n*.

patien|ce ['peiʃəns] Geduld; Ausdauer, Beharrlichkeit; Patience(spiel *n*) *f*; *in* ~~ geduldig; *to be out of* ~~ *with* aufgebracht sein gegen; *to have no* ~~ *with* nicht vertragen (können), nicht (länger) aushalten; *to play* ~~ Patiencen legen; *to possess o.'s soul in* ~~ sich in Geduld fassen; *the* ~~ *of Job* [dʒoub] e-e Engelsgeduld; ~~*-dock (bot)* Wiesenknöterich *m*, Natter-, Drachenwurz *f*; ~**t** ['-t] *a* geduldig; beharrlich, ausdauernd; zulassend, gestattend (*of s.th.* etw); *s* Patient *m*; *out-~~* ambulante(r) Patient *m*.

patina ['pætinə] Patina *f*.

patio ['pætiou, 'pɑ:-] *pl -s* Innenhof *m*.

patriarch ['peitriɑ:k] *rel* Erzvater; Patriarch *m a. fig*; ~**al** [peitri'ɑ:kəl] patriarchalisch; Patriarchen-; ehrwürdig; ~**ate** ['peitriɑ:kit] *rel* Patriarchat *n*.

patrician [pə'triʃən] *a* patrizisch; vornehm, aristokratisch; *s hist* Patrizier; *allg* Aristokrat *m*.

patricid|al [pætri'saidəl] vatermörderisch; ~**e** ['pætrisaid] Vatermord *m*.

patrimon|ial [pætri'mounjəl] *a* Patrimonial-; *fig* erblich, ererbt; ~**y** ['pætriməni] Patrimonium, väterliche(s) Erbe, Erbteil *n a. fig*; Stiftung *f*, Kirchengut *n*.

patriot ['peitriət, 'pæ-] Patriot *m*; ~**ic** [pætri'ɔtik, *Am* pei-] patriotisch; ~**ism** ['pætriətizm] Patriotismus *m*.

patrol [pə'troul] *s mil* Patrouille, Streife, Runde *f*; Spähtrupp *m*; *aero* Luftstreife *f*; Überwachungsflug *m*; *Am* (Polizei-)Revier *n*; *tr* abpatrouillieren; abfliegen; -gehen; *itr* patrouillieren, die Runde machen; Sperre fliegen; ~ **activity** Spähtrupptätigkeit *f*; ~ **boat, -vessel** Vorposten-, Wachschiff *n*; ~ **car** Streifen-, *mil* Spähwagen *m*; ~ **clash** Vorpostenkampf *m*; ~ **leader** Spähtruppführer *m*; ~**man** *Am* Streifenpolizist *m*; ~ **mission** Patrouillenflug *m*; ~ **plane** Überwachungs-, Sperrflugzeug *n*; ~ **report** Spähtruppmeldung *f*; ~ **service** Streifendienst *m*; ~ **wagon** *Am* Gefangenentransportwagen *m*.

patron ['peitrən] Schutz-, Patronatsherr; *(~ saint)* Schutzheilige(r), Patron; Schirmherr, Beschützer, Gönner, Wohltäter, Mäzen; Vorkämpfer, Verfechter, Vertreter; *com* (Stamm-) Kunde *m*; ~**age** ['pætrənidʒ, 'pei-] Patronat(srecht) *n*; Schirm-, Schutzherrschaft; Förderung, Unterstützung; Gunst, Gönnerschaft; Herablassung; (Stamm-)Kundschaft *f*; Geschäft *n*; ~~ *dividend* Rabattmarke *f*; ~**ess** ['peitrənis] Schutzherrin, -heilige; Schirmherrin *f*; ~**ize** ['pætrənaiz, *Am* 'pei-] *tr* beschützen, -schirmen, protegieren, unterstützen; begönnern; Stammgast, Kunde sein (*a shop* e-s Geschäftes); *theat* regelmäßig besuchen; ~**izer** ['pætrənaizə, *Am* 'pei-] Beschützer; *com* Kunde; Gönner *m*; ~**izing** ['pætrənaiziŋ, *Am* 'pei-] *a* gönnerhaft, herablassend.

patten ['pætn] Holzschuh *m*, -pantine *f*; *arch* Sockel, Säulenfuß *m*.

patter ['pætə] **1.** *itr* klatschen, klappen, prasseln; *(Füße)* trappeln, trampeln, trippeln; knirschen; peitschen; *tr* klatschen, klappen mit; *s* Klatschen, Klappen, Geprassel; Getrappel; *(Regen)* Peitschen; *(Schnee)* Knirschen *n*; **2.** *itr tr* (her)plappern, -leiern; *s* Geplapper, Geleier; Kauderwelsch *n*, Jargon *m*; *fam* Gewäsch, Geschwätz *n*.

pattern ['pætən] *s* Ideal, Vorbild; Muster, Modell *n*, Schablone, Vorlage; Bauart, Gußform *f*; *(paper ~)* Schnittmuster; (Muster-)Beispiel, Muster, Probe; Warenprobe *f*, Muster ohne Wert; *(Textil, Tapete)* Muster *n*, Zeichnung *f*; *fig* Vorbild, Muster; *mil* Trefferbild; *tech* Diagramm, Schaubild *n*; *Am* Stoff *m* zu e-m Kleidungsstück; *attr* Muster-; vorbildlich, ideal; *tr* bilden, formen, gestalten (*on, upon, after* nach); als Beispiel anführen; mustern, mit e-m Muster versehen; *to ~ o.s. on* sich richten nach; *according to ~* nach Muster; *by ~ post* als Warenprobe *f*, als Muster *n* ohne Wert; *to take a ~ by* sich ein Beispiel nehmen an, sich zum Vorbild nehmen; *behavio(u)r ~* Verhaltensweise *f*; ~**-articles** *pl* Massenware *f*; ~**-assortment** Musterkollektion *f*; ~**-bomb** *tr* e-n Bombenteppich legen auf; ~**-bombing** *aero* versetzte(r) Reihenwurf *m*; Flächenbombardierung *f*; Legen *n* e-s Bombenteppichs; ~**-book** Musterbuch *n*; ~**-card** Musterkarte *f*; ~**-designer** Modell-, Musterzeichner *m*; ~ **ga(u)ge** Formlehre *f*; ~ **husband** Mustergatte *m*; ~**-maker** Modellschreiner, -tischler *m*; ~ **pupil** Musterschüler *m*; ~**-shop** Modellwerkstätte *f*; ~ **painting** Tarnanstrich *m*.

patty ['pæti] kleine Pastete; Frikadelle *f*, Bratklops; kleine(r) flache(r) Kuchen *m*; ~**-cake** *s. pat-a-cake*; ~**-pan** kleine Pfanne *f*.

paucity ['pɔ:siti] geringe Menge *od* Anzahl; Knappheit *f*, Mangel *m*.

Paul [pɔ:l] Paul *m*; ~**a** ['-ə] Paula *f*; ~**ine** [pɔ:'li:n, '-] *s* Pauline *f*; *a* ['pɔ:lain] *rel* paulinisch; ~ **Pry** naseweise(r) Mensch *m*.

paunch [pɔ:ntʃ] Bauch; (Fett-)Wanst, Bier-, Hängebauch; *zoo* Pansen *m*; ~**y** ['-i] dickbäuchig, fettleibig.

pauper ['pɔ:pə] Arme(r); Unterstützungsempfänger; auf Armenrecht Klagende(r *m*; ~ **asylum** Armenhaus *n*; ~**ism** ['-rizm] (Massen-)Armut *f*; ~**ization** [pɔ:pərai'zeiʃən] Verarmung, Verelendung *f*; ~**ize** ['pɔ:pərais] *tr* an den Bettelstab bringen; ~ **relief** Armenunterstützung *f*.

pause [pɔ:z] *s* (Ruhe-)Pause *f*; Zögern *n*; Aufschub *m*, Unterbrechung *f*; *typ* Gedankenstrich *m*; *poet* Zäsur *f*; *mus* Verlängerungszeichen *n*, Fermate *f*; *itr* e-e Pause machen, pausieren; inne-, anhalten, zögern, überlegen; verweilen (*on, upon* bei); aushalten (*upon a note* e-n Ton); *without a ~* ununterbrochen, ohne Unterbrechung; *to give s.o. ~* jdn unsicher machen, zur Überlegung veranlassen.

pav|e [peiv] *tr* pflastern; asphaltieren, betonieren, ausbauen; be-, zudecken; *to ~~ the way for s.o. (fig)* jdm den Weg ebnen; ~*ed with good intentions* mit guten Vorsätzen gepflastert; ~**ement** ['-mənt] Pflaster *n*; Straßendecke; *Am* Fahrbahn, ausgebaute Straße *f*; Straßenbaumaterial *n*; *Br* Gehweg, Bürgersteig *m*, Trottoir *n*; ~~ *artist* Gehwegzeichner *m*; ~**er** ['-ə], ~**io(u)r** ['-jə] Steinsetzer; Platten-, Fliesenleger; *(~ing stone)* Pflasterstein *m*.

pavilion [pə'viljən] große(s) Zelt *n*; *(Ausstellungs-, Park-)* Pavillon; *arch* (Seiten-)Flügel *m*; Nebengebäude *n*.

paw [pɔ:] *s* Pfote, Tatze; *fam* Pfote, Hand *f*; *itr tr* stampfen, scharren (in); *fig* ungeschickt umgehen mit, unsanft anfassen; tätscheln; ~**ky** ['-ki] schlau.

pawl [pɔ:l] *tech* Sperrhaken *m*, -klinke; *mar* Palle *f*.

pawn [pɔ:n] **1.** *s (Schach)* Bauer *m*; *fig* Schachfigur, Puppe *f*, Werkzeug *n*; **2.** *s* Pfand(stück) *n*; Bürgschaft *f*; Bürge *m*; Verpfändung *f*; *tr* verpfänden; versetzen; lombardieren, als Sicherheit hinterlegen; ein-, aufs Spiel setzen, wagen; *at, in ~* verpfändet; versetzt; pfandweise, zur Sicherheit; *to give in ~* verpfänden; *to hold in ~* als Pfand behalten; *to ~ o.'s hono(u)r* s-e Ehre verpfänden; *to ~ o.'s word* sein Wort geben; ~**broker** Pfandleiher *m*; ~~*'s shop*, ~**shop** (Pfand-) Leihhaus *n*; ~**broking** Pfandleihe *f*; ~**ee** [pɔ:'ni:] Pfandinhaber *m*; ~**er** ['pɔ:nə] Pfandgeber *m*; ~**-ticket** Pfandschein *m*.

pay [pei] *irr paid, paid* [-d] **1.** *tr* (be)zahlen; *(Rechnung, Schulden)* begleichen; *(Kosten)* tragen, erstatten; *(Arbeit)* entlohnen; *mil* besolden; *mar* abmustern; *(Gewinn)* einbringen, abwerfen; *tech (Kabel)* abrollen, auslegen; *fig* ent-, vergelten, lohnen; dienlich, nützlich sein (*s.o.* jdm), befriedigen; *(Dank, e-n Besuch)* abstatten; *allg* entgegenbringen; *(Aufmerksamkeit)* schenken; **2.** *itr* (be)zahlen; Gewinn abwerfen, etwas einbringen, sich rentieren, sich bezahlt machen; büßen (*for* für); **3.** (Be-)Zahlung; Lohnzahlung, Entlohnung *f*; Lohn *m*, Gehalt *n*; *mil* Löhnung *f*, Sold *m*; Besoldung *f*; *fig* Entgelt *n, a. m*, Lohn *m*; **4.** *a Am mil* abbauwürdig; Münz-; *without ~* unbezahlt; ehrenamtlich; *to be in s.o.'s ~* bei jdm beschäftigt sein; *to draw o.'s ~* sein Gehalt beziehen; *to get less ~* sich (gehaltlich) verschlechtern; *to ~ afterwards* nachträglich, postnumerando bezahlen; *to ~ attention* achtgeben, achten; aufpassen, aufmerksam sein (*to* auf); *o.'s attention to s.o.* jdm den Hof machen; *to ~ beforehand* im voraus, pränumerando bezahlen; *to ~ a call, a visit* e-n Besuch machen; *to ~ a compliment* ein Kompliment machen; *to ~ court to s.o.* jdm den Hof machen; *to ~ damages* Schadenersatz leisten; *to ~ the debt of nature* das Zeitliche segnen; *to ~ o.'s footing* Lehrgeld bezahlen; *to ~ as you go (Am)* immer gleich bezahlen; *to ~ in instal(l)ments* (in Raten) abzahlen; *to ~ lip service to s.th.* e-r Sache nur äußerlich zustimmen; *to ~ the penalty* Strafe leiden, bestraft werden; *to ~ the piper (fig)* die Zeche bezahlen; *to ~ o.'s* *respects* e-n Höflichkeitsbesuch machen (*to s.o.* bei jdm); *to ~ through the nose* es teuer bezahlen müssen; Wucherpreise bezahlen; *to ~ o.'s way* alles bezahlen, keine Schulden machen; s-e eigenen Auslagen bestreiten; *that doesn't ~* das lohnt sich nicht; *there will be the devil to ~* es gibt e-n großen Klamauk; *basic ~* Grundgehalt *n*; *holidays with ~* bezahlte Ferien *pl*; *leave-~* Urlaubsgeld *n*; *monthly ~* Monatsgehalt *n*; *sick-~* Krankengeld *n*; *take-home ~* Nettogehalt *n*; *weekly ~* Wochenlohn *m*; *to ~* **away** *(Kabel)* abfieren, abrollen lassen; *to ~* **back** zurückzahlen, -erstatten; *fig* heimzahlen; *to ~ s.o. back in his own coin* in gleicher Münze zurückzahlen; *to ~* **down** bar bezahlen; anzahlen; *to ~* **for itself** sich bezahlt machen; *to ~ for with o.'s life* mit dem Leben bezahlen; *to ~* **in** ein(be)zahlen; *~~ a check* e-n Scheck einlösen; *to ~* **off** *tr (Schulden)* abbezahlen, tilgen; *(Gläubiger)* abfinden, befriedigen; *(Arbeiter)* entlohnen, auszahlen (u. entlassen); abgelten; *mar* abmustern; wiedergutmachen; Rache nehmen an *od* für; *itr* sich rentieren; Erfolg haben; *~~ old scores (fig)* e-e alte Rechnung begleichen; *to ~* **out** *(Geld)* ausgeben; aus(be)zahlen; abfinden; es heimzahlen (*s.o.* jdm); *mar (Tau)* auslassen, abrollen (lassen); *to ~* **up** voll bezahlen; abbezahlen, tilgen; **~able** ['-əbl] zahlbar, fällig; rentabel, lohnend; *accounts ~~* Passiva, Verbindlichkeiten *f pl*; *~~ to bearer* zahlbar an Überbringer; *~~ to order* an Order lautend; **~-as-you-earn** *Br* Lohnsteuerabzug *m*; **~-bill** Zahlungsanweisung *f*; **~-book** *mil* Soldbuch *n*; *~* **boost** *(Am sl)*, **raise** Gehaltserhöhung *f*; **~-box, -desk** Kasse(nschalter *m*) *f*; *~* **clerk** Rechnungsführer *m*; **~-day** Zahl-, Löhnungs-, Abrechnungs-, Verfallstag *m*; *~* **dirt** *Am min* abbauwürdige(s) Gestein *n*; *to strike ~~* sein Glück machen; **~ee** [-'iː] Zahlungsempfänger; Wechselnehmer, -inhaber *m*; **~-envelope** Lohntüte *f*; **~er** ['-ə] (Be-, Ein-)Zahler; *(Wechsel)* Trassat, Bezogene(r) *m*; *tax~~* Steuerzahler *m*; *~~-in* Einzahler *m*; *~* **grade** Besoldungsgruppe *f*; *~* **increase** Lohn-, Gehaltserhöhung *f*; **~ing** ['-iŋ] einträglich, ertragbringend, -reich; gewinnbringend, lohnend, rentabel; *(Geschäft)* vorteilhaft; *~~-back* Rückzahlung *f*; *~~-guest* Pensionär *m*; *~~-in* Einzahlung *f*; *~~-in slip (Br)* Einzahlungsbeleg *m*; *~(~) library* Leihbücherei *f*; *~~-off* Ab(be)zahlung; Aus(be)zahlung; Abfindung *f*; *~~-office* Zahlstelle *f*; *~~-out* Auszahlung; Abfindung *f*; *~~-up* volle Bezahlung; Tilgung *f*; **~-load** Nutzlast *f*; *~~ capacity* Ladefähigkeit *f*; **~master** Zahlmeister *m*; *~~'s office* Zahlmeisterei; Kasse *f*; **~ment** ['-mənt] (Be-)Zahlung, Entrichtung, Begleichung, Erstattung; *(Wechsel)* Einlösung; Rate; *(Anspruch)* Befriedigung; Entlohnung, Löhnung *f*, Lohn *m*, Gehalt *n*, Sold *m*; Belohnung *od* Strafe *f*; *in ~~ of* zum Ausgleich *gen*; *on ~~ of* nach Eingang *gen*; *to demand ~~* Zahlung verlangen; *to effect, to make a ~~* Zahlung leisten; *to refuse ~~* die Zahlung verweigern; *to stop, to suspend ~~s* die Zahlungen einstellen; *~~ received* Betrag erhalten; *additional ~~* Nachzahlung *f*; *advance ~~* Vorauszahlung *f*; *application, request for ~~* Zahlungsaufforderung *f*; *cash-~~* Barzahlung *f*; *date, day of ~~* Zahlungstermin *m*; *delay for ~~* Zahlungsaufschub *m*; *dividend-~~* Dividendenausschüttung *f*; *down ~~* sofortige Barzahlung *f*; *easy ~~* Zahlungserleichterungen *f pl*; *means of ~~* Zahlungsmittel *n pl*; *non-~~* Nichtbezahlung *f*; *order for ~~* Zahlungsanweisung *f*; *place of ~~* Erfüllungsort *m*; *promise of ~~* Zahlungsversprechen *n*; *refusal of ~~* Zahlungsverweigerung *f*; *salary-~~* Gehaltszahlung *f*; *wage-~~* Lohnzahlung *f*; *way of ~~* Zahlungsweise *f*; *~~ on account* Anzahlung *f*; Teil-, Abschlags-, Ratenzahlung *f*; *~~ in advance* Vorauszahlung *f*; *~~ by, in instal(l)ments* Ratenzahlung *f*; *~~ instructions (pl)* Zahlungsanweisungen *f pl*; *~~ in kind* Sach-, Naturalleistung *f*; *~~ terms (pl)* Zahlungsbedingungen *f pl*; *~~ load* Lohnkostenanteil *m*; **~-off** *fam* Abrechnung; *fig* Überraschung *f*, unerwartete(r) Höhepunkt, Knalleffekt; *fig* Lohn, Erfolg *m*; **~-office** Zahlstelle; Kasse(nschalter *m*) *f*; Lohnbüro *n*, -stelle; *mil* Zahlmeisterei *f*; **~ola** [-'oulə] *Am sl* Bestechungsgeld *n*; Lohnliste *f*; **~-parade** *mil* Löhnungsappell *m*; **~-roll, -sheet** Lohn-, *mil* Löhnungsliste; Lohnsumme *f*; *to be on the ~~* angestellt, beschäftigt sein; *~~ clerk* Lohnbuchhalter *m*; *~~ office* Lohnbuchhaltung *f*; *~* **seniority** Besoldungsdienstalter *n*; **~-sergeant** *mil* Rechnungsführer *m*; **~-slip** Lohnzettel *m*; *~* **station** öffentliche(r) Fernsprecher *m*; *~* **television** *Am* Münzfernsehen *n*.

pea [piː] Erbse *f*; *as like as two ~s* gleich wie ein Ei dem andern; *to jump about like a ~ on a drum* sich wie verrückt gebärden; *green, garden-~s(pl)* junge Erbsen *f pl*; *split ~s (pl)* getrocknete Erbsen *f pl*; *Sweet ~ (bot)* Garten-, Spanische Wicke *f*; **~-pod, ~se-cod** Erbsenschote *f*; **~-shooter** Blasrohr; *sl* MG, Maschinengewehr *n*; **~-soup** Erbsensuppe *f*; **~-souper** *fam* Waschküche *f*; **~-soupy** *(Nebel)* dick u. gelb.

peace [piːs] Friede(n); Frieden(sschluß, -vertrag) *m*; Ruhe (u. Ordnung); Eintracht; Ruhe, Stille; öffentliche Ordnung *f*; *(to be) at ~* in Frieden (leben) (*with* mit); *to break the ~* den Frieden brechen; die öffentliche Ruhe stören; *to give s.o. no ~* jdn nicht in Ruhe lassen; *to hold, to keep o.'s ~* sich ruhig verhalten, still sein; *to keep the ~* die öffentliche Sicherheit wahren; *to leave s.o. in ~* jdn in Ruhe lassen; *to make ~* Frieden schließen; *to make o.'s ~ with* sich versöhnen, sich vertragen mit; *~ be with you* der Friede sei mit dir; *breach of the ~* Ruhestörung *f*; *domestic ~* Hausfriede(n) *m*; *breach of the domestic ~* Hausfriedensbruch *m*; *industrial ~* Arbeitsfrieden *m*; *King's ~* Landfrieden *m*; *proposal of ~* Friedensvorschlag *m*; *public ~* öffentliche Ordnung *f*; *threat to ~* Bedrohung *f* des Friedens; *~ in the home* häusliche(r) Frieden *m*; *~ of mind* Seelenfrieden *m*, innere Ruhe *f*; **~able** ['-əbl] friedlich; **~-breaker** Friedensbrecher, Ruhestörer *m*; *~* **conditions, terms** *pl* Friedensbedingungen *f pl*; *~* **conference** Friedenskonferenz *f*; *~* **congress** Friedenskongreß *m*; *~* **establishment, footing** Friedensstärke *f*; **~ful** ['-ful] friedlich; friedliebend, verträglich; ruhig; gütlich; **~fulness** ['-fulnis] Friedlichkeit *f*; **~-loving** friedliebend; **~-maker** Friedensstifter *m*; *~* **negotiations, parleys** *pl* Friedensverhandlungen *f pl*; *~* **offer** Friedensangebot *n*; **~-offering** *rel* Sühnopfer *n*; Genugtuung *f*; Dankesopfer; Friedensangebot *n*; **~-officer** Sicherheitsbeamte(r); Sheriff; Schutzmann, Polizist *m*; **~-pipe** Friedenspfeife *f*; **~-time** Friedenszeit *f*; *~~ economy, production* Friedenswirtschaft, -produktion *f*; *~~ strength* Friedensstärke *f*; **~-treaty** Friedensvertrag *m*.

peach [piːtʃ] **1.** Pfirsich(baum *m*, -farbe *f*); *sl* Pfunds-, Prachtkerl; süße(r) Käfer *m*; nette(s) Ding *n (Mädchen)*; Pfunds-, prima Sache *f*; **~-blossom** Pfirsichblüte *f*; **~y** ['-i] pfirsichfarben; samtweich; *sl* prächtig, prima, Klasse; reizend; auffallend; **~y-keen** *Am sl* bestens, in Ordnung; **2.** *itr sl* verpfeifen, angeben, verraten (*against, upon s.o.* jdn); **~er** ['-ə] *sl* Verräter *m*.

pea|chick ['piːtʃik] junge(r) Pfau *m*; **~cock** ['piːkɔk] *s* Pfau; *fig* aufgeblasene(r) Mensch *m*; *itr fig* sich aufblasen, sich aufblähen; *proud as a ~~* stolz wie ein Pfau; *~~-blue* pfauenblau; *~~ blue* Pfauenblau *n*; *~~-butterfly (ent)* Tagpfauenauge *n*; **~fowl** ['-faul], **~hen** Pfauhenne *f*; **~-jacket** *mar* Matrosenjacke *f*.

peak [piːk] **1.** Spitze *f*; (Berg-)Gipfel; Bergkegel; (Haar-)Wirbel; Mützenschirm; Scheitelpunkt; *fig* Gipfel *m*, Spitze *f a. el*; Höhepunkt; *(~ value)* Höchstwert *m*; *mar* Piek *f*; *tr itr* (sich) aufrichten; anspitzen; *to be at the ~ of o.'s power* auf dem Gipfel der Macht stehen; *to reach the ~* den höchsten Stand erreichen; *post-war ~* Nachkriegshöchststand *m*; *~ of production* Produktionsspitze *f*; *~* **capacity** Höchstleistungsgrenze *f*; **~ed** [-t] *a*, **~y** ['-i] spitz; *~* **hours** *pl* Verkehrsspitze *f*; *~* **level** Höchststand *m*; *~* **load** Spitzenbelastung *f*; *~* **output** Höchstproduktion *f*; *~* **power** *tech* Leistungsspitze *f*; *~* **season** Hochkonjunktur *f*; **~-traffic hours** *pl* Hauptverkehrszeit *f*; **2.** *itr (to ~ and pine)* kränkeln, dahinsiechen; **~ed** *a*, **~y** spitzig, schmächtig, kränklich, bleich.

peal [piːl] *s* (Glocken-)Läuten, Geläute; Glockenspiel; Dröhnen *n*, Lärm *m*, Getöse *n*; *itr tr* laut läuten, dröhnen, schallen, donnern, krachen (lassen); *~s of applause* Beifallssturm *m*; *~ of laughter* schallende(s) Gelächter *n*, Lachsalve *f*; *~ of rain* Platzregen *m*; *~ of thunder* Donnergetöse, -rollen *n*.

peanut ['piːnʌt] *s* Erdnuß *f*; *pl Am sl* unbedeutende Sache *f*; *a Am sl* unbedeutend; *~* **butter** Erdnußbutter *f*; *~* **gallery** *theat* Olymp *m*; *~* **oil** Erdnußöl *n*; *~* **politics** *pl mit sing Am* politische(s) Intrigenspiel *n*; *to play ~~ (Am)* (politisch) intrigieren.

pear [pɛə] Birne *f*; *(~-tree)* Birnbaum *m*.

pearl [pəːl] *s* Perle *a. allg u. fig*; Perlfarbe; *typ* Perl *f (Schriftgrad)*; *itr* Perlen fischen; *to cast (o.'s) ~s before swine* s-e Perlen vor die Säue werfen; *mother-of-~* Perlmutter *f*; *seed-~* Saatperle *f*; **~-ash** *chem* Pottasche *f*; **~-barley** Perlgraupen *f pl*; **~-button** Perlmutterknopf *m*; **~-diver, -fisher** Perlenfischer *m*; **~-fishery** Perlenfischerei *f*; **~-oyster** Perlmuschel *f*; **~-powder, -white** Schminkweiß *n*; **~-shell** Perlmutt(er *f*) *n*; **~y** ['-i] perlmutterartig; perlen-, perlmutterverziert.

peasant ['pezənt] *s* Landwirt, Kleinbauer; Land-, landwirtschaftliche(r) Arbeiter *m*; *a* (klein)bäuerlich; **~-boy, -girl** Bauernjunge *m*, -mädchen *n*;

~-leader Bauernführer *m*; **~-party** Bauernpartei *f*; **~ property-holding** kleinbäuerliche(r) Grundbesitz *m*; **~ proprietor** Kleinbauer *m*; **~ry** ['-ri] Landvolk; Kleinbauerntum *n*; Landarbeiterschaft *f*.
peat [pi:t] Torf *m*; *to cut, to make* ~ Torf stechen; **~-bog** Torfmoor *n*; **~-cutter, -digger** Torfstecher *m*; Torfbagger *m*; **~-sod** Torfsode *f*; **~y** ['-i] torfartig; Torf-.
pebbl|e ['pebl] *s* Kiesel(stein); (Linse *f* aus) Bergkristall *m*; *(Leder)* Narbe *f*; *tr (Leder, Papier)* narben; *you are not the only ~~ on the beach* man kann auch ohne dich auskommen; *~~ leather* Narbenleder *n*; **~y** ['-i] kiesig; genarbt.
pecan [pi'kæn] Pekannuß *f*, -baum *m*.
peccadillo [pekə'dilou] *pl -o(e)s* läßliche Sünde *f*.
peck [pek] **1.** *tr (Loch)* picken, hacken; *(Futter)* aufpicken; *fam* flüchtig küssen; *itr* picken, hacken (*at* nach); *fam* herumnaschen (*at* an); *fam (mit Worten)* herumhacken (*at* auf); *s* (Schnabel-)Hieb *m*; Loch *n*; Pickstelle *f*; flüchtige(r) Kuß *m*; *sl* Futter *n*, Fressalien *pl*; *to have s.th. to ~ at* etw zum Nagen u. zu Beißen haben; **~er** ['-ə] Picke, Haue *f*; *to keep o.'s ~~ up (sl)* den Kopf oben behalten; **~ing** ['-iŋ]: *~~ order* strenge soziale Rangordnung *f*; **~ish** ['-iʃ] *fam* hungrig; *Am* reizbar; **2.** Viertelscheffel *m (Trockenmaß, 9,1 l; Am 8,8 l)*; *fig* e-e Menge, Masse, ein Haufen *m*.
pectoral ['pektərəl] *a* Brust-; *s* Brustplatte *f*, -schild *m*; *rel* Pektorale *n*; Brustmuskel *m*, *(~~ fin)* -flosse *f*; *pharm* Brustmittel *n*.
peculat|e ['pekjuleit] *tr (öffentliche Gelder)* veruntreuen; unterschlagen; **~ion** [pekju'leiʃən] Veruntreuung, (Amts-)Unterschlagung *f*.
peculiar [pi'kju:ljə] *a* besonder, Sonder-; ausschließlich, eigen, eigentümlich (*to* für); einzigartig; charakteristisch (*to* für); sonderbar, eigenartig, seltsam; *s* Sondervermögen, -recht *n*; **~ity** [pikju:li'æriti] Besonderheit; Eigentümlichkeit, Eigenheit, Einzigartigkeit; Sonderbarkeit, Seltsamkeit, Eigenart *f*; *das* Besondere, Einzigartige, Sonderbare, Seltsame; kennzeichnende Eigenschaft *f*; Charakter-, Wesenszug *m*; **~ly** [-li] *adv* besonders; seltsam; persönlich.
pecuniary [pi'kju:njəri] pekuniär, geldlich; Geld-; **~ advantages** *pl* materielle Vorteile *m pl*; **~ affairs, matters** *pl* Geldangelegenheiten, -sachen *f pl*; **~ assistance** finanzielle Unterstützung *f*; **~ benefit**: *for ~~* in gewinnsüchtiger Absicht; **~ claim** Geldforderung *f*; **~ compensation** Geldentschädigung *f*; **~ embarrassments** *pl* Geldverlegenheit *f*; Zahlungsschwierigkeiten *f pl*; **~ loss** Vermögensverlust *m*; **~ penalty** Geldstrafe *f*; **~ present** Geldgeschenk *n*; **~ profit** finanzielle(r) Vorteil *m*; **~ request** Geldforderung *f*; **~ requirements** *pl* Geldbedarf *m*; **~ resources** *pl* Geldmittel *n pl*; **~ transactions** *pl* Geldgeschäfte *n pl*; **~ troubles** *pl* finanzielle Schwierigkeiten *f pl*.
pedagog|ic(al) [pedə'gɔdʒik(əl)] pädagogisch, erzieherisch; Erziehungs-; **~ics** [pedə'gɔdʒiks] *s pl mit sing s.* **~y**; **~(ue)** ['pedəgɔg] Pädagoge, Erzieher, Lehrer; *pej* Schulmeister *m*; **~y** ['pedəgɔgi, '-dʒi] Pädagogik, Erziehungswissenschaft *f*.
pedal ['pedl] *s tech mus* Pedal *n*; Fußhebel *m*; *a* [*a.* pi:dl] *zoo* Fuß-; Tret-; *itr* das Pedal, die Pedale bedienen; radfahren; *tr* mit e-m Pedal in Gang setzen; *(Rad)* fahren, treten; **~-boat, -craft, ~o** ['-əlou] Wassertretrad *n*; **~ brake** *mot* Fußbremse *f*.
pedant ['pedənt] Pedant, Kleinigkeitskrämer; Schulfuchs; Wissensprotz *m*; **~ic** [pi'dæntik] pedantisch, kleinlich; angeberisch; **~ry** ['pedəntri] Pedanterie *f*; Protzen *n* mit s-m Wissen.
peddl|e ['pedl] *itr* hausieren; (herum-) trödeln; sich mit Kleinigkeiten abgeben; *tr* hausieren mit *a. fig*; **~er(y)** *Am s. pedlar(y)*; **~ing** ['-iŋ] herumtrödelnd; *fig* geringfügig, unbedeutend.
pederast(y) *s. paederast(y)*.
pedest|al ['pedistl] Sockel *m*, Fußgestell *n*, Untersatz *m*, Piedestal *n*; *fig* Grundlage, Basis, Stütze *f*; **~rian** [pi'destriən] *a* zu Fuß (gehend); Fuß-; *fig (Stil)* prosaisch, langweilig, trocken, schwunglos, nüchtern; *s* Fußgänger *m*; *~~ crossing* Überweg *m*.
pediatr... *s. paediatr...*.
pedic|el ['pedisl], **~cle** [-kl] *zoo bot* (kleiner) Stiel; Blütenstengel *m*.
pedicure ['pedikjuə] Fußpfleger *m*; Fußpflege, Pediküre *f*.
pedigree ['pedigri:] Stammbaum *m*, *a. zoo*; Herkunft, Abstammung; Ahnentafel; *(Wort)* Ableitung *f*; *attr* u. **~d** ['-d] *a (Tier)* mit Stammbaum; Zucht-; **~ cattle** Zuchtvieh *n*; **~ dog** Rassehund *m*.
pediment ['pedimənt] *arch* Tympanum, *(flaches)* Giebelfeld *n*.
pedlar ['pedlə] Hausierer (*of* mit), ambulante(r) Gewerbetreibende(r) *m*; **~y** ['-ri] ambulante(s) Gewerbe *n*; Trödelkram *m*.
pedometer [pi'dɔmitə] Schrittzähler *m*.
peduncle [pi'dʌŋkl] Blumen-, Blütenstiel; *anat zoo* Stiel *m*.

*

pee [pi:] *itr fam* pinkeln.
peek [pi:k] *itr* gucken (*at* nach); spähen (*into* in); *s* schnelle(r), kurze(r) Blick *m*.
peel [pi:l] **1.** *tr* schälen; die Haut abziehen (*s.th.* e-r S); *(Kleider)* abstreifen; *itr* sich häuten; sich abschälen; abgehen, abblättern, abbröckeln; *sl* sich auspellen, sich ausziehen; *s* Schale, Haut *f (e-r Frucht)*; *to keep o.'s eyes ~ed (Am fam)* ein wachsames Auge, die Augen überall haben; *to ~ off (itr) (aero)* ausscheren; *sl* sich entblättern; abblättern, sich abschuppen; *Am sl* abhauen; *tr* ausziehen; abschälen; *candied ~* Zitronat *n*, Sukkade *f*; **~er** ['-ə] Schäler *m*; Striptease-Tänzerin *f*; **~ings** ['-iŋ] *pl* (Obst-, *bes.* Kartoffel-)Schalen *f pl*; **2.** (Brot-) Schieber *m (Gerät)*.
peep [pi:p] **1.** *itr* (verstohlen) gucken, lugen, spähen (*at* nach); teilweise *od* allmählich sichtbar werden; zum Vorschein kommen; *s* kurze(r), schnelle(r), flüchtige(r), heimliche(r) Blick; Durchblick *m*; erste(s) Erscheinen, Auftreten; Guckloch *n*; *at ~ of dawn, day* bei Tagesanbruch *m*; *to have a ~ at s.th.* nach etw verstohlen blicken; **~-bo** Guckguckspiel *n*; **~er** ['-ə] Zugucker, Späher, Beobachter, Neugierige(r) *m*; *pl fam* Augen *n pl*, Gucker *m pl*; **~hole** Guckloch *n*; **~ing -Tom** heimliche(r) Beobachter; Voyeur *m*; **~-show** Guckkasten *m*; *Am sl fig* Fleischbeschau *f*; **~-sight** *(Gewehr)* Lochvisier *n*; **2.** *itr* piepen; piepsen; *s* Piepen *n*; *Am sl* Piepser, Ton *m*, Wort *n*; **~er** Piep(s)ende(r) *m*.
peer [piə] **1.** *itr* angestrengt schauen, spähen, lugen (*at* auf; *into* in; *for* nach); auftauchen, in Erscheinung treten, sich zeigen, zum Vorschein kommen; *to ~ at* angucken; **2.** *s* Gleichgestellte(r), Ebenbürtige(r); Pair, Peer, Angehörige(r) *m* des hohen Adels; *~ of the realm (brit.)* Pair *m*; **~age** ['-ridʒ] Pairswürde *f*, -stand *m*; Adelsliste *f*; **~ess** ['-ris] Frau *f* e-s Pairs, weibliche(r) Pair *m*; **~less** ['-lis] unvergleichlich, ohnegleichen.
peev|e [pi:v] *fam tr* auf die Palme bringen, ärgern; **~ed** [-d] *a fam* ärgerlich, gereizt, gekränkt, verärgert, *fam* eingeschnappt (*about, at* über, wegen); **~ish** ['-iʃ] reizbar, launisch, ungeduldig; schlecht-, übelgelaunt.
peewit *s. pewit*.

*

peg [peg] *s* Pflock, Holznagel, Dübel, Bolzen *m*, Sprosse *f*, Splint, Keil *m*, Knagge *f*, Daumen, Haken *m*, Klammer *f*; Wirbel *m (e-s Saiteninstruments)*; *(clothes-~)* Wäscheklammer *f*; *(Zelt)* Hering *m*; Stufe *f*, Schritt; *fig* Vorwand *m*, Gelegenheit *f*; *fig* Aufhänger *m*; *fam* Stelze *f*, Bein *n*; *fam* Zahn; Whisky *m* (mit) Soda; *com* Kurs-, Marktstützung *f*; *tr* festpflökken, -stecken; abgrenzen, markieren; festsetzen; *(Schuhe)* nageln; durchstoßen; anhaken; *com (Preis)* halten, stabilisieren; *Am fam* erkennen, festlegen; *fam* werfen, schmeißen (*at* nach); *itr* schlagen, werfen (*at* nach); *off the ~ (Kleidung)* von der Stange; *to be a square ~ in a round hole* am falschen, verkehrten Platz sein; *to come down a ~ or two (fig)* e-n Pflock zurückstecken, gelindere Saiten aufziehen; *to take s.o. down a ~ or two* jdn demütigen; *a good ~ on which to hang a sermon* ein Grund *m* zum Reden; *tent-~* Zeltpflock *m*; *to ~* **along**, *to ~* **away** drauflos-, weiterarbeiten (*at* an); sich anstrengen; drauflosessen; *to ~* **down** festpflocken, befestigen; festmachen; *fig* festnageln; *to ~* **out** abgrenzen, abstecken; *fam* ins Gras beißen, sterben; erledigt *od* fertig sein; ausgehen; **~-house** *sl* Kneipe *f*; **~-leg** Stelzfuß *m*; **~-tooth** Stiftzahn *m*; **~-top** Kreisel *m*.
Peg(gy) ['peg(i)] Gretchen *n*.
peignoir ['peinwɑ:] Morgenrock; Frisier-, Bademantel *m*.
pejorative ['pi:dʒərətiv, pi'dʒɔrətiv] *(Wort)* herabsetzend, verschlechternd.
peke, Pekin(g)ese [pi:k, pi:ki'ni:z, -iŋ'i:z] *zoo* Pekinese *m*.
pelf [pelf] *pej* Mammon *m*.
pelican ['pelikən] *orn* Pelikan *m*.
pelisse [pe'li:s] *obs* Damen-, Kindermantel *m*.
pellet ['pelit] Kügelchen *n*; Pille *f*; Schrotkorn *n*.
pellicle ['pelikl] Häutchen *n*; dünne Hautschicht *f*.
pell-mell ['pel'mel] *adv* durcheinander; *a* hastig; verworren; *s* Durcheinander *n*, Unordnung *f*.
pellucid [pe'lju:sid] durchsichtig; *fig* klar, verständlich.
pelt [pelt] **1.** *tr* bewerfen, beschießen (*with* mit); werfen (*s.o. with s.th.* etw nach jdm); *(mit Fragen)* bombardieren; *itr* (nieder)prasseln, trommeln (*against the roof* auf das Dach); stürmen; *s* Wurf; Schlag *m*; Eile, Geschwindigkeit *f*; *to ~ down* nieder-, herunterprasseln; *at full ~* in voller Geschwindigkeit; *it was ~ing with rain* es goß; *~ing rain* Platzregen; Regenguß, -schauer *m*; **2.** Fell *n*, Haut *f*; Pelz *m*;

~ry ['-ri] Felle *n pl*, Häute; Pelzwaren *f pl*, Rauchwerk *n*.

pelv|ic ['pelvik] *a anat* Becken-; **~is** ['-is] *pl -ves* [-i:z] *anat* Becken *n*.

pem(m)ican ['pemikən] Pemmikan *m*.

pen [pen] **1.** *s* (Schreib-)Feder; *fig* Feder; Ausdrucksweise *f*, Stil *m*; Schreiben *n*, Schriftstellerei *f*; Schriftsteller *m*; *tr* schreiben, ver-, abfassen; entwerfen; *to put o.'s ~ to paper* zur Feder greifen; *ball(-point) ~* Kugelschreiber *m*; *fountain-~* Füllfeder (-halter *m*) *f*; *fountain-~ ink* Füllfedertinte *f*; *quill ~* Gänsefeder *f*; *steel-~* Stahlfeder *f*; *stroke of the ~* Federstrich *m*; *~ and ink* Schreibmaterial *n*; **~-and-ink** *a* Feder-, Schreib-; *~~-drawing* Federzeichnung *f*; **~-case** Federkasten *m*; **~holder** Federhalter *m*; **~knife** Feder-, Taschenmesser *n*; **~-man** Schreiber, Schreibkünstler; Schriftsteller *m*; **~manship** ['-mənʃip] Schreibkunst; Duktus, Schriftzug *m*; **~-name** Schriftstellername *m*, Pseudonym *n*; **~-nib** Federspitze *f*; **~-pal, -friend** *Am fam* Brieffreund *m*; **~-pusher** *fam* Schreiberling, Schreiberseele *f*; **~-tray** Federschale *f*; **2.** *s* Pferch *m*, Gehege *n*, Verschlag; (Schweine-, Hühner-)Stall *m*; *(play-~)* Laufställchen *n*; (U-Boot-)Bunker; *mil sl* Bunker, Bau, Arrest(lokal *n*) *m*; *Am fam* Kittchen *n*; *tr a. irr pent, pent* [pent] *(to ~ up, in)* einpferchen, -schließen, -sperren.

penal ['pi:nl] *a* Straf-; strafbar; *~* **act** strafbare Handlung *f*; *~* **action** öffentliche Anklage *f*; *~* **clause** Strafbestimmung *f*; *~* **code** Strafgesetzbuch *n*; *~* **colony, settlement** Strafkolonie *f*; *~* **confinement** Strafhaft *f*; *~* **duty** Strafzoll *m*, Zollstrafe *f*; *~* **establishment** Strafanstalt *f*; *~* **interest** Verzugszinsen *pl*; **~ization** [pi:nəlai'zeiʃən] Bestrafung; Benachteiligung *f*; **~ize** ['pi:nəlaiz] *tr* unter Strafe stellen, mit Strafe belegen; bestrafen, e-e Strafe verhängen über; benachteiligen, schlechter stellen, zurücksetzen; *sport* mit e-m Handicap, mit Strafpunkten belegen; *~* **jurisdiction** Strafrechtspflege *f*; *~* **law** Strafrecht *n*; *~* **legislation** Strafgesetzgebung *f*; *~* **offence** strafbare Handlung; Straftat *f*; *~* **provisions** *pl* Strafbestimmungen *f pl*; *~* **reform** Strafrechtsreform *f*; *~* **register** Strafregister *n*; *~* **servitude** Zuchthaus(strafe *f*) *n*; *~~ for life* lebenslängliche Zuchthausstrafe *f*; *~* **suit** Strafklage *f*; Strafprozeß *m*, -verfahren *n*; **~ty** ['penlti] Strafe *a. fig*; Geldbuße, -strafe; Benachteiligung *f*; *sport* Strafpunkt *m*; *fig* Folgen *f pl*; Kehrseite *f* (*of fame* des Ruhmes); *on, under ~~ of* bei ...strafe; *to incur a ~~* e-e Strafe verwirken; *to pay the ~~* die Folgen tragen (*of s.th.* e-r S); *aggravation of ~~* Strafverschärfung *f*; *in aggravation of ~~* strafverschärfend; *collective ~~* Kollektivstrafe *f*; *disciplinary ~~* Disziplinar-, Ordnungsstrafe *f*; *maximum, minimum ~~* Höchst-, Mindeststrafe *f*; *mitigation of ~~* Strafmilderung *f*; *in mitigation of ~~* strafmildernd; *remission of the ~~* Straferlaß *m*; *~ of death* Todesstrafe *f*; *~ for delay* Verzugsstrafe *f*; *~ of imprisonment* Gefängnisstrafe *f*; *~~ area (Fußball)* Strafraum *m*; *~~ box (Eishockey)* Strafbank *f*; *~~ clause* Strafklausel; Vertrags-, Konventionalstrafe *f*; *~~ kick (Fußball)* Strafstoß, Elfmeter *m*; *~~ postage* Strafporto *n*.

penance ['penəns] *rel u. allg* Buße *f* (*for* für); *to do ~* Buße tun.

penchant ['pɑ̃:ŋʃɑ̃:ŋ, *Am* 'pentʃənt] Vorliebe, Neigung *f*, Hang *m*, Lust *f* (*for* zu), Geschmack *m* (*for* für).

pencil ['pensl] *s* (Farb-, Blei-, Augenbrauen-)Stift, Griffel *m*; *(~ of rays)* Strahlenbündel *n*; *zoo* Haarpinsel *m*; *(Kunst)* Pinsel-, Strichführung *f*; *fig* Stift *m*; *tr* mit e-m (Blei-)Stift markieren *od* schreiben *od* zeichnen; *(Augenbrauen)* (nach)ziehen; *to write in ~* mit Bleistift schreiben; *colo(u)red ~* Buntstift *m*; *lead ~* Bleistift *m*; **~-case** Federkasten *m*; **~(l)ed** [-d] *a* gezeichnet; büschelig; *(Strahlen)* gebündelt; **~-sharpener** Bleistiftspitzer *m*; **~-sharpening machine** Bleistiftspitzmaschine *f*.

pend|ant, ~ent ['pendənt] Gehänge *n*, Anhänger *m*; Ohrgehänge *n*, -ring *m*; *(Taschenuhr)* Knopf u. Bügel *m*, Pendant *n*; Lampenzug *m*; Hängelampe *f*; *arch* Pendentif *n*, Zwickel; *mar* Wimpel *m*; *fig* Gegen-, Seitenstück, Pendant *n* (*to* zu); **~ency** ['pendənsi] *(Prozeß)* Schweben *n*; **~ent, ~ant** ['-ənt] hängend, schwebend; Hänge-; überhängend; *fig* unentschieden, schwebend; *~~ light* Hängeleuchte *f*; **~entive** [pen'dentiv] *arch* Zwickel *m*; **~ing** ['-iŋ] *a fig* schwebend, in der Schwebe, unentschieden, unerledigt; *jur* anhängig; *prp* während *gen*; bis zu, in Erwartung *gen*; *still ~~* noch nicht erledigt; noch in der Schwebe; *~~ further instructions, notice* bis auf weiteres; *to be ~~* schweben; **~ulate** ['pendjuleit] *itr* pendeln, schwingen; *fig* schwanken; unentschlossen, unentschieden sein; zögern; **~ulous** ['-juləs] (frei, lose, herab)hängend; pendelnd, schwingend; schwebend; **~ulum** ['-juləm] Pendel *n*; *the swing of the ~~* das Schwanken der öffentlichen Meinung; *~~ clock, length, motion, swing, test* Pendeluhr, -länge, -bewegung, -schwingung *f*, -versuch *m*.

*

penetr|ability [penitrə'biliti] Durchdringbarkeit, Durchlässigkeit *f*; **~able** ['penitrəbl] durchdringbar; **~alia** [peni'treiljə] *pl das* Innerste; *das* Allerheiligste; Geheimnis(se *pl*) *n*; **~ate** ['penitreit] *tr* dringen durch; vor-, eindringen in; durchdringen *a. fig* (*with* mit); durchstoßen; *fig* (geistig) durchdringen, durchschauen, erkennen, ergründen, erfassen; *itr* eindringen (*into* in), vordringen (*to* bis); durchdringen (*through* durch); durchstoßen; *aero* einfliegen; *fig* ergründen (*into s.th.* etw); **~ating** ['-eitiŋ] durchdringend, scharf, stark; tief; scharfsinnig, verständig, einsichtig; **~ation** [peni'treiʃən] Ein-, Durchdringen *n*; Ein-, Durchbruch *m*; Durchschlagskraft, Einschlagtiefe *f* *(e-s Geschosses)*; Durchstoß *m*; Durchdringen *n*, (politische u. wirtschaftliche) Durchdringung *f*; Scharfsinn, Verstand *m*, Einsicht *f*, Einfühlungsvermögen *n*; *aero* Einflug *m*; **~ative** ['penitreitiv] = *~ating*; *~~ power (Geschoß)* Durchschlagskraft *f*; *(Strahlen)* Eindringungsvermögen *n*.

penguin ['peŋwin] *orn* Pinguin *m*; *king ~* Königs-, Fettpinguin *m*.

penicillin [peni'silin] Penizillin *n*.

peninsul|a [pi'ninsjulə] Halbinsel *f*; **~ar** [-] halbinselförmig; Halbinsel-.

penis ['pi:nis] *anat* Penis *m*.

peniten|ce ['penitəns] Reue, Bußfertigkeit *f*; **~t** [-t] *a* reu(müt)ig, bußfertig; *s* reuige(r) Sünder(in *f*) *m*; Bußfertige(r *m*) *f*; Büßer(in *f*) *m*; **~tial** [peni'tenʃəl] *a* Buß-; bußfertig; *s* Büßer(in *f*) *m*; *(~~ book)* Bußbuch *n*; **~tiary** [-'tenʃəri] *a* Buß-; Besserungs-; *Am* strafbar; Straf-; *s* Besserungsanstalt, *Am* Strafanstalt *f*, Zuchthaus *n*; *rel* Apostolische Pönitentiarie *f*; *rel* Großpönitentiar *m*; *~~ system* Strafvollzug *m*.

pennant ['penənt] Stander, Wimpel *m*, Fähnchen *n*.

pennate *s. pinnate*.

penniless ['penilis] völlig mittellos, ohne e-n Pfennig.

pennon ['penən] *mil* Fähnlein *n*; Stander, Wimpel *m*; Schwinge *f*.

penny ['peni] *pl pence* [pens] *(Wert) u. pennies (Anzahl Münzen)* Penny *m* (*1/12 Schilling)*; Pennystück *n*; (*US* od *Kanada*) Cent; *fig* Heller *m*; *to take care of the pence* den Pfennig zehnmal umdrehen, ehe man ihn ausgibt; *to turn an honest ~* etwas (dazu-)verdienen; *the ~ dropped* der Groschen ist gefallen; *in for a ~, in for a pound (prov)* wer A sagt, muß auch B sagen; *a ~ for your thoughts* wo sind Sie mit Ihren Gedanken? *a pretty ~* e-e schöne Stange Geld; **~-a-liner** *pej* Zeilenschinder *m*; **~-dreadful** [peni'dredful] Schund-, Schauerroman *m*; **~-farthing** *Br* Hochrad *n*; **~-in-the-slot** automatisch; Automaten-; *~* **number**: *to do s.th. in ~~s* etw nicht auf einmal machen; **~royal** *bot* Poleiminze *f*; **~weight** Pennyweight *n (Gewicht,* = *1/20 Unze* od *1,42 g)*; **~wise**: *~~ and poundfoolish* sparsam im Kleinen u. verschwenderisch im Großen; **~wort** ['-wə:t]: *(Wall P~~)* Nabelkraut *n*; *(Marsh P~~, Water P~~) bot* Gemeine(r) Wassernabel *m*; **~worth, penn'orth** ['penəθ] Wert e-s Penny; kleine(r) Betrag *m*; *a good, bad ~~* ein guter, schlechter Kauf *m*.

penology [pi:'nɔlədʒi] Lehre *f* vom Strafvollzug.

pension ['penʃən] *s* Rente; Pension *f*, Ruhe-, Witwengehalt; ['pɑ̃:ŋsiɔ̃ŋ] Fremdenheim *n*, Pension *f*; Pensionat *n*; *tr* pensionieren, e-e Pension zahlen (*s.o.* jdm); *mil* verabschieden; *to ~ off* pensionieren; *to draw a ~* e-e Rente beziehen; *to live en ~* in e-r Pension wohnen; *to retire on a ~* in Pension gehen, sich pensionieren lassen; *disability ~* Invalidenrente *f*; *entitled to a ~* pensionsberechtigt; *old-age ~* Altersrente *f*; *retirement ~* Ruhegehalt *n*; *war ~* Militär-, Kriegsrente *f*; *widow's ~* Witwenrente *f*; *~ for orphans* Waisenrente *f*; **~able** ['-əbl] ruhegehalts-, pensionsberechtigt; *~~ age* Pensionsalter *n*; *~* **account** Pensionskasse *f*; **~ary** ['-əri] *a* Pensions-, Renten-; im Genuß e-r Pension; abhängig; *s u.* **~er** ['-ə] Pensionär, Ruhegehalts-, Rentenempfänger; *fig* Mietling *m*, Werkzeug *n*, Puppe *f*; **~aire** [pɑ̃:ŋsiə'nɛə] Pensionsgast; Pensionatsschüler(in *f*) *m*; *~* **plan** Altersversorgungsplan *m*.

pensive ['pensiv] nachdenklich, gedankenvoll; tiefsinnig; **~ness** ['-nis] Nachdenklichkeit *f*; Tiefsinn *m*.

penstock ['penstɔk] *tech* Wehr *n*, Schleuse *f*; *Am* Druckrohr *n*.

penta|gon ['pentəgən] Fünfeck *n*; *the P~~* das amerik. Verteidigungsministerium *(in Arlington, Virginia)*; **~gonal** [pen'tægənl] fünfeckig; **~gram** ['pentəgræm] Pentagramm *n*, Drudenfuß *m*; **~meter** [pen'tæmitə] Pentameter *m*; **P~teuch,** *the* ['pentətju:k] der Pentateuch, die 5 Bücher *m pl* Mosis; **~thlon** [pen'tæθlən] *sport* Fünfkampf *m*.

Pentecost ['pentikɔst] Pfingsten *n* od *pl*, Pfingstfest *n*.

penthouse ['penthaus] angebaute(r) Schuppen *m*; Schutz-, Wetterdach; Pultdach *n*; *Am* kleine Wohnung *f* auf dem Dach e-s Hochhauses.
pent-up ['pent'ʌp] *a* eingepfercht; *(Gefühl)* unterdrückt, angestaut; ~ **demand** *Am com* Nachholbedarf *m*.
penult [pi'nʌlt] vorletzte Silbe *f*; ~**imate** [-imit] *a* vorletzt(e Silbe *f*).
penumbra [pi'nʌmbrə] Halbschatten *m*.
penur|ious [pi'njuəriəs] karg, knapp, dürftig, ärmlich; knauserig, filzig, geizig; schäbig; ~**iousness** [-iəsnis] Kargheit, Knappheit, Dürftigkeit; Knauserigkeit *f*, Geiz *m*; ~**y** ['penjuri] (völlige) Armut *f*; (großer) Mangel *m* (*of* an).
peon ['pi:ən] *(in Lateinamerika)* Tagelöhner, Arbeiter; *(in Indien)* Infanterist, Fußsoldat; Polizist; Bote; Diener, Lakai *m*; ~**age** ['pi:ənidʒ] Tagelohn *m*; Schuldknechtschaft *f*.
peony ['piəni] Pfingstrose, Päonie *f*.
people ['pi:pl] *s pl* die Menschen; die Leute; die Be-, Einwohner; *(the common ~)* das gemeine Volk; *mit Possessivpron.*: Familie *f*, Leute *pl*, Angehörige *m pl*; *sing* (*pl* ~*s*) Volk *n*; Nation, Völkerschaft *f*; *tr* bevölkern (*with* mit); *what will ~ say?* was werden die Leute sagen? *many* ~ viele Leute; *man of the* ~ der Mann aus dem Volke; ~**'s bank** Volks-, Genossenschaftsbank *f*; ~**'s court** Volksgerichtshof *m*; **P~'s Democracy** Volksdemokratie *f*; ~**'s front** Volksfront *f*; ~**'s party** Volkspartei *f*.
pep [pep] *s Am sl* Mumm, Schmiß, Schwung *m*, Begeisterung; Kraft, Energie *f*; *tr*: *to ~ up (Am sl)* aufpulvern, aufmöbeln, ankurbeln, anfeuern, in Schwung bringen, aufputschen, begeistern; *to be ~ped up* mächtig in Fahrt sein; *to be ~ped out* erschöpft, erledigt sein; ~**py** ['-i] *sl* forsch, schmissig, schwungvoll, temperamentvoll *a. mot*; ~ **rally** Versammlung *f* mit aufmunternden Reden; ~ **talk** *sl* aufmunternde Rede *f*.
pepper ['pepə] *s* Pfeffer; Paprika; *Am sl* Schwung *m*, Energie *f*; *tr* pfeffern; dick bestreuen; *fig* hageln lassen auf, bombardieren (*with* mit); schlagen, verdreschen; ~**-and-salt** *attr* Pfeffer-u.-Salz- *(Muster)*; ~**-box, -pot, -castor,** *Am* **-shaker** Pfefferstreuer *m*; ~**corn** Pfefferkorn *n*; *fig* Kleinigkeit *f*; ~~ *rent* nominelle Miete *f*; ~**-mill** Pfeffermühle *f*; ~**mint** *bot* Pfefferminze *f*; Pfefferminzöl; (~~ *drop*) Pfefferminz(plätzchen) *n*; ~**-upper** *Am sl* jem, etw, das aufmöbelt; ~**y** ['-ri] gepfeffert; scharf, heftig; hitzig, heißblütig, reizbar.
pep|sin ['pepsin] *chem physiol* Pepsin *n*; ~**tic** ['-tik] *a* Verdauungs-; *s* verdauungsfördernde(s) Mittel *n*; ~~ *ulcer* Magengeschwür *n*; ~**tone** ['-toun] *pharm* Pepton *n*.

*

per [pə:] *prp* per, pro, je, für; durch, mit (Hilfe *gen)*; laut, gemäß; *as ~ usual (hum)* wie gewöhnlich, wie immer; *(as) ~ account* laut Rechnung; ~ *annum, diem, mensem* pro Jahr, Tag, Monat; ~ *capita* pro Kopf; ~~ *quota* Kopfbetrag *m*; ~ *cent* pro *od* vom Hundert; ~ *contra (adv)* dagegen; ~ *diem allowance* Tagessatz *m* für Reisespesen; ~ *hour, minute, second* pro *od* in der Stunde, Minute, Sekunde; ~ *man* pro *od* je Mann, Kopf; ~ *post* mit der Post; ~ *procuration* per Prokura; ~ *se* an (und für) sich, für sich (genommen).
peradventure [pərəd'ventʃə] *adv obs* vielleicht; *nach if u. lest*: zufällig.
perambulat|e [pə'ræmbjuleit] *tr* wandern, ziehen, reisen durch *od* um; besichtigen; *(Land)* begehen; *itr* umherwandern, -streifen, -ziehen; ~**ion** [pəræmbju'leiʃən] Durchwandern *n*; Besichtigung(sreise); Begehung *f*; Umherstreifen *n*; ~**or** ['præmbjuleitə] *Br* Kinderwagen *m*; *doll's* ~~ Puppenwagen *m*.
perceiv|able [pə'si:vəbl] wahrnehmbar; erkennbar; ~**e** [pə'si:v] *tr* wahrnehmen; spüren, (be)merken, erkennen, erfassen, verstehen.
percentage [pə'sentidʒ] Hundert-, Prozentsatz; (Prozent-)Gehalt, Anteil *m* (*of* an); Tantieme; *com* Provision *f*; Teil *m*.
percept|ibility [pəsepti'biliti] Wahrnehmbarkeit *f*; ~**ible** [pə'septibl] wahrnehmbar; merklich; ~**ion** [pə'sepʃən] Empfindungsvermögen *n*; Wahrnehmung, Einsicht, Einfühlung; Kenntnis, Vorstellung *f*; Bewußtsein *n*; ~**ive** [pə'septiv] *a* Wahrnehmungs-; wahrnehmend; scharfsichtig; ~**iveness** [-ivnis], ~**ivity** [pəsep'tiviti] Wahrnehmungsvermögen *n*.
perch [pə:tʃ] **1.** *s* Vogel-, *bes.* Hühnerstange *f*; Sitzplatz e-s Vogels; *fam* hohe(r), sichere(r) Platz; *(Wagen)* Langbaum *m*; *mar* Prick, Rute; Rute *(Längenmaß = 5½ yards* od *5,029 m)*; *(square ~)* (Quadrat-)Rute *f (= 30¼ square yards* od *25,29 qm)*; *itr* sich niederlassen, sich setzen (*on* auf); *aero sl* landen; (hoch) sitzen, stehen; *tr* (hoch hinauf)stellen; *to hop the ~ (sl)* das Zeitliche segnen, abkratzen; *to knock s.o. off his ~* jdn erledigen, besiegen, vernichten; *the bird takes its ~* der Vogel setzt sich; *come off your ~* spiel dich nicht so auf! ~**ed** [-t] *a* hochliegend, -gelegen; ~**er** ['-ə] Baumvogel *m*; **2.** Barsch *m (Fisch)*.
perchance [pə'tʃɑ:ns] *adv obs poet* vielleicht; zufällig.
percipien|ce, -cy [pə'sipiəns(i)] Wahrnehmung(svermögen *n*) *f*; ~**t** [-t] *a* wahrnehmend; *s* (durch Telepathie) Wahrnehmende(r) *m*.
percolat|e ['pə:kəleit] *tr* durchseihen, filtern; *(Kaffee)* in e-m Filter zubereiten; *itr* durchsickern *a. fig*; *Am mot* ruhig laufen; ~**ion** [pə:kə'leiʃən] Durchseihen, Filtern; Durchsickern *n*; ~**or** ['pə:kəleitə] Filter *m*; *(coffee-~~)* Kaffeefilter *m*.
percuss|ion [pə:'kʌʃən] Stoß, Schlag *m*; Erschütterung *f*; Aufschlagen *n*; *med* Perkussion; Klopfmassage *f*; *(~~ instruments) (mus)* Schlaginstrumente *n pl*; ~~ *cap* Zündhütchen *n*; ~~ *fuse* Aufschlagzünder *m*; ~~ *wave* Druckwelle *f*; ~**ive** [pə:'kʌsiv] *a* Schlag-, Stoß-.
perdition [pə:'diʃən] Ruin *m*; Verderben *n*; *rel* Verdammnis *f*.
perdu(e) [pə:'dju:] *a* versteckt, verborgen; auf der Lauer, im Hinterhalt.
peregrin|ate ['perigrineit] *tr (Strecke, Weg)* zurücklegen; entlang-, durchwandern; bereisen; *itr* wandern, ziehen, reisen; ~**ation** [perigri'neiʃən] Wanderung, Wanderschaft *f*.
peremptor|ily [pə'remptərili] *adv* unweigerlich; ein für allemal; ~**iness** [-inis] Endgültigkeit; Bestimmtheit, Entschiedenheit *f*; ~**y** [pə'rem(p)təri, 'perəm-] endgültig, definitiv, entscheidend; unabdingbar, unerläßlich, zwingend; unabänderlich, unaufschiebbar; bestimmt, entschieden.
perennial [pə'renjəl] *a* ein (ganzes) Jahr dauernd; langdauernd, beständig, immerwährend, ewig; (immer) wiederkehrend; *bot* ausdauernd, perennierend; *s* ausdauernde Pflanze *f*.
perfect ['pə:fikt] *a* vollendet, vollkommen, untadelig, tadellos, fehlerlos; vollständig, völlig, gänzlich; genau, exakt; *(Wettbewerb)* uneingeschränkt; *s gram (~ tense)* Perfekt *n*; *tr* [pə'fekt] vervollkommnen, vervollständigen; verbessern, (vollständig) ausbilden; auf beiden Seiten bedrucken; *he is a ~ stranger to me* er ist mir völlig unbekannt; *present ~ tense* Perfekt *n*; *past ~* Plusquamperfekt *n*; *future ~* 2. Futurum *n*; ~**ible** [pə'fektibl] vervollkommnungsfähig; ~**ion** [pə'fekʃən] Vervollkommnung; Vollendung, Vollkommenheit; Verkörperung *f*, Inbegriff; *fig* Gipfel, höchste(r) Grad *m*; *to ~~* vollkommen *adv*; *to bring to ~~* vollenden; vervollkommnen; ~**ionism** [-'fekʃnizm] Perfektionismus *m*; ~**ionist** [-'fekʃnist] Perfektionist *m*; ~**ly** ['-li] *adv* vollkommen, völlig, durchaus, absolut; tadellos; ~ **pitch** absolute(s) Gehör *n*; ~**o** [pə'fektou] *pl -os Am* dicke Zigarre *f* mit spitzen Enden; ~ **participle** Partizip *n* des Perfekts.
perfervid [pə:'fə:vid] glühend(heiß), glutvoll.
perfid|ious [pə(:)'fidiəs] verräterisch, treulos, perfid(e); ~**iousness** [pə(:)'fidiəsnis], ~**y** ['pə:fidi] Vertrauens-, Treubruch, Verrat *m*; Treulosigkeit *f*.
perforat|e ['pə:fəreit] *tr* durchbohren, -löchern; perforieren, lochen; *itr* (hinein)dringen (*into* in; *through* durch); *a* [-rit], ~**ed** [-reitid] *a* perforiert; ~*ed brick* Lochziegel *m*; ~*ed tape* Lochstreifen *m*; ~**ion** [pə:fə'reiʃən] Durchbohrung, -löcherung; *a. pl* Perforierung, Lochung *f*; Loch *n*; ~**ive** ['pə:fəreitiv, '-rətiv] *a* Perforier-; ~**or** ['-ə] Perforierer *(Person)*; *(paper ~~)* Locher *m*; Perforiermaschine *f*.
perforce [pə(:)'fɔ:s] *adv* notgedrungen.
perform [pə'fɔ:m] *tr* ausführen, verrichten, machen, tun, bewerkstelligen; zustande bringen, leisten; voll-, durchführen, einhalten, erfüllen; *theat* aufführen, spielen, vortragen, -führen; *(Rolle)* spielen *a. mus*; *(Handlung)* vornehmen; *(Pflicht, Versprechen)* erfüllen; *(Verpflichtung)* nachkommen; *itr (öffentlich)* auftreten, spielen; *tech* funktionieren; ~**ance** [-əns] Aus-, Durchführung, Verrichtung; Bewerkstelligung; Erfüllung; Funktion(ieren *n*); Leistung *f*, Werk *n*; Funktions-, Leistungsfähigkeit; Tat *f*, Werk *n*, Arbeit; *theat* Aufführung, Vorführung, Vorstellung, Darbietung *f*, Spiel *n*, Schau; *sport* Veranstaltung; Darstellung *f*; *afternoon, evening ~~* Nachmittags-, Abendvorstellung *f*; *first ~~* Premiere *f*; *~~ curve, graph* Leistungskurve *f*; *~~ in kind, in money* Sach-, Geldleistung *f*; *~~ level* Leistungsgrad *m*; *~~ report* Leistungsbericht *m*; *~~ test(ing)* Leistungsprüfung *f*; *~~-type glider (aero)* Leistungssegler *m*; ~**er** [-ə] Ausführende(r); Darsteller, Spieler; Künstler; Schausteller *m*; ~**ing** [-iŋ] *(Tier)* abgerichtet, dressiert.
perfum|e ['pə:fju:m] Duft, Wohlgeruch *m*; Parfüm *n*; Riech-, Duftstoff *m*; *tr* [pə'fju:m] parfümieren; *~~ flacon* Parfümfläschchen *n*; *~~-sprayer (Parfüm)* Zerstäuber *m*; ~**er** [pə'fju:mə] Parfümfabrikant; Parfümeriewarenhändler, Parfümeur *m*; ~**ery** [pə'fju:məri] Parfümfabrik; Parfümerie *f*; Parfümeriewaren(handel *m*) *f pl*; Parfüm *n*.

perfunctory [pəˈfʌŋktəri] mechanisch, routinemäßig, teilnahmslos; oberflächlich, flüchtig; gleichgültig, (nach-) lässig.

pergola [ˈpəːgələ] Pergola, Laube(ngang *m*) *f*.

perhaps [pəˈhæps, *fam* præps] *adv* vielleicht, eventuell; zufällig.

pericard|iac, ~ial [periˈkɑːdjæk, -əl] *a anat* Herzbeutel-; **~itis** [-kɑːˈdaitis] *med* Herzbeutelentzündung *f*; **~ium** [-ˈkɑːdjəm] *pl -dia* [-djə] *med* Herzbeutel *m*.

pericarp [ˈperikɑːp] *bot* Fruchthülle *f*.

peri|gee [ˈperidʒiː] *astr* Perigäum *n*, Erdnähe *f*; **~helion** [periˈhiːljən] *astr* Perihel(ium) *n*, Sonnennähe *f*.

peril [ˈperil] *s* Gefahr *f*, Risiko *n*; *tr* in Gefahr bringen, gefährden; riskieren, wagen; *at s.o.'s ~* auf jds Gefahr, Risiko, Verantwortung; *in ~ of o.'s life* in Lebensgefahr; *~ of war* Kriegsgefahr *f*; **~ous** [ˈ-əs] gefährlich, riskant.

perimeter [pəˈrimitə] *bes. math* Umfang, Umkreis *m*; *~ of defence (mil)* Verteidigungsgürtel *m*; **~ defence** Rundumverteidigung *f*; **~ track** *aero* Rollfeld-Ringstraße *f*.

perineum [periˈniːəm] *pl -nea* [-ˈniːə] *anat* Damm *m*.

period [ˈpiəriəd] *s astr* Umlaufszeit; *allg* Periode *f a. geol*, Zeit(raum, -abschnitt *m*) *f*, Abschnitt *m*; Epoche; Phase *f*, Stadium *n*; Dauer; Frist; *a. pl physiol* Periode, Regel, Menstruation *f*; Ende *n*, Schluß(punkt, -strich); *gram* (vollständiger) Satz *m*, Satzgefüge *n*; (Sprech-)Pause *f*; Punkt *m*; *(Metrik, mus math)* Periode; *Am* (Unterrichts-, Schul-)Stunde *f*; *a (Kunst)* zeitgenössisch; Stil-; *interj Am sl* Punkt damit! Schluß! (und damit) basta! *for a ~ of* für die Dauer von; *to put a ~ to* Schluß, ein Ende machen mit; *bright ~* Aufklärung *f*; *election ~ (parl)* Legislaturperiode *f*; *transition ~* Übergangszeit *f*; *~ of assessment* Veranlagungs-, Steuerperiode *f*; *~ of availability* Gültigkeitsdauer *f*; *~ of incubation (med)* Inkubationszeit *f*; *~ of office* Amtszeit *f*; *~ of notice, of prescription* Kündigungs-, Verjährungsfrist *f*; *~ of service* Dienstzeit *f*; *~ of validity* Gültigkeitsdauer *f*; **~ furniture** Stilmöbel *n pl*; **~ic(al)** [piəriˈɔdik(əl)] periodisch, regelmäßig auftretend *od* wiederkehrend; *~ical (s)* Zeitschrift *f*, Magazin *n*; **~icity** [piəriəˈdisiti] *scient* Periodizität; *el* Frequenz *f*; **~ novel** zeitgeschichtliche(r) Roman *m*; **~ play** Zeitstück *n*.

periost|eum [periˈɔstiəm] *anat* Knochenhaut *f*; *dental ~* Wurzelhaut *f*; **~itis** [periɔsˈtaitis] *med* Knochenhautentzündung *f*.

peripher|al [pəˈrifərəl] peripher(isch) *a. anat*; **~y** [-ˈrifəri] Umfang, Rand *m*; Oberfläche; Außenseite *f*, Umkreis *m*, Umgebung *f*; Stadtrand *m*.

periphras|e [ˈperifreis], **~is** [pəˈrifrəsis] *pl -es* [-siːz] Umschreibung *f*; **~tic** [periˈfræstik] umschreibend.

periscope [ˈperiskoup] *mar mil* Periskop, Sehrohr *n*.

perish [ˈperiʃ] *itr u. to be ~ed* eingehen, zugrunde gehen, umkommen (*by* durch; *of, with* an); *(Waren)* verderben; *tr* vernichten; *to ~ with cold (fam)* erfrieren; *to ~ from starvation* verhungern; *~ the thought!* daran darf man gar nicht denken; **~able** [ˈ-əbl] *a* vergänglich; *(Ware)* verderblich, dem Verderb ausgesetzt; *s pl* verderbliche Waren *f pl*; *~~ commodities (pl)* Verbrauchsgüter *pl*; **~er** [ˈ-ə] *sl* Lümmel *m*; **~ing** [ˈ-iŋ] *a* vernichtend; *sl* widerlich; *adv sl* verflixt, verdammt.

peristyle [ˈperistail] *arch* Säulenumgang *m*, -reihe *f*.

periton|(a)eum [perito(u)ˈniːəm] *pl -ea* [-ə] *anat* Bauchfell *n*; **~itis** [-təˈnaitis] *med* Bauchfellentzündung *f*.

periwig [ˈperiwig] Perücke *f*.

periwinkle [ˈperiwiŋkl] *bot* Immer-, Singrün *n*; *zoo* Uferschnecke *f*.

perjur|e [ˈpəːdʒə]: *tr: to ~~ o.s.* falsch schwören, meineidig werden; *to be ~ed* des Meineids überführt werden; **~ed** [ˈ-d] *a* meineidig; **~er** [ˈ-rə] Meineidige(r) *m*; **~y** [ˈ-ri] Falsch-, Meineid; Eidbruch *m*; *to commit ~~* e-n Meineid leisten.

perk [pəːk] **1.** *tr (to ~ up) (den Kopf)* aufwerfen, hochtragen; *(Ohren)* spitzen; *itr (to ~ up)* den Kopf aufwerfen; sich in die Brust werfen; wieder auf die Höhe kommen; lebhaft, munter werden; *Am mot* ruhig laufen; *to ~ o.s. (up)* sich herausputzen; **~iness** [ˈ-inis] Keckheit *f*, Übermut *m*; Munterkeit *f*; selbstbewußte(s) Auftreten *n*; **~y** [ˈ-i] unternehmungs-, angriffslustig; keck, frech; übermütig, munter, lustig; **2.** *s pl Br fam* Nebeneinkünfte, Sporteln *f pl*; **3.** *fam tr* durchseihen; *itr* durchsickern.

perm [pəːm] *s fam* Dauerwelle *f*; *tr: to have o.'s hair ~ed* sich Dauerwellen machen lassen.

permanen|ce [ˈpəːmənəns] (Fort-) Dauer; Dauerhaftigkeit; *tech* Konstanz *f*; **~cy** [ˈ-i] Dauer(haftigkeit) *f*; *das* Dauernde, Bleibende, Beständige; Dauerstellung *f*; **~t** [ˈ-t] *a* (fort)dauernd, bleibend; ständig; beständig, dauerhaft; auf Lebenszeit; *tech* ortsfest, massiv; *(Menschen)* ortsansässig, bodenständig; *s fam* Dauerwelle *f*; *~~ abode* ständige(r) Aufenthalt *m*; *~~ appointment* feste Anstellung *f*; *~~ assembly* ständige Versammlung *f*; *~~ assets, capital* Anlagevermögen, -kapital *n*; *~~ committee* ständige(r) Ausschuß *m*; *~~ establishment* ständige Einrichtung *f*; *~~ income* Kapitaleinkommen *n*; *~~ investment (fin)* Daueranlage *f*; *pl* langfristige Anlagegüter *pl*; *~~ position, situation* Lebens-, Dauerstellung *f*; *~~ residence* feste(r) Wohnsitz *m*; *~~ staff* Stammpersonal *m*; *~~ wave* Dauerwelle *f*; *~~ way (rail)* Oberbau, Bahnkörper *m*.

permangan|ate [pə(ː)ˈmæŋgənit] *chem* Permanganat *n*; *potassium ~~* Kaliumpermanganat *n*; **~ic** [pə(ː)mæŋˈgænik] *a*: *~~ acid* Übermangansäure *f*.

permea|bility [pəːmjəˈbiliti] Durchlässigkeit *f*; **~ble** [ˈpəːmjəbl] durchlässig (*to* für); **~te** [ˈpəːmieit] *tr (Flüssigkeit)* eindringen, -ziehen in; ziehen durch; *itr* eindringen, -ziehen (*into, among* in); dringen (*through* durch); sich verbreiten (*among* unter); **~tion** [pəːmiˈeiʃən] Durch-, Eindringen *n*.

Permian [ˈpəːmiən] *geol* Perm *n*.

permiss|ible [pəˈmisəbl] zulässig; **~ion** [pəˈmiʃən] Zustimmung, Genehmigung, Bewilligung, Erlaubnis *f*; Erlaubnisschein *m*; *by special ~~* mit besonderer Genehmigung; *without ~~* unbefugt; *to ask s.o.'s ~~, s.o. for ~~* jdn um Erlaubnis bitten; *to grant a ~~* e-e Erlaubnis erteilen; *to grant s.o. ~~ to speak* jdm das Wort erteilen; *grant of a ~~* Erlaubniserteilung *f*; *~~ by the authorities* behördliche Genehmigung *f*; **~ive** [pəˈmisiv] zulassend; zulässig, erlaubt; *jur* fakultativ.

permit [pəˈmit] *tr* erlauben, gestatten, zulassen, dulden; *itr* erlauben; *to ~ of (fig)* (es) zulassen; *s* [ˈpəːmit] Erlaubnis(schein *m*); Genehmigung, Bewilligung, Lizenz *f* (*to* für); Durchlaß-, Passierschein, Ausweis; Freigabe-, Zollerlaubnisschein *m*; *weather ~ting* bei günstigem Wetter; *to take out a ~* sich e-e Erlaubnis geben lassen; *building ~* Baugenehmigung *f*; *entry ~* Einreisebewilligung *f*; *exit ~* Ausreisebewilligung *f*; *export, import ~* Ausfuhr-, Einfuhrgenehmigung *f*; *labo(u)r ~* Arbeitserlaubnis *f*; *purchase ~* Bezug(s)schein *m*; *special ~* Sondergenehmigung *f*; *~ of residence, residence ~* Aufenthaltsbewilligung *f*; **~ted** [-id] *a* erlaubt, gestattet, genehmigt, zugelassen; *to be ~~* dürfen.

permut|ation [pəːmju(ː)ˈteiʃən] Wechsel *m*; Veränderung; Vertauschung; *math* Permutation *f*; *~~ lock* Buchstabenschloß *n*; **~e** [pəˈmjuːt] *tr* (ver)ändern; vertauschen.

pern [pəːn] *orn* Wespenbussard *m*.

pernicious [pə(ː)ˈniʃəs] schädlich, verderblich (*to* für); *med* bösartig; **~ anaemia** *med* perniziöse Anämie *f*; **~ness** [-nis] Verderblichkeit; Bösartigkeit *f*.

pernickety [pəˈnikiti] *fam* kleinlich, genau; *(Arbeit)* heikel.

perorat|e [ˈperəreit] *itr* e-e (lange) Rede halten; s-e Rede zs.fassen *od* abschließen; **~ion** [perəˈreiʃən] zs.fassende(r) Redeschluß *m*.

peroxid(e) [pəˈrɔksaid] *chem* Peroxyd; *(hydrogen ~)* Wasserstoffsuperoxyd *n*; **~ blonde** *fam* Wasserstoffblondine *f*.

perpendicular [pəːpənˈdikjulə] *a* senk-, lotrecht (*to* zu); sehr steil; *s math* Senkrechte *f*, Lot(rechte *f*); Lot *n*, Perpendikel *m od n*; aufrechte Stellung *f*; *out of the ~* schief, schräg, aus dem Lote; *P~ style* englische Spätgotik *f*.

perpetrat|e [ˈpəːpitreit] *tr (Fehler)* machen, begehen; *(Verbrechen)* verüben; **~ion** [pəːpiˈtreiʃən] Begehung, Verübung *f*; Vergehen *n*; **~or** [ˈpəːpitreitə] (Übel-)Täter, *lit* Frevler *m*.

perpetu|al [pəˈpetjuəl] *a* dauernd, (be)ständig, ewig; fortwährend, unaufhörlich, unablässig, ununterbrochen; lebenslänglich, auf Lebenszeit; unkündbar; *a u. s (~~ plant)* immerblühend(e Pflanze *f*); *~~ calendar* immerwährende(r) Kalender *m*; *~~ motion* (Bewegung *f* e-s) Perpetuum mobile *n*; *~~ snow* ewige(r) Schnee *m*; **~ate** [-eit] *tr* verewigen; der Vergessenheit entreißen; **~ation** [pəpetjuˈeiʃən] Verewigung; *jur* Sicherung *f*; **~ity** [pəːpiˈtju(ː)iti] (Be-)Ständigkeit, Dauer; Unaufhörlichkeit; Ewigkeit; Rente *f* auf Lebenszeit; dauernde(r) Genuß *m*; *in, for, to ~~* auf ewig.

perplex [pəˈpleks] *tr (Menschen)* unsicher, schwankend machen; aus der Fassung, durchea.bringen; verblüffen, verwirren; *(Sache)* verkomplizieren; **~ity** [-iti] Unsicherheit, Fassungslosigkeit; Verwirrung, Konfusion *f*; Durcheinander *n*; komplizierte Sache *f*.

perquisites [ˈpəːkwizits] *s pl* Nebeneinkünfte *f pl*, -bezüge *m pl*, Sporteln *f pl*.

persecut|e [ˈpəːsikjuːt] *tr* verfolgen; belästigen, drangsalieren, plagen, quälen (*with* mit); *to be ~ed* Verfolgungen erleiden *od* ausgesetzt sein; **~ion** [pəːsiˈkjuːʃən] Verfolgung; Belästigung *f*; *~~ mania (med)* Verfolgungswahn *m*; **~or** [ˈ-ə] Verfolger *m*.

persever|ance [pəːsiˈviərəns] Aus-, Durchhalten *n*; Ausdauer, Beharrlichkeit *f*; **~e** [pəːsiˈviə] *itr* aus-, durchhalten, ausharren, festhalten (*in* an); **~ing** [-riŋ] beharrlich, ausdauernd, standhaft.

Persia ['pə:ʃə] Persien *n*; **~n** ['-n] *a* persisch; *s* Perser(in *f*) *m*; (das) Persisch(e); *~~ blinds (pl)* Jalousie *f*; *~~ cat* Angorakatze *f*; *~~ lamb* Persianer *m* *(Pelz)*; *~~ rug, carpet* Perserteppich *m*.

persimmon [pə:'simən] Dattelpflaume *f*; *(~ tree)* Dattelpflaumenbaum *m*.

persist [pə'sist] *itr* beharren (*in* auf, bei), bestehen (*in* auf), nicht nachgeben; dabei bleiben, nicht aufhören (*in doing* zu tun); weiterarbeiten (*with* an); fortdauern, -bestehen, sich hartnäckig halten; **~ence, -cy** [-əns(i)] (hartnäckiges) Beharren *n* (*in* auf); Beharrlichkeit, Entschlossenheit, Hartnäckigkeit *f*; Anhalten *n*; Fortdauer *f*, -bestehen *n*; **~ent** [-ənt] beharrlich, unnachgiebig; unentwegt, (an)dauernd, beständig; wiederholt; *biol* bleibend.

*

person ['pə:sn] Person *f a. pej gram rel*; Individuum *n*; Persönlichkeit *f*; Mensch *m*, menschliche(s) Wesen *n*, Einzelmensch *m*, -wesen *n*; Gestalt, Erscheinung *f*, Äußere(s) *n*; *theat* Rolle *f*; *in ~* in Person, persönlich *adv*, selbst, leibhaftig; *in o.'s own ~* in eigener Person; *per ~* pro Person *od* Kopf; *without exception of ~s* ohne Ansehen der Person; *artificial, fictitious ~, ~ at law* juristische Person *f*; *authorized ~* Berechtigte(r) *m*; *average ~* Durchschnittsmensch *m*; *confidential ~* Vertrauensperson *f*; *the deceased ~* der, die Verstorbene; *natural ~* natürliche Person *f*; *private ~* Privatperson *f*; *a third ~* ein Dritter, e-e dritte Person; *unauthorized ~* Unbefugte(r) *m*; *a ~ unknown* ein Unbekannter, ein unbekannter Täter *m*; *against a ~ unknown, against ~s unknown (jur)* gegen Unbekannt; **~able** ['-əbl] stattlich, ansehnlich, gutaussehend, hübsch; *jur* prozeßfähig; **~age** ['-idʒ] Persönlichkeit; Person; *lit* Gestalt, Figur; *theat* Person *f*, Charakter *m*; **~al** ['-l] *a* persönlich; privat; Privat-; individuell; physisch, körperlich; *(Auskunft)* mündlich; *s Am (Zeitung)* persönliche Nachricht *f*; persönliche(s) Auftreten *n (e-s Filmstars)*; *jur* persönliche(r) Gegenstand *m*; *to become ~~ (in s-n Äußerungen)* persönlich, anzüglich werden; *~~ account* Privatkonto *n*; *~~ affair, matter* Privatangelegenheit, -sache *f*; *~~ background, history* Lebenslauf *m*; *~~ belongings, effects, estate, property* persönliche(r) Habe *f od* Besitz *m*; *~~ call (tele)* Gespräch *n* mit Voranmeldung; *~~ column (Zeitung)* Briefkasten *m*; *~~ data* Personalien *pl*; *~~ equation* Reaktionszeit *f*; *~~ files (pl)* Personalakten *f pl*; *~~ freedom, liberty* persönliche Freiheit *f*; *~~ hygiene* Körperpflege *f*; *~~ income* Privateinkommen *n*; *~~ injury (jur)* Körperverletzung *f*; *~~ life* Privatleben *n*; *~~ number* Wehrstammrolle *f*; *~~ opinion* Privatmeinung *f*; *~~ pronoun (gram)* Personalpronomen *n*; *~~ questionnaire* Personalbogen *m*; *~~ representative* gesetzliche(r) Vertreter *m*; *~~ share* Namensaktie *f*; *~~ status* Personenstand *m*; *~~ tax* Kopfsteuer *f*; *~~ union* Personalunion *f*; *articles (pl) for ~~ use* Gegenstände *m pl* des persönlichen Gebrauchs; **~ality** [pə:sə'næliti] Persönlichkeit, Individualität; (*bes.* hohe) Persönlichkeit, Person *f*; Wesen *n*; *pl* persönliche Bemerkungen, Anzüglichkeiten *f pl*; **~alize** ['pə:snəlaiz] *tr* auf e-e bestimmte Person beziehen; personifizieren; persönlich machen *od* gestalten; *~~d (service)* individuell(e) Bedienung *f*; **~alty** ['pə:snlti] *jur* persönliche(s) Eigentum *n*; **~ate** ['pə:səneit] *tr theat* spielen, darstellen, verkörpern; *lit poet* personifizieren; sich ausgeben, auftreten als; **~ated** ['-eitid] *a* gespielt, fingiert; **~ation** [pə:sə'neiʃən] Darstellung, Verkörperung; Personifikation; falsche Personenstandsangabe *f*; **~ification** [pə:sɔnifi'keiʃən] Verkörperung, Personifikation *f*; **~ify** [pə:'sɔnifai] *tr* verkörpern, personifizieren, versinnbildlichen; **~nel** [pə:sə'nel] Personal *n*; Belegschaft; *mil* Mannschaft(en *pl*); *mar* Besatzung *f*; *attr* Personal-, Belegschafts-, Mannschafts-; *to recruit ~~* Personal einstellen; *~~ carrier (mil)* Mannschaftswagen *m*; *~~ division, office* Personalabteilung *f*; *~~ strength* Kopfstärke *f*.

perspective [pə'spektiv] *s (Kunst)* Perspektive *f*; perspektivische(s) Bild *n*; Fernsicht *f*, -blick *m*; *fig* Perspektive, Aussicht *f*, -blick, Standpunkt *m*; *a* perspektivisch; *to view in ~ (fig)* mit Abstand betrachten.

perspex ['pə:speks] Plexiglas *n (Schutzmarke)*.

perspic|acious [pə:spi'keiʃəs] scharfsinnig, -blickend; **~acity** [-'kæsiti] Scharfsinn, -blick *m*; **~uity** [-'kju(:)iti] Klarheit, Deutlichkeit, Verständlichkeit *f*; **~uous** [pə'spikjuəs] klar, deutlich, verständlich.

perspir|ation [pə:spə'reiʃən] Schwitzen *n*; Ausdünstung *f*; Schweiß *m*; *~~ cure* Schwitzkur *f*; **~e** [pəs'paiə] *tr* ausschwitzen, -dünsten; *itr* schwitzen.

persua|de [pə'sweid] *tr* überreden (*of s.th.* zu e-r S); verleiten, dazu bringen (*to do, (Am) into doing* zu tun); überzeugen (*of s.th.* von e-r S); *to be ~~d of* überzeugt sein von; *to ~~ s.o. from s.th.* jdm etw ausreden; **~sion** [pə'sweiʒən] Überredung; Überzeugung(skraft); (feste) Überzeugung *f*, Glaube *m*, politische Überzeugung; *sl* Art, Sorte, Klasse *f*, Typ *m*, Geschlecht *n*; **~sive** [pə'sweisiv] redegewandt, überzeugend; **~siveness** [-sivnis] Überredungskunst, Redegewandtheit; Überzeugungskraft *f*.

pert [pə:t] vorlaut, keck, dreist, frech; schnippisch, naseweis; *dial u. Am* lebhaft, munter, lustig; **~ness** ['-nis] Keckheit, Dreistigkeit *f*.

pertain [pə(:)'tein] *itr* gehören (*to* zu), ein (wesentlicher) Bestandteil sein (*to* gen); passend, angebracht sein, sich gebühren, sich schicken (*to* für); zukommen (*to* dat); Zs.hang haben, in Zs.hang, in Verbindung stehen (*to* mit); betreffen (*to* acc); sich beziehen (*to* auf).

pertinac|eous [pə:ti'neiʃəs] entschlossen, beharrlich, standhaft; versessen, verbissen; eingewurzelt, festsitzend, hartnäckig, zäh; **~eousness** [-'neiʃəsnis], **~ity** [-'næsiti] Entschlossenheit, Beharrlichkeit, Standhaftigkeit; Hartnäckigkeit, Zähigkeit *f*.

pertinen|ce, -cy ['pə:tinəns(i)] Zugehörigkeit; Eignung (*to* für); Relevanz, Wichtigkeit *f*; **~t** ['-t] *a* in Zs.hang stehend (*to* mit), betreffend (*to* acc); sachdienlich, zur Sache (gehörig); einschlägig; *s pl* Zubehör *n*; *to be ~ to s.th.* sich auf etw beziehen.

perturb [pə'tə:b] *tr* verwirren; aufregen, beunruhigen; stören; **~ation** [pə:tə:'beiʃən] Verwirrung, Aufregung, Unruhe; Störung; *astr* Perturbation *f*.

peruke [pə'ru:k] Perücke *f*.

perus|al [pə'ru:zəl] Durchlesen *n*; (genaue) Durchsicht, Prüfung *f*; *for ~~* zur Einsicht; **~e** [pə'ru:z] *tr* (genau, sorgfältig) durchlesen; (prüfend) durchsehen, durchstudieren.

Peruvian [pə'ru:vjən] *a* peruanisch; *s* Peruaner(in *f*) *m*; *~* **bark** *pharm* Chinarinde *f*.

perva|de [pə:'veid] *tr* durchdringen *a. fig*; sich ausbreiten in; **~sion** [pə'veiʒən] Durchdringung *a. fig*; Ausbreitung *f*; **~sive** [pə'veisiv] durchdringend; *fig* beherrschend.

pervers|e [pə'və:s] verkehrt, falsch; pervers, widernatürlich; verderbt; böse, schlecht; störrisch, widerborstig, verstockt; **~eness** [-nis], **~ity** [-iti] Verkehrtheit; Perversität, Widernatürlichkeit; Verderbtheit; Schlechtigkeit; Widersetzlichkeit *f*, Eigensinn *m*; **~ion** [pə'və:ʃən] Um-, Verkehrung, Verdrehung, Perversion; Abkehr *(vom Glauben)*; Verderbtheit; Perversität *f*; *~~ of law* Rechtsbeugung *f*; **~ive** [pə'və:siv] *fig* verdrehend, entstellend, pervertierend (*to s.th.* etw); verderblich (*of* für).

pervert [pə'və:t] *tr* umkehren, verdrehen; mißdeuten, mißbrauchen; irreführen, verführen, verderben; *(Sinn)* entstellen; *s* ['pə:və:t] *rel* Abtrünnige(r); perverse(r) Mensch *m*.

pervious ['pə:vjəs] durchlässig (*to* für); *fig* beeinflußbar, zugänglich (*to* für).

pesky ['peski] *Am fam* dumm, blöde, vertrackt, verdammt, verteufelt.

pessary ['pesəri] *med* Pessar *n*.

pessim|ism ['pesimizm] Pessimismus *m*, Schwarzseherei *f*; **~ist** ['-ist] Pessimist, Schwarzseher *m*; **~istic** [pesi'mistik] *adv ~~ally* pessimistisch, schwarzseherisch.

pest [pest] Plagegeist *m*; Plage *f*; Schädling *m*; *obs* Pest, Seuche *f*; *~* **control** Schädlingsbekämpfung *f*; **~hole** Seuchenherd *m*; **~icide** ['-isaid] Schädlingsbekämpfungsmittel *n*; **~iferous** [pes'tifərəs] verseucht; verdorben, sittenverderbend; *fam* ärgerlich; **~ilence** ['pestiləns] Beulenpest; *allg* ansteckende Krankheit; Seuche *f a. fig*; **~ilent** ['-t] tödlich; verderbenbringend, verderblich; *fig* sittengefährdend; *fam* ärgerlich; **~ilential** [pesti'lenʃəl] ansteckend; gefährlich, tödlich, verderblich; sittengefährdend, -verderbend; abscheulich, widerwärtig; lästig; *fam* ärgerlich.

pester ['pestə] *tr* belästigen, quälen, plagen (*with* von, mit).

pestle ['pesl] *s* (Mörser-)Keule *f*, Stößel *m*; *tech* Stampfe(r *m*) *f*; *tr* zerstoßen, zerstampfen, zermahlen.

¯pet [pet] **1.** *s* Lieblingstier; Haustier *n*; Liebling *m*, Schoßkind, Schätzchen *n*; *a* Lieblings-; *hum* ganz speziell, ganz besonder; *tr* (ver)hätscheln; verwöhnen; *Am* liebkosen, streicheln; *fam* (ab)knutschen; *itr Am* sich in den Armen liegen, *fam* sich abknutschen; *~* **aversion**: *it is my ~~* das ist mir ein Greuel, das widert mich an; *~* **mistake** Lieblingsfehler *m*; *~* **name** Kosename *m*; *~* **shop** Tierhandlung *f*; *~* **subject** Steckenpferd *n*; **~ting party** *Am* Knutscherei *f*; **2.** *s* schlechte, üble Laune *f*; *itr: to be in a ~, to take (the) ~* schlechte Laune haben.

petal ['petl] *bot* Blumenblatt *n*.

petard [pe'tɑ:d] Knallfrosch; *mil hist* Sprengmörser *m*, Petarde *f*; *to be hoist with o.'s own ~* sich in der eigenen Schlinge gefangen haben.

Peter ['pi:tə] Peter, Petrus *m*; *to rob ~ to pay Paul* ein Loch aufreißen, um ein anderes zu verstopfen; *Blue ~*

(mar) blaue(r) Peter *m*; **~'s pence** Peterspfennig *m*.

peter ['pi:tə] *itr*: *to ~ out* immer schwächer werden; nachlassen, allmählich zu Ende gehen, dahinschwinden, versickern, versanden; sich totlaufen, zu nichts führen; *mot* absterben.

petiole ['petioul] *bot* Blattstiel *m*.

petition [pi'tiʃən] *s* Bitte *f*, Ersuchen *n*; Bittschrift, Eingabe *f*, Gesuch *n*; Forderung *f*; *jur* Antrag *m* (*for* auf); *tr* bitten, ersuchen (*s.o.* jdn); e-e Bittschrift richten (*s.o.* an jdn); bitten um, beantragen; *itr* einkommen, nachsuchen, bitten (*for* um); *to file a ~* e-n Antrag einreichen; *to file o.'s ~ in bankruptcy* Konkurs anmelden; *to grant a ~* e-n Antrag bewilligen; *to ~ for divorce* die Scheidung(sklage) einreichen; *to ~ for mercy, for pardon* ein Gnadengesuch einreichen; *counter-, cross-~ (jur)* Gegenantrag *m*; *election ~* Wahlanfechtung *f*, -einspruch *m*; *~ in bankruptcy* Konkurseröffnungsantrag *m*; *~ for divorce* Scheidungsklage *f*; *~ for mercy, for pardon, for reprieve* Gnadengesuch *n*; *~ for nullification* Nichtigkeitsbeschwerde *f*; *~ for revival (jur)* Erneuerungsantrag *m*; **~er** [-ʃnə] Bittsteller; *jur* Antragsteller; Kläger *m* (*bes. in Scheidungssachen*); **~ jobbing** *Am* Unterschriftensammeln *n*.

petrel ['petrəl] *orn* Sturmvogel *m*; *stormy ~ (fig)* unruhige(r) Geist *m*.

petr|ifaction [petri'fækʃən] Versteinerung *f*; *fig* lähmende(r) Schreck *m*, Bestürzung *f*, Entsetzen *n*; **~ify** ['petrifai] *tr* versteinern *a. fig*; *fig* erstarren lassen; *itr* versteinern; erstarren; *fig* starr werden vor Schreck; **~ography** [pe'trɔgrəfi], **~ology** [pe'trɔlədʒi] Gesteinskunde *f*.

petrol ['petrəl] *Br* Benzin *n*, Kraft-, Treibstoff *m*; **~ can** Benzinkanister *m*; **~ consumption** Benzinverbrauch *m*; **~ cooker** Benzinkocher *m*; **~ drum** Benzinfaß *n*; **~ dump** Benzinlager *n*; **~ engine** Benzinmotor *m*; **~eum** [pi'trouljəm] Roh-, Erdöl, Petroleum *n*; *~~ lamp* Petroleumlampe *f*; *~~ pitch* Erdpech *n*; **~ feed** Benzinzuführung *f*; **~ ga(u)ge** Benzinstandanzeiger *m*, -uhr *f*; **~ lorry** Tankwagen *m*; **~ pipe** Benzinleitung *f*; **~ point, station** Tankstelle *f*; **~ pump** Zapfstelle *f*; **~ voucher** Benzinscheck *m*.

pett|icoat ['petikout] *s* Unterrock *m*; *fam* Weib(sbild) *n*; *tech* Glocke *f*; *a* weiblich; Weiber-; *~~-chaser (Am fam)* Mädchenjäger *m*; *~~ government* Weiberregiment *n*, -herrschaft *f*; *~~ insulator* Isolierglocke *f*; **~ifogging** ['-fɔgiŋ] *a* unreell; kleinlich; unwesentlich; gemein; *s* Unehrlichkeit im kleinen; Haarspalterei; kleine Betrügerei *f*; **~iness** ['-inis] Geringfügigkeit *f*; **~ish** ['-iʃ] launisch, reizbar, verdrießlich; **~y** ['-i] klein, geringfügig, unbedeutend, nebensächlich; trivial, banal; kleinlich, engstirnig; gemein, niedrig; *~~ case (pl) jur* Bagatellsache *f*; *~~ cash* (Porto-)Kasse *f*, Geld *n* für kleine Ausgaben; *~~ dealer* Kleinhändler *m*; *~~ debts (pl)* Bagatellschulden *f pl*; *~~ jury* Urteilsjury *f*; *~~ larceny* Bagatelldiebstahl *m*; *~~-minded (a)* engstirnig; *~~ offence* Übertretung *f*; *~~ officer (mar)* Bootsmann *m*; *~~ trader, tradesman* kleine(r) Geschäftsmann *m*; *~~ wares (pl)* Kurzwaren *f pl*.

petulan|ce, -cy ['petjuləns(i)] Ungeduld, Reizbarkeit; Launenhaftigkeit *f*, mürrische(s) Wesen *n*; **~t** ['-t] ungeduldig, reizbar, empfindlich; launisch, verdrießlich, nörgelnd.

petunia [pi'tju:njə] *bot* Petunie *f*.

pew [pju:] Kirchenstuhl, -sitz *m*, -bank; *sl* Sitzgelegenheit *f*, Stuhl *m*.

pewee ['pi:wi:] *orn Am* Tyrann; Königswürger, -tyrann *m*.

pewit, peewit ['pi:wit] *orn* Kiebitz *m*; *(~ gull)* Lachmöwe *f*; *Am* Königswürger, -tyrann *m*.

pewter ['pju:tə] Hartzinn, Weißmetall; Zinn(geschirr, -gerät) *n*; *a* zinnern; Zinn-; *grey ~* Graumetall *n*; **~er** ['-rə] Zinngießer *m*; **~ pot** Zinnkanne *f*.

phaeton ['feitn] Phaeton; *mot* Reisewagen *m*.

phalanx ['fælæŋks, *Am* 'fei-] *pl a. phalanges* ['fæ-, fə'lændʒi:z] *hist u. fig* Phalanx; *fig* geschlossene Front *f*; *anat* Finger-, Zehenglied *n*.

phantasm ['fæntæzm] Trugbild *n*; **~agoria** [fæntæzmə'gɔriə] Truggebilde, Blendwerk *n*, Wahnvorstellung, Phantasmagorie *f*; **~al** [fæn'tæzməl] trügerisch, illusorisch, unwirklich.

phantom ['fæntəm] *s* Phantom *a. med*, Gespenst *n*, Geist *m*; Einbildung *f*, Hirngespinst; Vorstellungs-, Erinnerungsbild *n*; *a ~ of a ...* ein(e) angebliche(r, s); *attr* Schein-; Gespenster-; *itr* mitklingen; **~ circuit** *el* Viererleitung *f*.

Pharis|aic [færi'seiik] *rel hist* pharisäisch; *p~aic(al)* [-(əl)] *allg* pharisäisch, buchstabengerecht; scheinheilig; **~aism** ['færiseiizm] *rel hist* Pharisäertum *n*; *p~~ (allg)* Pharisäertum *n*, Buchstabengerechtigkeit; Scheinheiligkeit *f*; **~ee** ['færizi:] *rel hist* Pharisäer *m*; *p~~ (allg)* Pharisäer, Heuchler *m*.

pharmac|eutic(al) [fɑ:mə'sju:tik(əl)] pharmazeutisch; Heilmittel-; *~~ chemist* Apotheker *m*; **~eutics** [-s] *s pl mit sing* Pharmazeutik, Arzneimittelkunde *f*; **~ist** ['fɑ:məsist] Apotheker *m*; **~ology** [-'kɔlədʒi] Pharmakologie *f*; **~opoeia** [fɑ:məkə'pi:ə] amtliche(s) Arzneibuch *n*; **~y** ['fɑ:məsi] Pharmazie; Apotheke *f*.

pharyn|gal [fə'riŋgəl], **~geal** [-n-'dʒi:əl] *a anat* Rachen-, Schlund-; **~gitis** [færin'dʒaitis] Rachenkatarrh *m*; **~goscope** [fə'riŋgəskoup] *med* Rachenspiegel *m*; **~x** ['færiŋks] *anat* Rachen, Schlundkopf *m*.

phase [feiz] *astr phys* Phase; *allg* (Entwick(e)lungs-)Phase, Stufe *f*, Stadium *n*; Seite *f*, Aspekt *m*, Betrachtungsweise *f*; *mil* Abschnitt; *phys chem* Aggregatzustand *m*; *in ~* phasengleich; *~ of the moon* Mondphase *f*; **~ number, reversal, sequence, shift, voltage** Phasenzahl, -umkehrung, -folge, -verschiebung, -spannung *f*.

pheasant ['feznt] (*bes.* Edel-, Jagd-) Fasan *m*; *Gold(en) P~* Goldfasan *m*; **~ry** ['-ri] Fasanerie *f*.

phen|acetin(e) [fi'næsitin] *chem* Phenazetin *n*; **~ic** ['fi:nik]: *~~ acid*, **~ol** ['fi:nɔl] Phenol *n*, Karbolsäure *f*; **~yl** ['fenil, 'fi:nil] *chem* Phenyl *n*.

pheno|menal [fi'nɔminl] *a* Erscheinungs-; *fam* außergewöhnlich, -ordentlich, phänomenal; **~menalism** [-'nɔminəlizm] *philos* Phänomenalismus *m*; **~menology** [finɔmi'nɔlədzi] Phänomenologie *f*; **~menon** [fi-'nɔminən] *pl -na* [-ə] Erscheinung *f*; Vorgang *m*, Tatsache *f*; *fam* Phänomen, Genie, Wunder *n*; **~type** ['fi:nətaip] *biol* Phänotyp *m*.

phew [fju:] *interj* puh! pfui! ach!

phial ['faiəl] Phiole *f*; Fläschchen *n*.

philander [fi'lændə] *itr (Mann)* (herum)poussieren, flirten; **~er** [-rə] Poussierstengel, Schürzenjäger *m*.

philanthrop|ic(al) [filən'θrɔpik(əl)] philanthropisch, menschenfreundlich; **~ist** [fi'lænθrəpist] Philanthrop, Menschenfreund *m*; **~y** [-'lænθrəpi] Philanthropie, Menschenliebe *f*.

philatel|ic [filə'telik] philatelistisch; Briefmarken-; **~ist** [fi'lætəlist] Briefmarkensammler *m*; **~y** [-'lætəli] Briefmarkensammeln *n*.

philharmonic [filɑ:'mɔnik] musikliebend; philharmonisch; **~ pitch** Pariser Kammerton *m*.

Philip ['filip] Philipp(us) *m*; **p~pic** [fi'lipik] Philippika, Strafrede, *fam* Standpauke *f*; **P~pine** ['filipi:n] *a geog* philippinisch; *s pl u. ~~ Islands* die Philippinen *pl*.

Philistin|e ['filistain, *bes. Am* '-in] *s hist u. fig* Philister; *fig* Spießbürg)er *m*; *a fig* philisterhaft, philiströs, spießbürgerlich, spießig; **~ism** ['-inizm] Spießbürgertum *n*.

philodendron [filə'dendrən] *bot* Philodendron *n*.

philolog|ic(al) [filə'lɔdʒik(əl)] philologisch; **~ist** [fi'lɔlədʒist] Philologe *m*; **~y** ['-lɔlədʒi] Philologie *f*.

philosoph|er [fi'lɔsəfə] Philosoph *m*; *~~'s stone, a. ~~s' stone* Stein *m* der Weisen; **~ic(al)** [filə'sɔfik(əl)] philosophisch; *fig* weise, einsichtig, gelassen; **~ize** [fi'lɔsəfaiz] *itr* philosophieren; **~y** [fi'lɔsəfi] Philosophie; (Lebens-) Weisheit; Abgeklärtheit, Gelassenheit *f*, Gleichmut *m*; *moral ~~* Ethik *f*; *natural ~~* Naturwissenschaft *f*; *~~ of history* Geschichtsphilosophie *f*; *~~ (of life)* Lebens-, Weltanschauung *f*.

philtre, *Am* **philter** ['filtə] Liebestrank *m*.

phiz [fiz] *fam* Gesicht *n*, Visage, Fratze *f*.

phleb|itis [fli'baitis] Venenentzündung *f*; **~otomy** [fli'bɔtəmi] *med* Aderlaß *m*.

phlegm [flem] *physiol med* Schleim *m*; Phlegma *n*; *fig* Trägheit, Apathie, Ruhe *f*, Gleichmut *m*; **~atic(al)** [fleg'mætik(əl)] phlegmatisch, träge, stumpf, apathisch; *fig* ruhig, gleichmütig, unerschütterlich.

phlox [flɔks] Phlox, Flammenblume *f*.

phobia ['foubiə] krankhafte Furcht *f*.

Ph(o)enicia [fi'niʃiə] Phönizien *n*; **~n** [-n] *a* phönizisch; *s* Phönizier(in *f*) *m*.

ph(o)enix ['fi:niks] *(Mythologie)* Phönix *m*.

phon [fɔn] Phon *n*; **~e** [foun] *s (Sprache)* Laut *m*; *fam* Telephon *n*; *pl* Kopfhörer *m pl*; *itr* telephonieren, ein Ferngespräch führen; *tr* anrufen, *fam* anklingeln; *over the ~~* telephonisch *adv*; *to be on the ~~* am Apparat sein, sprechen; Telephon (-anschluß) haben; *to be wanted on the ~~* am Telephon verlangt werden; *~~ booth* Telephonzelle *f*; *~~ call (telephonischer)* Anruf *m*; **~eme** ['founi:m] *gram* Phonem *n*; **~emic** [fo(u)'ni:mik] Phonem-; **~etic** [fo(u)'netik] *a* phonetisch, Aussprache-; *~~ spelling* Lautschrift *f*; *s pl mit sing* Phonetik *f*; Lautsystem *n (e-r bestimmten Sprache)*; **~etician** [founi'tiʃən] Phonetiker *m*; **~ic** ['fo(u)nik] lautlich; Laut-; **~ogram** ['founəgræm] Lautzeichen *n*; Tonspur *f*; zugesprochene(s) Telegramm *n*; **~ograph** ['founəgrɑ:f] *Am* Phonograph *m*; Grammophon *n*, Plattenspieler *m*; *~~ pickup* Tonabnehmer *m*; *~~ radio* Kombinationsgerät, Rundfunkgerät *n* mit Plattenspieler; *~~ record* Schallplatte *f*; *~~ recorder* (Platten-)Aufnahmegerät *n*; **~ographic** [founə'græfik] phonographisch; **~ology** [fo(u)'nɔlədʒi] Lautlehre *f*; **~ometer** [fo(u)'nɔmitə] Lautstärkemesser *m*.

phon(e)y ['founi] *Am a sl* unecht, falsch, Schwindel-; *s* Schwindel *m*, Fälschung *f*; Schwindler, Hochstapler; Snob *m*.

phos|gene ['fɔzdʒi:n] *chem* Phosgen *n*; **~phate** ['fɔsfeit] *chem* Phosphat, phosphorsaure(s) Salz *n*; **~phatic** [fɔs'fætik] phosphathaltig; **~phorate** ['fɔsfəreit] *tr* mit Phosphor verbinden *od* imprägnieren; **~phoresce** [fɔsfə'res] *itr* phosphoreszieren; **~phorescence** [fɔsfə'resns] Phosphoreszenz *f*; *~~ of the sea* Meeresleuchten *n*; **~phorescent** [-'resnt] phosphoreszierend; Leucht-; **~phoric** [fɔs'fɔrik] *a* Phosphor-; *~~ acid* Phosphorsäure *f*; **~phorism** ['fɔsfərizm] Phosphorvergiftung *f*; **~phorous** ['fɔsfərəs] *a*: *~~ acid* phosphorige Säure *f*; **~phorus** [-] Phosphor *m*.

photo ['foutou, fouto(u), -tə] *in Zssgen* Licht-, Photo-; photographisch, Lichtbild-, Photo-; *s fam* Photo *n*, Photographie *f*; *tr fam* knipsen, photographieren; **~bacterium** Leuchtbakterie *f*; **~cell** photoelektrische Zelle *f*; **~chemical** photochemisch; **~chemistry** Photochemie *f*; **~chromy** ['-təkroumi] Farbphotographie *f*; **~copy** Photokopie *f*; **~ dealer** Photohändler *m*; **~drama** *Am* Film *m*, *fam* Kinostück *n*; **~electric(al)** photoelektrisch; *~~ cell* photoelektrische Zelle *f*; **~engraving** *typ* photomechanische Wiedergabe, Klischeeherstellung *f*; **~ finish** *Am sport* Finish *n*, Endkampf *m*, der nur durch Photographie entschieden werden kann; knappe(r) Sieg *n*; **~flash** Vakublitz *m*; *~~ bulb* Vakublitzlampe *f*; **~flood** *a*: *~~ bulb* Nitraphotlampe *f*; **~g** ['foutɔg] *Am sl* Photograph *m*; **~genic** [foutou'dʒenik] photogen, bildwirksam; *biol* phosphoreszierend; **~grammetry** [-tə'græmitri] Photogrammetrie *f*, Meßbildverfahren *n*; **~graph** ['foutəgrɑ:f] *s* Lichtbild *n*, Photographie *f*; *tr* photographieren, aufnehmen; *itr* photographieren; sich *(gut od schlecht)* photographieren lassen; *to take a ~~* e-e Aufnahme machen; **~grapher** [fə'tɔgrəfə] Photograph, Lichtbildner *m*; **~graphic** [foutə'græfik] *adv ~~ally* photographisch; *~~ copy* Photokopie *f*; *~~ flight, mission (aero)* Bildflug *m*; *~~ interpretation* Luftbildauswertung *f*; *~~ personnel (aero)* Bildpersonal *n*; *~~ plane* Bildflugzeug *n*; *~~ post* Bildstelle *f*; *~~ reconnaissance* Bildaufklärung *f*; *~~ report (mil)* Bildmeldung *f*; *~~ strip* Luftbildreihe *f*; **~graphy** [fə'tɔgrəfi] Photographie, Lichtbildkunst *f*; *natural-colo(u)r ~~* Farb(en)photographie *f*; **~gravure** [foutəgrə'vjuə] Kupfertiefdruck *m*, Heliogravüre *f*; **~ interpreter** *(Luft-)* Bildauswerter *m*; **~lithograph** Photolithographie *f*; **~map** Luftbildkarte *f*; **~maton** [fə'tɔmətən] Photomaton *n (Warenzeichen)*; **~mechanical** photomechanisch; **~meter** [fou'tɔmitə] Belichtungsmesser, Photometer *m*; **~metric(al)** [foutə'metrik(əl)] photometrisch; **~metry** [fou'tɔmitri] Photometrie *f*; **~micrograph** Mikrophotographie *f (Bild)*; **~micrography** Mikrophotographie *f (Verfahren)*; **~montage** Photomontage *f*; **~mural** Photoplakat *n*; **~n** ['foutɔn] *phys* Photon *n (Strahlungs-, Lichtquant)*; **~ observer** *aero* Bildbeobachter *m*; **~play** *Am* Film *m*, *fam* Kinostück *n*; **~print** Abzug *m*; Photokopie *f*; **~radiogram** Funkbild *n*; **~ reporter** Bildbericht(erstatt)er *m*; **~sensitive** lichtempfindlich; **~sphere** *astr* Photosphäre *f (der Sonne)*; **~stat** ['fouto(u)stæt] *s (Warenzeichen)* Photokopiergerät *n*; Photokopie, Lichtpause *f*; *tr* photokopieren; **~telegram** Bildtelegramm; Lichtsignal *n*; **~telegraphy** Bildtelegraphie *f*; **~therapeutics, ~therapy** *med* Phototherapie *f*, Lichtheilverfahren *n*; **~tropism** [fouto(u)'trɔpizm] *bot* Phototropismus *m*; **~tube** photoelektrische Zelle *f*; **~type** ['foutoutaip] *s* Lichtdruck(platte *f*) *m*; *tr* durch Lichtdruck vervielfältigen; **~typy** [fou'tɔtipi] Lichtdruck(verfahren *n*) *m*.

phrase [freiz] *s* Ausdrucksweise; Redensart *f*, Ausdruck; *gram* Satzteil *m*; Wortgruppe; *mus* Periode *f*, Satz *m*; *tr* in Worte kleiden; zum Ausdruck bringen; ausdrücken; *mus* in Sätze, Perioden einteilen; **~-monger** Phrasendrescher *m*; **~ology** [freizi'ɔlədʒi] Ausdrucks-, Redeweise, Phraseologie *f*.

phren|etic(al) [fri'netik(əl)] wild, tosend, tobend, rasend, toll, *fam* wahn-, irrsinnig; fanatisch; **~ic** ['frenik] *a* Zwerchfell-; **~ology** [fri'nɔlədʒi] Phrenologie, Schädellehre *f*.

phthis|ic(al) ['θaisik(əl), 'fθai-] schwindsüchtig; **~is** ['θaisis, 'fθai-, 'tai-] Schwindsucht, Tuberkulose *f*; *pulmonary ~~* Lungenschwindsucht *f*.

phut [fʌt] *interj* fft! *to go ~ (fam)* futsch-, draufgehen, dran glauben müssen.

phylloxera [filɔk'siərə] *pl -rae* [-ri:] *ent* Reblaus *f*.

phys|ic ['fisik] *s* Heilkunde *f*, ärztliche(r) Beruf *m*; *fam* Medizin, Arznei *f*, Heil-, *bes.* Abführmittel *n*; *pl mit sing* Physik *f*; *tr* (e-e) Medizin, *bes.* ein Abführmittel geben (*s.o.* jdm); heilen, kurieren; e-e günstige Heilwirkung haben auf; *experimental ~~s* Experimentalphysik *f*; **~ical** ['fizikəl] physisch, natürlich, materiell; körperlich, Leibes-; physikalisch; naturwissenschaftlich; *~~ chemistry* physikalische Chemie *f*; *~~ condition* Gesundheitszustand *m*, körperliche(s) Befinden *n*; *~~ culture* Körperpflege, -kultur *f*; *~~ defect* Körperfehler *m*, körperliche(s) Gebrechen *n*; *~~-disability benefit* Versehrten-, Unfallrente *f*; *~~ education* Turnunterricht *m*, Turnen *n*; *~~ fitness* Tauglichkeit *f*; *~~ geography* physikalische Geographie *f*; *~~ inspection (mil)* Gesundheitsappell *m*; *~~ inventory* Bestandsaufnahme *f*; *~~ reconditioning* Wiederherstellung *f* der Arbeitsfähigkeit; *~~ science* Physik *f*; Naturwissenschaften *f pl*; *~~ therapy* Naturheilkunde *f*; *~~ training, (fam) ~~ jerks (pl)* Leibesübungen *f pl*; **~ician** [fi'ziʃən] Arzt *m*; **~icist** ['fizisist] Physiker *m*; **~iocrat** ['fiziəkræt] Physiokrat *m*; **~iognomic** [fiziə'nɔmik] physiognomisch; **~iognomy** [fizi'ɔ(g)nəmi] Physiognomie *f*; Gesichtszüge *m pl*, -ausdruck *m*; **~iography** [fizi'ɔgrəfi] Naturbeschreibung; physikalische Geographie; *Am* Geomorphologie *f*; **~iologic(al)** [fiziə'lɔdʒik(əl)] physiologisch; **~iologist** [fizi'ɔlədʒist] Physiologe *m*; **~iology** [-'ɔlədʒi] Physiologie *f*; **~iotherapy** [fizio(u)'θerəpi] Naturheilkunde *f*; **~ique** [fi'zi:k] Körperbau *m*, -form, körperliche Erscheinung, Konstitution, Leibesbeschaffenheit *f*.

pi [pai] *sl (Schule)* artig, brav; **~ jaw** *sl* Gardinenpredigt, Standpauke *f*.

pian|ino [pi:ə'ni:nou] Pianino *n*; **~ist** ['pjænist, 'piə-] Pianist, Klavierspieler *m*; **~o 1.** ['pjɑ:nou] *a adv mus* piano; **2.** ['pjænou] *pl -os*, (*~~forte*) [pjæno(u)'fɔ:ti] Piano(forte); Klavier *n*; *to play (on) the ~~* Klavier spielen; *cottage ~~* Kleinklavier *n*; *grand ~~* Flügel *m*; *upright ~~* Klavier *n*; *~~ lesson, teacher* Klavierstunde *f*, -lehrer *m*; **~ola** [piə'noulə] Pianola *n*.

piazza [pi'ædzə, *Am* pi'æzə] (großer, viereckiger) Platz; *Am* Laubengang *m*, Arkaden *pl*; Veranda *f*.

pibroch ['pi:brɔk, -ɔx] Dudelsackstück *n*, -variationen *f pl*.

pica ['paikə] *typ* Cicero *f (Schriftgrad)*.

picaresque [pikə'resk] *a lit* Schelmen-.

picaroon [pikə'ru:n] Strolch; Dieb; Seeräuber, Pirat *m*; Piratenschiff *n*.

picayun|e [pikə'ju:n] *s Am* kleine Münze *f*, Groschen *m*; *fig* Kleinigkeit, Lappalie, Bagatelle *f*; *fam* Plunder, Dreck; unbedeutende(r) Mensch *m*, Null *f*; *a u.* **~ish** [-iʃ] *Am* gewöhnlich, billig, schäbig, *fam* lumpig, mies.

piccalilli ['pikəlili] mit scharfen Gewürzen eingemachte(s) Mischgemüse *n*; **piccaninny** ['pikənini] (Neger-) Kind *n*.

piccolo ['pikəlou] *pl -es* Pikkoloflöte *f*.

pick [pik] **1.** *tr (Boden, Gestein, Pflaster)* (auf)hacken, aufbrechen; aushöhlen; hacken, kratzen an; abkratzen, stochern an, ausstochern, sich stochern in *(den Zähnen)*; *(Naht)* auftrennen; *(Obst, Blumen)* pflücken; *(Baum)* leer pflücken; *(Ähren)* lesen; *(Geflügel)* rupfen; *(Vogel)* (auf)picken; (halb widerwillig) essen, herumpicken, -stochern in; ab-, benagen; (ausea.-, zer)zupfen, ziehen (*at* an); *Am mus (Saiten)* zupfen; *Am (Gitarre, Mandoline)* spielen; *(Schloß)* mit e-m Dietrich öffnen, aufbrechen; stehlen aus (*s.o.'s pocket* jds Tasche); suchen nach, heraussuchen, -lesen, -finden, ausfindig machen; *(Händel, Streit)* suchen; *(Streit)* vom Zaun brechen; *itr* hacken; Beeren, Blumen pflücken; sich pflücken lassen; widerwillig *od* zerstreut essen (*at* an); herumspielen, -fummeln (*at* an); herumsuchen, -wühlen; *(to ~ on)* auswählen; *Am fam* schikanieren, (herum)meckern (*at, on* an), anöden (*on s.o.* jdn), ärgern (*on s.o.* jdn); *s* Picken, Hacken; (Herum-)Suchen *n*; Fund *m*; *(the ~ of the bunch)* das Beste (von allem), das (Aller-)Beste; Auswahl *f*; *typ* Spieß *m*; Picke; Spitzhacke, Haue *f*; *meist in Zssgen*: Pickel, Stocher *m*; *to have a bone to ~ with s.o.* mit jdm ein Hühnchen zu rupfen haben; *to have, to take o.'s ~* s-e Wahl treffen; *to ~ s.o.'s brains* sich jds Ideen zunutze machen; *to ~ and choose* sorgfältig (her)aussuchen; *to ~ holes in s.th.* an e-r S herummeckern, etw auszusetzen haben; *to ~ a lock* ein Schloß knacken; *to ~ to pieces* kein gutes Haar lassen (*s.o.* an jdm); in Stücke reißen; zerpflücken; *to ~ pockets* Taschendiebstahl begehen; *to ~ a quarrel with s.o.* mit jdm e-n Streit vom Zaun brechen; *to ~ and steal* stibitzen; *to ~ o.'s teeth* sich in den Zähnen stochern; *to ~ o.'s way, o.'s steps* vorsichtig gehen, behutsam e-n Fuß vor den andern setzen; sich durchschlängeln; *to ~ o.'s words* die Worte wählen, gewählt sprechen; *to* **~ off** abpflücken; wegnehmen; abschießen; *to* **~ out** heraussuchen, (aus)wählen; ausfindig machen; *(Rätsel)* herausbekommen, *fam* -kriegen; *(Farbe)* hervorheben, zur Geltung bringen, absetzen (*with* gegen); *(Ton)* angeben, -schlagen; *to* **~ over** überprüfen; durchsehen; *to* **~ up** *tr* aufhacken; aufpicken, -heben, -lesen; auf-, mitnehmen *(a. Fahrgäste), fam* aufgabeln; finden, sammeln, zs.-bringen; *(billig, teuer)* erstehen; herausfinden, -bringen, in Erfahrung bringen, *fam* aufschnappen; verstehen, erfassen; *(Kenntnisse)* sich aneignen; *fam* zufällig kennenlernen, *s.o.* jds Bekanntschaft machen; *Am fam* verhaften; begeistert sein für; *(mit dem Scheinwerfer)* anleuchten; zu Gesicht, zu Gehör bekommen *(Funkspruch, Rundfunksendung)* aufnehmen; *(Zimmer)* aufräumen, sauber machen; *tech* abgreifen, aufnehmen; *itr* sich erholen, wieder zu Kräften kommen *(a. tr: to ~~ health, power, spirits)*; *(to ~~ efficiency)* aufholen; *mot* auf Touren kommen; *with s.o. (fam)* mit jdm Freundschaft schließen; *to ~ o.s. up* (wieder) aufstehen; *to ~~ courage* Mut fassen; *to ~~ a living* s-n Unterhalt finden, sich durchbringen; *to ~~ speed* an Geschwindigkeit gewinnen, schneller werden, in Fahrt kommen; **~-a-back** ['-əbæk] *adv* huckepack; *a*: *~~ airplane* Huckepackflugzeug *n*; **~-ax(e)** *s* Spitzhacke, Haue *f*; *itr tr* (auf)hacken; **~ed** [-t] *a* gepflückt; ausgewählt, -gesucht, -erlesen; aufgehackt; *~~ troops (pl)* Kern-, Elitetruppen *f pl*; **~er** ['-ə] Pflücker; (Beeren-)Sammler; *(Textil)* Fadenklauber *(Gerät)*; *min* Klaubhammer *m*; **~ing** ['-iŋ] Hacken, Stochern, Zupfen, Picken, Rupfen, Pflücken; Stehlen *n*; *pl* Abfälle, Reste *m pl*, Überbleibsel *n pl (bes. e-r Mahlzeit)*; gestohlene, *fam* geklaute Sachen *f pl*, Diebesgut *n*; Gewinn *m*; **~lock** Einbrecher, Dieb; Dietrich *m*; **~-me-up** *fam* (zwischendurch getrunkenes) Schnäpschen; Stärkungsmittel *n*; **~-off** *a Am* abmontierbar; **~pocket** Taschendieb *m*; *beware of ~~s!* vor Taschendieben wird gewarnt! **~-up** *sport* Aufheben *n (des Balles)*; *(Plattenspieler)* Tonabnehmer *m*; Abtastdose; Rundfunk-, Fernsehaufnahme(apparatur); Außenaufnahmestelle; Apparatur *f* zur Übertragung von Außenaufnahmen; *com* Gelegenheitskauf; *Am* kleine(r) Lieferwagen *m*; Beschleunigung(svermögen *n*) *f*; *fam* Gelegenheitsbekanntschaft; (kleine) Aufmunterung; Erholung *a. com*; *Am sl* Verhaftung *f*; *attr* Aufnahme-; Gelegenheits-; *air mail ~~* Luftpostaufnahme *f* im Flug; *~~ girl (Am sl)* leichte(s) Mädchen *n*; *~~ head* Tonabnehmerkopf *m*.

pickaninny *s. piccaninny*.

pickerel ['pikərəl] *zoo* junge(r) Grashecht *m*.

picket ['pikit] *s* Pflock, (Zaun-)Pfahl, Pfosten *m*; *mil* (Feld-)Wache *f*, (Wacht-)Posten; *bes. pl* Streikposten *m*; *tr* an e-n Pfahl binden; einzäunen; als Streikposten einsetzen, Streikposten stehen vor, durch Streikposten absperren; *mil* als Feldwache, Posten aufstellen; *itr* Streikposten, *mil* Feldwache stehen; **~ boat** Wach-, *Am* Hafenpolizeiboot *n*; **~ fence** Pfahlzaun *m*; **~ line** *mil* Vorposten-, Streikpostenlinie *f*; **~ pole** Meßlatte *f*, Fluchtstab *m*.

pickl|e ['pikl] *s* Pökel *m*, (Salz-)Lake, Würzbrühe; *tech* Beize *f*, Metall-, Holzbad *n*; *fam* unangenehme, peinliche Lage, Verlegenheit; schöne Bescherung; *fam* Range *f*, ungezogene(s) Kind *n*; *pl* eingelegte(s) Gemüse *n*; Essiggurken *f pl*; *tr* (ein-)pökeln, einmachen; marinieren; in Essig einlegen; *agr tech* beizen; *Am sl* ruinieren; *itr* Gurken einlegen; *to be in a nice, sad, sorry ~~ (fam)* ganz schön in der Patsche sitzen, in der Klemme sein; *to have a rod in ~~ for s.o.* für jdn e-e unangenehme Überraschung haben; *to put up ~~s* Gurken einlegen; *mixed ~~s (pl)* gemischtes Essiggemüse *n*; *onion ~~s (pl)* Essigzwiebeln *f pl*; *~~-herring* dumme(r) August, Clown *m*; **~ed** ['-d] *a* gepökelt, eingemacht; *sl* besoffen; *~~ herring* Salzhering *m*.

picnic ['piknik] *s* Landpartie *f*, Picknick; *fam* Kinderspiel; *sl* nette(s) Erlebnis, Vergnügen *n*, *fig* Kleinigkeit *f*; *itr (pp ~ked)* ein Picknick veranstalten; picknicken; **~ker** ['-ə] Ausflügler, Teilnehme(r) *m* an e-m Picknick.

picric ['pikrik] *a*: **~ acid** Pikrinsäure *f*.

picto|graph ['piktəgrɑ:f] Bildzeichen, (Schrift-)Symbol *n*; Bilderschrift *f*; **~rial** [pik'tɔ:riəl] *a* bildlich, bebildert, in Bildern, illustriert; bildhaft, malerisch; Bilder-; *s* Illustrierte *f*; *~~ advertising* Bildwerbung *f*.

picture ['piktʃə] *s* Bild; Gemälde *n*; Abbildung; *phot* Aufnahme *f*; *(moving ~)* Film(streifen) *m*; *fig* Ab-, Ebenbild *n*, Verkörperung; Vorstellung *f*, Bild *n*, Idee; Darstellung, Beschreibung, Schilderung, Wiedergabe *f*; *fam* etw Bildschöne; *pl fam (moving ~s)* Kino *n*; *tr* abbilden, malen, zeichnen; photographieren; (ver)filmen; illustrieren; *fig* anschaulich machen, schildern, beschreiben, wiedergeben, darstellen, -legen, erklären; sich vorstellen, sich e-n Begriff machen von; *to be a ~* bildschön sein; *not to come into the ~* außer Betracht bleiben; *to give a ~ of s.th.* ein Bild von etw geben, etw darstellen; *to go to the ~s* ins Kino gehen; *to look the ~ of health* wie das blühende Leben aussehen; *to put s.o. in the ~* jdn ins Bild setzen; *to take a ~* photographieren, aufnehmen; *silent, sound ~* Stumm-, Tonfilm *m*; **~ band** *video* Bildbereich *m*; **~-book** Bilderbuch *n*; **~-card** Bild *n (im Kartenspiel)*; **~ cartoon** Trickfilm *m*; **~ control** *video* Bildsteuerung *f*; **~-dealer** Kunsthändler *m*; **~-fastener** Bilderhaken *m*; **~-frame** Bilderrahmen *m*; **~-gallery** Gemäldegalerie *f*; *Am sl* Verbrecheralbum *n*; **~-goer** Kinobesucher *m*; **~-hat** breitrandige(r) (Damen-)Hut *m*, *hum* Wagenrad *n*; **~-house, -palace, -theatre** Lichtspielhaus, Lichtspiel-, Filmtheater *n*; **~-mo(u)lding** Bilderleiste *f*; **~ play** Film *m*; **~ postcard** Ansichtskarte *f*; **~ primer** Bilderfibel *f*; **~ puzzle** Bilderrätsel *n*; **~ reception** *video* Bildempfang *m*; **~-rail, -rod** Bilderschiene *f*; **~ show** Film(vorführung *f*) *m*; Kino *n*; **~ size** Bildformat *n*; **~-story** Bildergeschichte *f*; **~ telegraphy** Bildtelegraphie *f*; **~-transmission** Bildübertragung *f*, -funk *m*; **~-tube** *video* Bildröhre *f*; **~ window** Panoramafenster *n*; **~-writing** Bilderschrift *f*.

pictur|esque [piktʃə'resk] malerisch; *(Stil)* lebhaft, lebendig, anschaulich, plastisch; **~ization** *Am* [piktʃərai'zeiʃən] bildliche Darstellung; Verfilmung *f*; **~ize** ['piktʃəraiz] *tr Am* bildlich darstellen; verfilmen.

piddl|e ['pidl] *itr* vertrödeln; *fam* pinkeln; **~ing** ['-iŋ] unbedeutend, belanglos, *fam* lumpig.

pidgin ['pidʒin] *fam* Arbeit, Aufgabe, Angelegenheit *f*; **~ English** Pidgin-Englis(c)h *n*.

pie [pai] **1.** Pastete; *Am* Torte *f*; *Am sl* gefundene(s) Fressen *n*; Protektion *f*; *easy as ~* kinderleicht; *to eat humble ~* klein beigeben; *to have a finger in the ~* die Hand im Spiel haben; *apple-~* Apfeltorte *f*; *meat ~* Fleischpastete *f*; **~crust** Pastetenkruste, -hülle *f*; **~-dish** Pastetenform *f*; **~-eyed** *a Am sl* besoffen; **~man** ['-mən] Pastetenverkäufer *m*; **~plant** ['-plænt] *Am* Rhabarber *m*; **~ wagon** *Am sl* grüne Minna *f*; **2.** *(printer's ~) typ* Zwiebelfische *m pl*; *fig* Durcheinander *n*, Wirrwarr *m*; **3.** *(mag~) orn* Elster *f*; **~bald, ~d** *a* bunt, (bunt)scheckig; *the Pied Piper (of Hamelin)* der Rattenfänger von Hameln.

piece [pi:s] *s* Stück; Bruchstück *n*; Abschnitt *m*; Stelle *f (in e-m Buch)*; Einzelteil, -stück *(e-s Services, Satzes)*; *(~ of money)* Geldstück *n*, Münze *f*; *in Zssgen* -stück; *Am sl* Anteil; *(Brettspiel)* Stein *m*; *(Schach)* Figur *f (außer den Bauern)*, Offizier *m*; *(bes. in Zssgen)* Gewehr, Geschütz *n*; (Stoff-)Ballen *m*, (Tapeten-)Rolle; Stückarbeit *f*; (Musik-, Theater-)Stück, (literarisches, Kunst-)Werk; *sl* Mädchen *n*; *a ~ of...* ein(e) ...; *tr* anstücken *(on to* an); flicken; zs.stücken, -setzen, -flicken; verbinden; *itr Am fam* zwischen den Mahlzeiten essen; *by the ~* stückweise; im Akkord; *~ by ~* Stück für Stück, eins nach dem andern; *in ~s* entzwei, *fam* kaputt; *of 20 ~s (Service)* 20teilig; *of a, of one ~* aus e-m Stück, einheitlich, homogen; gleichmäßig, -artig; übereinstimmend *(with* mit); *all of a ~* aus e-m Stück; *to ~s* in Stücke; kaputt; *to be all of a ~ (fam)* vom selben Kaliber sein; *to fall to ~s* ausea.fallen; *to give s.o. a ~ of o.'s mind (fam)* jdm gehörig die Meinung *od* Bescheid sagen, jdn gehörig zurechtstutzen; *to go to ~s* zerbrechen; *fig* die Herrschaft über sich selbst verlieren; *to speak o.'s ~* s-e Meinung sagen; *to take to ~s* in Stücke teilen, zerlegen, ausea.nehmen; *(Kleid)* auftrennen; *to tear to ~s* zerreißen, zerpflücken *a. fig*; *a ~ of advice* ein Rat *m*; *a ~ of business* e-e Geschäftsangelegenheit *f*; *a ~ of change, of jack (Am sl)* e-e schöne Stange Geld; *a ~ of folly* e-e Dummheit, Torheit, ein Wahnsinn *m*; *a ~ of impudence* e-e Unverschämtheit; *a ~ of land* ein Grundstück; *a ~ of luck* ein Glück *n*; *a ~ of money* ein Geldstück; *a ~ of music* ein Musikstück; *a ~ of news* e-e Neuigkeit; *a ~ of nonsense* Unsinn *m*; *a ~ of painting* ein Bild *n*; *a ~ of poetry* ein Gedicht *n*; *a (fine) ~ of work* e-e saubere Arbeit; *pocket ~* Glückspfennig *m*; *to ~* **out** vervollständigen, ergänzen; *to ~* **together** zs.stücken, -setzen, -flikken; *to ~* **up** flicken, ausbessern; **~ cost** Stückkosten *pl*; **~er** ['-ə] Flicker(in *f*) *m*; **~-goods** *pl (Textil)* Meter-, Schnittware *f*; **~meal** ['-mi:l] *adv* stückweise; Stück für Stück, nach u. nach; *a* nach u. nach erfolgend; fragmentarisch; planlos, ohne Methode; **~-price** Stückpreis *m*; **~-rate** Akkordsatz *m*; **~-wages** *pl* Stück-, Akkordlohn *m*; **~-work** Stück-, Akkordarbeit *f*; *to do ~~* im Akkord arbeiten; **~-worker** Akkordarbeiter *m*.

pier [piə] Brückenpfeiler *m*; Landungsbrücke *f*, Landesteg; Pier *m u. mar f*; Ladebühne; Mole *f*, Hafendamm; *arch* (Fenster-, Strebe-)Pfeiler *m*; **~age** ['-ridʒ] Hafen-, Kaigebühren *f pl*; **~-glass** *(hoher)* Pfeilerspiegel *m*; **~-head** Molenkopf *m*.

pierc|e ['piəs] *tr* eindringen in; durchbohren, -dringen, -stoßen; ein Loch bohren in *od* durch; *(ein Loch)* machen, bohren; einbrechen in, brechen durch;

mil durchstoßen; *fig* durchdringen, -schauen; *(Sinne, Gefühle)* stark erregen; *itr* eindringen (*into* in); dringen (*through* durch); **~er** ['-ə] Bohrer *m*, Ahle *f*, Pfriem *m*; **~ing** ['-iŋ] durchdringend, schneidend, scharf; *(Schrei)* gellend.

piet|à [pie'tɑ:] *(Kunst)* Pietà, Schmerzensmutter *f*; **~ism** ['paiətizm] *rel* Pietismus *m*; **~ist** ['paiətist] Pietist *m*; **~istic(al)** [paiə'tistik(əl)] pietistisch; **~y** ['paiəti] Frömmigkeit; Pietät, kindliche Liebe, Achtung, Ehrfurcht *f* (*to* vor).

piffl|e ['pifl] *fam s* Quatsch, Blödsinn, Unsinn *m*, *sl* Blech *n*; *itr sl* dämlich quatschen; **~ing** ['-iŋ] *sl* unbedeutend, unwichtig; lächerlich.

pig [pig] *s* Schwein; Ferkel; Schweinefleisch; *fam pej* (Dreck-)Schwein *n*, Sau, Schlampe *f*; Dickschädel *m*; *Am sl* Mädchen *n*; *tech* Massel *f*, Roheisen(barren *m*) *n*; Mulde *f (Form für Bleiguß)*; *itr (Sau)* ferkeln; *(to ~ it, to ~ together)* wie (im) Schweine(stall) hausen; zs.gepfercht leben; *in a ~'s eye (Am sl)* keineswegs; denkste! *to bring o.'s ~s to a fine, pretty, the wrong market (fig iro)* an den Rechten kommen; *to buy a ~ in a poke (fig)* die Katze im Sack kaufen; *to make a ~ of o.s.* sich überfuttern; *~s might fly* es geschehen noch Wunder; *guinea-~* Meerschweinchen; *fig* Versuchskaninchen *n*; *sucking ~* Spanferkel *n*; **~ bed** *metal* Gießbett *n*; **~boat** *Am sl* U-Boot *n*; **~-breeder** Schweinezüchter *m*; **~-breeding** Schweinezucht *f*; **~-copper** Rohkupfer *n*; **~gery** ['-əri] Schweinezüchterei *f*; Schweinestall *m a. fig pej, fam* Saustall, -laden *m*; Schweinerei, Sauerei *f*; **~gish** ['-iʃ] schweinisch, säuisch; gierig; **~gy** ['-i] Schweinchen *n*; *Am sl* Zehe *f*; *~~-back* huckepack; *~~ bank* Sparschweinchen *n*; **~headed** ['-'--] *a* verbohrt, halsstarrig, störrisch, *fam* stur; **~headedness** Verbohrtheit, Halsstarrigkeit, *fam* Sturheit *f*; **~-iron** Roheisen *n*; **~let** ['-lit], **~ling** ['-liŋ] Schweinchen *n*; **~nut** *bot* Nußkümmel *m*; Erdkastanie, -nuß; *Am* Hickorynuß *f*; **~pen** Schweinestall *m*; **~skin** Schweinsleder *n*; *sl* Sattel *m*; *sl sport* Leder *n*; **~sticker** Hirschfänger; Schweineschlächter; Wildschweinjäger *m*; **~sticking** Sauhatz *f*; Schlachtfest, (Schweine-)Schlachten *n*; **~sty** Schweinestall; *fig pej* Schweine-, Saustall *m*; **~tail** Hängezopf *m*; Tabakrolle *f*; **~-trough, -tub** Schweinetrog *m*; **~wash** Drang *m*, Küchenabfälle *m pl (als Schweinefutter)*; *fig pej* Abwasch-, Spülwasser, Gesöff *n*.

pigeon ['pidʒin] *orn* Taube *f*; *fig* Täubchen *n*; *sl pej* Gimpel *m (Mensch)*; *carrier, homing ~* Brieftaube *f*; *clay-~* Tontaube *f*; *cock-~* Täuberich *m*; *wild ~* Wildtaube *f*; **~-breast** *med* Hühnerbrust *f*; **~-breeder, -fancier** Taubenzüchter *m*; **~-hawk** Sperber; Hühnerhabicht; *Am* Merlinfalke *m*; **~-hearted** *a* bange, ängstlich; **~hole** *s* Taubenloch *n*; (Ablege-, Brief-, Post-)Fach *n*; *tr (Papiere)* ablegen, einordnen; ordnen, klassifizieren; zurücklegen, aufheben (*for* für); beiseite legen, zurückstellen; unerledigt lassen, auf-, *fam* auf die lange Bank schieben, hinauszögern, *fam* ad acta, auf Eis legen; **~-house, -loft, ~ry** ['-ri] Taubenschlag *m*, -haus *n*; **~-livered** *a* feige; **~-toed** *a* mit einwärtsgekehrten Zehen.

pigment ['pigmənt] *biol* (Haut-)Pigment *n*; (unlöslicher) Farbstoff *m*, Farbe *f (in Pulverform)*; **~al** [pig'mentl], **~ary** [-əri] *a* Pigment-; **~ation** [pigmen'teiʃən] *biol med* Pigmentierung *f*.

pigmy *s. pygmy.*

pike [paik] *s* Pike *f*, Spieß *m*; (Speer-)Spitze *f*; *zoo* Hecht *m*; *(turn~)* Zollschranke *f*, Schlagbaum *m*; Mautstraße *f*; Straßen-, Wegzoll *m*; *Am* (Berg-)Spitze *f*; *Am pej* Hinterwäldler *m*; *tr* aufspießen; *itr Am sl* bescheiden *od* vorsichtig spielen *od* spekulieren; *Am sl (to ~ along)* flitzen, sausen; **~let** ['-lit] *Art* Teegebäck *n*; **~man** ['-mən] *mil hist* Pikenträger; *min* Häuer; Zolleinnehmer *m*; **~r** ['-ə] *Am sl* arme(r) Schlucker; Drückeberger; kleinliche(r) Mensch, Knicker; vorsichtige(r) Spieler *m*; **~staff**: *as plain as a ~~* sonnenklar.

pilaster [pi'læstə] *arch* Pilaster *m*.

pilch [piltʃ] Dreieckswindel *f*.

pilchard ['piltʃəd] *zoo* Sardine *f*.

pile [pail] **1.** *s* (Ramm-)Pfahl, Pfosten; (Brücken-)Pfeiler *m*; *tr* Pfähle schlagen *od* treiben in; mit Pfählen, Pfeilern stützen; **~-bent** Pfahljoch *n*; **~-bridge** Jochbrücke *f*; **~-driver** Pfahlramme *f*; **~-dweller** Pfahlbaubewohner *m*; **~-dwelling** Pfahlbau *m*; **~-grating** Pfahlrost *m*; **~-worm** Bohrwurm *m*; **piling** ['-iŋ] Verpfählung; Pfahlkonstruktion *f*; Pfähle *m pl*; **2.** *s* Haufen, Stoß, Stapel; Holzstoß; *(funeral ~)* Scheiterhaufen; (Kohlen-)Meiler; Häuserblock, Gebäudekomplex; *fam* (großer) Haufen *m*, Menge, Masse *f*; *sl (~ of money)* Haufen *m*, Masse *f* Geld; Riesenvermögen *n*; *el* galvanische Säule; Trokkenbatterie *f*; *(atomic, chain-reaction ~)* Atommeiler, Kernreaktor *m*; *tr (to ~ up)* aufhäufen, -stapeln, -türmen, anhäufen; (schwer) beladen; *itr (to ~ up)* e-n Haufen bilden, sich anhäufen, sich ansammeln; wimmeln; *to ~ in, to ~ up (aero sl)* Kleinholz machen; *mot* aufea.prallen; *to make o.'s ~ (fam)* sein Schäfchen ins trockene bringen (*in* mit, durch); *to ~ on the agony (fam)* die Sache (noch) schlimmer machen, als sie (schon) ist; *to ~ arms* die Gewehre zs.setzen; *to ~ it on (fam)* dick auftragen, übertreiben; *~ of arms* Gewehrpyramide *f*; **~-cloud** Haufenwolke *f*; **~-up** Massensturz *m*, -karambolage *f*; Autounfall *m*; **3.** *(Textil)* Noppe(nfläche) *f*; weiche(s) Haar, Fell *n*, Pelz *m*, Wolle, Daune *f*; Flor *m*; **4.** *pl. med* Hämorrhoiden *f pl*.

pilfer ['pilfə] *tr itr* stehlen, *fam* mausen, mopsen, stibitzen; **~age** ['-ridʒ], **~ing** ['-riŋ] Mausen *n*; Dieberei *f*, kleine(r) Diebstahl *m*; **~er** ['-rə] (kleiner) Dieb *m*.

pilgrim ['pilgrim] Pilger; Wanderer, Wandersmann; *Am* Neuankömmling *m*; *the P~s, the P~ Fathers (hist)* die Pilgerväter *m pl*; **~age** ['-idʒ] Pilger-, Wallfahrt *f* (*to* nach).

pill [pil] *s pharm* Pille, Tablette; *fig (bitter ~)* bittere Pille *f*; *sl sport* Ball *m*; *sl* (Billard-, Kanonen-)Kugel; *sl* Nervensäge *f*, Ekel *n*; *tr* (bei der Wahl) durchfallen lassen, ablehnen, nicht wählen; mit Pillen behandeln; *to gild the ~ (fig)* die Pille versüßen; *to swallow the ~ (fig)* die (bittere) Pille schlucken; *a ~ to cure an earthquake* ein Tropfen auf den heißen Stein; **~-box** Pillenschachtel; *mil* betonierte(r) MG-Stand, kleine(r) Betonbunker *m*; **~-bug** *zoo* Rollassel *f*.

pillag|e ['pilidʒ] *s* Plünderung, Beraubung; Beute *f*; *tr* plündern, (be-)rauben; *itr* plündern, rauben.

pillar ['pilə] *s* Pfeiler; Ständer *m*, Säule *a. fig*, Stütze *f*; *tr* mit Pfeilern abstützen; *driven from ~ to post (fig)* (ab-, hin u. her)gehetzt; *the P~s of Hercules* die Säulen *f pl* des Herkules; **~-box** Briefkasten *m*; **~ed** ['-d] *a* mit Pfeilern (abgestützt); säulenförmig; *bot* gestielt; **~-tap** *tech* Standhahn *m*.

pillion ['piljən] (zusätzliches) Sattelkissen *n*; *Br mot* Soziussitz, *fam* Sozius *m*; *to ride ~* (auf dem) Sozius (mit)fahren; im Damensitz mitreiten; **~ passenger** Soziusfahrer(in *f*) *m*.

pillory ['piləri] *s* Pranger, Schandpfahl *m*; *tr* an den Pranger stellen *a. fig*; *fig* anprangern; *in the ~* am Pranger.

pillow ['pilou] *s* Kopfkissen, -polster; *tech* (Zapfen-)Lager *n*; *(Mikroskop)* Stativsäule *f*; *tr* (aufs Kopfkissen) legen; als Kopfkissen dienen für; *to ~ up* hoch betten; *to take counsel of o.'s ~* e-e S beschlafen; **~-case, -slip** Kopfkissenbe-, -überzug *m*; **~-fight** Kissenschlacht *f*; **~-lace** Klöppelspitze *f*.

pilos|e ['pailous], **pilous** ['piləs] *bot zoo* (fein) behaart, flaumbedeckt.

pilot ['pailət] *s mar* Lotse; *aero* Pilot, Flugzeugführer; *fig* Führer *m*; *tech* Steuergerät *n*; Zündflamme, Kontrollampe *f*; *attr* Führungs-, Leit-; Versuchs-; *tr* lotsen; steuern; *aero* führen; *to drop the ~* den Lotsen absetzen; *fig* e-n bewährten Ratgeber gehen lassen; *automatic ~ (tech)* Selbststeuergerät *n*; *gyro-~* Kreiselsteuergerät *n*; *second ~* Kopilot *m*; **~age** ['-idʒ] Lotsendienst *m*, -geld *n*; *aero* Führung(stechnik); *fig* Führung, Lenkung *f*; *compulsory ~~* Lotsenzwang *m*; **~ balloon** Pilot-, *mete* Registrierballon *m*; **~ biscuit, bread** *Am* Schiffszwieback *m*; **~ boat** Lotsenboot *n*; **~ burner** Sparbrenner *m*; **~-cloth** *(Textil)* Flausch, Fries *m*; **~ engine** Leerlokomotive *f*; **~-fish** Lotsenfisch *m*; **~ flag** Lotsenflagge *f*; **~ instructor** Fluglehrer *m*; **~ jet** *tech* Leerlaufdüse *f*; **~ lamp** Kontroll-, Signal-, Warnlampe *f*; **~less** ['-lis] führerlos, unbemannt; **~ light** Zünd-, Kontroll-, Sparflamme *f*; *aero* Leitscheinwerfer *m*; **~ officer** *Br* Fliegerleutnant *m*; **~ pin** Führungsstift *m*; **~ plant** Versuchsanlage *f*; **~ scheme** Versuchsprojekt *n*; **~ school** Flugzeugführerschule *f*; **~'s licence** Flugzeugführerschein *m*; **~ stage** Entwicklungsstadium *n*; **~ train** Vorzug *m*; **~ trainee** Flugschüler *m*; **~ training** Flugzeugführerausbildung *f*.

pimento [pi'mentou] *pl -os* Piment, Nelken-, Jamaikapfeffer; Pimentbaum *m*.

pimp [pimp] *s* Kuppler(in *f*); *Am sl* Strichjunge *m*; *itr* Kuppelei treiben.

pimpernel ['pimpənel] *bot (common ~)* Pimpernelle, Bibernelle *f*; *(scarlet ~)* Gauchheil *m*.

pimpl|e ['pimpl] Pickel *m*, Pustel *f*, Mitesser *m*; Eiterbläschen *n*; **~ed** ['-d], **~y** ['-i] pick(e)lig, unrein.

pin [pin] *s* (Steck-)Nadel; Anstecknadel, Brosche *f*; *fam* Abzeichen *n*; *tech* Pinne *f*, Stift, Dorn, Bolzen *m*, (Reiß-)Zwecke *f*, Nagel, Kegel, Splint; *(Geige)* Wirbel; Kegel *m (des Spiels)*; *fig* Kleinigkeit *f*; *pl fam* Beine *m pl*; *tr* mit e-r Nadel, e-m Stift befestigen; festmachen, (an)heften, anstecken; (mit e-r Nadel) stechen, *fam* pik(s)en; (fest)halten; einklemmen; drücken (*against, to* gegen); *s.th. on s.o.* jdm etw zur Last legen, *fam* ankreiden; *to ~ down* niederhalten *a. mil*; *fig* festlegen, *fam* -nageln (*to* auf); *mil* fesseln; *to ~ on* anstecken (*for* an); sich anstecken; *to ~ together* zs.heften; *to ~ up* aufspießen; *(Saum)* abstecken; *(Haar)* aufstecken; mit Reißzwecken befestigen; *(Notiz)* anschlagen; *for two ~s* um e-e Kleinigkeit; *to sit on, to be ~s and needles* wie auf Nadeln, wie auf glühenden Kohlen sitzen; *to ~ o.'s ears back (sl)* die Ohren spitzen; *s.o.'s* jdn am Boden zerstören; *to ~ o.'s faith on, to* sein Vertrauen setzen, sich völlig verlassen auf; *to pull the ~* die Arbeit *od* Familie im Stich lassen; *I have (got) ~s and needles in my feet* mir sind die Füße eingeschlafen; *I don't care a ~* das ist mir (ganz) egal, einerlei, *fam* schnuppe, Wurst; *neat as a new ~* blitzsauber; *clothes-~ (Am)* Wäscheklammer *f*; *drawing-* Reißnadel *f*; *hair-~* Haarnadel *f*; *hat-~* Hutnadel *f*; *knitting ~* Stricknadel *f*; *neat as a new ~* (funkel)nagelneu; *nine-~* Kegel *m (des Spiels)*; *rolling-~* Teigrolle *f*, Wellholz *n*; *safety ~* Sicherheitsnadel *f*; *scarf-, tie-~* Krawattennadel *f*; *split ~* Splint *m*; **~afore** ['-əfɔ:] Kinder-, Kittelschürze *f*, Schürzenkleid *n*; **~ball machine** *Art* Spielautomat *m*; **~-bone** Hüftknochen *m*; **~ boy** *Am* Kegeljunge *m*; **~-cushion** Nadelkissen *n*; **~-feather** *orn* Stoppelfeder *f*; **~-head** Stecknadelknopf *m a. fig*; *fig* winzige(s) Bißchen *n*; Kleinigkeit *f*; Dummkopf *m*; **~-hole** winzige(s) Loch; Zapfenloch *n*; **~-money** Nadelgeld *n*; *com* Saison-, Heimarbeiterlohn *m*; **~-point** *s* Nadelspitze *f*; etwas völlig Belangloses, Unwichtiges *n*; *tr (Ziel)* markieren; genau treffen; *a* Punkt-; haarscharf; *~~ bombing (aero)* Bomben-, Punktzielwurf *m*; *~~ target* Punktziel *n*; **~-prick** Nadelstich *m a. fig*; *fig* spitze Bemerkung, kleine Schikane *f*; **~ punch** *tech* Durchschlag *m*; **~-stripe** *(Textil)* feine(r) helle(r) Streifen *m*; **~-tab** Fähnchen *n*; **~-table** *Art* Spielautomat *m*; **~-tooth** Stiftzahn *m*; **~-tuck** schmale Zierfalte *f*; **~-up** *s* hübsche(s) Mädchenphoto *n (in e-r Zeitung)*; *a* bevorzugt; hübsch; *~~ girl* Bild *n* e-s hübschen Mädchens *n*; **~-wheel** Windmühle *f (Spielzeug)*; Feuerrad *n*; **~-worm** *zoo* Pfriemenschwanz, Springwurm *m*.

pince-nez ['pɛ̃:nsnei] *opt* Kneifer, Klemmer, *fam* Zwicker *m*.

pincer|s ['pinsəz] *pl* (Kneif-, Beiß-) Zange; *med* Pinzette; *zoo* (Krebs-) Schere *f*; **~ movement, attack** *mil* Zangenbewegung *f*, -angriff *m*; **~shaped** *a* zangenförmig.

pinch [pintʃ] *tr* kneifen, zwicken; (ein-) klemmen, quetschen; *(Schuh, Kleidung)* zu eng sein (*s.o.* jdm), drücken; *fig* bedrücken, beklemmen; in die Enge treiben; darben lassen, kurz halten; *sl* klauen, stibitzen, mausen; *sl* in Nummer Sicher bringen, hinter Schloß u. Riegel setzen, einsperren; *mar* dicht am Wind halten; *to be ~ed* umkommen (*with hunger* vor Hunger); vergehen (*with cold* vor Kälte); *(for money)* in Geldnöten, -schwierigkeiten sein; knapp sein (*for, in, of* an); *itr* drücken, kneifen; sich einschränken; knausern, knauserig, geizig sein; Schwierigkeiten machen; *s* Kneifen *n*; Prise, Messerspitzevoll; *fig* Klemme, Enge, Schwierigkeit; Not(fall *m*) *f*, Druck; kritische(r) Augenblick *m*; *sl* Verhaftung; *sl* Klauerei *f*, Diebstahl; Knick *m*, Falte *f*; *to ~ off* abkneifen, abquetschen; *to ~ out (Pflanzentrieb)* auskneifen; *at, (Am) in a ~* in e-r schwierigen Lage; im Notfall; zur Not; in der Not; *to have ~ed o.'s finger* sich den Finger eingeklemmt haben; *to give s.o. a ~* jdn kneifen; *that's where the shoe ~es (fig)* da drückt der Schuh, das ist der wunde Punkt; *if it comes to the ~* notfalls; im kritischen Augenblick; *a ~ of salt, snuff* e-e Prise Salz, (Schnupf-)Tabak *m*; **~-bar** Brechstange *f*; **~-beck** *a* unecht; billig, minderwertig; *s* Tombak *m*; *fig* Talmi *n*; Schund, Tinnef, Plunder *m*; **~-cock** *tech* Quetschhahn *m*; **~ed** [-t] *a* zs.gedrückt; eng, schmal; schmächtig; hager; *~~ with cold* blaugefroren; **~er** ['-ə] Kneifende(r); *fig* Knauser, Knicker, Geizhals *m*; **~-hit** *itr Am* einspringen, eintreten (*for s.o.* für jdn), ersetzen (*for s.o.* jdn); *for s.o.* an jds Stelle treten; **~-hitter** *Am* (Stell-)Vertreter, Ersatz(mann) *m*.

pine [pain] **1.** Kiefer, Fichte, Föhre; Tanne *f*; Nadelbaum *m*; Pinie *f*; Fichten-, Kiefernholz *n*; *fam* Tannenzapfen *m*; *fam* Ananas *f*; **~al** ['piniəl] tannenzapfenförmig; *~~ gland (anat)* Zirbeldrüse *f*; **~-apple** Ananas; *sl* Handgranate; kleine Sprengbombe *f*; **~-cone, -nut** Kiefern-, Fichten-, Tannenzapfen *m*; **~-grove** Pinien-, Fichten-, Tannenwäldchen *n*; **~-kernel** Kiefernsamen *m*; **~-needle** Kiefern-, Fichten-, Tannennadel *f*; **~-resin** Kiefernharz *n*; **~ry** ['-əri] Kiefern-, Fichten-, Tannen-, Nadelwald *m*; Ananaspflanzung *f*, -treibhaus *n*; **~-siskin, -finch** *Am* Zeisig *m*; **~-tar** Kienteer *m*; **~-tree** Kiefer; Fichte; Tanne *f*; **~tum** [pai'ni:təm] *pl -ta* [-ə] Kiefern-, Tannenpflanzung *f*; **~-wood** Kiefern-, Fichten-, Tannen-, Nadelwald *m*; **2.** *itr (to ~ away)* umkommen (*with hunger* vor Hunger); vergehen (*with grief* vor Kummer); schmachten, vergehen vor Sehnsucht, sich sehnen (*for, after* nach).

pinfold ['pinfould] *s* Pferch *m*; *tr (Vieh)* einpferchen.

ping [piŋ] *s* Päng, Schwirren, Pfeifen *n*, Aufschlag *m (e-r Kugel)*; *mot* Klopfen *n*; *itr (Kugel)* pfeifen, aufschlagen; sausen, schwirren; *mot* klopfen.

ping-pong ['piŋpɔŋ] *(Warenzeichen)* Tischtennis, *fam* Pingpong *n*.

pinion ['pinjən] **1.** Flügelspitze *f*; Flügel *m*, Schwinge *a. fig*, Schwungfeder *f*; *tr* die Flügel beschneiden (*a bird* e-m Vogel); *(die Flügel)* (fest-) binden; *fig* die Hände binden (*s.o.* jdm); festbinden, fesseln (*to* an); einsperren; *fig* lähmen; **2.** *tech mot* (kleines) Getrieberad, Ritzel *n*.

pink [piŋk] **1.** *s bot* Nelke *f*; Blaßrot *n*; (roter) Jagdrock (der Fuchsjäger); Fuchsjäger *m*; *fig das* Beste, *die* Spitze, *der* Gipfel; *Am pej* Salonbolschewist *m*; *Am sl* Kraftfahrzeugpapiere *n pl*, Fahrerlaubnis *f*; *Am sl* Privatdetektiv *m*; *a* blaßrot; *pol* rosarot; *to be in the ~ (fam)* in bester Verfassung, in Form sein; *the very ~ of perfection* ein Muster *n* der Vollkommenheit; *rose-~* rosenrot, rosa; *salmon-~* lachsrot; **~ish** ['-iʃ] blaßrosa, rötlich *a. pol*; **~ slip** *tr* entlassen; *s* Entlassungsschreiben *n*; **~ tea** *Am fam* vornehmer Kaffeeklatsch *m*; **~y** ['-i] *Am fam* kleine(r) Finger *m*; **2.** *tr (to ~ out) (Leder)* punzen; durchbohren; auszacken; stechen; *(to ~ out)* verschönern, schmücken; **3.** *itr mot* klopfen, klingeln.

pinn|a ['pinə] *pl -ae* [-i:] *zoo* Feder *f*; Flügel *m*; Flosse; *anat* Ohrmuschel; *bot* Fieder *f*; **~ace** ['-is] *mar* Pinasse *f*; **~acle** ['-əkl] *s* Zinne; Fiale *f*, Spitztürmchen *n*; Turmhelm *m*, -spitze; Bergspitze *f*; *fig* Gipfel, Höhepunkt *m*; *tr* mit Zinnen verzieren; krönen, die Spitze bilden (*s.th.* e-r S); *at the ~~ of* auf der Spitze *gen*; **~ate** ['-it], **pennate** ['penit] *zoo bot (Blatt)* gefiedert; **~er, ~y** ['-ə, '-i] *fam* Schürze *f*; **~iped** ['-iped] *zoo* Flossenfüßler *m*, Robbe *f*.

pint [paint] Pinte *f* ($^1/_8$ *Gallone; Br 0,568 l, Am 0,473 l)*.

pintle ['pintl] (Dreh-)Zapfen; *(Steuerruder)* Fingerling *m*; **~-hook** *mot* Zughaken *m*.

pinto ['pintou] *pl -os Am a* (bunt-) scheckig; *s* Scheck(e) *m (Pferd)*; *(~ bean)* bunte Bohne *f*.

pioneer [paiə'niə] *s mil* Pionier *a. fig*; *fig* Vorkämpfer, Bahnbrecher *m*; *itr fig* Pionierarbeit leisten, die Bahn freimachen; den Weg bahnen; *tr (e-n Weg)* eröffnen; den Weg, die Bahn freimachen für; **~ work** Pionierarbeit *f*.

pious ['paiəs] fromm, gottesfürchtig; religiös.

pip [pip] **1.** *s* (Obst-)Kern; *bot* Ableger; *(~pin) sl* Bombenkerl *m*, -sache *f*; *a Am sl* ausgezeichnet, pfundig; **~less** ['-lis] kernlos; **~eroo** ['-əru:] *Am sl a* pfundig, hervorragend; *s* Schönheit *f*; **~ squeak** *sl* Schwachmatikus; miese(r) Kerl *m*, miese(s) Ding *n*; **2.** *(Spielkarten, Würfel, Dominosteine) Br* Auge *n*; *mil sl* Stern *m (Rangabzeichen)*; *(Tannenzapfen)* Deckschuppe; Blüte(nstengel *m*) *f*; **3.** Pips *m (Geflügelkrankheit)*; *hum* Wehwehchen *n*; *sl* miese Stimmung *f*; *I've the ~* mich ekelt alles an; ich bin nicht auf der Höhe; *that gives me the ~* das kotzt mich an, hängt mir zum Halse raus; **4.** *Br* Piepen *n*, Piepton; *radio* Kurzton *m*; Zeitzeichen; (Radar-)Zeichen *n*, Bildspur *f*; **5.** *tr fam* abblitzen, durchsausen lassen; abknallen; abhängen; *(Examen)* versauen; *sport* schlagen, besiegen; *to ~ off* abschalten; *itr: to ~ out* sterben.

pipe [paip] *s* Pfeife *(zum Blasen)*; Orgel-, Signalpfeife *f*; Pfeifenton *m*; Singstimme *f*; *(Vogel)* Ruf *m*; Rohr *n*, Röhre; *anat* (Luft-, Speise-)Röhre; *Am sl* Kehle; (Tabaks-)Pfeife; *com* Pipe *f (großes Faß n Br 477,3 l, Am 397,4 l)*; *fig Am sl* Kinderspiel *n*, Leichtigkeit; *Am sl* Besprechung, Unterredung; *pl* Panflöte *f*; Dudelsack(pfeife *f*) *m*; Atemwege *m pl*; *itr* pfeifen; *allg* quieken, quietschen; *tr (Lied)* pfeifen, anstimmen; schrill ausstoßen, ertönen lassen; heraus-, zs.pfeifen; mit Röhren versehen; durch ein Rohr, *tele* über den Draht leiten; paspelieren; *(Torte)* spritzen; *Am sl* reden, benachrichtigen, ausplaudern, bemerken, beobachten; *to ~ o.'s eye(s)* weinen, *fam* flennen; *put that in your ~ and smoke it (fig)* das kannst du dir hintern Spiegel stecken; *to ~* **away** das Startsignal geben für *(ein Boot)*; *to ~* **down** *tr mar* das Schlußsignal geben für; *itr sl* das Maul halten; klein beigeben; *to ~* **in** *fam* ein Wörtchen mitreden; *to ~* **off** auf die schwarze Liste setzen, ächten, denunzieren; *to ~* **up** *itr* loslegen, anfangen; *bag-~s (pl)* Dudelsack *m*; *blow-~* Blasebalg *m*; *feed-~ (tech)* Speiserohr *n*; *gas-~* Gasrohr *n*; *Pan's ~s (pl)* Panflöte *f*; *water-~* Wasserrohr *n*; *wind-~ (anat)* Luftröhre *f*; *~ of peace* Friedenspfeife *f*; **~-bend** Rohrbiegung *f*; **~-bowl** Pfeifenkopf *m*; **~-burst** Rohrbruch *m*; **~-clay** Pfeifenton *(Material)*; *mil sl* Barras, Kommiß *m*;

~-cleaner Pfeifenreiniger *m*; **~-clip, -clamp** Rohrschelle *f*; **~-coil** Rohrschlange *f*; **~-connection** Rohranschluß *m*; **~ course** *Am sl* leichte Übung *f*; **~-dream** *fam* Wunschtraum, fromme(r) Wunsch *m*, Luftschloß *n*, Wahnidee *f*; **~-fitter** Klempner, Rohrleger *m*; **~-fitting** Rohrmuffe *f*; **~ful** ['-ful] Pfeifevoll *f*; **~ inlet** Saugstutzen *m*; **~-layer** Rohrleger; *Am sl pol* Schieber, Drahtzieher *m*; **~-line** *s* Pipeline, Rohrleitung *f (für Wasser* od *Öl)*; *(~~ for information) Am* Nachrichten-, Informationsquelle; *mil* Nachschublinie *f*; *tr* durch ein Rohr leiten; *in the ~~* unterwegs, im Anzug *od* Kommen; *~~ system* Rohrnetz *n*; **~-organ** Orgel *f*; **~r** ['-ə] Pfeifer *m*; *to pay the ~~* die Zeche bezahlen; für alles gradestehen, die Konsequenzen tragen; **~-socket** Rohrstutzen *m*; **~-stem** Pfeifenrohr *n*; *pl* dünne Beine *n pl*; **~-wall** Rohrwand *f*; **~-wrench** Rohrschlüssel *m*.

pipette [pi'pet] *chem* Pipette *f*.

piping ['paipiŋ] *a* pfeifend; schrill, piepsend; friedlich, ruhig, idyllisch; *s* Pfeifen *n*, Pfiff *m*; Pfeifentöne *m pl*; schrille(r) Ton *m*, schrille Stimme *f*; Rohrnetz *n*, -leitung; *(Konditorei)* Garnitur *f*; feine(r) Zuckerguß(verzierung *f*) *m*; *(Schneiderei)* Biese, Paspelierung *f*; *in the ~ time(s) of peace* in Friedenszeiten; *the ~ times of yore* die gute alte Zeit; **~ hot** kochend, siedend heiß.

pipit ['pipit] *orn* Pieper *m*; Stelze *f*.

pipkin ['pipkin] kleine(r) irdene(r) Topf *m*.

pippin ['pipin] Pippinapfel; (Obst-)Kern; *sl* Bombenkerl *m*, -sache *f*, hübsche(r) Käfer *m*; **~-faced** *a* pausbäckig.

piqu|ancy ['pi:kənsi] *(Speise)* Pikantheit; *fig* Interessantheit *f*, Reiz *m*; **~ant** ['-t] pikant, appetitanregend; *fig* anregend, reizvoll, interessant; **~e** [pi:k] *s* (heimlicher) Groll, *fam* Pik *m*; plötzliche(s) Unlustgefühl *n*; *tr* (auf)reizen, verärgern, herausfordern; erregen; *to ~~ o.s. (up)on* sich etw zugute tun, stolz sein auf, sich brüsten mit; *to take a ~~ against s.o.* e-n Pik auf jdn haben.

pira|cy ['paiərəsi] Piraterie, Seeräuberei *f*; *fig* unberechtigte(r) Nachdruck; geistige(r) Diebstahl *m*; **~te** ['-rit] *s* Seeräuber, Pirat *m*; Piratenschiff *n*; Plagiator, Nachdrucker *m*; *itr* Seeräuberei, Piraterie treiben; geistigen Diebstahl begehen; *tr* rauben; plündern *a. fig*; (unberechtigt) nachdrucken; *radio (Welle)* unerlaubt benutzen; *~~ edition* Nachdruck *m*; *~~ listener* Schwarzhörer *m*; **~tic(al)** [pai'rætik(əl), pi-] *a* Piraten-, Raub-.

piragua [pi'rægwə], **pirogue** [-'roug] *mar* Piroge *f*, Einbaum *m*.

pirouette [piru'et] Pirouette *f*.

pisciculture ['pisikʌltʃə] Fischzucht *f*.

pish [piʃ] *interj* pfui! *s* Pfui *n*.

piss [pis] *itr* pissen; *s* Pisse *f*, Urin *m*; **~ed** [-t] *a sl* besoffen, voll; *~~ off (Am sl)* verärgert, erschöpft, unglücklich.

pistachio [pis'tɑ:ʃiou] *pl -os* Pistazie(nnuß) *f*.

pistil ['pistil] *bot* Fruchtknoten, Stempel *m*.

pistol ['pistl] *s* Pistole *f (Waffe)*; *tr* mit e-r Pistole erschießen; **~ grip, holster, shot** Pistolengriff *m*, -tasche *f*, -schuß *m*.

piston ['pistən] *tech* Kolben, Stempel, Bolzen *m*; **~-bearing** Kolbenlager *n*; **~-displacement** Kolbenverdrängung *f*, Hubraum *m*; **~-engine** Kolbenmotor *m*; **~-packing** Kolbenpackung, -liderung *f*; **~-pin** Kolbenbolzen *m*; **~-ring** Kolbenring *m*; **~-rod** Kolbenstange *f*; **~-stroke** Kolbenhub *m*; **~-wrench** Kolbenschlüssel *m*.

pit [pit] **1.** *s* Grube *f*, (Erd-)Loch *n*, Mulde, Vertiefung, Höhle *f*; Abgrund *m*; (Schacht *m* e-r) (Kohlen-)Grube, Zeche; Fallgrube; Hölle; *(working ~)* Arbeitsgrube; *fig* Grube, Falle *f a. sl mil (Bett)*; *fig* Abgrund *m*, Tiefe *f*; (Hirsch-)Graben, (Bären-)Zwinger; Kampfplatz *m (bei Hahnenkämpfen)*; *mot* Box *f*; *theat Br* Parterre, Parkett *n*; Orchesterraum *m*; *agr* (Kartoffel-)Miete; *Am com* Börse(nplatz *m*) *f*; *mil* Geschützstand *m*, Schützenloch *n*; *med* Vertiefung, Delle; (Magen-)Grube; (Pocken-)Narbe *f*; *tr agr* einmieten; Gruben graben in; *(Metall)* durchbohren; mit Narben überziehen; *tech* anfressen, angreifen; *(Hähne)* mitea. kämpfen lassen; ausspielen *(against* gegen); ea. gegenüberstellen; *to ~ o.s. against* sich messen mit; *arm-~* Achselhöhle *f*; *chalk-, clay-, coal-~* Kalk-, Ton-, Kohlengrube *f*; *refuse ~* Müllgrube *f*; **~-bracer** Grubenholz *n*; **~fall** Fallgrube *f*, *fig* -strick *m*; *fig* Falle *f*; **~-head** *min* Schachteingang *m*, Grubenhalde *f*; **~man** ['pitmən] *min* Bergmann, -arbeiter, Häuer *m*; **~-prop** *min* Stempel *m*; **~-saw** Schrotsäge *f*; **~ted** ['-id] *a* mit Narben (versehen); pockennarbig; **2.** *Am s* Stein *m (e-r Steinfrucht)*; *tr (Frucht)* entsteinen.

pit-(a-)pat ['pitə'pæt] *adv*: *to go ~* schnell klopfen, schlagen, trappeln; *s* Ticktack, Klippklapp *n*.

*

pitch [pitʃ] **1.** *tr* errichten, aufstellen; *(Zelt)* aufschlagen; werfen, schleudern, stoßen; aufladen; festsetzen, -legen; *(e-n Trumpf)* machen, bestimmen; *mus (Ton)* angeben; *(Instrument)* stimmen; *fig (Erwartungen)* hochschrauben; *Am sl* auf der Straße verhökern, anpreisen; *(e-e Party)* geben; *itr* ein Lager aufschlagen, Stellung beziehen; der Länge nach hinfallen, hinschlagen; verfallen *(on, upon* auf); (aus)wählen *(on, upon s.th.* etw); sich festlegen *(on, upon* auf), sich entscheiden *(on, upon* für); vornüberneigen, -kippen; *(to ~ down) aero* abkippen; *(Schiff)* stampfen; *fam* herfallen, sich hermachen *(into* über); *(mit Worten)* fertigmachen *(into s.o.* jdn); *Am sl* als Straßenverkäufer tätig sein, sich ins beste Licht setzen, übertreiben, aufschneiden; *to ~ in (fam)* sich schwer ins Zeug legen, sich tüchtig 'ran, an die Arbeit machen; loslegen, zupacken; *to ~ out* hinauswerfen; *to ~ upon* sich entscheiden für; *s* Wurf, Stoß *m*; Wurfweite, -höhe; Gesamtlänge; *mus* Tonhöhe; *fig* Höhe *f*, Grad *m*, Stufe *f*, Standort *m*; *fig Am sl* Annäherungsversuch *(for* an), Plan, Gesichtspunkt *m*; Neigung(swinkel *m*) *f a. geol arch*, Abfall *m*; (Dach-)Schräge; *tech* Steigung, Steig-, Ganghöhe *f*; Abstand, Zwischenraum *m (Rad, Schraube)*; *(Schiff)* Stampfen *n*; Stand(platz) *m (e-s Straßenhändlers)*; Warenangebot *n*, Anpreisung *f*; *sl* Rastplatz *m*; *(Kricket)* (Mittel-)Feld *n*; *at the ~ of her voice* so laut sie konnte; *to fly a high ~ (fig)* hoch hinauswollen, hochfliegende Pläne haben; *to queer s.o.'s ~* jds Pläne durchkreuzen; *to ~ it strong (fam)* aufschneiden, übertreiben; *to ~ o.'s tent (fig)* s-e Zelte aufschlagen, sich niederlassen, ansässig werden; *to ~ a yarn (fam)* e-e Geschichte vom Stapel lassen, ein Seemannsgarn spinnen; *excitement was raised to the highest ~* die Erregung hatte ihren Höhepunkt erreicht; *concert, philharmonic ~ (mus)* Pariser Kammerton *m*; *~-and-toss (Münze)* Kopf oder Schrift; **~ angle** Steigungswinkel *m*; **~-circle** *tech* Teilkreis *m*; **~ed** [-t] *a*: *~~ battle* regelrechte Schlacht *f*; **~er** ['-ə] Werfende(r), Werfer *m*; *Am* Kanne *f*, Krug *m*; **~fork** *s* Heu-, Mistgabel; Stimmgabel *f*; *tr* mit der Heugabel werfen *od* wenden; *fig (Menschen)* plötzlich versetzen *(into a position* in e-e Lage); hineinlancieren *(into a job* in e-e Stellung); **~man** ['-mən] *Am fam* Straßenhändler; Ansager *m* beim Werbefernsehen; **~-pipe** *mus* Stimmpfeife *f*; **~ speed** *aero* Steigungsgeschwindigkeit *f*; **2.** *s* Pech *n*; *tr* verpichen; *mar* teeren; *who touches ~ shall be defiled (prov)* wer Pech angreift, besudelt sich; *as dark as ~* schwarz wie die Nacht; *mineral ~* Erdpech *n*; **~-black** pechschwarz; **~-blende** ['-blend] Pechblende *f*; **~-dark** stockfinster; **~pine** *bot* Pechkiefer *f*; **~y** ['-i] mit Pech beschmiert; pechartig; pechschwarz.

piteous ['pitiəs] kläglich, jämmerlich.

pith [piθ] Mark *a. fig*; *med* Rückenmark *n*; *(Orange)* Haut *f*; *fig* Kern *m*, Substanz *f*, *das* Wesentliche, Quintessenz; Kraft, Stärke; Bedeutung *f*; **~ helmet** Tropenhelm *m*; **~iness** ['-inis] *fig* Kraft; Gedrängtheit *f*, Gehalt *m*; **~y** ['-] markig; *fig (Stil)* gedrängt; inhaltsreich, gehaltvoll, kraftvoll; *~~ sayings (pl)* Kraftsprüche *m pl*.

piti|able ['pitiəbl] bemitleidenswert; erbärmlich, jämmerlich, verächtlich; **~ful** ['-ful] mitleidig, mitleidsvoll; bemitleidens-, bejammernswert; erbärmlich, jämmerlich; **~less** ['-lis] mitleids-, erbarmungslos, unbarmherzig; **~lessness** ['-lisnis] Unbarmherzigkeit *f*.

pittance ['pitəns] (knappe) Zuteilung *f*; kleine(r) Betrag *od* Anteil *m*, Bißchen *n*; Hungerlohn *m*.

pituitary [pi'tju(:)itəri] *physiol* schleimig, Schleim-; Hypophysen-; **~ gland, body** *anat* Hypophyse *f*.

pity ['piti] *s* Mitleid, Erbarmen, Bedauern *n*; Jammer *m*; *tr* bemitleiden, bedauern; *in ~ of, out of ~* aus Mitleid; *to be in ~ of, to feel ~ for, to have, to take ~ on* Mitleid haben mit; *I ~ you* Sie tun mir leid; *what a ~!* wie schade! *it's a ~ (a thousand pities) that* es ist (ewig) schade, daß; *the ~ is that* es ist ein Jammer, daß; *for ~'s sake!* um('s) Himmels, um Gottes willen! **~ing** ['-iŋ] mitleidig.

pivot ['pivət] *s* Drehpunkt; (Dreh-)Zapfen *m*; Achse; (Tür-)Angel *f*; *mil* Flügelmann; *(~ing point)* Schwenkungspunkt; *fig* Dreh-, Angelpunkt *m*; Schlüsselfigur; Drehung, Kreisbewegung *f*; *a = ~al*; *tr* mit (e-m) Drehzapfen, mit Angeln versehen; drehbar lagern; schwenken; *itr* drehbar gelagert sein *(on* auf); sich drehen *(on, upon* um) *a. fig*; **~al** ['-l] als Zapfen, Achse dienend; Kardinal-, Haupt-; entscheidend, lebenswichtig; *the ~~ question* die Kernfrage; **~-arm** Schwenkarm *m*; **~-bearing** Zapfen-, Drehlager *n*; **~-bridge** Drehbrücke *f*; **~-industry** Schlüsselindustrie *f*; **~-pin** *mot* Achsbolzen *m*; **~ position**

Schlüsselstellung *f*; **~-ring** Drehring *m*; ~ **tooth** Stiftzahn *m*.

pix [piks] **1.** *s. pyx*; **2.** *pl (pictures) Am fam* Kino *n*; *(Zeitung)* Bilder *n pl*, Illustrationen *f pl*.

pixie, pixy ['piksi] Fee *f*, Elf(e *f*) *m*.

pixilated ['piksileitid] *a Am* verwirrt; *fam* durchgedreht, durcheinander; *Am sl* besoffen, blau.

plac|ability [plækə'biliti] Versöhnlichkeit, Nachgiebigkeit *f*; **~able** ['plækəbl] versöhnlich; nachgiebig; **~ate** [plə'keit, *Am* 'pleikeit] *tr* besänftigen, beruhigen; versöhnen; **~atory** ['-kətəri] versöhnend, versöhnlich.

placard ['plækɑ:d] *s* Plakat *n*, Anschlag(zettel) *m*; *tr* mit Plakaten, Zetteln bekleben; anschlagen, plakatieren, durch Anschlag bekanntmachen (*on* auf); *fig* (offen) zur Schau tragen; *itr* Zettel ankleben.

place [pleis] **1.** *s* Platz, Ort *m*, Stelle *f*, Raum *m*, *lit* Stätte; Lage *f*; *geog* Ort; Wohnort, -sitz *m*; Haus *n*, Wohnung *f*; *(~ in the country)* Landhaus; Lokal *n*; Fleckchen *n* Erde; (Sitz-, Theater-) Platz, Sitz *m*; (Schrift-, Buch-)Stelle; *fig* Stelle *f*, Platz *m (in e-r Ordnung, Reihenfolge)*; Stelle, (An-)Stellung *f (im Beruf)*; Stand, Rang *m*; Amt *n*; *fig* Lage *f*; Amtspflichten *f pl*, -geschäfte *n pl*, Aufgabe *f*; **2.** *adv Am fam in Zssgen*: ...wo; **3.** *tr* (auf)stellen, legen, setzen *a. fig (Vertrauen, Hoffnung)* (*in* auf); plazieren; unterbringen, ein-, anstellen; *(Ware)* absetzen; *(Gespräch)* anmelden; *(Geld)* anlegen; *(Geschäft)* abschließen; hintun, hinbringen, einordnen; *(Bestellung)* aufgeben; *(Auftrag)* erteilen; *fig* ein-, abschätzen; identifizieren; **4.** *itr sport (to be ~d)* unter den drei ersten, Besten sein; **5.** *all over the ~* überall, an allen Orten; *any ~ (Am fam)* irgendwo; *at this ~* hier; *com* am hiesigen Platze; *every ~ (Am fam)* überall; *from ~ to ~* von Ort zu Ort; *from this ~ (com)* ab hier; *in ~* an Ort u. Stelle; in Ordnung, angebracht, angemessen; *of s.o.* an jds Stelle, (an)statt jds, anstelle von; (stellvertretend) für jdn; *in all ~s* überall; *in my ~* an meiner Stelle, in meiner Lage; *in the first ~* in erster Linie, vor allem, zunächst (einmal); *no ~ (Am fam)* nirgendwo; *out of ~* nicht am (rechten) Platz; unangebracht; außer Dienst; stellenlos; *some ~ (Am fam)* irgendwo; **6.** *to be s.o.'s ~ to do s.th.* jds Sache, Aufgabe sein, etw zu tun; *to be awkwardly ~d* sich in e-r unangenehmen Lage befinden; *to calculate to five ~s (of decimals)* auf 5 (Dezimal-)Stellen berechnen; *to give ~* Platz machen (*to* für); *to go ~s (Am fam)* e-n Lokalitätenbummel machen; *Am sl* das Rennen machen; *to have lost o.'s ~* nicht mehr wissen, wo man aufgehört hatte zu lesen; *to hold a ~* e-e Stellung bekleiden; *to keep s.o. in his ~* jdn in Schranken halten; *to keep o.'s ~* s-e Stellung behaupten; *to know o.'s ~ (fig)* wissen, wo man hingehört; *to lay, to set a ~ for s.o.* für jdn ein Gedeck auflegen, für jdn decken; *to put s.o. to, in his ~* jdn in s-e Schranken verweisen; jdn zurechtweisen; *to take ~* stattfinden; *to take s.o.'s ~* jds Stelle einnehmen; an jds Stelle treten; **7.** *to ~ to account* in Rechnung stellen; *to ~ to s.o.'s credit* jdm gutschreiben; *to ~ to s.o.'s debit* jdn belasten (*s.th.* mit e-r S); *to ~ on file* zu den Akten nehmen; *to ~ a matter in s.o.'s hands* jdm die Erledigung e-r S übertragen; *to ~ in position* einbauen; *to ~ on record* notieren, auf-, verzeichnen; **8.** *his heart is in the right ~* er hat das Herz auf dem rechten Fleck; *she was out of ~* sie fiel aus dem Rahmen; *there is no ~ for doubt* es besteht kein Anlaß *od* Grund zum Zweifeln; *put yourself in my ~!* versetzen Sie sich in meine Lage! **9.** *birth~* Geburtsort *m*; *decimal ~* Dezimalstelle *f*; *market ~* Marktplatz *m*; *meeting ~* Treffpunkt *m*; *permanent ~* Dauerstellung *f*; *sore ~* wunde Stelle *f*; *watering ~* Badeort *m*; **10.** *~ of abode* Aufenthalt(sort) *m*; *~ of amusement* Vergnügungsstätte *f*; *~ of arrival* Ankunftsort *m*; *~ of business* Geschäft; Büro *n*; *~ of delivery* Zustell-, Erfüllungsort *m*; *~ of destination* Bestimmungsort *m*; *~ of employment, of work* Arbeitsplatz *m*; *~ of origin* Ursprungs-, Herkunfts-, Heimat-, Aufgabeort *m*; *~ of refuge* Zufluchtsort *m*; *~ of residence* Wohnort *m*; *~ of worship* Gotteshaus *n*; Kultstätte *f*; **~-card** Tisch-, Platzkarte *f*; **~-hunter** Stellenjäger *m*; **~-hunting** Stellenjägerei *f*; **~-kick** *(Fußball)* Abschlag *m (vom Tor)*; **~man** ['-mən] *pej* Stelleninhaber *m*; **~ment** ['-mənt] Unterbringung, Plazierung; Verwendung; Anlage, Investition *f*; Arbeitseinsatz *m*; *~~ service* Stellenvermittlung *f*; *~~ test* Einstufungsprüfung *f*; **~-name** Ortsname *m*; **~r** ['-ə] Stellende(r), Setzende(r); Börsen-, Effektenhändler *m*; *Am* (Gold-, Platin-)Ablagerung, Seife *f*; *~~ mining* Gold-, Platinwäscherei *f*; **placing** ['-iŋ] *fin* Anlage *f*.

placebo [plə'si:bou] *pl -os med* Placebo *n*; *fig* Beruhigungspille *f*.

placenta [plə'sentə] *pl -tae* [-i:] *anat* Mutterkuchen *m*.

placid ['plæsid] ruhig, gelassen, gesetzt, still, sanft(mütig); **~ity** [plæ'siditi] Ruhe, Gelassenheit, Gesetztheit, Sanftheit *f*, -mut *m*.

placket ['plækit] *(~ hole)* (Damen-) Rockschlitz *m*, -tasche *f*.

plagiar|ism ['pleidʒjərizm] Abschreiben, Plagiieren; Plagiat *n*; **~ist** ['-ist] Plagiator, literarische(r) Freibeuter *m*; **~ize** ['pleidʒjəraiz] *tr* abschreiben; plagiieren, kopieren, nachahmen.

plagu|e [pleig] *s* (Land-)Plage; (Gottes-)Geißel; *(tödliche)* Seuche; (Beulen-)Pest *f*; *fig* Quälgeist *m*; *fam* Plage *f*, Ärger *m*; *tr* heimsuchen; belästigen, quälen, schinden, peinigen, plagen; *to ~~ the life out of s.o.* jdn grün u. blau ärgern; *~~ on it!* verdammt noch mal! verflucht! verflixt! *~~-spot* Pestbeule *f a. fig*; verseuchte(s) Gebiet *n*; *fig* Schandfleck *m*; **~y** ['-i] *a fam* blöd(e), dumm, ärgerlich; *adv* sehr, äußerst.

plaice [pleis] *pl ~ zoo* Gemeine Scholle *f*, Goldbutt *m*.

plaid [plæd] (viereckiger, wollener) Überwurf *m* (der Schotten); (Wollstoff *m* mit) Schottenmuster *n*.

plain [plein] *a* flach, eben, ohne Hindernisse, offen, glatt; *(Textil)* ungeköpert, ungefärbt, ungemustert, einfarbig, uni; *(Alkohol)* unverdünnt; schmucklos, einfach, schlicht, gewöhnlich, reizlos, hausbacken, derb, platt, nicht schön, häßlich; einfach, unkompliziert, klar, offensichtlich, verständlich, deutlich; *(Essen)* einfach, bürgerlich; unzweideutig, offen, ehrlich, gerade, unverblümt; *(Worte)* unumwunden; *(Wahrheit)* rein, nackt, bloß; *adv* offen (u. ehrlich), frei, geradeheraus; *s* (weite) Ebene, freie Fläche *f*, freie(s) Feld *n*; *pl Am* Prärie *f*; *in ~ clothes* in Zivil; *in ~ English, in ~ word* auf gut deutsch, (frei u.) offen, geradeheraus; *to be ~, to use ~ language with s.o.* jdm die Wahrheit, offen s-e Meinung sagen, offen mit jdm sprechen; *to make ~* deutlich, verständlich machen, zu verstehen geben, klarmachen; *to tell the ~ truth* die volle Wahrheit sagen, reinen Wein einschenken; *I'm a ~ man* ich bin ein einfacher Mann; *that's as ~ as a pikestaff, as ~ as the nose on your face* das ist sonnenklar; ~ **bearing** Gleitlager *n*; **~-chant, -song** *rel* Gregorianische(r) Gesang *m*; **~-clothes man** Geheimpolizist, Detektiv *m*; ~ **country** Flachland *n*; ~ **dealing** aufrichtige, ehrliche, gerade Handlungsweise *f*; **~-dealing** *a* offen, ehrlich, gerade, aufrichtig; ~ **fare** Hausmannskost *f*; **~ly** ['-li] *adv* einfach, klar, offen; deutlich; *to put it ~~* um es klar auszudrücken; **~ness** ['-nis] Einfachheit, Schlichtheit, Gewöhnlichkeit, Reizlosigkeit, Derbheit, Plattheit, Häßlichkeit; Unkompliziertheit, Klarheit, Deutlichkeit; Offenheit, Geradheit, Ehrlichkeit *f*; ~ **sailing** e-e einfache Sache; *pred* (ganz) leicht, einfach; ~ **sewing** Weißnähen *n*; **~sman** ['-zmən] *Am* Präriebewohner *m*; ~ **speaking** freie Meinungsäußerung *f*; **~-spoken** *a* freimütig, offen; ~ **suit** *(Karten)* einfache(s) Spiel *n*; ~ **text** Klartext *m*; ~ **tile** Biberschwanz, Flachziegel *m*.

plaint [pleint] *jur u. poet* Klage; *jur* Beschwerde *f*; **~iff** ['-if] *jur* Kläger(in *f*) *m*, klagende Partei *f*; *joint ~~* Nebenkläger *m*; **~ive** ['-iv] klagend, trauernd, traurig, schmerzlich, kläglich.

plait [plæt, *Am* pleit] *s* Falte; Tresse; Flechte *f*, Zopf *m*; *tr* falten, fälteln; (zu e-m Zopf) flechten.

plan [plæn] *s* Entwurf *m*, Skizze *f*; *(~ view)* Grundriß, (Lage-)Plan *m*; Übersicht(stafel); *fig* Absicht *f*, Vorhaben *n*, Plan *m*, Projekt, Programm; Verfahren(sweise) *f*) *n*, Methode *f*; *itr* planen (*for s.th.* etw); *tr* entwerfen, skizzieren; *(to ~ out)* ausarbeiten, vorplanen; *Am* planen, vorhaben, beabsichtigen, (zu tun) gedenken, erwarten, (er)hoffen; *(Zeit)* einteilen; *to ~ on* rechnen mit, bauen auf; *in ~* im Grundriß; *to ~* nach Wunsch; *five-year ~* Fünfjahresplan *m*; *~ned economy* Planwirtschaft *f*; **~less** ['-lis] planlos; **~ner** ['-ə] Planer; *pej* Pläne-, Projektemacher *m*; **~ning** ['-iŋ] Planung, Ausarbeitung *f*; *family ~~* Geburtenkontrolle *f*; *town ~~* Stadtbebauungsplan *m*; *~~ office* Lenkungsstelle *f*; **~-position indicator** Radarschirm *m*; ~ **view** Draufsicht *f*.

plane [plein] **1.** *a* flach, eben *a. math*; *scient* plan-; *s* (glatte) Fläche, Ebene *f a. fig*; *fig* Niveau *n* (Entwicklungs-) Stufe, Höhe; *aero* Tragfläche *f*; Flugzeug *n*; *min* Förderstrecke *f*; *itr aero* gleiten; *to ~ down (aero)* niedergleiten, -schweben; *on the same ~* auf der gleichen Ebene (*as* wie); *inclined ~ (phys)* schiefe Ebene *f*; *~ of culture* Kulturstufe *f*; *~ of living* Lebensstandard *m*; **~-mirror** Planspiegel *m*; **~-spotter** Luftspäher *m*; **~-table** Meßtisch *m*; *~~ sheet* Meßtischblatt *n*; **~-ticket** Flugkarte *f*; **2.** *s* Verstreichkelle *f (des Maurers)*; Hobel *m*; *tr* verstreichen, hobeln, glätten; planieren; *to ~ off, away, down* ab-, weghobeln; **~r** ['-ə] Verstreicher; Hobler; Hobel (-maschine *f*) *m*; *typ* Klopfholz *n*; **3.** *(~-tree) bot* Platane *f*.

planet ['plænit] *astr* Planet, Wandelstern *m*; **~arium** [plæni'tɛəriəm] Planetarium *m*; **~ary** ['plænitəri] Planeten-; planetarisch; irdisch; in Bewegung (befindlich); *phys* sich in e-r Kreisbahn bewegend; **~~** *gear (mot)* Planetengetriebe *n*; **~oid** ['-ɔid] *astr* Planetoid *m*; **~-wheel** *tech* Planetenrad *n*.

planimet|er [plæ'nimitə] Planimeter *n*; **~ry** [plæ'nimətri] Planimetrie *f*.

planing ['pleiniŋ] *s* (Ab-, Be-)Hobeln; Planieren *n*; *attr* Hobel-; **~-bench** Hobelbank *f*; **~-machine** Hobelmaschine *f*.

planish ['plæniʃ] *tr* schlichten, glätten, polieren; *(Blech)* ausbeulen; *phot* satinieren.

plank [plæŋk] *s* Planke, Bohle, Diele *f*; Brett *n*; *(~ing)* Bohlen(holz *n*) *f pl*; *arch* Träger *m*, Stütze, Grundlage *f*; *Am pol* Grundsatz, (Partei-)Programmpunkt *m*; *tr* mit Planken, Bohlen, Dielen aus-, belegen; beplanken, verschalen; *(Fleisch, Fisch)* auf e-m Brett backen u. servieren; hinlegen; *to ~ down, to ~ out (fam)* blechen, (be)zahlen; *(Geld)* ausspucken; **~ bed** Pritsche *f*; **~ing** ['-iŋ] Bohlen-, Dielenlegen *n*; Bohlen, Dielen *f pl*; Verschalung *f*; *(Brücke)* Belag *m*.

plankton ['plæŋktən] *biol* Plankton *n*.

plant [plɑ:nt] *s bot* Pflanze *f*; *agr* Setzling *m*; Gewächs, Kraut *n*; Blume; *tech* Fabrik *f*, Werk(sanlage *f*) *n*, Betrieb(seinrichtung *f*) *m*; Apparatur, Anlage, Maschinerie *f*, Maschinenpark *m*, Gerät *n*; Gebäude *n pl*; *rail* Betriebsmaterial *n*; *min* Grubenanlage *f*; *sl* Betrug(smanöver *n*), Schwindel (-unternehmen *n*) *m*; Versteck *n*; *sl* Falle, Irreführung *f*, Spitzel *m*; *tr* pflanzen, setzen; fest (auf)stellen, einpflanzen; *(Fahne)* aufpflanzen; *fig* (im Gedächtnis) einprägen, -pflanzen, -impfen; *(Anschauungen, Gewohnheiten)* einbürgern; ansiedeln; (be)gründen, stiften; anlegen, einrichten; bestücken; *(junge Fische, Austern)* setzen; *sl (Schlag)* verpassen, versetzen; *sl (Menschen* od *Sache)* als Täuschung, als Falle aufstellen; *sl (Diebesgut)* hehlen, verstecken, verbergen; *sl (Menschen)* 'reinlegen; *sl (Ware)* andrehen *(on s.o.* jdm); *to ~ o.s.* sich aufstellen, *fam* sich hinpflanzen; *to lose ~* absterben; *assembly ~* Montagewerk *n*; *garden ~* Gartenpflanze *f*; *power ~* Kraftanlage *f*, -werk *n*; *tobacco ~* Tabakpflanze *f*; **~ation** [plæn'teiʃən] (An-)Pflanzung, Plantage *f*; Plantagenbetrieb *m*; Baumschule; *hist* Niederlassung, (An-)Siedlung, Kolonie *f*; *coffee, cotton, sugar ~~* Kaffee-, Baumwoll-, Zuckerplantage *f*; **~ capacity** Betriebskapazität *f*; **~er** ['plɑ:ntə] Pflanzer, Plantagenbesitzer; Siedler, Kolonist; Pionier *m*; Pflanz-, Setzmaschine *f*; **~ facilities** *pl* Betriebseinrichtungen *f pl*; **~-louse** Blattlaus *f*; **~ management** Betriebsführung *f*; **~ protection** Werkschutz *m*.

plantain ['plæntin] **1.** *bot* Wegerich; **2.** *bot* Pisang *m*; (Mehl-)Banane *f*.

plantigrade ['plæntigreid] *a zoo* auf den (Fuß-)Sohlen gehend; *s* Sohlengänger *m*.

plaque [plɑ:k] Platte *f*, Plättchen *n*; (Gedenk-)Tafel; Plakette; Brosche, Anstecknadel; (Ordens-)Schnalle *f*; *med* Fleck *m*, Platte *f*.

plash [plæʃ] **1.** *s* Pfütze *f*, Pfuhl *m*, Sumpfloch *n*; **~y** ['-i] naß, sumpfig; feucht; **2.** *itr* platschen; plätschern; planschen; *tr* platschen, klatschen auf; *s* Klatschen, Platschen; Plätschern *n*; **~y** ['-i] plätschernd, spritzend; feucht, sumpfig; **3.** *tr (Zweige)* mitea. verflechten; zu e-r Hecke flechten.

plasm ['plæzm], **~a** ['plæzmə] *biol min* Plasma *n*; *(proto~)* Protoplasma *n*; **~(at)ic** ['plæzmik, plæz'mætik] *a* Plasma-.

plaster ['plɑ:stə] *s arch* (Ver-)Putz, Bewurf *m*; *(~ paint)* Tünche *f*; *(~ of Paris)* Gips; Mörtel *m*; *med pharm* Pflaster *n*; *Am sl* Banknote, Vorladung *f*, *fig* Schatten *m*; *tr* verputzen, bewerfen, (ver-, ein)gipsen; tünchen; bepflastern, bekleben; *Am sl* verpfänden; *sticking ~* Heftpflaster *n*; **~-board** *arch* Gipsplatte *f*; **~-cast** *(Kunst)* Gipsabguß; *med* Gipsverband *m*; **~ed** ['-d] *sl* besoffen, (sternhagel)voll; **~er** ['-rə] Gipsarbeiter, Gipser, Stukkateur *m*; **~ing** ['-riŋ] (Be-)Pflastern *n*; Bewurf, Verputz *m*; Stukkatur *f*.

plastic ['plæstik] *a* bildend, formend, gestaltend; verformbar, knetbar, plastisch; biegsam, formbar, bildsam *a. fig*; *biol* veränderlich; *physiol (Gewebe)* erneuerungsfähig; *med* plastisch; *s (pl)* Kunststoff *m*, -harz *n*; **~ arts** *pl* bildende Kunst *f*; **~ clay** Knetton *m*; **~ compound** Preßstoff *m*; **~ effect** *phot* Tiefenwirkung *f*; **~ine** ['-si:n] Plastilin *n*, Knetmasse *f*; **~ity** [plæs'tisiti] Formbarkeit, Bildsamkeit; Gestaltungsfähigkeit, Nachgiebigkeit *f*; **~ize** ['plæstisaiz] *tr itr* knetbar, formbar machen *od* werden; **~ operation** *med* Hautplastik *f*; **~s industry** Kunststoffindustrie *f*; **~ surgery** plastische Chirurgie *f*.

plastron ['plæstrən] Brustharnisch; *(Fechten)* Paukschurz *m*.

plat [plæt] **1.** *s* Fleckchen *n* Erde, Stück *n* Land; *Am* Karte *f*, Plan *m*; *tr Am* e-e Karte, e-n Plan machen von; **~band** *arch* Kranzleiste *f*, (erhabener) Streifen, Sturz *m*; Blumenbeet *n*; **2.** *tr* (ver)flechten.

plate [pleit] *s* Platte, Tafel, Scheibe *f*; (Grob-)Blech *n*; Lamelle; (Metall-)Schuppe *f*; Schuppenpanzer *m*; Namens-, Firmen-, Metallschild(chen) *n*; *(Graphik)* Kupfer-, Stahl-, Druckplatte *f*; Kupfer(stich), Stahlstich *m*, Lithographie, Tafel *f*, Einschaltbild *n (in e-m Buch)*; *typ* Stereotypplatte; Bildseite, -tafel; *phot* Platte; *el* Anode, Elektrode; (Geschirr-)Platte *f*; Teller *m*; Tafel-, Silbergeschirr *n*; Tellervoll; *(Mahlzeit)* Gang *m*, Gedeck *n*; *sport* Pokal; Preis *m*; (Pferde-)Rennen *n*; *med (dental ~)* Zahn-, Gaumenplatte *f*; *anat zoo* Blatt *n*; *arch* Querbalken, Träger; *rel* Kollektenteller *m*; *Am sl* gut gekleidete, hübsche Frau *f*; *pl sl* Füße *m pl*; *tr (mit Metall)* überziehen, plattieren, dublieren; *(bes. Schiff)* panzern; *(Papier)* satinieren; *typ* stereotypieren; *dial ~ (tele)* Wählscheibe *f*; *door ~* Türschild *n*; *hot ~* Heizplatte *f*; *identification ~* Erkennungsmarke *f*; *number, (Am) license ~ (mot)* Nummerntafel *f*; *soup, dinner ~* Suppenteller *m*; **~-basket** Besteckkorb *m*; **~-battery** *el* Anodenbatterie *f*; **~-brass** Messingblech *n*; **~-circuit** *el* Anodenstromkreis *m*; **~-clutch** Scheibenkupplung *f*; **~-condenser** *el* Plattenkondensator *m*; **~-cover** Deckel *m (e-r Schüssel)*; **~-covering** Blechbelag *m*; **~-cutter** Blechschere *f*; **~d** ['-id] *a* gepanzert, Panzer-; mit Metall überzogen, plattiert; *chromium-~~* verchromt; *copper-~~* verkupfert; *electro-~~* galvanisiert; galvanisch versilbert; *gold-~~* vergoldet; *nickel-~~* vernickelt; *silver-~~* versilbert; *tin-~~* verzinnt; **~ful** ['-ful] Tellervoll *m*; **~-ga(u)ge** Blechlehre *f*; **~-glass** Dick-, Spiegelglas *n*; **~-glazer** Papiersatinierer *m*; **~-goods** *pl* plattierte, versilberte Ware *f*; **~-holder** *phot* Kassette *f*; **~-iron** Walzblech *n*; **~-layer** *rail* Schienenleger, Streckenarbeiter *m*; **~-lunch** Tellergericht *n*; **~-maker** Blechschmied *m*; **~-mark** Feingehaltsstempel *m*; **~-mill** (Eisen-)Walzwerk *n*; **~-powder** (Silber-)Putzpulver *n*; **~r** ['-ə] *tech* Plattierer *m*; *sport* (schlechtes) Rennpferd *n*; **~-race** *sport* Preisrennen *n*; **~-rack** Geschirrspülkorb *m*; **~-rail** Platt-, flache Schiene *f*; **~-roller** Blechwalzer *m*; **~-rolling mill** (Grobblech-)Walzwerk *n*; **~-shears** *pl* Blechschere *f*; **~-spring** Blattfeder *f*; **~-supply** Anodenspannung *f*; **~-warmer** Tellerwärmer *m*; **~-wheel** Radscheibe *f*.

plateau ['plætou, *Am* -'tou] *pl a.* -x [-z] Hochebene, -fläche *f*, Plateau, Tafelland *n*.

platen ['plætən] *typ* (Druck-)Tiegel *m*, Platte *f*; **~-press** Tiegeldruckpresse *f*; **~(-roller)** Schreibmaschinenwalze *f*.

platform ['plætfɔ:m] Plattform; Hochebene; Terrasse *f*; flache(s) Dach *n*; (Treppen-)Absatz *m*; Rampe *f*; *Br* Bahnsteig *m*; *tech* Laufbühne; *mar* Laufbrücke; *mil* Geschützbettung; *Am rail* Bühne, Wagenplattform *f*; Podium *n*, (Redner-)Tribüne *f*; *pol* (Partei-)Programm *n*; Grundsatzerklärung; *fig* Ebene *f*; *arrival, departure ~* Ankunfts-, Abgangsbahnsteig *m*; *charging-~ (tech)* Beschickungsbühne *f*; *end ~* Kopfbahnsteig *m*; *lifting ~* Hebebühne *f*; *loading-~* Ladebühne *f*; **~-balance** Brückenwaage *f*; **~-barrier** Bahnsteigsperre *f*; **~-car** *Am* Rungen-, offene(r) Güterwagen *m*; **~ refreshment stall** Büfett *n* auf dem Bahnsteig; **~ scale** Brückenwaage *f*; **~-ticket** Bahnsteigkarte *f*; **~-underpass** Bahnsteigunterführung *f*.

plating ['pleitiŋ] Panzerung; Plattierung *f*, Metallüberzug *m*; Beplankung *f*; **~-vat** Galvanisierbottich *m*.

platin|oid ['plætinɔid] *a* platinartig; *s* Platinlegierung *f*, Platinoid *n*; **~um** ['-əm] Platin *n*; **~~** *blonde (fam)* Platinblondine *f*.

platitud|e ['plætitju:d] Plattheit, Seichtheit *f*; Gemeinplatz *m*, Platitüde, Banalität *f*; **~inarian** [-'nɛəriən] Schwätzer *m*; **~inize** [plæti'tju:dinaiz] *itr* seichte Bemerkungen machen, *fam* (dämlich) quatschen; **~inous** [-'tju:dinəs] banal, seicht.

Platonic [plə'tɔnik] platonisch.

platoon [plə'tu:n] *mil* Zug *m*; *allg* Abteilung, Gruppe *f*, Aufgebot; *(Polizei)* Kommando *n*; *(Fußball)* Mannschaft *f*; **~ commander,** *Am* **officer** Zugführer *m*; **~ sergeant,** *Am* **leader** stellvertretende(r) Zugführer *m*.

platter ['plætə] *Am* (Braten-)Platte; flache Schüssel; *Am sl* (Schall-)Platte *f*; *Am sport* Diskus *m*.

plau|dits ['plɔ:dits] *pl* Beifallklatschen *n*, Applaus *m*; **~sibility** [plɔ:zə'biliti] Annehmbarkeit, Überzeugungskraft; Glaub-, Vertrauenswürdigkeit *f*; **~sible** ['plɔ:zəbl] annehmbar, überzeugend, einleuchtend, glaubhaft.

play [plei] **1.** *itr* spielen *a. fig (vom Sonnenlicht, Lächeln: on* auf, *over* über; *at a game* ein Spiel; *with s.o.* mit jdm *a. fig*; *fig on s.o.* sein Spiel mit jdm treiben); *mus* Musik machen, spielen *(on a violin* auf e-r Geige); *theat* spielen, auftreten; *(Musik-, Theater-*

stück) sich spielen lassen, zu spielen sein; tändeln, flirten; *tech* Spielraum haben; Wasser spritzen (*on s.th.* auf etw); beschießen (*on s.th.* etw); **2.** *tr (ein Spiel)* spielen; spielen gegen; *(e-n Spieler)* spielen lassen, einsetzen, verwenden (*as* als); wetten, setzen auf; *(Musik, ein Instrument, ein Theaterstück, e-e Rolle)* spielen; *(auf e-m Instrument)* begleiten; sich benehmen, auftreten als; *(Karte)* ausspielen; *(Theater)* spielen in *(e-r Stadt)*; spielen mit *(e-m Gegenstand)*; *(Licht-, Wasserstrahl)* spielen lassen (*on, over* über); *(Fisch an der Angel)* zappeln lassen; leicht, gewandt umgehen mit, handhaben; *Am sl* hofieren, gehen mit; Geschäftsverbindungen haben mit; **3.** *s* Spiel *n*; Spaß, Scherz *m*; Wette *f*; (Theater-)Spiel, Stück; Spielen *n (des Lichtes)*; freie Bewegung, Bewegungsfreiheit *f*, Spielraum *a. tech*; *fig* Umtrieb *m*, Aktivität, Tätigkeit; Kurzweil *f*; Verhalten *n*, Handlungsweise *f*; **4.** *as good as a* ~ unterhaltsam; *at* ~ beim Spiel; *at the* ~ im Theater; *in* ~ im Spaß, Scherz; *sport* im Spiel; *in full* ~ in vollem Gange; *out of* ~ *(sport)* aus (dem Spiel); **5.** *to allow full* ~ *to s.th.* e-r S freien Lauf lassen; *to bring into* ~ ins Spiel, in Gang bringen; Gebrauch machen von; *to come into* ~ s-e Tätigkeit entfalten; in Tätigkeit treten; *to give free, more* ~ *to s.th.* e-r S freien, mehr Spielraum lassen; *to go to the* ~ ins Theater gehen; *to make a* ~ *for (Am sl)* alles e-m zu Gebote Stehende tun, um zu; allen Charme aufbieten; *to* ~ *ball (Am sl)* zs.arbeiten; *to* ~ *to capacity audience (theat)* vor vollem Haus spielen; *to* ~ *at cards* Karten spielen; *to* ~ *o.'s cards well* das Beste aus der Sache herausholen; *to* ~ *at chess* Schach spielen; *to* ~ *ducks and drakes with s.th.* mit etw verschwenderisch umgehen; *to* ~ *by ear (mus)* nach Gehör spielen; *to* ~ *both ends against the middle* mit allem rechnen; die beiden Gegner gegenea. ausspielen; *to* ~ *fair* fair, ehrlich spielen; sich ordentlich, anständig benehmen; *to* ~ *s.o. false* jdn betrügen, hintergehen, *fam* jdn übers Ohr hauen; *to* ~ *fast and loose* rücksichtslos umgehen mit; *to* ~ *the second fiddle* in untergeordneter Stellung sein; die zweite Geige spielen (*to* bei); *to* ~ *the fool* sich albern benehmen; *to* ~ *football* Fußball spielen; *to* ~ *foul* unfair, falsch spielen; sich schlecht benehmen; *to* ~ *to the gallery* auf die Straße gehen, an den Pöbel appellieren; *to* ~ *the game* die Spielregeln einhalten; *to* ~ *games with s.o. (Am sl)* jdn hereinlegen; *to* ~ *hard (Am)* alle Mittel anwenden; *to* ~ *at hide-and-seek* Versteck spielen; *to* ~ *into the hands of s.o.* jdm in die Hände spielen; *to* ~ *(at) hockey* Hockey spielen; *to* ~ *it (low) on s.o.* jdn ausnützen; *to* ~ *for safety* auf Sicherheit gehen; sich vorsichtig verhalten; *to* ~ *tennis* Tennis spielen; *to* ~ *with edged tools* ein großes Risiko eingehen; *to* ~ *for time* Zeit zu gewinnen suchen; *to* ~ *truant, the wag, (Am) hooky* die Schule schwänzen; **6.** *it* ~*ed on our nerves* es ging uns auf die Nerven; *it is your* ~ Sie sind am Spiel; **7.** *child's* ~ Kinderspiel *n*, leichte, einfache Sache *f*; *fair* ~ ehrliche(s) Spiel; *fig* einwandfreie(s) Verhalten *n*; *foul* ~ regelwidrige(s) Spiel *n*; *fig* Betrug *m*; Gewalt *f*; *as good as* ~ sehr lustig, spaßig; ~ *of colo(u)rs* Farbenspiel *n*; ~ *on words* Wortspiel *n*; *to* ~ **about** herum-, umherspielen (*with s.th.* mit etw); *to* ~ **against** ausspielen gegen; *to* ~ **away** verspielen; *sport* auswärts spielen; *to* ~ **back** *(Platte)* abspielen; *to* ~ **down** geringen Wert beimessen (*s.th.* e-r S); herabsetzen; nicht viel reden über, beschönigen; *to s.o.* sich auf jds Ebene begeben; *to* ~ **for** spielen um (*s.th.* etw; *s.o.* für jdn); *to* ~ **off** *tr sport (Spiel)* beenden; (mit der Hand) abwehren; sich lustig machen über; betrügen um (*on s.o.* jdn); *s.o. against s.o. else* jdn gegen jdn anders ausspielen; *itr* ein Entscheidungsspiel spielen; *to* ~ **on** weiterspielen; *to* ~ **out** zu Ende spielen; mit Musik hinausbegleiten; ~*ed out* ausgespielt, erledigt; verbraucht, erschöpft, *fam* fertig; überholt, veraltet; *to* ~ **to** vorspielen (*s.o.* jdm); *to* ~ **up** *itr* sich (beim Spiel) zs.reißen; dem Beispiel folgen; *tr fam* breittreten, an die große Glocke hängen; besonders herausstellen; *fam* verärgern, aufbringen; *to s.o. (fam)* jdm Honig ums Maul schmieren; sich an jdn anpassen; *with s.th.* etw durcheinanderbringen; *to* ~ **upon** ausnützen (*s.o.* jdn); ~**able** ['-əbl] spielbar; bühnenreif; ~**-actor** *pej* Komödiant *m*; ~**back** Ab-, Rückspielen *n (e-r Tonaufnahme)*; ~**-bill** Theaterzettel *m*, -programm *n*; ~**-book** Textbuch; Schauspielbuch *n*; ~**-box** Spiel(zeug)kiste *f*; ~**-boy** *fam* Lebemann; Luftikus *m*; ~**-day** freie(r) Tag *m*; ~**-debt** Spielschuld *f*; ~**er** ['-ə] Spieler; *theat* Darsteller *m*; *chess-, football-, piano-*~~ Schach-, Fußball-, Klavierspieler *m*; ~~*-piano* elektrische(s) Klavier *n*; ~**fellow** Spielgefährte *m*; ~**ful** ['-ful] zu Scherz aufgelegt; lustig, fidel, spaßig, spaßhaft; ~**fulness** ['-fulnis] Mutwille *m*; Lustigkeit *f*; ~**game** Kinderspiel *n fig*; ~**goer** Theaterbesucher *m*; ~**ground** Spielplatz; Schulhof *m*; ~**house** Theater; *Am* Spielhaus *(für Kinder)*; *Am* Puppenhaus *n*; ~**ing** ['-iŋ] Spiel(en) *n*; ~~*-card* Spielkarte *f*; ~~*-field* Sportplatz *m*; ~**let** ['-lit] *theat* Dramolett *n*, Einakter *m*; ~**mate** Spielgefährte; Partner *m (im Spiel)*; ~**-off** Entscheidungs-, Wiederholungsspiel *n*; ~**-pen** Laufställchen *n*; ~**room** Spielzimmer *n*; ~**-suit** Strandanzug *m*; ~**thing** Spielzeug *n*; ~**time** Spielzeit; Pause *f*; ~**wright** ['-rait] Schauspieldirektor, Bühnenschriftsteller, Dramatiker *m*.

*

plea [pli:] Ausrede *f*, Vorwand *m*, Entschuldigung *f*; Einwand; *jur* Rechts-, Prozeßeinwand *m*, Einrede; *(counter* ~*)* Klagentgegnung, -erwiderung; Verteidigung(seinwand *m*); Rechtfertigung *f*; Prozeß, Rechtsstreit *m*; dringende Bitte *f*, Gesuch *n* (*for* um); *on the* ~ *of* unter dem Vorwand *gen*; *to enter, to put in, to tender a* ~ e-e Einrede erheben *od* einbringen; ~ *of guilty* Schuldbekenntnis *n*; ~ *of nullity* Nichtigkeitseinrede *f*.

plead [pli:d] *itr jur* plädieren, vortragen, verhandeln; *for s.th.* um etw bitten; sich für etw einsetzen, sich für etw verwenden (*with s.o.* bei jdm); anflehen (*with s.o.* jdn); *tr* verteidigen, vertreten; erörtern; einwenden, geltend machen, vorbringen, angeben, behaupten; vorschützen, sich entschuldigen mit; *to* ~ *the cause of s.o.* für jdn eintreten; jds S vertreten; *to* ~ *guilty* sich schuldig bekennen (*to* an); *to* ~ *not guilty* s-e Schuld bestreiten, leugnen; *to* ~ *ignorance* Unkenntnis vorschützen; *to* ~ *for mercy* um Gnade bitten; ~**er** ['-ə] Verteidiger, Fürsprecher; Sachwalter; Prozeßbevollmächtigte(r), Anwalt *m*; ~**ing** ['-iŋ] Plädoyer *n*, Verteidigung *f*; Bitten *n* (*for* um); *pl* Gerichtsverhandlungen *f pl*; Vorverhandlung *f*; Aussagen *f pl* der Prozeßparteien; (vorbereitende) Schriftsätze *m pl*; Prozeßakten *f pl*.

pleas|ant ['pleznt] angenehm, gefällig, erfreulich; umgänglich, liebenswürdig; heiter, fröhlich, lustig, gemütlich; scherzhaft, scherzend; ~**antness** ['plezntnis] Annehmlichkeit; Gemütlichkeit; Liebenswürdigkeit; Heiterkeit, Fröhlichkeit; Scherzhaftigkeit *f*; ~**antry** ['plezntri] Lustigkeit, Ausgelassenheit *f*; Scherz, Spaß *m*; ~**e** [pli:z] *tr* gefallen, angenehm sein (*s.o.* jdm), befriedigen; zufriedenstellen, recht machen; *itr* gefallen, angenehm sein, zufriedenstellen; *iro* geruhen, belieben; *to* ~ *o.s.* nach s-m Belieben tun *od* handeln; *to be* ~*ed* zufrieden sein (*with* mit); froh, erfreut sein (*with* über); *as* ~*ed as Punch* quietschvergnügt; *if you* ~~ denken Sie nur; wenn ich bitten darf; *it* ~*es me* es gefällt mir; *(if you)* ~~ bitte! ~~ *yourself, do as you* ~~ tun Sie ganz nach Belieben! ~~ *be seated* setzen Sie sich, bitte; ~~ *God* so Gott will; *hard to* ~~ wählerisch, anspruchsvoll; ~**ing** ['pli:ziŋ] angenehm; anziehend; ~**urable** ['pleʒərəbl] angenehm, erfreulich; ~**ure** ['pleʒə] Vergnügen *n*, Freude *f*; Gefallen *n*; Zufriedenheit *f*; Genuß *m*; *at* ~~ nach Belieben; *with* ~~ mit Vergnügen; *to afford great* ~~ großes Vergnügen machen; *to have the* ~~ *of doing* das Vergnügen haben, zu tun; *to take* ~~ *in* Gefallen finden an; *business comes before* ~~ zuerst die Arbeit, dann das Vergnügen; ~~*-boat* Vergnügungsdampfer *m*; ~~*-ground* Fest-, Spiel-, Sportplatz *m*; ~~ *party* Ausflug *m*; ~~*-principle (psychol)* Lustprinzip *n*; ~~ *resort* Vergnügungsort *m*; ~~*-trip* Vergnügungsreise *f*.

pleat [pli:t] *s* (Zier-)Falte *f*, Plissee *n*; *tr* in Falten legen, fälteln, plissieren.

pleb [pleb] *sl* Prolet *m*; ~**e** [pli:b] *Am das* (gemeine) Volk; ~**eian** [pli'bi(:)ən] *s hist* Plebejer; Proletarier; Prolet *m*; *a hist* plebejisch; proletarisch; proletenhaft; ~**iscite** ['plebisit, *Am* '-ait] Volksentscheid *m*, -abstimmung *f*.

plectrum ['plektrəm] *pl a. -tra* [-trə] *mus* Plektron *n*.

pledg|e [pledʒ] (Faust-)Pfand *n*, Bürgschaft, Sicherheit *f*; Geisel *m od f*; *fig* Unterpfand; Gelöbnis, Versprechen *n*, Zusage *f*; Trinkspruch, Toast; Novize *m*; *tr* verpfänden, *a. fig* als Pfand geben, versetzen; verpflichten; geloben, zusagen (*s.th.* etw); *s.o.* auf jdn e-n Trinkspruch ausbringen, jdm zutrinken; jdn verpflichten (*to* zu); jdn als Novizen, als neues Mitglied aufnehmen; *to* ~~ *o.s.* sich verbürgen, sich verpflichten (*to do* zu tun); *in* ~~ als, zum Pfand; *under the* ~~ *of secrecy* unter dem Siegel der Verschwiegenheit; *to hold in* ~~ als Pfand haben; *to put, to give in* ~~ als Pfand geben; *to take the* ~~ sich zur Abstinenz verpflichten; *to take in* ~~ als Pfand nehmen; *to take out of* ~~ auslösen; *to* ~~ *o.'s word* sein (Ehren-)Wort geben; *dead* ~~ Faustpfand *n*; *election* ~~ Wahlversprechen *n*; ~~*-holder s.* ~*ee*; ~**ed** [-d] *a* verpflichtet; ~**ee** [ple'dʒi:] Pfandnehmer, -halter, -inhaber, -gläubiger *m*; ~**er,** ~**or** ['-ə, '-ɔ:] Pfandgeber, -schuld-

ner *m*; **~et** ['-it] *med* Tampon *m*; **~ing** ['-iŋ] Verpfändung; Pfandbestellung *f*.
pleistocene ['pli:sto(u)si:n, 'plai-] *geol* Pleistozän *n*.
plen|ary ['pli:nəri] voll(ständig, -kommen); Voll-, Plenar-; *~~ assembly, meeting* Vollversammlung *f*; *~~ indulgence (rel)* vollkommene(r) Ablaß *m*; *~~ powers (pl)* (unbeschränkte) Vollmacht *f*; *~~ session* Voll-, Plenarsitzung *f*; **~ipotentiary** [plenipə'tenʃəri] *a* bevollmächtigt; Vollmacht-; *s* Bevollmächtigte(r) *m*; **~itude** ['plenitju:d] Fülle *f*, Reichtum *m* (*of* an); Vollständigkeit *f*; *~~ of faculties* Vollbesitz *m* der geistigen Kräfte; *~~ of power* Machtvollkommenheit *f*.
plent|eous ['plentjəs] reichlich; **~eousness** ['-jəsnis] (Über-)Fülle *f*, Überfluß *m*; **~iful** ['-iful] reichlich, im Überfluß; **~ifulness** ['-ifulnis] Überfülle *f*, -fluß, Reichtum *m* (*of* an); **~y** ['-i] *s* Reichtum *m*, Fülle *f*, Überfluß *m*; *Am a pred* reichlich, im Überfluß; *adv fam* reichlich; *~~ of* e-e Menge ...; reichlich; sehr viel; *~~ more* e-e Menge mehr; *in ~~* in Hülle u. Fülle, *fam* in rauhen Mengen; *horn of ~~* Füllhorn *n*; *land of ~~* Schlaraffenland *n*.
plenum ['pli:nəm] *phys* erfüllte(r) Raum *m*; Vollversammlung *f*, Plenum *n*; *~* **heating** Umwälzheizung *f*.
pleon|asm ['pli(:)ənæzm] Pleonasmus *m*; **~astic** [pliə'næstik] *adv ~~ally* pleonastisch.
plethor|a ['pleθərə] *med* Blutandrang *m*; *fig* Fülle, Überfüllung *f* (*of* an); **~ic** [ple'θɔrik] *adv ~~ally*; *med* vollblütig; *fig* übervoll; *(Stil)* geschwollen.
pleurisy ['pluərisi] Brustfell-, Rippenfellentzündung *f*.
plex|iglass ['pleksiglɑ:s] *(Warenzeichen)* Plexiglas *n*; **~us** [-əs] Netzwerk, Geflecht, Gewirr; *anat* (Gefäß-, Nerven-)Geflecht *n*.
pli|ability [plaiə'biliti] Biegsamkeit; Geschmeidigkeit *f a. fig*; **~able** ['plaiəbl] biegsam, formbar, geschmeidig *a. fig*; *fig* leicht zu beeinflussen(d) *od* zu überreden(d), nachgiebig, umgänglich, entgegenkommend; **~ancy** ['-ənsi] = *~ability*; **~ant** ['-ənt] = *~able*.
plica ['plaikə] *pl -ae* [-si:] *anat* Falte *f*; *med* Weichselzopf *m*; *bot* Verwachsung *f*; **~tion** [plai'keiʃən] *geol* Faltung *f*.
pliers ['plaiəz] *pl* (Draht-, Flach-) Zange *f*.
plight [plait] **1.** (*bes.* gefährliche *od* peinliche) Lage *f*; **2.** *tr* verpfänden; *to ~ o.s.* sich verpflichten, sich binden; sich verloben (*to* mit); *s* Verlobung *f*.
plinth [plinθ] *arch* Plinthe, Säulenplatte; Fußleiste *f*.
pliocene ['plaiəsi:n] *geol* Pliozän *n*.
plod [plɔd] *tr (to ~ (on) o.'s way)* (mühsam) daherstapfen; *itr* sta(m)pfen; mühsam vorwärtsschreiten; sich (ab)placken, schuften; *to ~ on* mühsam weitermachen; *s* schwere(r) Tritt *m*; Plackerei *f*; **~der** ['-ə] Packesel *fig*, Büffler; stumpfsinnige(r) Mensch *m*; **~ding** ['-iŋ] schwerfällig; ausdauernd.
plop [plɔp] *itr tr* plumpsen (lassen) (*into* in); *s* Plumps(en *n*) *m*; *(Kork)* Knallen *n*; *adv* plumpsend.
plosive ['plousiv] Verschlußlaut *m*.
plot [plɔt] **1.** *s* Fleck(chen *n*) *m* Erde *od* Land; Parzelle *f*; Platz *m*, Stelle *f*, Standort; *bes. Am* Grundriß, Plan *m*, Schaubild, Diagramm *n*, Karte, graphische Darstellung *f*; Plan, Anschlag *m*, böse Absicht, Intrige, Verschwörung; *lit* Handlung, Fabel, Verwick(e)lung, Intrige *f*; *tr* e-n Plan, e-e Karte machen von, graphisch darstellen *a. math*; ein-, aufzeichnen, auf-, eintragen; *(Kurs)* abstecken, absetzen; *(Plan)* aushecken, schmieden; *lit* ausdenken, entwerfen; *to ~ out* skizzieren, entwerfen; parzellieren; *itr* Ränke schmieden, intrigieren; konspirieren (*against* gegen); *to lay, to hatch a ~* e-e Verschwörung anzetteln *od* aushecken; *building ~* Bauplatz *m*; **~ter** ['-ə] Intrigant, Ränkeschmied; Verschwörer; *tech* Zeichner; Auswerter, Rechner *m*; **~ting** ['-iŋ] *aero* Eintragung, Auswertung *f*; Planen *n*; Darstellung *f*; *~~ table* Auswerte-, Koppeltisch *m*.
plough, *Am meist* **plow** [plau] *s* Pflug; *tech* Kehl-, *(Buchbinderei)* Beschneidhobel; *fig sl (Prüfung)* Mißerfolg *m*, Durchfallen *n*; *the P~ (astr)* der Große Bär, der Große Wagen; *tr* pflügen; *(Furche)* ziehen; (durch-) furchen; durchziehen; hobeln; *(Weg)* bahnen; *fig* durchfallen lassen; *to be ~ed* die Prüfung nicht bestehen, durchfallen; *to ~ back* unterpflügen; *itr* pflügen; sich pflügen lassen; ziehen (*through* durch); einherstapfen; *fig* sich vergraben (*into* in); durchackern (*through a book* ein Buch); *to ~ up* umpflügen; *to put o.'s hand to the ~* Hand anlegen; *to ~ a lonely furrow* alles allein machen; *to ~ the sands (fig)* sich vergebliche Mühe machen; *motor-~* Motorpflug *m*; *snow-~* Schneepflug *m*; **~boy** Pflüger; Bauernjunge *m*; **~-land** Hufe *f*; **~man** Pflüger; Landarbeiter *m*; **~share** Pflugschar *f*; **~-stock, -tail** Pflugsterz *m*.
plover ['plʌvə, *Am a.* 'plouvə] *orn* Regenpfeifer; *a.* Kiebitz *m*.
ploy [plɔi] List; Arbeit *f*.
pluck [plʌk] *tr* ab-, ausreißen; reißen, zerren; *(Geflügel)* rupfen; zupfen; *(Augenbrauen)* auszupfen; *(Blume)* pflücken, abreißen; *sl* rupfen, abstauben, begaunern; *Br sl (in e-r Prüfung)* durchfallen lassen; *itr* reißen, zerren, zupfen, ziehen (*at* an); schnappen (*at* nach); *s* Ruck, Zug *m*; Zerren, Reißen *n*; *fig* Beherztheit *f*, Mut *m*, Tapferkeit *f*; *(Tier)* Innereien *f pl*; *to ~ out, to ~ up* ausreißen; *(Unkraut)* jäten; *to ~ up (courage, heart, spirits)* Mut fassen; **~ed** [-t] *a* mutig; **~iness** ['-inis] Mut *m*, Kühnheit *f*; **~y** ['-i] mutig, kühn, beherzt.
plug [plʌg] *s* Pflock, Stöpsel, Pfropfen; *(Faß)* Spund; Zapfen, Dübel; Verschluß; *(~ of cotton)* Wattebausch; *el* Stöpsel, Stecker *m*; *mot (spark-~)* Zündkerze *f*; *(fire-~)* Hydrant; *(WC)* Druckspüler *m*; *med* Plombe, Füllung; *sl* Kugel; *Am sl (~ hat)* Angströhre *f*, Zylinder; *Am sl* (alter) Klepper *m*, Schindmähre *f*, alte(r) Kasten *m*, alte Mühle *f*, alte(r) Plunder, Ladenhüter; *(Buch)* Schmöker *m*; *Am sl* Reklame *f*, Werbespruch *m*, Empfehlung; *radio* eingeschaltete Werbesendung *f*; *tr (to ~ up)* zustopfen, -stöpseln; *(Faß)* zuspunden; hineinstecken; *(Zahn)* plombieren, füllen; ein Stück herausschneiden aus *(e-r Melone)*; *sl* e-e Kugel jagen in; mit der Faust schlagen auf, bearbeiten; *fam* die Werbetrommel rühren für; einhämmern, -bleuen, -trichtern; *s.th. on s.o.* jdm etw aufdrängen, anhängen; *to ~ away at (fam)* sich abquälen mit, herumschuften an, büffeln an; *to ~ in (el)* einstöpseln, hineinstecken; einschalten; *to ~ into connection* an die Steckdose anschließen; *to pull the ~* das Klo spülen; *Am sl* hängen lassen, Schwierigkeiten machen, verpfeifen; **~-box, -connector, -contact, -point, -socket** Steckdose *f*, -kontakt *m*; **~ger** ['-ə] *fam* Einhämmerer, -trichterer; begeisterte(r) Zuschauer; Arbeitsfanatiker, Büffler *m*; **~-ugly** *Am* Rowdy, Gangster *m*.
plum [plʌm] Pflaume *f*; *(~-tree)* Pflaumenbaum *m*; Rosine *f (im Kuchen* od *Pudding)*; *fig das* Beste, *die* Auslese, Spitze; *das* Glanzstück; *sl* Belohnung, gutbezahlte Stelle *f*; *sl* 100000 £; *to get the ~ (fig)* den Vogel abschießen; den Löwenanteil bekommen; *cherry-, dried, egg-~* Kirsch-, Back-, Zierpflaume *f*; *French ~* Damaszene(r Pflaume) *f*; *mussel-~* Zwetsch(g)e *f*; *sugar-~* Bonbon *m od n*; **~-cake** Rosinenkuchen *m*; **~-duff** (einfacher) Rosinenpudding *m*; **~-jam** Pflaumenmarmelade *f*; **~-pudding** Plumpudding *m*; *~~ stone (geol)* Puddingstein *m*; **~-tart** Zwetsch(g)enkuchen *m*, Pflaumentorte *f*.
plumage ['plu:midʒ] Gefieder *n*.
plumb [plʌm] *s (~-line, -bob)* Lot, Senkblei *n*; *a* lot-, senkrecht; aufrecht stehend; *fig* aufrecht, aufrichtig; *fam* vollkommen, völlig, absolut, glatt *(Unsinn)*; *adv* senkrecht; direkt; *Am fam* vollkommen, absolut, glatt, total; *tr* (aus)loten, sondieren *a. fig*; *fig* erforschen, herausbekommen, lösen, verstehen; lot-, senkrecht machen; mit Blei beschweren *od* versiegeln; *(als Klempner)* installieren, *(Rohre)* legen; *Am sl* völlig versauen; *out of ~, (Am) off ~* aus dem Lot, schief; **~ago** [-'beigou] *min* Graphit *m*; Bleistiftzeichnung; *bot* Bleiwurz *f*; **~eous** ['-biəs] bleiartig, -haltig, Blei-; bleiern; **~er** ['-ə] Klempner, Flaschner, Spengler; Rohrleger; Installateur *m*; **~ery** ['-əri] Klempnerei, Flaschnerei, Spenglerei; Installation *f*; Rohrlegen *n*; **~ic** ['-bik] *a chem* Plumbi-; *med* Blei-; **~iferous** [-'bifərəs] bleihaltig; **~ing** ['-iŋ] Lotung; Klempner-, Flaschner-, Spenglerarbeit *f*; Rohre u. Bindungen *pl*; **~ism** ['-bizm] Bleivergiftung *f*; **~-rule** Senk-, Lotwaage *f*.
plume [plu:m] *s* (*bes.* wehende, wallende, Straußen-)Feder *f*; Federbusch *m*; Gefieder *n*; *zoo* Feder; *Am* Trophäe *f*, Siegespreis *m*; *tr* mit Federn schmücken; *(Vogel das Gefieder)* glätten; *to ~ o.s. (Vogel)* sein Gefieder glätten; *fig* sich brüsten (*on* mit); *~ of smoke* Rauchfahne *f*.
plummet ['plʌmit] *s* Senkblei; *fig* Bleigewicht *n*; *itr* senkrecht hinunterfallen, (ab)stürzen.
plummy ['plʌmi] pflaumenreich, voller Pflaumen; pflaumenartig; *fam* pfundig, prima.
plumose ['plu:mous] gefiedert; flaumig, federartig.
plump [plʌmp] **1.** *a* rundlich, mollig; pausbäckig, *fam* pumm(e)lig; *tr itr (to ~ up, to ~ out)* aufschwellen; dick machen *od* werden; **~er** ['-ə] Bausch *m*; **~ness** ['-nis] Rundlichkeit *f*; **2.** *itr* plumpsen; stoßen; *fig* ausschließlich wählen *od* unterstützen (*for s.o.* jdn); *to ~ into* hineinplatzen in; *tr* plumpsen, fallen lassen; *(to ~ up) (Kissen)* aufschütteln; *fig* offen heraussagen (*with s.th.* etw); *s* schwere(r) Fall, Zs.stoß; Plumps(en *n*) *m*; *adv* plumpsend, heftig; gerade hinunter; gerade heraus, (ganz) offen; *a* gerade, offen, unverblümt; **~er** ['-ə] schwere(r) Fall, Plumps *m*; Wahl *f* nur e-s Kandidaten; plumpe Lüge *f*.
plumy ['plu:mi] *a* aus Federn; federgeschmückt; federartig.
plunder ['plʌndə] *tr* (aus)plündern;

itr plündern, stehlen; *s* Plünderung *f*, Diebstahl; Raub *m*, Beute *f*, Diebesgut *n*; *sl* Profit, Gewinn; *Am fam* Plunder *m*; **~er** ['-rə] Plünderer, Dieb *m*.

plung|e [plʌndʒ] *tr* tauchen, tunken; *(in e-e Flüssigkeit, e-e Waffe)* stoßen; *(in Schulden, in e-n Krieg)* stürzen (*in, into* in); *itr* tauchen, sich (hinein-) stürzen *a. fig* (*into* in); *(Pferd)* durchgehen; *(Schiff)* stampfen; *(Hang)* steil abfallen; *(Straße)* steil hinabführen; *fam* mit dem Geld um sich werfen, das Geld aus dem Fenster werfen; wild spekulieren; *s* Tauchen *n*; (Ab-)Sprung, Sturz *m*; Schwimmen; Schwimmbecken; *(Pferd)* Ausschlagen *n*; *fam* schnelle(r) Entschluß *m*, Investierung, Spekulation *f*; *to take the ~~* sich in ein Abenteuer stürzen; **~r** ['-ə] Taucher; *fam* Spekulant; *tech* Tauchkolben *m*.

plunk [plʌŋk] *tr* hinwerfen, umstoßen, -kippen; heftig werfen, hinschleudern; *mus (Instrument)* zupfen; *Am sl* umlegen; *itr* hinfallen, umfallen, -kippen; *(Saiteninstrument)* erklingen; *(sl) to ~ down (Geld)* auf den Tisch legen; blechen; *s mus* Zupfen; Erklingen *n*; *Am fam* (heftiger) Schlag, Stoß; *Am sl* Dollar *m*; *adv* mit e-m Plumps; genau.

pluperfect ['plu:'pə:fikt] *s gram* Plusquamperfekt *n*.

plural ['pluərəl] *a* mehrfach; *gram* pluralisch, Plural-; *s* Plural *m*, Mehrzahl *f*; **~ism** ['-izm] *philos* Pluralismus *m*; Vereinigung *f* mehrerer Ämter *od* Pfründen; **~istic** [pluərə'listik] *philos* pluralistisch; **~ity** [-'ræliti] Vielheit; *(Wahl)* Mehrheit; *(~~ of votes)* Stimmenmehrheit *f*; *~~ of gods* Vielgötterei *f*; *~~ of wives* Vielweiberei *f*.

plus [plʌs] *conj* und, plus; *prp* zuzüglich *gen*; *adv* dazu, außerdem, obendrein; *el* positiv; *a* Plus-; positiv; Extra-; *com* Haben-; *s* Plus, Mehr; *(~-sign)* Pluszeichen *n*; **~-fours** *pl* Golfhose *f*, Knickerbocker *pl*.

plush [plʌʃ] *s* Plüsch; *Am sl* luxuriöse(r) Gegenstand *m*; *a* aus Plüsch; *sl* luxuriös, üppig, schick, elegant; **~y** ['-i] *a* aus Plüsch; plüschartig; *sl* luxuriös, elegant.

plutocra|cy [plu:'tɔkrəsi] Plutokratie; Geldherrschaft; Geldaristokratie *f*; **~t** ['plu:təkræt] Plutokrat, Geldaristokrat, Großkapitalist; *fam* Geldprotz *m*; **~tic** [plu:tə'krætik] plutokratisch.

plutonium [plu:'tounjəm] *chem* Plutonium *n*.

pluv|ial ['plu:viəl], **~ious** ['-iəs] *a* Regen-; regenreich; regnerisch; **~iometer** [plu:vi'ɔmitə] Regenmesser *m*.

ply [plai] **1.** *tr* biegen, winden, falten, formen; *itr fig* nachgiebig, anpassungsfähig sein; nachgeben (*to s.o.* jdm), zustimmen (*to s.th.* e-r S); *s* Falte, Windung; Schicht, Lage; (Garn-) Strähne *f*, Strang *m*; Furnier *n*; *fig* Neigung *f*, Hang *m*; *three-~* dreifach; **~wood** Sperrholz *n*; *~~ covering, fairing* Sperrholzbeplankung *f*; *~~ sheet* Sperrholzplatte *f*; *~~ shelter* Finnenzelt *n*; **2.** *tr* gebrauchen, benutzen, (eifrig) handhaben; bearbeiten, arbeiten an (*with* mit); beschäftigt sein mit; *(Gewerbe)* ausüben, betreiben; *fig* bearbeiten, bestürmen (*with questions* mit Fragen); zusetzen (*s.o.* jdm); überhäufen (*with* mit); (regelmäßig) versorgen (*with* mit); *(Schiff)* (regelmäßig) überqueren, befahren; *itr* fleißig arbeiten (*at* an), dauernd beschäftigt sein (*at* mit); regelmäßig verkehren (*between* zwischen); *mar* lavieren, aufkreuzen.

pneum|atic [nju(:)'mætik] *adv ~~ally*; *a* pneumatisch; Luft-, Preß-, Druckluft-; Rohrpost-; mit Luftbereifung; luftgefüllt, Luft enthaltend; *s* Luftreifen *m*; Fahrzeug *n* mit Luftbereifung; *pl mit sing* Mechanik *f* der Gase; *~~ air* Preßluft *f*; *~~ boat* Schlauchboot *n*, Floßsack *m*; *~~ brake* Druckluftbremse *f*; *~~ chipper* Preßluftmeißel *m*; *~~ dispatch* Rohrpost *f*; *~~ drill, hammer* Druckluftbohrer, -hammer *m*; *~~ post* Rohrpost *f*; *~~ pump* Luftpumpe *f*; *~~ trough* pneumatische Wanne *f*; *~~ tube* Rohrpost *f*; *~~ tyre, (Am) tire* Luftreifen *m*; **~onia** [nju(:)'mounjə] Lungenentzündung *f*.

poach [poutʃ] **1.** *tr* zertrampeln, -treten, herumtrampeln auf; versumpfen; verdünnen; hineinstecken (*into* in); unbefugt betreten; *(Wild)* unberechtigt jagen; *(Fische)* unberechtigt fangen; stehlen, abgaunern; *itr (in weichen Boden)* einsinken; stapfen; zertreten, -trampelt, schmutzig werden; wildern; unberechtigt angeln; *to ~ on s.o.'s preserves* sich gegenüber jdm Übergriffe leisten; **~er** ['-ə] Wilddieb *m*; **~ing** ['-iŋ] Wilddieberei *f*; **~y** ['-i] *(Boden)* aufgeweicht, sumpfig; **2.** *tr (Ei)* pochieren; *~ed eggs (pl)* verlorene Eier *n pl*.

*

pock [pɔk] (Eiter-)Pustel; *(~-mark)* Pocken-, Blatternarbe *f*; **~-marked** *a* pocken-, blatternarbig.

pocket ['pɔkit] *s* Tasche *f*; Sack *m* (*= 76 kg*); Höhlung, Höhle *f*; *(Billard)* Loch; *(air-~)* Luftloch *n*, Fallbö *f*; *min* Erzlager, -nest *n*; *med* Tasche *f*, Beutel *m*, Höhle *f*; *fig* Geld(mittel *n pl*) *n*; *Am sl* Klemme *f*; *mil* Kessel *m*; Widerstandsnest *n*; *a* Taschen-; klein; *tr* in die Tasche stecken; einstecken; einwickeln, einheimsen; sich aneignen, *fam* stibitzen; *(Beleidigung)* einstecken; *(Stolz)* überwinden; nicht zeigen; *(Billard)* ins Loch spielen; *mil* einkesseln; *Am (Gesetz)* durch ein Veto ablehnen; *to be s.th. in (out of) ~* etw gewonnen, verloren haben; *to have s.o. in o.'s ~* jdn in der Gewalt haben; *to pick s.o.'s ~ of s.th.* jdn etw aus der Tasche stehlen; *to put o.'s hand in o.'s ~* in die Tasche greifen *a. fig*; *to put o.'s pride in o.'s ~* s-n Stolz überwinden; *to suffer in o.'s ~* Verluste einstecken; *back, breast ~* Gesäß-, Brusttasche *f*; *out-of-~ expenses (pl)* Barauslagen *pl*; *~* **battleship** *mar* Westentaschenkreuzer *m*; **~-book** Taschenbuch; Notizbuch *n*; *Am* Hand-, Brieftasche *f*; *~~ edition* Taschenausgabe *f*; **~-comb** Taschenkamm *m*; **~ful** ['-ful] Taschevoll *f*; **~-knife** Taschenmesser *n*; **~-lamp** Taschenlampe *f*; **~-lighter** Taschenfeuerzeug *n*; **~-money** Taschengeld *n*; **~-picking** Taschendiebstahl *m*; **~-size** Taschenformat *n*; *~* **veto** *Am* Verzögerung *f* e-s Gesetzes durch Nichtunterschreiben des Präsidenten.

*

pod [pɔd] **1.** *s bot* Schote, Hülse *f*; *(Seidenraupe)* Kokon; *vulg* Bauch *m*; *itr* Schoten tragen; *tr* enthülsen; **2.** *s zoo* Schule, Herde *f*; *tr (Tiere)* zs.-treiben; **~-net** Aalreuse *f*.

podgy ['pɔdʒi] *fam* untersetzt; klein u. dick.

poem ['po(u)im] Gedicht *n*.

poesy ['po(u)izi] *obs = poetry*.

poet ['po(u)it] Dichter, Poet *m*; **~ess** ['po(u)itis] Dichterin *f*; **~ic(al)** [po(u)-'etik(əl)] dichterisch, poetisch (veranlagt); *~ic licence* dichterische Freiheit *f*; **~ics** *pl mit sing* Poetik *f*; **~ize** ['po(u)itaiz] *itr* dichten; *tr* in Verse bringen; dichterisch gestalten; *~* **laureate** [-'lɔ:rieit] *pl ~s laureate, ~~s Br* Hofdichter *m*; **~ry** ['po(u)itri] Dichtkunst; Dichtung *f*; Gedichte *n pl*.

pogrom ['pɔgrəm, pə'grɔm, *Am* 'pougrəm] (*bes.* Juden-)Verfolgung *f*, Pogrom *m*.

poignan|cy ['pɔinənsi] Schärfe *a. fig*; Heftigkeit *f*; **~t** ['-t] scharf, beißend *a. fig*; pikant; schneidend, stechend, heftig; *Am* ergreifend.

point [pɔint] **1.** *s* Punkt *m*; Pünktchen *n*, Fleck(chen *n*) *m*; (genaue) Stelle *f*; Platz; (Zeit-)Punkt, Moment, Augenblick; (einzelner) Punkt *m (e-s Problems, e-s Gespräches, e-s Programms)*; Einzelheit *f*, Detail *n*, Einzelfrage, Sache *f*; *the ~* der Hauptpunkt, das Wesentliche, der springende Punkt, das Thema; *(Witz)* die Pointe; Punkt *m (e-r Einteilung, Skala, Bewertung, beim Spiel)*; Richtung *f*; *(Kompaß)* Strich, Grad *m*, Stufe *f*; *(Würfel)* Auge *n*; *typ (Schriftgrad)* Punkt *m*; (Unterscheidungs-)Merkmal, Charakteristikum *n (e-s Tieres)*; besondere, hervorstechende Eigenschaft *f*, Vorzug *m*; *fig* Seite, Stelle *f*; Sinn *m*, Absicht *f*, Zweck *m*; Spitze *f*, spitze(s) Ende *n*, spitze(r) Gegenstand *m*; *(Geweih)* Ende *n*; Radiernadel; *(pen-~)* Federspitze; *(~-lace)* genähte Spitze *f*; *el* Metallstift *m (e-s Steckers)*; Steckdose *f*; Anschluß(stelle *f*) *m*; Landzunge *f*, Vorgebirge, Kap; Vorstehen *n (des Jagdhundes)*; *pl rail* Weiche *f*; **2.** *tr* (an-, zu)spitzen; *(Werkzeug)* schärfen; *(to ~ up) Am* betonen, Nachdruck geben *od* verleihen (*s.th.* e-r S); unterstreichen; *(to ~ out)* zeigen, hinweisen, deuten, die Aufmerksamkeit, das Interesse richten auf; *(Waffe)* richten (*at* auf); *(Jagdhund)* stehen vor; *(Fugen)* verstreichen; *(Satz)* mit Satzzeichen versehen, interpunktieren; *(Rede)* durch Pausen gliedern; **3.** *itr* (hin)weisen, zeigen (*at* auf); die Aufmerksamkeit, das Interesse richten (*to* auf); gerichtet sein, (hin-) zielen (*to* auf); *(Jagdhund)* vorstehen; *(Geschwür)* reif werden; mit dem Winde segeln; *to ~ off (Dezimalstellen)* abstreichen; *to ~ toward* hinweisen, hindeuten auf; **4.** *at the ~ of* am Rande *gen*, dicht an; *at all ~s* in allen Punkten *od* Stücken; ganz (und gar), völlig, vollständig; *at this ~* in diesem Augenblick; *at the ~ of the sword* unter Androhung von Gewalt; *beside the ~* nebensächlich, unerheblich, belanglos; *in ~, to the ~* angebracht, passend, zur Sache, hierher gehörend, zutreffend; *in ~ of* in Hinsicht, mit Hinblick auf; *in ~ of fact* tatsächlich, in Wirklichkeit; *off the ~* nicht zur Sache gehörend; unzutreffend, unpassend, unangebracht; *on, upon the ~* im Begriff (*of doing* zu tun); *on ~s (sport)* nach Punkten; *on the ~ of o.'s toes* auf Zehenspitzen; *up to a certain ~* bis zu e-m gewissen Grade; *to the ~* zur Sache gehörig; *~ by ~* Punkt für Punkt; **5.** *to bring to a ~* zu Ende führen; *to carry, to gain o.'s ~* sein Ziel erreichen; s-e Auffassung durchdrücken; *to come to the ~* zur (Haupt-)Sache kommen; am entscheidenden Punkt ankommen; *to get the ~ (fam)* verstehen; *to get away from the ~* vom Thema abschweifen; *to give ~ to s.th.* etw Nachdruck verleihen; *to give ~s to s.o.* es mit jdm aufnehmen können; *to keep to the ~* bei der Sache bleiben; *to make a ~ of s.th.* auf etw bestehen, dringen, Wert legen; sich etw zur Richtschnur nehmen, sich etw zur Regel machen; sich etw als Aufgabe setzen, sich vornehmen; *to make, to score a ~ (fig)* e-n Punkt für sich buchen; *(Jagdhund)* stehen; *to miss the ~* die Pointe nicht kapieren; *to speak to the ~* zur Sache sprechen; offen reden; *to stretch, to strain a ~* ein Zugeständnis, e-e Ausnahme machen; *fam* fünfe gerade sein lassen; *to ~ the finger at* mit dem Finger zeigen auf; **6.** *I don't see your ~* ich weiß nicht, worauf Sie hinauswollen; *I see no ~ in (doing)* ich halte es für sinnlos zu; *it has come to the ~* es ist soweit; *there is no ~ in that* das hat keinen Sinn; *that's the ~!* da liegt der Hase im Pfeffer! *that's beside the ~* das gehört nicht zur Sache; *not to put too fine a ~ on it* rundheraus gesagt; **7.** *boiling-~* Siedepunkt *m*; *cardinal ~* Himmelsrichtung *f*; *a case in ~* ein gutes, treffendes Beispiel; *exclamation ~ (Am)* Ausrufezeichen *n*; *freezing-~* Gefrierpunkt *m*; *melting-~* Schmelzpunkt *m*; *saturation-~* Sättigungspunkt *m*; *sore ~* wunde(r) Punkt *m*; *stand~* Standpunkt *m*; *starting-~* Ausgangspunkt *m*; *strong ~* starke Seite, Stärke *f*; *turning-~* Wendepunkt *m*; **8.** *~ of aim (mil)* Ziel-, Haltepunkt *m*; Abkommen *n*; *~ of attack* Angriffspunkt *m*, -stelle *f*; *~ of balance* Schwerpunkt *m*; *~ of conscience* Gewissensfrage *f*; *~ of contact* Berührungspunkt *m*; *~ of controversy* Streitpunkt *m*; *~ of death* Todesstunde *f*; *~ of departure* Ausgangspunkt *m*, *mil* -stellung *f*; *~ of exclamation* Ausrufungszeichen *n*; *~ of fracture* Bruchstelle *f*; *~ of hono(u)r* Ehrensache *f*; *~ of impact* Treffpunkt, Einschlag *m*; *~ of ignition* Flammpunkt *m*; *~ of interrogation* Fragezeichen *n*; *~ of intersection* Schnittpunkt *m*; *~ of junction* Kreuzung *f*, Kreuz-, Knotenpunkt *m*; *mil* Nahtstelle *f*; *~ of land* Landspitze *f*; *~ of order (parl)* Frage *f* zur Geschäftsordnung; *~ of origin (Am)* Versandstation *f*; *~ of penetration (mil)* Durchbruchsstelle *f*; *~ of rest* Nullstellung *f*; *~ of support (Brücke)* Auflager *n*; *tech* Stützpunkt *m*; *~ of time* Zeitpunkt *m*; *~ of view* Gesichtswinkel, Standpunkt *m*; **~-blank** *a* schnurgerade; flach, horizontal; *fig* offen, direkt, gerade; glatt; *adv* aus großer Nähe; *fig* geradeheraus, (ganz) offen, unverblümt; *at ~~ range* auf Kernschußweite; *a ~~ refusal* e-e glatte Weigerung; **~-duty** *(Polizei)* Posten-, Verkehrsdienst *m*; *constable on ~~* Verkehrsschutzmann *m*; **~ed** ['-id] *a* (zuge-)spitz(t); *fig* scharf, beißend, treffend; *(Bemerkung)* anzüglich; betont, offen (-sichtlich); deutlich, auffällig; *~~ arch* Spitzbogen *m*; **~edness** ['-idnis] Schärfe, Bissigkeit; Anzüglichkeit; Offenheit, Deutlichkeit *f*; **~er** ['-ə] Zeiger, Weiser; Pfeil; Zeigestock; *mil* Richtschütze; Vorsteh-, Jagd-, Hühnerhund; *fam* Tip, Wink *m*; *~~ knob* Einstellknopf *m*; *~~ reading* Zeigerablesung *f*; **~ing** ['-iŋ] Interpunktion *f*; (An-)Spitzen *n*; Betonung *f*, Nachdruck; Hinweis *m*; Richten *(e-r Waffe)*; *(Ziegel)* Verstreichen *n*; **~less** ['-lis] stumpf *a. fig*; schwach, bedeutungs-, sinn-, witz-, zwecklos; *sport* ohne Punkte; **~-policeman** Verkehrsschutzmann, -polizist *m*; **~sman** ['-smən] *Br* Weichensteller; *Br* Verkehrspolizist *m*; **~-system** Punktsystem *n*; **~-to-~ communication** *tele* Direktverbindung *f*; **~-to-~ (race)** Querfeldeinrennen *n*.

poise [pɔiz] *s* Gleichgewicht *n*, Stabilität *f*; *fig* (inneres) Gleichgewicht *n*, (innere) Ausgeglichenheit, Ruhe, Gelassenheit; (Körper-, Kopf-)Haltung *f*; sichere(s) Auftreten *n*; Schwebe (-zustand *m*); Unentschlossenheit *f*, Schwanken *n*; *tr* im Gleichgewicht halten, balancieren; tragen; auswägen; *to be ~d*, *itr* u. *to ~ o.s.* im Gleichgewicht, in der Schwebe sein, schweben; sich halten; *to have a lot of ~* ein sicheres Auftreten haben; *to lose o.'s ~* die Fassung verlieren.

poison ['pɔizn] *s* Gift *n a. fig (to* für); *a* giftig; *tr* Gift geben (*s.o.* jdm), vergiften *a. fig*; *med* infizieren; *fig* verderben; *to ~ s.o.'s mind against* jdn aufhetzen gegen; *rat-~* Rattengift *n*; **~er** ['-ə] Giftmischer(in *f*) *m*; **~-fang** Giftzahn *m*; **~-gas** Giftgas *n*; Kampfstoff *m*; **~-hemlock** *Am* Schierling *m*; **~ing** ['-iŋ] Vergiftung *f*; **~-nut** Brechnuß *f*; **~ous** [-əs] giftig; *fam* ekelhaft, eklig *a. fam*; *fig* zersetzend.

pok|e [pouk] **1.** *tr* (an)stoßen, schubsen, knuffen; *Am sl* eine knallen (*s.o.* jdm); *(ein Loch)* bohren; wühlen, kratzen, stochern (*in* in); *(to ~~ up) (Feuer)* schüren; *Am sl* beeinflussen, in Schwung bringen; *(Baseball) (e-n Treffer)* erzielen; *itr* (herum)bohren (*at* in); sich (ein)mischen (*into* in); *(to ~~ about, around)* herumstöbern, -schnüffeln; *(to ~~ along)* herumbummeln, -schlendern; *s* Stoß, Schubs, Knuff *m*; Bohren, Wühlen *n*; *Am sl* Faustschlag; *Am* Faulenzer, Bummelant; *(~-bonnet)* Kapotthut *m*; *to ~~ fun at s.o.* sich über jdn lustig machen; *to ~~ o.'s nose into* s-e Nase stecken in; *to ~~ s.o. in the ribs* jdm e-n Rippenstoß geben; *~~-bonnet* Schute *f*, Kiepenhut *m*; *~~-out (Am sl)* Freßpaket; Essen *n* im Freien, Camping *n*; **~er** ['-ə] Feuerhaken *m*, Schüreisen; *(Spiel)* Poker *n*; *(Univ. Oxford u. Cambridge)* Pedell; *Am* Popanz *m*, Schreckgespenst *n*; *red-hot ~~ (Brandmalerei)* Brennstift *m*; *~~ face* eiserne(s) Gesicht *n*; *~~-work* Brandmalerei *f*; **~(e)y** ['-i] *a* bumm(e)lig; (eng u.) muffig; schäbig; langweilig; *s Am sl* Kittchen *n*; **2.** *obs u. Am sl* Beutel, Sack *m*, Tasche *f*; *Am sl* Cowboy, Langweiler *m*; *to buy a pig in a ~~ (fig)* die Katze im Sack kaufen.

Pol|and ['poulənd] Polen *n*; **~e** [poul] Pole *m*, Polin *f*; **~ish** ['-iʃ] *a* polnisch; *s* (das) Polnisch(e).

polar ['poulə] *a astr* Polar-; *fig* Leit-; *astr phys* polar; *fig* ea. entgegengesetzt, gegensätzlich; **~ air** arktische Kaltluft *f*; **~ bear** Eisbär *m*; **~ circle** Polarkreis *m*; **~ front** *mete* Polar-, Kaltluftfront *f*; **~ ice** Polareis *n*; **~ity** [po(u)'læriti] *phys el* Polarität *a. fig*; *fig* Gegensätzlichkeit *f*; **~ization** [poulərai'zeiʃən] *phys el* Polarisation *f*; **~ize** ['pouləraiz] *phys el tr* polarisieren; *fig* zs.fassen; **~ lights** *pl* Nordlicht *n*; **~ star** Polarstern *m*; **~ zone** Polargebiet *n*.

pole [poul] **1.** Pfahl, Pfosten, Mast *m*; Deichsel *f*; *sport* Stab; (Schi-)Stock *m*; (Balancier-)Stange; Rute *f (= 5½ yards = 5,029 m, bzw. 30¼ square yards = 25,29 qm)*; *tr (Boot, Floß)* staken; an Stangen binden; *itr* staken; *Am sl* abstimmen; *under bare ~s* vor Topp u. Takel; *fig* nackt, kahl, bloß; *up the ~ (sl)* in der Patsche; verrückt; entfallen, aus dem Gedächtnis; **~-ax(e)** Streitaxt *f*; Enterbeil *n*; **~-cat** *zoo* Iltis; *Am* Skunk *m*, Stinktier *n*; **~-jumping, vault** Stabhochsprung *m*; **~-jumper, vaulter** Stabhochspringer *m*; **2.** *geog* Pol *m a. phys el*; *North, South P~* Nord-, Südpol; *math philos* Bezugspunkt *m*; *to be ~s apart* himmelweit vonea. verschieden sein; *magnetic ~* magnetische(r) Pol *m*; **~-reversal** *el* Umpolung *f*; **~-shoe** Polschuh *m*; **~-star** Polar-, *fig* Leitstern *n*.

polem|ic [pɔ'lemik] *adv ~~ally*; *a* polemisch; streitsüchtig; *s* Ausea.setzung *f*, Streit; streitsüchtige(r), rechthaberische(r) Mensch *m*; *pl mit sing* Polemik *f*; Streitgespräch *n*.

police [pə'li:s] *s* Polizei *f*; Amt *n* für öffentliche Ordnung *f*; Polizisten *m pl*, Polizeiaufgebot *n*; *Am mil* Ordnungsdienst *m*; *tr* polizeilich be-, überwachen; schützen *od* in Ordnung halten; in Ordnung bringen; regulieren, regeln, verwalten; *(to ~ up) Am* säubern, sauberhalten; *auxiliary, frontier, harbour, local, military, railway, road, rural, secret, water ~* Hilfs-, Grenz-, Hafen-, Orts-, Feld- *od* Militär-, Bahn-, Straßen-, Feld-, Geheim-, Wasserpolizei *f*; *kitchen ~* Küchendienst *m*; **~-action** Polizeiaktion *f*; **~-authority** Polizeibehörde *f*; **~-commissioner, -superintendent** Polizeikommissar *m*; **~-court** Polizeigericht *n*; **~-decoy, -informer, -spy** Polizeispitzel *m*; **~-dog** Polizeihund *m*; **~-escort** Polizeibedeckung *f*; **~-force** Polizeitruppe *f*; **~-inquiry, -investigation** polizeiliche Untersuchung *f*; **~-inspector** Polizeiinspektor *m*; **~-intervention** polizeiliche(s) Einschreiten *n*; **~-magistrate** Polizeirichter *m*; **~man** [-mən], **~-constable** Polizist, Schutzmann *m*; **~-measure** polizeiliche Maßnahme *f*; **~-office** Polizeiverwaltung *f*, -präsidium, -büro *n*; **~-officer** Polizei-, Sicherheitsbeamte(r) *m*; **~-picket** Polizeiposten *m*, -streife *f*; **~-raid** Razzia *f*; **~-record** Strafregister *n*; **~-state** Polizeistaat *m*; **~-station** Polizeirevier *n*, -wache *f*; **~-supervision** Polizeiaufsicht *f*; *to be, to place under ~~* unter Polizeiaufsicht stehen, stellen; **~-surgeon** Gerichtsarzt *m*; **~-trap** Autofalle *f*; **~-van** Zellenwagen *m*, *sl* grüne Minna *f*; **~-woman** Polizistin, Polizeibeamtin *f*.

policlinic [pɔli'klinik] *med* Poliklinik *f*.

policy ['pɔlisi] **1.** Politik; Staats-, Regierungskunst; (Welt-)Gewandtheit; Diplomatie; Schlauheit, Vorsicht, List *f*; politische(s), umsichtige(s), kluge(s), geschickte(s) Verhalten *n*; klug, umsichtige, geschickte Staatsführung; *pl* (bestimmte) Politik *f*, politische Maßnahmen *f pl*; Grundsatz *m*, Absicht *f*, Ziel *n*, Plan *m*; Regierungshandlung *f*; *Am* Lotto *n*; *he makes it a ~ to* er hat es sich zum Grundsatz gemacht, es ist sein Prinzip zu; *commercial, domestic* od *home* od *internal, economic, financial, fiscal, foreign, social ~* Handels-, Innen-, Wirtschafts-, Finanz-, Steuer-, Außen-, Sozialpolitik *f*; *new alignment of ~* Neuorientierung *f* der Politik; *population ~* Bevölkerungspolitik *f*; *wage ~* Lohnpolitik *f*; *~ of alliances* Bündnispolitik *f*; *~ of appeasement* Beschwichtigungspolitik *f*; *~ of the open door* Politik *f* der offenen Tür; *~ of non-intervention* Nichteinmischungspolitik *f*; **2.** (Versicherungs-)Police *f*; *to take out a ~* e-e Versicherung abschließen *od* eingehen; *bearer ~*

Inhaberpolice *f*; *fire (insurance)* ~ Feuerversicherungspolice *f*; *life (insurance)* ~ Lebensversicherungspolice *f*; **~-holder** Policeninhaber, Versicherungsnehmer, Versicherte(r) *m*; ~ **number** Policennummer *f*.

polio(myelitis) ['pouliou(maiə'laitis)], (spinale) Kinderlähmung *f*.

polish ['pɔliʃ] *tr* polieren; blank reiben; verfeinern, *fam* aufpolieren; glätten, (ab)schleifen; bohnern, schmirgeln; *(Schuhe)* putzen, wichsen; verschönern, vervollkommnen, vollenden; *itr* glänzend, feiner, elegant werden; *s* Politur *f*, (Hoch-)Glanz *m*; Politur *f*, (flüssiges) Putzmittel *n*; Schuhcreme, -wichse *f*, Bohnerwachs *n*; Eleganz, Verfeinerung *f*, *fam* Schliff *m*; *to ~ off (fam)* schnell erledigen; *(Essen)* verwegputzen; *(Gegner)* erledigen, loswerden; *to ~ up (fam)* aufpolieren, aufmöbeln; *(Kenntnisse)* auffrischen; **~ed** ['-t] *a* poliert; glatt, glänzend; *fig* fein, elegant, manierlich; makel-, tadellos, fehlerfrei; *~~ plate glass* Spiegelglas *n*; **~er** ['-ə] Polierer *m*; Politur *f*, Putzmittel *n*; **~ing** ['-iŋ] *s* Polieren *n*; *attr* Polier-, Putz-, Glanz-; *~~ disk* Polierscheibe *f*; *~~ wax* Bohnerwachs *n*.

polite [pə'lait] (ver)fein(ert), elegant; korrekt; höflich, zuvorkommend (*to* gegen); **~ness** [-nis] Höflichkeit *f*.

politic ['pɔlitik] *a* politisch, diplomatisch *a. fig*; *fig* (welt)gewandt, klug, um-, vorsichtig, berechnend, schlau, gerissen, raffiniert; *s pl mit sing* Politik, Staatskunst, -wissenschaft *f*; Politik *f*, politische(s) Geschehen *n*; politische Angelegenheiten *od* Machenschaften *f pl*; *Am (politische)* Taktik; *(mit pl)* politische Überzeugung *f*, Grundsätze *m pl*, Verbindungen *f pl*; *to talk ~s* politisieren; *parish-pump ~s* Kirchturmpolitik *f*; *party-~s* Parteipolitik *f*; *power ~s* Machtpolitik *f*; *world ~s* Weltpolitik *f*; **~al** [pə'litikəl] politisch; staatspolitisch; Staats-, Regierungs-; *for ~~ reasons* aus politischen Gründen; *~~ activities (pl)* politische Betätigung *f*; *~~ economy* Volkswirtschaft, Nationalökonomie *f*; *~~ geography* politische Geographie *f*; *~~ liberties, rights (pl)* politische, staatsbürgerliche Rechte *n pl*; *~~ offence* politische(s) Vergehen *n*; *~~ police* (Geheime) Staatspolizei *f*; *~~ prisoner* politische(r) Gefangene(r) *od* Häftling *m*; *~~ science* Staatswissenschaft *f*, politische Wissenschaften *f pl*; *~~ strife* parteipolitische Ausea.-setzungen *f pl*; *~~ warfare* psychologische Kriegführung *f*, Propagandakrieg *m*; **~ian** [pɔli'tiʃən] Staatsmann; (Partei-)Politiker; *Am sl* gewandte(r) Bursche, Schmeichler, Radfahrer *m*; **~o** [pə'litikou] Politiker; *pej* politische(r) Ehrgeizling *m*.

polity ['pɔliti] politische, staatliche Organisation *f*; Staatsorgane *n pl*; Staatswesen *n*, -körper *m*; Gemeinwesen *n*.

polka ['pɔlkə, *Am* 'pou(l)kə] *s* Polka *f (Tanz)*; *itr* Polka tanzen; **~-dot** *Am* Pünktchen *(auf Stoff)*; (Stoff *m* mit) Punktmuster *n*.

poll [poul] **1.** *s* Kopf *m*, Person *f*; Namensverzeichnis *n*, *bes.* Wählerliste; *(politische)* Wahl, Abstimmung; Wahlbeteiligung *f*, -ergebnis; Stimmenzählen *n*, -zahl; Umfrage, Erhebung *f*; *pl Am* Wahllokal *n*; *tr* ab-, be-, kurz schneiden; stutzen, kappen; Wählerlisten anlegen von; erfassen, registrieren (*s.o.* jdn); *(Stimmen)* erhalten, auf sich vereinigen; befragen; *itr* s-e Stimme abgeben; stimmen (*for* für); abstimmen; wählen; *per ~* pro Kopf (der Bevölkerung); *to be defeated at the ~s* e-e Wahlniederlage erleiden; *to be at the head of the ~s* die meisten Stimmen auf sich vereinigt haben, an der Spitze liegen, führen; *to declare the ~* das Wahl-, Abstimmungsergebnis bekanntgeben; *to go to the ~s* zur Wahl gehen; *heavy, light ~* hohe, niedrige Wahlbeteiligung *f*; *public opinion ~* Meinungsumfrage *f*; **~-book** Wählerverzeichnis *n*, Wahlliste *f*; **~ed** [-d] *a* hornlos(es Rind *n*); **~ing** ['-iŋ] *s* Wahl(akt, -gang *m*, -handlung) *f*; *attr* Wahl-, Wähler-; *~~-book* Wahlliste *f*, Wählerverzeichnis *n*; *~~-booth* Wahlzelle *f*; *~~-clerk* (Wahl-)Beisitzer *m*; *~~-district, -section* Wahlbezirk *m*; *~~ enquiry* Meinungsbefragung *f*; *~~-station* Wahllokal *n*; **~ster** ['-stə] *Am* Meinungsforscher *m*; **~-tax** Kopfsteuer *f*; **2.** [pɔl] *(~-parrot)* Papagei *m*; *sl* Prostituierte *f*.

pollard ['pɔləd] *s* hornlose(s) Tier *n*; gekappte(r) Baum *m*; feine Kleie *f*; *tr (Baum)* kappen.

pollen ['pɔlin] Blütenstaub, Pollen *m*.

polliwog, pollywog ['pɔliwɔg] *dial u. Am* Kaulquappe *f*.

pollut|e [pə'lu:t] *tr* entweihen, schänden; besudeln, verunreinigen, beschmutzen; *(sittlich)* verderben; **~ion** [pə'lu:ʃən] *fig* Entweihung, Schändung; Befleckung; *physiol* Pollution; *tech* Verschmutzung, Verunreinigung *f*.

polo ['poulou] Polo(spiel) *n*; **~ist** ['-ist], **~-player** Polospieler *m*; **~-shirt, -stick** Polohemd *n*, -schläger *m*.

polonaise [pɔlə'neiz] Polonaise *f (Tanz)*.

polony [pə'louni] *Art* Jagdwurst *f*.

poltroon [pɔl'tru:n] Feigling *m*, Memme *f*; **~ery** [-əri] Feigheit *f*.

poly ['pɔli] *in Zssgen* Viel-, Mehr-, Poly-; **~andry** ['-ændri] Vielmännerei, Polyandrie *f*; **~chromatic** [pɔlikro(u)-'mætik] *adv ~ally*; *a* in vielen *od* wechselnden Farben; **~chrome** ['pɔlikroum] bunt, farbig; *(Kunst)* bemalt, polychrom; **~chromy** ['pɔlikroumi] Buntheit; *(Kunst)* Polychromie *f*; **~clinic** [pɔli'klinik] Poliklinik *f*; **~gamist** [pɔ-'ligəmist] Polygamist *m*; **~gamous** [-'ligəməs] polygam; **~gamy** [-'ligəmi] Polygamie, Vielweiberei, Viel-, Mehrehe *f*; **~glot** ['pɔliglɔt] *a* mehrsprachig, polyglott; *s* Polyglotte *m*; Polyglotte *f*; **~gon** ['pɔligən] *math* Vieleck, Polygon *n*; **~gonal** [pɔ'ligənl] vieleckig, polygonal; **~hedral** ['pɔli'hedrəl] *math* vielflächig, polyedrisch; **~hedron** ['-'hedrən] Vielflächner, Polyeder *m*; **~meric** [pɔli'merik] *chem* polymer; **~merism** ['-merizm] *chem biol* Polymerie *f*; **~merisation** [pɔlimeri'zeiʃən] Polymerisation *f*; **~merize** ['pɔliməraiz] *tr* polymerisieren; **~morphic** [pɔli-'mɔ:fik], **~morphous** [-'mɔ:fəs] vielgestaltig, polymorph; **~morphism** [-'mɔ:fizm] Vielgestaltigkeit *f*; **P~nesia** [pɔli'ni:zjə] Polynesien *n*; **P~nesian** [-'ni:zjən] *a* polynesisch; *s* Polynesier(in *f*) *m*; **~nomial** [pɔli-'noumjəl] *math* polynomisch, vielgliedrig; **~p** ['pɔlip] *zoo med* Polyp *m*; **~phase** ['pɔlifeiz] *el* mehrphasig; *~~ current* Drehstrom *m*; **~phonic** [pɔli'fɔnik] *mus* polyphon, mehr-, vielstimmig; **~phony** [pɔ'lifəni] polyphone(r) Satz, Kontrapunkt *m*; Polyphonie *f*; **~pous** ['pɔlipəs] *a* Polypen-; **~pus** [-] *pl a.* *-i* [-ai] = *~p*; **~syllabic(al)** ['pɔlisi-'læbik(əl)] mehrsilbig; **~syllable** ['-siləbl] mehrsilbige(s) Wort *n*; **~technic** [pɔli'teknik] *a* polytechnisch; *s* Polytechnikum *n*, Ingenieurschule *f*; **~theism** ['pɔliθi(:)izm] Polytheismus *m*, Vielgötterei *f*; **~theistic** [pɔliθi(:)'istik] polytheistisch; **~valent** [pɔli'vælənt] *chem* mehrwertig.

pom|ace ['pʌmis] Treber, Trester *pl*; **~ade** [pə'mɑ:d, *Am* pou'meid]; **~atum** [pə'meitəm] Pomade, (Haar-)Salbe *f*; **~e** [poum] Kernfrucht *f*; **~granate** ['pɔmgrænit] Granatapfel *m*; **~elo** ['pɔmilou] *pl -os* Pampelmuse *f*; **~iculture** ['poumikʌltʃə] Obstbaumkultur *f*; **~ology** [pə'mɔlədʒi] Obst(bau)kunde *f*.

Pomerania [pɔmə'reinjə] Pommern *n*; **~n** [-n] *a* pommer(i)sch; *s* Pommer(in *f*); *(~ dog)* Spitz *m*.

pommel ['pʌml] *s* (Degen-, Sattel-) Knopf *m*; *tr* mit der Faust schlagen; puffen, knuffen; *sword-~* Schwertknauf *m*.

pomp [pɔmp] Pomp, Prunk *m*, Gepränge *n*, Pracht *f*; **~osity** [pɔm'pɔsiti] Prunk; Schwulst *m*; Anmaßung *f*; **~ous** ['pɔmpəs] prunkvoll, pompös; *(Stil)* schwülstig, bombastisch, hochtrabend; hochfahrend, anmaßend; **~on** ['-ɔn] *(Mode)* Pompon *m*.

pom-pom ['pɔmpɔm] (automatisches) Schnellfeuergeschütz *n*; Maschinenflak *f*.

ponce [pɔns] *sl* Louis, Zuhälter *m*.

poncho ['pɔntʃou] *pl -os* Regencape *n*, -umhang *m*.

pond [pɔnd] Teich, Weiher *m*; *duck-~* Ententeich *m*; **~age** ['-idʒ] Staumenge *f*; **~-lily** Teich-, Seerose *f*; **~weed** Laichkraut *n*.

ponder ['pɔndə] *tr* erwägen, nachdenken über, sich überlegen; *itr* tief nachdenken, nachsinnen (*on* über); grübeln (*over* über); **~ability** [pɔndərə-'biliti] Wägbarkeit; *fig* Abschätzbarkeit *f*; **~able** ['pɔndərəbl] wägbar; *fig* zu ermessen(d), abzuschätzen(d); **~osity** [pɔndə'rɔsiti], **~ousness** ['pɔndərəsnis] Schwere; *fig* Schwerfälligkeit; Unbeholfenheit *f*; **~ous** ['pɔndərəs] schwer, massig; unhandlich; *fig* schwerfällig; mühsam, langweilig; *fig* unbeholfen, umständlich.

pone [poun] *Am* Maisbrot *n*.

poniard ['pɔnjəd] *s* Dolch *m*; *tr* erdolchen, -stechen.

pontif|f ['pɔntif] *rel (Altrom)* Pontifex; Hohe(r)priester; Bischof; Papst *m*; **~ical** [pɔn'tifikəl] Hohepriester-; pontifikal; bischöflich; päpstlich *a. fig*; *P~~ Mass* Pontifikalmesse *f*; **~icate** [pɔn'tifikit] *s* Pontifikat *n* od *m*; *itr* [-eit] geschwollen reden; *rel* ein Pontifikalamt zelebrieren.

pontoon [pɔn'tu:n] Ponton *m*; *mar* Kiell(e)ichter; *aero* Schwimmer *m*; *Br Art Kartenspiel*; **~-bridge** Ponton-, Schiffsbrücke *f*; ~ **train** Brükkenkolonne *f*.

pony ['pouni] *s* Pony *n*; *fig* Zwerg *m*; *sl (Wettrennen)* 25 £; *Am fam* Schnapsgläschen, kleine(s) Glas *n* Bier; *Am fam (Schule)* Klatsche, Eselsbrücke *f*, Schlauch *(Übersetzungshilfe)*, Spickzettel *m*; *Am sl* Revuetänzerin *f*, Rennpferd *n*; *tr itr Am sl (Schule)* spicken, e-e Eselsbrücke benutzen, abschreiben; *to ~ up (Am sl)* blechen, bezahlen; **~-edition** Kurzausgabe *f*; **~-engine** Rangierlokomotive *f*; **~-tail** (**hair-do**) Pferdeschwanz *m (Frisur)*.

pooch [pu:tʃ] *Am sl* Köter *m*.

poodle ['pu:dl] *zoo* Pudel *m*.

pooh [pu:] *interj* pah! bah! *tr Am sl* fertigmachen, erledigen *fig*; ~~-

[pu:'pu:] *tr* (mit e-r Handbewegung) abtun, lächerlich machen.

pool [pu:l] **1.** kleine(r) Teich, Pfuhl *m*, Wasserloch *n*, Lache *f*; *(swimming-~)* Schwimmbecken, -bassin *n*; *tech* Schmelze *f*; **2.** *s* Poule *f (Spieleinsatz, a. sport)*; *Art* Billard *n*; (Einsatz *m* für) gemeinsame(s) Spiel *n*; gemeinsame(r) Fonds *m*; Toto *m* od *n*; *com* Kartell *n*, Pool, Ring *m*, Interessengemeinschaft *f*; Park *m*, Lager; Wettbüro *n*, -annahme(stelle) *f*, Totalisator *m*; *tr itr* sich (zu e-m Pool) zs.schließen, (e-e Interessengemeinschaft) bilden; *(Gewinn)* teilen; *(Geld)* zs.werfen; *to ~ o.'s funds* die Kapitalien zs.legen; *to ~ the orders* die Aufträge kartellieren; *typists' ~* Sekretärinnenzimmer *n*, Schreibtisch *m*; **~-counter** Spielmarke *f*; **~-room** Billard-, Poulezimmer *n*; Totalisator *m*, Wettbüro *n*.

poop [pu:p] **1.** *s mar* Heck; *(~ deck)* Achterdeck *n*; *tr mar* über das Heck kommen; **2.** *s sl* Einfaltspinsel, blöde(r) Kerl *m*; **3.** *Am sl tr*: *to be ~ed* erschöpft sein; **4.** *s Am sl* Nachrichtenmaterial *n*, Tatsachen *f pl*; *(Kindersprache)* Häufchen *n*.

poor [puə] *a* arm, bedürftig, notleidend, wirtschaftlich schwach; ärmlich, dürftig, schlecht, schäbig; mangelhaft, schwach; *(Meinung)* gering; knapp, unzulänglich, unzureichend, kümmerlich; *(Ernte)* mager; *(Boden)* dürftig, dürr, unfruchtbar; *(Gestein)* taub; *(Körper)* ausgemergelt; armselig, minderwertig; *(Zeit)* schlecht, unangenehm, ungemütlich; *(Nacht)* unruhig, schlecht; unglücklich, bedauernswert, arm; *s pl*: *the ~* die Armen, die wirtschaftlich Schwachen *m pl*; *to be ~ in arithmetic* schwach im Rechnen sein; *to have a ~ opinion of s.o.* nicht viel von jdm halten; *to make but a ~ shift* sich kümmerlich durchschlagen; *that is a ~ consolation* das ist ein schwacher Trost; *~ me!* ich Ärmster! **~-box** Opferstock, Klingelbeutel *m (für die Armen)*; **~-boy** *Am* große(s), belegte(s) Brot *n*; **~-house,** *Am* **-farm** Armenhaus *n*; **~-law** Armenrecht *n*, -gesetzgebung *f*; **~ly** ['-li] *adv* schwach, knapp, unzulänglich, mangelhaft, dürftig; *a fam* kränklich, schwach; *to be ~~ off* übel dran sein; *to feel ~~* sich nicht wohl fühlen; *to think ~~ of s.o.* nicht viel von jdm halten; **~ness** ['-nis] Armut, Beschränktheit *f*, Mangel *m*, Dürftigkeit; *(Boden)* Unfruchtbarkeit *f*; **~-relief** (Armen-)Fürsorge, Wohlfahrt *f*; **~-spirited** *a* feig(e), ängstlich, bange; armselig, jämmerlich.

pop [pɔp] **1.** *s* Knall(en *n*); Schuß *m*; *fam* Brause *f*, Sprudel, Schampus *m*; *itr* puffen, knallen; (mit e-m Knall) (zer)springen, platzen; stoßen, bumsen, knallen, sausen, fliegen; *(Augen)* plötzlich groß werden; (mit e-m Gewehr) knallen (*at* auf); springen, huschen; *tr* puffen, knallen, aufspringen lassen; *bes. Am (Mais)* rösten; *(Pistole)* abfeuern; ab-, niederknallen; stoßen, knallen, feuern; *sl* verpfänden; *adv* mit e-m Knall; plötzlich; *to ~ in* hereinplatzen; *(Kopf)* hereinstrecken; *to ~ off* lossausen; abhauen; *sl* abkratzen, sterben; *sl (Worte)* heraussprudeln; *to ~ up* in die Höhe, hoch-, auffahren; plötzlich auftauchen; *~ to (Am mil sl)* stillgestanden! *in ~ (sl)* versetzt, im Leihhaus; *to go ~* platzen, losgehen; *to ~ the question (fam)* e-n Heiratsantrag machen; *his eyes ~ped* er riß die Augen weit auf; *ginger-~ (fam)* Ingwerbier *n*; **~-corn** *Am* Puffmais *m*; **~-eyed** *a Am* glotzäugig, mit Glotzaugen; *to be ~~ with* große Augen, Glotz-, Stielaugen machen vor; **~-eyes** *pl* Glotzaugen *n pl*; **~-gun** Knallbüchse *f*; **~over** *Am* Windbeutel *m (Gebäck)*; **~per** ['-ə] *Am* Maisröster *m*; **~shop** Leihhaus *n*; **2.** *Am sl* Papa; *fam hum* Alte(rchen *n*) *m*; **3.** *s* volkstümliche(s) Konzert *n*; *a* populär, volkstümlich; **~ music, song** volkstümliche Musik *f*; populäre(s) Lied *n*.

pop|e [poup] *(P) ~* Papst *m*; **~ery** ['-əri] *pej* Papisterei *f*; **~ish** ['-iʃ] *pej* papistisch; Pfaffen-.

popinjay ['pɔpindʒei] *fig* Fatzke *m*.

poplar ['pɔplə] Pappel *f*.

poplin ['pɔplin] Popelin(e *f*) *m (Stoff)*.

poppet ['pɔpit] *tech* Schlittenständer, Reitstock *m*; *(~-head) (Drehbank)* Docke *f*; *(~-leg) min* Strebe *f*, Pfosten, Schenkel *m*; *dial* Püppchen *n*; **~-valve** Schnarch-, Schnüffel-, Rohrventil *n*.

poppy ['pɔpi] Mohn(blume *f*) *m*; Hochrot *n*; *corn, field ~* Klatschmohn *m*; **~cock** *sl* Quatsch *m*; **~head** Mohnkapsel *f*; **~-seed** Mohnsamen *m*.

popsy(-wopsy) ['pɔpsi('wɔpsi)] *fam* Goldkäferchen, süße(s) Püppchen *n*.

popul|ace ['pɔpjuləs] Pöbel, Mob *m*; (gemeines) Volk *n*, (große) Masse *f*; **~ar** ['-ə] *a* allgemein; volkstümlich, populär; Volks-; *(Preis)* niedrig, erschwinglich, volkstümlich; gemeinverständlich; beliebt (*with* bei); *s* Platzkonzert *n*; *at ~~ prices* zu volkstümlichen Preisen; *to make o.s. ~~* sich beliebt machen (*with* bei); *~~ edition (Buch)* Volksausgabe *f*; *~~ etymology* Volksetymologie *f*; *~~ front (pol)* Volksfront *f*; *~~ hero* Volksheld *m*; *~~ insurrection* Volksaufstand *m*, -erhebung *f*; *~~ referendum, (Am) vote* Volksabstimmung *f*; *~~ song* Schlager *m*; *~~ tumult* Volksauflauf *m*; **~arity** [pɔpju'læriti] Volkstümlichkeit, Popularität, Beliebtheit *f* (*with* bei; *among* unter); **~arize** ['pɔpjuləraiz] *tr* populär, beliebt machen; popularisieren; gemeinverständlich darstellen; **~ate** ['pɔpjuleit] *tr* bevölkern, besiedeln; **~ation** [pɔpju'leiʃən] Bevölkerung, Einwohnerschaft; Einwohnerzahl; Bevölkerungsgruppe; Menge; *biol* Population *f*; Bestand *m*, Menge, Zahl *f*; *civil(ian) ~~* Zivilbevölkerung *f*; *fall, increase* od *rise in ~~* Bevölkerungsabnahme *f od* -rückgang *m*, -zunahme *f*; *rural, urban ~~* Land-, Stadtbevölkerung *f*; *surplus ~~* Bevölkerungsüberschuß *m*; *working-class ~~* werktätige Bevölkerung *f*; *~~ census* Volkszählung *f*; *~~ density* Bevölkerungsdichte *f*; *~~ policy* Bevölkerungspolitik *f*; *~~ pressure* Bevölkerungsdruck *m*; *~~ pyramid* Bevölkerungspyramide *f*; **~osity** [pɔpju'lɔsiti], **~ousness** ['pɔpjuləsnis] Volkreichtum *m*, dichte Bevölkerung *f*; **~ous** ['pɔpjuləs] volkreich, dicht bevölkert, dicht besiedelt.

porcelain ['pɔ:slin, -lein] Porzellan *n*; **~ cement, clay** Porzellanzement *m*, -erde *f*.

porch [pɔ:tʃ] Vor-, Säulenhalle *f*, Portikus *m*, Kolonnade *f*; *bes. Br* Kirchenquerschiff *n*; *Am* Veranda *f*; *the P~* die Stoa; **~-climber** *Am* Fassadenkletterer *m*.

porcine ['pɔ:sain] *a scient* Schweine-.

porcupine ['pɔ:kjupain] Stachelschwein *n*; *tech* Kamm-, Nadelwalze *f*; **~ ant-eater** Ameisenigel *m*.

pore [pɔ:] **1.** *itr* starren (*at, on, over* auf); vertieft sein (*over* in); (nach-) sinnen, -grübeln (*at, on, over* über); eifrig studieren (*over a book* ein Buch); **2.** Pore *f*.

pork [pɔ:k] Schweinefleisch *n*; *Am sl* Schmiergelder *n pl*, Pöstchen *n*; **~ barrel** *Am sl pol* Wahlgeschenk *n*; **~-butcher** Schweineschlächter, -metzger *m*; **~ chop** Schweinskotelett *n*; **~er** ['-ə] Mastschwein *n*; **~ling** ['-liŋ] Ferkel *n*; **~-pie** (Schweine-)Fleischpastete *f*; **~-rind** Schwarte *f*; **~y** ['-i] *a* Schweine(fleisch)-; *fam* fett, dick, korpulent; *Am sl* miserabel; *s Am fam* Stachelschwein *n*.

pornography [pɔ:'nɔgrəfi] Schmutz- u. Schundliteratur, Pornographie *f*.

por|osity [pɔ:'rɔsiti] Durchlässigkeit, Porosität *f*; **~ous** ['-əs] durchlässig, porös.

porphyry ['pɔ:firi] *min* Porphyr *m*.

porpoise ['pɔ:pəs] *zoo* Tümmler *m*.

porr|idge ['pɔridʒ] Milch-, Mehlsuppe *f*, -brei; Haferflockenbrei, Haferschleim *m*; **~inger** ['-indʒə] Suppen-, *mil* Eßnapf *m*.

port [pɔ:t] **1.** *tr (Waffe zur Inspektion)* über der Brust kreuzen; *s* Haltung *f*; Anstand *m*, Benehmen *n*; Bedeutung *f*, Zweck *m*; **~able** ['pɔ:təbl] fahrbar, tragbar, transportabel; beweglich; *~~ chair* Tragstuhl *m*; *~~ engine* Lokomobile *f*; *~~ gramophone* Koffergrammophon *n*; *~~ lamp* Handlampe *f*; *~~ railway* Feldbahn *f*; *~~ station* fahrbare Funkstation *f*; *~~ (type-writer)* Reise(schreib)maschine *f*; *~~ wireless-set* Kofferempfänger *m*; **~age** ['-idʒ] Tragen *n*, Transport *m*, Beförderung; Ladung, Fracht *f*; Transportkosten *pl*; *mar* Tragen *n (von Fluß zu Fluß)*; Landbrücke *f*; **~-crayon** Bleistifthalter *m*; **~er** ['-ə] (Gepäck-)Träger, Dienstmann; *Am* Hausdiener; *Am* Salon-, Schlafwagenschaffner *m*; Porter *n (Bier)*; Pförtner, Portier *m*; *Am (~~-house steak)* (Rinder-)Filet *n*; **~erage** ['-əridʒ] Tragen *n*, Beförderung *f*, Transport; Träger-, Botenlohn *m*, Zustellgebühr *f*; **~folio** [-'fouljou] Brieftasche; (Akten-, Brief-)Mappe *f*; Geschäftsbereich *m* (e-s Ministers); *minister without ~~* Minister *m* ohne Geschäftsbereich; *~~ of bills (com)* Wechselbestand *m*; *~~ investment* Wertpapierbestand *m*; **~liness** ['-linis] Korpulenz; Stattlichkeit *f*; **~ly** ['-li] korpulent, dick; stattlich; **~manteau** [-'mæntou] *pl a. -x* Klappkoffer *m*; *~~-word* Schachtelwort *n*; **2.** (See-)Hafen *m*; Hafenstadt *f*, -platz *m*; *fig* Zuflucht, Hilfe *f* in der Not; *to come into, to reach ~* in den Hafen einlaufen; *to get safely into ~, to reach ~ safely* den Hafen sicher erreichen; *to leave ~* auslaufen; *air-~* Flughafen *m*; *fishing-~* Fischereihafen *m*; *free, open ~* Freihafen *m*; *home-~* Heimathafen *m*; *inland-~* Binnenhafen *m*; *interdiction of a ~* Hafensperre *f*; *naval ~* Kriegshafen; Flottenstützpunkt *m*; *sea-~* Seehafen *m*; *~ of anchorage* Nothafen *m*; *~ of arrival* Ankunftshafen *m*; *~ of call* Anlauf-, Anflughafen *m*; *~ of clearance, of departure, of l(o)ading* Abgangshafen *m*; *~ of destination* Bestimmungshafen *m*; *~ of entry* Eingangs-, Einfuhrhafen *m*; *~ of exportation* Ausfuhrhafen *m*; *~ of registry* Heimathafen *m*; *~ of transit* Durchgangs-, Transithafen *m*; **~-authority** Hafenbehörde *f*; **~-charges, -dues, -duties** *pl* Hafengebühren *f pl*; **~ installations** *pl* Hafenanlagen *f pl*; **~ station** Hafenbahnhof *m*; **3.** *obs u. Scot* Tor(weg *m*) *n*; *mar (~hole)* Ladepforte, Pfortluke *f*; *tech* Durchlaß, Kanal *m*; **~al** ['-l] Tor(einfahrt *f*); Portal *n*, Haupteingang; *fig poet* Eingang *m (of* zu); *(~~ vein) anat* Pfortader; *tech* Öffnung *f*; **~cullis** [-'kʌlis] Fallgatter *n*; **4.** *s mar* Backbord *n*; *attr* Backbord-; *itr tr mar (das Steuer)* nach Backbord halten; **~-engine** *aero* Backbordmotor *m*; **~-light** *aero* Backbordlicht *n*; **~sider** Linkshänder *m*; **5.** Portwein *m*.

porten|d [pɔ:'tend] *tr* ankündigen, andeuten, anzeigen; **~t** ['pɔ:tent] (schlimme) Vorbedeutung *f*, böse(s) Vorzeichen, Omen; Wunder *n*; **~tous** [pɔ:-'tentəs] ominös, verhängnis-, unheilvoll; schrecklich, furchtbar; wunderbar, ungewöhnlich.

portico ['pɔ:tikou] *pl -o(e)s* Säulenhalle *f*, -gang *m*, Kolonnade *f*.

portion ['pɔ:ʃən] *s* (An-)Teil *m (of* an); Stück; Erbteil *n*; Mitgift, Aussteuer; (Essens-)Portion *f*, *fam* Schlag *m* (Essen); (zufallendes) Schicksal, Los *n*; *tr (to ~ out)* ein-, zu-, austeilen; *(Person)* ausstatten, -steuern; **~less** ['-lis] *a* ohne Anteil; ohne Mitgift.

portr|ait ['pɔ:trit] Bild(nis), Porträt *n*; *fig* Schilderung, Beschreibung *f*; *to get o.'s ~~ painted* sich malen lassen; *~~ painter*, **~aitist** ['-itist] Bildnis-Porträtmaler, Porträtist *m*; **~aiture** ['-itʃə] Bildnis-, Porträtmalerei *f*; Bildnis, Porträt *n*; **~ay** [pɔ:'trei] *tr* porträtieren; abmalen, -zeichnen; *fig* schildern, beschreiben; *theat* darstellen; **~ayal** [-'treiəl] Porträtieren; Abmalen, -zeichnen *n*; *fig* Schilderung, Beschreibung; *theat* Darstellung *f*.

Portug|al ['pɔ:tjugəl] Portugal *n*; **~uese** [pɔ:tju'gi:z] *a* portugiesisch; *s* Portugiese *m*, Portugiesin *f*; (das) Portugiesisch(e).

pose [pouz] **1.** *tr (Behauptung)* aufstellen; *(Anspruch)* stellen; *(Beweis)* liefern; *(Frage)* stellen, aufwerfen; ausgeben *(as* für); *(Modell, Objekt)* in e-e bestimmte Stellung bringen; *itr* Modell stehen, posieren, sich stellen *(for a photo* e-m Photographen); sich in Positur werfen, schauspielern; e-e bestimmte Haltung einnehmen; auftreten; sich ausgeben *(as* als); *s* Stellung *(e-s Modells)*, Pose *a. fig*; Haltung *f*, Auftreten *n*; **~r** ['-ə], **poseur** [po(u)'zə:] Poseur; affektierte(r) Mensch *m*; **2.** *tr* konfrontieren, behelligen, aus der Ruhe, in Verlegenheit bringen *(with* mit); verwirren; **~r** ['-ə] schwierige Frage; harte Nuß *f*.

posh [pɔʃ] *sl* großartig, prima, piekfein, tipptopp, Klasse.

posit ['pɔzit] *tr* voraussetzen, annehmen; behaupten; fordern, postulieren; **~ion** [pə'ziʃən] *s* Voraussetzung, Annahme; Behauptung; Forderung, Postulierung; Stellung, Lage; Anordnung, Disposition; Haltung, (innere) Einstellung *f*, Standpunkt; Standort *m*; *mil* Stellung; *mar* Position *f*, Besteck *n*; *mot* Begrenzungslichter *n pl*; gesellschaftliche Stellung; hohe Stellung; (feste) Stelle, Stellung, Position *f*, Amt *n (with* bei); *tr* in die (rechte) Lage bringen *od* versetzen; *tech* einstellen; *in, out of ~~* am rechten, falschen Platz; *in my ~~* in meiner Lage; *in a difficult, in an awkward ~~* in e-r schwierigen, schiefen Lage; *to be in a ~~ to do* in der Lage, imstande, fähig sein zu tun; *to define o.'s ~~* s-n Standpunkt darlegen; *to hold, to occupy a ~~* e-e Stelle haben, ein Amt bekleiden; *to place in a difficult ~~* in e-e schwierige Lage bringen; *to take up a ~~ (fig)* Stellung beziehen; *firm, permanent ~~* feste Stelle *f*; *legal ~~* Rechtslage *f*; *people of ~~* Leute *pl* von Rang u. Stand; *policy-making ~~* leitende Stellung *f*; *top ~~* Spitzenstellung *f*; *~~ for life* Lebensstellung *f*; *~~ of trust* Vertrauensstellung *f*; *~~-change* Standortänderung *f*; *~~-determination* Standortbestimmung *f*; *~~-finder* Ortungsgerät *n*; *~~-finder station* (Funk-)Peilstelle *f*; *~~-fixing, -finding* Ortung *f*; *~~-light (aero)* Positionslicht *n*; *~~-message, -report (aero)* Positions-, Standortmeldung *f*; *~~ warfare* Stellungskrieg *m*; **~ional** [pə-'ziʃənl] Stellungs-, Lage-; **~ive** ['pɔzətiv] *a* fest(stehend), (ganz) bestimmt, ganz sicher; genau, exakt, ausdrücklich; entschieden; selbstbewußt, -sicher; eigensinnig, von sich selbst überzeugt, dogmatisch; entschlossen; zustimmend, bejahend, positiv; konstruktiv, aufbauend; unabhängig, absolut; wirklich, tatsächlich, positiv; *scient* empirisch, praktisch, positiv; *(Angebot)* fest; *el phot math gram* positiv; *fam* vollkommen, komplett; *s phot* Positiv *n*; *gram* Positiv *m*; *to be ~~* ganz sicher sein *(that* daß); **~ivism** ['pɔzitivizm] *philos* Positivismus *m*; **~ivist** ['-ist] *philos* Positivist *m*; **~vistic** [pɔziti'vistik] *philos* positivistisch; **~iveness** ['pɔzətivnis] Bestimmtheit; Selbstbewußtsein *n*; Wirklichkeit, Realität *f*; **~ron** ['pɔzitrɔn] *phys* Positron *n (Kernteilchen)*.

posse ['pɔsi] (Polizei-)Aufgebot *n*; Haufe(n) *m*, Schar, Gruppe *f*.

possess [pə'zes] *tr* besitzen, (inne-) haben; *(Sprache)* beherrschen; *(Gedanke, e-n Menschen)* beherrschen, Besitz ergriffen haben von; in der Gewalt haben *fig*; in den Besitz setzen *(of* gen); *to ~ o.s. of s.th.* sich in den Besitz e-r S setzen, von e-r S Besitz ergreifen, sich e-r S bemächtigen; sich etw aneignen; *to be ~ed of* im Besitz sein *gen*; *with* ergriffen, (ganz) eingenommen sein; besessen sein von; *to ~ o.s. in patience* sich in Geduld fassen; *what ~ed you to do that?* was ist in Sie gefahren, so etwas zu tun? **~ed** [-t] *a* besessen *(by* von); erfüllt *(with* von); begabt *(of* mit); **~ion** [pə'zeʃən] Besitz *m*; Besitz-, Eigentum *n*; *pol* Besitzung; *fig (self-~~)* Selbstbeherrschung *f*; *pl* Besitz *m*, Habe *f*, Reichtum, Wohlstand *m*; *to be in ~~ of s.th., to have s.th. in o.'s ~~* im Besitz e-r S sein, etw in Besitz haben; *to be in ~~ of the House (parl)* das Wort haben; *to come, to enter into ~~ of s.th.* in den Besitz, Genuß e-r S kommen *od* gelangen; *to put s.o. in ~~ of s.th.* jdn in den Besitz e-r S setzen; *to take ~~ of* Besitz ergreifen von, in Besitz nehmen; **~ive** [pə'zesiv] *a* Besitz-; *gram* besitzanzeigend, possessiv; *s* u. *~~ case* Genitiv *m*; *~~ pronoun* Possessivpronomen, besitzanzeigende(s) Fürwort *n*; **~or** [-ə] Besitzer, Inhaber; Eigentümer *m*; **~ory** [-əri] *a* Besitz-; *~~ action, right* Besitzklage *f*, -recht *n*.

posset ['pɔsit] heiße Milch *f* mit Bier *od* Wein.

possib|ility [pɔsə'biliti] Möglichkeit *f* *(of doing* zu tun; *of* zu, für); **~le** ['pɔsibl] *a* möglich *(for* für; *with* bei); denkbar, geeignet; *fam* erträglich; *s sport* höchste Punkt-, Ringzahl *f*; in Frage kommende Person *od* Sache *f*; *as early, as soon as ~~* so früh, so bald wie möglich; *if (it is) ~~* wenn möglich; *to do o.'s ~~* sein möglichstes tun; **~ly** ['-li] *adv* möglicherweise, eventuell; nur; *if I ~~ can* wenn ich irgend kann; wenn es mir irgend möglich ist; *I cannot ~~ come* ich kann unmöglich kommen.

possum ['pɔsəm] *fam* Opossum *n*, Beutelratte *f*; *to play ~ (fam)* sich krank stellen; den Unschuldsengel spielen *(with s.o.* vor jdm).

post [poust] **1.** *s* Pfosten, Pfahl, Mast *m*; *tr (to ~ up)* ankleben, -schlagen; (durch Anschlag) bekanntgeben, -machen; *(mit Zetteln)* bekleben; mit e-m Verbotsschild versehen; *~ no bills* Ankleben verboten! *bed, gate, lamp~* Bett-, Tor-, Lampenpfosten *m*; *starting ~ (sport)* Start *m (Ort)*; *winning ~ (sport)* Ziel *n*; **~er** ['-ə] (Plakat-)Ankleber *m*; Plakat *n*, Anschlag *m*; *publicity ~~* Reklameplakat *n*; *~~ advertising* Plakatwerbung *f*; *~~ panel* Plakattafel *f*; **2.** *s mil* Posten(bereich), Platz *m*; Stellung *f*; Standort *m*, Garnison *f*; *(last ~)* Zapfenstreich; (Arbeits-)Platz *m*; Stelle, Stellung *f*; *(trading ~)* Handelsplatz; *com* Rechnungsposten *m*; *tr mil* als Posten aufstellen, (ab-) kommandieren; *to apply for a ~* sich um e-e Stellung bewerben; *first, last ~* (erstes, zweites Signal *n* des) Zapfenstreich(s); *~* **commander** *Am* Standortkommandant *m*; **3.** Post (-sendung) *f*, Postsachen *f pl*; *(~-office)* Post(amt *n*) *f*; Briefkasten *m*; *hist* Postkutsche *f*; Papierformat *n* 16 × 20 Zoll *(40,6 × 50,8 cm)*; *itr hist* mit der Post reisen; eilig reisen; sich beeilen; *tr* in den Briefkasten werfen; auf die Post geben; aufgeben, abschicken, -senden; *(to ~ up)* laufend unterrichten, auf dem laufenden halten; *com (to ~ up)* ins Hauptbuch ein-, übertragen, (ver-) buchen; *(Buchung)* vornehmen; ins reine schreiben; *to ~ o.s.* sich informieren, sich unterrichten; *adv* in Eile, eilig; *by ~* mit der Post; *by return of ~* postwendend; *by the same ~* mit gleicher Post; *by separate ~* in besonderem Umschlag; *to keep s.o. ~ed* jdn auf dem laufenden halten; *to take to the ~* zur Post bringen; *evening, letter, morning, parcel ~* Abend-, Brief-, Morgen-, Paketpost *f*; **~age** ['-idʒ] Porto *n*, (Post-)Gebühr *f*; *additional, extra ~~* Nachgebühr *f*, Strafporto *n*; *letter-~~* Briefporto *n*; *liable, subject to ~~* portopflichtig; *return-~~* Rückporto *n*; *~~-due* Nachgebühr *f*, Strafporto *n*; *~~-envelope* Freiumschlag *m*; *~~-free, -paid* gebühren-, portofrei, franko; frankiert; *~~-meter (Am)* Frankiermaschine *f*; *~~-rates (pl)* Postgebühren *f pl*, -tarif *m*; *~~-stamp* Briefmarke *f*, Postwertzeichen *n*; *~~ unpaid* unfrankiert; **~al** ['-əl] *a* postalisch; Post-; *s Am fam* (frankierte) Postkarte *f*, *rail* -wagen *m*; *~~ address* Postanschrift *f*; *~~ administration, authorities (pl)* Postverwaltung, -behörde *f*; *~~ agency* Postagentur, -hilfsstelle *f*; *~~ car (Am), rail* Postwagen *m*; *~~ card (Am)* Postkarte *f (mit aufgedruckter Freimarke)*; *~~ cheque* Postscheck *m*; *~~-cheque account* Postscheckkonto *n*; *~~ clerk, employee* Postangestellte(r) *m*; *~~ district* Zustellbezirk *m*; *~~ mailing (Am)* Poststreuversand *m*; *~~ matters (pl)* Postsachen *f pl*; *~~ note (Am), order (Br)* Postanweisung *f*; *~~ packet, parcel* Postpaket *n*; *~~ rates (pl), tariff* Posttarif, -gebührensatz *m*; *~~ reply coupon* Antwortschein *m*; *~~ service* Postdienst *m*; *~~ subscription fee* Bestellgeld *n*; *~~ tuition* Fernunterricht *m*; *Universal P~~ Union*

Weltpostverein *m*; ~~ *wrapper* Kreuz-, Streifband *n*; **~-bag** Postsack *m*; **~-box** Briefkasten *m*; **~-boy** *hist* Postreiter; Postillion *m*; **~card** Postkarte *f*; *picture* ~~ Ansichtspostkarte *f*; **~-chaise** Postkutsche *f*; **~ed** ['-id] *a*: *well* ~~ gut unterrichtet, gut informiert; **~e restante** ['poust 'restɑ:nt, *Am* '--'-] *adv* postlagernd; *s* Abteilung *f* für postlagernde Sendungen; **~ exchange** *(PX) Am mil* Marketenderei *f*; **~-free** portofrei, franko; frankiert, freigemacht; **~-haste** *adv* in großer Eile; **~il(l)ion** [pəs'tiljən] Postillion *m*; **~man** Briefträger *m*; ~~*'s horn* Posthorn *n*; **~mark** *s* Poststempel *m*; *tr* (ab)stempeln; **~master** Postmeister *m*; *P~~ General* Generalpostmeister *m*; **~-office** Postamt *n*; *auxiliary* ~~ Posthilfsstelle *f*; *branch* ~~ Zweigpostamt *n*; *general* ~~ Hauptpost; (Ober-)Postdirektion *f*; *railway* ~~ Bahnpostamt *n*; ~~ *box* Postschließfach *n*; ~~ *clerk* Postangestellte(r) *m*; *P~~ Department (Am)* Postministerium *n*; ~~ *hours (pl)* Schalterstunden *f pl*; ~~ *order* Postanweisung *f*; ~~ *receipt* Posteinlieferungsschein *m*; ~~ *savings-bank* Postsparkasse *f*; **~-package, -parcel** Postpaket *n*; **~-paid** *a* frankiert, freigemacht; ~~ *reply card* Werbeantwort *f*; **~-stamp** Poststempel *m*; **~-terminal** *Am* Bestimmungsort *m*; **4.** *prp u. in Zssgen* Nach-, nach-.

post|-date ['poust'deit] *tr* nachdatieren; folgen auf, später sein als; **~-entry** ['-'entri] nachträgliche Eintragung *od* Buchung *od* Verzollung *f*.

poster|ior [pɔs'tiəriə] *a* später (*to* als); folgend; hinter, rückwärtig, Rück-; *s fam* Hintere, Hintern *m*; **~ity** [pɔs'teriti] Nachkommen(schaft *f*), -fahren *pl*; Nachwelt *f*.

postern ['poustə:n] Hintertür *f a. fig.*

post-fix ['poustfiks] *s gram* Suffix *n*; *tr* [poust'fiks] *(e-m Wort)* anfügen; **~-graduate** ['-'grædjuit] *a (Studium)* nach dem Examen, vorgeschritten; *s* Doktorand *m*.

posthumous ['pɔstjuməs] nachgeboren, posthum; nachträglich; *(Buch)* nachgelassen; ~ **fame** Nachruhm *m*.

postlude [poust'lu:d] *mus* Postludium, Nachspiel *n*; **~-meridian** ['-mə'ridiən] nachmittägig; Nachmittags-; ~ **meridiem** ['poustmə'ridiəm] *(p.m.)* nachmittags; **~-mortem** ['-'mɔ:tem] *a* nach dem Tode (stattfindend *od* eingetreten *od* vollzogen); *s u.* ~~ *examination* Leichenöffnung, Autopsie *f*; **~-natal** ['-'neitl] nach der Geburt (stattfindend); **~-nuptial** ['-'nʌpʃəl] nach der Hochzeit (stattfindend); **~-obit** [-'ɔbit] *a u. s* nach dem Tode fällig(er Schuldschein *m*).

postpon|able [poust'pounəbl] aufschiebbar; **~e** [-'poun] *tr* auf-, verschieben, zurückstellen; *(Termin)* verlegen, vertagen; unterordnen (*to s.th.* e-r S), als weniger behandeln (*to* als); zurückstellen (*to* hinter); **~ement** [-mənt] Aufschub *m*, Zurückstellung; Vertagung; Unterordnung *f*.

post|position ['poustpə'ziʃən] *gram* Nachstellen *n*; nachgestellte Präposition *f*; **~positive** ['-'pɔzətiv] *gram* nachgestellt; **~prandial** [poust'prændiəl] nach dem Mittagessen (stattfindend); **~script** ['pous(s)kript] Nachschrift *f*; *(Buch)* Nachwort *n*; Rundfunkkommentar *m (nach den Nachrichten)*.

postul|ant ['pɔstjulənt] Bewerber, Kandidat *m*; **~ate** ['pɔstjuleit] *tr* (er-)fordern; voraussetzen, postulieren; (als selbstverständlich) annehmen; *itr* ersuchen (*for* um); *s* [-lit] (Grund-)Voraussetzung *f*, Postulat *n*; (selbstverständliche) Annahme *f*; **~ation** [pɔstju'leiʃən] Forderung *f*, Erfordernis *n*; Voraussetzung; Annahme *f*.

posture ['pɔstʃə] *s* (Körper-)Stellung, Lage, Haltung; (Geistes-)Haltung; Lage *f* (der Dinge), Zustand *m*, Umstände *m pl*, Verhältnisse *n pl*; *tr* in e-e bestimmte Stellung bringen; e-e Stellung einnehmen lassen; *itr* e-e bestimmte Stellung, *fig* Haltung einnehmen; posieren; auftreten (*as* als).

post-war ['poust'wɔ:] *a* Nachkriegs-; ~ **demands** *pl* Nachkriegsbedürfnisse *n pl*; ~ **years** *pl*, **period** Nachkriegszeit *f*.

posy ['pouzi] Blumenstrauß *m*.

pot [pɔt] Topf, Kessel *m*; Kanne *f*, Krug *m*, Kruke, Tonflasche *f*; Topfvoll *m*, Kannevoll *f*, Krugvoll *m*; Steingut *n*; Ton *m*; Portion *f*; (Krug) Schnaps *m*, Bier *n*, Wein; *sport sl* Preis, *bes.* (Silber-)Pokal; *fam* (Wett-)Einsatz *m*; *(~s of money) fam* Menge *f* Geld; *fam* mühelose(r) Schuß, Zufallstreffer *m*; *fam (big ~)* hohe(s) Tier *n (Mensch)*; *Am sl* rechthaberische Frau *f*; *Am sl* Motor *m*, Lokomotive *f*, Vergaser *m*; *Am sl* Marihuana *n*; *tr* in e-n Topf tun; einmachen; in e-m Topf kochen; *(Pflanzen)* eintopfen; (ab)schießen, *fam* abknallen; *fam* ein-, in die Tasche stecken, einwickeln *fig*; *fam* auf den Topf setzen; *itr fam* (herum)knallen; *at s.th.* auf etw losknallen; *(Billard)* ins Loch spielen; *to go to ~ (sl)* in den Eimer, in die Brüche gehen; *to keep the ~ boiling* sein Auskommen haben; die Sache in Gang halten; *to put a quart into a pint* ~ Unmögliches versuchen; *the ~ should not call the kettle black* wer im Glashaus sitzt, soll nicht mit Steinen werfen; *the ~ goes so long* od *so often to the well that it is broken at last (prov)* der Krug geht so lange zum Brunnen, bis er bricht; *chimney-~* Kaminaufsatz *m*; *coffee-~* Kaffeekanne *f*; *cooking-~* Kochtopf *m*; *fish-~* Fischreuse *f*; *flower-~* Blumentopf *m*; *ink-~* Tintenfaß *n*; *jam-~* Marmeladentopf *m*; *lobster-~* Hummerkorb *m*; *pint* ~ Maßkrug *m*; *tea-~* Teekanne *f*; *watering-~* Gießkanne *f*; **~-bellied** *a* dickbäuchig; **~-belly** Dickbauch, Wanst *m*; **~-boiler** *fam* Brotarbeit(er *m*) *f*; **~-boy** Kellner *m*; **~-cheese** *Am* Quark *m*; **~-hat** *fam* Melone *f (Hut)*; **~-herb** Gemüse, Küchenkraut *n*; **~-holder** Topflappen *m*; **~-hole** tiefe(s) runde(s) Loch; Schlagloch *n*; Gletschertopf *m*; **~-holer** Höhlenforscher *m*; **~-hook** Kesselhaken; *fam* Krakelfuß *m*; **~-house** *Br* Wirtschaft *f*, Lokal *n*, Kneipe *f*; ~~ *manners (pl)* rüpelhafte(s) Benehmen *n*; ~~ *politician* Biertischpolitiker *m*; **~-hunter** Jäger *m*, der jedes Wild abknallt; *sport* Preisjäger; *fig* materiell eingestellte(r) Mensch *m*; **~-ladle** Kochlöffel *m*; **~-lid** Topfdeckel *m*; **~-luck**: *to take* ~~ mit dem vorlieb nehmen, was es gerade gibt (*with s.o.* bei jdm); **~-pie** *Am* Topfsülze *f*; **~-roast** *Am* Schmorbraten *m*; **~-sherd** (Topf-)Scherbe *f*; **~-shot** mühelose(r) Schuß, Nahschuß, Glückstreffer *m*; *fig* leichte Sache *f*; **~ted** ['-id] *a* eingetopft, eingemacht; *fig* schlecht zs.gefaßt; *sl* besoffen; ~~ *meat* Pökelfleisch *n*; **~ter** ['-ə] **1.** Töpfer *m*; ~~*'s wheel* Töpferscheibe *f*; **~tery** ['-ri] Töpferei *f*; Töpferwaren *f pl*, irdene(s) Geschirr *n*; **~ty** ['-i] *a sl* winzig, puppig; läppisch; kinderleicht; verrückt (*about* über; *of* nach); *fam* Töpfchen *n*; **~-valiant**: *to be* ~~ sich Mut angetrunken haben.

pot|able ['poutəbl] *a* trinkbar; Trink-; *s pl* Getränke *n pl*; **~ation** [po(u)'teiʃən] Trinken, Zechen *n*; Zug *m*; Getränk *n*; Schnaps *m*; **~ion** ['pouʃən] Trunk; (Arznei-, Gift-)Trank *m*; *love-~~* Liebestrank *m*.

potash ['pɔtæʃ] *chem* Pottasche *f*; Kali *n*; *caustic* ~ Ätzkali *n*; ~ **lye, mine, salt** Kalilauge *f*, -bergwerk, -salz *n*.

potassium [pə'tæsjəm] *chem* Kalium *n*; ~ **chlorate** Kaliumchlorat, chlorsaure(s) Kalium *n*; ~ **chloride** Kaliumchlorid, Chlorkalium *n*; ~ **cyanide** Zyankali *n*; ~ **hydrate** Ätzkali *n*; ~ **permanganate** Kaliumpermanganat *n*.

potato [pə'teitou] *pl -es* Kartoffel; *Am sl* Rübe *f*, Dollar *m*; *boiled, a. steamed ~es* Salzkartoffeln *f pl*; *chipped ~es, (Am) French fried ~es (pl)* Pommes frites *pl*; *fried ~es (pl)* Brat-, Röstkartoffeln *f pl*; *mashed ~es (pl)* Kartoffelbrei *m*, -püree *n*; *sweet, Spanish* ~ Batate *f*, Süße Kartoffel *f*; *~es in the jacket* Pellkartoffeln *f pl*; ~ **beetle, bug** Kartoffelkäfer *m*; **~-blight, -disease, -rot** Kartoffelfäule *f*; ~ **chips** *pl* Kartoffelchips *pl*; ~ **cultivator** Hack-, Häufelpflug *m*; **~-digger** Kartoffelroder *m*, -rodemaschine *f*; **~-flour, -meal** Kartoffelmehl *n*; **~-starch** Kartoffelstärke *f*.

poteen [pɔ'ti:n] *(Irland)* heimlich gebrannte(r) Whisky *m*.

poten|ce, -cy ['poutəns(i)] Macht, Kraft, Stärke; Wirksamkeit; Überzeugungskraft; Wirkungsfähigkeit; *physiol* Potenz *f*; **~t** ['-t] mächtig, kraftvoll, stark, einflußreich; wirksam; überzeugend, zwingend; *physiol* potent; **~tate** ['poutənteit] Machthaber, Herrscher, Potentat *m*; **~tial** [pə'tenʃəl] *a* potentiell, möglich, denkbar, latent, im Keim vorhanden; noch unentwickelt, entwicklungsfähig, zukunftsträchtig; *phys el* potentiell; *gram* potential; *s* Potential *n a. phys*; Wirkungs-, Leistungsfähigkeit *f*; *gram (~~ mood)* Potentialis *m*; *el* Spannung *f*; *war* ~~ Kriegspotential *n*; ~~ *difference (math)* Potentialdifferenz *f*, -gefälle; *el* Spannungsgefälle *n*; ~~ *drop* Spannungsabfall *m*; ~~ *energy (phys)* potentielle Energie *f*; **~tiality** [pətenʃi'æliti] Möglichkeit, Denkbarkeit, Latenz; Keim-, Entwick(e)lungsfähigkeit; verborgene Kraft *od* Stärke *f*; *pl* (Entwicklungs-)Möglichkeiten *f pl*; **~tilla** [poutən'tilə] *bot* Fingerkraut *n*; **~tiometer** [pətenʃi'ɔmitə] *el* Potentiometer *n*, Spannungsteiler *m*.

pother ['pɔðə] *s* Rauch-, Staubwolke *f*; Aufruhr *m*, Durcheinander *n*, Lärm, Krach *m*; *tr* in Aufregung versetzen, *tr itr* (sich) aufregen; *to make a* ~ Krach schlagen (*about* um).

potpourri [po(u)'puri, *Am* pɔt'-] *mus* Potpourri *n*; *lit* Blütenlese *f*; Dufttopf *m*.

pottage ['pɔtidʒ] (dicke) Suppe *f*, Eintopf(essen *n*) *m*; *to sell o.'s birthright for a mess of* ~ sein Erstgeburtsrecht um ein Linsengericht verkaufen.

potter ['pɔtə] **2.** *itr (to ~ about)* herumtrödeln, -bummeln; herumpfuschen (*at* an); *tr (to ~ away)* vertrödeln, verbummeln, vertun; *s s. pot.*

pouch [pautʃ] *s* Beutel, (kleiner) Sack *m*, Tasche *a. bot*; *(ammunition ~)* Patronentasche *f*; *(tobacco-)* Tabaksbeutel; Postsack *m*; *Scot* Tasche *f (in der Kleidung)*; *zoo* Beutel *(der Beuteltiere)*; Kropf, Beutel *m (der*

Pelikane); Backentasche *f*; *med* Tränen-, Hodensack *m*; *tr* in e-n Beutel, in e-e Tasche stecken; einstecken; verschlingen; ausbauchen, bauschen; *fig* beschenken; *itr* sich bauschen, e-n Beutel bilden; *diplomatic* ~ Diplomatengepäck *n*; **~ed** [-t] *a* bauschig; *zoo* Beutel-.

poult [poult] *orn* Küken *n a. fig*; **~erer** ['-ərə] *bes. Br* Geflügelhändler *m*; **~ry** ['-ri] Geflügel, Federvieh *n*; *~~-farm* Geflügelfarm *f*.

poultice ['poultis] *s med* Breiumschlag *m*, Packung *f*; *tr* e-e warme Packung machen auf.

pounce [pauns] **1.** *s* Kralle, Klaue *f*; Herabstoßen *(e-s Raubvogels)*; Anspringen *n (e-s Raubtiers)*; *tr* (mit den Krallen) packen; *itr* herabstoßen, sich stürzen (*on, upon, at* auf); anspringen (*on, upon, at* auf); herfallen (*on, upon, at* über); *on the ~* sprungbereit; *to make a ~* sich stürzen (*on, upon, at* auf); **2.** *s hist* Bimsstein-, Löschpulver; Kohle-, Pauspulver *n*; *tr* abbimsen; (durch)pausen.

pound [paund] **1.** Pfund *(lbs., 16 Unzen = 453,592 g)*; *(~ sterling)* Pfund *n (£ = 20 Schilling)*; *by the ~~* pfundweise; *to exact o.'s ~ of flesh (fig)* auf s-m Recht bestehen; *in for a penny in for a ~ (prov)* wer A sagt, muß auch B sagen; *two shillings in the ~* zehn Prozent; *an ounce of prevention is worth a ~ of cure* Vorsicht ist besser als Nachsicht; **~age** ['-idʒ] Provision *f* pro Pfund; Pfundgeld *n*; **~-cake** *Art (schwerer)* Teekuchen *m*; **~er** ['-ə] *in Zssgen* -pfünder *m*; **~ foolish**: *penny wise and ~~* sparsam im Kleinen und verschwenderisch im Großen; **2.** *s* Pferch; Pfandstall *m*; Falle *f (für große Tiere)*; Fischkasten *m*; (Tier-)Asyl; Gefängnis *n*; *tr (Vieh)* einpferchen, -sperren; **3.** *tr* (zer)stoßen, (zer)stampfen, pulverisieren; schlagen, stoßen, trommeln auf *od* gegen; *itr* schlagen, stoßen, trommeln, hämmern (*at, on* auf, gegen); *(Maschine)* stampfen; *(Herz)* heftig schlagen; *to ~ about* herumstapfen; *to ~ along* mühsam gehen; *to ~ away* sich ins Zeug legen; heftig angreifen (*at s.o.* jdn); *to ~ the pavement (Am sl)* Arbeit suchen; s-e Runde machen; **~er** ['-ə] Schlagende(r), Stoßende(r); Schläger, Stößel *m*, Keule *f*; *Am sl* Polizist *m*.

pour [pɔ:(ə)] *tr* gießen, schütten (*out of, from* aus; *into* in; *on* auf; *over* über); *(Getränk)* eingießen, -schenken; verschwenden; *itr* fließen, strömen, sich ergießen; gießen, schütten, heftig regnen; *(Menschen)* sich (in Massen) stürzen; *s* Guß *m*; Strömen *n*; Regenguß; *tech* Einguß *m*; *to ~ it on (Am sl)* 'rangehen; *mot* Vollgas geben; *to ~ oil on troubled waters* die erhitzten Gemüter beruhigen; *to ~ cold water on s.o.* jdn ernüchtern; *it never rains but it ~s (fig)* es kommt immer alles zusammen; *the sweat ~ed off him* der Schweiß floß ihm (nur so) vom Leibe; *it's ~ing with rain* es gießt in Strömen; *to ~* **down** *tr* niedergehen lassen; *itr* herabstürzen; in Strömen fallen; *to ~* **forth** aus-, hervorstoßen; ertönen lassen; *to ~* **in** *itr* hereinströmen; *(Aufträge)* in großen Mengen eingehen; *tr* eingießen, -schenken; *to ~* **off** abgießen; *to ~* **out** *itr* herausströmen; *tr* ausgießen; *(sein Herz)* ausschütten; *he ~ed his troubles out to me* er hat mir sein Leid geklagt; **~ing** ['-riŋ] *a* strömend, triefend, in Strömen; *~~ defect (metal)* Gußfehler *m*; **~ point** *(Öl)* Stockpunkt; *(Metall)* Fließpunkt *m*.

pout [paut] *itr* die Lippen aufwerfen *od* spitzen; schmollen, ein böses Gesicht machen; vorstehen; *s* Schmollen *n*; *pl* (Anfall *m*) schlechte(r) Laune *f*; **~er** ['-ə] Schmoller *m*; Kropftaube *f*; **~ing** ['-iŋ] *a (Lippen)* aufgeworfen, dick; *s* Schmollen *n*; **~y** ['-i] *Am fam* übelnehmerisch, sauertöpfisch.

poverty ['pɔvəti] Armut, Dürftigkeit *f*; Elend *n*, Not(durft) *f*; Mangel *m* (*of, in* an); Mangelhaftigkeit, Minderwertigkeit *f*; *to be reduced to ~* verarmt sein; **~-stricken** *a* sehr arm; *fig* armselig, ärmlich, dürftig.

*

powder ['paudə] *s* Puder *m*, Pulver *n*, Staub *m*; *tr* (ein)pudern; bestreuen (*with* mit); pulverisieren; *itr* pulverförmig sein, stäuben; *(to ~ o.'s face)* sich pudern; *Am sl* abhauen, sich aus dem Staub machen = *to take a ~*; *to keep o.'s ~ dry (fig)* auf der Hut sein; *baby-~* Kinder-, Körperpuder *m*; *face-, foot-~* Gesichts-, Fußpuder *m*; *gun~* Schießpulver *n*; *smell of ~* Pulvergeruch *m*; *not worth ~ and shot* keinen Schuß Pulver wert; nicht der Mühe wert; **~ blue** rauchblau; **~-box, -com-pact** Puderdose *f*; **~ chamber** Pulverkammer *f*; Verbrennungsraum *m*; **~ charge** Pulverladung *f*; **~ed** ['-d] *a*: *~~ coal* Kohlenstaub *m*; *~~ egg* Eipulver, Trockenei *n*; *~~ coffee* Kaffeepulver *n*; *~~ sugar* Puder-, Staubzucker *m*; **~-flask, -horn** Pulverhorn *n*; **~ keg** Pulverfaß *n*; **~-magazine** Pulvermagazin *n*, -kammer *f*; **~-mill** Pulvermühle, Munitionsfabrik *f*; **~-puff** Puderquaste *f*; *Am sl* vorsichtige(r) Boxer *m*; **~ room** *Am* Damentoilette *f*; **~ smoke** Pulverqualm *m*; **~ sticks** *pl* Stangenpulver *n*; **~y** ['-ri] pulverförmig, pulverisiert; mürbe, leicht (zu Staub) zerfallend; staubig, staubbedeckt; *~~ snow* Pulverschnee *m*.

power ['pauə] (Handlungs-, Leistungs-)Fähigkeit *f*, Vermögen *n*; Kraft, Stärke, Energie; Gewalt; Herrschaft *f* (*over* über); Einfluß *m* (*with* auf); Vollmacht *(a. als Dokument)*, Berechtigung, Befugnis; *pol* Macht; *phys tech el* (Treib-)Kraft, Energie; Leistung, (Strom-)Stärke *f*; *el* Strom *m*; *opt* Vergrößerungskraft, Stärke; *min* Mächtigkeit; *math* Potenz; *fam* Menge, Masse *f* (*of money* Geld); *attr tech* Kraft-, Energie-; *pl* Behörden *f pl*; *pl* Rechte *n pl*, Vollmacht *f*; *tr tech* mit e-r Kraft-, Energiequelle versehen; antreiben; potenzieren; *fam* mit Gewalt durchsetzen; *in ~* an der Macht; im Amt; *to be in s.o.'s ~* in jds Gewalt sein; *to be within (beyond) s.o.'s ~* in (nicht in) jds Macht liegen; *to come into ~* an die Macht gelangen; *to do all in o.'s ~* alles in s-r Macht Stehende tun; *to give s.o. full ~s* jdm Vollmacht erteilen; jdm freie Hand lassen; *to have full ~s* Vollmacht haben; *to have s.o. in o.'s ~* jdn in der Gewalt haben; *he is losing his ~s* s-e Kräfte lassen nach; *more ~ to you* viel Erfolg! *abuse of ~* Amtsmißbrauch *m*; *accession, coming to, assumption of ~* Machtübernahme *f*; *balance of ~* Gleichgewicht *n* der Mächte; *borrowing ~* Kreditfähigkeit *f*; *buying ~* Kaufkraft *f*; *central ~* Zentralgewalt *f*; *colonial ~* Kolonialmacht *f*; *competitive ~* Konkurrenzfähigkeit *f*; *consuming ~* Konsumkraft *f*; *disciplinary ~* Disziplinargewalt *f*; *display of ~* Machtentfaltung *f*; *earning-~* Ertrags-, Erwerbsfähigkeit *f*; *economic ~* Wirtschaftspotential *n*; *electric ~* elektrische Energie *f*; *financial ~* Finanzkraft *f*; *full ~* Vollmacht *f*; *great ~* Großmacht *f*; *horse-~* Pferdestärke *f*; *increase of ~* Leistungssteigerung *f*; *land ~* Landmacht *f*; *military ~* Militär-, Kriegsmacht *f*; *occupational ~* Besatzungsmacht *f*; *parental ~* elterliche Gewalt *f*; *productive ~* Produktionskraft *f*; *purchasing ~* Kaufkraft *f*; *rated ~ (tech)* Nennleistung *f*; *sea ~* Seemacht *f*; *separation of ~s* Gewaltenteilung *f*; *signatory ~* Signatarmacht *f*; *source of ~* Kraft-, Energiequelle *f*; *sphere of ~* Machtsphäre *f*, Einflußbereich *m*; *water ~* Wasserkraft *f*; *will to ~* Machtwille; Wille *m* zur Macht; *world ~* Weltmacht *f*; *the ~s above* die himmlischen Mächte *f pl*; *~ of appointment* Ernennungsrecht *n*; *~ of attorney* (Handlungs-, Prozeß-)Vollmacht *f*; *~ of life and death* Gewalt über Leben u. Tod; *the ~s that be* die Machthaber *m pl*; die Obrigkeit; **~ amplifier** Leistungs-, Endverstärker *m*; **~-basin** Staubeckenanlage *f*; **~-boat** *Am* schnelle(s) Motorboot; *mil* Sturmboot *n*; **~ cable** Starkstromkabel *n*; **~-circuit** Starkstromleitung *f*; Kraftstromkreis *m*; **~ consumer** Stromabnehmer *m*; **~ consumption** Strom-, Kraftverbrauch *m*; **~ demand** Kraftbedarf *m*; **~-dive** *aero* Sturzflug *m* mit Vollgas; **~-driven** *a* mit Motorantrieb; **~ economy** Energiewirtschaft *f*; **~ed** ['-d] *a* angetrieben; *in Zssgen tech* Kraft-; *~~ glider (aero)* Motorsegler *m*; **~ factor** Leistungs-, Machtfaktor *m*; **~ failure** *aero* Motorausfall *m*; **~ frequency** Netzfrequenz *f*; **~ful** ['-ful] mächtig, stark, einflußreich; vermögend, wohlhabend; leistungsfähig; **~fully** ['-fuli] *adv fam* mächtig, gewaltig; **~ generation** Krafterzeugung *f*; **~-house** Kraftwerk *n*; *Am sl* Kraftprotz *m*, Kanone *f*; **~ increase** Leistungsanstieg *m*, -zunahme *f*; **~ input** Eingangsleistung *f*; **~less** ['-lis] kraft-, machtlos; **~lessness** ['-lisnis] Kraft-, Machtlosigkeit *f*; **~ level** Leistungspegel *m*; **~ line** Starkstrom-, Hochspannungsleitung *f*; **~ load** Kraftstrom *m*; Strombelastung *f*; **~-loom** mechanische(r) Webstuhl *m*; **~ loss** Energieverlust *m*; **~ mains** *pl* Kraftnetz *n*; **~ output** Ausgangsleistung *f*; **~ peak** Leistungsspitze *f*; **~ plant** Kraftwerk *n*; *tech* Maschinensatz *m*; *mot* Triebwerk *n*; **~ plug** Netzstecker *m*; **~-point** *el* Steckdose *f*; **~ politics** Machtpolitik *f*; **~ rail** Stromschiene *f*; **~ rating** Nennleistung *f*; **~ reserve** Kraftreserve *f*; **~ saw** Motorsäge *f*; **~ set** *el* Aggregat *n*; **~ shovel** Löffelbagger *m*; **~ shut-down** Stromsperre *f*; **~ source** Energie-, Kraftquelle *f*; **~ station** Kraftwerk *n*, -zentrale *f*; **~ steering** *mot* Servosteuerung *f*; **~ stroke** Arbeitshub *m*; **~ supply** Energie-, Stromversorgung *f*; *radio* Netzanschluß *m*; *~~ line* Zuführungsleitung *f*; **~ take-off** *tech* Abtrieb *m*; **~ traction** *mot* Kraftzug *m*; **~ transmission** *tech* Kraftübertragung *f*; **~ tube** Lautsprecherröhre *f*; **~ unit** Krafteinheit *f*.

powwow ['pauwau] *s Am* Medizinmann; *fam* Konferenz, Versammlung *f*; Fest *n*; *Br sl* Manöverbesprechung *f*; *itr (to hold a ~) Am fam* debattieren, konferieren (*about* über).

pox [pɔks] *(small~)* Pocken, Blattern *pl*; *fam* Syphilis *f*; *chicken, cow ~* Wind-, Kuhpocken *pl*.

pract|icability [præktikə'biliti], **~icableness** ['præktikəblnis] Aus-, Durchführbarkeit; Brauchbarkeit; Befahr-, Begehbarkeit *f*; **~icable** ['præktikəbl] aus-, durchführbar; brauchbar, benutzbar, gangbar; befahr-, begehbar; **~ical** ['præktikəl] praktisch; leicht zu handhaben(d); durchführbar; anwendbar; *(Vorschlag)* praktisch, brauchbar; nützlich; zweckmäßig; *(Können, Wissen)* praktisch, in der Praxis gewonnen; *(Wissenschaft)* angewandt; *(Mensch)* praktisch (veranlagt); erfahren; alltäglich, Alltags-, Umgangs-; tatsächlich, wirklich; wirklichkeitsnah, -verbunden; *~~ capacity* Betriebsoptimum *n*; *~~ chemist* Chemotechniker *m*; *~~ joke* handgreifliche(r) Spaß, Streich *m*; *~~ knowledge* Erfahrungswissen *n*; **~icality** [prækti'kæliti] einfache Handhabung; Brauchbarkeit; praktische Veranlagung; Wirklichkeitsnähe, -verbundenheit *f*; **~ically** ['præktikəli] *adv* in der Praxis; (in) praktisch(er) Weise, wirklichkeitsnah; ['præktikli] praktisch, faktisch, so gut wie, nahezu, beinahe, fast; *it's ~~ the same* es ist fast dasselbe; **~ice** ['præktis] Ausübung, Handhabung *f*, Verfahren *n*; praktische Tätigkeit, Praxis *(a. e-s Arztes* od *Rechtsanwalts)*; Klientel; Gewohnheit *f*, (Ge-)Brauch *m*, Sitte; Übung *a. mil*; praktische Erfahrung *f*; *pl pej* Praktiken *f pl*, Kniffe *m pl*, Schliche *pl*, Gaunereien *f pl*, Ränke *pl*; *v Am = ~ise*; *in ~~* in Wirklichkeit, tatsächlich; in (der) Übung; *out of ~~* aus der Übung; *to be in ~~ (Arzt, Anwalt)* praktizieren; *to make it a ~~ to do, to make a ~~ of doing* es sich zur Gewohnheit machen zu tun; *to put in(to) ~~* in die Tat umsetzen, wirklich machen, ausführen; *~~ makes perfect (prov)* Übung macht den Meister; *barrister's, law ~~* (Rechts-)Anwaltspraxis *f*; *doctor's ~~, ~~ of medicine* Arztpraxis *f*; *~~ alarm* Probealarm *m*; *~~ alert* Luftschutzübung *f*; *~~ ammunition (mil)* Übungsmunition *f*; *~~ cartridge* Exerzierpatrone *f*; *~~ firing* Übungsschießen *n*; *~~ ground* Schießstand *m*; *~~ target* Schießscheibe *f*; **~ician** [præk'tiʃən] Praktiker, Mann der Praxis, *fam* Praktikus; praktizierende(r) Arzt, Anwalt *m*; **~ise**, *Am meist* **~ice** ['præktis] *tr* ausüben, betreiben; es sich zur Gewohnheit machen; (ein)üben; (praktisch) anleiten, ausbilden; *itr* (sich) üben (*on* an, auf); praktisch tätig sein, praktizieren; *sport* trainieren; mißbrauchen, hintergehen, hereinlegen (*on, upon s.o.* jdn); *to ~~ law, as a lawyer* od *attorney* e-e Anwaltspraxis haben, als Anwalt tätig sein; *to ~~ medicine, as a doctor* e-e ärztliche Praxis haben, (als Arzt) praktizieren; **~ised**, *Am meist* **~iced** ['-t] *a* geübt, erfahren, bewandert, gewandt, geschickt; **~itioner** [præk'tiʃnə] Fachmann; Praktiker, Mann *m* der Praxis; *(general ~~)* praktische(r) Arzt *m*; *legal ~~* (praktizierender) Rechtsanwalt *m*.

pragmat|ic [præg'mætik] *pol hist philos* pragmatisch; **~ical** [-ikəl] geschäftig, aufdringlich; von sich selbst überzeugt, rechthaberisch, dogmatisch; *philos* pragmatisch; **~ism** ['prægmətizm] Tätigkeit *f*; Fleiß; Übereifer *m*, Geschäftigkeit; Sachlichkeit, Nüchternheit *f*; *philos* Pragmatismus *m*; **~ist** ['prægmətist] Pragmatiker *m*; **~ize** ['prægmətaiz] *tr* als wirklich ansehen *od* hinstellen; *(Mythus)* rational auslegen.

prairie ['prɛəri] Prärie, Grasebene *(bes. in Nordamerika)*; *Am* Wiese, *a.* Lichtung *f*; **~ chicken, hen** *orn* Präriehuhn *n*; **~ dog** Präriehund *m*; **~ oyster** Prärieauster *f (rohes Eigelb mit Tomatenmark u. Gewürzen)*; **~ schooner** *Am* (großer) Planwagen *m*; **~ wolf** Präriewolf *m*.

praise [preiz] *tr* preisen, loben (*for* wegen); bewundern; *s* Preis *m*, Lob *n*; Anerkennung, Bewunderung *f*; *to ~ up* rühmen; *to ~ to the skies (fam)* in den Himmel heben; über den grünen Klee loben; **~worthiness** ['-wə:ðinis] lobenswerte Eigenschaften *f pl*; **~worthy** ['-wə:ði] anerkennens-, lobenswert.

pram [præm] **1.** *mar* Prahm *m*; **2.** *fam* Kinderwagen *m*.

prance [prɑ:ns] *itr (Pferd)* sich aufbäumen, sich auf der Hinterhand aufrichten, e-e Levade, e-e Kurbette machen; *(Mensch) (auf e-m Pferde)* paradieren; *(vor Ungeduld)* stampfen; umherspringen; *fig* einherstolzieren; sich brüsten.

prang [præŋ] *s aero sl* Bruchlandung *f*; Bombenhagel, schwere(r) Luftangriff *m*; Heldentat *f*; *tr* bepflastern, schwer bombardieren; *(durch Bruchlandung)* kaputtmachen.

prank [præŋk] **1.** *s* (übler) Streich, Ulk, Possen, handgreifliche(r) Scherz; *(Tier)* übermütige(r), ausgelassene(r) Sprung *m*; *to play ~s on s.o.* jdm e-n Streich spielen; **2.** *tr itr (to ~ out, to ~ up)* (sich) ausstaffieren (*with* mit); *fig* herausstreichen.

prat [præt] *sl* Hinterteil *n*; **~fall**: *to have a ~~ (Am sl)* auf den Hintern fallen.

prat|e [preit] *itr* schwatzen, plappern; albern reden; *tr* daherreden; ausschwatzen; *s* Geschwätz, Gewäsch, Geplapper *n*; **~er** ['-ə] Schwätzer *m*; **~ing** ['-iŋ] geschwätzig.

praties ['preiti:z] *pl fam* Kartoffeln *f pl*.

prattl|e ['prætl] *itr* schwatzen, plappern, babbeln; quasseln; *s* Geschwätz *n*, Schwatz *m*; Geplapper; Gequassel; Gebabbel *n*; **~er** ['-ə] Schwätzer *m*, Plappermaul *n*; **~ing** ['-iŋ] schwatzhaft.

prawn [prɔ:n] *zoo* (Stein-)Garnele *f*.

pray [prei] *tr* beten, flehen um; erflehen; *to ~ s.o. to do s.th.* jdn bitten, etw zu tun; *itr* beten (*to* zu; *for* um); flehen(tlich bitten) (*for* um); *(I) ~ (you)* (ich) bitte (Sie); **~er** [prɛə] Gebet; Flehen *n*, flehentliche Bitte *f*; Bittgesuch *n*; *pl* Bittgottesdienst *m*; ['preiə] Bet(end)er *m*; *to say o.'s ~~s* sein Gebet verrichten; *he hasn't got a ~~ (Am sl)* er hat keine Chance; *the Book of Common P~* die Liturgie *f* der englischen Hochkirche; *the Lord's P~* das Vaterunser; *morning-, evening-~* Morgen-, Abendgebet *n*; *~~-book* Gebetbuch *n*; *~~-meeting* Betstunde *f*; *~~-rug, -mat* Gebetsteppich *m*; *~~-stool* Betstuhl *m*; *~~-wheel, -mill* Gebetsmühle *f*; **~ing** ['-iŋ]: *~~ mantis (ent)* Gottesanbeterin *f*.

pre [pri(:)] *pref* Vor(aus)-, vor(aus)-; Prä-, prä-; vorher(ig), früher.

preach [pri:tʃ] *itr* predigen *a. pej* (*to* vor); *tr* predigen; verfechten, sich einsetzen für; *(Predigt)* halten; *to ~ down* heruntermachen; *to ~ up* herausstreichen; *to ~ to deaf ears* tauben Ohren predigen; **~er** ['-ə] Prediger; salbungsvolle(r) Redner *m*; **~ify** ['-ifai] *itr fam* salbadern; **~ing** ['-iŋ] Predigen *n*; Predigt *f*; **~ment** ['-mənt] lang(weilig)e Predigt, Salbaderei *f*; **~y** ['-i] salbungsvoll.

preamble [pri:'æmbl] *jur pol* Präambel; Einleitung, Vorrede *f*, Vorwort *n*; *fig* Auftakt *m*.

prearrange ['pri:ə'reindʒ] *tr* vorher einrichten, festlegen, bestimmen; vorbereiten.

prebend ['prebənd] *rel* Pfründe *f*; **~ary** ['-əri] Pfründner; Domherr *m*.

precarious [pri'kɛəriəs] *jur* widerruflich; unsicher, ungewiß, schwankend; unbestätigt, unbewiesen; prekär, riskant, gefährlich.

precast [pri:'kɑ:st] *a (Beton)* Spann-; vorgefertigt; **~ pile** Betonmast *m*.

precaut|ion [pri'kɔ:ʃən] Vorsicht(smaßnahme, -maßregel); Umsicht *f*; *by way of ~~* aus Vorsicht; *to take ~~s* Vorsichtsmaßnahmen treffen; **~ionary** [-ʃnəri] *a* Vorsichts-, Warn(ungs)-; *~~ signal* Warnsignal *n*.

preced|e [pri(:)'si:d] *tr* voraus-, vorangehen (*s.o., s.th.* jdm, e-r S); *fig* vorausschicken; den Vorrang haben vor; bedeutender, wichtiger sein als; *itr* voran-, vorgehen; **~ence, ~ency** [pri(:)'si:dəns(i), 'presi-] Voraus-, Vorangehen *n*; Vorrang, -tritt, höhere(r) Rang *m*, höhere(s) Dienstalter, Vorrecht *n*; *to give s.o. ~~, to yield ~~ to s.o.*, jdm den Vortritt lassen; *order of ~~* Rangordnung *f*; **~ent** ['presidənt] *a* vorher-, voraus-, vorangehend; *s* Präzedenzfall *m*; *pl* Rechtsprechung *f (of a case* zu e-m Fall); *to become a ~~* ein Präzedenzfall werden.

precept ['pri:sept] Verordnung, Vorschrift; Anweisung, Verhaltensmaßregel; (Lebens-)Regel, Maxime; Richtschnur, Unterweisung; *jur* gerichtliche Anordnung *f*; *(Steuer)* Zahlungsauftrag *m*; **~ive** [pri'septiv], **~ory** [-əri] instruktiv, lehrhaft; **~or** [-'septə] Lehrer; *Am (Universität)* Tutor, Repetitor *m*; **~orial** [prisep'tɔ:riəl] *a* Lehrer-; **~ress** [-'septris] Lehrerin; Erzieherin *f*.

precinct ['pri:siŋkt] *Am* (Stadt-, Polizei-, Wahl-)Bezirk; *fig* Bereich *m* od *n*; Grenze *f*; *pl* Umkreis *m*, Umgebung, Nachbarschaft *f*.

precious ['preʃəs] *a* wertvoll (*to* für); kostbar *a. fig*; ausgezeichnet; (ge-)lieb(t), teuer; zierlich, geziert, affektiert; *fam* riesig, gewaltig; *adv fam* mächtig, schrecklich, sehr, höchst, äußerst; *s fam* Liebling *m*, Schätzchen *n*; **~ metal** Edelmetall *n*; **~ness** ['-nis] Kostbarkeit *f*, hohe(r) Wert *m*; Affektiertheit *f*; **~ stone** Edelstein *m*.

precip|ice ['presipis] Abgrund *a. fig*, Steilhang *m*; *fig* große, ungeheure Gefahr *f*; **~itance, -cy** [pri'sipitəns(i)] Überstürzung, Übereilung, Hast, große Eile, Unüberlegtheit *f*; **~itant** [pri'sipitənt] *a Am* kopfüber; *fig* überstürzt, übereilt; plötzlich, unerwartet; *s chem* Fällungsmittel *n*; **~itate** [pri'sipiteit] *tr* (kopfüber) hinabstürzen; niederstoßen, -werfen; *fig* überstürzen, übereilen, übers Knie brechen; stark beschleunigen; *chem mete* niederschlagen, kondensieren, fällen; *itr chem mete* sich niederschlagen; *a* [-tit] steil abfallend; (her-, hin)abstürzend; *fig* überstürzt, übereilt; *s chem mete* Niederschlag *m*; **~itation** [prisipi'teiʃən] (tiefer) Sturz, Absturz *m*; Überstürzung, Übereilung, Hast; *chem* Fällung *f*; *mete* Niederschläge *m pl*, Niederschlagsmenge *f*; *~~ area* Niederschlagsgebiet *n*; **~itous** [pri'sipitəs] abschüssig, steil (abfallend), jäh.

précis ['preisi:] *pl* ~ [-si:z] Abriß, Auszug *m*; (kurze) Zs.fassung, Übersicht *f*; **~-writing** *(Schule)* Nacherzählung *f*.

precis|e [pri'sais] genau, exakt, bestimmt, fest umrissen, deutlich, klar; gewissenhaft; pünktlich; pedantisch, umständlich; **~ely** [-li] *adv* genau;

stimmt, so ist es; **~eness** [-nis] Genauigkeit; Korrektheit; Pedanterie *f*; **~ian** [-'siʒən] Pedant *m*; **~ion** [pri'siʒən] *s* Genauigkeit, Exaktheit, Bestimmtheit; *tech* Präzision *f*; *attr* Präzisions-; *~~ balance* Präzisionswaage *f*; *~~ bombing* gezielte(r) Bombenwurf *m*; *~~ instrument* Präzisionsinstrument *n*; *~~ landing (aero)* Ziellandung *f*; *~~ mechanic* Feinmechaniker *m*; *pl* Feinmechanik *f*; *~~ tools (pl)* Präzisionswerkzeuge *n pl*.

preclu|de [pri'klu:d] *tr* ausschließen, -schalten, verhüten, vermeiden, (ver-)hindern (*from doing* etw zu tun); *to ~~ all doubt* jeden Zweifel ausschließen; **~sion** [-ʒən] Ausschluß *m* (*from* von); Ausschaltung, Verhütung, Vermeidung, Verhinderung *f*; **~sive** [-siv] *a* Verhütungs-; ausschließend, verhütend (*of s.th.* etw).

precoc|ious [pri'kouʃəs] frühreif *a. fig*; *med* Jugend-; **~iousness** [-nis], **~ity** [-'kɔsiti] Frühzeitigkeit, -reife *f*.

preconc|eive ['pri:kən'si:v] *tr* sich (schon) vorher Gedanken machen *od* e-e Meinung bilden über; vorwegnehmen; *~~d opinion* vorgefaßte Meinung *f*; **~eption** ['-'sepʃən] vorgefaßte Meinung *f*; Vorurteil *n*.

preconcert ['prikən'sə:t] *tr* vorher absprechen; **~ed** ['-id] *a* abgesprochen, abgekartet.

precurs|or [pri'kə:sə] Vorläufer, -bote; Vorgänger *m*; **~ory** [-əri] an-, verkündigend, Ankündigungs-; vorbereitend, einleitend, Eingangs-; *to be ~~ of s.th.* etw verkünden, anzeigen.

predatory ['predətəri] räuberisch, raubgierig; schädlich; *~~ bird* Raubvogel *m*.

predecessor ['pri:disesə] (Amts-)Vorgänger; Vorfahr(e), Ahn(herr) *m*.

predestin|ate [pri(:)'destineit] *tr rel* vorherbestimmen (*to* für); *a.* **~e** [-'destin] *tr allg* vorher festlegen; *a* [-nit] vorherbestimmt; **~ation** [pri(:)desti'neiʃən] Prädestination *f*.

predetermin|ation ['pri:ditə:mi'neiʃən] Vorherbestimmung *f*; **~e** ['pri:di'tə:min] *tr* vorher festlegen; *to ~~ s.o. to s.th.* jdn für etw vorbestimmen.

predic|able ['predikəbl] aussagbar, auszusagen(d) (*of* von, über); **~ament** [pri'dikəmənt] mißliche, üble, ungenehme, heikle Lage *f*; *philos* Kategorie *f*; **~ate** ['predikeit] *tr* aussagen (*of* über); feststellen; behaupten; einschließen, in sich begreifen, umfassen; *Am* (be)gründen (*on, upon* auf); abhängig machen (*on a condition* von e-r Bedingung); *itr* e-e Behauptung aufstellen, e-e Feststellung treffen; [-kit] *s gram (a. Logik)* Prädikat *n*; *a* Prädikats-; *~~ noun* Prädikatsnomen *n*; **~ation** [predi'keiʃən] Aussage *f*; **~ative** [pri'dikətiv] *a* Aussage-; *gram* prädikativ.

predict [pri'dikt] *tr* vorhersagen, prophezeien; **~ion** [pri'dikʃən] Vorhersage; Weissagung, Prophezeiung *f*; *~~ angle (mil)* Vorhaltewinkel *m*; **~ive** [pri'diktiv] in die Zukunft weisend; prophetisch; **~or** [pri'diktə] Prophet *m*; *(Flak)* Kommandogerät *n*.

predilection [pri:di'lekʃən] Vorliebe, Voreingenommenheit (*for* für).

predispos|e ['pri:dis'pouz] *tr* geneigt, empfänglich machen (*to* zu, für); günstig stimmen (*in s.o.'s favo(u)r* für jdn); empfänglich *a. med*, aufnahmebereit machen, prädisponieren (*to* für); **~ition** ['pri:dispə'ziʃən] Geneigtheit, Empfänglichkeit *a. med*; *med* Prädisposition *f* (*to* für).

predomin|ance, -cy [pri'dɔminəns(i)] Überlegenheit *f*, Übergewicht *n* (*over* über); Vorherrschaft *f*; Vorherrschen *n* (*over* über; *in* in); **~ant** [-ənt] überlegen, beherrschend; vorherrschend, überwiegend; **~ate** [-eit] *itr* überlegen sein; die Oberhand haben (*over* über); vorherrschen (*over* unter).

preem [pri:m] *Am theat sl s* Erstaufführung, Premiere *f*; *tr* erstaufführen; **~y** ['-i] *Am fam med* Frühgeburt *f*.

pre-eminen|ce [pri(:)'eminəns] Vorrang *m*, Überlegenheit *f* (*over* über); **~t** [-t] hervor-, überragend (*above* über).

pre-empt [pri(:)'empt] *tr* auf Grund e-s Vorkaufsrechts erwerben; *(Am) s.th.* sich das Vorkaufsrecht auf e-e S sichern; **~ion** [-'empʃən] Vorkauf(s-recht *n*) *m*; *~~ price* Vorkaufspreis *m*; **~ive** [-iv] Vorkaufs-.

preen [pri:n] *tr (Gefieder)* putzen, glätten; *itr* u. *to ~ o.s.* sich fein machen; *to ~ o.s.* sich etw einbilden (*on* auf).

pre-engage ['pri:in'geidʒ] *tr* im voraus verpflichten; *itr* sich im voraus verpflichten; *com* vorbestellen; **~ment** ['-mənt] frühere Verpflichtung *f*.

pre-exist ['pri:ig'zist] *itr* vorher existieren; **~ence** ['-əns] Präexistenz *f*.

*

prefab ['pri:'fæb] *tr fam* = *~ricate*; *s fam* Fertighaus *n*; **~ricate** ['-rikeit] *tr* vorfabrizieren; *(Haus)* fabrik-, serienmäßig, in genormten Fertigteilen herstellen; **~rication** ['-fæbri'keiʃən] Fertigbauweise *f*.

prefa|ce ['prefis] *s* Vorrede *f*, Vorwort *n*; Einleitung *f*; *tr* mit e-r Vorrede, Einleitung versehen; einleiten (*with* mit); einführen in; **~torial** [prefə'tɔ:riəl], **~tory** ['prefətəri] einleitend, -führend; *~tory note* Vorbemerkung *f*.

prefect ['pri:fekt] (Polizei-)Präfekt; *Br* Vertrauensschüler, Ordner *m*.

prefer [pri'fə:] *tr* vorziehen, bevorzugen; lieber tun *od* haben (*s.th. to s.th. else* etw als e-e andere S; *rather than* als); *(im Amt, Rang)* befördern (*to* zu); *(Bitte)* vortragen; in Vorschlag bringen, vor-, einbringen; *(Gesuch)* einreichen; *(Anspruch; Klage, Anschuldigung)* erheben (*against* gegen; *to* bei); **~able** ['prefərəbl] vorzuziehen(d), wünschenswerter (*to* als); **~ably** *adv* vorzugsweise, mit Vorliebe; besser, eher, lieber; **~ence** ['prefərəns] Bevorzugung (*over* vor); Vorliebe (*for* für); Vortritt *m*, Vorrecht *n*, höhere(r) *od* ältere(r) Anspruch *m*, Priorität(srecht *n*); Meistbegünstigung *f*, Vorzugstarif *m*; *pl* Vorzugsaktien *f pl*; *a* Vorzugs-, Präferenz-; bevorrechtigt, privilegiert; *by, for, from ~~* mit Vorliebe, besonders gern, vorzugsweise; *in ~~ to* lieber als; *to give ~~ to s.o.* jdm den Vorzug geben; *to have a ~~ for* e-e Vorliebe haben für; *what is your ~~?* was ziehen Sie vor? *I have no ~~* das ist mir einerlei; *~~ bonds (pl)* Prioritätsobligationen *f pl*; *~~ capital* Vorzugsaktienkapital *n*; *~~ loan* Prioritätsanleihe *f*; *~~ offer* Vorzugs-, Sonderangebot *n*; *~~ share, (Am) stock* Vorzugsaktie *f*; **~ential** [prefə'renʃəl] *a* Vorzugs-; bevorzugt, bevorrechtet; *~~ claim, debt* bevorrechtete Forderung *f*; *~~ creditor* Prioritätsgläubiger *m*; *~~ dividend* Vorzugsdividende *f*; *~~ duty* Vorzugszoll *m*; *~~ loan* Prioritätsanleihe *f*; *~~ offer* Vorzugs-, Sonderangebot *n*; *~~ price* Vorzugs-, Sonderpreis *m*; *~~ rate, tariff* Vorzugssatz, -tarif *m*; *~~ share, stock* Vorzugsaktie *f*; *~~ treatment* bevorzugte Behandlung, Bevorzugung *f*; **~entially** [prefə'renʃəli] *adv* vorzugsweise; **~ment** [pri'fə:mənt] Beförderung *(im Amt)*; höhere Stelle *f*; **~red** [pri'fə:d] *a* bevorzugt; Vorzugs-.

prefigur|ation [pri:figju'reiʃən] Andeutung, Vorwegnahme; vorherige Ausmalung *f*; Prototyp *m*, Urbild *n*; **~e** [pri(:)'figə] *tr* andeuten, vorwegnehmen; sich vorher ausmalen.

prefix ['pri:fiks] *s* Vorsilbe *f*, Präfix *n*; *tr* [pri:'fiks] als Vorsilbe, Präfix setzen vor; *fig* voranstellen, voransetzen.

pregnan|cy ['pregnənsi] *(Frau)* Schwangerschaft(sdauer); *(Tier)* Trächtigkeit(sdauer); *fig* Fruchtbarkeit *f*, Reichtum *m*, Gewichtigkeit; *(Ereignis)* Tragweite, Bedeutung *f*; **~t** ['-t] *(Frau)* schwanger; *(Tier)* trächtig; voll (*with* von); reich (*in* an); *fig* fruchtbar, gedankenreich; bedeutungsvoll, gewichtig; inhaltsreich.

preheat [pri:'hi:t] *tr* vorwärmen, vorerhitzen, anheizen.

prehensile [pri'hensail] *zoo* Greif-.

prehist|oric(al) ['pri:his'tɔrik(əl)] vor-, urgeschichtlich, prähistorisch; **~ory** ['pri:'histəri] Vor-, Urgeschichte *f*.

pre-ignition ['pri:ig'niʃən] *mot* Frühzündung *f*.

prejudg|e ['pri:'dʒʌdʒ] *tr* vorschnell ab-, verurteilen.

prejudic|e ['predʒudis] *s* Vorurteil *n*, vorgefaßte Meinung (*against* gegen); Voreingenommenheit (*in favo(u)r of* für); Beeinträchtigung, Schädigung *f*, Schaden, Nachteil *m*; *tr* ungünstig beeinflussen, einnehmen (*s.o. against* jdn gegen); sich nachteilig auswirken auf, Abbruch tun (*s.th.* e-r S); *to s.o.'s ~~* zu jds Nachteil, Schaden; *without ~~* unverbindlich, unter Vorbehalt, ohne Gewähr; *to s.th.* ohne e-r S vorzugreifen, unbeschadet e-r S; **~ed** ['-t] *a* voreingenommen (*in favo(u)r of* zugunsten); voller Vorurteile (*against* gegen); **~ial** [predʒu'diʃəl] nachteilig, schädlich (*to* für); *to be ~~ to* sich nachteilig auswirken auf.

prela|cy ['preləsi] Prälatenwürde *f*; Prälaten *m pl*; **~te** ['prelit] *rel* Prälat *m*.

prelect [pri'lekt] *itr (Univ.)* Vorlesungen halten (*on* über; *to* for); **~ion** [-'lekʃən] Vorlesung *f*; **~or** [-'lektə] Lektor, Dozent *m*.

prelim [pri'lim] *fam* Vor-, Aufnahmeprüfung *f*; *sport* Vorkampf *m*.

preliminary [pri'liminəri] *a* einleitend, -führend, vorbereitend; vorläufig, einstweilig; *s* Einleitung, Vorbereitung (*to* zu); Vorarbeit; vorbereitende Handlung *f*; Vorstadium *n*; *fam* Vorprüfung; *typ* Titelei *f*; *pl pol* Vorverhandlungen *f pl*, Präliminarien *pl*; *as a ~, by way of ~* einleitend, vorbereitend *adv*; *~* **advice, announcement, notice** Voranzeige *f*; *~* **agreement, contract** Vorvertrag *m*; *~* **custody** vorläufige Festnahme *f*; *~* **decision** Vorbe-, -entscheid *m*; *~* **decree** einstweilige Verfügung *f*; *~* **discussion** Vorbesprechung *f*; *~* **dressing** Notverband *m*; *~* **estimate** Voranschlag *m*; *~* **examination** Aufnahme-, Vorprüfung *f*; *~* **inquiry** Voranfrage *f*; *jur, a.* *~* **investigation** Voruntersuchung *f*; *~* **knowledge** vorherige Kenntnis *f*; Vorkenntnisse *f pl*, -bildung *f*; *~* **meeting** Vorversammlung *f*; *~* **plan** Vorentwurf *m*; *~* **question** Vorfrage *f*; *~* **report** Vorbericht *m*; Vorausmeldung *f*; *~* **round** *sport* Vorrundenspiel *n*; *~* **signal** Vorsignal *n*; *~* **state** Vorstadium *n*; *~* **step** erste(r) Schritt *m fig*; *~* **studies** *pl* Vorstudien *pl*; *~* **warning** Vorwarnung *f*; *~* **works** *pl* Vorarbeiten *f pl*.

prelude ['prelju:d] *s* Einleitung (*to* zu), Eröffnung *f* (*to* gen); *mus* Vorspiel, Präludium *n*; *fig* Auftakt *m*; *tr* einleiten, eröffnen; *itr* als Einleitung, *fig* als Auftakt dienen; *mus* präludieren.

prematur|e [preməˈtjuə, *Am* pri:-] vorzeitig, sehr früh, zu früh; *fig* voreilig; *med* frühreif; *~~ birth* Frühgeburt *f*; **~eness** [-nis], **~ity** [-riti] Vorzeitigkeit; Voreiligkeit; Frühreife *f*.

premeditat|e [pri(:)'mediteit] *tr* vorher bedenken; *tr itr* vorher überlegen; **~ion** [pri(:)medi'teiʃən] vorherige Überlegung *f*; Vorsatz *m*; *with ~~* überlegt *adv*, vorsätzlich.

premier ['premjə, *Am* pri'miə] *a* erst; frühest; *s* Premier(minister), Ministerpräsident; **~ship** ['-ʃip] Amt *n* des Premierministers.

première ['premiɛə, *Am* pri'miə] *theat film* Ur-, Erstaufführung *f*.

premise ['premis] *s* Prämisse, Voraussetzung *f*, *(Logik)* Vordersatz *m*; *the ~s (pl)* das Besagte, das Vorerwähnte, das Vorausgeschickte; die Vorbemerkungen *f pl*, die einleitenden Punkte *m pl* e-r Urkunde; das Grundstück, das Anwesen; die Geschäftsrämue, das Lokal; *tr* [pri'maiz] einleitend bemerken *od* feststellen, vorausschicken; *itr* e-e einleitende Bemerkung machen; *in the ~s* im Vorstehenden; *on the ~s* an Ort u. Stelle; *bank, factory ~s (pl)* Bank-, Fabrikgebäude *n*; *business ~s (pl)* Geschäftsgrundstück *n*, -räume *m pl*.

premium ['pri:mjəm] *com* Prämie *f*, Bonus *m*; Aufgeld, (Wechsel-)Agio *n*; Provision; Zugabe *f*; Lehrgeld *n*; (Versicherungs-)Prämie; Rabattmarke *f*; Preis *m*, Belohnung *f* (*on* auf); *fin* höhere(r) Realwert *m*; *at a ~ (fin)* über pari, mit Gewinn; *fig* sehr geschätzt, sehr gesucht; *to put a ~ on* e-e Belohnung setzen auf; *to sell at a ~* mit Gewinn verkaufen; *rate of ~* Prämiensatz *m*; *~ on exports* Ausfuhr-, Exportprämie *f*; *~* **pay** Zuschlag *m*; *~* **promotion** Zugabewesen *n*.

premonit|ion [pri:mə'niʃən] Warnung; Vorbedeutung; Vorahnung *f*; *med* Vorgefühl *n*; **~ory** [pri'mənitəri] warnend, ankündigend, -deutend; *~~ symptoms (pl)* erste Anzeichen *n pl*; *to be ~~ of s.th.* etw ankündigen.

pre-natal ['pri:'neitl] vor der Geburt; *~* **home** Heim *n* für werdende Mütter.

preoccup|ancy [pri:'əkjupənsi] (Recht *n* der) frühere(n) (In-)Besitznahme *f*; **~ation** [pri(:)əkju'peiʃən] vorherige, frühere(In-)Besitznahme; Inanspruchnahme *f*; Vertieftsein *n* (*with* in); Sorge; *(mental ~~)* Voreingenommenheit, Befangenheit *f*; **~ied** [pri(:)'əkjupaid] *a* in Anspruch genommen, beschäftigt; in Gedanken versunken; **~y** [pri(:)'əkjupai] *tr* vorher, früher in Besitz nehmen; ausschließlich (in Gedanken) beschäftigen, ganz beherrschen.

preordain ['pri:ɔ:'dein] *tr* vorher anordnen, bestimmen, festlegen.

prep [prep] *(= preparation) (Schule) fam* Hausaufgabe; *(= preparatory school) fam* Vorschule *f*.

prepaid ['pri:'peid] *a* (voraus)bezahlt; porto-, gebührenfrei; *~* **reply** Rückantwort bezahlt.

prepar|ation [prepə'reiʃən] Vor-, Zubereitung; Herstellung *f*; Vorkehrungsmaßnahmen *f pl*; Schularbeit *f*; *(Bericht)* Abfassen *n*; *mil* Rüstung; *tech* Aufbereitung *f*; *pharm* Präparat *n*; *med* Vorbehandlung *f*; *to make ~~s* Anstalten, Vorbereitungen treffen (*for* für); **~ative** [pri'pærətiv] *a* = *~atory*; *s* vorbereitende Maßnahme, Vorbereitung *f* (*for* auf; *to* zu); **~atory** [pri'pærətəri] *a* vorbereitend; Vorbereitungs-; einführend; *~~ to* vor; *s (~~ school, student)* (Schüler *m* e-r) private(n) Vorbereitungsschule *f*; *~~ command* Ankündigungskommando *n*; *~~ course* Vorbereitungslehrgang *m*; *~~ period* Vorbereitungszeit; *(Versicherung)* Wartezeit *f*; **~e** [pri'pɛə] *tr* vorbereiten (*for s.th.* auf etw; *to do* zu tun); Vorbereitungen, Vorkehrung(smaßnahm)en treffen für; *mil* sich rüsten auf; präparieren; fertigstellen; *tech* zurichten; *chem* darstellen; *(Erz)* aufbereiten; *(Essen)* zubereiten; *(Rechnung)* aufstellen; *(Vertrag)* entwerfen, anfertigen; *(Fragebogen)* ausfüllen; *itr* Vorbereitungen treffen, Anstalten machen; sich vorbereiten, sich anschicken; sich gefaßt machen (*for* auf); **~ed** [pri'pɛəd] *a* bereit, fertig (*for* für); *mil* kriegsbereit, gerüstet, einsatzbereit; (innerlich) vorbereitet, gefaßt (*for* auf; *to do* zu tun); präpariert; *to be ~~ to acknowledge, to admit* bereit sein, anzuerkennen, zuzugeben; *to be ~~ for the worst* auf das Schlimmste gefaßt sein; *I am not ~~ to say* ich möchte nicht behaupten; **~edness** [pri'pɛədnis, -ridnis] Bereitschaft (*for* zu); *mil* Einsatz-, Kriegsbereitschaft *f*.

prepay ['pri:'pei] *irr s. pay tr* im voraus, vorher bezahlen, vorauszahlen; *(Postsendung)* freimachen, frankieren; **~ment** ['-mənt] An-, Vorauszahlung; Freimachung *f*, Frankieren *n*.

prepense [pri'pens] vorbedacht, überlegt, vorsätzlich; *with malice ~~* in böser Absicht, vorsätzlich *adv*.

preponder|ance, -cy [pri'pɔndərəns(i)] Übergewicht *n a. fig*, -macht *f* (*over* über); **~ant** [-t] überwiegend, vorherrschend; *to be ~~* überwiegen; **~ate** [-eit] *itr* mehr wiegen, schwerer sein; das Übergewicht haben (*over s.th.* über etw); *(Waagschale)* sich neigen; *fig* überwiegen, vorherrschen.

preposit|ion [prepə'ziʃən] *gram* Präposition *f*; **~ional** [-ʃənl] *gram* präpositional.

prepossess [pri:pə'zes] *tr* von vornherein einnehmen (*in favo(u)r of* für); alles andere vergessen lassen; beeinflussen (*against* gegen); **~ing** [-iŋ] einnehmend, anziehend; **~ion** [pri:pə'zeʃən] Voreingenommenheit *f* (*in favo(u)r of* für; *against* gegen); Vorurteil *n* (*against* gegen).

preposterous [pri'pɔstərəs] unnatürlich, sinnwidrig, unsinnig; albern, lächerlich; *fam* hirnverbrannt.

prepot|ence, -cy [pri:'poutəns(i)] Vorherrschaft; Überlegenheit; *biol* Dominanz *f*; **~ent** [-t] vorherrschend, stärker, überlegen; *biol* dominant.

preprint ['pri:'print] Vorabdruck *m*.

prepuce ['pri:pju:s] *anat* Vorhaut *f*.

Pre-Raphaelite ['pri:'ræfəlait] *s (Kunst)* Präraffaelit *m*; *a* präraffaelitisch.

prerequisite ['pri:'rekwizit] *a* vorher erforderlich, notwendig (*to* für); *s* Vorbedingung, Voraussetzung *f* (*to, for* für).

prerogative [pri'rɔgətiv] *s* Vorrecht *n*, Prärogative *f*, Privileg; Hoheitsrecht *n*; *a* bevorrechtet, privilegiert.

presage ['presidʒ] *s* Vorzeichen *n*, -bedeutung *f*, Omen; Vorgefühl *n*, Vorahnung *f*; *tr* [*a.* pri'seidʒ] ein Vorzeichen sein für; bedeuten; ahnen; vorhersagen, prophezeien.

presbyop|ia [prezbi'oupjə] (Alters-) Weitsichtigkeit *f*; **~ic** [-'ɔpik] (alters-) weitsichtig.

presbyter ['prezbitə] Kirchenältester, *hist* Presbyter *m*; **P~ian** [prezbi'tiəriən] *a* presbyterianisch; *s* Presbyterianer *m*; **~y** ['prezbitəri] Altarplatz; Kirchenrat *m*; Presbyterium; *(röm.-kath.)* Pfarrhaus *n*.

prescien|ce ['presiəns, -ʃ-] Vorherwissen, -sehen *n*; **~t** [-t] vorherwissend, -sehend (*of* acc); *to be ~~ of s.th.* etw vorhersehen.

prescribe [pris'kraib] *tr* vorschreiben (*to s.o.* jdm); anordnen, -weisen, bestimmen; *med* verschreiben, verordnen (*s.th. for s.o.* jdm etw); *jur* für ungültig erklären, außer Kraft setzen; *itr* Vorschriften machen, Anweisungen geben; (ärztlich) beraten, behandeln (*for s.o.* jdn); verschreiben; *jur* ein Gewohnheitsrecht geltend machen (*to, for* auf); verjähren, ungültig werden, außer Kraft treten; **~d** [-d] *a* vorgeschrieben; *as ~~, in the ~~ form* vorschriftsmäßig, ordnungsgemäß, in der vorgeschriebenen Form; *in the ~~ time* fristgerecht, in der vorgesehenen Frist; *~~ by law* gesetzlich vorgeschrieben, obligatorisch.

prescript ['pri:skript] Vorschrift *f*; **~ion** [-'kripʃən] Vorschrift, Anordnung, Anweisung; *med* Verordnung *f*, Rezept *n*; *jur* Verjährung; Ersitzung *f*.

presence ['prezns] Gegenwart, Anwesenheit; (unmittelbare) Nähe, Umgebung; Begleitung *f*, Begleiter *m pl*; (hohe) Persönlichkeit, stattliche Erscheinung *f*, Äußere(s); Auftreten, Benehmen *n*; Geist(ererscheinung *f*) *m*; *min* Vorkommen *n*; *in the ~ of* im Beisein, in Gegenwart *gen*; *saving your ~* mit Verlaub (zu sagen); *your ~ is requested* Sie werden gebeten, sich einzufinden; *~ of mind* Geistesgegenwart *f*; **~-chamber** Audienzzimmer *n*.

present ['preznt] *a (räuml.)* anwesend, zugegen; *(räuml. u. zeitl.)* gegenwärtig; *(zeitl.)* augenblicklich, momentan; vorliegend; laufend; *s* Gegenwart *f*, augenblickliche(r) Zeitpunkt *m*; diese Gelegenheit *f*; *jur* vorliegende(s) Schriftstück; *gram* Präsens(form *f*) *n*, Gegenwart *f*; Geschenk, Präsent *n*, kleine Aufmerksamkeit *f*; *tr* [pri'zent] *(Person)* vorstellen; vortragen; vorlegen, (vor)zeigen; aufweisen; darbieten, vorführen, zur Schau stellen; *theat* spielen, aufführen; zu bedenken geben, anheimstellen; empfehlen, vorschlagen (*to* für); überreichen, schenken; beschenken (*with* mit); *jur parl* eingeben, vorlegen; einreichen; anklagen, Klage erheben gegen; *(Schwierigkeiten)* mit sich bringen, bieten; *(Gewehr)* anlegen, in Anschlag bringen; präsentieren; *at ~, at the ~ time* gegenwärtig, momentan *adv*, im Augenblick, zur Zeit, im gegenwärtigen Zeitpunkt; *by these ~s* mit der vorliegenden Urkunde; hiermit, hierdurch; *for the ~* vorerst, vorläufig; einstweilen; *in the ~ case* im vorliegenden Fall; *up to the ~ time* bis zum heutigen Tage, bis heute; *to be ~ at s.th.* bei e-r S anwesend, zugegen sein, e-r S beiwohnen; *to ~ o.'s apologies* sich entschuldigen; *to ~ arms* das Gewehr präsentieren; *to ~ o.s. at an examination* sich zu e-m Examen melden; *to ~ o.'s compliments to s.o.* sich jdm empfehlen, jdn grüßen, jdm Grüße ausrichten lassen; *all ~* alle Anwesenden; *~ arms!* präsentiert — das Gewehr! **~able** [pri'zentəbl] gesellschaftsfähig; würdig, ansehnlich, respektabel; **~ation** [prezen'teiʃən] Vorstellung; Vorlage, Vorzeigung; *theat* Darbietung,

Schaustellung, Vorführung; Aufführung *f*; Vortrag *m*, Darstellung; Überreichung; Schenkung *f*; Geschenk *n*; Eingabe, Vorlage *f*; Vorschlagsrecht *n*; *com* Aufmachung, Ausstattung; *med* Lage *f*; *mil* Anschlag *m*, Präsentieren *n*; *philos* Bewußtseinsinhalt *m*, Vorstellung *f*; *on* ~~ gegen Vorzeigung; ~~ *of claim* Anspruchserhebung *f*; ~~ *copy (Buch)* Frei-, Widmungsexemplar *n*; ~~ *of proof* Beweisantritt *m*; **~-day** gegenwärtig, heutig, zeitgenössisch; zeitgemäß, modern; **~ly** ['prezntli] *adv* bald, in kurzem, in Kürze; *Am* gegenwärtig; *obs* sofort, gleich; **~ment** [pri'zentmənt] Vorstellung, Aufführung; *theat* Darbietung, Vorführung, Schaustellung *f*; Schauobjekt *n*; Darlegung; *com fin* Vorzeigung, Vorlage; *jur* Anklage *f* von Amts wegen; *philos* Bewußtseinsinhalt *m*, Vorstellung *f*; ~ **participle** Mittelwort *n* der Gegenwart, Partizip *n* des Präsens; ~ **perfect** Perfekt *n*; ~ **tense** Präsens *n*, Gegenwart *f*; ~ **value** Realwert *m*.

presentiment [pri'zentimənt] Vorgefühl *n*, (*bes.* böse) (Vor-)Ahnung *f*.

preserv|able [pri'zə:vəbl] konservierbar; **~ation** [prezə(:)'veiʃən] Erhaltung, Konservierung; Beibehaltung, Aufrechterhaltung; *tech* Imprägnierung *f*; *state of* ~~ Erhaltungszustand *m*; *in good state of* ~~ gut erhalten; **~ative** [pri'zə:vətiv] *a* konservierend; Schutz-; *s* Konservierungs-, Schutzmittel; *med* Vorbeugungsmittel *n*, (*against, from* gegen); **~e** [pri'zə:v] *tr* bewahren, schützen (*from* vor); schonen; *(in gutem Zustand)* erhalten; instand halten; *(Nahrungsmittel)* einmachen, konservieren; *(Wild)* hegen; *tech* imprägnieren; *allg* beibehalten, aufrechterhalten; festhalten an; *(Frieden)* erhalten; *(Ruhe)* bewahren; *s (Wild, Fische)* Gehege *n*; *Br (game ~~)* Reservat, private(s) Jagdgebiet; Sonderrecht *n*; *meist pl* Eingemachte(s) *n*, Konserven *f pl*; Konfitüre, Marmelade *f*; *to encroach on s.o.'s ~~s* jdm ins Gehege kommen; *~~-jar* Einmach-, Marmeladenglas *n*; *~~ing salt* Pökelsalz *n*; **~ed** [-d] *a* konserviert, eingedost, eingemacht; *Am sl* betrunken; *well* ~~ noch gut aussehend, jünger erscheinend; ~~ *food* Konserven *f pl*; **~er** [-ə] Erhalter, Bewahrer (*from* von); Konservenfabrikant; Einkochapparat *m*; Konservierungsmittel *n*; *dress-~~ (Kleid)* Schweißblätter *n pl*.

pre-shrunk ['pri:'ʃrʌnk] *a (Textil)* nicht einlaufend, schrumpffest, krumpfecht.

presid|e [pri'zaid] *itr* vorsitzen (*over s.th.* e-r S); den Vorsitz, die Aufsicht führen, präsidieren (*over* über; *at* bei); leiten (*over s.th.* etw); die Macht in den Händen haben; *mus* führen *a. fig*; **~ency** ['prezidənsi] Vorsitz *m*, Präsidium *n*; (Ober-)Aufsicht; Präsidentschaft *f*; *Am* Rektorat *n (e-r Universität)*; **~ent** ['prezidənt] Vorsitzende(r), Präsident; Direktor; *Am (Universität)* Rektor *m*; **~ential** [prezi'denʃəl] *a* Präsidial-; Präsidenten-.

*

press [pres] **1.** *tr* drücken (*the button* auf den Knopf); pressen; *(Obst od Saft)* ausdrücken, -pressen; keltern; zs.drücken, -pressen; *(Hebel)* herunterdrücken, betätigen; plätten, bügeln; fest drücken (*to* an); dringend ersuchen, bestürmen, bitten (*to do* zu tun); nachdrücklich vorbringen; aufdrängen, -nötigen (*s.th. on s.o.* jdm etw); *(Auffassung)* durchsetzen; Nachdruck legen auf, hervorheben, betonen; drängen auf; energisch durchführen; bedrücken; *(to ~ hard)* bedrängen; zwingen, antreiben; *hist mil* pressen, gewaltsam anwerben; requirieren; *fig* an sich nehmen; **2.** *itr* e-n Druck ausüben, drücken (*on, upon* auf); vorwärtsdrängen, -stürmen; sich e-n Weg bahnen; drängen (*for s.th.* auf etw); bestehen (*for* auf); eindringen (*on, upon* auf); lasten (*against* auf); nötigen (*on, upon s.o.* jdn); dringlich sein; sich drängen; *to be ~ed for s.th.* an e-r S Mangel, nicht genug von e-r S haben, etw dringend brauchen; **3.** *s* Druck; Drang *m*, Dringlichkeit, Eile, Bedrängnis *f*; Andrang *m*, Gedränge *n*, (Menschen-)Menge; (Frucht-, Öl-)Presse, Stampfe; *(printing-~)* Druckpresse; (Buch-)Druckerei *f*; (Buch-)Druck *m*; Druckereigewerbe, -wesen; Druck- u. Verlagshaus *n*; Presse *f*, Zeitungen *f pl*; Zeitungs-, Pressewesen *n*; Journalismus *m*; Journalisten *m pl*; (Wäsche-, Bücher-)Schrank *(mit Regalen)*; *sport* Spanner *m*; *to ~ back* zurückdrängen, -drücken; *to ~ down* nieder-, zu Boden drücken; *to ~ in* eindrücken; *to ~ on, to ~ forward* weiter-, vorwärtseilen; vorwärts-, weiterdrängen; sich beeilen; *to ~ out* ausdrücken; ausbügeln; *to ~ upon* lasten auf; aufdrängen; **4.** *in the ~* in der Presse, im Druck; *to be hard ~ed* in großer Verlegenheit sein; *to have a good (bad) ~* e-e gute (schlechte) Presse haben, gut (schlecht) aufgenommen, beurteilt werden; *to ~ o.'s advantage* hinter s-m Vorteil her sein; *to ~ the button (el)* auf den Knopf, *fig* auf den Hebel drücken, den entscheidenden ersten Schritt tun; *to ~ s.o.'s hand* jdm die Hand drücken; *to ~ home* mit Nachdruck vertreten; energisch durchführen; *to ~ o.'s point* s-e Auffassung durchsetzen; *time ~es* die Zeit drängt, *fam* es pressiert; *I won't ~ the matter* ich möchte in dieser Sache nicht weiter drängen; *copying-~* Vervielfältigungsapparat *m*; *daily ~* Tagespresse *f*; *gutter ~* Skandalpresse *f*; *liberty of the ~* Pressefreiheit *f*; *linen-~* Wäscheschrank *m*; *local ~* Lokalpresse *f*; *rotary ~* Rotationspresse *f*; *trouser-~* Hosenbügler *m (Gerät)*; *wine-~* Kelter *f*; **~-agency** Nachrichtenbüro *n*, Presseagentur *f*; **~-agent** Presse-, Reklamechef, Werbeleiter *m*; ~ **attaché** Presseattaché *m*; **~-board** Preßspan *m*; **~-box** Presseloge *f*; **~-button** *el* (Druck-)Knopf *m*; *~~ control* Druckknopfsteuerung *f*; *~~ switch* Druckknopfschalter *m*; **~-campaign** Pressefeldzug *m*; **~-censorship** Pressezensur *f*; **~-clipping,** *Br* **-cutting** Zeitungsausschnitt *m*; *~-cutting agency* Zeitungsausschnittbüro *n*; ~ **commentary** Pressekommentar *m*; ~ **correspondent** Pressekorrespondent *m*; **~-conference** Pressekonferenz *f*; **~-copy** Durchschlag *m*; *(Buch)* Besprechungsexemplar *n*; ~ **date** Redaktionsschluß *m*; **~er** ['-ə] Presser, Drucker *m*; Presse, Stampfe, Quetsche; Druckwalze *f*; **~-fastener** Druckknopf *m (an der Kleidung)*; **~-fit** Preßsitz *m*; **~-gallery** Pressetribüne *f*; **~-guide** Zeitungskatalog *m*, -verzeichnis *n*; **~ing** ['-iŋ] *a* dringend, dringlich, eilig; aufdringlich; *s* Pressen *n*; *tech* Preßling *m*, -stück, -teil *n*, -matrize, -platte *f*; *(Papier)* Satinieren *n*; *~~-hammer* Preßhammer *m*; *~~-iron* Bügeleisen *n*; *~~-plant* Preßwerk *n*, -anlage *f*; *~~-roll* Preß-, Druckwalze *f*; ~ **item, notice** Pressenotiz *f*; **~-law** Pressegesetz *n*; **~man** ['-mən] Drucker; Journalist, Pressemann; *tech* Stanzer *m*; **~mark** *(Bibliotheksbuch)* Standortnummer *f*; ~ **opinions** *pl* Pressestimmen *f pl*; ~ **photographer** Pressephotograph *m*; **~-proof** *typ* Maschinenrevision *f*; **~-reader** Korrektor *m*; *~~'s mark* Korrekturzeichen *n*; ~ **release** Pressemitteilung *f*; **~-report** Presse-, Zeitungsbericht *m*; **~-reporter** Pressekorrespondent *m*; **~-room** *typ* Maschinensaal *m*; **~-service** Pressedienst *m*; **~-stud** Teppichnagel *m*; **~-up** *sport* Liegestütz *m*; **~-work** Druckarbeit; Berichterstattung *f*.

pressur|e ['preʃə] Druck *m a. phys tech*; *el* Spannung; *fig* Dringlichkeit *f*; Druck, Zwang *m*; Bedrückung, drükkende Lage, Bedrängnis, Not *f*; *under ~~* unter Druck *od* Zwang, unfreiwillig; *under the ~~ of circumstances* unter dem Druck der Verhältnisse; *under the ~~ of necessity* notgedrungen, der Not gehorchend; *to put ~~* Druck, Zwang ausüben (*on* auf); unter Druck setzen (*on s.o.* jdn); *to work at high ~~* mit Hochdruck arbeiten; *atmospheric ~~* Luftdruck *m*; *blood ~~* Blutdruck *m*; *economic ~~* wirtschaftliche(r) Druck *m*; *financial ~~* finanzielle Schwierigkeiten *f pl*; *gas(eous) ~~* Gasdruck *m*; *high, low ~~ (mete)* Hoch-, Tiefdruck *m*; *monetary ~~* Geldmangel *m*, -knappheit *f*; *tyre ~~* Reifendruck *m*; *~~ of business* Geschäftsdrang *m*; *~~ of the hand* Händedruck *m*; *~~ of money* Geldverlegenheit *f*; *~~ on space* Raummangel *m*; *~~ of taxation* Steuerdruck *m*; *~~ balance* Druckregler, -ausgleich *m*; *~~ cabin* Druckkabine *f*; *~~ compensation* Druckausgleich *m*; *~~ cooker* Schnellkochtopf *m*; *~~ distribution* Druckverteilung *f*; *~~ drop* Druck-, *el* Spannungsabfall *m*; *~~-ga(u)ge* Druckmesser *m*; *~~ gradient* Druckgefälle *n*; *~~ group* Interessengruppe *f*; *~~ head* Druckhöhe *f*, Staudruck *m*; *~~-hull* Druckkörper *m*; *~~ lubrication* Druckschmierung *f*; *~~ point (physiol)* Druckpunkt *m*; *~~-pump* Druckpumpe *f*; *~~ regulator* Druckregler *m*; *~~-sensitive (med)* druckempfindlich; *~~ suit* Druckanzug *m*; *~~ turbine* Druckturbine *f*; *~~ wave* Druckwelle *f*; **~ized** ['preʃəraizd] *a aero (Kabine)* mit Druckausgleich *(für Höhenflüge)*.

prestidigitat|ion ['prestididʒi'teiʃən] Taschenspielerkunst *f*; **~or** [presti'didʒiteitə] Taschenspieler *m*.

prestige [pres'ti:ʒ] Prestige *n*, Nimbus, Zauber *m*; *pol* Ansehen *n*, Einfluß *m*.

prestressed ['pri:'strest] *a*: ~ **concrete** Spannbeton *m*.

presum|able [pri'zju:məbl] vermutlich, mutmaßlich, sehr wahrscheinlich, voraussichtlich; **~e** [pri:'zju:m] *tr* annehmen, vermuten, mutmaßen, schließen (*from* aus); schließen lassen auf, wahrscheinlich machen; sich herausnehmen, sich erdreisten, sich anmaßen; *itr* vermuten; sich zuviel herausnehmen; sich etw einbilden, pochen (*on, upon* auf); ausnutzen (*on s.th.* etw); **~edly** [-idli] *adv* vermutlich, wie man annehmen muß; **~ing** [-iŋ] anmaßend, *lit* vermessen.

presumpt|ion [pri'zʌm(p)ʃən] Vermutung *a. jur*, Mutmaßung, Annahme *f*; Grund *m* zur Annahme; Wahrscheinlichkeit; Anmaßung, Vermessenheit, Unverschämtheit *f*; *on the ~~ that* in der Annahme, daß; **~ive** [-tiv] mutmaßlich; *~~ evidence* Indizienbeweis *m*; *~~ proof* Wahrscheinlichkeitsbeweis *m*; **~uous** [-tjuəs] überheblich, anmaßend, unverschämt.

presuppos|e [pri:sə'pouz] *tr* im voraus, von vornherein annehmen; voraussetzen; **~ition** [pri:sʌpə'ziʃən] Annahme; Voraussetzung *f*.

preten|ce, *Am* **pretense** [pri'tens] Anspruch *m* (*to* auf); Vorspiegelung *f*, Vorwand, Deckmantel *m*; Ausrede, -flucht; Heuchelei; Verstellung, Maske *f*, Spiel *n*; Anmaßung *f*; *on, under the ~~ of* unter dem Vorwand, unter der Maske *gen*; *on the slightest ~~* aus dem geringsten Anlaß; *(under) false ~~s* (unter) Vorspiegelung falscher Tatsachen; *to make a ~~ of s.th.* etw vorschützen, -täuschen; *at s.th.* Anspruch erheben auf (*to be, at being* zu sein); *devoid of all ~~* ohne Verstellung, offen, aufrichtig; **~d** [-d] *tr* beanspruchen; behaupten, vorgeben, -schützen; vortäuschen, heucheln; sich ausgeben als, spielen; *itr* Anspruch erheben (*to* auf); sich verstellen; (nur) so tun (*that* als ob); spielen; sich ausgeben (*that he is a doctor* als Arzt); *he's just ~~ing* er tut nur so; **~ded** [-did] *a* gespielt, geheuchelt; angeblich; vermeintlich; **~der** [-də] Ansprüche Erhebende(r); *(~~ to the throne)* (Kron-)Prätendent *m*; **~sion** [pri'tenʃən] Behauptung *f*, Vorwand; Anspruch *m* (*to* auf); Anmaßung *f*, Dünkel *m*, Überheblichkeit *f*; **~tious** [-ʃəs] anmaßend, überheblich; prahlerisch, prunkend; **~tiousness** [-ʃəsnis] Anmaßung *f*.

preterit|(e) ['pretərit] *(~ tense) gram* Präteritum *n*, erste Vergangenheit *f*.

preternatural [pri:tə'nætʃrəl] ungewöhnlich, abnorm; übernatürlich.

pretext ['pri:tekst] *s* Vorwand *m*, Ausrede, -flucht; Entschuldigung *f*; *tr* [pri:'tekst] vorschützen, -geben; *on, under the ~* unter dem Vorwand (*of doing* etw zu tun); *to make a ~ of s.th.* etw zum Vorwand nehmen (*in order to* um zu).

prett|ify ['pritifai] *tr* (oberflächlich) verschönern; **~iness** ['-inis] Gefälligkeit, Niedlichkeit *f*, reizende(s) Wesen *n*; *(Stil)* Geziertheit *f*; **~y** ['-i] *a* angenehm, gefällig; nett, hübsch, gut aussehend; niedlich, reizend, reizvoll; *iro* nett, sauber, reizend; geziert, geckenhaft; *fam, a. als adv* ziemlich, (ganz) ordentlich, anständig, ganz schön, beachtlich; *adv* recht; *s* Hübsche, Kleine *f*; *pl* hübsche Kleinigkeit *f*; *to be sitting ~~* sein Schäfchen im trockenen haben; *~~ bad* recht *od* ziemlich mies; *~~ good* (gar) nicht (so) übel; ganz gut; *~~ much* so ziemlich; *~~ near* beinah(e), fast; *a ~~ penny* e-e schöne Stange Geld; *I'm ~~ well* es geht mir ganz gut; *that's ~~ much the same (thing)* das läuft auf eins hinaus; *~~-~~* ganz entzückend, süß.

pretzel ['pretsl] (Salz-)Brezel *f*.

prevail [pri'veil] *itr* die Oberhand gewinnen, herrschen (*over, against* über); sich durchsetzen, sich behaupten (*against* gegen); Erfolg haben, erfolgreich sein; maßgebend sein; vorherrschen, überwiegen (*in* bei); veranlassen, dazu bewegen, überreden, verleiten, verführen (*on, upon, with s.o.* jdn); **~ing** [-iŋ] stärker, einflußreicher; (vor)herrschend, maßgebend, überwiegend; wirksam; *com* üblich, gangbar, geltend; *under the ~~ circumstances* unter den obwaltenden Umständen.

prevalen|ce ['prevələns] allgemeine *od* weite Verbreitung; Geltung *f*; Überhandnehmen *n*; **~t** [-t] allgemein *od* weit verbreitet; vorherrschend.

prevaricat|e [pri'værikeit] *itr* Ausflüchte machen, am Wesentlichen vorbeireden; flunkern; **~ion** [priværi'keiʃən] Ausflucht; Verdrehung; Unaufrichtigkeit; Lüge *f*; **~or** [pri'værikeitə] Wortverdreher; unaufrichtige(r) Mensch; Lügner *m*.

prevent [pri'vent] *tr* ab-, zurückhalten (*from doing s.th.* etw zu tun); verhindern, verhüten, vermeiden; zuvorkommen, vorbeugen; **~able, ~ible** [pri'ventəbl] vermeidbar; **~ion** [pri'venʃən] Verhinderung, Vermeidung, Vorbeugung, Verhütung *f*; *in case of ~~* im Fall der Verhinderung; *~~ is better than cure* Vorsicht ist besser als Nachsicht; *crime ~~* Verbrechensverhütung, -bekämpfung *f*; *~~ of accidents* Unfallverhütung *f*; *(society for the) ~~ of cruelty to animals* Tierschutz(verein) *m*; **~ive** [pri'ventiv] *a* verhütend; Verhütungs-, Schutz-; *bes. med* vorbeugend, prophylaktisch; Vorbeugungs-; *s* Schutzmaßnahme *f*; Schutz-, *bes. med* Vorbeugungsmittel *n* (*of* gegen); *~~ custody* Schutzhaft *f*; *~~ detention* Schutzhaft; Sicherungsverwahrung *f*; *~~ medicine* Gesundheitspflege *f*; Vorbeugungsmittel *n*; *~~ officer* Beamte(r) *m* des Zollfahndungsdienstes; *~~ war* Präventivkrieg *m*.

preview, *Am a.* **prevue** ['pri:'vju:] *theat film* private Voraufführung, Vorschau *f*; Vorabdruck *m*; vorherige Beurteilung *f*.

previous ['pri:vjəs] *a (zeitl.)* voraus-, vorhergehend, früher; letzt; *fam (too ~)* voreilig, -schnell; *prp*: *~ to* vor; *without ~ notice* ohne Vorankündigung; *~* **conviction** Vorstrafe *f*; *to have (no) ~~s* (nicht) vorbestraft sein; *~* **experience** Vorkenntnisse *pl*, Vorbildung *f*; *~* **history** *jur* Vorgeschichte *f*; *~* **holder** Vorbesitzer *m*; **~ly** ['-li] *adv* früher; vorher; *~* **month** Vormonat *m*; *~* **notice** Vorankündigung *f*; *~* **owner** Voreigentümer *m*; *~* **payment** Vorauszahlung *f*; *~* **question** Vorfrage; *Am parl* Frage *f*, ob über die Hauptfrage ohne weitere Debatte sofort abgestimmt werden soll; *to move the ~~ (parl)* den Übergang zur Tagesordnung beantragen.

prevision [pri(:)'viʒən] Ahnung *f*, Vorhersehen *n (der Zukunft)*.

pre-war ['pri:'wɔ:] *a* Vorkriegs-, Friedens-; *~* **years** *pl*, **period** Vorkriegszeit *f*.

prey [prei] *s* Beute(tier *n*) *f*; Raub *m*; Opfer *n fig*; *itr* plündern, rauben; herfallen (*on* über); nachstellen (*on, upon other animals* anderen Tieren); fangen (*on, upon* acc); leben (*on* von), fressen (*on s.th.* etw); *fig* lasten (*on, upon* auf); beeinträchtigen (*on, upon s.th.* etw); nagen, zehren (*on* an); *to fall a ~ to* zum Opfer fallen *dat*; *to fall an easy ~ to* e-e leichte Beute sein *dat*; *beast of ~* Raubtier *n*; *bird of ~* Raubvogel *m*.

price [prais] *s com* (Kauf-)Preis, Kosten(punkt *m*) *pl*; *(Börse)* Kurs; Wert *m*; Belohnung *f*; *tr* e-n Preis festsetzen für, bewerten; mit e-m Preis versehen, auszeichnen; *fam* nach dem Preis fragen, sich nach dem Preis erkundigen (*s.th.* e-r S); *above, beyond, without ~ (fig)* unbezahlbar; *at all ~s* in jeder Preislage; *at any ~ (fig)* um jeden Preis, auf jeden Fall, unter allen Umständen; koste es, was es wolle; *at half-~* zum halben Preis; *at a low ~* billig; *beyond, without ~* unbezahlbar; *under ~* unter Preis; *to fetch a ~* e-n Preis erzielen; *to have o.'s ~* käuflich sein; *to peg ~s* Preise stützen; *to put, to set a ~ on s.o.'s head* e-n Preis auf jds Kopf aussetzen; *to realize a good, a high ~* e-n hohen Preis erzielen; *~s have dropped, hardened* Kurse sind gefallen, haben angezogen; *what ~? (fam)* was halten Sie von? *bargain ~* Ausverkaufs-, Vorzugspreis *m*; *base, basis ~* Grundpreis *m*; *calculation of ~s* Preisbildung, Kalkulation *f*; *cash ~* Preis *m* bei Barzahlung; *class, range, schedule of ~s* Preisklasse *f*; *ceiling ~* amtliche(r) Höchstpreis *m*; *collapse of ~s* Kurssturz *m*; *consumer ~* Verbraucherpreis *m*; *cost, manufacturing ~* Herstellungspreis *m*; *cut, decline, fall in ~s* Preisrückgang *m*; *deduction, reduction in ~* Preisabschlag, Rabatt *m*; *difference in ~s* Preisunterschied *m*, -differenz *f*; *discount ~* Wiederverkaufspreis *m*; *domestic ~* Inlandspreis *m*; *estimated ~* Schätzwert *m*; *factory ~* Fabrikpreis *m*; *fancy ~* Liebhaber-, Phantasiepreis *m*; *firmness, stability of ~s* Preisstabilität *f*; *fixed ~* Festpreis *m*; *fluctuation in ~s* Preisschwankungen *f pl*; *gross ~* Bruttopreis *m*; *knock-down ~* Reklamepreis *m*; *list, table of ~s* Preisliste *f*; *market ~* Börsen-, amtliche(r) Kurs *m*; *maximum ~* Höchstpreis *m*; *net ~* Nettopreis *m*; *opening ~ (Börse)* Eröffnungskurs *m*; *preferential ~* Vorzugspreis *m*; *published, publishing ~ (Buch)* Verlagspreis *m*; *purchasing ~* Kauf-, Anschaffungspreis *m*; *quantity ~* Mengenpreis *m*; *quotation of ~s, quoted ~* Preisnotierung, -angabe *f*; *real-estate ~* Grundstückspreis *m*; *resale, reselling ~* Wiederverkaufspreis *m*; *reserved ~* Mindestpreis *m*; *retail ~* Kleinhandelspreis *m*; *sales ~* Verkaufspreis *m*; *special ~* Ausnahme-, Extra-, Sonderpreis *m*; *subscription ~* Subskriptions-, Bezugspreis *m*; *top ~* Höchstpreis *m*; *total ~* Gesamtpreis *m*; *uniform ~* Einheitspreis *m*; *wholesale ~* Großhandelspreis *m*; *world ~* Weltmarktpreis *m*; *~ of money* Kapitalmarktzins *m*; *~ at station* Preis *m* frei Bahnhof; *~ at works* Fabrikpreis *m*; **~-administration, -control** Preisüberwachung, -kontrolle *f*; **~-boost** Preissteigerung, -treiberei *f*; **~-calculation** Preisbildung, -gestaltung, Kalkulation *f*; **~-catalogue, -current, -list** Preisliste *f*; **~-curb** Preisdrosselung *f*; **~-cutting** Preissenkung, -drückerei *f*; **~d** [-t] *a* mit Preis versehen, ausgezeichnet (*at* mit); *economy-~* preisgünstig; *high-~~* teuer; *low-~~* billig; *~* **development** Preisentwicklung *f*; *~* **difference** Preisunterschied *m*; *~* **fixing** Preisfestsetzung *f*; *~* **fluctuations** *pl* Preis-, Kursschwankungen *f pl*; *~* **increase** Preiserhöhung, -steigerung *f*; **~-index** Preisindex *m*; *~~ number* Preisindexzahl *f*; **~less** ['-lis] unbezahlbar, unschätzbar, unvergleichlich; *Br* amüsant, aus dem Rahmen fallend, verrückt; **~-level** Preisniveau *n*; **~-limit** Preisgrenze *f*; **~-list** Preisliste *f*; *(Börse)* Kurszettel *m*; *~* **maintenance** Preisbindung *f*; *~* **margin** Preisspanne *f*; **~-mark** Preiszettel *m*; *~* **movement** Preis-, Kursbewegung *f*; **~-policy** Preispolitik *f*; *~* **quotation** Preisangabe *f*; *~* **range** Preislage; *(Börse)* Kursbildung *f*; *~* **regulation** Preislenkung *f*; *~* **tag** Preisschild *n*; **~y** ['-i] *fam* teuer.

prick [prik] *s* (Nadel-)Stich *m*; Punktur *f*, stechende(r) Schmerz; Dorn, Stachel *m*; Hasenspur *f*; *tr* stechen; *(Loch)* bohren; *(Blase)* aufstechen; punktieren; sich stechen (*o.'s hand* in die Hand); anstreichen, markieren, bezeichnen; *(Spur)* verfolgen; *fig* keine Ruhe lassen (*s.o.* jdm); wurmen; anspornen; *agr* pikieren; *itr (Schmerz, Wunde)* stechen; ein Stechen, Prickeln haben; prickeln (*with* von); dem Pferde die Sporen geben; *(Wein)* sauer werden; *to ~ in, to ~ off, to ~ out (Pflanzen)* versetzen; *to kick against the ~s (fig)* sich aufreiben, *lit* wider den Stachel löcken; *to ~ the bladder, bubble (fig)* die Illusion zerstören; *to ~ a chart (mar)* ein Besteck machen; *to ~ up o.'s ears* die Ohren spitzen; *~s of conscience* Gewissensbisse *m pl*; **~-ears** *pl* Stehohren *n pl*; **~er** ['-ə] Pfriem *m*, Ahle, Räumnadel *f*; **~et** ['-it] Kerzenhalter; Spießer *m (Hirsch im 2. Jahr)*; **~ing** ['-iŋ] stechend; prickelnd; in die Höhe stehend; *fig* anspornend; **~le** ['-l] *s* Stachel, Dorn *m*; Prickeln *n*; *tr* stechen; *tr itr* prickeln; **~ly** ['-li] stach(e)lig; prick(e)lig; *fig* reizbar; *~~ heat (med)* Hitzpickel *m pl*; *~~ pear (bot)* Feigendistel *f*.

pride [praid] *s* Stolz; Hochmut *m*, Überheblichkeit, Arroganz *f*, Dünkel *m*; *fig* Feuer *n (Pferd)*; *the ~* die Blüte *fig* (*of youth* der Jugend); *zoo* Rudel *n*, Schwarm *m*; *v: to ~ o.s. (up)on, to take (a) ~ in* stolz sein auf, sich viel einbilden auf, sich brüsten, *fam* angeben mit; *he is his father's ~* er ist der ganze Stolz s-s Vaters; *~ goes before a fall, ~ will have a fall (prov)* Hochmut kommt vor dem Fall; *~ of place* Standesbewußtsein *n*, -dünkel *m*.

priest [pri:st] Priester; Geistliche(r) *m*; **~ess** ['-is] Priesterin *f*; **~hood** ['-hud] Priesteramt *n*, -würde; Priesterschaft, Geistlichkeit *f*; **~ly** ['-li] priesterlich; **~'s pintle** *bot* Knabenkraut *n*.

prig [prig] *s* Pedant, Schulfuchs; Sittenrichter; *sl* Gauner, (Taschen-) Dieb *m*; *tr sl* stibitzen, stehlen; **~gery** ['-əri], **~ishness** ['-iʃnis] Pedanterie *f*; **~gish** ['-iʃ] pedantisch; dünkelhaft, besserwisserisch.

prim [prim] *a* steif, (über)korrekt, förmlich, genau, eigen, geziert; *(Lächeln)* gezwungen; *v: to ~ o.s.* sich zieren.

prima|donna ['pri:mə'dɔnə] *mus u. allg* Primadonna *f*; *~* **facie** ['praimə 'feiʃi(i:)] auf den ersten Blick; *~-facie evidence (jur)* Beweis *m* des ersten Anscheins.

prim|acy ['praiməsi] Vorrang(stellung *f*) *m*; Primat *m od n (des Papstes)*; **~aeval** *s.* *~eval*; **~al** ['-əl] erst; frühest; ursprünglich, primitiv; *fig* wesentlich, hauptsächlich; Haupt-; *~~ cause (fig)* Urgrund *m*; *~~ man* Urmensch *m*; **~ary** ['-əri] *a* erst, Erst-; frühest, anfänglich, Anfangs-; Ur-, ursprünglich, primär, Primär-; grundlegend, Grund-; elementar, Elementar-; fundamental, Fundamental-; hauptsächlich(st), wichtigst, Haupt-; *(Bedarf)* vordringlich; *s* Hauptsache; *(~~ colo(u)r)* Grundfarbe; Schwungfeder *f*; *(~~ planet)* Planet *m (e-r Sonne)*; *(~~ coil) el* Primärspule *f*; *(~~ assembly, meeting, elections)* Vorwahl(en *pl*), Urwählerversammlung *f*; *(~~ product)* Grundstoff *m*; *pl* erste Grundlagen *f pl*; *direct ~~ (pol)* direkte Kandidatenwahl *f*; *of ~~ importance* von größter Wichtigkeit; *~~ accent (gram)* Hauptton *m*; *~~ battery (el)* Primärbatterie *f*; *~~ cell (el)* Primärelement *n*; *~~ concern* Hauptsorge *f*; *~~ current (el)* Primärstrom *m*; *~~ education* Grundschul-, Elementarunterricht *m*; *~~ industry* Grundstoffindustrie *f*; *~~ material* Roh-, Ausgangsstoff *m*; *~~ meaning* Grundbedeutung *f (e-s Wortes)*; *~~ pressure (el)* Primärspannung *f*; *~~ receiver (radio)* Einkreisempfänger *m*; *~~ rock* Urgestein *n*; *~~ school* Grund-, Elementarschule *f*; *~~ share* Stammaktie *f*; *~~ target* Hauptziel *n*; *~~ trainer* Schulflugzeug *n*; *~~ winding (el)* Primärwick(e)lung *f*; **~ate** ['praimit] Primas, Erzbischof *m*; *pl* [-'meiti:z] *zoo* Primaten *m pl*; **~e** [praim] *a* erst; Haupt-, Ober-; bedeutendst, wichtigst, wesentlich; Haupt- *a. math*; erstklassig, erster, bester Qualität; ursprünglich; Grund-; *math* unteilbar; *s* Morgenstunde *f*; Anfang; Lenz *m* (des Lebens); *rel* Prime; Anfangs-, Frühzeit; Blüte(zeit) *f*, Höhepunkt *m*; *das* Beste, *die* Besten, *die* Auslese, Spitze; *math* Primzahl; *mus* Prim; *(Fechten)* Prime *f*; *tr* vorbereiten, fertigmachen; instand setzen; ausrüsten; betriebsfertig machen; *tr itr* (e-e Feuerwaffe) laden; (e-e Granate) schärfen; (e-e Pumpe) in Gang bringen, anstechen; *tech* Wasserdampf einströmen lassen; Benzin einspritzen; *(Malfläche)* grundieren; *fam (to ~~ up)* (e-n Menschen) vollaufen lassen, füttern; (jdn) (vorher) informieren; *in o.'s ~~* in der Blüte des Lebens; *~~ cost* Gestehungs-, Anschaffungs-, Selbstkosten *pl*; *~~ meridian* Nullmeridian *m*; *~~ minister* Premierminister, Ministerpräsident *m*; *~~ mourner* Hauptleidtragende(r) *m*; *~~ mover* Kraftquelle, Antriebskraft; *tech* Energie *f*; Motor *m*; Zugmaschine *f*, Schlepper *m*; *~~ number (math)* Primzahl *f*; **~ely** ['-li] *adv fam* prima, bestens; **~er** ['-ə, *Am a.* 'primə] Fibel *f*; Elementarbuch *n*; Leitfaden; Lehrgang; Grundierer; Zünddraht *m*, -nadel *f*, -hütchen *n*; Sprengkapsel *f*; *tech* Grundanstrich *m*; *mot* Einspritzpumpe *f*; *typ* ['primə] *great ~~* Schriftgrad *m* von 18 Punkten *(zwischen Tertia u. Text)*; *long ~~* Korpus, Garmond *f*; **~eval** [prai'mi:vəl] ursprünglich; urzeitlich, Ur-; *~~ forest* Urwald *m*; *~~ world* Urwelt *f*; **~ing** ['praimiŋ] *s* Grundierung; *(Feuerwaffe)* Zündung *f*; Zündstoff *m*, Pulver *n*; Gezeitenverfrühung *f*; *mot* Einspritzen *n* von Kraftstoff; *attr* Zünd-, Pulver-; *~~ composition* Zündsatz *m*; *~~ fuel* Anlaßkraftstoff *m*; *~~ pump* Einspritzpumpe *f*; **~itive** ['primitiv] *a* ursprünglich, urzeitlich, Ur-; *biol* Stamm-; primitiv, roh, einfach, unkultiviert; grundlegend, Grund-; primär; *s* Primitive(r), Naturmensch; *(Kunst)* frühe(r) Meister *m*; *gram* Stammwort *n*; *pl die* Primitiven *m pl*, *die* Naturvölker *n pl*; **~itiveness** ['primitivnis] Ursprünglichkeit; Primitivität, Einfachheit, Roheit, Unkultiviertheit *f*; **~ogeniture** [praimo(u)'dʒenitʃə] Erstgeburt(srecht *n*), Primogenitur *f*; **~ordial** [prai'mɔ:diəl] ursprünglich, Ur-; fundamental; *bes. biol* Stamm-; **~rose** ['primrouz] *s* Primel, Schlüsselblume *f*; Blaßgelb *n*; *a* Primel-; blaßgelb; **~ula** ['primjulə] Primel *f*.

primp [primp] *Am tr itr* (sich) herausputzen.

prince [prins] Fürst; Monarch, Herrscher; Prinz; *fig* Fürst, König; *Am fam* pfundige(r) Kerl *m*; *~ of the Church* Kirchenfürst *m*; *the P~ of Darkness* der Fürst der Finsternis, der Teufel; *the P~ of Peace* der Friede(ns)fürst, Christus *m*; *P~ of Wales (Titel des englischen Thronfolgers)*; *~* **consort** Prinzgemahl *m*; **~ling** ['-liŋ] Duodezfürst *m*; **~like** ['-laik], **~ly** ['-li] fürstlich; königlich; großzügig, edel(mütig), *fam* nobel, splendid; prächtig, verschwenderisch; *~* **regent** Prinzregent *m*; *~* **royal** Kronprinz *m*; **~ss** [prin'ses, *attr u. Am* 'prinses] Fürstin; Prinzessin *f*; *~~ royal* Kronprinzessin *f*; **~ss(e)** [prin'ses] Prinzeßrock *m*; *~~ dress* Prinzeßkleid *n*.

princip|al ['prinsəpəl] *a* oberst; wichtigst, bedeutendst; hauptsächlich, größt; Haupt-; *s* Hauptperson, -sache *f*, -punkt *m*; Oberhaupt *n*; Chef, Prinzipal; Vorsitzende(r); Geschäftsinhaber; *Am* Vorsteher, (Di-)Rektor, Schulleiter; *com* Auftraggeber; *theat* Hauptdarsteller; *mus* Solist; *jur* Haupttäter, -schuldige(r); Hauptschuldner *m*; Kapital *n*, Hauptsumme *f*; *arch* Träger, Binderbalken *m*; *(Orgel)* Prinzipal *n*; *sport* Duellant *m*; *~~s only!* Vermittler verbeten! *lady ~~* Schulleiterin, (Di-)Rektorin *f*; *~~ activity* Haupttätigkeit *f*; *~~ clause* Hauptsatz *m*; *~~ establishment* Stammhaus *n*; *~~ parts (pl)* Stammformen *f pl* (e-s Zeitworts); **~ality** [prinsi'pæliti] Fürstentum *n*; Fürstenrang *m*, -würde *f*; **~ally** ['prinsəp(ə)li] *adv* hauptsächlich, besonders, vor allem; **~le** ['prinsəpl] Ursprung *m*, Ursache *f*, Grund; Grundbestandteil *m*, -richtung *f*, Wesen(smerkmal *n*, -zug *m*) *n*; Grundwahrheit *f*, -gesetz *n*, -lage *f*, Grundsatz *m*, Prinzip *n*; (Grund-Lebens-)Regel *f*; Prinzipien *n pl*; *chem* (Haupt-)Bestandteil *m*; *in ~~* im Prinzip, im Grunde, im wesentlichen, grundsätzlich; *on ~~* aus Prinzip, grundsätzlich; *to hold a ~~* e-n Grundsatz haben; *to lay down a ~~* e-n Grundsatz aufstellen; *to make it a ~~* es sich zum Grundsatz machen (*to* zu); *a man of ~~(s)* ein Mann *m* von Prinzipien; *as a matter of ~~* grundsätzlich, prinzipiell.

prink [priŋk] *tr* anziehen, fertigmachen; *itr (to ~ o.s.)* sich anziehen; *(to ~ up)* sich herausputzen.

print [print] *s* (Ab-)Druck *m*; Druckstelle *f*, -mal *n*, Spur *f*; *fig* Spuren *f pl*; (Druck-)Form *f*, (Präge-)Stempel *m*, Siegel; *(Gießerei)* Gesenk; geformte(s) Stück *n (Butter)*; (Kleid *n* aus) bedruckte(m) Kattun *m*; gemusterte(s) Kleid *n*; *typ* Druck; *(Graphik, phot)* Abzug *m*; Radierung *f*, Stich *m*; Lichtpause; *phot* Kopie *f*, Positiv *n*; *Am* Druckwerk *n*, -schrift, Veröffentlichung; Zeitschrift, Zeitung; Auflage *f*; *(news~)* Zeitungspapier *n*; *tr* eindrücken, pressen, formen, prägen, stempeln, siegeln; *(Form, Stempel, Siegel)* drücken, pressen; *(Zeichen, Buchstaben)* einprägen, -schneiden, schnitzen, ritzen, einzeichnen (*on* in); *(Papier, Stoff)* bedrucken; *(Stoff)* mustern; *(Text)* (ab)drucken; in Druck geben; herausgeben, veröffentlichen, in Druckbuchstaben schreiben; *phot* abziehen, kopieren; *fig* einprägen; *itr* drucken, als Drucker tätig sein; *(Druckplatte, Negativ)* e-n Abdruck geben; in Druckschrift schreiben; *in ~* gedruckt, herausgegeben, veröffentlicht; *(Buch)* lieferbar; *in cold ~ (fig)* schwarz auf weiß; *out of ~* vergriffen; *to take a ~ from* e-n Abzug machen von; **~able** ['-əbl] druckfähig, -fertig; (gute) Abzüge liefernd; **~ed** ['-id] *a*: *~~ and mixed consignment* Postwurfsendung *f*; *~~ form* Vordruck *m*, Formular *n*; *~~ goods (pl)* bedruckte Stoffe *m pl*; *~~ matter* Drucksache *f*; **~er** ['-ə] (Buch-, *a.* Kattun-) Drucker; Druckereibesitzer; Kopierapparat *m*; *~~'s devil* Setzerlehrling *m*; *~~'s error* Druckfehler *m*; *~~'s flower* Vignette *f*; *~~'s ink* Druckerschwärze *f*; *~~'s* *mark* Druckerzeichen *n*; *~~'s pie (typ)* Zwiebelfische *m pl*; *~~'s reader* Korrektor *m*; **~ery** ['-əri] *bes. Am* Druckerei *f*; **~ing** ['-iŋ] Druck(en *n*); Buchdruck(erkunst *f*); Druck(werk *n*) *m*; Auflage; Druck-, Zierschrift *f*; *(~~ charges)* Druckkosten *pl*; *phot* Abziehen, Kopieren *n*; *(cloth ~~)* Zeugdruck *m*; *cylinder-, flat, hand ~~* Walzen-, Flach-, Handdruck *m*; *(copper-)plate ~~* (Kupfer-)Tiefdruck *m*; *~~ in black* Schwarzdruck *m*; *~~ in colo(u)rs* Bunt-, Farbdruck *m*; *~~-block* Klischee *n*; *~~-box* Druckkasten *m (zum Spielen)*; *~~-character, -letter, -type* (Druck-) Type, Letter *f*; *~~-cylinder* Auftragwalze *f*; *~~-frame* Kopierrahmen *m*; *~~-ink* Druckerschwärze *f*; *~~ laboratory* Kopieranstalt *f*; *~~ licence* Druckerlaubnis *f*; *~~-machine* (Buch-) Druckmaschine, Schnellpresse; *phot* Kopiermaschine *f*; *~~-office* (Buch-) Druckerei *f*; *~~-paper* Druckpapier; *phot* Kopierpapier *n*; *thin ~~-paper* Dünndruckpapier *n*; *~~-press* Druckpresse *f*; Maschinenraum *m*; Drukkerei *f*; *~~ process* Druckverfahren *n*; *~~ space* Satzspiegel *m*; *~~ trade* Druck(erei)gewerbe *n*; *~~ types (pl)* Lettern *f pl*; *~~-works (pl)* typographische Anstalt, Großdruckerei *f*; **~-shop** Kunsthandlung; *Am* Drukkerei *f*.

prior ['praiə] *a* voraus, voraufgehend, früher, älter (*to* als); bedeutender, wichtiger (*to* als); bevorzugt, Vorzugs-; *com* bevorrechtigt; *s rel* Prior *m*; *adv*: *~ to (prp)* vor; *~ to my arrival* vor meiner Ankunft; *~ to my buying the car* ehe, bevor ich den Wagen kaufte; *the ~ condition* die erste Voraussetzung (*for* für); **~ate** ['-rit] Priorat *n*, Priorei *f*; *~* **claim** ältere(r, s) Anspruch *m*, Recht *n*; **~ess** ['-ris] Priorin *f*; **~ity** [prai'ɔriti] *s* Priorität *f*, Vorrang *m*, Vorrecht (*over, to* vor); Dringlichkeit, -sstufe; *mot* Vorfahrt(srecht *n*) *f*; *attr* Vorzugs-; dringend; *of first ~~* von größter Dringlichkeit; *to claim ~~* den Vorrang beanspruchen; *to give ~~ to s.th.* e-r S den Vorrang geben; vordringlich behandeln; *to have, to take ~~* den Vorrang haben (*of* vor); *creditor by ~~* bevorrechtigte(r) Gläubiger *m*; *~~ of birth* Erstgeburt(srecht *n*) *f*; *~~ call* Vorranggespräch *n*; *~~ claim* Prioritätsanspruch *m*; *~~* list Dringlichkeitsliste *f*; *~~ message* dringende Meldung *f*; *~~ share* Vorzugsaktie *f*; **~y** ['-ri] Priorei *f*.

prism ['prizm] *math phys opt* Prisma *n*; **~atic** [priz'mætik] *adv ~~ally* prismatisch; Prismen-; *fig* glänzend; *~~ colo(u)rs (pl)* Regenbogenfarben *f pl*; **~-glass,** *~atic binoculars (pl)* Prismenglas *n*, -feldstecher *m*.

prison ['prizn] Gefängnis *n*; Straf-, Haftanstalt; *fig* Haft, Freiheitsstrafe *f*; *to be in ~* e-e Freiheitsstrafe verbüßen; *to be sentenced to go to ~* zu Gefängnis verurteilt werden; *to escape from ~* aus dem Gefängnis ausbrechen; *to go, to be sent to ~* eingesperrt, mit Gefängnis bestraft werden; *to send to ~* einsperren, inhaftieren, in Haft nehmen; **~-administration** Gefängnisverwaltung *f*; **~-breaker** Ausbrecher *m*; **~-breaking** Ausbrechen *n* (aus dem Gefängnis); **~-camp** Gefangenenlager *n*; **~er** ['-ə] Gefangene(r), Häftling; *(~~ at the bar, awaiting, before trial, on remand, on suspicion)* Angeklagte(r); Untersuchungsgefangene(r) *m*; *to be a ~~ to (fig)* gefesselt sein an; *to hold, to keep ~~* gefangenhalten; *to take ~~* gefangennehmen; *exchange of ~~s* Gefangenenaustausch *m*; *~~'s bars (pl), base (sport)* Barlauf *m*; *~~ of war* Kriegsgefangene(r) *m*; *~~-of-war camp* Kriegsgefangenenlager *n*; **~-governor** Gefängnisdirektor *m*; **~-van** Zellenwagen *m*; **~-warden** Gefängnisdirektor, -aufseher, -wärter *m*; **~-yard** Gefängnishof *m*.

prissy ['prisi] *Am fam* (über)genau, pusselig; zimperlich, affektiert.

pristine ['pristi(:)n, '-ain] ursprünglich; vormalig, früher; (noch) unberührt, unverdorben.

privacy ['praivəsi] private Sphäre, Intimsphäre; Stille, Zurückgezogenheit, Abgeschiedenheit *f*; Geheimnis *n*; Heimlichkeit, Geheimhaltung *f*; *in strict ~* im engsten Kreise; im Vertrauen; *to live in ~* ganz für sich, zurückgezogen leben.

privat|e ['praivit] *a* privat, persönlich, eigen, individuell; allein, einsam; privat, nicht öffentlich, Privat-; abgetrennt, abgeschlossen; *(Ort)* abgeschieden; geheim, vertraulich; *s* (einfacher) Soldat, Gemeine(r) *m*; *pl (~~ parts)* Geschlechtsteile *n pl*; *for s.o.'s ~~ ear* (ganz) im Vertrauen; vertraulich; *for ~~ use* für den eigenen Gebrauch; *in ~~* privat(im); im geheimen, insgeheim; unter vier Augen; *in o.'s ~~ capacity* als Privatmann, -person; *in ~~ hands* in Privathand; *to keep ~~* geheimhalten; *~~ account* Privat-, Geheimkonto *n*; *~~ affair, business, concerns, matter* Privatsache, -angelegenheit *f*; *~~ agreement* Privatabkommen *n*, -vertrag *m*; *~~ arrangement, settlement* private Vereinbarung; gütliche Einigung *f*; Privatvergleich *m*; *~~ audience* Privataudienz *f*; *~~ boarding-house* Privatpension *f*; *~~ box (Post)* Abholfach *n*; *~~ branch exchange* Fernsprechnebenstelle *f*; *~~ citizen* Privatperson *f*; *~~ clothes (pl)* Zivilkleidung; *in ~~ clothes* in Zivil; *~~ company* offene Handelsgesellschaft (OHG); Personalgesellschaft *f*; *~~ contract* Privatabkommen *n*, -vertrag *m*; *by ~~ contract* unter der Hand, freihändig; *~~ conversation* Privatgespräch *n*; *~~ customer* Privatkunde *m*; *~~ detective* Privatdetektiv *m*; *~~ enterprise* Privatunternehmen *n*, -betrieb *m*; *~~ first class (Am)* Gefreiter *m*; *~~ fortune* Privatvermögen *n*; *~~ gentleman* Privatmann, Rentier *m*; *~~ house* Privathaus *n*; *~~ income* Privatvermögen *n*; *~~ industry* Privatwirtschaft *f*; *~~ information* vertrauliche Mitteilung *f*; *~~ initiative* Privatinitiative *f*; *~~ law* Privat-, Zivilrecht *n*; *~~ lessons (pl)* Privatstunden *f pl*, -unterricht *m*; *~~ letter* Privatbrief *m*; *~~ life* Privatleben *n*; *~~ means (pl)* eigene Mittel *n pl*; Privateinkommen *n*; *~~ opinion* Privatmeinung *f*; *~~ property* Privateigentum *n*; *~~ residence* Privatwohnung *f*; *~~ road* Privatweg *m*; *~~ sale* freihändige(r) Verkauf *m*; *~~ school* Privatschule *f*; *~~ secretary* Privatsekretär *m*; *~~ soldier* gemeine(r) Soldat *m*; *~~ talks (pl)* interne Besprechungen *f pl*; *~~ theatre* Liebhabertheater *n*; *~~ view* Sonderführung *f (geladener Gäste auf e-r Ausstellung)*; **~eer** [praivə'tiə] *s* Kaperschiff *n*; *itr* Freibeuterei treiben; **~ion** [prai'veiʃən] Entzug; Verlust *m*; Not *f*, Mangel *m* (*of* an); *pl* Entbehrungen *f pl*; **~ive** ['privətiv] *a* ausschließend; *s gram* Privativum *n*.

privet ['privit] *bot* Liguster *m*.

priv|ilege ['privilidʒ] *s* Privileg, Vorrecht *n*, Vorrang *m*; *parl* Unverletzlichkeit, Immunität *f*; Monopol *n*; *tr* privilegieren, bevorzugen, bevorrechten; befreien, ausnehmen (*from* von); **~ileged** ['-d] *a* privilegiert, bevorrechtet; *to be ~~* das Vorrecht genießen (*to do s.th.* etw zu tun); **~ily** ['privili] *adv* heimlich, insgeheim, im geheimen; **~ity** ['-iti] Mitwisserschaft *f*; Rechtsgemeinschaft *f*; **~y** ['privi] *a jur* eingeweiht (*to* in); vertraut (*to* mit); beteiligt (*to* an); *s jur* Beteiligte(r), Teilhaber (*to* an); Abtritt, Abort *m*, Klosett *n (bes. im Freien)*; *to be ~~ to s.th.* in e-e S eingeweiht sein; *~~ council* Geheime(r) Staatsrat *m (Gremium)*; *~~ councillor* Staats-, Geheime(r) Rat *m (Person)*; *~~ parts (pl)* Geschlechtsteile *n pl*.

prize [praiz] **1.** *s* (Sieges-)Preis *m*, Prämie *f*; (Lotterie-)Gewinn, Treffer; *fig* Preis, Lohn *m*; *attr* Preis-; *a* preisgekrönt; *fam* ausgemacht, Erz-; *fam* hervorragend, erstklassig; *tr* e-n Preis setzen auf; (sehr) (hoch)schätzen; *to carry off, to take the ~* den Preis davontragen; *consolation ~* Trostpreis *m*; *first ~* Große(s) Los *n*; Hauptgewinn *m*; **~-competition, contest** Preisausschreiben *n*, Wettbewerb *m*; **~-drawing** Aus-, Verlosung *f*; **~-fight** (Berufs-)Boxkampf *m*; **~-fighter** Berufsboxer *m*; **~-fighting** Berufsboxen *n*; **~-giving** Preisverteilung *f*; **~-list** *(Lotterie)* Gewinnliste *f*; **~man, ~-winner** Preisträger, Gewinner *m*; **~-money** Geldpreis *m*; **~-question** Preisfrage *f*; **~-ring** (Box-)Ring; *fig* Wettkampf *m*; **~-winning** preisgekrönt; **2.** *s mar* Prise; (Kriegs-)Beute *f*; *tr (Schiff)* aufbringen; erbeuten; **~-court** Prisengericht *n*; **~-crew** Prisenkommando *n*; **~-master** Prisenkommandant *m*; **~-money, -bounty** Prisengeld *n*, -anteil *m*; **3.** *tr (to ~ open)* aufbrechen, gewaltsam öffnen; *s* Brechstange *f*, Hebel *m*.

pro [prou] *adv* dafür; *adj* günstig; *s pl -s* Befürworter, Verfechter, Vertreter *m*; *pl* Ja-Stimmen *f pl*; *the ~s and cons* das Für u. Wider; *to argue s.th. ~ and con* etw von allen Seiten beleuchten *fig*; *pref* Vor-, vor-, vorwärts; anstelle, anstatt; für, pro-, Pro-; *fam (für: ~fessional) sport a* Berufs-; *s* Profi, Berufssportler *m*; *~* **rata** [-'reitə, -'rɑ:tə] *a* verhältnismäßig; *~* **tem(pore)** *adv* zur Zeit, gegenwärtig, augenblicklich; *adv u. a* vorübergehend.

prob|ability [prɔbə'biliti] Wahrscheinlichkeit *f*; *in all ~~* aller Wahrscheinlichkeit nach; *what are the ~abilities?* welche Aussichten bestehen da? *the ~~ is that he will come* er wird wahrscheinlich kommen; *theory of ~~* Wahrscheinlichkeitsrechnung *f*; **~able** ['prɔbəbl] *a* wahrscheinlich; mutmaßlich, zu erwarten(d), anzunehmen(d); einleuchtend; *s* aussichtsreichste(r) Kandidat *m*; *~~ cause (jur)* hinreichende(r) Verdacht *m*; **~ate** ['proubit, *Am* -eit] *(gerichtliche)* Testamentseröffnung (u. -bestätigung); Erblegitimation *f*; *(~~ court, department, division)* Nachlaßgericht *n*; beglaubigte Abschrift *f* e-s gerichtlich bestätigten Testaments; *~~ duty* Erbschaft(s)-steuer *f*; **~ation** [prə'beiʃən] Prüfung, Erprobung; Probe(zeit); *jur* Bewährungsfrist, Strafaussetzung *f*, -nachlaß *m*; *on ~~* auf Probe; widerruflich; *jur* mit Bewährung(sfrist); *~~ officer* Bewährungshelfer *m*; **~ational** [prə'beiʃənl], **~ationary** [prə'beiʃnəri] *a*

Prüfungs-, Probe-; auf Probe; widerruflich; mit Bewährungsfrist; **~a***tionary employment* Probeanstellung *f*; **~ationer** [prə'beiʃnə] Prüfling, (Probe-)Kandidat, auf Probe Angestellte(r); Novize; *allg* Neuling *m*; *med* Lernschwester *f*; *jur* Strafentlassene(r) *m* mit Bewährungsfrist; **~ative** ['proubətiv] Prüfungs-, Probe-; *(Tatsache)* beweiserheblich; Beweis-; *a.* **~atory** ['proubətəri] als Beweis dienend (*of* für); **~e** [proub] *s tech med* Sonde; Sondierung; *Am jur* Untersuchung *f (durch e-n Ausschuß)*; *mil (~ing attack)* Sondierungsangriff *m*; *tr* sondieren; *tr itr fig* (eingehend) untersuchen (*into s.th.* etw); *~-scissors (pl)* Wundschere *f*.

probity ['prɔbiti, 'prou-] Rechtschaffenheit, Redlichkeit *f*.

problem ['prɔbləm] Problem *n*, Frage; Schwierigkeit *f*; Rätsel *n*; Sorge; *math* Aufgabe *f*; *a* Problem-; problematisch, schwierig; *to set a ~ to s.o.* jdn vor e-e schwierige Aufgabe stellen; *it is a ~ to me* das ist mir ein Rätsel; *that's your ~* das ist Ihre Sorge; **~atic(al)** [prɔbli'mætik(əl)] problematisch; fraglich, zweifelhaft, unsicher, ungewiß, fragwürdig; **~ child** schwierige(s) Kind *n*; **~ novel, play** Problemroman *m*, -stück *n*; **~ range** Problemkreis *m*.

probosc|idian [pro(u)bə'sidiən] Rüsseltier *n*; **~is** [prə'bɔsis] Rüssel; *hum* Zinken *m*, Nase *f*.

procedure [prə'si:dʒə] Verfahren, Verhalten, Vorgehen *n*, Vorgang *m*, Prozedur *f*; Verfahrens-, Verhaltens-, Handlungsweise, Verfahrensart *f*; *(code of) civil ~* Zivilprozeß(ordnung *f*) *m*; *(code of) criminal ~* Strafprozeß (-ordnung *f*) *m*; *disciplinary ~* Disziplinarverfahren *n*; *electory ~* Wahlmodus *m*; *law of ~* Prozeßrecht *n*; *legal ~* Gerichtsverfahren *n*, Prozeß *m*; *operating ~* Herstellungsverfahren *n*; *question of ~* Verfahrensfrage *f*; *rules (pl) of ~* Verfahrensbestimmungen *f pl*; *~ by arbitration* Schiedsgerichtsverfahren *n*.

proceed [prə'si:d] *itr* vorwärtsgehen, vorschreiten, vorrücken; s-n Weg machen, fortsetzen (*on a journey* e-e Reise); weitergehen, -fahren, -reisen; weitergehen, s-n Fortgang nehmen; weitermachen, fortfahren (*with, in* mit); fortsetzen, verfolgen (*to s.th.* etw); schreiten (*to* zu); in Angriff nehmen (*to s.th.* etw); anfangen, beginnen (*to s.th.* (mit) etw); übergehen (*to* zu); vorgehen, verfahren, handeln (*on a principle* nach e-m Grundsatz); vor sich gehen, sich vollziehen, sich entwickeln; sich ereignen; hervorgehen (*from* aus); erwerben (*to a degree* e-n Grad); gerichtlich vorgehen, e-n Prozeß anstrengen (*against s.o.* gegen jdn); verklagen, gerichtlich belangen (*against s.o.* jdn); *to ~ to blows* tätlich werden; *to ~ to business* zur Sache kommen; *to ~ to extremes* bis zum äußersten gehen; *to ~ to the order of the day* zur Tagesordnung übergehen; *to ~ to take evidence* in die Beweisaufnahme eintreten; *to ~ to violence* gewalttätig werden, zu Gewalttätigkeiten greifen; **~ing** [-iŋ] *s* Fortsetzung *f*, Fortgang, (weiterer) Verlauf *m*; Handlung(sweise) *f*, Verhalten, Vorgehen, Verfahren(sweise *f*) *n*, Maßnahme(n *pl*) *f*; *pl* (Gerichts-) Verfahren *n*, Verhandlungen; Beratungen *f pl*; Sitzungs-, Verhandlungsberichte *m pl*, Prozeßakten *f pl*; Prozeß *m*; *to commence, to initiate, to institute, to take legal ~~s* den Rechtsweg beschreiten, ein gerichtliches Verfahren einleiten, e-n Prozeß anstrengen; gerichtlich vorgehen, Klage erheben (*against s.o.* gegen jdn); *to stay ~~s* das Verfahren aussetzen; *to stop ~~s* das Verfahren einstellen; *arbitration ~~s* Schieds(gerichts)verfahren *n*; *bankruptcy ~~s* Konkursverfahren *n*; *civil ~~s* Zivilprozeß *m*; *criminal ~~s* Strafprozeß *m*; *disciplinary ~~s* Disziplinarverfahren *n*; *divorce ~~s* Scheidungsprozeß *m*; *execution ~~s* Zwangsvollstreckung *f*; *legal ~~s, ~~s at law* Gerichtsverfahren *n*, Prozeß *m*; *preparatory ~~s* Vorverfahren *n*; *reopening of the ~~s* Wiederaufnahme *f* des Verfahrens; *summary ~~s* Schnellverfahren *n*; **~s** ['prousi:dz] *s pl* Ergebnis, Resultat *n*; Ertrag, Erlös *m*, Einnahmen *f pl*, Gewinn *m* (*from* aus); *annual ~~* Jahresertrag *m*; *cash ~~* Barerlös *m*; *diminished, falling-off in ~~* Mindererertrag *m*; *gross ~~* Bruttoerlös, -ertrag *m*; *net ~~* Reinerlös, -ertrag, Nettoertrag *m*; *~~ of labo(u)r* Arbeitsertrag *m*.

process ['prouses, *Am* 'prɔ-] *s* Ab-, Verlauf *m*, Entwicklung *f*, Vorgang; Fortgang *m*, -schreiten *n*; (Ver-)Lauf *m* (der Zeit); (Arbeits-)Verfahren *n*, Arbeitsweise *f*, -gang *m*, Fabrikation *f*; *typ (~ printing)* photomechanische(s) Reproduktionsverfahren *n*; *chem* Prozeß; *jur* Prozeß, Rechtsstreit *m*, (Gerichts-)Verfahren *n*; *anat zoo bot* Fortsatz *m*; *a* (besonders) präpariert; *tr* (besonders) präparieren, (chemisch) behandeln; ver-, bearbeiten; e-r besonderen Behandlung, e-m besonderen (chemischen) Prozeß unterwerfen; veredeln; photomechanisch reproduzieren; *Am fig* abfertigen (*s.o.* jdn); *itr* [prə'ses] *fam* in e-r Prozession mitgehen; *in ~* im Gange; *in (the) ~ of* im (Ver-) Lauf *gen*; dabei; *in ~ of completion* in Arbeit; *in ~ of construction* im Bau (befindlich); *in ~ of time* im (Ver-)Lauf der Zeit; *to serve a ~ on s.o.* jdn gerichtlich vorladen; *Bessemer ~ (metal)* Bessemerverfahren *n*; *executory ~* Vollstreckungsverfahren *n*; *finishing ~* Veredelungsverfahren *n*; *manufacturing ~* Produktionsprozeß *m*; *~ of combustion* Verbrennungsvorgang *m*; *~ of digestion* Verdauungsvorgang *m*; *~ of distraint* Zwangsvollstreckungsverfahren *n*; *~ of growth (biol)* Wachstumsvorgänge *m pl*; *~ of manufacture* Arbeitsvorgang, -prozeß *m*; *~ of reproduction* Zeugungsvorgang *m*; **~ block** Klischee *n*; **~ cheese** Streichkäse *m*; **~ costing** Kostenrechnung *f* für Massenfertigung; **~ing** ['-iŋ] *agr tech* Veredelung; Verarbeitung, Behandlung; *tech* Aufbereitung; *fig* Bearbeitung *f*; *~~ cost* Fertigungskosten *pl*; *~~ industry* Veredelungsindustrie *f*; **~ion** [prə'seʃən] *s* Prozession, (feierlicher) Umzug; (Fest-)Zug *m*; *(~~ of the Holy Spirit)* Ausgießung *f* des Heiligen Geistes; *itr* sich in feierlichem Zug bewegen, in e-r Prozession gehen; e-n Zug bilden; *funeral ~~* Leichenzug *m*; *~~ caterpillar (ent)* Prozessionsspinnnerraupe *f*; *~~ moth* Prozessionsspinner *m*; **~ional** [-ʃənl] Prozessions-; **~ printing** Mehrfarbendruck *m*; **~ server** Zustellungsbeamte(r) *m*.

proclaim [prə'kleim] *tr* proklamieren, verkünden; ausrufen, erklären (*s.o. king* jdn zum König); *(Versammlung)* verbieten; ächten, in Acht u. Bann tun; den Belagerungszustand verhängen über; zeigen, erweisen (*s.o. master* jdn als Meister).

proclamation [prɔklə'meiʃən] Proklamation, Ausrufung, Bekanntmachung (*to* an); Ächtung *f*.

proclivity [prə'kliviti] Neigung *f*, Hang, Trieb *m* (*to, towards* zu).

proconsul [pro(u)'kɔnsəl] Statthalter; *hist* Prokonsul *m*.

procrastinat|e [pro(u)'kræstineit] *itr* zögern, zaudern; **~ion** [pro(u)kræsti'neiʃən] Aufschub *m*; Verzögerung *f*.

procre|ant ['proukriənt] sich fortpflanzend; (er)zeugend; fruchtbar; **~ate** ['-eit] *tr* (er)zeugen; hervorbringen; ins Leben rufen; *itr* sich fortpflanzen; **~ation** [proukri'eiʃən] Fortpflanzung; Zeugung; *fig* Hervorbringung *f*; **~ative** ['proukrieitiv] *a* Zeugungs-, Fortpflanzungs-; sich fortpflanzend, fruchtbar.

proctor ['prɔktə] Prokurator, bevollmächtigte(r) Vertreter; Anwalt *(vor e-m freiwilligen od Seegericht)*; *(Univ.)* Proktor; Aufsichtführende(r) *m* (bei Prüfungen).

procur|able [prə'kjuərəbl] erhältlich, zu beschaffen(d), zu besorgen(d); **~ation** [prɔkjuə'reiʃən] Verwaltung, Vertretung; Vollmacht, Prokura; Vollmachtsurkunde; Beschaffung, Besorgung; Kuppelei *f*; *(~~ fee)* Maklergebühr *f*, -lohn *m*; *per ~~* per Prokura; **~ator** ['prɔkjuəreitə] Sachwalter; *Am jur* (Prozeß-)Bevollmächtigte(r) *m*; **~e** [prə'kjuə] *tr (mühsam)* erhalten, erlangen, bekommen; ver-, beschaffen, besorgen; verkuppeln; *obs* zustande bringen, bewerkstelligen, herbeiführen, verursachen, veranlassen; *itr* kuppeln, Kuppelei treiben; **~ement** [-mənt] Erlangung; Beschaffung, Besorgung; Vermittlung *f*; *~~ division (Am)* Beschaffungsamt *n*; **~er** [-rə] Besorger; Kuppler *m*; **~ess** [-ris] Kupplerin *f*.

prod [prɔd] *tr* stechen; stoßen; *fig* an-, aufstacheln (*into* zu); *s* Stich; Stoß; Stachelstock *m*; Ahle *f*.

prodigal ['prɔdigəl] *a* verschwenderisch (*of* mit); *s* Verschwender *m*; *to be ~ of* verschwenden; nicht sparen mit; (nur so) um sich werfen mit; *the ~ son* der verlorene Sohn; **~ity** [prɔdi'gæliti] Verschwendung(ssucht); übertriebene Großzügigkeit; Fülle *f*, Überfluß *m* (*of* an); **~ize** ['prɔdigəlaiz] *tr* verschwenden.

prodig|ious [prə'didʒəs] wunderbar, -voll; erstaunlich; gewaltig; ungeheuer(lich); **~y** ['prɔdidʒi] Wunder (-ding, -werk), Weltwunder (*of* an); *(Mensch)* Phänomen; Ungeheuer; *infant ~~* Wunderkind *n*.

produc|e [prə'dju:s] *tr* vorführen, zeigen; *(Papiere)* vorzeigen, -weisen, -legen; *(Zeugen)* beibringen; *(Nachweis)* erbringen, führen; *(Gründe)* anführen; aufweisen; *agr* tragen, liefern, hervorbringen; erzeugen, produzieren, herstellen, fertigen, ausstoßen, fabrizieren; *(Eier)* legen; *min* fördern; *fig* hervorrufen, veranlassen, bewirken, zur Folge haben; *(Buch)* herausbringen, -geben, veröffentlichen; *theat* einstudieren, inszenieren, heraus-, auf die Bühne bringen; *film* drehen, produzieren; *(Aufnahme)* leiten; *math (Strecke)* verlängern (*to* bis); *(Fläche)* erweitern; *fin* abwerfen, einbringen; *itr* tragen; produzieren; *s* ['prɔdju:s] *nur sing bes. agr* Ertrag *m*, Erträgnis(se), Erzeugnis(se), Produkt(e) *n (pl)*; Ausbeute *f*; *brought to ~~* sortiert; *colonial ~~* Kolonialwaren *f pl*; *daily ~~* Tagesleistung *f*; *net ~~* Reinertrag *m*; *raw ~~* Rohstoffe *m pl*; *~~ business, dealer* od *merchant, ex-*

change, market Produktenhandel, -händler *m*, -börse *f*, -markt *od* Erzeugermarkt *m*; ~~ *of the country* Landesprodukte *n pl*; ~**er** [prə'dju:sə] Erzeuger, Hersteller, Produzent, Fabrikant, Lieferant *m*; Lieferfirma *f*; *theat film* Spielleiter, Regisseur; *theat* Direktor; *film* Produzent; *radio* Sendeleiter; *tech (~~ plant)* (Gas-)Generator *m*; ~~ *cooperative* Absatz-, Produktionsgenossenschaft *f*; ~~ *country* Erzeuger-, Herstellerland *n*; ~~ *gas* Generatorgas *n*; ~~*'s goods (pl)* Produktionsgüter *n pl*; ~~ *price* Erzeugerpreis *m*; ~**ible** [-ibl] zu erbringen(d), beizubringen(d); produzierbar, herstellbar; ~**ing** [-iŋ] *a* Erzeugungs-, Herstellungs-, Produktions-; produzierend; ertragbringend, produktiv; ~~*-charges, -costs (pl)* Herstellungs-, Gestehungskosten *pl*; ~~ *country* Erzeuger-, Herstellungsland *n*; ~~ *facilities (pl)* Fabrikationsanlagen *f pl*; ~~ *method* Produktionsweise *f*; ~~ *power* Leistungsfähigkeit, Kapazität *f*; ~~ *unit* Produktionseinheit *f*.

product ['prɔdəkt] Erzeugnis, Produkt; Werk *(geleistete Arbeit)*; *fig* Ergebnis, Resultat *n*, Folge, Frucht *f*; *com* Fabrikat *n*, Artikel *m*; *chem math* Produkt *n*; *by-~* Nebenprodukt *n*; *final* ~ Endprodukt *n*; *garden ~s (pl)* Gartenerzeugnisse *n pl*; *industrial* ~ *(pl)* Industrieerzeugnisse *n pl*; *national* ~ Sozialprodukt *n*; *primary ~s (pl)* Rohprodukte *n pl*; *semi-finished* ~ Halb(fertig)fabrikat *n*; *staple* ~ Hauptprodukt *n*; ~ *of combustion (chem)* Verbrennungsprodukt *n*; ~**ion** [prə'dʌkʃən] Erzeugung, Herstellung, Produktion, Fabrikation, Fertigung; *min* Förderung; Leistung, Kapazität *f*; Erzeugnis, Produkt, Fabrikat; *(geistige)* Produktion *f*, Werk *n*; *theat* Aufführung, Inszenierung; *theat film* Regie; *film* Produktion; *(Dokument)* Vorlage, Beibringung *f*; *to curb the* ~~ die Produktion drosseln; *to go into* ~~ die Produktion aufnehmen; *annual* ~~ Jahresproduktion *f*; *cost of* ~~ Herstellungskosten *pl*; *excess, surplus, over*~~ Produktionsüberschuß *m*; *loss of* ~~ Produktionsausfall *m*; *mass, quantity* ~~ Massenproduktion *f*; *means of* ~~ Produktionsmittel *n pl*; *method, way of* ~~ Produktionsweise *f*; ~~ *of current* Stromerzeugung *f*; ~~ *of goods* Gütererzeugung *f*; ~~ *of income* Einkommensbildung *f*; ~~ *area* Produktionsgebiet *n*; ~~ *bonus* Leistungsprämie *f*; ~~ *capacity* Leistungsfähigkeit; Produktionskapazität *f*; ~~ *car (mot)* Serienwagen *m*; ~~ *centre* Produktionszentrum *n*, Kostenstelle *f*; ~~ *control* Betriebsüberwachung, Fertigungskontrolle; Produktionsbeschränkung *f*; ~~ *costs (pl)* Herstellungs-, Gestehungskosten *pl*; ~~ *cut* Produktionseinschränkung *f*; ~~ *decrease* Produktionsrückgang *m*; ~~ *director (radio)* Sendeleiter *m*; ~~ *engineer* Betriebsingenieur *m*; ~~ *figures (pl)* Produktionszahlen *f pl*; ~~ *increase* Produktionssteigerung *f*; ~~ *index* Produktionsindex *m*; ~~ *line* Fließband *n*; ~~ *manager* Produktionsleiter *m*; ~~ *plan, schedule* Fertigungsplan *m*; ~~ *process* Herstellungsverfahren *n*, -prozeß *m*; ~~ *program(me)* Produktionsplan *m*, -programm *n*; ~~ *scheduling* Fertigungs-, Arbeitsplanung *f*; ~~ *surplus* Produktionsüberschuß *m*; ~~ *target* Produktionsziel *n*; ~~ *time* Arbeitszeit *f*; ~~ *volume* Produktionsumfang *m*; ~**ive** [prə'dʌktiv] *agr* ertragreich, ergiebig, fruchtbar (*of* an) *a. fig*; *min* abbauwürdig; *fig* produktiv, schöpferisch; Erzeugungs-, Produktions-; Ertrags-; gewinnbringend, rentabel; werteschaffend; *to be* ~~ *of* hervorrufen, zur Folge haben, die Ursache sein *gen*; erzeugen; ~~ *of interest* zinsbringend, -tragend; ~~ *capacity, power* Leistungsfähigkeit *f*; ~~ *industry* Produktionsmittelindustrie *f*; ~~ *labo(u)r* Fertigungslöhne *m pl*; ~~ *value* Ertragswert *m*; ~**iveness** [-'dʌktivnis], ~**ivity** [prɔdʌk'tiviti] Ertragfähigkeit, Ergiebigkeit, Rentabilität; Fruchtbarkeit; Produktivität, Leistungsfähigkeit *f*.

proem ['prouem] (kurze) Einführung, Einleitung, Vorrede *f*, -wort *n*.

prof, proff [prɔf] *fam* Professor *m*.

profan|ation [prɔfə'neiʃən] Entweihung, Schändung, Profanation *f*; ~**e** [prə'fein] *a* profan, weltlich; un(ein)geweiht (*to* in); ruchlos, gottlos; fluchend; *tr (Heiligtum)* miß-, verachten; entweihen, schänden, profanieren; ~~ *word* Fluch *m*; ~**eness** [prə'feinnis], ~**ity** [prə'fæniti] Weltlichkeit; Uneingeweihtheit; Ruchlosigkeit, Gottlosigkeit *f*; ruchlose, gottlose Worte *n pl*, Lästerung *f*; Fluchen *n*; *pl* Flüche *m pl*.

profess [prə'fes] *tr* gestehen, bekennen; versichern, erklären; sich bekennen zu; vorgeben, -täuschen, heucheln, spielen; *(Beruf)* ausüben; *(Fach)* vertreten, unterrichten, lehren; *itr rel* praktizieren; die (Ordens-)Gelübde ablegen; ~**ed** [-t] *a* erklärt, ausgesprochen, offen; vor-, angeblich, vorgetäuscht, geheuchelt, gespielt; ~**edly** [-idli] *adv* offen, unverhohlen; angeblich; ~**ion** [prə'feʃən] Erklärung, Versicherung *f*; Bekenntnis *n*; Glauben(sbekenntnis *n*); (geistiger) Beruf, Stand *m*; Berufsgruppe *f*, -vertreter *m pl*; (Ordens-)Gelübde *n pl*; *by* ~~ von Beruf; *to take up a* ~~ e-n Beruf ergreifen; *the learned ~~s (pl)* die akademischen Berufe *m pl*; ~~ *of faith* Glaubensbekenntnis *n*; ~**ional** [prə'feʃənl] *a* beruflich; berufsmäßig; gelernt; fachlich; freiberuflich tätig; Berufs-, Fach-; *s (~~ man)* Berufsangehörige(r), -vertreter; Akademiker; Berufskünstler; Berufssportler, -spieler, -boxer *m*; *to take* ~~ *advice on s.th.* e-n Fachmann um etw befragen; ~~ *business, work* Berufsarbeit *f*; ~~ *disease* Berufskrankheit *f*; ~~ *employee* höhere(r) Angestellte(r) *m*; ~~ *experience* Berufserfahrung *f*; ~~ *jealousy* Konkurrenz-, Brotneid *m*; ~~ *journal* Fachzeitschrift *f*; ~~ *player* Berufsspieler *m*; ~~ *secrecy, secret* Berufsgeheimnis *n*; ~~ *soldier* Berufssoldat *m*; ~~ *tax* Gewerbesteuer *f*; ~~ *training* Berufsausbildung *f*; ~**ionalism** [-'feʃnəlizm] fachliche Qualifikation *f*; Berufsstand *m*; *sport* Berufsspielertum *n*; ~**or** [prə'fesə] Bekenner; Professor, (Hochschul-)Lehrer *m* (*in the university* an der Universität); *Am fam hum* Kanone *f (Mensch)*; *Am sl* Klavierspieler *m*; *assistant* ~~ Dozent *m*; *associate* ~~ *(Am)* außerordentliche(r) Professor *m*; *full* ~~ *(Am)* ordentliche(r) Professor, Ordinarius *m*; ~**orial** [prɔfe'sɔ:riəl] *a* Professoren-; professoral, professorenhaft; ~**oriate** [-'sɔ:riit] Professorenschaft; Professur *f*; ~**orship** [prə'fesəʃip] Professur *f*; *to be appointed to a* ~~ e-e Professur erhalten.

proffer ['prɔfə] *tr lit* anbieten; *s* Anerbieten, Angebot *n*.

proficien|cy [prə'fiʃənsi] Erfahrenheit, Fähigkeit, Tüchtigkeit, Geschicklichkeit *f*; ~**t** [-t] *a* geübt, erfahren, fähig, tüchtig; *lit* kundig, *fam* bewandert (*in* in); *s* Experte, (erfahrener) Fachmann *m*.

profile ['proufi:l, -ail] *s* Profil *n*, Seitenansicht *f*; Querschnitt; Umriß *m*, Konturen *f pl*; Lebens-, biographische Skizze *f*; *arch* Aufriß *m*; *tr* im Profil darstellen *od* zeichnen; profilieren; *s.o.* jds Lebensbild entwerfen; *in* ~ im Profil; *wing, airfoil* ~ *(aero)* Flügelprofil *n*; ~ **cutter** Fassonfräser *m*.

profit ['prɔfit] *s* Gewinn, Ertrag, Verdienst, Nutzen, Vorteil *m*; *pl* Erträgnisse *pl*; Aufkommen *n*; Nutzung *f*; Einkünfte *pl*; *tr itr* Nutzen, Gewinn bringen; etw einbringen, eintragen (*s.o.* jdm); *itr* Nutzen ziehen, lernen (*by* aus, durch); profitieren, gewinnen (*by* an); *at a* ~ mit Gewinn; gewinn-, nutzbringend; vorteilhaft *adv*; *to bring, to show, to yield a* ~ e-n Gewinn abwerfen; Nutzen bringen; *to make a* ~ *on s.th.* aus etw Gewinn ziehen; *to turn to o.'s* ~ sich etw zunutze machen; *you* ~ *from your mistakes* durch Schaden wird man klug; *book* ~ Buchgewinn *m*; *chances (pl) of* ~ Gewinnaussichten, -chancen *f pl*; *clear, net* ~ Reingewinn *m*; *margin of* ~ Gewinnspanne *f*; *pecuniary* ~ Vermögensvorteil *m*; *share in the* ~*s* Gewinnanteil *m*; *war* ~ Kriegsgewinn *m*; ~ *and loss* Gewinne u. Verluste *pl*; ~**able** ['-əbl] gewinn-, nutzbringend, vorteilhaft, günstig, einträglich, lohnend, rentabel (*to* für); *to be* ~~ sich rentieren; ~**ableness** ['-əblnis] Einträglichkeit, Wirtschaftlichkeit, Rentabilität *f*; ~ **balance** Gewinnüberschuß *m*; ~-**earning** rentabel; ~**eer** [prɔfi'tiə] *s* Schieber, Wucherer *m*; *itr* schieben, unsaubere, Schiebergeschäfte machen; *war-*~~ Kriegsgewinnler *m*; ~**eering** [-'tiəriŋ] *s* Schieber-, Wuchergeschäfte *n pl*; Preistreiberei; Profitgier, Gewinnsucht *f*; *attr* Schieber-, Wucher-; ~ **forward** Gewinnvortrag *m*; ~**less** ['prɔfitlis] *a* ohne Gewinn, ohne Nutzen; nicht einträglich, unrentabel; ~ **margin** Gewinnspanne *f*; **-seeking, -making** auf Gewinn gerichtet; ~ **sharing** Gewinnbeteiligung *f (der Arbeitnehmer)*; ~-**sharing** *a* am Gewinn beteiligt.

proflig|acy ['prɔfligəsi] Verworfenheit, Verkommenheit, Lasterhaftigkeit; Verschwendung *f*; ~**ate** ['prɔfligit] *a* verworfen, verkommen, verdorben, lasterhaft, verschwenderisch; ausschweifend, liederlich; *s* verkommene(r) Mensch; Verschwender *m*.

profound [prə'faund] *(Schmerz, Schlaf, Schweigen)* tief; stark; tiefgründig, -schürfend, gründlich; unergründlich; *(Veränderungen)* tiefgreifend; schwerwiegend; ~**ness** [-nis], **profundity** [prə'fʌnditi] (große) Tiefe; Tiefgründigkeit; Stärke *f*.

profus|e [prə'fju:s] überreichlich, verschwenderisch (*of* an); in Hülle u. Fülle; (allzu) freigebig, sehr großzügig (*in, of* mit); ~**eness** [-nis], ~**ion** [prə'fju:ʒən] Überfluß *m*, -fülle, verschwenderische Fülle *f*, Luxus *m* (*of* an); Verschwendung(ssucht), Großzügigkeit *f*; *in* ~*ion* im Überfluß.

prog [prɔg] **1.** *s sl* Futter *n*, Fraß *m*; **2.** *a.* ~*gins* ['-inz] *sl (Oxford u. Cambridge)* Univ.-Proktor *m*.

progen|itive [pro(u)'dʒenitiv] zeugungs-, fortpflanzungsfähig; Zeugungs-, Fortpflanzungs-; ~**itor** [-itə] Vorfahr, Ahn(herr) *m*; ~**y** ['prɔdʒini]

Kinder *n pl*; Nachwuchs *m*; Nachkommen(schaft *f*) *m pl a. zoo bot*; *zoo* Brut; Abstammung *f*, Geschlecht *n*; *fig* Ergebnis *n*, Folge, Frucht *f*.

progno|sis [prɔg'nousis] *pl -ses* [-i:z] *bes. med* Prognose; Voraus-, Vorhersage *f*; **~stic** [prəg'nɔstik] *s* Vorzeichen *n a. med*; Vorhersage, Prognose *f*; **~sticate** [prəg'nɔstikeit] *tr* ein Vorzeichen sein für; voraus-, vorhersagen, prophezeien; *med* prognostizieren; **~stication** [prəgnɔsti'keiʃən] Voraus-, Vorhersage, Weissagung, Prophezeiung, Prognose *f a. med*.

program|(me) ['prougræm] Programm *n*, Spiel-, Vortragsfolge *f*, Festablauf; *theat* Spielplan, Theaterzettel *m*; *radio* Hör-, Sendefolge; Tanzkarte *f*; Lehr-, Arbeitsplan *m*; Tagesordnung *f*; *med* Diätplan *m*; *itr* ein Programm aufstellen; *tech* programmieren; *radio* das Programm gestalten; *what's on your ~* was haben Sie vor? *(emergency) aid(-) ~* (Sofort-)Hilfsprogramm *n*; *change of ~* Programmänderung *f*; *home construction, housing ~* Wohnungsbauprogramm *n*; *party ~* Parteiprogramm *n*; *production, manufacturing ~* Produktionsplan *m*; *reform ~* Reformprogramm *n*; *working ~* Arbeitsplan *m*; ~ **advertising** Theater-, Kinowerbung *f*; ~ **director** *radio* Sendeleiter *m*; **~mer** Programmierer *m*; **~matic** [prougrə'mætik] programmatisch; ~ **music** Programmusik *f*; ~ **picture** *Am* Beifilm *m*; ~ **seller** Programmverkäufer(in *f*) *m*.

progress ['prougres] *nur sing s* Vorrücken, Weiter-, Fortschreiten *n*; Fortschritt(e) *m (pl)*, (Weiter-)Entwick(e)lung *f*, Fortgang, Verlauf *m*; *itr* [prə'gres] vorrücken (*towards* gegen); weiter-, fortschreiten; vorwärtskommen; sich entwickeln; Fortschritte machen (*with* in, bei); *in ~* im Gange; in Vorbereitung; *to make ~* Fortschritte machen; vorankommen; *~ of events* Gang *m* der Dinge; **~ion** [prə'greʃən] Fortschreiten *n*, -schritt, Fortgang *m*; Vorrücken *n*; Verlauf *m*; *mus astr math* Progression; *math* Reihe *f*; *arithmetic, geometric ~~* arithmetische, geometrische Reihe *f*; **~ional** [prə'greʃənl] *a* Progressions-; fortschreitend; **~ionist** [prə'greʃnist] Fortschrittsgläubige(r), Fortschrittler *m*; **~ive** [prə'gresiv] vorrückend; fortschreitend, zunehmend; fortschrittlich; *med* progressiv; *(Steuer)* gestaffelt; *~~ assembly* Fließbandmontage *f*; *~~ form (gram)* Progressiv-, Dauerform *f*; ~ **report** Tätigkeitsbericht *m*.

prohibit [prə'hibit] *tr* verbieten (*s.o. from doing s.th.* jdm etw zu tun); verhindern, unterbinden; *~ed area* (Luft-) Sperrgebiet *n*; **~ion** [pro(u)i'biʃən] Verbot *n*; *hist* Prohibition *f*; **~ionist** [pro(u)i'biʃnist] Anhänger des Schutzzollsystems; *Am* Alkoholgegner *m*; **~ive** [prə'hibitiv], **~ory** [-əri] *a* verhindernd, ausschließend; Prohibitiv-, Hinderungs-; *fam* unerschwinglich; *~ive duty* Schutzzoll *m*; *~ive system* Schutzzollsystem *n*.

project ['prɔdʒekt] *s* Projekt *n*, Plan, Entwurf *m*; Vorhaben, Unternehmen *n*; *v* [prə'dʒekt] *tr* werfen, schleudern, feuern; vorstrecken, vorspringen lassen; *opt math psychol* projizieren (*on* auf); entwerfen, planen, vorhaben; *itr* vorspringen, hervorstehen; *arch* auskragen (*over* über); *to ~ o.s.* sich *(in Gedanken)* (hinein)versetzen (*into* in); *development ~* Entwicklungsvorhaben *n*; **~ile** ['prɔdʒiktail] *s* (Wurf-) Geschoß, Projektil *n*; *a* [prə'dʒektail] Wurf-, Geschoß-; antreibend; *zoo* ausstreckbar; **~ion** [prə'dʒekʃən] Wurf; Vorsprung, vorspringende(r) Teil *m*; *arch* Auskragung *f*; Entwurf, Plan *m*; *fig* Bild *n*, Auffassung *f*; *opt film (Karten-)* Projektion; *film* Vorführung *f*; *~~ room, (Am) booth* Vorführraum *m*; *~~ screen* Bildschirm *m*; **~ionist** [prə'dʒekʃənist] *film* Vorführer *m*; **~or** [prə'dʒektə] Projektenmacher; Pläneschmied; *com* Gründer; Scheinwerfer; Bildwerfer *m*, Projektions-, *film* Vorführgerät *n*.

prolapse ['proulæps] *s med* Vorfall *m*; *itr* vorfallen.

prolate ['prouleit] *(Körper)* (an den Polen) abgeplattet; länglich, gestreckt.

prolegomenon [proule'gɔminən] *meist pl*: *-a* [-ə] Vorbemerkung(en *pl*), Einführung, -leitung, Vorrede *f*.

proletari|an [proule'tɛəriən] *a* proletarisch; *s* Proletarier *m*; *~~ dictatorship* Diktatur *f* des Proletariats; **~at(e)** [-riət] Proletariat *n*.

proli|ferate [prə-, pro(u)'lifəreit] *itr biol* sprossen, sich vermehren; *med* wuchern; **~feration** [pro(u)lifə'reiʃən] Sprossung; Wucherung *f*; **~fic** [prə'lifik] *biol* fruchtbar *a. fig*; *fig* produktiv, reich (*of, in* an).

prolix ['prouliks] weitschweifig, langatmig, wortreich; **~ity** [pro(u)'liksiti] Weitschweifigkeit, Langatmigkeit *f*.

prolog(ue) ['proulɔg] *s* Prolog *m (bes. e-s Dramas)*, Vorspiel *n*, -spruch *m*, -rede, Einleitung *f* (*to* zu); *fig* Auftakt; *theat* Prologsprecher *m*; *to be the ~ to s.th.* zu etw den Auftakt bilden; *tr* durch e-n Prolog einleiten.

prolong [prə'lɔŋ] *tr* verlängern; aufschieben, hinauszögern; *(Wechsel)* prolongieren; **~ation** [proulɔŋ'geiʃən] Verlängerung; Hinauszögerung *f*; (Zahlungs-)Aufschub *m*; *(Wechsel)* Prolongierung *f*.

prom [prɔm] *fam* Promenadenkonzert *n*; *Am fam* Schüler-, Klassenball *m*, Tanzparty *f*.

promenade [prɔmi'nɑ:d, *Am* -'neid] *s* Spaziergang *m*; Promenade *f*, Spazierweg; Wandelgang *m*, -halle *f*; *Am* Ball *m*; Polonäse *f*, Einzug *m* der Ballgäste; *itr* spazieren(gehen), promenieren, *lit* lustwandeln; *tr* spazieren(gehen) in, durch, ... entlang; zur Schau tragen, paradieren mit; ~ **concert** Promenadenkonzert *n*; ~ **deck** *mar* Promenadendeck *n*.

prominen|ce, -cy ['prɔminəns(i)] Hervorragen, -stehen *n*; Vorsprung, vorspringende(r) Teil *m*, Protuberanz; Anhöhe; *fig* Bedeutung, Wichtigkeit *f*; **~ce** *fam* Prominente(r) *m*, prominente Persönlichkeit *f*; *to bring s.th. into ~ce* etw herausstellen; *to come into ~ce (fig)* in den Vordergrund treten; **~t** ['-t] vorstehend, -springend; *fig* hervorragend, bedeutend; auffällig; (wohl)bekannt, prominent.

promiscu|ity [prɔmis'kju(:)iti] (buntes) Durcheinander *n*, Wirrwarr *m*; Vermischung; Promiskuität *f*; **~ous** [prə'miskjuəs] (bunt) gemischt, wirr, durchea.geraten, -geworfen, -gewirbelt; wahl-, unterschiedslos; gemeinsam; (geschlechtlich) sehr frei; *fam* planlos, gelegentlich.

promis|e ['prɔmis] *s* Versprechen; Gelöbnis, Gelübde *n*; Verheißung; (feste) Zusage, Zusicherung; (feste) Aussicht, Hoffnung *f* (*of* auf); Eheversprechen *n*; *tr* versprechen, zusagen, in Aussicht stellen; *itr* Hoffnungen erwecken; zusagen; *to ~~ o.s.* sich freuen auf, erwarten; *of great ~~* vielversprechend; *to break o.'s ~~* sein Wort brechen; *to give, to make a ~~* ein Versprechen geben; *to go back on o.'s ~~* sein Versprechen zurücknehmen; *to keep o.'s ~~* sein Versprechen, sein Wort halten; *to redeem o.'s ~~* sein Versprechen einlösen; *to show great ~~* zu großen Hoffnungen Anlaß geben *od* berechtigen; *the day ~~s well* der Tag verspricht schön zu werden, sieht günstig aus; *breach of ~~* Wortbruch *m*; *empty ~~s (pl)* leere Versprechungen *f pl*; *P~ed Land* Gelobte(s) Land *m*; *~~ of payment* Zahlungsversprechen *n*; **~ee** [prɔmi'si:] Versprechensempfänger *m*; **~er**, *jur* **~or** ['prɔmisə, '-ɔ:] Versprechende(r) *m*; **~ing** ['-iŋ] vielversprechend, verheißungs-, hoffnungsvoll, aussichtsreich; erfolgversprechend; **~ory** ['-əri] ein Versprechen enthaltend; *to be ~~* andeuten; *~~ note* Schuldverschreibung *f*, -schein *m*; Eigen-, Solawechsel *m*.

promontory ['prɔməntri] Vorgebirge *n a. anat*.

promot|e [prə'mout] *tr* fördern, begünstigen, weiterbringen, unterstützen; arbeiten, eintreten, sich einsetzen für; befürworten, erleichtern; erregen, erwecken; *(e-r S)* Vorschub leisten; ins Werk setzen; *(Geschäft)* gründen; *(Gesetzentwurf)* einbringen; *(im Rang)* befördern; *Am (Schüler)* versetzen; *(Schach: Bauern zur Dame)* machen; *Am com* werben für *(e-n Artikel)*; *(Verkauf)* steigern; *Am sl* erbetteln, klauen, stibitzen; **~er** [-ə] Förderer, Befürworter; Urheber, geistige(r) Vater; Anstifter; (Geschäfts-)Gründer *(e-r AG)*; Organisator; *sport* Veranstalter; *tech* Katalysator *m*; *~~'s shares (pl)* Gründeraktien *f pl*; **~ion** [-ʃən] Förderung, Begünstigung, Unterstützung, Befürwortung, Erleichterung; *com* Gründung; Beförderung; *Am* Versetzung; *Am* Werbung, Reklame, Propaganda *f*; *to get o.'s ~~* befördert werden; *export ~~* Exportförderung *f*; *sales ~~* Verkaufsförderung, Absatzsteigerung *f*; *~~ of employment* Arbeitsbeschaffung *f*; *~~ manager* Reklamechef *m*; *~~ matter (Am)* Werbematerial *n*; **~ional** [-ʃənl] fördernd, Förderungs-; begünstigend, günstig; erleichternd, Erleichterungs-; *Am* Werbe-, Reklame-, Propaganda-; **~ive** [-iv] fördernd; *to be ~~ of s.th.* etw fördern.

prompt [prɔmpt] *a* bereit, fertig; zur Hand, griffbereit; umgehend, sofortig, unverzüglich, prompt; *(Bezahlung)* bar; *(Mensch)* schnell, fix, (sofort) bereit; bereitwillig; pünktlich; *s theat* Soufflieren *n*; *com* Zahlungsfrist *f*, Ziel *n*; *tr* anspornen, -treiben, veranlassen (*to* zu); auf die Sprünge helfen, *theat* soufflieren, einsagen (*s.o.* jdm); zuflüstern, eingeben, inspirieren (*s.o.* jdm; *with s.th.* etw); beeinflussen; *at six months ~* Ziel 6 Monate; *to be ~ in doing s.th.* pünktlich etw tun; **~-book** Soufflierbuch *n*; **~-box** Souffleurkasten *m*; **~er** ['-ə] Antreiber; Souffleur *m*, Souffleuse *f*; Anstifter, Inspirator *m*; **~ing** ['-iŋ] Antreiben; Soufflieren *n*; Eingebung, Inspiration *f*; Impuls *m*; **~itude** ['-itju:d] Bereitwilligkeit, Schnelligkeit, Fixigkeit, *com* Promptheit; Pünktlichkeit *f*; **~ly** ['-li] *adv* pünktlich; *to start ~~ at eight* Punkt 8 Uhr anfangen; ~ **note** Mahnzettel *m*.

promulgat|e ['prɔməlgeit] *tr* (öffentlich) bekanntmachen, -geben; *(a. Gesetz)* verkünden; aus-, verbreiten;

~ion [prɔməl'geiʃən] Bekanntmachung, -gabe, Verkündung; Aus-, Verbreitung *f*; **~or** ['-ə] Verkünder; Verbreiter *m*.

prone [proun] *a* vorgebeugt, vornübergeneigt; abschüssig; mit dem Gesicht auf dem Boden liegend, ausgestreckt; *fig* geneigt (*to* zu), empfänglich (*to* für); *to fall ~ to the floor* lang, flach auf den Boden fallen; **~ness** ['-nis] vorgebeugte Haltung *f*; Liegen *n* auf dem Gesicht; Hang *m*, Neigung (*to* zu), Empfänglichkeit *f* (*to* für); **~ position** Bauchlage *f*.

prong [prɔŋ] *(Gabel)* Zinke; Heu-, Mistgabel; *allg* Spitze, Zacke; *(Geweih)* Sprosse *f*; **~ed** [-d] *a* gezackt, spitz(ig).

pronominal [prə'nɔminl] *gram* pronominal.

pronoun ['prounaun] *gram* Pronomen, Fürwort *n*.

pronounc|e [prə'nauns] *tr* verkünden; *(feierlich)* erklären; *(Urteil)* abgeben, *jur* fällen; erklären (für); äußern; (richtig) aussprechen; *itr* sich erklären, sich aussprechen (*on* über; *for, in favo(u)r of* für; *against* gegen); **~eable** [-əbl] aussprechbar; **~ed** [-t] *a* ausgesprochen, deutlich; festgelegt, entschieden; *(Tendenz)* ausgeprägt; **~ement** [-mənt] Verkündung; (feierliche) Erklärung; Äußerung *f*; **~ing** [-iŋ] *a* Aussprache-.

pronto ['prɔntou] *adv Am fam* fix, rasch, schnell, sofort, gleich, dalli.

pronunciation [prənʌnsi'eiʃən] Aussprache *f*.

proof [pru:f] *s* Beweisführung, *jur* -aufnahme *f*; Nachweis, Beleg; Beweis (-mittel *n*) *m*; Begründung; Bestätigung; (Nach-)Prüfung *f*, Versuch *m*, (Kost-)Probe; Erprobung, Erprobtheit; Festigkeit, Stärke; *(Getränk)* Normalstärke *f*; *(Graphik, phot)* Probeabzug; *typ* Probedruck, Korrekturbogen *m*; *a* fest, sicher (*against* gegen); undurchdringlich, undurchlässig (*to, against* für); *fig* stichhaltig, gefeit (*against* gegen); unempfindlich (*against* für); Probe-; *(Alkohol)* probehaltig; *tr* prüfen; imprägnieren, wasserdicht machen; *by way of ~* als Beweis; *to furnish, to produce ~* den Beweis erbringen; *to give ~ of s.th.* etw unter Beweis stellen; *to put to (the) ~* auf die Probe stellen; *to read (the) ~s* Korrektur lesen (*on an article* e-s Artikels); *the ~ of the pudding is in the eating* Probieren geht über Studieren; *bomb-~* bombenfest, -sicher; *brush-~ (typ)* Bürstenabzug *m*; *bullet-~* kugelsicher; *burden, onus of ~* Beweislast *f*; *burglar-~* einbruchsicher; *fire-~* feuerfest; *fool-~* narrensicher; *galley-~ (typ)* Fahne *f*, Korrekturbogen *m*; *press-~* druckfertige(r) Korrekturbogen *m*; *revised ~ (typ)* Revision *f*, Umbruch *m*; *water-~* wasserdicht; *weather-~* wetterfest; *~ against bribe* unbestechlich; *~ by the evidence of witnesses* Zeugenbeweis *m*; *~ of origin* Herkunftsnachweis *m*; Ursprungszeugnis *n*; **~-correcting, -correction, -reading** Korrekturlesen *n*; **~-impression** Probeabzug *m*; **~ing** ['-iŋ] Imprägnierung *f*; **~less** ['-lis] unbewiesen; **~ load** Probebelastung *f*; **~-mark** Probestempel *m*; **~-puller** Fahnenabzieher *m*; **~read** *itr irr Am* Korrektur lesen; **~-reader** *typ* Korrektor *m*; *~'s marks (pl)* Korrekturzeichen *n pl*; **~ reading** Korrekturlesen *n*; **~-sheet** Korrekturbogen *m*, Druckfahne *f*; **~-spirit** Normalweingeist *m*; **~ test** Abnahmeprüfung *f*.

prop [prɔp] **1.** *s* Pfosten *m*, Stütze, Strebe *f*; *tech* Stempel *m*; *fig* Stütze, Säule *f*; *pl theat* Requisiten *pl*; *pl sl* Stelzen *pl*, Beine *n pl*; *tr (to ~ up)* (mit e-m Pfosten) stützen; verstreben; (an)lehnen (*against* an); *mot* aufbocken; *min* absteifen; *fig* (unter-) stützen; *sl* umlegen, niederschlagen; *to ~ o.s. against (fig)* sich stemmen gegen; **2.** *Am sl aero* Latte *f*, Propeller *m*; **3.** *(Schule) sl (mathematischer)* Lehrsatz *m*.

propag|anda [prɔpə'gændə] Propaganda(apparat *m*); Reklame, Werbung *f*; *to make ~~* Propaganda treiben *od* machen (*for* für); *election ~~* Wahlpropaganda *f*; *whispering-~~* Flüsterpropaganda *f*; *~~ film* Werbe-, Reklamefilm *m*; *~~ leaflet* Flugblatt *n*; *~~ week* Werbewoche *f*; **~andist** [-'gændist] Propagandist *m*; **~andistic** [prɔpəgæn'distik] propagandistisch; **~andize** [prɔpə'gændaiz] *tr (Idee, Lehre)* propagieren; werben für; *(Menschen)* mit Propaganda bearbeiten; *itr* Propaganda treiben; **~ate** ['prɔpəgeit] *tr (Pflanze, Tier)* züchten; *biol u. fig* fortpflanzen, übertragen; *phys opt* ausbreiten; *(Idee, Sitte)* aus-, verbreiten; *itr u. to ~~ itself (bot zoo)* sich fortpflanzen, sich vermehren; **~ation** [prɔpə'geiʃən] *biol* Fortpflanzung, Übertragung; Aus-, Verbreitung *f*; *~~ velocity* Fortpflanzungsgeschwindigkeit *f*; **~ator** ['prɔpəgeitə] Verbreiter *m*.

propane ['proupein] Propan(gas) *n*.

propel [prə'pel] *tr* vorwärts-, fort-, weitertreiben; in Bewegung setzen; **~lant** [-ənt] Treibstoff *m*, -mittel *n*, *mil* -ladung *f*; **~lent** [-] *a* (vorwärts-, an)treibend; Treib-; *s* Treibstoff *m*, -kraft *f*; Antrieb *m*; **~ler** [-ə] Propeller *m*, Schiffs-, Luftschraube *f*; *~~ blade* Propeller-, Luftschraubenblatt *n*; *~~ pitch* Ganghöhe *f*; *~~ shaft* Luftschraubenwelle; *Am mot* Kardanwelle; *~~ slipstream* Luftschraubenstrahl *m*; *~~ turbine* Propellerturbine *f*; *~~-turbine engine* Propellerturbinen-(Luftstrahl-)Triebwerk *n*; **~ling** [-iŋ] *a* treibend, Trieb-, Antriebs-; *~~ charge* Treibsatz *m*, -ladung *f*; *~~ nozzle (aero)* Schubdüse *f*; *~~ pencil* Drehbleistift *m*; *~~ power* Triebkraft *f*.

propensity [prə'pensiti] Neigung *f*, Hang *m* (*to, toward s.th.* zu etw; *for doing* zu tun).

proper ['prɔpə] *a* passend, angebracht, richtig, geeignet (*for* für); richtig, korrekt, gehörig, geziemend, ordnungsmäßig, ordnungsgemäß; sittsam, bescheiden, höflich; eigentümlich, charakteristisch (*to* für), eigen (*to* dat); besonder; *(häufig nachgestellt)* eigentlich, genau(genommen), im engeren Sinn, selbst; *fam* recht, richtig, wahr, gehörig; *in ~ condition* in gutem Zustand; *to deem ~ to* es für richtig halten zu; *that's not ~* das gehört sich nicht; *everything at the ~ time* alles zu s-r Zeit; **~ fraction** *math* echte(r) Bruch *m*; **~ly** ['-li] *adv* korrekt, richtig; *fam* durch u. durch, gründlich; *~~ speaking* genaugenommen, eigentlich, in Wirklichkeit; **~tied** ['-tid] *a* besitzend, begütert, vermögend; **~ty** ['-ti] Besitz *m*, Eigentum, Vermögen *n*; *(landed ~~)* Landbesitz *m*, Ländereien *f pl*; Grundstück, Stück Land, Gut *n*; Eigenschaft, Eigentümlichkeit, Besonderheit *f (e-r Sache)*; Merkmal *n*; *pl theat* Requisiten *n pl*; *to hold ~~* Eigentum besitzen; *enemy ~~* Feindvermögen *n*; *lost ~~ office* Fundbüro *n*; *private ~~* Privatvermögen *n*; *~~ agent* Grundstücksmakler *m*; *~~ assets (pl)* Vermögenswerte *m pl*; *~~ control* Vermögensaufsicht *f*; *~~ holder* Eigentümer *m*; *~~ insurance* Sachversicherung *f*; *~~ loss* Vermögensverlust *m*; *~~-man (theat)* Requisiteur *m*; *~~ market* Immobilienmarkt *m*; *~~ right* Eigentumsrecht *n*; *~~-room* Requisitenkammer *f*; *~~ tax* Grund-, Vermögen(s)steuer *f*.

prophe|cy ['prɔfisi] Prophezeiung, Weissagung; Vorhersage; prophetische Gabe *f*; **~sy** ['prɔfisai] *tr* prophezeien, weissagen (*s.th. for s.o.* jdm etw); vorhersagen; *itr* wahrsagen (*of s.th.* etw); **~t** ['prɔfit] *rel* Prophet *a. allg*, Wahrsager *m*; **~tess** ['-is] Prophetin *f*; **~tic(al)** [prə'fetik(əl)] prophetisch.

prophyl|actic [prɔfi'læktik] *a med* vorbeugend, prophylaktisch; Vorbeugungs-; *s* vorbeugende(s) Mittel *n*; *med* Sanierungsmittel *n*; *~~ aid centre, (Am) station* Sanierungsstelle *f*; **~axis** [-sis] *med* Vorbeugung(smaßnahme), vorbeugende Behandlung, Prophylaxe *f*.

propinquity [prə'piŋkwiti] Nähe; (nahe) Verwandtschaft *f*.

propiti|able [prə'piʃiəbl] versöhnlich; **~ate** [-eit] *tr* günstig, versöhnlich stimmen; versöhnen, besänftigen, beruhigen, befriedigen; **~ation** [prəpiʃi'eiʃən] Versöhnung, Beruhigung, Befriedigung; Sühne *f*; **~ative** [prə'piʃiətiv], **~atory** [-əri] versöhnlich (stimmend), beruhigend; Sühne-; **~ous** [prə'piʃəs] geneigt, günstig gesinnt, gnädig; *(Vorzeichen, Gelegenheit, Wetter, Wind)* günstig (*to, for* für).

proportion [prə'pɔ:ʃən] *s* (An-)Teil *m*, Quote *f*; (Größen-)Verhältnis *n*, Proportion *f a. math*; Ebenmaß *n*, Ausgeglichenheit, Ausgewogenheit, Harmonie; relative Größe *f*, Grad *m*; *pl* Dimensionen, Proportionen *f pl*; Ausmaße *n pl*; *tr* in das richtige Verhältnis bringen (*to* zu); abstimmen (*to* auf); anpassen (*to* an); einteilen, verhältnismäßig verteilen; *in ~* verhältnismäßig, anteilig; im Verhältnis (*to* zu); in dem Maße (*as* wie); *in due ~* wohlproportioniert; *out of ~* unverhältnismäßig; *out of all ~* in gar keinem Verhältnis (*to* zu); *~ of costs, of profit* Kosten-, Gewinnanteil *m*; **~al** [-ʃnəl] *s math* Proportionale *f*; *a* proportional *a. math*, im (richtigen) Verhältnis (*to* zu); entsprechend; verhältnismäßig, relativ; *~~ representation* Verhältniswahlsystem *n*; **~ate** [-ʃnit] proportional, im richtigen Verhältnis; anteilig; angemessen; ausgeglichen; **~ed** [prə'pɔ:ʃənd] *a* in bestimmtem Verhältnis; *well ~~* wohlproportioniert.

propos|al [prə'pouzəl] Vorschlag *m*, Anregung *f*; (*bes.* Heirats-)Antrag; Plan *m*, Absicht *f*, Vorhaben *n*; *upon the ~~ of* auf Vorschlag *gen*; *to place ~~s before s.o.* jdm Vorschläge unterbreiten; **~e** [prə'pouz] *tr* vorschlagen (*s.th. to s.o.* jdm etw, *doing s.th.* etw zu tun); *(Person)* in Vorschlag bringen (*for* zu); anregen; *(e-n Antrag)* stellen; *(to ~~ s.o.'s health)* e-n Toast ausbringen auf; *itr* e-n Vorschlag machen; beabsichtigen, e-n Plan, e-n Entschluß fassen *od* äußern; e-n Heiratsantrag machen (*to s.o.* jdm); anhalten (*for* um); *to ~~ o.s.* sich vornehmen; *to ~~ a vote of censure* e-n Mißtrauensantrag einbringen; *man ~~s, God disposes (prov)* der Mensch denkt, Gott lenkt; **~er** [-ə] *pol* Antragsteller *m*; **~ition** [prɔpə-

'ziʃən] Vorschlag *m*, Anregung *f*; Antrag; *fam* Liebesantrag; Plan *m*, Absicht *f*, Vorhaben *n*; *math* Lehrsatz *m*; Feststellung, Behauptung *f*; Thema; *com* Angebot; *Am fam* Projekt, *(geplantes)* Geschäft, Unternehmen *n*; *Am fam* Aufgabe, Frage, Sache, Angelegenheit *f*; *that's an expensive* ~~ das ist ein teures Vergnügen; *it's a different* ~~ das steht auf e-m andern Blatt; **~itional** [prɔpə'ziʃənl] *a* Vorschlags-, Antrags-; vorgeschlagen, beantragt.

propound [prə'paund] *tr* vorlegen, -tragen, -schlagen.

propriet|ary [prə'praiətəri] *a* Eigentums-; besitzend; *com* gesetzlich geschützt; *s* Eigentümer *m (pl)*; Eigentum(srecht) *n*; ~~ *article* Markenartikel *m*; ~~ *capital* Eigenkapital *n*; ~~ *possession* Eigenbesitz *m*; ~~ *rights (pl)* Eigentumsrecht *n*; **~or** [-ə] Eigentümer, Besitzer; (Geschäfts-)Inhaber *m*; *landed* ~~ Grundeigentümer, Grund-, Gutsbesitzer *m*; *sole* ~~ Alleininhaber *m*; **~orship** [-əʃip] Eigentum(srecht) *n* (*in* an); **~ress** [-ris] Eigentümerin, Besitzerin, Inhaberin *f*; **~y** [-i] Angebrachtheit, Angemessenheit; Schicklichkeit *f*, Anstand *m*; *the ~ies (pl)* die Anstandsformen *f pl*, das gute Benehmen; *breach of* ~~ Mangel *m* an Lebensart.

props [prɔps] *pl sl theat* Requisiten *n pl*.

propuls|ion [prə'pʌlʃən] *tech* Antrieb; *fig* Anstoß, Impuls *m*, treibende Kraft *f*; *jet* ~~ Strahl-, Düsenantrieb *m*; ~~ *equipment, unit* Triebwerk *n*; **~ive** [-siv] (an-, vorwärts)treibend; ~~ *charge* Treibsatz *m*; ~~ *effect* Treibwirkung *f*; ~~ *power* Vortriebsleistung *f*.

prorate [pro(u)'reit] *tr Am* anteilmäßig ver-, zuteilen.

prorog|ation [prourə'geiʃən] *parl* Vertagung *f*; **~ue** [prə'roug] *tr* vertagen.

prosaic(al) [pro(u)'zeiik(əl)] *a* Prosa-; *fig* prosaisch, nüchtern, trocken.

proscenium [pro(u)'si:njəm] *theat* Proszenium *n*.

proscri|be [pro(u)s'kraib] *tr* ächten, für vogelfrei erklären; *fig* verbannen, ausweisen; *fig* verbieten, untersagen; **~ption** [-'kripʃən] Ächtung; Acht; Verbannung *f*; *fig* Verbot *n*.

pros|e [prouz] *s* Prosa; Alltagssprache *f*, -ausdruck *m*; Alltäglichkeit *f*; *a* Prosa-; prosaisch, nüchtern; *itr tr* (in) Prosa schreiben; *itr* nüchtern, trocken, langweilig reden, sprechen (*about* über); ~~ *poem* Prosagedicht *n*; **~er** ['-ə] (langweiliger) Redner *m*.

prosecut|e ['prɔsikju:t] *tr (Absicht, Ziel, Anspruch)* verfolgen; *(Tätigkeit)* fortsetzen, ausüben; *(Studien)* eifrig betreiben, durchführen; *(Gewerbe)* nachgehen; *(Reise)* ausführen; gerichtlich, strafrechtlich verfolgen, belangen; ein (Straf-)Verfahren einleiten gegen (*for s.th.* wegen e-r S); *itr* Klage erheben; die Anklage vertreten; *trespassers will be ~ed* unbefugtes Betreten bei Strafe verboten; **~ing** ['-iŋ] *jur (Partei)* klagend; ~~ *attorney (Am)* Anklagevertreter, Staatsanwalt *m*; **~ion** [prɔsi'kju:ʃən] Verfolgung, Fortsetzung, Betreibung, Ausübung, Durchführung; Strafverfolgung *f*; *the* ~~ die Anklage(behörde), die Staatsanwaltschaft; *to start a* ~~ *against s.o.* gegen jdn gerichtlich vorgehen; *liable to* ~~ strafbar; ~~ *witness, witness for the* ~~ Belastungszeuge *m*; **~or** ['prɔsikju:tə] (An-)Kläger; *(public* ~~*)* Anklagevertreter, Staatsanwalt *m*.

proselyt|e ['prɔsilait] Neubekehrte(r), Proselyt *m*; **~ism** ['-litizm] Proselytentum *n*; Bekehrungseifer *m*; **~ize** ['-litaiz] *itr* Proselyten machen; *tr* bekehren.

prosody ['prɔsədi] Prosodie *f*.

prospect ['prɔspekt] *s* Aussicht *f*, -blick, Fernblick *m*; Ausschau, Vorwegnahme; Erwartung; Anwartschaft *f* (*of* auf); *Am* mögliche(r) Käufer, Interessent, Kunde, Anwärter, Kandidat *m*; *min* Schürfstelle *f*; *pl* Aussichten *f pl*; *itr tr* [prə'spekt] sich umsehen, Ausschau halten, suchen (nach); versprechen; *min* schürfen (*for* nach); *(Öl)* bohren; *in* ~ in Aussicht, erwartet; *to hold out the* ~ *of s.th.* etw in Aussicht stellen; *what are your ~s?* haben Sie Aussicht (*of doing s.th.* etw zu tun)?; **~ive** [prɔs'pektiv] vorausschauend, -blickend, weitsichtig; in die Zukunft weisend; voraussichtlich, in Aussicht stehend, zu erwarten(d), angehend, zu gewärtigen(d), zukünftig; ~~ *buyer, customer* Reflektant, Interessent *m*; **~or** [prə'spektə] *min* Schürfer *m*; **~us** [prə'spektəs] Prospekt *m*, Werbeschrift; Ankündigung, Voranzeige *f*.

prosper ['prɔspə] *itr* gedeihen, blühen, Fortschritte machen; weiter-, vorankommen; Erfolg, Glück haben, Erfolge erzielen (*in* bei); gutgehen; *tr* weiterbringen, begünstigen, zum Erfolg verhelfen (*s.o.* jdm); *he is ~ing* es geht ihm gut; **~ity** [prɔs'periti] Gedeihen; Glück *n*, Erfolg *m*, Wohlergehen *n*; Wohlstand *m*; **~ous** ['prɔspərəs] erfolgreich, blühend; wohlhabend, glücklich; gedeihlich, erfolgbringend, günstig, glücklich.

prostate ['prɔsteit] *s u. a.*: ~ **gland** *anat* Vorsteherdrüse, Prostata *f*.

pro-station ['prousteiʃən] *mil fam* = *prophylactic station*.

prosthesis ['prɔsθisis] *pl -es* [-i:z] *med* Prothese *f*.

prostitut|e ['prɔstitju:t] *tr* (*o.s.* sich) feilbieten, prostituieren; (*o.s.* sich) verkaufen, hergeben, erniedrigen, herabwürdigen (*to* zu); *s* Prostituierte, Dirne *f*; *fig* käufliche(r) Mensch *m*; **~ion** [prɔsti'tju:ʃən] Prostitution, gewerbsmäßige Unzucht; *fig* Herabwürdigung, Erniedrigung *f*.

prostrat|e ['prɔstreit, -it] *a* hingestreckt, mit dem Gesicht am Boden liegend; *bot* am Boden wachsend; *fig* fußfällig, unterwürfig, demütig; *fig* kraftlos, gebrochen; *tr* [prɔs'treit, *Am* '--] zu Boden, niederwerfen, hinstrecken; *fig* aller Kraft berauben, entkräften, niederschmettern; *to* ~ *o.s.* sich niederwerfen (*at a shrine* an e-m Altar; *before s.o.* vor jdm); sich demütigen (*before s.o.* vor jdm); **~ion** [prɔs'treiʃən] Demütigung; Niedergeschlagenheit; Entkräftung, (völlige) Erschöpfung *f*; Fußfall *m*.

prosy ['prouzi] prosaisch, gewöhnlich, nüchtern, trocken, langweilig.

protagonist [pro(u)'tægənist] *lit theat* Held *m*; *allg* Hauptperson *f*, führende(r) Kopf; *fig* Vorkämpfer *m*.

protean [pro(u)'ti:ən, 'proutjən] *fig* wandelbar.

protect [prə'tekt] *tr* schützen, bewahren (*from* vor); beschützen, verteidigen (*against* gegen); abschirmen, decken *a. mil*; (durch Schutzzölle) sichern; *fin (Wechsel)* honorieren, einlösen; *to* ~ *o.s.* sich sichern (*against* gegen); *to* ~ *s.o.'s interests* jds Interessen wahrnehmen *od* wahren; **~ion** [-'tekʃən] Schutz *m* (*from* vor), Abwehr *f*; Schutz-, Geleitbrief *m*; *mil* Abschirmung, Deckung *f*; *com* Schutzzoll(politik *f*) *m*; *(Interessen)* Wahrnehmung; *(Wechsel)* Honorierung, Einlösung *f*; ~~ *of registered design* Gebrauchsmusterschutz *m*; **~ionism** [-ʃənizm] Schutzzollsystem *n*; **~ionist** [-ʃənist] Vertreter, Verfechter *m* des Schutzzollsystems; **~ive** [prə'tektiv] schützend, Schutz-; Schutzzoll-; *mil* Deckungs-; ~~ *clothing* Schutzkleidung *f*; ~~ *coating* Schutzanstrich *m*; ~~ *colo(u)ring, coloration (biol)* Schutzfärbung *f*; ~~ *cover(ing)* Schutzhülle *f*; ~~ *custody* Schutzhaft *f*; ~~ *device* Schutzvorrichtung *f*; ~~ *duty, tariff* Schutzzoll *m*; ~~ *fire (mil)* Feuerschutz *m*; ~~ *goggles (pl)* Schutzbrille *f*; ~~ *inoculation* Schutzimpfung *f*; ~~ *measure* Schutzmaßnahme *f*; **~or** [-ə] Schutz-, Schirmherr, Beschützer; *hist* Protektor, Regent, Statthalter; Gönner *m*; Schutzmittel *n*, -vorrichtung, Sicherung *f*; **~orate** [-ərit] Schutz-, Schirmherrschaft *f*, Protektorat *n*; **~ory** [-əri] (Kinder-)Fürsorgeheim *n*; **~ress** [-ris] Schirmherrin, Beschützerin; Gönnerin *f*.

protégé *m*, **~e** *f* ['proutəʒei] Schützling *m*.

prote|in ['prouti:n, '-i(:)in] *chem* Protein *n*; *pl* Eiweißkörper, -stoffe *m pl*.

protest [prə'test] *tr* (feierlich) erklären, beteuern; (felsen)fest behaupten, versichern; *Am* protestieren gegen; *fin (Wechsel)* protestieren, zu Protest gehen lassen; *(Zeugen)* ablehnen; *itr* protestieren; Einspruch, Protest erheben *od* einlegen (*to s.o.* bei jdm); sich verwahren (*against* gegen); *s* ['proutest] Einspruch, Protest *m* (*against* gegen); *com* Reklamation *f*; *as a* ~, *in* ~ *against* als Protest gegen; *under* ~ unter Protest; unter Vorbehalt; *without* ~ widerspruchs-, vorbehaltlos; *to enter, to lodge, to make a* ~ Protest erheben, Verwahrung einlegen (*against s.th.* gegen etw; *with s.o.* bei jdm); **(P)~ant** ['prɔtistənt] *s rel* Protestant *m*; *a* protestantisch; **P~antism** ['prɔtistəntizm] Protestantismus *m*; **~ation** [proutes'teiʃən, prɔ-] Beteuerung, Erklärung, Behauptung, Versicherung *f*; Einspruch, Protest *m*.

prot(o)- ['prout(ə)] *in Zssgen* Proto-, Erst-, Ur-, Haupt-.

proto|col ['proutəkɔl] Protokoll *n a. pol*; (Verhandlungs-)Niederschrift *f*; *opening, final* ~~ Eröffnungs-, Schlußprotokoll *n*; *secret* ~~ Geheimprotokoll *n*; *to declare on the* ~~ zu Protokoll geben; *to draw up a* ~~ protokollieren; **~n** ['proutɔn] *phys* Proton *n*; **~plasm** ['-plæzm] *biol* Protoplasma *n*; **~plast** ['-plæst] Protoplast, Zellkörper *m*; **~type** ['-taip] Prototyp *m*, Urbild; Modell, Vorbild, Muster *n*; **~zoan** [proutə'zo(u)ən], **~zoon** [-] *pl ~zoa* [-'zo(u)ə] Protozoon, Urtierchen *n*.

protract [prə'trækt] *tr (zeitl.)* in die Länge (*od* hin)ziehen, verlängern, ausdehnen; hinauszögern, aufschieben, verschleppen; (maßstabgerecht) zeichnen, auftragen, -reißen; *zoo (Fühler)* ausstrecken; **~ed** [-id] *a* in die Länge gezogen; langatmig, weitschweifig; langwierig; *(Verteidigung)* hinhaltend; **~ile** [-ail] *zoo* ausstreckbar; **~ion** [-'trækʃən] Ausdehnung, Verzögerung *a. jur*, Aufschiebung, Verschleppung; (maßstabgerechte) Zeichnung *f*; Auftragen *n*; **~or** [-'træktə] Transporteur, Winkelmesser, Gradbogen; *anat* Streckmuskel *m*.

protru|de [prə'tru:d] *tr* heraus-, hervorstoßen, -strecken; *itr* herausragen, -treten, vorstoßen (*beyond* über); **~dent** [-ənt], **~ding** [-iŋ], **~sive** [-siv] herausragend, -tretend; vorspringend; *fig* aufdringlich; **~sion** [-'tru:ʒən] Herausragen, -treten *n*.

protuber|ance, -cy [prə'tju:bərəns(i)] Ausbauchung, -buchtung, (An-) Schwellung *f*, Höcker *m*; *astr* Protuberanz *f*; **~ant** [-t] heraustretend, -stehend; *~~ eyes (pl)* Glotzaugen *n pl*.

proud [praud] stolz (*of* auf); hochmütig, -fahrend, überheblich, eingebildet, arrogant; stolz, stattlich; prächtig; *to do s.o. ~* jdm Ehre antun, *od* erweisen; jdn königlich bewirten; **~ flesh** wilde(s) Fleisch *n*.

prov|able ['pru:vəbl] beweisbar, nachweisbar; **~e** [pru:v] *tr* erproben, (nach-) prüfen; erfahren, erleben; be-, er-, nachweisen; den Nachweis führen; unter Beweis stellen; bestätigen; beglaubigen, beurkunden; *math* die Probe machen auf; *itr* sich erweisen, sich herausstellen als; *(gut, schlecht)* ausfallen; *to ~~ out (Am)* sich bestätigen; *to ~~ up* die Richtigkeit dokumentarisch nachweisen; *to ~~ o.'s identity* sich ausweisen, sich legitimieren; *to ~ (to be) false (true)* sich (nicht) bestätigen, sich als falsch (richtig) herausstellen; *the exception ~s the rule* Ausnahmen bestätigen die Regel; **~ed** [-d] *a* be-, er-, nachgewiesen; erprobt, bewährt; **~en** ['-ən]: *verdict of not ~~ (jur)* Freispruch *m* wegen Mangels an Beweisen; **~ing** ['-iŋ] Erprobung *f*; *~~ flight* Probeflug *m*; *~~ ground* Versuchsgelände *n*.

provenance ['prɔvinəns] Herkunft *f*, Ursprung, Abstammung, -leitung *f*.

provender ['prɔvində] *agr* Trockenfutter; *fam hum* Futter, Essen *n*.

proverb ['prɔvəb] Sprichwort *n*; *to a ~ (nach: a)* bekannt als; sprichwörtlich; *to be a ~* sprichwörtlich, notorisch, berüchtigt sein; *he is a ~ for idleness* s-e Faulheit ist sprichwörtlich; *(the Book of) P~s (Bibel)* (die) Sprüche *m pl* (Salomos); **~ial** [prə'və:bjəl] sprichwörtlich *a. fig* (*for* wegen); *fig* bekannt, notorisch, berüchtigt.

provid|e [prə'vaid] *tr* beschaffen, besorgen; heranschaffen, liefern; zur Verfügung, bereitstellen; versorgen, versehen, ausstatten, beliefern (*with* mit); *itr* vorsorgen; Vorsorge, Vorbereitungen treffen (*for* für; *against* gegen); verhindern (*against s.th.* etw); sorgen (*for* für); vorsehen (*for* für); versorgen (*for s.o.* jdn); *fin* Deckung schaffen; *jur* bestimmen, festsetzen, vorsehen; *to ~~ o.s.* sich versorgen; **~ed** [-id] *a* vorbereitet (*for* für); versehen (*with* mit); vorgesehen; *(conj) ~~ (that)* vorausgesetzt, unter der Voraussetzung, daß; sofern; *unless otherwise ~~* sofern keine anderen Bestimmungen vorliegen; **~ence** ['prɔvidəns] Vorsorge; Vorsorglichkeit, weise Voraussicht; Sparsamkeit; *(P~~)* die Vorsehung, der Himmel, Gott; *a special ~~* e-e Fügung des Himmels; **~ent** ['prɔvidənt] vorsorglich; haushälterisch, wirtschaftlich, sparsam; *~~ bank* Sparkasse *f*; *~~ fund* Hilfs-, Unterstützungskasse *f*; *~~ reserve (fund)* Reservefonds *m*, Sicherheitsreserve, Sonderrücklage *f*; *~~ scheme* Hilfsaktion *f*; *~~ society* (Arbeiter-)Hilfs-, Unterstützungsverein *m*; **~ential** [prɔvi'denʃəl] von der Vorsehung beschlossen; glücklich; **~er** [prə'vaidə] Ernährer, Versorger; Lieferant *m*; *universal ~~* Waren-, Kaufhaus *n*; **~ing** [-iŋ] vorausgesetzt.

provinc|e ['prɔvins] Provinz *f a. fig*; Bezirk, Distrikt *m*, Gebiet *n*; (Kirchen-)Provinz; *(Tier-, Pflanzengeographie)* Subregion *f*; (Unterrichts-) Fach *n*; (Aufgaben-, Tätigkeits-)Bereich *m od n*; Arbeitsgebiet *n*; Verwaltungs-)Zweig, Sektor *m*; Amt, Ressort *n*; *to fall within s.o.'s ~~* zu jds Aufgabenbereich gehören; **~ial** [prə'vinʃəl] *a* Provinz-; provinziell, kleinstädtisch, ländlich; *fig* eng(stirnig), begrenzt; *s* Provinzbewohner; Provinzler *m*; *pl* Provinztruppen *f pl*; **~ialism** [prə'vinʃəlizm] Provinzlertum *n*, Spießigkeit *f*; Provinzialismus *m*.

provis|ion [prə'viʒən] *s* Vorsorge, Vorkehrung, Vorbereitung, Planung; Beschaffung, Besorgung, Lieferung, Bereitstellung *f*; Vorrat *m* (*of* an); *jur* Vorschrift, Bestimmung, Vereinbarung, Klausel; *fin* Deckung, Rückstellung, Rücklage, Reserve *f*; *pl* (Mund-)Vorrat, Proviant *m*; *tr* mit e-m Vorrat, *bes.* mit Nahrungsmitteln, mit Proviant versorgen; verproviantieren; *to fall within the ~~s of the law* unter die gesetzlichen Bestimmungen fallen; *to make ~~s for, against* Vorkehrungen, Anstalten treffen für, gegen; *~~ business* Lebensmittelhandel *m*, -branche *f*; *~~ dealer* Lebensmittelhändler *m*; *~~ industry* Nahrungsmittelindustrie *f*; *~~ merchant* Lebensmittelhändler *m*; *~~ store* Lebensmittelgeschäft *n*, Kolonialwarenhandlung *f*; **~ional** [-ʒənl] vorläufig, einstweilig; Interims-; provisorisch; bedingt; *~~ arrangement* Provisorium *n*; *~~ bill* Interimswechsel *m*; *~~ order* einstweilige Verfügung *f*; *~~ result (sport)* Zwischenergebnis *n*; **~o** [prə'vaizou] *pl -o(e)s jur* (Zusatz-) Bestimmung, Klausel *f*, Vorbehalt *m*; **~ory** [-'vaizəri] = *~ional.*

provocat|ion [prɔvə'keiʃən] Provozierung (*of s.th.* e-r S), Provokation, Herausforderung, Aufreizung *f* (*to* zu); Antrieb, Anreiz (*to* zu); Ärger *m*; **~ive** [prə'vɔkətiv] *a* provokatorisch; herausfordernd (*of s.th.* etw); aufreizend (*of th.* zu etw); *s* Herausforderung, Aufreizung *f (Sache)*; Reiz(mittel *n) m.*

provok|e [prə'vouk] *tr* provozieren, herausfordern; aufreizen, -stacheln; reizen, wütend machen, aufbringen; veranlassen, bewirken, hervor-, wachrufen; **~ing** [-iŋ] provozierend, herausfordernd, aufreizend; ärgerlich, unausstehlich.

provost ['prɔvəst] Vorsteher, Aufseher; *Scot* Bürgermeister *m*; *rel* Erste(r) Dom-, Stiftsherr; Hauptpastor; Direktor *(gewisser Schulen)*; *Am* (Univ.-)Kurator *m*; **~-marshal** [prə'vou'mɑ:ʃəl] Kommandeur *m* der Feldgendarmerie.

prow [prau] *mar* Bug *m*.

prowess ['prauis] Tapferkeit, Kühnheit; Heldentat; Überlegenheit *f*.

prowl [praul] *itr* herumschleichen, -suchen; *tr* durchstreifen, -suchen; *s* Umherstreifen *n*; *to be, to go on the ~* herumschleichen; **~ car** *Am* (Polizei-) Streifenwagen *m*; **~er** ['-ə] Landstreicher, Vagabund *m*.

proxim|ate ['prɔksimit] nächst; unmittelbar, direkt; **~ity** [prɔk'simiti] (unmittelbare) Nähe *f*; *~~ of blood* Blutsverwandtschaft *f*; *~~ fuze (Am mil)* Annäherungszünder *m*; **~o** ['prɔksimou] nächsten Monats.

proxy ['prɔksi] (Stell-)Vertretung; (schriftliche) Vollmacht, Vollmachtsurkunde *f*; (Stell-)Vertreter, Bevollmächtigte(r); Anwalt *m*; *Am (~ vote)* in Stellvertretung abgegebene Wahlstimme *f*; *by ~* in Vertretung; *to stand ~ for s.o.* jdn vertreten; *marriage by ~* Ferntrauung *f*.

prud|e [pru:d] spröde, prüde, zimperliche Person *f*; **~ery** ['-əri] Prüderie; Zimperlichkeit, Ziererei *f*; **~ish** ['-iʃ] prüde, spröde, zimperlich, geziert.

pruden|ce ['pru:dəns] (Lebens-)Klugheit, Verständigkeit *f*; kluge(s) Verhalten *n*; Um-, Vorsicht, Bedachtsamkeit *f*; **~t** ['-t] klug, verständig; um-, vorsichtig, vorausschauend, vorsorgend, haushälterisch; **~tial** [pru(:)'denʃəl] *a* Klugheits-; Vorsichts-; ratsam; klug, verständig; umsichtig.

prun|e [pru:n] **1.** *tr (Baum, Strauch)* beschneiden, ausputzen; *allg* sorgfältig entfernen; *fig (stilistisch)* (aus-) feilen; *to ~ away* ab-, wegschneiden; *fig* entfernen, ausmerzen; *to ~ down* zurückschneiden; **~ers** ['-əz] *pl* Baumschere *f*; **~ing** ['-iŋ]: *~~-hook, -shears (pl)* Heckensichel, Baumschere *f*; *~~-knife* Gartenmesser *n*; **2.** Backpflaume; *Am* Zwetsch(g)e *f*; **~ello** [pru(:)'nelou], *Am* **~elle** [-'nel] Prünelle *f*.

prури|ence, -cy ['pruəriəns(i)] Begehrlichkeit (*for* nach); Lüsternheit *f*, Kitzel *m*; Gier, Geilheit *f*; **~ent** ['-t] lüstern, gierig, geil; **~go** [-'raigou] *med* Juckflechte *f*, juckende(r) Ausschlag *m*.

Pruss|ia ['prʌʃə] Preußen *n*; **~ian** ['-n] *a* preußisch; *s* Preuße *m*, Preußin *f*; *~~ blue* Preußischblau *n*; **p~ic** ['prʌsik]: *~~ acid* Blausäure *f*.

pry [prai] **1.** *itr (to ~ about)* (umher-) spähen, herumspionieren, -schnüffeln, -horchen; s-e Nase stecken (*into* in); *s* Gucker *m*, neugierige Person *f*; **~ing** ['-iŋ] *a* herumspionierend, -schnüffelnd, -horchend; (sehr) neugierig; **2.** *s* Hebel *m*, Stemm-, Brecheisen *n*; Hebelwirkung, -kraft *f*; *tr (to ~ open)* auf-, erbrechen; *(to ~ up)* hochstemmen; *fig (Geheimnis)* herauspressen (*out of s.o.* aus jdm).

psalm [sɑ:m] Psalm *m*; *the (Book of) P~s* die Psalmen *m pl*; **~book** Psalter *m*; **~ist** ['-ist] Psalmist *m*; **~odic** [sæl'mɔdik] psalmodisch, psalmartig; **~odist** ['sælmədist] Psalmsänger *m*; **~ody** ['sælmədi] Psalmodie *f*, Psalmengesang *m*.

Psalter, the ['sɔ:ltə] der Psalter, die Psalmen *m pl*; **p~y** ['sɔ:ltəri] *rel mus* Psalter *m*.

pseudo ['(p)sju:dou] *in Zssgen* Pseudo-, falsch; **~nym** ['(p)sju:dənim] Pseudonym *n*, Deckname *m*; **~nymous** [(p)sju:'dɔniməs] pseudonym.

pshaw [pʃɔ:] *interj* pah! bah!

psittacosis [psitə'kousis] Papageienkrankheit *f*.

psoriasis [psɔ:'raiəsis] *med* Schuppenflechte *f*.

psych|e ['saiki(:)] Seele; *psychol* Psyche *f*; Geist *m*; **~iatric(al)** [saiki'ætrik(əl)] *a* psychiatrisch; **~iatrist** [sai'kaiətrist] Psychiater *m*; **~iatry** [sai'kaiətri] Psychiatrie *f*; **~ic(al)** ['saikik] *a* psychisch, seelisch; telepathisch; *s (Spiritismus)* (gutes) Medium *n*; *pl mit sing* Parapsychologie *f*; *~ic trauma* psychische(s) Trauma *n*, seelische(r) Schock *m*; **~o-analyse** [saiko(u)'ænəlaiz] *tr* psychoanalytisch behandeln; **~o-analysis** [saiko(u)-ə'næləsis] Psychoanalyse *f*; **~o-analyst** [saiko(u)'ænəlist] Psychoanalytiker *m*; **~o-analytic(al)** [saiko(u)-ænə'litik(əl)] psychoanalytisch; **~o-logic(al)** [saikə'lɔdʒik(əl)] psychologisch; *~ological moment* kritische(r) Moment, entscheidende(r) Augenblick *m*; *~ological warfare (fam: psy--war)* psychologische Kriegführung *f*, Propagandakrieg *m*, Kriegspropaganda *f*; **~ologist** [sai'kɔlədʒist] Psychologe *f*; **~ology** [sai'kɔlədʒi] Psychologie, Seelenkunde *f*; *applied ~~* angewandte Psychologie *f*; *child ~~* Kinderpsychologie *f*; *experimental, individual, social ~~* Experimental-, Individual-, Sozialpsychologie *f*; *~~ of the adolescent* Jugendpsychologie *f*; **~opath** ['saikəpæθ] Psychopath *m*; **~opathic** [saiko(u)'pæθik] psychopathisch; **~opathology** [saiko(u)pə'θɔlədʒi] Psychopathologie *f*; **~opathy** [sai'kɔpəθi] Geisteskrankheit *f*; **~osis** [sai'kousis] *pl -ses* [-i:z] Psychose *f*; **~osomatic** ['saiko(u)sou'mætik] psychosomatisch; **~otherapeutics** ['saiko(u)θerə'pju:tiks] *pl mit sing*, **~therapy** [-'θerəpi] Psychotherapie *f*.

*

ptarmigan ['tɑ:migən] *orn* (Alpen-) Schneehuhn *n*.

ptomain ['toumein] Leichengift *n*; **~ poisoning** Fleischvergiftung *f*.

pub [pʌb] *fam* Kneipe *f*, Wirtshaus *n*; **~-crawl** Bierreise *f*, Bummel *m*; **~-keeper** Gastwirt *m*.

pub|erty ['pju:bəti] Pubertät(szeit *f*, -alter *n*), *lit* Mannbarkeit *f*; **~escence** [pju(:)'besəns] Beginn *m* der Geschlechtsreife; *bot zoo* Haarflaum *m*, Flaumhaare *n pl*; **~escent** [pju(:)'besnt] mannbar (werdend); *bot zoo* mit Flaumhaaren bedeckt; **~ic** ['pju(:)bik] *a anat* Scham-; **~is** ['-is] *pl -es* ['-i:z] *anat* Schambein *n*.

public ['pʌblik] *a* öffentlich, allgemein, gemeinnützig; national, Volks-; staatlich, Staats-; städtisch, Stadt-, Gemeinde-; allgemein bekannt, offen (-kundig), notorisch; *s* Publikum *n*; *the ~* die Öffentlichkeit, die Allgemeinheit *f*, die Leute *pl*, die Welt *f*; *fam* Kneipe *f*, Lokal *n*; *in ~* offen, öffentlich *adv*, in der Öffentlichkeit, vor aller Welt; *to be in the ~ eye* im Brennpunkt des öffentlichen Lebens stehen; *to become ~* bekannt-offenkundig werden; sich herumsprechen; *to make, to render ~* öffentlich bekanntgeben, -machen; *the cinema-going, the theatre-going ~* das Film-, das Theaterpublikum; *notary ~* Notar *m*; *the reading ~* die Leserschaft; **~ accountant** *Am* Wirtschaftsprüfer *m*; **~ act** Gesetz *n*, Verordnung *f*; **~-address system** Lautsprecheranlage *f*; **~ administration** Staatsverwaltung *f*; **~ affairs** *pl* öffentliche Angelegenheiten *f pl*, Staatsgeschäfte *n pl*; **~an** ['-ən] Gast-, Schankwirt; *hist* Zöllner *m*; **~ appointment** Staatsanstellung *f*; **~ assistance** öffentliche Unterstützung *od* Fürsorge *f*; **~ation** [pʌbli'keiʃən] (öffentliche) Bekanntmachung; Veröffentlichung *(bes. e-s Buches)*, Herausgabe *f*, Erscheinen *n*; Publikation, Veröffentlichung *f*, (veröffentlichtes, Verlags-)Werk, Erscheinen *n*; *in course of ~~* im Erscheinen begriffen, im Druck; *list of ~~s* Verlagskatalog *m*; *monthly, weekly ~~* Monats-, Wochenschrift *f*; *new ~~* Neuerscheinung *f*; soeben erschienen; *~~ price* Ladenpreis *m (e-s Buches)*; **~ authority** Staatsgewalt; Behörde *f*; **~ body, corporation** Körperschaft *f* des öffentlichen Rechts; **~ bonds** *pl* Staatsanleihe *f*; **~ call-office** öffentliche(r), Münzfernsprecher *m*; **~ comfort-station, convenience** öffentliche Bedürfnisanstalt *f*; **~ conveyance** öffentliche(s) Verkehrsmittel *n*; **~ corporation** Körperschaft *f* des öffentlichen Rechts; **~ debt** Staatsschuld *f*; **~ domain** *Am* Staatseigentum *n*, staatliche(r) Grund u. Boden *m*; *in the ~~ (geistiges Eigentum)* frei (geworden); **~ enemy** *Am* Staatsfeind; Asoziale(r) *m*; **~ expenditure, expenses** *pl* Staatsausgaben *f pl*; *at the ~ expense* auf Staatskosten; **~ finance** Staatsfinanzen *f pl*; **~ funds** *pl* Staats-, öffentliche Gelder *n pl*; Staatspapiere *n pl*; **~ gallery** Zuschauertribüne *f*; **~ health** Volksgesundheit *f*; *~~ service* öffentliche Gesundheitspflege *f*; **~ holiday** gesetzliche(r) Feiertag *m*; **~ house** *Br* Wirts-, Gasthaus *n*, Gaststätte *f*; **~ information officer** Presseoffizier *m*; **~ indecency** öffentliche(s) Ärgernis *n*; **~ interest** öffentliche(s), Staatsinteresse *n*; **~ist** ['pʌblisist] Völkerrechtler; Publizist, politische(r), Tagesschriftsteller, Journalist; Werbefachmann *m*; **~ity** [pʌb'lisiti] Offenkundigkeit, Publizität *f*; öffentliche(s) Interesse *n*; Reklame, Werbung, Propaganda; Werbeabteilung *f*; *to give ~~ to s.th.* etw bekannt machen, einführen; veröffentlichen; *to give s.o. ~~, to make ~~ for s.o.* für jdn Reklame, Propaganda machen, werben; *outdoor ~~* Straßenreklame *f*; *~~-agent* Propagandist; Pressechef *m*; *~~-bureau, -agency* Werbebüro *n*, Inseratenannahme *f*; *~~-campaign* Werbefeldzug *m*; *~~-department* Werbeabteilung *f*; *~~-expenses, costs (pl)* Werbekosten *pl*; *~~-man* Werbefachmann *m*; *~~-manager* Werbeleiter, Reklamechef *m*; *~~ material* Werbematerial *n*; **~ize** ['pʌblisaiz] *tr* bekanntmachen; werben für, Reklame, Propaganda machen für; **~ law** Staatsrecht *n*; *under ~~* öffentlich-rechtlich; **~ lecture** öffentliche(r) Vortrag *m*; **~ ledger** Hauptbuch; Staatsschuldbuch *n*; **~ library** Staats-, Stadtbibliothek, Volksbücherei *f*; **~ life** öffentliche(s) Leben *n*; **~ loan** Staatsanleihe *f*; **~ man** Mann *m* im öffentlichen Leben; **~ nuisance** öffentliche(s) Ärgernis *n*; *fam* unbeliebte(r) Mensch *m*; **~ opinion** öffentliche Meinung *f*; *~~ analyst* Meinungsforscher *m*; *~~ poll* Meinungsbefragung, Umfrage *f*; **~ orator** *(Univ.)* Sprecher; Volksredner *m*; **~ property** Gemeingut *n*; **~ prosecutor, trustee** Staatsanwalt *m*; **~ records** *pl* Staatsarchiv *n*; **~ relations** *pl* Verhältnis *n* zur Öffentlichkeit; Vertrauenswerbung, Öffentlichkeitsarbeit *f*; **~-relations counsel,** *mil* **officer** Pressechef, -offizier *m*; **~ release** Presseverlautbarung *f*; **~ revenue** Staatseinkünfte *pl*, -einnahmen *f pl*; **~ school** *Br* (exklusives) Internat *n (für 13—18jährige)*; *Am* öffentliche, staatliche Schule *f*; **~ security, safety** Staats-, öffentliche Sicherheit *f*; **~ servant** Angestellte(r) im öffentlichen Dienst; Staatsbeamte(r) *m*; **~ service** Staatsdienst *m*; **~ spirit** Gemeinsinn *m*; **~-spirited, -minded** *a* sozial gesinnt; **~ telephone** öffentliche(r) Fernsprecher *m*; **~ treasure** Staatskasse *f*, Schatzamt *n*; **~ trial** *jur* öffentliche Verhandlung *f*; **~ utility** Gemeinnutz; (öffentlicher) Versorgungsbetrieb *m*, Stadtwerke *n pl*, Wasser-, Gas-, E(lektrizitäts)-werk *n*; **~ weal** Allgemeinwohl *n*; **~ welfare** allgemeine Wohlfahrt *f*; **~ works** *pl* öffentliche Arbeiten *f pl od* Bauvorhaben *n pl od* Einrichtungen *f pl*; **~ worship** öffentliche(r) Gottesdienst *m*.

publish ['pʌbliʃ] *tr* (öffentlich) bekanntgeben, -machen, publik machen; in Umlauf bringen, verbreiten; *(Buch)* veröffentlichen, herausgeben, -bringen, erscheinen lassen, verlegen; *to be ~ed in instal(l)ments* in Lieferungen herauskommen *od* erscheinen; *about to be ~ed* im Erscheinen begriffen, im Druck; *just ~ed* soeben erschienen; *to be ~ed shortly* erscheint in Kürze; *to ~ the bans* das Aufgebot bestellen; **~er** ['-ə] Herausgeber, Verleger, Verlags(buch)händler; *Am (newspaper ~~)* Zeitungsverleger *m*; *pl* Verlag(sanstalt *f*) *m*; *~~'s binding* Leineneinband *m*; *~~'s reader* (Verlags-)Lektor *m*; **~ing** ['-iŋ] Bekanntgabe; Verbreitung; Veröffentlichung, Herausgabe *f*, Verlag *m*; Erscheinen *n*; *~~ business, trade* Verlagsbuchhandel *m*, -geschäft *n*; *~~ firm, house* Verlag(s)buchhandlung *f*, -haus *n*) *m*.

puce [pju:s] flohfarben, rotbraun.

puck [pʌk] **1.** Kobold, Elf *m*; **2.** Eishockeyscheibe *f*, Puck *m*.

pucka ['pʌkə] gut, erstklassig; dauerhaft, echt, wirklich.

pucker ['pʌkə] *tr* (*itr* sich) falten, (sich) in Falten legen; *(Stirn)* (sich) runzeln; *s* Falte, Runzel; *fig fam* Verlegenheit, Aufregung *f* (*about* über); *pl* Krähenfüße *m pl (im Gesicht)*; **~y** ['-ri] faltig, runz(e)lig.

pudding ['pudiŋ] Süßspeise *f*, Pudding *m*; *dial u. Scot Art* Wurst *f*; *mar (= puddening)* Fender *m*; *batter, Yorkshire ~* Eierkuchen *m*; *black ~* Blutwurst *f*; *currant ~* Rosinenpudding *m*; *hog's ~* Schwartenmagen *m*; *milk, plum, rice ~* Milch-, Plum-, Reispudding *f*; *white ~* Preßsack *m*; **~-face** *fam* Vollmondgesicht *n*; **~-head** *fam* Dummkopf *m*; **~-stone** *geol* Puddingstein *m*; **~y** ['-i] dumm; fett.

puddl|e ['pʌdl] *s* (Wasser-)Lache, Pfütze *f*; *tech* Lehm-, Ton-, Lettenschlag *m*; *tr (Wasser)* trüben; verunreinigen; *(Lehm, Sand)* anrühren; (mit Lehmschlag) abdichten; *tech* puddeln; *itr (to ~~ about)* herumplanschen; *~ed iron* Puddeleisen *n*; **~er** ['-ə] *tech* Puddler *m*; **~ing** ['-iŋ] Puddeln *n*; *~~-furnace* Puddelofen *m*.

puden|cy ['pju:dənsi] Schamhaftigkeit *f*; **~da** [pju:'dendə] *pl* äußere Schamteile *pl*.

pudgy ['pʌdʒi] untersetzt, plump.

puer|ile ['pjuərail] kindisch, knabenhaft, unfertig; dumm, albern, nichtssagend; **~ility** [pjuə'riliti] kindische(s) Wesen *n*, Kinderei, Dummheit, Albernheit *f*; **~peral** [pju(:)'ə:pərəl] *a physiol med* Kindbett-; *~~ fever* Kindbettfieber *n*.

puff [pʌf] *s* Atem-, Windstoß *m*; Paffen *n*; ausgestoßene(r) Rauch; Zug *m (an e-r Zigarette)*; Blase, Geschwulst *f*; Bausch *m*; *(Frisur)* lockere Rolle; *(powder-~)* Puderquaste; Steppdecke *f*; Windbeutel *m (Gebäck)*; übertriebene(s) Lob *n*; marktschreierische Reklame *f*; *(Buch)* Waschzettel *m*; *sl* Lebensdauer *f*; *itr* puffen, (stoßweise) blasen; Rauch, Dampf ausstoßen, schnaufen, keuchen, heftig atmen; *(Raucher)* paffen (*at* an); sich aufblasen *a. fig*; *tr* ausstoßen, -puffen; aufblasen; außer Atem bringen; *fig* übertrieben loben *od* preisen, ein Loblied singen auf; (über Gebühr) herausstreichen; *(Preis)* in die Höhe treiben; *(Haar, Kleid)* bauschen; *to be out of ~*

(fam) außer Atem sein; *jam-~* mit Marmelade gefüllte Schillerlocke *f*; *to ~* **away** wegblasen, -pusten; *to ~* **out** *tr (Flamme)* ausblasen; *(Luft)* ausstoßen; *tr itr* (sich) aufblasen, -blähen; *to ~* **up** *itr (Rauch)* stoßweise aufsteigen; *fig* sich aufblähen, -plustern; *tr* aufgeblasen machen; *(Preise)* in die Höhe treiben; *~ed up (fig)* aufgeblasen, hochmütig; **~-adder** *zoo* Puffotter *f*; **~-ball** *bot* Bofist, Bovist *m (Pilz)*; **~-box** Puderdose *f*; **~er** ['-ə] Paffer; Schnaubende(r), Keuchende(r); *fig* Aufschneider; Marktschreier; Preistreiber *m*; *fam* Lokomotive *f*; **~ery** ['-əri] Aufschneiderei *f*; übertriebene(s) Lob *n*; marktschreierische Reklame *f*; **~in** ['-in] *zoo* Papageitaucher *m*; **~iness** ['-inis] geschwollene(r) Zustand *m*; *fig* Aufgeblasenheit *f*; **~ing** ['-iŋ] *a* marktschreierisch; *s* Aufblähung *f*; **~-paste** Blätterteig *m*; **~-pastry** Blätterteiggebäck *n*; **~-puff** *(Kindersprache)* Lokomotive; Eisenbahn *f*; **~y** ['-i] böig, in Stößen; keuchend; *fig* aufgeblasen, geschwollen; *(Gesicht)* aufgedunsen; dick, fett; *(Ärmel)* bauschig.

pug [pʌg] **1.** *(~-dog)* Mops *m*; **~gish** ['-iʃ], **~gy** ['-i] mops(art)ig; **~-nose** Stups-, Stumpfnase *f*; **~-nosed** *a* stups-, stumpfnasig; **2.** *s* Lehm, (feuchter) Ton *m*; *tr (Lehm, Ton)* anfeuchten, stampfen, kneten; mit schalldämpfendem Material ausfüllen; **~-mill** Mischtrommel *f*; **3.** (Fuß-)Spur *f (e-s Tieres)*; **4.** *sl* Boxer *m (Mensch)*.

pugil|ism ['pju:dʒilizm] Boxen *n*, Box-, Faustkampf *m*; **~ist** ['-list] Boxer, Faustkämpfer *m*.

pugnac|ious [pʌg'neiʃəs] kampflustig, kriegerisch; streitsüchtig; **~ity** [-'næsiti] Kampf(es)lust; Streitsucht *f*.

puisne ['pju:ni] *jur* niedriger im Rang; im Dienstalter nachstehend; jünger.

puke [pju:k] *itr* (sich er)brechen.

pulchritude ['pʌlkritju:d] *bes. Am* Schönheit *f*.

pule [pju:l] *itr* wimmern, winseln, (vor sich hin) weinen.

pull [pul] **1.** *tr* ziehen, zerren, reißen (*by the hair* an den Haaren); *(Zahn)* (aus-)ziehen; ausrupfen, -reißen; *(Blume, Frucht)* pflücken; ausea.-, zerreißen; *(Muskel)* zerren; *dial (Geflügel)* ausnehmen; *(Ruder)* anziehen; *(Boot)* rudern; *(Boot)* bewegt werden von, haben (*four oars* 4 Ruder); *typ* abziehen; *(Pferd beim Rennen)* zurückhalten; zurückhalten mit *(s-r Kraft, s-n Schlägen)*; *fam* abhalten, durchführen, veranstalten, machen; *sl* einbuchten, festnehmen, verhaften; *(Verbrecherbande, Unterschlupf)* ausheben; *(Verbrechen)* ausführen, begehen; **2.** *itr* ziehen, zerren, reißen (*at* an); *(Trinken, Rauchen)* e-n Zug machen; sich ziehen lassen; sich bewegen; *Am fam* den Daumen drücken (*for* für); **3.** *s* Zug, Ruck *m*; Zerren, Reißen *n*; (Zug-)Kraft, Stärke, Gewalt *f*; *(Trinken, Rauchen)* Zug *m*; Rudern *n*, Ruderfahrt; Anspannung, Anstrengung, Mühe *f*; (Tür-)Griff, Drücker, (Klingel-)Zug; Handgriff; *typ* (Probe-)Abzug *m*, Fahne *f*; Vorteil *m*, Chance *f*, Glück *n* (*of* gen); Werbe-, Zugkraft *f*; Einfluß *m* (*with* auf); Protektion *f*; *to ~ a boner* ins Fettnäpfchen treten; *to ~ s.o.'s chestnuts out of the fire* für jdn die Kastanien aus dem Feuer holen; *to ~ a face, to ~ faces* das Gesicht verziehen, Fratzen schneiden; *to ~ a fast one (sl)* hereinlegen (*on s.o.* jdn); *to ~ it (Am fam)* ausreißen, abhauen, türmen; *to ~ s.o.'s leg* jdn an der Nase herumführen, zum besten, zum Narren haben; *to ~ to pieces* in Stücke reißen, zerreißen; *to ~ a pistol (Am)* e-n Schuß abgeben, feuern (*on* auf); *to ~ o.'s punches (fig)* sich zurückhalten; *to ~ o.'s rank* s-e Stellung herauskehren; *to ~ the strings, wires (fig)* die Fäden in der Hand haben; *to ~ strings* Beziehungen spielen lassen; *to ~ a dirty trick on s.o.* jdm e-n bösen Streich spielen; *to ~ o.'s weight* sich ins Ruder legen; *fig* sich Mühe geben, sich anstrengen; *to ~ the wool over s.o.'s eyes* jdn hereinlegen; *to give a ~* rudern; *to have the ~* e-n Vorteil haben (*of, on, over* vor); *don't ~ any funny stuff!* machen Sie keine Geschichten! *political ~ (Am)* Beziehungen *f pl*, Vitamin B *n*, Protektion *f*; *to ~* **about** hin u. her zerren, -reißen, -stoßen; *to ~* **apart** *fig* zerreißen, zerrupfen, kein gutes Haar lassen an; *to ~* **away** weggehen, *fam* abhauen; *to ~* **back** zurückreißen, -stoßen; *fig* verzögern; *to ~* **down** nieder-, einreißen, demolieren; *(Jalousie)* herunterlassen; *(Person)* heruntermachen, kein gutes Haar lassen an; entmutigen; *(Preis)* herabsetzen; *(Geld)* verdienen; *(Regierung)* stürzen; *(Stellung)* ausfindig machen; *to ~* **in** *tr (Pferd u. fig)* zügeln; *(Gürtel)* enger schnallen; *fig* in Schranken halten; verhaften; *itr* sich be-, sich einschränken; *(Zug)* einfahren, ankommen; *mot* am Straßenrand halten; *~~ your ears, your neck (Am sl)* halt die Klappe! *to ~* **off** wegziehen, -reißen, -zerren; *(Boot)* abstoßen; ausziehen; *(Hut)* abnehmen; *(Handel)* abschließen; *fam* Glück haben mit, *sl (Sache)* schmeißen; *(Sieg)* davontragen; *to ~* **out** *tr* (her)ausziehen, -reißen; *itr bes. Am (Zug)* abfahren, *(fam a. von Menschen)* abdampfen; *(Mensch)* weggehen, *fam* abhauen; *to ~* **over** *mot fam (Wagen)* heranfahren (*to the side* auf die Seite); *to ~* **round** *tr (Kranken)* durchbringen, *fam* -kriegen; *itr* durchkommen, die Krankheit überstehen; *to ~* **through** *tr* (hin)durchziehen; *(Sache)* durchbringen, *fam* -kriegen, *sl* hinhauen; durchhelfen (*s.o.* jdm); *itr* sich durchschlagen, *(Kranker)* durchkommen; *to ~* **together** *fig* am gleichen Strang ziehen, (gut) zs.arbeiten; *to ~ o.s. together* sich zs.nehmen, sich zs.reißen, alle Kräfte anspannen; *to ~* **up** *tr* anhalten, zum Stehen bringen, stoppen; Einhalt gebieten (*s.o.* jdm); *(Pflanze)* herausreißen; *(Flagge)* aufziehen, hissen; heranrücken, -ziehen; *itr* anhalten, stehenbleiben (*at* an, bei, vor); einholen (*with s.o.* jdn); *sport* aufholen; *mot* vorfahren; *to ~ ~ short* plötzlich bremsen; *fig* plötzlich unterbrechen; *to ~ ~ stakes (sl)* abhauen, türmen, das Weite suchen; *~~!* halt! **~-back** Zurückziehen; Hindernis *n*; *tech* Hemmung *f (Vorrichtung)*; **~-down** Abbruch *m (e-s Hauses)*; **~ed** [-d] *a* gerupft, geschoren; *~~ chicken* Hühnerfrikassee *n*; *~~ figs (pl)* getrocknete u. gepackte Feigen *f pl*; **~er** ['-ə] Ziehende(r); Ruderer *m*; *Am sl* zugkräftige Anzeige *f*; **~-fastener** Reißverschluß *m*; **~-off** *(Gewehr)* Druckpunkt *m*; **~-out** *aero* Abfangen *n*; *~~ branch* Abfangbahn *f*; **~-over** Pullover *m*; **~-through** Gewehrreiniger; *sl* dünne(r) Mensch *m*; **~-up** Anhalten *n* (a. *~-in*) Halte-, Rastplatz *m*, Raststätte *f*, Absteigequartier *n*.

pullet ['pulit] Hühnchen *n*.

pulley ['puli] *tech* Rolle; Flasche *f*; Kloben, Block; Flaschenzug *m*; *mar* Talje *f*.

Pullman ['pulmən]: *(~ car) rail* Pullman-, Schlaf-, Salonwagen *m*.

pullulat|e ['pʌljuleit] *itr* keimen, sprossen; sich schnell u. stark vermehren; üppig gedeihen, wuchern; *fig* wimmeln; **~ion** ['-ʃən] Sprossen *n*.

pulmon|ary ['pʌlmənəri] *a scient* Lungen-; lungenkrank; *~~ artery* Lungenschlagader *f*; *~~ disease* Lungenkrankheit *f*; *~~ vein* Lungenvene *f*; **~ic** [pʌl'mɔnik] = *~ary*.

pulp [pʌlp] *s* breiige Masse *f*, Brei *m*; *bot* Fruchtfleisch, Mark; *anat* Zahnmark *n*, Pulpa *f*; *(paper-~)* Papierbrei *m*, Pulpe *f*; *fam (~ magazine)* Groschenheft *n*, billige (minderwertige) Zeitschrift *f*; *tr* zu Brei machen; einstampfen; das Mark, das Fleisch entfernen von; *itr* breiig werden; **~er** ['-ə] *(Papierfabrikation)* Holländer *m*; **~iness** ['-inis] breiige Beschaffenheit *f*; **~y** ['-i] breiartig, breiig.

pulpit ['pulpit] Kanzel *f*; Katheder *n*; *die* Geistlichen *m pl*, *die* Geistlichkeit *f*; Predigen *n*; *in the ~* auf der Kanzel; *~* **eloquence** Kanzelberedsamkeit *f*; *~* **orator** Kanzelredner *m*.

puls|ate ['pʌlseit, -'-] *itr* (regelmäßig) klopfen, schlagen, pochen; zittern, vibrieren; pulsieren (*with* von); **~atile** ['-sətail] klopfend, schlagend; *mus* Schlag-; **~atilla** [pʌlsə'tilə] *bot* Küchenschelle *f*; **~ation** [-'seiʃən] Klopfen, Schlagen, Vibrieren *n*; **~atory** ['pʌlsətəri] klopfend, schlagend; pulsierend; **~e** [pʌls] **1.** *s* Puls; *(~~ beat)* Pulsschlag *a. fig*; *phys el* Impuls; *el* (Strom-)Stoß *m*; *itr* pulsieren *a. fig*; *to feel, to take s.o.'s ~~* jdm den Puls, *fig* auf den Zahn fühlen; **2.** Hülsenfrüchte *f pl*.

pulver|ization [pʌlvərai'zeiʃən] Pulverisierung *f*; **~ize** ['pʌlvəraiz] *tr* pulverisieren, zermahlen, -stäuben; *fig* zermalmen; *itr* pulverisiert, zu Staub werden; **~izer** ['-aizə] Zerstäuber; Zerkleinerer *m*; **~ulent** [pʌl'verjulənt] pulverförmig; staubig; leicht zerfallend.

puma ['pju:mə] *zoo* Puma *m*.

pumice ['pʌmis] *(~-stone)* Bimsstein *m*.

pummel ['pʌml] *tr* mit der Faust schlagen, verprügeln.

pump [pʌmp] **1.** *s* Pumpe *f*; *Am sl* Herz *n*; *tr* pumpen; *(to ~ out)* ausleer pumpen *a. fig*; *fig* erschöpfen; ausholen, ausfragen; die Würmer aus der Nase ziehen (*s.o.* jdm); *to ~ up* aufpumpen; *fig (Wissen)* eintrichtern; *itr* pumpen; auf- u. abbewegen; *to ~ dry* leerpumpen; **~-fed lubrication** Druckschmierung *f*; **~-handle** *s* (Pumpen-)Schwengel *m*; *tr fam (Hand)* überschwenglich schütteln; **~ing** ['-iŋ] Pumpen *n*; *fig* Kunst *f* des Ausfragens; *~~ plant, station* Wasserwerk *n*, Pumpstation *f*; *~* **priming** *fig* Ankurbelung *f (d. Wirtschaft)*; **~-room** *(Kurort)* Trinkhalle *f*; **~-valve** Pumpenventil *n*; **~-water** Brunnenwasser *n*; **2.** *pl* Pumps *m*.

pumpernickel ['pumpənikl] Pumpernickel *m*.

pumpkin ['pʌmpkin] *bot* Kürbis; *Am sl* Kopf, Fußball *m*, Kaff *n*.

pun [pʌn] **1.** *s* Wortspiel *n*; *itr* ein Wortspiel machen (*on, upon* auf); witzeln (*on* über); **~ner** ['-ə], **~ster** ['-stə] Freund *m* von Wortspielen.

Punch [pʌntʃ] Hanswurst, dumme(r) August *m*; Kasperle *n*; *pleased as ~* hocherfreut; **~-and-Judy show** Kasperle-, Puppentheater *n*.

punch [pʌntʃ] **1.** *s* Locheisen *n*,

Locher, Durchschlag, Stempel, Körner, Dorn, Pfriem *m*, Punze *f*; Preßstempel *m*; *tr* durchbohren, lochen, körnen, stempeln, stanzen, punzen; **~-card** Lochkarte *f*; **~-clock** Kontrolluhr *f*; **~-cutter** Stempelschneider *m*; **~ed-tape** Lochstreifen *m*; **~er** ['-ə] Stanzer; Locher *m (Person)*; **~ing** ['-iŋ]: *~~ machine* Stanz-, Lochmaschine, Lochstanze *f*; **~-press** Stanze, Lochmaschine *f*; **2.** *tr* mit der Faust (an)stoßen, schlagen, knuffen; *Am* mit e-m Stock stoßen; *(Vieh)* treiben; *Am sl (Prüfung)* versieben, durchfallen; *s* Faustschlag, Stoß, Knuff, Puff; *Am fam* Schmiß, Schwung *m*, Energie, Tatkraft *f*; *to pull o.'s ~es (Boxen)* verhalten schlagen; *fig* sich zurückhalten; **~-drunk** *(Boxen)* angeschlagen, (wie) benommen *(von Schlägen)*; *fam* durchgedreht, durcheinander, verwirrt; **~er** ['-ə] Schläger, Knuffer; *Am (cow ~~)* Viehtreiber *m*; **~ing-bag, ~(ing-)ball** *(Boxen)* Sandsack, Punchingball *m*; **~-line** *fig* Höhe-, Schlußpunkt *m*; *Am* Pointe *f*; **~-up** *sl* Boxkampf *m*; **~y** ['-i] *Am sl* doof, benommen; kräftig, kraftvoll; **3.** gedrungene(s) Pferd *n*; **~y** ['-i] *fam* pumm(e)lig, klein u. dick; **4.** Punsch *m*; **~-bowl** Bowle *f (Gefäß)*; Loch *n (an e-m Berghang)*.

puncheon ['pʌntʃən] **1.** kurze(r) Pfosten; Stempel *m*, Stanze *f*, Pfriem, Dorn; Preßstempel; *Am* Riemen *m (e-s Fußbodens)*; **2.** (großes) (Bier-, Wein-)Faß *n (111,6 gallons = 324 l)*.

punct|ate(d) ['pʌŋkteit(id)] *a bot zoo* getüpfelt; **~ilio** [-'tiliou] *pl -s* Förmlichkeit, peinliche Genauigkeit *f*; kitz(e)lige(r) Punkt *m* der Etikette; Ehrensache *f*; **~ilious** [-'tiliəs] förmlich, steif; peinlich genau, sehr gewissenhaft; pedantisch; spitzfindig; **~iliousness** [-'tiliəsnis] Strenge, Förmlichkeit, Steifheit, Genauigkeit, Gewissenhaftigkeit, Pedanterie, Spitzfindigkeit *f*; **~ual** ['pʌŋktjuəl] genau; gewissenhaft; pünktlich (*in* bei); **~uality** [pʌŋktju'æliti] Pünktlichkeit *f*; **~uate** ['pʌŋktjueit] *tr* interpunktieren, mit Satzzeichen versehen; *fig* zeitweise unterbrechen; *fig* hervorheben, betonen; **~uation** [pʌŋktju'eiʃən] Interpunktion, Zeichensetzung *f*; Satzzeichen *n pl*; *~~ mark* Satzzeichen *n*; **~ure** ['pʌŋktʃə] *s* Stich *m*; Loch *n*; Stichwunde; *med* Punktur, Punktion; *mot* (Reifen-)Panne *f*, *fam* Plattfuß; *el* Durchschlag *m*; *tr* auf-, durchstechen; *(Sicherung)* durchschlagen; perforieren, durchlöchern; *fig* zum Platzen bringen; *(Hoffnungen)* vernichten; *med* punktieren; *itr (Reifen)* platzen; *to have a ~~ (mot)* e-e (Reifen-)Panne haben; *~~ outfit (mot)* Flickzeug *n*.

pundit ['pʌndit] Pandit; *allg* große(r) Gelehrte(r) *m*, *oft hum* gelehrte(s) Haus, wandelnde(s) Lexikon *n*.

pungenc|y ['pʌndʒənsi] Schärfe *bes. fig*; Schmerzhaftigkeit *f*; Scharfsinn *m*; **~t** ['-t] *(Geruch, Geschmack)* scharf, beißend *a. fig (Worte)*; prickelnd, stechend, schmerzhaft; *(Sorgen)* quälend; scharfsinnig; (stark) anregend.

punish ['pʌniʃ] *tr* (be)strafen (*for* für; *with* mit); *fam (körperlich)* fertig-, *sl* zur Sau machen; zusetzen (*s.o.* jdm); *sl (Essen)* 'runterputzen, verdrücken; *itr* strafen; **~able** ['-əbl] strafbar; *to make ~~* unter Strafe stellen; *~~ act* strafbare Handlung, Straftat *f*; **~ment** ['-mənt] Bestrafung, Züchtigung; Strafe; *fam* schlechte, rauhe Behandlung; Strapaze; *sport* Niederlage *f*; *as a ~~* zur Strafe; *to impose, to inflict a ~~ (up)on s.o.* gegen jdn e-e Strafe verhängen; *to take a lot of ~~* viel aushalten; *capital ~~* Todesstrafe *f*; *corporal ~~* körperliche Züchtigung *f*; *disciplinary ~~* Disziplinarstrafe *f*; *exemption from ~~* Straffreiheit *f*; *maximum ~~* Höchststrafe *f*; *mitigation of ~~* Strafmilderung *f*; *pecuniary ~~* Geldstrafe *f*.

punit|ive ['pju:nitiv], **~ory** ['-əri] *a* strafend; Straf-; *~~ damages (pl)* Buße *f*; *~~ power* Strafgewalt *f*.

punk [pʌŋk] *s Am* faule(s) Holz *n*, getrocknete Pilze *m pl*, Zunder *m*; *Am sl* Dreck, Mist; *sl* Unsinn, Quatsch; *sl* Rowdy *m*; *Am sl* Anfänger *m*, Nulpe *f*, Brot *n*; *a Am sl* mies, mau, schäbig, armselig; *I'm feeling ~ (sl)* mir ist mies.

punt [pʌnt] **1.** *s (Fußball)* Fallstoß *m*; *tr* e-n Fallstoß geben (*the ball* dem Ball), im Flug zurückschlagen; *itr* e-n Fallstoß machen; **2.** *s* Flachboot *n*, Stechkahn *m*; *tr (Boot)* staken; *itr* punten; **~ ferry** Kahnfähre *f*; **3.** *itr* (gegen den Bankhalter) wetten; *(auf ein Pferd)* wetten.

puny ['pju:ni] klein, schwach, unbedeutend.

pup [pʌp] *s* junge(r) Hund *od* Otter *od* Seehund; *fig* Laffe *m*; *Am sl* heiße Saitenwürstchen, Wiener *pl*; *Am sl* kleine Zugmaschine *f*; *itr (Hündin)* (Junge) werfen; *in ~* trächtig; *to sell s.o. a ~* jdn übers Ohr hauen, jdn betrügen; **~mobile** ['-mobi:l] *mot fam* Kleinwagen *m*, (Straßen-)Wanze *f*; **~py** ['-i] junge(r) Hund; *fig* Fatzke, Schnösel *m*; *pl Am sl* Füße *m pl*; *~~ cake, (Am) biscuit* Hundekuchen *m*; *~~-dog (Kindersprache)* kleine(r) Wauwau *m*; **~ tent** Einmannzelt *n*.

pup|a ['pju:pə] *pl -ae* [-i:] *ent* Puppe *f*; **~ate** ['-eit] *itr* sich verpuppen.

pupil ['pju:pl] Schüler, Zögling *m*; Mündel *n*; *anat* Pupille *f*; **~(l)age** ['-ilidʒ] Schulzeit; Minderjährigkeit *f*; *fig* Anfangsstadium *n*, Anfänge *m pl*; *to be still in o.'s ~~ (fig)* noch in den Kinderschuhen stecken; **~ teacher** Pädagogikstudent *m* in der Praxis.

puppet ['pʌpit] (Draht-)Puppe, Marionette *a. fig*; *fig* Puppe *f*, Strohmann *m*, Werkzeug *n*; **~eer** [pʌpi'tiə], **~ player** Puppenspieler *m*; **~ government** Marionettenregierung *f*; **~-show** Puppenspiel *n*.

purblind ['pə:blaind] halbblind, stark kurzsichtig; *fig* schwer von Begriff, blöde; *to be ~* e-e lange Leitung haben.

purchas|able ['pə:tʃəsəbl] käuflich; bestechlich; **~e** ['pə:tʃəs] *tr* (an-, auf-, ein)kaufen; (käuflich) erwerben; erstehen, anschaffen, besorgen; *fig* erkaufen; *tech* (an)heben, hochwinden; *s* (An-, Auf-, Ein-)Kauf; Erwerb *m*, Erstehung, Anschaffung, Besorgung *f*; Kaufobjekt; Einkommen *n*, (Jahres-)Ertrag *m*; (fester) (Zu-)Griff, Halt; Handgriff *m*; *tech* Greifvorrichtung *f*, Greifer *m*; *mar* Takel; *fig* Mittel *n*, Einfluß *m*; *pl com* Wareneingänge *m pl*; *by (way of) ~~* durch Kauf, käuflich; *to conclude, to effect, to make a ~~* e-n Kauf tätigen; *to ~~ at auction* ersteigern; *his life is not worth a day's ~~* sein Leben ist keinen Pfifferling wert; *cash-, ready money ~~* Barkauf *m*; *credit-~~* Kreditkauf *m*; *hire-~~* Abzahlungs-, Ratenzahlungsgeschäft *n*; *occasional ~~* Gelegenheitskauf *m*; *terms of ~~* Kaufbedingungen *f pl*; *~~ book* Einkaufsbuch *n*; *~~ contract-deed* Kaufvertrag *m*, -urkunde *f*; *~~-department* Einkaufsabteilung *f*; *~~-money, -price* Kauf-, Einkaufspreis *m*; *~~ order* Bestellung *f*; *~~ register* Kreditorenjournal *n*; *~~ requisition number* Bestellnummer *f*; *~~ tax* Warenumsatzsteuer *f*; **~er** ['-ə] Käufer, Abnehmer; Kunde; *(Auktion)* Ersteigerer *m*; *to find, to meet with ~~s* Käufer finden; *prospective ~~* Kauflustige(r) *m*; **~ing** ['-iŋ] Kauf, Erwerb *m*, Anschaffung; Beschaffung *f*; *~~-clerk* Einkäufer *m*; *~~ department* Einkaufsabteilung *f*; *~~ manager* Einkaufsleiter *m*; *~~-order* Kaufauftrag; Bestellschein *m*; *~~-power* Kaufkraft *f*; *excessive ~~-power* Kaufkraftüberhang *m*.

pure [pjuə] rein *a. rel philos biol*; lauter; sauber *fig*; untadelig, tadel(s)frei, -los, fehlerfrei; schuldlos, unschuldig; *jur* bedingungslos; rein, keusch, jungfräulich; unverfälscht; unge-, unvermischt, schier; *that's ~ nonsense* das ist reiner Unsinn; **~ blood** Vollblut *n*; **~bred** ['-bred] *a* reinrassig, rasserein; *s* reinrassige(s) Tier *n*; **~ gold** Feingold *n*; **~ly** ['-li] *adv* ausschließlich; **~ness** ['-nis] Reinheit, Lauterkeit *f*.

purée ['pjuərei] Püree *n*; Brei *m*.

purg|ation [pə:'geiʃən] Reinigung *a. fig rel*; *pol* Säuberung; *jur* Rechtfertigung *f*; *med* Abführen *n*; **~ative** ['pə:gətiv] *a* reinigend; *med* abführend, Abführ-; *s* Abführmittel *n*; **~atory** ['pə:gətəri] Fegefeuer *n a. fig*; **~e** [pə:dʒ] *tr* reinigen, säubern *a. fig*; *fig* befreien, frei machen (*of, from* von); *pol* säubern; *jur* rechtfertigen; *(Verbrechen)* sühnen; *fin* sanieren; *med* abführen; *s* Reinigung(smittel *n*); *pol* Säuberung(saktion) *f*; *med* Abführmittel *n*; *fin* Sanierung; *jur* Rechtfertigung *f*.

purif|ication [pjuərifi'keiʃən] Reinigung (*from* von) *a. fig rel*; *tech* Aufbereitung, Regenerierung *f*; *~~ plant* Kläranlage *f*; **~icatory** ['pjuərifikeitəri] reinigend; Reinigungs-; **~ier** ['pjuərifaiə] Reiniger *m*; Klär-, Reinigungsmittel *n*; **~y** ['pjuərifai] *tr* reinigen, läutern (*of, from* von) *a. fig rel*; säubern (*of, from* von); *tech* reinigen, waschen, klären; raffinieren, veredeln, aufbereiten.

pur|ism ['pjuərizm] Purismus *m*; **~ist** ['-ist] Purist *m*.

Puritan ['pjuəritən] *rel* Puritaner *m*; *a* puritanisch; **p~ic(al)** [pjuəri'tænik(əl)] puritanisch, sittenstreng; **P~ism** ['pjuəritənizm] Puritanismus *m*.

purity ['pjuəriti] Reinheit *f a. fig*.

purl [pə:l] **1.** *tr* säumen; linksstricken; *s* Saum *m*, (gestickte, Gold-, Silber-) Borte *f*; Linksstricken *n*; **2.** *itr (Wasser)* murmeln, plätschern; *s* Murmeln, Plätschern; warme(s) Bier *n* mit Gin; **3.** *tr itr fam* kopfüber stürzen; *itr* hinpurzeln; **~er** ['-ə] *s fam* Sturz, Fall; Schlag, Stoß *m*; *to come, to take a ~~* lang hinschlagen.

purlieus ['pə:lju:z] *pl* Grenzen *f pl*, Gebiet *n*; Umgebung *f*; Armenviertel *n (e-r Stadt)*, Slums *pl*; Stadtrand *m*.

purlin(e) ['pə:lin] *arch* Dachstuhlpfette *f*.

purloin [pə:'lɔin] *tr* stehlen, entwenden.

purple ['pə:pl] *s* Purpur(farbe *f*); *(~ robe)* Purpurmantel *m*; *zoo* Purpurschnecke *f*; *pl med* Purpura *pl*; *a (~ red)* purpur(farbe)n, purpurrot; *fig* glänzend; *Am fam* zotig; *tr itr* purpurn färben *od* werden; *born in the ~* von hoher Geburt; *(Order of the) P~ Heart (Am)* Verwundetenabzeichen *n*.

purport ['pə:pət] *s* Bedeutung *f*, Sinn, Inhalt; Wortlaut; Zweck *m*, Absicht *f*, Ziel *n*; *tr* [*a.* pə:'pə:t] den Eindruck machen, den Anschein erwecken; sich den Anschein geben; zu verstehen geben; besagen.

purpose ['pə:pəs] *s* Absicht *f*, Ziel, Vorhaben *n*; Entschluß *m*, Entscheidung; Entschlußkraft *f*; Zweck, Sinn *m*; Wirkung; Zweckbestimmung, Zielsetzung *f*; *tr* beabsichtigen, vorhaben, sich vornehmen, sich als Ziel setzen; *for that* ~ zu diesem Zweck, deswegen, deshalb; *for the* ~ *of* zum Zweck *gen*; *jur* im Sinne *gen*; *for what* ~*?* weshalb? *of set* ~, *on* ~ absichtlich, mit Absicht; *jur* vorsätzlich; *to* ~ nach Wunsch; *to all intents and* ~*s* in jeder Hinsicht *od* Beziehung; *to good* ~ mit guter Wirkung, wirkungsvoll; *to little* ~ mit geringer Wirkung; mit wenig Erfolg; *to no* ~ ohne Erfolg, wirkungslos; vergeblich; *to some* ~ mit einigem Erfolg; zweckentsprechend; *to the* ~ im beabsichtigten Sinne; zweckdienlich; zur Sache; *to answer, to serve the* ~ dem Zweck entsprechen *od* dienen; *to be to little* ~ wenig Zweck haben; *to serve no* ~ zwecklos sein; *to turn to good* ~ gut ausnützen; *business* ~ Geschäftszweck *m*; *novel with a* ~ Tendenzroman *m*; *weak, infirm of* ~ von mangelnder Entschlußkraft; ~**ful** ['-ful] zweck-, sinn-, bedeutungsvoll; entschlossen, zielbewußt; ~**fulness** ['-fulnis] Zweckhaftigkeit; Entschlossenheit *f*; ~**less** ['-lis] ziel-, zweck-, planlos; ~**lessness** ['-lisnis] Ziel-, Planlosigkeit *f*; ~**ly** ['-li] *adv* absichtlich, mit Absicht, vorsätzlich, (wohl)überlegt; ~**-novel** Tendenzroman *m*; ~**-trained** *a* mit Spezialausbildung; **purposive** ['-iv] absichtlich; zweckdienlich; auf ein Ziel gerichtet.

*

purr [pə:] *itr (Katze)* schnurren *a. fig*; *tech* surren, brummen; *tr* schnurrend sagen; *s* Schnurren; Surren *n*.

purse [pə:s] *s* Geldbeutel *m*, Börse *f a. sport*, Portemonnaie; Geld *n*, Finanzen *f pl*, Kasse *f*; Hilfsquellen *f pl*; Geldpreis *m*, -geschenk *n*; (Damen-)Handtasche *f*; Beutel *m*; *tr (to* ~ *up)* in Falten legen, zs.ziehen; *(Lippen)* schürzen; *beyond s.o.'s* ~ zu teuer; *to have a common* ~ *with s.o.* mit jdm gemeinsame Kasse machen; *to make up a* ~ *for s.th.* für etw Geld sammeln; *to* ~ *up o.'s mouth* den Mund verziehen; *o.'s forehead* die Stirn runzeln; *long, light* ~ volle, leere Kassen; *the public* ~ die Staatskasse, der Staatssäckel; ~**-net, -seine** Fischnetz *n*; ~**-proud** geldstolz; ~**r** ['-ə] *mar* Zahlmeister *m*; ~**strings** *pl*: *to hold the* ~~ übers Geld verfügen; *to loosen, to tighten the* ~~ mehr, weniger Geld 'rausrücken.

pursiness ['pə:sinis] Kurzatmigkeit, Engbrüstigkeit; Fettleibigkeit *f*.

purslane ['pə:slin] *bot* Portulak *m*.

pursu|ance [pə'sju(:)əns] Aus-, Durchführung, Verfolgung *f*; *in* ~~ *of* in Verfolg *gen*; gemäß *dat*; auf Grund *gen*; ~**ant** [-ənt]: ~~ *to* zufolge, entsprechend, gemäß *dat*; in Übereinstimmung mit; ~**e** [pə'sju:] *tr* verfolgen, jagen; *(Weg)* einschlagen; *(Plan, Absicht, Zweck)* verfolgen; streben nach, suchen; *(Tätigkeit, Beruf)* ausüben, nachgehen; *(Aufgaben)* erledigen; obliegen (*a study* e-m Studium); fortsetzen, -führen; nicht in Ruhe lassen; *itr* fortfahren, weitermachen; *to* ~~ *the subject* beim Thema bleiben; ~**er** [-ə] Verfolger; *jur* Kläger *m*; ~**it** [-t] Verfolgung, Jagd *f* (*of* auf); Streben, Trachten *n* (*of* nach); Beschäftigung, Tätigkeit, Arbeit, Laufbahn *f*; *pl* Bestrebungen *f pl*, Arbeit *f*, Beruf *m*; Geschäfte *n pl*; Beschäftigung *f*, Zeitvertreib *m*; Studien *f pl*; *in* ~~ *of* auf der Jagd nach; ~~*-flyer* Jagdflieger *m*; ~~*-plane* Jagdflugzeug *n*.

pursy ['pə:si] **1.** kurzatmig, engbrüstig; *(Pferd)* dämpfig, herzschlächtig; fett (-leibig); **2.** faltig; **3.** reich.

purulen|ce, -cy ['pjuərulens(i)] eit(e)rige(r) Zustand; Eiter *m*; ~**t** ['-t] eit(e)rig, Eiter-.

purvey [pə:'vei] *tr com (bes. Lebensmittel)* liefern (*to* an); an-, beschaffen; *itr* liefern (*for* für); beliefern, versorgen (*for s.o.* jdn); ~**ance** [-əns] Versorgung, Lieferung; Beschaffung; gelieferte Ware *f*; ~**or** [-ə] (*bes.* Lebensmittel-)Lieferant *m*; ~~ *to the Court* Hoflieferant *m*.

purview ['pə:vju:] *(Gesetz)* Geltungsbereich; Herrschafts-, Tätigkeitsbereich *m od n*, Wirkungskreis, Rahmen *m*, Sphäre *f*, Gebiet *n*; Gesichtskreis, Horizont *m*, Blickfeld; (geistiges) Fassungsvermögen *n*; wesentliche(r) Inhalt *m*.

pus [pʌs] Eiter *m*; ~**sy** ['-i] eit(e)rig.

push [puʃ] **1.** *tr* stoßen, drücken (auf), schieben; drängen, (an)treiben; eifrig, energisch betreiben; be-, vorantreiben, (eifrig) fördern, energisch verfolgen; *(Bekanntschaft)* pflegen; vorstoßen mit, ausdehnen (*to* bis zu); sich verwenden für, Reklame machen für; *Am fam* heranrücken an; *Am sl (Auto)* anschieben; *(Person)* umbringen; **2.** *itr* drücken, schieben, stoßen (*at* an); sich (sehr) anstrengen; sich vorwärtsschieben, sich vordrängen; *Am sl* zu weit gehen; **3.** *s* Stoß, Druck, Schub; Vorstoß (*for* auf) *a. mil*; Schubs; *tech* Drücker; *arch* Druck; (An-)Trieb, Drang, Schwung, Eifer *m*, Energie, Tatkraft, Anstrengung, Bemühung *f*; Schwierigkeiten *f pl*, Verlegenheit *f*, *fam* Druck; Not-, Ernstfall; *fam* Unternehmungsgeist *m*, Angriffslust; Protektion; *sl* (Menschen-)Masse *sl* (Verbrecher-)Bande *f*; **4.** *at a* ~ im Notfall; in (großer) Verlegenheit, in Schwierigkeiten; *at one* ~ mit e-m Ruck; auf einmal; *to be* ~*ed for (time, money)* in (Zeit-)Schwierigkeiten, in (Geld-)Verlegenheit sein; *to bring to the last* ~ aufs Äußerste, auf die Spitze treiben; *to get the* ~ *(sl)* ('raus)fliegen, 'rausgeschmissen, entlassen werden; *to give s.o. the* ~ jdn 'rausschmeißen, auf die Straße setzen; *to make a* ~ e-e Anstrengung, *mil* e-n Vorstoß machen; *to* ~ *o.'s advantage* s-n Vorteil wahrnehmen; *to* ~ *the blame on s.o.* die Schuld auf jdn abwälzen; *to* ~ *o.'s way* (im Leben) vorwärts-, vorankommen; sich e-n Weg bahnen; sich hineindrängeln (*into* in); *when it comes to the* ~ im entscheidenden Augenblick; *to* ~ **along** weiter-, vorwärtskommen; *to* ~ **around** herumstoßen; *fig* schlecht behandeln; *to* ~ **away** wegstoßen, -schieben; *to* ~ **back** zurückstoßen; *sl* hinunterschlucken; *to* ~ **down** hinab-, hinunter-, niederstoßen; herunterdrükken; *to* ~ **forward** weiterschieben, vortreiben; vorantreiben, beschleunigen; fördern; *to* ~ *o.s. forward* sich vordrängen; sich emporarbeiten; *to* ~ **in** *tr* hineinstoßen, -drücken, schieben; *itr* sich hineindrängeln; *to* ~ **off** *tr (Ware)* abstoßen, losschlagen; *(Boot)* abstoßen; *itr fam* abhauen, (weg-) gehen, -fahren, in See stechen; ~ *off!* los! mach zu! *to* ~ **on** *tr* vorwärts-, vorantreiben, *fig* -bringen; *itr* (mühsam) voran-, vorwärts-, weiterkommen; vordringen; *to* ~ **out** *tr* hinausstoßen, -drücken, -schieben, -drängen; *itr bot* treiben; *mar* in See stechen; *to* ~ **through** durchsetzen; *(Gesetz)* durchbringen; *fig* zu e-m guten Ende bringen; *to* ~ **up** hinaufschieben; drücken (*against* gegen); *(Preise)* hochtreiben, hinaufschrauben; *fig* sich verwenden für; ~**-and-pull** *a* im Pendelverkehr; ~**-ball** *sport* Pushball(spiel *n*) *m*; ~**-bike** *fam* Fahrrad *n*; ~ **button** *el* Drücker, Knopf *m*; (Druck-)Taste *f*; ~~ *switch* Druckknopfschalter *m*; ~~ *warfare* automatisch abrollende(r) Krieg *m*; ~**-cart** Schubkarren; *Am* Verkaufskarren *m*; ~**er** ['-ə] Stoßende(r), Schiebende(r); *fig* Streber, *fam* Radfahrer; Draufgänger; *metal* Ausdrücker; *min* (Wagen-)Aufschieber; Schieber *m (Kinderlöffel)*; *(*~~*-plane, -aircraft)* Flugzeug *n* mit Druckluftschraube *(*~~*-airscrew)*; ~**ful** ['-ful] energisch, rührig, unternehmungslustig, *fam* auf Draht; ~**ing** ['-iŋ] *a* unternehmend, unternehmungslustig, tatkräftig, energisch; auf-, zudringlich; ~ **key** Drucktaste *f*; ~**-off** *fam* Anfang *m*; ~**-over** *Am sl* Kinderspiel *n*, Kleinigkeit, leichte, einfache Sache *f*; *fig* Gimpel; *Am sl* Schwächling *m*; ~**pin** *Am* Reißzwecke *f*; ~**-pull** Gegentakt *m*; ~~ *communication (tele)* Gegentaktverkehr *m*; ~**-rod** Stoßstange *f*; ~**-up** *sport* Liegestütz *m*; ~**y** ['-i] *Am s* Streber, Emporkömmling *m*; *a* anmaßend.

pusillanim|ity [pju:silə'nimiti] Zaghaftigkeit, Schüchternheit *f*; ~**ous** [pju:si'læniməs] kleinmütig, furchtsam, ängstlich, zaghaft.

puss [pus] Pussi, Miez(e), (Mieze-)Katze *f*; Häschen, -lein *n*, Meister *m* Lampe; *fig* Katze *f*; *Am sl* Gesicht *n*, Fresse, Grimasse *f*; ~ *in boots* der Gestiefelte Kater; ~ *in the corner* Drittenabschlagen *n (Kinderspiel)*; ~**-moth** *ent* Gabelschwanz *m*; ~**y** ['-i] *(*~~*-cat)* Mieze(katze) *f*; *bot* (Weiden-)Kätzchen *n*; ~**yfoot** ['-ifut] *sl Am itr* schleichen; *fig* sich (herum)drücken, der Entscheidung aus dem Wege gehen; nicht mit der Sprache herauswollen, heimlichtun, sich ausschweigen (*on* über); *pol* keine klare Stellung beziehen; *s* Schleicher, Kriecher, Leisetreter, Heimlichtuer *m*; *a* kriecherisch, heimlichtuend; ~**y-willow** *bot* Salweide *f*.

pustul|ate ['pʌstjuleit] *tr* Pusteln verursachen; *itr* in Pusteln übergehen; ~**ation** [pʌstju'leiʃən] Pustelbildung *f*; ~**e** ['pʌstju:l] Pustel *f*, Pickel *m*, Eiterbläschen *n*; *bot zoo* Warze *f*.

put [put] *irr put, put* **1.** *tr* setzen, stellen, legen; stecken (*into* in; *at* an); anbringen (*to* an); *fig* (in e-e Lage) bringen, versetzen; *(Jungen)* geben (*to shoemaking* in die Schuhmacherlehre); einfügen, hineinlegen *a. fig* (*into* in); ausdrücken (*it mildly* sich gelinde); kleiden (*into words* in Worte); übersetzen (*into French* ins Französische); *(Frage)* stellen; vorlegen, unterbreiten; *(Steuer)* legen (*on* auf), auferlegen (*on s.o.* jdm); festsetzen (*on* für); ansetzen, berechnen (*at* mit, zu); zur Last legen (*on s.o.* jdm); tun, hinzufügen (*to* zu); *(Unterschrift)* setzen (*to* unter; *on* auf); *(Pferd)* spannen (*to* vor); bestimmen (*to* für); stoßen, werfen, schleudern; treiben, zwingen; **2.** *itr* gehen, fahren, sich begeben, (ab)reisen (*for* nach; *to* zu); **3.** *s* Stoß; Wurf; *com* Terminverkauf *m*, Prämiengeschäft *n*; **4.** *a fam* unbeweglich; **5.** *to be (hard) ~ to it* in e-r schwierigen Lage *od* Situation sein; *to feel ~ upon, out* sich ungerecht behandelt, sich ausgenützt fühlen; ungehalten sein; *to ~ to account* in Rechnung stellen; *to ~ out of action* außer Betrieb setzen; *mil* kampfunfähig machen; *to ~ on airs* sich aufs hohe Roß setzen; *to ~ to bed* zu Bett bringen; *to ~ the blame on s.o.* jdm die Schuld zuschieben; *to ~ to blush* schamrot machen, beschämen; *to ~ (money) into a business* Geld in ein Geschäft stecken; *to ~ in two cents (Am)* s-n Senf dazu beisteuern; *to ~ clearly* klarlegen, -stellen; *to ~ in commission* in Dienst stellen; *to ~ the date on s.th.* etw datieren; *to ~ to death* umbringen; hinrichten; *to ~ all o.'s eggs in one basket* alles auf e-e Karte setzen; *to ~ an end to s.th.* ein Ende machen mit e-r S; *to o.s., to o.'s life* sich das Leben nehmen; *to ~ s.o. to expense* jdm Unkosten verursachen; *to ~ s.o. on his feet* jdn auf die Beine bringen; *to ~ up a fight* e-n Kampf liefern; Widerstand leisten; sich wehren; *to ~ to flight* in die Flucht schlagen; *to ~ o.'s foot down* energisch auftreten; *to ~ in force* in Kraft setzen; *to ~ in hand (fig)* in die Hand nehmen; *to ~ s.th. in(to) s.o.'s hands* etw in jds Hände legen, jdm etw überlassen; *to ~ o.'s hand in o.'s pocket* die Hand in die Tasche stecken; *to ~ s.th. out of o.'s head* sich etw aus dem Kopf schlagen; *to ~ o.'s heads together* die Köpfe zs.stecken; *to ~ s.o. in a hole (fig)* jdn in e-e schiefe Lage bringen; *to ~ it to s.o.* es jdm anheimstellen *od* überlassen; *to ~ s.o. to it* jdm schwer zusetzen, *fam* jdm auf den Pelz rücken; *to ~ it there (Am sl)* sich die Hand reichen; *to ~ it upon s.th.* es ankommen lassen auf; *to ~ the lid on it* noch den letzten Schlag versetzen; *to ~ on the market* auf den Markt bringen; *to ~ o.'s mind on s.th.* sich konzentrieren auf; jds Aufmerksamkeit richten auf; *to ~ in mind of* erinnern an; *to ~ in motion* in Bewegung setzen; *to ~ s.o. on his oath* jdn unter Eid nehmen; *to ~ in order* in Ordnung bringen; *to ~ s.o. through his paces* jdn auf die Probe stellen, jdm auf den Zahn fühlen; *to ~ in possession* in Besitz setzen, versehen (*of* mit); *to ~ into practice* in die Praxis umsetzen; *to ~ the question* die Frage stellen; *parl* zur Abstimmung schreiten; *to ~ s.o. to ransom* ein Lösegeld für jdn fordern; *to ~ right* verbessern; in Ordnung bringen; *to ~ to sea* in See stechen; *to ~ into service* in Dienst stellen; *to ~ s.o. in good shape* jdn in gute Verfassung bringen; *to ~ a stop to* Schluß, ein Ende machen mit; *to ~ to trial* vor Gericht bringen; *to ~ to a good use* gut verwenden; *to ~ to the vote* zur Abstimmung stellen; *to ~ on weight* an Gewicht zunehmen, dicker werden; *to ~ s.o. out of the way* jdn beiseite schaffen; *to ~ the weight, the shot (sport)* die Kugel stoßen; *to ~ wise (Am)* enttäuschen; aufklären; informieren; *to ~ in a word for s.o.* für jdn ein gutes Wort einlegen; *to ~* **about** *tr (Schiff)* herumlegen; *(Flasche)* herumgehen lassen; *(Nachricht)* verbreiten; in Umlauf setzen; *s.o.* jdn in Aufregung versetzen; *to be ~~* Ärger, Scherereien haben; *itr* e-e andere Richtung einschlagen; *(Schiff)* beidrehen; *to ~* **across** *mar* übersetzen; *sl* fertig-, durchkriegen; erledigen; durch-, zustande bringen, lancieren; verkaufen; *theat film* zu e-m (Publikums-)Erfolg machen; *to s.th., it across s.o. (sl)* jdn übers Ohr hauen; jdn verdreschen; *s.th. to s.o.* jdm etw beibringen; *to ~* **aside** zurücklegen, aufheben; *(Geld)* auf die Seite, *fam* auf die hohe Kante legen; aus der Hand, weg-, beiseite legen; *to ~* **away** *tr* weg-, an s-n Platz legen *od* stellen; zur Seite, zurücklegen, sparen; sich aus dem Kopf schlagen; *fam* aus dem Wege räumen; an s-n Platz legen *od* stellen; zur Seite, zurücklegen, sparen; sich aus dem Kopf schlagen; aus dem Wege räumen; *sl (Essen)* verdrücken, 'runterputzen; konsumieren; *sl* beseitigen, umbringen; *itr (Schiff)* sich entfernen (*from* von); *to ~* **back** *tr (an s-n Platz)* zurücklegen, -stellen; *(für später)* zurücklegen; *(Uhr)* zurückstellen; zurücksteuern; *(Schüler)* zurückversetzen; Einhalt gebieten (*s.th.* e-r S), *fam* abbremsen; *tele* wieder verbinden (*to* mit); *itr* zurückkehren, *mar* -fahren; *to ~* **before** dar-, vorlegen; *to ~* **by** *(für später)* zurücklegen, -stellen; zur Seite legen, ablegen, -schieben, übergehen; *to ~* **down** *tr* niedersetzen, -stellen, -legen; *(Vorhang)* herunterlassen; *(Schirm)* zumachen; nieder-, unterdrücken; *(Aufstand)* niederschlagen; abschaffen, aufheben; zum Schweigen bringen, mundtot machen; tadeln, herabsetzen, erniedrigen, demütigen; verringern, verkleinern, herabsetzen; *(in writing)* nieder-, aufschreiben, notieren; buchen; (jdn) vormerken (*for* für); anschreiben (*to s.o.* jdm), in Rechnung stellen (*to s.o., to s.o.'s account* jdm); zuschreiben (*s.th. to s.o.* jdm etw); halten (*as, for* für); ansehen, betrachten (*as, for* als); *(Lager, Vorrat)* anlegen; *itr mar aero* landen; *to ~* **forth** *tr bot* hervorbringen, treiben; *(Kraft, Mühe)* an-, aufwenden, aufbieten; herausstellen, vorbringen, vorschlagen, anbieten; von sich geben, behaupten; *(Behauptung)* aufstellen; *(Ansicht)* vorbringen; ausgeben (*as* als); herausgeben, -bringen, veröffentlichen; *itr mar* in See stechen, auslaufen; *bot* keimen; *to ~* **forward** vorschlagen, in Vorschlag bringen (*o.s.* sich); unterbreiten, vorlegen; *(Bitte)* vorbringen; *(Uhr)* vorstellen; *to ~* **in** *tr* hineinbringen, einführen, -stellen; *(Glasscheibe)* einsetzen; vorlegen, unterbreiten, vorschlagen; einreichen; *(Papiere)* vorzeigen, -weisen; *(Kandidaten)* aufstellen; *(Zeit)* verwenden, hineinstecken; *(Extrastunde)* einlegen; einfügen, -schalten, -rücken; *(Bemerkung)* einwerfen; *(Anzeige in die Zeitung; Geld)* setzen; *fam (Zeit)* verbringen; *(Schlag)* anbringen, versetzen; *itr mar* anlaufen (*at* acc); sich bewerben (*for* um); *to ~~ an appearance* in Erscheinung treten; kurz halten (*at* bei, an); *to ~~ a claim* Anspruch erheben, anmelden (*for* auf); *to ~~ a plea* e-n Rechtseinwand erheben; *to ~~ a word* ein (gutes) Wort einlegen (*for* für); *to ~~ writing* schriftlich machen; *to ~* **off** *tr* auf-, hinaus-, verschieben, zurückstellen, auf die lange Bank schieben; *(jdn)* hinhalten, abschieben, vertrösten, abspeisen, *fam* abwimmeln (*with fine words* mit schönen Worten); *(jdn)* abhalten, -bringen, davon zurückhalten, daran hindern; ablegen, beiseite lassen; *(Pferd)* ausspannen; *(Kleidungsstück)* ausziehen, ablegen; *(Hut)* absetzen; *itr mar* auslaufen, abfahren; *(Tischtuch)* auflegen; *to ~* **on** *(Kleidung)* anlegen, anziehen; *(Hut)* aufsetzen; *(Uhr)* vorstellen; *(Zeiger)* vorrücken; *tech (Bremse)* anziehen; in Gang setzen, anlassen; *(Pfeife)* anstecken; vermehren, erhöhen, auflegen; einlegen; *(Zug)* zusätzlich fahren lassen; *(Wasser auf dem Herd)* aufsetzen; *(Briefmarken)* aufkleben; *theat* heraus-, auf die Bühne bringen; *(Darbietung)* bringen; mitteilen (*to s.o.* jdm); *(Haltung)* annehmen; heucheln, vorgeben; *(an Gewicht)* zunehmen, sich zulegen; *to ~* **out** *tr* hinauswerfen, vor die Tür setzen, entlassen; *(Hand)* ausstrecken; aus der (gewohnten, normalen) Lage bringen, ausrenken; *(Licht, Feuer)* ausmachen, löschen; fertig-, herstellen, hervorbringen, produzieren; *(Arbeit)* vergeben; *(Geld)* ver-, ausleihen, anlegen; *(öffentlich)* ausschreiben, in Submission geben; stören, verärgern, verstimmen, in Verlegenheit, in Verwirrung bringen; *itr mar* auslaufen, in See stechen; abfahren, -fliegen; *to ~ o.s. out* sich Umstände machen; *to ~* **over** *tr* aufschieben, zurückstellen; *fam* durchbringen, -setzen; *theat film* e-n Publikumserfolg sichern für; an den Mann bringen; *itr mar* hinüberfahren (*to* zu); *to ~ s.th. over on s.o.* jdm etw weis-, vormachen; *to ~* **past**: *I wouldn't ~ it past him* ich traue es ihm zu (*to* zu); *to ~* **through** (glücklich) durchführen, vollenden, *fam* fertigkriegen; durchgeben, mitteilen; *tele* verbinden (*with* mit); *to ~* **together** zs.setzen, -stellen, -stecken; aufbauen, montieren; *to ~* **up** *tr* hochheben, -halten; *(Flagge)* hissen; *(Vorhang)* hochziehen; auf-, errichten, (auf)bauen, aufstellen, montieren, einrichten, installieren; *(Preis)* ausschreiben; beiseite tun, -stellen, beiseite-, weglegen, einstecken; *(Schirm)* aufspannen; *(Waren)* anbieten (*for sale* zum Verkauf); weglegen, *fam* verstauen, einpacken (u. verwahren); verpacken; *(Haar)* aufstecken; *(Denkmal)* errichten; *(Lebensmittel)* einmachen; *(Geld)* aufbringen; *(Person)* unterbringen, beherbergen; *(Wild)* aufscheuchen, aufspüren; herausstellen, hervorkehren, -heben, zeigen; *(als Kandidaten)* vorschlagen, in Vorschlag bringen, aufstellen; *theat* zur Aufführung, auf die Bühne bringen; *(Gebet)* richten (*to* an); *(Preis)* erhöhen, heraufsetzen; informieren (*to* über), unterrichten (*to* von); *fam (jdn)* bringen, (auf)reizen, verführen, aufhetzen (*to* zu); *fam* im Schilde führen; *itr* einkehren, absteigen (*at* in); wohnen (*with* bei); sich bewerben (*for* um); *with s.th.* sich mit e-r S abfinden, mit e-r S fertigwerden; **6. ~-off** Ausrede, -flucht *f*, Vorwand; Aufschub *m*; **~-on** *a* scheinbar; angeblich, vorgetäuscht; *s* Kniff *m*, Täuschungsmanöver *n*; **~-put** *sl mot* Knatterkiste *f*; Tuckern *n*; **~ting** ['-iŋ] Stoß, Wurf *m*; *~~ the weight, the shot* Kugelstoßen *n*; **~-up** *fam* abgemacht, abgekartet.

putative ['pju:tətiv] angenommen, vermeintlich, mutmaßlich; *jur* putativ.

putlog ['putlɔg], **putlock** ['-lɔk] kurze(r) Tragbalken *m*, Rüststange *f*.

putr|efaction [pju:tri'fækʃən] Fäulnis; Verwesung; Zersetzung *f*; faulige Stoffe *m pl*; Moder *m*; **~efactive** [-'fæktiv] fäulniserregend; Fäulnis-; **~efier** ['pju:trifaiə] Fäulniserreger *m*; **~efy** ['pju:trifai] *itr tr* (ver)faulen, verwesen, sich zersetzen (lassen); **~escence** [pju:'tresns] Fäulnis, Verwesung *f*; faulige(s) Zeug *n*, Moder *m*; *fig* Sittenverderbnis, Korruption *f*; **~escent** [-'tresnt] (ver)faulend, faulig; Fäulnis-; **~id** ['pju:trid] faul(ig); verwest; zersetzt; fäulniserregend, Fäulnis-; *fig (sittlich)* verdorben, verkommen; *fam* ekelhaft, scheußlich, miserabel; **~idity** [pju:'triditi], **~idness** ['pju:tridnis] Fäule, Fäulnis; *fig* (Sitten-)Verderbtheit *f*.

putt [pʌt] *tr itr (Golfball)* putten; **~er** ['-ə] **1.** *(Golf)* Putter, Schläger *m*; **~ing** ['-iŋ] *(Golf)* Putten *n*; *~~-green* Grün *n*; *~~-hole* (Golf-)Loch *n*.

puttee ['pʌti] (Reit-, Leder-, Wickel-) Gamasche *f*.

putter ['pʌtə] **2.** *Am itr* geschäftig tun; (herum)trödeln (*over* mit); *tr* verbummeln, vertrödeln.

putty ['pʌti] *s* (Öl-, Harz-, Leim-Gummi-)Kitt *m*; *tr (to ~ up)* (ver-)kitten; **~-knife** Spa(ch)tel *m*.

puzzle ['pʌzl] *tr* durchea.bringen, verwirren, in Verlegenheit bringen; konfus, verwirrt, verlegen machen; *itr* durchea., verwirrt, konfus, perplex, bestürzt, verlegen, in Verlegenheit sein; sich den Kopf zerbrechen (*about, over* über); knobeln (*over* an); *s* Verwirrung, Konfusion, Verlegenheit; schwierige, knifflige Frage *f*, schwierige(s) Problem; Rätsel; Geduldsspiel *n*; *to ~ out* austüfteln, -sinnen, *fam* -klamüsern, -knobeln; *(Schrift)* entziffern; *(Problem)* lösen; *to ~ over* sich den Kopf zerbrechen über, *fam* herumknobeln an; *to ~ o.'s brains* sich den Kopf zerbrechen (*over* über); *it ~s me* es läßt mir keine Ruhe, will mir nicht aus dem Kopf; **~-headed** ['-hedid] *a*: *to be ~~* unklare Vorstellungen haben, nicht klar denken (können); **~-lock** Vexier-, Kombinationsschloß *n*; **~ment** ['-mənt] Verwirrung, Konfusion, Bestürzung *f*; **~r** ['-ə] schwierige(s) Problem *n*.

*

pyelitis [paii'laitis] Nierenbeckenentzündung *f*.

pygm|(a)en [pig'mi:ən] zwergenhaft; **~y** ['pigmi] *s* Pygmäe; Zwerg *m a. fig*; *a* zwergenhaft; unbedeutend, belanglos.

pyjamas, *Am* **pajamas** [pə'dʒɑ:məz] *pl* Schlafanzug, Pyjama *m*.

pylon ['pailən] *arch* Eingangstor *n*; *tech* Standpfeiler, Pylon; (Licht-, Leitungs-)Mast *m*; *aero* Wendemarke *f*.

pylorus [pai'lɔ:rəs] *pl -ri anat* Pförtner *m*.

pyo|genesis [paiou'dʒenisis], **~sis** [-'ousis] Vereiterung *f*; **~rrh(o)ea** [paiə'riə] Eiterfluß *m*; Paradentose *f*.

pyramid ['pirəmid] *math min arch bot* Pyramide *f*; **~al** [pi'ræmidl] pyramidal, pyramidenförmig.

pyre ['paiə] Scheiterhaufen *m*.

Pyren|ean [pirə'ni:ən] pyrenäisch; *the* **~ees** [-'ni:z] *pl* die Pyrenäen *pl*.

pyretic [pai'retik] *a* Fieber-; *s* Fiebermittel *n*.

pyrex ['paireks] *Am (Warenzeichen) Art (feuerfestes)* Jenaer Glas *n*; **~ia** [-'reksiə] Fieberanfall, -zustand *m*.

pyrites [pai'raiti:z] *min* Pyrit, Schwefel-, Eisenkies *m*.

pyro ['paiəro(u)] *in Zssgen* Feuer-, Brand-; Wärme-; **~graphy** [pai'rɔgrəfi] Brandmalerei *f*; **~ligneous** ['paiərə'ligniəs] *a*: *~~ acid* Holzessig *m*; **~mania** [paiəro(u)'meinjə] *(krankhafter)* Brandstiftungstrieb *m*; **~meter** [pai'rɔmitə] Pyrometer *n*, Hitzemesser *m*; **~pe** [pai'roup] *min* böhmische(r) Granat *m*; **~technic** [paiəro(u)'teknik] *a* pyrotechnisch; Feuerwerks-; *fig* blendend; *s pl mit sing* Feuerwerkerei *f*; *(~~ display)* Feuerwerk *n a. fig*; *fig* Glanz-, Prachtentfaltung *f*; **~technist** [-'teknist] Feuerwerker *m*; **~xylin(e)** [pai'rɔksilin] Kollodiumwolle *f*.

Pyrrhic ['pirik]: *~* **victory** Pyrrhussieg *m*.

Pythagorean [paiθægə'ri:ən] *a* pythogoreisch; *s* Pythagoreer *m*.

python ['paiθən] Python-, *allg* Riesenschlange *f*; **~ess** ['-is] Wahrsagerin *f*.

pyx [piks] *rel* Monstranz *f*; Münzbehälter *m (der brit. Münze)*; **~idium** [-'sidiəm] *pl -ia* [-iə] *bot* Deckelkapsel *f*; *~ie* ['-i] *bot* Blühende(s) Moos *n*; *~is* ['-is] (Juwelen-)Kästchen *n*.

Q

Q [kju:] *pl ~'s* Q, q *n*; **~-boat, -ship** U-Boot-Falle *f*.

quack [kwæk] **1.** *itr (Ente)* quaken *a. fig*; *s* Gequake *n a. fig*; **2.** *s* Quacksalber, Scharlatan, Kurpfuscher; *allg* Schaumschläger *m*; *a* marktschreierisch, großsprecherisch, angeberisch; quacksalberisch; Schwindel-; *~* **doctor** Kurpfuscher *m*; **~ery** ['-əri] Quacksalberei, Kurpfuscherei; Marktschreierei, Schaumschlägerei *f*; Schwindel *m*; *~* **medicine** Wundermittel *n*.

quad [kwɔd] *fam (Schule)* Viereck *n*; *fam* Vierling; *Br sl* Knast *m*, Gefängnis; *typ* Quadrat *n*.

quadr|agenarian [kwɔdrədʒi'nɛəriən] *a* vierzigjährig; *s* Vierzigjährige(r *m*) *f*; **Q~agesima** [kwɔdrə'dʒesimə *(~~ Sunday)* Invokavit *m (1. Fastensonntag)*; **~angle** ['kwɔdræŋgl] Viereck *n*; (viereckiger) (*bes.* Schul-, Gefängnis-)Hof; Baublock *m (um e-n Hof)*; **~angular** [kwɔ'dræŋgjulə] viereckig; **~ant** ['kwɔdrənt] *math astr mar* Quadrant; Viertelkreis *m*; **~at** ['kwɔdræt] *typ* Quadrat *n*; **~ate** ['-it] *a* quadratisch; rechteckig; *s* Quadrat; Rechteck *n*; [kwɔ'dreit] *tr* passend machen (*to* zu), anpassen (*to* an); *itr* passen (*with* zu); übereinstimmen (*with* mit); **~atic** [kwə'drætik] *a* quadratisch; *s* quadratische Gleichung *f*; **~ature** ['kwɔdrətʃə] Quadratur *f a. astr*; **~ennial** [kwɔ'dreniəl] vierjährig; alle vier Jahre stattfindend; **~ilateral** [kwɔdri'lætərəl] *a* vierseitig; *s* Viereck *n*; **~ille** [kwə'dril] Quadrille *f (Tanz)*; **~illion** [kwɔ'driljən] *Br* Quadrillion, *Am* Billiarde *f*; **~ipartite** [kwɔdri'pɑ:tait] vierteilig; *pol (Verhandlung, Vertrag)* vierseitig; *~~ treaty* Viermächteabkommen *n*; **~oon** [kwɔ'dru:n] Viertelneger(in *f*) *m*; **~uped** ['kwɔdruped] *zoo* Vierfüß(l)er *m*; **~uple** ['kwɔdrupl] *a* vierfach; viermal so groß (*to* wie); Vierer-; *s* Vierfache(s) *n*; *tr itr* (sich) vervierfachen; **~uplet** ['kwɔdruplit, -et] Vierling *m*; **~uplicate** [kwɔ'dru:plikit] *a* vierfach; *s*: *in ~~* in vierfacher Ausfertigung; *tr* [-eit] *tr* vervierfachen; vierfach ausfertigen.

quaff [kwɑ:f, kwɔ(:)f] *itr tr* in langen Zügen, begierig trinken; *tr (to ~ off)* hinunterstürzen.

quag [kwæg], *meist* **~mire** ['-maiə] Sumpf(boden), Morast *m*, Moor *n*; *fig (~mire)* Klemme, Patsche *f*; **~gy** ['-i] sumpfig, morastig, moorig; weich, schlaff, nachgiebig.

quail [kweil] **1.** *itr* (ver)zagen; *(Herz)* erzittern; zaghaft, ängstlich sein; zurückschrecken (*to, before* vor); **2.** *orn* Wachtel *f*; *Am sl* Mädchen *n*.

quaint [kweint] altmodisch; sonderbar, seltsam, eigenartig; launisch; **~ness** ['-nis] Seltsamkeit, Absonderlichkeit *f*; *das* Altmodische.

quake [kweik] *itr* (er)beben, schwanken; zittern (*with cold, fear* vor Kälte, Angst); *s* Zittern, Beben; *(earth~)* Erdbeben *n*.

Quaker ['kweikə] *rel* Quäker *m*; **~dom** ['-dəm], **~ism** ['-rizm] Quäkertum *n*; **~ess** ['-ris] Quäkerin *f*.

qual|ifiable ['kwɔlifaiəbl] qualifizierbar; **~ification** [kwɔlifi'keiʃən] genaue Beschreibung *f*, genaue Angaben *f pl*; Befähigung, Eignung, Qualifizierung, Qualifikation (*for an office, for a profession* für ein Amt, für e-n Beruf); Berechtigung *f*; gestellte Anforderungen *f pl*; erforderliche, notwendige Voraussetzung *f*, Erfordernis *n*, (Vor-)Bedingung (*of, for* für); Modifikation, Einschränkung *f*, Vorbehalt *m*, Klausel *f*; *subject to ~~* Änderungen vorbehalten; *without ~~* vorbehaltlos; *~~ test* Eignungsprüfung *f*; **~ified** ['kwɔlifaid] *a* befähigt, geeignet; qualifiziert, kompetent, zuständig (*for* für); *(Mehrheit)* qualifiziert; *(Diebstahl)* schwer; berechtigt, ermächtigt (*for* zu); amtlich geprüft; eingeschränkt, bedingt, mit Vorbehalt, verklausuliert; *in a ~~ sense* mit Einschränkung(en), eingeschränkt, beschränkt; *to be ~~ to vote* stimmberechtigt sein; *duly, legally ~~ (Arzt)* approbiert; *fully ~~* vollberechtigt; *~~ approval* bedingte Zustimmung *f*; *~~ to inherit* erbberechtigt; *~~ seaman* Maat *m*; *~~ voter* Wahlberechtigte(r) *m*; *~~ worker* Facharbeiter *m*; **~ify** ['-ifai] *tr* genau beschreiben, bestimmen; genaue, nähere Angaben machen über; befähigen, geeignet machen, ausbilden (*for* für); berechtigen (*for* zu); modifizieren, be-, einschränken; mäßigen, abschwächen; *(Getränk)* verdünnen; *(Urteil)* mildern; *itr* die erforderliche Befähigung erwerben, besitzen *od* nachweisen; sich eignen (*for* für); die Bestimmungen erfüllen (*for* für); sich qualifizieren (*for* für); *to ~ as a doctor* die Approbation erwerben; **~ifying** ['-ifaiiŋ] *a* berichtigend; *~~ certificate*

Befähigungsnachweis *m*; ~~ *examination* Eignungs-, Aufnahmeprüfung *f*; ~~ *period* Probezeit *f*; ~~ *round (sport)* Ausscheidungsspiele *n pl*; **~itative** ['-iteitiv, -tə-] qualitativ; **~ity** ['kwɔliti] Beschaffenheit, Eigenschaft, Eigenart *f*, Charakter *m*, Wesen *n*, Natur; (hohe) Qualität, Güte, Besonderheit *f*, (besonderer) Wert *m*; *mus* Klangfarbe; hohe soziale Stellung; *com* Sorte, Marke *f*; *in the* ~~ *of* als; *of the best* ~~ erste Wahl; beste Qualität; ~~ *area* Güteklasse *f*; ~~ *inspection* Güte-, Abnahmeprüfung *f*; ~~ *label, mark* Gütezeichen *n*; ~~ *product* Qualitätserzeugnis *n*.

qualm [kwɔ:m, kwɑ:m] (Krankheits-, Schwäche-)Anfall, Anfall *m* von Übelkeit; *fig* (plötzliches) unangenehme(s) Gefühl *n*, böse Ahnung *f*, (plötzlicher) Zweifel *m*; *pl* Gewissensbisse *m pl*; **~ish** ['-iʃ] unwohl; Schwäche-; Übelkeit erregend.

quandary ['kwɔndəri] Ungewißheit; unangenehme, schwierige Lage; Verlegenheit *f*; *in a* ~ in Verlegenheit, in der Klemme.

quant|itative ['kwɔntitətiv, -tei-] quantitativ, mengen-, zahlenmäßig; meß-, zählbar; *gram* Quantitäts-; ~~ *analysis (chem)* Maßanalyse *f*; **~ity** ['kwɔntiti] Quantität, Menge, Größe, Zahl *f*, Umfang *m*; Masse *f*; Quantum *n*; große Menge *od* Zahl; meßbare Größe; *philos math mus gram* Quantität *f*; *in* ~~ in großen Mengen; *to produce in large ~ities* in großen Mengen herstellen; *unknown* ~~ *(math)* Unbekannte *f*; ~~ *discount* Mengenrabatt *m*; ~~ *production* Massenproduktion *f*; ~~*surveyor (Br)* Bausachverständige(r) *m*; **~um** [-əm] *pl -a* [-ə] Quantum *n*, Menge *f*, Betrag *m*; bestimmte Menge *od* Größe *f*; *phys* Energiequantum *n*; ~~ *mechanics (pl)* Quantenmechanik *f*; ~~ *theory* Quantentheorie *f*.

*

quarantine ['kwɔrənti:n] *s med* Quarantäne *f*; *tr (to put under* ~*)* unter Quarantäne stellen; *fig* (politisch, wirtschaftlich) isolieren.

quarrel ['kwɔrəl] **1.** *s* Streit *m*, Meinungsverschiedenheit, Ausea.setzung *f* (*against, with* mit); Zank *m*, Gezänk *n*; Streit-, strittige(r) Punkt *m*; Entfremdung *f*, Bruch *m* der Freundschaft; *itr* streiten, zanken, sich ausea.setzen (*with* mit; *about* um, über; *for* wegen); etw auszusetzen haben (*with* an); sich beklagen (*with* über); brechen (*with s.o.* mit jdm); in Widerspruch stehen (*with* zu); *to fight s.o.'s ~s for s.o.* sich für jdn einsetzen, für jdn eintreten; *to seek, to pick a* ~ *with s.o.* mit jdm Streit anfangen, Händel suchen; *to take up, to espouse s.o.'s* ~ jds Partei ergreifen; *to* ~ *with o.'s bread and butter (fig)* sich ins eigene Fleisch schneiden; *I have no* ~ *with him* ich habe nichts gegen ihn; **~(l)er** ['-ə] Zänker, streitsüchtige(r) Mensch *m*; **~some** ['-səm] streit-, zanksüchtig, zänkisch; **2.** *s* rautenförmige kleine Glasscheibe *f*; Pfeil, Bolzen; Steinmetzmeißel; Glaserdiamant *m*.

quarry ['kwɔri] **1.** *s* Steinbruch *m*; *fig* Fundgrube, (Informations-)Quelle *f*; *tr (to* ~ *out)* (aus e-m Steinbruch) gewinnen, hauen, brechen; *fig* mühsam suchen, stöbern nach; durchstöbern, -wühlen; *itr* Steine hauen *od* brechen; *fig* stöbern, wühlen, forschen (*in* in); **~man** [-mən], **quarrier** ['kwɔriə] Steinbrucharbeiter *m*; **~-stone** Bruchstein *m*; **2.** verfolgte(s) Wild *n*, Jagdbeute *f*; *fig* Opfer, verfolgte(s) Ziel *n*.

quart [kwɔ:t] Quart *n*, Viertelgallone *(Br 1,14 l, Am 0,95 l)*; *mus* Quart(e); [kɑ:t] *(Fechtkunst, Karten)* Quart *f*; **~an** ['-n] *a u. s* viertägig(es Fieber *n*).

quarter ['kwɔ:tə] *s* Viertel *n (a. e-s Schlachttieres)*; Viertelzentner *m (28 engl. bzw. 25 amerik. Pfund)*; 8 Scheffel *m pl (Vierteltonne = 291 l)*; Viertelmeile *(402,34 m)*; Spanne, Viertelelle *f (22,8 cm)*; Vierteljahr, Quartal; *(Uhr)* Viertel *n*, volle Viertelstunde *f*; *Am (~ dollar)* Vierteldollar *m*, 25 Cent (-stück *n*); Himmelsrichtung; Weltgegend *f*; (Mond-)Viertel; (Stadt-) Viertel *n*, Stadtteil *m*; *mar* Achterschiff *n*; *mil* Gnade, Schonung *f*; Wappenfeld *n*; *fig* Quelle *f*; Ort *m*, Stelle; *pl* Wohnung, Unterkunft, Bleibe *f*, Nachtquartier; *mil* Quartier *n*, Ortsunterkunft *f*; *(Personen-)* Kreise *m pl*; *tr* in vier (gleiche) Teile teilen, vierteln; *(Verbrecher)* vierteilen; ein Quartier beschaffen *od* besorgen für; einquartieren, unterbringen; *to* ~ *o.s. upon s.o.* sich bei jdm einquartieren; *itr (to be ~ed)* im Quartier liegen, untergebracht sein, wohnen (*at, with* bei); *at a* ~ *to (Am of) three* um Viertel vor drei; *at close ~s* dicht zs.(gedrängt); dicht dabei, nahebei; *from all ~s, from every* ~ von allen Seiten, von überallher; *from another* ~ von anderer Seite, anderswoher; *from official ~s* von amtlicher Seite; *from a reliable* ~ aus zuverlässiger Quelle; *in close ~s* (be)eng(t) *adv*; *in this* ~ in dieser Gegend, hier(zulande); *not a* ~ nicht annähernd; *to ask for* ~, *to cry* ~ um Gnade bitten; *to come to close ~s* handgemein werden; *to change o.'s ~s* umziehen, das Quartier, *fam* die Tapeten wechseln; *to find no* ~ keine Gnade finden (*with* bei); *to give* ~ Gnade, Schonung gewähren; *to receive* ~ Gnade finden; *to take up o.'s ~s at, with s.o.* bei jdm Unterkunft, e-e Bleibe finden; sich bei jdm einquartieren; *collective ~s (pl)* Sammelunterkunft *f*; *fore, hind* ~ *(Schlachttier)* Vorder-, Hinterviertel *n*; *manufacturing* ~ Fabrikviertel *n*; *poor* ~ Armenviertel *n*; *residential* ~ Wohnviertel *n*; *winter ~s (pl)* Winterquartier *n*; ~ *of the century* Vierteljahrhundert *n*; ~ *of an hour* Viertelstunde *f*; *a bad* ~~ ein unangenehmes Erlebnis; *~s in kind* freie Unterkunft; **~age** ['-ridʒ] Vierteljahrszahlung, -miete *f*; *mil* Quartier *n*; Einquartierung *f*; Quartiergeld *n*; **~back** *Am s (Fußball)* Verteidiger *m*; *tr* leiten, dirigieren; **~-binding** Halbleder-, Halbfranzband *m*; **~-day** Quartals-, Mietzahltag *m*; **~-deck** *mar* Achterdeck *n*; *fig mar* Offiziere *m pl*; **~ed** ['-d] *a* in vier Teile geteilt, vierteilig; untergebracht; ~~ *in barracks* kaserniert; **~-hour** Viertelstunde *f*; **~ing** ['-riŋ] Teilung in vier Teile; Quartierbeschaffung, *mil* Einquartierung *f*; **~ly** ['-li] *a* vierteljährlich, Vierteljahrs-; ein Viertel ausmachend; *adv* alle Vierteljahre; vierteljährlich; *s* Vierteljahrsschrift *f*; **~master** *mil* Quartiermeister, Verpflegungsoffizier; *mar* Steuerer *m*; *Q~~ Corps (Am mil)* Versorgungstruppen *f pl*; *Q~ General* Generalquartiermeister *m*; **~-note, -tone** *mus* Viertelnote *f*; ~ **section** *Am* Viertelquadratmeile *f (etwa 65 Hektar)*; **~-sessions** *pl* vierteljährlich zs.-tretende(s) Friedensgericht *n*.

quart|ern ['kwɔ:tən] Viertel *n*; Viertelpinte *f (Br 0,142 l, Am 0,118 l)*; Viertelstein *m (= 1,588 kg)*; *(~~ loaf)* Vierpfundbrot *n*; **~et(te)** [kwɔ:'tet] *mus* Quartett *n*; **~o** ['kwɔ:tou] *pl -os* Quartformat *n*, -band *m*.

quartz [kwɔ:ts] *min* Quarz *m*; **~-lamp** Quarzlampe *f*.

quash [kwɔʃ] *tr* zerdrücken, -quetschen, -malmen; *fig* unterdrücken; *(Aufstand)* niederwerfen; *jur* kassieren, aufheben; *(Verfahren)* niederschlagen.

quasi ['kwɑ:zi(:)] *adv* gewissermaßen, gleichsam, *fam* quasi; beinahe, fast; *a*: *a* ~ . . . e-e Art . . .; *in Zssgen* Schein-, Halb-; **~-official** halbamtlich.

quaternary [kwə'tə:nəri] *a* aus vier bestehend; durch vier teilbar; quaternär *a. chem*; Vier(er)-; *geol* Quartär-; *s* Vierzahl, Vierergruppe *f*; *the Q~ (Period) (geol)* das Quartär.

quatrain ['kwɔtrein] Vierzeiler *m*.

quaver ['kweivə] *itr* zittern; *(Stimme)* tremolieren; *mus* trillern *a. tr*; *tr* zitternd hervorbringen *od* sagen; *s mus* Tremolo *n*; *Br* Achtelnote *f*.

quay [ki:] (Schiffs-)Landeplatz, Kai; Ufer-, Hafendamm *m*; Uferstraße *f*; *alongside the* ~ längseits Kai; **~age** ['-idʒ] Kaigeld *n*, -gebühr *f*.

queas|iness ['kwi:zinis] Ek(e)ligkeit; Übelkeit; große Empfindlichkeit *f*; **~y** ['kwi:zi] ek(e)lig, ekelerregend; unwohl; empfindlich.

queen [kwi:n] *s* Königin *a. fig ent*; *(Schach, Kartenspiel)* Dame; *Am sl* Pfundsfrau *f*; *tr* zur Königin, *(Schach)* zur Dame machen; *(Bienen)* beweiseln; *itr* Königin sein, als Königin regieren; *to* ~ *it* die große Dame, die führende Rolle spielen; ~ *of hearts (Karten)* Herzkönigin; *allg* schöne Frau *f*; *Q~ of Heaven* Himmelskönigin *f*; ~ *of the May* Maienkönigin *f*; **~-bee** Bienenkönigin *f*; **~-cake** kleine(r) Rosinenkuchen *m*; ~ **dowager** Königinwitwe *f*; **~like** ['-laik], **~ly** ['-li] königlich; **Q~ Mab** Feenkönigin *f*; ~ **mother** Königinmutter *f*; **~'s metal** Weiß-, Lagermetall *n*; **~'s ware** kremfarbene(s) Wedgwood *n (Steingut)*.

queer [kwiə] *a* ungewöhnlich, absonderlich, sonderbar, ausgefallen, eigenartig, seltsam, merkwürdig; wunderlich, schrullig, schrullenhaft; *fam* unwohl, von Übelkeit befallen; *fam* anrüchig, verdächtig, nicht astrein; *sl* nachgemacht, unecht; *sl* nicht ganz bei Trost, nicht ganz klar im Kopf; *sl* schwul; *tr sl* versauen, vermasseln; vermiesen; verrückt machen, durchea.bringen; *to* ~ *o.s. (sl)* sich was (Schönes) einbrocken; sich in die Nesseln setzen; *s sl* Blüte *f*, Falschgeld *n*; *sl* Schwule(r) *m*; *to* ~ *s.o.'s pitch* jds Pläne durchkreuzen, jdm e-n Strich durch die Rechnung machen; *to be in Q~ Street* in schlechten Verhältnissen sein; finanziell schlecht dran sein; **~ness** ['-nis] Eigenart, Absonderlichkeit, Seltsamkeit, Merkwürdigkeit, Schrull(enhaft)igkeit *f*.

quell [kwel] *tr lit poet* unterdrücken.

quench [kwentʃ] *tr* (aus)löschen; *(Begeisterung)* abkühlen; *tech* löschen; *(Metall)* abschrecken; *(Durst)* löschen, stillen; befriedigen, beruhigen, dämpfen; *(Rührung)* unterdrücken; *fam* den Mund stopfen (*s.o.* jdm); **~er** ['-ə] *fam* Schluck *m*; **~less** ['-lis] unauslöschlich.

quer|ist ['kwerist] Fragesteller *m*; **~ulous** ['kweruləs] mürrisch, nörgelnd, verdrossen, *fam* mäk(e)lig, meck(e)rig; ~~ *person* Querulant, Nörgler, *fam* Meckerer *m*; **~y** ['kwiəri] *s* Frage(zeichen *n*) *f*; Zweifel *m*; *tr* (be-, aus)fragen; fragen nach, in Frage stellen; bezweifeln, mit e-m Fragezeichen versehen *a. typ.*

quern [kwə:n] Hand-, Pfeffermühle *f*.

quest [kwest] *s* Suche, Jagd (*for, of* nach); abenteuerliche Fahrt; Nachforschung *f*; *itr (Jagd)* e-e Spur verfolgen; *in ~ of* auf der Suche nach.

question ['kwestʃən] *s* Frage *f*; Zweifel *m* (*of* an); Ungewißheit, Unsicherheit; (Streit-)Frage *f*, Problem *n*, Streitpunkt *m*; *jur* Streitsache *f*, -objekt *n*; *parl* Anfrage, Interpellation; Folter *f*; *tr* (aus-, be)fragen, verhören; bezweifeln, in Zweifel ziehen; in Frage stellen; herausfordern; *itr* e-e Frage, Fragen stellen; *beside the ~* nicht zur Debatte stehend; *beyond (all) ~, out of (the) ~* (völlig) außer Frage (stehend), ausgeschlossen; *in ~* fraglich, zur Debatte stehend; betreffend; *without, past ~* ohne Frage, fraglos, ohne Zweifel; *to answer a ~* e-e Frage beantworten; *to ask, to put, to raise a ~* e-e Frage stellen; *to be out of the ~* nicht in Frage kommen; ganz ausgeschlossen sein; *to call for the ~ (parl)* um Abstimmung bitten; Schluß der Debatte verlangen; *to call in ~* in Frage stellen, in Zweifel ziehen; *to come into ~* in Frage kommen; besprochen werden; *fam* aufs Tapet kommen; *to enter into a ~* auf e-e Frage eingehen; *to put the ~ (parl)* e-e Frage zur Abstimmung stellen, die Debatte schließen; *to put to the ~* foltern; *to shoot ~s at s.o. (fam)* jdn mit Fragen bombardieren; *what is the ~?* worum geht es, handelt es sich, *fam* dreht es sich? was steht zur Debatte? *there is no ~ but* es steht außer Zweifel, daß; *~!* zur Sache! *contentious ~* Streitfrage *f*; *cross-~* Gegenfrage *f*; *economic ~* Wirtschaftsproblem *n*; *leading ~* Suggestivfrage *f*; *legal ~* Rechtsfrage *f*; *preliminary, previous ~* Vorfrage *f*; *a sixty-four-dollar ~ (Am fam)* e-e ganz verzwickte Sache; *technical ~* Verfahrensfrage *f*; *~ of confidence* Vertrauensfrage *f*; *~ of guilt* Schuldfrage *f*; *~ of money* Geldfrage *f*; *~ of procedure* Verfahrensfrage *f*; *~ of time* Zeitfrage *f*; **~able** ['-əbl] fraglich, zweifelhaft; fragwürdig, bedenklich, verdächtig; **~ary** ['-nəri] *a* fragend; Frage-; *s* = *~naire*; *~* **box** *(Zeitung)* Briefkasten *m*; **~er** ['-nə] Fragende(r), Fragesteller *m*; **~ing** ['-niŋ] *a* fragend; *s* Befragung *f*; Verhör *n*; **~-mark** Fragezeichen *n*; **~naire** [kwestiə'nɛə, *Am* -tʃə-] Fragebogen *m*; *to fill in a ~~* e-n Fragebogen ausfüllen; *~* **time, period** Fragestunde *f*.

queue [kju:] *s hist* Zopf *m*; *fig* Schlange *f* (*at a ticket window* vor e-m Fahrkartenschalter); *tr (Haar)* in e-n Zopf flechten; *itr (to ~ up)* sich anstellen, e-e Schlange bilden; *to fall in at the end of the ~* sich hinten anstellen; *to form a ~* e-e Schlange bilden; *to stand, to wait in a ~* Schlange stehen, anstehen; *to take o.'s place in a ~* sich anstellen; **~ing** ['-iŋ] Schlange-, Anstehen *n*.

quibbl|e ['kwibl] *s* Wortspiel *n*; Spitzfindigkeit, Wortklauberei; Ausflucht, Ausrede *f*; *itr* Wortspiele gebrauchen; ausweichen(d) antworten, Ausflüchte machen, sich herausreden; **~er** ['-ə] Wortklauber *m*; **~ing** ['-iŋ] spitzfindig.

quick [kwik] *a* schnell, rasch, flink; behende, gewandt, geschickt; aufgeweckt, schlagfertig; munter, lebhaft, quicklebendig; unruhig, ungeduldig; *(~ with child)* (hoch)schwanger; *(Auge, Geruch)* scharf; *(Ohr)* fein; *min* ergiebig; *zoo* lebend; *adv* schnell, rasch; *s* lebende(s) Fleisch *n*, empfindliche (Körper-)Stelle *f*; *the ~ (and the dead) (pl)* die Lebenden (u. die Toten) *pl*; *at a ~ trot* in schnellem Schritt; *to the ~* tief *adv (schmerzen, verletzen)*; zutiefst, in tiefster Seele, im Innersten; bis ins Mark; *~ on the draw (Am)* impulsiv; *to be ~* sich beeilen, *fam* schnell machen (*about* mit); *at doing s.th.* rasch etw tun; *to be ~ of scent* e-e feine, gute Nase haben; *to cut to the ~* tief kränken, *fam* schwer beleidigen; **~-action closure** Schnellverschluß *m*; **~-change artist** Verwandlungskünstler *m*; **~en** ['-ən] *tr* (neu) beleben; auf-, ermuntern; munter, lebendig machen; anregen, an-, aufreizen; entfachen; *(Gang)* beschleunigen; *itr* sich (neu) beleben; wieder lebendig, wieder munter werden; *(Fötus)* sich zu regen beginnen; sich beschleunigen, schneller werden; **~-eyed** *a* scharfäugig; *~* **fire, -firing** *mil* Schnellfeuer *n*; **~-fire gun** Schnellfeuergewehr *n*; **~-freeze** *tr* tiefkühlen; **~-freezing** Tiefkühlung *f*; **~ie** ['-i] *s* ein paar (kurze) Worte *n pl od* Zeilen *f pl*; kurze(r) Schluck; schnelle(r) Happen; schnell, hergestellte(r), billige(r) Film; *com* Ramsch(ware *f*) *m*; **~lime** ungelöschte(r) Kalk *m*; *~* **lunch** *Am* schnelle(s) Mittagessen *n*; *~~ counter* Schnellgaststätte, Imbiß-, Frühstückstube *f*; **~ly** ['-li] *adv* schnell, rasch, geschwind, eilig, in Eile; *to go off ~~* reißenden Absatz finden; *~* **march, ~step, ~time** *mil* Eilmarsch; Schnellschritt *m*; *~ time, march!* Im Gleichschritt, marsch! *~* **match** Zündschnur *f*; **~-motion apparatus** *film* Zeitraffer *m*; **~ness** ['-nis] Schnelligkeit, Fixigkeit, Gewandtheit; Wendigkeit, schnelle Auffassungsgabe; Lebendigkeit, Lebhaftigkeit, Munterkeit; Hitzigkeit; Schärfe, Feinheit *f*; **~-release** *aero* Schnellablaß *m*; *~~ cord* Reißschnur *f*; *~~ fastener* Schnellverschluß *m*; *~~ hook* Sicherungshaken *m*; **~-repair service** Schnellreparaturdienst *m*, -werkstatt *f*; **~sand** Treib-, Trieb-, Flugsand *m*; **~-service restaurant** *Am* Schnellgaststätte *f*; **~set** Setzling; Heckenstrauch; Weißdorn *m*; *(~~ hedge)* (lebende) Hecke *f*; **~sighted** *a* mit scharfen Augen; **~silver** Quecksilber *n a. fig*; **~step** = *~ march*; Quickstep *m (Tanz)*; **~-tempered** *a* leicht erregbar, reizbar; jähzornig; **~-witted** *a* schlagfertig, *fam* nicht auf den Mund gefallen.

quid [kwid] **1.** Priem *m (Kautabak)*; **2.** *sl* Pfund *n (Sterling)*.

quiddity ['kwiditi] Wesen *n*, Kern *m*; *fig* Wortklauberei, Spitzfindigkeit *f*.

quidnunc ['kwidnʌŋk] Neuigkeitskrämer *m*; Klatschmaul *n*; Bierbankpolitiker *m*.

quid pro quo ['kwid pro(u) 'kwou] *pl -os* Gegenleistung *f*, Entgelt *n*, Lohn *m*; *to return a ~* heimzahlen.

quiescen|ce, -cy [kwai'esns(i)] Ruhe, Stille; Reglosigkeit, Untätigkeit *f*; **~t** [-t] ruhig, still; *gram* stumm; reglos; untätig, in Ruhe.

quiet ['kwaiət] *a* ruhig, still; laut-, geräuschlos; reg(ungs)-, bewegungslos; friedlich; *(Genuß)* ungestört; schlicht, einfach; unauffällig, unaufdringlich, zurückhaltend; versteckt, geheim; *com* lustlos, flau; *s* Ruhe, Stille; Laut-, Geräuschlosigkeit; Untätigkeit; Seelenruhe *f*, Frieden *m*; *tr* beruhigen; besänftigen, befriedigen; *itr (to ~ down)* ruhig(er) werden, sich beruhigen; *(Aufregung)* sich legen; *on the ~, (sl) on the q.t.* ['kju:'ti:] (ganz) heimlich; insgeheim; *fam* klammheimlich; *to keep ~ (tr)* geheimhalten; *itr* schweigen; **~en** ['-n] *tr itr* (sich) beruhigen; **~ism** ['-izm] *rel* Quietismus *m*; **~ist** ['-ist] *s* Quietist *m*; *a* quietistisch; **~ness** ['-nis], **~ude** ['kwaiitju:d] (*bes.* innere) Ruhe, Seelenruhe, Unbewegtheit, Ausgeglichenheit *f*, Gleichmut *m*.

quietus [kwai'i:təs] (Schluß-)Quittung *f*; Tod(esstoß); Schluß *m*, Ende *n*; *to get o.'s ~* den Rest kriegen *fig*; *to give s.o. his ~* jdm den Rest geben.

quiff [kwif] Stirnlocke *f*; *sl* Dreh *m*.

quill [kwil] *s* Federkiel *m*; *(~-feather)* Kielfeder *f*; Stachel *(d. Igels od Stachelschweins)*; Federkiel *m*; *mus* Plektron *n*; Rohrpfeife; *tech* Hülse; (Garn-)Spule; *(Zimt)* Stange *f*; *(Angel)* Schwimmer *m*; *tr* in bauschige Falten legen, fälteln; aufspulen; **~-driver** Federfuchser, Schreiberling *m*; **~ing** ['-iŋ] Rüsche *f*.

quilt [kwilt] *s* Steppdecke *f*; Steppstich *m*; *pl* Stepp- u. Bettdecken *f pl*; *tr* steppen; wattieren; einnähen; auspolstern; ausstopfen; *fig* zs.stoppeln; **~ing** ['-iŋ] Steppen; Steppmaterial *n*, -arbeit *f*; Pikee *m* od *n*; Wattierung *f*; *~~ bee (Am)* Handarbeitskränzchen *n*.

quince [kwins] *bot* Quitte *f*.

quinine [kwi'ni:n, *Am* 'kwainain] Chinin *n*.

quinqu|agenarian [kwiŋkwədʒi'nɛəriən] *a* fünfzigjährig; *s* Fünfzigjährige(r) *m*; **Q~agesima** [kwiŋkwə'dʒesimə] Quinquagesima *f (7. Sonntag vor Ostern)*; **~ennial** [kwiŋ'kweniəl] fünfjährig; alle fünf Jahre stattfindend; **~ennium** [-'kweniəm] *pl -ia* [-iə] Jahrfünft *n*.

quins [kwinz] *pl fam* Fünflinge *m pl*.

quinsy ['kwinzi] Angina, Mandelentzündung *f*.

quint [kwint] *mus* Quint(e) *f*; *fam* Fünfling *m*; **~al** ['-l] Doppelzentner *m (Br 112 Pfund, Am 100 Pfund)*; **~essence** [kwin'tesns] Quintessenz *f*; *fig* Kern *m*, Hauptsache *f*, Grundgedanke *m*; **~et(te)** [-'tet] *mus* Quintett *n*; **~uple** ['kwintjupl] *a* fünffach; *s* Fünffache(s) *n*; *tr itr* (sich) verfünffachen; **~uplets** ['kwintjuplits] *pl* Fünflinge *m pl*.

quip [kwip] *s* geistreiche, witzige, spöttische, bissige Bemerkung; Stichelei *f*; *itr* spotten, sticheln.

quire ['kwaiə] *typ* Buch *n (= 24 od 25 Bogen)*; Lage *f*.

quirk [kwə:k] Finte *f*, Kniff *m*, Ausflucht, -rede; geschickte Wendung *(in der Rede)*; Anwandlung *f*, Einfall *m*; Eigenart, -heit *f*; Schnörkel *m a. fig*; *arch* Hohlkehle *f*; *aero* Anfänger, Flugschüler *m*.

quirt [kwə:t] *Am Art* Reitpeitsche *f*.

quisling ['kwizliŋ] Kollaborateur, Quisling; *fam* Verräter *m*.

quit [kwit] *tr (Stellung)* aufgeben; *(Amt)* niederlegen; *(Arbeit)* einstellen; aus den Händen, weggeben; endgültig verlassen; räumen; *(Schuld)* streichen; *fam* aufhören mit, unterbrechen (*doing s.th.* etw zu tun); *poet* lohnen, vergelten; *itr* weg-, fortgehen; aufhören; *fam* s-e Stelle aufgeben, den Dienst quittieren; *Am* schlapp machen; *to ~ o.s.* sich frei machen (*of* von); *a* quitt, erledigt; frei, los (*of* von); *(~ of charges)* spesenfrei; *to ~ hold of* loslassen; *to ~ the service* den Abschied nehmen; *notice to ~* Kündigung *f*; *to give notice to* ~ kündigen; ~ *it!* Schluß damit! ~**claim** *s* Verzicht (-leistung, -erklärung *f*) *m*; *itr* verzichten, Verzicht leisten; ~**s** [-s] *a*: *to be* ~~ quitt sein (*with* mit); *to cry* ~~ erklären, daß man quitt ist; ~**tance** ['-əns] Streichung (e-r Schuld); *com* Quittung *f*; *poet* Lohn *m*, Vergeltung *f*; ~**ter** ['-ə] *Am fam* Schlappschwanz, Waschlappen *m*; ~**ting** ['-iŋ]: ~~ *time (Am)* Geschäftsschluß *m*.

quite [kwait] *adv* ganz, völlig, vollständig; durchaus; sehr wohl; *(~ so)* wirklich, tatsächlich, allerdings; ganz recht! *fam* ziemlich, recht; sehr; ~ *a few* nicht wenig(e); eine ziemliche Anzahl.

quiver ['kwivə] **1.** *itr* zittern, beben (*with* vor); *(Augenlider)* flattern; *s* Zittern, Flattern *n*; *to ~ its wings* mit den Flügeln schlagen; **2.** Köcher (-voll) *m*.

quixotic [kwik'sɔtik] überspannt; welt-, wirklichkeitsfremd.

quiz [kwiz] *pl -zes* ['-iz] *s obs* Scherz, Ulk *m*; (Reihe *f* von) Fragen *f pl*; *(unterhaltsame)* Befragung, Prüfung *f*, Frage-und-Antwort-Spiel, Quiz *n*; *Am (Schule)* Prüfung(sarbeit), Klassenarbeit *f*, Examen *n*; *tr obs* verspotten, verulken, aufziehen, hänseln, necken; frech angucken, -schauen; *(a. Schule)* ab-, befragen, prüfen; ~**master** Frage(n)steller, Prüfende(r), Quizmaster *m*; ~ **program(me)** *radio video* Quizsendung *f*; ~**zical** ['-ikəl] komisch, ulkig; eigenartig, sonderbar; spottlustig.

*

quod [kwɔd] *s Br sl* Knast *m*, Gefängnis *n*; *tr sl* einlochen, -sperren; *in* ~ hinter schwedischen Gardinen; *out of* ~ auf freiem Fuß.

quoin [k(w)ɔin] *s arch* Ecke *f*; Eckstein; *typ* Keil *m*; *tr* mit Ecken versehen; verkeilen.

quoit [kɔit, *Am* kwɔit] *sport* Wurfscheibe *f*, -ring *m*; *pl mit sing* Wurfscheibenspiel *n*.

Quonset hut ['kwɔnsit 'hʌt] Nissenhütte *f*.

quorum ['kwɔ:rəm] *parl* Zahl *f* der zur Beschlußfähigkeit erforderlichen Abgeordneten; *to constitute, to form, to have a* ~ beschlußfähig sein; *to lack a* ~ beschlußunfähig sein; *there is a (no)* ~ die Versammlung ist beschluß-(un)fähig.

quota ['kwoutə] Anteil *m*, Quote *f*, Kontingent; (Lieferungs-)Soll *n*; Beitrag *m*; *to fix, to establish* ~*s* kontingentieren (*for s.th.* etw); *export, import* ~ Ausfuhr-, Einfuhrkontingent *n*; *fixing of* ~*s* Kontingentierung *f*; *immigration* ~ Einwanderungsquote *f*; ~ **goods** *pl* kontingentierte Waren *f pl*.

quot|able ['kwoutəbl] zitierbar, anführbar; *com* notierbar; ~**ation** [kwo(u)'teiʃən] Zitieren *n*, Anführung; angeführte Stelle *f*, Zitat *n*; Beleg *m*; Börsen-, Kurs-, Preisnotierung *f*; Kurs; Kostenanschlag *m*; *pl* gehandelte Kurse *m pl*; *asked, bid* ~~*s (pl)* Brief-, Geldkurs *m*; *closing* ~~ *(com)* Schlußnotierung *f*; *familiar* ~~ geflügelte(s) Wort *n*; *market* ~~, ~~ *of the day* Tagesnotierung *f*, Marktkurs *m*; *price* ~~ Preisangabe *f*; ~~ *board* Kurstafel *f*; ~~ *marks (pl)* Anführungszeichen, *fam* Gänsefüßchen *n pl*; ~**e** [kwout] *tr* anführen, zitieren (*from* aus); angeben; *com* notieren (*at* mit); *(Preis)* feststellen, nennen, veranschlagen; *typ* in Anführungszeichen setzen; *s fam* Zitat, *fam* Gänsefüßchen, Anführungszeichen *n*; ~~ ich zitiere *(in e-r Rede)*; ~*ed list* amtliche(r) Kurszettel *m*; ~*ed price* Preisangebot *n*; *(officially)* ~*ed shares (pl)* (amtlich) notierte Aktien *f pl*; ~*ed value* Kurswert *m*.

quoth [kwouθ] *obs (mit nachfolgendem Subjekt)* sagte.

quotidian [kwɔ'tidiən] *a* täglich; *s med* Quotidianfieber *n*.

quotient ['kwouʃənt] *math* Quotient *m*.

R

R [ɑ:] *pl* ~*'s* R, r *n*; *the three* ~*'s* Lesen, Schreiben u. Rechnen *n*.

rabbet ['ræbit] *s tech* Fuge, Nute *f*, Falz *m*; *tr* nuten, falzen; ein-, zs.-fügen; ~**-plane** Falzhobel *m*.

rabbi ['ræbai] Rabbi(ner) *m*.

rabbit ['ræbit] Kaninchen *n*; *Am* Hase *m*; *(Welsh ~)* Röstbrot *n* mit Schmelzkäse; *sl sport* Niete, Flasche *f*; *Am sl* grüne(r) Salat *m*; *buck-*~ Rammler *m*; geröstete(s) Käsebrot mit Ei; ~**-burrow, -hole** Kaninchenbau *m*; ~ **fever** *med* Tularämie, Hasenpest *f*; ~**-hutch** Kaninchenstall *m*; ~ **punch** *(Boxen)* Nackenschlag *m*; ~**-warren** (offenes) Kaninchengehege *n*; *fig* überfüllte(r) Raum *m*; ~**y** ['-i] Kaninchen-; *(Mensch)fam* mickerig; wertlos.

rabble ['ræbl] **1.** *s* Pöbelhaufen *m*, Volksmenge *f*; *the* ~ der Mob; ~ **rouser** *Am* Volksverhetzer, Demagoge *m*; **2.** *s metal* Kratze, Rührstange *f*; *tr (Metall)* umrühren.

rabid ['ræbid] toll, rasend, wütend; *(Haß)* wild; *(Durst)* brennend; fanatisch, übereifrig; *(Hund)* tollwütig; ~**ness** ['ræbidnis] Tollheit, Wut, Raserei *f*; Fanatismus, Übereifer *m*.

rabies ['reibii:z, 'ræ-](Hunds-)Tollwut *f*.

*

rac(c)oon [rə'ku:n] Waschbär *m*.

rac|e [reis] **1.** *s* (Wett-)Rennen *n*, Wettlauf *a. fig*, Wettflug; Wettbewerb, Kampf *m* (*for* um); *fig* Jagd *f*; Lauf *m*, ständige Bewegung; *(Wasser)* Strömung *f*; *Am (~way)* (Wasser-) Rinne *f*, Kanal; *(mill-~)* Mühlgraben *m*; *tech* Gleit-, Lauf-, Führungsrinne *f*; Laufring; *aero* Nachstrom *m*; *pl* (Pferde-)Rennen *n*; *itr* an e-m (Wett-)Rennen teilnehmen; um die Wette laufen (*against, with* mit); rennen, jagen, rasen; Rennpferde halten; *tech* durchgehen; *tr* um die Wette rennen mit; an e-m Rennen teilnehmen lassen, rennen lassen; jagen; *(Gesetz)* durchpeitschen; *tech* durchgehen lassen; *mot* hochjagen; *(to ~~ up)* abbremsen; *his ~~ is nearly run (fig)* es geht mit ihm zu Ende; *bicycle* ~~ Radrennen *n*; ~~*-boat* Rennboot *n*; ~~*-card* Rennprogramm *n*, -folge *f*; ~~*course, (Am) -track* Rennbahn *f*, -platz *m*; ~~*horse* Rennpferd *n*; ~~*-meeting* (Pferde-)Rennen *n*; ~~ *for power (pol)* Machtkampf *m*; ~**er** ['-ə] Rennfahrer, -wagen *m*, -boot, -flugzeug, -pferd *n*; ~**ing** ['-iŋ] *s* (Wett-, Pferde-)Rennen *n*; Rennsport *m*; *a* Renn-; **2.** (Menschen-)Rasse; Menschengruppe *f*, Volk *n*, Nation *f*, Stamm, (Menschen-)Schlag *m*; Rassenzugehörigkeit *f*, -merkmale *n pl*; Geschlecht *n*, Stamm *m*, Sippe, Familie *f*, *fig* Geschlecht *n*; *zoo* Unter-, Spielart, Varietät; *agr* Zucht *f*, Schlag *m*, Rasse *f*; *(Wein)* charakteristische(r) Geschmack *m*; *fig* geistige Prägung, Lebhaftigkeit *f*, Feuer *n*; *the human* ~ das Menschengeschlecht; ~~ *conflict, riot* Rassenkampf *m*; ~~ *conscious* rassebewußt; ~~ *consciousness* Rassebewußtsein *n*; ~~ *hatred* Rassenhaß *m*; ~~ *segregation* Rassentrennung *f*; ~**ial** ['reiʃəl] rassisch; Rassen-; ~~ *policy* Rassenpolitik *f*; ~**(ial)ism** ['-ʃəlizm, 'reisism] Rassenbewußtsein *n*, -standpunkt *m*, -überheblichkeit *f*; ~**iness** ['reisinis] Urwüchsigkeit, Kraft, Stärke; Lebhaftigkeit, geistvolle Art; *Am* Gewagtheit *f*; ~**ist** ['reisist] *a* rassenbewußt; *s* Anhänger *m* des Rassenstandpunktes; ~**y** ['reisi] rassig, ur-, eigenwüchsig; kraftvoll, stark; lebensvoll, lebhaft, lebendig, geistvoll; anregend, pikant; *Am* gewagt, zweideutig, etwas frei.

racem|e [ræ'si:m, '--] *bot* Traube *f (als Blütenstand)*.

rach|is ['reikis] *pl -ides* ['ræ-, 'reikidi:z] *scient* Wirbelsäule; *bot (Blütenstand)* Hauptachse, Spindel *f*; *zoo (Feder)* Schaft *m*; ~**itic** [ræ'kitik, rə'k-] rachitisch; ~**itis** [ræ'kaitis, rə'k-] Rachitis, Englische Krankheit *f*.

rack [ræk] **1.** *s* Gestell, Gerüst *n*; (Futter-)Raufe *f*; Kleiderrechen, Garderobenständer *m*; *rail* Gepäckablage *f*, -netz *n*; Ablage *f*, Regal *n* (mit Fächern); Wagenleiter; *typ* (Setzer-)Regal; *aero* (Steuer-)Gestell *n*; *aero (bomb-~)* Bombenträger *m*; *tech* Zahnstange; Folterbank *f*; *(plate-~)* Spülkorb *m*; *fig* Folter, Qual *f*; Sturm(wirbel), heftige(r) Wind(stoß) *m*; *tr* (aus-) strecken, recken; auf ein Gestell legen; *(Raufe)* füllen; auf die Folter spannen *a. fig*; *fig* foltern, quälen; *(wirtschaftlich)* auspressen, aussaugen; *(Miete)* hochschrauben; *to be ~ed with* gequält werden von, leiden an; *to be on the* ~ gefoltert werden; *fig* Folterqualen leiden; *to put s.o. on the* ~ jdn auf die Folter spannen; *to ~ o.'s brains (fig)* sich den Kopf zerbrechen; *bicycle* ~ Fahrradständer *m*; *hat* ~ Hutständer *m*; *roof-*~ Gepäckträger, Kuli *m*; ~**-railway** Zahnradbahn *f*; ~**-rent** *s* Wuchermiete, -pacht *f*; *tr* e-e Wuchermiete verlangen (*s.o.* von jdm); ~**-wheel** Zahnrad *n*; **2.** *to go to ~ and ruin* völlig zugrunde gehen; **3.** *s* treibende(s), dahinziehende(s) Gewölk *n*; *itr (Gewölk)* dahinziehen, treiben; **4.** *tr (to ~ off) (Wein, Most)* abziehen; **5.** *s (Pferd)* Schritt *od* Paßgang *m*; **6.** *s* Arrak *m*; ~ **punch** Grog *m* von Arrak.

racket ['rækit] **1.** *s* Lärm, Tumult, Aufruhr; (Fest-)Trubel, Spektakel, Radau, Rummel *m*, laute Lustbarkeit, Ausgelassenheit; *fig* Nervenprobe; *sl* Schiebung, Gaunerei, Halsabschneiderei; *fam* Erpressung *f*; *fam* Geschäft(emacherei *f*) *n*, (leichter) Job *m*; *itr* lärmen, (herum)toben; *(to ~ about)* sich austoben; *to go on the ~* ein lockeres Leben führen; *to make a ~* Krach schlagen, lärmen, Radau machen; *to stand the ~* die Folgen tragen, die Verantwortung auf sich nehmen; die Sache durchstehen; **~eer** [ræki'tiə] Erpresser; Schmuggler, Schieber, Spekulant *m*; **~eering** [-'tiəriŋ] Erpressung; Schiebung(en *pl*) *f*; **~y** ['rækiti] lärmend, tumultartig; ausgelassen; vergnügungssüchtig; **2.** *(a. racquet)* (Tennis-)Schläger *m*, Rakett *n*; Schneereifen *m*; *pl* Rakettspiel *n*.

radar ['reidə, -a:] Radar *m* od *n*, Funkmeßtechnik *f*, -verfahren; Radar-, Funkmeßgerät *n*; *attr* Radar-; *to be on the ~* auf dem Radarschirm zu sehen sein; *to pick up, to spot by ~* mit dem Radargerät erfassen, orten; *long-range-~* Großraumübersichtsgerät *n*; ~ **altimeter** *aero* Radarhöhenmesser *m*; ~ **beacon** Radarfunkfeuer *n*; **~scope** Radarschirmbild *n*; **~screen** Radar(leucht)schirm *m*; ~ **station** Radarstation *f*.

raddle ['rædl] *s* Rötel, Roteisenstein *m*; *tr* mit Rötel färben.

radi|al ['reidjəl] *a* strahlig, radial; Radial-; *anat* Schienbein- *od* Speichen-; *s med* Radialarterie *f*; *(~~ engine)* Sternmotor *m*; *~~ bearing* Querlager *n*; *~~ bone (med)* Speiche *f*; **~an** ['-ən] *math* Bogengrad *m*; **~ance, -cy** ['reidiəns(i)] Strahlen *n*, Glanz *a. fig*, (heller) Schein *m*; **~ant** [-ənt] *a* strahlend (*with* vor, von) *a. fig*; glänzend, (hell)scheinend, leuchtend, glühend; (freude)strahlend; *s* Strahlungspunkt *m*; *to be ~~ with joy* vor Freude strahlen; *~~ energy* Strahlungsenergie *f*; *~~ heat* Strahlungswärme *f*; *~~-heat lamp (med)* Höhensonne *f*; **~ate** ['reidieit] *itr (Licht, Wärme, Glück)* (aus)strahlen (*from* von); sich strahlenförmig ausbreiten; strahlenförmig verlaufen; *tr (Licht, Wärme)* ausstrahlen; *a* ['-iit] strahlig, radial; *zoo, a. s* radialsymmetrisch(es Tier *n*); *~~d beam* Richtstrahl *m*; *~~d field* Strahlungsfeld *n*; **~ation** [reidi'eiʃən] (Aus-)Strahlung *f*; Strahlen *m pl*; *med* Bestrahlung; strahlenförmige Anordnung *f*; *cosmic ~~* Höhenstrahlung *f*; **~ator** ['reidieitə] Heizkörper *m*; Heizsonne *f*, elektrische(s) Heizgerät *n*; *mot* Kühler *m*; *~~-cap, cover, shutter* Kühlerverschluß *m*, -haube, -jalousie *f*.

radical ['rædikəl] *a* Wurzel-, Grund-; wesentlich, grundlegend, gründlich, grundsätzlich; fundamental; ursprünglich; angeboren; *bot math* Wurzel-; *pol* radikal; *s* Grundbestandteil *m*; Grundlage *f*, Fundament; *chem* Radikal *n*; *(Wort)* Wurzel *f*, Stamm; *mus* Grundton; *pol* Radikale(r) *m*; *to make ~ changes in s.th.* bei etw grundsätzliche Änderungen vornehmen; ~ **error, evil** Grundirrtum *m*, -übel *n*; **~ism** [-izm] *pol* Radikalismus *m*; ~ **sign** *math* Wurzelzeichen *n*.

radicle ['rædikl] *anat* Haargefäß *n*, Kapillare *f*; (Nerven-)Ast *m*; *bot* Wurzelfaser *f*; *chem* Radikal *n*.

radio ['reidiou] *pl -os s* (Rund-)Funk *m*, drahtlose Telegraphie *f*; (Rund-)Funknetz *n*; Rundfunk *m*, *fam* Radio (-apparat *m*) *n*; Funkspruch *m*; Hochfrequenztechnik *f*; *in Zssgen*: Radio-, Strahlungs-; (Rund-)Funk-; *itr* funken; *tr* funken, drahtlos übermitteln; (im Rundfunk)senden; in Funkverbindung stehen (*s.o.* mit jdm); e-e Röntgenaufnahme machen von; durchleuchten; *by ~, on the ~* im Rundfunk; *to announce over the ~* im Rundfunk durchgeben; *to go on the ~* im Rundfunk sprechen; *to turn off, on, the ~* das Radio an-, abschalten; *voice-~* Sprechfunk *m*; **~active** ['-'æktiv] radioaktiv; *~~ contamination* radioaktive Verseuchung *f*; *~~ decay* radioaktive(r) Zerfall *m*; *~~ deposit* radioaktive(r) Niederschlag *m*; **~activity** [-æk'tiviti] Radioaktivität *f*; ~ **address** Rundfunkansprache *f*; ~ **advertising** Funkwerbung *f*; ~ **apparatus, set** (Rund-)Funkgerät *n*, Radioapparat *m*; ~ **beacon** Funkbake *f*, -feuer *n*; ~ **beam** Funk-, Leitstrahl *m*; ~ **bearing** Funkpeilung *f*; **~(broad)cast** *irr (s. cast) Am tr* senden, durch Rundfunk verbreiten; **~(broad)casting** *Am* (Rundfunk-)Sendung; Verbreitung *f* durch den Rundfunk; ~ **buoy** Funkboje *f*; ~ **call-sign** Funkrufzeichen *n*; ~ **car, truck** Funkwagen *m*; ~ **censorship, monitoring** Funküberwachung *f*; ~ **circuit** Funknetz *n*; Hochfrequenzkanal *m*; ~ **commentator** Rundfunkkommentator *m*; ~ **communication** Funkverbindung *f*, -verkehr *m*; ~ **control** Fernlenkung, -steuerung *f*; ~ **dealer** Rundfunkhändler *m*; ~ **direction-finder** Funkpeilgerät *n*; ~ **drama, play** Hörspiel *n*; **~element** radioaktive(s) Element *n*; ~ **engineer, technician** Funktechniker *m*; ~ **engineering, technology** Hochfrequenz-, Funktechnik *f*; ~ **equipment** Funkausrüstung *f*; ~ **frequency** Hochfrequenz *f*; **~gram** ['reidio(u)græm] Funkspruch *m*; *Br* Röntgenaufnahme *f*; *Br* Rundfunkgerät mit Plattenspieler; Musiktruhe *f*; **~graph** ['-gra:f] *s* u. *tr* (e-e) Röntgenaufnahme *f* (machen von); **~graphy** [reidi'ɔgrəfi] Röntgenphotographie *f*; ~ **hookup** Ringsendung *f*; ~ **installation** Funkanlage *f*; ~ **interference, jamming** Funkstörung *f*; ~ **location** Funkortung *f*; **~logic(al)** [reidio(u)-'lɔdʒik(əl)] radiologisch; **~logist** [reidi-'ɔlədʒist] Röntgenologe *m*; **~logy** [reidi'ɔlədʒi] Röntgenologie *f*; ~ **mast** Funkmast *m*; ~ **mechanic** Funkwart *m*; ~ **message** Funkspruch *m*; **~meteorograph, sonde** *mete* Radiosonde *f*; **~meter** [reidi'ɔmitə] Strahlungsmesser *m*; **~metry** [-'ɔmitri] Strahlungsmessung *f*; **~mobile** *radio* Aufnahmewagen *m*; ~ **navigation** Funknavigation *f*; ~ **net(work)** Funknetz *n*; ~ **noise** Funkstörpegel *m*; ~ **officer** Funkoffizier *m*; ~ **operator** Funker, *aero* Bordfunker *m*; ~ **orientation** Funkortung *f*; **~phone** = *~telephone*; **~phonograph** *Am* Musiktruhe *f*; **~-photogram** Funkbild *n*; ~ **range** Peilfeld *n (e-s Flugplatzes)*; ~ **receiver** (Rundfunk-)Empfänger *m*, Empfangsgerät *n*; ~ **reception** (Rundfunk-)Empfang *m*; **~scopy** [reidi'ɔskəpi] Röntgenuntersuchung, Durchleuchtung *f*; ~ **section** *mil* Funktrupp *m*; ~ **signal** Funksignal *n*; ~ **silence** Funkstille *f*; ~ **station** Rundfunkstation; Funkstelle *f*; **~(tele)gram** ['reidio(u)('teli)græm] Funktelegramm *n*; **~telegraphy** ['reidio(u)ti'legrəfi] Funktelegraphie *f*; **~(tele)phone** Sprechfunkgerät *n*; **~telephony** ['reidio(u)ti'lefəni] Sprechfunk *m*; ~ **teleprinter, teletypewriter** Funk-Fernschreibgerät *n*; **~therapeutics** [reidio(u)θerə'pju:tiks] *pl mit sing* **~therapy** [-'θerəpi] *med* Röntgentherapie *f*; ~ **tower** Funkturm *m*; ~ **tracer** Aufspürer *m* radioaktiver Stoffe; ~ **traffic** Funkverkehr *m*; ~ **transmitter** (Funk-)Sender *m*, Sendegerät *n*; **~trician** ['reidio(u)-'triʃən] *Am* Radioelektriker, -fachmann *m*; ~ **tube** (Radio-)Röhre *f*; ~ **wave** Funkwelle *f*; ~ **weather-station** Funkwetterwarte *f*.

radish ['rædiʃ] Rettich *m*.

radium ['reidjəm] *s chem* Radium *n*; ~ **disintegration** radioaktive(r) Zerfall *m*; ~ **emanation** = *radon* (s.d.); ~ **paint** Leuchtfarbe *f*; ~ **radiation** radioaktive Strahlung *f*; ~ **rays** *pl* radioaktive Strahlen *m pl*; **~therapy** ['-θerəpi] *med* Radiumtherapie *f*.

radius ['reidiəs] *pl radii* ['-ai] Strahl *m*; (Rad-)Speiche *f*; *math* Halbmesser, Radius; Umkreis; *fig* (Erfahrungs-) Bereich *m*; *anat* Speiche *f*; *cruising ~ (aero)* Flugbereich *m*; *steering ~ (mot)* Wendekreis *m*; *~ of curvature* Krümmungsradius *m*.

radix ['reidiks] *pl -dices* ['-si:z] *math bot gram fig* Wurzel *f*; *fig* Ursprung *m*.

radon ['reidən] *chem* Radon *n*, (Radium-)Emanation *f*.

raffia ['ræfiə] Raphiabast *m*; *(~ palm)* Raphiapalme *f*.

raffish ['ræfiʃ] gemein, niedrig; pöbelhaft; liederlich.

raffle ['ræfl] *s* Aus-, Verlosung; Lotterie, Tombola *f*; *tr (to ~ off)* verlosen.

raft [ra:ft] **1.** *s* Floß *n*; *tr* flößen; zu e-m Floß zs.zimmern; auf e-m Floß befördern, überqueren; **~er** ['-ə], **~sman** ['-smən] Flößer *m*; **2.** [ræft] *Am fam* (große) Menge, Masse *f*.

rafter ['ra:ftə] *s arch* (Dach-)Sparren *m*; *tr arch* mit Sparren versehen; *agr* halbschichtig pflügen.

rag [ræg] **1.** Lumpen, Lappen, Fetzen, Flicken; Staub-, Wisch-, Putz-, Abwaschlappen *m*; *fig* Bruchstück, bißchen; Abfall, Plunder *m*; *fam* Zunge *f*; *fam* Fetzen *m (Kleid)*, Fahne *f*, Käseblatt *n*; *pl* Lumpen *(altes Zeug)*; *hum* Klamotten *f pl*; *a* Lumpen-; *in ~s (and tatters)* zerrissen; in Lumpen, zerlumpt; *in o.'s glad ~s* im Sonntagsstaat; *like a red ~ to a bull (fig)* ein rotes Tuch; *to be all in ~s* in Lumpen gehen; ganz abgerissen sein; *to chew the ~ (fam)* quasseln, quatschen, reden; *not to have a ~ to put on o.'s back* nichts anzuziehen haben; **~amuffin** ['rægəmʌfin] Lump, Strolch, Rowdy; Straßenjunge *m*; **~-and-bone-man, ~man, -picker** Lumpensammler *m*; **~-bag** Flickenbeutel *m*; *fig* Durcheinander *n*; **~-book** unzerreißbare(s) Bilderbuch *n*; **~-chewing** *Am* Geschwätz *n*; **~-fair** Trödelmarkt *m*; **~ged** ['-id] *a* abgetragen; zerlumpt, schäbig; schartig, rauh; spitzig; zottig, strähnig; *(Stimme)* rauh; unfertig, (noch) roh; *(Stil)* ungefeilt; *on the ~~ edge (fig)* auf der schiefen Ebene, am Rande des Abgrunds; *~~ robin* Kuckucksblume *f*; **~-paper** Lumpenpapier *n*; **~-tag**: *~~ and bobtail* Krethi u. Plethi *pl*, Hinz u. Kunz *m*; **~time** *s mus* Ragtime *m*; *a sl* lustig; **~wort** ['-wə:t] Jakobskraut *n*; **2.** *arch* grobe(r) (Dach-)Schiefer; *geol* Kalkstein *m*; **3.** *tr sl* fertig-, 'runtermachen; durch den Kakao ziehen; e-n Streich spielen, übel mitspielen (*s.o.* jdm;) *s* Krach, Radau, Tumult; Streich, Ulk *m*.

rage [reidʒ] *s* Wut *f*, Toben *n a. fig (d. Elemente)*; Raserei; Gefühlswallung *f*, Sturm *m* der Begeisterung; Sucht, Gier (*for* nach); Leidenschaft *f*; Modeschrei *m*; *itr* wüten, rasen, toben *a. fig* (*against* gegen; *at* über); *(Krankheit)* wüten; *to fly into a* ~ in e-e Wut geraten; *she is all the* ~ man reißt sich um sie.

ragout ['rægu:] *s* Ragout *n*.

raid [reid] *s* (feindlicher) Überfall *m* (*into* auf); Stoßtruppunternehmen *n*; *aero* Luftangriff, Feindflug *m*; (Polizei-)Razzia *f* (*on* auf); *fig* Ansturm (*on* auf); *tr* überfallen, e-n Überfall machen auf; plündern; *com (den Markt)* drücken; *(Reserven)* angreifen; ~ *on a bank* Banküberfall, -raub *m*; ~**er** ['-ə] Plünderer, Einbrecher *m*; Kaperschiff *n*; *aero* Bomber *m*; *Am mil* für den Nahkampf ausgebildete(r) Marinekorpssoldat *m*; ~~*s past signal* Entwarnung *f*; ~**ing party** *mil* Stoßtrupp *m*; *aero* Jagdkommando *n*; (Polizei-)Streife *f*.

rail [reil] *s* Geländer(stange *f*) *n*; Handlauf *m*; *mar* Reling *f*, Zaun *m*, Gitter; *rail* Gleis *n*; Schiene(nstrang, -weg *m*); (Wagen-)Leiter; (waagerecht angebrachte) Stange *f*; Querholz *n*, -balken; Riegel *m*; *pl* Eisenbahnaktien *f pl*; Schienennetz *n*; *tr (to* ~ *off)* mit e-m Geländer versehen; *(to* ~ *in)* einzäunen, -friedigen; absperren; mit Schienen versehen; *Br* mit der Bahn befördern; *by* ~ auf dem Schienenwege, mit der (Eisen-)Bahn; *off the* ~*s* entgleist; *fig* in Unordnung, im Irrtum; *to run off the* ~*s* entgleisen; *hand*-~ Geländerstange *f*; ~-**bus** Schienen(omni)bus *m*; ~-**ga(u)ge** Spurweite *f*; ~-**head** Schienenkopf *m*; Endstation *f*; Zentral-, Sammel-, Kopfbahnhof *m*; Umschlagstelle *f*; ~**ing** ['-iŋ] Geländer *n*; *mar* Reling *f*; Schienen(material *n*) *f pl*; ~ **joint** Schienenstoß *m*; ~-**lifter** Gleisheber *m*; ~-**motor,** *Am* **car** Triebwagen *m*; ~ **post** Geländerpfosten *m*; ~ **traffic vehicle** Schienenfahrzeug *n*; ~ **train** *tech* Walzenstraße *f*; **2.** *itr* schimpfen, losziehen (*against, at* auf, über); ~**er** ['-ə] *fig* böse Zunge *f*; ~**ing** ['-iŋ] Schimpfen, Geschimpfe *n*; ~**lery** ['-əri] Gespött *n*, Spott *m*; **3.** *orn* Ralle *f*.

railway ['reilwei], *Am* **railroad** ['-roud] *s* Eisenbahn *f*; *tr (to* ~*road) Am fam (Antrag)* durchpeitschen; *circular* ~ Ringbahn *f*; *elevated* ~ Hochbahn *f*; *standard gauge* ~ Normalspurbahn *f*; ~-**accident** Eisenbahnunglück *n*; ~-**administration** Eisenbahnverwaltung *f*; ~ **bookstall** Bahnhofsbuchhandlung *f*; ~ **bridge** Eisenbahnbrücke *f*; ~-**car, -carriage** Eisenbahnwagen *m*; ~-**company** Eisenbahngesellschaft *f*; ~-**conductor** Zugführer *m*; ~ **crossing** Bahnübergang *m*; ~-**engine** Lokomotive *f*; **railroad engineer** *Am* Lokomotivführer *m*; ~ **fares** *pl* (Eisen-)Bahntarif *m*; ~ **ferry** Eisenbahnfähre *f*; ~ **freight rate** Gütertarif *m*; ~-**guard** Zugbegleiter, Schaffner; Zugführer *m*; ~-**guide** Kursbuch *n*; ~-**junction** Eisenbahnknotenpunkt *m*; ~-**line** Eisenbahnlinie *f*; ~-**man** (Eisen-)Bahnbeamte(r) *m*; ~-**net** Eisenbahnnetz *n*; ~-**plant** Bahnanlage *f*, Bahn-, Gleiskörper *m*; ~ **post-office** Bahnpostamt *n*; ~ **service** Eisenbahnbetrieb *m*; ~ **siding** Anschluß-, Abstellgleis *n*; ~-**station** Bahnhof *m*; ~-**terminus** Endbahnhof *m*; ~-**traffic** Eisenbahnverkehr *m*; ~-**transport** Bahntransport *m*; ~-**truck** offene(r) Güterwagen *m*; ~ **warrant** Militärfahrschein *m*; ~-**worker** Bahnarbeiter *m*; ~ **workshop, repairshop** Eisenbahnausbesserungswerk *n*.

raiment ['reimənt] *poet* Gewand *n*.

rain [rein] *s* Regen *a. fig*; *fig* Erguß; *(Tränen)* Strom; *(Pfeile)* Hagel *m*; *the* ~*s* Regenzeit *f (in den Tropen)*; *itr tr* regnen *a. fig*; *(Tränen)* strömen; herabfließen (*on* auf); *(Schläge)* hageln lassen; ~ *or shine* ob Regen oder Sonnenschein; *it* ~*s cats and dogs, it is pouring with* ~ es regnet in Strömen; *it never* ~*s but it pours (prov)* ein Unglück kommt selten allein; *it looks like* ~ es sieht nach Regen aus; *drizzling* ~ Nieselregen *m*; *golden* ~ *(bot)* Goldregen *m*; *shower of* ~ Regenschauer *m*; ~ *of ashes* Aschenregen *m*; ~ *of bullets* Kugelregen *m*; ~**bow** ['-bou] Regenbogen *m*; ~~ *trout* Regenbogenforelle *f*; ~ **check** Eintrittskarte, Einladung *f* für e-e (wegen Regen) ausgefallene Veranstaltung; ~-**cloud** Regenwolke *f*; ~**coat** Regenmantel *m*; ~**drop** Regentropfen *m*; ~**fall** Regenschauer *m*; Regenmenge *f*; ~-**ga(u)ge** ['-geidʒ] Regenmesser *m*; ~**iness** ['-inis] Regenwetter *n*; ~ **insurance** Regenversicherung *f*; ~**proof** *a* regendicht; *s* Regenmantel *m*; *tr* gegen Regen abdichten, wasserdicht machen; ~ **shower** Regenschauer *m*; ~-**soaked** *a* (vom Regen) durchnäßt, *fam* durchgeregnet; ~**water** Regenwasser *n*; ~ **wear** Regenkleidung *f*; ~**y** ['-i] regnerisch, naß, trüb(e); ~~ *day* regnerische(r) Tag *m*; *fig* schwierige Zeit *f*; ~~ *weather* Regenwetter *n*.

rais|e [reiz] *tr* (auf-, er-, hoch)heben; auf-, hochziehen; auf-, errichten *(a. ein Gebäude)*; aufrecht hinstellen; *(Häuser)* bauen; *(Teig)* gehen lassen; *(Staub)* aufwirbeln; *(Kohle)* fördern; *(Hut)* lüften (*to s.o.* vor jdm); vergrößern, erhöhen, heraufsetzen, steigern, anheben *(a. Preis)*; *(Scheck)* abändern; *(geistig, sittlich, sozial)* heben; vermehren; verstärken; *(Ruf)* festigen; *fig* befördern; erregen; *(Gefühl, Hoffnung)* erwecken; in Gang bringen *od* setzen; ins Leben rufen; anfeuern, antreiben; wieder ins Leben rufen, auferwecken (*from the dead* von den Toten); aufwiegeln, aufputschen (*against* gegen); auf-, zs.-bringen, auf die Beine stellen; *(Beiträge, Steuern)* erheben; *(Anleihe)* aufnehmen; *(Geld)* aufbringen, borgen; *(Gewinn)* einbringen; *(Frage)* stellen, aufwerfen, erörtern; *(Forderung)* geltend machen; *(Geschrei, Einspruch)* erheben; *(Gelächter)* verursachen; *(Schrei)* ausstoßen; *(Truppen)* aufstellen; *(Verbot)* aufheben; *(Belagerung)* abbrechen, beenden; *agr* anbauen, ziehen; *Am (Kinder)* groß-, aufziehen; *(Tiere)* züchten; *(Familie)* ernähren; *(Tuch)* aufrauhen; *(Dampf)* aufmachen; *Scot* auf-, in Harnisch bringen, aufregen; *mar* sichten; *itr fam* spucken müssen; *s* Erhebung; *(~ in wages) Am* (*bes.* Lohn-, Gehalts-) Erhöhung, Aufbesserung *f*; *to* ~~ *Cain, the devil, hell, the roof, a row, a rumpus, a stink* Krach schlagen; *to* ~~ *a dust* Staub aufwirbeln; *to* ~~ *s.o.'s hair (Am)* jdn skalpieren; *to* ~~ *land (mar)* Land sichten; *to* ~~ *from the ranks* in den Offiziersstand erheben; *to* ~~ *s.o.'s spirits* jdm wieder Mut machen; *to* ~~ *o.'s voice against* s-e Stimme erheben gegen; *to* ~~ *the wind (sl)* das *(nötige)* Geld auftreiben; das Schiff wieder flottmachen *fig*; ~**ed** [-d] *a* überhöht; *(Kunst)* erhaben, reliefartig; *(Gebäck) (durch Hefe* od *Backpulver)* locker (gebacken); ~**er** ['-ə] *Am* Pflanzer; Züchter *m*.

raisin ['reizn] Rosine *f*.

rak|e [reik] **1.** *s* Rechen *m*, Harke *f*; Schür-, Stochereisen *n*; *fam* Kamm, Lausrechen *m*; *tr* zs.harken, -rechen; *fig* zs.kratzen, (mühsam) zs.bringen, zs.raffen; (glatt) harken; *(Feuer)* schüren; abkämmen, -suchen; durchstöbern (*for* nach); *mil* bestreichen; *(mit den Augen)* mustern; *itr* harken (*over, across* über); *fig* wühlen, stöbern; *to* ~~ *in (Geld)* scheffeln; in großen Mengen einnehmen; *to* ~~ *through* durchwühlen, -stöbern; *to* ~~ *up* durchwühlen; aufstöbern, wieder ans Licht bringen; zs.bringen; *to* ~~ *s.o. over the coals (Am fam)* jdn ausschimpfen, jdm die Meinung sagen, jdn herunterlaufen lassen; ~~*-off (sl)* Ramsch, Profit, Gewinn, Vorteil; Anteil *m*, Gewinnbeteiligung *f*; **2.** Wüstling *m*; ~**ish** ['-iʃ] wüst, liederlich, ausschweifend; **3.** *itr* geneigt, schräg, schief sein; schief, nicht gerade stehen; überhangen; sich neigen; Fall haben; *tr* geneigt, schief stellen; *s* Schiefe, Neigung, Abschrägung *f*, Überhangen *n*; *at a* ~~ *of* bei e-r Neigung von; ~**ish** ['-iʃ] *(bes. Schiff)* schnittig; *fig* schneidig; schick, elegant.

rally ['ræli] **1.** *tr bes. mil* wieder sammeln; versammeln, zs.bringen; scharen (*round, to* um); *fig (Kräfte)* sammeln, aufbieten; aufmuntern; *itr* sich wieder sammeln; zs.kommen, sich zs.finden, sich versammeln; sich zs.nehmen; sich scharen (*round, to* um); zu Hilfe kommen (*to s.o.* jdm); sich anschließen (*to s.o.'s opinion* jds Meinung); sich (wieder) erholen (*from* von); *(Preise)* wieder anziehen, steigen; *s mil* Sammeln *n*; Versammlung, Zs.kunft, Tagung *f*, Treffen *n*; *com* Erholung *f*, Anziehen *n (der Preise)*; *sport* Schlagwechsel; mehrmalige(r) Ballwechsel *m*; *mot* Sternfahrt *f*; ~**ing** ['-iŋ] *mil* Sammeln *n*; ~~ *point* Sammelplatz *m*; ~~ *position* Aufnahmestellung *f*; **2.** *tr obs* sich lustig machen über, auslachen, verspotten.

ram [ræm] *zoo* Widder, Schafbock; *hist mil* Widder, Sturmbock; Rammbock, -bär *m*, Ramme *f*; Stößel, Preßstempel; Fallblock *m*; hydraulische Presse *f*; Tauchkolben; *aero* Staudruck *m*; *Am* Fliegerrakete *f* mit starker Durchschlagskraft; *the R*~ *(astr)* der Widder; *tr* rammen; stoßen (*against* gegen); hineinstoßen, -drücken, -pressen; *(to* ~ *up)* vollstopfen, verrammeln (*with* mit); *fam* schmeißen; *fig* eintrichtern; *to* ~ *home (fig)* ausführlich immer wieder darlegen; ~-**air** *aero* Luftstrom *m*; ~-**effect** Stauwirkung *f*; ~-**jet** *Am aero* Staustrahl-, Lorintriebwerk *n*; ~**med concrete** Stampfbeton *m*; ~**mer** ['-ə] Rammer; Rammbock; Fallblock *m*; = ~*rod*; ~**rod** *(Gewehr)* Ladestock *m*; *as stiff as a* ~~ steif wie ein Besenstiel.

rambl|e ['ræmbl] *itr* umherschweifen, (umher)streifen; dahinschlendern; *fig (beim Reden* od *Schreiben)* vom Hundertsten ins Tausendste kommen; abschweifen; *bot* ranken, wuchern; *s* Umherschweifen, -streifen *n*; Bummel *m*; *fig* Zs.hanglosigkeit *f*; *to go for a* ~~ e-n Spaziergang machen; ~**er** ['-ə] unstete(r) Mensch *m*; *(crimson* ~~*)* Kletterrose *f*; ~**ing** ['-iŋ] umherschweifend, -streifend; *fig* weitschweifig, sich verlierend, zs.hanglos; abschweifend; *(Haus)* planlos gebaut; *(Weg)* gewunden; *bot* rankend, kletternd.

rambunctious [ræm'bʌŋkʃəs] *Am fam* frech, laut, krakeelend, randalierend.

ram|ification [ræmifi'keiʃən] Verzweigung, Verästelung *f*; Zweig *m a. fig*; *fig* Abzweigung; Auswirkung, Folge; *com* Zweiggesellschaft *f*; **~ify** ['-fai] *itr tr* (sich) verzweigen, (sich) verästeln.

ramp [ræmp] **1.** *s* Rampe, Auf-, Abfahrt; schräge(s) Straßen-, Weg-, Verbindungsstück *n*; *(Treppengeländer)* Krümmling *m*; *arch* Abdachung; *mot* Hebebühne *f*; *fam* Wutanfall, -ausbruch *m*; *tr* mit e-r Rampe, mit Auf- u. Abfahrt versehen; *itr* e-n Niveauunterschied überwinden; sich auf die Hinterbeine, sich zum Sprung erheben; *fig* e-e drohende Haltung einnehmen; *hum (to ~ about)* (herum)wüten, -toben; *bot* sich ranken (*on* an); **~age** [-'peidʒ] *itr* (herum)tollen, -toben, wüten; *s*: *to be on the ~~* sich austoben; e-n Tobsuchtsanfall haben; **~ageous** [ræm'peidʒəs] tobsüchtig, wild, unbeherrscht, unbändig; *(Farbe)* schreiend; **~ancy** ['ræmpənsi] Zügellosigkeit, Wildheit, Heftigkeit *f*; **~ant** ['-ənt] *arch* schräg, steigend; sich (drohend) aufrichtend; *bot* wuchernd; *allg* überhandnehmend; zügellos, wild, heftig; *to be ~~* um sich greifen; **2.** *sl s* Betrugsmanöver *n*, Schwindel, Wucher *m*.

rampart ['ræmpɑ:t] *s* Wall *m a. fig*.

rampion ['ræmpjən] *bot* Rapunze(l) *f*.

ramshackle ['ræmʃækl] wack(e)lig, altersschwach, baufällig.

ran [ræn] **1.** *pret u. pp von run*; *also ~* ferner liefen *a. fig*; **2.** Stück *n*, Strick *m*; Schnur; Docke *f*.

ranch [rɑ:n(t)ʃ, *Am* ræn(t)ʃ] Viehfarm, Ranch *f*; *itr* e-e Ranch bewirtschaften, auf e-r Ranch arbeiten; **~er** ['-ə], **~man** ['-mən] Viehzüchter; Farmer *m*.

rancid ['rænsid] ranzig; **~ity** [ræn'siditi], **~ness** ['-nis] ranzige(r) Geruch *m*.

ranc|orous ['ræŋkərəs] grollend, erbittert; böswillig, boshaft, gehässig; **~o(u)r** ['ræŋkə] Groll *m*, Bosheit; Gehässigkeit *f*.

rand [rænd] Rand; Bergrücken *m*; **~an** ['-ən] *sl* Sauferei *f*; **~y** lärmend; *fam* lüstern.

random ['rændəm] *a* zufällig; Zufalls-; absichtslos, unabsichtlich, ziel-, planlos; *s*: *at ~* aufs Geratewohl; auf gut Glück; *to talk at ~* bald von diesem, bald von jenem reden; **~ sample, selection, test** Stichprobe *f*; **~ shot** Schuß *m* ins Blaue.

range [reindʒ] **1.** *tr* arrangieren, einreihen, einrangieren; in e-r Reihe anordnen *od* aufstellen; (systematisch) ordnen, klassifizieren; (jdn, sich) in e-e Reihe stellen (*with* mit), einreihen (*with* in); *mil* einschießen (*on* auf); *(Fernrohr)* einstellen; *(Geschütz)* richten (*on* auf); durchstreifen, -ziehen, -wandern; *(Vieh)* auf die Weide bringen; *(Ankertau)* ausea.rollen; *mar* entlangfahren; **2.** *itr* sich erstrecken, sich ausdehnen, sich ausbreiten; reichen bis, e-e Reichweite haben (*over* von); *(in der Größe, im Gewicht, im Alter, im Preis)* schwanken, sich bewegen (*from ... to* zwischen ... und); im gleichen Rang stehen (*with* mit); *bot zoo* vorkommen; *mil* sich einschießen; schweifen, streifen (*through* durch); *to ~ along (mar)* entlangfahren; **3.** *s* Reihe, Linie; Gruppe, Klasse; *(~ of mountains)* (Berg-)Kette *f*, Gebirgszug *m*; *(Feuerwaffe)* Schuß-, Reichweite *f*; *(rifle-~)* Schießplatz, -stand *m*; Entfernung *f*; *allg* Reich-, Tragweite *f*, Aktionsradius, Wirkungsbereich *m*; (Arbeits-)Feld *n*; Spielraum, Umfang *m*, Bereich *m od n*, Spanne, Schwankung; Differenz; (Farben-)Skala *f*; (Umher-)Schweifen, (Umher-)Streifen *n*; Fläche, Ausdehnung *f*; Weidegründe, -plätze *m pl*, -fläche *f*; *zoo bot* Verbreitungsgebiet *n*; *(kitchen-~)* (Koch-, Küchen-)Herd *m*; *com* Kollektion, Sammlung, Auswahl *f*; **4.** *at a ~ of* in e-r Entfernung von; *at close, wide ~* auf kurze, weite Entfernung; *in ~ with* in e-r Reihe mit; *out of ~* außer Hör-, Reich-, Schußweite; *within the ~ of s.o. (fig)* für jdn verständlich; *to give free ~* freien Lauf lassen (*to s.th.* dat); *annual, daily ~ (mete)* Tages-, Jahresschwankung *f*; *long, short ~* große, geringe Reichweite *f*; *price ~* Preislage, -klasse, -bewegung; *(Börse)* Kursbewegung *f*; *~ of application* Anwendungsbereich *m*; *~ of flight* Flugreichweite *f*; *~ of reception (radio)* Empfangsbereich *m*; *~ of transmission (radio)* Sendebereich *m*; *~ of vision* Sichtweite *f*, Gesichtsfeld *n*; **~-finder** Entfernungsmesser *m (Gerät)*; **~-pole** Meßlatte *f*; **~r** ['-ə] *Am* Förster; *Br* Aufseher e-s königlichen Forstes; *(Pfadfinder)* Ranger *m*; *pl Am* Kommandotruppe *f*; **rangy** ['-i] *bes. Am* weiträumig; *(Vieh)* umherschweifend; sehnig, straff.

rank [ræŋk] **1.** *s* Reihe, Linie; (An-)Ordnung; Stellung, Klasse *f*, Stand, Rang *m*; hohe Stellung *f*, hohe(r) Rang; *mil* (Dienst-)Grad *m*; *mil* Glied *n*; *pl* Heer *n*, Armee *f*; *the ~s* der Mannschaftsstand; *tr* einreihen, -ordnen, klassifizieren; einschätzen (*as* als); rechnen, zählen (*with* zu); stellen *fig* (*above* über; *below* unter); kommen, rangieren (*s.o.* vor jdm); *Am* den Vorrang haben vor; *Am sl* ärgern, belästigen, verraten; *itr* gelten (*among* als); gerechnet werden, zählen, gehören (*among* zu); einnehmen, haben (*third* den 3. Platz); *Am* die erste Stelle, den höchsten Rang einnehmen; *to ~ above, below* über, unter stehen; *at the head of the ~* an der Spitze; *of the very first ~* erste(r) Ordnung; *to ~ high* großes Ansehen genießen; *to break ~(s) (mil)* wegtreten; *to fall in ~ (mil)* antreten; ins Glied treten; *fig* in Ordnung kommen; *to pull o.'s ~ (Am)* autoritär auftreten; *to reduce to the ~s* degradieren; *to rise from the ~s (mil u. allg)* von der Pike auf dienen; *fig* es zu etw bringen; *to take ~ of s.o.* vor jdm den Vorrang haben; *with s.o.* mit jdm auf e-r Stufe stehen; *front, rear ~ (mil)* Vorder-, hintere(s) Glied *n*; *taxi-~* Droschkenhalteplatz *m*; *the ~ and file (mil)* Unteroffiziere u. Mannschaften; *allg* die gewöhnlichen Sterblichen *m pl*; **~er** ['-ə] Rangälteste(r); einfache(r) Soldat; aus dem Mannschaftsstand hervorgegangene(r) Offizier *m*; **~ing** ['-iŋ] erste(r), höchste(r); **2.** *(Pflanzenwuchs)* wuchernd, üppig; überwuchert (*with* von); *(Boden)* fruchtbar, fett; *(Tier)* brünstig; stinkend, übelriechend, ranzig; anstößig, unanständig; *pej* kraß, glatt, rein, schier; Erz-; **~ness** ['-nis] Üppigkeit, Fruchtbarkeit *f*; üble(r) Geruch *m*; Unanständigkeit *f*.

rankle ['ræŋkl] *itr fig* nagen, fressen (*with s.o.* an jdm); unter der Oberfläche schwelen.

ransack ['rænsæk] *tr* durchsuchen, -wühlen (*for* nach); (aus)plündern.

ransom ['rænsəm] *s* Freikauf *m*; Lösegeld *n a. fig rel*; *fig* Gegenleistung; *rel* Erlösung *f*; *tr* los-, freikaufen; *(Gegenstand)* auslösen; gegen ein Lösegeld freilassen; *rel* erlösen; *to exact a ~ from s.o.* von jdm ein Lösegeld erpressen; *to hold s.o. to ~* gegen ein Lösegeld festhalten; *a king's ~* e-e Riesensumme.

rant [rænt] *itr* großspurig reden; prahlen; (laut) eifern, brüllen, toben; *tr (to ~ out)* hinausschreien; übertrieben deklamieren; *s* (laute) Prahlerei *f*, hochtrabende Reden *f pl*; Wortschwall *m*; **~ankerous** [-'tæŋkərəs] *Am fam* rechthaberisch; mürrisch; **~er** ['-ə] Schreihals, Schreier, Prahlhans *m*.

ranunculus [rə'nʌŋkjuləs] *pl a. -li* [-lai] *bot* Hahnenfuß *m*; Butterblume *f*.

rap [ræp] **1.** *tr itr* klopfen, schlagen, stoßen (*at* an); *Am fam* tadeln, kritisieren; *Am sl* verhaften, verurteilen, identifizieren; *s* Klaps, Schlag (*on* auf); Stoß; *sl Am* Rüffel, Tadel *m*; Strafe; Identifizierung; Verurteilung *f*; *to ~ out* hervor-, ausstoßen; durch Klopfen ausdrücken; *to beat the ~ (Am sl)* freikommen; *to give s.o. a ~ on the knuckles* jdm auf die Finger klopfen; *fig* jdn auf s-n Platz verweisen; *to take the ~ (sl)* bestraft werden; e-n Anpfiff einstecken; *there was a ~ at the door* es klopfte an der Tür; **2.** *s*: *not to give a ~ for* keinen Heller geben für; *I don't care a ~* das ist mir völlig egal.

rapac|ious [rə'peiʃəs] raubend, plündernd; *fig* (raub-,hab)gierig; *zoo* Raub-; **~ity** [-'pæsiti] (Raub-, Hab-)Gier *f*.

rape [reip] **1.** *s* Raub *m*, Entführung; *jur* Vergewaltigung, Notzucht *f*; *tr* rauben, entführen; *jur* vergewaltigen; *attempted ~* Notzucht(s)versuch *m*; *statutory ~* Unzucht *f* mit Minderjährigen; *~ and murder, ~ slaying* Lustmord *m*; **2.** *bot* Raps *m*; **~-oil, ~seed oil** Rüböl *n*; **~seed** Rübs(am)en *m*; **3.** Trester, Treber *pl*.

rapid ['ræpid] *a* schnell, flink, eilig; *(Fluß)* reißend; *(Abhang)* steil; *phot* lichtstark; *s pl* Stromschnellen *f pl*; **~ity** [rə'piditi] Schnelligkeit; Geschwindigkeit *f*.

rapier ['reipjə] Rapier *n*; **~-thrust** *fig* Nadelstich *m*.

rapine ['ræp(a)in] *lit* Raub *m*, Plünderung *f*.

rapist ['reipist] Vergewaltiger *m*.

rapport [ræ'pɔ:(t)] (*bes.* enge) Beziehung *f*, (enges) Verhältnis *n*; Übereinstimmung, Freundschaft *f*; *in ~ with* in Übereinstimmung, in enger Verbindung mit; **~eur** [ræpɔ'tə:] Berichterstatter *m*.

rapprochement [ræ'prɔʃmɑ:(ŋ)] *pol* (*bes.* Wieder-)Annäherung *f*.

rapt [ræpt] *fig* versunken (*in* in); ent-, verzückt; **~ure** ['ræptʃə] Entzücken, Hingerissensein *n*; Verzückung *f*; *to go into ~~s over s.th.* über etw in Entzücken geraten; **~urous** ['ræptʃərəs] ver-, entzückt, hingerissen; *(Beifall)* stürmisch.

rare [rɛə] selten, ungewöhnlich, rar; dünn, fein; *fam fig* unbezahlbar, herrlich; *(Fleisch)* nicht durchgebraten; **~faction** [rɛəri'fækʃən] Verdünnung; Verfeinerung *f*; **~fy** ['rɛərifai] *tr itr* (sich) verdünnen; *fig* (sich) verfeinern; **~ gas** Edelgas *n*; **~ness** ['-nis], **rarity** ['rɛəriti] Seltenheit, Ungewöhnlichkeit; Kostbarkeit; Dünnheit, Feinheit; Rarität *f*.

rarebit ['rɛəbit]: *Welsh ~* überbackene Käseschnitte *f*.

raree-show ['rɛəri:ʃou] Guckkasten *m*; Jahrmarktsschau, -veranstaltung *f*.

rascal ['rɑ:skəl] Schurke, Schuft; *fam hum* (kleiner) Schelm, Schlingel *m*; **~ity** [rɑ:s'kæliti] Schurkenhaftigkeit,

Schuftigkeit *f*; **~ly** ['rɑːskəli] *a adv* schuftig; gemein, erbärmlich.

rase *s. raze.*

rash [ræʃ] **1.** zu schnell, (zu) rasch, eilig, hastig; vorschnell, übereilt, unbesonnen; tollkühn; **~ness** ['-nis] Eile, Hast; Übereiltheit, Unbesonnenheit *f*; **2.** Hautausschlag *m* (*on o.'s face* im Gesicht); *fig* Ansammlung *f*; *heat-~* Hitzebläschen *n pl*.

rasher ['ræʃə] Speck-, -schnitte *f*.

rasp [rɑːsp] *tr tech* raspeln; *(Brot)* reiben; krächzen; *fig* reizen, irritieren; *itr* kratzen *(a. akustisch)*; *s* Raspel *f*, Reibeisen; Raspeln; Kratzen *n*; *to ~ s.o.'s nerves* jdm auf die Nerven gehen; **~ing** ['-iŋ] *a* kratzend, rauh; aufreizend; *s* Raspeln; Kratzen *n*; *pl* Raspelspäne *m pl*.

raspberry ['rɑːzbəri] Himbeere *f*; *(~ bush)* Himbeerstrauch *m*; *sl* verächtliche Mundbewegung *f*, Zischen; *sl* Mißfallen *n*; *vulg* Furz *m*; *to give s.o. the ~* jdm e-n Rüffel erteilen; jdn auspfeifen; **~-cane** Himbeerranke *f*.

rat [ræt] *s* Ratte *f*; *fig* Abtrünnige(r), Überläufer, Verräter, Gesinnungslump; *Br fam* Streikbrecher; Lockspitzel; *sl* gemeine(r) Kerl, Schuft, Lump, Gauner; falsche(r) Fünfziger; *Am fam* Haarpolster *n*, -einlage *f*; *itr* Ratten fangen; fahnenflüchtig werden, die Gesinnung wechseln, überlaufen; Streikbrecher *od* Lockspitzel sein; unter Tarif arbeiten; *to ~ on s.o. (Am sl)* jdn verpetzen; jdn im Stich lassen; *to ~ out (Am sl)* abhauen; *like a drowned ~* pudel-, patschnaß; *to smell a ~ (fig)* Lunte, *fam* den Braten riechen; *~s! sl* Quatsch! Blödsinn! *black, old-English ~* Hausratte *f*; *brown, grey, Norway ~* Wanderratte *f*; *musk-~* Bisamratte *f*; *water-~* Wasserratte *f*; **~-catcher** Rattenfänger *m (Mensch)*; **~-cheese** *Am* einfache(r) Käse *m* (vom Stück); **~-face** *Am sl* hinterlistige(r) Bursche *m*; **~-hole** *tr* hamstern; **~-poison** Rattengift *n*; **~-race** *sl* rücksichtslose(r) Wettstreit *m*; soziale Angeberei *f*; **~sbane** Rattengift *n*; **~'s-tail** Nadel-, Lochfeile *f*; **~-trap** Rattenfalle *f*; rücksichtslose(s) Strebertum *n*; *Am fig* Falle *f*; **~ty** ['-i] rattenartig, Ratten-; voller Ratten; *sl* mies, schäbig, elend, Ratten-; *sl* (leicht) eingeschnappt (*about* über).

rat|ability [reitə'biliti] **1.** Ab-, Einschätzbarkeit; Umlage-, Steuerpflicht; Zollpflichtigkeit *f*; **~able** ['reitəbl] ab-, einschätzbar; gebühren-, umlage-, steuer-, zollpflichtig; anteilsmäßig; **~al** ['reitəl] *fin* Meßbetrag, Veranlagungswert *m*; **~e** [reit] **1.** *s* Betrag *m*, Höhe *f*, Grad *m*; Geschwindigkeit; Ziffer, Quote *f*, Anteil *m*, Rate; Quote *f*, Verhältnis *n*, Maßstab; Kurs *m*, Taxe *f*, Prämien-, Gebührensatz, Tarif *m*, Veranschlagung *f*; *(postal ~~)* Posttarif *m*, Porto *n*; Gebühr *f*, Preis; *(Zeitung)* Anzeigenpreis *m*; Klasse *f*, Rang *m*, Stufe *f*; *pl* Gemeindesteuer *f*, -abgaben *f pl*; *tr* ab-, einschätzen, taxieren (*at* auf); bewerten; einstufen, rechnen (*among* zu); bemessen; *(Steuern)* veranlagen; zu e-r Umlage heranziehen, besteuern; *mar* einstufen; *Am sl* Anspruch haben auf; *itr* angesehen werden, gelten (*as* als); *at any ~~* auf jdn Fall, auf alle Fälle, jedenfalls; zu jedem Preis; *at that ~~* wenn dem so ist; dann; *at this ~~* auf diese Weise; so; unter den gegenwärtigen Umständen; *at the ~~ of* zum Kurse von; mit e-r Geschwindigkeit von; *at a low, high ~~* zu e-m niedrigen, hohen Kurs *od* (Gebühren-)Satz; *at a terrific ~* mit wahnsinniger Geschwindigkeit; *to be ~ed as* eingeschätzt werden als; *asked, buying ~~* Brief-, Geldkurs *m*; *assessment, tax ~~* Steuersatz *m*; *basic salary ~~* Grundgehalt *n*; *birth ~~* Geburtenziffer *f*; *church ~~* Kirchensteuer *f*; *clearing ~~* Verrechnungskurs *m*; *death ~~* Sterbeziffer *f*; *dog ~~* Hundesteuer *f*; *first-~~* erstklassig; *flat ~~* Pauschalsatz *m*; *forced ~~* Zwangskurs *m*; *inofficial ~~* Freiverkehrs-, außerbörsliche(r) Kurs *m*; *market ~~* Börsen-, amtliche(r) Kurs *m*; *marriage ~~* Heiratsziffer *f*; *maximum, minimum ~~* Höchst-, Mindestsatz *m*; *mortality ~~* Sterblichkeitsziffer *f*; *preferential ~~* Vorzugstarif *m*; *subscription ~~* Abonnementspreis *m*; *supplementary ~~* Zuschlag *m*; *telephone ~~* Grundgebühr *f*; *water ~~* Wassergeld *n*; *~~-aided (a)* von der Gemeinde gefördert; *~~-book* Preisliste; Steuerrolle *f*; *~~-card* Anzeigentarif *m*; *~~ of climb* Steiggeschwindigkeit *f*; *~~ of conversion* Umrechnungskurs *m*; *~~-cutting* Tarifkürzung *f*; *~~d load* Nennleistung *f*; *~~ voltage* Nennspannung *f*; *~~ of the day* Tageskurs *m*, -notierung *f*; *~~ of discount* Diskontsatz *m*; *~~ of duty* Zollsatz *m*; *~~ of exchange* Wechselkurs *m*; *~~ of insurance* Versicherungsprämie *f*; *~~ of interest* Zinssatz, -fuß *m*; *~~ of living* Lebenshaltung *f*, -standard *m*; *~~-office* (Gemeinde-)Steueramt *n*; *~~-payer* Steuerzahler *m*; *~~ of subscription* Bezugspreis *m*; Teilnehmergebühr *f*; *~~ of wages* Lohnsatz *m*; **2.** *tr* ausschimpfen, heruntermachen (*for* wegen); *itr* schimpfen, wüten, toben (*at* gegen); **~ing** ['-iŋ] **1.** (Ein-)Schätzung, Bewertung, Bemessung; Einstufung; *Am* Note, Zensur; Heranziehung zu e-r Umlage, Besteuerung; Erhebung *f* e-r Umlage; Umlagen-, Steuerbetrag *m*; Einteilung *f* in (Rang-)Klassen; *mar* Rang, (Dienst-)Grad; *mar* Mannschaftsdienstgrad *m*; *tech* Leistung(sfähigkeit) *f*; *credit ~~* Einschätzung *f* der Kreditwürdigkeit; *~~ assessment* Umlagenverteilung *f*; **2.** Schimpfen *n*; strenge(r) Tadel, Verweis *m*.

ratch [rætʃ] Sperrstange, -klinke, -vorrichtung *f*; **~et** ['-it] Ratsche, Knarre; *(~~ release)* (Sperrad-)Auslösung *f*; *~~-wheel* Sperrad *n*.

rather ['rɑːðə] *adv* lieber; eher; richtiger, genauer, besser; im Gegenteil, dagegen, vielmehr; fast, beinahe; ziemlich, nicht wenig; *fam (als Antwort)* klar, natürlich, selbstverständlich; *the ~ that* um so mehr, als; *I would, I had ~* ich würde, hätte lieber, eher; *a ~ failure* fast ein Reinfall.

ratif|ication [rætifi'keiʃən] Billigung, Genehmigung; Bestätigung; *pol* Ratifizierung, Ratifikation(surkunde) *f*; **~y** ['rætifai] *tr* billigen, genehmigen; anerkennen, bestätigen, ratifizieren.

ratio ['reiʃiou] *pl -os* (zahlenmäßiges, Größen-, Stärke-)Verhältnis *n a. math*; *math* Quotient; Anteil *m*; *tech* Übersetzungsverhältnis *n*; *in the ~ of 2 to 3* im Verhältnis 2 zu 3; *in the inverse ~* im umgekehrten Verhältnis; *current ~* Liquiditätsgrad *m*; *~ of distribution* Verteilungsschlüssel *m*; **~cination** [rætiəsi'neiʃən] Schlußfolgerung *f*, (logischer) Schluß *m*.

ration ['ræʃən] *s* Ration; Zuteilung *f*; *mil (~ scale)* (Tages-)Verpflegungssatz *m*; *pl sl mil* Nahrung(smittel *n pl*) *f*; *tr mil* verpflegen, versorgen; *com* einteilen, rationieren, bewirtschaften; *on the ~* rationiert; *to be on short ~s* auf schmale Kost gesetzt sein; *to put s.o. on ~s* jdn auf Rationen setzen; *out of ~s* jdn von der Verpflegung absetzen; *iron ~* eiserne Ration *f*; *~s in kind* Naturalverpflegung *f*; *~* **allowance** Verpflegungsgeld *n*; **~-book, -card** Lebensmittelkarte *f*; *clothing ~~* Kleiderkarte *f*; **~-depot, -dump** Verpflegungslager *n*; *~* **distribution point** Verpflegungsausgabestelle *f*; **~ing** ['-iŋ] Zuteilung; Rationierung, Bewirtschaftung *f*; **~-party** Essenholer *m pl*; **~-strength** *mil* Verpflegungsstärke *f*; *~* **ticket** Lebensmittelmarke *f*.

rational ['ræʃənl] vernunftgemäß, vernünftig, verständig; rational, Vernunft-; denkfähig; zweckmäßig, rationell; *math* rational; **~e** [ræʃiə'nɑːli] logische Grundlage; vernünftige Erklärung *f*; **~ism** ['ræʃnəlizm] Rationalismus *m*; **~ist** [-ist] Rationalist *m*; **~istic** [ræʃnə'listik] rationalistisch; **~ity** [ræʃə'næliti] Vernunft; Vernünftigkeit; Denkfähigkeit *f*; **~ization** [ræʃnəlai'zeiʃən] Rationalisierung, wirtschaftlichere Gestaltung *f*; *industrial ~~* betriebswirtschaftliche Rationalisierung *f*; **~ize** ['ræʃnəlaiz] *tr* mit der Vernunft in Einklang bringen; rational erklären; *com* rationalisieren, wirtschaftlicher gestalten; *math* die Wurzel(n) auflösen (*an equation* e-r Gleichung).

rat-tat(-tat) ['ræt'tæt, '-tətæt] *s* Knallen, Geknatter *n*; *itr* klopfen, knattern.

rattl|e ['rætl] *itr* klappern, rattern, rasseln, knarren, poltern; röcheln; klopfen (*at* an); plappern, *fam* quasseln (*on* über); *to ~~ down* herunterprasseln; *to ~~ on* daherplappern; *tr* klappern, rasseln mit; *mus (to ~~ off)* herunterrasseln; rütteln *(the doorknob* an der Tür); *Am fam* durchea.-, aus dem Konzept bringen; auf die Palme bringen; *(to ~~ through) (Gesetz)* durchpeitschen; *s* Geklapper, Gerassel, Gepolter; Röcheln; Geplapper, *fam* Gequassel *n*; (Kinder-)Klapper, Rassel, Schnarre *f*; *to get s.o. ~ed* jdn aus dem Konzept bringen; *~~-box (Am)* Plappermaul *n*, *fam* Quasselstrippe; Schnarre *f*; *bot* Klappertopf *m*; *~~-brain, -head, -pate* Hohlkopf, Windbeutel, *fam* Luftikus, Schwätzer *m*; *~~-brained, -headed, -pated (a)* hohl(köpfig), dumm; windbeutelig, leichtsinnig; geschwätzig, schwatzhaft; *~~-snake* Klapperschlange *f*; *~~-trap* Klapperkasten *m (altes Fahrzeug)*; *sl* Quasselstrippe *f*, Quatschmaul *n*; *sl* Fresse *f*, Maul *n*; *pl* Tand, Krimskrams *m*, Klamotten *f pl*; **~er** ['-ə] Schwätzer *m*, Klatschmaul *n*, -base; *sl* Klappe *f*; (heftiger) Schlag, Stoß; (schwerer) Sturz *m*; *fam* prima Sache *f*, Pfundskerl *m*; *Am* Klapperschlange *f*; *Am fam* (Güter-)Zug *m*; **~ing** ['-iŋ] *a* klappernd, ratternd, rasselnd; *fam (Tempo)* flott, lebhaft, rasend, toll; phänomenal, unglaublich; *(Geschäft)* florierend; *adv* mächtig, gewaltig, kolossal.

raucous ['rɔːkəs] rauh, heiser.

ravag|e ['rævidʒ] *s* Verwüstung, Verheerung, Zerstörung *f a. fig*; Ruin *m*; *tr* verwüsten, verheeren, zerstören; plündern; *itr* Verwüstungen anrichten (*among* unter); *~~s of time* Zahn *m* der Zeit.

rav|e [reiv] *itr med* im Fieberwahn reden, phantasieren; *fig* schwärmen (*about, of* von); wüten, toben, rasen (*about, at* über; *against* gegen); *(Meer)* tosen, heulen; *s* Phantasieren *n*; *Am fam* überwältigende Begeisterung; Schwärmerei *f*, Gefasel *n*; *Am sl* Liebling *m*; *~~ review* tolle Kritik *f*; völlige(r) Verriß *m*; **~ing** ['-iŋ] *a* phantasierend, faselnd; *fam* hinreißend, bezaubernd; *adv*: *~~ mad* vollkommen übergeschnappt; *s (oft pl)* Fieberwahn *m*, Gefasel *n*.

ravel ['ræv(ə)l] *tr* verwickeln, verwirren; *fig* komplizieren, kompliziert machen; *(to ~ out)* abwickeln, aufziehen, -trennen, zerfasern; *fig* entwirren; *itr* sich verwickeln, sich verwirren; *fig* kompliziert werden; aufgehen, zerfasern; *(to ~ out)* ausfransen; *fig* sich aufklären; *s* lose(r) Faden *m*; *fig* Verwirrung; Schwierigkeit, Verwicklung *f*; ausgefranste(s) Ende *n*; **~(l)ing** ['-liŋ] Aufziehen, -trennen *n*; aufgezogene(r) Faden *m*; **~ment** ['-mənt] Verwick(e)lung, Komplikation *f*.

raven ['reivn], *a.* **ravin** ['rævin] **1.** *s* (Kolk-)Rabe *m*; *a* rabenschwarz, schwarzglänzend; **2.** *itr* ['rævn] plündern, rauben; gierig (fr)essen; von Raub leben; e-n Heißhunger haben, sich sehnen (*for* nach); *tr* (gierig) ver-, hinunterschlingen *a. fig*; *s* Raub *m*, Plünderung; Beute; Gefräßigkeit *f*; **~ous** ['rævinəs] räuberisch; raubgierig; gefräßig, heißhungrig; gierig (*for* nach); versessen (*for* auf).

ravine [rə'vi:n] Schlucht, Klamm *f*.

ravish ['rævíʃ] *tr fig* hinreißen, entzücken; *obs* rauben, entführen, entreißen (*from* aus); *obs* vergewaltigen, schänden, entehren; **~er** ['-ə] Räuber; Schänder *m*; **~ing** ['-iŋ] *a* hinreißend, bezaubernd, entzückend; **~ment** ['-mənt] *fig* Hingerissenheit, Ekstase, Begeisterung *f*, Entzücken *n*; *obs* Entführung; Vergewaltigung, Schändung *f*.

raw [rɔ:] *a (Nahrung)* roh; *(Material)* roh, unver-, unbearbeitet; *(Alkohol)* unverdünnt, rein; *fig* unausgebildet, unerfahren, ungeschult; ungebildet, unreif; *(Haut)* abgeschürft, wund, entzündet; *(Wind, Wetter, Klima)* rauh, unwirtlich, naßkalt; *fam* unanständig; *sl* roh, grob; *s* wunde, entzündete Stelle *f*; *pl com* Rohstoffe *m pl*; *in the ~* im Naturzustand; unverändert, unbearbeitet; *Am sl* nackt; *to touch s.o. on the ~ (fig)* jds wunden Punkt berühren; jdn an der empfindlichsten Stelle treffen; **~-boned** *a* grobknochig, hager, mager; **~ deal** *fam* miserable, schlechte Behandlung *f*; *he got, he was handed a ~~* ihm wurde übel mitgespielt; **~ hide** Rohhaut; Reitpeitsche *f*; **~ material** Rohmaterial *n*, -stoff *m*; *~~ market, shortage* Rohstoffmarkt *m*, -knappheit *f*; **~ness** ['-nis] Roheit *f*; Rohzustand *m*; *fig* Reinheit; Unerfahrenheit, Unreife; Rauheit, Rauhigkeit *f*; *med* Wundsein *n*; **~ silk** Rohseide *f*; **~ spirit** reine(r) Alkohol *m*; **~ steel** Rohstahl *m*; **~ sugar** Roh-, braune(r) Zucker *m*.

ray [rei] **1.** *s* (Licht-)Strahl *a. fig*; Lichtstreifen; (schwacher) Schimmer; *phys* Strahl *m*; *fig* Spur *f*, Schimmer *m*; *itr* (aus)strahlen *a. fig*; *tr* ausstrahlen *a. fig*; *phys med* bestrahlen; mit Strahlen verzieren; *Am fam* ein Röntgenbild machen von; *heat-~s (pl)* Wärmestrahlen *m pl*; *X-~s (pl)* Röntgenstrahlen *m pl*; *a ~ of hope* ein Hoffnungsschimmer, Lichtstreifen *m* am Horizont; **~less** ['-lis] ohne Strahlen; dunkel, düster; **~-treatment** *med* Bestrahlung *f*; **2.** *s zoo* Rochen *m*; *electric ~* Zitterrochen *m*.

rayon ['reiɔn] Kunstseide *f*, Reyon *m* od *n*; **~ staple** Zellwolle *f*.

raze, rase [reiz] *tr* völlig zerstören, dem Erdboden gleich machen; *mil* schleifen; *fig (aus dem Gedächtnis)* (aus)tilgen, -löschen, -merzen.

razor ['reizə] *s* Rasiermesser *n*; *on the ~'s edge (fig)* auf des Messers Schneide; *to strop o.'s ~* das Rasiermesser abziehen; *electric ~* elektrische(r) Rasierapparat *m*; *(safety) ~* Rasierapparat *m*; *tr*: *a well-~ed chin* ein glattes Kinn *n*; **~-back** *zoo* Finnwal *m*; *Am (Südstaaten)* Wildschwein *n*; *Am sl* (Hand-)Arbeiter *m*; **~-backed** *a* scharfkantig; mit hervorstehendem Rückgrat; **~-blade** Rasierklinge *f*; **~-edge** scharfe Schneide *f*; scharfe(r) Bergkamm; *fig* kritische(r) Punkt *m*; **~-strop** Streichriemen *m*.

razz [ræz] *sl tr* durch den Kakao ziehen, aufziehen, lächerlich machen; *itr* witzeln, spotten; *s* verächtliche Mundbewegung *f*; Rüffel *m*.

razzia ['ræziə] Raubzug *m* (*on* auf).

razzle-dazzle ['ræzldæzl] *s sl* Rummel *m*, Remmidemmi *n*, Besäufnis, Sauferei *f*; *Am sl* Durcheinander *n*, Trubel; Schwindel *m*; *a* glänzend, toll; *to go on the ~* sich ins Vergnügen stürzen.

*

re [ri:] **1.** *s mus* D *n*; re *n*; **2.** *prp (s: in ~) (Schriftverkehr)* mit Bezug auf, betreffend; *jur* in Sachen; **3.** *pref* zurück; wieder, noch einmal.

reach [ri:tʃ] *tr (to ~ out)* (dar)reichen, hinhalten, ausstrecken; (herüber)reichen, geben; herankommen an, (hin)reichen bis (zu); *(Gerücht)* dringen bis zu; ergreifen, berühren, treffen; erreichen, erlangen; einholen; treffen, erzielen (*an agreement* e-e Vereinbarung); kommen nach, ankommen in; Verbindung haben mit, Beziehungen haben zu, in Berührung, in Kontakt kommen mit; *typ (e-e Auflage)* erleben; *(e-n Schlag)* versetzen; *fig* begreifen, erfassen; *itr* die Hand, den Fuß ausstrecken; greifen, *fam* langen (*for, after* nach; *into o.'s pocket* in die Tasche); reichen, gehen, sich erstrecken (*to* bis; *into* bis in ... hinein); gelangen (*to* nach); sich belaufen (*to* auf); zu erreichen, zu erlangen suchen, erstreben, etw (geistig) zu erfassen versuchen (*after s.th.* etw); *(to ~ down)* herunterreichen; *to ~ out, forth* ausstrecken; *to ~ up to* reichen bis zu; *s* Ausstrecken *n*; Berührung; Erreichung; Reich-, Tragweite *f*, Fassungsvermögen *n*, -kraft *f*; Bereich *m* od *n*, Spielraum *m*; Strecke (Weg); Strecke Land, Landzunge; Flußstrecke *f*, Meeresarm *m*; *as far as the eye can ~* soweit das Auge reicht; *out of ~* unerreichbar; *within ~* in Reichweite; erschwinglich; *to be beyond the ~ of s.o.* für jdn unerreichbar sein; nicht in jds Macht stehen; *to be within easy ~ of* leicht zu erreichen, nicht weit (entfernt) sein von; *to be ~ed* erfaßt werden (*by* von); *to ~ a high price* e-n hohen Preis erzielen; *he was beyond the ~ of human help* niemand konnte ihm (mehr) helfen; *to have a long ~ (fig)* e-n langen Arm haben; **~able** ['-əbl] erreichbar; **~less** ['-lis] unerreichbar; **~-me-down** *s fam* Anzug *m*, Kleid *n* von der Stange; *pl* Konfektion(sware) *f*; *a* billig; Konfektions-; von der Stange.

react [ri(:)'ækt] *itr* zurückwirken (*on, upon* auf; *against* gegen); in der entgegengesetzten Richtung wirken; entgegenarbeiten; zurückgehen; reagieren (*to* auf) *a. chem*; **~ance** [-əns] *el* Reaktanz *f*, Blindwiderstand *m*; **~ion** [-'ækʃən] Rück-, Gegenwirkung *f* (*against* gegen); Rückschlag; Gegendruck; Rückschritt *m*; Reaktion (*to, on* auf) *a. pol u. chem physiol psychol*; *fig* Stellungnahme *f*, Verhalten *n*, Einstellung; *el* Rückkoppelung *f*; *mil* Gegenstoß, -schlag; *(Waffe)* Rückstoß *m*; *~~ time (psychol)* Reaktionszeit *f*; **~ionary** [-'ækʃnəri] *a pol* reaktionär, rückschrittlich; *com* rückläufig; *s* Reaktionär *m*; **~ivate** [-'æktiveit] *tr* reaktivieren; **~ive** [-'æktiv] rückwirkend; reagierend (*to* auf); empfänglich (*to* für); *el* Blind-; **~or** [-'æktə] *el radio* Drossel(spule) *f*; *phys* Reaktor *m*; *nuclear ~~* Kernreaktor *m*.

re-act [ri(:)'ækt] *tr theat* wieder aufführen.

read [ri:d] *irr read, read* [red] *tr* lesen; ver-, vorlesen (*to s.o.* jdm); *(Buch)* aus-, durchlesen; *(to ~ off)* ablesen; entziffern; *fig* ablesen (*in s.o.'s face* aus jds Gesicht); auslegen, deuten, interpretieren; verstehen (*as* als); hineinlesen (*in, into* in); *(die Zukunft)* vorhersagen; *(Rätsel)* lösen; hören, erfahren; *Br* studieren; *(als Lesart)* haben, lauten; *(Meßgerät)* anzeigen; *Am sl* durchschauen, sorgfältig prüfen; *itr* (laut) lesen; hören, erfahren (*about, of* von); lernen, studieren; Vorlesungen halten; sich vorbereiten (*for s.th.* auf etw); lauten; sich lesen (lassen) (*like* wie); *s* Lesen *n*, Lektüre; Zeit *f* zum Lesen; *to ~ between the lines* zwischen den Zeilen lesen; *to ~ a will* ein Testament eröffnen; *to have a quiet ~* Zeit zum ruhigen Lesen haben; *to ~* **on** weiterlesen; *to ~* **out** laut lesen; zu Ende lesen; *to ~* **over**, *to ~* **through** durchlesen; *to ~* **up** sich einarbeiten (*on* in); **~able** ['ri:dəbl] lesbar; **~er** ['-ə] Leser; Vorleser *a. rel*; (Verlags-)Lektor; *typ* Korrektor; Dozent, außerordentliche(r) Professor; Ableser *m (von Meßgeräten)*; Lesebuch; (Mikrofilm-)Ablesegerät *n*; *Am sl* Steckbrief *m*, Lizenz *f*; *pl Am sl* gezinkte Karten *f pl*; *~~'s mark* Korrekturzeichen *n*; **~ership** ['-əʃip] Leserkreis *m*; Dozentur *f*; **~ing** ['-iŋ] *a* Lese-; *s* Lesen *n*, Lektüre *f*; Vorlesen *n*, Vorlesung *f*; Studium *n*; Belesenheit *f*; Lesestoff *m*, Lektüre; Lesart, Variante; Auslegung, Deutung, Erklärung, Interpretation; *parl* Lesung *f*; *tech* Ablesen *n*; *(Meßgerät, Zähler)* Stand *m*; *a book that makes a good ~~* ein interessantes, ein anregend geschriebenes Buch *n*; *proof ~~* Korrekturlesen *n*; *~~-desk* Lesepult *n*; *~~-glasses (pl)* Lesebrille *f*; *~~-lamp* Leselampe *f*; *~~ matter* Lesestoff *m*; *~~ public* Leserschaft *f*; *~~-room* Leseraum *m*, -zimmer *n*.

read|ily ['redili] *adv* bereitwillig, ohne Zögern, ohne weiteres, *fam* anstandslos; gleich, sofort; (ganz) leicht, ohne Schwierigkeit; **~iness** ['redinis] Bereitschaft; Bereitwilligkeit, Geneigtheit; Geschicktheit, Gewandtheit, Wendigkeit; Fertigkeit; Schnelligkeit, Fixigkeit *f*; *to keep in ~~* bereithalten; *~~ of mind* Geistesgegenwart *f*; **~y** ['redi] *a (Person* od *Sache)* bereit, fertig (*for* für; *to* zu); prompt; *mar* klar; *(Geld)* verfügbar, flüssig; bereit, willens, willig, geneigt (*to* zu); *(Markt)* aufnahmebereit; geschickt, gewandt, wendig; schnell, rasch, flink, fix; griffbereit, zur Hand, zur Verfügung (stehend), bequem; *adv mit pp* fertig; *s (Gewehr)* Anschlag *m*; *the ~~* das Bargeld, die Kasse; *tr to make ~~* vorbereiten, fertigmachen; *to ~~ o.s.* sich vorbereiten, sich fertigmachen; *to find a ~~ market (com)* gut gehen; rasch Absatz finden; *at the ~~ (Sache)* in Bereitschaft, bereit, *fam* gezückt; *(Gewehr)* schußbereit, in Anschlag; *I feel ~~ for dinner* mich plagt der Hunger; *he's always ~~ with an excuse* er ist immer mit e-r Entschuldigung bei der Hand; *~~ for judg(e)ment (jur)* spruchreif; *~~ for printing* druckreif; *~~ for sea* seeklar; *~~ for take-off (aero)* startklar; *~~ for working* betriebsfertig; *~~ cash, money* Bargeld *n*, -zahlung *f*; *~~-made (a)* Konfektions-*(Kleidung)*; *fig* Klischee-, stereotyp; unoriginell, unpersönlich; *~~ reckoner* Rechentabelle *f*; *~~ room (aero)* Bereitschaftsraum *m (für fliegendes Personal)*; *~~-to-eat* kochfertig; *~~-to-wear a* Konfektions-*(Kleidung)*; *~~-witted (a)* von schneller Auffassungsgabe, schlagfertig.

readjust ['ri:ə'dʒʌst] *tr* wieder in Ordnung bringen; neu ordnen; *tech* nachstellen; **~ment** ['-mənt] Neuordnung, -orientierung; Reorganisation; Sanierung *f*.

readmi|ssion ['ri:əd'miʃən] Wiederzulassung *f (to* zu); **~t** ['-'mit] *tr* wiederzulassen *(to* zu); **~ttance** ['-əns] Wiederzulassung *f*.

reaffirm ['ri:ə'fə:m] *tr* nochmals versichern; erneut bestätigen; **~ation** [-æfə:'meiʃən] nochmalige Versicherung *f*.

reafforest ['ri:æ'fɔrist] *tr* wiederaufforsten; **~ation** [-æfɔris'teiʃən] Wiederaufforstung *f*.

reagent [ri(:)'eidʒənt] *chem* Reagens *n*; *fig* Wirkung *f (against* gegen).

real ['riəl] *a* wirklich, tatsächlich, real, wahr, effektiv; echt, authentisch; *(Blumen)* natürlich; *jur* dinglich, Sach-; unbeweglich; Grund-, Land-; *phys* reell; *adv Am fam* mächtig, gewaltig, kolossal; *the ~ McCoy* das Eigentliche, Echte, Unübertreffliche; *it's the ~ thing* das ist das einzig Wahre; **~ action** *jur* dingliche Klage *f*; **~ assets** *pl*, **earnings** *pl* Realeinkommen *n*; **~ estate** Grundbesitz *m*, -vermögen *n*, Immobilien, Liegenschaften *pl*, Grund u. Boden *m*; **~-estate** *attr*: *~~ agent, broker* Grundstücksmakler *m*; *~~ mortgage* Hypothek *f*; *~~ price* Grundstückspreis *m*; *~~ recording-office (Am)* Grundbuchamt *n*; *~~ register (Am)* Grundbuch *n*; *~~ security* hypothekarische Sicherheit *f*; **~ injury** Körperverletzung *f*; **~ investment** Sachanlage *f*; **~ism** ['-izm] Realismus *m*; **~ist** ['-ist] Realist *m*; **~istic** [riə'listik] realistisch; sachlich, wirklichkeitsnah, nüchtern, praktisch; **~ity** [ri(:)'æliti] Wirklichkeit, Realität *f*; *in ~~* in Wirklichkeit; **~izable** ['riəlaizəbl] aus-, durchführbar, realisierbar; erkennbar, verständlich; *fin* realisierbar, verkäuflich, flüssig zu machen(d); kapitalisierbar; verwertbar; *(Börse)* börsengängig; **~ization** [riəlai'zeiʃən] Verwirklichung, Realisation; Einsicht *f*, Verständnis *n (of* gen); Vorstellungskraft; lebendige Vorstellung; *com* Flüssigmachung, Liquidation; Verwertung *f*, Verkauf *m*, Glattstellung; Kapitalisierung *f*; **~ize** ['riəlaiz] *tr* verwirklichen, wirklich machen, realisieren, in die Tat umsetzen; einsehen, verstehen, erkennen, sich vergegenwärtigen, (er-)fassen; sich lebhaft vorstellen; *fin* flüssig, zu Geld machen, veräußern; glattstellen; *(Gewinn)* erzielen, machen, *fam* einstecken; **~ly** ['riəli] *adv* wirklich, tatsächlich, in Wirklichkeit, in der Tat, wahrhaftig; eigentlich; **~ property** = *~ estate*; **~ servitude** Grunddienstbarkeit *f*; **~ silk** Naturseide *f*; **~tor** ['-tə] *Am* Grundstücksmakler *m*; **~ty** ['-ti] = *~ estate*; **~ value** Sachwert *m*; **~ wages** *pl* Reallohn *m*.

realm [relm] Königreich; *fig* Reich *n*, Sphäre *f*, Bereich *m* od *n*, Gebiet *n*.

ream [ri:m] **1.** Ries *n (480 od 516 Bogen)*; *pl fam* e-e (ganze) Menge, e-e Masse; **2.** *tr (to ~ out) (Loch, Öffnung)* erweitern; (aus)räumen; *(Zitrone, Apfelsine)* ausdrücken, -pressen; **~er** ['-ə] Reibahle *f*.

reanimat|e [ri:'ænimeit] *tr* ins Leben zurückrufen, wieder ins Leben rufen; *fig* wieder, neu beleben.

reap [ri:p] *tr (Getreide)* schneiden, mähen; (ein)ernten; *(Acker)* abernten; *(Nutzen)* ziehen; *fig* ernten; *itr* ernten *a. fig*; *to sow the wind and ~ the whirlwind (fig)* Wind säen u. Sturm ernten; *to ~ where one has not sown (fig)* ernten, wo man nicht gesät hat; **~er** ['-ə] Schnitter, Mäher *m*; Mähmaschine *f*; *the (Grim) R~~* der Schnitter Tod; *~~-binder* Mähbinder *m*; **~ing-hook** Sichel *f*; **~ing-machine** Mähmaschine *f*.

reappear ['ri:ə'piə] *itr* wiedererscheinen; **~ance** ['-rəns] Wiedererscheinen *n*.

reappl|ication ['ri:æpli'keiʃən] Wiederanwendung *f*; erneute(s) Gesuch *n*; **~y** ['ri:ə'plai] *tr* wieder anwenden; erneut einreichen; *itr* sich erneut bewerben *(for* um).

reappoint ['ri:ə'pɔint] *tr* wiederanstellen; **~ment** ['-mənt] Wiederanstellung, -ernennung *f*.

rear ['riə] **1.** hintere(r), rückwärtige(r) Teil *m*; Rückseite *f*; Hintergrund; *fig* Schwanz *m (e-r Schlange)*; *mil* die rückwärtigen Linien *od* Stellungen *f pl*; *(~-guard)* Nachhut *f*; *fam* Hinterteil; *fam* Klo *n*; *in the ~* hinten; *to attack, to take in (the) ~* von hinten angreifen; *to be in the ~, to bring up the ~* der letzte sein, den Schluß bilden; **~-admiral** *mar* Konteradmiral *m*; **~ army area** rückwärtige(s) Armeegebiet *n*; **~-axle** Hinterachse *f*; *~~ drive* Hinterradantrieb *m*; **~ communications** *pl mil* rückwärtige Verbindungen *f pl*; **~ cover** Rückendeckung *f*; **~ drive** *mot* Heckantrieb *m*; **~ engine** *mot* Heckmotor *m*; **~ gunner** Heckschütze *m*; **~-lamp, -light** *mot* Rücklicht *n*; **~most** hinterst, letzt; **~ party** Nachkommando *n*; **~ position** *mil* rückwärtige, Auffangstellung *f*; **~ rank** *mil* hintere(s) Glied *n*; **~ sight** *(Geschütz)* Aufsatz *m*; *(Gewehr)* Kimme *f*; **~ view mirror** Rückspiegel *m*; **~ wall** Rückwand *f*; **~ward** ['-wə(:)d] *a* hinter, rückwärtig; *adv a. ~~s* rückwärts, zurück; nach hinten; **~ wheel** Hinterrad *n*; **~-window** *mot* Rückfenster *n*; **2.** *tr* aufrichten, heben; errichten, (er-)bauen; *agr* ziehen, züchten; *(Kind)* auf-, erziehen; *itr (Pferd)* sich (auf-)bäumen; *(to ~ up) (im Zorn)* auffahren; *(Berg)* sich erheben.

rearm ['ri:'ɑ:m] *tr* wiederbewaffnen; *itr* (wieder)aufrüsten; **~ament** ['-əmənt] (Wieder-)Aufrüstung *f*.

rearrange ['ri:ə'reindʒ] *tr* neu (an)ordnen; umgruppieren; **~ment** [-mənt] Neuordnung; neue Anordnung; Umwandlung; Änderung; *chem* Umlagerung *f*.

reason ['ri:zn] *s* Vernunft *f*; Verstand *m*; Vernünftigkeit, Verständigkeit, Einsicht *f*, gesunde(r) Menschenverstand *m*; Erklärung, Begründung *f (of* für); Grund *m*, Ursache *f*, Anlaß *m (of* für; *for doing s.th.* etw zu tun); *itr* logisch denken; Schlußfolgerungen, Schlüsse ziehen *(from* aus); vernünftig denken *od* urteilen *od* reden *(on, about* über); gut zureden *(with s.o.* jdm); *tr* untersuchen, durchdenken, überlegen; folgern *(that* daß); begründen; erörtern, diskutieren *(with* mit); überzeugen *(into* von); abbringen *(out, of* von); ausreden *(s.o. out of s.th.* jdm etw); einreden *(s.o. into s.th.* jdm etw); *to ~ away* wegdiskutieren; *by ~ of* wegen; auf Grund *gen*; *for this ~* aus diesem Grunde; *for no particular ~* aus keinem besonderen Grund; *in ~* begründetermaßen; in vernünftiger Weise; *out of all ~* (ganz) unvernünftig, sinnlos; völlig unberechtigt; *with ~* mit (Fug u.) Recht; *without rhyme or ~* ohne Sinn u. Verstand; *without any ~* grundlos; *the ~ why* weswegen; deswegen; *to bring to ~* zur Vernunft bringen; *to give a ~* e-n Grund angeben; *to listen to ~* Vernunft annehmen; *to lose o.'s ~* den Verstand verlieren; *to stand to ~* Sinn u. Verstand, Hand u. Fuß haben; einleuchtend sein; *there is ~ to believe that* es besteht Grund zur Annahme, daß; *for what ~?* aus welchem Grund? **~able** [-əbl] vernünftig; verständig, verständnisvoll; sinnvoll; *(Frist)* angemessen; *(Zweifel)* berechtigt; (sich) in (vernünftigen) Grenzen, in Maßen (halten), nicht übertrieben, mäßig; *(Preis)* vernünftig, tragbar, angemessen, gangbar, annehmbar; *(Forderung)* billig; **~ableness** ['-əblnis] Vernünftigkeit; Verständigkeit; Annehmbarkeit *f*; **~ably** ['-əbli] *adv* vernünftig(erweise); einigermaßen, leidlich, ziemlich; **~ing** ['-iŋ] *s* Folgern, Urteilen *n*; Schlußfolgerungen *f pl*, Beweisführung; Urteilskraft *f*, -vermögen *n*; (Vernunft-)Gründe *m pl*; *a* vernunftbegabt.

reassembl|e ['ri:ə'sembl] *tr itr* (sich) wieder versammeln; *tr tech* wieder zs.setzen; **~y** [-i] *parl* Wiederzs.tritt *m*.

reassert ['ri:ə'sə:t] *tr* wieder, aufs neue behaupten; wieder geltend machen.

reassign ['ri:ə'sain] *tr* wieder abtreten, zurückübertragen; wieder zuteilen.

reassur|ance [ri:ə'ʃuərəns] Beruhigung; erneute Versicherung; Rückversicherung *f*; **~e** [-'ʃuə] *tr* (wieder) beruhigen; aufs neue versichern; *fin* wieder versichern; rückversichern; **~ing** [-riŋ] beruhigend.

rebapt|ism ['ri:'bæptizm] Wiedertaufe *f*; **~ize** ['-bæp'taiz] *tr* noch einmal taufen; umtaufen, -benennen.

rebate ['ri:beit] **1.** *s* (Preis-)Nachlaß, Abschlag, Abzug *m*, Ermäßigung, Verbilligung *f*, Rabatt *m (on* auf); *(Bank)* Bonifikation *f*; *tr* [ri:'beit] *tr (Preis)* herabsetzen; verringern, vermindern; **2.** *s* ['ræbit] u. *v* [ri:'beit] = *rabbet*.

rebel ['rebl] *s* Rebell, Aufrührer, Aufständische(r) *m*; *a* aufrührerisch, aufständisch; Rebellen-; *tech* spröde; *itr* [ri'bel] *itr* sich empören, rebellieren *(against* gegen) *a. fig*; **~lion** [ri'beljən] Empörung, Rebellion *f*, Aufruhr, Aufstand *m (against* gegen); **~lious** [ri'beljəs] aufrührerisch, aufständisch; rebellisch, widersetzlich; widerspenstig.

re|birth ['ri:'bə:θ] Wiedergeburt *f a. fig*; **~born** ['-'bɔ:n] wiedergeboren *a. fig*.

rebound [ri'baund] *itr* ab-, zurückprallen; *fig* zurückfallen *(on, upon s.o.* auf jdn); *fig (Gesundheit)* wiederhergestellt werden; *(Lebensgeister, -mut)* zurückkehren; *s* Rückprall *(from* von); *fig* Rückschlag, Umschwung *m*, Reaktion *f*; *to catch, to take s.o. at,*

on the ~~ jdn (nach e-m Fehlschlag) vom Gegenteil überzeugen.
rebuff [ri'bʌf] *s* Zurückweisung; (schroffe) Ablehnung, Abfuhr *f*; *tr* abweisen, *fam* e-e Abfuhr erteilen (*s.o.* jdm); *(Person, Sache)* ab-, zurückweisen; *(Sache)* ablehnen; *to meet with a ~* e-e Zurückweisung erfahren (*from* von).
rebuild ['ri:'bild] *irr s. build*; *tr* wieder auf-, zs.bauen.
rebuke [ri'bju:k] *tr* zurechtweisen, tadeln, *fam* abkanzeln (*s.o. for s.th.* jdn wegen etw); *s* Zurechtweisung *f*, Tadel *m*, *fam* Zigarre *f*.
rebus ['ri:bəs] Bilderrätsel *n*, Rebus *m* od *n*.
rebut [ri'bʌt] *tr* zurückweisen, ablehnen; widerlegen; *(Vermutung)* entkräften; **~tal** [-l] *jur* Widerlegung; Entkräftung *f*; Gegenbeweis *m*; **~er** ['-ə] Ablehnende(r) *m*; *jur* Quadruplik *f*.
recalcitr|ance, -cy [ri'kælsitrəns(i)] Widerspenstigkeit *f*, störrische(s) Wesen *n*; **~ant** [-t] widerspenstig, störrisch.
recall [ri'kɔ:l] *tr* zurückrufen; erinnern (*to* an); sich ins Gedächtnis zurückrufen, sich (wieder) erinnern an; zurücknehmen, -ziehen, widerrufen; *com* (auf)kündigen; ab-, zurückberufen; *jur (Urteil)* aufheben; *mil* wieder einberufen; *s* Zurücknahme *f*, Widerruf *m*; *com* Aufkündigung; *Am* (Recht *n* der) Abberufung *f* (durch Volksentscheid); *mil* Signal *n* zum Sammeln; *tele* Rückruf *m*; *beyond, past ~* unwiederbringlich, unwiderruflich; (völlig) vergessen; *until ~led* bis auf Widerruf.
recant [ri'kænt] *itr tr* (*bes.* öffentlich, feierlich) widerrufen; **~ation** [ri:kæn'teiʃən] Widerruf *m*.
recap ['ri:'kæp] *tr (Reifen, Lauffläche)* runderneuern; vulkanisieren; *fam* kurz zs.fassen.
recapitulat|e [ri:kə'pitjuleit] *tr* kurz wiederholen, rekapitulieren; kurz zs.-fassen; **~ion** ['ri:kəpitju'leiʃən] kurze Wiederholung, kurze Zs.fassung *f*.
recapture ['ri:'kæptʃə] *tr* zurück-, wieder in Besitz nehmen; wieder besetzen; ins Gedächtnis zurückrufen; *s* Zurücknahme; Wiedererlangung; Wiederbesetzung *f*.
recast ['ri:'ka:st] *tr* umschmelzen, -gießen; *fig* umformen; um-, neu gestalten, umarbeiten; neu formulieren, umschreiben; nachrechnen, -zählen; überprüfen; *theat* neu besetzen; *s* Umschmelzung; Umformung, -arbeitung, Neugestaltung *f*; neue(r) Entwurf *m*; *theat* Neubesetzung *f*.
recce, reccy ['reki], **recco** ['rekou], **recon** ['rekən] *sl mil (= reconnaissance)* *s* Aufklärung, Erkundung *f*; *attr* Aufklärungs-; *tr (= reconnoitre)* aufklären, erkunden.
reced|e [ri(:)'si:d] *itr* zurückweichen, -treten; entschwinden; *fig* sich zurückziehen, zurücktreten (*from* von); Abstand nehmen (*from* von); verzichten (*from* auf); aufgeben (*from o.'s opinion* s-e Meinung); *(Preise)* nachgeben; *(to ~~ into the background)* in den Hintergrund treten; *(aus dem Gedächtnis)* entschwinden; *a ~ing chin, forehead* ein fliehendes Kinn, e-e fliehende Stirn.
receipt [ri'si:t] *s* (Koch-)Rezept *n*; Empfang *m*, Annahme *f*, Erhalt *m*; Quittung, Empfangsbestätigung *f*; Beleg *m*; *pl* Einnahme(n *pl*) *f*, Eingänge *m pl*; eingehende Waren *f pl*; *(tax ~s)* Steueraufkommen *n*; *tr itr* quittieren; den Empfang bestätigen (*s.th.* e-r S); *against ~* gegen Quittung; *(up)on ~* bei Empfang, nach Eingang; gegen Quittung; *to acknowledge ~* den Empfang bestätigen; *to give s.o. a ~* jdm e-e Quittung ausstellen; *accountable ~* Rechnungsbeleg *m*; *daily, day's ~* Tageseinnahme, -kasse *f*; *date, day of ~* Eingangsdatum *n*; *delivery ~* Lagerschein *m*; *luggage-~* Gepäckschein *m*; *net ~s (pl)* Nettoeinkommen *n*; Betriebsüberschüsse *m pl*; *return ~* Rück-, Empfangsschein *m*; *warehouse-~* Lagerschein *m*; *~ of money* Geldempfang, -eingang *m*; **~-book** Rezept-, Quittungsbuch *n*; **~-form** Quittungsformular *n*.
receiv|able [ri'si:vəbl] *a* annehmbar, zulässig; *com* (noch) zu zahlen(d), ausstehend, fällig; *pl Am* Außenstände *m pl*; *accounts ~~ (pl)* Außenstände *pl*, Forderungen, Aktivschulden *f pl*; *bills ~~* Wechselforderungen *f pl*; *mortgages ~~* Hypothekenforderungen *f pl*; **~e** [ri'si:v] *tr* erhalten, bekommen; empfangen, in Empfang nehmen; *(Besucher)* bewillkommnen; an-, auf-, einnehmen; entgegen-, hinnehmen; *(Geld)* vereinnahmen; *(Gehalt)* beziehen; hinnehmen müssen, erfahren, erleiden; anhören; anerkennen; *jur* hehlen; *itr* Besuch empfangen; *rel* das Abendmahl empfangen; **~ed** [-d] *a* erhalten, empfangen; (allgemein) anerkannt, herrschend; echt, gültig, vorschriftsmäßig; *when ~~* nach Erhalt; **~er** [-ə] Empfänger, Adressat; (Steuer-)Einnehmer; Hehler; *(~~ in bankruptcy)* Zwangs-, Konkursverwalter; Liquidator; Treuhänder; *tech* Behälter; *chem* Rezipient; *tele* Hörer; *radio video* Empfänger *m*; *head-~~ (radio)* Kopfhörer *m*; *hook of the ~~* Hörergabel *f*; *~~ of a loan* Darlehensnehmer *m*; *~~ of stolen goods* Hehler *m*; *~~-shell (tele)* Hörermuschel *f*; **~ership** [-əʃip] Zwangs-, Konkursverwaltung *f*; *(temporary ~~)* Geschäftsaufsicht *f*; *under ~~* in Konkurs; **~ing** [-iŋ] Ab-, Annahme *f*, Empfang *m a. radio*; *(~~ department)* Warenannahmestelle; *jur* Hehlerei *f*; *~~-office* Annahmestelle *f*; *~~-order* Konkurseröffnungsbeschluß *m*; *~~-room (radio)* Empfangsraum *m*; *com* Wareneingangsstelle *f*; *~~-set (radio video)* Empfänger *m*, Empfangsgerät *n*; *~~-station* Empfangsstation *f*.
recen|cy ['ri:snsi] Neuheit *f*; **~t** ['-t] *a* neu, frisch, jung, modern; *(Nachrichten)* letzt; *ours is a ~~ acquaintance* wir kennen uns erst seit kurzem; **~tly** ['-tli] *adv* neulich, kürzlich, vor kurzem, unlängst, *lit* jüngst; *until quite ~~* bis vor kurzem; **~tness** ['-tnis] Neuheit *f*.
recension [ri'senʃən] (Text-)Revision, kritische Durchsicht *f*; kritisch durchgesehene(r), revidierte(r) Text *m*.
recept|acle [ri'septəkl] Behälter *m*, Gefäß *n*; *el* Stecker *m*, Steckdose *f*; *bot (floral ~~)* Blütenboden *m*; **~ible** [ri'septibl] aufnahmefähig; **~ion** [ri'sepʃən] Aufnahme *f*, Empfang *m*; An-, Hinnahme, Billigung; Zulassung *f*; *tele radio* Empfang *m*; *fig* Aufnahmefähigkeit *f*; *to give s.o. a warm ~~* jdm e-n warmen Empfang bereiten; *to meet with a favo(u)rable ~~* günstig aufgenommen werden; *state ~~* Staatsempfang *m*; *~~ area, camp, centre* Aufnahmegebiet, -lager, -zentrum *n*; *~~-clerk (Am)* Empfangschef *m*; *~~-desk* Empfang(sbüro *n*) *m*; *~~ hall* Empfangshalle *f*; *~~-office* Empfangsbüro *n*; *~~ order (med)* Entmündigungsbeschluß *m*; *~~-room* Empfangsraum *m*, -zimmer *n*, Salon *m*; **~ionist** [-ʃənist] Empfangschef *m*, -dame; Sprechstundenhilfe *f*; **~ive** [ri'septiv] Empfangs-; empfangs-, aufnahmebereit; empfänglich (*of* für); **~iveness** [-ivnis], **~ivity** [risep'tiviti] Empfangs-, Aufnahmebereitschaft; Empfänglichkeit *f* (*of* für).
recess [ri'ses] *s* kurze Unterbrechung *od* Pause *f*; (Schul-, Gerichts-, Parlaments-)Ferien *pl*; *arch* Vertiefung; Nische *f*, Alkoven *m*; *geog* Depression *f*; *anat* (kleiner) Hohlraum *m*, Vertiefung, Abgeschiedenheit *f*, Schlupfwinkel *m*; *pl fig* geheime Winkel *m pl*, Falten *f pl*; *tr* zurücksetzen; einsenken, aussparen, -schneiden; *itr Am jur* sich vertagen; **~ion** [-'seʃən] Zurücktreten, -weichen *n*; *com* Rückgang, Rückschlag *m*, Flaute, Rezession, Depression *f*; **~ional** [-'seʃənl] *a* Rücktritts-; *parl* Ferien-; *s rel* Schlußgesang *m*; **~ive** [ri'sesiv] zurückgehend, nachlassend; *biol (Vererbung)* rezessiv.
recidiv|ism [ri'sidivizm] *jur* (gewohnheitsmäßige) Rückfälligkeit *f*; **~ist** [-ist] rückfällige(r), Gewohnheitsverbrecher *m*; **~ous** [-əs] rückfällig.
recipe ['resipi] *med pharm allg* Rezept; *fig* Mittel *n*.
recipient [ri'sipiənt] *s* Empfänger *m*; *a* empfangsbereit, empfänglich.
reciproc|al [ri'siprəkl] *a* gegen-, wechselseitig, entsprechend; *bes. math* reziprok; *s* Gegenstück *n*, Ergänzung *f*; *math* reziproke(r) Wert, Kehrwert *m*; *~~ insurance* Versicherung *f* auf Gegenseitigkeit; *~~ trade agreement* Handelsabkommen *n* mit Meistbegünstigungsklausel; **~ate** [-keit] *tr* austauschen, wechseln; *(Gefühle)* erwidern (*with* mit); *itr tech* pendeln; *fig* e-n Gegendienst leisten; sich erkenntlich zeigen (*for* für; *with* mit); **~ating**: [-keitiŋ]: *~~ engine* Kolbenmotor *m*; **~ation** [risiprə'keiʃən] *tech* Pendeln *n*; Wechselwirkung; Entsprechung *f*; Austausch *m*; Erwiderung *f*; **~ity** [resi'prɔsiti] Wechsel-, Gegenseitigkeit *a. pl*; Wechselwirkung *f*.
recit|al [ri'saitl] Auf-, Hersagen *n*; Aufzählung, Schilderung (der Einzelheiten); *jur* Darlegung des Sachverhalts; Wiedergabe *f*, Bericht; *mus* (Solo-)Vortrag *m*, Darbietung; Hörfolge *f*, Programm *n*; **~ation** [resi'teiʃən] Auf-, Hersagen *n*, Deklamation *f*, Vortrag *m*; Vortragsstück *n*; *(Schule) Am* Übungsstunde *f*, Abfragen *n*; *~~ room (Am)* Klassenzimmer *n*; **~ative** [resitə'ti:v] *s mus* Rezitativ *n*; *a mus* rezitativ; deklamatorisch; **~e** [ri'sait] *tr itr* auf-, hersagen, deklamieren, vortragen; *tr* aufzählen; genau schildern, darstellen; **~er** [-ə] Rezitator, Deklamator, Vortragende(r) *m*; Vortragsbuch *n*.
reckless ['reklis] nachlässig, achtlos, sorglos, unbekümmert (*of* um); rücksichtslos, unverantwortlich; *jur* grob fahrlässig; **~ness** ['-nis] Nachlässigkeit, Unbekümmertheit (*of* um); Sorglosigkeit; Rücksichtslosigkeit; *jur* grobe Fahrlässigkeit *f*.
reckon ['rekən] *tr* zählen, (er)rechnen; be-, anrechnen, in Ansatz bringen (*s.th. to s.o.* jdm etw); *com* berechnen, kalkulieren; zählen (*among, with* zu); rechnen (*among, with* unter); einstufen, einschätzen, ansehen, betrachten (*as* als); halten (*for* für); einschätzen, beurteilen; *itr* zählen, gelten, etwas ausmachen; rechnen, sich verlassen (*on, upon* auf); (ab)rechnen (*with* mit); *fam* denken, meinen, annehmen, vermuten; *to ~ for* berücksichtigen; *to ~ in* einbeziehen; einrechnen; *to ~ over* nachrechnen; *to ~ up* aus-, zs.-

rechnen; auf-, verrechnen; *to ~ without o.'s host (fig)* die Rechnung ohne den Wirt machen; *to be ~ed* gelten; **~er** ['-ə] Rechner *m*; *(ready ~~)* Rechentabellen *f pl*; **~ing** ['-iŋ] Zählung, (Be-)Rechnung *f*; Berechnungen, Vermutungen *f pl*; An-, Abrechnung; *(zu bezahlende)* Rechnung *f*; *mar* Besteck; *(dead ~~)* gegißte(s) Besteck *n*; *to the best of my ~~* nach bestem Wissen u. Gewissen; *to be out in o.'s ~~* sich verrechnet haben *a. fig*; *to pay the ~~* die Rechnung bezahlen *a. fig*; *fig* die Suppe auslöffeln; *day of ~~* Zahltag; *rel* Tag des Gerichts, Jüngste(r) Tag; *pol* Tag *m* der Abrechnung.

reclaim [ri'kleim] *tr* zurückgewinnen; *(Ödland)* kultivieren, urbar machen; *(Neuland)* gewinnen; *(aus Abfällen)* rückgewinnen; *tech* regenerieren; *(Tiere)* zähmen; *(Menschen)* bekehren; kulturell, sittlich heben *od* bessern; zurückbringen (*from* von); zurückfordern, herausverlangen; **~able** [-əbl] regenerier-, kultur-, (ver)besserungsfähig.

reclamation [reklə'meiʃən] Nutzbarmachung, Kultivierung, Urbarmachung; (Neu-)Gewinnung; *tech* Rückgewinnung; *Am* Berichtigung; *fig* kulturelle, sittliche Hebung, Besserung; *jur* Zurückforderung *f*; Einspruch, Einwand *m*, Beanstandung, Reklamation *f*.

recline [ri'klain] *tr itr* (sich) zurücklehnen (*on* auf; *against* gegen); (sich) niederlegen; *itr fig* sich verlassen (*on, upon* auf).

recluse [ri'klu:s, *Am* 're-] *s* Klausner, Eremit; Einsiedler *m*; *a* zurückgezogen lebend; eremitenhaft.

recogn|ition [rekəg'niʃən] (Wieder-)Erkennen *n*; Anerkennung *(e-r Leistung, e-s Staates)*; Bestätigung, Ratifizierung *f*; *beyond ~~* bis zur Unkenntlichkeit *(entstellt)*; *in ~~ of* als Anerkennung für; **~izable** ['rekəgnaizəbl] erkennbar, kenntlich, wiederzuerkennen(d); **~izance** [ri'kɔgnizəns] *jur* (schriftliche) Verpflichtung; Sicherheitsleistung, Kaution *f*; Schuldschein *m*; Anerkennung *f*; Geständnis *n*; *to enter into ~~s* Kaution stellen; **~ize** ['rekəgnaiz] *tr* wieder(er)kennen (*as* als); erkennen (*by* an); *(Leistung, Staat)* anerkennen; beachten, grüßen; *Am* das Wort erteilen (*s.o.* jdm).

recoil [ri'kɔil] *itr* sich zurückziehen; zurückfahren, -prallen; zurückschnellen; *fig* zurückfallen (*on, upon* auf); zurückschrecken (*from* vor); *s* Rückzug *m*; Zurückprallen, -schnellen *n*; *(Feuerwaffe)* Rückstoß *m*; *fig* Zurückschaudern *n* (*from* vor); Abscheu, Widerwillen *m* (*from* vor); **~less** [-lis] *(Geschütz)* ohne Rückstoß.

recollect [rekə'lekt] *tr itr* sich besinnen auf, sich erinnern an, ins Gedächtnis zurückrufen; **~ion** [-'lekʃən] Erinnerung (*of* an); *fig* Sammlung, Fassung *f*; *within my ~~* soweit ich mich erinnern kann; *~~s of youth* Jugenderinnerungen *f pl*.

re-collect ['ri:kə'lekt] *tr* wieder (auf-, zs.)sammeln, wieder zs.bringen; *to re-collect o.s.* sich sammeln, sich fassen, wieder zu sich kommen.

recommence ['ri:kə'mens] *tr itr* wieder, neu anfangen *od* beginnen.

recommend [rekə'mend] *tr* (an)empfehlen (*for* für; *as* als; *to do* zu tun); vorschlagen, befürworten; raten (*s.th.* zu e-r S); anvertrauen (*to s.o.* jdm); **~able** [-əbl] empfehlenswert, zu empfehlen(d); **~ation** [rekəmen'deiʃən] Empfehlung, Befürwortung *f*; Vorschlag, Rat(schlag) *m*; *letter of ~~* Empfehlungsschreiben *n*; **~atory** [-'mendətəri] empfehlend; Empfehlungs-.

recommission ['ri:kə'miʃən] *tr (Schiff, Flugzeug)* wieder in Dienst stellen; *(Offizier)* reaktivieren.

recommit [ri:kə'mit] *tr* wieder übergeben; *(Verbrechen)* wieder begehen *od* verüben; *(Gesetzentwurf)* an e-n Ausschuß zurückverweisen; *to ~ to prison* wieder festnehmen.

recompense ['rekəmpens] *tr* belohnen, entschädigen (*for* für; *with* mit; *by* durch); vergüten, vergelten; zurückerstatten, ersetzen, wiedergutmachen; *s* Belohnung, Entschädigung *f*, Entgelt *n*, Vergütung (*for* für); Rückerstattung *f*; (Schaden-)Ersatz *m*.

recompos|e ['ri:kəm'pouz] *tr* wieder, neu zs.setzen *od* anordnen *od* umgruppieren; *typ* neu setzen; *fig* wieder beruhigen.

reconcil|able ['rekənsailəbl] versöhnlich; vereinbar, verträglich (*with* mit); **~e** ['-sail] *tr* (wieder) versöhnen, aussöhnen (*to s.th., with s.o.* mit etw, jdm); *(Streit)* beilegen, schlichten; aufea. abstimmen; in Einklang, in Übereinstimmung bringen (*with, a. to* mit); *to be ~ed, to ~~ o.s.* sich abfinden, sich aussöhnen (*to* mit; *to doing s.th.* etw zu tun); **~iation** [rekənsili'eiʃən] Ver-, (Wieder-)Aussöhnung *f* (*to, with* mit); *attempt at ~~ (jur)* Sühneversuch *m*.

recondite [ri'kɔndait, rə'k-, 're-] geheim; dunkel, schwer(verständlich), tief(gründig).

recondition ['ri:kən'diʃən] *tr* (wieder) instand setzen; wiederherstellen; überholen; *(Werkzeuge)* aufarbeiten, zurichten.

reconnaissance [ri'kɔnisəns] *mil mar aero* Aufklärung, Erkundung; *fig* Untersuchung *f*; *attr* Aufklärungs-, Erkundungs-; *~ in force* gewaltsame Aufklärung *f*; **~ aircraft** Aufklärungsflugzeug *n*; **~ area** Aufklärungsraum *m*; **~ car** Spähwagen *m*; **~ flight** Aufklärungsflug *m*; **~ patrol** Spähtrupp *m*.

reconnoit|re, *Am* -er [rekə'nɔitə] *tr itr mil mar aero* erkunden, erforschen, auskundschaften.

reconque|r ['ri:'kɔŋkə] *tr* wieder erobern (*from* von); **~st** ['-'kɔŋkwest] Wiedereroberung *f*.

reconsider ['ri:kən'sidə] *tr* wieder in Betracht ziehen, wieder erwägen *od* erörtern; überdenken; nachprüfen; *(erledigte Sache)* wieder aufgreifen; **~ation** ['-sidə'reiʃən] nochmalige Erwägung *f*.

reconstruct ['ri:kən'strʌkt] *tr* wieder aufbauen, wiederherstellen; umbauen; rekonstruieren; *com* sanieren; **~ion** ['-'strʌkʃən] Wiederaufbau *m a. fig*; Wiederherstellung; *com* Reorganisation, Sanierung *f*; Umbau *m*.

reconver|sion ['ri:kən'və:ʃən] Umstellung *f*; **~t** ['-'və:t] *tr* umstellen; umwandeln.

record [ri'kɔ:d] *tr* auf-, verzeichnen, zu Papier bringen, niederschreiben, protokollieren; buchen, eintragen, registrieren; festhalten; dokumentieren, urkundlich belegen, beurkunden; (auf Schall-, Wachsplatte) aufnehmen; (an)zeigen, angeben; *s* ['rekɔ:d, *Am* 'rekəd] Aufzeichnung, Niederschrift *f*; Bericht *m*; Verzeichnis *n*, Aufstellung; Urkunde *f*, Dokument; Protokoll; *com* Kontobuch *n*; *pl* (Parlaments-, Gerichts-, Polizei-, Personal-)Akten *f pl*; Unterlage *f*, Beleg *m*; (Ton-)Aufnahme, (Schall-)Platte *f*; Rekord *m*, Höchst-, Bestleistung *f*; *fig* Ruf *m*, Vorleben *n*, Vergangenheit *f*; *attr* Rekord-; *at ~ speed* mit Rekordgeschwindigkeit; *off the ~ (Am)* nicht für die Öffentlichkeit (bestimmt); *on ~* schriftlich niedergelegt, zu Protokoll genommen; belegt, nachgewiesen; *Am* öffentlich bekanntgegeben; *to bear ~ to* bezeugen; *to beat, to break, to cut a ~* e-n Rekord brechen *od* schlagen; *to enter in the ~* im Protokoll vermerken; *to go on ~ (Am)* offen s-e Meinung sagen; s-e Stimme abgeben; zu Protokoll genommen werden; *to keep a ~ of s.th.* über etw Buch führen; *to make a ~ of s.th.* etw zu Protokoll nehmen; *to place, to take down on ~* zu Protokoll geben, nehmen; *to set up a ~* e-n Rekord aufstellen; *he has a good (bad) ~* s-e Papiere sind (nicht) in Ordnung; er wird (nicht) gut beurteilt; er hat ein gutes(schlechtes) Schulzeugnis; *gramophone ~* Grammophonplatte *f*; *a matter of ~* verbürgte Tatsache *f*; *criminal ~* Vorstrafenverzeichnis *n*; *~ of attendance* Anwesenheitsliste *f*; *~ of the proceedings* Sitzungsprotokoll *n*; **~ card** Karteikarte *f*; **~-changer** Plattenwechsler *m*; **~ crop** Rekordernte *f*; **~ dealer** Schallplattenhändler *m*; **~ed** [ri'kɔ:did] *a*: *~~ music* Schallplattenmusik *f*, -konzert *n*; **~er** [ri'kɔ:də] Protokollführer; Registrator; Archivar; Stadtrichter; *tech* (Gang-)Zähler, Registrierapparat *m*; (Ton-)Aufnahmegerät *n*; *mus* Blockflöte *f*; *tape ~~* Magnetophongerät *n*; **~ film** Dokumentarfilm *m*; **~ holder** Rekordhalter *m*; **~ing** [ri'kɔ:diŋ] *a* Registrier-; *s* Aufzeichnung, Registrierung; (Ton-)Aufnahme; *(radio)* Bandsendung *f*; *~~ of accidents* Unfallstatistik *f*; *~~ barometer* Höhenschreiber *m*; *~~-car (radio)* Aufnahmewagen *m*; *~~ tape* Tonband *n*; **~ library** Schallplattenarchiv *n*; **~ output** Rekordproduktion *f*; **~ player, turntable** Plattenspieler *m*; **~ time** Rekordzeit *f*; **~ smasher, breaker** Rekordbrecher *m*.

recount [ri'kaunt] *tr* im einzelnen erzählen; ['ri:'kaunt] *tr* nachzählen.

recoup [ri'ku:p] *tr (Verlust)* wieder einbringen, decken; entschädigen, schadlos halten (*for* für); zurückzahlen; *jur* einbehalten, abziehen; *to ~ s.o. for injury* jdn schadenersatzpflichtig machen.

recourse [ri'kɔ:s] *s* Zuflucht *f* (*to* zu); Rückhalt; *jur* Regreß, Rückgriff *m*; *liable to ~* regreßpflichtig; *to have ~ to* Zuflucht suchen bei; *jur* regreßpflichtig machen; *right of ~* Rückgriffsrecht *n*.

recover [ri'kʌvə] *tr* zurückbekommen, -erhalten; *(s-e Gesundheit)* wiedererlangen, -gewinnen; *(das Bewußtsein)* wieder-, zurückerlangen; *(Verlust)* wiedereinbringen, decken, aufholen; wiedergutmachen; eintreiben, -ziehen; *(Pfand)* einlösen; *(Land, Abfallprodukte)* gewinnen; *(verlorene Zeit)* wieder aufholen; *(Krankheit)* überwinden; *itr (to ~ o.s.)* sich erholen (*from* von); wieder zu sich kommen; *com (Markt)* sich wiederbeleben; *(to ~ o.s.)* sich im letzten Augenblick, sich gerade noch halten; *(Fechten)* in Paradestellung zurückkommen; *jur* entschädigt werden; sich schadlos halten, Regreß nehmen; gewinnen (*in a suit* e-n Prozeß); *to ~ o.'s breath* wieder zu Atem kommen; *to ~ o.'s legs* wieder hoch-, wieder auf die Beine kommen; *he ~ed himself from a stumble* er wäre beinahe gestolpert; **~able** [-rəbl] wiederzuerlangen(d), zurückzugewinnen(d); besserungsfähig;

(Gesundheit) wiederherzustellen(d); *tech* regenerierbar; *com* beitreibbar, einziehbar; **~y** [-ri] Zurück-, Wiedererlangung, Wieder-, Rückgewinnung *a. tech; jur* Einziehung, Eintreibung; *tech* Gewinnung; Genesung, Erholung; Wiedererlangung des Bewußtseins; *com* (Wieder-)Belebung, Erholung *f; past ~~* unrettbar verloren; *to be on the road to ~~* auf dem Wege der Besserung sein; *right of ~~* Regreßrecht *n; ~~ of damages* Erlangung *f*, Erhalt *m* von Schadenersatz; *~~ measures (pl)* Wiederaufbaumaßnahmen *f pl; ~~ plant (tech)* Rückgewinnungsanlage *f; ~~ program(me)* Wiederaufbauplan *m; ~~ service (mot)* Abschleppdienst *m; ~~ vehicle* Abschleppwagen *m*.

re-cover ['ri:'kʌvə] *tr* wieder bedecken.

recreant ['rekriənt] *a* feige; abtrünnig, verräterisch; *s* Feigling; Abtrünnige(r), Verräter *m*.

recreat|e ['rekrieit] *tr* erfrischen, *lit poet* erquicken; entspannen; aufmuntern; unterhalten; *itr* u. *to ~ o.s.* sich erfrischen, sich entspannen, wieder munter werden, sich erholen; sich amüsieren (*with* mit); **~ion** [rekri'eiʃən] Erfrischung, Erholung, Entspannung; Aufmunterung, -heiterung; Belustigung, Unterhaltung *f; ~~ center (Am)* Soldatenheim *n; ~~ ground* Sport-, Spielplatz *m; ~~ leave* Erholungsurlaub *m; ~~ room* Erholungs-, Unterhaltungsraum *m;* **~ional** [-'eiʃənl], **~ive** ['-tiv] erfrischend, entspannend, erholsam; erheiternd.

re-create ['ri:kri'eit] *tr* neu (er)schaffen.

recriminat|e [ri'krimineit] *itr* Gegenbeschuldigungen vorbringen; **~ion** [rikrimi'neiʃən] Gegen(an)klage *f*.

recrudesc|e [ri:kru:'des] *itr med* sich wieder verschlimmern; *fig* von neuem ausbrechen; *(Wunde)* wieder aufbrechen; **~ence, -cy** [-sns(i)] *med* Verschlimmerung *f*, Rückfall, Wiederausbruch *m a. fig*.

recruit [ri'kru:t] *tr mil u. allg* rekrutieren, ergänzen, verstärken; *(zum Heeresdienst)* einziehen, ausheben; *(d. Gesundheit)* wiederherstellen; *(Anhänger)* gewinnen; *(Nachschub)* sicherstellen; *itr* Rekruten einziehen; sich neu versorgen; sich (wieder) erholen; *s* Rekrut *m; fig* neue(s) Mitglied *n;* **~ing** [-iŋ] *s mil* Aushebung; (personelle) Ergänzung; *med* Wiederherstellung *f; ~~ administration* Wehrersatzverwaltung *f; ~~ board* Musterungskommission *f; ~~ centre, office, station* Rekrutierungsstelle *f*.

rect|al ['rektəl] *a anat med* Mastdarm-; rektal; *~~ syringe* Klistierspritze *f;* **~angle** ['-æŋgl] Rechteck *n;* **~angular** [rek'tæŋgjulə] rechtwinklig; *~~ block* Quader *m; ~~ timber* Kantholz *n;* **~angularity** [-tæŋgju'læriti] Rechtwinkligkeit *f;* **~ifiable** ['rektifaiəbl] zu berichtigen(d), richtigzustellen(d); *math* rektifizierbar; **~ification** [rektifi'keiʃən] Berichtigung, Richtigstellung; *el* Gleichrichtung; *math chem* Rektifikation; *(Luftbild)* Entzerrung *f;* **~ifier** ['rektifaiə] Berichtiger; *el* Gleichrichter *m; phot* Entzerrungsgerät *n; chem* Rektifikator *m;* **~ify** ['rektifai] *tr* berichtigen, richtigstellen, korrigieren, verbessern; *el* gleichrichten; *math chem* rektifizieren; **~ilineal** [rekti'liniəl], **~ilinear** [-'liniə] geradlinig; **~itude** ['rektitju:d] Redlichkeit; Geradheit, Korrektheit *f;* **~o** ['rektou] *typ* Vorder-, rechte, ung(e)rade Seite *f*, Rekto *n;* **~or** ['rektə] Pfarrer, Pastor; *(Schule, College)* Direktor; *(Univ.)* Rektor *m;* **~orate** ['-ərit], **~orship** ['-əʃip] Pfarrstelle *f*, -amt; (Di-)Rektorat *n;* **~ory** ['rektəri] Pfarrhaus *n*, -stelle *f;* **~um** ['-əm] *anat* Mastdarm *m*.

recumben|ce, -cy [ri'kʌmbəns(i)] zurückgelehnte Haltung; Ruhelage *f;* **~t** [-t] liegend; zurückgelehnt; (aus-)ruhend.

recuperat|e [ri'kju:pəreit] *tr* wieder zu Kräften bringen; *(Gesundheit)* wiederherstellen; wiedergewinnen, -erlangen; *itr* sich (wieder) erholen *a. fin*, wieder zu Kräften kommen; **~ion** [rikju:pə'reiʃən] Wiederherstellung, -erlangung; *med* Erholung, Genesung *f;* **~ive** [-rətiv], **~ory** [-ətəri] erholsam; *med* stärkend, kräftigend; *tech* rekuperativ.

recur [ri'kə:] *itr* zurückkehren *fig* (*to* zu); wieder zurückkommen (*to* auf); wieder auftreten, wieder auftauchen, sich wieder ergeben; *(Frage)* sich wieder stellen; wieder einfallen (*to s.o.'s mind* jdm); *(Ereignis)* sich wiederholen; *(Gelegenheit)* sich wieder bieten; regelmäßig, periodisch wiederkehren; **~rence** [-'kʌrəns] Zurückkommen (*to* auf); Wiederauftauchen, -treten *n*, Rückkehr, Wiederholung *f; med* Rückfall *m;* **~rent** [-'kʌrənt] sich wiederholend, regelmäßig, periodisch wiederkehrend; *anat* rückläufig; *~~ fever* Rückfallfieber *n*.

recurve [ri:'kə:v] *tr* zurückbiegen.

recusant ['rekju-, ri'kju:zənt] widerspenstig (*against* gegen).

red [red] *a* rot; rothaarig; von rötlicher Hautfarbe; gerötet (*with* von); *(R~) pol* rot, radikal, revolutionär, kommunistisch; *(Fleisch)* blutend; *s* Rot *n;* rote(r) Farbstoff; *(R~) pol* Rote(r) *m; the ~s (pl)* die Rothäute *f pl; to be in the ~ (Am fam)* in Schulden stecken; *to be out of the ~ (Am fam)* s-e Schulden los sein; *to become, to go ~ in the face* erröten, rot werden, rot anlaufen; *to paint the town ~* die Stadt auf den Kopf stellen; *to see ~* rot sehen; wild, wütend werden; sich vergessen *(vor Wut); she makes me see ~* sie wirkt auf mich wie ein rotes Tuch; *with ~ hands* blutbefleckt; *~ with anger* rot vor Zorn; **~bird** *orn* Dompfaff *m;* **~-blooded** *a* lebendig, lebhaft; kraftstrotzend; **~breast,** *robin ~~ (orn)* Rotkehlchen *n;* **~ cabbage** Rotkohl *m;* **~cap** *orn* Stieglitz, Distelfink; *Br fam* Militärpolizist, Feldgendarm; *Am* Dienstmann, Gepäckträger *m;* **~ carpet** *a* elegant; *s fig* große(r) Bahnhof *m; to roll out the ~~ for s.o.* jdn großartig empfangen; **~cent** *Am fam: not a ~~* keinen roten Heller; *the* **R~ Cross** das Rote Kreuz; **~ current** Johannisbeere *f;* **~ deer** Rotwild *n;* **~den** ['-ən] *tr* röten, rot färben; *itr* rot werden, erröten (*with* vor; *at* über); **~dish** ['-iʃ] rötlich; **R~ Ensign** britische Handelsflagge *f; the* **R~ Flag** die Rote Fahne; **~ fox** Rotfuchs *m;* **~-handed** *a* blutbefleckt; *to be caught ~~* auf frischer Tat ertappt werden; **~ head** rothaarige(r) Mensch; *(College)* Fuchs *m;* **~headed** *a* rothaarig; **~ heat** Rotglut *f;* **~ herring** Bückling *m; to draw a ~~ across the path* ein Ablenkungsmanöver unternehmen; *neither fish, flesh, nor good ~ herring (fig)* weder Fisch noch Fleisch; undefinierbar; **~-hot** *a* rotglühend; *fig* aufgeregt; begeistert; *fig (Nachricht)* brühwarm; *s Am sl* Frankfurter Würstchen *n;* **R~ Indian** Rothaut *f;* **~ lead** Mennige *f;* **~-letter day** Fest-, Feiertag; *fig* Glückstag *m;* **~ light** *(Verkehr)* rote(s) Licht; Warnsignal *n; to see the ~~ (fig)* die Gefahr erkennen; *~~ district (Am)* Bordellviertel *n;* **~ man, ~skin** Rothaut *f;* **~ meat** Rind- u. Hammelfleisch *n;* **~ ochre** Rötel, Roteisenstein *m;* **~ rag** rote(s) Tuch *n; it's like a ~~ to him* es wirkt auf ihn wie ein rotes Tuch; *the* **R~ Sea** das Rote Meer; **~start** *orn* Rotschwänzchen *n;* **~ tape** Bürokratismus, Amtsschimmel *m;* **~ tapist** Bürokrat *m;* **~wing** *orn* Rot-, Weindrossel *f;* **~wood** *bot* Mammutbaum *m*.

redact [ri'dækt] *tr* abfassen, redigieren, bearbeiten, herausgeben; **~ion** [-'dækʃən] Abfassung, Bearbeitung, Redaktion, Revision, Herausgabe; (*bes.* Neu-)Ausgabe *f*.

reddle ['redl] Rötel *m*.

redeem [ri:'di:m] *tr* zurückkaufen, -erwerben; ein-, ablösen, (ab)bezahlen, amortisieren, tilgen; *(Schulden)* abtragen; *(Wechsel)* honorieren; auslösen, los-, freikaufen; wettmachen; *rel* erlösen; *(Sünde)* abbüßen; *(Versprechen)* einlösen, erfüllen; wiedergutmachen, Schadenersatz leisten für; *~ing feature* ausgleichende(s) Element *n;* versöhnende(r) Zug *m;* **~able** [-əbl] rückzahlbar, amortisierbar, tilgbar, kündbar, ab-, einlösbar; rückkaufbar; *~~ loan* Tilgungsdarlehen *n;* **~er** [-ə] Rückkäufer, Einlöser *m; the R~~* der Erlöser, der Heiland.

redempt|ion [-'dempʃən] Rückkauf, -erwerb *m;* Ein-, Ablösung, (Ab-)Bezahlung, Amortisation, Tilgung; Auslosung *f;* Los-, Freikauf *m; rel* Erlösung (*from* von); Einlösung, Erfüllung; Sühne, Wiedergutmachung *f;* Lösegeld *n;* Ausgleich *m* (*of* für); *beyond, past ~~* nicht wiedergutzumachen(d); unrettbar verloren; *in the year of our ~~* im Jahre des Heils; *~~ capital* Ablösungssumme *f*, -betrag *m; ~~ fund* Tilgungskasse *f; ~~ plan, table* Tilgungs-, Amortisationsplan *m; ~~ rate* Ein-, Ablösungskurs *m;* Tilgungssatz *m*, -quote *f; ~~ service* Anleihedienst *m; ~~ value* Rückkaufs-, Einlösungswert *m; ~~ voucher* Einlösungsschein *m;* **~ive** [-iv] Rückkaufs-, Einlösungs-, Amortisations-, Tilgungs-; *rel* erlösend.

redeploy ['ri:di'plɔi] *tr (Truppen)* verlegen, umgruppieren; **~ment** ['-mənt] *mil* Verlegung; Umgruppierung *f*.

redintegrate [re'dintigreit] *tr* wieder vervollständigen, wieder ergänzen; wiederherstellen, erneuern.

redirect ['ri:di'rekt] *tr* umadressieren, nachsenden.

redistribut|e ['ri:'dis'tribju(:)t] *tr* neu verteilen; **~ion** [-'bju:ʃən] Neuverteilung *f*.

redo ['ri:'du:] *irr s. do; tr* neu machen, erneuern, renovieren.

redolen|ce, -cy ['redo(u)ləns(i)] Wohlgeruch, Duft *m;* **~t** ['-t] wohlriechend; duftend (*of* nach); *to be ~~ of s.th.* an etw erinnern.

redouble [ri(:)'dʌbl] *tr* verdoppeln; wiederholen; nachhallen lassen; doppelt falten, zs.legen; *itr* sich verdoppeln; stärker werden; nachhallen.

redoubt [ri'daut] *mil* Feldschanze *f;* Stützpunkt *m;* **~able** [-əbl] furchtbar, schrecklich.

redound [ri'daund] *itr* gereichen, führen (*to* zu); zur Folge haben, bewirken (*to s.th.* etw); Einfluß haben (*to* auf); zurückfallen, zurückwirken (*upon* auf).

redraft ['ri:'drɑ:ft] *s* Neu-, neue(r) Entwurf; *fin* Rückwechsel *m*; *tr* neu entwerfen.
redress [ri'dres] *tr* wiedergutmachen, Abhilfe schaffen für, abhelfen (*s.th.* e-r S); *(Fehler)* abstellen; *(Schaden)* beseitigen; *(Übel)* beheben; wiederherstellen; *tech* aufbereiten; *s* Wiedergutmachung, Genugtuung, Abhilfe *f*, Regreß *m*; *beyond* ~ nicht wiedergutzumachend; *legal* ~ Rechtshilfe *f*; *self-*~ (Akt *m* der) Selbsthilfe *f*.

*

reduc|e [ri'dju:s] *tr* verringern, vermindern, abbauen, herunter-, herabsetzen, abschwächen, reduzieren (*to* auf); *(Preis)* senken, ermäßigen; ab-, nachlassen; einschränken, verkleinern; verdünnen; erniedrigen; *(Produktion)* drosseln; ordnen, ein-, aufteilen; um-, verwandeln (*to* in); zurückführen (*to* auf); *(Geld)* umrechnen; *(in e-e Form, zur Vernunft, zum Gehorsam, in s-e Gewalt, in Not)* bringen (*to* zu); machen (*to* zu); *(in e-e Lage)* versetzen; *mil* degradieren; *(Feind)* niederkämpfen; zwingen (*to doing s.th.* etw zu tun); *math* kürzen; *chem* reduzieren; *med* einrenken, in s-e normale Lage bringen; *itr* abnehmen, abmagern; *at ~ed prices* zu zurückgesetzten Preisen; verbilligt; *to ~~ to an absurdity* ad absurdum führen; *to ~~ to nothing* zunichte machen; *to ~~ s.o. to poverty* jdn an den Bettelstab bringen; *to ~~ to silence* zum Schweigen bringen, den Mund stopfen (*s.o.* jdm); *to ~~ to a system* in ein System bringen; *to ~~ to tears* zu Tränen rühren; *to ~~ in value* entwerten; *to ~~ to writing* zu Papier bringen, schriftlich niederlegen; *~ed circumstances (pl)* beschränkte Verhältnisse *n pl*; **~er** [-ə] *chem* Reduktions-, Abmagerungsmittel *n*; *phot* Abschwächer *m*; *tech* Reduzierstück *n*; **~ible** [ri'dju:səbl] zurückführbar, reduzierbar (*to* auf); **~ing** [ri:'dju:siŋ]: *~~-agent (chem)* Reduktionsmittel *n*; *~~ diet* Abmagerungs-, Hungerkur *f*; *~~-glass (opt)* Verkleinerungslinse *f*; *~~ scale* verkürzte(r) Maßstab *m*; *~~ valve* Reduzierventil *n*.
reduction [ri'dʌkʃən] Verringerung, Verminderung, Kürzung, Verkleinerung, Verdünnung *f*; *(Personal)* Abbau *m*; Herabsetzung, (Preis-)Ermäßigung, Senkung *f*, Nachlaß, Abbau, Rabatt *m*; (Lohn-, Gehalts-)Kürzung; *(Produktion)* Drosselung; Reduktion, Zurückführung, Umwandlung, Umrechnung (*to* auf); *mil* Degradierung; *(Produktion)* Drosselung; Reduktion, Zurückführung, Umwandlung, Umrechnung; *mil* Degradierung; *(Feind)* Niederkämpfung; *(Land)* Eroberung; *math* Kürzung; *(Zeichnung)* verkleinerte Wiedergabe; *chem* Reduktion; *phot* Abschwächung; *med* Einrenkung; Abmagerung *f*; *to grant, to make a ~* e-e Ermäßigung einräumen; *tax ~* Steuerermäßigung *f*, -nachlaß *m*; *wage ~* Lohnsenkung *f*, -abbau *m*; *~ in the discount rate* Diskontherabsetzung *f*; *~ of fare* Fahrpreisermäßigung *f*; *~ in, of numbers* zahlenmäßige Verringerung *f*; *~ of a penalty* Strafmilderung *f*; *~ in prices* Preisabbau, -sturz *m*; *~ of staff* Personaleinschränkung *f*, -abbau *m*; *~ in value* Wertminderung, Abwertung *f*; *~ of working hours* Arbeitszeitverkürzung *f*.
redundan|ce, -cy [ri'dʌndəns(i)] Überfluß *m*, Fülle *f* (*of* an); Überflüssigkeit; Weitschweifigkeit *f*; **~t** [-t] im Überfluß vorhanden, überreichlich, übermäßig; überflüssig, unnötig; wortreich, weitschweifig; *(Stil)* überladen; *com* entlassen, arbeitslos.
reduplicat|e [ri'dju:plikeit] *tr* verdoppeln; *a* [-kit] (ver)doppelt; **~ion** [ridju:pli'keiʃən] Verdoppelung; *gram* Reduplikation *f*.
re-echo [ri(:)'ekou] *tr itr* noch einmal widerhallen; *s* doppelte(s) Echo *n*.
reed [ri:d] *s* Riedgras; Ried, Rohr *n*; *poet* (Rohr-)Flöte *f*, Pfeil *m*; *mus* Zunge; *(~-pipe)* (Orgel-)Pfeife *f*; *arch* Stab; Weberkamm *m*; *pl* Dachstroh *n*; *the ~s* die Zungeninstrumente; *broken ~ (fig)* schwanke(s) Rohr *n*; **~-bird** *orn* Bobolink *m*; **~-bunting, -sparrow** *orn* Rohrammer *f*; **~ing** ['-iŋ] *arch* Stabverzierung; *(Münze)* Ränftelung *f*; **~ling** ['-liŋ] *orn* Bartmeise *f*; **~-organ** Harmonium *n*; **~-warbler, -wren** *orn* Teichrohrsänger *m*; **~y** ['-i] riedbestanden, schilfreich; Rohr-, rohrartig; *(Ton)* flötend, dünn.
re-edit ['ri:'edit] *tr (Buch)* neu herausgeben.
re-educat|e ['ri:'edju(:)keit] *tr* umerziehen, umschulen; **~ion** ['ri:edju(:)'keiʃən] Umschulung, Umerziehung *f*.
reef [ri:f] **1.** *s* (Felsen-)Riff *n*; Untiefe; *min* Ader *f*; **2.** *s mar* Reff; Reffen *n*; *tr* reffen; **~er** ['-ə] zweireihige (Seemanns-, *a.* Damen-)Jacke *f*; *mar* Reffer; *mar sl* Seekadett *m*; *sl* Marihuanazigarette *f*; *sl* Kühlwagen, -schrank *m*.
reek [ri:k] *s* Dampf, Dunst; Gestank *m*; *itr* dampfen, rauchen; übel riechen, stinken (*of* nach); bedeckt sein (*of, with* mit); **~y** ['-i] dampfend, dunstig; übelriechend; schmutzig.
reel [ri:l] **1.** *s* Rolle, Spule, Winde, Haspel, Trommel, Walze; Filmrolle *f*, -streifen *m*; Angelschnurrolle *f*; *tr* rollen, spulen, winden, haspeln, wickeln; *off the ~ (fig)* wie am Schnürchen; in einem fort; *to ~* **in** aufrollen, -spulen, -winden, -haspeln, -wickeln; *to ~* **off** *fig* herunterleiern, -rasseln; spielend erledigen; *to ~* **out** abrollen, -haspeln, -wickeln; **2.** *itr* (sch)wanken; wirbeln; taumeln; *I'm ~ing* mir dreht sich alles, mir schwindelt.
re-elect ['ri:i'lekt] *tr* wiederwählen; **~ion** ['-'lekʃən] Wiederwahl *f*.
re-eligible ['ri:'elidʒəbl] wiederwählbar.
re-enact ['ri:i'nækt] *tr* wieder in Kraft setzen; *theat* wiederaufführen, neu inszenieren.
re-engage ['ri:in'geidʒ] *tr* wiedereinstellen, neu verpflichten; *tech* wiedereinrücken.
re-enlist ['ri:in'list] *itr mil* dienen, sich weiterverpflichten, kapitulieren.
re-ent|er ['ri:'entə] *itr* wieder eintreten (*into* in); *tr* wieder betreten; wieder an-, wieder in Besitz nehmen; wieder eintragen; **~ry** [ri'entri] Wiedereintreten *n*; *fig* Wiedereintritt *m*; Wiederannahme *f*.
reeve [ri:v] *a. irr rove, rove tr mar* einscheren; *(Tau)* spannen; *s hist* Vogt *m*.
re-exchange ['ri:iks'tʃeindʒ] Rücktausch; *fin* Rückwechsel, Rikambio *m*.
re-export ['ri:eks'pɔ:t] *tr com* wiederausführen; *s* ['-'ekspɔ:t] Wiederausfuhr *f*.
refect|ion [ri'fekʃən] Erfrischung *f*, Imbiß *m*; **~ory** [-təri] Refektorium *n*, Speisesaal *m (in e-m Kloster)*.
refer [ri'fə:] *tr* zuschreiben, -rechnen, -zählen (*to s.th.* e-r S); zurückführen, beziehen (*to* auf); verweisen (*to s.o.* an jdn); vorlegen, unterbreiten (*s.th. to s.o.* jdm etw); übergeben, überweisen (*to* an); *itr* sich berufen, sich beziehen, Bezug nehmen (*to* auf); sich befassen (*to* mit); aufmerksam machen, hinweisen, verweisen (*to* auf); erwähnen (*to s.th.* etw); anspielen (*to* auf); sich *(rat-, hilfesuchend)* wenden (*to* an); *(Buch)* nachschlagen (*to s.th.* etw); *to ~ back to* zurückverweisen an; **~able** [-rəbl, 'refərəbl] zuzuschreiben(d), -rechnen(d), -zählen(d) (*to s.th.* e-r S); bezüglich (*to* auf); **~ee** [refə'ri:] Referent, Sachverständige(r); *jur* Schiedsrichter, -mann; Unparteiische(r), Schlichter; *sport* Schieds-, Ringrichter *m*; *~~'s court* Schiedsgericht *n*; **~ence** ['refrəns] Berufung *f*, Bezug(nahme *f*) *m*; Verweisung; Anspielung (*to* auf), Erwähnung (*to s.th.* e-r S); Quellenangabe *f*, erwähnte(s) Werk *n od* Stelle *f*; Verweisungszeichen *n*; Vorgang *m*; Aktennummer *f*, -zeichen *n*; Empfehlung, Referenz *f (a. Person)*; Gewährsmann *m*; (Dienst-)Zeugnis; Nachschlagen *n*; *jur* Zuständigkeit; Notadresse *f*; *attr* Nachschlage-; *for ~~* zur Unterrichtung; *in, with ~~ to* in bezug, mit Bezug auf, betreffend, betreffs *gen*, hinsichtlich *gen*; *without ~~ to* ohne Bezug auf, unabhängig von; *to give s.o. as a ~~* jdn als Referenz angeben; *to have no ~~ to* nichts zu tun haben mit; *to make ~~ to* sich beziehen, Bezug nehmen, anspielen auf, erwähnen; *to take up s.o.'s ~~s* über jdn Referenzen einholen; *cross ~~* Querverweis *m*; *terms of ~~* Richtlinien *f pl*; *~~ book* Nachschlagewerk *n*; *~~ files (pl)* Handakten *f pl*; *~~ library* Handbücherei *f*; *~~ mark* Verweisungszeichen; Einstellmarke; Bezeichnung *f*; *~~-number* Aktenzeichen *n*; Geschäftsnummer *f*; *~~ point* Bezugspunkt *m*; *~~ room* Nachschlageraum *m*; **~endum** [refə'rendəm] Volksabstimmung *f*, -entscheid *m* (*on* über).
refill ['ri:'fil] *tr* wieder (an)füllen, nachfüllen; *itr mot* auftanken; *s* ['ri:fil] Nachfüllung; *(Drehbleistift)* Ersatzmine, -füllung *f*; Ersatzfilm *m*, -batterie *f*, -blätter *n pl*; **~ing station** Tankstelle *f*.
refin|e [ri'fain] *tr* reinigen, läutern *a. fig*; klären, raffinieren; verfeinern; veredeln; *tech* frischen; *fig* verfeinern, kultivieren; *itr* rein, klar werden; sich reinigen; feiner, eleganter werden; sich geziert benehmen; *(to ~~ upon words)* geziert sprechen; *to ~~ on, upon* verfeinern, verbessern; grübeln über, herumtüfteln an; **~ed** ['-d] *a* gereinigt; (ver)fein(ert); *~~ copper* Raffinatkupfer *m*; *~~ manners (pl)* feine Manieren *f pl*; **~ement** [-mənt] Reinigung, Klärung; Verfeinerung *a. fig*; *fig* Läuterung; Feinheit, Eleganz, Gewähltheit, Geziertheit; Grübelei *f*; **~er** [-ə] Raffineur; *metal* Frischmeister *m*; *metal* Walzenreibmaschine *f*; **~ery** [-əri] Raffinerie *f*; *sugar ~~* Zuckerraffinerie *f*; **~ing** [-iŋ]: *~~ industry* Veredelungsindustrie *f*; *~~ process* Frischverfahren *n*.
refit ['ri:'fit] *tr* wieder in Ordnung bringen; überholen, wiederherstellen; wiederher-, einrichten; wieder ausrüsten; *itr* überholt, wiederhergestellt werden; *s* Überholung, Wiederherstellung, Wiederinstandsetzung, Ausbesserung *f*.
reflect [ri'flekt] *tr* zurückwerfen, -strahlen, widerspiegeln *a. fig*, reflektieren; zur Folge haben (*on* für); einbringen (*on s.o.* jdm); *fig* zeigen, ausdrücken; *itr* zurückgeworfen, reflektiert werden; zurückfallen, -strahlen; reflektieren, spiegeln; *fig*

nachdenken (*on, upon* über); überlegen, erwägen, in Betracht ziehen (*on, upon s.th.* etw); in Zweifel ziehen (*on s.th.* etw); sich nachteilig äußern (*on, upon* über); tadeln (*on, upon s.th.* etw); ein schlechtes Licht werfen, sich nachteilig auswirken (*on* auf); **~ing** [-iŋ] zurückwerfend; *~~ projector* Epidiaskop *n*; *~~ telescope* Spiegelteleskop *n*; **~ion, reflexion** [-'flekʃən] (Zu-)Rückstrahlung *f*, Reflex(ion *f*) *m*, (Wider-)Spiegelung *f*; Bild; *fig* Nachdenken *n*, Betrachtung, Überlegung, Reflexion *f* (*on* über); Gedanke *m*, Äußerung; abfällige Bemerkung *f*, Vorwurf, Tadel *m*; *on ~~* nach gründlicher Überlegung; *to cast ~~s on s.o.* jdn in ein schlechtes Licht setzen; **~ive** [-'flektiv] reflektierend, spiegelnd; *gram* reflexiv; nachdenklich, gedankenvoll; **~or** [ri'flektə] Reflektor, Hohlspiegel; Scheinwerfer *m*; Spiegelteleskop *n*; *mot* Rückstrahler *m*; Katzenauge *n*.

reflex ['ri:fleks] *s* Widerschein *m* (*from* von); (Wider-)Spiegelung *f*, Spiegelbild *n*, Reflex *(a. Kunst)*; *physiol* Reflex(handlung *f*) *m*; *a* zurückgeworfen, -gestrahlt, reflektiert; reflektierend; rückwirkend; *physiol* Reflex-; *bot* zurückgebogen; **~ action** Reflexbewegung *f*; ~ (**camera**) Spiegelreflexkamera *f*; **~ion** *s. reflection*; **~ive** [ri'fleksiv] *a* reflektierend; reflektiert; rückwirkend; *gram* rückbezüglich, reflexiv; *s* (*~~ pronoun*) Reflexivpronomen *n*.

reflu|ent ['-ənt] zurückflutend, verebbend; **~x** ['ri:flʌks] Zurückfluten *n*, Ebbe *f*; *tech com* Rückfluß, Rücklauf *m*.

reforest ['ri:'fɔrist] *tr itr* wiederaufforsten; **~ation** ['ri:fɔris'teiʃən] Wiederaufforstung *f*.

reform [ri'fɔ:m] *tr* um-, neugestalten, umbauen, reformieren, verbessern; *(Mißbrauch)* abstellen; *(Mißstand)* beseitigen, abschaffen; *(Menschen)* bessern; *itr* sich bessern; *s* Reform, Umgestaltung; (Ver-)Besserung *f*; Reformbestrebungen *f pl*, -bewegung *f*; *land ~* Bodenreform *f*; *penal ~* Strafrechtsreform *f*; **~ation** [refə'meiʃən] Um-, Neugestaltung; (Ver-)Besserung; *(R~~) rel hist* Reformation *f*; **~atory** [-ətəri] *a* Reform-, Besserungs-; *s* Besserungsanstalt *f*; **~er** [ri'fɔ:mə] Reformer; *rel hist* Reformator *m*; **~ school** Besserungsanstalt *f*.

re-form ['ri:'fɔ:m] *tr itr* (sich) neu bilden; *tr mil* neu gliedern.

refract [ri'frækt] *tr phys (Strahlen)* brechen, ablenken; *~ing angle* Brechungswinkel *m*; *~ing telescope = ~or*; **~ion** [-'frækʃən] Strahlen-, Lichtbrechung; *astr* Refraktion *f*; **~ive** [-'fræktiv] lichtbrechend; Brechungs-; **~or** [-'fræktə] *opt* Refraktor *m*; **~oriness** [-ərinis] Widerspenstigkeit; Hartnäckigkeit, Widerstandsfähigkeit *a. med*; Hitzebeständigkeit, Feuerfestigkeit; Strengflüssigkeit *f*; **~ory** [-əri] widerspenstig (*to* gegen); *chem* strengflüssig; *med* hartnäckig; widerstandsfähig; feuerfest, hitzebeständig; *~~ brick* Schamottestein *m*.

refrain [ri'frein] **1.** *tr itr* (sich) zurückhalten (*from doing s.th.* etw zu tun); *itr* sich enthalten (*from s.th.* e-r S); sich zurückhalten, absehen (*from* von); **2.** Kehrreim, Refrain *m*.

refrangib|ility [rifrændʒi'biliti] *opt* Brechbarkeit *f*; **~le** [-'frændʒibl] brechbar.

refresh [ri'freʃ] *tr* erfrischen, stärken; erneuern; auffrischen *(a. Kenntnisse)*, beleben; *itr* sich erfrischen, sich stärken; wiederaufleben, sich erneuern; **~er** [-ə] Erneuerung, (Neu-)Belebung; *(Wissen)* Wiederauffrischung; *sport* Wiederaufnahme; *fam* Erfrischung, Stärkung *f*, Imbiß *m*, Gläschen *n*, Schluck *m*; Zuschlagshonorar *n (für e-n Anwalt)*; *attr*: *~~ course* Wiederholungs-, Auffrischungskurs *m*; **~ing** [-iŋ] erfrischend, belebend, anregend; **~ment** [-mənt] Erfrischung, *f*; *pl* Erfrischungen *f pl*; *~~-room* Erfrischungsraum *m*.

refriger|ant [ri'fridʒərənt] *a* kühlend; Kühl-, Gefrier-; *s pharm* kühlende(s) Mittel *n*; *tech* Kälteträger *m*; **~ate** [-eit] *tr* kühlen, gefrieren lassen; kühl halten, aufbewahren; **~ation** [rifridʒə'reiʃən] (Ab-)Kühlung; Kälteerzeugung; Kühlhaltung *f*; **~ator** [-reitə] Kühlanlage *f*, -raum, -schrank; Eisschrank *m*; *~~ lorry, (Am) car (rail)* Kühlwagen *m*.

refuel [ri:'fjuəl] *tr itr* auftanken.

refug|e ['refju:dʒ] *s* Zuflucht(sort *m*) *f*, Obdach *n*; Beschützer; Schutz *m*, Sicherung (*from* von); Sicherheitsmaßnahme *f*; *fig* Ausweg *m*, -flucht *f*, Hilfsmittel *n*; *Br* Verkehrsinsel; Schutzhütte *f*; *tr* Zuflucht gewähren; *itr* Zuflucht suchen; *to seek, to take ~~* Zuflucht suchen (*in, at a place* an e-m Ort; *for* vor; *with s.o.* bei jdm); **~ee** [refju(:)'dʒi:] Flüchtling *m*; *~~ camp* Flüchtlingslager *n*.

refulgen|ce, -cy [ri'fʌldʒəns(i)] Schimmer, Glanz *m*; Pracht *f*; **~t** [-t] leuchtend, schimmernd, strahlend.

refund [ri:'fʌnd] **1.** *tr* zurückzahlen, -erstatten, begleichen; rückvergüten; die Auslagen ersetzen (*s.o.* jdm); *s* ['ri:fʌnd] Rückzahlung, -vergütung, (Rück-)Erstattung *f*; erstattete(s) Geld *n*; **2.** ['ri:'fʌnd] *tr* neu finanzieren.

refurbish ['ri:'fə:biʃ] *tr* (wieder)aufpolieren; erneuern.

refus|al [ri'fju:zəl] (Ver-)Weigerung, Ablehnung; Absage *f*, abschlägige(r) Bescheid *m*, Antwort *f* (*from* von); *com* Vorkauf(srecht *n*) *m*; *first ~~ of* erste(s) Anrecht *n* auf; *in case of ~~* im Weigerungsfalle; *to meet with a ~~* e-e abschlägige Antwort erhalten; *to take no ~~* sich nicht abweisen lassen; *~~ of acceptance* Annahmeverweigerung *f*; **~e** [ri'fju:z] *tr* ablehnen, zurückweisen, nicht annehmen, verweigern, versagen; abschlagen (*to do* zu tun; *s.o. s.th.* jdm etw); *(Gesuch)* abfällig bescheiden; *(Angebot)* ausschlagen; *itr* die Annahme, s-e Einwilligung verweigern, sich weigern; *(Pferd)* nicht über die Hürde gehen; *I ~~ to let you go* ich lasse dich nicht gehen; ['refju:s] *s* Abfälle *m pl*, Abfall, Müll; Ramsch, Ausschuß *m*; *a* wertlos; ausgemustert; *household ~~* Haushaltsabfälle *m pl*; *~~ bin* Mülleimer *m*; *~~ dump* Abfallhaufen *m*.

refut|able ['refjutəbl] widerlegbar; **~ation** [refju'teiʃən] Widerlegung *f*; **~e** [ri'fju:t] *tr* widerlegen; zurückweisen.

regain [ri'gein] *tr* zurück-, wiederbekommen, -erhalten, -erlangen; wieder-, zurückgewinnen; *(Ort)* wiedererreichen; *to ~ o.'s footing* wieder auf die Beine kommen.

regal ['ri:gəl] königlich; majestätisch, prunkvoll, prächtig; **~e** [ri'geil] *tr* festlich bewirten, unterhalten, erfreuen (*with* mit); e-e große Freude machen (*s.o.* jdm); *to ~~ o.s. on s.th.* sich an etw erfreuen; **~ia** [ri'geiljə] *pl hist* Hoheitsrechte, Regalien *n pl*; Krönungsinsignien *pl*, Kronjuwelen *n pl*; Ordensattribute *n pl*.

regard [ri'gɑ:d] *tr* (aufmerksam, fest) ansehen, -schauen, betrachten (*with suspicion* mit Mißtrauen); in Betracht ziehen, erwägen, berücksichtigen; beachten, Beachtung schenken (*s.th.* e-r S); achten, schätzen; ansehen, betrachten (*as* als), halten (*as* für); angehen, betreffen; *s* feste(r) Blick *m*; Aufmerksamkeit (*to, for* für); Rücksicht, Berücksichtigung; (Hoch-)Achtung, Wertschätzung *f*; Bezug *m*, Beziehung *f* (*to* auf); *pl (Brief)* Grüße, Wünsche *m pl*; Empfehlungen *f pl*; *as ~s* was ... betrifft; *in ~ to* od *of, with ~ to* in bezug, mit Bezug auf, mit Rücksicht auf; *in this ~* in dieser Hinsicht; *with kind ~s* mit freundlichen, herzlichen Grüßen (*to* an); *without ~ to, for* ohne Rücksicht auf; *to pay ~ to* Rücksicht nehmen auf; *give my ~s to ...* Grüße an ...; grüßen Sie ...; *this does not ~ me at all* das geht mich überhaupt nichts an; *she has no ~ for others* sie nimmt auf andere keine Rücksicht; **~ful** [-ful] aufmerksam (*of* auf); rücksichtsvoll (*of* gegen); **~ing** [-iŋ] *prp* betreffend, betreffs, hinsichtlich *gen*; **~less** [-lis] *a* unaufmerksam, unachtsam, rücksichtslos, achtlos (*of* auf); *adv fam* ohne Rücksicht auf die Kosten *od* Folgen.

regatta [ri'gætə] Regatta *f*.

regen|cy ['ri:dʒənsi] Regentschaft; *(Kunst)* Régence(stil *m*) *f*; **~t** ['-t] *s* Regent *m*; *prince ~~* Prinzregent *m*.

regenerat|e [ri'dʒenəreit] *tr rel* zu neuem Leben erwecken; zu e-m besseren Menschen machen; wieder ins Leben rufen, auf e-e neue Grundlage stellen; verjüngen; *biol* regenerieren; *chem* reinigen; *el (Strom)* zurückgewinnen; *tech* regenerieren, auffrischen; *radio* rückkoppeln; *itr* geistig wiedergeboren werden; ein besserer Mensch werden; sich erneuern; sich regenerieren; *biol* nachwachsen; *a* ['-rit] wiedergeboren *fig*; (innerlich) erneuert; verjüngt; **~ion** [ridʒenə'reiʃən] *rel* Wiedergeburt; geistige Erneuerung; *biol chem tech el* Regeneration; Auffrischung, Wiedergewinnung; *radio* Rückkopplung *f*.

regicide ['redʒisaid] Königsmörder, -mord *m*.

regim|e, régime [rei'ʒi:m] Regime *n*, Regierungsform *f*, politische(s) System *n*; *geog* Wasserstandsverhältnisse *n pl*; **~en** ['redʒimen] Lebensweise, Diät; *gram* Rektion *f*.

regiment ['redʒimənt] *s mil* Regiment *n*; *fig* große Zahl, Schar *f*; *tr* ['-ment] zu e-m Regiment zs.stellen; organisieren; e-r strengen Zucht *od* Disziplin unterwerfen; bevormunden; **~al** [-'mentl] *a* Regiments-; *s pl mil* (*hist* Regiments-)Uniform *f*; *~~ command post* Regimentsgefechtsstand *m*; *~~ officer (Br)* Truppenoffizier *m*; *~~ sector* Regimentsabschnitt *m*; **~ation** [redʒimen'teiʃən] Organisation; Bevormundung, strenge Zucht, Disziplin *f*.

region ['ri:dʒən] Gegend *f*, Gebiet *n a. fig*, Landstrich *m*, Region *f a. zoo bot*; Bezirk, Bereich *m*; **~al** ['-l] *a* lokal, regional; Gebiets-, Bezirks-, Distrikts-; örtlich, Orts-; *s radio* Bezirkssender *m*.

register ['redʒistə] *s* Liste *f*, Verzeichnis, Register *n*, Rolle, Matrikel *f*; Kontobuch; Inhaltsverzeichnis *n*, Index *m*; Tabelle, Zahlentafel *f*; Zählwerk *n*, Zähler, Zähl-, Registrierapparat *m*; Registrierung *f*; Protokoll; Fremdenbuch; *typ* Register; *jur* Grundbuch *n*, Kataster *m*; *phot* (Entfernungs-)Einstellung *f*; *tech* (Regulier-)Schieber *m*, Zug-, Luftklappe *f*, Ventil; *mus* Register *n*, Tonlage *f*,

Stimmumfang *m*; *tr* eintragen, -schreiben, registrieren, auf-, verzeichnen, protokollieren; einschreiben, -tragen lassen; (an)melden (*with* bei); *Am* immatrikulieren; *(Gepäck)* aufgeben; *(Brief)* einschreiben (lassen); *(Meßgerät, Zähler)* anzeigen; *tech* einpassen; *(Gesicht)* zeigen, ausdrücken, zum Ausdruck bringen; *itr* sich eintragen, sich einschreiben (lassen); sich (an)melden (*with* bei); *Am parl* sich in die Wahlliste eintragen; die Orgelregister ziehen; *mil* sich einschießen; *tech* in Eingriff stehen; *fam* Eindruck machen *od* schinden; *to keep the* ~ Protokoll führen; *baptismal* ~ Taufregister *n*; *cash* ~ Registrierkasse *f*; *church, parish* ~ Kirchenbuch *n*; *commercial, trade* ~, ~ *of companies* Handelsregister *n*; *firm* ~ Firmenregister *n*; *land* ~ Grundbuch *n*; *Lloyd's* ~ (englisches) Schiffsregister *n*; *patent* ~ Patentregister *n*, -rolle *f*; *parliamentary* ~, ~ *of electors* Wählerliste *f*; ~ *of associations* Vereinsregister *n*; ~ *of births* Geburtsregister *n*; ~ *of births, marriages and deaths* Personenstandsregister *n pl*; ~ *of deaths* Sterberegister *n*; ~ *of marriages* Heiratsregister *n*; ~ *of members* Mitgliederverzeichnis *n*; ~ *of voters* Wählerliste *f*; **~ed** ['-d] *a (amtlich)* eingetragen, gesetzlich geschützt; staatlich geprüft; *(Brief)* eingeschrieben, ‚Einschreiben'; *to be* ~~ auf den Namen lauten; ~~ *charge* Grundschuld *f*; ~~ *club, firm* eingetragene(r) Verein *m*, Firma *f*; ~~ *customer* Stammkunde *m*; ~~ *design* Gebrauchsmuster *n*; ~~ *letter* Einschreibbrief; Wertbrief *m*; ~~ *parcel* Einschreibpäckchen *n*; ~~ *shares (pl), stock* Namensaktien *f pl*; ~~ *trade-mark* eingetragene(s) Warenzeichen *n*, Schutzmarke *f*.

registr|ar [redʒis'trɑ:, 'redʒistrɑ:] Registraturbeamte(r), Registrator; Archivar; Gerichtsschreiber, Urkundsbeamte(r); Standesbeamte(r) *m*; Register *n*; *to get married before the* ~~ sich standesamtlich trauen lassen; *R~~ General (Br)* Leiter *m* des Statistischen Amtes; ~~ *of mortgages* Grundbuch(amt); Hypothekenamt *n*; Grundbuchrichter *m*; ~~*'s licence* Heiratslizenz *f*; ~~*'s office* Standesamt; *Am* Universitätssekretariat *n*; ~~ *of societies* Vereinsregister *n*; **~ation** [redʒis'treiʃən] Einschreibung, Registrierung; Anmeldung *f*; Eintrag(ung *f*) *m*; Listen-, Registerführung *f*; *(Gepäck)* Aufgeben; *(Brief)* Einschreiben *n*; *mot* Zulassung *f*; *compulsory* ~~ Meldepflicht *f*; ~~ *certificate* Zulassung, Genehmigung, (Aufenthalts-)Bewilligung *f*; ~~ *fee* Eintragungs-, Einschreibgebühr *f*; ~~ *form* Meldeschein, -bogen *m*, Anmeldeformular *n*; ~~ *number* Matrikelnummer *f*; *mot* polizeiliche(s) Kennzeichen *n*, Wagennummer *f*; ~~ *office* Meldestelle *f*, Einwohnermeldeamt *n*; ~~ *plate (mot)* Nummernschild *n*; ~~ *window* Gepäckschalter *m*; **~y** ['redʒistri] Eintragung, Registrierung *f*; Verzeichnis *n*, Liste *f*, Register *n*; Registratur *f*; *(~~ office)* Register-, Standesamt *n*, Gerichtsschreiberei, Stellenvermitt(e)lung *f*; *land* ~~ *(Br)* Grundbuch(amt) *n*; *port of* ~~ Heimathafen *m*.

reglet ['reglit] *arch* schmale, flache Leiste; *typ* Reglette *f*, Durchschuß *m*.

regnant ['regnənt] regierend, herrschend; *fig* vorherrschend.

regress ['ri:gres] *s* Rückkehr *f*; Rückschritt *m*; *itr* [ri'gres] zurückkehren; sich rückwärts, rückläufig bewegen; **~ion** [ri'greʃən] Rückkehr; Rückwärtsbewegung *f*; Rückgang, -fall *m*; *biol* Rückentwick(e)lung; *psychol* Regression *f*; **~ive** [ri'gresiv] rückläufig; *(Steuer)* regressiv *a. biol.*

regret [ri'gret] *tr* bedauern, beklagen, betrauern, (schmerzlich) vermissen; *s* Bedauern *n* (*at* über); Reue *f*; Schmerz *m*, Trauer *f* (*for* um); *to express* ~ sein Bedauern aussprechen (*for* über); *to have* ~*s* bereuen; *I* ~ es tut mir leid; *it is to be* ~*ted* es ist bedauerlich, schade (*that* daß); **~ful** [-ful] bedauernd; reue-, kummervoll, traurig; **~table** [-əbl] bedauerlich; bemitleidenswert.

regroup ['ri:'gru:p] *tr* umgruppieren, -schichten.

regul|ar ['regjulə] *a* regelmäßig; geordnet, geregelt; vorschriftsmäßig, ordentlich; geprüft, gelernt; regulär, gewöhnlich, üblich, gebräuchlich, normal; *rail* fahrplanmäßig; *(Bewegung)* gleichförmig, -mäßig; periodisch; symmetrisch; *math gram* regelmäßig; *mil* aktiv; *rel* Ordens-; *Am pol* linientreu; *fam* regelrecht, Erz-; *Am fam* pfundig, patent; *s* Ordensgeistliche(r), -angehörige(r); *(~~ soldier)* Berufssoldat; *fam* Festangestellte(r); *fam* Stammkunde, -gast *m*; *Am* linientreue(s) Parteimitglied *n*; ~~ *army* stehende(s) Heer *n*; *a* ~~ *guy (Am fam)* ein Pfunds-, Prachtkerl, ein prächtiger Bursche *m*; ~~ *officer* Berufsoffizier *m*; **~arity** [regju'læriti] Regelmäßigkeit; Ordnung; Vorschriftsmäßigkeit *f*; **~arize** ['regjuləraiz] *tr* gesetzlich *od* amtlich festlegen; **~ate** ['regju:leit] *tr tech* steuern, regeln; regulieren, nach-, einstellen; vereinheitlichen, ordnen; anpassen; ~*ating screw* Stellschraube *f*; **~ation** [regju'leiʃən] *s* Regelung, Regulierung, Einstellung, Vereinheitlichung, Ordnung; Regel *f*, Prinzip, System *n*; Vorschrift, Anordnung, Anweisung *f*; *pl* (Ausführungs-)Bestimmungen, Statuten, Satzungen *f pl*; *a* angeordnet, vorgeschrieben, vorschriftsmäßig; regulär, normal, üblich, gewöhnlich; *contrary to* ~~*s* unvorschriftsmäßig; *currency* ~~*s (pl)* Devisenbestimmungen *f pl*; *price* ~~*s (pl)* Preisbestimmungen *f pl*; *road, traffic* ~~*s (pl)* Verkehrsvorschriften *f pl*, Straßenverkehrsordnung *f*; *safety* ~~*s (pl)* Sicherheitsbestimmungen *f pl*; *shop, working* ~~*s (pl)* Arbeitsordnung *f*; *trade* ~~*s (pl)* Gewerbeordnung *f*; **~ative** ['regjulətiv] regulierend; **~ator** ['-leitə] Ordner *(Person)*; *tech* Regler; Regulator *m*, Wanduhr *f*.

regurgitat|e [ri'gə:dʒiteit] *itr* zurückströmen, -fluten; *tr* erbrechen; *(Wiederkäuer)* zurückschlucken.

rehabilitat|e [ri:ə'biliteit] *tr* wiedereinsetzen, -gliedern (*in* in); rehabilitieren; normalisieren; wieder auf die Beine stellen *fig*; *com* sanieren; *(Truppen)* auffrischen; **~ion** ['ri:əbili'teiʃən] Wiedereinsetzung, -gliederung; Normalisierung; Ehrenrettung; *com* Sanierung; *med* Wiederherstellung (der Arbeitsfähigkeit); *(Truppen)* Wiederauffrischung *f*; ~~ *relief* soziale Fürsorge *f*.

rehash ['ri:'hæʃ] *tr fig* wieder aufwärmen; wiederholen; *s* Wiederaufwärmen *n*, Wiederholung *f*.

rehears|al [ri'hə:səl] Wiederholung *f*, Hersagen *n*; Bericht *m*; *theat* Probe *f*; *dress* ~~ Haupt-, Kostüm-, Generalprobe *f*; **~e** [ri'hə:s] *tr* (laut) wiederholen, hersagen; genau erzählen, haarklein ausea.setzen; *theat* einüben, -studieren, proben; *(jdn)* eintrainieren.

reign [rein] *s* Regierung(szeit); Herrschaft *f a. fig*; *itr* regieren, herrschen (*over* über) *a. fig*; *in the* ~ *of* während der Regierungszeit *gen*; ~ *of law* Rechtsstaatlichkeit *f*; *R~ of Terror (hist)* Schreckensherrschaft *f*.

reimburse [ri:im'bə:s] *tr* zurückzahlen, (zurück)erstatten; entschädigen (*s.o. s.th.* jdn für etw); vergüten, ersetzen (*s.o. (for) s.th.* jdm etw); *(Kosten)* decken; *to* ~ *o.s.* sich schadlos halten (*for* für; *on* an); **~ment** [-mənt] Rückvergütung, Rückzahlung, (Rück-)Erstattung; Entschädigung *f*, Ersatz *m*; ~~ *credit* Rembourskredit *m*.

rein [rein] *s* Zügel, Zaum *m*; *pl fig* Zügel *m pl*; *tr* zügeln; *fig* kontrollieren, beherrschen; *to* ~ *in* zurückhalten; *to* ~ *up, back (Pferd)* zum Stehen bringen; *to assume the* ~*s of government* die Regierung antreten *od* übernehmen; *to draw* ~ anhalten; *fig* langsamer voranmachen; zügeln; *to give (the)* ~*(s)* die Zügel locker *od* schießen lassen (*to* dat); *to hold the* ~*s (fig)* das Heft in der Hand haben; *to keep a tight* ~ *on s.o.* jdn fest in der Gewalt *od* Hand haben.

reincarnation ['ri:inkɑ:'neiʃən] *rel* Wiedergeburt, Reinkarnation *f*.

reindeer ['reindiə] Ren, Ren(n)tier *n*.

reinforce [ri:in'fɔ:s] *tr* verstärken *a. mil u. fig*, erhöhen; *(Beton)* armieren; *arch* absteifen; *fig* Nachdruck verleihen (*s.th.* dat); *s* Verstärkung *f*; ~*d concrete* Stahlbeton *m*; **~ment** [-mənt] Verstärkung *a. mil*; Verfestigung; *arch* Absteifung; *pl mil* Verstärkung *f*.

reinstall ['ri:in'stɔ:l], **reinstate** ['-'steit] *tr* wiedereinsetzen (*in* in); *(Versicherung)* wiederaufleben lassen; wiederherstellen; **~ment** ['-mənt], **reinstatement** ['-mənt] Wiedereinsetzung; Wiederherstellung *f*.

reinsur|ance ['ri:in'ʃuərəns] Wieder-, Rückversicherung *f*; **~e** ['-'ʃuə] *tr* rückversichern; **~er** ['-'ʃuərə] Rückversicherer *m*.

reissue ['ri:'isju:, *Am* '-'iʃu:] *s* Neuausgabe, -auflage; *fin* Neuemission; *film* Reprise *f*; *tr typ* neu herausgeben; wieder ausgeben.

reiterat|e [ri:'itəreit] *tr* (oft) wiederholen; **~ion** ['ri:itə'reiʃən] Wiederholung *f*; **~ive** [-rətiv] wiederholend.

reject [ri'dʒekt] *tr* ablehnen, ausschlagen, zurückweisen; *(Plan)* verwerfen; ausscheiden, ausmustern, abstoßen, ausrangieren; *com* als Ausschuß verkaufen; *med* erbrechen; *s* ['ri:dʒekt] *com* Ausschuß; *mil* Ausgemusterte(r) *m*; **~ion** [-'dʒekʃən] Ablehnung, Zurückweisung; *com* Annahmeverweigerung *f*; *pl* Ausschuß, Abfall *m*; *med* Exkremente *n pl*.

rejig [ri:'dʒig] *tr tech fam* auf neu bringen; neu ausrüsten.

rejoic|e [ri'dʒɔis] *tr* erfreuen (*by* durch); *itr* sich freuen (*at, over* über, an); sich erfreuen (*in s.th.* e-r S); **~ing** [-iŋ] *s* Freude *f*; *(oft pl)* Vergnügen *n*, Lustbarkeit, Feier *f*; *a* erfreulich; fröhlich, frohlockend (*at, in* über).

rejoin 1. ['ri:'dʒɔin] *tr itr* wieder zs.-kommen, -treffen mit; wieder verein(ig)en (*to, with* mit); wieder eintreten in; **2.** [ri'dʒɔin] *tr itr* erwidern, entgegenhalten; *jur* duplizieren; **~der** [-də] Erwiderung; *jur* Duplik *f*.

rejuven|ate [ri'dʒu:vineit] *tr* (wieder) verjüngen; *itr* sich verjüngen; **~ation** [ridʒu:vi'neiʃən], **~escence** [-'nesns] Verjüngung *f a. biol.*

rekindle ['ri:'kindl] *tr* wieder an-, entzünden; *fig* neu beleben.

relapse [ri'læps] *itr med* e-n Rückfall erleiden (*into* in); zurückfallen, -sinken, nachlassen; *rel* rückfällig sein; *s* Rückfall (*into* in) *a. med rel*; Rückschlag *m*, Zurücksinken *n*.

relat|e [ri'leit] *tr* berichten, erzählen; wiedergeben, schildern; verbinden, verknüpfen, verein(ig)en (*to* mit); in Verbindung bringen, in Beziehung setzen (*with* mit); *itr* Verbindung haben, in Verbindung stehen (*to* mit); Bezug haben, sich beziehen (*to* auf); **~ed** [-id] *a* verwandt (*to* mit); *to be ~~ to* verbunden, verwandt sein mit; *~~ by marriage* verschwägert (*to* mit); **~ion** [ri'leiʃən] Bericht *m*, Erzählung; Wiedergabe; Beziehung *f*, Verhältnis *n*; Verwandtschaft; Verschwägerung *f*; Verwandte(r) *m*; *pl pol com* Beziehungen *f pl*; *in, with ~~ to* in bezug, mit Bezug auf; *to be out of (all) ~~ to, to bear no ~~ to* keinerlei Beziehung haben zu, nichts zu tun haben mit; *to enter into ~~s with s.o.* zu jdm in Verbindung treten; *to entertain, to have, to maintain ~s to* Beziehungen unterhalten, in Beziehungen stehen (*to* mit); *~~ between cause and effect* Kausalzs.hang *m*; *amicable* od *friendly, business, commercial* od *trade, diplomatic, economic ~~s (pl)* freundschaftliche, Geschäfts-, Handels-, diplomatische, Wirtschaftsbeziehungen *f pl*; *blood ~~* Blutsverwandtschaft *f*; *human ~~s (pl)* Kontaktpflege *f*; *public ~~s (pl)* Öffentlichkeitsarbeit *f*; **~ionship** [-'leiʃənʃip] Verbindung; Beziehung (*to* zu); Verwandtschaft; *(~~ by marriage)* Verschwägerung *f*; *fiduciary ~~* Treuhandverhältnis *n*; **~ive** ['relətiv] *a* sich beziehend, in Bezug (*to* auf); in Beziehung (stehend) (*to* mit); *~~ ... to* auf ... bezüglich; relativ, bezüglich, sich beziehend (*to* auf); vergleichsweise, bedingt; entsprechend; verhältnismäßig; *gram* rückbezüglich, relativ; *s gram* Relativ(pronomen) *n*; Verwandte(r) *m*; *to be ~~ to* in Beziehung stehen zu, sich beziehen auf, zu tun haben mit; *~~ clause* Relativsatz *m*; *~~ pronoun* Relativpronomen *n*; **~ively** ['relətivli] *adv* verhältnismäßig; im Verhältnis (*to* zu); **~ivism** ['relətivizm] Relativismus *m*; **~ivity** [relə'tiviti] Relativität, Bezüglichkeit, Bedingtheit *f*; *theory of ~~* Relativitätstheorie *f*.

relax [ri'læks] *tr* lockern; *(Muskeln, Geist)* entspannen; erschlaffen lassen, verweichlichen; mildern, abschwächen; vermindern, verringern; *med* laxieren; *itr* sich lockern; sich erholen, sich entspannen, ausspannen, sich Ruhe gönnen; sich beruhigen; ausruhen; *(Miene)* sich aufheitern; erschlaffen; nachlassen, sich abschwächen, sich mildern; *to ~ the bowels (med)* abführen; **~ation** [ri:læk'seiʃən] Lockerung; Erholung, Entspannung; Zerstreuung *f*, Vergnügen; Ausruhen *n*; Erschlaffung *f*; Nachlassen *n*, Abschwächung, Milderung *f*.

relay [ri:'lei] *s* (frischer) Vorspann *m*; Ersatzpferde *n pl*, -hunde *m pl*; Ablösung(smannschaft) *f*; ['ri:lei] *sport* Staffel, Stafette *f*; *(~ race)* Staffel-, Stafettenlauf *m*; *tele radio* Relais *n*, Verstärker *m*; *tr* ['-'-] *(bei e-r Tätigkeit)* ablösen; *tele radio* verstärken; anschließen; *(Sendung)* (mit Relais) übertragen; *~* **point** Umschlagstelle *f*; *~* **station, transmitter** *radio* Relaisstation *f*, Zwischensender *m*.

re-lay, relay ['ri:'lei] *irr s. lay, tr* neu, wieder legen.

release [ri'li:s] *tr* frei-, entlassen, freigeben (*from* von); loslassen; fallen, abgehen lassen; *tech* auslösen; *(Bremse)* lösen; *(Bomben)* abwerfen; *(Gase)* freisetzen, abblasen; *fig* befreien, frei machen (*from* von); *(Recht, Anspruch)* aufgeben; verzichten auf; *(Schuld, Steuer, Strafe)* erlassen; *(Kapital)* flüssig machen; *(zur Veröffentlichung, Verbreitung)* freigeben; zulassen; *film* zur Aufführung zulassen; *s* Frei-, Entlassung (*from* aus); Entlastung, Entpflichtung, Befreiung, Entbindung *f* (*from* von); Verzicht *m*, Aufgabe; Verzichtleistung, -erklärung, -urkunde *f*; Erlaß *m (e-r Schuld)*; *(Beschlagnahme)* Aufhebung; Quittung *f*; Freigabeschein *m*; Freigabe *(zur Veröffentlichung, Verbreitung, e-s Sperrkontos)*; Zulassung; *(Konto)* Entsperrung; *tech* Auslösung *f*; (Bomben-)Abwurf; *phot* Auslöser *m (Vorrichtung)*; *to ~ the clutch* auskuppeln; *conditional ~* bedingte, vorläufige Ent-, Freilassung *f*; *first ~ (film)* Uraufführung *f*; *press ~* freigegebene Nachricht *f* für die Presse; *~ from custody* Haftentlassung *f*; *~ of mortgage* Löschung *f* e-r Hypothek; *~ upon word of honour, (Am) on parole* Freilassung *f* auf Ehrenwort, bedingte Begnadigung *f*; *~* **button** Auslöseknopf *m*.

relegat|e ['religeit] *tr* verbannen (*to* nach; *out of* aus); versetzen, verweisen (*to* auf); einordnen, -stufen; über-, verweisen (*to s.o.* an jdn).

relent [ri'lent] *itr* gelindere Saiten aufziehen, sich erweichen lassen; **~less** [-lis] mitleidlos; unerbittlich, unnachgiebig.

relevan|ce, -cy ['relivəns(i)] Sachdienlichkeit; Bedeutung, Relevanz *f* (*to* für); **~t** ['-t] sachdienlich; erheblich, wichtig, relevant (*to* für).

reli|ability [rilaiə'biliti] Zuverlässigkeit, Verläßlichkeit, Glaubwürdigkeit; *tech* Betriebssicherheit *f*; **~able** [ri'laiəbl] zuverlässig, verläßlich, vertrauens-, glaubwürdig; *tech* betriebssicher; *com* solide, kreditwürdig; **~ance** [-'laiəns] Ver-, Zutrauen *n*; *to have, to place, to put ~~ in, (up)on* Vertrauen setzen in *od* auf, Vertrauen schenken (*s.o.* jdm); **~ant** [-'laiənt] vertrauensvoll, zuversichtlich.

relic ['relik] Überrest *m*, -bleibsel; Andenken *n*; *rel* Reliquie *f*; **~t** ['-t] Witwe *f*.

relief [ri'li:f] Erleichterung, Befreiung, Linderung (*from* von); *fig* Erholung; (geistige) Abwechs(e)lung; Wohltat (*to* für); Hilfe *f*, Beistand *m*, *(Arbeitslosen-)*Unterstützung, Fürsorge; Abhilfe; Entlastung, Ablösung *f a. mil*; *mil* Entsatz; *jur* (Straf-)Erlaß *m*; Rechtshilfe *f*; Schadenersatz *m*; *(Kunst)* Relief(arbeit *f*) *n*; *(Landkarte)* (Höhen-)Schraffierung *f*; *lit allg* Gegensatz, Kontrast *m*; *to be on ~* Unterstützung beziehen; *to bring, to throw into ~* hervortreten lassen; *to stand out in ~ against* in Gegensatz stehen zu, sich scharf abheben von; *to throw into ~* hervortreten lassen *a. fig*; *old-age ~* Altersfürsorge, -unterstützung *f*; *poor ~* Armenunterstützung *f*; *tax ~* Steuererleichterung, -befreiung *f*; *unemployment ~* Arbeitslosenunterstützung *f*; *~ for refugees* Flüchtlingshilfe *f*; *~ of tension* Entspannung *f*; *~* **attack** Entlastungsangriff *m*; *~* **committee** Hilfsausschuß *m*; *~* **credits** *pl* Hilfskredite *m pl*; *~* **driver** *mot* Beifahrer *m*; *~* **fund** Unterstützungs-, Hilfsfonds *m*; *~* **map** Reliefkarte *f*; *~* **measure** Hilfsmaßnahme *f*; *~* **road** Entlastungsstraße *f*; *~* **train** *rail* Vor-, Entlastungszug *m*; *~* **valve** Überdruckventil *n*; *~* **work** Hilfswerk *n*; *pl* Notstandsarbeiten *f pl*.

relieve [ri'li:v] *tr (Los)* erleichtern; entlasten (*from* von); *(Krankheit, Schmerz, Not)* lindern, mildern; Erleichterung verschaffen (*a part of the body* e-m Körperteil); entheben, befreien, entbinden (*from* von); *tech* entspannen, auslösen; *hum* erleichtern (*of* um, von); *(belagerte Stadt)* entsetzen; *(Wache)* ablösen; *(Lage)* entspannen; unterstützen, beistehen, helfen (*s.o.* jdm); abhelfen; Abwechs(e)lung bringen in, angenehm unterbrechen; beleben (*with* mit); abheben (*from* von); hervorheben (*against* gegen); *to ~ one another* sich gegenseitig abwechseln; *to ~ o.s., to ~ nature (physiol)* sich Erleichterung verschaffen; austreten; *to ~ o.'s feelings* s-n Gefühlen freien Lauf lassen; sich Luft machen; *to ~ s.o.'s mind* jdn beruhigen; *to feel ~~d* sich erleichtert fühlen.

relig|ion [ri'lidʒən] Religion *f*, Glaube(n) *m*; Gottesfurcht, Frömmigkeit, Gottseligkeit *f*; gottselige(s) Leben; höchste(s) Gebot *n*, oberste Richtschnur *f*; *to be in ~* im Kloster sein; *to make a ~ of s.th.* sich ein Gewissen aus etw machen; *freedom of ~* Religionsfreiheit *f*; *State, Established ~* Staatsreligion *f*; *war of ~* Religionskrieg *m*; **~iosity** [-dʒi'əsiti], **~iousness** [ri'lidʒəsnis] Religiosität; Frömmigkeit *f*; **~ious** [ri'lidʒəs] *a* religiös; gottesfürchtig, fromm; mönchisch; Mönchs-, Ordens-; gewissenhaft; *s* Ordensgeistliche(r *m*) *f*.

relinquish [ri'liŋkwiʃ] *tr* aufgeben, preisgeben, verzichten; *(Recht)* abtreten; *(Erbschaft)* ausschlagen; *(Plan)* aufgeben.

reliquary ['relikwəri] *rel* Reliquienschrein *m*.

relish ['reliʃ] *s* (angenehmer) Geschmack *m*; Würze *f*; Appetitanreger, -happen; Genuß *m*, Vergnügen *n* (*for* an); Lust, Neigung *f* (*for* zu); Sinn *m* (*for* für); Anregung *f*, Reiz; Beigeschmack *m* (*of* von); *fig* Andeutung *f*, Anflug *m*, Spur *f* (*of* von); *tr* würzen; genießen; gern mögen; angenehm finden; Geschmack finden an (*having to do* daran finden, etw zu tun); *itr* schmecken (*of* nach); *to have a ~ for* e-e Vorliebe haben für.

relocation [rilo(u)'keiʃən] Verlagerung, Verlegung; (Zwangs-)Umsiedlung *f*; *~ centre* Umsiedlerlager *n*.

reluctan|ce, -cy [ri'lʌktəns(i)] Abneigung *f*, Widerwille *m*, Widerstreben *n* (*to* gegen; *to do s.th.* etw zu tun); *tech* magnetische(r) Widerstand *m*; **~t** [-t] abgeneigt, widerstrebend, ungern, un-, widerwillig (*to* zu).

rely [ri'lai] *itr* sich verlassen, bauen, zählen (*on, upon* auf); vertrauen, glauben (*on, upon s.o.* jdm); *~ing on* im Vertrauen auf.

remain [ri'mein] *itr* (ver)bleiben; fortdauern, bestehenbleiben; übrigbleiben; *s pl* Überbleibsel *n pl*, Rest *m*; Reste *m pl*, Trümmer *pl*; Überlebende *m pl*; hinterlassene Werke *n pl*; *die* sterblichen Reste *m pl*; *there ~s nothing else to do but to* es bleibt nichts anderes übrig als zu; *that ~s to be seen* das wird sich zeigen; **~der** [-də] *s* Rest *a. math*; Rückstand *m*; *(Buchhandel)* Restauflage *f*, -bestand *m*; *jur* Anwartschaft (auf ein Nacherbe); Servitut *f*; *pl* Reste *m pl*; *a* übrig, verbleibend; *tr* als Restauflage, im modernen Antiquariat verkaufen;

without a ~~ restlos; *~~ shop* moderne(s) Antiquariat *n*; **~ing** [-iŋ] übrig(geblieben), restlich, verbleibend.
remake ['ri:'meik] *irr s. make*; *tr* noch einmal, neu machen; *s* Neuverfilmung *f*.
remand [ri'mɑ:nd] *tr (to ~ in custody)* wieder in Untersuchungshaft nehmen; an die untere Instanz zurückverweisen; zurückstellen (*for a week* e-e Woche); *s* Rücksendung; Untersuchungshaft *f*; Untersuchungsgefangene(r) *m*; *to be on ~* in Untersuchungshaft sein; *prisoner on ~* Untersuchungsgefangene(r) *m*; *~* **home** Anstalt *f* für jugendliche Straffällige vor ihrer Aburteilung.
remark [ri'mɑ:k] *tr* bemerken, beobachten, feststellen (*that* daß); *(mündlich* od *schriftlich)* bemerken, äußern, erwähnen; *itr* e-e Bemerkung machen (*on, upon* über); *s* Beobachtung, Feststellung; Beachtung; (kurze) Bemerkung (*on* über); Anmerkung *f*; *concluding ~* Schlußbemerkung *f*; *preliminary ~* Vorbemerkung *f*; *worthy of ~* der Beachtung wert; **~able** [-əbl] bemerkenswert, beachtlich, auffallend, auffällig, ungewöhnlich (*about* an).
remarr|iage ['ri:'mæridʒ] Wiederverheiratung *f*; **~y** ['ri:'mæri] *itr tr* (sich) wieder (ver)heiraten (*to, with* mit).
remed|iable [ri'mi:djəbl] heilbar; **~ial** [-jəl] *a* Heil-; heilend; heilkräftig; abhelfend; *~~ gymnastics (pl)* Heilgymnastik *f*; *~~ measure* Abhilfsmaßnahme *f*; **~y** ['remidi] *s* Heilmittel *n*, Arznei, Medizin *f* (*for* gegen); Hilfs-, Gegenmittel *n* (*for* gegen); (wirksame) Hilfe, Abhilfe; *(Münze)* Toleranz *f*; *jur* Rechtsmittel *n*, -hilfe *f*; *tr* heilen; (wieder) in Ordnung bringen; abhelfen (*s.th.* e-r S), Abhilfe schaffen (*s.th.* für etw); *(Übelstand)* abstellen (*s.th.* etw); *(Mängel)* beseitigen; *household ~~* Hausmittel *n*.
rememb|er [ri'membə] *tr* sich (wieder) erinnern an; sich ins Gedächtnis zurückrufen, sich merken, behalten; *lit* eingedenk sein (*s.th.* e-r S); daran denken; (wohlwollend) denken an; *(mit etw Gutem)* bedenken; ein Trinkgeld geben (*the waiter* dem Kellner); empfehlen; *itr* sich erinnern, sich entsinnen; *~~ me to your father* grüßen Sie Ihren Vater von mir! **~rance** [-rəns] Erinnerung *f* (*of* an); Gedächtnis *n*; Erinnerung(sstück *n*) *f*, Andenken *n*; *pl* Grüße *m pl (im Brief)*; *in ~~ of* zur Erinnerung an; *within the ~~ of man* seit Menschengedenken; *R~~ Day* Waffenstillstandstag *(11. Nov.)*.
remind [ri'maind] *tr* erinnern, mahnen (*of* an; *to do* zu tun; *that* daß); *that ~s me* dabei fällt mir ein; *~ me about it* erinnere mich daran; **~er** [-ə] Gedächtnisstütze, Mahnung *f*, Wink *m*.
reminisc|e [remi'nis] *itr* in Erinnerungen schwelgen; **~ence** [-ns] Erinnerung *f* (*of* an); Gedächtnis *n*; Spur *f*; *pl* (Lebens-)Erinnerungen *f pl*; **~ent** [-nt] sich erinnernd (*of* an).
remise [ri'maiz] *tr jur (Recht)* aufgeben, abtreten; *s* Rechtsverzicht; [rə'mi:z] Wagenschuppen; *(Fechten)* Nachstoß *m*.
remiss [ri'mis] nachlässig, sorglos (*in* bei); *(Arbeit)* schlampig, schlud(e)rig; lässig, schlaff, energielos; **~ible** [-əbl] verzeihlich; *(Sünde)* läßlich; **~ion** [ri'miʃən] Vergebung *(von Sünden)*; Erlassung *(von Schulden, Steuern, Strafen)*; Befreiung *(von Gebühren)*; Ermäßigung *f*; Nachlassen *n*, Abschwächung *f*, Rückgang *m*, Verminderung, Verringerung; *med* vorübergehende Besserung *f*.
remit [ri'mit] *tr (Sünde)* vergeben; verzeihen; *(Strafe, Schuld, Steuer)* erlassen, streichen; verzichten auf; überlassen, abtreten; verringern, vermindern, herabsetzen, nachlassen in, mäßigen; verweisen (*to s.o.* an jdn); *jur* (*an e-e untere Instanz*) zurückverweisen; vertagen, verschieben; *(bes. Geld)* schicken, (über)senden, überweisen; *(Wechsel)* einlösen; zurücklegen, -stellen, auf-, verschieben (*till, to* bis); *itr* abnehmen, nachlassen; Geld senden; *com* remittieren; **~tal** [-l] Vergebung; Erlassung; *jur* Zurückverweisung; *com* Überweisung *f*; **~tance** [-əns] *(Geld)* Sendung, Überweisung *f*; *fam* Wechsel *m*; *upon ~~ of* gegen Einsendung von; *to provide for, to make ~~ (com)* Deckung anschaffen; *~~ account, form, order* Überweisungskonto, -formular *n*, -auftrag *m*; **~tee** [rimi'ti:] Empfänger *m (e-r Überweisung)*; **~tent** [ri'mitənt] vorübergehend nachlassend; **~ter** [ri'mitə] *(Geld)* Absender, Einzahler; Remittent *m*; *jur* Zurückverweisung; Wiedereinsetzung *f* (*to* in).
remnant ['remnənt] (schwacher) Rest, Überrest *m*, Überbleibsel *n* (*of* gen); Stoffrest *m*; *fig* Spur *f* (*of* von); *~* **sale** Resteverkauf *m*.
remodel ['ri:'mɔdl] *tr* umbilden, -gestalten, -formen; erneuern.
remonstr|ance [ri'mɔnstrəns] Einwand *m*, Beschwerde *f*, Vorwurf, Protest *m*; **~ant** [-t] *a* protestierend, Einwände machend; *s* Beschwerdeführer *m*; **~ate** [-eit] *itr* Einwendungen machen, (*against* gegen), vorstellig werden (*on* wegen), sich beschweren (*on* über; *with* bei).
remorse [ri'mɔ:s] Gewissensbisse *m pl* (*at* über; *for* wegen); *without ~* mitleids-, erbarmungslos; *to feel ~* Gewissensbisse haben; **~ful** [-ful] reumütig; **~less** [-lis] mitleids-, erbarmungslos, rücksichtslos.
remote [ri'mout] *a* entfernt, entlegen, abgelegen (*from* von); *(zeitl.)* weit zurück- *od* in ferner Zukunft liegend; *(Vergangenheit, Zukunft)* fern; *(Gedanke)* fernliegend; *(Verwandter)* entfernt; *(Verwandtschaft)* weitläufig; *(Ähnlichkeit, Aussichten)* schwach; unbedeutend, gering; *(Mensch)* zurückhaltend; *s pl* Fernsehaufnahmen *f pl* außerhalb des Senderaumes; *I haven't the ~st idea* ich habe nicht die mindeste Vorstellung; *~* **control** *tech* Fernbedienung, -steuerung, -lenkung *f*; **~-controlled** *a* ferngelenkt, -gesteuert; **~ness** [-nis] Entlegenheit, Abgeschiedenheit *f*.
remount [ri:'maunt] *tr* wieder besteigen; *mil* mit frischen Pferden versehen; *(Bild, Karte)* neu aufziehen; *(Fluß)* hinauffahren; *itr* wieder aufsteigen, wieder hinaufgehen; wieder be-, ersteigen; *fig* zurückgehen (*to* auf); *s* ['ri:maunt] frische (Reit-) Pferd(e *pl*) *n*.
remov|able [ri'mu:vəbl] heraus-, abnehmbar; abstell-, behebbar; auswechselbar; absetzbar; **~al** [-əl] Entfernung *f*; Wegräumen, Weg-, Fortschaffen *n*, Wegnahme; Abschaffung, -stellung, Beseitigung; Entlassung, Versetzung *f* (*from* von); Umzug (*to* in, nach); Ortswechsel *m*; Verlegung *f*; *tech* Ausbau *m*; *~~ from office* Amtsenthebung *f*; *~~ van* Möbelwagen *m*; **~e** [ri:'mu:v] *tr* entfernen, beseitigen, wegschaffen, -nehmen; forträumen, woanders hinbringen, -schaffen; *tech* abmontieren; *(Geschäft)* verlegen; *(von der Universität)* relegieren; *(Kleidung)* ausziehen, ablegen; *(Hut)* absetzen; *(Einrichtung)* abschaffen; *(Schwierigkeiten)* beseitigen; *(Mißbrauch)* abstellen, beheben; *(Name)* streichen; *(Pflanze)* versetzen; *(Zweifel)* zerstreuen, aus der Welt schaffen; *(Beamten)* entlassen, aus dem Amt entfernen, absetzen; versetzen; entfernen, beseitigen, aus dem Wege räumen, umbringen; *med* ausschneiden, exstirpieren; *(Verband)* abnehmen; *itr* umziehen (*to* nach); *s* Entfernung, Beseitigung; Entlassung; *(Schule)* Versetzung *f*; Verwandtschaftsgrad *m*; Strecke *f*, Abschnitt, Grad *m*; *to ~~ from the agenda* von der Tagesordnung absetzen; *to ~~ to (the) hospital* ins Krankenhaus bringen; *not to get o.'s ~~ (Schule)* sitzenbleiben; *to ~~ a pupil from school* e-n Schüler aus der Schule nehmen; **~er** [ri'mu:və] (Möbel-)Spediteur, Transporteur *m*; **~ing** [ri'mu:viŋ]: *~~ cream* Abschminkcreme *f*; *~~ expenses (pl)* Umzugskosten *pl*.
remunerat|e [ri'mju:nəreit] *tr (Menschen)* belohnen, entschädigen (*for* für); *(Bemühungen)* vergüten; *(Unkosten)* erstatten; **~ion** [rimju:nə'reiʃən] Belohnung; Entschädigung *f*, Entgelt *n*; Vergütung *f*; Lohn *m*; Honorar *n*; Erstattung *f*; **~ive** [-ətiv] *a* Entschädigungs-, Vergütungs-; lohnend, einträglich, vorteilhaft.
Renaissance [ri'neisəns, *Am* 'renəsɑ:ns] *s* Renaissance *f*; *a* Renaissance-.
renal ['ri:nl] *a scient* Nieren-; *~* **calculus** *med* Nierenstein *m*; *~* **colic** Nieren(stein)kolik *f*.
rename ['ri:'neim] *tr* umbenennen; neu benennen.
renascen|ce [ri'næsns] Wiedergeburt *f*, Wiederaufleben *n fig*; *R~~* Renaissance *f*; **~t** [-t] wiederauflebend, -blühend, sich erneuernd.
rend [rend] *irr rent, rent tr* (weg)reißen (*from* von); zerreißen *bes. fig*; *(Land)* zerstückeln; *to ~ away* wegreißen.
render ['rendə] *tr* ab-, übergeben *a. mil*, überreichen; vorlegen, unterbreiten; übersenden, überweisen; *(Rechenschaft)* ablegen; *(to ~ back)* zurückgeben, erstatten; *(Dank)* abstatten; *(Gehorsam, e-n Dienst)* erweisen; *(Hilfe)* leisten; *(Nutzen, Gewinn)* bringen, abwerfen; machen *mit a*; verwandeln in; *lit Kunst mus* wiedergeben; *mus* vortragen; *theat* darstellen, spielen; *(Thema)* behandeln; *(Gründe)* angeben; *(in Worten)* ausdrücken, erzählen, sagen; übertragen, übersetzen (*into* in); *(Gutachten)* erstatten; *(Fett)* auslassen; *arch* verputzen, bewerfen; *jur (Urteil)* verkünden; *mar* durchscheren; *s arch* (Roh-)Bewurf *m*; *to ~ an account of* Rechenschaft ablegen über; berichten über; *to ~ difficult* erschweren; **~ing** ['-riŋ] Übertragung, Übersetzung (*into* in); Darstellung; *mus* Wiedergabe *f*; *arch* (Roh-)Bewurf *m*; *~~ of account* Rechnungslegung *f*.
rendezvous ['rɔndivu:, 'rɑ:nd-] *pl ~* ['-z] Treffpunkt *m a. mil*, Stelldichein *n*, Verabredung *f*; *mil* Sammelplatz *m*.
rendition [ren'diʃən] *mus* Wiedergabe, Interpretation; *theat* Verkörperung; Übertragung, -setzung; *Am* (Urteils-) Verkündigung *f*.
reneg|ade ['renigeid] *s rel* Renegat, Apostat; *allg* Abtrünnige(r) *m*; **~(u)e** [ri'ni(:)g] *itr (Kartenspiel)* nicht bedienen; *Am fam* nicht Wort halten; nicht einhalten (*on a promise* ein Versprechen).

renew [ri'nju:] *tr* erneuern; *tech* auswechseln; auffrischen; ermuntern; erneuen, wiederaufnehmen, -greifen; *(Versuch)* wiederholen; *(Vorräte)* erneuern, auffrischen; *(Lager)* ergänzen; *(Vertrag)* verlängern; *(Wechsel)* prolongieren; **~al** [-l] Erneuerung *f*; *tech* Ersatz *m*; Auffrischung; *(Wechsel)* Prolongation; Wiederaufnahme; Verlängerung *f*.

renn|et ['renit] **1.** (Kälber-)Lab *n*; **2.** Renette *f (Apfel)*.

renounce [ri'nauns] *tr* verzichten auf, aufgeben; entsagen (*s.th.* e-r S); *(Erbschaft)* ausschlagen, ablehnen; sich lossagen von, verleugnen; *(Schuld)* nicht anerkennen; *(Karte)* nicht bedienen; *(Vertrag)* aufkündigen, zurücktreten von; *itr* (auf sein Recht) verzichten; *(Kartenspiel)* nicht bedienen, passen.

renovat|e ['reno(u)veit] *tr* erneuern, (wieder) instand setzen, renovieren; **~ion** [reno(u)'veiʃən] Erneuerung, Instandsetzung, Renovierung *f*; **~or** ['-ə] Erneuerer *m*.

renown [ri'naun] Ruf *m*, Berühmtheit *f*, Renommee *n*; **~ed** [-d] *a* bekannt, berühmt, namhaft, angesehen (*for* wegen).

rent [rent] **1.** *pp von rend*; *s* Riß *a. fig*; Sprung, Spalt; *fig* Bruch *m*, Spaltung *f*; **2.** *s* Miete *f*, (Miet-)Zins *m*, Pacht (-zins *m*) *f*; Einkommen *n*, Rente; *Am fam* Wohnung *f*; *tr* mieten, pachten (*from* von); *Am* (aus)leihen; *Am* (*to ~ out*) vermieten, verpachten; *itr* zu mieten sein (*at, for* für); sich verzinsen (*at* zu); *for ~ (Am)* zu vermieten(d); zu verleihen; *ground ~* Grundrente; Reallast *f*; **~able** ['-əbl] zu vermieten(d); **~al** ['rentl] Mietbetrag *m*; Miete, Pacht(summe) *f*; Mietsaufkommen; Mietbuch; *Am* Miethaus *n*, -wohnung *f*; *subscriber's ~~* Fernsprechanschlußgebühr *f*; *~~ allowance* Wohnungsgeld *n*, Mietzuschuß *m*; *~~ control* Mietpreisüberwachung *f*; *~~ library (Am)* Leihbücherei, -bibliothek *f*; **~-day** Miet-, Pachtzahlungstag *m*; **~er** ['-ə] Mieter, Pächter; Vermieter, Eigentümer; (Film-)Verleiher *m*; **~-free** pachtfrei; **~less** ['-lis] ertrag-, zinslos; **~-roll** Pachtverzeichnis; Mietaufkommen *n*, -einnahmen *f pl*.

renunciation [rinʌnsi'eiʃən] Verzicht *m* (*of* auf); Aufgabe; Ablehnung *(e-r Erbschaft)*; (Selbst-)Verleugnung *f*.

reopen ['ri:'oupən] *tr itr* wieder (er-)öffnen; wieder aufnehmen *od* anfangen.

reorganiz|ation ['ri:ɔ:gənai'zeiʃən] Neu-, Umgestaltung, Neugliederung, Reform, Reorganisation; *fin* Sanierung *f*; *Am* Gläubigervergleich *m*; **~e** ['ri:'ɔ:gənaiz] *tr* neu-, umgestalten, reorganisieren; *fin* sanieren.

reorientation ['ri:ɔ:rien'teiʃən] Neuorientierung *f*.

rep [rep] **1.** *(a. repp, reps)* Rips *m*; **2.** *sl* Flittchen *n*; Wüstling *m*; *Am sl* Ruf *m*; **3.** *sl (Schule) (= repetition)* Auswendiggelernte(s) *n*; **4.** *sl mil* Anschiß *m*; **5.** Repertoiretheater *n*.

repair [ri'pɛə] **1.** *tr* (wieder) ausbessern, reparieren, instand setzen; erneuern, wiederherstellen; *(Fehler)* berichtigen, richtigstellen; abhelfen (*s.th.* e-r S); *(Unrecht)* wiedergutmachen; *(Verlust)* wettmachen; *s* Ausbesserung, Reparatur *f*; bauliche(r) Zustand *m*; *pl* Instandsetzungsarbeiten *f pl*; *beyond ~* nicht mehr zu reparieren; *in good ~* in gutem Zustand; *out of ~* nicht in Ordnung; baufällig; *under ~* in Reparatur; *to keep in ~* instand halten; *closed during ~s* wegen Renovierung geschlossen; *road ~s (pl)* Straßeninstandsetzungsarbeiten *f pl*; **~able** [-rəbl] (noch) zu reparieren(d); reparaturbedürftig; **~er** [-rə], **~man** [-mən] Mechaniker *m*; **~ kit, outfit** Reparaturwerkzeug *n*, Werkzeugkasten *m*; **~ order** Reparaturauftrag *m*; **~ service** Kundendienst *m*; **~ shop** Reparaturwerkstatt *f*; **2.** *itr* sich (häufig *od* zahlreich) begeben (*to* nach); sich wenden (*to* an; *for* wegen).

repar|able ['repərəbl] wiedergutzumachen(d); ersetzbar; **~ation** [repə'reiʃən] Ausbesserung, Instandsetzung, Reparatur, Wiederherstellung; Wiedergutmachung; Entschädigung *f*, Ersatz *m*; *meist pl* Reparationen *f pl*, Kriegsentschädigung *f*.

repartee [repɑ:'ti:, *Am* repə'ti:] schnelle, geschickte Entgegnung *od* Erwiderung; Schlagfertigkeit *f*; *to be good at ~* schlagfertig sein.

repartition [ri:pɑ:'tiʃən] Auf-, Ein-, Verteilung; Neuein-, Neuverteilung *f*.

repast [ri'pɑ:st] Essen *n*; Mahlzeit *f*.

repatriat|e [ri:'pætrieit, *Am* -pei-] *tr* ins Heimatland zurückbringen, -führen, -senden, repatriieren; *s* [ri:'pætriət] Repatriierte(r *m*) *f*; **~ion** ['ri:pætri'eiʃən] Rückführung *f*.

repay [ri:'pei] *irr s. pay tr* zurückzahlen, (zurück)erstatten (*s.o.* jdm); ersetzen; entschädigen (*for* für); *(Kredit)* abdecken; *(Gefälligkeit, Besuch)* erwidern; *(Unrecht)* vergelten; *(Mühe)* belohnen; **~able** [-əbl] rückzahlbar; **~ment** [-mənt] Rückzahlung, Erstattung, Vergütung; *(Kredit)* Abdeckung, Tilgung; Erwiderung; Vergeltung *f*.

repeal [ri'pi:l] *tr* widerrufen, zurücknehmen, -ziehen, aufheben; *(Gesetz)* außer Kraft setzen; *s* Widerruf *m*, Zurückziehung, Aufhebung *f*.

repeat [ri'pi:t] *tr* wiederholen; nachsagen, -sprechen; auf-, hersagen; ausplaudern; wiederholen; noch einmal tun; *itr* u. *to ~ o.s.* sich wiederholen; *med* aufstoßen; *itr Am* mehr als eine (Wahl-)Stimme abgeben; e-e Klasse wiederholen; *to ~ after* nachsprechen, -sagen; *s* Wiederholung *f a. mus radio*; *mus* Wiederholungszeichen *n*; *com (~ order)* Nachbestellung *f*; **~ed** [-id] *a* wiederholt, mehrmalig; **~edly** [-idli] *adv* (zu) wiederholt(en Malen); **~er** [-ə] Wiederholende(r); *Am (Schule)* Sitzengebliebene(r); *Am (Gefängnis)* Rückfälliger *m*; *Am* jem, der mehr als e-e (Wahl-)Stimme abgibt; Repetieruhr *f*, *Am (~ing rifle)* -gewehr *n*; *tele* Übertrager; Verstärker; *(~ing decimal)* periodische(r) Dezimalbruch *m*.

repel [ri'pel] *tr* zurückschlagen, -stoßen, -treiben; ab-, zurückweisen; *(Flüssigkeit)* abstoßen *a. fig*; anwidern; **~ent** [-ənt] zurück-, abstoßend *a. fig*; wasserdicht; *fig* widerwärtig.

repent [ri'pent] *itr tr* bereuen; Reue empfinden (*of* über); *I ~ it* es reut mich, es tut mir leid; **~ance** [-əns] Reue; Bußfertigkeit *f*; **~ant** [-ənt] reuig (*of* über); bußfertig.

repeople ['ri:'pi:pl] *tr* wieder bevölkern.

repercussion [ri:pə:'kʌʃən] Rückprall, -stoß; Widerhall *m*, Echo *n*; *fig* Rückwirkung *f* (*on* auf); *pl fig* Reaktionen, Auswirkungen *f pl*.

repertoire ['repətwɑ:] *theat* Repertoire *n*, Spielplan *m*.

repertory ['repətəri] *fig* Fundgrube, Schatzkammer *f*; *theat* Repertoire *n*; **~ theatre** Repertoirebühne *f*.

repetit|ion [repi'tiʃən] Wiederholung *f*; Auf-, Hersagen *n*; Nachbildung, Zweitanfertigung; *(Kunst)* Kopie; *com* Kollationierung *f*; *~~ work* Serienherstellung *f*; **~ive** [ri'petitiv] Wiederholungs-; sich wiederholend.

repin|e [ri'pain] *itr* mißvergnügt, unzufrieden sein (*against* mit); murren, sich beklagen (*at* über); **~ing** [-iŋ] unzufrieden, mißgestimmt, -vergnügt.

replace [ri'pleis] *tr* wieder hinsetzen, -stellen, -legen; an die Stelle treten (*s.o., s.th.* jds, e-r S); ersetzen (*by* durch) *a. tech*; auswechseln, erneuern (*by* durch); *(Schaden)* ersetzen; zurückerstatten, rückvergüten; *to ~ the receiver* den Hörer auflegen; **~able** [-əbl] ersetzbar; auswechselbar; **~ment** [-mənt] Ersatz *m*; Wiederbeschaffung; Vertretung *f*, Vertreter; *mil* Ersatzmann *m*; Ergänzung, Reserve *f*; *(~~ part)* Ersatzteil *n*, *a. m*; *com* Ersatzbeschaffung; *(Lager)* Auffüllung *f*; *pl mil* Verstärkungen *f pl*; *stock of ~~s* Ersatzteillager *n*; *~~ engine* Austauschmotor *m*; *~~ price* Wiederbeschaffungspreis *m*.

replant ['ri:'plɑ:nt] *tr* umpflanzen; neu pflanzen.

replay ['ri:plei] *sport* Wiederholungsspiel *n*.

replenish [ri'pleniʃ] *tr* (wieder) auffüllen (*with* mit); *(Vorrat)* ergänzen, vervollständigen; **~ment** [-mənt] Auffüllung; Ergänzung *f*; Nachschub *m*.

replet|e [ri'pli:t] (wohl)gefüllt, voll (*with* von); vollgestopft, bis zum Platzen voll (*with* mit); **~ion** [-'pli:ʃən] (Über-)Fülle *f*; *to eat to ~~* sich vollessen; *filled to ~~* randvoll.

replica ['replikə] Kopie *f*; *fig* Ebenbild *n*; **~tion** [repli'keiʃən] *jur* Erwiderung, Replik *f*; Widerhall *m*, Echo *n*; *(Kunst)* Kopie *f*.

reply [ri'plai] *itr* antworten, (e-e) Antwort geben, entgegnen (*to* auf); *(Tätigkeit, mil: Feuer)* erwidern (*to s.th.* etw); widerhallen; *tr* beantworten, erwidern, entgegnen; *s* Antwort, Entgegnung (*to* auf); Erwiderung; *jur* Replik *f*; Antwortschreiben *n*, Rückäußerung *f*; *in ~ to* in Erwiderung auf; *to make no ~* keine Antwort geben; *intermediate ~* Zwischenbescheid *m*; **~-card** Antwortkarte *f*; **~-coupon** Antwortschein *m*; **~-postage** Rückporto *n*.

report [ri'pɔ:t] *tr* berichten (über), Bericht erstatten über; erzählen; vortragen; verbreiten; *(Nachricht, Meldung)* (über)bringen; melden, anzeigen, angeben, denunzieren (*for* wegen; *to the police* bei der Polizei); *(Zoll)* deklarieren, anmelden; *itr* e-n Bericht machen, Bericht erstatten, berichten (*on* über; *for* wegen); als Berichter(statter) tätig sein (*for* für); sich melden, Meldung machen (*to* bei); sich stellen; *to ~ upon s.th.* über etw referieren; *s* Bericht *m* (*of, on* über); Meldung *f*; Protokoll *n*; Vortrag *m*, Referat *n*; Rechenschaftsbericht *m*; Überbringung *f*; Gerücht, Gerede *n*, Klatsch; Ruf, Leumund; Knall *m* (*bei e-r Explosion*); (Schul-)Zeugnis *n*; Zolldeklaration *f*; *pl* Akten *f pl*; *to make, to give a ~* Bericht erstatten; *to make a progress ~* über den Stand e-r Angelegenheit berichten; *to prepare a ~* e-n Bericht abfassen; *annual, monthly, weekly ~* Jahres-, Monats-, Wochenbericht *m*; *committee ~* Ausschußbericht *m*; *damage ~* Schadensmeldung *f*; *financial ~* Geschäftsbericht *m*; *market ~* Marktbericht *m*; *money-market ~* Börsen-, Kursbericht *m*; *negative ~*

Fehlmeldung *f*; *newspaper* ~ Zeitungsbericht *m*; *official* ~ amtliche(r) Bericht *m*, Protokoll *n*; *period, month, year under* ~ Berichtszeit *f*, -monat *m*, -jahr *n*; *press* ~ Pressemeldung *f*; *sick* ~ Krankenzustandsbericht *m*; *treasurer's* ~ Kassenbericht *m*; *weather* ~ Wetterbericht *m*; ~*ed speech* indirekte Rede *f*; ~ **card** *Am* (Schul-)Zeugnis *n*; ~**er** [-ə] Bericht(erstatt)er, Reporter; *jur* Protokollführer *m*; ~~*'s gallery* Pressetribüne *f*; ~ **stage** *parl* Berichtsstadium *n*.

repose [ri'pouz] **1.** *tr* (zur Ruhe) legen, ausruhen; niederlegen (*on* auf); *itr* liegen, ruhen (*on* auf); *fig* beruhen (*on* auf); *to* ~ *o.s.* sich ausruhen; schlafen; *s* Ausruhen *n*, Erholung (*from* von); Ruhe; Stille *f*; Schlaf *m*; Gelassenheit *f*; ~**ful** [-ful] ruhig, erholsam; **2.** *tr (Vertrauen)* setzen (*in* auf).

repository [ri'pɔzitəri] Aufbewahrungsort *m*; Ablage *f*; (Waren-)Lager *n*, Niederlage *f*; Speicher, Lagerraum *m*, -haus, Magazin *n*; Behälter; *allg* Sammelplatz *m*, -lager; Grab(gewölbe); *min* Lager *n*; *fig* Fundgrube *f*; *fig* Vertraute(r) *m*, Vertrauensperson *f*.

repp *s. rep.*

reprehen|d [repri'hend] *tr* tadeln, rügen, etwas auszusetzen haben an, (scharf) kritisieren; ~**sible** [-'hensəbl] tadelnswert; ~**sion** [-'henʃən] Tadel *m*, Rüge *f*, Verweis *m*, (scharfe) Kritik *f*.

represent [repri'zent] *tr (geistig)* vorstellen; darlegen, darstellen, schildern, begreiflich machen, ausmalen, hinstellen (*as* als); behaupten, vorgeben; *(Bild)* darstellen, wiedergeben; *(Zeichen)* bedeuten; *(durch Zeichen)* ausdrücken; sein, bedeuten (*to s.o.* jdm); verkörpern, repräsentieren, vertreten; *theat* darstellen, spielen; aufführen; *com pol* vertreten; als Beispiel dienen für; ~**ation** [reprizen'teiʃən] Vorstellung; Darstellung, Schilderung; Wiedergabe; Abbildung *f*, Bild *n*; *theat* Aufführung, Vorstellung; (Stell-)Vertretung *f*; *oft pl* Vorstellungen, Vorhaltungen, (Er-)Mahnungen *f pl*, Proteste *m pl*; *to make* ~~*s* Vorstellungen erheben (*to* bei); ~**ative** [-'zentətiv] *a* vor-, darstellend, wiedergebend; (stell)vertretend (*of* für); repräsentativ; parlamentarisch; typisch, symbolisch (*of* für); *s allg com pol* Vertreter; Repräsentant; Beauftragte(r); Abgeordnete(r), Volksvertreter *m*; typische(s) Beispiel *n* (*of* für); *commercial, sales* ~~ Handelsvertreter *m*; *diplomatic* ~~ diplomatische(r) Vertreter *m*; *general* ~~ Generalvertreter *m*; *House of* ~~*s* Abgeordneten-, *(Am)* Repräsentantenhaus *n*; *legal, personal* ~~ Rechtsvertreter; Vormund *m*; *sole* ~~ Alleinvertreter *m*; *special* ~~ Sonderbeauftragte(r) *m*; ~~ *assembly* Abgeordnetenversammlung *f*; ~~ *government* parlamentarische Regierungsform *f*; ~~ *sample* Serienmuster *n*.

repress [ri'pres] *tr (Aufruhr)* unterdrücken; unterwerfen, -jochen; zügeln; *psychol* verdrängen; *(Gefühl)* nicht aufkommen lassen; ~**ion** [-'preʃən] Unterdrückung; Zügelung; *psychol* Verdrängung *f*; ~**ive** [ri'presiv] *a* Unterdrückungs-; hemmend; ~~ *measures (pl)* Unterdrückungsmaßnahmen *f pl*.

reprieve [ri'pri:v] *tr* Strafaufschub, e-e Gnadenfrist gewähren (*s.o.* jdm); *(Unangenehmes)* aufschieben; *s* Begnadigung *f*; Strafaufschub *m*; Gnadenfrist, vorübergehende Befreiung, Erleichterung; *fig* Atempause *f*; *right of* ~ Begnadigungsrecht *n*.

reprimand ['reprimα:nd] *s* (strenger) Verweis, Tadel *m*; *tr* [-, repri'mα:nd] e-n (strengen) Verweis erteilen (*s.o.* jdm), zurechtweisen.

reprint ['ri:'print] *tr* wieder (ab)drukken, neu auflegen; *s* [*a.* '--] Neudruck *m*, -ausgabe *f*; *cheap* ~ Volksausgabe *f*.

reprisal [ri'praizəl] Repressalie; Vergeltung(smaßnahme) *f*; *as* ~*s for* als Vergeltung für; *to make* ~*s* Repressalien ergreifen (*(up)on* gegen).

reproach [ri'proutʃ] *tr* vorwerfen (*s.o. with s.th.* jdm etw); Vorwürfe, Vorhaltungen machen (*s.o. with s.th.* jdm wegen e-r S); schelten, tadeln (*for* wegen); Unehre machen, Schande bringen (*s.o.* jdm); *s* Vorwurf *m*, Vorhaltung *f*, Tadel *m*; Unehre, Schande *f* (*to* für); *to be a* ~ *to s.o.* für jdn ein Schandfleck sein; ~**ful** [-ful] vorwurfsvoll; tadelnswert, schändlich.

reprob|ate ['repro(u)beit] *a* verderbt, verkommen; laster-, frevelhaft; ruchlos, verworfen; *rel* verdammt, verloren; *s* verkommene(r), lasterhafte(r) Mensch; *rel* Verdammte(r) *m*; *tr* mißbilligen, verurteilen; verwerfen; *rel* verdammen; ~**ation** [repro(u)'beiʃən] Mißbilligung; *rel* Verdammnis *f*.

reproduc|e [ri:prə'dju:s] *tr biol* hervorbringen; *(die Art)* fortpflanzen; *(verlorenen Körperteil)* regenerieren; *agr* züchten; reproduzieren, nachbilden, kopieren, vervielfältigen; *tech* wiedergeben; wiederholen; *theat* neuinszenieren; wiederaufführen; *itr* sich fortpflanzen; ~**eable**, ~**ible** [-əbl] reproduzierbar; wiederholbar; ~**er** [-ə] Züchter; Vervielfältiger *m*; *tech* Wiedergabegerät *n*; ~**tion** [ri:prə'dʌkʃən] Wiederholung; Nachbildung, Reproduktion, Vervielfältigung; Wiedergabe; Kopie; *biol* Fortpflanzung; Züchtung *f*; ~~ *cost* Wiederbeschaffungs-, Veredlungskosten *pl*; ~**tive** [-'dʌktiv] sich wiederholend; sich fortpflanzend; Fortpflanzungs-, Zucht-.

reproof [ri'pru:f] Mißbilligung, Beanstandung *f*; Tadel, Vorwurf *m*.

re-proof ['ri:'pru:f] *tr* neu imprägnieren.

reprov|able [ri'pru:vəbl] zu beanstanden(d); tadelnswert; ~**al** [-əl] = *reproof*; ~**e** [ri'pru:v] *tr* mißbilligen, beanstanden; zurechtweisen, tadeln.

reps *s. rep 1.*

rept|ant ['reptənt] *zoo bot* kriechend; ~**ile** ['-tail] *s* Reptil, Kriechtier *n*; *fig* Kriecher, Schleicher *m*; *a* reptilartig; kriechend; *fig* kriecherisch; ~**ilian** [rep'tiliən] *a* Reptilien-; reptilartig; *fig* kriecherisch, hinterhältig, niederträchtig; *s* Reptil, Kriechtier *n*.

republic [ri'pʌblik] Republik *f a. fig*, Freistaat *m*; *the* ~ *of letters* die Gelehrtenrepublik; ~**an** [-ən] *a* republikanisch; *s* Republikaner *m*; ~**anism** [-ənizm] republikanische Prinzipien *n pl od* Gesinnung *od* Staatsform *f*.

republ|ication ['ri:pʌbli'keiʃən] *(Buch)* Wiederherausgabe; Neuausgabe, -auflage *f*; ~**ish** ['ri:'pʌbliʃ] *tr* neu herausgeben *od* auflegen.

repudiat|e [ri'pju:dieit] *tr (Frau, Sohn)* verstoßen; verwerfen, ablehnen, zurückweisen; nicht anerkennen, in Abrede stellen; ~**ion** [ripjudi'eiʃən] Verstoßung; Verwerfung, Ablehnung, Zurückweisung, Nichtanerkennung; *com* Erfüllungsverweigerung *f*.

repugn|ance, -cy [ri'pʌgnəns(i)] Widerspruch (*to, with* mit); Gegensatz *m*, -sätzlichkeit; Unvereinbarkeit (*between* zwischen); Ungereimtheit *f*; Widerwille *m*, (heftige) Abneigung *f* (*against, to* gegen); ~**ant** [-ənt] unvereinbar (*to* mit), im Widerspruch stehend (*to* zu); gegensätzlich, Gegen-; widerlich, abstoßend, unangenehm.

repuls|e [ri'pʌls] *tr (Angriff)* zurückschlagen; zurück-, abweisen; zurückstoßen; ablehnen; *s* Abweisung; Verweigerung; Ablehnung *f*; *phys* Rückstoß *m*; *to meet with a* ~~ abgewiesen werden; ~**ion** [-'pʌlʃən] Zurückschlagen *n*, Abweisung *f*; Widerwille *m*, (starke, heftige) Abneigung; *phys* Abstoßung *f*; ~**ive** [-'pʌlsiv] abweisend; abstoßend *a. phys*; *fig* widerlich, widerwärtig.

repurchase ['ri:'pə:tʃəs] *tr* zurückkaufen, -erwerben; *s* Rückkauf *m*; ~ **value** Rückkaufwert *m*.

reput|able ['repjutəbl] angesehen, achtbar, respektabel; anständig; ~**ation** [repju(:)'teiʃən] Leumund, Ruf, Name *m*; Ansehen *n*, Achtung *f*; *of good, high* ~~ von gutem Ruf; *to have a* ~~ *for beauty* als schön gelten; wegen s-r Schönheit bekannt sein; *to have the* ~~ *of being lazy* in dem Ruf stehen, faul zu sein; *to lose o.'s* ~~ in schlechten Ruf kommen; ~**e** [ri'pju:t] *tr*: *to be* ~*ed* in dem Ruf stehen (*to be* ... ... zu sein); *s* = ~*ation*; ~**ed** [-'pju:tid] *a* vermeintlich; angeblich.

request [ri'kwest] *s* Bitte *f*, An-, Ersuchen, Verlangen *n*, Nachfrage *f*; Gesuch *n*; Auf-, Anforderung *f*; *tr* bitten, er-, nachsuchen (*s.th. of s.o.* jdn um etw); einkommen um; beantragen; *to* ~ *s.o. to do s.th., that s.th. is done* jdn bitten, etw zu tun; *to* ~ *s.th. from s.o.* etw von jdm erbitten; *as* ~*ed* wie gewünscht; *at s.o.'s* ~ auf jds Bitte, Wunsch; *by, on* ~ auf Wunsch; auf Verlangen *od* Ansuchen; *in* ~ gesucht, gefragt, beliebt, geschätzt; *to be in* ~ gefragt sein; *to grant, to refuse a* ~ e-m Gesuch stattgeben; ein Gesuch ablehnen; *to make a* ~ ein Gesuch einreichen; e-e Forderung stellen; *to* ~ *permission* um Erlaubnis bitten; *it is* ~*ed* es wird gebeten (*to do* zu tun); *she is much in* ~ man reißt sich um sie; ~ *for extradition* Auslieferungsantrag *m*; ~ *for payment* Zahlungsaufforderung *f*; ~ *for respite* Stundungsgesuch *n*; ~ **book** Beschwerdebuch *n*; ~ **form** Antragsformular *n*; Bestellschein *m*; ~ **program(me)** Wunschkonzert *n*; ~ **stop** Bedarfshaltestelle *f*.

requiem ['rekwiem] Requiem *n a. mus*, Seelen-, Totenmesse *f*.

require [ri'kwaiə] *tr* fordern, verlangen (*s.th. of s.o.* etw von jdm); bedürfen; befehlen, den Befehl, die Anweisung geben (*s.o. to do s.th.* jdm etw zu tun); erforderlich sein zu, erfordern, nötig haben, brauchen, Bedarf haben an; *itr* nötig sein; *if* ~*d* falls nötig; nötigenfalls; *that* ~*s some time* das kostet einige Zeit; ~**ment** [-mənt] (An-)Forderung *f*, Verlangen *n*; Vorschrift *f*; Erfordernis *n*, Bedingung *f*; Bedürfnis *n*, Notwendigkeit; erforderliche Eigenschaft, Voraussetzung *f*; *pl* Bedarf *m*; *pl Am* Pflichtfächer *n pl*; *according to* ~~ nach Bedarf; *to fulfil, to meet the* ~~*s* die Bedingungen erfüllen; den Anforderungen entsprechen.

requisit|e ['rekwisit] *a* erforderlich, notwendig, unerläßlich (*for* für); *s* Erfordernis *n*, Bedingung, Notwendigkeit *f* (*for* für); *pl com* Bedarfsartikel, Gebrauchsgegenstände *m pl*; *office* ~~*s (pl)* Büroartikel *m pl*; ~**ion** [rekwi'ziʃən] *s* (Auf-)Forderung *f*, Ersuchen *n* (*on s.o.* an jdn); Anweisung *f*; Antrag *m*; Gesuch; Erfordernis *n*; *jur* (*~~ for extradition*) Auslieferungsantrag *m*; *com* Zahlungsaufforderung *f*; Verlangen *n*, Bedarf *m*; *mil* Beschlagnahme, Requirierung, Erfassung *f* (*for* von); *tr mil* requirieren, beschlagnahmen, erfassen; anfordern, beanspruchen; zu Lieferungen, Abgaben heranziehen; *in ~~* dringend benötigt, gesucht; *to call into, to put in ~~* beschlagnahmen, requirieren; *~~ blank, form* Anforderungsformular *n*; *~~ number* Bestellnummer *f*.

requit|al [ri'kwaitl] Belohnung (*for* für); Vergütung, Erstattung (*for* für); Kompensation; Vergeltung *f*; *in ~~ of, for* als Belohnung für; **~e** [ri'kwait] *tr* belohnen (*with* mit); vergüten, erstatten; kompensieren; (*Beleidigung*) heimzahlen, vergelten, rächen.

resale ['ri:'seil] Weiterverkauf *m*; **~ price** Wiederverkaufspreis *m*.

resci|nd [ri'sind] *tr* annullieren, aufheben, abschaffen; zurücknehmen, rückgängig machen; für ungültig erklären; (*Urteil*) kassieren; zurücktreten (*a bargain* von e-m Geschäft); **~ssion** [ri'siʒən] Annullierung, Aufhebung, Abschaffung; Zurücknahme, Rückgängigmachung; Ungültigkeitserklärung *f*; *action for ~~* Anfechtungsklage *f*; *~~ of a contract* Rücktritt *m* von e-m Vertrag.

rescript ['ri:skript] Erlaß *m*.

rescue ['reskju:] *tr* (er)retten, befreien (*from* aus); bergen; (*Gefangenen*) gewaltsam befreien; entreißen (*from* aus); *s* (Er-)Rettung, Hilfe, Befreiung; Bergung; gewaltsame Befreiung *f*; Pfandbruch *m*; *to ~ from oblivion* der Vergessenheit entreißen; *to come to the ~ of s.o.* jdm zu Hilfe kommen; **~ party** Bergungstrupp *m*; **~r** ['-ə] Retter, Befreier *m*.

research [ri'sə:tʃ] *s oft pl* Untersuchung, Nachforschung (*after, for* nach); Forschung(sarbeit) (*on* über) *f*; *itr* Untersuchungen anstellen (*on* über); untersuchen (*into s.th.* etw); Forschungen treiben; *to be engaged in ~ work* in der Forschung tätig sein; *to make ~es* Nachforschungen anstellen; *business, industrial ~* Konjunkturforschung *f*; *market ~* Marktanalyse *f*; **~er** [-ə], **~ worker** Forscher *m*; **~ expenditures** *pl* Forschungsausgaben *f pl*; **~ laboratory** Forschungslaboratorium *n*; **~ plant, station** Forschungsstelle *f*; **~ work** Forschungsarbeit *f*.

reseat ['ri'si:t] *tr* wieder setzen; mit neuen Sitzen versehen; (*Ventile*) nachschleifen.

resect [ri:'sekt] *med* herausschneiden, -sägen; **~ion** [-'sekʃən] *med* Resektion *f*.

reseda [ri'si:də] *s bot* Reseda *f*; *a* resedafarben.

resembl|ance [ri'zembləns] Ähnlichkeit (*to* mit; *between* zwischen); *to bear great ~~* e-e große Ähnlichkeit haben (*to* mit); **~e** [ri'zembl] *tr* ähneln, ähnlich sehen, gleichen (*s.o.* jdm).

resent [ri'zent] *tr* übelnehmen; verübeln (*s.o.* jdm; *doing s.th.* etw zu tun); sich ärgern über; **~ful** [-ful] beleidigt, *fam* eingeschnappt; aufgebracht (*against, of* gegen); empfindlich; **~ment** [-mənt] Verdruß, Ärger, Groll *m*, Verstimmung *f*; *to bear no ~~ against s.o.* jdm nicht böse sein, nichts gegen jdn haben.

reserv|ation [rezə'veiʃən] Vorbehalt *m*, Einschränkung *f*; Reservat(recht *n*, -bestimmung *f*); *Am* (*staatl.*) Reservat(gebiet); *Am* Reservieren *n*, Vorbestellung *f*; Zurücklegen *n* (*von Theater-, Fahrkarten*); vorbestellte(s) Zimmer *n*, vorbestellte(r) Platz *m*, vorbestellte Karte; Platzkarte *f*; *with ~~s* unter Vorbehalt; *with ~~ of* vorbehaltlich *gen*; *without ~~* vorbehaltlos, uneingeschränkt; ohne Hintergedanken; *to make o.'s ~~* e-e Platzkarte, ein Zimmer bestellen; *mar* e-n Platz buchen; *mental ~~s (pl)* geistige(r) Vorbehalt *m*; **~e** [ri'zə:v] *tr* zurücklegen, -behalten, zurückstellen; aufbewahren, aufheben, aufsparen (*for* für); reservieren, vorbestellen (*to, for* für); sich (*ein Recht*) vorbehalten; *to ~~ o.s.* sich schonen (*for* für); *s* Rücklage, Reserve *f*, Vorrat; Rückhalt *m*; Begrenzung, Einschränkung, -engung *f*; Vorbehalt *m*; *fig* Zurückhaltung, Reserviertheit; Verschwiegenheit *f*, Schweigen *n*; (*Stil*) Einfachheit, Schlichtheit; *fin* Reserve *f*; *mil* Reservetruppen, -einheiten *f pl*; Reserve *f*; *sport* Ersatzspieler *m*; *Am* Reservat(land) *n*; *pl* Rücklagen *f pl*; *in ~~* in Reserve; vorrätig; *under ~~* unter Vorbehalt, vorbehaltlich; *with all (due) ~~s* mit allem *od* unter ausdrücklichem Vorbehalt; *without (any) ~~* ohne (jeden) Vorbehalt; *to build up ~~s* Rücklagen bilden; *to dig into s.o.'s ~~s* jds Reserven angreifen; *to exercise, to observe ~~* Zurückhaltung üben; *to place, to put a ~~ on s.th.* etw e-r Einschränkung unterwerfen; *bank(er's) ~~* Bankreserve *f*; *capital ~~* Kapitalreserve *f*; *cash ~~* Barbestand *m*; *gold ~~* Goldreserve *f*, -bestand *m*; *operating ~~* Betriebsreserve *f*; *power ~~* Kraft-, Leistungsreserve *f*; *secret ~~* stille Reserve *f*; *statutory ~~* Mindestreserve *f*; *tax ~~* Steuerrücklage *f*; *~~ fund* Reservefonds *m*, Rücklagen *f pl*; *~~ position* Auffangstellung *f*; *~~ price* Mindestpreis *m*; *~~ seat* Notsitz *m*; *~~ tank* Reservebehälter *m*; **~ed** [-d] *a* reserviert, zurückgelegt, vorbestellt, belegt; (*Urteil*) ausgesetzt; (*Preise*) bescheiden; (*Rücklagen*) zweckgebunden; *mil* zurückgestellt; zurückhaltend, reserviert; verschwiegen; *all rights ~~* alle Rechte vorbehalten; *~~ area* Sperrgebiet *n*; *~~ surplus* Gewinnvortrag *m*; **~ist** [-ist] *mil* Reservist *m*; **~oir** ['rezəvwɑ:] Wasserbecken; Staubecken *n*, -see *m*; (Flüssigkeits-)Reservoir; Reservoir *n*, große Reserven *f pl* (*of* an) *a. fig*.

reset ['ri:'set] *tr* (*Knochen*) wieder einrenken; *tech* umrichten, nachstellen; (*Edelstein*) neu fassen; (*Uhr*) stellen; *typ* neu setzen; *agr* neu bepflanzen.

resettle ['ri:'setl] *tr* um-, neu ansiedeln; *fig* wieder eingliedern; *itr* sich niederlassen; *tr itr* (sich) wieder setzen; (sich) (wieder) beruhigen.

reshuffle ['ri:'ʃʌfl] *tr* (*Spielkarten*) neu mischen; umordnen, -sortieren, -stellen, -gruppieren; (*Regierung*) umbilden; *s* Umstellung, -gruppierung, -bildung *f*; *Cabinet ~* Regierungsumbildung *f*.

resid|e [ri'zaid] *itr* s-n Wohnsitz haben, wohnen, leben, sich aufhalten (*in, at* in); *fig* (*Eigenschaft*) innewohnen, sich finden (*in s.th.* e-r S); liegen (*in* bei); (*Kraft, Recht*) beruhen (*in* auf); **~ence** ['rezidəns] Aufenthalt; Aufenthaltsort, Wohnsitz, -ort *m*; Wohnung; Residenzpflicht *f*; (großes) (Wohn-)Haus *n*; (*official ~~*) Amtssitz *m*; *in ~~* am Ort; (*Student*) in e-m Wohnheim wohnend; *to change o.'s ~~* die Wohnung wechseln, umziehen; *to have o.'s ~~* wohnen (*in* in); *to take up o.'s ~~* s-n Wohnsitz aufschlagen (*at* in); *change of ~~* Wohnungswechsel, Umzug *m*; *delivery at ~~* Lieferung *f* ins Haus; *permanent ~~* feste(r) Wohnsitz *m*; *private ~~* Privatwohnung *f*; *~~ of a company* Gesellschaftssitz *m*; *~~ insurance* Gebäudeversicherung *f*; **~ency** ['rezidənsi] Wohn-, Amtssitz *m*, Residenz *f*; **~ent** ['rezidənt] *a* wohnhaft, ansässig (*in* in); Anstalts-; (*Eigenschaft*) innewohnend; *zoo biol* einheimisch; *s* Be-, Einwohner, Einheimische(r), Ortsansässige(r); *pol* Resident *m*; *to be ~~* ansässig sein; *~~ agent (com)* Platzvertreter *m*; *~~ bird* Standvogel *m*; *the ~~ population* die ortsansässige Bevölkerung; **~ential** [rezi'denʃəl] *a* Wohn-; im Hause wohnend; herrschaftlich; *~~ allowance* Ortszulage *f*; *~~ area* Wohngegend *f*; *~~ estate, property* Wohngrundstück *n*; *~~ hotel* Familienpension *f*; *~~ quarter, (Am) district* Wohnviertel *n*; *~~ rent* Wohnungsmiete *f*.

residu|al [ri'zidjuəl] *a* zurückbleibend, restlich, Rest-; *s* Rest *m*, Differenz *f a. math* (*~~ quantity*); *~~ product* Abfallprodukt *n*; *~~ sound* Nachklang *m*; **~ary** [-əri] übrig(geblieben, -gelassen), restlich; **~e** ['rezidju:] Rest(betrag); *chem* Rückstand *m*; *jur* dem Haupterben verbleibende Erbmasse *f*; **~um** [ri'zidjuəm] *pl -ua* [-juə] *chem* Rückstand *m*, Residuum *n*; *fig* Abschaum *m*.

resign [ri'zain] *tr* verzichten auf (*e-n Anspruch*); (*Amt*) niederlegen, aufgeben; zurücktreten von (*e-m Amt*); (*e-e Stelle*) aufgeben; abtreten; *itr* zurücktreten (*from* von); (*König*) abdanken; *pol* demissionieren; verzichten; e-e Stelle aufgeben, ein Amt niederlegen; austreten (*from* aus); *to ~ o.s.* Verzicht leisten, resignieren; sich fügen (*to s.o.* jdm); sich ergeben, sich schicken (*to* in); sich abfinden (*to* mit); **~ation** [rezig'neiʃən] Verzicht (-leistung *f*); Rücktritt *m*; Niederlegung; Abtretung *f*; Austritt(serklärung *f*) *m*; Ergebung (*to* in); Resignation *f*; *to hand in o.'s ~~* um s-e Entlassung einkommen, sein Entlassungsgesuch einreichen; **~ed** [ri'zaind] *a* ergeben, resigniert.

resil|ience, -cy [ri'ziliəns(i)] Elastizität, Spannkraft *f a. fig* (*e-s Menschen*); *fig* Schwung *m*; Federung *f*; **~ient** [-'ziliənt] elastisch, federnd; *fig* unverwüstlich.

resin ['rezin] *s bot* Harz *n*; *tr* mit Harz behandeln; **~ous** ['-əs] harzig.

resist [ri'zist] *tr itr* widerstehen (*s.th.* e-r S; *doing s.th.* etw zu tun); sich widersetzen, Widerstand leisten (*s.o.* jdm); *tech* entgegenwirken; *s* Schutzbeize *f*; *to ~ temptation* der Versuchung widerstehen; **~ance** [-əns] Widerstand *m* (*to* gegen) *a. fig u. el*; *tech* Festigkeit; Beständigkeit *f*; (*R*)*~~ (pol)* Widerstand(sbewegung *f*) *m*; *to offer ~~ to s.o.* jdm Widerstand entgegensetzen; *to take the line of least ~~* der Linie des geringsten Widerstands folgen; *~~-coil (el)* Widerstandsrolle *f*; *~~ to heat* Hitzebeständigkeit *f*; *~~ movement* Widerstandsbewegung *f*; *~~ to wear* Verschleißfestigkeit *f*; **~ant** [-ənt] widerstehend, Widerstand leistend; widerstandsfähig (*to* gegen); *~~ to acids, to cold* säure-, kältebeständig; **~ive** [-ive] widerstrebend; Widerstands-; **~ivity** [rizis'tiviti] *el* spezifische(r) Widerstand *m*; **~or** [-ə] *el* Widerstand *m*.

resole ['ri:'soul] *tr* (*Schuh*) neu besohlen.

resoluble ['rezəljubl, ri'zə-] lösbar (*into* in) *a. fig*.

resolut|e ['rezəlu:t] entschlossen, beherzt; fest, unerschütterlich, *fam* resolut; **~eness** ['-nis] Entschlossenheit, Festigkeit, Unerschütterlichkeit *f*; **~ion** [rezə'lu:ʃən] Auflösung *a. mus math med*; *(Geschwulst)* Zerteilung *f*; Be-, Entschluß *m*, Entschließung, Beschlußfassung, Entscheidung; Resolution; Entschlossenheit, Standhaftigkeit; Lösung *f (e-r Frage)*; *to adopt a ~~* e-n Beschluß annehmen; *to make good ~~s* gute Vorsätze fassen; *~~ of the majority* Mehrheitsbeschluß *m*.

resolv|able [ri'zɔlvəbl] (auf)lösbar (*into* in); **~e** [ri'zɔlv] *tr* auflösen, zerlegen, analysieren; zu dem Entschluß bringen (*to do* zu tun); beschließen (*on, upon s.th.* etw); sich entschließen (*to do* zu tun); entscheiden; *(Problem)* lösen; *(Frage)* klären; *(Zweifel)* beheben, beseitigen; *mus med* auflösen (*into* in); *opt* zerlegen; *itr* sich auflösen (*into, to* in); sich entschließen (*upon s.th.* zu etw); *to ~~ o.s. into* sich umwandeln in; sich konstituieren als; *s* Be-, Entschluß *m*; Resolution; *Am* Beschlußfassung *f*; *to ~~ itself into a committee* sich als Ausschuß konstituieren; **~ed** [-d] *a* entschlossen; **~ent** [-ənt] *a u. s med* auflösend(es Mittel *n*).

resonan|ce ['reznəns] *mus phys el* Resonanz *f*, Mitschwingen *n*; *fig* Widerhall, Anklang *m*; **~t** ['-t] mittönend, -schwingend; *(Stimme)* volltönend; wieder-, nachhallend (*with* von).

resor|b [ri'sɔ:b, -z-] *tr* resorbieren, auf-, einsaugen; **~ption** [-'sɔ:pʃən] Resorption, Aufsaugung *f*.

resort [ri'zɔ:t] *itr* (häufig, regelmäßig) gehen (*to* in, zu, nach); (oft, regelmäßig) auf-, besuchen (*to s.th.* etw); *fig* greifen, s-e Zuflucht nehmen (*to* zu); *s* Treffpunkt; Ferien-, Ausflugsort *m*, Erholungsstätte; Zuflucht (*to* zu); Hilfe *f*, Mittel *n*; *in the last ~ (fig)* wenn alle Stricke reißen; *jur* in letzter Instanz; *to have ~ to* s-e Zuflucht nehmen zu; *to ~ to force, to drastic measures* zur Gewalt, zu drastischen Maßnahmen greifen; *health ~* (Luft-) Kurort *m*; *holiday ~* Ferien-, Urlaubsort *m*; *mountain ~* Höhenkurort *m*; *seaside ~* Seebad *n*; *summer ~* Sommerfrische *f*; *winter ~* Winterkurort *m*.

resound [ri'zaund] *itr* ertönen, erschallen, widerhallen (*with* von); *fig* Widerhall, ein Echo finden; *tr* widerhallen lassen; *fig* (laut) verkünden.

resource [ri'sɔ:s] Hilfsquelle *f*, -mittel *n*; Zuflucht *f*, Ausweg *m*; Findigkeit *f*; *pl* (Geld-)Mittel *n pl*; Hilfsquellen *f pl (e-s Landes)*; Unterhaltung *f*, Zeitvertreib *m*; *as a last ~* als letzter Ausweg; *without ~* mittellos; *to be at the end of o.'s ~s* am Ende s-r Kunst sein, nicht mehr weiter wissen; *to exhaust all ~s* alle Mittel erschöpfen; *to tap, to open up new ~s* neue Hilfsquellen erschließen; **~ful** [-ful] reich an Hilfsquellen, -mitteln; findig, *sl* auf Draht; *to be ~~* sich zu helfen wissen.

*

respect [ris'pekt] *tr* achten, respektieren; Achtung zollen (*s.o.* jdm); Rücksicht nehmen auf; betreffen, angehen, sich beziehen auf; *s* (Hoch-) Achtung *f*, Respekt *m* (*for* vor); Rücksicht *f* (*to, of* auf); *pl* Grüße *m pl*, Empfehlungen *f pl*; *in ~ of, to* in Hinsicht, in bezug, mit Rücksicht auf; *in ~ that* in Anbetracht dessen *od* der Tatsache, daß; *in every ~* in jeder Hinsicht *od* Beziehung; *in many ~s* in mancher Beziehung, in vieler Hinsicht; *in this ~* in dieser Hinsicht; *with ~ to* was ... betrifft; *to have ~ to s.th.* etw betreffen; *to enforce ~* Achtung verschaffen (*for s.th.* dat); *to pay o.'s ~s to s.o.* jdm s-e Aufwartung machen; *without ~ to persons* ohne Ansehung der Person; *~ for the law* Achtung *f* vor dem Gesetz; **~ability** [rispektə'biliti] Achtbarkeit *f*; gute(r) Ruf *m*, Ansehen *n*, gesellschaftliche Stellung *f*; *pl* Respektspersonen *f pl*; *meist pl* Anstandsregeln *f pl*; **~able** [ris'pektəbl] achtbar, schätzenswert, angesehen, *com* solide, reell; beachtlich, ansehnlich; nennenswert; *(Kleidung)* korrekt; konventionell, förmlich; **~er** [-ə]: *to be no ~~ of* keine Rücksicht nehmen auf; *no ~~ of persons* jem, der ohne Ansehen der Person handelt; **~ful** [-ful] ehrerbietig, respektvoll (*towards* gegen); **~fully** [-fuli] *adv* höflichst; *yours ~~* hochachtungsvoll; **~ing** [-iŋ] *prp* hinsichtlich *gen*, in bezug auf, betreffs *gen*; **~ive** [-iv] *a attr* jeweilige, einzelne; **~ively** [-ivli] *adv* jeweils, im einzelnen; beziehungsweise.

respir|able ['respirəbl] einatembar; atemfähig; **~ation** [respə'reiʃən] Atmen *n*; Atmung, *scient* Respiration *f*; **~ator** ['-reitə] Atemgerät *n*; Gasmaske *f*; **~atory** [ris'paiərətəri, 'respirətəri] *a* Atmungs-; Atem-; **~e** [ris'paiə] *itr* atmen; (wieder) Luft schöpfen; *fig* aufatmen.

respite ['respait, *a.* '-it] *s jur* Aufschub *m*, Frist, Stundung *f* (*for* für); Strafaufschub *m*; Atempause; *med* Erholung *f* (*for* von); *tr* e-n Aufschub, e-e Frist gewähren (*s.o.* jdm); auf-, verschieben; *med* Erleichterung geben; *days of ~ (fin)* Respekttage *m pl*.

resplenden|ce, -cy [ris'plendəns(i)] Glanz *a. fig*; *fig* Pracht *f*; **~t** [-t] strahlend, glänzend; *fig* prächtig.

respon|d [ris'pɔnd] *itr* antworten (*to* auf); erwidern (*with* mit); *physiol psychol* reagieren, ansprechen (*to* auf); eingehen (*to* auf); *Am* verantwortlich, haftbar sein (*to* für); *s rel* Responsorium *n*; *arch* Strebepfeiler *m*; **~dent** [-ənt] *a* antwortend; reagierend (*to* auf); *s jur* (Scheidungs-)Beklagte(r) *m*; **~se** [ris'pɔns] Antwort; Erwiderung; *jur* Klagebeantwortung *f*; *physiol psychol* Ansprechen *n a. tech*, Reaktion (*to* auf); Empfindlichkeit *f* (*to* für); *rel* Responsorium *n*; *in ~~ to* als Antwort auf; *to meet with a ~~* beantwortet werden; *with a warm ~~* herzliche Aufnahme finden; **~sibility** [rispɔnsə'biliti] Verantwortung (*for, of* für); Verantwortlichkeit; Verpflichtung, Haftung, Haftpflicht, Haftbarkeit; *com* Zahlungsfähigkeit *f*; *on o.'s own ~~* auf eigene Verantwortung; *without ~~* ohne Gewähr; *to accept, to assume, to take the ~~ for s.th.* die Verantwortung für etw übernehmen; *to decline, to disclaim the ~~* die Verantwortung ablehnen; *sense of ~~* Verantwortungsgefühl *n*; **~sible** [ris'pɔnsəbl] verantwortlich (*for* für); verantwortungsvoll, -bewußt; haftbar (*for* für); schuld (*for* an); *jur* zurechnungsfähig; *com* zahlungsfähig; *to be ~~* verantwortlich sein, die Ursache sein (*for* für); zurechnungsfähig sein; *to be held ~~* verantwortlich gemacht werden (*for* für); *~~ partner* persönlich haftende(r) Gesellschafter *m*; **~sive** [-siv] *a* Antwort-; entsprechend; leicht reagierend (*to* auf); *(Motor)* temperamentvoll; verständnisvoll, empfänglich (*to* für); *to be ~~ to* ansprechen, eingehen auf.

rest [rest] **1.** *s* Ruhe *f*, Schlaf *m*; Rast *f*, Ausruhen *n*, Erholung; Arbeits-, Ruhepause; (seelische) Entspannung; innere Ruhe; letzte, ewige Ruhe *f*; Reg-, Bewegungslosigkeit, Ruhe(zustand *m*) *f*; Rastplatz, Ruhepunkt; *tech* Halter *m*, Stütze, Auflage *f*; *(Brille)* Steg *m*; Telephongabel; *mus* Pause *f*; Pausenzeichen *n*; *(Vers)* Zäsur *f*; *itr* ruhen, (sich) ausruhen, sich erholen, (sich aus-)schlafen, *fam* ausspannen; nicht arbeiten, feiern; (be)ruhig(t) sein; ruhen, die ewige Ruhe haben, tot sein; *(Augen, Blick)* ruhen (*on* auf); *(Sache, Arbeit)* ruhen; auf sich beruhen; beruhen (*in, on, upon* auf); *(Last, Verantwortung)* ruhen (*on, upon s.o.* auf jdm); liegen *fig* (*with* an, bei); abhängen (*on, upon* von); sich verlassen (*on, upon* auf); (da)bleiben; *agr* brachliegen; *Am jur* sein Plädoyer schließen; *tr* Ruhe gewähren (*s.o.* jdm); (aus)ruhen lassen; sich ausruhen, sich erholen, schlafen lassen; legen, stützen (*on* auf); basieren (*on* auf), begründen (*on* mit); lehnen (*against* an); *(s-e Augen)* ruhen lassen (*on* auf); anhalten; *Am jur* schließen (*o.'s case* sein Plädoyer); *at ~* in Ruhe; tot; *to be at ~* ruhig sein, stehen; beruhigt sein; ruhen; *to be laid to ~* zur ewigen Ruhe gebettet werden; *to come to ~* stehenbleiben; *to give s.th. a ~* etw Ruhe gönnen; *to go, to retire to ~* zu Bett, schlafen gehen; *to put (s.)o.'s mind, to set (s.)o.'s heart at ~* jdn, sich beruhigen; *to take a ~* sich ausruhen; *to ~ on o.'s oars* die Ruderschläge unterbrechen; *fig* sich e-e Ruhepause gönnen; einschlafen; *let the matter ~* lassen Sie die Sache auf sich beruhen; *a good night's ~* e-e gute Nacht; *arm-~* Armstütze *f*; **~-cure** Liegekur *f*; **~ful** ['-ful] ruhig, friedlich; beruhigend; **~-house** Rasthaus *n*; **~ing** ['-iŋ] Ruhe(n *n*) *f*; *~~-place* Ruheplatz *m*; **~less** ['-lis] ruhelos; unruhig; unstet; unzufrieden; **~lessness** ['-lisnis] Ruhelosigkeit; Unruhe *f*; **~-room** *Am* Toilette *f*; Aufenthaltsraum *m*; **2.** *s* Rest *m*, Übriggebliebene(s) *n*; *(the ~)* das übrige, die übrigen; *fin* Saldo; Reservefonds; *com* Rechnungs-, Bücherabschluß *m*; *itr* bleiben; lasten (*on* auf); liegen *fig* (*with* bei); *for the ~* im übrigen; *it ~s with you* es liegt (ganz) bei Ihnen, Sie haben die Entscheidung; *you may ~ assured* seien Sie versichert; *(all) the ~ (of it)* alles andere; alles übrige; *(all) the ~ of us (mit pl)* wir andern, wir übrigen.

restate ['ri:'steit] *tr* neu formulieren.

restaur|ant ['restərɔ:ŋ, *Am* '-rənt] Restaurant *n*, Speisewirtschaft *f*, -lokal *n*; *~~-car (rail)* Speisewagen *m*.

restitution [resti'tju:ʃən] Rückerstattung, Wiederherausgabe; Wiedergutmachung, Entschädigung *f*; Ersatz *m*; Wiederherstellung, -einsetzung; *phys* Rückstellung; *phot* Entzerrung *f*; *to make ~* Ersatz leisten (*of* für).

restive ['restiv] störrisch, bockig; widerspenstig; unruhig, nervös (*over* über); **~ness** ['-nis] Widerspenstigkeit; Nervosität, Aufgeregtheit *f*.

restock ['ri:'stɔk] *tr* wieder, neu versorgen (*with* mit); *(Lager)* wieder auffüllen.

restor|ation [restə'reiʃən] (Rück-)Erstattung, Rückgabe; Wiederherstellung, -einsetzung (*to* in); Wiedergutmachung; Restaurierung; Instandsetzung; *com* Sanierung; *med* Heilung *f*; *the R~~* die *(englische)* Restauration *(der Stuarts* 1660); **~ative** [ri'stɔrətiv] *a* heilend, stärkend, kräftigend; *s* Heil-, Stärkungs-, Wiederbelebungsmittel *n*; **~e** [ris'tɔ:] *tr* zurückgeben, -erstatten, ersetzen; wiedereinsetzen (*to an office* in ein Amt); wiederherstellen, restaurieren; erneuern, instand setzen; wieder gesund machen, stärken, kräftigen, heilen; *(to ~~ to life)* wieder ins Leben rufen; *to ~~ to its former condition* den früheren Zustand wiederherstellen; *to ~~ s.o. to liberty* jdm die Freiheit schenken, jdn (wieder) auf freien Fuß setzen; *~ed to health* geheilt; **~er** [ris'tɔ:rə] Restaurator *m*; *(hair-~~)* Haarwuchsmittel *n*.

restrain [ris'trein] *tr* ab-, zurückhalten (*from doing s.th.* etw zu tun); hindern (*from* an); einschränken, in Schranken halten; *(Gefühl)* unterdrücken; *(Neugier)* bezähmen; *(Befugnisse)* einschränken; *(Produktion)* drosseln; einsperren; **~ed** [-d] *a* zurückhaltend; maßvoll; beherrscht; **~edly** [-dli] *adv* mit Zurückhaltung; **~t** [-t] Be-, Einschränkung *f*; Hemmnis *n*, Unterdrückung *f*, Zwang *m*; Zwangsmaßnahme *f*, -mittel *n*; Freiheitsbeschränkung *f*, -entzug *m*; Zurückhaltung *f*; *under ~~* in e-r Anstalt untergebracht; in Gewahrsam; *without ~~* rückhaltlos, bedenkenlos; *~~-jacket* Zwangsjacke *f*; *~~ of trade* Konkurrenz-, Handelsbeschränkungen *f pl*.

restrict [ris'trikt] *tr* be-, einschränken, begrenzen (*to* auf); **~ed** [-id] *a* eingeschränkt, begrenzt; nur für den Dienstgebrauch; *com* bewirtschaftet; *(Geld)* zweckgebunden; *Am* nur für Weiße; *locally ~~* örtlich begrenzt; *~~ area* Sperrgebiet; *mot* Gebiet *n* mit Geschwindigkeitsbegrenzung; **~ion** [-'trikʃən] Be-, Einschränkung, Begrenzung *f*; Vorbehalt *m*; *mil* Ausgehverbot *n*; *to be subject to ~~s* Beschränkungen unterliegen; *credit ~~* Kreditrestriktion *f*; *export, import ~~* Ausfuhr-, Einfuhrbeschränkung *f*; *rent ~~s (pl) (Br)* Mieterschutzbestimmungen *f pl*; *zoning ~~s (pl)* Baubeschränkungen *f pl*; *~~ of production* Produktionsbeschränkung *f*; *~~ on sales* Verkaufsbeschränkung *f*; **~ive** [ris'triktiv] be-, einschränkend (*of s.th.* etw) *a. gram*.

result [ri'zʌlt] *itr* hervorgehen, herrühren, sich ergeben, folgen, erwachsen, resultieren (*from* aus); führen (*in* zu), hinauslaufen (*in* auf), enden (*in* in, mit); *jur* zurückfallen (*to* an); *s* Ergebnis *n*, Ausgang *m*, Resultat *n a. math*, Wirkung, Folge *f*; *pl* Erfolg *m*; *as a ~ of* als Folge *gen*; *without ~* ergebnislos; *to bring, to yield good ~s* gute Ergebnisse bringen *od* zeitigen; *to obtain a good ~* ein gutes Ergebnis erzielen; *to ~ in a profit* mit Gewinn abschließen; e-n Gewinn abwerfen; *the ~ is that* die Folge (davon) ist, daß; *election ~s (pl)* Wahlergebnis *n*; *final ~* Schlußergebnis *n*; *football ~s (pl)* Fußballergebnis *n*; *total ~* Gesamtergebnis *n*; **~ant** [-ənt] *a* sich ergebend; resultierend (*from* aus); *s* Resultat, Ergebnis *n*; *phys* Resultante *f*; **~ fee** *Br* Erfolgshonorar *n*; **~ing** [-iŋ] *a* herrührend (*from* von).

resum|e [ri'zju:m] *tr* wieder (an-, auf-, ein)nehmen, zurücknehmen; wiedererlangen, zurückbekommen, -erhalten, -gewinnen; *(Inhalt)* rekapitulieren, zs.fassen; *tr itr* wieder beginnen, wieder anfangen; *itr* fortfahren; *to ~~ o.'s seat* sich wieder setzen; s-n Platz wieder einnehmen; **~ption** [-'zʌmpʃən] Zurücknahme; Wiederaufnahme *f*, -beginn *m*; Wiederannahme *f*.

resurg|ence [ri'sə:dʒəns] Wiederaufstieg *m*, -aufleben *n*; **~ent** [-ənt] *a* wieder auftauchend; wieder auflebend; sich wieder erhebend.

resurrect [rezə'rekt] *tr* ausgraben, exhumieren; *fig* zu neuem Leben erwekken; wieder aufleben lassen; **~ion** [-'rekʃən] Auferstehung *f*; Wiederaufleben *n*; *jur* Exhumierung *f*; *the R~~* die Auferstehung der Toten *od* Jesu.

resuscitat|e [ri'sʌsiteit] *tr itr* wieder zu sich bringen, kommen; *tr fig* wiederbeleben, -erwecken; *itr fig* wieder aufleben, wieder lebendig werden; das Bewußtsein wiedererlangen; **~ion** [risʌsi'teiʃən] Wiederbelebung *f a. fig*; *fig* Wiederaufleben *n*.

*

ret [ret] *tr (Flachs)* rösten, rötten.

retail ['ri:teil] *s* Einzel-, Kleinhandel *m*; *attr* Einzelhandels-, Wiederverkaufs-; *itr* [ri:'teil] im Einzelhandel verkauft werden (*at* um); ein Einzelhandelsgeschäft betreiben; *tr* im kleinen, an den Verbraucher verkaufen; *fig* weitererzählen; breittreten; detaillieren; *by ~, (Am) at ~* im kleinen, stückweise, en detail, im Einzelhandel; *to sell ~* im Einzelhandel verkaufen; **~ bookseller** Sortiment(sbuchhändl)er *m*; **~ book-trade** Sortiment(sbuchhandel *m*) *n*; **~ business** Einzelhandelsgeschäft *n*; **~ customer** Einzelhandelskunde *m*; **~ dealer** Einzelhändler *m*; **~er** [ri:'teilə] Einzelhändler, Wiederverkäufer *m*; *fig* Klatschmaul *n*; **~ market** Einzel-, Kleinhandel *m*; **~ price** Einzelhandels-, Ladenpreis *m*; **~ sale** Ladenverkauf *m*; **~ store** Einzelhandelsgeschäft *n*.

retain [ri'tein] *tr* zurück-, festhalten; (ein-, zurück)behalten; *(Platz)* belegen; (im Gedächtnis) behalten; *(Gebräuche)* beibehalten; *tech* halten; bleiben bei; (mit Beschlag) belegen; *(für Dienste)* in Anspruch nehmen; *(e-n Anwalt)* sich nehmen; *to ~ s.o.'s services* sich jds Dienste versichern; *~ing wall* Stütz-, Staumauer *f*; **~er** [-ə] *hist* Gefolgs-, Dienstmann; *tech* Spannring, Mitnehmer *m*; Bestellung, Inanspruchnahme *f (bes. e-s Rechtsanwalts)*; Rechtsanwaltsvorschuß *m*, Pauschalgebühr *f*, -honorar *n*; Prozeßvollmacht *f*; *tech* Läppkäfig *m*; *old ~~* alte(s) Faktotum *n*.

retake ['ri:'teik] *irr s. take tr* wieder, zurücknehmen; *Am phot* noch einmal aufnehmen; *film* noch einmal drehen; *s Am* Neu-, zweite Aufnahme *f*.

retaliat|e [ri'tælieit] *itr* Vergeltung üben, sich rächen (*on* an); *tr* vergelten; **~ion** [ritæli'eiʃən] (Wieder-)Vergeltung *f*; *pl* Vergeltungsmaßnahmen *f pl*; **~ive** [ri'tæliətiv], **~ory** [-iətəri] *a* Vergeltungs-; *~~ measures (pl)* Repressalien *pl*.

retard [ri'tɑ:d] *tr* verzögern, aufhalten, hinausschieben; verlangsamen, hemmen; *tech* retardieren *a. biol*, bremsen; *(Zündung)* nachstellen; *mentally ~ed* geistig zurückgeblieben; *~ed ignition* Spätzündung *f*; **~ation** [ri:tɑ:'deiʃən] Verzögerung *f*, Aufschub *m*, Verlangsamung; *phys biol* Retardation *f*; Hemmnis *n*; *tech* (Ab-)Bremsung, Nacheilung *f*; **~ing** [-iŋ]: *~~ field, force, torque* Bremsfeld *n*, -kraft *f*, -moment *n*.

retch [ri:tʃ] *itr* würgen, sich erbrechen (wollen), e-n Brechreiz haben.

retell ['ri:'tel] *irr s. tell tr* noch einmal erzählen.

retent|ion [ri'tenʃən] Behalten, Zurückhalten *n*; Beibehaltung; Bewahrung; *(Harn)* Verhaltung; Erinnerung *f*, (gutes) Gedächtnis *n*; *right of ~~* Zurückbehaltungsrecht *n*; **~ive** [-tiv] (zurück)haltend; bewahrend; *(Gedächtnis)* gut, treu.

reticen|ce, -cy ['retisens(i)] Schweigsamkeit; Verschwiegenheit; Zurückhaltung, Reserviertheit *f*; **~t** ['-t] schweigsam; verschwiegen (*on, about* über); zurückhaltend, reserviert.

reti|cle ['retikl] *opt* Fadenkreuz *n*; **~cular** [ri'tikjulə] netzartig; **~culate** [ri'tikjuleit] *tr* netzartig einteilen; *a* ['-it] netzartig; *~~d glass* Filigranglas *n*; **~culation** [ritikju'leiʃən] Netzwerk *n a. fig*; **~cule** ['retikju:l] Handtäschchen; Fadenkreuz *n*; **~form** ['ri:tifɔ:m] netzförmig, -artig; **~na** ['retinə] *pl a. -ae* ['-i:] *anat* Netzhaut *f*; **~nitis** [reti'naitis] Netzhautentzündung *f*.

retinue ['retinju:] Gefolge *n*, Begleitung *f*.

retir|e [ri'taiə] *itr* sich zurückziehen *a. mil*; sich entfernen (*from* von, aus); zu Bett, schlafen gehen; sich aus dem Geschäftsleben zurückziehen, sich zur Ruhe setzen; *(von e-m Amt)* zurücktreten, ausscheiden; niederlegen (*from o.'s office* sein Amt); sich pensionieren lassen; in Pension gehen; *tr* zurückziehen *a. mil*; *(Truppen)* zurücknehmen; in den Ruhestand versetzen, pensionieren, entlassen; verabschieden; *com* ausbuchen; *(Anleihe)* zurückkaufen; *fin* aus dem Verkehr ziehen; zurückzahlen; *(Wechsel)* einlösen; *to ~~ into o.s. (fig)* sich verschließen; **~ed** [-d] *a* zurückgezogen; abgeschieden, einsam; verborgen; im Ruhestand, außer Dienst, pensioniert, ausgeschieden; Ruhestands-; *com* ausgebucht; *to be placed on the ~~ list* in den Ruhestand versetzt werden; *~~ pay* Ruhegehalt *n*; **~ement** [-mənt] Ausscheiden *n*, Austritt (*from* aus); Rücktritt *m*, Pensionierung *f*; Ruhestand *m*; Zurückgezogenheit, Einsamkeit; *fin* Rückzahlung, Ablösung *f*; *mil* Rückzug *m*; *compulsory ~~* Zwangspensionierung *f*; *~~ age limit* Pensionierungsgrenze *f*; **~ing** [-riŋ] zurückhaltend, reserviert; bescheiden; schüchtern, scheu; (aus)scheidend; Ruhestands-; *to reach ~~ age* das Pensionierungsalter erreichen; *~~ allowance, pension* Ruhegehalt *n*; *~~ place* Zufluchtsort *m*.

retort [ri'tɔ:t] **1.** *tr (Beleidigung, Schlag)* zurückgeben (*upon s.o.* jdm); vergelten, heimzahlen; gehörig beantworten, erwidern; *itr* schlagfertig antworten, nicht auf den Mund gefallen sein; *s* schlagfertige Antwort *od* Erwiderung *f*; **~ion** [ri'tɔ:ʃən] Umkehrung; Vergeltung(smaßnahmen *f pl*) *f*, Repressalien *pl*; **2.** *chem* Retorte *f*.

retouch ['ri:'tʌtʃ] *tr* überarbeiten; *phot* retuschieren; *s phot* Retusche *f*.

retrace [ri'treis] *tr* zurückverfolgen; zurückführen (*to* auf); noch einmal durchgehen, sich in die Erinnerung zurückrufen; nachgehen (*s.th.* e-r S); ['ri:'treis] *tr* nachzeichnen; *to ~ o.'s steps* den gleichen Weg zurückgehen; *fig* etw ungeschehen machen.

retract [ri'trækt] *tr* zurück-, einziehen; *(Äußerung)* zurücknehmen; *(Fahrgestell)* einziehen, einfahren; *itr* sich zurück-, einziehen lassen; *fig* zurücktreten (*from* von); *tr itr* widerrufen; **~able** [-əbl], **~ile** [-ail] zurück-, einziehbar; *aero* einfahrbar; *~able landing-gear, undercarriage (aero)* Einziehfahrwerk, einziehbare(s) Fahrgestell *n*; **~ation** [ritræk'teiʃən], **~ion** [ri'trækʃən] Zurücknahme *f*; Widerruf *m*; Zurück-, Einziehen *n*; *zoo med* Retraktion *f*; **~or** [-ə] *anat* Retraktionsmuskel; *med* Retraktor *m*.

retread ['ri:'tred] *tr (Autoreifen)* runderneuern; *s* runderneuerte(r) Reifen *m*.

retreat [ri'tri:t] *s* Rückzug *m a. mil*; Rückzugssignal *n*; Zapfenstreich *m*; *(Meer)* Zurückweichen *n*; *fig* Zurückgezogenheit *f*; Zuflucht(sort *m*) *f*, Versteck *n*; Heilanstalt *f*, Asyl *n*; *itr* sich zurückziehen; den Rückzug antreten; zurückweichen; *tr (Schachfigur)* zurückziehen; *to beat a* ~ sich zurückziehen *a. fig*; *to sound the* ~ zum Rückzug blasen.

retrench [ri'trentʃ] *tr (Ausgaben)* einschränken, kürzen, herabsetzen; *(Rechte)* beschneiden, schmälern; *(Teil e-s Buches)* herausschneiden, entfernen, unterdrücken, streichen; *itr* sich einschränken; sparen; *to* ~ *o.'s expenses* Einsparungen vornehmen; **~ment** [-mənt] Einschränkung; Kürzung, Verminderung; Einsparung; Beschneidung *f*; Abbau *m*; Streichung; *mil* Auffangstellung *f*.

retrial ['ri:'traiəl] *jur* neue Verhandlung *f*; Wiederaufnahmeverfahren *n*.

retribut|ion [retri'bju:ʃən] Vergeltung; Strafe; *rel* ausgleichende Gerechtigkeit *f*; **~ive** [ri'tribjutiv] Vergeltungs-.

retriev|able [ri'tri:vəbl] ersetzbar; **~al** [-əl] Wiedererlangung; Wiederherstellung, Neubelebung; Wiedergutmachung; Genesung *f*; *beyond, past* ~~ unheilbar; **~e** [-'tri:v] *tr* wiedererlangen, zurückerhalten, -bekommen; wiederherstellen, auffrischen, neubeleben; retten (*from* aus); wiedergutmachen; *(Schaden)* ersetzen; *(Verlust)* wettmachen; bewahren (*from* vor); *(Irrtum)* richtigstellen; sich ins Gedächtnis zurückrufen; *tr itr (Jagdhund)* apportieren; *s* = *~al*; **~er** [-ə] Apportierhund *m*.

retro [(')retro(u), (')ri:tro(u)] *in Zssgen* (zu)rück-.

retroact [retro(u)'ækt] *itr* zurückwirken, rückwirkende Kraft haben (*on* auf); **~ion** [-'ækʃən] Rückwirkung, rückwirkende Kraft *f* (*on* auf); **~ive** [-'æktiv] rückwirkend (*on* auf); *with* ~~ *effect* mit rückwirkender Kraft (*as from* von).

retroce|de [retro(u)'si:d] *itr* zurückgehen; *med* nach innen schlagen; *tr* zurückgeben, -erstatten, wiederabtreten (*to* an); **~ssion** [retro(u)'seʃən] Zurückgehen, -weichen *n*; Rückgabe, -erstattung; Rückübertragung, Wiederabtretung *f*.

retrograd|ation [retro(u)grə'deiʃən] Rückwärtsbewegung *f*; *fig* Rückschritt, Rückgang, Verfall *m*; *astr* rückläufige Bewegung *f*; **~e** ['-greid] *a* zurückgehend; Rückwärts-; *com* rückgängig; *astr* rückläufig *a. fig*; *fig* rückschrittlich; *itr* rückwärtsgehen; *astr* sich rückläufig bewegen; *fig* sich verschlechtern, absinken; verfallen; *biol* entarten.

retrogress [retro(u)'gres] *itr* zurückgehen *bes. fig*; *fig* ab-, verfallen, absinken, degenerieren; **~ion** [-'greʃən] Rückwärtsbewegung *f*; *fig* Rückgang, Verfall *m*; *biol* Degeneration; *astr* rückläufige Bewegung *f*; **~ive** [-'gresiv] *a* Verfalls-; degenerativ; Degenerations-.

retrospect ['retro(u)spekt] *fig* Rückblick *m* (*of, on s.th.* auf etw); *in (the)* ~ rückblickend, -schauend; **~ion** [retro(u)'spekʃən] Rückblick *m*, -schau (*of* auf); Erinnerung *f* (*of* an); **~ive** [-'spektiv] rückblickend, -schauend; rückwärts gerichtet; *jur* rückwirkend.

*

return [ri'tə:n] **1.** *itr* zurückkehren (*to* zu) *a. fig*; *fig* wiederkehren; zurück-, wiederkommen (*to* auf); wieder werden (*to* zu); *jur* zurückfallen (*to* an); antworten, e-e Antwort geben; *tech* zurückschalten (*to* auf); **2.** *tr* zurückgeben, -bringen, -schicken, -senden, -stellen; wieder zustellen; zurückerstatten, -zahlen; *(Gruß, Besuch, Liebe, Gefälligkeit)* erwidern; *(Farbe im Kartenspiel)* bedienen; *(Gewinn)* einbringen, -tragen, abwerfen; *(Kapital)* umsetzen; sich verzinsen (5 % mit 5 %); *(Schreiben an e-e Behörde)* einreichen; *(Bericht)* erstatten; *(offiziell, amtlich)* mitteilen, berichten, melden, verlautbaren, verkünden, bekanntgeben, -machen; *com* retournieren, zurückgehen lassen; *pol* (wieder)wählen (*to Parliament* ins Parlament); *jur (Urteil)* fällen, verhängen, aussprechen; *(Ball)* zurückschlagen; *(von der Bahn)* ablenken; *tech* zurücklaufen lassen; *(Ton)* zurückwerfen; **3.** *s* Rückkehr, -kunft; *fig* Wiederkehr; Rückgabe *f*; Zurückschicken, -senden *n*; Rückerstattung, -zahlung, Entschädigung *f*, Ersatz *m*; Rücknahme; Erwiderung *f (e-r Freundlichkeit)*; *(Kartenspiel)* Bedienen *n*; Ertrag, Gewinn, Nutzen; *(Kapital)* Umsatz; Geldverkehr, Bankausweis *m*; Aufstellung, Übersicht *f*, -blick *m*; (Bestands-)Nachweisung *f*; (amtlicher) Bericht *m*, Meldung, Mitteilung, Verlautbarung; *jur* Stellungnahme; (Steuer-)Erklärung; (Termin-)Meldung; Wahlmeldung *f*, -bericht *m*; Volkszählung; Wiederwahl *f*; *(Tennis)* Rückschlag; *med* Rückfall; *tech* Rücklauf, -schlag *m*; *el* Rückleitung *f*; *(Radar)* Echo *n*; *arch* Einkehle *f*, Knick, Seitenflügel *m*; *pl* Einnahmen *f pl*, Einkünfte *pl*, Gewinn, Ertrag *m*, Ergebnis *n*, Gegenwert, (Kapital-, Geld-)Umsatz *m*; (statistische) Angaben *f pl*; Aufstellung *f*; *(bes.* Wahl-)Bericht *m*; *(election ~s)* Wahlergebnis *n*; **4.** *by* ~ *(of post)*, *(Am) by* ~ *mail* umgehend, postwendend; *in* ~ dafür; als Gegenleistung, -gabe (*for* für); in Erwiderung (*for* gen); *on* ~ nach der Rückkehr; *to send on sale or* ~ in Kommission geben; *to* ~ *to dust* wieder zu Staub werden; *to* ~ *guilty* schuldig sprechen; *to* ~ *thanks* Dank sagen; das Dankgebet (nach Tisch) sprechen; e-n Toast erwidern; *many happy ~s (of the day)!* viel Glück (zum Geburts-, Hochzeitstag)! *annual, quarterly, monthly, weekly* ~ Jahres-, Vierteljahrs-, Monats-, Wochenbericht *m*; *bank* ~ Bankausweis *m*; *(income-tax)* ~ (Einkommen-)Steuererklärung; *to make, to file a tax* ~ e-e Steuererklärung abgeben; *nil* ~ Fehlmeldung *f*; ~ *on sales* Gewinnspanne *f*; **~able** [-əbl] rückgabepflichtig; rückzahlbar; *parl* wählbar; *not* ~~ nicht umtauschbar; ~ **card** (Rück-)Antwortkarte *f*; ~ **cargo, freight** Rückfracht *f*; ~ **copies** *pl* Remittenden *f pl*; ~ **fare** Fahrgeld *n* für Hin- u. Rückfahrt *f*; ~ **flight** Rückflug *m*; ~ **gear** *tech* Rücklaufgetriebe *n*; **~ing** [-iŋ] Rückkehr, -gabe, -sendung, -erstattung; Wahl *f*; *on* ~~ bei Rückgabe; *~~-officer* Wahlleiter, -vorsteher *m*; ~ **journey, voyage** Rückreise *f*; ~ **match** *sport* Rückspiel *n*; ~ **payment** Rückzahlung *f*; ~ **postage** Rückporto *n*; ~ **receipt** Rück-, Empfangsschein *m*; ~ **ticket** Rückfahr-, -flugkarte *f*; ~ **transport(ation)** Rücktransport *m*, -beförderung *f*; ~ **valve** Rückschlagventil *n*; ~ **visit** Gegenbesuch *m*; ~ **wire** *el* Nulleiter *m*.

reunification ['ri:ju:nifi'keiʃən] *pol* Wiedervereinigung *f*.

reun|ion ['ri:'ju:njən] Wiedervereinigung; Zs.kunft *f*, Treffen *n*, Wiedersehensfeier *f*; **~ite** ['ri:ju:'nait] *tr itr* (sich) wiedervereinigen; wieder zs.-bringen, -kommen.

rev [rev] *s fam tech* Drehzahl, Umdrehung *f*; *tr fam (to* ~ *up) (Motor)* auf Touren bringen; *itr* auf Touren kommen.

reval|orization ['ri:vælərai'zeiʃən] *fin* Aufwertung *f*; **~orize** ['ri:'væləraiz] *tr* (wieder)aufwerten; **~uate** ['-'væljueit] *tr* neu bewerten; aufwerten; **~e** ['ri:'vælju:] *tr* aufwerten; nochmals schätzen.

revamp ['ri:'væmp] *tr Am* vorschuhen; *fam* flicken, ausbessern, erneuern; *fig fam* aufpolieren.

reveal [ri'vi:l] **1.** *tr bes. rel* offenbaren; bekanntgeben, -machen; enthüllen, verraten; zeigen, zur Schau stellen; *~ed religion* Offenbarungsreligion *f*; **2.** *arch* (Fenster-, Tür-)Wange *f*, Pfosten *m*, Leibung *f*; *mot* Fensterrahmen *m*.

reveille [ri'væli, *Am* 'reveli] *mil* Wecken *n*; Frühappell *m*.

revel ['revl] *itr* sich amüsieren, lustig sein, (lärmend) feiern; sein Vergnügen, s-e Freude haben, schwelgen (*in* in); *s u.* **~ry** ['-ri] (laute) Feier *f*, (Zech-)Gelage *n*, Lustbarkeit *f*, Rummel *m*; **~(l)er** ['-ə] (lustiger) Zecher, Zechbruder *m*.

revelation [revi'leiʃən] (sensationelle) Enthüllung; *bes. rel* Offenbarung *f a. fig*; *the R~ (of Saint John the Divine) (Bibel)* die Offenbarung (St. Johannis).

revenge [ri'vendʒ] *tr* Rache nehmen für; *(Person)* rächen; *to be ~d, to* ~ *o.s.* sich rächen (*on s.o.* an jdm; *for s.th.* für etw); *s* Rache *f*; Racheakt; Rachedurst *m*, Rachsucht; Revanche (-spiel *n*) *f*; *in* ~ aus Rache (*for* für); *to meditate* ~ auf Rache sinnen; *to take* ~ *on s.o. for s.th.* sich an jdm wegen etw rächen; *thirsting for* ~ rachedürstend; **~ful** [-ful] rachsüchtig; **~fulness** [-fulnis] Rachsucht *f*.

revenue ['revinju:] Einkommen *n*, Einkünfte *pl*; Einkommensquelle; Einnahme *f*, Ertrag *m*; *(tax, (Am) internal ~)* Steuereinnahmen *f pl*, -aufkommen *n*; *(national, public ~)* Staatseinkommen *n*, -einkünfte *pl*; Finanzverwaltung *f*; *yearly* ~ Jahreseinkommen *n*; ~ **agent** *Am* Steuer-, Finanz-, Zollbeamte(r) *m*; ~ **board** Finanzamt *n*; ~ **cutter** Zollboot *n*, -kutter *m*; ~ **duty** Finanzzoll *m*; **~-earning** gewinnbringend, einträglich; ~ **laws** *pl* Steuergesetzgebung *f*; Zollbestimmungen *f pl*; ~ **offence** Steuerhinterziehung *f*; Zollvergehen *n*; ~ **office** Finanzamt *n*; Finanz-, Steuerkasse *f*; Zollamt *n*; ~ **officer** Steuer-, Finanz-, Zollbeamte(r) *m*; **~r** ['-ə] *Am sl* Steuer-, Zollbeamte(r) *m*; ~ **receipts** *pl* Steueraufkommen *n*; ~ **stamp** Steuer-, Stempelmarke, Banderole *f*.

reverber|ate [ri:'və:bəreit] *tr (Schall)* zurückwerfen; *(Licht)* reflektieren, zurückstrahlen; *(Hitze im Flammofen)* ablenken; *itr (Schall)* widerhallen; *(Licht)* reflektiert, zurückgestrahlt werden; *(Hitze)* abgelenkt werden; *fig* Widerhall erwecken (*to* bei); **~ation** [rivə:bə'reiʃən] Widerhall *m*, Echo *n a. fig*; Rückstrahlung, Reflexion; Ablenkung *f (der Hitze im Flammofen)*; *(Flamme)* Zurückschlagen *n*; **~ator** [-eitə] Reflektor; Hohlspiegel; Scheinwerfer; Flammofen *m*; **~atory** [-ətəri] *a* zurückstrahlend, -gestrahlt; nachhallend; *(Hitze)* abgelenkt; *s u.* ~~ *furnace (tech)* Flammofen *m*.

rever|e [ri'viə] *tr* verehren, achten, hochschätzen; **~ence** ['revərəns] *s* Verehrung, Hochachtung (*for* für); Ehrfurcht (*for* vor); Verbeugung *f*; *tr* (ver-)ehren; **~end** ['revərənd] *a* (verehrungs-)würdig; *s fam* Pastor, Pfarrer *m*; *the Rev. John Jones, the Rev. Mr Jones* Pastor, Pfarrer J.; *the Right Rev. the Bishop of A.* S. Exzellenz der Bischof von A.; **~ent** ['revərənt], **~ential** [revə'renʃəl] ehrerbietig, ehrfurchtsvoll.

reverie, -ry ['revəri] Träumerei *f a. mus*; *lost in ~* in Träumen versunken.

revers|al [ri'və:səl] Umkehr(ung) *f a. el*; *jur* Widerruf *m*, Aufhebung, Annullierung; *com* Stornierung *f*; *fig* Umschwung *m*, Änderung; *mot* Rückwärtsschaltung *f*; *~~ point* Wendepunkt *m*; **~e** [ri'və:s] *a* umgekehrt, entgegengesetzt (*to* zu); *tech* Rückwärts-, Rück-; *s* Gegenteil *n*; Rück-, Kehrseite; Umkehrung *f*; Rückschlag, Schicksals-, harte(r) Schlag *m*; Niederlage, *fam* Schlappe *f*; Verlust *m*; *pl* Mißgeschick, Unglück *n*; *tech* Rückwärts-, rückläufige Bewegung *f*; *tech mot (~~ gear, speed)* Rückwärtsgang *m*; *tr* umkehren, umdrehen; das Innere nach außen, das Obere zuunterst kehren; ins Gegenteil verkehren, verwandeln; umstellen; *mot* zurückstoßen, zurücksetzen, rückwärts fahren; *tech* umsteuern; *jur* umstoßen, widerrufen, aufheben, annullieren; *itr* sich umwenden, sich rückwärts bewegen; *mot* auf Rückwärtsgang schalten; *in the ~~ order* in umgekehrter Reihenfolge; *on the ~~* umstehend; auf der Rückseite; *to go into ~~* rückwärts fahren; *fig* den Krebsgang gehen; *to suffer a ~~* e-n Rückschlag erleiden; *~~ side* linke, Rückseite *f*; *~~ slope* Hinterhang *m*; **~ible** [ri'və:səbl] umkehrbar *a. chem phys*; drehbar; *tech* umsteuerbar; *(Kleidung)* doppelseitig; *chem (Prozeß)* umkehrbar; **~ion** [ri'və:ʃən] Umkehrung (*to* zu); *el* Umpolung; Rückkehr *f (in e-n früheren Zustand)*; *biol* Atavismus *m*; *jur* Anwartschaft *f*, Heimfall *m* (*to* an); **~ionary** [ri'və:ʃnəri] *jur* zu erwarten(d), Anwartschafts-; *biol* atavistisch; *~~ heir* Nacherbe *m*; **~ioner** [re'və:ʃnə] Anwärter; Nacherbe *m*.

revert [ri'və:t] *itr* umkehren; zurückkommen, -greifen (*to* auf); *biol* zurückschlagen (*to* zu); wieder zurückfallen (*to* in); sich zurückverwandeln (*to* zu, in); *jur* heim-, zurückfallen (*to s.o.* an jdn); *tr (Blick)* zurückwenden; **~ible** [-əbl] *a jur* heimfällig (*to* an).

revet [ri'vet] *tr (Mauer)* verkleiden; abstützen; **~ment** [-mənt] Verkleidung; Futtermauer *f*.

review [ri'vju:] *s* Rückblick (*of* auf); (nochmaliger) Blick *m*; Überfliegen *n*; (nochmalige) Durchsicht; *jur* (nochmalige) Überprüfung, Nachprüfung, Revision; Besprechung *(in e-r Zeitschrift)*, Kritik, Rezension *f*; Überblick *m* (*of* über); Rundschau, kritische Zeitschrift; *theat s. revue*; *mil* Besichtigung, Truppenschau, (Truppen-)Parade *f*; *tr* zurückblicken, e-n Rückblick werfen auf; e-n Überblick geben über; noch einmal überblicken, überfliegen; kritisch durchsehen; an sich vorbeiziehen lassen; *jur* (nochmals) überprüfen, nachprüfen, revidieren, e-r Revision unterziehen; *(Auffassung)* berichtigen; besprechen, rezensieren; *(Truppen)* besichtigen, inspizieren; *(Schule)* abhören (*a lesson* e-e Aufgabe); *itr* Besprechungen, Kritiken schreiben; *in ~ing our records* bei Durchsicht unserer Bücher; *to come under ~* e-r Prüfung unterzogen werden; erwogen werden; *to hold the ~* die Parade abnehmen; *to pass in ~* mustern; *fig* an seinem geistigen Auge vorüberziehen lassen; *to take the ~ (mil)* die Front abschreiten; *market ~* Marktbericht *m*; *weekly, monthly ~* Wochen-, Monatsbericht *m*; *week, month, year under ~* Berichtswoche *f*, -monat *m*, -jahr *n*; **~ board** Prüfungsausschuß *m*; **~ copy** *(Buch)* Besprechungsexemplar *n*; **~er** [-ə] (Über-)Prüf(end)er; Rezensent, Kritiker *m*; *~~'s copy* Rezensionsexemplar *n*; **~ lesson** *Am* Wiederholungs-, Hausaufgabe *f*.

revile [ri'vail] *tr itr* sich abfällig äußern, abfällige Bemerkungen machen, herziehen (*at, against* über); *lit* schmähen.

revis|al [ri'vaizəl] Durchsicht, Überprüfung, Revision *f a. typ*; **~e** [ri'vaiz] *tr* durchsehen, überprüfen, revidieren; (ab)ändern, verbessern; be-, überarbeiten; *typ* Revision lesen von; *s* Durchsicht; Revision; *typ* zweite Korrektur, Revision *f*; *R~ed Version* Durchgesehene(r) *(engl.)* (Bibel-)Text *m*; **~er, ~or** [-ə] Über-, Nachprüf(end)er; *typ* Korrektor *m*; **~ion** [ri'viʒən] (erneute) Durchsicht; Revision; Änderung; Be-, Überarbeitung; *jur* erneute Verhandlung *f*.

revitalize ['ri:'vaitəlaiz] *tr* neu beleben, wieder Leben bringen in.

reviv|al [ri'vaivəl] Wiederbelebung *f a. fig*; *fig* Wiederaufleben, -blühen *n*; *com* Belebung *f*, Aufschwung *m*; *rel* Erweckung(sbewegung); *theat* Neueinstudierung; *theat film* Wiederaufführung, -aufnahme; *(Buch)* Neuausgabe; *jur* Erneuerung *f*, Wiederinkraftsetzen, -treten *n*; *the R~~ of Learning* der Humanismus; **~e** [ri'vaiv] *itr* ins Leben zurückkehren, wieder lebendig werden; wieder zu sich kommen, das Bewußtsein zurückerlangen; *fig* zu neuem Leben erwachen, wieder aufleben, wieder aufblühen; wieder auf-, in Gebrauch kommen; *jur* wieder in Kraft treten; *com* sich wiederbeleben; *(Aktien)* sich erholen; *tr* ins Leben zurückrufen; wieder zu sich bringen; *fig* zu neuem Leben erwecken, wiedererwecken, -beleben; wiederaufleben lassen; wieder in Erinnerung bringen; *(Brauch, Gesetz, Vertrag)* erneuern; wieder auffrischen; wieder in Kraft setzen; *chem* frischen; *theat* wieder einstudieren; *theat film* wieder aufführen; **~er** [-ə] Erneuerer *m*; Auffrischungsmittel *n*; *com* Aufmunterungsspritze; *sl* Stärkung *f*, Schnäpschen *n*; **~ify** [ri(:)'vivifai] *tr* wiederbeleben.

revoc|able ['revəkəbl] widerruflich; **~ation** [revə'keiʃən] Widerruf *m*, Zurücknahme, Aufhebung *f*; Entzug *m*.

revoke [ri'vouk] *tr* widerrufen, zurücknehmen, -ziehen, aufheben; *(Auftrag)* rückgängig machen, annullieren; *itr (Kartenspiel)* nicht Farbe bekennen.

revolt [ri'voult] *s* Revolte *f*, Aufruhr *m*, Empörung, Rebellion *f*, Aufstand *m*, Aufsässigkeit, Meuterei *f* (*against* gegen); *itr* revoltieren, rebellieren, sich empören, sich erheben; meutern (*against* gegen); überlaufen (*to* zu); angewidert, angeekelt abkehren, -wenden (*from* von); angewidert, angeekelt werden (*at, against, from* von); *tr fig* anwidern, -ekeln, abstoßen; *to rise in ~* sich erheben (*against* gegen); *to stir up to ~* aufwiegeln (*against* gegen); **~ing** [-iŋ] *fig* abstoßend, widerlich.

revolution [revə'lu:ʃən] *astr* Kreisbewegung *f*, Umlauf(szeit *f*) *m*; *phys* Umdrehung, Rotation *f*; *fig* Ablauf *m (d. Ereignisse)*; Umwälzung *f*, Umschwung; *pol* Umsturz *m*, Revolution *f*; **~ary** [-ʃnəri] *s* Revolutionär *m*; *a* revolutionär, umstürzlerisch; *fig* umwälzend; Revolutions-, Umsturz-; **~ counter** Umdrehungszähler *m*; **~ist** [-ʃnist] Revolutionär *m*; **~ize** [-ʃnaiz] *tr* revolutionieren, von Grund auf um-, neugestalten.

revolv|e [ri'vɔlv] *tr* kreisen, rotieren lassen; *fig* hin u. her überlegen; *fig* überdenken, im Kopf wälzen; *itr* kreisen, sich drehen (*round* um); rotieren (*about, round* um); periodisch ablaufen *od* wiederkehren; **~er** [-ə] Revolver *m*; **~ing** [-iŋ] *a tech* Dreh-; rotierend, umlaufend, wiederkehrend; *~~ assets (pl)* Umlaufvermögen *n*; *~~ bookstand* drehbare(r) Bücherständer *m*; *~~ chair* Drehstuhl *m*; *~~ crane* Drehkran *m*; *~~ door* Drehtür(e) *f*; *~~ light* Drehfeuer *n*; *~~ pencil* Drehbleistift *m*; *~~ shutter* Rolladen *m*; *~~ stage* Drehbühne *f*; *~~ turret (mil)* MG-Turm, Drehkranz *m*.

revue [ri'vju:] *theat* Revue *f*, Ausstattungsstück *n*.

revuls|ion [ri'vʌlʃən] *fig* Gefühlsumschwung *m*; heftige Reaktion; *med* Ableitung *f*; **~ive** [-siv] *a u. s (med)* ableitend(es Mittel *n*).

reward [ri'wɔ:d] *s* Belohnung *f*, *poet* Lohn *m*; Entgelt *n*, Entschädigung; Vergütung *f*; Gewinn, Ertrag *m*; *tr (Person* od *Dienst)* belohnen, vergelten (*with* mit; *for* für); *as a ~ for* zum Dank für; als Belohnung für; *for ~* gegen Entgelt; **~ing** [-iŋ] lohnend *a. fig*.

reword ['ri:'wə:d] *tr* in andere Worte kleiden, neu formulieren; wiederholen.

rewrite ['ri:'rait] *irr s. write tr* abschreiben; um-, neu schreiben; *(Geschriebenes)* abändern, umarbeiten; *(Presseberichte)* bearbeiten; *s* bearbeitete(r) Pressebericht *od* Artikel *m*; **~ man** *Am (Presse)* Bearbeiter *m*.

rhapsod|ic(al) [ræp'sɔdik(əl)] rhapsodisch; *fig* ekstatisch, überschwenglich; **~ist** ['ræpsədist] Rhapsode, Schwärmer *m*; **~ize** ['-aiz] *tr itr* rhapsodieren; *itr* schwärmen (*on, over, about* von); **~y** ['-i] Rhapsodie *f a. mus*; *fam* überschwengliche(r) Vortrag *m*; *to go into ~ies over* in Ekstase geraten über.

rheostat ['ri:o(u)stæt] *el* Rheostat *m*.

rhesus ['ri:səs] Rhesusaffe *m*; *R~ factor (med)* Rh-, Rhesusfaktor *m*.

rhetor|ic ['retərik] Rhetorik, Redekunst *f*; **~ical** [ri'tɔrikəl] rhetorisch; *~~ question* rhetorische Frage *f*; **~ician** [retə'riʃən] gute(r) Redner; Schönredner *m*.

rheum|atic [ru(:)'mætik] *a* rheumatisch; *s* Rheumatiker, Rheumaleidende(r) *m*; *pl* u. **~atism** ['ru(:)mətizm] Rheuma(tismus *m*) *n*.

rhin|al ['rainl] *a scient* Nasen-; **~o** ['-ou] *sl* Zaster *m*, Moneten *pl*; **~oceros** [-'nɔsərəs], *fam* **~o** Nashorn, Rhinozeros *n*.

Rhine, *the* [rain] der Rhein; **~land,** *the* [-lænd, -lənd] das Rheinland; **r~stone** *min* Rheinkiesel *m*; **~ wine** Rheinwein *m*.

rhizome ['raizoum] *bot* Wurzelstock *m*.

rhododendron [roudə'dendrən] *pl a. -dra bot* Rhododendron *n, a. m*.

rhomb [rɔm] *math* Rhombus *m*, Raute *f*; **~ic(al)** ['rɔmbik(əl)] rhombisch, rautenförmig; **~oid** ['rɔmbɔid] *math* Parallelogramm *n*; **~us** ['-əs] = **~**.

rhubarb ['ru:bɑ:b] *bot* Rhabarber; *Am sl* Streit, Krach *m*.

rhumb [rʌm] Kompaßstrich *m*; **~-line** Loxodrome, Kompaßlinie *f*.

rhym|e, rime [raim] *s* Reim (*to* auf); (gereimter) Vers *m*; Poesie *f*; *itr* sich reimen (*to* auf; *with* mit); reimen, dichten, Gedichte machen; *tr* reimen; in Verse bringen; *without* ~~ *nor reason* ohne Sinn u. Verstand; *nursery* ~~ Kindervers *m*, -lied *n*; ~~ *scheme* Reimschema *n*; **~eless** ['-lis] reimlos; **~er** ['-ə], **~ester** ['-stə] Verseschmied *m*.

rhythm ['riδ(ə)m, -θ-] Rhythmus; Takt *m*; ~ *of speech* Redefluß *m*; **~ic(al)** ['riδmik(əl), -θ-] rhythmisch; taktmäßig; **~ics** ['-miks] *pl mit sing* Rhythmik *f*.

rib [rib] *s anat bot tech* Rippe; *tech* Leiste *f*, Spant *m*; *arch* (Gewölbe-) Rippe; *fam* bessere Hälfte; *Am sl* witzige Bemerkung *f*; *tr* mit Rippen versehen; versteifen, verstärken; *sl* sich lustig machen über, durch den Kakao ziehen; *to dig, to poke s.o. in the* ~*s* jdm e-n Rippenstoß geben; **~-grass, ~wort** ['-wə:t] *bot* Spitzwegerich *m*.

ribald ['ribəld] *a* zotig, obszön; *s* Zotenreißer *m*; **~ry** ['-ri] zotige Reden *f pl*; Zoten(reißerei *f*) *f pl*.

ribbon ['ribən], **riband** ['ribənd] Band *n*; Borte *f*; Ordensband; *(typewriter* ~*)* Farbband; Metallband *n*, -streifen *m*; *(*~*-saw)* Bandsäge *f*; *Am sl* Mikrophon *n*; *fig* (Farb-)Streifen *m*; *pl* Fetzen *m pl*; *pl* Zügel *m pl*; **~-building, -development** Stadtrandsiedlung *f* (entlang e-r Ausfallstraße).

rice [rais] Reis *m*; **~-field** Reisfeld *n*; **~-flour** Reismehl *n*; **~-growing** Reisanbau *m*; **~-milk** Milchreis *m*; **~-paper** Reispapier *n*; **~-pudding** Reispudding *m*; **~-straw** Reisstroh *n*; **~-wine** Sake *m*.

rich [ritʃ] *a* reich, wohlhabend; *allg* reich (*in, with* an); reichlich; wertvoll, kostbar; prächtig, prachtvoll, herrlich, stattlich; luxuriös, üppig; nahrhaft, kräftig, fett; *(Wein)* vollmundig; schwer; duftend; *(Stimme)* voll, klangreich; *(Farben)* satt, kräftig; *(Ton)* voll; *(Boden)* fruchtbar, *allg* ergiebig; *mot* fett; *fam* ulkig, spaßig; *sl* unanständig; *s*: *the* ~ die Reichen *m pl*; **~es** ['-iz] *pl* Reichtum, Wohlstand *m*; Reichtümer, Schätze *m pl*; **~ness** ['-nis] Reichtum *m* (*in* an); Pracht, Herrlichkeit; Üppigkeit *f*, Luxus *m*; Kraft, Fülle, Sattheit; Klangfülle; Fruchtbarkeit *f*.

rick [rik] **1.** Heuhaufen, -schober *m*; Strohmiete *f*; **2.** *s. wrick.*

ricket|s ['rikits] *pl mit sing* Rachitis, englische Krankheit *f*; **~y** ['-i] *med* rachitisch; schwach, wack(e)lig.

ricochet ['rikəʃet] *s* Abprall; *mil* Querschläger, Abpraller *m*; *itr* abprallen.

rid [rid] *a. irr rid, rid tr* frei machen, befreien (*of* von); *to* ~ *o.s. of s.o., s.th.* sich jdn, etw vom Halse schaffen; *to be* ~ *of s.o., s.th.* jdn, etw los sein, vom Halse haben; *to get* ~ *of s.o., s.th.* jdn, etw loswerden; sich jdn, etw vom Halse schaffen; **~dance** ['-əns] Befreiung *f* (*of* von); Loswerden *n* (*of* gen); *good* ~~*!* den wäre ich glücklich los!

ridden ['ridn] *pp von ride*; *(in Zssgen)* beherrscht, besessen, verfolgt (*by* von); *hag-*~ (wie) besessen, irr-, wahnsinnig; *police-*~ von der Polizei verfolgt.

riddle ['ridl] **1.** *s* Rätsel *n a. fig*; *tr (Rätsel)* lösen; erklären; enträtseln; *itr* Rätsel aufgeben; *fig* in Rätseln sprechen; **2.** *s* Rätter *m (großes Sieb)*; *tr* rättern; durchlöchern, -bohren; *fig* heruntermachen, zerpflücken.

ride [raid] *irr rode, ridden itr* reiten; fahren (*on a bicycle* auf e-m Rad; *in a train* mit e-m Zug); sich bewegen (*on, upon* auf); gleiten, getragen werden; schwimmen; *(Wolken)* schweben, dahinziehen; *(to* ~ *at anchor)* vor Anker liegen; sich reiten, fahren, tragen lassen; *(Straße, Boden)* sich befahren lassen; sich überschneiden, sich kreuzen; *sl* (auf sich be)ruhen; *tr* reiten; *(Fahrrad)* fahren; fahren auf, in *(e-m Fahrzeug)*; reiten, fahren auf *(e-r Straße)*; reiten, fahren lassen; rittlings sitzen (lassen) auf; *(Schiff)* vor Anker liegen lassen; *Am fig* beherrschen, tyrannisieren, bedrücken, quälen *(meist pp mit by)*; *fam* fertigmachen, durch den Kakao ziehen, piesacken; *s* Ritt *m*; Fahrt; Radfahrt *f*; Reitweg *m*, Schneise; *Am sl* leichte Arbeit *f*, Vergnügen *n*; *to give s.o. a* ~ jdn (im Auto) mitnehmen; *to go for a* ~ e-e (Auto-)Fahrt unternehmen; *to let s.th.* ~ sich mit etw abfinden; *to take for a* ~ *(Am sl) (im Auto)* entführen u. umbringen; hochnehmen (*s.o.* jdn); sich lustig machen (*s.o.* über jdn); *to* ~ *an airline* e-e Fluglinie benutzen; *to* ~ *for a fall* nachlässig *od* rücksichtslos reiten; *fig* in sein Verderben rennen; *to* ~ *to hounds* auf Fuchsjagd gehen; *to* ~ *roughshod* sich rücksichtslos hinwegsetzen (*over* über); *to* ~ **away** wegreiten, -fahren; *to* ~ **down** niederreiten; überfahren; *(Flüchtigen)* stellen; einholen, erreichen; *to* ~ **out** *(Schiff)* gut (hindurch)kommen durch; *fig* gut überstehen; *to* ~ **up** sich verschieben, verrutschen; **~r** ['-ə] Reiter; (Motor-)Radfahrer; *tech* Reiter *m*, Laufgewicht *n*; *math* knifflige Aufgabe *f*; Zusatz, Nachtrag *m*; Zusatzklausel; (Wechsel-)Allonge *f*; *pl mar* Binnenspanten *n pl*; *to be no* ~~ nicht reiten (können); **~rless** ['-lis] ohne Reiter.

ridge [ridʒ] *s* Rücken *(e-s Tieres; der Nase)*; (Berg-)Rücken, Grat; (Wellen-)Kamm *m*; Untiefe *f*, Riff *n*; (Erd-)Wall *m*; Berg-, Hügelkette; Wasserscheide *f*; (Dach-)First; *mete* Hochdruckrücken; *(*~*-plough)* Häufelpflug *m*; Ackerfurche *f*; *tr itr* (an)häufeln; (sich) furchen; **~-piece, -pole** Firstbalken *m*, -stange *f (Zelt)*; **~-roof** Satteldach *n*; ~ **soaring** Hangsegeln *n*; **~-tile** Firstziegel *m*.

ridicul|e ['ridikju:l] *s* Hohn, Spott *m*; *tr* verspotten; *to turn into* ~~, *to hold up to* ~~ lächerlich machen; **~ous** [ri'dikjuləs] lächerlich; **~ousness** [-'dikjuləsnis] Lächerlichkeit *f*.

riding ['raidiŋ] *a* reitend; fahrend; Reit-; *s* Ritt *m*, Fahrt *f*; *mar* Ankern *n*; *mot* Federung *f*; Reitweg *m*; *sport* Reiten *n*; **~-boots** *pl* Reitstiefel *m pl*; **~-breeches** *pl* Reithose *f*; **~-crop, -whip** Reitpeitsche *f*; **~-habit** Reitkostüm *n*; **~-light** Anker-, Positionslicht *n*; **~-master** Reitlehrer *m*; **~-school** Reitschule *f*.

rif [rif] *Am sl tr* entlassen, auf die Straße setzen; **~f** [-] *Am sl s* Improvisation *f*; unwahre(s) Gerede *n*.

rife [raif] *a pred* häufig, (weit)verbreitet, allgemein, (vor)herrschend; *with* voll (-gestopft) mit, voller, reich an.

riffle ['rifl] *Am* Untiefe *(in e-m Wasserlauf)*, Furt, Stromschnelle; Riefelung; *(Goldwäscherei)* Riffel *f*; *(Karten)* Stechen *n*; *tr (Buch)* (schnell) durchblättern; *tech* riffeln; *(Karten)* stechen; **~r** ['-ə] Lochfeile *f*.

riff-raff ['rifræf] Pöbel, Mob *m*, Gesindel, (Lumpen-)Pack *n*, Abschaum *m*.

rifle ['raifl] **1.** *s* Gewehr *n (mit gezogenem Lauf)*; Büchse, Flinte *f*; *pl* Schützen *m pl*; *tr (Gewehrlauf)* ziehen; ausplündern, berauben; durchwühlen; ~ **barrel, butt** Gewehrlauf, -kolben *m*; ~ **company** Schützenkompanie *f*; ~ **exercise** (Gewehr-) Griffe *m pl*; ~ **grenade** Gewehrgranate *f*; ~ **inspection** Waffenappell *m*; **~man** ['-mən] Schütze, Jäger, Grenadier; Scharfschütze *m*; ~ **pit** Schützenloch *n*; ~ **rack** Gewehrgestell *n*; **~-range** Schießstand *m*; Schußweite *f*; *within, out of* ~~ in, außer Schußweite; **~-shot** Büchsenschuß *m*; Schußweite *f*; gute(r) Schütze *m*; ~ **sling** Gewehrriemen *m*; ~ **stock** Gewehrschaft *m*; ~ **target** Ringscheibe *f*; ~ **training** Schießausbildung *f*.

rift [rift] *s* Riß *a. fig*; Spalt *m*, Ritze *f*, Sprung, *fam* Knacks *m*; *tr* (zer)spalten, rissig machen; *itr* reißen, sich spalten, rissig werden, springen; ~ **valley** *geol* Senkungsgraben *m*.

rig [rig] *tr mar* (auf)takeln; *aero* (auf-) rüsten; *(to* ~ *out, to* ~ *up)* ausrüsten, einrichten; montieren; *(to* ~ *up)* eilig, behelfsmäßig *od* provisorisch herrichten; *(Preise)* künstlich hochschrauben; *fig* betrügerisch handhaben, manipulieren, fälschen; *(Markt)* künstlich beeinflussen; *fam (to* ~ *out, to* ~ *up)* auftakeln, (wie e-n Pfingstochsen) herausputzen; *s mar* Takelage *f*, Takelwerk *n*, Takelung; Auf-, Ausrüstung, Einrichtung; Anlage, Maschinerie *f*; *Am* Gespann *n*; *fig* Manipulation *f*, Trick, Schwindel, Betrug *m*; Börsenmanöver *n*; *fam* Aufputz, -zug *m*, -machung *f (auffällige Kleidung)*; *fam* Streich, Possen *m*; *to* ~ *the market* die Preise manipulieren, künstlich hochtreiben *od* drücken; **~ger** ['-ə] *mar* Tak(e)ler; *aero* (Rüst-) Mechaniker *m*; *arch* Schutzgerüst *n (an e-m Neubau)*; *tech* Bandscheibe *f*; Betrüger, Schwindler; *(Börse)* Kurs-, Preistreiber *m*; **~ging** ['-iŋ] *mar* Takelage *f*, Takelwerk *n*; Takelung *f*; *aero* (Auf-)Rüsten *n*; *tech* Montage *f*; *~~-band (aero)* Ballon-, Traggurt *m*; *~~-line* Fallschirm-, Fangleine *f*; *~~-loft (theat)* Schnürboden *m*; **~-out** *fam* Toilette *f*, Kleider *n pl*; **~-up** Hilfskonstruktion *f*.

right [rait] **1.** *a* gerade; aufrecht(stehend); (ge)recht, aufrecht, tugendhaft, gut; normal, gesund; richtig, korrekt; in Ordnung; passend, geeignet, angebracht; rechtmäßig; geeignetste(r, s), günstigste(r, s); *(Stoffseite)* recht; *(Edelstein)* echt; **2.** *s das* Rechte, Gute, Richtige; (An-, Vor-)Recht *n*, Berechtigung *f*; *die* Rechte, rechte Seite; *(Boxen) die* Rechte, rechte Hand; Schlag *m* mit der Rechten; *(the R*~*) pol* die Rechte; **3.** *adv* (auf) gerade(m Wege), geradeswegs; direkt, genau, ganz, gleich; gerade; recht, richtig, ordentlich, wie es sich gehört; völlig, vollständig, ganz; sehr, recht, ganz; gleich, sofort; **4.** *tr* (wieder) aufrichten; berichtigen, verbessern, korrigieren; in Ordnung bringen, aufräumen; Recht widerfahren, zuteil werden lassen, zu s-m Recht verhelfen (*s.o.* jdm); wiedergutmachen; **5.** *itr mar* sich (wieder) aufrichten; **6.** *at the* ~ *time* zur rechten Zeit; *by* ~*(s)* mit Recht; von Rechts wegen; *by* ~ *of* auf Grund, kraft, mittels, vermöge, mit Hilfe *gen*; *in o.'s own* ~ unabhängig; *on the* ~ rechts, zur Rechten; *on the* ~ *side of 50* (noch) nicht über 50 (Jahre alt); *to* ~*s (Am fam)* in Ordnung; ~ *along (Am)* immer geradeaus; ~ *away, now, off (Am)* gleich, sofort; ~ *down (fam)* voll u. ganz; ~ *into (Am)* direkt hinein; ~ *and left* auf, nach beiden

Seiten; überall; ~ *on (Am)* immer geradeaus; ~ *through* durch u. durch; ~ *to (Am)* gerade drauflos; *the ~ way* in der rechten Weise; **7.** *to abandon, to acquire, to alienate, to claim, to dispute, to forfeit, to grant, to reserve, to vindicate a ~* ein Recht aufgeben, erwerben, veräußern, beanspruchen, bestreiten, verwirken, verleihen, vorbehalten, geltend machen; *to assert o.'s ~s, to stand on o.'s ~s* sein Recht behaupten; *to be ~* recht haben; richtig sein, stimmen, zutreffen; auf dem richtigen Wege sein (*for* nach); *to be in the ~* im Recht sein; *to be in o.'s ~ mind, senses* bei klarem Verstand sein; *to get ~* klarstellen; *to go ~* in Ordnung, gutgehen; *not to go ~* schiefgehen; *to keep to the ~* sich rechts halten; *to put s.th. to ~s* etw in Ordnung bringen; *to put o.'s ~ hand to the work* tüchtig arbeiten; *to put, to set ~* (wieder) in Ordnung bringen; *to turn out all ~* gut ausgehen, in Ordnung kommen; *to waive o.'s ~s* auf s-e Rechte verzichten; **8.** *I never got to know the ~s of it* ich bin niemals ganz dahintergekommen; *it serves him ~* das geschieht ihm recht; *you can't be in your ~ mind* Sie sind wohl nicht richtig im Kopf; *have you the ~ time on you?* haben Sie genaue Zeit? *what is the ~ time?* wie spät ist es genau? *all ~!* in Ordnung! schön! gut! *eyes ~! (mil)* Augen rechts! ~ *you are! (fam)*, ~ *oh! (sl)* da hast du (ganz) recht! *go ~ straight ahead* gehen Sie nur geradeaus; ~ *enough!* sicher! einverstanden! **9.** *bill of ~s* Grundrechte *n pl*; *birth ~* Geburtsrecht *n*; *the civic ~s (pl)* die bürgerlichen Rechte *n pl*; *contractual ~* Vertragsrecht *n*; *dramatic ~s (pl)* Aufführungs-, Bühnenrechte *n pl*; *exercise of a ~* Ausübung *f* e-s Rechtes; *natural ~s (pl)* Grundrechte *n pl*; *patent ~* Patentrecht *n*; *sovereign ~* Hoheitsrecht *n*; ~ *of action* Klagerecht *n*; ~ *of appeal* Beschwerderecht *n*; ~ *of assembly* Versammlungsrecht *n*; ~ *of asylum* Asylrecht *n*; ~ *of control* Aufsichtsrecht *n*; *the ~s of man* die Menschenrechte *n pl*; *the ~ man at the ~ place* der rechte Mann am rechten Platz; ~ *of passage* Durchmarschrecht *n*; ~ *of pre-emption* Vorkaufsrecht *n*; ~ *of priority* Priorität(srecht *n*) *f*; ~ *of property* Eigentum(srecht) *n*; ~ *as rain, as a trivet (fam)* prima; ~ *of repurchase* Rückkaufsrecht *n*; ~ *of residence* Wohn-, Aufenthaltsrecht *n*; ~ *of reversion* Rückfallsrecht *n*; ~ *of succession* Erbrecht *n*; ~ *of usufruct* Nießbrauch *m*; ~ *of victory* Recht *n* des Siegers; ~ *of voting* Wahl-, Stimmrecht *n*; ~ *of way* Wegerecht *n*; Vorfahrt *f*; **~-about** *a* entgegengesetzt; *adv* in der entgegengesetzten, in die entgegengesetzte Richtung; *s* Kehrtwendung *f*; *to send s.o. to the ~~* jdn wegschicken, -jagen, entlassen; *~~ turn! (mil)* ganze Abteilung – kehrt! *~~ turn, face* Kehrtwendung *f*; **~-angled** *a* rechtwinklig; ~ **arm**: *to be s.o.'s ~~ (fig)* jds rechte Hand sein; ~ **ascension** *astr* Rektaszension *f*; **~-down** *a adv* völlig, durch u. durch; **~eous** ['raitʃəs] recht(schaffen), gerecht, ehrlich, gerade, tugendhaft; *Am fam* selbstgerecht, hochnäsig; *Am sl* furchtbar; **~eousness** ['-tʃəsnis] Rechtschaffenheit, Gerechtigkeit, Geradheit; recht(schaffen)e Tat *f*; **~ful** ['-ful] (ge)recht; berechtigt, rechtmäßig; **~fulness** ['-fulnis] Gerechtigkeit; Berechtigung, Rechtmäßigkeit *f*; **~-hand** *a* recht, rechtsseitig, -gerichtet; rechtshändig; *tech* rechtsläufig; *fig* tüchtig, zuverlässig; *to be s.o.'s ~~ man (fig)* jds rechte Hand sein; **~-handed** *a* rechtshändig; Rechts-; im Uhrzeigersinn; **~-hander** Rechtshänder *m*; **~ist** ['-ist] *s* Konservative(r); Rechtsradikale(r); *a* konservativ; rechtsradikal; **~ly** ['-li] *adv* rechtmäßig; richtig, korrekt; wie es sich gehört; **~-minded** *a* wohlmeinend; rechtlich; gerecht denkend *od* empfindend; **~ness** ['-nis] Geradheit; Gerechtigkeit; Richtigkeit, Korrektheit *f*; ~ **turn** Rechtswendung *f*; *~~!* rechts um!

rigid ['ridʒid] steif, starr; unelastisch, unbeweglich, fest; *fig* unnachgiebig, unbeugsam, hart, streng; *(Bestimmung, Regel)* streng; *(Luftschiff)* starr; **~ity** [ri'dʒiditi] Starrheit; Festigkeit, Unbeweglichkeit; *fig* Unnachgiebigkeit, Härte, Strenge *f*.

rigmarole ['rigməroul] dumme(s) Geschwätz, Gerede, Gewäsch *n*; Unsinn *m*.

rig|or ['raigɔ:, *Am a.* 'rigə] *med* Schüttelfrost *m*; *Am* ['rigə] = **~our**; *~~ mortis* [-'mɔ:tis] Leichenstarre *f*; **~orous** ['rigərəs] rigoros, streng, strikt, scharf, hart; *(Wetter, Klima)* rauh; streng, genau, exakt; **~our** ['rigə] Härte, Strenge, Unbeugsamkeit; Genauigkeit; *(Wetter, Klima)* Rauheit *f*.

rile [rail] *tr fam* ärgern.

rill [ril] *s* Bächlein *n*.

rim [rim] *s* Rand *m*, Kante *f*, Reif; Randstreifen *m*; Hutkrempe; *(Brille)* Fassung; *(Rad)* Felge; *arch* Zarge *f*; *tr* mit e-m Rand, Reif versehen; **~less** ['-lis] randlos; ~ **zone** Randzone *f*.

rim|e [raim] **1.** *s lit* (Rauh-)Reif *m*; *tr* mit (Rauh-)Reif überziehen; **~y** ['-i] bereift; **2.** *s. rhyme.*

rim|ose ['raimous], **~ous** ['-əs] *bot zoo* zerklüftet, rissig, schrundig.

rind [raind] *s* (Baum-, Käse-)Rinde; Kruste; Hülse; Schale; Speckschwarte *f*; *tr* entrinden, abschälen.

ring [riŋ] **1.** *irr rang (selten: rung), rung* [ræŋ, rʌŋ] *itr (Glocke)* läuten; *(Person)* läuten, klingeln (*for* nach); schellen; klingen; erklingen, erschallen, ertönen, widerhallen (*with, of* von) *a. fig*; nachklingen; *tr (Glocke)* läuten (lassen); erklingen, erschallen, ertönen lassen; *(durch Geläut)* verkünden; *(Münze)* klingen lassen; *tele (to ~ up)* anrufen; *s* Geläut(e) *n*; Glockenklang, -ton *m*, -zeichen; Klingelzeichen, Klingeln, Geklingel *n*; Schall, Widerhall; Klang *a. fig*; *tele* Anruf *m*; Rufzeichen *n*; *to give s.o. a ~ (tele)* jdn anrufen; *to ~ the bell (fam)* es geschafft haben; *allg* klingeln, läuten; *to ~ a bell (fig)* vertraut klingen; *to ~ the changes on s.th.* immer wieder auf etw zurückkommen; *to ~ the knell of s.th. (fig)* etw zu Grabe läuten; *to ~ s.o.'s praises* jds Lob singen *od* verkünden; *a ~ of laughter* ein schallendes Gelächter; *there was a ~* es hat geläutet; *to ~* **back** *tele* zurückrufen; *to ~* **down** abblasen; *to ~~ the curtain (theat)* das Klingelzeichen für die Pause geben; *to ~* **in** *tr* einläuten; *sl* einschmuggeln; *itr* die Ankunft auf der Kontrolluhr markieren; *sl* sich einschmuggeln (*on* bei), ungebeten erscheinen (*on* bei); *to ~* **off** *tele* den Hörer auflegen; *to ~* **out** *tr (Feiertag)* ausläuten; *itr* den Weggang auf der Kontrolluhr markieren; verhallen; ertönen, erklingen; *to ~* **up** *tele* anrufen; *to ~~ the curtain (theat)* das Klingelzeichen für den Aktbeginn geben; **~er** ['-ə] Läutende(r), Glöckner *m*; Läutwerk *n*; *Am* eingeschmuggelte(r) Mitspieler, Mitbewerber (*a. Rennpferd*); Doppelgänger *m*; *to be a ~~ for s.o.* jds Doppelgänger sein; **~ing** ['-iŋ] *a* schallend, dröhnend; *~~ tone* Rufzeichen *n*; **2.** *s* Ring (*on o.'s finger* am Finger); Reif; Kreis; Rand; *(Mond)* Hof; Spiralring *m*; runde (Tanz-)Fläche *f*; *(Zirkus)* Ring *m*, Manege, Arena *f*; (Box-)Ring *m*; Boxen *n*, Boxsport; *(Rennplatz)* Totalisator *m*; *die* Buchmacher *m pl*; *com* Interessengemeinschaft *f*, Kartell *n*, Ring *m*, Syndikat *n*; Gruppe, Bande *f*; *math* Kreisring; *chem* Ring *m*; *tr* im Kreis aufstellen; *(Vogel)* beringen; e-n Ring durch die Nase ziehen (*an animal* e-m Tier); einkreisen; zs.treiben; *itr* e-n Kreis beschreiben; *to have ~s round the eyes* Ringe um die Augen haben; *to make, to run ~s round s.o.* jdn übertreffen; *to toss o.'s hat in the ~* als Kandidat auftreten; *annual ~ (Baum)* Jahresring *m*; *circus-~* Zirkusring *m*; *ear-~* Ohrring *m*; *key-~* Schlüsselring *m*; *napkin-~* Serviettenring *m*; *prize-~* Boxring *m*; *wedding ~* Ehering *m*; **~-a-~-a-roses, ~-game** Ringelreihen *m (Kinderspiel)*; **~-connection** *el* Ringschaltung *f*; **~-dove** Lach-, Ringeltaube *f*; **~ed** [-d] *a* beringt; **~-finger** Ringfinger *m*; **~leader** Rädelsführer *m*; **~let** ['-lit] Ringlein *n*; (Hänge-)Locke *f*; **~-mail** Kettenpanzer *m*; **~-master** Zirkusdirektor *m*; **~-net** Schmetterlingsnetz *n*; **~-road** Ringstraße *f*; **~-shaped** *a* ringförmig; **~side** Platz *m* in den vordersten Reihen; **~-snake** Ringelnatter *f*; **~ster** ['-stə] *fam pol* Mietglied *n* e-s politischen Kreises; **~worm** *med* scherende Flechte *f*.

rink [riŋk] (künstliche) Eis-, Rollschuhbahn *f*; Spielfeld *n*.

rins|e [rins] *tr* (ab-, aus)spülen; *s u.* **~ing** ['-iŋ] Spülen; *pl* Spülicht *n*; *~~ bath, vessel, water* Spülbad, -gefäß, -wasser *n*.

riot ['raiət] *s* Tumult; (Volks-)Auflauf, Aufruhr; *jur* Landfriedensbruch *m*; Zs.rottung *f*; Trubel *m*, laute Lustbarkeit, Feier; Orgie *f a. fig*; *Am fam* tolle Sache *f*, amüsante(r) Kerl *m*; *pl* Unruhen, Ausschreitungen *f pl*; *itr* (herum)toben, randalieren; lebhaft, laut feiern; umherschwärmen; ein wüstes Leben führen; sich austoben (*in* in); *to be a ~ (theat)* Furore machen, das größte Aufsehen erregen; zum Brüllen sein; *to read the R~ Act (fig fam)* warnen (*to s.o.* jdn); *to run ~* sich austoben, sich über alle Schranken hinwegsetzen; *bot* wuchern; *a ~ of colo(u)rs* ein prächtiges Farbenspiel; *a ~ of laughter* ein schallendes Gelächter, e-e Lachsalve; **~er** ['-ə] Aufrührer, Krawallmacher; Saufbruder, -kumpan *m*; **~ous** ['-əs] aufrührerisch; tobend, lärmend, ausgelassen; liederlich; ~ **squad** *Am* Überfallkommando *n*.

rip [rip] **1.** *tr* auf-, ein-, zerreißen, auftrennen; *(Holz)* spalten, der Länge nach sägen; *itr* (ein-, zer)reißen; *fam* durch die Gegend sausen, herumrasen, -toben; fluchen, vor Wut platzen; *s* Riß, Schlitz *m*; *like ~s (Am fam)* energisch *adv*; *let her ~ (mot)* laß ihn laufen *od* sausen! gib Vollgas! *to let s.o. ~* jdn auf die Palme bringen; *let things ~* mach dir keine Gedanken! ~ *of laughter (Am)* schallende(s) Gelächter *n*; *to ~* **away** zerreißen; *to ~* **off** wegreißen; *to ~* **open** aufschlitzen; *to ~* **out** herausreißen; *fig* herausplatzen mit; fahren lassen; *to ~* **up** auftrennen; *(Holz)* spalten;

aufschlitzen; **~-cord** *aero* Reißleine *f*; **~hook** Faschinenmesser *n*; **~per** ['-ə] Aufschlitzer *m*; Zerreißmaschine *f*; *Am* Doppelschlitten; *sl* Prachtkerl *m*, -ding *n*; **~ping** ['-iŋ] *a* Trenn-, Reiß-; *sl* prächtig, prima, Klasse; *adv sl* toll, unheimlich; **~-roaring** *Am sl* tobend, lärmend, laut, ausgelassen, feuchtfröhlich; **~saw** Langsäge *f*; **~-snorter** *Am sl* tolle Sache *f*; tolle(r) Kerl *m*; **2.** *(~-tide)* Kabbelung, gekräuselte Wasserfläche; starke Strömung *f*; Strudel *m*; **3.** Luftikus, Taugenichts *m*; Schindmähre *f*; Schund *m*.

riparian [rai'pɛəriən] *a* Ufer-; *s* Uferbewohner, -anlieger *m*.

ripe [raip] *(Frucht, Käse)* reif; *(Wein)* ausgereift, abgelagert; *(Vieh)* schlachtreif; *(Tier)* ausgewachsen; *(Mensch)* erwachsen; reif, in den besten Jahren, (lebens)erfahren; *(Alter)* hoch, gereift; *(Geschwür)* reif; *(Angelegenheit)* genügend fortgeschritten *od* gediehen, ausgereift; *(Zeit)* reif, gekommen (*for* für); *(Lippen)* voll; *(Schönheit)* vollendet; bereit (*for* zu); *sl* zum Brüllen, obszön, besoffen; *of ~ age (Mensch)* reif; *of ~(r) years* reiferen Alters; *soon ~, soon rotten (prov)* gut Ding will Weile; **~n** ['-ən] *itr tr* reifen; *itr* heranreifen, sich entwickeln (*into* zu); **~ness** ['-nis] Reife *f a. fig.*

ripost(e) [ri'poust] *s (Fechten u. fig)* Nach-, Gegenstoß *m*; *fig* schlagfertige Antwort *f*; *itr* e-n Gegenstoß führen; *fig* die Antwort nicht schuldig bleiben.

rippl|e ['ripl] *itr (bewegliche Fläche)* sich (leicht) kräuseln, sanft wogen; *(Wasser)* rieseln; murmeln, plätschern; *(Laut)* vibrieren; *(Unterhaltung)* dahinplätschern; *tr* (leicht) kräuseln, sanft bewegen; wellenförmig machen *od* gestalten; *(Haar)* ondulieren; *s* kleine Welle *f*; Kräuseln; Geriesel; Geplätscher, Gemurmel *n*; Haarwelle *f*; *~~ mark* Wellenlinie *f* im Sand; *~~ of laughter* perlende(s) Gelächter *n*; **~y** ['-i] leicht gekräuselt, sanft wellig; rieselnd; murmelnd; **2.** *tr (Flachs)* riffeln, kämmen, aufrauhen; *s* Riffel *f*, Flachs-, Reffkamm *m*.

rise [raiz] *irr rose, risen* **1.** *itr* aufstehen, sich erheben; *(von den Toten)* auferstehen; aufbrechen, weggehen; *(Vögel)* wegfliegen; *(Versammlung)* ausea.gehen, sich vertagen; sich erheben, revoltieren, sich empören; e-n Aufstand machen (*against* gegen); *(to ~ up)* aufsteigen; *(Gestirn, Vorhang)* aufgehen; *(Weg)* aufwärts gehen, ansteigen; *(Wasser)* steigen, ansteigen, -schwellen; *fig* aufsteigen; reich, berühmt werden; *(Gebäude, Berg)* sich erheben; sichtbar werden, aufsteigen; *(Ton)* sich heben; größer werden, wachsen, zunehmen; werden (*into* zu); *(Preise)* anziehen, ansteigen, in die Höhe gehen; lauter, stärker, lebhafter werden; *(Teig)* (auf)gehen; heraus-, hervorstehen; s-n Anfang, Ursprung haben; *(Fluß)* entspringen; entstehen; sich ergeben; *(Zweifel)* sich erheben; **2.** *tr (Vögel)* aufjagen; *(Fische)* anbeißen lassen; **3.** *s* (Auf-)Steigen *n*, Aufwärtsbewegung *f*; *(Wasser)* Ansteigen *n*; *(Gestirn)* Aufgang *m*; *(Vorhang)* Aufgehen *n*; Auferstehung *f*; (An-)Wachsen, Anschwellen *n*; (Boden-)Erhebung, Anhöhe, Höhe *f*; Aufschwung *m*; Zunahme; (Gehalts-)Erhöhung; *(Preise)* Steigerung *f*, Ansteigen, Anziehen *n*; *arch* Stich *m*; *tech* Ganghöhe *f*; (sozialer) Aufstieg *m*; Beförderung *f*; Anlaß, Anstoß *m*, Veranlassung, Ursache, Quelle *f*, Ursprung, Anfang, Beginn *m*; **4.** *to ask for a ~* um Gehaltserhöhung bitten; *to be on the ~* im Steigen begriffen sein; *to buy for a ~ (fin)* auf Hausse spekulieren; *to give ~ to* veranlassen, Anlaß, Veranlassung geben zu; herbeiführen, bewirken; *to have, to take o.'s ~ (Fluß)* entspringen (*in* in; *from* aus); *to take, to get a ~ out of s.o.* jdn hoch-, *fam* auf die Palme bringen; *to ~ with the lark* mit den Hühnern aufstehen; *to ~ to the occasion* sich der Lage gewachsen zeigen; *to ~ to order* zu der Geschäftsordnung sprechen; *I did not get a ~* es hat kein Fisch angebissen; *he rose from the ranks* er hat von der Pike auf gedient; *~ in the bank-rate* Diskonterhöhung *f*; *~ in population* Bevölkerungszunahme *f*; *~ to power* Machtübernahme *f*; *~ in prices* Preissteigerung, -erhöhung *f*; *~ in temperature* Temperaturerhöhung *f*, -anstieg *m*; Erwärmung *f*; *~ in value* Wertzuwachs *m*; *~ of wages* Steigen *n* der Löhne; Lohnerhöhung *f*; **~r** ['-ə] *metal* Steiger *m*; (Kollektor-)Fahne *f*; Steigrohr; *(Treppenstufe)* Setz-, Futterbrett *n*; *early ~~* Frühaufsteher *m*; *~~ pipe* Steigrohr *n*.

risib|ility [rizi'biliti] Lachlust *f*; *meist pl* Sinn *m* für Humor; **~le** ['rizibl] Lach-; lachlustig, lachhaft, spaßig, lustig.

rising ['raiziŋ] *a* (auf-, an)steigend; *(Gestirn)* aufgehend; heranwachsend; aufstrebend; *fig* kommend; *s* (Auf-, An-)Steigen; Aufstehen *n*; Auf-, Anstieg *m*; Steigung; Erhöhung, Zunahme, Steigerung *f*; Anschwellen *n*; Erhebung *f*, Aufstand, Aufruhr; Aufbruch *m*; *parl* Vertagung; Anhöhe *f*; *astr theat* Aufgehen *n*; *med* Eiterpickel *m*, -beule, Pustel *f*; *min* Aufbau *m*; *rel* Auferstehung *f*; *prp Am fam* über, mehr als; gegen, an die (*fifty* fünfzig); *the ~ generation* die kommende Generation; **~ floor, platform, stage** Hebebühne *f*; **~ ground** Bodenerhebung *f*; **~ gust** Steigbö *f*.

risk [risk] *s* Gefahr *f*, Wagnis, Risiko *n a. fin*; *fin* Versicherungsgegenstand *m*; *tr* wagen, *fam* riskieren (*to do s.th.* etw zu tun); in Gefahr bringen, aufs Spiel setzen; *at the ~ of* auf die Gefahr *gen*; *o.'s life* unter Lebensgefahr; *at s.o.'s ~s* auf jds Verantwortung; *at all ~s* auf jede Gefahr hin; *at o.'s own ~* auf eigene Gefahr; *without ~* gefahr-, risikolos; *to assume a ~* ein Risiko übernehmen; *to run, to take the ~* Gefahr laufen (*of doing s.th.* etw zu tun); *~ of breakage* Bruchgefahr *f*; **~y** ['-i] gefährlich, gewagt, heikel.

rissole ['risoul] Frikadelle *f*, deutsche(s) Beefsteak *n*.

rit|e [rait] feierliche Handlung *f*; Ritus *a. rel*; Brauch *m*; *rel* Liturgie, gottesdienstliche Ordnung *f*; *marriage ~~s (pl)* Hochzeitsbräuche *m pl*; **~ual** ['ritjuəl] *a* rituell; feierlich; *s* Ritual, Zeremoniell; Zeremonienbuch *n*.

ritzy ['ritsi] *Am sl, oft iro* super-, hochelegant, piekfein; übergeschnappt.

rival ['raivəl] *s* Mitbewerber, Rivale, Nebenbuhler, Konkurrent *m*; *a* rivalisierend; *tr* rivalisieren, in Wettbewerb treten, wetteifern mit; *(to be a ~ of)* es aufnehmen (können) mit; ausstechen (*s.o.* jdn); *itr* wetteifern (*with* mit); **~ry** ['-ri] Rivalität, Nebenbuhlerschaft, Konkurrenz *f*; *to enter into ~~ with s.o.* mit jdm in Wettbewerb treten, jdm Konkurrenz machen.

rive [raiv] *irr pp a. ~n tr* zerreißen; spalten; *itr* reißen (*at* an); bersten; *fig (Herz)* brechen; sich spalten; *to ~ away, off* weg-, herausreißen.

river ['rivə] Fluß; Strom *m*; *up, down the ~* stromauf-, abwärts; *to sell s.o. down the ~ (sl)* jdn verraten; *the ~ Thames* die Themse; *~s of blood* Ströme *m pl* von Blut; *~ of lava* Lavastrom *m*; **~-basin** Stromgebiet *n*; **~-bed** Flußbett *n*; **~-borne** *a* auf dem Fluß befördert; **~-fish** Flußfisch *m*; **~-god** Flußgott *m*; **~-head** Quelle *f*; **~-horse** *zoo* Fluß-, Nilpferd *n*; **~ine** ['-rain], **~ain** ['-rein] *a* Fluß-; **~-navigation** Flußschiffahrt *f*; **~-police** Wasserpolizei *f*; **~-port** Flußhafen *m*; **~side** *s* Flußufer *n*; *a* (Fluß-)Ufer-; *by the ~~* am Fluß(ufer); **~-steamer** Flußdampfer *m*.

rivet ['rivit] *s tech* Niet(e *f*) *m*; *tr* (ver-)nieten; festmachen, befestigen *a. fig* (*to* an); *(den Blick)* heften, *(die Aufmerksamkeit)* richten (*on* auf).

rivulet ['rivjulit] Flüßchen *n*, Bach *m*.

roach [routʃ] **1.** Plötze, Rotfeder *f*, -auge *n (Fisch)*; *as sound as a ~* gesund wie ein Fisch; **2.** *(cock~) ent* (Küchen-)Schabe *f*; **3.** *mar* Gilling *f*.

road [roud] (Land-)Straße *f*; *fig* Weg *m* (*to power* zur Macht; *to success* zum Erfolg); *Am (rail~)* Eisenbahn; *meist pl (~stead) mar* Reede *f*; *min* Strecke *f*; *a* Straßen-, Weg-; *by ~* auf der Landstraße; im Straßentransport, per Achse; *in the ~* auf der Landstraße; auf der Reede; *to be on the ~* auf der Straße, unterwegs sein; *to get in s.o.'s ~ (fig)* jdm in den Weg, in die Quere kommen; *out of o.'s ~* aus dem Weg gehen; *to give s.o. the ~* jdn vorbeilassen; *to go on the ~* auf Tour, *theat* auf Tournee gehen; *to hit the ~ (Am)* sich aus dem Staub machen; *to ride at the ~* auf der Reede liegen; *to take the ~* sich auf den Weg machen; losfahren; *where does this ~ go to?* wohin führt diese Straße? *it's your ~* Sie haben Vorfahrt; *get out of the ~* geh mir aus dem Weg! *~ closed ahead* gesperrt für den Durchgangsverkehr! *accomodation ~* Zufahrtsstraße *f*; *royal ~* leichte(r) Weg (*to* zu); *rule of the ~* Straßenverkehrsordnung *f*; *side ~* Seitenstraße *f*; **~ability** [-ə'biliti] *mot* Straßenlage *f*; **~ accident** Verkehrsunfall *m*; **~ agent** *Am* Straßenräuber *m*; **~bed** *Am* Bahnkörper *m*; **~bend, ~curve** (Straßen-)Biegung, Kurve *f*; **~block** *mil* Straßensperre *f*; **~ book** Straßenführer *m (Buch)*; **~ carpet** Straßendecke *f*; **~ conditions** *pl* Straßenzustand *m*; **~ construction** Straßenbau *m*; **~ hog** Kilometerfresser, rücksichtslose(r) Fahrer *m*; **~ holding** Straßenlage *f*; **~ hole** Schlagloch *n*; **~house** Rasthaus *n*; Kneipe *f*; **~ intersection** Straßenkreuzung *f*; **~ jam** Verkehrsstockung *f*; **~ junction** (Straßen-)Stern, Knotenpunkt *m*; **~man, ~mender** Straßenarbeiter *m*; **~ map** Straßen-, Autokarte *f*; **~ metal** Straßenbaumaterial *n*, Schotter, Steinschlag *m*; **~ net** Straßennetz *n*; **~-roller** Straßenwalze *f*; **~-sense** Fahrtüchtigkeit *f*; **~ show** Wanderschau, -bühne *f*; **~side** *s* Straßenrand *m*; *attr* an der (Land-)Straße; Straßen-; *~~ inn* Rasthaus *n*; **~sign** Wegweiser *m*; **~stead** *mar* Reede *f*; **~ster** ['-stə] *mot* (offener) Sportzweisitzer *m*; Reit-, Reisepferd; Tourenrad *n*; auf der Reede liegende(s) Schiff *n*; **~-stud** Straßennagel *m*; **~ surface** Straßendecke *f*; **~ test** *Am mot* Probefahrt *f*; **~-up** Baustelle, Straßensperre *f*; **~ user** Verkehrsteilnehmer *m*; **~way** Landstraße *f*; Fahrweg *m*, -bahn *f*.

roam [roum] *itr (to ~ about)* umherschweifen; *tr* durchstreifen *a. fig*; sich herumtreiben (*the streets* auf den Straßen); *s* Umherschweifen *n*; **~er** ['-ə] Landstreicher *m*.

roan [roun] **1.** *a (Pferd)* falb *od* rotbraun; mit grauen *od* weißen Flecken; *s* Gelb-, Braun-, Rot-, Muskatschimmel *m*; **2.** (sumachgegerbtes) Schafleder *n (bes. für Bucheinbände)*.

roar[rɔː] *itr* brüllen (*with* vor); schreien, laut reden; schallend, laut lachen (*at* über); *vet (Pferd)* keuchen; *(Maschine)* rattern, rasseln; Krach machen; dröhnen (*with* von); donnern; *(Sturm)* brausen, heulen, gellen, toben; *(Geschütze)* krachen; *(Donner)* grollen; *tr (to ~ out)* (hinaus)brüllen, schreien; *to ~ down* niederschreien, -brüllen; *s* Gebrüll; Geschrei; laute(s) Gelächter *n*; Lärm, Spektakel *m*; Getöse; *(Sturm)* Toben, Heulen; *(Wasserfall)* Brausen *n*; *to ~ o.s. hoarse* sich heiser schreien; *to ~ with laughter* vor Lachen brüllen; **~er** ['-rə] keuchende(s) Pferd *n*; *Am fam* plötzlich fließende Ölquelle *f*; **~ing** ['-riŋ] *a* brüllend (*with* vor); donnernd, tosend, brausend, heulend; *(Nacht)* stürmisch; *fam* flott, lebhaft, glänzend, großartig; *(Handel)* schwunghaft; *s* Gebrüll *n*; *vet (Pferd)* Keuchen *n*; *to be in ~~ health* vor Gesundheit strotzen.

roast [roust] *tr* braten, rösten, schmoren *a. fig*; *(Kaffee)* rösten; erhitzen; *metal* rösten, ausglühen, abschwelen; *fam* herunter-, fertigmachen; *fam* auf-, durch den Kakao ziehen, hänseln; *itr* braten, rösten, schmoren *a. fig*; *to ~ o.s.* sich aufwärmen; *s* (Stück *n*) Braten *m*; Bratenfleisch; Braten; *fam* Picknick *n*; *fam* Anpfiff; Spott, Hohn *m*; *a* gebraten, geröstet; Brat-, Röst-; *~ (of) pork, veal* Schweins-, Kalbsbraten *m*; **~ beef** Roastbeef *n*, Rinder-, Rostbraten *m*; *Am fam* Zigarre *f*, Anpfiff *m*; **~ chicken** Brathuhn *n*; **~er** ['-ə] (Brat-)Rost *m*; Röstmaschine *f*; Bratgeflügel; Spanferkel *n*; **~ing** ['-iŋ] Braten; *(Kaffee)* Rösten *a. tech*; *fam* Spotten *n*; *Am fam* Abreibung *f*; *~~-jack* Bratspieß *m*, Bratenwender *m*; **~ meat** Braten (-fleisch *n*) *m*; **~ venison** Rehbraten *m*.

*

rob [rɔb] *tr (Sache)* rauben; *(Person)* berauben; *s.o. of s.th.* jdm etw rauben; jdn e-r S berauben; jdm etw ab-, wegnehmen; plündern, ausrauben; *itr* räubern; **~ber** ['-ə] Räuber *m*; *~~ baron* Raubritter *m*; *~~ farming* Raubbau *m*; **~bery** ['-əri] Raub(überfall) *m*; *fig* Räuberei *f*; *highway ~~* Straßenraub *m*.

robe [roub] *s* (Ober-)Gewand, Kleid *n*, Mantel *m*; Robe *f*, Talar; Morgen-, Hausrock, *Am (bath, slumber ~)* Bademantel *m*; *(elegantes)* (Damen-)Kleid *n*; *Am* Decke *f*, Fell *n*; *pl* Kleider *n pl*, Kleidung *f*; *tr itr* (sich) e-n Talar, Morgenrock überziehen; (sich) ankleiden; *baby's ~* Kinderkleid *n*; *night ~ (Am)* Nachthemd *n*; *the gentlemen of the ~* die Juristen *m pl*; *~ of office* Amtstracht *f*.

robin ['rɔbin] *(~ redbreast) orn* Rotkehlchen *n*; *Am* Wanderdrossel *f*.

roborant ['roubərənt] *a pharm* stärkend; *s* Stärkungsmittel, Tonikum *n*.

robot ['roubɔt] *s* Roboter *a. fig*; Maschinenmensch; *tech* Automat *m*; *(~ pilot) aero* Selbststeuergerät *n*; *attr* Roboter-; mechanisch, automatisch.

robust [rə'bʌst, *Am* 'roub-] stark, kräftig, kraftvoll, robust; kräftig gebaut, muskulös; *(Arbeit)* schwer; *fig* selbstsicher; *(Humor)* derb; **~ness** [-nis] Stärke, Kraft, Robustheit *f*.

rock [rɔk] **1.** Gestein(smasse *f*) *n*; Fels(en) *m*, Klippe *f*; *Am fam* Stein; *fig* Felsen, Rückhalt *m*, feste Burg; *fig* gefährliche Klippe *f*, Gefahrenpunkt *m*; Lutschstange *f*, Kandis *m*; *pl sl* (Edel-)Stein *m*, Geldstück *n*, Zaster *m*; *the R~* Gibraltar *n*; *on the ~s (fam)* aufgeschmissen; blank, ohne Geld; *(Getränk)* mit Eiswürfeln; *as firm as a ~* felsenfest, unerschütterlich; **~-bottom** *a (bes. Preis)* sehr, äußerst niedrig; **~ bottom** *s fig* Tiefpunkt *m*; *to go down to ~~* der Sache auf den Grund gehen; **~ burst** *min* Gebirgsschlag *m*; **~-cake** *Art* kleine(r) trockene(r) Kuchen *m*; **~-candy** Kandiszucker *m*; **~-crusher** Stein-, Erzbrecher *m*; **~-crystal** Bergkristall *m*; **~ debris** *geol* Felsgeröll *n*; **~-drill** Gesteinsbohrmaschine *f*; **~-garden, ~ery** Steingarten *m*; **~-gas** Erdgas *n*; **~iness** ['-inis] felsige, steinige Beschaffenheit *f*; **~-oil** Petroleum *n*; **~-plant** Stein-, Felsen-, Alpenpflanze *f*; **~ pressure** *min* Gebirgsdruck *m*; **~-salt** Steinsalz *n*; **~-slide** Felsrutsch *m*; **~y** ['-i] felsig; steinig; steinhart; *fig* hart wie Stein; **2.** (Spinn-)Rocken *m*; **3.** *tr* schaukeln, wiegen; kippen; *(Kind)* einwiegen *a. fig*; *fig* einlullen; rütteln, erschüttern; *(Sand, Kies durch ein Sieb)* schütteln; *sl* aufschrecken; *itr* schaukeln; schwanken(*on* auf); wackeln, wippen; (er)zittern; *(durch ein Sieb)* geschüttelt werden; *(Schiff)* schlingern; *to make ~* erschüttern; *to ~ asleep* in den Schlaf wiegen; *to ~ the boat (fig)* das Unternehmen gefährden; **~-and-roll, ~'n 'roll** Rock 'n' Roll *m*; **~er** ['-ə] Wiegen-, Schaukelstuhlkufe *f*; *Am* Schaukelstuhl; *tech (~~ arm)* Schwing-, Kipphebel *m*; Wippe *f*; *pl* ungepflegte(r) Halbstarke(r) *m*; *to go off o.'s ~~ (fam)* den Verstand verlieren; **~ing** ['-iŋ] *a* schaukelnd; Schaukel-; *~~-chair* Schaukelstuhl *m*; *~~-horse* Schaukelpferd *n*; **~y** ['-i] *fam* schaukelnd, schwankend, wack(e)lig *a. fig*.

rocket ['rɔkit] **1.** *s* Rakete *f*; *mil sl* scharfe(r) Verweis *m*; *itr (Vogel)* senkrecht aufsteigen; pfeilschnell davonschießen; wie aus der Pistole geschossen kommen; *(Filmstar)* über Nacht berühmt werden; *(Preise)* rasch steigen, hochschnellen; *tr* mit Raketen beschießen; **~ aircraft, plane** Raketenflugzeug *n*; **~ battery** *mil* Raketenbatterie *f*; **~ bomb** V-Waffe, Raketenbombe *f*; **~ drive, power** Raketenantrieb *m*; **~eer** [-'tiə] Raketenforscher *m*; **~ engine, jet, motor** Raketentriebwerk *n*; **~-launching site** Raketenabschußbasis *f*; **~-propelled** *a* mit Raketenantrieb; *supersonic ~~ fighter* Überschallraketenjäger *m*; **~ propulsion** Raketenantrieb *m*; **~ range** Raketenversuchsgelände *n*; **~ry** ['-ri] Raketentechnik *f*; **2.** *bot* Senf-, Raukenkohl *m*; (*bes.* Rote) Nachtviole *f*.

*

rococo [rə'koukou] *s* Rokoko *n*; *a* Rokoko-; verschnörkelt.

rod [rɔd] Rute, Gerte *f*; *(biblisch)* Reis *n*; (Rund-)Stab, Stock *m*, Stange *f*; *tech* (Schweiß-)Draht *m*; Rute *f*, Rohrstock *m*; *fig* Strafe *f*; Herrscherstab *m*, Zepter *n*; Macht, (Gewalt-) Herrschaft; *(fishing-~)* Angelrute; Meßstange, -latte; Rute *(16½ Fuß od 5,03 m)*; (Quadrat-)Rute *f (26,7 qm)*; *anat (Netzhaut)* Stäbchen *n*; Bakterie *f*; *Am sl* Schießeisen *n*; *pl tech* Gestänge *n*; *to have a ~ in pickle for s.o. (fig)* mit jdm ein Hühnchen zu rupfen haben; *to kiss the ~ (fig)* die Hand, die e-n schlägt, küssen; *to make a ~ for o.'s own back* sich das Leben (unnütz) schwer machen; sich etw selbst einbrocken; *curtain-~* Gardinenstange *f*; *lightning ~* Blitzableiter *m*; *measuring-~* Meßlatte *f*; *piston ~ (tech)* Kolbenstange *f*, Pleuel *m*; **~ antenna** Stabantenne *f*; **~ bacterium** Stäbchenbakterie *f*; **~ grid** Stabgitter *n*; **~-iron** Stabeisen *n*; **~ magnet** Stabmagnet *m*; **~-shaft** Pumpenschacht *m*; **~-shaped** *a* stabförmig; **~-winding** *el* Stabwick(e)lung *f*.

rodent ['roudənt] *a* nagend; *med* fressend; *s* Nagetier *n*; *fam* Ratte, Maus *f*.

rodeo [ro(u)'deiou, 'roudiou] *pl -os Am* Viehauftrieb; Sammelplatz *m* (für Vieh); Wildwestschau *f*.

rodomontade [rɔdə'mɔnteid, -'teid] Prahlerei, Aufschneiderei *f*.

roe [rou] **1.** *(~ deer)* Reh *n*; **~buck** Rehbock *m*; **2.** *(hard ~)* (Fisch-) Rogen *m*; *soft ~* Milch *f*.

Roentgen ['rɔntjən, 'rʌnt-, -gən] *attr* Röntgen-; **r~ize** ['-aiz] *tr* röntgen, durchleuchten; **r~ogram** [rɔnt'genəgræm] Röntgenbild *n*, -aufnahme *f*; **r~oscope** [-ə'skoup] Röntgenschirm *m*; **r~otherapy** [rɔntjəno(u)'θerəpi] Röntgentherapie, -behandlung *f*; **~ rays** *pl* Röntgenstrahlen *m pl*.

rogation [ro(u)'geiʃən] *meist pl rel* Bittgesang *m*; *R~ days* die drei Tage *m pl* vor Himmelfahrt; *R~ Sunday* (Sonntag) Rogate *m*; *R~ week* Himmelfahrtswoche *f*.

rogu|e [roug] Schuft, Schurke, Strolch; *hum* Schelm; Spaßvogel; *zoo* Einzelgänger *m*; widerspenstige(s) Pferd *n*; *biol* Mißbildung *f*; *~~s' gallery (Am)* Verbrecheralbum *n*; *~~'s march (Am)* unehrenhafte Entlassung *f*; **~ery** ['-əri] Schurkenstreich *m*; Schurkerei, Schuftigkeit *f*; *pl* Streiche *m pl*; **~ish** ['-iʃ] schurkenhaft, schurkisch, schuftig; gewissenlos; schelmisch.

roil [rɔil] *tr Am (Flüssigkeit)* trüben; *fam* ärgern, aufbringen, reizen, auf die Nerven gehen *od* fallen (*s.o.* jdm); **~y** ['-i] *Am* trübe; *fig* ärgerlich, gereizt.

roister ['rɔistə] *itr fam* großtun, *fam* angeben; lärmen, toben; **~er** ['-rə] Krakeeler *m*.

role, rôle [roul] *theat fig* Rolle *f*; Amt *n*, Funktion *f*; *to play a ~* e-e Rolle spielen; *leading ~* Hauptrolle *f*; *title-~* Titelrolle *f*.

roll [roul] *itr* rollen *(a. Augen, Wogen, Donner)*; (auf Rädern) laufen, fahren; auf der Walze sein, wandern; rotieren; *(Trommel)* wirbeln; *(Himmelskörper)* kreisen; *(Schiff)* schlingern; *(im Gehen)* schwanken, dahinschlenkern; vorwärts-, vorankommen; *(Zeit, Wogen)* dahinrollen; *(Meer)* wogen; sich rollen, sich wälzen; *tr* rollen, wälzen; *(Straße, Eisen)* walzen; rotieren, kreisen lassen; zs.rollen, (auf)wickeln (*into* in); einwickeln (*in* in); *(Zigarette)* drehen; *(die Augen)* rollen, verdrehen; *(Teig)* (aus)rollen; *(Rasen)* walzen; *(Wäsche)* rollen, mangeln; *(Ärmel)* ohne Falte bügeln; *tech* kalandern, walzvergüten; *typ* einschwärzen; *gram* rollend (aus)sprechen; *Am sl* bestehlen, berauben, *theat* anfangen; *s* Rollen *n*; Rolle; Walze; Tapeten-, Papier-, Pergamentrolle *f*; *jur* Terminkalender *m*; Mutter-, Stammrolle *f*, Register, Verzeichnis *n*, Liste; Akte, Urkunde *f*; Brötchen *n*, Semmel *f*, Rundstück *n*; *(Küche)* Roulade *f*; (Fett-)Wulst *m*; *(Schiff)* Schlingern *n; arch* Schnörkel *m; sport aero* Rolle *f;* (Trommel-)Wirbel *m;* Grollen, Rollen *n (d. Donners);* (Rede-)Fluß *m; pl* Archiv; *sl* Moos *n,* Zaster *m,* Moneten *pl,* Stange *f* Geld; *to call the ~* die Namen verlesen; *to keep the ~s* Protokoll führen; *to strike off the ~s (Rechtsanwalt)* von der Liste streichen; disqualifizieren; *to ~ in money* im Geld schwimmen; *~ed gold, glass, plate, steel* Walzgold, -glas, -blech *n,* -stahl *m; death-~* Liste *f* der Toten; *membership ~* Mitgliederliste *f; pay ~* Lohn-, Gehaltsliste *f; to ~* **about** umherrollen; *to ~* **along** entlangrollen; *fam* eintrudeln; *to ~* **away** (sich) entfernen; wegrollen; *to ~* **back** *(Preise)* herabsetzen; festlegen; zurückrollen; *to ~* **by** vorbeirollen; *to ~* **down** herunterrollen, -kullern; *to ~* **in** anrollen; hereinströmen; (an Land) wogen; *fam (Geld)* sich anhäufen; *fam* zu Bett gehen; *to ~* **off** abrollen; *to ~* **on** *itr* weiterrollen; *(Zeit)* verfließen; *tr (Kleidungsstück)* überziehen; *to ~* **out** *tr* aus(ea.)rollen; *itr fig* schwankend hinausgehen; *fam* aufstehen; *to ~~ the red carpet (fig)* jdn feierlich, mit e-m großen Bahnhof empfangen; *to ~* **over** sich umdrehen; sich kugeln, kopfüber hinfallen; *to ~* **round** *(wie im Kreis)* zurückkehren, wiederkommen; *to ~* **up** *tr* auf-, zs.rollen; zs.falten; einwickeln; anhäufen; *(Ärmel)* aufkrempeln; *itr fam* anrollen; sich aufhäufen; hereinströmen; kommen, erscheinen; **~away** *a (Möbel)* Roll-; **~-back** *Am* Preissenkung, -festsetzung *f;* (Personal-, Gehalts-)Abbau *m;* **~-call** *mil* Anwesenheitsappell, Namensaufruf *m;* **~-collar** Rollkragen *m;* **~-film** Rollfilm *m;* **~-fronted cabinet** Rollschrank *m;* **~-on (belt)** Hüfthalter *m,* Kors(el)ett *n;* **~-top desk** Rollschreibtisch *m;* **~-train** Walzenstraße *f;* **~-up** Abbrechen *n,* Abbau *m;* **~-way** Roll-, Gleitbahn *f.*

roller ['roulə] *tech* Trag-, Laufrolle; Rolle, Walze *a. typ; (~-bandage)* Rollbinde; *mar* Woge, Sturzsee *f; orn* Purzler, Tümmler *m (Taube); road ~* Dampfwalze *f;* **~ bearing** *Am tech* Rollenlager *n;* **~ blind** Rollvorhang *m,* Marquise *f;* **~ coaster** *Am* Achter-; Berg-und-Talbahn *f;* **~-skate** *s* Rollschuh *m; itr* Rollschuh laufen; **~ towel** Rollhandtuch *n.*

rollick ['rɔlik] *itr* fröhlich, ausgelassen, übermütig sein, (herum)tollen; **~ing** ['-iŋ] fröhlich, lustig, ausgelassen.

rolling ['rouliŋ] *a* rollend *(a. Ton, Donner);* sich drehend; *mar* schlingernd; *(Gang)* schwankend, unsicher; wogend; *(Rauch)* dick; *(Gelände)* wellig, wellenförmig; *(See)* hohl; *s* Rollen, Walzen; *mar* Schlingern; *(Donner)* Rollen *n;* **~ capital** Betriebskapital *n;* **~ chair** Rollstuhl *m;* **~ collar** Rollkragen *m;* **~ door** Rolltür *f;* **~ machine** Kalander *m;* **~-mill** Walzwerk *n;* **~-pin** Teigrolle *f,* Wellholz *n;* **~ press** Rotations(druck)presse *f;* **~ stock** *rail* rollende(s) Material *n,* Wagenpark *m;* **~ train** Walzstraße *f.*

roly-poly ['rouli'pouli] *a* dick u. rund, rundlich, untersetzt, *fam* pumm(e)lig; *s* Pummelchen *n; Br* Schinkenrolle *f.*

Roman ['roumən] *a* römisch; römisch-katholisch; *s* Römer(in *f*); römische(r) Katholik *m; r~ (typ)* Antiqua *f;* **~-Catholic** römisch-katholisch; **~-ization** [roumənai'zeiʃən] Romanisierung *f;* **~ize** ['roumənaiz] *tr* romanisieren; **~ nose** Adlernase *f;* **~ numerals** *pl* römische Ziffern *f pl;* **~ road** Römerstraße *f.*

Romance [rə'mæns] *a (Sprache)* romanisch; *s* romanische Sprachen *f pl.*

romance [rə'mæns] *s* Ritter-, Abenteuer-, Liebesroman *m;* Abenteuer *n (pl); fig* Romantik; Übertreibung, Erfindung; Liebesgeschichte; *fig* Poesie; *mus* Romanze *f; itr* abenteuerliche Geschichten erzählen; übertreiben, aufschneiden; *tr fam* den Hof machen (*a girl* e-m Mädchen).

Romanesque [roumə'nesk] *a* romanisch; *s* Romanik *f,* romanische(r) (Bau-)Stil *m.*

Romanic [ro(u)'mænik] *(Sprache)* romanisch.

romantic [rə'mæntik] *a* romantisch; unwirklich, erdichtet; wirklichkeitsfremd, unrealistisch; *s* Romantiker *m;* **~ism** [-tisizm] romantische(s) Wesen *n,* romantische(r) Geist *m;* Romantik *f;* **~ist** [-tisist] *(Kunst)* Romantiker *m.*

Romany ['rɔməni] Zigeuner(sprache *f*) *m.*

Rom|e [roum] Rom *n;* römische Kirche *f; when in ~~, do as the Romans do* man muß mit den Wölfen heulen; **~ish** ['-iʃ] *pej* römisch(-katholisch), päpstlich.

romp [rɔmp] *itr* herumtollen, sich *(im Spiel)* austoben, ausgelassen sein; *sl* rasen; *s* Range, Göre *f,* Wildfang *m;* Herumtollen; lärmende(s) Spiel *n; to ~ home, in (fam)* mühelos gewinnen; **~er** ['-ə] *meist pl* Spielhöschen *n.*

röntgen ['rɔntjən] *s. Roentgen.*

roneo ['rouniou] *s* Vervielfältigungsapparat *m (Schutzmarke); tr* vervielfältigen.

rood [ru:d] Kreuz (Christi); Kruzifix *n;* Rute *f (etwa 5—7 m);* Viertelsmorgen *m (40 (Quadrat-)Ruten = 10,7 a);* **~-loft** Lettnerempore *f;* **~-screen** *arch rel* Lettner *m.*

roof [ru:f] *s* Dach (*over o.'s head* über dem Kopf) *a. fig; fig* Haus, Heim *n;* (Altar-)Himmel *m; mot* Verdeck *n; aero* Gipfelhöhe *f; min* Hangende(s) *n,* First(e *f*) *m; tr* mit e-m Dach versehen; bedachen, decken; *fig* unterbringen, beherbergen; *to ~ over* überdachen; *under s.o.'s ~* unter jds Dach, in jds vier Wänden, bei jdm zu Hause; *to raise the ~ (Am fam)* Krach machen *od* schlagen; sich über alles hinwegsetzen; *the ~ of heaven* das Himmelszelt; *the ~ of the mouth* der harte Gaumen; *the ~ of the world* das Dach der Welt, hochgelegene(s) Tafelland *n;* **~ covering** Dachdeckerarbeiten *f pl;* Dachhaut *f;* **~ed-in** *a* überdacht; **~er** ['-ə] Dachdecker *m; fam* Dankbrief *m;* **~-garden** Dachgarten *m;* **~ing** ['-iŋ] Bedachung(smaterial *n*) *f;* Dach *n,* -haut *f; ~~-felt, -paper* Dachpappe *f; ~~-tile* Dachziegel *m;* **~less** ['-lis] *a* ohne Dach; *fig* obdachlos; **~ light** *mot* Decken-, Innenleuchte *f;* Oberlicht *n;* **~ tile** Dachziegel *m;* **~-tree** Firstbalken *m; fig* Dach *n;* **~ truss** Dachstuhl *m.*

rook [ruk] **1.** *s* Saatkrähe *f; fig* Schwindler, Betrüger *m; itr tr* betrügen; *fam* hereinlegen, übervorteilen; **~ery** ['-əri] (Saatkrähen-)Brutkolonie *f,* Krähenhorst *m; fig* alte Mietskaserne *f;* Elendsviertel *n;* **2.** *(Schach)* Turm *m.*

rookie ['ruki] *sl mil* Rekrut; *allg* Neuling, Anfänger *m.*

room [ru(:)m] *s* Raum, Platz; (Wohn-) Raum *m,* Zimmer *n; fig* Raum, Grund, Anlaß *m,* Gelegenheit (*for* für); *pl* Wohnung *f; itr Am* (möbliert) wohnen (*at* in; *with* bei; *together* zusammen); *tr Am* unterbringen; *in s.o.'s ~* an jds Stelle, statt jds; *to make ~ for* Platz schaffen für; *to take too much ~* zuviel Platz einnehmen *od* beanspruchen; *there is ~ for improvement* es ließe sich noch manches verbessern; *~s to let* Zimmer zu vermieten; *bed, dining-, living-~* Schlaf-, Eß-, Wohnzimmer *n; reception ~* Empfangsraum *m; show ~s (pl)* Ausstellungsräume *m pl; state ~ (mar)* Kabine *f; strong ~* Banktresor *m; waiting ~* Wartezimmer *n; ~ and board* Unterkunft u. Verpflegung; **~ clerk** *Am* Empfangschef *m (im Hotel);* **~ed** [-d] *a in Zssgen: two-~~, three-~~ flat* Zwei-, Dreizimmerwohnung *f;* **~er** ['-ə] *Am* (Unter-)Mieter *m;* **~ette** [ru'met] *Am rail* Einzelabteil *n* (im Schlafwagen); **~ful** ['-ful] Zimmervoll *n* (*of people* Leute); **~iness** ['-inis] Geräumigkeit *f;* **~ing house** *Am* Mietshaus *n* mit möblierten Wohnungen; **~-mate** Stubengenosse, Kamerad *m;* **~-temperature** Zimmertemperatur *f;* **~y** ['-i] geräumig.

roorback, roorbach ['ru:əbæk] *Am pol* verleumderische(s) Gerücht *n.*

roost [ru:st] *s* Hühnerstange *f,* -stall *m; fam* Ruheplätzchen *n,* Schlafstelle *f; itr (Vogel)* sich auf die Stange setzen; *(Mensch)* zu Bett, schlafen gehen; schlafen; übernachten; hausen, wohnen; *at ~* auf der Stange; *fig* im Bett, schlafend; *to come home to ~ (fig)* auf den Urheber zurückfallen; *to go to ~* zu Bett, schlafen gehen; *to rule the ~* das Regiment führen; **~er** ['-ə] Hahn *m.*

root [ru:t] **1.** *s bot* Wurzel; Wurzelknolle; (Haar-, Zahn-)Wurzel *f; fig* Ahnherr *m,* Vorfahren *m pl;* Fundament *n,* Basis, Grundlage *f;* Kern *m fig;* Quelle *f,* Ursprung *m,* Ursache *f;* Urgrund *m; math* Wurzel *f; mus* Grundton *m; (Wort)* Wurzel *f,* Stamm *m; pl (~-crops)* Knollengewächse *n pl; itr* Wurzeln, *fig* Wurzel schlagen; beruhen (*in* auf); *tr* (ein)pflanzen; *fig* ansiedeln, einrichten; einimpfen, verankern (*in* in); *to ~ up, out, away* mit der Wurzel ausreißen; *fig* ausrotten, -merzen; *~ and branch (fig)* mit Stumpf u. Stiel, ganz u. gar, vollkommen; *to go to the ~ of s.th.* e-r S auf den Grund gehen; *to strike at the ~ of s.th. (fig)* etw an der Wurzel packen *od* angreifen; *to take, to strike ~* Wurzeln, *fig* Wurzel schlagen; *fig* sich einbürgern; *fear ~ed him to the ground* er stand vor Furcht wie angewurzelt; *square, cube, fourth ~ (math)* Quadrat-, Kubik-, 4. Wurzel *f;* **~age** ['-idz] Verwurzelung *f,* Wurzelwerk *n;* **~ beer** *Am* leichte(s) nichtalkoholische(s) Getränk *n;* **~ed** ['-id] *a* fest-, eingewurzelt; bodenständig; *~~ to the spot (fig)* festgewurzelt; **~-fallen** *a (Getreide durch Regen)* liegend; **~ hair** Haarwurzel *f;* **~less** ['-lis] wurzellos; **~let** ['-lit] Würzelchen *n,* Wurzelfaser *f;* **~ sign** *math* Wurzelzeichen *n;* **~stalk, ~stock** Wurzelstock *m a. fig;* **~y** ['-i] stark verwurzelt; wurzelartig; **2.** *tr (mit der Schnauze)* aufwühlen; durchwühlen; *itr* wühlen (*through* in); *fam* schuften; *Am sl sport* (durch laute Zurufe) anfeuern, anspornen (*for s.o.* jdn); applaudieren (*for s.o.* jdm); *to ~ about* herumwühlen in; *to ~ up* aufstöbern; **~er** ['-ə] *Am sport* Anfeuerer *m;* **~ing-tooting** *Am sl* lärmend; aufregend; *(Geschichte)* handlungsreich.

rope [roup] *s* Seil, Tau; *mar* (Tau-)Ende *n;* Strick, Strang *m;* Schnur *f;* Tod *m* durch Erhängen; *Am* Lasso *m* od *n; (Zwiebeln)* Bund *m; (~ team)* Seilschaft *f; (Getränke)* Fadenziehen *n,* Zähflüssigkeit *f; pl* Tauwerk; *(Boxen)*

Seil *n*; *tr* mit e-m Seil befestigen, zs.binden, fesseln; *(Bergsport)* anseilen; *Am* mit dem Lasso fangen; *itr (Flüssigkeit)* Fäden ziehen; *to ~ down* (sich) abseilen; *to ~ in* einschließen; *s.o.* jdn (ein)fangen, *sl* einwickeln; bei e-r Razzia fangen; *to ~ off, to ~ out* mit e-m Seil absperren; *fig* ausschließen; abspenstig machen; *on the ~* angeseilt; *on the ~s (Boxen)* im Seil; *sl* erschossen, fertig, erledigt; *on the high ~s* in gehobener Stimmung; hochfahrend; *to be at the end of o.'s ~* am Ende sein, nicht mehr können; *to give s.o. (plenty of) ~* jdm die Zügel schießen, jdm Spielraum lassen; *to know the ~s (fam)* die Schliche kennen; genau Bescheid wissen; *to put on the ~* sich anseilen; *to show s.o. the ~s* jdn einweihen; *~ of pearls* Perlenschnur *f*; *a ~ of sand (fig)* ein schwacher Halt *m*; **~-dancer, -walker** Seiltänzer *m*; **~-end, ~'s end** Tauende *n*; **~-ferry** Seilfähre *f*; **~-ladder** Strickleiter *f*; **~-maker** Seiler, Reepschläger *m*; **~ry** ['-əri], **-walk, -yard** Seilerei; Seilerbahn *f*; **~way** (Draht-)Seilbahn *f*; **~-yarn** Kabelgarn *n*; *fig* Bagatelle *f*; **ropiness** ['-inis] Klebrigkeit, Zähigkeit *f*; **ropy** ['-i] Fäden ziehend, klebrig, zäh; tau-, seilartig.

ros|aceous [ro(u)'zeiʃəs] *a bot* Rosazeen-; rosenartig; rosenfarben, rosig; **~ary** ['rouzəri] Rosenbeet *n*, -garten; *rel* Rosenkranz *m*; **~e** [rouz] *s bot* Rose; Rosenfarbe *f*, Rosa *n*; *mar* Windrose; *(Gießkanne)* Brause(nkopf *m*); Rosette; Fensterrose; *med* Wundrose; *fig* Schönheit *f*; *a* rosenfarben, rosig, rosa; *tr* röten, e-n rosigen Hauch geben (*the cheeks* den Wangen); *under the ~~* heimlich, im Vertrauen; *no bed of ~~s* kein reines Vergnügen; *not to be all ~~s* nicht vollkommen sein; *not to be on a bed of ~s* nicht auf Rosen gebettet sein; *to gather (life's) ~~s* das Leben genießen; *no ~~ without a thorn* keine Rose ohne Dornen; *climbing, rambler ~~* Kletterrose *f*; *~~-beetle* Rosenkäfer *m*; *~~-bud* Rosenknospe *f*; *Am* hübsche(s) Mädchen *n*; *~~-bush* Rosenstrauch *m*; *~~-colo(u)red (a)* rosenfarben, rosig; *fig* schön, anziehend; *~~-garden* Rosengarten *m*; *~~-hips (pl)* Hagebutten *f pl*; *~~ leaf* Rosenblatt *n*; *~~-oil* Rosenöl *n*; *~~-pink* rosarot; *~~-tree* Rosenstock *m*; *~~-water* Rosenwasser *n*; *~~-window* Fensterrose *f*; *~~-wood* Palisander-, Rosenholz *n*; **~eate** ['rouziit] rosenfarben, rosa; Rosen-; *fig* rosig, optimistisch; **~emary** ['rouzməri] *bot* Rosmarin *m*; **~eola** [ro(u)'zi:ələ] Röteln *pl*; **~ette** [ro(u)'zet] Rosette *f a. arch*; **~iness** ['rouzinis] rosenrote Farbe *f*; rosige(r) Zustand *m*; **~y** ['rouzi] rosenrot, rosig *a. fig*; mit Rosen geschmückt; blühend; *fig* vielversprechend; optimistisch.

rosin ['rɔzin] *s* (*bes.* Geigen-)Harz, Kolophonium *n*; *tr* mit Kolophonium einreiben; **~y** ['-i] harzig; harzartig.

roster ['roustə, *Am* 'rɔ-] *bes. mil* Namens-, Dienstliste *f*; *(duty ~)* Dienstplan *m*; Tabelle *f*.

rostr|al ['rɔstrəl] *a* schnabelförmig; Schnabel-; **~um** ['-əm] *pl a. -a* ['-ə] *hist* Schiffsschnabel *m*; Rednerbühne; Tribüne *f*; Rednerpult *n*, Kanzel *f*; Dirigentenpult *n*; *zoo* Rüssel, Schnabel *m*.

rot [rɔt] *itr* (ver)faulen, vermodern, verwesen; *fig* (sittlich) verkommen, verderben, sinken; entarten; *geol* verwittern; *sl* quatschen; *tr* verfaulen lassen; *(Flachs)* rösten; *tech* verderben, angreifen; *sl* durch den Kakao ziehen; hänseln; *s* Fäulnis, Verwesung *f*; Moder *m*; *fig* Demoralisierung; Pechsträhne; *zoo bot* Fäule *f (Krankheit)*; *sl* Un-, Blödsinn, Quatsch *m*; *interj* Quatsch! *to ~ away, to ~ off* dahinschwinden, verfaulen; *to talk ~ (sl)* Unsinn, Kohl reden; **~-gut** *sl* Fusel *m*.

rot|a ['routə] *rel* Rota; Runde *f*, Umlauf *m*; Routine; Dienstliste *f*; **R~arian** [rou'tɛəriən] Rotarier *m*; **~ary** ['-əri] *a* rotierend, sich drehend, kreisend; *s (~~ machine)* Rotationsmaschine *f*; *Am* Kreisverkehr *m*; *R~~ Club* Rotary-Club *m*; *~~ current* Drehstrom *m*; *~~ engine* Umlaufmotor *m*; *R~~ International* Weltvereinigung *f* der Rotary-Clubs; *~~ momentum* Drehmoment *n*; *~~ motion* Kreis-, Drehbewegung *f*; *~~ press (typ)* Rotationspresse *f*; *~~ pump* Umlaufpumpe *f*; *~~ switch* Drehschalter *m*; *~~ tower crane* Turmdrehkran *m*; *~~ traffic* Kreisverkehr *m*; *~~ wing* Drehflügel *m*; **~ate** [ro(u)'teit] *itr* rotieren, sich drehen; umlaufen; *fig* turnusmäßig abwechseln; *tr* rotieren lassen; *fig* turnusmäßig wechseln lassen; *to ~~ crops* im Fruchtwechsel anbauen; **~ation** [-'teiʃən] Umdrehung, Rotation *f*; *(Geschoß)* Drall; *fig* Kreislauf, turnusmäßige(r) Wechsel, Turnus *m*; *by, in ~~* turnusmäßig, im Turnus; *~~ of crops (agr)* Fruchtwechsel *m*; **~ative** ['routətiv], **~atory** ['-tətəri, -'tei-] rotierend; *fig* turnusmäßig wechselnd, abwechselnd; *~atory storm* Wirbelsturm *m*; **~ogravure** [routəgrə'vjuə] (Kupfer-)Tiefdruck *m*; **~or** ['routə] Rotor, Drehzylinder, Induktor; *aero* Drehflügel *m*; *~~ core* Anker(kern) *m*; *~~ plane* Drehflügelflugzeug *n*, Hubschrauber *m*; **~umbulator** [rou'tʌmbjuleitə] *film* Kamerawagen *m*; **~und** [ro(u)'tʌnd] rundlich; *(Stimme)* voll, wohltönend; *(Stil)* hochtrabend; **~unda** [ro(u)'tʌndə] Rund-, *bes.* Kuppelbau *m*, Rotunde *f*; **~undity** [ro(u)'tʌnditi] Rundlichkeit *f*; rundliche(r) Gegenstand *m*.

rote [rout] **1.** *s*: *by ~* mechanisch, gedankenlos, wie aufgezogen; **2.** *s Am* Meeresrauschen *n*.

rott|en ['rɔtən] *a* (ver)faul(t), verfallen, zersetzt, verdorben; *(Zahn)* faulig; weich; brüchig; *(Balken)* morsch; *fig (sittlich)* verdorben, heruntergekommen; niederträchtig, gemein; bestechlich; *sl* scheußlich, gräßlich, ekelhaft; *to feel ~~ (sl)* auf dem Hund sein; **~er** ['-ə] *sl* Lump, gemeine(r) Kerl *m*.

rouge [ru:ʒ] *s* Rouge *n*, rote Schminke *f*; *tech* Polierrot *n*; *tr* schminken; *itr* sich schminken, Rouge auflegen.

rough [rʌf] **1.** *a* rauh, uneben, holp(e)rig; rauh(haarig), zottig; rauh, heftig; *(Wetter)* stürmisch; *(See)* aufgewühlt, rauh, stark bewegt; *(Wein)* herb; ungestüm, wild; roh, grob, ungehobelt, *fam* ungeschliffen; ungefügig; mißtönend; heftig, hart, scharf; roh, unbearbeitet, ungehobelt; primitiv, einfach; *(Edelstein)* ungeschliffen; unausgewogen, unausgeglichen; annähernd, ungefähr; *fam* scheußlich, ungemütlich; *(Phonetik)* aspiriert; *sl* ungenießbar; *Am fam* gefährlich, schwierig, unangenehm; **2.** *adv* grob, roh; **3.** *s* unebene(r) Boden *m*; Rohmaterial *n*; rohe(r) Zustand, Rohzustand *m*; *das* Rauhe, Grobe, Harte *(e-r S)*; *das* Unfertige; Abfall; *fig* Grobian, Flegel, Rüpel, Lümmel, Rowdy *m*; **4.** *tr* (auf-)rauhen, roh behauen; *sport (to ~ up)* rauh, roh, grob behandeln; zureiten; *tech* vorbehandeln, -drehen, schruppen; *(to ~ in, to ~ out)* in groben Zügen, im Umriß, roh entwerfen, skizzieren; **5.** *itr* rauh werden; sich flegel-, lümmelhaft, rüpelig benehmen; **6.** *at a ~ estimate* grob geschätzt; über den Daumen gepeilt; *in the ~* unfertig; im Rohzustand; *adv* ungefähr, in groben Umrissen *od* Zügen; *to be ~ on s.th.* für etw nachteilig sein; *to take the ~ with the smooth* die Dinge nehmen, wie sie kommen; *to treat s.o. ~* jdn derb anfassen; *to ~ it* sich roh benehmen; sich (mühsam) durchschlagen; *Am* ohne jede Bequemlichkeit, ganz primitiv leben; *it's ~ on him* er hat kein Glück; alles hackt auf ihm herum; *the ~ of life* die Beschwerlichkeiten, die Mühsale des Lebens; **~-and-ready** ungefähr, über den Daumen gepeilt; Überschlags-; *(Mensch)* urwüchsig; *(Arbeit)* zs.gepfuscht; **~-and-tumble** *s* Schlägerei *f*; *fig* Wirren *pl*; *a* wüst, wirr, regellos, wild; **~ adjustment** Grobeinstellung *f*; **~age** ['-idʒ] rohe(s), grobe(s) Material; *bes.* grobe(s), zellulosereiche(s) Futter *n*, grobe Nahrungsmittel *n pl*; **~calculation** Überschlag *m*; *on a ~~* nach ungefährer Berechnung; **~-cast** *s arch* Roh(ver)putz; Roh-, erste(r) Entwurf *m*; *a* roh verputzt; *fig* im Entwurf; *tr arch* (roh)verputzen; roh, in den Umrissen entwerfen; **~-coated** *a zoo* langhaarig; **~ copy** erste(r) Entwurf *m*, Skizze *f*; **~ customer** grobe(r) Klotz, freche(r) Kerl *m*; **~-cut:** *~~ tobacco* Grobschnitt *m*; **~ diamond** ungeschliffene(r) Diamant *m*; *fig* Rauhbein *n*; **~ draft** Rohentwurf *m*; **~-drill** *tr tech* vorbohren; **~-dry** *tr (Wäsche)* (nur) trocknen lassen *(ohne zu bügeln)*; **~en** ['-n] *tr* (auf)rauhen; *itr* rauh werden; **~ estimate, guess** ungefähre Schätzung *f*, Überschlag *m*; **~-grained** *a* grobkörnig; **~-handle** mißhandeln; **~-hew** *irr tr* grob behauen; *fig* grob umreißen, flüchtig entwerfen; **~ house** *sl* Krach, Krawall *m*, Schlägerei *f*; **~-house** *tr* e-n Streich spielen (*s.o.* jdm); *itr* randalieren; **~ly** ['-li] *adv* rauh, grob; barsch; ungefähr, annähernd, überschlägig, etwa; **~-machine** *tr tech* vor(be)arbeiten, schruppen; **~-neck** *Am sl* Rowdy *m*; **~ness** ['-nis] Rauheit, Unebenheit; Heftigkeit *f*, Ungestüm *n*, Wildheit; Roheit, Grobheit; Härte, Schärfe; *(Wein)* Herbheit; Roheit, Einfachheit *f*; **~-plane** *tr* vorhobeln; **~-rider** Be-, Zureiter *m*; **~-shod** *a (Pferd)* scharf beschlagen; *to ride ~~ over s.o.* jdn rücksichtslos behandeln; **~-spoken** *a* grobschnäuzig; **~-up** *sl* Schlägerei *f*.

roul|ade [ru:'lɑ:d] *(mus u. Küche)* Roulade *f*; **~ette** [ru:'let] Roulett *n (Glücksspiel)*.

R(o)umania [ru(:)'meinjə] Rumänien *n*; **~n** ['-ən] *a* rumänisch; *s* Rumäne *m*, Rumänin *f*; (das) Rumänisch(e).

round [raund] **1.** *a* rund, kreis-, kugelförmig, zylindrisch; gerundet; rundlich; im Kreis herumgehend; *(Vokal)* offen; *(Zahl)* ganz; voll, rund; abgerundet, abgeschlossen; Rund-; ungefähr; beträchtlich, ansehnlich, bedeutend; *(Stil)* vollendet, gefeilt; ausgereift; *(Stimme)* voll, wohlklingend; lebhaft, schnell; *(Schritt)* ausgreifend; *(Rede)* offen, klar, bestimmt; eindeutig; uneingeschränkt; *(Lüge)* frech; **2.** *s* Rundteil *n*; Scheibe *(Brot)*; Rundung *f*; Kreis *m*; (Leiter-)Sprosse; *(~ of beef)* (Rinder-)Keule; Rundheit; Runde *(Menschen u. Getränke)*; Kreisbewegung *f*; Rundtanz, Reigen; Rundgesang *m*; Runde *f*, Um-, Ablauf *m*, Folge, Serie *f*; (ganzer) Umfang *m*, Gesamtheit *f*; Rundgang *m*, *mil* Runde; *mil* Salve *f*; Schuß *m (Munition)*; *(Schußwaffe)* Ladung; Lachsalve; *(Bier)* Lage; *(Brot)* Scheibe; *sport* Runde *f*; *mus* Kanon; *astr* Umlauf *m*; **3.** *tr* runden, rund machen; *fig* offen aussprechen; abrunden, vollenden; herumgehen, -fahren, -reiten um; umgeben, einschließen; sich im Kreise bewegen lassen; herumdrehen (*towards* nach); **4.** *itr* sich im Kreise bewegen, e-n Kreis(bogen) beschreiben; sich umdrehen, kehrtmachen; sich runden, rund werden; sich abrunden (*into* zu); herfallen (*on, upon* über), verraten (*on s.o.* jdn); anfahren (*on s.o.* jdn); **5.** *adv* im Kreise; (rings)herum; rund(her)um; auf, nach allen Seiten, in allen Richtungen, allgemein, auf der ganzen Linie; hier u. dort, da; annähernd, nahezu, beinahe, fast; **6.** *prp* um (... herum); durch alle Teile *gen*; überall in; *(zeitlich)* während; **7.** *to ~ off (tech)* abrunden *a. com, fig*; *to ~ out (fig)* abrunden, vervollständigen; *to ~ up (Vieh)* zs.treiben; *fam (Menschen)* zs.bringen; **8.** *all, right ~* ganz herum; *all the year ~, the whole year ~* das ganze Jahr über; *in ~ numbers* rund, ungefähr *adv*; *in the ~ (fig)* vollständig; realistisch; *taken all ~* alles insgesamt; *~ and ~* immer wieder herum; *the other way ~* anders herum; **9.** *to bring ~* wieder zu sich kommen lassen; *to come ~* herüberkommen; *s.o.* jdn überlisten, *fam* einwickeln; sich bei jdm einschmeicheln, lieb Kind machen; *to get s.o. ~* jdn herumkriegen; *to go ~ (fig)* umgehen; herumgehen (*in a circle* in e-m Kreis); *to go, to make o.'s ~s* s-e Runde, s-n Rundgang machen; *to go the ~ (fig)* die Runde machen (*of* in); *to hand ~* herumreichen; *to look ~* sich *(in e-r Stadt)* umsehen; sich *(nach hinten)* umsehen, -schauen; *to make the ~s* die Runde machen; *to show s.o. ~* jdn herumführen; *to take s.th. all ~* etw von allen Seiten betrachten; *to turn ~* sich umdrehen; *is there enough tea to go ~?* reicht der Tee für alle? *what are you hanging ~ for?* was stehen Sie hier 'rum? worauf warten Sie? *the daily ~* die täglichen Pflichten; *~-the-clock* ganztägig; *~ of beef* Rinderkeule *f*; **~about** *a* umständlich, weitschweifig; umgebend, einschließend; *s (~~ way)* Umweg *m*; Umschweife *pl*; kurze, enge (Herren-, Knaben-)Jacke *f*; *Br* Karussell *n*; *Br* Kreisverkehr *m*; *to hear s.th. in a ~~ way* etw hintenherum hören; **~ dance** Rundtanz *m*; **~el** ['raundl] (kleine) runde Scheibe *f*, Medaillon *n*; (Flugzeug-)Kokarde *f*, Erkennungszeichen; Rondell *n*; **~elay** ['raundilei] Rundgesang *m*; **~er** ['-ə] *Am sl* Verschwender, Lebemann, Trunkenbold, Berufsverbrecher *m*; *tech* Rundmaschine *f*; *pl mit sing* Schlagball *m*; **~ game** Gesellschaftsspiel *n*; **~-hand** Rundschrift *f*; **R~head** *hist* Rundkopf *m (engl. Puritaner des 17. Jhs. mit kurzer Haartracht)*; **~-house** *s mar* (Achter-)Hütte, Latrine *f*; *Am rail* Lokomotivschuppen *m*; *a Am sl* weitausholend; **~ing** ['-iŋ] Rundung *f*, Bogen *m*; Auf-, Abrundung *f*; **~ly** ['-li] rundweg, rund heraus; ehrlich, offen; gründlich; in Kreisform; **~ness** ['-nis] Rundheit; *fig* Aufrichtigkeit, Geradheit; *(Stil)* Ausgeglichenheit *f*; **~ oath** kräftige(r) Fluch *n*; **~ robin** Beschwerde-, Bittschrift *f* mit kreisförmig angeordneten Unterschriften; *Am sport* Wettspiel *n* im Rahmen e-r Gruppe; **~ rod** Rundstab *m*; **~-shot** Kanonen-, Gewehrkugel *f*; **~shouldered** *a* mit runden Schultern; **~sman** ['-zmən] Laufjunge, -bursche; Austräger; *Am (Polizei)* Unterwachtmeister *m*; **~-table** runde(r) Tisch *m*; Tafelrunde *f*; *~~ conference* Konferenz *f* am runden Tisch; **~ trip, tour, voyage** Rundfahrt; *Am* Hin- u. Rückfahrt *f*; *aero* Hin- u. Rückflug *m*; *~~ ticket* Rückfahrkarte *f*; **~-up** zs.getriebene(s) Vieh *n*, Auftrieb *m*; Treffen *n*, Versammlung; zs.getriebene Menschengruppe; Razzia; *Am sl* gewalttätige Beilegung *f* e-s Streites.

roup [ru:p] Pips *m (Geflügelkrankheit)*; **~y** ['-i] pipsig.

rous|e [rauz] *tr (Wild)* aufscheuchen; aufwecken (*from* aus); aus der Ruhe, in Bewegung bringen; Leben bringen in, in Unruhe versetzen; aufregen, anstacheln, antreiben, aufmuntern (*to* zu); (auf)wecken; Bewußtsein zurückbringen; *(Bewunderung)* erregen, erwecken; *(Entrüstung)* hervorrufen; *itr (Wild)* die Flucht ergreifen; *(to ~~ up)* auf-, erwachen; wach, aktiv, lebendig werden; *s mil* Wecken *n*; Weckruf *m*; *to ~~ to action* zur Tat anstacheln; **~er** ['-ə] *fam* unverschämte, freche Lüge; Sensation *f*; **~ing** ['-iŋ] laut; zündend, aufwühlend; aktiv, lebhaft; *fam* gewaltig; erstaunlich; frech; *(Beifall)* brausend.

roust [raust] *tr Am sl* verhaften; *(to ~ up) fam* auf die Palme bringen; *(to ~ out) fam* 'rausschmeißen.

roustabout ['raustəbaut] *Am* Wander-, Gelegenheits-, ungelernte(r) Arbeiter, Handlanger *m bes. mar.*

rout [raut] **1.** *s* Pöbel, Mob *m*; Menschenmasse *f*, Volkshaufen *m*, Rotte; *jur* Zs.rottung, Friedensstörung; *mil* wilde Flucht; völlige Niederlage; Verwirrung *f*; *tr (to put to ~)* in die Flucht schlagen; **2.** *itr (Schwein)* im Boden wühlen; *(to ~ about)* herumstöbern; *tr (den Boden)* aufwühlen; *(to ~ out, to ~ up)* aufstöbern; *tech* ausfräsen, -holen; *to ~ out of bed* aus dem Bett holen.

route [ru:t, *mil a.* raut] *s* Weg *m*, Straße, Strecke, Linie, Route *f*; Transportweg *m*; *Am* feste Kunden *m pl*, (Kunden-)Tour *f*; *mil* Marschbefehl *m*, -richtung; *tele* Verbindung *f*; *tr* transportieren (*via* über); in Marsch setzen, schicken, senden, leiten (*via* über); mit Leitvermerk versehen; *fig* leiten (*through* über); *~ step, march!* ohne Tritt, marsch! *air, overland, sea, shipping ~* Luft-, Land-, See-, Schifffahrtsweg *m*; *bus ~* Omnibusstrecke *f*; *~ of advance (mil)* Vormarschstraße *f*; *~ of approach* Anmarschweg *m*; *~ of transmission* Transportweg *m*; **~ card** Arbeitsablaufkarte *f*; **~ column** Marschkolonne, -ordnung *f*; **~ lightning** Streckenbefeuerung *f*; **~ map** Straßenkarte *f*; **~-march** Übungsmarsch; Marsch *m* mit Marscherleichterung; **~ signing** Streckenmarkierung *f*.

routine [ru:'ti:n] *s* (gewöhnlicher, normaler) Geschäftsgang *m*; Schablone, Routine(arbeit) *f*; *mil* Dienstbetrieb *m*; *a* routine-, gewohnheitsmäßig; mechanisch; laufend, gewöhnlich, normal, üblich; *to do s.th. as a matter of ~* etw routinemäßig tun; *to make a ~ of s.th.* etw zur Regel machen; **~-board** Dienstplan *m*; **~ inquiry, report** Routineanfrage *f*, -bericht *m*; **~ work** Routinearbeit *f*.

roux [ru:] *(Küche)* Mehlschwitze *f*.

rov|e [rouv] **1.** *itr* umherschweifen, -streifen, -irren; *tr* durchstreifen; herumirren in; *s* Wandern, Umherschweifen *n*; *to be on the ~~* herumvagabundieren; auf der Wanderschaft sein; **~er** ['-ə] Wanderer; *(sea-~~)* Seeräuber, Pirat; Rover *m (Pfadfinderführer)*; *fig* Fernziel *n*; **2.** *tr (Fasern)* vorspinnen; *(Wolle)* krempeln, ausfasern; *s* Vorgespinst(garn) *n*; **~er** ['-ə] Vorspinnmaschine *f*.

row 1. [rou] Reihe *a. agr*; *theat* (Sitz-)Reihe; (Auto-)Schlange; Häuserreihe, Zeile, Straße *f*; *in ~s* reihenweise; *in a ~* hintereinander; *a hard, long ~ to hoe (Am)* ein schweres, *iro* schönes Stück Arbeit; *to set in a ~* der Reihe nach aufstellen; **2.** [-] *itr tr* rudern; *s* Rudern *n*; Ruderfahrt, -strecke *f*; *to ~ down (tr)* beim (Wett-)Rudern überholen; *to ~ stroke* Bootsführer sein; *to go for a ~* rudern gehen; **~er** ['-ə] Ruderer *m*; **~(ing) boat** Ruderboot *n*; **~ing club** Ruderklub *m*; **~lock** Ruderklampe *f*; **3.** [rau] *s fam* Krawall, Tumult; Krach *m*; *fig fam* Abreibung *f*, scharfe(r) Tadel *m*; *itr fam* randalieren; streiten (*with* mit); *fam* 'runtermachen, -putzen; *to get into a ~* eins auf den Deckel kriegen; *to have a ~ with s.o.* mit jdm Krach haben; *to kick up a ~* Krach schlagen; *hold your ~ (pop)* halt den Schnabel!

rowan ['rauən] *(~-tree)* Eberesche *f*, Vogelbeerbaum *m*; **~-berry** Vogelbeere *f*.

row-de-dow, rowdydow ['raudi'dau] Radau, Lärm *m*.

rowd|iness ['raudinis] Rauflust; Rüpelhaftigkeit *f*; **~y** ['raudi] *s* Raufbold, Rabauke, Rowdy, Rüpel *m*; *a* rauflustig; rüpelhaft; gewalttätig, roh; **~yism** ['-iizm] Rauflust; Rüpelhaftigkeit *f*; rüpelhafte(s) Benehmen *n*.

rowel ['rauəl] *s* Spornrädchen *n*; *tr* die Sporen geben (*a horse* e-m Pferd).

rowen ['rauən] *Am agr* Grum(me)t *n*.

royal ['rɔiəl] *a* königlich; *fig* fürstlich, prächtig, prunkvoll; majestätisch, stattlich, edel; extra groß *od* fein; *s fam* Mitglied *n* der königlichen Familie; *Papierformat (20 × 25 Zoll = 50,8 × 63,5 cm als Druck-, 19 × 24 Zoll = 48,26 × 60,96 cm als Schreibpapier)*; *(~ sail, main ~)* Oberbramsegel *n*; *(Hirschgeweih)* Sprosse *f*; kapitale(r) Hirsch *m*; **~ fern** *bot* Königsfarn *m*; **R~ Highness**: *Your, His, Her ~~* Ew., S-e, Ihre Königliche Hoheit *f*; **~ism** ['-izm] Monarchismus *m*; Königstreue *f*; **~ist** ['-ist] Monarchist; Royalist; Königstreue(r) *m*; **~ mast** Großmast *m*; **~ palm** Königspalme *f*; **~ stag** *zoo* Zwölfender *m*; **~ty** ['-ti] Königtum *n*, Königswürde *f*, königliche(r) Rang *m*; *(Träger der)* Krone *f*; Königreich *n*; Majestät *f*; *meist pl* Kronrecht; Regal, Hoheitsrecht *n*; Abgaben, Lasten *f pl*; Lizenz(abgabe, -gebühr) *f*, Ertrags-, Gewinnanteil *m*, Tantieme *f*; Verfasserhonorar *n*, Autorenanteil *m*; *min (mining ~ties)* Förderabgaben *f pl*; *on a ~~ basis* gegen Zahlung e-r Lizenz.

rozzer ['rɔzə] *sl* Schupo *m*.

*

rub [rʌb] *tr* (ab-, ein)reiben; *(to ~ together)* anea.reiben; *(Pferd)* abreiben; (ab)wischen, scheuern, frottieren, reiben, polieren, bohnern, fegen; streifen (*s.th. against* mit etw an); wundreiben, -scheuern; einreiben (*in, into* in); *(Geweih)* fegen; *itr* (sich) reiben, scheuern (*against, on* an); sich abnutzen; *s* Reiben, Scheuern *n*; rauh- *od* wundgeriebene, durchgescheuerte

Stelle *f*; *fig* Hindernis *n*; Schwierigkeit; Unannehmlichkeit, ärgerliche Sache *od fam* Geschichte *f*; *Am fam das* Wesentliche, *die* Pointe; *to give s.th. a ~ up* etw abstauben; *to ~ o.'s hands (together)* sich (zufrieden) die Hände reiben; *to ~ shoulders, elbows with s.o.* mit jdm verkehren; *to ~ s.o. the wrong way* bei jdm anecken, Anstoß erregen; *there's the ~ (fam)* da liegt der Hase im Pfeffer; *there's a ~ in it (fam)* die Sache hat e-n Haken; *to ~* **along** *fam* sich durchschlagen; *~~ together* mitea. auskommen; *to ~* **down** abreiben, frottieren; massieren; zerreiben; blank, glatt reiben, scheuern; *fam* durchsuchen, filzen; *to ~* **in** einreiben (*the salve* die Salbe; *into the skin* in die Haut); *fig* einbleuen, -trichtern, -pauken; *to ~ it in* jdm etw unter die Nase reiben; *to ~* **off** *tr* wegreiben, -scheuern; abstreifen (*on* auf); *itr* sich abnutzen; *Am fam* abhauen; *to ~* **out** ausradieren; *Am sl* abmurksen, killen; *to ~* **through** *fig* durchstehen, überstehen; *to ~* **up** blank reiben; (auf)polieren; *fig (Kenntnisse)* auffrischen; *~~ against s.o. (fam)* mit jdm verkehren; **~bing** ['-iŋ] Reiben, Frottieren, Scheuern, Polieren, Putzen *n*; *~~-away* Abnutzung *f*; *~~-cloth* Frottiertuch *n*; *~~-down* Abnutzung *f*; Abreiben *n*; *~~-up* Putzen, Wichsen *n*; *~~ varnish* Schleiflack *m*; *~~-wax* Bohnerwachs *n*; **~-down** Abreiben, Frottieren *n*; Abreibung *a. fig*; Massage *f*; **~-joint** *Am sl* billige(s) Tanzlokal *n*; **~-stone** Schleifstein *m*; **~-out** *Am sl* Mord *m*.

rub-a-dub ['rʌbədʌb] *s* Rumtata, Getrommel *n*, Trommelwirbel *m*.

rubber ['rʌbə] *s* Polierer; Masseur *m*; Frottier-, Poliertuch *n*; Reibfläche *f*, -kissen *n*; *(india-~)* Gummi *m* od *n*, Kautschuk; Radiergummi *m*; *(~-band)* Gummiband *n*; *(Rad)* Gummireifen; *(Karten)* Robber *m*; *Am pop* Präservativ *n*; *pl* Gummi-, Überschuhe *m pl*; *itr Am sl* Stielaugen machen; *tr* mit Gummi überziehen; *hard ~* Hartgummi *m* od *n*; **~-articles, -goods** *pl* Gummiwaren *f pl*; **~-blanket** Gummituch *n*; **~-boots** *pl* Gummistiefel *m pl*; **~ check** *Am* gefälschte(r) Scheck *m*; **~ coating** Gummierung *f*; **~-cover** Gummiüberzug *m*; **~-dinghy** Schlauchboot *n*; **~-gasket, -joint, packing** Gummidichtung *f*; **~-glove** Gummihandschuh *m*; **~-heel** Gummiabsatz *m*; **~-hose** Gummischlauch *m*; **~ize** ['-raiz] *tr* mit Gummi überziehen *od* imprägnieren; gummieren; **~neck** *Am sl* Gaffer, neugierige(r) Mensch; Tourist *m*; *a* Touristen-, Reise-; *itr* sich den Hals ausrecken; interessiert besichtigen; **~-plant** Gummibaum *m*; **~-ring** Gummiring *m*; **~-roll** Gummiwalze *f*; **~-solution** Gummilösung *f*; **~-stamp** *s* Gummistempel *m*; *fam* abgedroschene Phrase *f*; sture(r) Beamte(r), Jasager *m*; *tr* (ab)stempeln; *fam* automatisch genehmigen; **~ stopper** Gummipfropfen *m*; **~ tape** Isolierband *n*; **~-tree** Gummibaum *m*; **~-truncheon** Gummiknüppel *m*; **~-tube** *(Rad)* Gummischlauch *m*; **~-tyre, tire** *mot* Gummireifen *m*, -decke *f*; **~y** ['-ri] gummiartig, dehnbar, zäh.

rubbish ['rʌbiʃ] Schutt, Abfall, Schund; *min* Abraum *m*, taube(s) Gestein; *fig* dumme(s) Zeug *n*, Blödsinn, Quatsch *m*; *interj* Unsinn! *to be all ~* nichts wert sein, nichts taugen; **~y** ['-i] nichts (mehr) wert, wertlos; minderwertig; *fam* blödsinnig.

rubbl|e ['rʌbl] (Bau-)Schutt *m*; *(~~-work)* Bruchsteinmauerwerk; *geol* Geschiebe *n*; **~y** ['-i] Schutt-; voller Schutt.

rube [ru:b] *Am sl* Bauer(ntölpel) *m*.

rub|efacient [ru:bi'feiʃ(j)ənt] *a s med* Rötung der Haut bewirkend(es Mittel *n*); **~efaction** [-'fækʃən] Rötung *f* der Haut; **~efy** ['ru:bifai] *tr (die Haut)* röten; **~ella** [ru'belə] *med* Röteln *pl*; **~icund** ['ru:bikənd] rötlich; *(Gesichtsfarbe)* frisch u. rot; **~y** ['ru:bi] *s min* Rubin *m*; Rubinfarbe *f*; *typ* Parisienne *f*; *a* rubinrot; *(Nase)* kupferrot.

rubric ['ru:brik] *s* Rubrik, Überschrift *f*, Titel, Paragraph *m*; liturgische, gottesdienstliche Regel *f*; *a* rot gedruckt *od* geschrieben; **~ate** ['-eit] *tr (Buch)* rot illuminieren; rubrizieren.

ruche [ru:ʃ] Rüsche *f*.

ruck [rʌk] **1.** *s* (große) Menge *f*; *fig (the common ~)* der große Haufen, die (Volks-)Massen *f pl*; *(Rennen)* übrige(s) Feld *n*; **2.** *s* Falte *f*, Kniff, Knick *m*; *tr itr* (sich) falten, (sich) kniffen; (zer)knittern; *to ~ up* zerknüllen, zerknautschen.

rucksack ['ruksæk, 'rʌk-] Rucksack *m*.

ruckus ['rʌkəs] *Am fam* Spektakel, Krawall, Tumult, Hexensabbat *m*.

ruction ['rʌkʃən] *sl* Krawall, Aufruhr *m* (*about* wegen).

rudder ['rʌdə] *mar* Steuer-, *aero* Seitenruder *n*; *fig* Richtschnur *f*.

rudd|iness ['rʌdinis] Röte; gesunde Farbe *f*; **~y** ['rʌdi] *a (Gesichtsfarbe)* frisch u. rot; gesund; rötlich; rot; *sl* verdammt, verflixt.

rude [ru:d] roh, primitiv, kunstlos; *(Entwurf)* flüchtig; barbarisch, unzivilisiert; primitiv; robust; bäu(e)risch, tölpelhaft; unhöflich, patzig, frech; unverschämt, ungezogen (*to* gegen); rauh, heftig, stark, kräftig, ungestüm, unsanft, heftig; *(Worte)* unpassend, unanständig; **~ness** ['-nis] Roheit; Primitivität; Grobheit, Unhöflichkeit *f*.

rudiment ['ru:dimənt] *biol* Rudiment *n*; *meist pl* Anfänge *m pl*, Elemente *n pl*, Anfangsgründe *m pl*; *zoo* erste(r) Ansatz, Ausgangspunkt *m* (*of* zu); **~al** [ru:di'mentl], **~ary** [-'mentəri] *biol* rudimentär; elementar, Anfangs-.

rue [ru:] **1.** *tr* bereuen, bedauern, beklagen; *you'll live to ~ it* du wirst es e-s Tages noch bereuen; **~ful** ['-ful] bedauerns-, beklagenswert; traurig, kummervoll, bekümmert, wehmütig; *the Knight of the R~~ Countenance* der Ritter von der traurigen Gestalt; **~fulness** ['-fulnis] Trauer *f*, Gram, Kummer, Jammer *m*; **2.** *bot* (*bes.* Garten-)Raute *f*.

ruff [rʌf] **1.** *hist* Halskrause *f*; *zoo* Halsgefieder *n*, Kragen *m*; (Blumentopf-) Manschette; Perückentaube *f*; Kampfhahn, -läufer *(Schnepfe)*; *(a. ~e)* Kaulbarsch *m (Fisch)*; *~ed grouse* nordamerik. Haselhuhn *n*; **2.** *itr (Karten)* mit Trumpf stechen; *tr (Trumpf)* ausspielen; *s* Stechen *n*.

ruffian ['rʌfjən] *s* Raufbold, Rohling, brutale(r) Mensch *m*.

ruffle ['rʌfl] **1.** *tr* kräuseln, fälteln; zerknittern; falten, in Falten legen; spreizen; *fig* aufregen, aufwühlen; *(Buch)* schnell umblättern; *(Karten)* mischen; *(Gefieder)* sträuben; *itr* sich kräuseln, faltig werden, Falten schlagen; *fig* sich aufplustern; sich aufspielen; sich aufregen; lärmen, Krach machen; *s* Kräuselung *f*; *(Wasser)* Kräuseln *n*; Rüsche *f (am Kleid)*; *zoo* Kragen *m*, Feder-, Haarkrause; *fig* Aufregung, Unruhe, Störung *f*; Lärm, Tumult *m*; **~r** ['-ə] Unruhestifter *m*; **2.** Trommelwirbel *m*; *tr itr* (e-n Trommelwirbel) schlagen.

rug [rʌg] *(kleinerer)* Teppich, Läufer *m*, Brücke *f*; *(travelling ~)* (Reise-)Decke; *(bedside ~)* Bettvorlage *f*; **~ joint** *Am sl* teure(r) Nachtklub *m*.

Rugby ['rʌgbi], **~ football** *sport* Rugby *n*.

rugged ['rʌgid] uneben, rauh, holp(e)rig; unregelmäßig, eckig, scharf; *(Fels)* zerklüftet; *(Gesicht)* runzelig, zerfurcht; rauh, hart, streng; kraß; *fig* grob, barsch, unhöflich; *Am* stark, kräftig, robust; **~ness** ['-nis] Unebenheit; Rauheit; Unregelmäßigkeit; Härte; Grobheit; *Am* Widerstandsfähigkeit, Robustheit *f*.

Rugger ['rʌgə] *sl* = *Rugby*.

ruin ['ru(:)in] *s* Ruine *f a. fig*; *pl* Trümmer *pl*, Trümmerhaufen *m*; *fig* menschliche(s) Wrack *n*; Verwüstung, Zerstörung *f*; *(a. wirtschaftl., sittl.)* Verfall; Ruin, Zs.bruch, Untergang *m*; *tr* verwüsten, zerstören, vernichten; *(to bring to ~)* ruinieren, zugrunde richten; *(Pläne)* zunichte machen; *(sittlich)* verderben; *(Gesundheit)* zerrütten; *(Mädchen)* verführen; *to go to ~* verfallen; **~ation** [rui'neiʃən] Zerstörung *f*; *fam* Verderben *n*; **~ous** ['-əs] einstürzend, verfallen(d), baufällig; zerstörerisch, verderblich, verheerend; verlustbringend; ruinös; *~~ price* Schleuderpreis *m*.

rul|e [ru:l] **1.** *s* Regel *a. math*; (Ordens-) Regel *f*; Grundsatz, Brauch *m*; Richtschnur; Gepflogenheit, Gewohnheit, Sitte; *com* Usance *f*; *die* Regel, *das* Übliche, *das* Gewöhnliche; Rechtsgrundsatz *m*; (Gesetzes-)Bestimmung, Vorschrift *f*; (Gerichts-)Entscheid *m*, Verfügung, Verordnung; Herrschaft, Regierung, Verwaltung, Leitung *f*; Lineal *n*, Zollstock *m*, Maß(stab *m*) *n*; *typ* Linie *f (Material)*; *pl* Satzungen *f pl*, Ordnung *f*; **2.** *tr* regeln, festlegen, -setzen, anordnen, bestimmen, entscheiden; regieren, verwalten, leiten, lenken; beherrschen; in Schranken halten, einschränken; verringern, herabsetzen; lini(i)eren; *(Linie)* ziehen; *itr* herrschen, regieren (*over* über); vorherrschen; gelten, gültig, in Kraft sein; *jur* e-n Entscheid treffen; *com (Preise)* notieren; *to ~~ off* e-n Schlußstrich ziehen unter, abschließen; *to ~~ out* (durch)streichen; ausschließen; für unzulässig erklären; **3.** *against the ~s* regelwidrig; *as a ~~* in der Regel, gewöhnlich *adv*, normalerweise; **4.** *to ~~ high (com)* ein hohes Kurs-, Preisniveau behaupten; *to ~~ the roost* den Ton angeben, *fam* die Hosen anhaben; Hahn im Korb sein; *to be against the ~~s* gegen die Regeln verstoßen; *to make it a ~~* es sich zur Regel machen (*to do s.th.* etw zu tun); *to make an exception to a ~~* e-e Ausnahme von der Regel sein; *to stick to the ~~s* sich an die Vorschriften halten; *the exception proves the ~~* die Ausnahme bestätigt die Regel; **5.** *home ~~* Selbstverwaltung *f*; *standing ~~* stehende Regel; Geschäftsordnung; Satzung *f*; *~~ of application* Durchführungsbestimmung *f*; *~~s of conduct* Verhaltensmaßregeln *f pl*; *~~s of the court* Prozeßordnung *f*; *~~s of the game* Spielregeln *f pl*; *~~ of law* Rechtsstaatlichkeit *f*; *~~ of the road* Verkehrsvorschrift *f*; *~~ of three (math)* Dreisatz *m*, Regeldetri *f*; *~~ of thumb* Faustregel *f*, Erfahrungssatz *m*; *by ~~ of thumb* über den Daumen gepeilt; *~~-joint* Scharniergelenk *n*; *~~-tape* Meßband *n*; **~er** ['-ə] Herrscher (*of, over* über), Beherrscher (*of, over* gen), Souverän *m*; Lineal *n*; Liniermaschine *f*; **~ing** ['-iŋ] *a* (vor)herrschend; geltend, gültig; maßgebend; *s* Beherrschung, Herrschaft, Regierung, Verwaltung *f*; *(~~ of the court)* Gerichtsentscheid *m*, (gerichtliche) Entscheidung; Lini(i)erung *f*, Gitterstrich *m*; *~~ pen* Reißfeder *f*; *~~ price* Tages-, Marktpreis *m*.

rum [rʌm] **1.** Rum; *Am allg pej* Schnaps, Alkohol *m*; **~dum** ['-dʌm] *Am sl* Säufer *m*; **~my** ['-i] *Am sl* Säufer *m*; **2.** *(a. ~my) sl* komisch, ulkig, eigenartig; *he is a ~ customer* mit dem ist nicht gut Kirschen essen.

Rumania(n) *s. Roumania(n).*

rumba ['rʌmbə] Rumba *m* od *f (Tanz)*.

rumbl|e ['rʌmbl] *itr (Donner)* rollen; poltern, rumpeln, rasseln, rattern; *(Magen)* knurren; *tr* rollen, rumpeln lassen; *(Laut)* rollen; *tech* in e-r Trommel mischen; *Am sl* kommen sehen, riechen; spitzkriegen; *to ~~ out* polternd, brummend sagen; *s* Rollen; Rumpeln, Gepolter *n*; *(Kutsche)* Bedientensitz; *mot (Am: ~~ seat)* Not-, Klappsitz *m*; *tech* Poliertrommel; *Am* Anzeige *f*, Polizeiaktion, Ausea.setzung *f* Jugendlicher.

rumbustious [rʌm'bʌstjəs, -tʃəs] *fam* grölend, randalierend.

rumen ['ru:mən] *pl -mina* ['-minə] Pansen, Vordermagen *m* (der Wiederkäuer).

rumin|ant ['ru:minənt] *a* wiederkäuend; Wiederkäuer-; *fig* nachdenklich; *s* Wiederkäuer *m*; **~ate** ['-eit] *itr tr* wiederkäuen; *fig* hin u. her überlegen; *itr fig* nachdenken, -sinnen (*about, upon, over* über); *to ~~ revenge* auf Rache sinnen; **~ation** [ru:mi'neiʃən] Wiederkäuen; *fig* Nachdenken, -sinnen *n*; **~ative** ['ru:minətiv, -eitiv] wiederkäuend; *fig* nachdenklich, grüblerisch.

rummage ['rʌmidʒ] *s* Trödel(kram), Ausschuß, Ramsch *m*; Durchstöbern, -suchen *n*; *(~ sale)* Ramsch-, Ausverkauf; Wohltätigkeitsbazar *m*; *tr* durchstöbern; (zollamtlich) durchsuchen; *(to ~ out, to ~ up)* aufstöbern, auskramen; *itr (to ~ about)* herumstöbern (*among, in* in); suchen (*for* nach).

rummer ['rʌmə] Humpen, Römer *m*.

rummy ['rʌmi] Rommé *n (Kartenspiel)*; *s. rum* 1. *u.* 2.

rumour ['ru:mə] *s* Gerede, Geschwätz; Gerücht *n* (*of* über); *tr* gerüchtweise (weiter-, herum)erzählen; *~ has it that, it is ~ed that* es geht das Gerücht, man munkelt, daß; *the ~ spread like wildfire* das Gerücht verbreitete sich wie ein Lauffeuer.

rump [rʌmp] *(Vieh)* Schwanz-, Nierenstück *n*, Lende *f*; *(Vogel)* Bürzel *m*; *Am = ~-steak*; *(Mensch)* Kreuz; Gesäß; *fig* Überbleibsel *n*, Rest *m*; *(~ parliament)* Rumpfparlament *n*; **~-steak** ['-steik] Rumpsteak *n*.

rumple ['rʌmpl] *tr* zerknittern, zerknüllen; runzeln; *(Haar)* zerzausen; *fam* verärgern.

rumpus ['rʌmpəs] *fam* Krawall, Krach *m*; *to kick up a ~~* Spektakel machen; *~* **room** *Am* Spielzimmer *n*.

*

run [rʌn] *irr ran* [ræn], *run* **1.** *itr* laufen, rennen, eilen, jagen; (sich) stürzen; schnell fahren, reisen; gleiten (*over* über); sich frei, ungehindert bewegen, sich entwickeln, wachsen; weglaufen, -rennen, enteilen, (ent)fliehen *(a. Zeit)*; *(Zeit)* verfließen, vergehen, zerrinnen; um die Wette laufen, an e-m (Wett-)Rennen, Wettbewerb teilnehmen, sich bewerben, als Kandidat auftreten; *(als erster, zweiter)* durchs Ziel gehen; *(Verkehrsmittel)* fahren, verkehren; *(Ball)* rollen; *(Rad)* sich drehen; *(Fisch) (regelmäßig zum Laichen)* schwimmen, wandern; *(Pflanze)* kriechen, klettern; *(Wind)* gehen, wehen; *(Gerücht)* umgehen, im Umlauf sein, sich (schnell) verbreiten; *(zeitlich)* gehen, führen, reichen; fortwährend in Bewegung sein, beständig gehen; *(Blut, Geld)* zirkulieren; *(Geld)* sich im Umlauf befinden; *(Zinsen, Wechsel)* laufen; *(Ausgaben)* sich belaufen (*to* auf); *(Verluste)* gehen (*into the thousands* in die Tausende); *(Geschäft, Maschine)* gehen, laufen, in Betrieb sein, arbeiten; *(Maschine)* funktionieren; *(Veranstaltung)* stattfinden, abgehalten werden, ihren Verlauf nehmen; ablaufen, vor sich gehen, s-n Fortgang nehmen, (an-)dauern; *theat* sich auf dem Spielplan halten (*for a year* ein Jahr lang); in Kraft, gültig sein, gelten; *(Text)* lauten, den Wortlaut haben; sich erstrecken, verlaufen, gehen, führen; *(Gewässer)* fließen, strömen, fluten; *(Fluß)* sich ergießen, münden (*into* in); *(Straße)* vorbeiführen (*by* an); *(Tränen)* rinnen; *(Nase)* laufen; *(Geschwür)* offen sein; schmelzen, zergehen; zerfließen; *(Farbe)* auslaufen; abgleiten, -prallen (*off s.o.* von jdm); nachlaufen (*after s.o., s.th.* jdm, e-r S); sich bemühen (*after, for* um); zufällig treffen (*into, (Am) across s.o.* jdn); stoßen (*into* auf); geraten (*into* an, in); durchmachen, erleben (*through s.th.* etw); sich beziehen (*on, upon* auf); sich befassen (*on, upon* mit); handeln (*on, upon* von); übereinstimmen (*with* mit); **2.** *tr* entlanggehen, -laufen, verfolgen, durchlaufen, -eilen, zurücklegen; *(Strecke)* rennen, laufen; *(Rennen)* laufen; verlassen; entgehen, entkommen, ausweichen, aus dem Wege gehen (*s.th.* e-r S), vermeiden, fliehen; *(Gefahr)* heraufbeschwören, riskieren; sich *(e-e Krankheit)* zuziehen; *(Tier)* treiben, jagen, verfolgen; weiden, auf die Weide führen; um die Wette laufen, in Wettbewerb treten mit; *(Pferd bei e-m Rennen)* laufen lassen; *(Kandidaten für e-e Wahl)* aufstellen; laufen, rollen, verkehren, umlaufen lassen; in Betrieb, in Gang halten; gelten, gültig sein, in Kraft lassen; machen, bringen (*into* zu; *into difficulties* in Schwierigkeiten); versetzen (*into a situation* in e-e Lage); befördern, transportieren; schmuggeln; zwängen, treiben, stoßen, drücken, stecken, stechen (*against* gegen; *into* in); *(Splitter in die Hand)* reißen; *(Seil)* hindurchziehen (*through* durch); *(Kabel)* verlegen; heften, schnell nähen; laufen, fließen lassen; eingießen; *metal* schmelzen, gießen; von sich geben, ausspeien; *(Geschäft)* betreiben, führen, leiten; *(Unternehmen, Versuch)* durchführen; *(Prüfung)* vornehmen; *(Maschine)* bedienen, handhaben; *(Blockade)* brechen; *(Haushalt)* führen; erscheinen lassen, veröffentlichen; *(Linie)* ziehen, einzeichnen; *(Spur)* verfolgen; *to ~ o.s.* sich stürzen (*into* in); **3.** *s* Lauf(en *n*) *m*, Rennen *n*; Laufschritt, schnelle(r) Gang *m*; Schnelligkeit *f* (im Laufen); (im Lauf) zurückgelegte Strecke; *theat* Spiel-, Laufzeit *f*; Ausflug *m*, Tour *(a. e-s Austrägers)*, (kurze *od* einmalige) Fahrt, Reise *f*; Verlauf, Fortschritt *m*; Richtung, Tendenz; (starke, anhaltende) Nachfrage *f*, (großer) Zustrom, Ansturm, Run *m* (*on* auf); (Hoch-)Konjunktur, Vogue, Mode; (ununterbrochene) Folge, Reihe, Serie *f*; Fluß, Strom *m a. fig*; *Am* Flüßchen *n*, Bach *m*, Bächlein *n*; Zeit, die e-e Flüssigkeit läuft; ausgelaufene Menge; *tech* Funktionsdauer, Betriebs-, Arbeitszeit *f*; Nutzeffekt *m*, -leistung; (Waren-)Gattung, Sorte, Klasse *f*; Weg, Gang, Kanal *m*, Rohr *n*; Weide, Trift *f*; *(Hühner)* Auslauf *m*; Bewegungsfreiheit *f*, freie(r) Verkehr *m*; Herde (in Bewegung befindlicher) Tiere; Laufmasche *f*; *mus* Lauf; *sport* Anlauf *m*; *aero* Rollstrecke *f*; *(bombing ~)* (Bomben-)Zielanflug *m*; **4.** *a* geschmolzen; *metal* gegossen; *(Honig)* Schleuder- *od* Leck-; *fam* geschmuggelt, Schmuggel-; **5.** *at a ~* in (großer) Eile; *in the long ~* auf die Dauer; *on the ~* auf den Beinen; auf der Flucht; *fig* in Betrieb; *with a ~* plötzlich, über Nacht; **6.** *the common ~* das Gewöhnliche, der Durchschnitt; *the ~ of events* der Gang der Ereignisse; *~ of ill luck* Pechsträhne *f*; *~ of the mill* Durchschnitt *m*; *~ of a wheel* Radkranz *m*; **7.** *to have the ~ of s.th. (fam)* freien Zugang zu etw haben; *to have a ~ for o.'s money* sich mächtig anstrengen müssen; *to have a considerable ~* sehr gefragt sein; *to take a ~* e-n Anlauf nehmen; **8.** *to ~ an advertisement* mehrmals inserieren; *to ~ to s.o.'s aid* jdm zu Hilfe eilen; *to ~ a blockade* e-e Blockade brechen; *to ~ in s.o.'s blood* jdm im Blut liegen; *to ~ s.o. close* jdm auf den Fersen sein; *fig* jdm gleichkommen; *to ~ cold (Blut)* gerinnen *fig*; *to ~ into danger* sich in Gefahr bringen; *to ~ into debt* in Schulden geraten; sich in Schulden stürzen; *to ~ dry* aus-, vertrocknen; *to ~ into, through ten editions (Buch)* die 10. Auflage erreichen; *to ~ errands, messages* Botengänge verrichten; *to ~ it fine* gerade aus-, hinkommen; *to ~ first, second* als erster, zweiter durchs Ziel gehen; *to ~ foul of* auflaufen auf *(ein Schiff)*; *fig* sich streiten mit; Schwierigkeiten bekommen mit; *to ~ the gauntlet* Spießruten laufen *a. fig*; *to ~ s.o. hard* jdm tüchtig zusetzen, *fam* einheizen; *to ~ with the hare and hunt with the hounds (fig)* auf beiden Schultern Wasser tragen; *to ~ o.'s head against a wall, into a post, a brick wall (fig)* mit dem Kopf durch die Wand wollen; *to ~ high (Preise)* steigen, in die Höhe gehen; *(Gefühle)* lebhaft, erregt werden; *to ~ hot* sich heißlaufen; *to ~ idle, light* Leerlauf haben; *to ~ low* zur Neige, zu Ende gehen; *to ~ mad* verrückt werden; *to ~ a match, a race* e-n Wettlauf machen, um die Wette laufen; *to ~ in s.o.'s mind* jdm im Kopf herumgehen; *to ~ a race* ein Rennen laufen; *to ~ off the rails* entgleisen; *to ~ riot* sich wie ein Verrückter benehmen; *bot* ins Kraut schießen, wuchern; *to ~ the risk* Gefahr laufen (*of being killed* ermordet zu werden); *to ~ to seed (fam)* aus der Art schlagen, entarten; *to ~ a ship on the rocks* ein Schiff auf den Felsen auflaufen lassen; *to ~ short* zu Ende gehen (*of s.th.* etw); *to ~ the show (sl)* der Chef vom Ganzen sein; den Laden schmeißen; *to ~ the streets* sich auf der Straße herumtreiben; *to ~ a temperature* Übertemperatur, leichtes Fieber haben; *to ~ wild* über die Stränge schlagen; völlig ausarten; verwildern; **9.** *I'm ~ning short of cash* mir geht das Bargeld aus; *he ran with tears* die Tränen liefen ihm über die Wangen; *he's ~ning a high fever* er hat hohes Fieber; *my blood ran cold (fig)* es lief mir eiskalt über den Rücken; *the play had a long ~* das Stück hielt sich lange auf dem Spielplan; *he who ~s may read* das leuchtet ohne weiteres ein; *the road ~s up the hill* die Straße zieht sich den Berg hinauf; *the tide is ~ning out* es wird Ebbe; **10.** *to ~* **about** herum-, umherlaufen; *(Kind)* herumspielen; *to ~* **across** begegnen, treffen (*s.o.* jdn), über den Weg laufen (*s.o.* jdm); *to ~* **after** hinterherlaufen; *to ~* **aground** auf Grund (auf)laufen; *to ~* **around** *Am* sich herumtreiben; *to ~* **away** weglaufen, -rennen, -fahren; *with* durchbrennen mit, durchgehen mit; verbrauchen, aufzehren; (zu) schnell überzeugt sein von, voreilig annehmen; *(Gefühl)* durchgehen mit; *(Mitbewerber)* abhängen, *fam* in die Tasche stecken; *(Preis)* haushoch gewinnen; *to ~* **back** zurückverfolgen; *to ~* **down** *itr (Mechanismus)* ablaufen; ermüden, (gesundheitlich) herunterkommen, nachlassen; *tr* umlaufen, -rennen, -reiten, -fahren; *(Schiff)* versenken; *(Menschen)* überfahren; erjagen, fangen, fassen, *fam* kriegen, schnappen; *(Zitat)* finden, aufspüren; herunter-, verkommen, auf den Hund kommen lassen; *(mit Worten)* schlecht-, heruntermachen, durch den Schmutz ziehen; *(Schrift)* überfliegen; *(Stelle)* (heraus)finden; *(Spur)* nachgehen; *to ~* **for** kandidieren für; *to ~* **in** *itr* hineinlaufen; vorbeikommen (*to s.o.* bei jdm); *tr mot* einfahren; (mit) einschließen, einbeziehen; *sl* in Nummer Sicher bringen, hinter Schloß u. Riegel setzen; *to ~ in the family (fig)* in der Familie liegen; *to ~* **into** stoßen auf, zs.stoßen mit; geraten in; unerwartet treffen; *to ~* **off** *itr* weglaufen, -rennen; *(Tier)* entlaufen; *with s.th.* mit e-r S durchgehen, -brennen; ablaufen; *tr (Wasser)* ablaufen lassen; abfließen von; *(Auswendiggelerntes)* herunterschnurren; *typ* abziehen, Abzüge machen von, drücken; *sport (durch e-n Entscheidungskampf)* entscheiden; *(Lager)* räumen; *to ~* **on** weitergehen, sich fortsetzen; weitermachen, fortfahren; (immer) weiterreden, nicht aufhören zu reden; (ohne Unterbrechung, *(Text)* ohne Absatz) fortlaufen; *(Schulden)* auflaufen; *to ~* **out** *itr* zu Ende gehen; *(Ware)* ausgehen; *(Bescheinigung)* ablaufen; hinausragen; *tr (Ware)* ausverkaufen; hinaus-, wegjagen, vertreiben; *on s.o.* jdn im Stich lassen; *to be ~~* am Ende *od* ausverkauft sein; *he ran out of supplies* die Vorräte gingen ihm aus; *to ~* **over** *itr* überlaufen, überfließen; *tr* überfahren; *(mit den Augen)* überfliegen, schnell durchsehen, (noch einmal) durchgehen, wiederholen; *to ~* **through** *tr* überfliegen, schnell durchsehen; durchbohren, erstechen; völlig verbrauchen; *(Vermögen)* durchbringen, verschwenden; *(Theaterstück)* proben; *itr (Zug)* durchfahren; *to ~* **up** *itr* hinauflaufen, -eilen; rasch anwachsen; sich summieren, sich belaufen (*to* auf); stoßen (*against* auf); im Preise steigen, anziehen; *tr* auf-, hochziehen; *(Flagge)* hissen; *mot* warmlaufen lassen; *fig* hinauftreiben, in die Höhe treiben, steigern, (rasch) anwachsen lassen; schnell errichten *od* bauen; *(Rechnungen)* auflaufen lassen; **~about** Landstreicher, Vagabund; kleine(r) Sportwagen *m*; kleine(s) Motorboot *n*; **~-around** *Am sl* ausweichende Antwort *f*; Hinhalten *n*; *to get the ~~* keine vernünftige Antwort kriegen; *to give the ~~* dumme Reden führen, um den heißen Brei herumreden, Ausflüchte machen; **~away** *s* Ausreißer; Deserteur; Flüchtige(r) *m*; wild gewordene(s) Pferd *n*; *a* flüchtig, entlaufen; schnell (an)steigend; hemmungslos; leicht errungen *od* gewonnen; entscheidend, Entscheidungs-; **~-down** *a (Mechanismus)* abgelaufen; *(gesundheitlich)* heruntergekommen, elend, *fam* kaputt; in schlechtem Zustand; verfallen; *s* kurze Zs.fassung; Reportage *f*; genaue(r) Bericht *m*; **~-in** *sport* Einlauf; *Am fam* Klamauk, Krach, Streit *m*; **~let** ['-lit], **~nel** ['-əl] Bächlein *n*, (kleiner) Wassergraben *m*, Rinnsal *n*; **~-off** Ablaufwasser *n*; Abfall, Ausschuß; *sport* Entscheidungslauf *m*, -spiel *n*; **~-through** summarische Wiederholung *f*; **~-on** *a typ* fortlaufend; *s* fortlaufend Gedruckte(s) *n*; **~-out** *sl* Abhauen, Entweichen *n*; **~way** (Wasser-)Rinne *f*; (Trampel-)Pfad, Wildwechsel *m*; Schneise; *sport* An-, Ablaufbahn; Fahr-, Rollbahn; Rampe *f*; Laufsteg *m*; *aero* Start-, Landebahn *f*; *~~ funnel* Anflug-, Landeschneise *f*; *~~ lighting* Start- u. Landebahnbefeuerung *f*; *~~ lights (pl)* Start- u. Landebahnfeuer *n*.

rundle ['rʌndl] (Leiter-)Sprosse *f*.

run|e [ru:n] Rune *a. fig*; Runen(in)schrift *f*; **~ic** ['ru:nik] *a* Runen-.

rung [rʌŋ] **1.** Querbalken *m*; Sprosse, Runge, Speiche; *fig* Stufe *f*; **2.** *pret u. pp von ring* 2.

runner ['rʌnə] Läufer, Renner *m*; Rennpferd *n*; Laufjunge, -bursche; *(bank ~)* (Bank-)Bote; *mil* Meldegänger; *sport* Sprinter *m*; Rennpferd *n*; (Kunden-)Werber, Schlepper; gängige(r) Artikel; *Am* Geschäftsführer; Makler; Schmuggler *m*; Schmuggelschiff *n*; Blockadebrecher; Bediener (e-r Maschine); *tech* Läufer *m*, Laufrolle, -walze *f*, -ring *m*, -rad *n*, *(~ rail)* -schiene *f*, Schieber *m*; (Schlitten-, Lande-)Kufe *f*; (Boden-, Tisch-)Läufer *m*; Laufmasche *f*; *bot* Ausläufer; *zoo* Laufvogel; Rotfuß *m*, Wasserralle *f*; *blockade-~* Blockadebrecher *m*; **~-bean** Stangen-, Laufbohne *f*; **~-up** *sport* zweite(r) Sieger *m*.

running ['rʌniŋ] *s* Laufen, Rennen *n*; *fam* Tour; (Autobus-)Strecke; Tätigkeit, Bedienung; Leitung, Führung *a. tech*; Kraft, Fähigkeit *f* zum Laufen; *tech* Einguß, Einlauf *m*; auslaufende, -gelaufene Flüssigkeit(smenge); *jur* Schmuggelware; *com* Laufzeit, Gültigkeitsdauer *f*; *a* sich schnell bewegend; *(Wasser)* fließend; schmelzend, sich verflüssigend, zergehend; *(Wunde)* eiternd; *(Handschrift)* flüssig; *(Pflanze)* kletternd, Kletter-; gerade, geradlinig; beweglich, gleitend; tätig, in Tätigkeit, in Betrieb; *(Konto)* laufend; fortlaufend, ununterbrochen; *(nachgestellt)* nach-, hinterea.; *in ~ order* betriebsfähig; *in, out of the ~* im, aus dem Rennen; *to be ~~* verkehren; *to make the ~~* das Rennen machen; das Tempo angeben; *fig* den Ton angeben; *to take up the ~~ (a. fig)* die Führung übernehmen; **~-board** *mot* Trittbrett *n*; *~* **commentary** laufende(r) Kommentar, fortlaufende(r) Bericht *m*; Funkreportage *f*, Hörbericht *m*; *~* **costs** *pl* Betriebsunkosten *pl*; *~* **end** freie(s) (Tau-)Ende *n*; *~* **fight** *mil* Rückzugsgefecht *n*; *~* **fire** *mil* Trommel-, *fig* Lauffeuer *n*; *~* **gear** *rail* Laufwerk *n*; *~* **hand** Kurrentschrift *f*; *~* **head, title** *typ* lebende(r) Kolumnentitel *m*; **~-in test** Probelauf *m*; *~* **knot, noose** Schlinge *f*; *~* **speed** Fahr-, Umlaufgeschwindigkeit *f*; *~* **start** fliegende(r) Start *m*; *~* **stone** Mahlstein *m*; *~* **time** Laufzeit *f*.

runt [rʌnt] *fam* Zwerg, Liliputaner *m*; lächerliche(r) Mensch, Knilch *m*; *zoo* Zwergrind *n*; *Art* Taube *f*.

rupee [ru:'pi:] Rupie *f (Münze)*.

rupture ['rʌptʃə] *s* Bruch *m*, Zerbrechen *n*; *med* (Eingeweide-)Bruch *m*, *(Gefäß)* Platzen *n*; *(Muskel)* Riß; *fig* Bruch, Abbruch *m (der Beziehungen)*; *tr itr* zerbrechen; zerreißen; *fig* abbrechen; *itr* sich e-n Bruch zuziehen.

rural ['ruərəl] *a* ländlich; bäurisch; landwirtschaftlich; Land-; **~ize** ['ruərəlaiz] *tr itr* verländlichen; *itr* auf dem Lande leben; verbauen.

ruse [ru:z] List *f*, Kniff, Trick *m*; *pl* Schliche *pl*.

rush [rʌʃ] **1.** *itr* (daher)stürmen, rasen, brausen, stürzen (*to* zu); hinein-, herabstürzen; sich stürzen (*into* in; *on, upon* auf); losschießen (*at s.o.* auf jdn); *tr* (schnell *od* heftig) drängen, stoßen, treiben, jagen, erledigen; schnell befördern, transportieren, schaffen (*to the hospital* in das Krankenhaus); *(Arbeit)* überstürzen; sich stürzen auf; im Sturm niederwerfen *od* nehmen; *(Fußball)* vorwärtsstürmen mit *(dem Ball)*; *sl* betrügen, hereinlegen; zu viel verlangen (*s.o.* von jdm; *for* für), neppen; *Am sl* sich heftig bewerben, sich nahezu umbringen um *(e-e Geliebte)*; *Am sl* angreifen (*s.o.* jdn); *Am sl (Studenten)* keilen; *to ~ o.s.* sich überstürzen; *to ~ s.o. for s.th.* jdn dringend um etw bitten; *s* Stürmen, Rasen, (Sich-)Stürzen *n*; Ausbruch; große(r) Andrang, Ansturm (*for* auf); (Geschäfts-, Verkehrs-)Stoß, Hochbetrieb *m*; lebhafte Nachfrage (*for* nach); Geschäftigkeit, Hast, Eile *f*; Rummel *m*; *(Fußball)* Vor(wärts)stürmen *n*; *(~ of current)* (Strom-)Stoß; *Am (Schule, Univ.) Art* Wettstreit, -bewerb *m*; *(~ act)* heftige(s) Werben *n*; *meist pl* erste Vorführung *f* (e-r Filmszene); *on the ~ (fam)* in aller Eile; *with a ~* plötzlich; *to ~ up (Preis)* hochtreiben; *to ~ s.o. off his feet (fig)* jdn überfahren; *to ~ headlong* sich Hals über Kopf stürzen; *to ~ through (fig)* durchpeitschen; *the blood ~ed to his face* das Blut stieg ihm ins Gesicht; *what's your ~?* wozu die Eile? **~ee** ['-i:] *Am sl* Keilfuchs *m*; **~er** ['-ə] *(Fußball)* Stürmer *m*; *~* **hour(s** *pl)* Hauptgeschäfts-, Hauptverkehrszeit *f*; *~* **job** eilige Arbeit *f*; *~* **order** Eilauftrag *m*; *~* **work** dringliche *od* schnell erledigte Arbeit *f*; **2.** *bot* Binse *f*, Rohr *n*; *not to be worth a ~* keinen Pfifferling wert sein; **~y** ['-i] mit Rohr bestanden; rohrartig; Rohr-.

rusk [rʌsk] Zwieback *m*.

russet ['rʌsit] *s* Gelb- *od* Rotbraun *n*; Rötling *m (Apfelsorte)*; *a* gelb- *od* rotbraun.

Russia ['rʌʃə] Rußland *n*; *(~ leather)* Juchten(leder *n*) *m* od *n*; **~n** ['-n] *a* russisch; *s* Russe *m*, Russin *f*; (das) Russisch(e); *~~ wolfhound* Barsoi, russische(r) Windhund *m*; **~nize** ['-naiz] *tr* russifizieren.

rust [rʌst] *s (iron ~)* Rost *m*; Rostfarbe *f*; *fig* verrottete(r) Zustand *m*, Verkommenheit *f*; *bot* Rost(krankheit *f*); Mehltau, Brand, Rostpilz *m*; *itr* verrosten; *bot* brandig werden; *fig* einrosten; *to rub the ~ off* entrosten; *fig* geschmeidig werden; **~iness** ['-inis] rostige(r) Zustand *m*; **~less** ['-lis], **~proof** rostfrei; **~-preventative** Rostschutzmittel *n*; **~-resisting** rostbeständig, nichtrostend; **~y** ['-i] rostig, verrostet; *bot* rostbefallen; *(Stimme)* rauh; *(Stoff)* verschossen; Rost-; *fig* eingerostet, eingeschlafen, vernachlässigt, aus der Übung, außer Gebrauch (gekommen), steif (geworden); rostfarben; heruntergekommen, schäbig; *to get ~~* rosten; *to turn ~~ (fig sl)* ärgerlich werden.

rustic ['rʌstik] *a* ländlich; Land-; bäurisch, schlicht, kunst-, schmucklos; *arch* roh bearbeitet; *s* Bauer *m*; **~ate** ['-eit] *itr* aufs Land gehen; auf dem Lande leben; *tr* aufs Land schicken; *(Studenten, Schüler)* (vorübergehend) relegieren; *arch* roh bearbeiten; **~ation** [rʌsti'keiʃən] Landleben *n*; Relegation *f*; **~ity** [rʌs'tisiti] Ländlichkeit, ländliche Art; Schlichtheit, Einfachheit, Kunst-, Schmucklosigkeit; Plumpheit *f*, linkische(s) Wesen; Landleben *n*; **~ work** *arch* Rustika *f*, Bossenwerk *n*.

rustl|e ['rʌsl] **1.** *itr* rascheln, rauschen; *(Seide)* knistern; *tr* rascheln mit; *s* Geraschel, Knistern, Rauschen *n*; **2.** *Am fam itr* sehr rührig sein; *tr* energisch anpacken; *tr itr* (Vieh) zs.-treiben *od fam* stehlen; *s Am fam* Schlüsselkind *n*; *to ~~ up (Am fam)* besorgen, auftreiben; rasch hinhauen; **~er** ['-ə] *Am fam* geschäftige(r) Mensch; *Am fam* Viehdieb *m*.

rut [rʌt] **1.** *s* (Wagen-)Spur, Furche *f*, G(e)leis(e) *n*; *fig* alte(s) Geleise, alte(r) Trott; *tr* furchen; *full of ~s*, **~ted** ['-id], **~ty** ['-i] *(Weg)* ausgefahren; *to get into a ~* in e-n Trott verfallen; *to lift s.o. out of the ~* jdn aus s-m Trott herausreißen; **2.** *s* Brunst; *(Jagd)* Brunft, Brunstzeit *f*; *itr* brünstig sein; **~tish** ['-iʃ] brünstig.

rutabaga [ru:tə'beigə, -'bɑ:gə] *Am* Kohl-, Steckrübe *f*.

ruthless ['ru:θlis] erbarmungs-, mitleid(s)los, unbarmherzig; **~ness** ['-nis] Unbarmherzigkeit, Mitleid(s)losigkeit *f*.

rye [rai] Roggen; *Am* (Roggen-) Whisky *m*.

S

S, s [es] *pl* **~'s** ['esiz] S, s *n*.

Sabbat|h ['sæbəθ] *rel* Sabbat; Sonntag *m*; *to keep (to break) the ~~* den Feiertag (ent)heiligen; *witches' ~~* Hexensabbat *m*; **~ic(al)** [sə'bætik(əl)] *a* Sabbat-; feier-, sonntäglich; *~~ year, leave* einjährige(r) Urlaub *m (Univ.)*.

sable ['seibl] *s zoo* Zobel(pelz) *m*; *(Heraldik)* Schwarz *n*; *pl* Trauerkleidung *f*; *a* Zobel-; *(Heraldik)* schwarz.

sabot ['sæbou] Holzschuh, (Holz-) Pantine *f*; **~age** ['sæbətɑ:ʒ] *s* Sabotage *f*; *tr* sabotieren; zerstören; *itr* Sabotage treiben; **~eur** ['-bətə:] Saboteur *m*.

sabre, *Am* **saber** ['seibə] *s* Säbel *m*; *tr* niedersäbeln; **~-rattling** *fig* Säbelrasseln *n*.

sabulous ['sæbjuləs] sandig.

sac [sæk] *anat zoo bot* Tasche *f*, Beutel *m*, Säckchen *n*.

sacchar|iferous [sækə'rifərəs] zuckerhaltig; **~ify** [sə'kærifai] *tr chem* verzuckern; **~imeter** [sækə'rimitə] Zukkergehaltsmesser *m*; **~in** ['sækərin] Süßstoff *m*, Sa(c)charin *n*; **~ine** ['sækəri:n, -ain] *a* zuckerhaltig; Zucker-; *fig iro* zukkersüß; *s* ['-i(:)n] Sa(c)charin *n*; **~ose** ['-rous] (Rohr- *od* Rüben-)Zucker *m*.

sacerdotal [sæsə'doutl] priesterlich; Priester-; **~ism** [-əlizm] Priesterwesen *n*.

sachem ['seitʃəm] Indianerhäuptling *m*; *fig* hohe(s) Tier *n*.

sachet ['sæʃei] Duftkissen *n*.

sack [sæk] **1.** *s* Sack; *(~ coat)* Umhang, Überwurf; weite(r), lose(r) Mantel *m*; Sackkleid *n*; *fam* Entlassung *f*; *Am sl* Schlafsack *m*; *Am sl* Falle *f*, Bett *n*; *tr* in e-n Sack tun; einsacken; *fam* den Laufpaß geben (*s.o.* jdm); *fam* ein-, in die Tasche stecken (*s.o.* jdn); *to ~ in, out, to hit the ~ (Am sl mil)* sich in die Falle, sich hinhauen; *to give the ~ (fam)* an die Luft setzen, entlassen; *to hold the ~ (Am fam)* in die Röhre, in den Mond gucken; **~cloth** Sacktuch *n*, -leinwand *f*; *in ~~ and ashes* in Sack und Asche; **~ coat** Sakko *m*; **~ful** ['-ful] Sackvoll *m*; **~ing** ['-iŋ] = *~cloth*; **~ race** Sackhüpfen *n*; **~ time** *Am sl* Schlafenszeit *f*; **2.** *s mil* Plünderung *f*; *tr (to put to ~)* plündern; **3.** trockene(r) spanische(r) Weißwein *m*.

sacr|al ['seikrəl] *rel anat* sakral; **~ament** ['sækrəmənt]: *the Blessed (Holy) S~* Abendmahl *n*, Kommunion *f*; *rel* Sakrament *n*; *to take the ~~* das Abendmahl nehmen, kommunizieren; **~amental** [sækrə'mentl] *rel* sakramental; Sakrament-; **~ed** ['seikrid] *a* heilig; biblisch; geweiht, unverletzlich; verehrt; ehrwürdig; *~~-music* Kirchenmusik *f*; **~edness** ['seikridnis] Heiligkeit; Unverletzlichkeit; Ehrwürdigkeit *f*; **~ifice** ['sækrifais] *s* Opfer *n a. fig*; *com* Verlust(geschäft *n*), Schaden *m*; *tr* opfern (*s.th. to s.o.* etw jdm) *a. fig*; *(to sell at a ~~) com* mit Verlust verkaufen; *itr* ein Opfer bringen; *to ~~ o.s.* sich (auf-) opfern (*for* für); *to give as a ~~* zum Opfer bringen; *to make ~~s* Opfer bringen; *self-~~* Selbstaufopferung *f*; *the supreme ~~* die Hingabe des Lebens; *~~ price* Verlustpreis *m*; *~~ of time* Zeitaufwand *m*; **~ificial** [sækri'fiʃəl] *a* Opfer-; Verlust-; **~ilege** ['sækrilidʒ] Sakrileg *n*; Kirchenraub; Frevel *m*, Entheiligung, -weihung *f*; **~ilegious** [sækri'lidʒəs] frevlerisch, schänderisch; gotteslästerlich; **~istan** ['sækristən] Sakristan, Küster, Mesner, Kirchendiener *m*; **~isty** ['sækristi] Sakristei *f*; **~osanct** ['sækro(u)sæŋ(k)t] sakrosankt, hochheilig, unverletzlich; **~um** ['seikrəm] *anat* Kreuzbein *n*.

*

sad [sæ(:)d] traurig, betrübt (*at* über); niedergeschlagen, kummervoll, bekümmert, unglücklich; traurig, betrüblich, trostlos; ernst, schlimm, unheilvoll; *(Fehler)* bedauerlich; *(Ort)* düster; trüb(e), dunkel; *fam* mies, *(übertreibend)* scheußlich, gräßlich; *~ to say* bedauerlicherweise; **~den** ['-n] *tr* traurig machen, betrüben; *itr* traurig, betrübt werden (*at* über); **~ness** ['-nis] Traurigkeit, Betrübtheit, Niedergeschlagenheit; Trostlosigkeit *f*.

saddle ['sædl] *s* Sattel *a. tech*; *(Tier)* Rücken *m*, Kreuz *n*; Bergsattel *m*; *mar* Klampe *f*; *tech* Schlitten *m*; *tr* satteln; bepacken, beladen, belasten *a. fig*; aufpacken, *fig* auferlegen (*on, upon s.o.* jdm); *to ~ s.o. with s.th.* jdm etw aufhalsen; *in the ~* im Sattel; *(fig)* in einflußreicher Stellung; *to be ~d with* belastet sein mit; **~back** hohle(r) Rücken; Bergsattel *m*; Nebelkrähe *f*; **~-bag** Satteltasche *f*; **~-blanket, -cloth** Woilach *m*; **~-bow** Sattelbogen *m*; **~-horse** Reitpferd *n*; **~r** ['-ə] Sattler *m*; **~-roof** Satteldach *n*; **~ry** ['-əri] Sattlerei *f*; (Pferde-)Geschirr *n*.

sad|ism ['sædizm, 'sei-, 'sɑ:-] Sadismus *m*; **~ist** ['-st] Sadist *m*; **~istic** [sæ'distik] sadistisch.

safari [sə'fɑ:ri] Safari, Großwildjagd *f*.

safe [seif] *a* heil, unversehrt, unbeschädigt; sicher (*from* vor); schützend; ungefährlich, gefahrlos; unversehrt; zuverlässig; sicher, geheuer; geschützt (*from* vor); vorsichtig; *(Ankunft)* glücklich; *tech* tragfest, -sicher; *s* Speiseschrank; Geld-, Panzerschrank, Safe, Tresor; *allg* Schutzbehälter *m*; *from a ~ quarter* aus zuverlässiger Quelle; *to be ~* in Sicherheit sein; *to be ~ to do s.th.* ganz sicher, bestimmt, mit Sicherheit etw tun; *(so as) to be on the ~ side* um ganz sicher zu gehen; *it is ~ to say* man kann ruhig sagen; *~ and sound* heil u. gesund; gesund u. munter; *cold ~* Gefrierfach *n*; **~-blower** *Am*, **~-breaker, -cracker** Geldschrankknacker *m*; **~-conduct** Schutzbrief *m*; sichere(s) Geleit *n*; **~-custody** *jur* sichere(r) Gewahrsam *m*; *(Bank)* Wertpapierdepot *n*; **~-deposit** *(~~ vault)* Tresor(raum) *m*, Stahlkammer *f*; *~~ box* Safe, Schließ-, Bankfach *n*; *~~ department* Tresorabteilung *f*; *~~ fee* Schließfachgebühr *f*; **~guard** ['-gɑ:d] *s* Schutz *m a. fig* (*against* vor); Sicherung, Vorsichtsmaßnahme *f* (*against* gegen); Schutzbrief *m*, Sicherstellung; *jur* Garantie, Sicherheit *f*, Schutzbestimmungen *f pl*; sichere(s) Geleit *n*; Schutzvorrichtung *f*; *tr* schützen, sichern (*against* vor); sicherstellen; in Verwahrung nehmen; **~keeping** sichere(r) Gewahrsam *m*; **~ness** ['-nis] Verwahrung *f*; **~ty** ['-ti] Sicherheit, Zuverlässigkeit; Gefahrlosigkeit *f*; *in ~~* in Sicherheit; *to bring (in)to ~~* in Sicherheit bringen; *to play for ~~* sichergehen, kein Risiko eingehen wollen; *~~ first* Sicherheit ist das wichtigste; Unfallschutz *m*; *~~-belt* Rettungsgürtel *m*; Sicherheits-, Anschnallgurt *f a. aero*; *~~ buoy* Rettungsboje *f*; *~~-catch* Sicherung(svorrichtung) *f*; *to release the ~~-catch (Gewehr)* entsichern; *~~-curtain (theat)* eiserne(r) Vorhang *m*; *~~ factor* Sicherheitsfaktor *m*; *~~-fuse (el)* Sicherung *f*; *~~-glass* nicht splitternde(s) Glas *n*; *~~ island, zone* Verkehrsinsel *f*; *~~-lamp* Sicherheits-, *bes.* Grubenlampe *f*; *~~-load* zulässige Belastung *f*; *~~-lock* Sicherheitsschloß *n*; *~~-match* Sicherheitsstreichholz *n*; *~~-measures (pl)* Sicherheitsmaßnahmen *f pl*; *~~-pin* Sicherheitsnadel *f*; *~~-razor* Rasierapparat *m*; *~~-regulations (pl)* Sicherheitsbestimmungen *f pl*; *~~-sheet* Sprungtuch *n*; *~~-valve* Sicherheitsventil *n*; *to sit on the ~~-valve (fig)* e-e Politik der Unterdrückung betreiben.

saffron ['sæfrən] *s bot* Safran *m*; Safrangelb *n*; *a* safrangelb.

sag [sæg] *itr* durchhängen, -sacken; lose hängen; *fig* schwächer werden, nachlassen; *(Preis)* nachgeben, sinken, sich abschwächen; *mar* abtreiben; *s* Durchhängen *n*, Senkung *f*; *fig* Nachlassen, Schwächerwerden *n*; Wertminderung *f*; *(Preise)* Sinken; *mar* Abtreiben *n*.

saga ['sɑ:gə] *(altnordische)* Saga; Heldengeschichte *f*; *~* **novel** (Familien-) Chronik *f (Romangattung)*.

sagac|ious [sə'geiʃəs] scharfsinnig, klug; **~ity** [sə'gæsiti] Scharfsinn *m*, Klugheit *f*.

sage [seidʒ] **1.** *a* weise, klug; *s* Weise(r) *m*; **2.** *bot* Salbei *m* od *f*; **~brush** *bot* Beifuß *m*.

Sagittarius [sædʒi'tɛəriəs] *astr* Schütze *m*.

said [sed, səd] *pret u. pp von say*; *a* besagt, vor-, oben erwähnt; *he is ~ to have done* er soll getan haben; es heißt, daß er getan hat, er habe getan; *it is ~ that* es heißt, man sagt, daß; *sooner ~ than done* das ist leicht gesagt!

sail [seil] *s* Segel *n*; *die* Segel *n pl*; Segelschiff(e *pl*) *n*; Schiff-, Seefahrt *f*; (Windmühlen-)Flügel *m*; *itr* segeln (*on the sea* auf dem Meer); fahren (*for* nach; *by* auf); zur See fahren; abfahren, auslaufen (*for, to* nach); in See stechen (*at* um); *(durch die Luft)* gleiten, schweben; *aero* segeln; fliegen; *fam* kräftig anpacken *fig* (*in s.th.* etw); *fam* anfahren, ausschimpfen (*into s.o.* jdn); *fam* stolz daherschreiten; hereinrauschen (*into* in); *tr (Schiff)* fahren, steuern; (auf e-m Schiff) befördern, fahren; *to ~ through (Am sl)* rasch, mühelos erledigen; *in full ~* mit vollen Segeln; *under ~* unter Segel; *to go for a ~* segeln gehen; *to lower ~* die Segel streichen; *to make, to set ~* die Segel setzen; in See stechen (*for* nach); *to shorten, to take in ~* die Segel einziehen, reffen; *fig* nachlassen, mit halbem Winde segeln; *fig* zurückstecken; *to take the wind out of s.o.'s ~s* jdm den Wind aus den Segeln nehmen; *to ~ against, close to, near (to) the wind (fig)* mit Schwierigkeiten zu kämpfen haben; sich am Rande des Erlaubten bewegen; **~-arm** Windmühlenflügel *m*; **~-boat** Segelboot, -schiff *n*; **~-cloth** Segeltuch *n*; **~er** ['-ə] Segler *m (Schiff)*; **~ing** ['-iŋ] *s* Segeln *n*; (Segel-)Schiffahrt; (Ab-)Fahrt *f* (*for* nach); *a* Segel-; Schiff(ahrt)s-; *plain ~~ (fig)* klare Sache *f*; *~~-boat, -ship, -vessel* Segelboot, -schiff *n*; **~or** ['-ə] Seemann, Matrose; flache(r) Strohhut *m*; *to be a good (bad) ~~* (nicht) seefest sein; *~~ blouse, collar, hat, suit* Matrosenbluse *f*, -kragen, -hut, -anzug *m*; *~~'s home* Seemannsheim *n*; **~plane** Segelflugzeug *n*; *~~ model* Segelflugmodell *n*; *~~ pilot* Segelflieger *m*; **~planing** Segelflug *m*; **~-sledge** Segelschlitten *m*.

sainfoin ['sænfɔin] *bot* Esparsette *f*.

saint [seint] *s* Heilige(r) *m*; *a* heilig; *St, S (vor e-m Namen)* [sənt, sint, snt] der heilige, Sankt, St.; **St Bernard** Bernhardiner *m (Hunderasse)*; **~ed** ['-id] *a* geheiligt, heilig(gehalten); heiliggesprochen; **~hood** ['-hud] Heiligkeit *f*; **~liness** ['-linis] Heiligkeit, Frömmigkeit *f*; **~ly** ['-li] *a* heilig, fromm; **St Vitus's dance** *med* Veitstanz *m*.

sake [seik]: *for s.o.'s ~, for the ~ of s.th.* um jds, um e-r S willen; *for my, your ~* meinet-, deinetwegen; *for goodness', heaven's ~* um Himmels willen.

sal [sæl] *scient* Salz *n*; **~-ammoniac** Salmiak *m*; **~-volatile** [-və'lætəli] Hirschhorn-, Riechsalz *n*.

salab|ility, saleability [seilə'biliti] *com* Gangbarkeit *f*; **~le, saleable** ['seiləbl] verkäuflich, gangbar, absetzbar; *~~ value* Verkehrswert *m*.

salac|eous [sə'leiʃəs] geil, wollüstig; schlüpfrig, obszön; *(Witz)* gepfeffert; **~ity** [sə'læsiti] Geilheit; Schlüpfrigkeit *f*.

salad ['sæləd] Salat(pflanze *f*), *bes.* (Kopf-)Salat *m*; *fruit-~* Obstsalat *m*; **~-bowl** Salatschüssel *f*; **~-days** *pl* unreife Jugend *f*; **~-dressing** Salatsoße, -tunke *f*; **~-oil** Speise-, Salatöl *n*; **~-servers** *pl* Salatbesteck *n*.

salamander ['sæləmændə] Salamander; Feuergeist *m*; jem, der große Hitze liebt *od* verträgt; Schüreisen *n*; *tech* Ofensau *f*.

salar|ied ['sælərid] *a* besoldet, bezahlt; (fest)angestellt; *~~ clerk* Büroangestellte(r) *m*; *~~ employee* Gehaltsempfänger *m*; **~y** ['sæləri] *s* Gehalt *n*, Besoldung *f*; *tr* besolden; *to draw a ~~* Gehalt beziehen; *to live, to manage on a ~~* von e-m Gehalt leben; mit e-m Gehalt auskommen; *annual, yearly ~~* Jahresgehalt *n*; *fixed, regular ~~* feste(s) Gehalt *n*; *increase of ~~* Gehaltserhöhung, -aufbesserung *f*; *initial ~~* Anfangsgehalt *n*; *monthly ~~* Monatsgehalt *n*; *reduction of ~~* Gehaltskürzung *f*; *~~ account* Gehaltskonto *n*; *~~ bonus* Gehaltszulage *f*; *~~ bracket* Gehaltsstufe *f*; *~~ cut* Gehaltskürzung *f*; *~~ demand* Gehaltsforderung *f*; *~~ earner* Gehaltsempfänger *m*; *~~ payment* Gehaltszahlung *f*; *~~ roll* Besoldungsliste *f*; *~~ scale* Besoldungsordnung, Gehaltsskala *f*.

sale [seil] Verkauf *m*, Veräußerung *f*; Vertrieb; Absatz; Inventur-, Aus-, Schlußverkauf *m*; Versteigerung, Auktion *f*; *pl* Umsatz, Absatz *m*; *for, on ~* zu verkaufen(d), verkäuflich; *not for ~* unverkäuflich; *to effect a ~* e-n Verkauf abschließen; *to find ready ~, to have a, to meet with a ready ~* sich gut verkaufen, e-n guten Absatz haben; *to find a quick ~* rasch e-n Käufer finden; *to have on, to keep, to offer, to put up for ~* zum Verkauf anbieten, feilhalten; *~ or return* Verkauf *m* mit Rückgaberecht; Kommissionsgeschäft *n*; *~ of work* Wohltätigkeitsbasar *m*; *cash ~* Barverkauf *m*; *clearance ~* Aus-, Räumungsverkauf *m*; *to buy s.th. at a ~~* etw im Ausverkauf kaufen; *closing-down ~* Totalausverkauf *m*; *compulsory, forced ~* Zwangsverkauf *m*; *contract, deed of ~* Kaufvertrag, -brief *m*; *summer, winter ~* Sommer-, Winterschlußverkauf *m*; *white ~* Weiße Woche *f*; *~* **contract** Verkaufsvertrag *m*; *~* **goods** *pl* Ramschwaren *f pl*; **~-price** (Aus-)Verkaufspreis *m*; **~-room** Auktionslokal *n*; **~scheck** Kassenzettel *m*; **~sclerk** *Am* Verkäufer *m*; **~s commission** Verkaufsprovision *f*; **~s department** Verkaufsabteilung *f*; **~s figures** *pl* Verkaufszahlen *f pl*; **~sgirl, ~slady, ~swoman** Verkäuferin *f*; **~sman** Verkäufer; *(travel(l)ing ~~) Am com* Vertreter; Effektenmakler *m*; **~s manager** Verkaufsleiter *m*; **~smanship** Geschäftstüchtigkeit *f*; **~speople** Verkaufspersonal *n*; **~sperson** Verkäufer(in *f*) *m*; **~s promotion** Absatzförderung *f*; *~~ officer* Werbeleiter *m*; **~s representative** Handelsvertreter *m*; **~s resistance** Kaufabneigung, -unlust *f*; **~s-room** Verkaufsraum *m*, Auktionslokal *n*; **~s situation** Absatz-, Marktlage *f*; **~s tax** Umsatzsteuer *f*; **~s terms** *pl Am* Verkaufsbedingungen *f pl*; **~s ticket** Kassenzettel *m*; **~s value** Verkaufswert *m*.

salicylic [sæli'silik]: *~* **acid** Salizylsäure *f*.

salient ['seiljənt] *a* vorspringend, (hinaus)ragend; *fig* hervorragend, in die Augen springend, hervorstechend, auffällig, bemerkenswert; *s* Vorsprung *m*, vorstehende Ecke *f*; *mil* Frontvorsprung, (Front-)Keil *m*.

saliferous [sə'lifərəs] salzhaltig.

salin|e ['seilain, 'sæl-, sə'lain] *a* salz(halt)ig; Salz-; *s* [sə'lain] Saline; Salzquelle *f*; *~~ (solution)* Salzlösung *f*; **~ity** [sə'liniti] Salzgehalt *m*.

saliv|a [sə'laivə] Speichel *m*; **~ary** ['sælivəri] Speichel-; *~~ gland* Speicheldrüse *f*; **~ate** ['sæliveit] *tr* zu vermehrter Speichelabsonderung anregen; *itr* Speichel absondern; **~ation** [sæli'veiʃən] (vermehrter) Speichelfluß *m*, -absonderung *f*.

sallow ['sælou] **1.** *a* fahl, gelb, bläßlich; **~ness** ['-nis] Fahlheit *f*, fahle(s) Aussehen *n*, bläßliche, kränkliche Farbe *f*; **2.** *bot* Salweide *f*.

sally ['sæli] *s mil* Ausfall; *arch* Vorsprung; *fig* plötzliche(r) Ausbruch, Geistesblitz; Seitenhieb *m*; *itr (to ~ forth, to ~ out) mil* e-n Ausfall machen; hervorbrechen, -springen; sich aufmachen, aufbrechen; **~-lunn** *Art* Teekuchen *m*.

salmagundi [sælmə'gʌndi] Ragout; *fig* Gemisch *n*, Mischmasch *m*.

salmon ['sæmən] *pl -s* Lachs, Salm *m*; Lachsfarbe *f*, -rot *n*; *a u. ~* **pink** lachsrot, -farben; *~* **trout** Lachsforelle *f*.

salon ['sælɔn] (Empfangs-)Salon *m*; Ausstellungsraum *m*, -halle; (Kunst-) Ausstellung *f*.

saloon [sə'lu:n] Salon, Gesellschaftsraum, Saal *m*, (Hotel-)Halle; *Am* Schankwirtschaft *f*, Gasthaus *n*, -stätte, *fam* Kneipe, Schenke; *mot (~ car)* Limousine *f*; *Br rail* Salonwagen *m*; *billiard ~* Billardzimmer *n*; *dancing ~* Tanzsaal *m*; *dining-~ (bes. auf Schiffen)* Speisesaal, -raum; *hairdressing, shaving-~ (Am)* Frisier-, Rasiersalon *m*; *~* **bar** Gastzimmer *n* *(e-s Gasthauses)*; *~* **cabin** *mar* Kabine *f* 1. Klasse; **~-car(riage)** *Br rail* Salonwagen *m*; *~* **deck** Salondeck *n*; **~keeper** *Am* Gast-, Schankwirt *m*.

salsify ['sælsifi] *bot* (lauchblättriger) Bocksbart *m*.

salt [sɔ:lt] *s* Salz *a. chem*; Salzfaß *n*; *fig* Würze *f*, beißende(r) Witz *m*; Bitterkeit *f*; *fam (old ~)* alte(r) Seebär *m*; *pl* (Mineral-)Salze *n pl*; *(smelling ~s)* Riechsalz *n*; *a* salz(halt)ig; gesalzen, gepökelt; scharf, stechend, beißend; *(Preis)* gepfeffert, gesalzen; *fig* bitter; *tr* salzen; *(to ~ down)* einsalzen *a. fig*, pökeln; *fig* würzen (*with* mit); *com* überteuern; *sl (Rechnung)* salzen; *s.th.* etw frisieren, aufmöbeln, anreichern; *to ~ away (Am fam)* auf die Seite schaffen; auf die hohe Kante legen; *above, below the ~* oben, unten am Tisch; *with a grain of ~ (fig)* mit einiger Einschränkung, cum grano salis; *not to be worth o.'s* ~ zu nichts nutze sein; *the* ~ *of the earth (Bibel)* das Salz der Erde; die Elite *f*; *the* ~ *of life* die Würze des Lebens; *kitchen* ~ Kochsalz *n*; *rock, sea* ~ Stein-, Meersalz *n*; **~-cellar,** *Am* **shaker** Salzstreuer *m*, -fäßchen *n*; **~ed** ['-id] *a* (ein)gesalzen; *fig fam* ausgekocht, abgebrüht; **~ern** ['-ən], **~works** *pl* Saline *f*; **~iness** ['-inis] Salzigkeit *f*; **~-lake** Salzsee *m*; ~ **lick** Salzlecke *f*; *Am* salzige(r) Boden *m*; **~-pan** Verdunstungsbassin *n*; **~petre,** *Am* **~peter** ['-pi:tə] Salpeter *m*; **~-pit, -mine** Salzbergwerk *n*, Saline *f*; ~ **solution** Salzlösung *f*; **~-spring** Sole, Salzquelle *f*; **~-water** Salz-, Meerwasser *n*; ~~ *fish* Salzwasserfisch *m*; **~y** ['-i] salz(halt)ig; See-; *fig* beißend, scharf; gepfeffert.

salt|ant ['sæltənt] springend, tanzend; **~ation** [sæl'teiʃən] Springen *n*, Tanz(en *n*) *m*; *physiol* Klopfen *n*; *fig* Sprung *m (in der Entwicklung)*; *biol* Mutation *f*; **~atorial** [sæltə'tɔ:riəl], **~atory** ['sæltətəri] springend; Sprung-.

salubr|ious [sə'lu:briəs] gesund, zuträglich, bekömmlich; **~ity** [-iti] Zuträglichkeit, Bekömmlichkeit *f*.

salutar|iness ['sæljutərinis] Gesundheit, Zuträglichkeit; *fig* Heilsamkeit *f*; **~y** ['sæljutəri] gesund, zuträglich (*to* für); *fig* heilsam.

salut|ation [sælju(:)'teiʃən] Gruß *m*, Begrüßung; *(Brief)* Anrede *f*; *in* ~~ zur Begrüßung; *angelic* ~~ *(rel)* englische(r) Gruß *m*, Ave Maria *n*; **~atorian** [-tə'tɔ:riən] *Am* Schüler *m*, der e-e Begrüßungsansprache hält; **~atory** [sə'lju:tətəri] *a* Begrüßungs-, Gruß-; *Am* Eröffnungs-; *s Am (Schule)* Begrüßungsansprache *f*; **~e** [sə'lu:t] *tr* (be)grüßen; *mil* grüßen, salutieren (*s.o.* vor jdm); *itr* grüßen; *mil* salutieren (*to* vor); *s* Gruß *m*, Begrüßung *f*; (Begrüßungs-)Kuß *m*; *mil* Ehrenbezeigung *f*; Salut(schuß) *m*; *in* ~~ zum Gruß; *to stand at the* ~~ e-e Ehrenbezeigung machen; salutieren; *to take the* ~~ die Parade abnehmen; den Gruß erwidern.

salv|age ['sælvidʒ] *s* Rettung; *bes. mar* Bergung *f*; Bergungsgut *n*; *(~ money)* Bergungsprämie; Verwertung, Ausschlachtung *f*; Altmaterial *n*; *tr* retten; *bes. mar* bergen; *mil* sammeln; verwerten, ausschlachten; *Am sl mil* organisieren; ~~ *boat, ship* Bergungsdampfer *m*; ~~ *company* Bergungsgesellschaft *f*; ~~ *crane* Abschleppkran *m*; ~~ *depot (mil)* Materialsammelstelle *f*; ~~ *service* Seenotdienst *m*; ~~ *squad* Bergungskolonne *f*; ~~ *value* Schrottwert *m*; ~~ *work* Aufräumungsarbeiten *f pl*; **~ation** [sæl'veiʃən] (Er-)Rettung *f*; Retter *m*; *rel* Erlösung *f*; *the S~~ Army* die Heilsarmee *f*; **~e 1.** [sælv] *tr* retten; bergen; *interj* ['sælvi] Heil! **~or** ['sælvə] Bergungsarbeiter *m*, -schiff *n*.

salve 2. [sɑ:v, sælv] *s* Salbe *f*; *fig* Balsam, Trost(pflästerchen *n*) *m*; *Am* Schmeichelei *f*; *tr (Schmerz)* lindern, beruhigen; *fig* beschwichtigen; beschönigen; *Am* schmeicheln (*s.o.* jdm).

salver ['sælvə] Präsentierteller *m*, Tablett *n*.

salvo ['sælvou] **1.** *pl -o(e)s mil* Salve *f*; Beifallssturm *m*; ~ **release** *aero* Massenabwurf *m*; **2.** *pl -os jur* Vorbehalt *m*; Ausflucht *f*.

Sam [sæm]: *to stand* ~ *(sl)* die Zeche bezahlen.

Samaritan [sə'mæritn] Samariter *m*.

same [seim] *a prn adv: the* ~ der-, die-, dasselbe, der, die, das gleiche; ebenso; *at the* ~ *time* gleichzeitig, zur gleichen Zeit; *the very* ~, *one and the* ~ genau, ebender-, die-, dasselbe; *all, just the* ~ trotzdem, dennoch, nichtsdestoweniger; ganz gleich, ganz einerlei; *to come to the* ~ *thing* auf eins hinauslaufen; *it's all, just the* ~ das ist, bleibt sich gleich; *we're the* ~ *age* wir sind gleichaltrig; *(thanks, the)* ~ *to you* (danke,) gleichfalls; **~ness** ['-nis] Identität; Ein-, Gleichförmigkeit, Monotonie *f*.

samovar ['sæmo(u)vɑ:] Samowar *m*.

samp [sæmp] *Am* grobe(s) Maismehl *n*.

sampl|e ['sɑ:mpl] *s* Probe *f*, Muster *n*; *(Statistik)* Stichprobe, Auswahl *f*; Versuchsstück; Präparat; *fig* Beispiel *n*, Probe *f*; *tr* e-e Probe nehmen von; *(Speise)* probieren; er-, ausprobieren; *by* ~~ *post* als Muster ohne Wert; *up to* ~~ der Probe, dem Muster entsprechend; *to buy s.th. from* ~~ etw nach dem Muster kaufen; *pattern* ~~ Musterstück *n*; ~~ *area* Versuchsfeld *n*; ~~*bag, book, card* Musterkoffer *m*, -buch *n*, -karte *f*; ~~ *room* Ausstellungsraum *m*; ~~ *signature* Unterschriftsprobe *f*; ~~ *stock* Musterlager *n*; **~er** ['-ə] Sticktuch *n*; **~ing** ['-iŋ] Musterkollektion; Bemusterung; Verkaufsförderung durch Musterverteilung; Marktforschung *f* durch Untersuchung e-r repräsentativen Käuferschicht; *random* ~~ Entnahme *f* von Stichproben; ~~ *inspection* Stichprobenkontrolle *f*.

sanat|ive ['sænətiv] = *~ory*; **~orium** [sænə'tɔ:riəm] *pl a. -oria* [-ə] Sanatorium *n*, Heilstätte, -anstalt *f*, Genesungsheim *n*; (Höhen-)Luftkurort *m*; **~ory** ['sænətəri] heilkräftig, heilend.

sanct|ification [sæŋktifi'keiʃən] Heiligung; Weihe *f*; **~ify** ['sæŋktifai] *tr* heiligen; weihen; (von Sünden) lossprechen; **~imonious** [sæŋkti'mounjəs] scheinheilig; **~imoniousness** [-'mounjəsnis], **~imony** ['sæŋktiməni] Scheinheiligkeit, religiöse Heuchelei *f*; **~ion** ['sæŋkʃən] *s* Sanktion; Bestätigung, Genehmigung; Billigung, Unterstützung; Autorisation, Sanktionierung *f*; Beschluß *m*, Gesetz *n*; *meist pl* Sanktionen, Sicherungs-, Zwangs-, Strafmaßnahmen *f pl*; *tr* sanktionieren, bestätigen, Gesetzeskraft verleihen (*s.th.* e-r S); genehmigen, billigen, gutheißen, unterstützen; **~ity** ['sæŋktiti] Heiligkeit; Unverletzlichkeit *f*; ~~ *of the mail* Postgeheimnis *n*; **~uary** ['sæŋktjuəri] Heiligtum; Allerheiligste(s) *n*, Altarraum *m*; Asyl *n*, Freistatt *f*; Schongebiet *n (für Tiere)*; *bird* ~~ Vogelschutzgebiet *n*; **~um** ['-əm] heilige, geweihte Stätte *f*; *fig* Privat-, Studier-, Arbeitszimmer *n*.

sand [sænd] *s* Sand *m*; Sandfarbe; Sandbank *f*; *Am sl* Mumm, Schneid *m*; *pl* Sandfläche, sandige Ebene *f*, Strand *m*; *fig* Augenblicke, Momente *m pl*; *tr* mit Sand bestreuen, bedecken, anfüllen, abreiben; abschmirgeln; mit Sand (ver)mischen; *to build on* ~ *(fig)* auf Sand bauen; *to make ropes of* ~ *(fig)* Unmögliches wollen; *to plough the* ~ *(fig)* s-e Mühe verschwenden; **~bag** *s* Sandsack *m*; *tr* mit Sandsäcken abschirmen *od* beschweren; *Am* niederschlagen, hinterrücks überfallen; *Am fam* zwingen; **~bank, -bar** Sandbank *f*; **~-blast** *tech* Sandstrahlgebläse *n*; ~ **bowl** *Am* Sandbüchse *f*; Steppengebiete *n pl*; **~box** Sandkasten *m*, -form *f*; **~boy:** *as hapy as a* ~~ kreuzfidel; **~-drift** Sandtreiben *n*; **~ed** ['-id] *a* mit Sand bedeckt *od* angefüllt; sandig; sandfarben; **~-flea, -hopper** Sandfloh *m*; **~glass** Sanduhr *f*, Stundenglas *n*; **~-hill** Düne *f*; **~man** ['-mən] Sandmännchen *n*; **~paper** Sand-, Schmirgelpapier *n*; **~piper** *orn* Strandläufer *m*; **~-pit** Sandgrube *f*; **~shoe** Strandschuh *m*; **~stone** Sandstein *m*; **~-storm** Sandsturm *m*; **~-table** *mil* Sandkasten *m*; **~y** ['-i] sandig; sandbedeckt, voller Sand; sandfarben; *fig* beweglich, unbeständig.

sandal ['sændl] **1.** Sandale *f*; **2.** = **~wood** Sandelholz *n*.

sandwich ['sænwidʃ] *s* Sandwich *n*; *tr* einschieben, -klemmen; dazwischenschichten, dazwischentun; einzwängen (*between* zwischen); **~-board** Plakattafel *f (e-s Plakatträgers)*; **~-counter** *Am* Imbißhalle *f*; **~-man** ['-mæn] Plakatträger *m*; **~-paper** Butterbrotpapier *n*.

sane [sein] geistig normal; *fig* vernünftig, sinnvoll, gesund.

sanforize ['sænfəraiz] *tr (Wäsche)* sanforisieren.

sanguin|ary ['sæŋgwinəri] blutig; blutbefleckt; blutdürstig, -gierig; grausam; **~e** ['sæŋgwin] *s* Rötel *m*; *a* blutrot; *(Haut)* rot, gerötet; *psychol* sanguinisch, heißblütig, lebhaft; leichtblütig, stets heiter, zufrieden, zuversichtlich, optimistisch; *to feel* ~~ *about s.th.* etw zuversichtlich entgegensehen; **~eous** [sæŋ'gwinjəs] *a* Blut-; (blut)rot; blutig; blutdürstig.

sanit|arian [sæni'tɛəriən] *a* sanitär, hygienisch; *s* Hygieniker; Gesundheitsprediger, -apostel *m*; **~arium** [-əm] *pl a. -ia bes. Am* = *sanatorium*; **~ary** ['sænitəri] sanitär, hygienisch (einwandfrei), sauber, gesund; ~~ *engineering* Installation *f*; ~~ *napkin, (Am) towel* Damen-, Monatsbinde *f*; ~~ *police* Gesundheitspolizei *f*; **~ation** [sæni'teiʃən] Hygiene, Gesundheitspflege *f*, -wesen *n*; Kanalisation *f*; sanitäre Anlagen *f pl*; **~y** ['sæniti] (geistige) Gesundheit; Vernunft *f*, gesunde(r) Menschenverstand *m*.

sank [sæŋk] *pret von sink*.

Santa Claus [sæntə'klɔ:z] Nikolaus *od* Weihnachtsmann *m*.

sap [sæp] **1.** *s bot* Saft; *allg* Lebenssaft *m*; *fig* (Lebens-)Kraft, Vitalität, Energie, Stärke *f*; *fam (~-head)* Esel, Schafskopf *m*, Kamel *n*; *sl (Schule)* Streber *m*; *Am sl* Keule *f*; *tr (Baumstamm)* anzapfen; *fig* entkräften, schwächen; *sl* ochsen, büffeln, pauken; *Am sl* niederschlagen; **~-happy** *Am sl* betrunken; **~less** ['-lis] saftlos, trocken; *fig* (saft- u.) kraftlos, fade, seicht; **~ling** ['-liŋ] junge(r) Baum; *fig* (junger) Bursche; junge(r) Windhund *m*; **~piness** ['-inis] Saftigkeit; *fig* (Lebens-)Kraft, Stärke *f*; **~py** ['-i] saftig, frisch, zart, jung; *fig* kräftig, kraftvoll, energisch; *sl* doof, blöd(e), dumm; ~ **wood** Splint *m*; **2.** *s mil* Lauf-, Annäherungsgraben *m*; *tr* unterminieren, -graben *a. fig*; *(Überzeugung)* erschüttern; **~per** ['-ə] *mil* Pionier *m*.

sapid ['sæpid] schmackhaft; *fig* einladend, interessant.

sapien|ce, -cy ['seipjəns] (Schein-)Weisheit *f*; **~t** ['-t] *oft iro* weise, klug.

sapon|aceous [sæpo(u)'neiʃəs] seifig; *fig* salbungsvoll; **~ification** [sæpɔnifi'keiʃən, sə-] Verseifung, Seifenbildung *f*; **~ify** [sæ'pɔnifai, sə-] *tr itr* verseifen.

sapphire ['sæfaiə] *min* Saphir *m*.

sarc|asm ['sɑ:kæzm] Sarkasmus, beißende(r) Spott, bittere(r) Hohn *m*; **~astic** [sɑ:'kæstik] sarkastisch; **~oma** [sɑ:'koumə] *pl -mata* [-mətə] *med* Sar-

kom *n*; ~**ophagus** [sɑː'kɔfəgəs] *pl a. -gi* [-gai, -dʒai] Sarkophag *m.*
sardine [sɑː'diːn] Sardine *f*; *oil* ~ Ölsardine *f*; *packed like* ~*s* dichtgedrängt, wie Heringe; *tin, (Am) can of* ~*s* Büchse, Dose *f* Ölsardinen.
Sardinia [sɑː'dinjə] Sardinien *n*; ~**n** [-n] *a* sard(in)isch; *s* Sardinier(in *f*) *m.*
sardonic [sɑː'dɔnik]: ~ **laugh, smile** sardonische(s), höhnische(s) Lachen *n.*
sartori|al [sɑː'tɔːriəl] Schneider-; Kleider-; ~**us** [-əs] *anat* Schneidermuskel *m.*
sash [sæʃ] **1.** Schärpe *f*; **2.** (Schiebe-) Fensterrahmen *m*; ~ **window** Schiebefenster *n.*
sass [sæs] *s Am fam* freche, unverschämte Reden *f pl*; *tr* frech, unverschämt reden mit.
Satan ['seitən] Satan *m*; **s**~**ic(al)** [sə'tænik(əl)] satanisch, teuflisch.
satchel ['sætʃəl] Handtasche *f*; Schulranzen *m.*
sate [seit] *tr* vollständig, vollauf befriedigen; übersättigen (*with* mit).
sateen [sæ'tiːn] Baumwollsatin *m.*
satellite ['sætəlait] Gefolgsmann, Trabant *a. pej*; *astr* Satellit, Trabant, Mond *allg*; *tech (künstlicher)* (Erd-) Satellit *m*; *pol (~ nation)* Satellit(enstaat), *hist* Vasallenstaat *m*; ~ **airfield, landing-ground** Ausweich-, Feld-, Arbeitsflugplatz *m*; ~ **line** Nebenlinie *f*; ~ **town** Trabantenstadt *f.*
sati|ate ['seiʃieit] *tr meist im Passiv*: *to be* ~~*d* (vollauf) genug haben, übersättigt sein (*with* mit) *a. fig*; *a* (über-) satt, übersättigt; ~**ation** [seiʃi'eiʃən] (Über-)Sättigung; Sattheit *f*; ~**ety** [sə'taiəti] Sattheit; *fig* Übersättigung *f* (*of* mit); Überdruß *m* (*of* an); *to (the point of)* ~~ bis zum Überdruß.
satin ['sætin] *s* (Seiden-)Satin, Seidenatlas *m*; *a* seidenglatt; glänzend; ~**et(te)** [sæti'net] Baumwollsatin, -atlas *m*; ~ **paper** Atlaspapier *n.*
satir|e ['sætaiə] Satire *f* (*upon* auf); (beißender) Spott *m*; ~**ic(al)** [sə'tirik(əl)] satirisch, spöttisch, beißend; ~**ist** ['sætərist] Satiriker, Spötter *m*; ~**ize** ['sætəraiz] *tr* verspotten.
satisf|action [sætis'fækʃən] Genugtuung (*at, with* über); Befriedigung, Zufriedenheit (*at, with* mit); Freude (*at, with* über); *rel jur* Buße, Sühne; *com* Begleichung, Bezahlung; Erfüllung *(e-r Bedingung)*; Quittung *f*; *to s.o.'s* ~~ zu jds Zufriedenheit; *to demand, to give, to obtain* ~~ Genugtuung verlangen, geben, erlangen; *to enter* ~~ e-e Hypothek im Grundbuch löschen; *to get* ~~ *out of s.th.* in etw Befriedigung finden; *to give* ~~ *to s.o.* jdn zufriedenstellen; jdm Recht geben; ~**actory** [-'fæktəri] zufriedenstellend, befriedigend (*to* für); den Erwartungen entsprechend; annehmbar; hinreichend; *not to be* ~~ zu wünschen übriglassen; *to give a* ~~ *account of s.th.* etw rechtfertigen; ~**y** ['sætisfai] *tr* zufriedenstellen, befriedigen; genügen (*s.o.* jdm); *(Hunger)* stillen; *(Bedingungen, Verpflichtungen)* erfüllen, nachkommen; *(Regeln)* entsprechen; *(Anforderungen)* genügen, Genüge leisten (*s.th.* e-r S); *(e-m Bedürfnis)* abhelfen; *(Zweifel)* beheben; *(Problem)* lösen; überzeugen (*of* von); *(Schuld)* begleichen, bezahlen; sühnen, büßen; Genugtuung geben (*s.o.* jdm); *to be* ~*ied* befriedigt, zufrieden, einverstanden sein (*with* mit); sich begnügen (*with* mit); überzeugt sein (*of* von; *that* daß); ~**fying** ['sætisfaiiŋ] zufriedenstellend, befriedigend.
satrap ['sætrəp] *hist u. fig* Satrap *m.*
satur|ate ['sætʃəreit, -tjur-] *tr bes. chem* sättigen; *fig* völlig durchdringen, erfüllen (*with* mit); *mil* mit e-m Bombenteppich belegen; ~**ated** ['-id] *a chem (Lösung)* gesättigt; ~**ation** [-'reiʃən] Sättigung; Durchdringung *f* (*with* mit); *degree of* ~~ Sättigungsgrad *m*; ~~ *bombing (aero)* Bombenteppich *m*; ~~ *point (chem)* Sättigungspunkt *m.*
Satur|day ['sætədi] Sonnabend, Samstag *m*; *on* ~~ am Sonnabend; ~**n** ['sætə(ː)n] *rel hist u. astr* Saturn *m*; **s**~**nine** ['sætə(ː)nain] düster, trüb(e), traurig, ernst, schweigsam; **s**~**nism** ['sætə(ː)nizm] Bleivergiftung *f.*
satyr ['sætə] *rel hist* Satyr *m a. fig.*
sauc|e [sɔːs] *s* Soße, Tunke *f*; *Am* Mus, Kompott *n*; *fig* Würze; *fam* Frechheit, Unverschämtheit *f*; *Am sl* Whisky *m*; *tr* Soße geben zu; würzen (*with* mit); *fam* frech, unverschämt sein zu; *to be on the* ~~ *(Am sl)* saufen wie ein Loch; *hunger is the best* ~~ *(prov)* Hunger ist der beste Koch; *apple* ~~ Apfelkompott *n*; *Am fam interj* Unsinn! *chocolate* ~~ Schokoladekreme *f*; *tomato* ~~ Tomatensauce *f*; ~~*-boat, -tureen* Sauciere, Soßenschüssel *f*; ~~*-box (fam)* Frechdachs *m*; ~~*dish (Am)* Kompottschüssel *f*; ~~*pan* Tiegel, Kochtopf *m*; ~**er** ['-ə] Untertasse *f*; *flying* ~~ fliegende Untertasse *f* ~~ *eyes (pl)* Kuller-, Glotzaugen *n pl*; ~**iness** ['-inis] Frechheit, Unverschämtheit, Impertinenz *f*; *fam* Schick *m*; ~**y** ['-i] frech, unverschämt; *fam* schick, keß.
sauerkraut ['sauəkraut] Sauerkraut *n.*
sauna ['saunə] Sauna *f.*
saunter ['sɔːntə] *itr* umherschlendern, -bummeln; *s* (Herum-)Schlendern *n*, Bummel *m*; ~**er** ['-rə] Bummler *m.*
saurian ['sɔːriən] *a* Eidechsen-; *s* Eidechse; Echse *f*; Saurier *m.*
sausage ['sɔsidʒ] Wurst *f*; *(~ balloon) mil sl* Fesselballon *m*; *luncheon* ~ (Schnitt-, Streich-)Wurst *f*; ~ **meat** (Wurst-)Brät *n*; ~ **roll** Wurstpastete *f.*
savage ['sævidʒ] *a* wild; unbebaut; *(Tier)* ungezähmt, ungebändigt; *(Mensch)* primitiv, barbarisch; *fig* roh, ungebildet, ungeschliffen; grausam; *fam* wütend; *s* Wilde(r); Rohling; Grobian *m*; ~**ness** ['-nis] Wildheit; Roheit; Grausamkeit *f*; ~**ry** ['-ri] Wildheit; Barbarei, Grausamkeit *f.*
savanna(h) [sə'vænə] *geog* Savanne *f.*
savant ['sævənt, *Am a.* sə'vænt] Gelehrte(r) *m.*
sav|e [seiv] **1.** *tr* erretten, befreien; bewahren (*from* vor; *from doing s.th.* etw zu tun); retten (*from* von); *rel* erlösen; *mar* bergen; *(to ~ up)* aufheben, aufbewahren, zurücklegen; *(Sitz)* reservieren; horten; *(Geld, Kosten, Mühe, Zeit)* sparen; ersparen (*s.o.* jdm); *(Briefmarken)* sammeln; *(Kleidung, Augen)* schonen; **2.** *itr* sparsam, haushälterisch sein; sparen, horten; Bestand haben, bleiben; *(Nahrungsmittel)* sich halten; *sport* den Ball auffangen; **3.** *s sport* Abfangen, Stoppen *n* des Balles; **4.** *prp* außer *dat*, ausgenommen *acc*; ~~ *for* abgesehen von; *all* ~~ *him* er allein; **5.** *conj* außer daß, es sei denn, daß; *to* ~~ *s.o. from himself* jdn vor Dummheiten bewahren; *to* ~~ *appearances* den Schein wahren; *to* ~~ *o.'s bacon (fam)* entwischen, davonkommen; *to* ~~ *o.'s face* das Gesicht wahren; *to* ~~ *the goal (sport)* den Ball abfangen; *to* ~~ *s.o.'s life* jdm das Leben retten; *to* ~~ *the situation* die Situation retten; *to* ~~ *o.'s skin (fig)* (mit) heil(er Haut) davonkommen; *it* ~~*s me time* dabei spare ich Zeit; ~~*-all* Arbeitshose *f*; (Schlabber-)Lätzchen *n*; Tropfenfänger *m*; Sparbüchse *f*; ~**er** ['-ə] Retter; Sparer *m*; *in Zssgen*: zeit-, arbeitsparende(s) Gerät *n*; *this device is a time-*~~ diese Vorrichtung spart Zeit; *the small* ~~*s* die kleinen Sparer *m pl*; ~**ing** ['-iŋ] *a* sparsam, wirtschaftlich, haushälterisch (*of* mit); rettend, erlösend; Rettungs-; Erlösungs-; Spar-; Ausnahme-; *in Zssgen*: -sparend; *s* Rettung *f*; Sparen *n*; Einsparung, Ersparnis *f*; *com* Konsumverzicht; *jur* Vorbehalt *m*, Ausnahme *f*; *rel* Heil *n*; *pl* Ersparte(s) *n*, Ersparnisse, Spareinlagen *f pl*; *prp u. conj = save prp u. conj*; ~~ *clause* einschränkende Bestimmung; Vorbehalts-, Sicherheitsklausel *f*; ~~*s account (Am)* Sparkonto *n*; ~~*s-bank* Sparkasse *f*; *postal, post-office* ~~*s-bank* Postsparkasse *f*; ~~*s-bank book* Sparkassenbuch *n*; ~~*s-deposits (pl)* Spareinlagen *f pl*; ~**io(u)r** ['seivjə] Retter *m*; *the S*~~ der Erlöser, der Heiland.
saveloy ['sævilɔi] Zervelatwurst *f.*
savory ['seivəri] *bot* Bohnenkraut *n.*
savo(u)r ['seivə] *s* Geschmack; Geruch, Duft *m*, Aroma *n*; *fig* Eigenheit, -art *f*; Beigeschmack, (An-)Hauch *m*, Spur *f*, Anflug; Reiz *m*, *das* Anziehende; *itr* schmecken, riechen (*of* nach) *a. fig*; erkennen lassen (*of s.th.* etw); e-n Anstrich haben (*of* von); *tr* e-n bestimmten Geschmack *od* Geruch geben (*s.th.* e-r S); schmecken, riechen nach; erkennen lassen; genießen, auskosten; ~**iness** ['-rinis] Schmackhaftigkeit *f*, Wohlgeschmack; Wohlgeruch, Duft *m*; ~**less** ['-lis] geschmack-, geruch-, reizlos; ~**y** ['-ri] *a* wohlschmekkend, schmackhaft, appetitanregend; pikant; wohlriechend, duftend; angenehm, gefällig, ansprechend; (ehr-) würdig; *s* Appetithappen *m*, pikante(s) Gericht *n*; Vor-, Nachspeise *f.*
Savoy [sə'vɔi] Savoyen *n*; **s**~ Wirsingkohl *m.*
savvy ['sævi] *itr sl* kapieren, begreifen; *s* Grips, (Sinn u.) Verstand *m.*
saw [sɔː] **1.** *s* Säge; Sägemaschine; *Am sl* alte Geschichte *f*; *itr tr irr pp meist sawn* [sɔːn] sägen; *(Holz)* sich sägen lassen; *to* ~ *down, off* um-, absägen; *to* ~ *up* zersägen; *to* ~ *the air* in der Luft herumfuchteln; *to* ~ *wood* (Holz) sägen *a. fig*; *fig* schnarchen; ~**-blade** Sägeblatt *n*; ~ **buck** *Am*, **-horse** Sägebock *m*; ~**dust** Sägemehl *n*, -späne *m pl*; ~~ *parlor (Am sl)* billige(s) Lokal *n*; ~**ed-off** *Am fam* untersetzt; *fig* abgesägt, ausgestoßen; ~**fish** Sägefisch *m*; ~**-mill** Sägemühle *f*; ~**ney** ['-ni] Schotte; *sl* Trottel *m*; ~ **timber** Schnittholz *n*; ~**tooth** Sägezahn *m*; ~**yer** ['-jə] Säger *m*; **2.** Spruch *m*, Sprichwort *n*; **3.** *pret von see.*
saxifrage ['sæksifridʒ] *bot* Steinbrech *m.*
Saxon ['sæksn] *s hist* Angelsachse; Sachse *m*, Sächsin *f*; *a* sächsisch; angelsächsisch; ~**y** ['-i] Sachsen *n.*
saxophon|e ['sæksəfoun] *mus* Saxophon *n*; ~**ist** [sæk'sɔfənist] Saxophonist *m.*
say [sei] *irr said, said* [sed] *tr* sagen, äußern, (aus)sprechen, ausdrücken; bemerken; mit Bestimmtheit sagen, bestimmen, befehlen; feststellen, erklären; *(to ~ over)* auf-, hersagen; annehmen; behaupten; *itr* (s-e Meinung) sagen, sprechen; bedeuten; *s* Rede *f*, Wort *n*; *(the ~)* das letzte Wort, die Entscheidung; *to have o.'s* ~ s-e Meinung sagen (*to* zu; *on* über); *to have a, no, not much* ~ viel, nichts, nicht viel zu sagen haben; *to* ~ *good-by(e) to* sich verabschieden von; *to* ~ *mass*

die Messe lesen; *to ~ a prayer* ein Gebet sprechen; *to ~ the word (Am fam)* einverstanden sein; s-e Zustimmung geben; *no sooner said than done* gesagt, getan; *(let's) ~* sagen wir; angenommen; *I should ~* ich möchte annehmen; *I say! you don't ~!* so! na, hör, hören Sie mal! *he had nothing to ~ for himself* er hatte keine Entschuldigung; *she is said to be clever* sie soll klug sein; *it goes without ~ing* das ist selbstverständlich, versteht sich von selbst; *there's much to be said for his suggestion* sein Vorschlag hat viel für sich; *that is to ~* das heißt, mit anderen Worten; *to ~ nothing of* ganz zu schweigen von; gar nicht zu reden von; *the paper ~s* in der Zeitung steht; **~ing** *s* Rede(n *n*) *f*; Spruch *m*, Sprichwort *n*, Maxime *f*; *as the ~~ goes* wie man zu sagen pflegt; **~-so** *sl* Entscheidung; Behauptung *f*; *the final ~~* die entscheidende Autorität.

scab [skæb] *s* Schorf, Grind *m*; *vet* (Schaf-)Räude *f*; *bot* Brand-, Rostfleck; *fig* nichtorganisierte(r) Arbeiter; Streikbrecher; *Am sl* Schuft *m*; *itr* von der Räude *od* Pilzkrankheit befallen werden; *fig (Arbeiter)* nicht organisiert, Streikbrecher sein; **~by** ['-i] *fig* schäbig, gemein, schuftig, schurkisch; *med* schorfig; räudig.

scabbard ['skæbəd] *s* (Schwert-)Scheide *f*.

scabi|es ['skeibii:z] Krätze, Räude *f*; **~ous** ['-iəs] *a* krätzig, räudig; *s bot* Skabiose *f*.

scabrous ['skeibrəs] rauh, uneben, holprig; *(Haut)* schuppig, grindig; *fig* schwierig; *(Frage)* kniff(e)lig; gewagt, anstößig, anzüglich.

scads [skædz] *pl Am fam* ein Haufen *m*, e-e Masse, e-e Menge.

scaffold ['skæfəld] *s* (Bau-)Gerüst; Schafott *n*; (provisorische) Tribüne *f*; *anat* Knochengerüst, Skelett *n*; *tr* einrüsten, mit e-m Gerüst versehen; **~ing** ['-iŋ] Rüstzeug; (Bau-)Gerüst *n*; *~~-pole* Gerüststange *f*.

scalawag *s. scallawag.*

scald [skɔ:ld] *tr* verbrühen; abbrühen; ab-, aus-, aufkochen (lassen); *s* Verbrühung, Verbrennung *f*; **~-head** *med* Grindkopf *m*; **~ing** ['-iŋ] *a* siedend, brennend heiß; *s* Ab-, Auskochen; *med* Brennen; Verbrühen *n*; *~~ tears (pl)* heiße Tränen *f pl*.

scal|e [skeil] **1.** *s* Skala, Gradeinteilung *f*; Meßgerät *n* mit e-r Skala; Maßstab *m*; Ausmaß *n*, Umfang *m*; *fig (soziale)* Stufenleiter; *(Lohn-)* Skala *f*, Tarif; Stundenlohn *m*; Stufe *f*; *math* (Zahlen-)System *n*, Zahlenreihe; *mus* Tonleiter *f*; *typ* Kolumnenmaß *n*; *tr* ersteigen, -klettern; maßstabgerecht machen; den Maßstab festsetzen für; messen; *itr* klettern, steigen; *(Thermometer)* hochklettern, steigen; *to ~~ up, down* (maßstabgerecht) vergrößern, verkleinern; *Am* die Preise herauf-, herabsetzen; erhöhen; verkleinern, reduzieren; fallen; *(according) to ~~* maßstabgerecht, -getreu; *on the ~~ of ... to* im Maßstab ... zu; *on a large, small ~~* in großem, kleinem Maßstab; *on a descending ~~ (fin)* degressiv; *chromatic, diatonic, major, minor ~~ (mus)* chromatische, diatonische, Dur-, Molltonleiter *f*; *pay ~~* Gehaltskala *f*; *sliding ~~* gleitende Skala *f*; *social ~~* soziale Stellung *f*, gesellschaftliche(r) Rang *m*; *taxation ~~* Steuer-, Hebesatz *m*; *wage ~~* Lohnskala *f*; *~~ beam* Waagebalken *m*; *~~ dial* Skalenscheibe *f*; *~~ division* Skaleneinteilung *f*; *~~ of charges, fees* Gebührentarif *m*, -ordnung *f*; *~~ line* Teilstrich *m*; *~~ pan* Waagschale *f*; *~~ paper* Millimeterpapier *n*; *~~ of prices* Preistabelle *f*; *~~ of production* Produktionsumfang *f*; *~~ reading* Skalenablesung *f*; *~~ unit* Maßstabeinheit *f*; **2.** *s zoo med* Schuppe *f*; dünne(r) Überzug *m*, dünne äußere Schicht *f*; Kessel-, Zahnstein *m*; *tr* abschuppen, -schalen; abstreifen, -lösen; von Kessel-, Zahnstein befreien; mit Schuppen, e-r Kruste bedecken; *itr* abblättern, sich ablösen (*off s.th.* von etw); sich mit Schuppen bedecken; Kessel-, Zahnstein ansetzen; *to remove the ~~s from s.o.'s eyes (fig)* jdm die Augen öffnen; *~~s dropped, fell from my eyes* es fiel mir wie Schuppen von den Augen; **~ing** ['-iŋ] Abschuppung, Abschieferung; *(Metall)* Verzunderung *f*; *~~-ladder (mil hist)* Sturm-, Feuerleiter *f*; **~y** ['-i] schuppig; *sl* schäbig; **3.** *s* Waagschale *a. fig*; *meist pl* Waage *f*; *a pair of ~~s* e-e Waage; *tr (auf e-r Waage)* wiegen; wiegen, schwer sein (*one pound* ein Pfund); *fig* abwägen; *itr* gewogen werden; *the S~~s (astr)* die Waage; *to hold the ~~s even (fig)* gerecht urteilen; *to throw into the ~~ (fig)* in die Waagschale werfen; *to turn the ~~s (fig)* den Ausschlag geben; *fam* wiegen (*at 80 lb* 80 Pfund); *kitchen ~~s (pl)* Küchenwaage *f*.

scalene ['skeili:n] *math* ungleichseitig.

scal(l)awag, scallywag ['skæləwæg, -i-] *zoo* Kümmerling; *sl* Schuft *m*.

scallion ['skæljən] *bot* Schalotte *f*.

scallop ['skɔləp] *s zoo* Kammuschel; *(Küche)* Muschelform, -schale *f*; *pl* Langetten *f pl*; *tr (Küche)* überbacken; *arch* auszacken, muschelartig verzieren; *(Nähen)* langettieren.

scalp [skælp] *s* Kopfhaut *f*; Skalp *m*; *fig* Trophäe; *geogr* (kahle) Bergkuppe *f*; *tr* skalpieren; *fig* kein gutes Haar lassen an; *Am* betrügen; *Am fam (bes. Theater-, Eintrittskarten)* mit Gewinn wieder verkaufen; **~er** ['-ə] Skalpjäger *m*; Schabemesser *n*; *Am sl* Spekulant *m*.

scalpel ['skælpəl] *med* Skalpell *n*.

scamp [skæmp] *tr* zs.pfuschen, zs.-schlampern; schlampig herstellen; *s* Lump, Schuft *m*; **~er** ['-ə] **1.** Pfuscher *m*; **2.** *itr* rennen, laufen; *(to ~~ about)* herum-, umherlaufen, -schweifen, umhertollen, -springen; *(to ~~ away, off)* weglaufen, ausrücken; *s* Galopp, Lauf *m*; schnelle Flucht *f*.

scan [skæn] *tr (Vers)* skandieren; prüfend, forschend betrachten; e-n flüchtigen Blick werfen auf; absuchen; rasch durchblättern, überfliegen; *video* abtasten, rastern; *itr* (die Verse) skandieren; sich skandieren lassen; *video* rastern; *s video* Abtastung *f*.

scandal ['skændl] *s* Ärgernis *n*, Stein des Anstoßes; Skandal *m*; Schande; üble Nachrede *f*; *to talk ~ about s.o.* über jdn losziehen, klatschen; **~ize** ['-dəlaiz] *tr* Anstoß erregen (*s.o.* bei jdm), schockieren; *to be ~~d* Anstoß nehmen (*at, by* an); empört sein (*at* über); **~monger** ['-mʌŋgə] Lästermaul *n*, -zunge *f*; **~ous** ['-dələs] skandalös, anstößig, schändlich, schimpflich; verleumderisch; klatschsüchtig.

Scandinavia [skændi'neivjə] Skandinavien *n*; **~n** [-n] *a* skandinavisch; *s* Skandinavier(in *f*) *m*.

scansion ['skænʃən] Skandieren *n*.

scant [skænt] knapp (*of* an); (etwas) zu klein, unzureichend; *(Erfolg)* mager; *(Pflanzenwuchs)* dürftig; **~iness** ['-inis] Knappheit; Unzulänglichkeit; Dürftigkeit; Armseligkeit *f*; **~y** ['-i] knapp, dürftig, mager; unzureichend, unzulänglich, ungenügend, nicht ausreichend; eng, schmal, klein.

scantling ['skæntliŋ] kleine *od* (unbedingt) erforderliche Menge *f*; Halbholz *n*; (Roh-)Entwurf *m*.

scape [skeip] *arch* Säulenschaft; *zoo bot* Stiel, Schaft *m*; **~goat** ['-gout] *rel u. fig* Sündenbock *m*; **~grace** ['-greis] Taugenichts, Lump, Strolch *m*.

scapular ['skæpjulə] *a scient* Schulter-(-blatt-); *s rel (~y)* Skapulier; *med* Schultertragband *n*.

scar [skɑ:] **1.** *s* Narbe *a. bot fig*; Schramme *f*, *fam* Kratzer *m*; *fig* Spur *f*; *tr* (ver)schrammen; verunstalten; *itr (to ~ over)* vernarben; **~red** ['-d] *a* vernarbt; voller Narben; **2.** Fels-, Steilhang *m*, Klippe *f*.

scarab ['skærəb] (Mist-)Käfer, Pillendreher; Skarabäus *m a. Schmuck*.

scarc|e [skɛəs] selten, spärlich, rar, nicht alltäglich; knapp, nicht ausreichend vorhanden, schwer zu bekommen(d); *to make o.s. ~~ (fam)* sich selten machen; **~ely** ['-li] *adv* gerade (so) eben; kaum, schwerlich; *~~ anything* kaum etwas, fast nichts; **~eness** ['-nis], **~ity** ['-iti] Verknappung, Knappheit *f*, Mangel *m* (*of* an); *fig* Seltenheit, Ungewöhnlichkeit *f*; *~~ of goods, of provisions, of raw materials* Güter-, Lebensmittel-, Rohstoffmangel *m*; *~~ value* Seltenheitswert *m*.

scar|e [skɛə] *tr* Schrecken einjagen (*s.o.* jdm); er-, aufschrecken; *(to ~~ away, off)* auf-, verscheuchen; *to ~~ up (Geld)* auftreiben; *(Wild)* aufscheuchen; *itr* erschrecken; Angst haben, sich fürchten; *s* Schreck(en) *m*; Entsetzen *n*; Panik, Psychose, Angst *f*; *to create a ~~* e-e Panik verursachen; *to give s.o. a ~~* jdm e-n Schrecken einjagen; *war ~~* Kriegspsychose, -furcht *f*; *~~ buying* Angstkauf *m*, -käufe *m pl*; **~crow** ['-krou] Vogelscheuche *f a. hum*; *fig* Schreckgespenst *n*; **~-headline** sensationelle Schlagzeile *f*; **~monger** Miesmacher *m*; **~-news** Greuelnachricht *f*; **~strap** *sl aero* Sicherheitsgurt *m*; **~y** ['-ri] *fam* Schreck einjagend; (über)ängstlich, (furchtbar) bange.

scarf [skɑ:f] *pl a. scarves* **1.** Hals-, Kopftuch *n*, Schal *m*; Krawatte, Schleife, Halsbinde; *mil* Schärpe *f*; *Am* (Tisch-)Läufer *m*; **~-pin** Krawattennadel *f*; **~skin** *anat* Epidermis, Oberhaut *f*; **2.** *(~-joint) pl -s tech* Laschung, (Ver-)Blattung *f*; Blatt *n*; *mar* Scherbe *f*, Lasch *n*.

scarif|ication [skɛərifi'keiʃən] *agr* Aufreißen *n (des Ackerbodens)*; *med* Skarifizierung *f*; **~ier** ['-faiə] *agr* Reißpflug *m*; *med* Impfmesser *n*; **~y** ['-fai] *tr agr* aufreißen; eggen; *med* skarifizieren; *fig* verreißen, scharf kritisieren; *(Gefühle)* verletzen.

scarlatina [skɑ:lə'ti:nə] *med* Scharlach *m*.

scarlet ['skɑ:lit] *s* Scharlach(farbe *f*) *m*; scharlachfarbene(r, s) Stoff *m od* Kleid *n*; *a* scharlachfarben, -rot; *fig* sündig, unzüchtig; **~ fever** *med* Scharlach *m*; **~ hat** Kardinalshut *m*; **~ runner** Feuer-, Türkische Bohne *f*.

scarp [skɑ:p] *s* Steilhang *m*; Böschung *f*; *tr* (steil) abschrägen; abböschen; **~ed** [-t] *a* steil, abschüssig.

scat [skæt] *itr fam* abhauen; *mus* unverständliche Wörter singen; **~ty** ['-ti] *fam* plemplem.

scath|e [skeið] *tr fig* herunterreißen, -machen; **~ing** ['-iŋ] *fig* verletzend, beißend, scharf.

scatter ['skætə] *tr (to ~ about)* ver-, umher-, ausea.streuen; bestreuen; *(Nachrichten)* verbreiten; zerstreuen *a. phys; (Menschen)* ausea.jagen, versprengen; verschwenden, vergeuden; *itr (Menschenansammlung)* sich zerstreuen, sich verteilen, sich auflösen; **~-brain** flatterhafte(r) Mensch, Wirrkopf *m*; **~-brained** *a* flatterhaft, fahrig; **~ed** ['-d] *a* ver-, zerstreut, vereinzelt, einzeln(stehend); *tech* gestreut, diffus; **~ gun** *Am* Schrotflinte *f*; **~ing** ['-riŋ] *a Am parl (Stimmen)* zersplittert; *s tech* Streuung *f*; **~ rug** *Am* Brücke *f (Teppich)*.
scaveng|e ['skævindʒ] *tr (die Straße)* kehren, reinigen; *mot* spülen; *itr* die Straße kehren; **~er** ['-ə] Straßenkehrer *m*, -reinigungsmaschine *f*; *zoo* Aasfresser *m*.
scenar|io [si'nɑ:riou] *pl -os theat* Szenarium; *film* Drehbuch *n*; **~ist** ['si:nərist] *(~~ writer)* Drehbuchautor *m*.
scen|e [si:n] *allg u. theat* Schauplatz *m*; *theat* Szene *f*, (Bühnen-)Bild *n*; Szene *f*, Auftritt *m a. allg*; *allg* Bild *n*; Szene *f*, erregte(r) Auftritt *m*; Handlung; Szenerie *f*; *pl* Kulissen *f pl*; *behind the ~~s (a. fig)* hinter den Kulissen; *to come on the ~~* auf-, in Erscheinung treten; *the ~~ is laid in London* die Szene spielt in London; *change of ~~* Szenenwechsel *m*; *fig* Luftveränderung *f*; *~~ of accident, crime* Unfall-, Tatort *m*; *~~-dock (theat)* Requisitenraum *m*; *~~-painter* Bühnen-, Dekorationsmaler *m*; *~~-shifter* Kulissenschieber *m*; **~ery** ['-əri] *theat* Bühnenbild *n*, Dekoration, Ausstattung; *allg* Szenerie; Landschaft *f*; **~ic(al)** ['si:nik(əl)] *a* dramatisch, Theater-; szenisch, Szenen-, Bühnen-; landschaftlich, Landschafts-; landschaftlich reizvoll, malerisch; *s* Heimatfilm *m*; *~~ artist* Bühnenmaler *m*; *~~ railway* Berg-u.-Tal-Bahn *f*.
scent [sent] *tr* riechen; *(Tier)* wittern; *fig* ahnen, wittern, *fam* riechen; mit (s-m) Duft erfüllen; parfümieren *(with* mit); *itr* wittern; duften, riechen *(of* nach); *s* (Wohl-)Geruch, Duft *m*; Parfüm *n*; Duft-, Riechstoff; Geruchssinn *m*; *(Tier)* Witterung, Fährte, Spur *f*; *fig* Spürsinn, *fam* Riecher *m*, gute Nase; Ahnung *f*, Verdacht *m*; (Geruchs-)Spur *f*; *to get ~ of s.th.* von etw Wind bekommen; *to put on a false ~* auf e-e falsche Fährte locken; *to throw s.o. off the ~ (fig)* jdn von der richtigen Fährte ablenken; **~-bottle** Riech-, Parfümflasche *f*; **~ed** ['-id] *a* parfümiert, wohlriechend, duftend; **~less** ['-lis] geruchlos.
sceptic ['skeptik] Skeptiker, Zweifler *m*; **~al** ['-əl] skeptisch, zweifelnd; **~ism** ['-sizm] Skeptizismus *m*.
sceptre, *Am* **scepter** ['septə] *s* Zepter *n*.
schedule ['ʃedju:l, *Am* 'skedʒul] *s* Liste *f*, Katalog *m*, Verzeichnis, Inventar *n*, Auf-, Zs.stellung, Übersicht, Tabelle *f*; Schema; Formblatt *n*, Vordruck; *Am* Stunden-, Fahr-, *allg* Zeit-, Dienst-, Arbeitsplan; (erklärender) Zusatz, Zusatzparagraph, -artikel *m*; Begleitschreiben *n*; Anlage *f*, -hang *m*; *com* Konkursbilanz *f*, Inventar *n*; *(tax ~)* (Steuer-)Klasse *f*; *tr* (in die Liste) eintragen; (in Tabellenform) auf-, zs.stellen; e-n Plan, ein Programm machen für; *Am* fest-, ansetzen, vorsehen *(on* auf; *for tomorrow* für morgen); anfügen, -hängen, als Anhang beigeben; *(according) to ~ (Am)* programmgemäß; (fahr)planmäßig; *to arrive on ~* fahrplanmäßig, pünktlich ankommen; *production ~* Produktionsprogramm *n*; *train ~* Zugfolge *f*; *wage ~* Lohntarif *m*; *work ~* Arbeitsplan *m*; *~ of arrivals and departures* Tafel *f* der ankommenden u. abfahrenden Züge; *~ of fees* Gebührenordnung *f*; *~ of expenses* Kostenaufstellung *f*; *~ of prices* Preisverzeichnis *n*; *~ of rates* Frachttarif *m*; *~ of speakers (Am)* Rednerliste *f*; **~ed** ['-d] *a*: *as ~~* fahrplanmäßig; *to be ~~ for* vorgesehen sein für; *(Am) to be ~~ to arrive at* fahrplanmäßig ankommen um; *~~ price* Listenpreis *m*; **~ time** Abfahrts-, Ankunftszeit *f*; Beginn *m*.
schem|a ['ski:mə] Schema *n*, (systematische) Anordnung *f*; Entwurf, Plan *m*, Übersicht *f*; **~atic** [ski'mætik] schematisch; **~atize** ['ski:mətaiz] *tr* schematisieren; **~e** [ski:m] *s* (Aktions-)Plan *m*, Projekt *n*, Entwurf *m*; Intrige; Vision, Utopie *f*; System, Schema *n*; Aufstellung, Tabelle *f*; Diagramm *n*, graphische Darstellung *f*; *tr* planen, entwerfen; betreiben; ausdenken; aushecken, anzetteln; intrigieren; *itr* Pläne machen *od* schmieden *(for s.th.* zu etw); intrigieren, Ränke schmieden; *allocation, pension ~~* Zuteilungs-, Pensionsplan *m*; *bubble ~~* Schwindelunternehmen *n*; *colo(u)r ~~* Farbzusammenstellung *f*; *~~ of work* Arbeitsplan *m*; **~er** ['-ə] Pläne-, Ränkeschmied *m*; **~ing** ['-iŋ] intrigant.
schism ['sizəm] Schisma *n*, Kirchenspaltung *f*; **~atic(al)** [siz'mætik(əl)] *a* schismatisch; **~atic** *s* Schismatiker *m*.
schist [ʃist] *geol* Schiefer *m allg*.
schizophren|ia [skitso(u)'fri:njə] Schizophrenie *f*; **~ic** [-'frenik] schizophren.
schnorkle, schnorkel ['ʃnɔ:kl] *s. snorkel u. snort*.
schol|ar ['skɔlə] Gelehrte(r), Wissenschaftler; Kenner; Lernende(r); *(Univ.)* Stipendiat *m*; *sl* jem, der lesen u. schreiben kann; *to be bred a ~~* studiert haben; *not to be much of a ~~* kaum lesen u. schreiben können; **~arly** ['-əli] *a adv* gelehrt, wissenschaftlich (gebildet); lernbegierig, eifrig (im Lernen); **~arship** ['-əʃip] Gelehrsamkeit; Wissen(schaft *f*) *n*, Bildung *f*; Stipendium *n*; *to win a ~~* ein Stipendium erhalten *(to* für); **~astic** [skə'læstik] *adv ~~ally (a)* akademisch; Universitäts-, Schul-, Bildungs-, Erziehungs-; *rel hist* scholastisch; formalistisch, dogmatisch, pedantisch; *s* Gelehrte(r), Schulmann; Pedant; Scholastiker *m*; *~~ profession* Lehrberuf *m*; **~asticism** [skə'læstisizm] Scholastik *f*.
school [sku:l] *s* Schule *f a. fig*; *Am* College *n*, Hochschule *f*; Schulgebäude *n (pl)*; (Schul-)Unterricht *m*, Unterrichtsstunden *f pl*; Fakultät *f*; *zoo* (Fisch-)Schwarm *m*; *fig* Schule, Richtung; (Lebens-)Art *f*, Stil *m*; *tr* schulen, unterrichten, -weisen, erziehen; gewöhnen *(to* an); in s-e Gewalt bringen; *(Zunge)* zügeln; *itr zoo* in Schwärmen zs.leben; *at ~* in der Schule, im Unterricht; *of the old ~* von der alten Schule, von altem Schrot u. Korn; *to go to ~* zur Schule gehen; die Schule besuchen; *to graduate at (Am from) a ~* ein Abschlußexamen ablegen; *to keep ~* Unterricht erteilen, Schule halten; *to leave ~* die Schule verlassen, (von der Schule) abgehen; *to send to ~* in die Schule schicken; *boarding ~* Internat *n*; *commercial ~* Handelsschule *f*; *continuation ~* Fortbildungsschule *f*; *dancing ~* Tanzschule *f*; *day ~* Tagesschule *f*; *denominational, parochial ~* Konfessionsschule *f*; *driving ~* Fahrschule *f*; *grammar ~* Gymnasium *n*, Lateinschule *f*; *language ~* Sprachenschule *f*; *night, evening ~* Abendschule *f*; *primary ~* Volks-, Grundschule *f*; *private ~* Privatschule *f*; *public ~ (England)* (exklusive) höhere (Internats-)Schule; *Am* Volksschule *f*; *secondary, high ~* höhere, Oberschule *f*; *summer-~* Ferienkurs *m*; *Sunday ~* Sonntagsschule *f*, Kindergottesdienst *m*; *vocational ~* Berufsschule *f*; **~able** ['-əbl] schulpflichtig; **~ age** schulpflichtige(s) Alter *n*; *of ~~* schulpflichtig; **~-board** *Am* Schulbeirat *m*; **~-book** Schulbuch *n*; **~-boy** Schuljunge, Schüler *m*; **~-days** *pl* Schulzeit *f*; **~-edition** Schulausgabe *f*; **~-fee** Schulgeld *n*; **~fellow, mate** Schulkamerad, Mitschüler *m*; **~-girl** Schulmädchen *n*, Schülerin *f*; **~-house** Schulhaus, -gebäude *n*; ['-'-] Wohnhaus *n* des Schulleiters; **~ing** ['-iŋ] Schulunterricht *m*; Ausbildung, Schulung *f*; Schulgeld; *(Pferd)* Zureiten *n*; **~-leaving certificate** Abgangszeugnis *n*; **~-magazine** Schülerzeitung *f*; **~-master** (Schul-)Lehrer, (Di-)Rektor *m*; **~-mistress,** *fam* **~-ma'm, ~-marm** ['-mɑ:m] Lehrerin *f*; **~room** Schul-, Klassenzimmer *n*; **~ session** *Am* Unterrichtszeit *f*; **~-teacher** Schullehrer(in *f*) *m*; **~-work** Schularbeit *f*; **~-yard** *Am* Schulhof *m*; **~-year** Schuljahr *n*.
schooner ['sku:nə] *mar* Schoner *m*; *Am* Planwagen; Deckelschoppen *m*.
sciatic [sai'ætik] *a* Hüft-; **~a** ['-ə] *med* Ischias *f*.
scien|ce ['saiəns] Wissen(schaft *f*) *n*; *(einzelne)* Wissenschaft; Kunde; *sport* Technik, Geschicklichkeit *f*; *Christian S~~* Christliche Wissenschaft *f*; *exact, pure ~~* exakte, reine Wissenschaft *f*; *natural, physical ~~* Naturwissenschaft *f*; *political ~* Staatswissenschaft *f*; *social ~~* Soziologie, Sozialwissenschaft *f*; *~~ of industrial administration* Betriebswirtschaftslehre *f*; *~~ of music* Musikwissenschaft *f*; *~~ fiction* Zukunftsroman *m*; **~tific** [saiən'tifik] wissenschaftlich; systematisch; *sport* geschult, trainiert; **~tist** ['saiəntist] *(bes.* Natur-)Wissenschaftler *m*.
scimitar ['simitə] Krummsäbel *m*.
scintill|a [sin'tilə] *fig* Funke(n) *m*; *not a ~~ of truth* nicht ein Fünkchen Wahrheit; **~ate** ['sintileit] *itr* funkeln; Funken sprühen; *fig* glänzen *(with* mit); **~ation** [sinti'leiʃən] Flimmern, Funkeln; *fig* Glänzen *n*.
sciol|ism ['saiəlizm] Halbwissen *n*, -bildung *f*; Scharlatanismus *m*; **~ist** ['-ist] Halbgebildete(r); Blender *m*.
scion ['saiən] *bot* Schößling *m*; Pfropfreis *n*; *fig* Sproß, Sprößling *m*.
sciss|el ['sisl] Metallspäne *m pl*; **~ion** ['siʒən] Zerschneiden, Spalten, (Zer-)Trennen *n*; Schnitt, Riß, Spalt *m*; Trennung *f a. fig*; **~ors** ['sizəz] *pl*: *a pair of ~~* e-e Schere *f*; **~ure** ['siʒə] Riß, Spalt, (Ein-)Schnitt *m*; *med* Fissur *f*.
scler|osis [skliə'rousis] *pl -oses* [-i:z] *med* Sklerose, Verkalkung *f*; *~~ of the arteries* Arterienverkalkung *f*; **~otic** [-'rɔtik], **~ous** ['skliərəs] sklerotisch, verhärtet; *~~ (coat)* Lederhaut *f* (des Auges).
scoff [skɔf] *s* Spott, Hohn *(at* über); Zielscheibe *f* des Spottes; *sl* Fraß *m*; *itr* spotten *(at* über); *to be ~~ed at* Ziel des Spottes sein; **~er** ['-ə] Spötter *m*; **~ing** ['-iŋ] spöttisch, höhnisch.
scold [skould] *s* zänkische(s) Weib *n*, Xanthippe *f*; *tr* ausschimpfen; *itr* schelten, zanken; keifen, schimpfen; **~ing** ['-iŋ] *a* schimpfend; zänkisch;

s Schelte *f*; *to give s.o. a ~~* jdn schelten (*for being late* weil er sich verspätete).

sconce [skɔns] **1.** *fam* Birne *f*; *fam* Köpfchen *n*, Grips *m*; **2.** Leuchterarm; Arm-, Wandleuchter; Kerzenhalter *m*; **3.** *(Univ., bes. Oxford) tr (zu e-r Strafe)* verdonnern; *s* Strafe *f*.

scon(e) [skɔn, skoun] flache(s), runde(s) Teegebäck *n*.

scoop [sku:p] *s* Schaufel, Schippe; (Schöpf-)Kelle *f*; Käsemesser *n*; Schöpflöffel; *med* Spa(ch)tel *m*; (Waag-)Schale; *(~ful)* Schaufel-, Löffel-, Kelle(voll); Mulde, Senke, Bodensenkung *f*; *fig fam* große(r) Spekulationsgewinn; Fischzug *m*; *Am sl (Zeitung)* Erst-, Alleinmeldung *f*; *tr (to ~ out)* ausschaufeln, -schöpfen, -graben, -höhlen; *med* auskratzen; *fam (to ~ in, up)* einheimsen, -stecken; zs.scharren; *Am sl* ausstechen, übertrumpfen, mit e-r Erstnachricht schlagen; *to ~ up* an-, auf-, häufen; *(Geld)* scheffeln; *in one ~ (fig)* mit e-m Schlag; **~-wheel** Schöpfrad *n*.

scoot [sku:t] *itr fam* abhauen, türmen (gehen); **~er** ['-ə] (Kinder-)Roller; *(motor ~~)* (Motor-)Roller *m*; *Am* Eisjacht *f*; *Am* (schnelles) Motorboot *n*.

scope [skoup] Fassungs-, Begriffsvermögen *n*; Horizont, Gesichtskreis; Spielraum *m*, Gelegenheit *f*; Ausblick *m*, -sicht; Reichweite *f*; Bereich *m* od *n*, Umfang, Rahmen *m*; Ausdehnung, Länge *f*; Betätigungsfeld *n*; *(riding~) mar* Kabellänge *f*; *to give s.o. free ~* jdm freie Hand lassen (*to do* zu tun); *to give o.'s fancy full ~* s-r Phantasie die Zügel schießen lassen; *it comes within my ~* es schlägt in mein Fach.

scorbutic [skɔ:'bju:tik] *med a* skorbutisch; *s* Skorbutkranke(r) *m*.

scorch [skɔ:tʃ] *tr* an-, versengen; *(die Haut)* verbrennen; (aus)dörren; *fig (mit Worten)* verletzen; *itr* versengt werden, verbrennen; ausdörren; *sl mot* sausen, rasen, rücksichtslos fahren; *s* verbrannte Stelle *f*; *mot* Rasen *n*; **~ed** [-t] *a* versengt, verbrannt; *~~-earth (policy)* (Politik der) verbrannte(n) Erde *f*; **~er** ['-ə] *fam* heiße(r) Tag *m*, Bollen-, Bullenhitze; bissige Bemerkung *f*; rücksichtslose(r) Fahrer; *sl* Knüller *m*, Sensation *f*, tolle(r) Kerl *m*; **~ing** ['-iŋ] *a* sengend; glühend heiß; *fig* scharf, bissig, verletzend.

score [skɔ:] *s* Einschnitt, Riß *m*, Ritze, Kerbe, Schramme *f*, *fam* Kratzer *m*; Rille, Rinne; markierte Linie, Markierung *f*, Strich *m*; *fig* Zeche, Rechnung, Schuld *f*; *fig* Groll *m*; Treffer-, Punktzahl *f*, Spielergebnis *n*; Stiege *f*, 20 Stück *n pl*; *fam* Dusel *m*, große(s) Glück *n*; *mus* Partitur; Musikbegleitung; *film* Begleitmusik *f*; *Am sl* Fischzug *m*, reiche Beute *f*; *pl* sehr viele, e-e ganze Menge; Scharen (*of* von); *tr* mit Kerben versehen; einkerben; mit Linien versehen; unterstreichen; *(to ~ up)* ankerben, -kreiden, -streichen; markieren, notieren, anschreiben, auf die Rechnung setzen; *(Spiel)* für sich buchen; zählen, gerechnet werden als; einstufen; *(Punkte)* erzielen; *sport (Tor)* schießen; *(Gewinn)* verbuchen, *fam* einstecken, -streichen; *mus* instrumentieren; *sl Am* scharf kritisieren, es (tüchtig) geben (*s.o.* jdm); *to ~ off* ausstechen, übertrumpfen; *to ~ out* ausstreichen; *itr* (e-n Punkt, Punkte) gewinnen; *(beim Schießen)* treffen; e-n Vorsprung gewinnen; mitgerechnet werden; *fig* Erfolg, Glück haben; *on the ~* wegen (*of s.th.* e-r S); *on that ~* aus d(ies)em Grunde; was das betrifft; darüber; deswegen; *to ~ a hit* e-n Treffer erzielen; *to know the ~ (Am)* Bescheid wissen; auf Draht sein; *to make a ~ off s.o. (fam)* jdm eins auswischen; *to run up a ~* Schulden machen; *to settle a ~ with s.o.* mit jdm abrechnen; mit jdm e-e Rechnung zu begleichen haben; *what's the ~?* wie steht das Spiel? was ist los? **~r** ['-rə] *sport* Torschütze; Punktrichter *m*.

scori|a ['skɔ:riə] *pl -ae* ['-ii:] *metal* Schlacke *f*; **~fy** ['skɔ:rifai] *tr* verschlacken.

scorn [skɔ:n] *s* Verachtung; Schmähung, Verhöhnung *f*; Hohn, Spott; verächtliche(r) Mensch *m*; *tr* verachten, geringschätzen; verschmähen, als unwürdig ablehnen (*to do, doing* zu tun); *to laugh to ~* auslachen; *to think ~ of, to hold in ~* verachten; **~ful** ['-ful] verächtlich, spöttisch.

scorpion ['skɔ:pjən] *zoo* Skorpion *m*.

Scot [skɔt] Schotte *m*, Schottin *f*; **~ch** [-ʃ] *a* schottisch; *sl* geizig; *s* schottische(r) Dialekt; *(~~ whisky)* schottische(r) Whisky *m*; *the ~~ (pl)* die Schotten *m pl*; *~~ tape* Klebstreifen *m*; *~~ terrier* Scotchterrier *m (Hunderasse)*; **~chman** ['-ʃmən] *oft pej* Schotte *m*; **~land** ['-lənd] Schottland *n*; *~~ Yard* die Londoner Kriminalpolizei *f*; **~s** [skɔts] *a* schottisch; *s* (das) Schottisch(e); **~sman** ['-smən] *pl ~smen (geog)* Schotte *m*; **~swoman** ['-swumən] *pl ~swomen* Schottin *f*; **~tish** ['-iʃ] *bes. lit* schottisch.

scot [skɔt] Steuer(geld *n*), Abgabe *f*, (erhobener) Beitrag *m*; *to pay o.'s ~* s-n Anteil bezahlen; *to pay ~ and lot* alles auf Heller u. Pfennig bezahlen; **~free** *fig* ungestraft; *to get off ~~* ungestraft, unverletzt davonkommen.

scotch [skɔtʃ] **1.** *tr* (leicht) verletzen, verwunden; *fig* unterdrücken, unschädlich machen; *s* (Ein-)Schnitt, Riß *m*; Kerbe; Rille *f*; **2.** *tr* (ab)bremsen; verkeilen; *(Rad)* feststellen; *fig* vereiteln; *s* Bremsklotz *m a. fig.*

scoundrel ['skaundrəl] Schurke, Schuft, Lump, Gauner *m*; *a u.* **~ly** ['-i] schurkisch; Schurken-.

scour ['skauə] **1.** *tr* (ab)scheuern, -schrubben; (gründlich) reinigen; (ab)spülen; schlämmen; ab-, wegwaschen; *med* purgieren, spülen; wegwischen, -fegen, entfernen; *(Wolle)* entfetten; *fig* befreien, säubern (*of* von); *itr* scheuern, schrubben; blankgescheuert werden; *s* Scheuern, Schrubben *n*; *(Wolle)* Entfettung *f*; Scheuerpulver *n*; starke Strömung *f*; *zoo* Durchfall *m*; **2.** *tr* ab-, durchsuchen, abkämmen, durchstöbern (*for* nach); *itr (to ~ about)* herumsuchen, rennen.

scourge [skɔ:dʒ] *s* Peitsche, Geißel *a. fig*; *fig* Strafe, Plage *f*; *tr* (aus)peitschen, geißeln; züchtigen; *fig* quälen, peinigen, plagen.

scout [skaut] *s* Späher, Kundschafter *m*; *mar* Aufklärungsfahrzeug *n*; *aero* Aufklärer; *(boy ~)* Pfadfinder; *sl* Bursche, Kerl; *(Oxford)* College-aufwärter, -diener *m*; *(England)* Straßenwacht *f*; *itr mil* aufklären; auf der Suche sein (*for* nach); Pfadfinder sein; *to ~ about, around* herumsuchen; *on the ~* auf Kundschaft, auf der Suche; *~* **car** (Panzer-)Spähwagen *m*; **~master** Pfadfinderführer *m*; **2.** *tr* verächtlich abtun, *fam* pfeifen auf.

scow [skau] Schute *f*, Leichter *m*.

scowl [skaul] *itr* finster dreinschauen; die Stirn runzeln; *to ~ at s.o.* jdn schief ansehen; *s* finstere(r) Blick *m*, böse(s) Gesicht; Stirnrunzeln *n*.

scrabble ['skræbl] *itr* scharren, kratzen; kritzeln; *to ~ about* herumsuchen (*for* nach); *to ~ for s.th.* etw überall zs.-suchen, zs.scharren.

scrag [skræg] *s fig* Gerippe *n*; *(Schaf, sl Mensch)* Hals *m*; *tr sl* den Hals umdrehen (*s.o.* jdm); **~giness** ['-inis] Hagerkeit, Magerkeit *f*; **~gy** ['-i] mager, hager, dürr, knochig.

scram [skræm] *itr Am sl* sich verdünnisieren, verschwinden; *meist: ~!* hau ab! mach, daß du wegkommst!

scramble ['skræmbl] *itr* klettern, krabbeln; sich (katz)balgen, sich reißen (*for* um); *tr* durchea.werfen; *(to ~ up)* zs.-raffen, zs.scharren; *s* Klettern *n*; Balgerei *f* (*for* um); *fig* Kampf *m* (*for* um), Jagd *f* (*for* nach); *Am sl* Wettrennen *n*, Tanz *m* Jugendlicher; *~d eggs (pl)* Rühreier *n pl*.

scrap [skræp] **1.** *s* Stück(chen), ein bißchen *n*; *(~ of paper)* (Papier-)Fetzen; Abfall; Schrott; *(Text)* Auszug, Abschnitt *m*, Stelle *f*; Zeitungsausschnitt *m*; *pl* Brocken (Essen) *m pl*; (Speck-)Grieben *f pl*; (in ein Buch geklebte) Andenken *n pl*; Reste *m pl*, Trümmer *pl*; *a* bruchstückhaft; *tr* verschrotten; *fig* zum alten Eisen werfen; (achtlos) beiseite-, wegwerfen, ausrangieren; abmontieren; *not a ~* kein bißchen; **~book** Sammelbuch, -album *n*; **~-heap** Müll-, Abfall-, Schutt-, Schrotthaufen *m*; **~-iron** Alteisen *n*, Eisenschrott *m*; **~py** ['-i] *a* zs.geflickt; bruchstückhaft; zs.gestoppelt; *~* **value** Schrottwert *m*; **2.** *fam s* Rauferei, Keilerei *f*, Streit *m*; *itr* sich raufen, sich streiten, sich balgen (*with* mit); **~per** ['-ə] *fam* Raufbold *m*; **~py** *a fam* rauflustig.

scrap|e [skreip] *tr* (ab)kratzen, -bürsten; glatt, sauber bürsten; (ab)schaben; abstreifen; (wund)scheuern, aufschürfen; *itr* kratzen, scheuern; scharren; sich reiben (*against* an); e-n Kratzfuß machen; *s* Kratzen, Scharren *n*; Kratzfuß; dünne(r) (Brot-)Aufstrich; Kratzer *m*; Schramme; *fig* Klemme, Patsche *f*; *in a ~~* in Verlegenheit (*about* um); *to ~~ along, to ~~ a living* sich (mühsam) durchschlagen; *to ~~ off, out* aus-, ab-, herauskratzen; *to ~~ through* gerade noch durchkommen; *to ~~ up, together (a. fig)* zs.kratzen, -scharren; *to bow and ~~* e-n Kratzfuß machen; *to get into a ~~* sich in die Nesseln setzen; *to ~~ (up) acquaintance with s.o.* sich an jdn heranmachen, sich anbiedern; *to ~~ the fiddle* auf der Violine kratzen; **~er** ['-ə] *tech* Abstreifer, Schaber; Schrapper *m*; Kratzbürste *f*, -eisen *n*; Fußabstreifer *m*; Schäleisen *n*; Schrupphobel *m*; Ziehklinge; Reißnadel *f*; *fig* Geizhals *m*; **~ing** ['-iŋ] *a* kratzend, scharrend; *fig* geizig; *s* Kratzen *n*; *meist pl* Abfall, *fig* Abschaum *m*; *fig* Zs.gekratzte(s), mühsam Ersparte(s) *n*.

scratch [skrætʃ] *tr* (zer)kratzen, ritzen, verschrammen; scheuern, (wund)reiben; kritzeln; *(Zündholz)* anstreichen; *bes. pol sport (Namen)* streichen, zurückziehen; *itr* (sich) kratzen; *(Huhn)* scharren; *fig* Schwierigkeiten haben; zurücktreten, s-e Meldung zurückziehen; *s* Kratzen *n*; Schramme *f*, *fam* Kratzer *m*; Riß *m*; Kratzwunde *f*; Gekritzel *n*; *Am film* Arbeitstitel *m*; *sport* Startlinie *f*; *Am sl* Geld *n*, Nulpe *f*; günstige(r) Eindruck *m*; *a* Gelegenheits-, Zufalls-; zufällig, improvisiert, rasch zs.gestellt, zs.gewürfelt; *sport* ohne Vorgabe; *to ~ for* mühsam zs.-suchen; *to ~ off* abkratzen; *to ~ out, through* (aus)streichen, ausradieren; *to ~ up* zs.kratzen, mühsam zs.-

bringen; *at, from, on* ~ von der Startlinie aus; ohne Vorgabe; *from* ~ von Grund auf, ganz von vorne; *up to* ~ startbereit; *fam* auf dem Sprunge; *fam* auf der Höhe; *to come up to* ~ s-n Verpflichtungen nachkommen, s-e Pflicht erfüllen; den Erwartungen entsprechen; *to start from* ~ *(fig)* mit nichts anfangen; *to* ~ *out s.o.'s eyes* jdm die Augen auskratzen; *to* ~ *o.'s head* sich den Kopf kratzen; *to* ~ *the surface (fig)* an der Oberfläche bleiben; *a* ~ *of the pen* ein paar (flüchtig geschriebene) Worte *n pl*; ~ **hardness** *tech* Ritzhärte *f*; ~ **pad** *Am* Notizblock *m*; ~ **paper** Konzept-, Schmierpapier *n*; ~ **race** Rennen *n*, Wettlauf *m* ohne Vorgabe; ~**y** ['-i] *(Stoff, Geräusch)* kratzend; gekritzelt; (schnell) zs.gekratzt; *(Mannschaft)* zs.gewürfelt; *fam* leicht aufbrausend.

scrawl [skrɔ:l] *tr itr* (be)kritzeln; *s* Gekritzel *n*, Kritzelei *f*.

scrawny ['skrɔ:ni] dünn, mager.

scray [skrei] *zoo* Seeschwalbe *f*.

scream [skri:m] *itr* (laut auf)schreien (*with fright* vor Angst); kreischen; zetern; *(to* ~ *with laughter)* schallend lachen; *(Wind)* heulen; *fig* zum Himmel schreien; *Am sl* sich rasch bewegen; *tr* (hinaus)schreien; *to* ~ *o.s. (hoarse)* sich (heiser) schreien; *s* (Auf-, Angst-)Schrei *m*, (lautes) Geschrei; Heulen *n*; *fam* ulkige(r) Kerl *m*, seltsame(s) Ding *n*; *he's a* ~ *(fam)* er ist zum Brüllen; ~**er** ['-ə] Schreihals; *orn* Wehrvogel; *sl* Teufelskerl *m*, Mordsding *n*, -spaß *m*; *sl typ* Ausrufezeichen *n*; *Am sl* sensationelle Schlagzeile, Reklametafel, tolle Geschichte *f*, Krimi *m*; ~**ing** ['-iŋ] schreiend, kreischend, schrill; himmelschreiend; *sl* toll, phänomenal; *sl* urkomisch, ulkig.

scree [skri:] *geol* Geröll *n*.

screech [skri:tʃ] *itr tr* kreischen, schreien; *(Fahrzeug)* quietschen; *(Lokomotive)* pfeifen; *tr* kreischend ausstoßen; *s* schrille(r) Schrei, Angstschrei *m*; Kreischen *n*; ~-**owl** Käuzchen *n*.

screed [skri:d] lange(r) Brief *m*; Tirade *f*; lange(r) Auszug *m*.

screen [skri:n] *s* Licht-, Wand-, Wind-, Ofenschirm *m*; spanische Wand *f*; Vorhang *m*; Schutzwand; *Br* (Wind-)Schutzscheibe *f*; *fig* Schutz *m*; *mil* Deckung, Tarnung; Verschleierung, Nebelwand, Tarnoperation *f*, (Sicherungs-)Schleier *m*; *aero* Abschirmung *f*; (Jagd-)Schutz *m*; (grobes) Sieb *n*, (Draht-)Gaze *f*, Fliegenfenster *n*; *typ photo* Raster *m*; *film* Leinwand *f*; *fig* Film; *(Radar)* Bildschirm *m*; *el* Schirmgitter *n*; *phys* Blende *f*, Filter *n*; *tr* abschirmen, -decken; verdecken, verhüllen, verschleiern; *fig* schützen; *mot* abblenden; *mil* tarnen, ein-, vernebeln; (durch-)sieben; durchleuchten; *(to* ~ *out) (Menschen)* überprüfen, auslesen; *(Sache)* sichten; *(auf e-e Leinwand)* projizieren; *(Film)* vorführen; (mit der Filmkamera) aufnehmen; verfilmen; *itr* verfilmt werden; sich verfilmen lassen; *to* ~ *off* abschirmen; abteilen; *on the* ~ auf der Leinwand, im Film; *to bring to the* ~, *to put on the* ~ verfilmen; *air-raid* ~ Verdunkelung *f (am Fenster)*; *fire-*~ Kaminschirm *m*; ~ **adaptation** Filmbearbeitung *f*; ~ **advertising** Kinoreklame *f*; ~ **defroster** *mot* Frostschutzscheibe *f*; ~ **dot** Rasterpunkt *m*; ~**ed** [-d] *a el* abgeschirmt; ~ **grid** Schirmgitter *n*; ~**ing** ['-iŋ] Abschirmung *f*; Durchsieben *n*; Durchleuchtung; *fig* Überprüfung *f*; *pl* Rückstand, Abfall *m* beim Sieben; (Durch-)Gesiebte(s) *n*; ~~ *test* Eignungsprüfung *f*; ~**play** Drehbuch *n*; ~ **reporter** Wochenschaureporter *m*; ~ **rights** *pl* Verfilmungsrechte *n pl*; ~-**test** *tr film* Probeaufnahmen machen (*s.o.* von jdm); ~ **washer** Scheibenwaschanlage *f*; ~-**wiper** Scheibenwischer *m*; ~-**wire** Maschendraht *m*; ~-**writer** Drehbuchautor *m*.

screw [skru:] *s (male, external* ~*)* Schraube; Schraubendrehung; Schiffsschraube *f*; *aero* Propeller; *(Ball)* Effet *m*; *Br sl* Tütchen *n* Tabak; *Br* (Konfekt-)Tüte; *Br* Schindmähre *f*; *Br* Knikker, Geizhals; gerissene(r) Händler; *Br sl* Gefängniswärter; *Br sl* (Arbeits-)Lohn *m*; *tr* (fest-, zu)schrauben, festdrehen (*on, to* an); (ver)drehen; *fig* e-n Druck ausüben auf, unter Druck setzen, zwingen; erpressen; *itr* sich (zu)drehen lassen; *fig* sich drehen; *fig* geizig sein; *Am sl* abhauen, verschwinden; *to* ~ *off* abschrauben; *to* ~ *up* aufschrauben; *to* ~ *up o.'s courage* sich zs.reißen; Mut fassen; *to* ~ *up o.'s face, features, eyes* das Gesicht verziehen; *to give another turn to the* ~ die Schraube anziehen *a. fig*; *to have o.'s head* ~*ed on the right way (fig)* nicht auf den Kopf gefallen sein; *to put the* ~ *on s.o.* jdn unter Druck setzen; *to tighten a* ~ e-e Schraube anziehen; *he has a* ~ *loose (fig)* bei ihm ist e-e Schraube locker; *there's a* ~ *loose somewhere* da ist irgendwas nicht in Ordnung; ~**ball** *sl s* komische(r) Kauz; *sport* Effetball *m*; *a* (ein bißchen) komisch, verrückt; ~-**cap** Verschraubung *f*, Schraubdeckel *m*; ~-**clamp** Schraubzwinge *f*; ~-**conveyer** Förderschnecke *f*; ~**driver** Schraubenzieher *m*; ~**ed** [-d] *a* gewunden; verschraubt; *sl* besoffen; *Am sl* hereingelegt; ~~ *fitting* Schraubmuffe *f*; ~ **jack** Wagenheber *m*; ~ **joint** Verschraubung *f*; ~-**nut** Schraubenmutter *f*; ~-**plate** Gewindekluppe *f*; ~-**propeller** Schiffsschraube *f*; ~-**tap** Gewindebohrer *m*; ~-**thread** Schraubengang *m*; ~-**wrench** Schraubenschlüssel *m*; ~**y** ['-i] *sl* komisch, eigenartig; *Am* verrückt; knickerig; *sl* betrunken.

scrib|al ['skraibəl] *a* Schreib-; ~~ *error* Schreibfehler *m*; ~**e** [skraib] *tr tech* (an)reißen; *s hist* (Buch-)Schreiber; *rel hist* Schriftgelehrte(r); *Am* Schriftsteller, Autor *m*; ~**er** ['-ə] *tech* Reißnadel *f*.

scribbl|e ['skribl] *tr* (hin-, be)kritzeln; *fig* flüchtig hinwerfen, eilig zu Papier bringen; *(Textil)* krempeln; *itr* kritzeln; *to* ~~ *up* bekritzeln; *s* Gekritzel *n*; (literarisches) Machwerk *n*; ~**er** ['-ə] Schmierfink; Sudler; Schreiberling *m*; *(Textil)* Krempelmaschine *f*; ~**ing** ['-iŋ] Kritzeln *n*; ~~ *block, pad* Notizblock *m*.

scrimmage ['skrimidʒ] Handgemenge *n*, Rauferei *f*; *(Fußball) Am* Raufen *n*; ~**r** ['-ə] *(Rugby)* Stürmer *m*.

scrimp [skrimp] *tr* zu klein, zu kurz, zu eng machen; *fig* knapp halten; *itr* knausern, (sehr) sparsam sein (*on* mit); *a u.* ~**y** ['-i] beschnitten; knapp, dürftig; *fig* knauserig.

scrimshank ['skrimʃæŋk] *itr Br sl mil* sich drücken.

scrip [skrip] **1.** *obs* Ränzel *n*, Tasche *f*; **2.** Zettel, Schein; Gut-, Interims-, Zwischenschein *m*; ~ **company** *Am* Kommanditgesellschaft *f* auf Aktien; ~ **money** Interims-, *Am* Besatzungsgeld *n*.

script [skript] (Hand-)Schrift *f*, Schriftstück, Manuskript *n*; *jur* Urschrift *f*, Original *n*; *typ* Schreibschrift *f*; *theat* Text(buch *n*) *m*; *film* Drehbuch *n*; Prüfungsarbeit *f*; ~**er** ['-ə], ~-**writer** *film* Drehbuchautor; *radio* Hörspielverfasser *m*; ~-**girl** *film* Scriptgirl *n*; ~**ural** ['skriptʃərəl] *a* Schrift-; biblisch; ~**ure** ['skriptʃə] Schriftstück, Manuskript, Dokument *n*; *(the) Holy S*~~*(s) (pl)* die Heilige Schrift *f*; ~~ *lesson* Religionsstunde *f*.

scroful|a ['skrɔfjulə] *med* Skrofel, Skrofulose *f*; ~**ous** ['-əs] skrofulös.

scroll [skroul] *hist* (Schrift-)Rolle; Liste *f*, Verzeichnis *n*; *arch* Spirale, Schnecke, Volute *f*; *fam* Schnörkel *m*; *(Heraldik)* Spruchband *n*; (Geigen-)Schnecke *f*; ~-**saw** Laubsäge *f*; ~-**work** Schnörkel(verzierungen *f pl*) *m pl*; Laubsägearbeit *f*.

scrotum ['skroutəm] *pl -ta* ['-tə] *anat* Hodensack *m*.

scrounge [skraundʒ] *tr itr sl* mausen, mopsen, stibitzen, *mil* organisieren; *Am sl* anpumpen; ~**r** ['-ə] *sl* Organisierer, Dieb *m*; *Am sl* Pumpgenie *n*.

scrub [skrʌb] **1.** *s* Buschwerk, Gestrüpp, Krüppelholz *n*; Busch(wald); abgenutzte(r) Besen; Krüppel *m*, Kümmerform *f*; *fam* Zwerg, Knirps; *Am sport* Ersatzspieler, -mann *m*; *pl* Ersatzmannschaft *f*; *a* zurückgeblieben, verkümmert; kümmerlich, armselig; *sport* Ersatz-; ~**by** ['-i] verkümmert; buschbestanden; klein; armselig, schäbig; struppig; ~-**team** *Am sport* zweite Garnitur *f*; **2.** *tr* (ab)schrubben, scheuern; (ab)bürsten; *itr* schrubben, scheuern; *fig* sich placken, sich (ab-)quälen; *s* Schrubben, Scheuern *n*; Plackerei, Quälerei *f*; Packesel *m fig*; *to* ~ *out an order (com sl)* e-n Auftrag annullieren; ~**ber** ['-ə] Scheuerfrau *f*; Schrubber; *tech* Berieselungsturm *m*; ~**bing-brush** Scheuerbürste *f*; ~**woman** *Am* Scheuerfrau *f*.

scruff [skrʌf] Genick *n*, Nacken *m*; *to take by the* ~ *of the neck* im Genick beim Kragen packen.

scrummage ['skrʌmidʒ] *(Rugby)* Raufen *n* (um den Ball).

scrumptious ['skrʌmpʃəs] *fam* prima, Klasse; *(Speise)* köstlich; prima in Schale; bombig; Bomben-; großartig.

scrunch [skrʌntʃ] *tr* zerkauen, zermalmen, zerknacken, zerbeißen; *itr* knirschen; *s* Knirschen *n*.

scrup|le ['skru:pl] *s fig* Zweifel *m*, Bedenken *n*, innere Unsicherheit *f*; ganz kleine Menge *f*; *pharm* Skrupel *n* (= *1,296 g)*; *itr* zweifeln (*about, at* an); zögern, Bedenken tragen (*to do* zu tun); sich ein Gewissen machen (*at* aus); ~**ulous** ['skru:pjuləs] voller Zweifel; bedenklich (*about* in); (über)gewissenhaft, genau, exakt; ängstlich.

scrutin|ize ['skru:tinaiz] *tr* genau erforschen, prüfen, untersuchen; *(Wahlstimmen)* zählen; ~**izer**, ~**eer** ['-aizə, -'ni:ə] (Wahl-)Prüfer *m*; ~**y** ['-i] prüfende(r) Blick *m*; genaue Prüfung *od* Untersuchung; Wahlprüfung *f*.

scud [skʌd] *itr* laufen, eilen; rasch (dahin)gleiten; *mar* lenzen; *s* Lauf *m*, schnelle Bewegung *f*; *sl* schnelle(r) Läufer *m*; Bö *f*; Regenschauer *m*; *mar* Wolkenfetzen *m pl*; *Am sl* langweilige Arbeit *f*.

scuff [skʌf] *tr* abscheuern, abnutzen; *(Fuß)* nachziehen; *itr* schlurfen.

scuffle ['skʌfl] *itr* sich balgen, sich herumschlagen (*with* mit); schlurfen; *s* Balgerei *f*, Handgemenge; Schlurfen *n*.

scull [skʌl] *s mar* Wriggriemen; *(~er)* Skuller *m*; *itr tr* wriggen.

scullery ['skʌləri] Spül-, Abwaschküche *f*; ~-**maid** Küchenmädchen *n*, -hilfe *f*.

sculpt|or ['skʌlptə] Bildhauer *m*; **~ress** ['-ris] Bildhauerin *f*; **~ural** ['-tʃərəl] *a* Bildhauer-; Skulpturen-; **~ure** ['-tʃə] *s* Bildhauerei, Plastik *f*; Bildwerk *n*, Skulptur *f*; *tr* (aus)meißeln, -hauen; gießen; modellieren (*in, out of* in); *geol* auswaschen.

scum [skʌm] *s tech* Abstrich; *fig* Abschaum *m* (*of the earth* der Menschheit); **~my** ['-i] schäumend, schaumbedeckt; schaumig; *fig* wertlos, gemein, niedrig.

scupper ['skʌpə] **1.** *mar* Speigatt *n*; **2.** *tr sl* erledigen (*s.o.* jdn); *(Plan)* sabotieren, ruinieren.

scurf [skə:f] Grind *m*, (Kopf-)Schuppen *f pl*; Kruste *f*; *tech* Kesselstein *m*; Schuppenkleid *n*; **~y** ['-i] grindig, schorfig; schuppig.

scurril|ity [skʌ'riliti] Gemeinheit; Unanständigkeit *f*; **~ous** ['skʌriləs] ordinär, gemein, unanständig; zotig.

scurry ['skʌri] *itr* hasten *a. fig*, rennen; trippeln, hoppeln; *to ~ away, off* sich aus dem Staub machen; *s* Rennen *n*, Eile *f*; Hoppeln, Trippeln *n*; (Regen-, Schnee-)Schauer *m*.

scurvy ['skə:vi] *s med* Skorbut *m*; *a* niederträchtig; **~ grass** *bot* Löffelkraut *n*.

scut [skʌt] Stummelschwanz *m*; *(Hase)* Blume *f*; *Am sl* Neuling, gemeine(r) Kerl *m*.

scutch [skʌtʃ] *tr (Flachs)* schwingen; *s* Flachsschwinge *f*.

scutcheon ['skʌtʃən] Wappenschild; Namen-, Türschild; Schloßblech *n*.

scute [sk(j)u:t] *zoo* Schuppe *f*.

scuttle ['skʌtl] **1.** Kohleneimer, -kasten *m*; **2.** *s* (Dach-)Luke; *mar* Springluke *f*; *tr (Schiff)* anbohren (u. versenken); *fig* vernichten; **~-butt** *mar* Trinkwasserfaß; *Am sl* Gerücht *n*, Latrinenparole *f*; **3.** *itr* schnell laufen, rennen; *to ~ away, off* weglaufen, sich in Sicherheit bringen; *s* überstürzte Flucht *f*, Aufbruch *m*; *policy of ~* Verzichtpolitik *f*.

scythe [saið] *s* Sense *f*; *tr* (ab)mähen.

sea [si:] See *f*, Meer *n*; Ozean *m*; Seegang *m*, hohe Welle, Woge; Dünung; *fig* große Menge *f*, Ströme *m pl*; *across, beyond the ~(s)* in, nach Übersee; *at ~* auf (hoher) See; auf dem Meere; *fig* ratlos, aufgeregt; *by the ~* an der See; *by ~ and land, land and ~* zu Wasser u. zu Lande; *on the ~* auf dem Meer; auf See; am Meer; *to ~* zur See; *to follow the ~* zur See fahren, Seemann sein; *to go to ~* zur See gehen, Seemann werden; sich einschiffen; *to put to ~* in See stechen; *the freedom of the ~s* die Freiheit der Meere; *half ~s over* betrunken; *the high ~s (pl)* die Hochsee *f*; **~ air** Seeluft *f*; **~ anchor** Treibanker *m*; **~ anemone** *zoo* Seeanemone *f*; **~ bag** Seesack *m*; **~ battle** Seeschlacht *f*; **~bird, -fowl** Seevogel *m*; **~ biscuit** Schiffszwieback *m*; **~board** *s* Küste(nstrich *m*) *f*; *a* Küsten-; **~-borne** *a* auf dem Seeweg befördert; *(Schiff)* auf See befindlich; **~-calf** Seehund *m*; **~-captain** Schiffskapitän *m*; **~ chart** Seekarte *f*; **~ chest** Seekiste *f*; **~-coast** (Meeres-) Küste *f*; **~-cow** Walroß *n*; Seekuh *f*; Flußpferd *n*; **~ cucumber** *zoo* Seegurke *f*; **~ damages** *pl* Seeschaden *m*; **~-dog** Hundshai; Seehund; *fig* Seebär *m*; **~drome** Wasserflughafen *m*; **~-eagle** Seeadler *m*; **~ elephant** See-Elefant *m*; **~farer** ['-fɛərə] Seefahrer *m*; **~faring** ['-fɛəriŋ] *a* seefahrend; *s* Seefahrt *f*; **~-fight** Seeschlacht *f*; **~-fire** Meeresleuchten *n*; **~-fish** Meerfisch *m*; **~-floor** Meeresboden *m*; **~ food** *Am* eßbare Seetiere *n pl*; **~-fowl** Seevogel *m*; **~-front** Seefront, -seite *(e-r Hafenstadt)*; Uferstraße *f*; **~ ga(u)ge** Tiefgang *m (e-s Schiffes)*; **~-girt** meerumschlungen; **~-god** Meeresgott *m*; **~-going** seefahrend; Hochsee-; seetüchtig; **~-green** seegrün; **~-gull, -mew** Seemöwe *f*; **~-hog** *zoo* Tümmler *m*; **~-horse** Walroß; Seepferdchen *n*; **~ insurance** Seeversicherung *f*; **~ jet** Marinedüsenjäger *m*; **~-kale** *bot* Meerkohl *m*; **~-legs** *pl*: *to get, to find o.'s ~~* sich an den Seegang gewöhnen; **~ letter** Schiffspaß *m*; **~-level** Meeresspiegel *m*; **~-lion** Seelöwe *m*; **seaman** ['-mən] *pl -men* Seemann; Matrose; *Am mil mar* Obergefreite(r) *m*; **~-mark** Seezeichen *n*; **~-mile** Seemeile *f (1852 m)*; **~-nettle** Qualle *f*; **~ pen** *zoo* Seefeder *f*; **~plane** Wasserflugzeug *n*; **~~ base** Seefliegerhorst *m*; **~~ carrier** Flugzeugträger *m*; **~port** Seehafen *m*; **~-power** Seestreitkräfte *f pl*; *pol* Seemacht *f*; **~-proof** seetüchtig; **~quake** Seebeben *n*; **~ rescue-service** Seenotdienst *m*; **~ road** *Am* Schiffahrtsweg *m*; **~ robber** Seeräuber *m*; **~-rover** Pirat(enschiff *n*); *fam* Hering *m*; **~-salt** Meersalz *n*; **~scape** *(Malerei)* Seestück *n*; **~-serpent** Seeschlange *f*; **~shell** Seemuschel *f*; **~shore** Meeresküste *f*; **~sick** seekrank; **~sickness** Seekrankheit *f*; **~side** ['-'said] *s* Meeresküste; *a* See-; *to go to the ~~* an die See gehen; **~~ place, resort** Seebad *n*; **~-swallow** Seeschwalbe *f*; Sturmvogel *m*; **~-tangle, ~weed** Seegras *n*, Tang *m*; **~-town** Hafenstadt *f*; **~-trip** Schiffsreise *f*; **~-urchin** Seeigel *m*; **~-voyage** Seereise *f*; **~-wall** Deich *m*; **~ward** ['si:wəd] *s* Richtung *f* aufs Meer; Land *n* am Meer; *a* seewärts; am Meer gelegen; Meer-, See-; **~ward(s)** *adv* seewärts; **~-water** Seewasser *n*; **~-way** Seegang *m*; Kielwasser *n*; *Am* Seeweg *m*; **~weed** Seetang *m*; **~ wind** Seewind *m*; **~worthy** ['si:wə:ði] seetüchtig.

seal [si:l] **1.** *s* Siegel *n a. fig*; Plombe *f*, Verschluß; Stempel *m*, Petschaft *n*, Siegelring; Abdruck *m*, Fußspur; *fig* Bekräftigung, Bestätigung; *tech* Dichtung *f*, Wasserverschluß, Verguß *m*; *tr* (be-, ver)siegeln; (ab)stempeln; plombieren; *(Brief)* zukleben; *fig* bekräftigen, bestätigen; (rechtskräftig) übergeben, abtreten; endgültig, unwiderruflich entscheiden, festlegen; *jur* pfänden; *tech* luftdicht verschließen, abdichten, verlöten, zuschmelzen; *to ~ up* versiegeln; *to set o.'s ~ on s.th.* sein Siegel auf etw drücken; etw genehmigen; etw s-n Stempel aufdrücken; *to ~ s.o.'s fate* jds Schicksal besiegeln; *to ~ with lead* plombieren; *given under ~ of office, public ~* Dienstsiegel *n*; **~ed** [-d] *a* versiegelt; verschlossen; plombiert; dicht; *a ~~ book (fig)* ein Buch mit sieben Siegeln; **~ing** Versiegeln, Plombieren *n*; Abschluß *m*; **~~ pliers (pl)** Plombierzange *f*; **~~ wax** Siegellack *m*; **~~ wire** Abschmelzdraht *m*; **~ ring** Siegelring *m*; **2.** Seehund *m*, Robbe *f*; *fur ~* Pelzseehund *m*, -robbe *f*; **~er** ['-ə] Robbenfänger *m*; **~ery** ['-əri], **~ing** ['-iŋ] Robbenfang *m*; **~skin** Seehund(fell *n*); Seal *m*.

seam [si:m] *s* Saum *m*, Naht; Fuge, Furche; Verbindungslinie *f*; Spalt *m*, Rille *f*, Einschnitt *m*; Runzel, Narbe *f*; *min (Kohle)* Flöz, *(Erz)* Lager *n*; *geol* Schicht; *med* Knochennaht, Sutur *f*; *tr* säumen; zs.nähen; zs.fügen; (durch-) furchen *a. fig*, ritzen, schrammen; **~less** ['-lis] nahtlos; **~stress** ['semstris, *Am* 'si:m-] Näherin *f*; **~ welding** Nahtschweißung *f*; **~y** ['-i] gesäumt; *the ~~ side (Kleidung)* die linke Seite; *fig* die Schattenseite *f*.

sear [siə] *a lit* versengt, dürr, trocken; *fig* gefühllos; *tr* versengen, verbrennen; ausdörren, -trocknen; brandmarken; *a. fig*; schwielig machen; *fig* verhärten, abstumpfen; *med* ätzen.

search [sə:tʃ] *tr* durchsuchen, -forschen, -stöbern; durchdringen, fahren durch; *(Gewissen)* erforschen; *itr* suchen, forschen, stöbern (*for, after* nach); *fig* zu ergründen suchen (*into s.th.* etw); *s* Suche, Durchsuchung, Durchforschung, genaue Untersuchung; Leibesvisitation; Nachforschung *f* (*for* nach); *to ~ out* ausfindig machen, aufstöbern; *in ~ of* auf der Suche nach; *to ~ o.'s heart (fig)* sein Herz prüfen; *to go in ~ of* auf die Suche gehen nach; *to make a thorough ~* e-e gründliche Durchsuchung vornehmen; *~ me! (Am)* keine Ahnung! *house-~* Hausdurchsuchung *f*; *right of ~* Durchsuchungs-, Haussuchungsrecht *n*; **~er** ['-ə] Durchsuchende(r); Durchsuchungs-, Zollbeamte(r) *m*; *med* Sonde *f*; **~ing** ['-iŋ] *a* eindringlich, gründlich, tiefschürfend; durchdringend; *(Wind)* schneidend, scharf; *s* Haussuchung; Zollrevision; Durch-, Untersuchung *f*; **~~ fire (mil)** Streufeuer *n*; **~light** Scheinwerfer *m*; **~-party** Rettungs-, Bergungsmannschaft *f*; **~-warrant** Haussuchungsbefehl *m*.

season ['si:zn] *s* Jahreszeit; Saison *a. theat*; Kurzeit; (bestimmte kürzere) passende Zeit *f*; *Am com* Fälligkeitstermin *m*; Dauerkarte *f*; *tr* reifen lassen; gewöhnen (*to* an); *mil* abhärten; mildern, abschwächen; *(Speise)* würzen; *(Fleisch)* abhängen lassen; *(Holz)* lufttrocknen; *fig* interessant machen; würzen, salzen; *itr* reifen; *(Holz)* ablagern; sich abhärten; *for a ~* für e-e Weile, e-e Zeit; *in ~* an der Zeit; zur rechten Zeit; fristgerecht; *zoo* in der Brunstzeit; *out of ~* nicht an der Zeit; zu ungelegener Zeit; *fig* am falschen Platz; *in ~ and out of ~* zu jeder Zeit, jederzeit; *in good ~* rechtzeitig *adv*; *in the off-~s* außerhalb der Saison; *with the best compliments for the ~!* mit den besten Wünschen zum Fest! *dead, dull ~* Sauregurkenzeit *f*; *holiday ~* Ferienzeit *f*; *late ~* Nachsaison *f*; *peak, busy ~* Hochsaison *f*; *theatrical ~* Spielzeit *f*; *tourist ~* Reisezeit *f*; **~able** ['-əbl] *a* an der Zeit; der Jahreszeit angemessen; zeitgemäß; rechtzeitig, gelegen, passend, angebracht; **~al** ['-l] jahreszeitlich; saisonbedingt, Saison-; periodisch, regelmäßig wiederkehrend; **~~ commodity, item** Saisonartikel *m*; **~~ fluctuations, variations (pl)** Saison-, Konjunkturschwankungen *f pl*; **~~ trade** Saisongewerbe *n*; **~~ worker** Saisonarbeiter *m*; **~ed** ['-d] *a* gewürzt; abgelagert; *fig* kampferprobt; *com* renommiert; **~ing** ['-niŋ] Würze *f a. fig*; Gewürz *n*; *tech* Alterung; *(Mensch)* Abhärtung, Angewöhnung; Milderung *f*; **~-ticket** *Br* Zeit-, Dauerkarte *f*; **~~ holder** Inhaber *m* e-r Dauerkarte.

seat [si:t] *s* Sitz(weise, -gelegenheit *f*, -platz); (Theater-)Platz; Sitz, Stuhl, Hocker, Sessel *m*; Sitzfläche *f*; Hinterteil, Gesäß *n*; Schauplatz; *parl* (Abgeordneten-)Sitz *m*, Mandat *n*; Mitgliedschaft *f*; (Regierungs-, Amts-, Verwaltungs-, Wohn-, Land-)Sitz; *med* Herd *m*, Stelle *f*; *tech* Lager *n*; (Fahrrad-)Sattel *m*; *com* Hauptniederlassung *f*, Sitz *m*; *tr* (hin)setzen; zu e-m Sitz(platz) verhelfen, e-n Sitz (-platz) verschaffen *od* anweisen (*s.o.* jdm); *(Raum)* Sitzgelegenheit bieten für, Platz haben für, fassen; *(Möbel)* mit e-r (neuen) Sitzfläche versehen; *(Menschen)* machen, erheben zu; *tech* lagern; *(Ventil)* einschleifen; *to ~ o.s* sich (hin)setzen; *to be ~ed* sich (hin-, nieder)setzen, sich niederlassen; sitzen; s-n (Wohn-)Sitz, sein Amt haben; *to be in the driver's ~ (fig)* die Zügel in den Händen halten; *to have a ~ on a committee* e-n Sitz im Ausschuß haben; *to have a good ~ (Reiten)* gut im Sattel sitzen; *to keep o.'s ~* Platz behalten, sitzenbleiben; *to take a ~* sich (hin)setzen; Platz nehmen; *to take o.'s ~* s-n Platz einnehmen, sich setzen; *to win, to lose a ~ (parl)* e-n Sitz gewinnen, verlieren; *take your ~s!* einsteigen! *to ~ 40 passengers* 40 Sitzplätze haben; *emergency, (Am) jump ~* Notsitz *m*; *folding ~* Klappsitz *m*; **~er** ['-ə] *in Zssgen mot* -sitzer *m*; *four-~~* Viersitzer *m*; **~ing** ['-iŋ] Platzanweisung, Unterbringung; Sitzanordnung, Platzverteilung *f*; Polster(material); *tech* Lager; Fundament *n*, Auflage(fläche) *f*; *~~ accommodation capacity* Sitzzahl *f*; *~~ pad (Am)* Sitzpolster *n*; *~~ room* Sitzplätze *m pl*.

sebaceous [si'beiʃəs] *a scient* Fett-, Talg-; talgig; *~* **gland** Talgdrüse *f*.

secant ['si:kənt] *math a* schneidend; *s* Sekante *f*.

sece|de [si'si:d] *itr* sich trennen (*from* von); austreten (*from* aus); übertreten (*to* zu); **~ssion** [si'seʃən] Abfall *m*, Lossagung, Sezession *f*; **~ssional** [si'seʃənl] *a* Sonder(bunds)-; **~ssionist** [si'seʃnist] Abtrünnige(r), Sonderbündler *m*.

seclu|de [si'klu:d] *tr* abtrennen, -sondern, isolieren (*from* von); **~ded** [-id] *a* isoliert; abgelegen; einsam; **~sion** [-'klu:ʒən] Absonderung; Isolation; Zurückgezogenheit *f*; *to live in ~~* zurückgezogen, einsam leben.

second ['sekənd] *a* zweit *a. mus*, nächst, weiter, ander, noch ein; *vor Superlativ*: zweit-; geringer (*to* als); untergeordnet (*to* dat); *s* Zweite(r), Nächste(r) *m*; *com* zweite Sorte *od* Güte *f*; Sekundant *m*; Sekunde *f a. mus*; Augenblick *m*; *rail* zweite Klasse *f*; *pl* Mittelsorte *f*, Waren *f pl* zweiter Güte; *tr bes. parl* unterstützen; helfen, beistehen, assistieren, sekundieren (*s.o.* jdm); fördern, stärken; *parl (Antrag)* unterstützen; [si'kɔnd] *Br mil* (ab)kommandieren (*for service on a staff* zum Dienst bei e-m Stab); *(Beamten)* abstellen; *adv* an zweiter Stelle, als zweite(r, s); *for the ~ time* zum zweitenmal; *in the ~ place* an zweiter Stelle, zweitens; *on ~ thoughts* bei nochmaliger Überlegung; *to be ~ to none* niemandem nachstehen; *to come ~* an zweiter Stelle kommen; *to get o.'s ~ wind (Am fam)* sich wieder erholen; wieder zu Kräften kommen; *to play ~ fiddle* die zweite Geige spielen *a. fig*; *wait a ~* warten Sie e-n Augenblick; *~ of exchange* Sekundawechsel *m*; **~ariness** ['-ərinis] Untergeordnetheit, Zweitrangigkeit *f*; **~ary** ['-əri] zweitrangig, untergeordnet, geringer, Neben-; *scient* sekundär, Sekundär-; *~~ accent (Wort)* Nebenton *m*; *~~ action, effect* Nebenwirkung *f*; *~~ education* höhere(s) Schulwesen *n*, -bildung *f*; *~~ era (geol)* Erdmittelalter, Mesozoikum *n*; *~~ liability* Haftungsschuld *f*; *~~ line* Nebenbahn *f*; *~~ objective (mil)* Ausweichziel *n*; Nebenabsicht *f*; *~~ school* höhere Schule *f*; *~~ target* Nebenziel *n*; *~* **ballot** Stichwahl *f*; **~-best** zweitbest; *to come off ~~ (fig)* den kürzeren ziehen; *~* **cabin** *mar* Kabine *f* 2. Klasse; *~* **chamber** *parl* Oberhaus *n*; **~-class** *a adv* zweiter Klasse; *~~ matter (Am)* Drucksache *f*; *~* **cousin** Vetter *m*, Base *f* zweiten Grades; *~* **floor** zweite(r), *Am* erste(r) Stock *m*; *on the ~~* im zweiten, *Am* ersten Stock; *~* **gear** *mot* zweite(r) Gang *m*; **~-hand** *a* aus zweiter Hand; gebraucht; *(Kleider)* getragen; *(Buch)* antiquarisch; *to have o.'s information at ~~* Nachrichten aus zweiter Hand haben; *~~ bookseller* Antiquar *m*; *~~ bookshop* Antiquariat *n*; *~~ material* Altmaterial *n*; *~* **hand** Sekundenzeiger *m*; *~* **lieutenant** Leutnant *m*; **~ly** ['-li] *adv* zweitens; *~* **nature** zweite Natur, feste Gewohnheit *f*; **~-rate** *a* zweitrangig, -klassig; von geringerer Qualität, minderwertig; *~* **sight** zweite(s) Gesicht *n*.

secre|cy ['si:krisi] Geheimhaltung; Verschwiegenheit; Heimlichkeit, Verborgenheit; Abgeschiedenheit; Schweigepflicht *f*; *in, with ~~* insgeheim, im geheimen, heimlich; *under pledge of ~~* unter dem Siegel der Verschwiegenheit; *breach of ~~* Vertrauensbruch *m*; *official, professional ~~* Amts-, Berufsgeheimnis *n*; *(violation of the) ~~ of letters* (Verletzung *f* des) Briefgeheimnis(ses) *n*; *~~ of vote, voting, ballot* Wahlgeheimnis *n*, geheime Wahl *f*; **~t** ['si:krit] *a* geheim, heimlich; Geheim-; verborgen, versteckt, einsam, abgelegen; verschwiegen, verschlossen, zurückhaltend; geheimnisvoll, mysteriös; *com (Teilhaberschaft, Reserven)* still; *s* Geheimnis (*from* vor); Mysterium *n*; *in ~~* insgeheim, im geheimen; *to be in the ~~* eingeweiht sein; *to keep, to betray a ~~* ein Geheimnis bewahren, verraten; *to keep ~~* verheimlichen, geheimhalten; *to let s.o. into the ~~* jdn einweihen; *bank ~~* Bankgeheimnis *n*; *official ~~* Staatsgeheimnis *n*; *an open ~~* ein offenes Geheimnis *n*; *professional, trade ~~* Berufs-, Geschäftsgeheimnis *n*; *~~ agent* Geheimagent *m*; *~~ ballot* geheime Abstimmung *f*; *~~ clause* Geheimklausel *f*; *~~ drawer* Geheimfach *n*; *~~ partner* stille(r) Teilhaber *m*; *~~ service* Geheim-, Nachrichtendienst *m*; *~~ society* Geheimbund *m*; *~~ traffic* Schleichhandel *m*; *~~ treaty* Geheimvertrag *m*, -abkommen *n*; *~~ understanding* geheime(s) Einvernehmen *n*; *~~ writing* Geheimschrift *f*; **~tarial** [sekrə'tɛəriəl] Büro-; *~~ clerk* Büroangestellte(r) *m*; **~tariat(e)** [sekrə'tɛəriət] Sekretariat *n*; **~tary** ['sekrətri] Sekretär; *com* Geschäftsführer; Schriftführer; (Staats-)Sekretär; *Am* Minister; Sekretär, Schreibtisch *m* mit Aufsatz; *private ~~* Privatsekretär *m*; *~~-bird (orn)* Sekretär *m*; *~~ of embassy, legation* Botschafts-, Legationssekretär *m*; *~~-general* Generalsekretär *m*; *S~~ of State* Staatssekretär; Minister; *Am* Außenminister *m*; *S~~ of State for Foreign Affairs, for Home Affairs, for War* Außen-, Innen-, Kriegsminister *m*; *S~~ of the Interior (Am)* Innenminister *m*; **~taryship** ['sekrətriʃip] Sekretärsstelle *f*; Schriftführeramt *n*; **~te** [si'kri:t] *tr* verstecken, verbergen, verheimlichen (*from* vor); *physiol* absondern, ausscheiden; **~tion** [si'kri:ʃən] Verheimlichung; *physiol* Absonderung, Ausscheidung, Sekretion *f*; **~tive** [si'kri:tiv] zurückhaltend, verschwiegen; geheim, verborgen; *physiol* sekretorisch; **~tiveness** [si'kri:tivnis] Zurückhaltung, Verschwiegenheit *f*.

sect [sekt] *bes. rel* Sekte; Gruppe, Schule, Richtung, Partei *f*; **~arian** [sek'tɛəriən] *a* sektiererisch; *fig* engstirnig; bigott; *s* Sektierer *m*; **~arianism** [sek'tɛəriənizm] Sektierertum *n*; **~ion** ['sekʃən] *s* Zerschneiden *n*, Schnitt *m*, Durchschneidung *f*; Ausschnitt *m*; Abgeschnittene(s) *n*; (dünne) Scheibe; *(Bevölkerung)* Schicht *f*; *(Buch)* Abschnitt, Paragraph *m*; Abteilung, Sektion *f*, Referat, Dezernat; Glied *n*, Teil *m*; (Anbau-)Einheit *f*; *Am rail* Abteil; Fach *a. fig*; *fig* Gebiet *n*, Distrikt, (Verwaltungs-)Bezirk; *Am* Stadtteil *m*, -viertel *n*; Parzelle *f*; *(cross-~~)* Querschnitt *m*; *arch* Profil *n*; Strecke(nabschnitt *m*), Teilstrecke *f*; *mil* Abschnitt *m*; *mil* Gruppe, Korporalschaft *f*, *Am* Halbzug; *math* Schnitt *m*; *med* Sektion, Leichenöffnung, Obduktion *f*; *tr* in Abschnitte zerlegen, unterteilen; *commercial, residential ~~* Geschäfts-, Wohnviertel *n*; *polling ~~* Wahlbezirk *m*; *~~ gang (rail)* Rotte *f*, Streckenarbeiter *m pl*; *~~ iron* Profileisen *n*; *~~ leader (Br)* Gruppen-, *Am* Halbzugführer *m*; *~~ mark* Paragraphenzeichen *n*; **~ional** ['sekʃənl] in Abschnitte eingeteilt; abgeteilt; zs.setzbar; Lokal-, Gebiets-, Bezirks-, Distrikts-; *~~ interests (pl)* Lokalinteressen *n pl*; *~~ view* Schnittbild *n*; **~ionalism** ['sekʃnəlizm] Partikularismus *m*; **~or** ['sektə] *math* Sektor, Ausschnitt; *mil* Abschnitt *m*; (Besatzungs-)Zone *f*; *postal ~~* Postbezirk *m*; *~~ boundary, line (mil)* Abschnittsgrenze *f*.

secular ['sekjulə] *a* weltlich, profan; weltgeistlich; alle hundert Jahre vorkommend *od* geschehend; säkular; hundertjährig; uralt; *s* Weltgeistliche(r) *m*; **~ization** [sekjulərai'zeiʃən] Säkularisierung; Verweltlichung *f*; **~ize** ['sekjuləraiz] *tr* säkularisieren; verweltlichen.

secur|e [si'kjuə] *a* sicher (*from* vor); vertrauensvoll, unbesorgt, sorgenfrei; gefahrlos; furchtlos; sicher, in Sicherheit; gesichert, beständig, fest, stark; *tech* zuverlässig, verläßlich, fest; *tr* sichern, in Sicherheit bringen, verwahren, schützen (*from, against* vor); sicherstellen; in Gewahrsam bringen; garantieren (*s.th. to s.o., s.o. s.th.* jdm etw); decken, Sicherheit bieten für; bewahren (*from* vor); sichern, festmachen, befestigen, feststellen; *(Türe)* (fest) verschließen; sich verschaffen, erwerben, bekommen, erhalten, erlangen; *(Zimmer)* bestellen; *(Platz)* belegen; *(Geschäft)* zustande bringen; *(Preis)* erzielen; *mil* decken; *to make ~~* festmachen, befestigen; *to ~~ a profit* e-n Gewinn erzielen; **~ed** [-d] *a* (ge)sicher(t), geschützt, gedeckt; *(Forderung)* bevorrechtet; **~ity** [-riti] Sicherheit (*against, from* vor); Unbesorgtheit, Furchtlosigkeit; Gewißheit, Überzeugtheit; Sorglosigkeit *f*; Schutz *m* (*against, from* vor); *tech* Festigkeit, Stabilität; Sicherheit, Gewißheit; Gewähr, Sicherheit, Sicherung, *jur* Bürgschaft, Garantie, Kaution *f*, Pfand *n*, Hypothek *f*; Bürge *m*; *mil* Sicherung, Abwehr *f*; *pl* Wertpapiere *n pl*, Effekten *pl*; *in ~~* in Sicherheit; *on, against ~~* gegen Sicherheit; *without ~~* ungesichert, ohne Sicherheit; *to furnish, to lodge ~~* Kaution stellen, Bürgschaft leisten; *to give ~~ for* Sicherheit bieten, Bürgschaft leisten (*for* für); *able to put up ~~* kautionsfähig; *additional, collateral ~~* zusätzliche Sicherheit *f*; *bearer ~ities (pl)* Inhaberpapiere *n pl*; *guilt-edged ~ities (pl)* mündelsichere Wertpapiere *n pl*; *investment ~ities (pl)* Anlagewerte *m pl*; *public ~ities (pl)* Staatspapiere *n pl*; *stock-exchange ~ities (pl)* Börsenpapiere *n pl*, -titel *m pl*; *~~ bond* Bürgschaftsschein *m*; *S~~ Council (pol)* Sicherheitsrat *m*; *~~ dealer* Effektenhändler *m*; *~~ market* Effekten-, Wertpapiermarkt *m*; *~~ measure* Sicherheitsmaßnahme *f*; *~~ sales (pl)* Wertpapierverkäufe *m pl*.

sedan [si'dæn] *(~-chair)* Sänfte; *mot* Limousine *f*.

sedat|e [si'deit] gesetzt, ruhig, gelassen; nüchtern; ernst; **~eness** [-nis] Gelassenheit, Gesetztheit, Ruhe *f*; Ernst *m*; **~ion** [si'deiʃən] *med* Beruhigung *f*; **~ive** ['sedətiv] *a* beruhigend, schmerzstillend; *s* Beruhigungs-, schmerzstillende(s) Mittel *n*.

sedentar|iness ['sedntərinis] sitzende Lebensweise; Seßhaftigkeit *f*; **~y** ['sedntəri] sitzend; seßhaft, ortsgebunden, an-, festgewachsen; *to lead a ~~ life* e-e sitzende Lebensweise haben.

sedge [sedʒ] Schilf-, Riedgras *n*.

sediment ['sedimənt] Niederschlag, (Boden-)Satz *m*; *geol* Ablagerung *f*, Sediment *n*; **~ary** [sedi'mentəri] *geol* sedimentär; Sediment-; *~~ rock* Sedimentgestein *n*; **~ation** [sedimen'teiʃən] Sedimentbildung *f*; *blood ~~* Blutsenkung *f*.

sedit|ion [si'diʃən] Aufwiegelung, Verhetzung *f*; Aufstand, Aufruhr *m*, Meuterei *f*; **~ious** [si'diʃəs] aufrührerisch; aufwieglerisch, hetzerisch; Hetz-.

seduc|e [si'dju:s] *tr* verführen; verlocken, verleiten (*into doing s.th.* dazu etw zu tun); korrumpieren; abbringen (*from* von); **~ement** [-mənt], **~tion** [si'dʌkʃən] Verführung; Verlockung *f*; **~er** [si'dju:sə] Verführer *m*; **~tive** [si'dʌktiv] verführerisch, verlockend; anziehend, reizvoll.

sedul|ity [si'dju:liti], **~ousness** ['sedjuləsnis] Emsigkeit *f*, Fleiß *m*; **~ous** ['sedjuləs] emsig, fleißig, eifrig.

see [si:] **1.** *irr saw* [sɔ:], *seen* [si:n] *tr* sehen, erblicken; ansehen, -schauen, betrachten, beobachten, prüfen; einsehen, verstehen, begreifen; herausbekommen, ausfindig machen, in Erfahrung bringen; erleben, erfahren; treffen, begegnen (*s.o.* jdm); be-, aufsuchen, um Rat fragen, zu Rate ziehen, konsultieren, gehen (*s.o.* zu jdm); sich wenden (*s.o.* an jdn); *(Besuch)* empfangen; *(Theaterstück, Film)* sehen; begleiten (*to* nach); dafür sorgen, darauf achten (*that* daß); *itr* sehen (können); sich ansehen, besichtigen, prüfen (*over s.th.* etw); verstehen, begreifen; *into s.th.* etw durchschauen, nachsehen, -schauen; sehen (*about, into* nach); überlegen, nachdenken; achtgeben, achten (*about, after, to* auf); sorgen, Sorge tragen (*about, after, to* für); sich kümmern (*about, after, to* um); *about doing s.th.* daß etw getan wird); *to come, to go to ~* besuchen; *to have ~n better days* bessere Tage gesehen haben; *to live to ~* erleben; *to ~ s.o.'s back* jdn von hinten, jdn (weg)gehen sehen; *to ~ daylight (fig)* das Ende absehen; etw klar sehen; *to ~ double* doppelt sehen; *to ~ fit* für richtig halten; *to ~ s.o. home* jdn nach Hause begleiten *od* bringen; *to ~ a joke* e-n Spaß vertragen; *to ~ the last of s.o.* jdn nicht mehr wiedersehen; *of s.th.* mit e-r S fertig sein, etw hinter sich haben; das Ende e-r S erleben; *to ~ a lot of s.o.* mit jdm häufig zs.sein; *to ~ red* rot sehen; *he makes me ~ red* er wirkt auf mich wie ein rotes Tuch; *to ~ service* etw von der S verstehen; in Benutzung sein (*for* seit); *mil* dienen; *to ~ things* Halluzinationen haben; *to ~ the use, advantage, good, fun of s.th.* den Zweck e-r S einsehen; *to ~ visions* hellsehen; *to ~ o.'s way to do(ing) s.th.* mit etw umzugehen, etw anzufassen wissen, zu etw aufgelegt sein; es für möglich halten, etw zu tun; *to ~ how the wind lies* sehen, woher der Wind weht; *as I ~ it* so, wie ich es sehe; *as far as I can ~* soweit ich sehe, wie mir scheint; *I'll ~ about it* ich werde es mir überlegen; *I ~* ich verstehe, allerdings; ach so; *~ to it that* sehen Sie zu, daß; sorgen Sie dafür, daß; *you ~* sehen Sie! wie Sie wissen! *~!* sieh, schau mal! *wait and ~!* abwarten (u. Tee trinken)! immer mit der Ruhe! *just let me ~!* e-n Augenblick (mal)! *that remains to be ~n* das wird sich zeigen; *~ you again* auf Wiedersehen! *~ me tomorrow* kommen Sie morgen zu mir; *to ~* **off** zur Bahn bringen, fortbegleiten; *to ~* **out** fertigbringen, beenden; bis zum Ende bleiben (*s.th.* e-r S); *s.o.* jdn hinausbegleiten; *to ~* **over** *s.th.* sich etw genau ansehen; über etw hinwegsehen; *to ~* **through** *tr* durchschauen; überstehen; durchhelfen (*s.o. with s.th.* jdm bei e-r S); *to ~ s.th. through* etw durchsetzen, abwickeln, erledigen (*on time* rechtzeitig); *itr fam* durchhalten; **~ing** ['-iŋ] *a* sehend; *s* Sehen *n*; Sehkraft *f*; Gesichtssinn *m*; *conj: ~~ that* in Anbetracht der Tatsache, daß; insofern; *~~-eye dog* Blindenhund *m*; **~r** ['-ə] Sehende(r); Visionär, Seher, Prophet *m*; **2.** Bischofssitz *m*, -amt *n*; *Holy, Papal S~* Päpstliche(r) Stuhl *m*.

seed [si:d] *s* Same(n) *m*; Samenkorn *n*; *(Orange)* Kern *m*; Saat *f*; *physiol* Samen; *(Bibel)* Samen *m*, Nachkommen(schaft *f*) *m pl*; *fig* Keim *m*, (erste) Anlage *f*, Ursprung *m*; *pl* Sämereien *f pl*, Saatgut *n*; *tr* (be)säen; *(Frucht)* entkernen, -steinen, -samen; *sport* auswählen, setzen *(Spieler)*; *itr* Samen tragen; sich aussäen; *to go, to run to ~* in Samen schießen; *fig* nachlassen, herunterkommen; verkümmern; verblühen; **~bed** Saatbeet *n*; **~ bulb** Samenzwiebel *f*; **~-cake** Kümmelkuchen *n*; **~case, -vessel** *bot* Samenkapsel *f*; **~-corn** Saatkorn, -gut *n*; **~-drill** Drillmaschine *f*; **~er** ['-ə] Sämann *m*; Sämaschine *f*; Entkerner, -steiner *m (Gerät)*; **~-grower** Saatzüchter *m*; **~iness** ['-inis] Samenfülle *f*, Kernreichtum *m*; *fam* Unpäßlichkeit; *fam* Schäbigkeit *f*; **~-leaf** Keimblatt *n*; **~less** ['-lis] samen-, kernlos; **~ling** ['-liŋ] *bot* Sämling *m*; **~ pearl** Saatperle *f*; **~-plot** Saatbeet *n*; Pflanzschule; *fig* Brutstätte *f*; **~-potato** Saat-, Pflanzkartoffel *f*; **~(s)man** ['-zmən] Sämann; Samenhändler *m*; **~-time** Saatzeit *f*; **~y** ['-i] kernreich; in Samen geschossen; *(Glas)* mit Bläschen; *fam* schäbig; *fam* mies, elend; *to look ~~* schlecht aussehen.

seek [si:k] *irr sought, sought tr* (auf-)suchen; suchen nach; *(Rat)* einholen; versuchen (*to* zu); durchsuchen, erkunden, erforschen; zu bekommen versuchen; begehren, streben, trachten nach, verfolgen; verlangen; *to do s.th.* etw zu tun suchen; sich bewerben (*employment* um e-e Stelle); *itr* suchen, auf der Suche sein (*after, for* nach); *to ~ out* ausfindig machen, herausbekommen; heraussuchen; *to ~ through* durchsuchen; *to ~ the good offices of s.o.* jds Vermittlung erbitten; *to ~ a quarrel* Streit suchen *od* anfangen; *to ~ shelter* Schutz suchen; *it is not far to ~* das liegt nahe, auf der Hand; *little, much sought after* wenig, stark gesucht, gefragt; **~er** ['-ə] Sucher *m* (*after* nach).

seem [si:m] *itr* (er)scheinen, vorkommen; den Eindruck haben *od* machen; **~ing** ['-iŋ] *a* anscheinend, scheinbar, angeblich; **~ingly** ['-iŋli] *adv* allem Anschein nach; anscheinend; **~liness** ['-linis] Schicklichkeit *f*, Anstand *m*; Angebrachtheit *f*; **~ly** ['-li] *a adv* schicklich, anständig; passend, angebracht; *it is not ~~* es gehört sich nicht.

seep [si:p] *itr* sickern, lecken; *s* Sickerstelle *f (im Boden)*; **~age** ['-idʒ] (Durch-)Sickern, Lecken; Sickerwasser *n*.

seersucker ['siəsʌkə] leichte gestreifte Leinwand *f* (*od* Baumwollstoff *m*).

seesaw ['si:'sɔ:] *s* Schaukelbrett *n*, Wippe *f*; Schaukeln *a. fig*, *fig* Hin u. Her, Auf u. Ab *n*; *tr itr (to play at ~)* schaukeln, wippen; (sich) auf- u. ab-, hin- u. herbewegen *a. fig*; *fig* schwanken, zögern.

seethe [si:ð] *itr* sieden, kochen; sprudeln, schäumen (*with* vor) *a. fig*; er-, aufgeregt sein.

segment ['segmənt] *s* Abschnitt, Teil *m*; *biol* Glied; *math* Segment *n*; *tech* Lamelle *f*; *tr* (in Abschnitte) einteilen; *itr biol* sich teilen; **~al** [seg'mentl] segmentartig; in Abschnitte eingeteilt; Abschnitt-; **~ation** [segmən'teiʃən] Einteilung in Abschnitte; *biol* Furchung, Zellteilung *f*.

segregat|e ['segrigeit] *tr* isolieren, absondern; trennen; *tech* ausseigern; *itr* sich absondern; *biol* mendeln; *a* ['segrigit] getrennt, abgesondert, isoliert; **~ion** [segri'geiʃən] (Rassen-)Trennung; Absonderung, Isolierung; *biol* Aufspaltung; *tech* Ausseigerung *f*.

seine [sein, si:n] Schleppnetz *n*.

seise *s. seize.*

seism|al ['saizml], **~ic(al)** ['-ik(əl)] seismisch; Erdbeben-; **~ogram** ['-əgræm] Seismogramm *n*; **~ograph** ['-əgrɑ:f] Seismograph *m*; **~ology** [saiz'mɔlədʒi] Erdbebenkunde *f*; **~ometer** [-'mɔmitə] Seismometer *n*.

seiz|e, *jur a.* **seise** [si:z] *tr* Besitz ergreifen *od* nehmen von; sich bemächtigen (*s.th.* e-r S), sich aneignen; beschlagnahmen, konfiszieren, einziehen; pfänden; gefangen-, festnehmen, verhaften; (er)greifen, fassen, packen; *fig (Gelegenheit)* (beim Schopf) ergreifen *od* fassen; *fig* begreifen, verstehen, fassen; *mar* befestigen, festzurren; *itr* sich festklemmen; *to be ~ed by, with s.th.* von e-r S ergriffen, befallen werden; *to ~~ up (tech)* sich festfressen; *to ~~ (up)on s.th.* sich e-r S bemächtigen, von e-r S Besitz ergreifen; **~in, seisin** ['-in] Besitz(ergreifung *f*) *m*; *(Immobilien)* Besitzrecht *n*; **~ing** ['-iŋ] Beschlagnahme; Ergreifung *f*; *mar* Zurring *m*; *pl* Zurrtau; *tech* Festfressen *n*; **~ure** ['si:ʒə] Besitzergreifung, Inbesitznahme; Beschlagnahmung, Einziehung, Konfiskation; Pfändung; Gefangen-, Festnahme, Verhaftung; Ergreifung *f*; *med* (plötzlicher) Anfall *m*, Attacke *f*; *to be under ~~* beschlagnahmt sein.

seldom ['seldəm] *adv* selten.

select [si'lekt] *tr* (her)aussuchen, auslesen, auswählen (*from* aus); *a* ausgewählt, auserlesen; *(Publikum)* geladen; hervorragend, erstklassig; exklusiv; wählerisch; ~ **committee** Sonderausschuß *m*; ~**ee** [silek'ti:] *Am mil* Einberufene(r) *m*; ~**ion** [si'lekʃən] Auswahl, -lese *f* (*from* aus); *(natural)* ~~ *(biol)* (natürliche) Zuchtwahl *f*; ~~ *principle* Auswahlprinzip *n*; ~**ive** [-tiv] *a* Auswahl-, Auslese-; auswählend; wahlweise; *radio* trennscharf; ~~ *circuit* Trennkreis *m*; ~~ *service (Am)* Wehrdienstpflicht *f*; ~**ivity** [silek'tiviti] *radio* Trennschärfe *f*; ~**man** [si'lektmən] *pl -men (Neuengland)* Stadtrat, Senator *m*; ~**or** [-ə] Auswählende(r); Wahlmann; *tele* Wähler *m*; ~~ *dial* Wählscheibe *f*.

selen|ium [si'li:njəm] *chem* Selen(ium) *n*; ~**ography** [seli'nɔgrəfi] Mondbeschreibung *f*.

self [self] *pl selves* [selvz] *s* Selbst, Ich *n*, Person, Individualität *f*; *prn fam* = *my~ etc. a* (der-, die-, das)selbe, (der, die, das) gleiche; *in Zssgen* Selbst-, Eigen-; automatisch; *to be o.'s old* ~ wieder der alte sein; *my poor* ~ meine Wenigkeit; *his better* ~ s-e bessere Natur, sein besseres Ich; *thought of* ~ Selbstsucht *f*; ~-**abasement** Selbsterniedrigung *f*; ~-**absorbed** *a* nur mit sich selbst beschäftigt; eigensüchtig; ~-**abuse** Selbstbefriedigung *f*; ~-**acting** selbsttätig; *tech* automatisch; ~-**appointed** *a* selbsternannt; ~-**assertion** Selbstbehauptung *f*; anmaßende(s) Auftreten *n*; ~-**assertive** anmaßend; ~-**assurance** Selbstbewußtsein *n*, -sicherheit *f*; ~-**assured** *a* selbstbewußt, -sicher; ~-**cent(e)red** *a* egozentrisch; selbstsüchtig; ~-**colo(u)red** *a* naturfarben; Ton in Ton; ~-**command** Selbstbeherrschung *f*; ~-**complacent** selbstgefällig; ~-**conceit** Überheblichkeit *f*, Dünkel *m*; ~-**conceited** *a* überheblich, dünkelhaft; ~-**confidence** Selbstvertrauen *n*, Selbstsicherheit *f*; ~-**conscious** befangen; *psychol* bewußt; *to make s.o.* ~~ jdn einschüchtern; ~-**consciousness** Befangenheit *f*; *psychol* Bewußtsein *n*; ~-**contained** *a fig* beherrscht, zurückhaltend, verschlossen; *tech* (in sich) abgeschlossen, selbständig; Einbau-; ~~ *house* Einfamilienhaus *n*; ~-**control** Selbstbeherrschung *f*; ~-**deceit, -deception,** ~-**delusion** Selbsttäuschung *f*; ~-**defence, -se** Selbstverteidigung *f*; *in* ~~ in Notwehr; *the art of* ~~ die Kunst *f* der Selbstverteidigung; ~-**denial** Selbstverleugnung *f*; ~-**denying** *a* sich selbst verleugnend; ~-**destruction** Selbstmord *m*; ~-**determination** *pol* Selbstbestimmung *f*; freie(r) Wille *m*; ~-**distrust** mangelnde(s) Selbstvertrauen *n*; ~-**educated** *a*: ~~ *man* Autodidakt *m*; ~-**esteem** Selbstachtung *f*; ~-**evident** selbstverständlich; *it is* ~~ es versteht sich von selbst; ~-**examination** Selbstprüfung *f*; ~-**excited** *a tech* selbsterregt; ~-**explanatory** unmittelbar verständlich; ~-**expression** Ausdruck *m* der eigenen Persönlichkeit; ~-**feeder** Dauerbrandofen *m*; ~-**fertilization** Selbstbefruchtung *f*; ~-**glorification** Selbstverherrlichung *f*; ~-**governing** autonom; ~-**government** Selbstverwaltung; Unabhängigkeit *f*; ~-**help** Selbsthilfe *f*; ~-**ignition** *mot* Selbstzündung *f*; ~-**important** eingebildet; ~-**indulgence** Sichgehenlassen *n*; Zügellosigkeit, Hemmungslosigkeit *f*; ~-**indulgent** sich gehenlassend; ungehemmt, zügellos; ~-**interest** Eigennutz *m*; ~**ish** ['-iʃ] selbstsüchtig; eigennützig; ~**ishness** ['-iʃnis] Selbstsucht *f*; ~-**knowledge** Selbsterkenntnis *f*; ~**less** ['-lis] selbstlos; ~-**love** Eigenliebe *f*; ~-**made** *a* selbstgemacht; ~~ *man* jdm, der es durch eigene Kraft zu etw gebracht hat; ~-**opinionated** *a* rechthaberisch; ~-**portrait** Selbstporträt *n*; ~-**possessed** *a* selbstbeherrscht; gefaßt; ~-**preservation** Selbsterhaltung *f*; *instinct of* ~~ Selbsterhaltungstrieb *m*; ~-**propelled, -propelling** *a tech* Selbstfahr-; mit eigenem Antrieb; ~-**realization** Selbstverwirklichung *f*; ~-**regard** Eigennutz *m*; ~-**reliance** Selbstvertrauen *n*; ~-**reliant** *a* voll(er) Selbstvertrauen; ~-**respect** Selbstachtung *f*; ~-**respecting** *a* voll(er) Selbstachtung; *no* ~~ *man* keiner, der etw auf sich hält; ~-**restraint** Selbstbeherrschung *f*; ~-**righteous** selbstgerecht; ~-**righteousness** Selbstgerechtigkeit *f*; ~-**sacrifice** Selbstaufopferung *f*; ~-**sacrificing** sich selbst (auf)opfernd; *the* ~**same** ebenderselbe, eben, genau der; ~-**sealing** *tech* selbstabdichtend; ~-**seeker** Egoist, selbstsüchtige(r) Mensch *m*; ~-**seeking** eigennützig, selbstsüchtig; ~-**service** *com* Selbstbedienung *f*; ~~ *shop, store* Selbstbedienungsgeschäft *n*; ~-**starter** *mot* automatische(r) Anlasser *m*; ~-**styled** *a (vor e-m Titel)* angeblich; ~-**sufficiency** Unabhängigkeit, Selbständigkeit; Autarkie; Überheblichkeit *f*; ~-**sufficient** unabhängig, selbständig; autark; überheblich; ~-**supplier, -supporter** Selbstversorger *m*; ~-**supply** Selbstversorgung *f*; ~-**supporting, -sustaining** materiell, finanziell unabhängig; autark; *com* sich selbst tragend; *tech* freistehend, -tragend; ~-**taught** = ~-*educated*; ~-**timer** *phot* Selbstauslöser *m*; ~-**willed** *a* eigenwillig, -sinnig; ~-**winding** *(Uhr)* automatisch.

sell [sel] *irr sold, sold* [sould] *tr* verkaufen (*to* an); veräußern, absetzen, unterbringen (*at a profit* mit Gewinn); handeln, Handel treiben mit, vertreiben; *Am* werben (*s.th.* für etw; *to* bei); *(Person* od *Sache)* verraten (*to the enemy* an den Feind); *(s-e Ehre)* verkaufen; *fam* an den Mann bringen, anbringen, loswerden, losschlagen; *Am fam* 'rumkriegen, überreden (*on* zu), gewinnen (*on* für), überzeugen (*on* von); *(to ~ s.o. a pup)* andrehen (*s.th. to s.o.* jdm etw); popularisieren; *sl* bescheißen, an-, hinters Licht führen; *itr* handeln, Handel treiben; verkauft werden (*at* um; *for* für); kosten (*for s.th.* etw); *(to ~ well)* sich gut verkaufen, gut gehen, guten Absatz finden; *fam* (allgemein) Anklang finden; *s sl* Geschäftstüchtigkeit *f*; Trick; Kniff; Reinfall *m*, Enttäuschung *f*; *to be sold on s.o. (pop)* in jdn vernarrt sein; *to ~ by auction* versteigern; *to ~ like hot cakes (fam)* wie warme Semmeln abgehen; *to ~ for cash, on credit, at a loss* bar, auf Kredit, mit Verlust verkaufen; *to ~ cheap, dear* billig, teuer verkaufen; *to ~ on commission* in Kommission geben; im Auftrag verkaufen; *to ~ s.o. a bill of goods (fam)* jdm e-n Ladenhüter andrehen; *to ~ the pass (fam)* s-e Partei im Stich lassen; *to ~ s.o. down the river (Am fam)* jdn im Stich lassen; *to ~ short difficult, hard to ~* schwer verkäuflich, abzusetzen(d); *to ~* **off** verramschen, verschleudern; *to ~* **out** ausverkaufen; realisieren (*at a great discount* zu stark zurückgesetzten Preisen); *Am fam* verraten; abhauen; *to ~* **up** restlos absetzen, ausverkaufen; alles verkaufen; *(Schuldner)* (aus)pfänden; ~**er** ['-ə] Verkäufer; *(good ~~)* (Verkaufs-)Schlager *m*; ~~*'s market* Verkäufermarkt *m*; ~**ing** ['-iŋ] Verkauf, Vertrieb, Absatz *m*; ~~ *agent* Verkaufskommissionär *m*; ~~ *cost* Vertriebskosten *pl*; ~~*-off* Ausverkauf *m*; ~~*-out* Ausverkauf; *Am fam* Verrat *m*; ~~ *price* Verkaufspreis; *(Börse)* Briefkurs *m*; ~~ *right* Verkaufsrecht *n*; ~~ *territory* Verkaufsgebiet *n*; ~~ *value* Verkaufswert *m*; ~-**out** *Am fam* große(r) Erfolg, Schlager; *Am sl* Verrat *m*.

seltzer ['seltsə] Selterswasser *n*.

selvage, selvedge ['selvidʒ] Salleiste *f*, (Web-)Kante, Borte *f*; Schließblech *n (e-s Schlosses)*.

semantic [si'mæntik] *a* semantisch; *s pl mit sing* Semantik, Wortbedeutungslehre *f*.

semaphore ['seməfɔ:] *s* Semaphor *n (a. m)*, optische(r) Telegraph *m*; *rail* Flügelsignal *n*; *itr tr* signalisieren, winken.

semblance ['sembləns] Aussehen *n*, Erscheinung *f*, Anblick *m*, Gestalt; Ähnlichkeit *f* (*to* mit); Ebenbild; (Ab-)Bild *n*, Darstellung; täuschende Ähnlichkeit, Täuschung *f*; Anschein, (bloßer, hohler) Schein *m*; *in ~* scheinbar; *to put on a ~ of gaiety* sich den Anschein geben, fröhlich zu sein.

semen ['si:men] *physiol* Samen(flüssigkeit *f*) *m*.

semester [si'mestə] *bes. Am* Semester *n*.

semi ['semi] *pref* halb-, Halb-, semi, Semi-; ~-**annual** halbjährlich, -jährig; ~-**automatic** halbautomatisch; ~**breve** ['-bri:v] *Br mus* ganze Note *f*; ~~ *rest* ganze Pause *f*; ~**circle** Halbkreis *m*; ~**circular** halbkreisförmig; ~~ *arch* Rundbogen *m*; ~**colon** ['semi'koulən] Semikolon *n*, Strichpunkt *m*; ~-**conductor** *phys* Halbleiter *m*; ~-**detached** *a*: ~~ *houses pl* Doppelhaus *n*; ~-**durable** beschränkt haltbar; ~~ *goods (pl)* Konsumgüter *n pl* mit beschränkter Haltbarkeit; ~-**final** *sport* Vorschlußrunde *f*; ~-**finalist** Teilnehmer *m* an der Vorschlußrunde; ~-**finished** *a* halbfertig; ~~ *products (pl)* Halbfabrikate *n pl*; ~**fluid** = ~*solid*; ~-**manufactured** *a* Halbfertig-; ~~ *goods (pl)* Halbfabrikate *n pl*; ~-**monthly** *a adv* halbmonatlich; *s* Halbmonatsschrift *f*; ~-**official** halbamtlich, offiziös; ~-**precious**: ~~ *stone* Halbedelstein *m*; ~**quaver** *Br mus* Sechzehntelnote *f*; ~-**skilled** *a (Arbeiter)* angelernt; ~**solid** halbfest; gallertartig; ~**tone** Halbton *m*; ~**trailer** *mot* Sattelschlepper *m*; ~-**tropical** subtropisch; ~**vowel** Halbvokal *m*; ~-**weekly** *a adv* halbwöchentlich.

semin|al ['si:minl, 'seminl] *a* Samen-, Keim-, Zeugungs-; *fig* Quellen-, Herkunfts-; zukunftsträchtig; *in the ~~ state* noch unentwickelt, in den Anfängen (befindlich); ~~ *fluid (physiol)* Samenflüssigkeit *f*; ~~ *power* Zeugungskraft *f*; ~**ar** ['semina:] *(Univ.)* Seminar *n*; ~**arist** ['seminərist] *rel* Seminarist *m*; ~**ary** ['seminəri] Pflanz-, *pej* Brutstätte *f*; *(bes.* Priester-)Seminar *n*.

Semit|e ['si:mait] Semit *m*; ~**ic** [si'mitik] semitisch.

semolina [semə'li:nə] (Weizen-)Grieß *m*.

sempiternal [sempi'tə:nl] ewig.

sempstress ['sem(p)stris] Näherin *f*.

sen|ate ['senit] Senat *m*; *the S~~* der (amerik.) Senat; ~**ator** ['senətə] Senator *m*, Senatsmitglied *n*; ~**atorial**

[senə'tɔ:riəl] senatorisch; Senatoren-, Senats-; *(Wahlbezirk)* zur Wahl e-s *(amerik.)* Senators berechtigt; **~escence** [si'nesns] Altern *n*; **~escent** [si'nesnt] alternd; **~ile** ['si:nail] greisenhaft, senil; Alters-; **~ility** [si'niliti] Greisenhaftigkeit, Senilität, Vergreisung *f*; Greisenalter *n*; **~ior** ['si:njə] *a* älter (*to* als); dienstälter; ranghöher; übergeordnet; *(Schüler)* der obersten Klasse; *(Student)* des letzten Studienjahres; *(nach e-m Namen)* der Ältere, senior; *s* Ältere(r); Senior; Schüler, Student *m* des letzten Studienjahres; Rangältere(r) *m*; *~~ clerk* Bürovorsteher *m*; *~~ partner* Hauptteilhaber, Seniorpartner *m*; *~~ year (Am)* letzte(s) Studienjahr *n*; **~iority** [si:ni'ɔriti] höhere(s) (Dienst-) Alter *n*, höhere(r) Rang *m*; *~~ list* Dienstrangliste *f*.

send [send] *irr sent, sent* [sent] *tr* senden, schicken; in Bewegung setzen, stoßen, treiben, befördern; *(Telegramm)* aufgeben; *(Stein)* werfen; *(Pfeil)* schießen; *mil* in Marsch setzen; *(mit a)* machen; *itr*: *to ~ for s.o.* jdn kommen lassen; *mil tele* geben, senden, funken; *to ~ to Coventry (fig)* jdn links liegenlassen; *to ~ s.o. flying* jdm Beine machen; *to send s.o. o.'s love* jdn herzlich grüßen (lassen); *to ~ mad* verrückt machen; *to ~ s.o. out of his mind* jdn um den Verstand bringen; *to ~ o.'s regards* jdn grüßen lassen; *to ~ packing, to the right-about (fig)* 'rauswerfen; fortjagen; *to ~ to sleep* ins Bett schicken; *to ~ s.o. word* jdm Nachricht geben; *to ~* **after** nachschicken; *to ~* **away** entlassen; fort-, wegschicken; *to ~* **back** zurückschicken; *to ~* **down** fallen, sinken lassen; hinunterschicken; *(Preise)* drücken; *(Univ.)* relegieren; *to ~* **forth** von sich geben; ausstoßen, -senden, -strahlen; hervorbringen; erscheinen lassen, veröffentlichen; *to ~* **in** einschicken, -senden, -reichen; *~~ o.'s name* sich anmelden; *~~ o.'s papers* s-e Entlassung einreichen; *~~ o.'s resignation* s-n Rücktritt erklären; *to ~* **off** abschicken, -senden; entlassen; fortbegleiten; *~~ by post* zur Post geben; *to ~* **on** (voraus)schicken; *(Brief)* nachschicken; *to ~* **out** aussenden, -strahlen; *bot* treiben; (fort-) schicken (*for* um); ausgehen lassen, bekanntmachen, veröffentlichen; *to ~* **round** in Umlauf setzen; umherschicken; *to ~* **up** weiterleiten; *(Preise)* in die Höhe treiben; *Am fam* einlochen, -sperren; **~er** ['-ə] (Ab-)Sender; *tele* Geber, Sender *m*; *return to ~~* an den Absender zurück; **~ing** ['-iŋ] Schicken, Absenden *n*, Versand *m*; Sendung *f*; *~~ end (el)* Eingang(sseite *f*) *m*; *~~ station* Aufgabestelle *f*; **~-off** *fam* Abschiedsfeier *f*, -wünsche *m pl*; neue(r) Beginn, Start *m*.

sens|ation [sen'seiʃən] *physiol* Sinn *m*; Sinneswahrnehmung, -empfindung; Empfindung *f*, Eindruck *m*; Empfinden, Gefühl *n*; Sensation *f*, Aufsehen *n*; *to create, to make a ~~* Aufsehen erregen; **~ational** [-l]*a* Sinnes-, Empfindungs-; sensationell, aufsehenerregend; **~e** [sens] *physiol* Sinn *m*; sinnliche Wahrnehmung *f*, Sinnesleben *n*; Wahrnehmung, Empfindung *f*, Eindruck *m*, Gefühl *n*; *fig* Sinn (*of* für); Verstand *m*; Vernunft *f*; Verständnis *n*; allgemeine Meinung *od* Einstellung; *(Wort)* Bedeutung *f*; *(Äußerung)* Sinn *m*; Richtung, Tendenz *f*; *pl* Verstand *m*; *tr* wahrnehmen, gewahr werden, empfinden, fühlen; *fam* begreifen, verstehen; *in a ~~* in gewissem Sinne; gewissermaßen; *the five ~~s* die fünf Sinne; *in the best ~~ of the term* im wahrsten Sinne des Wortes; *in o.'s right ~~s* bei (Sinn u.) Verstand; *to be out of o.'s ~~s* ganz aus dem Häuschen sein; *to bring s.o. to his ~~s* jdn zur Vernunft bringen; *to come to o.'s ~~s* (wieder) zur Vernunft kommen; *to frighten s.o. out of his ~~s* jdn zu Tode erschrecken; *to lose, to regain o.'s ~~s* das Bewußtsein verlieren; wieder zu(m) Bewußtsein kommen; *fig* wieder Vernunft annehmen; *to make ~~* Sinn haben; *of s.th.* etw begreifen; aus etw schlau werden; *to take leave of o.'s ~~s* den Verstand verlieren; *to talk ~~* vernünftig reden; *there's no ~~ in doing it* es hat keinen Sinn, ist zwecklos, das zu tun; *common ~~* gesunde(r) Menschenverstand *m*; *moral ~~* sittliche(s) Empfinden *n*; *sixth ~~* sechste(r) Sinn *m*, hellseherische Begabung *f*; *~~ of direction, locality* Richtungs-, Ortssinn *m*; *~~ of duty, guilt* Pflicht-, Schuldgefühl *n*; *~~ of hearing, of smell* Gehör-, Geschmackssinn *m*; *~~ of humo(u)r* Sinn *m* für Humor; *~~-organ* Sinnesorgan *n*; *~~-perception* Sinneswahrnehmung *f*; *~~ of warmth* Wärmegefühl *n*; **~eless** ['-lis] bewußtlos; dumm, töricht; unvernünftig, sinnlos; **~elessness** ['-lisnis] Bewußtlosigkeit; Dummheit, Torheit; Unvernunft, Sinnlosigkeit *f*; **~ibility** [sensi'biliti] Wahrnehmungs-, Empfindungsvermögen *n* (*to* für); Reaktionsfähigkeit *f*; *oft pl* Gefühl *n*, Ansprechbarkeit *f*; Feingefühl, Einfühlungsvermögen, Verständnis *n*; **~ible** ['sensibl] sinnlich wahrnehmbar, fühlbar; verständlich; sinn-, augenfällig; begreiflich; empfindungsfähig, empfänglich, ansprechbar, feinfühlend, verständig, verständnisvoll; vernünftig, klug, weise; *to be ~~ of s.th.* sich e-r S bewußt sein; **~ibleness** ['-iblnis] Feingefühl, Verständnis *n*; Vernunft *f*; **~itive** ['sensitiv] *physiol* sinnlich, Sinnes-; wahrnehmungs-, empfindungsfähig; feinfühlig, empfindlich, reizbar (*about* in); empfindlich, empfänglich (*to* für); *~~ to light* lichtempfindlich (*to* für); *~~ plant (bot)* Mimose *f*; **~itiveness** ['-itivnis] Feingefühl *n*, Empfindlichkeit, Reizbarkeit; Empfänglichkeit *f*; **~itize** ['sensitaiz] *tr* lichtempfindlich machen; *med* sensibilisieren; **~orial** [sen'sɔ:riəl], **~ory** ['sensəri] *physiol* sinnlich, Sinnes-; **~orium** [sen'sɔ:riəm] *anat* Sinnesapparat *m*; Empfindungsvermögen *n*; **~ual** ['sensjuəl, *Am* '-ʃuəl] sinnlich; wollüstig, geil; **~ualism** ['-izm] Sinnlichkeit *f*; *philos* Sensualismus *m*; **~ualist** ['-juəlist] sinnliche(r) Mensch, Lüstling; *philos* Sensualist *m*; **~uality** [sensju'æliti] Sinnlichkeit; Geilheit *f*; **~ualize** ['sensjuəlaiz] *tr* sinnlich machen; **~uous** ['sensjuəs, *Am* '-ʃuəs] sinnlich, Sinnes-; sinnen-, genußfreudig, genießerisch.

senten|ce ['sentəns] *s* Richterspruch *m*, Gerichtsurteil; (Straf-)Urteil *n*; Strafe *f*; *gram mus* Satz; *obs* Ausspruch *m*, Sentenz, Maxime *f*; *tr (Angeklagten)* ver-, aburteilen (*to* zu); *under ~~ of death* zum Tode verurteilt; *to be ~~d to five years at hard labour* zu fünf Jahren Zuchthaus verurteilt werden; *to pass ~~* ein Urteil fällen (*on s.o.* über jdn); *to quash a ~~* ein Urteil aufheben *od* kassieren; *to serve o.'s ~~* s-e Strafe verbüßen, *fam* absitzen; *to submit to a ~~* ein Urteil annehmen; *to suspend a ~~* die Strafvollstreckung aussetzen; *commutation of ~~* Strafumwandlung *f*; *life ~~* lebenslängliche Gefängnis-, Zuchthausstrafe *f*; *maximum ~~* Höchststrafe *f*; *~~ of death* Todesurteil *n*; *~~ of imprisonment* Freiheits-, Gefängnisstrafe *f*; *~~ stress (gram)* Satzton *m*; **~tious** [sen'tenʃəs] kurz, knapp, inhaltsreich, markant, lapidar; sentenzenreich, sentenziös; *pej* affektiert, salbungsvoll, geschwollen; **~tiousness** [-'tenʃəsnis] Gedrängtheit; Geschwollenheit *f*.

senti|ence, ~ency ['senʃəns(i)] Gefühl, Empfinden *n*; Wahrnehmung(sfähigkeit) *f*; **~ent** ['-t] empfindend, fühlend, wahrnehmend; **~ment** ['sentimənt] Gefühl, Empfinden *n*; Meinung, Ansicht *f* (*on* über); Gedanke *m*, Auffassung (*on* von); Empfindsamkeit, Gefühlsbetontheit *f*; Zartgefühl *n*; Sentimentalität, Gefühlsduselei *f*; *pl* Einstellung, Gesinnung, Haltung *f*; **~mental** [senti'mentl] empfindsam, gefühlvoll; sentimental; gefühlsbetont, rührselig; *~~ value* Liebhaberwert *m*; **~mentalism** [-izm], **~mentality** [sentimen'tæliti] Sentimentalität, Gefühlsduselei *f*; **~mentalist** [senti'mentəlist] Gefühlsmensch *m*; **~mentalize** [-'mentəlaiz] *tr* sentimental, gefühlvoll machen *od* stimmen; gefühlsmäßig auffassen; *itr* sentimental sein *od* reden (*about* über).

sent|inel ['sentinl] Wache *f*, (Wach-) Posten *m*; *to stand ~~ (over) (lit)* bewachen; **~ry** ['-tri] (Wach-)Posten *m*; Wache *f*; *to go on ~~* auf Wache ziehen; *to keep ~~* Wache haben, *sl* schieben; *~~-box* Schilderhaus *n*; *~~-go* Postengang *m*; *~~-squad* Wachmannschaft *f*.

*

sepal ['sepəl, *Am* 'si:-] *bot* Kelchblatt *n*.

separ|able ['sepərəbl] trennbar, -fähig; **~ate** ['sepəreit] *tr* (ab)trennen; (zer)teilen (*into* in); ausea.halten, unterscheiden; *(Gruppe)* einteilen (*into* in); absondern, trennen (*from* von); *tech* ausea.schneiden; *tech* zentrifugieren; *Am mil* entlassen; *Am (Ehe)* scheiden; *itr* sich trennen, scheiden, sich lossagen (*from* von); *Am mil* den Abschied nehmen; *tech* sich abscheiden; *a* ['seprit] (ab)getrennt, gesondert (*from* von); einzeln; *(Zimmer)* separat, getrennt; besonder; verschieden; Sonder-, Einzel-; selbständig, unabhängig; Eigen-; *s* ['-prit] Sonderdruck *m*; *to keep ~~* ausea.halten; *to be ~~d* getrennt, geschieden sein; *~~ edition, print* Sonderausgabe *f*, -druck *m*; *~~ excitation (el)* Fremderregung *f*; **~ation** [sepə'reiʃən] Trennung, Teilung; Absonderung *f*; Zwischenraum, Abstand *m*; Trenn(ungs)-, Bruchstelle; *tech* Abscheidung; *(judicial ~~)* Aufhebung *f* der ehelichen Gemeinschaft; *tele* Trennschärfe; *Am mil* Entlassung; Demobilisierung *f*, Abschied *m*; *to live in ~~* getrennt leben (*from* von); *~~ allowance, indemnity* Trennungsentschädigung *f*; *~~ center (Am mil)* Entlassungslager *n*; *~~ of powers* Gewaltentrennung *f*; **~atism** ['sepərətizm] Separatismus *m*; **~atist** ['sepərətist] Separatist *m*; **~ative** ['sepərətiv] trennend; Trenn(ungs)-; **~ator** ['sepəreitə] Trennende(r); *tech* (Ab-)Scheider *m*; Schleuder, Zentrifuge *f*.

sepia ['si:pjə] *s* Tintenfisch *m*; Sepia (-braun *n*) *f*; *a* Sepia-; sepiabraun.

sepoy ['si:pɔi] *hist* Sepoy *m*.

sep|sis ['sepsis], **~tic(a)emia** [septi'si:miə] Blutvergiftung *f*; **~tic** ['septik]

a septisch; sl widerlich; s Fäulniserreger m; ~~ tank Klärbehälter m.
sept|al ['septl] a Scheide-; **~um** ['-əm] pl -a ['-ə] Scheidewand f.
Sept|ember [səp'tembə] September m; **s~enary** ['-tənəri, -'ti(:)nəri] a Sieben(er)-; siebenjährig; s Sieben(ergruppe) f; **~ennial** [sep'tenjəl] siebenjährig; alle sieben Jahre stattfindend; **~uagenarian** [septjuədʒi'nɛəriən] a siebzigjährig; s Siebzig(jährig)er m; **S~uagesima** [-'dʒesimə] Septuagesima f (9. Sonntag vor Ostern); **S~uagint** ['septjuədʒint] Septuaginta f.
sepul|chral [si'pʌlkrəl] a Grab-, Beerdigungs-, Toten-; fig düster, finster, unheimlich; ~~ vault Grabgewölbe n; ~~ voice Grabesstimme f; **~chre,** Am **~cher** ['sepəlkə] s Grab(stätte f, -gewölbe) n, Gruft f; tr begraben, bestatten, beisetzen; the Holy S~~ das Heilige Grab (Jesu); **~ture** ['sepəltʃə] Beerdigung, Bestattung f.
sequ|el ['si:kwəl] Fortsetzung; Folge f, Ergebnis n, Folgeerscheinung, Wirkung f; Nachspiel n; lit (in sich abgeschlossener) Teil m e-s Zyklus; in the ~~ der Reihe nach; in der Folge, danach; ~~ of war Kriegsfolge f; **~ence** ['-əns] Reihe(nfolge), Serie, Folge; Anordnung; Folge f, Ergebnis n; (Kartenspiel, mus, rel) Sequenz; film Szene f; **~ent** ['-t] a (nach)folgend, sich ergebend; s Folge f, Ergebnis n; **~ential** [-'kwenʃəl] folgend (to auf); folgerichtig.
sequest|er [si'kwestə] tr abtrennen, -sondern (from von); beschlagnahmen, einziehen, sequestrieren, unter Zwangsverwaltung stellen; to ~~ o.s. sich zurückziehen (from von); a ~~ed life ein zurückgezogenes Leben, ruhiges Dasein n; a ~~ed spot ein stilles Plätzchen n; **~ration** [si:kwes'treiʃən] Abtrennung, -sonderung; Zurückgezogenheit; jur Beschlagnahme, Sequestration; Zwangsverwaltung f; **~rator** ['si:kwestreitə] Zwangsverwalter m.
sequin ['si:kwin] Metallschuppe, -scheibe; Zechine f (Münze).
sequoia [si'kwɔiə] Mammutbaum m.
seraglio [se'rɑ:liou] pl -os Serail n.
serape [sə'rɑ:pi] Am (bunter) Umhang.
seraph ['serəf] pl -im ['-im] rel Seraph m; **~ic(al)** [se'ræfik(əl)] seraphisch.
Serb|ia ['sə:bjə] Serbien n; **~(ian)** ['-bjən] a serbisch; s Serbe m, Serbin f; (das) Serbisch(e); **~o-Croatian** ['sə:boukrou'eiʃən] s (das) Serbokroatisch(e); a serbokroatisch.
sere s. sear.
serenade [seri'neid] mus Ständchen n; Serenade f.
seren|e [si'ri:n] heiter, klar, rein; (Meer) ruhig, still; (Himmel) hell, klar; fig froh, heiter, gelassen; His S~~ Highness Seine Durchlaucht f; **~ity** [si'reniti] Heiterkeit, Klarheit; Ruhe, Stille; fig Gemütsruhe, Gelassenheit f; S~~ Durchlaucht f.
serf [sə:f] Leibeigene(r); bes. fig Sklave m; **~age** ['-idʒ], **~dom** ['-dəm] Leibeigenschaft; fig Sklaverei f.
serge [sə:dʒ] (Textil) Serge, Sersche f.
sergeant, serjeant ['sɑ:dʒənt] Feldwebel; Wachtmeister m (a. d. Polizei); master ~ (Am) Stabsfeldwebel, -wachtmeister m; **~-at-arms** Art Ordnungsbeamte(r) m; **~-at-law** Justizrat m; **~-major** Br Oberfeldwebel, -wachtmeister m; company ~~ Hauptfeldwebel, -wachtmeister m.
seri|al ['siəriəl] a fortlaufend; reihenweise, laufend; Reihen-; in Lieferungen, periodisch erscheinend; s Fortsetzungsroman, -bericht m; Artikelreihe, -serie; radio Sendefolge; Wochen-, Monatsschrift, Zeitschrift f; Lieferungs-, Fortsetzungswerk n; mil Marschgruppe f; ~~ house Reihenhaus n; ~~ novel Fortsetzungs-, Feuilletonroman m; ~~ number laufende Nummer; com Fabrikationsnummer; mil Matrikel-, Stamm-, Wehrnummer f; ~~ photograph Reihenbild n; ~~ production Serien-, Reihenfertigung, Massenproduktion f; ~~ writer Feuilletonist m; **~alize** ['-iəlaiz] tr in Fortsetzungen veröffentlichen; com serienmäßig herstellen; **~ate** ['-eit] tr aufreihen, ordnen; a ['-it] u. **~ated** ['-eitid] aufgereiht; serienweise; **~atim** [siəri'eitim] adv der Reihe nach; **~es** ['siəri:z] pl ~~ Reihe, Folge, Serie f; Zyklus m; math Reihe; biol Gruppe f; in ~~ reihen-, serienweise, serienmäßig; el hintereа.geschaltet; ~~-circuit, -connection (el) Reihenschaltung f; ~~ control Reihensteuerung f; ~~ motor Reihenschlußmotor m; ~~ of observations, tests Beobachtungs-, Versuchsreihe f; ~~ production Serienherstellung, Massenproduktion f; ~~ of reactions Kettenreaktion f; ~~ resistance (el) Vorwiderstand m; ~~ winding Reihen-, Hauptschlußwicklung f.
seri|ceous [si'riʃəs] seidig; **~culture** ['serikʌltʃə] Seidenraupenzucht f.
serio-comic(al) ['siərio(u)'kɔmik(əl)] tragikomisch.
serious ['siəriəs] ernst; (Irrtum) grob; (Fehler) schwer(wiegend); ernsthaft, aufrichtig, ehrlich; wichtig, bedeutend, bedeutsam, schwerwiegend; you can't be ~ das kann nicht Ihr Ernst sein; **~ly** ['-li] adv ernst; im Ernst; ~~ now Spaß beiseite; to take ~~ ernst nehmen; **~ness** ['-nis] Ernst m; Ernsthaftigkeit, Aufrichtigkeit; Wichtigkeit, Bedeutung f.
sermon ['sə:mən] Predigt; pej Gardinen-, Strafpredigt f; the S~ on the Mount die Bergpredigt; **~ize** ['sə:mənaiz] itr predigen a. pej; tr e-e Strafpredigt halten (s.o. jdm).
ser|ology [siə'rɔlədʒi] med Serologie f; **~osity** [-'rɔsiti], **~um** ['siərəm] med Serum n; **~ous** ['-rəs] med serös.
serpent ['sə:pənt] (Gift-)Schlange f a. fig astr; **~-charmer** Schlangenbeschwörer m; **~ine** ['sə:pəntain] a Schlangen-; schlangenartig, -förmig; sich schlängelnd, gewunden; fig falsch, hinterlistig, -hältig; s min Serpentin m; Schlangenlinie; Kehre, Serpentine f; ~~-cooler Kühlschlange f.
serpigo [sə:'paigou] med fressende Flechte f.
serrat|e ['serit], **~ed** [se'reitid] a (aus-)gezackt, gezähnt, gekerbt; zackig; **~ion** [se'reiʃən] Auszackung f.
serried ['serid] a (dicht) gedrängt, massiert, kompakt; (Reihe) geschlossen.
serv|ant ['sə:vənt] (domestic ~~) (Haus-)Diener, Bediente(r), Hausangestellte(r); fig eifrige(r) Anhänger m; pl Dienstboten m pl; civil, public ~~ Beamte(r) m; ~~-girl Hausmädchen n, -angestellte f; **~e** [sə:v] tr dienen (s.o. jdm; God Gott; o.'s country s-m Lande); e-n Dienst, Dienste erweisen; von Nutzen, dienlich sein, helfen (s.o. jdm); dienen (as a substitute als Ersatz); (Amt) ausüben, verwalten; (Kunden) bedienen; beliefern; (Gebiet) versorgen; (to ~~ out) ausgeben; (Essen, Getränk) servieren, auftragen; (Getränk) herumreichen; (Gast) bedienen; Essen auftragen (s.o. jdm); (Suppe) austeilen; (Dienst) ausüben; (Lehrzeit) ableisten; (Strafe) verbüßen, fam absitzen; (Zweck) erfüllen, entsprechen; da sein für; behandeln; jur (ein Schreiben) zustellen (s.th. on s.o., s.o. with s.th. etw jdm); ein Schreiben zustellen (s.o. jdm); sport (Ball) anschlagen; zoo (weibl. Tier) decken; tech (Kabel) armieren; itr dienen, Dienst tun (as als); tätig sein (with s.o. bei jdm); gebraucht werden, brauchbar, dienlich sein, sich verwenden lassen; funktionieren; von Nutzen sein, den Zweck erfüllen; (Kellner) bedienen; rel als Meßgehilfe fungieren; sport anspielen, -schlagen; s sport Anschlag m, Angabe f; to ~~ s.o. out es jdm heimzahlen; to ~~ s.o. badly jdn schlecht behandeln; to ~~ on a committee e-m Ausschuß angehören; Mitglied e-s Ausschusses sein; to ~~ two masters zwei Herren dienen; to ~~ notice on s.o. jdn vorladen; to ~~ time, a term in prison e-e Gefängnisstrafe absitzen; to ~~ no purpose zwecklos sein; to ~~ a trick on s.o. jdm e-n Streich spielen; as the occasion, as the time ~~s bei (passender) Gelegenheit; (that) serve(s) you right! das geschieht dir recht! **~er** ['-ə] Dienende(r), Diensttuende(r); jur Zustellungsbeamte(r); sport Anspielende(r), Aufschläger m; Tablett n; rel Ministrant m; **~ice** ['-is] **1.** Dienst m; Arbeitsleistung; Beschäftigung f; Amt n; (civil, public ~~) Staatsdienst; Wehr-, Militärdienst m; (a. pl) Wehrmacht f; tech Service m, Wartung f, Kundendienst m; Dienststelle f, Amt n; öffentliche Dienste m pl od Versorgung f; (repair, telephone, train ~~) (Reparatur-, Telephon-, Fahr-)Dienst; (bus ~~) (Bus-)Verkehr; Kundendienst m, Belieferung f; Betrieb; (Liebes-)Dienst m, Gefälligkeit f, Entgegenkommen n, Hilfe f; Nutzen, Vorteil m; Servieren n, Bedienung f (bei Tisch); (Eß-, Tee-)Service n; (divine ~~) Gottesdienst m; jur Zustellung f; com Zinsendienst; sport Aufschlag m; mil Truppengattung; (~~ troops) Versorgungstruppe f; zoo (Tiere) Decken n; tr versorgen, bedienen; instand halten, setzen; reparieren, überholen; of ~~ von Nutzen; out of ~~ außer Dienst; to attend ~~ den Gottesdienst besuchen; to be at s.o.'s ~~ jdm zu Diensten stehen; to be in ~~ (Mädchen) in Stellung sein; to be in, on active ~~ dienen, Soldat sein; to go into, to go out to ~~ (Mädchen) in Stellung gehen; to be of ~~ behilflich sein; to make use of s.o.'s ~~ von jds Angebot Gebrauch machen; to put into ~~ in Dienst stellen; to render s.o. a ~~ jdm e-n Dienst erweisen od leisten; to retire from ~~ in den Ruhestand treten; to see ~~ dienstliche Erfahrungen haben; air ~~ Luftverkehr, Flugdienst m; civil ~~ Staatsdienst m; clerical ~~ Bürotätigkeit f; compulsory ~~ Dienstpflicht f; Consular, Diplomatic, Secret S~~ Konsularische(r), Diplomatische(r), Geheimdienst m; contract of ~~ Dienstvertrag m; delivery ~~ Zustelldienst m; dinner, tea ~~ Eß-, Teeservice n; field ~~ Außendienst; mil Frontdienst m; fit for ~~ dienstfähig, -tauglich; intelligence ~~ Nachrichtendienst m; labo(u)r ~~ Arbeitsdienst m; marriage ~~ Trauung f; ready for ~~ dienst-, einsatzbereit; train ~~ Zugverkehr m, -folge f; travel ~~ Reisedienst m; ~~ area (radio) Sendegebiet; Liefergebiet n; ~~ book Gesangbuch n; ~~ brake Betriebsbremse f; ~~ cable Versorgungs-, Zulei-

tungskabel *n*; ~~ *call (tele)* Dienstgespräch *n*; ~~ *cap (mil)* Dienstmütze *f*; ~~ *centre* Reparaturwerkstätte *f*; ~~ *charge* Bedienungsgeld *n*; Verwaltungsgebühr *f*; ~~ *coat* Waffenrock *m*; ~~ *colo(u)r* Waffenfarbe *f*; *S~~ Command (Am)* Wehrkreis *m*; ~~ *company (Am)* Versorgungs- u. Instandsetzungskompanie *f*; ~~ *condition* Betriebsbedingung *f*; ~~ *control* Dienstaufsicht; ~~ *department* Kundendienstabteilung; *f*; Hilfsbetrieb *m*; ~~ *dress (mil)* Dienstanzug *m*; ~~ *entrance* Eingang *m* für Personal u. Lieferanten; *tech* Hausanschluß *m*; ~~ *fee* Zustellungsgebühr *f*; ~~ *hatch* Durchreiche *f*; ~~*-instructions (pl)* Betriebsanweisung, -vorschrift *f*; ~~ *life* Nutzungsdauer, Haltbarkeit *f*; ~~ *load* Nutzlast *f*; ~~*man* ['-mən] *pl -men* Soldat *m*; ~~ *period* Dienstzeit *f*; ~~ *pipe* Anschlußrohr *n*; ~~ *record (Am)* Wehrstammrolle *f*; *Am* (Führungs-) Zeugnis *n*; ~~ *requirements (pl)* Betriebserfordernisse *n pl*; ~~ *road* Zugang *m*; ~~ *station (Am)* (*bes.* Auto-) Reparaturwerkstätte; Tankstelle *f*; ~~ *voltage* Betriebsspannung *f*; ~~ *work* Betriebsfürsorge *f*; **~iceable** ['-isəbl] verwendbar, tauglich (*to* für, zu); brauchbar, dienlich, nützlich; betriebsfähig, gebrauchs-, verwendungsfähig; vorteilhaft; **~icing** ['-isiŋ] *mot* Wartung *f*; **~iette** [sə:vi'et] Serviette *f*; **~ile** ['-ail] *s* Sklaven-; sklavisch, knechtisch, servil, kriecherisch, unterwürfig; ~~ *revolt* Sklavenaufstand *m*; **~ility** [sə:'viliti] Unterwürfigkeit *f*; **~ing** ['-iŋ] *Am fam* Schlag *m*, Portion; *jur* Zustellung; *tech* Umwicklung *f*; **~itor** ['-itə] Anhänger; *obs* Gefolgsmann, Diener; *hist (Oxforder)* Stipendiat *m*; **~itude** ['-itju:d] Sklaverei *a. fig*; *fig* Knechtschaft; *jur* Dienstbarkeit, Servitut *f*; *penal* ~~ Zuchthaus (-strafe *f*) *n*; **~o-motor** ['sə:vo(u)'moutə] Servo-, Stellmotor *m*.

service ['sə:vis] **2.** (*~~-tree*) Eberesche *f*.

sesame ['sesəmi] *bot* Sesam *m*; *open ~* Sesam, öffne dich! *(Zauberformel)*.

sesqui- ['seskwi] *in Zssgen* anderthalb-; **~pedalian** ['-pi'deiljən] *a* anderthalbfüßig; *(Wort)* (sehr) lang; *fig* langatmig, geschwollen, schwülstig; *s* lange(s) Wort, Wortungetüm *n*.

sess|ile ['sesil, '-ail] *bot* stiellos; *zoo* ungestielt; **~ion** ['seʃən] *jur parl* Sitzung; Tagung; Sitzungsperiode *f*; *(Univ., bes. Scot u. Am)* Semester, *Br* akademische(s) Jahr *n*; Blockstunden *f pl*; *in full ~~* in öffentlicher Sitzung; *to be in ~~* e-e Sitzung haben, tagen; *closing ~~* Schlußsitzung *f*; *opening ~~* Eröffnungssitzung *f*; *plenary ~~* Plenar-, Vollsitzung *f*; *secret ~~* Geheimsitzung *f*; *~~ of legislature* Legislaturperiode *f*; **~ional** ['seʃənl] *a* Sitzungs-, Tagungs-.

set [set] *irr set, set* **1.** *tr* (hin)setzen; hinlegen, hin-, aufstellen; aufziehen, -pflanzen; *(Segel)* beisetzen; anbringen, applizieren; (ein-, her)richten, zurecht-, fertigmachen; *(Messer)* abziehen, schärfen; *(Tisch)* decken; *(Edelstein)* fassen; *(mit Edelsteinen)* besetzen; *(Glasscheibe)* einsetzen; *med* einrenken; *(Falle, Uhr)* stellen; *radio* einstellen; *tech* justieren; *(Grenze)* festlegen; *(Datum, Zeitpunkt, Menge, Preis, Strafe)* festsetzen; *(die Mode)* bestimmen, einführen; *(den Ton)* angeben; *(Beispiel)* geben; anberaumen, bestimmen, festsetzen (*at* auf); aufzeichnen, niederschreiben, (schriftlich) festlegen, fixieren; *(Unterschrift)* setzen (*to* unter); *(Frage)* stellen; vergleichen (*against* mit); *mus (Text)* zugrunde legen; vertonen; *typ* setzen; *theat (den Schauplatz)* verlegen (*in* nach); *(Mode)* kreieren; pflanzen, setzen; *(Henne zum Brüten)* setzen; *(Eier zum Bebrüten)* unterlegen; *(Hund, allg)* hetzen, loslassen auf; *theat (Szene)* aufbauen; **2.** *itr* sich setzen; *(Henne auf Eiern, Kleidung)* sitzen; *(Henne)* brüten; *(Sonne)* untergehen; *fig* vergehen, abnehmen, nachlassen; fest, hart werden, gerinnen, erstarren; *(Gips)* abbinden; *(Frucht)* ansetzen; reifen; *(Jagdhund)* vorstehen; fließen, wehen; sich in Bewegung setzen, sich aufmachen, aufbrechen; sich (heran-) machen (*about, to* an); eindringen (*on, upon* auf), bestürmen (*on, upon s.o.* jdn; *with* mit); **3.** *a* festgesetzt, -gelegt, bestimmt; angeordnet, vorgeschrieben, befohlen; im voraus, vorher festgelegt; geplant, beabsichtigt, absichtlich, (wohl)überlegt; fest, starr, unbeweglich, reg(ungs)los; (fest) entschlossen, unnachgiebig, hartnäckig; versessen (*on* auf); bereit, fertig; fest, hart, steif; *in Zssgen (körperlich)* gebaut; **4.** *s* Hinsetzen, -stellen *n*; Aufstellung *f*; Stehen; *(Hund)* Vorstehen *n*; (Sonnen-)Untergang *m*; Hart-, Festwerden *n*; Pflasterstein *m*; Stellung, Richtung, Neigung; Strömung *a. fig*; *(psychol, Körper)* Haltung *f*; *(Kleidung)* Sitz, Schnitt; *agr* Setzling *m*; *theat* Requisiten *n pl*, Kulissen *f pl*; Szenerie *f*, Bühnenbild *n*; (Tanz-, Menschen-)Gruppe, Gesellschaft; Bande *f*; Satz *m*, Garnitur *f*, Service, Besteck *n*; *(Bücher)* Reihe; Sammlung, Kollektion, Zs.stellung *f*; *(bes. Radio-)* Apparat *m*, (Rundfunk-)Gerät *n*; *astr* Untergang; *sport* Satz *m*; **5.** *to be ~* versessen sein (*on* auf); *to be dead ~ against s.th.* gegen etw eingestellt sein; *to be ~ in o.'s ways (fig)* festgefahren sein; *to make a dead ~ at s.o.* über jdn herfallen; jdn zu gewinnen suchen; *to ~ o.'s affection, o.'s heart on s.th.* sein Herz an etw hängen; auf etw versessen sein; *to ~ the axe to (lit fig)* die Axt legen an; *to ~ o.'s cap at s.o.* ein Auge werfen auf; es auf jdn abgesehen haben; *to ~ s.o., s.th. at defiance* jdm, e-r S Trotz bieten; jdn, e-e S herausfordern; *to ~ by the ears, at loggerheads, at variance* aufhetzen; *to ~ at ease, at rest* beruhigen; *to ~ on end* aufstellen, -richten; *to ~ eyes on* erblicken; *to ~ o.'s face against s.th.* sich e-r S heftig widersetzen; *to ~ s.o. on his feet (fig)* jdn auf die Beine stellen; *to ~ on fire, to ~ fire to* in Brand stecken; anzünden; *to ~ foot in s.th.* etw betreten; *to ~ on foot, to ~ going* in Gang bringen; *to ~ free* freilassen; *to ~ o.'s hand to* sich machen an; *to ~ o.'s hand to the plough (fig)* Hand ans Werk legen; *to ~ o.'s hope on* s-e Hoffnung richten auf; *to ~ laughing* zum Lachen bringen; *to ~ at liberty* in Freiheit setzen; *to ~ o.'s mind on doing s.th.* sich entschließen, etw zu tun; *to ~ s.th. to music* etw vertonen; *to ~ at naught* aus-, verlachen, geringschätzen, mißachten; *to ~ the pace (fig)* den Ton, das Tempo angeben; *to ~ at rest* beruhigen; beseitigen; *to ~ right* zurechtweisen; *to ~ to rights* richtigstellen, in Ordnung bringen; *to ~ sail (Schiff)* auslaufen (*for* nach); *to ~ the seal on s.th.* etw besiegeln; *to ~ a sentry* e-e Wache aufstellen; *to ~ great, little, no store by* großen, wenig, keinen Wert legen auf; *to ~ o.'s teeth* fest entschlossen sein; *to ~ s.o.'s teeth on edge* jdm auf die Nerven gehen; *to ~ the Thames on fire (fig)* alles auf den Kopf stellen; *to ~ to work* sich ans Werk, an die Arbeit machen; *everything is all ~* alles ist fix u. fertig; **6.** *beach ~* Strandanzug *m*; *thick-~* untersetzt, stämmig; *well-~* gutgebaut; **7.** *to ~* **about** in Umlauf setzen, verbreiten; in Angriff nehmen, anfangen; *fam* angreifen (*s.o.* jdn), anfallen; *to ~* **afloat** vom Stapel lassen; *fig* in Bewegung setzen; *to ~* **ahead** *(Uhr)* vorstellen; *to ~* **apart** beiseite stellen, zurücklegen, reservieren; aussondern; *to ~* **ashore** an Land setzen; *to ~* **aside** beiseite setzen *od* legen *od* stellen; reservieren; absondern; nicht beachten; *(Angebot)* ablehnen; *(Betrag)* absetzen; ablehnen; *jur* aufheben, annullieren, kassieren, für ungültig erklären, außer Kraft setzen; *(Klage)* abweisen; *to ~* **back** *(Uhr)* zurückstellen; *(in der Entwicklung)* hemmen, zurückbringen; nicht berücksichtigen; *fam* kosten; *to ~* **by** auf die Seite, zurücklegen; *to ~* **down** nieder-, absetzen; hinstellen; aussteigen lassen; *(to ~~ in writing)* niederschreiben; eintragen; ansehen, betrachten (*as* als); zuschreiben (*to s.o.* jdm); niederlegen, festsetzen; *(Termin)* anberaumen (*for* auf); *fam fig* anfahren, 'runtermachen; *to ~* **for** *(Uhr)* stellen auf; festsetzen auf; *to ~* **forth** *tr* zum Ausdruck bringen, ausdrücken, feststellen, darlegen, ausea.setzen, erklären, erläutern, vortragen; veröffentlichen, bekanntmachen; *itr* aufbrechen, abreisen; *to ~* **forward** *tr* bekanntmachen, äußern, vorbringen; *itr* aufbrechen, vorrücken; *to ~* **in** *tr* einsetzen, anfangen, beginnen; *itr* sich einstellen; *to ~* **off** *tr* starten, beginnen; *(Reise)* antreten; veranlassen, bewegen; zur Geltung bringen, hervorheben; explodieren lassen, in die Luft jagen; *com* an-, aufrechnen, absetzen; *itr* abfahren (*for* nach); sich in Marsch setzen; *to ~* **on** *tr* vorwärts-, antreiben, aufhetzen; hetzen (*to s.o.* auf jdn); *itr* vorrücken, angreifen; *to ~* **out** *tr* abstecken, begrenzen, festlegen; verzeichnen, enthalten, aufführen; planen, entwerfen; dekorieren, schmükken; pflanzen; (zum Verkauf) ausstellen, feilbieten; *itr* abfahren, aufbrechen, sich auf den Weg machen (*for* nach); anfangen; *to ~* **straight** aufklären (*s.o. on s.th.* jdn über etw); *to ~* **up** *tr* aufstellen, auf-, errichten; erheben (*over* über); zur Macht bringen; beginnen, anfangen; eröffnen, gründen; einrichten; *com (Rückstellung)* bilden; ausstatten, versorgen (*with* mit); anregen; veranlassen; *Am fam* zu e-m Gläschen einladen; *(Theorie, Grundsatz)* aufstellen; *(Geschrei)* erheben; *(Schrei)* ausstoßen; (gesundheitlich) auf die Höhe bringen; *itr* sich niederlassen (*as* als); sich selbständig machen; *to be ~~* sich aufspielen; *to ~~ o.s. as* sich aufspielen, sich ausgeben als; *to ~~ for o.s.* sich selbständig machen; **8. ~-back** Rückschlag *m*, Verschlechterung, Schlappe *f*; *arch* Absatz *m*, Stufe, Kante *f*; Strudel *m (im Wasser)*; *to have a ~~* e-n Rückschlag erleiden; *~~ in production* Produktionsrückgang *m*; **~-chisel** Setzmeißel *m*; **~-designer** Bühnenbildner *m*; **~-down** *fam* Anschnauzer *m*, Zigarre *f*; **~ form** Formular *n*; **~-hammer** Setz-, Flachhammer *m*; **~-off** ['-'ɔ:f] Gegengewicht *n*, Ausgleich *m*, Kompensation *f*; Kontrast; Schmuck (*to* für); *com* Ausgleichsposten *m*, Gegenforderung, -rechnung, Aufrechnung *f*; *arch* Absatz *m*, Stufe; Berme *f*; **~-out** ['-'-] Schaustellung; Aufmachung, Ausstattung *f*; Anfang *m*, Vorbereitung *f*; **~-pin, -screw** Stellstift *m*, -schraube *f*; **~-square** Dreieck *n (Lineal)*; **~-to** ['-'tu:] *fam* Schlägerei, Rauferei *f*; Streit *m*, Ausea.setzung *f*; *to have a ~~* sich in die Haare geraten; **~-up** *a* gut entwickelt; *s* Plan *m*, Anordnung, Einrichtung, Anlage *f*; *Am* Aufbau *m*, Gliederung, Organisation; (Körper-)Haltung *f*; (Soda-)Wasser, Eis *n*; *Am sl* Schiebung *f*, *allg* abgekartete(s) Spiel *n*; *~~ time* Anlaufzeit *f*.

setaceous [si'teiʃəs] borstig.

settee [se'ti:] kleine(s) Sofa *n*, Polsterbank *f*.

setter ['setə] *zoo* Setter; Einsetzer; *(type-~)* Setzer; *arch* Steinsetzer *m*; **~-on** (Auf-)Hetzer, Anstifter *m*.

setting ['setiŋ] *s* (Ein-)Setzen; Festsetzen, Bestimmen *n*; (Sonnen-)Untergang *m*; *(Ruhm)* Verblassen; Fest-, Hartwerden, Erstarren, Abbinden *n*; *tech* Ein-, Aufstellung, Montage, Einrichtung; Justierung; Aufspannung; Bettung *f*; *typ* (Schrift-)Satz *m*; (Ein-)Fassung *(a. e-s Edelsteines)*; Umrahmung *f*, Rahmen *m*, Einkleidung, Ausstattung, Szenerie; Bühnenausstattung, Inszenierung; Anlage; Vertonung *f*; Bruteier *n pl*; *mar* Richtung *f*; *med* Einrenken; *(Küche)* Gedeck *n*; **~ apart** Bereitstellung *f*; **~ aside** Verwerfung, Zurückweisung; Außerachtlassung *f*; **~-down** *fam* Rüffel, Anschnauzer *m*; **~-lotion** (Haar-)Fixativ *n*; **~-mark** Einstellmarke *f*; **~-off** Gegenforderung *f*; **~-point** Erstarrungs-, Einstellpunkt *m*; **~-rule** *typ* Setzlinie *f*; **~-stick** *typ* Winkelhaken *m*; **~-time** Abbindezeit *f*; **~-up** Aufstellung; Errichtung, Gründung *f*; *~~ cost* Aufstellungskosten *pl*; *~~-exercises (pl) Am* Freiübung, Gymnastik *f*.

settl|e ['setl] **1.** *tr (Staub)* sich setzen lassen; *(Flüssigkeit)* abklaren, klären; in Ordnung bringen, aufräumen, regeln; *fig* beruhigen; unterbringen, versorgen, verheiraten; *(Kolonie)* gründen; festigen, stärken; fest in den Sattel setzen; regeln, entscheiden, erledigen; ab-, ausmachen; *(Streit)* beilegen, schlichten; *(Frage)* entscheiden; *(Schuld)* begleichen, bezahlen; *(Ansprüche)* befriedigen; *(Rechnung)* bezahlen; *(Konto)* ausgleichen, abrechnen, saldieren; *(Geschäft)* abwikkeln, liquidieren, erledigen, abschließen; *(Rente)* aussetzen; *(Eigentum)* übertragen, vermachen, übereignen, verschreiben (*on s.o.* jdm); *fam* eins auf den Deckel geben (*s.o.* jdm); *Am sl* erledigen (*s.o.* jdn); *itr* sich setzen (*on* auf); sich niederlassen; sich ansiedeln; sich etablieren; *(Nebel, Erdboden)* sich senken; sich zs.ziehen; einsinken; *(Bauwerk)* sich senken; *(Staub)* sich legen; sich niederschlagen; *(Flüssigkeit)* sich (ab)klären; *(Tee)* sich setzen; sich beruhigen, zur Ruhe kommen, beständig(er) werden *(a. Wetter)*; *(Unwetter)* nachlassen; sich niederlassen, s-n (dauernden) Wohnsitz nehmen (*in* in); sich entscheiden, sich entschließen (*on* zu); sich einigen, sich vergleichen (*with s.o. on, upon s.th.* mit jdm über etw); zahlen; *to ~~ o.s.* es sich bequem machen; *to ~~ down* sich senken; sich (endgültig) niederlassen (*as* als); *(Aufregung)* sich legen; beständiger, ruhiger, gesetzter werden; sich hineinfinden (*to* in); sich gewöhnen (*to* an); *to ~~ for* sich einigen auf; *to ~~ in (itr)* einziehen, sich (häuslich) einrichten; *tr* (gut) unterbringen; *to ~~ out of* sich niederschlagen in; *to ~~ up* die Rechnung begleichen (*with s.o.* bei jdm); *to have an account, a score to ~~ with s.o.* mit jdm ein Hühnchen zu rupfen haben; *to ~~ o.'s accounts* abrechnen; *to ~~ o.'s affairs* s-e Angelegenheiten regeln; *to ~~ s.o.'s hash* jdn klein kriegen; *to ~~ to a task* sich an e-e Aufgabe machen; *that ~~s the matter* damit ist die Sache erledigt; **~ed** ['-d] *a* entschieden, abgemacht, abgewickelt, erledigt; bezahlt, beglichen; ausgeglichen; *(Entschluß)* fest; fest, dauerhaft, beständig; festverwurzelt; seßhaft; ansässig; verheiratet, versorgt; **~ement** ['-mənt] Regelung; Stabilisierung; Unterbringung, Versorgung; (Geschäfts-)Gründung; Festigung; Entscheidung, Erledigung; Beilegung, Schlichtung; Abmachung *f*, Übereinkommen *n*; Ausgleich *m*, Abrechnung; Begleichung, Bezahlung; Abwick(e)lung, Liquidation; Abfindung; Verständigung *f*, Vergleich *m*; *jur* Übertragung; *(Rente)* Aussetzung *f*; Vermächtnis *n*; Festsetzung, Bestimmung; Niederlassung; Kolonie; Siedlung *f*; Wohnsitz *m*; *Am (~~ house)* Gemeinde-, Kulturzentrum *n*; *das* Sichsenken *(e-s Baues* od *Bauteiles)*; *to make a ~~ with s.o.* mit jdm e-n Vergleich abschließen; *to reach a ~~* zu e-m Vergleich kommen; sich verständigen; *cash, financial ~~* Bar-, Kapitalabfindung *f*; *compulsory ~~* Zwangsvergleich *m*; *final ~~* Schlußabrechnung *f*; *marriage ~~* Ehevertrag *m*; *~~ of damages* Schadenfeststellung *f*; *~~ of an estate* Nachlaßregulierung *f*; **~er** ['-ə] (An-)Siedler, Kolonist, Pflanzer; Stifter; *sl* Knalleffekt *m*; **~ing** ['-iŋ] Regelung; Erledigung; Entscheidung; Schlichtung, Beilegung, Abrechnung; *(Rente)* Aussetzung; Niederlassung *f*; *pl* Niederschlag *(in e-r Flüssigkeit)*, (Boden-)Satz *m*; *~~-basin* Klärbecken *n*; *~~-day* Abrechnungstag *m*; **2.** (Sitz-)Bank *(mit hoher Rückenlehne)*, Truhenbank *f*.

seven ['sevn] *a* sieben; *s* Sieben(er *m*) *f*; *at sixes and ~s* durcheinander; *to have sailed the ~ seas* kreuz u. quer, in der ganzen Welt herumgekommen sein; **~fold** ['-fould] siebenfach; **~-league boots** *pl* Siebenmeilenstiefel *m pl*; **~teen** ['-'ti:n] siebzehn; *sweet ~~* Backfischzeit *f*; **~teenth** ['-'ti:nθ] *a* siebzehnt; *s* Siebzehntel *n*; **~th** ['sevnθ] *a* siebent; *s* Siebentel *n*; *mus* Septime *f*; **~thly** ['-θli] *adv* sieb(en)tens; **~tieth** ['-tiiθ] *a* siebzigst; *s* Siebzigstel *n*; **~ty** ['-ti] *a* siebzig; *s die* Siebzig; *the ~~ties (pl)* die siebziger Jahre *(e-s Jahrhunderts)*; die Siebzigerjahre *n pl (e-s Menschenlebens)*.

sever ['sevə] *tr* (ab)trennen (*from* von); zertrennen, -teilen, -reißen; abbrechen, ein Ende machen (*s.th.* e-r S); *(Vertrag)* auflösen; *(Beziehungen)* abbrechen; *(Verbindungen)* lösen; *itr* sich trennen; (zer)reißen; ausea.-, zu Ende gehen; **~ance** ['-rəns] Trennung *f* (*from* von); Abbruch *m*, Ende *n*; *~~ allowance* Trennungsentschädigung *f*; *~~ pay* Härteausgleich *m*; Abfindung *f*; *~~ of relations* Abbruch *m* der Beziehungen.

several ['sevrəl] *a u. prn pl* verschiedene, unterschiedliche, besondere; verschiedene, einzelne, einige, mehrere; Sonder-; *s* mehrere; *joint and ~ debt, liability* od *obligation* Gesamtschuld, -verbindlichkeit *f*; **~ly** ['-i] *adv* einzeln, getrennt, für sich; besonders; jeweils; *jointly and ~~* gesamtschuldnerisch; **~ times** mehrmals, ein paarmal.

sever|e [si'viə] streng, hart (*upon* gegen); strikt; ernst; unerbittlich, unnachgiebig; gewissenhaft, sorgfältig, genau, gründlich; schlicht, einfach, streng *(in der Linienführung)*; *(Schmerz)* heftig, stark; schwierig, schwer, streng; *(Krankheit)* schwer; **~ity** [si'veriti] Strenge, Härte (*on* gegen); Striktheit *f*; Ernst *m*, Unerbittlichkeit; Gewissenhaftigkeit; Schlichtheit, Einfachheit; Heftigkeit, Stärke; Schwierigkeit *f*.

*

sew [sou] *irr ~ed* [-d], *~ed* od *~n* [-n] *tr itr* nähen; *tr (Buch)* heften, broschieren; *to ~ in* einheften; *to ~ on* annähen; *to ~ up* zs.-, einnähen; *Am fam* beenden, (erfolgreich) abschließen; **~er** ['-ə] Näher(in *f*) *m*; **~ing** ['-iŋ] *s* Nähen; Nähzeug *n*; Handarbeit *f*; *~~ circle* Handarbeitskränzchen *n*; *~~-kit* Nähzeug *n*; *~~-machine* Nähmaschine *f*; *~~-needle* Nähnadel *f*; *~~-silk* Nähseide *f*.

sew|age ['sju(:)idʒ] Abwässer *n pl*; Abwasseranlage *f*; *~~-farm* Rieselfelder *n pl*; **~er** ['sjuə] Abzugsrohr *n*, -kanal *m*; Kloake *f*; *~~ gas* Sumpfgas *n*; **~erage** ['sjuəridʒ] Kanalisation *f*; Abwässer *n pl*; *~~ plant* Abwasserkläranlage *f*.

sex [seks] *s* Geschlecht *n*; *attr* Geschlechts-, Sexual-; sexuell, geschlechtlich; *tr* das Geschlecht bestimmen von; *of both ~es* beiderlei Geschlechts; **~ appeal** Sex-Appeal *m*, geschlechtliche Anziehungskraft *f*; **~ed** [-t] geschlechtlich; **~ education** sexuelle Aufklärung *f*; **~iness** ['-inis] *sl* Geilheit *f*; Reiz *m*; **~less** ['-lis] geschlechtslos; **~-linked** *biol* an die Geschlechtschromosomen gebunden; **~ology** [sek'sɔlədʒi] Sexualwissenschaft *f*; **~ual** ['seksjuəl] sexuell; geschlechtlich; Geschlechts-, Sexual-; *~~ desire* Geschlechtstrieb *m*; *~~ intercourse* Geschlechtsverkehr *m*; *~~ life* Geschlechtsleben *n*; **~uality** [seksju'æliti] Sexualität, Geschlechtlichkeit *f*; **~-urge** Geschlechtstrieb *m*; **~y** ['seksi] *sl* aufreizend; scharf; geil.

sex|agenarian [seksədʒi'nɛəriən] *a* sechzigjährig; *s* Sechzig(jährig)er *m*; **S~agesima** [-'dʒesimə] Sexagesima *f (8. Sonntag vor Ostern)*; **~angular** [seks'æŋgjulə] sechseckig; **~ennial** [sek'seniəl] sechsjährig; alle sechs Jahre stattfindend; **~partite** [seks'pɑ:tait] sechsteilig; **~tain** ['sekstein] Sechszeiler *m (Gedicht)*; **~tant** ['-tənt] *astr* Sextant *m*; **~tet(te)** [seks'tet] *mus* Sextett *n*; **~todecimo** ['seksto(u)'desimou] Sedezformat *n*, -band *m*; *a* Sedez-; **~tuple** ['sekstjupl] *a* sechsfach; *tr itr* (sich) versechsfachen.

sexton ['sekstən] Küster (u. Totengräber) *m*; **~-beetle** Aaskäfer *m*.

shabb|iness ['ʃæbinis] Schäbigkeit *f a. fig*; **~y** ['ʃæbi] schäbig, fadenscheinig, abgenutzt, verbraucht; zerlumpt, armselig; lumpig, schäbig, wertlos; gemein, erbärmlich, knausrig, *sl* schofel; *~~-genteel (a)* von verschämter Armut.

shack [ʃæk] *Am s* (elende) Hütte, (Bretter-)Bude *f*; *itr*: *to ~ up (sl)* schlafen (*with* mit).

shackle ['ʃækl] *s mar* Schake *f*, Schäkel *m*; Kettenglied *n*, Ring *m*; Traglasche; *fig* Fessel *f*; *pl* Fesseln, Handschellen *f pl*; *tr* fesseln; *fig* in s-r Freiheit be-, einschränken (*s.o.* jdn); hemmen; *mar* schäkeln.

shad [ʃæd] Alse *f (Fisch)*; **~berry** *Am* Vogelbeere *f*; **~bush** *Am* Vogelbeerbaum *m.*

shaddock ['ʃædək] *Art* Pampelmuse *f.*

shad|e [ʃeid] *s* Schatten *m*; dunkle Stelle *f*, Dunkel *n*; Schattierung, Tönung, Nuance; *fig* Spur, Andeutung *f*; Phantom, Gespenst *n*, Geist; (Licht-)Schirm *m*; *Am* Rouleau *n*; *pl* schattige(r), dunkle(r) Platz *m*; ruhige(s), stille(s) Plätzchen *n*; Weinkeller *m*; *lit poet* Unterwelt; Dunkel(heit *f*) *n*; *tr* beschatten; abschirmen, schützen; verdunkeln; verhüllen, bedecken; *(Kunst)* schattieren, abtönen; schraffieren, schummern; abstufen; *(Preis)* geringfügig, allmählich senken; *itr* sich geringfügig ändern, sich leicht abwandeln, unmerklich übergehen (*to* zu; *into* in); *to ~~ away, off* allmählich verschwinden; *of every ~~ and hue (fig fam)* jeder Sorte; *to put, to throw into the ~~ (fig)* in den Schatten stellen; *eye-~~* Scheuklappe *f*; *lamp-~~* Lampenschirm *m*; *sun-~~* Sonnenschirm *m*; **~iness** ['-inis] Schatten *m*, Dunkelheit; *fig* Anrüchigkeit *f*; **~ing** ['-iŋ] Abschirmung *f*, Licht-, Wärme-, Sonnenschutz *m*; *(Kunst)* Schattierung *a. fig*, Schummerung, Schraffierung; *fig* Abstufung *f*; **~ow** ['ʃædou] (Schlag-)Schatten; Schutz, Schirm *m*; Dunkelheit, Düsterkeit, düstere Stimmung *f*; Spiegelbild *n*; Schatten(bild *n*) *m*, Erscheinung *f*, Geist *m*; *fig* (Vor-)Ahnung; Andeutung, Spur, Kleinigkeit *f*; *fig* Schatten, ständige(r) Begleiter; Detektiv, Spion; Schutz; *Am pej sl* Neger, Schwarze(r) *m*; *tr* beschatten; verdunkeln, -düstern, umwölken; *(to ~~ forth)* ahnen lassen; andeuten; *(Kunst)* schattieren; *fig* beständig folgen (*s.o.* jdm), beschatten, unauffällig beobachten; *in the ~~ of s.th.* im Schatten, am Rande e-r S; *under the ~~ of s.th.* im Schatten, unter der Drohung e-r S; *to have ~~s under the eyes* dunkle Ringe um die Augen haben; *to pursue a ~* hinter e-m Schatten herjagen; *coming events cast their ~~s before (them)* kommende Ereignisse werfen ihre Schatten voraus; *not a ~~ of doubt* nicht der leiseste Zweifel; *~~-boxing* Scheinboxen *n*; *~~ cabinet (pol)* Schattenkabinett *n*; *~~-factory (mil)* Ausweich-, Tarnbetrieb *m*; **~owless** ['ʃædoulis] schattenlos; **~owy** ['ʃædoui] schattig, beschattet; trüb(e), undeutlich, verschwommen; *fig* verschwimmend, schattenhaft, illusorisch; **~y** ['ʃeidi] schattig; schattenhaft, undeutlich; *fig* verhüllt, dunkel, geheim; *fam* zweifelhaft, anrüchig, faul.

shaft [ʃɑːft] Schaft; Speer *m*, Lanze *f*; Pfeil; (Licht-)Strahl; Griff, Stiel *m*; Deichsel; (Fahnen-)Stange; *tech* Spindel, Welle, Achse *f*; *min tech* Schacht; *arch* Pfeiler, Säulenschaft; *bot* Stamm; *fig* Hohn *m*; **~ bottom** Schachtsohle *f*; **~ drive** Antriebswelle *f*; **~ furnace** Schachtofen *m.*

shag [ʃæg] **1.** *s* Zotte(l) *f*; zottige(s) Haar *n*; *(Textil)* Plüsch *m*; wirre(s) Büschel *n*; Grobschnitt, Shag(tabak) *m*; *tr* zottig machen; *Am sl* wegjagen, heruntermachen; *itr Am sl* abhauen; **~gy** ['-i] zottig, struppig; *(Haare)* zott(e)lig; plüschartig, rauh; wirr; **2.** *orn* Krähenscharbe *f.*

shagreen [ʃæ'griːn] Chagrin(leder) *n.*

shah [ʃɑː] Schah *m.*

shak|e [ʃeik] *irr shook, shaken tr* schütteln, rütteln (an); erschüttern *(a. seelisch)*; *fig* schwankend, unsicher machen; *(Fahne, Fackel)* schwingen, schwenken; *Am fam* abschütteln, entkommen (*s.o.* jdm); *itr* (er)zittern, -beben (*with* vor); (sch)wanken *a. fig*; vibrieren; *mus* trillern; *(Segel)* flattern; *to ~~ o.s.* sich schütteln; *s* Schütteln, Gerüttel; Zittern, Beben; Vibrieren *n*; Erschütterung *f*; Stoß; *mus* Triller; Sprung *(im Stein)*; Riß *m (im Holz)*; *fam* Erdbeben *n*; *fam* Moment, Augenblick; *Am* Shake *m (Getränk)*; *Am sl* Abschütteln *n*; *pl* Zittern *n*; *to ~~ down (tr)* herunterschütteln; zs.rütteln; hinstreuen; *fig* eingewöhnen; *sl (durch Erpressung)* ausquetschen, -pressen; durchsuchen; *itr* sich setzen, zs.-rutschen, *fam* -sacken; sich gewöhnen, sich beruhigen, ruhig(er) werden; *in a couple of ~~s, in a ~~* im Handumdrehen, im Nu; *to ~~ off (Lästiges)* (von sich) abschütteln; losbekommen; *to ~~ off the dust from o.'s feet* den Staub von s-n Füßen schütteln; *to ~~ out* herausschütteln; *(Staubtuch, Teppich)* ausschütteln; *(Flagge)* entrollen; *to ~~ up* durchea.schütteln; *(durch Schütteln)* mischen; durchea.-, *fig* aufrütteln; *badly ~en-up* arg, bös(e) mitgenommen; *to give s.o., s.th. the ~~ (Am sl)* jdm, e-r S aus dem Weg gehen; jdn, etw loswerden; *to ~~ o.'s finger, o.'s fist at s.o.* jdm mit dem Finger, mit der Faust drohen; *to ~~ o.'s head over, at* den Kopf schütteln über; *to ~~ hands with s.o., to ~~ s.o.'s hand, to ~~ s.o. by the hand* jdm die Hand drücken *od* geben; *to ~~ o.'s sides with laughter* sich schütteln vor Lachen; *I'm all shook (up)* ich bin ganz durchea.; *~~ it up, ~~ a leg* beeil dich; *no great ~~s (fam)* nichts Besonderes *n*; nicht viel wert; *~~-down (s)* Strohschütte, Streu *f*, Not-, Behelfs-, Nachtlager *n*; *Am sl* Erpressung, Durchsuchung *f*; *a fam* Eingewöhnungs-; *~~-hands* Händedruck *m*; *~~-up* Aufrüttelung; (große) Umwälzung, Umgruppierung *f*, Umschwung *m*; **~er** ['-ə] Schüttler; *rel* Shaker; (Salz-, Gewürz-)Streuer; *(cocktail ~~)* Mixbecher *m*; *~~ conveyor* Schüttelrutsche *f*; **~iness** ['-inis] Zitt(e)rigkeit, Wack(e)ligkeit, Schwäche; Unsicherheit; Brüchigkeit *f*; **~ing** ['-iŋ] Schütteln; Zittern *n*; *~~ palsy* Parkinsonsche Krankheit *f*; *~~ screen* Schüttelsieb *n*; **~y** ['-i] zitternd, zitt(e)rig; wack(e)lig, schwach, ungesund; fragwürdig, unsicher, unzuverlässig; brüchig; *(Holz)* kernrissig.

shale [ʃeil] Tonschiefer *m.*

shall [ʃæl; ʃəl, ʃl] *irr (nur pr u. pret) pret: should* soll; *(bei der Bildung des Futurs)* werde; *he ~ not leave* er darf nicht weg; *I should say so!* das will ich meinen! *I should like to go* ich möchte, ich würde gerne gehen.

shallop ['ʃæləp] *mar* Schaluppe *f.*

shallot [ʃə'lɔt] Schalotte *f.*

shallow ['ʃælou] *a* flach; seicht; *fig* oberflächlich, nichtssagend, belanglos; *s (~ water)* seichte Stelle, Untiefe; *pl* Sandbank *f*, Watten *n pl*; *tr itr* (sich) verflachen; **~-brained** einfältig; **~ness** ['-nis] Flachheit, Seichtheit *f a. fig.*

sham [ʃæm] *s* Fälschung; Nachahmung; Imitation; Attrappe *f*; Wichtigtuer, *fam* Angeber; Hochstapler *m*; *a* falsch, unecht, Schein-; fingiert, fiktiv; *(Entschuldigung)* leer; *tr* vortäuschen, -geben, -spielen; *itr* sich verstellen, simulieren, *fam* so tun, als ob; angeben; *to ~ sleep* sich schlafend stellen; **~ fight,** *Am* **battle** Scheingefecht *n*; **~ package** Schaupackung *f*; **~ title page** Schmutzseite *f*; **~ purchase** Scheinkauf *m.*

shambl|e ['ʃæmbl] *itr* schlenkern, schlürfen, watscheln; *s* schlürfende(r), watschelnde(r) Gang *m.*

shambles ['ʃæmblz] *pl meist mit sing* Schlachthaus *n*, Fleischbank *f*; Schlachtfeld *bes. fig*; Trümmerfeld *n*, -haufen *m*, wüste(s) Durcheinander *n.*

shame [ʃeim] *s* Scham(gefühl *n*); Schande *f* (*to* für); Schandfleck *m*; *tr* beschämen, schamrot machen; Schande bereiten *od* machen (*s.o.* jdm) *od* bringen (*s.o.* über jdn); durch Appellieren an das Schamgefühl bringen (*into* zu), abbringen (*out of* von); *to s.o.'s ~* zu jds Schande; *without ~* schamlos; *to bring ~ on* Schande bringen über; *to cry ~* pfui rufen (*on s.o.* über jdn); *to flush with ~* schamrot werden; *to have lost all sense of ~* schamlos sein; *to put to ~* beschämen; *it's a ~, what a ~* jammerschade! es ist e-e Schande! *~ on you!* schäm dich! **~faced** ['-feist] *a* schamhaft, verschämt, scheu, schüchtern; **~facedness** ['-feistnis] Schamhaftigkeit, Verschämtheit, Schüchternheit *f*; **~ful** ['-ful] schändlich; schamlos; schimpflich; **~fulness** ['-fulnis] Schändlichkeit; Schamlosigkeit *f*; **~less** ['-lis] schamlos; unverschämt; **~lessness** ['-lisnis] Schamlosigkeit *f.*

shammy ['ʃæmi] *(~-leather)* Sämischleder *n.*

shampoo [ʃæm'puː] *tr (den Kopf, die Haare)* waschen; *s.o.* jdm die Haare waschen; *s* Haar-, Kopfwäsche *f*; Schampun *n*; **~ing** ['-iŋ] Kopfwäsche *f.*

shamrock ['ʃæmrɔk] *bot* dreiblätterige(r) (*bes.* Acker-, Hasen-)Klee *m*; Kleeblatt *n (irisches Symbol).*

shandy(gaff) ['ʃændigæf] *Br* Bier *n* u. Limonade gemischt.

shanghai [ʃæŋ'hai] *tr mar* gewaltsam (an)heuern; zwingen.

shank [ʃæŋk] *s* Unterschenkel *m*; Schienbein *n*; *(Vogel)* Schenkel *m*; *(Schlachttier)* Haxe *f*; *bot* Stengel; *tech* Griff, Stiel, Schaft *m*; *(Strumpf)* Beinlänge *f*; *(Schuh)* Gelenk; (Pfeifen-)Rohr *n*; *typ* (Schrift-)Kegel; *arch* (Säulen-)Schaft *m*; *itr bot*: *to ~ off* abfallen; *on Sh~'s pony, mare* auf Schusters Rappen; **~-painter** *mar* Rüstleine *f.*

shan't [ʃɑːnt] = *shall not.*

shanty ['ʃænti] **1.** Schuppen *m*, Bude; (ärmliche) Hütte *f*; **~-town** Barackenstadt *f*; **2.** Seemannslied *n.*

shape [ʃeip] *s* Form; Gestalt *f*; Wuchs *m*; Umrisse *m pl*; *tech* Form *f*, Modell, Muster *n*; Pudding *m* (aus e-r Form); Fasson; *fig* Gestalt, (Erscheinungs-)Form, äußere Erscheinung; Verkleidung; *fam* Form *f*, Zustand *m*, (*bes.* gesundheitliche) Verfassung; Ordnung *f*; *theat* Kostüm *n*; *Am* Gruppe *f* von Hafenarbeitern; *tr* formen, bilden, gestalten *a. fig*; *fig* anordnen, (ein-)richten; ausdrücken, zum Ausdruck bringen; anpassen; *(sein Leben)* führen; *itr fam* auslaufen (*into* in); sich entwickeln (*into* zu); *to ~ up (fam)* sich abrunden; sich gut machen; feste Formen annehmen; drohend losgehen (*to* auf); *in the ~ of* in Form, Gestalt *gen*; in der Maske *gen*; *in any ~ or form* irgendwie; *in a great ~ (fam)* glänzend in Form; *to be in bad ~* in schlechter Verfassung sein; *to be out of ~* aus der Form, aus der Fasson sein; *to be shaping well (fig)* sich gut anlassen, vielversprechend sein; *to put into ~* formen, gestalten; *to take ~* Gestalt annehmen; *to ~ the course (mar)* den Kurs absetzen; zusteuern (*towards* auf); **~d** [-t]: **~~** *charge* Hohlgeschoß *n*; **~less** ['-lis] form-, gestaltlos; unförmig, ungestalt; *fig* zwecklos, ziellos; **~lessness** ['-lisnis] Gestaltlosigkeit *f*; **~ly** ['-li] *a* wohlgestaltet, gut proportioniert; gefällig, angenehm; *s pl* Büstenformer *m*; **~ rolling mill** Profilwalzwerk *n*.

shard [ʃɑːd] (*bes.* Topf-)Scherbe; *(Käfer)* Flügeldecke *f*.

share [ʃɛə] **1.** *s* Anteil *m*, Teil *n u. m*; volle(s) Maß *n*; Beitrag *m*; Kontingent *n*, Quote *f*; Gewinnanteil *m*, Dividende; Aktie *f*, Anteilschein *m*; Beteiligung *f*; *tr* (aus-, ver)teilen (*among* unter); teilhaben, sich beteiligen an; *itr* teilhaben, teilnehmen (*in* an); *with s.o. in s.th.* sich mit jdm in e-e S teilen; *in equal ~s, ~ and ~ alike* zu gleichen Teilen; *on ~s* mit Beteiligung; *to come in for a ~ of s.th.* s-n Anteil an etw bekommen; *to fall to s.o.'s ~* jdm als Anteil zufallen; *to give s.o. a ~ in s.th.* jdn an e-r S beteiligen; *to go ~s with s.o.* mit jdm gemeinsame Sache machen; mit jdm teilen; *to have a ~ in s.th.* an e-r S teilhaben, beteiligt sein, an etw teilnehmen; *to hold ~s* Aktionär sein (*in a company* e-r Gesellschaft); *to take a ~ in s.th.* sich an e-r S beteiligen; *to ~ and ~ alike* zu gleichen Teilen teilen; *baby ~* Kleinaktie *f*; *bearer ~* Inhaberaktie *f*; *common (Am), ordinary, original (Br), primary ~* Stammaktie *f*; *legal ~* Pflichtteil *n*; *lion's ~* Löwenanteil *m*; *mining ~* Kux *f*; *preference, preferred ~* Vorzugsaktie *f*; *~ in a business, of stock* Geschäftsanteil *m*; *~ of capital* Geschäftseinlage *f*; **~ boom** Aktienhausse *f*; **~ broker, dealer** Effektenhändler, Börsenmakler *m*; **~ capital** Aktien-, Stammkapital *n*; **~cropper** Deputant, Pächter *m*, der als Pacht e-n Teil der Ernte abliefert; **~holder** Aktieninhaber, Aktionär *m*; *chief, principal ~~* Hauptaktionär *m*; **~ index** Aktienindex *m*; **~ list** Kurszettel *m*; Aktienregister *n*; **~ market** Aktien-, Effektenmarkt *m*; **~ price** Aktienkurs *m*; **~ quotation** Aktiennotierung *f*; **~r** ['-rə] Beteiligte(r), Interessent, Teilhaber *m*; **~ transaction** Börsentransaktion *f*; **2.** *s* Pflugschar *f*.

shark [ʃɑːk] *s* Hai(fisch); *fig* Schurke, Schuft, Gauner; *Am fam* Experte *m*; **~skin** Haifischleder *n*; Haifischhaut *f*, leichte(r) Baumwoll- *od* Chemiefaserstoff *m*.

sharp [ʃɑːp] *a* scharf; spitz; unvermittelt, abrupt; *(Kurve)* scharf; eckig; klar, scharf umrissen, deutlich; hart, streng; *(Abhang)* steil, jäh abfallend; schnell, fix, durchdringend, scharfsinnig, schlau, verschlagen; *fam* gerissen, auf Draht; hellhörig, aufmerksam; scharf, heftig, hitzig; kräftig, kraftvoll, lebhaft; energisch; schneidend, scharf, beißend, stechend, heftig, stark; durchdringend, schrill; *(Phonetik)* stimmlos; *mus* e-n halben Ton höher; *Am sl* rassig, schnittig, elegant, gutaussehend; *s mus* e-n halben Ton höhere Note *f*; *mus* Kreuz *n*; stimmlose(r) Konsonant; *fam* Kenner, Experte; *fam* Gauner, Schwindler *m*; *meist pl* besonders spitze Nähnadel *f*; *tr mus* um e-e halbe Note erhöhen; *sl* 'reinlegen; *itr* e-e halbe Note höher singen *od* spielen; *adv* plötzlich, unvermittelt; aufmerksam; durchdringend; *mus* e-e halbe Note höher; pünktlich, genau; *C ~ (mus)* Cis *n*; *to keep a ~ eye on s.o.* jdn scharf im Auge behalten; **~-cut** *a* geschärft, gespitzt; scharfgeschnitten; **~-eared** *a* mit spitzen Ohren; hellhörig; **~-edged** *a* scharf(kantig); **~en** ['ʃɑːpən] *tr* schärfen, spitzen, schleifen, wetzen; scharf machen *a. fig*; *(Appetit)* anregen; *fig* reizen, an-, aufstacheln; schmerzlicher machen; *mus* um e-e halbe Note erhöhen; *itr* schärfer werden *a. fig*; **~ener** ['ʃɑːpnə] *(pencil-~~)* Bleistift-, Anspitzer *m*; **~er** ['ʃɑːpə] Gauner, Schwindler *m*; **~-eyed** *a* scharfsichtig; **~ness** ['ʃɑːpnis] Schneide; Schärfe; Härte; Heftigkeit, Lebhaftigkeit, Stärke; Härte; Bitterkeit *f*; Scharfsinn *m*, Schlauheit *f*; **~-set** *a* hungrig; begierig; erpicht, *fam* scharf (*on* auf); **~shooter** Scharfschütze *m*; **~-sighted** *a* scharfsichtig *a. fig*; **~-witted** *a* scharfsinnig *fig*; gewitzt.

shatter ['ʃætə] *tr* zerschmettern, zerbrechen; *(Knochen)* zersplittern; *fig* zerstören, vernichten, zunichte machen; erschüttern, *(Gesundheit)* untergraben, *(Nerven)* zerrütten; *itr* zerbrechen, bersten, entzweigehen; *fig* (übel) mitgenommen werden; *s pl*: *in, into, to ~s* in (tausend) Stücke; **~-proof** splittersicher.

shav|e [ʃeiv] *irr*: *pp a.* **~en** ['-n] *tr* abschaben, -hobeln; ab-, aufspalten, in (dünne) Scheiben schneiden; rasieren; *(Gras)* ganz kurz schneiden; *(Haar)* kurz scheren; dicht (hin)wegfahren über; knapp vorbeikommen an; (leicht) streifen, kaum berühren; *(Leder)* falzen; *fam (Preis)* etwas senken; ein bißchen billiger erstehen; *(Voranschlag)* kürzen; *sl* ausnehmen, abstauben; erpressen; *Am sl* überrunden, überlisten; *itr* sich rasieren; nichts verschenken; *to ~~ through* knapp durchkommen; *s* Rasieren *n*, Rasur *f*; Abschabsel *n pl*; Zieh-, Schälmesser; leichte(s) Streifen; knappe(s) Entkommen *n*; Gaunerei *f*, Schwindel; Wucherzins *m*; *by a ~~* um ein Haar; *to get a ~~* sich rasieren lassen; *to give a clean, close ~~* gut, sauber rasieren; *to have a close, narrow, near ~~ (fig)* mit knapper Not davonkommen; *a ~~, please!* rasieren, bitte! *that was a close ~~ (fam)* das hätte ins Auge gehen können; *a clean ~~ (Am)* e-e saubere, gründliche Arbeit; **~en** *a* (kahl)geschoren; *(clean ~~)* glattrasiert; **~er** ['-ə] Barbier, Friseur; Rasierapparat; *sl (young ~~)* Grünschnabel, junge(r) Bengel, Springer *m*; **~etail** ['-teil] *Am sl* frischgebackene(r) Leutnant *m*; **~ing** ['-iŋ] Rasur *f*; Späne *m pl*, Abschabsel *n pl*; *~~-brush* Rasierpinsel *m*; *~~-cream* Rasierkreme *f*; *~~-mirror* Rasierspiegel *m*; *~~-plane* Flachhobel *m*; *~~-soap, stick* Rasierseife *f*.

shawl [ʃɔːl] Schal *m*, Hals-, Kopftuch *n*.

shawm [ʃɔːm] *mus obs* Schalmei *f*.

she [ʃiː, ʃi] *prn* sie; *s*: *a ~* e-e Sie, ein weibliches Wesen; *zoo* Weibchen *n*; *in Zssgen* weiblich; **~-ass, -bear, -dog, -goat** Eselin, Bärin, Hündin, Ziege *od* Geiß *n*; **~-cat, -devil** Xanthippe, Teufelin *f*.

sheaf [ʃiːf] *pl sheaves* Garbe *f*; Bündel *n*; Bund *m*.

shear [ʃiə] *irr*: *pp a. shorn tr* scheren; *(to ~ off)* abschneiden; berauben (*of s.th.* e-r S); *lit poet* abschlagen, -hauen; *s phys* Scherung; *(Tier)* Schur *f*; *pl* große, *bes.* Metallschere *f*; *to be shorn* beraubt sein (*of s.th.* e-r S); **~er** ['-rə] Schafscherer; Schnitter *m*; **~ force** Scher-, Schubkraft *f*; **~ing** ['-riŋ] Scheren *n*, Schur *f*; *pl* Schurwolle *f*; **~ legs** *pl mit sing* Scherenkran *m*; **~ling** ['-liŋ] jährige(s) Schaf *n*, Jährling *m*; **~ pin** Scherbolzen *m*; **~ stress** Scherbeanspruchung *f*.

sheath [ʃiːθ] Scheide *f a. bot zoo anat*; Futteral *n*, Hülle, Decke *f a. zoo*, Überzug *m*; **~e** [ʃiːð] *tr* in die Scheide stecken; überziehen, einhüllen; *(die Krallen)* ein-, zurückziehen; *tech* umkleiden, umhüllen; *(Kabel)* armieren; **~ing** ['-ðiŋ] Schutzhülle, Verkleidung, Ummantelung; *arch* Verschalung; *mar* Kupferhaut *f*; **~-knife** Fahrtenmesser *m*.

sheave [ʃiːv] **1.** *tech* (Lauf-)Rolle, (Seil-)Scheibe *f*; **2.** *tr* in Garben binden; bündeln.

she|bang [ʃə'bæŋ] *Am sl* Kram, Klumpatsch *m*; Bude *f*; *the whole ~* der ganze Kram; **~been** [-'biːn] Kneipe *f*.

shed [ʃed] **1.** *tr* aus-, vergießen; *fig* ausströmen, -strahlen, verbreiten; *(Feuchtigkeit)* abstoßen; *(Licht)* werfen (*on* auf); *(Blätter, Haut)* abstoßen, -werfen; von sich werfen, sich entledigen (*s.th.* e-r S); *(Haare)* verlieren; *to ~ blood, tears* Blut, Tränen vergießen; **2.** Schutz-, Wetterdach *n*; Verschlag, Schuppen *m*; (Lager-)Halle *f*; **~ building, construction** Hallenbau *m*; **~-roof** Pultdach *n*.

sheen [ʃiːn] *s* Glanz, Schimmer *m*.

sheep [ʃiːp] *pl sheep* Schaf *n a. fig*; *rel* Herde, Gemeinde(mitglied *n*) *f*; *to cast, make ~'s eyes at s.o.* auf jdn verliebte Blicke werfen; jdn anhimmeln; *to separate the ~ from the goats (fig)* die Schafe von den Böcken sondern; *one may as well be hanged for a ~ as a lamb* wenn schon, denn schon; *a black, lost ~ (fig)* ein schwarzes, verlorenes Schaf; *a wolf in ~'s clothing (fig)* ein Wolf in Schafskleidern; **~-cot(e), -fold, -pen** Pferch *m*; **~-dog** Schäferhund *m*; **~-farmer, -breeder** Schafzüchter *m*; **~-hook** Hirtenstab *m*; **~ish** ['-iʃ] schüchtern, scheu; linkisch, ungeschickt; einfältig; **~man** *Am* Schafzüchter *m*; **~-run, -walk** Schafweide *f*; **~-shank** Hammelkeule *f*; *mar* Trompetenstek *m (Knoten)*; **~-shearing** Schafschur *f*; **~-skin** Schaffell, -leder; Pergament *n*, Urkunde *f*; *Am* Diplom *n*.

sheer [ʃiə] **1.** *a* unvermischt, rein; *fig* bloß, rein, schier, völlig; *(Textil)* dünn, durchsichtig; steil, senkrecht; *adv* völlig, vollständig, voll u. ganz, äußerst; steil, senkrecht; kerzengerade; **~ madness** helle(r) Wahnsinn *m*; **2.** *itr mar* ausscheren, gieren, ausweichen; *(to ~ off) fam* ausrücken, sich aus dem Staube machen; *s mar* Ausscheren *n*; *(Deck)* Sprung *m*; Schiffsprofil *n*; *pl* Ladekran *m*.

sheet [ʃiːt] **1.** *s* Bettuch, Laken; *poet* Segel *n*; Bogen *m* (Papier); Blatt *n*, Zeitung; Platte; (große) Fläche; Scheibe; *mar* Schote, Schot, Segelleine *f*; *(Boot)* Vorderteil *m od n*; *(~ metal)* Blech *n*; *pl* (große) Massen *f pl*; Druckbogen *m pl*; *tr (Bett)* beziehen; mit e-m Tuch bedecken, ein-, verhüllen; flächig massieren; *(Segel)* befestigen; *in ~s* ungefalzt, roh; *to stand in a white ~* als reuiger Sünder dastehen; *to ~ home (Segel)* aufziehen; *rain fell in ~s* es regnete in Strömen; *a ~ in the wind (fam)* (leicht) beschwipst, angeheitert; *three ~s in the wind (fam)* sternhagelvoll, völlig besoffen; *attendance-~* Anwesenheitsliste *f*; *proof ~* Bürstenabzug, Korrekturbogen *m*; *white as a ~* kreidebleich; *~ of flame* Feuermeer *n*; **~-anchor** *mar* Pflichtanker *m*; *fig* letzte Rettung *f*; **~-copper** Kupferblech *n*; **~-glass** Tafel-, Fensterglas *n*; **~ing** ['-iŋ] Bettuchstoff *m*; Verschalung, (Blech-)Verkleidung *f*, Belag *m*; **~-iron** Eisen-, Walzblech *n*; **~-lightning** Flächenblitz *m*; **~-mica** Plattenglimmer *m*; **~ mill** Blechwalzwerk *n*; **~-music** Notenblätter *n pl*; **~ panel** Blechtafel *f*; **~ steel** Stahlblech *n*.

sheik(h) [ʃeik] Scheich; *fig fam* Weiberheld, Herzensbrecher *m*.

sheldrake ['ʃeldreik] Brandente *f*.

shelf [ʃelf] *pl shelves* (Wand-)Brett, Regal; Gestell; Fach *n*; Sims; *allg* Saum *m*; Sandbank *f*, Riff *n*; *geol* (feste) Gesteinsschicht *f*; *on the ~ (fig)* abgestellt, -gelegt, ausrangiert, ausgedient; *com* auf Lager; *to be put on the ~ (Mädchen)* sitzengeblieben sein; ausrangiert sein; *to put on the ~ (fig)* beiseite schieben, auf die lange Bank schieben; *continental ~* Kontinentalsockel *m*; **~ life** Haltbarkeit *f*.

shell [ʃel] *s* Schale, Hülse, Kapsel; Muschel; *(Fisch)* Schuppe *f*; Schneckenhaus; Gehäuse *n*; *tech* Mantel *m*, Hülle; *aero* Schale *f*; *(racing-~)* Rennboot *n*; Bombe, Granate, Patrone *f*; *fig* äußere(r) Schein *m*, Scheu *f*; *tr (Ei)* schälen; *(Erbsen)* enthülsen; *(Nuß)* (auf)knacken; bombardieren, beschießen; unter Feuer nehmen; *itr* sich schälen lassen; *(to ~ off)* sich abschälen, abblättern; *to ~ out (fam) (bes. Geld)* 'rausrücken; *as easy as ~ing peas* kinderleicht; *to come out of o.'s ~* aus sich herausgehen; *to go, to retire into o.'s ~* sich in sich zurückziehen; *chance ~* Zufallstreffer *m*; **~-almond** Krach-, Knackmandel *f*; **~back** *sl* alte(r) Seebär *m*; **~ case** Geschoß-, Granathülse *f*; **~chuck** Schalenfutter *n*; **~ construction** Schalenbauweise *f*; **~-crater, -hole** Granatloch *n*, -trichter *m*; **~ed** [-d] *in Zssgen* -schalig; *hard-, soft-~~* hart-, weichschalig; *~~ area* Trichterfeld *n*; **~-egg** *com* Frischei *n*; **~-fire** Granatfeuer *n*; **~fish** Schaltier *n (Krebs, Muschel)*; **~ fragment, splinter** Granatsplitter *m*; **~-game** Schwindel, Betrug *m*; **~ hole** Granattrichter *m*; **~ing** ['-iŋ] Beschuß *m*; **~-proof** bombensicher; **~-shock** Kriegsneurose *f*; **~-work** Muschelwerk *n*.

shellac(k) [ʃə'læk] *s* Schellack *m*; *tr* mit Schellack überziehen; *Am sl* schlagen, verdreschen *a. fig sport.*

shelter ['ʃeltə] *s* Unterstellraum, Schuppen *m*; Schutzdach *n*, -hütte *f*; Unterschlupf *m*, Unterkunft *f*, Obdach *n*, Zuflucht(sort *m*) *f*; *mil* Bunker, Unterstand; *(air-raid ~)* (Luft-)Schutzraum; *fig* Schutz, Rückhalt *m*, Deckung *f*; *tr* beherbergen, Unterschlupf, Obdach gewähren (*s.o.* jdm); (be)schützen, beschirmen (*from* vor); *itr* sich unterstellen, Schutz suchen (*under* unter); *under ~* geschützt; *to take ~* Schutz suchen (*from* vor); *night ~* Nachtasyl *n*; **~ed** ['-d]: *~~ trade* durch Zölle geschützte(r) Handel *m*; **~ half** *Am* Zeltbahn *f*; **~less** ['-lis] schutz-, obdachlos; **~ tent** *mil* Zweimannzelt *n*.

shelv|e [ʃelv] *tr* mit Brettern, Fächern, Regalen versehen; auf ein Regal stellen; zu den Akten legen; *fam* ausrangieren; *fig* auf-, beiseite schieben, zurückstellen; *(Problem)* auf Eis legen; *(Beamten)* abstellen; zum alten Eisen werfen; *itr* sich leicht neigen; **~ing** ['-iŋ] *a* sich neigend; *s* Material *n* für Regale; Regale *n pl*.

shemozzle [ʃi'mɔzl] *sl* Krawall *m*.

shenanigan [ʃi'nænigən] *meist pl Am fam* Blödsinn, Quatsch, Mumpitz *m*.

shepherd ['ʃepəd] *s* Schäfer, Hirt; *fig* (Seelen-)Hirt, Seelsorger; Schäferhund *m*; *tr* leiten, führen; beaufsichtigen, sich kümmern um; *the Good S~* der gute Hirte *(Jesus)*; **~ess** ['-is] Schäferin *f*; **~'s clock** *bot* Pimpernell *m*; **~'s club** *bot* Königskerze *f*; **~'s dog** Schäferhund *m*; **~'s pie** *Art* Fleischpastete *f*; **~'s plaid** schwarzweiß karierte(r) Plaid *m*; **~'s purse** *bot* Hirtentäschel *n*.

sherbet ['ʃə:bət] Scherbett, Sorbett *m od n*; (Brause-)Limonade *f*; *Am* Speiseeis *n*.

sheriff ['ʃerif] *Br (ehrenamtlicher)* Landrat *(e-r Grafschaft)*; *Am* oberste(r) Polizeibeamte(r) *m (e-s county)*.

sherry ['ʃeri] Sherry *m (spanischer Wein)*; **~ cobbler** Sherry *m* mit Zitronensaft, Zucker u. Eisstückchen; **~-glass** Süßweinglas *n*.

shew [ʃou] *s. show.*

shibboleth ['ʃibəleθ] Kennwort, -zeichen *n*.

shield [ʃi:ld] *s mil hist* Schild *m*; Wappenschild *m* od *n*; Schutzschild *m*, -blech *n*, -wehr; Abschirmung *f*; *zoo* (Rücken-)Schild *m*; Schweißblatt *n*; *fig* Schutz, Schirm *m*; *tr* schützen (*from* vor); (be)schirmen, decken, bewahren, bewachen, verteidigen; *tech* abschirmen (*from* gegen); *(Kabel)* bewehren; *mil* decken; *sun-~ (mot)* Sonnenblende *f*; **~-bearer** *hist* Schildknappe *m*.

shift [ʃift] *tr* (ver-, weg-, ab-, von sich) schieben; umlegen, umstellen; (von sich) abwälzen, verlagern, verschieben; *tech* umschalten; (aus)wechseln, austauschen; *(Versammlung)* verlegen, verschieben; *(Meinung)* ändern; *mot* schalten (*the gear* den Gang); *to ~ off* sich vom Halse schaffen; *itr* sich verschieben; sich verlagern; sich ändern; *fam* abhauen; sich rasch bewegen; *(Wind)* umspringen, sich drehen; *(Wetter)* umschlagen; *mot (Gang)* sich (automatisch) umschalten; fertigwerden, sich (durch-, weiter)helfen, sich durchschlagen (*for o.s.* selbst); Ausflüchte machen; unaufrichtig handeln, betrügen; *s* Verschiebung *f*, Wechsel *m*, Veränderung *f*, Ersatz *m*; (Arbeits-)Schicht *f*; Arbeitstag *m*; *geol gram* Verschiebung *f*; Notbehelf, Ausweg, Kniff *m*; Ausflucht; List *f*, Trick *m*; *in ~s* umschichtig; *to drop ~s* Feierschichten einlegen; *to make (a) ~* fertig werden, es schaffen, sich behelfen (*with* mit); *to ~ o.'s ground* s-e Meinung ändern; *to ~ into second* in den zweiten Gang umschalten; *~ of crops* Fruchtwechsel *m*; *day-~* Tagesschicht *f*; *dropped ~* Feierschicht *f*; *night-~* Nachtschicht *f*; *vowel-~* Lautverschiebung *f*; **~er** ['-ə] *tech* Ausrücker, Umleger *m*; Rangiermaschine *f*; *scene-~~ (theat)* Kulissenschieber *m*; **~iness** ['-inis] Geschicktheit, Gewandtheit; Durchtriebenheit, Gerissenheit, Hinterhältigkeit, Falschheit *f*; **~ing** *a* veränderlich, beweglich; *fig* schlau, verschlagen; *s* Ortsveränderung; *tech* Schaltung; (Laut-)Verschiebung; Verlagerung *f*; *~~ beach* Treibsandgrund *m*; *~~ sand* Treib-, Trieb-, Flugsand *m*; **~-key** Umschalttaste *f (Schreibmaschine)*; **~less** ['-lis] hilflos, ungeschickt, ungewandt, unbehilflich, unfähig; faul, träge, gleichgültig; **~lessness** ['-lisnis] Hilflosigkeit, Faulheit, Trägheit *f*; **~man** Schichtarbeiter *m*; **~y** ['ʃifti] geschickt, gewandt, durchtrieben, gerissen, gerieben, hinterhältig, falsch.

shill [ʃil] *Am sl* Lockvogel, Schlepper *m*.

shilling ['ʃiliŋ] Schilling *m (= 12 pence)*; *to cut off with a ~* enterben; *a ~ in the pound* 5%; **~ shocker** Reißer, Schund-, Groschenroman *m*.

shilly-shally ['ʃiliʃæli] *a adv* unentschlossen, unentschieden, zögernd; *s* Unentschlossenheit *f*; *itr* schwanken, unentschlossen sein, zögern.

shim [ʃim] *tech* Einlage *f*; Futterholz *n*.

shimmer ['ʃimə] *itr* schimmern; *s* Schimmer; Lichtschein *m*; **~y** ['-ri] schimmernd.

shimm(e)y ['ʃimi] *s* Wackeln; *mot* Flattern *n*; Shimmy *m (Tanz)*; *fam* Hemd *n*; *itr* wackeln; *mot* flattern; Shimmy tanzen.

shin [ʃin] *s (~-bone)* Schienbein *n*; *itr (to ~ up)* hinaufklettern; *to ~ o.s.* sich am Schienbein stoßen; *to ~ around (Am sl)* Geld pumpen (wollen); **~-bone** Schienbein *n*.

shindig ['ʃindig] *Am fam* Schwof *m*, Tanzmusik *f*, -vergnügen *n*; Rummel *m*.

shindy ['ʃindi] *Am fam* Spektakel, Radau *m*; Rauferei, Schlägerei *f*; Schwof *m*; *to kick up a ~* Krach schlagen.

shin|e [ʃain] *irr shone, shone* [ʃɔn] *itr* scheinen, leuchten (*with joy* vor Freude); glänzen, glühen; funkeln; (aus)strahlen (*from* von); *fig* hervorragen, glänzen, sich hervortun (*at* bei); *tr* scheinen, leuchten lassen; glänzend machen; *Am (pret fam: ~ed) (Schuhe)* putzen, wichsen, polieren, *fam* wienern; *s* helle(r) Schein, Glanz *m a. fig*; *fig* Pracht *f*, glänzende(r) Eindruck; Glanz *m*, Politur *f*; *Am* Schuhputzen *n*; *(Kleidungsstück)* Glanz; *sl* Spektakel, Radau, Krach; *Am sl* Streich, Trick *m*; *to ~~ up to s.o.* mit jdm anzubändeln suchen, hinter jdm her sein; *to take the ~~ out of s.th.* das Neue, den Glanz von e-r S nehmen; *s.o.* jdn in den Schatten stellen; jdn abhängen; *to take a ~~ to s.o. (sl)* sich in jdn vergaffen; *to ~~ a torch on s.o.* jdn mit e-r Taschenlampe anleuchten; *I'll come, rain or ~~* ich komme bei jedem Wetter; *he's no ~ing light* er ist kein Kirchenlicht; **~er** ['-ə] Schuhputzer *m*; *fig* Leuchte *f*; *sl* Goldfuchs *m*, -stück; *Am sl* blaue(s) Auge *n*; **~ing** ['-iŋ] glänzend, leuchtend; **~y** ['-i] glänzend, leuchtend, strahlend; (glatt-)poliert; *to be ~~ (Stoff)* glänzen.

shingl|e ['ʃiŋgl] **1.** *s* (Dach-)Schindel *f*; Herrenschnitt *m (Damenfrisur)*; *Am fam* Schild *n (bes. e-s Arztes od Rechtsanwalts)*; *tr* mit Schindeln decken; *(Haar)* sehr kurz schneiden; *to hang out o.'s ~~ (Am fam) (Arzt, Rechtsanwalt)* e-e Praxis eröffnen; **2.** grobe(r) Kies; kiesige(r) Strand *m*; **~y** ['-i] *a* Kies-; kiesartig; kiesbedeckt; **3.** *pl mit sing med* Gürtelrose *f*.

*

ship [ʃip] *s* Schiff; Segelschiff *n*; (Schiffs-)Besatzung *f*; *bes. Am* Luftschiff, Flugzeug *n*; *tr* an Bord nehmen, einschiffen; *(Waren)* verschiffen; *Am allg* (ver)senden; *(Matrosen)* (an-)heuern; *fam* zum Teufel jagen; *fam* loswerden; *itr* sich einschiffen, an Bord gehen; sich (an)heuern lassen; *to ~ off* wegschicken; *by ~* mit dem Schiff; *on board ~* an Bord; *to launch a ~* ein Schiff vom Stapel lassen; *to take ~* an Bord gehen; sich einschiffen (*for* nach); *to ~ the oars* die Ruder einlegen; *to ~ a sea* Brecher übernehmen; *his ~ comes home* er hat sein Glück gemacht, s-e Hoffnungen haben sich erfüllt; *drill-~* Schulschiff *n*; *merchant-~* Handelsschiff *n*; *ocean-going* ~ Hochseedampfer *m*; *passenger* ~ Passagierschiff *n*; *refrigerator* ~ Kühlschiff *n*; ~ **biscuit** Schiffszwieback *m*; ~**board**: *on* ~~ an Bord; ~-**breaker** Schiffsschrotthändler *m*; ~-**broker** Schiffsmakler *m*; ~-**builder** Schiffbauer, Schiffbauingenieur *m*; ~-**building** Schiffbau *m*; ~~ *yard* = ~*yard*; ~-**canal** Schiffahrtkanal *m*; ~-**chandler** Schiffslieferant *m*; ~ **lift** Schiffshebewerk *n*; ~-**load** Schiffsladung *f*; ~**man,** -**master** *Am* Kapitän *m* (e-s Handelsschiffes); ~**mate** Bordkamerad *m*; ~**ment** ['-mənt] Verschiffung (*for* nach); *Am allg* Verladung *f*, Versand, Transport *m*; Schiffsladung; *Am allg* Ladung, Sendung *f*; ~**owner** Reeder *m*; ~**per** ['-ə] Schiffstransportunternehmer; *Am* Spediteur *m*; ~**ping** ['-iŋ] *s* Verschiffung; *Am allg* Verladung *f*, Versand, Transport *m*; Lieferung, Sendung; Handelsflotte *f*; Schiffe *n pl*, (Gesamt-)Tonnage *f*; *attr* Verschiffungs-, *Am* Transport-, Versand-; ~~-*agency* Schiffsagentur *f*; ~~-*agent* Schiffsmakler *m*; ~~ *articles (pl)* Scheuervertrag *m*; ~~ *box (Am)* Versandkiste *f*; ~~-*channel* Fahrwasser *n*; ~~ *clerk (Am)* Versandbuchhalter *m*; ~~-*company* Reederei *f*; ~~-*expenses (pl)* Transport-, Frachtkosten *pl*; ~~-*law* See(handels)recht *n*; ~~-*line* Schiffahrtslinie *f*; ~~-*office* Reederei *f*; Heuerbüro *n*; ~~-*register* Schiffsregister *n*; ~~ *room (Am)* Versandraum *m*; ~~ *routes (pl)* Schiffahrtswege *m pl*; ~**shape** *a* aufgeräumt, sauber, ordentlich; *adv* tadellos, einwandfrei; ~-**way** Helling *f*, Stapel *m*; ~**worm** Bohrmuschel *f*; ~**wreck** *s* Schiffbruch *m a. fig*; Wrack *n*; *tr* scheitern lassen *a. fig*; *fig* ruinieren; ~**wright** Schiffszimmermann; Schiffbauer *m*; ~**yard** (Schiffs-)Werft *f*.

shire ['ʃaiə] Grafschaft *f*, Bezirk *m*; ~-**horse** *(schweres)* Zug-, Ackerpferd *n*.

shirk [ʃə:k] *tr* vermeiden, umgehen; sich drücken vor, aus dem Wege gehen (*s.th.* e-r S); *itr* sich drücken (*from* vor); ~**er** ['-ə] Drückeberger *m*.

shirr [ʃə:] *Am* Fältelung *f*; Gummizug *m*; ~**ed** [-d] *a Am* gefältelt; mit Gummizug; ~~ *eggs (pl Am)* verlorene Eier *n pl* (in Buttersoße).

shirt [ʃə:t] (Ober-, Sport-, Nacht-) Hemd; Unterhemd *n*, -jacke; (~-*blouse*) Hemdbluse *f (für Damen)*; *to get s.o.'s* ~ *out (sl)* jdn auf die Palme bringen; *to give s.o. a wet* ~ jdn in Schweiß bringen; *to give s.o. the* ~ *off o.'s back* für jdn sein letztes Hemd (her)geben; *to keep o.'s* ~ *on (sl)* sich nicht aus der Fassung bringen lassen; *to put o.'s* ~ *(up)on (sl)* Hab u. Gut setzen auf; *he has lost his* ~ *(sl)* er hat alles verloren; *near is my* ~, *but nearer is my skin (prov)* das Hemd ist e-m näher als der Rock; *boiled* ~ gestärkte(s) (Frack-)Hemd *n*; *fam* eingebildete(r) Pinsel *m*; *night*-~ (Herren-)Nachthemd *n*; *stripped to the* ~ im (bloßen) Hemd; *stuffed* ~ *(Am fig)* Hohlkopf *m*; ~-**collar** Hemdkragen *m*; ~-**cuffs** *pl* Manschetten *f pl*; ~-**front** Hemdbrust *f*; ~**ing** ['-iŋ] Hemdenstoff *m*; ~**less** ['-lis] *a* ohne Hemd; *fig* bettelarm; ~**maker** Weißnäherin *f*; ~-**sleeve** *s* Hemd(s)ärmel *m*; *a Am* einfach, schlicht; hemdsärmelig, formlos, ungezwungen; *in o.'s* ~~*s* in Hemdsärmeln; ~-**stud** Hemdenknopf *m*; ~**waist** *Am* Hemdbluse *f*; ~**y** ['-i] *sl* (leicht) beleidigt, eingeschnappt; wütend.

shit [ʃit], **shite** [ʃait] *itr sl* scheißen; *s sl* Scheiße *f a. fig*.

shiver ['ʃivə] **1.** *itr* zittern *(with cold, fear* vor Kälte, Angst); beben; *I* ~ ich schauere, mir *od* mich schauert; *s* Zittern *n*; Schüttelfrost, Fieberschauer *m*; *I got, had the* ~*s (fam)* es lief mir eiskalt über den Rücken; *it gave me the* ~*s (fam)* das ließ mir das Blut in den Adern erstarren; ~ *my timbers!* verflixt nochmal! ~**y** ['-ri] zitternd, bebend; fröstelnd; erschauernd; **2.** Splitter; *tech* Span *m*; *tr* zersplittern; *itr* (zer)splittern.

shoal [ʃoul] **1.** *s* seichte Stelle, Untiefe; Sandbank *f*; *meist pl* lauernde Gefahr *f*, Haken *m fig*; *a* seicht, flach; *itr* flach(er), seicht(er) werden; **2.** *s* große Masse, Menge *f*, (*bes.* Fisch-)Schwarm, Zug *m*; Schule *f*; *itr (Fische)* e-n Schwarm, e-e Schule bilden; in e-m Schwarm ziehen *od* schwimmen; wimmeln; sich zs.drängen; *in* ~*s* in Unmengen, haufenweise; in Scharen.

shock [ʃɔk] **1.** *s* (heftiger) Stoß, Schlag; Zs.prall; (feindlicher) Vorstoß, Angriff *m*; plötzliche Er-, Aufregung, Erschütterung (*to* für); aufregende Sache *f*, Erlebnis *n*; *(electric* ~*)* (elektrischer) Schlag; *med* Nervenschock; *fam* Kollaps, Klaps *m*; *tr* (heftig) (an)stoßen, schlagen; e-n elektrischen Schlag versetzen (*s.o.* jdm); sehr auf-, erregen; Anstoß erregen bei, schockieren; *to be* ~*ed at, by* empört, aufgeregt, entsetzt sein über, schockiert sein von; *to be a great* ~ *to s.o.* für jdn ein schwerer Schlag sein; *earthquake* ~ Erdstoß *m*; *shell* ~ Kriegsneurose *f*; ~-**absorber** Stoßdämpfer *m*; ~**er** ['-ə] *fam* böse Überraschung; Sensation(snachricht) *f*; Schauerroman *m*; ~**ing** ['-iŋ] aufregend; Anstoß erregend, anstößig, schockierend; *fam* schlimm, schrecklich, entsetzlich; ~-**proof** stoßfest; mit Berührungsschutz; ~ **tactics** *pl*, *meist mit sing, mil* Überraschungsstrategie *f*; ~ **therapy, treatment** *med* Schockbehandlung *f*; ~ **troops** *pl* Stoßtruppen *f pl*; ~**wave** Druckwelle *f*; ~ **worker** Rekordarbeiter, *fam* Hennecke *m*; **2.** *s* (Korn-)Puppe *f*, Haufen *m*, Mandel, Garbe *f*; *tr itr* (das Korn) in Haufen stellen; **3.** dichte(r) (Haar-) Schopf *m*; ~-**headed** *a* strubb(e)lig.

shoddy ['ʃɔdi] *s* Shoddy-, Lumpenwolle *f*, -wollstoff; *fig* Schund, Tinnef; *Am* Neureiche(r) *m*; *a* aus Lumpenwolle; schäbig, minderwertig, Schund-; *Am* neureich, protzig, protzenhaft.

shoe [ʃu:] *s* (Halb-)Schuh *m*; *(horse* ~*)* Hufeisen *n*; (Metall-)Kappe *f (auf e-r Stange)*; Bremsschuh, -klotz *m*, -backe *f*; *arch* Lager *n*; Beschlag; Mantel *(e-s Gummireifens)*; *tech* Gleitschuh *m*; *el* Kontaktrolle *f*, Polschuh *m*; *tr irr shod, shod* [ʃɔd] mit Schuhen, e-r Metallkappe versehen; *(Pferd)* beschlagen; schienen; *to be in, to fill s.o.'s* ~*s* jds Platz, Stelle einnehmen; in jds Haut stecken; *to know where the* ~ *pinches* wissen, wo der Schuh drückt; *to shake in o.'s* ~*s* vor Angst schlottern; *that's another pair of* ~*s* das ist etw ganz anderes; *the* ~ *is on the other foot* das ist genau das Gegenteil; ~**black** Schuhputzer *m*; ~**horn, -lift** Schuhlöffel *m*; ~-**lace** Schnürsenkel, Schuhriemen *m*; ~-**leather** Schuhleder *n*; ~**maker** Schuhmacher *m*; ~**polish** Schuhwichse *f*; ~-**repair shop** Schuhreparaturwerkstätte *f*; ~-**scraper** Schuhabstreifer *m*; ~**shine** *Am* Schuhputzen *n*; *(*~~ *boy)* Schuhputzer *m*; ~~ *parlor* Schuhputzsalon *m*; ~-**shop,** *Am* -**store** Schuhladen *m*; ~-**string** Schnürsenkel *m*; *sl* geringe(s) Kapital *n*; *to start a business on a* ~~ ein Geschäft mit praktisch nichts anfangen; ~-**tree** Schuhspanner *m*.

shoo [ʃu:] *interj* sch! fort! weg! *itr* sch machen; *tr (to* ~ *away)* verscheuchen.

shook [ʃuk] **1.** Kistenbretter *n pl*; Faßdauben *f pl*; (Korn-)Puppe *f*, Haufen *m*; **2.** *pret von shake*.

shoot [ʃu:t] *irr shot, shot* [ʃɔt] *tr (to* ~ *past)* vorbeisausen, vorüberschießen an; (hin)wegsausen, -schießen über; überholen; ausgießen, -schütten; abladen; aus-, wegwerfen, (fort)schleudern; *(Riegel)* auf-, zuschieben; *(Anker)* auswerfen; *(Strahlen)* aussenden; *(Stromschnelle)* hinunterfahren; *bot* (hervor)treiben; *(Kohle)* hinunterbefördern (*into the cellar* in den Keller); *(Lippen)* vorstülpen; (ab)schießen, -feuern; *(Drohung, Blick)* schleudern, werfen; *(Frage)* aufwerfen, richten (*at* an); *(Wild)* schießen, jagen; *(Gebiet)* jagen in; treffen, er-, abschießen; aufnehmen, photographieren, *fam* knipsen; filmen; *sport (Ball, Tor)* schießen; *med (Einspritzung)* vornehmen; *sl* 'rausrücken, ('rüber-, her)schmeißen; *itr* sausen, schießen; *(Schmerz)* stechen, plötzlich auftreten; hervorschießen, -stürzen; *(Pflanzen)* auf-, in die Höhe schießen, sprossen, treiben; heranwachsen, emporschießen; vorragen, -stehen; *(Ball)* schlagen, schießen; schießen, feuern; *(Gewehr)* losgehen; jagen, auf die Jagd gehen; *phot* e-e Aufnahme machen, *fam* knipsen; drehen, filmen; *sport* schießen; *fam* es abgesehen haben (*at* auf); *s* Schuß *m*; Jagd *f*, -gebiet *n*, -gruppe *f*; schnelle(s) Wachstum *n*; *bot* Schößling, Trieb, Ableger; Schuß *m (Wasser)*; *min* Erzlager; Abflußrohr *n*, -graben *m*; Rutsche, Rutschbahn; Stromschnelle *f*; stechende(r) Schmerz *m*; *the whole* ~ *(fam)* alles; *to* ~ *the breeze (Am sl)* zwanglos plaudern; *to* ~ *the bull (Am sl)* schwätzen, schmeicheln, übertreiben; *to* ~ *a goal (fig)* ins Schwarze treffen; *to* ~ *a line (Am sl)* prahlen; *to* ~ *the moon (sl)* durchbrennen; *to be all shot (fig)* ganz herunter sein; *they shot their bolt* sie pfiffen auf dem letzten Loch; *his nerves are all shot* er ist mit den Nerven ganz herunter; ~*!* schieß los! leg los! *to* ~ **ahead** hervorschießen, -schnellen; davonschießen, -rennen; *to* ~ **away** *itr* weiterschießen; *tr (Munition)* verschießen; *to* ~ **down** ab-, herunter-, niederschießen; *to* ~~ *o.'s wad (Am sl)* alles auf e-e Karte setzen; *to* ~~ *the works (Am sl)* sein Letztes hergeben, sich verausgaben; alles ausplaudern; *to* ~ **off** ab-, wegschießen; *o.'s, at the mouth (sl)* drauflos reden; *to* ~ **out** *tr* ausstoßen, hinauswerfen; *itr (Flammen)* herausschlagen; *to* ~ **past** vorbeisausen (*s.o.* an jdm); *to* ~ **up** *itr* auf-, in die Höhe schießen, schnell wachsen; *(Flammen)* herausschlagen (*from* aus); wild herumschießen; *tr* durchlöchern; rasch hinaufbefördern; *Am fam (Ort)* terrorisieren; ~**er** ['-ə] Schütze; Revolver *m*; ~**ing** ['-iŋ] *s* Schießen *n*; Erschießung *f*; *(Schmerz)* plötzliche(s) Stechen; Jagen *n*, Jagd; Jagd(gebiet *n*) *f*; *(Stromschnelle)* Durchqueren *n*; *bot* Trieb, Ableger *m*; Filmen, Drehen *n*; *a (Schmerz)* stechend; vorstehend, -ragend; *to go* ~~ auf die Jagd gehen; *indoor, outdoor* ~~ Innen-, Außenaufnahmen *f pl*; *pistol* ~~ Pistolenschießen *n*; ~~-*boots (pl)* Jagdstiefel *m pl*; ~~-*box* Jagdhütte *f*; ~~ *of a film* Filmaufnahme *f*; ~~-*gallery* Schießstand *m*; ~~-*iron (sl)* Schießeisen *n*; ~~-*licence* Jagdschein *m*;

~~-*range (mil) (großer)* Schießstand *m*; Entfernung *f* (beim Filmen); ~~-*script* Drehbuch *n*; ~~ *season* Jagdzeit *f*; ~~ *star* Sternschnuppe *f*; ~~ *war* heiße(r) Krieg *m*; ~-**out** *Am sl* Pistolenduell *n*.

shop [ʃɔp] *s* Laden *m a. sl pej*; (Laden-) Geschäft *n*, Verkaufsstelle; *in Zssgen a.*: -handlung *f*; *sl* Kittchen *n*; Werkstatt, -stätte *f*, Betrieb *m*, Fabrik *f*; *itr (to go ~ping)* einkaufen (gehen); *Am a.* Schaufenstereinkäufe machen; sich in den Geschäften umsehen; *tr* einkaufen; *sl* verpfeifen (*s.o.* jdn), einlochen; *fam* entlassen; *all over the ~ (sl)* überall; wild durcheinander; *to come, to go to the wrong ~ (fig)* vor die falsche Tür, an den Unrechten kommen; *to keep a ~* ein Geschäft, e-n Laden haben; *to keep ~* das Geschäft führen; *to set up ~* e-n Laden aufmachen, ein Geschäft eröffnen; *to shut up ~* den Laden zumachen, das Geschäft schließen *od* aufgeben; Schluß machen; *to talk ~* fachsimpeln; *baker's ~* Bäckerladen *m*, Bäckerei *f*; *bargain ~* billige(r) Laden *m*; *chemist's ~* Drogerie *f*; *closed ~ (Am)* Betrieb *m*, der nur Gewerkschaftsmitglieder einstellt; *erecting ~* Montagehalle *f*; *flower-~* Blumengeschäft *n*; *gift-~* Geschenkartikel-, Galanteriewarengeschäft *n*; *grocer's ~* Kolonialwaren-, Delikatessengeschäft *n*, Feinkosthandlung *f*; *ironmonger's ~* Eisenhandlung u. Haushaltwarengeschäft *n*; *machine ~* mechanische Werkstatt *f*; *repair ~* Reparaturwerkstätte *f*; *shoemaker's ~* Schuhmacherwerkstatt *f*; *stationer's ~* Papierwarengeschäft *n*, -handlung *f*; *sweet-~* Süßwarengeschäft *n*; *toy-~* Spielwarengeschäft *n*; *union ~ (Am)* Betrieb *m*, dessen Angehörige Gewerkschaftsmitglieder sein *od* werden müssen; ~-**accident** Betriebsunfall *m*; ~-**assistant, -boy, -girl** Verkäufer(in *f*) *m*; Ladenmädchen *n*; ~-**bell** Ladenklingel *f*; ~-**door** Ladentür *f*; ~-**fittings** *pl* Ladeneinrichtung *f*; ~-**front** Ladenfront, Auslage *f*; ~-**hours** *pl* Laden-, Öffnungszeiten *f pl*; ~**keeper** Ladenbesitzer, Geschäftsinhaber; *sl* Ladenhüter *m*; ~**keeping** Ladenbetrieb; Kleinhandel *m*; ~ **language** Fachsprache *f*; ~**lifter** Ladendieb *m*; ~**lifting** Ladendiebstahl *m*; ~**man** Ladenbesitzer; Verkäufer; *Am* Arbeiter *m*; ~ **operation** Arbeitsgang *m*; ~**per** ['-ə] Einkäufer *m*; ~**ping** ['-iŋ] Einkauf(en *n*), Einkaufsbummel *m*; *to do o.'s ~~* Einkäufe, Besorgungen machen; *to go window-~~* Schaufenster ansehen; ~~ *bag* Einkaufstasche *f*; ~~ *centre* Geschäftszentrum, -viertel *n*; ~~ *expedition (Am)* Einkaufsbummel *m*; ~~ *hours (pl)* Einkaufsstunden *f pl*; ~~ *street* Geschäftsstraße *f*; ~ **price** Ladenpreis *m*; ~**py** ['-i] *a* voller Geschäfte, Geschäfts-; Einzelhandels-, Kleinverkaufs-; beruflich, Fach-; ~-**soiled, -worn** *a (Ware)* angestaubt; ~**steward, chairman** *Am* Betriebsobmann, Betriebsratsvorsitzende(r) *m*; ~**talk** Fachsimpelei *f*; ~**walker** Aufsichtführende(r) *m* in e-m Ladengeschäft; ~-**window** Schaufenster *n*; *to put all o.'s goods in the ~~ (fig)* glänzen wollen.

shore [ʃɔː] *s* Küste(nstreifen *m*, -gebiet, -land *n*) *f*; Ufer *n (a. e-s Flusses)*; Strand *m*, *lit poet* Gestade; Watt(enmeer); *mar* Land *n*; *in ~ (mar)* unter Land; *off ~* auf See, in Landnähe; *on ~* an Land; ~-**based** *a aero* an der Küste stationiert; ~-**battery** *mil* Küstenbatterie *f*; ~-**bird** Uferschwalbe *f*; ~-**dinner** *Am* Fisch-, Muschelessen *n*; ~ **leave** Landurlaub *m*; ~**less** ['-lis] *poet* uferlos; ~-**line** Küstenlinie *f*; ~ **patrol** *Am mar* Küstenstreife *f*; ~**ward** *adv* landwärts; ~ **wind** Seewind *m*; **2.** *s* Stütze, Strebe; *mar* Schore *f*; *tr (to ~ up)* (ab)stützen.

short [ʃɔːt] *a* kurz *(a. zeitlich)*; kurzfristig; niedrig; klein *(a. Personen)*; (zs.)gedrängt, knapp (gefaßt); knapp (*of* an), unzureichend, unzulänglich; nachstehend (*of* dat); kurz angebunden *fig*, barsch (*with* gegen); *(Gebäck, Metall)* mürbe, bröck(e)lig, krüm(e)lig; *(Getränk)* stark, unverdünnt; *(Taille)* hoch; *com* ungedeckt, ohne Deckung; *s* zu kurzer Schuß *m*; Kürze, kurze Silbe; *(Name)* Kurzform *f*; Kurzfilm; *el* Kurzschluß, *fam* Kurze(r); *com* Baissespekulant *m*; *Am sl* Auto, Taxi *n*; *(~ one)* Spritzer *m*; *pl* kurze Hose *f*, Shorts *pl*; kurze Unterhose; Kleie *f*; Abfälle, Reste *m pl*; *typ* Fehlabzüge *m pl*; *Am sl* Geldverlegenheit *f*; *adv* (zu) kurz; knapp; ganz kurz (*of* vor); kurz, in Kürze; barsch; plötzlich, unerwartet; *a ~ time ago* vor kurzem; *at ~ date, notice (fin)* kurzfristig (kündbar); *for ~* kurz *adv*, der Kürze halber *od* wegen; *in a ~ time* in kurzer Zeit; binnen kurzem; *in ~, the long and the ~ of it* (in) kurz(en, wenigen Worten); *in ~ order (Am)* schnell *adv*; *nothing ~ of* nichts weniger als; *to be ~* schlecht bei Kasse sein; *of s.th.* von etw nicht genug, zu wenig haben; *with s.o.* mit jdm kurz angebunden sein; *to be taken ~ (fam)* rasch austreten müssen; *to come, to fall ~* nicht (aus)reichen, nicht genügen; *(die Erwartungen)* enttäuschen, zurückbleiben hinter; *of s.th.* etw nicht erreichen; *to cut ~* unter-, (vorzeitig) abbrechen; *fig* das Wort abschneiden (*s.o.* jdm); *to give s.o. the ~ end of the stick (Am sl)* jdn schlecht behandeln; *to have a ~ temper* leicht aufbrausen, sehr reizbar sein; *to make it ~* sich kurz fassen; *to make ~ work, thrift of* kurzen Prozeß machen mit; *to make a long story ~* kurz gesagt, kurz u. gut; *to run ~* knapp sein, ausgehen; *of* nicht genug ... haben; *to sell ~* ohne Deckung verkaufen; *to stop ~* plötzlich stehenbleiben; *to strike ~* das Ziel verfehlen; *to turn ~* plötzlich kehrtmachen; *~ of breath* außer Atem; kurzatmig; *~ of cash* nicht bei Kasse; *~ of money* in Geldschwierigkeiten, -nöten, *fam* knapp bei Kasse; ~**age** ['-idʒ] Mangel *m*, Knappheit, Verknappung *f* (*of* an); Defizit *n*, Fehlbetrag, Abgang; Gewichtsverlust *m*; *to make up the ~~* den Fehlbetrag decken; *housing ~~* Wohnungsknappheit *f*; *labo(u)r ~~* Mangel *m* an Arbeitskräften; ~-**amount** Minderbetrag *m*; ~-**armed** *a* kurzarmig; ~ **bill** kurzfristige(r) Wechsel; Inkassowechsel *m*; ~**bread, -cake** Mürbeteig *m*, -gebäck *n*; Teekuchen *m*; ~**change** *tr itr Am* betrügen; ~ **circuit** ['-sɜːkit] *el s* Kurzschluß *m*; ~-**circuit** *tr* vereinfachen; *el* kurzschließen; ~-**coated** *a (Hund)* kurzhaarig; ~**coming** Fehler, Mangel, Defekt *m*; Versagen *n*, ungenügende Leistung; Pflichtversäumnis *f*; *pl* Unzulänglichkeit *f*; *(Person)* Schwächen *f pl*; ~~ *goods (pl)* Mangelwaren *f pl*; ~ **cut** Richt-, kürzere(r) Weg *m a. fig*; *fig* abgekürzte(s) Verfahren *n*; ~-**dated** *a* kurzfristig, auf kurze Sicht, mit kurzer Fälligkeit; ~ **delivery** Teillieferung *f*; ~**en** ['-n] *tr* (ab-, ver)kürzen, stutzen, vermindern, verringern; *(Aufträge)* zurückziehen; Backfett hinzufügen, -tun zu; *(Segel)* einziehen, raffen; *(Feuer)* zurückverlegen; *(Front)* verkürzen; *itr* kurz, kürzer werden; ~**ening** ['-niŋ] (Ab-, Ver-)Kürzung, Verminderung; *mil (Front)* Verkürzung *f*; *Am* Backfett *n*; ~~ *of working hours* Verkürzung *f* der Arbeitszeit; ~-**haired** *a* kurzhaarig; ~**hand** Kurzschrift, Stenographie *f*; *to take down in ~~* (mit)stenographieren; *to write ~~* stenographieren; ~~ *note* Stenogramm *n*; ~~ *notebook* Stenogrammheft *n*; ~~ *typist* Stenotypist(in*f*) *m*; ~~ *writer* Stenograph *m*; ~-**handed** *a*: *to be ~~* zu wenig Arbeitskräfte haben; ~-**haul traffic** Nahverkehr *m*; ~-**headed** *a* kurzköpfig; ~**horn** Kurzhorn *n (Rinderrasse)*; ~**ish** ['-iʃ] etwas kurz; ~ **leave** Kurzurlaub *m*; ~-**list** *tr* in die engere (Aus-)Wahl ziehen; ~-**lived** *a* kurzlebig *a. fig*; ~**ly** ['-li] *adv* in kurzem, bald; kurz, in Kürze, in wenigen Worten; scharf; barsch; ~~ *after* bald danach; ~**ness** ['-nis] Kürze; Knappheit *f*, Mangel *m* (*of* an); Unzulänglichkeit, Schwäche *f*; ~~ *of memory* Gedächtnisschwäche *f*; ~~ *of money* Geldknappheit *f*; ~~ *of sight* Kurzsichtigkeit *f*; ~ **order** *Am (Restaurant)* Schnellgericht *n*; ~ **pastry** Mürbeteig *m*, -gebäck *n*; ~-**range** *a* nicht weitreichend; kurzfristig; Nahkampf-; ~ **sight** Kurzsichtigkeit *f a. fig*; ~-**sighted** *a* kurzsichtig *a. fig*; ~-**spoken** *a* wortkarg; ~ **story** Novelette, Kurzgeschichte *f*; ~-**stroke** *mot* kurzhubig; ~-**tempered** *a* leicht aufbrausend, sehr reizbar, barsch, kurz angebunden; ~-**term** kurzfristig; ~ **time (work)** Kurzarbeit *f*; *to be on ~~* verkürzt arbeiten; ~ **ton** *2000 engl. Pfund = 907,184 kg*; ~**waist** hohe Taille *f*; ~-**waisted** *a* mit hoher Taille; ~ **wave** *radio* Kurzwelle *f*; ~-**wave** *a* Kurzwellen-; ~~ *set* Kurzwellengerät *n*; ~ **weight** *com* Unter-, Mindergewicht *n*; *to give ~~* knapp abwiegen; ~-**winded** ['-windid] *a* außer Atem; kurzatmig; ~-**witted** *a* einfältig, dumm.

shot [ʃɔt] *s* (Ab-)Schuß *m a. sport*; Schußweite; *fig* Reichweite *f*, Bereich *m od n*; *fig* Versuch *m*; Vermutung *f*; *fig* Seitenhieb *m*, bissige, kritische Bemerkung *f*; Geschoß *n*, Kugel; Munition *f*; Schrot *m*; *sport* Kugel *f*; *sport* Wurf, Stoß *m*; *min* Sprengung, Sprengladung *f*; Schütze *m*; *com* Postwerbeexemplar *n*; *phot film* Aufnahme; *med fam* Spritze, Einspritzung, Injektion *f*; *fam* Schuß, Schluck *m*; Zeche, Schuld *f*; Anteil *m*; *a (pp von shoot)* durchschossen, -setzt; *fam* hin(über), verbraucht, aus, vorbei; erschossen; gesprenkelt, schillernd; *~ through with* gespickt mit; *like a ~* sofort, wie der Blitz; *(off) like a ~* blitzschnell, wie der Blitz; *within ~* in Schußweite; *to be ~ to pieces (Am fam)* ruiniert sein; *to call o.'s ~s (fig)* kein Blatt vor den Mund nehmen; *to have a ~ at s.th.* etw probieren, versuchen; *to have a ~ in the locker (fam)* noch ein Eisen im Feuer haben; *to make, to take a ~* e-n Schuß abgeben, -feuern (*at* auf); *to make a bad ~* daneben-, vorbeischießen; *to need a ~ in the arm (fig)* e-e Spritze nötig haben; *to put the ~ (sport)* die Kugel stoßen; *good ~!* gut getroffen! *his question is a ~ in the dark* er fragt aufs Geratewohl; *a big ~ (fam)* ein hohes Tier *n*; *crack, dead ~* Scharfschütze *m*; *ear-~* Hörweite *f*; *good ~* Volltreffer *m*; *half ~ (fam)* angetrunken, angesäuselt; *long ~* aussichtslose(s) Unternehmen, hoffnungslose(r) Versuch; *fam* schwache(r) Kandidat *m*; *not by a long ~ (sl)* nicht im allergeringsten; *putting the ~* Kugelstoßen *n*;

random ~ ungezielte(r) Schuß *m*; *small* ~ Schrot *m* od *n*; ~**-gun** *s* Schrotflinte *f*; *a sl Am* erzwungen; ~**-hole** Sprengloch *n*; ~**-proof** kugelfest, -sicher; ~~ *jacket* Panzerweste *f*; ~**-put** Kugelstoßen *n*; ~**-putter** Kugelstoßer *m*.

should [ʃud] *s. shall.*

shoulder [ˈʃouldə] *s* Schulter, Achsel; Schulterpartie *f (a. d. Kleidung)*; *zoo* Vorderviertel, Blatt *n*, Bug *m*; *(Schlachttier)* Schulterstück *n*, Keule *f*; Vorsprung *m*, (kleine) Anhöhe; *mil* Schulterwehr *f*; *(Straße)* Bankett *n*; *arch* Brüstung *f*, Vorsprung, Absatz *m*; *tech* Widerlager *n*, Bund *m*, Bord *n*; *pl* Schultern *f pl bes. fig*, Rücken *m*; *tr* auf die Schulter nehmen; (auf der Schulter) tragen; sich *(e-n Weg)* mit den Schultern bahnen; *(Gewehr)* schultern; *tech* abstützen (*against* auf), absetzen; *fig* auf sich nehmen (*s.th.* etw); *straight from the ~ (Worte)* offen, unverblümt *a. adv (reden)*; ~ *to* ~ Schulter an Schulter; mit vereinten Kräften; *to be head and ~s above s.o.* jdn beträchtlich überragen; viel tüchtiger sein als jem; *to carry a chip on o.'s* ~ immer bei schlechter Laune sein; *to cry on s.o.'s* ~ sich bei jdm ausweinen; *to give, to turn s.o. the cold ~ (fig)* jdm die kalte Schulter zeigen; *to have a head on o.'s ~s* klug, gewandt sein; *to put o.'s ~ to the wheel* tüchtig zupacken, Hand anlegen; sich ordentlich ins Zeug legen; *to rub ~s with* an einem Tisch sitzen, engen Umgang haben mit; *to stand head and ~s above s.o. (fig)* jdn weit überragen; *to ~ o.'s way through a crowd* s-n Weg durch e-e Menge bahnen; ~ *arms!* das Gewehr über! ~**-belt** Schulterriemen *m*; Wehrgehänge *n*; ~**-blade** Schulterblatt *n*; ~**-joint** Schultergelenk *n*; ~**-knot** *mil* Schulterstück *n*; ~**-strap** Träger *m (an Damenunterwäsche)*; *mil* Schulterstück *n*.

shout [ʃaut] *s* Schrei *m*; Geschrei *n*, Lärm, Krach; Ruf *m*; *fam* (zu zahlende) Runde *f*; *tr* (hinaus)schreien *(for joy* vor Freude); *itr* schreien; jauchzen (*with* vor); *at s.o.* jdn anschreien; *for s.o.* nach jdm rufen; *to s.o.* jdm laut zurufen; *to ~ down* niederschreien, -brüllen; *~s of applause* Beifallsrufe *m pl*; ~**ing** [ˈ-iŋ] Geschrei, Brüllen; Rufen *n*; Jubel *m*; *to be all over but the ~ing* die Schlacht ist geschlagen.

shove [ʃʌv] *tr itr* schieben; (fest) stoßen; hineinstopfen (*into a drawer* in e-e Schublade); *itr* sich drängen; *sl* abhauen; *s* Schubs, Stoß *m*; *to ~ along* sich (langsam) weiterbewegen; *to ~ around (Am)* herumschubsen; *to ~ off (tr) (Boot vom Ufer)* abstoßen; *itr fam* abschieben, -hauen; *to ~ through* sich durchdränge(l)n; *to ~ the responsibility on to s.o.* jdm die Verantwortung zuschieben.

shovel [ˈʃʌvl] *s* Schaufel, Schippe; *(~ful)* Schaufel(voll) *f*; *(Bagger)* Löffel; *(~ hat)* flache(r) Hut *m (der Geistlichen)*; *tr* schaufeln, schippen; ~**-board** Beilkespiel *n*, -tafel *f*; ~**-dredger** Löffelbagger *m*; ~**ler** [ˈ-ə] *orn* Löffelente *f*.

show [ʃou] *irr showed, shown* od *(selten) showed* **1.** *tr* zeigen; zur Schau, ausstellen; weisen, den Weg zeigen, führen (*to* zu); sehen, durchblicken, erkennen lassen; aufweisen; an den Tag legen, enthüllen; aufzeigen, darlegen, klarstellen, erklären; ergeben; demonstrieren; nach-, er-, beweisen, den Nachweis erbringen (*that* daß); anzeigen, registrieren; *(Gunst, Gnade)* erweisen; *jur* dartun, -legen, angeben; *theat* spielen, geben; **2.** *itr* sich zeigen, auftreten, erscheinen; zu sehen sein; wirken; *theat* auftreten; *to ~ o.s.* sich (in der Öffentlichkeit) zeigen, öffentlich auftreten; sich blicken lassen; **3.** *s* Sichtbarwerden *n*; Erscheinung; (Pracht-)Entfaltung *f*, Prunken *n*, Repräsentation *f*; (großer) Aufzug *m*; Angabe *f*, falsche(r) Schein *m*; *fig* Bild *n*; Schau(stellung), Ausstellung, Vor-, *theat* Aufführung; *radio video* Sendung *f*; *Am* Zeigen, Sichtbarwerdenlassen *n*, Enthüllung; *Am* Darlegung *f*, Er-, Nachweis *m*, Arbeit; *fam* Chance; *fam* Sache, Angelegenheit *f*; *fam* Betrieb, Laden *m*; **4.** *all over the ~* in völliger Unordnung; *by (a) ~ of hands (parl)* durch Handerheben; *for ~* zum Schein; nur fürs Auge; *on ~* zur Besichtigung; ausgestellt; **5.** *to be on ~* gezeigt werden, ausgestellt sein; *to give s.o. a fair ~* jdm e-e Chance geben; *to give the (whole) ~ away (fig)* den Schleier, die Maske fallen lassen; *to go to ~* beweisen; *to make a ~ of doing s.th.* Miene machen, etw zu tun; *of s.th.* etw herausstellen; *to make a fine ~* gut aussehen, Eindruck machen *od fam* schinden; *to manage, to run the ~ (fam)* die Sache machen; das Ding drehen; den Laden, den Kram schmeißen; *to put on a ~* so tun als ob; heucheln; *to stand, to have a ~ (fam)* gewisse, schwache Aussichten haben; *to steal the ~* die Schau stehlen; *to ~ o.'s cards, hand* s-e Karten aufdecken; *to ~ cause* s-e Gründe darlegen *od* angeben; *to ~ o.s. in o.'s true colo(u)rs* sein wahres Gesicht zeigen; *to ~ the door to s.o.* jdm die Türe weisen, jdn hinauswerfen; *to ~ the white feather* das Hasenpanier ergreifen; *to ~ fight* Kampfgeist zeigen; *to ~ an improvement* e-n Fortschritt aufzuweisen haben; *to ~ interest* Interesse zeigen *od* bekunden (*in* an); *to ~ o.'s paces* zeigen, was man kann; *to ~ o.'s teeth* die Zähne zeigen; *I'll ~ them* ich werde es ihnen schon zeigen; *to ~* **(a)round** herumführen; **6.** *agricultural, dog ~* Landwirtschafts-, Hundeausstellung *f*; *dumb ~* Pantomime *f*; *flower ~* Blumenschau *f*; *motor ~* Autoausstellung *f*; *travelling ~* Wanderausstellung *f*; *to ~* **forth** verkündigen; *to ~* **in** (her)einführen; *to ~* **off** *tr* in vollem Glanz erstrahlen lassen, im besten Licht, von s-r besten Seite zeigen; Staat machen mit; *itr* sich brüsten, sich aufspielen, sich auffällig benehmen, die (allgemeine) Aufmerksamkeit auf sich ziehen; angeben (*with* mit); *to ~* **out** hinausführen, -geleiten; *to ~* **up** *tr* hinaufführen; ans Licht bringen; bloßlegen, -stellen; *fam* abhängen, aus dem Feld schlagen; *itr* ans Licht kommen, auftauchen, kommen, erscheinen, in Erscheinung treten; sich (deutlich) zeigen; sich abheben (*against* gegen); ~**-bill, -card** Anschlag(zettel) *m*, Plakat *n*; *(~-card)* Musterkarte *f*; ~**boat** Theaterschiff *n*; ~**-box, -case, -glass** Schau-, Guckkasten *m*, Vitrine *f*; ~**-business** Schaustellergewerbe *n*; Regiekunst; *Am* Unterhaltungsindustrie *f*; ~**-down** *Am fam a* entscheidend; *s* Aufdecken *n* der Karten *(im Spiel u. fig)*; *fig* Enthüllung *f (der wirklichen Absichten, Ziele)*; entscheidende(r), kritische(r) Augenblick; Wendepunkt *m*; Kraftprobe *f*; *to force a ~~* die Bekanntgabe der Absichten erzwingen; ~ **flat** Modellwohnung *f*; ~**-girl** Statistin; Varieté-Tänzerin *f*; ~**iness** [ˈ-inis] Auffälligkeit, (äußere) Pracht *f*; ~**ing** [ˈ-iŋ] Nachweis *m*, Darlegung, -stellung; *film* Vorführung *f*; Eindruck *m*, Bild *n*; *to make a good ~~* sich gut aus der Affäre ziehen; ~**man** [ˈ-mən] gewandte(r) Redner; Schausteller *m*; ~**manship** [ˈ-mənʃip] Schaustellergewerbe *n*; *fig* Kunst, (das allgemeine) Interesse zu erwecken; effektvolle Attraktion *f*; ~**-off** auffällige(s) Benehmen *n*; *fam* Angeber; Protz *m*; ~**piece** Schaustück, Muster *a. fig*; *fig* Musterexemplar *n*; ~**-place** Sehenswürdigkeit *f*; ~**-purpose** *com* Reklamezweck *m*; ~**room** Ausstellungsraum *m*; ~**-up** Entlarvung, Bloßstellung; *Am fam* Gegenüberstellung *f*; ~**-window** *Am* Schaufenster *n*; ~**y** [ˈ-i] *meist pej* auffällig, prächtig, grell; zugkräftig; angeberisch; Zug-.

shower [ˈʃauə] *s* (Regen-, Schnee-, Hagel-)Schauer; (Sprüh-)Regen *(a. Funken)*; (Er-)Guß *a. fig*; *(Pfeile)* Hagel; *fig* Schwall, Erguß, Regen *m*, Flut, Fülle; *(~-bath)* Dusche, Brause *f*, Brause-, Sturzbad *n*; *Am* Party *f*, bei der jeder Gast ein Geschenk mitbringt; *tr* be-, übergießen; be-, naßspritzen; *fig* überschütten (*s.th. upon s.o., (Am) s.o. with s.th.* jdn mit etw); *itr* nieder-, herabregnen; duschen, ein Brausebad nehmen; *to take a ~* sich duschen; ~**y** [ˈ-ri] *a* mit einzelnen Regenschauern; schauerartig.

shrapnel [ˈʃræpnl] *mil* Schrapnell *n*.

shred [ʃred] *s* Fetzen; Lappen *m*; *fig* Spur *f*, Fünkchen *n*, ein (klein) bißchen; *tr* zerfetzen, in Fetzen reißen; zerfasern; zerteilen; abschneiden; *to tear to ~s (fig)* keinen guten Faden lassen an.

shrew [ʃruː] Zankteufel *m*, Xanthippe *f*, böse(s), zänkische(s) Weib *n*; *(~-mouse)* Spitzmaus *f*; ~**ish** [ˈ-iʃ] boshaft, zänkisch.

shrewd [ʃruːd] *a* gewitzt, schlau, klug, scharfsinnig; *(Verstand, Wind)* scharf; *(Antwort)* treffend; *to make a ~ guess* der Wahrheit sehr nahe kommen; ~**ness** [ˈ-nis] Gewitztheit, Schlauheit, Klugheit *f*, Scharfsinn *m*.

shriek [ʃriːk] *itr* kreischen, schreien; *tr (to ~ out)* (hinaus)schreien; *s* (gellender durchdringender, Auf-)Schrei *m*; Geschrei, Gekreisch *n*; *to ~ with laughter* schreien vor Lachen.

shrievalty [ˈʃriːvəlti] Amt(szeit *f*) *n*, Bezirk *m* e-s Sheriffs.

shrift [ʃrift] *obs* (Ohren-)Beichte *f*; *to give short ~* kurzen Prozeß machen mit.

shrike [ʃraik] *orn* Würger *m*.

shrill [ʃril] schrill, gellend; *(Stimme)* durchdringend; ~**ness** [ˈ-nis] schrille(r) Klang *m*.

shrimp [ʃrimp] *zoo* Garnele, Krabbe *f*; *fam* Knirps *m*; ~**-cocktail** *Am* Krabben *f pl* mit Zutaten im Glas.

shrine [ʃrain] *s rel* (Reliquien-)Schrein *m*, Reliquiar *n*; Weihestätte *f*; *fig* Heiligtum *n*.

shrink [ʃriŋk] *irr shrank* [-æ-], *shrunk* [-ʌ-]; *itr* (ein-, zs.)schrumpfen, einlaufen, eingehen; *(Holz)* schwinden; *fig* abnehmen, nachlassen; sich verkriechen; zs.zucken; zurückschrecken (*from* vor); *to ~ from doing s.th.* etw höchst ungern tun; *tr* schrumpfen lassen, zs.ziehen; *(Textil)* krumpfen; *(Kopf)* zurückziehen; *s* Schrumpfung *f*; ~**age** [ˈ-idʒ] Schrumpfung *f*, Einlaufen; Krumpfmaß; Krumpfen *n*; Schwund *m*, Abnahme *f*, (Wert-)Verlust *m*, Verminderung *f*, Nachlassen *n*, Rückgang *m*, Schrumpfung *f*; ~**hole** *tech* Lunker *m*; ~**-proof** krumpffest.

shrive [ʃraiv] *irr shrived* od *shrove* [-ou-], *shrived* od *shriven* [ˈʃrivn] *tr obs*: *s.o.* jds Beichte hören (u. Absolution erteilen).

shrivel [ˈʃrivl] *itr tr* verwelken (lassen); runzelig werden; verschrumpeln; *fig* verkümmern (lassen).

shroud [ʃraud] *s* Leichentuch *n*; *fig* Hülle *f*, Mantel, Schutz *m*; *mar* Want; *tech* Verkleidung *f*; *mot* Windleitblech *n*; *tr (Leiche)* einhüllen; *fig* bedecken, verhüllen, verbergen; *tech* verkleiden.
Shrove|tide ['ʃrouvtaid] Fastnachtstage *m pl (vor Aschermittwoch)*; ~ **Tuesday** Fastnacht(dienstag *m*) *f*.
shrub [ʃrʌb] **1.** *bot* Strauch, Busch *m*; Staude *f*; ~**bery** ['-əri] Gebüsch, Gesträuch, Busch-, Strauchwerk *n*; ~**by** ['-i] strauchartig, buschig; **2.** *Art* Cocktail *m*.
shrug [ʃrʌg] *itr (tr: to ~ o.'s shoulders)* mit den Achseln zucken; *s* Achselzucken *n*; *to ~ s.th. off* etw mit e-m Achselzucken abtun.
shrunk(en) ['ʃrʌnkn] *a* eingeschrumpft, -gefallen; *(Haut)* verschrumpelt; abgemagert.
shuck [ʃʌk] *Am s* Schale, Hülse, Schote *f*; *tr* schälen, enthülsen, entkernen; abstreifen; *(Auster)* öffnen; *to ~ o.'s clothes* sich entblättern *hum*; *to ~ off* auf die lange Bank schieben; *not worth ~s* keinen Pfifferling wert; ~**s** *interj* Unsinn!
shudder ['ʃʌdə] *itr* (er)schaudern; *I ~* mich schaudert (*at the thought* bei dem Gedanken); *s* Schauder *m*.
shuffl|e ['ʃʌfl] *tr* schleifen, nachziehen; (weg)schieben; schubsen (*into* in; *out of* aus); durchea.schütteln, -bringen, -werfen; *(Spielkarten)* mischen; *itr (to ~~ o.'s feet)* schlurfen, die Füße nachziehen; sich hin- u. herbewegen; die (Spiel-)Karten mischen; sich mit List u. Tücke bringen (*into* in; *out of* aus); sich drücken; Ausflüchte machen; schwindeln, mogeln; *s* Schlurfen; Schieben, Schubsen; (Karten-)Mischen *n*; *(Tanz)* Schleifschritt *m*; *fig* Ausflüchte, Schliche *pl*, Trick, Kunstgriff, Schwindel *m*; *to ~~ away* auf die Seite schaffen, wegpraktizieren; *to ~~ off, on (Kleidung)* ab-, überstreifen; *to ~~ through (Arbeit)* flüchtig erledigen; *~~-board s. shovel-board*; ~**er** ['-ə] Schlurfer; (Karten-)Mischer; Ausflüchtemacher, Schwindler; *Am sl* Arbeitslose(r), Wanderarbeiter *m*; ~**ing** ['-iŋ] schlurfend, schleppend; *fig* ausweichend; unaufrichtig, unehrlich.
shun [ʃʌn] *tr* (geflissentlich, beharrlich) (ver)meiden, ausweichen (*s.th.* e-r S).
shunt [ʃʌnt] *tr* abstellen; *(Diskussion)* ablenken; *rail* auf ein Nebengleis schieben; *el* parallel schalten (*across* zu); *fig* kaltstellen; *fig* aufschieben; *s* Abstellen; Rangieren; Neben-, Abstellgleis *n*; Weiche *f*; *el* Neben(an)schluß *m*, -leitung *f*; ~**-circuit** Nebenschluß-, Feldstromkreis *m*; ~**er** ['-ə] Weichensteller *m*; ~**ing** ['-iŋ]: *~~ engine* Rangierlok(omotive) *f*; *~~-station, -yard* Verschiebebahnhof *m*.
shush [ʃʌʃ] *interj fam* sch! pst!
shut [ʃʌt] *irr shut, shut tr* schließen, zumachen; *(Vorhang)* herunterlassen; ver-, zuriegeln; versperren; einsperren, einschließen; *itr* sich schließen, zugehen; *to ~ the door in s.o.'s face* die Türe vor jds Nase zuschlagen; *to ~ the ears to the truth* die Ohren vor der Wahrheit verschließen; *to ~* **down** *tr* herunterlassen; *(Fabrik)* (vorübergehend) schließen, stillegen, den Betrieb einstellen; *sport Am* besiegen; *itr* die Arbeit beenden, aufhören, Schluß machen; *to be ~ down* stilliegen; *to ~* **in** einschließen, -sperren; umgeben, einschließen; die Aussicht nehmen (*s.o.* jdm); *to ~ o.'s finger in the door* den Finger in die Türe klemmen; *to ~* **off** ausschließen (*from* von); absperren, -schließen; *tech* ausschalten, zu-, abdrehen; *(Motor)* abstellen; *Am sport* besiegen; *to ~ o.s. off* sich absondern, seine eigenen Wege gehen; *to ~* **out** ausschließen, -sperren; *to ~* **up** (fest) zu-, verschließen; ein-, wegschließen; *fam* den Mund stopfen (*s.o.* jdm); *to ~ up shop* nicht mehr weiterarbeiten; *(fam) ~~!* halt den Mund! halt's Maul! ~**down** *Am* Arbeitsniederlegung; Stillegung (des Betriebes), Betriebseinstellung, -störung; Arbeitsunterbrechung *f*; ~**-eye** *sl* Schläfchen *n*; ~**-in** *s* ans Haus gefesselte(r) Kranke(r), Invalide *m*; *a (Kranker)* ans Haus gefesselt; *psychol* völlig introvertiert, in sich gekehrt; ~**-off cock** Absperrhahn *m*; ~**-out** Ausschluß *m a. sport*; *Am* Spiel *n*, bei dem der Gegner keinen Punkt erzielt; ~**ter** ['-ə] *s* Fenster-, Rolladen; *phot* Verschluß *m*; *pl Am* Augen *n pl*; *tr* mit Fensterläden versehen *od* verschließen; *arch* verschalen; *to put up the ~~s* den Laden zumachen; ~**tering** ['-əriŋ] *arch* Verschalung *f*.
shuttle ['ʃʌtl] *s* Weberschiff *n*, Schütze *m*; *(Nähmaschine)* Schiffchen *n*; *(~-traffic)* Pendelverkehr *m*; *tr itr* schnell hin- u. herbewegen, -gehen; ~**-bus** Autobus im Pendelverkehr, Zubringer(bus) *m*; ~**cock** Federball(spiel *n*) *m*; *fig* schwanke(s) Rohr *n*; ~**-service** Zubringerdienst, Pendelverkehr *m*; ~**-train** Pendelzug, Zubringer *m*.
shy [ʃai] **1.** *a* scheu, ängstlich; schüchtern, verschämt; argwöhnisch, mißtrauisch (*of* gegen); vorsichtig, zögernd (*of doing* zu tun); *agr* schwachtragend; *sl* knapp (*of* an); *sl (mit e-r Zahlung)* im Rückstand, schuldig; *itr* scheuen (*at* bei); zurückschrecken, -scheuen (*at* vor); *to ~ away from* zurückweichen, -schrecken vor; sich in acht nehmen vor; *to fight ~ of s.o., s.th.* jdm, e-r S aus dem Wege gehen; *work-~* arbeitsscheu; ~**ness** ['-nis] Scheu, Schüchternheit *f*; Argwohn *m*; Mißtrauen *n*; **2.** *tr itr* werfen, schleudern; *s* Wurf(ziel *n*); *fig fam* Seitenhieb *m*, bissige Bemerkung *f*; *fam* Versuch *m*; *to have a ~ at s.th. (fam)* etw probieren, versuchen.
shyster ['ʃaistə] *Am sl* Gauner; Winkeladvokat *m*.
Siam ['saiæm, sai'æm] Siam *n*; ~**ese** [saiə'mi:z] *a* siamesisch; *s* Siamese *m*, Siamesin *f*; *~~ twins (pl)* siamesische Zwillinge *m pl*.
Siberia [sai'biəriə] Sibirien *n*; ~**n** [-n] *a* sibirisch; *s* Sibirier(in *f*) *m*.
sibil|ance, -cy ['sibiləns(i)] Zischlaut *m*; ~**ant** ['-t] *a* zischend; *s* Zischlaut *m*; ~**ate** ['-eit] *itr tr* zischen (d aussprechen); auszischen; ~**ation** [sibi'leiʃən] Zischen *n*; Zischlaut *m*.
sibling ['sibliŋ] Bruder *m od* Schwester *f*; *pl* (Voll-)Geschwister *pl*.
sibyl ['sibil] *hist* Sibylle *f*; ~**line** [si'bilain, 'sib-] *hist* sibyllinisch; geheimnisvoll.
siccative ['sikətiv] *a u. s* trocknend(es Mittel *n*).
Sicil|ian [si'siljən] *a* sizilianisch; *s* Sizilianer(in *f*) *m*; ~**y** ['sisili] Sizilien *n*.
sick [sik] **1.** *a pred* krank (*of* an; *with* vor); unwohl *(Am, Br nur lit u. sl; sl mil a. attr)*; kränklich; *(~ and tired, ~ to death)* überdrüssig (*of* gen); krankhaft, ungesund, leidig, ärgerlich; *fam* wütend; enttäuschend; *fam* unglücklich (*at, about* über); schadhaft, schlecht; krank (vor Sehnsucht) (*for* nach); *fam* grausig; verdorben; *s*: *the ~* die Kranken *m pl*; *to be ~ (Br)* unwohl sein, sich brechen müssen; *Am* krank sein; *to be ~ of s.th.* etw satt, leid haben; *to be ~ in bed* krank zu Bett liegen; *to be taken ~* erkranken; *to fall ~* krank werden; *to get ~ and tired of s.th.* etw gründlich satt, über haben; *to go, to report ~ (mil)* sich krank melden; *to turn ~* sich übergeben müssen; *he's ~ with the flu* er hat Grippe; *I am, I feel ~* mir ist übel; *I'm getting ~ and tired of it* es hängt mir zum Hals heraus; ~**-allowance, -pay** Krankengeld *n*; ~**-bag** *aero* Spucktüte *f*; ~**-bay** Schiffslazarett *n*; ~**-bed** Krankenbett *n*; ~**-benefit** Krankenbeihilfe *f*, -geld *n*; ~**-certificate** Krankenschein *m*; ~**en** ['-n] *itr* krank werden, erkranken (*for* an); angewidert werden (*at* von); Ekel empfinden (*at* bei); satt haben (*of s.th.* etw), überdrüssig sein (*of s.th.* e-r S); *tr* Übelkeit verursachen (*s.o.* jdm); anwidern, -ekeln; ~**ening** ['-niŋ] *fig* widerlich; ekelhaft; ~ **fund** Krankenkasse *f*; ~ **headache** Kopfschmerz *m (bei Übelkeit)*, *fam* Schädelbrummen *n*; Migräne *f*; ~**-insurance** Krankenversicherung, -kasse *f*; ~**ish** ['-iʃ] kränklich; unwohl; Übelkeit erregend; ~**-leave** Genesungsurlaub *m*; ~**liness** ['-linis] Kränklichkeit, Schwächlichkeit; Krankhaftigkeit; Schwäche *f*; ~**-list** *mil* Krankenliste *f*; *to put on the ~~* krank schreiben; ~**ly** ['-li] kränklich, leidend, schwächlich; krankhaft; ungesund; Übelkeit erregend; widerlich; schwach, matt; süßlich, sentimental; *(Lächeln)* gezwungen; ~**ness** ['-nis] Krankheit; Übelkeit *f*, Erbrechen *n*; *~~ benefit, pay* Krankengeld *n*; *~~ insurance* Krankenversicherung *f*; ~ **nursing** Krankenpflege *f*; ~**-parade, -call** *mil* Revierstunde *f*; ~**-pay** Krankengeld *n*; ~**-report** Krankenbericht *m*; Krankmeldung *f*; *~~ book* Krankenbuch *n*; ~**-room, -chamber** Krankenzimmer *n*; ~**-ward** Krankenstation *f*; **2.** *tr (Hund)* hetzen (*on* auf); *~ him!* faß!
sickle ['sikl] Sichel *f*; ~**-feather** Schwanz-, Hahnenfeder *f*.
side [said] *s* Seite *a. anat math f*; Rand *m*, Ufer *n*; (Berg-)Hang *m*; Gegend *f*, Gebiet *n*; Richtung *f*; *sport* Spielfeld *n*; *fig* Seite *f*, Standpunkt *m*, Stellungnahme, Meinung; Seite, Partei; (väterliche, mütterliche) Seite *(der Vorfahren)*; Arroganz, Einbildung *f*; *attr* Seiten-; Neben-; *itr* Partei ergreifen (*with* für); *at, by my ~* an meiner Seite, mir zur Seite; *by the ~ of* neben, verglichen mit; *by the father's ~* väterlicherseits; *~ by ~* Seite an Seite, dicht zusammen; *from, on all ~s, every ~* von, auf allen Seiten; von überallher, überall; *on the ~ (fam)* nebenbei, -her; *on every ~* auf, von allen Seiten; *on his ~* seinerseits; *on the right, wrong ~ of 50* über, unter 50 (Jahre alt); *to be on the safe ~* um sicherzugehen; *to be a thorn in o.'s ~* jdm ein Dorn im Auge sein; *to get on s.o.'s good ~ (fam)* jdn herumkriegen; *to put on ~ (sl)* sich aufspielen, angeben; *to split o.'s ~s with laughter* vor Lachen (beinahe) platzen; *to stand by s.o.'s ~ (fig)* jdm zur Seite stehen; *to take ~s* Stellung nehmen, Partei ergreifen (*with* für); sich anschließen (*with s.o.* jdm); *this ~ up!* Vorsicht, nicht stürzen! ~**-arms** Seitenwaffen *f pl*; ~**-bar** *Am fam* zusätzlich; *~~ job* Nebenbeschäftigung *f*; ~**board** Büfett *n*, Anrichte *f*; Seitenbrett *n*, -wand *f*; ~**burns** *pl Am*, ~**whiskers** *pl Br* Koteletten *f pl (Frisur)*; ~**-car** *mot* Beiwagen *m*; ~**-chapel** Seitenkapelle *f*; ~**-cut** Seitenhieb *m*; ~**d** ['-id] *a in Zssgen* -seitig; ~**-dish** Zwischen-

gericht *n (bei Tisch)*; **~-door** Seitentür *f*; **~-effect** Nebenwirkung *f*; **~-elevation** *arch* Seitenansicht *f*; **~-entry** Seiteneingang *m*; **~-face** Seitenansicht *f*, Profil *n*; **~-glance** Seitenblick *m*; **~-issue** Nebenresultat *n*, -frage *f*; Randproblem *n*; **~-kick** *Am sl* Kumpel *m*; **~-light** Seitenlicht, -fenster; *mar aero* Positionslicht; *mot* Begrenzungslicht *n*; *pl fig* Streiflichter *n pl*; *to throw a ~~ on (fig)* ein Streiflicht werfen auf; **~-line** Seitenlinie *bes. sport*; *rail* Nebenlinie *f*; Nebenberuf *m*, -beschäftigung *f*; *com* Nebenartikel *m*; **~long** *a* seitlich; geneigt, schräg; *adv* seitwärts; auf der Seite; **~-pocket** Seitentasche *f*; **~-saddle** Damensattel *m*; **~-show** Nebenschau, -ausstellung; Nebenerscheinung; Episode *f*; unwesentliche(s) Ereignis *n*; **~-slip** *itr mot* schleudern; *aero* seitlich abrutschen *a. sport*, slippen; *s* Schleudern; Slippen *n*, Seitengleit-, Schiebeflug; *bot* Trieb *m*; **~-splitting** *(Lachen)* zwerchfellerschütternd; *(Sache)* zum Totlachen; **~-step** *s* Ausweichen *n*; *(Boxen)* Seitenschritt *m*; *itr* zur Seite treten; *tr* ausweichen *(s.th.* e-r S) *a. sport*; **~-stroke** Seitenschlag *m*; Seitenschwimmen *n*; **~-swipe** *itr tr* seitlich zs.stoßen (mit); **~-track** *bes. Am s* Nebengleis *n*; *tr* abstellen, auf ein Nebengleis fahren; *allg* beiseite schieben; *fig* ablenken; kaltstellen; *Am sl* festnehmen, verhaften; *to get on a ~~ (fig)* vom Thema abkommen; **~-view** Seitenblick *m*, -ansicht *f*; **~walk** *Am* Gehweg *m*; *to hit the ~~s (Am sl)* Arbeit suchen; **~way(s)**, **~wise** *a* seitlich; *adv* seitwärts; **~-wheeler** *Am sl* Linkshänder; Schrittmacher; Schaufelraddampfer *m*; **~-wind** Seitenwind *m*; **~winder** *Am sl* Schläger *m*.

sidereal [sai'diəriəl] *a scient* Stern-; **~ time** *astr* Sternzeit *f*.

siding ['saidiŋ] *rail* Nebengleis *n*, Gleisanschluß *m*, Abstellgleis *n*; *Am arch* Mauerbehang *m*; *fig* Parteinahme *f*.

sidle ['saidl] *itr* sich seitlich fortbewegen; *to ~ away from s.o.* sich vor jdm heimlich aus dem Staube machen; *to ~ up to s.o.* sich heimlich an jdn heranmachen.

siege [si:dʒ] Belagerung *f*; zähe(s) Ringen *n*; *to lay ~ to* belagern; zäh ringen um.

sieve [siv] *s* Sieb *n*; *fig* Klatschbase *f*; *tr itr* (durch)sieben.

sift [sift] *tr* (durch)sieben; aussondern; (aus)streuen *(on to* auf, über); *fig* sichten, prüfen; *(Problem)* vertiefen; trennen, unterscheiden; *itr* sieben; sichten; *to ~ out* aussieben, -sortieren *(from* aus); **~er** ['-ə] Sieb *n*; Streudose *f*; **~ing** ['-iŋ] Sieben *n*; *fig* (genaue) Untersuchung *f*; *pl* Streu *f*; Rückstände *m pl*.

sigh [sai] *itr* seufzen *(with* vor); ächzen *a. fig*; jammern, sich sehnen *(for* nach); *tr* seufzen über, bejammern; *s* Seufzer *m*.

sight [sait] **1.** *s* (An-)Sicht *f*, (An-)Blick *m*; Schau(spiel *n*) *f*; Sehen *n*, Blick *m*; Sehkraft *f*, Gesicht(ssinn *m*) *n*, *fig* Augen *n pl*; Blickfeld *n*; Blickpunkt *m*, Ziel; Visier(einrichtung *f*); geistige(s) Auge *n*, Vorstellung(skraft); Ansicht, Meinung *f*, Urteil *n*; *fam* Masse, Menge *f*; *fam* seltsame(r) Anblick *m*; *pl* Sehenswürdigkeiten *f pl*; **2.** *tr* beobachten, prüfend betrachten, ansehen, anschauen; sehen, erblicken; *(Land)* sichten; zielen nach, aufs Korn nehmen; das Visier einstellen *(s.th.* e-r S); mit e-m Visier versehen; *com* vorzeigen, präsentieren; **3.** *at, on ~* sofort, ohne weiteres; *mus* vom Blatt; *com* bei Sicht; *at the ~ of* beim Anblick *gen*; *at first ~* auf den ersten Blick; *by ~* vom Ansehen; *not by a long ~ (fam)* nicht im entferntesten, nicht im geringsten; *in, within ~* in Sicht, Sehweite; *com* vorhanden; *in s.o.'s ~* nach jds Ansicht, Meinung; *on ~* gegen Einsichtnahme; *out of ~* außer Sicht *od* Sehweite; weit weg; *fam* außer Reichweite, unerschwinglich; *~ unseen (Am)* ungesehen; **4.** *to be a ~ (fam)* fürchterlich, verheerend aussehen; *to be unable to bear the ~ of s.o.* jdn nicht ausstehen, *fam* riechen können; *to catch, to get (a) ~ of s.th.* etw zu Gesicht bekommen; erblicken; *to keep ~ of s.th.* etw im Auge behalten; *to know by ~* vom Sehen (her) kennen; *to lose ~ of s.th.* etw aus den Augen verlieren *a. fig*; *to shoot on ~* ohne vorherige Warnung schießen; *to take ~ of s.th.* etw anvisieren; **5.** *the end is not yet in ~* das Ende ist noch nicht abzusehen; *what a ~ you are!* wie siehst denn du aus! *out of ~, out of mind (prov)* aus den Augen, aus dem Sinn; *commercial ~* Handelsakzept *n*; *long, near ~* Weit-, Kurzsichtigkeit *f*; *second ~* zweite(s) Gesicht *n*, hellseherische Fähigkeiten *f pl*; *a ~ better (fam)* viel besser; *a ~ for sore eyes* ein erfreulicher Anblick *m*; **~-bill, draft** *fin* Sichtwechsel *m*; **~ed** ['-id] *a* mit Visier; *in Zssgen* -sehend, -schauend, -blickend; *far ~~* weitblickend; *keen-~~* scharfsichtig; **~ error** Zielfehler *m*; **~-hole** Sehschlitz *m*, Guckloch *n*; **~ing**: *~~-line* Visierlinie *f*; *~~-shot* An-, Probeschuß *m*; *~~ telescope* Zielfernrohr *n*; **~less** ['-lis] blind; ungesehen; unsichtbar; **~liness** ['-linis] Ansehnlichkeit, Stattlichkeit *f*; **~ly** ['-li] ansehnlich, stattlich; **~ notch** Kimme *f*; **~-read** *tr* vom Blatt spielen; **~seeing** Besuch *m* von Sehenswürdigkeiten; *~~ car* Rundfahrtwagen *m*; *~~ tour* Stadtrundfahrt *f*; **~seer** ['-si:ə] Tourist *m*.

sign [sain] *s* (Kenn-)Zeichen; (An-, Vor-)Zeichen, Symptom *n*; Spur *f*, Merkmal *n*; Andeutung *f*, Wink *m*, Zeichen, Symbol; (Tür-, Aushänge-) Schild; *math mus* Vorzeichen; *tele* Rufzeichen *n*; *tr* (durch ein Zeichen) zu verstehen geben; unterzeichnen, -schreiben, -fertigen, signieren; *(s-n Namen)* (als Unterschrift) daruntersetzen; *rel* bekreuzigen; *itr* ein Zeichen geben, winken; unterschreiben; *at the ~ of (the Red Lion)* im (Roten Löwen); *inn-~* Wirtshausschild *n*; *road ~* Wegweiser *m*; *traffic-~* Verkehrszeichen *n*; *the ~ of the cross* das Kreuzeszeichen; *~ of the zodiac (astr)* Tierkreiszeichen *n*; *to ~* **away**, *to ~* **over** (schriftlich) abtreten *tr*; *to ~* **in** sich einschreiben, sich eintragen, sich einzeichnen; *to ~* **off** *itr radio* das Programm beenden; *Am sl* keinen Ton mehr sagen; kündigen; *to ~* **on** *(radio) itr (Sender)* sich melden; *tr itr* (sich) engagieren (lassen), (sich) (vertraglich) verpflichten; anstellen; *to ~ o.s. on* sich (vertraglich) verpflichten; *to ~* **out** sich austragen; *to ~* **over** überschreiben; *to ~* **up** *tr* anstellen *(s.o.* jdn); *itr* sich anmelden *(for* für), belegen *(for s.th.* etw); **~-board** Schild *n*, Tafel *f*; **~er** ['-ə] Unterzeichner *m*; **~ language** Zeichensprache *f*; **~ manual** Handzeichen *n*, eigenhändige Unterschrift *f*; **~-off** *radio* Sendeschluß *m*; **~post** Wegweiser *m*.

signal ['signəl] *s* Zeichen *n*, Wink *m*; *(Verkehr, tele, radio)* Signal *n (for* zu); (Funk-)Spruch; Kartenreiter *m*; *pl* Nachrichten(truppe *f*) *f pl*; *a* Signal-; bemerkenswert, auffällig, auffallend, außerordentlich, ungewöhnlich; *tr* (ein) Zeichen geben *(s.o.* jdm); signalisieren; *itr* (ein) Zeichen, ein Signal, Signale geben; *to give, to make a ~* ein Zeichen geben; *the Royal Corps of S~s* die (brit.) Nachrichtentruppe *f*; **~-beam** Peilstrahl *m*; **~-box, tower** *rail* Stellwerk *n*; *the* **S~ Corps** die (amerik.) Nachrichtentruppe *f*; **~ engineering** Schwachstromtechnik *m*; **~-flag** Signalflagge *f*; **~ise**, *Am* **~ize** ['-aiz] *tr* auszeichnen, bemerkenswert machen; hervorheben, aufmerksam machen auf; *com* kenn-, auszeichnen; **~ lamp** Warn-, Blinklampe *f*; **~(l)er** ['-ə] Signalgeber, -gast *m*; **~man** ['-mən] *rail* Bahnwärter; *mar* Signalgast *m*; **~ment** ['-mənt] *Am* Steckbrief *m*; **~ panel** *aero* Flieger-, Signaltuch *n*; **~ pistol** Leuchtpistole *f*; **~ rocket** Leuchtrakete *f*; **~ service** Fernmeldedienst *m*; **~ strength** *el* Laut-, Feldstärke *f*; **~ wave** *tele* Arbeitswelle *f*.

signat|ory ['signətəri] *a* (mit)unterzeichnend; Vertrags-, Signatar-; *s* Unterzeichner *m*; *pl u. ~~ powers, states (pl)* Signatarmächte *f pl*, -staaten *m pl*; **~ure** ['signitʃə] *s* Unterschrift; Signatur; *typ* Bogenbezeichnung *f*; *mus* Vorzeichen; *radio (~~ tune)* Pausenzeichen *n*; *tr* signieren, unterzeichnen; bestätigen; *to put o.'s ~~ to s.th.* s-e Unterschrift unter etw setzen.

signet ['signit] Siegel *n*, *(bes.* Unterschriften-)Stempel *m*; **~-ring** Siegelring *m*; **~wafer** Siegelmarke *f*.

signif|icance, -cy [sig'nifikəns(i)] Bedeutung *f*, (tieferer) Sinn *m*; Ausdrucksfähigkeit, -kraft; Bedeutung, Bedeutsamkeit, Wichtigkeit *f*; **~icant** [-ikənt] bezeichnend *(of* für); bedeutungsvoll, bedeutsam, wichtig *(for* für); *(Blick)* vielsagend; **~ication** [signifi'keiʃən] Bedeutung *f*, Sinn; Hinweis *m*; **~ificative** [sig'nifikətiv] = *~icant*; **~ify** ['signifai] *tr* andeuten, anzeigen; bedeuten; bekanntmachen, -geben, zum Ausdruck bringen; bezeichnen; *itr* bedeuten; wichtig sein; *it doesn't ~~* es hat nichts zu bedeuten.

silage ['sailidʒ] Silofutter *n*.

silen|ce ['sailəns] *s* Schweigen *n*; Stille, Ruhe *f*; (Ver-)Schweigen *n (on s.th.* e-r S); Vergessen-, Versunkenheit *f*; *tr* zum Schweigen bringen *a. mil*; niederwerfen; meistern; *(Geräusch)* dämpfen; *interj* Ruhe! *in ~~* schweigend; *to keep ~~* Stillschweigen beobachten *(on* über); *to pass over in ~~* mit Stillschweigen übergehen; **~cer** ['-ə] Schalldämpfer; *mot* Auspufftopf *m*; **~t** ['-ənt] schweigend; stumm *a. gram*; schweigsam; still, ruhig, geräuschlos; untätig; *to be ~~* schweigsam, still sein, schweigen *(on* über); *to keep ~~* Stillschweigen bewahren, nichts sagen; *~~ film* Stummfilm *m*; *~~ partner Am com* stille(r) Teilhaber *m*.

Silesia [sai'li:zjə] Schlesien *n*; **~n** [-n] *a* schlesisch; *s* Schlesier(in *f*) *m*.

silex ['saileks] *min* Flint, Feuerstein *m*; feuerfeste(s) Glas *n*.

silhouette [silu(:)'et] *s* Schattenriß *m*, Silhouette *f*; *allg* Umriß *m*; *tr* silhouettieren; *itr u.*: *to be ~d* sich abheben *(against, on, upon* gegen, von).

silic|a ['silikə] *chem* Kieselerde *f*, Siliziumdioxyd *n*; *~~ lamp* Quarzlampe *f*; **~ate** ['-it] *chem* Silikat *n*; *potassium ~~* Kaliumsilikat, Wasserglas *n*; **~ated** ['-eitid] *a* kieselsauer; **~eous** [si'liʃəs] *a* Kiesel-; kieselhaltig, -artig; **~ic** [si'lisik]: *~~ acid* Kieselsäure *f*; **~ium** [si'lisiəm], **~on** ['silikən] *chem* Silizium *n*; *~~ steel* Siliziumstahl *m*; **~osis** [sili'kousis] *med* Silikose *f*.

silk [silk] *s* Seide(nstoff *m*) *f*; seidene(s) Kleid(ungsstück) *n*; seidene(r) Talar; *fam* Kronanwalt *m*; *pl sport* (Seiden-) Dress *m*; *a* seiden; *in ~s and satins (fig)* in Samt und Seide; *artificial ~* Kunstseide *f*; **~en** ['-ən] *lit* seiden; seidig; elegant, luxuriös; weich, sanft, zart, glatt; **~ hat** Zylinder *m (Hut)*; **~iness** ['-inis] seidige Beschaffenheit *f*; **~-paper** Seidenpapier *n*; **~-trade** Seidenhandel *m*; **~worm** Seidenraupe *f*; **~y** ['-i] seiden; seidig; *(Wein)* ölig; weich; glänzend; *fig* einschmeichelnd, sanft.

sill [sil] (Tür-)Schwelle *a. geol*; Fensterbank *f*, -brett *n*, Sims; *geol* Lagergang *m*.

sillabub, syllabub ['siləbʌb] süße(r) Milchschaum *m* mit Wein *(Nachtisch)*; *fig* Gefasel *n*.

sill|iness ['silinis] Dummheit; Torheit, Albernheit *f*; **~y** ['sili] *a* dumm; töricht, närrisch, albern; *s fam (~~-billy)* Dussel, Dummkopf *m*; *~~ season* Sauregurkenzeit *f*.

silo ['sailou] *pl -os* Grünfutterspeicher, Gärfutterbehälter, Silo *m*.

silt [silt] *s* Schlick, Schlamm *m*; *tr itr (to ~ up)* verschlammen; (sich) verstopfen.

silver ['silvə] *s* Silber(barren *m pl*, -geld); (Tafel-)Silber, Silbergeschirr, -zeug, Besteck; Silber(farbe *f*); *phot* Silbersalz *n*; *a* silbern; Silber-; silberhaltig; versilbert; silb(e)rig, silberglänzend; Silber-, 25jährig; *tr* versilbern; *itr* silb(e)rig werden; *to be born with a ~ spoon in o.'s mouth* Kind reicher Eltern, ein Glückskind sein; *every cloud has a ~ lining (prov)* auf Regen folgt Sonnenschein; **~-alloy** Silberlegierung *f*; **~-bar** Silberbarren *m*; **~-birch** Weißbirke *f*; **~-bromide** *chem* Silberbromid *n*; **~-chloride** *chem* Silberchlorid *n*; **~-colo(u)red** *a* silberfarben; **~-fir** Weiß-, Edeltanne *f*; **~-fish** Silberfisch *m*; *ent* Silberfischchen *n*; **~-foil, -leaf** Silberfolie *f*, Blattsilber *n*; **~-fox** Silberfuchs *m*; **~-gilt** vergoldete(s) Silber *n*; **~-glance** Schwefelsilber *n*; **~-grey** silbergrau; **~-haired, -headed** *a* silberhaarig, grauhaarig, -köpfig; **~ing** ['-riŋ] Versilbern *n*; **~ lining** *fig* Silberstreifen *m* am Horizont, Lichtblick *m*; **~-mine** Silbermine *f*; **~-nitrate** Silbernitrat *n*; *med* Höllenstein *m*; **~-ore** Silbererz *n*; **~-paper** Stanniolpapier *n*; **~-plate, ~ware** Silbergeschirr *n*, -sachen *f pl*; **~ screen** (Film-)Leinwand *f*; Film *m*; **~-side** *(Rind)* Schwanzstück *n*; **~smith** Silberschmied *m*; **~-tongued** *a* beredt, redegewandt; **~ wedding** silberne Hochzeit *f*; **~y** ['-ri] silb(e)rig, silberglänzend; *(Ton)* silberhell; silberhaltig, versilbert.

silviculture [silvi'kʌltʃə] Forstpflege, -kultur, -wissenschaft *f*.

simian ['simiən] *a* affenartig; *s* (Menschen-)Affe *m*.

simil|ar ['similə] ähnlich (*to* dat) *a. math*, gleich(artig); **~arity** [simi'læriti] Ähnlichkeit, Gleichartigkeit *f* (*to* mit); **~e** ['simili] *gram* Vergleich *m*; Gleichnis *n*; **~itude** [si'militju:d] Ähnlichkeit *f*; Bild *n*, Gestalt *f*; Gleichnis *n*, Parabel *f*.

simmer ['simə] *itr tr* bei schwacher Hitze kochen (lassen); *itr* (leicht) brodeln; *(Teewasser)* summen; *fig (vor Zorn)* kochen (*with* vor); *to ~ down* langsam verkochen; *meist fig* sich abkühlen, sich (wieder) beruhigen; *s*: *to keep at a* od *on the ~* am Kochen halten.

simnel ['simnl] englische(r) Teekuchen *m*.

simoleon [sə'mouliən] *Am sl* Dollar *m*.

Simon ['saimən] Simon *m*; *Simple ~* dumme(r) August *m*; *(the real) ~* **Pure** der wahre Jakob; **s~y** ['-i] *rel hist* Simonie *f*.

simoom [si'mu:m] *mete* Samum *m*.

simp [simp] *fam* blöde(r) Kerl *m*.

simper ['simpə] *itr* einfältig, selbstgefällig, geziert lächeln; *s* einfältige(s) selbstgefällige(s) Lächeln *n*.

simpl|e ['simpl] *a* einfach; unkompliziert, leicht; einfach, schlicht, anspruchslos; ungekünstelt, unverstellt, natürlich; *(Wahrheit)* rein, nackt; niedrig(gestellt), bescheiden, gewöhnlich, unbedeutend; einfältig, dumm, töricht; *attr* bloß, rein, *fam* pur; *s* Arzneipflanze *f*; *pure and ~~* voll u. ganz; *~~ equation* Gleichung *f* 1. Grades; *the ~~ fact* die bloße Tatsache *f*; *~~ fraction* gemeine(r) Bruch *m*; *a ~~ lifer (fam)* Naturapostel *m*; *~~-hearted a* offen(herzig), aufrichtig, grundehrlich; *~~-minded (a)* offen, ehrlich, bieder; arglos, einfältig; **~eton** ['-tən] Einfaltspinsel, Dummkopf *m*; **~icity** [sim'plisiti] Einfachheit; Unkompliziertheit; Schlichtheit, Anspruchslosigkeit, Natürlichkeit; Einfalt *f*; *for the sake of ~~* der Einfachheit halber; **~ification** [simplifi'keiʃən] Vereinfachung *f*; **~ify** ['simplifai] *tr* vereinfachen; erleichtern; **~y** ['-i] *adv* (ganz) einfach; bloß, nur, rund-, glattweg; rundheraus, ohne Umschweife; geradezu; *fam* vollkommen, völlig, absolut, nichts anderes als.

simul|acrum [simju'leikrəm] *pl -acra* [-ə] (Ab-)Bild *n*; Schein, Trug(bild *n*) *m*; **~ate** ['simjuleit] *tr* vorgeben, -täuschen, -spiegeln; heucheln, simulieren; nachahmen; **~ated** ['-eitid] *a* vorgetäuscht, geheuchelt, falsch; **~ation** [simju'leiʃən] Verstellung, Heuchelei *f*, falsche(s) Spiel *n fig*; Nachahmung *f*.

simultan|eity [siməltə'niəti], **~eousness** [-'teinjəsnis] Gleichzeitigkeit *f*; **~eous** [-'teinjəs] gleichzeitig (*with* mit).

sin [sin] *s rel* Sünde *f a. allg*; *fig* Vergehen *n* (*against* gegen); Versündigung *f*; *itr* sündigen *a. allg*, sich vergehen (*against* gegen, *lit* wider); sich versündigen (*against* an); *deadly, mortal ~* Todsünde *f*; *original ~* Erbsünde *f*; **~ful** ['-ful] sündig; böse; sündhaft; **~fulness** ['-fulnis] Sündhaftigkeit *f*; **~less** ['-lis] sündlos, ohne Sünde; **~lessness** ['-lisnis] Sündlosigkeit *f*; **~ner** ['-ə] Sünder *m*.

since [sins] *adv* seitdem, -her; vorher, zuvor, vordem; *ever ~* in der ganzen Zwischenzeit; seit der Zeit; *long ~* (seit) lange(m); *how long ~* wie lange? seit wann? *prp* seit; *conj* seitdem; da (...ja), weil, insofern, insoweit.

sincer|e [sin'siə] offen, ehrlich, aufrichtig; wirklich, tatsächlich, echt; *to be ~~ about s.th.* es mit etw ehrlich meinen; **~ely** [-li] *adv* aufrichtig, ehrlich, herzlich; *Yours ~~* Ihr ergebener; **~ity** [sin'seriti] Offenheit, Ehrlichkeit, Aufrichtigkeit, Echtheit *f*.

sinciput ['sinsipʌt] *anat* Vorderhaupt *n*.

sine [sain] **1.** *math* Sinus *m*; **2.** *prp* ['-i] ohne; *~ qua non* ['-ikwei'nən] unerläßliche Bedingung *f*.

sinecur|e ['sainikjuə] Sinekure *f*; *fig* mühelose(s), einträgliche(s) Amt *n*; *rel* Pfründe *f*.

sinew ['sinju:] Sehne; Flechse *f*; *oft pl* (Muskel-, Körper-)Kraft, Stärke; *pl* Kraftquelle *f*, Hilfsquellen *f pl*; *fig* Hauptstütze *f*; *~s of war (fig)* Geld *n*; **~y** ['-i] *(Fleisch u. fig)* sehnig; muskulös; kräftig, stark, kraftvoll.

sing [siŋ] *irr sang* [sæŋ], *sung* [sʌŋ] *itr* singen *(a. Singvögel)*; besingen (*of* acc); vorsingen; *(Ohr)* klingen; *(Bienen)* summen; surren, brummen, pfeifen; *(Wind)* heulen; *(Hahn)* krähen; jubeln, frohlocken; zwitschern; *sl* gestehen; *tr* (be)singen; vorsingen; *s* Summen, Surren, Pfeifen *n*; *Am fam* Singgruppe *f*, Gruppensingen *n*; *to ~ out* laut rufen, schreien, brüllen; *to ~ up* lauter singen; *to ~ s.o.'s praises* ein Loblied auf jdn singen; *to ~ to sleep* in den Schlaf singen; *to ~ small, to ~ another song, tune* klein beigeben, gelindere Saiten aufziehen; **~er** ['-ə] Sänger *m*; **~ing** ['-iŋ] Singen *n*, Gesang *m*; Summen, Brummen, Pfeifen *n*; *~~-bird* Singvogel *m*, *~~ book* Liederbuch *n*; *~~ club, society* Gesangverein *m*; *~~-lesson* Sing-, Gesangstunde *f*; *~~-master* Gesangslehrer *m*; *~~ voice* Singstimme *f*; **~song** Gemeinschaftssingen *n*; Singsang *m*.

singe [sindʒ] *tr* anbrennen, -sengen; (ver)sengen; *to ~ off* absengen; *s* leichte Verbrennung; Verletzung *f*.

Singhalese [siŋgə'li:z] *a* singhalesisch; *s* Singhalese *m*, Singhalesin *f*; (das) Singhalesisch(e).

singl|e ['siŋgl] *a* einzig, alleinig; allein, für sich, einsam; einzeln; Einzel- *a. sport*; getrennt, unverbunden; ledig, unverheiratet, alleinstehend; Junggesellen-; einfach; *fig* unerhört, ungewöhnlich; *fig* aufrichtig, ehrlich, selbstlos; *fig* gerecht; *(Bier)* schwach, dünn; *bot* einfach; *adv* allein, ohne Hilfe; *s* Einzelperson *f*; Einzelstück *n*; *(~~ ticket)* einfache Fahrkarte *f*; Einzelzimmer; *(~s) sport* Einzelspiel *n*; *tr (to ~~ out)* aussondern, -lesen, -wählen; herausgreifen (*from* aus); *in ~~s* einzeln; *in ~~ file* im Gänsemarsch; *ladies', men's ~(s) (Tennis)* Damen-, Herreneinzel *n*; *~~-acting (tech mil)* einfach wirkend; *~~ bed* Einzelbett *n*; *~~ bedroom* Einzelzimmer *n*; *~~ bill* Solawechsel *m*; *~~-breasted (a) (Jacke, Mantel)* einreihig; *~~ combat* Zweikampf *m*, Duell *n*; *~~-contact, -pole* einpolig; *~~-core (tech)* einadrig; *~~-eyed (a)* einäugig; *a. fig* offen, gerade, ehrlich; *~~-handed (a)* einhändig; Einzel-, Allein-; ohne Hilfe; allein, selbständig; *~~-hearted, -minded (a)* ehrenhaft, ehrlich, aufrichtig, zuverlässig, vertrauenswürdig; *~~ house* Einfamilienhaus *n*; *~~ life* Ledigenstand *m*; *~~ line* einspurige (Eisenbahn-)Linie *f*; *~~ man* Junggeselle *m*; *~~-o (Am sl) a* selbständig; unverheiratet; *adv* allein; *~~ obligation* Schuldversprechen *n*; *~~ payment* einmalige Zahlung *f*; *~~-phase(el)* einphasig; *~~ price* Einheitspreis *m*; *~~-price shop, (Am) store* Einheitspreisgeschäft *n*; *~-purpose* Einzweck-; *~~ room* Einzelzimmer *n*; *~~ seater* Einsitzer *m*; *~~-stage (tech)* einstufig; *~~ ticket* einfache(r) Fahr-, Flugschein *m*; *~~-track* eingleisig *a. fig*; *~~ woman* Junggesellin *f*; **~eness** ['-nis] Alleinsein *n*; Unvermähltheit; *fig* Redlichkeit, Aufrichtigkeit, Ehrlichkeit *f*; **~et** ['siŋglit] Unterhemd *n*, -jacke *f*; **~eton** ['-tən] *(Kartenspiel)* Singleton *m*; Einzelstück; Einzelkind *n*; Alleinstehende(r) *m*; *Am sl* einmalige Sache *f*; **~y** ['-i] *adv* allein; einzeln, besonders; stückweise; nacheinander; ohne Hilfe.

singular ['siŋgjulə] *a* einzig, Einzel-; einzeln, getrennt, individuell, persönlich, privat; ungewöhnlich, seltsam, sonderbar; außergewöhnlich, außerordentlich, einzigartig, bemerkenswert, beachtlich; selten; Ausnahme-;

gram Singular-; *s* Singular *m*, Einzahl *f*; **~ity** [siŋgju'læriti] Eigenheit; Ungewöhnlichkeit, Seltenheit; Seltsamkeit, Sonderbarkeit *f*; **~ize** ['-raiz] *tr* vereinzeln; besonders hervorheben; **~ly** ['-li] *adv* bemerkenswert; seltsam, sonderbar.

sinist|er ['sinistə] unheilverkündend, -voll; schlecht, böse, unselig; unglücklich, verderblich (*to* für); *(Heraldik)* link; **~ral** ['-trəl] linksherum gehend; linkshändig.

sink [siŋk] *irr sank* [sæŋk], *sunk* [sʌŋk] **1.** *itr* (ein-, ver)sinken; sinken, (langsam) fallen *a. fig*; *(Schiff)* sinken, untergehen; *fig* niedriger, schwächer werden, nachlassen, zurückgehen *(a. Preise)*; zs.brechen; *(in e-n Lehnstuhl)* sich fallen lassen (*into* in); *(Wangen)* einfallen, hohl(er) werden; *(in Schlaf, Verzweiflung)* fallen; *(gesundheitlich)* nachlassen; *(Tageslicht)* abnehmen; *(sittlich, sozial)* sinken, abfallen; Prestige verlieren; einsickern, -sinken, -dringen; *fig* sich einprägen; *(Gebäude)* sich senken; *(Boden)* nachgeben; *(Abhang)* abfallen; **2.** *tr* versenken, (ver)sinken lassen; stoßen, drücken (*in, into* in); sinken, (langsam) fallen lassen; in den Boden einlassen; *(Loch)* graben, aushöhlen, bohren; *min (Schacht)* abteufen; eingraben, (ein)ritzen, gravieren, stechen; *(Stempel)* schneiden; einschränken, verringern, vermindern; *(Preise, Stimme, Kopf)* senken; *(Geld)* anlegen; *(Geld durch schlechte Geschäfte)* verlieren; *(Schuld)* bezahlen, tilgen, begleichen; *(Streit)* beilegen; verheimlichen, unterdrücken; erniedrigen, herabsetzen; *to be sunk* ruiniert, erledigt sein; **3.** *s* Ausguß, Abfluß; Spültisch *m*, Spüle; *(~ hole)* Senkgrube; Kloake *f*; *fig* finstere(s) Loch *n*, Räuber-, Lasterhöhle; *geog* Doline *f*; *to ~ in (fam)* einleuchten; **4.** *~ or swim* friß Vogel oder stirb! *he's ~ing* s-e Kräfte nehmen ab; **~able** ['-əbl] versenkbar; **~er** ['-ə] Gräber; *min* Abteufer *m*; Senkblei *n*; *(Angel)* Senker; *Am fam* Berliner (Pfannkuchen), Krapfen *m*; **~ing** ['-iŋ] Sinken; Absinken, Nachlassen *n*, Rückgang *m*; Schwinden *n*; *med* Hunger-, Schwächegefühl *n*; Versenkung; Grabung, Bohrung, *min* Abteufung; Einschränkung, Verringerung, Verminderung; Vertiefung, Senke; *com* Tilgung, Geldanlage *f*; *~~ feeling* Beklommenheit *f*; *~~-fund* (Schulden-)Tilgungsfonds *m*.

sinolog|ical [sinə'lɔdʒikəl] sinologisch; **~ist** [si'nɔlədʒist], **~ue** ['sinəlɔg] Sinologe *m*; **~y** [si'nɔlədʒi] Sinologie, Chinakunde *f*.

sinter ['sintə] *s min* Sinter *m*; *tr* sintern.

sinu|osity [sinju'ɔsiti] Gewundenheit; Windung, Biegung, Krümmung *f*; **~ous** ['sinjuəs] sich windend, sich schlängelnd; *bot* ausgebuchtet; biegsam; *fig* unehrlich; **~s** ['sainəs] Windung, Biegung, Kurve; Ausbuchtung *f a. bot*; Hohlraum *m bes. zoo anat*; *anat* Höhle *f*; *scient* Sinus; *med* Fistelgang *m*; *fam* = *~usitis*; **~sitis** [sainə'saitis] Sinusitis; *(frontal ~~)* Stirnhöhlenvereiterung *f*.

sip [sip] *itr tr* schlürfen, nippen (*of* an); *s* Schlückchen *n*.

siphon, syphon ['saifən] *s* Saugheber; Siphon; *zoo* Sipho *m*; *tr* ausheben, entleeren *a. med*.

sippet ['sipit] (in Suppe *od* Soße getunktes) Stück Toast; *fig* Stückchen *n*.

sir [sə:] Herr *m (Anrede ohne Namen)*; *S~* Sir *m (Titel vor dem Vor- od vollen Namen e-s Angehörigen des niederen Adels)*; *yes, ~* jawohl!

sire ['saiə] *s* Ew. Majestät *(Anrede)*; *lit poet* Ahnherr, Ahne *m*; *(Säugetiere)* Vatertier *n*; *tr (Säugetier)* (er)zeugen.

siren ['saiərin] *(Mythologie u. tech)* Sirene; *fig* verführerische Frau, Circe *f*; *zoo* Siren, Armmolch *m*; **~ian** [sai'ri:niən] *zoo* Sirene, Seekuh *f*.

sirloin ['sə:lɔin] *(Rind)* Lendenstück *n*.

sirocco [si'rɔkou] *pl -os mete* Schirokko *m*.

sirup *s. syrup*.

sis [sis] *Am fam* Schwester(chen *n*) *f*; **~sy** ['-i] *bes. Am fam* weibische(r) Mann; Homosexuelle(r) *m*; *Am sl* kohlensäurehaltige(s) Getränk *n*.

sisal ['saisl, *a.* 'sisl], **~ hemp** Sisalhanf *m*.

siskin ['siskin] *orn* Zeisig *m*.

sister ['sistə] Schwester *a. rel*; *med* (Ober-)Schwester *f*; *brothers and ~s* Geschwister *pl*; *half-, step, foster-* Halb-, Stief-, Pflegeschwester *f*; **~hood** ['-hud] Schwesternschaft *f*; **~-in-law** ['-rinlɔ:] Schwägerin *f*; **~ly** ['-li] *a adv* schwesterlich; **~-stand-in** *film (weibl.)* Double *n*; **S~ Superior** *rel* Schwester *f* Oberin.

sit [sit] *irr sat, sat* [sæt] **1.** *itr* sitzen *a. zoo*; *(Vogel)* brüten; *(Henne)* sitzen; den Vorsitz führen; e-e Sitzung abhalten, tagen, beraten; Mitglied sein (*in Parliament* im Parlament; *on a committee* e-s Ausschusses); ruhen, untätig sein; sich befinden; *tech* aufliegen, ruhen; *(bes. Kleidungsstück)* sitzen, passen; stehen (*on s.o.* jdm); *fig* liegen, ruhen, lasten (*on* auf); *(to baby-~)* auf ein Kind aufpassen; *fam* niederdrücken, -halten, 'runtermachen, -putzen (*on s.o.* jdn); **2.** *tr* setzen; sitzen auf; *to ~ o.s.* sich setzen, Platz nehmen (*on* auf); **3.** *to make s.o. ~ up* jdn in Erstaunen versetzen, jdn verblüffen; *to ~ on the bench* als Richter amtieren; *to ~ in chambers (jur)* als Einzelrichter tätig sein; *to ~ on a committee* e-m Ausschuß angehören; *to ~ for a constituency* e-n Wahlkreis vertreten; *to ~ for an examination* sich e-r Prüfung unterziehen; *to ~ on the fence, rail (fam fig)* unentschlossen sein; sich zurückhalten; *to ~ on o.'s hands* nicht klatschen, nicht applaudieren; *to ~ in judg(e)ment (fig)* zu Gericht sitzen (*on* über); *to ~ on a jury* Geschworener sein; *to ~ for o.'s portrait, for, to a painter, artist* sich malen lassen; *to ~ pretty (Am fam)* gut dran sein; *to ~ tight* sich nicht (von der Stelle) rühren; *fam* sich nicht beirren lassen; *to ~ at work* fleißig arbeiten; **4.** *to ~* **back** sich zurücklehnen; *fig* abwarten *itr*; *to ~* **down** sich (hin-)setzen, Platz nehmen; *mil* in Stellung gehen; *over here* sich hierhersetzen; *under s.th.* sich etw gefallen lassen; etw hinnehmen; *to ~~ hard on (Am)* sich scharf wenden gegen; *to ~* **in** teilnehmen (*on* an); Babysitter sein; *to ~* **on** bleiben, sitzen; *Am fig* eins aufs Dach geben (*s.o.* jdm); *to ~* **out** *tr* bis zum Ende bleiben bei, auf, in; länger bleiben als; nicht mitmachen, nicht teilnehmen an, auslassen, überschlagen, -springen; *itr* im Freien sitzen; *to ~* **through** bis zum Ende anhören (*s.th.* etw); *to ~* **up** sich *(im Sitzen)* aufrichten; aufrecht sitzen; aufbleiben (*late* lange); *fam* e-n Schreck kriegen, auffahren; *for s.o.* auf jdn abends warten; *with s.o.* bei jdm wachen; *to ~~ and take notice (Am)* hellhörig werden; *to make s.o. ~~* jdn aufschrecken; **~-down (strike)** Sitzstreik *m*; **~ter** ['-ə] Sitzende(r) *m*; Modell *n (e-s Malers)*; *(baby-~~, ~~-in)* Babysitter *m*; Bruthenne *f*; *fam* Wohnzimmer *n*; *sl* leichte Arbeit, leichte Beute *f a. fig*; *sl* Dummkopf *m*; **~ting** ['-iŋ] Sitzen *n*; Sitzung *(a. bei e-m Maler)*, Tagung; *jur* Sitzungsperiode *f*; (bezahlter) Kirchenstuhl, -platz *m*; Brüten; Gelege *n*; *at one ~~ (fig)* in einem Zug; *~~ member* Sitzungsmitglied *n*; Abgeordnete(r) *m* (*for* für); *~~-room* Wohnzimmer *n*; **~-upon** *fam* Hinterteil *n*.

site [sait] *s* Lage *f*, Platz *m*; Gelände *n*; Stelle *f*; Standort *(e-r Industrie)*; Sitz *(e-r Firma)*; *(building-~)* Bauplatz *m*, -grundstück *n*; *tr* lokalisieren, placieren; *country ~* Landsitz *m*; **~ development** Baulanderschließung *f*; **~ owner** Grundstückseigentümer *m*; **~ plan** Lageplan *m*.

situat|e ['sitjueit] *tr* (hin-, unter)bringen, (auf)stellen; **~ed** ['-id] *a* gelegen, befindlich; *to be ~~* liegen, gelegen sein; sich befinden; *how is it ~~?* wie steht es damit? **~ion** [sitju'eiʃən] Lage; Stelle *f*, Platz, Ort *m*; Situation *f*, Umstände *m pl*, Verhältnisse *n pl*; *(Drama)* Wendepunkt *m*; Stelle, (An-)Stellung *f*, Arbeitsplatz *m*; *to be equal to the ~~* der Situation gewachsen sein; *~~ map, report* Lagekarte *f*, -bericht *m*; *~~s offered, wanted* Stellenangebote, -gesuche *n pl*.

six [siks] *a* sechs; *s* Sechs *f*; *at ~es and sevens (fam)* durcheinander; in Unordnung *od* Verwirrung; *to be at ~es and sevens* nicht zs.-, zuea. passen; uneinig sein (*about* über; *with* mit); *~ of one and half a dozen of the other* das ist Jacke wie Hose; **~fold** ['-fould] *a adv* sechsfach; sechsmal; **~-footer** *fam* (langer) Lulatsch *m*; **~pence** Sixpence(stück *n*), halbe(r) Schilling *m*; **~penny** Sixpence wert; *fig* billig; **~-shooter** *fam* sechsschüssige(r) Revolver *m*; **~teen** ['siks'ti:n] sechzehn; **~teenth** ['siks'ti:nθ] *a* sechzehnt; *s* Sechzehntel *n*; **~th** [siksθ] *a* sechst; *s* Sechstel *n*; *mus* Sexte *f*; **~thly** ['-θli] *adv* sechstens; **~tieth** ['-tiiθ] *a* sechzigste; *s* Sechzigstel *n*, Sechzigste(r) *m*; **~ty** ['-ti] *a* sechzig; *s* Sechzig *f*; *the ~ties (pl)* die sechziger Jahre *(e-s Jahrhunderts)*, die Sechzigerjahre *n pl (e-s Menschenlebens)*.

sizar ['saizə] Stipendiat *m* in Cambridge *od* am Trinity College, Dublin.

siz|e [saiz] **1.** *s* Größe *f*, Umfang *m*, Ausmaß *n*; *(Kleidung, Schuhe)* Größe, Nummer *f*; Maße *n pl*; *fig* Umfang *m*, Ausmaß *n*, Bedeutung *f*; (geistige) Fähigkeiten *f pl*, *fam* Format *n*; *tr* nach Größen, Nummern einteilen *od* ordnen; *to ~~ up (tr) (fam)* abschätzen, taxieren, richtig einschätzen; *itr fam* (aus)reichen, es tun; *next in ~~* nächstgrößere Nummer *f*; *of a ~~* gleich groß; *to arrange according to ~~* der Größe nach ordnen; *to be about the ~~ of* ungefähr so groß sein wie; *to take the ~~ of* Maß nehmen von; *what ~~ do you wear?* welche Größe tragen Sie? *that's about the ~~ of it (fam)* genau so war's; *life-~~* lebensgroß; *standard ~~* Normalgröße *f*; *~~ of type* Schriftgrad *m*; **~ed** [-d] *a in Zssgen*: *large-~~* in Großformat; *medium-~~* mittelgroß; **~(e)able** ['-əbl] umfangreich; beträchtlich; ansehnlich; **~e-up** *Am sl* Abschätzung *f*; **~er** ['-ə] Sortiermaschine *f*; **~ing** ['-iŋ] Klassierung, Sortierung; Größeneinteilung *f*; **2.** *s tech* Appretur *f*, (Auftrag-, Schlicht-) Leim *m*; *tr* appretieren, schlichten, leimen; *(Gemälde)* grundieren; **~ing** ['-iŋ] Leimen; Schlichten *n*.

sizz(le) ['sizl] *itr* zischen; *s* Zischen *n*.

skat|e [skeit] **1.** *s (ice-~~)* Schlittschuh; *(roller-~~)* Rollschuh; *Am sl* Kerl, Bursche *m*; *itr* Schlittschuh, Rollschuh laufen; *to ~~ on thin ice (fig)* in e-r schwierigen Lage sein; *to ~~ over thin ice (fig)* vorsichtig lavieren; **~er** ['-ə] Schlittschuh-, Rollschuhläufer *m*; **~ing** ['-iŋ] Schlittschuh-, Rollschuhlaufen *n*; *~~-rink* Eisbahn; Rollschuhbahn *f*; **2.** *zoo* Glattroche(n) *m*; **3.** *Am sl* Schindmähre *f*; *fig* alte(s) Haus *n*.

skedaddle [ski'dædl] *itr fam* türmen, abhauen, ausreißen; *s* Ausreißen *n*.

skee|sicks, ~zicks ['skisiks] *Am fam* Taugenichts, Strolch *m*.

skein [skein] Docke, Strähne *f (Garn)*; *orn* Zug, Schwarm, Flug *m*.

skeleton ['skelitn] Skelett, Gerippe *a. fig tech*; Gestell *n*, Rahmen *m*, Gerüst, Gebälk *n*; Umriß, Entwurf *m*; magere Überreste *m pl*; *(~ army) mil* Kader, Stamm(truppe *f*) *m*; *in ~ form* schematisch; *family ~, ~ in the cupboard, (Am) in the closet* Familiengeheimnis *n*; *~ at the feast (fig)* Spielverderber *m*; *steel ~ (arch)* Stahlskelett *n*; **~ agreement** Rahmenabkommen *n*; **~ bill** Wechselformular *n*; **~ construction** Skelettbauweise *f*; **~ crew, staff** Stammannschaft, -besatzung *f*; **~ize** ['-aiz] *tr (Tier)* präparieren; *fig* entwerfen, umreißen; *(zahlenmäßig)* einschränken, reduzieren; **~ key** Dietrich; Haupt-, Nachschlüssel *m*; **~ law** Rahmengesetz *n*; **~ map** Umrißkarte *f*; **~ service** Bereitschaftsdienst *m*.

skelp [skelp] *fam* Schlag, Klaps *m*.

skep [skep] (Weiden-, Bienen-)Korb *m*.

skept... *s. scept...*.

sketch [sketʃ] *s (Kunst, lit, mus, allg)* Skizze; *lit* Kurzgeschichte *f*; *theat* Sketch *m*; *allg* Umrisse *m pl*, Entwurf *m*; *com* überschlägige Berechnung *f*; *tr* skizzieren, umreißen, entwerfen; *itr* e-e Skizze machen; **~-block, -book** Skizzenblock *m*, -buch *n*; **~iness** ['-inis] Skizzenhaftigkeit *f*; **~ map** Kroki *n*; Lageskizze; Umrißkarte *f*; **~y** ['-i] skizzenhaft; flüchtig.

skew [skju:] *a* schräg; schief; gebogen, gewunden; unsymmetrisch; *tr* verschränken; *itr* schief, scheel blicken; *s* Abschrägung, Abdachung; Verdrehung *f*; **~back** *arch* Schrägfläche *f*; **~bald** *(Pferd)* scheckig; **~er** ['-ə] Fleischspieß *m*; **~-eyed** *a* schielend; **~-whiff** *fam* krumm, schief.

ski [ski:, *Br a.* ʃi:] *pl ~(s)* Schi, Ski, Schneeschuh *m*; *aero* Schneekufe *f*; *itr (pret ski'd, Am skied)* Schi laufen *od* fahren; *to bind on o.'s ~ (s)* die Schi anschnallen; **~-binding** Schibindung *f*; **~-boot** Schistiefel *m*; **~borne** *a mil* auf Schiern, Schi-; **~er** ['-ə] Schiläufer, -fahrer *m*; **~ing** ['-iŋ] Schisport *m*; *~~-grounds (pl)* Schigelände *n*; **~-joring** [-'jə:riŋ] *sport* Schikjöring *n*; **~-jump** Schisprung *m*; Sprungschanze *f*; **~-jumping** Schispringen *n*; **~-lift, ~mobile, ~tow** Schilift *m*; **~-pants** *pl* Schi-, Keilhose *f*; **~-plane** Flugzeug *n* mit Schneekufen; **~-stick** Schistock *m*; **~-suit** Schianzug *m*.

skid [skid] *s* Gleitkufe, -schiene; *aero* Schneekufe *f*, Sporn; Bremsklotz, Hemmschuh *m*, -kette *f*; Gleitschutz (-vorrichtung *f*); *mar* Fender *m*; *tr* hemmen, bremsen; *itr mot* rutschen, schleudern; *aero* schieben, (ab)rutschen; *non-~ (attr)* Gleitschutz-; **~ chain** Schneekette *f*; **~-lid** *mot* Sturzhelm *m*; **~ mark** Bremsspur *f*; **~ding** *mot* Schleudern *n*; **~proof** *a mot* Gleitschutz-; **~ row, road** *Am* Herumtreiberviertel *n*, -gegend *f (e-r Großstadt)*; billige(s) Viertel *n*.

skidoo [ski'du:] *itr*: *~! Am sl* hau ab!

skiff [skif] Skiff *n*; Renneiner *m*.

skilful, *Am* **skillful** ['skilful] geschickt, gewandt, fähig, tüchtig, erfahren (*at* in).

skill [skil] Geschicklichkeit; *Am* Fähigkeit, (Hand-)Fertigkeit (*in, at* in); Kunst *f*, Geschick; Können *n*; **~ed** [-d] *a* geschickt, gewandt (*in doing s.th.* im Tun); geübt, erfahren, erprobt; geschult; gelernt; Fach-; *to be ~~ in s.th.* in etw fachlich ausgebildet sein; *~~ labo(u)r, manpower* Fach-, gelernte Arbeiter *m pl*; *~~ work* Facharbeit *f*; *~~ worker* Fach-, gelernte(r) Arbeiter *m*; **~ful** *s. skilful*.

skillet ['skilit] Tiegel *m*, Kasserole *f*; *Am* Bratpfanne *f*.

skim [skim] *tr (Flüssigkeit)* abschäumen; *(Milch)* entrahmen; *(Schaum, Rahm)* abschöpfen *a. fig*, -nehmen, entfernen; *fig* leicht (hin)streifen, -fahren über; flüchtig berühren *a. fig*; flüchtig lesen, überfliegen; *itr* gleiten, fliegen (*through* durch; *over* über; *along* an...entlang); hinwegfliegen, -sausen (*over* über); durchblättern (*through a book* ein Buch); diagonallesen; *to ~ the surface (fig)* an der Oberfläche bleiben (*of s.th.* e-r S); **~mer** ['-ə] Schaumlöffel, Abstreifer *m*; **~-milk** Magermilch *f*; **~mings** ['-iŋz] *pl* Schaum *m*; *das* Abgeschöpfte; Abstrich *m*.

skimp [skimp] *fam itr* knausern, geizen; pfuschen; *tr* hinpfuschen; sparen an; *(Person)* knapp halten; *a* knapp; **~iness** ['-inis] Knauserigkeit *f*, Geiz *m*; **~y** ['-i] knapp; knauserig, filzig, geizig; *(Portion)* mager, ungenügend; *(Kleid)* zu eng.

skin [skin] *s* Haut *f*; Fell *n*, Balg *m*; *allg* Schale, Hülse, Rinde; Außen-, Oberfläche, Außenseite *f*; (Wein-)Schlauch *m*; *tech* Hülle; *mar* Beplankung; *aero* Bespannung *f*; *Am sl* Knauser, Geizkragen, -hals; *Am sl* Klepper *m*; *tr* häuten, abziehen; schälen, enthülsen, entrinden; abschürfen; *sl* übers Ohr hauen; *itr* sich häuten; *(to ~ over)* sich mit Haut überziehen, verharschen, vernarben; *Am sl (to ~ through)* abhauen, türmen; *by the ~ of o.'s teeth* mit knapper (Müh u.) Not; *in, with a whole ~* mit heiler Haut; *to get under s.o.'s ~ (Am sl)* jdm auf den Wecker, auf die Nerven fallen; *s.o.* sich in jdn verlieben; *to have a thick ~ (fig)* ein dickes Fell haben, dickfellig sein; *to have a thin ~* feinfühlig sein; *to keep o.'s eyes ~ned (fam)* ein wachsames Auge haben; *to save o.'s ~ (fam)* mit heiler Haut davonkommen; *to strip to the ~* (sich) splitternackt ausziehen; *to ~ alive* schinden; *fam fig* fertigmachen; *to ~ a flint* geizig sein; *give me some ~ (Am sl)* gib mir die Flosse! *it's no ~ off my back (Am sl)* das kann mir gestohlen bleiben; das geht mich nichts an; *gold-beater's ~* Goldschlägerhäutchen *n*; *wet to the ~* naß bis auf die Haut; **~-deep** *a adv* oberflächlich, flüchtig; **~-disease** Hautkrankheit *f*; **~-diving** Sporttauchen *n*; **~flint** Geizhals, Knauser *m*; **~ful** ['-ful] *fam* Bauchvoll *m*; **~ game** *Am fam* Gaunerei *f*, Schwindel *m*; **~ grafting** *med* Hauttransplantation *f*; **~ner** ['-ə] Gerber; Rauchwarenhändler *m*; **~ny** ['-i] häutig; Haut-; hager, mager, dürr, knochig; geizig, knauserig; **~tight** *(Kleidung)* hauteng.

skint [skint] *sl* völlig abgebrannt.

skip [skip] *itr* hüpfen, springen; seilhüpfen; *fig* e-n kurzen Sprung machen (*to* nach); *(Schule)* e-e Klasse überspringen; *(in e-m Buch)* überschlagen, überspringen; *fam (to ~ off)* türmen, abhauen; *to ~ about* herumhüpfen; *tr* hüpfen, springen über; *(Buchseite)* übergehen, -springen, -schlagen, auslassen; *(Klasse)* überspringen; *fam* fluchtartig verlassen; *(Schule)* schwänzen; *s* Sprung *m*; Hüpfen; Überspringen, Auslassen *n*; *fam* Schwof; *tech* Kippwagen *m*, Lore *f*; *to ~ rope* seilhüpfen; **~ distance** *radio* tote Zone *f*; **~jack** Stehaufmännchen *n*; Schnellkäfer; *Art* fliegende(r) Fisch *m*; **~per** ['-ə] **1.** Hüpfende(r), Springer *m*; *Am* Käsemade *f*; **2.** *mar aero* Kapitän; *allg* Führer, Leiter; *sport* Mannschaftsführer *m*; **~ping-rope** Springseil *n (Spielzeug)*.

skirl [skə:l] *s u. itr* (ein) pfeifendes Geräusch *n* (machen).

skirmish ['skə:miʃ] *s* Scharmützel, Vorpostengefecht *n*; *allg* kleine(r) Konflikt *m*, Geplänkel *n*; *itr* plänkeln; **~ line** *mil* Schützenlinie *f*; **~er** ['-ə] Plänkler *m*.

skirt [skə:t] *s* (Kleider-)Rock; Rockschoß *m*; *sl* Weibsbild *n*; *pl* Rand (-gebiet *n*); Stadtrand; (Wald-)Rand *m*; *tr* einfassen, umgeben, säumen; sich am Rande hinziehen (*s.th.* e-r S); am Rand entlanggehen (*s.th.* e-r S); herumgehen um, umgehen; **~ing** ['-iŋ] Kostümstoff *m*; *~~-board* Scheuerleiste *f*.

skit [skit] Spott *m*, Stichelei; kleine Satire, Spottschrift *f* (*on s.o.* auf jdn); *theat* satirische(r) Sketch *m*; **~tish** ['-iʃ] lebhaft, lustig, ausgelassen; reizbar, nervös; ängstlich, scheu *(a. Pferd)*; wankelmütig, unzuverlässig.

skitter ['skitə] *itr tr* über das Wasser schnellen (lassen).

skittle ['skitl] *s* Kegel *m*; *pl mit sing* Kegeln *n*; *tr*: *to ~ away* vertrödeln, -tun; *to play at ~s* kegeln, *fam* kegelschieben; *it is not all beer and ~s* das ist kein reines Vergnügen; *~s!* Unsinn! Quatsch! **~-alley, -ground** Kegelbahn *f*; **~-ball** Kegelkugel *f*.

skive [skaiv] *tr (Leder)* spalten; *(Edelstein)* schleifen; **~r** ['-ə] Spaltleder *n*.

skivvy ['skivi] *fam pej* Dienstmädchen *n*; *pl Am sl* Unterwäsche *f*.

skivy ['skaivi] *sl* unehrlich.

skulduggery [skʌl'dʌgəri] *Am fam* Gaunerei *f*.

skulk [skʌlk] *itr* umherschleichen; sich verbergen; lauern; *fam* sich (herum-) drücken; *s u.* **~er** ['-ə] Schleicher; Drückeberger *m*.

skull [skʌl] Hirnschale *f*, Schädel; *Am sl* Chef (vom Ganzen), Intellektuelle(r); *(Schule)* Primus *m*; *to have a thick ~* Stroh im Kopf haben; *~ and crossbones* Totenkopf *m (Zeichen)*; **~ bone** Schädelknochen *m*; **~-cap** (Seiden-) Käppchen; *anat* Schädeldach *n*.

skunk [skʌŋk] *s zoo* Skunk *m*, Stinktier *n*; Skunk(s *pl*) *(Pelz)*; *fam* Lump, Strolch, Gauner *m*; *tr Am sl sport* haushoch schlagen; *Am sl (Schuld)* nicht bezahlen; *to ~ s.o. out of s.th. (Am sl)* jdm etw abgaunern.

sky [skai] *s oft pl (sichtbarer)* Himmel *m*; Himmelszelt, Firmament; Wetter, Klima *n*; Gegend *f*, Himmelsstrich *m*; *tr (Ball)* in die Höhe schlagen; hoch aufhängen; *in the ~* am Himmel; *out of a clear ~ (fig)* aus heiterem Himmel; *under the open ~* unter freiem Himmel, im Freien; *to praise to the skies (fig)* in den Himmel heben; **~-blue** himmelblau; **~-high** *a adv* himmelhoch; **~-hook** *Am* Registrierballon *m*; **~lark** *s* Feldlerche *f*; *fig* Ulk *m*; *itr* herumtollen; dumme Streiche machen; **~lift** Luftbrücke *f*; **~light** Dachluke *f*, Oberlicht *n*; Deckenbeleuchtung *f*; **~-line** Horizont *m*; (Stadt-)Silhouette *f*; **~-piece** *Am sl* Mütze *f*, Hut *m*; **~-pilot** *sl* Pfaffe, Schwarzrock; *sl* Flieger *m*; **~-rocket** *s (Feuerwerk)* Rakete; *mil* Signalrakete *f*; *itr Am fam* schnell steigen; *(Preise)* in die Höhe klettern, emporschnellen; **~-scraper** Wolkenkratzer *m*; *Am sl* dicke(s), belegte(s) Brot *n*; **~-sign** (Neon-)Reklameschild *n*; **~ward(s)** ['-wəd(z)] *adv* himmelan; **~-way** Luftfahrtweg, Flugstrecke *f*; **~-writing** Himmelsschrift *f*.

slab [slæb] *s* Platte, Tafel, Scheibe, Fliese; *(Brot)* Scheibe *f*; (halbrundes) Schalbrett *n*, Schwarte; Bramme *f*; *sl* Operationstisch *m*.

slabber *s. slobber.*

slack [slæk] **1.** *a* langsam, träge, müßig, lässig (*at* bei); flau, matt, ruhig, still; *rail* verkehrsarm; schlaff, locker, lose; schlapp, schwach, haltlos; nachlässig, sorglos, gleichgültig; *com* flau, lustlos; *(Geschäft)* ruhig; *adv in Zssgen* (zu) schwach, ungenügend, langsam; *s mar* Lose *n*; Schlaffheit, Lockerheit *f*; Stillstand *m*, Flaute *a. com*; Mattheit *f*; *tech* Spiel *n*; *pl* weite *(Herren-* od *Damen-)* Hose *f*; *tr* lockern; vermindern; *(Kalk)* löschen; *itr* locker, lose werden; *to ~ off, up* langsamer werden, nachlassen; sich ausruhen; *to be ~ (tech)* Spiel haben; **~en** ['slækən] *itr* schwächer werden, nachlassen, abflauen; sich verlangsamen; schlaffer, lockerer werden; *(Widerstand)* erlahmen; *com* flau werden, stocken; *tr* abschwächen, mäßigen, verringern, vermindern; lockern; *mar* fieren; **~er** ['-ə] Drückeberger *m*; **~ joint** Wackelkontakt *m*; **~ness** ['-nis] Trägheit; Flaute; Schlaffheit *f*; *tech* Spiel *n*; *~~ of trade* Geschäftsstockung *f*; **~ water** *mar* Still-, Stauwasser *n*; **2.** Kohlengrus *m*, Staubkohle *f*.

slag [slæg] *s metal geol* Schlacke *f*; *tr itr* verschlacken; **~gy** ['-i] schlackig; **~-heap** Schlackenhaufen *m*.

slake [sleik] *tr (Feuer, Kalk, Koks, Durst)* löschen; *(Verlangen)* stillen.

slam [slæm] *tr (Tür)* zuschlagen (lassen); heftig werfen, *fam* zuknallen, zupfeffern; *fam* 'runtermachen, -putzen; *to ~ down* auf die Erde schleudern; *itr (Tür)* zuschlagen; krachen; *(Whist)* Schlemm werden; *s* (Zu-)Schlagen *n*; Schlag; Knall; *fam* Anschnauzer *m*, Zigarre; vernichtende Kritik *f*; *(Whist, Bridge)* Schlemm *m*; *to ~ the door in s.o.'s face* jdm die Tür vor der Nase zuschlagen.

slander ['slɑːndə] *s* Verleumdung, üble Nachrede *f*; *tr* verleumden; **~ action** Verleumdungsklage *f*; **~er** ['-rə] Verleumder *m*; **~ous** ['-rəs] verleumderisch.

slang [slæŋ] *s* Slang *m*; Sonder-, Zunftsprache *f*, Jargon *m*; *tr* anschreien, beschimpfen, beleidigen; **~iness** ['-inis] Derbheit *f*; **~y** ['-i] *a* Slang-; volkstümlich, derb; Slang redend.

slant [slɑːnt] *tr* schräg stellen, kippen; abschrägen; abböschen; *Am fam* tendenziös färben; *itr* schräg sein; sich neigen; *Am fam* voreingenommen sein, tendieren (*towards* zu); *s* Hang *m*; schiefe Ebene *od* Fläche; Schräge, Neigung *f*; *Am fam* schnelle(r) Blick *m*; *Am fam* Ansicht(ssache), Meinung, Einstellung *f*; *a (on the ~, on a ~)* schräg, schief, geneigt; **~-eyed** *a* schlitzäugig; **~ing** ['-iŋ] *a* schief, geneigt, schräg; *s* Schräge *f*; Abschräger *m*; **~ways** ['-weiz] *adv* = **~wise** ['-waiz] *adv a* schräg, schief.

slap [slæp] *s* Klaps, Schlag *m*; *fig* Beleidigung, Zurücksetzung *f*; *tr* schlagen, e-n Klaps geben (*s.o.* jdm; *s.o.'s hand* auf die Hand); klatschen; *adv fam* stracks, gerade(swegs); *to ~ down (fam)* hinhauen, -knallen; *to ~ s.o.'s face* jdn ohrfeigen; *a ~ in the eye, face (fam)* Ohrfeige *f*; *fig* ein Schlag *m* ins Kontor, (große) Enttäuschung *f*; **~-bang** *adv fam* haste, was kannste; holterdiepolter; **~-dash** *a* eilig, hastig, flüchtig; *(Arbeit)* schlampig; *adv* in Eile, Hals über Kopf; mit e-m Schlag; *s fam* Schlamperei, Pfuscherei *f*; **~-happy** *Am sl* (wie) besoffen; verrückt; **~jack** *Am* Pfannkuchen *m*; **~stick** *s* (Narren-)Pritsche; Burleske *f*, Schwank *m*, Posse *f*; *a* burlesk, possenhaft; **~-up** *a sl* erstklassig, prima.

slash [slæʃ] **1.** *tr* (auf)schlitzen, ritzen, zerschneiden; *(Bäume)* fällen; peitschen, geißeln *a. fig*; *fam* scharf kritisieren; *(Preise)* heruntersetzen; *Am fig* drastisch kürzen, zs.streichen; *itr (to ~ out)* um sich hauen; hauen (*at* nach); losschlagen (*at* auf); *s* Hieb *m*; Schnitt-, Hiebwunde, Schmarre *f*, Schmiß; Schnitt, Schlitz *(a. als Zierde)*; Peitschenschlag; *(Wald)* Einschlag; Windbruch *m*; Baumtrümmer *pl*; *~ed sleeve* Schlitzärmel *m*; **~ing** ['-iŋ] streng, heftig, erbarmungslos; schneidig, schnittig; *(Kritik)* vernichtend; *fam (übertreibend)* gewaltig; *price ~~* Preisherabsetzung *f*; **2.** *Am* Sumpf(wald) *m*.

slat [slæt] *s* Latte, Leiste *f*; *pl sl* Rippen *f pl*; *Am sl* dürre Zicke, Hopfenstange *f*.

slat|e [sleit] *s geol* Schiefer *m*; Schieferplatte, -tafel *f*; Schiefergrau *n*; *film* Klappe; *Am* Kandidatenliste *f*; *a (~-coloured)* schiefergrau; *tr* mit Schiefer decken; *Am* auf die Kandidatenliste setzen, vormerken; *fam* es geben (*s.o.* jdm), fertigmachen, vermöbeln; 'runtermachen, -putzen; *on the ~~ (fam)* auf Kredit; *to have a clean ~~ (fig)* e-e reine Weste haben; *to start with a clean ~~* e-n neuen Anfang machen; *~~-board* Schiefertafel *f*; *~~-club* Weihnachtssparverein *m*; *~~-gray* schiefergrau; *~~-pencil* Griffel *m*; *~~-quarry* Schieferbruch *m*; **~er** ['-ə] Schieferdecker *m*; **~(e)y** ['-i] schieferartig, -haltig; *~~ marl* Schiefermergel *m*; **~ing** ['-iŋ] Decken *n* mit Schiefer; Schieferplatten *f pl (zum Dachdecken)*; *fam* vernichtende Kritik, Strafpredigt *f*.

slattern ['slætən] Schlampe *f*; **~liness** ['-linis] Schlampigkeit *f*; **~ly** ['-li] *a adv* schlampig.

slaughter ['slɔːtə] *s* Schlachten *n (von Vieh)*; bestialische(r) Mord *m*; Gemetzel, Blutbad *n*; *Am com* Verschleuderung *f*; *tr (Vieh)* schlachten; *(Menschen)* hinschlachten, niedermetzeln, -machen; *Am* (durch Raubbau) vernichten, zerstören; *Am com* mit Verlust verkaufen, verschleudern; *Am fam* erledigen; **~er** ['-rə] Schlachter, Schlächter *m*; **~house** Schlachthaus *n*, *fig* -bank *f*; **~ous** ['-rəs] mörderisch; **~ price** Schleuderpreis *m*.

Slav [slɑːv] *s* Slawe *m*, Slawin *f*; *a* slawisch; **~ic, ~onic** ['slævik, slə'vɔnik] *a* slawisch.

slav|e [sleiv] *s* Sklave *m*, Sklavin *f*; *fig* Sklave, Knecht (*to, of a vice* e-s Lasters); *fig* Packesel *m*; *itr* schuften, sich plakken, sich schinden, sich abmühen; *to be a ~~ to duty* nur s-e Pflicht kennen; *to make a ~~ of s.o.* jdn versklaven; *white-~~ trade* Mädchenhandel *m*; *~~-driver* Sklavenaufseher *m*; *fig* Leuteschinder *m*; *~~-holder* Sklavenhalter *m*; *~~ labo(u)r* Sklaven-, Zwangsarbeit *f*; *~~-ship* Sklavenschiff *n*; *~~-trade, -traffic* Sklavenhandel *m*; **~er** ['-ə] Sklavenjäger, -händler *m*, -schiff *n*; **~ery** ['-əri] Sklaverei *a. fig*; *fig* sklavische Hingabe; Schinderei, Plackerei *f*; *white-~~* Mädchenhandel *m*; **~ey** ['-i] *fam* Dienstmädchen *n*; **~ish** ['-iʃ] sklavisch; servil, untertänig; **~ishness** ['-iʃnis] Untertänigkeit, Servilität *f*.

slaver ['slævə] *itr* sabbern, schlabbern, geifern; *tr* begeifern; *s* Geifer; *fig* Unsinn *m*; **~y** ['-ri] geifernd.

slaw [slɔː] *Am* Kohl-, Krautsalat *m*.

slay [slei] *irr slew* [sluː], *slain* [slein] *tr lit u. Am* erschlagen *a. fig*; **~er** ['-ə] Totschläger *m*.

sleave [sliːv] *s* (feiner) Seidenfaden *m*; Flockseide *f*; Garngewirr *n*; *tr (Seide)* haspeln; *(Garnknäuel)* entwirren.

sleazy ['sliːzi] *(Gewebe)* dünn, schwach, locker, wenig haltbar; *Am sl* schmutzig, heruntergekommen, minderwertig.

sled [sled], **~ge** [-ʒ] **1.** *s* Schlitten *m*; *itr tr* (auf, in e-m) Schlitten fahren, befördern *od* transportieren; **~ding** ['-iŋ] Schlittenfahrt *f*.

sledge [sledʒ] **2.** *(~-hammer)* Schmiede-, Vorschlag-, *fig* Holzhammer *m*; *a* wuchtig.

sleek [sliːk] *a (Haar, Fell, Pelz, Gefieder)* weich, glatt u. glänzend; *(Tier)* gepflegt, wohlgenährt; *fig* salbungsvoll, honigsüß; *tr* glätten, pflegen.

sleep [sliːp] *s* Schlaf *m a. fig*; *v irr slept, slept* [slept] *itr* schlafen *a. fig*; überschlafen (*on, over s.th.* etw); *tr* schlafen; Unterkunft bieten für; unterbringen; *to get to ~* einschlafen können; *to go to ~* schlafen gehen; einschlafen; *to put to ~* einschläfern; *to ~ the clock round* volle 12 Stunden schlafen; *to ~ like a log, top* wie ein Murmeltier, ein Sack schlafen; *to ~ the ~ of the just* den Schlaf des Gerechten schlafen; *my leg has gone to ~* mein Bein ist eingeschlafen; *he didn't ~ a wink* er hat kein Auge zugetan; *the last ~* die letzte Ruhe, der Tod; *want of ~* Schlaflosigkeit *f*; *to ~* **away** verschlafen *tr*; *to ~* **in** zu Hause schlafen; *to ~* **off** ausschlafen *tr*; *to ~* **on** weiterschlafen; *to ~* **out** auswärts schlafen; **~er** ['-ə] Schläfer *m*; *bes. rail* Schwelle *f*; Schlafwagen; *Am* überraschende(r) Erfolg *m*; *to be a good, bad ~~* (immer) gut, schlecht schlafen; *to be a heavy, light, sound ~~* e-n festen, leisen, gesunden Schlaf haben; *~~ plane* Flugzeug *n* mit Schlafkojen; **~iness** ['-inis] Schläfrigkeit *f*; **~ing** ['-iŋ] *a* schlafend; *~~-accomodation* Schlafgelegenheit *f*; *~~-bag* Schlafsack *m*; *the S~~ Beauty* Dornröschen *n*; *~~-berth (rail aero)* Schlafkoje *f*; *~~-car (rail)* Schlafwagen *m*; *~~-draught, -pill (pharm)* Schlafmittel *n*; *~~ partner (com)* stille(r) Teilhaber *m*; *~~-sickness* Schlafkrankheit *f*; *~~-suit* Schlafanzug, Pyjama *m*; **~less** ['-lis] schlaflos; unruhig; wachsam; rastlos, ununterbrochen; **~lessness** ['-lisnis] Schlaflosigkeit; Rastlosigkeit *f*; **~-walker** Schlaf-, Nachtwandler *m*; **~-walking** Schlaf-, Nachtwandeln *n*; **~y** ['-i] schläfrig, müde; verschlafen; *fig* still, ruhig, tot; einschläfernd; *(Frucht)* überreif; **~yhead** *fig* Schlafmütze *f*.

sleet [sliːt] *s mete* Schloßen, Graupeln *f pl*; *Am* Hagel *m*; *itr* graupeln; *shower of ~* Graupelschauer *m*; **~y** ['-i] graupelig.

sleeve [sliːv] Ärmel *m*; *tech* Muffe, Buchse, Hülse, Tülle *f*; *aero* Windsack *m*; *to have s.th., a card up o.'s ~* etw auf Lager, in Reserve, in petto haben; etw im Schilde führen; *to laugh up o.'s ~* sich ins Fäustchen lachen; *to wear o.'s heart on o.'s ~* das Herz auf der Zunge haben; **~-ball** *mot* Preßnippel *m*; **~-band** Ärmelhalter *m*; **~-button, -link** Manschettenknopf *m*; **~d** [-d] *a* mit Ärmeln (versehen); *in Zssgen* -ärm(e)lig, mit...Ärmeln; *long-, short-~~* lang-, kurzärm(e)lig; mit langen, kurzen Ärmeln; **~-fish** *zoo* Kalmar *m (Tintenfisch)*; **~ information** *fam* vertrauliche Information *f*; **~less** ['-lis] ärmellos, ohne Ärmel; **~-valve** Muffenventil *n*.

sleigh [slei] *s* (Pferde-)Schlitten *m*; *itr* Schlitten fahren; **~ bells** *pl* Schlittenglöckchen *n pl*; **~ing** ['-iŋ], *~~-party* Schlittenfahrt, -partie *f*.

sleight [slait] Kunstgriff *m*; Geschicklichkeit, Gewandtheit *f*; *~-of-hand* Fingerfertigkeit *f*; (Zauber-)Kunststück(chen) *n*; Trick *m a. fig*.

slender ['slendə] schlank, schmächtig, dünn; *fig* mager, dürftig; schwach; *(Mittel)* unzureichend; *(Ton)* dünn; **~ize** ['-raiz] *tr Am* schlank machen, schlank(er) erscheinen lassen; *itr* schlank(er) werden; **~ness** ['-nis] Schlankheit; *fig* Dürftigkeit *f*.

sleugh *s. slew* **3**.

sleuth [slu:θ] *s (~-hound)* Polizei-, *a. fig* Spür-, Bluthund; *fam hum* Detektiv *m*; *itr* e-r Spur nachgehen.

slew [slu:] **1.** *pret von slay*; **2.** *a.* **slue** *(to ~ round) tr itr* (sich) drehen; *s* Drehung *f* (um die eigene Achse); **3.** *a.* **slue, sleugh** *Am* Sumpf(loch *n*) *m*; **4.** *a.* **slue** *Am fam* (gewaltige) Menge, Masse *f*.

slic|e [slais] *s* Scheibe, Schnitte, Tranche *f*; *fig* Stück *n*, (An-)Teil *m*; Kelle, Schaufel *(Tischgerät)*; Spa(ch)tel *f*; *(Golf)* Schlag *m* mit Rechtsdrall; *fig* Querschnitt *m*; *tr* aufschneiden, (in Scheiben) abschneiden; zerschneiden, (zer)teilen; zerlegen, einteilen; **~er** ['-ə] (Brot-, Wurst-)Schneidemaschine *f*.

slick [slik] *a* (spiegel)glatt; schlüpfrig; vollkommen, klug, erfinderisch, raffiniert; wendig, gewandt; *fam* (be)trügerisch; *fam* trügerisch, falsch; *sl* großartig, phantastisch, herrlich, prima; *sl* entzückend, süß; elegant; *adv fam* schnurstracks, spornstreichs, geradewegs; *s* breite(r), flache(r) Meißel; *Am* Ölfleck *m (a. d. Wasser)*; *(~ paper) Am sl* Zeitschrift *f* auf Kunstdruckpapier; *tr* glätten, glatt, glänzend machen; *(to ~ up) Am fam* aufpolieren; sich erfrischen; **~ chick** *Am sl* gutgekleidete(s), hübsche(s) Mädchen *n*; **~er** ['-ə] *Am* Ölhaut *f (Regenmantel)*; *Am fam* gerissene(r) Kerl, Schwindler *m*.

slid|e [slaid] *irr slid, slid* [slid] *itr* gleiten *(from* aus); rutschen; schlittern; kriechen; schleichen; ausgleiten, -rutschen; *fig* geraten *(into* in); *tr* gleiten lassen *(in, into* in); *fig* einfließen lassen; *s* Gleiten *n*, Gleitbewegung ;Rutsch-, Schlitterbahn; Gleitfläche *f*; Schlitten, Schieber *m*; (Haar-)Spange *f*; Objektträger *m*, Deckglas *(für mikroskopische Präparate)*; *(lantern ~~)* Lichtbild, Diapositiv, *fam* Dia *n*; Berg-, Erdrutsch *m*; Lawine *f*; *to ~~ down* herunterrutschen; *(Preise)* abrutschen; *to ~~ in* hineinschieben; *to ~~ over (fig)* hinweggehen über, übergehen; *to let ~~* laufenlassen, sich nicht kümmern um; *to let things ~~* die Dinge laufenlassen; *~~-fastener* Reißverschluß *m*; *~~-gauge* Schublehre *f*; *~~-knot* Schlinge *f*; *~~-projector* Bildwerfer *m*; *~~-rest tech* Support *m*; *~~-rule* Rechenschieber *m*; *~~-valve* Schieberventil *n*; *~~-way* Gleitfläche; Auffahrt *f*; **~ing** ['-iŋ] *a fig* gleitend; *tech* Gleit-; *~~ contact* Schleifkontakt *m*; *~~ door* Schiebetür *f*; *~~ roof (mot)* Schiebedach *n*; *~~ rule* Rechenschieber *m*; *~~ scale* gleitende (Lohn-, Preis-)Skala *f*; *~~ seat* Gleit-, Rollsitz *m*; *~~ stage* Schiebebühne *f*; *~~ table* Ausziehtisch *m*; *~~ weight* Laufgewicht *n*; *~~ window* Schiebefenster *n*.

slight [slait] *a* schlank, dünn, schmächtig; *(Person)* zerbrechlich, zart, schwach; *(Erkältung)* leicht; klein, geringfügig, unbedeutend, unwesentlich, belanglos; *(Eindruck)* oberflächlich; *(Unterschied)* klein; *tr* vernachlässigen; mißachten; zurücksetzen, geringschätzig behandeln; *s* Mißachtung; geringschätzige Behandlung; Zurücksetzung *f*; *not in the ~est* nicht im geringsten; **~ing** ['-iŋ] geringschätzig; verächtlich; **~ly** ['-li] *adv* ein wenig; **~ness** ['-nis] Schmächtigkeit; Zartheit, Schwäche; Geringfügigkeit, Belanglosigkeit *f*.

slily = *slyly (adv zu sly)*.

slim [slim] *a* schlank, schmächtig, schmal, dünn; *Am* gering(fügig), schwach, klein; *Br* schlau, pfiffig, gerissen; *tr itr* schlank machen, werden; **~ming** ['-iŋ] *Br* Entfettungs-, Abmagerungskur *f*; *~~ diet* Abmagerungsdiät *f*; **~ness** ['-nis] Schmächtigkeit; Geringfügigkeit; Gerissenheit *f*.

slim|e [slaim] *s bot zoo* Schleim; Schlamm, Schlick; *Am sl fig* Abschaum *m*; *tr* schleimig machen; *~~ fungus, mold* Schleimpilz *m*; *~~ pit* Schlammgrube *f*; **~y** ['-i] schleimig *a. fig*, verschleimt; schlammig, verschlammt; *fig* schmutzig, widerlich, ekelhaft; *Am sl* obszön.

slim(p)sy [slimzi,-psi] *Am fam* schwach, dünn, fadenscheinig *fig*.

sling [sliŋ] **1.** *s* (Stein-)Schleuder *f*; Schleudern *n*, Wurf *m*; Schlinge; Binde *f*; (Gewehr-, Trag-)Riemen *m*; *tr irr slung, slung* [slʌŋ] schleudern, werfen; hochziehen; *(Gewehr)* um-, überhängen; aufhängen; *med* in die Schlinge legen; *mar* laschen; *to ~ o.'s hook (fam)* abhauen; *to ~ mud at s.o.* jdn mit Schmutz bewerfen; **~shot** Schleuder *f*; *Am* Katapult *m* od *n*; **2.** *Am* Eiswasser *n*, Schnaps u. Zitronensaft.

slink [sliŋk] **1.** *irr slunk, slunk* [slʌŋk] *itr* schleichen; *to ~ about* umherschleichen; *to ~ away, off* wegschleichen; sich davonstehlen; **~y** ['-i] *fam (Kleider)* hauteng; schlank; graziös; **2.** *tr itr* zu früh (Junge) werfen; verwerfen; *s (bes. Kalb)* Früh-, Fehlgeburt *f*; *a* zu früh geboren.

slip [slip] *itr* schlüpfen *(into a coat* in e-n Mantel); schleichen; gleiten *(through the water* durch das Wasser); rutschen; ausgleiten, -rutschen *(on the ice* auf dem Eis); *fig* sich versehen, sich irren; sich versprechen, sich verschreiben; abgleiten, absinken, nachlassen; entgleiten, entschlüpfen, *(dem Gedächtnis)* entfallen; *aero* slip(p)en; *tr* gleiten lassen; hineinstecken *(into* in); schnell, unbemerkt stecken, drücken *(into* in); *(Geld)* zustecken; *(Maschen)* fallen lassen; *(Bemerkung)* nicht unterdrükken können; übersehen, verpassen, sich entgehen lassen; entschwinden, entfallen *(the mind, memory* dem Gedächtnis); sich befreien, sich freimachen von; *(Keramik)* engobieren; *(Junges)* zu früh gebären; *s* Ausgleiten, -rutschen *n*; Un(glücks)fall; Fehltritt; Irrtum *m*, Versehen *n*, Schnitzer, Fehler *m*; Versprechen; Verschreiben *n*; *tech aero* Schlupf; *mar* Lande-, Anlegeplatz *m*, Landungsbrücke *f*, Pier *m* od *f*; *mar* Helling; (Hunde-) Koppel *f*; Unter-, Prinzeßrock *m*; Kinderschürze *f*; (Kissen-)Bezug, Überzug *m*; *pl* Badehose *f*; Sproß, Trieb, Schößling *m*, Steckreis; Brett(chen) *n*; Zettel; *com* Beleg, Abschnitt *m*; *typ* Fahne; *theat* Kulisse *f*; *to give s.o. the ~* jdm entwischen, ausweichen; *to let s.th. ~ through o.'s fingers* sich etw entgehen lassen; *to ~ a cog (Am fam)* sich verhauen, e-n Fehler machen; Pech haben; *I let it ~* das ist mir (so) entfahren; *don't let the chance ~* lassen Sie sich die Gelegenheit nicht entgehen; *there's many a ~ ('twixt the cup and the lip)* bis dahin fließt noch viel Wasser ins Meer; *it was a ~ of the tongue* ich habe mich versprochen; *a (mere) ~ of a boy, girl* ein schmächtiges Kerlchen, zartes Ding *n*; *~ (of paper)* Zettel *m*; *~ of the pen* Schreibfehler *m*; *check ~* Kontrollabschnitt *m*; *wage ~* Lohnzettel *m*; *to* **~ away,** *to* **~ past** entschlüpfen, entgleiten; sich drücken, sich fortschleichen; *to* **~ by,** *to* **~ away,** *to* **~ past** *(Zeit)* enteilen, entschwinden, vergehen; *(Fluß)* vorbeifließen; *to* **~ in** *tr (Wort)* einfließen lassen; *itr* sich einschleichen; *to* **~ off** hinausschlüpfen aus *(e-m Kleidungsstück)*; ausziehen; *to* **~ on** hineinschlüpfen in *(ein Kleidungsstück)*; *to* **~ out** *itr* ausschlüpfen; ausrutschen *(of* aus); *tr* herausziehen; *to* **~ over on s.o.** *Am fam* jdn hinters Licht führen, übers Ohr hauen; *to* **~ up on** *Am fam* sich verhauen bei; auf dem Holzwege sein mit; Pech haben mit; übersehen; **~-carriage, -coach** *rail* abhängbare(r) Wagen *m*; **~-case** Buchhülle *f*; **~-cover** Überzug *m*, Schutzhülle *f*; **~-fastener** Reißverschluß *m*; **~-knot** Laufknoten *m*; **~-noose** Schlinge *f*; **~-on, -over** *Am a u. s* über den Kopf zu ziehend(es Kleidungsstück *n*), Pullover, Sweater *m*; Korsett *n*; **~per** ['-ə] *(carpet-~~)* Hausschuh; *(bedroom-~~)* Pantoffel; Brems-, Hemmschuh *m*; *~~-slopper* sentimental; **~periness** ['-ərinis] Glätte; mangelnde Festigkeit; *fig* Gerissenheit, Unzuverlässigkeit *f*; **~pery** ['-əri] schlüpfrig, glatt, glitschig; nicht ganz fest, ohne festen Halt, lose; *fig* unsicher, unzuverlässig, gerissen; **~-proof** *typ* Fahnenkorrektur *f*; **~py** ['-i] *fam* glatt, schlüpfrig; behende, flink; **~-ring** *el* Schleifring *m*; **~shod** ['-ʃɔd] *a fig* schlampig, nachlässig, gleichgültig; **~slop** *a* fade; *s* Gesöff; *fig* Gewäsch *n*; **~-stream** *aero* Luftschraubenstrahl *m*; **~-tank** Abwurfbehälter *m*; **~-up** *fam* Schnitzer, Bock, Fehler *m*, Versehen *n*; **~way** *mar* Helling *f*.

slit [slit] *irr slit, slit tr* (auf)schlitzen, aufschneiden, spalten; in Streifen schneiden; *s* Schlitz, Spalt, Riß *m*, Fuge *f*; **~-eyed** *a* schlitzäugig; **~ trench** *mil* Splitter-, Laufgraben *m*.

slither ['sliðə] *itr* (aus)rutschen, -gleiten; *(Schlange)* kriechen; **~y** ['-ri] schlüpfrig, glatt.

sliver ['slivə] *s* Splitter, Span *m*; Faser (-band *n*); Schnitte *f*; *tr* (zer)spalten, zerschneiden, zerhacken; *itr* zersplittern; sich loslösen *(from* von).

slob [slɔb] *dial* Schlamm, Matsch; *Am fam* Schmutzfink; Trottel; Durchschnittsmensch *m*.

slobber ['slɔbə], **slabber** ['-æ-] *itr* schlabbern, sabbern, geifern; *fig* vor Rührung vergehen; *(to ~ over s.o.)* jdn abküssen; *tr* besabbern, begeifern; *fig* anhimmeln; *s* Geifer *m*; *fig* Gefühlsduselei, Salbaderei *f*; **~y** ['-ri] schlabb(e)rig, schleimig, glitschig; *fig* gefühlstriefend, salbadernd.

sloe [slou] Schlehe *f*; Schlehen-, Schwarzdorn *m*.

slog [slɔg] *itr tr* (hart) schlagen; treffen; (ver)prügeln; schwer arbeiten (an); *fam* schuften (an); schwerfällig gehen; *to ~ away, along* tüchtig weiterarbeiten (*at* an); *s* (heftiger) Schlag *m*; schwere Arbeit, *fam* Schufterei *f*; **~ger** ['-ə] (harter) Schläger, Boxer; tüchtige(r), gute(r) Arbeiter *m*.

slogan ['slougən] *Scot* Schlachtruf *m*; *allg* Motto *n*, Wahlspruch *m*; Schlagwort *n*; *com* Werbespruch *m*.

sloid, slojd, sloyd [slɔid] Werkunterricht *m*.

sloop [slu:p] *mar* Schaluppe *f*; Geleitboot *n*.

slop [slɔp] **1.** *s* Lache, Pfütze *f*; *pl* Schmutzwasser; Abwasch-, Spülwasser *a. fig*, Spülicht *n*; Schlempe; (dünne) Suppe, Milch; *fig* Gefühlsduselei; *sing* Schlampe; *Am sl* Kneipe *f*; *itr (to ~ over)* überlaufen, -fließen, -schwappen; spritzen; *fig* sentimental werden, schwärmen; *tr* verschütten, vergießen; verspritzen; beschmutzen; **~-basin** Schale *f* für Teeblätter; **~-jar** *Am*, **-pail** Spül-, Schmutzeimer *m*; **~piness** ['-inis] Nässe *f*; Matsch *m*; *fig* Schlamperei; *fam* Gefühlsduselei *f*; **~py** ['-i] matschig, schmutzig, naß, bespritzt; *fam* schlampig, unsauber, liederlich; *fam* übertrieben sentimental, schnulzenhaft; *to do ~~ work* pfuschen; **2.** *s pl* billige Konfektionskleidung, Kleidung *f* von der Stange; *mar* Kleider *n pl* u. Bettzeug *n*; **~ chest** *mar* Kleiderkiste *f*; **~-room** *mar* Kleiderkammer *f*; **~-seller** Konfektionshändler *m*; **~-shop** billige(s) Konfektionsgeschäft *n*; **~-work** Konfektion; Pfuscharbeit, Pfuscherei, Schlamperei *f*; **3.** *sl* Schupo, Polizist *m*.

slop|e [sloup] *s* (Ab-)Hang *m*, Böschung; Schräge, Abdachung, Neigung(swinkel *m*) *f*; *rail* Gefälle *n*; *itr* schräg abfallen; sich senken *od* (an)steigen; sich neigen; *sl (to ~~ off)* abhauen, türmen, stiftengehen; *tr* abschrägen, abdachen, abflachen; *on the ~~* abschüssig; *~~ arms!* das Gewehr über! *~~ angle* Böschungswinkel *m*; **~ing** ['-iŋ] schräg, geneigt, schief, abfallend.

slosh [slɔʃ] **1.** *s. slush*; **2.** *tr sl* verdreschen; **~ing** ['-iŋ] Tracht *f* Prügel; **3.** *itr* herumpatschen; *Am* herumbummeln, -lungern; **~ed** [-ʃt] *a sl* besoffen.

slot [slɔt] **1.** *s* Kerbe *f*, Einschnitt *m*, Nut(e), Fuge *f*; Schlitz, (Münz-)Einwurf *m*; *theat* Versenkung *f*; *tr* schlitzen, nuten; *to insert a penny in the ~* e-n Penny einwerfen; **~-machine** (Waren-, Spiel-)Automat *m*; **~-meter** Münzzähler *m*; **2.** Fährte *f*.

sloth [slouθ] Faulheit, Trägheit *f*; *zoo* Faultier, Ai *n*; **~ful** ['-ful] faul, träge.

slouch [slautʃ] *itr* schlaff herabhängen; schlottern; sich gehenlassen; lässig, schlacksig herumsitzen, -stehen; sich hinflegeln; herumschlendern, latschen; *s* schlaffe, schlechte Haltung *f*; schwerfällige(r) Gang; *(~-hat)* Schlapphut *m*; *Am sl* Flasche, Niete *f*; *to be no ~ (Am fam)* was loshaben (*at* in); *to walk with a ~* latschen.

slough [slʌf] **1.** *s* (*bes.* abgeworfene Schlangen-)Haut *f*; *med* Schorf *m*; *itr (to ~ off, away)* sich ablösen, *fam* abgehen; sich häuten, sich schälen; *med* sich verschorfen; *tr (to ~ off)* abwerfen, -stoßen; *(Tier)* abbalgen; *fig (Angewohnheit)* ablegen, loswerden; *Am sl* einsperren, verbieten, schlagen; **~y** ['-i] häutig; schorfig; Schorf-; **2.** [slau] Sumpf, Morast *m*; *Am* [slu] Sumpfloch *n*; *fig* Hoffnungs-, Mutlosigkeit *f*; **~y** ['-i] sumpfig, morastig.

Slovak ['slouvæk] *s* Slowake *m*, Slowakin *f*; *a* slowakisch; **~ia** [slo(u)'vækiə] Slowakei *f*; **~ian** [-'vækiən] = *Slovak*.

sloven ['slʌvn] Schmier-, Schmutzfink *m*; **~liness** ['-linis] Unsauberkeit; Liederlichkeit *f*; **~ly** ['-li] *a adv* unsauber, schlampig, liederlich; schlud(e)rig.

Sloven|e ['slouvi:n] *s* Slowene *m*, Slowenin *f*; *a* slowenisch; **~ia** [slo(u)'vi:njə] Slowenien *n*; **~ian** [-'vi:njən] = *~e*.

slow [slou] *a* langsam (*to* zu); schleppend, träge; *fam* langweilig; *(Markt)* flau; schwerfällig, *fam* schwer von Begriff; nicht (recht) vorankommend; spät; die Entwicklung (be)hindernd, hemmend; *(Uhr)* nachgehend; *(Fieber)* schleichend; *(Feuer)* schwach; *(Zahler)* faul, säumig, unpünktlich; *tr (to ~ up, down)* verlangsamen; aufhalten; *itr (to ~ up, down)* (immer) langsamer werden; *(in der Arbeit)* nachlassen; *adv* langsam; *to be ~ (Uhr)* nachgehen; *to do s.th.* etwas widerwillig tun; *to cook over a ~ fire* auf kleiner Flamme kochen; *to go ~* vorsichtig sein; *he's ~ in catching on, (Am sl) on the draw* er hat e-e lange Leitung; *take it ~ (Am sl)* sei vorsichtig; **~-coach** Schlafmütze *f*, Trottel *m*; *to be a ~~ (fam)* hinterm Monde leben; **~-down** Drosselung *f*; **~-match** Lunte, Zündschnur *f*; **~-motion** *attr film u. allg* Zeitlupen-; *~~ picture* Zeitlupenaufnahme *f*; **~-moving** langsam vorankommend; schwer verkäuflich; **~ness** ['-nis] Langsamkeit; Trägheit; Schwerfälligkeit *f*; *(Uhr)* Nachgehen *n*; **~poke** *Am fam* Schlafmütze *f*, Trottel *m*; **~ time** *mil* (langsames) Marschtempo *n*; **~ train** Bummelzug *m*; **~-witted** *a* schwerfällig; **~worm** *zoo* Blindschleiche *f*.

sloyd *s. sloid.*

sludge [slʌdʒ] (Schnee-)Matsch; *tech* (Klär-)Schlamm *m*; Fettreste *m pl*.

slue *s. slew 2—4.*

slug [slʌg] **1.** Acker-, Wegschnecke; *fig* Schnecke; *tech* Wurmschraube *f*; **~abed** ['-əbed] Langschläfer *m*; **~gard** ['-əd] *s* Faulpelz *m*; *a* faul; **~gish** ['-iʃ] faul, träge; langsam; schlaff, schwach; *com* schleppend; *tech* zähflüssig; **2.** *tech* Barren, Rohling *m*; Gewehr-, Blei-, Schrotkugel; Spiel-, Automatenmarke *f*; *typ* Zeilenguß *m*, Reglette *f*, *pl* Durchschuß *m*; *phys* Masseneinheit *f*; **3.** *Am fam tr* verdreschen, schlagen, boxen; *s* (Faust-)Schlag *m*; *to put the ~ on s.o.* jdm eins versetzen; **~-fest** *Am sl* Boxkampf *m*; **~ger** ['-ə] *Am fam* Schläger *(Person)*; Boxer *m*; **4.** *Am sl* Schluck *m* (Schnaps); Dollar; Berliner Pfannkuchen; Kerl *m*; **~-nutty** *Am sl* besoffen.

sluice [slu:s] *s* Schleuse *f*; Gerinne, Schleusenwasser *n*; *(~-way)* Kanal, (Wasser-)Graben *m*; *Am* (Gold-)Waschrinne *f*; *itr* herausströmen; *tr* waschen; abspritzen; ab-, auswaschen, ausspülen; *(Teich)* ablassen; **~-gate** Schleusentor *n*.

slum [slʌm] *s* schmutzige Straße *od* Gasse *f*; *Am sl* Eintopf, Fraß, Schund *m*; *pl* Elendsviertel *n*; *itr*: *to go ~ming* Slums aufsuchen; **~-clearance** Altstadtsanierung *f*; **~ gudgen, ~gullion** *Am sl* Eintopf *m*.

slumber ['slʌmbə] *lit itr* schlummern, schlafen *a. fig*; *tr (to ~ away)* verschlafen, verbummeln; *s (oft pl)* Schlummer *m*; *to fall into a ~* einschlummern; **~ous** ['-rəs], **slumbrous** ['slʌmbrəs] schläfrig, verschlafen; einschläfernd; **~ wear** Nachtzeug *n*.

slump [slʌmp] **1.** *itr (plötzlich, mit Wucht)* stürzen, fallen, sinken; *Am (durch das Eis)* einbrechen (*into* in); zs.brechen; *fig (bes. Preise)* (plötzlich) fallen, sinken, nachlassen; Schiffbruch erleiden *fig*; sich fallen lassen (*down on a sofa* auf ein Sofa); *s* Sturz, heftige(r) Fall *m*; (plötzliches) Nachlassen, Absinken; (Preis-, Kurs-) Sturz *m*, Depression, Rezession, Krise *f*; *~ in production* Produktionsrückgang *m*; **2.** *s*: *by, in (the) ~* in Bausch u. Bogen.

slur [slə:] *tr* undeutlich, nachlässig aussprechen; *(in der Aussprache)* zs.-ziehen; undeutlich, flüchtig schreiben, *a. typ* verschmieren; *mus* binden, halten; *mus* mit e-m Haltezeichen versehen; *(a. itr: to ~ over)* stillschweigend übergehen, hinweggehen über; *s* undeutliche Aussprache *f*; *typ* verschmierte Stelle *f*; (Schmutz-)Fleck *m*; *fig* Verunglimpfung *f*; Vorwurf, Tadel *m*; *mus* Bindung *f*; *mus* Bindebogen *m*; **~p** [-p] *Am sl itr tr* laut schmatzen; schmatzend essen *od* trinken.

slush [slʌʃ], **slosh** [slɔʃ] *s* (Schnee-) Matsch, Schlamm *m*; *mar (Küche)* Fettreste *m pl*, Lebensmittel *pl*; Schmierfett, -öl *n*; *fig* Gefühlsduselei *f*, Geschwafel *n*; Unsinn *m*; *tr* bespritzen; abschmieren; *arch* verputzen; *(to ~ in mud)* durch Matsch waten; **~ fund** *Am* Bestechungs-, Schmiergelder *n pl*; **~ joint** *Am sl* Eisdiele *f*; **~y** ['-] schmutzig, verschmutzt; *fig* billig, kitschig.

slut [slʌt] Schlampe *f*; Flittchen *n*; *Am* Hündin *f*; **~tish** ['-iʃ] schlampig.

sly [slai] schlau, verschlagen; falsch, hinterhältig; *on the ~* heimlich; **~boots** *fam* Schlauberger *m*; **~ minx** *fam* schlaue(s) Luder *n*; **~ness** ['-nis] Schlauheit; Falschheit *f*.

smack [smæk] **1.** *s* (leichter) Geschmack, Beigeschmack *m a. fig* (*of* von); *fig* (schwache) Spur, Andeutung *f*, Anflug *m*, *fam* Idee *f*, ein bißchen; *itr* schmecken, *fig* riechen (*of* nach); e-n Anflug haben (*of* von); e-n Eindruck machen (*of* gen); **2.** *s (~ on the lips)* Schmatz, laute(r) Kuß *m*; Schmatzen; *(Peitsche)* Knallen *n*; Klaps, Schlag; *fam* Angriff, Versuch *m*; *tr* (klatschend) schlagen; ohrfeigen; *itr* klatschen; knallen; schmatzen; *to ~ down (Am sl)* zs.stauchen, herunterkanzeln; *adv* heftig; schnurstracks, geradewegs; *interj* schwupp! bums! *to ~ o.'s lips* schmatzen; *to have a ~ at s.th. (fam)* etw probieren; *a ~ in the eye (fam)* ein Schlag ins Kontor, ein Mißerfolg *m*; **~er** ['-ə] klatschende(r) Schlag; Schmatz; *Am sl* Dollar *m*; **~ing** ['-iŋ] *a* lebhaft, scharf, heftig, stark; *s* Schläge *m pl*; *a good ~~* e-e tüchtige Tracht Prügel; **3.** *mar* Schmacke *f*.

small [smɔ:l] *a* klein, beschränkt, gering; *(Zahl)* niedrig; *(Vermögen)* bescheiden; *(Trost)* schwach, schlecht; geringfügig, unbedeutend; gewöhnlich; *(Mensch)* kleinlich; *(Ton)* weich, sanft; *(Stimme)* schwach; *(Getränk, bes. Bier)* schwach, dünn; *s pl (Oxford)* erste(s) Examen *n* für den B.A.; Kleinanzeigen *f pl*; *fam* Leibwäsche *f*; *in a ~ way* (in) bescheiden(em Umfang, -en Grenzen); *on the ~ side* ein bißchen, etwas zu klein; *to feel ~* kleinlaut sein; *to look ~* nach nichts aussehen; *to sing ~* klein beigeben; *the ~ of the back (anat)* Kreuz *n*; **~ arms** *pl* Handfeuerwaffen *f pl*; **~ beer** *fig* Kleinigkeit *f*; kleine(r) Wicht *m*; *to think no ~~ of o.s.* keine geringe Meinung von sich haben; *it's ~~ (fig)* das sind kleine Fische; **~-bore rifle** Kleinkalibergewehr *n*; **~ change** Klein-, Wechselgeld *n*; *fig* leere Redensarten *f pl*; seichte Unterhaltung *f*; **~ coal** Kohlengrus *m*; **~ farmer, holder** Kleinbauer *m*;

~ **fry** kleine Fische *m pl a. fig*; kleine Kinder *n pl*; *fig* kleine Leute *pl*; Nebensächlichkeiten *f pl*; ~ **hand** gewöhnliche Handschrift *f*; ~ **holding** Kleinbesitz *m*; *the* ~ **hours** *pl* die frühen Morgenstunden; ~ **intestine** Dünndarm *m*; **~ish** ['-iʃ] ein bißchen, etwas klein; ~ **letter** Kleinbuchstabe *f*; ~ **matter** Kleinigkeit *f*; **~-minded** *a* kleinlich, engstirnig; **~ness** ['-nis] Kleinheit; Beschränktheit; Geringfügigkeit; Kleinlichkeit *f*; ~ **potatoes** *pl Am fam* Nebenfigur, -sache *f*; kleine Leute *pl*; Belanglosigkeiten *f pl*; kleine Fische *m pl*; **~pox** Pocken, Blattern *pl*; **~-screen** Fernseh-; ~ **stock** Kleinvieh *n*; **~sword** Degen *m*, Rapier *n*; ~ **talk** Plauderei *f*; **~-time** *a fam* klein; Klein-, Neben-; nebensächlich, belanglos, unbedeutend; **~-town** *a* kleinstädtisch; ~ **tradesman, trader** kleine(r) Geschäftsmann *m*; ~ **tradespeople** *pl* kleine Geschäftsleute *pl*.

smalt [smɔ:lt] Kobalt-, Blauglas *n*; Schmalte *f*.

smarmy ['smɑ:mi] *fam* kriecherisch.

smart [smɑ:t] *itr* (heftig) schmerzen, (sehr) weh tun (*from* von); Schmerz empfinden, leiden (*under* unter); *fig* grollen; büßen müssen (*for* für); *s* Schmerz *m*; Leid *n*, Kummer *m*; *a* schmerzend; heftig, scharf, kräftig; lebhaft, munter; flink, gewandt, tüchtig, klug, gescheit; schlau, gerissen, gewitzt; unverschämt, frech; frisch, sauber; schmuck, fesch, elegant, schick, modern, *fam* schmissig, spritzig; *fam* tüchtig, gewaltig, beträchtlich; ~ **alec(k)** ['-ælek] *Am* Neunmalkluge(r), Besserwisser *m*; **~en** ['-n] *tr (to ~ up)* auffrischen, -polieren, herausputzen; in Schwung bringen; *itr* frisch, sauber, schöner werden; aufleben, in Schwung kommen; *to ~~ o.s. up* sich schön machen; **~-money** Schmerzensgeld *n*; **~ness** ['-nis] Heftigkeit, Schärfe; Lebhaftigkeit; Gewandtheit *f*, Schneid *m*, Tüchtigkeit; Schlauheit, Gerissenheit; Unverschämtheit; Frische, Sauberkeit; Eleganz *f*; *the* ~ **set** die elegante Welt *f*; **~y** ['-i] *Am sl* Klugscheißer *m*.

smash [smæʃ] *tr (to ~ up)* zerschmettern, zerschlagen; *(Fenster)* einwerfen, -schlagen, -hauen; (vernichtend) schlagen, (schwer) treffen, ruinieren; *(Tennis)* schmettern; *itr* in Stücke gehen, zerbrechen; zs.brechen, zerschellen; (heftig) aufea.prallen, zs.stoßen; *fig* Bank(e)rott, *fam* Pleite machen, pleite gehen; *s* heftige(r) Schlag; *(Tennis)* Schmetterball *m*; Zerbrechen, Zerkrachen *n*; Krach, Knall; *(~-up)* heftige(r) Zs.stoß, -prall, *fig* Zs.bruch, Ruin, Bank(e)rott *m*, Pleite *f*; Pfefferminzwasser *n* mit Schnaps; *(Zeitung) Am sl* sensationelle Nachricht *f*; *Am sl* tolle(r) Erfolg *m*; *adv* krachend; *to ~ down, in (Tür)* einschlagen; *all to ~* in tausend Stücke; *to come, to go to ~ (fam)* in Stücke, *fig* in die Brüche gehen; *to ~ to bits* in tausend Stücke zerbrechen, zerschlagen; **~-and-grab raid** Schaufenstereinbruch *m*; **~er** ['-ə] *sl* (Zs.-)Knall, Bums; *fig* schwere(r) Schlag; Knüller *m*, Bomben-, Pfundssache *f*, Ding *n* mit 'nem Pfiff; Pfundskerl *m*, Prachtmädel *n*; ~ **hit** *theat* Bombenerfolg *m*; **~ing** ['-iŋ] *a* niederschmetternd; *(Kritik)* vernichtend; *(Schlag)* heftig; *sl* toll, gewaltig, mächtig, phantastisch; **~-up** Zs.stoß; Zs.bruch *m*.

smattering ['smætəriŋ] Halbbildung; oberflächliche Kenntnis *f* (*in, of* gen).

smear [smiə] *tr* beschmieren (*with* mit); *(Fett)* auftragen, schmieren (*on* auf); einschmieren (*with* mit); *fig* beschmutzen, verleumden; *Am sl (jdn)* (vollständig) fertigmachen, erledigen; *Am sl* bestechen (*s.o.* jdn), schmieren (*s.o.* jdm); *itr* schmierig werden *od* sein; sich verwischen; *s* (Schmier-, Schmutz-) Fleck *m*; Geschmier *n*; *med* Abstrich *m*; *fig (~ campaign)* Verleumdung(sfeldzug *m*) *f*; **~case** *Am* Quark *m*; ~ **word** Anzüglichkeit *f*; **~y** ['-ri] schmierig, schmutzig; fettig.

smell [smel] *irr smelt, smelt* [smelt] *tr* riechen; wittern *a. fig*; beriechen, schnüffeln an; *itr* riechen (*at* an; *of* nach); duften; stinken *a. fig*; *Am sl* nichts los haben, nichts taugen, unangenehm sein; *s* Geruch(ssinn); Geruch, Duft; Gestank *m*; *to have, to take a ~ at s.th.* etw beriechen *a. fig*; *to ~ to high heaven* zum Himmel stinken; *to ~ of the lamp* augewandte Mühe erkennen lassen; *to ~ a rat* Lunte, *fam* den Braten riechen; *to ~* **about,** *to ~* **round** herumschnüffeln *a. fig*; *to ~* **out** aufstöbern, ausfindig machen; *fig* herausfinden; *to ~* **up** verpesten; **~er** ['-ə] *fig* Spürnase; *pop* Nase; übelriechende Sache *od* Person *f*; **~ing-bottle** Riechfläschchen *n*; **~ing-salt** Riechsalz *n*; **~y** ['-i] *fam* übelriechend.

smelt [smelt] **1.** *pret u. pp* von *smell*; **2.** *tr metal* (aus)schmelzen, verhütten; *to ~ down* einschmelzen; **~ing** ['-iŋ] Schmelzen, Verhütten *n*; *~~-furnace* Schmelzofen *m*; *~~-plant (min)* Hütte *f*; *~~-pot* Schmelztiegel *m*; **3.** *zoo* Stint *m*.

smil|e [smail] *tr* lächelnd ausdrücken; *itr* lächeln; anlächeln (*at, on, upon s.o.* jdn); zulächeln (*at s.o.* jdm); *s* Lächeln *n a. fig*; *pl* Gunst *f*; *to ~~ approval* zustimmend lächeln; *he is all ~~s* er lacht übers ganze Gesicht; **~ing** ['-iŋ] lächelnd; *fig* lachend.

*

smirch [smə:tʃ] *tr* beschmieren; beschmutzen, besudeln *a. fig*; *fig* Unehre, Schande machen (*s.o.* jdm); *s* (Schmutz-) Fleck; *fig* Schandfleck *m*.

smirk [smə:k] *itr* hämisch lächeln; *s* Grinsen *n*.

smite [smait] *irr smote, smitten tr* (heftig) schlagen, treffen; überwältigen, niederwerfen, (be)strafen, vernichten; *(to ~ dead)* erschlagen, töten; überfallen, heimsuchen; *fig* ergreifen, hin-, mitreißen, begeistern, entflammen; beunruhigen, plagen; *itr* schlagen, einschlagen (*on, upon* auf); treffen (*on, upon* auf); *to ~* **down** niederschlagen; *to ~* **off** abschlagen, -hauen; *to ~ hip and thigh* vernichtend schlagen; *my conscience smote me* es tat mir außerordentlich leid; *my heart smote me* es gab mir e-n Stich (ins Herz).

smith [smiθ] Schmied *m*; **~ery** ['smiðəri] Schmiedehandwerk *n*; Schmiede *f*; **~y** ['smiði] *Am* Schmiede *f*.

smither|eens [smiðə'ri:nz] *pl* Stückchen *n pl*, Splitter *m pl*; *to go to ~~* in die Brüche, *fam* kaputtgehen; *to smash (in)to ~~* in Stücke schlagen; **~s** ['smiðəz] *fam* = *~eens*.

smitten ['smitn] *pp* von *smite a* (seelisch) gebrochen, geknickt, sehr mitgenommen; begeistert, hingerissen, Feuer u. Flamme (*with* von); *fam* verknallt, verschossen, verliebt (*by, with* in).

smock [smɔk] *s* (Arbeits-)Kittel *m*; Schürzenbluse *f*; **~-frock** Bauernkittel *m*; **~ing** ['-iŋ] Smokarbeit *f*.

smog [smɔg] rauchgeschwängerte(r) Industrienebel *m*.

smok|e [smouk] *s* Rauch, Qualm; Dampf, Nebel(schwaden) *m*; *(Tabak-)* Rauchen *n*; *fig* Schall u. Rauch *m*; (dunkle) Wetterwolken *f pl fig*; *fam* Zigarette, Zigarre, Pfeife *f* Tabak; *pl fam* Tabakwaren *f pl*; *itr (Feuer u. Raucher)* rauchen, *fam* paffen; qualmen; dampfen; *Am sl* wütend sein, kochen; *tr* an-, verräuchern; *(mit Rauch)* schwärzen; *(to ~ out) (Ungeziefer)* ausräuchern *a. mil*, *fam* hinausekeln, entlarven; *mil* einnebeln; *(Fleisch, Fisch)* räuchern; *(Tabak)* rauchen; *to end, to go up in ~~ (fig)* in Rauch aufgehen; ergebnislos verlaufen; *to have a ~~* e-e Zigarettenpause machen; *no ~~ without a fire* keine Wirkung ohne Ursache; *~~-bomb* Rauchbombe *f*; *~~-cloud* Nebel-, Rauchwolke *f*; *~~-consumer* Rauchverzehrer *m*; *~~-dried (a) (Fleisch, Fisch)* geräuchert; *~~ dust* Flugasche *f*; *~~ house* Räucherkammer *f*; *~~ pot* Nebeltopf *m*; *~~-projector (mil)* Nebelwerfer *m*; *~~-room* = *~ing-room*; *~~-screen (mil)* Rauch-, Nebelwand; *fig* Vernebelung *f*; *~~-signal* Rauchsignal *n*; *~~-shell* Nebelgranate *f*; *~~ stack* (Fabrik-)Schornstein, Schlot *m*; *~~-stained (a)* rauchgeschwärzt; **~eless** ['-lis] rauchlos; **~er** ['-ə] Raucher *m a. rail*; = *~ing concert*; *Am* Herrengesellschaft *f*, -abend *m*; **~ing** ['-iŋ] Rauchen; Räuchern *n*; *no ~~* Rauchen verboten! *~~-car(riage)* Raucherwagen *m*; *~~-compartment* Raucherabteil *n*; *~~-concert* Konzert *n*, bei dem geraucht werden darf; *~~-jacket* Hausjacke *f*; *~~-room* Rauchzimmer *n*; **~y** ['-i] *(Feuer)* qualmend; rauchig; verräuchert; rauchgeschwärzt; rauchfarben; nebelartig; *~~ quartz (min)* Rauchtopas *m*.

smooch, smooge [smu:tʃ, smu:dʒ] *Am sl tr* ausborgen; küssen, streicheln; **~er** ['-ə] *Am sl* Nassauer; Schmuser *m*.

smooth [smu:ð] *a* glatt; eben; abgenutzt; gleichmäßig, ruhig, ungestört, reibungslos *a. tech*; geschmeidig; weich, sanft, mild(e); *(Worte)* glatt, einschmeichelnd; angenehm; *(Wein)* mild; *Am sl* perfekt, großartig, hervorragend, hübsch, gutaussehend; *tr* glätten; ebnen *a. fig*; *tech* planieren; *fig* beruhigen, besänftigen; *adv* glatt; *fig* ohne Schwierigkeit(en); *s* glatte, ebene Stelle; *fig* mühelose Sache *f*; *to give o.'s hair a ~* das Haar glattstreichen; *to have a ~ manner, tongue* katzenfreundlich sein; *to make things ~ for s.o.* jdm die Schwierigkeiten aus dem Weg räumen; *to take the rough with the ~* das Gute wie das Böse hinnehmen; *to ~* **away** *(Schwierigkeiten)* beseitigen; *to ~* **down** *tr* glätten, bügeln; *fig* beruhigen, beschwichtigen; *itr* sich glätten; *to ~* **over** bemänteln, beschönigen; **~-bore** *(Geschützrohr)* glatt; **~-faced** *a* glattwangig, bartlos; *fig* katzenfreundlich; **~ie, ~y** ['-i] *Am sl* hübsche(r) Käfer *m*; **~ing-iron** Plätt-, Bügeleisen *n*; **~ing-plane** Schlichthobel *m*; ~ **muscle** glattgestrichene(r) Muskel *m*; **~ness** ['-nis] Glätte; Geschmeidigkeit; Sanftheit *f*; **~-shaven** *a* glattrasiert; **~-spoken, -tongued** *a* katzenfreundlich; schmeichlerisch.

smother ['smʌðə] *tr* ersticken; überschütten, überhäufen, ganz zudecken (*in, with* mit); *fig* unterdrücken; *s* (dicker) Qualm, dichte(r) Nebel *m*.

smo(u)lder ['smouldə] *itr* schwelen, glimmen *a. fig*; *fig* glühen (*with* vor); *s* Schwelen *n*; Qualm *m*; **~ing plant** Schwelanlage *f*.

smudg|e [smʌdʒ] *s* Schmutzfleck *m*; *bes. Am* qualmende(s) Feuer *n*; *tr* beschmutzen, beschmieren; verwischen; *itr* schmutzig werden; klecksen; **~y** ['-i] schmutzig, schmierig; verwischt.

smug [smʌg] *a* selbstzufrieden, -gefällig; eingebildet; blasiert; geziert; *s sl* Streber *m*; **~ness** ['-nis] Selbstzufriedenheit, Blasiertheit *f*.

smuggl|e ['smʌgl] *tr itr* schmuggeln (*s.th. into England* etw nach England); *to ~~ away* verschwinden lassen; **~er** ['-ə] Schmuggler, Schleichhändler *m*; **~ing** ['-iŋ] Schmuggel(n *n*), Schleichhandel *m*.

smut [smʌt] *s* Ruß(flocke *f*); Schmutzfleck *m*; *fig* Zoten *f pl*; *bot* Brand; Brandpilz *m*; *tr* beschmutzen *a. fig*; *bot* brandig machen; *typ* unsauber abziehen; *itr* schmutzig, *bot* brandig werden; **~ty** ['-i] schmutzig *a. fig*; *fig* zotig, unanständig; *bot* brandig.

smutch [smʌtʃ] *tr* beschmutzen; *s* Schmutz(fleck); Ruß *m*.

snack [snæk] Imbiß *m*; **~-bar, -counter** Imbißhalle, Frühstücksstube, Schnellgaststätte *f*.

snaffle ['snæfl] **1.** *s (~-bit) (Zaum)* Trense(ngebiß *n*) *f*; *tr (Pferd)* an die Trense nehmen; im Zaume halten; *to ride on the ~ (fig)* die Zügel schießen lassen (*s.o.* jdm); **2.** *tr sl* organisieren, stibitzen, klauen; verhaften.

snafu ['snæfu:, snæ'fu:] *adv Am mil sl* in der üblichen Unordnung; *tr* durchea.bringen; *s* Durcheinander *n*, Dummheit *f*.

snag [snæg] *s* Zacke(n *m*) *f*; Baum-, Aststumpf; *med* Raffzahn, Zahnstumpf; Riß *m (im Strumpf)*; *fig fam* (unerwartetes) Hindernis *n*, verborgene Schwierigkeit *f*, Nachteil, *fam* Haken *m*; *tr Am (Schiff)* durch e-n Baumstumpf im Gewässer beschädigen; *Am (Gewässer)* von Baumstümpfen befreien; *tech* grobschleifen; *(Strumpf)* beschädigen; *fig* e-n Stein in den Weg legen (*s.o.* jdm); *to strike a ~ (fam)* auf e-e Schwierigkeit, ein Hindernis stoßen (*in carrying out a plan* bei der Ausführung e-s Planes); **~ged** [-d], **~gy** ['-i] *a* knorrig, zackig; voller Baumstümpfe.

snail [sneil] (Schnirkel-)Schnecke *f*; *fig* Faulpelz *m*; *at a ~'s pace* im Schneckentempo; **~-shell** Schneckenhaus *n*; **~-wheel** *tech* Schneckenrad *n*.

snak|e [sneik] *s* Schlange *f a. fig tech*; *itr* sich schlängeln, sich winden; *tr Am fam* ziehen; zerren, reißen (an); *a ~~ in the grass (fig)* ein hinterhältiger, heimtückischer Mensch *m*; *common, grass-~~* Blindschleiche *f*; *~~-bite* Schlangenbiß *m*; *~~-charmer* Schlangenbeschwörer *m*; *~~-poison, -venom* Schlangengift *n*; *~~-ranch* Schlangenfarm *f*; *Am sl* Bordell *n*; *~~-skin* Schlangenhaut *f (Leder)*; **~y** ['-i] schlangenartig; sich schlängelnd; voller Schlangen; *fig* falsch, hinterlistig.

snap [snæp] *itr* schnappen (*at* nach); zuschnappen; rasch zupacken; *at s.o.* jdn anfahren, -kläffen; platzen, (zer)springen, (zer)reißen; knallen, knacken, knistern, knipsen; *(to ~ shut) (Tür, Schloß)* zuschlagen, zuschnappen; *tr (to ~ up)* (auf)schnappen; fassen, greifen, haschen; zerbrechen, -reißen; zuklappen, zuknallen; knallen lassen; *(to ~ out)* herausfahren mit; *(Worte)* hervorstoßen; knipsen *bes. phot*; *s* (Zu-)Schnappen, Zubeißen *n*; schnelle(r) (Zu-)Griff *m*; Platzen, (Zer-)Springen *n*, Knacks; Knall *m*, Knackgeräusch; Geblaffe *n*; *(cold ~)* Kältewelle *f*; (Knusper-)Keks *m*; Schnappschloß *n*; Druckknopf; *Am* Schnappschuß *m*; *Am fam* Zackigkeit *f*, Mumm, Schneid, Schwung *m*; *Am sl* Kinderspiel *n*, leichte Arbeit, sichere Sache, einmalige Gelegenheit *f*; *Am sl fig* Waschlappen *m*; *attr* schnell, eilig, rasch, unüberlegt, übereilt; Schnapp-; *sl* simpel, kinderleicht; *adv Am* mit e-m Knall; *to ~ away* wegschnappen; entreißen; *to ~ in* einrasten; *to ~ off* wegschnappen; zerbrechen; *to ~ s.o.'s head, nose off* jdn ankläffen, -brüllen, -fahren, zs.stauchen; *to ~ on (el)* anknipsen; *to ~ out* ärgerlich sagen; *(Befehl)* schneidig erteilen; *el* ausknipsen; *to ~ out of it* sich aufrappeln; *Am* sich zs.reißen, sich an die Arbeit machen; *~ out of it! (Am fam)* nimm dich zs.! *to ~ up* anbrüllen; das Wort abschneiden (*s.o.* jdm); unüberlegt kaufen; *to ~ o.'s fingers at s.o.* jdn über die Achsel ansehen, links liegen, unbeachtet lassen; *not to give the ~ of o.'s fingers for* sich keinen Deut kümmern um; *~ into it! (fam)* los! an die Arbeit! *not a ~* nicht ein Fünkchen, nicht e-e Spur *od* Idee; *don't make ~ judg(e)ments (Am fam)* urteile nicht vorschnell! **~-bolt, -lock** Schnappschloß *n*; **~dragon** *bot* Löwenmaul; Herausfischen *n* von Rosinen u. ä. aus brennendem Branntwein *(Weihnachtsspiel)*; **~-fastener** Druckknopf *m*; **~pish** ['-iʃ] bissig, scharf; *fig* reizbar, unwirsch, barsch; schnippisch; **~pishness** ['-iʃnis] Bissigkeit; Barschheit *f*; schnippische(s) Wesen *n*; **~py** ['-i] bissig *a. fig*; *fam* lebhaft, munter, flott, zackig, schneidig, auf Draht; *Am sl* hübsch, anziehend, elegant; *make it ~~! (fam)* fix! los, los! lebhaft! zackig! **~-ring** Sprengring *m*; **~shot** *s* Schnappschuß *m*, Momentaufnahme *f*; *tr itr* knipsen; **~-vote** Blitzabstimmung *f*.

snar|e [snɛə] *s* Schlinge, Falle *f a. fig*; *fig* Fallstrick *m*; *tr* in e-r Schlinge fangen; *fig* e-e Falle stellen (*s.o.* jdm); **~ky** ['snɑ:ki] *fam* schlecht gelaunt.

snarl [snɑ:l] **1.** *itr* (an)knurren (*at s.o.* jdn) *a. fig*; die Zähne fletschen; *fig* schimpfen; *tr (to ~ out)* knurrend, brummend sagen; *s* Zähnefletschen; Knurren; *fig* Murren *n*; **2.** *tr* verwirren, *itr* durchea.geraten *a. fig*; *fig* sich verwickeln, sich komplizieren; *s* Knoten *m*; *fig* Durcheinander, Gewirr *n*; Verwirrung, Verwick(e)lung; *(traffic ~)* Verkehrsstockung *f*.

snatch [snætʃ] *tr* schnappen; (er)greifen, fassen, (er)haschen, erwischen *a. fig, fam* ergattern; entreißen; *(Kuß)* rauben; wegnehmen (*from* von); *(Gelegenheit)* beim Schopf ergreifen; *Am sl* kidnappen; *itr* schnappen, haschen, rasch zugreifen (*at* nach); *s* Schnappen, Zupacken *n*, schnelle(r) Griff *m*; Stück (-chen) *n*, Brocken; *fig* Augenblick, Moment(chen *n*); *Am sl* Kindesraub, Diebstahl *m*; *by, in ~es* stoß-, ruckweise, mit Unterbrechungen; *to ~ away, off* wegschnappen; *to ~ up* rasch packen, aufgreifen; *to put the ~ on (Am sl)* Besitz ergreifen von; festnehmen (*s.o.* jdn); **~y** ['-i] unzs.hängend, unregelmäßig, unterbrochen.

sneak [sni:k] *itr* schleichen, kriechen *a. fig* (*into* in); sich davonmachen, *sl* petzen; *tr sl (Schule)* angeben, verpetzen; *sl* mausen; *s* Schleichen *n*; = *~er*; *to ~ in* sich einschleichen; *to ~ off, past, round* weg-, vorbei-, herumschleichen; *to ~ out* sich herausschleichen (*of* aus); *fig* sich drücken (*of* von); **~er** ['-ə] Schleicher, Kriecher; *sl* Petzer *m*; *pl Am fam* Turnschuhe *m pl*; **~ing** ['-iŋ] heimlich, geheim; hinterlistig; **~-thief** Gelegenheitsdieb *m*; **~y** ['-i] heimlich; heimtückisch; feige.

sneer [sniə] *itr* höhnisch lächeln; höhnen, spotten (*at* über); *tr* höhnisch (lächelnd) sagen; verspotten, verhöhnen; *s* Hohn(lachen, -gelächter *n*), Spott *m*; höhnische Bemerkung *f*; **~ing** ['-riŋ] höhnisch, spöttisch.

sneeze [sni:z] *itr* niesen; *tr Am sl* packen, entführen; *s* Niesen *n*; *it is not to be ~d at (fam)* das ist nicht so ohne.

snick [snik] **1.** *s* Kerbe *f*, Ritz *m*; *tr* ritzen, einkerben; **2.** *tr* leicht anschlagen.

snicker *s. snigger*.

snid|e [snaid] *fam* falsch, nachgemacht, billig; *fig* gemein; **~y** ['-i] *sl* schlau.

sniff [snif] *itr* schnauben; schniefen; schnüffeln, schnuppern (*at* an); die Nase rümpfen (*at* über); *tr* in die Nase einziehen; beschnüffeln, beriechen; riechen an; *fig* wittern; *s* Schnauben, Schnüffeln *n*; Brise *f (Seeluft)*; **~y** ['-i] verächtlich, schnippisch; hochnäsig; übelriechend.

sniffle ['snifl] *itr* schniefen, schnauben; *s* Geschnüffel, Geschnaube *n*; *pl Am fam* Schnupfen *m*.

snifter ['sniftə] *Am* Kognakschwenker *m*; *fam* Schnäpschen *n*.

snigger ['snigə] *itr* kichern (*at, over* über); *(Pferd)* wiehern.

snip [snip] *tr* schnippen, (ab)schnippeln; schneiden; *itr* schnippe(l)n; *to ~ off* abschneiden; *s* kleine(r) Schnitt, Einschnitt; Schnipsel, Schnippel *m od s*; *fam* Schneider; *Am fam* Knirps; *fam* gute(r) (Ein-)Kauf *m*, günstige Gelegenheit; *pl* Metallschere *f*; **~pet** ['-it] Schnipsel, Schnippel *m od s*; *Am fam* Knirps *m*; *pl* Bruchstücke *n pl*.

snip|e [snaip] *s orn* Schnepfe *f*; *fig* Tropf, Trottel; Schuß *m* aus dem Hinterhalt; *Am sl* Kippe *f*; *itr tr* Schnepfen jagen *od* schießen; *mil* aus dem Hinterhalt (ab)schießen (*at* auf); **~er** ['-ə] Hecken-, Scharfschütze *m*.

snitch [snitʃ] *sl tr itr* stibitzen, mausen; *itr* angeben, verpfeifen (*on s.o.* jdn).

snivel ['snivl] *itr* (dauernd) schnüffeln; heulen, schluchzen; Krokodilstränen weinen; *s* Nasenschleim, Rotz *m*; Schnüffeln *n*; Heulerei *f*; *I ~* mir läuft die Nase; **~(l)er** ['-ə] weinerliche(r) Mensch *m*, Heulsuse *f*; **~(l)ing** ['-iŋ] Rotz-; weinerlich; wehleidig.

snob [snɔb] Snob, Protz *m*; **~bery** ['-əri] protzenhafte(s) Benehmen *n*, Großtuerei *f*; **~bish** ['-iʃ] protzenhaft, großtuerisch; aufgeblasen, dünkelhaft.

snood [snu:d] Haarband, -netz *n*.

snook [snu:k] *itr: to cock a ~ at s.o.* jdm e-e lange Nase machen; **~er** ['-ə] *(Art)* Billard *n*.

snoop [snu:p] *itr fam (to ~ around)* herumschnüffeln, -spionieren; *s* Herumschnüffeln *n*; **~er** ['-ə] Schnüffler *m*.

snoot [snu:t] *Am fam s* Nase; Schnute, Fratze *f*; *tr* verächtlich behandeln; *to have a ~ full* besoffen sein; **~y** ['-i] *fam* hochnäsig, von sich überzogen.

snooze [snu:z] *s fam* Nickerchen *n*; *itr fam* ein Nickerchen machen.

snore [snɔ:] *itr* schnarchen; *s* Schnarchen, Geschnarche *n*.

snorkel ['snɔ:kəl] Schnorchel *m*.

snort [snɔ:t] *itr* schnauben (*with rage* vor Wut); schnaufen; prusten; *s* Schnauben, Schnaufen *n*; *mar mil* Schnorchel; *Am sl* Schluck *m* Whisky; **~er** ['-ə] *fam* heftige(r) Sturm *m*; tolle Sache *f*; Anschnauzer *m*; **~y** ['-i] *fam* gereizt.

snot [snɔt] *sl* Rotz *m*; **~ty** ['-i] *sl* rotzig, Rotz-; lümmelhaft, frech; gereizt; gemein, verächtlich; *Am sl* patzig.

snout [snaut] Schnauze *f a. fig*, Rüssel *m*; *fam* Nase *f*, Zinken *m*; *tech* Auslaufrinne *f*; **~-beetle** Rüsselkäfer *m*.

snow [snou] *s* Schnee *a. fig*; Schneefall *m*; *pl* Schneemassen *f pl*; *sl* Koks *m*; *itr* schneien; *(to ~ in)* hereinströmen; *tr fig* ausschütten; *~ed in, up, (Am) under* eingeschneit, *fig Am* überschüttet, überhäuft (*with* mit); *to be ~ed under with (fig)* ersticken in; überhäuft sein mit; **~ball** *s* Schneeball; *bot* Schneeball(strauch) *m*; *itr* (sich) schneeballen; *fig* lawinenartig anwachsen; *tr* mit Schneebällen werfen nach; **~bank** Schneeverwehung *f*; **~berry** *bot* Schneebeere *f*; **~bird** *orn* Schneeammer *f*, Lerchenfink *m*; *sl* Kokain-, Heroinsüchtige(r) *m*; **~-blind** schneeblind; **~-blindness** Schneeblindheit *f*; **~-boot** Schneestiefel *m*; **~-bound** *a* eingeschneit; **~-broth** Schmelzwasser *n*; **~ bunny** *fam* Schihaserl *n*; **~-bunting, -finch** *orn* Schneeammer *f*, Lerchenfink *m*; **~cap** Schneekappe *f (e-s Berges)*; **~-capped** *a (Berg)* schneebedeckt; **~-chain** Schneekette *f*; **~-cloud** Schneewolke *f*; **~ cover** Schneedecke *f*; **~-drift** Schneewehe *f*; **~drop** *bot* Schneeglöckchen *n*; **~fall** Schneefall *m*, -menge *f*; **~ fence** Schneezaun *m*; **~-field** Schneefläche *f*, -feld *n*; **~flake** Schneeflocke; *orn* Schneeammer *f*; *bot* Große(s) Schnee-, Märzglöckchen *n*; **~-flurry** Schneegestöber, -treiben *n*; **~-goggles** *pl* Schneebrille *f*; **~-grouse, -hen** *orn* Schneehuhn *n*; **~-job** *Am sl* verlogene(s) Geschwätz *n*, Aufschneiderei *f*; **~-line, -limit** Schneegrenze *f (im Gebirge)*; **~-man** Schneemann *m*; **~mobile, ~ weasel** *Am* Motorschlitten *m*, Schneeauto *n*; Schneetraktor *m*; **~ pit** Schneeloch *n*; **~-plough,** *Am* **~plow** Schneepflug *m*; **~ pudding** Schaumpudding *m*; **~ region** Schneeregion *f*; **~shed** *Am rail* Lawinengalerie *f*; **~shoe** Schneeteller, -schuh *m*; **~-slab** Schneebrett *n*; **~slide** *Am*, **~slip** Lawine *f*; **~storm** Schneesturm *m*; **~ tyre, tire** Winterreifen *m*; **~ water** Schmelz-, Schneewasser *n*; **~-white** schneeweiß; **~y** ['-i] schneeig; Schnee-; verschneit; schneeweiß; rein.

snub [snʌb] *tr* anfahren, ausschimpfen, anschnauzen; verächtlich, von oben herab behandeln; *mar (abrollendes Tau, Kabel)* (mit e-m Ruck) anhalten; *s* Anpfiff, Anschnauzer *m*; Zurücksetzung; Beleidigung *f*; **~ nose** Stupsnase *f*; **~-nosed** *a* stupsnasig.

snuff [snʌf] **1.** *tr* in die Nase einziehen; beschnüffeln; *fig* wittern; *itr* schnüffeln (*at* an); schnauben, schnaufen; (Tabak) schnupfen; *s* Schnauben, Schnaufen; Geschnüffel *n*; Schnupftabak *m*; Prise *f* (Tabak); Schnupfpulver *n*; *up to ~ (fam)* auf der Höhe, auf Draht; *pinch of ~* Prise *f* (Tabak); **~-box** Schnupftabak(s)dose *f*; **~-colo(u)red** gelbbraun; **~le** ['-l] *itr* schnauben, schnaufen; schniefen; *s pl* (Stock-) Schnupfen *m*; **~-stick** Kautabak, Priem *m*; **~y** ['-i] schnupftabakartig; Schnupftabak gebrauchend; mit Schnupftabak beschmutzt; *fig* unangenehm, reizlos; schlecht-, übelgelaunt, verschnupft; **2.** *s* Lichtschnuppe *f*; *tr (Licht)* putzen; *(Zigarette)* ausdrücken; *to ~ out (tr)* (aus)löschen; *fig* auslöschen, vernichten, zerstören, ein Ende bereiten (*s.th.* e-r S); *itr fam* abkratzen, sterben; **~fers** ['-əz] *pl* Lichtputzschere *f*.

snug [snʌg] *a* geborgen, geschützt; behaglich, gemütlich; nett, sauber; *(Kleidung)* genau passend, eng(anliegend); *(Einkommen)* auskömmlich, reichlich; *(Stellung)* einträglich; *(Schiff)* seetüchtig; *(Hafen)* geschützt; versteckt, verborgen; *adv* behaglich; *tr* gemütlich machen *od* einrichten; *to ~ down (mar)* sturmklar machen; es sich behaglich machen; *as ~ as a bug in a rug* wie ein Fisch im Wasser; **~-fitting** eng anliegend; **~gery** ['-əri] gemütliche(s) Heim *od* Zimmer *n*; gute Stelle *f*; **~gle** ['-l] *itr* sich kuscheln; sich anschmiegen (*to* an); *tr* kuscheln; (schützend) an sich schmiegen; an sich drükken; *to ~~ down* es sich gemütlich machen; **~ness** ['-nis] Bequemlichkeit *f*, Wohlbefinden *n*.

so [sou; so, sə] **1.** *adv* so; *(ever ~) fam* dermaßen, -art, so (sehr); *~ late, long, many (that)* so spät, so lange, so viele (, daß); *not ~ ... as* nicht so ... wie; *~ ... as to* so ... daß; *~ did I* ich auch; *~ I did* ja, das habe ich getan; *~ be it* amen! *~ it was* ja, so war es; *~ they say* so heißt es; man sagt so; *and ~ on, and ~ forth, ~ on and ~ forth* und so weiter; *is that ~?* wirklich? *be ~ kind as to* sei so freundlich und ... ; *or ~ (nachgestellt)* oder so, etwa; *~ far* bis jetzt, bisher; soweit; *~ far as* soviel, soweit *conj*; *~ far from* weit davon entfernt, zu; *~ far, ~ good* so weit ganz gut; *~ long as* solange *conj*; *~ long! (fam)* auf Wiedersehen! *~ much as* sogar; *not ~ much as* nicht einmal; *~ much for* soviel über; *~ much ~ that* derart, daß; *~ much nonsense, rubbish!* alles Unsinn! alles Quatsch! *~ I hope, I hope ~* das hoffe ich, ich hoffe es; *~ I see* ich seh's, das sehe ich; *you don't say ~! do you say ~?* wirklich? *I told you ~* ich sagte es doch! sagte ich es nicht? *just ~! quite ~!* ganz richtig! *thanks ever ~ much* vielen Dank! *~ help me God!* so wahr mir Gott helfe! **2.** *conj* so; also, darum, deshalb, daher; folglich; *~ that* so daß, damit; *~ as* so daß; vorausgesetzt, daß; *~ as to* um zu; *~ that's that (fam)* so, das wär's! damit Schluß! *~ what? (fam)* ja, und? **~-and-~** ['so(u)ənsou] *adv* soundso; *Mr S~~* Herr Soundso; **~-called** *a* sogenannt; **~-so** *adv* soso, lala; so einigermaßen; *a* ganz leidlich.

soak [souk] *tr* einweichen, tränken, durchnässen, -feuchten; *(to ~ up, in)* auf-, einsaugen; *sl fig* schröpfen; *sl* saufen; *sl* besoffen machen; *Am sl* (tüchtig) eine langen (*s.o.* jdm), durchprügeln; *Am sl* tüchtig übers Ohr hauen; *Am sl (als Pfand)* versetzen; *itr* durchnäßt, naß, feucht werden; *(to ~ through)* (ein)sickern *a. fig*; *fig* eindringen, Fuß fassen *(into* in); *fam* saufen; *to ~ o.s. in (fig)* sich versenken in; *s* Ein-, Durchweichen, Feucht-, Naßwerden *n*; Einweichbrühe *f*; Regenguß *m*; *sl* Sauferei *f*; *sl* Säufer; *sl Am* mächtige(r) Schlag *m*; *in ~ (Am sl)* versetzt, auf dem Leihhaus; *~ed to the skin* naß bis auf die Haut, völlig durchnäßt; klatschnaß; **~age** ['-idʒ] Sickerwasser *n*; **~er** ['-ə] (tüchtiger) Regenguß; *sl* Säufer *m*; Babyhöschen *n*; **~ing** ['-iŋ] klatschnaß; *(Regenguß)* heftig.

soap [soup] *s* Seife *f a. chem*; *sl Am (bes.* Bestechungs-)Geld *n*; *tr* einseifen; *fig fam* Honig ums Maul schmieren (*s.o.* jdm); *to ~ o.s. down* sich abseifen; *no ~! (Am sl)* kommt nicht in die Tüte *od* in Frage! *a cake of ~* ein Stück Seife; *scented ~* Toilettenseife *f*; *soft ~* Schmierseife; *fig* Schmeichelei *f*; **~-boiler, -maker** Seifensieder *m*; **~box** *s* Seifenkiste; *Am* (Kiste als) behelfsmäßige Rednertribüne *f*; *itr Am* e-e Straßenrede halten; *a Am: ~~ orator* Straßenredner *m*; *~~ race* Seifenkistenrennen *n*; *~~ speech* Straßenrede *f*; **~-bubble** Seifenblase *f*; **~-dish** Seifenschale *f*; **~-flakes, -chips** *pl* Seifenflocken *f pl*; **~ opera** *Am radio fam* rührselige(s) Hörspiel *n*; **~-powder** Seifenpulver *n*; **~-solution** Seifenlösung *f*; **~stone** Speckstein *m*; **~-suds** *pl* Seifenlauge *f*; **~-works, -factory** Seifenfabrik *f*; **~wort** ['-wəːt] Seifenkraut *n*; **~y** ['-i] seifig; *fig sl* dick aufgetragen, ölig, schmeichelhaft.

soar [sɔː, sɔə] *itr* sich (in die Luft) erheben, steigen *a. fig*; *fig* ansteigen; schweben, gleiten; *aero* segeln; *(Preise)* steigen, in die Höhe schnellen; *fig* sich herausheben, hervorragen; **~ing** ['-riŋ] *a* (auf)steigend; auf-, emporstrebend *a. fig*; *com* steigend; *s* Segelfliegen *n*; Segelfliegerei *f*; *~~-certificate* Segelflugschein *m*; *~~-flight* Segelflug *m*; *~~-flyer, -pilot* Segelflieger *m*; *~~-plane* Segelflugzeug *n*; *~~-site* Segelfluggelände *n*.

sob [sɔb] *itr* schluchzen; *tr (to ~ out)* schluchzend sagen; *s* Schluchzen *n*; *attr Am sl* rührselig; Rühr-; sentimental; Kitsch-; *to ~ o.'s heart out* heiße Tränen, bitterlich weinen; *to ~ o.s. to sleep* sich in den Schlaf weinen; **~ sister** *Am sl* Journalistin *f* (die auf die Tränendrüse drückt); **~ story** *Am sl* rührselige, sentimentale Geschichte *f*; **~ stuff** *fam* Kitsch *m*; Schnulze *f*.

sober ['soubə] *a* nüchtern; mäßig, maßhaltend; gesetzt, ruhig, besonnen, ernst; einfach, schlicht; *(Farbe)* ruhig; vernünftig, gesund; bloß, rein; *tr itr (to ~ up, down)* nüchtern machen *od* ernüchtern; (wieder) nüchtern werden; *in ~ earnest* in vollem Ernst; *in o.'s ~ senses* bei klarem Verstand *od* Kopf; **~-minded** *a* ruhig, besonnen; **~ness** ['-nis], **sobriety** [so(u)'braiəti, sə-'] Nüchternheit; Mäßigkeit; Gesetztheit, Besonnenheit *f*, Ernst *m*; Schlichtheit, Einfachheit *f*; **~ sides** *fam* ernste(r), gesetzte(r) Mensch; Trauerkloß *m*.

sobriquet, soubriquet ['soubrikei] Spitzname *m*.

soccer, socker ['sɔkə] *fam* Fußballspiel *n*.

soci|ability [souʃə'biliti] Geselligkeit; Umgänglichkeit *f*; **~able** ['souʃəbl] *a* gesellig; umgänglich, freundlich, nett; *(Beisammensein)* gemütlich, ungezwungen; *s* Kremser *m*; Tandem; S-förmige(s) Sofa; *Am* gesellige(s) Beisammensein *n*, zwanglose Zs.kunft *f*; *~~ game* Gesellschaftsspiel *n*; **~al** ['souʃəl] *a* sozial; Sozial-, Gesellschafts-; gesellschaftlich; gesellig, umgänglich; Geselligkeits-; *s* gesellige(s), zwanglose(s) Beisammensein *n*; *~~ advancement* soziale(r) Aufstieg *m*; *~~ animal* Gesellschaftswesen *n*; *~~ climber* Streber *m*; *~~ contract, compact (pol)* Gesellschaftsvertrag *m*; *~~ evening* gesellige(r) Abend *m*; *~~ evil* Prostitution *f*; *~~ gathering* gesellige(s) Beisammensein *n*; *~~ income* Volkseinkommen *n*; *~~ insurance* Sozialversicherung *f*; *~~ legislation* Sozialgesetzgebung *f*; *~~ order, system* Sozial-, Gesellschaftsordnung *f*; *~~ policy* Sozialpolitik *f*; *~~-political* sozialpolitisch; *~~ position, rank, status* soziale, gesellschaftliche Rang(stufe *f*) *m*, Stellung *f*; *~~ problem* soziale Frage *f*; *~~ reform* Sozialreform *f*; *~~ reformer* Sozialreformer *m*; *~~ science* Sozialwissenschaften *f pl*; *~~ security* soziale Sicherheit; *Am* Sozialversicherung *f*; *~~ service, work* Fürsorge, Wohlfahrt *f*; *~~ services (pl)* soziale Einrichtungen *f pl*; *~~ stock* Gesellschaftskapital, -vermögen *n*; *~~ structure* Sozial-, gesellschaftliche Struktur *f*; *~~ studies (pl)* Gemeinschaftskunde *f*; *~~ welfare* soziale Fürsorge *f*; *~~ worker* Wohlfahrtspfleger, Fürsorger *m*; **~alism** ['-ʃəlizm] Sozialismus *m*; **~alist** ['-ʃəlist] *s* Sozialist *m*; **~alist(ic)** [souʃə'listik] sozialistisch; **~alite** ['souʃəlait] *Am fam* Angehörige(r) *m* der oberen Gesellschaftsklasse; **~ality** [souʃi'æliti] Geselligkeit *f*; **~alization** [souʃəlai'zeiʃən] Sozialisierung, Verstaatlichung *f*; **~alize** ['souʃəlaiz] *tr* gesellig machen; *pol* sozialisieren, verstaatlichen; *itr Am fam* verkehren (*with* mit); **~ety** [sə'saiəti] Gesellschaft; vornehme Welt *f*; Verein(igung *f*); Umgang *m*, Beziehungen *f pl*; *com* Gesellschaft, Genossenschaft *f*; Verband *m*; *building* **~~** Baugenossenschaft *f*; *co-operative* **~~** Konsumverein *m*; **~~** *column (Zeitung)* Nachrichten *f pl* aus der (hohen) Gesellschaft; **~~** *gossip* Gesellschaftsklatsch *m*; *the S~ of Friends* die Quäker; *the S~ of Jesus* die Gesellschaft Jesu, der Jesuitenorden; **~~** *man, woman* Mann *m*, Dame *f* der Gesellschaft; **~ological** [sousjə'lɔdʒikəl] soziologisch; **~ologist** [sousi'ɔlədʒist] Soziologe *m*; **~ology** [sousi'ɔlədʒi] Soziologie *f*.

sock [sɔk] **1.** Socke; Einlegesohle *f*; *Am sl* Sparstrumpf *m*, nette Stange *f* Geld; **2.** *to pull up o.'s ~s (fam)* sich ins Zeug legen; **3.** *sl tr* eine knallen, schmieren, 'runterhauen (*s.o.* jdm); verprügeln; *s* (Faust-)Schlag *a. fig*; *Am* tolle(r) Erfolg *m*; *adv* direkt, glatt; *to give s.o. a ~ on the jaw* jdm e-e 'runterhauen.

socker *s. soccer.*

socket ['sɔkit] *s* Hülse, Tülle, Muffe *f*; Rohransatz, -stutzen *m*; *el* Fassung; (*~ outlet*) Steckdose *f*; *radio* Sockel *m*; *anat* (Augen-)Höhle; (Gelenk-)Pfanne *f*; **~ joint** Kugelgelenk *m*; **~ wrench** Steckschlüssel *m*.

socle ['sɔkl] *arch* Sockel, Unterbau *m*.

sod [sɔd] **1.** *s* Rasen(stück *n*) *m*; *tr* mit Rasen(stücken) bedecken; *under the ~* unter der Erde; **2.** *vulg* Saukerl *m*.

soda ['soudə] Soda *f* od *n*, kohlensaure(s) Natrium; (*~ water*) Soda-, Selterswasser *n*; **~ biscuit, cracker** *Am (einfacher, ungesüßter)* Sodabiskuit *n*, -keks *m*; **~ clerk,** *Am* **jerk** *Am sl* Verkäufer(in *f*) *m* in e-r Erfrischungshalle; **~ fountain** *Am* Erfrischungshalle, Eisbar *f*; Mineralwasserausschank; Siphon *m*; **~ lye** *chem* Natronlauge *f*; **~ mint** Selterswasser *n* mit Pfefferminzgeschmack; **~ pop** Brause *f*, süße(r) Sprudel *m*; **~-water** Sodawasser *n*; Sprudel *m*.

sodden ['sɔdn] durchweicht, durchnäßt; *(Brot)* teigig, nicht durchgebakken; benommen, dumpf; blöde *(vom Trinken)*; aufgedunsen, käsig.

sodium ['soudjəm] *chem* Natrium *n*; **~ bicarbonate** doppeltkohlensaure(s) Natrium *n*; **~ carbonate** Natriumkarbonat *n*; **~ chlorate** Natriumchlorat *n*; **~ chloride** Natriumchlorid, Stein-, Kochsalz *n*; **~ hydroxide** Ätznatron *n*; **~ nitrate** Chilesalpeter *m*; **~ sulfate** Natriumsulfat, Glaubersalz *n*.

sodomy ['sɔdəmi] Sodomie *f*.

sofa ['soufə] Sofa, Kanapee *n*; **~ bed** Bettcouch *f*.

soffit [sɔfit] *arch* Laibung; Soffitte *f*.

soft [sɔft] *a* weich, nachgebend, formbar; zart, mild, sanft; weichlich, schwächlich; zaghaft; *(Arbeit)* leicht, angenehm, bequem; *com (Markt)* nachgiebig; sanft, nachgiebig, entgegenkommend, gutmütig, gütig, mitleidig, mitfühlend; zärtlich, liebevoll; weichlich; leicht zu beeinflussen(d), lenksam; einfältig, dumm; *(Farbe)* matt, sanft; *(Linie)* weich, sanft; *(Licht)* matt; *(Flamme)* kühl; *(Röhre)* gashaltig; *(Ton)* schwach, leise; *(Stimme)* weich; *(Getränk)* alkoholfrei; *adv* sacht, leise; *s* (gutmütiger) Tropf, Einfaltspinsel *m*; *to be ~ on s.o.* in jdn verliebt sein; *to get ~* weich werden; verweichlichen; sich erweichen lassen; *to have a ~ spot for* ein Herz haben für; *pretty ~ for him! (Am fam)* er hat es gut! *~ as butter* butterweich; **~ball** *Am* Hallenbaseball (-spiel *n*), Softball *m*; **~-boiled** *a (Ei)* weichgekocht; **~-brained, -headed, -witted** *a* albern, blöd(e), dumm; **~ coal** Braunkohle *f*; **~en** ['sɔ(:)fn] *tr* weich machen; lindern, mildern; erweichen, besänftigen; *itr* weich werden; *to ~~ up* zermürben; *~~ing plant* Enthärtungsanlage *f*; **~ener** ['sɔfnə] Wasserenthärtungsmittel *n*; Weichmacher *m*; **~ening** ['sɔfniŋ] Erweichung; (*~~ of the brain*) *med* Gehirnerweichung *f a. fam*; **~ goods** *pl* Textilien *pl*; kurzlebige Verbrauchsgüter *n pl*; **~head** Simpel, Einfaltspinsel *m*; **~-hearted** *a* weichherzig, gutmütig; **~ie** ['-i] = *~y*; **~ iron** Weicheisen *n*; **~ job** angenehme Stelle *od* Tätigkeit *f*; **~ money** Papiergeld *n*; **~ness** ['-nis] Weichheit, Zartheit, Milde, Sanftheit; Weichlichkeit, Zaghaftigkeit, Schwäche; Gutmütigkeit; Zärtlichkeit; Einfalt, Dummheit *f*; **~ nothings** *pl* Tändeleien *f pl*; **~ palate** *anat* weiche(r) Gaumen *m*; **~ pedal** Piano-Pedal *n*; **~-pedal** *tr mus* abschwächen, dämpfen; *fam* eins auf den Deckel geben (*s.o.* jdm); zurückhaltender vorbringen; **~ roe** *(Fisch)* Milchner *m*; **~ sawder** Schmeichelei *f*; **~-shelled** *a zoo* weichschalig; *Am fam* nicht streng; **~ soap** Schmierseife; *fig* Schmeichelei *f*; **~-soap** *tr fam* schmeicheln (*s.o.* jdm); **~-soldering** Weichlöten *n*; **~-spoken** *a* leise; friedlich; gewinnend, einschmeichelnd; **~ thing** *sl* Pfundssache *f*, Bombengeschäft *n*; Masche *f*; **~ tissues** *pl anat* Weichteile *pl*; **~wood** Nadel-, Weichholz *n*; **~y** ['-i] *a fam* schlapp; blöd(e); *s* Schwächling; Trottel *m*.

soggy ['sɔgi] feucht, durchweicht, durchnäßt; sumpfig; pappig; teigig, nicht durchgebacken *(Brot)*.

soil [sɔil] **1.** (Erd-)Boden *m*, Erdreich *n*; Scholle *f*, Boden *m*, Land *n*; *fig* Nährboden *m*; *on native ~* in der Heimat; *foreign ~* fremde(r) Boden *m*; **~ tilling** Bodenbearbeitung *f*; **2.** *tr* beschmieren, beschmutzen; *agr* düngen; *fig* beflekken, Schande machen (*s.th.* e-r S); *itr* fleckig, schmutzig werden; *s* Schmutz (-fleck); Kot, Mist; Dünger *m*; Beschmutzung *f*; *to ~ o.'s hand with s.th.* sich die Hände bei e-r S schmutzig machen; **~ conservation** Bodenkonservierung *f*; **~ improvement** Melioration *f*; **~less** ['-lis] fleckenlos; **~-pipe** Fallrohr *n*; **3.** *tr (Vieh)* mit Grünfutter füttern.

soirée, soiree ['swa:rei] Abendgesellschaft *f*.

sojourn ['sɔdʒə(:)n] *itr* sich aufhalten, *lit poet* weilen (*at, in* in; *with* bei); *s* (kurzer) Aufenthalt, Besuch *m*.

solace ['sɔlis] *s* Trost *m*; *tr* trösten; *(Schmerz)* lindern; *to ~ o.s. with* sich trösten mit; *to find ~ in* Trost finden in.

solanum [so(u)'leinəm] *bot* Nachtschatten *m*.

solar ['soulə] *a astr* Sonnen-; **~ day, eclipse, energy, flare, system, time, year** Sonnentag *m*, -finsternis, -energie, -fackel *f*, -system *n*, -zeit *f*, -jahr *n*; **~ium** [so(u)'lɛəriəm] Sonnenterrasse *f*; **~ize** ['souləraiz] *tr* überbelichten; **~ plexus** *anat* Sonnengeflecht *n*; **~ radiation** Sonnenstrahlung *f*.

solder ['sɔ(l)də] *s* Lötmittel, -zinn *n*; *fig* Kitt *m*, Bindemittel *n*; *tr* löten; *fig* binden, zs.halten; **~ing iron** Lötkolben *m*; **~ing torch** Lötlampe *f*; **~ seam** Lötstelle *f*.

soldier ['souldʒə] *s* Soldat *m a. ent*, Krieger; Kämpfer *m*; *Am sl* leere (Bier-)Flasche *f*; *fam* Bückling *m*; *itr* (als Soldat) dienen; *Am sl* sich drücken; *to be an old ~* mit allen Hunden gehetzt, mit allen Wassern gewaschen sein; *to play at ~s* Soldaten spielen; *toy ~* Zinnsoldat *m*; *~ of fortune* Glücksritter *m*; **~ing** ['-riŋ] Soldatenleben *n*; **~like** ['-laik], **~ly** ['-li] soldatisch, kriegerisch, kämpferisch; diszipliniert; **~'s pay** (Wehr-)Sold *m*; **~y** ['-ri] Soldaten *m pl*, Militär *n*; Soldateska *f*.

sole [soul] **1.** *s* (Fuß-, Schuh-)Sohle *f a. allg*; *tr* (be)sohlen; **~-leather** Sohlenleder *n*; **~-plate** *tech* Fußplatte *f*; **2.** *zoo* Seezunge, Scholle *f*; **3.** *a* einzig, alleinig; *for the ~ purpose of* einzig u. allein um; *feme ~* ledige Person *f*; **~ agency** Alleinvertretung *f*; **~ bill** Solawechsel *m*; **~ heir** Alleinerbe *m*; **~ judge** Einzelrichter *m*; **~ly** ['-li] *adv* allein, nur, bloß; einzig u. allein; **~ owner** Alleineigentümer *m*; **~ proprietor** Alleininhaber *m*.

solecism ['sɔlisizm] Sprachschnitzer *m*; Unschicklichkeit *f*, Verstoß *m*.

solemn ['sɔləm] feierlich, festlich, zeremoniell; formell; heilig, weihevoll; *(Ausdruck)* ernst; *(Tatsache)* schwerwiegend; feierlich, eindrucksvoll; **~ity** [sə'lemniti] feierliche Handlung *f*, Ritual *n*; Feierlichkeit, Weihe *f*, Ernst *m*; *pl jur* Formalitäten *f pl*; **~ize** ['sɔləmnaiz] *tr* feiern, festlich begehen; (feierlich) vollziehen; e-n ernsten Charakter geben (*s.th.* e-r S).

solenoid ['soulinɔid] Spule *f*; **~ switch** Magnetschalter *m*.

sol-fa [sɔl'fa:] Tonleiter *f*.

solicit [sə'lisit] *tr* dringend bitten, anhalten, ersuchen (*for* um); erbitten (*s.th. of, from* etw von); *(Prostituierte)* ansprechen; sich bewerben um; *com (Aufträge)* sammeln; *(Abonnenten)* werben; *itr* Männer ansprechen; **~ation** [səlisi'teiʃən] dringende Bitte *f*, An-, Ersuchen; Ansprechen, Belästigen *n*; Aufreizung, Verlockung; *com* Werbung *f*; **~or** [sə'lisitə] (nicht plädierender) (Rechts-)Anwalt; Rechtskonsulent, -beistand; *Am* Bitt-, Antragsteller, Bewerber; *Am* Werber, Agent, Handelsvertreter *m*; *S~~ General (Br)* Zweite(r) Kronanwalt; *Am* stellvertretende(r) Justizminister *m*; **~ous** [-əs] (eifrig) besorgt (*about, for, of* um); (eifrig) bestrebt (*to do* zu tun); sehr besorgt, in Aufregung (*for* um); **~ude** [-ju:d] Besorgtheit, Sorge, Besorgnis, Unruhe *f* (*about, for* um).

solid ['sɔlid] *a (Körper)* fest; massiv; Kubik-; *(Nebel)* dick, dicht; fest, solide, derb, tragfähig, haltbar, dauerhaft, zuverlässig, sicher; kreditfähig; *(Geschäft)* reell; begründet; gründlich; *(Grund)* triftig, stichhaltig; ununterbrochen, durchgehend; *fam* voll, ganz, geschlagen *(Stunde)*; einheitlich; *(Edelmetall)* rein, gediegen, pur; echt, wirklich; einmütig, -hellig; *typ* kompreß; *Am fam* treu wie Gold, verläßlich, zuverlässig; *Am sl* erstklassig, ausgezeichnet, tadellos; *adv* einstimmig, einmütig; *Am fam* einverstanden, sicherlich; *s phys* feste(r) Körper; *math* Körper *m*; *pl* feste Nahrung *f*; *to be frozen ~* fest zugefroren sein; *to be on ~*

ground (a. fig) festen Boden unter den Füßen haben; *to vote ~ for s.th.* etw einstimmig annehmen; **~arity** [sɔli'dæriti] Solidarität *f*, Zs.halt *m*, Zs.gehörigkeitsgefühl *n*, Gemeinschaftsgeist, Gemeinsinn *m*; *jur* Gesamtschuldnerschaft *f*; **~ geometry** Stereometrie *f*; **~ification** [sɔlidifi'keiʃən] Verdichtung; Festigung; Kristallisation *f*; **~ify** [sə'lidifai] *tr itr* (sich) verdichten, (sich) konkretisieren, (sich) festigen; (sich) kristallisieren; erstarren; **~ity** [sə'liditi] Festigkeit, Solidität; Haltbarkeit, Dauerhaftigkeit, Zuverlässigkeit, Sicherheit; *com* Kreditfähigkeit; *(Grund)* Stichhaltigkeit; *(Metall)* Reinheit, Gediegenheit; Echtheit; Einmütigkeit *f*; *math* Rauminhalt *m*, Volumen *n*; **~ leather** Kernleder *n*; **~ sender** *Am sl* prächtige(r) Kerl *m*; **~ spirit** Hartspiritus *m*; **~ tyre** Vollgummireifen *m*.

soliloqu|ize [sə'liləkwaiz] *itr* ein Selbstgespräch führen; **~y** [sə'liləkwi] Selbstgespräch *n*; *theat* Monolog *m*.

solit|aire [sɔli'tɛə, *Am* 'sɔ-] Solitär *m*; Patience *f*; **~ary** ['sɔlitəri] *a* alleinstehend; einsiedlerisch; einsam; einzeln; *fig* einzig; abgelegen; *bot zoo* solitär; *s* Einsiedler, Eremit *m*; *fam* Einzelhaft *f*; **~ude** ['-ju:d] Einsamkeit, Abgeschieden-, Abgelegenheit; Einöde *f*.

solo ['soulou] *pl a. soli* ['-li] *s mus* Solo *n*; *theat* Alleinauftritt *m*; Patience(spiel *n*) *f*; *aero* Alleinflug *m*; *a* Solo-; *adv* allein; *itr aero* allein fliegen; **~ist** ['-ist] *mus* Solist *m*.

solstice ['sɔlstis] Sonnenwende *f*; *summer, winter ~* Sommer-, Wintersonnenwende *f*.

solu|bility [sɔlju'biliti] *chem* Löslichkeit *f*; **~ble** ['sɔljubl] löslich; **~tion** [sə'lu:ʃən] *(Rätsel)* (Auf-)Lösung, *(Problem, Aufgabe)* Lösung; *(Frage)* Klärung; *chem pharm* Lösung; Auflösung *(e-r Einheit)*; *med* Heilung; *med* Krise; *(rubber ~~)* Gummilösung *f*.

solv|e ['sɔlv] *tr (Rätsel, Aufgabe)* lösen, *fam* 'rauskriegen; (er)klären; *(Schwierigkeit)* beseitigen; **~ency** ['-ənsi] Zahlungsfähigkeit, Solvenz, Liquidität *f*; **~ent** ['-ənt] *a* zahlungsfähig, solvent, liquid; *chem* lösend, Lösungs-; *s chem* Lösungsmittel *n*.

somatic [so(u)'mætik] *scient* somatisch, körperlich; Körper-; **~ cell** *biol* Körperzelle *f*.

sombre, *Am* **somber** ['sɔmbə] düster, dunkel *a. fig*; *fig* niederdrückend, unheilvoll, finster, traurig, melancholisch.

sombrero [sɔm'brɛərou] *pl -os* Sombrero *m (Hut)*.

some [sʌm, səm] *prn a* (irgend)ein, ein gewisser; *pl* gewisse, manche; einige, ein paar; *(vor e-r unbestimmten Mengenangabe)* etwas, ein wenig; beträchtlich; *Am fam* beachtlich; *~ meal* ein tolles Essen! *prn s* einige, ein paar, manche, gewisse Leute *pl*; (irgend) etwas, ein wenig, ein bißchen (davon); *prn adv (vor e-r Zahl)* einige, etwa, ungefähr; *Am fam (vor Komparativ)* ein (ganz) schönes Stück(chen), eine Menge; *Am fam* (ganz) tüchtig; *~ day (or other)* eines (schönen) Tages; *in ~ book or other* in irgendeinem der Bücher; *to ~ extent* bis zu e-m gewissen Grade; *~ few* einige wenige; *~ more* noch ein paar; noch etwas; *~ place (Am)* irgendwo; *(at) ~ time (or other)* (irgendwann) einmal; *for ~ time* (für) einige Zeit, eine Zeitlang; *~ time ago* vor einiger Zeit; *in ~ way or other* irgendwie; **~body** ['sʌmbədi] (irgend) jemand, irgendwer; *~~ else* jemand (*fam* wer) anders; *to be a ~~ (Person)* etwas Besonderes sein; **~how,** *~~ or other* irgendwie, auf irgendeine Weise, *fam* so oder so; **~one** (irgend) jemand; **~place** *adv Am* irgendwo (-hin); **~thing,** *~~ or other* (irgend) etwas; etwas Besonderes; *fam* schon was (Besonderes); *~~ like* ungefähr; so etw wie; *fam* wirklich; beachtlich; *there's a ~~* da muß schon was dran sein; *~~ else for you?* (soll es) sonst noch etwas sein)? *that's ~~ to think about* das muß man sich mal überlegen; **~time** *adv*, *at ~~ or other* (ein)mal; irgendwann; gelegentlich; *a* früher, ehemalig; **~times** *adv* manchmal, ab und zu, gelegentlich; **~what** etwas, ein wenig; *~~ of* so (et)was wie, eine Art; *to be ~~ (fam)* was sein; **~where** *adv* irgendwo(hin); *~~ else* anderswo, irgendwo anders.

somersault ['sʌməsɔ:lt] *s* Purzelbaum *m*; *mot* Überschlagen *n*, Überschlag *m*; *itr (to turn a ~)* e-n Purzelbaum schlagen; *aero* sich *(beim Landen)* überschlagen.

somn|ambulant [sɔm'næmbjulənt] **~ambulist** [-ist] Nachtwandler *m*; **~ambulate** [-eit] *itr* nachtwandeln; **~ambulism** [sɔm'næmbjulizm] Nachtwandeln *n*, Somnambulismus *m*; **~ambulistic** [sɔmnæmbju'listik] nachtwandlerisch; **~iferous** [sɔm'nifərəs] einschläfernd; **~olence** ['sɔmnələns] Schläfrigkeit *f*; **~olent** ['sɔmnələnt] schläfrig; einschläfernd.

*

son [sʌn] Sohn *m a. fig*; *S~ of God, Man* Sohn Gottes, Menschensohn *m (Christus)*; *a ~ of the soil* ein Kind *n* des Landes; **~-in-law** Schwiegersohn *m*; **~ny** ['-i] *fam (bes. als Anrede)* Söhnchen *n*; **~-of-a-bitch** *bes. Am vulg* Hundesohn, Scheißkerl *m*; **~-of-a-gun** *fam* Tausendsas(s)a, Schwerenöter *m*.

sonan|ce ['sounəns] Stimmhaftigkeit *f*; **~t** ['-t] *(Phonetik) a* stimmhaft; *s* stimmhafte(r) Laut *m*.

sonar ['souna:] (Unterwasser-)Schallmeßgerät, S-Gerät *n*.

sonat|a [sə'na:tə] *mus* Sonate *f*; **~ina** [sɔnə'ti:nə] *mus* Sonatine *f*.

song [sɔŋ] Gesang *m*; Lied; (kurzes) Gedicht *n*; Poesie, Dichtung *f*; *for a (mere) ~* für ein Butterbrot *od* e-n Spottpreis; spottbillig; *to burst into ~* zu singen beginnen; *nothing to make a ~ about* nicht der Rede wert; *~ and dance (that)* Gesang u. Tanz; *fig* Getue *n (about* um); *the S~ of Solomon, the S~ of S~s* das Hohelied (Salomonis); **~-bird** Singvogel *m*; **~-book** Liederbuch *n*; **~-hit** Schlager(melodie *f*) *m*; **~ster** ['-stə] Sänger; *fig* Dichter; *zoo* Singvogel *m*; **~stress** ['-stris] Sängerin *f*; **~-thrush** *orn* Singdrossel *f*.

sonic ['sɔnik] *a* Schall-; **~ bang** Knall *m* beim Durchbrechen der Schallmauer; **~ barrier** Schallmauer *f*; **~ speed** Schallgeschwindigkeit *f*; **~ threshold** Schallwelle *f*.

sonnet ['sɔnit] Sonett *n*; **~ier** [-'tiə] Sonettdichter; Dichterling *m*.

sonor|ity [sə'nɔriti] Klang *m*, -fülle *f*; Wohlklang *m*; *gram* (Ton-)Stärke *f*; **~ous** [sə'nɔ:rəs] klangvoll, -reich, wohltönend; *(Ton)* voll.

soon [su:n] *adv* bald; früh, zeitig; rasch; gern; *as ~ as (conj)* sobald, sowie; *as ~ as possible* sobald wie möglich; *just as ~* genauso gern; **~er** *adv (Komparativ)* eher, früher, zeitiger, schneller; lieber; *~~ or later* früher oder später, schließlich doch einmal; *the ~~ the better* je eher desto besser; *no ~~ ... than* kaum ..., als; *no ~~ said than done* gesagt, getan; *I had, would ~~ leave* ich möchte lieber gehen; ich ginge genauso gern; **~est** *adv (Superlativ)*: *least said, ~~ mended (prov)* Reden ist Silber, Schweigen ist Gold.

soot [su:t] *s* Ruß *m*; *tr* berußen; *to ~ up* verrußen; **~iness** ['-inis] Rußigkeit, Schwärze *f*; **~y** ['-i] *a* Ruß-; rußig, verrußt; schwarz, dunkel.

sooth [su:θ] *obs*: *in ~* fürwahr; **~e** [su:ð] *tr* beruhigen, besänftigen; *(Schmerz)* lindern, mildern; *(der Eitelkeit)* schmeicheln; **~ing** ['-ðiŋ] beruhigend, besänftigend; lindernd, mildernd; **~sayer** ['-seiə] Wahrsager *m*; *zoo* Gottesanbeterin *f*.

sop [sɔp] *s* eingetunkte(s) Stück *n* (Brot); kleine Belohnung; Beruhigungspille *f*, *fam* Drachenfutter; Bestechungsgeld *n*; Weichling, *fam* Waschlappen; *Am sl* Säufer *m*; *tr* eintunken, -weichen; *(to ~ up) (Flüssigkeit)* aufsaugen, -wischen; *itr (to ~ in)* einsickern; völlig durchnäßt werden *od* sein; triefen (*with* vor); **~ping, ~py** ['-iŋ, '-i] naß, feucht; regnerisch; *sl* rührselig, kitschig, schnulzenhaft.

soph [sɔf] *fam* = *~ister* od *~omore*; **~ism** ['sɔfizm] Trugschluß, Sophismus *m*; **~ist** ['-ist] *hist u. allg* Sophist *m*; **~ister** ['-istə] *(Univ.)*: *junior, senior ~~* Student *m* im 2., 3. Studienjahr; **~istic(al)** [sə'fistik(əl)] sophistisch; **~isticate** [sə'fistikeit] *tr* verführen, verderben; verfälschen; **~icated** [sə'fistikeitid] *a* (hoch)entwickelt, kultiviert, verfeinert, fortgeschritten; aufgeklärt, weltklug, -gewandt; weltmännisch; unehrlich, enttäuschend; intellektuell; blasiert; künstlich; **~istication** [səfisti'keiʃən] (weltmännische) Verfeinerung, Kultiviertheit, Weltklugheit; Spitzfindigkeit; Blasiertheit; Fälschung *f*; **~istry** ['sɔfistri] Spitzfindigkeit, Sophisterei *f*; Trugschluß *m*; **~omore** ['sɔfəmɔ:] *Am* Student *m* im 2. Studienjahr; *fig* Besserwisser *m*.

soporific [soupə'rifik] *a* einschläfernd; *s* Schlafmittel *n*.

soprano [sə'pra:nou] *pl -os mus* Sopran *m*; Sopranistin *f*.

*

sorb [sɔ:b] Eberesche *f*, Vogelbeerbaum *m*; *(~-apple)* Vogelbeere *f*.

sorcer|er ['sɔ:sərə] Zauberer, Hexenmeister *m*; **~ess** ['-ris] Zauberin, Hexe *f*; **~ous** ['-rəs] *a* Zauber-; **~y** ['-ri] Zauberei, Hexerei *f*.

sordid ['sɔ:did] schmutzig, verfilzt; elend, miserabel; gemein, niedrig; geizig, knauserig, *fam* filzig; **~ness** ['-nis] Schmutz *m*; Elend *n*; Gemeinheit *f*; schmutzige(r) Geiz *m*, Knauserigkeit *f*.

sore [sɔ:] *a* schmerzhaft, schmerzend; weh, wund, entzündet; schlimm, krank; (schmerz)empfindlich; reizbar; *fig* beleidigt, verärgert, bekümmert, traurig, schmerzbewegt; schmerzlich, betrüblich; peinlich; leidig, ärgerlich (*about* über, wegen); *Am fam* ärgerlich, verärgert, gereizt, böse; *fig* groß, stark, heftig; *(Not)* äußerst; *(Gewissen)* böse; *s* wunde Stelle, Verletzung *f*; *fig* wunde(r) Punkt *m*; *like a bear with a ~ head (fig)* brummig; *to be ~ at* böse sein auf; *to have a ~ throat* Halsweh haben; *to touch a ~ spot* e-n wunden Punkt berühren; **~head** *Am fam* Brummbär, Enttäuschte(r), Verbitterte(r) *m*; **~ly** ['-li] *adv* stark; äußerst; heftig.

sorg|hum ['sɔ:gəm], **~o** ['-ou] *bot* Sorghum *s*, Sorgho *m*, Mohren-, Kaffernhirse *f*.

sorority [sə'rɔriti] *Am* Studentinnenverbindung *f*, -klub *m*.

sorrel ['sɔrəl] **1.** *bot* Sauerampfer *m*; **2.** *s* Rotbraun *n*; Fuchs *m (Pferd)*; *a* rotbraun.

sorrow ['sɔrou] *s* Kummer *m*, Leid *n*, Gram *m*, Betrübnis *f*, Jammer, Schmerz *m* (*at* über; *for* um); Reue (*for* über); Trauer *f*; Klagen *n*; *itr* Kummer haben, sich grämen, sich härmen (*at, for, over* um); Reue empfinden; klagen, trauern (*at, over, for, after* um, wegen); *to my* ~ zu meinem Bedauern; *the Man of S~s* der Schmerzensmann (*Christus*); **~ful** ['-ful] bekümmert, betrübt, vergrämt, traurig; düster; elend; kummervoll.
sorry ['sɔri] *a* betrübt, bekümmert; traurig, kläglich; kümmerlich, armselig; erbärmlich, jämmerlich, elend, traurig; *I am ~ to* ... es tut mir leid zu ..., daß ...; leider (muß ich ...); *I'm really ~* es tut mir wirklich leid; *I am ~ for you* es tut mir leid um Sie; Sie tun mir leid; *I am ~ for it* es tut mir leid; *I am so ~* es tut mir so leid; entschuldigen Sie vielmals; *~!* Verzeihung! leider nicht! schade!
sort [sɔ:t] *s* Sorte, Art, Gattung, Klasse *f*; Charakter *m*, Natur *f*, Typ *m*; Güte, Qualität; *mot* Marke *f*; *tr* sortieren, sichten, ordnen; *(to ~ out)* aussortieren, -lesen, heraussuchen; trennen (*from* von); *itr* harmonisieren (*with* mit); passen (*with* zu); sich schicken; *after a ~, in a ~* bis zu e-m gewissen Grade; *of ~s, of a ~* so was wie; *of all ~s* aller Art(en); *out of ~s (fam) (gesundheitlich)* nicht auf dem Posten; *fam* schlechter Laune; *~ of (fam)* gewissermaßen, eigentlich, irgendwie; *I am ~ of glad* ich bin eigentlich, im Grunde froh; *I have ~ of a hunch* ich habe so eine Ahnung; *I ~ of knew that* ... ich habe es irgendwie gewußt, daß ...; *she is ~ of interesting* sie ist nicht uninteressant, sie hat so etwas Gewisses; *all ~s of things* alles mögliche; *nothing of the ~* nichts Derartiges, nichts dergleichen; *such ~ of thing* etwas Derartiges, so (et)was; *what ~ of ...?* was für ein ...? *not a bad ~* (gar) nicht so übel; *a decent ~* ein anständiger Kerl *m*; **~able** ['-əbl] sortierbar; **~er** ['-ə] Sortierer *m*.
sortie ['sɔ:ti] *mil* Ausfall; *aero* Feindflug, Einzelauftrag *m*; *mar* Auslaufen *n*; *daylight ~ (aero)* Tageseinsatz *m*.
sortilege ['sɔ:tilidʒ] Loswerfen *n*.
sot [sɔt] *s* Säufer, Trunkenbold *m*; *itr* (gewohnheitsmäßig) saufen; **~tish** ['-iʃ] versoffen; (ver)blöde(t); *to be ~~* s-n Verstand versoffen haben.
soubrette [su:'bret] *theat* Soubrette *f*.
soubriquet *s. sobriquet.*
sough [sau] *s* Säuseln, Rauschen, Rascheln *n*; *itr* säuseln, rauschen, rascheln.
sought [sɔ:t] *pret u. pp von seek*; (*~-after, ~-for*) gesucht, gefragt, begehrt.
soul [soul] Seele *f a. fig*; Herz *fig*, Gemüt; *(Kunst)* Leben *n*, Wärme *f*; Wesen *n*, Inbegriff *m*; Verkörperung; *fig* Triebfeder *f*; *pl (mit Zahlwort)* Seelen *f pl*, Menschen *m pl*; *not a ~* nicht eine lebende Seele; *with all my ~* von ganzem Herzen; *to keep body and ~ together* Leib u. Seele zs.halten; *she's in it heart and ~* sie ist mit Leib u. Seele dabei; *he cannot call his ~ his own* er steht ganz unter (fremdem) Einfluß; *upon my ~!* Donnerwetter! *All S~s' Day* Allerseelen *n*; *good, simple ~* gute(r), einfache(r) Mensch *m*; *poor ~* arme(r) Teufel *m*; *poor little ~* arme(s) Ding *n*; **~-destroying** geisttötend; **~ed** [-d] *in Zssgen.* -herzig; *high-~~* hochherzig; **~ful** ['-ful] seelenvoll; **~less** ['-lis] seelenlos; **~-stirring** herzergreifend.
sound [saund] **1.** *a* gesund; einwandfrei, fehlerfrei, -los, unbeschädigt, unversehrt, in gutem Zustand, solide; unverdorben; (seelisch, innerlich) gesund, lebensfähig, kräftig, stark, widerstandsfähig; *(Schiff)* seetüchtig; fest, sicher, (finanziell) gesichert; *(Anspruch)* (wohl)begründet; *(Grund)* triftig; zuverlässig, verläßlich; vernünftig, verständig, verständnis-, sinnvoll, klug, weise; stichhaltig; *(Rat)* gut; gründlich, tiefschürfend; sittenrein, -streng, ehrbar, ehrenhaft, korrekt; recht-, strenggläubig, orthodox; konservativ; *jur* rechtskräftig, -gültig; *com* kreditfähig; *(Schlaf)* tief, fest, gesund; *adv* gesund; tief, fest; *to be ~ asleep* fest schlafen; *as ~ as a bell* kerngesund; *of ~ mind* geschäftsfähig; *of ~ and disposing mind* testierfähig; *~ and safe* heil u. gesund; gesund u. munter; *~* **health** gute Gesundheit *f*; **~ness** ['-nis] Gesundheit; Unversehrtheit; Vernünftigkeit, Klugheit *f*; **2.** *s* Laut, Schall, Ton, Klang *m*; Geräusch *n*; Stimme; Hörweite; Klangwirkung *f*; *itr* (er)tönen, erschallen, (er)klingen; *fig* klingen, erscheinen, wirken, vorkommen; e-n ... Eindruck machen, sich anhören (*as if* als wenn); *(Bericht)* lauten; *tr* ertönen, erklingen, erschallen lassen; *(Instrument)* schlagen, blasen, spielen; aussprechen; verbreiten; abhorchen, abhören; *to ~ off* abwechselnd, der Reihe nach sprechen; *Am sl* herausplatzen (*on* mit); das große Wort führen; sich beklagen; *within ~ of* in Hörweite *gen*; *to ~ the horn (mot)* hupen; *to ~ the retreat* zum Rückzug blasen; *that ~s fishy to me* das kommt mir nicht geheuer vor; **~-absorbing** schallschluckend, -dämmend; *~* **barrier** Schallgrenze *f*; **~-board** = *~ing-board*; **~-box** Schalldose; *film* Abhörkabine *f*; **~-camera** Tonkamera *f*; **~-channel** Tonkanal *m*; **~-damping** Schalldämmung *f*; **~-detector** Horchgerät *n*; **~-effects** *pl* Geräuschkulisse *f*; **~-engineer** Toningenieur *m*; **~er** ['-ə] *tele* Taste *f*, Klopfer *m*; *mar* Lot *n*; **~-film** Tonfilm *m*; *~~ projector* Tonfilmvorführapparat *m*; **~ing** ['-iŋ] tönend, klingend; klangvoll *a. fig*; *fig* hochtrabend, bombastisch; *~~-board* Resonanzboden *m*; *~* **intensity** Schallstärke *f*; **~less** ['-lis] geräusch-, lautlos, still; *~* **level** Schallpegel *m*; **~-locator** *mil* Horchgerät *n*; **~-man** *film radio* Geräuschoperateur *m*; **~-proof** *a* schalldicht; *tr* schalldicht machen; *~* **ranging** Schallmeßverfahren *n*; *~~-instrument* Schallmeßgerät *n*; *~~ team* (Schall-)Meßtrupp *m*; **~-reception** Höraufnahme *f*; **~-recording** Schallaufzeichnung, -aufnahme *f*; **~-reproduction** Tonwiedergabe *f*; **~-shift** *(Linguistik)* Lautverschiebung *f*; **~-source** Schallquelle *f*; **~-track** *film* Tonstreifen *m*, -band *n*, -spur *f*; **~-truck** Lautsprecherwagen *m*; **~-velocity** Schallgeschwindigkeit *f*; **~-vibration** Schallschwingung *f*; **~-volume** Lautstärke *f*; **~-wave** Schallwelle *f*; **3.** *tr mar* (aus)loten, sondieren *a. fig*; *med* abhorchen; *(to ~ out)* aushorchen, erkunden; auf den Zahn fühlen (*s.o.* jdm); *itr* loten; *fig* s-e Fühler ausstrecken; *s mar* Lotung *f*; *med* Abhorchen *n*; *med* Sonde *f*; **~ing** *mar* Lotung, gelotete Tiefe *f*; *pl* Ankergrund *m*; *~~-balloon* Ballonsonde *f*, Registrierballon *m*; *~~-device (aero)* Peilanlage *f*; *~~-lead* Senkblei, Lot *n*; *~~-line* Lotleine *f*; **3.** Meerenge *f*; Meeresarm *m*; Fischblase *f*.
soup [su:p] *s* Suppe, Brühe *f*; *sl* Nitroglyzerin *n*; *phot sl* Entwickler; *sl aero* dicke(r) Nebel *m*; *sl mot aero* Pusse, Kraft *f*, PS *pl*, Kraftstoff *m*; *tr sl (to ~ up)* mehr herausholen (*an engine, a motor* aus e-r Maschine, e-m Motor); hochzüchten; *in the ~ (fam)* in der Tinte, in Schwierigkeiten, in der Patsche; *chicken, pea, tomato, vegetable ~* Hühner-, Erbsen-, Tomaten-, Gemüsesuppe *f*; *clear ~* Kraftbrühe *f*; **~-and-fish** *sl* volle(r) Dreß *m*; **~-kitchen** Volksküche; *mil* Feldküche, *sl* Gulaschkanone *f*; **~-plate** Suppenteller *m*; **~-spoon, -ladle** Suppenlöffel *m*; **~-terrine** Suppenschüssel *f*; **~y** ['-i] *fam* sentimental; *(Stimme)* zitternd.
soupçon ['su:psɔ̃:ŋ] Spur *f*, Anflug *m*, Andeutung *f* (*of* von).
sour ['sauə] *a* sauer; säuerlich; ranzig; bitter; *fig* verärgert, verstimmt, übelgelaunt, mißmutig, mürrisch, verdrießlich, verbittert; ungenügend, schlecht; unangenehm; *(Boden)* übersäuert; *Am fam* ungesetzlich, unrecht, verdächtig; *tr* sauer werden lassen; *fig* verärgern, verstimmen, verbittern; *itr* sauer, ranzig, bitter werden; *fig* ärgerlich, mißmutig, verbittert werden; *in ~ (Am sl)* in der Tinte; *to turn ~* sauer werden; *~* **grapes** *fig* saure Trauben *f pl*; **~ish** ['-riʃ] säuerlich; **~ness** ['-nis] Säure; Bitterkeit; Verstimmtheit, Verbittertheit, Mißlaunigkeit *f*; **~puss** *fam* Sauertopf, Griesgram, Trauerkloß *m*.
source [sɔ:s] Quelle *f a. fig*; *com* Lieferant *m*; *el* Strom-, Energiequelle *f*; *med* Herd; *fig* Ursprung *m*, Wurzel *f*; *to have its ~* s-n Ursprung haben (*in* in); *to take its ~* entspringen (*from* aus); *~ of errors* Fehlerquelle *f*; *~ of income* Einkommensquelle *f*; *~ of light* Lichtquelle *f*.
souse [saus] **1.** *s.* Pökelfleisch *n*; Salzlake *f*; (Ein-)Pökeln; *allg* Eintauchen; Eisbein *n*; *Am sl* Säufer *m*; *tr* (ein)pökeln; in Salzlake legen; ein-, untertauchen; ins Wasser werfen; (völlig) durchnässen; *Am sl* besoffen machen; *itr* (völlig) durchnäßt, ganz naß werden; ins Wasser fallen; *Am sl* sich besaufen; **~d** [-t] *a sl* besoffen, blau; **2.** *(Falknerei) s* Aufsteigen *(des gejagten Vogels)*; Herabstoßen *n (des Falken)*; *itr* herabstoßen (*on* auf); *tr* herabstoßen auf; *adv* schwupp, plumps.
south [sauθ] *s* Süd(en) *m*; Süd-, südliche Richtung *f*, Südkurs *m*; Südseite *f*; *the S~* der Süden, die Südstaaten *m pl (der US)*; *a* südlich (*of* von); Süd-; *adv* im Süden; südwärts, in südlicher Richtung; nach Süden; **S~ Africa** Südafrika *n*, die Südafrikanische Union *f*; **S~ African** südafrikanisch; **S~ America** Südamerika *n*; **S~ American** südamerikanisch; **~-east** ['-'i:st] *s* Südost(en) *m*; *a* südöstlich, Südost-; *adv* in, aus Südost, südostwärts; **~-easter** [sauθ'i:stə] (starker) Südostwind *m*; **~-easterly** [-'i:stəli] *a adv* südöstlich; aus Südost; **~-eastern** [-'i:stən] *a* südöstlich; aus Südost; **~-eastward** [-wəd] *a adv* südöstlich; **~-eastwardly** [-'i:stwədli] = *~easterly*; **~-eastwards** [-'i:stwədz] *adv* südöstlich; **~erly** ['sʌðəli], **~ern** ['sʌðən] *a* südlich; aus Süden; Süd-; *s* = *~erner*; *the S~~ Hemisphere* die Südhalbkugel *f (der Erde)*; **~erner** ['sʌðənə] Südländer *m*; *S~~* Südstaatler *m*; **~ernmost** ['sʌðənmoust] *a* südlichst; **~ing** ['sauðiŋ] (Bewegung in) südliche(r) Richtung; *astr* südliche Deklination *f*; **~paw** *Am sl sport s* Linkshänder *m*; *a* linkshändig; **S~ Pole** Südpol *m*; **S~ Sea Islander** Südseeinsulaner *m*; *the* **S~ Seas** *pl* die Süd-

see *f*; **~-east** *s* Südsüdost *m*; *a adv* südsüdöstlich; aus Südsüdost; **~-west** *s* Südsüdwest *m*; *a adv* südsüdwestlich; aus Südsüdwest; **~ward** ['-wəd] *a adv* südlich; aus Süden; **~wardly** ['-wədli] *a adv* südlich; **~wards** ['-wədz] *adv* südlich; aus Süden; **~-west** ['-'west] *s* Südwest *m*; *a* südwestlich, Südwest-; *adv* in, aus Südwest, südwestwärts; **~-wester** [sauθ'westə] (starker) Südwestwind; Südwester *m (Hut)*; **~-westerly** [-'westəli] *a adv* südwestlich; aus Südwest; **~-western** [-'westən] *a* südwestlich; aus Südwest; **~-westward** [-'westwəd] *a adv* südwestlich; **~-westwardly** [-'westwədli] = *~westerly*; **~-westwards** [-'westwədz] *adv* südwestlich; **~ wind** Südwind *m*.

souvenir ['su:vəniə] (Reise-)Andenken *n*.

sou'wester [sau'westə] Südwester *m*.

sovereign ['sɔvrin] *a* höchst, oberst, Haupt-, Ober-; ranghöchst, an der Spitze stehend; regierend; souverän, unabhängig; ausgezeichnet, vortrefflich, vorzüglich; *med pharm* sehr wirksam; *s* Monarch, Herrscher, (Landes-) Fürst, Souverän *m*; *(Großbritannien) (goldenes)* Zwanzigschillingstück *n*; **~ rights** *pl* Hoheitsrechte *n pl*; **~ territory** Hoheitsgebiet *n*; **~ty** ['-ənti] Regierungsgewalt, Herrschaft, oberste Staatsgewalt; unumschränkte Gewalt, Souveränität *f*, Hoheitsrechte *n pl*.

soviet ['souviet] *s* Sowjet *m*; *a* Sowjet-; sowjetisch; *the Supreme S~* der Oberste Sowjet; **~ism** ['-izm] Sowjetsystem *n*; **~ization** [souvietai'zeiʃən] Sowjetisierung *f*; **~ize** ['souvietaiz] *tr* sowjetisieren; **S~ Russia** Sowjetrußland *n*; *the* **S~ Union** die Sowjetunion *f*.

sow 1. [sou] *irr ~ed, ~n* od *~ed tr (Saat)* (aus)säen; *(Acker)* bestellen; *fig (Nachricht)* ausstreuen, verbreiten; *fig* einpflanzen, -schärfen; *itr* den Acker bestellen; *to ~ o.'s wild oats (fig)* sich die Hörner abstoßen; *to ~ (the seeds of) dissension* Zwietracht säen; *to ~ the wind and reap the whirlwind* Wind säen u. Sturm ernten; *as a man ~s, so shall he reap (prov)* wie die Saat, so die Ernte; **~er** ['-ə] Sämann *m*; Sämaschine *f*; *fig* Anstifter *m*; **~ing** ['-iŋ] Säen *n*; Aussaat *f*; *~~ machine* Sämaschine *f*; **2.** [sau] *zoo* Sau; *metal* Sau *f*, Eisenklumpen; Masselgraben *m*; **~-belly** *Am fam* Pökelfleisch *n*; **~ bug** *zoo* Bohrassel *f*; **~'s ear** Schweinsohr *n*; **~-thistle** *bot* Saudistel *f*.

soya, *Am* **soja** ['sɔiə] *bot* Sojabohne *f*.

sozzled ['sɔzld] *a sl* blau, besoffen.

*

spa [spɑ:] Mineral-, Heilquelle *f*; (Heil-)Bad *n*; Kurort *m*.

spac|e [speis] *s* Raum, Platz; Zwischenraum *a. mus*, Abstand *m*; *typ* Spatium *n*; Zeit(raum *m*), Frist *f*; *(outer ~~)* Weltraum *m*; *pl typ* Blindmaterial *n*; *tr* mit Abstand, in Abständen, in Zwischenräumen anordnen *od* aufstellen; verteilen, staffeln; *typ* spati(on)ieren; räumlich gliedern; *to ~~ out (typ)* sperren; *to occupy, to take up ~~* Platz einnehmen; *to set in ~ed type* gesperrt drucken; *to stare (out) into ~~* in die Luft starren; *a short ~~* ein Weilchen, eine kurze Zeit; *for a ~~* eine Zeitlang; *with ~~ (typ)* durchschossen; *within the ~~ of* innerhalb; *advertising ~~* Reklamefläche *f*; *blank ~~* freie Stelle *f*; *floor ~~* Bodenfläche *f*; *living ~~* Lebensraum *m*; *office ~~* Bürofläche *f*; *parking ~~* Platz *m* zum Parken; *~~-bar, -key (Schreibmaschine)* Leer-, Zwischenraumtaste *f*; *~~ diagram* Lageplan *m*; Raumbild *n*; *~~ effect* Raumwirkung *f*; *~~ fiction* Raumfahrtromane *m pl*; *~~-flight, -travel* Raumfahrt *f*; *~~-filling* raumfüllend; *~~ line (typ)* Durchschuß *m*; *~~man* Raumfahrer *m*; *~~ research* Raumforschung *f*; *~~-saving* raumsparend; *~~ship* Raumschiff, -fahrzeug *n*; *~~ station* Raumstation *f*; *~~-time (continuum)* Raum-Zeit-Einheit *f*; *~~-traveller* Raumfahrer *m*; *~~ writer* Zeilenschinder *m*; **~er** ['-ə] Leertaste *f*; *tech* Abstandsstück *n*; **~ial** ['speiʃəl] *s. spatial*; **~ing** ['-iŋ] Zwischenraum, Abstand *m*, *typ* Spatium *n*; *single-, double-~~* kleine(r), große(r) Zeilenabstand *m*; **~ious** ['speiʃəs] geräumig; ausgedehnt, weit; unbegrenzt; umfangreich *a. fig*; **~iousness** ['-ʃəsnis] Geräumigkeit; Ausgedehntheit, Weite *f*, Ausmaß *n*; Unbegrenztheit *f*.

spade [speid] *s* Spaten *m*; *pl (Kartenspiel)* Pik, Schippen *n*; *tr* umgraben; *itr* graben; *to call a ~ a ~ (fig)* das Kind beim (rechten) Namen nennen; **~ful** ['-ful] Spatenvoll *m*; **~-work** mühevolle Vorarbeit(en *pl*) *f*.

spadix ['speidiks] *pl a. -dices* [-'daisi:z] *bot* Kolben *m (Blütenstand)*.

Spain [spein] Spanien *n*; *castles (pl) in ~* Luftschlösser *n pl*.

spall [spɔ:l] *s (bes.* Stein-)Splitter *m*; *pl* Bruchsteine *m pl*; *tr* aufsplittern, zerspalten; *itr* (zer)splittern; *tr itr* zerbröckeln, -krümeln, zerkleinern.

spam [spæm] *(spiced ham)* amerikanische(s) Büchsenfleisch *n*.

span [spæn] **1.** *s* Spanne *f (= 9 Zoll* od *22,85 cm)*; Abstand *m*; *(~-length)* Spannweite; *arch* lichte Weite; *(~ of time)* Zeitspanne; Spanne *f* Zeit; *(Am, Südafrika)* Gespann *n*; *tr* (um-, über-) spannen; überbrücken; *(bes.* mit der Hand) (ab)messen; *mar* mit Tauen festzurren; *fig* umfassen; *~ of life* Lebensspanne *f*; **~ner** ['-ə] Spanner *(Gerät)*; Schraubenschlüssel *m*; *a ~~ in the works (fam)* Sand im Getriebe; **~-roof** Satteldach *n*; **~-wire** Abspanndraht *m*; **2.** *obs pret* von *spin (s.d.)*.

spangl|e ['spæŋgl] *s* Metallsplitter *m*, -folie *f*; Flitter *m*, Paillette *f*; *tr* mit Flitter besetzen *od* bestreuen; *fig* übersäen (*with* mit); *itr* flimmern, glitzern; **~ed** ['-d]: *~~ with stars* mit Sternen be-, übersät; *the star-~~ banner* Flagge *f* der USA.

Spaniard ['spænjəd] Spanier(in *f*) *m*.

spaniel ['spænjəl] *zoo* Wachtelhund, Spaniel; *fig* Kriecher, Schmeichler *m*.

Spanish ['spæniʃ] *a* spanisch; *s* (das) Spanisch(e); *the ~* die Spanier *m pl*; **~ chestnut** echte Kastanie *f*; **~ fly** *ent* Spanische Fliege *f*; **~ moss** Floridamoos *n*.

spank [spæŋk] *tr* (das Hinterteil) versohlen; verprügeln; *sport* schlagen; *itr (to ~ along)* dahinrasen, -flitzen; *s* (tüchtiger) Klaps *m*; **~er** ['-ə] *fam* tüchtige(r) Schlag *m*; *fam* gewaltige Sache *f*, Pfundskerl; *fam* Renner *m*, Rennpferd *n*; *mar* Besansegel *n*; **~ing** ['-iŋ] *a* schnell; *(Wind)* lebhaft, frisch, kräftig; *fam* großartig, gewaltig, prächtig, herrlich, phantastisch; *adv* außerordentlich; *s* Schläge *m pl*.

spar [spɑ:] **1.** *mar* Spiere *f*, Rundholz *n*; *aero* Holm *m*; **2.** *min* Spat *m*; **3.** *itr (Hahn)* mit den Sporen kämpfen; zanken, streiten; *sport* sparren, trainieren; *s* Hahnenkampf; *sport* Boxkampf *m*, Boxen, Sparren *n*; Streit, Zank *m*, Ausea.setzung *f*; **~ring** ['-riŋ] (Trainings-) Boxen *n*; *~~ match* (Freundschafts-, Trainings-)Boxkampf *m*; *~~ partner* Trainingspartner *m* (beim Boxen).

spar|e [spɛə] *tr* aufsparen; (ver)schonen, Nachsicht üben gegen, rücksichtsvoll, nachsichtig behandeln; ersparen (*s.o. s.th., from s.th.* jdm etw), verschonen mit; *(s-e Kräfte)* sparen zurückhalten mit; entbehren, erübrigen, übrig haben (*s.o. s.th.* etw für jdn); *to be ~d* am Leben bleiben; *itr* sparen, sparsam sein; sich zurückhalten; nachsichtig sein, Nachsicht üben; *a* zur Verfügung (stehend); Ersatz-; frei, übrig, überzählig, überflüssig; sparsam, bescheiden, einfach, schlicht, knapp, karg; mager, hager, dürr; *s (~~ piece)* Ersatzteil, -stück *n*; Reserve-, Ersatz-; *to ~~* übrig, über; *enough and to ~~* mehr als genug, reichlich; *to ~~ no expense* keine Kosten scheuen; *to ~~ for nothing* es an nichts fehlen lassen; *not to ~~ o.s.* sich nicht schonen, keine Mühe scheuen; *~~ me the details* verschonen Sie mich mit den Einzelheiten; *do you have a minute to ~~* haben Sie e-e Minute Zeit? *can you ~~ me a cigarette?* hast du e-e Zigarette für mich (über)? *~~ anchor* Notanker *m*; *~~ fuse* Ersatzsicherung *f*; *~~ hours (pl)* Mußestunden *f pl*; *~~ money* Notgroschen *m*; *~~ parts (pl)* Ersatzteile *pl*; *~~ parts catalogue* Ersatzteilliste *f*; *~~ parts depot* Ersatzteillager *n*; *~~ rib* Rippenspeer *m*; *~~ room* Gastzimmer *n*; *~~ seat* Notsitz *m*; *~~ time* Freizeit *f*; *~~-time job* Freizeitbeschäftigung *f*; *~~ tire* Reservereifen *m*; *Am sl* fünfte(s) Rad *n* am Wagen, Fettwulst *m* um den Bauch; *~~ wheel* Ersatzrad *n*; **~eness** ['-nis] Knappheit; Magerkeit *f*; **~ing** ['-riŋ] sparsam, haushälterisch (*of* mit); sorgfältig, -sam, einfach, schlicht; karg, mager; begrenzt, eingeschränkt; **~ingness** ['-riŋnis] Sparsamkeit; Sorgfalt; Einfachheit; Kargheit *f*.

spark [spɑ:k] **1.** *s* Funke(n) *m a. el*; *fig* Fünkchen *n*, Spur *f*, zündende(r) Funke; Lebensfunke *m*; *pl* (Schiffs-) Funker *m*; *itr* Funken sprühen; *mot* zünden; *tr fig* elektrisieren, anfeuern, -treiben, -regen, begeistern; *to ~ out (sl)* ohnmächtig werden; **~ arrester** *el* Funkenfang *m*; **~ coil** Zündspule *f*; **~ discharge** Funkenentladung *f*; **~ gap** Funkenstrecke *f*; **~ing** ['-iŋ] Funkenbildung *f*; **~ing-plug,** *Am* **~-plug** *mot* Zündkerze *f*; *Am sl* Seele *f* des Ganzen; **~over** *el* Überschlag *m*; **~ timing** Zündeinstellung *f*; **2.** *s* flotte(r) junge(r) Mann; *tr* den Hof machen.

sparkl|e ['spɑ:kl] *itr* (Funken) sprühen; funkeln, blitzen, glitzern (*with* vor); *(Flüssigkeit)* sprudeln, perlen, schäumen; *tr* sprühen, funkeln lassen; *s* Funke(n) *m*; Funkeln, Glitzern *n*; Glanz *m*; **~er** ['-ə] *fig* Glanzstück *n*; glänzende Erscheinung *f (Person)*; *pl fam* blitzende Augen *n pl*, Diamanten *m pl*; **~ing** ['-iŋ] funkelnd, glitzernd; sprudelnd; *(Wein)* perlend; lebhaft; *(Geist)* sprühend; *~~ water* Sprudel *m*.

sparrow ['spærou] *zoo* Sperling, Spatz *m*; **~-hawk** Sperber *m*.

spars|e [spɑ:s] dünn, (weit) verstreut; spärlich, selten; **~eness, ~ity** ['-iti] Spärlichkeit *f*.

spartan ['spɑ:tən] *fig* spartanisch.

spasm [spæzm] *med* Krampf, Spasmus, Anfall *m*; *cardiac ~* Herzkrampf *m*; **~odic** [-'mɔdik] krampfhaft, spastisch; Krampf-; *fig* sprunghaft.

spat [spæt] **1.** *s* Schaltierlaich *m*; junge Auster(n *pl*) *f*; *itr (Auster)* laichen; **2.** *meist pl (kurze)* Gamaschen *f pl*; **3.** *pret u. pp* von *spit (s.d.)*; **4.** *Am fam s*

Klaps, Zank, Wortwechsel *m*; *itr* klatschen; *fig* streiten; *tr* e-n Klaps geben (*s.o.* jdm).
spatchcock ['spætʃkɔk] *s* rasch gekochte(s) Geflügel *n*; *tr fig (Textteil)* einschieben (*into, in* in); *fam* einflicken.
spate [speit] Überschwemmung *f*; Hochwasser *n*; Wolkenbruch; *fig* Wortschwall *m*; *a ~ of* e-e Menge *gen.*
spatial, *Am a.* **spacial** ['speiʃəl] räumlich; Raum-; *~* **distribution** Raumverteilung *f*.
spatter ['spætə] *tr* (be)spritzen (*with* mit); *fig* beschmutzen; *itr* spritzen; *(Regen)* (nieder)prasseln; *s* Spritzen *n*; Spritzfleck; Spritzer; *fig* Hagel *m*.
spatul|a ['spætjulə] Spa(ch)tel *m*; **~ar** ['-ə] spatelartig; Spatel-.
spavin ['spævin] *vet* Spat *m (d. Pferde)*; **~ed** ['-d] *a (Pferd)* spatig.
spawn [spɔ:n] *itr* laichen; *fam* sich hemmungslos vermehren; *tr (Laich)* ablegen; ausbrüten *a. fig*; *(Eier)* legen; *fig pej* in Massen, am laufenden Band produzieren; *s* Laich, Rogen *m*; *pej* Brut *f*, Gezücht *n*; *bot* Myzel(ium) *n*; **~er** ['-ə] *zoo* Rog(e)ner *m*.
spay [spei] *tr (weibl. Tier)* verschneiden.

*

speak [spi:k] *irr spoke* [spouk], *spoken* ['spoukən] *itr* sprechen (*of* von; *on, about* über; *to* mit, zu; *for* für); reden (*of* von über); sich äußern (*of* über); e-e Rede, e-n Vortrag halten; sich unterhalten; *mus* ertönen; *zoo* Laut geben; *tr* (aus)sprechen, sagen, äußern, ausdrücken; *(Sprache)* sprechen; bekanntgeben; anreden; zeugen von; *(Schiff)* ansprechen; *to ~ out, up* laut, deutlich sprechen; frei, offen reden, *fam* den Mund aufmachen; *to ~ (up) for* eintreten für; *not to ~ of* ganz zu schweigen von; *nothing to ~ of* nicht der Rede wert; *so to ~* sozusagen, gewissermaßen; *to ~ comfort to s.o.* jdm Trost zusprechen; *to ~ s.o. fair* jdm gut zureden, jdm gute Worte geben; *to ~ o.'s piece (Am fam)* sich beklagen, meckern; *to ~ to the point* zur Sache sprechen; *to ~ volumes (fig)* Bände sprechen (*for* für); *to ~ well for s.o.* zu jds Gunsten sprechen; *of s.o.* Gutes von jdm sagen; **~-easy** *Am sl* (nicht lizenzierte) Kneipe *f*; **~er** ['-ə] Sprecher; Vorsitzende(r); Redner; *(loud-~~)* Lautsprecher; *(parl) S~~* Präsident, Sprecher *m*; **~ing** ['-iŋ] *a* Sprech-; *fig* sprechend, beredt, ausdrucksvoll, lebendig; sprechend ähnlich; *s* Sprechen *n*, Rede, Äußerung *f*; *generally ~~* im allgemeinen; im großen u. ganzen; *strictly ~~* genaugenommen; *not to be on ~~ terms with s.o.* mit jdm nicht (mehr) sprechen; jdn nicht näher kennen; *~~-key (tele)* Sprechtaste *f*; *~~-trumpet, -tube* Sprachrohr *n*.
spear [spiə] *s* Speer, Spieß *m*, Lanze; Speer-, Lanzenspitze *f*; *poet* Speerkämpfer; *bot* Halm, Schaft *m*; *tr* durchbohren, aufspießen; *itr bot* sprießen; **~head** *s* Speer-, Lanzenspitze *f*; *fig* führende(r) Kopf *m*; *mil* Angriffsspitze, Vorhut, Vorausabteilung *f*, Stoßkeil *m*; *tr* an der Spitze stehen von; **~mint** *bot* Grüne Minze *f*; *~* **side** männliche Linie *f*.
spec [spek] *(= speculation) fam* Spekulation *f*; *on ~* auf Verdacht.
spec|ial ['speʃəl] *a* besonder; un-, außergewöhnlich, außerordentlich; Ausnahme-; speziell; Sonder-, Extra-, Spezial-; *s* Sonderbeauftragte(r); Sonderdruck *m*, -ausgabe, -nummer *f*; Extrablatt *n*; Sonderzug *m*; *Am* Spezialität *f* (des Hauses); *for ~~ duty* zu besonderer Verwendung; *~~ area (Br)* Notstandsgebiet *n*; *~~ attorney* Sonderbevollmächtigte(r) *m*; *~~ bargain* Sonderangebot *n*, Gelegenheitskauf *m*; *~~ body (mot)* Spezialkarosserie *f*; *~~ case* Sonder-, Spezialfall *m*; *~~ committee* Sonderausschuß *m*; *~~ constable* Hilfspolizist *m*; *~~ correspondent* Sonderberichterstatter *m*; *~~ delivery (Am)* Eilzustellung *f*; *~~ design* Sonderausführung *f*; *~~ desire* Sonderwunsch *m*; *~~ dictionary* Fach-, Spezialwörterbuch *m*; *~~ edition* Sonderausgabe *f*; *~~ election (Am)* Nachwahl *f*; *~~ fee* Sondergebühr *f*; *~~ leave* Sonderurlaub *m*; *~~ message* Sondermeldung *f*; *~~ messenger* Expreßbote; *mil* Kurier *m*; *~~ mission* Sonderauftrag *m*; *~~ offer (com)* Sonderangebot *n*; *~~ permit* Sondergenehmigung *f*; *~~ power* Sondervollmacht *f*; *~~ price* Vorzugspreis *m*; *~~ reduction* Sonderrabatt *m*; *~~ regulation* Sonderbestimmung *f*; *~~ right* Sonder-, Vorrecht *n*; *~~ services (Am mil)* Truppenbetreuung *f*; *~~ subject* Sonder-, Fachgebiet; Wahlfach *n*; *~~ treaty* Sonderabkommen *n*; **~ialism** ['-izm] Fach(gebiet *n*, -richtung *f*) *n*; **~ialist** ['-ist] Spezialist, Fachmann, -gelehrte(r), -arzt *m*; **~ialistic** [speʃə'listik] fachlich, -männisch; Fach-; **~iality** [speʃi'æliti] Besonderheit *f*, Charakteristikum *n*; Spezialartikel *m*; = *~ialty*; *pl* Besonder-, Einzelheiten *f pl*; **~ialization** [speʃəlai'zeiʃən] Spezialisierung *f*; **~ialize** ['speʃəlaiz] *tr* spezialisieren; besonders einrichten (*for* für); *itr* sich spezialisieren (*in* in, auf); sich einseitig festlegen; *biol* sich anpassen; **~ialty** ['speʃəlti] Besonderheit *f*; Fach (-gebiet *n*, -richtung *f*) *n*; Spezialität; *com* Neuheit *f*, Spezialartikel *m*; *jur* vertragliche Vereinbarung, notarielle Urkunde *f*; **~ie** ['spi:ʃi:] Hart-, Metallgeld *n*; *in ~~* in Hartgeld; in bar; **~ies** ['spi:ʃi:z] *pl ~~* Art *f bes. zoo bot*; *allg* Sorte, Gattung *f*; **~ific** [spi'sifik] *a* genau festgelegt, begrenzt, bestimmt; artgemäß; besonder, charakteristisch, *scient* spezifisch; *s bes. med* Spezifikum *n*; *in each ~~ case* in jedem Einzelfall; *to be ~~* in Einzelheiten gehen; *~~ gravity, heat (phys)* spezifische(s) Gewicht *n*, Wärme *f*; *~~ name* Artbezeichnung, -name *f*; *~~ order* Sonderauftrag *m*; **~ification** [spesifikeiʃən] Spezifizierung, genaue Angabe, Aufführung, Bezeichnung, Detaillierung *f*; Einzelnachweis *m*; *jur* Patentbeschreibung; *arch* Baubeschreibung *f*; *tech* technische Daten *pl*; *pl* Beschreibung *f* der Einzelheiten; *arch* Ausschreibungsbedingungen *f pl*, Baukostenvoranschlag *m*; *~~ test* Abnahmeprüfung *f*; **~ify** ['spesifai] *tr* darlegen, einzeln, genau angeben, an-, aufführen, spezifizieren; *for a ~ified purpose* für e-n bestimmten Zweck; **~imen** ['spesimin] Muster *n*, Probe(stück *n*) *f*, Exemplar *n*; *fam* Typ, Kerl, Bursche *m*; *Am fam* Harnprobe *f*; *attr* Muster-, Probe-; *to take a blood ~~* e-e Blutprobe machen; *~~ book* Musterbuch *n*; *~~ copy* Belegexemplar *n*; *~~ page* Probeseite *f*; *~~ signature* Unterschriftsprobe *f*; **~ious** ['spi:ʃəs] scheinbar, Schein-; trügerisch, bestechend; **~iousness** ['spi:ʃəsnis] bloße(r), äußere(r) Schein, Trug *m*, täuschende Fassade *f*.
speck [spek] Fleck(chen *n*) *m*; *a ~* ein bißchen, ein (klein) wenig; *~ of dust* Stäubchen *n*; **~le** ['-l] *s* (Farb-)Fleck *m*, Tüpfel *m* od *n*; *tr* tüpfeln, sprenkeln; **~led** ['-ld] *a* getüpfelt, gesprenkelt; *(Holz)* maserig; **~less** ['-lis] fleckenlos, rein.
specs [speks] *pl fam* Brille *f*; *fam com* detaillierte Angaben *f pl*, Data *pl*.
spect|acle ['spektəkl] ungewöhnliche(r) Anblick *m*; Schauspiel *n*, Erscheinung; Schau(spiel *n*) *f*; *pl (pair of ~~s)* Brille *f*; *to look through rose-colo(u)red ~~ (fig)* alles durch e-e rosige Brille sehen; *~~-case* Brillenfutteral *n*; *~~ lens* Brillenglas *n*; **~acled** ['-d] brillentragend; *zoo* Brillen-; **~acular** [spek'tækjulə] *a* auffällig, ungewöhnlich; auf Wirkung berechnet; theatralisch; prächtig, stattlich; *s Am* große Fernsehschau; große Zeitungsanzeige *f*; **~ator** [-'teitə] Zuschauer *m*.
spectr|al ['spektrəl] gespenstisch, geisterhaft; Spektral-; *~~ analysis* Spektralanalyse *f*; **~e,** *Am* **specter** ['spektə] Gespenst *n*, Geist *m*, Phantom *n*, Erscheinung *f*; *fig* Schreckgespenst *n*; *~~-lemur (zoo)* Koboldmaki *m*; **~ogram** ['spektrəgræm] Spektrogramm *n*; **~ograph** ['-əgrɑ:f] Spektrograph *m*; **~ometer** [spek'trɔmitə] Spektrometer *n*; **~oscope** ['spektrəskoup] Spektroskop *n*; **~oscopic(al)** [spektrəs'kɔpik(-əl)] spektroskopisch; **~um** ['-əm] *pl a.-a* ['-ə] *opt* Spektrum *n*; *fig* Skala *f*; *solar ~~* Sonnenspektrum *n*; *~~ analysis* Spektralanalyse *f*.
specul|ar ['spekjulə] spiegelnd; Spiegel-; **~ate** ['spekjuleit] *itr* nachdenken, (nach)sinnen, grübeln (*on, upon, about* über); theoretisieren; *com* spekulieren, gewagte Geschäfte machen (*in* in); **~ation** [spekju'leiʃən] Nachdenken, (Nach-)Sinnen, Grübeln *n* (*on* über); Vermutung; *a. com* Spekulation *f*; *bear, bull ~~* Baisse-, Haussespekulation *f*; *~~ in stocks* Aktienspekulation *f*; **~ative** ['spekjulətiv] *philos* spekulativ; theoretisch; vermutet, mutmaßlich; *com* Spekulations-; gewagt, riskant; *~~ gain* Spekulationsgewinn *m*; **~ator** ['-leitə] Theoretiker; Spekulant *m*; **~um** ['-ləm] *pl -la* [-lə] (*bes.* Metall-)Spiegel; *zoo* Spiegel *m*.
speech [spi:tʃ] Sprache *f*; Sprech-, Ausdrucksvermögen *n*, -weise *f*; Worte *n pl*, Äußerung, Bemerkung *f*; Ansprache, Rede; Sprache *f*, Idiom *n*, Dialekt *m*; *to deliver, to make a ~* e-e Rede halten (*on, about* über; *to* vor); *~ is silver but silence is golden (prov)* Reden ist Silber, Schweigen ist Gold; *after-dinner ~* Tischrede *f*; *freedom of ~* Redefreiheit *f*; *maiden ~* Jungfernrede *f*; *~* **clinic** *(Am)* Abteilung *f* für Sprachgestörte; *~* **community** Sprachgemeinschaft *f*; *~* **current** Sprechstrom *m*; **~-day** *Br* (Schul-)Schlußfeier *f*; *~* **disorder** Sprachstörung *f*; **~ifier** ['-ifaiə] Schwätzer *m*; **~ify** ['-ifai] *itr hum* große Reden schwingen, *pej* große Bogen spucken; **~less** ['-lis] stumm; sprachlos (*with* vor); **~-training** Sprecherziehung *f*.
speed [spi:d] *s* Schnelligkeit, Fixigkeit; *(bestimmte)* Geschwindigkeit *f*; Tempo *n*; *tech* Drehzahl *f*; *mot* Gang *m*; *film* Empfindlichkeit *f*; *itr irr sped, sped* [sped] zu schnell fahren; *tr* in schnelle Bewegung setzen; *(to ~ up)* beschleunigen; *fig* anspornen; fördern, unterstützen; die Geschwindigkeit einstellen (*a machine* e-r Maschine); *at a ~ of* mit e-r Geschwindigkeit von; *at full, top ~* mit Höchstgeschwindigkeit; *God ~ you! good ~! (obs)* Gott segne dich, gehab dich wohl! *more haste, less ~ (prov)* Eile mit Weile! *cruising ~* Reisegeschwindigkeit *f*; **~boat** Rennboot *n*; *~* **control** Geschwindigkeitskontrolle; *tech* Drehzahlsteuerung *f*; **~-cop** Verkehrsstreife *f (Polizist)*; **~er** ['-ə] Kilometerfresser *m*, *fam* Rennsau *f*; **~iness** ['-inis] Schnellig-

keit; Eile, Hast *f*; **~ing** ['-iŋ] *mot* zu schnelle(s) Fahren *n*; **~ limit** Höchstgeschwindigkeit, Geschwindigkeitsbegrenzung *f*; **~ merchant** *sl* Kilometerfresser *m*; **~ometer** [spi'dɔmitə], **~ indicator** Geschwindigkeitsmesser *m*; **~ range** Drehzahlbereich *m*; **~ restriction** Geschwindigkeitsbegrenzung *f*; **~ster** ['-stə] Kilometerfresser; Rennwagen *m*; Schnellboot *n*; **~ trap** *Am* Straßenfalle *f*; **~-up** Beschleunigung; Produktions-, Leistungssteigerung *f*; **~ wag(g)on** *mot* Lieferwagen *m*; **~way** *Am* Rennstrecke; Autobahn *f*; **~well** *bot* Ehrenpreis *n* od *m*; **~y** ['-i] schnell; prompt, unverzüglich, schlagartig.

spel|eologist [spi:li'ɔlədʒist] Höhlenforscher *m*; **~eology** [-li'ɔlədʒi] Höhlenforschung *f*.

spell [spel] **1.** Zauberwort *n*, -formel *f*, -spruch; Zauber, Reiz *m*, Anziehungskraft, Faszination, Wirkung *f*; *to be under s.o.'s ~* verzaubert, gebannt sein; in jds Bann stehen; *to cast a ~ on* verzaubern; ganz für sich einnehmen; **~bind** *irr (s. bind) tr* ver-, bezaubern, bannen, faszinieren, fesseln; **~binder** *fam* mitreißende(r), faszinierende(r) Redner *m*; **~bound** *a* verzaubert, gebannt, fasziniert, mit-, hingerissen; **2.** *a. irr spelt, spelt* [spelt] *tr* buchstabieren; (richtig) schreiben (*with* mit); *(Wort)* bilden; bedeuten, gleichkommen (*s.th.* e-r S); *itr* orthographisch schreiben; *to ~ out* entziffern, herausbekommen; *Am sl* ausea.-klamüsern; **~down** *Am* orthographische(r) Wettbewerb *m*; **~er** ['-ə] Buchstabierende(r) *m*; Fibel *f*; *to be a bad ~~* viele Rechtschreibfehler machen; **~ing** ['-iŋ] Buchstabieren *n*; Rechtschreibung, Orthographie *f*; *~~-bee (Am)* orthographische(r) Wettbewerb *m*; *~~-book* Fibel *f*; **3.** *s* Ablösung (bei der Arbeit); Schicht, Arbeitszeit; (kurze) Zeit, (Zeit-)Dauer, Periode *f*; *fam* Weilchen *n*, Moment, Augenblick; *Am fam* Katzensprung *fig*; *Am fam* (Krankheits-)Anfall *m*; *(bes. Australien)* Ruhepause *f*; *at a ~* in einem fort, ununterbrochen; *by ~s* dann u. wann; *for a ~* e-e Weile; *~ and ~* abwechselnd; *to take ~s* sich ablösen; *cold, hot ~* Kälte-, Hitzewelle *f*; *fresh ~* Ablösung(smannschaft) *f*; neue Arbeitskräfte *f pl*.

spelt [spelt] **1.** *pret u. pp* von *spell*; **2.** Dinkel(weizen), Spelz *m*.

spelter ['speltə] Hartlot; Zink(barren *m*) *n*.

spelunker [spi'lʌŋkə] *Am fam* (Amateur-)Höhlenforscher *m*.

spencer ['spensə] **1.** kurze *(Herren-* od *Damen-)* Wolljacke *f*; **2.** *mar* Gaffelsegel *n*.

spend [spend] *irr spent, spent tr* verbrauchen, erschöpfen; *(Geld)* ausgeben, verausgaben; verbrauchen; auf-, verwenden (*on, upon* für); widmen (*on s.th.* e-r S); *(Zeit)* ver-, zubringen; verschwenden, vergeuden; *(Vermögen)* durchbringen; *mar* verlieren; *itr* (sein) Geld ausgeben; (sich) verbrauchen, sich verzehren; *zoo* laichen; *to ~ money like water* sein Geld zum Fenster hinauswerfen; **~ing** ['-iŋ] Ausgabe *f*; *deficit ~~* öffentliche Verschuldung *f* durch Aufnahme von Anleihen; *~~ capacity, power* Kaufkraft *f*; *~~ money* Taschengeld *n*; *~~ period* Haushaltsperiode *f*; **~thrift** ['-θrift] *s* Verschwender *m*; *a* verschwenderisch.

spent [spent] *a* erschöpft, abgespannt, entkräftet, ermattet; *tech* verbraucht, abgenutzt.

sperm [spə:m] Sperma *n*, männliche(r) Samen *m*, Samenflüssigkeit *f*; Walrat *m* od *n*; Pottwal *m*; **~aceti** [spə:mə'seti] Walrat *m* od *n*; **~ary** ['-əri] *anat* Samendrüse *f*; **~atic** [spə:'mætik] *scient* Samen-; *~~ cord (anat)* Samenstrang *m*; **~atozoon** [spə:məto(u)'zouɔn] *pl -zoa* [-'zouə] *physiol* Samentierchen *n*; **~ oil** Walöl *n*; **~ whale** Pottwal *m*.

spew, spue [spju:] *tr itr (to ~ up, out)* erbrechen.

*

sphagnum ['sfægnəm] *bot* Torfmoos *n*.

sphen|ic ['sfenik], **~oid** ['sfi:nɔid] *scient a* keilförmig; **~oid** *s med* Keilbein *n*.

spher|e ['sfiə] *math* Kugel *f*; *astr* Himmelskörper; Himmel(sgewölbe *n*) *m*; *(~~ of life) fig* Sphäre *f*, Lebensbereich *m*, Gebiet *n*, Wirkungskreis *m*, Umwelt *f*, Milieu *n*; *pl* Sphären *f pl*; *~~ of influence, of interest (pol)* Einflußbereich *m*, Interessensphäre *f*; *~~ of operation* Wirkungsbereich *m*; **~ic(al)** ['sferik(əl)] kugelförmig, sphärisch; **~icity** [sfe'risiti] Kugelgestalt *f*; **~oid** ['-rɔid] *s* Sphäroid, Rotationsellipsoid *n*.

sphincter ['sfiŋktə] *anat* Schließmuskel *m*.

sphinx [sfiŋks] Sphinx *f a. fig*.

*

spic|e [spais] *s* Gewürz *n*; Würze *f*; Aroma *n*, Duft *m*; *fig* Würze; *fig* Spur, Andeutung *f*; *tr* würzen *a. fig*; **~ed** [-t] *a* gewürzt; würzig; **~ery** ['-əri] Gewürz *n (kollektiv)*; **~iness** ['-inis] *das* Würzige, Pikante, Reizvolle; **~y** ['-i] (stark) gewürzt; würzig, aromatisch; *fig* pikant, anregend, reizvoll, rassig; gewagt; schick.

spick-and-span ['spikn'spæn] (funkel)nagelneu; wie aus dem Ei gepellt.

spider ['spaidə] *zoo* Spinne *f a. tech*; Dreibein *n*, -fuß *m*; *mot* Kardangelenk; Drehkreuz *n*; *Am* Bratpfanne *f*; **~-catcher** *zoo* Mauerspecht *m*; **~-crab** *zoo* Seespinne *f*; **~like** ['-laik] spinnenartig; **~ lines** *pl tech* Fadenkreuz *n*; **~-monkey** *zoo* Klammeraffe *m*; **~('s)-web** Spinn(en)gewebe *n*; **~y** ['-ri] spinnenartig; voller Spinnen.

spiel [spi:l] *Am sl s* Gequassel *n*; *itr* quasseln; **~er** ['-ə] *sl* Schwindler *m*.

spif(f)licate ['spiflikeit] *tr sl* wüst umgehen mit; vermurksen.

spiffy ['spifi], **spiffing** ['-iŋ] *sl* schnieke, tipptopp, fesch.

spigot ['spigət] Spund, Zapfen, (Faß-)Hahn *m*.

spik|e [spaik] *s* (Metall-)Spitze *f*; Dorn *(unter Rennschuhen)*; *(~~ nail)* Spieker, große(r) Nagel; *(Hirsch)* Spieß; *bot* Kolben *m*, Ähre *f*; *pl* Rennschuhe *m pl*; *tr* fest-, vernageln; durchbohren; verletzen; *fig* durchkreuzen, vereiteln, verhindern; *Am sl* e-n Schuß Alkohol tun in; *~~ lavender* Lavendel *m*; **~y** ['-i] (lang u.) spitz, spitzig; *fig* empfindlich.

spikenard ['spaikna:d] *bot* Narde *f*; Narden-, Lavendelöl *n*.

spile [spail] *s* Pflock, Zapfen, Spund, Zapfhahn; Pfahl *m (in sumpfigem Baugrund)*; *tr* mit Pflöcken versehen; verspunden; anzapfen; verpfählen.

spill [spil] **1.** *a. irr spilt, spilt* [-t] *tr* aus-, verschütten, vergießen; ver-, ausstreuen; gießen (*on* über); *fam* unter die Leute bringen, verbreiten; *fam (Reiter, Last)* abwerfen; *Am fam* hinfallen lassen, ein Bein stellen; *itr (to ~ over)* überlaufen, -fließen; *Am sl* s-e Meinung sagen; *s* Überfließen, -laufen *n*; *fam* Sturz *m (vom Pferd, Rad)*; *(~way)* Abflußrinne *f*, -rohr *n*; *to take a ~* herunter-, hinfallen; *to ~ the beans (Am sl)* das Geheimnis verraten; *to ~ blood* Blut vergießen; *there is no use crying over spilt milk* es hat keinen Sinn, Vergangenem nachzuweinen; **2.** Splitter; Fidibus; kleine(r) Zapfen, Stöpsel *m*.

spin [spin] *irr spun (obs: span), spun* [spʌn] *tr* spinnen *a. zoo*; (schnell) drehen; herumwirbeln; *(to ~ out)* in die Länge ziehen *a. fig*; ausspinnen, ersinnen, erdichten; *aero* trudeln lassen; *itr* spinnen; *(to ~ round)* sich schnell drehen, im Kreis herumwirbeln; *aero* trudeln; *(to ~ along)* schnell dahinrollen; *to ~ round* sich im Kreise drehen; *s* Wirbeln *n*, schnelle Drehbewegung *f*; Dahinrollen *n*; kurze(r) Ritt *m od* Fahrt *f*; *aero* Trudeln *n*; *phys* Spin; *(Geschoß)* Drall *m*; *to go for a ~ (mot fam)* spazierenfahren; *to go into a ~ (aero)* abtrudeln; *to ~ a coin* Zahl oder Wappen spielen; *to ~ the top* Kreisel spielen *od* schlagen; *to ~ a yarn (fig)* ein Seemannsgarn spinnen; *my head is ~ning* mir dreht sich alles im Kopf; *flat ~ (fam)* Panik *f*; **~ drier** Trockenschleuder *f (für Wäsche)*; **~ner** ['-ə] Spinner(in *f*) *m a. fig*; Spinnmaschine *f*; Planierer *m*; Spinne; Spinndrüse *f*; *aero* Propellerhaube *f*; **~ning** ['-iŋ] Spinnen *n*, Spinnerei *f*; *tech* Drücken *n*; *~~-jenny* Jennymaschine *f*; *~~-lathe* Drück-, Planierbank *f*; *~~-machine* Spinnmaschine *f*; *~~-mill* Spinnerei *f*; *~~-wheel* Spinnrad *n*; **~ster** ['-stə] *jur* Ledige; alte Jungfer *f*.

spinach ['spinidʒ] Spinat; *Am sl* Unsinn *m*.

spin|al ['spainl] *a anat* Rückgrat-, Wirbel-; Rückenmarks-; *~~ canal (anat)* Wirbelkanal *m*; *~~ column* Wirbelsäule *f*; *~~ cord, marrow, medulla* Rückenmark *n*; *~~ curvature* Rückgratverkrümmung *f*; *~~ fluid* Rückenmarksflüssigkeit *f*; **~e** [spain] *bes. bot zoo* Stachel; Dorn *m*; Rückgrat *n*; Grat, (Berg-)Kamm; (Buch-)Rücken *m*; **~eless** ['-lis] rückgratlos *a. fig*; **~ose** ['spainous], **~ous** ['spainəs] stach(e)lig, dornig; (zuge)spitz(t); **~y** ['spaini] stach(e)lig, dornig *a. fig*; *fig* schwierig, mühsam, -selig; *(Thema)* heikel.

spindl|e ['spindl] *s tech* Spindel; *tech* Welle; Drehachse *f*, Schaft *m*; Stange; weibliche, mütterliche Linie *f*; *itr* hoch aufschießen; *~~-legged, -shanked (a)* mit dünnen Beinen; *~~-legs, -shanks* dünnbeinige(r) Mensch *m*; *~~-tree (bot)* Pfaffenhütchen *n*; **~ing** ['-iŋ], **~y** ['-i] spindeldürr.

spindrift ['spindrift] Gischt, Sprühnebel *m*.

spinet [spi'net] *mus hist* Spinett *n*.

spinney ['spini] Gehölz; Dickicht *n*.

spir|acle ['spaiərəkl] *bes. zoo* Luftloch *n*; *(Wale)* Atemgang *m*; **~ant** ['spaiərənt] Reibelaut *m*.

spiraea, *Am a.* **spirea** [spai'riə] *bot* Spiräe *f*, Spierstrauch *m*.

spir|al ['spaiərəl] *a* spiralig, schneckenod schraubenförmig; Spiral-, Schnekken-, Schrauben-; *s* Spirale; Spiral-, Schnecken-, Schraubenlinie; Spiralfeder *f*; *itr* sich in e-r Spirale bewegen; sich in die Höhe schrauben; *(Preise)* stetig steigen *od* fallen; e-e Spirale bilden; *tr* in die Höhe *od* hoch-, herunterschrauben; *(Preise)* allmählich steigern, ansteigen lassen; *~~ conveyor* Förderschnecke *f*; *~~ nebula (astr)* Spiralnebel *m*; *the ~~ of rising prices and wages* die Lohn-Preis-Spirale *f*; *~~ spring* Spiralfeder *f*; *~~ staircase* Wendeltreppe *f*; **~e** ['spaiə] **1.** *s* Spirale, Schnecken-, Schraubenlinie; Spiral-, Schraubenwindung *f*; **2.** *s* Turmspitze *f*, -helm *m*; Baumspitze *f*; (Gras-)Halm; (Berg-)Gipfel; *zoo* Halm, Schößling *m*;

itr emporschießen; spitz zulaufen, sich steil erheben; **~y** ['-ri] spiralig; gewunden; gelockt, lockig; spitz(zulaufend); turmartig; vieltürmig.

spirit ['spirit] *s* Lebensgeist *m*, Seele *f*; Geist; Gedanke; Geist *m*, Gespenst *n*; Fee *f*, Elf; Mensch *m (im guten Sinn)*; Geisteshaltung, Einstellung; Anlage, Veranlagung *f*; Temperament *n*, Gemütsart; Stimmung; Begeisterung *f*, Schwung *m*, Lebhaftigkeit, Lebendigkeit *f*; Mut *m*, Tatkraft *f*; Geist *m*, wirkliche Bedeutung, wahre Absicht *f*, Sinn; Spiritus, Alkohol *m*; *the S~* der (Heilige) Geist; Gott *m*; *pl* Spirituosen *pl*, geistige Getränke *n pl*; *tr*: *to ~ away, off* wegzaubern, verschwinden lassen; *to ~ up* aufmuntern; *in high, great ~s* in gehobener Stimmung, frohgelaunt, gut aufgelegt; *in poor, low ~s, out of ~s* niedergeschlagen, bedrückt, in gedrückter Stimmung, schlecht aufgelegt; *to be with s.o. in ~* in Gedanken bei jdm sein; *to enter into the ~ of s.th.* sich an etw anpassen; *to keep up o.'s ~s* sich nicht niederdrücken lassen; *the Holy S~* der Heilige Geist; *leading ~* führende(r) Kopf *m*; *public ~* Gemeinsinn *m*; *~ of enterprise* Unternehmungsgeist *m*; *~ of wine* Weingeist *m*; **~ed** ['-id] lebhaft, lebendig, feurig, energisch, kraftvoll, mutig; *high-~~* hochgestimmt, frohgelaunt; optimistisch; *low-~~* niedergeschlagen, be-, gedrückt; pessimistisch; **~edness** ['-idnis] Lebhaftigkeit *f*; Feuer *n*, Kraft *f*, Mut *m*; **~ism** ['-izm] Spiritismus *m*; **~less** ['-lis] träge, schläfrig, schlaff, kraft-, mut-, lustlos, niedergedrückt, -geschlagen; **~ level** Wasserwaage *f*; **~ual** ['-juəl] *a* geistig, seelisch, innerlich; geistlich, kirchlich, religiös, heilig; *s* (Neger-) Spiritual *n*; *the Lords S~~* die geistlichen Herren *(im brit. Oberhaus)*; **~ualism** ['-juəlizm] Spiritismus; *philos* Spiritualismus *m*; **~ualist** ['-juəlist] Spiritist *m*; **~ualistic** [spiritjuə'listik] spiritistisch; spiritualistisch; **~uality** [spiritju'æliti] geistige Natur, Geistigkeit; Unkörperlichkeit *f*; **~ualization** [-juəlai'zeiʃən] Vergeistigung *f*; **~ualize** ['spiritjuəlaiz] *tr* vergeistigen; **~uous** ['-juəs] alkoholisch; *~~ beverages (pl)* Spirituosen *pl*.

spirt *s. spurt.*

spit [spit] **1.** *s* Bratspieß *m*; Landzunge; Sandbank *f*, Riff *n*; *tr* aufspießen, durchbohren; **2.** *irr spat, spat tr* ausspeien, -spucken; *allg* ausstoßen; *(Worte)* heraussprudeln; *mil (Zünder)* anstecken; *itr* speien, spucken (*at, on, upon* auf *a. fig*); *(Regen)* klatschen, spritzen, sprühen; *(Feder)* spritzen; *(Katze)* zischen, fauchen; *s* Speien *n*; Speichel *m*, *fam* Spucke *f*; *ent* Schaum; Sprühregen *m*; *fam (~ting image)* Ebenbild *n*; *to be s.o.'s dead ~, s.o.'s ~ and image (fam)* jdm wie aus dem Gesicht geschnitten sein; *~ it out* nun sag's schon! **~ball** *Am* Papierkügelchen *n*; **~fire** Hitzkopf *m*; **~tle** ['-l] Speichel; *ent* Schaum *m*; **~toon** [spi'tu:n] Spucknapf *m*; **3.** Spatentiefe *f*, -stich *m*.

spite [spait] *s* Haß, Groll *m*, Bosheit *f*, böse(r) Wille *m* (*against* gegen); *tr* kränken, verletzen, ärgern, s-n Groll auslassen an; *from, out of ~* aus Bosheit; *in ~ of* trotz *gen*; *in ~ of the fact that* obgleich, obwohl; *to cut off o.'s nose to ~ o.'s face (fig)* sich ins eigene Fleisch schneiden; *to do s.th. to ~ s.o.* etw jdm zum Trotz tun; **~ful** ['-ful] gehässig, boshaft; *(Zunge)* giftig; **~fulness** ['-fulnis] Gehässigkeit, Bosheit, Boshaftigkeit *f*.

spiv [spiv] *Br sl* Arbeitsscheue(r), Drückeberger; Schieber; Schwarzhändler; Gauner, Strolch *m*.

splash [splæʃ] *tr* (ver)spritzen; planschen in; bespritzen; *Am sl* an die große Glocke hängen; *sl* in großer Aufmachung bringen; *sl* großzügig ausgeben; *itr* spritzen (*in all directions* nach allen Richtungen); *(Regen)* klatschen; *(to ~ o.'s way)* patschen (*into* in; *through* durch) *s* Spritzen *n*; *(Wellen)* Plätschern, Klatschen *n*; Spritzfleck, Spritzer; Klecks; Lichtfleck; *fam* Gesichtspuder; Plumps; *fam* Schuß *m* Sodawasser; *Am sl* Wasser, Bad *n*; *sl* Aufregung, Sensation, Aufmachung *f*; *to make a ~ (fig)* Furore machen, Aufsehen erregen; *~ of mud* Dreckspritzer *m*; **~-board** Spritzbrett; Schutzblech *n*; Schütze *f*; **~ lubrication** Tauchschmierung *f*; **~ news** *(Zeitung)* Blickfang *m*; **~ water** Spritzwasser *n*; **~y** ['-i] spritzend; naß, schmutzig; beschmutzt; *fig* in die Augen springend, *od* fallend, auffällig; *sl* sensationell.

splay [splei] *s* (abge)schräg(t)e Fläche; *arch* Ausschrägung, Fensterlaibung; Ausbreitung, -dehnung, Verbreiterung *f*; *a* (abge)schräg(t), sich ausdehnend, -breitend; breit u. flach; schief; *tr* abschrägen; ausbreiten, -dehnen, erweitern; *(Knochen)* verrenken; *itr (to ~ out)* sich ausbreiten, -dehnen, sich erweitern; sich abschrägen; **~foot** Spreizfuß *m*; **~footed** *a* mit Spreizfüßen.

spleen [spli:n] *anat* Milz; *fig* schlechte, üble Laune *f*, Ärger *m*, Verdrießlichkeit; Bosheit *f*; *obs* Spleen, verrückte(r) Einfall *m*, Melancholie *f*; *to vent o.'s ~* s-m Ärger Luft machen (*on* gegen); **~ish** ['-iʃ] schlechtgelaunt; boshaft.

splend|ent ['splendənt] glänzend; strahlend, prächtig; glanzvoll, berühmt; **~id** ['-id] prachtvoll, prächtig, glänzend; herrlich, großartig; glanzvoll, (hoch)berühmt; *fam (übertreibend)* großartig, prächtig, herrlich, ausgezeichnet, blendend; **~iferous** [splen'difərəs] *hum fam* glänzend; **~o(u)r** ['splendə] Glanz *m*, Pracht, Herrlichkeit, Größe *f*, Ruhm *m*.

splen|etic(al) [spli'netik(əl)] *a* Milz-; *fig* übelgelaunt, reizbar, mürrisch; gehässig; *s* Griesgram *m*; **~ic** [splenik] *a* Milz-; *~~ fever* Milzbrand *m*; **~itis** [spli'naitis] Milzentzündung *f*.

splice [splais] *tr mar* spleißen, splissen; *allg* verscheren, verzahnen, verbinden; *film* zs.kleben; *sl (Ehepaar)* zs.-bringen; *s* Splissung *f*.

spline [splain] *tr tech* verkeilen, sichern; nuten; *s* Keil, (Wellen-)Nut *m*.

splint [splint] *s* Holz-, Rohrstreifen *m*; Latte; *med* Schiene; *vet (Pferd)* Piephacke *f*; *(~-bone) (Pferd)* Griffel-, *(Mensch)* Wadenbein *n*; *tech* Splint, Keil *m*; *tr med* schienen; **~er** ['-ə] *tr* zersplittern; *itr* (zer)splittern; *s* Splitter, Span *m*; Sprengstück *n*, Granat-, Bombensplitter *m*; *~~-bomb* Splitterbombe *f*; *~~ party* Splitterpartei *f*; **~erless** ['-əlis] *(Glas)* nicht splitternd; **~erproof** ['-əpru:f] *(Glas)* splittersicher *a. mil*; **~ery** ['-əri] voller Splitter; leicht splitternd.

split [split] *irr split, split tr* spalten, aufsplittern; zerbrechen, zerreißen; *fig* trennen, (auf)spalten, entzweien; *(Kosten)* aufteilen; verteilen; aufgliedern, -teilen; sich teilen in; *chem phys* spalten; *(Aktien)* splitten; *itr* sich spalten, (zer)splittern (*into* in); (zer)brechen, (zer)reißen, bersten; sich spalten lassen; *fig* uneins werden, sich entzweien; *fam* den Gewinn teilen, Halbpart machen; *sl* verpfeifen, verraten (*on s.o.* jdn); *s* (Zer-)Splittern *n*; Spalt, Riß, Sprung; Splitter *m*; *fig* Entzweiung, Spaltung *a. pol*; *fam* halbe Flasche *f*, halbe(s) Glas *n (Schnaps)*; *sl* (Beute-)Anteil *m*; Spaltleder *n*; dünne(r) Holzstreifen; *(Sekunde)* Bruchteil *m*; halbe (Soda-)Flasche *f*, halbe(s) Glas Schnaps *n*; *pl (sport)* Spagat *m* od *n*; *a* Spalt-; (auf)geteilt; *to ~ off* absplittern, sich abspalten; *to ~ open* aufbrechen, -platzen; *to ~ up* sich aufspalten, zerfallen; sich trennen; *to ~ with s.o.* mit jdm endgültig brechen; *at full ~ (Am)* in Windeseile; *in a ~ second* im Bruchteil e-r Sekunde; *to ~ the difference* e-n Kompromiß schließen, sich auf der Mitte einigen; *to ~ hairs* Haarspalterei treiben; *to ~ o.'s sides (laughing, with laughter)* platzen vor Lachen; *my head is ~ting* mir platzt der Schädel, ich habe furchtbare Kopfschmerzen; *banana ~* Bananensplit *m*; **~ leather** Spaltleder *n*; **~ peas** *pl* gespaltene, halbe Erbsen *f pl*; **~ pin** Splint *m*; **~ plug** Bananenstecker *m*; **~ ring** Sprengring *m*; **~ter** ['-ə] Spaltende(r) *m*; **~ting** ['-iŋ] *a (bes. Kopfschmerzen)* stark, heftig, rasend; *(Lärm)* betäubend; *s* Spaltung, Teilung *f*; *(Steuer)* Splitting *n*; *ear-~~* ohrenzerreißend; *hair-~~* Haarspalterei *f*; **~-up** *Am sl* Trennung, Scheidung *f*.

splotch [splɔtʃ], **splodge** [-dʒ] *s* Fleck, Klecks *m*; *tr* beklecksen, beschmieren; **~y** ['-i] fleckig, bekleckst.

splurge [splə:dʒ] *Am fam s* Angeberei, Angabe *f*, Protzentum *n*; *itr* angeben; das Geld zum Fenster hinauswerfen.

splutter ['splʌtə] *itr* zischen; spritzen (*over* über); sprudeln, sprühen; *(Feder)* klecksen; *mot* kotzen; sich *(beim Sprechen)* überschlagen, sprudelnd reden; (vor Wut) stottern; *tr (to ~ out)* heraussprudeln; *s* Zischen; Spritzen, Sprühen; *mot* Kotzen; *(Feder)* Klecksen *n*.

spoil [spɔil] *a. irr spoilt, spoilt* [spɔilt] *tr* vernichten, zerstören; beschädigen; vereiteln; verderben, (stark) beeinträchtigen; *(Augen)* verderben; verwöhnen, verziehen; *obs lit* (be)rauben, (aus)plündern; *itr* verderben, verkommen, schlecht werden, (ver)faulen; *to be ~ing for* (ganz) verrückt sein nach; *s* Beute(stück *n*); ausgehobene Erde, Halde; *obs* Plünderung *f*, Raub; *obs* Schaden *m*, Schädigung; *pl* Beute *f*; Gewinn *m*; *pl Am pol* von der siegreichen Partei neu zu besetzende Posten *m pl*; *to ~ the fun for s.o.* jdm die Freude verderben; **~age** ['-idʒ] Abfall *m*, Abfälle *m pl*; *typ* Makulatur *f*, Ausschuß *m*; **~sman** ['-zmən] *Am* politische(r) Stellen-, Postenjäger *m*; **~-sport** Spiel-, Spaßverderber *m*; **~s system** *Am pol* System *n* der Futterkrippen.

spoke [spouk] **1.** *pret*, **~n** ['-ən] *pp* von *speak*; **~sman** ['-smən] Sprecher, Wortführer *m*; **2.** *s* Speiche; *(Leiter)* Sprosse; *mar* Spake *f*; *tr* mit Speichen, Sprossen versehen; *(Rad)* bremsen; *to put a ~ in s.o.'s wheel* jdm Steine in den Weg legen; **~-bone** *anat* Speiche *f*; **~-shave** Schabhobel *m*; **~-wheel** Speichenrad *n*; **~wise** ['-waiz] *a adv* strahlenartig.

spoliat|e ['spoulieit] *tr* plündern, rauben; **~ion** [spouli'eiʃən] Beraubung *f*, Raub *m*, Plünderung; *jur* Vernichtung, Beseitigung *f* von Urkunden; **~or** ['spoulieitə] Plünderer, Räuber *m*.

spondee ['spɔndi:] Spondeus *m*.

spong|e [spʌndʒ] *s* Schwamm *a. zoo*; (Gummi-, Kunststoff-)Schwamm;

(Gaze-, Watte-)Bausch; Brotteig; *Am* Schaumpudding *m*; *Am* = *~-cake* od *~-bath*; *fam* Nassauer, Schmarotzer, Parasit; *Am sl* Säufer *m*; *tr* mit e-m Schwamm abwischen *od* behandeln; abtupfen; *(to ~~ up)* aufsaugen; *fam* sich unter den Nagel reißen; *itr* Schwämme fischen; sich vollsaugen; *fig* schmarotzen (*on* bei); *on s.o.* auf jds Kosten leben; *to ~~ away, off, out* auswischen, -löschen; *to pass the ~~ over* vergessen wollen, nichts mehr wissen wollen von; *to throw, to toss up the ~~ (Boxen u. allg)* (den Kampf) aufgeben, die Flinte ins Korn werfen; *~~-bag* Kulturbeutel *m*; *~~-bath* (Ab-)Waschung *f*; *~~-cake* Sandtorte *f*; *~~-cloth* Flausch *m*; *~~-finger* Löffelbiskuit *m*; *~~-rubber* Schaumgummi *m* od *n*; *~~-tent (med)* Tampon *m*; **~er** ['-ə] Schmarotzer *m*; **~iness** ['-inis] Schwammigkeit; Porosität; Saugfähigkeit *f*; **~y** ['-i] schwammartig; schwammig; löch(e)rig, porös; saugfähig; weich, sumpfig.

spons|al ['spɔnsəl] *a* Hochzeits-, Ehe-; bräutlich; **~ion** ['-ʃən] Bürgschaft *f*; **~or** ['-sə] Bürge; Taufzeuge, Pate *m*, Patin *f*; Gönner, Förderer; *Am* Geldgeber *m*; *tr* fördern, unterstützen; garantieren; Pate stehen bei; *Am radio tele* (heraus)bringen, finanzieren.

spontan|eity [spɔntə'ni:iti] Unmittelbarkeit, Unbedingtheit, Spontaneität *f*; eigene(r) Antrieb *m*; Freiwilligkeit; impulsive, unüberlegte Handlung(sweise) *f*; **~eous** [spɔn'teinjəs] unmittelbar; spontan; impulsiv, unüberlegt, ohne Vorbedacht, (ganz) zwanglos, dem inneren Triebe folgend; *bot* wild(wachsend); *~~ ignition* Selbstentzündung *f*; *~~ generation* Urzeugung *f*.

spoof [spu:f] *sl s* Schwindel, Ulk, Fez *m*; *itr* schwindeln, Ulk machen; *tr* beschwindeln, verulken; *a* falsch.

spook [spu:k] *hum* Gespenst *n*, Geist, Spuk *m*; **~ish** ['-iʃ], **~y** ['-i] *a fam* spuk-, geister-, gespensterhaft.

spool [spu:l] *s* Spule; Rolle *f*; *tr* (auf)spulen, aufwickeln.

spoon [spu:n] *s* Löffel; *sl* Einfaltspinsel, Simpel; närrisch(er) Verliebte(r) *m*; *tr* (aus)löffeln; *itr sl* närrisch verliebt sein; sich abknutschen; *sport* mit Löffelköder angeln; *to be born with a silver-~ in o.'s mouth* ein Glückskind, -pilz sein; *dessert-, egg-, salt-, soup* od *table-, tea-~* Dessert-, Eier-, Salz-, Suppen- *od* Eß-, Teelöffel *m*; **~-bait** Löffelköder, Blinker *m*; **~-bill** Löffelreiher *m*; **~-dredge, -scraper** Löffelbagger, -schaber *m*; **~-drift** = *spindrift (s.d.)*; **~(e)y** ['-i] *sl a* läppisch, dämlich; bis über die Ohren, närrisch verliebt (*on, upon* in); *s* närrische(r) Kauz *m*; **~-fed** *a* aufgepäppelt, verweichlicht; *com* subventioniert; **~ful** ['-ful] Löffelvoll *m*.

spoor [spuə] Spur, Fährte *f*.

sporadic(al) [spə'rædik(əl)] sporadisch; *med* vereinzelt auftretend.

sporangium [spə'rændʒəm, spou-] *pl -gia* [-dʒə] *bot* Sporenkapsel *f*.

spore [spɔ:] *bot* Spore *f*; *biol* Keim *m a. fig*; *~* **case** Sporenkapsel *f*.

sport [spɔ:t] *s* Sport *m*; Spiel *n*; Unterhaltung, Belustigung *f*; Zeitvertreib *m*, Vergnügen *n*, Spaß *m*; Zielscheibe *f* des Spottes, *fig* Spielball *m*; Spielzeug *n*; *zoo bot* Spielart *f*; *fam* prima Kerl *m*; *pl* Sport(wett)kämpfe *m pl*; *itr* Sport treiben; spielen; sich unterhalten, sich belustigen; *biol* variieren, mutieren; *tr fam* zur Schau tragen, angeben, protzen mit; *a Am (bes. Kleidung)* Sport-; *in, for ~* zum Spaß; *to be a good (bad) ~* (keinen) Spaß verstehen; alles leicht (schwer) nehmen; *to go in for ~s* Sport treiben; *to make ~ of* sich lustig machen über; *to ~ o.'s oak (Br Universität)* die Türe abschließen; *be a (good) ~* sei ein netter Kerl! *athletic ~s (pl)* Leichtathletik *f*; *field ~s (pl)* Jagd *f*, Fischfang *m*, Pferderennen *n*; *poor ~* Spielverderber *m*; **~ing** ['-iŋ] *a* Sport-; sportlich; unternehmungslustig; *~~ chance (fam)* aussichtsreiche Chance *f*; *~~ goods (Am)* Sportartikel *m pl*; **~ive** ['-iv] lustig; spaßhaft; verspielt; **~s airplane** Sportflugzeug *n*; **~s car** Rennwagen *m*; **~scast** *Am radio video s* Sportübertragung; *itr* e-e Sportveranstaltung übertragen; **~scaster** *Am radio video* Sportberichter(statter) *m*; **~s coat, jacket** Sportsakko *m*; **~s field** Sportplatz *m*; **~sman** ['-smən] Sportler; Jäger; Angler; gute(r) Verlierer *m*; **~smanlike** ['-mənlaik], **~smanly** ['-mənli] sportlich; **~smanship** ['-smənʃip] Sportlichkeit, sportliche Haltung *f*; **~s suit** Sportanzug *m*, -kostüm *n*; **~s wear** Sportkleidung *f*; **~s woman** Sportlerin *f*; **~y** ['-i] sportlich; sportsmännisch; Sport-; *(Kleidung)* auffällig, elegant.

spot [spɔt] *s* Ort *m*, Örtlichkeit, Gegend; Stelle *f*; Fleck(en), Klecks *m*; *med* (Mutter-)Mal *n*, Pustel *f*; *fig* Schandfleck, Makel, (Charakter-)Fehler; *fam* Bissen *m*, Häppchen *n*, Schuß; *Am sl* Job *m*, Stelle *f*, Arbeitsplatz *m*; *Am sl* Vergnügungs-, Gaststätte *f*; *Am sl radio video* Platz *m* im Programm; *Am (Spiel)* Auge *n*; *pl* = *~ goods*; *tr* aufstellen; *fam* ausfindig machen; besudeln, besprenkeln, tüpfeln; *fig* beflecken; tadeln; die Flecken entfernen aus, (chemisch) reinigen; vormerken, -sehen; *fam (Punkte im Spiel)* vorgeben *od* abziehen; *fam* herausfinden, draufkommen auf, entdecken; *itr* fleckig werden; *in a ~ (sl)* in der Patsche; *on the ~* auf der Stelle; vom Fleck weg; *Am sl* in e-r üblen Lage, in Gefahr; *to be on the ~* zur Stelle sein; *fig fam* auf Draht sein; *Am* in der Klemme sitzen; *to be a hard ~ (fin)* eingefroren sein; *to hit the ~ (fam)* (gerade) das Richtige treffen; *to hit the high ~s (fam)* das Wichtigste herauspicken; *to put on the ~ (fam)* in Verlegenheit bringen; *sl* erledigen, auf die Seite schaffen, umbringen; *that's a sore ~ with him* das ist s-e wunde Stelle; *black ~* blaue(r) Fleck *m*; *the people on the ~* die Eingesessenen *pl*; *rooted to the ~* wie angewurzelt; *~ of ink* Tintenfleck *m*; *~* **announcement** Werbedurchsage *f*; *~* **business, deal** Bargeschäft *n*; *~* **cash** (sofortige) Barzahlung *f*; **~check** *Am* Stichprobe *f*; *~* **delivery** Kassalieferung *f*; *~* **elevation, height** *(Karte)* Höhenangabe *f*; *~* **film** Werbekurzfilm *m*; *~* **goods** *pl* sofort lieferbare Waren *f pl*; *~* **landing** Ziellandung *f*; **~less** ['-lis] flecken-, *fig* makellos; **~light** *s* Suchscheinwerfer(licht *n*) *m*; *tr* besonders herausstellen, in den Vordergrund spielen; *in the ~~* im Rampen-, Scheinwerferlicht der Öffentlichkeit; **~-market price** Platzkurs *m*; **~-news** *Am* Lokalnachrichten *f pl*; *~~ reporter* Lokalberichterstatter *m*; **~-on** *a fam* einwandfrei; **~-remover** Fleckentferner *m*; **~ted** ['-id] *a* gesprenkelt, gefleckt, getüpfelt; *fig* befleckt; *~~ fever* Fleckfieber *n*; **~ter** ['-ə] *mil* Aufklärer, (Artillerie-)Beobachter; *Am* (geheimer) Aufpasser, -seher *m*; **~ty** ['-i] gesprenkelt, gefleckt; ungleichmäßig, uneinheitlich; **~-weld** *tr tech* punktschweißen.

spous|al ['spauzl] *a* Hochzeits-, Ehe-; ehelich; **~e** [spauz] *s* Gatte *m*, Gattin *f*.

spout [spaut] *s* (Ausguß-)Röhre *f*, Röhrchen *n*; Tülle, Schnauze *f*; (Regen-)Guß, (Wasser-)Strahl *m*; Dachrinne, Traufe *f*, Ablaufrohr *n*; Wasserspeier *m*; *fam* Leihhaus *n*; *tr* (aus)gießen, -spritzen; *fig* zum besten, von sich geben; *fam* versetzen, verpfänden; *itr* herausschießen, -spritzen, -sprudeln; prusten; *(Gefäß)* spritzen; *fig* große Reden schwingen; *down the ~ (fam)* futsch; *up the ~ (fam)* versetzt, verpfändet; *fig* in Schwierigkeit; **~er** ['-ə] Ölquelle *f*; Wal(fisch); Walfänger; *fam* pathetische(r) Redner, Deklamator *m*.

sprag [spræg] *min* Spreizstempel, Keil, Bremsklotz *m*.

sprain [sprein] *tr* verrenken, verstauchen; *s* Verrenkung, Verstauchung *f*; *he ~ed his ankle* er hat sich den Fuß verstaucht.

sprat [spræt] *zoo* Sprotte *f*; *a ~ to catch a herring* ein kleines Zugeständnis, um ein größeres zu erlangen.

sprawl [sprɔ:l] *itr* sich recken, sich strecken; sich räkeln; krabbeln, kriechen; sich ausdehnen, sich erstrecken (*across* über); *bot* wuchern; *tr (to ~ out)* ausstrecken, -dehnen; *s* Räkeln *n*; wirre(r) Komplex *m*.

spray [sprei] **1.** *s* Sprüh-, Staubregen; Schaum, (feiner) Gischt, Sprühnebel *m*; zerstäubte Flüssigkeit *f*; *(~er)* Zerstäuber, Spray *m*; *(~ gun)* Spritzpistole; Spritzlackierung *f*; *tr* zerstäuben, spritzen; besprühen; *tech* spritzlackieren; *itr* sprühen; spritzen; *~* **nozzle** Spritzdüse *f*; **2.** (Blüten-, Frucht-)Zweig *m*; Vignette *f*.

spread [spred] *irr spread, spread tr* entfalten, ausbreiten, -spannen; spreizen; auslegen, zur Schau stellen; ausstrecken, dehnen, ausea.ziehen; aus-, ver-, zerstreuen; *(Brot)* bestreichen; streichen, schmieren (*on* auf); *(zeitlich)* ausdehnen, verteilen (*on* auf; *over several years* über mehrere Jahre); *(Nachricht, Krankheit)* verbreiten; bedecken, überziehen (*with* mit); *(den Tisch)* decken; *(Speise)* auftragen; zur Seite rücken; flach klopfen, breit schlagen; *to ~ out* ausbreiten; *itr* sich ausdehnen, -breiten; *(Feuer)* um sich greifen; sich aus-, verbreiten, bekannt werden; sich (auf)streichen, schmieren lassen; *to ~ o.s.* sich aufspielen; sich mächtig anstrengen; *s* (Aus-)Dehnung; Aus-, Verbreitung; Spreizung *f*; Umfang *m*, Spanne; *Am* Preisspanne, Marge *f*; *(bed-~)* Bettuch, -laken; Tischtuch *n*; *Am* (Brot-)Aufstrich *m*; *fam* Gelage *n*; *Am sl* (lobender) Zeitungsartikel *m*; doppelseitige Anzeige *f*; *Am typ* Doppelseite *f*; doppelseitige(r) Druck *m*; *aero* Spannweite *f*; *to spread the cloth, table* den Tisch decken; *to ~ it thick (sl)* auf großem Fuße leben; *to ~ o.s. thin (fig)* sich teilen mögen; sich klein machen; *middle-age ~ (fam)* Altersspeck *m*; *~* **eagle** Adler *m* mit ausgebreiteten Flügeln; *Am* Angeber *m*; **~-eagle** *tr* flach ausstrecken; *itr* die Arme ausbreiten; *a Am fam* bombastisch, chauvinistisch, prahlerisch; **~er** ['-ə] Zer-, Verteiler *m*; Streichmesser *n*; **~ing** ['-iŋ] *a* ausgedehnt, -gebreitet, ausladend, weit; *s* Streuung, Ausbreitung *f*.

spree [spri:] lustige(r) Abend *m*, ausgelassene Feier, Zecherei *f*, Zechgelage *n*; *fig* Welle *f*; *to go on the ~* e-n Lokalbummel machen.

sprig [sprig] *s* Zweig(lein *n*) *m*; Vignette *f*; (Metall-)Stift *m*; (dreieckiges Metall-)Plättchen *n*; *hum* Sprößling *(Sohn, Schüler)*; *fam* grüne(r) Junge *m*; *tr* mit e-r Vignette verzieren; mit Stiften befestigen.

sprightl|iness ['spraitlinis] Munterkeit, Lebendigkeit, Lebhaftigkeit *f*; **~y** ['-li] *a adv* munter, lebendig, lebhaft.

spring [spriŋ] *irr sprang, sprung itr* springen; (auf)schnellen, aufspringen (*from* von); *fig (to ~ up)* entspringen, entstehen, s-n Anfang nehmen (*from* aus); (her)stammen, herrühren (*from* von); sich erheben, auf-, emporragen; *tech* sich werfen, rissig werden, springen, platzen; explodieren, losgehen; sich werfen (*at* auf); eilen (*to arms* zu den Waffen); *Am sl* plötzlich auftauchen (*with* mit); *tr* aufscheuchen; springen über; ein-, zuschnappen lassen; *(Falle)* stellen; sprengen; zur Explosion bringen; (ab)federn; zum Vorschein kommen lassen; bekanntmachen; plötzlich herausplatzen mit; *(Geld)* springen lassen; *sl* aus der Haft freikriegen; *s* Sprung, Satz *m*; Hochschnellen *n*; Schnell-, Spannkraft; (Sprung-)Feder, Federung; Elastizität; Quelle *f*; *fig* Ursprung, Anfang; Grund *m*, Veranlassung *f*, Motiv *n*, Triebfeder *f*; Frühling *m*, Frühjahr *n*; *poet u. fig* Lenz; *mar* Spring *m*; *to ~ up* aufspringen, hochfahren; *(Gebäude)* aus der Erde schießen (*like mushrooms* wie Pilze); *(Wind)* aufkommen; *in (the) ~* im Frühjahr; *in the ~ of life* im Lenz des Lebens; *to take a ~* e-n Satz machen; *to ~ into existence* plötzlich dasein, auf-, ins Leben treten; *to ~ to o.'s feet* aufspringen; *to ~ to it (fam)* rasch handeln; *to ~ a leak* ein Leck bekommen, leck werden; *to ~ to s.o.'s lips* jdm über die Lippen kommen; *to ~ a surprise on s.o.* jdn überraschen; *to ~ s.th. on s.o.* jdn mit etw überraschen; *impulse ~* Antriebsfeder *f*; *spiral, watch ~* Spiral-, Uhrfeder *f*; **~-balance** Federwaage *f*; **~-bed, -mattress** Sprungfedermatratze *f*; **~ blade, leaf** Blattfeder *f*, Federblatt *n*; **~-board** *sport* Sprungbrett *n a. fig*; **~bok** ['-bɔk] *zoo* Springbock *m*; **~-bolt** Federriegel, -bolzen *m*; **~ catch** Schnapperschluß *m*; **~-cleaning** Frühjahrsreinigung *f*, -(haus)putz *m*; **~er** ['-ə] Springer; *arch* Kämpfer; *zoo* Springbock *m*; **~ fever, debility** Frühjahrsmüdigkeit *f*; **~head** Quelle *f*; **~ hook** Karabinerhaken *m*; **~iness** ['-inis] Elastizität, Sprungkraft *f*; **~ing** ['-iŋ] Federung *f*; **~ lock** Schnappschloß *n*; **~ shopping** Frühjahrseinkäufe *m pl*; **~tide** *(Ebbe u. Flut)* Springtide *f*; = **~time** Frühlingszeit *f*, -jahr *n*; **~-water** Quellwasser *n*; **~y** ['-i] elastisch; federnd.

springe [sprin(d)ʒ] *s* Schlinge *f (zum Tierfang)*; *tr* in e-r Schlinge fangen.

sprinkl|e ['spriŋkl] *tr* (ver)spritzen (*on* auf); besprengen, bespritzen; sprenkeln, bestreuen, übersäen (*with* mit); streuen (*on* auf); bestreuen (*s.th. with s.th.* etw mit etw); *itr* spritzen; sprühen; nieseln; *s* (Be-)Spritzen, (Be-)Sprengen *n*; Sprüh-, Nieselregen *m*; ein bißchen *(of)*; **~er** ['-ə] Gießkanne *f*; Rasensprenger; *(street-~~)* Sprengwagen *m*; Feuerlöschgerät *n*; Weih(wasser)wedel *m*; *~~ system* Rasenspreng-, Feuerlöschanlage *f*; **~ing** ['-iŋ] Spritzen, Sprengen *n*; *fig* Anstrich, Anhauch, Anflug *m*; *a ~~ of* ein bißchen; *~~ can (Am)* Gießkanne *f*; *~~ cart (Am)* Sprengwagen *m*; *~~ nozzle* Brause; Sprinklerdüse *f*.

sprint [sprint] *itr* sprinten; (End-)Spurt *a. fig*; *s* Kurzstreckenlauf *m*; **~er** ['-ə] Sprinter, Kurzstreckenläufer; *(Rad)* Flieger *m*.

sprit [sprit] *mar* (Bug-)Spriet *n*.

sprite [sprait] Kobold, Elf(e *f*) *m*, Fee *f*.

sprocket ['sprɔkit] *tech* (Kettenrad-)Zahn; **~ chain** Gelenk-, Laschenkette *f*; **~ wheel** Kettenrad *n*; *film* Führungsrolle *f*.

sprout [spraut] *itr* sprießen; aufschießen; keimen; schnell wachsen, sich schnell entwickeln; *tr* sprießen, keimen lassen; *s bot* u. *fig* (junger) Trieb, Sproß; Keim; *pl (Brussels ~s)* Rosenkohl *m*.

spruce [spruːs] **1.** *a* nett, blank, sauber; *v (to ~ up) tr* herausputzen; *itr* blank, sauber werden; sich herausputzen; **~ness** ['-nis] Sauberkeit; Eleganz *f*; **2.** Fichte, Rottanne *f*.

spry [sprai] lebhaft, quicklebendig, munter; flink, fix; gepflegt, elegant.

spud [spʌd] *s* Jäthacke; Gabel *f* (zum Kartoffelroden); Klumpen, Kloß *m*; *fam* Kartoffel *f*; *sl* Kumpel *m*.

spue *s. spew.*

spum|e [spjuːm] *s* Schaum, Gischt *m*; *itr* schäumen; **~ous** ['spjuːməs], **~y** ['-i] schaumig, schäumend, schaumbedeckt.

spun [spʌn] *pp* von *spin (s.d.)*; **~ casting** Schleuderguß *m*; **~ glass** Glaswolle *f*.

spunk [spʌŋk] Zunder *m*; Funke(n) *m*, Flämmchen *n*; *fam* Mumm *m*; *fam* hitzige(s) Temperament *n*; **~y** ['-i] *fam* couragiert, nicht bange; munter, lebhaft, hitzig.

spur [spəː] *s* Sporn *a. zoo bot*; *fig* Ansporn, Antrieb, Anreiz, *scient* Stimulus *m*; Steigeisen *n*; *tech* Sporn, Dorn *m*; scharfe Spitze *f*, Vorsprung; *(Gebirge)* Ausläufer *m*; *(Säule)* Eckblatt *n*; *arch* Strebe(pfeiler *m*) *f*; Stützbalken *m*, Knagge *f*; *mil hist* Außenwerk *n*; *(~ track) rail* Stichbahn *f*; *tr* spornen, die Sporen geben (*a horse* e-m Pferde); *fig* anspornen, -treiben, -reizen, stimulieren; mit Sporen versehen; *itr* die Sporen geben (*on* dat); galoppieren; *fig* drängen, (sich be)eilen; *on the ~ of the moment* in der Eingebung des Augenblicks, ohne Überlegung, vorschnell; *to win o.'s ~s* sich die Sporen verdienen; **~ gear** Stirn-, Zahnrad; *(~~ing)* Zahnradgetriebe *n*; **~ post** Prellstein *m*; **~red** [-d] *a* gespornt; **~ track** Neben-, Anschlußgleis *n*; **~ wheel** Zahnrad *n*.

spurge [spəːdʒ] *bot* Wolfsmilch *f*.

spurius ['spjuəriəs] falsch, unecht, nachgemacht; unehelich, illegitim; *(Gefühl)* geheuchelt; *zoo bot* Schein-; *tech* störend, unerwünscht; **~ness** ['-nis] Unechtheit; Illegitimität *f*.

spurn [spəːn] *tr* (verächtlich) mit dem Fuße wegstoßen; e-n Fußtritt versetzen; *fig* verschmähen, (verächtlich) abweisen.

spurr(e)y ['spʌri] *bot* Spergel *m*.

spurt, spirt [spəːt] *tr* ausstoßen, -spritzen, heraussprudeln; *to ~ out* herausspritzen; *itr* heraus-, entströmen, hervorsprudeln; *fig* sich plötzlich e-n Schwung geben, e-e plötzliche Anstrengung machen, sich zs.reißen; *sport* spurten; *com* plötzlich steigen; *s* plötzliche(s) Ausströmen *n*; starke(r) Strahl *m*; *fig* plötzliche Anstrengung *f*, Ruck; *sport* Spurt *m*; *com* plötzliche(s) Ansteigen *n*; *final ~* Endspurt *m*.

sputter ['spʌtə] *s. splutter.*

sputum ['spjuːtəm] Speichel *m*; Sputum *n*, Auswurf *m*.

spy [spai] *tr (to ~ out)* genau, sorgfältig beobachten; erspähen; *(to ~ out)* ausspionieren, -kundschaften; *itr* (herum)spionieren; ein wachsames Auge haben (*upon s.o.* auf jdn); (genau) unter die Lupe nehmen (*into s. th.* etw; *upon s.o.* jdn); *s* Späher; Spion *m*; *(~ing)* Spionage *f*; **~-glass** (kleines) Fernrohr *n*; **~-hole** Guckloch *n*, Spion *m*; **~-mirror** Fensterspiegel *m*; **~ ring** Spionageorganisation *f*; **~ trial** Spionageprozeß *m*.

squab [skwɔb] *s* ungefiederte Taube *f*; *fig* kleine(r) Fettkloß *m (Mensch)*; (Sitz-)Kissen; Sofa *n*, Couch *f*; *a (Vogel)* noch nicht flügge, ungefiedert; *(~by)* klein u. dick, plump, pumm(e)lig.

squabb|le ['skwɔbl] *itr* sich (herum-)zanken, sich streiten; *tr typ (Satz)* durchea.bringen, verrücken; *s* Zank, Streit *m*; **~er** ['-ə] Streithammel *m*.

squad [skwɔd] *mil Am* Gruppe, *(~ in barracks)* Korporalschaft *f*; (Arbeits-)Trupp *m*, Rotte; *sport* Mannschaft *f*, Team *n*, (Turn-)Riege *f*; *firing ~* Exekutionskommando *n*; **~ car** *Am* (Polizei-)Streifenwagen *m*; **~ column** Schützenreihe *f*; **~ leader** *mil Am* Gruppenführer *m*; **~ron** ['-rən] *(Kavallerie) obs* Schwadron *f*; *mar* Geschwader; *(Panzer)* Bataillon *n*; *aero* Staffel; *allg* Einheit *f*; *~~ commander (Am aero)* Staffelkapitän *m*; *~~ leader (Br aero)* Major *m* der Luftwaffe; *~~ wedge (aero)* Staffelkeil *m*.

squal|id ['skwɔlid] schmutzig, schmierig; *fig* dürftig, elend, ärmlich; **~idness** ['skwɔlidnis], **~or** ['skwɔlə] Schmutz *m*; Elend *n*.

squall [skwɔːl] **1.** *s* Bö *f*, (Regen-)Schauer; *fam* Wirbel, Krach, Streit *m*; **~y** ['-i] böig; stürmisch; *fig* drohend; **2.** *itr* laut schreien, grölen, aufkreischen; *tr* laut rufen; *s* Schrei *m*; Geschrei *n*; **~er** ['-ə] Schreihals *m*.

squam|a ['skweimə] *pl ~ae* ['-iː] *zoo bot* Schuppe *f*; **~ous** ['-əs] schuppig.

squander ['skwɔndə] *tr* verschwenden, vergeuden; *(Geld) fam* durchbringen; *itr* ein Verschwender sein; *s (~ing)* Verschwendung, Vergeudung *f*; **~er** ['-rə] Verschwender *m*; **~ing** ['-riŋ] verschwenderisch; **~mania** ['-'meinjə] *fam* Verschwendungssucht *f*.

square [skwɛə] *s math (a. Algebra)* Quadrat *n*; Quadratzahl *f*; *allg* Viereck, Rechteck *n*; 100 Quadratfuß (= *9,29 m²*); (viereckiger) Platz *m*; öffentliche Anlage *f*; Häuserblock *m*; *Am* Häuserreihe *f*; *mil* Karree *n*, Parade-, Exerzierplatz *m*; Glasscheibe *f*; Anschlagwinkel *m*, Winkelmaß *n*, -haken *m*; *(Schachbrett)* Feld; *arch* Sparrenfeld; *sl* gerade(r), ehrliche(r) Kerl; *sl* Hinterwäldler *m*; *a* quadratisch; viereckig; rechtwinklig; senkrecht (*to* zu, auf); quaderförmig, Quader-; *(Klammer)* eckig; gerade, eben, genau eingerichtet *od* passend; *com* ausgeglichen, quitt; *fig* gerade, redlich, ehrlich, gerecht, anständig, fair; klar, direkt, offen, unzweideutig, glatt; *(Algebra)* quadratisch, Quadrat-; *fam* ordentlich, solide, gut, reichlich; *fam* gerade, derb, vierschrötig; *Am sl* bieder, geistig nicht auf der Höhe; *adv* gerade, rechtwink(e)lig, viereckig; genau, direkt; fest, solide; offen, ehrlich; gerade (-heraus); *tr* quadratisch, viereckig, rechtwink(e)lig, -eckig machen; vierkantig zuschneiden *od* behauen; ausrichten, begradigen; *(to ~ off)* karieren, in Quadrate einteilen; *(Algebra)* quadrieren; einrichten, in Ordnung bringen, regeln; *com (to ~ up)* begleichen, aus-, bezahlen, saldieren; *s.o.* jds Verhältnisse regeln; anpassen (*with* an), in Übereinstimmung bringen (*with* mit); *sl* überreden, bestechen; *itr* aufea. passen, sich decken; passen, übereinstimmen (*with* mit); sich aufstellen, sich formieren; e-n rechten Winkel bilden; *to ~ o.s. (fam)* den (angerichteten) Schaden wiedergutmachen; *with s.o.* mit jdm wieder ins reine kommen; *to ~ off, up* Kampfstellung einnehmen (*to* gegen); *fig fam* nüchtern betrachten; *on the ~* im rechten Winkel; *fam* gerade, ehrlich, zuverlässig, echt *a u. adv*; *out of ~* schief; *fam* nicht passend, nicht übereinstimmend; ungenau; *to be a ~ peg in a round hole* falsch am Platz sein; wie die Faust aufs Auge passen; *to meet with a ~ refusal* e-e glatte Ablehnung erfahren; *to ~ accounts with (fig)* abrechnen mit; *to ~ the circle* die Quadratur des Zirkels finden; *fig* etwas Unmögliches tun (wollen); *to ~ o.'s conscience* sein Gewissen beruhigen; *he hasn't eaten a ~ meal in days* er hat seit Tagen nichts Anständiges gegessen; ~ **brackets** *pl* eckige Klammern *f pl*; **~-built** *a* breit(gebaut), vierschrötig; ~ **dance** Volkstanz *m*; **~-file** Vierkantfeile *f*; ~ **foot** Quadratfuß *m*; **~head** *Am sl pej* Quadratschädel *m*; ~ **inch** Quadratzoll *m*; ~ **knot** Weberknoten *m*; ~ **meal** anständige Mahlzeit *f*; ~ **measure** Flächenmaß *n*; ~ **mile** Quadratmeile *f*; **~ness** ['-nis] viereckige Gestalt; *fig* Geradheit, Anständigkeit, Ehrlichkeit *f*; ~ **number** Quadratzahl *f*; **~-rigged** *mar* mit den Rahsegeln getakelt; ~ **root** *math* Quadratwurzel *f*; **~sail** *mar* Rahsegel *n*; ~ **shooter** *Am fam* ordentliche(r) Kerl *m*; ~ **stone** Quader *m*; **~-toed** *a (Schuh)* breit; *fig* altmodisch; engstirnig; pedantisch; ~ **steel** Vierkantstahl *m*.

squash [skwɔʃ] **1.** *tr* zerdrücken, zermalmen; aus-, zerquetschen; zu Brei schlagen; *(Finger)* quetschen; *fig* unterdrücken, ersticken, zum Schweigen bringen; *fam* über den Mund fahren (*s.o.* jdm), über den Löffel barbieren; *itr* zerquetscht werden; (auf-) klatschen, platschen; sich zs.quetschen; *s* weiche, breiige Masse *f*; Fruchtsaft *m*; Zerquetschen; dumpfe(s) Geräusch, Platschen *n*; *fam* dichte Menge *f*; *sport Art* Ballspiel *n*; *lemon ~* Zitronenwasser *n*, Zitrone *f* naturell; **~iness** ['-inis] Saftigkeit *f*; **~y** ['-i] weich, saftig, matschig; zerknautscht, zerdrückt; **2.** *s* (*bes.* Turban-)Kürbis *m*.

squat [skwɔt] *itr* hocken; *zoo* (am Boden) kauern, sich ducken; *fam* sitzen, hocken; *Am* sich ohne Rechtstitel ansiedeln; *to ~ o.s.* niederhocken; sich niederkauern; *a (~ty)* hockend; kauernd; *fam* untersetzt, stämmig; *s* Hockstellung, *sport* Hocke *f*; **~ter** ['-ə] Siedler *m* ohne Rechtstitel; *(Australien)* Schafzüchter *m*.

squaw [skwɔ:] Indianerfrau *f*.

squawk [skwɔ:k] *itr* (heiser) schreien; *fam* (herum)zetern, laut meckern; *tr* schreien, ausstoßen; *s* heisere(r) Schrei *m*; *fam* Gezeter, Gemecker *n*.

squeak [skwi:k] *itr* quieken; quietschen, knarren; *sl* nicht dichthalten, angeben; *tr (to ~ out)* quiekend sagen; *sl* verpfeifen, verraten; *s* Gequiek(e); Quietschen, Kreischen; Gequietsch, Geknarre; *(Maus)* Piepsen; *(Kaninchen)* Pfeifen *n*; *to have a narrow ~* mit knapper Not davonkommen; **~er** ['-ə] Schreihals; *sl* Denunziant; junge(r) Vogel *m*, *bes.* Taube *f*; **~y** ['-i] quietschend, knarrend; kreischend.

squeal [skwi:l] *itr* schreien, quieken; quietschen (*with joy* vor Freude); *fam* meckern, protestieren; *sl* petzen, das Geheimnis verraten; *s* Geschrei, Gequiek(e) *n*; *Am sl* Schinken *m*, Schweinefleisch *n*; **~er** ['-ə] Verräter *m*.

squeamish ['skwi:miʃ] *a (Magen)* empfindlich; *fig* überempfindlich, feinfühlig; heikel; schnell beleidigt, zimperlich; *to be ~* nicht alles vertragen können; *fig* alles gleich übelnehmen.

squeegee ['skwi:'dʒi:] *s* Scheibenwischer; *typ phot* Rakel, Abstreicher *m*; *tr* abstreichen.

squeez|able ['skwi:zəbl] zs.-, ausdrückbar; *fig* zu erpressen(d); **~e** ['skwi:z] *tr* fest drücken, pressen, quetschen; *(to ~~ out)* ausdrücken, -pressen, -quetschen; pressen; hineinzwängen, hineinquetschen (*into* in); fest an sich drücken; *(Bild)* abklatschen; *fig fam (Menschen)* ausquetschen, -pressen; erpressen (*from* von); *to ~~ in (tr)* dazwischenquetschen; *itr* (sich) hineinquetschen; *itr* e-n Druck ausüben; (dem Druck) nachgeben; *to ~~ o.s. through* sich hindurchzwängen; *s (tight ~~)* (fester) Druck *m*, Quetschung *f*; (fester) Händedruck *m*, innige Umarmung *f*; Gedränge *n*; Abklatsch, -druck *m*; *tech* Presse; *fig* (Geld-)Verlegenheit, Klemme; *fam* Erpressung *f*; *to be in a tight ~~* in großer Verlegenheit sein, *fam* in der Klemme, Patsche sitzen; *to have a close, narrow, tight ~~* mit knapper Not davonkommen; *to put the ~~ on s.o. (fig)* jdm die Daumenschrauben anlegen; *~~ box (sl)* Schifferklavier *n*; **~er** ['-ə] Presse; Preßform-, Auspreßmaschine *f*; *metal* Preßwerk *n*; *fam* Erpresser *m*.

squelch [skweltʃ] *tr* zerdrücken, zermalmen; *fig* (völlig) unterdrücken; *fam* den Mund stopfen (*s.o.* jdm); *itr* platschen, quatschen; klucksen; durch Matsch waten; *s* Platschen; Glucksen *n*; Matsch *m*; *fam* schlagfertige Antwort *f*; **~er** ['-ə] *fig* schwere(r) Schlag *m*.

squib [skwib] Feuerwerkskörper; Schwärmer, Frosch *m*; *fig* bissige, witzige Bemerkung, Satire; *Am fam* Kleinanzeige *f*, witzige(r) Zwischentext *m*.

squid [skwid] Kalmar *(Tintenfisch)*; (tintenfischähnlicher) Köder *m*.

squiffy ['skwifi] *sl* besoffen, blau.

squill [skwil] *bot* Meerzwiebel *f*; Heuschreckenkrebs *m*.

squint [skwint] *itr* schielen (*at, on, upon* nach); mit den Augen zwinkern; e-e Vorliebe haben (*towards* für), ein Auge werfen (*at* auf); abweichen (*from* von); *tr (die Augen)* zukneifen; *(e-n Blick)* heimlich werfen; *s* Schielen *n*; Seitenblick *m*; Neigung *f*, Hang *m* (*towards* zu); Vorliebe, Schwäche *f*; *a (~-eyed)* schielend; *to take a ~ at* e-n Blick werfen auf; **~-eyed** *a fig* mißgünstig, boshaft.

squire ['skwaiə] *s hist* (Schild-)Knappe; (Land-)Junker, Gutsbesitzer; *Am* Friedensrichter, Gemeindevorsteher; Kavalier, Galan *m*; *tr* den Hof machen; **~archy** ['-rɑ:ki] Junkertum *n*.

squirm [skwə:m] *itr* sich winden, sich krümmen; *fig* in Bedrängnis, in Verlegenheit, in Verwirrung sein; Verlegenheit zeigen; *s* Windung, Krümmung; *mar* Kink *f*.

squirrel ['skwirəl, *Am* 'skwə:rəl] Eichhörnchen; Grauwerk *n*; *Am sl* Verrückte(r), Psychologe, Psychiater, *mot* rücksichtslose(r) Fahrer *m*; ~ **cage** *el* Käfiganker *m*.

squirt [skwə:t] *itr* spritzen; sprudeln; *tr* ausspritzen; bespritzen, naß machen; *to ~ out* heraussprudeln; *s* Spritze *f*; (Wasser-)Strahl, *fam* Spritzer; *fam* junge(r) Spritzer; *Am sl* Limonadeautomat *m*; *Am sl* Düsenflugzeug *n*; ~ **gun** Wasserpistole *f*.

squish [skwiʃ] *tr fam* zermantschen; *s fam* Brei *m*; *sl* Marmelade *f*.

squit [skwit] *sl fig* Null *f*; Schuft *m*; *vulg* Scheißdreck *m*.

stab [stæb] *tr (to ~ to death)* (er)stechen; *(Herz)* durchbohren; eindringen in; *(Mauer)* aufrauhen; *itr* stechen (*a. vom Schmerz*); e-n Dolchstoß versetzen (*at s.o.* jdm); *s* (Messer-)Stich, (Dolch-) Stoß; Stich(wunde *f*); *fig* Stich, plötzliche(r) Schmerz; *fig* schwere(r) Schlag; *fam* Versuch *m*; *to have a ~ at (sl)* versuchen zu; *to ~ in the back (fig)* in den Rücken fallen; **~ber** ['-ə] Messerstecher; Meuchelmörder *m*; Locheisen *n*; *mar* Pricker *m*; **~bing** ['-iŋ] stechend *a. Schmerz*.

stab|ility [stə'biliti], **~leness** ['steiblnis] (Stand-)Festigkeit, Stabilität, Widerstandsfähigkeit; *fig* Charakterfestigkeit, Standhaftigkeit; Beständigkeit, Dauerhaftigkeit; *(Lage)* Beruhigung *f*; **~ilization** [steibilai'zeiʃən] (Be-)Festigung; Stabilisierung *f*; **~ilize** ['steibilaiz] *tr* (be)festigen; *tech* stabilisieren *(a. Preise)*; *~~d warfare* Stellungskrieg *m*; **~ilizer** ['steibilaizə] Stabilisator *m*; *aero* Höhenflosse *f*; Rostschutzmittel *n*; **~le** ['steibl] **1.** *a* fest, stabil; *fig* (innerlich) gefestigt, (charakter)fest, standhaft; beständig, dauerhaft; *(Stellung)* fest; *(Waren)* haltbar; *(Regierung)* stabil.

stable ['steibl] **2.** *s* Stall; *Am sl* Saustall *m*; *tr* einstallen; **~-companion** Stallgefährte *m fam a. fig.*

stack [stæk] *s agr* Dieme *f*, Feim(en) *m*, Miete *f*, Schober; Stapel, Stoß, Haufen *m*; *Raummaß von 108 Kubikfuß (= 305,814 m³)*; Gewehrpyramide *f*; *(smoke-~)* Schornstein *m*; *Am* (Bücher-)Regal; *pl* (Buch-)Magazin *n*; *pl fam* große Menge *od* Zahl *f*, Haufen *m*; *Am sl* Antenne *f*; *tr* (auf)stapeln, -schichten; auf-, anhäufen; aufspeichern; *(die Gewehre)* zs.setzen; *to ~ the cards* die (Spiel-)Karten betrügerisch mischen; *the cards are, the deck is ~ed (Am fig)* das ist e-e abgekartete Sache; *well-~ed (Am sl) a* gut aussehend, gut gebaut; **~er** ['-ə] *Am* Stroh-, Heustapler *m (Maschine)*.

stadium ['steidjəm] *pl a. -ia* ['-ə] *sport med* Stadium *n*; Kampfbahn *f*.

staff [stɑ:f] **1.** *s* Stab, Stock *m*, Stange *f*, Schaft *m*; *fig* Stütze *f*; *mus (pl staves* [steivz] Notensystem *n*; *fig* (Führungs-, Mitarbeiter-, Beamten-) Stab *m*, Belegschaft *f*, (Betriebs-)Personal *n*; *(teaching ~)* (Lehr-)Körper *m*; *a* Stabs-; *tr* mit e-m Stab, mit Personal versehen; Personal einstellen für; *to be on the ~* zum Personal gehören; *clerical ~* Büropersonal *n*; *editorial ~* Schriftleitung *f*; *hotel ~* Hotelpersonal *n*; *the General S~ (mil)* der Generalstab; *nursing ~* Pflegepersonal *n*; *sales ~* Verkaufspersonal *n*; *shop ~* Betriebspersonal *n*; *the ~ of life* das tägliche Brot; ~ **college** Kriegsakademie *f*; ~ **executive** Leiter *m* der Personalabteilung; ~ **expenses** *pl* Personalkosten *pl*; ~ **magazine** Werkzeitschrift *f*; ~ **locator** Rufanlage *f*; ~ **officer** *mil* Stabsoffizier; *com* Betriebsberater *m*.

stag [stæg] *s* (Rot-)Hirsch; Bock, Bulle *m*; kastrierte(s) männliche(s) Tier *n*; Herr *m* ohne Damenbegleitung; *Am* Herrengesellschaft *f*; Aktien-, Börsenspekulant *m*; *a* ohne Dame; Herren-; *tr sl* beschatten, heimlich überwachen, nachspionieren (*s.o.* jdm); *(fam) to go* ~ ohne Damenbegleitung sein; *itr com* in Aktien spekulieren; **~-beetle** Hirschkäfer *m*; **~-dinner** Herrenessen *n*; **~-party** *fam* Herrengesellschaft, -partie *f*, -abend *m*.

stage [steidʒ] *s* Gerüst, Gestell *n*; Plattform; *theat* Bühne *f*; Theater (-laufbahn *f*) *n*; *fig* Schauplatz *m*; Tätigkeitsfeld *n*, Wirkungsbereich; Rastplatz *m*; Phase, Etappe; Teilstrecke, Haltestelle *f*, Abschnitt *m*; Stadium *n*, (Entwicklungs-)Stufe, Periode *f*; *(Mikroskop)* Objekttisch *m*; *(Rakete)* Stufe; *Am* Postkutsche *f*; Autobus *m*; *tr* auf die Bühne bringen, inszenieren; veranstalten; auf die Beine bringen, durchführen; *itr* aufführbar sein, sich aufführen lassen; *Am* mit der Postkutsche fahren; *at this* ~ in diesem Stadium; *by, in ~s* in Etappen, nicht auf einmal; *by easy ~s* mit vielen Unterbrechungen; *off* ~ hinter den Kulissen; *to be on the* ~ auf der Bühne stehen, Schauspieler sein; *to go on the* ~, *to take the* ~ zur Bühne gehen; *to have a clear* ~ freies Feld haben; *experimental* ~ Versuchsstadium *n*; *final ~s (pl)* Endstadien *n pl*; *~s of appeal* Instanzenweg *m*; ~ **adaptation** Bühnenbearbeitung *f*; **~-box** Proszeniumsloge *f*; **~-coach** Postkutsche *f*; **~-coachman** Postillion *m*; ~ **direction** Bühnenanweisung *f*; **~-door** Bühnenzugang; Künstlereingang *m*; **~-effect** Bühnenwirkung *f*; **~-fever** Theaterbegeisterung *f*; **~-fright** Lampenfieber *n*; **~-hand** Bühnenarbeiter, *pej* Kulissenschieber *m*; **~-lighting** Bühnenbeleuchtung *f*; **~-manager** Regisseur, Spielleiter *m*; **~-name** Künstlername *m*; **~-play** Bühnenstück *n*; **~-properties** *pl* Bühnenrequisiten *pl*; **~r** ['-ə]: *to be an old* ~ schon lange s-n Dienst tun; ein alter Praktikus sein; **~-right** Aufführungs-, Bühnenrechte *n pl*; **~-setter** Bühnentechniker *m*; **~-struck** *a* theaterbegeistert; **~-version** Bühnenbearbeitung *f*; ~ **whisper** Bühnen-, Scheingeflüster *n*; **~y, stagy** ['-i] theatralisch; affektiert, hochtrabend.

stagger ['stægə] *itr* (sch)wanken, taumeln; *fig* schwanken, unsicher sein, zaudern, zögern; *tr* ins Wanken, aus dem Gleichgewicht bringen *a. fig*; *fig* verblüffen; *tech* versetzt, im Zickzack anordnen; staffeln, (über e-n Zeitraum, gleichmäßig(er)) verteilen; *s* Wanken, Schwanken, Taumeln *n*; Zickzackanordnung; Staffelung *f a. aero*; *pl mit sing vet (blind ~s)* Drehkrankheit *f*, Koller *m*; *allg* Schwindel(gefühl *n*) *m*; **~ed** ['-d] *a* gestaffelt; *fam* überrascht, verblüfft; **~er** ['-rə] Schwankende(r) *m*; **~ing** ['-riŋ] *s* Staffelung *f*; *a* (sch)wankend, torkelnd; *(Schlag)* heftig; *fig* phantastisch; erschütternd.

stagn|ancy ['stægnənsi] Stagnation *f*, Stillstand *m*; *fig* Trägheit, Untätigkeit; *com* Flaute, Stockung, Lustlosigkeit *f*; **~ant** ['-ənt] *(Wasser)* stehend, stagnierend *a. fig*; *fig* dumpf, träge, untätig; *com* flau, stockend, lustlos; **~ate** ['-eit] *itr* stagnieren *a. fig*; träge, flau werden *od* sein, stocken, darniederliegen; **~ation** [stæg'neiʃən] Stagnation, Stockung; *com* Flaute, Lustlosigkeit *f*.

staid [steid] *a* gesetzt, ruhig, gelassen, nüchtern; **~ness** ['-nis] Gesetztheit, Ruhe *f*.

stain [stein] *tr* fleckig machen, beschmutzen, beschmieren; beizen; färben; *fig* beflecken, besudeln, verderben, entehren; färben *(a. mikroskopisches Präparat)*; *(Glas)* bemalen; *itr* abfärben; schmutzen; *s* (Farb-) Fleck; *fig* Schandfleck *m*, Schande; Farbe *f*, Farbstoff *m*; Beize *f*; *to be ~ed* fleckig sein; **~ed** [-d] *a* bunt; *~~ glass* Kirchenfensterglas *n*; **~er** ['-ə] Färber; Farbstoff *m*; **~less** ['-lis] flecken-, makellos *bes. fig*; *biol* farblos; *(Stahl)* rostfrei.

stair [stɛə] (Treppen-)Stufe; *pl* Treppe *f*; *below ~s* unten; *fig* beim Hauspersonal; *flight, pair of ~s* Treppenflucht *f*; **~-carpet** Treppenläufer *m*; **~case** Treppe(nflucht) *f*, -naufgang *m*, -nhaus *n*; *back ~~* Hintertreppe *f*; *moving ~~* Rolltreppe *f*; **~head, -landing** (oberster) Treppenabsatz *m*; ~ **lighting** Treppenbeleuchtung *f*; **~-rail** Treppengeländer *n*; **~-rod** Läuferstange *f*; **~way** Treppe(nflucht) *f*; Aufgang *m*; **~-well** Treppenspindel *f*.

stake [steik] *s* Pfahl, Pfosten, Pflock; (Pfahl des) Scheiterhaufen(s); *a. pl (Spiel)* Einsatz; Gewinn *m*; Risiko, Wagnis *n*; *tech* (Wagen-)Runge *f*; *(Amboß)* Stöckel *m*; *pl* Preiswettrennen *n*; Anteil *m*, finanzielle Beteiligung *f* (*in* an); Wetteinsatz *m*; *Am com* Sonderreserven *f pl*; *tr* anpfählen; durch (e-n) Pfosten stützen; *(Pfahl)* zuspitzen; *(to ~ off, out) (Grenze)* abstecken *a. fig*; *fig* ein-, aufs Spiel setzen, riskieren; *(Geld)* setzen (*on* auf); *Am fam* die nötigen Mittel geben (*s.o.* jdm); *to ~ in, up* einpfählen, -zäunen; *to ~ s.o. to s.th.* jdm für etw Geld geben; *to be at* ~ auf dem Spiele stehen; *to be sent, condemned to the* ~, *to suffer at the* ~ zum Feuertod verurteilt werden; den Feuertod erleiden; *to have a* ~ *in* interessiert sein an; *to pull up ~s (Am)* s-e Zelte abbrechen *fig*; *to sweep the ~s* den Gewinn einheimsen, den ganzen Gewinn einstreichen; *his life is at* ~ es geht um sein Leben; *I'd ~ my life on it* ich bin todsicher; **~holder** Verwahrer *m* der Wetteinsätze; Eigentümer *m* e-r Parzelle; **~-money** Einsatz *m*; **~-out** *Am sl* (Polizei-)Falle *f*.

stalac|mite ['stæləkmait] *geol* Stalagmit *m*; **~tite** ['-tait] Stalaktit *m*.

stale [steil] *a* schal, abgestanden; *(Brot)* altbacken; *(Fleisch, Ei)* nicht mehr ganz frisch; *(Brot)* trocken; *(Wasser, Luft)* verbraucht, sauerstoffarm; *fig* abgegriffen, abgedroschen, alltäglich, langweilig; nicht mehr neu; unmodern; *(körperlich* od *geistig)* nicht mehr auf der Höhe; überanstrengt, verbraucht; *jur* hinfällig (geworden); *s (Pferd, Rind)* Harn *m*; *itr tr* alt werden, veralten, abstehen (lassen); *itr (Pferd, Rind)* stallen, harnen; **~mate** ['-'meit] *s (Schach)* Patt *n*; *fig* Stillstand *m*; Sackgasse, ausweglose Situation *f*; *tr (Schach)* patt setzen; *fig* in die Enge, in e-e Sackgasse treiben; matt setzen.

stalk [stɔ:k] **1.** *itr* (einher)stolzieren; pirschen; *tr (Wild)* sich heranpirschen an; *fig* ziehen durch; *s* Stolzieren *n*; Pirsch(gang *m*) *f*, Beschleichen *n*; **~er** ['-ə] Pirschgänger *m*; **~ing-horse** *fig* Deckmantel, Vorwand; *pol* Strohmann *m*; **2.** *bot* Stengel, Halm; Stiel *a. Glas*; Schlot *m*; **~ed** [-t] *a* gestielt; **~-eyed** *a* mit Stielaugen; **~less** ['-lis] ungestielt; **~y** ['-i] stielartig; lang u. dünn, hoch aufgeschossen; langstielig; *sl* gerissen, schlau.

stall [stɔ:l] *s* Verschlag *m*, Box *f*, Stand; Parkplatz *m (für* ein *Fahrzeug)*; (Markt-)Bude *f*, (Verkaufs-) Stand; Kirchenstuhl; *theat Br* Sperrsitz *m*; *(finger-~)* Fingerling; *aero* überzogene(r) Flug(zustand) *m*; *Am sl* Komplize; *Am fam* Vorwand *m*; *tr* in den Stall bringen; im Stall halten, füttern, mästen; in den Dreck fahren *a. fig*; *(Flugzeug)* überziehen; *mot* abwürgen; *fig* aufschieben, hinhalten, vertrösten; *itr* im Stall stehen; e-n Stand einnehmen; steckenbleiben; *mot* stehenbleiben, aussetzen; *fig* abwarten, herumlungern; *aero* abrutschen, durchsacken; *to ~ off* aufschieben; *to ~ for time* Zeit gewinnen; *book-, flower-, fruit-, newspaper* ~ Bücher-, Blumen-, Obst-, Zeitungsstand *m*; **~age** ['-idʒ] Standgeld *n*; **~-fed** *a* stallgefüttert; **~-feed** *tr* im Stall füttern, mästen; **~-feeding** Stallfütterung *f*; **~-keeper** Standinhaber *m*; **~-money** Standgeld *n*.

stallion ['stæljən] (Zucht-)Hengst *m*.

stalwart ['stɔ:lwət] *a* stark, kräftig, kraftvoll, robust, handfest; wacker, tapfer; fest entschlossen, unentwegt, standhaft, unerschütterlich, treu; *(Erklärung)* geharnischt; *s* treue(r) Anhänger *m*.

stam|en ['steimen] *bot* Staubfaden *m*; **~ina** ['stæminə] Widerstandskraft, -fähigkeit; Ausdauer; Vitalität *f*.

stammer ['stæmə] *itr* stottern; *itr tr* stammeln; *s* Gestammel, Gestotter; Stottern *n*; *to ~ out* hervorstottern; **~er** ['-rə] Stotterer *m*.

stamp [stæmp] *tr* (zer)stampfen; aufstampfen mit; *(to ~ out)* (aus)stanzen; *(Münze)* prägen; stempeln *a. fig*; abstempeln, siegeln; *fig* deutlich kennzeichnen; stempeln, frankieren, freimachen; *itr* (mit dem Fuß) aufstampfen; trampeln (*on* auf); *s* Stampfen *n*; *tech* Stampfer; (Präge-) Stempel; Stempel(abdruck) *m*, Siegel *a. fig*; *fig* Gepräge *n*, Schlag *m*; *(postage-~)* Postwertzeichen *n*, Briefmarke; *(revenue ~)* Stempelmarke *f*; *to ~ down, flat* nieder-, plattstampfen; *to ~ out* zertreten, zermalmen; *fig* vernichten, zerstören; *of the same* ~ von derselben Art; *to put a ~ on a letter* e-n Brief freimachen; **~-album** Briefmarkenalbum *n*; **~-book** Portobuch *n*; **~-booklet** Briefmarkenheftchen *n*; **~-collector** Briefmarkensammler *m*; **~-dealer** Briefmarkenhändler *m*; **~-duty** Stempelsteuer *f*; **~ed** [-t] *a* gestempelt; frankiert, freigemacht; *~~ envelope* Freiumschlag *m*; **~er** ['-ə] Stampfer *m*, Ramme *f*; Stempler; Briefmarkenentwerter *m*; **~ing-ground** *fam* Lieblingsaufenthalt, Sammelplatz, Treffpunkt, beliebte(r) Kurort *m*; **~-machine** Briefmarkenautomat *m*; Stampfmaschine *f*; **~-mill** Pochwerk *n*; **~-office** Stempelamt *n*; **~-pad** Stempelkissen *n*; **~-paper** Stempelpapier *n*; **~-tax** Stempelsteuer *f*.

stampede [stæm'pi:d] *s* wilde Flucht; Panik *f*; *Am* Sturm *m*, Massenbewegung *f*; *Am Art Tanz*; *itr* in wilder Flucht davonrennen; den Kopf verlieren, kopflos werden; *tr* zu wilder Flucht veranlassen; in Panik versetzen, kopflos machen.

stanch *s. staunch.*

stanchion ['stɑːnʃən] *s* Stütze, Steife, Strebe; Stützstange *f*, -pfosten, -pfeiler, -balken *m*; *tr* mit Stützen versehen.

stand [stænd] *irr stood, stood* [stud] **1.** *itr* stehen; sich stellen; *fig* stehen, sich befinden, sein; beruhen (*on* auf); (still)stehen; stehen bleiben; bestehen, gültig, in Kraft sein; (an-) dauern; sich halten, bleiben, weiterbestehen; bestehen (*on* auf), verharren (*on, to* bei); stehen (*to* zu), sich einsetzen (*for, to* für); darstellen, bedeuten (*for s.th.* etw), stehen (*for* für); gelten; als Kandidat auftreten (*for* für); *(mit Maßangabe)* groß sein, messen; *mar* steuern, segeln (*for, to* nach); **2.** *tr* (hin)stellen, -setzen; ertragen, aushalten; *(Kälte)* vertragen; *(Menschen)* ausstehen, *fam* riechen, leiden können; widerstehen (*s.th.* e-r S); sich unterziehen müssen, unterliegen (*s.th.* e-r S); *fam* zum besten geben, spendieren, ausgeben, bezahlen; kosten (*a lot of money* viel Geld); **3.** *s* Stehenbleiben *n*, Stillstand, Halt *m*, Pause *f*, *Am* Aufenthalt(sort); Platz *m*, Stellung *f*, Standort *m*; *fig Am* Einstellung, Ansicht, Meinung *f*, Standpunkt (*on a matter* in e-r S); Ständer; (Verkaufs-, Markt-)Stand *m*, Bude; Tribüne; Ernte *f* auf dem Halm; *Am jur* Zeugenstand; *mot* Parkstreifen, -platz, Halteplatz *m*; **4.** *to know where one ~s* wissen, wo man dran ist; *to make a ~* zum Stehen kommen; sich festlegen; Widerstand leisten (*against* gegen); *for s.o.* sich für jdn einsetzen; *to take the ~ (Am jur)* den Zeugenstand betreten; *to ~ aghast* bestürzt sein; *to ~ alone* allein (da)stehen; nicht seinesgleichen haben; *to ~ aloof* sich zurückhalten; *to ~ at attention (mil)* stillstehen; *to ~ at bay* kampfbereit sein; *to ~ on ceremony* sich förmlich benehmen; *to ~ a chance, show* e-e Chance, Aussicht, Hoffnung haben; *to ~ clear* zurücktreten; *to ~ condemned, convicted* überführt sein; *to ~ corrected* sein Unrecht einsehen; *to ~ on end (Haare)* zu Berge stehen; *to ~ on o.'s own feet* auf eigenen Füßen stehen; *to ~ fire (mil)* dem (feindlichen) Ansturm standhalten; *to ~ firm, fast, o.'s ground* nicht nachgeben, unnachgiebig sein; s-n Mann stehen; *to ~ guard* Wache stehen, *fam* schieben; *to ~ it that* dabei bleiben, daß; *to ~ idle (Fabrik)* stillstehen; *to ~ good (Angebot)* bestehenbleiben; *to ~ in good* gutstehen (*with* mit); *to ~ the loss* für den Verlust aufkommen; *to ~ in need of* nötig haben, brauchen, *lit* bedürfen *gen*; *to ~ no nonsense* keine Albernheiten dulden; *to ~ pat (Am fam)* nicht locker lassen; *to ~ to reason* sich von selbst verstehen, (ohne weiteres) einleuchten; *to ~ s.o. in good stead* jdm dienlich, nützlich, von Nutzen sein; *to ~ the test* sich bewähren; *to ~ treat, sam (fam)* freihalten; *to ~ (o.'s) trial (jur)* vernommen werden; *to ~ well with s.o.* mit jdm gutstehen; *~ at attention!* stillgestanden! *~ easy!* rührt euch! *~ back! ~ aside! ~ clear!* Vorsicht! Zurücktreten! *please ~ away from platform edge!* bitte von der Bahnsteigkante zurücktreten! *~ out of my sight!* geh mir aus den Augen! *he wants to know where he ~s* er will wissen, wie er dran ist; *he ~s six foot two* er ist 6 Fuß 2 Zoll groß; *the matter ~s thus* so liegen die Dinge; *as it ~s* so wie es ist, wie es liegt u. steht; *~ and deliver* Geld oder Leben! **5.** *cab-~* Droschkenhalteplatz, -stand *m*; *flower-~* Blumenständer, -tisch *m*; *grand-~* Zuschauertribüne *f*; *hat-, coat-~* Garderobenständer *m*; *ink~* Tintenfaß *n*; *music-~* Notenständer *m*; *umbrella-~* Schirmständer *m*; *wash-, hand-~* Waschständer *m*; **6.** *to ~* **aside** auf die Seite treten, beiseite treten; *to ~* **back** zurücktreten; *(Haus)* zurückstehen; *to ~* **between** dazwischenstehen; *to ~* **by** dabeisein; dabei-, danebenstehen; herumstehen; bereit sein, zur Verfügung stehen, in Bereitschaft sein (*for* für); beistehen (*s.o.* jdm); helfen, Hand anlegen; bleiben (*a decision* bei e-r Entscheidung); stehen (*a word* zu e-m Wort); *radio* sendebereit *od* eingeschaltet sein *od* bleiben; *to ~* **down** sich zurückziehen; *mil* den Dienst quittieren; *Am* den Zeugenstand verlassen; *to ~* **for** eintreten für; bedeuten, heißen; sich gefallen lassen, dulden, hinnehmen; *Br* kandidieren für; *to ~* **in** *fam* zu stehen kommen; sich beteiligen; einspringen (*for s.o.* für jdn); *with s.o.* jdm unter die Arme greifen; sich gut mit jdm stehen; *to ~* **off** abseits stehen *a. fig*; *fig* nicht mitmachen, sich zurück-, sich fernhalten von; *mar* die Küste meiden; *to ~* **on** bestehen auf; *to ~* **out** (her-) vorstehen, vorragen; hinausragen (*into the sea* ins Meer); deutlich (zu erkennen) sein; auffallen; sich deutlich abheben; *fig* heraus-, hervorragen (*from* aus), glänzen (*in languages* in Sprachen); Widerstand leisten; *to ~* **over** zurückbleiben, zurückgestellt, aufgeschoben sein; *to ~* **up** *itr* aufstehen, sich erheben; sich als brauchbar erweisen, Strapazen aushalten; *for* unterstützen, verteidigen; Partei nehmen für, eintreten für; *to* entgegentreten, die Stirn bieten, die Meinung sagen (*s.o.* jdm); *tr Am fam* versetzen, (auf)sitzenlassen; **7. ~-backer** *fam* Drückeberger *m*; **~-by** *s* zuverlässige, stets bereite, brauchbare, gute Hilfe *f*; Ersatzmann *m*; *sport* Hilfestellung *f*; *com* zuverlässige Ware *f*; *tech* Zubehör *n*; *a* Reserve-; *~~ equipment* Reserveausrüstung *f*; *~~ time* Wartezeit *f*; **~-easy** Ruhe-, Erholungspause *f*; **~ee** [stæn'diː] *Am fam*, **~er** ['stændə] Stehende(r), Stehplatzinhaber *m*; *~~-by* Zuschauer, Unbeteiligte(r) *m*; *~~-up* Parteigänger, Anhänger; *Am fam* unzuverlässige(r) Mensch *m*; **~-in** *film* Double *n*; Ersatzmann *m*; **~ing** ['-iŋ] *a* stehend, aufrecht; *sport* aus dem Stand; *(Gewässer)* stehend, still; fest(stehend), unbeweglich; untätig, außer Betrieb; dauernd; Dauer-; beständig; *(Getreide)* auf dem Halm; *s* Stehen *n*; Stand *m*, Stellung *f*; *(~ room)* Stehplatz *m*; *(soziale)* Stellung *f*, Stand, Rang; Ruf *m*, Reputation; (Zeit-)Dauer *f*, Bestand *m*; *of long ~~* lang(dauernd), anhaltend; seit langem, von alters her; *~~ army* stehende(s) Heer *n*; *~~ committee* ständige(r) Ausschuß *m*; *~~ composition (typ)* Stehsatz *m*; *~~ corn* Getreide *n* auf dem Halm; *~~ desk* Stehpult *n*; *~~ jump (sport)* Sprung *m* aus dem Stand; *~~ lamp* Stehlampe *f*; *~~ order (com fin)* Dauerauftrag *m*; *pl parl* Geschäftsordnung *f*; *~~ rigging (mar)* stehende(s), feste(s) Gut *n*; *~~ room* Stehplatz *m*; *~~ rope* Tragseil *n*; *~~ rule* stehende, feste Regel *f*; *~~ timber* Nutzholz *n*; **~-off** *s* Abseitsstehen; Gegengewicht *n*; Widerstand *m*; *(Spiel, Sport)* Unentschieden *n*; *a* u. **~-offish** abseitsstehend, unbeteiligt; zurückhaltend, reserviert; hochmütig; **~-out** *Am* Außenseiter; *sport* Favorit *m*; Genie *n*; glänzende Sache *f*; **~pat** *Am fam* reaktionär, konservativ; **~patter** *Am fam* Reaktionär, Konservative(r) *m*; **~pipe** *tech* Standrohr *n*; **~point** Standpunkt *a. fig*; *fig* Gesichtspunkt *m*; **~still** Stillstand *m*; *sport* Stehvermögen *n*; *to be at a ~~* stocken; ruhen, stillstehen; *to come to a ~~* ins Stocken geraten, zum Stillstand kommen; *~~ agreement* Stillhalteabkommen *n*; **~-up** *a* aufrecht (stehend); im Stehen *(nachgestellt)*; *Am fam* tapfer; *~~ collar* Stehkragen *m*; *~~ fight* regelrechte Schlacht *f*.

standard ['stændəd] *s* Standarte *f*, Banner *n a. fig*; (Maß-, Währungs-, Wert-) Einheit; Währung, Valuta *f*, Münzfuß *m*; Niveau *n*, Grad; Maßstab *m*, Regel, Norm, Richtschnur *f*, Anforderungen *f pl*; Durchschnitt *m*; Muster, Vorbild *n*; Stütze *f*, Ständer, Schaft, Pfosten, Pfeiler; *agr* freistehende(r) Hochstamm *m*; *el* Stehlampe *f*; *a* genormt; Norm-; normal, regelrecht, muster-, beispielhaft, vorschriftsmäßig; klassisch; Standard-; maßgebend, führend; aufrecht, stehend; *agr* hochstämmig; *above, below ~* über-, unterdurchschnittlich; über dem Durchschnitt, den Anforderungen nicht genügend; *to be up to ~* den Anforderungen entsprechen; *to raise the ~ (fig)* das Banner erheben (*of* gen); *gold, silver ~* Gold-, Silberwährung *f*; *~ of beauty* Schönheitsideal *n*; *~ of intelligence* geistige(s) Niveau *n*; *~ of knowledge, learning* Bildungsgrad *m*, -stufe *f*; *~ of life, living* Lebensstandard *m*; *~ of prices* Preisniveau *n*, -spiegel *m*; *~ of wages* Lohnniveau *n*; **~ author** Klassiker *m*; **~-bearer** Bannerträger *m a. fig*; **~ book** Standardwerk; Normenbuch *n*; **~ candle** *tech* Normalkerze *f*; **~ component** Normbauteil *m*; **~ English** gute(s) Englisch *n*; **~ film** Normalfilm *m*; **~ gauge** *rail* Normalspur(weite) *f*; **~-gauge** *a rail* normalspurig, Normalspur-; **~ gold** Münzgold *n*; **~ization** [stændədai'zeiʃən] Normung, Normierung, Normalisierung, Uniformierung, Vereinheitlichung *f*; **~ize** ['stændədaiz] *tr* normen, normieren, normalisieren, uniformieren, vereinheitlichen; **~ lamp** Stehlampe; *el* Normallampe *f*; **~ measure** Normalmaß *n*; **~ price** Grund-, Richtpreis *m*; **~ production** Durchschnittsproduktion *f*; **~ rate** Normalkurs, -tarif *m*, Grundgebühr *f*; **~ size** Normalgröße, gängige Größe *f*; **~ solution** Normallösung *f*; **~ specification** Normvorschrift *f*; **~ time** Normalzeit *f*; **~-type car** Serienwagen *m*; **~ value** Einheitswert *m*.

St Andrew's Cross [snt'ændruːz 'krɔs] Andreas-, liegende(s) Kreuz *n*.

stann|ic ['stænik], **~ous** ['-əs] *a* Zinn-; zinnhaltig; *~~ chloride, oxide* Zinnchlorid, -oxyd *n*; *~ous oxide* Zinnoxydul *n*; **~iferous** [stæ'nifərəs] zinnhaltig; **~um** ['stænəm] *scient* Zinn *n*.

stanza ['stænzə] Stanze, Strophe *f*.

staple ['steipl] **1.** Krampe, (Draht-) Öse *f*, *(~ hook)* Schließhaken *m*, Haspe; *tech* Schelle *f*; Stützbein *n*; *(Buchbinderei)* Heftklammer *f*; **stapling-machine, ~r** ['-ə] Heftmaschine *f*; **2.** *s* Haupterzeugnis *n*; Hauptgegenstand *m*, -sache *f*, *das* Wesentliche; Rohstoff *m*, -material *n*; (Haupt-) Handelsware *f*; Stapel; Stapelplatz *m*; (Woll-, Baumwoll-, Flachs-)Faser; Faser(beschaffenheit, -länge) *f*; *pl*

Stapelwaren *f pl*, Massenartikel *m pl*; *a* Haupt-, Stapel-; marktgängig; ~ **house** Lagerhaus *n*; ~ **industries** *pl* Hauptindustriezweige *m pl*; ~ **fibre** Zellwolle *f*; ~ **place** Hauptniederlage *f*; ~**r** ['-ə] Stapelhändler; (Woll-)Stapler *m*; ~ **trade** Stapelhandel *m*.

star [stɑ:] *s* Stern (*in the sky* am Himmel); *(fixed ~)* Fixstern; Himmelskörper *m*; *pl a. die* Gestirne *pl*; Stern *m (Figur)*; *typ* Sternchen *n*; Glücksstern *m*; *oft pl* Schicksal, Geschick *n*; Bühnen-, *bes.* Filmgröße *f*, (Film-)Star *m*; Leuchtkugel *f*; *tech (~ connection)* Sternschaltung *f*; *tr* mit Sternen verzieren; *typ* mit e-m Sternchen versehen *od* auszeichnen; e-e Hauptrolle übertragen (*an actor* e-m Schauspieler); in e-r Hauptrolle herausbringen, präsentieren; *itr theat film* glänzen, in e-r Glanzrolle auftreten, die Hauptrolle spielen; *under an unlucky ~* unter e-m ungünstigen Stern; *to see ~s* Funken (tanzen) sehen; *to thank o.'s (lucky) ~s* dem Schicksal danken; *his ~ is in the ascendant* sein Stern ist im Steigen; *film ~* Filmstar *m*; *the ~s and stripes, the ~-spangled banner* das Sternenbanner *(der US)*; ~**-billing** *Am* Starreklame *f*; **S~ Chamber** *hist* Sternenkammer *f*; ~**-crossed** *a poet* vom Schicksal verfolgt; ~**dom** ['-dəm] Berühmtheit *f* beim Theater *od* Film; die Größen *f pl* von Theater u. Film; ~**-dust** Sternnebel, Nebelstern *m*; *fig* Illusion *f*; ~**fish** *zoo* Seestern *m*; ~**-gaze** *itr* nach den Sternen schauen; träumen; ~**-gazer** *hum* Sterngucker *m*; ~**-gazing** Sternguckerei; geistige Abwesenheit; Träumerei *f*; ~**less** ['-lis] *(Himmel)* sternlos, schwarz; ~**let** ['-lit] *theat film* Starlet(t), *hum* Sternchen *n*; ~**light** *s* Sternenlicht *n*, -schein *m*; *a* sternhell, -klar; ~ **lighting** Vorverdunkelung *f*; ~**like** ['-laik] glänzend, funkelnd *(wie ein Stern)*; sternförmig; ~**ling** ['-liŋ] *orn* Star *m*; *(Brücke)* Pfeilerhaupt *n*, -kopf *m*; ~**lit** *a* sternhell, -klar; ~**red** [-d] *a* sternbesät, gestirnt; sternförmig; unter dem Einfluß der Gestirne; *theat film* als Star herausgestellt; mit e-m Ordensstern; *typ* mit Sternchen; ~**ring** ['-iŋ]: *~~ X.* mit X. in der Hauptrolle; ~ **role** Starrolle *f*; ~**ry** ['-i] sternbesät; (stern)hell, glänzend, leuchtend; sternförmig; Stern-; *~~-eyed (fam)* verträumt, träumerisch; unpraktisch, wirklichkeitsfremd; ~**-shaped** *a* sternförmig; ~ **shell** *mil* Leuchtgranate *f*; ~**-turn** *fam* Clou *m*.

starboard ['stɑ:bəd] *mar s* Steuerbord *n*; *a* Steuerbord-; *tr itr* (das Ruder) steuerbord legen.

starch [stɑ:tʃ] *s (Kartoffel-, Weizen-, Reis-)* Stärke *f*, -mehl *n*; *fig* Steifheit *f*; *Am fam* Mumm *m*, Energie, Kraft *f*; *tr (Wäsche)* stärken; ~ **content** Stärkegehalt *m*; ~ **formation** Stärkebildung *f*; ~**iness** ['-inis] Steifheit, Förmlichkeit *f*; ~**y** ['-i] stärkeartig, -haltig; *(Wäsche)* gestärkt; *fig* steif, förmlich, formell.

star|e [stɛə] *itr (mit den Augen)* starren, *fam* glotzen; große Augen machen, die Augen weit aufreißen; staunen; *(Haare, Stacheln)* starren, aufgerichtet stehen; anstarren (*at s.o.* jdn); *tr* anstarren *n*, *fam* -glotzen; *(mit den Augen)* fixieren; *s* Starren *n*, starre(r) Blick *m*; Staunen *n*; *to ~~ down, out of countenance* durch Anstarren aus der Fassung bringen; *to make s.o. ~~* jdn aufs höchste überraschen; *to ~~ s.o. in the face* jdn anstarren *(a. von Sachen)*; *fig* jdm in die Augen springen; ~**ing** ['-riŋ] *a* in die Augen fallend; auffallend, -fällig; *(Farbe)* grell, schreiend.

stark [stɑ:k] *a* starr, steif, unbeweglich; todesstarr; *fig* rein, völlig; sachlich; nackt, kahl; leer, öde; *adv* völlig, gänzlich; ~**-naked** *a* splitter-(faser)nackt.

start [stɑ:t] *itr* auf-, hochfahren, plötzlich aufspringen (*at* vor, bei); e-e plötzliche Bewegung machen, stutzen; los-, ab-, aufgehen, sich verschieben; *(Naht)* aufgehen; vorspringen, -stehen, heraustreten *a. fig*; anfangen, beginnen, s-n Anfang nehmen, losgehen, entstehen; aufbrechen (*on a journey* zu e-r Reise); weggehen, abfahren, -fliegen, -reisen (*for* nach); *bes. sport* starten (*from* von); *(Motor)* anspringen; *(Produktion)* anlaufen; *tr* auf-, hochfahren lassen, aufjagen, -scheuchen; stutzig machen; *(Wild)* aufstöbern; *(Einwendungen)* erheben; ab-, aufgehen, platzen lassen, verziehen, -rücken; anfangen (*singing* zu singen); in Bewegung setzen, ankurbeln, in Gang bringen (*a. Gespräch)*, ins Leben rufen; *(Gerücht)* unter die Leute bringen, in die Welt setzen; *(Frage)* aufwerfen; *(Thema)* anschneiden; *(Geschäft)* gründen, eröffnen; *(Gefäß)* anzapfen; *(Feuer)* anzünden, machen; *(Kessel)* anheizen; *(Reise)* antreten; *sport* das Startsignal geben für; *rail* abfahren lassen, das Zeichen zur Abfahrt geben; *mot* anlassen, -werfen, starten; *s* plötzliche(r) Schreck, Ruck *m*; Anfahren, Anspringen *n*; Beginn, Anfang; Aufbruch, Abmarsch *m*; Abreise, Abfahrt *f*; *aero* Abflug, Aufstieg; *sport* Start *m*; Startsignal *n*, -platz *m*; *tech* Anlaufenlassen, Ingangsetzen *n*; *allg* Ausgangspunkt *m*; günstige Gelegenheit *f*; Vorsprung *m*, Vorgabe *f*; *at the ~* bei Beginn; *by fits and ~s* (in) unregelmäßig(en Abständen); *by ~s* ruckweise; *from ~ to finish* von Anfang bis (zu) Ende; *to ~ from scratch (Am fam)* (wieder) ganz von vorne anfangen; *to ~ to skid* ins Rutschen kommen; *to ~ with* zunächst (einmal); für den Anfang; *to get the ~ of s.o.* jdm zuvorkommen, e-n Vorsprung vor jdm gewinnen; *to give s.o. a ~* jdn erschrecken; *to make a fresh ~* von neuem anfangen; *to ~* **back** zurückfahren, -schrecken, -springen; *to ~* **in** *fam* anfangen (*with* mit; *to do* zu tun); *to ~* **off** anfangen, beginnen (*with* mit); *mot* anfahren; *rail* sich in Bewegung setzen, abfahren; *to ~* **out** *fam* sich auf den Weg machen; anfangen, losgehen; sich anschicken; sich vornehmen; *to ~* **up** *itr* auffahren, -springen; (plötzlich) in Erscheinung treten, dasein; sich in Bewegung setzen; die Arbeit aufnehmen; sich entwickeln; *tr* in Gang bringen, in Bewegung setzen, ankurbeln; *he'll ~ the ball rolling* er wird die Sache ins Rollen bringen; *false ~* Fehlstart *m*; *ready to ~* abfahrbereit; ~**er** ['-ə] Teilnehmer (an e-m Rennen); Begründer, Urheber; *sport* Starter, Rennwart; *mot* Starter, Anlasser *m*; *to be a slow ~~* sich langsam in Bewegung setzen; *~~ flag* Startflagge *f*; *~~ push-button* Anlaßknopf *m*; ~**ing** ['-iŋ] *s mot* Anlassen; Anspringen *n*; Anlauf *m*; Inbetriebnahme *f*; Abmarsch; Abflug *m*; *in Zssgen* Anfangs-, Eröffnungs-; *a* ab; *~~ today* ab heute, von heute an; *~~-crank, -handle (mot)* Anlasserkurbel *f*; *~~ period* Anlaufzeit *f*; *~~-pit (sport)* Startgrube *f*; *~~ platform* Abfahrtsbahnsteig *m*; *~~ of production* Produktionsbeginn *m*; *~~-point* Ausgangspunkt *m*; *~~-post, -line* Startpfosten *m*, -linie *f*; *~~-price (Rennen)* Eröffnungseinsatz, *(Börse)* -kurs *m*; *~~-run (aero)* Anlauf(strecke *f*) *m*; *~~ salary* Anfangsgehalt *n*; *~~-signal* Startzeichen; Abfahrtssignal *n*; *~~-time* Abfahrtszeit *f*; ~**-up** *tech* Anlauf *m*.

startl|e ['stɑ:tl] *tr* er-, aufschrecken, e-n Schrecken einjagen (*s.o.* jdm); auffahren lassen; aufscheuchen; aufs äußerste überraschen, äußerst stutzig machen; ~**ing** ['-iŋ] erschreckend, überraschend.

starv|ation [stɑ:'veiʃən] Verhungern *n*, Hungertod *m*; *fig* Elend *n*, (furchtbare) Not *f*; *~~ wages (pl)* Hungerlohn *m*; ~**e** [stɑ:v] *itr* verhungern, *lit* Hungers sterben; am Verhungern sein; *fig* im Elend leben, Not leiden; *fam* furchtbaren Hunger haben; *fig* sich sehnen (*for* nach); *tr (to ~~ to death)* verhungern lassen; aushungern; durch Hunger zwingen (*into* zu); *to be ~ed* Not leiden, hungern; *of s.th.* an etw knapp sein; *we're simply ~ing (for food)* wir kommen fast um vor Hunger; ~**eling** ['-liŋ] *a* hungernd, ausgehungert; elend, notleidend; jämmerlich, kümmerlich, dürftig; *s* Hungerleider *m*; halb verhungerte(s) Tier *n*.

stash [stæʃ] *Am fam tr* (sich heimlich) weg-, zurücklegen; verbergen; *itr* sich heimliche Vorräte, e-e geheime Reserve anlegen; *sl* aufhören.

state [steit] *s* Zustand *m*, Lage *f*, Gegebenheiten *f pl*, Verhältnisse *n pl*; *zoo med* Stadium *n*; Stand, Rang *m*, (soziale) Stellung *f*; Pomp, Aufzug *m*, Zeremonie *f*, Glanz *m*, Pracht, Würde, Stattlichkeit *f*; *(S~)* Staat(skörper *m*, -verwaltung *f*, -gebiet *n*) *m*; *pl* (Land-)Stände *m pl*; *the S~s* die (Vereinigten) Staaten (von Amerika); *a* zeremoniell; *(S~)* Staats-, staatlich; *tr* festsetzen, -legen, anordnen, bestimmen, feststellen; aussagen, erklären, darlegen, versichern; berichten, melden; *(Rechnung)* spezifizieren; *(Problem)* stellen; *in ~* mit allen Feierlichkeiten; *in bad ~* in schlechtem Zustand; *in(to) a ~* in Unordnung, in Aufregung; *in the present ~ of things* unter den gegebenen Umständen; *to ~ full particulars* genaue Einzelheiten angeben; *to be (not) in a ~ to* imstande, außerstande sein zu; *to get in a ~* in Erregung geraten (*about, over* über); *to lie in ~* aufgebahrt liegen; *to put in a ~ of* in den Stand versetzen zu; *affairs (pl) of ~* Staatsgeschäfte *n pl*, öffentliche Angelegenheiten *f pl*; *buffer ~* Pufferstaat *m*; *confederation of ~s* Staatenbund *m*; *federal ~* Bundesstaat *m*; *finances (pl) of the ~* Staatsfinanzen *f pl*; *satellite ~* Satellitenstaat *m*; *Secretary of S~ (Am)* Außenminister *m*; *~ of affairs* Lage *f*, Stand *m* der Dinge; Sachlage *f*; Zustand *m*; *~ of alert* Alarmzustand *m*; *~ of business* Geschäftslage *f*; *~ of the case* Sachverhalt *m*; *the S~s of the Church* der Kirchenstaat; *~ of emergency* Ausnahmezustand; Notstand *m*; *~ of health* Gesundheitszustand *m*; *~ of life* Lebenslage *f*; *~ of mind* Geisteszustand *m*, -verfassung *f*; *~ of repair* Unterhaltungszustand *m*; *~ of siege* Belagerungs-, Ausnahmezustand *m*; *~ of trade* Konjunktur-, Geschäftslage *f*; *~ of war* Kriegszustand *m*;

~ administration Staatsverwaltung *f*; **~ aid** Subvention, staatliche Unterstützung *f*; **~ archives** *pl* Staatsarchiv *n*; **~ authority** Staatsautorität *f*; **~ capitalism** Staatskapitalismus *m*; **~ church** Staatskirche *f*; **~ coach** Staatskutsche *f*; **~ constitution** Staatsverfassung *f*; **~ control** Staatsaufsicht; *(~~led economy)* Zwangswirtschaft *f*; **~craft** Staatskunst *f*; **~d** ['-id] *a* festgesetzt, -gelegt, bestimmt; *(Rechnung)* spezifiziert; *(Gehalt)* fest; *as ~~* wie erwähnt; *S~ Department (Am)* Außenministerium *n*; **~ documents** *pl* amtliche Schriftstücke *n pl*; **~ funds** *pl* Staatsgelder *n pl*; **~ grant** Staatszuschuß *m*; **~ help** Staatsbeihilfe *f*; **~hood** Eigenstaatlichkeit *f*; **S~house** Parlamentsgebäude *n* (e-s amerikanischen Bundesstaates); **~less** ['-lis] staatenlos; **~lessness** ['-lisnis] Staatenlosigkeit *f*; **~liness** ['-linis] Stattlichkeit, Würde, Erhabenheit, Majestät *f*; **~ly** ['-li] stattlich, würdig, würdevoll, erhaben, majestätisch, eindrucksvoll, imposant; bedächtig, überlegt; **~ official** Staatsbeamte(r) *m*; **~-papers** *pl* Staatspapiere *n pl*, -akten *f pl*; **~ prison** Staatsgefängnis *n*; **~ prisoner** Staatsgefangene(r), politische(r) Häftling *m*; **~ property** Staatseigentum *n*; **~ revenue** Staatseinnahmen *f pl*; **S~ rights, S~s' rights** *pl Am* Rechte *n pl* u. Machtbefugnisse *f pl* der Einzelstaaten; **~room** Prunk-, Repräsentationsraum *m*; *Am mar* Luxuskabine *f*; *rail* Salonabteil *n*; **S~'s attorney** *Am* Staatsanwalt *m*; **~'s evidence** *Am jur* belastende Aussage *f*; *to turn ~~* als Kronzeuge auftreten; **~side** ['-said] *Am fam a* (typisch) amerikanisch; *adv* in, nach den Vereinigten Staaten; **~sman** ['-smən] Staatsmann; Politiker *m*; **~smanlike** ['-smənlaik], **~smanly** ['-smənli] staatsmännisch; **~smanship** ['-smənʃip] politische Fähigkeiten *f pl*; Staatskunst *f*; **~ socialism** Staatssozialismus *m*; **~ structure** Staatsgefüge *n*; **~ territory** Staatsgebiet *n*; **S~ trial** Staatsprozeß *m*; **~ witness** Belastungszeuge *m*.

statement ['steitmənt] Feststellung, Erklärung, Darlegung, Behauptung, Aussage *f*; *Am* Bericht *m*, Aufstellung, Übersicht *f*, Verzeichnis *n*, Liste *f*, (Konto-)Auszug, Ausweis *m*, Bilanz; Abrechnung *f*; *to give, to make a ~* e-e Erklärung abgeben; *to make (knowingly) false ~s* (wissentlich, bewußt) falsche Angaben machen; *annual ~* Jahresbericht *m*; *bank ~* Bankausweis *m*; *certified ~* Feststellung *f*; *final ~* Schlußabrechnung *f*; *monthly ~* Monatsausweis *m*; *official ~ to the press* amtliche Pressemitteilung *f*; *~ of affairs* Vermögensaufstellung, -übersicht *f*; Konkursstatus *m*; *~ of charges* Kostenaufstellung, -(ab)rechnung *f*; *~ of claim* Klageschrift *f*; *~ of clearance* Unbedenklichkeitserklärung *f*; *~ of costs* Kostenaufstellung *f*; *~ of defence* Klagebeantwortung, -erwiderung *f*; *~ of facts* Tatbericht; Sachverhalt, Tatbestand *m*; *~ of fees* Gebührentarif *m*; *~ of finances* Finanzbericht *m*; *~ of the market* Marktbericht *m*; *~ of prices* Preisliste *f*; *~ of revenue and expenditure* Gewinn- u. Verlustrechnung *f*; **~ analysis** *Am* Bilanzanalyse *f*; **~ wages** *pl* Akkordlohn *m*.

static ['stætik] *a phys* statisch; *fig* feststehend, unbeweglich, untätig, stationär; elektrostatisch; *Am radio* Störungs-; *s pl radio* atmosphärische Störung *f*; *(~ noise)* Störgeräusch *n*; *pl mit sing* Statik *f*.

station ['steiʃən] *s* Standort *m*, Stellung, Lage *f*, Platz; *bot zoo* Standort *m*, Vorkommen *n*; Stelle, Station *f*, Posten; trigonometrische(r) Punkt *m*; *radio* Funk-, Sende-, Empfangsstelle *f*; Sender; Standort *m*, *mil* Basis *f*, Stützpunkt; *mil aero* Fliegerhorst *m*; *mar* Position; Haltestelle, Station *f*; *rail* Bahnhof *m*; *Am (filling-~)* Tankstelle; *(Australien)* (Schafzucht-)Farm; (soziale) Stellung *f*, Rang, Stand *m*; *tr* aufstellen; stationieren; unterbringen; postieren; *at the ~* auf dem Bahnhof; *broadcasting, radio ~* Sender *m*; *bus-, coach-~* Autobusbahnhof *m*; *fire-~* Feuerwache *f*; *first-aid ~* Unfallstation *f*; *frontier ~* Grenzbahnhof *m*; *goods ~* Güterbahnhof *m*; *home ~* Heimatbahnhof *m*; *intermediate ~ (rail)* Zwischenstation *f*; *main, central ~* Hauptbahnhof *m*; *passenger ~* Personenbahnhof *m*; *petrol-~* Tankstelle *f*; *police-~* Polizeiwache *f*, -revier *n*; *polling ~* Wahllokal *n*; *postal ~* Post(hilfs)stelle, -station *f*, *power ~* Kraftwerk *n*; *railway-, (Am) railroad ~* Bahnhof *m*; *shunting ~* Verschiebebahnhof *m*; *weather ~* Wetterstation *f*; *~ of attachment* Heimatbahnhof *m*; *~ of destination* Bestimmungsbahnhof *m*; **~ announcement, signal** *radio* Pausenzeichen *n*; **~ary** ['steiʃnəri] fest(stehend) *a. fig*, ruhend, stationär, ortsgebunden, -fest; sich gleichbleibend; **~er** ['steiʃnə] Schreibwarenhändler *m*; *S~~s' Hall* Buchhändlerbörse *f*; *~~'s shop (Br)* Schreibwaren-, Papierwarengeschäft *n*; **~ery** ['-ʃnəri] Schreib-, Papierwaren *f pl*, *bes.* Briefpapier *n*; Bürobedarf *m*; *~~ store (Am)* Schreibwaren-, Papierwarengeschäft *n*; **~ hall** Bahnhofshalle *f*; **~-house** *rail* Stationsgebäude *f*; *Am* Polizeiwache, -dienststelle; Feuerwache *f*; **~-master,** *Am a.* **-agent** *rail* Bahnhofsvorsteher *m*; **~ premises** *pl* Bahnhofsgelände *n*; **~ wagon** *mot* Kombi(wagen) *m*.

statistic|(al) [stə'tistik(əl)] statistisch; **~ian** [stætis'tiʃən] Statistiker *m*; **~s** [stə'tistiks] *pl* statistische(s) Material *n*, Statistik; *mit sing* Statistik *f (Wissenschaft)*.

statu|ary ['stætjuəri] *a* statuarisch; statuenmäßig; *s* Bildwerke *n pl*; Bildhauerkunst *f*; Bildhauer *m*; **~e** ['stætju:] Standbild *n*, Statue, Bildsäule *f*, -werk *n*; *the S~ of Liberty* die Freiheitsstatue *(in New York)*; **~esque** [stætju'esk] statuenhaft; *fig* stattlich; würdig; **~ette** [-'et] Statuette *f*.

stature ['stætʃə] Statur, Gestalt *f*, Wuchs *m*, Größe *f*; *fig* Format *n*, Bedeutung *f*.

status ['steitəs] Zustand *m*, Lage; Stellung *f*, Stand, Rang; *jur* Status *m*; *civil, personal ~* Personenstand *m*; *equality of ~* politische Gleichberechtigung *f*; *legal ~* Rechtsfähigkeit *f*; *marital ~* Familienstand *m*; *social ~* soziale Stellung *f*; *~ of affairs* Lage *f* der Dinge; **~ symbol** Statussymbol *n*.

statut|able ['stætjutəbl] = *~ory*; **~e** ['stætju:t] Gesetz(esbestimmung, -vorschrift *f*); Statut *n*; *pl* Statuten *n pl*, Satzung(en *pl*) *f*; Gesellschaftsvertrag *m*; *~~ book* Gesetzbuch *n*, Gesetzessammlung *f*; *~~ law* geschriebene(s) Recht *n*; *~~ of limitations* Verjährungsgesetz *n*; **~ory** ['-əri] gesetzlich; satzungs-, bestimmungsgemäß; *~~ company, corporation* Körperschaft *f* des öffentlichen Rechts; *~~ declaration* eidesstattliche Erklärung *f*; *~~ holiday* gesetzliche(r) Feiertag *m*.

sta(u)nch [stɑ:n(t)ʃ, stɔ:n(t)ʃ] *tr (Blut)* stillen; *(Tränen, Wunde)* trocknen; *a* dicht, undurchlässig; *(Schiff)* seetüchtig; *fig* zuverlässig, vertrauenswürdig, treu; stark, fest, solide.

stave [steiv] *s. a. staff s* (Faß-)Daube *f*; Stab, Stock *m*; *(Leiter)* Sprosse; *mus* (Noten-)Linie; Strophe *f*; *tr (to ~ in)* einstoßen, -drücken; durchbrechen, den Boden ausschlagen (*s.th.* e-r S); *~ in (itr)* zerbrechen; in Trümmer gehen; *~ off* abwehren, hinhalten, hinaus-, aufschieben, hinauszögern; **~ maker** Küfer, Faßbinder *m*; **~ rhyme** Stabreim *m*.

stay [stei] **1.** *itr* bleiben (*with s.o.* bei jdm); sich aufhalten, *lit* verweilen, wohnen, leben (*with s.o.* bei jdm); absteigen (*at a hotel* in e-m Hotel); stehenbleiben, anhalten; e-n Halt, e-e Pause machen, pausieren, warten (*for* auf); *fam* durchhalten; *fam* mitkommen, Schritt halten; *tr* an-, fest-, zurückhalten; hemmen; abhalten (*from* von), hindern (*from* an); aufschieben, zurückstellen, *jur* aussetzen, einstellen; *(to ~ out)* durch-, aushalten, vertragen; beruhigen, befriedigen; *(Hunger, Durst)* stillen; *(Streit)* schlichten, beilegen; *s* Halt *m*, Pause; Stockung *f*; Aufenthalt *m*, *lit* Verweilen *n*; Zurückstellung, Verschiebung *f*, Aufschub *m*; *jur* Aussetzung, Einstellung *f*; *to come to ~* (für immer) bleiben; *to ~ in bed* das Bett hüten; *to ~ the course (fig)* durchhalten; *to ~ put (fam)* sich nicht von der Stelle rühren, an Ort u. Stelle bleiben; *to ~ after school* nachsitzen; *to* **~ away** wegbleiben; *to* **~ down** e-e Klasse wiederholen; *to* **~ in** zu Hause, daheim bleiben; das Haus nicht verlassen; *(Schule)* nachsitzen müssen; *to* **~ on** fortdauern; noch bleiben, noch nicht fortgehen; *to* **~ out** draußen bleiben; nicht hineingehen, nicht hereinkommen; sich fernhalten (*of* von); von zu Hause wegbleiben; *to* **~ up** aufbleiben, nicht zu Bett gehen; *to* **~ with** wohnen bei; **~-at-home** Stubenhocker *m*; **~er** ['-ə] *sport* Steher *m*; **~-in strike** Sitzstreik *m*; **~ing-power** Ausdauer *f*; Stehvermögen *n*; **2.** *s* Stütze, Strebe *f*; Bügel, Steg *m*; Abspannseil *n*; Korsettstange *f*; *mar* Stag, Stütztau; *pl* Korsett *n*; *tr* stützen; stärken; beruhigen; ruhen lassen (*on, upon* auf; *in* in); mit Stegen, Stangen stützen; verstreben, abspannen; *(Mast)* stagen; *(Schiff)* wenden; **~ wire** Abspanndraht *m*.

*

stead [sted] *s*: *in s.o.'s ~* an jds Stelle; *to stand s.o. in good ~* jdm gut zustatten kommen; für jdn von Nutzen, Vorteil sein; **~fast** ['-fəst] fest(gegründet); beständig; unentwegt, standhaft, zielbewußt; **~fastness** ['-fəstnis] Festigkeit; Beständigkeit; Standhaftigkeit *f*; **~iness** ['-inis] Festigkeit; Beständigkeit; Gesetztheit, Beherrschtheit, Besonnenheit; Verläßlichkeit, Zuverlässigkeit *f*; **~y** ['-i] *a* fest, unbeweglich; beständig, gleich-, regelmäßig, (an)dauernd, unentwegt, stetig; sich (immer) gleichbleibend; *tech* konstant; verläßlich, zuverlässig; ruhig, beherrscht, unerschütterlich, sicher; gesetzt, nüchtern, ernst, besonnen, beherrscht;

com stabil; *interj* immer mit der Ruhe! *itr tr* ruhig werden *od* machen; sich festigen; *(Preise)* sich behaupten; *tr (to keep ~~) (Schiff)* fest in der Gewalt haben; *s Am sl* feste(s) Verhältnis *n*, feste(r) Freund *m*; *to go ~~ (Am sl)* zs. gehen, ein (festes) Verhältnis haben; *~~ customer* Stammkunde *m*; *~~ work* Dauerstellung *f*.

steak [steik] Steak; (Fisch-)Filet *n*.

steal [sti:l] *irr stole* [stoul], *stolen* ['stoulən] *tr* stehlen *a. fig*, (heimlich) entwenden, sich heimlich aneignen; erschleichen; *(Blick)* erhaschen; *itr* stehlen, ein Dieb sein; sich stehlen, schleichen; *to ~ away* sich wegschleichen, sich fortstehlen; *to ~ upon* sachte gelangen an; *s fam* Diebstahl *m*; Diebesgut *n*; *Am fam* gute(r) Fund *m*, gefundene(s) Fressen *n*; *to ~ a look at* e-n Blick werfen auf; *to ~ a march upon s.o.* jdm e-n Vorsprung abgewinnen; jdm zuvorkommen; *to ~ the show* den Erfolg davontragen; **~er** ['-ə] Dieb *m*; *deer ~~* Wilddieb *m*; **~ing** ['-iŋ] *a* diebisch; *s* Diebstahl *m*; *pl* Diebesgut *n*; **~th** [stelθ], **~thiness** ['stelθinis] Heimlichkeit; Heimlichtuerei *f*; *by ~~* heimlich, insgeheim; **~y** ['stelθi] heimlich, geheim, verstohlen; *with ~~ tread* auf Katzenpfoten.

steam [sti:m] *s* (Wasser-)Dampf; Dunst *m*; Dampfkraft; *fam* Kraft, Stärke, Energie *f*; *attr* Dampf-; *itr* (ver)dampfen; *(Fenster, Brille)* sich beschlagen; Dampf erzeugen *od* ablassen; mit Dampf (an)getrieben werden; *(Zug)* dampfen, fahren; *tr* dämpfen, dünsten; ausdünsten; *to ~ up (fam)* auf Touren bringen, *itr* kommen; *to be ~ed up (fam)* vor Wut kochen (*about* wegen); *at full ~, full ~ ahead* (mit) Volldampf voraus; *to blow off, to let off, to work off ~ (fam)* sich austoben; s-m Zorn Luft machen; *to get up ~ (fam)* Kräfte sammeln; *to put on ~ (fig)* Dampf dahintermachen; *tech* Dampf anlassen; *exhaust, waste ~* Abdampf *m*; **~-bath** Dampfbad *n*; **~boat, ~er** ['-ə], **~ship** Dampfschiff *n*, Dampfer *m*; **~-boiler** Dampfkessel *m*; **~-engine** Dampfmaschine *f*; **~-fitter** Heizungsmechaniker, -installateur *m*; **~-ga(u)ge** Manometer *n*; **~-generating plant** Kesselanlage *f*; **~-hammer** Dampfhammer *m*; **~-heat(ing)** Dampfheizung *f*; **~iness** ['-inis] Dunstigkeit *f*; **~-jet** Dampfstrahl *m*; **~-pipe** Dampfleitungsrohr *n*; **~-power** Dampfkraft *f*; **~-roller** *s* Dampfwalze *f a. fig, bes. pol*; *tr fig* niederwalzen; *(Antrag)* durchpeitschen; **~-shovel** Dampfbagger *m*; **~-tug** Schleppdampfer *m*; **~-turbine** Dampfturbine *f*; **~y** ['-i] dampfig, Dampf-; dampferfüllt; *(Glas)* beschlagen; dampfend, verdunstend.

stear|ic [sti'ærik] *a* Stearin-; *~~ acid* Stearinsäure *f*; **~in** ['stiərin] Stearin *n*.

stedfast *s. steadfast.*

steed [sti:d] *lit* od *hum* (Streit-)Roß *n*.

steel [sti:l] *s* Stahl *a. fig*; Dolch; (Wetz-)Stahl *m*; Drahtstange *f*; *fig* Härte *f*; *a* stählern, stahlhart; Stahl-; *tr* (ver)stählen; *fig* stählen, abhärten; hart, gefühllos machen; *to ~ o.s. against* sich wappnen gegen; *an enemy worthy of o.'s ~* ein würdiger Gegner *m*; *alloy ~* legierte(r) Stahl *m*; *Bessemer ~* Bessemerstahl *m*; *cast ~* Gußstahl *m*; *damask ~* Damaszenerstahl *m*; *forging-~* Schmiedeeisen *n*; *hard-~* Hartstahl *m*; *ingot, medium carbon-~* Flußstahl *m*; *mild, soft ~* Flußeisen *n*; *nickel-~* Nickelstahl *m*; *puddled ~* Puddelstahl *m*; *raw ~* Rohstahl *m*; *rolled ~* Walzstahl *m*; *structural ~* Baustahl *m*; *superrefined ~* Edelstahl *m*; *tool-~* Werkzeugstahl *m*; **~ alloy** Stahllegierung *f*; **~-armoured, -clad, -plated** *a* stahlgepanzert; **~ articles** *pl* Stahlwaren *f pl*; **~ band** Stahlband *n*; **~ bar** Stahlstange *f*; **~ blade** Stahlklinge *f*; **~-blue** stahlblau; **~ bottle** Stahlflasche *f*; **~ concrete** Stahlbeton *m*; **~ conduit** Stahlrohr *n*; **~ construction** Stahlbau *m*; **~ engraving** Stahlstich *m*; **~ foundry** Stahlgießerei *f*; **~ frame** Stahlgerüst, -skelett *n*; **~-gray** stahlgrau; **~ industry** Stahlindustrie *f*; **~ing** ['-iŋ] Verstählung *f*; **~ ingot** Stahlbarren *m*; **~ mill, works** *pl, a. mit sing* Stahlwerk(e *n*) *pl*; **~ output** Stahlproduktion *f*; **~ plate** Stahlplatte *f*, -blech *n*; **~ production** Stahlerzeugung *f*; **~ rope** Stahlseil *n*; **~ spring** Stahlfeder *f*; **~ tower** Stahlmast *m*; **~ tubing** Stahlrohr *n*; **~ vault** Stahlkammer *f*; **~ wire** Stahldraht *m*; **~ wool** Stahlwolle *f*; **~y** ['-i] stählern *a. fig*; Stahl-; **~yard** Laufgewichts-, Schnellwaage *f*.

steep [sti:p] **1.** *a* steil, abschüssig; jäh; *fam* gewaltig, mächtig; *fam (Preis)* gesalzen, exorbitant, happig; *(Geschichte)* unwahrscheinlich; *s lit* Steilhang *m*; **~en** ['-ən] *tr itr* steil(er) machen, werden; *(Preise)* anziehen; **~ness** ['-nis] Steilheit *f*; **~ slope** Steilabhang *m*; **2.** *tr* einweichen, -tunken; sich vollsaugen lassen; imprägnieren (*in, with* mit); *(Tee)* ziehen lassen; *itr* eingeweicht werden; *to ~ o.s. (fig)* sich versenken (*in* in); *s* Einweichen *n*; Lauge *f*; **~ed** [-t] *a* gesättigt (*in* mit).

steeple ['sti:pl] (Kirch-)Turm *m*; Turmspitze, -haube *f*; **~chase** Hindernisrennen *n*; Querfeldeinlauf *m*.

steer [stiə] **1.** *tr* steuern *a. fig*; *fig* lenken, leiten, führen; *(Schritte)* richten, lenken (*to* nach, auf); *itr* steuern, lenken; sich steuern, lenken lassen; Kurs nehmen *od* halten (*for* auf); *s Am sl* Tip, Wink *m*; *to ~ clear of s.o.* jdm aus dem Weg gehen; **~able** ['-rəbl] lenkbar; **~age** ['-ridʒ] Steuerung *f*; *mar* Zwischendeck *n*; *~~ passenger* Zwischendeckpassagier *m*; **~ing** ['-riŋ] Steuerung *f*; *~~ axle* Lenkachse *f*; *~~ column (mot)* Lenksäule *f*; *~~ committee* Lenkungs-, Organisationsausschuß *m*; *~~-gear* Steuer-, Lenkvorrichtung; *mot* Spurstange; *mar* Ruderanlage *f*; *~~ lock (mot)* Lenkradschloß *n*; *~~-play (mot)* tote(r) Gang *m*; *~~-wheel* Lenk-, Steuerrad *m*; **~less** ['-lis] steuerlos; **~sman** ['-zmən] Steuermann *m*; **2.** junge(r) Ochse, *(seltener)* Bulle; *Am* Mastochse *m*.

stein [stain] *Am* Bier-, Maßkrug *m*.

stell|ar ['stelə] *a* Stern-; *theat film* Star-, Haupt-; führend; hervorragend; **~ate** ['-it] sternförmig.

stem [stem] *s bot* Stamm; Stengel; Stiel *a. allg*; Schaft; *(Glas)* Fuß *m*; *(Pfeife)* Rohr *n*; *(Note)* Hals; *(Buchstabe)* Grundstrich; *(Wort)* Stamm *m*, Wurzel *f*; *mar* (Vorder-)Steven; Bug; *sport* Schneepflug *m*; *pl Am sl* Beine *n pl*; *tr (Früchte)* entstielen; ankommen, -kämpfen gegen; hemmen, aufhalten; *(Blut)* stillen; *itr* stammen, herrühren, kommen (*from* von); *from ~ to stern* von vorn bis hinten; **~less** ['-lis] ungestielt; **~ turn** Stemmbogen *m*; **~-winder** *Am* Remontoiruhr *f*; *Am fam* As *n*; Knüller *m*.

stench [stentʃ] Gestank *m*; **~-trap** Siphon *m (Kanalisation)*.

stencil ['stensl] *s* Schablone; Schablonenarbeit *f*, -druck *m*; *(Maschinenschreiben)* Matrize *f*; *tr* mit e-r Schablone herstellen; auf Matrize(n) schreiben; *to type ~s* Matrizen schreiben.

steno ['stenou] *tr itr fam* stenographieren; **~g** ['-əg] *Am sl s* Stenotypistin *f*; *tr itr* stenographieren.

steno|graph ['stenəgra:f] *tr itr* stenographieren; *s* Stenogramm; stenographische(s) Zeichen *n*; Stenographiermaschine *f*; **~grapher** [ste'nɔgrəfə] Stenograph(in *f*) *m*; **~grapher-typist** *Am* Stenotypist(in *f*) *m*; **~graphic(al)** [stenə'græfik(əl)] stenographisch; **~graphy** [ste'nɔgrəfi] Stenographie, Kurzschrift *f*; **~type** ['stenətaip] Stenographiermaschine *f*; Abkürzung *f*, Sigel *n*; **~typist** ['stenətaipist] Maschinenstenograph(in *f*) *m*.

step [step] **1.** *s* Schritt, Tritt *m*; kurze Strecke *f*; Katzensprung *fig*; Gang *(Art zu gehen)*; (*schwerer* od *fester, leichter*) Schritt, Tritt; Fuß(s)tapfen; Tanzschritt; Tritt(brett *n*) *m*, Stufe; *fig* Stufe *f*, Grad, Schritt; *fig* Schritt *m*, Unternehmen, Wagnis; *mus* Intervall *n*; *itr* schreiten, treten; stapfen; gehen, kommen; (hinein-)treten, (hinein)geraten (*into* in); *(absichtlich* od *unabsichtlich)* treten (*on* auf); *tr (Schritt)* machen; auftreten mit *(dem Fuß)*; *(Tanz)* tanzen; *(Tanzschritt)* ausführen; *(to ~ off)* abschreiten, -messen; mit Stufen versehen; *fig* abstufen; *mar (Mast)* einsetzen; *~ by ~* schritt-, stufenweise; Schritt für Schritt, nach u. nach; *in ~* im Gleichschritt (*with* mit); *in ~s* stufenweise; *out of ~* ohne Tritt, nicht im Gleichschritt; *a ~ in advance* ein Schritt vorwärts; *to be out of ~* nicht Schritt halten (*with* mit); *to break ~* aus dem Schritt kommen; *to fall in ~ (mil)* Tritt fassen; *to follow, to tread in s.o.'s ~s (fig)* in jds Fußtapfen treten; *to get out of ~* aus dem Schritt kommen; *to keep ~ with* Schritt halten mit; *to make a long ~ (fig)* e-n tüchtigen Schritt vorwärtskommen; *to retrace o.'s ~s* den gleichen Weg zurück-, noch einmal gehen; *to take ~s* Schritte unternehmen; *to watch o.'s ~* vorsichtig gehen, *fig* sein; aufpassen; *to ~ on the gas, to ~ on it (mot)* Gas geben *a. fig*; sich beeilen; *(to ~ high* die Füße hochziehen; *to ~ it* tanzen; *to ~ on s.o.'s toes (fig)* jdm auf die Füße treten; jdn beleidigen; *~ in! (Am)* herein! *~ lively!* mach schnell, *fam* zu! weitergehen, bitte! *~ this way* komm (hier)her! *mind the ~!* Vorsicht, Stufe! *quick ~* Geschwindschritt *m*; *to ~* **along** einherschreiten; *to ~* **aside** zur Seite treten, ausweichen; *fig* abschweifen; *to ~* **back** zurücktreten; *to ~* **down** *itr* hinuntergehen; zurücktreten, s-n Abschied nehmen; abnehmen; *tr* herabsetzen; *el* herabtransformieren, umspannen; *to ~* **forward** vortreten; *to ~* **in** hereinkommen, hineingehen; *fig* sich einschalten, -mischen, sich ins Mittel legen, eingreifen; *to ~* **off** aussteigen; *Am sl* ins Gras beißen; *~~ the carpet (Am sl)* heiraten; *to ~* **out** kurz hinausgehen; aussteigen; tüchtig ausschreiten, sich beeilen; *Am fam* s-e Stellung aufgeben; *Am fam* ausgehen, sich mal amüsieren, ein Stelldichein haben; *on s.o.* mit jdm e-n Seitensprung machen; *to ~* **up** *itr* hinaufgehen; näherkommen, sich nähern, zugehen (*to s.o.* auf jdn); vorwärts-, weiterkommen; zunehmen; *tr* steigern;

vermehren; beschleunigen; *el* hochtransformieren; **~-dance** Steptanz *m*; **~-ins** *pl fam* (Damen-)Schlüpfer *m*; Pantoffeln, Slippers *m pl*; **~-ladder** Trittleiter *f*; **~mobile** schnelle(r) Wagen *m*; **~-off** *s Am* Absinken; Abtropfen *n*; **~ping-stone** Trittstein *m*; *fig* Sprungbrett *n*; **~-switch** Stufenschalter *m*; **~-up** *a* stufenweise erhöhend; **~wise** schritt-, stufenweise **2.** Stief-; **~brother, child, daughter, father, mother, sister, son** Stiefbruder *m*, -kind *n*, -tochter *f*, -vater *m*, -mutter, -schwester *f*, -sohn *m*.

Stephen ['sti:vn] Stephan *m*.

steppe [step] Steppe *f*.

stereo|chemistry [stiəriə'kemistri, steriо(u)'-] Stereochemie *f*; **~chromy** ['stiəriəkroumi] Stereochromie *f*; **~graphy** [stiəri'ɔgrəfi] Stereographie *f*; **~metric(al)** [stiəriə'metrik(əl)] stereometrisch; **~metry** [stiəri'ɔmitri] Stereometrie *f*; **~phonic** [stiəriə'fɔnik] *(Tonübertragung)* stereophon(isch); *~~ record* stereophone Schallplatte *f*; **~scope** ['stiəriəskoup, 'steriə-] Stereoskop *n*; **~scopic(al)** [stiəriə'skɔpik(əl)] stereoskopisch; **~type** ['stiəriətaip] *s typ* Druckplatte *f*, Klischee *n a. fig*; = *~typy*; *tr* stereotypieren; *fig* e-e feste Form geben (*s.th.* e-r S), ein für allemal festlegen; **~typed** ['-t] *a* stereotyp, stets gleichbleibend, unveränderlich; **~typy** ['stiəriətaipi] Stereotypgießerei *f*, -druck *m*.

steril|e ['sterail] unfruchtbar *a. fig*; steril; keimfrei; *fig* wirkungslos; fruchtlos, nutzlos; langweilig; **~ity** [ste'riliti] Unfruchtbarkeit; Sterilität; Keimfreiheit *f*; **~ization** [sterilai'zeiʃən] Unfruchtbarmachung; Sterilisierung; Entkeimung *f*; **~ize** ['sterilaiz] *tr* unfruchtbar machen; sterilisieren; entkeimen.

sterling ['stə:liŋ] echt, unverfälscht; *(Metall)* gediegen; vollwertig; *a pound ~* ein Pfund Sterling; *~* **area** Sterlinggebiet *n*.

stern [stə:n] **1.** ernst, streng, hart; *(Blick)* finster; abstoßend; *fig* unnachgiebig, unerbittlich; **~ness** ['-nis] Ernst *m*, Strenge *f*; **2.** *mar* Heck *n*; *allg* hintere(r) Teil *m*; **~-heavy** *aero* schwanzlastig; **~post** Achtersteven *m*; *~* **sheets** *pl (Boot)* Achtersitze *m pl*.

stern|al ['stə:nl] *a anat* Brustbein-; **~um** ['-əm] *pl a.* **~a** ['-ə] Brustbein *n*.

stertor ['stə:tə] *med* Röcheln, Schnarchen *n*; **~ous** ['-rəs] *med* röchelnd, schnarchend.

stet [stet] *imp typ* bleibt!

stethoscope ['steθəskoup] *med* Hörrohr *n*.

Stetson ['stetsən] *(~ hat) (Warenzeichen) Am Art* breitkrempige(r) Filzhut *m (der Cowboys)*.

stevedore ['sti:vidɔ:] *mar* Stauer *m*.

stew [stju:] **1.** *tr* schmoren *a. fig*; dämpfen; *tr itr* langsam kochen, bei schwacher Hitze kochen (lassen); *fig fam* (sich) ärgern; *s* Eintopf(essen *n*); *fam* Ärger *m*, Wut *f*; *Am sl* Säufer *m*, Besäufnis *f*, Durcheinander *n*; *pl* Bordell *n*; *to be in a ~* vor Wut kochen; außer sich sein; *to ~ in o.'s own juice (fig)* im eigenen Saft schmoren; *Irish ~* Hammelfleisch *n* mit Kartoffeln u. Zwiebeln; **~ed** [-d] *a* geschmort, gedämpft; *Am sl* besoffen; *~~ fruit* Kompott *n*; **~pan, ~pot** Schmor-, Kochtopf *m*; **2.** Fischkasten, -teich; Austernpark *m*.

steward ['stjuəd] Haushofmeister; (Grundstücks-)Verwalter; Sportkommissar, (Fest-)Ordner; *mar* Proviantmeister; *mar aero* Steward *m*; *shop ~* Betriebsrat(svorsitzende(r)) *m*; **~ess** ['-is] Verwalterin, Beschließerin; *mar aero* Stewardeß *f*.

stick [stik] *irr stuck, stuck* [stʌk] *tr* (durch)stechen; durchbohren; ab-, er-, totstechen; schlachten; sich stechen in; *(spitzen Gegenstand)* stechen, stecken, stoßen (*into* in); anstecken, -heften; bestecken; (an)kleben; *agr* mit Stangen versehen, anpfählen; *fam* (hinein)stecken, tun, legen (*into* in); *fam* beschmieren, schmierig, klebrig machen; *fam* verblüffen, aus der Fassung bringen, vor den Kopf stoßen; *sl* was Schönes aufhalsen, -laden (*s.o.* jdm); *sl* das Geld aus der Tasche ziehen *fig* (*s.o.* jdm); *sl* 'reinlegen; *sl* vertragen, aushalten, -stehen; *itr (heraus-, hervor)*stehen; stecken(bleiben), kleben(bleiben), haften (*to* an), picken; haften-, hängenbleiben *a. fig*; sich genau halten (*to the text* an den Wortlaut); *fig* hängen, festhalten (*at, to* an); verbunden sein (*at, to* mit); durchhalten; sich halten (*to* an), bleiben (*to* bei), beibehalten (*to s.th.* etw); *tech* nicht mehr funktionieren (wollen); *(Türe)* klemmen; *fig* stecken-, hängenbleiben, nicht weiter, nicht zum Ziel kommen; *(unverkauft)* liegenbleiben; im Zweifel, unschlüssig sein; zögern, zaudern, zurückschrecken (*at* vor); *s* Stock, Stecken, Knüppel; Stab *m*, Stange *f*; Stäbchen *n*, Stift *m*; Stück *n* (Seife); (Schokolade-)Riegel; Schaft; Stengel; (Takt-)Stock; (Hockey-)Schläger *m*; *sport* Hürde *f*; *(joy ~) aero* Steuerknüppel; *mar* Mast; *typ* Winkelhaken *m*; Schriftzeile *f*; Stich *m*; Klebkraft *f*; Schuß *(Alkohol in e-m Getränk)*; *(~ of bombs)* (Bomben-)Reihenabwurf; *fam* Sack, blöde(r) Kerl, Tranpott; *Am sl* Zahn *m*, (hohes) Tempo; *Am sl* Pech *n*; *Am sl* Zigarette *f*; *Am sl* Croupier *m*; *pl Br sl* bescheidene(s) Mobiliar *n*; *Am sl* Provinz, ländliche Gegend *f*; *in a cleft ~* in der Klemme; *in the ~s (Am fam)* j. w. d., wo sich Füchse u. Hasen gute Nacht sagen; *through ~ and stone* über Stock u. Stein; *to be stuck (fig)* in der Tinte, Patsche sitzen; *(Am sl)* versessen sein (*on* auf); vernarrt sein (*on* in); *to be from the ~s (Am sl)* aus der Provinz kommen; *to beat to ~s* kurz u. klein schlagen; *fig* abhängen; *to get stuck* steckenbleiben, festfahren (*in the mud* im Schlamm); *fig* hereinfallen; *to get, to have hold of the wrong end of the ~* die Sache nicht mitkriegen; *to go to ~s and staves* in die Brüche, in Scherben gehen; *to take a ~ to s.o.* jdn verprügeln; *to want the ~* Schläge brauchen; *to ~ to o.'s guns* s-n Standpunkt vertreten; *to ~ o.'s hands in o.'s pocket* die Hände in die Tasche stecken; *to ~ it on (sl)* den Mund mächtig vollnehmen, tüchtig angeben; *to ~ it out (Am fam)* es aushalten, durchhalten; *to ~ out a mile* offensichtlich sein; *to ~ o.'s neck out* sich herausfordernd benehmen; etw riskieren; *to ~ o.'s nose into s.th.* s-e Nase in etw stecken; *to ~ at nothing* vor nichts zurückschrecken; *to ~ to o.'s promise* sein Versprechen halten; *to ~ to o.'s ribs (Am sl)* sich vollschlagen; *to ~ to s.o.'s throat* jdm im Halse steckenbleiben; *~ no bills* (Zettel-)Ankleben verboten; *not a ~ was left standing* es blieb kein Stein auf dem andern; *~ them up! (Am sl)* Hände hoch! *broom~* Besenstiel *m*; *composing-~ (typ)* Winkelhaken *m*; *drum-~* Trommelstock *m*; *fiddle-~* Geigenbogen *m*; *lip~* Lippenstift *m*; *small ~s (pl)* Reisig *n*; *walking ~* Spazierstock *m*; *a ~ of sealing-wax* e-e Stange Siegellack; *a ~ of shaving-soap* ein Stück Rasierseife; *to ~* **around** *sl* in der Nähe bleiben; *to ~* **by** *fam* zur Stange halten; *to ~* **down** zukleben, verschließen (*an envelope* e-n Briefumschlag); *to ~* **out** *itr (Nagel)* herausstehen; bestehen (*for* auf); *fig* deutlich sichtbar sein; *tr* heraus-st(r)ecken; *to ~* **together** *fig* zs.-halten; *to ~* **up** *itr* hoch-, aufrecht stehen, aufragen; *(Nagel)* herausstehen; *fam* sich ins Zeug legen (*for* für); *tr* aufrichten; *sl* (überfallen u.) be-, ausrauben; *to be stuck up (fam)* die Nase hochheben, hochnäsig sein; *to ~ o.s. up (fam)* sich herausstreichen; **~er** ['-ə] Schlachter, Schlächter; Ankleber; *fam* zähe(r) Bursche, hartnäckige(r) Mensch *m*; Klette *f*; Dorn, Stachel; *Am* Klebe-, Aufklebzettel *m*; *fam* schwierige Sache *f*, Rätsel, Problem *n*; bissige Bemerkung *f*; *com* Ladenhüter *m*; **~ful** ['-ful] *typ* Schriftzeile *f*; **~iness** ['-inis] Klebrigkeit *f*; **~ing** ['-iŋ] *s* Stechen, Stecken; Kleben, Heften *n*; *~~-place, -point (fig)* entscheidende(r) Augenblick *m*; Entscheidung *f*; *~~-plaster* Heftpflaster *n*; **~-in-the-mud** *fam* Schlafmütze *f*, Trauerkloß *m*; **~jaw** klebrige(r, s) Bonbon *m* od *n*; **~-out** *Am sl* hervorragende Sache *f*; überlegene(r) Mensch *m*; **~pin** *Am* Krawattennadel *f*; **~-to-itiveness** [-'tu:itivnis] *Am fam* Ausdauer, Zähigkeit *f*; **~um** ['-ʌm] *Am fam* Klebstoff *m*; **~-up** *fam* Vatermörder, Stehkragen; *sl* Raubüberfall *m*; **~y** ['-i] klebrig; *fam (Wetter)* schwül, drükkend, dämpfig; *sl* schwierig, ungefällig, linkisch; *I feel ~~ (Am sl)* mir ist (so) mies; *~~ charge* Haftmine; Hafthohlladung *f*; *~~-fingered (Am sl a)* mit langen Fingern; knickig; *~~ label* Klebezettel *m*; *~~ wicket (Br sl)* schwierige Lage, Patsche *f*

stickle ['stikl] *itr* etwas einzuwenden haben; Schwierigkeiten machen; streiten, zanken (*about* um); **~back** *zoo* Stichling *m*; **~r** ['-ə] Eiferer (*for* für), (hartnäckiger, eifriger) Verfechter (*for* gen); *fam* (alter) Meckerer, Nörgler, Pedant *m* (*for* mit).

stiff [stif] *a* steif, starr; schwer beweglich; (ge)straff(t), gespannt; steifgefroren, gliedersteif, unbeweglich, schwerfällig; *(Schaum)* steif, fest; *(Arznei, alkoholische Getränke)* stark; *(Grog)* steif; *(Wind)* heftig; *(Brise)* steif; *(Examen)* schwer; *(Strafe)* schwer, hart; ungeschickt, gezwungen, steif, förmlich; *(~-necked)* hartnäckig, halsstarrig, verbissen, unbeugsam; *fam (Preis)* hoch, überhöht; *fam* schwierig, kompliziert; *sl* voll (*with* von); *sl* außerordentlich; *Am sl* besoffen; *Am sl (Scheck)* gefälscht; *s Am sl* Wisch; Kassiber *m*; Leiche *f*; Besoffene(r) *m*, Bierleiche *f*; *(big ~)* blöde(r) Kerl; linkische(r), steife(r), förmliche(r) Mensch; (Wander-)Arbeiter; Versager; Strolch, Landstreicher *m*; *~ as a poker, a ramrod* steif wie ein Besenstiel; *to bear s.o. ~ (sl)* jdn zu Tode langweilen; *to keep a ~ upper lip* die Ohren steifhalten; **~en** ['stifn] *tr* versteifen, straffen; *(Preise)* ansteigen lassen; *(Flüssigkeit)* verdicken; *itr* steif, hart werden; sich verfestigen, sich verhärten; erstarren; *(Preise)* anziehen, sich festigen; *fig* sich versteifen; **~ener** ['-nə] feste Einlage; Versteifung; *fam* Stärkung *f*, Schnäpschen *n*; Schuß *m*

(Alkohol); *sport Am sl* Entscheidungskampf *m*, Siegestor *n*, K.-o.-Schlag *m*; **~ening** ['-niŋ] Versteifung, Verstärkung *f*; *(Preise)* Anziehen *n*; **~-necked** *a fig* halsstarrig; **~ness** ['-nis] Steife, Steifheit *a. fig*; Hartnäckigkeit *f*.
stifl|e ['staifl] **1.** *tr* ersticken *a. fig*; *fig* unterdrücken; *(Hoffnung)* zerstören; *itr* ersticken; (vor Hitze) umkommen; **~ing** ['-iŋ] *(Hitze)* erstickend; **2.** *s (Pferd, Hund)* Kniegelenk *n*.
stigma ['stigmə] *pl a.* *-ta* ['-tə] *fig* Schandfleck *m*, Stigma *n*; *rel pl (-ta)* Wundmale *n pl* (Christi); *med* Symptom *n*; *bot* Narbe; *zoo* Tracheenöffnung *f*; **~tization** [stigmətai'zeiʃən] Brandmarkung; Stigmatisierung *f*; **~tize** ['stigmətaiz] *tr* brandmarken; stigmatisieren.
stile [stail] Zauntritt, -übergang *m*.
stiletto [sti'letou] *pl -o(e)s* Stilett *n*; Pfriem *m*; **~ (heel)** Pfennigabsatz *m*.
still [stil] **1.** *a* still, ruhig, schweigend; leise; ruhig, bewegungs-, reglos, unbewegt; *(Wein)* nicht schäumend; *(Wasser)* stehend; *phot* Stand-, Steh-; *s poet* Ruhe, Stille *f*; *phot* Stehbild, Standphoto; *fam (Kunst)* Stilleben *n*; *tr* zum Schweigen, zur Ruhe bringen; beruhigen, erleichtern; *adv* (immer) noch; nach wie vor; *vor Komparativ*: noch; *a. conj* (den)noch; trotzdem; *to hold ~* stillhalten; *to keep ~* schweigen; *to sit ~* stillsitzen; **~ birth** Totgeburt *f*; **~-born** *a* totgeboren; **~ hunt** *Am* Pirsch *f*; **~-hunt** *Am itr* pirschen; *tr* beschleichen; **~-life** *pl ~-lifes (Kunst)* Stilleben *n*; **~ more** noch mehr; **~ness** ['-nis] Stille, Ruhe *f*; **~ projector** Bildwerfer, Projektionsapparat *m*; **~y** ['-i] *a poet* still, ruhig; **2.** Destillierapparat *m*; Brennerei, *fam* Destille *f*; **~er** ['-ə] Brenner *m*; **~-room** Destillierraum *m*, Hausbrennerei *f*; Vorratsraum *m*.
stilt [stilt] Stelze *f*; *arch* Pfahl *m*; **~ed** ['-id] *a fig* hochtrabend, gespreizt, anspruchsvoll; *arch* auf Pfählen.
stimul|ant ['stimjulənt] *a* anregend, stimulierend; erregend; *s* Ansporn, Antrieb, Anreiz *m* (*of* für); Reizmittel, Stimulans *n*; **~ate** ['-eit] *tr* anspornen (*to* zu); anreizen, -regen (*s.o. into s.th.* jdn zu etw); stimulieren; erregen, beleben; **~ation** [stimju'leiʃən] Ansporn, Anreiz, Kitzel *m*; Belebung *f*; **~ative** ['stimjuleitiv] *a* anregend, stimulierend; *s* Anreiz *m*; Reizmittel *n*; **~us** ['-əs] *pl -i* ['-ai] Ansporn, Anreiz *m*; Aufmunterung *f*; Reizmittel *n*; *med* Reiz *m*; *~~ threshold* Reizschwelle *f*.
sting [stiŋ] *irr stung, stung* [stʌŋ] *tr* stechen (*on the cheek* in die Wange); beißen, brennen; schmerzen; *fig* verwunden, verletzen; *fig* an-, aufstacheln (*intozu*); *meist Passiv*: 'reingelegt werden; *sl* anpumpen; (*for* um); *itr* stechen; brennen, prickeln, schmerzen, weh tun; *s* Stechen *n*; Stich; Biß; stechende(r) Schmerz; *zoo bot (Gerät)* Stachel *m*; *bot* Brennhaar *n*; *fig* Schärfe *f*; starke(r) Anreiz, Ansporn; *(Gewissen)* Stachel *m*; **~aree** ['-əri:] *zoo* Stechrochen *m*, Feuer-, Giftflunder *f*; **~er** ['-ə] Stechende(r) *m*; stechende(s) Tier *n*, stechende Pflanze *f*; Stachel; *fam* heftige(r), starke(r) Schlag *m*; *fam* beißende, bissige Bemerkung *f*; *sl* (Glas *n*) Whisky mit Soda; *Am* Pfefferminzlikör *m* mit Eis; *Am sl* ungelöste(s) Problem *n*; **~ing** ['-iŋ] stechend; *~~ hair (bot)* Brennhaar *n*; *~~-nettle* Brennessel *f*; **~o** ['-gou] *sl* starke(s) Bier *n*; *fig* Mumm *m*, Kraft *f*; **~-ray** = *~aree*.
sting|iness ['stindʒinis] Knauserigkeit *f*, Geiz *m*; **~y** ['stindʒi] geizig, knauserig, knickig, filzig; dürftig, mager.
stink [stiŋk] *irr stank* [-æ-] od *stunk* [-ʌ-], *stunk itr* stinken (*of* nach) *a. fig*; widerlich, gräßlich, scheußlich, nicht in Ordnung sein; *Am sl* nichts taugen, nicht viel wert sein; *tr (to ~ up)* verstänkern, verpesten; *(to ~ out)* durch Gestank vertreiben; *s* Gestank, üble(r) Geruch; *Am* Skandal *m*; *pl sl (Schule)* Chemie *f*; *to raise a ~ (sl)* Stunk machen; *to ~ of money* Geld wie Heu haben; **~ard** ['-ə:d] Stinker; *sl* Scheißkerl; *sl* grobe(r) Brief *m*; **~-bomb** Stinkbombe *f*; **~er** ['-ə] *fam* widerliche(r) Kerl, Stinker *m*; etw Widerliches *n*; **~eroo** ['-əru:] *Am sl* langweilig; minderwertig; **~ing** ['-iŋ] *a* stinkend, übelriechend; *fam* gemein, elend, mies, gräßlich, furchtbar, scheußlich; *sl* besoffen; *Am sl* nach Geld stinkend; **~-pot** *fig* widerliche(r) Kerl, Stinker *m*.
stint [stint] *tr* be-, einschränken, in Schranken, knapphalten (*in, of* mit); *to ~ s.o. of s.th.* jdm etw verweigern, knauserig zuteilen; *itr* knausern, *fam* knapsen; *to ~ o.s.* sich einschränken; *s* Ein-, Beschränkung, Einengung, Begrenzung, Grenze; begrenzte Menge; bestimmte Arbeit, tägliche Aufgabe; *min* Schicht *f*; *without ~* freigebig.
stipend ['staipend] *jur rel* (festes) Gehalt *n*, Besoldung; Pension *f*; **~iary** [stai'pendjəri] *a* fest besoldet; *s* Festbesoldete(r); *Br* Polizeirichter *m*.
stipple ['stipl] *tr* tüpfeln; *(Kunst)* in Punktiermanier malen; *s (Kunst)* Punktiermanier *f*.
stipulat|e ['stipjuleit] *tr* ausbedingen, aus-, abmachen, vereinbaren (*in writing* schriftlich); bestimmen, festsetzen, -legen, vorsehen; *(Bedingungen)* stellen; *as ~ed* wie vereinbart; **~ion** [stipju'leiʃən] Bedingung, Klausel, Bestimmung; Vereinbarung, Abmachung *f*; *on the ~~ that* unter der Bedingung, daß.
stir [stə:] **1.** *tr* (leicht, sanft) (hin u. her) bewegen; *fig* aufrühren, -rütteln; *(Flüssigkeit)* um-, *(Pulver)* durchea.-rühren; *(Feuer)* schüren; *fig* (innerlich, seelisch) aufwühlen; erregen; *(to ~ up)* auf-, wachrütteln; (an)reizen, an-, aufstacheln, aufhetzen (*to* zu); *(Haß)* schüren; *itr* sich rühren; sich regen, *fam* sich mucksen; in Bewegung kommen *od* geraten; auf(gestanden), in Bewegung, in Tätigkeit sein; im Gange, *lit* im Schwange sein, s-n Gang gehen, s-n Verlauf nehmen; sich um-, verrühren lassen; *to ~ out* aus dem Haus gehen; *s* Umrühren *n*; Bewegung, Tätigkeit; Bewegung, Erregung, Unruhe *f*; Aufruhr *m*; Getümmel, Gedränge *n*; *to make a ~* Aufsehen erregen; *to ~ s.o.'s bile* jdn ärgerlich machen; *to ~ s.o.'s blood* jds Blut in Wallung bringen; *not to ~ an eyelid* nicht mit der Wimper zucken; *not to ~ a finger* keinen Finger krumm machen *od* rühren; *to ~ o.'s stumps (fam)* die Beine unter den Arm nehmen; Energie zeigen; *to ~ s.o.'s wrath* jdn in Wut bringen; **~about** ['-rəbaut] Mehlsuppe; *fam* Aufregung *f*; **~ring** ['-riŋ] tätig, rührig, geschäftig; er-, aufregend, aufwühlend; **2.** *sl* Kittchen, Gefängnis *n*.
stirps [stə:ps] *pl stirpes* ['-i:z] Stamm, Zweig *m (e-r Familie)*, Geschlecht *n*; Stammvater *m*; *biol* Erbmaterial *n*, -faktoren *m pl*.
stirrup ['stirəp] Steigbügel *m*; **~-bone** *anat (Ohr)* Steigbügel *m*; **~-cup** Abschiedstrunk *m*; **~-leather, -strap** Steigriemen *m*; **~-pump** Handfeuerspritze *f*.
stitch [stitʃ] *s (Handarbeiten)* Stich *m*; Masche *f*; *med (~ in the side)* (Seiten-)Stiche *m pl*, Stechen *n*; *med* Naht *f*; *itr tr* nähen *a. med*; *tr* steppen; *(Buch)* heften; *to ~ on* annähen; *itr* sticken (*on* auf); *to be in ~es (fam Am)* sich die Seiten vor Lachen halten; *to drop* od *to lose, to take up a ~* e-e Masche fallen lassen, aufnehmen; *to have not a ~ on* (gar) nichts anhaben; *to have not a dry ~ on one* keinen Faden Trockenes am Leibe haben; *to put ~es in a wound* e-e Wunde nähen; *she hasn't done a ~ of work today* sie hat heute noch keinen Finger gerührt; *a ~ in time saves nine* gleich getan, viel getan; *buttonhole-~* Knopflochstich *m*; **~-proof** maschensicher.
stiver ['staivə] *hist* Stüber *m (Münze)*; *without a ~* ohne e-n Pfennig (Geld); *not to care a ~ for s.th.* sich nichts, *fam* e-n Dreck aus etw machen.
stoat [stout] Hermelin *(bes. im braunen Sommerfell)*; Wiesel *n*.
stock [stɔk] **1.** *s* (Baum-)Stamm; *bot* (Wurzel-)Stock; Stengel, Strunk *m*; (Pfropf-)Unterlage *f*; *fig* Stammvater, Stammbaum *m*, Nachkommenschaft, Familie *f*; *(Anthropologie)* Stamm *m*, Abstammungsgruppe, Rasse *f*; (Tier-, Pflanzen-)Stamm; Sprachstamm; *tech* Klotz, Block, Kolben; (Gewehr-)Schaft; (Peitschen-)Stock *m*, (Angel-)Rute *f*; Griff; Stiel; *com* Rohstoff *m*, -material *n*; (Papier-)Stoff; (Suppen-, Soßen-)Fond; Vorrat, (Lager-, Waren-)Bestand *m*, Lager *n*, Stapel, Stoß; Viehbestand *m*; Inventar *n*; *(Kartenspiel)* Haufen *m*; *Br* (Stamm-)Kapital; *Am* Aktienkapital; *theat* Repertoire *n*; *zoo* Kolonie *(niederer Tiere)*; *bot* Levkoje *f*; *mar* Ankerstock; *fig* Dummkopf, Klotz *m*; *pl hist* Stock *(Strafe)*; *mar* Stapel *m*, Helling *f*; (Stamm-)Aktien *f pl*; *Br* Obligationen *f pl*, Staatspapiere *n pl*; **2.** *a* Stamm-; Lager-; stets vorrätig, auf Lager; üblich, gewöhnlich; ständig; stereotyp; **3.** *tr* mit e-m Kolben, Schaft, Griff versehen; *(Anker)* stocken; *(Gewehr)* schäften; *(Waren)* führen; mit Material, (neuen) Waren, e-m Lagerbestand versehen; auf Lager halten *od* nehmen; einlagern; **4.** *itr bot* neue Schößlinge treiben; *com* s-n Lagerbestand erneuern *od* auffrischen; *to ~ up on s.th.* sich mit etw eindecken; **5.** *in ~* vorrätig, auf, am Lager; *on the ~s (Schiff)* auf der Helling, im Bau; in Reparatur; *out of ~* ausverkauft, nicht auf Lager; **6.** *to be in ~* bei Kasse sein; *to be out of ~* nicht vorrätig haben; *to have, to keep in ~* auf Lager *od* vorrätig, zur Verfügung haben; *to lay in a ~ of s.th.* sich von etw e-n Vorrat anlegen; *to put much ~ in s.th.* auf etw viel Wert legen; *to take ~* Inventur, Bestandsaufnahme machen; Aktien kaufen (*in* bei); *in s.th. (fam)* Wert auf etw legen, Interesse an etw haben; *of s.th.* etw in Betracht, in Erwägung ziehen; sich über etw klar werden; **7.** *actual ~* Ist-Bestand *m*; *dead ~* tote(s) Inventar *n*; *fat ~* schlachtreife(s) Vieh *n*; *a laughing ~* e-e Zielscheibe des Spottes; *live ~* lebende(s) Inventar *n*, Viehbestand *m*; *preference ~* Vorzugsaktie *f*; *remainder of ~* Restbestand *m*; *rolling ~* rollende(s), Betriebsmaterial *n*; *~ in bank* Bankguthaben *n*; *~-in-hand* Warenbestand *m*; *~-in-trade*

Warenvorrat, Lagerbestand *m*; Stamm-, Betriebskapital *n*; *fig* feste(r) Bestand *m*; ~ *of goods* Warenlager *n*; ~ *of plays (theat)* Repertoire *n*, Spielplan *m*; ~ *of shares* Aktien-, Effektenbestand *m*; ~*s and stones* Ölgötzen *m pl*; ~**-account** Waren-, Lager-, Kapitalkonto *n*; ~**-book** Lager-, Bestandsbuch; Aktionärsbuch *n*; ~**-breeder, -farmer, -raiser** Viehzüchter *m*; ~**-breeding, -farming, -raising** Viehzucht *f*; ~**-broker** Börsenmakler, Effektenhändler *m*; ~**-broking** Börsen-, Effektenhandel *m*; ~**-business** Effektengeschäft *n*; ~**-capital** Anlage-, Grund-, Aktienkapital *n*; ~**-car** *Am rail* Viehwagen; *mot* Serienwagen *m*; ~**-certificate** Aktienzertifikat *n*; ~**-check** Bestandsaufnahme *f*; ~**-company** Repertoiregruppe; *com* Aktiengesellschaft *f*; ~**-deposit** *Br* Wertpapierdepot *n*; ~**-exchange** Wertpapier-, Aktienbörse *f*; ~~*dealings (pl)* Börsengeschäfte *n pl*; ~~ *list* Börsenzettel *m*; ~~ *news (pl mit sing)* Börsenbericht *m*; ~**-farm** Zuchtfarm *f (Vieh)*; ~**fish** Stockfisch *m*; ~**holder** *Am* Aktionär *m*; Effektenbesitzer *m*; ~**ist** ['-ist] Fachhändler *m*; ~**-jobber** Börsenspekulant *m*; ~**-jobbing** Börsenspekulation *f*; ~**-keeper** Lagerhalter *m*; ~**-keeping** Lagerhaltung *f*; ~**-list** *Am* Kurszettel *m*; ~**man** *(Am, Australien)* Viehzüchter; *Am* Lagerist *m*; ~**-market** Effektenmarkt *m*; Wertpapierbörse *f*; ~~ *crash* Börsenkrach *m*; ~~ *credit* Lombardkredit *m*; ~**pile** *Am s* große(r) Vorrat *m*, Reserve(vorrat *m*) *f*; *itr* (sich) große Vorräte anlegen; *tr* sammeln, anhäufen, (auf)stapeln; auf Lager nehmen; ~**-play, -piece** *theat* Repertoirestück *n*; ~ **price** *Am* Aktienkurs *m*; ~**-receipt** Wareneingang *m*; ~**-record** Lagerkarte *f*; Aktienregister *n*; ~**-room** Vorrats-, Lagerraum *m*; ~**-size** Normalgröße *f*; ~**-still** (mucks)mäuschenstill; ~**-taking** Bestandsaufnahme, Inventur; *fig* Orientierung *f*; ~~ *sale* Inventurausverkauf *m*; ~**-transfer tax** Börsenumsatzsteuer *f*; ~**-warrant** = ~*-certificate*; ~**y** ['-i] stämmig, untersetzt; ~**-yard** Viehhof *m*.

stockade [stɔ'keid] *s* Palisade; Einfried(ig)ung *f*, (Latten-)Zaun *m*; *tr* mit e-r Palisade umgeben, einfried(ig)en.

stockinet [stɔki'net] Stockinett *n*.

stocking ['stɔkiŋ] Strumpf *m*; *in o.'s* ~*ed feet* in Strümpfen, ohne Schuhe; ~ **suspender** Strumpfhalter *m*; ~**-trade** Wirk- u. Strickwarenhandel *m*; ~**-weaver** Strumpfwirker *m*.

stodg|e [stɔdʒ] *sl s* fette(s) Essen *n*; *fig* schwere(r) Brocken *m*; *itr* sich den Bauch vollschlagen, sich vollstopfen (*with* mit); ~**y** ['-i] *(Essen)* fett, schwer (-verdaulich); vollgestopft, -gepfropft, gepackt; stämmig, untersetzt, dick; *fig* schwerfällig, langweilig, spießig.

stogie, stog(e)y ['stougi] *Am* billige Zigarre *f*; klobige(r) Schuh *m*.

stoic ['sto(u)ik] Stoiker *m*; ~**(al)** ['-(əl)] stoisch; ~**ism** ['-isizm] Stoizismus *m*.

stoke [stouk] *tr (Feuer)* schüren; *(Ofen)* (an)heizen, *tech* beschicken; *(Essen)* hineinstopfen; *itr* heizen; *(to ~ up) fam* sich vollschlagen; ~**hold** *mar* Heizraum *m*; ~**hole** Schürloch *n*; *mar* Heizraum *m*; ~**r** ['-ə] Heizer *m*.

stole [stoul] **1.** *pret von steal*; **2.** Stola *f*.

stolid ['stɔlid] blöd(e), stupide, stumpf (-sinnig), schwerfällig; ~**ity** [stɔ'liditi] Blödheit, Stupidität, Stumpfheit *f*, -sinn *m*, Schwerfälligkeit *f*.

stomach ['stʌmək] *s* Magen; Bauch, (Unter-)Leib; *fig* Appetit *m*, Eßlust; Begierde *f*, Wunsch *m*, Verlangen *n* (*for* nach); *tr* vertragen, verdauen können; ertragen, aushalten (können); *(Beleidigung)* einstecken; *fam* schmekken, riechen können (*s.o.* jdn); *on a full, an empty* ~ auf vollen, leeren Magen; *to turn o.'s* ~ jdn anekeln; *I have no* ~ *for it* ich habe keine Lust dazu; ~**-ache** Magen-, Leibschmerzen *m pl*, Leib-, Bauchweh *n*; ~**ic(al)** [stə'mækik(əl)] *a* Magen-; magenstärkend; *s* magenstärkende(s) Mittel *n*; ~~ *dilatation* Magenerweiterung *f*; ~ **ulcer** Magengeschwür *n*.

ston|e [stoun] *s* Stein *m*; Gestein *n*; (Bau-, Pflaster-, Mühl-, Wetz-, Meilen-, Grenz-, Grab-)Stein; *(precious* ~~*)* (Edel-)Stein *m*; Hagelkorn *n*; *(Obst)* Kern; *med (Gallen-)*Stein; Stein *m (= 14 Pfund = 6,35 kg)*; *a* steinern; Stein-; Steingut-; *tr* mit Steinen werfen (nach), steinigen; mit Steinen pflastern; *(Frucht)* entsteinen; *to cast, to throw* ~~*s at s.o. (fig)* mit Steinen nach jdm werfen; *to cast the first* ~~ *(fig)* den ersten Stein werfen; *to harden into* ~~ verhärten, zu Stein werden lassen; *to leave no* ~~ *unturned (fig)* alle Hebel in Bewegung setzen; *to mark with a white* ~~ rot im Kalender anstreichen; *a* ~~*'s cast, throw* ein Steinwurf (weit), *fam* ein Katzensprung; *gall-*~~ *(med)* Gallenstein *m*; *paving-*~~ Pflasterstein *m*; *philosopher's* ~~ Stein *m* der Weisen; *stepping-*~~ Trittstein *m*; *S*~~ *Age* Steinzeit *f*; ~~*-bedding (tech)* Steinbettung *f*; ~~*-blind* stockblind; ~~*-break (bot)* Steinbrech *m*; ~*-broke (a Am sl)* völlig abgebrannt, ohne e-n Pfennig (Geld); ~~*chat* ['-tʃæt] *orn* Schwarzkehlchen *n*; ~~*crop (bot)* Mauerpfeffer *m*; ~~*-crusher* Steinbrecher *m*; ~~*-cutter* Steinmetz, -hauer *m*; ~~*-dead* mausetot; ~~*-deaf* stocktaub; ~~*-floor* Steinfußboden *m*; ~~*-fruit* Steinobst *n*; ~~*-jug* Steinkrug *m*; ~~*-marten* Steinmarder *m*; ~~*-mason* Steinmetz *m*; ~~*-pine (bot)* Pinie *f*; ~~*-pit* Steinbruch *m*; ~~*-wall(ing)* Obstruktion(spolitik) *f*; *sport* Mauern *n*; ~~*ware* Steingut *n*; ~~*work* Mauerwerk *n*; ~**y** ['-i] steinig; steinhart; *poet* steinern; *fig (*~~*-hearted)* hart(herzig), mitleidlos, kalt; *fam* pleite, abgebrannt.

stooge [stu:dʒ] *s Am fam theat* Partner *m*, der Stichworte liefert; *pej* Helfershelfer, Trabant, Lakai; Strohmann, Sündenbock *m*; *itr fam* Lakaiendienste tun (*for* für); als Strohmann tätig sein; *to* ~ *around (sl)* ziellos umherwandern.

stool [stu:l] *s* Hocker, Schemel *m*; *(foot-*~*)* Fußbank; *arch* Fensterbank; *obs* Toilette *f*, Klosett *n*; *med* Stuhl (-gang); *bot* Schößling, Baumstumpf; Lockvogel(stange *f*) *m*; *to fall between two* ~*s (fig)* sich zwischen zwei Stühle setzen; *folding* ~ Faltstuhl *m*; *music-*~ Klavierhocker *m*; *night-*~ Nachtstuhl *m*, Zimmerklosett *n*; *office-*~ Bürohocker *m*; *three-legged* ~ Dreibein *m*; ~**-pigeon** Locktaube *f*; *fig* Lockvogel, Spitzel *m*.

stoop [stu:p] **1.** *itr* sich bücken, sich beugen, sich neigen; sich niederhocken; gebeugt, vornübergeneigt gehen; *fig* sich demütigen, sich erniedrigen, *(sittlich)* sinken; sich herablassen, sich hergeben (*to* zu); *(Vogel)* herabstoßen (*on* auf); *tr (Kopf)* beugen, neigen; *s* Beugen, Bücken; Niederhocken *n*; gebeugte (Körper-) Haltung; *fig* Herablassung *f*; *(Vogel)* Herabstoßen *n*; *to walk with a* ~ gebeugt gehen; **2.** *Am* Veranda; Vortreppe, Terrasse *f*.

stop [stɔp] *tr* (ver-, zu)stopfen; *(Weg)* (ver)sperren; *(Gefäß, bes. Flasche, Öffnung)* verschließen; *(Zahn)* füllen, plombieren; an-, auf-, abhalten (*s.o. doing s.th.* jdn etw zu tun; *from* von); zum Halten, Stehen, Stillstand bringen; *(Blut)* stillen; abfangen, unterbinden, verhindern, unterdrücken; unterbrechen (*s.o.* jdn); hindern (*from* an); *(Schlag)* parieren; beenden, aufhören mit, aufhören (*doing* zu tun); aussetzen; *com (Auftrag)* zurücknehmen; *(Zahlung)* einstellen; *(Scheck)* sperren; *mus (Saite)* greifen; e-e Sinnpause folgen lassen auf; *Br* interpunktieren; *itr* stehenbleiben, anhalten, stillstehen; (e-n) Halt, e-e Pause machen; aufhören (*to do* zu tun); *tech* aussetzen; *fig* steckenbleiben; sich aufhalten, bleiben (*at* in); warten (*for* auf); zu Besuch sein (*with* bei); absteigen (*at a hotel* in e-m Hotel); *s* Halt, Stillstand *m*; Pause, Unterbrechung *f*; Ende *n*, Schluß; Aufenthalt *m*; Haltestelle *f*, -punkt *m*; Hindernis, Hemmnis *n*, Hemmung; Sperrung, Sperre *f*; *tech* Sperrhebel *m*, -klinke *f*; Riegel, Anschlag *m*; *phot* Blende *f*; *mus* Ventil *n*, Klappe *f*; *(Saiteninstrument)* Wirbel; *(Geige)* Griff *m*; *(Orgel)* Register *n*; *(Phonetik)* Verschlußlaut *m*; Satzzeichen *n*, *bes.* Punkt *m*; *com* Zurücknahme; (Zahlungs-)Einstellung *f*; *to bring s.th. to a* ~, *to put a* ~ *to s.th.* mit etw Schluß machen; *mot* zum Halten, zum Stehen bringen; *to come to a full* ~ am Ende sein, nicht mehr weiter können; *to get off at the next* ~ bei der nächsten Haltestelle aussteigen; *to* ~ *dead, short* plötzlich aufhören, anhalten; das Wort abschneiden (*s.o.* jdm); *to* ~ *for a drink* einkehren; *to* ~ *o.'s ears* sich die Ohren zuhalten; *to* ~ *a gap* e-e Lücke schließen; *to* ~ *s.o.'s mouth* jdn zum Schweigen bringen; *to* ~ *wages* Lohn einbehalten; *he* ~*s at nothing* er schreckt vor nichts zurück; er geht über Leichen; *bus-*~ Autobushaltestelle *f*; *full* ~ Punkt *m*; *request, conditional* ~ Bedarfshaltestelle *f*; *to* ~ **away** wegbleiben; *to* ~ **by, in** *Am* (mal) hereinschauen, e-n kleinen Besuch machen; *to* ~ **down** abblenden; *to* ~ **in** zu Hause bleiben; *to* ~ **off** *Am* e-n kurzen Halt machen, (unterwegs) kurz anhalten; *to* ~ **on** länger bleiben; *to* ~ **over** *Am* e-e Weile bleiben; die Reise unterbrechen; vorbeikommen (*at* bei); *to* ~ **up** zu-, verstopfen, schließen; füllen; *fam* aufbleiben; ~**-butt** Kugelfang *m*; ~**cock** Absperr-, Abstellhahn *m*; ~**gap** Lückenbüßer, (Not-)Behelf, Ersatz *m*; ~~ *advertisement* Füller *m*; ~~ *aid* Soforthilfe *f*; ~**-go, -sign** Verkehrsampel *f*; ~**-light** *(Verkehr)* rote(s) Licht; Bremslicht *n*; ~**-list** schwarze Liste *f*; ~**-opening** *phot* Blende *f*; ~**-order** limitierte Order *f*; ~**over** *Am* (Fahrt-, Flug-)Unterbrechung *f*, Aufenthalt *m*; Zwischenlandung *f*; ~**-press (news)** *(Zeitung)* letzte Meldungen *f pl*; ~**-screw** *tech* Stell-, Anschlagschraube *f*; ~**-valve** Absperrventil *n*; ~**-watch, -clock** Stoppuhr *f*.

stopp|age ['stɔpidʒ] *med* Verstopfung; Unterbrechung *f*; Stillstand *m*, Stokkung; Stillegung; Unterbindung, Verhinderung, Unterdrückung; Beendigung; Zurücknahme; *com el* Sperre; *(Arbeits-, Zahlungs-)*Einstellung; (Betriebs-)Störung *f*; Gehaltsabzug *m*; Verkehrsstockung; *mil* Ladehemmung *f*; *~~ of leave* Urlaubssperre *f*; **~er** ['-ə] *s* Hindernis *n*; Pfropf, Stöpsel; *mar* Stopper *m*; *tech* Hemmstange *f*, Ausrücker; *(Zeitung)* Blickfang *m*; *tr* zustöpseln, -korken; *~~ circuit (el)* Sperrkreis *m*; **~ing** ['-iŋ] *s* (Zahn-)Füllung, Plombe *f*; *~~ condenser* Blockkondensator *m*; *~~-distance* Bremsweg *m*; *~~-power* Bremsvermögen *n*; *~~ train (fam)* Bummelzug *m*.

stopple ['stɔpl] *s* Stöpsel *m*; *tr* zustöpseln.

stor|age ['stɔ:ridʒ] (Ein-)Lagerung *f*, (Auf-)Speichern *n*; Lagerplatz, -raum *m*, -haus *n*, Speicher *m*; Lagergeld *n*, -gebühren *f pl*; *el (Batterie)* Aufladung *f*; *in cold ~~* im Kühlraum; *to put in ~~ (Möbel)* auf den Speicher stellen; *to put a plan into cold ~~* e-n Plan auf Eis legen; *cold ~~* Kühlhauslagerung *f*; *~~ accommodation* Lagerungsmöglichkeit *f*; *~~ battery* Akku(mulator) *m*; *~~ bin* Silo *m*; *~~ building* Lagergebäude *n*; *~~ capacity* Fassungs-, Lagervermögen *n*; *~~ room* Lagerraum *m*; *mar* Schiffspackraum *m*; *~~ shed* Lagerschuppen *m*; *~~ site* Lagerplatz *m*; *~~ time* Lagerzeit *f*; *~~ track* Abstellgleis *n*; *~~ warehouse (Am)* Möbelspeicher *m*; *~~ yard* Lagerplatz *m*; **~e** [stɔ:] *s* Vorrat, *(Waren-)*Bestand *m*, Reserve *f* (*of* an); *(~house)* Lagerhaus, Magazin; Depot *n*, Niederlage *f*; *Br (departmental ~~)* Waren-, Kaufhaus *n*; *Am* Laden *m*, Geschäft *n*; *pl bes. mil* Nachschub, Proviant *m*, Vorräte *m pl*; *tr* (ein)lagern; aufspeichern, -bewahren; *(Möbel)* auf den Speicher stellen; *(Ernte)* einbringen; versehen, versorgen (*with* mit); *phys* speichern; *(Schiff)* verproviantieren, bevorraten; *to ~ away* beiseite legen; *to ~~ up* aufspeichern, einlagern; *in ~~* vorrätig, vorhanden, bereit, gebrauchsfertig; *to be in ~~ for s.o.* jdm bevorstehen, jdn erwarten; *to have in ~~ for s.o.* für jdn bereithalten, -haben; *to lay in ~~* Vorrat anlegen; *to set ~~ by* Wert legen auf; *to set no great ~ by* keinen großen Wert legen auf, nicht viel halten von; *the Cooperative S~* der Konsum; *fashion ~~s (pl)* Modewaren *f pl*; *five-and-ten ~~ (Am)* Einheitspreisgeschäft *n*; *retail ~~ (Am)* Einzelhandelsgeschäft *n*; *~~ of energy* Energiereserve *f*; *~~-cattle* Mastvieh *n*; *~~ clothes (Am pl)* Fertigkleidung *f*; *~~-cupboard* Vorratsschrank *m*; *~~-food (Am)* fertige Speisen *f pl*; *~~house* Lagerhaus *n*, Speicher *m*; *fig* Fundgrube *f*; *~~keeper* Lager-, Magazinverwalter; *Am* Laden-, Geschäftsinhaber, -besitzer *m*; *~~-room* Lager-, Vorratsraum *m*.

stor|(e)y ['stɔ:ri] Stockwerk *n*, Etage *f*; *to be weak in the upper ~~ (sl)* nicht ganz richtig im Kopf sein; **~eyed, ~ied** [-d] *a in Zssgen* -stöckig; *three-~~* dreistöckig; **~ied** *a* geschichtlich berühmt; sagenumwoben; mit Darstellungen aus der Sage *od* Geschichte verziert; **~y** *s* Darstellung *f*, Bericht *m*; Erzählung, Geschichte *f*, Märchen *n*; Erzählkunst; *lit* Handlung *f*; Gerücht, Gerede *n*; *fam* Schwindel *m*, Flunkerei *f*; *Am sl* (Stoff zu e-m) Zeitungsartikel *m*; *to cut a long ~~ short* um es kurz zu machen; *this is not the whole ~~* das ist (noch) nicht alles; *it's always the same old ~~* es ist immer das alte Lied; *that's another ~~* das ist ein Kapitel für sich; *short ~~* Kurzgeschichte, Erzählung *f*; *~~-book* Märchenbuch *n*; *~~-teller* Märchen-, Geschichtenerzähler; *fam* Aufschneider, Lügner *m*.

stork [stɔ:k] Storch *m*; **~'s bill** *bot* Storchschnabel *m*.

storm [stɔ:m] *s* Sturm *m a. fig mil*; Unwetter *n*; *(Pfeile)* Hagel *m*; *itr* stürmen *a. fig*; *fig* wüten (*at* gegen); *tr mil* (be)stürmen; *to take by ~* im Sturm erobern *a. fig*; *a ~ in a teacup (fig)* ein Sturm im Wasserglas, viel Lärm um nichts; *~ of applause* Beifallssturm *m*; *brain-~* verrückte(r) Einfall *m*; *Am* glänzende Idee *f*; **~-beaten, -tossed** *a* sturmgepeitscht; **~-bound** *a* durch Stürme festgehalten; **~ cellar** *Am* Schutzkeller *m* gegen Wirbelstürme; **~-centre** *mete* Sturmzentrum *n*; *fig* Unruheherd, -stifter *m*; **~-cloud** Sturm-, Wetterwolke *f*; **~cock, ~thrush** *orn* Misteldrossel *f*; **~-cone, -signal, -warning** Sturmkegel *m*, -signal *n*, -warnung *f*; **~ door** *Am* äußere, Doppeltür *f*; **~iness** ['-inis] stürmische(s) Wetter *n*; **~ing** Sturmangriff *m*; *~~ party* Sturmabteilung *f*; **~-lantern** Sturmlaterne *f*; **~-proof** sturmsicher, wasserdicht; **~-sail** Sturmsegel *n*; **~-troops** *pl* Sturmtruppen *f pl*; **~-window** äußere(s), Doppelfenster *n*; **~y** ['-i] stürmisch *a. fig*; *fig* leidenschaftlich, heftig; *~~ petrel* Sturmvogel; *fig* Unruhestifter *m*.

stoup [stu:p] *obs u. Scot* Trinkgefäß *n*; Eimer, Kübel *m*; *rel* Weihwasserbecken *n*.

stout [staut] *a* stämmig, kräftig, stark; untersetzt, beleibt; massig, dick; fest, widerstandsfähig; *tech* solide; *(Karton)* steif; mutig, beherzt, mannhaft, entschlossen; *s* Starkbier *n*; **~-hearted** *a* beherzt, wacker, tapfer; **~-heartedness** Beherztheit, Tapferkeit *f*; **~ness** ['-nis] Korpulenz; Stärke; Kraft; Beherztheit, Tapferkeit, Mannhaftigkeit *f*.

stove [stouv] Ofen *m*; Heiz-, Kochgerät *n*, Kocher; Brennofen; Trockenraum *m*; Treibhaus *n*; **~-fitter** Ofensetzer *m*; **~-pipe** Ofenrohr *n*; *~~ hat (Am fam)* Angströhre *f*, Zylinder *m*.

stow [stou] *tr* verstauen, -packen, wegpacken; vollpacken, füllen (*with* mit); *(Raum, Behälter)* fassen; *sl* aufhören mit; *to ~ away* verstecken, verbergen; beiseite legen; *~ it! (fam)* halt die Klappe! **~age** ['-idʒ] *mar* Lade-, Stauraum *m*; *mar* Verstauen; Staugeld *n*; **~away** blinde(r) Passagier *m*.

strabismus [strə'bizməs] *med* Schielen *n*.

straddle ['strædl] *tr* sich rittlings setzen auf; rittlings sitzen auf; *(die Beine)* spreizen; *mil* eingabeln, dekken; *Am fam* sich nicht festlegen auf (*s.th.* e-r S); *itr* die Beine spreizen; rittlings sitzen; *Am fam* sich nicht festlegen, es mit keinem verderben (wollen); nicht wissen, was man will; *s* Beinspreizen *n*; *Am fam* schwankende Haltung; Schaukelpolitik; *fin* Stellage *f*.

straf|e [strɑ:f, *Am* streif] *tr aero* mit Bordwaffen beschießen; mit Bomben belegen, bombardieren; *fam* (be)strafen, ausschimpfen; **~er** ['-ə] *fam* Tiefflieger *m*; **~ing** ['-iŋ] *fam* Bordwaffenbeschuß; *fig* Anschnauzer *m*.

straggl|e ['strægl] *itr* (vom Wege) abschweifen, -weichen, sich von der Masse trennen; *mil* von der Truppe abkommen; umherschweifen, -streifen; (hier u. da) verstreut sein; in unregelmäßigen Abständen vorkommen; *bot* kriechen, ranken, wuchern; **~er** ['-ə] *mil* Nachzügler, Versprengte(r) *m*; *bot* Ranke *f*; *~~ collecting point* Versprengtensammelstelle *f*; **~ing** ['-iŋ], **~y** ['-i] *bot* rankend, wuchernd; *(Häuser)* verstreut; *(Stadtbezirk)* aufgelockert.

straight [streit] *a* g(e)rade; *(Haar)* glatt; aufrecht; unmittelbar, direkt, fortlaufend, ununterbrochen; geradlinig, konsequent, methodisch, systematisch; *Am pol* linientreu; sauber, aufgeräumt; *fig* redlich, ehrlich, aufrichtig, offen; *fam* brauchbar, in Ordnung, zuverlässig; *(Tip)* gut; *Am (Getränk)* unverdünnt, unvermischt; *Am (nach Preisangabe)* ohne Mengenrabatt; ohne Abzug; *adv* (in) gerade(r Linie), geradlinig; aufrecht; geradeswegs, direkt, ohne Umschweife, (schnur)stracks; *fig* klar; *s sport* (Ziel-) Gerade; *(Poker)* Sequenz *f*; *as ~ as an arrow* schnurgerade; *out of the ~* ung(e)rade, gekrümmt; verbogen; *~ ahead* immer geradeaus; *~ away, off* sofort, unverzüglich; *~ on* geradeaus; *~ out* offenheraus; *~ through* geradedurch; *to come ~ to the point* keine Umschweife machen; *not to get s.th. ~ (fam)* etw nicht (richtig, ganz) mitkriegen; *to get an information ~ from the horse's mouth* e-e Nachricht direkt von der Quelle haben; *to go, to keep, to run ~ (fig)* s-n geraden Weg gehen; *to give it to s.o. ~ (Am)* jdm die ungeschminkte Wahrheit sagen; *to keep a ~ face* keine Miene verziehen; *to put ~* aufräumen, ordnen, in Ordnung bringen *a. fig*; *is my hat on ~?* sitzt mein Hut richtig? *he hits ~ from the shoulder* wo er hinhaut, wächst kein Gras mehr; *fig* er nimmt kein Blatt vor den Mund; **~ angle** gestreckte(r) Winkel *m* (von 180°); **~-edge** Richtscheit, Lineal *n*; **~en** ['-n] *tr* begradigen, gerade machen *od* ziehen; *(Tuch)* glattziehen; *tech* geradebiegen *a. fig*; *fig (to ~~ out)* in Ordnung bringen; *to ~~ up* aufräumen; *itr* gerade werden; sich aufrichten; *fig* in Ordnung kommen; **~ engine** Reihenmotor *m*; **~ fight** Wahlkampf *m* zwischen zwei Kandidaten; **~ forward** [-'fɔ:wəd] *a* gerade(ausgehend); direkt; einfach; offen, frei, ehrlich; **~forwardness** [-'fɔ:wədnis] Ehrlichkeit *f*; **~ line** Gerade *f*; **~-line** geradlinig; **~ matter** *typ* glatte(r) Satz *m*; **~ness** ['-nis] Geradheit; Konsequenz; Ehrlichkeit, Offenheit *f*; **~-out** *a Am fam* direkt, glatt, uneingeschränkt; **~ ticket** *Am* Parteiprogramm *n*; *to vote a ~~* Kandidaten nur einer Partei wählen; **~way** *adv* sofort, unverzüglich, auf der Stelle.

strain [strein] **1.** *tr* strecken, spannen; (aufs äußerste) anspannen, (über)anstrengen; *med* verrenken, verstauchen; stark mitnehmen, in Mitleidenschaft ziehen, überfordern; *tech* beanspruchen; verbiegen; zu sehr in die Länge ziehen, zu stark weiten; *(an die Brust)* ziehen; durchseihen, -sieben, filtern, filtrieren; *itr* sich zs.-reißen, sich anstrengen, sich Mühe geben; streben (*after, for* nach); fest ziehen, zerren (*at* an); her sein (*after s.th.* hinter etw); *fig* nicht fassen können (*at s.th.* etw); durchsickern; *to ~ o.s.* sich überanstrengen; *s* (An-) Spannung, Belastung (*on* für); (Über-)Anstrengung, Überlastung (*on s.th.* e-r S); *med* Verrenkung, Verstauchung; Verbiegung; Weitung *f*; Druck *m*, Spannung; *(Text)* Verdrehung; *fig* (seelische) Überforderung *f*; *to be a ~ on s.o.'s nerves* jdm auf die Nerven gehen; *to stand the ~* die Anstrengung aushalten; *to ~ o.'s eyes* sich die Augen verderben; *to ~ every* *nerve* sein Äußerstes tun; *to ~ o.'s point (fig)* zu weit gehen; *to ~ the truth* übertreiben; *to ~ o.'s voice* sich die Lunge aus dem Leibe, sich heiser schreien; *I must ~ every effort* ich muß alle Kräfte anstrengen (*to* um); *a ~ on the credit* e-e Kreditanspannung; **~ed** [-d] *a* überspannt, unnatürlich, gezwungen; **~er** ['-ə] Spanner *m*; Seihtuch *n*, Filter *m*; **2.** *s* Abstammung *f*; Vorfahren; Nachkommen (-schaft *f*) *m pl*; Geschlecht *n*, Rasse; (Zucht-)Reihe *f*; *(Bakterien)* Stamm *m*; (Erb-)Eigenschaft, (Rasse-)Eigentümlichkeit *f*, Merkmal *n*; Anlage, Veranlagung *f*; Hang *m*, Neigung *f* (*of* zu); Redeschwall *m*; *fig* Ausdrucksweise *f*, Stil *m*; *oft pl* Melodie *f*.

strait [streit] *s meist pl* Meerenge, Straße *f*; *fig* Schwierigkeiten *f pl*; unangenehme Lage, peinliche Situation, Verlegenheit, *fam* Klemme *f*; *financial ~s (pl)* finanzielle, geldliche Schwierigkeiten *f pl*; **~en** ['-n] *tr* verenge(r)n; *in ~~ed circumstances* in beschränkten Verhältnissen; **~-jacket, -waistcoat** Zwangsjacke *f a. fig*; **~-laced** *a* engherzig, -stirnig, kleinlich, pedantisch; prüde.

strake [streik] *mar* Planken-, Plattengang *m*.

strand [strænd] **1.** *s* Strand *m*, Küste(nstreifen *m*) *f*, Gestade, Seeufer *n*; *tr* auf den Strand setzen; *fig* stranden lassen; *itr* stranden *a. fig*; **~ed** ['-id] *a fig* gestrandet, hilflos, festgefahren; in Not; *mot* liegengeblieben; **~ line** Küstenlinie *f*; **2.** (Haar-)Strähne *f*; Strang *m*; Ader, (Seil-)Litze; *biol* Faser; Schnur *f*, Faden *m*; *~ of pearls, beads* Perlenschnur, -kette *f*.

strang|e [streindʒ] fremd(artig), unbekannt; nicht vertraut (*to* mit); ungewöhnlich, außerordentlich; eigentümlich, seltsam, komisch, merkwürdig; nicht gewöhnt (*to* an); unerfahren (*to* in); *to feel ~~* sich nicht wohl fühlen; *~~ to say* seltsamerweise; **~eness** ['-nis] Fremdheit, Fremdartigkeit; Ungewöhnlichkeit, Seltsamkeit, Merkwürdigkeit; Unerfahrenheit *f*; **~er** ['-ə] Fremde(r), Unbekannte(r); Neuling (*to* in); *jur* Dritte(r), Unbeteiligte(r) *m* (*to* an); *to be no ~~ to poverty* die Armut kennengelernt haben; *don't be such a ~~* machen Sie sich nicht so rar!

strang|le ['stræŋgl] *tr* erwürgen, erdrosseln; ersticken lassen, die Luft nehmen (*s.o.* jdm); *fig* unterdrücken; *~~-hold* Würgegriff *m a. fig*; **~les** ['-z] *pl mit sing vet* Druse *f (der Pferde)*; **~ulate** ['-juleit] *tr* erwürgen, strangulieren; *med (Gefäß, Gang)* abschnüren, -binden; **~ulation** [stræŋgju'leiʃən] Erdrosselung, Strangulierung; *med* Abschnürung; *(Bruch)* Einklemmung *f*; **~ury** ['-gjuəri] Harnzwang *m*.

strap [stræp] *s* (Leder-)Riemen, Gurt *m*; (Metall-)Band *n*; Lasche *f*; Schulter-, Trag-, Streichriemen; *(Kleid)* Träger; (Halte-)Griff *m*; *bot* Blatthäutchen *n*; *tr* festschnallen; (*to* an); *(Koppel)* umschnallen; mit e-m Riemen züchtigen; *(Rasiermesser)* abstreichen, -ziehen; **~-hanger** *fam* Stehende(r) *m* in e-r Straßenbahn, e-m Autobus; **~ped** [-t] *a Am sl* ohne e-n Pfennig; **~per** ['-ə] *fam* stramme(r) Kerl *m*; **~ping** ['-iŋ] *fam* stramm, stämmig, kräftig.

strat|agem ['strætidʒəm] Kriegslist *f*; *allg* Kunstgriff, Trick *m*; **~egic(al)** [strə'ti:dʒik(əl)] *mil* strategisch, operativ; kriegswichtig; *~~ map (Am)* Generalstabskarte *f*; **~egics** [strə'ti:dʒiks] *pl mit sing = ~egy*; **~egist** ['-idʒist] Stratege *m*; **~egy** ['-idʒi] Strategie, Kriegskunst; *fig* Taktik; *allg* Wendigkeit, Gewandtheit, List *f*.

strat|ify ['strætifai] *tr* schichten; *agr* mit Torfmull bedecken; *~ified rock* Schichtgestein *n*; **~o-cruiser** ['-o(u)-kru:zə] Stratosphärenflugzeug *n*; **~osphere** ['stræto(u)sfiə] Stratosphäre *f*; *~~ aircraft* Stratosphärenflugzeug *n*; *~~ flight* Stratosphärenflug *m*; **~ospheric** [stræto(u)'sferik] stratosphärisch; Stratosphären-; **~um** ['streitəm, strα:-] *pl -a geol* Schicht *a. fig*, Ablagerung *f*; *min* Flöz *m*; *anat* Gewebeschicht *f*; *~~ of society* Gesellschaftsschicht *f*; **~us** ['streitəs] *pl -ti* [-tai] Schichtwolke *f*.

straw [strɔ:] *s* Stroh *n*; Strohhalm *m*; *(~ hat)* Strohhut *m*; *a* Stroh-; strohfarben, -blond; *not to be worth a ~* keinen Pfifferling wert sein; *not to care a ~* sich nicht das geringste daraus machen; *to catch, to clutch, to grasp at a ~ (fig)* sich an e-n Strohhalm klammern; *to try to make bricks without ~ (fig)* mit ungenügenden Voraussetzungen an die Arbeit gehen; *to turn on a ~ (fig)* an e-m seidenen Faden hängen; *that's the last ~ (fig)* jetzt reicht es aber; das schlägt dem Faß den Boden aus; *there is a ~ in the wind (fig)* es liegt etw in der Luft; *a man of ~* ein Strohmann *m*; **~berry** ['-bəri] Erdbeere *f*; *~~ blonde (Am)* Rotblonde *f*; *~~ bush* Erdbeerpflanze *f*; *~~ mark* Muttermal *n*; **~ bid** *Am* Scheingebot *n*; **~-board** Strohpappe *f*; **~ boss** *Am sl* Vorarbeiter *m*; **~ cat** *Am sl* Wanderarbeiter *m*; **~-colo(u)red** *a* blaßgelb, strohfarben; **~ mattress** Strohsack *m*; **~ vote** Probeabstimmung *f*.

stray [strei] *itr* umherschweifen, -irren; sich verirren; *fig* in die Irre gehen; abirren, abschweifen, sich verlieren; *el* vagabundieren; *s* Heimat-, Obdachlose(r), Streune(r) *m*; verirrte(s) *od* wildernde(s) Haustier *n*; *el* Streukapazität *f*; *pl radio* atmosphärische Störungen *f pl*; *a* verirrt, verlaufen, verloren; herrenlos, streunend; gelegentlich, vereinzelt, verstreut, einzeln; *el* vagabundierend.

streak [stri:k] *s* Streifen, Strich *m*; Maserung; *geol* Ader *f*, Schicht; *min* Schliere; (Fett-)Schicht *f*; *fig* Anflug, Hang *m*, Neigung *f*; *tr* mit Streifen versehen, markieren; *itr* Streifen bilden, streifig werden; *(to ~ along)* vorbeisausen; *like a ~ (of lightning)* wie der Blitz, blitzschnell; *a ~ of good, bad luck* e-e Glücks-, Pechsträhne *f*; **~y** ['-i] streifig; gemasert, geädert; Schicht-; *(Fleisch, Speck)* durchwachsen; *fig* ungleich(mäßig), schwankend.

stream [stri:m] *s* Wasserlauf; Bach, Fluß; Strom *m*, Strömung *f*; (Luft-)Zug; (Licht-)Strahl; Strom *(von Passanten, Wagen)*; Lauf, Gang *m (der Ereignisse)*; *itr* strömen, fließen, rinnen; *(Licht)* fluten; *(im Winde)* flattern, wehen; *against the ~* gegen den Strom; *up, down the ~* stromauf-, abwärts; *to go with the ~ (fig)* mit dem Strom schwimmen; *~ of consciousness (psychol)* Bewußtseinsstrom *m*; **~er** ['-ə] Wimpel *m*, Banner; hängende(s) Band *n*; *el* Leuchtfaden, Lichtstrahl *m*; Papierschlange; (ganzseitige) Schlagzeile *f*; **~let** ['-lit] Bächlein *n*; **~line** *s phys* Stromlinie *f*; *tr* e-e Stromlinienform geben (*s.th.* e-r S); *fig* modernisieren; rationalisieren; verbessern; **~line(d)** *a* stromlinienförmig; schnittig; rationell, modern, zeitgemäß; **~liner** *Am* Schienenzepp *m*.

street [stri:t] Straße *f*; Fahrdamm; *(Börse)* Freiverkehr *m*; *in (Am), on the ~* auf der Straße; *up o.'s ~ (fam)* in jds Bereich; *to be on the ~s (Frau)* auf die Straße gehen; arbeitslos sein; *to be on easy ~s (Am)* in guten Verhältnissen leben; *not to be in the same ~ with s.o.* sich mit jdm nicht messen, es mit jdm nicht aufnehmen können; *to be ~s ahead, better (sl)* weit voraus, überlegen sein (*of s.o.* jdm); *to get, to have the key of the ~s* ausgesperrt sein; kein Zuhause haben; *to look on the ~ (Fenster)* auf die Straße gehen; *to walk the ~(s)* e-n Stadtbummel machen; *(Frau)* auf die Straße gehen; *business ~* Geschäftsstraße *f*; *dead-end ~* Sackgasse *f*; *main ~* Hauptstraße *f*; *the man in the ~* der Mann auf der Straße, der Durchschnittsmensch; *off-~* Nebenstraße *f*; *one-way ~* Einbahnstraße *f*; *residential ~* Wohnstraße *f*; *village ~* Dorfstraße *f*; *water ~* Wasserstraße *f*, -weg *m*; **~ accident** Verkehrsunfall *m*; **~ Arab, -boy, -urchin** Straßen-, Gassenjunge *m*; **~car** *Am* Straßenbahn(wagen *m*) *f*; **~ collection** Straßensammlung *f*; **~-door** Haustür *f*; **~ hawker** Straßenhändler *m*; **~ lamp** Straßenlaterne *f*; **~ lighting** Straßenbeleuchtung *f*; **~ market** *com* Nachbörse *f*; **~-sweeper,** *Am* **-cleaner** Straßenkehrer, -kehrmaschine *f*; **~-sweeping,** *Am* **-cleaning** Straßenreinigung *f*; **~-walker** Straßendirne *f*.

strength [streŋθ] Kraft, Stärke *a. fig*; Widerstandskraft, -fähigkeit; Zähigkeit; *(Flüssigkeit, bes. Getränk)* Stärke *f*, Gehalt *m*, Wirkung *f*; *mil (actual ~)* Truppen-, Mannschafts-, Ist-Stärke; *com* Festigkeit (der Preise); Kraftquelle *f*; *at full ~* mit voller Kraft; *on the ~ of* auf Grund *gen*, im Vertrauen auf; *up to (below) ~* (nicht) vollzählig; *to gather ~* wieder zu Kräften kommen; *that is beyond human ~* das übersteigt menschliche Kraft; *that is too much for my ~* das geht über meine Kräfte; **~en** ['-ən] *tr* kräftigen, stärken; verstärken; *fig* bestärken; *itr* stärker, kräftig(er) werden, erstarken; *to ~~ s.o.'s hands (fig)* jdm den Rücken steifen; **~ener** ['-ənə] Stärkung(smittel *n*) *f*; *tech* Verstärker *m*; Einlage *f*; **~ report, return** Stärkemeldung *f*; **~ test** Kraftprobe; *tech* Festigkeitsprüfung *f*.

strenuous ['strenjuəs] mühsam, mühevoll, anstrengend; zäh, eifrig (bemüht), rastlos (tätig), emsig; energisch; **~ly** ['-li] *adv* mit Feuereifer; **~ness** ['-nis] Zähigkeit *f*, Eifer *m*, Rastlosigkeit, Emsigkeit *f*.

strepto|coccus [strepto(u)'kɔkəs] *pl -ci* [-kai] *med* Streptokokkus *m*; **~mycin** [-'maisin] *pharm* Streptomyzin *n*.

stress [stres] *s* Druck *m*; *tech* Beanspruchung, Belastung *f*; Zug *m*, Spannung; *el* Feldstärke *f*; Widerstand(skraft *f*); *fig* Nachdruck *m* (*on* auf); Bedeutung, Wichtigkeit; *med* (seelische) Belastung, Spannung *f*, Streß *m*; *(Phonetik, poet)* Betonung *f*, (Wort-)Ton *m*; *tr* Nachdruck legen auf; betonen; hervorheben; *tech* (auf Zug) beanspruchen; *to lay ~ on s.th.* auf etw Wert legen; *strong, light ~* Haupt-, Nebenton *m*; *times of ~* Krisenzeiten *f pl*; *zero ~* Tonlosigkeit *f*; **~ disease** nervöse Überreiztheit *f*; **~less** ['-lis] tonlos; **~ limit** Bruchgrenze *f*; **~-mark** Betonungszeichen *n*.

stretch [stretʃ] *tr* ausstrecken; strekken, recken, dehnen; ausspannen, -breiten, -dehnen; *(Seil)* spannen;

weiten, ausdehnen; *fig* dehnen; *fig* überspannen; übertreiben; *(Muskel)* spannen; *(Kredit)* überschreiten; *(Vorrecht)* mißbrauchen; *sl* niederschlagen, zu Boden strecken; *itr* sich (aus)dehnen, sich strecken, sich recken; sich erstrecken; dehnbar, elastisch sein; sich ausstrecken (*on the bed* auf dem Bett); *fam* übertreiben; *sl* (auf)gehängt werden; *s* (Aus-)Strekken *n*, Streckung, Dehnung, Dehnbarkeit; (An-)Spannung; Anstrengung; (Gesamt-)Ausdehnung, volle Weite, ganze Fläche; (ganze) Strecke; Richtung; Zeitstrecke, -spanne; (*~ of land*) Strecke *f*, Gebiet *n*; *fig* Mißbrauch; *sl* Knast *m*, Gefängnis (-strafe *f*) *n*; *to ~ away* sich erstrecken (*for miles* meilenweit); *to ~ out* sich ausstrecken; (sich) zu Boden werfen; sich erstrecken, sich ausdehnen; *at a ~* in e-m Zuge, ohne Unterbrechung; nach-, hinterea., auf einmal; *at full ~* auf Hochtouren; *on the ~* angespannt; *to be fully ~ed* mit Anspannung aller Kräfte arbeiten; *to give a ~* sich strecken; *to ~ o.'s legs* sich die Beine vertreten; *to ~ o.'s neck* den Hals recken; *to ~ a point (fig)* ein Auge zudrücken; *to ~ tight* straff spannen; *to ~ the truth* es mit der Wahrheit nicht (so) genau nehmen; **~ed** [-t] *a* ausgestreckt; **~er** ['-ə] *tech* Strecker, Spanner *m*, Spannvorrichtung *f*, -stab *m*; *med* Trag-, Krankenbahre; *mar* Fußlatte; *sl* Übertreibung, Angabe *f*; *~~-bearer* Krankenträger *m*; **~-out** *Am fam* Mehrarbeit *f*; Überstunden *f pl* ohne Lohnerhöhung; **~y** ['-i] dehnbar, über(be)ansprucht.

strew [stru:] *irr pp a. strewn* [stru:n] *tr* (aus-, ver)streuen; bestreuen (*with* mit); verstreut, ausgebreitet sein über.

stri|a ['straiə] *pl -ae* ['-i:] Rille, Riefe *f*; Streifen; *geol* Schrammen *m*; **~ate** ['-it], **~ated** [-'eitid] *a* gerillt, geriefelt; *med* gestreift; **~ation** [-'eiʃən] Riefelung; Streifung; *geol* Schrammung; *chem* Schlierenbildung *f*.

stricken ['strikən] *pp von strike*; *a* getroffen; *fig* geschlagen, bedrückt, heimgesucht (*with* von); schwergeprüft; *(Gefäß)* gestrichen voll; *~ out (Am)* ausgestrichen, annulliert; *terror-~* vor Schreck wie gelähmt; *~ in years* (hoch)betagt.

strict [strikt] genau, (genau) fest(gelegt); streng, strikt, rigoros (*with* gegen); ganz, vollkommen, absolut; *~ly speaking* strenggenommen; **~ness** ['-nis] Genauigkeit; Strenge, Striktheit *f*; **~ure** ['-ʃə] kritische Bemerkung *f* (*on, upon* über), Tadel *m*; *med* Verengung *f*.

stride [straid] *irr strode, stridden itr* einherschreiten, -stolzieren; *(to ~ along)* (tüchtig) ausschreiten; *to ~ over s.th.* über etw hinwegschreiten; *tr* entlangschreiten an, abschreiten; hinwegschreiten über; rittlings sitzen auf; *s* Schreiten, Stolzieren *n*; (langer) Schritt; *meist pl* Fortschritt *m*; *to hit o.'s ~* (richtig) in Gang, auf Touren kommen; *to make great ~s* große Fortschritte machen; *to take s.th. in o.'s ~ (fig)* etw spielend erledigen.

strident ['straidnt] schrill, kreischend.

strife [straif] (Wett-)Streit; Zank, Hader; Kampf *m*.

strike [straik] *irr struck, struck* [strʌk] *od (Am gelegentlich) stricken* ['strikən] **1.** *tr* schlagen; treffen; *(Schlag)* versetzen; stoßen, stechen, stanzen; *(Münzen)* schlagen, prägen; harpunieren; angeln; *(Ton)* anschlagen; *(die Stunde)* schlagen; stoßen (an, auf); *(Streichholz)* an-, entzünden, anstecken; *(Licht)* (an)machen *od* ausmachen; *(Schlange)* beißen; *mar* auffahren auf; angreifen; fallen auf; *(das Ohr)* treffen; stoßen auf, erreichen; finden, entdecken; *(Anblick)* treffen; *(Gedanke)* einfallen (*s.o.* jdm); *s.o.* jds Aufmerksamkeit erregen, jdm auffallen, jdn beeindrucken; erscheinen (*s.o.* jdm; *as silly* dumm); *mit a* machen; *(Gefühl)* hervorrufen, bewirken; *(Schreck)* einjagen (*to s.o.* jdm); *(Geschäft, Vertrag)* abschließen; *(Bilanz)* ziehen, machen; *(Saldo, Durchschnitt)* ziehen; *(Dividende)* ausschütten; *(Namen)* streichen (*off a list* von e-r Liste); *(Segel, Flagge)* einholen, *(Flagge)* streichen; bestreiken; *(Haltung)* einnehmen; *(Wurzeln)* schlagen; *theat (Szene)* wechseln, abbauen; *sl* unerwartet stoßen auf; anhauen (*for* um); *to be struck with s.th.* von etw sehr beeindruckt sein; **2.** *itr* schlagen (*at* nach); angreifen, e-n Angriff machen; *(Uhr, Glocke, Stunde)* schlagen; stoßen, treffen (*against, on, upon* gegen, auf); *(Streichholz)* aufflammen, sich entzünden; *(Fisch)* schnappen (*at* nach), anbeißen; *(auf e-e Beute)* losfahren, -schießen; zufällig kommen, stoßen (*on, upon* auf); die Segel einziehen; die Flagge streichen (*to* vor); die Arbeit einstellen *od* niederlegen, streiken; Wurzeln schlagen; *(Blitz)* einschlagen; sich wenden; schießen, sausen; sich schlagen (*into the woods* in die Wälder); **3.** *s* Schlag, Stoß; Streik, Ausstand; *bes. min* Fund; Glücksfall, unerwartete(r) Erfolg *m*; Abstreichholz *n*; *aero* Luftangriff *m*; *min* Streichen *n*; *Am parl (~ bill)* Scheinantrag *m*; **4.** *to be on ~* streiken, im Ausstand sein; *to call, to proclaim a ~* e-n Streik ausrufen; *to go, to come out on ~* in den Ausstand treten; *to ~ an attitude* e-e Haltung einnehmen; *to ~ a bargain* handelseinig werden; *to ~ blind, dumb* mit Blindheit, Taubheit schlagen; *to ~ camp* die Zelte abbrechen; *to ~ dead* erschlagen; *to ~ o.'s eye (fig)* ins Auge fallen; *to ~ o.'s fancy* jdm angenehm auffallen; *to ~ up a friendship (Am)* sich anfreunden; *to ~ hands* sich die Hand drücken; sich einig werden; *to ~ home (fig)* empfindlich treffen; *to ~ it lucky, (Am) rich, oil (fam)* Glück haben; *to ~ a happy medium* den goldenen Mittelweg wählen; *to ~ a snag (fam)* auf e-e Schwierigkeit stoßen; *to ~ a warning note* e-n warnenden Ton anschlagen; *to ~ the right path, the track* den rechten Weg finden; *to ~ root* Wurzeln schlagen; *to ~ the root of the trouble* das Übel an der Wurzel packen; **5.** *I was struck speechless* es verschlug mir die Sprache; *it has struck two* es hat zwei geschlagen; *his hour has struck (fig)* s-n Stündlein hat geschlagen; *it ~s me that* es kommt mir vor, als ob; *how does it ~ you?* was halten Sie davon? *does that ~ a familiar note?* kommt Ihnen das bekannt vor? *it ~s my fancy* es gefällt mir; *~ me dead! (sl, zur Bekräftigung)* du kannst mich totschlagen, (wenn ...); *~ while the iron is hot* man muß das Eisen schmieden, solange es heiß ist; **6.** *buyer's ~* Käuferstreik *m*; *freedom of ~* Streikrecht *n*; *general ~* Generalstreik *m*; *hunger ~* Hungerstreik *m*; *a lucky ~* ein Glückstreffer, glückliche(r) Fund *m*; *protest ~* Proteststreik *m*; *sitdown ~* Sitzstreik *m*; *slowdown ~* Bummelstreik *m*; *sympathy ~, ~ of solidarity* Sympathiestreik *m*; *warning ~* Warnstreik *m*; *wave of ~s* Streikwelle *f*; *wildcat ~* wilde(r) Streik *m*; *to ~* **at** zielen auf; *to ~* **down** niederschlagen; *to ~* **in** unterbrechen; sich einschalten; übereinstimmen (*with* mit); *to ~* **into** *(Schrecken)* einjagen; plötzlich verfallen in; stoßen in; *to ~* **off** abschlagen, -hauen; *(Geschriebenes)* (aus-, durch)streichen; *typ* abziehen *a. com*; *(Auktion)* zuschlagen; *to ~* **out** *itr* aus-, um sich, drauflosschlagen; anfangen, sich in Bewegung setzen; loslaufen, -schwimmen (*for* in Richtung auf); *com* sich selbständig machen; *tr* ausstreichen; hervorbringen; ausdenken, ersinnen; *to ~* **through** durchstreichen; durchschlagen; *to ~* **up** *tr* anstimmen; (zu spielen) beginnen; *(Bekanntschaft)* machen, anknüpfen; *(Freundschaft)* schließen (*with* mit); boss(el)ieren; *itr (Musik)* einsetzen; *to ~* **upon** plötzlich verfallen auf; *~* **benefit** Streikunterstützung *f*; **~-bound** *a* bestreikt; **~-breaker** Streikbrecher *m*; *~* **committee** Streikleitung *f*; *~* **movement** Streikbewegung *f*; **~-pay** Streikgeld *n*; **~r** ['-ə] Schläger; Streikende(r); *el* Zünder *m*; *~~ on picket duty* Streikposten *m*; *~* **threat** Streikdrohung *f*; *~* **wave** Streikwelle *f*.

striking ['straikiŋ] schlagend, treffend; auffallend, -fällig; eindrucksvoll, beachtlich, beachtens-, bemerkenswert, außerordentlich; *~* **power** Schlag-, Stoßkraft *f*.

string [striŋ] *s* Strang *m*, Schnur *f*, (dicker) Bindfaden, *(Österreich)* Spagat *m*; (dünnes) Seil; Band *n*; *mus* Saite; *(Bogen)* Sehne; *bot* Faser *f*, Faden *m*; *anat* Sehne, Flechse; *fig* Kette, Reihe, Folge, Serie, Gruppe; *sport* Riege, Mannschaft *f*; Aufgebot *n*; *(Rennen)* (Pferde *n pl* aus e-m) Stall *m*; *Am fam* Bedingung *f*, Vorbehalt *m*, Einschränkung *f*; *Am fam* Scherz, Spaß; *(shoe~) Am* Schuhnestel, Schnürsenkel *m*; *pl mus* Saiteninstrumente *n pl*; Streicher *m pl*; *v irr strung, strung* [strʌŋ] *tr (Instrument)* besaiten; (auf e-e Schnur) aufziehen, aufreihen; zs.-, verschnüren; an-, festbinden, befestigen; *(Bohnen)* abziehen; ausstrecken, spannen; anspannen, -ziehen, straffen, verstärken; *mus* stimmen; *(Bogen)* spannen; *fig (to ~ up)* er-, aufregen, nervös machen; *Am fam (to ~ along)* sich lustig machen über; hinhalten (*s.o.* jdn); *itr* faserig werden; Fäden ziehen; sich ausstrecken, sich erstrecken; *to ~ along with s.o.* mittun, -arbeiten; jdm treu ergeben sein; jdm vertrauen; *to ~ out (tr)* in e-e (lange) Reihe legen; aufstellen (*along s.th.* entlang e-r S); *itr* sich in e-r Reihe ausea.ziehen; *to ~ up (fam) (Menschen)* aufhängen; *on a ~* (völlig) abhängig; hilflos; unter Aufsicht; *fam* am Bändel; *with no ~s attached (Am)* bedingungslos; *to be attached to o.'s mother's apron ~s* der Mutter am Rockzipfel hängen; *to harp on one, the same ~* nur ein Thema haben; *to have two ~s to o.'s bow (fig)* zwei Eisen im Feuer haben; *to have s.o. on the ~ (fam)* jdn am Bändel haben; *to pull ~s (fig)* s-e Hand im Spiel haben; der Drahtzieher sein; *to touch the ~s* die Saiten anschlagen; *fig* den wunden Punkt berühren; *~ of pearls* Perlenkette *f*; **~-bag** Einkaufsnetz *n*; **~-band, -orchestra** Streichorchester *n*; **~-bean** *Am* grüne Bohne *f*; **~-board** Treppenwange *f*; **~ed** [-d] *a mus* Saiten-; Streich-; **~er, ~piece** Stütz-,

Trag-, Querbalken *m*; **~iness** ['-inis] *(Fleisch)* Zähigkeit, Faserigkeit *f*; **~ quartet** Streichquartett *n*; **~y** ['-i] faserig; zäh; verfilzt; lang u. dünn.

stringen|cy ['strindʒənsi] Strenge, Genauigkeit; *com* Knappheit; *(Geldmarkt)* Gedrücktheit; Nachdrücklichkeit; zwingende, bindende Kraft *f*; **~t** ['-t] streng, genau, strikt; knapp, bündig; *(Beweis)* zwingend, bindend; *(Regel)* fest; nach-, ausdrücklich; *(Maßnahmen)* streng, energisch; überzeugend; *com (Markt)* gedrückt, angespannt; *(Geld)* knapp.

strip [strip] *tr* ausziehen, entkleiden, entblößen (*to the waist* bis auf den Gürtel); abziehen, abstreifen; *(Draht)* abisolieren; *fig* berauben (*of s.th.* e-r S); *mil* degradieren; (weg)nehmen (*s.th. off s.o.* jdm etw); (aus)plündern; *(Decke)* herunterziehen, -reißen; abreißen, -schälen; bloßlegen; schälen; kahlfressen; *tech* ausea.nehmen, demontieren; *mar* abtakeln; *(Gebäude)* ausschalen; *(Tabak)* entrippen; *(Federn)* schleißen; *itr* sich ausziehen, sich entkleiden; *tech* sich lockern, locker werden; *s* (schmaler) Streifen *m*, Band *n*; *(air-, landing-~) aero* (Start- u.) Landestreifen *m*; *arch* Lasche *f*; *(comic ~, ~ cartoon)* Bildgeschichte *f*, Comic Strips *pl*; *to cut into ~s* in Streifen schneiden; **~ cropping, planting** *Am agr* Anbau *m* in schmalen, abwechselnden Streifen; **~ iron** Bandeisen *n*; **~ling** ['-liŋ] junge(r) Bursche *m*; **~ map** Marschskizze; *aero* Flugstreckenkarte *f*; **~ mill** Bandwalzwerk *n*; **~ mining** *Am min* Tagebau *m*; **~per** ['-ə] Öldestillator *m*; Schälmaschine *f*; *sl* = *~teaser*; **~ steel** Bandstahl *m*; **~-tease** *theat* Entkleidungsszene *f*, -akt *m*, -nummer *f*; **~teaser** Nackttänzerin *f*.

strip|e [straip] *s* Streif(en) *m*; Strieme(n *m*) *f*; (Peitschen-)Hieb *m*; *mil* Tresse; (kennzeichnende) Farbe *f*; Kennzeichen *n*; *Am* Art, Sorte, Gattung *f*, Schlag, Typ *m*; *Am* politische *od* religiöse Gruppe *f*; *tr* streifen; in Streifen teilen; *to get o.'s ~~s* (zum Unteroffizier) befördert werden; **~ed** [-t] *a* gestreift, streifig.

strive [straiv] *irr strove* [-ou-], *striven* [strivn] *itr* sich große Mühe geben, sich sehr bemühen, sich anstrengen, wetteifern (*for* um; *to do s.th.* etw zu tun); streben (*after* nach); ringen, kämpfen (*against* gegen; *with* mit).

stroke [strouk] *s* Schlag *a. fig*, Hieb, (Schwert-)Streich, Stoß *a. fig*; (Herz-)Schlag; *med* Anfall, *bes.* Schlag(anfall); (Glocken-, Stunden-)Schlag; *(Ballspiel)* Schlag; (Schwimm-)Stoß; (Pinsel-, Feder-, Bogen-)Strich *m*; Streicheln *n*; *fig* Einfall; *tech* Stoß, (Kolben-)Hub; *(Skala)* Gradstrich; *(Rudern)* (Platz des) Schlagmann(es) *m*; *tr* streicheln; *(Rudern)* den Schlag angeben für; *at one ~* mit e-m Schlag; *on the ~* pünktlich; mit dem Glockenschlag; *with a ~ of the pen* mit e-m Federstrich; *not to do a ~ of work* keinen Finger rühren; *to ~ s.o. the wrong way* jdn vor den Kopf stoßen; *sun-~* Hitzschlag *m*; *~ of fate* Schicksalsschlag *m*; *~ of lightning* Blitzschlag *m*; *~ of luck* Glücksfall, glückliche(r) Zufall *m*; **~-oar** *(Rudern)* Schlagriemen; Vormann *m*.

stroll [stroul] *itr* umherschlendern, -bummeln, -streifen, -ziehen; *tr* durchstreifen, -ziehen; *s* Spaziergang, Bummel *m*; *to take a ~* e-n Bummel machen (*through the town* durch die Stadt); **~er** ['-ə] Landstreicher; Bummler; Schausteller, Schmierenkomödiant; *Am (Kinder-)* Sportwagen *m*.

strong [strɔŋ] *a* stark, kräftig, kraftvoll, robust, kraftstrotzend; *fam* stramm; gesund (u. stark), kräftig; *(~-minded)* charakterfest, willensstark, zielbewußt; scharfsinnig, klardenkend; stark, tüchtig (*in, at, (sl) on languages* in Sprachen); *(Augen)* scharf; *(Gegenstände)* stark, fest, stabil, dauerhaft; *(Festung)* stark, schwer einnehmbar; stark *(an Zahl, Mitteln)*; streng, drastisch; *(Wind)* stark, heftig; *(Flüssigkeit, bes. Getränk, Geruch, Licht)* stark; *(Geräusch)* laut; *(Brille)* scharf; *(Fett)* ranzig; *(Gefühl)* stark; *(Äußerung)* heftig, energisch; *(Stimme)* laut; *(Meinung)* fest; überzeugt; *(Grund)* triftig; klar, deutlich, scharf; *(Ähnlichkeit)* groß; *com* stark anziehend; *(Börse)* fest; *gram (Verb)* stark; *adv* sehr, mit Nachdruck; *to be going ~* kräftig weitermachen; noch auf der Höhe sein; *to come, to go it rather ~* übertreiben; sich auffällig benehmen; *to feel ~ again* wieder bei Kräften, gesundheitlich wieder auf der Höhe sein; *to feel ~ about* sich aufregen, sich ärgern über; *to use ~ language* fluchen; *that is my ~ point* das ist meine Stärke; **~-arm** *fam a* gewalttätig; Gewalt-; *tr* Gewalt anwenden gegenüber; **~-box** Geldkassette *f*; Geld-, Panzerschrank *m*; **~ drink** Schnaps *m*; **~hold** Festung, Feste *f*; *fig* Bollwerk *n*, Hochburg *f*; **~ly** ['-li] *adv* nachdrücklich, sehr; **~-minded** *a* willensstark; entschlossen; *(Frau)* emanzipiert; **~-point** *mil* Stützpunkt *m*; **~-room** Stahlkammer *f*, Tresor *m*, Panzergewölbe *n*.

strontium ['strɔnʃiəm] *chem* Strontium *n*.

strop [strɔp] *s mar* Stropp; Streichriemen *m*; *tr (Rasiermesser)* abziehen.

stroph|e ['stroufi] *poet* Strophe *f*; **~ic(al)** ['strɔfik(l)] strophisch.

struck [strʌk] *pret u. pp von strike*; *a* betroffen (*with* von); wie vor den Kopf geschlagen, *fam* platt; versessen (*on* auf); *(~ up) (fam)* verschossen, verknallt (*on* in); bestreikt; *to be ~* gerührt sein (*at* über).

structur|al ['strʌktʃərəl] strukturell; Struktur-; *geol* tektonisch; *arch* baulich, Bau-; *med (Leiden)* organisch; *~~ alterations (pl)* bauliche Veränderungen *f pl*; *~~ defect* Konstruktionsfehler *m*; *~~ element* Bauelement *n*; *~~ engineer* Statiker *m*; *~~ engineering* Ingenieurbau *m*; *~~ material* Baustoff *m*, -material *n*; *~~ member* Bauwerksteil *m*, -glied *n*; *~~ part* Bauteil *m*; *~~ steel* Baustahl *m*; *~~ steelwork* Stahlkonstruktion *f*, Stahlbau *m*; *~~ strength* Baufestigkeit *f*; *~~ weight* Rüst-, Konstruktionsgewicht *n*; *~~ work* Stahlbau *m*; *pl* bauliche Anlagen, Baukonstruktionen *f pl*; **~e** ['strʌktʃə] Struktur *f*, Gefüge *n*, Aufbau; Bau *m*, Gebilde, Gerüst *n*; Bauweise, Konstruktion *f*; *aero* Flugwerk *n*; Zelle *f*; *med* Körper-, Knochenbau; *biol* Organismus *m*; *cost ~~* Kostengefüge *n*; *economic ~~* Wirtschaftssystem *n*; *iron ~~* Eisenkonstruktion *f*; *price ~~* Preisgefüge *n*; **~eless** ['-əlis] *geol* amorph; *fig* ohne Gliederung.

struggle ['strʌgl] *itr* sich zur Wehr setzen, sich sträuben (*against* gegen); ringen (*for* um); (an)kämpfen (*against* gegen; *with* mit); sich durchschlagen; sich (ab)mühen, sich anstrengen (*with* mit; *to do* zu tun); *to ~ along* mühsam vorankommen; *to ~ up* sich mit Mühe erheben; *s* heftige Anstrengung(en *pl*) *f*, eifrige Bemühungen *f pl*, Streben *n*; (Wett-)Streit *m*, Ringen *n*, Kampf *m* (*with* mit; *for* um); *the ~ for life, existence (biol)* der Kampf ums Dasein; **~r** ['-ə] Kämpfer *m*.

strum [strʌm] *itr tr* klimpern, herumhämmern (*on* auf); *s* Geklimper *n*.

struma ['stru:mə] *pl* *-ae* ['-i:] *med* Kropf *m*; Skrofel *f*.

strumpet ['strʌmpit] *fam* Dirne *f*.

strung [strʌŋ] *pret u. pp von string*; *a*: *highly ~ (fig)* zart besaitet, nervös.

strut [strʌt] *itr* (herum)stolzieren; *tr* (ab)stützen, absteifen, verstreben; *s* Stolzieren *n*, stolze(r) Gang *m*; Strebe, Stütze *f*, Stützbalken *m*; **~ter** ['-ə] *fig* stolze(r) Pfau *m*; **~ting** ['-iŋ] *s* Verstrebung, Absteifung *f*; *a* prahlerisch.

strychnine ['strikni:n] *chem* Strychnin *n*.

stub [stʌb] *s* (Baum-)Stumpf, Stubben *m*; Endchen *n*, (Bleistift-, Zigarren-, Zigaretten-)Stummel *m*; *fam* Kippe; *el* Stichleitung *f*; *Am* Kupon, (Kontroll-)Abschnitt *m*; *tr* ausroden, -reißen; *(Land)* roden; *(o.'s toe)* mit der Zehe stoßen (*against s.th.* an etw); *(to ~ out) (Zigarre, Zigarette)* ausdrücken; **~by** ['-i] untersetzt, stämmig, kräftig.

stubbl|e ['stʌbl] *meist pl (Getreide-, Bart-)* Stoppeln; Borsten *f pl*; *~~ field* Stoppelfeld *n*; **~y** ['-i] stopp(e)lig; borstig.

stubborn ['stʌbən] widerspenstig, -borstig; eigensinnig, hartnäckig; halsstarrig, *fam* stur; *(Wille)* unbeugsam; zäh; *tech* spröde, hart; *(Metall)* streng-, schwerflüssig; **~ness** ['-nis] Widerspenstigkeit *f*, Eigensinn *m*, Hartnäckigkeit *f*.

stucco ['stʌkou] *pl* *-(e)s* *s* Stuck *m*; *(~work)* Stuckarbeit, Stukkatur *f*; *tr* mit Stuck verzieren.

stuck [stʌk] *pret u. pp von stick (fam)* verschossen, vernarrt (*on s.o.* in jdn); (ganz) erpicht (*on s.th.* auf etw); *to get ~* festfahren; übers Ohr gehauen werden; **~-up** *a fam* hochnäsig, eingebildet, überheblich, arrogant.

stud [stʌd] **1.** *s* Beschlag-, Ziernagel; Kragen-, Hemdknopf *m*; *tech* Stiftschraube, Warze *f*, Knauf, Zapfen; Stift; Ständer; Pfosten; *mar* Amboß; (Ketten-)Steg *m*; *tr* mit Nägeln beschlagen; übersäen; mit Pfosten, Ständern versehen; **~ding** ['-iŋ] Fachwerk *n*, Pfosten *m pl (e-s Hauses)*; *~~-sail* Leesegel *n*; **2.** Stall *m*, Gestüt *n*; *Am* = *~-horse*; **~-book** Zucht-, Stutbuch *n*; **~-farm** Gestüt *n*; **~-horse, -mare** Zuchthengst *m*, -stute *f*.

stud|ent ['stju:dənt] Student, Schüler; Gelehrte(r); Forscher; Fachmann, Kenner; *in Zssgen*: Kundige(r), Erforscher *m gen*; *~~ of birds* Vogelkundige(r) *m*; *~~ of human behavio(u)r* Verhaltensforscher *m*; *Bible ~~* Bibelforscher *m (Sektierer)*; *~~ lamp (Am)* Studierlampe *f*; **~entship** ['-ʃip] Studentenzeit *f*; Stipendium *n*; **~ied** [stʌdid] *a* einstudiert, -geübt; sorgfältig vorbereitet; durchdacht, wohlüberlegt; geplant, absichtlich; gesucht, affektiert; studiert, gelehrt; **~io** ['stju:diou] *pl* *-s* Atelier *n*; *film* Aufnahmeraum; *radio video* Senderaum *m*; *~~ couch (Am)* Schlaf-, Bettcouch *f*; **~ious** ['stju:djəs] lernbegierig, -beflissen; eifrig (studierend); sorgfältig, aufmerksam; bedacht (*of* auf); überlegt, absichtlich; **~iousness** ['-djəsnis] Lerneifer *m*; Beflissenheit, Sorgfalt *f*; **~y** ['stʌdi] *s* Studieren, Studium;

Fach(gebiet) *n*; Studie, wissenschaftliche Arbeit, Analyse *f* (*in, of* über); Entwurf *m*; *mus* Etüde *f*; Studier-, Arbeitszimmer *n*; *allg* Bemühung *f*, Streben *n*, Absicht *f*; tiefe(s) Nachdenken *n*, Versunkenheit *f*; *tr* studieren (*at the university* an der Universität); lernen; betreiben; sich befassen mit; eingehend untersuchen, (genau) studieren, prüfen; einstudieren, auswendig lernen, memorieren; sich bemühen, sich befleißigen (*to* zu); bedacht sein auf; *itr* studieren (*for s.th.* etw); Student sein; nachdenken, -sinnen, überlegen; *to ~ for an examination* ein Examen vorbereiten; *to make a ~~ of s.th.* etw eifrig studieren; *in a brown ~~* in Gedanken versunken; *~~ bag* Schultasche *f*; *~~ group* Arbeitsgemeinschaft *f*, -ausschuß *m*; *~~ hall (Schule)* Arbeitsraum *m*.

stuff [stʌf] *s* (Roh-)Stoff *m*, (Roh-)Material *n*; *allg* Stoff *m*, Materie; *fig* (Wesens-)Art *f*, Schlag *m*, Zeug *n* (*of* zu); (Woll-)Stoff; Hausrat, *fam* Kram *m*, Sachen *f pl*; Plunder, Dreck, Krimskrams *m*; dumme(s) Zeug, Gerede, Geschwätz *n*, Unsinn *m*; *(doctor's ~)* Medizin *f*; *tr (bes. Kissen)* stopfen, füllen; *(Möbel)* polstern; *(Tierbalg)* ausstopfen; *(Braten)* füllen; *(Gans)* nudeln, stopfen; vollstopfen, -pfropfen *a. fig*; *(to ~ up)* voll-, verstopfen; *(Leder)* einfetten; drücken, pressen, stopfen, stecken (*into* in); *Am* gefälschte Stimmzettel stecken in; *to be good, sorry ~* etwas, nichts taugen; *he knows his ~* er kennt sich aus; *do your ~! (Am sl)* zeige, was du kannst! *food-~s (pl)* Lebensmittel *n pl*; *garden, green ~* Grünzeug, Gemüse *n*; *household ~* Hausgerät *n*; **~ed** [-t] *a*: *~~ shirt (fam)* Angeber, aufgeblasene(r) Kerl *m*; **~er** ['-ə] *(gedruckte)* Beilage *f*; **~iness** ['-inis] Dumpfheit; *fig* Stumpfheit; Schlafmützigkeit *f*; **~ing** ['-iŋ] (Voll-)Stopfen *n*; Füllung *f*, Füllsel *(a. Küche)*; Polstermaterial *n*; *to knock the ~~ out of s.o. (fam)* jdn kleinkriegen; jdn. fertigmachen; *~~-box (tech)* Stopfbüchse *f*; **~y** ['-i] stickig, dumpf; *(Luft)* schwül; (leicht) verschnupft; *fam* langweilig, stumpf (-sinnig); *fam fig* tranig, schlafmützig; *Am fam* steif; altmodisch; verbohrt; trüb(sinnig).

stultif|ication [stʌltifi'keiʃən] Lächerlichmachen *n*, Verspottung *f*; **~y** ['stʌltifai] *tr* zum Narren haben, *fam* für dumm verkaufen; lächerlich machen; zuschanden, illusorisch, wirkungslos machen; widerlegen; *jur* für unzurechnungsfähig erklären.

stumbl|e ['stʌmbl] *itr* stolpern, straucheln (*over* über); torkeln, schwanken; stottern, stammeln; *fig (sittlich)* straucheln; *fig* stolpern (*across, (up)on* über); zufällig stoßen (*on* auf); *Am sl* e-e Dummheit machen; Pech haben; zurückschrecken (*at* vor); *s* Straucheln, Stolpern *n*; *fig* Fehltritt, Fehler *m*; **~ing-block** Hindernis *n*, Stein *m* des Anstoßes (*to* für).

stumer ['stju:mə] *sl* gefälschte(r) Scheck *m*; Blüte, falsche Banknote; falsche Münze *f*; Ruin *m*.

stump [stʌmp] *s* (Baum-)Stumpf; Stummel; (Kraut-)Strunk; *fig* Dickmops; *(Zeichnen)* Wischer *m*; Rednertribüne *f*; *sport (Kricket)* Torstab *m*; *Am* Herausforderung *f*; *Am sl* Telegraphenmast *m*; *pl Am sl* Stelzen *f pl*, Beine *n pl*; *tr* bis auf e-n Stumpf abhauen, -nutzen, verbrauchen; *(Baumstümpfe)* roden; *(Zeichnung)* wischen; stoßen (*one's toes* sich die Zehe); *(Land)* als Wahlredner bereisen; *Am fam* vor den Kopf stoßen, stutzig machen; aus der Fassung bringen; vereiteln, zunichte machen, durchkreuzen; *Am* herausfordern; *to ~ up (fam)* blechen, bezahlen; *itr* schwerfällig, unbeholfen, steif gehen; sta(m)pfen; herumreisen u. Wahlreden halten; *to ~ about, along* umherstapfen; *on the ~ (Wahlredner)* auf Tournee; *up a ~ = ~ed*; *to stir o.'s ~s (fam)* die Beine unter die Arme nehmen; *to ~ it (fam)* sich auf die Socken, sich aus dem Staube machen; **~ed** [-t] *a* verwirrt, verblüfft, außer Fassung, in Verlegenheit; **~er** ['-ə] *Am fam* Fangfrage, harte Nuß *f*; **~ orator, speaker** Propaganda-, Volksredner *m*; **~ oratory, speech** Propaganda-, Volksrede *f*; **~ work** Kurzwort *n*; **~y** ['-i] *a* stämmig, untersetzt.

stun [stʌn] *tr* betäuben, lähmen; aus der Fassung bringen, überwältigen, *fam* umhauen; **~ned** [-d] *a* benommen; verdutzt, verblüfft; *fam* erschlagen (*with* von); **~ner** ['-ə] *fam* Pracht-, Pfundskerl *m*; tolle Frau; Pfunds-, prima Sache *f*; Mordsding *n*; **~ning** ['-iŋ] betäubend; atemraubend; verblüffend; *fam* prächtig, toll, blendend.

stunt [stʌnt] **1.** *tr* verkümmern lassen, in der Entwicklung hemmen *a. fig*; *(Entwicklung, Wachstum)* hemmen, hindern; **~ed** ['-id] *a* verkümmert, zurückgeblieben; **2.** *fam s* Kraft-, Kunststück *n*; Heldentat; Glanzleistung; Sensation *f*; Reklameschlager, Knüller, Geschäftstrick *m*; *itr* ein Kunststück vorführen; **~er** ['-ə] *fam* Kunstflieger *m*; **~ film** Trickfilm *m*; **~-flying** Kunstfliegen *n*; **~-man** *film* Double *n*; **~-press** Sensationspresse *f*.

stupe [stju:p] *s* feuchtwarme(r) Umschlag; *Am sl* Dummkopf *m*; *tr* bähen; mit e-m warmen Umschlag behandeln.

stup|efacient [stj:upi'feiʃənt] Narkotikum, Rausch-, Betäubungsmittel *n*; **~efaction** [-'fækʃən] Betäubung; *fig* Verblüffung; Verwirrung *f*; Erstaunen *n*; **~efy** ['stu:pifai] *tr* betäuben; *fig* verblüffen, verwundern; verwirren; abstumpfen; **~endous** [stju(:)'pendəs] überwältigend; gewaltig, ungeheuer; **~id** ['stju:pid] *a* dumm, einfältig, stupid(e); blöd(e), dämlich; sinnlos; langweilig, stumpfsinnig; *s* Dummkopf *m*; **~idity** [stju(:)'piditi] Dummheit, Einfalt, Blödheit, Dämlichkeit *f*; Stumpfsinn *m*; **~or** ['stju:pə] Benommenheit, Starre; Stumpfheit *f*, Stumpfsinn; *med* Stupor *m*.

sturd|iness ['stə:dinis] Stärke, Kraft; Robustheit, Derbheit *f*; **~y** ['stə:di] stark, kräftig, derb, handfest; *(Pflanze)* wetterhart; *fig* fest, entschlossen, unnachgiebig.

sturgeon ['stə:dʒən] *zoo* Stör *m*.

stutter ['stʌtə] *tr itr* stottern; stammeln; *s* Stottern, Gestotter, Gestammel *n*; **~er** ['-rə] Stotterer *m*; **~ingly** ['-riŋli] *adv* stotternd, stammelnd.

sty [stai] *(pig~)* Schweinestall *m a. fig*.

sty(e) [stai] *med* Gerstenkorn *n*.

styl|e [stail] *fig* Stil *m*, Ausdrucksweise *f*; *(Kunst)* Stil *m*; Lebensart *f*, Geschmack *m*, Eleganz, Vornehmheit; Fasson, Machart; Mode *f*; Titel *m*, Anrede *f*; *com* Firmenname *m*; -bezeichnung; Art u. Weise, (Spiel-)Art *f*, Typ *m*; Rechtschreibung, Orthographie *f*; *hist* Grabstichel, Griffel *m* *(Schreibgerät)*; Radier-, Grammophonnadel *f*; *bot* Griffel; *tech* Gnomon *m*; *tr* stilisieren; entwerfen; *typ* vereinheitlichen; nennen, bezeichnen als; betiteln, anreden; *in ~~* stil-, geschmackvoll; großzügig; *in the ~~ of* in der Art *gen*; *under the ~~ of* unter dem Namen, der Firma *gen*; *to be in ~* Mode sein; *to live in ~~* ein großes Haus führen, Aufwand treiben; *there is no ~~ about her* sie versteht es nicht, etwas aus sich zu machen; *that's the ~~* das ist das richtige; *good, bad ~~* gute(r), schlechte(r) Geschmack *m*; *latest ~~* neueste Mode *f*; *Norman, early English, decorated, perpendicular ~~ (etwa)* romanische(r), früh-, hoch-, spätgotische(r) Stil *m*; *old, new ~~* Julianische(r), Gregorianische(r) Kalender *m*; *poor ~~* schlechte(r) Stil *m*; *~~-book* Anstandsbuch; Modeheft; Rechtschreibbuch *n*; Druckvorschrift *f*; **~er** ['-ə] *Am* Modeschöpfer *m*; **~et** ['-it] Stilett *n*; *med* feine Sonde *f*; **~ish** ['-iʃ] modisch, elegant; stilvoll; geschmackvoll, passend; **~ist** ['-ist] gute(r) Stilist; eigenwillige(r) Schriftsteller; Modezeichner, -berater; Formgestalter; Innendekorateur *m*; *hair-~~* Damenfrisör *m*; **~istic(al)** [stai'listik(əl)] stilistisch; **~ization** [staili'zeiʃən] Stilisierung *f*; **~ize** ['stailaiz] *tr* stilisieren; **~o** ['-ou], **~ograph** ['-əgrɑ:f] Tintenkuli; Füllfederhalter, *fam* Füller *m*; **~us** ['-ə] Griffel; Kopierstift *m*; Grammophonnadel *f*.

stymie ['staimi] *Am fam tr* (be-, ver)hindern; *(Plan)* durchkreuzen, vereiteln; *fig* lahmlegen.

styptic ['stiptik] *a u. s* blutstillend(es Mittel *n*).

Styria ['stiriə] die Steiermark.

suab|ility [sju(:)ə'biliti] *jur* (Ein-)Klagbarkeit, Prozeßfähigkeit *f*; **~le** ['sju(:)əbl] (ein)klagbar; prozeßfähig.

suas|ion ['sweiʒən] *jur (moral ~~)* Zureden *n*, Überredung *f*; **~ive** ['-siv] *a* Überredungs-; überzeugend (*of* für).

suav|e [sweiv, swɑ:v] höflich, verbindlich; einschmeichelnd, glatt; *(Wein)* mild; *pej* süßlich; **~ity** ['swæviti] Höflichkeit, Verbindlichkeit *f*; Zuvorkommenheit, Freundlichkeit *f*.

sub [sʌb] *pref* Unter-, Neben-, (Aus-) Hilfs-; Sub- *a. math chem*; *tr* einspringen (*for* für); *~ judice* [-'dʒu:disi] vor Gericht; schwebend, noch nicht entschieden; *~ poena* [səb'pi:nə] *jur* bei, unter Strafe; *~ rosa* vertraulich; *~ verbo, voce* unter dem angegebenen Wort.

subacid ['sʌb'æsid] (leicht) säuerlich; *fig (Bemerkung)* bissig, scharf.

subagen|cy ['sʌb'eidʒənsi] Unteragentur, -vertretung *f*; **~t** ['-t] Untervertreter *m*.

subaltern ['sʌbltən] *a* untergeordnet; (rang)niedriger; subaltern; *s* Subalternbeamte(r), -offizier; Untergebene(r) *m*.

sub|area ['sʌb'ɛəriə] Teilgebiet *n*; **~assembly** ['-əsembli] Teilmontage *f*; *~~ line* Teilmontagestraße *f*.

subbranch ['sʌb'brɑ:ntʃ] Fachgruppe, Unterabteilung; Zweigstelle *f*.

subcalibre [sʌb'kælibə] Kleinkaliber *n*; *~~ ammunition* Kleinkalibermunition *f*.

subcommittee ['sʌbkəmiti:] Unterausschuß *m*.

subconscious ['sʌb'kɔnʃəs] *a* unterbewußt; halb bewußt; *s (the ~)* das Unterbewußte; **~ness** ['-nis] Unterbewußtsein *n*.

subcontinent [sʌb'kɔntinənt] *geog* Subkontinent *m*.

subcontract [sʌb'kɔntrækt] *s* Unter-, Nebenvertrag *m*; *itr (tr)* e-n Nebenvertrag abschließen (über); als Zulieferant übernehmen; **~or** [-kən'træktə] Unterkontrahent, Zulieferant *m*.

subcutaneous ['sʌbkju:'teinjəs] *med* subkutan, unter der *od* die Haut.
subdeb [sʌb'deb] *Am fam* junge(s) Mädchen *n* vor der Einführung in die Gesellschaft *(= subdebutante)*; Backfisch, Teenager *m*.
subdivi|de ['sʌbdi'vaid] *tr itr* (sich) unterteilen, untergliedern; *(Land)* parzellieren; **~sion** ['-viʒən] Unterteilung; Unterabteilung; Parzellierung *f*.
subdue [səb'dju:] *tr* besiegen, unterwerfen, -jochen, -drücken; beherrschen, in s-r Gewalt haben; *(Stimme)* senken; abschwächen, mildern, vermindern; *(Gefühl)* unterdrücken; *(Licht, Ton)* dämpfen; *(Land)* bestellen, bearbeiten.
subeditor ['sʌb'editə] zweite(r) Redakteur; *Br* Korrektor *m*.
subhead ['sʌbhed] stellvertretende(r) (Schul-)Leiter; *(~ing)* Untertitel *m*.
subjacent [sʌb'dʒeisənt] darunter befindlich; *fig* zugrunde liegend; niedriger (liegend).
subject ['sʌbdʒikt] *a* unterworfen; anfällig (*to* für), ausgesetzt (*to* dat); abhängig (*to* von); *s fig* Gegenstand *m*, Thema *n*, Stoff *m* (*for* für); *mus* Thema *n*; Anlaß *m*, Veranlassung *f*, Grund *m* (*for* zu), Ursache *f* (*for* für); Fach(gebiet) *n*; Unterrichtsgegenstand *m*, -fach *n*; *gram* Subjekt *n*, Satzgegenstand *m*; *philos* Subjekt *n*; Untertan; Staatsbürger, -angehörige(r) *m*; *med* (zu sezierende) Leiche *f*; *med* Patient *m*; *tr* [səb'dʒekt] unterwerfen, -jochen; aussetzen (*to* dat); *(e-r Prüfung)* unterziehen (*to* dat); *on the ~ of* betreffs *gen*; *to be ~ to* unterworfen sein; *(Krankheit)* neigen zu, leicht bekommen; *to change the ~* das Thema wechseln; *to wander from the ~* vom Thema abkommen; *compulsory ~* Pflichtfach *n*; *~ to alteration, change* Änderungen vorbehalten; freibleibend; *~ of deliberation* Beratungsgegenstand *m*; *~ to duty* zollpflichtig; **~ catalogue** Schlagwortkatalog *m*; **~ entry** Stichworteintragung *f*; **~ index** Sachregister *n*; **~ion** [səb'dʒekʃən] Unterwerfung; Abhängigkeit *f* (*of* von); **~ive** [səb'dʒektiv] *bes. philos psychol* subjektiv; **~ivity** [sʌbdʒek'tiviti] Subjektivität, persönliche Betrachtungsweise *f*; **~ matter** (Verhandlungs-)Gegenstand; Inhalt *(e-s Buches)*; Lehrstoff *m*.
subjoin ['sub'dʒɔin] *tr* bei-, hinzufügen; **~der** [səb'dʒɔində] Anhang *m*.
subjugat|e ['sʌbdʒugeit] *tr* unterjochen, -werfen; bezwingen; *fig* gefügig machen; **~ion** [sʌbdʒu'geiʃən] Unterjochung, -werfung *f*.
subjunctive [səb'dʒʌŋktiv] *s u. a*: *~ mood* Konjunktiv *m*.
sub|lease ['sʌb'li:s] *s* Unterpacht, -miete *f*; *tr* ['-'-] weiterverpachten, untervermieten; **~lessee** ['-le'si:] Unterpächter, -mieter *m*; **~lessor** ['-le'sɔ:] Untervermieter *m*.
sublet ['sʌb'let] *irr s. let tr* unter-, weiterverpachten, -vermieten; *(Arbeit)* weitervergeben.
sublieutenant ['sʌble(f)'tenənt, *Am* 'sʌblu:'tenənt] *Br* Oberleutnant *m* z. S.
sublim|ate ['sʌblimeit] *tr chem* sublimieren *a. fig psychol*; *fig* vergeistigen; veredeln; verfeinern; ['-it] *a* sublimiert; *s* Sublimat *n*; **~ation** [sʌbli'meiʃən] Sublimierung *f a. fig*; Sublimat *n*; *fig* Vergeistigung *f*; **~e** [sə'blaim] *a* erhaben, edel, *poet* hehr; überragend, unvergleichlich; vollendet; *fam* kraß; *s (the ~~)* das Erhabene; *tr* läutern, veredeln; *chem* sublimieren; **~inal** [sʌb'liminl] *psychol* unterschwellig; unterbewußt; **~ity** [sə'blimiti] Erhabenheit *f*.
submachine-gun ['sʌbmə'ʃi:ngʌn] Maschinenpistole *f*.
submarine ['sʌbməri:n] *a* Unterwasser-; unterseeisch; *s* Meerespflanze *f*; Seetier; Unterseeboot, U-Boot *n*; **~ arm** U-Boot-Waffe *f*; **~ base** U-Boot-Stützpunkt *m*; **~ berth** U-Boot-Liegeplatz *m*; **~ campaign** U-Boot-Krieg *m*; **~ chaser** U-Boot-Jäger *m*; **~ detector** U-Boot-Ortungsgerät *n*; **~ mine** Unterwassermine *f*; **~ net** Unterseebootnetz *n*; **~ pack** U-Boot-Rudel *n*; **~ pen** U-Boot-Bunker *m*; **~ war(fare)** U-Boot-Krieg *m*.
submer|ge [səb'mə:dʒ] *tr* untertauchen; überschwemmen, -fluten; eintauchen; *fig* verbergen; unterdrücken; *itr* (unter)tauchen; **~gence** ['-əns], **~sion** [-'mə:ʃən] Untertauchen *n*; Überschwemmung, -flutung *f*.
submi|ssion [səb'miʃən] Unterwerfung (*to* unter); Unterwürfigkeit, Nachgiebigkeit; *jur* Unterbreitung, Vorlage; *jur* Auffassung *f*; *~~ of arbitration* Schiedsgerichtsvereinbarung *f*; **~ssive** [-siv] unterwürfig, nachgiebig, fügsam; **~ssiveness** [-sivnis] Unterwürfigkeit, Nachgiebigkeit, Fügsamkeit *f*; **~t** [-'mit] *tr* vorlegen, unterbreiten, einreichen; *(Zeugnis)* beibringen; vorschlagen, anheimstellen, zu bedenken geben; abtreten (*to* an), übergeben; verweisen; *itr* sich unterwerfen, sich fügen (*to* dat), nachgeben; sich unterziehen (*to an operation* e-r Operation); sich gefallen lassen (*to s.th.* etw); sich damit abfinden (*to doing s.th.* etw zu tun); *to ~~ o.s.* nachgeben, sich fügen (*to* in).
subnormal ['sʌb'nɔ:məl] unternormal; *psych* minderbegabt.
subordinat|e [sə'bɔ:dnit] *a* untergeordnet, zweitrangig; untergeben; unterwürfig, fügsam; *s* Untergebene(r) *m*; untergeordnete Sache *f*; *tr* [-dineit] *tr* unterordnen; zurückstellen; als zweitrangig behandeln; *to be ~~* unterstehen (*to s.o.* jdm); *~~ clause* Nebensatz *m*; **~ion** [səbɔ:di'neiʃən] Unterordnung (*to* unter); Unterstellung *f*.
suborn [sʌ'bɔ:n] *tr* anstiften, -zetteln; bestehen, verleiten; **~ation** [sʌbɔ:'neiʃən] Anstiftung, Anzettelung; Bestechung, Verleitung *f*; **~er** [sʌ'bɔ:nə] Anstifter (*of* zu) *m*.
subpoena [səb'pi:nə] *jur s* Vorladung *f*; *tr* vorladen.
subrogat|e ['sʌbrəgeit] *tr jur* an die Stelle setzen (*for s.o.* gen); **~ion** [sʌbrə'geiʃən] *jur* Ersetzung *f* (des Gläubigers), Rechts-, Forderungsübergang *m*.
subscribe [səb'skraib] *tr* unterschreiben, (unter)zeichnen; zustimmen, beistimmen, billigen, beipflichten (*s.th.* e-r S); sich einsetzen, eintreten für; *(Geld)* zeichnen (*to* für *e-e Sache*; *for* für *Aktien*); *itr* unterschreiben, -zeichnen; beistimmen, -pflichten (*to s.th.* e-r S); sich (zu e-r Zahlung) verpflichten; e-n Beitrag zahlen (*to* an); abonnieren (*to s.th.* etw); abonniert sein (*to* auf); vorausbestellen (*for a book* ein Buch); belegen (*to lectures* Vorlesungen); **~r** [-ə] Subskribent, Unterzeichner (*to* gen); Abonnent, Bezieher; *(telephone ~~)* (Fernsprech-)Teilnehmer; *(Anleihe)* Zeichner *m*; *~~'s line* Fernsprechanschluß *m*; *~~'s number* Teilnehmernummer *f*.
subscription [səb'skripʃən] Unterzeichnung; Unterschrift; (schriftliche) Zustimmung, Einwilligung (*to* in); *com* Zeichnung *f*; gezeichnete(r) Betrag *m*, Summe *f*, (Mitglieds-)Beitrag *m* (*to* für); Abonnement *n* (*to* auf), Bezug; *(~ price)* Bezugspreis *m*; Vorbestellung *f*; *tele* Anschluß *m*; Grundgebühr *f*; *by ~* im Abonnement; *open for ~* zur Zeichnung aufgelegt; *to drop o.'s ~* sein Abonnement aufgeben; *to take out a ~* sich abonnieren (*to* auf); *conditions of ~* Bezugsbedingungen *f pl*; **~ form** Bestellschein *m*; **~ library** Leihbücherei *f*; **~ list** Subskriptions-, Zeichnungsliste *f*; **~ office** Zeichnungsstelle *f*; **~ period** Zeichnungsfrist *f*; **~ ticket** Dauerkarte *f*.
subsection ['sʌbsekʃən] Unterabschnitt *m*, -abteilung *f*.
subsequen|t ['sʌbsikwənt] (nach)folgend; nachträglich, später; *~~ to* später als, folgend auf; *~~ assessment* Nachveranlagung *f*; *~~ clause* Zusatzartikel *m*; *~~ delivery* Nachlieferung *f*; *~~ order* Nachbestellung *f*; *~~ payment* Nachzahlung *f*; **~tly** ['-tli] *adv* darauf, danach, später.
subserv|e [səb'sə:v] *tr* dienen, dienlich, förderlich, nützlich, von Nutzen, behilflich sein (*s.th.* e-r S); fördern; **~ience, -cy** [-iəns(i)] Dienlichkeit, Förderlichkeit, Nützlichkeit (*to* für); Dienstfertigkeit, -bereitschaft; Unterwürfigkeit *f*; **~ient** [-jənt] dienlich, förderlich, nützlich (*to* für); behilflich; dienstfertig, -bereit; übereifrig, unterwürfig (*to* gegenüber).
subsid|e [səb'said] *itr (Flüssigkeit)* sich setzen, sich niederschlagen; sinken; *(Boden)* sich senken; sich niederlassen (*into a chair* auf e-m Stuhl); *fig* nachlassen, abklingen, schwächer werden, sich beruhigen; *(Wind)* abflauen; **~ence** [səb'saidəns] Sinken *n*; (Boden-)Senkung *f*; *fig* Nachlassen, Abflauen *n*, Beruhigung *f*.
subsid|iary [səb'sidjəri] *a* (Aus-)Hilfs-, Neben-, Ersatz-; stellvertretend, *jur* subsidiär (*to* für); zweitrangig, sekundär; untergeordnet; Subventions-; subventioniert; *s* Hilfe, Unterstützung, Stütze; *(~~ company)* Tochtergesellschaft *f*; *to be ~~ to s.th.* etw ergänzen; *~~ income, employment* Nebeneinkommen *n*, -beschäftigung *f*; *~~ office* Nebenstelle *f*; **~ize** ['sʌbsidaiz] *tr* finanziell unterstützen, subventionieren; **~y** ['sʌbsidi] finanzielle Unterstützung, Beihilfe, Subvention *f*; *meist pl* Subsidien *pl*.
subsist [səb'sist] *itr* (weiter)bestehen, existieren; leben, sich ernähren (*on, by* von); bestehen (*in* in); **~ence** [-əns] (Da-)Sein *n*, Existenz *f*; Fort-, Weiterbestehen *n*, Bestand *m*; Unterstützung; *mil* Versorgung *f*; (Lebens-)Unterhalt *m*, Auskommen *n*; *to earn a bare ~~* das nackte Dasein fristen; *~~ allowance* Unterhaltszuschuß *m*; *~~ level* Existenzminimum *n*; *~~ money* (Lohn-)Vorschuß *m*; *~~ wages (pl)* Existenzlohn *m*.
subsoil ['sʌbsɔil] Untergrund *m*.
subsonic ['sʌb'sɔnik] *a* unter Schallgeschwindigkeit.
substan|ce ['sʌbstəns] Wesen *n*, Substanz *f*, Körper, Kern *m*; *das* Wesentliche, Hauptsache *f*; Inhalt *m*; Wirklichkeit, Realität *f*, Bestand *m*; Materie *f*, Stoff *m*; (Hilfs-)Mittel *n pl*, Vermögen, Kapital *n*; Besitz, Wohlstand *m*; *in ~~* im wesentlichen; wirklich; *of ~~* vermögend; **~tial** [səb'stænʃəl] *a* wesentlich; wirklich, real, tatsächlich; solide, fest, stark, kräftig; wohlhabend, reich; *(Beweis)* schlüssig; *(Grund)* stichhaltig; beträchtlich, be-

deutend, umfangreich, ansehnlich; wichtig; wertvoll; *com* zahlungskräftig; *s pl* Gegenstand *m*; *to be in ~~ agreement* im wesentlichen übereinstimmen; **~tiality** [səbstænʃi'æliti] Wesen(haftigkeit *f*) *n*; Wirklichkeit, Tatsächlichkeit, Realität; Echtheit; Festigkeit, Stärke, Solidität; Nahrhaftigkeit *f*; **~tially** [səb'stænʃəli] *adv* fest, mit Festigkeit *od* Bestimmtheit; weitgehend; im wesentlichen, in der Hauptsache; wirklich, tatsächlich; **~tiate** [səb'stænʃieit] *tr* konkretisieren, realisieren; nach-, beweisen, dartun, -legen, begründen, glaubhaft machen; bestätigen, erhärten; **~tival** [sʌbstən-'taivəl] *gram* substantivisch; **~tive** ['sʌbstəntiv] *a* selbständig; beträchtlich, bedeutend; wirklich, tatsächlich, real, wesentlich; *(Recht)* materiell; *gram* substantivisch; *s gram* Substantiv, Hauptwort *n*.

substandard [sʌb'stændəd] *(Sprache)* unfein, ungebildet, gewöhnlich, ordinär; *tech* unter der Norm; *(Qualität)* minderwertig.

substation ['sʌbsteiʃən] Nebenstelle *f*; *tech* Unterwerk *n*; *Am* Teilnehmeranschluß *m*.

substitut|e ['sʌbstitju:t] *s* Ersatz (-mittel *n*, -mann *m*); Stellvertreter; Ersatzstoff *m*, Surrogat; *gram* Hilfswort *n*; *tr* an die Stelle setzen (*for* gen); austauschen (*for* gegen); *for s.th.* anstelle e-r S gebrauchen *od* nehmen; die Stelle einnehmen (*s.th.* e-r S); ersetzen (*by* durch); *itr Am* stellvertretend handeln, einspringen (*for* für); vertreten (*for s.o.* jdn); *a* stellvertretend; *to be appointed s.o.'s ~~* zu jds Stellvertreter ernannt werden; **~ion** [sʌbsti'tju:ʃən] Ersatz *m*, Ersetzung, Substituierung, Substitution; Stellvertretung *f*; **~ional** [-'tju:ʃənl] stellvertretend; Ersatz-.

substratum ['sʌb'strɑ:təm, *Am* '-'strei-] *pl -ta* ['-ə] Unter-, Grundlage *f*, Fundament *n a. fig*; *agr* Mutterboden; *biol* Nährboden *m*; *gram* Substrat *n*; *philos* Substanz *f*.

substruct|ion ['sʌbstrʌkʃən], **~ure** ['-ə] Unterbau *m*, Grundlage *a. fig*; Basis *f*, Fundament *n*.

subsum|e [səb'sju:m] *tr* zs.fassen, ordnen, klassifizieren (*under* unter); unter ein Prinzip, e-e Regel bringen; subsumieren; **~ption** [-'sʌmpʃən] Zs.-fassung, Klassifizierung; Subsumtion *f* (*under* unter); **~ptive** [-'sʌmptiv] zs.fassend; subsumierend.

subtenan|cy ['sʌb'tenənsi] Unterpacht, -miete *f*; **~t** [-t] Unterpächter, -mieter *m*.

subtend [səb'tend] *tr* sich hinziehen unter, gegenüber; *math* gegenüberliegen (*s.th.* e-r S).

subterfuge ['sʌbtəfju:dʒ] Vorwand *m*, Ausflucht *f*; Trick *m*.

subterran|e [sʌbtə'rein] unterirdische(r) Raum *m*, Höhle *f*; **~ean** [-jən], **~eous** [-jəs] unterirdisch; *fig* verborgen, heimlich; *~~ diplomacy* Geheimdiplomatie *f*; *~~ waters (pl)* Grundwasser *n*; *~~ workings (pl)* Tiefbauarbeiten *f pl*.

subtil|ization [sʌtilai'zeiʃən] Verdünnung, Verflüchtigung *f*; Feinerwerden *n*, Verfeinerung; Spitzfindigkeit; *chem* Verflüchtigung *f*; **~ize** ['sʌtilaiz] *tr* verfeinern; *fig* ausklügeln; *chem* verflüchtigen; *itr* dünner, feiner werden; *fig* spitzfindig argumentieren.

subtitle ['sʌbtaitl] Untertitel *m*.

subtle ['sʌtl] dünn; fein, zart; scharf (-sinnig), durchdringend, spitzfindig; schlau, klug, geschickt, kunstfertig; kunstvoll, sinnreich; kniff(e)lig, verzwickt, schwierig; **~ty** ['-ti] Feinheit *f*; Scharfsinn *m*; Spitzfindigkeit; Verschlagenheit *f*.

subtopia [sʌb'toupjə] verstädterte Landschaft *f*; Vorstadtgebiet *n*.

subtract [səb'trækt] *tr itr* abziehen, subtrahieren (*from* von); **~ion** [-'trækʃən] Abziehen *n*, Subtraktion *f* (*from* von).

subtropic(al) ['sʌb'trɔpik(əl)] subtropisch.

suburb ['sʌbə:b] Vorstadt *f*, -ort *m*; Stadtrandsiedlung *f*; *pl* Rand-, Außengebiete *n pl*; Stadtrand *m*; **~an** [sə'bə:bən] *a* vorstädtisch; kleinbürgerlich; Vorstadt-, Vorort-; *s* = *~anite*; *~~ area* Vorstadtgebiet *n*; *~~ line* Vorortstrecke *f*; *~~ residence* Vorstadtwohnung *f*; *~~ traffic, train* Vorortverkehr, -zug *m*; **~anite** [sə'bə:bənait] Vorstädter, Vorortbewohner *m*; **~ia** [sə'bə:bjə] Stadtrandbezirke *m pl*; Vorstadt; Lebenseinstellung *f* der Vororte.

subvention [sʌb'venʃən] (staatliche) Unterstützung, (Bei-)Hilfe; Bewilligung *f*, Zuschuß *m*, Subvention *f*.

subver|sion [sʌb'və:ʃən] Umsturz *m*; Zerrüttung, Untergrabung *f*; **~sive** [-siv] umstürzlerisch, revolutionär; Umsturz-; gefährdend (*of* acc); **~t** [sʌb'və:t] *tr* umstürzen, zerstören; untergraben, -minieren, erschüttern; (sittlich) verderben, korrumpieren.

subway ['sʌbwei] unterirdische(r) Gang; Tunnel *m*; (Straßen-, Bahn-, Fußgänger-)Unterführung; *Am* Untergrundbahn, U-Bahn *f*; **~ rider** *Am* U-Bahn-Benützer *m*.

*

succeed [sək'si:d] *itr* folgen (*to* auf); nachfolgen; aufrücken; an die Stelle treten (*to s.o.* jds); antreten (*to an office* ein Amt); beerben (*to s.o.* jdn); Glück, Erfolg haben (*in an examination* bei e-r Prüfung); glücken, gelingen; *with s.o.* sich bei jdm durchsetzen; *tr* an die Stelle treten (*s.o.* jds); beerben (*s.o.* jdn); folgen (*s.th.* auf etw); *I ~* es gelingt mir (*in doing* zu tun); *to ~ to a business* ein Geschäft übernehmen; *to ~ to the throne* die Thronfolge antreten; **~ing** [-iŋ] aufea.-, nachfolgend.

success [sək'ses] Erfolg *m*, (glückliches) Gelingen *n*; erfolgreiche(r) Mensch *m*; *to be a ~*, *to meet with ~* Erfolg haben, erfolgreich sein; *to make s.th. a ~* etw zum Erfolg führen; mit etw Erfolg haben; *box-office ~* Kassenerfolg *m*; **~ful** [-ful] erfolgreich (*in everything* bei allem); glücklich; *to be entirely ~* e-n vollen Erfolg davontragen; **~ion** [-'seʃən] Nachrücken *n*, -folge; *jur* Erbschaft *f*, -recht *n*; Reihe(nfolge), (Aufea.-)Folge (*of* von); *in ~~* der Reihe nach; nach-, hintereinander; *law of ~~* Erbrecht *n*; *~~ of crops (agr)* Fruchtwechsel *m*; *~~ duty* Erbschaft(s)steuer *f*; *~~ in law* Rechtsnachfolge *f*; *~~ state* Nachfolgestaat *m*; *~~ to the throne* Thronfolge *f*; **~ive** [-'sesiv] aufea.folgend; Nachfolge-; **~or** [-ə] Nachfolger (*to* für); Erbe *m*.

succinct [sək'siŋ(k)t] kurz (u. bündig), knapp; kurzgefaßt, gedrängt; **~ness** [-nis] Kürze, Bündigkeit, Gedrängtheit *f*.

succory ['sʌkəri] *bot* Zichorie *f*.

succotash ['sʌkətæʃ] *Am* Gericht *n* aus Bohnen u. Maiskörnern.

succo(u)r ['sʌkə] *tr* helfen, Hilfe leisten (*s.o.* jdm), unterstützen; *s* Hilfe (-leistung), Unterstützung *f*, Beistand *m*.

succulen|ce, -cy ['sʌkjuləns(i)] Saftigkeit *f*; **~t** ['-t] saftig *a. bot*; *bot* fleischig; *fig* lebendig, frisch, anregend.

succumb [sə'kʌm] *itr* unterlegen sein; unterliegen, nachgeben (*to* dat); weichen (*before* vor); erliegen (*to a disease* e-r Krankheit); überwältigt werden (*to* von).

succursal [sə'kə:səl] Filial-, Tochter-, Zweig-; *rel* Hilfs-.

such [sʌtʃ, sətʃ] *a* solch, derartig, so(lch) ein(e); *adv* so, solch; *prn* so einer, solche (Leute) *pl*; so etwas, solche Sachen *f pl*; *Mr ~ a one* Herr Soundso; *~-and-~* solche, derartige *pl*; *no ~ thing* nichts Derartiges, nichts dergleichen; *as ~* als solche(r, s); so, entsprechend; *and ~* usw.; *some ~ thing* so etw ähnliches; *~ as* wie z.B., wie etwa; *~ as to*, *~ that* so, daß; derart, daß; *~ a thing* so etwas; *~ a long time* so lange (her); **~like** ['-laik] *a fam* dergleichen.

suck [sʌk] *tr* saugen (*from, out of* aus); *(Bonbon, Eis)* lutschen; saugen, lutschen an; *(Vorteil)* ziehen (*out of* aus); *itr* lutschen (*at* an); saugen; *s* Saugen, Lutschen; saugende(s) Geräusch *n*; *fam* Schluck; *sl* Reinfall *m*; *to ~ in* einsaugen; *Am sl* aussaugen, -nutzen; täuschen; *to ~ up* aufsaugen; *to s.o. (fam)* jdm Honig ums Maul schmieren; sich bei jdm einschmeicheln; *to give ~ to (e-m Kinde)* die Brust geben; *to ~ s.o.'s brains* jdn ausnutzen; jdn ausholen; *to ~ dry* völlig aussaugen; *to ~ o.'s thumb* am Daumen lutschen; **~er** ['-ə] *s* Saugende(r) *m*; *tech (~ing pipe)* Saugrohr *n*, -röhre, -scheibe *f*; Pumpenschuh *m*; *zoo* Saugscheibe *f*, -napf; *zoo* Seehase *m*; *bot* Saugwurzel *f (der Schmarotzer)*; Schößling; *fam* Bonbon *m od n*; *sl* Gimpel, Dussel *m*; *tr Am sl* 'reinlegen, für dumm verkaufen; **~ing** ['-iŋ] *zoo* saugend; *fig* unerfahren; *~~-disk (zoo)* Saugnapf *m*; *~~ pig* Spanferkel *n*.

suckl|e ['sʌkl] *tr* säugen; stillen; nähren, aufziehen; **~ing** ['-iŋ] Säugling *m*; Jungtier *n*; *fig* Anfänger *m*.

sucrose ['sju:krous] *chem* (Rohr-, Rüben-)Zucker *m*.

suction ['sʌkʃən] Saugen *n*; Sog; *mot* Hub *m*; **~ line** Absaugleitung *f*; **~ pipe, plate, pump, stroke, valve** Ansaugrohr *n*, Saugplatte, -pumpe *f*, -hub *m*, -ventil *n*.

*

Sudanese [su:də'ni:z] *s* Sudanese *m*, Sudanesin *f*; *a* sudanesisch.

sud|arium [sju(:)'dɛəriəm] *rel* Schweißtuch *n*; **~atorium** [-də'tɔriəm] *pl -ria* [-riə] Schwitzbad *n*; **~atory** ['sju:dətəri] *a* schweißtreibend; Schwitz-; *s* schweißtreibende(s) Mittel; Schwitzbad *n*.

sudden ['sʌdən] *a* plötzlich, jäh; unerwartet, unvorhergesehen; *s*: *all of a ~* (ganz) plötzlich; **~ly** ['-li] *adv* plötzlich, auf einmal; **~ness** ['-nis] Plötzlichkeit *f*.

sudori|ferous [sju:də'rifərəs] *med* schweißabsondernd; **~fic** [-fik] *a u. s* schweißtreibend(es Mittel *n*).

suds [sʌdz] *pl* Seifenwasser *n*, -lauge *f*, -schaum *m*; *Am sl* Bier *n*, *a.* Kaffee *m*; **~y** ['-i] *Am* schaumig.

sue [sju:] *tr* appellieren, ein Gesuch richten an; bitten (*for* um); gerichtlich verfolgen, belangen, verklagen (*for* auf); *itr* ein Gesuch einreichen; nachsuchen, -kommen, angehen, bitten (*to s.o. for* jdn um); klagen (*for* auf); *to ~ for a divorce* auf Scheidung klagen.

suède [sweid] Wildleder *n*.

suet ['sju:it] Nierentalg *m*, -fett *n* *(von Rindern* od *Schafen)*; **~y** ['-i] talgig.

suffer ['sʌfə] *tr* erleiden, -dulden; ertragen; erfahren, über sich ergehen lassen (müssen); dulden, zulassen, gestatten, erlauben; *itr* leiden (*from* an); Schaden nehmen, leiden (*from* durch); bestraft werden (*for* wegen); büßen (*for* für); *to ~ death* den Tod erleiden; *to ~ pain* Schmerz ertragen; **~able** ['-rəbl] erträglich; auszuhalten(d); tragbar, zulässig, statthaft; **~ance** ['-rəns] Leidensfähigkeit; Duldung *f*; *on ~~* (nur) geduldet; *to leave a bill in ~~* e-n Wechsel nicht einlösen; **~er** ['-rə] Leidende(r), Dulder; *med* Patient; *com* Geschädigte(r) *m*; **~ing** ['-riŋ] Dulden; Leiden *n*.

suffic|e [sə'fais] *itr tr* genügen, ausreichen (*for* für); befriedigen; **~iency** [sə'fiʃənsi] (e-e) genügende Menge *f* (*a ~~ of water* Wasser); genügende, ausreichende Mittel *n pl*, hinlängliche(s) Auskommen *n*; erforderliche Fähigkeit *f*; **~ient** [sə'fiʃənt] genügend, aus-, hinreichend, genug (*for* für); *he has ~~* es reicht ihm.

suffix ['sʌfiks] *s* Nachsilbe *f*, Suffix *n*.

suffocat|e ['sʌfəkeit] *tr* ersticken *a. fig*; *fig* unterdrücken; *itr* ersticken *a. fig* (*with* an); **~ion** [sʌfə'keiʃən] Ersticken *n*.

suffrag|an ['sʌfrəgən] Suffragan-, Weihbischof *m* (*to* für); **~e** ['sʌfridʒ] (Wahl-)Stimme; Zustimmung *f*; Stimmrecht *n*; Abstimmung; *rel* Fürbitte *f*; *woman ~~* Frauenstimmrecht *n*; **~ette** [sʌfrə'dʒet] Frauenrechtlerin, Suffragette *f*.

suffus|e [sə'fju:z] *tr* überfluten, übergießen, erfüllen, bedecken (*with* mit); eintauchen, hüllen (*with* in) *bes. fig*; *~~d with tears* tränenüberströmt; **~ion** [sə'fju:ʒən] Übergießen; *fig* Erröten *n*, Schamröte *f*; *med* Bluterguß *m*.

sugar ['ʃugə] *s* Zucker *m*; *fig* zuckersüße Worte *n pl*, Schmeichelei *f*; *Am sl* Moos, (leichtverdientes) Geld *n*; *Am sl* Liebling *m*; *tr* (über)zuckern; (ver)süßen; mit Zucker bestreuen; *fig* beschönigen, versüßen; *itr Am* Ahornzucker gewinnen; *sl* bummeln, bumm(e)lig arbeiten, sich von der Arbeit drücken; *to be all ~ (fig)* honigsüß sein; *to ~ the pill (a. fig)* die Pille versüßen; *beet-, cane-~* Rüben-, Rohrzucker *m*; *brown ~* braune(r) Zucker *m*; *caster, castor ~* Sandzucker *m*; *lump, cube, loaf ~* Würfelzucker *m*; *powdered ~* Puderzucker *m*; *~ of milk* Milchzucker *m*; **~-basin,** *Am* **-bowl** Zuckerdose *f*; **~-beet** Zuckerrübe *f*; **~-candy** Kandis(zucker) *m*; **~-cane** Zuckerrohr *n*; **~-coated** *a* mit Zucker überzogen, glasiert; *fig* zuckersüß, mundgerecht; **~-coating** Zuckerguß *m*, -glasur *f*; *fig* Schmeichelworte *n pl*; Beschönigung *f*; **~-daddy** *sl* ältere(r), großzügige(r) Liebhaber *m*; **~ed** ['-d] *a* gezuckert, (mit Zucker) gesüßt; *fig* verzuckert, mundgerecht; **~-icing** Zuckerguß *m*; **~-loaf** Zuckerhut *m*; **~-maple** *(nordamerik.)* Zuckerahorn *m*; **~-mill** *(Rohr-)* Zuckerfabrik *f*; **~-plum** *(harter, s)* Bonbon *m* od *n*; *fig* Schmeichelei *f*; **~-refinery** Zuckerraffinerie, -fabrik *f*; **~ report** *Am sl* Liebesbrief *m*; **~-tongs** *pl* Zuckerzange *f*; **~y** ['-ri] *a* Zucker-; süß; körnig; *fig* zuckersüß.

suggest [sə'dʒest, *Am* səg'dʒest] *tr* zu bedenken, zu verstehen geben; vorbringen, -schlagen (*doing* zu tun; *that* daß); anregen; nahelegen, einflüstern, suggerieren; andeuten, die Vorstellung *gen* erwecken; denken lassen, erinnern an; vermuten lassen, schließen lassen auf, deuten auf; meinen (*that* daß); *does this ~ anything to you?* können Sie sich etwas darunter vorstellen? **~ible** [-ibl] beeinflußbar; suggerierbar; **~ion** [-ʃən] Vorschlag *m*; Anregung; Einflüsterung *f*, Wink *m*; Gedankenverbindung; Andeutung, (schwache) Spur *f*, Anzeichen *n*, *fam* Idee (*of* von); Vermutung; Suggestion; Suggestividee *f*; *at his ~~* auf s-n Vorschlag hin; **~ive** [-iv] nachdenklich (stimmend), anregend, zu denken gebend; andeutend (*of* an); zweideutig, pikant, schlüpf(e)rig, lasziv; *psychol* suggestiv.

suicid|al [sjui'saidl] selbstmörderisch *a. fig*; Selbstmord-; **~e** ['sjuisaid] Selbstmord *a. fig*; Selbstmörder *m*; *to commit ~~* Selbstmord begehen.

suit [sju:t] *s* Ausrüstung, Garnitur *f*; *(~ of clothes)* (Herren-)Anzug *m*; (Damen-)Kostüm *n*; Satz *m*, Garnitur; *(Kartenspiel)* Farbe *f*; *Am fam (~ of hair)* Haarwuchs *m*; *(~ of teeth)* Zahnreihe *f*; *jur (law~, ~ at law)* (Zivil-)Prozeß *m*, Klage, Rechtsstreitigkeit *f*; Gesuch *n*, Antrag *m*, Eingabe; Werbung *f*, Heiratsantrag *m*; *tr* den Bedürfnissen entsprechen (*s.o.* jds), passend sein für, passen (*s.o.* jdm); (zu Gesicht) stehen (*s.o.* jdm), kleiden; passend machen, anpassen (*to* dat, an); es recht machen, gefallen (*s.o.* jdm); passend, recht, angenehm sein (*s.o.* jdm); etwas Passendes finden für; (ein)kleiden; *itr* passend, recht, brauchbar, angemessen sein; passen (*with* zu); übereinstimmen (*with* mit); *to ~ o.s.* nach s-m eigenen Willen handeln; *to ~ s.o.'s book (fam)* für jdn vorteilhaft sein; *to ~ s.o. down to the ground (fam)* wie gerufen kommen; haargenau richtig sein; *to ~ the action to the word* das Wort in die Tat umsetzen; *to bring ~ (jur)* Klage führen, prozessieren (*against* gegen); *to follow ~ (Kartenspiel)* bedienen, Farbe bekennen; *fig* sich nach (den) anderen richten, alles nachmachen, es auch tun; *to press o.'s ~* nicht nach-, *fam* nicht lockerlassen; *~ yourself* wie Sie wollen; *birthday ~ (hum)* Adamskostüm *n*; *civil, criminal ~* Zivil-, Strafprozeß *m*; **~ability** [-ə'biliti] = *~ableness*; **~able** ['-əbl] passend, geeignet, brauchbar (*for, to* für); angemessen, entsprechend (*for, to* dat); angebracht, schicklich; **~ableness** ['-əblnis] Geeignetheit, Brauchbarkeit; Angemessenheit; Angebrachtheit, Schicklichkeit *f*; **~case** Hand-, Reisekoffer *m*; **~ed** ['-id] *a* passend, geeignet (*for* für; *to be* als); *to be ~~ for* sich eignen für; sich qualifizieren als; **~ing** ['-iŋ] Anzugstoff *m*; **~or** ['-ə] *jur* Kläger *m*, Partei *f*; Bittsteller, Bewerber; Werber, Freier *m*.

suite [swi:t] Gefolge, Personal *n*, Stab; Satz *m (zs.gehörender Dinge)*, Reihe; *(~ of furniture)* Zimmereinrichtung, -garnitur; *mus* Suite; *(~ of rooms)* Zimmerflucht *f*.

sulf ... *Am s. sulph ...*

sulk [sʌlk] *itr* schlechte Laune haben, schlecht gelaunt, schlecht aufgelegt, verdrießlich sein; *(Frau)* schmollen (*with* mit); *(Kind)* trotzen; *s pl* üble Laune *f*; *to be in the ~s* schlechte Laune haben, mißgestimmt sein; **~iness** ['-inis] üble Laune; Mißgestimmtheit *f*; **~y** ['-i] *a* übel-, schlechtgelaunt, schlecht aufgelegt, mißgestimmt; schmollend; *s* leichter, zweirädrige(r) Wagen *m* mit nur e-m Sitz; *sport* Sulky *n*.

sullen ['sʌlən] verdrießlich, mürrisch, unfreundlich, eigensinnig; niederdrückend, dumpf, düster, trüb(e), traurig; träge; unheimlich, drohend; **~ness** ['-nis] Verdrießlichkeit, Unfreundlichkeit *f*; düstere(s), unheimliche(s) Wesen *n*.

sully ['sʌli] *tr fig* beflecken.

sulph|ate ['sʌlfeit] *s chem* Sulfat, schwefelsaure(s) Salz *n*; *tr agr* mit Vitriol spritzen; sulfatieren; *aluminium ~~* schwefelsaure Tonerde *f*; *copper ~~* Kupfersulfat *n*; *~~ of magnesia, of sodium* Bitter-, Glaubersalz *n*; *~~ paper* Natronpapier *n*; **~ide** ['-aid] *chem* Sulfid *n*; *hydrogen ~~* Schwefelwasserstoff *m*; **~ite** ['-ait] *chem* Sulfit *n*; **~onamide** [sʌl'fɔnəmaid, *Am a.* sʌlfə'næmid] *pharm* Sulphonamid *n*; **~ur** ['sʌlfə] *s* Schwefel *m*; *tr* ausschwefeln; *~~ dioxide* Schwefeldioxyd *n*; *~~ flower* Schwefelblüte *f*; **~urate** ['-fjureit] *tr* schwefeln; *chem* mit Schwefel verbinden; **~ureous** [sʌl'fjuəriəs] schwefel(halt)ig; schwefel-, grüngelb; **~uretted** ['sʌlfjuretid] *a*: *~~ hydrogen* Schwefelwasserstoff *m*; **~uric** [sʌl'fjuərik]: *~~ acid* Schwefelsäure *f*; **~urization** [sʌlfjuərai'zeiʃən] Schwefelung; Vulkanisierung *f*; **~urize** ['sʌlfjuəraiz] *tr* schwefeln; vulkanisieren; **~urous** ['sʌlfərəs, -fju-] schwefel(halt)ig; Schwefel-; *fig* höllisch; *fig* hitzig.

sultan ['sʌltən] Sultan *m*; **~a** [sʌl'tɑ:nə] Sultanin *f*; *orn* Purpurhuhn *n*; [səl'tɑ:nə] Sultanine *f*; **~ate** ['sʌltənit] Sultanat *n*.

sultr|iness ['sʌltrinis] Schwüle, drückende Hitze *f*; **~y** ['sʌltri] schwül *a. fig*; drückend; glühendheiß; *fig* feurig, glühend, hitzig; leidenschaftlich (erregt).

sum [sʌm] *s* (Geld-)Summe *f*, Betrag *m*; (Gesamt-)Ergebnis, Resultat *n*; Inbegriff *m*, Wesen *n*, Hauptinhalt, Höhepunkt *m*; *math* Summe; Rechenaufgabe *f*; *pl (Kindersprache)* Rechnen *n*; *tr* zs.zählen, -rechnen, addieren, summieren; zs.fassen, rekapitulieren; *itr* sich belaufen (*to* auf); *to ~ up (tr)* zs.zählen; zs.fassen, rekapitulieren; *adv* kurz u. gut, mit e-m Wort, alles in allem; *in ~* kurz (gesagt); in kurzen, in wenigen Worten, summa summarum; *to be good at ~s* gut im Rechnen sein; *to do ~s* rechnen; *lump ~* Pauschalsumme *f*; *~ of digits* Quersumme *f*; **~marization** [sʌmərai'zeiʃən] Zs.fassung *f*; **~marize** ['sʌməraiz] *tr itr* (kurz) zs.fassen; kurz darlegen; e-e (kurze) Zs.fassung sein (*s.th.* e-r S); **~mary** ['sʌməri] *a* kurz (zs.gefaßt), gedrängt; *jur* summarisch; *s* (kurze) Zs.fassung, Zs.stellung *f*; Abriß, Auszug *m*; *~~ of contents* Inhaltsangabe *f*; *~~ jurisdiction, proceedings (pl), procedure* Schnellverfahren *n*; *court of ~~ jurisdiction* Schnellgericht *n*; **~mation** [sə'meiʃən] *math* Addition *f*; **~ming-up** Zs.fassung *f*; **~ total** Gesamtsumme *f*, -betrag; *fig* eigentliche(r) Gehalt *m*, Wesen *n*.

summer ['sʌmə] **1.** *s* Sommer *m a. fig*; *a* Sommer-; sommerlich; *itr* den Sommer verbringen; *in (the) ~* im Sommer; *in the ~ of ...* im Sommer ...; *Indian, St Martin's, St Luke's ~* Altweibersommer *m*; **~ clothes** *pl* Sommerkleidung *f*; **~ day** Sommertag *m*; **~-house** Gartenhaus; Sommer-, Land-, Ferienhaus *n*; **~ holidays** *pl* Sommerferien *pl*; **~ lightning** Wetterleuchten *n*; **~like** ['-laik], **~ly**

['-li], **~y** ['-ri] sommerlich; Sommer-; **~ resort** Sommerfrische *f*; **~-school** Ferienkurs *m*; **~ solstice** Sommersonnenwende *f*; **~ term** Sommersemester *n*; **~time** Sommerszeit *f*; **~ time** Sommerzeit *f*; **2.** *arch* Tragbalken *m*, Träger-, Oberschwelle *f*; Kämpfer *m*.

summit ['sʌmit] Gipfel *m*, Spitze *f a. fig*; *fig* Höhepunkt *m*; *S~ (pol)* Gipfelkonferenz *f*; **~-level** *(Straße)* höchste Erhebung *f*; *at ~~ (pol)* auf höchster Ebene; **~ meeting, talk** Gipfeltreffen *n*, -besprechung *f*.

summon ['sʌmən] *tr (Sitzung)* einberufen; *jur* vor Gericht laden, vorladen; (zu sich) bestellen; holen, kommen lassen, rufen; *mil* zur Übergabe auffordern; *to ~ s.o. for s.th.* jdn wegen etw verklagen; *to ~ (up) o.'s strength* s-e Kräfte zs.nehmen; sich zs.reißen, alle Kraft aufbieten; **~s** ['-z], *pl -ses* ['-ziz] *jur* (Vor-)Ladung; Aufforderung *f*; *to serve a ~~ on s.o.* jdm e-e Ladung zustellen; *to take out a ~~ against s.o.* jdn vorladen lassen.

sump [sʌmp] Senkgrube *f*; Klärbecken *n*; *tech min* Sumpf *m*; *mot* Ölwanne *f*.

sumpter ['sʌm(p)tə] Saumtier; Packpferd *n*.

sumptu|ary ['sʌm(p)tjuəri] *a* Aufwands-, Luxus-; **~ous** ['-əs] kostspielig, verschwenderisch; prächtig, prunkvoll, pompös; **~ousness** ['-əsnis] Aufwand *m*; Pracht *f*, Prunk, Pomp *m*.

*

sun [sʌn] *s* Sonne; Sonne(nschein *m*, -nlicht *n*) *f*; *tr* sonnen; *itr* u. *to ~ o.s.* sich sonnen; *against the ~* gegen den Uhrzeigersinn; *in the ~* im Sonnenschein, in der Sonne; *under the ~ (fig)* unter der Sonne; auf der Welt; *to rise with the ~* mit der Sonne, in aller Herrgottsfrühe aufstehen; *to take, to shoot the ~ (mar)* den Sonnenstand messen; *his ~ is set (fig)* sein Stern ist erloschen; *midnight ~* Mitternachtssonne *f*; *a place in the ~* ein Platz an der Sonne; **~-arc, -lamp** *film* Jupiterlampe *f*; **~-bath** Sonnenbad *n*; **~-bathing** Sonnenbaden *n*, -bäder *n pl*; **~beam** Sonnenstrahl *m a. fig*; **~bird** *orn* Honigsauger *m*; **~-blind** Jalousie; Markise *f*; **~bow** *poet* Regenbogen *m*; **~burn** Sonnenbrand *m*; **~burned, ~burnt** ['-bə:nt] *a* sonn(en)verbrannt, braun(gebrannt); **~ cream** Sonnenkreme *f*; **~-cured, -dried** *a* in der Sonne getrocknet; **~ deck** *mar* Sonnendeck *n*; **~dew** *bot* Sonnentau *m*; **~dial** Sonnenuhr *f*; **~dog** Nebensonne *f*; **~down** *(dial, Am u. Übersee)* Sonnenuntergang *m*; **~downer** *(Am u. Übersee, fam)* Landstreicher; Dämmerschoppen; *mil sl* strenge(r) Offizier *m*; **~fast** *Am* lichtecht; **~flower** Sonnenblume *f*; **~-frock** Strand-, schulterfreie(s), leichte(s) Sommerkleid *n*; **~-glass** Brennglas *n*; *pl* Sonnenbrille *f*; **~-god** Sonnengott *m*; **~-hat, -helmet** Tropenhelm *m*; **~ irradiation** Sonnenbestrahlung *f*; **~ lamp** = *~-ray lamp*; **~less** ['-lis] *a* ohne Sonne; lichtarm; dunkel; **~light** Sonnenlicht *n*; **~lit** *a* von der Sonne beschienen; **~ lotion** Salbe *f* gegen Sonnenbrand; **~niness** ['-inis] Sonnigkeit; *fig* Heiterkeit *f*; **~ny** ['-i] sonnig; Sonnen-; *fig* warm, heiter, freundlich; *~~ side* Sonnen-, Lichtseite *f*; *on the ~~ side of* 50 noch keine, noch unter 50; *~~-side up (Am fam)* Spiegeleier *n pl*; **~ parlo(u)r, room, porch** Wintergarten *m*; **~proof** lichtfest; sonnenundurchlässig; **~-ray** Sonnenstrahl *m*; *~~ lamp* Höhensonne *f*; *~~ treatment* Bestrahlung *f* mit der Höhensonne; **~rise** Sonnenaufgang *m*; *at ~~* bei S.; **~set** Sonnenuntergang *m*; *at ~~* bei S.; **~shade** Sonnenschirm; breitrandige(r) Hut *m*; Sonnendach *n*, Markise; *phot* Gegenlichtblende *f*; **~ shield** Sonnenblende *f*; **~shine** Sonnenschein *m a. fig*; *~~ roof (mot)* Schiebedach *n*; **~shiny** sonnig *a. fig*; *fig* warm, hell, freundlich; **~spot** *astr* Sonnenfleck *m*; **~stricken, ~struck** *a*: *to be ~~* e-n Sonnenstich haben; **~stroke** Sonnenstich *m*; **~-tan** Sonnenbräune *f*; **~-up** *Am* Sonnenaufgang *m*; **~ visor** *mot* Sonnenblende *f*; **~-worshipper** Sonnenanbeter *m*.

sundae ['sʌndei] *bes. Am* Eiskrem *f* mit Zuckerguß, Früchten, Nüssen, Schlagsahne *od* Schokolade.

Sunday ['sʌndi] Sonntag *m*; *on ~(s)* am Sonntag, sonntags; **~ best, clothes** *pl fam* Sonntagsstaat *m*; **~ edition** Sonntagsausgabe *f*; **~ -go--to-meeting** *a Am fam* Sonntags-; *(Kleidung)* sonntäglich; **~ paper** Sonntagsblatt *n*; **~-school** Sonntagsschule *f*, Kindergottesdienst *m*; **~ supplement** Sonntagsbeilage *f*; **~ work** Sonntagsarbeit *f*.

sunder ['sʌndə] *poet lit tr (itr)* (sich) trennen (*from* von); entzweien; *s*: *in ~ (poet lit)* auseinander.

sundry ['sʌndri] *a* verschiedene, gemischte, mannigfache, diverse; allerlei, -hand; *s pl*: *sundries* Diverses *n*; alles mögliche; *com* diverse Unkosten *pl*; *all and ~* jedermann, ein jeder; alle miteinander.

sunken ['sʌŋkən] *a* versunken, untergegangen; eingesunken; tiefer gelegen, Hohl-; *(Wangen)* eingefallen; *(Augen)* tiefliegend; **~ road** Hohlweg *m*.

sup [sʌp] **1.** *itr tr* schlürfen, nippen (an); *s* Schluck *m*, Schlückchen *n*; *neither bite nor ~* nichts zu nagen u. nichts zu beißen; **2.** *itr* zu Abend essen (*on, off s.th.* etw).

super ['sju:pə] *s theat fam* Statist; *com fam* Super *m*, Spitzenprodukt *n*, -marke *f*, Supermarkt, (großer) Selbstbedienungsladen; *fam* Superintendent *m*; *a oft iro sl* Super-; super, piekfein, erstklassig, brillant, prima; *in Zssgen*: Über-, über, Super-, super-; Ober-.

superable ['sju:pərəbl] besiegbar, nicht unüberwindbar.

superabound [sju:pərə'baund] *itr* im Überfluß, reichlich vorhanden sein; Überfluß haben (*with, in* an).

superabundan|ce [sju:pərə'bʌndəns] Überfluß (*of* an); Überschuß *m*; **~t** [-t] im Überfluß vorhanden, (über)reichlich; überschwenglich.

superadd [sju:pər'æd] *tr* noch hinzutun, -fügen (*to* zu).

superannuat|e [sju:pə'rænjueit] *tr* pensionieren, in den Ruhestand versetzen; als veraltet abtun, *fam* zum alten Eisen werfen; **~ed** [-id] *a* pensioniert, ausgedient; altersschwach, veraltet, altmodisch, aus der Mode; verbraucht, abgenutzt; **~ion** [-rænju'eiʃən] Pensionierung; Pension *f*, Ruhegehalt *n*; *~~ fund* Pensionskasse *f*.

superb [sju(:)'pə:b] großartig, prächtig, stattlich; luxuriös, elegant; ausgezeichnet, hervorragend.

supercargo ['sju:pəka:gou] *pl -oes mar* Ladungsaufseher *m*.

supercharg|e ['sju:pətʃa:dʒ] *tr mot* vor-, überverdichten; aufladen; **~er** ['-ə] *mot* Vor-, Überverdichter, Kompressor *m*.

supercili|ary [sju:pə'siliəri] *a anat* Augenbrauen-; **~ous** [-əs] hochmütig, -näsig, anmaßend, arrogant, verächtlich; **~ousness** [-nis] Hochnäsigkeit; Herablassung *f*.

superduper ['sju:pədju:pə] *a Am sl* Super-, Riesen-, Bomben-; ganz groß, Klasse-.

supereminen|ce [sju:pər'eminəns] überragende Eigenschaft *f*; Vorrang *m*; **~t** [-t] weitaus überragend.

supererogat|e [sju:pər'erəgeit] *itr* über das Ziel hinausgehen, *fam* -schießen; **~ion** [-erə'geiʃən] zusätzliche, höhere Leistung *f*; *the works of ~~ (rel)* der Schatz der guten Werke; **~ory** [-e'rɔgətəri] zusätzlich; überzählig, -schüssig; überflüssig, unnötig.

superfici|al [sju:pə'fiʃəl] *a* Oberflächen-; *(Maß)* Flächen-; *fig* oberflächlich, flach, flüchtig; äußerlich, scheinbar, Schein-; **~ality** [-fiʃi'æliti] Oberflächlichkeit, Flachheit, Flüchtigkeit; Äußerlichkeit *f*; **~es** [-'fiʃi:z] Oberfläche *f a. fig*; *das* Äußere.

superfine ['sju:pəfain] überfeinert; hochfein.

superflu|ity [sju:pə'flu(:)iti] Überflüssigkeit *f*; Überfluß *m* (*of* an); **~ous** [s(j)u(:)'pə:fluəs] reichlich, überflüssig.

superheat [sju:pə'hi:t] *tr (Dampf)* überhitzen.

superhet ['sju:pə'het] *radio* Superhet(erodynempfänger) *m*.

superhighway [su:pə'haiwei] *Am* Autobahn *f*.

superhuman [sju:pə'hju:mən] übermenschlich.

superimpose ['sju:pərim'pouz] *tr* darauf-, darüberlegen (*on* auf); dazutun; *el* überlagern; *(Titel)* überdrucken; **~ition** [-pə'ziʃən] *tech* Überlagerung *f*.

superincumbent ['sju:pərin'kʌmbənt] darüberliegend, -hängend.

superinduce ['sju:pərin'dju:s] *tr* hinzufügen, -tun (*on* zu).

superintend [sju:prin'tend] *tr* die Oberaufsicht führen über; leiten, beaufsichtigen; überwachen; **~ence, -cy** [-əns(i)] Oberaufsicht (*over* über); (Betriebs-)Leitung *f* (*of* gen); **~ent** [-ənt] Aufsichtsbeamte(r); (Betriebs-) Leiter, Direktor, Manager; *Am* Hausverwalter *m*; *~~ officer* Amtsvorstand; Polizeidirektor *m*.

superior [sju(:)'piəriə] *a* höher, ober; besser (*to* als); überdurchschnittlich; hervorragend, vorzüglich; überlegen (*to* dat); anmaßend, arrogant; *(Wort, Plan)* umfassender; *s* Ranghöhere(r); Vorgesetzte(r); *rel* Prior *m*; *to be ~* übertreffen (*in* an); *~ in numbers* zahlenmäßig überlegen; *mother ~ (rel)* Oberin *f*; *three ~ (math)* hoch drei; **~ forces** *pl* Übermacht *f*; **~ity** [-piəri'ɔriti] höhere(r) Rang, Vorrang *m*; Überlegenheit (*to, over* über; *in* an); Anmaßung, Arroganz *f*; *~~ complex (psychol)* Machtkomplex *m*; **~ officer** Dienstvorgesetzte(r) *m*.

*

superlative [sju(:)'pə:lətiv] *a* höchst, best; hervorragend; äußerst, übertrieben; *gram* superlativisch; *s* höchste(r) Grad, Gipfel, Höhepunkt *m*; *gram* Superlativ *m*; *to speak in ~s* in Superlativen reden.

super|man ['sju:pəmæn] Übermensch *m*; **~market** ['-ma:kit] Supermarkt *m*, große(s) Selbstbedienungsgeschäft *n*.

supernal [sju(:)'pə:nl] *poet lit* hoch, hehr, erhaben.

super|natural [sju:pə'nætʃrəl] übernatürlich; **~normal** ['-'nɔ:məl] überdurchschnittlich; ungewöhnlich.

supernumerary [sju:pə'nju:mərəri] *a* überzählig; überflüssig; überplanmäßig; *s* überzählige Person *od* Sache *f*; *theat* Statist; Beamte(r) *m* auf Probe.

superpos|e ['sju:pə'pouz] *tr* darauf-, darüberlegen (*on* auf); auf-, überea.-legen; *el* überlagern; **~ition** [-pə'ziʃən] *geol* Schichtung; *el* Überlagerung *f*.

supersaturat|e [sjupə'sætʃu:reit] *tr scient* übersättigen; **~ion** [-sætʃu:'reiʃən] Übersättigung *f*.

superscri|be ['sju:pə'skraib] *tr* beschriften; **~pt** ['-skript] *math* Exponent *m*; **~ption** [sju:pə'skripʃən] Aufschrift; Adresse *f*.

superse|de [sju:pə'si:d] *tr* verdrängen; abschaffen, aufheben; an die Stelle treten (*s.o.* jds); ersetzen (*by* durch); *(Beamten)* ablösen, aus dem Amt entfernen; **~ssion** [-'seʃən] Aufhebung; Er-, Absetzung *f*.

super|sensible [sju:pə'sensəbl] (mit den Sinnen) nicht wahrnehmbar; **~sensitive** [-'sensitiv] hoch-, überempfindlich.

supersonic ['sju:pə'sɔnik] *a* Überschall-; *to fly at ~ speed* mit Überschallgeschwindigkeit fliegen; *~~ bang, flight, speed* od *velocity* Überschallknall, -flug *m*, -geschwindigkeit *f*; *~~ rocket-propelled fighter (aero)* Überschallraketenjäger *m*.

superstit|ion [sju:pə'stiʃən] Aberglaube *m*; **~ious** [-əs] abergläubisch.

superstruct|ion ['sju:pəstrʌkʃən], **~ure** ['-tʃə] Auf-, Ober-, Überbau *m*.

superven|e [sju:pə'vi:n] *itr* (noch) hinzukommen, -treten; unerwartet geschehen *od* eintreten, sich ereignen.

supervis|e ['s(j)u:pəvaiz] *tr* beaufsichtigen, die Aufsicht führen *od* haben über; kontrollieren, überwachen; **~ion** [sju:pə'viʒən] Beaufsichtigung, (Ober-)Aufsicht, Kontrolle (*of* über); Leitung, Direktion *f*; *to keep under ~~ (Kinder)* beaufsichtigen; **~or** ['-vaizə] Aufseher, Aufsichtsbeamte(r), Inspektor, Kontrolleur; Leiter, Direktor *m*; **~ory** [-'vaizəri] *a* Aufsichts-; leitend; *as a ~~ measure* zur Kontrolle; *~~ committee* Kontrollausschuß *m*.

supine [sju:'pain] *a* auf dem Rücken liegend; *poet* zurückgelehnt; *fig* passiv, gleichgültig, lässig, träge; *(Hand)* erhoben; *s* ['sju:pain] *gram* Supinum *n*.

supper ['sʌpə] Abendessen, -brot; Nachtmahl *n*; *to have ~* zu Abend essen; *the Last S~* das letzte Abendmahl; *the Lord's S~* das Abendmahl, die Kommunion, die Eucharistie.

supplant [sə'plɑ:nt] *tr* verdrängen; ausstechen, ersetzen (*by* durch); *s.o.* sich an jds Stelle setzen, jds Stelle einnehmen.

supple ['sʌpl] *a* biegsam, geschmeidig, elastisch *a. fig*, anpassungsfähig; gelenkig, wendig, behende; nachgiebig, entgegenkommend, gefällig; willfährig; servil, unterwürfig, kriechend; *tr* geschmeidig machen; *(Pferd)* zureiten; **~ness** ['-nis] Biegsamkeit, Geschmeidigkeit, Elastizität *a. fig*; Unterwürfigkeit *f*.

supplement ['sʌplimənt] *s* Ergänzung *f*, Zusatz (*to* zu); *(Buch)* Nachtrag, Anhang; Ergänzungsband *m*; *(Zeitung)* (Unterhaltungs-)Beilage *f*; *math* Ergänzungswinkel *m*; *tr* ['-ment] ergänzen; e-n Nachtrag liefern, e-n Zusatz machen zu; *to ~ a budget* den Nachtragshaushalt vorlegen; *literary ~* Literaturbeilage *f*; **~al** [səpli'mentl], **~ary** [-'mentəri] ergänzend; Zusatz-, Nachtrags-; *~ary agreement* Zusatzabkommen *n*; *~ary angle* Ergänzungswinkel *m*; *~ary claim* Nachforderung *f*; *~ary volume* Ergänzungsband *m*; *~ary wages (pl)* Lohnzulage *f*; **~ation** [-'teiʃən] Ergänzung, Vervollständigung, Erweiterung *f*.

suppli|ant ['sʌpliənt], **~cant** ['-kənt] *a* demütig bittend, flehend, beschwörend, eindringlich; *s* Bittsteller *m*; **~cate** ['-keit] *tr* demütig, inständig, flehentlich bitten (*s.o. for s.th.* jdn um etw); anflehen; *itr* nachsuchen (*for* um); **~cation** [sʌpli'keiʃən] demütige, inständige Bitte(n *n*) *f* (*for* um); Flehen; Bittgesuch *n*, -schrift *f*; **~catory** ['sʌplikətəri] demütig; flehend, bittend; Bitt-.

suppl|ier [sə'plaiə] Lieferant *m*, Lieferfirma *f*; *~~'s ledger* Wareneingangsbuch *n*; **~y** [sə'plai] *tr* liefern; be-, heranschaffen, besorgen, zur Verfügung stellen; verkaufen; ausstatten, beliefern, versorgen, versehen (*with* mit); *(Bedarf)* befriedigen, decken; *(Mangel)* ausgleichen, kompensieren, abhelfen (*s.th.* e-r S); ersetzen, ergänzen; nachzahlen; *(Stelle)* ausfüllen, besetzen; *(Platz)* einnehmen; vertreten (*s.o.* jdn); *(Familie)* unterhalten; *tech el* speisen; *a* Hilfs-; Lieferungs-, Versorgungs-, Nachschub-; *el* Speise-; *s* Lieferung (*to* an); Beschaffung; Zu-, Anfuhr, Belieferung, Versorgung (*of* mit); Ausstattung *f*; Vorrat, (Lager-)Bestand *m*; Lager; (Waren-)Angebot *n*; Proviant *m*; Nachzahlung *f*; Ersatz(mann), (Stell-)Vertreter *m*; Stellvertretung *f*; Unterhaltszuschuß; *el* (Netz-)Anschluß *m*; *pl* Zufuhren *f pl*; Vorräte *m pl*; Nachschub *m bes. mil*; *mil* Verstärkungen *f pl*; *parl* bewilligte(r) Etat *m*; *to ~~ the place of s.o.* jdn vertreten; *to vote ~~ (Br)* den Etat bewilligen; *bill of ~~ (parl)* Nachtragshaushaltsvorlage *f*; *committee of ~~* Haushaltsausschuß *m*; *electric ~~* Stromversorgung *f*; *food ~~* Lebensmittel *n pl*; *power ~~* Energieversorgung *f*; *source of ~~* Versorgungsquelle *f*; *~~ agreement* Liefervertrag *m*; *~~ and demand* Angebot u. Nachfrage; *~~ area* Versorgungsgebiet *n*; *~~ base* Nachschubbasis *f*; *~~ current* Netzstrom *m*; *~~ dump* Materialdepot *n*; *~~ of goods* Güterversorgung *f*; *~~ line* Versorgungslinie; Zuleitung *f*; *~~ main* Stromnetz *n*; *~~-pipe* Zuführungsrohr *n*, Zuleitung *f*; *~~ plant* Lieferwerk *n*; *~~ sergeant* Kammerunteroffizier *m*; *~-waggon* Lieferwagen *m*; *~~ of water* Wasserversorgung *f*.

support [sə'pɔ:t] *tr arch* (ab)stützen, tragen, halten; absteifen; *fig* unterstützen, tragen, fördern, begünstigen, billigen, verteidigen; befürworten; sich aussprechen für; (be)stärken, ermutigen; unterhalten, tragen, sorgen für; ernähren, unterstützen; *(Aussage)* stützen, bekräftigen, bestätigen; ertragen, aushalten, sich fügen, sich schicken in; aufrecht-, in Gang halten; *theat (Rolle)* spielen; zs.spielen mit; *to ~ o.s.* s-n Unterhalt selbst verdienen, sich ernähren; *s* Stützung; Halterung, Stütze, Strebe, Absteifung *f*, Träger, Mast, Untersatz *m*, Bettung, Auflage, Unterlage *f*, Lager; Stativ *n*; *(~ point)* Unterstützungspunkt *m*; (Schuh-)Einlage; *com* Stützungsaktion; *fig* Unterstützung *f*, Beistand *m*, Hilfe *f*, Rückhalt *m*; Befürwortung *f*; Versorger, Träger *(e-s Unternehmens)*; *theat* Partner; (Lebens-)Unterhalt *m*, Auskommen *n*, (Existenz-)Mittel *n pl*; *mil* Verstärkung *f*; *pl tech* Tragkonstruktion *f*; *in ~ of* zur Unterstützung, zur Begründung *gen*; als Beleg für; *close ~* Infanterieunterstützung *f*; *inability to ~ o.s.* Erwerbsunfähigkeit *f*; **~able** [-əbl] tragbar; erträglich, auszuhalten(d); **~ company** Bereitschaftskompanie *f*; **~ costs** *pl mil* Stationierungskosten *pl*; **~er** [-ə] Verfechter, Vertreter, Anhänger, Parteigänger, Förderer, Gönner *m*; Stütze *f*, Ernährer *m*; *tech* Stütze *f*, Träger, Halter *m*; Binde *f*, Bruchband *n*; **~ing** [-iŋ] *a* Unterstützungs-, Hilfs-; tragend, Stütz-; *~~ beam, cable, frame* Tragbalken *m*, -seil, -gerüst *f*; *~~ programme (film)* Beiprogramm *n*; *~~ strap* Traggurt *m*; *~~ tower* Abspannturm, -mast *m*.

suppos|e [sə'pouz] *tr* voraussetzen; annehmen, meinen, glauben, denken, der Ansicht sein; den Fall setzen; *~~* gesetzt den Fall, angenommen, falls; *I'm ~ed to do* es wird von mir erwartet, angenommen, daß ich tue; ich soll tun; *he's ~ed to be rich* er gilt als reich; *I ~~ so* vermutlich, wahrscheinlich; **~ed** [-d] *a* vermutet, vermutlich, angenommen, angeblich; **~edly** [-idli] *adv* mutmaßlich; angeblich; **~ing** [-iŋ] angenommen; **~ition** [sʌpə'ziʃən] Voraussetzung; Meinung, Vermutung, Annahme; Hypothese *f*; *on the ~~ that* unter der Annahme, daß; **~itional** [sʌpə'ziʃənl] mutmaßlich, angenommen, hypothetisch; **~ititious** [səpɔzi'tiʃəs] untergeschoben; falsch, unecht, nachgemacht, erfunden, erdichtet; angenommen, hypothetisch; **~itory** [sə'pɔzitəri] *med* Zäpfchen *n*.

suppress [sə'pres] *tr* unterdrücken; *(Gefühl)* ersticken; abschaffen; geheimhalten, verheimlichen, verschweigen; *(Skandal)* vertuschen; nicht (zur Veröffentlichung) freigeben, (durch-)streichen; unterbinden; *(Dokument)* unterschlagen; anhalten, zum Stehen bringen; *(Lachen)* verbeißen; *psychol* verdrängen; *med (Blutung)* stillen; **~ion** [sə'preʃən] Unterdrückung; *(Dokument)* Unterschlagung; Abschaffung; Geheimhaltung; *med* (Blut-)Stillung; *psychol* Verdrängung *f*; **~ive** [sə'presiv] *a* Unterdrückungs-; *~~ measures (pl)* Unterdrückungsmaßnahmen *f pl*; **~or** [-ə] *el* Entstörkondensator; Dämpfer *m*, Bremse *f*.

suppurat|e ['sʌpju(ə)reit] *itr* eitern, schwären; **~ion** [sʌpju(ə)'reiʃən] Vereiterung *f*; Eitern *n*; Eiter *m*; **~ive** ['sʌpjuəreitiv, -rətiv] *a* Eiter-; eitrig.

supra|mundane ['sju:prə'mʌndein] überweltlich; **~national** ['-'næʃənl] übernational.

suprem|acy [sju'preməsi] Vorrang *m*, Überlegenheit, überragende Stellung; Oberhoheit, höchste Gewalt *f*; *air, naval ~~* Luft-, Seeherrschaft *f*; **~e** [sju(:)'pri:m] (rang)höchst, oberst; vorzüglichst, best, ganz ausgezeichnet; größt, äußerst; letzt; *the ~~ authority* die Regierungsgewalt *f*; *the S~~ Being* das höchste Wesen, Gott *m*; *the ~~ command (mil)* der Oberbefehl, das Oberkommando; *~~ commander* Oberbefehlshaber *m*; *the S~~ Court (of Justice, of Judicature)* der Oberste Gerichtshof; *~~ punishment* Todesstrafe *f*; *the ~~ sacrifice* die Hingabe des Lebens; *the S~~ Soviet* der Oberste Sowjet.

surcharge [sə:'tʃɑ:dʒ] *tr* zuviel verlangen für, überteuern; überladen, -lasten *a. el*; mit Zuschlag, mit e-r

Strafgebühr belegen; *(Briefmarke)* überdrucken; *s* ['sə:tʃɑ:dʒ] Überbelastung, Überladung *a. el*; Überforderung, -teuerung; Sondergebühr *f*, Zuschlag *m*; Strafgebühr *f*; Nachporto *n*; *(Briefmarke)* Überdruck *m*.

surcingle ['sə:siŋl, -'-] Sattelgurt; *(Kutte)* Gürtel *m*.

surd [sə:d] *a math* irrational; *(Konsonant)* stimmlos; *s math* irrationale Größe *f*; stimmlose(r) Konsonant *m*.

sure [ʃuə, ʃɔə, ʃɔ:, ʃə:] *a pred* sicher, gewiß; feststehend; unfehlbar; zuverlässig; *adv fam* wirklich, sicher(lich), natürlich, selbstverständlich; allerdings; *for ~* sicherlich; *(fam) ~ enough* gewiß, sicher(lich), bestimmt, zweifellos; wirklich; *as ~ as* so sicher wie; *to be ~* wohl, zwar, sicherlich; *to be ~ of s.th.* e-r S sicher sein (*of winning* zu gewinnen); *to be, to feel ~ of o.s.* s-r selbst sicher sein, Selbstvertrauen haben; *to make ~* sich vergewissern (*of s.th.* e-r S; *that* daß); dafür sorgen, zusehen (*that* daß); um sicher zu gehen; *he is ~ to come* er wird sicher(lich) kommen; *be ~ not to forget your book* vergessen Sie ja Ihr Buch nicht; *are you ~ you won't come?* wollen Sie wirklich nicht kommen? *to be ~* wahrhaftig! **~-fire** *Am fam* todsicher; **~-footed** *a*: *to be ~~* e-n sicheren, festen Tritt haben; **~ly** ['ʃuəli] *adv* sicher(lich), gewiß, ohne Zweifel, bestimmt; *fam* vermutlich; *he ~~ ought to know that* das müßte er doch wissen; **~ness** ['ʃuənis] Sicherheit, Gewißheit *f*; **~ty** ['ʃuəti] *jur* Sicherheit, Garantie, Bürgschaft, Kaution *f*, Pfand *n*; Bürge, Garant *m*; *to become, to go, to stand ~~* Bürgschaft leisten (*for* für); *~~ bond* Kautions-, Garantieverpflichtung *f*; *~~ warrant* Bürgschaftserklärung *f*.

surf [sə:f] Brandung *f*; **~board** Brett *n* zum Wellenreiten; **~boat** Brandungsboot *n*; **~-riding** Wellenreiten *n*.

surface ['sə:fis] *s* Oberfläche *a. fig*; Außenfläche, -seite *f*; *fig das* Äußere; *math* Fläche; *aero* Tragfläche *f*; *a* oberflächlich; äußerlich; zu Wasser, zu Lande; *min* im Tagebau; *tr* oberflächlich bearbeiten; *(Straße)* mit e-m Belag versehen; *tech* glätten, polieren, plandrehen; *(U-Boot)* auftauchen lassen; *itr* auftauchen; e-e Straßendecke herstellen; *Am min* im Tagebau arbeiten; *on the ~* äußerlich; bei oberflächlicher Betrachtung; *min* über Tag; *under the ~* bei genauer Untersuchung; *to rise to the ~* an die Oberfläche kommen; **~ area** *math* Flächeninhalt *m*; **~ car** *Am* Straßenbahn(wagen *m*) *f*; **~ condition(s** *pl)* Oberflächenbeschaffenheit *f*; **~-craft** Überwasserfahrzeug *n*; **~-diggings** *pl*, **-mining** *Am min* Tagebau *m*; **~-grinding** Planschleifen *n*; **~-leakage** *el* Kriechstrom *m*; **~-line** *math* Mantellinie; *tele* Bodenleitung *f*; **~-mail** auf dem Landweg beförderte Post *f*; **~man** *rail* Streckenarbeiter *m*; **~-noise** *(Schallplatte)* Reibungsgeräusch *n*; **~ owner** Grundeigentümer *m*; **~ plate** *tech* Richtplatte; Planscheibe *f*; **~ printing** Walzendruck *m*; **~ soil** Mutterboden *m*; **~ tension** *phys* Oberflächenspannung *f*; **~ unit** Flächeneinheit *f*; **~ water** Straßenabwässer *n pl*; *min* Tagewasser *n*; **~ wave** *radio* Bodenwelle *f*; **~ wind** Bodenwind *m*.

surfeit ['sə:fit] *s* Übermaß (*of* an); Völlegefühl *n*; *fig* Übersättigung *f*, -druß, Ekel *m*; *tr* übersättigen, überfüttern; *to be ~ed* übersättigt sein (*with* von); *to ~* bis zum Überdruß.

surge [sə:dʒ] *s* Welle, Woge *a. fig*; Brandung, Sturzsee *f*; *el (~ of current)* Stromstoß *m*; *fig* Flut *f*, Wogen *f pl*; *itr* wogen, branden; *(Gefühl)* (auf-) wallen; *el* anschwellen, schwanken.

surg|eon ['sə:dʒən] Arzt, Chirurg; *mil* Sanitätsoffizier *m*; *dental ~~* Zahnarzt *m*; *~~ captain* Stabsarzt *m*; *S~~ General (Am mil)* Inspekteur *m* des Sanitätswesens; *~~ lieutenant (mil)* Oberarzt *m*; *~~ major (Br)* Oberstabsarzt *m*; **~ery** ['-əri] Chirurgie, operative Heilbehandlung *f*; Operationszimmer; Sprechzimmer *n*; *~~ hours (pl)* Sprechzeit, -stunde(n *pl*) *f*; **~ical** ['-ikəl] chirurgisch; orthopädisch; *~~ chest* Sanitätskasten *m*; *~~ cotton* (Verband-)Watte *f*; *~~ scissors (pl)* Wundschere *f*.

surl|iness ['sə:linis] mürrische(s) Wesen *n*; Schroffheit, Unfreundlichkeit *f*; **~y** ['sə:li] schlecht-, übelgelaunt, mürrisch; grob, unfreundlich, unhöflich.

surmise ['sə:mai:z] *s* Vermutung, (bloße) Annahme *f*; Argwohn *m*; *tr* [sə:'maiz] vermuten, annehmen; argwöhnen; *itr* Vermutungen anstellen; Argwohn hegen.

surmount [sə:'maunt] *tr* übersteigen, -treffen, -ragen; steigen, klettern über; *fig* überwinden, schlagen; *to be ~ed* gekrönt sein (*by, with* von); **~able** [-əbl] übersteigbar; *fig* überwindlich, schlagbar.

surname ['sə:neim] *s* Familien-, Zuname; Beiname *m*; *tr* e-n Beinamen geben (*s.o.* jdm).

surpass [sə:'pɑ:s] *tr* übertreffen, -ragen, -steigen (*in* an) *(a. quantitativ)*; hinausgehen über, mehr sein als; **~ing** [-iŋ] überdurchschnittlich, unübertroffen, ungewöhnlich; hervorragend.

surplice ['sə:pləs] *rel* Chorhemd *n*.

surplus ['sə:pləs] *s* Überschuß *m* (*of* an); Rest; *Am (~ profit)* Mehrertrag *m*, -einnahme *f*, Gewinnüberschuß *m*; Zugabe *f*; *a* überschüssig, -zählig; *accumulated ~* Kapitalreserve *f*; *appropriated ~* Gewinnrücklage *f*; *budget ~* Haushaltsüberschuß *m*; *cash ~* Kassenüberschuß *m*; *export, import ~* Ausfuhr-, Einfuhrüberschuß *m*; *operating ~* Betriebsüberschuß *m*; *~ of goods* Warenüberfluß *m*; *~ (of) money* Geldüberhang *m*; *~ in taxes* Steuerüberschuß *m*; **~age** ['-idʒ] Überschuß *m* (*of* an); überflüssige Worte *n pl*; *jur* unerhebliche(r) Einwand *m*; **~ area** Überschußgebiet *n*; **~ brought forward** *com* Gewinnübertrag *m*; **~ copies** *pl* Remittenden *f pl*; **~ interests** *pl* Zinsgewinn *m*; **~ load** Mehrbelastung *f*; **~ population** Bevölkerungsüberschuß *m*; **~ price** Mehrpreis *m*; **~ production** Überproduktion *f*; **~ revenue** Mehreinkommen *n*; **~ stock** Mehrbestand *m*; **~ supply** Überangebot *n*; **~ value** Mehrwert *m*; **~ weight** Über-, Mehrgewicht *n*.

surpris|e [sə'praiz] *tr* überraschen; (plötzlich) überfallen, überrumpeln; in Erstaunen *od* Verwunderung versetzen, erstaunen, verwundern, befremden; *s.o.* jdn Hals über Kopf veranlassen (*into doing* zu tun); *s.th. from s.o.* jdm etw abluchsen; *s* Überraschung, Überrumpelung *f*; plötzliche(r) Angriff, Überfall *m*; Erstaunen *n*, Verwunderung *f* (*at* über); *attr* Überraschungs-; überraschend; *(much) to my ~~* zu meiner (großen) Überraschung; *to be ~ed* überrascht sein; *at s.th.* sich wundern, staunen über; *to be ~ ed to see* staunen; *to catch, to take by ~~* überraschen; plötzlich überfallen; *to give s.o. a ~~* jdm e-e Überraschung bereiten; *to ~~ in the act* auf frischer Tat ertappen; *I should not be ~ed* es würde mich nicht überraschen; *you'll get the ~~ of your life* Sie werden Ihr blaues Wunder erleben; *nothing ~~s me any more* ich wundere mich über nichts mehr; *~~ attack* Überrumpelungsangriff *m*; *~~ party* nicht vorgesehene Tanzveranstaltung *f*; **~edly** [-idli] *adv* überraschend, ganz plötzlich; **~ing** [-iŋ] erstaunlich, überraschend.

surreal|ism [sə'riəlizm] Surrealismus *m*; **~ist** [-ist] *a* surrealistisch; *s* Surrealist *m*.

surrender [sə'rendə] *tr* übergeben, ausliefern, aushändigen; abtreten, überlassen, überantworten (*to* dat); verzichten auf; *(Hoffnung)* aufgeben; *(Versicherungspolice)* zurückkaufen; *(Grundstück)* auflassen; *itr* sich ergeben; *jur* sich stellen; *mil* kapitulieren, die Waffen strecken; *to ~ o.s. (fig)* sich *(e-m Gefühl)* hingeben (*to* dat); *s* Über-, Aufgabe, Aushändigung, Auslieferung; Preisgabe; Ergebung; Abtretung (*of* gen); *jur* Auflassung *f*; (Versicherungs-)Rückkauf *m*; *mil* Kapitulation, Waffenstreckung *f*; *to ~ to the police* sich der Polizei stellen; **~ value** Rückkaufswert *m*.

surreptitious [sʌrəp'tiʃəs] heimlich, erschlichen, unrechtmäßig, unecht; *(Blick)* verstohlen; **~ edition** *(unrechtmäßiger)* Nachdruck *m*.

surrogate ['sʌrəgit] *bes. rel* Stellvertreter; Nachlaßrichter; Ersatz *m*, Surrogat *n* (*of, for* für).

surround [sə'raund] *tr* umgeben, -fassen, einschließen *a. mil*, umzingeln; herumstehen um; *s* Umfassung, Einschließung; *Am* Treibjagd *f*; *to be ~ed with, by* umringt sein von; **~ing** [-iŋ] *a* umliegend; *s meist pl* Umgebung *f*; Milieu *n*, Umwelt *f*; *~~ circumstances (pl)* Begleitumstände *m pl*.

surtax ['sə:tæks] *s* Steuerzuschlag *m*; Sondersteuer *f*; *tr* e-n Steuerzuschlag erheben auf.

surveillance [sə:'veiləns] Überwachung, Beaufsichtigung; (Ober-)Aufsicht *f*; *under ~* unter Aufsicht; *police ~* Polizeiaufsicht *f*.

survey [sə:'vei] *tr* e-r eingehenden Prüfung unterziehen, genau prüfen, in Augenschein nehmen; übersehen, überblicken; besichtigen, prüfen(d betrachten), (über)prüfen, inspizieren; *(Land)* vermessen; *s* ['sə:vei] eingehende Prüfung; Besichtigung, Inspektion; Überprüfung, Begutachtung; (allgemeine) Übersicht *f*, Überblick *m* (*of* über); Landmessung, Vermessung *f*; vermessene(s) Land(stück) *n*; Grundriß, (Lage-)Plan *m*; *year under ~* Berichtsjahr *n*; *~ and valuation register* Kataster, Grundbuch *n*; **~or** [sə(:)'veiə] Feldmesser, Vermessungsbeamte(r), Geometer; Aufsichtsbeamte(r), Inspekteur, Inspektor; Sachverständige(r), Gutachter; *Am* Zollaufseher, -inspektor *m*; *~~ chain* Meßkette *f*; *~~ of mines (min)* Markscheider *m*; *~~'s office* Hochbauamt *n*, Bau(aufsichts)behörde *f*; *~~'s tape* Meßband *n*.

surviv|al [sə'vaivəl] Überleben *n*; Überrest *m*, -bleibsel *n*; *~ of the fittest (biol)* natürliche Zuchtwahl *f*; *~~ rate* Geburtenüberschuß *m*; **~e**

[sə'vaiv] *tr* überleben, -dauern; überstehen; *itr* fort-, überleben, am Leben bleiben; weiterbestehen; übrigbleiben; **~ing** [-iŋ] überlebend, hinterblieben; übrigbleibend; **~or,** *Am a.* **~er** ['-ə] Überlebende(r); Hinterbliebene(r) *m*; *~~s' insurance* Hinterbliebenenversicherung *f*.

suscept|ibility [səseptə'biliti] Beeinflußbarkeit; *med* Empfänglichkeit, Anfälligkeit (*to* für); Reizbarkeit *f*; *pl fig* empfindliche Stelle *f*; **~ible** [sə'septəbl] leicht beeinflußbar; aufnahmefähig; reizbar; *med* empfänglich, anfällig (*to* für); empfindlich (*to* gegen); geeignet (*of* für); fähig (*of* zu); *~~ of error* Irrtümern unterworfen; **~ive** [-iv] empfänglich; aufnahmefähig; **~ivity** [səsep'tiviti] Empfänglichkeit; Aufnahmefähigkeit *f*.

suspect [səs'pekt] *tr* verdächtigen, beargwöhnen, in Verdacht haben; Mißtrauen haben gegen, mißtrauen (*s.o.* jdm); argwöhnen, vermuten, annehmen; mutmaßen; *s* ['sʌspekt] *bes. jur* Verdächtigte(r) *m*; *a* verdächtig; *to be ~ed* im Verdacht stehen (*of doing* zu tun); *to be ~ of s.th.* verdächtig sein *gen*; *I ~ed as much* das dachte ich mir.

suspen|d [səs'pend] *tr* (frei) (auf-) hängen (*from* an); in der Schwebe halten, *fig* lassen; herabhängen lassen (*from* von); *fig* unentschieden lassen; ver-, aufschieben; (zeitweise) einstellen, unterbrechen; *(Vorschrift)* außer Kraft setzen; *(Verhandlung)* aussetzen; *(Beamter)* des Amtes entheben, suspendieren; *sport* (zeitweilig) ausschließen, sperren; *mil (Feindseligkeiten)* einstellen; *to be ~ded* schweben, hängen; *to ~~ payment* die Zahlungen einstellen; **~ded** *a*: *~~ animation* Scheintod *m*; *~~ ash* Flugasche *f*; *~~ ceiling* Hängedecke *f*; *~~ railway* Schwebebahn *f*; **~der** [-ə] Strumpfband *n*, -halter *m*; *pl Am* Hosenträger *m pl*; *~~-belt* Hüftgürtel *m*; **~se** [səs'pens] Unentschiedenheit, Ungewißheit; Unentschlossenheit; Spannung; Unsicherheit *f*; *jur* Vollstreckungsaufschub *m*; *in ~~* uneingelöst, unbezahlt; *to be, to keep, to remain in ~~* in der Schwebe, unentschieden sein, lassen, bleiben; *don't keep me in ~~ any longer* spanne mich nicht länger auf die Folter; *~~ entry* vorläufige Buchung *f*; **~sion** [səs'penʃən] Aufhängen *n*; Aufhängung, Aufhängevorrichtung; *mot* Federung; *chem* Suspension *f*; *mus* Vorhalt *m*, Halten *n (e-s Tones)*; *(Zahlungs-)* Aufschub *m*; (zeitweilige) Einstellung *f*; (zeitweiliger) Ausschluß *m*; *jur* Aufhebung *(e-s Gesetzes)*, Aussetzung, vorläufige Einstellung; (vorläufige) Amtsenthebung *f*; *sport* (zeitweiliger) Ausschluß *m*; *~~ of judg(e)ment* Urteilsaussetzung *f*; *~~ of payment* Zahlungseinstellung *f*; *~~ of work* Arbeitseinstellung *f*; *~~-bridge* Hängebrücke *f*; *~~-brooch* Ordensschnalle *f*; *~~-crane* Hängekran *m*; *~~ points (pl)* Auslassungspunkte *m pl*; *~~-railway* Schwebebahn *f*; *~~-strand* Tragseil *n*; **~sive** [-siv] aufschiebend; unentschlossen, unschlüssig; unsicher; **~sory** [-səri] *a* Hänge-; aufschiebend; *s (~~ bandage) med* Bruchband; Suspensorium *n*.

suspic|ion [səs'piʃən] *s* Verdacht, Argwohn *m* (*of, about* gegen); Ahnung *f*, Vorgefühl *n*; *fig* Andeutung, Spur *f*, Hauch *m* (*of* von); *tr Am fam* verdächtigen; *above ~~* über jeden Verdacht erhaben; *on (the) ~~* unter dem Verdacht (*of having done s.th.* etw getan zu haben); *to be under ~~* unter Verdacht stehen; **~ious** [-əs] verdächtig (*to* dat); argwöhnisch, mißtrauisch (*of s.o.* gegen jdn; *about, of s.th.* gegen etw); **~iousness** [-əsnis] Argwohn *m*, Mißtrauen *n* (*of* gegen).

sustain [səs'tein] *tr* stützen, tragen, halten; (aufrechter)halten; erhalten; unterstützen, -halten, sorgen für, ernähren; e-e Stütze, ein Trost sein für; (seelisch) stärken, ermutigen, trösten; Kraft geben (*s.o.* jdm); aushalten, ertragen, widerstehen (*s.th.* e-r S), durchstehen; durchmachen, erfahren; *(Verlust)* erleiden; *(Antrag)* annehmen; *(e-r Klage)* stattgeben; *(Behauptung, Anspruch)* stützen, bekräftigen, erhärten, bestätigen, beweisen; anerkennen; *(Vergleich)* aushalten; *(Interesse)* wachhalten; *theat (Rolle)* spielen; *mus (Note)* aushalten; **~able** [-əbl] zu halten(d); tragbar; ertragbar; **~ed** [-d] *a mus* getragen; *~~ fire (mil)* Dauerfeuer *n*; *~~ power* Dauerleistung *f*; *~~ signal* Dauerzeichen *n*; **~ing** [-iŋ] *a*: *~~ power* Steh-, Durchhaltevermögen *n*; *~~ program (Am radio)* Programm *n* (ohne Reklameeinschaltungen); *~~ wall* Stützmauer *f*.

sustenance ['sʌstinəns] Unterhalt *m*, Versorgung, Ernährung; Nahrung, Speise *f*, Essen *n*; Nährwert *m*.

sustentation [sʌstən'teiʃən] Unterstützung, Aufrechterhaltung; Unterhaltung, Versorgung, Ernährung *f*; (Lebens-)Unterhalt *m*, Nahrung *f*; **~ fund** Unterstützungsfonds *m*.

sutler ['sʌtlə] Marketender(in *f*) *m*.

suture ['sju:tʃə] *s med* (Zs.-)Nähen *n*; Naht *f a. anat bot*; *tr med* (zs.)nähen.

suzerain ['su:zərein] *hist* Lehns-, Oberherr *m*; **~ty** ['-ti] Lehns-, Oberherrschaft *f*.

svelte [svelt] schlank; anmutig; graziös, gewandt, geschmeidig.

swab [swɔb] *s* Mop, *mar* Schwabber *m*; Abstaubtuch *n*, Wischlappen *m*; *mil Art* Gewehrreinigungsgerät *n*; *med* Wattebausch *m*, Schwämmchen *n*, Tupfer; *med* Abstrich; *sl* Tolpatsch, Tölpel; *mar sl* Matrose *m*; *tr* scheuern, aufwischen; *med* abtupfen; *to ~ down (Am sl)* sich reinigen, baden; **~ber** ['-ə] Scheuernde(r *m*) *f*; *sl* Tolpatsch; Mop *m*.

Swabia ['sweibjə] Schwaben *n*; **~n** ['-n] *a* schwäbisch; *s* Schwabe *m*, Schwäbin *f*.

swack [swæk] *tr sl (to ~ up)* betrügen, hereinlegen; **~ed** [-t] *a sl* besoffen.

swaddl|e ['swɔdl] *tr* bandagieren; *(Säugling)* wickeln, in Windeln legen; *s pl Am* Windeln *f pl*; **~ing** ['-iŋ] Wickeln *n*; *~~-bands, -clothes, -clouts (pl)* Windeln *f pl*; *to be still in o.'s ~~-clothes (fig)* noch in den Anfängen stecken.

swag [swæg] *s sl* Diebesgut *n*; Beute *f*; unrechtmäßige(r) Gewinn *m*; *(Australien)* (Reise-)Bündel *n*; *itr obs u. Am* schwingen, schlenkern; *Am* zs.sacken, sich setzen; *(Australien)* trampen.

swage [sweidʒ] *s tech* Gesenk *n*; *tr* im Gesenk schmieden; hämmern.

swagger ['swægə] *itr* (einher)stolzieren; großtun, prahlen, aufschneiden, *fam* angeben (*about* mit); *sl* große Bogen spucken; *s* Stolzieren *n*; Prahlerei, *fam* Angabe *f*; *a fam* schick, fesch; **~-cane, -stick** *mil* (Ausgeh-) Stöckchen *n*; **~er** ['-rə] Prahler, Prahlhans, Aufschneider, *fam* Angeber *m*.

Swahili [swɑ:'hi:li] Suaheli *n*.

swain [swein] *poet* Bauernbursch(e); Schäfer, *hum* Liebhaber *m*.

swallow ['swɔlou] **1.** *zoo* Schwalbe *f*; **~-dive** *Br sport* Kopfsprung *m*; **~-tail** *ent tech* Schwalbenschwanz *m*; = **~-tailed coat** Frack *m*, *fam* Schwalbenschwanz *m*; **2.** *tr* (hinunter-, ver)schlucken, verschlingen; *fig (to ~ up)* aufnehmen, umfassen, verschlingen, auffressen, aufbrauchen; *(Gesagtes)* zurücknehmen; *(Beleidigung)* (hinunter)schlucken, einstekken; *(Gefühlsregung)* unterdrücken; glauben, für bare Münze nehmen; *itr* schlucken; *s* Schlucken *n*; Schluck *a. tech*; Schlund, Rachen *m*, Kehle *f*.

swamp [swɔmp] *s* Sumpf, Morast *m*, Moor *n*; *tr* versenken; überschwemmen, -fluten, unter Wasser setzen; *mar* vollaufen lassen; *fig* zugrunde richten, ruinieren; *Am pol (Gesetz)* zu Fall bringen; *fam* zudecken, überhäufen (*with work* mit Arbeit); *itr* versinken, untergehen; *mar* vollaufen, vollschlagen; **~er** ['-ə] *Am sl* (Lastwagen-)Beifahrer; Gepäckträger *m*; **~ fever** Sumpffieber *n*, Malaria *f*; **~land** Sumpfland *n*; **~y** ['-i] sumpfig, morastig.

swan [swɔn] Schwan *m*; *black ~ (fig)* weiße(r) Rabe *m*; **~ dive** *Am* Kopfsprung *m*; **~ maiden** *(Mythologie)* Schwanenjungfrau *f*; **~-neck** Schwanenhals *m a. tech*; **~'s down** Schwanendaunen *f pl*; *Art* feine(r), dicke(r) Wollstoff *m*; **~-skin** Weichflanell *m*; **~-song** Schwanengesang *m*.

swank [swæŋk] *s* protzige(s) Benehmen *n*; Angeberei; *Am sl* Eleganz *f*; Angeber *m*; *a Br sl* protzig, aufgedonnert, -getakelt; *Am sl* elegant; *itr sl* protzen, angeben; **~y** ['-i] *Br sl* protzig, protzenhaft; *Am sl* betont elegant; luxuriös.

swap, swop [swɔp] *tr fam* (um)tauschen (*for* für); *fam* entlassen, auf die Straße setzen; *itr* Tauschgeschäfte machen; *s fam* Tausch(geschäft *n*) *m*.

sward [swɔ:d] *lit* Rasen *m*.

swarm [swɔ:m] **1.** *s* (Bienen-, Insekten-, Menschen-)Schwarm *m*; *fig* Gewimmel, Getümmel, Gedränge *n*; *itr (Bienen)* schwärmen; schwirren, sich drängen (*into* in); zs.strömen; wimmeln (*with* von); *tr fig* überschwemmen; **2.** *itr* klettern; *tr* erklettern, erklimmen.

swarth|iness ['swɔ:ðinis] dunkle Hautfarbe *f*; **~y** ['swɔ:ði] dunkel(häutig).

swash [swɔʃ] *itr* platschen, klatschen, planschen; *(Wasser)* rauschen; spritzen, zischen; *tr* schlagen gegen, bespritzen; *s* Platschen, Klatschen, Planschen, Spritzen *n*; Sturzbach *m*; **~buckler** ['-bʌklə] Eisenfresser, Bramarbas, Renommist *m*; **~buckling** ['-bʌkliŋ] *a* prahlerisch; *s* Renommieren *n*.

swastika ['swæstikə, 'swɔstikə] Hakenkreuz *n*.

swat, swot [swɔt] **1.** *tr fam* schlagen, knallen, klappen, klatschen; *s fam* Schlag, Klaps *m*; **~ter** ['-ə] Schlagende(r) *m*; *(fly-~~)* Fliegenklappe *f*; **2.** *s. swot* 1.

swath [swɔ:θ, *pl* -ðz] *(Mähen)* Schwaden; Streifen *m*, Reihe *f*.

swathe [sweið] *tr* (um)wickeln, bandagieren (*with* mit); *(Band)* wickeln; (ein)hüllen (*in* in); *s* Binde, Bandage; *med* feuchte Packung *f*.

sway [swei] *itr* schwanken, schwingen; sich neigen, sich lehnen; *fig* (hin-) neigen, tendieren (*towards* zu); herrschen; *tr* schwingen, schwenken; neigen; *fig* geneigt machen (*towards* für); beeinflussen; zum Schwanken, ins Wanken bringen; mitreißen;

s Schwanken, Schwingen; *(Korn)* Wogen *n*; *fig* Schwung *m*, Kraft, Gewalt, Macht, Herrschaft *f*, Einfluß; Herrschaftsbereich *m*; *to be easily ~ed* leicht beeinflußbar sein; *to hold ~ over s.o.* jdn in der Gewalt haben.

swear [swɛə] *irr swore* [swɔ:], *sworn* [swɔ:n] *itr* schwören (*by* bei, auf); *jur* unter Eid aussagen; beschwören (*to s.th.* etw; *to having done s.th.* etw getan zu haben); fluchen (*at s.th.* auf etw); beschimpfen (*at s.o.* jdn); *tr* (be)schwören (*s.th. against s.o.* etw gegen jdn); *(Eid)* leisten; vereidigen (*s.o. in s.th.* jdn in e-r S; *to s.th.* auf etw); *to ~ in s.o.* jdm den Diensteid abnehmen; *to ~ off (fam)* abschwören; aufgeben; **~ing** ['-riŋ] Schwören; Fluchen *n*; Eidesleistung *f*; *~~-in* Be-, Vereidigung *f*; **~-word** Fluch *m*.

sweat [swet] *itr* schwitzen (*with* vor) *a. allg*; *(Gefäß, Scheibe)* sich beschlagen; *fam* schwitzen, schuften, schwer arbeiten; *tr* ausschwitzen *a. allg*; schwitzen lassen, zum Schwitzen bringen *a. allg*; *(Kleidung)* durchschwitzen; *(to ~ out)* ausschwitzen; schuften lassen; *(Arbeiter)* ausbeuten, schinden, schlecht bezahlen; *fam* ausquetschen, zu e-m Geständnis bringen, auspressen; *tech* schmelzen; schweißen, löten; *s* Schweiß *m*; Schweißwasser; Schwitzen *n*; *fig* Plackerei; Ungeduld, Unruhe, Aufregung *f*; *sl fig* alte(r) Hase *m*; *to ~ down (Am fam)* zs.schmelzen lassen; zs.pressen; *to ~ all over* am ganzen Körper schwitzen; *to ~ out* geduldig abwarten; herauspressen (*s.o.* aus jdm); *to ~ it out (Am sl)* e-e schwierige Zeit durchstehen; *by the ~ of his brow* im Schweiße s-s Angesichts; *in a ~, (fam) all of a ~* schweißtriefend; in Schweiß gebadet; *in a cold ~* mit Angstschweiß auf der Stirn; *to be in a ~* in Schweiß gebadet sein; *to wipe the ~ from o.'s brow* den Schweiß von der Stirne wischen; *to ~ blood (fig)* Blut u. Wasser schwitzen; **~-band** Schweißband *n*; **~-cloth** Schweißblatt *n*; **~-duct** Schweißpore *f*; **~ed** ['-id] *a* für Hungerlöhne hergestellt; *(Arbeit)* schlecht bezahlt; *(Arbeiter)* ausgebeutet; **~er** ['-ə] Sweater, Pullover *m*; schweißtreibende(s) Mittel *n*; Leuteschinder *m*; **~-gland** Schweißdrüse *f*; **~ing** ['-iŋ] Schwitzen; *Am* verschärfte(s) Verhör *n*; Ausbeutung *f*; *~~-bath* Schwitzbad *n*; *~~-system* Ausbeutungssystem *n*; *~~-thimble* Lötschuh *m*; **~-producing** schweißtreibend; **~-shirt** Trainingsbluse *f*; **~-shop** Ausbeuterbetrieb *m*; **~y** ['-i] schwitzend; schweißbedeckt; *(Hand)* feucht; Schweiß-; schweißtreibend; *(Arbeit)* anstrengend; *~~ odour* Schweißgeruch *m*.

Swed|e [swi:d] Schwede *m*; Schwedin *f*; **~en** ['-n] Schweden *n*; **~ish** ['-iʃ] schwedisch(e Sprache *f*).

sweep [swi:p] *irr swept, swept* [swept] **1.** *tr (Raum)* (aus)fegen, -kehren; *(Tisch)* abwischen; *(Schmutz)* wegfegen, -kehren, -wischen; *allg* (hin)wegfegen, -blasen; fahren (*s.th. through s.th.* mit e-r S durch etw); fegen, fahren über, streifen; durchstreifen, absuchen; *(Grund e-s Gewässers)* mit dem Netz absuchen; *mil (mit Feuer)* bestreichen; *(mit e-m Scheinwerfer)* absuchen; *(Minen)* räumen; *(Knicks)* machen; *fam (Spiel)* machen, gewinnen; *(Wahl)* haushoch gewinnen; im Sturm erobern, überall populär werden (*the country* im Land); **2.** *itr* (dahin)fegen, -fahren; (vorbei-, vorüber)rauschen; *(Frau)* hinausrauschen (*out of a room* aus e-m Zimmer); *(Kleid)* schleppen; sich in weitem Bogen winden (*round* um); **3.** *s* Fegen, Kehren; Sausen *n*, Schwung; Schlag *m*; Schleppen, Vorüberrauschen *n*; Bereich *m* od *n*, Spielraum *m*; *tech* Schwenken *n*; Schußweite *f*, -feld *n*; Ausdehnung, Strecke, Fläche *f*; weite(r) Bogen *m*, Kurve, Krümmung, fließende Linie; schwungvolle Handbewegung; Auffahrt *f*; Gewinnen *n* aller Einzelspiele *od* Entscheidungen; Gesamt-, vollkommene(r), glänzende(r) Sieg; *aero* Streifen-, Angriffsflug; *(Radar)* Abtaststrahl *m*, Strahlablenkung *f*; *(chimney ~)* Schornstein-, Kaminkehrer *m*; lange(s) Ruder *n*; (Brunnen-)Schwengel; *sl* Schuft *m*; *pl* Kehricht *m* od *n*; **4.** *to ~ away, off* (hin)wegfegen, -raffen; wegschwemmen; *fig* mitreißen; *to ~ back* zurückfluten; *to ~ up* auffegen, zs.-kehren; *to be swept off o.'s feet (fig)* nicht (mehr) an sich halten können; ganz mitgerissen sein; *to give s.th. a ~* etw kehren; *to make a clean ~ of (fig)* reinen Tisch machen, aufräumen mit; e-n durchschlagenden Erfolg davontragen bei; *to ~ all before one* immer, ununterbrochen Erfolg haben; *to ~ the board* alles gewinnen, e-n vollen Erfolg haben; *a new broom ~s clean (prov)* neue Besen kehren gut; *as black as a ~* pechschwarz; **~er** ['-ə] Straßenkehrer, -feger *m*; Kehrmaschine *f*; Kohlentrimmer *m*; *mar* Räumboot *n*; *carpet-~~* Teppichkehrmaschine *f*; **~-gate** Flügeltor *n*; **~ing** ['-iŋ] *a* ausgedehnt, weitreichend, (weit) ausgreifend, weittragend; gründlich, umfassend, durchgreifend, vollständig, überwältigend; radikal; *s pl* Kehricht *m* od *n*; *fig* Hefe *f*; *~~ fire (mil)* Streu-, Strichfeuer *n*; *~~-gear* Minensuch-, -räumgerät *n*; **~-net** Schmetterlings-, Schleppnetz *n*; **~stake** *Art* Lotterie *f* (bei der der Gesamteinsatz an die Spieler ausgezahlt wird); *pl* (Haupt-)Gewinn *m*.

sweet [swi:t] *a* süß *a. fig*; *fig* angenehm, lieblich, duftig; gefällig, anmutig, hübsch; lieb, freundlich (*to* gegenüber, zu); frisch, unverbraucht; *(Boden)* fruchttragend, -bar; *fam* reizend, goldig; *chem* säure-, schwefelfrei; *s* Süße; Süßigkeit; Süßspeise *f*, Nachtisch; *fig* Liebling *m*, Liebchen *n*; *pl* Süßigkeiten *f pl*, Bonbons *m* od *n pl*; *at his own ~ will* ganz nach s-m Belieben; *to be ~ (fam)* verknallt, verschossen, verliebt sein (*on* in); duften (*with* nach); *to taste the ~s of success* den Erfolg auskosten; **~bread** *(Küche)* (Kalbs-)Bröschen *n*; **~brier, ~briar** ['-'braiə] Hecken-, Hundsrose *f*; **~ chestnut** Eßkastanie *f*; **~ cider** Süßmost *m*; **~ clover** *bot* Honig-, Steinklee *m*; **~-corn** *bot* Süßkorn *n*, Zuckermais *m*; **~en** ['-n] *tr* süßen, zuckern; *fig* versüßen; *sl* bestechen; mildern, abschwächen; *Am fin fam* aufbessern, nachhelfen (*s.th.* e-r S); *to ~ up (Am sl)* um den Bart streichen (*s.o.* jdm); **~ening** ['-niŋ] Versüßen; Mittel *n* zum Süßen; **~heart** Liebchen *n*; **~ie** ['-i] *fam* Schleckerei *f*; *fam* Herzchen *n*; **~ing** ['-iŋ] Johannisapfel *m*; *~~ agent* Süßstoff *m*; **~ish** ['-iʃ] süßlich; **~meat** Süßigkeit *f*, Bonbon *m*, *bes.* kandierte Frucht *f*; **~ness** ['-nis] Süßigkeit *f*; Wohlgeschmack; Duft *m*; *fig* Lieblichkeit, Anmut, Süße; Frische; Reinheit *f*; **~ oil** Olivenöl *n*; **~pea** *bot* Garten-, spanische Wicke *f*; *Am sl* Liebling; *Am sl* Tölpel *m*; **~ potato** Süßkartoffel, Batate *f*; **~-scented** *a* wohlriechend, duftend; **~shop** Schokoladengeschäft *n*; **~-talk** *Am sl itr* Süßholz raspeln; *tr* Schmeicheleien sagen (*s.o.* jdm); **~-tempered** *a* sanft(mütig); **~ tooth**: *to have a ~~ (fam)* ein Schlecker, Süßmaul sein; **~ water** Süßwasser *n*; **~-william** *bot* Bartnelke *f*.

swell [swel] *irr ~ed, ~ed* od *swollen itr (to ~ up, out)* (an)schwellen (*into* zu; *with* von); sich (auf)blähen *a. fig* (*with* vor); sich bauschen, sich ausbauchen; sich ausdehnen; zunehmen, stärker werden, anwachsen (*to* zu); sich steigern; *fig* bersten (*with* vor); *fig* sich brüsten; *tr* aufblasen, -blähen (*with* vor) *a. fig*; anschwellen lassen; erweitern, vergrößern, ausweiten; verstärken; ausbauchen; *s* (An-)Schwellung; Beule; Ausbauchung; Stauung *f*; Anwachsen *n*, Zunahme, Verstärkung *f*, Stärkerwerden; *mus* Anschwellen, Crescendo *n*; Orgelschweller *m*; *mar* Dünung *f*; *fam* Stutzer, Dandy *m*; hohe(s) Tier *n*; *fig* Kanone *f* (*at* in); *a fam* flott, fesch, elegant; *Am fam* prima, pfundig, glänzend, großartig; liebenswürdig, reizend; *to come the heavy ~ over s.o. (sl)* bei jdm durch lautes Tönen Eindruck schinden; *to have a, to suffer from a ~ed head (fam)* an Größenwahn leiden; *he has a ~ed head* ihm ist der Kamm geschwollen; **~ing** ['-iŋ] *s* Anschwellen *n*, Zunahme, Verstärkung; Wölbung, Schwellung, Geschwulst, Beule *f*; *tech* Wulst *m*; *a* geschwollen *a. fig*; geschwungen; ausgebaucht, -gebeult; **~-mob(sman)** ['-mɔb(zmən)] *sl* Hochstapler, Taschendieb *m*.

swelt|er ['sweltə] *itr fig* vor Hitze umkommen *od* vergehen *od* zerfließen; drückend heiß sein; *(Person)* in Schweiß gebadet sein; *s* fürchterliche(s) Schwitzen *n*; Glut-, Backofenhitze *f*; **~ering** ['-riŋ], **~ry** ['-ri] drückend, glühend heiß; schwül.

swept [swept] *pret u. pp von sweep*; **~(-back) wing** *aero* Pfeilflügel *m*; **~ volume** *mot* Hubraum *m*.

swerve [swə:v] *itr* abweichen, -schweifen, -gehen, -kommen (*from* von); *mot* schleudern; *tr* abbringen, ablenken (*from* von); *sport (Ball)* schneiden; *s* Drehung *f*.

swift [swift] *a* schnell, rasch, flink, eilig, hurtig; *(Zeit)* flüchtig; unverzüglich; *lit* schnell bereit (*to* zu); *s tech* Trommel, Haspel *f*; *orn* Segler *m*; *zoo* Eidechse *f*; Molch *m*; *chimney ~* Mauer-, Turmsegler *m*, -schwalbe *f*; **~-footed** *a* schnellfüßig; **~-handed** *a* geschickt; **~ly** ['-li] *adv* geschwind, schnell; **~ness** ['-nis] Schnelligkeit *f*.

swig [swig] *tr itr fam* saufen; *itr* zechen; *s fam* tüchtige(r) Schluck, lange(r) Zug *m* (*at a bottle* aus e-r Flasche).

swill [swil] *tr* spülen, abwaschen; hinunterspülen; *sl* saufen; *itr sl* saufen; *to ~ out* ausspülen; *s* Spülwasser, Spülicht; Spülen, Abwaschen *n*; Schweinefutter; *fam* Gesöff *n*, Fraß *m*; *to give s.th. a ~ out* etw tüchtig ausspülen.

swim [swim] *irr swam* [swæm], *swum* [swʌm] *itr* schwimmen (*on* auf) *a. fig*; *(auf d. Wasser)* treiben; triefen, überfließen, unter Wasser stehen; *med* schwindlig sein; sich drehen (*before o.'s eyes* vor jds Augen); *tr* schwimmen in; hinüber-, durchschwimmen; schwimmen lassen; um die Wette schwimmen (*s.o.* mit jdm);

(Pferd) in die Schwemme reiten; *s* Schwimmen *n*; geschwommene Strecke; Schwimmblase *f*; fischreiche(s) Gewässer; *med fam* Schwindelgefühl *n*; *to be in (out of) the ~* (nicht) auf dem laufenden, auf der Höhe, im Bilde sein; *to have, to take, to go for a ~* schwimmen, baden (gehen); *to ~ with the tide (fig)* mit dem Strom schwimmen; *his eyes were ~ming with tears* die Augen standen ihm voller Tränen; *my head is ~ming* mir dreht sich alles, mir schwindelt; es schwimmt mir alles vor den Augen; **~mer** ['-ə] Schwimmer *m*; *zoo* Schwimmblase *f*; **~ming** ['-iŋ] *s* Schwimmen; *(~~ of the head)* Schwindelgefühl *n*; *a* schwimmend; *(Augen)* in Tränen gebadet; schwind(e)lig; *fig* glatt, reibungslos; *~~-bath, -pool* Schwimmbad, -becken *n*; *~~-belt* Schwimmgürtel *m*; *~(~)-bladder* Schwimmblase *f (d. Fische)*; *~~ costume* Badeanzug *m*; *~~ gala* Wassersportfest *n*; *~~ match* Wettschwimmen *n*; **~mingly** ['-iŋli] *adv* spielend, wie am Schnürchen; glatt, leicht; *everything went ~~* alles ging glatt (vonstatten); **~ suit** Badeanzug *m*.

swindl|e ['swindl] *tr* beschwindeln, betrügen (*s.o. out of s.th., s.th. out of s.o.* jdn um etw); erschwindeln (*s.th. out of s.o.* etw von jdm); *s* Schwindel, Betrug *m*; *Am sl* Geschäft *n*; **~er** ['-ə] Schwindler, Betrüger; Hochstapler *m*.

swin|e [swain] *inv* Schwein *n a. fig pej*; *pej* Sau *f fig*; *~~-bread* Trüffel *f*; *~~-herd* Schweinehirt *m*; **~ish** ['-iʃ] *pej* schweinisch, säuisch, schmutzig.

swing [swiŋ] *irr swung, swung* [swʌŋ] *itr* schwingen; sich frei bewegen, schlenkern, baumeln, schaukeln, schwanken; hängen (*for* wegen) *(a. am Galgen)*; sich drehen; (sich) schaukeln; rhythmisch gehen; *mar* schwojen; *Am sl* aus sich selbst heraus entstehen; *to ~ to and fro* hin- u. herschwingen, pendeln; *tr* schwingen, (herum)schwenken; schaukeln; schlenkern, schleudern; (auf)hängen; *(Propeller)* durchdrehen; *fam (Sache)* schaukeln, drehen, verstehen; *Am fam* beeinflussen, umstimmen; *mus* als Swing bearbeiten *od* spielen; *to ~ (a)round* (sich) herumdrehen; *to ~ in* einschwenken; *to ~ out* ausschwenken; *s* Schwingen *n*, Schwingung, Drehung *f*, Schlenkern, Baumeln, Schaukeln, Schwanken *n*; (weit) ausholende(r) Schlag; *(Skala)* Ausschlag; Schwung(kraft *f*) *m*; freie Bewegung, Bewegungsfreiheit *f*; *fig* Umschwung; Spielraum *m*, freie Hand *f*; Gang, Verlauf *m (d. Ereignisse, d. Entwicklung)*; Schaukel *f*; Swing *(Tanz)*; *mus* Rhythmus; *(Boxen)* Schwinger; *tech* Drehdurchmesser *m*; *(Kran)* Ausladung; *Am sl* (Arbeits-)Pause; *Am fam* Konjunktur *f*; *in full ~* in vollem Gange; reibungslos arbeitend; *to get into ~* in Schwung kommen; *to go with a ~* Schwung, *fam* Schmiß haben; *fig* glatt über die Bühne gehen; *to ~ round the circle (Am)* e-e politische Rundreise machen; *to ~ o.'s hips* mit den Hüften schaukeln; *to ~ the lead (sl)* sich drücken; *this is no room to ~ a cat in* man kann sich hier nicht umdrehen; *the ~ of the pendulum (fig)* der Pendelschlag; *market ~ (Am)* Konjunkturumschwung *m*; **~-back** *phot* Einstellscheibe *f*; *fig* Umschwung *m* (*to* zu); **~-boat** Schiffschaukel *f*; **~-bridge** Drehbrücke *f*; **~-crane** Drehkran *m*; **~-door** Drehtüre *f*; **~-gate** Drehkreuz *n*; **~ing** ['-iŋ] *a* schwingend; schwankend; *fig* beschwingt, schwungvoll; rhythmisch; *tech* schwenkbar; *~~ chair* Schaukelstuhl *m*; *~~ door* Drehtür *f*; **~ room** *Am sl* Kantine *f*; **~-round** *mot* Drehung *f* um die eigene Achse; **~ shift** *Am fam* Spätschicht *f*.

swingeing ['swindʒiŋ] *a fam* gewaltig, mächtig, enorm, ungeheuer; *fam* prima, tadellos, phantastisch.

swingle ['swiŋl] *tr (Flachs)* schwingen; *s* Flachsschwinge *f*; **~-bar, ~-tree** *(Wagen)* Ortscheit *n*.

swipe [swaip] *s* (Pumpen-)Schwengel; Griff; *sport* harte(r) Schlag, Hieb *m*; *s pl sl* Dünnbier, Gesöff *n*; *tr fam* e-n tüchtigen Schlag, Hieb versetzen (*s.o.* jdm); *sport* aus vollem Arm schlagen; *sl* mausen; *itr fam* dreinschlagen; kräftig schlagen (*at* nach).

swirl [swə:l] *itr tr* herumwirbeln (*about the street* in der Straße); *itr (Kopf)* sich drehen; *(Wasser)* Strudel bilden; *s* Wirbel, Strudel *m*.

swish [swiʃ] **1.** *itr* schwirren, surren, zischen, sausen; rascheln, rauschen; *to ~ in* hereinrauschen; *tr* schwirren *od* sausen lassen; wedeln (*its tail* mit dem Schwanz); *fam* (aus)peitschen, verdreschen (*with* mit); *s* Surren, Rascheln, Zischen *n*; Rohrstock; Peitschenhieb; *Am sl* Homosexuelle(r) *m*; *a fam* schick, fesch.

Swiss [swis] *a* schweizerisch; *s inv* Schweizer(in *f*) *m*; **~ cheese** Emmentaler *m*; **~ roll** Biskuitrolle *f*.

switch [switʃ] *s* Gerte, Rute *f*, Rohrstock *m*; (Schwanz-)Quaste *f*; falsche(r) Zopf *m*; schnelle, rasche Bewegung *f*; (Licht-)Schalter *m*; (Sprech-)Taste; *rail* Weiche *f*; Weichenstellen *n*; *fig* Wechsel *m*; *tr* mit dem Stock schlagen; peitschen; ver-, weg-, abschieben; abbiegen, -lenken, -ändern; (plötzlich) wegnehmen; *(mit dem Schwanz)* wedeln; *el* um-, ab-, anschalten; *rail* (um)rangieren (*on to* auf); *(Produktion)* umstellen; *fam* (um)tauschen, wechseln (*to* auf); verwechseln, vertauschen; *to ~ back* zurückschalten (*to* auf); *to ~ on, off (el)* ein- *od* an-, aus- *od* abschalten; *tele* verbinden, trennen; *riding ~* Reitgerte *f*; **~back** Serpentine; Berg-, Gebirgsbahn (in Serpentinen); Berg-u.-Tal-Bahn *f*; **~board** *el* Schalttafel *f*; *tele* Klappenschrank *m*; *~~ cord* Vermittlungsschnur *f*; *~~ operator* Telephonfräulein *n*, Vermittlung *f*; **~box** Schaltkasten; Vermittlungsschrank *m*; Stellwerk *n*; **~ contact** Schaltkontakt *m*; **~gear** Schaltanlage *f*; **~ing** ['-iŋ] Schalten; Rangieren *n*; *~~ engine* Rangierlok(omotive) *f*; **~-key** Kippschalter *m*; **~-lever** *el mot* Schalthebel *m*; **~man** ['-mən] Weichensteller *m*; **~tower** *Am rail* Stellwerk *n*; **~yard** *Am* Rangierbahnhof *m*; *el* Freiluftschaltanlage *f*.

Switzerland ['switsələnd] die Schweiz.

swivel ['swivl] *s tech* Drehring *m*, -lager *n*; *(~-hook)* Karabiner-, Wirbelhaken; *mar* Kettenwirbel *m*; *attr* Dreh-; *tr* schwenken, herumdrehen; *itr* sich drehen; **~-bridge** Drehbrücke *f*; **~-chair** Drehstuhl *m*; *~~ activity (fam)* Bürodienst *m*; **~-eyed** *a fam* schielend; **~-joint** Universalgelenk *n*; **~-mounted** *a* schwenkbar; **~-table** Drehtisch *m*.

swiz [swiz] *fam* schreckliche Enttäuschung *f*, Reinfall *m*.

swizzle ['swizl] (alkohol.) Mischgetränk *n*, Cocktail; *sl* Schwindel, Betrug *m*, Enttäuschung *f*; **~-stick** Rührstäbchen *n (für Mischgetränke)*.

swoon [swu:n] *itr* ohnmächtig werden, das Bewußtsein verlieren (*with* vor); *mus* ver-, ausklingen; *s* Ohnmacht *f*.

swoop [swu:p] *itr (to ~ down) (Raubvogel)* herabschießen (*on* auf); herfallen (*on* über); *tr (to ~ up)* (weg-)schnappen; *s* Herabschießen *n*; *fig* plötzliche(r) Angriff *m*; *at one (fell) ~* mit e-m Schlag.

swoosh [swu:ʃ] *itr Am aero* (hin)wegbrausen, -sausen, fegen (*over* über).

swop *s. swap.*

sword [sɔ:d] Schwert *n a. fig*; Säbel, Degen *m*; *fig* (Militär-)Macht *f*; Wehrstand; Krieg *m*; *at the point of the ~* unter ständiger Bedrohung; unter Lebensgefahr; *by fire and ~* mit Feuer u. Schwert; *to be at ~'s points (Am)* mit gezücktem Schwert dastehen; *to cross, measure ~s (a. fig)* die Klingen kreuzen (*with* mit); *to draw, to sheathe the ~* das Schwert ziehen *od* zücken, in die Scheide stecken; *to put to the ~* über die Klinge springen lassen; **~-belt** Wehrgehenk *n*; Degenkoppel *f*; **~-blade** Degenklinge *f*; **~-cane, -stick** Stockdegen *m*; **~craft** Fechtkunst; Kriegskunst *f*; **~-cut** Säbelhieb *m*; **~-dance** Schwerttanz *m*; **~fish** Schwertfisch *m*; **~-grass** Riedgras *n*; **~guard** Stichblatt *n*; **~ hilt** Degengriff *m*; **~-knot** Portepee *n*, Degenquaste *f*; **~-lily** *bot* Schwertlilie, Gladiole *f*; **~-play** Fechten *n*; *fig* geschickte Antwort; Schlagfertigkeit *f*; **~-point** Degenspitze *f*; **~(s)man** ['-(z)mən] Fechter *m*; **~smanship** ['-zmənʃip] Fechtkunst *f*.

swot, swat [swɔt] **1.** *itr Br sl* ochsen, büffeln, pauken (*for an exam* auf e-e Prüfung); *to ~ up o.'s geometry* Geometrie büffeln; *s* Streber *m*; Büffelei *f*, Schlauch *m*; **2.** *s. swat* 1.

sybarit|e ['sibərait] *fig* Schlemmer *m*; **~ic** [sibə'ritik] genußsüchtig.

Sybil ['sibil] Sibylle *f*.

sycamore ['sikəmɔ:] *(~-tree) bot Br* Sykomore *f*, Bergahorn *m*; *(Vorderer Orient)* Maulbeerfeigenbaum *m*; *Am* Abendländische Platane, Wasserbuche *f*.

syce *s. sice* 2.

sycophan|cy ['sikəfənsi] Kriecherei, Speichelleckerei *f*; **~t** ['-t] Schmeichler, Speichellecker, Kriecher *m*.

sycosis [sai'kousis] *med* Bartflechte *f*.

syllab|ary ['siləbəri] Silbentafel, -schrift *f*; **~ic** [si'læbik] *a* Silben-; silbisch; **~icate** [si'læbikeit], **~ify** [si'læbifai], **~ize** ['siləbaiz] *tr* nach Silben abteilen; **~ication** [silæbi'keiʃən], **~ification** [-fi'keiʃən] Silbenteilung *f*; **~le** ['siləbl] *s* Silbe *f*; *tr* nach Silben aussprechen.

syllabub *s. sillabub.*

syllabus ['siləbəs] *pl a. -bi* ['-ai] Zs.fassung *f*, Kompendium *n*, Abriß, Auszug *m*; Übersicht *f*, (Lehr-, Stunden-)Plan *m*, (Inhalts-, Vorlesungs-)Verzeichnis, Programm *n*.

syllogism ['silədʒizm] Syllogismus, Vernunftschluß *m*.

sylph [silf] Sylphe, Luftgeist *m*; *fig* schlanke(s) Mädchen *n*.

sylvan ['silvən] Wald-; bewaldet, waldig.

symbiosis [simb(a)i'ousis] *biol* Symbiose *f*.

symbol ['simbəl] Sinnbild, Symbol; Zeichen *n*; **~ic(al)** [sim'bɔlik(əl)] sinnbildlich, symbolisch (*of* für); **~ics** [sim'bɔliks] *pl mit sing rel* Symbolik *f*;

~ism ['simbəlizm] *lit* Symbolismus *m*; Symbolik *f*; **~ization** [simbəlai'zeiʃən] Versinnbildlichung *f*; **~ize** ['simbəlaiz] *tr* symbolisch, sinnbildlich darstellen, symbolisieren, versinnbildlichen.
symmetr|ic(al) [si'metrik(əl)] symmetrisch; **~ize** ['simitraiz] *tr* symmetrisch machen; **~y** ['-i] Symmetrie *f*.
sympath|etic [simpə'θetik] gleichgestimmt, ähnlich empfindend *od* fühlend; mitfühlend; teilnehmend; empfänglich (*to* für); sympathisch *a. anat u. physiol*; *fam* einverstanden (*to* mit), geneigt (*towards* dat); **~~** *ink* Geheimtinte *f*; **~~** *nerve (anat)* Sympathikus *m*; **~~** *strike* Sympathiestreik *m*; **~ize** ['simpəθaiz] *itr* mitempfinden, -fühlen, sympathisieren (*with* mit); angetan sein (*with* von); Verständnis haben (*with* für); bedauern; sein Bedauern, sein Beileid aussprechen (*with s.o.* jdm); **~izer** ['simpəθaizə] *pol* Mitläufer *m*, förderndes(s) Mitglied *n*; Mitfühlende(r) *m*; **~y** ['-i] Seelenverwandtschaft, Harmonie *f*; gegenseitige(s) Einverständnis, gute(s) Einvernehmen *n*; Sympathie *f*, Mitgefühl, -empfinden, Mitleid (*with, for* mit, für); *pl* Beileid *n*, Anteilnahme; *physiol phys* Sympathie *f*; *in* **~~** *with* im Einverständnis mit; *to be out of* **~~** *with* mit jdm nicht einverstanden sein; *letter of* **~~** Beileidsschreiben *n*.
symphon|ic [sim'fɔnik] *mus* sinfonisch; **~~** *poem* sinfonische Dichtung *f*; **~ious** [-'founiəs] harmonisch; in Harmonie (*to, with* mit); **~y** ['simfəni] Sinfonie *f*; **~~** *concert, orchestra* Sinfoniekonzert, -orchester *n*.
symposium [sim'pouzjəm] *pl -sia* ['-iə] Sammlung *f* von Beiträgen; Konferenz *f*; *hist* Festmahl *n*.
symptom ['simptəm] Symptom, Anzeichen, Merkmal *n* (*of* für); **~atic(al)** [simptə'mætik(əl)] symptomatisch, kenn-, bezeichnend, charakteristisch (*of* für).
synagogue ['sinəgɔg] *rel* Synagoge *f*.
synchro|flash ['siŋkro(u)flæʃ]: **~~** *gun (phot)* Blitz(licht)gerät *n*; **~mesh** ['-meʃ] (**~~** *gear, gear system) mot* Synchrongetriebe *n*; **~tron** ['siŋkro(u)trən] Synchrotron *n*.
synchron|al ['siŋkrənəl], **~ic(al)** [siŋ'krənik(əl)] = **~***ous*; **~ism** ['siŋkrənizm] Gleichzeitigkeit; chronologische Übersicht, Zeittafel, (vergleichende) Geschichtstabelle *f*; **~istic(al)** [siŋkrə'nistik(əl)] = **~***ous*; **~ization** [siŋkrənai'zeiʃən] Synchronisierung *f*; **~ize** ['siŋkrənaiz] *tr (Geräte, bes. Uhren)* aufea. abstimmen, regulieren; *(Ereignisse)* zs.-, in Zs.hang bringen; chronologisch ordnen, zs.-stellen; *film* synchronisieren; *itr* gleichzeitig sein *od* ablaufen; *mot* gleichlaufen; *(Uhren)* gleichgehen; *film* synchronisiert sein; **~~***d flash contact (phot)* (Blitzlicht-)Synchronkontakt *m*; **~~***d shifting (mot)* Synchrongetriebe *n*; **~ous** ['siŋkrənəs] gleichzeitig (*with* mit); gleichlaufend, -phasig, synchron; **~~** *machine* Synchronmaschine *f*.
syncop|ation [siŋkə'peiʃən] *mus gram* Synkope *f*; **~ate** ['-eit] *mus gram tr* synkopieren; **~e** ['siŋkəpi] *med* Ohnmacht; *mus gram* Synkope *f*.
syndic ['sindik] Syndikus; Masseverwalter *m*; **~alism** ['sindikəlizm] *pol* Syndikalismus *m*; **~alist** ['-əlist] *s* Syndikalist *m*; *a u.* **~***alistic* [sindikə'listik] syndikalistisch; **~ate** ['sindikit] *s* Syndikat *n*, Ring, Verband *m*, Konsortium *n*, Gruppe; Nachrichtenagentur *f*; *tr itr* ['sindikeit] (sich) zu e-m Syndikat, Verband zs.schließen, vereinigen; als Syndikus tätig sein; *(Artikel, Beitrag)* an mehrere Zeitungen zu gleichzeitiger Veröffentlichung verkaufen; **~ation** [sindi'keiʃən] Zs.schluß *m* zu e-m Syndikat; Ringbildung *f*.
synod ['sinəd] Synode, Kirchenversammlung; *allg* Versammlung *f*; **~al** ['-əl] *a* Synodal-; **~~** *decree* Synodalbeschluß *m*; **~ic(al)** [si'nɔdik(əl)] *astr* synodisch; *rel* Synodal-.
synonym ['sinənim] Synonym, sinnverwandte(s) Wort *n*; **~ic(al)** [sinə'nimik(əl)], **~ous** [si'nɔniməs] synonym, sinnverwandt; gleichbedeutend (*with* mit).
synop|sis [si'nɔpsis] *pl -ses* [-i:z] Übersicht, Zs.fassung *f*, Abriß *m*, Inhaltsangabe *f*; **~tic(al)** [si'nɔptik(əl)] übersichtlich, zs.fassend; *rel* synoptisch; **~***tic chart* Übersichtskarte; Wetterkarte *f*; *the* **~***tic Gospels* die synoptischen Evangelien *n pl (Matthäus-, Markus- u. Lukasevangelium)*; **~***tic table* Übersichtstabelle *f*; **~***tic view* Gesamtüberblick *m*.
synovia [si'nouviə] *physiol* Gelenkschmiere *f*.
synta|ctic(al) [sin'tæktik(əl)] syntaktisch; Syntax-; **~x** ['sintæks] Syntax *f*.
synthe|sis ['sinθisis] *pl -ses* ['-si:z] Synthese *f a. chem*; *chem* Aufbau *m*; *fig* Zs.schau *f*; **~size** ['sinθisaiz] *tr* (mitea.) vereinigen; aufbauen; *(Stoff)* synthetisch, künstlich herstellen (*from* aus); **~tic(al)** [sin'θetik(əl)] synthetisch *a. gram chem*; *(Stoff)* künstlich; **~***tic resin* Kunstharz *n*; **~tic** *s* Kunststoff *m*; **~tize** = **~***size*.
synton|ic [sin'tɔnik] *a radio* Abstimmungs-; abgestimmt; **~ize** ['sintənaiz] *tr radio obs* abstimmen; **~y** ['sintəni] *radio obs* Resonanz *f*.
syphil|is ['sifilis] *med* Syphilis *f*; **~itic** [sifi'litik] syphilitisch.
syphon *s. siphon.*
Syria ['siriə] Syrien *n*; **~n** ['-ən] *a* syrisch; *s* Syrer(in *f*) *m*.
syringa [si'riŋgə] *bot* Syringe *f*, Flieder *m*.
syringe ['sirindʒ] *s med tech* Spritze *f*; *tr* ausspülen, einspritzen, injizieren.
syrinx ['siriŋks] *mus* Pan(s)flöte; *med* Eustachische Röhre; Fistel *f*.
syrup, sirup ['sirəp] Zuckerlösung *f*; Sirup *m*; *(fruit-~)* (eingedickter, stark gesüßter) Frucht-, Obstsaft *m*; **~y** ['-i] klebrig; *fam fig* süßlich.
system ['sistəm] System *n*; Anordnung *f*, Plan *m*, Verfahren *n*; Einrichtung, Gliederung *f*; Universum, Welt(all *n*); *geol* Formation *f*; *biol* Organismus *m*; *tech* Netz *n*; *circulatory, digestive, respiratory* **~** Kreislauf-, Verdauungs-, Atmungsorgane *n pl*; *carboniferous* **~** Steinkohlenformation *f*; *railway* **~** Eisenbahnnetz *n*; **~atic(al)** [sisti'mætik(əl)] systematisch; planmäßig; methodisch, folgerichtig; **~atics** [-'mætiks] *s pl mit sing* Systematik *f*; **~atization** [sistimətai'zeiʃən] Systematisierung *f*; **~(at)ize** ['sistim(ət)aiz] *tr* systematisieren, in ein System bringen, nach e-m System (an)ordnen.
systole ['sistəli] *physiol* Systole *f*.

T

T, t [ti:] *pl* **~'s** T, t; *tech* T-Stück *n*; *to a* **~** ganz genau, aufs Haar; *in Zssgen*: T-förmig; **~-bandage** *med* T-Binde *f*; **~-beam, -girder, -iron** T-Träger *m*, T-Eisen *n*; **~-joint** *el* Abzweigmuffe *f*; **~-shirt** Sporthemd, Trikot(hemd) *n*; **~-square** Reißschiene *f*.

*

ta [tɑ:] *interj fam* danke! **~-~** ['tæ'tɑ:] *(fam)* auf Wiedersehen!
tab [tæb] Schnürband *n*, Aufhänger, Henkel *m*, Öse *f*, Öhr *n*, Lasche *f*; Besatzstück; Etikett, Kennschild *n*; (Karten-)Reiter; *tech* Drucktastenauslöser *m*; *Am fam* Liste, Aufstellung, Rechnung; Kontrolle *f*; *aero* Trimmruder *n*; *mil* Kragenspiegel *m*; *Am sl* unbezahlte Rechnung *f*; *pl sl theat* Vorhang *m*; *to keep a* **~** od **~***s on (fam)* nicht aus den Augen lassen; genau kontrollieren.
tabard ['tæbəd] *hist* Überrock; Heroldsrock *m*.
tabby ['tæbi] *s* gestreifte(r) *od* moirierte(r) Seidentaft *m*; *(grau- od braungestreifte)* Katze; *fam* alte Jungfer; *fam* Klatschbase *f*; *a* moiriert; dunkelgestreift; scheckig; *tr (Seide)* moirieren.

*

tabernacle ['tæbə(:)nækl] *rel* Stiftshütte *f*; Tempel *m*; Gottes-, Bethaus; Sakramentshäuschen *n*; Tabernakel *n* od *m*; Ziborium *n*; *poet* Wohnung *f*; (Evangelisten-)Zelt *n*; *Feast of T***~***s* Laubhüttenfest *n*.
tab|es ['teibi:z] Schwindsucht, Auszehrung *f*; *(tabes dorsalis)* Rückenmarksschwindsucht *f*; **~etic** [tə'betik], **~id** ['tæbid] schwindsüchtig, tabisch.
table ['teibl] *s* Tafel, Platte *f*; Tisch; (gedeckter) Tisch *m*, Tafel *f*; Fest(-essen) *n*; Tischgesellschaft, Tafelrunde; (Übersichts-)Tafel, Tabelle, Liste, Aufstellung *f*, Verzeichnis; *geog* Tafelland, Plateau *n*; *geol arch* Tafel *f*; *tech* Tisch *m*; Planke *f*; *pl* Puffspiel *n*; *tr* auf den Tisch legen; in e-e Liste aufnehmen; *Br parl* einbringen; *Am parl* ad acta legen; vertagen; *at* **~** bei Tisch; *to* **~** *a motion (Am)* die Entscheidung über e-n Antrag verschieben; *to lay (clear) the* **~** den Tisch (ab)decken; *to lay on the* **~** zur Diskussion vorschlagen; *parl* auf die lange Bank schieben; *to put on the* **~** aufs Tapet, zur Sprache bringen; vorbringen,

anschneiden; *to turn the ~s (fig)* den Spieß umkehren, -drehen (*on s.o.* gegenüber jdm); *the ~s have turned* das Blatt hat sich gewendet; *bedside-, dining-room, dressing-, kitchen-, occasional, operating-, tea-, writing-~* Nacht-, Eß-, Frisier-, Küchen-, Anstell-, Operations-, Tee-, Schreibtisch *m*; *billiard-~* Billard *n*; *time-~* Fahr-, Stundenplan *m*; *~ of contents (Buch)* Inhaltsverzeichnis *n*; *~ of interest, of wages* Zins-, Lohntabelle *f*; *the two ~s, the ~s of the law* od *covenant* od *testimony (rel)* die Gesetzestafeln *f pl*; *the twelve ~s (hist)* die Zwölftafelgesetze *n pl*; ~ **board** Verpflegung *f*, Essen *n (Dienstleistung)*; **~-cloth** Tischtuch *n*; *pl* u. **~-linen** Tischwäsche *f*; **~knife** Tafelmesser *n*; **~-lamp** Tischlampe *f*; **~land** *geog* Tafelland, Plateau *n*; **~-lifting, -rapping, -turning** Tischrücken *n (der Spiritisten)*; **~-mat** Untersatz *m*; **~-napkin** Serviette *f*; **~-radio** Kofferradio *n*; **~-salt** Tafel-, Speisesalz *n*; **~-spoon** Eßlöffel *m*; **~-talk** Tischgespräch *n*; **~-tennis** Tischtennis, Pingpong *n*; **~-terminal** Tischklemme *f*; **~-top** Tischplatte *f*; **~-track** *tech* Führungsschiene *f*; **~-tray** Serviertisch *m*; **~-ware** Tafelgeschirr *n*; **~-water** Tafelwasser *n*.

tablet ['tæblit] Platte, Tafel; Gedenktafel; *hist* Schreibtafel *f*; Schreib-, Notizblock *m*; *pharm* Tablette; *math* Tabelle *f*; *(Seife)* Stück *n*; *throat ~* Hustenbonbon *n*.

tabloid ['tæblɔid] *s pharm* Tablette *f*; *Am (kleinformatige)* Bildzeitung *f*, Revolverblatt *n*; *a* zs.-, kurzgefaßt, gedrängt; *in ~ form* konzentriert; ~ **journalism** Sensationspresse *f*.

taboo [tə'bu:] *s* Tabu *a. fig*; Verbot *n*; *a* tabu, unverletzbar, verboten; geächtet; *tr* für tabu erklären.

tabo(u)r ['teibə] Handtrommel *f*; **~in(e)** ['tæbəri:n] *mus* Tamburin *n*.

tabo(u)ret ['tæbərit] Hocker; Stickrahmen *m*.

tabul|ar ['tæbjulə] *a* tafelförmig, flach; tabellarisch (berechnet); *in ~~ form* in Tabellenform; *~~ value* Tabellenwert *m*; **~ate** ['-leit] *tr* abflachen; tabellarisch anordnen; in Tabellenform bringen; *a* flach; dünn geschichtet; **~ation** [tæbju'leiʃən] tabellarische Anordnung *f*; **~ator** ['-eitə] Tabelliermaschine *f*; Tabulator *m*.

tach|ometer [tæ'kɔmitə] Tachometer *n, a. m*, Geschwindigkeits-, Drehzahlmesser *m*; **~ycardia** [tæki'kɑ:diə] *med* Tachykardie, hohe Pulsfrequenz *f*.

tacit ['tæsit] still, lautlos; *jur* stillschweigend; **~urn** ['-ə:n] schweigsam, wortkarg; **~urnity** [tæsi'tə:niti] Schweigsamkeit, Wortkargheit *f*.

tack [tæk] **1.** *s* Stift *(Nagel)*; *(thumb-~)* Reißbrettstift *m*, Heftzwecke *f*; Heftstich *m*; Heften *n*; Zickzack(bewegung *f*); *pol* Zickzackkurs; *pol* Zusatzantrag; *mar* Hals *m*, Haltetau *n*; *mar* Gang, Schlag *m*, Lavieren, Aufkreuzen *n (gegen den Wind)*; *fig* Kurs, Weg *m*; *tr* mit Stiften befestigen; (an-, fest-) heften, -nähen; *fig* anhängen, hinzufügen (*on to s.th.* an etw); *mar* halsen, lavieren; *to ~ together* zs.fügen *a. fig*; *itr* sich im Zickzack bewegen; *pol* e-n Kurswechsel vornehmen; *mar* lavieren; *mar* über Stag gehen; *on the wrong ~ (fig)* auf dem Holzweg, auf der falschen Fährte; *to come down to brass ~s (fam)* zur Sache kommen; ~ **board** *Am* Anschlagtafel *f*, Schwarze(s) Brett *n*; **~er** ['-ə] (An-)Hefter *m*; **~iness** ['-inis] Klebrigkeit *f*; **~y** ['-i] klebrig; *Am fam* mies, mau, schäbig; schlampig, vulgär; **2.** *sl* Essen *n*, Fraß *m*; *hard ~* Schiffszwieback *m*.

tackle ['tækl] *s* Ausrüstung, Einrichtung *f*; Gerät *n*, Apparat; Flaschenzug *m*; *mar* Talje *f*, Takel *n*; Takelung, Takelage *f*; *Am (Fußball)* Angreifen *n*; Stürmer; *sport* Angreifer *m*; *sl* Essen *n*, Fraß *m*; *tr mar* (auf)takeln; *(Pferd)* anschirren; *allg* ergreifen, packen; *sport* angreifen; *(Problem)* anpacken, in Angriff nehmen, herangehen an; angehen (*s.o. over* od *about s.th.* jdn wegen etw); *fishing ~* Angelgerät *n*; *writing ~* Schreibzeug *n*.

tact [tækt] Takt *m*, Fein-, Fingerspitzengefühl *n* (*of* für); **~ful** ['-ful] taktvoll; **~ile** ['tæktail, *Am* '-til] fühlbar; Tast-; *~~ sense* Tastsinn *m*; **~ility** [tæk'tiliti] Fühlbarkeit *f*; **~less** ['tæktlis] taktlos; **~lessness** ['-lisnis] Taktlosigkeit *f*; **~ual** ['tæktjuəl] *a physiol* Tast-.

tactic|al ['tæktik(əl)] *mil* taktisch *a. fig*; **~ian** [tæk'tiʃ(ə)n] *mil* Taktiker *m a. fig*; **~s** ['tæktiks] *pl a. mit sing mil* Taktik *f a. fig*.

tad [tæd] *Am das* Kleine *(Kind)*; **~pole** ['-poul] *zoo* Kaulquappe *f*.

taffeta ['tæfitə] Taft *m*.

Taffy ['tæfi] *fam* Waliser *m*.

taffy ['tæfi] *Am* Sahnekaramelle *f*.

tag [tæg] *s* Zipfel *m*; lose(s) Ende, Anhängsel *n*; Spitze *f*, Zacken *m*; Schnürbandhülse *f*; Stift; Anhänger *m*; Etikett *n*, Preiszettel *m*; *Am mot fam* Nummernschild *n*; An-, Aufhänger *m*, Öse *f*; Schnörkel *m*; stehende Redensart *f*; *(Rede)* Schlußworte *n pl*, -wendung, -floskel *f*; *theat* Stichwort *n*; Kriegen(spielen) *n*; *Am sl* Kassiber; Haftbefehl *m*; *(identification ~)* Erkennungsmarke *f*; *tr* mit e-m Stift *od* e-r Öse befestigen; zs.heften; hinzufügen (*to* an); mit e-m Anhänger, e-m Schildchen versehen; *com* auszeichnen, etikettieren; *(Rede)* ausschmücken, mit e-r Floskel, schwungvoll enden; *(im Spiel)* fangen, kriegen, haschen; *(to ~ along)* nachlaufen (*s.o.* jdm); *itr* hinterher-, nachlaufen (*after s.o.* jdm); *to ~ around with s.o.* jds ständiger Begleiter sein; *~, rag, and bobtail* Krethi u. Plethi, der große Haufen, das Lumpenpack, das Gesindel; *price ~* Preisschild *n*; *question ~ (gram)* Frageanhängsel *n*; **~ end** lose(s) Ende; Anhängsel; letzte(s) Ende; Überbleibsel *n*, Rest *m*; **~ger** ['-ə] Anhefter, -binder *m*; Blechscheibe, -platte *f*; ~ **lines** *pl* (abgedroschene) Redensart *f*.

tail [teil] *s* Schwanz, Schweif *m a. fig*; *fig* (Schwanz-, unteres) Ende *n*; Rockschoß; Rückstand *m*, Abfälle *pl*; Zopf; Kometenschweif *m*; *Am* Schlange *f (beim Anstehen)*; *aero* Rumpfende, Heck *n*; *pl (Münze)* Wappenseite *f*; *pl fam* Frack *m*; *tr* mit e-m Schwanz versehen; den Schwanz abschneiden (*s.th.* e-r S); *(Früchte)* den Stiel wegmachen; das Ende, den Schluß bilden (*s.th.* e-r S); anhängen; festmachen (*to* an); *sl* nachschleichen (*s.o.* jdm), beschatten; *itr* sich ausea.ziehen; *(to ~ away, off)* schwächer werden, abnehmen, nachlassen, abklingen; *after s.o.* dicht hinter jdm hergehen; *Am* hinter jdm herschleichen; *~s up* in guter Laune; *to wag o.s. ~* mit dem Schwanz wedeln; *to put o.'s ~ between o.'s legs (fig)* den Schwanz einziehen; *to turn ~* Reißaus nehmen; *to twist s.o.'s ~* jdn verrückt, wahnsinnig machen; *to watch s.o. with the ~ of o.'s eye* jdn verstohlen betrachten; *I can't make head or ~ of it* daraus werde ich nicht schlau, das begreife ich nicht; *head(s) or ~(s)?* Kopf oder Wappen? **~board, ~gate** *(Karren, Lastwagen)* (Lade-)Klappe *f*; **~-coat** Frack *m*; **~ed** *a in Zssgen*: = schwänzig; **~-end** hintere(s), untere(s) Ende *n*; Schluß *m*; *at the ~~* ganz am Schluß; **~ender** *Am fam* Schlußlicht *n (bei e-m Wettbewerb)*; ~ **fin** *aero* Seitenflosse *f*; ~ **gunner** *aero* Heckschütze *m*; **~heavy** *aero* schwanzlastig; **~ing** ['-iŋ] *arch* eingelassene(s) Ende *n*; *pl tech* Abfälle, Rückstände *m pl*; **~-lamp, -light** *mot* Schlußlicht; *aero* Hecklicht *n*; **~less** ['-lis] schwanzlos, ohne Schwanz; *~~ airplane* schwanzlose(s), Nurflügelflugzeug *n*; **~piece** End-, Schlußstück *n*; *(Geige)* Saitenhalter *m*; *typ* (Schluß-)Vignette *f*; **~-plane** *aero* Höhenflosse *f*; **~-skid** *aero* Schwanzsporn *m*; **~-spin** *s aero* Trudeln *n*; *fig* Panik *f*; *itr (to go into a ~~)* abtrudeln; **~stock** *tech* Reitstock *m*; ~ **turret** *aero* Heck(gefechts)stand, Heckturm *m*; ~ **unit** *aero* Leitwerk *n*; ~ **wheel** *aero* Spornrad *n*; ~ **wind** *aero* Rücken-, Schiebewind *m*.

tailor ['teilə] *s* Schneider *m*; *tr itr* schneidern; *tr (Schneider)* arbeiten für; kleiden, anziehen (*s.o.* jdn); *allg* zuschneiden (*to* auf); **~-bird** *orn* Schneidervogel *m*; **~ess** ['-ris] Schneiderin *f*; **~-made** *a (Damenkleidung)* vom Schneider gemacht; gut sitzend; *(Herrenkleidung)* Maß-; nach Maß angefertigt; *allg* zugeschnitten (*for* auf); *Am sl* fabrikmäßig, nach Norm hergestellt; *s* Schneiderkostüm *n*.

taint [teint] *tr physisch u. fig* anstecken, verseuchen, besudeln, verderben (*with* durch); *fig* beflecken, vergiften; *itr* angesteckt, verseucht, vergiftet werden; verderben; *s* Makel, (Schand-)Fleck *m*; Spur *f*; Gift *n*, Seuche *f*; (krankhafte) Anlage (*of* zu); Ansteckung, Verseuchung, Verderbnis *f*; **~less** ['-lis] makel-, fleckenlos; unbefleckt, rein.

*

take [teik] *irr took* [tuk], *taken* ['teikən] **1.** *tr* (weg)nehmen; an sich nehmen *od* reißen; mitnehmen (*to* zu, nach); bringen, führen, begleiten (*to* zu, nach); *(Verantwortung)* auf sich nehmen; *(Spiel)* gewinnen; *(Figur, Stein im Brettspiel)* nehmen; *(Tier)* fangen; ergreifen, packen, fassen, ertappen, *fam* schnappen; gefangennehmen; treffen (*in* in; *on* an); antreffen, *fam* erwischen (*at* bei); 'reinlegen, anführen, betrügen; für sich einnehmen, gewinnen, bezaubern; zu sich nehmen, essen, trinken; *(Arznei)* einnehmen; *(Temperatur)* messen; *(ins Haus)* aufnehmen; (hin)nehmen, bringen; behalten, kaufen; mieten, pachten; *(im Abonnement)* beziehen; an-, über-, *(on, upon o.s.)* auf sich nehmen; dulden, aushalten; *(Strafe)* hinnehmen, über sich ergehen lassen; *(e-r Behandlung)* sich unterziehen; *gram (Attribut, Objekt)* haben; nehmen, (aus)wählen, sich entscheiden für, sich entschließen zu; greifen zu, gebrauchen, benutzen; hinnehmen, auffassen, ansehen (*for* als), halten (*for* für); verstehen, begreifen; glauben; erfordern, in Anspruch nehmen, beanspruchen; brauchen; kosten; dauern; *(Preis)* gewinnen; *(Belohnung)* annehmen; *(Krankheit)* sich zuziehen; *(Hindernis)* nehmen, sich hinwegsetzen über; *fig* überwinden; **2.** *itr* Besitz ergreifen; *tech* anhaken, festhängen; hängenbleiben; anwachsen, Wurzeln schlagen; *(Feuer)* um sich greifen; Anklang, Beifall finden; wirken, wirksam sein; Abbruch tun, abträglich sein (*from* dat); gehen (*to* zu, nach); sich gewöhnen (*to* an); e-e Vorliebe entwickeln (*to* für), sich legen (*to* auf); kommen (*after* nach), aussehen, sich verhalten (*after* wie); *to ~ o.s.* gehen (*to* zu, nach); *(Karten)* stechen; **3.** *s* Nehmen *n*; Einnahme *f*; Fang; *Am sl* große(r) Gewinn *m*; *film* Aufnahme; *(Schallplatte)* Probeaufnahme *f*; *typ* Manuskript *n*; **4.** *to ~ into account* in Betracht ziehen; *to ~ advantage of* Gebrauch machen von; sich zunutze machen, Nutzen ziehen aus; wahrnehmen; *s.o.* jdn ausnutzen; *to ~ advice* sich Rat holen; *s.o.'s* auf jds Rat hören; *to ~ legal advice* zum Rechtsanwalt gehen; *to ~ the air* an die (frische) Luft gehen; *sl* abhauen; *aero* (auf)steigen; *to ~ alarm at* sich beunruhigen über; *to ~ s.o.'s arm* jds Arm nehmen, *fam* jdn einhaken; *to ~ s.o. to o.'s arms, breast* jdn umarmen, an die Brust drücken; *to ~ (up) arms* zu den Waffen greifen; *to ~ a back seat (fig)* sich im Hintergrund halten; *to ~ o.'s bearings* sich orientieren; Umschau halten; *to ~ to bed* sich (wegen Krankheit) zu Bett legen; *to ~ the blame* die Schuld auf sich nehmen; *to ~ a bow* sich verbeugen; *to ~ a break (Am)* e-e Pause machen; *to ~ breath* Atem schöpfen, Luft holen *a. fig*; *to ~ a deep breath* tief Atem holen; *to ~ the cake (Am)* den Vogel abschießen; den Sieg davontragen; *to ~ care* aufpassen, sich in acht nehmen, sich vorsehen; *of* achtgeben auf, sorgen für; sich annehmen um; *of o.s.* sich schonen; *to ~ a chair, seat* sich setzen, Platz nehmen; *to ~ the chair* den Vorsitz übernehmen; *to ~ a chance* wagen, riskieren; *to ~ o.'s chance* das Glück beim Schopf ergreifen; *to ~ charge of* sich kümmern um, achtgeben auf; übernehmen; die Leitung in die Hand nehmen; *to ~ a cold* sich erkälten; *to ~ comfort* sich trösten; *to ~ command (mil)* das Kommando führen; *to ~ compassion on* Mitleid haben mit; *to ~ into confidence* ins Vertrauen ziehen; *to ~ into consideration* in Erwägung ziehen; *to ~ counsel* beratschlagen (*with* mit); *to ~ courage* Mut fassen; *to ~ cover* Schutz suchen, in Deckung gehen; *to ~ a short cut* den Weg abkürzen; *to ~ a degree* promovieren *itr*; *to ~ s.o. at a disadvantage (Am)* jdn unvorbereitet treffen; jdn überraschen; *to have ~n a dislike to s.o.* jdn nicht mehr (leiden) mögen; *to ~ a drive* ausfahren; *to ~ in earnest* ernst nehmen; *to ~ easy* leicht, nicht tragisch nehmen; *to ~ effect* wirksam werden, wirken, Erfolg haben, gelingen; *to ~ an examination* e-e Prüfung machen *od* ablegen; *to ~ exception to (Am)* Einwände erheben gegen; *to ~ exercise* sich Bewegung machen; *to ~ s.o.'s fancy* jdm gefallen, zusagen; *to ~ a fancy to* eingenommen sein, e-e Schwäche haben für; *to ~ fire* Feuer fangen; *fig* wütend werden (*at* über); *to ~ the floor (parl)* das Wort ergreifen; *to ~ for granted* als Tatsache hinnehmen, gelten lassen; *to ~ a hand in s.th. (Am)* sich an etw beteiligen; *to ~ s.o.'s hand* jdn bei der Hand nehmen; *to ~ s.th. in hand (fig)* etw in die Hand nehmen, für etw sorgen; *to ~ s.th. into o.'s head* sich etw in den Kopf setzen; *to ~ heart* Mut fassen; *to ~ s.th. to heart* sich etw zu Herzen nehmen; *to ~ a hint* e-n Wink verstehen; *to ~ hold of s.th.* etw ergreifen, festhalten, sich e-r S bemächtigen, von e-r S Besitz ergreifen; anfassen, packen; *to ~ a holiday* Urlaub nehmen; *to ~ horse* aufsitzen; *to ~ ill, sick (fam)* krank werden; *to ~ interest in* Interesse haben an, sich interessieren für; *to ~ issue* sich in e-e Ausea.setzung einlassen (*with* mit); *to ~ a joke on o.s. (Am)* e-n Spaß vertragen können; *to ~ o.'s leave* sich verabschieden (*of* von); *to ~ liberties* sich Freiheiten herausnehmen; *to ~ the liberty* sich die Freiheit nehmen, sich erlauben; *to ~ o.'s own life* sich das Leben nehmen; *to ~ a liking to s.o.* sich zu jdm hingezogen fühlen; *to ~ a look* e-n Blick werfen (*at* auf); *to ~ measures* Maßnahmen ergreifen; *to ~ s.o.'s measure* jdm Maß nehmen; *fig* jdn abschätzen, -wägen; *to ~ a nap* ein Nickerchen machen; *to ~ a note of s.th.* etw notieren, aufschreiben; *fig* bemerken; *to ~ notes* sich Notizen machen; *to ~ notice of* beachten, Notiz nehmen von; *to ~ an oath* e-n Eid leisten, schwören; *to ~ observations* Beobachtungen anstellen; *to ~ an objection* e-n Einwand erheben *od* machen; *to ~ offence at* sich beleidigt fühlen durch; *to ~ orders* gehorchen; *to ~ pains* sich Mühe geben (*with* mit); *to ~ part in* teilnehmen an; *to ~ a photograph, picture* e-e Aufnahme, ein Bild machen; *to ~ s.o.'s picture* jdn aufnehmen, photographieren; *to ~ to pieces* ausea.nehmen; in Stücke zerlegen; *to ~ pity on* Mitleid haben mit; *to ~ place* stattfinden; *to ~ s.o.'s place* an jds Stelle treten, jdn ersetzen; *to ~ pleasure in* Vergnügen haben, finden an; *to ~ a poll* e-e Abstimmung vornehmen; *to ~ possession of* Besitz ergreifen von; *to ~ a pride in* stolz sein auf; *to ~ a resolution* e-n Entschluß fassen; *to ~ a rest* sich ausruhen; *to ~ revenge* sich rächen; *to ~ rise* entstehen, s-n Ausgang nehmen; *to ~ root (fig)* Fuß fassen; Wurzeln schlagen; *to ~ a shine to each other (Am)* sich gegenseitig angezogen fühlen; *to ~ ship* sich einschiffen (*for* nach); *to ~ a stand (Am)* e-n klaren Standpunkt einnehmen (*against* gegen); *to ~ by storm* im Sturm nehmen; *to ~ s.th. in o.'s stride (Am)* gelassen auf sich nehmen; *to ~ by surprise* überraschen; *to ~ to task* kritisieren; *to ~ by the throat* am Kragen packen; *to ~ time* Zeit benötigen *od* brauchen; *to ~ o.'s time* sich Zeit lassen (*to* zu); *to ~ time off (Am)* der Arbeit fernbleiben; *to ~ time out (Am)* die Arbeit unterbrechen; *to ~ trouble* sich Mühe machen, sich abmühen; *to ~ the trouble* sich die Mühe machen, sich bemühen (*to* zu); *to ~ a turn* sich Bewegung machen; auch mal zupacken (*at* an, bei); *to ~ turns* (sich) abwechseln; *to ~ a turn for the better, worse* e-e Wendung zum Besseren, Schlechteren nehmen; *to ~ a view of s.th.* etw e-r Prüfung unterziehen, prüfen; *to ~ views* Aufnahmen machen (*of* von); *to ~ a walk* e-n Spaziergang machen, spazierengehen; *to ~ the water (mar)* vom Stapel laufen; *to ~ well* sich gut photographieren lassen; *to ~ a wife* ein Weib nehmen, freien, heiraten; *to ~ s.o. at his word* jdn beim Wort nehmen; jdm glauben; *to ~ s.o. wrong* jdn falsch verstehen; **5.** *~ it easy!* mach dir nichts daraus! laß dir keine grauen Haare darum wachsen! *he does not ~ well* er läßt sich nicht gut photographieren; *he ~s a size nine shoe* er hat (Schuh-)Größe 9; *~ your seats!* (bitte) einsteigen! *that doesn't ~ much brains* dazu gehört nicht viel Verstand; **6.** *to ~* **after** geraten nach, nachschlagen (*s.o.* jdm); nachmachen; nachlaufen (*s.o.* jdm); *to ~* **along** *(Person)* mitnehmen; *to ~* **amiss** falsch auffassen; *fam* in den falschen Hals kriegen; *to ~* **apart** ausea.-nehmen; *to ~* **away** weg-, mitnehmen; *(Gefangenen)* abführen; *(Kunden)* abfangen; *(Speise in e-m Geschäft)* zum Mitnehmen, über die Straße; *to ~* **back** zurücknehmen *(a. Gesagtes)*; *(Ware)* zurückbringen; *fig* zurückversetzen (*to the time* in die Zeit); *to ~* **down** herunternehmen; abnehmen, -machen; ab-, einreißen; demütigen; aufnehmen, aufschreiben, zu Papier bringen, notieren; *tech* zerlegen; *I took him down a peg or two* ich habe ihm e-n Dämpfer aufgesetzt; *to ~* **for** halten für; *to ~* **from** entnehmen; vermindern; beeinträchtigen; *to ~* **in** annehmen, empfangen; *(Segel)* einziehen; *(Zeitung)* beziehen; zs.ziehen, verkleinern; *(Kleid)* enger, kürzer machen; einschließen, einbegreifen, umfassen; *(Land)* gewinnen; (mit e-m Blick) erfassen, aufnehmen; verstehen, auffassen, begreifen; täuschen, betrügen, hereinlegen; *(e-e Dame in das Speisezimmer)* hineinführen; an-, übernehmen; zu sich nehmen, in Pflege nehmen; aufnehmen; empfangen; *Am* besuchen; *to ~* **off** *tr* wegnehmen, -führen; *(Kleidung)* ausziehen; *(Hut)* abnehmen; *(vom Preis)* nachlassen; abziehen, subtrahieren; *(Zug)* ausfallen lassen; *com* aus dem Markt nehmen; abschreiben, kopieren, nachbilden; wegbringen (*s.o.* jdn); umbringen; *fam* nachmachen, -äffen; *itr* sich entfernen; *aero, a. allg fam* starten; *(Regen)* aufhören; *to ~ o.s. off* weggehen, *fam* abhauen; *to ~ a day off* sich e-n Tag freinehmen; *to ~ s.th. off o.'s hands* jdm etw abnehmen, abkaufen; *to ~* **on** *tr* annehmen, erwerben; mieten; beschäftigen, einstellen; *rail (Wagen)* ankuppeln, beistellen; übernehmen; unternehmen; auf sich nehmen; spielen gegen; einsteigen lassen; *itr fam* sich aufspielen; *fam* sich furchtbar ärgern; sich aufregen, klagen; *fam* Anklang finden, volkstümlich werden, in Mode kommen (*among* bei); *to ~* **out** herausnehmen, (her)ausziehen, entfernen; *(Pfand)* auslösen; sich *(ein Papier)* geben, ausstellen lassen; *(Patent)* nehmen; *(Versicherung)* abschließen; *(Führerschein)* machen; *fam* ausführen, begleiten; *(Bridge)* überbieten; *to ~ it out* sich schadlos halten (*in* an); *to ~ it out of s.o. (fam)* jdn fertigmachen, umhauen; es aus jdm herausholen; *to ~ it out on s.o.* s-n Ärger, s-e Wut an jdm auslassen; *to ~* **over** *(Geschäft, Amt)* übernehmen; hinübernehmen; *tele* verbinden; *to ~* **to** *(jdn)* ausführen; bringen zu; warm werden bei; Gefallen finden an; *(Vorschlag)* aufnehmen, sich stellen zu; Zuflucht nehmen zu; sich beschäftigen mit; sich verlegen auf; *to ~* **up** *tr* aufnehmen; hochheben; aufsaugen, absorbieren; *chem* auflösen; *(Platz)* einnehmen; *(Zeit)* verschlingen, in Anspruch nehmen; annehmen; verhaften; aufkaufen; *(Wechsel)* akzeptieren; *(Rock)* kürzer machen; *(Masche)* aufnehmen; in s-n Schutz nehmen; ab-, zurückweisen; wieder aufnehmen; zusteigen lassen; *(Redner)* unterbrechen, berichtigen; *(Woh-*

nung) beziehen; *(Gedanken)* aufgreifen, Interesse bekommen *od* finden an; beschäftigen, ausfüllen; studieren; sich beschäftigen mit; fördern, in s-e Obhut nehmen; besprechen (*with* mit); *itr* sich anfreunden, in Verkehr treten, sich in Verbindung setzen, Umgang suchen, sich einlassen, es halten (*with* mit); *I'll ~ you up on that* ich nehme Sie beim Wort; *the weather is taking up (fam)* das Wetter wird schön; **7. ~-down** *s* Ausea.nehmen *n*, Demontage; *fam* Demütigung; Enttäuschung *f*; *a* (leicht) demontierbar; zerlegbar; **~-home-pay** (*od* **-wages**) Nettolohn *m*; **~-in** *fam* Schwindel *m*, Gaunerei *f*, Betrug *m*; **~-off** Absprung; *aero* Abflug, Start *m a. fig*; *fam* Nachmachen, -äffen *n*, -äfferei *f*; Karikieren *n*, Karikatur *f*; *~~ clearance, distance, point, speed* Startfreigabe, -strecke, -stelle, -geschwindigkeit *f*; **~-out** *Am sl* Fertiggericht *n* zum Mitnehmen; **~-over bid** Übernahmeangebot *n*; **~-up:** *~~ roller (tech)* Aufroll-, Aufwickelvorrichtung *f*; **~y** ['-i] *Am fam* gewinnend, anziehend, an-, für sich sprechend.

taken ['teikən] *pp von take*; *a* entzückt (*with* von); *to be ~ aback* überrascht sein; *to be ~ ill* krank werden, erkranken; *to be ~ in* reinfallen, der Dumme sein; *to be ~ up with* beschäftigt sein, sich befassen mit.

taker ['teikə] Abnehmer; Käufer, Kunde; Mieter; Wettende(r) *m*; *ticket ~* Fahrkartenkontrolleur *m*; *~ of a bill* Wechselnehmer *m*; **~-in** Heimarbeiter; Betrüger *m*; **~-off** Abnahmebeamte(r) *m*.

taking ['teikiŋ] *a* anziehend, verlockend, attraktiv, interessant; *fam (Krankheit)* ansteckend; *s* (Hin-)Nehmen *n*, Hinnahme; Entnahme; *mil* Einnahme; Gefangennahme; *phot* Aufnahme *f*; Fang *m*; *fam* Ansteckung; *fam* Aufregung, Unruhe *f*; *pl* Einnahmen *f pl*; Gewinne *m pl*; Einkünfte *pl*; Verdienst *m*; *on ~* bei Entnahme; *day's ~s (pl)* Tageseinnahmen *f pl*; *stock ~* Inventur *f*; **~-away** Wegnahme *f*; **~-back** Zurücknahme *f*; **~ charge** Übernahme *f*; **~-in** Einnahme *f*; *fam* Hereinlegen *n*; **~-off** Wegnahme *f*; Weggehen, Scheiden *n*; **~-over** Übernahme *f*; **~-up** *com* Aufnahme *f*; *tech* Aufwickeln *n*.

talc [tælk] *min* Talk *m*; **~um** ['-əm] *(~~ powder)* Talkum *n*, Körperpuder *m*.

tale [teil] Erzählung, Geschichte *f*, Märchen *n*; Bericht *m*; Lüge, Erfindung *f*; dumme(s) Geschwätz, Gerede, Gerücht *n*; *obs poet* Zahl, Gesamtheit, -zahl *f*; *to tell ~s* klatschen, (aus)plaudern, schwätzen; *to tell o.'s own ~ (fig)* für sich selbst sprechen; **~-bearer, -teller** Klatschmaul *n*, -base *f*, Zuträger *m*; **~-bearing, -telling** Klatsch *m*, Zuträgerei *f*.

talent ['tælənt] Talent *n*, Begabung, (besondere) Anlage, Befähigung, Fähigkeit *f*; *die* Begabten *m pl*; *hist* Talent *n (Gewicht u. Geldeinheit)*; *to have a ~ for*, begabt sein für; **~ed** ['-id] *a* talentiert, begabt, gut veranlagt, befähigt; **~less** ['-lis] unbegabt.

tales ['teili:z] *pl jur* Ersatzgeschworene *m pl*; *pl mit sing* Vorladung *f* an Ersatzgeschworene; **~man** ['-mən] Ersatzgeschworene(r) *m*.

talipe|d ['tæliped] *a* klumpfüßig; *s* Klumpfuß *m* (Person); **~s** ['-i:z] *med* Klumpfuß *m*.

talisman ['tælismən] Talisman, Glücksbringer *m*.

talk [tɔ:k] *itr* sprechen, reden (*about, of, on* von, über; *to, with s.o.* mit jdm); *at s.o.* jdn meinen; *fam* ausschimpfen (*to s.o.* jdn); plaudern, schwatzen; schwätzen, klatschen; *tr* äußern, sagen; reden, sprechen (über), besprechen, diskutieren; überreden, beschwatzen (*into doing s.th.* etw zu tun); *s.o. into s.th.* jdm etw einreden; abbringen (*out of* von); *s.o. out of s.th.* jdm etw ausreden; *s* Rede *f*, Vortrag *m*; Gespräch *n*, Unterhaltung; Diskussion, Aussprache, Unterredung; Plauderei *f*; Gerede, Geschwätz *n*, Klatsch *m*; Redeweise *f*; *fam* Dialekt *m*; *to be all ~* immer nur reden; *to be the ~ of the town* Stadtgespräch, in aller Munde sein; *to be ~ed about* od *of* ins Gerede kommen; *to make ~* drauflos reden; von sich reden machen; *to ~ o.s. into believing that* sich einreden, daß; *to ~ big (sl)* den Mund vollnehmen, angeben, prahlen; *to ~ to death (sl)* sich totreden; *s.o.* jdn durch sein Reden verrückt machen; *to ~ through o.'s hat (sl)* Unsinn, dummes Zeug reden; *to ~ o.'s head, arm off* sich den Mund fusselig reden; *to ~ o.s. hoarse* sich heiser reden; *to ~ scandal* klatschen; *to ~ sense* vernünftig reden; *to ~ shop* fachsimpeln; *to ~ (cold) turkey (Am)* kein Blatt vor den Mund nehmen (*to s.o.* bei jdm); *there is ~ of* man spricht von, sagt; *big ~ (sl)* Angeberei, Prahlerei *f*; *heart-to-heart ~* Aussprache *f*; *small ~* Plauderei *f*; *now you are ~ing!* das läßt sich hören! *to ~* **away** *tr (Zeit)* verschwatzen; *itr* ununterbrochen reden; *to ~* **back** (scharf) erwidern, antworten; *Am* e-e dumme Antwort geben; frech, grob sein; *to ~* **down** *tr* niederschreien, durch langes Reden fertigmachen, (schließlich) überreden; zum Schweigen bringen; *(Argument)* zerreden; *(Tatsache)* verkleinern; *aero* heruntersprechen; *itr: to s.o.* sich zu jdm herablassen; herablassend reden mit; *to ~* **out** *(tr) (Thema)* erschöpfen(d behandeln); *parl* durch lange Debatten hinauszögern; *itr fam* laut u. deutlich sprechen; *o.s.* sich aussprechen; *to ~ s.o. out of s.th.* jdn von etw abbringen; *to ~ it out* sein Herz ausschütten; *to ~* **over** be-, durchsprechen (*with s.o.* mit jdm); überreden, überzeugen; *to ~* **round** überreden, überzeugen, gewinnen; herumreden (*s.th.* um etw); *to ~* **up** *tr* viel reden von, bei jeder Gelegenheit loben; frei herausreden; *itr fam* laut u. deutlich sprechen, den Mund vollnehmen; **~ative** ['-ətiv] gesprächig, redselig; geschwätzig; **~ativeness** ['-ətivnis] Gesprächigkeit, Redseligkeit; Geschwätzigkeit *f*; **~ee-talkee** ['tɔ:ki'tɔ:ki] *fam* endlose(s) Gerede, Gewäsch; Kauderwelsch *n*; **~er** ['-ə] Sprecher, Redner; Schwätzer *m*; **~ie** ['-i] *bes. Am fam* Tonfilm *m*; *pl* Tonfilmindustrie *f*; **~ing** ['-iŋ] *a* sprechend; *s* Rede *f*, Gespräch *n*, Unterhaltung *f*; Geplauder *n*; *~~ film, picture* Tonfilm *m*; *~~-point* Gesprächsgegenstand *m*; *~~ test* Sprech-, Leitungsprobe *f*; *~~-to (fam)* Schimpfe, Schelte *f*; Anschnauzer, -pfiff *m*; **~y** ['-i] redselig, geschwätzig, schwatzhaft; *~~-talk (fam)* Geschwätz *n*.

tall [tɔ:l] *a* groß (u. schlank), hoch(gewachsen), lang (aufgeschossen); *fam* gewaltig, großartig; *fam* großspurig, -sprecherisch, hochtrabend, geschwollen; *fam* unglaublich; *adv sl* prahlerisch; **~boy** hohe Kommode; hohe Schornsteinkappe *f*; **~ish** ['-iʃ] etwas groß, hoch; **~ness** ['-nis] Größe, Höhe, Länge *f*; **~ order** *fam* Zumutung; schwierige Aufgabe *f*; **~ story** *fam* Lügengeschichte *f*.

tallow ['tælou] *s* Talg *m*, Rinder-, Hammelfett *n*; *tr* mit Talg einschmieren, -fetten; *(Tier)* mästen; **~y** ['-i] talg(art)ig; kremfarben, blaßgelb; fett.

tally ['tæli] *s hist* Kerbholz; Anschreibbuch, -heft *n*, -block *m*, -tafel; (Ab-)Rechnung; Zählkerbe *f*, -strich *m*, -zeichen; Gegenstück, Pendant *n* (*of* zu); Entsprechung, Übereinstimmung *f*; Kontrollzeichen; Kontogegenbuch; Schild, Etikett *n*, Anhänger *m*; *attr* Abzahlungs-; *tr* ankerben, -kreiden, -schreiben; *(to ~ up)* (zs.-, durch-, nach)zählen, -rechnen; abhaken, nachprüfen; stückweise nachzählen; in Übereinstimmung bringen; etikettieren, (be)zeichnen; *(Waren)* auszeichnen; registrieren, buchen; *itr* anschreiben; übereinstimmen (*with* mit), sich entsprechen; *by the ~ (com)* stückweise; *to keep ~ of s.th.* etw abhaken; **~ clerk, keeper** Kontrolleur *m*; **~man** Inhaber *m* e-s Abzahlungsgeschäftes; Kontrolleur *m*; **~meter** Fernmeßinstrument *n*; **~ sheet** Kontrollzettel *m*, -liste *f*; Zählbogen *m*; *Am* (Wahl-)Protokoll *n*; **~-shop, -trade** Abzahlungsgeschäft *n*; **~ system** Abzahlungssystem *n*.

tally-ho ['tæli'hou] *interj*, *s u. itr (Jagd)* hallo (rufen).

talon ['tælən] *orn* Kralle; *tech* Klaue, Kralle; *arch* Kehlleiste *f*; *fin* Talon, Erneuerungsschein; *(Kartenspiel)* Talon *m*.

talus ['teiləs] *pl -li* ['-lai] *anat* Sprungbein *n*; Böschung; Schutthalde *f*.

tam|ability [teimə'biliti], **~ableness** ['teiməblnis] Zähmbarkeit *f*; **~able** ['-əbl] zähmbar; **~e** [teim] *a* zahm; gezähmt; sanft; gelehrig; unterwürfig, knechtisch; mut-, kraftlos, schlaff; matt, fade, schal; *(Witz)* harmlos; *(Land) Am* bebaut; *tr* (be)zähmen; *fig* gefügig machen; *to ~~ down* gesetzter werden; **~eness** ['-nis] Zahmheit; Sanftheit; Gelehrigkeit; Unterwürfigkeit *f*; **~er** ['-ə] (Tier-)Bändiger, Dompteur *m*.

tamale [tə'mɑ:li] *Art* Hackfleisch *n* mit Paprika u. Maismehl.

tamarack ['tæmərӕk] *bot* Amerikanische Lärche *f*.

tamar|ind ['tæmərind] *bot* Tamarinde *f*; **~isk** ['-risk] *bot* Tamariske *f*.

tambour ['tæmbuə] *s mus* Trommel; *arch* Säulentrommel *f*; Untersatz *m* e-r Kuppel, Tambour; Stickrahmen *m*; Rahmenstickerei *f*; *tr itr* tambourieren; **~ine** [tæmbə'ri:n] Schellen-, kleine Handtrommel *f*.

Tammany ['tæməni] *fig* politische Korruption *f*; *(~ Hall)* demokratische Parteiorganisation *f* in New York.

tam-o'-shanter [tæmə'ʃæntə] (runde) Schottenmütze *f*.

tamp [tæmp] *tr mil (mit Sandsäcken)* ab-, verdämmen; *(Beton)* rammen; *allg* feststampfen, -klopfen; *s u.* **~er** ['-ə] **1.** Stampfer *m*, Ramme; Verdämmung *f*; **~ing** ['-iŋ] Verdämmungsmaterial *n*; **~er 2.** Tamper, Rückstreumantel, Reflektor *m (d. Atombombe)*; **3.** *itr* intrigieren, die Hand im Spiel haben (*with* bei); *with s.th.* in etw hineinreden, sich in etw einmischen; etw ändern, fälschen; *with s.o.* mit jdm unter e-r Decke stecken; jdn bestechen; jdn verführen, verderben.

tampon ['tæmpən] *med* Tampon, Watte-, Mullbausch *m.*
tan [tæn] *s (Gerberei)* Lohe; Lohbrühe; gelbbraune Farbe; Sonnenbräune *f (der Haut)*; *a* lohfarben; *tr* gerben; beizen; *(in der Sonne)* bräunen; *fam* verdreschen, versohlen; *itr (in der Sonne)* braun werden; *to ~ s.o.'s hide (fam)* jdm das Fell gerben; *to get a good ~* e-e gute Farbe bekommen; **~bark** (Gerber-)Lohe *f*; **~-mill** Lohmühle *f*; **~ned** [-d] *a* braun, sonn(en)-verbrannt; **~ner** ['-ə] Gerber *m*; *fam* Sixpencestück *n*; **~nery** ['-əri] Gerberei *f*; **~nic** ['-ik] *a* Gerb(säure)-; *~~ acid*, **~nin** ['-in] Gerbsäure *f*; **~ning** ['-iŋ] (Loh-)Gerberei *f (Handwerk)*; Bräunen *n* in der Sonne; *fam* Dresche, Wichse *f*; **~-yard** Lohgerberei *f*.
tandem ['tændəm] *s* Tandem *n*; *tech* Reihe *f*; *adv* hintereinander; **~ connexion** *el* Kaskadenschaltung *f*; **~ office** Fernvermittlungsamt *n.*
tang [tæŋ] **1.** (Heft-)Zapfen, Dorn; penetrante(r) Geruch, scharfe(r) Geschmack; Beigeschmack *m*, Spur *a. fig* (*of* von); *fig* besondere Note, Eigentümlichkeit *f*; Anflug *m*; **~y** ['-i] stark riechend; **2.** *bot* (See-)Tang *m*; **3.** *itr tr* laut erklingen, ertönen, erschallen (lassen); *s* scharfe(r) Ton *m.*
tang|ent ['tændʒənt] *math a* berührend; Berührungs-; *s* Tangente *f*; *to fly, to go off at, on a ~~ (fig)* e-n Gedankensprung machen; vom Thema abkommen; plötzlich das Gegenteil tun; **~ential** [tæn'dʒenʃəl] *a math* Tangential-; *allg* abweichend; nur streifend, berührend; oberflächlich; abschweifend; *fig* sprunghaft; **~ibility** [tændʒi'biliti] Greifbarkeit; *fig* Verständlichkeit; Sachlichkeit *f*; **~ible** ['tændʒibl] fühl-, greifbar; *fig* verständlich, sachlich, endgültig; materiell; schätzenswert, wertvoll; *~~ property* Sachvermögen *n.*
tangerine [tændʒə'ri:n] *bot* Mandarine *f.*
tangle ['tæŋgl] **1.** *tr* verwickeln, verwirren; verschlingen, verknoten; *itr* sich verwickeln, sich verwirren; sich verfilzen, sich verheddern; *sl* sich in die Wolle geraten (*with* mit); *s* wirre(s) Knäuel *n*; *fig* Wirrwarr *m*, Durcheinander *n*; Verwirrung *f.*
tango ['tæŋgou] *pl -s s* Tango *m*; *itr* Tango tanzen.
tank [tæŋk] *s* Zisterne *f*; Tank, Behälter; *mil* Panzer(wagen), Tank, Kampfwagen *m*; *phot* Wanne *f*; *fam* Brotbeutel; *Am sl* Säufer *m*, Untersuchungsgefängnis *n*, Magen *m*; *tr* tanken; in e-n Behälter füllen; *itr* tanken; *Am sl* saufen, sich vollaufen lassen; *~ed up (sl)* besoffen, sternhagelvoll; **~age** ['-idʒ] Behälterinhalt *m*; Tankgebühr *f*; *agr* Fleischmehl *n*; **~ attack** Panzerangriff *m*; **~ barricade, barrier** Panzersperre *f*; **~ battle** Panzerschlacht *f*; **~ buster** Panzerknacker *m*; **~-busting** panzerbrechend; **~ car, wagon** *Am rail* Kesselwagen *m*; **~ circuit** Anodenschwingkreis *m*; **~ crew** Panzerbesatzung *f*; **~ destroyer** Zerstörerpanzer, Panzerjäger *m*; **~ ditch** Panzergraben *m*; **~ driver** Panzerfahrer *m*; **~ engine** Tenderlokomotive *f*; **~er** ['-ə] Tanker *m*, Tankschiff *n*; *(flying ~~)* Tankerflugzeug *n*; *rail* Kesselwagen; *mot* Tankwagen; *Am* Panzersoldat *m*; **~ farm** *mil* Tanklager *n*; **~ farming** *agr* Wasserkultur *f*; **~ fittings** *pl* Kesselarmaturen *f pl*; **~ fleet** Tankerflotte *f*; **~ force** Panzerwaffe *f*; **~ gunner** Panzerschütze *m*; **~ kill** Panzerabschuß *m*; **~-landing craft** Panzerlandungsboot *n*; **~ obstacle** Panzerhindernis *n*; **~ point, spearhead** Panzerspitze *f*; **~-proof** *a tr* panzersicher (machen); **~ road-block** Panzersperre *f*; **~ (town)** *Am* Kleinstadt *f*; **~ track** Panzerkette *f*; **~ trap** Panzerfalle *f*; **~ truck** *mot* Tankwagen *m*; **~ turret** Panzerturm *m*, -kuppel *f*.
tankard ['tæŋkəd] Maß(krug *m*) *n*, (Deckel-)Kanne *f.*
tansy ['tænsi] *bot* Rainfarn *m.*
tantaliz|e ['tæntəlaiz] *tr* auf die Folter spannen; foppen; quälen; **~ing** ['-iŋ] verlockend, quälend.
tantalum ['tæntələm] *chem* Tantal *n.*
tantamount ['tæntəmaunt] gleich(wertig), gleichbedeutend (*to* mit); *to be ~* gleichkommen (*to* dat).
tantivy [tæn'tivi] *adv* in voller Eile, überstürzt; *a* eilig, schnell, galoppierend; *s* Galopp *m*; *(Jagd)* Hussa *n.*
tantrum ['tæntrəm] *meist pl fam* Wutanfall *m*; schlechte Laune *f*; *she is in her ~s* mit ihr ist im Augenblick nichts anzufangen.
tap [tæp] **1.** *s* Zapfen, Spund, (Faß-, Wasser-)Hahn *m*; Zapfstelle; *(~-room) fam* Schankstube *f*, (Bier-)Lokal *n*; Anstich *m*, Bier *n*; *tech* Gewindebohrer; *tech* Abstich *m*; *el* Anzapfung *f*, Abgriff *m*; *fam* Sorte, Marke *f*; *tr* anzapfen *a. el*; *med* punktieren; abhorchen, -hören; *(Nachricht)* abfangen; abzweigen; *fam* anpumpen, -hauen (*for* um); aushorchen; *(Markt)* erschließen; *tech* ein Gewinde schneiden in; *to ~ into (sl)* dazwischenschalten; *on ~ (Bier)* im Anstich, angestochen; vom Faß; *fig* verfügbar; *to turn a ~ on, off* e-n Hahn auf-, zudrehen; **~hole** *min* Abstichloch *n*; **~-house, -room** Schankwirtschaft, -stube *f*; **~-root** *bot* Pfahlwurzel *f*; **~ster** ['-stə] Schankkellner, Büfettier *m*; **~-water** Leitungswasser *n*; **2.** *tr* (be-, ab)klopfen (*on the shoulder* auf die Schulter); *s.th. against s.th.* mit e-r S an etw klopfen; antippen; *(in e-e Maschine)* tippen; *(Schuhe)* flicken; *itr* klopfen (*at, on* an); *to ~ out (Am sl)* alles verlieren; bankrott gehen; *s* Klopfen (*on the window* an das Fenster; *at the door* an die Tür); Klopfgeräusch *n*; Flicken; leichte(r) Schlag *m*; *pl Am mil* Zapfenstreich *m*; *to ~ o.'s foot on the floor* mit dem Fuß auf den Boden stampfen; **~-dance** *itr* steppen.
tape [teip] *s* (Stoff-, Metall-)Band *n*; (Papier-)Streifen; *tele* Lochstreifen *m*; Maßband; *(streifenförmiges)* Heftpflaster; Tonband; Isolierband; *sport* Zielband *n*; *tr* mit e-m Band befestigen; auf Band sprechen *od* aufnehmen; *el* umwickeln; *to breast the ~* das Ziel erreichen; das Rennen gewinnen, *fam* machen; *to have s.th. ~d (fam)* etw gründlich kennen; *to record on ~* auf Band aufnehmen; *adhesive ~* Klebstreifen *m*; *red ~* Bürokratie *f*; Amtsschimmel *m*; **~ antenna** Bandantenne *f*; **~-line, measure** Maßband, Bandmaß *n*; **~ quotations** *pl com* Kabelnotierungen *f pl*; **~-record** *tr* auf Band aufnehmen; **~-recorder** Bandaufnahmegerät *n*; **~recording** Bandaufnahme *f*; **~worm** Bandwurm *m.*
taper ['teipə] *s* dünne (Wachs-)Kerze *f*; *tech* Konus, Kegel *m*; Konizität; Verjüngung *f*, Spitzzulaufen *n*; *fig* allmähliche Abnahme *f*; *a* spitz zulaufend; *fam fig* abnehmend; *tr* spitz zulaufen lassen, verringern; auslaufen lassen; *itr* spitz zulaufen, sich verjüngen; abnehmen; *to ~ off* spitz zulaufen, sich verjüngen; abklingen; zum Stillstand kommen; auslaufen.
tap|estry ['tæpistri] Wandbehang, -teppich, Gobelin *m*, Tapisserie, gewirkte Tapete *f*; **~is** ['tæpi:]: *to be on the ~~* zur Rede *od* Debatte stehen; *to come on the ~~* aufs Tapet gebracht werden, zur Sprache kommen.
tapioca [tæpi'oukə] Tapioka(mehl *n*) *f.*
tapir ['teipə] *zoo* Tapir *m.*
tappet ['tæpit] *tech* Stößel, Nocken, Daumen, Mitnehmer, Anschlag *m*; **~ switch** Kippschalter *m.*
tar [tɑ:] *s* Teer *m*; *fam* Teerjacke *f (Matrose)*; *tr* teeren; *to ~ and feather s.o.* jdn *(zur Strafe)* mit Teer bestreichen u. mit Federn bestreuen; *they are ~red with the same brush, stick* e-r ist nicht mehr wert als der andere; **~-board** Dach-, Teerpappe *f*; **~mac** ['-mæk] Teerschotter, Asphalt *m*; *aero* asphaltierte(s) Rollfeld *n*; **~ry 1.** ['-ri] *a* Teer; teerartig; teerig.
taradiddle ['tærədidl] *fam* Schwindel *m*, Lüge *f.*
tarant|ella [tærən'telə] Tarantella *f (Tanz)*; **~ula** [tə'ræntjulə] *zoo* Tarantel *f.*
tard|iness ['tɑ:dinis] Langsamkeit; *Am* Verspätung *f*; **~y** ['tɑ:di] langsam; spät; säumig, verspätet; hinhaltend; *to be ~~ for s.th.* zu etw zu spät kommen.
tare [tɛə] **1.** *bot* Wicke *f*; *(Bibel)* Unkraut *n*; **2.** *s* Tara *f*; *tr* tarieren; *customs ~* Zollgewicht *n.*
target ['tɑ:git] Schieß-, Zielscheibe *f*; Zielpunkt *m*; (Angriffs-)Ziel *n a. fig*; *fig* Zielscheibe *f* (des Spottes); *rail* Scheibensignal *n*; *el* Antikat(h)ode *f*; *phys* Ziel *(beim Kernbeschuß)*; *fig a. pol com* Ziel; Soll *n*, Planziffer *f*; *output ~* Produktionsziel *n*; **~ area** *aero* Zielraum *m*; **~ bombing** Bombenzielwurf *m*; **~ butt** Kugelfang *m*; **~ cost** vorkalkulierte Kosten *pl*; **~ date** *com* Ziel(tag *m*), Fälligkeitsdatum *n*, Lieferfrist *f*; **~ designation** Zielansprache *f*; **~ figures** *pl* Sollzahlen *f pl*; **~ flare** Zielmarkierungsbombe *f*; **~ indicator** *aero* (Boden-)Zielmarkierung *f*; **~ information** *aero* Zielunterlagen *f pl*; **~ marking** Zielmarkierung *f*; **~ pit** Anzeigerdeckung *f*; **~-practice** Scheibenschießen *n*; **~ range** Schießstand *m*; **~ reconnaissance** Zielerkundung *f*; **~ ship** Artillerieversuchs-, Zielschiff *n*; **~ shooting** *sport* Scheibenschießen *n*; **~ simulation** Zieldarstellung *f.*
tariff ['tærif] *s* (Zoll-)Tarif; Zoll(satz); Gebührensatz *m*, -verzeichnis *n*; *tele* Gesprächsgebühr; Preisliste *f*; Preis *m*; *tr* e-n Zolltarif aufstellen für; den Preis errechnen für; *to raise, to lower the ~s* die Zölle erhöhen, senken; *freight ~* Gütertarif *m*, Frachtsätze *m pl*; *fundamental ~* Grundtarif *m*; *hostile ~s (pl)* Zollschranken *f pl*; *preferential ~* Vorzugszoll *m*; *protection ~* Schutzzoll *m*; *railway ~* Eisenbahntarif *m*; *uniform ~* Einheitssatz *m*; **~ laws, regulations** *pl* Zollbestimmungen *f pl*; **~ legislation** Zollgesetzgebung *f*; **~ negotiations** *pl* Zollverhandlungen *f pl*; **~ policy** Zollpolitik *f*; **~ rates** *pl* Zolltarif *m*; **~ reform** Tarif-, Zollreform; *Br* Schutzzollpolitik, *Am* Freihandelspolitik *f*; **~ revenue** Zolleinnahmen *f pl*; **~ system** Tarif-, Zollsystem *n*; **~ union** Zollverein *m*, -union *f*; **~ wall** Zollschranken *f pl.*
tarn [tɑ:n] Bergsee *m.*

tarnish ['tɑ:niʃ] *tr (glatte Fläche)* trüben; *fig* beflecken, beschmutzen; *tech* mattieren; *itr* s-n Glanz verlieren; trübe, matt werden, anlaufen; *s* Trübung *f*, Mattwerden *n*; trübe (Ober-) Fläche *f*; *fig* Fleck, Makel *m*.

tarpaulin [tɑ:'pɔ:lin] Persenning *f*; Ölzeug *n*; Zeltplane, -bahn, Wagenplane *f*; Ölhut *m*.

tarragon ['tærəgən] *bot* Estragon *m*.

tarry 2. ['tæri] *lit itr* zögern, zaudern; bleiben, sich aufhalten; warten.

tarsus ['tɑ:səs] *pl -si* ['-ai] *anat* Fußwurzel *f*.

tart [tɑ:t] **1.** scharf, herb, sauer; *fig* scharf, beißend; **~ness** ['-nis] Schärfe *f a. fig*; **2.** Obsttorte *f*; *Am* Törtchen *n*; *apple-, cherry-~* Apfel-, Kirschtorte *f*; **~let** ['-lit] Törtchen *n*; **3.** *s sl* Dirne, Nutte *f*; *tr sl* herausstaffieren.

tartan ['tɑ:tən] (Wollstoff *m*, Decke *f* mit) Schottenmuster *n*.

Ta(r)tar ['tɑ:tə] *s* Ta(r)tar *m*; *a* ta(r)tarisch; *t~* Heißsporn, Querkopf *m*; *to catch a t~* an den Unrechten kommen; e-n Extragewinn einstreichen.

tartar ['tɑ:tə] Wein-, Zahnstein *m*; **~ic** [tɑ:'tærik] *a* Weinstein-; *~~ acid* Weinsteinsäure *f*.

task [tɑ:sk] *s* (schwierige) Aufgabe, Arbeit *f*, Tagewerk *n*; Pflicht *f*; Auftrag *m*; Unternehmen, -fangen *n*; Schulaufgabe; *(Fabrik)* Mindestleistung *f*; *tr* e-e Aufgabe stellen (*s.o.* jdm); e-e (bestimmte) Arbeit verlangen von; beschäftigen, in Anspruch nehmen; anstrengen; *to take to ~* zur Rede stellen, zurechtweisen, tadeln (*for, about* wegen); **~ force** *mil* Kampfgruppe (für Sonderunternehmen), Sondereinheit *f*; **~master** Zuchtmeister; (Arbeits-)Aufseher *m*; **~ wages** *pl* Stück-, Akkordlohn *m*; **~-work** unangenehme Arbeit; Stück-, Akkordarbeit *f*.

tassel ['tæsl] *s* Troddel, Quaste *f*; Büschel *n*; *tr* mit Quasten verzieren.

tast|e [teist] *tr (Speise, Getränk)* kosten, probieren, versuchen; prüfen; (ab-) schmecken; zu sich nehmen, essen; *fig* kosten, zu spüren bekommen; erfahren, erleben; nur e-n Vorgeschmack haben von; *itr* schmecken (*of* nach); versuchen, genießen (*of s.th.* etw); *fig* ein Vorgefühl, e-e Ahnung haben *gen*, *fam* e-n Riecher haben für; *s* Geschmack(ssinn); Geschmack *m (e-r Speise)*; Probieren *n*; Kostprobe *f*, Bissen *m*; *fig* Vorgeschmack; Hauch *m*, Andeutung, Spur *f* (*of* von); (guter) Geschmack *m*; Vorliebe (*for* für); Neigung *f* (*for* zu), Sinn *m* (*for* für); *in (good) ~~* geschmack-, taktvoll; *in bad, poor ~~* geschmacklos; *to ~ (Küche)* nach Geschmack; *to s.o.'s ~~* nach jds Geschmack; *to leave a bad ~~ in o.'s mouth (a. fig)* e-n schlechten Nachgeschmack haben; *~~ bud (anat)* Geschmacksknospe *f*, Schmeckbecher *m*; **~eful** ['-ful] geschmackvoll; **~efulness** ['-fulnis] gute(r) Geschmack *m*; **~eless** ['-lis] fade, nach nichts schmeckend; *fig* langweilig, uninteressant; geschmacklos; **~elessness** ['-lisnis] Fadheit; *fig* Geschmacklosigkeit *f*; **~er** ['-ə] (Wein-, Tee-) Schmecker, Prüfer, Probierer; *fam fig* (Verlags-)Lektor *m*; Pipette *f*, Prüfgerät *n*; *to give s.o. a ~~ of s.th.* jdm e-e Kostprobe von etw geben; **~iness** ['-inis] *(Speise)* Schmackhaftigkeit *f*; Geschmack *m*; **~y** ['-i] wohlschmeckend; *sl* geschmackvoll.

tat [tæt] **1.** *s: to give tit for ~* mit gleicher Münze heimzahlen; **2.** *tr itr* (in) Schiffchenarbeit herstellen; **3.** *pl sl* Lumpen *m pl*.

Tatar *s. Tartar.*

tatter ['tætə] Fetzen; Lumpen *m*; *pl* Lumpen *m pl*, abgerissene Kleidung *f*; *to tear to ~s (fig)* zerfetzen, zerreißen; **~demalion** [tætədə'meiljən] zerlumpte(r) Kerl *m*; **~ed** ['tætəd] *a* zerlumpt, abgerissen.

tattle ['tætl] *itr* plaudern, schwatzen; klatschen; *tr* ausplaudern, klatschen über; *s* Klatsch *m*; **~r** ['-ə] Schwätzer *m*; Klatschbase *f*; *orn* Wasserläufer; *Am sl* Wecker, Wachmann *m*; **~tale** *Am* Schwätzer *m*; Klatschbase *f*.

tattoo [tə'tu:] **1.** *mil* Zapfenstreich *m*; *allg* Trommeln, Klopfen *n*; *itr* trommeln, klopfen; *to beat, to sound the ~* den Zapfenstreich blasen; *to beat the devil's ~* ungeduldig mit den Fingern trommeln; *torchlight ~* Parade *f* bei Nacht mit Musik; **2.** *tr* tätowieren; *s* Tätowierung *f*.

tatty ['tæti] *fam* schäbig.

taunt [tɔ:nt] *tr* spotten, sich lustig machen über; verspotten, verhöhnen (*with cowardice* wegen Feigheit); *s* Spott, Hohn *m*, spöttische Bemerkung *f*; Tadel *m*; **~ingly** ['-iŋli] *adv* spöttisch, höhnisch.

Taurus ['tɔ:rəs] *astr* Stier *m*.

taut [tɔ:t] gespannt, straff, angezogen; *(Gesicht)* starr, steif; sauber, schmuck; *to haul a rope ~* ein Seil straff spannen; **~en** ['-n] *tr itr* (sich) straffen, (sich) spannen.

tautolog|ical [tɔ:tə'lɔdʒikəl] tautologisch; **~y** [tɔ:'tɔlədʒi] Tautologie *f*.

tavern ['tævən] Schenke *f*, Lokal *n*, Kneipe *f*.

taw [tɔ:] **1.** *tr* weißgerben; **~er** ['-ə] Weißgerber *m*; **2.** Murmel *f*; Murmelspiel *n*; *Am sl* Einsatz, große(r) Geldbetrag *m*.

tawdr|iness ['tɔ:drinis] Flitterhaftigkeit; Geschmacklosigkeit; Billigkeit *f*; **~y** ['tɔ:dri] flitterhaft, billig, geschmacklos; kitschig.

tawn|iness ['tɔ:ninis] Lohfarbe *f*; **~y** ['tɔ:ni] lohfarben, gelbbraun.

tax [tæks] *tr* (steuerlich) veranlagen, besteuern; mit e-r Gebühr belegen, belasten; auf die Probe stellen; stark in Anspruch nehmen, anstrengen; schätzen (*at* auf), einstufen; beschuldigen (*with* gen); *s* Steuer, Abgabe (*on* auf); Gebühr; Besteuerung (*on* auf); Last, Belastung, Beanspruchung, Inanspruchnahme *f* (*on* gen); *pl fam* Finanzamt *n*; *after, less ~es* nach Abzug der Steuern; *to cut a ~* e-e Steuer senken; *to collect ~es* Steuern erheben *od* einziehen; *to impose, to lay, to levy, to put a ~ on* mit e-r Steuer belegen, besteuern; *to pay* 100 £ *in ~es* 100 £ Steuern zahlen; *to prepare an income ~ return* e-e Einkommen(s)steuererklärung ausfüllen; *abatement of ~es* Steuernachlaß *m*; *amount of the ~* Steuerbetrag *m*; *automobile, motor-car ~* Kraftfahrzeugsteuer *f*; *beverage ~* Getränkesteuer *f*; *capital ~* Vermögen(s)steuer *f*; *church ~* Kirchensteuer *f*; *communal, local, municipal ~* Gemeindesteuer *f*; *dog ~* Hundesteuer *f*; *entertainment ~* Vergnügung(s)steuer *f*; *free of ~, of all ~es* steuerfrei; *income ~* Einkommen(s)steuer *f*; *increment value ~* Wertzuwachssteuer *f*; *indirect ~* indirekte, Verbrauch(s)steuer *f*; *inheritance ~* Erbschaft(s)steuer *f*; *luxury ~* Luxussteuer *f*; *non-resident ~* Kurtaxe *f*; *personal, poll ~* Kopfsteuer *f*; *property ~* Vermögen(s)-, Grundsteuer *f*; *purchase ~* Verkauf(s)steuer *f*; *salary ~* Lohnsteuer *f*; *trade ~* Gewerbesteuer *f*; *turnover ~* Umsatzsteuer *f*; *~ on sales* Umsatzsteuer *f*; **~able** ['-əbl] steuerpflichtig; *~~ period* Veranlagungszeitraum *m*; **~ation** [tæk'seiʃən] Besteuerung, Steuerveranlagung; (Kosten-)Festsetzung *f*; Steuern, Abgaben *f pl*; Einschätzung *f*; *~~ legislation* Steuergesetzgebung *f*; *~~ period* Steuerperiode; Veranlagungszeit *f*; **~ authority** Steuerbehörde, Finanzverwaltung *f*; **~ avoidance,** *Am* **evasion** Steuerhinterziehung *f*; **~ bond, certificate** Steuergutschein *m*; **~ bracket** Steuerklasse *f*; **~ burden** Steuerlast *f*; **~ claim** Steuerforderung *f*; **~-collector, -gatherer** Steuereinnehmer *m*; **~ evader** *Am* Steuerhinterzieher *m*; **~-exempt** steuer-, abgabenfrei; **~ exemption** Steuerfreiheit, -erleichterung *f*, -freibetrag *m*; **~-free** steuerfrei; **~ing** ['-iŋ] Festsetzung *f*; **~ law** Steuergesetz *n*; **~ liability** Steuerpflicht *f*; **~ list** Steuerliste *f*; **~ load** Steuerlast *f*; **~-payer** Steuerzahler *m*; *~~'s strike* Steuerstreik *m*; **~-paying capacity** Steuerkraft *f*; **~ rate** Steuersatz *m*; **~ receipts** *pl* Steueraufkommen *n*; **~ reduction** Steuerermäßigung *f*, -nachlaß *m*; **~ refund** Steuerrückerstattung *f*; **~ regulation** Steuervorschrift *f*; **~ (re)source** Steuerquelle *f*; **~ return** Steuererklärung *f*; **~ revenue** Steuereinnahmen *f pl*; **~ revision** Steuerreform *f*; **~ stamp** Steuermarke *f*; **~ year** Steuerjahr *n*.

taxi ['tæksi] *s (~cab)* Taxe *f*, Taxi *n*; *itr (to take a ~)* mit e-r Taxe fahren; *aero* rollen; *tr aero* rollen lassen; *to ~ off, out* abrollen; *to ~ to a standstill (aero)* ausrollen; **~-dancer, -girl** Taxigirl *n*; **~-driver** Taxifahrer, -chauffeur *m*; **~ing** ['-iŋ] *aero* Rollen *n (am Boden)*; **~meter** ['tæksimi:tə] Taxameter *m*; **~plane** Mietflugzeug *n*, Flugtaxe *f*; **~-rank,** *Am* **-stand** Haltestelle *f* für Taxen, Taxistand *m*; **~ strip, track, way** *aero* Rollstreifen *m*, -bahn *f*.

taxidermy ['tæksidə:mi] Taxidermie *f*.

tea [ti:] *s* Tee *m*; *to have ~* Tee trinken; *to make (the) ~* Tee zubereiten; *not my cup of ~ (fig fam)* nicht mein Fall; *beef ~* Fleisch-, Kraftbrühe *f*; *camomile, peppermint ~* Kamillen-, Pfefferminztee *m*; *five-o'-clock ~* Fünfuhrtee *m*; *herbal ~* Kräutertee *m*; *high, meat ~* frühe(s) Abendbrot, -essen *n*; *instant ~* Teepulver *n*; *~ for two, three* 2, 3 Portionen *f pl* Tee; **~-bag** Teebeutel *m*; **~-ball** *Am* Tee-Ei *n*; **~ biscuit** Teekuchen *m*; **~-break** Teepause *f*; **~-caddy** Teebüchse *f*; **~-cake** (warmer) Teekuchen *m*; **~-cart** Teewagen *m*; **~-chest** *com* Teekiste *f*; **~-cloth** (kleine) Tischdecke *f*; Geschirrtuch *n*; **~-cosy** Teewärmer *m*; **~cup** Teetasse *f*; *a storm in a ~~* ein Sturm im Wasserglas; **~cupful** Tassevoll *f*; **~-dance** Tanztee *m*; **~-garden** Gartenrestaurant *n*, Kaffeegarten *m*; Teepflanzung *f*; **~-gown** Nachmittagskleid *n*; **~house** Teehaus *n*; **~-kettle** Teekessel *m*; **~-leaves** *pl* Teesatz *m*; *to tell s.o.'s fortune from the ~~* das Glück aus dem Kaffeesatz lesen; **~-party, -fight** *sl* Teegesellschaft *f*; **~-pot** Teekanne *f*; **~-room, -shop** Konditorei *f*, *Art* Tagescafé *(mit Tee als Hauptgetränk)*; Teezimmer *n (e-s Restaurants)*; **~-rose** *bot* Teerose *f*; **~-service, -set** Teeservice *n*; **~spoon** Teelöffel *m*; **~spoonful** Teelöffelvoll *m*; **~-strainer** Teesieb *n*; **~-table** Teetisch *m*; *~~ conversation*

Tischgespräch *n*; **~-taster** Teeprüfer *m*; **~-things** *pl fam* Teegeschirr *n*; **~-time** Teestunde *f*; **~-tray** Teetablett *n*; **~-urn** Teemaschine *f*; **~-wag(g)on, -trolley** Teewagen *m*.
teach [ti:tʃ] *irr taught, taught* [tɔ:t] *tr* (be)lehren, unterrichten; beibringen; *(Tier)* dressieren; *itr* Unterricht geben *od* erteilen; unterrichten; **~able** ['ti:tʃəbl] lehrbar; gelehrig; **~er** ['-ə] Lehrer(in *f*) *m*; **~ing** ['-iŋ] Unterricht; Lehrberuf *m*; *pl* Lehre(n *f pl*) *f*; *~~ staff* Lehrkörper *m*.
teak [ti:k] Tiekbaum *m*, -holz *n*.
teal [ti:l] Kriekente *f*.
team [ti:m] *s* Gespann *n*; *sport* Mannschaft *f*; Team *n*, Arbeitsgruppe, Kolonne, Schicht *f*; *itr*: *to ~ up with (fam)* zs.arbeiten mit; sich zs.tun; *football ~* Fußballmannschaft *f*; **~ captain** Mannschaftsführer *m*; **~mate** Mannschafts-, Arbeits-, Gruppenkamerad *m*; **~ play** Zs.spiel *n*; **~ spirit** Mannschaftsgeist *m*; **~ster** ['-stə] Fuhrmann; Lastwagenfahrer *m*; **~-work** Zs.-, Gemeinschaftsarbeit *f*; *theat* gute(s) Zs.spiel *n*.
tear 1. [tɛə] *irr tore* [tɔ:], *torn* [tɔ:n] *tr* zerreißen (*on a nail* an e-m Nagel); *(Loch, Riß)* reißen; ein-, aufreißen; herausreißen (*from* aus); *(Haare)* sich raufen; *fig* (auf)spalten; zersplittern; *(innerlich)* hin- u. herreißen; *itr* (zer-) reißen; zerren, reißen (*at* an); rasen, sausen, toben; *s* (Zer-)Reißen *n*; Riß *m*; Toben *n*, Raserei *f*; *Am sl* Remmidemmi *n*, lustige(r) Abend *m*, Zecherei *f*; *to mend a ~* e-n Riß ausbessern; *to ~ o.'s hair* sich die Haare raufen; *to ~ to pieces, to bits* in Stücke reißen; *to ~ in two* in der Mitte durchreißen; *to ~* **about** herumtoben; *to ~* **along** dahinsausen, -rasen; *to ~* **around** herumrennen (*from ... to* von ... zu); *to ~* **away** los-, wegreißen; *he couldn't ~ away from* er konnte sich nicht trennen von; *to ~* **down** abreißen, abbrechen; herunterreißen (*from* von); *to ~* **off** abreißen; *the button tore off* der Knopf ist ab(gerissen); *to ~* **open** aufreißen; *to ~* **out** (her)ausreißen; *to ~ out of o.'s hand* aus der Hand reißen; *to ~* **up** zerreißen; auf-, ausreißen; *fig* untergraben; **~ing** ['-riŋ] *a* wild; wütend; **~-off calendar** Abreißkalender *m*; **~ sheet** *com* Belegstück *n*; **2.** [tiə] Träne *f*; *in ~s* in Tränen (aufgelöst), weinend; *to burst into ~s* in Tränen ausbrechen; *to move to ~s* zu Tränen rühren; *to shed ~s* Tränen vergießen; *to weep bitter ~s* heiße Tränen weinen; *crocodile ~s (pl)* Krokodilstränen *f pl*; **~ bomb** Tränengasbombe *f*; **~-drop** Träne *f*; **~ful** ['-ful] weinend; traurig; schmerzlich; *(Gesicht)* tränenüberströmt; **~-gas** Tränengas *n*; *~~ bomb* Tränengasbombe *f*; **~-jerker** *Am sl* sentimentale(r) Film *m*; Schnulze *f*; **~less** ['-lis] tränenlos; **~-stained** *a* tränenbenetzt; **~y** ['-ri] tränennaß; zu Tränen rührend.
teas|e [ti:z] *tr* hänseln, necken, aufziehen, frotzeln (*about* wegen); quälen, plagen; belästigen, in den Ohren liegen (*s.o.* jdm; *for* wegen); *tech* zerfasern, strähnen; *(Flachs)* hecheln; *(Wolle)* krempeln; *(Tuch)* kardieren; *(Werg)* auszupfen; *itr* sticheln, frotzeln; *s* Plagegeist; Hänsler *m*; Necken, Sticheln; *tech* Zerfasern *n*; **~er** ['-ə] Plagegeist, Hänsler *m*; *fam* schwierige(s) Problem *n*, harte Nuß *f*.
teasel ['ti:zl] *s bot* Kardendistel; *tech* Karde *f*; *tr (Tuch)* krempeln.
teat [ti:t] *med* Brustwarze; *zoo* Zitze *f*.

tec [tek] *sl* Detektiv *m*.
techn|ic ['teknik] *s* = *~ique*; *pl mit sing* Technik *f*, Ingenieurwissenschaften *f pl*; **~ical** ['-ikəl] technisch; ingenieurwissenschaftlich; fachlich; *com* manipuliert; *~~ bureau* Konstruktionsbüro *n*; *~~ college* technische Hochschule *f*; *~~ personnel* Fachkräfte *f pl*; *~~ question* Verfahrensfrage *f*; *~~ school* (Poly-)Technikum *n*; *~~ skill* Kunstfertigkeit, Technik *f*; *~~ term* Fachausdruck *m*; *~~ training* Berufsausbildung *f*; **~icality** [tekni'kæliti] Kunstfertigkeit; Technik; technische Seite *od* Frage *od* Einzelheit *f*; technische(r) Ausdruck *m*; **~ician** [tek'niʃən] Fachmann, Experte; Facharbeiter; Könner *m*; **~icolor** ['teknikʌlə] Technikolor(verfahren) *n*; **~ique** [tek'ni:k] Technik *f*, Verfahren; Geschick *n*, Kunstfertigkeit *f*; **~o-chemistry** [teknə'kemistri] Chemotechnik, Industriechemie *f*; **~ocracy** [tek'nɔkrəsi] Technokratie *f*; **~ologic(al)** [teknə'lɔdʒik(əl)] technologisch; **~ology** [tek'nɔlədʒi] Technologie, Gewerbekunde *f*; *school of ~~* technische Hochschule *f*.
techy *s. tetchy.*
tectonic [tek'tɔnik] *a geol* tektonisch; *biol* strukturell; *s pl mit sing geol* Tektonik *f*.
ted [ted] *tr (Heu)* wenden; **~der** ['-ə] Heuwender *m*.
Ted(dy) ['ted(i)] *fam* Theo(dor) *m*; *t~ bear* Teddybär *m*; *t~ boy* Halbstarke(r) *m*.
tedi|ous ['ti:djəs] langweilig, -wierig, ermüdend, uninteressant; umständlich; **~ousness** ['-əsnis], **~um** ['-əm] Langweiligkeit, -wierigkeit, Uninteressantheit; Umständlichkeit *f*.
tee [ti:] **1.** *s* T-Profil *n*; *tr el* abzweigen; **2.** *s* (*Golf*) Abschlagplatz *m*; Ausgangsstellung *f (des Spielers)*; *sport allg* Mal, Ziel *n*; *tr*: *to ~ off (Golfball)* abschlagen; *itr fig* anfangen.
teem [ti:m] *itr* im Überfluß vorhanden sein; strotzen, wimmeln (*with* von); **~ing** ['-iŋ] wimmelnd (*with* von).
teen|-age ['ti:neidʒ] *a* Teenager-; jugendlich; **~-ager** ['-ə] Teenager *m (zwischen 13 u. 19)*; **~s** [ti:ns] Alter *n* zwischen 13 u. 19; *she is still in her ~~* sie ist noch nicht 20.
teeny ['ti:ni], **~-weeny** winzig.
teepee *s. tepee.*
teeter ['ti:tə] *Am itr tr* schaukeln, wippen; *itr* schwanken, zittern; *s (~-board)* Schaukel(brett *n*), Wippe *f*.
teeth [ti:θ] *s. tooth*; **~e** [ti:ð] *itr* zahnen, Zähne bekommen; **~ing** ['-iŋ] *s* Zahnen *n*; *~~-troubles (pl) fig* Kinderkrankheiten *f pl*.
teetotal [ti:'toutl] abstinent; *fam* völlig, vollständig, -kommen; **~(l)er** [-ə] Abstinenzler, Alkoholgegner *m*; **~ism** [-izm] Abstinenz *f*.
teetotum ['ti:to(u)'tʌm, ti:'toutəm] Kreisel *m*; *fig* kleine(s) Ding *n*.
tegument ['tegjumənt] *anat zoo bot* Bedeckung, Decke, Hülle *f*.

*

telautogra|m [te'lɔ:təgræm] Bildtelegramm *n*; **~ph** [-æf] Bildtelegraph, -fernschreiber *m*.
tele-archics [teli'a:kiks] *pl mit sing* Fernsteuerung *f*.
tele ['teli] *pref* Fern-, Tele-; *bes.* Fernseh-; **~camera** [-'kæmərə] Kamera *f* mit Teleobjektiv; Fernsehkamera *f*.
telecast ['telikɑ:st] *pret u. pp ~* od *~ed tr* im Fernsehen senden *od* übertragen; *s* Fernsehsendung, -übertragung *f*; **~er** ['-ə] Mitwirkende(r) *m* in e-r Fernsehsendung.

teleceiver ['telisi:və] Fernsehempfänger *m*.
tele|communication ['telikəmju(:)ni'keiʃən] *s* Nachrichtenverbindung *f*; *pl* Fernmeldewesen *n*; *attr* Fernmelde-; **~control** ['-kəntroul] Fernsteuerung *f*; **~course** ['-kɔ:s] Fernsehunterricht, -kurs *m*; **~fan** ['-fæn] *Am* Fernsehnarr *m*; **~film** ['-film] Fernsehfilm *m*; **~genic** [teli'dʒenik] telegen.
telegram ['teligræm] Telegramm *n*; *to hand in a ~* ein T. aufgeben; *by ~* telegraphisch; *cipher ~* Schlüsseltelegramm *m*; *radio, wireless ~* Funktelegramm *n*; *~ delivered by mail* Brieftelegramm *n*; **~ form** Telegrammformular *n*.
telegraph ['teligrɑ:f] *s* Telegraph *m*; Telegramm *n*; *tr itr* telegraphieren; *sport (Spielstand)* anzeigen; **~-board** *sport* Anzeigetafel *f*; **~er** [ti'legrəfə], **~ist** [-ist] Telegraphist *m*; **~ese** ['teləgrɑ:'fi:z] Telegrammstil *m*; **~ form** Telegrammformular *n*; **~ic(al)** [teli'græfik] telegraphisch; Telegramm-; *~ic address* Telegrammadresse, Drahtanschrift *f*; *~ic answer* Drahtantwort *f*; *~ic news* Drahtbericht *m*; *~ic style* Telegrammstil *m*; **~ key** Klopfertaste *f*; **~ line** Telegraphenleitung *f*; **~ office** Telegraphenamt *n*; **~-pole, -post** Telegraphenstange *f*; **~y** [ti'legrəfi] Telegraphie *f*.
tele|kinesis [telikai'ni:sis] Telekinese *f*; **~lectric** [-'lektrik] *a* elektrische Übertragungs-; **~meter** [ti'lemitə] Fernmeßinstrument *n*; **~mobile** [-'moubail] Fernsprechwagen *m*.

*

teleolog|ical [teliə'lɔdʒikəl] *philos* teleologisch; **~y** [teli'ɔlədʒi] Teleologie *f*.
telepath|ic [teli'pæθik] telepathisch; **~y** [ti'lepəθi] Telepathie *f*.
telephon|e ['telifoun] *s* Fernsprecher *m*, Telephon *n*; (Fernsprech-)Apparat *m*; *itr* telephonieren; anrufen, -läuten; *tr (Nachricht)* telephonisch durchgeben, -sagen; *(Person)* anrufen, -läuten, -klingeln, -telephonieren (*s.o.* jdm); telephonisch, fernmündlich sprechen (mit); *by ~~* telephonisch, fernmündlich; *on the ~~* durch Fernsprecher; *to answer the ~~ bell* ans Telephon gehen; *to be on the ~~* Fernsprechanschluß haben; am Apparat sein; *to ring s.o. up on the ~~* jdn anrufen; *he is wanted on the ~~* er wird am Telephon verlangt; *automatic ~~* (Apparat im) Selbstwählbetrieb *m*; *coin collector ~~* Münzfernsprecher *m*; *desk ~~* Tischapparat *m*; *subscriber's ~~* Telephonanschluß *m*; *~~-booth, -box* Telephon-, Fernsprechzelle *f*; *~~-call* (Telephon-)Anruf *m*, -gespräch, *fam* Telefonat *n*; *~~-connection* Telephon-, Fernsprechverbindung *f*, -anschluß *m*; *~~-conversation* Telephon-, Ferngespräch *n*; *~~-directory* Fernsprech-, Teilnehmerverzeichnis, Telephonbuch *n*; *~~-exchange* Telephon-, Fernsprechvermitt(e)lung, -zentrale *f*; *~~-fees, -rates (pl)* Fernsprechgebühren *f pl*; *~~-line* Fernsprechleitung *f*; *~~-message* telephonische Nachricht, Durchsage *f*; *~~-number* Telephon-, Rufnummer *f*; *~~-office* Fernsprechamt *n*; *~~-operator* Telephonist(in *f*) *m*; *~~-receiver* (Telephon-)Hörer *m*; *~~-subscriber* Fernsprechteilnehmer *m*; *~~-wire* Telephondraht *m*; **~ee** [telifo(u)'ni:] Angerufene(r) *m*; **~ic** [teli'fɔnik] telephonisch, fernmündlich; Telephon-, Fernsprech-; *~~ communication* Telephonverbindung *f*; **~ist** [ti'lefənist] Tele-

phonist(in *f*) *m*; **~y** [ti'lefəni] Fernsprechwesen *n*, Telephonie *f*.

telephot|e ['telifout] photoelektrische Fernkamera *f*; **~o** ['-'foutou] *a* telephotographisch; Teleobjektiv-; *s* Draht-, Funkbild; Telebild *n*; *~~ lens* Teleobjektiv *n*; **~ograph** ['teli-'foutəgrɑ:f] *s* Telebild; Draht-, Funkbild *n*; *tr itr* mit Teleobjektiv *od* photoelektrischer Kamera aufnehmen; **~ographic** ['telifoutə'græfik] telephotographisch; Draht-, Funkbild-; **~ography** ['telifə'tɔgrəfi] Telephotographie; Bildtelegraphie *f*, -funk *m*.

teleprint ['teliprint] *(Warenzeichen) tr* als Fernschreiben übermitteln; **~er** ['-ə] Fernschreiber *m (Gerät)*; *to send s.o. a message over ~~* jdm e-e Nachricht durch Fernschreiber übermitteln.

tele|ran ['teliræn] *(= television radar air navigation)* Teleran *n*, Flugnavigation *f* mit Fernsehen u. Radar; **~recording** ['-ri'kɔ:diŋ] (Fernseh-) Aufzeichnung *f*.

telescop|e ['teliskoup] *s* Fernrohr, Teleskop *n*; *itr* sich inea.schieben; *tr* inea.schieben; *fig* verkürzen, verdichten; *a* ausziehbar; *reflecting ~~* Spiegelreflektor *m*; *~~ table* Ausziehtisch *m*; **~ic** [telis'kɔpik] teleskopisch; Fernrohr-; ausziehbar, inea.schiebbar; *~~ eyes (zoo)* Teleskopaugen *n pl*; *~~ lens* Teleobjektiv *n*; *~~ view-finder* Fernrohrsucher *m*.

tele|screen ['teliskri:n] *tele* Bildschirm *m*; **~scriptor** [-'skriptə] Fernschreiber *m*; **~station** ['-steiʃən] Fernsehsender *m*; **~thermometer** ['-θə-'mɔmitə] Fernthermometer *n*.

teletype ['telitaip] *s (Warenzeichen)* Fernschreiber *m*; Fernschreibverbindung *f*; *tr* als Fernschreiben übermitteln; *itr* (als) Fernschreiber (tätig) sein; ~ **exchange** Fernschreibvermittlung *f*; ~ **net** Fernschreibnetz *n*; **~r** ['-ə], **~writer** Fernschreiber *m*; **~setter** Fernschreibsetzmaschine *f*.

televi|ew ['telivju:] *tr* im Fernsehen, auf dem Bildschirm sehen; *itr* am Bildschirm sitzen; beim Fernsehen zuschauen; *fam* fernsehen; **~ewer** ['-vju:ə] (Fernseh-)Zuschauer *m*; **~se** ['-vaiz] *tr* im Fernsehen übertragen; auf dem Bildschirm sehen; **~sion** ['teliviʒən] Fernsehen *n*, Bildfunk; *fam* Fernseher *m (Gerät)*; *to see s.th. on ~~* etw im Fernsehen sehen; *~~ announcer* Fernsehsprecher, -ansager *m*; *~~ broadcast* Fernsehsendung *f*; *~~ camera* Fernsehkamera *f*; *~~ image, picture* Fernsehbild *n*; *~~ program(me), show* Fernsehprogramm *n*; *~~ receiver, set* Fernsehempfänger *m*, -gerät *n*, -apparat *m*; *~~ studio* Fernsehsenderaum *m*; *~~ transmitter* Fernsehsender *m*; *~~ viewer* (Fernseh-)Zuschauer *m*; *~~ wave* Bildwelle *f*; **~sor** ['telivaizə] Fernsehgerät *n*, -apparat, -empfänger *m*.

tell [tel] *irr told, told* [tould] *tr* erzählen, berichten, wiedergeben; sagen; mitteilen; bestellen, ausrichten; ankündigen, bekanntmachen, -geben; an den Tag, zum Ausdruck bringen, deutlich machen, enthüllen, bloßlegen; sehen, erkennen, feststellen; unterscheiden, ausea.halten (*from* von); ersuchen, anweisen, beauftragen, befehlen (*s.o.* jdm); versichern, die Versicherung geben (*s.o.* jdm); *obs* (ab)zählen; *to have been told* gehört haben; *itr* erzählen, berichten (*of* von; *about* über); hinweisen, -deuten (*of* auf); andeuten, beweisen (*of s.th.* etw); wissen; zählen, Bedeutung, Gewicht haben; Einfluß, Wirkung haben, wirken, sich auswirken (*on* auf); mitnehmen (*on s.o.* jdn); *to ~ apart* ausea.halten, unterscheiden; *to ~ off* ab-, auszählen; abkommandieren; *fam* anschnauzen; den Standpunkt klarmachen; *to ~ on s.o.* jdn verraten; *to ~ in advance* voraussagen; *all told* alles in allem, summa summarum; *to ~ fortunes from cards* aus den Karten wahrsagen; *to ~ the tale (fam)* e-e Geschichte erzählen, um Mitleid zu erwecken; *to ~ tales out of school* aus der Schule plaudern; *to ~ s.o. the time* jdm sagen, wie spät es ist; die Zeit angeben; *to ~ the truth* die Wahrheit sagen; ehrlich gesagt; *to ~ the world (sl)* lauthals verkünden; *I'll ~ you what!* ich will Ihnen was sagen! *I told you so* wie ich (Ihnen) sagte; *I can't ~ it* das weiß ich nicht; *you are ~ing me! (sl)* wem sagen Sie das! *you never can ~* man kann nie wissen; *who can ~?* wer weiß? **~er** ['-ə] Erzähler; (Aus-, Stimm-)Zähler; Kassenbeamte(r) *m*; *fortune-~~* Wahrsager(in *f*) *m*; **~ing** ['-iŋ] *a* wirkungsvoll, wirksam, nachdrücklich; *s: there is no ~~ what may happen* man weiß nie, was alles passieren kann; **~tale** *s* Klatschmaul *n*; Zuträger; Verräter *(a. Sache)*; Registrierapparat; *in Zssgen* Anzeiger *m*, Uhr *f*; *a* verräterisch; *~~ lamp, light* Warn-, Kontrollampe *f*; *~~ picture* Anschauungsbild *n*.

telly ['teli] *fam* Fernsehen *n*, -seher *m*.

telpher ['telfə] *s (~ line)* (Lasten-) Hängebahn; Hauspost *f*; **~age** ['-ridʒ] Lastenbeförderung *f* mit Hängebahn.

Telstar ['telstɑ:] Telstar *m (Nachrichtensatellit)*.

temer|arious [temə'rɛəriəs] *lit* rücksichtslos, vorschnell, -eilig; tollkühn; **~ity** [ti'meriti] Tollkühnheit, Unbesonnenheit; Voreiligkeit, Rücksichtslosigkeit *f*.

temper ['tempə] *tr* abstimmen (*with* mit); mäßigen, mildern, abschwächen (*with* durch); *tech (durch Beimischung)* veredeln; tempern, anlassen; *(Stahl)* härten; *(Eisen)* ablöschen; *(Farbe)* anrühren, mischen; *mus* temperieren; *itr* sich abschwächen, sich mäßigen, sich ausgleichen; *s tech* Härtegrad *m*; richtige Mischung; *fig* Laune, Stimmung, *bes. (bad ~)* schlechte, üble Laune *f*; Temperament *n*, Charakter *m*; Gereiztheit *f*; Ärger *m*, Wut *f*; *to be in a ~* wütend sein; *to be out of ~ with s.o.* jdm böse, auf jdn ärgerlich sein; *to get, to fly into a ~ about* ärgerlich werden über; *to keep, to control o.'s ~* ruhig Blut bewahren, sich beherrschen; *to lose o.'s ~* die Nerven verlieren; **~a** ['-rə] Temperamalerei *f*, -farben *f pl*; **~ament** ['-rəmənt] Temperament *n*; Charakter *m*, Gemütsbeschaffenheit *f*; Feuer, Lebhaftigkeit *f*; **~amental** [-rə'mentl] eigenwillig; anlagemäßig; **~ance** ['-rəns] Mäßigkeit; Abstinenz *f*; **~ate** ['-rit] mäßig; abstinent, enthaltsam; bedächtig, besonnen, zurückhaltend; *(Klima)* gemäßigt; *mus* wohltemperiert; **~ature** ['tempritʃə] Temperatur *f a. physiol med*; *to have, to run a ~~* Fieber haben; *to take the ~~* die Temperatur messen; *~~ chart* Fieberkurve *f*; *~~ gradient* Temperaturabnahme *f* mit der Höhe; **~ed** ['-d] *a (Stahl)* gehärtet; gemäßigt; *in Zssgen* -artig, -mütig, gelaunt; *mus* wohltemperiert.

tempest ['tempist] Sturm *m a. fig*; Unwetter, Gewitter *n*; **~-beaten, -swept, -tossed** *a* sturmgepeitscht; **~uous** [tem'pestjuəs] stürmisch *a. fig*; *fig* heftig, wild, ungestüm.

templ|ar, T~~ ['templə] Templer, Tempelritter, -herr; Anwalt *od* Student *m* (d. Rechte) am Londoner Temple; **~e** ['templ] **1.** Tempel *m*; Kirche *f*; **2.** *(Weberei)* Spannstock *m*; **~ate, ~et** ['-it] *arch* Pfette; *tech* Lehre, Schablone *f*; **3.** *anat* Schläfe *f*; *to get grey at the ~~s* an den Schläfen grau werden.

tempo ['tempou] *pl -s, mus -pi* ['-pi] *mus u. allg* Tempo *n*.

tempor|al ['tempərəl] **1.** *a anat* Schläfen-; *~~ bone* Schläfenbein *n*; **2.** zeitlich; vergänglich; weltlich; *gram* temporal, Temporal-; **~ality** [tempə'ræliti] Vergänglichkeit; Zeitbedingtheit *f*; *pl* weltliche(r) Besitz *m (d. Kirche)*; **~arily** ['tempərərili] *adv* vorübergehend, (nur) e-n Augenblick; **~ariness** ['-rərinis] Zeitbestimmtheit, -weiligkeit, zeitliche Beschränkung *f*; **~ary** ['-rəri] zeitlich begrenzt, vorübergehend, zeitweilig, vorläufig, provisorisch; Behelfs-, Aushilfs-, Not-; *~~ credit* Zwischenkredit *m*; **~ization** [tempərai'zeiʃən] zeitweilige Anpassung; Hinhaltetaktik *f*; Zeitgewinn *m*; Hinauszögerung *f*; **~ize** ['tempəraiz] *itr* sich nach den Umständen *od* Gegebenheiten richten; sich zeitweilig anbequemen, -passen, e-e Weile mitmachen; Zeit (zu) gewinnen (suchen); hinhalten (*with s.o.* jdn); e-n Kompromiß schließen (*with s.o.* mit jdm); ausgleichend wirken (*between* auf).

tempt [tempt] *tr* versuchen, verlocken; zu verführen, verleiten, überreden suchen (*to do* zu tun); in Versuchung führen; reizen, locken; *(das Schicksal)* herausfordern; *to be ~ed to* geneigt sein zu; in die Versuchung kommen zu; *to ~ the appetite* den Appetit anregen; *a ~ing offer* ein verlockendes Angebot; **~ation** [temp'teiʃən] Versuchung, Verlockung *f*, (An-)Reiz *m*; *to lead into ~~* in Versuchung führen; **~er** ['temptə] Versucher *m*; *the T~~* der Versucher, der Teufel; **~ing** ['-iŋ] *a* verführerisch, (ver)lockend, an-, aufreizend; **~ress** ['-ris] Verführerin *f*.

*

ten [ten] *a* zehn; *s (die)* Zehn; *by* od *in ~s* zu je zehn; *~ times (mit Komparativ) fam* zehnmal, viel, e-e Menge; *the upper ~ (thousand)* die oberen Zehntausend *pl*; **~fold** ['-fould] *a* zehnteilig; *a u. adv* zehnfach; **~-gallon hat** *Am* breitrandige(r) (Cowboy-) Filzhut *m*; **~ner** ['-ə] *fam* Zehnpfund-, *Am* -dollarschein *m*; **~-strike** *Am* alle neune *(bei 10 Kegeln)*; *allg* Meisterwurf, -schuß, *fam* Volltreffer *m*.

ten|able ['tenəbl] zu halten(d) *a. mil*, haltbar; *mil* verteidigungsfähig; *(Amt)* verliehen (*for* für, auf); **~acious** [ti'neiʃəs] *(Griff)* fest, eisern; hart, zäh; festsitzend, haftend (*of* an); *fig* eisern, zäh, unbeugsam, unermüdlich, beharrlich; *(Gedächtnis)* gut; **~acity** [ti'næsiti] Festigkeit; Zähigkeit; Beharrlichkeit; *(Gedächtnis)* Zuverlässigkeit; *phys* Zugfestigkeit *f*; **~ancy** ['tenənsi] Pacht-, Mietverhältnis *n*, -dauer *f*, -besitz; *jur* Besitz *m*; **~ant** ['-ənt] *s* Pächter, Mieter; Inhaber; Bewohner; *jur* Besitzer; *hist* Lehensmann *m*; *tr* in Pacht, Miete haben; verpachten; bewohnen; beherbergen; *jur* besitzen; *~~ farm* Pachthof *m*; *~~ farmer* Pächter *m*; *~~ rights (pl)* Rechte *n pl* des Pächters *od* Mieters; **~antless** ['-əntlis] unverpachtet, -vermietet, leerstehend, unbewohnt; **~antry** ['-əntri] Pächter *m*, Mieter *m pl*; Pachtverhältnis *n*.

tench [tentʃ] Schleie *f (Fisch)*.

tend [tend] **1.** *itr* gehen, führen, gerichtet sein (*towards* nach); *fig* neigen, geneigt sein (*to, towards* zu); *fig* führen (*to, towards* zu), gerichtet sein, abziehen, hinarbeiten (*to, towards* auf); **~encious** = *~entious*; **~ency** ['-ənsi] *fig* Hang *m*, Neigung, Geneigtheit *f*, Zug *m* (*to, towards* zu); *lit* Tendenz *f*, Zweck *m*; **~entious** [ten'denʃəs] *lit* tendenziös; Tendenz-, Zweck-; **~er** ['-ə] **1.** *tr* anbieten; zur Verfügung stellen; *(Beweis)* antreten, erbringen; *(Eid)* zuschieben; *(Gesuch)* einreichen; *itr* ein Angebot machen; *s* Anerbieten, Angebot *n*; Kostenanschlag *m*; *by ~~* in Submission; *to invite ~~s for s.th.* etw ausschreiben; *~~ exact fare!* Fahrgeld abgezählt bereithalten! *lawful, legal ~~* gesetzliche(s) Zahlungsmittel *n*; *~~ of consent* Beitrittserklärung *f*; *~~ of payment* Zahlungsangebot *n*; *~~ of resignation* Rücktrittsgesuch *n*; *~~ period* Einreichungsfrist *f*; **2.** (Auf-)Wärter(in *f*); *mar* Lichter, Leichter (-schiff *n*) *m*; Begleitschiff *n*, Tender; *rail* Kohlenwagen, Tender *m*; *aero* (Flugzeug-)Mutterschiff *n*; *bar ~~* Barmixer *m*.

tender ['tendə] **3.** weich, mürbe, zart, saftig; zerbrechlich, empfindlich; schwächlich, anfällig; *(Wunde)* (schmerz)empfindlich; sensibel; *(Alter, Farbton)* zart; *fig* sanft; zärtlich, liebevoll; mitfühlend; besorgt (*of* um); feinfühlig; *(Gefühl)* zart; *(Gewissen)* empfindlich; *(Herz)* weich; *(Thema)* heikel, kitzlig; *to touch s.o. on a ~ spot* jds wunden Punkt berühren; **~foot** *pl -s* Neuling, Anfänger *m*; **~hearted** *a* weichherzig, gutmütig; **~loin** ['-lɔin] *(Küche)* Filet *n*; *(T)~~ (Am)* Verbrecherviertel *n*; **~ness** ['-nis] Zartheit; Empfindlichkeit; Zärtlichkeit *f* (*to* gegen, zu); Mit-, Feingefühl *n*.

tendon ['tendən] *anat* Sehne *f*; **~-sheath** Sehnenscheide *f*.

tendril ['tendril] *bot* Ranke *f*.

tenement ['tenimənt] Pachtgut; (Pacht-)Grundstück *n*; Besitz *m*; Miet-, Wohnhaus *n*; Mietwohnung; *poet* Wohnung *f*; **~ house** Mietshaus *n*, -kaserne *f*.

tenet ['ti:net, 'ten-, -nit] Lehre, Doktrin, These, Lehrmeinung *f*.

tennis ['tenis] *(lawn-~)* Tennis *n*; **~-ball, -court, -racket, -shoes** *pl* Tennisball, -platz, -schläger *m*, -schuhe *m pl*.

tenon ['tenən] *s tech* Zapfen *m*; *tr* verzapfen; **~-saw** Zapfen-, Furniersäge *f*.

tenonitis [tenə'naitis] *med* Sehnenentzündung *f*.

tenor ['tenə] Wesen *n*, Charakter *m*, Art; Grundhaltung, -tendenz *f*; Verlauf, Gang; wesentliche(r) Inhalt; *mus* Tenor *m*.

tenpin ['tenpin] *Am (Spiel)* Kegel *m*; *pl mit sing* Kegelspiel, Kegeln *n*.

*

tens|e [tens] **1.** *a* gestreckt, gespannt *a. gram*, straff; *fig* spannungsgeladen, -voll; *(Lage)* gespannt; *tr itr* (sich) straffen, (sich) anspannen; **~eness** ['-nis], **~ity** ['-iti] Straffheit; Abgespanntheit; *fig* Spannung *f*; **~ibility** [tensi'biliti] Dehnbarkeit, Streckbarkeit *f*; **~ible** ['tensəbl] dehnbar, streckbar; **~ile** ['-ail, *Am* '-il] *a* Streck-, Spann-; straffend; streckbar, dehnbar; *~~ strength* Zugfestigkeit *f*; **~ion** ['tenʃən] Spannung *a. fig*; *fig* Anspannung, Angespanntheit; *pol* Gespanntheit, gespannte Lage; *phys el* Spannung *f*; Zug; *(Dampf)* Druck *m*; *high ~~ (el)* Hochspannung *f*; **~ional** ['-ʃənl] *a* Spannungs-; **~or** ['-ə] Spannmuskel; *math* Tensor *m*; **2.** *gram* Tempus *n*, Zeit(form) *f*.

tent [tent] **1.** *s* Zelt *n a. med*; *itr* zelten; *to pitch, to strike a ~* ein Zelt aufschlagen, abbrechen; *bell, circular ~* Rundzelt *n*; **~-bed** Feldbett; Himmelbett *n*; **~-equipment** Zeltausrüstung *f*; **~-peg** Zeltpflock, Hering *m*; **~-pole** Zeltstange *f*; **~-rope** Zeltleine *f*; **~-section, -square** Zeltbahn *f*; **2.** *s med* Watte-, Mullbausch, -pfropfen *m*; **3.** *(~ wine)* Tinto *m (dunkler spanischer Wein)*.

tent|acle ['tentəkl] *zoo* Fühler *a. fig*; Greifarm; *mil* Verbindungstrupp *m*; **~acled** ['-d] *a* mit Fühlern versehen; **~acular** [ten'tækjulə] *a* Fühler-; **~ative** ['tentətiv] *a* Versuchs-; versuchend; vorläufig, provisorisch; *s scient* Arbeitshypothese, Theorie *f*; Versuch *m*, Probe *f*; **~atively** ['-li] *adv* versuchsweise.

tenter ['tentə] *tech* Spannrahmen *m*; **~hook** *tech* Spannhaken *m*; *to be on ~~s (fig)* wie auf glühenden *od* heißen Kohlen sitzen; *to keep s.o. on ~~s (fig)* jdn auf die Folter spannen.

tenth [tenθ] *a* zehnt; zehntel; *s* Zehntel *n*; *der, die, das* Zehnte; **~ly** ['-li] *adv* zehntens.

tenuous ['tenjuəs] dünn, fein; (ver-)dünn(t), spärlich, dürftig; *fig* unbedeutend, unwesentlich.

tenure ['tenjuə] Besitz *m*; Amt *n*, Bestallung, Anstellung; Besitzart *f*, -recht *n*, Anspruch *m*; *(~ of office)* (Amts-)Dauer *f*.

tepee, *a.* **teepee** ['ti:pi:] Indianer-, Spitzzelt *n*.

tep|id ['tepid] lau(warm); **~idity** [te'piditi], **~idness** ['tepidnis] Lauheit *f*.

tercentenary [tə:sən'ti:nəri, *Am* -'sɛntənɛri] *s* 300. Jahrestag *m*; Dreihundertjahrfeier *f*; *a* Dreihundertjahr-.

tercet ['tə:sit] *mus* Triole; *(Metrik)* Terzine *f*.

tergiversat|e ['tə:dʒivəseit] *itr* Ausflüchte machen, sich drehen und wenden; e-r Sache den Rücken kehren, untreu werden, abfallen; s-e Meinung ändern; **~ion** [tə:dʒivə:'seiʃən] Ausrede, Ausflucht *f*; *fig* Schwanken *n*.

term [tə:m] *s* (Zahlungs-, Kündigungs-) Termin *m*; Frist, Dauer *f*, Zeitraum *m*; Laufzeit; *jur* (Sitzungs-)Periode; *(~ of office)* Amtsdauer, -zeit *f*; *(Schule, Univ.)* Trimester, Semester *n*; (Militär-)Dienstzeit; Strafzeit *f*; *gram* Ausdruck, Terminus; *math* Ausdruck, Posten *m*, Glied *n*; *med* Menstruation, Schwangerschaftszeit *f*; *pl* (Rede-) Wendungen; (Vertrags-, Geschäfts-, Zahlungs-)Bedingungen; Gebühren *f pl*; Preise *m pl*; *(nur in bestimmten Wendungen)* (persönliche) Beziehungen *f pl*, Verhältnis *n*; *tr* (be)nennen; *in ~s of* im Sinne von, vom Standpunkt *gen*; in Form von; *on easy ~s* zu günstigen Bedingungen; *to be on good, bad ~s with s.o.* sich mit jdm gut, nicht gut stehen; mit jdm auf gutem, gespanntem Fuße stehen; *to bring s.o. to ~s (fig)* jdn in die Knie zwingen; *to come to ~s, to make ~s* sich einig werden, sich einigen (*with s.o.* mit jdm); *to meet s.o. on equal ~s* mit jdm auf gleichem Fuß verkehren; *to serve o.'s ~* s-e Strafe verbüßen; *we are not on speaking ~s* wir sprechen nicht miteinander; *end-of-~ examination* Prüfung *f* zu Semesterende; *technical ~* Fachausdruck *m*; *~ of delivery* Lieferzeit, -frist *f*; *~ of notice* Kündigungsfrist *f*; *~ of notification* Anmeldefrist *f*; *~s of payment* Zahlungsbedingungen *f pl*; *~s of reference* Aufgabenbereich *m*; *~s of surrender* Übergabebedingungen *f pl*; *~s of trade* Terms *pl* of Trade; *~ of validity* Gültigkeitsdauer *f*; **~ day** Zahltag; Termin *m*.

termagant ['tə:məgənt] *s* Zankteufel *m*, Xanthippe *f*; *a* zänkisch.

termin|ability [tə:minə'biliti] Begrenzbarkeit; Kündbarkeit *f*; **~able** ['tə:minəbl] *(zeitlich)* begrenzbar, befristet; kündbar; rückzahlbar; **~al** ['tə:minl] *a* letzt; End-, Abschluß-; beschließend; Grenz-; Semester-; terminmäßig, -gemäß; *bot* gipfelständig; *s* äußerste(s) Ende *n*, Extremität *f*, Endstück *n a. arch*; Kopf; *el* Pol(klemme *f*) *m*; Anschlußklemme *f*; *(~~ station)* Endstation *f*; *aero* Bestimmungsflughafen *m*; *~~ board* Klemmleiste *f*; *~~ building* Flughafengebäude *n*; *~~ examination* Abschlußprüfung *f*; *~~ moraine* Endmoräne *f*; *~~ repeater* Endverstärker *m*; *~~ speed* Endgeschwindigkeit *f*; *~~ voltage* Klemmenspannung *f*; **~ate** ['tə:mineit] *tr* aufhören mit, beend(ig)en, enden, beschließen; zum Abschluß bringen; begrenzen; *itr* aufhören (*in* mit); enden (*in* auf); abschließen (*in* mit); **~ation** [tə:mi'neiʃən] Beendigung *f*; Ende *n*, Schluß *m*, Grenze *f*; Ab-, Beschluß *m*; *gram* Endung, Endsilbe *f*, -laut *m*; *to bring s.th. to a ~~* etw zum Abschluß bringen; *to put a ~~ to s.th.* e-r S ein Ende machen; **~ative** ['tə:minətiv] *a* End-; *s gram* Suffix *n*; **~ological** [tə:minə'lɔdʒikəl] terminologisch; **~ology** [tə:mi'nɔlədʒi] Terminologie *f*; **~us** ['tə:minəs] *pl meist -ni* ['-nai] Ende *n*, Schluß, Endpunkt *m*, Ziel *n*; Grenzstein *m*; Endstation *f*, Kopfbahnhof *m*.

termite ['tə:mait] *ent* Termite *f*.

tern [tə:n] *orn* Seeschwalbe *f*; Dreiergruppe *f*.

ternary ['tə:nəri] dreiteilig, -fach; *chem* ternär, dreistoffig; *bot* dreizählig.

terrace ['terəs] *s* Terrasse *f*; Altan, Söller *m*; Flachdach *n*; (Straße mit) höher gelegene(r) Häuserreihe *f*; *Am* Grünstreifen *m*; *tr* terrassenförmig anlegen; **~-house** Reihenhaus *n*.

terr|acotta ['terə'kɔtə] Terrakotta *f*; **~ain** ['terein] Gelände, Gebiet *n*; *~~ analysis, compartment, cut, exercise, point (mil)* Geländebeurteilung *f*, -abschnitt, -einschnitt *m*, -übung *f*, -punkt *m*; **~aneous** [tə'reiniəs] *a bot* Land-; **~apin** ['terəpin] Dosenschildkröte *f*.

terr|ene [te'ri:n] *a* aus Erde, Erd-; irdisch, weltlich; **~estrial** [ti'restriəl] *a* irdisch, weltlich; Erd-; Land- *a. bot zoo*; zoo Boden-; *s* Erdbewohner *m*; *~~ globe, magnetism* Erdkugel *f*, -magnetismus *m*.

terr|ible ['terəbl] schrecklich, furchtbar, fürchterlich *(a. fam übertreibend)*; gewaltig, gräßlich, schrecklich; **~ibly** ['-ibli] *adv* furchtbar, schrecklich; *fam* außerordentlich, phantastisch; **~ific** [tə'rifik] schrecklich, furchtbar, fürchterlich; *fam* gewaltig, großartig, phantastisch, Mords-; **~ify** ['-ifai] *tr* erschrecken; **~ifying** ['-ifaiiŋ] fürchterlich, erschreckend; **~or** ['terə] Entsetzen *n*, Schreck(en); Terror *m*; schreckliche Angst (*of* vor); *(T~~, Reign of T~~) hist* Schreckensherrschaft *f*; *fam* schreckliche(r), furchtbare(r) Mensch; Alptraum *m*; *~~-stricken, -struck (a)* (zu Tode) erschreckt *od* erschrokken; **~orism** ['-ərizm] Terrorismus *m*; Schreckensherrschaft *f*; **~orist** ['-ərist] Terrorist *m*; **~oristic** [terə-

'ristik] terroristisch; **~orization** [-ərai'zeiʃən] Terrorisierung *f*; **~orize** ['terəraiz] *tr* terrorisieren.

terrier ['teriə] **1.** Terrier *m (Hunderasse)*; **2.** Grundbuch *n.*

territor|ial [teri'tɔ:riəl] *a* territorial; Territorial-, Land-, Gebiets-; Grund-, Boden-; *T~~Army* Landwehr *f*; *T~~* Landwehrmann *m*; *~~ changes (pl), claims (pl), violation* Gebietsveränderungen *f pl*, -ansprüche *m pl*, -verletzung *f*; *~~ waters (pl)* Hoheitsgewässer *n pl*; **~y** ['teritəri] Gebiet, Territorium *n*, Geltungsbereich *m*; Vertretergebiet *n*; *sport* Spielfeldhälfte *f*; *cession, enlargement, exchange of ~~* Gebietsabtretung, -erweiterung *f*, -tausch *m*; *colonial ~ies (pl)* Kolonialgebiete *n pl*; *customs ~~* Zollgebiet *n*; *mandated, national, occupied ~~* Mandats-, Hoheits-, Besatzungs- *od* besetzte(s) Gebiet *n*; *sales ~~* Absatzgebiet *n*; *section of a ~~* Gebietsteil *m*.

terry ['teri] *(Textil)* Schlinge, Schleife *f*; Frottee; ungeschnittene(s), ungeritzte(s) Gewebe *n*.

terse [tə:s] *(Stil)* gedrängt, knapp, kurz u. bündig; **~ness** ['-nis] Gedrängtheit, Knappheit, Kürze *f*.

terti|an ['tə:ʃən] *a* dreitägig; *s (~~ fever)* Tertianfieber *n*; **~ary** ['tə:ʃəri] *a scient* tertiär; Tertiär-; *s rel* Tertiarier *m*; *T~~ (geol)* Tertiär *n*.

*

tessellate(d) ['tesilit, -eit(id)] *a* mosaikartig ausgelegt.

test [test] *s tech* Prüfschale *f*, -tiegel *m*; Metallprüfung; *allg* Prüfung, Probe, Untersuchung, Erprobung *f*, Versuch, Test *m a. psychol*; Probe-, Prüfungsarbeit; *(Schule)* Klassenarbeit *f*; *fig* Prüfstein *m*, Probe *f*; Prüfungsmaßstab *m*, Kriterium *n*; *chem* Analyse *f*; Reagenz *n*; *tr* prüfen, erproben; untersuchen, testen (*for* auf ... hin); überprüfen, nachkontrollieren; *chem* analysieren; *math* die Probe machen auf; *to ~ under break load (mot)* abbremsen; *to make ~s* Stichproben machen; *to put to the ~* auf die Probe stellen; *to stand, to pass a ~* e-e Prüfung, Probe bestehen; *to take a ~* e-e Prüfung ablegen; *aptitude ~* Eignungsprüfung *f*; *blood ~* Blutprobe *f*; *driving ~* Fahrprüfung *f*; *endurance ~* Dauerversuch *m*; *intelligence ~* Intelligenztest *m*; *~* **ban** Atomstopp *m*; *~* **bench** Prüfstand *m*; *~* **call** Leitungsprobe *f*; *~* **case** Probe-, *jur* Präzedenzfall; Musterprozeß *m*; Schulbeispiel *n*; *~* **certificate** Abnahmeprotokoll *n*; *~* **drive** Probefahrt *f*; **~er** ['-ə] **1.** Prüf(end)er *m*; Prüfgerät *n*; *~* **flight** Probeflug *m*; **~ing** ['-iŋ] *a* Prüf-, Probe-, Versuch-; Meß-; *s* (Über-)Prüfung, Erprobung *f*; *~~-apparatus* Prüfgerät *n*; *~~-battery (el)* Meßbatterie *f*; *~~-circuit* Meß-, Prüfstromkreis *m*; *~~-ground* Versuchsgelände *n*; *~~-machine* (Werkstoff-)Prüfmaschine *f*; *~~-plant* Versuchseinrichtung *f*; *~~-result* Prüfungsergebnis *n*; *~~-stand, -bench* Prüfstand *m*; *~~-wire (el)* Prüfdraht *m*; *~* **kitchen** Versuchsküche *f*; *~* **lamp** Prüflampe *f*; *~* **load** Probebelastung *f*; *~* (**match**) internationale(s) Vergleichsspiel *n*; *~* **method** Prüfverfahren *n*; *~* **paper** *chem* Reagenzpapier *n*; *(Schule)* Klassenarbeit *f*; *~* **piece** Probestück *n*; *~* **pilot** *aero* Versuchs-, Einflieger *m*; *~* **report** Prüfbericht *m*; *~* **result** Prüfungsergebnis *n*; *~* **run** *mot* Probelauf *m*; *~* **track, road** Versuchsstrecke *f*; **~-tube** Reagenzglas *n*; *~~ baby* durch künstliche Befruchtung erzeugte(s) Kind *n*.

testaceous [tes'teiʃəs] *zoo* hartschalig; Schalen-.

test|ament ['testəmənt] *(last will and ~~)* Testament *n*, letztwillige Verfügung *f*, letzte(r) Wille *m*; *rel* Testament *n*; *by ~~* letztwillig *adv*; **~amentary** [testə'mentəri] *a* Testaments-; testamentarisch, letztwillig; *~~ capacity (jur)* Testierfähigkeit *f*; *~~ disposition* Testamentsbestimmung, -klausel; letztwillige Verfügung *f*; **~ator** [tes'teitə] Erblasser *m*; **~atrix** [-'teitriks] *pl -trices* [-trisi:z] Erblasserin *f*; **~ification** [testifi'keiʃən] Zeugenaussage *f*; Zeugnis *n*; Beweis *m* (*to, of* für); **~ify** ['-ifai] *tr* bezeugen, aussagen über (*in s.o.'s favour, on s.o.'s behalf* zu jds Gunsten; *against s.o.* gegen jdn); bekunden; bekennen; *itr* ein Zeugnis ablegen (*of* von); *to ~~ to s.th.* etw bezeugen; etw bestätigen; *to refuse to ~~* die Aussage verweigern; *refusal to ~~* Aussageverweigerung *f*; **~imonial** [testi'mounjəl] Zeugnis *n*, Beurteilung *f*; Empfehlungsschreiben *n*; Ehrengabe *f*, Gedenkzeichen *n*; **~imony** ['testiməni] Zeugenaussage; Erklärung; Bestätigung *f*; Zeichen *n*, Beweis *m* (*of* für); *rel* Gesetzestafeln *f pl*; *in ~~ whereof* urkundlich dessen; *to be called in ~~* als Zeuge benannt werden; *to bear ~~* Zeugnis ablegen (*to* für).

tester ['testə] **2.** Betthimmel; *arch* Baldachin *m*.

testicle ['testikl] Hode(n *m*) *m* od *f*.

test|iness ['testinis] Reizbarkeit *f*; launische(s) Wesen *n*; **~y** ['-i] reizbar, empfindlich; launisch.

testudo [tes'tju:dou] *pl -os* Landschildkröte *f*; *hist mil, min* Schutzdach *n*.

tetanus ['tetənəs] (Wund-)Starrkrampf, Tetanus *m*.

tetchy ['tetʃi] empfindlich, reizbar; mürrisch.

tether ['teðə] *s* Strick *m*, Kette *f*; *tr (Tier)* anbinden (*to* an); an die Kette legen; *to be at the end of o.'s ~ (fig)* am Ende s-r Kräfte sein, nicht mehr weiter wissen.

tetra|gon ['tetrəgən] Viereck *n*; **~gonal** [te'trægənl] viereckig; **~hedron** ['tetrə'hedrən] *math* Tetraeder *n*; **~logy** [te'trælədʒi] *lit theat* Tetralogie *f*; **~pod** ['-pɔd] Vierfüßer *m*.

tetter ['tetə] *med* Ausschlag *m*, Flechte *f*, Ekzem *n*.

Teuton ['tju:tən] *hist* Teutone; Germane; *fam pej* Deutsche(r) *m*; **~ic** [tju:'tɔnik] *hist* teutonisch; germanisch; deutsch; *the T~~ Order (hist)* der Deutsche Ritterorden.

text [tekst] Text *m*; Bibelstelle *f*, -spruch *m*; Thema *n*, Gegenstand *m*; *(~book)* Lehrbuch *n*; *(~hand)* große Schreibschrift; *typ* Frakturschrift *f*; **~ile** ['-ail, *Am* '-il] *a* Textil-; Gewebe-; gewebt; *s* Webmaterial *n*; *pl (~~ fabrics, materials)* Textilien *pl*, Webwaren *f pl*, Spinnstoffe *m pl*; *~~ factory* Textilfabrik; *~~ industry* Textilindustrie *f*; **~ual** ['tekstjuəl] *a* Text-; wörtlich; **~ural** ['-tʃərəl] strukturell; Struktur-; **~ure** ['-ʃə] Gewebe *n a. fig*; Struktur *f*, Gefüge *n*, Bau *m*; Beschaffenheit; *(Holz)* Maserung *f*; *lit* Aufbau *m*, Gestaltung, Anordnung, Gliederung *f*.

Thames [temz] Themse *f*; *she won't set the ~ on fire (fig)* sie hat das Pulver nicht erfunden.

than [ðæn, ðən] *conj* als *(beim Komparativ)*; *you are taller ~ he (is), (fam) ~ him* du bist größer als er; *nothing else ~* nichts anderes als; völlig; *no other ~* kein anderer als.

thane [θein] *hist* Lehnsmann, Ministeriale *m*.

thank [θæŋk] *tr* danken (*s.o.* jdm); sich bedanken (*s.o.* bei jdm; *for s.th.* für etw); *s pl* Dank *m*; *interj (~s very much)* danke (schön)! vielen Dank! *~s to (prp)* dank *dat*; *in ~s for* zum Dank für; *small ~s to s.o.* ohne jds Hilfe; *to have o.s. to ~ for s.th.* sich etw selbst zuzuschreiben haben; *to return ~s* danksagen; *(I) ~ you (very much)* (ich) danke (Ihnen)! danke sehr, vielmals! besten Dank! *no, ~ you, (fam) ~s* danke, nein! *I will ~ you to, for* ich wäre Ihnen dankbar, wenn Sie ...; **~ful** ['-ful] dankbar (*for* für); **~less** ['-lis] undankbar; **~-offering** Gabe *f* als Zeichen des Dankes; *rel* Sühneopfer *n*; **~sgiving** ['-sgiviŋ] Danksagung *f*; *T~~ (Day) (Am)* Dankfest *n (letzter Donnerstag im November)*; **~worthy** ['-wə:ði] dankenswert.

that [ðæt] *prn (demonstrativ; pl those* [ðouz] jene(r, s); der-, die-, das(jenige); *(alleinstehend)* das; *at ~* (noch) obendrein; *fam* dabei; *~'s ~!* so, das wäre erledigt *od* geschafft! so ist es eben! *(relativ)* [ðæt, ðət] der, die, das; welche(r, s); *conj* [ðət] daß; damit; *in ~* darum weil; insofern als; als, da; *adv fam* so; *~ much* so viel; *this way or ~ way* so oder so.

thatch [θætʃ] *s* Stroh-, Binsen-, Blätterdach; Dachstroh *n*; *hum* (Haar-)Schopf *m*; *tr* mit Stroh decken; **~ed** [-t] *a* strohgedeckt; *~~ roof* Strohdach *n*; **~ing** ['-iŋ] Dachdecken (mit Stroh); Dachstroh *n*.

thaw [θɔ:] *itr* (auf)tauen; *fig* auftauen, warm werden; *it is ~ing* es taut; *tr (to ~ out)* auftauen *a. fig*; *s* (Auf-)Tauen; Tauwetter *a. fig*; *fig* Auftauen, Warmwerden *n*.

the [ðə, ð *(vor Konsonanten)*, ði *(vor Vokalen)*, ði: *(mit Nachdruck)*] *(bestimmter Artikel)* der, die, das; *adv*: *~ ... ~* je ... desto ...; *all ~ better, worse* um so besser, schlimmer; *~ sooner ~ better* je eher, je lieber.

theatr|e, *Am* **theater** ['θiətə] Theater; Schauspielhaus; *lit* Theater, Drama *n*; Hörsaal *(mit ansteigenden Sitzreihen)*; *fig* Schauplatz *m*; *to go to the ~* in das Theater gehen; *open-air ~~* Freilichtbühne *f*; *operating ~~* Operationssaal *m*; *picture ~~* Filmtheater *n*; *~~ glass* Opernglas *n*; *~~-goer* Theaterbesucher *m*; *~~ of operations* Operations-, Einsatzgebiet *n*; *~~ of war* Kriegsschauplatz *m*; *~~ poster* Theaterplakat *n*; **~ic(al)** [θi'ætrik(əl)] *a* Theater-, Bühnen-; bühnenmäßig; dramatisch; *fig* theatralisch, pomphaft, affektiert; *s pl* Theateraufführungen *f pl*, *bes.* Laienspiele *n pl*; *~~ company* Schauspieltruppe *f*; *~~ performance* Theatervorstellung *f*.

thee [ði:, ði] *prn obs poet* dich; dir; *of ~* dein.

theft [θeft] Diebstahl *m* (*from* aus; *from s.o.* an jdm).

theine ['θi:in] *chem* Thein *n*.

their [ðεə, vor Vokalen *a.* ðər] *prn* ihr(e) *(bei mehreren Besitzern)*; *fam* sein(e); **~s** ['-z] der, die, das ihre, ihrige, die ihren, ihrigen *pl*; *a friend of ~~* e-r ihrer Freunde; *it's ~~* es gehört ihnen.

the|ism ['θi:izm] Theismus *m*; **~ist** ['-ist] Theist *m*; **~istic(al)** [θi:'istik(əl)] theistisch.

them [ðem, ðəm] sie; *(to ~)* ihnen; *vulg* diese; *of ~* ihrer; *that's ~ (fam)* das sind sie; **~selves** [ðəm'selvz] *prn pl*:

they ... ~~ sie ... selbst; *reflexiv:* sich (selbst); *to* ~~ zu sich (selbst).

theme [θi:m] Thema *n a. mus*, Gegenstand; (Schul-)Aufsatz; *gram* (Wort-)Stamm *m*; *(~ song) radio* Kennmelodie *f*, Hauptschlager *m (e-s Films)*.

then [ðen] *adv* dann; darauf, da; damals; demnach, dann; dann, als nächste(r, s), weiter(hin), des weiteren, ferner; dann, in d(ies)em Fall; darum, folglich, also; außerdem; *a* damalig; *before* ~ vorher, zuvor; *but* ~ aber dann, dann jedoch, hinwiederum; *by* ~ zu der Zeit; bis dahin; *(every) now and* ~ dann u. wann; hin u. wieder; ab u. zu; von Zeit zu Zeit; *from* ~ *onwards* von da an; *until* ~ bis dahin; ~ *and there, there and* ~ gleich, sofort, auf der Stelle; *what* ~ ? was dann?

thence [ðens] *adv* von dort, da; von da an; deshalb, infolgedessen; daraus; **~forth** ['ðens'fɔ:θ], **~forward(s)** ['-'fɔ:wəd(z)] von da an, seitdem, danach.

theo|centric [θiə'sentrik] theozentrisch; **~cracy** [θi'ɔkrəsi] Theokratie *f*; **~cratic(al)** [θiə'krætik(əl)] theokratisch; **~dolite** [θi'ɔdəlait] Theodolit *m*; **~gony** [θi'ɔgəni] Theogonie *f*; **~logian** [θiə'loudʒjən] Theologe *m*; **~logic(al)** [-'lɔdʒik(əl)] theologisch; **~logy** [θi'ɔlədʒi] Theologie *f*; **~phany** [θi'ɔfəni] Theophanie, (Gottes-)Erscheinung *f*; **~sophic(al)** [θiə'sɔfik(əl)] theosophisch; **~sophist** [θi'ɔsəfist] Theosoph *m*; **~sophy** [θi'ɔsəfi] Theosophie *f*.

theor|em ['θiərəm] Lehrsatz *m*; **~etic(al)** [θiə'retik(əl)] theoretisch; spekulativ; **~etician** [θiəre'tiʃən], **~ist** ['θiərist] Theoretiker *m*; **~ize** ['θiəraiz] *itr* theoretisieren (*about* über); e-e Theorie aufstellen; **~y** ['θiəri] Theorie; *fam* Einbildung, Idee, Annahme *f*; ~~ *of history* Geschichtsphilosophie *f*; ~~ *of relativity* Relativitätstheorie *f*.

therap|eutic(al) [θerə'pju:tik(əl)] therapeutisch; **~eutics** [-iks] *pl mit sing* Therapeutik, Heilkunde *f*; **~ist** ['θerəpist] Therapeut *m*; **~y** ['θerəpi] Therapie *f*, Heilverfahren *n*; *occupational* ~~ Beschäftigungstherapie *f*.

there [ðɛə] **1.** *adv* dort, da; dort-, dahin; da, dann; gerade; in d(ies)em Punkt, darin; *(unbestimmt)* es; *here and* ~ hier u. da, dort; gelegentlich; *over* ~ dort drüben; *then and* ~, ~ *and then* hier u. jetzt; auf der Stelle; ~ *and back* hin u. zurück; ~ *is, are* es ist, sind; es gibt; ~ *you are!* da hast du's! da sind Sie ja! ~*'s a fine fellow!* na, also! ich bitte dich! ~ *is no one* ~ es ist niemand da; ~ *can be no doubt about it* es kann kein Zweifel daran bestehen; **2.** *interj* nanu! aber ich bitte dich! na also! sagte ich es nicht! da haben wir es! ~, ~! schon gut! ~, *that's enough* so, nun ist's aber genug; **~about(s)** ['ðɛərəbauts] *adv* in der Gegend, da herum; so etwa; **~after** [ðɛər'ɑ:ftə] danach; demzufolge, -gemäß; **~against** [-ə'genst] im Gegensatz dazu, dagegen; **~at** [ðɛər'æt] *obs lit* dort; da, dann; darum, deshalb; **~by** ['ðɛə'bai] dadurch; dabei; daran; da herum; *to come* ~~ darankommen; **~for** [ðɛə'fɔ:] *obs jur* dafür; **~fore** ['--] *adv conj* deshalb, -wegen, darum; demnach, infolgedessen, folglich; **~from** [ðɛə'frɔm] daher; davon; **~in** [ðɛər'in] darin; dahinein; in dieser Sache; **~inafter** [ðɛərin'ɑ:ftə] *jur* im folgenden; **~of** [ðɛər'ɔv] davon, darüber; dessen, deren; daher; **~on** [ðɛər'ɔn] *obs* diesbezüglich; darauf; deshalb; **~to** [ðɛə'tu:] = **~unto**; **~under** [ðɛər'ʌndə] darunter *a. fig*; **~unto** [ðɛər'ʌntu(:)] *obs* dazu; **~upon** ['ðɛərə'pɔn] darauf, danach; demzufolge, daraufhin; **~with** [ðɛə'wiθ] damit; dazu; darauf; **~withal** [ðɛəwi'ðɔ:l] überdies, darüber hinaus, zusätzlich.

therm|(e) [θə:m] kleine *od* große Kalorie(n *pl*) *f*; *(Gas)* 100000 Wärmeeinheiten *f pl*; **~al** ['θə:məl] *a* Thermal-; Wärme-, Hitze-; thermisch; warm, heiß; *s meist pl (aero) (warmer)* Aufwind *m*; Thermik *f*; ~~ *barrier* Hitzemauer *f*; ~~ *conductor* Wärmeleiter *m*; ~~ *efficiency* thermische(r) Wirkungsgrad *m*; ~~ *shock* Temperatursturz *m*; ~~ *springs (pl)* heiße Quelle *f pl*; ~~ *(power) station* Wärmekraftwerk *n*; ~~ *unit (phys)* Wärmeeinheit *f*; ~~ *up-current* Wärmeaufwind *m*; **~ic** ['-ik] *a* Wärme-, Hitze-; thermisch; **~ionic** [-i'ɔnik] Elektronen-; thermionisch; **~it(e)** ['-it, '-ait] *chem* Thermit *n*; **~o-couple** ['θə:mo(u)'kʌpl] = **~electric** *couple*; **~dynamic** ['-dai'næmik] *a* thermodynamisch; *s pl mit sing* Thermodynamik *f*; **~oelectric** ['-i'lektrik]: ~~ *couple* Thermoelement *n*; **~ometer** [θə'mɔmitə] Thermometer *n*; ~~ *scale* Thermometerskala *f*; **~o-nuclear** ['θə:mo(u)'nju:kliə]: ~~ *weapons (pl)* thermonukleare Waffen *f pl*; **~opile** ['-pail] Thermosäule *f*; **~o-plastic** ['-'plæstik] thermoplastisch; **~os** ['θə:mɔs]: ~~ *bottle, flask, jug* Thermosflasche *f*; **~ostat** ['θə:məstæt] Thermostat, Wärmeregler; *med* Brutschrank *m*.

thesaurus [θi(:)'sɔ:rəs] *pl a. -ri* [-rai] Wortschatz *m*; Wörterbuch *n*.

these [ði:z] *s. this.*

thesis ['θi:sis] *pl -ses* ['-si:z] These, Behauptung *f*; Thema *n*; Dissertation; *mus* Betonung; ['θesis] *poet* Hebung *f*; **~-play** *theat* Thesenstück *n*.

thew|s [θju:z] *s pl* Muskeln *m pl*, Sehnen *f pl*; *fig* Kraft *f*; **~y** ['-i] muskulös, sehnig, kräftig, stark.

they [ðei] *prn* sie *pl*; man; es; ~ *who* diejenigen, welche.

*

thick [θik] *a* dick, massig, stark; fest; dicht, füllig, üppig; gedrängt, geballt; *with* voller, voll von; dicht bedeckt mit; breiig; trübe, schmutzig, schlammig; neblig, verhangen; *(Stimme)* rauh, heiser; *(Flöz)* mächtig; *fig* dumm, stupide, stumpfsinnig; *fam (Freundschaft)* dick; eng befreundet (*with* mit); *fam* mächtig, gewaltig, toll; *adv* dicht; dick; *s* dickste(r), dichteste(r) Teil; *fam* Dummkopf; *sl* Kakao *m*; *in the* ~ *of* mitten in; im dichtesten; *through* ~ *and thin* durch dick u. dünn; *to be as* ~ *as thieves (fam)* dicke Freunde sein; *to come* ~ *and fast* Schlag auf Schlag gehen; *to lay it on* ~ *(fam fig)* dick auftragen, übertreiben; *it's a bit* ~ *(fam)* das ist ein starkes Stück; **~-coated** *a* dickschalig, -rindig; **~en** ['-ən] *tr itr* dicker machen, werden; (sich) verdicken; eindicken; dichter machen, werden; (sich) verdichten; (sich) verstärken; heftiger werden; sich verwickeln, sich verwirren; *the plot* ~~*s* der Knoten schürzt sich; **~ening** ['-iŋ] Verdikkung; Verdichtung *f*; *(Küche)* Eindickmittel *n*; *med* Anschwellung *f*; **~et** ['-it] Dickicht *n*; **~head** ['-hed] Dummkopf *m*; **~headed** ['-hedid] *a* blöd(e), dumm; **~ness** ['-nis] Dicke, Stärke; Dichtheit, Dichtigkeit; Undurchsichtigkeit; Lage, Schicht *f*; Verschwommenheit; *(Flöz)* Mächtigkeit *f*; **~-set** ['-'set] *a* dicht gepflanzt *od* gewachsen *od* besetzt; untersetzt, dick, stark; *s* ['--] Dickicht *n*; dichte Hecke *f*; **~-skinned** ['-'skind] *a* dickhäutig; *fig* dickfellig; **~-skulled** ['-'skʌld], **~-witted** ['-'witid] *a* dumm.

thief [θi:f] *pl thieves* Dieb *m*; *thieves' Latin* Gaunersprache *f*; *stop* ~*!* haltet den Dieb! **~-proof** diebessicher.

thiev|e [θi:v] *tr itr* stehlen; **~ery** ['-əri] Stehlen *n*, Dieberei *f*; Diebstahl *m*; **~ish** ['-iʃ] diebisch; verstohlen, heimlich.

thigh [θai] (Ober-)Schenkel *m*; **~-bone** Oberschenkelknochen *m*.

thill [θil] (Gabel-)Deichsel *f*; **~er** ['-ə], **~-horse** Gabelpferd *n*.

thimble ['θimbl] Fingerhut *m*; *mar* Kausche *f*; *tech* Meßring *m*; **~ful** ['-ful] Fingerhutvoll *m*; *a* ~~ ein bißchen; **~rig** ['-rig] *s Art* Spiel *n*; *tr* betrügen, beschwindeln; **~-rigger** ['-rigə] Taschenspieler; Schwindler, Betrüger *m*.

thin [θin] *a* dünn; flach; mager, hager; *(Gesicht)* schmal; fein (verteilt); schwach (besetzt); spärlich, dürftig; dünn, wäss(e)rig; *(Farbe)* blaß; *(Boden)* unfruchtbar; *(Buch)* seicht; *(Gewebe)* (hauch)dünn, fein, zart; *fig* durchsichtig; *(Beweis, Ausrede)* schwach; fadenscheinig; *phot* matt, undeutlich; *sl* mies, faul; *adv* dünn; schwach; *tr itr* dünn(er) machen, werden; verdünnen; (sich) lichten; *(to* ~ *down)* (sich) vermindern, (sich) verringern; *to* ~ *out (itr)* sich verlaufen, sich verlieren; *tr* ausforsten; *to have a* ~ *time (fam)* e-e üble Zeit durchmachen; **~-bodied** ['-'bɔdid] *a* dünnflüssig; ~ **flame** Stichflamme *f*; **~ness** ['-nis] Dünnheit; Magerkeit; Spärlichkeit, Dürftigkeit; *fig* Dürftigkeit *f*; ~ **sheet** Feinblech *n*; **~-skinned** ['-'skind] *a* dünnhäutig; *fig* feinfühlig, empfindlich, leicht beleidigt.

thine [ðain] *prn obs* der, die, das deine, deinige; *(vor Vokalen)* dein.

thing [θiŋ] Ding *n*, Sache *f a. jur*; Gegenstand *m*; Stück *n*; *the* ~ die Hauptsache, der Hauptpunkt, das Wesentliche, das Ziel; die (große) Sache; *fam (kleines, armes)* Ding, Hascherl; *fam* Ding, Ding(s)da *n*; *sl* Zuneigung *f*, Widerwillen *m*; *pl* Sachen *f pl*, Kleider *n pl*; Lage, Situation *f*; Umstände *m pl*, Verhältnisse *n pl*; es; *among other* ~*s* unter anderem; *as a general, usual* ~ (für) gewöhnlich; *first* ~ zuerst, zuallererst, zunächst (einmal), als erstes; *for one* ~ einmal, vor allem; *in all* ~*s* in jeder Hinsicht; *of all* ~*s* ausgerechnet *adv*; na so was! *no such* ~ nichts dergleichen; *no small* ~ keine Kleinigkeit; *quite the* ~ die Sache; *the real* ~ das Richtige; *an understood* ~ e-e abgemachte, *fam* abgekartete Sache; *the very* ~ genau das; *a* ~ *like that* so etwas, *fam* sowas; *a* ~ *or two* (schon) einiges, (so) allerhand; *to know a* ~ *or two* einiges *od* was loshaben; was können; *not to feel* od *look quite the* ~ nicht (so) besonders aussehen; nicht auf der Höhe sein; *to make a good* ~ *of s.th.* Nutzen ziehen aus; *to see* ~*s* Gespenster sehen; *that was a near* ~*!* das ist noch mal gut-, wäre beinahe schiefgegangen; *how are* ~*s?* wie geht's? wie steht's? *I'm going to tell him a* ~ *or two* dem werde ich was erzählen *od* den Marsch blasen! *there is no such* ~ so was gibt es nicht; *I don't know the first* ~ *about it* ich habe keinen blassen Dunst davon; **~amy, ~ummy** ['-əmi], **~um(a)bob** ['-əm(i)bɔb], **~umajig** ['-əmidʒig] Dingsda *n*; **~-in-itself** Ding *n* an sich; ~ **real** *jur* Grundstück *n*.

think [θiŋk] *irr thought, thought* [θɔ:t] *tr* (aus)denken, ersinnen; sich vorstellen; sich einbilden; halten für, ansehen als; glauben, meinen, finden, der Ansicht, Meinung sein (*that* daß); planen, die Absicht haben, beabsichtigen (*to do* zu tun); (dauernd) denken an, überlegen; *itr* denken (*of* an; *about* über); nachdenken, -sinnen (*about, on, upon* über); (sich) überlegen, sich durch den Kopf gehen lassen (*about s.th.* etw); meinen (*about* zu); halten (*of* von); bedacht sein (*of* auf); sich mit dem Gedanken tragen (*of doing* zu tun); sich erinnern (*of* an), sich besinnen (*of* auf); *o.s. into s.th.* sich in etw hineindenken, -versetzen; *to ~ aloud* laut denken, Selbstgespräche führen; *to ~ better of s.th.* sich etw nochmal, sich sehr überlegen; sich e-s Besseren besinnen; e-e bessere Meinung von etw haben; *to ~ fit, good to do* es für gut halten, zu tun; *to ~ highly, much of* viel halten von; *to ~ nothing of* nichts halten von; als nichts Besonderes ansehen; *to ~ twice* sich nochmal überlegen; *I ~ so* ich denke schon; *that's what you ~* so siehst du aus! *~ nothing of it!* es ist nicht der Rede wert! *to ~* **away** wegdenken; *to ~* **out** sich gut überlegen; ausdenken; *(Problem)* lösen; *to ~* **over** überdenken, -legen; sich durch den Kopf gehen lassen; *to ~* **through** durchdenken; *to ~* **up** (sich) ausdenken, ersinnen; **~able** ['-əbl] denk-, vorstellbar; **~box** *Am fam* (Hirn-)Schädel, Kasten *m*; **~er** ['-ə] Denker *m*; **~ing** ['-iŋ] *a* denkend, vernünftig; nachdenklich; *s* Denken; Nachdenken *n*; Meinung *f*; *to my ~~* meiner Meinung nach, meines Erachtens; *to put o.'s ~~-cap on (fam)* über etw nachdenken; *that's wishful ~~* das ist ein frommer Wunsch; *way of ~~* Gesichtspunkt *m*, Auffassung *f*; *~~ time* Schrecksekunde *f*; **~piece** *Am* erfundene(r) (Presse-)Bericht *m*.

third [θə:d] *a* dritt; *s der, die, das* Dritte; Drittel *n*; *(Zeugnis)* Drei *f*; *mot* dritte(r) Gang *m*; *mus* Terz *f*; **~-class** *a* drittklassig; **~-degree** *a* drittrangig; *tr Am (Polizei)* foltern; **~ degree** *s* dritte(r) Grad *m*; *Am* (polizeiliche) Folterung *f*; **~ eyelid** *zoo* Nickhaut *f*; **~ly** ['-li] *adv* drittens; **~ party** *jur* Dritte(r) *m*, dritte Person *f*; *~~ insurance* Haftpflichtversicherung *f*; *~~ risk* Haftpflicht *f*; **~ rail** *el* Stromschiene *f*; *Am sl* unbestechliche(r) Mensch *m*; **~-rate** *a* drittrangig; *fig* armselig; **~-rater** *fam* kleine(s) Licht *n (Mensch)*; **~ wheel** *Am fam fig* fünfte(s) Rad *n* am Wagen.

thirst [θə:st] *s* Durst *m a. fig*; *fig* Verlangen *n*, Sehnsucht *f* (*for* nach); *itr* Durst haben, *lit* dürsten; *fig* verlangen, sich sehnen (*for* nach); *to satisfy, to quench o.'s ~* den Durst löschen; *I ~ for (fig)* mich dürstet, verlangt nach; *it gives me a ~* es macht mich durstig; **~y** ['-i] durstig; *fig* begierig (*for, after* nach); *to be ~~ for rain* nach Regen lechzen.

thirt|een ['θə:'ti:n] *a* dreizehn; *s* Dreizehn *f*; **~eenth** ['-'-θ] *a* dreizehnt; *s* Dreizehntel *n*; **~ieth** ['θə:tiiθ] *a* dreißigst; *s* Dreißigstel *n*; **~y** ['-ti] dreißig; *s* Dreißig *f*; *Am fam* Ende *n*; *the ~ies (pl)* die dreißiger Jahre *(e-s Jahrhunderts)*; die Dreißigerjahre *(e-s Menschenlebens)*.

this [ðis] *pl these* [ði:z] *prn a* dies(er, e), diese; *(alleinstehend)* dies; *~ one (substantivisch)* diese(r, s); *adv* so; *at, with ~* hiermit; *by ~ (time)* jetzt; *for ~* dafür, hierfür; *from ~* daraus; davon; *with ~* damit; *~ day* heute; *~ day week* heute in acht Tagen; *~ minute* augenblicklich; *~ morning, evening, night* heute morgen, abend, nacht; *~ time* diesmal.

thistl|e ['θisl] Distel *f*; *~~-butterfly* Distelfalter *m*; *~~-down (bot)* Distelwolle *f*; *~~-finch* Distelfink, Stieglitz *m*; **~y** ['-i] stach(e)lig.

thither ['ðiðə] *adv obs* dort-, dahin.

tho(') [ðou, ðo] = *though*.

thole [θoul] *mar (~pin)* Ruderpflock *m*.

thong [θɔŋ] Lederstreifen, -riemen; Peitschenriemen *m*.

thor|acic [θɔ:'ræsik] *a* Brust(kasten-, -korb)-; **~ax** ['θɔ:ræks] *pl -es anat* Brust(kasten *m*, -korb *m*) *f*; *ent* Bruststück *n*.

thorn [θɔ:n] Dorn *a. zoo*; Dornbusch, -strauch *m*; *fig* dornige, schwierige Angelegenheit *f*; *that's a ~ in my flesh, side (fig)* das ist mir ein Dorn im Auge; *there's no rose without ~ (prov)* keine Rose ohne Dorn; **~y** ['-i] dornig *a. fig*; stach(e)lig, scharf; *fig* mühevoll, beschwerlich; schwierig; heikel.

thorough, *Am a.* **thoro** ['θʌrə] *a* vollständig, völlig; vollendet; sorgfältig, gründlich, genau; **~-bass** ['-'beis] *mus* Generalbaß *m*; **~bred** *a* Vollblut-; blaublütig, aristokratisch, vornehm, edel; kultiviert; *s* Vollblut(pferd) *n*; Aristokrat, Edelmann *m*; **~fare** ['-fɛə] Durchgang *m*, -fahrt; Durchfahrts-, Hauptverkehrsstraße; Verkehrsader *f*; *no ~~!* keine Durchfahrt! **~-going** *a* vollständig, vollkommen, vollendet; kompromißlos; durch u. durch; **~ly** ['-li] *adv* eingehend, gründlich; gänzlich; völlig; **~ness** ['-nis] Vollendung; Sorgfalt, Gründlichkeit *f*; **~-paced** *a fig* völlig, vollkommen; abgefeimt, ausgekocht; *(Pferd)* in allen Gangarten geübt.

those *s. that*.

thou [ðau] *prn obs poet rel* du.

though [ðou] *conj* obgleich, obwohl; wenn auch; trotzdem, dennoch; aber; *adv* indessen, doch; *fam (am Satzende)* immerhin, doch; *as ~* als ob; *even ~* obwohl, obgleich; *what ~?* was macht, tut das? was kommt darauf an?

thought [θɔ:t] *s* (Nach-)Denken, Sinnen *n* (u. Trachten); Überlegung, Reflexion; Denkfähigkeit *f*, Verstand *m*, Einbildungskraft *f*; Gedanke, Einfall *m*, Vorstellung, Meinung, Ansicht; Erwägung; Auffassung (*in* von), Vorstellungsweise, Einstellung (*in* zu); Denkweise *f*; Geistesleben *n*; Aufmerksamkeit, Rücksicht; Absicht, Erwartung *f*; *a ~* ein bißchen, etwas, *fam* e-e Idee; *v pret u. pp von think (s.d.)*; *after serious ~, on second ~s* nach reiflicher Überlegung; *in ~* in Gedanken (versunken); *without ~* gedankenlos; *to be lost in ~* in Gedanken versunken sein; *to give ~ to* nachdenken über; sich Gedanken machen über; *to show ~ for* Rücksicht nehmen auf; *to take ~ for (the morrow)* (an die Zukunft) denken; *I had no ~ of it* ich dachte gar nicht daran; *of doing it* ich hatte nicht im geringsten die Absicht, das zu tun; *I had some ~ of going to ...* halb u. halb hatte ich die Absicht, nach ... zu gehen; *a happy ~* e-e gute Idee; **~ful** ['-ful] gedankenvoll, nachdenklich; gedankenreich, gehaltvoll; aufmerksam, rücksichtsvoll, zuvorkommend; bedacht (*of* auf); besorgt (*of* um); **~fulness** ['-fulnis] Nachdenklichkeit *f*; Gedankenreichtum *m*; Aufmerksamkeit, Zuvorkommenheit, Besorgtheit *f*; **~less** ['-lis] gedankenlos, achtlos, unaufmerksam, sorglos; übereilt, unbesonnen; rücksichtslos (*of* gegen); unbekümmert (*of* um); dumm; **~lessness** ['-lisnis] Gedankenlosigkeit, Achtlosigkeit; Unaufmerksamkeit, Sorglosigkeit; Übereiltheit, Unbesonnenheit; Rücksichtslosigkeit; Unbekümmertheit; Dummheit *f*; **~-reader** Gedankenleser *m*; **~-reading** Gedankenlesen *n*; **~-transference** Gedankenübertragung, Telepathie *f*.

thousand ['θauzənd] *a (a ~)* tausend; *s* Tausend *n*; *one ~* eintausend; *a ~ thanks* tausend Dank; *a ~ times* tausendmal; **~fold** ['-fould] *a adv* tausendfach, -fältig; **~th** ['-nθ] *a* tausendst; tausendstel; *s* Tausendste; Tausendstel *n*.

thral(l)dom ['θrɔ:ldəm] Knechtschaft, Sklaverei *f a. fig*.

thrall [θrɔ:l] Knecht, Sklave *m a. fig* (*to his passions* s-r Leidenschaften).

thrash [θræʃ], **thresh** [θreʃ] *tr* schlagen, peitschen; *fam* zu Boden werfen, besiegen; *(meist: thresh)* dreschen; *itr (to ~ about)* mit Händen u. Füßen um sich schlagen; umherfahren, -zappeln; *mar* sich vorwärtsquälen; *(meist: thresh)* dreschen; *to ~ out (Thema)* gründlich erörtern, erledigen; **~er** ['-ə], **thresher** ['θreʃə] Drescher *m*; Dreschmaschine *f*; *zoo* Fuchshai *m*; *zoo* Spottdrossel *f*; **~ing** ['-iŋ], **threshing** ['θreʃiŋ] Schläge *m pl*, Tracht *f* Prügel, *fam* Dresche; *fig* völlige Niederlage *f*; *agr* Drusch *m*; *to give s.o. a good ~~* jdm e-e tüchtige Tracht Prügel verabreichen; *fig* jdn vernichtend schlagen; *~~-flail* Dreschflegel *m*; *~~-floor* (Dresch-)Tenne *f*; *~~-machine* Dreschmaschine *f*.

thread [θred] *s (Textil)* Faden *m a. fig*; Faser, Fiber *f*; Zwirn *m*; (Näh-)Garn *n*; *(Licht)* Strahl; Schraubengang *m*, Gewinde *n* (*on a screw* an e-r Schraube); *tr* einfädeln; auf e-n Faden ziehen, aufreihen; *fig* durchziehen, sich ziehen durch; sich durchschlängeln, sich durchwinden durch; *(Schraube)* mit e-m Gewinde versehen; *(Film)* einlegen; *itr* sich (hin)durchwinden; sich durchziehen (*through* durch); *to hang by a ~ (fig)* am seidenen Faden hängen; *to lose the ~ (fig)* den Faden verlieren; *to resume, to pick up the ~s (fig)* den Faden wieder aufnehmen; *to ~ o.'s way* sich durchschlagen; **~bare** ['-bɛə] fadenscheinig; *fig* abgedroschen, -gegriffen; *(Mensch)* schäbig, abgerissen; **~ing** ['-iŋ] Gewindeschneiden; Einfädeln *n*; *~~ head* Schneidkopf *m*; **~like** fadenförmig; **~worm** Fadenwurm *m*; **~y** ['-i] faserig; seimig; *fig* dünn, schwach.

threat [θret] *s* Drohung *f* (*of* mit; *to* gegen); *to utter a ~ against s.o.* gegen jdn e-e Drohung ausstoßen; *a ~ of rain* ein drohender Regen *m*; *~ of war* Kriegsdrohung *f*; **~en** ['-n] *tr (jdn)* bedrohen (*with* mit); androhen (*s.o. with s.th.* jdm etw); drohend ankündigen; drohen (*s.th.* mit etw; *to do* zu tun); *itr* drohen; **~ening** ['-niŋ] drohend, bedrohlich; *~~ letter* Drohbrief *m*.

three [θri:] *a* drei; *s* Drei *f*; **~-cornered** *a* dreieckig; zu dreien; **~-colo(u)r process** Dreifarbendruck *m*; **~-core** *tech* dreiaderig; **~-D** dreidimensional; **~-decker** *mar hist u. allg fam* Dreidecker *m*; **~fold** ['-fould] *a adv* dreifach; **~-leaved** *a bot* dreiblätterig; **~-legged** *a* dreibeinig; **~-master** *mar* Dreimaster *m*; **~ O** ['-'ou] *mar* dritte(r) Offizier *m*; **~pence** ['θrepəns, 'θrip-] *s* 3 Pence *pl*;

Dreipencestück *n*; **~penny** ['θrepəni] *a* Dreipence-; *fig* billig; *~~-bit* Dreipencestück *n*; **~-phase current** *el* Drehstrom *m*; **~-piece** dreiteilig; **~-ply** ['θri:plai] *a* dreifach; *s* Sperrholz *n*; **~-point landing,** *fam* **~-pointer** *aero* Dreipunkt-, *fam* saubere Landung *f*; **~-quarter** *a* dreiviertel, Dreiviertel-; **~score** ['θri:'skɔ:] sechzig; **~some** ['-səm] Dreier (-spiel), *fam* Trio *n*; **~-stage** *tech* dreistufig; **~-storied** *a* dreistöckig; **~-valve receiver** *radio* Dreiröhrenempfänger *m*; **~-way switch** Dreifachumschalter *m*; **~-wheeled** *a* Dreirad-.

thresh *s. thrash.*

threshold ['θreʃ(h)ould] (Tür-)Schwelle *f a. fig u. physiol psychol*; *fig* Anfang, Beginn *m*; *at the ~ of an era* an der Schwelle e-s Zeitalters; *to be on the ~ of o.'s career* am Anfang s-r Laufbahn stehen; *~ of consciousness* Bewußtseinsschwelle *f*; *~* **value** Grenzwert *m*.

thrice [θrais] *adv* dreimal, -fach; *fig* sehr, höchst, äußerst.

thrift [θrift], **~iness** ['-inis] Sparsamkeit, Wirtschaftlichkeit *f*; **~less** ['-lis] unwirtschaftlich; verschwenderisch; **~y** ['-i] sparsam (*of, with* mit); wirtschaftlich; vorsorglich; *Am* (gut) gedeihend, blühend.

thrill [θril] *tr* erschauern lassen (*with* vor); (innerlich) erregen, packen, aufwühlen; erzittern, erbeben lassen; *itr* erregt, aufgewühlt sein; zittern, beben (*with* vor); *s* Schauer *m*, Erregung; (Hoch-)Spannung; *sl* Schauergeschichte, Sensation *f*; Zittern, Beben *n*; *to give s.o. a ~* jdn in Erregung versetzen; *a ~ of joy* e-e freudige Erregung; **~er** ['-ə] Schauer-, Sensationsroman *m*, -drama *n*, -film *m*; **~ing** ['-iŋ] aufregend, aufwühlend; packend, spannend, sensationell.

thriv|e [θraiv] *meist irr throve* [θrouv], *thriven* ['θrivn] *itr* (gut) gedeihen *a. fig* (*on good food* bei guter Nahrung); *fig* blühen; reich werden; Erfolg haben; **~ing** ['-iŋ] *fig* (gut) gedeihend, blühend.

thro(') [θru:] = *through.*

throat [θrout] *s* Kehle, Gurgel *f*; Rachen, Schlund; Hals *a. fig*; *fig* enge(r) Durch-, Eingang; *tech* Hals *m*; *min* Gicht *f*; Bruchquerschnitt *m*; *arch* (Hohl-)Kehle *f*; *to clear o.'s ~* sich räuspern; *to cut one another's ~s (fam com)* sich gegenseitig kaputtmachen; *to cut o.'s own ~ (fig)* sich sein eigenes Grab schaufeln; *to grip s.o. by the ~* jdn an der Kehle packen; *to jump down s.o.'s ~ (fig fam)* jdm an die Gurgel fahren, ins Gesicht springen; *to ram, to thrust s.th. down s.o.'s ~* jdm etw aufzwingen; *to stick in s.o.'s ~ (a. fig)* jdm im Halse steckenbleiben; *my ~ is parched* mir klebt die Zunge am Gaumen; *a lump in the ~ (fig)* ein Kloß im Halse; *sore ~* Halsweh *n*; **~latch** *(Zaum)* Kehlriemen *m*; **~-phone** Kehlkopfmikrophon *n*; **~-pipe** *anat tech* Luftröhre *f*; *~* **register** Bruststimme *f*; **~y** ['-i] *(Stimme)* belegt, rauh; guttural; *(a. Mensch)* heiser.

throb [θrɔb] *itr (Herz)* (heftig) schlagen, klopfen, pochen, hämmern; zucken (*with* vor); *s* (Herz-, Puls-) Schlag *m*; *fig* (heftige, innere) Erregung *f*; Zittern, Dröhnen *n*; *his head ~bed* sein Kopf dröhnte.

throe [θrou] (heftiger, plötzlicher) Schmerz *m*; *pl* (Geburts-)Wehen *f pl*; Todeskampf *m a. fig*; *to be in the ~s of s.th.* etw durchzumachen, durchzustehen, durchzukämpfen haben.

thrombosis [θrɔm'bousis] *med* Thrombose *f*.

throne [θroun] *s* Thron *m a. fig*; *tr* inthronisieren; *to come to the ~* den Thron besteigen.

throng [θrɔŋ] *s* Gedränge, Gewühl *n*, Andrang *m*; (Menschen-)Menge, Masse; *allg* große Schar, Menge *f*; *itr* sich zs.drängen, (sich) drängen; strömen; *tr* bedrängen; zs.drängen; vollpfropfen, -stopfen.

throstle ['θrɔsl] *dial* od *lit* (*bes.* Sing-) Drossel *f*; *(~-frame) (Spinnerei)* Drosselstuhl *m*, -maschine *f*.

throttle ['θrɔtl] *s* Kehle, Luftröhre *f*; *(~-valve)* Drosselventil *n*; *tr* erdrosseln, erwürgen; *fig* ersticken, unterdrücken; *(to ~ down)* drosseln; *mot* (ab)drosseln; *(Wagen)* abbremsen; *itr* ersticken; *at full ~, with the ~ full open* mit Vollgas; *to close the ~* das Gas wegnehmen; *to open (out) the ~* Gas geben; *~* **flap** Drosselklappe *f*; **~-lever** *mot* Gashebel *m*.

through, thro', thro [θru:] *prp (räumlich)* durch; *(zeitlich, nachgestellt)* über; *Am* bis einschließlich; *(kausal)* durch, aus, vor, infolge *gen*; (ver-) mittels, mit Hilfe *gen*; *adv* durch, zu Ende; *a Am* durch, (ein für allemal) fertig (*with* mit); *(Verkehrsverbindung)* durchgehend; *~ and ~* durch u. durch, völlig, vollständig *adv*; *all ~* die ganze Zeit; *wet ~* patschnaß; *to be ~* durch, fertig sein, abgeschlossen haben (*with* mit); *fam* satt haben (*with s.th.* etw); *tele* Verbindung haben; *you are ~* ich verbinde; *to carry ~* zu Ende bringen *od* führen; *to drop, to fall ~* es nicht schaffen; nicht zustande kommen; ins Wasser fallen; *to get ~* durchkommen durch; *with (fam)* zu Ende kommen mit; *to go ~* durchgehen, -sehen (*with s.th.* etw); *(Schule)* durchmachen; *to put ~ (tele)* verbinden (*to s.o.* mit jdm); *to read, to see, to sleep ~* durchlesen, -sehen *od* -schauen, -schlafen; *~-and-~ (bullet-)wound (med)* Durchschuß *m*; *~* **car, carriage, coach** *rail* Kurswagen *m*; **~out** *prp* überall in; während; *adv* überall; die ganze Zeit (über); durchaus, ganz (u. gar), völlig, vollständig; *famous ~~ the world* in der ganzen Welt berühmt; *~* **passenger** Durchreisende(r) *m*; **~-put** *tech* Durchgangsleistung *f*; Durchsatz *m*; *~* **station** Durchgangsbahnhof *m*; *~* **street** Durchgangs-, Hauptverkehrsstraße *f*; *~* **ticket** *rail* durchgehende Fahrkarte *f*; *~* **traffic** Durchgangsverkehr *m*; *~* **train** durchgehende(r) Zug *m*.

throw [θrou] *irr threw* [θru:], *thrown* [θroun] *tr* (hin)werfen (*to the ground* auf den Boden); schleudern, *fam* schmeißen (*at* nach); zu Boden werfen *od* strecken; *(vom Pferd)* abwerfen; fallen lassen, verlieren; *(Karte)* ausspielen; *(Blick)* zuwerfen (*at me* mir); *(in e-e bestimmte Lage)* bringen, versetzen, werfen; ein-, ausschalten; *(Brücke)* schlagen (*over, across* über); *(Junge)* werfen; *(Haut)* abwerfen; *(auf der Drehscheibe)* drehen; *(Rohseide)* spinnen, zwirnen; *Am fam (Spiel, Rennen)* verlieren; *Am sl (Party)* geben, schmeißen; *itr* werfen; *to ~ o.s. at s.o. (fig)* sich jdm an den Hals werfen; *into s.th. (fig)* sich auf etw stürzen; *(up)on s.th.* sein Vertrauen auf etw setzen; *to be ~n upon o.s.* auf sich selbst angewiesen sein; *s* Wurf *m (a. beim Würfeln)*; Wagnis, Risiko *n*; Überwurf *m*, Decke; *geol* Verwerfung; *tech* Ausladung *f*, Hub, Ausschlag *m*, Kröpfung *f*; *to ~ blame on s.o.* jdn tadeln; *to ~ the book at s.o. (Am fam)* jdn zu der Höchststrafe verurteilen; *to ~ into confusion, disorder* in Unordnung bringen; *to ~ dice* würfeln; *to ~ a fit (sl)* e-n Wutanfall bekommen; *to ~ a glance at* e-n Blick werfen auf; *to ~ influence into* Einfluß ausüben auf; *to ~ light on s.th.* Licht über etw verbreiten, etw aufklären; *to ~ a monkey, a wrench into s.th.* etw zum Stehen bringen, sabotieren; *to ~ obstacles before s.o.* jdm Hindernisse in den Weg legen; *to ~ s.th. open* weit öffnen; allgemein zugänglich machen; *to ~ overboard* über Bord werfen; *to ~ into prison* ins Gefängnis werfen; *to ~ shadow(s)* Schatten werfen; *to ~ a six* e-e Sechs werfen *od* würfeln; *to ~ in od up the sponge* die Flinte ins Korn werfen; *~ that light this way, please* bitte, leuchten Sie hierher; *a stone's ~* ein Steinwurf, ein Sprung (*from* von); *to ~* **about** *(Papier)* herumwerfen; *(Geld)* zum Fenster hinauswerfen; *to ~* **away** fort-, wegwerfen; verschwenden, vergeuden; *(Gelegenheit)* verpassen; in den Wind schlagen; *(Worte)* fallenlassen; *to ~* **back** auf e-n früheren, unvollkommeneren Stand zurückwerfen; *(Bild)* zurückstrahlen; *to be ~n back upon* angewiesen sein auf; *to ~* **down** nieder-, hinwerfen; niederreißen; *to ~* **in** *tech* einschalten, -schieben, -kuppeln; *com* mit in den Kauf, zugeben; hinzufügen; *(e-e Bemerkung)* einwerfen, -flechten; *to ~ in o.'s hand* s-e Karten hinwerfen; *fig* aufgeben; *to ~ in (o.'s lot) with s.o.* mit jdm gemeinsame Sache machen; *to ~ o.s.* **into** nachdrücklich *(mit der Arbeit)* beginnen; *to ~* **off** weg-, abwerfen, ablegen; hinauswerfen, vertreiben; *tech* ab-, auswerfen; *fam* so hinwerfen, aus dem Ärmel schütteln; *(Erkältung)* losbekommen; *(von e-r Spur)* ablenken; *to ~* **on** *(Kleidungsstück)* (schnell) überwerfen, -ziehen; *to ~* **open** *(Tür)* aufstoßen; freigeben; *to ~* **out** wegwerfen; hinauswerfen, *fam* -schmeißen; zurückstoßen; *(Bemerkung)* fallenlassen; *fig* verwirren, aus dem Konzept bringen; *(Wink)* geben; *(Gesetzesvorlage)* ablehnen; *tech* ausschalten; *arch* anbauen; *(Licht)* ausschalten; *to ~ out of court (Klage) jur* abweisen; *to ~ out of gear* auskuppeln; *to ~* **over** hinüber-, herüberwerfen; aufgeben, verstoßen; *(Theorie)* verwerfen; *(Liebhaber)* sitzenlassen; *to ~* **together** zs.stoppeln; *(Personen)* zs.bringen; *to ~* **up** hoch-, in die Höhe werfen, hochheben; *med* (sich) erbrechen, sich übergeben; *(Arbeit)* aufgeben; *(Vorsitz)* niederlegen; (schnell) hinhauen; vorwerfen, (immer wieder) vorhalten (*s.th. to s.o.* jdm etw); *(Frage)* aufwerfen; *to ~ up o.'s eyes (fig)* die Hände über dem Kopf zs.schlagen; **~away** *a* (scheinbar) achtlos; *s* Reklamezettel *m*; **~back** Abweisung, -fuhr *f*; Rückfall *a. fig*, Atavismus; *Am fam* Rückschlag *m*; *Am film* Rückblende *f*; **~er** ['-ə] Werfer; *tech* Dreher, Former; Zwirner *m*; *~~-up* Kegeljunge *m*; **~-in** *sport* Einwurf *m*; **~ing** ['-iŋ] *s* Werfen *n*; *~~ the hammer, the javelin (sport)* Hammer-, Speerwerfen *n*; **~n** *a* ab-, zu Boden geworfen; gezwirnt; **~-off** *tech* Auswurf; *fig* Beginn *m*; **~-out** Abfall; *tech* Auswerfer *m*; **~-over** Aus-, Verstoßung *f*; *(Kleidung)* Überwurf *m*; **~ster** ['-stə] Seidenspinner *m*.

thru *Am* = *through*; **~way** *Am* Schnellverkehrsstraße, Autobahn *f*.

thrum [θrʌm] **1.** Trumm *m* od *n*, Saum *m*, Fransen *f pl*; *pl* Garnabfälle *m pl*, Zotten *f pl*; *mar* Fuchsjes *pl*; *tr* befransen; *thread and ~* alles durchea.; **2.** *tr* klimpern, trommeln auf; herleiern; *itr* klimpern; trommeln (*on* auf).

thrush [θrʌʃ] **1.** *orn* Drossel *f*; **2.** *med* Sohr *m*, Mundfäule *f*, Schwämmchen *n*; *(Pferde)* Strahlfäule *f*.

thrust [θrʌst] *irr thrust, thrust tr* (heftig, fest) stoßen, *fam* schubsen; drängen; durchbohren; werfen; *(Nadel)* stecken (*into* in); *itr* stoßen, stechen (*at* nach); sich drängen (*into* in; *through* durch); sich recken, sich dehnen; *to ~ o.s.* sich werfen, sich stürzen (*at* auf); sich drängen (*into* in; *past* an ... vorbei); sich mit allen Mitteln verschaffen (*into s.th.* etw); *to ~ o.s. forward* sich in den Vordergrund drängen; *s* Stoß, Stich, Hieb; feste(r) Druck; *mil* Vorstoß (*towards* gegen); *fig fam* hemmungslose(r) Einsatz *m*, scharfe Bemerkung *f*; *tech* Schub *a. geol*; Axialdruck; Vor-, Rückstoß *m*; *to ~ o.'s hands into o.'s pockets* die Hände in die Tasche stecken; *to ~ o.'s way through* sich e-n Weg bahnen durch; *to ~* **on** *(Kleidung)* überwerfen; *to ~* **out** (hin)ausstoßen, -werfen, (her)ausstrecken; ~ **bearing** *tech* Drucklager *n*; ~ **collar, washer** Druckring *m*; **~er** ['-ə] Draufgänger *m*; **~ing** draufgängerisch; rücksichtslos; eingebildet; ~ (**performance**) Schubleistung *f*; ~ **weapon** *mil* Stich-, Stoßwaffe *f*.

thud [θʌd] *s* (dumpfer) Schlag *m*, (dumpfes) Geräusch *n*, *fam* Bums *m*; *itr* dumpf aufschlagen, -stoßen (*to* auf); *fam* bumsen; *(Kugeln)* dumpf einschlagen (*into* in).

thug [θʌg] Mörder, Gangster, Rowdy *m*.

thumb [θʌm] *s* Daumen *m*; *tr* mit dem Daumen berühren *od* drücken *od* bearbeiten; *(Buchseite)* (um)wenden, beschmutzen; *to ~ a lift, a ride (fam)* per Anhalter fahren, wollen; *to ~ through (Buch)* durchblättern; *under s.o.'s ~* in jds Hand, Gewalt, *fam* unter jds Fuchtel; *to ~ o.'s nose* ätsch, e-e lange Nase machen (*at* gegen); *his fingers are all ~s* er hat zwei linke Hände; *~s down!* pfui! *~s up!* bravo! Kopf hoch! *rule of ~* Faustregel *f*; **~ed** [-d] *a*: *well-~~ (Buch)* abgegriffen, zerlesen; **~-index** *(Buch)* Daumenregister *n*; **~nail** *s* Daumennagel *m*; *fig* ein kleines bißchen, ganz wenig; *a* winzig; *~~ sketch* rasch angefertigte Skizze *f*; **~-nut** Flügelmutter *f*; **~-print** Daumenabdruck *m*; **~-screw** Flügel-, *hist* Daumenschraube *f*; **~stall** Däumling *m*; **~tack** *Am* Heftzwecke *f*, Reißnagel *m*.

thump [θʌmp] *s* dumpfe(r) Schlag, Stoß, Klaps, Puff, Knuff; *fam* Bums *m*; *tr* puffen, knuffen; schlagen; verdreschen, verprügeln; *itr* dumpf aufschlagen, -prallen; heftig schlagen (*on, at* an, auf); *(Herz)* pochen (*with* vor); **~er** ['-ə] *fam* Kerl *m*; gewaltige Sache; faustdicke Lüge *f*; **~ing** ['-iŋ] *a* dumpf aufschlagend; *fam* riesig; *adv fam* gewaltig, mordsmäßig.

thunder ['θʌndə] *s* Donner(schlag) *m a. fig*; *(Kanonen)* Donnern; Getöse *n*; *fig* Drohung *f*; *itr* donnern *a. fig*; anbrüllen, andonnern (*at s.o.* jdn); *tr (Worte)* mit Donnerstimme brüllen; *clap, crash of ~* Donnerschlag *m*; *a ~ of applause* donnernde(r) Beifall *m*; *to steal s.o.'s ~ (fig)* jdm den Wind aus den Segeln nehmen; *it was ~ing and lightening* es donnerte u. blitzte; **~bolt** Blitz u. Donnerschlag; *fig* Blitz *m* aus heiterem Himmel; **~-clap, ~peal** Donnerschlag *m*; **~-cloud** Gewitterwolke *f a. fig*; **~er** ['-rə] Donnerer *m*; **~ing** ['-riŋ] *a* donnernd; *fam* gewaltig, riesig, mächtig, phantastisch; *adv fam* riesig; **~ous** ['-rəs] *a* donnernd *a. fig*; *fig* (laut) polternd; gewitt(e)rig, gewitterschwül; *fam* gewaltig, ungeheuer, mächtig; **~storm** Gewitter; Unwetter *n*; **~stricken, ~struck** *a fig* wie vom Schlag getroffen *od* Donner gerührt; **~-stroke** Donnerschlag *m*; **~y** ['-ri] donnernd; gewitt(e)rig.

Thursday ['θə:zdi] Donnerstag *m*; *on ~* am Donnerstag; *on ~s* donnerstags; *Maundy ~* Gründonnerstag *m*.

thus [ðʌs] *adv* so, auf diese Weise; in dem Maße; so, infolgedessen, deshalb; ~ **far** so weit; bis jetzt; ~ **much** so viel.

thwack [θwæk] *tr* durchwalken, verdreschen; *s* heftige(r) Schlag *m*.

thwart [θwɔ:t] *tr (Plan)* durchkreuzen; *(Absicht)* vereiteln; *s.o.* jds Pläne durchkreuzen *od* Absichten vereiteln; jdm e-n Strich durch die Rechnung machen; *s mar* Ruderbank, Ducht *f*.

thy [ðai] *obs poet* dein; **~self** [ðai'self] *obs poet* du, dir, dich selbst.

thyme [taim] *bot* Thymian *m*.

thymus ['θaiməs] *(~ gland) anat* Thymus-, innere Brustdrüse *f*.

thyr(e)oid ['θai(ə)rɔid] *a* Schilddrüsen-; *s u. ~ gland* Schilddrüse *f*.

*

tiara [ti'ɑ:rə] Tiara *f*; Stirnreif *m*.

tibia ['tibiə] *pl -ae* ['-ii:] Schienbein *n*.

tic [tik] *med* Gesichts-, Muskelzucken *n*.

tick [tik] **1.** *s* Ticken; Häkchen *n* (Vermerk-)Strich; *fam* Moment, Augenblick *m*, Sekunde *f*; *itr* ticken; *fam* funktionieren, arbeiten; *tr* in e-r Strichliste vermerken; abhaken, anstreichen; *to ~ off* abhaken; *fam* anschnauzen, abkanzeln (*s.o.* jdn); *to ~ over (mot)* leerlaufen *a. fig*; *in a ~, in two ~s* gleich, sofort; *on, to the ~* auf die Minute, ganz pünktlich; *half a ~!* sofort! *to give s.o. a good ~ing-off (fam fig)* jdm ordentlich den Kopf waschen; *what makes it ~? (fam)* was steckt dahinter? **~er** ['-ə] *tele* Börsentelegraph, Ticker *m*; *fam* Uhr *f*; *sl* Herz *n*, Mut *m*; *to get a ~~-tape reception* mit e-m Konfettiregen empfangen werden; **~-tack** ['-'tæk] *s* Ticktack *n*; *(Buchmacher)* Handzeichen *n pl*; **~-tock** ['-'tɔk] *s* Ticken *n*; **2.** *ent* Zecke *f*; *fig* widerliche(r) Kerl *m*; **3.** Inlett *n*, Bezug *m*; **~ing** ['-iŋ] Inlett *n (Stoff)*; **4.** *s fam* Pump, Kredit *m*; *tr (to buy on ~)* auf Pump kaufen; Kredit geben (*s.o.* jdm).

ticket ['tikit] *s* (Eintritts-, Theater-, Fahr-, Flug-)Karte *f*; Fahrschein *m*; (Lotterie-)Los; Etikett, Schildchen *n*; Preiszettel *m*; (Lebensmittel-)Marke *f*; Ausweis(karte *f*); Merkzettel *m*; *Am parl* Kandidatenliste *f*; Wahlprogramm *n*; *Am fam* Strafmandat *n*, gebührenpflichtige Verwarnung *f*; *tr* etikettieren; *(Waren)* auszeichnen; *to buy, to take a ~* e-e Fahrkarte lösen; *to vote the straight ~* die Parteiliste wählen; *that's the ~! (fam)* das ist d i e Sache! *admission-~* Eintrittskarte *f*; *airplane-~* Flugkarte *f*; *circular-tour ~* Rundreisefahrkarte *f*; *cloakroom-~* Garderobenmarke *f*; Gepäck(aufbewahrungs)schein *m*; *complimentary ~* Freifahrschein *m*; *go-as-you-please ~* Netzkarte *f*; *landing ~* Landungskarte *f*; *lottery-~* Lotterielos *n*; *luggage-~, (Am) baggage-~* Gepäckschein *m*; *monthly ~* Monatskarte *f*; *pawn-~* Pfandschein *m*; *platform-~* Bahnsteigkarte *f*; *reserved-seat ~ (rail)* Platzkarte *f*; *return-~, (Am) round-trip ~* Rückfahrkarte *f* (*to* nach); *season-~* Dauer-, Zeitkarte *f*; *single ~* einfache Fahrkarte *f*; *supplementary ~* Zuschlagkarte *f*; *theatre ~* Theaterkarte *f*; *weekly ~* Wochenkarte *f*; *~ of leave (jur)* Schein *m* über vorzeitige, bedingte Entlassung (e-s Strafgefangenen); *on ~~* unter Polizeiaufsicht; **~-agent** Kartenagent(ur *f*); Schalterbeamte(r) *m*; **~-book** Fahrscheinheft *n*; **~-collector** Bahnsteigschaffner *m*; **~-day** *com* Abrechnungstag *m*; **~-gate** Bahnsteigsperre *f*; **~-inspector** Zugschaffner; Fahrkartenkontrolleur *m*; **~-number** *(Lotterie)* Losnummer *f*; **~-office, -window** Fahrkartenschalter *m*; **~-punch** Lochzange *f*.

tickl|e ['tikl] *tr* kitzeln *a. fig (die Sinne, den Gaumen)*; schmeicheln, gefallen, angenehm sein (*s.o.* jdm); erheitern; *itr* kitzeln, jucken; kitz(e)lig sein; *s* Kitzel *m*; *to ~ pink (sl)* sich halb totlachen; *I was ~ed to death (fam)* ich habe mich wahnsinnig amüsiert (*at* über); **~er** ['-ə] Kitzelnde(r) *m*; Feder *f* zum Kitzeln; Schüreisen *n*, Feuerhaken *m*; *fig* kitzlige Frage *f*, Problem *n*; heikle Situation *f*; *Am* Notizblock *m*, -buch, Merkheft *n*, Terminkalender *m*; *Am com* Verfallbuch *n*; *~~ coil* Rückkopplungsspule *f*; **~ish** ['-iʃ] *(Mensch)* kitz(e)lig; reizbar, empfindlich; *(Sache)* heikel, schwierig.

tid|al ['taidl] *a* Gezeiten-; *~~ basin* Tide-, Flutbecken *n*; *~~ wave* Flutwelle; *fig* Flut, Woge *f*; **~e** [taid] *s* Ebbe u. Flut *f*, Gezeiten *pl*; *fig* Auf u. Ab *n*; *fig* Strom *m*, Strömung *f*; Haupt(geschäfts-, Verkehrs-)Zeit *f*; *a* Gezeiten-; *itr* mit dem Strom treiben; *fig* strömen, fluten; *tr* (mit der Strömung) treiben; *at high ~~* bei Flut; *to turn the ~~ (fig)* den Spieß umdrehen; *to ~~ over (fig)* überbrücken; hinwegkommen über; über Wasser halten; *~~ is up* es ist Flut; *the ~~ turns (fig)* das Blatt wendet sich; *ebb, low ~~* Ebbe *f*, Niedrigwasser *n*; *flood, high ~~* Flut *f*, Hochwasser *n*; *neap ~~* Nipptide *f*; *spring ~~* Springtide *f*; *turn of the ~~* Flut-, *fig* Glückswechsel; Umschwung *m*; *~~-gauge* Pegel *m*; *~~land* Watt(enmeer) *n*; *~~-mark* Gezeitenmarke *f*; *~~-rip* Stromwelle *f* der Gezeiten; *~~-table* Gezeitentafel *f*; *~~-water* Gezeitenwasser *n*; *~~-wave* Flutwelle *f*; *~~way* Flutkanal, -strom *m*; **~iness** ['-inis] Sauberkeit, Ordentlichkeit, Nettigkeit *f*; **~ings** ['-iŋz] *s pl a. mit sing* Neuigkeiten, Nachrichten, Informationen *f pl*; **~y** ['-i] *a* sauber, ordentlich, nett; *fam (Geldsumme)* ganz nett, hübsch; *tr* sauber, hübsch machen, ordnen; *(to ~~ up)* aufräumen; *s* Sofadeckchen *n*; (Flick-)Beutel *m*.

tidbit *s. titbit.*

tiddl(e)y ['tidli] *fam* angeheitert.

tiddle(d)ywinks ['tidl(d)iwinks] Flohhüpfen *n (Spiel)*.

tie [tai] *tr* (an-, fest-, zs.-, zu)binden (*to* an); zs.knoten; *(Paket)* zs.schnüren; *(Knoten)* machen; *(Bündel)* schnüren; e-n Knoten machen in, verknoten; *arch* verankern; *allg* verbinden, verknüpfen; *tech* (ab-, ver)spannen, abbinden; *fig* (unter)binden; be-, einschränken; (be-, ver)hindern; *(Geld)* festlegen; *(punkt-, zahlenmäßig)* gleichstehen (*s.o.* mit jdm); *fam* verheiraten; *itr* sich binden lassen; e-n Knoten machen; gleichstehen (*with* mit); *sport* punktgleich sein, unentschieden spielen; *s* Band *n a. fig*; *fig* Bindung, Verpflichtung; *fam* Last, Belastung *f*; Verbindungen *f pl*; *(neck~)* Krawatte *f*, Schlips *m*, Schleife *f*, Halstuch; *allg* Verbindungsstück *n*; *arch* Anker *m*; *Am rail* Schwelle *f*; *sport* Punkt-, *parl* Stimmengleichheit *f*; Ausscheidungsspiel *n*; *mus* Ligatur *f*; *to ~ down* begrenzen, einschränken, behindern; festlegen (*s.o.* jdn); *to ~ in with* einbauen in; *to ~ on* anknüpfen; *to ~ o.s. on (sl)* sich betrinken; *to ~ together* zs.binden; *to ~ up* festbinden, fest zs.binden, verknoten; verschnüren; *(Kapital)* festlegen; *mar* verankern; *(Boot)* festmachen; *fam* trauen, verheiraten; behindern; zum Stehen, zum Stillstand bringen; *(Fabrik)* stilllegen; *to be ~d up* beschäftigt, belegt sein; in Verbindung stehen (*with* mit); *to ~ s.o.'s hands (a. fig)* jdm die Hände binden; *my hands are ~d* mir sind die Hände gebunden; *the game ended in a ~* das Spiel endete unentschieden; *the ~ will be played off (sport)* das Spiel wird wiederholt; *business ~* Geschäftsverbindung *f*; *family ~s (pl)* familiäre Bindungen *f pl*; *~s of blood, of friendship* Bande *n pl* des Blutes, der Freundschaft; **~-beam** Zug-, Ankerbalken *m*; **~-in(-sale)** Kopp(e)lungsverkauf *m*; **~-on label** Anhängeadresse *f*; **~-pin** Krawattennadel *f*; **~-up** Stockung *f*, Stillstand *m*; Störung, Unterbrechung; (Betriebs-)Einstellung; Verbindung *f*; *fig* tote(r) Punkt; Streik, Ausstand *m*; **~r** ['-ə] **1.** Binder *(Person)*; *sport* Gleichstehende(r) *m*; Band *n*; *Am* Kinderschürze *f*.

tier ['taiə] **2.** *s* (Sitz-)Reihe *f*, Regal *n*; *theat* Rang *m*.

tierce [tiə(:)s] *(mus rel Fechten)* Terz *f*; Stückfaß *n (42 Gallonen)*; [tə:s] *(Karten)* Terz *f*.

tiff [tif] Verstimmung; Streiterei *f*, kleine(r) Streit *m*; *in a ~* übelgelaunt; **~in** ['-in] leichte(s) Frühstück *n*.

tiger ['taigə] Tiger *m a. fig*; *(Am sl) three cheers and a ~!* dreimal hoch u. e-n Tusch! **~-beetle** *zoo* Sandlaufkäfer *m*; **~-cat** Tigerkatze *f*; **~ish** ['-riʃ] tigerartig; *fig* grausam, blutrünstig, wild; **~-lily** Tigerlilie *f*.

tight [tait] *a* (luft-, wasser)dicht; dicht, eng; fest(gefügt); fest angebunden; straff, eng(anliegend), zu eng, knapp; *(Behälter)* prallvoll; *agr* wasserundurchlässig; *fig* streng; schwierig, kritisch; gezwungen; (fast) gleich; *com* knapp, angespannt; in Geldverlegenheit; *(Stil)* knapp, straff; *(Argument)* hieb- u. stichfest; *fam* knauserig, filzig, geizig; *sl* besoffen; *adv* eng, knapp; *s pl* Trikothose *f (der Artisten)*; *to hold ~* festhalten; *to shut ~* fest zumachen; *to sit ~* sich nicht rühren; *fig* hartnäckig sein; sich nachdrücklich behaupten; *the cork is too ~* der Korken sitzt zu fest; *air-, water-~* luft-, wasserdicht; **~ corner, place** schwierige Lage, Klemme, Zwickmühle *f*; **~en** ['-n] *tr* anziehen, straffen; zs.ziehen, enger machen; *(Gürtel)* enger schnallen; *tech* abdichten; *(Bestimmungen)* verschärfen; *itr (to ~~ up)* enger werden, sich zs.ziehen, einlaufen; sich straffen; *(Markt)* sich versteifen; **~-fisted** *a* filzig, knauserig; **~ fit** *tech* stramme(r) Sitz *m*; **~-fitting** eng anliegend; *tech* genau eingepaßt; **~-laced** *a* fest ge-, verschnürt; *fig* engherzig; **~-lipped** *a* mit zs.gepreßten Lippen; *fig* verschwiegen; **~ness** ['-nis] Dichte; Enge; Knappheit, Verknappung; Knauserigkeit *f*; **~rope** (festgespanntes) (Draht-)Seil *n*; **~~ dancer** Seiltänzer *m*; **~wad** [-'wæd, -wɔd] *sl* Knicker, Knauser *m*.

tigress ['taigris] Tigerin *f a. fig*.

tike *s. tyke*.

tilde ['tild(i)] *gram* Tilde *f*.

til|e [tail] *s* (Dach-)Ziegel *m (pl)*; Kachel, Fliese; Tonröhre *f*; *arch* Hohlstein *m*; *fam* Angströhre *f*, Zylinder *m*; *tr* mit Ziegeln decken; kacheln; *to be (out) on the ~~s (sl)* herumsumpfen; *to have a ~~ loose* nicht richtig im Oberstübchen sein; **~er** ['-ə] Ziegelbrenner; Plattenleger; Dachdecker *m*.

till [til] **1.** *prp (zeitlich)* bis (zu); *not ~* nicht vor; erst; *true ~ death* (ge)treu bis in den Tod; *~ now* bis jetzt, bisher; *~ then* bis dahin; dann; *conj* bis; *~ such time as* bis *conj*; **2.** *itr* den Boden bearbeiten, ackern; *tr* beackern, *(den Boden)* bearbeiten; **~age** ['-idʒ] Bodenbearbeitung *f*; bestellte(s) Land *n*; Ernte *f*; **~er** ['-ə] Pflüger; Bauer; Landarbeiter *m*; Ladenkasse *f (Schublade)*; *geol* Geschiebelehm *m*; *mar* Ruderpinne *f*; *tech* Griff *m*; *~~-rope (mar)* Steuerreep *n*.

tilt [tilt] **1.** *tr* kippen, (ver)kanten, neigen, schräg stellen; schief halten; umstoßen; *(Hut)* schief aufsetzen; *(Kopf)* neigen; *tech* mit dem Schwarzhammer bearbeiten; *(Turnier)* anrennen gegen; *itr* geneigt, schräg sein *od* stehen; sich neigen, umkippen; (mit der Lanze) stoßen, stechen (*at* nach); anrennen *a. fig* (*at* gegen); Lanzen brechen; am Turnier teilnehmen; *fig* disputieren, Streitgespräche führen; losziehen (*at* gegen); *s* Neigung, schiefe Lage; Schrägfläche *f*; Hang *m*; Wippe *f*, Schaukelbrett *n*; Stoß *m* mit der Lanze; Turnier *n*; *fig* Disput *m*, Debatte *f*, Streitgespräch *n*; *(at) full ~* mit voller Wucht *od* aller Gewalt; *on the ~* auf der Kippe; *to have a ~ at s.o. (fig)* jdn (freundschaftlich) angreifen; *to ~ back* zurücklehnen, -beugen; **~ angle** Neigungswinkel *m*; **~-cart** Kippkarren *m*; **~er** ['-ə] Kipper *m*, Kantvorrichtung *f*; *hist* Turnierkämpfer *m*; **~-hammer** Schwarzhammer *m*; **~ing** ['-iŋ] *a* Turnier-; *tech* Kipp-; *s tech* Neigung, Kippung *f*; *~~ movement* Kippbewegung *f*; **~yard** Turnierhof, -platz *m*; **2.** *s* Wagendecke, Plane *f*; *tr* mit e-r W., P. (ab)decken.

tilth [tilθ] Feldbestellung; Tiefe *f* der Ackerkrume; bebaute(s) Land *n*.

timbal ['timbəl] *mus* Kesselpauke *f*.

timber ['timbə] Bau-, Schnitt-, Nutzholz *n*; Balken *m*; *mar* Spant *n*; (Nutz-)Holz-, Baumbestand, Wald *m*; *Am* Waldgebiet *n*; *fig Am* (Menschen-)Schlag *m*, Kaliber *n*; *a man of his ~ (Am)* ein Mann von s-m Schlage; **~ed** ['-d] *a* gezimmert; Holz-, Fachwerk-; baumbestanden, bewaldet; *fig Am in Zssgen* von ... Schlage; *half-~~ (Haus)* Stein-, Fachwerk-; **~ framed building** Fachwerkhaus *n*; **~ing** ['-riŋ] Nutz-, Bauholz; Gebälk *n*, Holzkonstruktion *f*, Fachwerk *n*; **~land** *Am* (nutzbares) Waldland *n*; **~-line** *Am geog* Baumgrenze *f*; **~-toe(s)** *fam* (Mann *m* mit) Holzbein *n*; **~-work** Holzkonstruktion *f*, Gebälk, Fachwerk; *pl* Sägewerk *n*; **~-yard** Zimmerplatz *m*.

time [taim] **1.** *s* Zeit(raum *m*, -spanne), (Zeit-)Dauer; Arbeitszeit *f*, -lohn *m*; Lehrzeit *f*; Zeitmaß, Tempo *n*, Geschwindigkeit *f*; *mus* Takt, Rhythmus; Zeitpunkt *m*, genaue Zeit; rechte Zeit *f*, richtige(r) Augenblick, gegebene(r) Moment *m*; Frist *f*; Termin *m*; Mal *n*, Gelegenheit *f*; *meist pl* Zeiten *f pl*, Zeitläufte *pl*; *pl* Zeitalter *n*, Epoche *f*; *pl (nach Zahlen)* mal; **2.** *tr* zur rechten Zeit tun; zeitlich einrichten; einstellen (*to* nach); die Zeit bestimmen, angeben für; stunden; *mus* den Takt angeben für; *sport* (ab)stoppen; die Zeit messen von; **3.** *itr* die Zeit einhalten; den Zeitpunkt wählen; den Takt halten (*with* mit); Zeit abstoppen, nehmen; **4.** *a* Zeit-; **5.** *abreast of the ~s* auf der Höhe der Zeit; *against ~* gegen die Zeit, in größter Eile; *ahead of, before o.'s ~(s)* s-r Zeit voraus; *all the ~* die ganze Zeit (über); dauernd; ständig; *another ~* ein andermal; *any number of ~s* x-mal; *at ~s* zu Zeiten, manchmal; hin u. wieder, ab u. zu; *at a ~, the same ~* zur gleichen Zeit, gleichzeitig *adv*, zugleich; *at a given ~* zu e-m festgesetzten Zeitpunkt; *at no ~* nie; *at one ~* einmal, einst; *at that ~* damals, zu der Zeit; *at the same ~* zur selben Zeit, gleichzeitig; nichtsdestoweniger; *behind the ~s* hinter dem Mond; veraltet; *by that ~* bis dahin, inzwischen, unterdessen; *by this ~* bis jetzt; *a dozen ~s* immer wieder, dauernd; *every ~* jedesmal; *for a long ~* lange; *for the ~ being* im Augenblick; zur Zeit, vorerst, vorläufig, einstweilen, bis jetzt; *from ~ to ~* von Zeit zu Zeit, ab u. zu; *half the ~* die halbe Zeit; meist, fast immer; *in half the ~* in der halben Zeit; *in ~* rechtzeitig; mit der Zeit, zu gegebener Zeit; *in double-quick ~* in höchster Eile; *in due ~* termingemäß; *in good ~* zur rechten Zeit; beizeiten; schnell *adv*; *in no ~* im Nu; *in s.o.'s ~* zu jds (Leb-)Zeiten; *many ~s, many a ~* manchesmal, oft(mals); *next ~* das nächste Mal; *on ~* pünktlich *adv*; in Raten, auf Abzahlung; *on o.'s own ~* in der Freizeit; *out of ~* zur Unzeit, ungelegen *adv*; *mus* aus dem Takt; *several ~s* mehrmals; *this ~* diesmal; *up to this, the present ~* bis heute, bis zum heutigen Tage; *once upon a ~ (there was)* (es war) einmal; *~ after ~, ~ and (~) again* immer wieder; **6.** *to ask s.o. the ~ of day* jdn nach der Uhrzeit fragen; *to be behind ~* zu spät kommen, Verspätung haben; *to be paid by ~* stundenweise bezahlt werden; *to be pressed for ~* es eilig haben; *to beat ~* den Takt schlagen; *to do ~ (fam)* s-e Zeit absitzen; *to gain ~* Zeit gewinnen; *to have (no, not much) ~* (keine, nicht viel) Zeit haben (*for* für); *to have no ~ to lose* keine Zeit zu verlieren *od* übrig haben; *to have a ~ doing s.th.* Schwierigkeiten haben etw zu tun; *to have had o.'s ~, the ~ of o.'s life* die besten Jahre hinter sich haben; *to have a good ~* sich gut unterhalten; *to have the ~ of o.'s life* sich glänzend amüsieren; *to keep ~ (mus)* den Takt halten; *to keep good (bad) ~ (Uhr)* (un)genau gehen; *to lose ~* Zeit verlieren; *(Uhr)* zu langsam gehen; *to make ~* aufholen; ein hohes Tempo haben; *to take ~* Zeit erfordern *od* benötigen; *to work against ~* unter Zeitdruck arbeiten; *to work full ~* ganztägig arbeiten; **7.** *what ~ do we eat?* um wieviel Uhr essen wir? *I must bide my ~* ich muß mich in Geduld üben; *~ is up* die Zeit ist (her)um, vorbei; *take your ~ over it* lassen Sie sich Zeit dazu; *~ will tell* die Zeit wird es lehren; **8.** *broken ~* Arbeitszeitverlust *m*; *Father T~* Chronos *m*; *leisure ~* Freizeit *f*; *length of ~* Zeitdauer, -spanne *f*; *local ~* Ortszeit *f*; *loss of ~* Zeitverlust *m*; *a matter of ~* e-e Frage der Zeit; *point of* ~ Zeitpunkt *m*; *record* ~ Rekordzeit *f*; *saving of* ~ Zeitgewinn *m*; *solar* ~ *(astr)* Sonnenzeit *f*; *space and* ~ Raum u. Zeit; *spare* ~ Freizeit *f*; *standard* ~ Einheitszeit *f*; *summer* ~ Sommerzeit *f*; *waiting*-~ Wartezeit *f*; *waltz* ~ Walzertakt *m*; *working* ~ Arbeitszeit *f*; *want of* ~ Zeitmangel *m*; *waste of* ~ Zeitverschwendung *f*; ~ *of arrival, of departure* Ankunfts-, Abfahrtszeit *f*; *the* ~ *of day* die Tageszeit; *to pass the* ~ *of day* ea. e-n guten Tag wünschen; sich grüßen; ~ *of payment* Zahlungstermin *m*; ~ **announcement** Zeitansage *f*; ~-**bargain** Termingeschäft *n*; ~ **belt, zone** Zeitzone *f*; ~ **bomb** Zeitbombe *f*; ~-**card, -sheet** *Am* (Arbeitszeit-)Kontrollkarte *f*; ~ **clock** *Am* Stech-, Kontrolluhr *f*; ~-**consuming** zeitraubend; ~**d** [-d] *a* (zeitlich) festgesetzt, -gelegt (*to* auf); ~ **deposits** *pl* langfristige Einlagen *f pl*; ~-**elapse** Zeitraum *m*; ~-**expired** *a (Soldat)* ausgedient; ~-**exposure** *phot* Zeitaufnahme *f*; ~-**fuse** Zeitzünder *m*; ~-**history** zeitliche Folge *f*; ~-**hono(u)red** *a* altehrwürdig; ~ **immemorial** unvordenkliche Zeiten *f pl*; ~-**interval** Pause *f*; Zeitabschnitt *m*; ~**keeper** Chronometer *n*; *(Zeit-)* Kontrolleur; Lohnbuchhalter; *sport* Zeitnehmer *m*; ~-**lag** Verzögerung; zeitliche Verschiebung *f*; ~-**lens** Zeitlupe *f*; ~**less** ['-lis] endlos; unbefristet; ~-**limit** Zeitgrenze, -beschränkung; Frist; Redezeit *f*; ~~-*switch* Zeitschalter *m*; ~**liness** ['-linis] Rechtzeitigkeit; Angebrachtheit *f*; ~ **loan** Zeitanleihe *f*; ~**ly** ['-li] rechtzeitig, im rechten Augenblick erfolgend; (gut) angebracht, passend; *(Thema)* aktuell; ~-**out** *Am* Unterbrechung; ~-**payment** *Am* Ratenzahlung *f*; ~**piece** Chronometer *n*, Uhr *f*; ~ **poster** Aushängefahrplan *m*; ~**r** ['-ə] Zeitmesser *m*, Uhr *f*; *phot* (Zeit-)Auslöser; *sport* Zeitnehmer, Trainer; *tech* Impulsgeber *m*; *big* ~~ *(Am fam)* Großverdiener *m*; *full*-~~ Vollbeschäftigte(r) *m*; *half-, part*-~~ Halbtags-, Kurzarbeiter *m*; *small* ~~ *(Am fam)* kleine(r) Geschäftsmann *m*; ~-**rating** Versuchsdauer *f*; ~-**sanctioned** *a* durch die Zeit geheiligt; ~-**saving** zeitsparend; ~-**server** Opportunist *m*; ~-**serving** *a* opportunistisch; *s* Opportunismus *m*; ~-**signal** *radio* Zeitzeichen *n*; ~ **standard** Lohngrundlage *f*; ~-**table** Zeitplan; *rail* Fahrplan *m*; Kursbuch *n*; *aero* Flugplan; *(Schule)* Stundenplan *m*; ~-**tested** *a* (lange) erprobt; ~ **wage** Stundenlohn *m*; ~**work** Arbeit *f* gegen Stundenlohn; ~**worn** *a* abgenutzt, verbraucht.

tim|id ['timid] furchtsam, ängstlich (*of* vor); scheu, schüchtern; *(Verhalten, Frage)* zögernd; ~**idity** [ti'miditi], ~**idness** ['timidnis] Furchtsamkeit, Ängstlichkeit; Scheu, Schüchternheit *f*; ~**orous** ['-ərəs] = *timid.*

timing ['taimiŋ] (Zeit-)Einstellung, zeitliche Festlegung; Regulierung, Abstimmung, Synchronisierung; *mot* Zündeinstellung; *com* Zeitnahme *f*.

timpano ['timpənou] *pl -ni* [-ni] *mus* Kesselpauke *f*.

*

tin [tin] *s* Zinn; Weißblech *n*; Blechschachtel, -büchse, -dose, -kanne; Konservenbüchse, -dose *f*; *sl* Moos *n*, Zaster *m*, Geld *n*; *a* zinnern; Blech-; *fig* unecht; minderwertig; *tr* verzinnen; (in Büchsen, Dosen) einmachen, eindosen; konservieren; *sl* schriftlich festhalten; *sardine*-~ Sardinenbüchse *f*; ~-**can** Blechdose *f*; *Am mar sl* Zerstörer *m*; ~**fish** *mar sl* Aal, Torpedo *m*; ~ **foil** Stanniol, Silberpapier *n*; ~ **god** *fig* Götze *m*; *a little* ~~ *(fam)* ein kleiner Gernegroß *m*; ~ **hat** *sl mil* Blechdeckel, Stahlhelm *m*; *to put the* ~~ *on it (sl)* mit der Faust auf den Tisch hauen; ~**horn** *sl* schäbig, simpel; angeberisch; *Am sl* hochstaplerisch; ~ **Lizzie** *sl* Ford *m (Wagen)*; Klapperkiste *f*; ~**ned** [-d] *a* verzinnt; in Büchsen eingemacht; eingedost; ~~ *fruit* Obstkonserven *f pl*; ~~ *meat* Büchsenfleisch *n*; ~~ *music* Konservenmusik *f*; ~**ner** ['-ə] Zinngrubenarbeiter; Zinngießer; Klempner, Spengler, Flaschner, Blechner; Arbeiter *m* in e-r Konservenfabrik; ~**ny** ['-i] zinnhaltig; zinnartig; *fig (Ton)* blechern, hohl; aufgeputzt; *sl* schwerreich; ~-**opener** Büchsenöffner *m*; ~-**pan alley** *Am* (Straße *f od* Stadtviertel *n*, *bes.* in New York, in der viele) Schlagerkomponisten, -sänger, -verleger *m pl* (wohnen); ~-**plate** *s* Weißblech *n*; *tr* verzinnen; ~**pot** *pej* billig, minderwertig; *pred* Tinnef *m*; ~**(s)man, -smith** Klempner, Spengler, Flaschner, Blechner; Zinngießer *m*; ~-**solder** Lötzinn, Zinnlot *n*; ~**ware** Zinn-, Blechgeschirr *n*.

tinctur|e ['tiŋ(k)tʃə] *s* Färbung *f*, Farbton *m*, Tönung *f*; *fig* Anstrich *m*, (leichte) Spur *f*, Schatten, Hauch, Beigeschmack *m*; *med* Tinktur *f*; *tr* schwach färben, (leicht) tönen; *fig* e-n Anstrich geben (*with* von; *s.th.* e-r S); ~~ *of iodine* Jodtinktur *f*; ~**ed** ['-d] *a fig* mit e-m Schimmer, Anstrich (*with* von).

tinder ['tində] Zunder *m a. allg*; ~-**box** *hist* Zunderbüchse *f*; *fig* Brause-, Hitzkopf *m*; Pulverfaß *n*.

tine [tain] Zacke(n *m*), Zinke; *(Hirschgeweih)* Sprosse *f*.

ting [tiŋ] *s* helle(r) Klang *m*; *itr tr* hell klingen (lassen); klingeln; ~-**a-ling** Klingeling *n*.

tinge [tindʒ] *tr* (leicht) färben, tönen (*with* mit); *fig* e-n Anstrich, Anhauch, Beigeschmack geben (*s.th.* e-r S; *with* von); *s* leichte Färbung, Tönung; *fig* (leichte) Spur *f*, Anflug, Anhauch, Geruch, (Bei-)Geschmack *m* (*of* von).

tingle ['tiŋgl] *itr* prickeln, stechen, jucken, brennen; zittern, beben (*with excitement* vor Aufregung); (in den Ohren) klingeln, summen; *tr* prickeln, zittern, klingeln lassen; *fig* erregen; *s* Prickeln, Stechen; Kribbeln; Zittern; Klingeln *n*.

tinker ['tiŋkə] *s* Kesselflicker; Pfuscher *m*; Pfuscherei *f*; *tr* flicken, ausbessern; *itr* herumbasteln, -pfuschen (*with, to* ~ *away at* an); *not to care a* ~*'s damn, cuss about s.th.* sich keine grauen Haare um etw wachsen lassen; *not worth a* ~*'s damn* keinen Pfifferling, keinen Pfennig, roten Heller wert; *to have a* ~ *at s.th.* an etw herumbasteln.

tinkl|e ['tiŋkl] *itr tr* klingeln, läuten (lassen); klirren; *s u.* ~**ing** ['-iŋ] Geklingel, Läuten *n*.

tinnitus [ti'naitəs] *med* Ohrensausen *n*.

tinsel ['tinsəl] *s* Flitter(gold *n*) *m*; Lametta *n*; *fig* Firlefanz, falsche(r) Glanz, Kitsch *m*; *a* Flitter- *a. fig*; aufgeputzt; *tr* mit Flittergold verzieren; *fig* e-n falschen Glanz geben.

tint [tint] *s* Färbung, Tönung *f*, Farbton *m*; Schattierung; *typ* Grundierung *f*; *tr* leicht färben, tönen; ~**ed** ['-id] *a* getönt; ~~ *glass* Rauchglas *n*; ~~ *paper* Tonpapier *n*; ~**ing strength** Farbkraft *f*.

tintinnabulation ['tintinæbju'leiʃən] Läuten, Klinge(l)n *n*.

tiny ['taini] winzig; *(Stimme)* dünn.

tip [tip] **1.** *s* Spitze *f*, Ende *n*; Kappe, Zwinge *f*; *(Zigarette)* Mundstück *n*; *(Berg)* Spitze *f*; Gipfel *m*; *tr* mit e-r Spitze, Kappe versehen, beschlagen; als Spitze dienen für; *from* ~ *to toe* vom Scheitel bis zur Sohle; *I have it on the* ~ *of my tongue (fig)* es liegt, schwebt mir auf der Zunge; ~ *of the nose, tongue* Nasen-, Zungenspitze *f*; *asparagus* ~*s (pl)* Spargelspitzen *f pl*; *cork-, filter-* ~ Kork-, Filtermundstück *n*; *finger*-~ Fingerspitze *f*; ~**ped** [-t] *a in Zssgen* mit Mundstück; *cork-, filter-, gold*-~~ mit Kork-, Filter-, Goldmundstück; ~**pet** ['-it] (Pelz-)Kragen; Umhang *m*; Schärpe *f*; ~**staff** *obs* (Stab des) Gerichtsdiener(s) *m*; ~-**tilted nose** Stupsnase *f*; ~**toe** ['-tou] *adv u. s*: *on* ~~ auf Zehenspitzen; *fig* ungeduldig, nervös *adv* (*with* vor); *itr* auf Zehenspitzen gehen; ~**top** ['-'tɔp] *s* Gipfel, Höhepunkt *m*; *a fam* tipptopp, prima; **2.** *tr* e-n Klaps geben (*s.o.* jdm); (leicht) berühren; ein Trinkgeld geben (*s.o.* jdm); *(to* ~ *into)* hineingießen; *(to* ~ *off)* auskippen, *fig* e-n Tip, Wink geben (*s.o.* jdm), *sl* umbringen; *(to* ~ *over, up)* umkippen, kanten, schräg stellen; *(to* ~ *out)* ausgießen; *(den Hut zum Gruß)* lüften, leicht berühren (*to s.o.* vor jdm); *itr* e-n Tip geben; sich neigen; *(to* ~ *up)* umkippen; *s* Klaps *m*; Trinkgeld *n*; Tip, Wink *m*; geneigte Lage, Neigung, Schiefstellung *f*; *(refuse* ~*)* (Schutt-)Abladeplatz; Müll, Schutt *m*; Halde *f*; *to* ~ *the scale (fig)* den Ausschlag geben; *to* ~ *s.o. the wink (fam)* jdm ein Zeichen geben; jdn warnen; *to* ~ *the winner (Rennen)* auf den Sieger tippen; ~-**and-run** *s Art* Kricket; *a* blitzschnell (angreifend u. sich zurückziehend); Überraschungs-; ~-**cart** Sturz-, Kippkarren *m*; ~ **cat** *Art* Kinderspiel *n*; ~-**off** *sl* Wink, Tip *m*, Zeichen *n*; (kurze) Warnung *f* (*on* vor); ~**ster** ['-stə] *fam* Tipgeber; Berater *m* bei Pferderennen; ~-**up seat** Klappsitz *m*.

tipple ['tipl] **1.** *tr itr* (gewohnheitsmäßig) trinken, süffeln; *s* Schnaps *m*; *allg* Getränk *n*; ~**r** ['-ə] (Gewohnheits-)Trinker, Säufer *m*; **2.** *Am* Kippvorrichtung *f*; Abladeplatz *m*.

tips|ify ['tipsifai] *tr* betrunken machen; ~**iness** ['-nis] Trunkenheit *f*, *fam* Suff *m*; ~**y** ['-i] kipp(e)lig, wack(e)lig; krumm (u. schief); *fam* angeheitert, beschwipst.

tirade [tai'reid, ti-, *Am* 'tai-] Tirade *f*, Wortschwall *m*; Geschimpf(e) *n*, Schimpferei *f*.

tire ['taiə] **1.** *itr* müde werden (*of doing s.th.* etw zu tun); *of s.th.* e-r S überdrüssig werden; etw satt haben; *tr* müde machen, ermüden; langweilen; strapazieren; *to* ~ *out* völlig erschöpfen; ~**d** ['-d] *a* müde, abgespannt (*with, by* von); erschöpft; überdrüssig (*of s.th.* e-r S); *to be* ~~ *out* abgespannt, fertig sein (*from* von); ~**dness** ['-dnis] Müdigkeit, Übermüdung *f*; Überdruß *m*, Langeweile *f*; ~**less** ['-lis] unermüdlich; ~**some** ['-səm] ermüdend; langweilig; ~ **wear** Abnützung *f* im Gebrauch; **2.** *mot* Reifen *m*, Bereifung *f*, Mantel *m*; *tr* bereifen; *to put air in the* ~ den Reifen aufpumpen; *tubeless* ~ schlauchlose(r) Reifen *m*; ~ **casing, cover** Reifendecke *f*; ~ **chain** Schneekette *f*; ~ **flap** Felgenband *n*; ~-**ga(u)ge** Reifendruckmesser *m*; ~-**lever** *mot*

Montiereisen *n*; ~ **marks** *pl mot* Reifen-, Bremsspur(en *pl*) *f*; ~ **pressure** Reifendruck *m*; ~ **profile** Reifenprofil *n*; ~**-pump** Luftpumpe *f*; ~ **rim** Reifenwulst *m*; ~ **trouble** Reifenschaden *m*, Panne *f*; **3.** *s obs* (Kopf-)Putz *m*; *tr* putzen; ~**woman** Zofe *f*; **tiring-room** *theat* (Schauspieler-)Garderobe *f*.

tiro, tyro ['taiərou] *pl -os* Anfänger, Neuling *m*.

'tis [tiz] = *it is*.

tissue ['tisju:, 'tiʃ(j)u:] (feines) Gewebe; *fig* Gewebe, Netz; *(~ paper)* Seidenpapier; Papiertaschentuch; *biol* Gewebe *n*; *connective ~ (biol)* Bindegewebe *n*; *toilet ~* Toilettenpapier *n*; ~ **culture** *biol* Gewebs-, Gewebezüchtung *f*.

tit [tit] **1.** *s*: *to give ~ for tat* mit gleicher Münze heimzahlen; **2.** = ~*lark*, ~*mouse*; **3.** *fam* Zitze; *sl* Brust *f*; **4.** (Schind-)Mähre *f*; *sl* Weib(sbild, -sstück) *n*.

titan|ic [tai'tænik] titanisch, titanenhaft; *chem* Titan-; ~**ium** [-'teinjəm] *chem* Titan *n*.

titbit ['titbit], **tidbit** ['tidbit] Leckerbissen *m a. fig*.

titfer ['titfə:] *sl* Hut *m*.

tith|able ['taiðəbl] zehnt-, abgabepflichtig; ~**e** [taið] *s hist* (Kirchen-)Zehnte *m*; Zehntel *n*; Bruchteil *m*; *allg* Abgabe *f*; *tr* den Zehnten abgeben von, für; den Zehnten einziehen von; ~~*-barn* Zehntscheuer *f*.

titian ['tiʃiən] *a (Haar)* tizianrot.

titillat|e ['titileit] *tr* kitzeln *a. fig*; *fig* reizen; ~**ion** [titi'leiʃən] Kitzel(n *n*) *a. fig*; *fig* Reiz *m*.

tit|lark ['titla:k] *orn* Wiesenpieper *m*; ~**mouse** ['-maus] *pl -mice* ['-mais] Meise *f*.

title ['taitl] *s jur* Abschnitt; *(Buch, Person)* Titel *m*; *(Kapitel)* Überschrift *f*; Anrecht *n*, (Rechts-)Titel *m*, Recht(sanspruch *m*) *n* (*to* auf); *film* Untertitel *m*; *tr* betiteln; *film* mit Untertiteln versehen; *under the same ~* in der gleichen Rubrik; *bastard ~* Schmutztitel *m*; ~**d** ['-d] *a* mit e-m (Adels-)Titel, adlig; ~**-deed** Besitztitel *m*, -urkunde *f*; ~**-expectant** *sport* Titelanwärter *m*; ~**-holder** Titelinhaber, *sport* -verteidiger *m*; ~**-page** *(Buch)* Titel(blatt *n*, -seite *f*) *m*; ~**-part, -role** *theat film* Titelrolle *f*; ~**-retention** Eigentumsvorbehalt *m*.

titrat|e ['t(a)itreit] *tr chem* titrieren.

titter ['titə] *itr* kichern; *s* Gekicher *n*.

tit(t)ivate ['titiveit] *tr fam* herausputzen; *itr fam* u. *to ~ o.s.* sich hübsch machen.

tittle ['titl] (I-)Punkt *m*; Pünktchen *n*, Tüpfel(chen *n*) *m* od *n*; *not a ~*, *not one jot or ~ of* nicht ein Jota von; ~**-tattle** ['-tætl] *s* Geschwätz, Geklatsch *n*, Tratsch *m*; *itr* schwatzen, klatschen.

titular ['titjulə] *a* Titular-; Titel-; *s* Titelinhaber *m*; ~ **bishop** Titularbischof.

tizzy ['tizi] *sl* tolle Aufregung *f*.

to [tu:, tu, tə] **1.** *prp* zu; *(beim inf)* zu, um zu; *(zeitlich)* vor; bis; *(vor Ortsangaben)* nach;bis zu; in; *to go ~ school* zur Schule gehen; *~ the left* (nach) links; *~ the ground* zu Boden; *~ the light* ans Licht; *to apply ~ the skin* auf die Haut auftragen; *wet ~ the skin* naß bis auf die Haut; *to count ~ ten* bis zehn zählen; *~ a fault* bis auf e-n Fehler; *(all) ~ a man* bis auf den letzten Mann; *to speak ~ s.o.* mit jdm sprechen; *tied ~ a post* an e-n Pfosten gebunden; *~ grow ~ manhood* zum Mann heranwachsen; *~ rise ~ fame* zu Ruhm gelangen; *~ six o'clock* bis 6 Uhr; *ten (minutes) ~ six (o'clock)* 10 (Minuten) vor 6 (Uhr); *~ come ~ s.o.'s aid* jdm zu Hilfe kommen; *~ be ~ s.o.* jdn betreffen, angehen; *~ be open ~ attack* angreifbar sein; *~ my amazement* zu meiner Verwunderung; *~ s.o.'s cost* auf jds Kosten; *~ my knowledge* soviel ich weiß, meines Wissens; *torn ~ pieces* in Stücke gerissen; *~ add s.th. ~ s.th.* etw zu e-r S hinzufügen; *~ the music* nach der Musik; *set ~ music* in Musik gesetzt, vertont; *the key ~ the kitchen* der Schlüssel zur Küche, der Küchenschlüssel; *10 ~ 1* 10 zu 1; *~ s.o.'s taste* nach jds Geschmack; *twenty ~ the bushel* zwanzig auf den, e-n Scheffel; *~ s.o.'s health* auf jds Gesundheit; *~ prefer s.th. ~ s.th.* etw e-r S vorziehen; *true ~ life* lebenswahr; *~ this* dazu; *as ~* was ... betrifft; **2.** *adv* [tu:] zu, (drauf)los, vorwärts; zu, geschlossen; *close ~* dicht dabei; *~ and fro* hin u. her; *~ push the door ~* die Tür zuschlagen; *the door blew ~* die Tür schlug zu; *that brought him ~* das brachte ihn (wieder) zu sich; *buckle, fall ~!* 'ran an die Arbeit!

toad [toud] Kröte *f a. fig*; ~**-eater** *fig* Speichellecker *m*; ~**-in-the-hole** Fleischpastete *f*; ~**stool** (Gift-)Pilz *m*; ~**y** ['-i] *s* Speichellecker, Schmarotzer *m*; *itr* niedrig schmeicheln; sich anbiedern (*to s.o.* mit jdm); *tr* um den Bart gehen, *fam* Honig ums Maul schmieren (*s.o.* jdm).

toast [toust] **1.** *tr* rösten; *itr* braun u. knusprig werden; *to ~ o.s.* sich auf-, durchwärmen; *s* Toast *m*, Röstbrot *n*; ~**er** ['-ə] Brotröster *m*; **2.** *s* Zutrunk; Trinkspruch, Toast *m*; *tr* zutrinken (*s.o.* jdm); hochleben lassen; *to propose, to give a ~* e-n Toast ausbringen (*to s.o.* auf jdn); ~**master** Toastmeister *m*.

tobacco [tə'bækou] *pl -os* Tabak *m*; *chewing, smoking ~* Kau-, Rauchtabak *m*; ~ **heart** *med* Flatterherz *n*; ~**nist** [-'bækənist] Tabakhändler *m*; *~~'s (shop)* Tabakladen *m*; ~**-pipe** Tabakspfeife *f*; ~**-plant, -pouch** Tabakpflanze *f*, -beutel *m*; ~ **shop** *Am* Tabakladen, -warenhandlung *f*.

toboggan [tə'bɔgən] *s* Toboggan, Rodel(schlitten) *m*; *itr* rodeln, Schlitten fahren; *fig* rapide nachlassen; ~ **slide** Rodelbahn *f*.

toby ['toubi] *(~ jug)* Bierkrug, Humpen *m (in Form e-s dicken Mannes mit Dreispitz)*; *Am sl* billige, lange Zigarre *f*; ~ **collar** Halskrause *f*.

toco, toko ['toukou] *sl* Dresche, Tracht *f* Prügel.

tocsin ['tɔksin] Sturmglocke *f*; *allg* Warnsignal *n*.

today, to-day [tə'dei] *adv* heute; heutzutage; *s* heutige(r) Tag *m*; Gegenwart *f*; ~*'s* heutig; *of ~* von heute; *~'s rate (com)* Tageskurs *m*; ~ **week** heute in, vor acht Tagen.

toddl|e ['tɔdl] *itr* tappen, *fam* tapsen, watscheln; *fam* (herum)schlendern, bummeln; *fam (to ~~ off)* abhauen; *s* Gewatschel; *fam* Herumbummeln *n*; ~**er** ['-ə] kleine(s) Kind *n*; watschelnde(r) Mensch *m*.

toddy ['tɔdi] Palmwein; *Art* Grog *m (meist von Whisky)*.

to-do [tə'du:] (allgemeine) Unruhe *f*, Lärm *m*, Geschrei *n*; *to make much ~ about s.th.* viel Aufhebens von e-r S machen.

toe [tou] *s* Zehe; Fußspitze; *(Schuh)* Kappe *f*; *(Hufeisen)* Griff; *(Golf)* Löffel; *tech* Zapfen, Nocken *m*; *tr (Schuh)* mit e-r neuen Kappe, *(Strumpf)* mit e-r neuen Spitze versehen; vorschuhen, anstricken; mit den Zehen berühren, mit der Fußspitze, dem Fuß stoßen; *(Nagel)* schräg einschlagen; *to ~ in, out* nach innen *od (fam)* nach außen gehen; *from top to ~* von Kopf bis Fuß; *to be on o.'s ~s (fig)* auf Draht sein; auf dem Sprung sein; *to step, to tread on s.o.'s ~s (fig)* jdm zu nahe, *fam* auf die Hühneraugen treten; *to turn up o.'s ~s (fig sl)* ins Gras beißen; *to ~ the line (fig)* sich ausrichten, nicht aus der Reihe tanzen; *fam* spuren; *sport* sich an der Startlinie aufstellen; *ball of the ~* Zehenballen *m*; *great, little ~* große, kleine Zehe *f*; ~**-cap** *(Schuh)* Kappe *f*; ~**d** [-d] *a in Zssgen* -zehig; *(Nagel)* schräg eingeschlagen; mit schräg eingeschlagenen Nägeln; ~ **dance** *s* Spitzentanz *m*; ~**-dance** *itr* e-n Spitzentanz tanzen; ~**-hold** Zehenleiste *f*; *fig* Halt; Ansatzpunkt; *mil* Brückenkopf *m*; *to get a ~~ (fig)* festen Fuß fassen; ~**less** ['-lis] zehenlos; *(Schuh)* ohne Kappe; ~**-nail** Zehen-, Fußnagel *m*.

toff [tɔf] *sl* feine(r) Pinkel *m*.

toffee, toffy ['tɔfi] Karamelle *f*, Karamelbonbon *m* od *n*; ~ **apple** Apfel *m* mit Zuckerglasur.

tog [tɔg] *s meist pl fam* Kluft *f*, Klamotten *f pl*; *tr itr fam (to ~ o.s. up, out)* (sich) ausstaffieren, (sich) herausputzen; ~**gery** ['-əri] *fam* Klamotten *f pl*; Manufakturwaren-, Herrenartikelgeschäft *n*.

together [tə'geðə] *adv* zusammen (*with* mit); miteinander, gemeinsam, gemeinschaftlich; zugleich, zu gleicher Zeit; nach-, hintereinander, ohne Unterbrechung, ununterbrochen; *to call, to come, to knock ~* zs.rufen, -kommen, -stoßen; ~**ness** ['-nis] *Am* Zugehörigkeitsgefühl *n*.

toggle ['tɔgl] *s tech* Knebel, Kipphebel *m*; *(~ joint)* Knebel-, Kniegelenk *n*; *tr* mit e-m Knebel befestigen; ~ **lever** Kniehebel *m*; ~ **plate** Druckplatte *f*; ~ **switch** Kippschalter *m*.

toil [tɔil] **1.** *itr* sich (ab)mühen, sich plagen, sich placken, sich quälen (*at* mit); schwer arbeiten, *fam* schuften; sich schleppen; *s* Mühe, Plackerei, *fam* Schufterei *f*; *to ~ up* sich mühsam hochschleppen, mühsam hochklettern; ~**er** ['-ə] Schwerarbeiter *m*; ~**ful** ['-ful], ~**some** ['-səm] arbeitsam, fleißig; mühsam, -selig, schwer; ~**-worn** *a* abgearbeitet, abgemergelt; **2.** *s pl* Schlingen *f pl*, Netz *n*; *fig* Fallstrick *m*; *to be in the ~s* hilflos sein, sich nicht zu helfen wissen; *of s.o.* in jds Netze verstrickt sein.

toilet ['tɔilit] (Morgen-)Toilette; *(Abend-)*Toilette, Kleidung; *(~-table)* Frisiertoilette *f*, -tisch *m*; *Am* Badezimmer *n*; Toilette *f*, Klosett *n*; *to make o.'s ~* Toilette machen; ~**-case** Reisenecessaire *n*, Kulturbeutel *m*; ~**-paper** Klosett-, Toilettenpapier *n*; ~**-powder** Körper-, Gesichtspuder *m*; ~**-roll** Rolle *f* Klosettpapier; ~**ry** ['-ri] Toilettenartikel *m pl*; ~**-set** Toilettengarnitur *f*; ~**-soap** Toilettenseife *f*; ~**-water** Toiletten-, Gesichtswasser *n*.

toke [touk] *sl* was zu beißen; Brot *n*.

token ['toukən] *s* Zeichen, Symbol *n*, Beweis *m*; Kennzeichen, (Unterscheidungs-)Merkmal; Andenken *n*, Erinnerung(sstück *n*); (Wert-)Marke *f*; Gutschein, Bon *m*; Steuermarke *f*; *a* symbolisch, Zeichen-; nominell;

scheinbar, Schein-; *by this, the same ~* aus dem gleichen Grund; außerdem, überdies; *in, as a ~ of* zum Zeichen *gen*; ~ **money** Wertmarke *f*; Papier-, Notgeld *n*; ~ **payment** symbolische Zahlung *f* als Anerkenntnis e-r Schuld; ~ **strike** Warnstreik *m*; ~ **vote** *parl* Bewilligung *f* e-r Summe, die überschritten werden kann.

toko *s. toco.*

told [tould] *pret u. pp von tell*; *all ~* alles in allem.

toler|able ['tɔlərəbl] erträglich; leidlich; *fam* einigermaßen auf der Höhe; **~ably** ['-əbli] *adv* leidlich, ziemlich; **~ance** ['-əns] Duldung; Duldsamkeit, Toleranz *a. fin tech med*; *med* Widerstandsfähigkeit *f*; **~ant** ['-ənt] duldsam, tolerant (*of* gegen); *med* widerstandsfähig (*of* gegen); **~ate** ['-eit] *tr* geschehen lassen; dulden, zulassen; ertragen, aushalten; *med* vertragen; **~ation** [tɔlə'reiʃən] *bes. rel* Duldung *f*.

toll [toul] **1.** Brücken-, Wegegeld *n*, -zoll *m*; Markt-, Standgeld; Zollregal, -recht *n*, -hoheit *f*; Zuschlag *m*, Sonder-, Zustell-, Fernsprechgebühr *f*; *fig* Zoll, Tribut *m*; *to take ~ (fig)* Tribut fordern (*of* von); *it took a heavy ~ of life* es hat viele Menschenleben gekostet; *the ~ of the road* die Verkehrsopfer *n pl*; **~-bar, -gate** Schlagbaum *m*; **~-bridge** Zollbrücke *f*; **~-call** *tele* Ferngespräch *n*; **~-house** Maut-, Zollhaus *n*; **~-line** Schnellverkehrsleitung; *Am* Fernleitung *f*; ~ **road** gebührenpflichtige Autostraße *f*; **2.** *tr (Glocke)* läuten; *itr* läuten; schallen; *s* Glockengeläut *n*, -schlag *m*.

tom [tɔm] Männchen *n (einiger Tiere)*; *T~ (fam)* Thomas; *T~, Dick, and Harry* Hinz u. Kunz; *T~ and Jerry (Am)* Eiergrog *m*; **~boy** Range *f*, Wildfang *m*; **~cat** Kater *m*; **~fool** *s* Narr *m*; *a* närrisch, dämlich, dumm; **~foolery** [tɔm'fu:ləri] Dummheit *f*; Unsinn *m*; **T~my** ['-i] *fam* Thomas; *(~~ Atkins, t~~)* Tommy, britische(r) Soldat *m*; **~my** Naturallohn *m*; *sl* Verpflegung *f*, Brot *n*; *tech* Schraubenschlüssel *m*; *soft ~~ (mar)* frische(s) Brot *n*; *~~-bag* Brotbeutel *m*; *~~ bar* Brecheisen *n*; *~~-cooker* Kochapparat, Schnellkocher *m*; *~~-gun* Maschinenpistole *f*; *~~rot (sl)* Unsinn, Blödsinn, Quatsch *m*; *~~-shop* Verkaufskantine; Bäckerei *f*; **~-noddy** Dummkopf *m*; **~tit** ['tɔm'tit] Meise *f*; **T~ Thumb** Däumling *m*; **~-trot** Karamelbonbon *n*.

tomahawk ['tɔməhɔ:k] Kriegsbeil *n*, Tomahawk *m*.

tomato [tə'mɑ:tou, *Am* -'mei-] *pl -es* Tomate *f*; *Am sl* Frau *f*, attraktive(s) Mädchen *n*; ~ **juice** Tomatensaft *m*; ~ **ketchup** (Tomaten-)Ketchup *m* od *n*; ~ **soup** Tomatensuppe *f*.

tomb [tu:m] Grab(gewölbe); *(~stone)* Grabmal *n*, -stein *m*; *fig* Grab *n*, Tod *m*.

tombac, tomba(c)k ['tɔmbæk] *tech* Tombak *m*.

tombola ['tɔmbələ] Tombola *f*.

tome [toum] Band; (dicker) Wälzer *m*.

tomorrow, to-morrow [tə'mɔro(u)] *adv* morgen; *s der* morgige Tag; *the day after ~* übermorgen; ~ **morning, afternoon, night** morgen früh, nachmittag, abend; ~ **week** morgen in acht Tagen.

ton [tʌn] Tonne *f (Gewichtseinheit)*; *(long ~) Br 2240 lb.* = 1016,05 kg; *(short ~) (Am u. überseeisches Commonwealth) 2000 lb.* = 907,18 kg; *(metric ~)* 1000 kg *(2204,6 lb.)*; *mar* Registertonne *f (100 Kubikfuß* = 2,83 m³); *fam* Schwergewicht *n*; *sl mot* Geschwindigkeit *f* von 160 Meilen; *pl fam*: *~s of* e-e Menge, Masse; **~nage** ['-idʒ] Tonnage *f*, Schiffsraum *m*; *mar* Tonnengeld *n*.

ton|al ['tounl] *mus* tonal; **~ality** [to(u)'næliti] *mus* Tonart; Klangfarbe, Tonalität; *(Malerei)* Farbgebung *f*; **~e** [toun] *s* Ton, Laut; Klang *m*; Betonung *f*, (Wort-)Ton; Tonfall *m*, -höhe *f*; Ton *m*, Ausdrucksweise *(beim Sprechen)*; *fig* Note, Art, Klangfarbe; Atmosphäre, Haltung, Stimmung; besondere Note *f*; Stil, Charakter; *(Malerei)* Ton *m*, Tönung, Farbgebung *f*; *physiol* Tonus *m*; Spannkraft, Elastizität *f*; *tr* (ab-)tönen; *phot* tonen; e-n bestimmten Ton, e-e bestimmte Klangfarbe *od* Note geben (*s.th.* e-r S); umstimmen, verändern; *itr* e-n Ton, Klang annehmen; *to ~~ down (tr)* niedriger stimmen; dämpfen; abschwächen; *itr* schwächer werden; abnehmen; *to ~~ in* harmonieren (*with* mit); *to ~~ up (tr)* höher stimmen; (ver)stärken; *itr* steigen; anschwellen, stärker werden; *in an angry ~~* mit zorniger Stimme; *~~-arm* Tonarm *m*; *~~ colo(u)r* Klangfarbe *f*; *~~ control (radio)* Klangregler *m*, Tonblende *f*; *~~ pitch* Tonhöhe *f*; *~~ poem* symphonische Dichtung *f*; *~~ quality* Klangcharakter *m*; **~eless** ['-lis] ton-, farblos; **~ic** ['tɔnik] *a med* tonisch; *med* stärkend, anregend; *physiol* Tonus-; *mus* Grundton-; *(Phonetik)* betont; Ton-; *s mus* Grundton *m*, Tonika *f*; *gram* Wortton; *(Phonetik)* stimmhafte(r) Laut *m*; *pharm* Tonikum, Stärkungsmittel *n*; *~~ chord (mus)* Grundakkord *m*; *~~ spasm* Starrkrampf *m*; **~y** ['touni] *sl* elegant; *oft iro* überkandidelt, aufgedonnert.

tongs [tɔŋz] *pl a. mit sing* Zange *f*; *a pair of ~* e-e Zange; *coal, sugar ~* Kohlen-, Zuckerzange *f*.

tongue [tʌŋ] *anat* Zunge *(a. Küche u. fig)*; *fig* Sprache; Sprechweise *f*; Gerede *n*; *(Tier, bes. Jagdhund)* Laut *m*; *(Schuh)* Lasche, Zunge *f*; *(Glocke)* Klöppel; *(Schnalle)* Dorn *m*; *(Waage)* Zünglein *n*; Zeiger *m*; Deichsel *f*; *tech* Zapfen *m*, Feder; *rail* Zunge *(e-r Weiche)*; *geog* Landzunge; züngelnde Flamme *f*; *to be in everyone's ~* in aller Munde sein; *to find o.'s ~* die Sprache wiederfinden; *to give ~* laut sagen; schreien; *(Hund)* Laut geben, anschlagen; *to have lost o.'s ~* die Sprache verloren haben, kein Wort herausbringen; *to have o.'s ~ in o.'s cheek* ironisch sein; Hintergedanken haben; *to hold o.'s ~* den Mund halten; *to keep a civil ~ in o.'s head* höflich bleiben; *to loll out, to put out o.'s ~* die Zunge herausstrecken (*at s.o.* gegen jdn); *to throw ~ (Jagdhund)* Laut geben; *to wag o.'s ~* ein loses Mundwerk haben; tratschen; *it is on the tip of my ~* es liegt, schwebt mir auf der Zunge; *a slip of the ~* ein Lapsus; *native ~* Muttersprache *f*; **~-and-groove joint** *tech* Spundung *f*; **~-bone** *anat* Zungenbein *n*; **~d** [-d] *a in Zssgen* -zündig; *to be loose-~~* ein loses Mundwerk haben; **~-tied** *a*: *to be ~~* e-n Zungen-, Sprachfehler haben; *fig* mundfaul, sprachlos, *fam* platt sein; **~-twister** Zungenbrecher *m (Wort)*.

tonight, to-night [tə'nait] *adv* heute abend, heute nacht; *s* der heutige Abend; diese Nacht.

tonneau ['tɔnou] *mot* Fahrgast-, Innenraum *m*.

tonsil ['tɔns(i)l] *anat* Mandel *f*; **~lar** ['tɔnsilə] *a* Mandel-; **~litis** [-'laitis] Mandelentzündung *f*.

tonsorial [tɔn'sɔ:riəl] *meist hum* Frisör-.

tonsure ['tɔnʃə] *rel* Tonsur *f*.

tontine [tɔn'ti:n, '--] *fin* Tontine *f*.

too [tu:] *adv (vorangestellt)* zu, allzu, gar zu; *fam* überaus, sehr, höchst; *(nachgestellt)* auch, eben-, gleichfalls, gleicherweise; *all ~* viel zu; *none ~* nicht allzu.

tool [tu:l] *s* Werkzeug, Gerät; Instrument *n a. fig jur*; Drehstahl *m*, -bank *f*; *fig* Werkzeug *n (Mensch)*, Helfershelfer *m*; *pl* Handwerkszeug, (Arbeits-)Gerät *n*; *tr* bearbeiten; *(to ~ up)* mit Werkzeugen, Maschinen ausstatten; pressen in *(Bucheinband)*; *sl* kutschieren, fahren; *itr* ein Werkzeug, Werkzeuge benutzen; *sl (to ~ along)* herumfahren, -kutschieren; *machine ~* Werkzeugmaschine *f*; **~-bag** *od* **~satchel, -box** Werkzeugtasche *f*, -kasten *m*; ~ **grinder** Werkzeugschleifer *m*; **~ing** ['-iŋ] Bearbeitung; *(Buchbinderei)* Prägung; Einrichtung *f (e-r Fabrik mit Maschinen)*; *~~ costs (pl)* Bearbeitungskosten *pl*; **~kit** Werkzeugsatz, -kasten *m*; **~maker** Werkzeugmacher *m*; ~ **steel** Werkzeugstahl *m*.

toot [tu:t] *itr tr* tuten, hupen; blasen; pfeifen; *s* Tuten, Hupen *n*.

tooth [tu:θ] *s pl teeth* [ti:θ] Zahn *m a. tech fig*; *tr* mit Zähnen versehen; verzahnen; *in the teeth of* angesichts; zum Trotz; *(armed) to the teeth* bis an die Zähne (bewaffnet); *long in the ~* alt; *~ and nail (fig)* mit aller Gewalt; erbittert; *to cast, to throw s.th. in s.o.'s teeth (fig)* jdm etw ins Gesicht schleudern; *to cut o.'s teeth* zahnen; *to escape by, with the skin of o.'s teeth* mit knapper Not davonkommen; *to have a sweet ~* gern etw Süßes mögen; gern naschen; *to have a ~ out, (Am) pulled* sich e-n Zahn ziehen lassen; *to put teeth in (fig)* durchsetzen, erzwingen; *to set o.'s teeth (fig)* die Zähne zs.beißen; *to set s.o.'s teeth on edge* jdn rasend machen; *to show o.'s teeth (fig)* die Zähne zeigen; *milk, first ~* Milchgebiß *n*, -zähne *m pl*; *permanent, second ~* bleibende(s) Gebiß *n*; *set of teeth (natürliches)* Gebiß *n*; *(set of) false teeth (künstliches)* Gebiß *n*; *wisdom ~* Weisheitszahn *m*; **~ache** Zahnschmerzen *m pl*, -weh *n*; **~-brush** Zahnbürste *f*; **~comb** Staubkamm *m*; *to go through with a ~~* kritisch prüfen; **~ed** [-t] *a* mit Zähnen; *tech* gezahnt; *in Zssgen* mit ... Zähnen; **~ing** ['-iŋ] Zahnen *n*; Verzahnung *f*; **~-paste** Zahnpasta *f*; **~pick** Zahnstocher *m*; **~-powder** Zahnpulver *n*; **~some** ['-səm] wohlschmeckend, schmackhaft.

tootle ['tu:tl] *itr* (leise) tuten; *sl* quasseln; *s* Tuten, Gedudel *n*.

toots(y) ['tu:ts(i)] *Am fam* Schätzchen *n*.

top [tɔp] **1.** *s* Kopfende *n*; Kopf, Scheitel; *(Baum)* Gipfel, Wipfel *m*; *(Berg)* Spitze; Oberfläche, obere Seite *f*; Deckel *m*, Kappe, (Flaschen-)Kapsel; *(Stiefel)* Stulpe *f*; *Am mot* (Klapp-)Verdeck *n*; *mar* Mars *m*; *(big ~)* (Zirkus-)Zelt *n*; *fig* Gipfel, Höhepunkt *m*; höchste Stellung; Oberste(r) *m*; Spitze *f (Person)*; *das* Beste; Anfang, Beginn *m*; *pl bot* Kraut *n*, Blätter *n pl*; *a* oberst; höchst; Haupt-; best; *~s (pred) Am sl* Klasse, prima; *tr (Pflanze)* kappen, köpfen; verkapseln; die Spitze bilden (*s.th.* e-r S); maximal erreichen; sich belaufen auf; übertreffen; die Spitze erreichen, an der Spitze stehen (*s.th.* e-r S); *(e-e Liste)* anführen; *sl* hängen; *to ~ off* ab-, beschließen, beenden; den letzten Schliff geben (*s.th.* e-r S); *to ~ up* auffüllen; *at the ~ of the tree (fig)* auf der höchsten Sprosse; *at the ~ of o.'s voice, of o.'s lungs* aus vollem Halse; *from ~ to bottom* von oben bis unten; völlig; *from ~ to toe* von Kopf bis Fuß; *in ~ (gear)* mit dem höchsten Gang; *on ~* oben; *fig* obenauf; *on ~ of* auf, über; *fig* über ... hinaus; *on ~ of that* darüber hinaus, zusätzlich; *on ~ of the world (fam)* allem, allen voran; auf dem Höhepunkt; *to ~ it off* zu guter Letzt; *~ left, right (Buch)* oben links, rechts; *to blow o.'s ~ (sl fig)* in die Luft gehen; platzen; *to come to the ~ (fig)* an die Spitze kommen; sich durchsetzen; *to go over the ~* zum Angriff antreten; *fig* es wagen; *that ~s everything* das setzt allem die Krone auf; *you are ~s with me* bei mir sind Sie ganz groß angeschrieben; *bottle-~* Flaschenkapsel *f*; **~-beam** Hahnebalken; *(Brücke)* Kopfbalken, Holm *m*, Kappe *f*; **~-boots** *pl* Stulpenstiefel *m pl*; **~ brass** *Am sl mil* die hohen Tiere *n pl*; **~ cap** *s mot* neue(s) Reifenprofil *n*; *tech* Gitter-, Röhrenkappe *f*; *tr* mit e-m neuen Profil versehen; **~-coat** Überzieher, (leichter) Sommermantel *m*; **~-dog** *sl der* Erste; Oberbonze; Sieger *m*; erste Stelle *f*; **~-drawer** *a* Ober-; erstklassig; vornehm; **~-dressing** Oberflächenbeschotterung; *agr* Kopfdüngung *f*; **~ edge** Oberkante *f*; **~-flight** *a fam* Spitzen-, Höchst-; erstklassig; **~gallant** *s mar* Bramstenge, -rahe *f*, -segel, -stag *n*; *fig* Gipfel *m*, Spitze *f*, überragende(r) Teil *m*; *a* Bram-; erstklassig; **~ gear** *mot* Direktgang *m*; **~-hamper** *s mar* Oberbramstenge, -rahe *f*, -segel, -stag *n*; **~-hat** Zylinder *m*; **~-heavy** *mar* oberlastig; *aero* kopflastig; *sl* betrunken; *fig fin* überfinanziert, -bewertet; **~-hole** *a sl* prima, Klasse; **~knot** Haarschopf, -knoten *m*; *orn* Haube; *fam* Birne *f*, Kopf *m*; **~less** ['-lis] in die Wolken ragend; **~-level**: *on ~~* auf höchster Ebene; **~-liner** *fam* maßgebende(r) Mann *m*; **~lofty** *fam* hochtrabend; **~mast** *mar* Stenge *f*; **~most** oberst; vorzüglich; **~-notch** *fam* großartig, phantastisch, prima; **~per** ['-ə] *sl* hohe(s) Tier *n*; Angströhre *f*, Zylinder; Hut; Überzieher; Hänger *m*; *fam* nicht zu übertreffende Bemerkung; tolle Sache *f*; **~ping** ['-iŋ] *s* Be-, Überdeckung; Decke *f*; *(Bäume)* Kappen *n*; (Haar-)Schopf *m*; *a* ober, höher; hochaufragend; *fam* prächtig, großartig, phantastisch; elegant; *~~-out* Richtfest *n*; **~ price** Höchstpreis *m*; **~sail** ['tɔpsl, '-seil] Marssegel *n*; **~ salary** Spitzengehalt *n*; **~ secret** *Am* streng (vertraulich u.) geheim; **~ sergeant** *Am mil fam, sl* **~ kick** Spieß, Hauptfeldwebel *od* -wachtmeister *m*; **~side** *s* obere Seite; *mar* Schiffswand *f* über der Wasserlinie; *adv fam* auf Deck; *fig* an leitender Stelle; **~soil** Humusboden *m*, -schicht *f*; **~ speed**: *at ~~* mit Höchstgeschwindigkeit; **~-team** *sport* Spitzenmannschaft *f*; **2.** Kreisel *m*; *to sleep like a ~* wie ein Murmeltier schlafen; *to spin a ~* e-n Kreisel drehen.

topaz ['toupæz] *min* Topas *m*.

top|e [toup] *tr itr* (gewohnheitsmäßig) trinken; *s zoo* Glatthai *m*; **~er** ['-ə] (Gewohnheits-)Trinker *m*.

topi, topee ['toupi] Tropenhelm *m*.

topic ['tɔpik] Thema *n*, Gegenstand, Inhalt *m*; *to provide a ~ for discussion* ein Diskussionsthema abgeben; **~al** ['-əl] *a* örtlich, lokal; thematisch; aktuell; Tages-; *med* örtlich; *s* Zeitfilm; Zeitfunk *m*; *~~ allusion* Anspielung *f* auf das Tagesgeschehen; *~~ encyclop(a)edia* Sachwörterbuch *n*; *~~ news film* Film *m* über das Tagesgeschehen; Wochenschau *f*; *~~ talk* Gespräch *n* über Tagesfragen; Zeitfunk *m*.

topograph|er [tə'pɔgrəfə] Topograph *m*; **~ic(al)** [tɔpə'græfik(əl)] topographisch; **~y** [tə'pɔgrəfi] Topographie, Ortsbeschreibung *f*.

topple ['tɔpl] *itr (to ~ over)* (um)kippen, kopfüber fallen; stürzen; schief stehen; überhängen (*on, over* über); *tr* umkippen; (herunter)stürzen.

topsyturvy ['tɔpsi'tə:vi] *adv* kopfüber, das Oberste zuunterst; drunter u. drüber, durcheinander; *a* auf den Kopf gestellt; in Unordnung; *to turn ~* das Oberste zuunterst kehren.; *s u.* **~dom** ['-dəm], **~ness** ['-nis] (heillose) Durcheinander *n*.

toque [touk] *hist* Barett *n*; Toque *f*.

tor [tɔ:] Felsen *m*, Felskuppe *f*, -hang *m*.

torch [tɔ:tʃ] Fackel *f a. fig*; *fig* Licht *n*, Flamme *f*; *(plumber's ~)* (Schweiß-)Brenner *m*; *(~-lamp)* Lötlampe *f*; Blitzlicht *n*; *to carry a ~ for s.o. (Am sl)* in jdn verknallt sein; *to hand on the ~ (fig)* die Fackel weitergeben, die Verantwortung in die Hände e-s Jüngeren legen; *electric ~* Taschenlampe *f*; **~ battery** Taschenlampen-, Stabbatterie *f*; **~bearer** Fackelträger *m a. fig*; **~light** Fackelschein *m*; *~~ procession* Fackelzug *m*; **~-race** *hist* Fackellauf *m*; **~-singer** *Am* Bänkelsängerin *f*; **~-song** *Am* sentimentale(s) Lied *n*; **~wood** Kienholz *n*.

torment ['tɔ:ment] *s* Qual, Marter, Folter, Pein *f*, (schweres) Leiden *n*; *(Kind)* Quälgeist *m*; *tr* [tɔ:'ment] quälen, martern, foltern, peinigen (*with* mit); beunruhigen; *to be in ~* Qualen ausstehen; **~or** [tɔ:'mentə] Peiniger; *agr* Kultivator *m*.

tornado [tɔ:'neidou] *pl -(e)s* Wirbelsturm, Tornado; *fig* Orkan *m*.

torp|edo [tɔ:'pi:dou] *pl -es s zoo* Zitterrochen; *mil mar* Torpedo *m*; Knallerbse *f*; *tr* torpedieren *a. fig*; *fig* unterminieren, hintertreiben, lahmlegen, durchkreuzen, e-n Strich machen durch; *~~-boat* Torpedoboot *n*; *~~-boat destroyer* Torpedobootzerstörer *m*; *~~ hit* Torpedotreffer *m*; *~~-netting* Torpedo(schutz)netz *n*; *~~-track, -wake* Torpedobahn *f*; *~~-tube* Torpedorohr *n*; **~id** ['tɔ:pid] (er)starr(t), leblos, regungslos, benommen, betäubt; apathisch, stumpf; *med* träge; *zoo* bewegungsunfähig *(im Winterschlaf)*; **~idity** [tɔ:'piditi], **~idness** ['tɔ:pidnis], **~or** ['tɔ:pə] Erstarrung *a. zoo*, Leblosigkeit, Benommenheit, Betäubung; Stumpfheit, Trägheit *f*.

torque [tɔ:k] *phys* Drehmoment *n*, -beanspruchung *f*; **~ arm** Hebelarm *m*; *mot* Schubstange *f*; **~ rod** Kardanwelle *f*.

torr|efaction [tɔri'fækʃən] Dörren, Rösten *n*; **~efy** ['tɔrifai] *tr* dörren, rösten; **~id** ['tɔrid] ausgedörrt, -getrocknet, sonn(en)verbrannt; glühend heiß, sengend; *fig* glühend; *~~ zone* heiße Zone *f*; **~idity** [tɔ'riditi] Ausgedörrtheit; Gluthitze; *fig* Glut *f*.

torrent ['tɔrənt] Sturz-, Gießbach; *pl* Regenguß, Wolkenbruch; *fig* Strom *m*, Flut *f*, (Wort-)Schwall *m*; *it rains in ~s* es gießt in Strömen; **~ial** [tɔ'renʃəl] reißend; wolkenbruchartig; *fig* mitreißend, überwältigend; wortreich; *~~ rain* Wolkenbruch *m*.

torsion ['tɔ:ʃən] Torsion, (Ver-)Drehung *f*; **~al** ['-l] *a* Dreh(ungs)-; **~ balance, bar, galvanometer** Torsionswaage, -feder *f*, -galvanometer *n*.

torso ['tɔ:sou] *pl -os* Rumpf; *(Kunst)* Torso *m a. fig*.

tort [tɔ:t] *jur* unerlaubte Handlung; *jur* Kränkung *f*; *property ~* Vermögensschaden *m*.

tortilla [tɔ:'tija] *Am* Maisfladen *m*.

tortoise ['tɔ:təs] (*bes.* Land-)Schildkröte *f*; *as slow as a ~* so langsam wie e-e Schnecke; **~-shell** Schildpatt *n*.

tort|uosity [tɔ:tju'ɔsiti, *Am* -tʃu-] Gewundenheit *f*; Kurvenreichtum *m*; *fig* Unaufrichtigkeit *f*; **~uous** ['tɔ:tjuəs, *Am* -tʃu-] gewunden, kurvenreich, geschlängelt; *fig* unaufrichtig, unehrlich; **~ure** ['tɔ:tʃə] *s* Folter, Marter, Tortur *a. fig*; *fig* Qual *f*, Schmerz *m*, Pein *f*; *tr* foltern, martern; quälen *a. fig*; peinigen; *(Sinn)* verdrehen, entstellen; *to put to the ~~* auf die Folter spannen; **~urer** ['-rə] Folterknecht; *fig* Peiniger *m*.

Tory ['tɔ:ri] (engl.) Konservative(r) *m*; **~ism** [-izm] Konservativismus *m*, konservative Haltung *f*.

tosh [tɔʃ] *fam* Quatsch, Blödsinn *m*.

toss [tɔs] *tr (to ~ about)* umherstoßen, -schleudern, -werfen; schütteln, rütteln; emporschleudern, hoch-, in die Höhe werfen; zuwerfen; *(Reiter)* abwerfen; (plötzlich) aufrichten; *(Kopf)* hoch-, zurückwerfen; *(Pfannkuchen)* auf die andere Seite schleudern; *(Äste)* schütteln; *(mit e-r Münze)* auslosen (*for* für); *Am fam (e-e Veranstaltung)* schmeißen; *itr* umhergestoßen, -geschleudert, -geworfen werden; *(to ~ o.s. about)* sich (unruhig) hin- u. herwerfen, -wälzen; aufgeregt hin- u. hergehen; *(Schiff)* schlingern; *(to ~ up)* das Los werfen, losen (*for* um); *s* Wurf *m*; Hochschleudern, -werfen; (Aus-)Losen; *(Schiff)* Schlingern *n*; *to ~ off* hinunterstürzen, -spülen; *fig* aus dem Ärmel schütteln; rasch erledigen, *fam* hinhauen; *to ~ out of* hinausstürzen aus; *to ~ s.o. for s.th.* mit jdm um etw losen; *to be in a ~ (fam)* aufgeregt, in Nöten sein; *to take a ~* stürzen; (vom Pferd) abgeworfen werden; *to win, to lose the ~* beim Losen gewinnen, verlieren; *to ~ o.'s cookies (Am sl)* kotzen; *to ~ it in (Am sl)* aufgeben; *to ~ oars (Rudern)* die Riemen pieken; **~-pot** *sl* Säufer *m*; **~-up** Losen *n*; *fig* ungewisse Sache *f*; *it's a ~~* das hängt ganz vom Zufall ab (*whether* ob).

tot [tɔt] **1.** *fam* ein bißchen; *fam* Schluck *m (Schnaps)*; *fam* Knirps *m*; **2.** *fam tr (to ~ up)* zs.zählen, -rechnen; *to ~ up to* betragen, sich belaufen auf.

total ['toutl] *a* ganz, völlig, vollständig, -zählig, total, gesamt; Gesamt-; *s* Gesamtbetrag *m*, Summe *f*, *das* Ganze; *tr (to ~ up)* zs.zählen, -rechnen; betragen, ausmachen; *itr* sich belaufen, kommen (*to* auf); *what does the ~ come to?* wie hoch ist der Gesamtbetrag? *sum ~* Gesamtsumme *f*, -betrag *m*; **~ amount** Gesamtbetrag *m*; **~ costs** *pl* Gesamtkosten *pl*; **~isator** = *~izator*; **~itarian** [toutæli'tɛəriən] *pol* totalitär; **~itarianism** [toutæli'tɛəriənizm] Totalitarismus *m*; **~ity** [to(u)'tæliti] Gesamtheit; Vollständig-, -zähligkeit; Gesamtsumme *f*, -betrag *m*; *astr* totale Verfinsterung *f*; *in ~~* im ganzen, insgesamt; **~izator** ['toutəlaizeitə] Totalisator *m*; Zählwerk *n*; **~ize** ['toutəlaiz] *tr* zs.rechnen, -zählen, -fassen; **~ loss** Gesamtverlust; *(Feuer)* Totalschaden *m*; **~ly** *adv* völlig, vollständig, ganz; **~ output** Gesamterzeugung, -produktion, -leistung *f*; ~ **population** Gesamtbevölkerung *f*; ~ **receipts** *pl* Gesamteinnahmen *f pl*; ~ **tonnage** Gesamttonnage *f*; ~ **value** Gesamtwert *m*; ~ **war** totale(r) Krieg *m*; ~ **weight** Gesamtgewicht *n*.

tote [tout] **1.** *Am fam tr* schleppen; befördern; begleiten; sich belaufen auf; *s* Schlepperei; Last *f*; ~ **bag** Einkaufstasche *f*; **2.** *sl* Totalisator *m*.

totem ['toutəm] Totem *n*; ~-**pole** Totempfahl *m*.

totter ['tɔtə] *itr* schaukeln; torkeln, (sch)wanken; wackeln; ~**y** ['-ri] (sch)wankend; wack(e)lig.

toucan ['tu:kən] *orn* Tukan *m*.

touch [tʌtʃ] *tr* be-, anrühren, anfassen; anstoßen; rühren, stoßen an; in Berührung kommen mit; grenzen an; streifen; *(durch Berühren)* (ein)wirken auf, angreifen, schaden (*s.th.* e-r S); *(Saite)* anschlagen; *(to ~ up)* retuschieren; *(Ort)* berühren; *(Hafen)* anlaufen; Hand anlegen an, handhaben, benutzen, gebrauchen; fertigwerden mit; beschädigen; antasten; erreichen, gleichkommen (*s.th.* e-r S), *fam* mitkommen mit; *(Thema)* berühren; betreffen, angehen; abfärben, einwirken auf; *(seelisch)* rühren; reizen, ärgern, aufbringen, treffen (*to the quick* ins Mark); *sl* anhauen, -pumpen (*for* um); *itr* in Berührung kommen; sich nähern, nahekommen (*on, upon s.th.* e-r S); anea.stoßen; *(in der Rede)* flüchtig berühren, erwähnen (*on, upon s.th.* etw); angehen, betreffen (*on, upon s.th.* etw); sich auswirken (*upon* auf); *(Schiff, Reisender)* berühren (*at a port* e-n Hafen), anlegen (*at* in); *s* (leichte) Berührung *f*; Streifen *n*; Pinselstrich; Tastsinn *m*; Gefühl *n*; Empfindung; Empfindlichkeit; Rührung *f*, Eindruck *m*; Verbindung, Fühlung; Retusche *f*; Anflug, Hauch *m*, Idee, Spur *f*; *fig* Stil, Griff *m*, Hand; Eigenart *f*; *med* leichte(r) Anfall; Probierstein; Feingehalt; (Gold-)Stempel *m*; Probe *f*; Merkmal *n*; *mus* Anschlag *m*; *sl* Anhauen, Anpumpen *n*; *at a ~* bei bloßer Berührung; *to be, to keep in ~ with* in Verbindung stehen, bleiben mit; *to be out of ~ with* nicht mehr in Verbindung stehen mit; *to lose ~ with s.o.* die Verbindung mit jdm verlieren; *to put, to bring to the ~* auf die Probe stellen; *to ~ bottom (fig)* der Sache auf den Grund kommen; auf e-m Tiefpunkt ankommen; *to ~ o.'s hand to o.'s hat* die Hand zum Gruß an den Hut legen; *to ~ the spot (fam)* den Nagel auf den Kopf treffen; (gerade) das richtige sein; *it was a near ~* das wäre beinahe schiefgegangen; *to ~* **down** *aero* zwischenlanden; *sport* ein Tor erzielen; *to ~* **off** flüchtig wiedergeben, skizzieren; in die Luft jagen, abfeuern; in Gang bringen, veranlassen, hervorrufen, verursachen, auslösen, *fam* starten; *tele* auflegen; *to ~* **up** vervollkommnen; auffrischen; ~**able** ['-əbl] berührbar; ~-**and-go** *a* unsicher, riskant, gewagt; ~-**down** *aero* Landung *f*; *sport* Tor *n*; ~**ed** [-t] *a* gerührt, ergriffen (*with* von); mit e-m Anhauch, Anflug (*with* von); *a little ~~* etwas angegangen *(Fleisch)*; *(fam) ~~ (in the head)* nicht ganz klar im Kopf; ~**er** ['-ə] *sport u. fam* Treffer *m*; *to a ~~ (sl)* haargenau; ~**iness** ['-inis] Empfindlichkeit; Reizbarkeit *f*; ~**ing** ['-iŋ] *a* rührend, ergreifend; *s* Berührung *f*; Tastsinn *m*; *prp obs* betreffend; ~**line** *sport* Seitenlinie *f*; ~-**me-not** *bot* Rührmichnichtan *n*; ~**stone** *fig* Prüfstein *m*; ~ **system** *(Schreibmaschine)* Zehnfingersystem *n*; ~-**type** *tr itr* blindschreiben; ~**wood** Zunderholz *n*; ~**y** ['-i] empfindlich; reizbar; prekär, heikel, riskant.

tough [tʌf] *a* zäh; kräftig, stark, robust; widerstandsfähig; hartnäckig; verbohrt, *fam* stur; schwierig, schwer; *(Kampf)* verbissen; rauflustig, streitsüchtig; *Am sl* unübertrefflich; *s* Raufbold, Rabauke, Messerstecher *m*; *that's a ~ nut to crack* das ist e-e harte Nuß; ~ **customer** *fam* üble(r) Kunde *m*; ~**en** ['-n] *tr itr* zäh(er) machen, werden; ~**ie** ['-i] *Am sl s* schwierige(s) Problem *n*; *fam* schwierige(r) Patron *m*; ~ **luck** *Am fam* Pech, Unglück *n*; ~ **minded** *a* unsentimental; ~**ness** ['-nis] Zähigkeit; Widerstandsfähigkeit; Schwierigkeit *f*; *Am fam* Raubaukentum *n*.

toupee ['tu:pei, *Am* -'-] Toupet, Haarersatzstück *n*, Halbperücke *f*.

tour [tuə] *s* (Arbeits-)Schicht *f*; *mil* Dienststunden *f pl*, -zeit; Auslandsverpflichtung; *theat* Tournee, Gastspielreise; Rundreise, Besichtigungsfahrt, Tour *f*, Rundgang *m* (*of* durch); *itr* e-e (Rund-)Reise machen (*through, about* durch; *in* in); *tr* e-e R. machen durch; bereisen; *theat* auf Tournee gehen mit; *on ~* auf Tournee; *conducted ~* Gesellschaftsreise *f*; *motor-coach ~* Busreise *f*; ~**ing car** *mot* Tourenwagen *m*; ~**ing exhibition** Wanderausstellung *f*; ~**ism** ['-rizm] Fremdenverkehr *m*; ~**ist** ['-rist] *s* Tourist, Vergnügungsreisende(r) *m*; *a* Touristen-; *~~ advertising* Fremdenverkehrswerbung *f*; *~~ agency, office, (Am) bureau* Reisebüro *n*; *~~ baggage insurance* Reisegepäckversicherung *f*; *~~ class* Touristenklasse *f*; *~~ guide* Fremdenführer *m*; *~~ industry* Fremdenverkehr(sindustrie *f*) *m*; *~~ season* Reisezeit *f*; *~~ ticket* Rundreise(fahr)karte *f*; *~~ travel* Touristenverkehr *m*.

tourn|ament ['tuənəmənt, 'tɔ:-] Turnier *n a. sport*; ~**ey** ['tuəni, 'tɔ:-] *s hist* Turnier *n*; *itr* turnieren.

tourniquet ['tuənikei] *med* Aderpresse *f*.

tousle ['tauzl] *tr* zerzausen; in Unordnung, durchea.bringen.

tout [taut] *itr fam* auf Kunden-, Stimmenfang gehen (*for* für); *(to ~ round)* auf Pferderennen Tips verkaufen; *s* Schlepper *(Person)*; Tipgeber *m*.

tow [tou] **1.** *tr mot mar* (ab)schleppen; *mar* bugsieren; treideln; *s* Schleppen; *mar* Treideln *n*; *mar* Schleppzug *m*; *(~(ing)-line, ~(ing)-rope)* Schlepptau *n*; *to have, to take in ~* im Schlepptau haben, ins Schlepptau nehmen *a. fig*; *can we give you a ~* können wir Sie abschleppen? ~**age** ['-idʒ] (Ab-)Schleppen, *mar* Bugsieren *n*; Schleppgebühr *f*; ~**boat** Schlepper *m*; ~**ing** Schleppen, Treideln *n*; *~~ cable* Schleppseil *n*; *~(~)-path* Treidelpfad *m*; ~-**plane** Schleppflugzeug *n*; ~ **take-off** *aero* Schleppstart *m*; **2.** *s* Werg *n*; ~**headed** *a* strohblond.

toward(s) [tə'wɔ:d(z), tɔ:d(z), tɔəd(z)] *prp* auf ... zu, nach ... zu, in Richtung auf *a. fig*; gegenüber *dat*; auf ... hin; um ... willen; *(zeitlich)* kurz vor, gegen; *to run ~~ s.o.* auf jdn zulaufen; *to save ~~ s.th.* auf etw sparen.

towel ['tauəl] *s* Hand-, Badetuch *n*; *tr* abtrocknen, trockenreiben; *sl* e-e Abreibung geben (*s.o.* jdm), verdreschen (*s.o.* jdn); *to throw in the ~ (Boxen u. fig)* aufgeben, sich für besiegt erklären; *bath-~* Badetuch *n*; *endless, roller ~* Rollhandtuch *n*; *kitchen ~* Geschirrtuch *n*; *sanitary ~* Damenbinde *f*; ~-**horse, -rack** Handtuchständer *m*; ~**(l)ing** ['-iŋ] Frottee *n* od *m*; *sl* Abreibung, Dresche *f*; *~~ bathrobe* Bademantel *m*; ~-**rail** Handtuchhalter *m*.

tower ['tauə] *s* Turm; Zwinger; *(~ of strength) fig* (sicherer) Hort *m*; *itr* sich (auf)türmen (*to* zu); sich emporrecken (*over s.th.* über etw); überragen (*above s.o.* jdn); *water ~* Wasserturm *m*; ~ **clock** Turmuhr *f*; ~**ing** ['-riŋ] *a* sich (auf)türmend; überragend; *fig* gewaltig, heftig; *(Wut)* rasend.

town [taun] (kleinere) Stadt; Stadtbevölkerung *f*; *attr* Stadt-; *in ~* in der Stadt; *on the ~ (sl)* auf dem Bummel; *to be out of ~* verreist sein; *to go to ~* in die Stadt gehen; *(sl)* auf den Bummel gehen; sehr erfolgreich sein; auf die Pauke hauen; *to paint the ~ red (sl)* die Stadt auf den Kopf stellen; herumrandalieren; *it is the talk of the ~, the whole ~ knows of it* es ist Stadtgespräch; *a man about ~* Lebemann *m*; ~ **centre** Stadtzentrum *n*; ~-**clerk** Stadtschreiber, -syndikus *m*; ~-**council** (Stadt-)Rat *m*; ~-**council(l)or** Stadtrat, -verordnete(r) *m*; ~-**crier** *hist* Ausrufer *m*; ~**ee** [-'ni:] *sl* Bewohner *m* e-r Universitätsstadt; Städter *m*; ~-**hall** Rathaus *n*; ~ **house** Stadthaus *n*, -wohnung *f*; ~**ified** ['-ifaid] *a* verstädtert; ~ **major** *mil* Ortskommandant *m*; ~ **meeting** Bürgerversammlung *f*; *Am (Neuengland)* Urwählerversammlung *f*; ~-**planning** Stadtplanung *f*; ~**scape** ['-skeip] Stadtbild *n*; ~**ship** ['-ʃip] *hist* Stadtgemeinde *f*; *Am* (Amts-)Bezirk *m* *(Unterteilung e-s County)*; *Am (Landvermessung)* Flächeneinheit *f* von 6 Quadratmeilen; *(Südafrika)* Eingeborenenviertel *n*; ~-**sman** ['-zmən] Städter; *(fellow-~~)* Mitbürger *m*; ~**speople**, ~**sfolk** Städter *m pl*; ~**ward(s)** ['-wəd(z)] stadt(ein)wärts.

tox|(a)emia [tɔk'si:miə] *scient* Blutvergiftung *f*; ~**ic** ['tɔksik] *a* Gift-; giftig; ~**icant** ['-ənt] *a* giftig; *s* Giftstoff *m*; ~**icology** [tɔksi'kɔlədʒi] Toxikologie *f*; ~**in(e)** ['tɔksin] Toxin *n*.

toy [tɔi] *s* Spielsache *f*, -zeug *n*; Tand; Schnörkel *m*; *pl* Spielzeug *n*, -waren *f pl*; *a* Spiel-; klein, Zwerg-; *itr* spielen *a. fig*; *fig* tändeln (*with* mit); ~-**box** Spielzeugkasten *m*; ~-**dealer** Spielwarenhändler *m*; ~ **dog** Stoffhund; Schoßhund *m*; ~ **fish** Zierfisch *m*; ~ **garden** Vor-, Ziergarten *m*; ~**shop** Spielwarenhandlung *f*; ~ **soldier** Blei-, Zinnsoldat *m*.

trac|e [treis] **1.** *s* Fährte, (Fuß-)Spur *a. fig (meist pl)*; *(meist pl)* Spur, verschwindend geringe Menge *f a. chem*; Überrest *m*; Merkzeichen *n*; Aufzeichnung *(e-s Meßgeräts)*; Trasse *f*; *bes. Am* (Trampel-)Pfad *m*; *mil aero* Leuchtspur *f*; *psychol* bleibende(r) Eindruck *m*; *tr* folgen (*a path* e-m Pfad); nachgehen, -spüren (*s.o.* jdm); *(Ereignisse, Entwicklung)* zurückverfolgen, zurückführen (*to* auf); aufspüren, ausfindig machen; entdecken; nachweisen; zeichnen, entwerfen; graphisch darstellen; einzeichnen; trassieren; *(Meßgerät)* aufzeichnen; markieren, abstecken; *(Linie)* ziehen; durchpausen; (mühsam) schreiben; *itr* die Spur (zurück)verfolgen; *without a ~~* spurlos; *to ~~ back* zurückverfolgen (*to* bis, bis auf, bis zu); *to ~~ out* ausfindig machen, herausbekommen; aufzeichnen, aufschreiben; *(Kurve)* beschreiben; *(Plan)* entwerfen; *to leave o.'s ~~s* s-e Spuren zurück-, hinterlassen; ~~ *element* Spurenelement *n*; **~eable** ['treisəbl] *a* zurückzuverfolgen(d); auffindbar; nachweisbar; zurückführbar (*to* auf); **~er** ['-ə] Aufspürer; technische(r) Zeichner; *Am* Lauf-, Suchzettel *m*; Spurenelement *n*; (*radioactive* ~~) Isotopenindikator; Leuchtstoff *m (der Leuchtspurmunition)*; ~~ *ammunition* Leuchtspurmunition *f*; ~~ *bullet, shell* Leuchtspurgeschoß *n*; ~~ *composition, mixture* Leuchtsatz *m*; **~ery** ['-əri] *arch* Maßwerk *n*; **~ing** ['-iŋ] Aufspüren *n*; Suchdienst *m*; (Durch-)Pausen *n*; Pause; Aufzeichnung *f (e-s Meßgeräts)*; Trassieren *n*; ~~ *file* Suchkartei *f*; ~~*-paper* Pauspapier *n*; **2.** Strang *m*, Zugleine *f*, -seil *n*; *to kick over the ~s (fig)* über die Stränge schlagen.

trache|a [trə'ki(:)ə, 'trækiə] *pl -ae* [-i:i:] *anat* Luftröhre *f*; **~itis** [træki'aitis] *med* Luftröhrenentzündung *f*; **~otomy** [træki'ɔtəmi] *med* Luftröhrenschnitt *m*.

track [træk] *s* (Fuß-, Wild-, Wagen-) Spur, Fährte *f*, Geleise *n*; Pfad, Weg *m*; Bahn *f*, Gang *m*; (Renn-, Aschen-) Bahn *f*; Rennsport; *fig* (Gedanken-) Gang *m*; *rail* Gleis *n*, Schienenstrang *m*; Spurweite; *mil* Panzer-, Gleiskette; Gleitschiene *f*; *mar* Kielwasser *n*; *Am* Bahnsteig *m*; *tr (jdn, e-e Spur)* verfolgen, folgen (*s.o.* jdm); nachspüren (*s.th.* e-r S); aufspüren, ausfindig machen; betreten, -gehen; *(to ~ up)* Spuren hinterlassen in; *Am (Schmutz)* ausea.treten; mit Schienen, G(e)leisen versehen; e-e Spurweite von ... haben; *itr* Spur halten; aufea. ausgerichtet sein; *to ~ down* aufspüren, ausfindig machen; erjagen, stellen, zur Strecke bringen; *to ~ out* aufspüren; *to ~ up (Am)* mit den Schuhen beschmutzen; *in o.'s ~s (sl)* an Ort u. Stelle; *off the ~* auf falscher Fährte; *fig* auf dem Holzweg; *off the beaten ~* ungewöhnlich; wenig bekannt; *on ~* auf Achse; *to be on the ~ of s.o.* jdm auf der Spur, auf jds Spur sein; *to cover up o.'s ~s (fig)* s-e Spuren verwischen; *to go off the ~* entgleisen; *to keep ~ of s.o.* jdn im Auge behalten; *of s.th.* sich etw genau merken; *to lose ~ of s.o.* jdn aus den Augen verlieren; *to make ~s (fam)* abhauen *itr*; sich auf den Weg machen (*for* nach); *the beaten ~ (fig)* das ausgetretene Geleise; *cinder-~* Aschenbahn *f*; *motor-racing, cycling, running ~* Motorradrenn-, Radrenn-, Aschenbahn *f*; **~age** ['-idʒ] Treideln *n*; Gleisanlagen *f pl*; *Am* (Gebühr *f* für die) Benutzung *f* fremder Gleisanlagen; **~er** ['-ə] Spürhund; Jäger; Verfolger *m*; ~ **events** *pl sport* Laufdisziplinen *f pl*; ~ **hurdling** Hürdenlauf *m*; **~layer** Raupenfahrzeug *n*; *rail* Schienenleger *m*; **~less** ['-lis] spur-, pfadlos; nicht schienengebunden; ~~ *trolley bus* Obus *m*; **~man, ~walker** *Am rail* Streckenaufseher *m*; ~ **man** *Am* Leichtathlet *m*; ~ **meet** *Am* Leichtathletikwettkampf *m*; **~mobile** Schienentraktor *m*; **~-suit** *Am* Trainingsanzug *m*; **~-way** Fahrbahn *f*; Schienenstrang *m*.

tract [trækt] (Land-)Strich *m*, Strecke, Fläche *f*; Gebiet *n*; Parzelle *f*; Zeitraum; *anat* Apparat *m*, Organe *n pl*; *anat* Strang *m*, Bahn *f*; *bes. rel* Traktat *m*, *pej* Traktätchen *n*; Broschüre *f*; *digestive ~* Verdauungsapparat *m*; *respiratory ~* Atmungsorgane *n pl*; **~ability** [træktə'biliti] Lenkbar-, Lenksamkeit *f*; **~able** ['træktəbl] folgsam, lenksam, -bar, fügsam, umgänglich; *tech* leicht zu bearbeiten(d); **~ion** ['trækʃən] Zug *m a. med*; Ziehen *n (e-r Last)*; Beförderung *f*, Transport *m*; Zugkraft *f*; Reibungsdruck *m*; *(~~ of the road)* Bodenhaftung, Griffigkeit *f*; ~~ *switch* Fahrschalter *m*; **~ional** ['-ʃənl], **~ive** ['træktiv] *a* Zug-; *~ive power* Zugleistung *f*; **~or** ['-ə] Traktor, Trecker, Schlepper *m*, Zugmaschine *f*; *(~~ aircraft) aero* Zugschrauber; *med* Streckapparat *m*; ~~ *plough* Motorpflug *m*; ~~*-trailer train (mot)* Lastzug *m*; ~~ *truck (Am)* Sattelschlepper *m*.

trade [treid] *s* Gewerbe, Handwerk *n*; *com* Handel; Beruf(sstand) *m*; Fach (-arbeit *f*) *n*, Erwerbszweig *m*, Branche; Geschäftswelt *f*; *(the ~)* Brauereigewerbe *n*, Handel *m* in Spirituosen; *Am die* Kunden *m pl*, Kundschaft *f*; *Am (einzelnes)* Geschäft *n*, Handel, (Geschäfts-)Abschluß, Tausch(geschäft *n*) *m*; *Am* Abmachung, Vereinbarung *f*, Abkommen *n*; *the T~s (pl)* die Passatwinde *m pl*; *itr* handeln, Handel treiben (*in s.th.* mit e-r S; *with s.o.* mit jdm); in Geschäftsverbindung stehen (*with s.o.* mit jdm); *Am* Geschäfte machen (*with s.o.* mit jdm); *Am fam* kaufen, Kunde sein (*at* bei); Nutzen, Vorteile ziehen, Gewinn schlagen (*on, upon* aus); ausnutzen (*on, upon s.o., s.th.*, jdn, etw); *tr com* verkaufen; eintauschen (*s.th. for s.th.* etw für etw); *to ~ away, off* verschachern; *to ~ in* in Kauf, Zahlung geben (*for* für); *to ~ on s.th.* auf etw spekulieren; etw ausnutzen; *by ~* von Beruf; *to be in ~* Handel treiben; *to carry on a ~* ein Geschäft betreiben; *to drive a good ~* ein gutgehendes Geschäft haben; *no man is born a master of his ~* es ist noch kein Meister vom Himmel gefallen; *active, export ~* Aktiv-, Exporthandel *m*; *arms ~* Waffenhandel *m*; *balance of ~* Handelsbilanz *f*; *basic ~* Schlüsselindustrie *f*; *Board of T~ (brit.)* Handelsministerium *n*; *building ~* Baugewerbe *n*; *catering ~* Gaststättengewerbe *n*; *domestic, home ~* Binnenhandel *m*; *foreign, international ~* Außenhandel *m*; *free ~* Freihandel *m*; *the Free-T~ Area (pol)* die Freihandelszone *f*; *goods ~* Warenverkehr *m*; *horse ~ (fig)* Kuhhandel *m*; *illegal ~* Schleichhandel *m*; *itinerant ~* ambulante(s) Gewerbe *n*; *overseas ~* Überseehandel *m*; *passive, import ~* Passiv-, Importhandel *m*; *retail ~* Klein-, Einzelhandel *m*; *white-slave ~* Mädchenhandel *m*; *wholesale ~* Großhandel *m*; *world ~* Welthandel *m*; ~ **acceptance** Warenwechsel *m*; ~ **accord** Wirtschaftsabkommen *n*; ~ **association** Handels-, Arbeitgeberverband *m*; Berufsgenossenschaft *f*; ~ **bank** Handelsbank *f*; ~ **barriers** *pl* Handelsschranken *f pl*; **~-binding** *(Buch)* Verlags-, Verlegereinband *m*; **~-board, -council** Arbeitgeber-, Arbeitnehmerausschuß *m*; ~ **certificate, licence** Gewerbeschein *m*; ~ **connections** *pl* Handels-, geschäftliche Beziehungen *f pl*; ~ **control** Gewerbeaufsicht *f*; ~ **cycle** Konjunkturzyklus *m*; ~ **directory** Handelsadreßbuch *n*; ~ **discount** Händler-, Großhandelsrabatt *m*; ~ **disease** Berufskrankheit *f*; ~ **dispute** Handelsstreit *m*, Arbeitsstreitigkeiten *f pl*; ~ **edition** *(Buch)* allgemeine Ausgabe *f*; ~ **fair** Handelsmesse *f*; **~-in** *Am* in Zahlung gegebene(r) Gegenstand *m*; **~-in value** Handelswert *m*; ~ **index** Handelsindex *m*; ~ **jealousy** Konkurrenzneid *m*; ~ **journal** Handelsblatt *n*; ~ **law** Handelsrecht *n*; **~-mark** Handels-, Fabrik-, Schutzmarke *f*, Warenzeichen *n*; **~-name** Firmen-, Handelsbezeichnung *f*; ~ **partner** Handels-, Vertragspartner *m*; ~ **policy, politics** *pl* Handelspolitik *f*; ~ **price** Wiederverkaufs-, Großhandelspreis *m*; **~r** ['-ə] Kaufmann, Händler; Gewerbetreibende(r); *(Börse)* freie(r) Makler *m*; *mar* Handelsschiff *n*; ~ **reference** Geschäftsempfehlung; Kreditauskunft *f*; ~ **register** Handelsregister *n*; ~ **regulations** *pl* Gewerbeordnung *f*; Handelsbestimmungen *f pl*; ~ **relations** *pl* Handelsbeziehungen *f pl*; ~ **report** Handels-, Marktbericht *m*; **~research** Marktuntersuchungen *f pl*; ~ **route** Handelsstraße *f*, -weg *m*; ~ **school** Gewerbe-, Handelsschule *f*; ~ **secret** Geschäftsgeheimnis *n*; ~ **show** Filmvorschau *f (für Verleiher u. Kritiker)*; ~ **sign** Firmen-, Ladenschild *n*; **~sman** ['-zmən] Gewerbetreibende(r), Handwerker; Händler, kleiner Geschäftsmann, Ladeninhaber, -besitzer *m*; *~smen's entrance* Eingang *m* für Lieferanten; **~speople** *pl* Gewerbetreibende; Geschäftsleute, Händler *m pl*; ~ **statistics** *pl* Handelsstatistik *f*; ~ **tax** Gewerbesteuer *f*; ~ **treaty** Handelsvertrag *m*, -abkommen *n*; **~-union** Gewerkschaft *f*; *to form a ~~* sich gewerkschaftlich zs.schließen; *building ~~* Baugewerkschaft *f*; ~~ *movement* Gewerkschaftsbewegung *f*; ~~ *secretary* Gewerkschaftssekretär *m*; **~-unionism** Gewerkschaftswesen *n*; **~-unionist** Gewerkschaftler *m*; ~ **usage** Handelsbrauch *m*; ~ **value** Handelswert *m*; ~ **war** Handelskrieg *m*; **~-wind** Passatwind *m*.

trading ['treidiŋ] *a* handeltreibend; kaufmännisch; Handels-; *s* Handel *m* (*in s.th.* mit etw; *with s.o.* mit jdm); ~ **agent** Handelsagent *m*; ~ **area, market** Absatzgebiet *n*; ~ **assets, capital** Betriebskapital *n*; ~ **bank** Handelsbank *f*; ~ **company** Handelsgesellschaft *f*; ~ **concern** Wirtschaftsunternehmen *n*; ~ **estate** (geplantes) Industrieviertel *n*; ~ **firm** Handelshaus *n*; ~ **licence** Gewerbeschein *m*; ~ **partner** Teilhaber *m*; ~ **profit** Handelsspanne *f*; Geschäftsgewinn *m*; ~ **stamp** Rabattmarke *f*; ~ **stocks** *pl* Betriebswerte *m pl*; ~ **value** Handelswert *m*; ~ **volume** Handelsvolumen *n*; **~year** Geschäftsjahr *n*.

tradition [trə'diʃən] (mündliche) Überlieferung, Tradition *f*; (alter) Brauch *m*; *jur* (förmliche) Übergabe *f*; **~al** [-l] überliefert; traditionell, herkömmlich; üblich; **~alism** [trə'diʃnəlizm] *rel u. allg* Traditionalismus *m*; Festhalten *n* an der Überlieferung; Traditionsgebundenheit *f*; **~alist** [-ʃnəlist] Traditionalist *m*.

traduce [trə'dju:s] *tr* verleumden.

*

traffic ['træfik] *s* Güterverkehr; Handel *m* (*in* in, mit); Kunden *m pl*; Schleich-, Schwarzhandel; (Geschäfts-)Verkehr, Umgang; (öffentlicher, Straßen-, See-, Luft-)Verkehr *m*; Transport-, Verkehrswesen *n*; Verkehrsteilnehmer *m pl*; *a* Verkehrs-; *itr (bes.* Schwarz-, Schleich-)Handel treiben, handeln (*in s.th.* mit etw); Geschäfte machen, Verkehr, Umgang haben (*with* mit); *to ~ away* verschachern; *to ~ on* ausnutzen; *to direct the ~* den Verkehr regeln; *freight, goods, merchandise ~* Fracht-, Güterverkehr *m*; *frontier ~* Grenzverkehr *m*; *long-distance ~* Fernverkehr *m*; *motor* ~ Autoverkehr *m*; *ocean* ~ Seeverkehr *m*; *one-way* ~ Einbahnverkehr *m*, -straße *f*; *passenger* ~ Personenverkehr *m*; *railway* ~ (Eisen-) Bahnverkehr *m*; *road* ~ Straßenverkehr *m*; *road-~ office* Straßenverkehrsamt *n*; *short-distance, local* ~ Nahverkehr *m*; *through* ~ Durchgangsverkehr *m*; *tourist* ~ Fremdenverkehr *m*; *transit* ~ Durchgangs-, Transitverkehr *m*; *trunk* ~ Fern(sprech)verkehr *m*; **~able** ['-əbl] *com* gängig; *(Straße)* befahrbar; ~ **accident** Verkehrsunfall *m*; ~ **artery** Verkehrsader *f*; **~ator** ['træfikeitə] *mot* Winker *m*; ~ **block, congestion, hold-up, jam** Verkehrsstockung *f*; ~ **census** Verkehrszählung *f*; ~ **circulation map** Straßenverkehrskarte *f*; ~ **control** Verkehrsregelung *f*; *~~ tower (aero)* Kontrollturm *m*; ~ **density** Verkehrsdichte *f*; ~ **island** Verkehrsinsel *f*; **~ker** ['-ə] Schwarzhändler, Schieber; Intrigant, Zuträger *m*; ~ **light, signal** Verkehrsampel *f*; ~ **load** Verkehrsstärke *f*; ~ **manager** *rail* Fahrdienstleiter; *com* Versandleiter *m*; ~ **offence** Verstoß *m* gegen die Verkehrsregeln; ~ **patrol** Verkehrsstreife *f*; ~ **police** Verkehrspolizei *f*; ~ **policeman** Verkehrspolizist *m*; ~ **rates** *pl* Fracht(gebühren)sätze *m pl*; ~ **regulation** Verkehrsregelung *f*; *pl* Verkehrsvorschriften *f pl*; ~ **returns** *pl* Verkehrsziffern *f pl*, -statistik *f*; ~ **rules** *pl* Verkehrsregeln *f pl*; ~ **sign** Verkehrszeichen, -schild *n*; ~ **ticket** *Am* Strafmandat *n* (wegen e-s Verkehrsdeliktes); ~ **tower** Verkehrsturm *m*.

trag|edian [trə'dʒi:djən] Tragiker; *theat* Tragöde *m*; **~edienne** [trədʒi:di'en] Tragödin *f*; **~edy** ['trædʒidi] Trauerspiel *n*, Tragödie *f a. fig*; **~ic(al)** ['trædʒik(əl)] tragisch *a. fig*; *fig* (tief)traurig, unheilvoll; **~icomedy** ['trædʒi'kəmidi] Tragikomödie *f a. fig*; **~icomic** ['trædʒi'kəmik] tragikomisch.

trail [treil] *tr* nach-, hinter sich herschleifen; nachziehen, -schleppen; aufspüren, verfolgen; nachgehen, -fahren, herziehen (*s.o.* hinter jdm); *(Gras)* niedertreten; *itr* (auf dem Boden) schleppen, schleifen; *bot* ranken, kriechen; sich hinziehen, auslaufen, verwehen; kriechen, sich dahinschleppen; *(Hund)* e-e Spur verfolgen; *to ~ off* immer schwächer werden; sich verlieren; *s* Schleppe *f*, Schweif *m fig*; *(Rauch)* Fahne *f*; (Kondens-)Streifen *m*; Spur; Fußspur, Fährte *f*; (Trampel-)Pfad; (Lafetten-)Schwanz *m*; *(hot) on the ~* (dicht) auf der Spur; *to blaze the ~* den Weg bahnen *a. fig*; *to ~ o.'s coat (fig)* sich herausfordernd benehmen; *~ of blood* Blutspur *f*; **~-blazer** *Am* Pfadfinder; *fig* Pionier *m*; **~er** ['-ə] Verfolger; Spürhund *m*; *bot* Kletterpflanze *f*; *(~~ car)* Anhänger *(e-s Fahrzeuges)*; Wohnanhänger, -wagen *m*; (Film-)Vorschau *f*; *~~ camp, park (Am)* Platz *m* für parkende Wohnwagen; Wohnwagenkolonie *f*; **~erite** ['-ərait] (Dauer-)Bewohner *m* e-s Wohnwagens; ~ **ferry** Gierfähre *f*; **~ing** ['-iŋ]: *~~ aerial (aero)* Schleppantenne *f*; *~~ edge (aero)* Profilhinterkante *f*; *~~ rope* Schlepptau *n*; **~-net** Schleppnetz *n*.

train [trein] (Eisenbahn-)Zug *m*; Gefolge *n*, Begleitung *f*, Begleiter *m pl*; lange(r) Zug *m*, Karawane, Wagenkolonne *f*; *(~ of barges)* Schleppzug *m*; Schleppe *a. fig*; *fig* Reihe, Serie, Kette, Folge *f*; *mil* Train, Troß; *tech* Zug *m*, Kette; Walzenstrecke, -straße *f*; Rädersatz *m*; Zündlinie *f*; *zoo* Schwanz, Schweif *m*; *tr* auf-, erziehen; *(to ~ up)* schulen, ausbilden (*for* für); unterrichten; dressieren, abrichten (*to do* zu tun); einweisen, einarbeiten, vorbereiten; *sport* trainieren; *mil* ausbilden; richten, einstellen (*on* auf); *bot* (am Spalier auf)ziehen; *itr* (sich) üben; *sport* trainieren (*for* zu); *mil* exerzieren; *Am fam* verkehren (*with* mit); *to ~ off* sich überanstrengen; aus der Übung kommen; *by ~* mit dem Zuge, mit der Bahn; *in ~* vorbereitet (*for* für); im Gange; *in its ~ (fig)* in s-m Gefolge, nach sich; *to get into, to get on, (Am) to board a ~* in e-n Zug einsteigen; *to miss o.'s ~ connection* den Anschlußzug verpassen; *to put in ~* in Gang setzen; *to take a ~* e-n Zug benutzen (*to* nach); *the ~ is in* der Zug steht da, ist eingefahren; *ambulance, Red-Cross ~* Sanitätszug *m*; *boat ~* (Schiffs-)Anschlußzug *m*; *connecting, corresponding ~* Anschlußzug *m*; *corridor ~* Durchgangs-, D-Zug *m*; *early ~* Frühzug *m*; *extra-~* Sonderzug *m*; *fast ~* Eilzug *m*; *freight, goods ~* Güterzug *m*; *local ~* Vorortzug *m*; *passenger ~* Personenzug *m*; *slow ~* Personen-, *pej hum* Bummelzug *m*; *through ~* durchgehende(r) Zug *m*; *~ of rolls (tech)* Walzenstraße *f*; *~ of thought* Gedankengang *m*, -folge *f*; ~ **accident, disaster, smash, wreck** Eisenbahnunglück *n*; **~-bearer** Schleppenträger *m*; ~ **connection** Zugverbindung *f*; ~ **crew** Zugpersonal *n*; ~ **dispatcher** Fahrdienstleiter *m*; **~ed** [-d] *a* ausgebildet, geschult; trainiert; *house-~~ (Hund)* stubenrein; *~~ men* Fachkräfte *f pl*; **~ee** [trei'ni:] Lehrgangsteilnehmer; in Berufsausbildung Stehende(r); *Am* Rekrut *m*; **~er** ['-ə] Dresseur; Zureiter; Trainer, Sportlehrer; *mil* Ausbilder; Seitenrichtkanonier *m*; *(~~ aircraft)* Übungs-, Schulflugzeug *n*; **~-ferry** Eisenbahnfähre *f*; **~ing** ['-iŋ] Schulung, Ausbildung; Einweisung; Dressur *f*; (Ein-)Üben, Training; *mil* Seitenrichten *n*; *in, out of ~~ (sport)* in, aus der Übung; *to go into ~~* e-e Abmagerungskur unternehmen; *~~-camp* Ausbildungs-, Schulungslager *n*; *(teachers) ~~-college* Hochschule *f* für Lehrerbildung; *~~-course* Schulungskurs *m*; *~~-facilities (pl)* Ausbildungsmöglichkeiten *f pl*; *~~-film* Lehrfilm *m*; *~~-flight (aero)* Übungsflug *m*; *~~-ground* Exerzierplatz *m*; Ausbildungs-, Übungsgelände *n*; *~~- group* Lehrgruppe *f*; *~~-instructions (pl)* Ausbildungsvorschrift *f*; *~~-jump (aero)* Übungssprung *m*; *~~-objective* Ausbildungsziel *n*; *~~-personnel* Lehrpersonal *n*; *~~-program(me)* Ausbildungsprogramm *n*; *~~-regulations pl* Ausbildungsvorschriften *f pl*; *~~-school* Berufsschule *f*; *~~-ship* Schulschiff *n*; **~load** *rail* Zugladung *f*; **~man** ['-mən] *Am* Eisenbahner (im Fahrdienst), *bes.* Bremser *m*; **~-oil** (Fisch-)Tran *m*; ~ **reservation** Platzkarte *f*; ~ **schedule** Fahrplan *m*; ~ **service** Zug-, Eisenbahnverkehr *m*, Bahnverbindung *f*; *passenger ~~* Personenzugverkehr *m*.

traipse [treips] *s. trapes.*

trait [trei, *Am* treit] (Charakter-, Wesens-, Gesichts-)Zug *m*, Eigentümlichkeit *f*.

trait|or ['treitə] Verräter *m* (*to* an); **~orous** ['-ərəs] verräterisch; **~ress** ['-ris] Verräterin *f*.

trajectory ['trædʒiktəri, trə'dʒek-] Flugbahn, Wurfparabel *f*.

tram [træm] *min* Förderwagen, Hund; *(~-car)* Straßenbahnwagen; Schienenstrang; *pl* Stangenzirkel *m*; *to go by ~* mit der Straßenbahn fahren; **~head** Straßenbahnendstation *f*; **~-line** Straßenbahnschiene, -linie *f*; **~way** Straßenbahn(linie) *f*.

trammel ['træməl] *s (~ net)* Schleppnetz *n*; *Art* Fessel *f* (für Pferde); Kesselhaken; Ellipsen-, Stangenzirkel *m*; *pl fig* Fesseln *f pl*, Hemmschuh *m*; *tr (to ~ up)* verwickeln, verwirren; fesseln, behindern, einengen, hemmen.

tramp [træmp] *itr* fest auftreten, sta(m)pfen; wandern; *(to ~ it)* zu Fuß gehen, marschieren; trampen, herumvagabundieren; *tr* herumstampfen, -trampeln auf; feststampfen; durchwandern, -streifen; *s* Getrampel *n*; (schwerer) Tritt *m*; Wanderschaft *f*, Fußmarsch; Landstreicher, Tramp *m*; *Am* Hure *f*; *mar (~ steamer)* Trampschiff *n*; **~le** ['-l] *tr* zertrampeln; *itr (to ~ (up)on)* herumtreten, -stampfen, trampeln auf; *on s.o.* auf jdm *(seelisch)* herumtrampeln; *s* Getrampel, Getrappel *n*; **~oline** ['-pəlin] Trampolin(e *f*) *n*.

trance [trɑ:ns] Starre, Erstarrung; Verzückung; Trance(zustand *m*) *f*; *to send s.o. into a ~* jdn in Trance versetzen.

tranquil ['træŋkwil] ruhig, heiter, unbewegt; reglos, still; *(Wasser)* stehend; **~(l)ity** [træŋ'kwiliti] (Seelen-)Ruhe, Heiterkeit *f*; **~(l)ize** ['-aiz] *tr itr* (sich) beruhigen; **~(l)izer** ['-aizə] *pharm* Beruhigungsmittel *n*.

transact [træn'zækt, -'s-] *tr (Geschäfte)* aus-, durchführen, abschließen, tätigen; verhandeln (*with* mit); **~ion** -'zækʃən] Aus-, Durchführung *f*; Abschluß *m*, Tätigung *f*; Geschäft(sabschluß *m*) *n*, Transaktion *f*; *(legal ~~)* Rechtsgeschäft *n*; *pl* (Geschäfts-) Umsätze *m pl*; Verhandlungen *f pl*; Verhandlungsprotokoll *n*, Sitzungsbericht *m*; *banking ~~* Banktransaktion *f*; *barter ~~* Tauschgeschäft *n*; *cash ~~* Barverkauf *m*; *credit ~~* Kreditgeschäft *n*; *exchange ~~* Börsentransaktion *f*; Devisentermingeschäft *n*; *financial ~~* Geldgeschäft *n*; *~~ for the account* Termingeschäft *n*.

transalpine ['trænz'ælpain] transalpin.

transatlantic ['trænzət'læntik] transatlantisch; ~ **flight** Flug *m* über den Ozean; ~ **liner** Überseedampfer *m*.

transceiver [træns'si:və] *radio* Sende- u. Empfangsgerät *n*.

transcend [træn'send] *tr fig* überschreiten, -steigen, hinausgehen über; übertreffen; *rel philos* transzendieren; **~ence, -cy** [-əns(i)] Vorzüglichkeit, Vortrefflichkeit; Überlegenheit *f*; *rel philos* Transzendenz *f*; **~ent** [-ənt] vortrefflich, hervorragend; außerordentlich; *rel philos* transzendent; **~ental** [trænsen'dentl] *philos* transzendent(al); übernatürlich; *fam* abstrakt, unklar.

transcontinental ['trænzkənti'nentl] transkontinental.

transcribe [træns'kraib] *tr* abschreiben, kopieren; umschreiben, übertragen, transkribieren; *mus* umsetzen; *radio* auf Band aufnehmen.

transcript ['trænskript] Abschrift, Kopie; Reproduktion *f*; **~ion** [træns'kripʃən] Abschreiben, Kopieren *n*; Abschrift, Kopie; Übertragung; Umschrift; *mus* Umsetzung; *radio* Ton-, Bandaufnahme, Wiedergabe *f*; *~~ turntable (radio)* Abspieltisch *m*.

transept ['trænsept] *arch* Querschiff *n.*

transfer [træns'fə:] *tr* befördern, transportieren, verschicken, versenden; überbringen, -mitteln; verlegen *(from ... to* von ... nach); versetzen *(to* nach); *(Eigentum, Recht, fig)* übertragen; abtreten, zedieren; *(Geld)* überweisen *(to* an), *com* übertragen, vortragen, rück-, gegenbuchen; *typ* übertragen, umdrucken; *itr* versetzt werden *(to* zu, nach); *Am rail* umsteigen; *s* ['trænsfə(:)] Beförderung *f*, Transport *m*, Verschickung *f*, Versand *m*; Überbringung, -mitt(e)lung; Verlegung; Versetzung *(to* nach); *jur* Übertragung *(to* auf); Abtretung, Zession; *com* Überweisung *f*; Übertrag *m*, Rück-, Gegenbuchung *f*; *typ* Umdruck; Umschlag-, Versandplatz; *Am* Umsteigefahrschein *m*; Versetzungspapiere *n pl*; *cable* ~ Drahtüberweisung *f*; **~able** [-'fə:rəbl] übertragbar; **~ee** [-fə(:)'ri:] Versetzter); *jur* Übernehmer, Zessionar; *fin* Indossatar *m*; **~ence** ['trænsfərəns] Übertragung *a. psychol*; Verlegung; Versetzung *f (e-s Beamten)*; **~ential** [trænsfə'renʃəl] Übertragungs-; **~or** ['trænsfərə] *jur* Zedent; *fin* Indossant *m*; **~-picture** Abziehbild *n*; **~rer** [-'fə:rə] Übertragende(r) *m*; **~-ticket** Umsteigefahrschein; *com* Verrechnungsscheck *m.*

transfigur|ation [trænsfigju'reiʃən] Umgestaltung, Umwandlung *f*; *the T~~ (rel)* die Verklärung; **~e** [-'figə] *tr* umgestalten, umwandeln *(into* in); *rel fig* verklären.

transfix [træns'fiks] *tr* durchbohren; aufspießen; *fig* lähmen; **~ed** [-t] *a fig* starr *(with* vor).

transform [træns'fɔ:m] *tr* umgestalten, verwandeln; umbilden, umformen, umwandeln *(to* in) *a. math phys el*; *el* umspannen; verändern; **~able** [-əbl] verwandelbar; **~ation** [-fə'meiʃən] Umgestaltung, Verwandlung; Umbildung, Umformung, Umsetzung, *bes. scient* Umwandlung; *el* Umspannung; *zoo* Metamorphose; (Damen-)Perücke *f*; *atomic, nuclear ~~* Atom-, Kernumwandlung(sprozeß *m*) *f*; *~~ scene (theat)* Verwandlungsszene *f*; **~ative** [-'fɔ:mətiv] umgestaltend; **~er** [-'fɔ:mə] *el* Umformer *m.*

transfus|e [træns'fju:z] *tr (Flüssigkeit)* umgießen; durchtränken *a. fig (with* mit); *(Blut)* übertragen; **~ion** [-'fju:ʒən] Umgießung; *(blood ~~)* Bluttübertragung; *fig* Durchtränkung *f.*

transgress [træns'gres] *tr (Grenze)* überschreiten *a. fig*; *(Gesetz, Bestimmung)* übertreten, verstoßen gegen, verletzen; *itr* sich vergehen; sündigen; **~ion** [-'greʃən] Überschreitung; Übertretung *f*, Verstoß *m*, Vergehen *n*, Rechtsbruch *m*; **~or** [-ə] Übertreter; Rechtsbrecher; Sünder *m.*

tranship *s. transship.*

transien|ce, -cy ['trænziəns(i), *Am* -ʃəns(i)] Vergänglichkeit *f*; **~t** ['-t] *a* vergänglich; vorübergehend, kurz (-lebig), flüchtig; *Am* Durchgangs-; *s Am (~~ visitor)* Durchreisende(r) *m*; *el* Überspannung *f*; *~~ camp* Durchgangslager *n*; *~~ hotel (Am)* Hotel *n* für Durchreisende; *~~ worker* Gelegenheitsarbeiter *m.*

transistor [træn'sistə] *el* Transistor *m*; **~ize** *tr* mit Transistoren bestücken.

transit ['trænsit] Durchgang *a. astr*; Übergang *a. fig (to* zu); Wechsel *m (from* von); Transit, Transit-, Durchgangsverkehr *m*; Durchgangsstraße *f*; *in ~* unterwegs, auf dem Transport; *~* **business, trade** Transithandel *m*; *~* **camp** Durchgangslager *n*; *~* **duty** Durchgangszoll *m*; *~* **goods** *pl* Transitwaren *f pl*; **~ion** [træn'si'ʒən] Übergang *m*; *(period of ~~)* Übergangszeit; *gram mus* Überleitung *f*; *~~ stage* Übergangsstadium *n*; **~ional** [-'siʒənl] Übergangs-; **~ive** ['-sitiv] *a gram* transitiv; *~* **manifest, permit** Durchfuhrerklärung, -bewilligung *f*; **~ory** ['-əri] vorübergehend, zeitlich bedingt, kurzlebig; *~~ provision* Übergangsbestimmung *f*; *~* **pass** Passierschein *m*; *~* **traffic** Durchgangsverkehr *m*; *~* **visa** Durchreisevisum *n.*

*

translat|able [træns'leitəbl] übersetzbar; **~e** [-'leit] *tr* übersetzen, -tragen *(into German* ins Deutsche; *from (the) Italian* aus dem Italienischen); interpretieren, erklären, erläutern, auslegen, deuten; *(Telegramm)* dechiffrieren; *allg* umsetzen, -wandeln, übertragen *(into* in); versetzen; *tech* übersetzen, verschieben *(to* auf); *(Gebeine, Reliquien)* überführen; *(in den Himmel)* entrücken; *itr* sich übersetzen lassen; **~ion** [-'leiʃən] Übersetzung, -tragung; Erklärung; *tech* Übersetzung, Verschiebung *f*; **~or** [-'leitə] Übersetzer *m.*

transliterat|e [trænz'litəreit] *tr* transkribieren *(into* in); *(in ein anderes Alphabet)* umschreiben; **~ion** [-litə'reiʃən] Transkription *f.*

transluc|ence, -cy [trænz'lu:sns(i)] Lichtdurchlässigkeit *f*; **~ent** [-t] durchscheinend, lichtdurchlässig.

transmarine [trænzmə'ri:n] überseeisch; Übersee-.

transmigrat|e ['trænzmaigreit] *itr* über-, umsiedeln, auswandern; **~ion** [-'greiʃən] Umsiedlung, Auswanderung *f*; *~~ of the soul* Seelenwanderung *f.*

transmiss|ibility [trænzmisə'biliti] Übertragbarkeit; *phys* Durchlässigkeit *f*; **~ible** [-'misəbl] übertragbar *(to* auf); *phys* durchlässig; *biol* vererblich; **~ion** [-'miʃən] Übersendung, -mitt(e)lung; Übertragung *a. biol phys*, Vererbung; Fortpflanzung *a. phys*; *tech* Transmission *f*; (Übersetzungs-)Getriebe *n*; *phys* Durchlässigkeit; *radio* Übertragung, Sendung *f*; *~~ engineer* Funkingenieur *m*; *~~ gear* Wechselgetriebe *n*; *~~ line* Hochspannungsleitung *f*; *~~ of power* Kraftübertragung *f*; *~~ shaft* Getriebewelle *f.*

transmit [trænz'mit] *tr* übersenden, -mitteln; vermachen; übertragen, vererben *a. biol*; mitteilen; *phys* übertragen, leiten, fortpflanzen, durchlassen; *tech (Kraft)* übertragen; *radio* senden, übertragen; **~tal** [-l] Übersendung, -mitt(e)lung; Übertragung *f*; **~ter** [-ə] Übersender, -mitt(e)ler; Übertragende(r) *m*; *tele radio* Mikrophon; Sendegerät *n*, Sender *m*; **~ting** [-iŋ] *a* Sende-; *~~-aerial, -antenna* Sendeantenne *f*; *~~-circuit* Sendekreis *m*; *~~-current* Sendestrom *m*; *~~-power* Sendestärke *f*; *~~-room* Senderaum *m*; *~~-station* Sendestelle *f*; *~~-valve* Senderöhre *f.*

transmogrify [trænz'mɔgrifai] *tr hum fig* auf den Kopf stellen.

transmut|ability [trænzmju:tə'biliti] Umwandelbarkeit *f*; **~able** [-'mju:təbl] umwandelbar; **~ion** [trænzmju:'teiʃən] *chem* Umwandlung; *biol* Transmutation *f*; **~e** [-'mju:t] *scient* umwandeln *(into* in).

transoceanic ['trænzouʃi'ænik] überseeisch; Übersee, Ozean-.

transom ['trænsəm] Querbalken, -träger *m.*

transparen|ce, -cy [træns'pɛərəns(i)] Durchsichtigkeit, Transparenz *f*; Transparent, Diapositiv *n*; **~t** [-t] durchsichtig; *fig* klar, deutlich; offen, aufrichtig, ehrlich.

transpir|ation [trænspi'reiʃən] Ausdünstung, Transpiration *f*; Schweiß *m*; **~e** [-'paiə] *tr* ausdünsten, -schwitzen; *bot* verdunsten; *itr* schwitzen, transpirieren; ausgedünstet, ausgeschwitzt werden; *fig* durchsickern, verlauten, bekannt-, ruchbar werden; *fam* passieren, geschehen.

transplant [træns'plɑ:nt] *tr* umpflanzen; *(Menschen)* verpflanzen, umsiedeln *(to* nach); *med (Gewebe)* transplantieren; *itr* sich um-, verpflanzen, sich transplantieren lassen; *s* ['--] *u.* **~ation** [trænsplɑ:n'teiʃən] *bot* Umpflanzen *n*; *fig* Umsiedlung; *med* Transplantation *f.*

transport [træns'pɔ:t] *tr* befördern, transportieren; *hist (in e-e Strafkolonie)* deportieren; *to be ~ed* außer sich sein *(with* vor); *s* ['trænspɔrt] Beförderung, Überführung *f*, Transport *m*, Spedition *f*, Versand; *(~-ship)* Frachter *m*, Transportschiff *n*; *(troop-~)* Truppentransporter *m*; Transportflugzeug; Beförderungsmittel *n*; *com* Übertrag *m*; *fig* Begeisterung, Hingerissenheit, Ekstase *f*, Enthusiasmus *m*; *in a ~, in ~s of, ~ed with* außer sich, hingerissen vor; *air ~* Luftverkehr *m*; *door-to-door ~* Beförderung *f* von Haus zu Haus; *means of ~* Beförderungs-, Transportmittel *n*; *passenger ~* Personenbeförderung *f*; *road ~* Straßentransport *m*; *water-borne ~* Beförderung *f* auf dem Wasser; *~ by rail* Schienentransport *m*; **~able** [-əbl] transportierbar, versendbar; *~* **agent** Spediteur *m*; **~ation** [trænspɔ:'teiʃən] Beförderung *f*, Versand *m*; *Am* Beförderungs-, Transportmittel *n*; Versand-, Transportkosten *pl*; *Am (~~ ticket)* Fahrtausweis, Fahrschein *m*, -karte *f*; *hist* Deportation *f*; *~* **café** Gasthaus *n* für Fernverkehrsfahrer; *~* **charges** *pl* Transportkosten *pl*; **~er** [-ə] Laufkran *m*; Förderband *n*; *~* **insurance** Transportversicherung *f.*

transpos|e [træns'pouz] *tr* umsetzen, -stellen; auswechseln, -tauschen; *math mus* transponieren; *tech* verdrillen; **~ition** [trænspə'ziʃən] Umsetzung, -stellung, Auswechs(e)lung; *math mus* Transposition; *tech* Verdrillung *f.*

transship [træns'ʃip] *tr* umladen; **~ment** [-mənt] *mar* Umladung *f*; Umschlag *m.*

trans(s)onic [træns'sɔnik] *a* Überschall-.

transubstantiat|e [trænsəb'stænʃieit] *tr bes. rel (Brot u. Wein)* um-, verwandeln *(into* in); **~ion** ['trænsəbstænʃi'eiʃən] Um-, Verwandlung; *rel* Transsubstantiation *f.*

transvers|al [trænz'və:səl] *a* = **~e** *s math* Transversale *f*; **~e** ['trænzvə:s, -'-] *a* diagonal, quer laufend *(to* zu); *s* Querstück *n*; *~~ section* Querschnitt *m.*

*

trap [træp] **1.** *s* Falle *a. fig*; Fallgrube *f*, -strick *m a. fig*, Schlinge; *(~door)* Falltür, *theat* Versenkung; *tech* Klappe *f*, Siphon *m*; *sport* Schlagholz *n*; zweirädrige(r) Einspänner; *pej* Klapperkasten *m*; *sl* Schnauze *f*; *sl* Polizist *m*; *Am sl* Nachtlokal *n*; *tr* fangen; *tech* mit e-r Klappe, e-m Verschluß versehen; einfangen; (ab)fangen, festhalten; *fig* erwischen; ertappen; *mil* einschließen; *itr* Fallen stellen; *to set a ~ for s.o.* jdm e-e Falle stellen; *to fall, to walk into a ~* in e-e Falle gehen; **~-ball** Schlagball *m*; **~per** ['-ə] Fallensteller, Trapper *m*; **2.** *pl fam (fam* Sieben-)Sachen, Habseligkeiten

f pl, Krimskrams *m*; **~pings** ['-iŋz] *pl* verzierte (Pferde-)Decke *f*; *fig* (Sonntags-)Staat *m*, Abzeichen *n pl*.
trapes, traipse, trapse [treips] *itr (Frau)* (herum)watscheln; latschen.
trapez|e [trə'pi:z] *sport* Trapez *n*; **~ium** [trə'pi:zjəm] *math Br* Trapez; *Am* Trapezoid *n*; **~oid** ['træpizɔid] *math Br* Trapezoid; *Am* Trapez *n*.
trash [træʃ] *s Am* Abfall; Plunder; Schund; *fig* Unsinn, Blödsinn, Quatsch *m*; Pfuscharbeit *f*; *Am* Lump(enpack *n*) *m*; *white* ~ *(Am)* arme Weiße *m pl*; **~-can** *Am* Abfalleimer *m*; **~-dump** *Am* Schuttabladeplatz *m*; **~y** ['-i] wertlos; kitschig; Abfall-; Schund-, Pfusch-.
traum|a ['trɔ:mə] *pl a. -ata* ['-ətə] (schwere) Wunde, Verletzung *f*; *psychol* Trauma *n*; **~atic** [trɔ:'mætik] traumatisch.

*

travail ['træveil] *obs* Wehen *f pl*.
travel ['trævl] *itr* reisen *a. com* (*in* in); auf Reisen sein; gehen, laufen; fahren; *(Blick)* schweifen; *(to ~ over) fig* überfliegen; *tech* sich bewegen (können), Spielraum haben; sich ausbreiten, sich fortpflanzen; *tr* bereisen, reisen durch, durchziehen, -wandern; *(Strecke)* zurücklegen; *s* Reisen *n*, Reise; Bewegung *f*; Verkehr; *tech* Kolbenweg, Hub *m*; *pl* Reisen *f pl*; Reisebeschreibung *f*, -erlebnisse *n pl*; ~ **agency, bureau** Reisebüro *n*; ~ **book, guide** Reisehandbuch *n*, -führer *m*; ~ **case** Reisekoffer *m*; ~ **expenses** *pl* Reisekosten *pl*; ~ **folder** Reiseprospekt *m*; **~(l)ed** ['-d] *a* weitgereist, welterfahren; viel befahren, viel begangen; *geol* erratisch; **~(l)er** ['-ə] Reisende(r) *a. com*; *tech* Fahrkran *m*; *commercial* ~~ Handlungs-, Geschäftsreisende(r) *m*; *fellow* ~~ Reisegefährte, Mitreisende(r); *pol* Sympathisierende(r) *m*; *T~'s Aid (Am)* Bahnhofsmission *f*; *~'s cheque, (Am) check* Reisescheck *m*, -kreditbrief *m*; *~'s tale (fam)* Lügenmärchen *n*; **~(l)ing** Reise-; *~~-allowance* Reisekostenzuschuß *m*; *~~-bag* Reisetasche *f*; *~~-bridge* Verladebrücke *f*; *~~-clock* Reisewecker *m*; *~~ crane* Laufkran *m*; *~~-expenses (pl)* Reisekosten, -spesen *pl*; *~~-guide* Reiseführer *m*; *~~-insurance* Reiseversicherung *f*; *~~-kitchen (mil)* Feldküche *f*; *~~-library* Wanderbücherei *f*; *~~-requisites (pl)* Reiseutensilien *pl*; *~~-rug* Reisedecke *f*; *~~-salesman (Am)* Geschäftsreisende(r) *m*; *~~-stairs (pl)* Rolltreppe *f*; *~~-weight* Laufgewicht *n*; **~og(ue)** ['trævələ(:)g] Lichtbildervortrag *m* über Reiseerlebnisse; Reisefilm *m*; *(illustrierte)* Reisebeschreibung *f*; ~ **order** *Am mil* Marschbefehl *m*; ~ **restrictions** *pl* Reisebeschränkungen *f pl*.
traverse ['trævə(:)s] *tr* durch-, überqueren; durchreisen; *(Geschütz, Drehbank)* schwenken; *fig* durchkreuzen, e-n Strich machen durch; *(Fluß)* durchfließen; *jur* be-, abstreiten, leugnen; Einspruch erheben gegen; *mar* kreuzen; *s* Querlinie *f*, -stück *n*, -balken *m*, -schwelle *f*, -wall, -gang *m*, Traverse *f*; Durch-, Überqueren; *fig* Hindernis *n*; seitliche, schräge, Zickzack-, Drehbewegung *f*; *(Bergsteigen)* Queren *n*; *(Geschütz)* Schwenkbereich *m*, Schwenkung *f*; *mar* Koppelkurs *m*; *math* Schnittlinie *f*; *jur* Einspruch *m*.
travesty ['trævisti] *s* Travestie; *fig* Verzerrung, Entstellung *f*; *tr* travestieren; *fig* verzerren, entstellen.
trawl [trɔ:l] *s (~-net)* Schleppnetz *n*; *tr itr* (mit dem S.) fischen; **~er** ['-ə] (Schleppnetz-)Fischer(boot *n*) *m*.
tray [trei] Brett, Tablett *n*; Präsentierteller; Untersatz *m*; (flache) Schale *f*; Koffereinsatz; (Mörtel-, Sandstein-) Trog *m*; *ash-~* Aschenbecher *m*; *in-, out-~* (Kasten *m* für) eingehende, ausgehende Post; *pen-~* Federschale *f*; *tea-~* Teetablett *n*.
treacher|ous ['tretʃərəs] verräterisch, treulos, untreu (*to s.o.* jdm); hinterhältig, heimtückisch; täuschend, irreführend; unzuverlässig; *(Gedächtnis)* trügerisch; **~y** ['-əri] Treulosigkeit *f* (*to* gegen); Verrat *m* (*to* an).
treacl|e ['tri:kl] Sirup *m*; Melasse; *fig* Schmeichelei *f*; **~y** ['-i] sirupartig; *fig* zuckersüß, süßlich.
tread [tred] *irr trod* [trɔd], *trodden* ['trɔdn] *tr* betreten; gehen, schreiten auf; *(Takt)* treten; herumtreten, -trampeln auf *a. fig*; *(Erde)* festtreten; *(Pfad)* trampeln; *orn* treten; *itr* treten, schreiten, gehen, sich stellen (*on* auf); auftreten; herumtreten, -trampeln (*on, upon* auf); *(Vögel)* sich paaren; *s* Tritt, Schritt; Tritt(brett *n*) *m*, (Treppen-)Stufe; *(Leiter)* Sprosse; *(Schuhsohle, Rad)* Lauffläche *f*; *(Gummireifen)* Profil *n*; Spurweite *f*; *(Vogelei)* Hahnentritt *m*; *to ~ out (Feuer)* austreten; *fig* unterdrücken; *to ~ on air (fig)* im Glück schwimmen; *to ~ the boards* auf den Brettern stehen, Schauspieler sein; *to ~ in s.o.'s (foot)steps (fig)* in jds Fußstapfen treten; *to ~ on s.o.'s heels* jdm auf die Fersen, *fam* Hacken treten; *fig* jdm nicht von den Fersen gehen; *to ~ on s.o.'s toes, corns (fig)* jdm zu nahe treten; *to ~ water* Wasser treten; **~mill** Tretmühle *f a. fig*.
treadle ['tredl] *tech* (Fuß-)Tritt *m*, Pedal *n*; **~-drive, -operation** Fußantrieb *m*.
treason ['tri:zn] Verrat *m*, Verräterei *f* (*to* an); *(high ~, ~-felony)* Hochverrat *m*; **~able** ['-əbl] verräterisch; ~ **trial** Hochverratsprozeß *m*.
treasur|e ['treʒə] *s* Schatz *a. fig*; *fig* Hort *m*; *fig fam* Perle *f*; *tr (to ~~ up)* horten, anhäufen, sammeln, zs.tragen; *fig* sehr schätzen; *art-~~s (pl)* Kunstschätze *m pl*; *~~-house* Schatzkammer; *fig* Fundgrube *f*; *~~-hunter* Schatzsucher *m*; *~~-trove* wertvolle(r), kostbare(r) Fund *m*; **~er** ['-rə] Schatzmeister, Kassenverwalter, -wart *m*; *city ~~* Stadtkämmerer *m*; **~y** ['-ri] Schatzhaus *n*, -kammer; Kasse(nraum *m*); Finanz-, Staatskasse *f*; Fiskus *m*; *T~~ (Board), (Am) T~~ Department* Schatzamt, Finanzministerium *n*; (Klub-)Kasse *f*; *fig (Kunst, lit)* Schatz *m*, Sammlung; Fundgrube; *(Dichtung)* Anthologie, Blütenlese *f*; *First Lord of the T~~* Premierminister *m*; *the Lords of the T~~ (Br)* Finanzkollegium, -ministerium *n*; *~~ bench (parl)* Regierungsbank *f*; *~~ bill* kurzfristige(r) Schatzwechsel *m*; *~~ bond, -certificate* Schatzanweisung *f*; *~~ clerk* Finanzbeamte(r) *m*; *~~ licence* Devisenbewilligung *f*; *~~ note (Am)* Schatzwechsel *m*.
treat [tri:t] *tr* behandeln (*for* wegen; *with* mit) *a. med chem tech*; umgehen mit; ansehen, betrachten (*as* als); *(Thema)* sich befassen mit, behandeln; bewirten, freihalten (*to s.th.* mit etw); zukommen lassen, spendieren, zum besten geben (*s.o. to s.th.* jdm etw); *itr* handeln (*of* von); ver-, unterhandeln (*with* mit; *for* wegen); die Zeche (be)zahlen; *to ~ o.s. to s.th.* sich etw gönnen; *s* Bewirtung *f*; Schmaus *m*, Fest(essen) *n*; (Hoch-)Genuß *m*, Lust, Wonne, Freude *f*, Vergnügen *n*; *to stand ~ (fam)* die Zeche bezahlen; *to ~ lightly* auf die leichte Schulter nehmen; *I stand ~, it's my ~* das geht auf meine Rechnung, *fam* Kappe; *it's a real ~* das ist ein wahrer Genuß; *a children's, a school ~* ein Kinderfest; ein Schulausflug; **~ise** ['-iz] *(wissenschaftliche)* Abhandlung *f* (*upon, on* über); **~ment** ['-mənt] Behandlung *a. med chem tech* (*for* wegen); *tech* Bearbeitung, Aufbereitung *f*; *to be under ~~* in Behandlung stehen; **~y** ['-i] Unter-, Verhandlung *f*; Vertrag *m*, Abkommen *n*, Übereinkunft *f*; *to be in ~~ with s.o. for* mit jdm in Verhandlung stehen wegen; *to enter into a ~~ of commerce with s.o.* mit jdm e-n Handelsvertrag abschließen; *commercial ~~* Handelsabkommen *n*; *peace ~~* Friedensvertrag *m*; *~~ powers (pol pl)* Vertragsmächte *f pl*.
treble ['trebl] *a* dreifach; *mus* Diskant-; Sopran-; schrill; *s* Diskant, Sopran; schrille(r) Ton *m*; *tr itr* (sich) verdreifachen.
tree [tri:] *s* Baum *a. tech*; hochstämmige(r) Strauch; Pfosten *m*, Stange; *tech* Welle *f*; Leisten *m*; *tr* auf e-n Baum jagen; *fig* in die Enge treiben; *at the top of the ~ (fig)* auf dem Gipfel s-r Laufbahn; *up a ~ (fam)* in der Klemme; *family, genealogical ~* Stammbaum *m*; ~ **belt** Grünstreifen *m*; **~-climbers** *pl* Steigeisen *n*; **~-fern** *bot* Baumfarn *m*; **~-frog** *zoo* Laubfrosch *m*; **~less** ['-lis] baumlos; **~-louse** Blattlaus *f*; **~nail** Holznagel *m*; ~ **nursery** Baumschule *f*; **~-top** Baumwipfel *m*, -krone *f*.
trefoil ['trefoil, 'tri:-] Klee *m*; *arch* Kleeblatt *n*.
trek [trek] *itr (Südafrika)* trecken; *allg* langsam reisen *od* fahren; *s (Südafrika)* lange, mühsame Fahrt *f*.
trellis ['trelis] *s* Gitter(werk); Spalier *n*; *tr* vergittern; an e-m Spalier ziehen; **~-work** Gitterwerk, -netz *n*.
tremble ['trembl] *itr (vor Kälte, Erregung, Angst)* zittern, beben (*with* vor); vibrieren, zittern; sehr besorgt sein, zittern (*for* um); *s* Zittern *n*; Schauder *m*; *pl* Zitterkrankheit *f*; *to be all of a ~ (fam)* am ganzen Leibe zittern; *to ~ to think* vor dem Gedanken zurückschaudern; **~r** ['-ə] *el* Kontakthammer *m*.
tremendous [tri'mendəs] schrecklich, fürchterlich, furchtbar; *fam* gewaltig, riesig, ungeheuer(lich), aufregend.
trem|olo ['tremələu] *pl -os mus* Tremolo *n*; **~or** ['-ə] Zittern, Beben *n*; *med* Tremor *m*; *fig* (große innere) Erregung *f*, Schauder *m*; **~ulous** ['-juləs] zitternd, bebend; ängstlich, angstvoll; *in a ~~ voice* mit zitternder Stimme.
trench [trentʃ] *tr* schneiden (in); (ab-, ein-, zer)schneiden; durchfurchen; mit e-m Graben durchziehen; *agr* tief umpflügen; *mil* mit Gräben befestigen; *itr* (ein)schneiden; e-n Graben ziehen; eingreifen (*on, upon* in); übergreifen (*on, upon* auf); beeinträchtigen (*upon s.th.* etw); nahekommen (*on, upon* dat); *s* Graben *m a. geol*, Rinne *f*; *mil* Schützengraben; *pl fig* Kampf *m* in vorderster Linie; **~ancy** ['-ənsi] Schärfe; Wirksamkeit; Deutlichkeit *f*; **~ant** ['-ənt] scharf, schneidend; nachdrücklich, energisch; ~ **bottom** Grabensohle *f*; **~-coat** Regen-, Wettermantel *m*; **~er** ['-ə] *mil* Schanzarbeiter; *tech* Grabenbagger *m*; *(Küche)* Hackbrett; Brett *n* zum

Brotschneiden; *~~ cap (viereckige)* Studentenmütze *f*; **~erman** ['-əmən] Esser *m*; *~* **mortar** *mil* Granat-, Minenwerfer *m*; *~* **sector** *mil* Grabenabschnitt *m*; *~* **warfare** *mil* Stellungskrieg *m*.

trend [trend] *itr* sich wenden, sich ziehen, sich erstrecken, sich ausdehnen; e-e Richtung haben, sich hinneigen (*to* zu); *fig* gerichtet sein, streben, neigen, tendieren (*towards* nach; *away from* weg von); *geol* streichen (*to* nach); *s* (Haupt-)Richtung *f*, Verlauf, *com* Trend; *fig* Ab-, Verlauf, Gang *m (d. Ereignisse)*; Neigung, Tendenz, Entwicklung *f*; *cost ~* Kostenentwicklung *f*; *~ of affairs* Geschäftsgang *m*; *~* **analysis** Konjunkturanalyse *f*.

trepan [tri'pæn] *s tech* Bohrmaschine *f*; *tr med* trepanieren; *tech* kernbohren.

trephine [tri'fi:n, -'fain] *tr med* trepanieren, *(den Schädel)* aufmeißeln.

trepidation [trepi'deiʃən] Zittern, Beben *n*; Aufregung, Aufgeregtheit; Verzagtheit; Angst, Furcht *f*.

trespass ['trespəs] *itr* unbefugt, widerrechtlich betreten (*on, upon s.th.* etw); zu sehr in Anspruch nehmen (*on, upon s.o.'s time* jds Zeit); verstoßen, sich vergehen (*against* an); übertreten (*against s.th.* etw); *(Bibel)* sündigen (*against* gegen, wider); *s* unerlaubte(s) Betreten *n*; Übergriff (*on, upon* auf); Eingriff *m* (*on, upon s.o.'s rights* in jds Rechte); Übertretung *f*, Vergehen *n*; *(Bibel)* Sünde *f*; *no ~ing!* Betreten verboten! **~er** ['-ə] Rechtsverletzer, Übertreter; Sünder *m*; *~~s will be prosecuted!* Betreten bei Strafe verboten!

tress [tres] *poet* (Haar-)Flechte *f*, Zopf *m*; Locke *f*; *pl* (langes, offenes) Haar *n*.

trestle ['tresl] Bock *m*, Gestell; Brückengerüst *n*; **~-bridge** Bockbrücke *f*; **~work** Brückengerüst *n*; Gerüstkonstruktion, -brücke *f*.

triad ['traiəd, '-æd] Dreiheit; *math chem* Triade *f*; *mus* Dreiklang *m*.

trial ['traiəl] Versuch *m*; Probe (*of* mit); Untersuchung, Prüfung *f*; Experiment *n*, Versuch *m*; *jur* Gerichtsverfahren *n*; (Gerichts-)Verhandlung *f*, Prozeß *m*; *fig* Versuchung, Anfechtung; harte Prüfung, schwere Belastung, Last *f* (*to s.o.* für jdn); *by way of ~ and error* durch Ausprobieren; *on ~* auf, zur Probe; während der Probezeit; *to be on ~ for* vor Gericht stehen, sich zu verantworten haben wegen; *to bring to, to put on ~* vor Gericht, zur Verhandlung bringen; *to give a ~* ausprobieren, versuchen; auf Probe einstellen; *to put s.th. to further ~* etw weiterhin ausprobieren; *to send for ~* unter Anklage stellen; *to stand o.'s ~* sich vor Gericht verantworten; *civil, criminal ~* Zivil-, Strafprozeß *m*; *day of ~* Verhandlungstermin *m*; *monster, murder, spy, treason, witch ~* Monster-, Mord-, Spionage-, Hochverrats-, Hexenprozeß *m*; *year of ~* Probejahr *n*; *~ by jury* Schwurgerichtsverfahren *n*; *~ of strength* Kraftprobe *f*; *~* **balance** *com* Roh-, Zwischenbilanz *f*; *~* **balloon** Versuchsballon *m*; *~* **flight** Versuchsflug *m*; *~* **judge** Richter *m* der 1. Instanz; *~* **jury** Schöffen-, Geschworenenbank *f*; *~* **lawyer** *Am* Verteidiger *m*; *~* **lot** Probesendung *f*; *~* **match** *sport* Ausscheidungsspiel *n*; *~* **order** Probeauftrag *m*; *~* **period** Probezeit *f*; *~* **run, trip** Versuchs-, Probefahrt *f*.

triang|le ['traiæŋgl] Dreieck *n*; *mus* Triangel *m*; **~ular** [trai'æŋgjulə] dreieckig; Dreiecks-; *~~ file* Dreikantfeile *f*; **~ulation** [traiæŋgju'leiʃən] Triangulation *f*.

triassic [trai'æsik] *geol* Trias-.

trib|al ['traibəl] Stammes-; **~e** [traib] (Volks-)Stamm *m*; *biol* Tribus; *pej* Sippschaft *f*, Klüngel *m*; **~esman** ['traibzmən] Stammesangehörige(r) *m*.

tribulation [tribju'leiʃən] (großer) Kummer *m*, Trübsal; schwere Prüfung *f*, Leid *n*.

tribun|al [trai'bju:nl] Richterstuhl *m a. fig*; Gericht(shof *m*), Tribunal *n*; **~e** ['tribju:n] *hist* Tribun *m*; Tribüne *f*; Bischofsstuhl *m*; Rednerbühne *f*.

tribut|ary ['tribjutəri] *a* tributpflichtig (*to* dat); abhängig (*to* von); helfend; Tribut-; Hilfs-; *s* Tributpflichtige(r); *(~~ stream)* Nebenfluß *m*; **~e** ['tribju:t] Tribut *m a. fig*, Abgaben *f pl*; Beitrag *m*, Beisteuer; *fig* Hochachtung, Ehrengabe *f*, Lob *n*; *to lay s.o. under ~~* jdm e-n Tribut auferlegen; *to pay (a) ~~ to s.o.* jdm Anerkennung zollen.

tricar ['traika:] Dreiradlieferwagen *m*.

trice [trais] *tr (to ~ up)* heißen, aufziehen; *s (nur in:) in a ~* im Handumdrehen, im Nu.

trich|ina [tri'kainə] *pl -ae* [-i:] *zoo* Trichine *f*; **~inosis** [triki'nousis] *med* Trichinose *f*.

trick [trik] *s* Kniff *m*, kleine List *f*, Schlich, Kunstgriff, Trick *m*; Kunst (-stück *n*) *f*; Streich *m*, Tücke; dumme Sache, Dummheit; Angewohnheit, Eigenheit *f*; *(Kartenspiel)* Stich *m*; *Am fam* kleine(s), dumme(s) Ding *n (Kind, Mädchen)*; *mar (~ at the wheel)* Rudertörn *m*; *tr* beschwindeln, 'reinlegen, betrügen; an der Nase herumführen; *to ~ s.o. into doing s.th.* jdn dazu verleiten, etw zu tun; *to ~ s.o. out of s.th.* jdm etw abschwindeln; jdn um etw prellen; *to ~ out, up* herausputzen, ausstaffieren; *to do, to turn the ~ (fam)* die Sache schaukeln; *to get, to learn the ~ of it (sl)* den Dreh herausbekommen; *to play a mean, a dirty ~ on s.o.* jdm e-n gemeinen Streich spielen; *to take, to win a ~ (Kartenspiel)* e-n Stich machen; *I know a ~ worth two of that* das kann ich besser; *I'm on to his ~s* ich kenne s-e Schliche; *card ~* Kartenkunststück *n*; **~er** ['-ə], **~ster** ['-stə] Schwindler, Gauner, Betrüger *m*; **~ery** ['-əri] Schwindel, Betrug *m*, Gaunerei *f*; **~-film** *(gezeichneter)* Trickfilm *m*; **~-flier** Kunstflieger *m*; **~iness** ['-inis] Gerissenheit *f*; äußere(r) Schein *m*; Kompliziertheit *f*; **~sy** ['-si] schlau; mutwillig; zurechtgemacht, aufgeputzt; **~y** ['-i] gerissen, durchtrieben; trügerisch, illusorisch; kompliziert, verwickelt, verzwickt.

trickle ['trikl] *itr* tröpfeln *a. fig*; rieseln, rinnen; *tr* träufeln; *s* Tröpfeln; Geriesel; Rinnsal *n*; *to ~ away (Menge)* sich verlaufen, *fam* sich verkrümeln; *to ~ out* sich herumsprechen, durchsickern; *fig* herausströmen (*of* aus).

tricolo(u)r ['trikələ] Trikolore *f*.

tricycle ['traisikl] Dreirad *n*.

trident ['traidənt] Dreizack *m*.

triennial [trai'enjəl] alle drei Jahre stattfindend; dreijährig.

trier ['traiə] Prüfer, Prüfende(r), Untersuchende(r) *m*; Prüfgerät *n*; *fig* Probe *f*.

trifl|e ['traifl] *s* Kleinigkeit, Belanglosigkeit, Nebensache, Lappalie (*to* für); *Art* Nachspeise *f (Mürbegebäck in Wein mit Schlagsahne, Mandeln)*; Zinn(geschirr) *n*; *itr* Spaß machen, spaßen, scherzen; spielen, tändeln (*with* mit) *a. fig*; *tr (to ~ away) (Zeit)* vertändeln, vergeuden, *fam* verplempern; *a ~* ein bißchen, e-e Idee, ein wenig *a. als adv*; *he doesn't stick at ~s* er hält sich nicht mit Kleinigkeiten auf; **~er** ['-ə] Spaßmacher, Witzbold; Windbeutel, Luftikus *m*; **~ing** ['-iŋ] klein, gering(fügig), unbedeutend; seicht, albern, läppisch.

trifoli|ate [trai'fouliit] dreiblätt(e)rig; **~um** [-jəm] Klee *m*.

trig [trig] **1.** *a* nett, sauber; kräftig, stark; **2.** *tr* hemmen; absteifen, (ab-)stützen; **~ger** ['-ə] Hemmschuh; *(Gewehr)* Drücker, Abzug; *phot* Auslöser *m*; *quick on the ~~ (fig)* auf Draht; schlagfertig; *to ~~ off (fig)* auslösen; *to pull the ~~* abdrücken.

trigonometric(al) [trigənə'metrik(əl)] trigonometrisch; **~ometry** [trigə'nəmitri] Trigonometrie *f*.

trilateral ['trai'lætərəl] dreiseitig.

trilby ['trilbi] *fam* Schlapphut *m*.

trilingual ['trai'liŋgwəl] dreisprachig.

trill [tril] *s* Triller; gerollte(r) Konsonant *m*; *tr itr* trillern, trällern; (das *r*) rollen.

trillion ['triljən] *Br* Trillion; *Am* Billion *f*.

trilogy ['trilədʒi] *lit theat* Trilogie *f*.

trim [trim] *tr* in Ordnung bringen, ordnen, säubern, reinigen, putzen; ausputzen, beschneiden, stutzen; *(Hund)* trimmen; *(to ~ off)* ab-, herausschneiden; *(to ~ up)* aufputzen, schmücken, verzieren, besetzen, garnieren; *mar (Schiff, Kohlen)* trimmen; *(Segel)* brassen; *aero* (aus)trimmen; anpassen; *fam* herunterputzen, verdreschen, erledigen, fertigmachen, 'reinlegen; *to ~ o.s. up* sich herausputzen; *to ~ o.'s sails to every wind* u. *itr* sein Mäntelchen nach dem Winde hängen, sich durchlavieren; *itr (Schiff)* trimmen, das Gleichgewicht halten; *s* Ausputzen *n*; (richtige) Ordnung; Bereitschaft *f*; gute(r) Zustand *m*, gute Verfassung; Ausstattung, Einrichtung, Ausrüstung *f*; Staat, Zierat, Schmuck *m*; *Am* Schaufensterdekoration *f*; *mar* Trimm *m*; *aero* Trimmlage; *mot* Innenausstattung *f*; *film* herausgeschnittene(r) Teil *m*; *a* ordentlich; sauber, nett, hübsch, fesch; ausgeglichen, gut proportioniert; *in good, proper ~* in gutem Zustand; *fam* in Form; *out of ~* in schlechtem Zustand; *fam* nicht in Form; **~mer** ['-ə] *mar* (Kohlen-)Trimmer, Stauer *m*; Putzmacherin; *fig* Wetterfahne *f*; *tech* Trimmkondensator *m*, Beschneidemaschine *f*; **~ming** ['-iŋ] Aufräumen *n*; Reinigung *f*, Putz *m*; Beschneiden; *mar* Trimmen *n*; *fam* Schimpfe, Dresche, Niederlage *f*, Reinfall, Schwindel *m*; *pl* Zierat, Besatz *m*, Garnitur *f*; Zutaten *f pl*; Abfälle *m pl*; **~ness** ['-nis] Ordnung *f*, gute(r) Zustand *m*, Sauberkeit *f*.

trinitrotolu|ene, ~ol [trai'naitro(u)-'təljui:n, -əl] *chem mil* Trinitrotoluol *n*.

trinity ['triniti] Dreiheit; *(T~) rel* Dreieinigkeit *f*; *T~ (Sunday)* Sonntag *m* Trinitatis.

trinket ['triŋkit] kleine(s) Zier-, Schmuckstück *n*; *pl fig* Flitterkram, Tand *m*.

trinomial [trai'noumjəl] *a* dreinamig, -gliedrig; *math* trinomisch; *s math* Trinom *n*.

trio ['tri(:)ou] *pl -s mus* Trio *n a. fig*.

trip [trip] *itr* trippeln, tänzeln; stolpern, straucheln (*over* über); *fig* e-n Fehltritt tun, e-n Irrtum begehen, e-n Schnitzer machen; sich versprechen, stottern; *tr (to ~ up)* ein Bein stellen (*s.o.* jdm); zum Stolpern bringen; *fig* scheitern lassen, zu Fall bringen; *(to ~ up)* ertappen; kippen, kanten; *tech* in Gang setzen; auslösen, -klinken; *mar (Anker)* lichten; *bot* bestäuben; *s* Ausflug *m*, Fahrt, Reise *f* (*to* nach); Getrippel; Stolpern, Straucheln; Beinstellen *n*; Fehltritt *a. fig*; *fig* Fehler, Irrtum *m*, Versehen *n*; *tech* Auslöser; *(~ gearing)* Auslöse-, Ausklinkmechanismus *m*; *min* Grubenfahrt *f*; Kohlenzug *m*; *to catch s.o. ~ping* jdn bei e-m Fehler ertappen; *round ~ (Am)* Hin- u. Rückfahrt *f*; **~ back** Rückfahrt *f*; **~ dog** *tech* Anschlag *m*; **~ hammer** Schmiedehammer *m*; **~ lever** Schalthebel *m*; **~per** ['-ə] Ausflügler; Reisende(r) *m*; **~perish** ['-əriʃ] *fam* vielbesucht; **~pet** ['-it] *tech* Auslöser *m*; **~ping** ['-iŋ] *a* flink, behend(e), leichtfüßig; *s* Trippeln; Beinstellen *n*; **~-record book** *mot* Fahrtenbuch *n*; **~ there** Hinfahrt *f*; **~ ticket** Fahrbefehl, Dienstreiseausweis *m*; **~ wire** Stolperdraht *m*.

tripartite ['trai'pɑ:tait] dreiteilig, -fach; Dreier-.

tripe [traip] *(Küche)* Kaldaunen, Kutteln *f pl*; *sl fig* Quatsch, Schund, Kitsch *m*; *pl pop* Eingeweide *n (pl)*.

triphase ['traifeiz] *a* dreiphasig; *~~ current* Drehstrom *m*.

triphibious [trai'fibiəs] *mil* Land-, Wasser- u. Luft-.

tripl|e ['tripl] *a* dreifach; *tr itr* (sich) verdreifachen; *T~~ Alliance (hist)* Dreibund *m*; **~et** ['-it] Dreiergruppe *f*; Dreireim *m*; *mus* Triole *f*; *meist pl* Drillinge *m pl*; **~ex** ['-eks] *scient a* dreifach; *s* Dreiheit *f*; *~~ glass* Dreischicht-, Sicherheitsglas *n*; **~icate** ['-ikit] *a* dreifach; in dreifacher Ausfertigung; *s* dritte Ausfertigung *f*; *in ~~* in dreifacher Ausfertigung; *tr* ['-eit] *tr* verdreifachen; dreifach ausfertigen; **~ication** [tripli'keiʃən] Verdreifachung *f*.

tripod ['traipɔd] Dreibein *n*, -fuß *m*; *phot* Stativ *n*.

tripos ['traipɔs] *(Cambridge)* Honours-Prüfung *f* für den B.A.

triptych ['triptik] Triptychon *n*.

trisect [trai'sekt] *tr* in drei *(math* gleiche) Teile teilen.

trisyllab|ic ['traisi'læbik] dreisilbig; **~le** ['trai'siləbl] dreisilbige(s) Wort *n*.

trite [trait] abgedroschen, abgegriffen, alltäglich, platt; **~ness** ['-nis] Abgedroschenheit, Plattheit *f*.

triturate ['tritjureit] *tr* zerreiben; tüchtig kauen.

triumph ['traiəmf] *s* Triumph, Sieg (*over* über); große(r) Erfolg; Triumphzug, Siegeszug *m*, -feier *f*; *itr* triumphieren (*over* über); siegen; e-n Triumph feiern; *to win a ~ over s.o.* über jdn e-n Sieg davontragen; *shouts of ~* Triumphgeschrei *n*; **~al** [trai'ʌmfəl] triumphal; Triumph-, Sieges-; *~~ arch* Triumphbogen *m*; **~ant** [trai'ʌmfənt] triumphierend; siegreich; jubelnd.

triune ['traiju:n] *rel* dreieinig.

trivet ['trivit] Dreibein *n*; -fuß, eiserne(r) Halter; Untersetzer *m*; *as right as a ~ (fam)* in bester Ordnung.

trivial ['triviəl] alltäglich, trivial; belanglos, unwichtig, nichtssagend; unbedeutend, nebensächlich; *(Person)* oberflächlich; *the ~ round* der Alltag, der tägliche Trott; **~ity** [trivi'æliti] Belanglosigkeit, Nebensache; Plattheit, nichtssagende Bemerkung *f*.

troch|aic [tro(u)'keiik] *a* trochäisch; **~ee** ['trouki:] Trochäus *m (Versfuß)*.

troglodyte ['trɔglədait] *hist* Höhlenmensch; *fig* Einsiedler *m*.

Trojan ['troudʒən] *a* trojanisch; *s* Trojaner *m*; *to work like a ~* wie ein Pferd arbeiten.

troll [troul] *tr* im Rundgesang singen; trällern; *(mit der Schleppangel)* angeln; drehen; *itr* rollen, sich drehen, wirbeln; e-n Rundgesang singen; trällern; *(mit der Schleppangel)* angeln, fischen (*for s.th.* etw); **~ey, ~y** ['trɔli] Handkarren *m*; *rail* Draisine; *el (wheel-~~)* Kontaktrolle *f*; *(bow-~~)* Bügelstromabnehmer *m*; *min* Laufkatze *f*; *(Am a.: ~~ car)* Straßenbahnwagen *m*; *to be, to slip off o.'s ~~ (Am sl)* verrückt sein, werden; *~~-bus* Obus *m*; *~~ line* Obus-Linie; *(Am)* Straßenbahnlinie *f*; *~~-table* Teewagen *m*; *~~ wire* Fahrdraht *m*.

trollop ['trɔləp] Schlampe; Dirne *f*.

trombon|e [trɔm'boun] Posaune *f*; **~ist** [-ist] Posaunenbläser *m*.

troop [tru:p] *s* Gruppe *f*, Haufe(n), Trupp *m*, Schar, Herde; *mil* Batterie; *(Panzer)* Kompanie *f*; *(Pfadfinder)* Zug *m*; *meist pl* Truppe(n *pl*) *f*; *itr* e-e Gruppe bilden; *(to ~ up, together)* sich gruppieren, sich scharen, sich zs.rotten; *to ~ away, off* abziehen; *to ~ out of* scharenweise herauskommen aus; *~ing the colo(u)r* Fahnenparade *f*; **~-carrier** *aero* Truppentransportflugzeug, *mar* -schiff *n*; **~ commander** Truppenkommandeur *m*; **~er** ['-ə] Panzersoldat; *obs* Reiter, Kavallerist; berittene(r) Polizist *m*; *(~-horse)* Kavalleriepferd; *(~-ship)* Truppentransportschiff *n*, -transporter *m*; *to swear like a ~~* wie ein Kutscher fluchen; **~-plane, -train** Truppentransportflugzeug *n*, -zug *m*.

trop|e [troup] *gram* bildliche(r) Ausdruck *m*; **~ic** ['trɔpik] *s geog* Wendekreis *m*; *pl a. T~s* Tropen *pl*; *a* tropisch; *T~~ of Cancer, Capricorn* Wendekreis *m* des Krebses, des Steinbocks; **~ical** ['trɔpikəl] *a* tropisch; heiß *a. fig*; *gram* bildlich, übertragen; *s pl Am, (Br) ~~ clothing* Tropenkleidung *f*; *~~ disease* Tropenkrankheit *f*.

trophy ['troufi] Trophäe *f*; *sport* Preis *m*.

trot [trɔt] *itr* trotten, traben; eilen, rennen, laufen; *tr* traben lassen; *fig* in Trab bringen; *s* Trab *a. fig*; Dauer-, Waldlauf; *Am sl* Schlauch *m*, Klatsche; *sl* Hure *f*; *to ~ along, off (fam)* losziehen; *to ~ out (neues Kleid)* spazierenführen, bewundern lassen; zur Schau tragen; vorführen; zur Begutachtung vorlegen; *(Ansicht)* darlegen, anführen; *to ~ round (hum)* herumführen; mitnehmen (*s.o.* jdn); *to go for a ~ (fam)* sich die Füße vertreten; *to keep s.o. on the ~ (fig)* jdn in Trab halten; **~ter** ['-ə] Traber *m (Rennpferd)*; *pl (Küche)* Schweins-, Hammelfüße *m pl*; **~ting (race)** Trabrennen *n*.

troth [trouθ, -ɔ-] *s*: *in ~* wahrlich *adv*; *to plight o.'s ~* sein Wort verpfänden.

trouble ['trʌbl] *tr* beunruhigen, bedrücken, aufregen; quälen, plagen; belästigen, stören, bemühen (*for* um); ärgern; wehtun *a. fig*; Kummer, Sorgen machen, zu schaffen machen, Schwierigkeiten bereiten (*s.o.* jdm); *to be ~d* sich Sorgen machen (*about* wegen); *itr* sich bemühen (*to do* zu tun); beunruhigt sein, sich Sorgen, Gedanken machen (*about* über); *s* Mühe *f*, Umstände *m pl*, Unannehmlichkeiten *f pl*; Unruhe *f*, Sorgen *f pl*, Verdruß *m*; Schwierigkeit *f*, Problem; Unglück, Mißgeschick *n*, Kummer *m*; mißliche Lage; *med* Krankheit *f*, Leiden *n*; Aufregung, Unruhe *f*, Durcheinander *n*; *pol* Wirren *pl*; Ärgernis *n*, Stein *m* des Anstoßes; *tech* Störung *f*, Defekt *m*; *to ask, to look for ~ (fam)* sich ins Unglück stürzen; *to be in ~* in Schwierigkeiten sein; *to fish in ~d waters (fig)* im Trüben fischen; *to get into ~* sich Unannehmlichkeiten zuziehen; *s.o.* jdn in Schwierigkeiten bringen; *to give s.o. ~, to put s.o. to ~* jdm Mühe, Scherereien machen; jdm zu schaffen machen; *to have ~ with* Ärger, Scherereien haben mit; es zu tun haben mit; *to stir up ~* Unruhe stiften; *to take (the) ~* (sich) Mühe geben; *may I ~ you?* darf ich Sie bitten (*for* um; *to do* zu tun); *will it be much ~ to you?* macht es Ihnen viel aus? *don't put yourself to any ~* machen Sie sich keine Umstände; *(it will be) no ~ (at all)* das ist nicht der Rede wert; *what's the ~?* was ist los? wo fehlt's? *liver, heart ~* Leber-, Herzleiden *n*; **~maker** Unruhestifter *m*; **~-shooter** *Am* Störungssucher *m a. fig*; **~some** ['-səm] störend, lästig; beschwerlich, mühevoll; ärgerlich, unangenehm.

trough [trɔf] Trog *m*, Mulde, Rinne *f*, Regen-, Wasserablauf *m*; *(~ of the sea)* Wellental *n*; *~ of barometric depression* Tiefdruckrinne *f*.

trounc|e [trauns] *tr* verprügeln, verdreschen; *s.o.* es jdm geben *a. fig*; *fam* fertigmachen, erledigen; **~ing** ['-iŋ] Verprügeln *n*; *to give s.o. a good ~~* jdn tüchtig verprügeln.

troup|e [tru:p] (Schauspieler-, Artisten-, Musik-)Truppe *f*; **~er** ['-ə] Mitglied *n* e-r Truppe *f*; anständige(r), tüchtige(r) Kollege; *Am* alte(r), erfahrene(r) Schauspieler *m*.

trouser ['trauzə]: *pl (pair of ~s)* (lange) Hose *f*; **~ button, pocket, strap, stretcher** Hosenknopf *m*, -tasche *f*, -steg, -spanner *m*.

trousseau ['tru:sou] Aussteuer *f*.

trout [traut] *pl ~s* Forelle *f*; *sl* dumme(s), alte(s) Weib *n*; **~-coloured** *a*: *~~ white horse* Apfelschimmel *m*; **~-fishing** Forellenfang *m*; **~-fly** künstliche Fliege *f*; **~-stream** Forellenbach *m*.

trover ['trouvə] *(action for ~)* Klage *f* auf Herausgabe e-r widerrechtlich angeeigneten Sache.

trowel ['trauəl] *(brick-~)* Maurerkelle *f*; *to lay it on with a ~* (zu) dick auftragen; *garden-~* Gartenkelle *f*, Ausheber *m*; *cement-~* Verstreichbrett *n*.

troy [trɔi] *(~weight)* Troy-, Juwelengewicht *n (1 lb. = 12 ounces = 373,24 g)*.

truan|cy ['tru(:)ənsi] Müßiggang *m*, Bummelei; Drückebergerei *f*, Krankfeiern *n*; **~t** ['-t] *s* Müßiggänger, Bummler; Drückeberger *m*; *a* müßig, faul; schwänzend; Bummel-; *to play ~~* (die Schule) schwänzen.

truce [tru:s] *mil* Waffenstillstand *m*; *fig* Atempause *f* (*from* von); *a ~ to* Schluß mit; *political ~* Burgfriede(n) *m*.

truck [trʌk] **1.** *s* Blockrad *n*, Rolle; Flaggenknopfscheibe *f*; Schub-, Handkarren, Gepäckwagen *m*; Lore *f*; *min* Förderwagen, Hund; Rollwagen; *Am (motor ~)* Lastwagen *m*, -auto *n*; offene(r) Güterwagen *m*; *tr rail* in Güterwagen verladen; *mot* auf Lastwagen befördern; **~age** ['-idʒ] Spedition; *(~ charges)* Rollgeld *n*, Frachtgebühr *f*; **~-convoy** Lastwagenkolonne *f*; **~-driver** Last(kraft)wagenfahrer *m*; **~er** ['-ə], **~man** ['-mən] Lastwagenfahrer; Fuhrunternehmer, Spediteur *m*; **~ing** ['-iŋ] *s (~~ agency)* Spedition *f*, Fuhrgeschäft, -unternehmen *n*; **~ line** *Am* Überlandverkehr *m*; ~ **service** *Am* Rollfuhrdienst *m*; ~ **trailer** Lastkraftwagenanhänger *m*; **2.** *tr* (aus)tauschen (*for* für); *itr* Tauschhandel treiben (*for* um); *s* Tausch(geschäft *n*, -handel, -verkehr); *(~ system)* Naturallohn; *com* Kleinbedarf; *fam* Krimskrams; *fam* Quatsch *m*; *Am (garden ~)* Gemüse *n* für den Markt; *to have no ~ with s.o.* mit jdm nichts zu tun haben; ~ **economy** Tauschwirtschaft *f*; ~ **farm, garden** *Am* Gemüsegärtnerei *f*; ~ **farmer, gardener, grower** *Am* Gemüse-, Handelsgärtner *m*; ~ **farming, gardening,** ~**ing** Gemüsebau *m* für Handelszwecke.

truckl|e ['trʌkl] *s (~-bed)* niedrige(s) Roll-, Faltbett *n*; *itr fig* kriechen, sich erniedrigen (*to* vor); sich unterwerfen (*to s.o.* jdm); ~**er** ['-ə] *fig* Kriecher *m*.

truculen|ce, -cy ['trʌkjuləns(i)] Wildheit; Roheit; Grobheit *f*; ~**t** ['-t] wild; grausam; roh; rauh, grob; heftig.

trudge [trʌdʒ] *itr* sich schleppen, (mühsam) gehen, schleichen, sta(m)pfen (*through* durch); *s* lange(r) mühsame(r) Marsch *m*.

true [tru:] *a* wahr, treu, (wahrheits)getreu; recht, richtig, korrekt, genau, regelrecht; rechtmäßig, berechtigt, begründet; echt, wirklich, tatsächlich, wahrhaft; aufrichtig, ehrlich, (ge)treu, zuverlässig, verläßlich, sicher; *(Magnetnadel)* rechtweisend; *tech* maßhaltig; *(Abschrift)* gleichlautend; *biol* rasserein; *adv* wahrhaftig, wirklich; genau; *biol* reinrassig; *s das* Wahre, *die* Wahrheit; *tr (to ~ up)* (genau) passend machen; *tech* ausrichten; *(Rad)* zentrieren; *in ~* genau passend; *out of ~ (tech)* unrund; *to be ~ to o.'s word* an s-m Wort festhalten; *to come ~* Wirklichkeit werden, sich verwirklichen; sich bewahrheiten; *to prove ~* sich bewahrheiten, sich als wahr erweisen; *tell me ~* sag mir die Wahrheit! *~ to life* lebenswahr, -echt; *~ to nature, size* natur-, maßstabgerecht; *(it is) ~* allerdings, zwar; ~ **bill** *jur* begründete u. bestätigte Anklageschrift *f*; ~**-blue** zuverlässig; ~**-born** *a* gebürtig; echt; ~**-bred** *a* rasserein; *fig* wohlerzogen; ~**-hearted** *a* aufrichtig, ehrlich; (ge)treu; ~ **level** *geog* Meereshöhe *f*; ~**-love** Liebchen *n*, Geliebte(r *m*) *f*; ~**ness** ['-nis] Treue; Echtheit; Wirklichkeit; Aufrichtigkeit; *tech* Richtigkeit *f a. fig.*

truffle ['trʌfl] Trüffel *f*.

truism ['tru(:)izm] Binsenwahrheit *f*; Gemeinplatz *m*, Plattheit *f*.

truly ['tru:li] *adv* aufrichtig, wahrhaftig; wirklich, tatsächlich; *Yours ~, Very ~ yours* hochachtungsvoll.

trump [trʌmp] **1.** *s* Trumpf(karte *f*) *m a. fig*; *a. pl.* Trümpfe *m pl*, Trumpfreihe *f*; *fam* Prachtkerl *m*; *tr (Kartenspiel)* stechen; *fig* übertrumpfen, -bieten (*with* mit); *itr* Trumpf ausspielen; *to ~ up* erfinden, erdichten, schwindeln; *to play o.'s ~-card (fig)* s-e Trümpfe ausspielen; *to turn up ~s (fig fam)* alle Erwartungen übertreffen; Glück haben; **2.**: *the last ~, the ~ of doom* die Posaune des Jüngsten Gerichts; ~**et** ['-ət] *s* Trompete *f*; Trompeter; Trompetenstoß; Schalltrichter *m*, Sprachrohr *n*; *tech* Fangmutter *f*; *anat* Ohrtrompete, Eustachische Röhre *f*; *tr itr* trompeten; *tr (to ~~ forth) fig* ausposaunen; *to blow o.'s own ~~ (fig)* sein eigenes Lob singen; *~~-major (mil)* Stabstrompeter *m*; ~**eter** ['-itə] Trompeter *m a. mil.*

trumpery ['trʌmpəri] *s* Plunder, Trödel, Schund, *fam* Tinnef; *fig* Unsinn, Blödsinn *m*; *a* kitschig; wertlos, belanglos; Schund-.

truncat|e ['trʌŋkeit] *tr* stutzen, verkürzen; abschneiden, -hauen, -schlagen; verstümmeln; ~**ed** [trʌŋ'keitid, '---] *a* (abge)stumpf(t); *~~ cone* Kegelstumpf *m*.

truncheon ['trʌn(t)ʃən] Knüttel, (Gummi-)Knüppel *m*; *(Heraldik)* Befehls-, Kommandostab *m*.

trundle ['trʌndl] *s* Rolle *f*, Rädchen *n*; Rutsche *f*, kleine(r) Handkarren *m*; *(~-bed)* Rollbett; Rollen *n*; *itr* (dahin)rollen; sich drehen, rotieren; *tr* rollen, ziehen, schieben.

trunk [trʌŋk] *s* (Baum-)Stamm *a. fig*; (Säulen-)Schaft; *(Mensch, Tier)* Rumpf *m*; *(Insekt)* Bruststück *n*; *(Elefant)* Rüssel *m*; Röhre *f*, Rohr; Hauptrohr *n*, Rohrleitung; Hauptlinie, -strecke; *tele* Fernleitung *f*; (großer) Koffer; *mot* Kofferraum *m*; *pl* Turn-, Badehose *f*; *a (tele, Verkehr)* Haupt-; *bathing-~s (pl)* Badehose *f*; *cabin, steamer ~* Kabinenkoffer *m*; ~**-call** *tele* Ferngespräch *n*; ~ **connection** *tele* Fernverbindung *f*; ~**er** ['-ə] Fernfahrer *m*; ~**-exchange** *tele* Fernamt *n*; ~**-hose** *hist* Pluderhose *f*; ~**-line** *rail* Hauptlinie; *tele* Fernleitung *f*; ~**-road** Fern-, Autostraße *f*.

trunnion ['trʌnjən] (Dreh-)Zapfen *m*.

*

truss [trʌs] *tr* abstützen, -steifen; (zs.)binden, bündeln; fesseln; *(Küche)* wickeln, dressieren; *s* Bündel; Bund *(Heu* od *Stroh)*; (Eisen-)Band *n*, Klammer *f*; *arch* Tragbalken *m*; *med* Bruchband *n*; *bot* Dolde *f*; *(~ frame)* Fach-, Hängewerk *n*; ~**-bridge** Fachwerk-, Gitterbrücke *f*.

trust [trʌst] *s* Vertrauen (*in* auf); Zutrauen *n* (*in* zu); Zuversicht *f*, Glaube *m*, Hoffnung; Vertrauens-, Glaubwürdigkeit *f*; *fin com* Kredit *m*; Treue-, Treuhandverhältnis *n*, Treuepflicht *f*; anvertraute(s) Gut, Treuhandvermögen *n*; Stiftung *f*; Fideikommiß; Syndikat, Kartell *n*, Trust *m*; *itr* Vertrauen haben; voller Vertrauen, vertrauensvoll sein; vertrauen, bauen (*to* auf); (sein) Vertrauen setzen (*in* in), sich verlassen (*to* auf); (fest) hoffen (*for* auf); *tr* vertrauen (*s.o.* jdm); *s.th. to s.o., s.o. with s.th.* jdm etw anvertrauen; sicher sein, sich verlassen (*s.o. to do s.th.* darauf, daß jem etw tut; *to* auf); erwarten, hoffen, glauben; Kredit geben (*s.o.* jdm); *in ~* zu treuen Händen; *on ~* auf Treu u. Glauben; auf Kredit; *to put o.'s ~ in s.o.* auf jdn sein Vertrauen setzen; *bond, breach, position of ~* Vertrauensverhältnis *n*, -bruch *m*, -stellung *f*; ~**-company** Treuhandgesellschaft *f*; ~**-deed** Stiftungsurkunde *f*; ~**ee** [trʌs'ti:] Treuhänder, Depositar; Kurator, Pfleger, Sachwalter, Verwalter; Bevollmächtigte(r), Beauftragte(r), Vertrauensmann *m*; *under ~~* in Treuhänderschaft, unter treuhänderischer Verwaltung; *bankruptcy ~~* Konkursverwalter *m*; *board of ~~s* Kuratorium *n*; *~~ investment, securities (pl)* mündelsichere Anlage *f*, Papiere *n pl*; ~**eeship** [-'ti:ʃip] Treuhänderschaft; Pflegschaft, Kuratel *f*; ~ **estate** Treuhandvermögen *n*; ~**ful** ['-ful], ~**ing** ['-iŋ] vertrauensvoll; ~ **territory** Treuhandgebiet *n*; ~**worthiness** ['-wə:ðinis] Vertrauenswürdigkeit, Zuverlässigkeit *f*; ~**worthy** ['-wə:ði] vertrauenswürdig, zuverlässig; ~**y** ['-i] *a* = *~worthy*; *s Am* wegen guter Führung bevorrechtete(r) Sträfling *m*.

truth [tru:θ] Wahrheit; Wahrhaftigkeit, Aufrichtigkeit, Ehrlichkeit; Wirklichkeit, Echtheit; Richtigkeit, Korrektheit, Genauigkeit *f*; *in ~* in Wirklichkeit *od* Wahrheit; *out of ~ (tech)* ungenau; *to tell the ~* ehrlich gesagt; *I told him the plain ~* ich habe ihm reinen Wein eingeschenkt; *there is no (not a word of) ~ in it* es ist nichts Wahres daran; *fundamental ~* Grundwahrheit *f*; *home ~s (pl)* bittere Wahrheiten *f pl*; *~ to nature* Naturtreue *f*; ~**ful** ['-ful] wahrheitsliebend, aufrichtig, ehrlich; wirklichkeitsgetreu, lebenswahr; ~**fulness** ['-fulnis] Wahrheitsliebe, Aufrichtigkeit, Ehrlichkeit; Echtheit *f*.

try [trai] *tr* versuchen (*doing s.th.* etw zu tun); (aus)probieren, erproben, prüfen; untersuchen; auf die Probe stellen; *(durch Leid)* prüfen; schwer plagen, quälen, überfordern, überanstrengen, stark in Anspruch nehmen; *jur* vor Gericht, unter Anklage stellen; verhören; aburteilen; *jur* untersuchen; verhandeln, entscheiden; *Am (Prozeß)* führen; *(to ~ out) metal* (aus)scheiden, raffinieren, reinigen; *(Fett)* auslassen; *itr* e-n Versuch machen; sich bemühen (*to do, and do* zu tun; *for* um); zu erlangen suchen (*for s.th.* etw); *s* Versuch *m*, Probe *f*; *on the first ~* beim ersten Versuch; *to be tried* zur Verhandlung kommen; *to ~ on (Kleidung)* anprobieren; *to ~ it on with s.o. (fam)* es bei jdm probieren; *to ~ out* ausprobieren; auslesen, -wählen; *to ~ o.'s hand at s.th.* sich an etw versuchen; *to ~ o.'s hardest* sein Äußerstes tun; sein Letztes hergeben; *to ~ o.'s luck* sein Glück versuchen (*with s.o.* bei jdm); *let me have a ~ at it* laß es mich versuchen; *he had three tries* er konnte es dreimal versuchen; ~**-cock** Probier-, Wasserstandhahn *m*; ~**ing** ['-iŋ] quälend; anstrengend, mühsam, -selig, beschwerlich, lästig (*to* für); ~**-on** Anprobe *f*; *sl* Versuch *m*, Täuschungsmanöver *n*; ~**-out** *Am fam* Probe *f*; *sport* Ausscheidungskampf *m*, -spiel *n*; ~**-sail** ['traisl] *mar* Gaffelsegel *n*; ~**-square** *tech* Anschlagwinkel *m*.

tryst [traist, trist] *obs* Verabredung *f*.

tsar... *s. czar...*

tsetse ['tsetsi] *zoo* Tsetsefliege *f*.

tub [tʌb] *s* Tonne *f*, Faß *n*; Kübel; Zuber *m*; kleine(s) Stückfaß *n (etwa 4 Gallonen)*; *fam (wash-, bath-~)* (Wasch-, Bade-)Wanne *f*; (Wannen-)Bad *n*; *min* Förderwagen, Hund; *pej fam* Kasten, Kahn *m*; *sl* Kanzel; *sl* Wampe *f*, Bauch *m*; *sl* Tonne *f*, Fettsack, -mops *m*; *tr* in ein Faß tun; in e-n Kübel pflanzen; *fam* baden; *itr fam* baden, sich waschen; *sport sl* sich im Rudern üben; ~**bing** ['-iŋ] Verschalung *f*; *fam* Baden; *sl* (Übungs-)Rudern *n*; ~**by** ['-i] tonnenförmig; *fam* klein u. dick, dickbäuchig; *mus* dumpf; ~**-thumper** volkstümliche(r) (Kanzel-)Redner *m*; ~**-thumping** theatralisch.

tub|e [tju:b] Röhre *f*, Rohr *n*, Schlauch *m*; Tube *f*; Zylinder, Tunnel; Untergrund-, U-Bahn-Schacht *m*; *fam* U-Bahn; *Am el radio* Röhre *f*; *mot (inner ~~)* Schlauch *m*; *med* Röhre *f*, Kanal *m*; *bronchial ~~ (anat)* Bronchie *f*; *rubber ~~* Gummischlauch *m*; *~~ base* Röhrensockel *m*; *~~ railway* Untergrundbahn *f*; *~~ receiver (Am radio)* Röhrenempfänger *m*; *~~ station* U-Bahnhof *m*; ~**ing** ['-iŋ] Rohrlegen; Rohrsystem, Röhrenwerk *n*, Röhren *f pl*, Rohre *n pl*; Rohrmaterial; Stück *n*

Rohr; **~less** ['-lis] *mot* schlauchlos; **~ular** ['-julə] röhrenförmig; Röhren-; *(Klang)* hohl; *~~ boiler* Röhrenkessel *m*; *~~ furniture* Stahlrohrmöbel *n pl*; *~~ steel frame* Stahlrohrrahmen *m*.

tuber ['tju:bə] *bot* Knolle *f*; = *~cle*; **~cle** ['tju:bə:kl] *bot* Knolle *f*; *med* Knötchen *n*, Tuberkel *m*; *~~ bacillus* Tuberkelbazillus *m*; **~cular** [tju(:)-'bə:kjulə], **~culous** [-'bə:kjuləs] tuberkulös, schwindsüchtig; knotig; **~culosis** [tju(:)bə:kju'lousis] Tuberkulose, Tb(c), Schwindsucht *f*; *pulmonary ~~* Lungentuberkulose *f*; **~ose** ['tju:bərouz] *s bot* Tuberose *f*; **~ous** ['-bərəs] *med* knotig; *bot* knollig.

*

tuck [tʌk] *tr (to ~ up)* (auf)schürzen, raffen; *(Ärmel)* um-, aufkrempeln; *(to ~ in, up)* (zs.)falten, zs.legen; umnähen, e-n Saum nähen in; *(Bett)* zudecken; (weg)stecken, zwängen, pressen, drücken; *(to ~ in)* hineinstecken; *itr* Falten nähen; *sl* hineinhauen, tüchtig hineinbeißen (*into* in); *s* Saum, Abnäher *m*; *sl* Leckereien *f pl*; *Am fam* Energie *f*; *to ~ in (sl)* verdrükken, sich zu Gemüte führen; *to ~ up in bed* ins Bett stecken; **~er** ['-ə] **1.** Saumnäher(in *f*) *m*; *hist* Schultertuch *n*; *sl* Futter, Essen *n*; *s.o.'s best bib and ~~ (hum)* jds Sonntagsstaat *m*; **~-in** *fam* solide Mahlzeit *f*; **~-shop** *fam* Konditorei *f*, Süßwarengeschäft *n*.

tucker ['tʌkə] **2.** *tr (to ~ out) Am fam* erledigen, fertigmachen; **~ed** ['-d] *a* völlig fertig, erschossen.

Tuesday ['tju:zdi] Dienstag *m*; *on ~* am Dienstag; *on ~s* dienstags.

tufa ['tju:fə], **tuff** [tʌf] Tuff(stein), Kalktuff *m*.

tuft [tʌft] Büschel; Gebüsch *n*, Busch *m*; **~ed** ['-id] *a* buschartig; *~~ lark* Haubenlerche *f*; **~y** ['-i] büschelig.

tug [tʌg] *itr* sich (ab)mühen, sich placken, sich Mühe machen (*for* um); fest ziehen, zerren, reißen (*at* an); *tr* zerren, heftig ziehen (an); *mar* schleppen; *s* Zerren *n*, Ruck, Zug *m*; *fig* Anstrengung *f*, Kampf, Streit *m* (*for* um); Schlepptau *n*, -kette *f*; *mar (~boat)* Schlepper *m*; *~ of war (sport)* Tauziehen *n a. fig*; *~* **aircraft** Schleppflugzeug *n*.

tuition [tju(:)'iʃən] Unterricht *m*; Schulgeld *n*; *postal, private ~* Fern-, Privatunterricht *m*.

tulip ['tju:lip] Tulpe *f*.

tumbl|e ['tʌmbl] *itr* sich umhertummeln; (hin)purzeln, sich überschlagen, hinfallen, -schlagen; straucheln, stolpern (*over* über); umherstolpern, sich (umher)wälzen; fallen (*off a bicycle* vom Fahrrad; *out of a window* aus e-m Fenster); *com* stürzen; *fam* plötzlich kapieren (*to s. th.* etw); *tr* umstoßen, (um)stürzen; hin u. her stoßen; in Unordnung bringen; durchea.werfen; (herum)schleudern; *(Haar)* zerzausen; *s* Purzelbaum; Sturz, Fall *m*; Stolpern *n*; *fig* Unordnung *f*, Durcheinander *n*; wirre(r) Haufen *m*; *all in a ~~* völlig durcheinander; *to ~~ about (tr)* umherstoßen; *itr* umherstolpern; *to ~~ down, off* herunterpurzeln; *to ~~ in (fam)* in die Federn kriechen; *to ~~ out* hinauskippen, -werfen, -schleudern (*of* aus); *to give s.o. a ~~ (Am sl)* von jdm Notiz nehmen; *~~ bug (ent)* Pillendreher *m*; *~~-down* baufällig; **~er** ['-ə] Akrobat; Tümmler *m (Haustaubenrasse)*; Stehaufmännchen; *(fußloses)* Trink-, Becherglas *n*; *tech* Zuhaltung *f*; *~~ shaft* Nockenwelle *f*; *~~-switch* Kippschalter *m*; **~ing-box** Mischer *m*, Mischgerät *n*.

tumbrel ['tʌmbrəl], **tumbril** ['-il] (Kipp-, *hist* Schinder-)Karren *m*.

tum|efacient [tju:mi'feiʃənt] *a med* Schwellung bewirkend; **~escence** [tju:'mesns] Schwellung *f*; **~escent** [-'mesnt] schwellend; **~id** ['tju:mid] geschwollen *a. fig*; **~idity** [tju:'miditi] *med* Schwellung *f*; *fig* Schwulst *m*; **~o(u)r** ['tju:mə] *med* Geschwulst *f*, Tumor *m*.

tummy ['tʌmi] *(Kindersprache)* Bauch, Magen *m*; **~-ache** Bauchweh *n*.

tumult ['tju:mʌlt] Lärm, Tumult *m*, Verwirrung *f*, Durcheinander *n*; *fig* Aufregung, Erregung *f*; *to be in a ~* aufgeregt sein; **~uous** [-'mʌltjuəs] lärmend; turbulent, stürmisch; aufgeregt, erregt.

tumulus ['tju:mjuləs] *pl -li* ['-lai] Tumulus, Grabhügel *m*, Hügelgrab *n*.

tun [tʌn] Tonne *f*, (großes Wein-, Bier-)Faß *n (252 gallons = 1144,98 l)*.

tuna ['tju:nə] *(~ fish)* (amerik.) Thunfisch *m*; *bot* Opuntie *f*.

tundra ['tʌndrə] *geog* Tundra *f*.

tun|e ['tju:n] *s* Melodie, (Sing-)Weise *f*; Lied *n*; *mus* richtige Tonhöhe; *fig* Harmonie, Übereinstimmung *f*, Einklang *m*; Stimmung *f*; *tr (Musikinstrument)* stimmen; *(Stimme, Melodie)* modulieren; *tele* einstellen, einregulieren (*to* auf); *fig* (aufea.) abstimmen; musikalisch ausdrücken, zum Ausdruck bringen; *itr* (gut) gestimmt; *fig* abgestimmt sein, harmonisieren; *to ~~ in, on (radio)* einstellen, abstimmen (*to* auf); abhören, -horchen; zustimmen; *to ~~ out (radio)* abstellen, ausschalten; *to ~~ up (tr) (Musikinstrumente im Orchester)* (aufea. ab)stimmen; *tech* konditionieren, justieren, in Ordnung bringen; *aero* startbereit machen; *itr fam* zu spielen, singen, weinen anfangen; in Stimmung kommen; *in ~~ (mus)* (gut) gestimmt; aufea. abgestimmt; in Harmonie (*with* mit); in Ordnung; *aero* startbereit; *out of ~~ (mus)* verstimmt; falsch; *fig* im Widerspruch (*with* zu); *to the ~~ of (fam)* zum Preise, in Höhe von; *mus* nach der Melodie von; *to change o.'s ~~, to sing another ~~ (fig)* e-n anderen Ton anschlagen; *to dance to s.o.'s ~~ (fig)* nach jds Pfeife tanzen; *~~-up (tech mot)* Justierung *f*; **~eful** ['-ful] klangvoll, melodisch; **~eless** ['-lis] mißtönend; unmelodisch; stumm; **~er** ['-ə] *(piano ~~)* Klavierstimmer *m*; Stimmpfeife *f*; **~ing** ['-iŋ] *mus* Stimmen; *tele* Abstimmen, Einstellen *n*; *~~-coil (radio)* Abstimmspule *f*; *~~-fork* Stimmgabel *f*; *~~-in (radio)* Einstellung; Abstimmung *f*; Abhören, -horchen *n*; *~~ knob* Abstimmknopf *m*; *~~ range* Abstimmbereich *m*; **~y** ['-i] *fam* melodisch, melodienreich.

tungst|en ['tʌŋstən] *chem* Wolfram *n*; **~ic** ['-ik] *a* Wolfram-.

tunic ['tju:nik] *hist* Tunika; lange (Damen-)Bluse *f*; *mil* Waffenrock *m*; *bot zoo anat* Häutchen *n*.

tunnel ['tʌnl] *s* Tunnel *m*; Unterführung *f*; *min* Stollen *m*, Strecke *f*; *zoo* Bau; *tech* Windkanal *m*; *tr* untertunneln; *itr* e-n Tunnel anlegen (*through* durch; *into* in).

tunny ['tʌni] *zoo* Thunfisch *m*.

tup [tʌp] *tech* (Schlag-)Bär *m*.

tuppence *s. twopence.*

turban ['tə:bən] Turban *m*.

turb|id ['tə:bid] *(Flüssigkeit)* dick(flüssig), trüb(e), schmutzig; *fig* wirr, konfus; **~idity** [tə:'biditi], **~idness** ['-idnis] Trübung; Dichte; *fig* Verworrenheit *f*; **~ulence** ['tə:bjuləns] Unruhe *f*, Ungestüm *n*, Wildheit *f*; wilde(s) Durcheinander *n*, Turbulenz *f a. phys*, Aufruhr *m*; *(Wetter)* Böigkeit *f*; **~ulent** ['tə:bjulənt] unruhig, ungestüm, aufrührerisch; wirr, stürmisch, aufgewühlt, aufgeregt, wild; *phys* turbulent; *(Wetter)* böig; *aero* verwirbelt.

turb|ine ['tə:bin, '-bain] Turbine *f*; *hot-air, steam, water ~~* Heißluft-, Dampf-, Wasserturbine *f*; *~~ airplane* Turbinenflugzeug *n*; *~~ boat, steamer* Turbinendampfer *m*; *~~ shaft* Turbinenwelle *f*; **~o** ['tə:bo(u)] *in Zssgen* Turbo-, Turbinen-; *~~blower* Turbo-, Turbinengebläse *n*; *~~car* Turbinenauto *n*; *~~generator* Turbogenerator *m*; *~~jet (aero)* Strahlturbine *f*; *~~jet fighter, plane* Turbostrahl-, Turbinenjäger *m*; *~~liner* Düsenverkehrsflugzeug *n*; *~~prop(eller engine)* Propellerturbinen-, Luftstrahltriebwerk *n*; *~~reactor* Turboreakt(ionsmot)or *m*.

turbot ['tə:bət] *zoo* (Stein-)Butt *m*.

turd [tə:d] *sl* Kacke *f*, Kot *m*.

tureen [tə'ri:n] Terrine, Suppenschüssel *f*.

turf [tə:f] *s* Grasnarbe *f*, Rasen *m*; Rasenstück *n*, Sode *f*; *(Irland) pl a. turves* Torf(stück *n*, -sode *f*) *m*; *the ~* die (Pferde-)Rennbahn; das Pferderennen; *tr* mit Rasen(stücken) bedecken; *to ~ out (sl)* 'rausschmeißen; *~* **accountant** Buchmacher *m*; **~man** ['-mən] Rennplatzbesucher, Rennbegeisterte(r) *m*; **~y** ['-i] gras-, rasenbedeckt; Gras-; torf(art)ig; *fig* Renn(sport)-.

turg|escence [tə:'dʒesns] *med* Schwellung; Geschwulst *f*; **~id** ['tə:dʒid] *med* geschwollen *a. fig*, aufgebläht; *fig* schwülstig; **~idity** [tə:'dʒiditi] geschwollene(r) Zustand *m*; *fig* Schwulst, Bombast *m*.

Turk [tə:k] Türke *m*, Türkin *f*; *hum* Wildfang *m*; **~estan** [tə:ki'stɑ:n] Turkestan *n*; **~ey** ['tə:ki] die Türkei; *~~ corn* Mais *m*; *~~ red* Türkischrot *n*; **~ish** ['-iʃ] *a* türkisch; *s* (das) Türkisch(e); *~~ bath* Schwitzbad *n*; *~~ delight, paste* Türkische(r) Honig *m*; *~~ towel* Frottee-, Frottiertuch *n*; **~oman** ['tə:kəmən] *pl -mens* Turkomane *m*.

turkey ['tə:ki] *(~-cock)* Puter, Truthahn; *fig* Fatzke *m*; Pute *f*; *Am sl* Pleite *f*, Versager *m*; *to talk ~ (Am sl)* kein Blatt vor den Mund nehmen; *(as) red as a ~* puterrot; *~* **buzzard, vulture** Truthahngeier *m*.

turmeric ['tə:mərik] Kurkuma *f*.

turmoil ['tə:mɔil] Tumult *m*, Getümmel *n*, Aufruhr *m*, Durcheinander *n*.

turn [tə:n] **1.** *tr (im Kreise)* drehen; drechseln *a. fig*; *fig* formen, bilden, gestalten, machen; *fig (to ~ over, in o.'s mind)* hin u. her überlegen, gründlich durchdenken; *(auf die andere Seite)* umdrehen, (um)wenden, umkehren; auf den Kopf stellen; *agr (den Boden)* wenden, (um)pflügen; *fig (den Magen)* umdrehen, -kehren; herumgehen um; *mil (Feind)* umgehen; abwenden, abbiegen, ablenken; *fig* abwenden, abweisen, abschlagen; *fig* abbringen (*from* von); aufbringen (*against* gegen); richten, lenken; *fig* führen, leiten (*to* auf; *against* gegen); anbringen, verwenden (*to* auf, für); um-, verwandeln (*into* in), machen (*into* zu); umtauschen (*into* in), austauschen (*into* gegen); umschreiben, wiedergeben, übertragen, -setzen; *fig* auf andere Gedanken bringen, zerstreuen; *fig* eingebildet, verrückt machen; *fig* ausschlaggebend sein für; sauer werden lassen; **2.** *itr* sich drehen, rotieren, wirbeln (*on* um); *fig* sich drehen (*on* um), abhängen (*on* von); drechseln; gedrechselt werden; sich biegen; sich umdrehen, -wenden, -kehren; *(Buch)* umblättern; sich abwenden, sich abkehren, abbiegen, abweichen; *aero mar* abdrehen; die entgegengesetzte Richtung einschlagen; gehen, sich begeben (*to* nach, zu); sich wenden (*to* zu, an; *against* gegen); sich richten (*on, upon* gegen); *(Wetter)* umschlagen; werden (*soldier* Soldat; *fifty* 50 Jahre alt; *2 o'clock* 2 Uhr; *sour* sauer; *to s.th.* zu etw); sich wandeln, sich um-, verwandeln (*into* in); sauer, ranzig, faul, schlecht werden; die Farbe wechseln *od* verändern, verschießen; *(Blätter)* verfärben; *(Schraube)* durchdrehen; **3.** *s* (Um-)Drehung, Rotation *f*; Richtungswechsel *m*, Wendung; Windung, Biegung, Krümmung, Kurve; Runde *f*, Rundgang, Spaziergang, -ritt *m*, -fahrt; *fig* Wendung, Veränderung *f*, Wechsel, Umschwung *m*; *(Jahrhundert-)* Wende *f*; Wendepunkt; *fam* Schock, Schreck *m*; Übelkeit *f*; (Krankheits-)Anfall *m*; Handlung *f*; (guter) Dienst; Versuch *m*; Anrecht *n*, Anspruch *m*; (Zirkus-, Programm-)Nummer; (Arbeits-)Schicht *f*, Arbeitsgang; *com* Vorteil, Nutzen, Profit *m*; Eigenschaft, -heit, Beschaffenheit, Art, Gestalt, Form *f*, Charakter *m*; Neigung, Veranlagung, Tendenz *f*, Zug *m*; (Rede-)Wendung; Deutung, Auslegung, Erklärung, Interpretation *f*; **4.** *at every ~* auf Schritt u. Tritt, alle Augenblicke; *by ~s* abwechselnd; *in ~* der Reihe nach, nacheinander, umschichtig; *on the ~ (fam)* im Begriff, sich zu ändern, *(Milch)* sauer zu werden; *out of ~* außer der Reihe; zur Unzeit; *fam* Hals über Kopf; unüberlegt; *to a ~* ganz genau, vollkommen, aufs Haar; gerade recht; *~ and ~ about* abwechselnd; **5.** *to do s.o. a good ~* jdm e-n Dienst erweisen; *to give, to take a new ~* e-e neue Wendung nehmen; *to have a ~ for business* e-e kaufmännische Ader haben; *to serve s.o.'s ~s* jds Zwecken dienen; *to take ~s* (sich, mitea.) abwechseln; umschichtig arbeiten; **6.** *to ~ s.th. to account* etw ausnutzen, sich etw zunutze machen; *to ~ o.'s back (up)on s.o.* jdm den Rücken kehren; *to ~ s.o.'s brain* jdn verrückt machen; *to ~ into a brawl* in e-e Schlägerei ausarten; *to ~ o.'s coat (fig)* die Farbe wechseln; *to ~ the corner* um die Ecke biegen; *fig* e-n Umschwung verzeichnen; *to ~ s.o.'s flank (fig)* jdn aus dem Felde schlagen; *mil* die Flanke aufrollen; *to be able to ~ o.'s hand to anything* zu allem zu gebrauchen sein; *to ~ s.o.'s head (fig)* jdm den Kopf verdrehen; *to ~ it over in o.'s mind* es sich durch den Kopf gehen lassen; *to ~ up o.'s nose* die Nase rümpfen; *to ~ inside out* das Innere nach außen kehren; *to ~ an honest penny* von s-r Hände Arbeit leben; *to ~ to ridicule* lächerlich machen; *to ~ the scale (fig)* den Ausschlag geben; *to ~ short* kurz abbrechen; *to ~ a somersault* e-n Purzelbaum schießen; *to ~ tail* kehrtmachen, das Weite suchen, Reißaus nehmen; *to ~ upside down* das Oberste zuunterst kehren; auf den Kopf stellen; *to ~ up trumps (fig)* von unerwarteter Hilfe sein; *my stomach ~s* der Magen dreht sich mir um; mir wird übel; *now the tables are ~ed* jetzt hat sich das Blatt gewendet; *it is my ~* ich bin an der Reihe *od* dran; *the corner is ~ed (fig)* wir sind über den Berg; *one good ~ deserves another* e-e Hand wäscht die andere; **7.** *to ~* **about** *tr itr* (sich) umdrehen, -wenden, -kehren, kehrtmachen; *about ~! (mil)* ganze Abteilung — kehrt! *to ~* **around** *Am* (sich) umdrehen; *to ~* **aside** *tr itr* (sich) abwenden, -lenken; *to ~* **away** *tr* fort-, wegschicken, -jagen, vertreiben; entlassen; *(Gesicht)* wegwenden; *itr* sich abwenden, weggehen; *to ~* **back** *tr* zurück-, abweisen, abschlagen; *itr* umdrehen, umkehren; *to ~* **down** *tr* herunterschlagen, -klappen; *(Bild)* umdrehen, auf den Kopf legen; *(Flamme)* zurückdrehen, -schrauben, kleinstellen; *(Sache)* abschlagen, -lehnen; *(Radio)* leiser stellen; *(Person)* ab-, zurückweisen; e-n Korb geben; *itr* einbiegen in *(e-e Straße)*; heruntergeklappt werden (können); (herunter)hängen; *to ~* **in** *tr* einwärts kehren; falten; einreichen, abgeben, einhändigen; ab-, zurückgeben; *itr fam* sich hinlegen, zu Bett gehen, schlafen gehen; *to ~* **off** *tr (Wasser, Gas)* abstellen, abdrehen; *(Strom)* ab-, *(Licht)* ausschalten, ausmachen; ablenken, -leiten; *(Angestellten)* entlassen; *sl* aufhängen; *itr* vom Wege abbiegen; *(Straße)* abzweigen, -biegen; *to ~* **on** *(Wasser)* aufdrehen; *(el. Gerät)* einschalten; *(Licht)* anmachen; *s.o.* sich gegen jdn wenden; *s.th.* von etw abhängen; *to ~* **out** *tr* nach außen, *(Tasche)* umkehren; (aus)leeren, ausräumen; hinauswerfen, -jagen, -treiben; austreiben; wegjagen, entlassen; *(Regierung)* stürzen; *(Wache)* heraustreten lassen; *(Licht)* ausmachen; ausstatten, -staffieren; hervorbringen, produzieren, ausstoßen, herstellen, liefern; machen zu; *(Saldo)* aufweisen; *itr* (heraus)kommen (*for* zu); *(Wache)* heraustreten; antreten; erscheinen; sich ergeben, die Folge sein, resultieren, daraus hervorgehen; sich erweisen, sich herausstellen (*to be good* als gut), ausgehen, ausfallen, werden (*wet* regnerisch); *(well)* gut gelingen, geraten, glücken; *fam (aus dem Bett)* aufstehen; *for* sich einstellen bei; *I ~ed out to be right* es stellte sich heraus, daß ich recht hatte; *to ~* **over** *tr* umdrehen; umwenden, -kehren, -werfen; übergeben, abliefern, aushändigen; überweisen; übertragen, -lassen; *(Warenbestand)* erneuern; *com* umsetzen, verkaufen; umstellen (*to* auf); nachdenken über, überdenken, (gut) überlegen; *itr* sich umdrehen, sich auf die andere Seite legen; sich überschlagen, umkippen; *to ~* **round** *tr itr* (sich) umdrehen; rotieren um; *itr* s-e Ansicht, Meinung ändern; neue Wege gehen, e-e neue Politik verfolgen; *to ~* **up** *tr* umschlagen, -klappen; auf-, einschlagen, säumen; *(auf die linke Seite)* umschlagen, wenden; *(Spielkarte)* aufdecken; *sl (die Arbeit)* niederlegen; ausgraben, freilegen, ans Licht bringen; nachschlagen; *(Wasser)* aufdrehen; *(Radio)* lauter drehen *od* stellen; *a street* in e-e Straße einbiegen u. hinaufgehen; *fam* den Kaffee hochkommen lassen (*s.o.* jdm); *itr* nach oben gehen *od* führen; steigen, sich erheben; zustande kommen, sich ereignen, geschehen; auf-, in Erscheinung treten, sich zeigen; sich erweisen; *~ it up!* halt die Klappe! **~about** Kehrtwendung *f a. fig*; *Am* Karussell *n*; *fig* Umschwung *m*; *~~-face* Meinungsänderung *f*, Abfall *m*; **~-around** Wendeplatte; *mot* Überholung; Rundreise *f*; **~-bench** Drehbank *f*; **~-bridge** Drehbrücke *f*; **~-buckle** *tech* Spannschloß *n*; **~coat** Überläufer, Abtrünnige(r), Renegat *m*; **~cock** Drehhahn *m*; **~down** *a* Umlege-; *s* Absage *f*; *~~ collar* Umlegkragen *m*; **~er** ['-ə] Drechsler; Dreher *m*; **~ery** ['-əri] Drechslerei *f*; **~-in** Einsendung; Vorlage *f*; *~~ slip* Rückgabeschein *m*; **~ indicator** *mot* (Fahrt-)Richtungsanzeiger, Winker *m*; **~ing** ['-iŋ] *s* Drehung, Wendung, Biegung, Windung, Krümmung; Kurve; Straßenecke; Drechslerei; *lit* Gestaltung, Formung *f*; *pl* Drehspäne *m pl*; *~~ circle* Drehkreis *m*; *~~ effect, moment* Drehmoment *n*; *~~ lathe* Drehbank *f*; *~~ point* Wendepunkt *m a. fig*, -marke *f*; **~key** Gefangenenwärter *m*; **~-off** (Straßen-)Gabelung, Abzweigung *f*; **~-out** Umkehrung; Leerung, Räumung; Vertreibung; Zusammenkunft *f*, Treffen *n*; Besuch(er *pl*) *m*; Schauspiel *n*; Ausweichstelle; *rail* Weiche *f*; Gespann *n*, Kutsche; Ausrüstung, Einrichtung, Ausstaffierung, Ausstattung; Produktion *f*, (Gesamt-)Ertrag *m*; Arbeitseinstellung *f*, Streik, Ausstand *m*; **~over** Drehung, Wendung *f*; Umschwung *m*; Übergabe *f*, -gang; Wechsel *m*, Verschiebung *f*; *com* Umsatz, Umschlag *m*; Umorganisation *f*; (Obst-)Törtchen *n*; *el* Umpolung *f*; *~~ tax* Umsatzsteuer *f*; **~pike** Schlagbaum *m*; Zahlschranke *f*; *Am* (gebührenpflichtige) Autobahn *f*; **~plate** = *~table*; **~-round** *mar* Umschlag *m*; *aero* Abfertigung *f*; **~-screw** Schraubenzieher *m*; **~spit** Bratenwender *m*; **~stile** Drehkreuz *n*; **~switch** *el* Drehschalter *m*; **~table** *rail* Drehscheibe *f*; Plattenteller *m*; **~-up** Um-, *(Hose)* Aufschlag *m*; *fam* Aufregung, Unruhe; Schlägerei *f*; plötzliche(s) Erscheinen *n*.

turnip ['tə:nip] Kohl-, Steckrübe *f*.

turpentine ['tə:pəntain] Terpentin *n*.

turpitude ['tə:pitju:d] Schändlichkeit, Schlechtigkeit, Gemeinheit *f*.

turps [tə:ps] *fam* = *turpentine*.

turquoise ['tə:kwɑ:z, '-ɔiz, '-kɔiz] *min* Türkis *m*.

turret ['tʌrit; *Am* 'tə:rit] Türmchen *n*; *mil* Geschütz-, Panzerturm *m*; *aero mil* Kanzel *f*; *tech (~head)* Revolverkopf *m*; **~ lathe** Revolverdrehbank *f*.

turtle ['tə:tl] **1.** Schildkröte *f*; *to turn ~* umkippen, -stürzen; sich überschlagen; *mar* kentern; **~ neck** Hals *m* der Schildkröte; Rollkragen *m*; **~-shell** Schildpatt *n*; *(mock)* **~-soup** (falsche) Schildkrötensuppe *f*; **2.** *meist* **~dove** Turteltaube *f*.

Tuscan ['tʌskən] *a* toskanisch; *s* Toskaner(in *f*) *m*; **~y** ['-i] die Toskana.

tush [tʌʃ] *interj* ha! pah!

tusk [tʌsk] Eck-, Augen-, Fang-, Stoßzahn; Hauer *m*.

tussle ['tʌsl] *itr* (heftig) kämpfen, ringen, sich balgen, sich raufen; *fig* streiten (*with* mit); *s* (heftiger) Kampf *m*, Rauferei, Balgerei *f*; *fig* Streit *m*.

tussock ['tʌsək] (Gras-)Büschel *n*.

tut [tʌt] **1.** *interj* pfui! *~-!* Unsinn! **2.** *min* Akkord *m*.

tut|ee [tju'ti:] *Am* (Privat-)Schüler *m*; **~elage** ['tju:tilidʒ] Vormundschaft *f*; Schutz *m*; Unmündigkeit, Minderjährigkeit *f*; (Privat-)Unterricht *m*; **~elar(y)** ['-ilər(i)] Vormundschafts-, Schutz-; vormundschaftlich; **~or** ['tju:tə] *s jur* Vormund; Privat-, Nachhilfe-, Hauslehrer; Erzieher; *(Univ.)* Tutor, *Am* Assistent *m*; *tr* Privatunterricht geben (*s.o.* jdm); erziehen; *(Leidenschaft)* zügeln; **~orial** [tju-

'tɔ:riəl] *a* Vormundschaft-; Hauslehrer-, Erzieher-; *s* Übung *f*; ~~ *system* Unterricht *m* durch Tutoren.
tutti-frutti ['tuti'fruti] gemischte(s) Kompott *n*; Obstsalat *m*; gemischte(s) Fruchteis *n*.
tux(edo) [tʌks, tʌk'si:dou] *pl -os Am* Smoking *m*.
TV-mobile ['ti'vi:moubail] Fernsehaufnahmewagen *m*.
twaddle ['twɔdl] *s* (dummes) Geschwätz, Gerede; Gewäsch *n*; *tr itr* schwatzen, daherreden.
twain [twein] *obs poet* zwei.
twang [twæŋ] *s* Schwirren; Näseln *n*; *itr* schwirren; losschwirren; klimpern; näseln; *tr* (los)schwirren lassen; näseln(d aussprechen).
'twas [twɔz, -ə-] = *it was*.
tweak [twi:k] *tr* zwicken, kneifen.
tweed [twi:d] *(Textil)* Tweed *m* *(Wollstoff)*.
'tween [twi:n] = *between*; **~-decks** *adv* im Zwischendeck.
tweeny ['twi:ni] *fam* junge Hausgehilfin *f*; Zigarillo *m* od *n*.
tweezers ['twi:zəz] *pl (a pair of ~)* Pinzette *f*.
twel|fth [twelfθ] *a* zwölft; *s der, die, das* Zwölfte; Zwölftel *n*; *T~~-day* Erscheinungsfest *n*; *T~~-night* Dreikönigsabend *m*; **~ve** [twelv] zwölf; **~vefold** ['-vfould] *a adv* zwölffach; **~vemonth** ['-vmʌnθ] Jahresfrist *f*.
twent|ieth ['twentiiθ] *a* zwanzigst; *s der, die, das* Zwanzigste; Zwanzigstel *n*; **~y** ['-i] zwanzig; *the ~ies (s pl)* die zwanziger Jahre *(e-s Jahrhunderts)*, die Zwanzigerjahre *n pl (e-s Menschenlebens)*; **~yfold** ['-ifould] *a adv* zwanzigfach.
twerp [twə:p] *sl* Stoffel, Lümmel, Prolet; blöde(r) Kerl *m*.
twice [twais] *adv* zweimal; doppelt, zwei-, zwiefach; *~ the amount* der doppelte Betrag; *~ as much, many* doppelt, noch einmal soviel(e); *to think ~ about s.th.* sich etw zweimal überlegen; **~-told** *a* zweimal, oft erzählt; abgedroschen.
twiddle ['twidl] *tr* zwischen den Fingern drehen, (herum)spielen mit; *itr* herumspielen, -trödeln, die Zeit vertrödeln (*with* mit); *to ~ o.'s thumbs* Däumchen drehen; den lieben Gott e-n guten Mann sein lassen.
twig [twig] **1.** Zweig(lein *n*) *m*, Ästchen *n*; **2.** *tr fam* kapieren, begreifen; sehen, bemerken.
twilight ['twailait] Zwielicht *n*; (*bes.* Abend-)Dämmerung *f*, Halbdunkel; *fig* Dunkel *n*; *the T~ of the Gods* die Götterdämmerung *f*; *~* **sleep** *med* Dämmerschlaf *m*.
twill [twil] *(Textil)* Köper *m*; **~ed** [-d] *a* geköpert.
twin [twin] *a* paarig, doppelt; Doppel-; Zwillings- *a. allg*; *phot* zweiäugig; *bot* gepaart; *s* Zwilling *m*; *fig* Gegenstück *n*; *fraternal, identical ~s (pl)* zwei-, eineiige Zwillinge *m pl*; *~* **barrel** Zwillingsrohr *n*; *~* **beds** *pl* zwei Einzelbetten *n pl*; *~* **brother, sister** Zwillingsbruder *m*, -schwester *f*; *~* **conductor** Doppelleiter *m*; *~* **engine** *aero* Zwillingstriebwerk *n*; **~-engined** *a aero* zweimotorig; *~* **fuselage** *aero* Doppelrumpf *m*; **~-set** Twinset *m* od *n*; *~* **tail** *aero* Doppelleitwerk *n*; *~* **turret** *mil* Zwillingsturm *m*.
twin|e [twain] *s* Bindfaden *m*, Schnur *f*; Zwirn, *(Österreich)* Spagat *m*; Wikkelung, Windung *f*; Wulst *m*, wirre(s) Knäuel *n*; *tr* umea.winden, verflechten; zwirnen; winden (*s.th. round s.th.* etw um etw winden); umfassen, umschlingen; *itr* sich verflechten (*with* mit); sich winden, sich schlängeln; **~er** ['-ə] *tech* Zwirnmaschine; *bot* Schlingpflanze *f*.
twinge [twindʒ] *tr* zwicken, zwacken, kneifen, stechen; *itr* stechen, heftig schmerzen; *s* Stechen *n*, Stich; stechende(r), heftige(r) Schmerz *m*; *~s(pl) of conscience* Gewissensbisse *m pl*.
twinkl|e ['twiŋkl] *itr* blinken, flimmern, blitzen, funkeln, glitzern; *(Augen)* aufleuchten, blitzen; *fig* schnell hin u. her tanzen, huschen; *s* Blinzeln, Zwinkern; Flimmern, Flackern; Funkeln *m*; **~ing** ['-iŋ] Funkeln; Aufblitzen *n*; *in a ~~, in the ~~ of an eye* im Handumdrehen, im Nu.
twirl [twə:l] *itr tr* herumwirbeln, (sich) im Kreise drehen; *(Bart)* zwirbeln; *Am (Baseball)* werfen; *s* Wirbel(n *n*) *m*, schnelle Umdrehung; Windung *f*; Schnörkel *m*; *to ~ o.'s thumbs* Däumchen drehen; **~ing-stick** Quirl *m*.
twist [twist] *tr* umea.drehen, -winden; flechten; zwirnen; winden (*around* um); *(Blumen)* binden; verdrehen, verdrillen; verrenken; biegen, krümmen; *(den Kopf)* umdrehen; *(das Gesicht)* verziehen, verzerren; *(Fuß)* vertreten; *fig* quälen, martern, foltern; *fig* verdrehen, entstellen; *(e-m Ball)* e-n Drall geben; *itr* sich drehen, sich winden *a. fig*; sich biegen; rotieren; *(Rauch)* sich ringeln; *(Tanz)* twisten; *sl* betrügen; *s* (Bind-) Faden *m*, Garn *n*; Twist *m (Tanz)*; (gedrehte) Tabakrolle *f*; (Hefe-) Zopf *m (Gebäck)*; (Um-)Drehung, Rotation *f*; *tech* Drall *m*; Biegung, Windung; Verdrehung; Verrenkung; Verzerrung *(des Gesichts)*; *fig* Verdrehung, (Sinn-)Entstellung; Neigung, (persönliche) Note, Eigenheit, Schrulle *f*; *to ~ off (Draht)* abdrehen; *(Kappe)* abschrauben; *to ~ out of* sich herauswinden aus; *to ~ up* zu e-r Spirale aufrollen; *to ~ s.o.'s arm, neck* jdm den Arm ver-, den Hals umdrehen; *she can ~ him round her little finger* sie kann ihn um den (kleinen) Finger wickeln; **~er** ['-ə] Garnwinder, Zwirner *m*; Zwirnmaschine *f*; *sport* geschnittene(r) Ball; *Am* Wirbelsturm, Tornado; Träger, Tragbalken *m*; *fig* Schwierigkeit *f*; schwierige(s) Problem *n*; *fam* Schwindler *m*; *tongue-~~* Zungenbrecher *m*; **~y** ['-i] gewunden; verdreht; *fig* unaufrichtig.
twit [twit] *tr* verspotten; *s.o. with, about s.th.* jdn mit etw aufziehen; jdm etw vorwerfen; *s sl* Depp *m*.
twitch [twitʃ] *tr* zwicken, zwacken, kneifen; zupfen, zerren; *itr* (zs.-) zucken (*with* vor); *s* Ruck *m*; (Zs.-) Zucken; Zupfen; Nervenzucken *n*; Stich *m*.
twitter ['twitə] *itr* zwitschern, piep(s)en; *fig* tuscheln, schnattern; (vor Erregung) zittern; kichern; *s* Gezwitscher, Gepiep(s)e; *fig* Geschnatter (aufgeregtes) Zittern *n*; *all of a ~, in a ~* aufgeregt.
'twixt ['twikst] = *betwixt*.
two [tu:] *a* zwei; beide; *s* Zwei *f (a. in Spielen)*; *by, in ~s, ~ and ~* zu zweit, zu zweien, paarweise; *in ~* entzwei; *in a day or ~* in ein paar Tagen; *one or ~* ein paar; *the ~ of us* wir beide; *to be in ~ minds about doing s.th.* nicht wissen, ob man etw tun soll; *to cut in ~* halbieren; *to put ~ and ~ together* sich die Sache zs.reimen; **~-bit** *Am sl* billig, mies; bestechlich; *~* **bits** *pl Am sl* 25 Cents *pl*; **~-by-four** *Am fam* klein, eng, beschränkt, vollgepfropft; **~-colo(u)r** zweifarbig; **~-core cable** zweiadrige(s) Kabel *n*; **~-cycle** *s* Zweitaktmotor *m*; *a* Zweitakt-; **~-edged** *a* zweischneidig *a. fig*; **~-faced** *a* doppelseitig; *fig* falsch, heuchlerisch, verräterisch; **~-fisted** *a fam* stark, kräftig, stramm, männlich; **~fold** *a adv* zweifach, doppelt; **~-four** *mus* Zweivierteltakt *m*; **~-handed** *a* zweihändig; **~-job man** Doppelverdiener *m*; **~-legged** *a* zweibeinig; **~-party system** Zweiparteiensystem *n*; **~pence**, *fam* **tuppence** ['tʌpəns] zwei Pence *m pl*; **~penny** ['tʌpni] *a* Zweipence-; *fig* billig, wertlos; *~~-halfpenny (fig)* nebensächlich, verächtlich, unbedeutend; **~-phase** zweiphasig; **~-piece** *a* zweiteilig; *s* Komplet *n*; *~~ bathing-suit* zweiteilige(r) Badeanzug, Bikini *m*; **~-ply** zweifädig; in zwei Lagen; **~-seater** *mot* Zweisitzer *m*; **~-sided** *a* zweiseitig; *fig* von doppeltem Aspekt; *pol* bilateral; **~some** ['-səm] *s* (Liebes-)Paar, Pärchen; Spiel *n* für zwei Spieler; *a* Zweier-; Doppel-; für zwei; zu zweien; **~-speed gear** *mot* Zweiganggetriebe *n*; **~-step** Twostep *m (Tanz)*; **~-stroke engine** Zweitaktmotor *m*; **~-thirds majority** *parl* Zweidrittelmehrheit *f*; **~-time** *tr Am sl (in der Liebe)* betrügen; **~-way** *a tech* Doppel-, Zweiweg-; *radio* Sende- u. Empfangs-; *~~ switch* Umschalter *m*; *~~ traffic* Gegenverkehr *m*.
tycoon [tai'ku:n] *fam* Schlotbaron, Industriemagnat *m*.
tyke, tike [taik] Köter; Lümmel *m*.
tympan ['timpən] Membran *f*; *typ* Preßdeckel *m*; *arch* = *~um*; **~ic** [tim'pænik]: *~~ membrane (anat)* Trommelfell *n*; **~itis** [-'naitis] *med* Mittelohrentzündung *f*; **~um** ['timpənəm] *pl a. -na* ['-nə] Mittelohr; Trommelfell *n*; *mus* Trommel(fell *n*) *f*; *arch* Giebelfeld, Tympanon *n*; *tele* Membran *f*; *hist* Pauke *f*; *tech* Schöpfrad *n*.
typ|e [taip] *s* Typ(us) *m*, Type *f*; Muster(beispiel) *n*; Art, Gattung *f*, Modell *n*, Sorte *f*; Symbol, Sinnbild, Emblem, (Kenn-)Zeichen *n* (*of* für); *typ* Type, Letter *f*; (gedruckter) Buchstabe; Druck *m*, Schrift *f*; *fam* Kaliber *n*, Schlag *m*, Type *f*; *tr* mit der Maschine schreiben, *fam* tippen; klassifizieren, gruppieren; typisch werden; *in ~~* (ab)gesetzt, fertig im Satz; gedruckt; *black-letter, German-text ~~* Fraktur *f*; *blood ~~* Blutgruppe *f*; *bold ~* Fettdruck *m*; *italic ~* Kursive *f*; *roman ~* Antiqua *f*; *~~-area (typ)* Satzspiegel *m*; *~~-bar (gegossene)* Zeile *f*; Typenhebel *m*; *~~cast (irr s. cast) tr theat* nach typischen Merkmalen auswählen; *~~-caster, -founder* Schriftgießer *m*; *~~ face* Schriftbild *n*, -art *f*; *~~-foundry* Schriftgießerei *f*; *~~ metal* Letternmetall *n*; *~~ page* Satzspiegel *m*; *~~script* Schreibmaschinenmanuskript *n*; Durchschrift *f*, -schlag *m*, Kopie *f*; *~~-setter* Schriftsetzer *m*; Setzmaschine *f*; *~~-setting* Setzen *n*, Satz *m*; *a* Satz-; *~~ size* Schriftgröße *f*; *~~write (irr)* mit der Maschine schreiben; *~~writer* Schreibmaschine *f*; Maschinenschreiber(in *f*) *m*; *~~writer ribbon* Farbband *n*; *~~writing* Maschinenschreiben *n*, -schrift *f*; *~~writing-paper* Schreibmaschinenpapier *n*; *~~written (a)* mit der Maschine geschrieben; *~~ copy* Durchschlag *m*, -schrift *f*; **~ic(al)** ['tipik(əl)] typisch, charakteristisch, beispielhaft, kennzeichnend (*of* für);

~ify ['tipifai] *tr* symbolisieren, bezeichnen, bedeuten; typisch, kennzeichnend, ein Beispiel sein für; **~ing-paper** Durchschlagpapier *n*; **~ist** ['taipist] Maschinenschreiber(in *f*) *m*; **~o** ['taipou] *sl* (Buch-)Drucker *m*; **~ographer** [tai'pɔgrəfə] Buchdrucker *m*; **~ographic(al)** [taipə'græfik(əl)] *a* Druck-; *~~ error* Druckfehler *m*; **~ography** [tai'pɔgrəfi] Buchdruck(erkunst *f*) *m*.
typh|oid ['taifɔid] *a* typhusartig; Typhus-; *~~ bacillus* Typhusbazillus *m*; *~~ (fever)* Typhus *m*; **~ous** ['taifəs] flecktyphusartig; Flecktyphus-; **~us** [-] Flecktyphus *m*.
typhoon [tai'fu:n] *mete* Taifun *m*.
tyrann|ic(al) [ti'rænik(əl), tai-] tyrannisch, despotisch; **~ize** ['tirənaiz] *itr* e-e Gewaltherrschaft ausüben (*over* über); tyrannisch, grausam, ungerecht herrschen *od* regieren; *tr* tyrannisieren; unter-, bedrücken; **~ous** ['tirənəs] = *~ic*; **~y** ['-i] Gewaltherrschaft *f*, Despotismus *m*, Tyrannei; Härte, Strenge, Grausamkeit *f*;
tyrant ['taiərənt] Tyrann *a. fig*, Despot, Gewaltherrscher, -haber *m*.
tyre *s. tire.*
tyro *s. tiro.*
Tyrol ['tairəl] Tirol *n*; **~ese** [tirə'li:z] *a* tirolisch; *s* Tiroler(in *f*) *m*.
Tyrrhenian [ti'ri:njən] *a*: *the ~ Sea* das Tyrrhenische Meer.
tzar... *s. czar...*
tzetze ['tsetsi] *s. tsetse.*

U

U, u [ju:] *pl ~'s* U, u *n*; *U-turn (mot)* Drehung um 180°, Kehrtwendung *f*.
ubiquit|ous [ju(:)'bikwitəs] allgegenwärtig; **~y** ['-i] Allgegenwart *f*.
udder ['ʌdə] Euter *n*.
udometer [ju(:)'dɔmitə] *mete* Regenmesser *m*.
ugh [u:x, uh] *interj* äh! hu! pfui!
ugl|ify ['ʌglifai] *tr* häßlich machen; entstellen; **~iness** ['ʌglinis] Häßlichkeit *f*; **~y** ['ʌgli] häßlich, widerlich, scheußlich, gräßlich; *fig* gemein, abstoßend, greulich; bedrohlich, unheilvoll, gefährlich; *Am fam* streitsüchtig, zänkisch; *~~ customer (fam)* üble(r) Kunde *m*.
ukase [ju:'keiz, -s] *hist u. allg* Ukas; Erlaß *m*, Verordnung *f*.
Ukrain|e, *the* [ju(:)'krein] die Ukraine *f*; **~ian** [-iən] *a* ukrainisch; *s* Ukrainer(in *f*) *m*; (das) Ukrainisch(e).
ukulele [ju:kə'leili] *mus* Ukulele *n*.
ulcer ['ʌlsə] *med* Geschwür *n a. fig*; *gastric ~* Magengeschwür *n*; **~ate** ['-reit] *med tr* vereitern; *itr* eitern, schwären; **~ation** [ʌlsə'reiʃən] Eitern *n*, Vereiterung *f*; **~ous** ['-rəs] *med* geschwürartig; eiternd; *fig* korrupt.
ullage ['ʌlidʒ] *com* Leckage *f*; Gewichtsverlust; *fam* Rest *m*.
ulna ['ʌlnə] *pl a. -ae* ['-i:] *anat* Elle *f*.
ulster ['ʌlstə] Ulster *m (weiter Herrenmantel)*.
ult|erior [ʌl'tiəriə] jenseitig; später, (zu)künftig; folgend, weiter, ferner, fernerliegend; *fig* uneingestanden, verborgen, versteckt; *the ~~ motive* der wirkliche Grund; **~imate** ['ʌltimit] (ent)fern(te)st, weitest, äußerst; endlich, schließlich, letzt; elementar, fundamental, grundlegend, primär; maximal, größt(möglich); *~~ consumer* Endverbraucher *m*; **~imately** ['ʌltimitli] *adv* schließlich, endlich, am Ende; **~imatum** [ʌlti'meitəm] *pl a. -ta* [-ə] *pol* Ultimatum (*to* an); letzte(s) Angebot *n*, letzte(r) Vorschlag *m*; **~imo** ['ʌltimou] *adv* letzten Monats.
ultra ['ʌltrə] *a* radikal, extrem; *s* Radikale(r), Extremist *m*; *pref* jenseitig, über ... hinausgehend, Über-, Ultra-.
ultramodern ['ʌltrə'mɔdən] supermodern.
ultrahigh frequency ['ʌltrə'hai 'fri:kwənsi] Ultrakurzwellenbereich *m*, dm-Wellen *f pl*.
ultramarine [ʌltrəmə'ri:n] *a* ultramarin; *s* Ultramarin *n (Farbe)*.
ultramontane [ʌltrə'mɔntein] *rel* ultramontan.
ultramundane ['ʌltrə'mʌndein] außerweltlich.
ultrared ['ʌltrə'red] ultra-, infrarot.
ultra-short wave ['ʌltrə 'ʃɔ:tweiv] *radio* Ultrakurzwelle *f*.
ultrasonic ['ʌltrə'sɔnik] *a* Über-, Ultraschall-.
ultra-violet ['ʌltrə'vaiəlit] *phys* ultraviolett.
ultra vires ['ʌltrə 'vaiəri:z] *adv pred a jur* über die Befugnisse, die Vollmacht(en) hinausgehend.
ululate ['ju:ljuleit] *itr* heulen; laut jammern; **~ation** [ju:lju'leiʃən] Geheul, Geschrei *n*.
umbel ['ʌmbəl] *bot* Dolde *f*.
umber ['ʌmbə] *s* Umber *m*, Umbra *(Farbstoff)*; Siena(erde) *f*; *a* dunkelbraun.
umbilical [ʌm'bilikəl, *med* -'ləi-] *a* Nabel- *a. allg*; *~~ cord* Nabelschnur *f*.
umbr|a ['ʌmbrə] *pl -ae* ['-i:] *scient* (Kern-, Erd-)Schatten *m*; **~age** ['-idʒ]: *to take ~~* Anstoß, Ärgernis nehmen (*at* an); **~ageous** [-'breidʒəs] schattig; *fig* leicht beleidigt, empfindlich; **~ella** [-'brelə] (Regen-)Schirm *a. fig*; *mil sl* Fallschirm; *fig* Schutz *m*, Abschirmung *f*; *mil aero* Jagdschutz *m*; *mil* Feuerglocke *f*; *under the ~~ of* unter dem Schutz *gen*; *to put up an ~~* e-n Schirm aufspannen; *~~ aerial (radio)* Schirm-, Fächerantenne *f*; *~~ case, cover* Schirmhülle *f*; *~~ stand* Schirmständer *m*.
umpire ['ʌmpaiə] *s* Schiedsrichter *m*; *tr* (durch Schiedsspruch) schlichten; *sport* als Schiedsrichter leiten; *itr* Schiedsrichter sein (*in a dispute* bei e-m Streit).
umpt|een, umpsteen ['ʌm(p)(s)ti:n] *sl* zig, e-e Menge, Masse; **~eenth** ['-ti:nθ], **~ieth** ['-tiiθ] *sl* zigst, soundsovielte; **~y** ['ʌmpti] *a sl* zig; *s tele sl* Strich *m (des Morsealphabets)*.
un [ʌn] *pref* un-, Un-, nicht; ohne; *vor v*: ent-; **'un** [ən] = *one*.
unabashed ['ʌnə'bæʃt] *a* nicht bange, beherzt, mutig, furchtlos.
unabat|ed ['ʌnə'beitid] *a* unvermindert; **~ing** ['-iŋ] nicht nachlassend, nicht schwächer werdend.
unabbreviated ['ʌnə'bri:vieitid] unabgekürzt, unverkürzt.
unable ['ʌn'eibl] untauglich, unfähig; nicht in der Lage, nicht imstande (*to* zu); *to be ~* außerstande sein; *~ to pay* zahlungsunfähig.
unabridged ['ʌnə'bridʒd] *a (Text)* ungekürzt, vollständig.
unaccented ['ʌnæk'sentid] *a* unbetont.
unacceptable ['ʌnək'septəbl] unannehmbar (*to* für).
unaccommodat|ed ['ʌnə'kɔmədeitid] *a* nicht angepaßt; unpassend; **~ing** ['-iŋ] nicht entgegenkommend; zurückhaltend; unverbindlich; unfreundlich.
unaccompanied ['ʌnə'kʌmpənid] *a* unbegleitet, ohne Begleitung *a. mus*.
unaccomplished ['ʌnə'kɔmpliʃt] *a* unvollendet; *fig* ungebildet.
unaccount|able ['ʌnə'kauntəbl] unerklärlich, geheimnisvoll; nicht verantwortlich; **~ed(-for)** *a* uner-, unaufgeklärt; *com* nicht ausgewiesen.
unaccustomed ['ʌnə'kʌstəmd] *a* nicht gewöhnt (*to* an), nicht gewohnt (*to s.th.* etw); ungewöhnlich, seltsam, sonderbar.
unachievable ['ʌnə'tʃi:vəbl] unvollendbar; nicht ausführbar.
unacknowledged ['ʌnək'nɔlidʒd] *a* nicht anerkannt; unbestätigt.
unacquainted ['ʌnə'kweintid] *a* nicht vertraut (*with* mit); unkundig (*with s.th.* e-r S).
unadaptable ['ʌnə'dæptəbl] nicht anpaßbar; *(Mensch)* nicht anpassungsfähig.
unaddressed ['ʌnə'drest] *a* ohne Anschrift.
unadjusted ['ʌnə'dʒʌstid] *a* ungeregelt, unerledigt, (noch) schwebend; *(seelisch)* unausgeglichen.
unadopted ['ʌnə'dɔptid] *a* nicht angenommen; *(Straße)* nicht unterhalten.
unadorned ['ʌnə'dɔ:nd] *a* schmucklos.
unadulterated [ʌnə'dʌltəreitid] *a* unverfälscht, rein.
unadvis|ability ['ʌnədvaizə'biliti] Unratsamkeit *f*; **~able** ['-əbl] nicht ratsam; **~ed** ['-zd] *a* unberaten, unbedacht, unbesonnen.
unaffected ['ʌnə'fektid] *a* unberührt, unbeeinflußt (*by* von); unverändert; [--'--] ungekünstelt, einfach, natürlich.
unafraid ['ʌnə'freid] furchtlos, ohne Furcht (*of* vor).
unaided ['ʌn'eidid] *a* ohne Hilfe *od* Unterstützung (*by* von); *(Auge)* unbewaffnet.
unalienable ['ʌn'eiliənəbl] unveräußerlich.
unalloyed ['ʌnə'lɔid] *a* unvermischt; *fig* ungetrübt.
unalter|ably [ʌn'ɔ:ltərəbli] *adv* unveränderlich; **~ed** ['ʌn'ɔ:ltəd] *a* unverändert.
unambiguous ['ʌnæm'bigjuəs] unzweideutig.
unambitious ['ʌnæm'biʃəs] nicht ehrgeizig; anspruchslos, bescheiden.

unamenable ['ʌnə'mi:nəbl] *(Mensch)* unzugänglich (*to* für); nicht verantwortlich (*to* gegenüber).
unamendable ['ʌnə'mendəbl] unverbesserlich.
un-American ['ʌnə'merikən] unamerikanisch.
unamiable ['ʌn'eimiəbl] unliebenswürdig, kühl, abweisend.
unanim|ity [ju:nə'nimiti] Einmütigkeit; *parl* Einstimmigkeit *f*; **~ous** [ju(:)'nænimәs] einmütig; *parl* einstimmig.
unannounced ['ʌnə'naunst] *a* unangekündigt, ohne Ankündigung.
unanswer|able [ʌn'ɑ:nsərəbl] unbestreitbar, unwiderleglich; **~ed** [-əd] *a* unbeantwortet, ohne Antwort.
unappalled ['ʌnə'pɔ:ld] *a* unerschrocken, furchtlos.
unappealable ['ʌnə'pi:ləbl]: *the case is ~* es kann keine Berufung eingelegt werden.
unappeasable ['ʌnə'pi:zəbl] nicht zu beruhigen(d); unversöhnlich.
unappetizing ['ʌn'æpitaiziŋ] unappetitlich.
unappreci|able [ʌnə'pri:ʃəbl] unschätzbar; unmerklich; **~ated** ['ʌnə'pri:ʃieitid] *a* nicht geschätzt.
unapproachable [ʌnə'proutʃəbl] unzugänglich, fern; unerreichbar.
unappropriated ['ʌnə'prouprieitid] *a* herrenlos; *(Gewinn)* (noch) nicht ausgeschüttet; ungenutzt; *(Kapital)* tot.
unapt ['ʌn'æpt] ungeeignet, unbrauchbar, untauglich (*for* für, zu); unpassend; ungeschickt, schwerfällig (*at* bei); *to be ~ to* nicht geneigt zu.
unargued ['ʌn'ɑ:gju:d] *a* ohne Debatte (angenommen).
unarmed ['ʌn'ɑ:md] *a* unbewaffnet.
unartistic ['ʌnɑ:'tistik] unkünstlerisch.
unascertain|able ['ʌnæsə'teinəbl] nicht feststellbar; **~ed** ['-d] *a* unermittelt, nicht festgestellt.
unashamed ['ʌnə'ʃeimd] *a* ungeniert; schamlos; *to be ~ of s.th.* sich e-r S nicht schämen.
unasked ['ʌn'ɑ:skt] *a* ungefragt; ungebeten.
unaspir|ated ['ʌn'æspəreitid] *a* nicht begehrt; *gram* nicht aspiriert; **~ing** ['-'pairiŋ] *a* bescheiden.
unassailable [ʌnə'seiləbl] unangreifbar *a. fig.*
unassignable ['ʌnə'sainəbl] *jur* nicht übertragbar.
unassisted ['ʌnə'sistid] *a* ohne Hilfe, ohne Unterstützung, allein.
unassuming ['ʌnə'sju:miŋ] anspruchslos, zurückhaltend, bescheiden.
unattached ['ʌnə'tætʃt] *a* unbefestigt, lose (*to* an); ungebunden, unabhängig, frei; ohne Anhang; *mil* zur Disposition (stehend); *(Student)* nicht inkorporiert.
unattainable ['ʌnə'teinəbl] unerreichbar.
unattempted ['ʌnə'temptid] *a* unversucht.
unattended ['ʌnə'tendid] *a* ohne Bedienung *od* Pflege; *(to)* vernachlässigt; *(Kinder)* unbeaufsichtigt; unbegleitet.
unattested ['ʌnə'testid] *a* unbezeugt; nicht überprüft.
unattractive [ʌnə'træktiv] nicht, wenig anziehend.
unauthenticated ['ʌnɔ:'θentikeitid] *a* unbeglaubigt, unbestätigt, unverbürgt.
unauthorized ['ʌn'ɔ:θəraizd] *a* unberechtigt, unbefugt, nicht ermächtigt; *~* **persons** *pl* Unbefugte *m pl.*
unavail|able ['ʌnə'veiləbl] nicht vorhanden *od* verfügbar *od* erreichbar; **~ing** ['-iŋ] nutzlos, unnütz, vergeblich.
unavoidable [ʌnə'vɔidəbl] unvermeidlich; *~* **cost** feste Kosten *pl.*
unawakened ['ʌnə'weikənd] *a* noch schlafend; *fig* latent.
unaware ['ʌnə'wɛə] *a* unbewußt (*of s.th.* e-r S); nicht ahnend (*of s.th.* etw); unaufmerksam, unachtsam, gedankenlos; *to be ~ of* nicht ahnen; nicht wissen; **~s** ['-z] *adv* ahnungslos, unabsichtlich; versehentlich; unversehens, unerwartet, (ganz) plötzlich; *to catch, to take ~~* überraschen.
unbacked ['ʌn'bækt] *a* nicht unterstützt; *fin* nicht indossiert; *(Pferd)* nicht zugeritten; *~* **horse** Pferd *n*, auf das keine Wette abgeschlossen wurde.
unbag ['ʌn'bæg] *tr* aus dem Sack lassen; ausschütten.
unbaked ['ʌn'beikt] *a* ungar; *fig* unreif.
unbalanc|e ['ʌn'bæləns] *tr* aus dem Gleichgewicht bringen *a. fig*; *s* Unausgeglichenheit *f*; **~ed** ['-t] *a* nicht im Gleichgewicht; *fig u. com* unausgeglichen; *fig* verwirrt.
unbaptized ['ʌnbæp'taizd] *a* ungetauft.
unbar ['ʌn'bɑ:] *tr* aufschließen.
unbearable [ʌn'bɛərəbl] unerträglich.
unbeaten ['ʌn'bi:tn] *a* ungeschlagen *a. fig*; *fig* unbesiegt; *(Weg)* unbetreten.
unbecoming ['ʌnbi'kʌmiŋ] unangebracht, unpassend, unkleidsam; *fig* unschicklich, ungehörig (*to, for* für).
unbefitting ['ʌnbi'fitiŋ] unpassend, ungeeignet.
unbefriended ['ʌnbi'frendid] *a* ohne Freund; verlassen, einsam; hilflos.
unbeknown(st *fam*) ['ʌnbi'noun(st)] *pred a fam* unbekannt (*to s.o.* jdm).
unbelie|f ['ʌnbi'li:f] *rel* Unglaube(n) *m*; **~vable** [-vəbl] unglaublich; **~ver** ['ʌnbi'li:və] *rel* Ungläubige(r), Glaubenslose(r); *allg* Zweifler *m*; **~ing** ['-'li:viŋ] ungläubig; skeptisch, zweifelnd.
unbend ['ʌn'bend] *irr s. bend tr* lockern, entspannen *a. fig*; glattstreichen, glätten; *mar (Seil)* lockern; *(Segel)* abschlagen; *itr* gerade werden, sich glätten; *fig* sich entspannen; aus sich herausgehen; **~ing** ['-iŋ] *a* starr, steif, unbiegsam; *fig* fest, entschlossen.
unbias(s)ed ['ʌn'baiəst] *a* vorurteilsfrei, unvoreingenommen, unbefangen, unparteiisch.
unbidden ['ʌn'bidn] *a* ungebeten; unbestellt.
unbind ['ʌn'baind] *irr s. bind tr* losbinden, -machen, lösen; aufknoten; befreien.
unbleached ['ʌn'bli:tʃt] *a* ungebleicht.
unblemished [ʌn'blemiʃt] *a fig* unbefleckt, untadelig.
unblessed, unblest ['ʌn'blest] *a* ungeweiht; ungesegnet; verflucht, böse; unselig, unglücklich, elend.
unblushing [ʌn'blʌʃiŋ] *fig* schamlos.
unbolt ['ʌn'boult] *tr* aufriegeln, -schließen, öffnen; *(Gewehr)* entsichern; **~ed** ['-id] *a* **1.** unverriegelt, unverschlossen, offen; **2.** *(Mehl)* ungebeutelt.
unborn ['ʌn'bɔ:n] *a* ungeboren; *fig* (zu)künftig.
unbosom [ʌn'buzəm] *tr* erzählen, enthüllen, freien Lauf lassen (*o.'s feelings* s-n Gefühlen); *itr* u. *to ~ o.s.* sein Herz ausschütten (*to s.o.* jdm).
unbound ['ʌn'baund, *attr a.* 'ʌnbaund] *a (Buch)* ungebunden, broschiert, geheftet; *fig* ohne Verpflichtung.
unbounded [ʌn'baundid] *a* unbegrenzt; *fig* grenzen-, schrankenlos.
unbowed ['ʌn'baud] *a* nicht gebogen; *fig* ungebeugt.
unbraid ['ʌn'breid] *tr* aufflechten.
unbreakable ['ʌn'breikəbl] unzerbrechlich.
unbribable ['ʌn'braibəbl] unbestechlich.
unbridled [ʌn'braidld] *a* ungezäumt; *fig* zügellos, unbeherrscht; *~~ tongue* lose(s) Mundwerk *n.*
unbroken ['ʌn'broukən] *a* unge-, unzerbrochen, heil, ganz; *fig* ungebrochen, gleichbleibend; ununterbrochen; intakt, unbeschädigt; *agr* nicht umgebrochen; *(Pferd)* nicht zugeritten.
unbrotherly ['ʌn'brʌðəli] unbrüderlich.
unbuckle ['ʌn'bʌkl] *tr* auf-, los-, abschnallen.
unburden [ʌn'bə:dn] *tr* entlasten *a. fig*; *fig* sich frei machen, sich befreien von, sich erleichtern um; *to ~ o.s.* sein Herz ausschütten.
unburied ['ʌn'berid] *a* unbegraben.
unbusinesslike [ʌn'biznislaik] nicht geschäftstüchtig.
unbutton ['ʌn'bʌtn] *tr* aufknöpfen; **~ed** ['-d] *a fig* zwanglos.

*

uncage ['ʌn'keidʒ] *tr* aus dem Käfig lassen, befreien *a. fig.*
uncalled ['ʌn'kɔ:ld] *a* ungerufen, unaufgefordert, uneingeladen; **~-for** ['-'k-] ungebeten, unverlangt, unangebracht, unverschämt; überflüssig.
uncanny [ʌn'kæni] unheimlich *a. fig.*
uncared-for ['ʌn'kɛədfɔ:] *a* vernachlässigt.
uncase ['ʌn'keis] *tr* herausnehmen; *(Schwert)* ziehen; *(Fahne)* entfalten.
unceasing [ʌn'si:ziŋ] unaufhörlich, pausenlos.
uncensored ['ʌn'sensəd] *a* unzensiert; ohne Einspruch.
unceremonious ['ʌnseri'mounjəs] zwanglos; unfreundlich.
uncert|ain [ʌn'sə:tn] ungewiß, unbestimmt *(a. Wetter)*, unsicher, problematisch, fraglich, zweifelhaft; vage, ungenau; unzuverlässig, wechselhaft, unbeständig *(a. Wetter)*; *in no ~~ terms* unverblümt, klipp u. klar; **~ainty** [-tnti] Ungewißheit, Unbestimmtheit, Unsicherheit, Fragwürdigkeit; Unzuverlässigkeit, Unbeständigkeit *f*; **~ified** ['-ifaid] *a* unbeglaubigt, unbestätigt.
unchain ['ʌn'tʃein] *tr* losketten; *fig* entfesseln.
unchalleng|eable ['ʌn'tʃælindʒəbl] unbestreitbar, unwiderlegbar, -lich; **~ed** ['-d] *a* unbestritten, unangefochten, unbeanstandet.
unchangeable [ʌn'tʃeindʒəbl] unveränderlich; **~ing** [ʌn'tʃeindʒiŋ] (immer) gleichbleibend.
uncharged ['ʌn'tʃɑ:dʒd] *a* un-, nicht belastet; *jur* nicht angeklagt; *el* ungeladen; *(Konto)* unbelastet.
uncharitable [ʌn'tʃæritəbl] streng, unbarmherzig, lieblos, kalt.
uncharted ['ʌn'tʃɑ:tid] *a* kartographisch (noch) nicht erfaßt.
unchast|e ['ʌn'tʃeist] unkeusch; **~ity** ['-'tʃæstiti] Unkeuschheit *f.*
unchecked ['ʌn'tʃekt] *a* unbe-, ungehindert; unkontrolliert.
unchivalrous ['ʌn'ʃivəlrəs] unritterlich.
unchristian ['ʌn'kristjən] unchristlich *a. fig.*
uncial ['ʌnsiəl, -ʃ-] *a* Unzial-; *s* Unziale, Unzialschrift *f.*
uncircumcised ['ʌn'sə:kəmsaizd] *a rel* unbeschnitten.

uncivil ['ʌn'sivl] ungesittet, roh; unhöflich, ungeschliffen; **~ized** ['-ilaizd] *a* barbarisch, wild, roh, ungesittet; ungebildet.
unclad ['ʌn'klæd] *a* unbekleidet, nackt.
unclaimed ['ʌn'kleimd] *a* nicht bestellt, unverlangt; herrenlos; *(Brief)* nicht abgeholt, unzustellbar.
unclasp ['ʌn'klɑːsp] *tr* auf-, loshaken; loslassen; öffnen; *itr* aufgehen, sich lösen.
unclassified ['ʌn'klæsifaid] *a* unklassifiziert, nicht geordnet; *mil* nicht geheim, offen.
uncle ['ʌŋkl] Onkel; *sl* Pfandleiher *m*.
unclean ['ʌn'kliːn] *a*. *fig rel* unrein.
unclench, unclinch ['ʌn'klentʃ, -i-] *tr itr (die Faust)* (sich) öffnen.
uncloak ['ʌn'klouk] *tr* den Mantel ausziehen (*s.o.* jdm); *fig* freilegen; enthüllen, entlarven; *itr* sich den Mantel ausziehen.
unclose ['ʌn'klouz] *tr* öffnen; *fig* enthüllen, offenbaren; *itr* sich öffnen.
uncloth|e ['ʌn'klouð] *tr* entkleiden, ausziehen, entblößen; *fig* enthüllen; **~ed** ['-d] *a* unbekleidet.
unclouded ['ʌn'klaudid] *a* unbewölkt, wolkenlos; *fig* unbekümmert.

*

uncocked ['ʌn'kɔkt] *a (Gewehr)* entspannt.
uncoil ['ʌn'kɔil] *tr itr* (sich) abwickeln, abspulen.
uncollected ['ʌnkə'lektid] ungesammelt; *(Gebühren)* nicht erhoben.
uncolo(u)red ['ʌn'kʌləd] *a* ungefärbt, farblos; *fig* ungeschminkt.
un-come-at-able ['ʌnkʌm'ætəbl] *fam* unzugänglich; unerreichbar.
uncomely ['ʌn'kʌmli] unschön, häßlich.
uncomfortable [ʌn'kʌmfətəbl] unbehaglich; unangenehm; verlegen; *to be ~* sich nicht wohl fühlen.
uncommercial ['ʌnkə'məːʃəl] unkaufmännisch.
uncommitted ['ʌnkə'mitid] *a (Verbrechen)* nicht begangen; nicht verpflichtet (*to* zu); nicht gebunden (*to* an); ungebunden, frei; auf freiem Fuß; *pol* bündnis-, blockfrei.
uncommon [ʌn'kɔmən] *a* ungewöhnlich, selten; *adv fam* außergewöhnlich, außerordentlich, selten; **~ly** [-li] *adv* bemerkenswert, ungewöhnlich.
uncommunic|able ['ʌnkə'mjuːnikəbl] nicht mitteilbar; **~ative** ['-ətiv] nicht, wenig mitteilsam; zurückhaltend.
uncomplaining ['ʌnkəm'pleiniŋ] nicht klagend; klaglos.
uncompleted ['ʌnkəm'pliːtid] *a* unfertig, unvollendet.
uncomplicated ['ʌn'kɔmplikeitid] *a* unkompliziert, einfach.
uncompromising [ʌn'kɔmprəmaiziŋ] nicht kompromißbereit, unnachgiebig, unbeugsam; (fest) entschlossen, entschieden.
unconcern ['ʌnkən'səːn] Interesselosigkeit, Sorglosigkeit, Gleichgültigkeit *f*; **~ed** ['-d] *a* interesselos, uninteressiert (*with* an); gleichgültig, teilnahmslos (*about* an).
uncondition|al ['ʌnkən'diʃənl] bedingungs-, vorbehaltlos; uneingeschränkt; **~ed** ['-ʃnd] *a* nicht bedingt; *psychol* unbedingt, angeboren.
unconfined ['ʌnkən'faind] *a* uneingeschränkt, unbegrenzt.
unconfirmed ['ʌnkən'fəːmd] *a* unbestätigt, unverbürgt; *rel* nicht konfirmiert, nicht gefirmt.
uncongenial ['ʌnkən'dʒiːnjəl] ungleichartig; ungünstig; fremd(artig), unsympathisch.
unconnected ['ʌnkə'nektid] *a* unverbunden, getrennt; *(Bericht)* unzs.hängend.
unconquerable [ʌn'kɔŋkərəbl] unbesiegbar; unüberwindlich.
unconscionable [ʌn'kɔnʃnəbl] gewissen-, skrupellos; unvernünftig, maßlos, unmäßig, übertrieben; *jur* unbillig.
unconscious [ʌn'kɔnʃəs] *a* unbewußt (*of s.th.* e-r S) *a. psychol*; unabsichtlich; bewußtlos, ohnmächtig; *s psychol das* Unbewußte; *to be ~ of s.th.* sich e-r S nicht bewußt sein; **~ly** [-li] *adv* unbewußt; **~ness** [-nis] Unbewußtheit; *med* Bewußtlosigkeit, Ohnmacht *f*.
unconsecrated ['ʌn'kɔnsikreitid] *a* ungeweiht.
unconsidered ['ʌnkən'sidəd] *a* unbedacht, gedankenlos; unbeachtet.
unconstitutional ['ʌnkɔnsti'tjuːʃənl] verfassungswidrig.
unconstrained ['ʌnkən'streind] *a* ungezwungen, zwanglos.
uncontaminated ['ʌnkən'tæmineitid] *a* nicht verunreinigt; nicht angesteckt; *fig* unverdorben.
uncontested ['ʌnkən'testid] *a* unbestritten; *(Wahl)* ohne Gegenkandidaten.
uncontradict|able ['ʌnkɔntrə'diktəbl] unbestreitbar; **~ed** ['-id] *a* unwidersprochen, unbestritten.
uncontroll|able [ʌnkən'trouləbl] unkontrollierbar; unbändig; **~ed** ['ʌnkən'trould] *a* unbeaufsichtigt; zügellos.
unconventional ['ʌnkən'venʃənl] unkonventionell, formlos, ungezwungen.
unconvert|ed ['ʌnkən'vəːtid] *a rel* unbekehrt; *fin* nicht konvertiert; **~ible** ['-ibl] nicht vertauschbar; *fin* nicht konvertierbar.
unconvinc|ed ['ʌnkən'vinst] *a* nicht überzeugt; **~ing** ['-siŋ] nicht überzeugend.
uncooked ['ʌn'kukt] *a* ungar, roh.
uncork ['ʌn'kɔːk] *tr* entkorken.
uncorrected ['ʌnkə'rektid] *a* unverbessert, unkorrigiert.
uncorrupt|(ed) ['ʌnkə'rʌpt(id)] *a* unverdorben; unbestochen; **~ible** ['-ibl] unbestechlich.
uncountable ['ʌn'kauntəbl] unzählbar, unzählig.
uncouple ['ʌn'kʌpl] *tr (Hunde)* loskoppeln; *tech* auskuppeln, -rücken; *el* trennen, ausschalten.
uncourt|eous ['ʌn'kəːtjəs] *a* unhöflich; **~ly** ['ʌn'kəːtli] *adv* unhöflich.
uncouth [ʌn'kuːθ] ungeschlacht; ungeschickt, unbeholfen; ungebildet.
uncover [ʌn'kʌvə] *tr* auf-, abdecken; *(das Haupt)* entblößen; *(Hut)* abnehmen; *fig* enthüllen, aufdecken.
uncritical ['ʌn'kritikəl] unkritisch.
uncrowned ['ʌn'kraund, *attr* '--] *a* ungekrönt, ohne Krone.
unct|ion ['ʌŋkʃən] *rel* Salbung; *med* Einreibung *f*; *rel* Salböl *n*; *med* Salbe *f*, Einreibmittel *n*; *fig* Trost *m*, Erleichterung (*to* für); salbungsvolle Ausdrucksweise *f*; Pathos *n*; *with (much) ~~* (sehr) salbungsvoll; *the Extreme U~~ (rel)* die Letzte Ölung; **~uous** ['ʌŋktjuəs] ölig, fett(ig); *fig* salbungsvoll.
uncult|ivated ['ʌn'kʌltiveitid] *a (Boden)* unbebaut, unbestellt; *(Pflanze)* wild; *fig* ungepflegt, vernachlässigt; **~ured** ['ʌn'kʌltʃəd] *a* ungebildet, unkultiviert *a. agr*.
uncurbed ['ʌn'kəːbd] *a* unverbogen, gerade; *fig* zügellos.
uncurl ['ʌn'kəːl] *tr itr* entkräuseln, (sich) glätten.
uncut ['ʌn'kʌt] *a (Haare)* ungeschnitten; *(Buch)* unbeschnitten; *(Stein)* ungeschliffen; *fig* ungekürzt.
undamaged ['ʌn'dæmidʒd] *a* unbeschädigt.
undamped ['ʌn'dæmpt] *a fig* unentwegt, nicht entmutigt; *mus el* ungedämpft.
undated ['ʌndeitid] *a* **1.** gewellt, wellig; **2.** ['-'--] undatiert, ohne Datum.
undaunted [ʌn'dɔːntid] *a* unerschrocken, furchtlos.
undazzled ['ʌn'dæzld] *a* ungeblendet.
undeceive ['ʌndi'siːv] *tr*: *to ~ s.o.* jdm die Augen öffnen, jdm reinen *od* klaren Wein einschenken (*of s.th.* über etw).
undecided ['ʌndi'saidid] *a* unentschieden; unschlüssig, unentschlossen, schwankend.
undecipherable ['ʌndi'saifərəbl] unentzifferbar; rätselhaft.
undeclared ['ʌndi'klɛəd] *a* nicht erklärt; *(Zoll)* nicht deklariert.
undefended ['ʌndi'fendid] *a* unverteidigt *a. jur*.
undefiled ['ʌndi'faild] *a fig* unbefleckt, fleckenlos, rein.
undefin|able [ʌndi'fainəbl] unbestimmbar, undefinierbar; **~ed** [-d] *a* nicht abgegrenzt; unbestimmt.
undeliverable ['ʌndi'livərəbl] *(Post)* unzustellbar.
undemonstrative ['ʌndi'mɔnstrətiv] zurückhaltend.
undeniable [ʌndi'naiəbl] unleugbar.
undenominational ['ʌndinɔmi'neiʃənl] an keine (bestimmte) Konfession gebunden, interkonfessionell; **~ school** Gemeinschaftsschule *f*.
under ['ʌndə] **1.** *prp* unter *a. fig*; unterhalb *gen*; am Fuße *gen*; unter ... her; *(zeitlich)* unter, während; unter, weniger als; geringer als; *(Acker)* bestellt mit; *jur* gemäß, laut, nach; *from ~* unter ... hervor; *~ an act* auf Grund e-s Gesetzes; *~ age* unmündig, minderjährig; *~ an alias (fig)* unter falscher Flagge *od* falschem Namen; *~ an anaesthetic* in Narkose; *~ o.'s breath* flüsternd, leise; *~ these circumstances, conditions* unter diesen Umständen *od* Bedingungen; *~ construction* im Bau (befindlich); *~ cover* geschützt; im Umschlag; *~ separate cover* mit getrennter Post; *~ discussion* zur Debatte; *~ s.o.'s (very) eyes* vor jds (eigenen) Augen; *~ fire (mil)* unter Feuer; *~ the impression* unter dem Eindruck; *~ the lee of* im Windschatten *gen*; *~ lock and key* hinter Schloß u. Riegel; *~ a mistake* im Irrtum; *~ s.o.'s name* unter jds Namen; *~ oath* unter Eid; *~ pain of death* bei Todesstrafe; *~ repair* in Reparatur; *~ sail* unter Segel; *~ sentence of death* zum Tode verurteilt; *~ s.o.'s signature* mit jds Unterschrift; *~ treatment* in Behandlung; *~ the treaty* laut Vertrag; *~ way (mar)* in Fahrt, unterwegs; *to be ~ control* in Ordnung sein, *fam* klappen; *to be ~ the impression* den Eindruck haben (*that* daß); *to come ~ s.th.* unter etw fallen; **2.** *adv* unten; nach unten; (dar)unter; *to be snowed ~ (fig)* überhäuft sein; mit großer Mehrheit überstimmt werden; *to go ~* scheitern; fallen, sinken; *(Firma)* eingehen; *to knuckle ~ (fam)* klein beigeben, sich fügen; **3.** *a* unter; Unter-; *pred* geringer; *pred* untergeordnet; *in Zssgen* Unter-, unter-; Minder-, minder-.
under|act ['ʌndər'ækt] *tr itr* verhalten, schlecht spielen; **~bid** ['-'bid] *irr s. bid*

tr com unterbieten *a. Bridge*; **~bred** ['-'bred] *a* schlecht erzogen, ungebildet; *(Tier)* nicht reinrassig; **~brush** ['-brʌʃ] Unterholz *n*; **~carriage** ['-kæridʒ] *mot* Fahrgestell, *aero* -werk *n*; **~charge** ['-'tʃɑ:dʒ] *tr* zu wenig berechnen (*s.o.* jdm); ungenügend (be)laden; *s* ungenügende Ladung, zu geringe Berechnung *f*; **~clothes** ['-klouðz] *pl*, **~clothing** ['-klouðiŋ] Unterkleidung; Unter-, Leibwäsche *f*; **~coat** ['-kout] Unterjacke *f*; *zoo* Flaum-, Wollhaare *n pl*; *tech* Grundanstrich *m*; **~cover** ['-kʌvə] geheim; *~~ agent* Spitzel, Geheimagent *m*; *~~ payments (pl)* Bestechungsgelder *n pl*; **~croft** ['-krɔft] *arch* Krypta *f*; **~current** ['-kʌrənt] Unterströmung *f a. fig*; **~cut** ['-'kʌt] *irr s. cut* unterhöhlen; *com* unterbieten; *s* ['--] (Rinder-)Filet *n*; *(Boxen)* Körperhaken *m*; **~developed** ['-di'veləpt] *a* unterentwickelt; **~dog** ['-dɔg] *fig* Verlierer, Benachteiligte(r), Unterlegene(r) *m*; **~done** ['-'dʌn, *attr* '--] *a* nicht gar; **~estimate** ['-ər'estimeit] *tr* unterschätzen; *s* ['-mit] Unterbewertung, Unterschätzung *f*; **~expose** ['-əriks'pouz] *tr phot* unterbelichten; **~exposure** ['-ə riks'pouʒə] *phot* Unterbelichtung *f*; **~fed** ['-'fed] *a* unterernährt; **~feeding** ['-'fi:diŋ] Unterernährung *f*; **~foot** [-'fut] *adv* am Boden (liegend), im Wege; **~garment** ['-gɑ:mənt] Unterkleid *n*, Leibwäsche *f*; **~go** [-'gou] *irr s. go tr* erfahren, erleben; durchmachen, erdulden, erleiden; sich unterziehen (müssen) (*s.th.* e-r S); **~graduate** [-'grædjuit] Student(in *f*) *m (der ersten Semester)*.

under|ground ['ʌndəgraund] *s* Untergrund; unterirdische(r) Raum, Gang *m*; *fig (~~ movement)* Untergrund-, Widerstandsbewegung; *(~~ railway)* Untergrundbahn *f*; *a* unterirdisch, Untergrund-; *fig* geheim; *adv* [-'-] unter der Erdoberfläche, *min* unter Tage; *fig* insgeheim, im geheimen; *to travel by ~~* mit der U-Bahn fahren; *station on the ~~* U-Bahn-Station *f*; *~~ engineering* Tiefbau *m*; *~~ mining* Untertagebau *m*; *~~ shelter* Unterstand; Tiefbunker *m*; *~~ water* Grundwasser *n*; **~growth** ['-grouθ] Unterholz *n*; **~hand** ['-hænd] *a* heimlich, geheim; trügerisch, täuschend; *adv* im geheimen; hinterhältig; **~handed** ['-hændid] *a* heimlich; *com* knapp an Arbeitskräften; **~hung** ['-'hʌŋ] *a med* mit vorstehendem Unterkiefer; **~lay** [-'lei] *irr s. lay tr* unterlegen (*with* mit); (dar)unterlegen; absteifen, -stützen; *typ* zurichten; *s* ['--] *typ* Zurichten *n*; **~-lease** ['-li:s] Unterverpachtung, -miete *f*; **~let** ['-'let] *irr s. let tr* weitervermieten, -verpachten; zu billig vermieten, verpachten; **~lie** [-'lai] *irr s. lie tr* liegen unter; zugrunde liegen (*s.th.* e-r S); die Grundlage bilden (*s.th.* für etw); **~line** [-'lain] *tr* unterstreichen *a. fig*; *fig* betonen, hervorheben; *theat* vorankündigen; *s* ['--] Unterstreichung *f*; Bildtext *m*; *theat* Vorankündigung *f (am unteren Ende e-s Theaterzettels)*; *pl* Linienblatt *n*; **~linen** ['-linin] Unter-, Leibwäsche *f*; **~ling** ['-liŋ] Untergebene(r), kleine(r) Angestellte(r), Handlanger *m*; **~lying** [-'laiiŋ] *a* zugrunde liegend; *fig* grundlegend; *fin* Vorrang-; **~manned** ['-'mænd] *a* ungenügend bemannt; **~mentioned** ['-'menʃənd] *a* unten erwähnt; **~mine** [-'main] *tr* unterminieren; auswaschen; *fig* untergraben, (unmerklich) schwächen; **~most** ['-moust] *a* unterst; *adv* zuunterst; **~neath** [-'ni:θ] *adv* unten, darunter; unterhalb; *prp* unter(halb); **~nourished** ['-'nʌriʃt] *a* unterernährt; **~pass** ['-pɑ:s] *Am* Unterführung *f*; **~pay** ['-'pei] *irr s. pay tr* unterbezahlen; **~pin** [-'pin] *tr* abstützen, -steifen, untermauern, -fangen; *fig* stützen, bekräftigen; *~pinning arch* Unterfangung, Untermauerung; *fig* Stütze *f*; *pl fam* Beine *n pl*, Fahrgestell *n*; **~populated** ['-'pɔpjuleitid] *a* dünn besiedelt; **~privileged** ['-'privilidʒd] *a* benachteiligt; schlecht(er) gestellt; *the ~~* die Entrechteten *m pl*; **~production** ['-prə'dʌkʃən] *com* Unterproduktion *f*; **~quote** ['-'kwout] *tr* niedriger berechnen; **~rate** [-'reit] *tr* unterschätzen *a. fig*; **~score** [-'skɔ:] *tr* unterstreichen; *fig* hervorheben, betonen; *s* ['--] Unterstreichung *f*; **~sea** ['-si:] *a* unterseeisch; Untersee-; *adv u.* *~~s* [-'si:z] *adv* unter der Meeresoberfläche; **~secretary** ['-'sekrətəri] *pol* Unterstaatssekretär *m*; **~sell** ['-'sel] *irr s. sell tr* unterbieten; verschleudern; unter dem Preis verkaufen; **~shirt** ['-ʃə:t] Unterhemd *n*, -jacke *f*; **~shoot** ['-'ʃu:t] *tr aero* zu kurz hereinkommen; **~shot** ['-ʃɔt] *a (Wasserrad)* unterschlächtig; **~signed** [-'saind] *a* unterzeichnet; *s* ['--] Unterzeichnete(r) *m*; **~sized** ['-'saizd] *a* unter Normalgröße; verkrüppelt, winzig; **~skirt** ['-skə:t] Unterrock *m*; **~staffed** ['-'stɑ:ft] *a* unterbesetzt; *to be ~~* an Personalmangel leiden.

understand [ʌndə'stænd] *irr s. stand tr* verstehen (*by* unter); begreifen, einsehen; annehmen, voraussetzen; entnehmen, schließen (*from* aus); erklären, deuten, auslegen; an-, hinnehmen; (sich) hinzudenken; hören, vernehmen, erfahren, in Erfahrung bringen; sich verstehen auf, sich auskennen in; können, beherrschen, verstehen *(Sprache)*; *itr* Verständnis, Einsicht haben; Bescheid wissen; *to ~ one another* sich, ea. (gut) verstehen; *to give s.o. to ~* jdm zu verstehen geben; *to make o.s. understood* sich verständlich machen; *I ~* wie ich höre; *it's understood* es ist selbstverständlich, es versteht sich von selbst (*that* daß); *(now) ~ me* verstehen Sie mich recht, hören Sie mal; **~able** [-əbl] verständlich; deutlich, klar; einzusehen(d); **~ing** [-iŋ] *s* Verstehen, Begreifen *n*, Einsicht *f*; Können; Verständnis *n* (*of* für); Einsicht *f* (*of* in); Einfühlungsvermögen *n*; Geist, Verstand *m*; Auffassung, Auslegung, Deutung; Absprache *f*, Übereinkommen *n*, Verständigung *f*, Einverständnis, Einvernehmen *n* (*between* zwischen); *pl sl* Beine *n pl*, Füße, Schuhe, Stiefel *m pl*; *a* verständnis-, einsichtsvoll, einsichtig, verständig, klug; *on this ~~* unter dieser Voraussetzung; *on the ~~ that* unter der Voraussetzung, daß; *without ~~* verständnislos; *to come to, to reach an ~~* zu e-r Verständigung kommen *od* gelangen (*with* mit); sich einigen; *to disturb the (good) ~~* das (gute) Einvernehmen stören (*between* zwischen).

under|state ['ʌndə'steit] *tr* zu niedrig angeben; abschwächen; untertreiben; **~statement** ['-'steitmənt] zu niedrige Angabe; Untertreibung *f*; **~stocked** ['-stɔkt] *a* ungenügend mit Waren versorgt; **~strapper** ['-stræpə] *fig* kleine(r) Mann; Untergebene(r) *m*; **~study** ['-stʌdi] *s theat* Ersatzdarsteller; *allg* Ersatzmann *m*; *itr tr* Ersatzdarsteller sein (für); einspringen für; als E. einstudieren.

undertak|e [ʌndə'teik] *irr s. take tr (Aufgabe, Verantwortung)* übernehmen; *(Pflicht)* auf sich nehmen; *(Risiko)* eingehen; es übernehmen, sich verpflichten (*to do* zu tun); sich verbürgen, bestätigen, versprechen, garantieren; *(Arbeit, Reise)* unternehmen; **~er** ['ʌndəteikə] Leichenbestatter *m*; **~ing** [-iŋ] Übernahme, Verpflichtung; Bürgschaft, Sicherheitsleistung *f*; Unternehmen *n*, Betrieb *m*; ['ʌndəteikiŋ] Beerdigungsinstitut *n*.

under|tenant ['ʌndə'tenənt] Untermieter *m*; **~tone** ['-toun] schwache(r) Ton *m od* Stimme *f*; matte(r) Farbton; *fig* Unterton; *(Börse)* Grundton *m*, Tendenz *f*; *to talk in ~~s* mit gedämpfter Stimme reden; **~tow** ['-tou] *mar* Sog *m*; **~valuation** ['-vælju'eiʃən] zu niedrige Schätzung; *fig* Unterschätzung, -bewertung *f*; **~value** ['-'vælju:] *tr* zu niedrig schätzen, unterbewerten; *fig* unterschätzen; den Wert verringern (*s.th.* e-r S); **~vest** ['-vest] Unterhemd *n*; **~wear** ['-wɛə] Unterkleidung, -wäsche *f*; **~weight** ['-weit] Untergewicht *n*, Gewichtsausfall *m*; **~wood** ['-wud] Gestrüpp, Unterholz *n*; **~world** ['-wə:ld] Unterwelt *f*; **~write** [-'rait, '--] *irr s. write tr* unterschreiben; *(Summe)* zeichnen; bestellen; unterschreiben, gutheißen, billigen; die Haftung übernehmen für; *fin* gutsagen für; *(Versicherung)* übernehmen, abschließen; **~writer** ['-raitə] Garant; Versicherungsagent, Versicherer *m*; **~writing** ['-raitiŋ] Übernahme *f* von (See-)Versicherungen.

undescribable ['ʌndis'kraibəbl] unbeschreiblich.

undeserv|ed ['ʌndi'zə:vd] unverdient; **~ing** ['-iŋ] unwürdig; schuldlos; *to be ~~ s.th.* etw nicht verdient haben.

undesign|ed ['ʌndi'zaind] *a* unbeabsichtigt; **~ing** ['-iŋ] gerade, offen, ehrlich.

undesirab|ility ['ʌndizaiərə'biliti] Unerwünschtheit *f*; **~le** ['ʌndi'zaiərəbl] *a* nicht erwünscht, unerwünscht; *s* unerwünschte Person *f*.

undetected ['ʌndi'tektid] *a* unentdeckt.

undetermin|able ['ʌndi'tə:minəbl] unbestimmbar; **~ate** ['-it], **~ed** ['-nd] *a* unbestimmt; unentschlossen; **~ation** ['ʌnditə:mi'neiʃən] Unbestimmtheit; Unentschlossenheit *f*.

undeterred ['ʌndi'tə:d] *a* nicht abgeschreckt (*by* von).

undeveloped ['ʌndi'veləpt] *a* unentwickelt; *com* unerschlossen.

undeviating [ʌn'di:vieitiŋ] nicht abweichend *a. fig*, gerade; beständig.

undies ['ʌndiz] *pl fam (Damen-)* Unterwäsche *f*.

undifferentiated ['ʌndifə'renʃieitid] *a* undifferenziert, nicht (genau) unterschieden.

undigest|ed ['ʌndi'dʒestid] *a* unverdaut *a. fig*; *fig* verworren; **~ible** ['-ibl] unverdaulich.

undignified [ʌn'dignifaid] *a* unwürdig (*by*, *with s.th.* e-r S).

undiminish|able ['ʌndi'miniʃəbl] unverminderbar; **~ed** ['-ʃt] *a* unvermindert.

undimmed ['ʌn'dimd] *a* ungetrübt; *(Scheinwerfer)* nicht abgeblendet.

undiplomatic ['ʌndiplə'mætik] undiplomatisch *a. fig*.

undirected ['ʌndi'rektid] *a* ungeleitet, ungeführt; unadressiert.

undiscern|ed ['ʌndi'sə:nd] *a* unbe-

merkt; **~ible** ['-ibl] unmerklich; **~ing** ['-iŋ] wenig scharfsinnig, urteilslos.
undischarged ['ʌndis'tʃɑːdʒd] *a* unbezahlt; unerledigt; nicht (von der Verpflichtung) befreit; *mil* nicht abgefeuert; *mar* nicht entladen; *com* nicht entlastet.
undisciplined [ʌn'disiplind] *a* undiszipliniert, zuchtlos; ungeschult, ungeübt.
undisclosed ['ʌndis'klouzd] *a* nicht enthüllt, nicht aufgedeckt; verheimlicht.
undiscouraged ['ʌndis'kʌridʒd] *a* nicht entmutigt.
undiscover|able ['ʌndis'kʌvərəbl] unauffindbar; **~ed** ['-əd] *a* unentdeckt; unbemerkt.
undiscriminating ['ʌndis'krimineitiŋ] *a* unterschiedslos; unkritisch.
undiscussed ['ʌndis'kʌst] *a* unerörtert.
undisguised ['ʌndis'gaizd] *a* unverstellt; unverkleidet; *fig* offen.
undismayed ['ʌndis'meid] *a* unerschrocken, unverzagt.
undisposed ['ʌndis'pouzd] *a*: *~-of* unvergeben, unverkauft; nicht geneigt zu, unwillig (*to do* zu tun); *it remains ~ of* es ist nicht darüber verfügt worden.
undisputed ['ʌndis'pjuːtid] *a* unbestritten.
undissolv|able ['ʌndi'zɔlvəbl] unauflöslich; **~ed** ['-d] *a* unaufgelöst.
undistinguish|able ['ʌndis'tiŋgwiʃəbl] nicht unterscheidbar (*from* von); undeutlich; **~ed** ['-t] *a* nicht unterschieden (*from* von); unbekannt.
undisturbed ['ʌndis'təːbd] *a* ungestört, ohne Störung; in (aller) Ruhe, gelassen.
undivided ['ʌndi'vaidid] *a* ungeteilt; *com* nicht verteilt; *(Verantwortung)* alleinig; *(Meinung)* einhellig.
undo ['ʌn'du] *irr s. do tr* aufmachen; *(Verschluß)* öffnen; *(Knoten)* lösen; *(Paket, Tür)* aufmachen, öffnen; aufknöpfen; zerstören, vernichten; *fam* rückgängig, ungeschehen machen, streichen; ein Ende machen mit, ruinieren; *what is done cannot be ~ne* geschehen ist geschehen; **~ing** ['-iŋ] Rückgängigmachung; Streichung; Vernichtung, Zerstörung *f*; Verderben, Unglück *n*; **~ne** ['-'dʌn] *a* vernichtet, zerstört, ruiniert; *(Arbeit)* unerledigt; *to come ~~* aufgehen; *to leave nothing ~~* nichts unversucht lassen.
undomesticated ['ʌndə'mestikeitid] *a* ungezähmt, wild.
undoubt|ed [ʌn'dautid] *a* unbestritten, unbezweifelt; **~edly** [-li] *adv* zweifellos, gewiß, sicher.
undramatic ['ʌndrə'mætik] undramatisch.
undream|ed, ~t [ʌn'dremt] *a*: *~~-of* ungeahnt, unerwartet.
undress ['ʌn'dres] *tr* entkleiden, ausziehen; des Schmuckes berauben; den Verband abnehmen (*a wound* von e-r Wunde); *itr* sich ausziehen, s-e Kleider ablegen; *s* Negligé, Hauskleid(ung *f*) *n*, Haus-, Schlaf-, Morgenrock; Straßenanzug *m*; *mil* Arbeitszeug *n*; **~ed** ['-t] *a* unbekleidet; im Negligé; *(Wunde)* unverbunden; *(Häute)* ungegerbt; *(Stein)* unbehauen.
undrinkable ['ʌn'driŋkəbl] nicht trinkbar; **~ water** kein Trinkwasser.
undu|e ['ʌn'djuː] *a fin* noch nicht fällig; unpassend; ungerecht(fertigt), unberechtigt; unzulässig; übermäßig, maßlos, unverschämt; *to use ~~ influence* e-n Druck ausüben (*on* auf).
undulat|e ['ʌndjuleit] *itr* wogen; wellig sein; *a* ['-it] *u.* **~ed** ['-eitid] *a* wellenförmig, gewellt, wellig; *~~ sheet iron* Wellblech *n*; **~ing** ['-iŋ] wogend; **~ion** [ʌndju'leiʃən] Wellenbewegung, -linie; Schwankung *f*; **~ory** ['-lətəri, -lei-] wellenförmig; Wellen-.
undutiful ['ʌn'djutiful] pflichtvergessen; unehrerbietig.
undyed ['ʌn'daid] *a* ungefärbt.
undying [ʌn'daiiŋ] unsterblich; nicht endend, unvergänglich, ewig.
unearned ['ʌn'əːnd] *a (Geld)* nicht verdient; *fig (Lob)* unverdient; **~ income** Kapitaleinkommen *n*; **~ increment** Wertzuwachs *m*.
unearth ['ʌn'əːθ] *tr* ausgraben; *fig* aufstöbern, ausfindig machen, entdecken; aufdecken, enthüllen; **~ly** [ʌn'əːθli] un-, überirdisch, übernatürlich, geisterhaft, gespenstisch; unheimlich, schauerlich; *fam* phantastisch, unvernünftig.
uneas|iness [ʌn'iːzinis] Aufgeregtheit, Unruhe; Verlegenheit *f*, Unbehagen *n*; **~y** [-i] ungeschickt, unbeholfen, linkisch; aufgeregt, unruhig (*about* wegen); besorgt (*about* um); verlegen; unsicher; unbehaglich; *to be ~~* sich in s-r Haut nicht wohl fühlen; *I feel ~~* mir ist unbehaglich (zumute) (*about s.th.* wegen etw).
uneat|able ['ʌn'iːtəbl] ungenießbar; **~en** ['-'iːtn] *a* ungegessen, ungenossen.
uneconomic(al) ['ʌniːkə'nɔmik(l)] unwirtschaftlich.
unedifying ['ʌn'edifaiiŋ] *fig* unerquicklich.
uneduc|able ['ʌn'edjukəbl] schwer erziehbar; **~ated** ['-eitid] *a* unerzogen, ungebildet.
unembarrassed ['ʌnim'bærəst] *a* unge-, unbehindert; ungezwungen, zwanglos, frei; ohne Geldsorgen.
unemotional ['ʌni'mouʃənl] leidenschaftslos, kühl, nüchtern, sachlich, trocken.
unemploy|able ['ʌnim'plɔiəbl] *a* unbrauchbar; *(Mensch)* arbeitsunfähig; *s* Arbeitsunfähige(r) *m*; **~ed** ['-ɔid] *a* unbeschäftigt; arbeitslos, stellenlos; unbe-, ungenutzt; *(Kapital)* tot; *the ~~ (pl)* die Arbeitslosen *m pl*; *~~ person* Arbeits-, Stellenlose(r) *m*; **~ment** ['-mənt] Erwerbs-, Arbeitslosigkeit *f*; *~~ assistance, benefit, compensation, pay, relief* Arbeitslosenunterstützung *f*; *~~ insurance* Arbeitslosenversicherung *f*.
unencumbered ['ʌnin'kʌmbəd] *a* unbehindert (*by* durch); unbelastet, hypothekenfrei.
unending [ʌn'endiŋ] endlos, unaufhörlich.
unendurable ['ʌnin'djuərəbl] unerträglich.
unenforceable ['ʌnin'fɔːsəbl] nicht erzwingbar; nicht vollstreckbar; nicht klagbar.
unengaged ['ʌnin'geidʒd] *a* nicht verpflichtet; ohne (dauernde) Beschäftigung; frei, verfügbar; nicht verlobt; *mil* nicht im Einsatz.
un-English ['ʌn'iŋglish] unenglisch.
unenlightened ['ʌnin'laitnd] *a fig* unaufgeklärt; ungebildet.
unenterprising ['ʌn'entəpraiziŋ] ohne Unternehmungslust.
unenviable ['ʌn'enviəbl] nicht zu beneiden(d), wenig beneidenswert.
unequal ['ʌn'iːkwəl] ungleich; unsymmetrisch; unausgeglichen; nicht gewachsen (*to a task* e-r Aufgabe); unbillig, ungerecht; *(Zahl)* ungerade; **~(l)ed** ['-d] *a* einzig(artig); beispiellos; unübertroffen; *to be ~~* seinesgleichen suchen.
unequivocal ['ʌni'kwivəkəl] unzweideutig; eindeutig.
unerring ['ʌn'əːriŋ] unfehlbar; untrüglich.
unescapable ['ʌnis'keipəbl] unentrinnbar; unausweichlich.
unessential ['ʌni'senʃəl] *a* unwesentlich, unbedeutend, belanglos; *s* Belanglosigkeit *f*.
uneven ['ʌn'iːvən] uneben; ungleich; *fig* uneinheitlich, schwankend, unausgeglichen; *(Zahl)* ung(e)rade; **~ness** ['-nis] Unebenheit, Unregelmäßigkeit; Unausgeglichenheit *f*.
uneventf[illegible] ['ʌni'ventful] ereignislos, still, ruhig.
unexaggerated ['ʌnig'zædʒəreitid] *a* nicht übertrieben.
unexampled ['ʌnig'zɑːmpld] *a* beispiellos, einzig (dastehend), einmalig.
unexception|able [ʌnik'sepʃnəbl] untadelig, tadellos, einwandfrei; **~al** ['-l] gewöhnlich; ausnahmslos; einwandfrei.
unexchangeable ['ʌniks'tʃeindʒəbl] nicht austauschbar, nicht auswechselbar.
unexciting ['ʌnik'saitiŋ] reizlos; langweilig.
unexhausted ['ʌnig'zɔːstid] *a* unerschöpflich.
unexpected ['ʌniks'pektid] *a* unerwartet, unvorhergesehen.
unexperienced ['ʌniks'piəriənst] *a* unerfahren; unerprobt.
unexpired ['ʌniks'paiəd] *a* noch nicht abgelaufen, noch gültig; noch nicht fällig.
unexplain|able ['ʌniks'pleinəbl] unerklärlich; **~ed** ['-d] *a* unerklärt.
unexplored ['ʌniks'plɔːd] *a* unerforscht.
unexpress|ed ['ʌniks'prest] nicht ausgedrückt; unausgesprochen; **~ive** ['-iv] wenig ausdrucksfähig, ausdruckslos.
unfad|able [ʌn'feidəbl] unverwelklich; **~ed** [-id] *a* unverwelkt *a. fig*; unverblichen, farbfrisch; **~ing** [-iŋ] bleibend, (farb)echt; unvergänglich.
unfailing [ʌn'feiliŋ] *a* unfehlbar; unerschöpflich; verläßlich, zuverlässig.
unfair ['ʌn'fɛə] unbillig, ungerecht; unsportlich, unfair; parteiisch; unredlich, unehrenhaft, anrüchig, unlauter (*to* gegenüber); **~ness** ['-nis] Unbilligkeit; Unredlichkeit *f*; unsportliche(s) Verhalten *n*.
unfaithful ['ʌn'feiθful] un(ge)treu, treulos; unzuverlässig; untreu (*to* gegenüber); **~ness** ['-nis] Treulosigkeit *f*.
unfaltering [ʌn'fɔːltəriŋ] nicht wankend, fest; *fig* unerschütterlich.
unfamiliar ['ʌnfə'miljə] ungewohnt, fremd(artig); nicht vertraut (*with* mit).
unfashionable ['ʌn'fæʃnəbl] unmodern.
unfasten ['ʌn'fɑːsn] *tr* los-, aufmachen.
unfathom|able [ʌn'fæðəməbl] unergründlich, unerforschlich; **~ed** [-d] *a* unergründet, unerforscht.
unfavo(u)rable ['ʌn'feivərəbl] ungünstig, unvorteilhaft (*for, to* für); widrig; *(Bilanz)* passiv.
unfeasible ['ʌn'fiːzibl] unaus-, undurchführbar.
unfeathered ['ʌn'feðəd] *a* ungefiedert; ohne Federn.
unfeeling [ʌn'fiːliŋ] fühl-, empfindungslos.
unfeigned [ʌn'feind] *a* unverstellt, echt, wirklich, aufrichtig, offen.
unfelt ['ʌn'felt] *a* ungefühlt.
unfeminine ['ʌn'feminin] unweiblich.
unfenced ['ʌn'fenst] *a* uneingefriedigt; unbefestigt.

unfermented ['ʌnfə(:)'mentid] *a (Getränk)* unvergoren.
unfetter ['ʌn'fetə] *tr* losketten; *fig* befreien; **~ed** ['-d] *fig* frei.
unfilial ['ʌn'filjəl] unkindlich; pflichtvergessen.
unfilled ['ʌn'fild] *a* ungefüllt; *(Stelle)* unbesetzt.
unfiltered ['ʌn'filtəd] *a* ungefiltert.
unfinished ['ʌn'finiʃt] *a* nicht beendet; unerledigt; unfertig, unvollendet.
unfit ['ʌn'fit] *a* unfähig, untüchtig; untauglich (*for* für); ungeeignet, unpassend; *tr* [ʌn'fit] untauglich machen; **~ting** ['-iŋ] nicht passend, ungeeignet; unpassend.
unfix ['ʌn'fiks] *tr* los-, abmachen, lösen; **~ed** ['-t] *a* beweglich; *fig* schwankend; nicht festgelegt.
unflagging [ʌn'flægiŋ] unermüdlich.
unflattering ['ʌn'flætəriŋ] ungeschmeichelt, ungeschminkt, frei u. offen.
unflavo(u)red ['ʌn'fleivəd] *a* ungewürzt.
unfledged ['ʌn'fledʒd] *a* noch ohne Federn, noch nicht flügge; *fig* unreif.
unflinching [ʌn'flin(t)ʃiŋ] unnachgiebig, fest, entschlossen, unbeugsam, unerschütterlich.
unflyable ['ʌn'flaiəbl] *a*: **~** *weather (aero)* kein Flugwetter.
unfold ['ʌn'fould] *tr* entfalten, ausbreiten; [-'-] *fig* offen darlegen, enthüllen; erklären; entwickeln; *itr* sich entfalten, sich ausbreiten, bekanntwerden; *(Knospe)* sich öffnen.
unforced ['ʌn'fɔ:st] *a* ungezwungen, zwanglos, frei, natürlich.
unforeseen ['ʌnfɔ:'si:n] *a* unvorhergesehen.
unforgettable ['ʌnfə'getəbl] unvergeßlich.
unforgiv|able ['ʌnfə'givəbl] unverzeihlich; **~en** ['-ən] *a* unverziehen; **~ing** [-iŋ] unversöhnlich, nachtragend.
unforgotten ['ʌnfə'gɔtn] *a* unvergessen.
unformed ['ʌn'fɔ:md, *attr* 'ʌnfɔ:md] *a* form-, gestaltlos; ungestaltet, unentwickelt.
unformulated ['ʌn'fɔ:mjuleitid] *a* nicht formuliert.
unfortified ['ʌn'fɔ:tifaid] *a* unbefestigt.
unfortunate [ʌn'fɔ:tʃnit] *a* unglücklich; verhängnisvoll; bedauerlich; erfolg-, aussichtslos; Unglücks-; *s* Pechvogel *m*; **~ly** [-li] *adv* unglücklicherweise, leider.
unfounded ['ʌn'faundid] *a* unbegründet, grundlos.
unframed ['ʌn'freimd] *a* ungerahmt.
unfree ['ʌn'fri:] unfrei.
unfrequented ['ʌnfri'kwentid] *a* wenig besucht, menschenleer, einsam.
unfriend|ed ['ʌn'frendid] *a* freundlos; **~liness** ['-linis] Unfreundlichkeit *f*; **~ly** ['-li] unfreundlich (*to* gegen); ungünstig (*for, to* für).
unfrock ['ʌn'frɔk] *tr* der Priesterwürde entkleiden.
unfruitful ['ʌn'fru:tful] unfruchtbar; ergebnislos.
unfulfilled ['ʌnful'fild] *a* unerfüllt.
unfunded ['ʌn'fʌndid] *a fin* nicht fundiert.
unfurl [ʌn'fə:l] *tr* aufspannen, -rollen; *tr itr* (sich) entfalten, (sich) ausbreiten.
unfurnished ['ʌn'fə:niʃt] *a* nicht ausgestattet, nicht eingerichtet (*with* mit); unmöbliert, leer.
ungainly [ʌn'geinli] unbeholfen, plump.
ungallant ['ʌn'gælənt] ungalant (*to* gegenüber); feige.
ungarnished ['ʌn'gɑ:niʃt] *a* unverziert.
ungear ['ʌn'giə] *tr (Pferd)* ausschirren; *tech (Getriebe)* auskuppeln.
ungenerous ['ʌn'dʒenərəs] kleinlich, engherzig; knauserig.
ungenial ['ʌn'dʒi:njəl] ungünstig; unfreundlich; *(Witterung)* rauh.
ungent|eel ['ʌndʒen'ti:l] unfein, wenig vornehm; unelegant; unhöflich; **~le** ['ʌn'dʒentl] kleinlich; unfreundlich; unsanft; **~lemanliness** [ʌn'dʒentlmənlinis] unfeine(s) Benehmen *n*, mangelnde(r) Anstand *m*; **~lemanly** [ʌn'dʒentlmənli] unfein, ungebildet.
un-get-at-able ['ʌnget'ætəbl] schwer erreichbar, unerreichbar.
ungird ['ʌn'gə:d] *tr* den Gürtel abnehmen (*s.o.* jdm); ab-, losgurten.
unglazed ['ʌn'gleizd] *a* unverglast; unglasiert.
ungloved ['ʌn'glʌvd] *a* ohne Handschuhe.
ungodl|iness [ʌn'gɔdlinis] Gottlosigkeit *f*; **~y** [-i] *a* ungläubig, gottlos; verrucht; *fam* verdammt; abscheulich.
ungovern|able [ʌn'gʌvənəbl] unlenksam; unbändig, wild, zügellos; **~ed** [-d] *a* unbeherrscht, ungezügelt.
ungra|ceful ['ʌn'greisful] *a* ohne Anmut, plump; reiz-, ausdruckslos; **~cious** ['ʌn'greiʃəs] abstoßend; abweisend, ungnädig, unhöflich; **~teful** [ʌn'greitful] undankbar (*to* gegen); **~tified** ['-'grætifaid] *a* unbefriedigt.
ungrammatical ['ʌngrə'mætikəl] ungrammatisch.
ungrounded [ʌn'graundid] *a* unbegründet, grundlos; *el* nicht geerdet.
ungrudging ['ʌn'grʌdʒiŋ] (bereit)willig, entgegenkommend; großzügig; **~ly** [ʌn'grʌdʒiŋli] *adv* ohne Murren, gern.
ung|ual ['ʌŋgwəl] *a* Nagel-, Krallen-, Klauen-, Huf-; **~ula** ['ʌŋgjulə] *pl -lae* ['-li:] Huf *m*, Klaue, Kralle *f*, Nagel; *math* Huf *m*; **~ulate** ['-it, -eit] *a* hufartig; Huf-; *s* Huftier *n*.
unguarded ['ʌn'gɑ:did] *a* unbewacht, unbeschützt; *sport* ungedeckt; sorglos, nachlässig.
unguent ['ʌŋgwənt] Salbe *f*.
unguided ['ʌn'gaidid] *a* ungeleitet, ohne Führung.
unhallowed [ʌn'hæloud] *a* ungeweiht; unheilig, böse.
unhampered ['ʌn'hæmpəd] *a* ungehindert.
unhand [ʌn'hænd] *obs tr* loslassen; **~iness** ['ʌn'hændinis] Unhandlichkeit *f*; Ungeschick *n*; **~some** ['ʌn'hænsəm] unschön; unpassend; **~y** ['ʌn'hændi] unhandlich, unpraktisch; unbeholfen; ungeschickt, linkisch.
unhapp|iness [ʌn'hæpinis] Unglück; Leid(en) *n*; **~y** [-i] unglücklich; elend; traurig, betrübt; leidig; unpassend.
unharmonious ['ʌnhɑ:'mounjəs] unharmonisch *a. fig.*
unharness ['ʌn'hɑ:nis] *tr (Pferd)* abschirren.
unhealth|ful [ʌn'helθful] = **~y**; **~iness** [-inis] Kränklichkeit *f*; **~y** [-i] *a* kränklich; unwohl; ungesund *a. fig*; schädlich.
unheard ['ʌn'hə:d] *a* ungehört; **~-of** [ʌn'hə:dɔv] *a* unerhört.
unheed|ed ['ʌn'hi:did] *a* unbeachtet; **~ful** ['-ful], **~ing** ['-iŋ] unachtsam, unaufmerksam, nachlässig.
unhesitating [ʌn'heziteitiŋ] nicht zögernd; bereitwillig.
unhinge [ʌn'hindʒ] *tr* aus den Angeln heben *a. fig*; herauslösen, -nehmen; *fig* verwirren; aus dem Gleichgewicht, ins Wanken bringen; zerrütten.
unhistoric(al) ['ʌnhis'tɔrik(əl)] ungeschichtlich.
unhitch ['ʌn'hitʃ] *tr* losmachen, ablösen, -trennen.
unholy [ʌn'houli] ungeweiht; gottlos, böse; *fam* entsetzlich, schrecklich.
unhono(u)red ['ʌn'ɔnəd] *a* nicht geehrt; *fin* uneingelöst, nicht honoriert.
unhook ['ʌn'huk] *tr itr* (sich) los-, aus-, ab-, aufhaken.
unhoped-for [ʌn'houptfɔ:] *a* unverhofft, unerwartet; Glücks-.
unhorse ['ʌn'hɔ:s] *tr* aus dem Sattel heben *od* werfen; sein(e) Pferd(e) wegnehmen (*s.o.* jdm); *fig* aus der Fassung, aus dem Konzept, in Verwirrung bringen.
unhous|e ['ʌn'hauz] *tr* aus dem Hause jagen; vor die Tür setzen; **~ed** ['-d] *a* obdachlos.

*

unicameral ['ju:ni'kæmərəl] *a pol* Einkammer-.
unicellular ['ju:ni'seljulə] *biol* einzellig; **~ animal** Einzeller *m*.
unicorn ['ju:nikɔ:n] Einhorn *n*.
unidentified ['ʌnai'dentifaid] *a* nicht identifiziert.
unidiomatic ['ʌnidiə'mætik] *a* nicht idiomatisch.
unif|ication [ju:nifi'keiʃən] Vereinheitlichung; Vereinigung; Konsolidierung *f*; **~y** ['ju:nifai] *tr* vereinheitlichen; verein(ig)en; konsolidieren.
uniform ['ju:nifɔ:m] *a* gleich(bleibend), gleichförmig, -mäßig; einförmig; einheitlich; übereinstimmend (*with* mit); *s* Uniform *f*; **~ed** ['-d] *a* in Uniform; **~ity** [ju:ni'fɔ:miti] Gleichförmig-, Gleichmäßigkeit; Übereinstimmung; Einförmigkeit; Einheitlichkeit *f*; **~ price, tariff** Einheitspreis, -tarif *m*.
unilateral ['ju:ni'lætərəl] einseitig.
unimagin|able [ʌni'mædʒinəbl] un(aus)denkbar; **~ative** ['ʌni'mædʒinətiv] phantasielos.
unimpaired ['ʌnim'pɛəd] *a* unbeschädigt, unbeeinträchtigt; ungeschwächt, unvermindert.
unimpeachable [ʌnim'pi:tʃəbl] unanfechtbar; einwandfrei, untadelig.
unimpeded ['ʌnim'pi:did] *a* unge-, unbehindert.
unimportan|ce ['ʌnim'pɔ:təns] Unwichtigkeit, Belanglosigkeit, Bedeutungslosigkeit *f*; **~t** ['-t] unwichtig, unbedeutend, belanglos.
unimpress|ed ['ʌnim'prest] *a* unbeeindruckt; **~ive** ['-siv] wenig eindrucksvoll, unscheinbar.
unimproved ['ʌnim'pru:vd] *a* unverbessert; *agr* unbebaut; ungenutzt; *(Gesundheit)* ungebessert.
uninfluenced ['ʌn'influənst] *a* unbeeinflußt (*by* von, durch).
uninformed ['ʌnin'fɔ:md] *a* nicht unterrichtet, nicht informiert (*on* über).
uninhabit|able ['ʌnin'hæbitəbl] unbewohnbar; **~ed** ['-id] *a* unbewohnt, menschenleer.
uninjured ['ʌn'indʒəd] *a* unbeschädigt, unverletzt.
uninspired ['ʌnin'spaiəd] *a fig* schwunglos, nicht angeregt.
uninstructed ['ʌnin'strʌktid] *a* ohne Anweisung(en), ohne Instruktion(en); unwissend.
uninsur|able ['ʌnin'ʃuərəbl] nicht versicherbar; **~ed** ['-uəd] *a* unversichert.
unintellig|ent ['ʌnin'telidʒənt] unintelligent; dumm; **~ible** ['-dʒəbl] unverständlich.
uninten|ded ['ʌnin'tendid] *a* unbeabsichtigt; **~tional** ['-ʃənl] unabsichtlich; **~tionally** ['-ʃnəli] *adv* unbeabsichtigt, ohne Absicht.

uninterest|ed ['ʌn'intristid] *a* uninteressiert (*in* an); unaufmerksam; **~ing** ['-iŋ] uninteressant.

uninterrupted ['ʌnintə'rʌptid] *a* ununterbrochen, unausgesetzt; **~ service, working-hours** *pl* durchgehende(r) Betrieb *m*, fortlaufende Arbeitszeit *f*.

uninvit|ed ['ʌnin'vaitid] *a* un(ein)geladen; **~ing** ['-iŋ] wenig einladend; abstoßend.

union ['ju:njən] Vereinigung, Kombination *f*, Zs.schluß *m*, Verschmelzung; Einheit, Einigkeit, Eintracht *f*; (Staaten-)Bund *m*, Union, Liga *f*, Verein(igung *f*) *m*; *(trade ~)* Gewerkschaft; Ehe; *mar* Gösch; *tech (pipe ~)* (Röhren-)Kupp(e)lung *f*; *(Textil)* gemischte(s) Gewebe *n*; *the U~* die US(A) *pl*; *hist* die Nordstaaten; *in perfect ~* in voller Eintracht; *~ is strength (prov)* Einigkeit macht stark; *Universal Postal U~* Weltpostverein *m*; *the U~ of South Africa* die Südafrikanische Union *f*; *the U~ of Soviet Socialist Republics (USSR)* die Union der Sozialistischen Sowjetrepubliken, die Sowjetunion *f (UdSSR)*; **~ card** Gewerkschaftsausweis *m*; **~ dues** *pl* Gewerkschaftsbeiträge *m pl*; **~ism** ['-izm] Einheitsprinzip *n*; Einheitsbestrebungen *f pl*; Gewerkschaftssystem *n*; **~ist** ['-ist] *pol* Unionsanhänger; Gewerkschaftler *m*; **~ize** ['-aiz] *tr* gewerkschaftlich organisieren; **U~ Jack,** *the* die britische Nationalflagge; **~man** Gewerkschaftsmitglied *n*; **~ movement** Gewerkschaftsbewegung *f*; **~ shop** Betrieb *m*, der nur Gewerkschaftsmitglieder einstellt; **~ station** *Am* gemeinsame(r) Bahnhof verschiedener Eisenbahngesellschaften, Hauptbahnhof *m*; **~ steward** Betriebsrat *m*; **~ suit** *Am* Hemdhose *f*.

unipolar [ju:ni'poulə] *el anat* einpolig.

unique [ju:'ni:k] einzig; einzigartig, ungewöhnlich, außerordentlich; *fam* großartig, toll; **~ness** [-nis] Einzigartigkeit *f*.

unison ['ju:nizn] Einklang *m*, Übereinstimmung, Eintracht, Harmonie *f*; *mus* Gleichklang *m*; *in ~ (mus)* im Gleichklang; *with* in Einklang mit; **~ous** [ju:'nisənəs] *a* in Einklang (befindlich); *fig* übereinstimmend; *mus* einstimmig.

unit ['ju:nit] Eins *f*, Einer *m*; Einheit *f a. math mil*; Einzelteil; Stück; Einzelwesen *n*, -person *f*; *fig* Kern *m*; *tech* Anlage *f*, Aggregat *n*, Satz, Bauteil *m*, -element *n*; *mil* Truppenteil, -verband *m*; *board of trade ~* Kilowattstunde *f*; *monetary ~* Münzeinheit *f*; *thermal ~* Wärmeeinheit *f*; *~ of account* Verrechnungseinheit *f*; *~ of measure, of power, of time, of value* Maß-, Leistungs-, Zeit-, Währungseinheit *f*; **U~arian** [ju:ni'tɛəriən] *rel s* Unitarier *m*; *a* unitarisch; *u~~* u. **~ary** ['ju:nitəri] einheitlich; Einheits-; **~ character** *biol* Erbanlage *f*; **~e** [ju:'nait] *tr itr* (sich) verein(ig)en, (sich) zs.schließen; zs.wachsen; sich verbinden (*with* mit); *tr* in sich verein(ig)en; zs.bringen; verbinden *a. chem*; ehelich verbinden, trauen; **~ed** [ju:'naitid] *a* verein(ig)t; geeint; gemeinsam; *the U~~ Kingdom* das Vereinigte Königreich (*Großbritannien u. Nordirland*; U.K.); *the U~~ Nations (Organization) (UN, UNO)* die (Organisation *f* der) Vereinten Nationen *f pl*; *the U~ Nations Security Council* der Sicherheitsrat der Vereinten Nationen; *the U~~ States (of America) (U.S., U.S.A.) pl mit sing* die Vereinigten Staaten (von Amerika); **~ factor** *biol* Erbfaktor *m*; **~ furniture** Anbaumöbel *pl*; **~ive** ['-iv] *a* Einheits-; verbindend; **~ price** Stück-, Einheitspreis *m*; **~ wage** Stücklohn *m*; **~y** ['-i] Einheit *a. math*; Einigkeit, Eintracht, Solidarität, Harmonie; Vereinigung; Ganzheit; Einheitlichkeit; innere Festigkeit, Geschlossenheit *f*; *in ~~ with* in Übereinstimmung mit.

univers|al [ju:ni'və:səl] *a* allgemein, allumfassend, universal; Welt-; Universal-, Allzweck-; allgemeingültig, universell; *s* Allgemeinbegriff *m*; allgemeine Aussage *f*; *~~ agent* Generalvertreter, -bevollmächtigte(r) *m*; *~~ conscription, (Am) military training (U.M.T.)* allgemeine Wehrpflicht *f*; *~~ heir* Alleinerbe *m*; *~~ joint, coupling (tech)* Kreuz-, Universalgelenk *n*, -kupplung *f*; *~~ language* Weltsprache *f*; *U~~ Postal Union* Weltpostverein *m*; *~~ screw-wrench (tech)* Engländer *m*; *~~ successor* Universalerbe *m*; *~~ suffrage* allgemeine(s) Wahlrecht *n*; **~ality** [-və:'sæliti] Allgemeinheit, Universalität; Allgemeingültigkeit; Vielseitigkeit, große Allgemeinbildung *f*, vielseitige(s) Interesse *n*; **~alize** [-'və:səlaiz] *tr* verallgemeinern; **~e** ['ju:nivə:s] Welt(all *n*) *f*, Universum *n*; Welt *f*; **~ity** [ju:ni'və:siti] Universität, Hochschule *f*; *attr* Universitäts-, Hochschul-; *to be at the ~~* die Universität besuchen, studieren; *~~ education* akademische Bildung *f*; *~~ extension* Volkshochschule *f*; *~~ lecture* Vorlesung *f*; *~~ library* Universitätsbibliothek *f*; *~~ professor* Universitätsprofessor *m*; *~~ student* Student *m*; *~~ town* Universitätsstadt *f*.

univocal ['ju:ni'voukəl] ein-, unzweideutig.

unjoint ['ʌn'dʒɔint] *tr* ausrenken, aus den Fugen bringen; trennen.

unjust ['ʌn'dʒʌst] un(ge)recht (*to* gegen); **~ifiable** [ʌn'dʒʌstifaiəbl] unverantwortlich, unentschuldbar; **~ified** [-'dʒʌstifaid] *a* ungerechtfertigt, unbegründet; unberechtigt; **~ly** ['-li] *adv* zu Unrecht; **~ness** ['-nis] Ungerechtigkeit *f*.

*

unkempt ['ʌn'kempt] *a* ungekämmt, zerzaust; unordentlich; *fig* grob.

unkind [ʌn'kaind] unfreundlich, abweisend, herzlos; **~ly** [-li] *a adv* hart, rauh; unfreundlich; **~ness** [-nis] Unfreundlichkeit *f*.

unknit ['ʌn'nit] *tr (Gestricktes)* auftrennen, -ziehen; glätten, glattstreichen; *fig* zerstreuen, auflösen, zerstören; entspannen; (ab)schwächen.

unknot ['ʌn'nɔt] *tr* aufknoten.

unknow|able ['ʌn'no(u)əbl] unerkennbar; **~ing** ['-iŋ] unwissend; nichts wissend (*of* von); **~n** ['-'noun] *a* unbekannt, fremd (*to s.o.* jdm).

unlabel(l)ed ['ʌn'leibld] *a* nicht etikettiert; nicht beschriftet; ohne Zettel.

unlabo(u)red ['ʌn'leibəd] *a* nicht ausgearbeitet, nicht gefeilt; mühelos; *agr* unbebaut.

unlace ['ʌn'leis] *tr* aufschnüren; ausziehen.

unlade ['ʌn'leid] *irr s. lade tr* entladen; *tr itr* ab-, ausladen (*from* von); *mar* (die Ladung) löschen; **~n** ['-n] *a* unbeladen; *fig* unbelastet.

unladylike ['ʌn'leidilaik] nicht damenhaft; unfein.

unlaid ['ʌn'leid] *a* ungelegt; nicht geglättet *fig*; *(Tisch)* ungedeckt; *(Papier)* ungerippt.

unlamented ['ʌnlə'mentid] *a* unbeklagt.

unlatch ['ʌn'lætʃ] *tr* aufklinken.

unlawful ['ʌn'lɔ:ful] widerrechtlich, ungesetzlich, illegal; unehelich.

unlearn ['ʌn'lə:n] *irr s. learn tr* verlernen, vergessen; **~ed** ['-id] *a* ungebildet, unwissend; ['-d] *a* ungelernt.

unleash ['ʌn'li:ʃ] *tr* loskoppeln, -binden, -lassen; *fig* freilassen, befreien; entfesseln.

unleavened ['ʌn'levnd] *a (Brot)* ungesäuert; *fig* unbeeinflußt.

unless [ən'les] *conj* wenn nicht; außer wenn; es sei denn, daß; unter der Voraussetzung, vorausgesetzt, daß; *prp* außer.

unlettered ['ʌn'letəd] *a* ungebildet, unwissend.

unlicensed ['ʌn'laisənst] *a* unerlaubt; unkonzessioniert; unbefugt.

unlicked ['ʌn'likt] *a fig* unbeleckt, roh, ungebildet; unreif.

unlike ['ʌn'laik] *a* ungleich-, verschieden(artig); nicht ähnlich; *prp* unähnlich (*s.o.* jdm); ver-, unterschieden von; im Gegensatz zu; **~lihood** [ʌn'laiklihud], **~likeliness** [-nis] Unwahrscheinlichkeit *f*; **~ly** [ʌn'laikli] *a adv* unwahrscheinlich.

unlimber [ʌn'limbə] *tr itr mil* abprotzen; *fig* (sich) fertigmachen.

unlimited [ʌn'limitid] *a* unbegrenzt; unbe-, uneingeschränkt; unbestimmt; *fig* grenzenlos; **~ liability** unbeschränkte Haftung *f*.

unliquidated ['ʌn'likwideitid] *a* nicht abgerechnet, unbezahlt, unbeglichen.

unlink ['ʌn'liŋk] *tr (Kette)* ausea.-nehmen; *allg* trennen, ausea.nehmen.

unlined ['ʌn'laind] *a (Kleidung)* ungefüttert; unliniert.

unload ['ʌn'loud] *tr itr (Ladung)* ab-, ausladen; *mar* löschen; *tr (Fahrzeug, Gewehr)* entladen; *fig* von e-r Last befreien; *com* abstoßen.

unlock ['ʌn'lɔk] *tr* aufschließen, -sperren; *(Gewehr)* entsichern; *allg* öffnen; *fig* aufdecken, enthüllen; *itr* sich öffnen, aufgehen; **~ed** ['-t] *a* unverschlossen.

unlooked-for [ʌn'luktfɔ:] *a* unerwartet, überraschend, plötzlich.

unloos|e ['ʌn'lu:s], **~en** [ʌn'lu:sn] *tr* losmachen, lösen, auf-, abmachen.

unlov|(e)able ['ʌn'lʌvəbl] unliebenswürdig; **~ed** ['-d] *a* ungeliebt; **~ely** ['-li] reizlos; **~ing** ['-iŋ] lieblos, kalt (-herzig).

unlucky [ʌn'lʌki] unglücklich; ungünstig; unheilvoll; Unglücks-; *to be ~~* Pech haben.

unmailable ['ʌn'meiləbl] *(Post)* unbestellbar.

unmake ['ʌn'meik] *irr s. make tr* zerstören, vernichten; *(Person)* absetzen; rückgängig machen, zurücknehmen, widerrufen; umbilden, völlig verändern.

unman ['ʌn'mæn] *tr* entmannen, kastrieren; entwürdigen; schwach, mutlos machen, entmutigen; **~ned** ['-d] *a* unbemannt; **~liness** ['-linis] Unmännlichkeit *f*; **~ly** ['-li] *a* unmännlich.

unmanageable [ʌn'mænidʒəbl] schwer zu lenken(d); schwierig, eigenwillig, -sinnig, widersetzlich, -spenstig.

unmanner|ed [ʌn'mænəd], **~ly** [-əli] *a* ungesittet, unmanierlich; **~liness** [-nis] schlechte(s) Benehmen *n*, Ungezogenheit *f*.

unmanufactured ['ʌnmænju'fæktʃəd] *a* unver-, unbearbeitet, roh.

unmarked ['ʌn'mɑ:kt] *a* unbezeichnet, unmarkiert; unbemerkt, unbeobachtet.
unmarketable ['ʌn'mɑ:kitəbl] *com* nicht marktfähig, unverkäuflich.
unmarri|ageable ['ʌn'mæridʒəbl] nicht *od* schwer zu verheiraten(d); unvereinbar; **~ed** ['-id] *a* unverheiratet, ledig.
unmask ['ʌn'mɑ:sk] *tr* demaskieren *a. fig*; *fig* entlarven, bloßstellen; *itr* sich demaskieren; *fig* die Maske fallen lassen.
unmastered ['ʌn'mɑ:stəd] *a* unbezwungen, ungemeistert.
unmatch|able ['ʌn'mætʃəbl] unerreichbar; **~ed** ['-tʃt] *a* unerreicht, unübertroffen, ohnegleichen, unvergleichlich.
unmean|ing [ʌn'mi:niŋ] nichtssagend, bedeutungs-, ausdruckslos, leer; **~t** ['ʌn'ment] *a* unbeabsichtigt, ungewollt.
unmeasur|able [ʌn'meʒərəbl] unermeßlich; **~ed** [-əd] *a* ungemessen, unermeßlich; maßlos, zügellos.
unmelodious ['ʌnmi'loudjəs] unmelodisch.
unmention|able [ʌn'menʃnəbl] unaussprechbar; **~ed** [-d] *a* unerwähnt.
unmerchantable ['ʌn'mə:tʃəntəbl] unverkäuflich, nicht abzusetzen(d).
unmerciful [ʌn'mə:siful] unbarmherzig, mitleidlos.
unmerited ['ʌn'meritid] *a* unverdient.
unmethodical ['ʌnmi'θɔdikəl] unmethodisch, unsystematisch.
unmilitary ['ʌn'militəri] unmilitärisch.
unmindful [ʌn'maindful] vergeßlich; sorglos; unachtsam, unbedacht, unaufmerksam; rücksichtslos, ohne Rücksicht (*of* auf).
unmistak(e)able ['ʌnmis'teikəbl] unverkennbar; unmißverständlich.
unmitigated [ʌn'mitigeitid] *a* ungemildert, unvermindert; rein, vollkommen, völlig; vollendet; Erz-.
unmixed ['ʌn'mikst] *a* unge-, unvermischt; *fig* rein.
unmodifi|able ['ʌn'mɔdifaiəbl] unabänderlich; **~ed** ['-aid] *a* unverändert.
unmolested ['ʌnmo(u)'lestid] *a* unbelästigt, unbehelligt.
unmoor ['ʌn'muə] *tr* (*Schiff*) flottmachen; *itr* die Anker lichten.
unmoral ['ʌn'mɔrəl] unmoralisch, unsittlich; amoralisch.
unmortgaged ['ʌn'mɔ:gidʒd] *a* unverpfändet; (*Grundstück*) unbelastet, hypothekenfrei.
unmotivated ['ʌn'moutiveitid] *a* unmotiviert, grundlos.
unmounted ['ʌn'mauntid] *a* unberitten; (*Geschütz*) abgeprotzt; (*Edelstein*) ungefaßt; (*Bild*) ungerahmt, nicht aufgezogen; *tech* nicht montiert.
unmourned ['ʌn'mɔ:nd] *a* unbetrauert.
unmov|eable ['ʌn'mu:vəbl] unbeweglich; **~ed** ['-d] *a* unbewegt; *fig* ungerührt; *fig* standhaft; **~ing** ['-iŋ] bewegungs-, reglos.
unmusical ['ʌn'mju:sikəl] (*Musik*) disharmonisch; (*Mensch*) unmusikalisch.
unmuzzle ['ʌn'mʌzl] *tr* den Maulkorb abnehmen (*a dog* e-m Hunde); *fig* freie Meinungsäußerung gewähren (*s.o.* jdm), die Zensur aufheben für.
unnam|(e)able ['ʌn'neiməbl] unnennbar; **~ed** ['-d] *a* unge-, unbenannt, namenlos.
unnatural [ʌn'nætʃrəl] unnatürlich, widernatürlich, unnormal, abnorm; gekünstelt, affektiert, gequält, unecht; abscheulich.
unnavigable ['ʌn'nævigəbl] nicht schiffbar.
unnecessar|ily [ʌn'nesisərili] *adv* unnötigerweise; **~y** [-i] unnötig, unnütz, überflüssig.
unneeded ['ʌn'ni:did] *a* nicht erforderlich, nicht nötig, nutzlos.
unneighbo(u)rly ['ʌn'neibəli] nicht gutnachbarlich.
unnerve ['ʌn'nə:v] *tr* entnerven, zermürben; die Kraft, das Selbstvertrauen, den Mut nehmen (*s.o.* jdm).
unnot|ed ['ʌn'noutid] *a* unbemerkt; nicht berühmt; **~iceable** ['-isəbl] unbemerkbar, unauffällig; **~iced** ['-t] *a* unbemerkt, unbeobachtet.
unnumbered ['ʌn'nʌmbəd] *a* ungezählt, zahllos; unnumeriert.

*

unobjectionable ['ʌnəb'dʒekʃnəbl] einwandfrei, tadellos.
unobliging ['ʌnə'blaidʒiŋ] unverbindlich; ungefällig.
unobserv|ance ['ʌnəb'zə:vəns] Unachtsamkeit *f*; **~ant** ['-t] unachtsam, unaufmerksam; **~ed** ['-'zə:vd] *a* unbemerkt, unbeobachtet.
unobstructed ['ʌnəb'strʌktid] *a* unversperrt, offen; (*Verkehr*) ungehindert; *fig* ohne Störung.
unobtainable ['ʌnəb'teinəbl] nicht zu bekommen(d), nicht zu erlangen(d), unerreichbar.
unobtrusive ['ʌnəb'tru:siv] (*Sache*) unaufdringlich; (*Mensch*) zurückhaltend, bescheiden; **~ness** ['-nis] Unaufdringlichkeit; Zurückhaltung, Bescheidenheit *f*.
unoccupied ['ʌn'ɔkjupaid] *a* unbesetzt, frei, leer; unbewohnt; unbeschäftigt, müßig.
unoffen|ding ['ʌnə'fendiŋ], **~sive** ['-siv] nicht aggressiv, harmlos, unschädlich.
unofficial ['ʌnə'fiʃəl] inoffiziell, nichtamtlich.
unopened ['ʌn'oupənd] *a* ungeöffnet, (noch) verschlossen; *com* unerschlossen.
unopposed ['ʌnə'pouzd] *a* ungehindert; ohne Widerstand (zu finden) (*by* bei).
unorganized ['ʌn'ɔ:gənaizd] *a* nichtorganisch; nicht organisiert; ungeordnet, unorganisch.
unorthodox ['ʌn'ɔ:θədɔks] nicht recht-, strenggläubig; *by ~ methods, through ~ channels* unter der Hand.
unostentatious ['ʌnɔsten'teiʃəs] unaufdringlich, zurückhaltend, bescheiden, anspruchslos, schlicht.
unowned ['ʌn'ound] *a* herrenlos; nicht anerkannt.

*

unpack ['ʌn'pæk] *tr itr* auspacken, -laden.
unpaid ['ʌn'peid] *a* unbezahlt; unfrankiert; nicht entlohnt; (*Stellung*) ehrenamtlich.
unpaired ['ʌn'pɛəd] *a zoo* unpaarig; (*Schuh, Strumpf, Handschuh*) einzeln.
unpalatable [ʌn'pælətəbl] fad(e); *fig* unangenehm.
unparallel(l)ed [ʌn'pærəleld] *a* unerreicht, unvergleichlich, einmalig.
unpardonable [ʌn'pɑ:dnəbl] unverzeihlich.
unparliamentary ['ʌnpɑ:lə'mentəri] unparlamentarisch.
unpatented ['ʌn'peitəntid, -pæt-] *a* nicht patentiert.
unpatriotic ['ʌnpætri'ɔtik] unpatriotisch.
unpaved ['ʌn'peivd] *a* ungepflastert.
unpeople ['ʌn'pi:pl] *tr* entvölkern.
unperceiv|able ['ʌnpə'si:vəbl] unmerklich; **~ed** ['-d] *a* unbemerkt.
unperplexed ['ʌnpə'plekst] *a* nicht verwirrt.
unperturbed ['ʌnpə(:)'tə:bd] *a* unerschüttert, gelassen.
unperused ['ʌnpə'ru:zd] *a* ungelesen.
unphilosophic(al) ['ʌnfilə'sɔfik(əl)] unphilosophisch.
unpick ['ʌn'pik] *tr* (*Schloß, Tür*) erbrechen; (*Naht*) auftrennen; **~ed** ['-t] *a* ungepflückt; unverlesen, unsortiert.
unpin ['ʌn'pin] *tr* die Stecknadeln ziehen aus; losmachen.
unpit|ied ['ʌn'pitid] *a* unbemitleidet; **~ying** [-'-iiŋ] mitleidlos, unbarmherzig.
unplaced ['ʌn'pleist] *a* ohne festen Platz; nicht (fest) angestellt; (*Pferderennen*) unplaziert.
unplait ['ʌn'plæt] *tr* (*Zopf*) aufflechten.
unpleas|ant [ʌn'pleznt] unangenehm; langweilig; ungefällig, unfreundlich; **~antness** [-ntnis] gespannte(s) Verhältnis *n*; Unstimmigkeit; Unannehmlichkeit *f*; **~ing** ['ʌn'pli:ziŋ] ungefällig; unerfreulich (*to* für).
unpledged ['ʌn'pledʒd] *a* nicht verpfändet.
unplumbed ['ʌn'plʌmd] *a* unerforscht; *tech* ungelötet, unplombiert.
unpoetic(al) ['ʌnpo(u)'etik(əl)] prosaisch *fig*.
unpolished ['ʌn'pɔliʃt] *a* unpoliert, rauh *a. fig*; *fig* grob, ungehobelt, unausgeglichen.
unpolitic(al) ['ʌn'pɔlitik, -pə'litikəl] unpolitisch.
unpolled ['ʌn'pould] *a* (*Wahlstimme*) nicht erfaßt, nicht registriert; **~ voter** Nichtwähler *m*.
unpolluted ['ʌnpə'lu:tid] *fig* unbefleckt; rein; (*Wasser*) nicht verunreinigt.
unpopular ['ʌn'pɔpjulə] unbeliebt, unpopulär; **~ity** ['ʌnpɔpju'læriti] Unbeliebtheit *f*.
unpossessed ['ʌnpə'zest] *a* herrenlos; ungenutzt; *to be ~ of s.th.* nicht im Besitz e-r S sein.
unposted ['ʌn'poustid] *a* (*Brief*) liegengeblieben, nicht abgeschickt; nicht unterrichtet, nicht informiert.
unpract|ical ['ʌn'præktikəl] unpraktisch; **~ised, *Am* ~iced** [-'-tist] *a* nicht üblich, nicht *od* wenig gehandhabt *od* benutzt; ungeübt, unerfahren (*in* in).
unprecedented [ʌn'presidəntid] *a* ohne Vorgang, einmalig, beispiellos, unerhört; *jur* ohne Präzedenzfall.
unpredictable ['ʌnpri'diktəbl] *a* nicht vorherzusagen(d).
unprejudiced [ʌn'predʒudist] *a* vorurteilsfrei, -los, unbefangen, unvoreingenommen, unparteiisch.
unpremeditated ['ʌnpri'mediteitid] *a* unvorbedacht, unüberlegt; improvisiert, aus dem Stegreif.
unprepared ['ʌnpri'pɛəd] *a* unvorbereitet (*for* auf).
unprepossess|ed ['ʌnpri:pə'zest] unvoreingenommen; **~ing** ['-iŋ] *a* reizlos.
unpresentable ['ʌnpri'zentəbl] wenig repräsentabel, unansehnlich.
unpresum|ing ['ʌnpri'zju:miŋ], **~ptuous** [-'zʌmptjuəs] anspruchslos, bescheiden.
unpreten|ding ['ʌnpri'tendiŋ], **~tious** ['-'tenʃəs] zurückhaltend, bescheiden.
unpreventable ['ʌnpri'ventəbl] unvermeidlich.
unprincipled [ʌn'prinsəpld] *a* ohne Grundsätze, prinzipienlos, ohne (festen) sittlichen Halt, gewissenlos.
unprint|able ['ʌn'printəbl] nicht für den Druck geeignet; **~ed** ['-id] *a* unge-, unbedruckt.
unprivileged ['ʌn'privilidʒd] *a* nicht bevorrechtet.
unproductive ['ʌnprə'dʌktiv] unproduktiv, unfruchtbar, unergiebig (*of* an); steril; wenig einträglich; **~ness**

['-nis] mangelnde Produktivität; geringe Ergiebigkeit; Unfruchtbarkeit *f*.
unprofessional ['ʌnprə'feʃənl] berufsfremd, laienhaft; berufswidrig.
unprofitable [ʌn'prɔfitəbl] wenig einträglich, von geringem Nutzen, unvorteilhaft; zwecklos.
unpromising ['ʌn'prɔmisiŋ] wenig versprechend, wenig verheißungsvoll, wenig aussichtsreich.
unprompted ['ʌn'prɔmptid] *a* aus eigenem Antrieb; unbeeinflußt (*by* von).
unpronounceable ['ʌnprə'naunsəbl] nicht aussprechbar.
unpropitious ['ʌnprə'piʃəs] ungeeignet; unheilvoll.
unproportion|ate ['ʌnprə'pɔ:ʃnit], **~ed** ['-ənd] *a* unproportional.
unprotected ['ʌnprə'tektid] *a* ungeschützt.
unproved ['ʌn'pru:vd] *a* unbe-, unerwiesen.
unprovided ['ʌnprə'vaidid] *a* nicht versehen, nicht ausgestattet (*with* mit); unversorgt; unvorbereitet, nicht fertig; (*~ for)* unvorhergesehen.
unprovoked ['ʌnprə'voukt] *a* unprovoziert, durch nichts veranlaßt, grundlos.
unpublished ['ʌn'pʌbliʃt] *a* unveröffentlicht.
unpunctual ['ʌn'pʌŋktjuəl] unpünktlich.
unpunished ['ʌn'pʌniʃt] *a* ungestraft; straffrei, -los; *to come off ~~* straffrei ausgehen.
unpurchas(e)able ['ʌn'pə:tʃisəbl] nicht käuflich.
unqualified ['ʌn'kwɔlifaid] *a* unqualifiziert, ungeeignet, nicht befähigt; [-'---] unbe-, uneingeschränkt, vorbehaltlos; völlig, vollkommen, absolut.
unquenchable [ʌn'kwen(t)ʃəbl] *(Feuer, Durst)* nicht zu löschen(d); *(Durst)* nicht zu stillen(d); *fig (Verlangen)* unauslöschlich; *(Sehnsucht)* unstillbar.
unquestion|able [ʌn'kwestʃənəbl] unzweifelhaft, unbestreitbar, sicher; einwandfrei, tadellos; **~ed** [-d] *a* unbezweifelt, unbestritten, unangefochten; **~ing** ['-iŋ] bedingungslos, blind.
unquiet ['ʌn'kwaiət] unruhig, ruhelos; ängstlich, besorgt.
unquot|e ['ʌn'kwout] *tr (Zitat)* beenden; **~ed** ['-id] *a (Börse)* nicht notiert.

*

unratified ['ʌn'rætifaid] *a pol* nicht ratifiziert.
unravel [ʌn'rævəl] *tr* auftrennen, -ziehen, ausfasern; *(Fäden)* entwirren *a. fig*; *fig* klären, lösen; *itr* zerfasern; sich auflösen.
unread ['ʌn'red] *a* ungelesen; wenig belesen; **~able** ['ʌn'ri:dəbl] unleserlich, unlesbar.
unread|iness ['ʌn'redinis] mangelnde Bereitschaft *f*; **~y** ['ʌn'redi] nicht bereit (*for* zu); nicht fertig; langsam, säumig, bumm(e)lig.
unreal ['ʌn'riəl] unwirklich, wirklichkeitsfremd; phantastisch, visionär, imaginär, eingebildet; **~istic** ['ʌnriə'listik] unrealistisch; **~ity** ['ʌnri'æliti] Unwirklichkeit; Einbildung *f*; **~izable** ['ʌn'riəlaizəbl] nicht zu verwirklichen(d), nicht realisierbar; *com* unverkäuflich; **~ized** ['ʌn'riəlaizd] *a* nicht verwirklicht; nicht erkannt, nicht verstanden.
unreason ['ʌn'ri:zn] Unvernunft *f*, Unsinn *m*, Dummheit *f*; **~able** [ʌn'ri:znəbl] unvernünftig; unsinnig, dumm; unmäßig, unbescheiden, übertrieben, exorbitant; **~ing** [-iŋ] unvernünftig, gedankenlos, blind.
unreceived ['ʌnri'si:vd] *a* nicht erhalten.
unreclaim|able ['ʌnri'kleiməbl] nicht zurückzufordern(d); unverbesserlich; **~ed** ['-d] *a* nicht zurückgefordert; *(Mensch)* ungebessert; *(Land)* unbebaut; *~~ land* Ödland *n*.
unrecogniz|able ['ʌn'rekəgnaizəbl] nicht wiederzuerkennen(d); **~ed** ['-d] *a* unerkannt; nicht anerkannt.
unrecompensed ['ʌn'rekəmpenst] *a* unbelohnt.
unreconcil|able ['ʌn'rekənsailəbl] unversöhnlich; **~ed** ['-d] *a* unversöhnt (*to* mit).
unrecorded ['ʌnri'kɔ:did] *a* nicht eingetragen, nicht vermerkt; nicht aufgezeichnet; nicht aufgenommen.
unrecoverable ['ʌnri'kʌvərəbl] *med* nicht wiederherstellbar; *com* nicht beitreibbar.
unredeem|able ['ʌnri'di:məbl] nicht wiedergutzumachen(d); nicht einlösbar; uneinbringlich; **~ed** ['-d] *a rel* unerlöst; nicht eingelöst, unbezahlt; *(Versprechen)* nicht erfüllt; ungemildert (*by* durch).
unredressed ['ʌnri'drest] *a* ungesühnt, nicht wiedergutgemacht.
unreel ['ʌn'ri:l] *tr* abhaspeln, -spulen.
unrefined ['ʌnri'faind] *a tech* ungereinigt, roh; *fig* unfein, ungebildet.
unreflect|ed ['ʌnri'flektid] *a (Wort, Tat)* unüberlegt, unbedacht; **~ing** ['-iŋ] *phys* nichtreflektierend; *(Mensch)* unbedacht, gedankenlos.
unreformed ['ʌnri'fɔ:md] *a* ungebessert.
unrefuted ['ʌnri'fju:tid] *a* unwiderlegt.
unregard|ed ['ʌnri'gɑ:did] *a* unbeachtet; unberücksichtigt; **~ful** ['-ful], **~ing** ['-iŋ] unachtsam, unaufmerksam; rücksichtslos.
unregener|acy ['ʌnri'dʒenərəsi] *rel* Sündhaftigkeit *f*; **~ate** ['-it], **~ated** ['-eitid] *a* nicht wiedergeboren; sündig.
unregistered ['ʌn'redʒistəd] *a* nicht eingetragen, nicht registriert; *(Brief)* nicht eingeschrieben; *(Arzt)* nicht approbiert.
unregretted ['ʌnri'gretid] *a* unbetrauert, unbeklagt.
unrehearsed ['ʌnri'hə:st] *a theat* ungeprobt; spontan.
unrelated ['ʌnri'leitid] *a* unverbunden, unbezogen (*to* auf); nicht verwandt (*with* mit).
unrelax|ed ['ʌnri'lækst] *a* unentspannt, unerholt; **~ing** ['-iŋ] nicht *od* wenig erholsam; nicht nachlassend.
unrelenting ['ʌnri'lentiŋ] unermüdlich; unnachgiebig, unbeugsam.
unreliab|ility ['ʌnrilaiə'biliti] Unzuverlässigkeit *f*; **~le** ['-'laiəbl] unzuverlässig; *com* unsolide.
unrelieved ['ʌnri'li:vd] *a* ununterbrochen; nicht befreit, nicht entbunden, nicht entlastet; *mil* nicht abgelöst; langweilig.
unreligious ['ʌnri'lidʒəs] ungläubig; religionslos.
unremitt|ed [ʌnri'mitid] *a (Schuld)* nicht erlassen; *(Bemühungen)* beständig; *(Mensch)* hartnäckig; **~ing** [-iŋ] unablässig, unaufhörlich, ununterbrochen, fortwährend, beständig; ausdauernd (*in* bei); erbarmungslos.
unremoved ['ʌnri'mu:vd] *a* unverrückt; **unremunerative** ['ʌnri'mju:nərətiv] unrentabel.
unrepaired ['ʌnri'pɛəd] *a* nicht repariert; **unrepealed** ['ʌnri'pi:ld] *a* nicht widerrufen, nicht aufgehoben.
unrepent|ant ['ʌnri'pentənt], **~ing** ['-iŋ] ohne Reue; verstockt; **~ed** ['-id] *a* unbereut.
unrepresent|ed ['ʌnrepri'zentid] *a* nicht dargestellt; nicht vertreten; **~ative** ['-ətiv] nicht repräsentativ.
unrequited ['ʌnri'kwaitid] *a (Dienste)* ungelohnt; *(Liebe)* unerwidert.
unreserved ['ʌnri'zə:vd] *a* unbe-, uneingeschränkt; nicht reserviert; frei, offen; **~ly** ['-vidli] *adv* rückhaltlos.
unresist|ant ['ʌnri'zistənt], **~ing** ['-iŋ] widerstandslos; ohne Widerstand; **~ed** ['-id] *a* ungehindert.
unresolved ['ʌnri'zɔlvd] *a* unentschlossen, unschlüssig; ungelöst; *chem mus* unaufgelöst.
unresponsive ['ʌnris'pɔnsiv] nicht reagierend; teilnahmslos; *to s.th.* wenig bereit, auf etw einzugehen.
unrest ['ʌn'rest] Unruhe, Ruhelosigkeit *f*; **~ful** ['-ful] unruhig, ruhelos; **~ing** ['-iŋ] rastlos.
unrestrain|ed ['ʌnris'treind] *a* unbeherrscht, ungezügelt, zügellos; unbe-, uneingeschränkt; **~t** ['-t] Hemmungslosigkeit; Zwanglosigkeit *f*.
unrestricted ['ʌnris'triktid] *a* unbe-, uneingeschränkt; *(Geschwindigkeit)* unbegrenzt.
unreturned ['ʌnri'tə:nd] *a* nicht zurückgegeben; nicht zurückgekehrt; unerwidert; *parl* nicht gewählt.
unrevealed ['ʌnri'vi:ld] *a* nicht enthüllt; verborgen.
unrevenged ['ʌnri'vendʒd] *a* ungerächt.
unrevised ['ʌnri'vaizd] *a* nicht durchgesehen, nicht revidiert.
unrewarded ['ʌnri'wɔ:did] *a* unbelohnt.
unrhymed ['ʌn'raimd] *a* ungereimt, reimlos.
unriddle ['ʌn'ridl] *tr* enträtseln.
unrig ['ʌn'rig] *tr mar* abtakeln; *allg* abmontieren; *fam* auskleiden.
unrighteous [ʌn'raitʃəs] *rel* sündig, sündhaft; un(ge)recht, unfair; unredlich; **~ness** ['-nis] *rel* Sündhaftigkeit; Ungerechtigkeit *f*.
unrip ['ʌn'rip] *tr* auftrennen, -reißen.
unripe ['ʌn'raip] unreif.
unrival(l)ed ['ʌn'raivəld] *a* ohne Nebenbuhler, konkurrenzlos; unvergleichlich, einzigartig.
unroll ['ʌn'roul] *tr* aufrollen *a. fig*; *fig* entwickeln, darlegen; *itr* sich entfalten.
unromantic ['ʌnrə'mæntik] unromantisch, prosaisch, nüchtern.
unroof ['ʌn'ru:f] *tr* das Dach abdecken (*a house* e-s Hauses).
unruffled ['ʌn'rʌfld] *a (See)* unbewegt, glatt, ruhig; *fig* (seelen)ruhig, unerschüttert.
unrul|iness [ʌn'rulinis] Widersetzlichkeit; Undiszipliniertheit *f*; **~y** [-i] widersetzlich, undiszipliniert, ungehorsam, aufsässig.

*

unsaddle ['ʌn'sædl] *tr (Pferd)* absatteln; aus dem Sattel werfen.
unsafe ['ʌn'seif] unsicher; gefährdet; gefährlich; unzuverlässig.
unsaid ['ʌn'sed] *a* ungesagt, unausgesprochen.
unsalaried ['ʌn'sælərid] *a (Arbeit, Volontär)* unbezahlt; ehrenamtlich.
unsal(e)able ['ʌn'seiləbl] unverkäuflich; *(Waren)* nicht gangbar.
unsalted ['ʌn'sɔ:ltid] *a* ungesalzen.
unsanct|ified ['ʌn'sæŋktifaid] *a* ungeweiht; **~ioned** ['-kʃənd] *a (Urkunde)* nicht bestätigt; nicht genehmigt.

unsanitary ['ʌn'sænitəri] ungesund; unhygienisch.
unsatisf|actory ['ʌnsætis'fæktəri], **~ying** ['ʌn'sætisfaiiŋ] unbefriedigend; **~ied** ['ʌn'sætisfaid] *a* unbefriedigt; nicht zufrieden(gestellt) (*with* mit); nicht erledigt, unbereinigt; *com* unbezahlt.
unsavo(u)r|iness ['ʌn'seivərinis] Geschmacklosigkeit, Fadheit; Widerlichkeit *f*; **~y** ['-i] geschmacklos, fad(e); widerlich *a. fig*; *fig* abstoßend.
unsay ['ʌn'sei] *irr s. say tr (Gesagtes)* zurücknehmen, widerrufen.
unscaled ['ʌn'skeild] *a* abgeschuppt.
unscathed ['ʌn'skeiðd] *a* unbeschädigt, unverletzt.
unscholarly ['ʌn'skɔləli] *a* ungebildet.
unschooled ['ʌn'sku:ld] *a* ungeschult, unausgebildet; ungebildet.
unscientific ['ʌnsaiən'tifik] *adv ~ally* ['-əli] unwissenschaftlich.
unscramble ['ʌn'skræmbl] *tr fam* (wieder) Ordnung bringen in; in s-e Bestandteile zerlegen; entziffern.
unscrew ['ʌn'skru:] *tr* los-, ab-, aufschrauben; *itr (Festgeschraubtes)* sich lockern.
unscriptural ['ʌn'skriptʃərəl] unbiblisch.
unscrupulous [ʌn'skru:pjuləs] skrupel-, gewissenlos.
unseal ['ʌn'si:l] *tr* entsiegeln; *(Brief, Behälter)* erbrechen; *(Lippen)* öffnen; *fig* enthüllen; **~ed** ['-d] *a* unversiegelt.
unsearchable [ʌn'sə:tʃəbl] unerforschlich, unergründlich.
unseason|able [ʌn'si:znəbl] unzeitig; unangebracht, unpassend; **~ed** ['-nd] *a* unausgereift; *(bes. Holz)* nicht abgelagert; *fig* (noch) unerfahren; *(Speise)* ungewürzt.
unseat ['ʌn'si:t] *tr* des Amtes entheben, absetzen; *parl* s-n Sitz nehmen (*s.o.* jdm); aus dem Sattel heben, abwerfen.
unseaworthy ['ʌn'si:wə:ði] *(Schiff)* nicht seetüchtig.
unsecured ['ʌnsi'kjuəd] *a* ungesichert; *com* ungedeckt.
unseeing ['ʌn'si:iŋ] nicht sehend; *fig* blind.
unseem|liness [ʌn'si:mlinis] Unschicklich-, Unziemlich-, Unanständigkeit *f*; **~ly** [-li] unpassend, unschicklich, unziemlich, unanständig.
unseen ['ʌn'si:n] *a* ungesehen; unbemerkt, unbeobachtet, unentdeckt; unsichtbar; noch nie dagewesen; *s* (Übersetzung *f* e-s) unbekannte(n) *(fremdsprachigen)* Text(es); Klausur (-arbeit) *f*; *the ~* das Jenseits.
unselfish ['ʌn'selfiʃ] selbstlos, uneigennützig; **~ness** ['-nis] Selbstlosigkeit, Uneigennützigkeit *f*.
unsentimental ['ʌnsenti'mentl] unsentimental.
unserviceable ['ʌn'sə:visəbl] nicht dienlich; unbrauchbar, unverwendbar, unnütz (*to* für).
unsettl|e ['ʌn'setl] *tr* in Unordnung, *fig* durchea.bringen; unsicher machen; **~ed** ['-d] *a* nicht seßhaft, ohne festen Wohnsitz; in unsicherer Stellung; unbesiedelt, unbevölkert; *fig* unordentlich, durcheinander; wechselnd, schwankend, unbeständig, ungewiß; uneinheitlich; unbestimmt, nicht festgelegt, -gesetzt; ungeregelt, unerledigt; *com* unbezahlt, unbeglichen.
unsex ['ʌn'seks] *tr* unweiblich, unfraulich machen; der weiblichen Reize berauben, vermännlichen.
unshackle ['ʌn'ʃækl] *tr* die Fesseln abnehmen (*s.o.* jdm); *mar* ausschäkeln.
unshaded ['ʌn'ʃeidid] *a* unbeschattet; ungetrübt; nicht schattiert.
unshak|able [ʌn'ʃeikəbl] unerschütterlich, unbeirrbar; **~en** ['ʌn'ʃeikən] *a* unerschüttert, unbeirrt, fest.
unshap|ed ['ʌn'ʃeipt] *a* ungeformt, formlos; **~ely** ['ʌn'ʃeipli] *a* unförmig, mißgestalt.
unshaven ['ʌn'ʃeivn] *a* unrasiert.
unsheathe ['ʌn'ʃi:ð] *tr* (aus der Scheide) ziehen.
unshed ['ʌn'ʃed] *a (Tränen)* unvergossen; *(Blätter)* nicht abgeworfen.
unshell ['ʌn'ʃel] *tr* schälen, enthülsen; *fig* befreien.
unsheltered ['ʌn'ʃeltəd] *a* ungeschützt, schutzlos; obdachlos.
unship ['ʌn'ʃip] *tr mar (Ladung)* löschen; *(Passagiere)* ausschiffen; *tech* ab-, ausbauen; *fam fig* ausbooten.
unshod ['ʌn'ʃɔd] *a* unbeschuht, barfuß; *(Pferd)* unbeschlagen.
unshorn ['ʌn'ʃɔ:n] *a* ungeschoren.
unshrink|able ['ʌn'ʃriŋkəbl] nicht schrumpfend; *(Gewebe)* nicht einlaufend; **~ing** [-'-iŋ] vor nichts zurückschreckend, furchtlos, unverzagt.
unsifted ['ʌn'siftid] *a* ungesiebt; *fig* ungeordnet, ungeprüft.
unsight|ed ['ʌn'saitid] *a* (noch) nicht gesichtet; **~ly** [-'-li] *a* unansehnlich, häßlich.
unsigned ['ʌn'saind, *attr a.* 'ʌnsaind] *a* nicht unterzeichnet.
unsized ['ʌn'saizd] *a* **1.** nicht nach Maß gemacht; nicht nach Größen sortiert; **2.** ungestärkt, -geleimt; nicht grundiert.
unskil|led ['ʌn'skild] *a* ungelernt, ungeübt; *~~ labo(u)r* einfache Handarbeit; die ungelernten Arbeiter *m pl*; *~~ labo(u)rer, worker* ungelernte(r) Arbeiter *m*; **~(l)ful** ['ʌn'skilful] ungeschickt, linkisch.
unskimmed ['ʌn'skimd] *a* nicht entrahmt; *~* **milk** Vollmilch *f*.
unslaked ['ʌn'sleikt] *a (Feuer, Durst, Kalk)* ungelöscht.
unsling ['ʌn'sliŋ] *tr* ab-, losschnallen; *(Gewehr)* abnehmen.
unsnarl ['ʌn'snɑ:l] *tr* entwirren.
unsoci|ability ['ʌnsouʃə'biliti] Ungeselligkeit *f*; **~able** [ʌn'souʃəbl] ungesellig; **~al** ['ʌn'souʃəl] unsozial; gesellschaftsfeindlich.
unsoiled ['ʌn'sɔild] *a* nicht beschmutzt, sauber; *fig* unbefleckt.
unsold ['ʌn'sould] *a* unverkauft, nicht abgesetzt.
unsolder ['ʌn'sɔldə] *tr* los-, ablöten.
unsoldier|like ['ʌn'souldʒəlaik] **~ly** ['-li] *a* unsoldatisch.
unsolicited ['ʌnsə'lisitid] *a* unverlangt; unaufgefordert, ungefragt, ungebeten.
unsolved ['ʌn'sɔlvd] *a* ungelöst.
unsophisticated ['ʌnsə'fistikeitid] *a* unverfälscht, echt; natürlich, ungekünstelt.
unsorted ['ʌn'sɔ:tid] *a* unsortiert.
unsought ['ʌn'sɔ:t] *a* ungesucht; ungebeten.
unsound ['ʌn'sound] ungesund, krankhaft, verdorben *a. fig*; unvollkommen; unvollständig; *fig* falsch; unecht, unwahr; *com* unzuverlässig; *(Grund)* nicht stichhaltig, fadenscheinig; *(Ausrede)* faul; *(Schlaf)* unruhig; *(Obst)* faul; *in an ~ state of mind* im Zustand geistiger Umnachtung; *of ~ mind* geisteskrank; *~* **doctrine** Irrlehre *f*.
unsparing [ʌn'spɛəriŋ] verschwenderisch, freigebig (*of* mit); reichlich, großzügig (*of* mit); schonungslos (*of* gegen); *to be ~ in o.'s efforts* keine Mühe scheuen.
unspeakable [ʌn'spi:kəbl] unaussprechlich, unsagbar; gräßlich.
unspecified ['ʌn'spesifaid] *a* nicht spezifiziert, nicht einzeln angegeben.
unspent ['ʌn'spent] *a* nicht ausgegeben, unverbraucht *a. fig*; *fig* ungeschwächt.
unspoil|ed ['ʌn'spɔild], **~t** ['-t] *a* unverdorben.
unsport|smanlike ['ʌn'spɔ:tsmənlaik], *fam* **~ing** ['-iŋ] unsportlich; unweidmännisch; unritterlich.
unspoken ['ʌn'spoukən] *a* ungesagt, unausgesprochen; *~-of* unerwähnt.
unspotted ['ʌn'spɔtid] *a bes. zoo* ungefleckt; *fig* unbefleckt, rein; unentdeckt.
unstable ['ʌn'steibl] labil; unsicher, schwankend *a. fig*; *fig* wankelmütig, unzuverlässig; *fig* unbeständig *a. chem (Verbindung)*.
unstained ['ʌn'steind] *a* fleckenlos *a. fig*; *fig* unbefleckt; ungefärbt.
unstamped ['ʌn'stæmpt] *a* ungestempelt; unfrankiert.
unstatesmanlike ['ʌn'steitsmənlaik] nicht staatsmännisch.
unsteady ['ʌn'stedi] wack(e)lig; unregelmäßig; *fig* unbeständig, schwankend, unzuverlässig *a. com*.
unstick ['ʌn'stik] *itr (Geklebtes)* sich lösen *a. fig*; *aero* sich vom (Erd-)Boden abheben.
unstint|ed [ʌn'stintid] *a* unbeschränkt, unbegrenzt; nicht bestimmt, nicht festgesetzt; **~ing** [-iŋ] großzügig, freigebig.
unstitch ['ʌn'stitʃ] *tr (Genähtes)* auftrennen; *to come ~ed (Naht)* aufgehen.
unstop ['ʌn'stɔp] *tr* aufstöpseln, -spunden; entkorken; *(Verstopftes)* frei machen.
unstrained ['ʌn'streind] *a* locker, lose; *fig* ungezwungen, zwanglos; nicht gesiebt, unfiltriert.
unstrap ['ʌn'stræp] *tr* losbinden, -schnallen.
unstressed ['ʌn'strest] *a (Silbe, Wort)* unbetont; *tech* unbelastet.
un|string ['ʌn'striŋ] *irr s. string tr* lockern, losbinden, entspannen; *fig* lockern, mildern; *(Nerven)* überanstrengen; nervös machen; **~strung** ['-'strʌŋ] *a* (ge)locker(t), lose; *(Perlen)* abgereiht; *fig* aufgelöst, aufgeregt; schwach, kraftlos; nervös.
unstuck ['ʌn'stʌk] *a* nicht fest; lose; *to come ~* sich lösen; *sl (Plan)* ins Wasser fallen.
unstudied ['ʌn'stʌdid] *a* ungekünstelt; natürlich, ungezwungen, spontan; ungebildet, unbewandert (*in* in).
unsubdued ['ʌnsəb'dju:d] *a* nicht unterjocht, -worfen, unbesiegt.
unsubmissive ['ʌnsəb'misiv] widersetzlich, -spenstig.
unsubstant|ial ['ʌnsəb'stænʃəl] unkörperlich, immateriell, substanzlos; schwach; gehaltlos; *fig* haltlos, unbegründet; **~iated** ['-ieitid] *a* unbegründet.
unsuccess ['ʌnsək'ses] Mißerfolg *m*; **~ful** ['-ful] erfolglos.
unsuitable ['ʌn'sju:təbl] unpassend, unangebracht, ungeeignet (*to, for* für); **~ed** ['-id] *a* ungeeignet, unpassend (*to, for* für).
unsullied ['ʌn'sʌlid] *a* sauber, rein; *fig* unbefleckt.
unsung ['ʌn'sʌŋ] *a lit* nicht besungen.
unsupport|able ['ʌnsə'pɔ:təbl] unerträglich; **~ed** ['-id] *a* nicht unterstützt (*by* von); nicht bestärkt, bestätigt, bekräftigt (*by* durch).
unsuppressed ['ʌnsə'prest] *a* nicht unterdrückt.

unsure ['ʌn'ʃuə] unsicher, ungewiß; zweifelhaft, im Zweifel (*of* über; *whether* ob); schwankend.
unsurmountable ['ʌnsə(:)'mauntəbl] unübersteigbar, unüberwindlich *a. fig.*
unsurpass|able ['ʌnsə(:)'pɑ:səbl] unübertrefflich; **~ed** ['-t] *a* unübertroffen.
unsuspect|ed ['ʌnsəs'pektid] *a* unverdächtig; unvermutet, ungeahnt; **~ing** ['-iŋ] nichtsahnend, ahnungslos; arglos.
unsuspicious ['ʌnsəs'piʃəs] unverdächtig; nicht argwöhnisch.
unsweetened ['ʌn'swi:tnd] *a* ungesüßt.
unswerving [ʌn'swə:viŋ] fest, unerschütterlich, standhaft.
unsworn ['ʌn'swɔ:n] *a* unvereidigt.
unsymmetrical ['ʌnsi'metrikəl] unsymmetrisch.
unsympathetic ['ʌnsimpə'θetik] *adv* **~ally** ['-əli] unsympathisch; teilnahmslos.
unsystematic ['ʌnsisti'mætik] *adv* **~ally** ['-əli] unsystematisch.
untack ['ʌn'tæk] *tr* los-, abmachen; abtrennen.
untainted ['ʌn'teintid] *a* fleckenlos, rein; unverdorben; *fig* makellos.
untam|able ['ʌn'teiməbl] un(be)zähmbar; **~ed** ['-d] *a* ungezähmt *a. fig.*
untangle ['ʌn'tæŋgl] *tr* entwirren *a. fig*; *fig* Ordnung bringen in, bereinigen, aufklären.
untanned ['ʌn'tænd] *a* ungegerbt; *(Gesicht)* ungebräunt.
untarnished ['ʌn'tɑ:niʃt] *a* ungetrübt; *fig* unbefleckt.
untaught ['ʌn'tɔ:t] *a* ungebildet, unwissend; angeboren, natürlich.
untax|able ['ʌn'tæksəbl] nicht besteuerungsfähig; **~ed** ['-t] *a* unbesteuert, steuerfrei.
unteachable ['ʌn'ti:tʃəbl] unbelehrbar; *(Sache)* unlehrbar.
untempered ['ʌn'tempəd] *a* ungeordnet, unbeherrscht, unbeeinflußt (*by* durch); *metal* ungehärtet; *fig* ungemildert (*with, by* durch).
untenable ['ʌn'tenəbl] *fig* unhaltbar.
untenanted ['ʌn'tenəntid] *a* unvermietet; leerstehend, unbewohnt.
untended ['ʌn'tendid] *a* ohne Pflege, ohne Wartung; vernachlässigt.
untested ['ʌn'testid] *a* ungeprüft; nicht erprobt.
unthankful ['ʌn'θæŋkful] undankbar.
un|thinkable [ʌn'θiŋkəbl] undenkbar; **~thinking** ['-'θiŋkiŋ] gedankenlos; unbedacht; **~thought-of** [-'θɔ:tɔv] unvermutet, ungeahnt.
unthread ['ʌn'θred] *tr* den Faden ziehen aus; ausfasern; aufziehen, -trennen; entwirren *a. fig*; *fig* s-n Weg finden durch.
unthrifty ['ʌn'θrifti] verschwenderisch; nicht gedeihend; unwirtschaftlich.
untid|iness [ʌn'taidinis] Unsauberkeit, Unordnung *f*; **~y** [-i] unsauber, unordentlich.
untie ['ʌn'tai] *tr* aufbinden, -knoten; *(Problem)* lösen; *(Schwierigkeit)* meistern; *(von e-m Zwang)* befreien; *itr (Schleife, Knoten)* aufgehen; *fig* klar werden.
until [ən'til, ʌn'til] *prp (zeitlich)* bis, bis zu; *not ... ~* nicht vor; erst; *~ further notice* bis auf Widerruf, bis auf weiteres; *conj* bis (daß); *not ... ~* nicht bevor; nicht ehe; erst als, erst wenn.
untilled ['ʌn'tild] *a (Land)* unbebaut, *(Acker)* unbestellt.
untime|liness [ʌn'taimlinis] Ungelegenheit, Unangebrachtheit; Vorzeitigkeit *f*; **~ly** [-li] *a adv* unzeitig, ungelegen, unangebracht, unpassend; vorzeitig, verfrüht.
untiring [ʌn'taiəriŋ] unermüdlich.
untitled [ʌn'taitld] *a (Mensch, Buch)* ohne Titel; ohne Anspruch, Anrecht, unberechtigt.
unto ['ʌntu] *prp obs poet lit* zu; bis (zu); in; bei.
untold ['ʌn'tould] *a* nicht erzählt; unaussprechlich; ungezählt, unzählig, zahllos; *(Reichtum)* unermeßlich.
untouchable [ʌn'tʌtʃəbl] *rel* unberührbar; unerreichbar; unangreifbar; **~ed** ['ʌn'tʌtʃt] *a* unberührt *a. fig*; unverletzt, intakt; unangetastet; ungerührt; unbeeinflußt; *fig* ungeschminkt; *phot* unretuschiert.
untoward [ʌn'to(u)əd] *obs* eigensinnig, widerspenstig; unpassend, ungünstig, unglücklich; unschicklich, unziemlich.
untraceable ['ʌn'treisəbl] unaufspürbar, unauffindbar; nicht zurückführbar (*to* auf).
untrained ['ʌn'treind] *a* ungeschult, unausgebildet; nicht eingearbeitet, unvorbereitet; nicht dressiert, nicht abgerichtet; *sport* untrainiert.
untrammel(l)ed [ʌn'træməld] *a* unge-, unbehindert *a. fig*; *fig* ohne Verwick(e)lungen.
untransferable ['ʌntræns'fə:rəbl] nicht übertragbar.
untranslatable ['ʌntræns'leitəbl] unübersetzbar.
untravel(l)ed ['ʌn'trævəld] *a* un-, wenig befahren; nicht bereist; wenig (in der Welt) herumgekommen.
untried ['ʌn'traid] *a* unversucht; unerprobt, ungeprüft; *jur* nicht untersucht, nicht verhandelt, nicht entschieden, nicht abgeurteilt.
untrimmed ['ʌn'trimd] *a* ungepflegt, ungeputzt, ungeschmückt; *(Hecke)* unbeschnitten.
untrodden ['ʌn'trɔdn] *a* unbetreten, unbegangen.
untroubled ['ʌn'trʌbld] *a* ungestört, unbelästigt, ruhig (verlaufen).
untru|e ['ʌn'tru:] unwahr, unrichtig, falsch; abweichend (*to* von); nicht den Anforderungen, Vorschriften *od* Maßen entsprechend; unrichtig, unvollkommen; un(ge)treu, treulos (*to* dat); *tech* unrund; **~ly** ['-li] *adv* irrtümlicherweise; **~th** ['-θ] Unwahrheit; Lüge *f*; **~thful** ['-ful] unwahr, falsch; unwahrhaft, unaufrichtig, lügenhaft, lügnerisch.
untruss ['ʌn'trʌs] *tr* aufbinden, -machen; ausziehen, aus-, entkleiden.
untrustworth|iness ['ʌn'trʌstwə:ðinis] Unzuverlässigkeit *f*; **~y** ['-i] nicht vertrauenswürdig; unzuverlässig.
untunable ['ʌn'tju:nəbl] mißklingend, -tönend, diskordant.
unturned ['ʌn'tə:nd] *a* ungewendet; *to leave no stone ~ (fig)* kein Mittel unversucht lassen.
untutored ['ʌn'tju:təd] *a* unbeaufsichtigt; unerzogen, ungebildet; unverbildet, natürlich, schlicht, einfach.
untwine ['ʌn'twain], **untwist** ['ʌn'twist] *tr* aufflechten, -drehen, -winden; aufmachen; entwirren *a. fig*; *itr (Geflochtenes, Gedrehtes)* aufgehen.

unus|ed ['ʌn'ju:zd] *a* ungebraucht, unbenutzt; *(Kredit)* nicht beansprucht; ['-st] ungewohnt; nicht gewohnt (*to* an); nicht gewohnt (*to doing* zu tun); **~ual** [ʌn'ju:ʒuəl] ungewöhnlich, seltsam, selten, Ausnahme-.
unutter|able [ʌn'ʌtərəbl] unaussprechlich *a. fig*; unbeschreiblich; **~ed** ['-əd] *a* ungeäußert, unausgesprochen.
unvaccinated ['ʌn'væksineitid] *a* ungeimpft.
unvalued ['ʌn'vælju:d] *a* nicht geschätzt, nicht geachtet; unbewertet, nicht taxiert.
unvaried [ʌn'vɛərid] *a* unverändert.
unvarnished ['ʌn'vɑ:niʃt] *a* nicht gefirnißt; [ʌn'v-] unverziert, schmucklos, schlicht, einfach; *(Wahrheit)* ungeschminkt.
unveil [ʌn'veil] *tr* entschleiern, enthüllen, aufdecken *a. fig*; *fig* ans Licht, an den Tag bringen, den Schleier lüften über; *itr* den Schleier fallen lassen *od* abnehmen; *fig* sich entpuppen (*as* als).
unventilated ['ʌn'ventileitid] *a* ungelüftet; *fig* nicht ventiliert, unbesprochen.
unverified ['ʌn'verifaid] *a* unbestätigt.
unversed ['ʌn'və:st] *a* unbewandert, unkundig, unerfahren (*in* in).
unvisited ['ʌn'vizitid] *a* nicht besucht.
unvitrified ['ʌn'vitrifaid] *a* unverglast.
unvoiced ['ʌn'vɔist] *a* nicht (aus)gesprochen; *(Konsonant)* stimmlos.
unwanted ['ʌn'wɔntid] *a* unge-, unerwünscht.
unwar|iness [ʌn'wɛərinis] Unvorsichtigkeit *f*; **~y** [-i] unachtsam, unaufmerksam; sorglos, unbekümmert; voreilig, übereilt.
unwarlike ['ʌn'wɔ:laik] unkriegerisch.
unwarrant|able [ʌn'wɔrəntəbl] unverantwortlich; ungesetzlich; *(Behauptung)* unhaltbar; **~ed** [ʌn'wɔrəntid] *a* ungerechtfertigt, unbegründet, grundlos; unberechtigt, unbefugt; ['ʌn'w-] unverbürgt, unbestätigt.
unwashed ['ʌn'wɔʃt] *a* ungewaschen.
unwatch|ed ['ʌn'wɔtʃt] *a* unbewacht; **~ful** ['-tʃful] nicht wachsam; unbekümmert.
unwavering [ʌn'weivəriŋ] unerschütterlich, standhaft, fest.
unwearied [ʌn'wiərid] *a* nicht müde.
unweathered ['ʌn'weðəd] *a* noch nicht verwittert.
unwed(ded) ['ʌn'wed(id)] *a* unverheiratet, ledig.
unweigh|ed ['ʌn'weid] *a* ungewogen; **~ted** ['-'weitid] *a* entlastet.
unwelcome [ʌn'welkəm] unwillkommen.
unwell ['ʌn'wel] unwohl; unpäßlich; unzuträglich *a. fig.*
unwept ['ʌn'wept] *a* unbeweint; *(Tränen)* unvergossen.
unwholesome ['ʌn'houlsəm] ungesund, unzuträglich; leidend; *fig (sittlich)* verderblich.
unwield|iness [ʌn'wi:ldinis] Unhandlichkeit; Ungeschicktheit *f*; **~y** [-i] unhandlich, sperrig; ungeschickt, schwerfällig.
unwill|ed ['ʌn'wild] *a* nicht gewillt; ungewollt; **~ing** ['-iŋ] un-, widerwillig, abgeneigt, nicht geneigt; *to be ~~* keine Lust haben (*to do* zu tun); **~ingly** [-'wiliŋli] *adv* ungern, wider Willen; **~ingness** [-'wiliŋnis] Widerwille *m*; Abgeneigtheit *f*.
unwind ['ʌn'waind] *irr s. wind tr* abwinden, -wickeln *a. fig*; *fig* glätten, (wieder) in Ordnung bringen; *itr* sich abwickeln.
unwise ['ʌn'waiz] töricht, dumm, unklug.
unwitting [ʌn'witiŋ] ahnungslos; unbewußt; unabsichtlich; **~ly** [-li] *adv* unwissentlich; in Gedanken; ohne Absicht.
unwoman|liness [ʌn'wumənlinis] Unweiblichkeit *f*; **~ly** [-li] unweiblich.

unwonted [ʌn'wountid] *a* ungewohnt (*to do* zu tun); nicht gewöhnt (*to* an); ungewöhnlich, selten.
unwork|able ['ʌn'wə:kəbl] nicht funktionierend, nicht funktions-, betriebsfähig; nicht durchführbar, nicht zu bewältigen(d); *(Plan)* unausführbar; *(Material)* nicht zu bearbeiten(d), unbrauchbar; *min* nicht abbauwürdig, nicht zu verhütten(d); **~ed** ['-t] *a* unbe-, unverarbeitet; *min* (noch) nicht abgebaut; *(Kohle)* anstehend; **~manlike** ['-mənlaik] unfachmännisch, stümperhaft.
unworld|liness ['ʌn'wə:ldlinis] Weltabgewandtheit *f*; **~ly** ['-li] *a* weltabgewandt; geistig; überirdisch, himmlisch.
unworn ['ʌn'wɔ:n] *a (Kleidung)* ungetragen; nicht abgetragen.
unworth|iness [ʌn'wə:ðinis] Unwürdigkeit; Würdelosigkeit *f*; **~y** [-i] unwürdig; nicht wert (*of s.th.* etw); würdelos, schändlich; *to be ~~ of belief* keinen Glauben verdienen.
unwounded ['ʌn'wu:ndid] *a* unverwundet, unverletzt.
unwrap ['ʌn'ræp] *tr* auswickeln, -packen.
unwrinkle ['ʌn'riŋkl] *tr* glattstreichen, glätten.
unwritten ['ʌn'ritn] *a* ungeschrieben, nicht niedergeschrieben; *~* **law** Gewohnheitsrecht *n*; *the ~~* das ungeschriebene Gesetz; das (gesunde) Volksempfinden.
unwrought ['ʌn'rɔ:t] *a* unbe-, unverarbeitet; Roh-; *~* **goods** *pl* Rohstoffe *m pl*; *~* **iron** Roheisen *n*.
unwrung ['ʌn'rʌŋ] *a* nicht ausgewrungen; nicht verzerrt, nicht verzogen; *my withers are ~ (fig)* das macht keinen Eindruck auf mich, *fam* das imponiert mir nicht.
unyielding [ʌn'ji:ldiŋ] nicht nachgebend, starr; *fig* unnachgiebig.
unyoke ['ʌn'jouk] *tr (Zugtier)* ausspannen; *allg* trennen, lösen; *fig* befreien.
unzip ['ʌn'zip] *tr*: *to ~ s.th.* den Reißverschluß e-r S öffnen; *to ~ a zipper* e-n Reißverschluß aufmachen.

*

up [ʌp] **1.** *adv* auf; aufwärts, hinauf, nach oben, empor *a. fig*; her (*to me* zu mir); oben, droben; hoch *a. fig; and ~ (nach Preisangaben)* und darüber, und mehr; aufrecht, aufgerichtet, erhoben; *(aus dem Bett)* auf(gestanden); (her)um, vorbei, abgelaufen; aus; **2.** *~ against (prp)* gegenüber; *~ against it (fam)* in (*bes.* finanziellen) Schwierigkeiten; *to be ~ against great difficulties* mit großen Schwierigkeiten zu kämpfen haben; *~ and doing* im Gange, geschäftig, tätig; *~ and down* überall hin; auf u. ab, hin u. her *a. fig*; von oben bis unten; *~ for election* auf der Wahlliste; *~ for trial* vor Gericht; *~ to* bis (zu); bei; *~ to the present day* bis zum heutigen Tage; bis heute; *to be ~ to s.th.* etw tun, machen; etw im Sinn, vorhaben, planen; *fam* im Schilde führen; e-r S gleichkommen, entsprechen, gewachsen sein; *~ to date* auf der Höhe der Zeit, modern; *~ to the eyes in (fig)* zugedeckt mit (*work* Arbeit); *~ to the mark, to scratch, to snuff* den Erfordernissen entsprechend, auf der Höhe; *~ to the minute* hochmodern, der (aller)letzte Schrei; *not ~ to much* nicht viel wert; *it is not ~ to much* damit ist nicht viel los, damit ist es nicht weit her; *~ to now* bisher, bis jetzt; *~ to par* vollwertig, auf der Höhe, auf dem Posten; *~ to standard* den Anforderungen entsprechend, auf der Höhe; *~ to s.o.* jds Sache, Angelegenheit, Aufgabe, Pflicht; *it's ~ to him* es hängt von ihm ab; *if it were ~ to him ...* wenn es nach ihm ginge ...; *~ and ~* immer weiter nach oben, immer höher; *~ with* auf gleicher Höhe mit, wie; *~ with the times* auf der Höhe der Zeit; **3.** *to be ~ and about, (Am) ~ around* wieder auf dem Damm, auf dem Posten sein; *to be hard ~* übel d(a)ran sein; *to be ~ in* od *on a subject (fam)* in e-m Fach gut beschlagen sein; *to come ~ to s.th.* bis an etw heranreichen, e-r S gleichkommen; entsprechen; *to feel ~ to s.th.* sich e-r S gewachsen fühlen; *to get ~* aufstehen, sich erheben; *to go ~* in die Höhe gehen, hinaufgehen; *to go ~ to town, to university* in die Stadt gehen *od* fahren, zur Universität gehen; *to use ~* aufbrauchen; *to walk ~* hinaufgehen; *it's all ~ with him (fam)* es ist aus mit ihm, er ist erledigt; *what's ~? (fam)* was ist los? was gibt's? *there's s.th. ~ (fig)* es liegt etw in der Luft; *chin ~!* Kopf hoch! *Parliament is ~* das Parlament hat sich vertagt; **4.** *prp* ... hinauf, an ... empor; in ... *(ein Land)* hinein; *~ the wind* gegen den Wind; **5.** *s* Steigung *(im Gelände)*; aufsteigende Linie *f*, *fam* Ast *m fig*; Ansteigen *n* (der Preise), steigende(r) Kurs *m*; in die Stadt, ins Stadtzentrum fahrende(r) Zug *(~ train)*, Bus *m*; *on the ~ and ~ (sl)* offen (u. ehrlich), gerade; *the ~s and downs* das Auf u. Ab, die Wechselfälle *m pl* des Lebens; **6.** *tr fam* auf-, hochheben; *(bes. Preise)* in die Höhe treiben; *(Auktion)* hochtreiben; *itr fam* in die Höhe fahren, aufspringen, -stehen.
up-and-coming ['ʌpən'kʌmiŋ] *fam* unternehmungslustig, tüchtig.
up-and-down ['ʌpən'daun] *a* auf- u. absteigend; hin u. zurück; schwankend, unregelmäßig; *Am fam* ehrlich.
upas ['ju:pəs] *pl -es* ['-iz] *(~-tree)* Upas-, Giftbaum *m*; Upas Antiar *(Pfeilgift)*; *fig* Gift *n*, verderbliche(r) Einfluß *m*, Übel *n*.
upbeat ['ʌpbi:t] *s mus* Auftakt *m*; *a Am fam* unterhaltsam; Unterhaltungs-.
up-bow ['ʌpbou] *mus* Aufstrich *m*.
upbraid [ʌp'breid] *tr* ausschimpfen, schelten, tadeln (*for, with* wegen); *s.o.* jdm vorwerfen, -halten (*with s.th.* etw; *for doing s.th.* etw zu tun); *itr* schimpfen; **~ing** [-iŋ] *s* Tadel *m*, Vorhaltungen *f pl*, Vorwurf *m*; *a* tadelnd, vorwurfsvoll.
upbringing ['ʌpbriŋiŋ] Aufzucht; Erziehung *f*.
upcast ['ʌpkɑ:st] *s (~ shaft) min* Luftschacht *m*; *a* [-'-] in die Höhe geworfen; auf-, emporgerichtet; *(Augen)* aufgeschlagen.
upchuck ['ʌptʃʌk] *itr Am fam* sich erbrechen.
up-country ['ʌp'kʌntri] *s* Binnenland, Landinnere(s) *n*; *a* binnenländisch; *Am pej* bäu(e)risch; *adv* [-'-] landeinwärts.
up-current ['ʌpkʌrənt] *aero* Aufwind *m*.
update [ʌp'deit] *tr Am* auf den neuesten Stand bringen, modernisieren.
updo ['ʌpdu:] *fam* Hochfrisur *f*.
updraught, *Am* **updraft** ['ʌpdrɑ:ft] *aero* Aufwind *m*.
up-end [ʌp'end] *tr* umstülpen; auf den Kopf, hochkant stellen; *itr* hochkant, auf dem Kopf stehen.
up-grade ['ʌpgreid] *s* Steigung *f (im Gelände)*; *a* ansteigend; *adv* bergauf; *tr* [ʌp'greid] *(Beamten)* befördern; höher einstufen; *on the ~* ansteigend; *fig* aufsteigend, fortschreitend, im Aufstieg (begriffen); *com* sich erholend; *(Preis)* steigend.
upgrowth ['ʌpgrouθ] Wachstum *n*; Entwick(e)lung *f*; Wuchs, Trieb, Schößling *m*.
upheav|al [ʌp'hi:vəl] *geol* plötzliche Umgestaltung; *fig* Umwälzung *f*, Umsturz *m*; **~e** [-'hi:v] *irr s. heave tr* (hoch-, empor)heben; *geol* aufwerfen; *itr* sich (plötzlich) heben.
uphill ['ʌp'hil] *s* Steigung, (Boden-)Erhebung *f*; *a* ['--] (an)steigend; *fig* mühselig, anstrengend; *adv* ['--, -'-] bergauf, -an.
uphold [ʌp'hould] *irr s. hold tr* hochheben, -halten; aufrecht halten, stützen; in gutem Zustand erhalten; *fig* Mut machen (*s.o.* jdm); *fig* unterstützen, verteidigen, billigen; **~er** [-ə] Stütze *f (Person)*; Verteidiger, Verfechter *m*.
upholster [ʌp'houlstə] *tr (Sitzmöbel)* polstern (*in, with* mit); *(Raum)* dekorieren; **~er** [-rə] Polsterer; Dekorateur, Innenausstatter *m*; **~y** [-ri] Polstermaterial *n*; Polsterung; Dekoration, Innenausstattung *f*; Polster-, Dekorations-, Teppich- u. Gardinengeschäft *n*.
upkeep ['ʌpki:p] Instandhaltung, Erhaltung *(e-s Gebäudes)*, Unterhaltung *f*; (baulicher) Erhaltungszustand *m*; Instandhaltungs-, Unterhaltungskosten *pl*.
upland ['ʌplənd] *oft pl s* Hoch-, Oberland *n*; *attr* Hoch-; hochgelegen.
uplift [ʌp'lift] *tr* hoch-, emporheben; *fig* (sittlich, geistig, gesellschaftlich) (er)heben; *s* ['ʌplift] *fig* (sittliche) Hebung *f*, (geistiger) Fortschritt; (sozialer) Aufstieg, Aufschwung *m*; (sittliche, geistige) Erneuerung(sbewegung); Besserung; *geol* Aufwölbung *f*; *(~ brassiere) Am* Büstenhalter *m*; *on the ~ (Am fam)* im Aufstieg, auf dem aufsteigenden Ast; **~er** ['-ə] *Am* (Sozial-) Reformer; Fürsorgebeamte(r) *m*.
up-line ['ʌplain] Gleis *n* in Richtung London.
upmost ['ʌpmoust] *a* oberst, höchst.
upon [ə'pɔn, əpən] *prp = on (meist lit)*; *once ~ a time* es war einmal; *~ inquiry* nach Erkundigung, auf Erkundigungen hin; *~ this* hierauf, danach, dann; *~ my word* auf mein Wort.
upper ['ʌpə] *a* höher, ober *a. geol fig*; *(Kleidung)* Ober-; *s (shoe ~)* Oberleder; *fam* obere(s) Bett *n*, obere Koje *f*; *med* Oberkiefer *m*; *to be (down) on o.'s ~s (fam)* völlig abgerissen sein; auf dem letzten Loch pfeifen; *to get, to have the ~ hand of* die Oberhand gewinnen, haben über; *the ~ case (typ)* die Versalien, großen Anfangsbuchstaben; *the ~ circle (theat)* der erste Rang; *the U~ House (parl)* das Oberhaus; *the ~ storey (fam)* das Oberstübchen, der Hirnkasten, der Verstand; *the ~ ten (thousand), (fam) the ~ crust* die oberen Zehntausend; *~* **arm** Oberarm *m*; *~* **beds** *pl min* Hangende(s) *n*; **~-bracket** *a* Höchst-, Spitzen-; in der oberen Einkommensgruppe; **~-case** *a* Groß-*(Buchstabe)*; *~* **class** Oberklasse *f (Gesellschaft, höhere Schule)*; **~-class** *a* Oberklassen-; **~cut** *s (Boxen)* Kinnhaken *m*; *tr* e-n K. versetzen (*s.o.* jdm); *~* **deck** *mar* Oberdeck *n*; *~* **jaw** Oberkiefer *m*; *~* **leather** Oberleder *n (Material)*; *~* **lip** Oberlippe *f*; **~most** ['-moust] *a* oberst, höchst; *adv* am höchsten; ganz oben; *to say whatever*

comes ~~ sagen, was e-m gerade einfällt.

upp|ish ['ʌpiʃ], *Am fam* **~ity** ['-iti] *a* dünkelhaft, überheblich, *fam* von sich selbst überzogen, hochnäsig.

up-platform ['ʌp-'plætfɔ:m] Ankunftbahnsteig *m (in London).*

upraised [*pred* ʌp'reizd, *attr* 'ʌpreizd] *a* erhoben, hochgehoben.

uprear [ʌp'riə] *tr* aufrichten; auf-, großziehen; *fig* in den Himmel heben.

upright *a* ['ʌp'rait] aufrecht, aufgerichtet, senkrecht; ['ʌprait] aufrecht, g(e)rade, ehrenhaft, -wert, rechtschaffen; *adv* ['ʌp'rait] auf-, senkrecht; in die Höhe; *s* ['--] aufrechte Stellung, Haltung *f*; Ständer, Pfosten *m*; *mus (~ piano)* Pianino *n*; *pl sport* Torpfosten *m pl*; **~ness** ['-nis] G(e)radheit, Ehrenhaftigkeit, Rechtschaffenheit *f*; **~ size** Hochformat *n.*

upris|e [ʌp'raiz] *irr s. rise itr lit* sich erheben, aufstehen, auf-, hoch-, ansteigen; sich aufrichten; aufrecht stehen; zunehmen, sich ausdehnen; *(Ton)* anschwellen; *fig* in Erscheinung, ins Leben, in Tätigkeit treten; sich *(zu e-m Aufstand)* erheben; *s* ['--] Aufstehen *n*; Auf-, Anstieg; *(Sonne)* Aufgang *m*; Zunahme, Ausdehnung; Steigung *f (im Gelände)*; **~ing** [-iŋ] *s* = *~e (s)*; Erhebung *f*, Aufstand *m.*

uproar ['ʌprɔ:] Aufruhr, Tumult; Lärm, Spektakel *m*; **~ious** [ʌp'rɔ:riəs] aufrührerisch; tobend, lärmend, laut.

uproot [ʌp'ru:t] *tr* entwurzeln; ausreißen (*from* aus); *allg* ausmerzen; völlig, gründlich vernichten, zerstören; aus der Welt schaffen; *fig* versetzen, verpflanzen.

upset [ʌp'set] *irr s. set tr* umstürzen, -kippen, -werfen, -stoßen; auf den Kopf stellen *a. fig*; *fig* durchea.-, völlig in Unordnung bringen; *fig* über den Haufen werfen, umstoßen, vereiteln; aus der Fassung, aus dem Gleichgewicht bringen, fassungslos machen; *tech* stauchen, quetschen; *mar* zum Kentern bringen; *itr* (um-)stürzen, -kippen, sich überschlagen; *(Boot)* kentern; *s* Umkippen, Umfallen *n*; Sturz; *fig* Fehlschlag *m*; Unordnung *f*, Durcheinander *n*, Verwirrung; Verstimmung, Uneinigkeit *f*, Streit *m*; *sport* unerwartete(s) Ergebnis *n*, Überraschung *f*; *(Boot)* Kentern; *tech* Gesenk *n*, Wulst *m*, Verdickung *f*; *min* Aufhieb *m*; *a* umgekippt, (um)gestürzt; in Unordnung (gebracht); *(Magen)* verstimmt; *fig* durchea.gebracht, aufgeregt, außer Fassung, bestürzt; fest(gesetzt); *to ~ the Government* die Regierung stürzen; **~ price** Anschlagspreis *m.*

upshot ['ʌpʃɔt] Ausgang *m*, Ende *n*, (Be-)Schluß *m*, Ergebnis, Resultat *n*; *in the ~* schließlich u. endlich, letzten Endes.

upside ['upsaid] obere Seite *f*, obere(r) Teil; Bahnsteig *m* (in Richtung London); **~-down** ['--'-] *adv* kopfüber, das Unterste zuoberst; verkehrt; *fig* drunter u. drüber, völlig durchea., in völliger Unordnung; *to turn s.th.* ~~ etw auf den Kopf stellen; **~s** ['-z] *adv fig fam* eben (*with* mit).

upstage ['ʌp'steidʒ] *adv* im Hintergrund der Bühne (befindlich); *a* [-'-] *fam* eingebildet, übergeschnappt, dünkelhaft, hochmütig.

upstairs ['ʌp'stɛəz] *adv* oben, im oberen Stock(werk); (die Treppe) hinauf, treppauf, nach oben, in den oberen Stock; *a* ['--] im oberen Stockwerk (befindlich); ober; *aero sl* in der Luft; *s* Oberstock *m*, obere Stockwerke *n pl*; *to go ~* nach oben, hinaufgehen; *aero sl* aufsteigen; *to kick s.o. ~ (Am fam)* jdn wegloben.

upstanding [ʌp'stændiŋ] aufgerichtet, stehend; stattlich; *fig* aufrecht.

•

upstart ['ʌpstɑ:t] *s* Emporkömmling, Neureiche(r), Parvenü *m*; *a* neureich; parvenühaft.

upstate ['ʌp'steit] *Am s* Hinterland *n (bes. von New York)*; *a* aus dem Hinterland; Hinterland-; *adv* im *od* ins Hinterland.

upstream ['ʌp'stri:m] *adv a* fluß-, stromaufwärts (gelegen); gegen den Strom (schwimmend).

upstroke ['ʌpstrouk] Auf-, Haarstrich *(e-s Buchstabens)*; *tech* (Aufwärts-) Hub *m.*

upsurge [ʌp'sə:dʒ] *itr* aufwallen; *s* ['--] Aufwallung *f.*

upsweep [ʌp'swi:p] *irr s. sweep tr* nach oben richten *od* kehren; *itr* nach oben gerichtet, gekehrt sein; *s* ['--] nach oben, aufwärts geschwungene Linie *od* Kurve; *(upswept hair-do)* Hochfrisur *f.*

upswing ['ʌpswiŋ] *s* Aufwärtsbewegung *f*, Aufschwung *m a. fig.*

uptake ['ʌpteik] Verständnis *n*; *tech* Fuchs *m*, Lüftungsrohr *n*, Luftschacht *m*; *to be quick, slow on the ~* schnell begreifen; schwer von Begriff sein.

upthrow ['ʌpθrou] *geol* Verwerfung; *fig* Erschütterung, Umwälzung *f.*

up-to-|date *a* [*pred* 'ʌptə'deit; *attr* 'ʌptədeit] *pred up to date* bis zur Gegenwart reichend; auf dem laufenden; auf der Höhe der Zeit stehend, modern; aktuell; **~the-minute** *a* modernst, letzt.

up-town ['ʌp'taun] *adv* in die, in den höhergelegenen Stadtteile(n); *Am* ins, im Wohnviertel; *a* ['--] in der Oberstadt, *Am* im Wohnviertel gelegen, ansässig *od* zu Hause.

up-train ['ʌptrein] nach London fahrende(r) Zug *m.*

upturn [ʌp'tə:n] *tr* umschlagen, -klappen, -kippen; *s* ['--] Ansteigen *n*; aufsteigende Linie *od* Kurve; *fig* Besserung *f*, Aufschwung *m*; **~ed** ['ʌp'tə:nd] *a* umgedreht, -gestülpt; (an)steigend; nach oben gebogen; ~~ *nose* Stupsnase *f.*

upward ['ʌpwəd] *a* nach oben gerichtet; oben befindlich; ansteigend; *adv (a.: ~s)* nach oben, aufwärts *a. fig*; stromaufwärts; im Laufe des Lebens; *and ~s* u. mehr, u. darüber; *~s of* mehr als; von ... an; *to go ~s* in die Höhe gehen; **~ trend** Aufwärtsbewegung *f.*

ur|(a)emia [juə'ri:mjə] *med* Urämie, Harnvergiftung *f*; **~ea** ['juəriə] *chem* Harnstoff *m*; **~eter** [-'ri:tə] *anat* Harnleiter *m*; **~ethra** [-'ri:θrə] *pl a. -ae* ['-i:] Harnröhre *f.*

uran|ite ['juərənait] Uranglimmer *m*, Uranit *n*; **~ium** [-'reinjəm] *chem* Uran *n*; ~~ *deposit, fission, ore, pile* Uranvorkommen *n*, -spaltung *f*, -erz *n*, -brenner *m*; **~ography** [juərə'nɔgrəfi] Himmelsbeschreibung *f.*

urban ['ə:bən] städtisch; Stadt-; **~ area** Stadtgebiet *n*; **~ district** Stadtbezirk *m*; **~e** [ə:'bein] höflich; elegant; weltmännisch; **~ity** [ə:'bæniti] Kultiviertheit; Höflichkeit *f*; *pl* gute Umgangsformen *f pl*; **~ization** [ə:bənai'zeiʃən] Verstädterung *f*; **~ize** ['ə:bənaiz] *tr* verstädtern, e-n städtischen Charakter verleihen (*s.th.* e-r S); **~ planning** Städteplanung *f.*

urchin ['ə:tʃin] *zoo* Seeigel; Lausbub, Lausejunge *m*, Balg *m od n.*

urg|e [ə:dʒ] *tr* treiben, drängen, stoßen; *(fig)* (an)treiben, drängen, zwingen, nötigen; aufdrängen, -nötigen (*s.th. upon s.o.* jdm etw); zureden (*s.o.* jdm); Nachdruck legen auf, geltend machen; nahelegen, vor Augen führen (*s.th. upon s.o.* jdm etw); dringend bitten; kräftig gebrauchen, handhaben; *s* Drängen, Treiben *n*; (An-)Trieb, Drang, Impuls *m*; starke Lust *f* (*to do* zu tun); *to* ~~ *on(ward), forward* vorwärtstreiben, -drängen; *to feel the* ~~ *to* Lust verspüren zu; ~~ *to battle* Kampf(es)lust *f*; **~ency** ['-ənsi] Dringlichkeit, Notwendigkeit; dringende Bitte *f*, Drängen *n*, Nachdruck *m*; *pl* dringende Vorstellungen *f pl*; *to demand a vote of* ~~ *(parl)* e-n Dringlichkeitsantrag stellen; *measure of* ~~ Dringlichkeitsmaßnahme *f*; **~ent** ['-ənt] dringend, (vor)dringlich, eilig; drängend, nachdrücklich; *to be* ~~ darauf drängen (*for s.o. to do* daß jem tut).

urin|al ['juərinl] Harnglas; Urinbecken; Pissoir *n*, Bedürfnisanstalt *f* (für Männer); **~ary** ['-əri] *a* Harn-, Urin-; *s mil* Latrine *f*; ~~ *bladder* Harnblase *f*; ~~ *calculus (med)* Harnstein *m*; **~ate** ['-eit] *itr* urinieren, harnen, Wasser lassen; **~e** ['juərin] Urin, Harn *m*; ~~ *analysis* Harnuntersuchung *f*; **~ogenital** [juərəno(u)-'dʒenitl] *a* Harn- u. Geschlechts-.

urn [ə:n] Vase; *(funeral ~)* (Toten-)Urne *f*; *fig* Grab *n*; Tee-, Kaffeemaschine *f*; *bot* Sporensack *m* (des Mooses).

urogenital [ju:ro(u)'dʒenitl] = *urinogenital.*

Urs|a ['ə:sə] *astr (~ Major)* der Große Bär *od* Wagen; *(~ Minor)* der Kleine Bär *od* Wagen; **u~ine** ['-ain] *a* Bären-; bärenartig.

Uruguay ['urugwai] Uruguay *n*; **~an** [uru'gwaiən] *a* uruguayisch; *s* Uruguayer(in *f*) *m.*

us [ʌs] uns *(dat u. acc)*; *all of ~* wir alle; *both of ~* wir beide; *that's ~ (fam)* wir sind's.

usable ['ju:zəbl] brauchbar, verwendbar, benutzbar, passend, geeignet; **~age** ['ju:zidʒ] Brauch *m*, Herkommen *n*, Sitte, Gewohnheit *f*; (Sprach-)Gebrauch *m*; *tech* Beanspruchung *f*; *to come into* ~~ üblich werden; *that's local* ~~ das ist ortsüblich; das ist so Brauch; *commercial* ~~ Handelsbrauch, Geschäftsgebrauch *m*; *~~s and customs* Sitten u. Gebräuche; **~ance** ['ju:zəns] *fin* Wechselfrist; *com* Usance *f*; *bill at* ~~ Usowechsel *m.*

use [ju:z] *tr* gebrauchen, benützen, an-, verwenden, Gebrauch machen von; sich bedienen (*s.th.* e-r S); *(Menschen)* behandeln, umgehen mit; *(to ~ up)* ver-, aufbrauchen, abnutzen; *fam (Menschen)* ausnutzen; *(ein Recht)* ausüben; *to be ~d* [ju:st] gewohnt sein, pflegen (*to do* zu tun); *s* [ju:s] Gebrauch *m*, Benutzung, An-, Verwendung; Verwertung; *(Name)* Führung; Nutzung, Nutznießung *f*; Nutzen, Vorteil *m*; Benutzungsrecht *n*; Verwendung(szweck *m*) *f*, Nutzen, Zweck *m*; Funktion; Liturgie, Gottesdienstordnung *f*; *fit for ~* brauchbar; *for ~* zum Gebrauch; *in, out of ~* in, außer Gebrauch; *in common ~* allgemein gebräuchlich; *with ~* durch den Gebrauch, mit der Zeit; *to be of no ~* keinen Zweck haben, sinnlos sein (*doing, to do* zu tun); *to come into ~* in Gebrauch, aufkommen; *to come to* *be ~d to each other* sich anea. gewöhnen; *to fall, to go out of ~* außer Gebrauch kommen; *to get ~d to* (sich) gewöhnen an; *to give s.o. the ~ of s.th.* jdm etw zur Verfügung stellen; *to have no ~ for* keine Verwendung haben für, nicht (ge)brauchen können; *fam* nichts zu tun haben wollen mit; nicht leiden mögen, nicht ausstehen, *fam* riechen können; *to make ~ of, to put to ~* Gebrauch machen von; ausnutzen; *there isn't much ~ for it* das hat nicht viel Zweck; *it's no ~ doing it* es hat keinen Zweck, das zu tun; *what's the ~?* wozu (denn, eigentlich)? *improper ~* Mißbrauch *m*; *~d up (a)* verbraucht; abgenutzt; *fam* kaputt, fertig, erschöpft; *~d car* Gebrauchtwagen *m*; **~ful** ['ju:sful] nützlich, brauchbar; vorteilhaft; *fam* gut; tüchtig; *to prove (to be) ~~* sich als nützlich erweisen; *~~ capacity, load* Nutzlast *f*; *~~ efficiency* Nutzeffekt *m*; *~~ life (tech)* Lebensdauer *f*; *~~ output* Nutzleistung *f*; *~~ plant* Nutzpflanze *f*; **~fulness** ['ju:sfulnis] Nützlichkeit, Brauchbarkeit, Verwendbarkeit; Vorteilhaftigkeit *f*; **~less** ['ju:slis] nutzlos, unnütz, zwecklos; unbrauchbar; *fam* erschöpft; **~lessness** ['ju:slisnis] Nutzlosigkeit, Unbrauchbarkeit *f*.

user ['ju:zə] Benutzer; *com* Verbraucher, Abnehmer *m*; *jur* Nutzung(srecht *n*) *f*; *ultimate ~* Letzt-, Endverbraucher *m*.

usher ['ʌʃə] *s* Türhüter, -steher, Portier; Platzanweiser; *jur* Gerichtsdiener; *pej hum* Schulmeister, Pauker *m*; *tr* (ein)führen, (ge)leiten (*into* in); *fig* (an)melden, einleiten; *to ~ in (fig)* ankünd(ig)en, den Weg bereiten (*s.th.* e-r S); **~ette** [ʌʃə'ret] Platzanweiserin *f*.

usual ['ju:ʒuəl] gewöhnlich, üblich, herkömmlich, normal; *as ~* wie gewöhnlich, wie immer, wie sonst; **~ly** ['-i] *adv* gewöhnlich, im allgemeinen, normalerweise.

usufruct ['ju:sju(:)frʌkt, 'ju:z-] *jur* Nießbrauch *m*; **~uary** [ju:sju'frʌktjuəri] *s* Nutznießer *m*; *a: ~~ right* Nutzungsrecht *n*.

usur|er ['ju:ʒərə] Wucherer *m*; **~ious** [ju:'zjuəriəs] wucherisch; Wucher-; *~~ interest* Wucherzinsen *m pl*; **~y** ['ju:ʒuri] Wucher(zinsen *m pl*) *m*.

usurp [ju:'zə:p] *tr* widerrechtlich Besitz ergreifen von; an sich reißen, usurpieren; sich bemächtigen (*s.th.* e-r S); **~ation** [ju:zə:'peiʃən] widerrechtliche, gewaltsame Besitznahme *f*; **~atory** [ju:'zə:pətəri], **~ing** [-iŋ] widerrechtlich, gewaltsam; **~er** [ju:'zə:pə] Usurpator *m*.

utensil [ju:'tens(i)l] Gerät, Werkzeug *n*, Gebrauchsgegenstand *m*; *pl* Geschirr *n*, Utensilien *pl*; *cooking-, kitchen-~s (pl)* Küchengeräte *n pl*, -geschirr *n*; *writing ~s (pl)* Schreibutensilien *pl*.

uter|ine ['ju:tərain] *a anat* Gebärmutter-; *~~ brother, sister* Halbbruder *m*, -schwester *f* mütterlicherseits; **~us** ['-rəs] *pl -i* ['-ai] *anat* Gebärmutter *f*.

util|itarian [ju:tili'tɛəriən] *a* Nützlichkeits-; utilitaristisch; *s* Utilitarist *m*; *~~ principle* Nützlichkeitsprinzip *n*; **~itarianism** [-'tɛəriənizm] Utilitarismus, Nützlichkeitsstandpunkt *m*; **~ity** [ju:'tiliti] Nützlichkeit *f*, Nutzen *m*, Brauchbarkeit *f*, Nutzwert (*to* für); Gebrauchsgegenstand *m*; *(public ~~)* öffentliche, gemeinnützige Einrichtung *f*, (öffentlicher) Versorgungsbetrieb *m*; Stadtwerke *n pl*; *(~~ company, corporation)* gemeinnützige Gesellschaft *od* Anstalt *f od* Unternehmen *n*; *(~~-man) theat* Spieler, Darsteller *m* von Nebenrollen; *Am* Gelegenheitsarbeiter *m*; *pl* Aktien *f pl*, Wertpapiere *n pl* gemeinnütziger Gesellschaften *od* öffentlicher Versorgungsbetriebe; *attr* Gebrauchs-; einfach, billig; Volks-; *marginal ~~* Grenznutzen *m*; *~~ car* Gebrauchswagen *m*; *~~ department* Kraftwerk *n*; *~~ goods (pl)* Gebrauchsgüter *pl*; *~~ room* Neben-, Dienst-, Anrichteraum *m*, Office *n*; **~izable** ['ju:tilaizəbl] verwertbar; auswert-, anwendbar; **~ization** [ju:tilai'zeiʃən] Verwendung, Nutzbarmachung; Auswertung, Ausnützung; Anwendung, Nutzanweisung *f*; **~ize** ['ju:tilaiz] *tr* nutzbar machen; (aus-)nutzen, ver-, auswerten, anwenden, Gebrauch machen von.

utmost ['ʌtmoust] *a* (ent)fern(te)st, ent-, abgelegenst; äußerst *a. fig*; *fig* höchst, größt; *s das* Äußerste, Höchste; *of the ~ importance* von größter Wichtigkeit; *to the ~* (aufs) äußerst(e); *to the ~ of o.'s power* nach besten Kräften; *to do o.'s ~* sein äußerstes, möglichstes tun; *I did my ~* ich habe alles getan, was in meinen Kräften stand.

utopia [ju:'toupjə] Wunsch-, Traum-, Idealland *n*; Utopie *f*, Hirngespinst *n*; **~n** [-n] *a* utopisch, phantastisch, wirklichkeitsfremd, unrealistisch; *s* Utopist, Phantast *m*.

utricle ['ju:trikl] *anat* Utrikulus *m*; *bot* Schlauchfrucht *f*.

utter ['ʌtə] **1.** *a* völlig, vollkommen, vollständig, gänzlich, total; **~ly** ['-li] *adv* ganz u. gar; entschieden; **~most** ['-moust] = *utmost*; **2.** *tr* äußern, aussprechen, sagen; ausdrücken, zum Ausdruck bringen; *(Wort)* hervorbringen; bekanntmachen, verbreiten; unter die Leute, in Umlauf bringen *(a. Geld)*; **~ance** ['-rəns] Äußerung; Aussprache; Sprechweise, Ausdrucksfähigkeit *f*; *to give ~~ to s.th. (fig)* Luft machen *dat*.

uvul|a ['ju:vjulə] *pl a. -ae* ['-i:] *anat* Zäpfchen *n*; **~ar** ['-] *a (anat, Phonetik)* Zäpfchen-.

uxorious [ʌk'sɔ:riəs] unter dem Pantoffel (stehend).

V

V, v [vi:] *pl ~'s* [vi:z] *s* V, v *n*; *Am fam* Fünfdollarschein *m*; *attr (~-shaped) in Zssgen* V-förmig.

vac [væk] *fam* Ferien *pl*; *Am fam* = *vacuum cleaner*; **~ancy** ['veikənsi] Leere *f*, leere(r) Raum *m*; leere Stelle *f*, leere(r) Platz *m*, Lücke; leer(stehend)e Wohnung *f*; *Am (Hotel)* freie(s) Zimmer *n*; offene Stelle; *fig* geistige Leere, Geistesabwesenheit *f*; *to fill a ~~* e-e Stelle (neu) besetzen; *~ancies (Zeitung)* Stellenangebot *n*; *(an e-m Hotel)* Zimmer frei; **~ant** ['veikənt] leer; *(Raum, Wohnung, Haus)* leerstehend, unbewohnt; *(Platz)* frei; *(Land)* unbebaut; *(Stelle)* unbesetzt, frei; untätig, (arbeits)frei; *tele (Leitung)* frei, nicht besetzt; *fig* geistesabwesend; gedanken-, geist-, interesselos; *to be ~~* leerstehen; *~~ possession (Haus)* sofort beziehbar; **~ate** [və'keit, *Am* 'veik-] *tr (Wohnung)* räumen; leer machen; *(Wohnung, Stelle)* freimachen, aufgeben; *(Amt)* niederlegen, zur Verfügung stellen; *jur* annullieren, aufheben, rückgängig machen, für ungültig erklären; **~ation** [və'keiʃən] *s* Räumung; Aufgabe (e-r Stelle), (Amts-)Niederlegung *f*; (*bes.* Schul-, Gerichts-)Ferien *pl*, Urlaub *m*; Freizeit, Ruhe *f*; *itr Am* s-n Urlaub, Ferien verbringen (*in, at* in); *on ~~* in Urlaub; *Christmas, Easter, Whitsun, long* od *summer ~~* Weihnachts-, Oster-, Pfingst-, Sommerferien *pl*; *~~ season* Urlaubszeit *f*; **~ationist** [və'keiʃnist] *Am* Urlauber, Feriengast, -reisende(r) *m*; **~ationize** [və'keiʃənaiz] *itr Am* Ferien, Urlaub machen; **~uity** [væ'kju(:)iti], **~uousness** ['vækjuəsnis] Leere *f*; leere(r) Raum *od* Platz *m*, leere Stelle; *fig* Gedanken-, Geist-, Interesselosigkeit; Ausdruckslosigkeit; Dummheit *f*; *pl* Platitüden *f pl*; **~uous** ['vækjuəs] leer; ausdruckslos; gedanken-, geist-, interesselos, dumm; müßig, zwecklos; *~~ space* Hohlraum *m*; **~uum** ['vækjuəm] *pl a. -ua* ['-ə] (luft)leere(r) Raum *m*, Vakuum *n*; *fig* Lücke; (geistige) Leere *f*; *Am fam* = *~~ cleaner*; *~~ bottle, flask* Thermosflasche *f*; *~~ cleaner* Staubsauger *m*; *~~ tube, valve (phys)* Geißlersche Röhre; *radio* (Vakuum-)Röhre *f*.

vaccin|al ['væksinl] *a* Impf-; **~ate** ['-eit] *tr* impfen (*against* gegen); **~ation** [væksi'neiʃən] (Pocken-)Impfung; *(~~ scar)* Impfnarbe *f*; **~ator** ['væksineitə] Impfarzt *m*, -nadel *f*; **~e** ['væksi:n] *a* Kuhpocken-; Impf-; *s* (*bes.* Pocken-)Impfstoff *m*, Lymphe *f*; **~ia** [væk'siniə] Kuhpocken *pl*.

vacillat|e ['væsileit] *itr* wanken, wackeln, schwanken *a. fig (between* zwischen); **~ion** [væsi'leiʃən] Wanken *n*, schwankende(r) Gang *m*; *fig* Schwanken *n*, Unschlüssigkeit *f*.

vade-mecum ['veidi'mi:kəm] Vademekum *n*, Leitfaden *m*, Taschenbuch *n*.

vagabond ['vægəbənd] *a* vagabundierend; Vagabunden-; nichtsnutzig; (planlos) (umher)treibend; unstet; *s* Landstreicher, Stromer, Lump *m*.

vagary ['veigəri, və'gɛəri] Laune, Grille, Schrulle, (dumme) Idee *f*, (seltsamer) Einfall *m*.

vagin|a [və'dʒainə] *pl a. -ae* [-i:] *anat bot* Scheide *f*; **~al** [-əl] scheidenförmig;

anat Scheiden-; **~itis** [vædʒi'naitis] *med* Scheidenentzündung *f*.
vagran|cy ['veigrənsi] Vagabundieren *n*, Landstreicherei *f*; **~t** ['-t] *s* Wanderbursche; Landstreicher, Vagabund *m*; *a* vagabundierend, fahrend; umherirrend; *fig* unstet, unbeständig.
vague [veig] vage, unbestimmt; ungenau, unklar, verschwommen; *not the ~st idea* nicht die leiseste Ahnung; **~ness** ['-nis] Unbestimmtheit, Unklarheit, Verschwommenheit *f*.
vain [vein] leer, nichtig, wertlos, hohl; wirkungs-, zweck-, nutzlos, vergeblich; eitel, selbstgefällig, eingebildet, überheblich (*of* auf); *in ~* umsonst, vergeblich, vergebens; *to take s.o.'s name in ~* respektlos, leichtfertig von jdm sprechen; **~glorious** [-'glɔ:riəs] großsprecherisch, prahlerisch; **~glory** [-'glɔ:ri] Prahlerei *f*.
valance ['væləns] kurze(r) Volant *m*.
vale [veil] *poet* Tal *n*.
valedict|ion [væli'dikʃən] Abschied *m*, Lebewohl *n*; Abschiedsworte *n pl*, *Am* -rede *f*; **~orian** [vælidik'tɔ:riən] *Am* Schüler *m*, der die Abschiedsrede (bei der Entlaßfeier) hält; **~ory** [væli'diktəri] *Am a* Abschieds-; *s* Abschiedsrede *f* (*bes.* e-s Schülers).
valenc|e, -y ['veiləns(i)] *chem* Wertigkeit *f*.
Valentine ['væləntain] Valentin *m*; *v~* am Valentinstage *(14. Februar)* erwählte(r) Schatz *m*; Postkarte *f od* Geschenk *n* zum Valentinstag.
valerian [və'liəriən] *bot pharm* Baldrian *m*.
valet ['vælit, 'væli, 'vælei] *s* (Kammer-)Diener; Hoteldiener *m*; *tr* bedienen; **~(ing) service** *(Hotel)* persönliche Dienstleistungen *f pl*.
valetudinarian ['vælitju:di'nɛəriən] *a* kränklich; hypochondrisch; *s* kränkliche(r) Mensch; Hypochonder *m*.
valiant ['væljənt] tapfer, mutig.
valid ['vælid] (rechts)gültig, rechtskräftig; *(Grund)* stichhaltig, triftig; schlüssig; wirksam, zwingend; *to become ~* Rechtskraft erlangen; *to remain ~* Geltung behalten; **~ate** ['-eit] *tr* legalisieren, rechtskräftig machen; für gültig erklären, bestätigen; die Gültigkeit nachweisen (*s.th.* e-r S); **~ation** [væli'deiʃən] Gültigkeitserklärung; Bestätigung *f*, Nachweis *m*; **~ity** [və'liditi] Gültigkeit, Rechtswirksamkeit; Stichhaltigkeit *f*.
valise [və'li:z, *Am* -i:s] kleine(r) Hand-, Stadtkoffer *m*; Reisetasche *f*; *mil* Tornister, Kleidersack *m*.
vall|ation [və'leiʃən] *mil* Umwallung *f*, (Erd-)Wall *m*; **~ey** ['væli] (*bes.* Fluß-) Tal *n*; *arch* Dachkehle *f*.
valoriz|ation [vælərai'zeiʃən] *fin* Aufwertung; *Am* Preisstabilisierung *f*; **~e** ['væləraiz] *tr fin* aufwerten.
val|orous ['vælərəs] tapfer; **~o(u)r** ['vælə] *lit poet* Tapferkeit *f*, Mut *m*.
valu|able ['væljuəbl] *a* wertvoll, kostbar; geschätzt; *s meist pl* Wertgegenstände *m pl*, -objekte *n pl*; **~ation** [vælju'eiʃən] (Ab-)Schätzung, Wertermittlung; Veranschlagung, Bewertung, Wertfestsetzung, -bestimmung *f*; Schätz-, Taxwert *m*; *fig* Wert-, Hochschätzung *f*; *~~ basis* Bewertungsgrundlage *f*; **~ator** ['væljueitə, -'eitə] Taxator, Schätzer *m*; **~e** ['vælju] *s* (Gegen-)Wert; Preis *m*; Kaufkraft *f*; Sachwert; Nutzen *m*; *(Wort)* Bedeutung *f*, Wert; *(Phonetik)* Lautwert; *math* Wert *m*; *mus* Quantität; *(Kunst)* Intensität *f*, Helligkeitsgrad *m*; *tr* (ab)schätzen, taxieren (*at* auf); (ein)schätzen; (wert)schätzen; *com* trassieren, ziehen; *at ~~* zum Tageskurs; *for ~~ received* Betrag erhalten; *of lasting ~~* von bleibendem Wert; *of no, little ~~* nichts, wenig wert; *to the ~~ of* im Werte von; *to attach ~~ to s.th.* e-r S Wert, Bedeutung beimessen; *to be of little ~~* geringwertig sein; *to give good ~~* reell bedienen (*to s.o.* jdn); gut wiegen; den Gegenwert geben (*for* für); *to go down in ~~* an Wert verlieren; *to set (great) ~~ on* (großen) Wert legen auf; *book ~~* Buchwert *m*; *commercial, trading, market ~~* Handelswert *m*; *exchange ~~* Gegenwert *m*, -leistung *f*; *increase in ~~, increment ~~* Wertzuwachs *m*; *loss of ~~* Wertverlust *m*, Entwertung *f*; *nominal ~~* Nennwert *m*; *nutritive ~~* Nährwert *m*; *scarcity ~~* Seltenheitswert *m*; *statement of the ~~* Wertangabe *f*; *total ~~* Gesamtwert *m*; *utility ~~* Nutzungswert *m*; *~~ date* Wertstellungstermin *m*; **~ed** ['-d] *a* geschätzt; **~eless** ['-lis] wertlos; **~er** ['-ə] Schätzer, Taxator *m*.
valv|e [vælv] *anat bot* Klappe *f*; Ventil *n*, Schieber *m*; Schleusentor *n*; *radio Br* Röhre *f*; *~~ head* Ventilkegel *m*; **~ular** ['-julə] *anat bot* klappenartig; Klappen-; **~ulitis** [vælvju'laitis] Herzklappenentzündung *f*.
vamo(o)se [və'mu:s, -'mous] *sl itr* abhauen, türmen (gehen); *tr* fluchtartig verlassen.
vamp [væmp] **1.** *s* Oberleder *n*; Flicken *m*; *fig* Flickwerk *n*; improvisierte Begleitmusik *f*; *tr* vorschuhen; *(to ~ up)* flicken, ausbessern, reparieren; *fig* zs.stoppeln; *itr tr mus* e-e Begleitung improvisieren (zu); **2.** *sl s* Vamp *m*; *tr* bezirzen.
vampire ['væmpaiə] Vampir *a. zoo*; *fig* Blutsauger *m*; *theat* Falltüre *f*.
van [væn] **1.** Last-, Möbelwagen; *rail* Güterwagen; Wohn-, Zigeunerwagen; Zellen-, Gefängniswagen *m*; *delivery ~* Lieferwagen *m*; *furniture ~* Möbelwagen *m*; *luggage ~ (rail)* Packwagen *m*; *mail ~* Postauto *n*; **2.** *s poet* Schwinge *f*, Flügel *m*; *tr min* sieben; **3.** = *vanguard*; *(Tennis)* Vorteil *m*.
vanadium [və'neidjəm] *chem* Vanadium *n*.
Vandal ['vændəl] *s hist* Vandale *m*; *v ~ (fig)* Barbar *m*; *a* u. **~ic** [væn'dælik] vandalisch; *(v~(~)) fig* barbarisch; **v~ism** ['-izm] Vandalismus *m*.
vandyke [væn'daik] *(~ collar)* Spitzenkragen *m*; *(~ beard)* Spitz-, Knebelbart *m*.
vane [vein] Wetterfahne *f*, -hahn; Windmühlenflügel; Flügel *m (e-s Propellers)*; *tech* Schaufel; *(Feder)* Fahne *f*; Visier, Diopter *n*.
vanguard ['vængɑ:d] *mil* Vorhut; *fig* Avantgarde *f*, Vorkämpfer *m pl*.
vanill|a [və'nilə] *bot* Vanille *f*.
vanish ['væniʃ] *itr* verschwinden *a. math*; (dahin)schwinden, vergehen; *~ing cream* Tagescreme *f*; *~ing line, point* Fluchtlinie *f*, -punkt *m*.
vanity ['væniti] Nichtigkeit; Eitelkeit, Selbstgefälligkeit, Eingebildetheit, Überheblichkeit *f*; (Gegenstand des) Stolz(es) *m*; **~ bag, case** Hand-, Ziertäschchen *n*; **V~ Fair** *poet* Jahrmarkt *m* der Eitelkeit.
vanquish ['væŋkwiʃ] *tr* besiegen, nieder-, unterwerfen; *fig* aus dem Felde schlagen; widerlegen; *(Gefühl)* überwinden, unterdrücken; **~er** ['-ə] Sieger; Eroberer; Überwinder *m*.
vantage ['vɑ:ntidʒ] Vorteil *m (a. Tennis)*; Überlegenheit *f*; *(~ ground)* vorteilhafte, günstigere Lage *od* Stellung *od* (Ausgangs-)Position *f*; **~ point** Aussichtspunkt; *fig* günstige(r) Ausgangspunkt *m*.
vapid ['væpid] fad(e), schal, geschmacklos; *fig* langweilig, uninteressant; geistlos; **~ity** [væ'piditi], **~ness** ['-nis] Fadheit; *fig* Geistlosigkeit; Eintönigkeit *f*.
vapor|ific [veipə'rifik] dampferzeugend; = *~ous*; **~ization** [veipərai'zeiʃən] Verdampfung; Verdunstung; *med* Dampfbehandlung *f*; **~ize** ['veipəraiz] *tr itr* verdampfen; *itr* verdunsten; *tech* vergasen; **~izer** ['-raizə] Zerstäuber; *tech mot* Vergaser *m*; **~osity** [veipə'rɔsiti], **~ousness** ['veipərəsnis] Dunstigkeit; Nebelhaftig-, Verschwommenheit; *fig* Unklarheit, Undeutlichkeit; Einbildung *f*; **~ous** ['veipərəs] dampfend; dampfig; dunstig; *fig* nebelhaft, verschwommen; *(Mensch)* eingebildet; *(Gewebe)* duftig.
vapo(u)r ['veipə] *s* Dampf, Dunst *m*; *fig* Einbildung *f*, Wahn(vorstellung *f*, -gebilde *n pl*) *m*; *itr* (ver)dampfen; *fig* schwatzen, prahlen; *tr* verdampfen; *water ~* Wasserdampf *m*; **~ bath** Wasserbad *n*; **~ings** ['-riŋz] *pl* Geschwätz *n*; **~ish** ['-riʃ] dampfartig; dampfig, dampfgefüllt; *fig* niedergeschlagen, gedrückt; **~ lamp** Quecksilberdampf-, Kohlenwasserstofflampe *f*; **~ pressure, tension** Dampfdruck *m*; **~ trails** *pl aero* Kondensstreifen *m pl*; **~y** ['-ri] = *vaporous*.
vaquero [va'kɛərou] *pl -os Am (Südweststaaten)* Kuhhirt, Cowboy *m*.
vari|ability [vɛəriə'biliti], **~ableness** ['vɛəriəblnis] Veränderlichkeit, Unbeständigkeit *a. fig*; *math biol* Variabilität *f*; **~able** ['vɛəriəbl] *a* veränderlich; unbeständig; *tech* variabel; *fig* schwankend; *s math* Variable *f*; *~~ capacitor* Drehkondensator *m*; **~ance** ['vɛəriəns] Veränderlichkeit; Veränderung *f*; Unterschied; Widerspruch *m*, Unvereinbarkeit; Meinungsverschiedenheit, Differenz, Uneinigkeit *f*; Streit *m*; *math* Streuung *f*; *at ~~ (Sachen)* im Widerspruch (*with* zu); im Gegensatz (*with* zu); *(Personen)* in Streit (*with* mit); **~ant** ['vɛəriənt] *a* abweichend; verschiedenartig; veränderlich; *s* Spielart; Sonderform; Variante, abweichende Fassung *f*; **~ation** [vɛəri'eiʃən] Veränderung, (Ab-)Wandlung; Abweichung *f*, Unterschied *m*; abweichende(s) Exemplar *n*; *astr* Abweichung; *gram* Flexion; *astr math mus biol* Variation *f*; *~~ of pressure, of temperature* Druck-, Temperaturschwankung *f*; *~~ in voltage* Spannungsschwankung *f*; **~cose** ['værikous] *med* varikös; Krampfadern-; **~colo(u)red** ['vɛərikʌləd] *a* mehr-, verschiedenfarbig; bunt; **~ed** ['vɛərid] *a* mannigfach, verschiedenartig, bunt; variiert; **~egate** ['vɛəri(ə)geit] *tr* Abwechslung bringen in, variieren, verschieden gestalten, abwandeln; bunt machen; **~egated** ['-tid] *a* bunt, farbenreich, -prächtig; *fig* mannigfaltig, abwechslungsreich; **~egation** [vɛəri(ə)'geiʃən] Buntheit *f*, Farbenreichtum *m*, -pracht, Mannigfaltigkeit *f*; **~ety** [və'raiəti] Mannigfaltigkeit, Abwechslung; Verschiedenartigkeit; Vielfalt, Auswahl; Art, Sorte; Erscheinungsform, Spielart, Variante, Verschiedenheit; (bunte) Zs.stellung, Auswahl *f*; *theat* Varieté *n*; *by way of, for the sake of ~~* zur Abwechslung; *for a ~~ of reasons* aus verschiedenen Gründen; *~~-artist* Artist *m*; *~~-show, -theatre* Varietévorstellung *f*, -theater *n*; **~form** ['vɛərifɔ:m] vielgestaltig; **~ola**

[və'raiələ] *med* Pocken, Blattern *pl*; **~ometer** [vɛəri'ɔmitə] Variometer *n*; **~orum** [vɛəri'ɔ:rəm] *(~~ edition) (Buch)* Ausgabe *f* mit Anmerkungen verschiedener Kommentatoren *od* mit verschiedenen Lesarten; **~ous** ['vɛəriəs] verschieden(artig); verschiedene; *fam* viele; *at ~~ times* zu verschiedenen Zeiten; *for ~~ reasons* aus verschiedenen Gründen.

varix ['vɛəriks] *pl varices* ['-si:z] Krampfader *f*.

varlet ['vɑ:lit] *obs* Page; *hist* Knappe; *obs* Schuft *m*.

varmint, varment ['vɑ:mint] *fam* Lausbube, Rowdy; *sl* Fuchs *m*.

varnish ['vɑ:niʃ] *s* Firnis *m*, Glasur, Politur *f*, Lack; *fig* (äußerer) Schein *m*, Tünche *f*; *tr* firnissen; glasieren, polieren, lackieren; (auf)polieren; *fig*; auffrisieren, anziehend(er) machen; beschönigen.

varsity ['vɑ:siti] *fam* Uni(versität) *f*; *sport* Universitäts-, Schulmannschaft *f*.

vary ['vɛəri] *tr* abwandeln, -ändern; verschieden machen; abwechslungsreich gestalten; *mus* variieren; *itr* sich wandeln, sich (ver)ändern, veränderlich sein; variieren; schwanken; verschieden sein; abweichen, sich unterscheiden (*from* von); abwechseln.

vascul|ar ['væskjulə] *a anat zoo bot* Gefäß-; **~um** ['-əm] *pl -a* ['-ə] Botanisiertrommel *f*.

vase [vɑ:z, *Am* veiz] (Blumen-)Vase *f*.

vaseline ['væsili:n] Vaseline *f (Warenzeichen)*.

vaso|constrictor ['veizo(u)kən'striktə] *physiol* gefäßverengend; **~dilator** ['-dai'leitə] *physiol* gefäßerweiternd; **~motor** ['-'moutə] *physiol* vasomotorisch.

vassal ['væsəl] *hist* Vasall, Lehnsmann; Untergebene(r) *m*; **~age** ['-idʒ] *hist* Lehnspflicht (*to* gegenüber); *allg* Abhängigkeit(sverhältnis *n*) *f*; Lehen *n*; Lehnsleute *pl*.

vast [vɑ:st] *a* weit(reichend), ausgedehnt; *fam* gewaltig, ungeheuer, enorm; beträchtlich, umfangreich, umfassend; *s poet* Weite *f*; **~ly** ['-li] *adv* in hohem Maße; äußerst; sehr, weit; **~ness** ['-nis] Weite, Ausgedehntheit; große Zahl; gewaltige Größe *f*, Umfang *m*.

vat [væt] *s* (großes) Faß *n*, Bottich *m*; Küpe *f*, Färbebad *n*; *tr* in ein Faß, e-n Bottich füllen.

Vatican, *the* ['vætikən] der Vatikan *m*; *the ~ City* die Vatikanstadt *f*.

vaticinate [væ'tisineit] *tr itr* prophezeien.

vaudeville ['voudəvil] Varieté(vorstellung *f*) *n*.

vault [vɔ:lt] **1.** *s* (Dach-, Keller-)Gewölbe *n a. biol*, Wölbung *f*; Keller *m*; Gruft; Stahlkammer *f*, Tresor (-raum); *(the ~ of heaven)* Himmel(sgewölbe, -zelt *n*) *m*; *tr* (ein-, über)wölben; *itr* sich wölben; *cranial ~* Schädeldecke *f*; *family ~* Familiengruft *f*; *wine-~s (pl)* Weinkeller *m*; **~ed** ['-id] *a* gewölbt; *~~ roof* Dachgewölbe *n*; **~ing** ['-iŋ] *s* Gewölbe *n*; **2.** *itr* springen (*over* über); *tr* springen über; *s* Sprung, Satz *m*; **~er** ['-ə] Springer *m*; **~ing** *a fig* übertrieben, selbstbewußt; hemmungslos; *~~-horse (sport)* Pferd *n (Gerät)*.

vaunt [vɔ:nt] *itr* prahlen (*of* mit); *tr* prahlen mit; *s* Prahlerei *f*; **~ing** ['-iŋ] prahlerisch.

*

veal [vi:l] Kalbfleisch *n*; *roast ~* Kalbsbraten *m*; *~* **cutlet** Kalbskotelett *n*.

vector ['vektə] *s math phys astr* Vektor; *med* (Bazillen-)Träger *m*; *tr (Flugzeug)* mittels Funk *od* Radar einweisen; **~ial** [vek'tɔ:riəl] *a math* Vektoren-.

vedette [vi'det] *mil obs* berittene(r) (Wacht-)Posten *m*; *(~ boat)* Wachtboot *n*; Filmstar *m*.

veep [vi:p] *Am sl* Vizepräsident *m*.

veer [viə] **1.** *itr* sich drehen, sich wenden; *mar* (ab)drehen; *fig* s-e Meinung, Haltung ändern, umschwenken (*to* zu); *tr* drehen *a. mar*, wenden; *s* Drehung, Wendung, Schwenkung *f*; **2.** *(to ~ out) tr mar* (ab)fieren; *(Tau)* schießen lassen.

veget|able ['vedʒitəbl] *a* pflanzlich; Pflanzen-, Gemüse-; *s* Pflanze *f*; Gemüse(pflanze *f*) *n*; *~~ butter* Pflanzenfett *n*; *~~ food* Pflanzenkost, pflanzliche Nahrung *f*; *~~ garden, soup* Gemüsegarten *m*, -suppe *f*; *~~ kingdom* Pflanzenreich *n*; *~~ oil* Pflanzenöl *n*; **~al** ['vedʒitl] pflanzlich, Pflanzen-; *physiol* vegetativ; **~arian** [vedʒi'tɛəriən] *s* Vegetarier *m*; *a* vegetarisch; Pflanzen-; **~ate** ['vedʒiteit] *itr* wachsen; *med* wuchern; *fig* (dahin)vegetieren; **~ation** [vedʒi'teiʃən] Pflanzenwuchs *m*, Vegetation; *med* Wucherung *f*; **~ative** ['vedʒitətiv] *a* Pflanzen-; wachstumsfördernd; *physiol* vegetativ *a. fig*.

vehemen|ce ['vi:iməns] Heftigkeit, Stärke, Gewalt, Vehemenz; *fig* Leidenschaft, Glut *f*, Feuer *n*; **~t** ['-t] heftig, stark, gewaltig, gewaltsam, hitzig; *fig* glühend, leidenschaftlich.

vehic|le ['vi:ikl] Fahrzeug, Beförderungs-, Transportmittel *n*; *fig* Träger; Vermittler; Verbreiter *m*; Medium, Mittel *n*; *motor, railed ~~* Motor-, Schienenfahrzeug *n*; *~~ of, for propaganda* Propagandamittel *n*; **~ular** [vi(:)'hikjulə] *a* Fahrzeug-, Beförderungs-, Transport-; *fig* Träger-; *~~ traffic* Fahrzeugverkehr *m*.

veil [veil] *s* Schleier *a. fig*; Vorhang *m*; *fig* Verhüllung *f*, Deckmantel *m*; *tr* mit e-m Schleier bedecken, verhüllen; *fig* verschleiern, verhüllen, verbergen, be-, verdecken; *beyond the ~* nach dem Tode; *under the ~ of (fig)* unter dem Schleier, unter dem Deckmantel *gen*; *to draw a ~ over (fig)* e-n Schleier ziehen über; *to raise the ~* den Schleier lüften; *to take the ~ (Frau)* ins Kloster gehen; **~ed** [-d] *a* verschleiert *a. phot*; **~ing** ['-iŋ] Verschleierung *f*; Schleier; Schleierstoff *m*.

vein [vein] *s anat* Vene; *bot zoo min* Ader; *(Holz)* Faser; *fig* Ader, Anlage, Veranlagung, Neigung (*of* zu); *fig* Spur; Stimmung *f*, Ton *m*; *tr* ädern, marmorieren; **~ed** [-d] *a* geädert; **~ing** ['-iŋ] Äderung, Maserung *f*; **~let** ['-lit] Äderchen *n*.

vel|ar ['vi:lə] *a* Gaumensegel-; velar; *s* Velar(laut) *m*; **~um** ['-əm] *pl -a* ['-ə] *anat* Gaumensegel *n*.

veld(t) [velt, f-] Grasland *n (in Südafrika)*.

vellum ['veləm] Velin *(feines Pergament)*; *(~-paper)* Velin(papier) *n*.

veloc|ipede [vi'lɔsipi:d] *Am* (Kinder-) Dreirad *n*; *rail* Draisine *f*; *hist* Hochrad *n*; **~ity** [-iti] Schnelligkeit; Geschwindigkeit *f*; *at the ~~ of* mit der Geschwindigkeit von; *initial, final od terminal ~~* Anfangs-, Endgeschwindigkeit *f*; *~~ of fall, of light* Fall-, Lichtgeschwindigkeit *f*; *~~ per hour* Stundengeschwindigkeit *f*; *~~ of sound* Schallgeschwindigkeit *f*; *~~ microphone (radio)* Bandmikrophon *n*.

velvet ['velvit] Samt *a. fig*; *(Geweih)* Bast; *Am sl* Reibach, Gewinn *m*; *a* Samt-; samtartig, -weich; *fig* sanft, glatt; *to be on ~ (fam)* des Erfolgs sicher sein; großartig leben; *~ glove (fig)* Samthandschuh *m*; *ribbed ~* Rippsamt, Kord *m*; **~een** ['velvi'ti:n] Baumwollsamt, Manchester *m*; **~y** ['-i] samtweich; *(Likör)* süß.

venal ['vi:nl] käuflich *a. pej*; *pej* bestechlich, feil; *med* Ader-; **~ity** [vi:'næliti] Käuflichkeit; Bestechlichkeit *f*.

venation [vi:'neiʃən] Äderung *f*, Geäder *n a. zoo*; *bot* Nervatur *f*.

vend [vend] *tr jur* verkaufen; handeln mit; *fig* veröffentlichen, offen äußern; **~ee** [-'di:] Käufer *m*; **~er, ~or** ['-ə] Verkäufer *m*; **~ible** ['vendibl] verkäuflich, absatzfähig, gängig; käuflich, bestechlich; **~ing machine** Verkaufs-, Warenautomat *m*; **~ue** [-'dju:] *Am* Auktion *f*, öffentliche Versteigerung *f*.

veneer [vi'niə] *tr* furnieren; *(Töpfe)* (mit e-r Schicht) überziehen; *allg* verschönern; *fig* übertünchen; *s (~ing)* Fournier *n*; Sperrholzlage *f*; *fig* äußere(r) Anstrich *m*, Tünche *f*, Firnis *m*.

vener|ability [venərə'biliti] Verehrungswürdigkeit *f*; **~able** ['venərəbl] *a* (ver)ehr(ungs)würdig; *(V~~ Sir) rel* Hochwürden *m*; **~ate** ['-eit] *tr* verehren, hochachten; **~ation** [venə'reiʃən] Verehrung, Hochachtung *f* (*for* für); **~ator** ['venəreitə] Verehrer *m*.

venereal [vi'niəriəl] geschlechtlich, sexuell; Geschlechts-, Sexual-; geschlechtskrank; *~* **disease** Geschlechtskrankheit *f*.

Venetian [vi'ni:ʃən] *a* venezianisch; *s* Venezianer(in *f*) *m*; *~* **(blind)** Jalousie *f*.

venge|ance ['ven(d)ʒəns] Rache, Strafe *f*; *with a ~~ (fam)* in gewaltigen, rauhen Mengen; wie toll, wie verrückt; gründlich; *to seek ~~ upon s.o. for s.th.* sich wegen etw an jdm rächen wollen; *to take ~~ (up)on s.o.* sich an jdm rächen; **~ful** ['-ful] rachsüchtig; Rache-.

venial ['vi:njəl] verzeihlich; *~* **sin** läßliche Sünde *f*.

venison ['ven(i)zn] Wild(bret) *n*.

venom ['venəm] *(bes.* tierisches*)* Gift *n*; *fig* Bosheit *f*; **~ous** ['-əs] giftig *bes. zoo*; *fig* boshaft, bösartig; *~~ snake* Giftschlange *f*.

ven|ose ['vi:nous], **~ous** ['-əs] *physiol* venös; Venen-; *bot* geädert.

vent [vent] *s (~-hole)* Öffnung *f*; Luft-, Spund-, Zündloch *n*; Krater(öffnung *f*); (Mantel-)Schlitz; *zoo* After *m*; *tech* Entweichen, Ausströmen *n*; Lüftungsklappe *f*; Belüftungsloch *n*; Rauchfang; *fig* Ausweg *m*; Erleichterung *f* (des Herzens), Erguß *m*; *tr* e-e Öffnung, ein Loch machen in; ent-, belüften; *(Gas, Flüssigkeit)* entweichen, ausströmen lassen; *(Gefühlen)* Luft machen, freien Lauf lassen; *(Ärger)* auslassen (*on s.o.* an jdm); von sich geben, äußern; *to ~ o.s.* s-m Herzen Luft machen; *to find ~ for, to give ~ to* Luft machen *dat*; freien Lauf lassen *dat*; **~age** ['ventidʒ] kleine Öffnung *f*, Luftloch *n*; *mus* Fingerloch *n*; *~* **cock** Entlüftungshahn *m*; **~iduct** ['-idʌkt] *arch* (unterirdischer) Luftschacht, -kanal *m*; **~ilate** ['-ileit] *tr* (aus-, ent-, be-, durch)lüften; *(Luft)* ventilieren in; *med* Sauerstoff zuführen; *fig (Frage)* ventilieren, erörtern; äußern; *~ilating fan* Ventilator *m*; **~ilation** [venti'leiʃən] Be-, Entlüftung, Ventilation; *min* Bewetterung; *fig* (freie) Aussprache *f*; **~ilator** ['ventileitə] Ventilator, Lüftungsanlage *f*.

venter ['ventə] *med zoo* Bauch; *zoo* Unter-, Hinterleib *m*; Ausbauchung *f*; Hohlraum; *jur* Mutterleib *m*.

ventr|al ['ventrəl] *a* Bauch-; Unterleibs-; **~icle** ['-ikl] *anat* Kammer;

bes. Herzkammer *f*, Ventrikel *m*; **~iloquism** [ven'triləkwizm] Bauchreden *n*; **~iloquist** [-'triləkwist] Bauchredner *m*; **~iloquize** [-'triləkwaiz] *itr* bauchreden.

ventur|e ['ventʃə] *s* Wagnis *n*, mutige(r) Einsatz *m*, gewagte(s) Unternehmen; Risiko; *com* Spekulationsobjekt; schwimmende(s) Gut *n*; *tr* wagen, einsetzen, aufs Spiel setzen, riskieren; herausfordern; (vorsichtig) äußern, bemerken; *itr* etw wagen, sich einsetzen; sich trauen, sich wagen, sich heranmachen (*on, upon s.th.* an etw); *to ~~ out* sich hinauswagen; *at a ~~* auf gut Glück; über den Daumen gepeilt; *may I ~~ my opinion* darf ich sagen, was ich darüber denke? *nothing ~~, nothing have (prov)* wer nicht wagt, der nicht gewinnt; **~esome** ['-səm], **~ous** ['-rəs] (wage-)mutig, einsatzfreudig, unternehmungslustig; *(Sache)* gewagt, riskant.

venue ['venju:] *jur* Tat-, Verhandlungsort; Gerichtsstand *m*, *(örtliche)* Zuständigkeit *f*; *fam* Treffpunkt *m*; *change of ~* Verweisung *f* an ein anderes Gericht zuständigkeitshalber.

Venus ['vi:nəs] Venus *f a. astr*; **~'s flytrap** *bot* Venusfliegenfalle *f*.

verac|eous [ve'reiʃəs] wahrhaft, aufrichtig, glaubwürdig, ehrlich; wahr, recht, richtig; **~ity** [ve'ræsiti] Wahrhaftigkeit, Aufrichtigkeit, Glaubwürdigkeit, Ehrlichkeit; Wahrheit *f*.

veranda(h) [və'rændə] Veranda *f*.

verb [və:b] *gram* Zeit-, Tätigkeitswort, Verb(um) *n*; **~al** ['-əl] *a* Wort-; mündlich; *(Übersetzung)* wörtlich; wortgetreu; im Wortlaut; *gram* Verb(al)-; *~~ inflexions (pl)* Verbformen *f pl*; *~~ memory* Wort-, Vokabelgedächtnis *n*; *~~ note (pol)* Verbalnote *f*; *~~ noun (gram)* Verbalsubstantiv *n*; **~alism** ['-əlizm] Wortklauberei *f*; Wortschwall *m*, bloße Worte *n pl*; (bloße) Redensart *f*; **~alist** ['-əlist] Wortklauber; gewandte(r) Redner *m*; **~alize** ['-əlaiz] *tr* in Worten ausdrücken; *gram* zum Verb machen; *itr* viele Worte machen; **~ally** ['-əli] *adv* in (bloßen) Worten; mündlich; Wort für Wort, wörtlich; **~atim** [və:'beitim] *adv a* wörtlich; Wort für Wort; **~iage** ['və:biidʒ] Wortreichtum, -schwall *m*; **~ose** [və:'bous] wortreich, weitschweifig; **~osity** [və:'bɔsiti] Wortreichtum, -schwall *m*.

verbena [və(:)'bi:nə] *bot* Eisenkraut *n*.

verd|ancy ['və:dənsi] *(bot) das* Grün(e); *fig* Unreife, Naivität; Unerfahrenheit *f*; **~ant** ['-ənt] grün, frisch; *fig* naiv, unreif, unerfahren, *fam* grün; **~igris** ['-igri(:)s] Grünspan *m*; **~ure** ['və:dʒə] *(bot) das* Grüne; Grün *n*, Vegetation *f*, Pflanzenwuchs *m*; *fig* Kraft, Blüte *f*.

verdict ['və:dikt] *jur* Wahrspruch *m*, Verdikt *n (der Geschworenen)*; *allg* Urteil *n*, Ansicht, Meinung (*on* über); Entscheidung *f*; *to arrive at a ~* zu e-m Spruch kommen; *to bring in, to return a ~* ein Urteil fällen; *to bring in, to deliver, to pronounce, to return a ~ of (not) guilty* (nicht) für schuldig befinden; *to give, to pass o.'s ~ (up)on s.th.* sein Urteil über etw abgeben; *~ of guilty* Schuldspruch *m*; *~ of not guilty* Freispruch *m*.

verge [və:dʒ] *s* Rand, Saum *m*; *agr* Einfassung; Grenze *f*; Bereich, Bezirk; *jur* Gerichtsbezirk *m*, Jurisdiktion *f*; (Amts-)Stab; (Säulen-)Schaft *m*; *itr* grenzen *a. fig* (*on* an); sich neigen (*towards* zu); sich nähern (*on s.th.* e-r S); *(Farben)* übergehen (*into* in); *on the ~ of (fig)* am Rande *gen*; nahe an; *to be on the ~ of doing* im Begriff, nahe daran sein zu tun; **~r** ['-ə] Kirchendiener; Stabträger *m*.

veri|fiable ['verifaiəbl] nachprüfbar, kontrollierbar; nachweisbar; **~fication** [verifi'keiʃən] Nach-, Überprüfung, Kontrolle *f*; Nachweis *m*, Bestätigung; Beurkundung *f*; *on ~~ of this* urkundlich dessen; **~fy** ['-fai] *tr (auf Echtheit, Richtigkeit)* prüfen, kontrollieren; als wahr, richtig erweisen; nachweisen, bestätigen, (urkundlich) belegen; beglaubigen; durch Eid bekräftigen; **~ly** ['-li] *obs* wahrlich; **~similar** [veri'similə] scheinbar; anscheinend; wahrscheinlich; **~similitude** [veri'similitju:d] Wahrscheinlichkeit *f*; **~table** ['-təbl] wahr(haft), wirklich; **~ty** ['-ti] Wahrheit; Wirklichkeit, Realität *f*.

verjuice ['və:dʒu:s] Saft *m* unreifer Früchte; Essig *m*.

vermeil ['və:meil] *s* Vermeil; feuervergoldete(s) Silber *n*; vergoldete Bronze *f*; *poet* Purpur(farbe f) *m*; *a poet* purpur(farbe)n.

verm|icelli [və:mi'seli] Fadennudeln *f pl*; **~icide** ['və:misaid] *pharm* Wurmmittel *n*; **~icular** [və:'mikjulə] wurmförmig; gewunden; wurmstichig, -zerfressen; Wurm-; **~iform** ['-ifɔ:m] wurmförmig; *~~ appendix (anat)* Wurmfortsatz *m*; **~ifuge** ['-ifju:dʒ] Wurmmittel *n*; **~in** ['-in] *sing mit pl* Ungeziefer *n*, Schädlinge *m pl*; Raubzeug; *fig* Gesindel *n*; **~inous** ['-inəs] *a* voller Ungeziefer; verlaust; verwanzt; Ungeziefer-.

vermilion [və'miljən] *s* Zinnober *m*; Zinnoberrot *n*; *a* zinnoberrot.

verm(o)uth ['və:məθ, -'mu:θ] Wermut (-wein) *m*.

vernacular [və'nækjulə] *a (Sprache)* Volks-, Landes-, Umgangs-; mundartlich; (ein)heimisch; *med* endemisch; *s* Volks-, Landes-, Umgangssprache *f*; Dialekt *m*; Fach-, Berufssprache *f*; Jargon *m*.

vernal ['və:nl] *lit* Frühlings-; frühlingshaft; *fig* jugendlich; **~ equinox** Frühjahrs-Tagundnachtgleiche *f (21. März)*.

vernier ['və:njə] Nonius; *tech* Feinsteller *m*.

veronica [vi'rɔnikə] *bot* Veronika *f*, Ehrenpreis *n* od *m*.

vers|ant ['və:sənt] *geol* (Berg-, Ab-)Hang *m*; **~atile** ['-ətail, *Am* -til] *tech* drehbar; *bot zoo* versatil; *fig* beweglich, wendig, gewandt, vielseitig; schwankend, unbeständig; **~atility** [və:sə'tiliti] *tech* Drehbarkeit; *fig* Beweglichkeit *a. bot zoo*, Wendigkeit, Gewandtheit, Vielseitigkeit; Unbeständigkeit *f*; **~e** [və:s] Vers *m (a. d. Bibel)*; Strophe *f*; Gedicht *n*; Poesie, *pej* Reimerei *f*; *to give chapter and ~ for* genau belegen; *blank ~~* Blankvers *m*; **~ed** [və:st] *a* erfahren, bewandert, versiert (*in* in); *(well ~~)* auf der Höhe; *math* umgekehrt; **~icolor** ['-ikʌlə], **~icoloured** ['-ikʌləd] *a* vielfarbig; schillernd; **~ification** [və:sifi'keiʃən] Verslehre, -kunst, -bildung *f*, -bau *m*; metrische Fassung *f*; **~ifier** ['və:sifaiə] Dichter; *pej* Reimschmied *m*; **~ify** ['-ifai] *itr* Verse machen, dichten; *tr* in Verse bringen; **~ion** ['və:ʃən] Übersetzung; *(Schule)* Hinübersetzung; Darstellung, Auffassung; Version, Gestalt(ung), Form *f*; **~o** ['və:sou] *(typ, Münze)* Rückseite *f*; **~us** ['-əs] *jur sport* gegen.

vert [və:t] **1.** *jur* Baumbestand *m*, (Unter-)Holz; Holzungsrecht *n*; **2.** *s fam rel* Konvertit(in *f*) *m*; *itr* konvertieren.

vert|ebra ['və:tibrə] *pl -ae* [-i:] Wirbel(knochen) *m*; **~ebral** ['-tibrəl] *a* Wirbel-; *~~ column* Wirbelsäule *f*, Rückgrat *n*; **~ebrate** ['-ibrit] *a* Wirbel-; *s* Wirbeltier *n*; **~ex** ['və:teks] *pl a. -ices* ['-isi:z] Spitze *f*, Gipfel *a. fig*; *math* Scheitel(punkt); *astr* Zenit *m*; **~ical** ['-ikəl] *a* senkrecht, lotrecht, vertikal; Gipfel- *a. fig fin*; *math anat zoo* Scheitel-; *s* Senkrechte, Vertikale *f*; *~~ clearance* lichte Höhe *f*; *~~ interval* Höhenunterschied *n*; *~~ take-off aircraft* Senkrechtstarter *m*; **~iginous** [və:'tidʒinəs] sich drehend, wirbelnd; schwind(e)lig; schwindelerregend; *fig* dauernd wechselnd, unbeständig, unstet; **~igo** ['və:tigou] *pl -o(e)s med* Schwindel(gefühl *n*) *m*; Höhenkrankheit *f*.

vertu *s. virtu.*

verve [və:v] Schwung *m*, Begeisterung *f*, Feuer *n*; Ausdruckskraft, -gewalt *f*.

Very ['viəri, 'veri]: **~ light** *mil* Leuchtzeichen *n*, -patrone *f*; **~ pistol** Leuchtpistole *f*; **~ signal** Leuchtzeichen, -signal *n*.

very ['veri] *adv* sehr; äußerst; gerade, (ganz) genau; völlig; *(beim Superlativ)* aller-; *a* genau, vollständig, völlig, absolut; bloß, allein, schon; sogar; selb, nämlich; *in the ~ act* auf frischer Tat; *to the ~ heart* tief ins Herz; *~ high frequency* Ultrakurzwelle *f*; *~ much* sehr; *~ well (adv)*, *~ good (a)* sehr gut; in Ordnung; *the ~ thought* der bloße Gedanke; *the ~ truth* die reine Wahrheit.

vesic|ate ['vesikeit] *tr* Blasen ziehen auf; *itr* Blasen ziehen; sich mit Blasen bedecken; **~atory** ['vesikeitəri] *a med* blasenziehend; *s* Zugpflaster *n*; **~cle** ['vesikl] *anat zoo bot* Bläschen *n*; *geol* Druse *f*; **~ular** [və'sikjulə] bläschenartig; Bläschen-.

vesper ['vespə] *(V~)* Abendstern; *poet* Abend *m*; *pl* Vesper, Abendandacht *f*, -gottesdienst *m*; **~-bell** Abendglocke *f*.

vessel ['vesl] Gefäß *n a. bot zoo anat*; Behälter *m*; *mar* Schiff; *aero* Luftschiff; *fig* Werkzeug *n*; *blood ~* Blutgefäß *n*.

vest [vest] *s* (Herren-)Unterhemd *n*, Unterjacke *f*; *(Damenkleid)* Einsatz *m*; *Am Br com* Weste *f*; *hist* (langes) Gewand *n*; *tr poet* (ein)kleiden; *(Rechte)* übertragen (*in s.o.* auf jdn); verleihen (*in s.o.* jdm); ausstatten (*s.o. with s.th.* jdn mit e-r S); *itr* sich ankleiden, -ziehen; *(Rechte, Eigentum)* übergehen (*in* auf); liegen (*in* bei); *~ed rights (pl)* wohlerworbene, verbriefte Rechte *n pl*; **~ibule** ['-ibju:l] Eingang(shalle *f*) *m*, Vestibül *n*; Vorraum; *Am rail* Durchgang *(d. D-Züge)*; *anat* Vorhof *m*; *~~ car (Am)* Durchgangs-, D-Zug-Wagen *m*; *~~ train (Am)* D-Zug *m*; **~ment** ['-mənt] (*bes.* Amts-)Gewand *n*, Tracht, Robe *f*; *rel* Meßgewand *n*; **~-pocket** *s* Westentasche *f*; *a* Westentaschen-, Miniatur-; *~~ edition (Buch)* Miniaturausgabe *f*; *~~ size* Westentaschenformat *n*; **~ry** ['-ri] *rel* Sakristei *f*; Kirchenrat *m*, Gemeindevertretung, -versammlung *f*, -haus *n*; *~~ book* Kirchenbuch *n*; *~~man* Kirchenälteste(r), -rat, Gemeindevertreter *m*; **~ure** ['vestʃə] *s poet* Gewand(ung *f*) *n*, Kleider *n pl*; Hülle *f*; *tr* (be)kleiden; bedecken.

vest|a ['vestə] (Wachs-)Zünd-, Streichholz *n*; **~al** ['-əl] *a rel hist* vestalisch, jungfräulich, rein, keusch; *s (~ virgin)* Vestalin; Jungfrau; Nonne *f*.

vestige ['vestidʒ] Spur *f*, Überrest *m*; *fig* Andeutung, Spur, Idee *f*; *biol* Rudiment *n*; *not a ~ of* keine Spur von.

vesuvian [vi'su:vjən] *a* vulkanisch; *V~ (geogr)* vesuvisch.
vet [vet] **1.** *s fam* Tierarzt *m*; *tr* tierärztlich untersuchen; *fam* auf Herz u. Nieren prüfen; sorgfältig durchkorrigieren; **2.** *Am fam* Veteran *m*; **~mobile** (Kriegs-)Versehrtenauto *n*.
vetch [vetʃ] *bot* Wicke *f*.
veteran ['vetərən] *s* Veteran; *fig* alte(r) Praktikus; *Am* ausgediente(r) Soldat; ehemalige(r) Frontkämpfer *m*; *a* (alt-, *bes.* kriegs)erfahren; *Am* Veteranen-.
veterinar|ian [vetəri'nɛəriən] Tierarzt, Veterinär *m*; **~y** ['vetərinəri, 'vetnri] *a* tierärztlich; Veterinär-; *s (~~ surgeon)* Tierarzt *m*; *~~ medicine* Tierheilkunde, Veterinärmedizin *f*.
veto ['vi:tou] *pl -oes s* Veto *n*, Einspruch *m*; *(power, right of ~)* Veto-, Einspruchsrecht *n*; *Am (~ message)* Begründung *f* e-s Vetos; *tr* sein Veto einlegen gegen; verbieten, untersagen; *to put a ~ on s.th.* gegen etw Einspruch erheben.
vex [veks] *tr* aus der Ruhe bringen, belästigen, stören, ärgern, reizen, aufregen, rasend machen; plagen, quälen *(a. von Krankheiten)*; *poet* aufwühlen; *to be ~ed at* verärgert sein über; *~ed question* e-e vieldiskutierte Frage; **~ation** [vek'seiʃən] Belästigung, Störung *f*, Ärger *m*, Aufregung; Plage, Qual, Sorge; Unannehmlichkeit *f*; **~atious** [vek'seiʃəs] lästig, störend, aufregend, ärgerlich, verdrießlich; quälend; *jur* schikanös.

*

via ['vaiə] *prp* über *(e-n Ort reisen)*; per; *s*: **V~ Lactea** *scient* Milchstraße *f*; **~ media** *fig* Mittelweg *m*.
viab|ility [vaiə'biliti] Lebensfähigkeit *f*; **~le** ['vaiəbl] lebensfähig *a. fig*.
viaduct ['vaiədʌkt] Viadukt *m*.
vial ['vaiəl] Phiole *f*, Fläschchen *n*; Ampulle *f*.
viands ['vaiəndz] *pl* Eßwaren *f pl*, Lebensmittel *n pl*, Delikatessen *f pl*.
viatic|(al) [vai'ætik(əl)] *a* Weg-, Reise-; **~um** [-əm] *pl meist -a* [-ə] Wegzehrung *f*; Zehrgeld *n*, -pfennig *m*; *rel* Viatikum, Sterbesakrament *n*.
vibr|ant ['vaibrənt] vibrierend, schwingend; zitternd (*with* vor); *fig* pulsierend, lebhaft; *(Phonetik)* stimmhaft; **~aphone** ['vaibrəfoun] *mus* Vibraphon *n*; **~ate** [-'breit, '--] *itr* vibrieren; schwingen, zittern (*with* vor); schwanken; *tr* in Schwingungen versetzen; *phys (Wellen)* ausstrahlen; messen; **~ation** [vai'breiʃən] Schwingung, Vibration *f*; **~ative** [vai'breitiv], **~atory** ['-ətəri] vibrierend, schwingend; Schwingungs-; **~ator** [vai'breitə] *(el. Klingel)* Klöppel; Vibrationsmassageapparat; *el* Summer, Zerhacker *m*.
viburnum [vai'bə:nəm] *bot* Schneeball *m*.
vicar ['vikə] *rel* (Stell-)Vertreter, Vikar, (Hilfs-)Geistliche(r); *Am* Pfarrer, Pastor *m*; **~age** ['-ridʒ] Pfarrhaus *n*; Vikar-, Pfarrstelle *f*; **~ious** [vai'kɛəriəs] stellvertretend; übertragen; *fig* nachempfunden.
vice [vais] **1.** Fehler *m*; Laster *n*, Untugend; Lasterhaftigkeit; *(Pferd)* Unart *f*; **2.** *(Am meist vise)* Schraubstock *m*; **3.** *fam* Vize(präsident) *m*; **4.** *prp* an Stelle, anstelle *gen*; *in Zssgen* ['-'-] stellvertretend, Vize-, Unter-; **~-admiral** Vizeadmiral *m*; **~-chairman** stellvertretende(r) Vorsitzende(r) *m*; **~-chancellor** Vizekanzler *m*; **~-consul** Vizekonsul *m*; **~-president** Vizepräsident *m*; **~regal** ['-'ri:gəl] vizeköniglich; **~roy** ['-rɔi] Vizekönig *m*; **4.**: **~ versa** ['vaisi'və:sə] *adv* umgekehrt.
vicin|age ['visinidʒ], **~ity** [vi'siniti] Nachbarschaft, Nähe *f*; *in close ~ity to* ganz nahe bei; **~al** ['visinl] benachbart, nah(e); *~~ road* Vizinalweg *m*.
vicious ['viʃəs] lasterhaft, verdorben, sittenlos; fehlerhaft, defekt; tückisch, bösartig, gefährlich; *(Hund)* bissig; boshaft; gemein, verächtlich; verderblich, unheilvoll; **~ circle** Teufelskreis, Circulus vitiosus *m*; **~ness** ['-nis] Lasterhaftigkeit; Bösartigkeit; Bosheit; Gemeinheit; Verderblichkeit *f*; defekte(r) Zustand *m*.
vicissitude [vi'sisitju:d] (regelmäßiger) Wechsel *m*; Unbeständigkeit *f*; *pl* Wechselfälle *m pl*, Auf u. Ab *n*.
victim ['viktim] Opfer(tier); *allg* Opfer *(Mensch) n*, Betroffene(r), Geschädigte(r); Geprellte(r), Hereingefallene(r) *m*; *~ of circumstances* Opfer *n* der Verhältnisse; *~ of war* Kriegsopfer *n*; **~ization** [viktimai'zeiʃən] Opferung; Bestrafung *f*; Hinopfern; Prellen *n*; **~ize** ['viktimaiz] *tr* opfern; hinopfern, -schlachten; bestrafen; prellen, hereinlegen, anführen.
victor ['viktə] *s* Sieger, Gewinner *m*; *V~* Viktor *m*; *a* siegreich; Sieger-; **V~ia** [vik'tɔ:riə] Viktoria *f*; *v~~* Kalesche *f*; *V~~ Cross* Viktoriakreuz *n (höchster brit. Militärorden)*; **V~ian** [-'tɔ:riən] *a hist* viktorianisch; *fig* spießbürgerlich, prüde; *s* Viktorianer *m*; **V~ianism** [-'tɔ:riənizm] *hist* Viktorianismus *m*; *fig* Spießbürgerlichkeit *f*; **~ious** [vik'tɔ:riəs] siegreich (*over* über); Sieger-, Sieges-; **~y** ['viktəri] Sieg *m a. fig*; *to gain, to win a ~~ over* e-n Sieg erringen über.
victual ['vitl] *s meist pl* Lebensmittel *n pl*; Vorräte *m pl*; *tr itr* (sich) verpflegen, (sich) verproviantieren; **~(l)er** ['-lə] Lebensmittelhändler, -lieferant; *(licensed ~~)* Schankwirt *m*; *mar* Proviantschiff *n*.
vicuña, vicu(g)na [vi'kju:nə] *zoo* Vikunja *f*; Vikunja-, Vigognewolle *f*; *(~ cloth)* Vikunja-, Vigognestoff *m*.
vide, v. ['vaidi(:), 'videi] siehe, s.; **v. infra** s. unten; **v. supra** s. oben.
videlicet, viz. [vi'di:liset] *(lies: namely)* nämlich; und zwar.
video ['vidiou] *a Am* Fernseh-; Bild-; *s* Fernsehen *n*; *(to make o.'s) ~ debut* (sein) Fernsehdebüt *n* (geben); **~ entertainment** Fernsehunterhaltung *f*; **~ frequency** Bildwelle *f*; **~ industry** Fernsehindustrie *f*; **~ set** Fernsehgerät *n*; **~ show** Fernsehprogramm *n*; **~ tape** Magnetbildband *n*; **~ transmission** Fernsehübertragung *f*; **~ transmitter** Fernsehsender *m*; **~ viewer** (Fernseh-)Zuschauer *m*.
vie [vai] *itr* wetteifern (*with s.o.* mit jdm; *for* um).
Vienn|a [vi'enə] Wien *n*; **~ waltz** Wiener Walzer *m*; **~ese** [viə'ni:z] *a* wienerisch, Wiener-; *s* Wiener(in *f*) *m*.
view [vju:] *s* Sehen, Schauen, Betrachten *n*, Besichtigung; Auf-, Vorführung; Untersuchung *a. jur*; (An-, Aus-)Sicht *f*; (An-, Aus-, Über-)Blick *m* (*of, over* auf); Blickfeld *n*, Sehbereich *m*, -weite *f*; Bild *n*, Skizze *f*, (Lage-)Plan *m*, *phot* Aufnahme; *fig* Ansicht, Anschauung, Auffassung, Meinung *f*, Urteil *n*; Absicht *f*, Plan *m*, Ziel *n*; Aussicht, Erwartung *f*; Überblick *m*, Zs.fassung *f*; *tr* an-, besehen, betrachten, anschauen, besichtigen, in Augenschein nehmen; prüfen, untersuchen; *fig* ins Auge fassen, überlegen, -denken, beurteilen; *itr video* fernsehen; *at first ~* auf den ersten Blick; *in ~* vor Augen *a. fig*, in Erinnerung; im Sinn; in Aussicht *od* Erwartung; *in ~ of* im Hinblick auf, in Anbetracht *gen*, angesichts *gen*; *in my ~* meines Erachtens, meiner Ansicht nach, nach meinem Dafürhalten; *on ~* zur Schau, zur Besichtigung; *on nearer ~* bei näherer Betrachtung; *out of ~* außer Sicht; *with a ~ to, with the ~ of* in der Absicht zu; mit der Aussicht auf; *to agree with s.o.'s ~s* jds Ansichten beipflichten; *to come in(to) ~* in Sicht kommen, auftauchen; *of s.th.* etw erblicken; *to fall in with s.o.'s ~s* sich jds Auffassung anschließen; *to have s.th. in ~* etw im Auge, vorhaben; beabsichtigen, planen; *to keep in ~* im Auge behalten; *to lose ~ of s.th.* etw aus den Augen verlieren; *to take a ~ of* e-e Aufnahme machen von; *fig* e-e Ansicht haben von; etw beurteilen; *I have it in ~* es schwebt mir vor; *aerial ~* Luftbild *n*; *broad ~s (pl)* liberale Ansichten *f pl*; *dim ~ (fam)* ungünstige(r) Eindruck *m*; *front, back, side ~* Vorder-, Rück-, Seitenansicht *f*; *point of ~ = ~point*; *sectional ~* Querschnitt *m*; **~er** ['-ə] Prüfer, Inspizient; (Fernseh-)Zuschauer *m*; **~-finder** *opt phot* Sucher *m*; *~ and range finder* Meßsucher *m*; **~ halloo** Halali *n (Jagdruf)*; **~ing** ['-iŋ] Inaugenscheinnahme, Besichtigung, Prüfung *f*; *~~ angle* Bildwinkel *m*; *~~ stand* Tribüne *f*; **~less** ['-lis] *a* ohne Aussicht; *lit* unsichtbar; *fig Am* ohne eigene Meinung, ohne eigenes Urteil; **~point** Gesichts-, Standpunkt *m*; **~y** ['-i] *fam* verstiegen, übergeschnappt; schrullig; *fam* in die Augen fallend; auffällig, protzig.

*

vigil ['vidʒil] Nachtwache *f*; *rel* Vorabend *m (e-s Festes)*; *rel* Vigilie *f*; *to hold, to keep ~* wachen (*over* bei); **~ance** ['-əns] Wachsamkeit; *med* Schlaflosigkeit *f*; *~~ committee (Am)* (ungesetzlicher) Ausschuß *m* zu polizeilicher u. rechtlicher Selbsthilfe (im Notstand); **~ant** ['-ənt] wachsam; **~ante** [vidʒi'lænti] *Am* Mitglied *n* e-s Vigilance committee.
vignette [vi'njet] *(Buch)* Vignette *f*, Zierstück *n*, -leiste, (Rand-)Verzierung; Charakterskizze *f*.
vig|orous ['vigərəs] stark, kräftig, kraftvoll, robust; energisch, vital, impulsiv; schlagkräftig; nachdrücklich, intensiv; **~o(u)r** ['vigə] Stärke, Kraft, Robustheit; Energie, Vitalität; Schlagkraft *f*; Nachdruck *m*, Intensität; *jur* Rechtskraft *f*.
viking ['vaikiŋ] Wiking(er) *m*.
vil|e [vail] *(sittlich)* schlecht, niedrig, gemein, verdorben, böse; abstoßend, widerlich, ekelhaft; herabwürdigend, gemein; *obs* wertlos; *fam* schlecht, abscheulich; **~eness** ['-nis] Schlechtigkeit, Niedrigkeit, Gemeinheit; Widerlichkeit *f*; **~ification** [vilifi'keiʃən] Verleumdung, Schmähung *f*; **~ify** ['vilifai] *tr* verleumden, schmähen, herabwürdigen, -setzen.
villag|e ['vilidʒ] Dorf *n*, (Land-)Gemeinde; Dorfgemeinschaft; *zoo* Siedlungsgebiet *f*; *~~ community* Dorfgemeinschaft *f*; *~~ inn* Dorfgasthaus *n*; **~er** ['-ə] Dorfbewohner, Dörfler *m*.
villain ['vilən] Schuft, Schurke; *hum* Schelm, Schlingel *m*; *hist (a.* **villein***)* Leibeigene(r) *m*; **~ous** ['-əs] schurkisch, gaunerhaft; schändlich, gemein; *fam* schlecht, scheußlich; **~y** ['-i] Schuftigkeit, Gemeinheit *f*.

vill|ose [vi'lous], **~ous** ['viləs] *zoo* zottig; *bot* haarig; **~us** ['-əs] *pl -i* ['-ai] *anat* (Darm-)Zotte *f*; *bot* Härchen *n*.

vim [vim] *fam bes. Am* Kraft, Energie *f*, Schwung, Schneid, Mumm *m*.

vinaigrette [vinei'gret] Riechfläschchen *n*.

vindic|ability [vindikə'biliti] Stichhaltigkeit *f*; **~able** ['vindikəbl] zu rechtfertigen(d); zu beanspruchen(d); **~ate** ['-eit] *tr* rechtfertigen, erhärten; verteidigen (*from* gegen); (unter)stützen; als Beweis *od* Bekräftigung dienen für; *jur* beanspruchen (*for* für); **~ation** [vindi'keiʃən] Rechtfertigung, Erhärtung; Verteidigung, Unterstützung; Bekräftigung *f*, Beweis *m*, Stütze *f*; Anspruch *m*; *in ~~ of* zur Rechtfertigung *gen*; **~ative** ['vindikətiv, vin'd-] rechtfertigend, stützend; **~ator** ['-eitə] Verteidiger; Beanspruchende(r) *m*; **~atory** ['-eitəri, *Am* '-ətəri] rechtfertigend; rächend, strafend; **~tive** [vin'diktiv] nachtragend; rachsüchtig; rächend; Rache-; **~tiveness** [-'diktivnis] Rachsucht *f*.

vine [vain] Weinstock *m*, Rebe *f*; *(grape-~)* echte(r) Weinstock *m*; *hop-~* Hopfen *m*; **~ branch** Weinranke *f*; **~-disease** Reblausbefall *m*; **~-dresser** Winzer *m*; **~-growing** Weinbau *m*; **~-louse, -pest** Reblaus *f*; **~ry** ['vainəri] Treibhaus *n* für Reben; **~yard** ['vinjəd] Weinberg, -garten *m*.

vinegar ['vinigə] (Wein-)Essig *m*; *aromatic ~* aromatische(r), Kräuteressig *m*; **~-eel** *zoo* Essigälchen *n*; **~y** ['-ri] (essig)sauer *a. fig.*

vini|cultural [vini'kʌltʃərəl] *a* Weinbau-; **~culture** ['vinikʌltʃə] Weinbau *m*.

vinous ['vainəs] wein(halt)ig; trunksüchtig; weinselig; weinrot.

vint|age ['vintidʒ] *s* (Wein-)Lese *f*; Wachstum *n*; Jahrgang *m*; *a* hervorragend; alt u. gut; *~~ car (mot)* Veteran *m*; *~~ wine* Qualitätswein *m*; **~ager** ['-idʒə] Winzer *m*; **~ner** ['-nə] Weinhändler *m*.

*

viol ['vaiəl] *hist* Fiedel, Viole; *allg* Geige *f*; *bass ~* Gambe *f*; **~a 1.** ['vaiələ] *bot* Veilchen, Stiefmütterchen *n*; **2.** [vi'oulə] Bratsche, Viola *f*; **~in** [vaiə'lin] Geige, Violine *f*; = **~inist**; *to play the ~~* Geige spielen; *~~ bow, case, string* Geigenbogen, -kasten *m*, -saite *f*; **~inist** ['vaiəlinist] Geiger *m*; **~oncellist** [vaiələn'tʃelist] Cellist *m*; **~oncello** [-ən'tʃelou] *pl -os* Cello *n*.

viol|able ['vaiələbl] verletzbar, -lich; **~ate** ['-eit] *tr (Recht)* verletzen; *(Gesetz)* übertreten, verstoßen gegen; *(Eid)* brechen; *(Versprechen)* nicht (ein)halten; *(Gefühl, Empfinden)* verletzen, beleidigen; *(Frieden)* stören; *(Heiligtum)* entweihen, schänden, profanieren; *(Frau)* schänden, entehren, vergewaltigen; **~ation** [vaiə'leiʃən] Verletzung; Übertretung, Zuwiderhandlung *f*; (Eid-)Bruch *m*; Nichteinhaltung; Beleidigung; Störung; Entweihung; Schändung; Vergewaltigung *f*; *~~ of trust* Vertrauensbruch *m*; **~ator** ['vaiəleitə] Verletzer; Übertreter; Rechts-, Eidbrecher; Schänder *m*; **~ence** ['-əns] Gewalt (-samkeit), Heftigkeit; Leidenschaftlichkeit *f*, Ungestüm *n*; Gewaltakt *m*, Gewaltanwendung *f*, gewaltsame(s) Vorgehen *n*; Schändung, Entweihung, Profanation *f*; *with ~~* unter Anwendung von Gewalt; *to do ~~ to s.o.* jdm Gewalt antun *a. fig.*; *crimes of ~~* Gewaltverbrechen *n pl*; **~ent** ['-ənt] gewaltsam, -tätig; heftig, stark; leidenschaftlich; *to meet a ~~ death* e-s gewaltsamen Todes sterben.

violet ['vaiəlit] *s* Veilchen; Violett *n*; *a* violett, veilchenblau.

V. I. P., VIP ['vi:ai'pi:] *(very important person) Am sl* hohe(s) Tier *n*.

viper ['vaipə] Viper; Natter; Giftschlange *a. fig*; *(common ~)* Kreuzotter; *fig* giftige Person, *fam* Giftnudel *f*; *Am sl* Rauschgiftsüchtige(r) *m*; **~ine** ['-rain, '-rin] viperartig; **~ish** ['-riʃ], **~ous** ['-rəs] *fig* giftig, hinterhältig.

virago [vi'rɑ:gou, -'reig-] *pl -o(e)s* Xanthippe *f*, Zankteufel *m*.

vir|eo ['viriou] *pl -os zoo Am* Laubwürger *m*; **~idescence** [viri'desns] grünliche Färbung *f*; **~idescent** [-i'desnt] grünlich; **~idity** [vi'riditi] *biol* grüne Farbe; *fig* Frische; Lebendig-, Lebhaftigkeit *f*.

virgin ['və:dʒin] *s* Jungfrau *f*; (junges) Mädchen *n*; *the (Blessed) V~ (Mary)* die Jungfrau Maria; *a* jungfräulich; Jungfrauen-; *fig* rein, keusch, unberührt; *allg* unberührt, unbenutzt, ungebraucht, unbetreten, unbefahren (*of* von); *(Boden)* ungepflügt; *min* gediegen; Jungfern-; **~al** ['-l] *a* jungfräulich; mädchenhaft; rein, frisch, unberührt; *zoo* unbefruchtet; *s mus* Virginal, Spinett *n*; *~~ membrane* Jungfernhäutchen *n*; **~ forest** Urwald *m*; **V~ia** [və'dʒinjə] Virginia *n*, -tabak *m*; *~~ creeper* wilde(r) Wein *m*, Jungfernrebe *f*; **~ity** [və:'dʒiniti] Jungfräulichkeit; Unberührtheit *f*.

Virgo ['və:gou] *astr* Jungfrau *f*.

viril|e ['virail, *Am* '-il] männlich; kraftvoll; zeugungskräftig; **~ity** [vi'riliti] Männlichkeit; Manneskraft; Zeugungskraft *f*.

virtu, vertu [və:'tu:] Kunstliebhaberei *f*; Kunstwert *m*; *(articles of ~)* Kunstgegenstände *m pl*.

virtu|al ['və:tjuəl] wirklich, tatsächlich, im Grunde (genommen), eigentlich; *tech* virtuell; *~~ value* Effektivwert *m*; **~e** ['və:tju:, *Am* '-tʃu:] sittliche(r) Wert *m*; Rechtschaffenheit, Tugend; Keuschheit *f*; Wert *m*, Verdienst *n*; besondere Eigenschaft, Qualität; Wirkung, Wirksamkeit *f*; *by, in ~~ of* kraft, auf Grund *gen*; (ver)mittels *(gen)*; *of easy ~~* von lockeren Sitten; *to make a ~~ of necessity (prov)* aus der Not e-e Tugend machen; **~osity** [və:tju'ɔsiti] Kunstsinn *m*, -verständnis *n*; Virtuosität; Kunstfertigkeit *f*; **~oso** [və:tju'ouzou] *pl a. -si* [-ai] Kunstliebhaber, -verständige(r), -kenner, -sammler; Virtuose *m*; **~ous** ['və:tjuəs, *Am* -tʃu-] tugendhaft, sittlich, rechtschaffen.

vir|ulence, -cy ['virulǝns(i)] Giftigkeit, Tödlichkeit; *med* Ansteckungsfähigkeit, Virulenz; *fig* Bosheit, Boshaftigkeit *f*; **~ulent** ['-ulənt] giftig, tödlich; *med* ansteckend, virulent; *fig* feindselig, haßerfüllt, gehässig; **~us** ['vaiərəs] Gift *a. fig*; *med* Virus *n, a. m.*

vis [vis] *pl vires* ['vaiəri:z] Kraft, Stärke *f*; **~ major** *jur* höhere Gewalt *f*; **~ viva** *phys* kinetische Energie *f*.

visa ['vi:zə], **visé** ['vi:zei] *s* Visum *n*, Sichtvermerk *m*; *tr* mit e-m Visum versehen; *entrance ~* Einreisevisum *n*.

visage ['vizidʒ] *lit* Antlitz *n*.

vis-à-vis ['vi:zɑ:vi:] *a* gegenüber (befindlich), gegenüberliegend; *adv prp* gegenüber (*to, with* von); *s* Gegenüber *n*; Gegner *m*.

viscer|a ['visərə] *pl anat* Eingeweide *n (pl)*, innere Organe *n pl*; **~al** ['-əl] *a anat* Eingeweide-.

visc|id ['visid] dick-, zäh(flüssig), klebrig *a. bot*; **~idity** [vi'siditi] Dick-, Zähflüssigkeit, Klebrigkeit *f*; **~ose** ['viskous] *s* Viskose *f*; **~osity** [vis'kɔsiti] Dick-, Zähflüssigkeit, Viskosität; Konsistenz *f*; **~ous** ['viskəs] dick-, zähflüssig, klebrig, viskos.

viscount ['vaikaunt] Vicomte *m*; **~ess** ['-is] Vicomtesse *f*.

vise *s. vice.*

visé *s. visa.*

visib|ility [vizi'biliti] Sichtbarkeit; Sicht(weite) *f*; *~~ of aim (Jagd)* Büchsenlicht *n*; **~le** ['vizəbl] sichtbar, wahrnehmbar; *fig* offensichtlich, deutlich, handgreiflich; greifbar, zur Verfügung stehend; *is he ~~?* ist er zu sprechen? *~~ horizon* Kimm *f*.

Visigoth ['vizigɔθ] Westgote *m*; **~ic** [vizi'gɔθik] westgotisch.

vision ['viʒən] Sehen *n*; Sehkraft *f*, -vermögen *n*; Vision *f*, Gesicht, Wunschbild *n*, Erscheinung *f*; Anblick *m*; Vorstellung(skraft), Phantasie; Voraussicht *f*, Weitblick *m*; (große) Schönheit *f (Frau)*; *field of ~* Gesichtsfeld *n*; **~ acuity** Sehschärfe *f*; **~ary** ['viʒnəri] *a* visionär, irreal, unwirklich, phantastisch; schwärmerisch, unpraktisch, undurchführbar; hellseherisch; *s* Visionär, Geister-, Hellseher; Phantast, Träumer *m*; **~ frequency** *video* Bildfrequenz *f*.

visit ['vizit] *tr* auf-, besuchen; auf Besuch sein bei; bereisen, besichtigen; unter-, durchsuchen, inspizieren; heimsuchen, (be)strafen; *itr* e-n Besuch machen (*with* bei); *Am fam* plaudern, schwatzen, tratschen, klatschen (*with* mit); *Am* wohnen (*at* in); sich aufhalten (*in Paris* in Paris); *obs* strafen, Rache üben (*upon* an); *s* Besuch *m* (*to* bei); Besichtigung; Unter-, Durchsuchung *f*; *Am fam* Geplauder *n*, Schwatz, Klatsch *m*; *to pay a ~ to s.o.* jdm e-n Besuch abstatten; *courtesy ~* Höflichkeitsbesuch *m*; **~ant** ['-ənt] Besucher, Gast; *zoo* Strich-, Durchzugsvogel *m*; **~ation** [vizi'teiʃən] Visitation, Inspektion, (offizielle) Besichtigung *f*; *rel* Besuch *m*; *jur* Durchsuchung; *fig* Heimsuchung *f*; *fam* zu langer Besuch *m*; **~(at)orial** [vizi'tɔ:riəl, -tə'tɔ:riəl] *a* Visitations-, Besichtigungs-; **~ing** ['-iŋ] *s* Besuchen *n*; *a* Besuchs-; *to be on ~~ terms* sich (gegenseitig) besuchen; *~~-card* Besucher-, Visitenkarte *f*; *~~ hours (pl)* Besuchszeit *f*; *~~-list* Besuchsliste *f*; **~or** ['-ə] Besucher, Gast; Inspizient *m*; *~~s' book* Fremden-, Gästebuch *n*.

visor, vizor ['vaizə] *hist (Helm)* Visier *n*; Maske *f*; Mützenschirm *m*; *mot (sun-~)* Sonnenblende *f*; **~ed** ['-d] *a* maskiert.

vista ['vistə] Durchblick *m*, Perspektive *f*; Ausblick *m*, -sicht *f*, Hintergrund; Korridor *m*; Einfassung *f*, Baum-, Häuserreihen *f pl*, Allee *f*; *fig* Ausblick *m*, Möglichkeit; Überschau, -sicht *f*, -blick *m*.

visual ['vizjuəl, -ʒjuəl] *a* Seh-; visuell; wahrnehmbar, sichtbar; visionär; optisch; Sicht-; *s (~ ray)* Blicklinie *f*; Augenmensch, optische(r) Typ *m*; **~ acuity** Sehschärfe *f*; **~ aids** *pl* Anschauungsmaterial *n*; **~ angle** Seh-, Gesichtswinkel *m*; **~ field** Gesichts-, Blickfeld *n*; **~ instruction** Anschauungsunterricht *m*; **~ization** [vizjuəlai'zeiʃən] lebendige Vorstellung *f*; geistige(s) Bild *n*; *faculty of ~~* Vorstellungsvermögen *n*; **~ize** ['vizjuəlaiz] *tr* sich vor Augen stellen, sich ein Bild, e-e Vorstellung machen von, sich ausmalen; sich vergegenwärtigen; **~izer**

['-aizə] *Am* visuelle(r) Typ; *(Werbung)* Ideenmann *m*; ~ **memory** visuelle(s) Gedächtnis *n*; ~ **nerve, organ** Sehnerv *m*, -organ *n*.
vital ['vaitl] *a* Lebens-; lebenswichtig, -notwendig; *fig* wesentlich, unersetzlich, entscheidend, unbedingt notwendig (*to* für); größt; tödlich; quicklebendig, tatkräftig, vital; *s pl* lebenswichtige Organe *n pl*; *fig das* Wesentliche, Unerläßliche; ~ **force** Lebenskraft *f*; **~ism** ['-izm] Vitalismus *m*; **~istic** [vaitə'listik] vitalistisch; **~ity** [vai'tæliti] Lebenskraft; Lebensfähigkeit; Vitalität, Energie *f*; **~ization** [vaitəlai'zeiʃən] Belebung *f*; **~ize** ['vaitəlaiz] *tr* beleben; lebendig gestalten, verlebendigen; ~ **statistics** *pl mit sing* Bevölkerungsstatistik *f*; *fam (Frau)* Körpermaße *n pl*.
vitamin(e) ['vitəmin, 'vait-] Vitamin *n*; ~ **deficiency, tablets** *pl* Vitaminmangel *m*, -tabletten *f pl*.
vitiat|e ['viʃieit] *tr* verderben, verfälschen, verunreinigen, verstümmeln; *(sittlich)* verderben, korrumpieren, erniedrigen; *jur* ungültig machen, für ungültig erklären, aufheben, annullieren; **~ion** [viʃi'eiʃən] Verfälschung, Verunreinigung, Verstümmelung; (Sitten-)Verderbnis; *jur* Ungültigmachung, Aufhebung *f*.
viticulture ['vitikʌltʃə] Weinbau *m*.
vitr|eous ['vitriəs] *a* Glas-; gläsern; glas(art)ig; *geol* glasig; ~~ *humo(u)r (Auge)* Glaskörper *m*; **~ifaction** [vitri'fækʃən], **~ification** [-fi'keiʃən] Glasherstellung *f*; Brennvorgang *m*; Sinterung *f*; **~fiable** ['vitrifaiəbl] zu Glas zu machen(d); **~ify** ['-ifai] *tr* zu Glas, glasig machen, verglasen; sintern; *itr* Glas, glasig werden; **~iol** ['vitriəl] *chem* Vitriol *n*; *(oil of* ~~*)* rauchende Schwefelsäure *f*; *fig* beißende(r) Spott *m*, bissige Worte *n pl*; Giftigkeit *f*; *blue, copper* ~~ Kupfervitriol*n*; **~iolic** [vitri'ɔlik] *a* Vitriol-; *fig* beißend, bissig, sarkastisch; **~iolize** ['vitriəlaiz] *tr chem* vitriolisieren; **mit** Vitriol verletzen *od* angreifen.
vituperat|e [vi'tju:pəreit] *tr* schmähen, heruntermachen, aus-, beschimpfen; **~ion** [vitju:pə'reiʃən] Beschimpfung, Schmähung *f*; Schmähworte *n pl*; **~ive** [vi'tju:pəreitiv, -rə-] schmähend; Schmäh-; **~or** [-'tju:pəreitə] Schmähende(r) *m*.
viv|aceous [vi'veiʃəs, vai-] lebhaft, (quick)lebendig, munter; **~acity** [vi'væsiti] Lebhaftigkeit, Lebendigkeit, Munterkeit *f*; **~arium** [vai'vɛəriəm] *pl a. -ia* [-iə] Vivarium, Aquarium *n* (mit Terrarium), Tierpark *m*; **~id** ['vivid] lebhaft, lebendig; *(Farbe)* leuchtend; *(Erinnerung)* frisch; **~idness** ['-idnis] Lebhaftigkeit, Lebendigkeit, Frische; Intensität *f*; **~ify** ['vivifai] *tr* beleben; intensivieren; **~iparous** [vi'vipərəs, vai-] *zoo* lebendgebärend; **~isect** [vivi'sekt] *tr* vivisezieren; **~isection** [-'sekʃən] Vivisektion *f*.
viva voce ['vaivə 'vousi] *adv a* mündlich; *s* mündliche Prüfung *f*.
vixen ['viksn] Füchsin; *fig* Xanthippe *f*, Zankteufel *m*; **~ish** ['-iʃ] *(Weib)* zänkisch.
voc|able ['voukəbl] *gram* Wort *n*; Vokabel *f*; **~abulary** [və'kæbjuləri] Wörterverzeichnis, Vokabular, Glossar *n*; Wortschatz *m*; **~al** ['voukəl] stimmlich; Stimm-, Vokal-, Gesangs-; mündlich; laut redend; redselig; tönend; *(Phonetik)* stimmhaft; vokalisch; *to become, (fam) to get* ~~ sich hören, s-e Stimme ertönen lassen; ~~ *chink* Stimmritze *f*; ~~ *cords (pl) anat* Stimmbänder *n pl*; ~~ *music* Vokalmusik *f*, Gesang *m*; ~~ *organ* Stimmorgan *n*; ~~ *part* Gesangspartie *f*; **~alic** [vo(u)'kælik] vokalisch; vokalreich; **~alism** ['voukəlizm] Vokalisation *f*; Vokalsystem *n (e-r Sprache)*, Vokalismus *m*; **~alist** ['-əlist] Sänger(in *f*) *m*; **~ality** [vo(u)'kæliti] Stimmbegabung; Stimmhaftigkeit *f*; **~alize** ['voukəlaiz] *tr itr* ausdrücken, sprechen, singen, rufen; *(Konsonanten)* vokalisieren; stimmhaft aussprechen; **~ally** ['voukəli] *adv* mit der Stimme; singend; mündlich; laut; **~ation** [vo(u)'keiʃən] Berufung; Neigung, Eignung *f* (*for* für); Beruf *m*, Laufbahn *f*; Gewerbe *n*, Beschäftigung, Tätigkeit *f*; *to mistake o.'s* ~~ s-n Beruf verfehlen; **~ational** [-'keiʃənl] beruflich; Berufs-; ~~ *adviser* Berufsberater *m*; ~~ *choice* Berufswahl *f*; ~~ *disease* Berufskrankheit *f*; ~~ *education* Berufsausbildung *f*; ~~ *guidance* Berufsberatung, -lenkung *f*; ~~ *school* Berufsschule *f*; ~~ *training* Berufsausbildung *f*; **~ative** ['vɔkətiv] *s u. a*: ~~ *case (gram)* Vokativ *m*; **~iferate** [vo(u)'sifəreit] *tr itr* schreien, brüllen, laut rufen; **~iferation** [vo(u)sifə'reiʃən] Geschrei, Gebrüll *n*; **~iferous** [vo(u)'sifərəs] schreiend, brüllend; laut.
vogue [voug] Mode; Beliebtheit, Volkstümlichkeit *f*; *to be in* ~ Mode sein; *to be all the* ~ große Mode sein, *to come into, to go out of* ~ in Mode, aus der Mode kommen.
voice [vɔis] *s* Stimme *a. mus fig pol*; Sprache *f*; Stimmrecht *n*; Ausdruck *m*, Äußerung; Meinung, Ansicht *f*; *gram* Genus *n* verbi; *(Phonetik)* stimmhafte(r) Laut; *mus* Gesang, Stimmton, Sänger *m*; *tr* äußern, zum Ausdruck bringen, ausdrücken; *mus (Instrument)* stimmen; stimmhaft aussprechen; *by a majority of* ~*s* mit Stimmenmehrheit; *in (good)* ~ stimmlich auf der Höhe; *in a loud* ~ mit lauter Stimme; *with one* ~ einstimmig; *to give* ~ *to s.th.* etw zum Ausdruck bringen; *to have a* ~ *in s.th.* bei e-r S (ein Wörtchen) mitzureden haben; *to lift up o.'s* ~ die Stimme erheben; protestieren; schreien; *I have no* ~ *in the matter* ich habe keine Entscheidungsbefugnis in der Angelegenheit; *active, passive* ~ *(gram)* Aktiv, Passiv *n*; *casting* ~ ausschlaggebende Stimme *f*; *chest, head* ~ Brust-, Kopfstimme *f*; **~-box** Kehlkopf; *Am sl* Lautsprecher *m*; **~cast** *tr Am* im Sprechfunk senden; ~ **current** Sprechstrom *m*; **~d** [vɔist] *a* stimmbegabt; *in Zssgen*: mit ... Stimme; *(Phonetik)* stimmhaft; **~less** ['-lis] stumm; schweigend; unausgesprochen; *parl* nicht stimmberechtigt; *(Phonetik)* stimmlos; ~ **modulation** Sprachmodulation *f*; ~ **part** Gesangspartie *f*; ~ **pipe, tube** Sprachrohr *n*; ~ **radio** Sprechfunk *m*; ~ **recorder** Tonaufnahmegerät *n*; ~ **training** Gesangsbildung *f*.

*

void [vɔid] *a* leer; frei, unbesetzt; unwirksam, wirkungs-, nutzlos; *jur* ungültig, nichtig; ~ *of* frei von, ohne; *s* Leere *f*, Vakuum *n*; *fig* (Gefühl *n* der) Leere; *fig* Lücke *f*; *tech* Loch *n*, Hohlraum *m*, Blase, Öffnung *f*; *tr* (aus-)leeren; *(Urin)* ausscheiden; *jur* ungültig machen, für ungültig, nichtig erklären; *null and* ~ null u. nichtig; *to become* ~ *(jur)* erlöschen; *a* ~ *(voting-)paper* ein leerer, ungültiger Stimmzettel *m*; **~able** ['-əbl] *jur* anfechtbar; annullierbar; **~ance** ['-əns] Räumung, Freigabe, Erledigung; Aufhebung, Annullierung *f*; **~ness** ['-nis] Leere; *jur* Ungültigkeit, Nichtigkeit *f*.
volatil|e ['vɔlətail, *Am* -til] *chem* flüchtig *a. fig*; *fig* flatterhaft, unbeständig, launenhaft; lebhaft, munter; **~ity** [vɔlə'tiliti] *chem* Flüchtigkeit *a. fig*; *fig* Flatterhaftigkeit, Unbeständigkeit, Launenhaftigkeit; Lebhaftigkeit, Fröhlichkeit *f*; **~ization** [vɔlætilai'zeiʃən] Verflüchtigung *f*; **~ize** [vɔ'lætilaiz] *tr itr* (sich) verflüchtigen.
volcan|ic [vɔl'kænik] *geol* vulkanisch; *fig* vulkanartig; ~~ *eruption* Vulkanausbruch *m*; ~~ *glass* Glaslava *f*, Obsidian *m*; ~~ *rock* Eruptivgestein *n*; **~ism** ['vɔlkənizm] Vulkanismus *m*; **~o** [vɔl'keinou] *pl meist -oes* Vulkan, feuerspeiende(r) Berg *m*; *fig* Pulverfaß *n*.
vole [voul] **1.** *(field-~)* Feldmaus *f*; *water-~* Wasserratte *f*; **2.** *s (Kartenspiel)* Vole *f*; *itr* alle Stiche gewinnen; *to go the* ~ *(fig)* alles aufs Spiel, auf eine Karte setzen.
volit|ion [vo(u)'liʃən] Wollen *n*, Wille *m*; Willensentscheidung; Willenskraft *f*; *to do s.th. of o.'s own* ~~ etw aus eigenem Antrieb tun; **~ional** ['-ʃənl], **~ive** ['vɔlitiv] *a* Willens-.
volley ['vɔli] *s mil* Salve *f*; *fig* Hagel *m*, Flut *f*, Sturm; *sport* Flugball *m*; *tr* (e-e Salve) abfeuern; (den Ball) im Fluge zurückschlagen, -stoßen; *itr* losbrechen, niedergehen, prasseln; *(Kanonen)* donnern; **~ball** Volleyball *m*.
volplane ['vɔlplein] *aero s* Gleitflug *m*; *itr* im Gleitflug niedergehen.
volt 1. [vɔlt] *(Reit- u. Fechtkunst)* Volte, Wendung *f*; **2.** [voult] *el* Volt *n*; **~age** ['-idʒ] (Strom-)Spannung *f*; ~~ *drop* Spannungsabfall *m*; ~~ *swing* Spannungsschwankung *f*; **~aic** [vɔl'teiik] galvanisch, voltaisch; **~ampere** ['voult'æmpɛə] Voltampere *n*; **~meter** ['voultmi:tə] Voltmeter *n*, Spannungsmesser *m*.
volte-face ['vɔlt'fɑ:s] *sport* (schnelle) Wendung *f*; *fig* Frontwechsel, (Meinungs-, Stimmungs-)Umschwung *m*.
volub|ility [vɔlju'biliti] Redegewandtheit, Zungenfertigkeit; Redseligkeit *f*; (Rede-)Fluß *m*; **~le** ['vɔljubl] gesprächig, redselig, geschwätzig; wortreich, zungenfertig; *(Rede)* flüssig.
volum|e ['vɔljum] Band *m*, Buch *n*; *(Zeitschrift)* Jahrgang; Rauminhalt *m*, Volumen *n*; Inhalt; (großer) Umfang *m*, Masse *f*, Betrag *m*; *el* Lautstärke; *mus* Klangfülle *f*; ~*s of* ein Schwall *gen*; *in three* ~~*s* in 3 Bänden; *to speak* ~~*s (fig)* Bände sprechen (*for* für); *aggregate* ~~ Gesamtvolumen *n*; *odd* ~~ Einzelband *m*; ~~ *of building, of business* Bau-, Geschäftsvolumen *n*; ~~ *control, regulator* Lautstärkeregler *m*; ~~ *discount* Mengenrabatt *m*; ~~ *production* Massenproduktion *f*; **~etric(al)** [-'metrik(əl)] *math chem* volumetrisch; **~inous** [və'lju:minəs] bändereich, -füllend; umfangreich; *(Rock)* bauschig; *(Verfasser)* vielschreibend, fruchtbar.
volunt|arily ['vɔləntərili] *adv* auf eigenen Wunsch, freiwillig; mit Absicht, absichtlich, vorsätzlich; **~ariness** ['-ərinis] Freiwilligkeit; Absichtlichkeit *f*; **~ary** ['vɔləntəri] *a* freiwillig; ungezwungen; absichtlich, vorsätzlich; *physiol* willkürlich; *psychol* spontan; *philos* mit Willensfreiheit begabt; *(Schule)* durch freiwillige Spenden unterhalten, privat; *jur* gütlich, außergerichtlich; *s* freiwillige Tat *od* Arbeit *f*; Orgelsolo *n*, -phantasie; *sport* Kür *f*; **~eer** [vɔlən'tiə] *s com* Volontär; *mil* Freiwillige(r) *m*; *a* frei-

willig (dienend); Freiwilligen-; freiwillig; *bot* wildwachsend; *tr* freiwillig zur Verfügung stellen; zum besten geben; *itr* freiwillig dienen *od* eintreten; als Volontär arbeiten; *(to ~~ o.'s services)* sich freiwillig melden (*for* zu).

voluptu|ary [və'lʌptjuəri] Genußmensch, Genießer *m*; **~ous** [-əs] sinnlich; lüstern; sinnenfreudig, genießerisch, genußsüchtig; wollüstig; **~ousness** [-əsnis] Sinnlichkeit; Lüsternheit *f*.

volut|e [və'lju:t] *arch* Volute, Schnecke; *allg* Spirale, Windung *f*; **~ed** [-id] *a* (auf)gerollt, spiralig, schneckenförmig; mit Voluten (versehen); **~ion** [-ʃən] *anat zoo* Windung; Spirale; *tech* Drehung *f*.

vomit ['vɔmit] *s med* (Er-)Brechen; Erbrochene(s); Brechmittel *n*; *itr* sich erbrechen; *allg* ausgestoßen werden; *(Vulkan)* Feuer speien; *tr* erbrechen, wieder von sich geben; *allg* ausstoßen; *(Feuer)* speien; **~ive** ['-iv], **~ory** ['-əri] *a* Brech-; *s* Brechmittel *n*.

voodoo ['wu:du:] *s* Zauberbuch, -ritual *n*; Zauberer *m*; *a* Zauber-; magisch; *tr* behexen, verzaubern.

vorac|ious [və'reiʃəs] gefräßig; gierig, unersättlich *a. fig*; **~iousness** [-ʃəsnis], **~ity** [vɔ'ræsiti] Gefräßigkeit; Gier, Unersättlichkeit *f a. fig* (*of* nach).

vort|ex ['vɔ:teks] *pl meist -ices* ['-isi:z] *(Wasser)* Strudel *a. fig*; *(Luft)* Wirbel(wind) *m*; **~ical** ['-ikəl], **~iginous** [vɔ:'tidʒinəs] strudelnd, wirbelnd.

vot|able, *a.* **~eable** ['voutəbl] e-r Abstimmung unterworfen; **~(a)ress** ['vout(ə)ris] Nonne, Geweihte; *fig* glühende Verehrerin, eifrige Anhängerin *f*; **~ary** ['-əri] Mönch, Geweihte(r); *fig* glühende(r) Verehrer, eifrige(r) Anhänger *m*; **~e** [vout] *s* Beschluß *m*; Wahl, Abstimmung; Stimmabgabe; (Wahl-)Stimme *f*; Wahlzettel *m*; Wahl-, Stimmrecht; Wahl-, Abstimmergebnis *n*; Bewilligung, bewilligte Summe *f*; *itr* abstimmen (*by head* nach der Kopfzahl; *on s.th.* über etw); wählen; s-e Stimme abgeben (*for* für); *tr* beschließen; bewilligen, genehmigen; wählen; stimmen, s-e Stimme abgeben für; unterstützen, eintreten für; allgemein ansehen als, erklären für; *fam* anregen, vorschlagen, in Vorschlag bringen (*that* daß); *to ~~ down* überstimmen; ablehnen; *to ~~ in* wählen (*s.o.* jdn); *to ~~ out* ablehnen; ausschließen; *by 5 ~~s to 3* mit 5 gegen 3 Stimmen; *by a majority of 2 ~~s* mit e-r Mehrheit von 2 Stimmen; *by a majority ~~* mit Stimmenmehrheit; *to bring, to put to the ~~* zur Abstimmung bringen; *to cast, to give, to record o.'s ~~* s-e Stimme abgeben, stimmen (*to, for* für); *to come to, to take the ~~, to take ~~s* zur Abstimmung schreiten, abstimmen lassen; *to count, to tell the ~~s* die Stimmen zählen; *to have a ~~* Stimmrecht haben (*in* bei); *to have the casting ~~* bei Stimmengleichheit entscheiden; *to pass a ~~ of s.th.* über etw abstimmen; *to take the ~~ on* abstimmen über; zur Abstimmung schreiten über; *to ~~ a bill through* e-n Gesetzesantrag durchbringen; *abstention from ~~* Stimmenthaltung *f*; *casting of ~~s* Stimmabgabe *f*; *counting of ~~s* Stimmenzählung *f*; *final ~~* Schlußabstimmung *f*; *majority ~~* Majoritätsbeschluß *m*; *number of ~~s* Stimmenzahl *f*; *popular ~~* Volksabstimmung, -befragung *f*; *secrecy of ~~* Wahlgeheimnis *n*; *straw ~~* Probeabstimmung *f*; *unanimity of ~~s* Einstimmigkeit *f*; *(total) ~~s cast* (Gesamt-)Stimmenzahl *f*; *~~ of confidence* Vertrauensvotum *n*; *to ask for a ~~ of confidence* die Vertrauensfrage stellen; *to pass a ~~ of confidence to s.o.* jdm das Vertrauen aussprechen; *~~ of no confidence* Mißtrauensvotum *n*; *~~ counter* Stimmenzähler *m*; *~~ hunter* Stimmenjäger *m*; *~~s (pl) polled, recorded* abgegebene Stimmen *f pl*; **~eless** ['-lis] nicht stimmberechtigt; **~er** ['-ə] Stimm-, Wahlberechtigte(r); Wähler *m*; *~~-getter (Am fam)* Stimmenfänger, zugkräftige(r) (Wahl-)Kandidat *m*; **~ing** ['-iŋ] Abstimmung, Wahl; Stimmabgabe *f*; Wahlgang *m*, -beteiligung *f*, -ergebnis *n*; *to abstain from ~~* sich der Stimme enthalten; *to return a blank ~~ paper* e-n leeren Stimmzettel abgeben; *manner, method of ~~* Wahlverfahren *n*, -modus *m*; *nominal ~~* Persönlichkeitswahl *f*; *secrecy of ~~* Wahlgeheimnis *n*; *system of ~~* Wahlsystem *n*; *~~-ballot, -card, -paper, -ticket* Wahl-, Stimmzettel *m*; *~~-booth* Wahlzelle *f*; *~~-machine* Stimmenzählmaschine *f*; *~~-powers (pl)* Stimm-, Wahlrecht *n*, Wahlberechtigung *f*; *~~ by rising and sitting* Abstimmung *f* durch Erheben von den Plätzen; *~~-steward* Wahlleiter *m*; *~~-test* Probewahl *f*; *~~-urn* Wahlurne *f*; **~ive** ['-iv] gelobt, geweiht; Votiv-; *~~ church, mass, offering, picture, tablet* Votivkirche, -messe, -gabe *f*, -bild *n*, -tafel *f*.

vouch [vautʃ] *itr* sich verbürgen, sich einsetzen, eintreten, garantieren (*for* für); bestätigen, bezeugen, verbürgen, einstehen, beweisen (*for s.th.* etw); **~er** ['-ə] Zeuge, Bürge *m*; Zeugnis *n*, Beleg(stück *n*), Nachweis *m*, Bescheinigung *f*, Schein *m*; Eintrittskarte; Empfangsbescheinigung, Quittung *f*; *to support by ~~* schriftlich nachweisen, dokumentarisch belegen; *baggage ~~* Gepäckschein *m*; *expense ~~* Ausgabenbeleg *m*; *pay ~~* Zahlungs-, Kassenanweisung *f*; *sick ~~* Krankenschein *m*; *~~ check (Am)* Verrechnungsscheck *m*; *~~ clerk* Kreditorenbuchhalter *m*; *~~ copy, number* Belegexemplar *n*, -nummer *f*; *~~ form* Belegformular *n*; **~safe** [vautʃ'seif] *tr* sich herablassen zu, gewähren; *he ~~d(me) no reply* er würdigte mich keiner Antwort.

vow [vau] *s* Gelübde; (Treue-)Gelöbnis *n*; Schwur, Eid *m*; *tr* geloben, weihen; feierlich erklären *od* versprechen; *to be under a ~* ein Gelübde getan haben (*of silence* nicht zu reden); *to make, to take a ~* ein Gelübde tun; *to take ~s* ins Kloster gehen; *to ~ and declare* feierlich versprechen *od* erklären; *marriage ~s (pl)* Eheversprechen *n*; *~ of chastity* Keuschheitsgelübde *n*.

vowel ['vauəl] Vokal, Selbstlaut *m*.

voyag|e ['vɔiidʒ, vɔidʒ] *s* (weite, See-, Flug-)Reise *f*; *itr* reisen, e-e (See-, Flug-)Reise machen; *tr* bereisen, reisen auf, über; *on the ~~ out, home* auf der Hin-, Rückreise; **~er** ['vɔiədʒə] Reisende(r); Seefahrer *m*.

vulcan|ite ['vʌlkənait] Hartgummi *m*, Ebonit *n*; **~ization** [vʌlkənai'zeiʃən] Vulkanisierung, Vulkanisation *f*; **~ize** ['vʌlkənaiz] *tr* vulkanisieren; *~izing factory, plant* Vulkanisieranstalt *f*; **~ized** ['-d] *a* vulkanisiert; *~~ fibre* Vulkanfiber *f*; **~izer** ['-aizə] Vulkanisierapparat *m*.

vulgar ['vʌlgə] gewöhnlich, allgemein; Volks-, Landes-; *(sprachlich)* Umgangs-; volkssprachlich; ungebildet; vulgär, gemein, roh, geschmacklos; unanständig; *the ~ herd* die große Masse; *~* **fraction** *math* gemeine(r) Bruch *m*; **~ian** [vʌl'gɛəriən] Banause; Neureiche(r), Parvenü, Protz *m*; **~ism** ['vʌlgərizm] vulgäre(r) Ausdruck *m*, vulgäre Redensart *f*; ungesittete(s) Benehmen *n*; **~ity** [vʌl'gæriti] Gemeinheit, Roheit *f*; **~ization** [vʌlgərai'zeiʃən] Vulgarisierung, weite Verbreitung *f*; **~ize** ['vʌlgəraiz] *tr* vulgarisieren, popularisieren, verbreiten.

Vulgate ['vʌlgit, '-eit] *rel die* Vulgata.

vulner|ability [vʌlnərə'biliti] Verwundbarkeit *f*; **~able** ['vʌlnərəbl] verwundbar *a. fig*; anfällig (*to* für); empfindlich; *fig* angreifbar; *to be ~~* Schwächen, schwache Stellen *od* Punkte haben; *to find o.'s ~~ spot* jds schwache Stelle treffen; **~ary** ['-rəri] *a* Wunden heilend; Wund(heil)-; *s* Wund(heil)mittel *n*.

vulpine ['vʌlpain] *a* Fuchs-; fuchsartig; *fig* listig, schlau, klug.

vulture ['vʌltʃə] Geier; *fig* Blutsauger *m*.

vulva ['vʌlvə] *pl -ae* ['-i:] *anat* (äußere) weibliche Scham, Vulva *f*.

vying ['vaiiŋ] *ppr von vie*; *a* wetteifernd.

W

W, w ['dʌblju(:)] *pl* **~'s** W, w *n.*
Waac [wæk] (Heeres-)Helferin *f (des britischen Women's Army Auxiliary Corps)* WAAC.
wabble *s. wobble.*
Wac [wæk] *Am* (Heeres-)Helferin *f (des amerik. Women's Army Corps)* WAC.
wack [wæk] *Am sl* verrückte(r) Kerl, Idiot *m*; **~y, whacky** ['-i] *Am sl* verrückt, blöd(e), übergeschnappt.
wad [wɔd] *s* Knäuel *m* od *n*, Bausch *m*; Büschel, (kleines) Bündel, Päckchen *n*, Stoß *m*; Klümpchen *n*, Pfropf(en); *(Kautabak)* Priem; *mil* Ladepfropf *m*; *Am fam* Bündel *n* Geldscheine; *Am sl* Haufen *m* Geld; *tr* zs.knüllen, -drükken; *Am (to ~ up)* zs.-, aufrollen; zu-, ausstopfen; füttern, wattieren, (aus-)polstern; **~ding** ['-iŋ] Füllsel *n*, Einlage, Fütterung, Wattierung, Watte *f.*
waddle ['wɔdl] *itr* watscheln, torkeln, wackeln(d gehen); *s* Watscheln *n*, torkelnde(r) Gang *m.*
wad|e [weid] *itr* waten, stapfen *(through* durch); *fig* sich (mühsam) (hin)durcharbeiten *(through* durch); *fam fig* sich hineinstürzen *(in, into* in), sich eifrig machen *(in, into* an); *tr* durchwaten; **~er** ['-ə] *zoo* Stelzvogel *m*; *pl* (hohe) Gummistiefel *m pl*; **~ing bird** Stelzvogel *m.*
Waf, WAF [wæf] (Luftwaffen-)Helferin *f (der amerik. Women in the Air Force).*
wafer ['weifə] *s* Waffel; *med* Oblate *a. rel*; *rel* Hostie; Siegelmarke *f*; *tr* (mit e-r Oblate) zukleben.
waffle ['wɔfl] **1.** *Am* Waffel *f*; **~ iron** Waffeleisen *n*; **2.** *itr fam* quasseln; *s* Gequassel *n.*
waft [wɔ(:)ft, wɑ:ft] *tr* (weg-, fort)wehen, -blasen, (fort)tragen; *itr* wehen, flattern; schweben; *s* Wehen; Flattern *n*; Hauch *a. fig*, Luftzug; Duft; (schwebender) Ton; *fig* Anflug *m*; *mar* Signalflagge *f*; Not-, Flaggensignal *n.*
wag [wæg] **1.** *tr (to set ~ging)* schwingen, wackeln, wedeln mit; *itr* wackeln, wedeln, hin- u. hergehen; *fam* abhauen, das Weite suchen; *s* Schwingen, Wackeln, Wedeln *n*; *to set tongues (chins, beards) ~ging* Anlaß zum Gerede geben; *to ~ o.'s finger at s.o.* jdm mit dem Finger drohen; **2.** *s* Witzbold, Schalk; *sl* Drückeberger, Schulschwänzer *m*; *itr sl* sich drücken; *(Schule)* schwänzen; **~gery** ['-əri] Mutwille, Spaß *m*; Flausen *f pl*; **~gish** ['-iʃ] lustig, spaßig, scherzhaft; **~gishness** ['-iʃnis] Spaßigkeit, Schalkhaftigkeit *f*; **~tail** Bachstelze *f.*
wage [weidʒ] **1.** *meist pl* (Arbeits-)Lohn *m*, Arbeitsentgelt *n*; Löhne *m pl*, Lohnaufkommen *n*, -anteil; *fig pl mit sing* Lohn, Sold *m*; *at a ~ of* bei e-m Gehalt von; *basic ~s (pl)* Grundlohn *m*; *hourly ~s (pl)* Stundenlohn *m*; *living ~* ausreichende(r) Lohn *m* zur Sicherung des Lebensunterhalts; Existenzminimum *n*; *piece(-work), job ~s (pl)* Stück-, Akkordlohn *m*; *real ~s (pl)* Reallohn *m*; **~ advance** Lohnvorauszahlung *f*; **~ agreement** Tarifvertrag *m*; **~ claims** *pl* Lohnansprüche *m pl*, -forderungen *f pl*; **~ cuts, reductions** *pl* Senkung *f* der Löhne, Lohnabbau *m*; **~ disputes** *pl* Lohnstreitigkeiten *f pl*; **~ earner** Lohnempfänger; Ernährer *m (e-r Familie)*; **~ freeze** Lohnstopp *m*; **~ group** Tarifgruppe *f*; **~ increase** Lohnerhöhung *f*; **~ level** Lohnniveau *n*; **~-packet** Lohntüte *f*; **~ payment** Lohnzahlung *f*; **~-price spiral** Lohn-Preis-Spirale *f*; **~ rates** *pl* Lohntarif *m*; **~s clerk** Lohnbuchhalter *m*; **~s policy** Lohnpolitik *f*; **~ scale** Lohnskala *f*, Tarif *m*; **~s schedule** Lohntabelle *f*; **~s sheet** Lohnliste *f*; **~ slip** Lohnstreifen *m*; **~s tax** Lohnsteuer *f*; **~worker** *Am* Lohnarbeiter *m*; **~working** *a Am* für Lohn arbeitend; **2.** *tr* (durch)führen; *to ~ war* Krieg führen.
wager ['weidʒə] *s* Wette *f*; *tr itr* wetten; *to lay, to make a ~* e-e Wette machen.
waggl|e ['wægl] *tr* (kräftig) schütteln; *itr* (heftig) wackeln; *s* (heftiges) Wakkeln *n*; **~y** ['-i] (heftig) wackelnd, stark schwankend, torkelnd.
wag(g)on ['wægən] (Fracht-, Last-) Wagen; *rail* offene(r) Güter-, Gepäckwagen, Waggon; *Am fam* Kinderwagen *m*; *Am fam (police, patrol ~)* grüne Minna *f*, (Polizei-)Gefangenenwagen *m*; *the W~ (astr)* der Große Wagen *od* Bär *m*; *by ~* per Achse, mit der Bahn; *to be on the (water) ~ (sl)* keinen Alkohol trinken; *to hitch o.'s ~ to a star (fig)* nach den Sternen greifen; **~age** ['-idʒ] Fuhre *f*; Fuhrlohn *m*; Wagen(park *m*) *m pl*; **~ bed** *Am* Wagenkasten *m*; **~-ceiling, vault** *arch* Tonnengewölbe *n*; **~er** ['-ə] Fuhrmann *m*; *the W~~ (astr)* der Fuhrmann; **~ette** [wægə'net] Break *m* od *n (kleiner Gesellschaftswagen)*; **~-load** Wagenladung *f*; **~ train** *Am* Güterzug; *Am mil* Versorgungszug *m.*
waif [weif] herrenlose(s) Gut *n*; Obdachlose(r) *m*; verwahrloste(s) Kind; herrenlose(s) Tier *n*, streunende(r) Hund *m*; *~s and strays* Gesindel *n*; verwahrloste Kinder *n pl*; herumliegende Sachen *f pl.*
wail [weil] *itr* wehklagen *(for* um; *over* über); *(Wind)* heulen; jammern *(with pain* vor Schmerzen); *tr* beklagen, bejammern; klagend rufen; *s* Wimmern, Jammern, Klagen *n*; **~ing** ['-iŋ] Wehklagen *n*; *W~~ Wall* Klagemauer *f.*
wain [wein] *poet* (Last-)Wagen *m*; *the W~, (meist) Charles's W~ (astr)* der Große Wagen *od* Bär *m.*
wainscot ['weinskət, 'wen-] *s* Holz-, Wandverkleidung *f*, Getäfel, Paneel *n*; *tr (Wand)* verkleiden, täfeln.
waist [weist] Taille *f (a. Kleidung)*; *Am* Oberteil *n (e-s Kleides)*, Bluse *f*; Leibchen, Mieder *n*, Büstenhalter *m*; *allg* schmal(st)e Stelle *f*, Einschnürung *f*, Einschnitt; *mar* mittlere(r) Teil *m* des Schiffes; *to be stripped to the ~* nackt bis auf die Hüften sein; *strip to the ~* machen Sie den Oberkörper frei; **~-band** (Rock-, Hosen-)Bund *m*; **~-belt** Leibriemen, Gürtel *m*; *mil* Koppel *n*; *aero* Anschnallgurt *m*; **~-cloth** Lendentuch *n*; **~coat** ['weiskout, *obs* 'weskət] Weste *f*; *hist* Wams *n*; **~-deep, -high** *a* bis an die Hüften (reichend); **~-line** Gürtellinie, Taille *f*; *to watch o.'s ~~* auf die schlanke Linie achten.
wait [weit] *itr* warten *(for* auf; *until* bis); er-, abwarten *(for s.th.* etw); lauern *(for* auf); fertig, bereit sein; *(Essen)* auf dem Tisch stehen; (auf Erledigung) warten, zurückstehen, unerledigt bleiben; aufwarten *(on s.o.* jdm; *at, (Am) on table* bei Tisch); bedienen *(on s.o.* jdn); s-e Aufwartung machen *(on s.o.* jdm); abhängen *(on s.th.* von etw); *mot* halten; *tr* warten auf, ab-, erwarten; *s* Warten *n*, Wartezeit *f*; *rail* Aufenthalt *m*; *pl* Weihnachtssänger u. -musikanten *m pl*; *to ~ up (fam)* aufbleiben *(for s.o.* bis jem kommt); *to keep ~ing* warten lassen; *to lie in ~* auf der Lauer liegen, auflauern *(for s.o.* jdm); *to ~ dinner* mit dem Essen warten *(for* auf); *to ~ and see* abwarten; *to ~ table* bei Tisch aufwarten, bedienen; *~ (Verkehrsampel)* warte; **~er** ['-ə] Wartende(r); Kellner *m*; Tablett *n*; *(head) ~~* Ober(kellner) *m*; *~~ the bill, (Am) check, please!* Ober, bitte zahlen! **~ing** ['-iŋ] *a* wartend, Warte-; aufwartend, Aufwarte-; *s* Warten *n*, Wartezeit; Aufwartung, Bedienung *f*; *in ~~* im Dienst; *mil* in Bereitschaft; *lady-in-~~* Hofdame *f*; *no ~~* Parken verboten; *~~-boy* Laufjunge, -bursche *m*; *~~ list* Warteliste *f*; *~~-maid* Kammermädchen *n*, Zofe; Aufwärterin *f*; *~~-room* Wartezimmer *n (beim Arzt)*; *rail* Warteraum, -saal *m*; *~~-woman* Kammerfrau *f*; **~ress** ['-ris] Kellnerin *f.*
waiv|e [weiv] *tr jur* verzichten auf, aufgeben, zurücktreten von; *(Schulden)* erlassen; zurückstellen, aufschieben; *to ~~ o.'s right to speak (parl)* auf das Wort verzichten; **~er** ['-ə] Verzicht(erklärung *f*) *m (of* auf).
wake [weik] **1.** *irr woke* [wouk] od *~d, woke* od *woken* ['-ən] od *~d itr (to ~ up)* auf-, erwachen, munter werden; wachen, wach, munter sein; *rel* auferstehen *(from the dead* von den Toten); aufmerksam werden *(to* auf); sich klar werden über; *tr (to ~ up)* (auf)wecken *a. fig*; *(Gefühl)* erwecken; *(Erinnerungen)* wachrufen; *(Ton, Echo)* hervorrufen; *(von den Toten)* auferwecken; *(obs, Irland)* Totenwache halten bei; *fig* anstacheln *(to* zu); *s* Kirchweih(fest *n*), Kirmes; *(Irland)* Totenwache *f*; *(Nordengland)* Urlaub *m*; *poet* Wachsein *n*; **~ful** ['-ful] wach(end); munter; wachsam; schlaflos; **~n** ['weikən] *itr* auf-, erwachen; munter werden; *fig* sich bewußt werden *(to s.th.* gen); *tr* (auf-)wecken *(from, out of* von, aus); *fig* auf-, ermuntern, antreiben; **~-robin** *bot* Aronsstab *m*; **~-up** *Am fam* Specht *m*; **~y** ['-i] *sl* aufwachen! **2.** Kielwasser *n a. fig*; Sog; *aero* Nachstrom, -lauf; Luftschraubenstrahl *m*; *in the ~ of (fig)* im Kielwasser, Gefolge *gen*; unmittelbar nach.
wale [weil] *s. a. weal* Strieme *f*; *(Textil)* Streifen *m*, Rippe, Salleiste *f*; *mar* Bergholz *n.*
walk [wɔ:k] *itr* (dahin-, einher-, entlang-, umher-, spazieren)gehen, zu Fuß gehen; wandern; *(Gespenst)* umgehen, spuken; *(Pferd)* (im) Schritt gehen; *allg* sich bewegen, hin- u. herschwanken; *fig* wandeln, leben; *sl* sich hermachen, herfallen *(into a sandwich* über e-e Stulle); *tr (e-e Straße)* entlanggehen; entlang *(gen)* gehen, gehen durch, über; auf u. ab gehen auf, in; durchwandern, -streifen; *(Strecke)* zurücklegen; *(kontrollierend)* abgehen; spazierenführen; *(Hund)* ausführen; *(Pferd)* (im)

Schritt gehen lassen; vorwärts-, antreiben; geleiten, begleiten; gehen, laufen lassen, auf den Beinen halten (*to exhaustion* bis zur Erschöpfung); *allg* in Bewegung setzen *od* halten; *s* Gehen *n*, Gang; Spaziergang *m*, Wanderung *f*; (Spazier-)Weg; *(an hour's)* ~ Weg *(von e-r Stunde)*; Gang(art *f*), Schritt *m*; *fig (~ of life)* Laufbahn *f*, Beruf, Lebensbereich *m*, (soziale) Stellung *f*; Arbeitsgebiet *n*; Lebensweise, -art *f*, Verhalten(sweise *f*) *n*; Spazierweg *m*, Promenade, Allee, Baumreihe; (*bes.* Schaf-)Weide *f*; Walddistrikt *m*; Wettgehen *n*; *com* Geschäftszweig *m*, Branche *f*; *(Post)* Zustellbezirk *m*; *(Polizei)* Runde *f*; *to go at a ~* (im) Schritt gehen; *to go for a ~, to take a ~* e-n Spaziergang machen, spazierengehen; *to ~ the hospitals* Medizin studieren; *to ~ the plank* über Bord gehen; *fig* zum Rücktritt gezwungen werden, zwangsweise demissionieren; *to ~ a round* e-e Runde machen; *to ~ s.o. Spanish (Am fam)* jdn zwingen, wegzugehen; *to ~ the streets (Prostituierte)* auf den Strich gehen; durch die Straße gehen; *it's a long ~* zu Fuß ist es ein weiter Weg; *constitutional ~* Verdauungsspaziergang *m*; *to ~* **about** *itr* umhergehen, -wandern, -streifen, *tr* -führen; *to ~* **along** dahingehen; weitergehen; *to ~* **away** *from s.o.* jdn hinter sich lassen, *fam* abhängen; *with s.th.* etw mitnehmen; leicht gewinnen; *to ~* **back** zurückgehen; *fam* e-n Rückzieher machen; *to ~* **down** hinuntergehen; *(Schuhe)* durchlaufen; *to ~* **into** *sl* tüchtig essen von, hineinhauen in; *s.o.* jdn ausschimpfen; über jdn herfallen; *to ~* **off** *itr* sich aus dem Staube machen, *fam* abhauen; *with s.th. (fam)* etw erwischen, (weg)schnappen; sich etw unter den Nagel reißen; klauen; *tr* wegführen; *to ~* **on** *theat* e-e Statistenrolle spielen; *to ~* **out** *fam* gehen, poussieren (*with* mit); *fam* streiken; *fam* im Stich, stehen-, sitzenlassen (*on s.o.* jdn); *to ~* **over** e-n leichten Sieg davontragen; *to ~ all over s.o.* jdn mißbrauchen; auf jdm herumtrampeln; *to ~* **up** herauf-, hinaufgehen; herankommen (*to* zu); **~-around** *Am Art* Negertanz *m*; **~athon** ['wɔ:kəθən] *sport* Marathongehen *n*; Dauertanz *m*; **~-away** leichte(r) Sieg *m*; **~-bill** *fin* Platzwechsel *m*; **~ charges** *pl* Inkassospesen *pl*; **~er** ['-ə] Fuß-, Spaziergänger; *sport* Geher; *dial* Walker; *(Jagd)* Treiber *m*; *~-on (theat)* Statist *m*; **~ie-lookie** tragbare Fernsehkamera *f*; **~ie-talkie, ~y-talky** ['-i-'tɔ:ki] tragbare(s) Sprechfunkgerät *n*; **~ing** ['-iŋ] *a* umherziehend, -wandernd; *(Vogel)* schreitend; *(Fahrzeug, Gerät)* Gespann-; sich hin- u. herbewegend; *s* Gehen *n*, Gang *m*; Wandern *n*; Wanderung *f*; Gang(art *f*) *m*; Begehbarkeit *f (e-s Weges, Bodens)*; *sport* Gehen *n*; *~~ crane* Laufkran *m*; *~~ delegate* (umher)reisende(r) Gewerkschaftsvertreter; *com* Geschäftsbevollmächtigte(r) *m*; *~~-dress* Straßenkleid *n*; *~~ gentleman, lady (theat)* Statist(in *f*) *m*; *~~ leaf (ent)* Wandelnde(s) Blatt *n*; *~~-on part* Statistenrolle *f*; *~~-papers (pl), -ticket* Entlassungspapiere *n pl*; *to give s.o. his ~~-papers* jdn entlassen; *~~ part* Statistenrolle *f*; *~~-shoes (pl)* Marschstiefel *m pl*; *~~-speed* Schrittgeschwindigkeit *f*; *~~-stick* Spazierstock *m*; *~~-tour* (Fuß-)Wanderung *f*; **~-on** *theat* Statistenrolle *f*; **~-out** *Am fam* Ausstand, Streik *m*; **~-over** *fig* leichte(r) Sieg *m*; *fig* Kleinigkeit *f*; **~-up** *Am fam* Mietshaus *n* ohne Fahrstuhl.

wall [wɔ:l] *s* Wand *a. anat*; Mauer *f a. fig*; Wall; Deich *m*; *allg* (Trenn-, Scheide-)Wand; *min* Sohle *f*; *tr (to ~ up)* ummauern; ein-, zumauern; *(to ~ off)* mit e-m Wall umgeben; durch Mauern abtrennen (*from* von); *fig* ein-, verschließen (*against* gegen); *with o.'s back to the ~ (fig)* in die Enge getrieben; *to drive, to push s.o. to the ~ (fig)* jdn an die Wand drücken; *to go to the ~ (fig)* an die Wand gedrückt werden; den kürzeren ziehen; pleite gehen, Bankrott machen; an die Wand gestellt, erschossen werden; *to hang s.th. on the ~* etw an die Wand hängen; *to run o.'s head against a ~ (fig)* mit dem Kopf gegen die Wand rennen; *to see through a brick ~ (fig)* das Gras wachsen hören; *~s have ears (prov)* Wände haben Ohren; *fire-proof ~* Brandmauer *f*; *tariff ~* Zollmauer *f*; *~ of partition* Scheidewand *f*; **~-bars** *pl sport* Sprossenwand *f*; **~board** *Am* Hartfaserplatte; Wandtafel *f*; **~ box** Briefkasten *m (an e-r Hauswand)*; **~ bracket** Konsole *f*, Wandarm *m*; **~ crack** Mauerriß *m*; **~-creeper** *orn* Mauerläufer, -specht *m*; **~-eye** *med vet* Glasauge; Glotzauge; *med* Leukom *n*; **~ fern** Mauerfarn *m*; **~flower** *bot* Goldlack *m*; *fig* Mauerblümchen *n*; **~-fruit** Spalierobst *n*; **~-map** Wandkarte *f*; **~-painting** Wandmalerei *f*, Fresko *n*; **~paper** Tapete *f*; **~-pepper** Mauerpfeffer *m*; **~-plate** *arch* Wandplatte *f*, -teller *m*; **~-plug, -socket** *el* Wandstecker *m*, Steckdose *f*; **W~ Street** *fig* die amerikanische Hochfinanz *f*; **~ tent** Steilwandzelt *n*; **~-tree** Spalierbaum *m*.

wallaby ['wɔləbi] Großfußkänguruh *n*; *pl fam* Australier *m pl*; *on the ~ (track)* auf der Walze, ohne Arbeit.

wallet ['wɔlit] (lederne) Werkzeugtasche; Brieftasche *f*; *obs* Mantelsack *m*, Reisetasche *f*.

Walloon [wɔ'lu:n] *s* Wallone *m*, Wallonin *f*; Wallonisch *n*; *a* wallonisch.

wallop ['wɔləp] *sl tr* schwer treffen; heftig schlagen; *fam* verdreschen, verprügeln; erledigen, fertigmachen (*s.o.* jdn); *itr fam* (daher)sta(m)pfen; trampeln, galoppieren; *s fam* heftige(r) Schlag *m*; Wucht, Kraft *f*; *fam* Sta(m)pfen; Galoppieren; *sl* Bier *n*; **~er** ['-ə] *fam* Schläger *m*; Riesending *n*, -sache *f*; **~ing** ['-iŋ] *a fam* mächtig, gewaltig, enorm, riesig; *s fam* Dresche *a fig*, Tracht *f* Prügel.

wallow ['wɔlou] *itr* sich wälzen; sich suhlen; *mar* rollen, schlingern; *(Nebel)* wogen; *(Flammen)* herausschlagen; *fig* schwelgen (*in* in); *s* Suhle *f*; *to ~ in money (fam)* im Gelde schwimmen.

walnut ['wɔ:lnʌt] Walnuß *f*; (Wal-)Nußbaum; Nußbaum(holz *n*) *m*.

walrus ['wɔ:lrəs] *zoo* Walroß *n*; **~ m(o)ustache** Hängeschnurrbart *m*.

waltz [wɔ:ls] *s* Walzer *m*; *itr* Walzer tanzen; herumwirbeln; *tr* Walzer tanzen mit.

wampum ['wɔmpəm] *Am sl* Moneten *pl*.

wan [wɔn] blaß, bleich; elend; müde, matt, schwach; **~ness** ['-nis] Blässe; Müdigkeit; Schwäche *f*.

wand [wɔnd] Rute, Gerte *f*; *mus* Taktstock; Amts-, Kommando-, Marschallstab; Zauberstab *m*; Wünschelrute *f*.

wander ['wɔndə] *itr* umherwandern, -streifen, -schweifen; abbiegen (*from* von); *(to ~ away)* sich verlaufen, sich verirren *a. fig*; phantasieren; *(to ~ off)* auf die Wanderschaft gehen; *fig (vom Thema)* abschweifen (*from* von); auf die schiefe Bahn *od* Ebene geraten; zs.hanglos sein; *(Blick)* umherschweifen, gleiten; *allg* sich schlängeln, sich winden; *tr poet* durchstreifen, wandern, ziehen durch; *his mind is ~ing* er ist geistig abwesend; **~er** ['-rə] Wanderer *m*; **~ing** ['-riŋ] *a* wandernd, umherstreifend, -schweifend, unstet; flatterhaft; nomadisch; sich schlängelnd, sich windend; *s* Wandern, Umherstreifen, -schweifen *n*; Abweichung *f* (*from* von); *pl* Wanderungen *f pl*, Wanderleben; Phantasieren; Irrereden *n*; *the W~~ Jew* der Ewige Jude; *~~ kidney (med)* Wanderniere *f*.

wane [wein] *itr (Mond)* abnehmen; *allg* schwächer werden, nachlassen *a. fig*; *(Farbe)* verblassen; *fig* vergehen, (dahin)schwinden, verfallen; zu Ende gehen, dem Ende zugehen; *s (Mond)* Abnehmen; *allg fig* Nachlassen, Vergehen, (Dahin-)Schwinden *n*, Verfall *m*; *to be on the ~* im Abnehmen sein.

wangle ['wæŋgl] *tr sl* hinkriegen, drehen, deichseln; 'rausschlagen, -schinden (*s.th. out of s.o.* etw aus jdm); ergattern; *sl* (zurecht)frisieren, -stutzen; hin- u. herschaukeln, -schwenken, -drehen; *itr Am fam* schummeln, mogeln; sich herauswinden (*out of* aus); sich zu helfen wissen; *s sl* Kniff, Dreh *m*.

want [wɔnt] *tr* Mangel haben *od* leiden an; es fehlen lassen an; nicht, kein(e, en) ... haben; *lit* ermangeln (*s.th.* e-r S); (ge)brauchen, benötigen, nötig haben, bedürfen; müssen, sollen; sich sehnen, Sehnsucht, Verlangen haben nach; wünschen (*to do* zu tun), wollen (*to do* tun); zu sprechen wünschen, sprechen wollen; verlangen, erfordern; *itr* (ge)brauchen, nötig haben (*for s.th.* etw); Mangel leiden; in Dürftigkeit, Armut leben; *s* Fehlen *n*, Mangel *m*; Knappheit; Dürftigkeit, Armut, Not *f*; Bedürfnis *n*, Bedarf *m* (*of* an); dringende Notwendigkeit *f*; Verlangen *n*, Sehnsucht *f*, Wunsch *m*; *pl* Bedürfnisse *n pl*, Wünsche *m pl*; *for, from ~ of* aus Mangel an; in Ermangelung *gen*; *to be ~ed* gesucht werden; *to be in ~ of s.th.* etw (ge)brauchen, nötig haben; *to ~ for nothing* alles haben, was man braucht; *I ~ you to do* ich möchte, daß Sie tun; *it ~s ...* es fehlt, es fehlen ...; *you ~ to do (fam)* du solltest tun; *your hair ~s cutting* Sie sollten Ihr Haar schneiden lassen; *a long-felt ~* ein langegehegter Wunsch; **~ ad** *fam* Klein-, Privatanzeige *f (in e-r Zeitung)*; Stellengesuch, -angebot *n*; **~age** ['-idʒ] *Am* Fehlbetrag *m*; **~ing** ['-iŋ] *a* fehlend, nicht vorhanden; *to be ~~* fehlen; nicht enthalten sein (*in* in); es fehlen lassen (*in* an), nicht haben (*in s.th.* etw), *lit* ermangeln (*in s.th.* e-r S); geistig zurückgeblieben sein; *weighed and found ~~* gewogen u. zu leicht befunden; *prp* ohne, in Ermangelung *gen*; außer, bis auf; weniger.

wanton ['wɔntən] *a* unbeherrscht, zügellos; ausschweifend, liederlich, lüstern; ausgelassen, mutwillig, übermütig; *(Kind)* ungezogen; böswillig, boshaft; rücksichtslos; extravagant, geziert; luxuriös, üppig *a. bot*; *s* Wüstling *m*; liederliche(s) Frauenzimmer *n*; *itr* tändeln, spielen; *(Pflanze)* üppig wachsen, ins Kraut schießen; **~ness** ['-nis] Unbeherrschtheit, Zügellosigkeit; Liederlichkeit; Geilheit, Lüsternheit; Ausgelassenheit *f*, Mutwille, Übermut *m*; Extravaganz, Üppigkeit *f*.

wapiti ['wɔpiti] Wapiti, Elk *m (nordamerik. Hirschart).*

war [wɔː] *s* Krieg *a. fig*; *fig* Kampf, Streit, Konflikt *m*; *(art of ~)* Kriegskunst, -wissenschaft *f*; *attr* Kriegs-; *itr* Krieg führen (*for* um); kämpfen, streiten (*against* gegen; *with* mit); *at ~* im Krieg(szustand) (befindlich) (*with* mit); *to be at ~ with* Krieg führen gegen; *fig* auf dem Kriegsfuß stehen (*with* mit); *in case, in the event of ~* im Kriegsfall; *in time(s) of ~* in Kriegszeiten; *on a ~ footing* in Kriegsstärke; *to agitate for ~* zum Krieg hetzen; *to carry the ~ into the enemy's country* den Krieg in Feindesland tragen; *fig* zum Gegenangriff übergehen; *to declare ~ (on a country)* (e-m Lande) den Krieg erklären; *fig (on s.o.)* jdm den Kampf ansagen; *to drift into ~* e-m Krieg zusteuern; *to fight a ~* e-n Krieg austragen; *fig* e-n Kampf ausfechten; *to go to ~* e-n Krieg beginnen (*against* gegen); in den Krieg ziehen; *to have been in the ~s (fig)* Schweres durchgemacht haben; *to make, to wage ~ (up)on* Krieg führen gegen; *to prepare ~* e-n Krieg vorbereiten; *act of ~* Kriegshandlung *f*; *civil ~* Bürgerkrieg *m*; *class ~* Klassenkampf *m*; *cost of ~* Kriegskosten *pl*; *declaration of ~* Kriegserklärung *f*; *liberation ~* Befreiungskrieg *m*; *naval, sea ~* Seekrieg *m*; *outbreak of ~* Kriegsausbruch *m*; *paper ~* Papierkrieg *m*; *preventive ~* Präventivkrieg *m*; *prisoner of ~* Kriegsgefangene(r) *m*; *psychological ~* Nervenkrieg *m*; *religious ~* Religionskrieg *m*; *Secretary of State for W~ (brit.)* Kriegs-, Verteidigungsminister *m*; *theatre of ~* Kriegsschauplatz *m*; *world ~* Weltkrieg *m*; *~ of aggression* Angriffskrieg *m*; *~ in the air* Luftkrieg *m*; *~ of attrition* Zermürbungskrieg *m*; *~ of conquest* Eroberungskrieg *m*; *~ of extermination* Vernichtungskrieg *m*; *~ of independence* Unabhängigkeitskrieg *m*; *~ to the knife* Krieg *m* bis aufs Messer; *~ of nerves* Nervenkrieg *m*; *~ of succession* Erbfolgekrieg *m*; **~ aims** *pl* Kriegsziele *n pl*; **~ armaments** *pl* Kriegsrüstungen *f pl*; **~ atrocities** *pl* Kriegsgreuel *m pl*; **~ baby** Kriegskind *n*; *Am fam* kriegsbedingte(r) Industrie(zweig *m*) *f*; **~-blinded** *a* kriegsblind; **~ bond** Kriegsschuldverschreibung *f*; **~ bonus** Kriegszulage *f*; **~-booty** Kriegsbeute *f*; **~-bride** Kriegsbraut *f*; **~ bulletin** Kriegsbericht *m*; **~-burden** Kriegslast *f*; **~-chest** Kriegskasse *f*; **~ correspondent** Kriegsberichter (-statter) *m*; **~ crime** Kriegsverbrechen *n*; **~ criminal** Kriegsverbrecher *m*; **~-cry** Schlachtruf *m a. fig*; **~ damages** *pl* Kriegsschäden *m pl*; **~-dance** Kriegstanz *m*; **~-debts** *pl* Kriegsschulden *f pl*; **W~ Department** Kriegsministerium *n (der US)*; **~ diary** Kriegstagebuch *n*; **~ disabled** *a* kriegsversehrt, -beschädigt; **~ economy** Kriegswirtschaft *f*; **~ efforts** *pl* Kriegsanstrengungen *f pl*; **~ establishment** Kriegsstärke *f*; **~ factory** Rüstungsbetrieb *m*; **~fare** ['-fɛə] Krieg(führung *f*) *m*; *economic ~~* Wirtschaftskriegführung *f*; *guerilla ~~* Guerilla-, Kleinkrieg *m*; *paper ~~* Papierkrieg *m*; *party ~~* Parteikämpfe *m pl*; *psychological ~~* Nervenkrieg *m*; **~faring** ['-fɛəriŋ] kriegführend; **~-flag** Kriegsflagge *f*; **~ footing**: *on a ~~ (mil)* kriegsstark; **~-game** Kriegsspiel *n*; **~-god** Kriegsgott *m*; **~-grave** Soldatengrab *n*; *pl* Kriegsgräber *n pl*; **~-guilt** Kriegsschuld *f*; **~-head** Sprengkopf *m*; **~-horse** Schlacht-, Streitroß *n*; *fig* alte(r) Haudegen, *allg* alte(r) Kämpfer *m*; **~ indemnification** Reparationen *f pl*; **~ industry** Rüstungsindustrie *f*; **~like** ['-laik] kriegerisch, feindselig; Kriegs-; *~~ operations (pl)* Kriegshandlungen *f pl*; **~ loan** Kriegsanleihe *f*; **~-lord** Kriegsherr *m*; **~ material** Kriegsmaterial *n*; **~monger** Kriegshetzer *m*; **~-nose** = *~-head*; **W~ Office** *(brit.)* Kriegsministerium *n*; **~ orphan** Kriegswaise *f*; **~ paint** Kriegsbemalung *f*; *fig* volle(s) Ornat *n*; **~-path**: *to be on the ~~* auf dem Kriegspfad sein *a. fig*; **~ pension** Kriegsrente *f*; **~ photographer** Kriegsberichter *m*; **~-plane** Kampfflugzeug *n*; **~ policy** Kriegs(treiber)-politik *f*; **~ potential** Kriegspotential *n*; **~ preparations** *pl* Kriegsvorbereitungen, Rüstungen *f pl*; **~ production** Kriegsproduktion *f*; **~ profiteer** Kriegsgewinnler *m*; **~ propaganda** Kriegspropaganda *f*; **~ring** ['-riŋ] *a* mitea. im Krieg befindlich; *fig* widerstreitend, entgegengesetzt; **~rior** ['wɔriə] Krieger *m*; **~scarred** *a* durch den Krieg zerrüttet; **~ship** Kriegsschiff *n*; **~ strength** Kriegsstärke *f*; **~time** Kriegszeit *f*; *attr* Kriegs-; *in ~~* in Kriegszeiten; *~~ propaganda* Kriegspropaganda *f*; **~-weary** kriegsmüde; **~-wedding** Kriegstrauung *f*; **~-whoop** Kriegsgeschrei *n (bes. d. Indianer)*; **~ widow** Kriegerwitwe *f*; **~-worn** *a* vom Krieg mitgenommen; kriegsmüde; **~ years** *pl* Kriegsjahre *n pl*; **~ zone** Kriegsgebiet *n*.

warbl|e ['wɔːbl] **1.** *itr (Vogel)* singen; *(Lerche)* trillern; *(Bach)* murmeln; *Am* jodeln; *tr* singen; besingen; zwitschern; *s* Gesang *m*, Lied *n*; Triller *m*; *Am* Jodeln *n*; **~er** ['-ə] Sänger *m*; *pl zoo* Sänger *m pl*; **2.** *vet* Dasselbeule; *ent (~ fly)* Dassel-, (Rinder-)Biesfliege, (Haut-)Bremse *f*.

ward [wɔːd] *s* Vormundschaft *f*; Mündel *n*; Schützling; Entmündigte(r) *m*; (Gefängnis-, Krankenhaus-)Abteilung; *med* Station *f*; (Stadt-, Verwaltungs-) Bezirk *m*; Schutzhaft, Verwahrung; *(Fechten)* Parade *f*; *tech (Schloß)* Besatzung; *(Schlüssel)* Aussparung, -nehmung *f*; *tr (to ~ off)* abwehren, fernhalten; *(in ein Gefängnis, Krankenhaus)* einliefern; *(in ein Heim)* aufnehmen; *in, under ~* unter Vormundschaft; *in watch and ~* hinter Schloß u. Riegel; *to keep watch and ~* bewachen; *casual ~* Asyl, Obdachlosenheim *n*; *electoral ~* Wahlbezirk *m*; *isolation ~ (med)* Isolierbaracke *f*, -pavillon *m*; **~en** ['-n] Wächter, Wärter, Aufseher; *Am* Gefängnisdirektor; Pförtner; Aufsichtsbeamte(r); (Amts-)Vorsteher, (Dienststellen-)Leiter; (Schul-)Leiter, (Di-)Rektor; Jugendherbergsvater *m*; *air-raid ~~* Luftschutzwart *m*; **~er** ['wɔːdə] Gefängniswärter *m*; **~ heeler** *Am pol fam pej* Werber, Wahlagent *m*; **~ress** ['wɔːdris] (Gefängnis-)Wärterin *f*; **~robe** ['wɔːdroub] Garderobe *f*; Kleiderschrank *m*; *spring ~~* Frühjahrsgarderobe *f*; *~~ trunk* Schrankkoffer *m*; **~room** *mar* Offiziersmesse *f*; **~ship** ['-ʃip] Vormundschaft (*of, over* über); Minderjährigkeit *f*.

war|e [wɛə] **1.** *s sing nur in Zssgen* -waren *f pl*, -artikel, -gegenstände *m pl*; *pl* Ware(n *pl*) *f*, Erzeugnisse *n pl*; irdene(s) Geschirr, Steingut *n*; **~ehouse** ['-haus] *s* (Waren-)Lager *n*, Niederlage *f*; Lagerhaus *n*, Speicher *m*; Großhandlung *f*; Waren-, Kaufhaus *n*; *tr* ['-hauz] einlagern, speichern; *bonded ~~* Zollspeicher *m*; *linen ~~* Wäschegeschäft *n*; *~~ book* Lager-, Bestandbuch *n*; *~~ certificate, receipt* Lagerschein *m*; *~~ charges (pl)* Lagergebühren *f pl*, -kosten *pl*; *~~keeper, ~~man* Lagerhalter, -verwalter, -aufseher; Lagerarbeiter, Lagerist *m*; *~~room* Laden(raum) *m*; Lager *n*; *~~ warrant* Lagerschein *m*; **2.** *tr* achtgeben, aufpassen auf, sich vorsehen vor; **~iness** ['wɛərinis] Vorsicht; Bedachtsamkeit *f*; **~y** ['wɛəri] vorsichtig, bedacht(sam), bedächtig, behutsam; *to be ~~ of s.th.* auf etw acht(geb)en.

warm [wɔːm] *a* warm *(a. von Farben)*; wärmend; erhitzt; *(Arbeit)* anstrengend, gefährlich; *fig* hitzig, erregt, aufgeregt; feurig, begeistert, übereifrig; heiß, lebhaft, lebendig; erregbar; leidenschaftlich, verliebt; mitfühlend; herzlich, freundlich; dankbar; aufrichtig; *(Spur)* frisch; *fam* unangenehm, ungemütlich; brenzlig; *fam* betucht, reich; *tr* (er)wärmen; *(to ~ up) (Speise)* aufwärmen, warm machen; *tech* hochheizen; *fig* erwärmen, erhitzen, begeistern (*to* für), erfreuen, erheitern; *sl* verdreschen; *itr (to ~ up)* warm werden, sich erwärmen *a. fig* (*to* für); *fig* sich erhitzen, sich begeistern, entflammen (*to* für); *s fam* Warmwerden *n*, Erwärmung *f*; *to ~ up (tr)* (er)wärmen; *(Essen)* an-, aufwärmen; *fig* in Schwung bringen, anfeuern, begeistern; *mot* warmlaufen lassen; *itr* warm, wärmer werden; in Schwung kommen, sich begeistern, sich erregen; *Am sport* sich in Form bringen, sich warm laufen; *in ~ blood* in der Erregung; in Leidenschaft; *to have a ~* sich aufwärmen; *to make it, things ~ for s.o. (fig)* jdm die Hölle heiß machen; **~-blooded** *a zoo* warmblütig; *fig* lebhaft, feurig, stürmisch, hitzig, (über)eifrig; **~er** ['-ə] *in Zssgen* -wärmer *m*; *foot-~~* Fußwärmer *m*; **~-hearted** *a* warmherzig, gütig, freundlich, mitfühlend, herzlich; **~ing** ['-iŋ] *a* (er)wärmend; *s* (Er-)Wärmen *n*, Erwärmung *f*; *tech* Anwärmer, Aufheizer *m*; *sl* Dresche *f*; *~~ pad* Heizkissen *n*; *~~-pan (hist)* Wärm-, Bettpfanne *f*; *~~-up period* Anwärmzeit *f*; **~ish** ['iʃ] lauwarm; **~th** [wɔːmθ] Wärme *a. fig*; *fig* Erregung; Herzlichkeit, Begeisterung *f*, Eifer; Ärger *m*; *~~ of the body* Körperwärme *f*; **~-up** *Am sport* Sichwarmlaufen; *mot* Warmlaufen *n*; *radio* Werbevorspann *m*.

warn [wɔːn] *tr* warnen (*of, against* vor); abraten (*of* von); (er)mahnen, erinnern (*of* an; *to do* zu tun); dringend raten; auffordern, anweisen; aufmerksam machen, hinweisen (*of* auf); vorher benachrichtigen, wissen lassen, Mitteilung machen (*s.o.* jdm), verständigen (*of* von); *to ~ off, out* auffordern, weg-, hinauszugehen; *to ~ to appear* vorladen; **~ing** ['-iŋ] *a* warnend; mahnend; *s* Warnung; (Er-) Mahnung; (Voraus-)Benachrichtigung, Mitteilung *f*, Wink *m*; Kündigung; Vorladung *f*; *at a minute's ~~* in kürzester Frist; fristlos; *without any ~~* überraschend, unerwartet; *to give s.o. a ~~, to give a ~~ to s.o.* jdn warnen; *to give (a month's) ~~* (zum nächsten Ersten) kündigen; *to take ~~ from s.th.* sich etw als Warnung dienen lassen; *gale ~~* Sturmwarnung *f*; *~~ light (tech)* Warnlicht *n*; *~~-shot* Warnschuß *m*; *~~-table* Warnschild *n*.

warp [wɔːp] *s* Verwerfung *(bes. im Holz)*; Biegung, Verkrümmung; *fig*

Verdrehung, Entstellung; Verdrehtheit, Absonderlichkeit; *agr* Anschwemmung, *f*, Schwemmland *n*, -boden, -sand *m*; *mar* Bugsier-, Warptau *n*; *(Weberei)* Kette *f*; *tr* verziehen, verzerren, verbiegen; *fig* verdrehen, entstellen; ablenken (*from* von); auf falsche Wege, auf die falsche Bahn führen; zs.binden; *(Weberei)* anscheren; *mar* bugsieren; *aero* verwinden; *(Land)* durch Überfluten düngen; *itr* sich werfen, sich wellen, sich verziehen, arbeiten, sich verbiegen; *fig* vom rechten Weg abweichen, krumme Wege gehen; *mar* werpen; *(Weberei)* (an)scheren, zetteln; **~ed** [-t] *a* krumm, verzogen; *fig* verschroben; *fig* parteiisch; **~ing** ['-iŋ] *geol* Verwerfung; *aero* Verwindung *f*; *tech* Verwerfen, Verziehen *n*.

warrant ['wɔrənt] *s* Begründung, Rechtfertigung; Berechtigung, Ermächtigung, Vollmacht; Unterlage *f*, Beleg *m*, Bescheinigung; Bürgschaft, Gewähr; Schatzanweisung, Quittung *f*; *com* Lagerschein; Befehl *m*, Verfügung *f*; *mil* Patent *n*, Beförderungsurkunde *f*; *tr* begründen, rechtfertigen; bestätigen, bescheinigen; berechtigen, ermächtigen, bevollmächtigen; garantieren, verbürgen, bürgen für, gewährleisten, belegen, bescheinigen; *fam* versichern, garantieren, sicher sein, daß; *not without* ~ nicht ohne gewisse Berechtigung; *to have a ~ for doing s.th.* ermächtigt sein, etw zu tun; *to take out a ~ against s.o.* e-n Haftbefehl gegen jdn erwirken; *a ~ is out against him* er wird steckbrieflich gesucht; *death* ~ Todesurteil *n*; *dividend* ~ Gewinnanteilschein *m*; *extradition* ~ Auslieferungsersuchen *n*; *search* ~ Haussuchungsbefehl *m*; ~ *of apprehension, of arrest* Haftbefehl *m*; ~ *of attorney* Prozeßvollmacht *f*; ~ *of distress* Beschlagnahmeverfügung *f*, Pfändungs-, Zwangsvollstreckungsbefehl *m*; ~ *for payment* gerichtliche(r) Zahlungsbefehl *m*; **~able** ['-əbl] begründbar, vertretbar; **~ably** ['-əbli] *adv* berechtigterweise, rechtmäßig, zu Recht; **~ed** ['-id] *a* garantiert, verbürgt; ermächtigt, berechtigt; **~ee** [wɔrən'ti:] Sicherheitsempfänger *m*; **~er, ~or** ['wɔrəntə, -tɔ:] Garant, Gewährsmann, Bürge *m*; **~-officer** *mil* Stabsfeldwebel; *mar* (Ober-)Stabsbootsmann *m*; **~y** ['-i] Rechtfertigung (*for* für), Berechtigung (*for* zu); Ermächtigung, Vollmacht (*for* zu); Gewähr, Bürgschaft, Garantie(schein *m*) *f*; ~~ *deed (Am)* Grundstücksübertragungsurkunde *f*.

warren ['wɔrin] Kaninchengehege *n*; *fig* Ameisenhaufen *m*, Mietskaserne *f*.

wart [wɔ:t] *bot zoo med* Warze *f*; ~ **hog** Warzenschwein *n*; **~y** ['-i] warzig.

wash [wɔʃ] *tr* (ab)waschen *a. rel*; reinigen; spülen, naß machen; an-, befeuchten; *(Fußboden)* aufwaschen; *(Wellen)* bespülen, schlagen gegen; (weg)spülen; *(Kunst)* lavieren; (mit Metall) überziehen; *chem geol* waschen; *tech* anstreichen; *itr (to ~ up)* sich waschen; *(Stoff)* sich waschen lassen; (Wäsche) waschen; bespült, ausgewaschen werden; *(Wellen)* branden, schlagen (*against* gegen); *fam* e-r Prüfung standhalten; *s* Waschen *n*; Wäsche *f*; Abwasch-, Spülwasser *n a. fig*; Wellenschlag *m*; *mar* Kielwasser *n*; *aero* Luftstrudel *m*; *geol* Auswaschung, Erosion *f*; Schwemmgut *n*, -sand *m*, -land *n*, Anschwemmung *f*; Überschwemmungsgebiet *n*, Marsch (-land *n*); (Wasser-)Lache *f*, Pfuhl *m*; Altwasser *n*; Fluß-, Meeresarm; Wasserlauf *m*, Rinnsal; *Am* trockene(s) Flußbett *n*; Wasserfarbe, Lavierung; Tünche *f*, Anstrich; (dünner) Metallüberzug *m*; *(Schönheits-, Haar-, Mund-)* Wasser *n*; flüssige Nahrung *f*; *fam* was zum Nachspülen *(e-s Schnapses)*; *to be at the ~* in der Wäsche sein; *to come out in the ~ (Am sl)* (mal) herauskommen; *to give s.th. a ~* etw (ab)waschen; *to have a ~* sich waschen; *to ~ the dishes* das Geschirr spülen; *to ~ o.'s hands of s.th.* mit e-r S nichts (mehr) zu tun haben wollen; *to ~* **away** wegspülen; fort-, wegschwemmen; *to ~* **down** (ab)spülen; *(Wagen)* waschen; *(Bissen)* hinunterspülen; *to ~* **off** weg-, abwaschen; *to ~* **out** *tr itr* (sich) wegwaschen (lassen); *fam* annullieren; *sl* auspunkten, erledigen; *to be ~ed out (fig)* am Ende sein; *to ~* **over** überstreichen, -pinseln; *to ~* **up** *(Geschirr)* ab-, aufwaschen, spülen; anschwemmen, anspülen; *Am fam* erledigen; *to be ~ed up (fig)* fertig, erledigt sein; **~able** ['-əbl] (ab)waschbar; **~-basin,** *Am* **~-bowl** Waschbecken *n*, -schüssel *f*; **~-board** Waschbrett *n*; Scheuerleiste *f*; *mar* Setzbord *n*; **~-boiler** Waschkessel *m*; **~-bottle** Spritz-, Waschflasche *f*; **~-cloth** Abwaschlappen; *Am* Waschlappen *m*; **~-day** Waschtag *m*; **~-down** *mot* (Wagen-) Waschen *n*; **~ed-out** *a (Farbe)* verwaschen, verblaßt; *fam* abgespannt, müde, schlapp, durchgedreht; **~ed-up** *a* abgewaschen; *fam* müde, kaputt; *sl* erledigt, hin; ausrangiert, abgetan; ruiniert; *(Pläne)* ins Wasser gefallen; **~er** ['-ə] Wäscher(in *f*) *m*; Waschmaschine; *tech* Unterlagscheibe *f*, Dichtungsring *m*; *dish-~~* Geschirrspülmaschine *f*; ~~ *woman* Wäscherin *f*; **~-hand-basin** = *~-basin*; **~-hand-stand** = *~-stand*; **~-house** Waschküche *f*, -haus *n*; **~iness** ['-inis] Wässerigkeit; *fig* Schwäche, Kraftlosigkeit; Fadheit, Abgeschmacktheit *f*; **~ing** ['-iŋ] *s* Waschen *n*; Wäsche *f*; Spülen, (Ab-)Waschen *n*; *geol* Unterspülung, Anschwemmung *f*; *min* Schlämmgut *n*; *tech* Farb-, Metallüberzug *m*; *meist pl* Spülwasser, Spülicht *n*; Abfall *m*, Abfälle *m pl*; *Am com* Scheinverkauf *m* von Börsenpapieren; *a* waschecht; Wasch-; *~~-board* Waschbrett *n*; *~~-day* Waschtag *m*; *~~-fluid* flüssige Seife *f*; *~~-machine* Waschmaschine *f*; *~~-powder* Waschpulver *n*; *~~-silk* Waschseide *f*; *~~-soda* Bleichsoda *f*; *~~-up* Abwaschen, Geschirrspülen *n*; **~-kitchen** Waschküche *f*; **~-leather** Fensterleder *n*; **~-out** *rail* Unterspülung; *med* Ausspülung; *(Straße)* ausgewaschene Stelle *f*; *sl* Reinfall *m*, Fiasko *n*; Niete *f (Mensch)*; **~-rag** = *~-cloth*; **~room** *Am* Toilette *f*; ~ **sale** *(Börse)* Scheingeschäft *n*; **~-stand** Waschtisch, -ständer *m*; **~-tub** Waschwanne *f*, -zuber *m*; **~woman** Waschfrau *f*; **~y** ['-i] wässerig, wäßrig; (ver)dünn(t), schwach *a. fig*; *fig* fad(e), geschmacklos, abgeschmackt, (saft- u.) kraftlos; *(Stil)* verwässert; *(Farbe)* matt, blaß.

wasp [wɔsp] Wespe *f*; **~ish** ['-iʃ] *fig* launisch, reizbar; *(Antwort)* scharf; **~'s nest** Wespennest *n*; **~-waisted** *a* mit e-r Wespentaille.

wassail ['wɔseil] *obs* Umtrunk *m*; gewürzte(s) Bier *n*.

wast|age ['weistidʒ] Abnutzung *f*, Schwund, Abgang, Verlust; Verbrauch *m*; Vergeudung, Verschwendung *f*; *tech* Ausschuß *m*; **~e** [weist] *tr* verschwenden, vergeuden, nutzlos vertun (*on* mit); verwüsten, verheeren; auf-, verbrauchen; auszehren, schwächen; *jur (Haus)* verkommen lassen; versäumen, verpassen; *to be ~ed* umsonst, vergeblich sein; wirkungslos sein (*on* auf); *itr (to ~~ away)* schwächer werden, nachlassen; abnehmen, weniger werden, dahinschwinden, vergehen; dahinsiechen; *(Zeit)* ungenutzt verstreichen; verschwendet, vergeudet werden; sich verzetteln (*in* in); *a* wüst, öde, verlassen; übrig(geblieben); ungenützt; unbrauchbar, unnütz (geworden), Alt-; Abfall-; überflüssig, -schüssig; *physiol* ausgeschieden; *tech* Abfluß-, Abzugs-; *s* Wüste, (Ein-)Öde *f*, Ödland *n*, Wildnis *f*; Schutthaufen; Müll; Schutt; Schrott, Abfall(produkt *n*) *m*, Abfälle *m pl*; Ausschuß *m*; Abwässer *pl*; *min* Abraum *m*; *geol* Geröll *n*; Überlauf; *(~ steam)* Abdampf; (allmählicher) Verlust, Abgang, Schwund *m*, Abnahme *f*; Verschleiß *m*, Abnutzung *f*; Verfall, Verderb *m*; *jur* Wertminderung; Verschwendung, Vergeudung *f*; *biol* Ausscheidungsprodukte *n pl*; *to go, to run to ~~* ungenutzt bleiben; verschwendet werden; *to lay ~~* zerstören, verwüsten, verheeren; *to lie ~~* brachliegen; *don't ~~ your breath* sparen Sie sich Ihre Worte; *haste makes ~~* Eile mit Weile; *~~ not, want not* spare in der Zeit, so hast du in der Not; *~~ of energy, money, time* Kraft-, Geld-, Zeitverschwendung *f*; *~~-basket* = *~~-paper-basket*; *~~ book* Kladde *f*, Konzeptheft *n*; *~~ cotton* Putzbaumwolle *f*; *~~-dump* Schutthalde *f*; *~~-flue* Abzugskanal *m*; *~~ gas* Abgas *n*; *~~ heat (tech)* Abhitze, -wärme *f*; *~~land* Ödland *n*; *~~ matter* Abfall *m*, Abfälle *m pl*; *~~ paper* Altpapier *n*, Makulatur *f a. fig*; *~~-paper basket* Papierkorb *m*; *~~-pipe* Abfluß-, Fallrohr *n*; *~~ product (tech)* Abfallprodukt *n*; *biol* Ausscheidungsstoff *m*; *~~ steam* Abdampf *m*; *~~ time* Leerlaufzeit *f*; *~~ water (tech)* Ab-, Kondenswasser *n*; *~~ wool* Putzwolle *f*; **~eful** ['-ful] verschwendungssüchtig; verschwenderisch (*of* mit); unrentabel; *~~ exploitation* Raubbau *m*; **~efulness** ['-fulnis] Verschwendungssucht; Kostspieligkeit *f*; **~er** ['-ə] Verschwender; *fam* Taugenichts, Nichtsnutz *m*; *com* fehlerhafte(s) Stück *n*; Ausschuß; *min* Fehlguß; *pl* Ausschuß(ware *f*) *m*; **~ing** ['-iŋ] *a* verheerend, vernichtend, zerstörerisch; schwindend; abnutzend, wertmindernd; *(Krankheit)* zehrend; **~rel** ['-rə] Verschwender; Taugenichts, Nichtsnutz; Straßenjunge *m*; *com* fehlerhaftes Stück *n*, Ausschuß(ware *f*) *m*; *(England)* Gemeindeland *n*.

*

watch [wɔtʃ] *s* Wache *a. mar*; Be-, Überwachung; (gespannte) Aufmerksamkeit, Wachsamkeit; Wache, Wachmannschaft *f*; Wachmann, Wächter, Wärter *m*; *obs* Nachtwache; Taschen-, Armbanduhr; *mar* (Schiffs-)Wache *f*; *itr* aufpassen, achtgeben (*over* auf); herschauen, -sehen; zusehen, beobachten; abpassen, -warten (*for s.th.* etw); auf der Lauer sein; wachen; Wache halten; *tr* bewachen, behüten, aufpassen auf, achtgeben auf; überwachen; nicht aus den Augen lassen; achten auf, beobachten; abwarten, -passen; *(Tiere)* hüten; *on ~* auf Wache; *on the ~* auf der Lauer; *to ~ out* auf der Hut sein, aufpassen, achtgeben; ausschauen (*for s.o.* nach jdm);

sich hüten (*for s.o.* vor jdm); *to be on the ~* auf der Hut sein; Ausschau halten (*for* nach); lauern (*for* auf); *to keep ~* Wache halten; aufpassen (*on* auf); *to ~ o.'s step* vorsichtig zu Werke gehen; *~ your step!* Achtung, Stufe! Seien Sie vorsichtig! *to ~ o.'s time* auf e-e günstige Gelegenheit warten; *he needs close ~ing* man muß ihm auf die Finger sehen; *by my ~ it's ten* nach meiner Uhr ist es zehn; *dress-, wrist-~* Taschen-, Armbanduhr *f*; *~* **band** Uhrarmband *n*; **~-boat** Wachtboot *n*; **~-box, -house** *(Übersee, Am)* Schilderhaus *n*; **~-bracelet** Uhrarmband *n*; **~-case** Uhrgehäuse *n*; **~-chain, -guard** Uhrkette *f*; **~-dog** Wachhund *m a. fig*; **~er** ['-ə] Wächter; Wärter; Aufpasser; Beobachter; Zuschauer *m*; **~-fire** Wachfeuer *n*; **~ful** ['-ful] wachsam, aufmerksam (*of* auf); behutsam, vorsichtig (*against* mit); *to be ~~ of s.th.* etw bewachen, beobachten; **~fulness** ['-fulnis] Wachsamkeit, Aufmerksamkeit, Behutsamkeit, Vorsicht *f*; **~-glass** Uhrglas *n*; *~* **hand** Uhrzeiger *m*; **~maker** Uhrmacher *m*; **~making** Uhrmacherei *f*; **~man** ['-mən] Wachmann, (Nacht-)Wächter *(in e-m Werk)*; Bahnwärter; *hist* Nachtwächter *m*; *~~'s clock* Stechuhr *f*; **~-meeting** Silvestergottesdienst *m*; **~-night** Silvesterabend *m*, -nacht *f*, -gottesdienst *m*; *~* **officer** Wachoffizier *m*; **~-pocket** Uhrtasche *f*; **~-spring** Uhrfeder *f*; **~-tower** Wachtturm *m*; **~-word** Schlagwort; Kennwort *n*, Losung, Parole *f a. hist mil.*

water ['wɔ:tə] *s* Wasser *n*; Wasserstand, -spiegel *m*; Flüssigkeit *f*; Aquarell *n*; *oft pl* Gewässer; *pl* Mineral-, Heilwasser *n*, (Sauer-)Brunnen *m*; *(Edelstein)* Wasser *n*; *tr (Vieh)* tränken; bewässern, begießen, sprengen; berieseln; *(to ~ down)* ein-, durchweichen, befeuchten; (mit Wasser) verdünnen; *(Milch)* pan(t)schen; *(Textil)* moirieren; *fig* verwässern; *itr (Tier)* saufen; Wasser einnehmen, tanken; sich mit Wasser versorgen; Wasser abgeben; *(Augen)* tränen; *aero* wassern; *to ~ down (fig)* verwässern, abschwächen, mildern; *above ~* über Wasser *a. fig*; *by ~* auf dem Wasserwege, zu Schiff; *like ~ (fig)* mit vollen Händen; am laufenden Band; *of the first, purest ~* reinsten Wassers; *on the ~* auf dem Wasser, in e-m Boot, auf e-m Schiff; *under ~* unter Wasser; *to back ~* rückwärts rudern; *to be in deep ~(s) (fig)* in Schwierigkeiten stecken; *to be like a fish out of ~ (fig)* sich fehl am Platz fühlen; *to be in low ~ (fig)* knapp bei Kasse sein; *to be in smooth ~ (fig)* gut vorankommen; *to cast, to throw o.'s bread upon the ~(s) (fig)* keinen Dank erwarten; *to drink the ~s* e-e Brunnenkur machen; *to get into hot ~ (fig)* in Teufels Küche kommen; *to go through fire and ~ (fig)* Schlimmes durchmachen (müssen); *to have ~ on the brain (fig)* den Verstand verloren haben, nicht bei Sinnen sein; *to hold ~* wasserdicht, *fig* stichhaltig sein; *to keep o.'s head above ~ (fig)* sich *(bes. finanziell)* über Wasser halten; *to let ~* Wasser durchlassen, nicht wasserdicht sein; *to make, to pass ~* Wasser lassen, urinieren; *mar* ein Leck haben; *to make s.o.'s mouth ~* jdm das Wasser im Munde zs.laufen lassen; *to throw cold ~ on s.th. (fig)* die Begeisterung für etw dämpfen; *I'm in low ~ (fam)* bei mir ist Ebbe; *my mouth ~s* mir läuft das Wasser im Munde zusammen; *the boat draws ten feet of ~* das Schiff hat 5 Fuß Tiefgang; *still ~s run deep (prov)* stille Wasser sind tief; *bath ~* Badewasser *n*; *drinking-~* Trinkwasser *n*; *ground-~* Grundwasser *n*; *~~ level* Grundwasserspiegel *m*; *high ~* Hochwasser *n*; Flut *f*; *holy ~* Weihwasser *n*; *low ~* Niedrigwasser *n*; Ebbe *f*; *mineral, table ~s (pl)* Mineralwasser *n*, Sauerbrunnen *m*; *tap ~* Leitungswasser *n*; *washing-~* Waschwasser *n*; *~ on the brain* Wasserkopf *m*; *~* **absorption** Wasseraufnahme *f*; *~* **adder** Wasserschlange *f*; **~age** ['-ridʒ] Transport *m* auf dem Wasserwege; *~* **bath** Wasserbad *n*; **~-beetle** Wasserkäfer *m*; **~-bird** Wasservogel *m*; **~-biscuit** Wasserzwieback *m*; **~-blister** *med* Wasserblase *f*; **~-boiler** Warmwasserspeicher *m*; **~-borne** *a* auf dem Wasserwege befördert; *med* durch Trinkwasser übertragen; **~-bottle** Wasserkaraffe; *Am mil* Feldflasche *f*; **~-brain** *vet* Drehkrankheit *f*; **~-brash** Sodbrennen *n*; **~buck** *zoo* Wasserbock *m*; **~-buffalo** Wasserbüffel *m*; **~-bug** Wasserwanze *f*, -käfer *m*; **~-butt** Regenwassertonne *f*; **W~-carrier** *astr der* Wassermann; **~-cart** Wasser-, Sprengwagen *m*; **~-chute** Wasserrutschbahn *f*; **~-clock** *hist* Wasseruhr *f*; **~-closet** ['-klɔzit] (Spül-, Wasser-)Klosett *n*; *~* **cock** Wasserhahn *m*; **~-colo(u)r** Wasserfarbe *f*; Aquarell *n*; *pl* Aquarellmalerei *f*; *~* **conduit** Wasserleitung *f*; *~* **content** Wassergehalt *m*; **~-cooled** *a tech* wassergekühlt; **~-cooling** *tech* Wasserkühlung *f*; **~course** Wasserlauf *m*; Fluß-, Kanalbett *n*; **~craft** Wasserfahrzeug(e *pl*) *n*; **~-cress** *bot* Brunnenkresse *f*; **~-cure** Wasser-, Kneippkur *f*; **~-diviner** = *~-finder*; **~-dog** *fig* Wasserratte *f*; alte(r) Seebär *m*; **~-drinker** Antialkoholiker, Abstinenzler *m*; **~drop** Wassertropfen *m*; **~ed** ['-d] *a* besprengt, bespritzt; bewässert; gewässert; verdünnt; moiriert; *fin* verwässert; **~fall** Wasserfall *m*; *~* **faucet** *Am* Wasserhahn *m*; *~* **feeding** *tech* Wasserzufuhr *f*; *~* **finder** Rutengänger *m*; *a.* = **~-finding instrument** Wünschelrute *f*; **~-flea** Wasserfloh *m*; **~fowl** (*bes.* jagdbare) Wasservögel *m pl*; *~* **front** *Am* Uferbezirk *m (e-r Stadt)*; Hafenviertel *n*; *~* **funk** *fam* wasserscheue(r) Mensch *m*; *~* **gap** *Am* tief eingeschnittene(s) Fluß- *od* Bachtal *n*; Schlucht, Klamm *f*; **~-gate** Flut-, Schleusentor, Schott *n*; *min* Sumpfstrecke *f*; **~-glass** *tech* Wasserstandsglas; *chem* Wasserglas *n*; **~-gauge** Pegel, Wasserstandsmesser *m*; *tech* Wasserstandsglas *n*, -stutzen *m*; **~-heater** Warmwasserbereiter *m*; **~-heating** Warmwasserbereitung *f*; **~-hen** Wasserhuhn *n*; **~-hole** Wasserloch *n*, -lache *f*; *~* **hose** Wasserschlauch *m*; **~-ice** Speiseeis *n* aus Wasser, Zucker u. Fruchtsaft; **~iness** ['-rinis] Wäßrigkeit *f*; **~ing** ['-riŋ] Sprengen, Begießen, (Be-)Wässern; *(Vieh)* Tränken *n*; *com* Verwässerung *f*; *~~-can* Gießkanne *f*; *~~-cart* Sprengwagen *m*; *~~-place* (Vieh-)Tränke, Wasserstelle; Schwemme *f*; Kurort *m*, (See-)Bad *n*; *~~-pot, -can* Gießkanne *f*; *~* **jacket** *tech* Wassermantel *m*; *~* **jet** Wasserstrahl *m*; **~-level** Wasseroberfläche *f*, -spiegel *m*; Wasserwaage; *mar* Wasserlinie *f*; **~-lily** Seerose *f*; **~-line** *mar* Wasserlinie *f*; **~-logged** ['-lɔgd] *a* voll(er) Wasser; vollgesogen; sumpfig; *sl* besoffen; *~* **main** Hauptwasserrohr *n*; *pl* Wasserleitungsnetz *n*; **~man** Fähr-, Bootsmann; *sport* Ruderer *m*; **~mark** *s* Hochwasserstandsmarke *f*; *(Papier)* Wasserzeichen *n*; *pl mar* Tiefgangsmarken *f pl*; *tr (Papier)* mit e-m Wasserzeichen versehen; *~* **meadow** *agr* Rieselwiese *f*; **~-melon** Wassermelone *f*; **~-meter** Wassermesser *m*, -uhr *f*; **~-mill** Wassermühle *f*; **~-motor** = *~-wheel*; **~-nymph** Wassernymphe, Najade *f*; **~-parting** Wasserscheide *f*; **~-pipe** Wasserrohr *n*; Wasserpfeife *f*; **~-plane** Flugboot, Wasserflugzeug *n*; **~-plant** Wasserpflanze *f*; **~-polo** Wasserball(spiel *n*) *m*; **~-power** Wasserkraft *f*; *~~ plant, station* Wasserkraftwerk *n*; **~-pox** *med* Wasser-, Windpocken *pl*; **~-press** hydraulische Presse *f*; *~* **pressure** Wasserdruck *m*; **~proof** *a* wasserdicht; *s* wasserdichte(r) Stoff *m*; Gummi-, *(wasserdichter)* Regenmantel *m*; *tr* imprägnieren; **~pump** Wasserpumpe *f*; *~* **purification** Wasseraufbereitung *f*; **~-rat** Wasserratte *f*; **~-rate** Wassergeld *n*, -zins *m*; **~-repellent** wasserabstoßend; **~scape** ['-skeip] *(Kunst)* Seestück *n*; **~shed** Wasserscheide *f*; Entwässerungs-, Stromgebiet *n*; *~* **shortage** Wassermangel *m*; **~-shoot** Regenrinne, Dachtraufe *f*; **~side** *s* Ufer *n*, Strand *m*; *a* Ufer-, Strand-; **~-ski** Wasserschi *m*; **~-skin** Wasserschlauch *m*; **~-snake** Wasserschlange *f*; **~-soak** *tr* sich mit Wasser vollsaugen lassen, mit Wasser sättigen; **~-softener** Enthärter *m*; **~-soluble** wasserlöslich; **~spout** Wasserspeier *m*, Abtraufe *f*, Ablaufrohr *n*; *mete* Wasserhose *f*; **~-sprite** Wassergeist *m*; **~-supply** Wasserversorgung, -leitung(ssystem, -netz *n*) *f*, -vorrat *m*; *~~ pipe* Wasserleitungsrohr *n*; *~~ point* Wasserstelle *f*; **~-system** Stromgebiet *n*; Wasserleitungsnetz *n*; **~-table** Grundwasserspiegel *m*; *arch* Wasserabflußleiste *f*; Rinnstein *m*; *~* **tank** Wasserbehälter *m*; **~-tap** Wasserhahn *m*; **~tight** wasserdicht; *fig* unmißverständlich; (absolut) zuverlässig; stichhaltig; **~-tower** Wasserturm *m*; *~* **tube** Wasserrohr *n*; *~* **vapo(u)r** Wasserdampf *m*; **~-vole** Wasserratte *f*; **~-wag(g)on**: *to be on the ~~ (sl)* auf dem Trockenen sitzen; keinen Alkohol trinken; **~-wave** *(Frisur)* Wasserwelle *f*; **~way** Wasserlauf, -weg; Schleppkanal *m*; Fahrrinne *f*; **~-wheel** Wasserrad *n*; **~-wings** *pl Art* Schwimmgürtel *m*; **~-witch** Wassernixe *f*; *s. ~-finder*; **~-works** *pl, oft mit sing* Wasserwerk *n*, -kunst; Pumpstation; *sl* Tränendrüse *f*; *to turn on the ~~ (sl)* auf die Tränendrüse drücken; losheulen; **~worn** *a (von fließendem Wasser)* glatt-, blankgewaschen; **~y** ['-ri] wässerig *(a. med, Farbe)*; wassergefüllt, naß, feucht; regnerisch; regenverkündend; tränenreich; weinend; schweißtriefend, schwitzend; *(Getränk, Suppe)* dünn; *fig* fad(e), schlaff, schlapp, weich.

Waterloo [wɔ:tə'lu:]: *to meet o.'s ~* vernichtend geschlagen werden.

watt [wɔt] *el* Watt *n*; **~age** ['-idʒ] Stromverbrauch *m (e-s Gerätes)*; (Watt-)Leistung *f*.

wattle ['wɔtl] *s* Flechtwerk, Geflecht *n*, Hürde; *bot* australische Akazie *f*; *zoo* Kehllappen *m (bes. d. Hahnes)*; *a* geflochten; Flecht-; *tr* zs.flechten.

waul, wawl [wɔ:l] *itr* schreien, heulen, miauen.

Wave, WAVE [weiv] *Am* (Marine-)

Helferin *f (der Women's Reserve of the United States Naval Reserve).*

wav|e [weiv] *itr* wogen; *(Fahne)* wehen, flattern; sich wellen; wellig, gewellt sein; (zu)winken (*to s.o.* jdm); Winkzeichen geben; *tr* schwingen, schwenken; winken (*a handkerchief* mit dem Taschentuch); durch Winkzeichen mitteilen; ondulieren, wellen, Wellen legen in; moirieren, flammen; *s* Welle *a. phys el radio u. fig*; Woge *a. fig*; *poet die* See; *fig* Flut *f*; Wogen, Wehen, Flattern *n*; Wink(zeichen *n*) *m*; *in ~~s* in aufea.folgenden Wellen; *to ~~ aside* beiseite schieben, (mit e-r lässigen Handbewegung) abtun; in den Wind schlagen; beiseite winken (*s.o.* jdn); *to ~~ s.o. away* jdm abwinken; jdn abweisen; *to ~~ o.'s hand to s.o.* jdm mit der Hand winken; *cold, heat ~~* Kälte-, Hitzewelle *f*; *a ~~ of indignation* e-e Flut der Entrüstung; *~~ of strikes* Streikwelle *f*; *~~ band* Frequenzband *n*; *~~-length (phys el radio)* Wellenlänge *f*; *~~-range (radio)* Wellenbereich *m*; *~~-trap (radio)* Sperrkreis *m*; **~y** ['-i] wellenförmig, wellig, gewellt; geschwungen, wogend; *fig* schwankend, unbeständig.

waver ['weivə] *itr* (hin- u. her)schwanken, flattern; *fig* schwanken, unschlüssig sein, zaudern; ins Wanken geraten, straucheln; *(Stimme)* zittern; *(Licht)* flackern, flimmern; *allg* fluktuieren, schwanken; **~er** ['-rə] Zauderer *m*; **~ing** ['-riŋ] *fig* unentschlossen, unschlüssig; schwankend *a. fig.*

wawl *s. waul.*

wax [wæks] **1.** *s (bees~)* (Bienen-)Wachs; *(ear-~)* Ohrenschmalz; *(paraffin ~)* Paraffin; *(cobbler's ~)* Schusterpech *n*; *(sealing-~)* Siegellack *m*; Schallplatte *f*; *tr* (ein)wachsen; bohnern; (aus)pichen, mit Pech verschmieren; *Am radio* auf (Wachs-)Platten aufnehmen = *to put on ~*; *a* Wachs-; wächsern; *to mould like ~ (fig)* wie Wachs formen; *~ed paper* = *~-paper*; **~-bean** Wachsbohne *f*; **~-candle, -light** Wachskerze *f*; **~cloth** Wachstuch *n*; **~-doll** Wachspuppe *f a. fig*; **~en** ['-ən] *obs* wächsern; **~-end** Pechdraht *m*; **~ figure** Wachsfigur *f*; **~ mould** Wachsmatrize *f*; **~-painting** Brandmalerei *f*; **~-paper** Wachspapier *n*; **~work** Wachsplastik, -figur *f*; *pl* Wachsfigurenkabinett *n*; **~y** ['-i] wachsartig; Wachs-; *fig* nachgiebig; **2.** *itr* wachsen; *(bes. Mond)* zunehmen; *obs* werden; *~ing moon* zunehmende(r) Mond *m*; **3.** *s sl* Wutanfall *m*; *to put s.o. into a ~* jdn rasend machen; **~y** ['-i] *sl* wütend, in Fahrt, leicht aufbrausend, jähzornig; **4.** *tr Am fam* jdn übertreffen, ausstechen.

way [wei] **1.** *s* Weg *m*, Straße *f*, Pfad *m*, Bahn; (Weg-)Strecke *f*; *(right of ~) jur* Wegerecht *n*; Richtung *f*; *mar* Kurs; Weg, Gang *m*, Fahrt *f*; *fig* Weg *m*, Handlungsweise *f*, Verfahren(sweise *f*) *n*; Verhaltensweise, Art u. Weise; *allg* Art, Weise; Möglichkeit, Gelegenheit; Hinsicht, Beziehung *f*, Punkt; Wille *m*; *fam* Gegend *f*, Umkreis *m*; *fam* Umstände *m pl*, Verhältnisse *n pl*, Lage *f*, Zustand *m*; *fam* Tätigkeit *f*, Beruf *m*; *tech* Gleitschiene, -fläche; *mar* Helling *f*; **2.** *adv fam Am (vor e-m adv des Ortes)* weit, ein tüchtiges Stück, e-e ganze Ecke, ganz; **3.** *across the ~* gegenüber; *any ~* auf jeden Fall; *by ~ of* über, durch; mittels, mit Hilfe *gen*; zwecks *gen*; als, zum, zur; *by the ~* auf dem Wege, unterwegs; *fig* nebenbei (gesagt), beiläufig; *in a ~* in gewisser Weise; gewissermaßen; *in the ~* im Wege, hinderlich, lästig; *of* hinsichtlich *gen*; *in no ~* in keiner Weise, durchaus nicht, keineswegs; *in a family ~* ohne Umstände, zwanglos; *in the family ~ (fam)* in andern Umständen; *in a small ~* bescheiden, unauffällig; *on the ~* auf dem Wege, unterwegs (*to* nach); *one ~ or another* irgendwie; *out of the ~* aus dem Wege, zur Seite; vom rechten Wege ab; falsch; ungewöhnlich, abwegig; *out-of-the-~* abgelegen; *that ~* so, auf diese Weise; *this ~* hierher; hier entlang, hindurch; *this ~ or that ~* so oder so; *to my ~ of thinking* meines Erachtens, meiner Meinung nach; *under ~* unterwegs, auf dem Wege; *fig* im Gang; *to be under ~ (fig)* vorankommen, Fortschritte machen; **4.** *~ back (Am fam)* weit, ein tüchtiges Stück zurück; *(zeitlich)* damals schon; *~ behind, down, up (Am fam)* ganz hinten, unten, oben; *a long ~ from* weit entfernt von; *a long ~ off, ~ off (Am fam)* weit, e-e ganze Ecke weg; *~ out, over (Am fam)* weit draußen, drüben; **5.** *to ask the ~* nach dem Weg fragen; *to be out of the ~* abgelegen sein; *to be on the ~ out (fig)* im Begriff unmodern zu werden; *to be in a good ~ of business (fig)* gute Geschäfte machen; *to come s.o.'s ~* jdm in den Weg kommen, begegnen; *to gather, to lose ~* s-e Geschwindigkeit erhöhen, vermindern; *to get, to have o.'s (own) ~* s-n Willen durchsetzen; *to get into the ~ of doing* in die Gewohnheit verfallen, etw zu tun; *to give ~* nachgeben *a. fig*; Platz machen (*to s.o.* jdm); *mar* sich in die Riemen legen; *to go o.'s ~(s), to take o.'s ~* s-r Wege gehen; *fig* s-n Lauf nehmen; *to go out of the ~, out of o.'s ~* sich große, besondere Mühe geben (*for* wegen); e-n Umweg machen; *to go, to take o.'s own (fig) ~* s-n eigenen Weg gehen; *to have a ~ with s.o.* mit jdm umzugehen verstehen; *to have it both ~s* es sich aussuchen können; *to lead the ~* vorangehen *a. fig*; *fig* ein Beispiel geben; *to make ~* Platz machen (*for* für); *(to make o.'s ~)* vorwärts-, weiter-, vorankommen *a. fig*; sich e-n Weg bahnen; *to make the best of o.'s ~* gehen, so schnell man kann, so schnell e-n s-e Beine tragen; *to pave the ~ for s.o. (fig)* jdm den Weg ebnen; *to put s.o. in the ~ of* jdm Gelegenheit geben zu; *to put s.o. out of the ~* jdn aus dem Wege räumen; *to put o.s. out of the ~* sich alle Mühe geben; tun, was man kann; *to see o.'s ~ (clear)* bereit sein; es für geraten, angebracht, möglich halten; *to work o.'s ~ through college* das Geld für das Studium selbst verdienen; *that's the ~ he wants it* so will er es haben; *where there's a will there's a ~ (prov)* wo ein Wille ist, ist auch ein Weg; **6.** *parting of the ~s (fig)* Wendepunkt *m*; *permanent ~* Bahnkörper, Schienenweg *m*; *right of ~* Wegerecht; Vorfahrtsrecht *n*; *the W~ of the Cross (rel, Kunst)* die Leidensstationen *f pl*, der Kalvarienberg; **7.** *~ home* Heimweg *m*; *~ in, out* Ein-, Ausgang *m*; *~s and means* Mittel u. Wege; **~bill** Frachtbrief *m*; Passagierliste *f*; **~farer** ['-fɛərə] Reisende(r), Wanderer *m*; **~faring** ['-fɛəriŋ] *s a* (auf der) Reise, Wanderschaft *f*; **~going** im Weggehen begriffen, beim Aufbruch; **~lay** ['-lei] *irr s. lay tr* auflauern (*s.o.* jdm); **~-leave** Wegerecht *n*; **~-out** *a sl* ungewöhnlich, aus dem Rahmen fallend; **~side** *s* Straßenrand *m*; *a* am Straßenrand, an der Straße (befindlich); *by the ~~* an der Straße; *~~ inn* Rasthaus *n*, -stätte *f*; **~ station** *Am rail* Blockstation, Bedarfshaltestelle *f*; **~ train** *Am* Personen-, *fam* Bummelzug *m*; **~-up** *a Am fam* ausgezeichnet; **~worn** *a* müde von der Reise.

wayward ['weiwəd] widerspenstig, eigensinnig, -willig; launisch, launenhaft; **~ness** ['-nis] Widerspenstigkeit *f*, Eigensinn *m*; Launenhaftigkeit *f*.

we [wi:, wi] *prn* wir.

weak [wi:k] schwach *a. gram*; schwächlich; *(Spieler)* schlecht; *(Flüssigkeit)* dünn; *(Gemisch)* arm; *fig* halt-, willenlos, unselbständig; *(Argument)* nicht überzeugend; *~ at the knees (fig)* weich in den Knien; *a ~ point* ein schwacher Punkt *m*; *the ~er sex* das schwache Geschlecht; *a ~ spot* e-e schwache Stelle *f*; **~en** ['-ən] *tr* schwächen; *(Flüssigkeit)* verdünnen; *itr* schwächer werden, nachlassen; **~-eyed, -sighted** *a* schwachsichtig; **~-headed** *a* dumm; **~-hearted** *a* weich(herzig); **~-kneed** *a* schwach in den Knien; *fig* halt-, willenlos, charakterschwach; **~ling** ['-liŋ] *s* Schwächling *m*; **~ly** ['-li] *a adv* schwächlich, schwach; **~-minded** *a* schwachsinnig; willens-, charakterschwach, haltlos; **~ness** ['-nis] Schwäche; Kränklichkeit; *fig* schwache Seite, Schwäche *f* (*for* für); **~-spirited** *a* mutlos, *lit* kleinmütig.

weal [wi:l] **1.** Strieme *f*; **2.** *obs* Wohl (-fahrt *f*, -stand *m*) *n*; *for the common, general, public ~* im allgemeinen Interesse; *~ and woe* gute u. schlechte Tage.

wealth [welθ] Wohlstand; Reichtum *m* (*of* an); *com* Vermögen *n*, Besitz; *fig* Überfluß *m*, -maß *n*; Fülle *f*; **~y** ['-i] reich (*in* an); vermögend, wohlhabend; *com* kapitalkräftig.

wean [wi:n] *tr (Kind)* entwöhnen; *s.o. from s.th.* jdm etw abgewöhnen; jdn von etw abbringen.

weapon ['wepən] Waffe *f a. fig*; *a double-edged ~ (fig)* ein zweischneidiges Schwert; *~ of attack* Angriffswaffe *f*; **~less** ['-lis] waffenlos, unbewaffnet.

wear [wɛə] *irr* wore [wɔ:], worn [wɔ:n] *tr (Kleidung, Schmuck, Brille, Namen)* tragen; anhaben; *(Haar)* tragen; *(Miene)* zur Schau tragen, zeigen, haben; *(Flagge)* führen, zeigen; gewöhnen (*into* an); *(to ~ away)* abtragen, -nutzen; *(schadhafte Stelle, Loch)* hervorrufen, machen; *(e-n Pfad)* treten; *(Gestein)* auswaschen; ermüden, müde machen; *(to ~ away, out) (die Zeit)* vertreiben, totschlagen; *itr (Kleidung)* sich tragen; lange halten; sich abtragen, -nutzen; fadenscheinig werden; *(to ~ away, on)* ver-, herumgehen; *s* Tragen *n*; Gebrauch *m*, Benutzung; Kleidung, Tracht, Mode; (Grad *m* der) Abnutzung *f*, Verschleiß *m*; Haltbarkeit *f*, Widerstand(skraft *f*) *m*; *for hard ~* strapazierfähig; *to be in ~* getragen werden, Mode sein; *to be the worse for ~* abgetragen, abgenutzt, verbraucht, mitgenommen, in schlechtem Zustand sein; *to ~ the breeches (fig) (Frau)* die Hosen anhaben; *to ~ s.th. into holes* etw tragen, bis es e-m vom Leibe fällt; *to ~ thin* fadenscheinig werden; *fig* sich erschöpfen; *to ~ well* sich gut tragen; *fig* (noch) gut aussehen; *there's still a lot of ~ left in these shoes* diese Schuhe kann man noch lange tragen; *the gloves show signs of ~* die Handschuhe sehen schon etwas abgetragen aus; *foot* ~ Fußbekleidung *f*, Schuhwerk *n*; *men's, women's, children's* ~ Herren-, Damen-, Kinder(be)kleidung *f*; *suit for everyday* ~ Alltagsanzug *m*; *summer, winter* ~ Sommer-, Winterkleidung *f*; *town* ~ Straßenkleidung *f*; ~ *and tear* Abnutzung *f*, Verschleiß *m*; *com* Abschreibung *f* für Wertminderung; *to* ~ **away** *tr itr* (sich) abtragen, -nutzen; *(Zeit)* vergehen; *(Inschrift)* verblassen; *to* ~ **down** *tr* abnutzen; *(Sohlen, Absätze)* abtreten; *(Stufe)* austreten; ermüden, müde, mürbe machen; *(Widerstand)* zermürben; *(Geduld)* erschöpfen; *to* ~ **off** *tr itr* (sich) abnutzen; *itr* vergehen, dahinschwinden; *(Aufregung)* sich legen; *(Eindruck)* sich verlieren; *to* ~ **on** *(Zeit)* (dahin)schleichen, nicht vergehen wollen; *to* ~ **out** *tr* abtragen, -nutzen; verbrauchen; *(Reifen)* abfahren; erschöpfen; ermüden; *o.s.* sich abhetzen; *to* ~~ *o.'s welcome (Besuch)* zu lange bleiben; zu oft kommen; ~**able** ['-rəbl] *a* zu tragen(d), anzuziehen(d); *s pl* Kleidung(sstücke *n pl*) *f*; ~**ing** ['-riŋ] *a* Kleidungs-; abnutzend; ermüdend; ~~ *apparel* Kleidung, Garderobe *f*.

wear|iness ['wiərinis] Müdigkeit, Ermüdung *f*; *fig* Überdruß *m*, Langeweile *f*; ~**isome** ['-səm] ermüdend, mühevoll, mühselig, -sam; langweilig, unangenehm, lästig; ~**y** ['-i] *a* (er)müde(t), abgespannt, erschöpft (*with* von); müde, überdrüssig (*of s.th.* e-r S); ermüdend; lästig, unangenehm; *tr* ermüden; anwidern, langweilen; *itr* müde werden (*of* von).

weasel ['wi:zl] *s zoo* Wiesel *n*; *fig* Schleicher *m*; *itr Am (to* ~ *out)* sich aus dem Staub machen; ~-**faced** *a* mit e-m Spitzmausgesicht.

weather ['weðə] *s* Wetter *n*, Witterung; *mar* Wetterseite, Luv(seite) *f*; *tr* verwittern lassen; *(Holz)* (aus)trocknen, ablagern lassen; *(Dach)* abschrägen; *mar* luvwärts umschiffen; vorbeifahren an; *fig (to* ~ *through)* gut überstehen; *itr* verwittern, verblassen; auswittern; *a* Luv-; *in wet* ~ bei nassem Wetter; *in all* ~*s* bei jeder Witterung; *under the* ~ *(fam)* nicht auf dem Posten *od* Damm; leicht beschwipst; in der Patsche; *under stress of* ~ wegen schlechten Wetters; *to keep o.'s* ~ *eye open (fig)* die Augen aufhaben, aufpassen; *to make good, bad* ~ *(mar)* gutes, schlechtes Wetter haben; *to make heavy* ~ *of s.th.* etw sehr ernst nehmen; etw schwierig finden; *April* ~ Aprilwetter *n a. fig*; ~-**beam** *mar* Luv(seite) *f*; ~-**beaten** *a* durch Witterungseinflüsse beschädigt *od* verdorben; sonnenverbrannt; wetterhart, abgehärtet; ~-**board** = ~-*beam*; *pl u.* ~-**boarding** Holzverschalung *f*; ~-**bound** *a mar aero* durch schlechtes Wetter an der Abfahrt *od* am Start, an der Weiterfahrt *od* am Weiterflug gehindert; ~-**box** Wetterhäuschen *n*; ~-**bureau, -service** Wetterwarte *f*, -amt *n*, -dienst *m*; ~-**chart, -map** Wetterkarte *f*; ~**cock, -vane** Wetterhahn *m*, -fahne *f a. fig*; ~-**conditions** *pl* Wetterlage *f*, -verhältnisse *n pl*; ~**ed** ['-d] *a* verwittert; ~-**forecast, -report** Wettervorhersage *f*, -bericht *m*; ~**glass** Wetterglas, Barometer *n*; ~**ing** ['-riŋ] *geol* Verwitterung; *arch* Abschrägung *f*; ~**man** ['-mən] *fam* Wetterfrosch, Meteorologe *m*; ~ **plane** Wetterflugzeug *n*; ~-**proof, -tight** wetterfest; ~-**ship** Schiff *n* des Wetterdienstes; ~ **station** Wetterwarte *f*; ~-**strip** *(Fenster, Tür)* Wetterleiste *f*; ~-**wise** *a*: *to be* ~~ das Wetter voraussagen können; *fig* ein Stimmungsbarometer sein; ~-**worn** = ~-*beaten*.

weav|e [wi:v] *irr wove* [wouv], *wove(n)* ['wouv(ə)n] *tr* weben, wirken; (ein-) flechten (*into* in); *fig* ausdenken, ersinnen, erfinden; *(in e-e Erzählung)* verflechten (*with* mit; *into* in, zu); *itr* weben; sich verflechten; sich hin- u. herbewegen; *(Weg)* sich schlängeln; *aero sl* ausweichen; *s* Gewebe *n*; *to* ~~ *o.'s way* sich durchlavieren (*through* durch); *to get* ~*ing (sl)* sich ins Zeug legen; ~**er** ['-ə] Weber *m*; ~~-*bird* Webervogel *m*; ~~'*s hitch, knot* Weberknoten *m*; ~**ing** ['-iŋ] Webkunst, Weberei *f*; ~~-*loom* Webstuhl *m*; ~~-*mill* Weberei *f*.

weazen *s. wizen.*

web [web] Gewebe; *(cob*~*)* Spinnengewebe, -netz *n*; *fig* komplizierte Gedankengänge *m pl*; *fig* Netz *n*; Gurt (-band *n*) *m*; *anat* Gewebe *n*, Haut; *zoo* Flug-, Schwimmhaut; *arch* Gewölbefläche *(zwischen den Rippen)*; *(Feder)* Fahne *f*; *(Schlüssel)* Bart *m*; (Säge-)Blatt *n*; *typ* Papierrolle *f*; ~ *of lies* Lügengewebe, -netz *n*; ~**bed** [-d] gewebeartig; aus Gurt-, Tragbändern; = ~-*footed*; ~**bing** ['-iŋ] Gurt-, Tragband *n*; ~**foot** *zoo* Schwimmfuß *m*; ~-**footed, -toed** *a* mit Schwimmfüßen versehen.

wed [wed] *tr* heiraten; trauen; *fig* eng verbinden, vereinigen (*with, to* mit); *itr* sich verheiraten, sich verehelichen; ~**ded** ['-id] *a* verheiratet; Ehe-; *fig* (ganz) hingegeben (*to* an); (eng) verbunden (*to* mit), gekettet (*to* an); ~**ding** ['-iŋ] Heirat, Hochzeit, Vermählung; Trauung(sfeierlichkeiten *f pl*) *f*; ~~ *breakfast* Hochzeitsessen *n*; ~~-*cake* Hochzeitskuchen *m*; ~~-*card* Heiratsanzeige *f*; ~~-*ceremony* Trauung *f*; ~~-*day, -dress, -guest, -present, -trip* Hochzeitstag *m*, -kleid *n*, -gast *m*, -geschenk *n*, -reise *f*; ~~-*ring* Ehe-, Trauring *m*; ~**lock** ['-lɔk] Ehe *f*; *born out of* ~~ unehelich geboren.

we'd [wi:d] *fam* = *we had, we should, we would.*

wedg|e [wedʒ] *s* Keil *m a mil u. fig*; *(keilförmiges)* Stück *n (Torte, Kuchen)*; *tr* (mit e-m Keil) spalten; verkeilen; *(to* ~ *in)* (hinein)stopfen, zs.pferchen; *itr* keilförmig stoßen; *to* ~~ *o.s. in* sich hineinzwängen, -drängen; *to be* ~~*d between* eingekeilt, eingezwängt sein zwischen; *the thin end of the* ~~ der erste Anfang, das Vorspiel; ~~ *formation (aero)* Keilformation *f*; ~~-*shaped (a)* keilförmig; ~~ *writing* Keilschrift *f*; ~**ie** ['-i] *Am fam* Keilabsatz *m*.

Wednesday ['wenzdi] Mittwoch *m*; *on* ~ am Mittwoch; *on* ~*s* mittwochs; *Ash* ~ Aschermittwoch *m*.

wee [wi:] *a* winzig(klein); *a* ~ *bit* ein bißchen, ein wenig; ziemlich.

weed [wi:d] *s* Unkraut *n a. fig*; *fig* Schwächling *m*; wertlose(s) Tier *n*; *fam* Glimmstengel; *fam* Tabak *m*; *tr (Garten)* jäten; *(to* ~ *out) fig* entfernen, ausmerzen; *fig* säubern, befreien (*of* von); *the garden is running to* ~*s* der Garten ist voller Unkraut; ~**er** ['-ə] Jäter *m*; Jäthacke *f*; ~-**killer** Unkrautvertilgungsmittel *n*; ~**y** ['-i] voller Unkraut; wie Unkraut wachsend; *fig* hager, dürr, schwächlich.

weeds [wi:dz] *pl* Trauerkleidung *f*; *(widow's* ~*)* Witwenkleider *n pl*.

week [wi:k] Woche *f*; *by the* ~ wochenweise; wöchentlich; *for* ~*s* wochenlang; *this day, yesterday, Sunday* ~ heute, gestern, Sonntag in *od* vor 8 Tagen; *a* ~ *from tomorrow* morgen in 8 Tagen; *once a* ~ (einmal) wöchentlich; ~ *after* ~, ~ *by* ~, ~ *in*, ~ *out* Woche für Woche, jede Woche; *a* ~ *or two* ein paar Wochen; *a* ~ *of Sundays* e-e (halbe) Ewigkeit! *what day of the* ~*?* an welchem Tag? *three* ~*s' leave* dreiwöchige(r) Urlaub *m*; ~ *under review* Berichtswoche *f*; ~-**day** Wochen-, Arbeitstag *m*; *on* ~~*s* werktäglich; ~-**end** *s* Wochenende *n*; *attr* Wochenend-; *itr* das Wochenende verbringen *od* verleben (*at, in* in); *long* ~~ verlängerte(s) Wochenende *n*; ~~ *ticket* Sonntagsrückfahrkarte *f*; ~~ *visit* Wochenendbesuch *m*; ~-**ender** Wochenendausflügler *m*; ~**ly** ['-li] *a* wöchentlich; *adv* wöchentlich, einmal in der Woche; *s* Wochenblatt *n*, -beilage *f*; ~~ *pay* Wochenlohn *m*; ~~ *report* Wochenbericht *m*.

ween [wi:n] *itr obs poet* wähnen, glauben, denken.

weenie, weeny ['wi:ni] *Am fam* Wiener (Würstchen) *n*.

weeny ['wi:ni] *fam* winzig.

weep [wi:p] *irr wept, wept* [wept] *itr* weinen, Tränen vergießen (*for* um; *at, over* über); beweinen (*for s.o.* jdn); *allg* schwitzen, triefen, tröpfeln; *tr* beweinen, beklagen; *(Tränen)* vergießen, weinen; *(Tropfen)* fallen lassen; *to* ~ *o.'s eyes out* sich die Augen ausweinen; *to* ~ *o.s. to sleep* sich in den Schlaf weinen; *to* ~ *for joy* vor Freude weinen; ~**er** ['-ə] Weinende(r), Trauernde(r); weinerliche(r) Mensch; Trauerflor, -schleier *m*, -abzeichen *n*; *pl sl* Backenbart *m*; *Am film* rührselige(r) Film *m*, Schnulze *f* = ~**ie**, ~**y** ['-i]; ~**ing** ['-iŋ] *a* weinend, jammernd; schwitzend, nässend, tröpfelnd; *bot* Trauer-; *s* Weinen, Wehklagen *n*; Trauer *f*; ~~ *willow* Trauerweide *f*.

weevil ['wi:vil] Rüsselkäfer, Rüßler *m*.

weft [weft] *(Weberei)* Einschlag *m*; Schußfäden *m pl*; Gewebe *n*; *fig* Dunst-, Nebel-, Wolkenschleier *m*.

weigh [wei] *tr* (ab)wiegen (*in the scales* auf der Waage); *(to* ~ *out)* auswiegen; *(to* ~ *up)* abwägen *a. fig*; *fig* (gut) überlegen; abschätzen; prüfen; gegenüberstellen (*against s.th.* e-r S); vergleichen (*against* mit); berücksichtigen; *itr* wiegen; *fig* Gewicht haben, von Bedeutung, ausschlaggebend sein (*with s.o.* bei jdm); drücken, e-n Druck ausüben, lasten (*on, upon* auf); *mar (to* ~ *anchor)* die Anker lichten, abfahren, in See stechen; *to* ~ *down* niederdrücken *a. fig*; *to* ~ *in (tr itr sport)* (ab)wiegen; *itr* anführen, vorbringen (*with s.th.* etw); *s*: *under* ~ *(mar)* unter Segel; *to* ~ *o.'s words* s-e Worte auf die Goldwaage legen; ~**able** ['-əbl] wägbar; ~-**beam** Waagebalken *m*; ~-**bridge** Brückenwaage *f*; ~**er** ['-ə] Waagemeister *m*; ~-**house** (Stadt-)Waage *f (Haus)*; ~-**in** *sport* Wiegen *n*; ~**ing-machine** Brückenwaage *f*.

weight [weit] *s* Gewicht *n a. fig*; *phys* Schwere; Gewichtseinheit *f*, -system; Gewichtstück; *sport* Gewicht *(zum Heben)*; (Uhr-)Gewicht *n*; *(paper*~*)* Briefbeschwerer *m*; *fig* (schwere) Last, Bürde; Wichtigkeit, Bedeutung; Macht *f*, Einfluß *m*, Ansehen *n*; *(Statistik)* Häufigkeit, Wertigkeit *f*; *tr* beschweren, belasten, Gewicht auflegen auf; *fig* belasten, bedrücken; *(Gewebe)* verstärken; *(Statistik)* Bedeutung beimessen (*s.th.* e-r S), bewerten; *to* ~ *down* beladen (*with* mit); *by* ~ nach Gewicht; *of* ~ gewichtig; *over, under* ~ zu schwer, zu leicht; *to attach ~ to s.th. (fig)* e-r S Gewicht beimessen; *to carry ~ (fig)* Gewicht, Macht, Einfluß haben (*with* auf); ins Gewicht fallen; *to fall short of ~* nicht das nötige Gewicht haben; *to lose ~* (an Gewicht) abnehmen; *to pull o.'s ~* s-e Pflicht tun; sein(en) Teil leisten; *to put the ~ (sport)* kugelstoßen; *to put on ~ (Mensch)* zunehmen, schwerer werden; *to throw o.'s ~ about (fam)* s-e Stellung, s-n Einfluß ausnutzen; *atomic ~ (chem)* Atomgewicht *n*; *dead ~* Leer-, Eigengewicht *n*; *excess, surplus ~* Übergewicht *n*; *gross, net ~* Brutto-, Nettogewicht *n*; **~iness** ['-inis] große(s) Gewicht *n*, Schwere *f a. fig*; *fig* Ernst *m*, Wichtigkeit, Bedeutung *f*; **~-lifting** *sport* Gewichtheben *n*; **~ loss** Gewichtsverlust *m*; **~ rod** Lastarm *m*; **~y** ['-i] schwer *a. fig*; *fig* (ge)wichtig, bedeutend; ernst; *(Grund)* triftig.

weir [wiə] Wehr *n*, Damm *m*; (Fisch-)Reuse *f*.

weird [wiəd] *a* unheimlich; übernatürlich; Schicksals-; *fam* komisch, ulkig, verrückt; *s bes. Scot* Schicksal *n*; *the W~ Sisters (pl)* die Parzen; **~ie** ['-i] *sl* komische(r) Kauz *m*.

welcome ['welkəm] *a* willkommen, gern gesehen; erfreulich, angenehm; *s* Willkomm(en *n*, *a. m*); Willkommensgruß *m*; *interj* willkommen! *tr* bewillkommnen, willkommen heißen; freudig begrüßen; *fig* begrüßen, gern sehen; *to bid ~ to s.o., to make s.o. ~* jdn willkommen heißen; *to give s.o. a warm ~* jdm e-n herzlichen Willkomm bereiten; *you are ~ to use my car* mein Wagen steht zu Ihrer Verfügung; *(you are) ~* bitte sehr, gern geschehen, nichts zu danken! *I should ~ it if ...* ich würde es begrüßen, wenn ...; *~ to England!* willkommen in England!

weld [weld] *tr tech* schweißen, löten; *fig* zs.schweißen, eng (mitea.) verbinden; *itr* sich schweißen lassen; *s* Schweißen *n*; Schweißstelle, -naht, -fläche *f*; **~able** ['-əbl] schweißbar; **~er** ['-ə] Schweißer *m*; **~ing** ['-iŋ] Schweißen *n*; *~~ seam, torch* Schweißnaht *f*, -brenner *m*.

welfare ['welfɛə] Wohlergehen *n*; Wohlfahrt; Fürsorge *f*; **~ centre** Wohlfahrtsamt *n*, Fürsorgestelle *f*; **~ department** Sozialabteilung *f*; **~ officer** Truppenbetreuungsoffizier *m*; **W~ State** Wohlfahrtsstaat *m*; **~ work** Wohlfahrtspflege, Fürsorge *f*; *industrial ~~* betriebliche Sozialfürsorge *f*; *~~ for the unemployed* Arbeitslosenfürsorge *f*; **~ worker** Wohlfahrtspfleger; *(Fabrik)* (Sozial-)Fürsorger *m*.

welkin ['welkin] *obs poet* Himmelszelt *n*; *to make the ~ ring (fig)* die Erde erzittern lassen (*with* mit).

well [wel] **1.** *s* Brunnen(schacht) *m*; *min* Bohrloch *n*, Schacht *m*; *poet* Quelle *f a. fig*; *arch* Treppenhaus *n*, Fahrstuhlschacht; Lichthof; *Br jur* eingefriedete(r) Platz *m* der Anwälte; (eingelassener) Behälter *m*, Reservoir *(für e-e Flüssigkeit)*; *mot* Felgenbett *n*, Kofferraum; *fig* Ursprung *m*, Quelle *f*; *itr* quellen, sprudeln, fließen, sich ergießen (*from* aus); *to ~ out* ausfließen, austreten; *to ~ over* überfließen; *to ~ up* aufsteigen; *tr* hervorquellen, -sprudeln lassen; *to drive, to sink a ~* e-n Brunnen bohren; *bucket-~* Ziehbrunnen *m*; *~ of information* Informations-, Nachrichtenquelle *f*; **~-head** Quelle *f*; **~-shaft** Brunnenschacht *m*; **~-spring** Quelle *f*; *fig* unerschöpfliche(r) Born *m*; **~-wag(g)on** Tiefladewagen *m*; **~-water** Brunnenwasser *n*; **2.** *adv* gut; durchaus, mit Recht, mit gutem Grund; weit, sehr; (ganz) genau; günstig; wohl; *a* gut, angebracht, recht, richtig; wohlauf, gesund; in Ordnung; *interj* hm! nun! nanu! na! leider! gut! schön! also! *s* Gute(s) *n*; *as ~* ebensogut *adv*; auch, ebenfalls; ebenso; *as ~ ... as* ebenfalls, auch; sowohl ... als auch; nicht nur ... sondern auch; *as ~ as* ebensogut wie; *~ enough* gut genug; *~ and good* schön u. gut; *~ away* gut vorangekommen; *sl* besoffen; *just as ~* ebensogut; *pretty ~* so ziemlich; *to be ~ out of s.th.* etw gut, heil überstehen; *to come off ~* Glück haben; gut abschneiden; *to do ~* wohlauf sein; gut daran tun; *to feel ~* sich wohl fühlen; *to get ~* gesund werden; *to let ~ alone* sich zufriedengeben; sich nicht einmischen; *to stand ~ with s.o.* sich mit jdm gutstehen; *he's doing very ~* es geht ihm sehr gut; *it's all very ~ (iro)* das ist alles ganz gut u. schön; *let ~ enough alone* lassen Sie's gut sein! *~ done!* recht so! gut (so)! *~ met!* gut getroffen! *all's ~ that ends ~* Ende gut, alles gut; **~-advised** *a (Handlung)* klug, wohlüberlegt; **~-appointed, -found** *a* gut ausgerüstet; **~-balanced** *a* wohl ausgewogen, gut ausgeglichen, im Gleichgewicht; **~-behaved** *a* von gutem Benehmen; artig, brav; **~-being** Wohl(befinden, -sein) *n*; **~born** *a* von guter Herkunft; **~-bred** *a* wohlerzogen; *(Pferd)* von edler Rasse; Rasse-; **~-built** *a* gut gebaut; **~-chosen** *a* gut (aus)gewählt, passend; **~-conducted** *a* von guter Führung; **~-connected** *a* mit guten verwandtschaftlichen Beziehungen; **~-content** durchaus zufrieden; **~-deserved** *a* wohlverdient; **~-disposed** *a* wohlgesinnt *(towards* dat); **~-doer** gute(r) Mensch *m*; **~-doing** Rechtschaffenheit *f*; **~-done** *a* wohlgetan; *(Fleisch)* gar, *fam* gut durch; *interj* gut (so)! **~-dressed** *a* gut angezogen *od* gekleidet; **~-established** *a* wohlerworben; **~-favo(u)red** *a* gut aussehend, nett, hübsch; **~-fed** *a* wohlgenährt, rund (-lich); **~-fixed** *a Am fam* in angenehmen Verhältnissen (lebend); **~-founded** *a* (wohl)begründet; **~-groomed** *a (Pferd, Mensch)* gut gepflegt; **~-grounded** *a* mit gründlichen Kenntnissen; wohlbegründet; **~-handled** *a* gut geführt; **~-heeled** *a sl* steinreich; **~-informed** *a* gut unterrichtet; **~-intentioned, -meaning** *a* wohlmeinend; **~-kept** *a* gepflegt; **~-knit, -set** *a* gut gebaut; **~-known** *a* (wohl)bekannt; **~-made** *a* gut gebaut, proportioniert; *lit* kunstvoll (gestaltet); **~-mannered** *a* von guten Manieren, gutem Benehmen, höflich; **~-meant** *a* wohlgemeint; **~-met** *a* gut zs.passend, wie fürea. geschaffen; **~-nigh** ['welnai] *adv* beinahe, fast; **~-off** *a* in guten Verhältnissen; wohlhabend; **~-oiled** *a sl* besoffen; *fig* schmeichelhaft; **~-ordered** *a* (wohl)geordnet, in guter Ordnung; **~-paid** *a* wohlbezahlt; **~-preserved** *a* gut erhalten, in gutem Zustand; **~-priced** *a* preisgünstig; **~-proportioned** *a* wohlproportioniert; **~-read** *a* belesen; *fam* bewandert, beschlagen (*in* in); **~-rounded** *a* abgerundet, ebenmäßig; **~ set-up** *a* standhaft, fest; **~-spoken** *a* gut gesprochen; redegewandt; sich höflich ausdrückend; **~-thought-of** *a* von gutem Ruf; **~-timed** *a* im rechten Augenblick gesagt *od* getan; geeignet, passend; **~-to-do** wohlhabend, **~-tried** *a* erprobt; bewährt; **~-trodden** *a* vielbenutzt; **~-turned** *a fig* gut ausgedrückt, abgerundet; **~-wisher** Wohlgesinnte(r), Gönner, Freund *m*; **~-worn** *a* viel getragen; abgenutzt; *fig* abgedroschen.

we'll [wi:l] *fam* = we shall, we will.

Welsh [welʃ] *a* walisisch; *s* (das) Walisisch(e); **~man, ~woman** Waliser(in *f*) *m*; **~ rabbit, ~ rarebit** Toast *m* mit zerlassenem Käse.

welsh [welʃ] *tr itr* (um den Wettgewinn) betrügen; **~er** ['-ə] Betrüger, Schwindler *m*.

welt [welt] *s* Saum *m*, Einfassung *f*, Rand *m*; Stoßkante; Strieme(n *m*) *f*; (Peitschen-)Hieb, Schlag *m*; *tr* säumen, einfassen; *fam* verdreschen.

welter ['weltə] **1.** *itr* sich wälzen (*in* in); *(Wellen)* sich überschlagen, rollen; *s* Rollen, Sichüberschlagen; *fig* Durcheinander *n*, Wirrwarr *m*; **2.** Weltergewicht(ler *m*) *n (Reiter* od *Boxer)*; *fam* mächtige(s) Ding, Riesenbiest *n*; **~weight** Weltergewicht(sboxer *m*) *n*.

wen [wen] gutartige Geschwulst *(bes. am Kopf)*; *fig* Bevölkerungsballung, Weltstadt *f*; *the great ~* London *n*.

wench [wentʃ] *obs hum* (Bauern-)Mädchen *n*, Landpomeranze; Dirne *f*.

wend [wend] *tr*: *to ~ o.'s way to* s-e Schritte lenken nach.

were [wə:, wɛə, wə] *2. sing u. 1.–3. pl Indikativ pret od Konjunktiv pret von to be*; *as it ~* gewissermaßen, gleichsam, sozusagen; *as you ~! (mil)* Kommando zurück!

we're [wiə] = *we are.*

weren't [wə:nt] = *were not.*

west [west] *s* West(en) *m*; *the W~* die westliche Hemisphäre *f*; das Abendland; *Am* die Weststaaten; *a* westlich; West-; *adv* im Westen; nach dem Westen, in westlicher Richtung; *~ of* westlich von; *to go ~ (sl)* abkratzen; **~bound** *a* nach Westen gehend *od* fahrend; *the* **W~ End** das Westend *(vornehmes Wohnviertel von London)*; **~erly** ['-əli] *a* westlich; *(Wind)* West-; aus westlicher Richtung; *s* Westwind *m*; *adv* nach *od* aus Westen; **~ern** ['-ən] *a* westlich; westwärts; *(Wind)* West-; *W~~* westlich, abendländisch; *s* = *~erner*; Wildwestgeschichte *f*, -roman, -film *m*; *the W~~ Empire (hist)* das Weströmische Reich; **~erner** ['-ənə] Abendländer(in *f*) *m*; *W~~ (amerik.)* Weststaatler(in *f*) *m*; **~ernize** ['-ənaiz] *tr* verwestlichen; **~ernmost** ['-ənmoust] am weitesten nach Westen gelegen; *the* **W~ Indies** *pl* Westindien *n*; **~-north-~** *s* Westnordwest *m*; *a adv* westnordwestlich; Westnordwest-; **W~phalia** [west'feiljə] Westfalen *n*; **W~phalian** [-'feiljən] *a* westfälisch; *s* Westfale *m*, -fälin *f*; **~-south-~** *s* Westsüdwest *m*; *a adv* westsüdwestlich; Westsüdwest-; **~ward** ['-wəd] *a* nach Westen gerichtet; West-; *adv* westwärts; *s* westliche Richtung *f*; Westen *m*; **~wards** ['-wədz] *adv* westwärts, nach Westen.

wet [wet] *a* naß, feucht (*with* von); regennaß, -feucht, regnerisch, neb(e)lig; *(Farbe)* frisch; *tech* Naß-; *dial sl* dem Suff ergeben; *sl* verrückt; unsympathisch, widerlich; sentimental; *Am* das Alkoholverbot ablehnend; *s* Nässe, Feuchtigkeit *f*; Regen(wetter *n*); *sl* Schluck Schnaps; *sl* blöde(r), sentimentale(r) Kerl; *Am* Nasser, Gegner *m* des Alkoholverbots; *tr itr* (*to ~ through, down*) naß machen, werden; *tr* durchfeuchten; naß machen; *sl* begießen; *all ~ (Am sl)* auf dem Holzwege; *~ to the skin* naß bis auf die Haut; *~ with tears* tränenfeucht; *to be ~ through (and through)* durch u. durch naß sein; *to ~ o.'s whistle (fam)* e-n hinter die Binde kippen; *~ paint!* frisch gestrichen! **~back** *Am fam* illegale(r) Einwanderer *m* aus Mexiko; *~* **blanket** *med* feuchte(r) Umschlag *m*; *fig fam* kalte Dusche *f*, Dämpfer; Spaß-, Spielverderber; Miesmacher *m*; **~-blanket** *tr (Sache)* vermiesen, verekeln; den Spaß nehmen an; die Lust nehmen zu; *~* **dock** Flutbecken *n*; **~ness** ['-nis] Nässe, Feuchtigkeit; Schmierigkeit *f*; *~* **nurse** Amme *f*; **~-nurse** *tr* als Amme säugen; *fig* verhätscheln; *~* **pack** *med* feuchte Packung *f*, Umschläge *m pl*, Kompressen *f pl*; *~* **season** Regenzeit *f*; **~ting** ['-iŋ] Dusche *f*, (Regen-)Guß *m*; *to get a ~~* durchnäßt, naß werden; **~tish** ['-iʃ] etwas feucht.

wether ['weðə] *zoo* Hammel, Schöps *m*.

we've [wi:v] = *we have*.

whack [(h)wæk] *tr itr* klatschen, kräftig schlagen; *fam* besiegen; *fam* aus-, verteilen; *sl (to ~ up)* beschleunigen; *s fam* heftige(r) Schlag, Knall, Bums; *sl* Versuch; *fam* Anteil *m*; *out of ~ (Am sl)* nicht in Ordnung, hin(über), kaputt; *to have a ~ at s.th. (Am sl)* sich an was 'ranmachen; **~er** ['-ə] *sl* dicke(r) Brocken *m*, mächtige(s) Ding *n*; faustdicke Lüge *f*; **~ing** ['-iŋ] *a fam* dick, gewaltig, mächtig, kolossal; *adv fam* mächtig, gewaltig, mordsmäßig; *s* Tracht Prügel, Dresche *f*; **~o** ['wækou] *interj sl* großartig, famos.

whacky *s. wacky.*

whal|e [(h)weil] **1.** *s* Wal(fisch) *m*; *itr (to go ~ing)* auf Walfang gehen; *a ~~ at (fam)* ein Fachmann in; *a ~~ for (fam)* scharf auf; *a ~~ of a (fam)* e-e wahnsinnige Menge *gen*; *~~-boat* Walfänger *m (Boot)*; *~~bone* Fischbein *n*; *~~-calf* junge(r) Wal *m*; *~~man* Walfänger *m (Mensch)* *~~-oil* Walfischtran *m*; **~er** ['-ə] Walfänger; *Am sl* Mordskerl *m*; **~ing** ['-iŋ] *s* Walfang *m*; *a Am sl* riesig, kolossal; *~~ gun* Harpunengeschütz *n*; **2.** *tr fam* verdreschen, versohlen, verprügeln; **~ing** ['-iŋ] *s fam* Dresche *f*.

whang [(h)wæŋ] *fam tr* schlagen, knallen, klatschen; *itr* knallen, krachen, bumsen; *s* Knall, Bums *m*.

whap *s. whop.*

wharf [(h)wɔ:f] *s pl ~s* od *wharves* ['-vz] Kai, Pier, Hafendamm *m*; Landungsbrücke *f*; *tr (Schiff)* anlegen; löschen, ausladen; **~age** ['-idʒ] Anlegen; Löschen *n*; Kaigebühr *f*, -geld *n*, -anlagen *f pl*; **~inger** ['-indʒə] Kaieigentümer, -meister *m*; *~* **rat** *Am* Wanderratte *f*; *sl* Hafendieb *m*.

what [(h)wɔt] *prn (fragend u. ausrufend)* was, wie; was für (ein); welche(r, s); *(relativ)* was; das, was; so viel(e) wie; *a* was für ein, welch; *and ~ not* u. was nicht noch alles; *but ~ (fam)* außer dem, der, daß; *~ about, of?* wie steht es mit ...? wie wäre es mit ...? was macht ...? *~ for?* warum? weshalb? wozu? wofür? zu welchem Zweck? *~ have you (Am fam)* dergleichen; *~ if* (u.) was geschieht, soll geschehen, wenn ...? *~ is more* außerdem; darüber hinaus; dazu kommt noch; zwar; *~ price?* wie teuer? *~ it takes (Am fam)* was man so braucht; *~ though* wenn ... auch; *~ with ... and (~ with)* teils durch ... u. teils durch ...; *to know ~'s ~* wissen, was los ist; sich zu helfen wissen; *~'s your name?* wie heißen Sie? *~ is he like?* wie sieht er aus? wie ist er? *~ next?* was nun? *~ of it!* was ist schon dabei! *~ is up?* was ist (denn) los? *that's just ~* gerade das; *I don't know ~'s ~ any more* ich kenne mich nicht mehr aus; *~'s that to you?* was geht Sie das an? *~ time is it?* wieviel Uhr ist es? *the ~'s ~* der wirkliche Sachverhalt; *Mr ~-d'you-call-him, Mr ~'s-his-name* Herr Dingsda, Herr Soundso; **~ever,** *betont* **~soever,** *poet* **~e'er,** *poet betont* **~soe'er** was auch (immer), alles, was; was für ... auch (immer); was in der Welt; welche(r, s) ... auch (immer); überhaupt; *no ... ~~* überhaupt kein; *~~ you say* nach Belieben; **~-for** *fam* Prügel *m pl*, Dresche *f*; **~-is-it,whassit** ['wɔsit] *Am* Dings(da) *n*; **~not** Etagere; Kleinigkeit *f*.

wheal [(h)wi:l] **1.** Pickel *m*, Pustel *f*; Insektenstich *m*; Strieme *f*; **2.** = *wale*.

wheat [(h)wi:t] Weizen *m*; *field of ~* Weizenfeld *n*; *shredded ~* Weizenflocken *f pl*; *~* **belt** *Am* Weizengürtel *m*; *~* **ear** Weizenähre *f*; **~en** ['-n] *a* Weizen-; *~* **flour** Weizenmehl *n*; *~* **harvest** Weizenernte *f*.

wheedle ['(h)wi:dl] *tr* schmeicheln (*s.o.* jdm); beschwatzen (*into doing s.th.* etw zu tun); abschmeicheln, abschwatzen (*s.th. out of s.o.* jdm etw).

wheel [(h)wi:l] *s* Rad; *(Pyrotechnik)* Feuerrad; *mar* Steuerrad; *mot (steering ~)* Steuer(rad), Lenkrad; *(spinning-~)* Spinnrad *n*; *(potter's ~)* Töpferscheibe *f*; *Am fam* (Fahr-)Rad *n*; *Am fam* Dollar(stück *n*) *m*; (Um-)Drehung; *mil* Schwenkung; *fig* Wiederholung, Wiederkehr *f*; Kehrreim, Refrain *m*; *fig* Ruder; *pl* Räderwerk, Getriebe *n*; *tr* rollen; transportieren; fahren; drehen, rotieren lassen; *(Rad, Kreis)* schlagen; *(Wagen)* ziehen, schieben; *itr (to ~ round)* sich drehen, rotieren; ein Rad schlagen; *fig (to ~ about)* e-e Schwenkung machen; rollen, fahren; auf Rädern laufen; *fam* radeln; *to ~ about (itr)* sich herumdrehen; *fig* s-e Meinung ändern; *tr* herumfahren; *at the ~* am Steuer; *fig* am Ruder; *on ~s* auf Rädern; *fig* reibungslos; *on the ~* auf Achse; *to break on the ~ (hist)* rädern *(Strafe)*; *to put o.'s shoulders to the ~ (fig)* Hand ans Werk legen; *to put a spoke in s.o.'s ~* jdm e-n Stein in den Weg legen; *the man at the ~* der Fahrer; *~ and axle (tech)* Winde *f*; *the ~ of fortune* das Glücksrad *n*; die Wechselfälle *m pl* des Lebens; *~s within ~s* komplizierte(r) Vorgang *m*, komplizierte Verhältnisse *n pl*; **~barrow** Schubkarren *m*; **~-base** *mot* Rad-, Achsstand *m*; *~* **bearing** Radlager *n*; *~* **cap** Radkappe *f*; **~-chair** Rollstuhl *m*; *~* **deflection** Radausschlag *m*; **~-drag** Hemmschuh *m*; **~ed** [-d] *a (in Zssg mit e-m Zahlwort)* -rädrig; **~er** ['-ə] *(~-horse)* Stangenpferd *n*; *(in Zssg mit e-m Zahlwort)* -rädrige(s) Fahrzeug *n*; Stellmacher; Fahrer *m*; *~* **gear** Zahnradgetriebe *n*; **~-horse** Stangenpferd; *Am fig* Arbeitstier *n*; **~-house** *mar* Ruderhaus *n*; *~* **hub** Radnabe *f*; **~ing** ['-iŋ] Fahren; *Am* Radfahren *n*; (Um-)Drehung *f*; Straßenzustand *m*; **~man** ['-mən] *fam* Radfahrer *m*; *~* **nut** Radmutter *f*; *~* **rim** Radkranz *m*, -felge *f*; **~sman** *Am mar* Steuermann *m*; *~* **track** Radspur *f*; **~-window** *arch* Radfenster *n*; **~wright** ['-rait] Stellmacher, Wagner *m*.

wheez|e [(h)wi:z] *itr* keuchen; *tr (to ~ out) (Worte)* pfeifend herausbringen; *(Töne)* quietschend von sich geben; *s* pfeifende(s) Geräusch, Keuchen *n*; *bes. theat* Scherz, Witz *m*, witzige Bemerkung; lustige Geschichte *f*; *Am sl* faule(r) Witz *m*, abgedroschene Redensart *f*; schlaue(r), raffinierte(r) Plan *m*; **~y** ['-i] pfeifend; keuchend.

whelk [welk] **1.** *zoo* Wellhornschnecke *f*; **2.** Pickel *m*, Pustel *f*.

whelp [(h)welp] junge(r) Hund, Welpe; *pej* Bengel, Bursche *m*, Bürschchen *n*; *tr itr* (Junge) werfen; *pej (Kind)* in die Welt setzen.

when [(h)wen] *adv (fragend)* wann; *(relativ)* als, wo, da; *since, until ~* seit, bis wann? *conj* als; wenn, nachdem; obwohl, obgleich; während, wo ... doch; (jedesmal) wenn, sobald; u. dann; *s* Zeitpunkt, Umstand *m*; *the ~ and where of s.th.* die zeitlichen u. örtlichen Umstände e-r S; **~ever** [-'evə], *(betont)* **~soever** [-so(u)'evə], *poet* **~e'er** ['-εə] *adv conj* wann auch immer.

whence [(h)wens] *adv obs* woher, von wo *a. fig*; *fig* wovon, wodurch; *~ comes it that?* wie kommt es, daß; *conj* von woher; *fig* weshalb.

where [(h)wεə] *adv (fragend u. relativ)* wo; wohin; worin; inwiefern; *conj* dorthin wo; **~about(s)** ['-rə'baut(s)] *adv* wo(herum); wohin; *s pl mit sing od pl* ['---] Aufenthalt(sort) *m*; **~as** [-r'æz] während, wohingegen; *jur* nachdem, da nun; mit Rücksicht darauf, daß; **~at** [-r'æt] *adv obs* wobei, worauf, worüber; **~by** [-'bai] *adv* wodurch, wie; **~'er** [-r'εə] *poet* = *~ver*; **~fore** ['-fɔ:] *adv conj* warum; weshalb; wofür; wozu; zu welchem Zweck; **~from** [-'frɔm] *adv conj* woher; von wo; **~in** [-r'in] *adv* worin; in dem, der; *~~ am I mistaken?* was habe ich falsch gemacht? **~of** [-r'ɔv] *adv conj* wovon, von was; **~on** [-r'ɔn] *adv conj* worauf; auf was; *(relativ)* auf dem, der; **~soe'er** [-sou'εə] *poet*, **~soever** [-'evə] *(betont) adv* wo(hin) auch immer; **~to** [-'tu:] *adv* wohin; wozu; **~upon** [-rə'pɔn] *adv conj* worauf; woraufhin; **~ver** [-r'evə] *adv* wo(hin) auch immer; **~with** [-'wiθ] *adv obs* womit; **~withal** [-wi'ðɔ:l] *adv obs* = *~with*; *s: the ~~* ['-wiðɔ:l] die (erforderlichen) Mittel *n pl*.

wherry ['(h)weri] Jolle *f*; Fährschiff *n*; Lastkahn *m*; Barke *f*.

whet [(h)wet] *tr* wetzen, schleifen, schärfen; *fig* anspornen, -treiben, aufstacheln; *(den Appetit)* anregen; *s* Wetzen, Schleifen *n*; *fig* Ansporn *m*, Anregung *f*; Reizmittel *n*; Appetitanreger, Aperitif *m*; **~stone** Wetz-, Schleifstein *m*.

whether ['(h)weðə] *conj* ob; *~ ... or (~)* ob ... oder (ob); *~ ... or not* ob ... oder (ob) nicht; *~ or no* auf jeden Fall, auf alle Fälle, so oder so.

whew [ju:, hwu:] *interj* hu! oh!

whey [(h)wei] Molke *f*; **~ey** ['-i] käsig; Molke-; **~-faced** *a (Mensch)* käsig.

which [(h)witʃ] *prn (relativ)* der, die, das; welche(r, s); was *(relativ)*; *(fragend)* welche(r, s); *a* welche(r, s); **~ever** [-'evə], *betont* **~soever** [-so(u)'evə] *prn* welche(r, s) auch immer.

whiff [(h)wif] *s* leichte(r) Windstoß, (Wind-)Hauch, (Luft-)Zug; plötzliche(r) *od* vorüberstreichende(r) Geruch *m*; (kleine) Dampf-, Rauch-, Qualmwolke *f*; Zug *m (an e-r Zigarette)*; *fam* Zigarillo *m od n*; *itr tr* blasen, paffen; unangenehm riechen; *tr* weg-

blasen; **~le** ['-l] *itr (Wind)* blasen; treiben, flattern, zucken, schwanken; **~y** ['-i] übelriechend.
Whig [(h)wig] *s (England)* Whig, Liberale(r); *(US, hist)* Revolutionär *(im Unabhängigkeitskrieg)*; Anhänger *m* e-r antidemokratischen Oppositionspartei *(um 1850)*; *attr* Whig-; liberal.
while [(h)wail] *s* Weile, Zeit(spanne) *f*; *tr (to ~ away) (Zeit)* (angenehm) verbringen, sich vertreiben; *conj a. whilst* ['-st] während, solange (wie, als), indem; während, wohingegen; obwohl, obgleich; *all this ~* die ganze Zeit; dauernd; *between ~s* dann u. wann, hin u. wieder, ab u. zu; *for a ~* e-e Zeitlang; *for a long ~* seit langem; *in a little ~* bald, in kurzem; *once in a ~* gelegentlich, bei Gelegenheit; *the ~* (gerade) in dem Augenblick; währenddessen; *a short ~* e-e kleine Weile *f*; *to be worth ~* der Mühe wert sein, sich lohnen.
whim [(h)wim] Einfall *m*, Grille, Laune *f*; *tech* Göpel *m*.
whimper ['(h)wimpə] *itr tr* wimmern; winseln; *s* Gewimmer; Gewinsel *n*.
whims|ical ['(h)wimzikəl] launisch, launenhaft, schrullig, wunderlich; komisch, ausgefallen, sonderbar, unaußergewöhnlich; **~icality** [(h)wimzi'kæliti], **~icalness** ['(h)wimzikəlnis] Wunderlichkeit; Ungewöhnlichkeit; Laune, Grille *f*; **~y** ['(h)wimzi] Laune, Grille *f*; sonderbare(r) Humor *m*.
whin [(h)win] **1.** *bot* (Stech-)Ginster *m*; **2.** *(~sill, ~stone)* Felsgestein *n*, *bes.* Basalt *m*.
whin|e [(h)wain] *itr* wimmern; winseln; jammern; *tr* weinerlich sagen; *s* Gewimmer, Gejammer; *mot* Jaulen *n*; **~y** ['-i] weinerlich; jammernd.
whinny ['(h)wini] *itr* leise wiehern; *s* leise(s) Wiehern *n*.
whip [(h)wip] *tr* peitschen, schlagen; reißen, zerren, schnappen; ent-, wegreißen *(from s.o.* jdm); *(Regen an das Fenster)* klatschen; (mit Gewalt) treiben, zwingen, nötigen; *(mit Worten)* geißeln; *(Sahne, Eiweiß)* (zu Schaum, Schnee) schlagen; *(Gewässer)* abangeln; *mar* hochwinden, aufziehen; (mit e-m Bindfaden) umwickeln; (um-) säumen, überwendlich nähen; *fam fig* abhängen, schlagen; *itr* rennen, rasen, flitzen; rasch handeln; *(Fahne)* flattern; die Angel werfen; *s* Peitsche, Geißel *f a. fig*; Peitschenschlag, -hieb, Geißelhieb *m*; heftige Bewegung *f*; Kutscher, Reitknecht, Reiter; *(Jagd)* Pikör; *parl* Einpeitscher; *allg* Trommler *fig*; *parl* Appell *m*, Aufforderung; schriftliche Mitteilung *f*, Rundschreiben *n*; Früchte *f pl* mit Schlagsahne *od* Ei(er)schnee; *tech* Winde *f*; Saum *m*, überwendliche Naht *f*; *to ~* **in** zs.-, hineintreiben; *fig* zs.trommeln; *to ~* **off** wegreißen, -wischen; *(Kleider)* herunterreißen; *(Getränk)* hinunterstürzen; *to ~* **on** *(Pferde durch Peitschenhiebe)* antreiben; *to ~* **out** herausreißen; *(Worte)* hervorstoßen; *to ~* **together** zs.peitschen, -treiben; *to ~* **up** aufpeitschen, -stacheln, antreiben; hochreißen; *fam (Speise)* schnell zs.hauen, in aller Eile zubereiten; **~-cord** Peitschenschnur *f*; Whipcord *m (Gewebe)*; Katgut *n*; **~crane** *tech* Wippkran *m*; **~graft** *tr bot* kopulieren; **~-hand**: *to have the ~~ (fig)* das Heft in der Hand haben; *of s.o.* jdn in s-r Gewalt haben; **~ handle** Peitschenstiel *m*; **~-lash** Peitschenschnur *f*; **~ped cream** Schlagsahne *f*, -rahm *m*; *(Österreich)* Schlagobers *n*; **~per** ['-ə] Peitschende(r); Kohlentrimmer *m*; *~~-in* ['wipər'in] *(Jagd)* Pikör; *parl* Einpeitscher *m*; *~~-snapper* Grünschnabel, Dreikäsehoch, kleine(r) Angeber *m*; **~pet** ['-it] Whippet *m (Rennhund)*; **~ping** ['-iŋ] Peitschen *n*; Peitschenhiebe *m pl (als Strafe)*, Prügelstrafe; Parteidisziplin; (Peitschen-)Schnur *f*, Bindfaden *m*; *(Buch)* Heften *n*; *~~-boy* Prügelknabe; Sündenbock *m*; *~~-in (parl)* Einpeitschen *n*; *~~-post* Schandpfahl, Pranger *m*; *~~-top* Kreisel *m*; **~pletree** ['-ltri:] *(Wagen)* Ortscheit *n*; **~py** ['-i] biegsam, geschmeidig; *fam* behend(e); **~ round** (Geld-)Sammlung *f*; **~saw** *s* Trumm-, Quersäge *f*; *tr Am* ab-, zersägen; *fig* doppelt schlagen *od* hereinlegen; *itr* e-n doppelten Vorteil haben; **~stick, ~stock** Peitschenstiel *m*; **~stitch** *tr itr* überwendlich nähen; *(Buch)* heften; *s* überwendliche Naht *f*.
whippoorwill ['(h)wippuəwil] *orn* Ziegenmelker *m*.
whirl [(h)wə:l] *itr* wirbeln, sich schnell (im Kreise) drehen, rotieren; *fig (Gedanken)* durchea.wirbeln; *(Sinne)* schwinden; rasen, sausen; *tr* wirbeln; *s* Wirbeln *n*, Kreiselbewegung, schnelle Drehung *f*; kurze(r) Weg; Wirbel *m a. fig*; Schwindel(gefühl *n*); *fig* Trubel *m*; wilde(s) Durcheinander, geschäftige(s) Hin u. Her *n*; *to ~ about* herumwirbeln; *to be in a ~* sich drehen, herumwirbeln; *~ of dust* Staubwirbel *m*; **~igig** ['-igig] Kreisel *m*; Karussell; Schnurrädchen *n*; Kreiselbewegung *f*; *fig* Wirbel, rasche(r) Wandel *m*; **~pool** ['-pu:l] Strudel *m a. fig*; **~wind** Wirbelwind *m*, Windhose *f*; *fig* Wirbel, Sturm, schnelle(r) Untergang *m*; *to reap the ~~ (fig, biblisch)* Sturm ernten.
whir(r) [(h)wə:] *itr* schwirren, surren; *s* Schwirren, Surren *n*.
whisk [(h)wisk] *tr* (weg)wischen, fegen, kehren; rasch (weg)nehmen; abstauben; *(Sahne, Eiweiß)* schlagen; *itr* fegen, sausen, huschen; *s* Fegen, Wischen *n*; schnelle Bewegung *f*; kurze(r) Besen, (Stroh-)Wisch; (Staub-)Wedel *m*; *(~-broom)* Kleiderbürste *f*; Schneebesen, Schaumschläger *m*; *in a ~* im Nu; *to ~ away, off* weg-, abwischen; rasch mitnehmen; *to ~ out* ausschütteln, -klopfen; *to ~ up* rasch hinaufbefördern; **~ers** ['-əz] *pl* Backenbart *m*; *zoo (bes. Katze)* Schnurrhaare *n pl*.
whisk(e)y ['(h)wiski] Whisky *m*.
whisper ['(h)wispə] *itr tr* wispern, flüstern; *(Wind)* rauschen, raunen; *tr* ausplaudern, weitererzählen; zuflüstern *(to s.o.* jdm); *s* Geflüster *n*; Heimlichkeit *f*, Tuscheln; Gerücht; Gewisper; Rascheln *n*; *to talk in a ~* im Flüsterton reden; **~er** ['-rə] Flüsterer; Ausplauderer, Zuträger *m*; **~ing** ['-riŋ] Geflüster *n*; Flüsterrede *f*; *~~-campaign (pol)* Flüsterkampagne *f*; *~~-gallery* Flüstergalerie *f*.
whist [(h)wist] **1.** *interj obs* pst! still! **2.** Whist *n (Kartenspiel)*; **~-drive** Whistturnier *n*.
whistle ['(h)wisl] *itr* pfeifen *(to s.o.* jdm); kreischen, schreien; *fig fam* sich die Hacken schief laufen, sich vergeblich bemühen *(for* um); *tr (Ton, Lied)* pfeifen; pfeifen *(s.o.* jdm); *s* (Signal-)Pfeife *f*; Pfeifen *n*; Pfiff, Pfeifton *m*; *to wet o.'s ~ (fam)* sich die Kehle anfeuchten, e-n heben; *to ~ for s.th.* vergeblich auf etw warten; **~ stop** *Am fam* (kleines) Nest *n*.
Whit [(h)wit] *a* Pfingst-; **~-Monday** Pfingstmontag *m*; **~-week** Pfingstwoche *f*.
whit [(h)wit] *s*: *no ~, not a ~* nicht ein bißchen, kein Jota, keine Spur von; nicht im geringsten, nicht die Spur.
white [(h)wait] *a* weiß; hell, silber(farbe)n, schneeig; blaß, (kreide)bleich *(with terror* vor Schrecken); weißgekleidet; *typ* blank, leer; *(Nacht)* schlaflos; *fig* rein, unschuldig, fleckenmakellos, untadelig; *fam* anständig, zuverlässig; *sl* in Weißglut, auf der Palme; *s* Weiß *n*; helle Hautfarbe; *fig* Reinheit, Unschuld, Flecken-, Makellosigkeit *f*; *das* Weiße *(of the eye* im Auge); *(~ of egg)* Eiweiß *n*; *(Buch)* leere Stelle, Lücke *f*; weiße(r) Stoff *m*, weiße Kleidung *f*; Weiße(r), Weißwein *m*; Weiß-, Auszugmehl *n*; Weiße(r) *(rassisch u. pol)*; *pl med* Leukorrhöe *f*, weiße(r) Fluß *m*; *sport* weiße(r) Dress *m*; *tr* weißen; *(to ~ out) (Buch)* aus-, frei lassen; *to bleed ~ (fig)* zum Weißbluten bringen, völlig aussaugen, schröpfen; *to turn up the ~ of o.'s eyes (fig)* (heuchlerisch) die Augen aufschlagen; *~ as a sheet* kreidebleich; *black or ~?* mit oder ohne Milch? **~ alloy** Weißmetall *n*; **~ ant** *ent* Termite *f*; **~bait** ['-beit] Sprotte *f*; Weißfisch *m*; **~ bear** Eisbär *m*; **~beard** Weiß-, Graubart *m (Mann)*; **~ birch** Weißbirke *f*; **~ book** *pol* Weißbuch *n*; **~ bread** Weißbrot *n*; **~-caps** *pl* Wellen *f pl* mit Schaumkronen; **~ clover** Weiß-, Steinklee *m*; **~ coal** weiße Kohle, Wasserkraft *f*; **~ coffee** Milchkaffee, Kaffee *m* mit Milch; **~-collar** *a*: *~~ union* Angestelltengewerkschaft *f*; *~~ worker* Büroangestellte(r) *m*; **~ corpuscle** weiße(s) Blutkörperchen *n*; **~ day** Glückstag *m*; **~ elephant** weiße(r) Elefant *m*; *fig* Ehrenamt; unrentable(s) Geschäft *n*; nutzlose(r) Besitz *m*; **~ ensign** *mar* Kriegsflagge *f (Englands)*; **~-faced** *a (Mensch)* blaß, bleich; *(Tier)* mit weißem Fleck über den Augen; **~ feather** weiße Feder *f*; *to show the ~~* sich feige benehmen; **~fish** Weißfisch; Weißwal *m*; **~ flag** weiße Fahne, Parlamentärflagge *f*; *to hoist the ~~* die weiße Fahne zeigen, sich ergeben; **W~ Friar** *rel* Karmeliter *m*; **~ frost** Rauhreif *m*; **W~hall** ['-'-] *fig* die britische Regierung; **~-headed** *a* weißhaarig; *zoo* weißköpfig; flachshaarig; *fam* Lieblings-; **~ heat** Weißglut *a. fig*; *fig* helle Erregung; fieberhafte Eile *f*; **~ horse** Schimmel *m*; *pl* Schaumkronen *f pl (auf den Wellen)*; **~-hot** weißglühend; *fig* in Weißglut *od* heller Aufregung; fieberhaft; *the* **W~ House** das Weiße Haus *(Regierungssitz des Präsidenten der US)*; **~ lead** Bleiweiß *n*; **~ lie** Notlüge *f*; **~ light** Tageslicht *n*; *fig* Vorurteilslosigkeit, Unvoreingenommenheit *f*; *~~ district* Vergnügungsviertel *n*; **~-lipped** *a* schreckensbleich; **~-livered** *a* blaß, *fam* käsig; ängstlich, feige; *the ~* **man** der weiße Mann, die Weißen *m pl*; **~ meat** Geflügel, Kalb- u. Schweinefleisch *n*; **~ metal** Lager-, Weißmetall *n*; **~ness** ['-nis] weiße Farbe *od* Färbung *od* Tönung; Blässe; Fleckenlosigkeit, Reinheit *a. fig*; *fig* Unschuld *f*; **~ paper** Weißbuch *n*; *com* erstklassige(r) Wechsel *m*; **~ poplar** Silberpappel *f*; **~ sale** *com* Weiße Woche *f*; **~ sheet** Büßerhemd *n*; **~-slave** *a*: *~~ traffic* Mädchenhandel *m*; **~smith** Blechschmied, Klempner, Spengler, Flaschner *m*; **~ squall** Sturmbö *f* aus heiterem Himmel *(in*

den Tropen); **~thorn** bot Weißdorn m; **~throat** orn Weißkehlchen n; **~ trash** Am arme(r) Weißer m; **~ war** Wirtschaftskrieg m; **~wash** s Tünche f; Kalk(anstrich) m; fig Mohrenwäsche, Entlastung, Ehrenrettung; Am fam sport haushohe Niederlage f; tr tünchen, weißen; fig reinwaschen, rehabilitieren; (Sache) bemänteln, beschönigen; Am fam sport haushoch schlagen, **~ wine** Weißwein m.

whiten ['(h)waitn] tr weiß, heller machen, bleichen; weißen, tünchen; fig reinwaschen; itr weiß, heller, bleicher werden; (Haar) ergrauen; **~ing** ['-iŋ] Bleichen; Weißen, Tünchen n; Tünche; Schlämmkreide f.

whither ['(h)wiðə] adv poet lit wohin; **~soever** [-so(u)'evə] betont adv wohin auch immer.

whiting ['(h)waitiŋ] **1.** Schlämmkreide; Silberbronze f; **2.** Wittling, Merlan m (Fisch).

whitish ['(h)waitiʃ] weißlich.

whitlow ['(h)witlou] Nagelgeschwür n.

Whitsun ['(h)witsn] a Pfingst-; **~day** ['(h)wit'sʌndi] Pfingstsonntag m; **~tide** ['(h)witsntaid] Pfingsten n od pl; **~ week** Pfingstwoche f.

whittle ['(h)witl] tr schnitzen (an); (to ~ away, down) in Stückchen schneiden; fig verringern, vermindern; itr herumschnitze(l)n (at an).

whiz(z) [(h)wiz] itr zischen, surren, pfeifen; sausen, rasen; s Zischen, Surren, Pfeifen n; Am sl fig Kanone, Wucht f, Knüller, Mumm m; it is a ~ abgemacht! gee ~! oh je! ach herrje! Donnerwetter! **~-bang** mil sl Ratschbum n; **~er** ['-ə] fam Zentrifuge; Trockenschleuder f; to pull a ~~ (Am sl) e-e krumme Tour drehen.

who [hu:] prn wer; der, die, das; welche(r, s); fam wen, wem; to know ~'s ~ die Personen kennen; ~ would have thought it? wer hätte das gedacht! **~dun(n)it** [hu:'dʌnit] sl Krimi (-nalroman, -film) m; **~ever** [hu(:)-'evə], (betont) **~soever** [hu:so(u)'evə], poet **~(so)e'er** [hu(:)'ɛə, hu:so(u)'ɛə] wer auch (immer); jeder, der; ~ever (fam) wer ... denn? wer zum Kuckuck?

whoa [wou] halt! brr!

whole [houl] a ganz, heil, intakt, vollständig; (Bibel) gesund; attr ganz; Voll-; s das Ganze, Gesamtheit; Einheit f; the ~ of der, die, das ganze; alle(s); (taken) as a ~ als Ganzes, im ganzen, als e-e Einheit; (up)on the ~ im ganzen gesehen, alles in allem; with o.'s ~ heart von ganzem Herzen; to get off, to escape with a ~ skin mit heiler Haut davonkommen; to go the ~ hog (fam) aufs Ganze gehen; made out of ~ cloth (Am fam) völlig falsch, pred reine Einbildung; **~ blood** (Pferd) Vollblut n; **~-footed** a plattfüßig; fam freimütig; **~-hearted** a aufrichtig, ernst; pred von ganzem Herzen; **~-hogger** sl Hundertfünfzigprozentige(r) m; **~-length** a (Bildnis) in voller Figur; Voll-, Ganz-; **~meal** a Vollkorn-; ~~ bread Vollkornbrot n; **~ milk** Vollmilch f; **~ness** ['-nis] Ganzheit, Intaktheit, Vollständigkeit f; **~ number** math ganze Zahl f; **~sale** s Großhandel m; a Großhandels-, Engros-, Groß-; allg vollständig, -kommen, total; allgemein; com partienweise, in Bausch u. Bogen; massenhaft, Massen-; adv im großen, en gros; tr en gros, im großen verkaufen; by, (Am) at ~~ im großen, en gros; im Großhandel; zum Großhandelspreis; ~~ and retail Groß- u. Einzelhandel; ~~ arrests, destruction, execution Massenverhaftungen f pl, -vernichtung f, -hinrichtungen f pl; ~~ business, enterprise Großhandelsgeschäft, -unternehmen n; ~~ buyer Großeinkäufer m; ~~ commerce, trade Großhandel m; ~~ dealer, merchant, trader Großhändler, Grossist m; ~~ manufacture Serienfabrikation f; ~~ market Großhandelsmarkt m; ~~ price Großhandels-, Grossistenpreis m; ~~ purchase Großeinkauf m; **~saler** Großhändler, -kaufmann m; **~seas** a fam total besoffen, mit Schlagseite; **~some** ['-səm] gesund (-heitsfördernd), zuträglich, wohltuend; heilsam, lehrreich, nützlich; gesund, kräftig, kraftvoll; **~-time** a ganztägig, Ganztags-; hauptberuflich; ~~ work Ganztagsarbeit; ganztägige Beschäftigung f; **~-timer** ganztägig, hauptberuflich beschäftigte Arbeitskraft f; **wholly** ['houlli] adv ganz, gänzlich, vollständig, völlig.

whom [hu:m] pron wen; (to ~) wem; den, die, das; welche(n, s); dem, der; welchem, welcher; **~ever** [-'evə], (betont) **~soever** [-so(u)'evə] wen, wem auch (immer); jeden, jedem, der.

whoop [hu:p] s Geschrei, Geheul, Gebrüll n; Schrei (e-s Tieres); med Inspirationsstridor m, fam Ziehen n; itr schreien, heulen, brüllen; med keuchen; tr schreien, brüllen; anbrüllen; to ~ out mit Schimpf u. Schande davonjagen; to ~ it, things up (Am sl) ein großes Remmidemmi machen; viel Sums, Aufhebens machen (for s.o., s.th. um jdn, etw); not worth a ~ keinen Pfifferling, keinen roten Heller wert; ~(s pl) of joy Freudengeheul n; **~ee** ['wu:pi:] Am interj juchhe! juchheirassa! s sl Remidemmi, Tamtam n; to make ~~ (sl) Rabatz machen; **~ing-cough** Keuch-, Stickhusten m; **~s** ['-s] Am interj hoppla!

whop, whap [(h)wɔp] tr sl verdreschen, versohlen; Am hinwerfen; to ~ o.s (Am) hinplumpsen, zs.sacken; **~per** ['-ə] fam Riesenbiest, Mordsding n; faustdicke Lücke f; **~ping** ['-iŋ] a adv fam gewaltig, riesig, Riesen-, Mords-; (Lüge) faustdick.

whore [hɔ:] s Hure f; itr (herum)huren.

whorl [(h)wɔ:l] (Spinn-)Wirtel m a. bot; anat zoo Windung f, Ring m; **~ed** [-d] a spiralig, geringelt, gewunden.

whortleberry ['(h)wɔ:tlberi] bot Heidelbeere f; red ~ Preiselbeere f.

who's [hu:z] = who is.

whose [hu:z] prn wessen; dessen, deren; **~soever** [-so(u)'evə] wessen ... auch (immer).

why [(h)wai] adv warum, weshalb, wofür; wieso; aus welchem Grunde; zu welchem Zweck; deshalb, darum; interj sieh da! nun! ~, yes! natürlich! s: the ~ and wherefore das Warum u. Wieso.

wick [wik] Docht m.

wicked ['wikid] a böse, schlecht, gottlos, verrucht; boshaft; fam schelmisch, schalkhaft; (Sache) böse, übel; (Schlag) schlimm; Am sl doll; **~ness** ['-nis] Schlechtigkeit, Gottlosigkeit, Verruchtheit; Bosheit f.

wicker ['wikə] s Weide(nrute) f; Flechtwerk; Geflecht n; a Weiden-, Flecht-, Korb-; **~ basket** Weidenkorb m; **~ bottle** Korbflasche f; **~ chair** Korbstuhl m; **~ furniture** Korbmöbel pl; **~work** Flechtwerk n, Korbwaren f pl.

wicket ['wikit] (~-door, -gate) Pförtchen; Drehkreuz; Schalterfenster n; (Kricket) Dreistab m, Spielfeld; Tor n; **~-keeper** (Kricket) Torhüter m.

wide [waid] a weit; breit; groß; (Augen) aufgerissen; fig umfangreich, umfassend, großzügig; tolerant, vorurteilslos, -frei; sl aufgeweckt; (Kleidung) weit, lose, locker fallend; (Auswahl) reich; (Pause) lang; (Interessen) vielseitig; (Preise) unterschiedlich; weit ab (of von), fig (Antwort) danebengeschossen, verfehlt; adv (~ of) weit (weg), fern; weitab; s poet Weite, weite Welt f; (Kricket) Fehlball m; far and ~ weit u. breit; to the ~ äußerst, völlig; to give s.o. a ~ berth (fam) jdm aus dem Wege gehen; **~-angle** a phot film Weitwinkel-; Breitwand-; **~-awake** a ganz, völlig wach; wachsam, aufmerksam (to auf); fig schlau; aufgeweckt; s ['---] Schlapphut m; **~-eyed** a mit großen Augen; to look at s.o. ~~ jdn groß anschauen; **~ly** ['-li] adv weit; weit ausea.; weit u. breit; in hohem Maße, sehr; to differ ~~ sehr verschieden sein; sehr verschiedener Meinung sein; **~n** ['-n] tr itr (sich) weiten, (sich) erweitern, (sich) verbreitern; (Kluft) (sich) vertiefen; **~ness** ['-nis] Weite, Breite f; Umfang m; fig Vorurteilslosigkeit, Toleranz f; **~ning** ['-niŋ]: road ~~ Straßenverbreiterung f; **~-open** a weit offen, geöffnet; Am lax; **~-screen** film Breitwand-; **~spread** a weit ausgebreitet od ausgedehnt; weit verbreitet; **~-stretched** a ausgedehnt.

widgeon ['widʒən] zoo Schwimmente f.

widow ['widou] s Witwe f; tr fig berauben (of gen); **~ed** ['-d] a verwitwet; **~er** ['-ə] Witwer m; **~hood** ['-hud] Witwenschaft f, -stand m, -zeit f; **~'s allowance** Witwengeld n; **~'s pension** Witwenpension f.

width [widθ] Weite, Breite; (Stoff-) Breite, Bahn; arch lichte Weite; geol Mächtigkeit; fig Größe, Weite f; to be 10 feet in ~ 10 Fuß breit sein.

wield [wi:ld] tr handhaben, gebrauchen; (Macht) ausüben (over über).

wiener ['wi:nə], **~wurst** ['-wə:st] Am Wiener (Würstchen) n.

wife [waif] pl wives [waivz] (Ehe-) Frau, Gattin f; to take to ~ zur Frau nehmen, heiraten; old wives' tale Altweibergeschichte f; **~ly** ['-li] weiblich; fraulich.

wig [wig] s (peri~) Perücke f; tr fam anschnauzen, 'runterputzen, fertigmachen; ~s on the green (fam) Streit m, Rauferei f; **~ged** [-d] a e-e Perücke tragend; **~ging** ['-iŋ] fam Anschnauzer m, Zigarre f.

wiggle ['wigl] tr wackeln mit; mar wricken; itr (hin- u. her)wackeln; sich schlängeln (through durch); Am sl tanzen; to get a ~~ on (Am sl) sich beschleunigen.

wight [wait] hum Wicht m, Kerlchen n.

wigwam ['wigwæm] Wigwam m, (konische) Indianerhütte f.

wild [waild] a wild(lebend, -wachsend); unbewohnt, unbebaut, öde; wild, primitiv, unzivilisiert; unbändig, zügellos; (Schmerz, Wut) rasend; ausgelassen, bacchantisch, toll; stürmisch (erregt); erregt, aufgeregt, erhitzt, (leidenschaftlich) begeistert; wild, tobend, verrückt, wahnsinnig (with vor); fam wütend (about über); unordentlich, ungekämmt; draufgängerisch; plan-, ziellos; abenteuerlich, phantastisch; (Tiere) gefährlich, scheu, ungezähmt; adv wild drauflos, ins Blaue; verworren; aufs Geratewohl; s meist pl Wildnis, (freie) Natur f; to be ~ about s.th. auf etw wild od erpicht sein; to drive s.o. ~ jdn zur Raserei bringen; to go ~

wild werden; *to run ~* sich austoben; ins Kraut schießen; verwildern; *to sow o.'s ~ oats* sich die Hörner abstoßen; *reserve for the preservation of ~ life* Naturschutzgebiet *n*; *~* **beast** Raubtier *n*; *~~ show* Raubtierschau *f*; **~-boar** Wildschwein *n*; **~cat** *s* Wildkatze *f*; *fig* Hitzkopf *m*; *com* Schwindelunternehmen *n*; *Am* neue Ölquelle, Probeschürfung; *Am* allein fahrende Lokomotive *f*; *a* (finanziell) ungesund, unreell, schwindelhaft; riskant, abenteuerlich; Schwindel-; *rail* nicht fahrplanmäßig; *(Bohrung)* unsicher; *~~ company* Schwindelgesellschaft *f*; *~~ strike* wilde(r) Streik *m*; **~catter** *Am* Schwindelunternehmer, Spekulant; Ölsucher *m*; **~-duck** Wildente *f*; **~erness** ['wildənis] Wildnis, Wüste *f a. fig*, Ödland; *fig* Gewirr, Durcheinander *n*; **~-eyed** *a* mit stierem Blick; **~fire** verheerende(s) Feuer; *hist* griechische(s) Feuer *n*; *to spread like ~~ (fig)* sich wie ein Lauffeuer verbreiten; **~-fowl** Wildvögel *m pl*; **~-goose** Wildgans *f*; *~~ chase (fig)* vergebliche(s) Bemühen *n*; *~* **horse** Wildpferd *n*; **~ing** ['-iŋ] *bot* Wildling; *fig* Außenseiter *m*; **~ly** ['-li] *adv* wild, wütend, stürmisch, heftig; **~ness** ['-nis] Wildheit, Unbändigkeit, Zügellosigkeit *f*.

wil|e [wail] *s* List *f*, Trick; Betrug *m*, Tücke *f*; *tr* (ver)locken *(s.o. into doing s.th.* jdn etw zu tun); umgarnen, überlisten, betrügen; *to ~~ away time* sich die Zeit vertreiben; **~iness** ['-inis] Verschlagenheit; List *f*; **~y** ['-i] listig, verschlagen, schlau.

wilful, *Am* **willful** ['wilful] absichtlich, vorsätzlich; eigensinnig, halsstarrig, hartnäckig; *~~ homicide* vorsätzliche Tötung *f*; *~~ murder* Mord *m*; **~ness** ['-nis] Absichtlichkeit, Vorsätzlichkeit *f*; Eigensinn *m*, Halsstarrigkeit, Hartnäckigkeit *f*.

will [wil] *(Hilfsverb) (nur) Präsens Indikativ; (pret) would* werden; wollen; *tr itr* will; wünsche, möchte; befehle, ordne an; bestimme, setze fest; pflege; *tr* vermachen; *s* Wille; Wunsch *m*, Verlangen *n*; Befehl *m*, Anordnung, Anweisung *f*; *(last ~ and testament)* letzte(r) Wille *m*, Testament *n*; *against s.o.'s ~* gegen jds Willen; *at ~* nach Wunsch *od* Belieben; *jur* auf Widerruf; *by ~* durch Testament, letztwillig; *with a ~* mit festem Vorsatz, fest entschlossen; *to do s.o.'s ~* jdm s-n Willen tun; *to have no ~ of o.'s own* keinen eigenen Willen haben; *to read a ~* ein Testament eröffnen; *to work o.'s ~ on s.o.* s-n Willen bei jdm durchsetzen; *I won't be a minute* ich bin gleich wieder da; *where there's a ~ there's a way (prov)* wo ein Wille ist, ist auch ein Weg; *this window won't open* dieses Fenster läßt sich nicht öffnen; *freedom of the ~* Willensfreiheit *f*; *good, ill ~* gute(r), böse(r) Wille *m*; **~ed** [-d] *a in Zssgen* mit ... Willen, ...willig; *self-~~* eigenwillig; **~ing** ['-iŋ] willig, geneigt; bereitwillig; freiwillig; Willens-; **~ingness** ['-iŋnis] Willigkeit, Geneigtheit; Bereitwilligkeit; Freiwilligkeit *f*; **~-power** Willenskraft *f*.

willies ['wiliz] *pl sl* Kribbeligkeit, Nervosität *f*.

will-o'-the-wisp ['wiləðwisp] Irrlicht *n a. fig*; *fig* Täuschung *f*.

willow ['wilou] *s bot (~-tree)* Weide *f*; Weidenholz *n*, -rute *f*; *fam* Kricket-, *Am* Baseballschläger; *tech* Reißwolf *m*; *a* Weiden-; *~* **herb** *bot* Weiderich *m*; Weidenröschen *n*; **~y** ['-i] mit Weiden bestanden; *fig* schlank, graziös.

willy-nilly ['wili'nili] *adv* wohl oder übel, notgedrungen, gezwungenermaßen; *a* schwankend, unentschlossen.

wilt [wilt] **1.** *obs poet (du)* willst; **2.** *itr* (ver)welken; *fig* erschlaffen; den Mut verlieren; *tr* (ver)welken, erschlaffen lassen.

wimble ['wimbl] Drill-, Frittbohrer *m*.

wimple ['wimpl] *hist u. rel* Haube *f (der Nonnen)*, Schleier *m*.

win [win] *irr won, won* [wʌn] *itr* gewinnen, siegen, triumphieren, Erfolg haben; *(mit adv)* gelangen, kommen *(to* an); *tr* erringen, gewinnen *(from s.o.* von jdm); siegen in; erreichen, erlangen; überreden *(to do* zu tun); *(to ~ over to)* (für sich) gewinnen, auf s-e Seite ziehen; *min metal* gewinnen; *sl* klauen; *s fam* Sieg *m*; Gewinne *m pl*; *to ~ away, (Am) out, over, through* weg-, hinaus-, hinüber-, durchkommen; *to ~ the day, field* den Sieg davontragen, siegreich sein; *to ~ free* sich befreien, die Freiheit erlangen; sich durchkämpfen; *to ~ hands down (fam)* leichtes Spiel haben; **~ner** ['-ə] Gewinner, Sieger *m*; *sl* totsichere Sache *f*; **~ning** ['-iŋ] *a* siegreich; *fig* gewinnend, einnehmend, anziehend; *s* Sieg *m*; *min* Gewinnung, Förderung *f*, Abbau *m*, Ausbeute *f*; *pl* (Geld-)Gewinn *m*; *~~ of iron* Eisengewinnung *f*; *~~-post (sport)* Ziel *n*; **~some** ['-səm] gewinnend, anziehend, gefällig, reizend, reizvoll.

wince [wins] *itr* zs.fahren, zs.-, zurückzucken *(under a blow* unter e-m Hieb; *at an insult* bei e-r Beleidigung); *s* Zs.-, Zurückzucken *n*; *without a ~* ohne e-e Miene zu verziehen.

winch [wintʃ] Winde, Haspel, Kurbel *f*, Kran *m*; **~ester** ['-estə] Winchesterbüchse; große Flasche *f*.

wind 1. [wind, *poet a.* waind] *s* Wind, Luftzug *m*, Brise *f*, Sturm; *(Jagd)* Wind; Atem *m*; Blähung *f*, Wind *m*; *(Boxen) sl* Magengrube *f*; *fig* dumme(s) Gerede, Geschwätz *n*, Unsinn *m*, Aufschneiderei *f*; *pl mus* Blasinstrumente *n pl*; *tr* an der Luft trocknen, lüften; *(Jagd)* wittern, aufspüren; außer Atem bringen; sich verschnaufen; *(Tier)* sich auslaufen lassen; *between ~ and water (fig)* an e-r empfindlichen Stelle; *down, off the ~* mit dem Wind; *in the teeth of the ~, in the ~'s eye* od *into, on, up the ~* gegen den Wind; *to the four ~s* in alle Winde, in alle vier Himmelsrichtungen; *to cast, to fling to the ~s (fig)* in den Wind schlagen; vergeuden; *to find out how the ~ blows* die Stimmung erkunden; *to get, to have ~ of s.th.* von e-r S Wind kriegen, haben; *to get o.'s second ~* wieder zu Atem kommen; *to know how the ~ blows (fig)* wissen, woher der Wind weht; *to put s.o. the ~ up (fig sl)* jdm bange machen; *to raise the ~ (sl)* das Geld heranschaffen; *to sail close to the ~ (mar)* hoch an den Wind gehen; *fig* mit e-m Fuß im Zuchthaus stehen; *to speak to the ~* in den Wind reden; *to take the ~ out of s.o.'s sails (fig)* jdm den Wind aus den Segeln nehmen; jdn verwirren; *I got the ~ up (sl)* das Herz fiel mir in die Hose; *there's s.th. in the ~ (fig)* es liegt etw in der Luft; *sound in ~ and limb* kerngesund; **~age** ['-idʒ] Geschoßablenkung *f*; *phys* Luftwiderstand *m*; *mar* Windseite; *tech* Belüftung, Ventilation *f*; **~bag** *fam fig* Windbeutel *m (Mensch)*; **~-blown** *a* vom Winde verweht; *(Baum)* wettergebeugt; *(Frisur)* Windstoß-; *~~ haircut* Windstoßfrisur *f*; **~bound** *a mar* durch widrige Winde fest-, zurückgehalten; **~break** Windschutz *m (Mauer, Hecke, Baumreihe)*; **~breaker** *Am (Warenzeichen)* warme Sport-, Windjacke *f*; **~broken** *a vet (Pferd)* dämpfig; **~cheater** Anorak *m*; **~-cone, -sleeve, -sock** *aero* Windsack *m*; **~ed** ['-id] *a* außer Atem, atemlos; *~* **egg** Windei *n*; **~fall** Fallobst *n*; *fig* Glücksfall, glückliche(r) Zufall *m*, unverhoffte(s) Glück *n*; *Am* Windbruch *m*; **~flow** Windstoß *m*; **~flower** (Busch-)Windröschen *n*, Anemone *f*; *~* **gap** Einschnitt *m* in e-m Bergrücken; **~-ga(u)ge** Windmesser *m*; **~hover, ~fanner** *orn* Turmfalke *m*; **~iness** ['-inis] windige(s) Wetter *n*; *fig* stürmische(r) Charakter *m*; wetterwendische(s) Wesen *n*; Empfindlichkeit; Redseligkeit; Aufgeblasenheit *f*; *~* **instrument** *mus* Blasinstrument *n*; **~jammer** *sl* Windjammer *m*, -jacke *f*; Matrose auf e-m Segelschiff; *Am sl* Schwätzer *m*, Klatschbase *f*; **~mill** Windmühle *f*; *to fight, to tilt at ~s (fig)* gegen Windmühlen kämpfen; **~pipe** ['-paip] *anat* Luftröhre *f*; **~-pollinated** *a bot* windbestäubt; **~row** *s* (Gras-, Getreide-) Schwade(n *m*) *f*; Verwehung; *agr* Furche *f*; *tr* in Schwaden legen; *(welkes Laub)* zs.fegen, verwehen; *~* **scale** Windskala *f*; **~-screen,** *Am* **-shield** *mot* Windschutzscheibe *f*; *~~ wiper* Scheibenwischer *m*; **~-swept** *a* sturmgepeitscht; **~tight** luftdicht; **~-tunnel** *aero* Windkanal, -tunnel *m*; **~ward** ['-wəd] *adv* gegen den Wind; *a* gegen den Wind gerichtet, auf der Windseite (befindlich); *s* Windseite, Luv *f*; **~y** ['-i] windig; *fig* stürmisch; wetterwendisch; *fam* ängstlich, nervös; redselig; aufgeblasen, pompös; *med* blähend; **2.** [waind] *irr wound, wound* [waund] *tr* drehen, kurbeln; winden, (auf)wickeln, spulen; umwinden, -wickeln; umschlingen; *(Saite)* spannen; *film* transportieren; *fig* einfließen lassen, anbringen, einflechten; *(to ~ up)* hochwinden; *(Uhr)* aufziehen; *itr* sich winden *(about, around* um); sich schlängeln; e-n Haken schlagen; *fig* Umwege machen, krumme Wege gehen; *(Holz)* sich werfen, arbeiten; *(Uhr)* sich aufziehen lassen; *s* Drehen, Winden, (Auf-)Wikkeln *n*; Drehung; Windung, Schlinge, Kurve *f*; *to ~ off* abwickeln, -spulen; *to ~ up (tr)* aufwickeln; hochwinden; *(Uhr)* aufziehen; *fig* gespannt machen, erregen; ankurbeln; ab-, beschließen, beenden, zu Ende bringen; *(Geschäft)* abwickeln, liquidieren, auflösen; *itr (Rede)* abschließen; *Am fam* enden, landen; *to ~ s.o. round o.'s (little) finger (fig)* jdn um den (kleinen) Finger wikkeln; **~er** ['-ə] Haspler *m (Arbeiter)*; Winde; Rolle; Kurbel; Stufe (e-r Wendeltreppe); *bot* Schlingpflanze *f*; **~ing** ['-iŋ] *s* Drehung *f*; Winden; (Auf-)Wickeln *n*; gewundene(r) (Ver-) Lauf *od* Weg *m*; *fig* Umwege *m pl*, *fam* krumme Touren *f pl*; *el* Wickelung, Spulung *f*; Wickeldraht *m*; *(einzelne)* Windung *f*; *(Holz)* Arbeiten *n*; *a* sich windend, sich schlängelnd, gewunden; *fig* krumm; *~~-rope* Förderseil *n*; *~~-shaft* Förderschacht *m*; *~~-sheet* Leichentuch *n*; *~~-tower* Förderturm *m*; *~~-up* Aufwickeln; Hochwinden, Aufziehen *n*; *fig* Beendigung *f*, Abschluß *m*, Abwick(e)lung *f*; **~up** ['-ʌp] (Ab-)Schluß *m*, Ende *n*; **3.** *a. irr wound, wound* [waund] *tr (Horn* od *Signal)* blasen.

windlass ['windləs] *s* Winde, Haspel; *mar* Schiffswinde *f*, Gangspill *n*.

window ['windou] *s* Fenster *n (a. e-s Briefumschlages)*; Schalter; *aero*

(Radar) Düppel(streifen) *m*, Störfolie *f*; *(shop-~)* Schaufenster *n*, Auslage *f*; *to dress a ~* ein Schaufenster dekorieren; *ticket ~* Fahrkartenschalter *m*; **~ advertising** Schaufensterreklame *f*; **~ blind** Jalousie *f*; **~ board** Fensterbrett *n*; **~-box** Blumenkasten *m*; **~ card** Schaufensterplakat *n*; **~ delivery** Schalterdienst *m*; **~-display** (Schaufenster-)Auslage *f*; *~~ competition* Schaufensterwettbewerb *m*; **~-dresser** Schaufensterdekorateur *m*; **~-dressing** Schaufensterdekoration; *fig* Aufmachung, Reklame, Mache; Vorspiegelung falscher Tatsachen; *com* Bilanzverschleierung *f*; **~ed** ['-d] *a* mit Fenstern versehen; **~ envelope** Fenster(brief)umschlag *m*; **~-frame** Fensterrahmen *m*; **~ goods** *pl* Schaufenster-, Dekorationsware *f*; **~ glass** Fensterglas *n*; **~-ledge** Fensterbrüstung *f*; **~less** ['-lis] fensterlos; **~ mirror** Spion, Fensterspiegel *m*; **~-pane** Fensterscheibe *f*; **~-screen** Fliegenfenster *n*; **~ seat** Fensterbank *f*; **~-shopping** Schaufensterbummel *m*; *to go ~~* e-n Schaufensterbummel machen; **~ shutter** Fensterladen *m*; **~-sill** Fensterbank *f*; **~-winder** *mot* Fensterkurbel *f*.

wine [wain] *s* Wein *m*; *tr* mit Wein bewirten; Wein einschenken (*s.o.* jdm); *Adam's ~ (hum)* Gänsewein *m*, Wasser *n*; *green ~* neue(r) Wein *m*; *new ~ in old bottles (fig)* neue(r) Wein in alten Schläuchen; *spirit of ~* Weingeist *m*; *white, red, sweet ~* Weiß-, Rot-, Süßwein *m*; **~bibber** (großer) Weintrinker, (Wein-)Säufer *m*; **~bottle** Weinflasche *f*; **~ cask** Weinfaß *n*; **~-cellar, -vault** Weinkeller *m*; **~-colo(u)red** *a* weinrot; **~-cooler** Sektkühler *m*; **~glass** Weinglas *n*; **~grower** Winzer, Weinbauer *m*; **~growing** Weinbau *m*; **~-merchant** Weinhändler *m*; **~press** Kelter *f*; **~ry** ['-ri] Weinkellerei *f*; **~shop** Weinhandlung *f*; **~skin** Weinschlauch *m*; **~stone** Weinstein *m*; **winy** ['-i] weinartig.

wing [wiŋ] *s* Flügel, *lit* Fittich *m*, Schwinge; *aero* Tragfläche *f*; *mot* Kotflügel; (Tür-, Fenster-)Flügel *m*; *theat (stage ~)* Kulisse *f*; *arch* (Seiten-)Flügel; *(Sessel)* Ohrenbacken *m*; *fig* (rechter, linker) Flügel *m (e-r Partei)*; *aero* Gruppe *f (fliegender Verband)*, *Am* Geschwader *n*; *hum* Arm *m*; *pl* Pilotenabzeichen *n*; *tr* durch-, überfliegen; mit Flügeln versehen; *fig* beflügeln; fliegen, auf dem Luftwege transportieren; *(Eilbrief)* abschicken; *arch* Seitenflügel anbauen an; in den Flügel treffen; *fam* in den Arm schießen; *itr* fliegen; *in the ~s (fam)* in Reserve; *on the ~* im Fluge; dauernd auf den Beinen, unterwegs; *on the ~s of the wind* mit Windeseile; *under s.o.'s ~s (fig)* unter jds Fittichen; *to clip s.o.'s ~s (fig)* jdm die Flügel beschneiden, jdn kurz halten; *to lend, to add ~s to s.th. (fig)* e-r S Flügel verleihen, etw beschleunigen; *to s.o.* jds Schritte beflügeln *od* beschleunigen; *to take ~* davonfliegen; aufbrechen; *to take to itself ~s (fig)* spurlos verschwinden; **~ assembly, unit** *aero* Tragwerk *n*; **~-beat, -stroke** Flügelschlag *m*; **~-case, -sheath** *ent* Flügeldecke *f*; **~ chair** Ohrensessel *m*; **~ commander** *aero* Gruppenkommandeur, Oberstleutnant; *Am* Geschwaderkommodore *m*; **~ed** [-d] *a* geflügelt *a. bot*; *fig* beflügelt, beschwingt, schnell; erhaben, fein, vornehm; am Flügel verletzt; *fam* am Arm, leicht verletzt; **~ feather** Schwungfeder *f*; **~ flap** Landeklappe *f*; **~less** ['-lis] ungeflügelt, flügellos; **~ load(ing)** *aero* (Trag-)Flächenbelastung *f*; **~ nut** Flügelmutter *f*; **~ shot** Schuß *m* auf e-n fliegenden Vogel; **~ skeleton** *aero* Tragflächengerippe *n*; **~-spread** *aero* (Tragflächen-)Spannweite; *orn* Flügelweite *f*; **~-tip** Flügelspitze *f*; *aero* Tragflächenende *n*; **~-weary** flügellahm *a. fig*; **~-width** *aero* Tragflächenweite *f*.

wink [wiŋk] *itr* blinzeln; mit den Augen zwinkern; *at s.o.* jdm zuzwinkern, zublinzeln; *at s.th.* etw geflissentlich übersehen; *(Stern)* flimmern; *tr* blinzeln, zwinkern mit *(den Augen)*; *s.o.* jdm zuzwinkern; *(Tränen) (to ~ away)* zurückhalten; *s* Blinzeln, Zwinkern *n*; Blick, Wink; Augenblick *m*; *mot* Blinken *n*; *to give s.o. a ~* jdm e-n Blick zuwerfen; *to tip s.o. the ~ (sl)* jdm e-n Wink geben; *I did not sleep a ~, I could not get a ~ of sleep (all night)* ich habe (die ganze Nacht) kein Auge zugetan; *forty ~s (pl) fam* Nickerchen, Schläfchen *n*; **~er** ['-ə] Blinzelnde(r) *m*; Scheuklappe *f*; *fam* Auge *n*, Wimper *f*; *pl mot* Blinklicht *n*; **~ing** ['-iŋ] Zwinkern, Blinzeln *n*; *as easy as ~~ (fam)* kinderleicht; *like ~~ (fam)* rasend, heftig.

winkle ['wiŋkl] *s* (Gemeine) Uferschnecke *f*; *tr*: *to ~ out* herausholen (*from* aus); **~-pickers** *pl fam* spitz zulaufende Schuhe *m pl*.

winnow ['winou] *tr (Getreide)* schwingen, worfeln; ver-, zerstreuen; sieben, sichten; aussortieren, -scheiden; trennen (*from* von); schlagen (*the wings* mit den Flügeln); *s* Worfeln, Schwingen; Schwingbrett *n*.

winter ['wintə] *s* Winter *m a. fig*; *itr tr* überwintern (*in, at* in); **~ apple** Winterapfel *m*; **~berry** Stechpalme *f*; **~crop** Wintergetreide *n*; **~feed** *tr* den Winter über füttern; **~ garden** Wintergarten *m*; **~green** *bot* Sin-, Immer-, Wintergrün *n*; **~ize** *tr* winterfest machen; **~kill** *itr tr Am bot* erfrieren (lassen); *itr (Saat)* auswintern; **~ quarters** *pl* Winterquartier *n*; **~ season** Wintersaison *f*; **~ sleep** Winterschlaf *m*; **~ solstice** Wintersonnenwende *f*; **~ sports** *pl* Wintersport *m*; **~time** Winterzeit *f*; **~ wheat** Winterweizen *m*; **~y** ['-ri], **wintry** ['wintri] winterlich; *fig* frostig; **wintriness** [-nis] Winterwetter *n*; Frostigkeit *f*.

wipe [waip] *tr* (ab)wischen, abreiben, -trocknen (*on a towel* an e-m Handtuch); säubern, reinigen; putzen (*o.'s nose* die Nase); reiben (*into* in); *sl* schlagen; *s* (Ab-)Wischen *n*; *sl* Schlag, Hieb; *fam* Seitenhieb *m*, spöttische, höhnische Bemerkung *f*; *sl* Rotzlappen *m*, Taschentuch *n*; *to ~ dry* trockenwischen; *to ~ the floor with s.o. (sl)* jdn völlig fertigmachen; *to* **~ away,** *to* **~ off** weg-, abwischen; *com* abbuchen, abschreiben; *(Schulden)* abtragen; *to* **~ out** *tr* auswischen, -löschen; tilgen; völlig vernichten, zerstören, dem Erdboden gleichmachen; *itr* sich aufheben; *to* **~ up** aufwischen, -nehmen; **~ contact** Schleifkontakt *m*; **~-out area** *radio* Schwundbereich *m*; **~r** ['-ə] Wischer *m*; Wischtuch *n*, -lappen *m*; *sl* Taschentuch *n*; *mot (windscreen ~~)* Scheibenwischer *m*; *tech* Abstreifung *f*; *el* Kontaktarm; *geol* Wackelstein *m*.

wire ['waiə] *s* Draht *m*; Drahtnetz *n*, -verhau *m*; (Draht-)Schlinge *f*; Leitungs-, Telephondraht *m*; (Kabel-)Ader *f*; Telegraph *m*; *fam* Telegramm *n*; *attr* Draht-; *tr* mit Draht versehen, verbinden, einfassen, befestigen; *(Jagd)* mit e-r (Draht-)Schlinge fangen; *el* e-e Leitung legen in; einrollen; anschließen (*to* an); *tr itr fam* telegraphieren, drahten; *by ~* telegraphisch; *to ~ in (fam)* loslegen, sich dranmachen; *to get under the ~ (Am)* es gerade noch schaffen; *to hold the ~ (tele)* am Apparat bleiben; *to pull (the) ~s (fig)* die Fäden in der Hand haben; *live ~* Hochspannungsdraht; *fig* lebhafte(r), energische(r) Mensch *m*; **~ address** Telegrammanschrift *f*; **~ bow** Drahtbügel *m*; **~-bridge** Drahtseilbrücke *f*; **~ broadcasting** Drahtfunk *m*; **~-cloth, -gauze, -netting** (feiner) Maschendraht *m*; **~ coil** Drahtspule *f*; **~ cutters** *pl* Drahtschere *f*; **~ dancer** Seiltänzer *m*; **~draw** *irr s. draw tr* drahtziehen; *fig* in die Länge ziehen; *fig* überspitzen; **~-edge** *(Schneide)* Grat *m*; **~ entanglement** Drahtverhau *m*; **~fence** Drahtzaun *m*; **~ ga(u)ge** Drahtlehre *f (Meßgerät)*; **~ glass** Drahtglas *n*; **~hair, -haired terrier** Drahthaarterrier *m (Hunderasse)*; **~ nail** Drahtstift *m*; **~ nippers, -pliers** *pl* Drahtzange *f*; **~photo** Bildtelegramm *n*; **~-puller** *fig* Drahtzieher *m*; **~pulling** *Am fig* Spiel *n* hinter den Kulissen, Drahtzieher *n*; **~ recorder** *el* Drahtmagnetophon *n*; **~ rod** Walzdraht *m*; **~-rope** Drahtseil *n*; **~ ropeway** Drahtseilbahn *f*; **~ service** *Am* telegraphische(r) Nachrichtendienst *m (der Presse)*; **~spun** *a* zu Draht gezogen; *fig* zu fein ausgesponnen, zu spitzfindig; **~ staple** (Draht-)Heftklammer *f*; **~-stitched** *a (Buch)* drahtgeheftet, broschiert; **~-stitching machine** Drahtheftmaschine *f*; **~ tack** Drahtstift *m*; **~ tapper** *tele* Abhörer; *fam (Rennen)* Tippgeber, Schwindler *m*; **~ tapping** *tele* Abhören *n*; **~-walker** Seiltänzer *m*; **~works** *pl, a. mit sing* Drahtzieherei, -fabrik *f*; **~worm** Drahtwurm; *Am* Tausendfüß(l)er *m*; **~-wove** *a* aus Draht geflochten; Velin-; *~~ mattress* Sprungfedermatratze *f*; *~~ paper* Velin(papier) *n*.

wireless ['waiəlis] *a* drahtlos; Funk-; Radio-; *s* drahtlose Telegraphie *od* Telephonie *f*; (Rund-)Funk *m*, Radio (-apparat *m*) *n*; *tr itr* funken; *by ~* durch Funkspruch, funktelegraphisch; *on, over the ~* im Rundfunk *od* Radio; *to listen to a concert over the ~* ein Konzert im Rundfunk anhören; *wired ~* Drahtfunk *m*; **~ aerial** Rundfunkantenne *f*; **~ beacon** Funkbake *f*, Peilsender *m*; **~ car** Funkstreifenwagen *m*; **~ communication** Funkverbindung *f*; **~ control** Fernlenkung *f*; **~ direction finder** (Funk-)Peilgerät *n*; **~ engineering** Funktechnik *f*; **~ equipment** Funkgerät *n*; **~ interception station** Abhörstelle *f*; **~ message** Funkspruch *m*; **~ operator** (*aero* Bord-)Funker *m*; **~ picture telegraphy** Bildfunk *m*; **~ pirate** Schwarzhörer *m*; **~ receiver** *radio* Empfänger *m*; **~ set** Funkgerät *n*; **~ silence** Funkstille *f*; **~ station** Funkstelle, -station *f*, (Rundfunk-)Sender *m*; **~ telegraphy** drahtlose Telegraphie *f*, Tastfunk *m*; **~ telephony** drahtlose Telephonie *f*, Sprechfunk *m*; **~ traffic** Funkverkehr *m*; **~ transmitter** Sendegerät *n*.

wir|iness ['waiərinis] drahtartige *od* sehnige Beschaffenheit; Straffheit *f*; **~ing** ['-riŋ] Verdrahtung *f a. tele*;

Draht-,(elektr.) Leitungsnetz *n*; Installation *f*; *aero* Bordnetz *n*; *~~ diagram* Leitungs-, Schaltplan *m*; **~y** ['-i] drahtartig, straff; Draht-; *fig* sehnig; *(Ton)* surrend.

wisdom ['wizdəm] Weisheit, Klugheit *f*; **~ tooth** Weisheitszahn *m*; *to cut o.'s ~ teeth (fig)* vernünftig werden.

wise [waiz] **1.** *a* weise, klug, vernünftig; verständig, verständnisvoll; gelehrt, gebildet; gewitzt, schlau, gerissen; *sl* alt-, neunmal-, überklug; vorlaut; *v*: *to ~ up (Am sl) tr* aufklären, informieren; *itr* schlau, klug werden; *to be non the ~r for s.th.* durch etw nicht schlauer geworden sein; *to be, to get ~ to s.th. (sl)* über etw im Bilde sein; von etw e-e Ahnung haben; *to crack ~ = ~crack*; *to get ~ (Am sl)* kapieren, begreifen; frech werden; *to put s.o. ~ to s.th. (sl)* jdm ein Licht aufstecken; *I get ~* mir geht ein Licht auf; *the Three W~ Men* die Drei Weisen aus dem Morgenland, die Heiligen Drei Könige *m pl*; **~acre** ['-eikə] Neunmalkluge(r), Klugschnacker, Angeber *m*; **~crack** *fam s* schnippische *od* spöttische *od* witzige Bemerkung *od* Antwort *f*; *itr* schnippisch, spöttisch, witzig reden; **~cracker, ~ guy, ~head, ~(n)heimer** *Am sl* Klugschnacker, -scheißer, Neunmalkluge(r), Angeber *m*; **2.** *obs* Weise, Art *f*.

wish [wiʃ] *tr* (sich) wünschen; wollen; sich sehnen nach; hoffen; *(Glück)* wünschen; bitten, ersuchen; auferlegen, aufhalsen (*on s.o.* jdm); *itr* wünschen; sich sehnen (*for* nach); e-n Wunsch äußern; *s* Wunsch; (sehnlicher, Herzens-)Wunsch; Wille *m*; Bitte *f* (*for* um), Ersuchen, Verlangen *n* (*for* nach); *pl (good ~es)* Glückwünsche *m pl*; *with best ~es* mit herzlichen Glückwünschen; *to ~ s.o. (good) luck* jdm Glück wünschen; *to ~ s.o. well, ill* jdm wohl-, übelwollen; *I ~* ich möchte *od* wollte; *the ~ is father to the thought (prov)* der Wunsch ist der Vater des Gedankens; **~bone, ~ing-bone** *(Vogel)* Gabelbein *n*; **~-dream** Wunschtraum *m*; **~ful** ['-ful] sehnsüchtig, sehnlich, verlangend; *~~ thinking* Wunschdenken *n*; **~ing cap** Zauberkappe *f*.

wish|-wash ['wiʃwɔʃ] Gesöff; Gewäsch, Geschwätz *n*; **~y-washy** ['wiʃiwɔʃi] wässerig, dünn; *fig* seicht, fad(e), schwach.

wisp [wisp] Büschel, Bündel *n*; Wisch, Fetzen; Streifen *m*; Fetzchen, Stückchen; Irrlicht *n*; Handfeger *m*; *a ~ of a girl* ein schmächtiges Ding; *~ of hair* Haarsträhne *f*; *~ of smoke* Rauchfetzen *m*; **~y** ['-i] klein, dünn, leicht; *(Haar)* büschelig.

wistaria [wis'tɛəriə], **wisteria** [-'tiəriə] *bot* Glyzine *f*.

wistful ['wistful] sehnsuchtsvoll, sehnsüchtig, verlangend; nachdenklich.

wit [wit] *a. pl* Verstand *m*, geistige Fähigkeiten *f pl*; Intelligenz *f*; Geist, Witz; witzige(r) Kopf *m*; *v obs nur noch in*: *to ~* das heißt, nämlich; *to be at o.'s ~s' end* am Ende s-r Kunst sein, *to be out of o.'s ~s* außer sich, ganz aus dem Häuschen sein (*with* vor); *to have, to keep o.'s ~s about one* e-n klaren Kopf behalten; *to live by o.'s ~s* sich (geschickt) durchs Leben schlagen; auf Kosten anderer leben; *he's no great ~* er ist kein großes Licht; **~less** ['-lis] geist-, witzlos; dumm, närrisch, albern; **~ticism** ['-isizm] geistreiche, witzige Bemerkung, Witzelei *f*; **~tiness** ['-inis] Witzigkeit *f*; **~tingly** ['-iŋli] *adv* wissentlich, absichtlich, vorsätzlich; **~ty** ['-i] geistreich, witzig.

witch [witʃ] *s* Hexe, Zauberin; *fig* bezaubernde Frau *f*; *tr* be-, verhexen; **~craft** ['-krɑ:ft], **~ery** ['-əri] Hexerei, Zauberei, Zauberkunst; Magie *f*; Zauber, Reiz *m*, (magische) Anziehungskraft *f*; **~-doctor** Medizinmann *m*; **~-hunt(ing)** *fig pol* Hexenverfolgung *f*; **~ing** ['-iŋ] *s* Zauberei, Zauberkraft *f*; *a* bezaubernd; *the ~~ hour of night* die Geisterstunde.

with [wið] *prp* mit; *(instrumental)* durch; *(kausal)* durch, an, vor; mit ... zusammen; nebst; bei; auf; trotz; vor; *~ the window open* bei offenem Fenster; *~ all his faults* bei all s-n Fehlern; trotz all s-r Fehler; *to be ~ it (fam)* auf Draht sein; *to have s.th. ~ one* bei sich haben; *to part ~* sich trennen von; *~ all the work he has done* nach dem, was er getan hat; *~ anger, love, hunger* vor Ärger, Liebe, Hunger; *~ smiles* lächelnd, mit e-m Lächeln; *~ this, that* hier-, damit, darauf; *away, down, off ~!* weg, nieder, herunter mit! *in ~* einig, verbunden mit.

withal [wi'ðɔ:l] *obs adv* zudem, überdies; ferner; darauf; dadurch; *prp (nach dem s u. am Satzende)* mit.

withdraw [wið'drɔ:] *irr s. draw tr* zurückziehen, -nehmen (*from* von, aus); *s.th. from s.o.* jdm etw entziehen; *(Geld)* abheben; *(Truppen)* abziehen; *itr* sich zurückziehen; sich entfernen; austreten, ausscheiden (*from* von); *parl* s-n Antrag zurücknehmen; *mil* sich absetzen; *to ~ from circulation (Geld)* aus dem Verkehr ziehen; *to ~ from school* von der Schule nehmen; **~al** [-əl] Zurücknahme, -ziehung (*from* von); Entnahme; Abhebung *f (vom Konto)*; Ausscheiden *n*, Rücktritt (*from* von); Widerruf; *mil* Rückzug, Abzug *m*; *~~ route* Rückzugsstraße *f*.

with|e [wiθ, wið, waið] Weidenrute *f*; **~y** ['wiði] *s* (Strick *m* aus) Weidenrute(n) *f*; *a* fest u. biegsam; *(Mensch)* zäh.

wither ['wiðə] *itr (to ~ up)* (ver)welken, verdorren, vertrocknen; (zs.) schrumpfen; *fig* s-e Kraft, Frische verlieren, vergehen; *(to ~ away)* (dahin)schwinden, dahinsinken; *tr (to ~ up)* vertrocknen, verdorren lassen; *fig* (vor Scham) in den Boden sinken lassen; einschüchtern (*with a look* mit e-m Blick); **~ing** ['-riŋ] *(Blick)* vernichtend.

withers ['wiðəz] *pl anat (Pferd)* Widerrist *m*; *my ~ are unwrung (fig)* ich wasche meine Hände in Unschuld.

withhold [wið'hould] *irr s. hold tr* zurückhalten, hindern; verweigern, vorenthalten (*s.th. from s.o.* jdm etw); verhindern; *(Steuern)* einbehalten.

within [wið'in] *adv* innen (drin), drin(nen), im Innern *(a. d. Herzens, der Seele)*, innerlich; daheim, zu Hause; nach innen, hinein, ins Innere; *from ~* von innen (her), aus dem Innern; *prp* in; innerhalb *gen (a. zeitl. u. graduell)*, im Bereich *gen*; in den Grenzen, im Rahmen *gen*; *(zeitl.)* binnen; *~ o.'s income* im Rahmen s-s Einkommens; *to be ~ walking distance of* zu Fuß gehen können zu; *~ call, hearing, reach, sight* in Ruf-, Hör-, Reich-, Sichtweite; *s das* Innere.

without [wið'aut] *adv* (dr)außen; äußerlich; außerhalb; *from ~* von außen (her); *prp* außerhalb *gen*, über ... hinaus; jenseits; ohne (*doing* zu tun); frei von; *~ delay* unverzüglich; *~ doubt* zweifellos; *~ fail* unweigerlich; *~ prejudice to* unbeschadet *gen*; *to do, to go ~ s.th.* ohne etw auskommen *od* fertigwerden; *that goes ~ saying* das versteht sich von selbst; *s das* Äußere.

withstand [wið'stænd] *irr s. stand tr itr* sich widersetzen, widerstehen (*s.o., s.th.* jdm, e-r S); aus-, standhalten (*hard wear* starker Beanspruchung).

witness ['witnis] *s* Zeugnis *n*; Zeuge *m* (*to* für); Urkundsperson *f*; Beweis (-stück, -mittel *n*) *m* (*to* für); *tr* bezeugen, bekunden; erkennen lassen; als Beweis(mittel) dienen für, beurkunden, bestätigen, beglaubigen; sich (persönlich) überzeugen von, selbst in Augenschein nehmen; Augenzeuge sein *gen*, gesehen haben; zuschauen, zusehen; *itr* Zeugnis geben *od* ablegen, Zeuge sein (*against, for s.o.* gegen, für jdn); bezeugen (*to s.th.* etw); als Zeugnis, Beweis dienen, Beweis sein (*to* für); *in ~ thereof, whereof* zu Urkund dessen; *to be a ~ to s.th.* für etw Zeuge, ein Zeichen sein; *to bear ~* Zeugnis ablegen (*of, to s.th.* von e-r S; *against, for s.o.* gegen, für jdn); *to call as, to ~* als Zeugen benennen *od* vorladen; *to hear a ~* e-n Zeugen vernehmen *od* verhören; *to summon a ~* e-n Zeugen vorladen; *to take to ~* als Zeugen anrufen *od* benennen; *evidence by ~es* Zeugenbeweis *m*; *eye-~* Augenzeuge *m*; *hearing of ~es* Zeugenvernehmung, Beweisaufnahme *f*; *marriage ~* Trauzeuge *m*; *principal ~* Haupt-, Kronzeuge *m*; *~ of an accident* Unfallzeuge *m*; *~ in court* Zeuge *m* vor Gericht; *~ for the defence, prosecution* Ent-, Belastungszeuge *m*; *~ on oath* vereidigte(r) Zeuge *m*; **~-box,** *Am* **stand** Zeugenstand *m*; **~ fee** Zeugengebühr *f*.

wive [waiv] *obs tr itr (Mann)* (sich ver)heiraten.

wizard ['wizəd] *s* Zauberer, Hexenmeister *a. fig*; *fam* patente(r) Kerl *m*; *a* magisch; *sl* blendend, prachtvoll, ganz groß, prima; **~ry** ['-ri] Zauberei, Magie *f a. fig*.

wizen(ed) ['wizn(d)] *a* vertrocknet, verwelkt; verhutzelt.

wo [wou] *s. whoa*.

woad [woud] *bot* (Färber-)Waid *m*.

wobbl|e ['wɔbl] *itr* wackeln, watscheln, (sch)wanken; *(Knie)* schlottern; *fam* schwabbeln; *mot* flattern; *fig* hin- u. herschwanken (*between* zwischen); *tr* ins Schwanken bringen; **~ing** ['-iŋ], **~y** ['-i] (sch)wankend, wack(e)lig.

wodge [wɔdʒ] *fam* Klumpen, Klotz *m*.

woe [wou] *s bes. poet, a. hum* Weh, Leid *n*, Schmerz *m*; (großes) Übel *n*; *pl* Übel *n pl*, Nöte *f pl*; *interj* wehe! *in weal and ~* in Wohl u. Wehe; *~ is me!* weh mir! *~ (be) to him!* wehe ihm! **~begone** ['-bigɔn] *a* jammervoll, jämmerlich, traurig, elend, erbärmlich; **~ful** ['-ful] traurig, betrüblich; elend, bejammerns-, beklagenswert; jämmerlich.

wold [would] Heide *f*, Ödland *n*.

wolf [wulf] *pl wolves* [wulvz] *s* Wolf; *fig* Bluthund; *sl* Schürzenjäger *m*; *tr (to ~ down)* hinunterschlingen; *to cry ~ (fig)* blinden Alarm schlagen; *to keep the ~ from the door (fig)* dafür sorgen, daß der Schornstein raucht; *a ~ in sheep's clothing (fig)* ein Wolf im Schafspelz; **~-call, -whistle** bewundernde(r) Zuruf, Pfiff *m* für e-e Schöne; **~-cub** junge(r) Wolf; Jungpfadfinder *m*; **~-dog, -hound** Schäfer-, Wolfshund *m*; **~ish** ['-iʃ] wölfisch; Wolfs-; *fig* räuberisch, (hab)gierig, gefräßig; *~~ appetite* Wolfs-, Bärenhunger *m*; **~sbane** *bot* Eisenhut *m*; **~'s-claws** *bot* Bärlapp *m*; **~'s milk** *bot* Wolfsmilch *f*.

wolfram ['wulfrəm] *chem* Wolfram *n*; **~ite** ['-ait] Wolfram(it) *n*.

wolver|ene, ~ine ['wulvəri:n] *zoo* Vielfraß; Wolverine *m (Pelz)*.

woman ['wumən] *pl women* ['wimin] *s* Weib *n*, Frau; Zofe *f*; *(ohne Artikel)* das weibliche Geschlecht, die Frauen; *the* ~ das typische Weib, die weibliche Art; *a* weiblich; Frauen-; *single* ~ Junggesellin *f*; ~ **doctor** Ärztin *f*; ~ **driver** *mot* Fahrerin *f*; ~-**hater** Weiberfeind *m*; ~**hood** ['-hud] Weiblichkeit, Fraulichkeit *f*; *to reach* ~~ *(Mädchen)* heranwachsen; ~**ish** ['-iʃ] weiblich; weibisch; ~**ize** ['-aiz] *tr* verweichlichen; *itr fam* es mit den Frauen haben; ~**kind** ['-'kaind] die Frauen *f pl*, das weibliche Geschlecht; ~**less** ['-lis] frauenlos; ~**like** ['-laik] (typisch) weiblich; ~**liness** ['-linis] Weiblichkeit *f*; ~**ly** ['-li] *a* weiblich, fraulich; ~ **suffrage** Frauenstimmrecht *n*; ~-**suffragist** Frauenrechtlerin *f*.

womb [wu:m] *anat* Gebärmutter *f*; Mutterleib; *fig* Schoß *m*; *in the* ~ *of time* im Schoße der Zeit; *falling of* ~ *(med)* Gebärmuttervorfall *m*.

wombat ['wɔmbət, -æt] *zoo* Wombat *m*, Beutelmaus *f*.

womenfolk ['wiminfouk] *die* Frauen; *fam das* Weibervolk *(in e-r Familie)*.

wonder ['wʌndə] *s* Wunder *a. fig*, -werk *n*; Verwunderung *f*, Erstaunen *n*; *itr* sich (ver)wundern; verwundert, erstaunt sein (*at, about* über); neugierig, gespannt sein; im Zweifel, unsicher sein; sich fragen; sich überlegen; gern wissen mögen *od* wollen; *for a* ~ überraschender-, erstaunlicherweise; *to be filled with* ~ ganz verwundert sein; *to work* ~*s* Wunder wirken; *(it is) no* ~ *(that)* es ist kein Wunder, es überrascht (mich) nicht, daß; *a nine days'* ~ e-e Sensation; *signs and* ~*s* Zeichen u. Wunder; ~**ful** ['-ful] wundervoll, -bar, erstaunlich; ~**ing** ['-riŋ] verwundert, erstaunt; ~**land** Wunder-, Zauber-, Märchenland *a. fig*; *fig* (Märchen-)Paradies *n*; ~**ment** ['-mənt] Verwunderung *f*, Erstaunen *n*; ~-**stricken, -struck** *a* verwundert, überrascht, erstaunt, verblüfft, hingerissen (*at* von); ~-**worker** Wundertäter *m*; **wondrous** ['wʌndrəs] *a adv lit* wunderbar.

wonky ['wɔŋki] *sl* wack(e)lig, kipp(e)lig, unsicher; *fig* unecht.

wont [wount, *Am* wʌnt] *pred a* gewohnt (*to* an); *s* Gewohnheit *f*; *to be* ~ gewohnt, gewöhnt sein, pflegen (*to do* zu tun); *use and* ~ Brauch u. Sitte; ~**ed** ['-id] *a* gewohnt, gewöhnt; gewöhnlich, üblich, normal.

won't [wount] = *will not*.

woo [wu:] *tr* (sich be)werben um, den Hof machen (*a woman* e-r Frau), umwerben; *fig* streben nach, trachten nach, zu gewinnen suchen; drängen (*s.o.* jdn); ~**er** ['-ə] Freier, Bewerber *m*; ~**ing** ['-iŋ] *a* werbend; verlockend, aufreizend, verführerisch; *s* Werbung *f* (*of* um); *to go a-*~~ auf Freiersfüßen gehen.

wood [wud] *s a. pl* Wald(ung *f*) *m*, Gehölz, Holz; Holzfaß; *mus* hölzerne(s) Blasinstrument *n*; *the* ~ die Holzblasinstrumente *n pl*; *sport* Holzkugel *f*; *a* hölzern; Holz-; Wald-; *in (the)* ~ *(Wein)* vom Faß; *out of the* ~*(s) (fam fig)* über den Berg; *to be unable to see the* ~ *for the trees (fig)* den Wald vor (lauter) Bäumen nicht sehen; *touch* ~*!* unberufen! *wine in the* ~ Faßwein *m*; ~-**alcohol** Methylalkohol *m*; ~-**anemone** *bot* Buschwindröschen *n*; ~-**ant** (rote) Waldameise *f*; ~-**ashes** *pl* Holzasche *f*; ~**bin** Holzkasten *m (für Brennholz)*; ~**bind** ['-baind], ~**bine** ['-bain] *bot* Geißblatt *n*; *Am* wilde(r) Wein *m*; ~-**block** Holzblock, -klotz; *typ* Druckblock; Blockdruck *m*; ~ **burner** *mot* Holzgaser *m*; ~-**burning** Holzfeuerung *f*; ~-**carver** Holzschnitzer *m*; ~ **ceiling** Holzdecke *f*; ~**chuck** *(amerik.)* Waldmurmeltier *n*; ~**coal** *min* Braun-, Holzkohle *f*; ~**cock** *orn* Wald-, Holz-, Bergschnepfe *f*; *fig* Einfaltspinsel *m*; ~**craft** ['-krɑ:ft] Kenntnis *f* des Waldes; Jägerei *f*; ~**cut** ['-kʌt] Holzschnitt *m*; ~**cutter** ['-kʌtə] Holzfäller; *(Kunst)* Holzschneider *m*; ~**cutting** ['-kʌtiŋ] Holzfällen *n*; Holzschneidekunst *f*; ~**ed** ['wudid] *a* bewaldet; waldreich; baumbestanden; ~**en** ['wudn] hölzern *a. fig*; *fig* steif, kalt, ausdruckslos, langweilig; dumm, borniert; Holz-; ~~ *construction* Holzkonstruktion *f*; ~~ *floor* Holzfußboden *m*; ~~ *headed (a)* dumm, doof; ~-**engraver** *(Kunst)* Holzschneider *m*; *ent* Buchdrucker, Fichtenborkenkäfer *m*; ~-**engraving** Holzschneidekunst *f*; Holzschnitt *m*; ~ **fibre slab** Holzfaserplatte *f*; ~-**free** holzfrei; ~-**gas** Holzgas *n*; ~**horse** *Am* Sägebock *m*; ~-**house**, ~**shed** Holzschuppen *m*; ~**iness** ['-inis] Waldreichtum *m*; holzige Beschaffenheit *f*; ~**land** Wald(land *n*) *m*, Waldung *f*; ~~ *scenery* Waldlandschaft *f*; ~-**lark** Heide-, Holz-, Baumlerche *f*; ~**less** ['-lis] unbewaldet, wald-, baumlos; ~**louse** *pl -lice zoo* Bohrassel *f*; ~**man** ['-mən] Förster; Holzfäller, -hacker; Waldbewohner *m*; ~ **panelling** Holztäfelung *f*; ~ **nymph** Waldnymphe *f*; ~**pecker** ['-pekə] Specht *m*; ~ **peg** Holzpflock *m*; ~-**pigeon** Wald-, Ringeltaube *f*; ~**pile** Holzstoß *m*, -miete *f*; ~-**pulp** Holzschliff, -stoff *m*; ~ **reeve** Forstwart *m*; ~**ruff** *bot* Waldmeister *m*; ~ **shavings** *pl* Hobelspäne *m pl*; ~**sman** ['-zmən] Waldarbeiter, -bewohner *m*; ~-**spirit** Holzgeist *m*; ~**sy** ['-zi] *Am* waldig; Wald-; ~-**tar** Holzteer *m*; ~-**tick** *zoo* Holzbock *m*; ~-**turner** Drechsler *m*; ~-**turning** Drechseln *n*, Drechslerei *f*; ~ **vinegar** Holzessig *m*; ~ **wind** *(pl)* (Holz-)Blasinstrument(e *pl*) *n*; ~-**wool** Holzwolle; *med* Zellstoffwatte *f*; ~**work** Holzarbeiten *n*; hölzerne Bauteile *m pl*, Balkenwerk *n*; ~-**working** Holzbearbeitung *f*; ~~ *machine, machinery* Holzbearbeitungsmaschine *f*, -maschinen *f pl*; ~**worm** *Am* Holzwurm *m*; ~**y** ['-i] bewaldet, waldig; holzig; Holz-; ~-**yard** Holzplatz, -hof *m*.

woof [wu:f] *(Weberei)* Schuß, Einschlag *m*; Gewebe *n*, Stoff *m*, Tuch *n*.

wool [wul] Wolle *f*; Wollgarn *n*, -stoff, Faserstoff *m*; (Neger-)Haar *n*; *against the* ~ *(fig)* gegen den Strich; *to go for* ~ *and come home shorn (fig)* e-n Reinfall erleben; *to lose o.'s* ~ *(fig)* aus der Haut fahren; *to pull the* ~ *over s.o.'s eyes (fig)* jdm das Fell über die Ohren ziehen, jdn hinters Licht führen; *much cry and little* ~ *(prov)* viel Geschrei und wenig Wolle; *keep your* ~ *on* nur keine Aufregung! *all* ~ *and a yard wide (fig)* echt; großartig; *dyed in the* ~ in der Wolle gefärbt; *fig* waschecht; *cotton* ~ Rohbaumwolle *f*; ~ **blanket** Wolldecke *f*; ~-**clip** jährliche(r) Wollertrag *m*; ~-**dyed** *a tech* in der Wolle gefärbt; ~-**fat, -oil** Wollfett, Lanolin *n*; ~**gathering** *s fig* Geistesabwesenheit, Zerstreutheit *f*; Tagtraum *m*; *a* geistesabwesend, in Gedanken versunken; ~**grower** Schafzüchter *m*; ~**(l)en** ['-in] *a* wollen; Woll-; *s pl (*~~ *goods)* Wollwaren, -sachen, Strickwaren *f pl*; ~~*-draper* Woll-, Strickwarenhändler *m*; ~**liness** ['-inis] wollige, weiche Beschaffenheit; *fig fam* Unklarheit *f*; ~**ly** ['-i] *a* wollen; wollig, flauschig, weich; Wolle tragend; Wollen-; *(Stimme)* dumpf, rauh, heiser, belegt; *(Bild)* verschwommen *a. fig*; *fig* nebelhaft; verworren; *fam* ungebildet; *s (bes.* flauschiges) wollene(s) Kleidungsstück; *Am (Weststaaten)* Schaf *n*; ~~*-headed (a)* mit dichtem Haar; *fig* verworren, unklar; ~**pack** Wollballen *m*; *mete* Haufenwolke *f*; ~**sack** Wollsack *m (Sitz des britischen Lordkanzlers im Oberhaus)*; ~ **scouring** Wollwäsche *f*; ~-**stapler** Wollhändler, -sortierer *m*; ~ **trade** Wollhandel *m*; ~ **yarn** Wollgarn *n*.

woozy ['wu:zi] *Am sl* besoffen.

wop [wɔp] **1.** *Am sl pej* Itaker *m*; ~ **house** *Am sl* italienische(s) Lokal *n*; ~ **special** *Am sl* Spaghetti *pl*; **2.** *sl mil* Funker *m*.

word [wə:d] *s* Wort *n*; Vokabel *f*; *mil* Befehl *m*, Kennwort *n*, Parole; *fig* Losung; kurze Äußerung *od* Bemerkung (*about* über); Rede *f*, Spruch *m*; Zusage *f*, (Ehren-)Wort *n*; Bescheid *m*, Meldung, Nachricht; *tech* Buchstabengruppe *f*; *pl* Wortwechsel, Disput, Streit; *pl* Text *m (e-r Melodie)*; *tr* in Worten ausdrücken, in Worte kleiden, formulieren; *at a* ~ auf e-n Wink, sofort; *by* ~ *of mouth* mündlich; *in a, one* ~ mit e-m Wort, kurz (u. gut) *adv*; *in other* ~*s* mit anderen Worten; *in so many* ~*s* genauso, wörtlich *adv*; *of few* ~*s* von wenig Worten, kurz angebunden, wortkarg; *of many* ~*s* redselig, gesprächig; *on, with the* ~ kaum gesagt; ~ *for* ~ Wort für Wort, wörtlich *adv*; *not to be the* ~ *for s.th.* etw nicht richtig ausdrücken *od* wiedergeben; *to break, to keep o.'s* ~ sein Wort brechen, halten; *to eat o.'s* ~*s* s-e Worte zurücknehmen, sich entschuldigen; *to give o.'s* ~ *upon s.th.* sein Wort auf etw geben; *to hang on s.o.'s* ~*s (fig)* an jds Lippen hängen; *to have a* ~ *with s.o.* kurz mit jdm sprechen; *to have* ~ *from* Nachricht haben von; *to have* ~*s with s.o.* sich mit jdm ausea.setzen, mit jdm e-n Wortwechsel haben; *to have no* ~*s for s.th.* für etw keine Worte haben *od* finden; *to have the last* ~ das letzte Wort haben; *to leave* ~ eine Nachricht, Bescheid hinter-, zurücklassen (*with* bei; *at the office* im Büro); *to put into* ~*s* in Worte kleiden; *to put in, to say a (good)* ~ *for s.o.* für jdn ein gutes Wort einlegen; *to send* ~ e-e Nachricht zukommen lassen (*to s.o.* jdm); *to suit the action to the* ~ das Wort in die Tat umsetzen; *to take s.o. at his* ~ jdn beim Wort nehmen; *to take the* ~*s out of s.o.'s mouth* jdm das Wort aus dem Munde nehmen; *I don't mince my* ~*s* ich nehme kein Blatt vor den Mund; *he is as good as his* ~ man kann sich auf ihn verlassen; *the last* ~ *has not yet been said on this matter* darüber ist das letzte Wort noch nicht gesprochen; *he didn't say a* ~ *about it* er hat kein Wort, keinen Ton davon gesagt, nichts darüber verlauten lassen; *upon my* ~*!* auf mein Wort! das ist ja allerhand! *my* ~ *upon it!* auf meine Ehre! *big* ~*s* große Worte *n pl*; *God's W*~, *the W*~ *of God* Gottes Wort, das Wort Gottes, die Bibel *f*; *the last* ~ *(fig)* der letzte Schrei; *on s.th.* das letzte Wort in e-r Angelegenheit; *a man of* ~*s* ein Mann von Wort; *play upon* ~*s* Wortspiel *n*; ~ *of hono(u)r* Ehrenwort *n*; *a* ~ *in season* ein gutes Wort zur rechten Zeit; ~-**book** Wörter-, Text-, Liederbuch *n*; ~-**formation** Wortbildung *f*; ~**iness** ['-inis] Wortschwall *m*; ~**ing** ['-iŋ] Wortwahl, Formulierung *f*; Wortlaut *m*; Überschrift; Wortstellung; Ausdrucksweise *f*; Inhalt *m*; ~**less** ['-lis] wort-, sprachlos; ~ **order** *gram* Wortstellung *f*; ~-**painting** Wortmalerei, anschauliche Schilderung *f*; ~-**perfect**: *to be* ~~ das Gedicht, s-e Rolle auswendig können; ~ **picture** lebhafte Schilderung *f*; ~ **power** Wortschatz *m*; ~-**play** Wortspiel *n*; ~-**splitting** *fig* Haarspalterei *f*; ~**y** ['-i] *a* Wort-; wortreich; ~~ *warfare* Wortstreit *m*.

work [wə:k] **1.** *s* Arbeit, Tätigkeit; Beschäftigung *f*, Geschäft; Handwerk *n*, Beruf(sarbeit *f*) *m*; Pflicht, Aufgabe *f*; Unternehmen; Werk *n*, (Arbeits-)Leistung *f*; (Kunst-)Werk; (Arbeits-)Material; Werkstück *n*; *phys* Kraftübertragung, Arbeit *f*; *pl* Werke *n pl a. rel*, Taten *f pl*; Werke *n pl (e-s Dichters)*; (Werk-, Industrie-, Festungs-)Anlage(n *f pl*) *f*; *arch* Baustelle *f*; (Uhr-)Werk, Getriebe *n*; *pl mit sing* Werk(e *pl*) *n*, Fabrik, Anstalt *f*, Hütten *f pl*; *a* Arbeits-, Werk-; **2.** *itr* arbeiten (*at* an); schaffen, wirken, beschäftigt, tätig sein (*at* mit); funktionieren; wirksam sein; Einfluß ausüben (*on, upon* auf); zu überreden suchen (*on, upon s.o.* jdn); sich be-, verarbeiten lassen; sich abmühen, sich plagen; in lebhafter Tätigkeit, in Bewegung, in Erregung sein; *(Pläne)* glücken, gelingen; *(los-, kaputt)* gehen; *(durch etw hindurch)* kommen; gären; *(Wind)* sich drehen (*to* nach); **3.** *tr* be-, ver-, erarbeiten, ausarbeiten; *(Aufgabe)* lösen, ausrechnen; zustande bringen, bewerkstelligen; hervorbringen, -rufen, auslösen, (be-)wirken; arbeiten mit, betätigen, in Betrieb setzen, in Gang bringen; *(Pferd)* zureiten; betätigen; gebrauchen; *(Maschine, Geschütz)* bedienen; lenken; arbeiten lassen; *(Maschine)* beanspruchen; bearbeiten, beeinflussen; *(Betrieb)* leiten; *(Gut)* bewirtschaften; *(Gebiet)* bereisen, bearbeiten; *(zu etw)* bringen; *(s-n Weg)* bahnen; *fam* spielen lassen, ausnutzen, Gebrauch machen von; *(jdn)* ausnutzen; *(etw)* herausschlagen; *to* ~ *o.s.* sich (hinein)steigern (*into* in); **4.** *at* ~ bei der Arbeit, beschäftigt (*upon* mit); in Betrieb, im Gange, tätig; *fit for* ~ arbeitsfähig; *in* ~ in Arbeit (*u. Brot*); *out of* ~ ohne Arbeit, arbeitslos; *without* ~ beschäftigungslos; **5.** *to* ~ *at a trade* ein Gewerbe ausüben; *to get the* ~*s (sl)* sein Fett bekommen; *to give s.o. the* ~*s (sl)* jdn fertigmachen; jdn über die Klinge springen lassen; *to have o.'s* ~ *cut out for one* schwer arbeiten, *fam* schuften, 'ran müssen; *to make sad* ~ *of* übel umgehen mit; *to make short, quick* ~ *of* kurzen Prozeß machen mit; *to set, to get to* ~ sich an die Arbeit machen, ans Werk gehen; *to shoot the* ~*s (Am sl)* aufs Ganze gehen; e-n letzten Versuch machen; *to* ~ *it (sl)* es fertig bringen, es schaffen; *to* ~ *loose* lose werden, los-, abgehen; *to* ~ *o.'s will* s-n Willen durchsetzen; *to* ~ *wonders* Wunder wirken; **6.** *brain, head, mental* ~ Kopf-, geistige Arbeit *f*; *brick* ~*s (pl)* Ziegelei *f*; *cessation of* ~ Arbeitsniederlegung *f*; *clerical* ~ Büroarbeit *f*; *conditions (pl) for* ~ Arbeitsbedingungen *f pl*; *course of* ~ Geschäftsgang *m*; *extension of* ~*s* Betriebserweiterung *f*; *factory* ~ Fabrikarbeit *f*; *farm* ~ Landarbeit *f*; *gas* ~*s (pl)* Gasanstalt *f*, -werk *n*; *home* ~ Heimarbeit *f*; *iron* ~*s (pl)* Eisenhütte *f*, -werk *n*; *job* ~ Stückarbeit *f*; *lack of* ~ Arbeitsmangel *m*; *man of all* ~ Faktotum *n*; *manual* ~ Handarbeit *f*; *piece of* ~ Stück *n* Arbeit; *public* ~*s (pl)* Stadt-, Versorgungswerke *n pl*; *research* ~ Forschungstätigkeit *f*; *skilled* ~ Facharbeit *f*; *sparetime* ~ Nebenbeschäftigung *f*; *speed of* ~ Arbeitstempo *n*; *team* ~ Gemeinschafts-, Gruppenarbeit *f*; *water* ~*s (pl)* Wasserwerk *n*, -kunst, Pumpstation *f*; ~ *of art* Kunstwerk *n*; ~ *on the books* Auftragsbestand *m*; *to* ~ **away,** *to* ~ **on** darauflos-, weiterarbeiten (*at* an); *to* ~ **in** *tr* einfügen, -flechten; einarbeiten; *itr* sich einfügen (*with* in); sich einarbeiten; *to* ~ **off** *tr* aufarbeiten; loswerden; wegtun; erledigen; *(Gefühl)* abreagieren; *itr* allmählich lösen; *to* ~ **on** bearbeiten (*s.o.* jdn); arbeiten an; *to* ~ **out** *tr* ausarbeiten, entwickeln, in die Praxis umsetzen; be-, zs.rechnen; erhöhen (*at* auf); lösen; fertigstellen, beenden, vollenden; aufbrauchen, erschöpfen; *(Schuld)* abarbeiten; *min* abbauen; *itr* heraustreten, sich herauslösen; (dabei) herauskommen, sich entwickeln, sich ergeben; sich auswirken; *to* ~ **over** überarbeiten; *s.o.* jdn mitnehmen *fig*; *to* ~ **round** sich mühsam durcharbeiten (*to* nach); sich wieder erholen; *to* ~ **up** *tr* auf-, durch-, ver-, ausarbeiten (*into* zu); entwickeln; erregen, hervorrufen; *(Appetit)* sich machen; verbrauchen; *itr* voran-, vorwärtskommen, aufsteigen (*to* zu); sich einarbeiten (*at* in); ~**able** ['-əbl] bearbeitbar; zu gebrauchen(d), brauchbar, praktizierbar, durchführbar; *min* abbaufähig, -würdig; ~**aday** ['-ədei] werktäglich, Alltags-; *allg* alltäglich, gewöhnlich, abgedroschen; ~-**bag, -basket, -box** Nähbeutel, -korb, -kasten *m*; ~**bench** Werkbank *f*; ~**book** Arbeitsübersicht *f*, -plan *m*, -anweisung *f*; Übungsbuch *n*; ~ **contract** Arbeitsvertrag *m*; ~**day** *s* Arbeits-, Werk-, Wochentag *m*; *a* werktäglich; *on* ~~*s* an Wochen-, Werktagen, werktäglich *adv*; ~**er** ['-ə] Arbeiter *m*; *zoo (~~ bee)* Arbeiterin *f*; *brain, head, intellectual* ~~ Kopf-, geistige(r) Arbeiter *m*; *clerical, office* ~~ Büroangestellte(r) *m*; *factory, industrial* ~~ Fabrikarbeiter *m*; *heavy* ~~ Schwerarbeiter *m*; *home, out-*~~ Heimarbeiter(in *f*) *m*; *itinerant, migratory* ~~ Wanderarbeiter *m*; *manual* ~~ Handarbeiter *m*; *part-time* ~~ Kurzarbeiter *m*; *seasonal* ~~ Saisonarbeiter *m*; *semi-skilled* ~~ angelernte(r) Arbeiter *m*; *social* ~~ Fürsorge(beamte)r, Wohlfahrtspfleger *m*; *(un)skilled* ~~ (un)gelernte(r) Arbeiter *m*; *wage-*~~ *(Am)* Lohnarbeiter *m*; ~ **force** Belegschaft *f*; ~**house** Armenhaus; *Am* Arbeitshaus *n*; ~**ing** ['-iŋ] *a* arbeitend; werktätig; Arbeits-, Werk-; betriebs-, arbeitsfähig *(a.parl. Mehrheit)*; praktisch, ausreichend; *(Gesicht)* in (sichtbarer) Erregung (befindlich); *(not)* ~~ in (außer) Betrieb; *s* Arbeit(en *n*) *f*, Schaffen, Wirken *n*, Tätigkeit; Funktion *f*, Gang *m*; Wirksamkeit *f*, Einfluß *m*; Verarbeitung *f*; Abbau *m*; Mühe *f*, Bemühungen *f pl*; lebhafte Tätigkeit, sichtbare Erregung; Gärung *f*; *min* Abbau *m*, Grube *f*; ~~ *accident* Betriebsunfall *m*; ~~ *agreement, arrangement* Arbeitsabkommen *n*; ~~ *capacity* Arbeits-, Leistungsfähigkeit *f*; ~~ *capital* Betriebskapital *n*; ~~ *class* Arbeiterklasse *f*; ~~-*class family* Arbeiterfamilie *f*; ~~ *clothes (pl)* Arbeitskleidung *f*, -zeug *n*; ~~ *committee* Arbeitsausschuß *m*; ~~ *condition* Arbeits-, Gebrauchs-, Betriebsfähigkeit *f*; *pl* Arbeitsbedingungen *f pl*; ~~ *costs, expenses (pl)* Betriebskosten *pl*; ~~ *current* Betriebsstrom *m*; ~~ *day* Arbeits-, Werktag *m*; ~~ *drawing* Arbeitsskizze, Vorlage; Bauzeichnung *f*; ~~ *hours (pl)* Arbeitszeit *f*; *extension, shortening of* ~~-*hours* Arbeitszeitverlängerung, -kürzung *f*; ~~ *instructions, regulations (pl)* Arbeitsordnung *f*; ~~ *load* Nutzlast *f*; ~~ *lunch (pol)* Arbeitsessen *n*; ~~ *man* (Fabrik-)Arbeiter *m*; ~~ *method* Arbeitsweise *f*; ~~ *operation* Arbeitsgang *m*; ~~ *order* Gebrauchs-, Betriebsfähigkeit *f*; *in* ~~ *order* (in) gebrauchs-, betriebsfähig(em Zustand); ~~-*out* Ausarbeitung; Berechnung; Beendigung, Fertigstellung *f*; ~~ *party* Arbeitsausschuß; *mil* Arbeitstrupp *m*; ~~ *place* Arbeitsplatz *m*; ~~ *plant* Betriebsanlage *f*; ~~ *power* Arbeitskraft *f*; ~~ *print* Werkstattpause *f*; ~~ *process* Arbeitsprozeß, -vorgang *m*; ~~-*program(me), -schedule* Arbeitsprogramm *n*, -plan *m*; ~~ *substance* Betriebsstoff *m*; ~~ *time* Arbeits-, Betriebszeit *f*; ~~-*up* Auf-, Ver-, Ausarbeitung *f*; ~~ *voltage* Betriebsspannung *f*; ~~ *woman* (Fabrik-)Arbeiterin *f*; ~~ *year* Betriebs-, Rechnungsjahr *n*; ~ **law** Energieprinzip *n*; ~**less** ['-lis] arbeits-, stellenlos; ~**man** ['-mən] Arbeiter *m*; *skilled* ~~ Facharbeiter *m*; ~**manlike,** ~**manly** *a* werk-, kunstgerecht, fachmännisch; ~**manship** Kunstfertigkeit; Facharbeit, Wertarbeit; Ausführung, Arbeit, Leistung *f*; *(jds)* Werk *n*; ~**material** Werkstoff *m*; ~-**piece** Werkstück *n*; ~ **room** Werkstatt *f*; ~-**out** *Am fam* Training *n*, Übung *f*; Probelauf *m*; mühevolle Arbeit *f*; ~**shop** Werkstatt, -stätte, Arbeitsstätte *f*, -platz *m*; Arbeitsgruppe *f*, -kreis; (Sommer-)Kurs *m*, Seminar *n*; ~~ *for repair work* Reparaturwerkstatt *f*; ~-**shy** arbeitsscheu; ~ **study** Zeitstudie *f*; ~ **table** Arbeitstisch *m*; Nähtischchen *n*; ~-**to-rule campaign** Bummelstreik *m*; ~-**up** *typ* Spieß *m*; ~**woman** Arbeiterin *f*.

world [wə:ld] Welt(all *n*); Welt, Erde *f*, Stern, Planet *m*; Menschheit; (Welt-)Öffentlichkeit; *die* Menschen; *das* Leben; (bekannte) Welt *f*; (Kultur-)Kreis *m*; Gebiet; (Natur-)Reich *n*; (Lebens-)Bereich *m*, (Um-)Welt, Sphäre *f*; (geistiger) Horizont *m*; *a* ~, ~*s (pl) of* e-e Menge, sehr viel; *all the* ~ die ganze Welt; *all the* ~ *over* in der ganzen Welt; *dead to the* ~ *(sl)* sternhagelvoll; *for (all) the* ~, *for the whole* ~ um alles in der Welt; *for all the* ~ *like* ganz genau wie; *in the* ~ in aller Welt; *on top of the* ~ *(Am sl)* ganz aus dem Häuschen; *out of this* ~ *(fam)* ganz besonder; phantastisch; *to the* ~ *(sl)* aufs äußerste; gänzlich; *to the* ~*'s end* bis ans Ende der Welt; *to be all the* ~ *to s.o.* jds ein und alles sein; *to begin the* ~ s-e Laufbahn beginnen; *to bring into the* ~ zur Welt bringen; *to carry the* ~ *before one* sich (schnell) durchsetzen; *to come into the* ~ zur Welt kommen, das Licht der Welt erblicken; *to know, to have seen the* ~ die Welt kennen, große (Lebens-)Erfahrung haben; *to make a noise in the* ~ viel von sich reden machen; *to think the* ~ *of* große Stücke halten auf; *how goes the* ~ *with you?* wie steht's? wie geht's? *the ancient* ~ die Alte Welt *f*; *a citizen of the* ~ ein Weltbürger; *history of the* ~ Weltgeschichte *f*; *the lower* ~ die Unterwelt *f*; *a man of the* ~ ein Mann *m* von Welt; *the Old, New W*~ die Alte, Neue Welt *f*; ~ **congress** Weltkongreß *m*; **W**~ **Court** Internationale(r) Ständige(r) Gerichtshof *m*; ~ **depression** Weltwirtschaftskrise *f*; ~ **domination** Weltherrschaft *f*; ~ **economy** Weltwirtschaft *f*; ~ **fair** Weltausstellung *f*; ~**-famous** weltberühmt; ~ **federation** Weltverband *m*; ~ **language** Weltsprache *f*; ~ **league** Weltliga *f*; ~**liness** ['-linis] Weltlichkeit, weltliche Gesinnung *f*; ~**ling** ['-liŋ] Weltkind *n*; **ly** ['-li] *a* weltlich, irdisch, diesseitig; Welt-; weltzugewandt; weltklug; ~~*-minded (a)* weltlich gesinnt; ~~*-mindedness* weltliche Gesinnung *f*; ~~*-wise* weltklug; ~ **market** Weltmarkt *m*; ~**-old** uralt; ~ **output, production** Welterzeugung, -produktion *f*; ~ **peace** Weltfrieden *m*; ~ **politics** *pl* Weltpolitik *f*; ~ **power** Weltmacht *f*; ~ **record** Weltrekord *m*; ~ **revolution** Weltrevolution *f*; ~('s) **series** *Am* Baseball-Meisterschaftsspiele *n pl*; ~ **soul** Weltseele *f*; ~ **thrift day** Weltspartag *m (31. Okt.)*; ~ **trade** Welthandel *m*; ~ **view** Weltanschauung *f*; **W~ War**: *First, Second* ~~, *(Am)* ~~ *I, II* Erste(r), Zweite(r) Weltkrieg *m*; ~**-weary** lebensmüde; ~**-wide** weltweit, -umspannend; ~~ *reputation* Weltruf *m*.

worm [wə:m] *s* Wurm *a. fig*; *fig* (elender) Wicht; widerliche(r) Bursche *m*; (Schrauben-)Gewinde *n*; Schraube, Schnecke; Kühlschlange *f*; *pl med* Würmer *m pl*; *itr* sich krümmen, sich winden, sich schlängeln; kriechen, schleichen; *tr* mit e-m Wurmmittel behandeln; *fig* herausziehen, -locken (*s.th., a secret out of s.o.* etw, ein Geheimnis aus jdm); *to* ~ *o.s., to* ~ *o.'s way in* sich einschleichen; *through* sich hindurchwinden; *to be food for* ~*s* von den Würmern gefressen werden, tot sein; ~**-cast** Erdhäufchen *n*; ~ **conveyor** Förderschnecke *f*; ~**-drive** *tech* Schneckenantrieb *m*; ~**-eaten** *a* wurmstichig; verbraucht, abgenutzt; morsch, veraltet; ~**-gear** Schneckengetriebe *n*; ~**-hole** Wurmloch *n (in e-m Möbelstück)*; ~**-powder** Wurmpulver *n*; ~**root** Wurmkraut *n*; ~**'s eye view** Froschperspektive *f*; ~**seed** *bot* Wurmsamen *m*; ~**-wheel** *tech* Schneckenrad *n*; ~**wood** *bot* Wermut; *fig* Wermutstropfen *m*; ~**y** ['-i] wurmig; wurmstichig; wurmartig; *fig* kriecherisch, gemein.

worn [wɔ:n] *pp von wear a* verbraucht, abgenutzt; abgetragen; geschwächt, erschöpft; abgespannt; verängstigt; *fig* abgedroschen; ~**-out** ['-'aut] *a* unbrauchbar (geworden); ermüdet, erschöpft, abgespannt.

worr|iment ['wʌrimənt, *Am* 'wə:ri-] *Am fam* Quälerei, innere Unruhe, Angst *f*; Ärger *m*, ärgerliche Sache, Verdrießlichkeit *f*; ~**isome** ['-səm] ärgerlich, verdrießlich; aufregend; unruhig; selbstquälerisch; ~**it** [-it] *sl* = ~*y*; ~**y** ['-i] *tr* beunruhigen, Sorgen machen; belästigen, reizen, ärgern, aufregen, quälen, zur Verzweiflung bringen, verängstigen; schütteln; zerren an; *(Problem)* immer wieder anpacken; herausknobeln; *itr* besorgt, beunruhigt sein, sich Sorgen machen; verzweifelt, in Unruhe, in Ängsten sein (*about* um); zerren, zausen, reißen (*at* an); *s* Quälerei, Unruhe, Angst *f*; Ärger, Verdruß *m*; *to* ~~ *about* befürchten; sich kümmern um; *to* ~~ *along, through* sich durchschlagen, -beißen, *fam* -wursteln; *to be* ~*ied* besorgt, unruhig sein; *don't* ~~ seien Sie ohne Sorge! *I won't let that* ~~ *me (Am)* darüber lasse ich mir keine grauen Haare wachsen; ~**ying** ['-iiŋ] beunruhigend, quälend.

worse [wə:s] *a (Komparativ von bad)* schlechter, übler, schlimmer, ärger; *(~ off)* schlechter, übler dran; kränker; *adv* schlimmer, ärger; *s* Schlimmere(s), Ärgere(s) *n*; *all, so much the* ~ um so schlimmer; *from bad to* ~ vom Regen in die Traufe; *none the* ~ nicht weniger, (noch) mehr; ~ *and* ~ immer schlimmer; *I'm* ~ *(off)* es geht mir *(gesundheitlich)* schlechter; *he's none the* ~ *for it* es hat ihm nichts geschadet; ~ *was to follow* es sollte noch schlimmer *od* Schlimmeres kommen; *my shoes are the* ~ *for wear* meine Schuhe sind ganz abgetragen; ~ *luck!* leider! unglücklicherweise! *a change for the* ~ e-e Wendung zum Schlechteren; ~**n** ['-n] *tr itr* (sich) verschlimmern, (sich) verschlechtern.

worship ['wə:ʃip] *s bes. rel* Verehrung, Anbetung *f*; Gebet *n*, Gottesdienst *m*; tiefe Hingabe *f*; *tr* verehren, anbeten, vergöttern; *itr* s-e religiösen Pflichten erfüllen; beten; *Your, His W*~ Ew., Se. Gnaden; ~**ful** ['-ful] ehrwürdig; ehrfürchtig, ehrfurchtsvoll; verehrend; ~**(p)er** ['-ə] Verehrer, Anbeter *m*; *pl* Kirchgänger *m pl*; ~~ *of idols* Götzendiener *m*; ~**(p)ing** ['-iŋ] Verehrung, Anbetung *f*.

worst ['wə:st] *a (Superlativ von bad)* schlechtest, übelst, schlimmst, ärgst; *adv* am schlimmsten, am ärgsten; *s das* Schlechteste, Schlimmste; *tr* überwältigen, besiegen; *at (the)* ~ schlimmstenfalls; *at his, her, its* ~ im ungünstigsten Moment; *if (the)* ~ *comes to (the)* ~ im allerschlimmsten Fall; *(in) the* ~ *way (Am sl)* ganz mächtig, ganz gewaltig *adv*; *to be* ~ *off* am schlimmsten dran sein; *to be prepared for the* ~ auf das Schlimmste gefaßt sein; *to get the* ~ *of it* den kürzeren ziehen; *to make the* ~ *of s.th.* e-r S keine großen Chancen geben; *the* ~ *of it is that* ... das Schlimmste daran ist, daß ...; *do your* ~*!* mach, was du willst! *let him do his* ~*!* laß ihn gewähren! kümmere dich nicht um ihn! *the* ~ *is yet to come* das dicke Ende kommt noch nach.

worsted ['wustid] *s* Kammgarn(stoff *m*) *n*; *a* Kammgarn-; Woll-; ~ **mill** Kammgarnspinnerei *f*; ~ **shag, velvet** Wollplüsch, -samt *m*; ~ **stocking** Wollstrumpf *m*; ~**work** Wollstickerei *f*.

wort [wə:t] **1.** (Bier-)Würze *f*; ~ **copper** Würzepfanne *f*; **2.** *in Zssgen bot* -wurz(el) *f*, -kraut *n*.

worth [wə:θ] *s (bes.* Geld-)Wert; Gegenwert; *fig* Wert(schätzung *f*) *m*, Verdienst, Ansehen *n*, Bedeutung, (Ge-)Wichtigkeit *f*; *pred a (e-e bestimmte Summe)* wert; *fig* (e-r S) wert, würdig; *a shilling's* ~ [wəθ] *of apples* für 1 sh Äpfel; *for all one is* ~ *(fam)* so gut man irgend kann, so gut es irgend geht; *for what it is* ~ so wie es da ist; ohne Garantie; *to be* ~ *it (fam)* der Mühe wert sein; *to be a million* ~ Millionär sein; *to be* ~ *the money* preiswert sein; *to put in o.'s two cents* ~ *(Am)* s-n Senf dazu geben, mitreden; *did you get your money's* ~ sind Sie auf Ihre Kosten gekommen? *it's* ~ *the trouble* es lohnt die Mühe; ~**iness** ['-inis] Würdigkeit *f*; ~**less** ['-lis] wertlos; *fig* unwürdig; ~ **mentioning** der Rede wert; ~ **reading** lesenswert; ~ **seeing** sehenswert; ~**-while** *a* der Mühe wert; ~**y** ['wə:ði] *a* würdig, wert (*of s.th.* e-r S); verdienst-, ehrenvoll; *hum* trefflich; *s fig obs* Größe *f*; *hum* wackere(r) Mann *m*; ~~ *of credit* glaub-, *com* kreditwürdig.

would [wud] *pret von will* würde; möchte; wollte; ~**-be** [-bi] *a attr* angeblich; Schein-, falsch; beabsichtigt, gewollt; zukünftig; *s* Angeber; Gernegroß *m*; ~~ *poet* Dichterling *m*; ~**n't** ['-nt] = ~ *not*.

wound 1. [wu:nd] *s* Wunde *(in the arm* am Arm); Verletzung *a. fig*; *fig* Kränkung, Beleidigung *f (to* für); *tr* verwunden, verletzen *a. fig*; *fig* kränken, beleidigen; *to* ~ *to death* tödlich verwunden; *incised, sword, punctured, contused, lacerated, gunshot* ~ Schnitt-, Hieb-, Stich-, Quetsch-, Riß-, Schußwunde *f*; *open, festering* ~ offene, eiternde Wunde *f*; *war* ~ Kriegsverletzung *f*; ~ *of entry, exit* Ein-, Ausschuß *m (e-r Schußwunde)*; ~**ed** ['-id] *a* verwundet, verletzt *a. fig*; *(Eitelkeit)* gekränkt; *seriously, walking* ~~ schwer-, leichtverletzt; ~~ *person, soldier* Verletzte(r), Verwundete(r) *m*; *the* ~~ die Verwundeten; **2.** [waund] *pret u. pp v. wind* 2.

wow [wau] **1.** *Am interj* ei! au! ach! *s* Mordsspaß; tolle(r) Kerl *m*, tolle Frau *f*; *bes. theat* Bombenerfolg *m*; *tr* hin-, mitreißen; **2.** Wimmern *n*.

wowser ['wauzə] *(Australien)* (strenger) Puritaner; *Am sl* Spielverderber, Miesmacher *m*.

wrack [ræk] **1.** Wrack *n*, Schiffstrümmer *pl*; an Land gespülte(r) Tang *m*; *to go to* ~ *and ruin* in die Brüche gehen; **2.** = *rack*.

wraith [reiθ] Geist *m (bes. e-s Sterbenden od soeben Verstorbenen)*.

wrangl|e ['ræŋgl] *itr* (sich) zanken, (sich) streiten, disputieren (*with s.o. about, over s.th.* mit jdm über etw); *tr Am (Weststaaten) (Vieh)* zs.treiben; *s* Zank, Streit, Wortwechsel *m*; ~**er** ['-ə] Streithahn *m*, streitsüchtige Person *f*; *Am* Cowboy; *(senior* ~~) *(Cambridge)* (bester) Mathematikstudent *m* bei der Abschlußprüfung.

wrap [ræp] *tr* herumwickeln, hineintun (*in* in); falten; *(to* ~ *up)* umwickeln (*round* um); einwickeln, -schlagen, ein-, verpacken (*in* in); *fig* (ein-, ver-)hüllen, verbergen, -stecken; *itr* sich einhüllen; *s* Hülle *f*, Umschlag *m*; *meist pl* Umschlagtuch *n*, Umhang, weite(r) Mantel, Pelz *m*; *under* ~*s* im Verborgenen, versteckt, geheim; *to* ~ *up well* sich gut anziehen; *to be* ~*ped up in* völlig in Anspruch genommen sein von, ganz aufgehen in; verborgen sein in; ~**-around windshield** *mot Am* Panoramascheibe *f*; ~**page** ['-idʒ] = ~*ing(s)*; ~**per** ['-ə] Packer(in *f*) *m*; Hülle *f*, Überzug *m*; Streif-, Kreuzband *n*; *(Buch)* Schutzumschlag *m*; *(Zigarre)* Deckblatt *n*; *(leichter)* Morgenrock *m*; ~**ping** ['-iŋ] Einwickeln *n*; *meist pl* Verpackung(smaterial *n*), Hülle *f*; ~~ *paper* Packpapier *n*.

wrath [rɔ:θ, *Am* ræθ] Zorn *m*, Wut *f*, Grimm *m*; ~**ful** ['-ful] zornig, wütend, grimmig; ~**y** ['-i, *Am* 'ræθi] *fam* wütend, in Fahrt.

wreak [ri:k] *tr (s-n Ärger, Zorn)* auslassen, *(Rache)* üben (*on, upon* an).

wreath [ri:θ] *pl* ~*s* [ri:ðz] Gewinde *n*, Girlande *f*, (lockerer) Kranz *m*; (Seil-)Windung *f*; (Nebel-)Schleier *m*; ~ *of smoke* Rauchfahne *f*; ~ *of snow* Schneewehe *f*; ~**e** [ri:ð] *tr* winden, flechten (*into a* ~ zu e-m Kranz); bekränzen; einhüllen; verdrehen; *itr* sich winden, sich kräuseln; sich ringeln (*round* um).

wreck [rek] *s* Wrack; *jur* Strandgut *n*; *allg* Trümmer *pl*, Ruine *f*; *fig* (elendes) Wrack *n*, Jammergestalt *f*; *mar* Schiffbruch *m*; *allg* Unglück, Verderben *n*, Zs.bruch, Untergang, Ruin *m*, Zerstörung *f*; *tr* zerstören *a. fig*; zertrümmern, zerschlagen; ein-, abreißen, abbrechen; *rail* entgleisen lassen; *fig* ruinieren, zugrunde richten *(a. gesundheitlich)*; *(Pläne)* vernichten; *itr (to be* ~*ed)* scheitern, *allg* in Trümmer gehen, zs.brechen, zugrunde gehen; *to be a* *mere ~ of o.'s former self* nur noch ein Schatten seiner selbst sein; *train ~* Zugunglück *n*; **~age** ['-idʒ] Schiffbruch; Zs.bruch *m*; Trümmer *pl*; Strandgut *n a. fig*; **~er** ['-ə] Strandräuber; Plünderer; Zerstörer; Abbrucharbeiter, -unternehmer; *Am* Bergungsdampfer; *mot* Abschleppwagen *m*; *pl* Bergungsmannschaft *f*, -trupp *m*; *~~service (Am mot)* Abschleppdienst *m*; **~ing** ['-iŋ] *s* Abbruch(arbeiten *f pl*); Strandraub *m*; *Am* Bergung(sarbeiten *f pl*) *f*, Abschleppen *n*; *a* vernichtend; *Am* Bergungs-, Abschlepp-; Abbruch-; *~~ company (Am)* Abbruchunternehmen *n*; *~~ crew (Am)* Bergungsmannschaft *f*; *~~ train (Am)* Hilfszug *m*; *~~ truck (Am)* Abschleppwagen *m*.

Wren [ren] (= *Women's Royal Naval Service) fam Br* Marinehelferin *f*.

wren [ren] *orn* Zaunkönig *m*.

wrench [rentʃ] *s* (plötzlicher) Ruck *m*; *med* (Ver-)Zerrung, Verrenkung, Verstauchung *f*; *fig* Stich *(ins Herz)*, Abschiedsschmerz; *tech* Schraubenschlüssel *m*; *phys* Torsion *f*; *tr* plötzlich *od* heftig reißen, ziehen (*from* von); zerren; verdrehen, -zerren; *med* verrenken, -stauchen; *fig (Sinn)* verzerren, verdrehen, entstellen; *to ~ away* wegreißen; entreißen (*from s.o.* jdm); *to ~ open* aufreißen; *to give o.'s ankle a ~* sich den Knöchel verstauchen; *monkey ~* Universalschraubenschlüssel, *fam* Engländer *m*; **~ing-iron** Brecheisen *n*.

wrest [rest] *tr* (ver)drehen, winden, zerren an; entwinden, -reißen (*from s.o.* jdm); abringen *a. fig*; *fig* verzerren, entstellen; *s* Verdrehung, -zerrung, -renkung *f*; Ruck; *mus* Stimmschlüssel *m*.

wrestl|e ['resl] *itr* ringen *a. fig*; *allg* kämpfen (*for* um; *with* mit); sich herumschlagen, sich abquälen (*with* mit); *tr* ringen mit; *(Ringkampf)* austragen; *s* Ringkampf; *allg* Streit *m*; *fig* Ringen *n*; **~er** [-ə] Ring(kämpf)er *m*; **~ing** ['-iŋ] Ringen *n a. fig*; *~~-bout, match* Ringkampf *m*.

wretch [retʃ] unglückliche(r) Mensch, *fam* Unglückswurm; (elender) Wicht; Schelm *m*; **~ed** ['-id] *a* unglücklich; elend; schlecht; lumpig, erbärmlich, jämmerlich, scheußlich; **~edness** ['-idnis] Elend *n*, Jammer *m*; Erbärmlichkeit, Jämmerlichkeit *f*.

wrick [rik] *tr* verdrehen, -renken; *s* Verdrehung, -renkung, -zerrung *f*.

wriggl|e ['rigl] *itr* sich winden; sich unruhig hin u. her bewegen; *fig* sich (drehen u.) winden; sich unbehaglich fühlen; *tr* in e-e drehende Bewegung versetzen; *to ~~ o.s.* sich winden; *s* Winden *n*; Krümmung *f*; *to ~~ (o.s.) out, to ~ o.'s way out* sich herauswinden (*of s.th.* aus etw); *to ~~ o.s. free* sich loswinden; **~er** ['-ə] aalglatte(r) Mensch *m*, Schlange; Mückenlarve *f*.

wright [rait] *s in Zssgen* -macher, -bauer *m*.

wring [riŋ] *irr wrung, wrung* [rʌŋ] *tr (to ~ out)* auswringen, -drücken, -pressen, -quetschen; *(to ~ out)* herausdrücken, -pressen; *(Bekenntnis)* abringen, erpressen (*from, out of* von); verdrehen, -ziehen, -zerren; entreißen, abnötigen (*from s.o.* jdm); *(Hals)* umdrehen; *fig* ängstigen, quälen; *itr* drehen, zerren; sich krümmen; *s* Wringen, Quetschen, Pressen *n*; *to ~ off* abdrehen; *to ~ s.o.'s hand* jdm herzlich die Hand drücken; *to ~ o.'s hands* die Hände ringen; *to ~ s.o.'s heart* jdm (großen) Kummer machen; jdm ans Herz greifen; *to give s.th. a ~* etw auswinden; **~er** ['-ə] *fig* Erpresser *m*; *tech* Wringmaschine *f*; *to put s.o. through the ~~ (Am sl)* jdn auf Herz u. Nieren prüfen; **~ing** ['-iŋ] *s* Wringen, Drücken *n*; *a* drückend; *fig* quälend; *~~ wet* triefend (naß).

wrinkl|e ['riŋkl] **1.** *s* Falte, Runzel *f*; *(Papier)* Kniff *m*; *tr itr* (sich) falten; *(to ~ up)* in Falten legen; (sich) runzeln; Runzeln bekommen; *(Stoff)* knittern; *(Gesicht)* sich verziehen; **~y** ['-i] runz(e)lig, faltig; *(Stoff)* leicht knitternd; **2.** *fam* gute Idee *f*, kluge(r) Schachzug, Trick, Kniff; gute(r) Rat *m*; *to give s.o. a ~~, to put s.o. up to a ~~* jdm e-n Wink geben.

wrist [rist] Handgelenk *n*; **~band** (feste) Manschette *f*; **~bone** Handwurzelknochen *m*; **~let** ['-lit] Armband *n*; Pulswärmer; *sport* Handgelenkschützer *m*; *pl sl* Handschellen *f pl*; **~lock** *(Ringen)* Schulterdrehgriff *m*; **~-pin** *tech* Kolbenbolzen *m*; **~-watch** Armbanduhr *f*; *~~ strap* Uhrenarmband *n*.

writ [rit] *jur* Verfügung *f*, Erlaß *m*; *(~ of summons)* Vorladung; *Br* Wahlausschreibung; *obs* Urkunde *f*; *to issue a ~ against s.o., to serve a ~ (up)on s.o.* jdm e-e Vorladung zustellen; *to take out a ~ against s.o.* e-e Vorladung gegen jdn erwirken; *Holy W~* Heilige Schrift *f*; *~ of assistance, of sequestration* Beschlagnahmeverfügung *f*; *~ of attachment* Haftbefehl *m*; *~ of execution* Vollstreckungs-, Zahlungsbefehl *m*.

write [rait] *irr wrote* [rout], *written* ['ritn] *tr* schreiben; schriftlich niederlegen, auf-, niederschreiben, zu Papier bringen; aufzeichnen, ab-, verfassen; *jur* aufsetzen; *(Bescheinigung, Scheck)* ausstellen; *(Scheck)* ausschreiben; *(Formular)* ausfüllen; *(Papier)* beschreiben; *(Vertrag)* aufsetzen; (schriftlich, brieflich) mitteilen (*s.th. to s.o., s.o. s.th.* jdm etw); unterschreiben, signieren; (schriftlich) bezeichnen (*acc* als); *fig* zeichnen, graben in; *itr* schreiben; *(Bücher)* schreiben, schriftstellern, Schreibarbeiten machen; bestellen, kommen lassen (*for s.th.* etw); *to ~ in full* ausschreiben; *to ~ o.s. a man* volljährig sein; *to ~ shorthand* stenographieren; *to ~* **down** nieder-, aufschreiben, schriftlich niederlegen; herziehen, schlecht schreiben über; *com* abschreiben; *to ~* **in** *it* eintragen; *itr* sich schriftlich bewerben (*for* um); *to ~* **off** rasch niederschreiben; *com u. fig* abschreiben; *to ~* **out** (voll)ausschreiben; abschreiben; *to ~ o.s. out* alles zum Ausdruck bringen; *to ~* **up** e-n schriftlichen Bericht machen über, eingehend berichten; zu Ende schreiben; *(schriftlich)* aufs laufende bringen; *(Wert)* höher einsetzen; *(in e-m Schreiben)* herausstreichen, sehr loben; Reklame machen; **~-down, -off** *com* Abschreibung *f*; **~-up** *com* Heraufsetzung *f* des Buchwertes; (positiver) Pressebericht *m*; Anpreisung *f*.

writ|er ['raitə] Schreiber *m*; Schreibkraft *f*; Buchhalter; Schriftsteller, Verfasser *m*; *Scot (~~ to the signet)* Rechtsanwalt *m*; *serial ~~* Feuilletonist *m*; *text ~~* Kommentator *m*; *~~'s cramp* Schreibkrampf *m*; **~ing** ['-iŋ] Schreiben; Schriftstück *n*, Urkunde *f*, Dokument; ausgefüllte(s) Formular *n*; (Hand-)Schrift; Schrift *f*, Buch, Werk *n*, Aufsatz *m*; Schriftstellerei *f*, Stil *m*; *in ~~* schriftlich; *to put in ~~* niederschreiben; *~~-block* Schreibblock *m*; *~~-case* Schreibmappe *f*; *~~-desk* Schreibpult *n*, -tisch *m*; *~~-ink* Tinte *f*; *~~-kit* Schreibzeug *n*; *~~-pad* Schreibunterlage *f*; Notiz-, Briefblock *m*; *student's ~~-pad* Schul-, Kollegheft *n*; *~~-paper, -room, -table* Schreibpapier, -zimmer *n*, -tisch *m*.

writhe [raið] *itr* sich *(in Schmerz, Ängsten)* winden (*with* vor); leiden (*under* unter).

written ['ritn] *pp von write a* schriftlich; *~ in water (fig)* in den Sand geschrieben; *~* **evidence** *jur* Urkundenbeweis *m*; *~* **examination** schriftliche Prüfung *f*; *~* **language** Schriftsprache *f*.

wrong [rɔŋ] *a* verkehrt, falsch; irrig, irrtümlich; unrecht, unbillig; unangebracht, unpassend, fehl am Platz; nicht in Ordnung, unbefriedigend; *(Gewebe)* links; *adv* falsch, nicht richtig, nicht recht; *s* Unrecht *n*; *jur* Rechtsbruch *m*; *tr* ein Unrecht zufügen (*s.o.* jdm); ungerecht behandeln, benachteiligen, beeinträchtigen; schaden (*s.o., s.th.* jdm, e-r S); mißverstehen; verkennen, Unrecht tun (*s.o.* jdm); beleidigen, kränken; *on the ~ side of 50* über 50 (Jahre); *~ side out* mit der Innenseite nach außen; *to be ~* unrecht haben; sich irren; nicht in Ordnung sein, nicht stimmen (*with s.th.* etw); *to be in the ~* im Unrecht sein; *to be in the ~ box* im Nachteil sein; in der Klemme stecken; fehl am Platze sein; *to do ~* Unrecht tun (*to s.o.* jdm); sich etw zuschulden kommen lassen; *s.th.* etw falsch, verkehrt machen; *to get, to go ~* schiefgehen, scheitern; nicht richtig funktionieren; auf die schiefe Ebene geraten; *to get s.o. in ~ (Am fam)* jdn in Mißkredit bringen; *to get in ~ with s.o. (Am fam)* bei jdm in Mißkredit kommen; *to get it ~* sich verrechnen; es falsch verstehen; *to get on the ~ side of s.o.* sich jdn zum Gegner machen; *to have, to get hold of the ~ end of the stick (fig)* auf dem Holzwege sein; *to put in the ~* ins Unrecht setzen; *to suffer ~* unrecht leiden; *to take s.th. ~* etw übelnehmen; *to take the ~ turning, path (fig)* auf Abwege geraten; *he got out on the ~ side of the bed* er ist mit dem falschen Fuß aufgestanden; *there is s.th. ~* da stimmt etw nicht (*with* mit); *what's ~? (fam)* stimmt was nicht? ist was nicht in Ordnung? *sorry, ~ number! (tele)* Verzeihung, (ich bin) falsch verbunden! *two ~s do not make a right (prov)* man kann sein Unrecht nicht durch ein anderes wiedergutmachen; **~doer** Übel-, Missetäter; Rechtsbrecher *m*; **~doing** Übertretung, Rechtsverletzung *f*, -bruch *m*; Sünde *f*; **~ful** ['-ful] unrecht, ungesetzlich, unerlaubt, gesetz-, rechtswidrig; **~fulness** ['-fulnis] Ungesetzlichkeit, Unerlaubtheit, Gesetzwidrigkeit *f*; **~-headed** *a* starrsinnig, querköpfig, halsstarrig, verbohrt; **~ly** ['-li] *adv* falsch, unrichtig; zu Unrecht; **~ness** ['-nis] Unrecht *n*; Verkehrtheit; Unbilligkeit *f*.

wroth [rouθ, rɔ:θ] *pred a poet* ergrimmt, zornig; *hum* in Rage.

wrought [rɔ:t] *pret u. pp von work a* be-, ge-, verarbeitet, verfertigt, hergestellt; geschmiedet, gehämmert; sorgfältig (aus)gearbeitet; *~* **goods** *pl* Fertigwaren *f pl*, -fabrikate *n pl*; *~* **iron** Schmiedeeisen *n*, Schweißstahl *m*; **~-up** *a* erregt; aufgeregt, -gewühlt.

wry [rai] *(bes. Gesicht, Mund)* verzogen, verzerrt, schief; *fig* verdreht, verzerrt, schief, falsch; *(Lächeln)* gezwungen; *to make a ~ face* das Gesicht verziehen, Grimassen schneiden; **~-mouthed** *a fig* ironisch, spitz; **~neck** *orn* Wendehals; *med* Schiefhals *m*; **~ness** ['-nis] Verdreht-, Verzerrtheit *f*.

X

X, x [eks] *pl* ~*'s* X, x *n*; (X-förmige) Krampe *f*; Unbekannte(r) *m*; *math* unbekannte Größe *a. fig*; Abszisse *f*; *tr: to* ~ *out (fam)* ausixen; **X-chromosome** *biol* X-, Geschlechtschromosom *n*; **X-formation** *mil* sich überschneidende (taktische) Aufstellung *f*; **X-ray** *s* Röntgenaufnahme *f*, Röntgen-, Schirmbild *n*; *pl* Röntgenstrahlen *m pl*; *a* Röntgen-; *tr* röntgen, durchleuchten; mit Röntgenstrahlen behandeln; ~~ *apparatus* Röntgenapparat *m*; ~~ *department* Röntgenstation *f*; ~~ *diagnosis, examination, test* Röntgenuntersuchung *f*; ~~ *therapy* Röntgentherapie *f*; ~~ *tube* Röntgenröhre *f*.

Xanthippe [zæn'θipi] Xanthippe *f*.

xeno|gamy [zi(:)'nɔgəmi] *bot* Fremdbestäubung *f*; ~**phobia** [zenə'foubjə] Fremdenhaß *m*.

xero|philous [zi'rɔfiləs] *bot* xerophil; ~**phyte** ['zerəfait] Xerophyt *m*, Dürrpflanze *f*.

Xmas ['krisməs, *fam* 'eks-] *fam* = Christmas.

xyl|em ['zailəm] *bot* Xylem *n*; ~**ograph** ['-əgra:f] Holzschnitt *m*; ~**ographer** [zai'lɔgrəfə] Holzschneider *m*; ~**ographic(al)** [zailə'græfik(əl)] Holzschnitt-, -schneide-; ~**ography** [zai'lɔgrəfi] Holzschneidekunst, Xylographie *f*; ~**onite** ['-ənait] *Art* Zelluloid *n (Handelsmarke)*; ~**ophone** ['-əfoun] *mus* Xylophon *n*; ~**ose** ['-ous] *chem* Xylose *f*, Holzzucker *m*.

Y

Y, y [wai] *pl* ~*'s* Y, y *n*; *tech* Gabel; *math* 2. Unbekannte; Ordinate *f*; ~**-connection** *el* Sternschaltung *f*; ~**-drain** gabelförmige(s) Entwässerungsrohr *n*; ~**-pipe, -tube** Rohrgabel *f*, Y-Rohr *n*; ~**-track** Gleisgabel *f*.

yacht [jɔt] *s mar* (Segel-, Motor-)Jacht *f*; *itr* auf e-r Jacht fahren; ~**-club** Jachtklub *m*; ~**ing** ['-iŋ] Jachtsport *m*, -segeln *n*; ~**sman** ['-smən] Jachtfahrer, -besitzer *m*.

yah [ja:] *interj* pfui! äh!

yahoo [jə'hu:] Scheusal *n*; Rohling *m*.

yak [jæk] **1.** *s* Jak, Grunzochse *m*; **2.** *Am itr* quasseln; *s* Gequassel; Gelächter *n*.

yam [jæm] *bot* Jamswurzel; *Scot* Kartoffel; *Am dial* Süße Kartoffel *f*.

yank [jæŋk] *fam itr* plötzlich auffahren; *tr* heftig ziehen an; *s* Ruck, kräftige(r) Zug *m*; *Y*~ *s. Yankee*; *to* ~ *out, off* mit e-m Ruck heraus-, wegreißen.

Yankee ['jæŋki] *s Am* Neuengländer; Nordstaatler; *bes. Br* Amerikaner, Yankee *m*; *a* typisch amerikanisch.

yap [jæp] *itr* kläffen *a. fig*; *sl* schwätzen; (dumm) quatschen; *s* Gekläff; *sl* dumme(s) Geschwätz, Gequatsche *n*; *Am sl* Quatschkopf *m*; *Am sl* Maul *n*.

yard [ja:d] **1.** Yard *n (= 0,914 m)*; *mar* Rahe *f*; *square* ~ Quadratyard *n*; ~**age** ['-idʒ] Ausmessung, Länge *f* in Yards; ~**-arm** *mar* Rahnock *m*; ~**-measure** Yardmaß *n*; ~**-stick** Yardstock *m*, Elle *f*; *fig* Maßstab *m*; **2.** Hof; (Werk-)Platz; Pferch *m*, Gehege *n*; *(railway* ~*)* Rangierbahnhof; *Am* (Haus-)Garten *m*; ~**age** Lagerung; Lagergebühr *f*; ~**bird** *Am sl* Rekrut *m*; ~**man** ['-mən] Bahn-, Werftarbeiter; Viehknecht *m*; ~**master** *rail* Rangiermeister *m*.

yarn [ja:n] *s* Garn *n*, Faden *m*; *fig fam* Seemannsgarn *n*; *itr* reden; plaudern; erzählen; *(a.: to spin a* ~*) (fam)* ein Seemannsgarn spinnen, Märchen erzählen (*about* über); *wool(l)en* ~ Wollgarn *n*; ~ **beam** Kettenbaum *m*; ~**-dyed** *a* im Garn gefärbt.

yarrow ['jærou] *bot* Schafgarbe *f*.

yaup *s. yawp.*

yaw [jɔ:] *itr mar aero* gieren; *(Geschoß)* von der Bahn abweichen; *fig* schwanken; *s* (Kurs-)Abweichung *f*; *fig* Schwanken *n*.

yawl [jɔ:l] **1.** *mar* Jolle *f*; **2.** *s. jowl.*

yawn [jɔ:n] *itr* gähnen *a. fig*; *fig* klaffen, sich öffnen; *tr* gähnend sagen; *s* Gähnen *n*; ~**ing** ['-iŋ] *a* gähnend *a. fig.*

yawp [jɔ:p] *Am fam itr* brüllen; quasseln; hörbar gähnen; *s* Gequassel *n*; Schrei *m*.

ye [ji:] **1.** *prn obs* ihr; du; dir; **2.** *the.*

yea [jei] *adv* ja (doch); gewiß, sicher, freilich, in der Tat; *s* Ja *n*; Jastimme *f*; ~**h** [je, jæ, ja:] *adv Am fam* ja.

yean [ji:n] *itr (Schaf, Ziege)* lammen, zickeln; ~**ling** ['-liŋ] Lamm; Zicklein *n*.

year [jə:, jiə] Jahr; *pl* Alter *n*; *all the* ~ *round* das ganze Jahr über; *for, in* ~*s* seit Jahren, jahrelang; *for his* ~*s* für sein Alter; *in the* ~ *1837* im Jahre 1837; *last, this, next* ~ letztes *od* vergangenes, dieses, nächstes Jahr; *the* ~ *one (hum)* zu Olims Zeiten; ~ *after (od by)* ~ Jahr für Jahr; ~*s ago* vor Jahren; ~ *in,* ~ *out* jahraus, jahrein; ~ *of birth* Geburtsjahr *n*; ~*s of discretion* gesetzte(s) Alter *n*; ~ *of the grace* Jahr *n* des Herrn; ~ *of manufacture* Baujahr *n*; ~ *under report* Berichtsjahr *n*; ~*s of service* Dienstjahre *n pl*; ~**-book** Jahrbuch *n*; ~**ling** ['-liŋ] *zoo* Jährling *m*; ~**-long** *a* ein volles Jahr dauernd; ~**ly** ['-li] *a adv* jährlich; ~~ *income, output, subscription* Jahreseinkommen *n*, -produktion *f*, -beitrag *m*.

yearn [jə:n] *itr* sich sehnen, verlangen (*for, after* nach; *to do* zu tun); ~**ing** ['-iŋ] *s* Sehnsucht *f*, Verlangen *n*; *a* sehnsuchtsvoll, verlangend.

yeast [ji:st] Hefe *f*; *(*~*-plant)* Hefepilz; *fig* Schaum *m*, Gischt *m, a. f*; *fig* Sauerteig *m*, Ferment *n*; ~**-cake** (Back-)Hefe *f*; ~**-powder** Backpulver *n*; ~**y** ['-i] hefig; schaumig, schäumend; *fig* gärend, bewegt, unruhig; leichtfertig, oberflächlich.

yegg(man) [jeg, '-mən] *Am sl* Geldschrankknacker, Bankräuber; Einbrecher; Gangster, Verbrecher *m*.

yell [jel] *itr* (auf)schreien (*with* vor); *itr tr* (gellend) schreien (*for help* um Hilfe); laut lachen; *s* Auf-, gellende(r) Schrei; *fam* etw zum Totlachen; *Am sport* anfeuernde(r) Zuruf *m*; *pl* Geheul *n*; *to let out a* ~ e-n Schrei ausstoßen.

yellow ['jelou] *a* gelb; vergilbt; *fig* neidisch, eifersüchtig; *Am* melancholisch; *Am (Zeitung)* sensationslüstern, reißerisch; *fam* feige; *s* Gelb *n*, gelbe Farbe *f*; gelbe(r) Farbstoff *m*; Eigelb *n*; *pl bot zoo* Gelbsucht; *fam* Feigheit *f*; *tr* gelb färben; *itr* gelb werden; vergilben; ~**-band street** Straße *f* mit Parkverbot; ~**bird** *amerik.* Goldfink *m*; Gelbe Grasmücke *f*; ~ **book** *pol* Gelbbuch *n*; ~ **dog** *Am* Lump, Schuft; Köter *m*; ~**-dog** *a Am* gewerkschaftsfeindlich; ~ **earth** Ocker *m od n*; Melinit *m*; ~ **fever** *med* Gelbfieber *n*; ~**-green** *a* grüngelb; *s* grüngelbe Farbe *f*, Grüngelb *n*; ~**-haired** *a* flachshaarig; ~**-(h)ammer** *orn* Goldammer *f*; ~**ish** ['-iʃ] gelblich; ~ **jack** *Am* Gelbfieber *n*; (gelbe) Quarantäneflagge *f*; ~**jacket** *Am fam* Wespe *f*; ~ **journal** Revolverblatt *n*; ~ **metal** Gold; Messing *n*; *the* ~ **peril** *pol* die gelbe Gefahr *f*; ~ **press** *Am* Hetz-, Sensationspresse *f*; ~ **sickness** Gelbsucht *f*; ~ **spot** *anat* Gelbe(r) Fleck *m* im Auge; ~ **streak** (Zug *m* von) Feigheit, Ängstlichkeit, Schüchternheit *f*; *he has a* ~~ *in him (fam)* er hat leicht die Hosen voll; ~**y** ['-i] gelblich.

yelp [jelp] *itr* kläffen; aufschreien; *s* kurze(s) Bellen *n*; Aufschrei *m*.

yen [jen] *Am fam s* Sehnsucht *f*; heiße(r) Wunsch *m*; *itr* vergehen vor Sehnsucht (*for* nach).

yeoman ['joumən] *pl* ~*men hist* Freisasse; kleine(r) Grundbesitzer; berittene(r) Milizsoldat *m*; *mar Am* Schreibstubenunteroffizier *m*; *Y*~ *of the Guard* Leibgardist *m*; ~ *of signals (mar)* Signalmaat *m*; ~ *of stores* Kammerunteroffizier *m*; ~**ly** ['-li] *a adv* treu, wacker, brav; einfach, schlicht; ~**ry** ['-ri] bäuerliche(r) Mittelstand *m*; berittene Miliz *f*; ~**('s) service** gute(r) Dienst *m*, treue Dienste *m pl*.

yep [jep] *Am sl* ja.

yes [jes] *adv* ja, jawohl; *s* Ja; Jasagen *n*; *itr tr* ja sagen (zu); ~**-man** *Am sl* Jasager *m*.

yester|day ['jestədi, -dei] *adv* gestern; *a* gestrig, letzt; *s* der gestrige Tag; *pl* die Vergangenheit *f*, vergangene Zeiten *f pl*; *of* ~~ von gestern, gestrig; *the day before* ~~ vorgestern; ~~ *morning, afternoon, night* gestern morgen, nachmittag, nacht; ~~*'s paper* die gestrige Zeitung; ~~ *week* vor acht Tagen.

yet [jet] *adv (zeitlich)* noch; jetzt; schon; schon noch; *(vor e-m Komparativ)* noch, sogar; außerdem; trotzdem; *as* ~ bis jetzt; *nor* ~ *(nach e-r Verneinung)* ja, nicht einmal; noch; *not* ~

noch nicht; *I have ~ to see it myself* ich habe es selbst noch nicht gesehen; *conj* (je)doch, dennoch, aber, indessen, trotzdem, nichtsdestoweniger.
yew [ju:] *(a. ~-tree) bot* Eibe *f*; Eibenholz *n*.
Yiddish ['jidiʃ] *a* jiddisch; *s* (das) Jiddisch(e).
yield [ji:ld] *tr* hervorbringen, liefern; einbringen, abwerfen, (her)geben; *(to ~ up)* auf-, her-, hin-, abgeben; *(Zinsen)* gewähren; *fig* zugestehen, gewähren (*to s.o.* jdm); *mil* übergeben; *itr agr* tragen; *(to ~ o.s. up)* sich fügen; es auf-, nach-, sich ergeben; sich hingeben (*to s.th.* e-r S); *tech* federn; *com* Zinsen tragen; *mil* weichen; *s* Ertrag, (erzielter) Gewinn *m*; Ernte; Ausbeute *f*, Einkünfte *pl*; *com* Rendite *f*; *to ~ to conditions* auf Bedingungen eingehen; *to ~ o.'s consent* sich einverstanden erklären; *to ~ to force* der Gewalt weichen; *to ~ up the ghost* den Geist aufgeben; *to ~ to none* niemandem nach-, hinter niemandem zurückstehen; *to ~ a point* in einem Punkt nachgeben (*to s.o.* jdm); *to ~ no return* keinen Ertrag bringen; *to ~ to submission* sich unterwerfen; **~ing** ['-iŋ] biegsam; *fig* nachgiebig; unterwürfig; ergiebig, einträglich.
yip [jip] *Am fam (Hund) itr* jaulen, wimmern; *s* Gejaule, Jaulen *n*.

*

yob [jɔb] *sl* Kerl *m*.
yodel, yodle ['joudl] *itr* jodeln; *s* Jodler *m*.
yog|a ['jougə] Joga *m*; **~(h)ourt** ['-ə:t] Joghurt *m*; **~i** ['-i:] Jogi *m (Anhänger des Joga)*.
yo-(heave-)ho ['jou(hi:v-)'hou, jo(u)-'hou] *interj mar* hau ruck!
yoicks [jɔiks] *interj (Jagd)* hussa!
yoke [jouk] *s agr tech fig* Joch *n*; *fig (~ of servitude)* Knechtschaft; *(Kleid)* Passe *f*; *mot* Gabelgelenk *n*; Schultertrage *f*; *tr (Zugtiere)* anjochen, anspannen (*to* an); *fig* koppeln, verbinden (*to* mit); verheiraten; *itr fig* verbunden sein; *(to ~ together)* zs.arbeiten; *to come, to pass under the ~ (fig)* sich unterwerfen, sich (unter das Joch) beugen; *to throw off the ~ (fig)* das Joch abschütteln; *five ~ of oxen* fünf Joch Ochsen; **~-bone** *anat* Jochbein *n*; **~-fellow, -mate** Arbeitsgenosse, Partner; Lebensgefährte *m*, -gefährtin *f*.
yokel ['joukəl] *pej* Bauerntölpel *m*.
yolk [jouk] Dotter *m od n*, Eigelb; *biol* Protoplasma; Wollfett *n*; *to beat up the ~* das Eigelb schlagen.
yon [jɔn] *a prn obs u. dial* = *~der*; **~der** ['-də] *prn* jene(r, s) dort; *adv* dort (drüben).
yore [jɔ:] *adv obs u. s*: *of ~* einst(mals), ehedem, vor Zeiten.
you [ju:, ju, jə] *prn* ihr, euch; du, dir, dich; Sie, Ihnen; *fam* man; einen.
young [jʌŋ] *a* jung *a. geol*; jugendlich; frisch, kräftig, stark, lebendig, lebhaft; neu; unerfahren, (noch) unwissend; *pol* fortschrittlich; Jung-; *s zoo* Junge(s) *n*; *the ~* die Jungen, die jungen Leute *pl*; *in o.'s ~er days* in der Jugend; *with ~ (Tier)* trächtig; *my ~ (wo)man* mein Liebling; *~ Miller* der junge Müller, Müller junior; *the night is still ~* der Abend hat erst angefangen; **~ animal** Jungtier *n*; **~ blood** Jugend; frische Kraft *f*; neue Ideen *f pl*; **~-eyed** *a* mit frischem Blick; (jugend)frisch; begeistert; **~ish** ['-iʃ] etwas jung; **~ people** Jugend *f*, junge Leute *pl*; **~ persons** *pl* Jugendliche *m pl*; **~ster** ['-stə] Junge, Bursche *m*.
your [jɔ:, jɔə, juə] *prn* euer, eu(e)re; dein(e); Ihr(e); **~s** der, die, das eu(e)re, eurige, deine; *(Höflichkeitsform)* Ihr(ig)e; *Am com* Ihr Schreiben; *a friend of ~s* einer deiner, Eu(e)rer Freunde; *a book of ~s* eins von deinen, Ihren Büchern; *this book is ~s* dies Buch gehört dir, euch, Ihnen; *~s truly* hochachtungsvoll; *fam* meine Wenigkeit; **~self** [-'self] *pl -selves* [-'selvz] *prn* (ihr, euch, du, dir, dich, Sie, sich, man) selbst; allein; *(all) by ~* selbständig allein; einsam, allein; *be ~~! (fam)* reiß dich zs.
you're [juə] = *you are*.
youth [ju:θ] Jugend; Jugendlichkeit, -frische *f*; *(mit sing od pl)* junge Leute *pl*; *(pl ~s* [ju:ðz]) junge(r) Mann, Jugendliche(r) *m*; *fig* Frühzeit *f*; *the friends of his ~* s-e Jugendfreunde *m pl*; *vigour of ~* Jugendkraft *f*; **~ centre, club** Haus *n* der Jugend; **~ful** ['-ful] jung *a. geol*; jugendlich; **~fulness** ['-fulnis] Jugendlichkeit *f*; **~ hostel** Jugendherberge *f*; **~ movement** Jugendbewegung *f*.
you've [ju:v] = *you have*.
yowl [jaul] *tr itr* jaulen.
yucca ['jʌkə] *bot* Yucca, Palmlilie *f*.
Yugoslav ['ju:go(u)slɑ:v] *s* Jugoslawe *m*, Jugoslawin *f*; *a* jugoslawisch; **~ia** [-'slɑ:vjə] Jugoslawien *n*.
yule [ju:l] Weihnacht(en *n od pl*) *f*; **~-log** Weihnachtsscheit *n*; **Y~tide** Weihnachtszeit *f*.

Z

Z, z [zed, *Am* zi:] *pl ~'s s* Z, z *n*.
zany ['zeini] *hist* (dummer) August, Hanswurst *m a. fig*.
zeal [zi:l] Eifer *m* (*for* für; *in* bei); Begeisterung *f*, Enthusiasmus *m* (*for* für); große(s) Interesse *n* (*for* an); **~ot** ['zelət] Eiferer, Fanatiker; *rel hist* Zelot *m*; **~otry** ['zelətri] übertriebene(r) Eifer, Fanatismus *m*; **~ous** ['zeləs] eifrig, begeistert, enthusiastisch (*to do* zu tun; *for* für).
zebra ['zi:brə] Zebra *n*; **~ crossing** Zebrastreifen, Fußgängerüberweg *m*.
zebu ['zi:bu:] Zebu, Buckelochse *m*.
zed [zed], *Am* **zee** [zi:] Zet *n (Buchstabe)*.
zenith ['zeniθ] Zenit *a. fig*; *fig* Höhepunkt, Gipfel *m*; *at the ~ of* auf dem Höhepunkt *gen*.
zephyr ['zefə] Westwind; *poet* leichte(r) Wind, Zephyr *m*; *(~ worsted)* feine Wolle *f*; *(~ cloth)* feine(r) Wollstoff *m*; (Sport-)Trikot *m od n*.
zero ['ziərou] *pl -os s* Null *f*; Nullpunkt *(e-r Skala)*; Gefrierpunkt; *fig* Null-, Tiefpunkt, -stand *m*; Nichts *n a. fig*; *tr (to adjust to ~) (Gerät)* genau einstellen, justieren; *to ~ in (Gewehr)* justieren; *to be at ~* auf Null stehen; *to fall to ~* auf 0 Grad fallen; *to fly at ~ (aero)* unter 300 m, in Bodennähe fliegen; *to reduce to ~* zuschanden machen, vernichten, zerstören; *to sink to ~ (fig)* auf e-n Tiefpunkt sinken; *absolute ~ (phys)* absolute(r) Nullpunkt *m (—273° Celsius)*; **~ adjustment** Nullstellung *f*; **~ altitude** *aero* Bodennähe *f*; **~ conductor** *el* Nulleiter *m*; **~ hour** *mil* X-Zeit *f*; Tiefpunkt der Produktion(sleistung); *allg* kritische(r) Moment, entscheidende(r) Augenblick *m*; **~ mark** Nullstrich *m*; **~ point** Nullpunkt *m*; **~ position** *tech* Nullstellung *f*; **~ voltage** Nullspannung *f*; **~-zero (condition)** *aero sl* dicke(r) Nebel *m*.
zest [zest] Würze *f bes. fig*; *fig* Beigeschmack, besondere(r) Reiz; Geschmack, Genuß *m*; Lust *f* (*for* an); Neigung (*for* zu), Begeisterung *f*, Eifer *m* (*for* für); *with ~* mit Eifer, Begeisterung; eifrig, begeistert; *to add, to give (a) ~ to s.th.* e-r S Würze verleihen, e-e S interessant machen; *~ for life* Lebenshunger *m*; **~ful** ['-ful] würzig, anregend, reizvoll; genußreich; begeistert, eifrig.

*

zigzag ['zigzæg] *s* Zickzack(linie *f*, -weg) *m*; *a* im Zickzack (ver)laufend; *adv* im Zickzack; *itr tr* im Zickzack (ver)laufen *od* gehen; **~ path** Zickzackweg *m*.
zinc [ziŋk] *s* Zink *n*; *tr* verzinken; **~ blende** Zinkblende *f*; **~ographer** [-'kɔgrəfə] Zinkograph *m*; **~ ointment** Zinksalbe *f*; **~ous** ['ziŋkəs] Zink-; **~ oxide** Zinkoxyd *n*; **~ white** Zinkweiß *n*.
zing [ziŋ] *interj sl* surr! *itr* (vorbei)surren, -zischen; *a Am sl* anziehend; *s Am sl* Kraft, Energie *f*.
zinnia ['zinjə] *bot* Zinnie *f*.
Zion ['zaiən] *(Bibel)* Zion *n*; **~ism** ['-izm] Zionismus *m*; **~ist** ['-ist] Zionist *m*.
zip [zip] *s* Pfeifen *(e-r Gewehrkugel)*; Zischen, Surren *n*; *fig fam* Dynamik *f*, Schwung; Reißverschluß *m*; *itr* pfeifen, schwirren, surren; *Am fam* herum-, durch die Gegend sausen, schwirren; *Am fam* Wind machen, auf die Tube drücken; *tr* mit e-m Reißverschluß schließen; *(to ~ open)* den R. aufmachen (*s.th.* e-r S); *fam* mit Schwung tun; **~-fastener** Reißverschluß *m*; **~per** ['-ə] Reißverschluß; *fam* vitale(r) Mensch *m*; *~~ bag, case* Tasche *f* mit Reißverschluß; **~py** ['-i] *fam* schwungvoll, lebhaft, energiegeladen.
zither ['ziθə] *mus* Zither *f*.
zodiac ['zoudiæk] *astr* Tierkreis *m*; *sign of the ~* Tierkreiszeichen *n*; **~al** [zo(u)'daiəkəl] *a* Zodiakal-, Tierkreis-; *~~ constellation* Tierkreissternbild *n*; *~~ light (mete)* Zodiakallicht *n*.
zombi(e) ['zɔmbi] *Am (Westindien)* Zauberkraft *f*; wandelnde(r) Leichnam; widerliche(r) Kerl; *Am sl* Depp *m*; *Art* Cocktail *m*.
zon|al ['zounl] zonenartig; zonal; Zonen-; **~e** [zoun] *s* Streifen *m*; *geog u. allg* Zone *f*; *allg* Gebiet(sstreifen *m*) *n*,

Bereich, Gürtel; (Post-)Bezirk *m*, *Am* Gebührenzone; *geol* Schicht *f*; *tr* in Zonen *od* Bezirke einteilen; mit e-m Gürtel umgeben; streifen; *cotton* ~~ *(geog)* Baumwollgebiet *n*; *danger* ~~ Gefahrenzone *f*, -bereich *m*; *frigid, temperate, torrid* ~~ kalte, gemäßigte, heiße Zone *f*; *wheat* ~~ *(geog)* Weizengürtel *m*; ~~ *of occupation* Besatzungsgebiet *n*; **~ing** ['-iŋ] Flächenaufteilung *f*; ~~ *ordinance* Bebauungsplan *m*.
zoo [zu:] Zoo *m*.
zoolog|ic(al) [zo(u)ə'lɔdʒik(əl)] zoologisch; *~ical garden(s)* [zu'l-] zoologische(r) Garten, Tierpark *m*; **~ist** [-'ɔlədʒist] Zoologe *m*; **~y** [-'ɔlədʒi] Zoologie, Tierkunde *f*.
zoom [zu:m] *itr* summen, surren; *aero* plötzlich steil aufsteigen; *(Flugzeug)* hochreißen; *tr aero* steil nach oben ziehen, hochreißen; *s aero* Kerze *f*, steile(r) Aufstieg *m*; plötzliche(r) Preisanstieg *m*; **~ lens** Gummilinse *f*.
zoophyte ['zo(u)əfait] *zoo* Zoophyt *m*, Hohltier *n*.
zoot [zu:t] *sl* fesch; farbenprächtig.
zounds [zaundz] *interj obs* sapperlot! ei der Tausend!
zygoma [zai'goumə] *pl -ta anat* Joch-, Wangenbein *n*; Jochbogen *m*.
zym|ase ['zaimeis] *chem* Zymase *f* *(Gärungsferment)*; **~osis** [-'mousis] *pl -ses* [-si:z] Gärung; *med* Infektionskrankheit *f*; **~otic** [-'mɔtik] zymotisch, gärend; Gär-.

Abkürzungen – Abbreviations

A

a about; account; accusative; acre; address; adjective; adult; aerial; after; afternoon; age; air; among; ampere; Angstrom; approved; arrival; artillery; at; atomic; attention; aviation
AAA American Automobile Association; anti-aircraft artillery; Amateur Athletic Association
AAAS American Association for the Advancement of Science
AAM air-to-air missile
AB able-bodied seaman; Bachelor of Arts
ABA American Bar Association
abbr, abbrev abbreviation
ABC American Broadcasting Company; Argentina, Brazil, and Chile
A-bomb atomic bomb
ac alternating current
a/c account (current)
acc accept; according; account; accusative
A-Com-in-C Air-Commodore-in-Chief
ACRA Associate of the Corporation of Registered Accountants
ACS American Cancer Society; American Chemical Society
a/cs pay accounts payable
a/cs rec accounts receivable
ACT Air Cargo Transport
actg acting
act. wt. actual weight
ACU Association of College Unions
a d active duty; adapted; adverb; advertisement;
AD Air Defence; Air Division; Armament Depot; Army Dental Corps; Anno Domini
ADA American Dairy Association; American Dental Association
add. addition; address
ADG Assistant Director General
ADGB Air Defence of Great Britain
adj adjacent; adjective; adjourned; adjustment
adm admission; administration
adv advance; adverb; advertisement; advisory
AEA American Economic Association
AEC Atomic Energy Commission
AEF Allied Expeditionary Force
AF Admiral of the Fleet; Air Force
AFA Academy of Fine Arts; American Forestry Association
AFB Air Force Base
AFBF American Farm Bureau Federation
a f c automatic frequency control
AFC Air Force Cross; Association Football Club
AFF Army Field Forces
AFL American Federation of Labo(u)r
AFLD air field
AFM Air Force Medal
AFN American Forces Network
AFS American Field Service
AFT American Federation of Teachers
AFUS Air Force of the United States
AG Accountant General; Adjutant General; Agent General; Attorney General
Agcy agency
AGM Annual General Meeting
AHA American Historical Association
AHEA American Home Economics Association
AHQ Air, *Am* Army Headquarters
AIA American Institute of Accountants; Archaeological Institute of America
AIAA Association of International Advertising Agencies
AID Army Intelligence Department
AIF Allied Invasion Forces
AIG Assistant Inspector General
AIWM American Institute of Weights and Measures
AJRC American Junior Red Cross
AL Air Lines; American Legion
ALA American Library Association; Authors' League of America
Ala Alabama
Alas Alaska
ALC American Lutheran Church
a.m. before noon
AM Air Marshal; air medal; Master of Arts
AMA American Medical Association; *Am* Automobile Manufacturers Association
Amb Ambassador; ambulance
AMC Army Medical Centre
AMG Allied Military Government
amp ampere
AMPH amphibious
AMS American Mathematical Society; Army Map Service
AMWA American Medical Women's Association
ANA Australian National Airways
anc(t) ancient
ANPA American Newspaper Publishers Association
ANRC American National Red Cross
ANS Admiralty Naval Staff
AO Accounting, Administration Officer
a/c account of
AOD Army Ordnance Department
a p accounts payable; apothecary; atmospheric pressure; atomic power
AP Associated Press
APC alien property custodian; American Parents Committee
APO Army Post Office
APS American Philosophical Society; American Physical Society; Army Postal Service
ar arrive(s)
a/r all rail; all risks
ARC American Red Cross
arch. archaic; architect
ARAMCO Arabian-American Oil Company
Ariz Arizona
Ark Arkansas
art. article; artillery
ARU American Railway Union
ARW Air Raid Warden
AS Academy of Science; Agricultural, Anthropological Society
ASA American Standards Association
ASC Allied Supreme Council
ASCAP American Society of Composers, Authors, and Publishers
ASCE American Society of Civil Engineers
ASF Army Service Forces
ASP ammunition supply point
ASSC Air Service Signal Corps
ASU American Students Union
at. atmosphere; atomic; attorney
ATA American Teachers Association
ATC Air Traffic Control; Air Training Corps
atm pr atmospheric pressure
ATS American Television Service; Army Transport Service
ATTN attention
AUS Army of the United States
AUT Association of University Teachers
a/v average
avdp. avoirdupois
AVWW II American Veterans of World War II
a/w actual weight
AWA American Women's Association
AWC American Women's Club
AWS Aircraft Warning Service; Air Weather Service
AYH(A) American Youth Hostels (Association)

B

BA Bachelor of Arts; British Academy; British Army
BAA Basketball Association of America; British Archaeological, Astronomical Association
BABS beam approach beacon system
BAC British Association of Chemists
bact bacteriology
BAI Bachelor of Engineering
BAOR British Army of the Rhine
bar. barometer; barrel; barrister
Bart Baronet
bat. battalion; battery; battle(ship)
b b bail bond; balloon barrage
BBA Bachelor of Business Administration; Big Brothers of America; British Bankers' Association
BBC British Broadcasting Corporation
b c bank clearing; battery commander
BC Bachelor of Chemistry, of the Classics, of Commerce, of Surgery; British Columbia; British Council; before Christ
b/c bill for collection
BCA Boys' Clubs of America; British Caravan Association; British Continental Airways
BCE Bachelor of Chemical Engineering, of Civil Engineering
BCL Bachelor of Canon Law, of Civil Law
BCS Bachelor of Chemical Science, of Commercial Science
BD Bachelor of Divinity
b d bankdebits; bank, back dividends
Bde brigade
BE Bachelor of Education, of Engineering; Bank of England; Bill of Exchange; Board of Education; British Empire
BEA (C) British European Airways (Corporation)
BEF British Employers' Federation; British Expeditionary Force
b f brought forward
BF Bachelor of Finance, of Forestry; British Forces
BFA British Football Association
BFBPW British Federation of Business and Professional Women
BFI British Film Institute
BFN British Forces Network
BFPO British Field Post Office
BFUW British Federation of University Women

B Gen Brigadier-General
B/H bill of health
b h p brake horse-power
BIIA British Institute of Industrial Art
BIOWAR biological warfare
BISF British Iron and Steel Federation
bk bank; book
BL Bachelor of Law, of Letters
B/L bill of lading
BLA Bachelor of Liberal Arts
bl(d)g building
BM Bachelor of Medicine; British Museum
BMA British Medical Association
BME Bachelor of Mechanical Engineering, of Mining Engineering
b o back order; branch office; buyer's option
b/o brought over
BOA(C) British Overseas Airways (Corporation)
BOE Board of Education
BOT Board of Trade
b p bill payable; boiling point
BP Bachelor of Pharmacy, of Philosophy; British Petroleum (Company)
b r bank rate
br branch; bridge; brief; brother
BR British Railways
B/R bills receivable
BRA Boy Rangers of America
BRCS British Red Cross Society
Brig.Gen Brigadier General
Brit Britain; British
bros brothers
b s balance sheet; battle squadron; broadcasting station
BS Bachelor of Science, of Surgery; Boy Scouts
b/s bags; bales; bill of sale
BSA Boy Scouts of America; Boy Scouts' Association
BSG British Standard Gauge
BSGA British Sports and Games Association
bsh bushel
B/St bill of sight
BST British summer time
b t board of trade; boat; bought
BTC Bicycle Touring Club
BTAF British Tactical Air Force
BTC British Transport Commission
btn battalion
BUP British United Press
by c battery commander

C

c calorie; candle; cent; century; city; corps; cubic
C Celsius; Centigrade; coefficient
c a consular agent; credit account; current account
CA Chartered Accountant; Chief Accountant; Commercial Aviation
CAC Civilian Affairs Committee; Coast Artillery Corps; Criminal Appeal Court
CAF Cost-Assurance-Freight
Cal(if) California
CALTEX California-Texas Oil Corporation
CAPT captain
capy capacity
CARE Co-operative for American Remittances to Everywhere
CB Companion of the Order of the Bath; Construction Battalion; county borough
CBC Canadian, Columbia Broadcasting Corporation; County Borough Council
c b d cash before delivery
CBE Commander of the Order of the British Empire
CBS Columbia Broadcasting System
cc carbon copy; cash credit; continuous current
CC Chamber of Commerce; City Council(or); Civil Court
CCP Code of Civil Procedure; Court of Common Pleas
CCrP Code of Criminal Procedure
CCUS Chamber of Commerce of the United States
cd cash discount; command; commissioned
CD Chief of Division; Civil Defence; Coast Defence; Diplomatic Corps
CDA Catholic Daughters of America; Civil Defence Act; Coast Defence Artillery
CDS cash on delivery service
CE Chancellor of the Exchequer; Chief Engineer; Church of England; counter-espionage
CEA County Education Authority; European Confederation of Agriculture
CEC Civil Engineering Corps
CED Committee for Economic Development
cert certain; certificate; certify
CET Central European Time
cf compare
c f cost and freight
CFA cost-freight-assurance
CFGI Camp Fire Girls, Inc
c f i cost, freight, and insurance
CG Consul-General
CGM Conspicuous Gallantry Medal
CGS centimeter-gramme-second
ch chairman; chapter, chief
CI Chief Inspector; cost-insurance; counter-intelligence
CIA Central Intelligence Agency
CIC Commander in Chief; Counter-Intelligence Corps
CID Criminal Investigation Department
c i f cost, insurance, and freight
CINC Commander in Chief
CIO Congress of Industrial Organizations
cir circuit; circular; circulation
civ civil; civilian
CJ Chief Judge
c n circular, credit note
CO Colonial Office; Commanding Officer; Criminal Office
c/o care of; carried over; cash order
COC Chamber of Commerce; Crown Office in Chancery
COD cash on delivery; Chamber of Deputies; collect on delivery; Concise Oxford Dictionary
COFS Chief of Staff
COFT Chief of Transportation
COI Central Office of Information
col collected; college; colonel; column; counsel
Colo Colorado
coll collateral; collect; college; colloquial
com commander; commercial; committee; commonly; commutator
COMDOF Commanding Officer
COMINCH Commander in Chief
comp companion; comparative; compare; compiled; compound; comprising
con concerning; concentrate; connection; consolidated
conf compare; conference
Conn. Connecticut
conn. connected
Consols Consolidated Annuities
const constable; constant; constitution
cont containing; continuous; contract; contrary; control
contd contained; continued
contr contract; contradiction; contrary
COO Chief Ordnance Officer
co-op co-operation; co-operative
cop. copper
COS Chief of Staff
cp candle power; carriage paid; compare
CP Car Park; Cardinal Point; Civil Procedure; Common Prayer; Communist Party
CPA Certified Public Accountant; Chartered Patent Agent
cpd compound
c p s cycles per second
CQM Chief Quartermaster
cr credit
CRALOG Council of Relief Agencies Licensed for Operations in Germany
CRCC Canadian Red Cross Committee
CRECON counter-reconnaissance
c r m counter radar measures
ct carat; cent; circuit; county; court
CT Central time; combat team
ctf certificate; certified
cu in. cubic inch
CUP Cambridge University Press
cur. currency; current
cu yd cubic yard
cv chief value
CV combat vehicle
CVO Commander of the Royal Victorian Order
CWAC Canadian Women's Army Corps; Christian Women's Association of Canada
CWS Chemical Warfare Service
cwt hundredweight (=112 pounds, *Am* 100 pounds)
cy capacity; county; currency; cycle
CYMS Catholic Young Men's Society of Great Britain
CZ Canal Zone; combat zone

D

d date; daughter; day; debit; deceased; degree; departure
d a deposit account
DA Department of Agriculture; District Attorney
D/A days after acceptance; deposit account
DAB Dictionary of American Biography
Dak Dakota
DAD Deputy Assistant Director
DAE Dictionary of American English
DAP documents against payment
DAR Daughters of the American Revolution
DAS delivered alongside ship
D/B date of birth
d c direct current; double column
DC Deputy Chief; Direct Current; District Court; District of Columbia
DCL Doctor of Civil Law
DCM Distinguished Conduct Medal
d d days after date; delayed delivery; demand draft
dd delivered
DD Department of Defence; Doctor of Divinity
d/d dated; domicile to domicile
D-day date of Allied invasion of France
DDD Direct Distance Dialing
DDG Deputy Director General
DDM Doctor of Dental Medicine

DDS Doctor of Dental Surgery
DDT dichloro-diphenyl-trichloro-ethane
DE Doctor of Education
deb debenture; debutante; debit
Dec December
dec deceased; decimal; declared
def defendant; deficit; definite
deg degree
Del Delaware
del delegate; delete
dely delivery
dem demand; democracy
dep department; departure; deposit; deputy
dept department; depot; deputy
det detachment; detail; determine
DFC Distinguished Flying Cross
diam diameter
dioc diocese
disc. discount; discovery
Dist Atty District Attorney
DL day letter; Doctor of Law
D Lit Doctor of Literature
DM Doctor of Medicine
DNB Dictionary of National Biography
doz dozen
D/PA Director of Personnel and Administration
DPR Director of Public Relations
DS Defence Secretary; Dental Surgeon; Deputy Secretary; detached service
DS(c) Doctor of Science
DSC Distinguished Service Cross
DSM Distinguished Service Medal
DSS Doctor of Social Science
DST Double Summer Time; Daylight Saving Time
DT(h) Doctor of Theology
dup(l) duplicate
d w dead weight
dwt pennyweight
dz dozen

E

e efficiency; errors; excellent
E Earl; East; English; 2nd class
EA Economic Adviser; English Association
EC East Coast; Eastern Command; Electric Current; Engineering Corps; Episcopal Church; Established Church
ECE Economic Commission for Europe
ECG EKG
ECLA United Nations Economic Commission for Latin America
econ economy
ECOSOC United Nations Economic and Social Council
ECSC European Coal and Steel Community
ed edition; extra duty
ED Doctor of Engineering; Education Department; Engineering Division
Ed B Bachelor of Education
EDC European Defence Community
EDT Eastern daylight time
EE Electrical Engineer; Employment Exchange; errors excepted
EEC European Economic Community
EETS Early English Text Society
EF Expeditionary Force
EFF effective
effy efficiency
EFTA European Free Trade Association
e.g. for example
ehp effective horsepower
el elevated (railway)
ELCA Evangelical Lutheran Church of America
elec electricity
EMA European Monetary Agreement
enc(l) enclosure
ency encyclopaedia
end. endorse
eng engaged; engineer
Eng D Doctor of Engineering
ENIAC Electronic Numerical Integrator and Computor
enl enlarged; enlisted
ENL enlist
ENT entrance
EO errors and omissions; Executive Officer
Epis Episcopalian
EPU European Payments Union
eq equal; equipment; equity
ERC English Red Cross; Enlisted Reserve Corps
ERP European Recovery Program
Esq(r) Esquire
ESRO European Space Research Organization
est established; estimated; estuary
EST Eastern Standard Time; Eastern Summer Time
ET Eastern Time; Educational Training
etc and so forth
ETO European Theater of Operations; European Transport Organization
EUCOM European Command
EURATOM European Atomic Energy Community
eve. evening
exec executed; executive
exp expedition; expense; export; express

F

f family; father; female; foot
F Fahrenheit
FA Field Artillery; Football Association
FACCA Fellow of the Association of Certified and Corporate Accountants
FAD free air delivered
FAGS Fellow of the American Geographical Society
FAIA Fellow of the American Institute of Architects
fam family; field ambulance
FAO finish all over; Food and Agriculture Organization
fas free alongside ship
FB freight bill
FBA Fellow of the British Academy
FBAA Fellow of the British Association of Accountants and Auditors
FBI Federal Bureau of Investigation; Federation of British Industries
FC Farmers' Club; fire control; Football Club; Forestry Commission
FCC Federal Communications Commission; Food Control Committee; Four Corners Club; Free Church Council
FCO Fire Control Officer; Flying Control Officer
fd field; fund
Fd Bty Field Battery
FDC fire direction centre
FEA Federal Economic Administration
FG Federal Government; field gun
f i c freight, insurance, carriage
FID Field Intelligence Department
fig. figurative; figure
fin. finance; finished
f i o free in and out
FL Flight Lieutenant; Flotilla Leader
FLA First Lord of the Admiralty
Fla Florida
FLD field
FM Field Manual; Field Marshal; Foreign Mission; Frequency Modulation
fo firm offer; for orders; fuel oil; [folio
FO Flying Officer; Foreign Office
f o b free on board
FOBS Fractional Orbit Bombardment System
f o c free of charge
f o d free of damage
fol folio
f o q free on quay
f o r free on rail; free on road
for. foreign; forestry
f o s free on steamer
f o w free on waggon
f p fixed price; fully paid
FPA Family Planning Association; Food Production Administration; Foreign Press Association
F/R Fighter Reconnaissance
FRCS Fellow of the Royal College of Surgeons
freq frequent
FS Field Service
F/S financial statement
ft foot
FTA Future Teachers of America
FTC Federal Trade Commission

G

g acceleration of gravity; general intelligence; gram
G-1, 2, 3, 4 *Am mil* personnel and administration; intelligence; operations and training; logistics
Ga Georgia
GA General Agent; General Assembly; Geographical Association
gal. gallon
GATT General Agreement on Tariffs and Trade
GB Great Britain
GBS Government Bureau of Standards; George Bernard Shaw
GCB Knight Grand Cross of the Order of the Bath
gen general; genitive
Gen General
gent gentleman
GFR German Federal Republic
GFTU General Federation of Trade Unions
GHQ General Headquarters
GM General Manager; General Motors; guided missile
GMT Greenwich mean time
gn guinea
GOC General Officer Commanding
gov(t) government
g p general practitioner
gp group
GPO General Post Office; Government Printing Office
gr grain; grammar; gramme; gravity
grad graduate
Gr Br Great Britain
GROBDM General Register Office for Births, Deaths and Marriages
gr wt gross weight
GS General Secretary; General Service; General Staff; Geographical Society; Girl Scouts
GSO General Staff Officer
GSUSA General Staff, United States Army
Gt Br Great Britain
gtd guaranteed

H

h heat; high; hour; intensity of magnetic field
HBM His (Her) Britannic Majesty
HC High Church; High Commissioner; High Court; House of Commons
HCJ High Court of Justice
HD Home Defence
hdqrs headquarters
HE high explosive; His Eminence; His Excellency
HF high frequency; Home Fleet; Home Forces
HFA Heavy Field Artillery
h f c high-frequency current
hgt height
HL House of Lords
HM His (Her) Majesty
HMS His (Her) Majesty's Service; His (Her) Majesty's Ship
HMSO His (Her) Majesty's Stationery Office
HO Head Office; Home Office
Hon Honorary; Hono(u)rable
hons honours
hosp hospital
h p high pressure; hire purchase; horse-power
HQ Headquarters
HR Home Rule; House of Representatives
HRH His (Her) Royal Highness
hrs hours
HS high school; Home Secretary; hospital ship
ht high tension
hts heights
HV high voltage

I

I. Idaho; interpreter; island
Ia Iowa
IA first quality; Imperial Airways; Iraqi Airlines
IAAF International Amateur Athletic Federation
IAC Inter-American Conference
IAES International Association of Exchange Students
IAF International Aeronautical *od* Automobile Association
IAM(AP) International Association of Meteorology and Atmospheric Physics
IARU International Amateur Radio Union
IATA International Air Transport Association
IAU International Association of Universities
IAW International Alliance of Women
IB Intelligence Branch; Invoice Book
IBA Institute of British Architects
IBE Institute of British Engineers; International Bureau of Education
IBM International Business Machines; international ballistic missile
IBO International Broadcasting Organization
IBRD International Bank for Reconstruction and Development
i/c in charge of
IC Information Center; Intelligence Corps; International Conference
ICAO International Civil Aviation Organization
ICBM intercontinental ballistic missile
ICC International Chamber of Commerce
ICEF International Children's Emergency Fund
ICFTU International Confederation of Free Trade Unions
ICPC International Criminal Police Commission
ICRC International Committee of the Red Cross
ICRF International Cancer Research Foundation
ID Intelligence Department
i.e. that is
IEFC International Emergency Food Committee
IETA International Federation of Teachers' Associations
IFTU International Federation of Trade Unions
IFUW International Federation of University Women
IFYHA International Federation of Youth Hostels Association
ihp indicated horse-power
ill. illustrated
Ill Illinois
ILO International Labo(u)r Office *od* Organization
IMF International Monetary Fund
IMO International Meteorological Organization
imp. imperative; imperfect; import; imprimatur
INA Indian National Airways
inc. inch
Inc Incorporated; Inclosure
incl including
incog incognito
Ind Indiana
indef indefinite
inf infantry; infinitive; below
ins inches; insulated; insurance
INS International News Service
inst instant; institute; institution
int interior; intermediate; international; interpreter
inv invoice
IO Intelligence Officer; Interpreter Officer
IOC International Olympic Committee
IOU I owe you
IPA International Phonetic Association
IQ intelligence quotient
Ir, Ire Ireland
IRC International Red Cross
IRD Internal Revenue Department
IRO International Refugee Organization
IS Intelligence Service
ISO Imperial Service Order; International Standards Organization
ISS International Student Service
ITO International Trade Organization
IUS International Union of Students
IUSY International Union of Socialist Youth
IVSP International Voluntary Service for Peace
IWW Industrial Workers of the World
IYRU International Youth Hostel Federation

J

J Judge; Justice
jato jet-assisted take-off
JC Jesus Christ
JCD Doctor of Civil Law
jct junction
JD Doctor of Law; Justice Department
JP Justice of the Peace; jet pilot
JUD Doctor of Civil and Canon Law
jun. junior

K

k karat; kilo
K Knight; Kiwanis Club
Kan(s) Kansas
KB King's Bench; Knight of the Bath
KC King's Counsel; Kiwanis Club; Knights of Columbus; Knight Commander
kc kilocycles
KCB Knight Commander of the Order of the Bath
Ken. Kentucky
kg kilogram
KG Knight of the Order of the Garter
KIA killed in action
KKK Ku Klux Klan
km kilometre
k o knock-out
kv kilovolt
kw(hr) kilowatt(-hour)
Ky Kentucky

L

l lake; league; left; length; liner; link; litre
L elevated railway
£ pound sterling
LA Law *od* Library Association
La Louisiana
lab. laboratory
Lab. Labo(u)r
LAC Leading Aircraftman
Lancs Lancashire
lat(d) latitude
LAUK Library Association of the United Kingdom
lb letter box; pound; local board
l b w leg before wicket *(cricket)*
l c letter card; letter of credit
LC deferred *(telegram)*; Library of Congress; Lieutenant Commander; Lord Chamberlain; Lower California *od* Canada
LCC London Chamber of Commerce; London County Council
LCJ Lord Chief Justice
Ldn London
Legco Legislative Council
Leics Leicestershire
l f c low-frequency current
Lib. Liberal
Lieut Lieutenant
Lieut Col, Gen, Gov Lieutenant Colonel, General, Governor
Lincs Lincolnshire
lino linotype
lit. litre; literal; literary
Lit(t)D Doctor of Letters
LJ Lord Justice
ll lines
LL Lending Library; Limited Liability
LLD Doctor of Laws
LM Legion of Merit; Lord Mayor
LMC Labo(u)r Management Committee
LMS London Mathematical Society; London Medical Society; London Missionary Society
LMT local mean time
LO Liaison Officer
loc cit at the place mentioned
long. longitude
LP Labo(u)r Party; long playing *(record)*; Lord of the Privy Council
l p low pressure
LRRO Land Revenue Record Office
LRS Lloyd's Register of Shipping
LSE London School of Economics; London Stock Exchange
LSO London Symphony Orchestra
LSS Life Saving Service
LST local standard time

lt lieutenant; local time; low tension
Lt Lieutenant
Lt Col, Gen Lieutenant Colonel, General
Ltd Limited
Luth Lutheran
LW long wave; low water

M

m male; married; member; metre; mile; minor; minute; month
M nautical mile; atomic weight; Majesty; member; Monday; Mountain
MA Master of Arts; Middle Ages; Military Academy
MAA Master of Arms; Mathematical Association of America
Maj(Gen) Major (General)
Mar. March
mar. marine; maritime; married
Mass. Massachusetts
Matric matriculation
MATS Military Air Transport Service
max. maxim; maximum
MB Bachelor of Medicine; Medical Board
MBE Member of the Order of the British Empire
MBS Master of Business Science; Mutual Broadcasting System
mc megacycle; millicurie; motorcycle
MC marriage certificate; Master of Ceremonies; Medical Corps; Member of Congress; Methodist Church; Military Cross
MD Doctor of Medicine; Managing Director; military district
Md Maryland
M-day Mobilization day
Me Maine
ME Middle East; Middle English; Mining Engineer
MED Master of Education
med medical; medium
memo memorandum
MET meteorology
MG Major General; Military Government
mg milligram
MGC Machine-Gun Company
MGT management
MH Medal of Honour; Most Honourable
MHR Member of the House of Representatives
MI Military Intelligence
Mich Michigan
min minim; minimum; minor, minute
Minn Minnesota
misc miscellaneous
Miss. Mississippi
ML Master of Laws; Ministry of Labour
MLAA Modern Language Association of America
mm millimetre
m o mail order; money order; motor operated
MO Medical Officer; Meteorological Office
Mo Missouri
MOH Medical Officer of Health; Ministry of Health
Mon Monday; Monitor; Montana
m p melting point; months after payment
MP Member of Parliament; Metropolitan Police; Military Police
mpg miles per gallon
mph miles per hour
MPO Military Post Office
Mr Mister
Mrs Mistress
m s mail steamer; motor ship
ms manuscript
MS Manuscript; Master of Science *od* Surgery; Metric System
MSC Medical Service Corps
M Sgt Master Sergeant
mss manuscripts
Mt Mountain
MT mean time; Motor Transport
mth month
mts mountains
Mx Middlesex

N

n nominative; noon; number; neuter; noun
N Name; North(ern)
NA Naval Attaché; Naval Aviation; North America; not available
NAA National Automobile Association
NAAFI Navy, Army and Air Force Institutes
n a d no appreciable disease
NAS National Academy of Science
NASA National Aeronautics and Space Administration
NASU National Association of State Universities
NATO North Atlantic Treaty Organization
naut nautical
NAVCENT Allied Naval Forces Central Europe
NBA National Bar Association *od* Basketball Association *od* Boxing Association
NBC National Broadcasting Company
NBS National Bureau of Standards
NC North Carolina
NCB National Coal Board
NCO non-commissioned officer
NCW National Council of Women
n d no date
N Dak North Dakota
NEA National Education Association
Neb Nebraska
NEC National Emergency *od* Economic Coucil
NED New English Dictionary
Nev Nevada
N/F no funds
NFL National Football League
NFPW National Federation of Professional Workers
NFU National Farmers' Union
NG National Guard; no good
NGS National Geographic Society
NH Naval Hospital; New Hampshire
NHA National Health Association; National Housing Agency
NI Naval Intelligence; Northern Ireland
NIC National Industrial Council
NJ New Jersey
NLF National Labor Federation
NLI National Lifeboat Institution
NLTA National League of Teachers Association
NM New Mexico
NMA National Medical Association
NMB National Maritime Board
no. number
NO naval officer; Navigation Officer
nom nominal; nominative
Notts Nottinghamshire
Nov November
NPA National Petroleum Association; National Planning Association; Newspaper Proprietors' Association
n p or d no place or date
n r a d no risk after discharge
NRF National Relief Fund
n/s not sufficient
NSA National Student Association
NSPCA National Society for the Prevention of Cruelty to Animals
NT New Testament
NTO Naval Transport Officer
nt wt net weight
NUEA National University Extension Association
NUM National Union of Manufacturers; National Union of Mine-Workers
NUR National Union of Railwaymen
NUS National Union of Students
NUT National Union of Teachers
NUWT National Union of Women Teachers
NUWW National Union of Women Workers
NW northwest
NY New Year; New York
NZ New Zealand

O

O Ohio
o/a on account of
OAPC Office of Alien Property Custodian
OAS On Active Service; Organization of American States
ob died [Bath
OB Order of Battle; Order of the
OBE Officer of the Order of the British Empire
o c office copy; in the work cited; order cancelled
OC Officer Commanding; Ordnance Corps
Oct October
oct octavo
OD Officer of the Day; Ordnance Department; overdraft
OECD Organization for Economic Co-operation and Development
OED Oxford English Dictionary
OH on hand
OHMS On His (Her) Majesty's Service
OK all correct
Okla Oklahoma
ONA Overseas News Agency
ONS Overseas News Service
Ont Ontario
OO Observation Officer; Operation Order; Orderly Officer
op operation; opus
OPC(A) Overseas Press Club (of America)
op cit in the work quoted
OPI Office of Public Information
opp opposite
o r owner's risk
Ore(g) Oregon
orig origine; original
OT Old Testament
OUP Oxford University Press
Oxon of Oxford
oz ounce

P

p perch; pint; pole
Pa Pennsylvania
p a yearly
PA Press Association; Public Address
PAA Pan American Airways
PAC Pan-American Congress
par. paragraph; parish
parl. parliament(ary)
pat. patent
PAU Pan American Union
payt payment
PB Prayer Book

PC Parish Council(lor); Police Constable; Post Card; Privy Council(lor); Provincial Commissioner
p c per cent
P/C price(s) current
PCIJ Permanent Court of International Justice
pcl parcel
pcs pieces
pd paid
p d by the day, per diem
PD Personnel Department; Police Department; Postal District
Pd D Doctor of Pedagogy
PEN (International Association of) Poets, Playwrights, Editors, Essayists, and Novelists
Penn Pennsylvania
per an by the year
per cap. each
per pro by proxy
Pfc private first class
PG paying guest
PH Public Health; Purple Heart
Ph D Doctor of Philosophy
PID Political *od* Press Intelligence Department; Public Information Division
pk pack; peak; peck
pl place; plain; platoon; plural
P/L profit and loss
PM Prime Minister; Provost Marshal
p m after noon; post-mortem
PMG Paymaster General; Postmaster General; Provost Marshal General
PMLA Publications of the Modern Language Association
PO Pacific Ocean; Patent Office; Petty Officer; Pilot Officer; post office; postal order
POB Post Office Box
POD pay on delivery
POO Post Office Order
pop. population
POSB Post Office Savings Bank
POW Prisoner of War
p p parcel post; past participle; by proxy
pp pages; prepaid
PPC Passport Control; to take leave
p pr present participle
P/R pay roll
pref preface; preference
Pres President
pret preterit(e)
Prof professor
pro tem for the time
prox of the next month
pr p present participle
PS passenger steamer; postscript
pseud pseudonym
PST Pacific Standard Time
PT physical training; preferential tariffs
p t past tense
pt payment; pint; point; port
PTA Parent Teachers' Association
PTO please turn over
pts parts
PW(C) Prisoner of War (Camp)
PWD Psychological Warfare Department; Public Works Department
PX Post Exchange

Q

q query; question
Q Queen
QC Queen's Counsel
QM Quartermaster
qr quarter
qt *on the qt* privately
qt quart; quantity
qto quarto

R

R Railway; Regina; Rex; River; Road
r railway; recipe; retired; right
RA(A) Royal Academy (of Arts)
RAC Royal Automobile Club
RADWAR radiological warfare
RAF Royal Air Force
RAM Royal Academy of Music
RAS Royal Academy of Science
RATO Rocket Assisted Take-off
RC Recruiting Centre; Red Cross; Reply Coupon; Roman Catholic
RCA Radio Corporation of America
RCAF Royal Canadian Air Force
rcpt receipt
rd road
RD Refer to Drawer; rural district
Re rupee
recd received
ref refer(ence)
regd registered
Regt Regiment
R Eng Royal Engineers
resp respective(ly)
ret retired; return
Rev Reverend
r f radio frequency; range finder; rent free
RFC Rugby Football Club
RFE Radio Free Europe
RGS Royal Geographical Society
Rgt Regiment
RI Rhode Island; Rotary International
RIBA Royal Institute of British Architects
RM(S) Royal Mail (Service)
RN Royal Navy
ROTC Reserve Officers' Training Camp
RP reply paid
rpm revolutions per minute
RR railroad
RS Royal Society
RSFSR Russian Socialist Federated Soviet Republic
RT radiotelegraphy
Rt Hon Right Hono(u)rable
RTO Rail(way) Transport(ation) Officer
Rt Rev Right Reverend
RU Rugby Union
RV Revised Version
ry railway

S

s second; section; shilling; solo; son; southern; steamer; substantive
S Saint; Saturday; South; Sunday
SA Salvation Army; South Africa
Sa Saturday
SAC Standing Armaments Committee; Strategic Air Command; Supreme Allied Commander
SACEUR Supreme Allied Commander Europe
SACLANT Supreme Allied Commander Atlantic
SAE Standard of Automotive Engineers
SAF Strategic Air Force
SAPA South African Press Association
SAS Scandinavian Airlines System
Sat Saturday
SB sales book; Savings Bank; Bachelor of Science
SC Security Council; Sanitary Corps; Signal Corps; South Carolina; Supreme Court
Sc D Doctor of Science
sch school
SD Secretary of Defense; State Department
S Dak South Dakota
SE southeast; Stock Exchange
SEATO South-East Asia Treaty Organization
Sec Secretary
sec second(ary); secretary; section
Sen(r) Senior
Sep(t) September
S(er)gt Sergeant
sh shilling
SHAPE Supreme Headquarters Allied Powers in Europe
sing. singular
SITA Students' International Travel Association
SIU Seafarer's International Union
SLt Sub-Lieutenant
SM Master of Science; Sergeant Major
SN Seaman; Secretary of the Navy; service number; shipping note
So. south(ern)
soc society
SOED Shorter Oxford English Dictionary
SOP Standing Operating Procedure
SOS *(Internationales Seenotzeichen)*
sov sovereign
SPCA Society for the Prevention of Cruelty to Animals
SPCK Society for Promoting Christian Knowledge
spec special; specimen
sp gr specific gravity
SPQR small profits — quick returns
Sq Squadron; Square
sq sequence
sq ft square foot
Sr Senior
S/S steamship
SSGT, S/Sgt Staff Sergeant
s t short ton
st stone; street; stumped
St Saint; strait; street
ST Standard Time
STD subscriber trunk dialling
stg sterling
STO Sea Transport Officer
St Ex Stock Exchange
sub submarine; subscription; substitute; subway
subj subject; subjunctive
subst substantive
Sun. Sunday
sup superb; superlative
suppl supplement
Supt Superintendent
Suss Sussex
SW South Wales; South West
SWG Standard Wire Ga(u)ge
Sx Sussex
syn synonym(ous)

T

t terminal; territory; time; ton; town; train
T Testament; Tuesday
TA telegraphic address; Territorial Army
TAA Technical Assistance Administration
TAB Technical Assistance Board
TAC Tactical Air Command; Technical Assistance Committee
TAF Tactical Air Force
TAUN Technical Assistance of the United Nations
TB, Tb tuberculosis
TC Technical College; Touring Club; Town Council(l)or; Training Centre; Transport Command
TD Treasury Department

TELERAN televisionradarnavigation
Tenn Tennessee
Tex Texas
TF Territorial Force(s)
TGWU Transport and General Workers' Union
tgm telegram
Thurs Thursday
TIIAL The International Institute of Applied Linguistics
TKO technical knock-out
TMO telegraph money order
TNT trinitrotoluene
TO technical officer; Telegraph Office; Transport Officer; turn over
tr transferred; transitive; translated; transport(ation)
treas treasurer; treasury
T/Sgt Technical Sergeant
TT teetotal(l)er; teletypewriter
TU Trade(s) Union(s)
TUC Trade(s) Union Congress *od* Council
Tues Tuesday
TV television; terminal velocity
TVA Tennessee Valley Authority
TWA Trans World Airlines
TWU Transport Workers' Union

U

U Union; universal; University; Utah
UAB Unemployment Assistance Board
UAR United Arab Republic
UAW United Automobile Workers
UDC Universal Decimal Classification
UDC Urban District Council
UEFA Union of European Football Associations
UFC United Free Church
UFO unidentified flying objects
UHF ultrahigh-frequency
UI Unemployment Insurance
UK United Kingdom
UKAEA United Kingdom Atomic Energy Authority
ULP University of London Press
ult ultimate(ly)
UMT Universal Military Training
UMW United Mine Workers
UN United Nations
UNAEC United Nations Atomic Energy Commission
UNEF United Nations Emergency Force
UNESCO United Nations Educational, Scientific and Cultural Organisation
UNIC United Nations Information Centre
UNICEF United Nations International Children's Emergency Fund
UNIVAC Universal Automatic Computer
UNSC United Nations Security Council
UPC Universal Postal Convention
UPI United Press International
UPU Universal Postal Union
USA United States of America
USAEC United States Atomic Energy Commission
USAF(E) United States Air Force (Europe)
USDA United States Department of Agriculture
USF United States Forces
USIS United States Information Service
USM United States Mail *od* Marine(s)
USN United States Navy
USO United States Organization(s)
USPHS United States Public Health Service
USS United States Ship *od* Steamer
USSC United States Supreme Court
USSR Union of Socialist Soviet Republics
USW United Steel Workers

V

V Viscount
v see; velocity; verb; versus; volt
Va Virginia
vb verb(al)
VC Veterinary Corps; Vice-Chairman; Vice-Chancellor; Victoria Cross
VD venereal disease
vg very good
VHF very high frequency
VIP very important person
Vis(c) Viscount, Viscountess
viz namely
VLF very low frequency
VOA Voice of America
vol volcano; volume; voluntary
VP Vice-President
v p p value payable (on delivery by) post
vs versus
v s see above
Vt Vermont
VTO(L) vertical take-off (and landing) (aircraft)
v v interchanged
vv verses

W

W watt; Wales; Wednesday; Welsh; West(ern)
w watt; week(s); weight; west(ern); wife; work
WAAE World Association for Adult Education
WAGGGS World Association of Girl Guides and Girl Scouts
War(w). Warwickshire
Wash Washington
WATA World Association of Travel Agencies
WC water closet; West Central
WCC World Council of Churches
W/Cdr Wing Commander
WEA Workers' Educational Association
Wed. Wednesday
WET Western European Time
WEU Western European Union
WFPA World Federation for the Protection of Animals
WFTU World Federation of Teachers' *od* Trade Union
WHO World Health Organization
Wis(c) Wisconsin
WL water line; wave length
WMO World Meteorological Organization
WO War Office; Warrant Officer
Worcs Worcestershire
w r t with reference to
WS Wireless Set
WSC World Security Council
WSR World Students' Relief
WIT Wireless Telegraphy *od* Telephony
wt weight
WVa West Virginia
Wy(o) Wyoming

X

Xm, Xmas Christmas
Xroads cross roads
Xt Christ

Y

yd(s) yard(s)
YH(A) Youth Hostel(s' Association)
Yks Yorkshire
YMCA Young Men's Christian Association
Yorks Yorkshire
yr year
yrs years; yours
YWCA Young Women's Christian Association

Z

Z zero; zone; atomic number

Eigennamen – Proper Names

A

Aaron ['ɛərən]
A Becket [ə'bekit]
Abraham ['eibrəhæm]
Achilles [ə'kili:z]
Ada ['eidə]
Adam(s) ['ædəm(z)]
Adelaide ['ædəleid]
Aden ['eidn]
Aeneas [i(:)'ni:æs]
Aeschylus ['i:skiləs]
Aethiopia [i:θi'oupjə]
Agate ['eigət]
Agincourt ['ædʒinkɔ:t]
Alabama [ælə'bɑ:mə]
Alaska [ə'læskə]
Albania [æl'beinjə]
Albert ['ælbət]
Alexander, -dra [ælig'zɑ:ndə, -drə]
Alfred ['ælfrid]
Algeria [æl'dʒiəriə] Algerien *n*
Algiers [æl'dʒiəz] Algier *n*
Alice ['ælis]
Allardice ['ælədais]
Allegheny ['æligeni]
Alsace ['ælsæs], **Alsatia** [æl'seiʃiə] Elsaß *n*
Amazon ['æməzən] Amazonas *m*
Amelia [ə'mi:ljə] Amalie
Andes ['ændi:z] Anden *pl*
Andreas ['ændriæs]
Andrew(s) ['ændru:(z)]
Anglesea ['æŋglsi]
Anglia ['æŋgliə]
Ann(a) ['æn(ə)]
Annabel ['ænəbel]
Anthony ['æntəni]
Antigone [æn'tigəni]
Antilles [æn'tili:z]
Antonia [æn'touniə]
Apennines ['æpinainz] Apenninen *pl*
Appalachian [æpə'lei(t)ʃiən]
Aquinas [ə'kwainəs]
Arabia [ə'reibjə] Arabien *n*
Arbuthnot [ɑ:'bʌθnət]
Arcadia [ɑ:'keidiə]
Archibald ['ɑ:tʃibəld]
Archimedes [ɑ:ki'mi:di:z]
Ariadne [æri'ædni]
Aristotle ['æristɔtl]
Arizona [æri'zounə]
Arkansas ['ɑ:kənsɔ:] *(Staat)*, [ɑ:'kænsəs] *(Stadt)*
Arkwright ['ɑ:krait]
Armenia [ɑ:'mi:njə] Armenien *n*
Arthur ['ɑ:θə]
Assyria [ə'siriə] Assyrien *n*
Athens ['æθinz] *sg* Athen *n*
Atlanta [ət'læntə]
Atlantis [ət'læntis]
Augustin(e) [ɔ:'gʌstin]
Augustus [ɔ:'gʌstəs]
Avon ['eivən, 'ævən]
Azores [ə'zɔ:z] *pl* Azoren *pl*

B

Babylon ['bæbilən]
Bacchus ['bækəs]
Baden-Powell ['beidn'pouəl]
Bahamas [bə'hɑ:məz] *pl* Bahama-Inseln *f pl*
Balfour ['bælf(u)ə]
Bal(l)iol ['beiljəl]
Balmoral [bæl'mɔrəl]
Baltimore ['bɔ:ltimɔ:]
Barabbas [bə'ræbəs]
Barbado(e)s [bɑ:'beidouz, -dəs]
Barbara ['bɑ:bərə]
Bartholomew [bɑ:'θɔləmju:]
Basle, Bâle [bɑ:l] Basel *n*
Bathsheba ['bæθʃibə]
Baton Rouge ['bætən'ru:ʒ]
Baugh [bɔ:]
Beatrice, -trix ['biətris, -triks]
Beattie ['bi:ti]
Beauchamp ['bi:tʃəm]
Bede [bi:d] Beda
Belfast ['belfɑ:st]
Belgrade [bel'greid]
Beluchistan [bə'lu:kistæn]
Bengal [beŋ'gɔ:l] Bengalen *n*
Benjamin ['bendʒəmin]
Ben Nevis [ben'nevis]
Beowulf ['beiəwulf, 'biə-]
Berkeley ['bɑ:kli, *Am* 'bə:kli]
Bermudas [bə(:)'mjudəz] *pl* Bermuda-Inseln *f pl*
Bernard ['bə:nəd]
Bertha ['bə:θə]
Berwick(shire) ['berik(ʃiə)]
Bethesda [be'θezdə]
Bethlehem ['beθlihem]
Beverly ['bevəli]
Bill(y) ['bil(i)] Willi
Birmingham ['bə:miŋəm]
Biscay ['biskei] Biskaya *f*
Blenheim ['blenim]
Boadicea [bouədi'siə]
Boccaccio [bɔ'kɑ:tʃiou]
Boethius [bou'i:θiəs]
Bohemia [bou'hi:mjə] Böhmen *n*
Boleyn ['bulin]
Bolingbroke ['bɔliŋbruk]
Bombay [bɔm'bei]
Boniface ['bɔnifeis] Bonifatius
Bosphorus, Bosporus ['bɔsfərəs, -pərəs]
Bournemouth ['bɔ:nməθ]
Bridget ['bridʒit] Brigitte
Brisbane ['brisbən]
Brontë ['brɔnti]
Brooklyn ['bruklin]
Buchanan [bju(:)'kænən]
Buckingham(shire) ['bʌkiŋəm(ʃiə)]
Bysshe [biʃ]
Byzantium [bai'zæntiəm] Byzanz *n*

C

Caedmon ['kædmən]
Cambridge ['keimbridʒ]
Canterbury ['kæntəbəri]
Canute [kə'nju:t]
Carlisle [kɑ:'lail]
Carnegie [kɑ:'negi]
Carpathians [kɑ:'peiθjənz] Karpaten *pl*
Carthage ['kɑ:θidʒ]
Castlerea(gh) ['kɑ:slrei]
Catalonia [kætə'lounjə] Katalonien *n*
Catullus [kə'tʌləs]
Caxton ['kækstən]
Cecily ['sesili] Cäcilie
Celibes [se'li:bez]
Celcius ['selsjəs]
Ceres ['siəri:z]
Charing Cross ['tʃæriŋ'krɔs]
Charlotte ['ʃɑ:lət]
Chatham ['tʃætəm]
Chaucer ['tʃɔ:sə]
Chequers ['tʃekəz]
Cherokee [tʃerə'ki:]
Chesapeake ['tʃesəpi:k]
Cheshire ['tʃeʃə]
Cheviot ['tʃeviət]
Chicago [ʃi'kɑ:gou]
Christina [kris'ti:nə] Christine
Christopher ['kristəfə]
Chuzzlewit ['tʃʌzlwit]
Cicero ['sisərou]
Circe ['sə:si]
Cissi, -sy ['sisi]
Clapham ['klæpəm]
Clara, -re ['klɛərə, klɛə]
Clarence ['klærəns]
Clarendon ['klærəndən]
Clarissa [klə'risə]
Claudia, -dius ['klɔ:diə(s)]
Clementina [klemən'ti:nə]
Clementine ['kleməntain]
Cleopatra [kliə'pɑ:trə]
Cleveland ['kli:vlənd]
Clive [klaiv]
Clyde [klaid]
Coleridge ['koulridʒ]
Cologne [kə'loun] Köln
Colombo [kə'lʌmbou]
Colorado [kɔlə'rɑ:dou]
Columbia [kə'lʌmbiə] Kolumbien *n*
Columbus [kə'lʌmbəs]
Confucius [kən'fju:ʃiəs]
Connecticut [kə'netikət]
Connie, -ny ['kɔni] Konstanze
Conrad ['kɔnræd]
Constance ['kɔnstəns]
Constantinople [kɔnstænti'noupl]
Copenhagen [koupn'heign]
Cordelia [kɔ:'di:liə]
Cordilleras [kɔ:di'ljɛərəz] *pl* Kordilleren *pl*
Corea [kə'riə]
Corinth ['kɔrinθ]
Coriolanus [kɔriə'leinəs]
Cornelia [kɔ:'ni:ljə]
Cornell [kɔ:'nel]
Cornwall ['kɔ:nwəl]
Cotswold ['kɔtswould]
Coventry ['kɔvəntri]
Crete [kri:t] Kreta *n*
Crimea [krai'miə] Krim *f*
Croatia [krou'eiʃiə] Kroatien *n*
Croesus ['kri:səs]
Crusoe ['kru:sou]
Cuba ['kju:bə]
Cumberland ['kʌmbələnd]
Cymbeline ['simbili:n]

D

Dahomey [də'houmi]
Dakota [də'koutə]
Dallas ['dæləs]
Dalmatia [dæl'meiʃiə] Dalmatien *n*
Dalton ['dɔ:ltən]
Damascus [də'mæskəs]
Damocles ['dæməkli:z]
Daniel ['dænjəl]
Dante ['dænti]
Daphne ['dæfni]
Dardanelles [dɑ:də'nelz] *pl* Dardanellen *pl*
Darius [də'raiəs]
Dartmoor ['dɑ:tmuə]
David ['deivid]
Defoe [də'fou]
Delaware ['deləwɛə]
Delhi ['deli]
Demeter, -trius [di'mi:tə, -triəs]
Demosthenes [di'mɔsθəni:z]
Denmark ['denmɑ:k] Dänemark *n*
Derby(shire) ['dɑ:bi(ʃiə)]
Desdemona [dezdi'mounə]
Detroit [də'trɔit]
Devon(shire) ['devn(ʃiə)]
Dewey ['dju(:)i]
Diana [dai'ænə]
Dick [dik] Richard
Dido ['daidou]
Diogenes [dai'ɔdʒini:z]
Disraeli [diz'reili]

Donald ['dɔnəld]
Donne [dʌn]
Don Quixote ['dɔn 'kwiksout]
Dora ['dɔ:rə]
Doris ['dɔris]
Dorothy ['dɔrəθi]
Dorset(shire) ['dɔ:sit(ʃiə)]
Douglas ['dʌgləs]
Dover ['douvə]
Downing ['dauniŋ]
Dryden ['draidn]
Dublin ['dʌblin]
Duluth [dju:'lu:θ]
Du Maurier [dju(:) 'mɔ:riei]
Dumfries [dʌm'fri:s]
Duncan ['dʌnkən]
Dunkirk [dʌn'kə:k]
Duquesne [dju:'kein]
D'Urbervilles ['də:bəvilz]
Durham ['dʌrəm]

E

Ebenezer [ebi'ni:zə]
Ecuador [ekwə'dɔ:]
Eddy, -dy ['edi]
Edinburgh ['edinbərə]
Edith ['i:diθ]
Edmund ['edmənd]
Edward ['edwəd]
Eleanor ['elinə]
Eleusis [e'lju:sis]
Elias [i'laiəs]
Elinor ['elinə]
Eliza [i'laizə] Elise
Elvira [el'vaiərə]
Ely ['i:li]
Emily ['emili]
Emma ['emə]
Epipsychidion [episai'kidiən]
Erie ['iəri]
Ernest ['ə:nist]
Essex ['esiks]
Ethel ['eθəl]
Eudora [ju:'dɔrə]
Eugene ['ju:dʒi:n, -'-]
Eunice ['ju:nis]
Euphrates [ju:'freiti:z] Euphrat *m*
Euphues ['ju:fju(:)i:z]
Euripides [juə'ripidi:z]
Euridice [juə'ridisi(:)]
Evelyn ['i:vlin]
Everest ['evərist]
Exeter ['eksətə]

F

Fagin ['feigin]
Fahrenheit ['færənhait]
Falkland ['fɔ:klənd]
Falmouth ['fælməθ]
Falstaff ['fɔ:lstɑ:f]
Fanny ['fæni]
Faulkner ['fɔ:knə]
Faustus ['fɔ:stəs] Faust
Fawkes [fɔ:ks]
Felicia [fi'lisiə]
Florida ['flɔridə]
Flushing ['flʌʃiŋ] Vlissingen
Folkestone ['foukstən]
Formosa [fɔ:'mousə]
Fortinbras ['fɔ:tinbræs]
Fred, -dy ['fred(i)] Friedrich
Frederic(k) ['fredrik] Friedrich

G

Gabriel ['geibriəl]
Gainsborough ['geinzbərə]
Galilee ['gælili:]
Gallup ['gæləp]
Galveston(e) ['gælvistən]
Gandhi ['gændi:]
Ganges ['gæn(d)ʒi:z]
Genoa ['dʒeno(u)ə] Genua
Geoffry ['dʒefri] Gottfried
Georgina [dʒɔ:'dʒi:nə]
Geraldine ['dʒerəldi:n]
Gertrude ['gə:tru:d]
Gethsemane [geθ'seməni]
Gettysburg ['getizbə:g]
Ghana ['gɑ:nə]
Giaour ['dʒauə]
Gibraltar [dʒi'brɔ:ltə]
Gielgud ['gi(:)lgud]
Giles [dʒailz] Julius
Gladstone ['glædstən]
Gladys ['glædis]
Glamis [glɑ:mz]
Glasgow ['glɑ:sgou]
Gloucester(shire) ['glɔstə(ʃiə)]
Godfree, -frey ['gɔdfri] Gottfried
Goldsmith ['gouldsmiθ]
Golgatha ['gɔlgəθə]
Goliath [gə'laiəθ]
Grace [greis]
Graham(e) ['greiəm]
Grasmere ['grɑ:smiə]
Gregory ['gregəri] Gregor
Grosvenor ['grouvnə]
Guernsey ['gə:nzi]
Guiana [gi'ɑ:nə]
Guinea ['gini]
Guinevere ['gwiniviə]
Guiness ['ginis]
Gulliver ['gʌlivə]
Gustavus [gus'tɑ:vəs] Gustav
Guy [gai]
Gwendolen ['gwendəlin]

H

Haarlem ['hɑ:lem]
Hades ['heidi:z]
Hadrian ['heidriən]
Hague [heig], *the* der Haag
Haiti ['heiti]
Hakluyt ['hæklu:t]
Hampshire ['hæmpʃiə]
Hampstead ['hæm(p)stid]
Hanover ['hænəvə]
Hargreaves ['hɑ:gri:vz]
Harold ['hærəld] Harald
Harrow ['hærou]
Harwich ['hæridʒ]
Hastings ['heistiŋz]
Hathaway ['hæθəwei]
Hawaii [hɑ:'waii:]
Hawthorne ['hɔ:θɔ:n]
Hebrides ['hebridi:z] *pl* Hebriden *pl*
Helen ['helin] Helene
Heligoland ['heligo(u)lænd]
Hellas ['helæs]
Henry ['henri] Heinrich
Herbert ['hə:bət]
Hercules ['hə:kjuli:z]
Hereford(shire) ['herifəd(ʃiə)]
Hermes ['hə:mi:z]
Hermione [hə:'maiəni]
Herod ['herəd] Herodes
Herodotus [he'rɔdətəs]
Hertford(shire) ['hɑ:(t)fəd(ʃiə)]
Hesperides [hes'peridi:z]
Hiawatha [haiə'wɔθə]
Hieronymus [haiə'rɔniməs]
Highgate ['haigit]
Hilda ['hildə]
Himalaya [himə'leiə]
Hindustan [hindu'stɑ:n]
Hobbes [hɔbz]
Hoboken ['houboukən]
Hogarth ['hougɑ:θ]
Holborn ['houbən]
Holmes [houmz]
Homer ['houmə]
Honduras [hɔn'djuərəs]
Horace ['hɔrəs] Horaz
Horatio [hɔ'reiʃiou]
Houston ['hu:stən]
Hudson ['hʌdsn]
Hugh [hju:] Hugo
Hull [hʌl]
Humphrey ['hʌmfri]
Huron ['hjuərən]
Huygens ['haigənz]
Hyde Park ['haid'pɑ:k]

I

Idaho ['aidəhou]
Ignatius [ig'neiʃiəs]
Ilfracombe [ilfrə'ku:m]
Illinois [ili'nɔi]
Indiana [indi'ænə]
Iona [ai'ounə]
Iowa ['aio(u)wə]
Iphigenia [ifidʒi'naiə] Iphigenie
Irene [ai'ri:ni]
Iroquois ['irəkwɔi]
Isaac ['aizək]
Isabel ['izəbel]
Isaiah [ai'zaiə] Jesaias
Iscariot [is'kæriət] Ischariot
Isis ['aisis]

J

Jacqueline ['dʒækli:n]
Jago ['dʒeigou]
Jasper ['dʒæspə] Kaspar
Java ['dʒɑ:və]
Jean [dʒi:n]
Jeremy ['dʒerimi]
Jerome ['dʒerəm]
Jersey ['dʒə:zi]
Jerusalem [dʒə'ru:sələm]
Jess(ica) ['dʒes(ikə)]
Jim(my) [dʒim] Jakob
Jordania [dʒɔ:'deiniə] Jordanien *n*
Joseph ['dʒouzif] Joseph
Joshua ['dʒɔʃwə] Josua
Joyce [dʒɔis]
Judith ['dʒu:diθ]
Julia, -an, -iet ['dʒu:ljə, -n, -ljət]

K

Kansas ['kænzəs]
Kashmir [kæʃ'miə]
Katharina, -ne [kæθə'ri:nə, 'kæθərin]
Kathleen ['kæθli:n]
Keats [ki:ts]
Keith [ki:θ]
Kensington ['kenziŋtən]
Kentucky [kən'tʌki]
Kenya ['ki:njə, 'keniə]
Kerguelen ['kə:gilin]
Keynes [keinz]
Khyber ['kaibə]

L

Labrador ['læbrədɔ:]
Lancashire ['læŋkəʃiə]
Lancaster ['læŋkəstə]
Latium ['leiʃiəm]
Laurence, Lawrence ['lɔrəns]
Lazarus ['læzərəs]
Lear [liə]
Leeds [li:dz]
Leicester(shire) ['lestə(ʃiə)]
Leigh [li:]
Leila ['li:lə]
Leonard ['lenəd]
Leslie ['lezli]
Libya ['libiə]
Lilian ['liliən]
Lilliput ['lilipʌt]
Lincoln(shire) ['liŋkən(ʃiə)]
Lindisfarne ['lindisfɑ:n]

Lionel ['lainl]
Lisbon ['lizbən] Lissabon
Liverpool ['livəpu:l]
Livy ['livi] Livius
Liz(zie, -y) ['liz(i)] Elisabeth
Llewel(l)yn [lu(:)'elin]
Lloyd [lɔid]
Longfellow ['lɔŋfelou]
Los Angeles [lɔs'ændʒili:z]
Louis(a), -se ['lu(:)i(s), -zə, -i:z]
Louisiana [lu(:)i:zi'ænə]
Lucerne [lu:'sə:n] Luzern *n*
Lucia, -cy ['lu:sjə, -si]
Ludgate ['lʌdgit]
Luther ['lu:θə]
Luxembourg ['lʌksəmbə:g]
Luxor ['lʌksɔ:]
Lydia ['lidiə] Lydia
Lyly ['lili]
Lyons ['laiənz] *sing* Lyon *n*

M

Mabel ['meibəl]
Macbeth [mæk'beθ]
Mackenzie [mə'kenzi]
Macmillan [mək'milən]
Macpherson [mək'fə:sn]
Madeira [mə'diərə]
Madge [mædʒ] Margarete
Madison ['mædisn]
Madras [mə'drɑ:s]
Magdalen ['mægdəlin] Magdalene; *(College)* ['mɔ:dlin]
Magellan [mə'gelən]
Maine [mein]
Malacca [mə'lækə] Malakka
Mali ['mɑ:li]
Manchester ['mæntʃistə]
Manhattan [mæn'hætən]
Manitoba [mæni'toubə]
Margate ['mɑ:git]
Margery ['mɑ:dʒəri]
Marlborough ['mɔ:lbərə]
Marlowe ['mɑ:lou]
Martha ['mɑ:θə]
Mary ['mɛəri] Maria
Maryland [*Am* 'merilənd]
Marylebone ['mærələbən]
Massachusetts [mæsə'tʃu:sets]
Mathew(s) ['mæθju:(z)] Matthäus
Maugham [mɔ:m]
Maurice ['mɔris]
Mauritius [mə'riʃjəs]
May [mei] Maria
Meg [meg] Gretchen
Melbourne ['melbən]
Mercedes [mə:'si:diz]
Mercia ['mə:ʃiə]
Mercutio [mə:'kju:ʃjou]
Mesopotamia [mesəpə'teimjə] Mesopotamien *n*
Messiah [mi'saiə] Messias
Miami [mai'æmi]
Michigan ['miʃigən]
Midas ['maidæs]
Middlesex ['midlseks]
Milan [mi'læn] Mailand *n*
Mildred ['mildrid]
Milton ['miltən]
Milwaukee [mil'wɔ:ki(:)]
Minneapolis [mini'æpəlis]
Minnesota [mini'soutə]
Mississippi [misi'sipi]
Missouri [mi'zuəri]
Moll(y) ['mɔli] Mariechen
Monmouth(shire) ['mɔnməθ(ʃiə)]
Monroe [mən'rou]
Montagu(e) ['mɔntəgju:]
Montana [mɔn'tɑ:nə]
Montgomery [mənt'gʌməri]
Montreal [mɔntri'ɔ:l]
Moravia [mə'reivjə] Mähren *n*
Moscow ['mɔskou] Moskau *n*
Moses ['mouziz]
Munich ['mju:nik] München *n*
Murray ['mʌri]
Mycenae [mai'si:ni(:)]

N

Nancy ['nænsi]
Naomi ['neiəmi]
Naples ['neiplz] Neapel *n*
Natal [nə'tæl] Natal *n*
Nathan ['neiθən]
Nathaniel [nə'θænjəl] Nathaniel
Nazareth ['næzəriθ]
Nebraska [ni'bræskə]
Nell [nel] Lenchen
Nelson ['nelsn]
Nevada [ne'vɑ:də]
Newark ['nju(:)ək]
Newcastle ['nju:kɑ:sl]
New Orleans [nju:'ɔ:liəns]
Newton ['nju:tn]
New York ['nju:'jɔ:k]
New Zealand [nju:'zi:lənd] Neuseeland *n*
Niagara [nai'ægərə]
Nicholas ['nikələs] Nikolas
Niger ['naidʒə]
Nigeria [nai'dʒiəriə]
Nile [nail] Nil *m*
Noah ['nouə]
Nobel [no(u)'bel]
Norfolk ['nɔfək]
Northampton(shire) [nɔ:'θæmptən [(-ʃiə)]
Northumberland [nɔ:'θʌmbələnd]
Northumbria [nɔ:'θʌmbriə]
Norwich ['nɔridʒ, *Am* 'nɔ:witʃ]
Nottingham(shire) ['nɔtiŋəm(ʃiə)]
Nova Scotia ['nouvə'skouʃə] Neuschottland *n*
Nuremberg ['njuərəmbə:g] Nürnberg

O

Oakland ['ouklənd]
Ogilvie ['ouglvi]
Ohio [o(u)'haiou]
Oklahoma [ouklə'houmə]
Oldham ['ouldəm]
Oliver ['ɔlivə] Oliver
Omaha [oumə'hɑ:]
O'Neill [o(u)'ni:l]
Ontario [ɔn'tɛəriou]
Ophelia [ɔ'fi:ljə]
Orange ['ɔrindʒ] Oranien
Oregon ['ɔrigən]
Orestes [ɔ'resti:z]
Orion [ə'raiən]
Orkney ['ɔ:kni]
Oscar ['ɔskə]
Osiris [o(u)'saiəris]
Ossian ['ɔsiən]
Ostend [ɔs'tend]
Oswald ['ɔzwəld]
Othello [o(u)'θelou]
Ottawa ['ɔtəwə]
Ouse [u:z]
Ovid ['ɔvid]
Ozark ['ouzɑ:k]

P

Pekin(g) [pi:'kin(ŋ)]
Pembroke(shire) ['pembruk(ʃiə)]
Pendennis [pen'denis]
Pall Mall ['pæl 'mæl]
Palmyra [pæl'maiərə]
Pamela ['pæmilə]
Parnassus [pɑ:'næsəs]
Patricia [pə'triʃə]
Patrick ['pætrik]
Pearl Harbor ['pə:l'hɑ:bə]
Peg(gy) ['peg(i)] Gretchen
Peggothy ['pegəti]
Penelope [pi'neləpi]
Pennsylvania [pensil'veinjə]
Penzance [pen'zæns]
Pepys [pi:ps]
Perceval ['pə:sivəl]
Percy ['pə:si]
Peshawar [pə'ʃɔ:ə]
Peterborough ['pi:təbrə]
Petrarch ['petrɑ:k] Petrarca
Philadelphia [filə'delfjə]
Piccadilly [pikə'dili]
Piedmont ['pi:dmənt]
Pilate ['pailət]
Pilatus [pi'lɑ:təs]
Pindar ['pində]
Piraeus [pai'ri(:)əs]
Pittsburgh ['pitsbə:g]
Plantagenet [plæn'tædʒinit]
Plato ['pleitou]
Plautus ['plɔ:təs]
Pliny ['plini] Plinius
Plymouth ['pliməθ]
Poe [pou]
Pompeii [pɔm'pi:ai] Pompeji
Pontius ['pɔnʃəs]
Portsmouth ['pɔ:tsməθ]
Potomac [pə'toumæk]
Powell ['pouəl]
Prague [prɑ:g]
Pretoria [pri'tɔ:riə]
Priam ['praiəm] Priamus
Princeton ['prinstən]
Prometheus [prə'mi:θju:s]
Propertius [prə'pə:ʃiəs] Properz
Ptolemy ['tɔləmi] Ptolemäus
Punjab ['pʌndʒɑ:b]
Purcell ['pə:sl]
Putnam ['pʌtnəm]
Pythagoras [pai'θægəræs]

Q

Quebec [kwi'bek]
Queensland ['kwi:nz(lənd)]

R

Rachel ['reitʃəl]
Raleigh ['rɔ:li, 'rɑ:li, 'ræli]
Ralph [reif, rælf]
Randolph ['rændɔlf]
Ratisbon ['rætizbən] Regensburg
Reading ['rediŋ]
Rebecca [ri'bekə] Rebekka
Reuben ['ru:bin] Ruben
Reynolds ['renldz]
Rhode Island ['roud 'ailənd]
Rhodes [roudz]
Rhodesia [ro(u)'di:zjə]
Richard ['ritʃəd]
Richmond ['ritʃmənd]
Rob(ert) ['rɔb(ət)]
Robin Hood ['rɔbin'hud]
Rockefeller ['rɔkifelə]
Roderick ['rɔdərik] Roderich
Roger ['rɔdʒə, 'roudʒə] Rüdiger
Romeo ['roumiou]
Roosevelt [*Am* 'rouzəvelt; *Br* 'ru:svelt]
Rosalind ['rɔzəlind] Rosalinde
Rosemary ['rouzməri] Rosemarie
Rosy ['rouzi] Röschen
Rothschild ['rɔθtʃaild]
Rudyard ['rʌdjəd]
Russel ['rʌsl]
Ruth [ru:θ]
Rutherford ['rʌðəfəd]
Rutland(shire) ['rʌtlənd(ʃiə)]

S

Sahara [sə'hɑ:rə]
Salem ['seilem]

Salisbury ['sɔ:lzbəri]
Sallust ['sæləst]
Sally ['sæli] Sarah
Salome [sə'loumi]
Sam(uel) ['sæm(juəl)]
San Francisco [sænfrən'siskou]
Sara(h) ['sɛərə]
Saskatchewan [sæs'kætʃiwæn]
Saul [sɔ:l]
Saxe-Coburg-Gotha ['sæks'koubə:g'gouθə]
Schenectady [ski'nektədi]
Scone [sku:n]
Seattle [si'ætl]
Senegal [seni'gɔ:l]
Seoul [soul]
Severn ['sevə(:)n]
Seymour ['si:mɔ:, 'sei-]
Shaftesbury ['ʃæftsbəri]
Shakespeare ['ʃeikspiə]
Sheba ['ʃi:bə]
Sheffield ['ʃefi:ld]
Sheila ['ʃi:lə]
Shelley ['ʃeli]
Shetlands ['ʃetləndz] *pl* Shetlandinseln *f pl*
Shirley ['ʃə:li]
Shrewsbury ['ʃru:zbəri, 'ʃrouz-]
Shylock ['ʃailɔk]
Sidney ['sidni]
Silas ['sailəs]
Silvia ['silviə]
Simon ['saimən]
Sinai ['sainiai]
Sinclair ['siŋklɛə]
Singapore [siŋgə'pɔ:]
Sinn Fein ['ʃin'fein]
Sion ['saiən] Zion
Sis(sy) ['sis(i)] Cäcilie
Sioux [su:]
Smollet ['smɔlit]
Snowdon ['snoudn]
Soames [soumz]
Socrates ['sɔkrəti:z]
Soho ['souhou]
Solomon ['sɔləmən]
Somerset(shire) ['sʌməsit(ʃiə)]
Sophia, -phy [sə'faiə, 'soufi] Sophie
Sophocles ['sɔfəkli:z]
Sotheby ['sʌðəbi]
Southampton [sauθ'æmptən]
Southwark ['sʌðək, 'sauθwək]
Stafford(shire) ['stæfəd(ʃiə)]
St Albans [snt'ɔ:lbənz]
Steinbeck ['stainbek]
Stevenson ['sti:vnsn]
St Helena [senti'li:nə] *Insel*
Stonehenge ['stoun'hendʒ]
Strachey ['streitʃi]
Stratford on Avon ['strætfəd ɔn 'eivən]
Stuart ['stjuət]
Sudan [su(:)'dɑ:n]
Suez ['su(:)iz]
Suffolk ['sʌfək]
Sumatra [su(:)'mɑ:trə]
Surrey ['sʌri]
Susan ['su:zn]
Susquehanna [sʌskwi'hænə]
Sussex ['sʌsiks]
Swansea ['swɔnzi]
Sydney ['sidni]
Synge [siŋ]

T

Tacitus ['tæsitəs]
Tagus ['teigəs] Tajo *m*
Talbot ['tɔ:lbət]
Tanganyika [tæŋgə'nji:kə]
Tangier [tæn'dʒiə] Tanger
Tattersall ['tætəsɔ:l]
Tavistock ['tævistɔk]
Tennessee [tene'si:]
Tennyson ['tenisn]
Terence ['terəns] Terenz
Tess [tes] Therese
Texas ['teksəs]
Thackeray ['θækəri]
Thailand ['tailænd]
Thebes [θi:bz] Theben *n*
Theobald ['θiəbɔ:ld] Theobald
Theodore ['θiədɔ:] Theodor
Theresa [tə'ri:zə] Therese
Thermopylae [θə:'mɔpili:] Thermopylen *pl*
Thomas ['tɔməs]
Thoreau ['θɔ:rou]
Tiber ['taibə] Tiber *m*
Tigris ['taigris]
Tim(my), Timothy ['tim(i), '-əθi]
Tintagel [tin'tædʒəl]
Tipperary [tipə'rɛəri]
Titian ['tiʃiən] Tizian
Tobias, Toby [tə'baiəs, 'toubi] Tobias
Toronto [tə'rɔntou]
Torquay ['tɔ:'ki:]
Tottenham ['tɔtnəm]
Trafalgar [trə'fælgə]
Trajan ['treidʒən]
Treves [tri:vz] Trier *n*
Trinidad ['trinidæd]
Tristan ['tristæn]
Troad ['trouæd]
Troy [trɔi] Troja *n*
Tudor ['tju:də]
Tunis ['tju:nis] Tunis *n*
Tussaud's [tə'sɔ:dz]
Tyne [tain]

U

Uganda [ju(:)'gændə]
Ulster ['ʌlstə]
Ulysses [ju(:)'lisi:z]
Upton ['ʌptən]
Ural ['juərəl]
Uriah [juə'raiə] Urias
Uruguay ['urugwai]
Utah ['ju:tɑ:]
Utopia [ju:'toupjə]

V

Valentine ['væləntain]
Vancouver [væn'ku:və]
Vaughan [vɔ:n]
Vauxhall ['vɔks'hɔ:l]
Venezuela [vene'zweilə] Venezuela *n*
Venice ['venis] Venedig *n*
Venus ['vi:nəs]
Vermont [və:'mɔnt]
Vernon ['və:nən]
Vesuvius [vi'su:viəs] Vesuv *m*
Virginia [və'dʒinjə]
Vistula ['vistjulə] Weichsel *f*
Vivian ['viviən]
Volga ['vɔlgə] Wolga *f*
Volpone [vɔl'pouni]
Vosges [vouʒ] *pl* Vogesen *pl*

W

Walden ['wɔ:ldən]
Waldo ['wɔ:ldou]
Wales [weilz]
Wallace ['wɔləs]
Walter ['wɔltə]
Warsaw ['wɔ:sɔ:] Warschau *n*
Warwick(shire) ['wɔrik(ʃiə)]
Washington ['wɔʃiŋtən]
Waterloo [wɔ:tə'lu:]
Waugh [wɔ:]
Wedgwood ['wedʒwud]
Wellington ['weliŋtən]
Wesley ['wezli]
Wessex ['wesiks]
Westminster ['wes(t)minstə]
Westphalia [west'feiljə] Westfalen *n*
Whitechapel ['waittʃæpl]
Whitehall ['wait'hɔ:l]
Wight [wait]
Will(iam) ['wil(jəm)] Wilhelm
Wiltshire ['wiltʃiə]
Wimbledon ['wimbldən]
Winchester ['wintʃistə]
Windermere ['windəmiə]
Windsor ['winzə]
Winnipeg ['winipeg]
Wisconsin [wis'kɔnsin]
Wollstonecraft ['wulstənkrɑ:ft]
Wolsey ['wulzi]
Woodrow ['wudrou]
Worcester(shire) ['wustə(ʃiə)]
Wordsworth ['wə:dzwə(:)θ]
Wyclif(fe) ['wiklif]
Wyoming [wai'oumiŋ]

X

Xanthippe [zæn'tipi]
Xenophon ['zenəfən]
Xerxes ['zə:ksi:z]

Y

Yale [jeil]
Yeat(e)s [jeits]
Yellowstone ['jeloustoun]
Yemen ['jeimən]
York(shire) ['jɔ:kʃ(iə)]
Yosemite [jou'semiti]

Z

Zachariah, -ary [zækə'raiə, 'zækəri]
Zurich ['zjuərik] Zürich *n*

PART II

German — English

Revised by Dr. Erwin Weis

and Dr. Erich Weis

EXPLANATIONS

1. Arrangement

Main headwords are in bold type and placed in alphabetical order. Words with the same stem and in certain cases with the same prefix have been placed together in groups.

Example: ***falt|bar*** ...; ~ **e** ...; ~ **en** ...;
durch|backen ...; ~**beißen** ...

Compounds are treated in the same way.

Example: ***Misch|apparat*** ...; ~**farbe** ...;
~ **wald** ...

Synonyms under the same main headword have also been grouped together.

Example: ***Brut*** ...;
~**apparat** *m*,~ **maschine** *f*,
~ **ofen** *m* ...

The strict alphabetical order also applies in principle to words with the same spelling but of different origin, gender or type.

Example: ***Ton*** ...;~**abnehmer** ...;~**erde** ...

Exceptions to this rule have been made in certain individual cases for the sake of convenience. In these cases the words have been printed separately and marked by superior numbers[1] and [2].

Example: ***Leit|artikel*** ...; ~**er**[1] ...;
Leiter[2] ...

The umlaut has not been exploded, i.e. into ae, oe, ue. Words containing an umlaut are therefore to be found in their alphabetical position regardless of the umlaut.

Example: ***Dusche*** ...;
Düse ...;
Dusel ...;
Dussel ...;
düster ...;

Main headwords, whose articles are particularly long, have been divided up for the sake of clarity.

2. Tilde (~) and double tilde (~~)

The tilde in bold print (~) repeats the boldly printed main headword or the first part of it which is divided off by a vertical stroke (|).

Example: ***Eimer*** ...; ~**bagger** ...;
Einwander|er ...; ~**n**...;
~ **ung** ...

Apart from the headword, the tilde also occurs in those German parts of the text printed in italics (expressions, idioms and explanatory matter). In this case it (~) also stands for the main headword or for those letters in it preceding the vertical stroke.

Example: ***Einwand*** ...;
e-n ~ erheben ...;
Klatsch...;
den ~ mäulern Stoff zum ~ en geben...

The double tilde (~ ~) repeats the immediately preceding bold headword.

Example: ***Klein|anzeigen*** ...;
~ **bürger**...; ~ ~ **lich** ...

In those parts of the German text printed in italics, the double tilde stands (a) for the main headword where this is divided by a vertical stroke and the passage refers to the main headword, or (b) for the preceding headword.

Example: ***Reserv|e*** ...;
in ~ ...;
Halt ...; ~ **en** ...;
wir ~ ~ es für ratsam ...

In italic passages the tilde can also be followed by endings.

Example: ***hart*** ...;
ein ~es Los ...

In a few cases headwords are fitted into a larger article to which they belong in principle, but from which they would normally be excluded, often because of an umlaut. In such cases a tilde cannot be used.

Example: ***Schwefel*** ...; ~ **zinn** ...;
schweflig ...

3. Vertical stroke(|)

The vertical stroke indicates up to which letter the headword is repeated by a tilde in the following group of headwords. Convenience dictates where the vertical stroke is placed in individual cases. As a rule, the principles of word formation are adhered to. Hence the vertical stroke does not indicate syllabification.

Example: ***Schweb|e*** ...;
Schweig|egeld ...;

4. Hyphen (-)

Current usage has been taken into account in the use of the hyphen in English. However it must be pointed out that usage varies. In order to avoid mistakes resulting from the division of a hyphenated word at that point where the hyphen would occur if the word were not divided, the hyphen is repeated at the beginning of the new line.

Example: ***freight-***
-carrying...

5. Capital and small initial letters

In an article under a main headword the order of the headwords takes no account of capital or small initial letters. Whether the word is written with a small initial or a capital can be seen from the grammatical classification which immediately follows it. An *m*, *f* or *n* means that the word is a noun and therefore written with a capital, all other classifications mean that the words are written with a small letter.

Example: ***Schwenk|achse*** *f* . . .;
~antrieb *m* = Schwenkantrieb;
~bar *a* = schwenkbar;
~en *tr* = schwenken.

6. Stress mark(ˈ)

The stress mark is given in the German where the meaning changes with the stress. In contrast with the intonation mark for English pronunciation in Part I, it follows the relevant syllable.

Example: ***durch' schreiten*** . . .;
durchschrei' ten . . .

7. Layout of the individual articles

Distinctions between the different meanings and uses of the German word are made in various ways in the English translations.
The semi-colon indicates that the word or words following translate a different sense of the German word.
The comma separates English words which translate the same sense of the German word.

Example: ***breit*** . . .;
extensive, vast, ample; diffuse.

The full stop stands at the end of each article. The different areas of meaning of the German word are indicated by explanations in the English. The explanations can take the form of abbreviations printed in italics—see list of abbreviations —or of bracketed synonyms or references printed in italics, which precede the relevant English translation.

Example: ***Kurs*** *m mar* course;
(*Peilung*) bearing; (*Weg, Richtung*) tack.

Translations of numerous phrases, idioms and sentences amplify and illustrate the range of meaning of the German word.
With verbs, transitive and intransitive use is carefully differentiated. Characteristically American translations are given side by side with the English ones and labelled *Am*.
Grammatical details are given to indicate special constructions.

Example: ***nehmen*** . . .
to take (*jdm etw* s.th from (s.o.).

German strong verbs are indicated as such by the abbreviation *irr*, which immediately follows the verb.

List of Abbreviations
Liste der Abkürzungen

a *Adjektiv, Eigenschaftswort* adjective
Abk *Abkürzung, abgekürzt* abbreviation
acc *Akkusativ, Wenfall* accusative
adv *Adverb, Umstandswort* adverb
aero *Luftfahrt* aeronautics
allg *allgemein(e, -er, -es)* commonly
Am *Amerikanismus* Americanism
anat *Anatomie* anatomy
arch *Architektur* architecture
astr *Astronomie* astronomy
attr *attributiv, beifügend* attributive
aux *Hilfs-, Hilfsverb* auxiliary
bes. *besonder(s), besondere* particular(ly)
bet *betont* stress(ed)
bot *Botanik, Pflanzenkunde* botany
chem *Chemie* chemistry
com *Handel(swesen)* commerce, commercial
conj *Konjunktion, Bindewort* conjunction
d. *der, die, das, den des, dem* the, of the, to the
dat *Dativ, Wemfall* dative
dial *Dialekt(form)* dialect(al)
dim *Diminutiv, Verkleinerungswort* diminutive
eccl *kirchlich, geistlich* ecclesiastical
e-e, *e-r*, *e-m*, *etc* *eine, einer, einem etc* (of, to) a(n)
el *Elektrotechnik, Elektrizität* electricity
Engl *englisch, britisch* English, British
etc *und so weiter* et cetera
etw *etwas* something
f *Femininum, weiblich* feminine gender
fam *Umgangssprache, familiär* familiar; colloquial
fig *bildlich, übertragen* figurative(ly)
film *Lichtspielwesen, Film* film
geog *Geographie, Erdkunde* geography
geol *Geologie, Gesteinskunde* geology
gram *Grammatik, Sprachlehre* grammar
hist *Geschichte* history
hum *humoristisch* humorously
imp *unpersönlich* impersonal
interj *Ausruf(ewort)* interjection
irr *unregelmäßig* irregular
itr *intransitives Verb, nicht zielendes Zeitwort* intransitive verb
jem, *jdm*, *jdn*, *jds* *jemand(em, en, es)* someone, somebody
jur *juristisch, Rechtswesen* jurisprudence, law term
m *Maskulinum, männlich* masculine gender
mar *Seefahrt* marine
math *Mathematik* mathematics
med *Medizin, Heilkunde* medicine
mil *Militärwesen* military
min *Mineralogie od Bergbau* mineralogy or mining
mot *Kraftfahrwesen* motoring
mus *Musik* music(al)
n *Neutrum, sächlich* neuter gender
od *oder* or
opt *Optik* optics
orn *Vogelkunde* ornithology
o.s. *selbst* oneself
p *Person* person
parl *parlamentarisch, Parlamentarismus* parliamentary
pharm *Arzneimittellehre* pharmacology
phot *Photographie* photography
phys *Physik* physics
pl *Plural, Mehrzahl* plural
pl mit sing *Plural mit Singularkonstruktion* plural with singular construction
poet *Dichtkunst, Poesie* poetry, poetical
pol *Politik, politisch* politics, political
pp *Partizip (Mittelwort) der Vergangenheit* past participle
ppr *Partizip (Mittelwort) der Gegenwart* present participle
pred *prädikativ, zur Satzaussage gehörig* predicative(ly)
pref *Vorsilbe* prefix
pret *Präteritum, Vergangenheit* preterite
prn *Pronomen, Fürwort* pronoun
prov *Sprichwort* proverb
prp *Präposition, Verhältniswort* preposition
r *reflexiv, rückbezüglich* reflexive
radio *Rundfunk* radio, wireless
rail *Eisenbahn* railway, railroad
reg *regelmäßig* regular
rel prn *Relativpronomen, bezügliches Fürwort* relative pronoun
s *Substantiv, Hauptwort* substantive
schott *schottisch* Scotch
sing *Singular, Einzahl* singular
sl *Slang, Berufssprache* slang
s.o. *jemand* someone
sport *Sport* sports
s.th. *etwas* something
tech *Technik, technisch* technical
tele *Telefon, Telegraf, Fernsehen* telephony, telegraphy, television
th. *Ding, Sache* thing
theat *Theater* theatre
tr *transitives Verb, zielendes Zeitwort* transitive verb
typ *Buchdruckerwesen* typography
u. *und* and
US *Vereinigte Staaten von Amerika* The United States of America
usw *und so weiter* and so on
v *Verb, Zeitwort* verb
vulg *vulgär* vulgar
z.B. *zum Beispiel* for instance
zoo *Zoologie* zoology
zus. *zusammen* together
Zssg *Zusammensetzung(en)* compound(s).

Cardinal Numbers
Grundzahlen

0 *null* nought, naught, zero, cipher
1 *eins* one
2 *zwei* two
3 *drei* three
4 *vier* four
5 *fünf* five
6 *sechs* six
7 *sieben* seven
8 *acht* eight
9 *neun* nine
10 *zehn* ten
11 *elf* eleven
12 *zwölf* twelve
13 *dreizehn* thirteen
14 *vierzehn* fourteen
15 *fünfzehn* fifteen
16 *sechzehn* sixteen
17 *siebzehn* seventeen
18 *achtzehn* eighteen
19 *neunzehn* nineteen
20 *zwanzig* twenty
21 *einundzwanzig* twenty-one
22 *zweiundzwanzig* twenty-two
23 *dreiundzwanzig* twenty-three
24 *vierundzwanzig* twenty-four
30 *dreißig* thirty
31 *einunddreißig* thirty-one
40 *vierzig* forty
41 *einundvierzig* forty-one
50 *fünfzig* fifty
51 *einundfünfzig* fifty-one
60 *sechzig* sixty
61 *einundsechzig* sixty-one
70 *siebzig* seventy
71 *einundsiebzig* seventy-one
80 *achtzig* eighty
81 *einundachtzig* eighty-one
90 *neunzig* ninety
91 *einundneunzig* ninety-one
99 *neunundneunzig* ninety-nine
100 *hundert* a (*od* one) hundred
101 *hundert(und)eins* one hundred and one
200 *zweihundert* two hundred
300 *dreihundert* three hundred
400 *vierhundert* four hundred
764 *siebenhundert(und)vierundsechzig* seven hundred and sixty-four
1 000 *tausend* a (*od* one) thousand
1 001 *tausendundeins* one thousand and one
1 150 *eintausendeinhundert(und)fünfzig* one thousand one hundred and fifty
2 000 *zweitausend* two thousand
1 000 000 *eine Million* a (*od* one) million
5 000 000 *fünf Millionen* five million
1 Milliarde one milliard, *Am* one billion

Ordinal Numbers
Ordnungszahlen

1. *erste* first 1st
2. *zweite* second 2nd
3. *dritte* third 3rd
4. *vierte* fourth 4th
5. *fünfte* fifth 5th
6. *sechste* sixth 6th
7. *sieb(en)te* seventh 7th
8. *achte* eighth 8th
9. *neunte* ninth 9th
10. *zehnte* tenth 10th
11. *elfte* eleventh 11th
12. *zwölfte* twelfth 12th
13. *dreizehnte* thirteenth 13th
14. *vierzehnte* fourteenth 14th
15. *fünfzehnte* fifteenth 15th
16. *sechzehnte* sixteenth 16th
17. *siebzehnte* seventeenth 17th
18. *achtzehnte* eighteenth 18th
19. *neunzehnte* nineteenth 19th
20. *zwanzigste* twentieth 20th
21. *einundzwanzigste* twenty-first 21st
22. *zweiundzwanzigste* twenty-second 22nd
23. *dreiundzwanzigste* twenty-third 23rd
30. *dreißigste* thirtieth 30th
31. *einunddreißigste* thirty-first 31st
40. *vierzigste* fortieth 40th
41. *einundvierzigste* forty-first 41st
50. *fünfzigste* fiftieth 50th
51. *einundfünfzigste* fifty-first 51st
60. *sechzigste* sixtieth 60th
61. *einundsechzigste* sixty-first 61st
70. *siebzigste* seventieth 70th
71. *einundsiebzigste* seventy-first 71st
80. *achtzigste* eightieth 80th
81. *einundachtzigste* eighty-first 81st
90. *neunzigste* ninetieth 90th
99. *neunundneunzigste* ninety-ninth 99th
100. *hundertste* (one) hundredth 100th
101. *hundert(und)erste* one hundred and first 101st
200. *zweihundertste* two hundredth 200th
300. *dreihundertste* three hundredth 300th
400. *vierhundertste* four hundredth 400th
764. *siebenhundertvierundsechzigste* seven hundred and sixty-fourth 764th
1 000. *tausendste* (one) thousandth 1 000th
1 001. *tausendunderste* thousand and first 1 001st
1 150. *tausendeinhundert(und)fünfzigste* thousand one hundred and fiftieth 1 150th
2 000. *zweitausendste* two thousandth 2 000th
1 000 000. *millionste* millionth 1 000 000th
5 000 000. *fünfmillionste* five millionth 5 000 000th

Weights and Measures
Maße und Gewichte

Gewicht – Weight *(Avoirdupois)*

grain (gr.) = 0,64 g
dram (dr.) = 27 grains = 1 772 g
ounce (oz.) = 28,35 g
pound (lb.) = 16 oz. = 453,592 g
stone (st.) = 14 lb. = 6,350 kg
quarter (Qr.) = 28 lb. = 12,695 kg
hundredweight (cwt) = 112 lb. = 50,8 kg
ton (t.) = 20 cwts = 1017 kg
25 pounds (Am) = 11,34 kg
100 pounds (Am) = 45,36 kg
short ton (Am) = 907,18 kg
quintal (Am) = 45,36 kg

Troy Weight

grain (gr.) = 0,064 g
pennyweight (dwt) = 24 grains = 1,555 g
ounce troy = 20 dwts = 31,10 g
pound troy = 12 oz. = 373,23 g

Längenmaße – Long Measure

inch (in.) = 12 lines = 0,0254 m
foot (ft.) = 12 inches = 0,3048 m
yard (yd.) = 3 feet = 0,9144 m
fathom (fthm.) = 6 feet = 1,8288 m
pole, rod, perch = 5,5 yards = 5,0292 m
chain = 4 poles = 20,116 m
rood, furlong = 40 poles = 201,16 m
mile (m.) = 8 furlongs = 1609,432 m
knot, nautical mile = 2025 yards = 1853 m
league = 3 miles = 4,827 km

Flächenmaße – Square Measure

square inch (sq. in.) = 6,451 cm^2
square foot (sq. ft.) = 144 square inches = 929 cm^2
square yard (sq. yd.) = 9 square feet = 0,8361 m^2
rood = 40 square rods (sq. r.) = 10,11 a
acre = 4 roods = 40,46 a

Raummaße – Cubic Measure

cubic inch (cu. in.) = 16,387 cm^3
cubic foot (cu. ft.) = 1728 cubic inches = 0,02832 m^3
cubic yard (cu. yd.) = 27 cubic feet = 0,7646 m^3

Hohlmaße – Measure of Capacity

gill (gi.) = 0,142 l
pint (pt.) = 4 gills = 0,568 l
quart (qt.) = 2 pints = 1,136 l
gallon (gal.) = 4 quarts = 4,5459 l
peck (pk.) = 2 gallons = 9,092 l
bushel (bu.) = 4 pecks = 36,368 l
quarter = 8 bushels = 290,935 l
barrel (bl.) = 36 gallons = 163,656 l, (Seife) 116,12 kg

Amerikanisch – American

gill = 0,1183 l
pint = 4 gills = 0,4732 l, *(dry)* = 0,5506 l
quart = 2 pints = 0,9464 l, *(dry)* = 1,1012 l
gallon = 4 quarts = 3,7853 l, *(dry)* = 4,405 l
peck = 2 gallons = *(dry)* 8,8096 l
bushel = 4 pecks = *(dry)* 35,2383 l
bushel barley = 48 pounds = 21,772 kg
bushel wheat = 60 pounds = 27,216 kg
barrel = 31.5 gallons = 119,228 l
barrel petroleum = 42 gallons = 158,97 l
hogshead (hhd.) = 2 barrels = 238,456 l

Metrische Maße und Gewichte
Metric Weights and Measures

gr = 5.432 grains
kg = 1000 gr = 2.204 pounds
dz = 100 kg = 220.46 pounds
t = 1000 kg = 19 cwts 2 grs, 23 lb

mm = 0.039 inch
cm = 10 mm = 0.393 inch
m = 100 cm = 1.0936 yard
km = 1000 m = 1,095 yard = 0.6214 mile

cm^2 = 100 mm^2 = 0.15499 square inch
m^2 = 10.000 cm^2 = 1.19599 square yard
km^2 = 10.000 m^2 = 247.11 acres = 0.3861 square mile
a = 100 m^2 = 119.5993 square yards
ha = 100 a = 2.4711 acres

cm^3 = 1000 mm^3 = 0.061023 cubic inch
m^3 = 1 Million cm^3 = 35.315 cubic feet = 1.3079 cubic yard

l (Liter) = 1.76 pint
hl = 100 l = 22.01 gallons = 2.75 bushels

Thermometer – Thermometer

0° Centigrade = 0° Reaumur = 32° Fahrenheit
100° Centigrade (Celsius) = 80° Reaumur = 212° Fahrenheit

In order to convert Fahrenheit into Centigrade, deduct 32, multiply by 5 and divide by 9. In order to convert Centigrade into Fahrenheit, multiply by 9, divide by 5 and add 32.

A

A *Abk mit* ***A*** *siehe Liste der Abk. Wer ~ sagt, muß auch B sagen* you can't say A without saying B; in for a penny, in for a pound; *das ~ u. das O* the beginning and the end; *von ~ bis Z* from beginning to end; **~-dur** A major; **~-moll** A minor.

a at; each; *~ Konto* on account.

Aal *m* eel; *mil sl* (*Geschoß*) torpedo; tin fish; **~en** *itr* to fish for eels; *r* (*faulenzen*) to relax, to laze, to be lazy, to have a good time; **~glatt** *a* slippery as an eel; *fig* elusive; **~quappe, ~raupe** *f* burbot; eel-pout; **~reuse** *f* eel-buck.

Aar *m poet* eagle.

Aas *n* carrion; (*Köder*) lure; (*Tierleiche*) carcass; (*Schimpfwort*) bitch; rascal; **~en** *itr* to graze; *fam* (*verschwenden*) to waste, to lavish, to squander; **~fliege** *f* dung- (*od* carrion-) fly; **~geier** *m* carrion-kite, carrion-vulture; **~geruch** *m* cadaverous odo(u)r; **~ig** *a* cadaverous, foul, dirty; **~käfer** *m* carrion-beetle; **~seite** *f* (*e-r Haut*) flesh side.

*

ab *adv* off; down; away; from; *Hut ~!* hat(s) off! *Gewehr ~!* order arms! *~!* off! *von da ~* from that time; *weit ~* far off; *~ und zu* now and then; *von heute ~* from this day; *~ und zu gehen* to go backwards and forwards; *auf und ~ gehen* to walk up and down; *prp ~ Hamburg* from Hamburg; *~ dort* to be delivered at yours; *~ Fabrik* ex works; *~ 1. April* on and after the 1st of April; *von nun ~*, *von jetzt ~* from now on; *~ heute* from today; *~ Lager* ex warehouse; *~ an Unkosten* charges to be deducted, off charges; *~ sein fam* to be exhausted, to be all in.

abänder|lich *a* modifiable, alterable; **~n** *tr* to change, to modify; to alter; (*verbessern*) to improve; to correct, to rectify; *seine Ansicht ~~* to change o.'s mind; (*Gesetz*) to amend (a bill); **~ung** *f* change; (*geringfügig*) modification; (*Gesetz*) amendment; *e-n ~~santrag einbringen* to move an amendment.

abängstigen *r* to be in mortal dread, to be alarmed; to fret, to be worried, to worry o. s. in anxiety.

abarbeiten *tr* to work off; to overtask; (*Schuld*) to repay by working; *das Gröbste ~* to rough-work; *r* to sweat; to overwork o. s.; (*abnützen*) to wear off.

abärgern *r* to be annoyed, to feel vexed.

Abart *f* variety; (*Sorte*) species; (*Variation*) variation; **~en** *itr* to vary; to form a new variety; (*entarten, schlechter werden*) to degenerate; (*abweichen*) to deviate; **~ung** *f* variety; variation; (*Entartung*) degeneration.

abästen *tr* to lop, to disbranch.

abbalgen *tr* to skin, to flay; *sich ~* to (have a) tussle with s. o.

Abbau *m min* working; (*Preis*) reduction; cut, cutting down; *chem* (*Auflösung, Trennung*) disintegration, decomposition; separation, reduction; (*Gesetze*) withdrawal; (*Zwangsbewirtschaftung*) decontrol; (*Fabrikeinrichtung*) dismantling; (*Beamte, Haushalt*) axe; dismissal; *Am* cutback; **~en** *tr min* to work; (*Gebäude*) to take down, to remove, to demolish; (*Preis*) to reduce; (*Beamte*) to dismiss, to discharge, to axe; (*zeitweilig entlassen*) *Am* to lay off; (*Maschinen*) to dismantle; *chem* to reduce, to decompose, to disintegrate; **~produkt** *n chem* decomposition product; **~strecke** *f min* board, stall, gate-road; **~würdig** *a min* payable, worthy of being worked, workable.

abbefördern *tr* (*Möbel*) to remove; (*räumen*) to evacuate; (*abschieben*) to deport.

abbeißen *irr tr* to bite off; *sich vor Lachen die Zunge ~* to burst with laughing.

abbekommen *irr tr* to get a share of; to participate in; *etw ~* (*verletzt werden*) to get damaged; *du wirst was ~!* you'll catch it!

abberuf|en *irr tr* to call home; (*Gesandten*) to recall; *in die Ewigkeit ~~* to summon home; **~ung** *f* recall.

abbestell|en *tr* to countermand; to cancel, to revoke, to annul (an order); (*Abonnement*) to discontinue; to cancel a newspaper subscription; **~ung** *f* revocation, cancellation (of an order); counter-order.

abbetteln *tr* to wheedle s. th. out of s. o.

abbezahlen *tr* to pay off; (*ratenweise*) to pay by instal(l)ments.

abbiegen *irr tr* to bend off; *itr* to take a turning; to branch off; *vom Wege ~* to turn aside from.

Abbild *n* copy; likeness; image; **~en** *tr* to copy, to portray; to model; **~ung** *f* copying; sketch; image; picture; illustration; *mit ~~en versehen* to illustrate.

abbinden *irr tr* to unbind; to untie; *med* to underbind, to tie off, to apply a tourniquet to.

Abbitte *f* apology; excuse, plea; *~ leisten* to apologize (for); *~ tun* to beg pardon; to apologize (*bei* to); to eat humble-pie, *Am* to eat crow; **~n** *irr tr* to beg pardon for, to apologize.

abblasen *irr tr* to blow off; (*Angriff*) to break off; (*Dampf*) to exhaust, to blow off; to release; *fig* (*e-e Veranstaltung*) to cancel, to break off.

abblättern *itr* to lose the leaves; (*sich abschälen*) to scale off; to peel off.

abblend|en *tr* (*Licht*) to screen; *mot* to dim o.'s (head-)lights; *phot* to stop down; to (set the) diaphragm; to dim (out); *radio, film* to fade out; *der Wagen hatte nicht abgeblendet* the car had not dimmed its lights; **~licht** *n* dim(med *od* dip) light; **~schalter** *m mot* dip switch; dipper; **~ung** *f* dim-out.

abblitzen: *jdn ~ lassen* to snub s. o.; to rebuff.

abblühen *itr* to cease blooming; *fig* to fade, to wither.

abböschen *tr* to slope.

abbrauchen *tr* to use up; to wear out.

abbrausen *tr* (*duschen*) to douche; *itr fam* (*wegfahren*) to start with a rushing noise.

abbrechen *irr tr* (*pflücken*) to pick, to pluck; (*wegbrechen*) to break off; (*Häuser*) to pull down; (*aufhören*) to cease, to stop; to cut short; (*Zelte*) to strike the tents; (*Thema*) to drop (a subject); (*Unterhandlungen*) to break off negotiations; *ein Lager ~* to break (up the) camp; *alle Brücken hinter sich ~* to burn o.'s boats; *itr* to break off; *kurz ~* to stop short; *wir wollen da ~!* let us drop the subject!

abbremsen *tr, itr mot* to brake; (*verzögern*) to retard; *den Motor ~* to make a brake test; (*Flugmotor vor dem Start*) to run up the engine.

abbrennen *irr tr* to burn down, to destroy by fire; *ein Feuerwerk ~* to display fire-works; *itr* to be destroyed by fire; *abgebrannt sein* to have suffered damage by fire; *fam* to be out of cash, to be broke.

abbringen *irr tr* to take off, to remove, to get off; *mar* to unmoor; *jdn von etw ~* to divert s. o.'s thoughts from, to dissuade.

abbröckeln *itr* to fall off in small pieces, to crumble off; *die Kurse bröckelten ab* prices declined.

Abbruch *m* (*Haus*) breaking off, pulling down; (*Beziehungen*) breaking off, rupture; (*Schaden*) damage, injury; *~ tun* to injure, to prejudice, to be prejudicial to; *sich ~ tun* to hurt o. s.; *auf ~ verkaufen* to sell for the materials; **~reif** *a* dilapidated; **~swert** *m* break-up value.

abbrühen *tr* to boil; (*Schweine*) to scald; *abgebrüht* indifferent; callous.

abbrummen *tr: fam e-e Gefängnisstrafe ~ fam* to do o.'s time; *ein Jahr ~* to serve one year in jail.

abbuch|en *tr* (*Verlust*) to write off; to deduct; **~ung** *f* (*Abschreibung*) deduction.

abbürsten *tr* to brush off; (*Rock*) to brush.

abbüß|en *tr* to expiate, to atone for; (*Strafe*) to serve; **~ung** *f* expiation, atonement.

Abc *n* ABC, alphabet; **~buch** *n* spelling-book, primer; **~schüler, ~schütz(e)** *m* abecedarian, beginner.

Abdachung *f* slope, declivity.

abdämmen *tr* to dam (up).

Abdampf *m* exhaust steam; waste steam.

abdampfen *tr, itr* to evaporate, to steam off; *fam* to depart; *Am* (*Zug*) to pull out; **abdämpfen** *tr* (*kochen*) to stew (well); *fig* (*Ton etc*) to tone down, to soften.

abdank|en *tr* to discharge, to dismiss, to send off; *mil* to cashier; *itr* (*Amt aufgeben*) to resign; (*Fürsten*) to abdicate; **~ung** *f* discharge, pensioning off; resignation; abdication.

abdarben *r* to stint o. s. of; to deny o.s. s. th.; to deprive o.s. of s.th.

abdeck|en *tr* to uncover; (*Dach*) to untile; (*Haus*) to unroof; (*Tisch*) to remove the cloth, to clear the table; (*ver-, zudecken*) to mask; to cover; (*Vieh*) to skin, to flay; (*Bett*) to turn down; (*Kredit*) to repay, to pay back; **~er** *m* flayer; **~erei** *f* flaying-place, knacker's yard, *Am* boneyard.

abdicht|en *tr* to make tight; to seal; (*Loch*) to plug (up); (*mit weichem Material*) to pack; (*kalfatern*) to cau(l)k; (*mit Kitt*) to lute; (*luftdicht machen*) to make air-tight (*od* air-proof); to make gas-tight; **~ung** *f* sealing; **~~smaterial** *n* packing (*od* sealing) material; **~~sring** *m* (*aus Gummi*) rubber washer.

abdienen *tr* to serve o.'s time.

abdingen *tr* to abate (*od* to beat down) the price by bargaining.

ab|dorren *itr* to wither and fall off; **~dörren** *tr* to dry up.

abdrängen *tr* to force away; (*vom Platz*) to push s. o. off (*od* aside).

abdrehen *tr* to wring off; (*Gas*) to

turn off; (*el Licht*) to switch off; *itr aero, mar* (*vom Feind*) to turn away from enemy (*od* target); to break away; (*ausscheren*) to sheer off; to veer.
abdreschen *irr tr* to thrash; *fig abgedroschen* trivial; (*Redensart*) commonplace, empty, trite.
abdrossel|n *tr mot* to throttle down; (*el Strom*) to choke; **~ung** *f mot* throttling down.
Abdruck *m* (*Kopie*) copy; print; reprint; (*Abzug*) proof; (*e-s Stempels, e-s Stiefels etc*) mark, stamp; impression; *phot* (*Abzug*) print; (*Gips~*) (plaster) cast; (*Finger~*) finger-print; *fig* (*Abbild*) image; **~en** *tr* to print off, to strike off; (*wieder ~~*) to reprint; (*veröffentlichen*) to publish; (*aufdrücken*) to imprint; (*abformen*) to impress; **~srecht** *n* copyright.
abdrücken *tr, itr* (*durch Druck entfernen*) to squeeze off; (*Gewehr*) to pull (*od* to press) the trigger; to fire, to shoot.
abdunkel|n *tr* to black out, to darken; (*Farben*) to deepen; **~ung** *f* (*Verdunklung*) black out.
abebben *itr* to ebb away; *fig* (*sich beruhigen*) to die down; to quieten.
Abend *m* (*von 15 — 20 h*) evening; (*ab 20 h*) night; (*Lebens~*) end; (*Vor~*) eve; (*Westen*) west, occident; *der Heilige ~* Christmas Eve; *am ~* in the evening; *am folgenden ~* on the following evening; *gegen ~* towards evening; *heute ~* this evening, to-night, tonight; *gestern ~* last night; *morgen ~* tomorrow evening; *es wird ~* it grows dark, night approaches; *am ~ des Lebens sein* to be in the decline of life; *es ist noch nicht aller Tage ~* time will show; *man soll den Tag nicht vor dem ~ loben* the evening crowns the day; *zu ~ essen* to have supper; **~andacht** *f* even-song; **~anzug** *m* evening-dress; **~blatt** *n* evening paper; **~brot, ~essen** *n* supper; **~dämmerung** *f* dusk; **~gebet** *n*, **~segen** *m* evening prayer; **~gesellschaft** *f* evening party; **~glocke** *f* evening bell; angelus; **~himmel** *m* evening sky; **~kasse** *f* box-office for evening performances; **~kleid** *n* evening-dress; **~kühle** *f* cool of the evening, evening breeze; **~land** *n* occident; west; **~länder** *m* inhabitant of a western country; **~ländisch** occidental, western; **~luft** *f* night-air; **~mahl** *n* the Lord's supper, communion; *zum ~~ gehen* to partake of the Lord's table; **~mantel** *m* evening coat; **~messe** *f* vespers *pl*; **~musik** *f*, **~ständchen** *n* serenade; **~röte** *f* sunset glow, sunset-light; **~s** *adv* in the evening, of an evening; at night, *Am* evenings; **~schule** *f* evening school, *Am* night school; **~seite** *f* western aspect; **~sonne** *f* setting sun; **~toilette** *f* formal clothes *pl*; **~stern** *m* evening-star, Venus; **~wärts** *adv* to the west, westward; **~wind** *m* evening breeze, west wind; **~zeitung** *f* evening paper.
Abenteu|er *n* adventure, perilous enterprise; *auf ~~ ausgehen* to seek adventures; **~erlich** *a* adventurous, fantastic; strange, wonderful, venturesome; **~~keit** *f* adventurousness, fantasticalness; **~rer** *m* adventurer; swindler; *fam* crook; **~rerin** *f* adventuress.
aber *conj* (*Gegensatz*) but; (*jedoch*) however; (*Verwunderung*) *nein ~* I say; *nun ~* but now; *oder ~* or else, otherwise; *die Sache hat ein ~* there's a 'but' in it; *ohne Wenn u. ~* without any ifs and buts; *hundert u. ~ hundert* hundreds and hundreds; **~glaube** *m* superstition; **~gläubisch** *a* superstitious.
aberkenn|en *irr tr* to deprive of; *jur* to disallow, to dispossess by judg(e)ment, to abjudicate; **~ung** *f* abjudication; (*bürgerlicher Ehrenrechte*) deprivation (*od* loss) of civil rights, civic degradation.
aber|malig *a* repeated; **~mals** *adv* again; once more; anew.
abernten *tr* to reap; *itr* to finish reaping.
Aberwitz *m* madness, craziness, folly; **~ig** *a* foolish, crazy, cracked.
abessen *tr* to clear; *itr* to finish eating.
abfädeln *tr* to string (beans).
abfahr|en *irr itr* to start (from, for), to leave; to depart for; (*Schiff*) to set off, to clear for; to sail; (*Ski*) to glissade; *~~! rail* ready! go! *tr* to carry away, to move; (*Räder*) to drive the wheels off; to wear away, to use by driving (*od* cycling); *jdn ~~ lassen fig* to snub; **~t** *f* departure; (*Schiff*) setting out, putting to sea; (*beim Skifahren*) run down, down-hill running, glissade, descent; **~~bahnsteig** *m* departure platform; **~~bereit** *a* ready to depart (*od* to start); **~~slauf** *m* down-hill run; glissade, descent; **~~spunkt** *m* starting point; **~~sstrecke** *f* down-hill course; **~~station** *f* station of departure; **~~zeit** *f* time of departure.
Abfall *m* fall, slope; (*Lossagung*) desertion; (*Sinken*) decrease; (*Überbleibsel*) waste, refuse; (*Müll*) rubbish, garbage; (*Schund*) offal; (*Ausschuß*) discard; (*Blätter*) fall; *min* dip; (*vom Glauben*) apostasy; (*Aufstand*) revolt, insurrection; **~behälter** *m* (*auf der Straße*) litter (*od* refuse) bin; **~eimer** *m* dust-bin; *Am* ash-can; (*für gebrauchte Verbände*) refuse-pail (for used dressings); **~en** *irr itr* to fall down; (*schräg sein*) to slope; (*unbrauchbar*) to be wasted, to go to waste; (*sich trennen*) to desert; to quit (a party); (*Gewinn*) to yield a profit; (*weniger werden*) to decrease; (*Glauben*) to apostatize; (*übrigbleiben*) to be left; (*davonlaufen, revoltieren*) to desert, to revolt; **~papier** *n* waste-paper; **~produkte** *n pl* waste-products *pl*.
abfällig *a* sloping; *fig* disapproving; derogatory; *jdn ~ beurteilen* to criticize s. o. severely; *von jdm ~ sprechen* to speak disparagingly (*od* slightingly) of s. o.; to slander s. o., to run down s. o.; *~e Bemerkungen machen* to make derogatory (*od* disparaging) remarks; *~ bescheiden* to give a negative answer to s. o., to refuse a request, to give s.o. a rebuff.
abfangen *irr tr* (*erwischen*) to catch, to seize; (*Jagd*) to kill with the knife; to stab; (*Briefe, Meldungen*) to intercept; *tech* (*stützen*) to prop, to support; *aero* to flatten out, to pull out of a dive.
abfärben *itr* to stain, to lose colo(u)r; *~ auf jdn* to influence s. o.
abfass|en *tr* to catch, to arrest; (*verfassen*) to compose, to write; to draw up; **~ung** *f* writing, composition.
abfaulen *itr* to decay and drop off; to putrefy, to rot off.
abfedern *tr* to cushion; to spring.
abfegen *tr* to cleanse, to dust; to sweep off.
abfeilen *tr* to clip; to file off.
abfertig|en *tr* to dispatch, to expedite; (*bedienen im Laden*) to serve; to deal with; (*Gegner*) *sport fam* to trim; to get rid off; *fig* (*kurz*) to snub; **~ung** *f* dispatch, expedition; rebuff; (*Bedienung*) service; **~~sschein** *m* (*Zollamt*) permit.
abfeuern *tr* to fire off, to discharge.
abfinden *irr tr* to satisfy, to pay off; *r* to settle, to agree; to put up with; to make the best of; to be resigned (to); *sich mit jdm ~* to come to terms with.
Abfindung *f* (*Übereinkommen*) arrangement, settlement, agreement; (*Vergleich*) composition, compromise; (*Entschädigung*) indemnification, compensation; **~ssumme** *f* indemnity, (amount of) compensation; (*Begleichung*) acquittance; **~svertrag** *m* agreement, compromise; **~szahlung** *f* composition payment.
abflauen *tr tech* to wash, to buddle; (*Tuchmacherei*) to rinse; *itr* (*Wind*) to drop, to calm down; (*Börse*) to droop, to ease off, to give way, to sag, to slacken; *die Kurse flauen ab* prices are drooping (*od* giving way, sagging); (*Streik*) to begin to collapse.
ab|fliegen *irr itr* to fly off, to start; *aero* to take off; (*Raum*) to patrol; **~fließen** *irr itr* to flow away (*od* off); to ebb, to run off; (*sich verlaufen*) to drain off.
Abflug *m aero* take-off, taking-off, start; (*Zugvögel*) flying off, departure; **~deck** *n aero* flightdeck; **~geschwindigkeit** *f aero* take-off speed; **~hafen** *m* (air)port of departure; **~kurs** *m* heading; **~leistung** *f* take-off power; **~ort** *m* place of departure; **~punkt** *m* point of departure.
Abfluß *m* drain; flowing off; outlet; *med* defluxion; **~graben** *m* culvert; **~röhre** *f* waste-pipe; (*Straße*) sewer, gutter; (*Küche*) sink; **~wasser** *n* waste water.
ab|fordern *tr* to ask for, to come for; **~formen** *tr* to model, to copy; **~forsten** *tr* to clear of trees; **~fragen** *irr tr* to examine; (*im Examen, in Denksportaufgaben*) *Am* to quiz; (*Aufgaben*) to hear; **~fressen** *irr tr* to eat away, to graze; (*abäsen*) to browse; *der Gram frißt ihm das Herz ab* the grief is breaking his heart
abfrieren *irr itr* to freeze off, to be nipped by frost; to be frostbitten.
Abfuhr *f* carrying away; removal; transportation; (*Rollabfuhr*) cartage; (*von Müll*) garbage-service; *fam fig* (*Rüge*) snub, rebuff; *Am sl* brush-off.
abführ|en *tr* to lead off; to clear off (a debt); (*Geld*) to deliver (to); (*Kehricht*) to remove; (*Häftling*) to take away, to be marched off to prison; *jdn ~~* to check; *itr med* to purge; **~end** *a* purgative, cathartic; **~ung** *f* transport; clearing; purgation; **~(ungs)mittel** *n* aperient, purgative, purge, laxative.
abfüll|en *tr* to fill out; (*abziehen*) to rack; (*in Flaschen*) to bottle; (*Bier*) to draw off; (*Wein*) to decant; **~anlage** *f* (*in Brauerei*) filling plant; racker; **~ung** *f* filling out; **~station** *f* filling station.
abfüttern *tr* (*Vieh*) to feed, to give the provender to; *fam* to give a big feed; (*Anzug*) to line.
Abgabe *f* delivery; (*Geld*) levy; contribution; (*Steuer*) duty, rate, tax; (*soziale*) social duty; **~druck** *m com* sales pressure; **~nfrei** *a* free from duty, exempt from taxes; **~npflichtig** *a* taxable, liable to duty.
Abgang *m* departure, starting; (*Bühne*) exit; (*Verlust*) loss; *Am* (*Defizit*) wantage; *med* emission; (*Abort*) *med* miscarriage; *typ* waste paper; (*Tod*) death, decease; (*Amt*) retirement; (*Schule*) leaving; (*Handel*) market; **~sprüfung** *f* final examination, leaving examination; **~spunkt** *m* starting-point; **~swinkel** *m* angle of departure; **~szeit** *f* time of departure; (*e-r Meldung*) time of dispatch; **~szeugnis** *n* leaving certificate.

Abgas *n mot* exhaust gas, waste gas; **~kanal** *m mot* exhaust passage; **~turbine** *f mot* exhaust turbine.

abgeben *irr tr* to give up, to hand over; (*Brief*) to leave a note (*bei jdm* with); *abzugeben bei* care of, (*abgekürzt auf Adresse*) c/o; (*Gepäck*) to deposit; (*Amt aufgeben*) to resign; (*Urteil*) to pass judg(e)ment; *seine Meinung ~ über* to express o.'s opinion about; (*Beruf*) to make; *er gibt e-n guten Matrosen ab* he'll make a good sailor; (*Ware*) to sell, to dispose of, to let have, to supply; *jdm etw ~* to let share in; to let have; *sich mit etw ~* to meddle with; to have to do with; to bother o. s. with; *sich mit jdm ~* to associate with.

abge|brannt *a* burnt out; *fig* without money, broken; *sl* broke; stony-broke; **~brüht** *a fig* hardened; **~droschen** *a fig* commonplace, trivial; **~feimt** *a* crafty, cunning; (*durchtrieben*) arrant; (*völlig*) downright; **~grast** *a fig* (*Gebiet*) well-covered; **~griffen** *a* (*Buch*) well-thumbed; (*Münzen*) worn.

abge|härtet *a* hardy, hardened (against, to); **~hackt** *a* (*Stil*) broken, abrupt.

abgehen *irr itr* to go away, to walk off; (*Bühne*) to make o.'s exit; (*Zug*) to start; (*Straße*) to branch off; (*vom rechten Wege*) to go astray; (*von e-r Meinung*) to change o.'s opinion; (*mit Tode*) to die, to decease; (*vom Amt*) to resign; (*von Schule*) to leave; (*Waren*) to sell, to find a ready sale; (*Preis*) to reduce; (*Richtung, Gesprächsgegenstand*) to swerve from; (*Knopf*) to come off; (*von Plan*) to relinquish; *mar* to set sail (for); (*Schuß*) to fire; *es ist alles gut abgegangen* everything went (*od* passed) off well; *ich kann nicht davon ~* I must insist upon it; *reißend ~* to sell like hot cakes; *~ lassen* to expedite, to forward, to dispatch (*od* despatch); *er läßt sich nichts ~* he indulges every enjoyment; *es geht ihm nichts ab* he has all he wants.

abge|kartet *a* (*~~e Sache*) put-up job; **~klärt** *a* (*Alter, Urteil*) mellow, wise; **~knickt** *a* bent, flexed; (*Eingeweide*) kinked; **~kürzt** *a* abridged, shortened.

abge|lagert *a* (*Wein*) matured; (*Holz*) seasoned; **~laufen** *a* (*Wechsel*) due, payable; (*Zeit*) up, expired; (*Uhr*) run down; **~lebt** *a* decrepit; worn out, used up; **~legen** *a* remote; out of the way; *~~e Straße* by-way; (*einsam*) retired; **~~heit** *f* remoteness, distance; **~macht!** 'tis a bargain! agreed! all right! *Am* O.K.! quits! *das ist e-e ~~e Sache* that's settled; **~magert** *a* emaciated; **~messen** *a* measured; reserved; **~neigt** *a* reluctant; averse; disinclined; *nicht ~~* ready; **~~heit** *f* aversion; disinclination; dislike; **~nutzt** *a* used up, worn out; (*Ausdruck*) trite.

abgelt|en *tr* (*Schuld*) to pay; (*befriedigen*) satisfy; to discharge; **~ung** *f* repayment, settlement; (*Ersatz*) compensation delivery.

Abgeordnet|e(r) *m* deputy; (*Verein*) delegate; Member of Parliament (M. P.); *Am* congressman, representative, (*abgekürzt vor Name*) Rep.· *der Herr ~e X.* the honourable member for ... (constituency), *Am* the gentleman from ... (*Staat*); **~enhaus** *n* House of Commons; chamber of deputies; *Am* House of Representatives.

abge|rissen *a* ragged, torn off; (*Kleider*) shabby; *fig* disconnected, abrupt; **~rundet** *a* rounded; **~sandte(r)** *m* delegate; ambassador; **~schabt** *a* threadbare, shabby; **~schieden** *a* solitary, remote; (*tot*) defunct, deceased; **~schiedenheit** *f* retirement, seclusion.

abge|schliffen *a fig* polished; **~schlossen** *a fig* isolated; exclusive; **~~heit** *f* reserve, exclusiveness; **~schmackt** *a* tasteless; insipid; absurd; *fig* flat, dull; **~~heit** *f* insipidity, dul(l)ness; bad taste; **~sehen** *von prp* apart from; leaving (*od* setting) aside; irrespective of; without regard to; *es ~~ haben auf* to aim at; *~~ davon, daß ...* without mentioning that; **~sondert** *a* separated (*von* from); **~spannt** *a* (*müde*) fatigued, run down, tired out; (*erschöpft*) exhausted; **~standen** *a* flat; (*Getränk*) stale; **~storben** *a* torpid, dead; **~stumpft** *a* blunt, obtuse; *fig* (*geistig*) dull, indifferent to; **~treten** *a* (*Absatz*) run-down.

abge|winnen *irr tr* to win, to carry off; *e-r Sache Geschmack ~~* to get a taste for; to get to like; **~wöhnen** *tr* to wean; *sich etw ~~* to get rid of (a bad habit); (*Rauchen*) to give up; to break o. s. of the habit of; *jdm etw ~~* to break s. o. from a custom; **~zehrt** *a* wasted, emaciated.

abgießen *irr tr* to pour off; to spray (off); *tech* to cast; *chem* to decant.

Abglanz *m* reflection; *fig* image.

ab|gleiten *irr*, **~*glitschen*** *itr* to glide off, to slide off; *mot* to skid.

Abgott *m* idol.

Abgött|erei *f* idolatry; **~isch** *a* idolatrous; *~~ verehren* to idolize.

abgraben *irr tr* to dig off; (*ableiten*) to draw off; (*Teich*) to drain (a pond).

abgrämen *r* to pine away (with grief).

abgrasen *tr* to graze off.

abgrenz|en *tr* to mark off, to limit; to define; **~ung** *f* demarcation.

Abgrund *m* abyss, gulf, precipice.

abgründig *a* precipitous; *fig* inscrutable, impenetrable.

abgucken *tr* to learn by watching.

Abguß *m* pouring off; (*Gießen*) founding; (*abgegossenes Bild*) cast, copy.

ab|hacken *tr* to chop off, to cut off; **~haken** *tr* to unhook; (*abstreichen auf Liste*) to tick off.

abhalftern *tr* to unharness; *fig* (*entlassen*) to dismiss; *fam* to sack, to give the sack to.

abhalt|en *irr tr* to keep off; (*Feind*) to check the enemy; (*Sitzung*) to hold; (*Kind*) to hold out; (*verhindern*) to hinder, to detain, to restrain, to stop; (*ausreden, etw zu tun*) to dissuade; (*Fest*) to celebrate; (*vom Land*) to bear off the land; *ich werde mich nicht ~~ lassen* that shall not deter me; **~ung** *f* (*Hindernis*) hindrance; prevention; (*Versammlung*) holding.

ab|handeln *tr* to purchase; (*vom Preise*) to abate; to beat down; to bargain; (*erörtern*) to treat of, to debate on; **~handen** *adv*: *~~ sein* to be missing; *~~ kommen* to get lost; **~handlung** *f* treatise, essay, dissertation; (*gesammelte ~~en e-r gelehrten Gesellschaft*) transactions *pl.*

Abhang *m* slope, declivity.

abhäng|en *tr* to take down; to detach; to hang off; (*Zug*) to uncouple; *tele* to take off the receiver; *tech* to disconnect; (*nach d. Überholen*) to overtake and leave behind; *irr itr* to depend on; to hinge; **~ig** *a* inclined; *gram* indirect; *~~e Rede* indirect speech; (*von e-r Person*) dependent; **~~keit** *f* (*von Personen*) dependence, dependency; *gegenseitige ~~* interdependence; (*Beziehung*) relation(ship); function; *gram* subordination.

abhärmen *r* to pine away, to grieve (*über* at).

abhärt|en *tr* to harden; *r fig* to inure o. s. (*gegen* to); to temper; **~ung** *f* hardening; inurement.

abhaspeln *tr* to reel off; *fig* (*Rede etc*) to rattle off.

ab|hauen *irr tr* to cut off; (*Bäume*) to fell; *itr sl* (*weggehen*) to knock off, to take off; *hau ab! sl* scram! **~häuten** *tr* to skin; to flay; *sich ~~ med* to excoriate, to peel; (*Schlange*) to slough.

abheben *irr tr* to take off; to lift off, to remove; to skim off, to siphon off; (*trennen*) to separate; *aero* (*Maschine vom Boden*) to take off, to unstick; to become air-borne; (*Karten*) to cut; (*Geld*) to take out; to withdraw; *sich ~* to detach o. s.; to stand out (against).

abheilen *itr* to heal up.

abhelfen *irr itr* to remedy, to redress (wrongs); to remove (a difficulty); to correct (an error); *e-r Sache ~* to remedy s. th.; *dem ist nicht abzuhelfen* it cannot be helped.

abherzen *tr* to hug and kiss.

abhetzen *tr* to run down; *fig* to overwork; *r* to worry o. s., to rush about, to wear o. s. out.

Abhilfe *f* redress, help, remedy; **~maßnahmen** *f pl* corrective measures *pl.*

abhobeln *tr* to plane off, to smooth; *fig* to polish off.

abhold *a* unfavo(u)rable; averse (to).

abhol|en *tr* to fetch away, to call for; (*jdn am Bahnhof*) to go to meet s. o. at the train; (*einsammeln*) to collect; *das Auto wird mich abholen* the car will come for me; *~~ lassen* to send for; *abzuholen bei* to be called for at; **~ung** *f* fetching; (*Güter*) collection.

abholz|en *tr* to cut down; (*ganze Gebiete*) to deforest; to clear; **~ung** *f* clearing.

abhorchen *tr med* to auscult(ate), to sound, to listen.

abhör|en *tr* to hear a pupil's lesson, *Am* to recite a pupil; (*Zeugen*) to interrogate; (*abfangen*) to intercept; to pick up; to overhear; *itr* to listen to; *radio* to listen in; **~box** *f* (*Tonfilm*) control box (for sound recording); **~raum** *m radio* control-room, listening-room; **~station** *f* listening station.

*

abirr|en *itr* to lose o.'s way; to go astray; to deviate, to swerve (*von* from); *fig* to err; **~ung** *f* deviation; aberration.

Abiturient *m* candidate for the final examination of a college in Germany; candidate for school leaving examination (*in England statt Abitur Aufnahmeprüfung im College, in USA Testprüfung bei Eintritt in Hochschule*), *Am etwa* (high school) graduate.

abjagen *tr* to jade, to founder, to override, to overdrive (a horse); *jdm etw ~* to retrieve, to rescue, to recover s. th. from; *r* to tire o. s. by running.

abkämmen *tr* to comb off.

abkanzeln *tr* to reprimand, to rebuke, *Am sl* to bawl out.

abkarten *tr* to pre-arrange, to plot; *abgekartetes Spiel* a preconcerted plan, *Am* a put-up job.

Abkauf *m* purchase; **~en** *tr* to buy, to purchase from.

Abkäufer *m* purchaser, buyer.

Abkehr *f* turning away; (*Kehrtwendung*) about-face; (*Entfremdung*) alienation; (*von Gott*) estrangement from God; (*Abneigung*) aversion.

abkehren *tr* (*mit Besen*) to brush, to sweep; *fig* to withdraw; *r* to turn away.

abklappern *tr* (*von Haus zu Haus*

gehen) to scour; to rove; *abgeklappert* (*Ausdruck, Redensart*) hackneyed.
abklär|en *itr* to clear, to clarify; (*Wein*) to fine; **~ung** *f* clarification.
Abklatsch *m* cast; (*Abdruck*) copy, proof; impression; *typ* stereo(type-plate); *fig* poor imitation; **~en** *tr typ* to stereotype; (*Korrekturbogen*) to print off, to strike off a proof.
abkling|eln *itr tele* to ring off; (*Straßenbahn*) to give starting signal; **~en** *irr itr mus* to die away; (*Schmerz etc*) to fade away.
abklopfen *tr* to knock off; (*vom Arzt*) to tap, to auscultate; (*Teppich*) to beat out, to dust off; (*Bettler e-e Gegend*) to scour; *itr mus* (*Dirigent*) to stop music by rapping with the baton.
abknabbern *tr* to nibble off, to pick.
abknallen *tr* to shoot down; to fire off.
abkneifen *irr*, ***abknipsen*** *tr* to pinch off, to nip off.
abknicken *tr* to break (*od* to snap) off.
abknöpfen *tr* to unbutton; *jdm etw ~ fam* to cheat, to swindle s.o. out of s.th., to get s.th. from s.o.
abknüpfen *tr* to unbind, to untie.
abknutschen *tr fam* to hug and kiss.
abkochen *tr* to boil; (*Milch*) to scald; *itr mil* to cook.
abkommandieren *tr* to detach, to detail.
abkommen *irr itr* to come off; to lose o.'s way; (*aus der Mode kommen*) to grow out of fashion; (*von etw*) to give up, to alter o.'s plan; *mil* (*beim Schießen*) to mark; *nicht ~ können* not to be able to get away (*od* to disengage o.s.); *~ n fig* settlement, agreement; (*Vertrag*) deal; *ein ~ treffen* to come to an agreement with; *gütliches ~* amicable arrangement.
abkömmlich *a* not wanted, who can be spared, unnecessary; free, having spare time; *~ sein* to be dispensed with; to have spare time.
Abkömmling *m* descendant, offspring; *chem* derivate.
abkonterfeien *tr* to portray.
abköpfen *tr* to decapitate; (*Bäume*) to top.
abkoppeln *tr* to uncouple.
abkratzen *tr* to scrape (*od* scratch) off; *itr vulg* (*sterben*) to die.
abkriegen *tr* to get (a share of); (*verletzt werden*) to get hurt; (*bestraft werden*) to be punished.
abkühl|en *tr* to chill, to ice; *fig* to cool; *r* to cool down; **~ung** *f* cooling; **~~smittel** *n* refrigerant; cooling agent.
Abkunft *f* origin, descent; family; breed; birth.
abkürz|en *tr* to shorten; to abridge; to abbreviate; to reduce; (*Weg*) to take a short cut; (*beschneiden*) to curtail; **~ung** *f* abbreviation; shortening; reduction.
abküssen *tr* to kiss heartily.
ablad|en *irr tr* to unload, to unpack; to dump; **~eplatz** *m* dumping-ground; (*Lagerplatz*) goods-yard; *mil* (*Depot*) dump; **~ung** *f* unloading; discharging.
Ablage *f* place of deposit; depot, warehouse; dump; (*Kleider~*) cloak-room, *Am* check-room.
ablager|n *tr* to deposit; (*Bier*) to settle; *~n lassen* to improve by storage; **~ung** *f* storage; *geol* sediment; deposit.
Ablaß *m* (*Abfluß*) drain; *eccl* indulgence; **~brief** *m* letter of indulgence; **~hahn** *m* (*Kessel*) safety-valve; delivery-cock; **~krämer** *m* seller of indulgences.
ablassen *irr itr* to leave off, to cease; *von etw ~* to abandon, to desist from, to let go; *vom Preise ~* to abate off the price; *tr* (*Zug*) to start; (*Teich*) to drain; (*Faß*) to tap; (*Dampf*) to let off; (*käuflich*) to sell.
Ablativ *m* ablative (case).
ablauern *tr* to watch for; to lie in wait for.
Ablauf *m* flowing off, drain; (*e-s Wechsels*) maturity of a bill (of exchange); (*e-r Frist*) expiration; *nach ~* at the end of; (*Ausfall*) end, result; (*Ort des ~s*) outlet, drain; (*~loch, ~rohr*) waste channel, waste-pipe; (*Ausguß in Küche*) sink; (*Gosse, Kandel, Dachrinne*) gutter; **~berg** *m rail* double incline; *Am* hump; **~en** *irr itr* to run off (*od* down); (*e-r Frist*) to expire; (*Uhr*) to run down, to stop; (*Wechsel*) to fall due; (*e-n Ausgang nehmen*) to end, to come off; *sport* to start; *tr* to wear out by running; *jdm den Rang ~~* to outdo s. o.; *sich ~~* to tire o. s. out by running; *sich die Hörner ~~* to grow wise by experience; **~zeit** *f* time of expiration.
ablauschen *tr* to learn by listening (*od* by eavesdropping); *radio* to pick up, to intercept.
Ablaut *m* vowel-gradation, vowel-permutation; ablaut.
abläuten *itr tele* to ring off; (*Zug*) to give starting signal.
abläutern *tr* to clarify, to refine.
Ableben *n* decease, death.
ablecken *tr* to lick off.
ableg|en *tr* (*Kleider*) to take off; (*Gewohnheiten*) to give up; (*Last*) to lay down; (*Karten*) to discard; (*von Briefen*) to file; *typ* to distribute; (*wegwerfen*) to cast off; *e-n Eid ~~* to take an oath; *e-e Probe ~~* to give a proof of; *e-e Prüfung ~~* to pass an examination; *Rechnung ~~* to give an account of; *Zeugnis ~~* to bear witness to; **~er** *m bot* shoot, layer, scion; *fig* branch.
ablehn|en *tr* to decline; to reject; to refuse, *Am* to turn down; (*Antrag bei Abstimmung*) to defeat; *jur* (*Zeugen*) to challenge; (*Richter, als befangen*) to recuse; **~end** *a* negative; reserved; **~ung** *f* declining, refusal, non-acceptance, *Am* declination; rejection.
ableiern *tr fig* to drawl out; (*Gedicht*) to recite in a tedious manner.
ableisten *tr: e-n Eid ~* to take an oath; *das Probejahr ~* to pass the probationary year; *Wehrdienst ~* to serve o.'s time.
ableit|en *tr* to turn off; (*Wasser*) to drain; (*Feuchtigkeit*) to draw off; (*Wort*) to derive from; (*Fluß*) to divert; (*irreleiten*) to mislead, to misguide; (*folgern*) to deduct; *el* to shunt; **~er** *m el* conductor; (*Röhre*) conduit pipe, channel; **~ung** *f* turning-off; (*e-s Flusses*) diversion; (*Wasser*) drainage; (*Folgerung*) deduction; (*Wortabstammung*) etymology, derivation; *el* branch-circuit, shuntwire; (*Rohr*) off-take, delivery pipe; **~~sgraben** *m* ditch, sewer; **~~ssilbe** *f* derivative affix.
ablenk|en *tr* to turn away, to divert; to deflect; (*Licht*) to diffract; **~ung** *f* diversion; (*der Magnetnadel*) deviation; *fig* distraction, recreation; (*Überredung*) dissuasion; **~~smanöver** *n* red-herring.
ablernen *tr* to learn from; *jdm etw ~* to imitate s. o. in s. th.
ablese|n *irr tr* (*Früchte*) to gather; to pick off, to pluck off; (*Namen*) to call over; *itr* (*von e-m Blatt*) to read from; **~marke** *f* index line, index mark; **~fehler** *m* index error; reading error.
ableugn|en *tr* to disclaim, to disavow; *jur* to traverse, to deny; **~ung** *f* denying, denial, disavowal; *jur* traverse; **~ungseid** *m jur* oath of abnegation.
abliefer|n *tr* to deliver, to consign; **~ung** *f* delivery; *bei ~~* on delivery; **~~sschein** *m* certificate of delivery; **~~ssoll** *n* delivery quota, delivery target; **~~stermin** *m* term of delivery; **~~szeit** *f* time of delivery.
abliegen *irr itr* to be far off, to lie out of the way, to lie remote; (*Früchte*) to ripen, to grow ripe; (*Wein*) to mature.
ablisten *tr* to trick s. o. out of; (*herausholen aus jdm*) to pump s. o.
ablocken *tr* to obtain s. th. from s. o. by flattery (*od* by coaxing).
ablohn|en *tr* to pay off, to discharge; **~ung** *f* discharge.
ablöschen *tr* to extinguish, to blot out; to quench.
ablösbar *a* (*trennbar*) separable; (*Schulden*) redeemable.
ablös|en *tr* to uncling, to detach; to loosen, to remove; *mil* to relieve; (*Schulden*) to discharge, to pay off; *jdn ~~* to replace; *sich, einander ~~* to relieve one another; *sich ~~* to come off; (*Haut*) to peel off, to scale off; **~ung** *f* detaching; *mil* relief; *med* amputation; (*Schulden*) redemption of debts; (*Renten*) commutation; **~~smannschaft** *f* relief, relays *pl* of fresh hands.
abmach|en *tr* to take off, to detach; (*Geschäft*) to adjust; to settle, to arrange; *das ist e-e abgemachte Sache* that's a settled affair; **~ung** *f* loosening; settling, arrangement; *gegenseitige ~~* mutual agreement; (*im Vertrag*) stipulation.
abmager|n *itr* to grow thin, to lose flesh; **~ung** *f* emaciation.
abmähen *tr* to mow off, to cut down.
abmahnen *tr* to dissuade from; to caution against, to warn; to advise to the contrary.
abmalen *tr* to paint, to portray; (*kopieren*) to copy; *fig* to depict.
Abmangel *m* deficit; deficiency; *e-n ~ decken* to make good a deficiency.
Abmarsch *m* marching off, departure, start; **~bereit** *a* ready to start; **~ieren** *itr* to march off, to decamp.
abmatt|en *itr* to harass; to fatigue, to exhaust; **~ung** *f* exhaustion.
abmeld|en *tr* to countermand; to give notice; *r* to announce o.'s departure; **~ung** *f* countermand, notice; **~~sbescheinigung** *f* certificate, notice of departure; **~~sformular** *n* registration form.
abmess|en *irr tr* to measure off, to survey; *seine Worte ~~* to measure o.'s terms, to weigh o.'s words; *ein abgemessenes Verhalten* reserve; **~ung** *f* measuring, measurement; survey; *tech* dimension, size, ga(u)ge.
abmiet|en *tr* to hire, to rent from; **~er(in)** *m* (*f*) hirer, lessee, holder, tenant.
abminder|n *tr* to lessen, to diminish; **~ung** *f* lessening, diminution, reduction.
abmontieren *tr* to dismantle, to dismount, to knock down, to take to pieces; *aero sl* to break up in the air.
abmühen: *sich ~* to labour at, to exert oneself.
abmustern *tr mar* to pay off.
abnagen *tr* to nibble; to gnaw off.
abnähen *tr* to quilt, to stitch in.
Abnahme *f* taking away; *med* amputation; (*Eid*) administering; (*Absatz*) sale; (*Verminderung*) diminution, decay; (*der Tage*) shortening; (*des Mondes*) wane; *tech* acceptance (test); (*Gewicht*) loss; **~fahrt** *f mot* test-drive;

~**prüfung** *f tech* (*von Werkstoffen*) inspection test; (*allgemein*) acceptance test; ~**verweigerung** *f tech* rejection; ~**vorschrift** *f tech* quality specification; ~**wesen** *n tech* quality inspection.
abnehm|en *irr tr, itr* (*jdm etw* ~~) to take s.th. from; (*etw* ~~) to take off; (*an Länge*) to shorten; *den Bart* ~~ to shave; (*Hörer*) *tele* to remove (*od* to lift, to take off) the receiver; *den Hut* ~~ to take off o.'s hat; (*Glied*) to amputate; (*abkaufen*) to purchase from; (*Maschen*) to narrow; *jdm e-n Eid* ~~ to administer an oath to s. o.; (*Parade*) to hold (a review); *an Zahl* ~~ to decrease; *an Größe od Bedeutung* ~~ to diminish; (*Wasser*) to sink; (*Kräfte*) to begin to fail; (*geringer werden*) to slack(en); (*an Gewicht*) to lose weight; (*Mond*) to wane; (*Preise*) to lower; (*Sturm*) to abate; (*Zeit*) to pass away; (*Karten*) to cut; (*schwinden*) to dwindle; (*Tage*) to grow shorter; ~**er** *m* buyer, customer, purchaser, consumer.
Abneigung *f* dislike, aversion, antipathy, reluctance.
abnorm *a* abnormal, irregular; (*außergewöhnlich*) exceptional.
abnötigen *tr* to wring from, to extort from.
abnutz|en *tr* to use up, to wear out; *sich* ~~ to get worn out; ~**ung** *f* wear and tear; (*Wertverminderung*) depreciation; attrition; ~~**skrieg** *m* war of attrition; ~~**sstrategie** *f* strategy of attrition.
Abonn|ement *n* subscription (to); *aus dem* ~~ *treten* to drop (*od* to discontinue) o.'s subscription; ~**ent** *m* subscriber; (*Eisenbahn, Straßenbahn*) season-ticket-holder, *Am* commuter; ~**ieren** *tr, itr* (*auf*) to subscribe, to become a subscriber to.
abordn|en *tr* to depute, to delegate; ~**ung** *f* deputation, delegation.
Abort *m* privy, lavatory, water-closet (W.C.); ladies' (cloak-)room, *Am* toilet; *med* (*Abortus*) abortion, miscarriage.
abpachten *tr* to rent from.
abpacken *tr* to unpack, to unload.
abpassen *tr* to fit, to adapt to, to adjust; to watch for an opportunity.
abpflücken *tr* to pick, to pluck off, to gather, to crop; ~ *n* cropping, gathering.
abplagen: *sich* ~ to drudge, to toil.
abplatten *tr* to flatten.
abprägen *tr* to stamp, to give an impression; *r* to leave an impress.
abprallen *itr* to fly off, to recoil, to ricochet, to bounce off; *fig* to glance off.
abpressen *tr* to squeeze off; *jdm etw* ~ to wring, to wrest from.
abprotzen *tr* to unlimber.
abputzen *tr* to clean (off), to polish; (*mit Hobel*) to plane; (*Haus*) to plaster
abquälen *r* to harass, to drudge, to toil; (*sich sorgen*) to worry o. s.
abquetschen *tr* to crush off, to squeeze off.
abrackern *r* to slave, to drudge, to toil.
abrahmen *tr* to skim (milk); *abgerahmte Milch* (*Magermilch*) skim(med) milk.
abrasieren *tr* to shave off.
abraspeln *tr* to rasp off.
abraten *irr itr* to dissuade from, to warn, to advise against.
Abraum *m* rubble, rubbish, waste.
abräumen *tr* to remove, to clear away; (*Tisch*) to clear the table.
abrechn|en *tr* (*abziehen*) to discount, to deduct; (*mit jdm* ~~) to settle with s. o.; to settle accounts with s. o.; *abgerechnet von* apart from; ~**ung** *f* deduction, discount; settlement; liquidation; (*Bank*) statement; clearing; *nach* ~~ *von* after deduction of; *auf* ~~ on account; ~~ *halten* to balance accounts; *in* ~~ *bringen* to take off; ~~**skurs** *m* making-up price; ~~**sstelle** *f* clearing house; ~~**sverfahren** *n* clearing; ~~**sverkehr** *m* clearing-system.
Abrede *f* agreement; *in* ~ *stellen* to deny, to disown; ~**n** *tr* (*vereinbaren*) to agree; *jdm etw* ~**n** to dissuade from.
Abregnen *n* (*vom Flugzeug*) aerial spraying.
abreib|en *irr tr* to rub off, to efface (colo(u)rs), to brush; ~**ung** *f* rubbing (off); abrasion; (*Abwaschung*) ablution; friction.
Abreise *f* departure, setting out; *bei meiner* ~ *von hier* on leaving this place; ~**n** *itr* to depart, to leave (for), to set out; to start (for).
abreiß|en *irr tr* to tear off; to pull down (a house), to wear away (clothes); *itr* to break off; to rend off; ~**kalender** *m* block-almanac; block-calendar, tear-off calendar, date-block, *Am* pad calendar; ~**schnur** *f* (*Fallschirm*) breaking cord.
abreiten *irr itr* to set out on horseback; *tr* (*Pferd*) to override a horse; *die Front* ~ to ride down the front.
abrennen *irr: sich* ~ to fatigue o. s. by running; *sich die Beine* ~ to run o. s. off o.'s feet.
abrichten *tr* (*Tiere*) to teach, to train; (*Pferde*) to break in; *jdn zu etw* ~ to drill s. o. into s. th.; (*Schiff*) to rig out a vessel; *tech* (*passend machen*) to adjust, to fit, to smooth, to straighten.
abriegel|n *tr* (*Tür*) to bolt; (*Straße*) to block; (*Frontstelle*) to bar, to shut off, to seal off, to contain; ~**ungsfeuer** *n mil* box barrage.
abrieseln *tr, itr* to trickle down; to spray.
abrinden *tr* to bark.
abringen *irr tr* to wrest (from).
abrinnen *irr itr* to flow down.
Abriß *m* sketch; draft; (*Auszug*) abstract, abridgement; design, outline, plan; (*Vermessungskunde*) lay-out; (*kurzer* ~) summary.
abrollen *tr* to roll off; to unroll; to uncoil; *film* to unwind; *fig* to unfold, to unroll.
abrücken *itr* to remove, to withdraw, to move off; (*fig*) to draw back; *mil* to start, to march off; *tr* to move off.
Abruf *m* call; (*Abberufung*) recall; *auf* ~ on (*od* at) call; ~**en** *irr tr* to call away, to call off; to remove; (*Börse*) to call; *tele* to ring off; (*Zug*) to call out; ~**ung** *f* recall.
abrund|en *tr* to make round; *fig* to round off; ~**ung** *f* rounding; *fig* polish, finish.
abrupfen *tr* to pluck off, to plume.
abrüst|en *tr* to take down (a scaffold); (*Heer*) to disarm; to demobilize; (*Schiff*) to unrig and lay up; ~**ung** *f* disarmament; ~~**skonferenz** *f* disarmament conference; ~**wagen** *m mot* breakdown lorry.
abrutschen *itr* to slide down (*od* off); *aero* to glide down; to side-slip; (*in der Kurve*) to skid; (*seitlich*) to fall off.

*

absäbeln *tr fam* to hack off; to sabre off.
absacken *itr* to sink, to sag down; *aero* to pancake; to stall.
Absag|e, ~**ung** *f* countermand, refusal; excuse; ~**en** *tr* to countermand, to renounce; to refuse; to call off, to cancel; to recall (an invitation); to break with s. o.; ~~ *lassen* to send word not to be able to.
absägen *tr* to saw off; *fam* to sack, to axe.
absahnen *siehe abrahmen.*
absatteln *tr* to unsaddle.
Absatz *m* (*Abschnitt*) intermission, stop; break, paragraph, section; (*Diktat, Druck*) new line; (*Musik*) pause; (*Bodensatz*) sediment; (*Schuh*~) heel; (*Waren*~) (ready) sale, market; outlet; (*Treppe*) landing; (*Berg*) shelf; (*Weinberg*) terrace; (*Zeitung*) circulation; *ohne* ~ without intervals; ~**gebiet** *n* market; outlet for export goods; ~**weise** *adv* at intervals.
absaufen *irr itr aero sl* to lose height owing to lack of up-currents; *mar* to go down, to drown.
absaugen *tr* to suck off.
abschab|en *tr* to scrape off; to wear out; *abgeschabt a* (*Anzug*) shabby, threadbare; ~**sel** *n* scrapings *pl*, parings *pl*.
abschaff|en *tr* to abolish, to do away with; to dismiss (servants); to give up keeping (horses); (*Gesetz*) to repeal, to rescind; (*Mißbrauch*) to remedy; ~**ung** *f* abolition; (*Mißstände*) removal of abuses; (*Gesetz*) repeal, abrogation; (*Entlassung*) dismissal.
abschälen *tr* to peel; to pare; to blanch (almonds); to bark (a tree).
abschalten *tr el* to switch off (out), to turn off, to cut out, to break; *radio* to delete part of a broadcasting programme; *tele* to disconnect.
abschätz|en *tr* to appraise, to size up; (*zur Besteuerung*) to assess; to estimate; to tax, to value; ~**er** *m* appraiser; valuer; ~**ig** *a* derogatory, disparaging; ~**ung** *f* taxation; valuation, estimation; assessment.
Ab|schaum *m* dross, scum; dregs *pl* of society, outcast; ~**schäumen** *tr* to scum, to skim (off).
abscheid|en *irr tr* to divide, to part; to separate; *itr* to die, to depart, to decease; *sich* ~~ *chem* to be deposited (*od* precipitated); ~~ *n* departure; decease, death.
abscheren *tr* to shave off; (*Haare*) to cut; (*Schafe*) to shear (sheep).
Abscheu *m* abhorrence, detestation, disgust; (*Ekel*) loathing at; horror; aversion (*vor* to); ~**lich** *a* detestable, abominable, atrocious; ~~**keit** *f* detestableness, horribleness, atrocity.
abscheuern *tr* to scour (off); to scrub; *sich* ~ to wear off.
abschicken *tr* to send away (*od* off), to dispatch; to delegate; (*Post*) to post, *Am* to mail.
abschieben *irr tr* to shove off, to push away; *jdn* ~ to pack off; to deport; *itr fam* to cut off, to buzz off.
Abschied *m* parting, departure, farewell; leave; (*Entlassung*) dismissal, discharge; ~ *nehmen* to take leave of, to bid farewell; *seinen* ~ *nehmen* to quit the service; *den* ~ *erhalten* to be dismissed; ~**sbesuch** *m* farewell visit; ~**sfeier** *f* farewell party; ~**sgesuch** *n* resignation; ~**skuß** *m* parting-kiss; ~**srede** *f* valedictory (speech); *Schüler, der e-e* ~~ *hält Am* valedictorian; ~**sschmaus** *m* parting-treat; ~**sstunde** *f* parting-hour.
abschießen *irr tr* to shoot off, to discharge; (*Pfeil*) to shoot; (*Gewehr*) to fire; (*Flugzeug*) to down; *den Vogel* ~ to hit the mark, to win the prize.
abschinden *irr tr* to flay; *r* to drudge.

abschirm|en *tr radio* to screen, to shield; **~ung** *f* screening.

abschirren *tr* to unharness.

abschlachten *tr* to slaughter, to butcher; to stick (a pig).

Abschlag *m* chips *pl*, fragments *pl*; *sport* place-kick; (*Hockey*) bully, *Am* face; (*Golf*) tee shot; (*Billard*) rebound; (*Abzug*) drain; (*Handel*) abatement, reduction, allowance, deduction, decline; fall; *auf* ~ on account; by instal(l)ments; **~szahlung** *f* part-payment; instal(l)ment; advance.

abschlagen *irr tr* to strike off, to cut off; (*Angriff*) to parry, to repulse, to contain; (*verweigern*) to deny, to turn down; (*Zelt*) to strike; (*Bettstelle*) to take down a bed(stead); *itr* (*Billard*) to rebound; (*Preise*) to sink, to fall.

abschläg|ig *a* denying, negative; *~~e Antwort* refusal, denial.

abschleifen *irr tr* to grind off, to rub off, to polish; *fig* to refine; *sich* ~ to refine.

abschlepp|en *tr* to drag, to carry off; (*Auto*) to tow (off), to take in tow; **~kran** *m* salvage crane, *Am* wrecking crane; **~seil** *n* towing rope; **~wagen** *m* breakdown lorry, *Am* wrecking car.

abschließen *irr tr* to lock up; to close; to separate; to isolate; to conclude (a treaty); to settle (a business); (*Vergleich*) to compound (with); (*geschäftliche Transaktion*) to carry through; (*Verkauf*) to effect; (*Fall*) to close the files on; (*Bücher*) to balance; (*Konto*) to adjust; (*Versicherung*) to effect; *sich* ~~ to keep back, to retire, to seclude o. s.; **~d** *a* final, definitive.

Abschluß *m* conclusion, termination, settlement, balance; balancing, closing; *com* sale, business, deal, transaction; (*Vertrag*) contract; **~meldung** *f* final report; **~prüfung** *f* final(s *pl*); **~rechnung** *f* final account; **~tag** *m* settling-day.

abschmecken *tr* (*Speisen*) to taste.

abschmeicheln *tr* (*jdm etw* ~) to coax (*od* wheedle) s. th. out of s. o.

abschmelz|en *tr* to melt off, to separate by melting; *el* (*Sicherung*) to fuse, to blow; **~sicherung** *f* safety-fuse.

abschmieren *tr* to transcribe (*od* copy) negligently; *mot* to grease.

abschminken: *sich* ~ to take off o.'s make up.

abschnallen *tr* to ungird; to unbuckle.

abschnappen *itr* (*plötzlich abbrechen*) to snap off; (*plötzlich aufhören*) to stop short; *tr* (*fangen*) to catch.

abschneiden *irr tr* to cut away (*od* off); to clip; (*Brot*) to cut; (*Bart*) to trim; *med* to amputate; (*Rede*) to interrupt; (*Ehre*) to injure; to slander; *gut* (*schlecht*) ~ to do well (badly), to come off well (badly); ~ *n* amputation, cutting off.

Abschnitt *m* cut, cutting; *mil* sector, section; *math* segment; (*Buch*) chapter; paragraph, passage; item; (*auf Lebensmittelkarte*) coupon, point, ticket; (*Lebens~*) period of life; (*Zeit~*) epoch.

abschnüren *tr med* to tie off.

abschöpfen *tr* to skim; *fig* to take the cream off; *überschüssige Kaufkraft* ~ to siphon off excess purchasing power.

abschrägen *tr* to bevel, to slant, to slope; to plane; to chamfer.

abschrauben *tr* to unscrew, to screw off.

abschreck|en *tr* to frighten (away); to deter from, to intimidate; (*kühlen*) to chill; **~end** *a* deterrent; **~ung** *f* discouragement.

abschreib|en *irr tr* to copy, to write out; *jur* to engross; *fig* to imitate, to plagiarize; (*Schule*) to crib from; (*absagen*) to revoke; *com* (*Forderung*) to write off; (*Anlagen*) to write down, to deduct; **~er** *m* copyist; plagiarist; **~erei** *f* plagiarism; **~ung** *f* transcription; *com* writing off, depreciation.

abschreiten *irr tr* to stride up and down; to measure by steps; to step off, to pace off; (*Front*) to pace down.

Abschrift *f* copy, duplicate; *gleichlautende* ~ true copy; certified true copy; *beglaubigte* ~ certified copy, exemplification; legally attested copy; **~lich** *a* copied, in duplicate.

abschuften: *sich* ~ to toil, to slave, to drudge.

abschuppen *tr* to scale (off); to scrape.

abschürf|en *tr* to scratch off, to scrape off; (*Haut*) to rub off o.'s skin; **~ung** *f* abrasion.

Abschuß *m* (*e-r Waffe*) firing, discharge; (*Raketengeschoß, Torpedo*) launching; (*e-s Flugzeuges*) bringing down, downing; (*e-s Panzers*) knocking out.

abschüssig *a* steep, precipitous; **~keit** *f* steepness, precipitousness, declivity.

ab|schütteln *tr* to shake off, to cas off; **~schütten** *tr* to pour off.

ab|schwächen *tr* to weaken, to lessen, to diminish; (*beschönigen*) to extenuate; **~schwatzen** *tr* to obtain s.th. by talking; *jdm etw* ~~ to talk s. o. out of s. th.; **~schwefeln** *tr* to desulphurate.

abschweif|en *itr* to deviate, to stray; (*vom Thema, improvisieren*) to ad-lib, to ramble; to digress; **~ung** *f* deviation; digression.

abschwellen *irr itr med* to go down; (*Ton etc*) to grow less.

ab|schwemmen *tr* to wash away, (*vom Wasser*) to carry off; to clean; **~schwenken** *tr* (*abwaschen*) to clean by rinsing; to wash off; *itr mil* to wheel aside; **~schwindeln** *tr* to swindle s. o. out of; **~schwören** *tr* (*durch Eid leugnen*) to deny upon oath; (*durch Schwur verzichten*) to abjure; (*widerrufen*) to recant; **~schwörung** *f* abjuration; recantation.

absegeln *itr* to set sail for, to depart.

abseh|bar *a* within reach of the eyes, within sight; (*Zeit*) before long; imaginable; *nicht* ~~ immeasurable, inconceivable; **~en** *irr tr* to turn o.'s eyes from; (*überblicken*) to see; (*vorwegnehmen*) to anticipate; (*Ende*) to (fore)see, to foretell; (*begreifen*) to conceive; (*sich enthalten*) to refrain from; to leave out of consideration; *die Gelegenheit* ~~ to watch for an opportunity; *jdm etw* ~~ to perceive, to learn from; *jdm etw an den Augen* ~~ to please, to read in s. o.'s eyes; *es auf etw abgesehen haben* to aim at, to drive at; *davon abgesehen* apart from this.

abseifen *tr* to soap.

abseihen *tr* to strain, to filter off.

abseilen *tr* (*Bergsteigerei*) to rope down; *itr* to descend on rope.

absein *irr itr* (*abgetrennt*) to be off; *fam* (*müde sein*) to be exhausted, to be tired out.

abseits *adv* aside, apart; (*Fußball*) offside.

absend|en *irr tr* to send (off); (*Briefe*) to forward, to post, *Am* to mail; *com* to dispatch, to expedite; *mil* to detach; **~er** *m* sender; *com* dispatcher, consignor, *Am* shipper; **~ung** *f* dispatch(ing), shipping, sending.

absengen *tr* to scorch, to singe off.

absetz|en *tr* to put down, to deposit; (*von Fahrzeugen; Fallschirmtruppen*) to drop; (*Hut*) to take off; (*abwerfen*) to dismount; (*verkaufen*) to sell; (*entsetzen*) to dismiss; to remove; (*König*) to dethrone; *typ* to compose; (*unterbrechen*) to stop, to intermit; *ohne abzusetzen* without intermission; (*Betrag abschreiben*) to deduct; *sich* ~~ *mil* to disengage o. s., to retreat; **~bar** *a* removable; *com* sal(e)able, marketable; **~ung** *f* (*Amt*) removal, deposition, (*einstweilig*) suspension; (*Pause*) break, halt, interruption; *typ* setting-up; **~zone** *f* (*Luftlandeoperationen*) landing-zone (for airborne troops and gliders).

Absicht *f* intention, view; *mit* ~ on purpose, intentionally; **~lich** *a* intentional, wilful; *adv* on purpose; **~~keit** *f* intentionality, purpose; **~slos** *a* unintentional, designless.

absieben *tr* to sift off.

absieden *irr tr* to boil, to decoct; (*Eier*) to poach.

absingen *irr tr* to sing at sight; to sing to the end.

Absinth *m* absinth.

absitzen *irr itr* to get off; to dismount; (*Strafe*) to serve a sentence, to serve time, to do o.'s time.

absol|ut *a* absolute; **~vent** *m* graduate; **~vieren** *tr* to acquit, to accomplish; (*Studien*) to finish; (*höhere Schule*) to graduate from.

absonder|lich *a* peculiar, strange; **~~keit** *f* peculiarity, strangeness; **~n** *tr* to separate, to isolate; *med* to secrete; *sich* ~~ to withdraw; **~ung** *f* separation; secretion.

absorbieren *tr* to absorb; **~d** *a* absorbing; *~~e Mittel n pl* absorbents *pl*.

abspalten *tr* to split off, to cleave off; to separate.

abspann|en *tr* to unbend; to unharness; (*lockern*) to relax, to loose; (*Kunden* ~~) to alienate, to entice (away) customers; *abgespannt a* (*müde*) tired out, exhausted; **~ung** *f* unbending; relaxation, exhaustion.

absparen: *sich etw am Munde* ~ to stint o. s. of s. th.

abspeisen *tr* to finish a meal; (*mit etw*) to feed on s. th.; *jdn mit leeren Worten* ~ to put s. o. off with fair words.

abspenstig *a* unfaithful, disloyal; *jdm* ~ *werden* to fall off, to desert; ~ *machen* to alienate; to estrange, to entice away.

absperr|en *tr* (*durch Polizei, Truppen*) to cordon off; (*Straße*) to block; to barricade; (*Gashahn*) to turn off; (*Tür*) to lock; (*abschließen von der Außenwelt*) to separate, to isolate; to shut off, to confine; **~hahn** *m* stopcock; **~ung** *f* barring cordon; stoppage; (*Stromsperre*) stoppage of current; (*Straßensperre*) blocking; barricade; (*Isolierung*) seclusion, isolation, confinement.

abspiegel|n *tr* to reflect; *sich* ~~ to be reflected; **~ung** *f* reflection.

abspielen *tr* (*Musik*) to perform, to play; *sich* ~ (*fig*) to take place, to occur.

absplittern *tr* to splinter, to split off.

absprech|en *irr tr* to contest, to dispute, to refuse; *es läßt sich nicht* ~~ there's no denying; *jdm das Leben* ~~ to condemn to death; **~end, ~erisch** *a* deprecatory, slighting.

absprengen *tr* to burst, to blast, to blow up with gunpowder; (*von Truppe*) to cut off; (*Blumen*) to sprinkle.

abspringen *irr itr* to jump off, to leap off; (*mit Fallschirm*) to bail (*od* bale) out; (*wegfliegen*) to fly off, to reel off; (*Glasur*) to chip off; (*abprallen*) to rebound; (*abfallen*) to fall off, to desert; to change abruptly; *fig* to digress.

Absprung *m* leap; *aero* (*Start*) take-off; (*Fallschirm*) descent, drop, jump, baling out; **~gebiet** *n* descent-area; **~punkt** *m* jump-off point.

ab|spulen *tr* to unwind; **~spülen** *tr* to wash off, to cleanse; to rinse; (*Geschirr*) to wash up.

abstamm|en *itr* to descend from; (*sprachlich*) to be derived from; *~~d aus* native of; **~ung** *f* descent, birth; lineage; derivation, etymology.

Abstand *m* distance, interval; *fig* contrast; (*Verzicht*) abandonment; *von e-r Sache ~ nehmen* to desist from s. th., to renounce, to give up; **~sgeld** *n* (sum of) compensation; **~szünder** *m mil* proximity fuse.

abstatten *tr* to discharge, to render, to pay; (*Bericht*) to report; *Dank ~* to return thanks; *jdm e-n Besuch ~* to call upon.

abstäuben *tr* to free from dust, to dust.

abstech|en *irr tr* to kill, to stick; to pierce; (*Rasen*) to cut green sods; (*Teich*) to drain a pond; *itr* to contrast with; **~er** *m* excursion, ramble, trip; *fig* digression.

absteck|en *tr* to unpin, to unfasten; (*Straße*) to lay out; (*Bahnlinie*) to trace; (*Lager*) to mark out; (*Kleid*) to pin; **~leine** *f* tracing-line; **~pfahl** *m* pole, picket; **~ung** *f* marking out, staking out.

abstehen *irr itr* to stand off from; (*schal werden*) to grow (*od* to get) stale; (*verzichten*) to abstain from.

absteifen *tr* to support, to prop up; to stiffen.

absteig|en *irr itr* to descend, to step out, to get off o.'s horse; (*vom Wagen*) to alight; (*im Gasthof*) to put up at; **~equartier** *n* lodging house; hotel; accommodation.

abstell|en *tr* to put down; (*Maschine*) to stop; (*Dampf*) to turn off; (*Gas, Wasser*) to disconnect; (*Motor*) to shut off, to stall; (*Radio*) to switch off; (*parken*) to park; (*Zug*) to marshal; *fig* (*Mißstände*) to abolish, to put an end to, to redress, to reform; **~geleise** *n pl rail* railway sidings; marshalling yards *pl*; **~hahn** *m* regulator tap; stop cock; **~ung** *f* stopping; reformation, abolition.

abstempel|n *tr* to stamp, to check; (*Marke*) to obliterate; **~ung** *f* cancellation.

absteppen *tr* to stitch, to quilt.

absterben *irr itr* to die away, to wither; *med* to mortify; *~ n* decease, death.

Abstieg *m* descent.

abstimm|en *tr* to tune; *radio* to tune (in) to; (*in Einklang bringen*) to harmonize; (*Farben*) to shade off; *itr* to vote, to poll, (*geheim*) to ballot; *über jdn ~~ lassen* to put to the vote; **~knopf** *m radio* tuning knob, tuner; **~schärfe** *f radio* sharpness of tuning; **~skala** *f radio* tuning dial, tuning scale; **~ung** *f* voting; (*durch Handaufheben*) show of hands; (*Volks~~*) plebiscite, referendum; *parl* division; *mus* tuning; *radio* tuning-in; *zur ~~ bringen* to put to the vote; *geheime ~~* ballot; *namentliche ~~* poll, polling; *sich der ~~ enthalten* to abstain from voting; **~~stag** *m* voting-day; **~~szettel** *m* voting-paper; ballot.

Abstinenzler *m* total abstainer, teetotal(l)er.

abstoßen *irr tr* to push off; to discharge (a debt); to get rid of; (*Waren*) to dispose of; *fig* to repel; *sich die Hörner ~ fig* to sow o.'s wild oats; *sich ~* to get worn out at the edges; **~d** *a* repulsive, repugnant, repellent.

abstrahieren *tr* to abstract.

abstrakt *a* abstract.

abstreich|en *irr tr* to wipe off; (*abhaken*) to tick off; (*ausstreichen*) to cancel, to strike out; (*e-e Summe*) to deduct; (*Rasiermesser*) to strop; **~er** *m*, **~brett** *n* door-scraper.

abstreifen *tr* to strip off; (*Schuhe*) to wipe; *itr* to wander aside, to deviate.

abstreiten *irr tr* to wrest from, to dispute, to contest; (*leugnen*) to deny.

Abstrich *m* deduction; cut; *med* (*bei Diphtherie*) swab; *e-n ~ machen* to take a swab; *com* to make cuts; (*Unkosten*) curtailment; (*Streichung*) cancellation; (*in der Schrift*) down-stroke.

abstuf|en *tr* to form into steps, to modify; *sich ~* to graduate; **~ung** *f* graduation, modification; grade.

abstumpfen *tr* to truncate, to blunt; *fig* to weaken, to stupefy.

Ab|sturz *m* violent downfall, steep descent; fall; precipice; *aero* crash; *zum ~~ bringen aero* to down (a plane); to shoot down; **~stürzen** *itr* to fall down; to precipitate; (*Flugzeug*) to crash, to have a crash.

abstutzen *tr* to cut off, to cut short, to curtail; to lop.

absuchen *tr* to search and take off; (*Raupen*) to pick off; (*durchstöbern*) to search all over; (*Scheinwerfer*) to sweep (the sky).

Absud *m* decoction; extract.

Abszeß *m med* abscess.

Abt *m* abbot.

abtakeln *tr* to dismantle; to unrig.

abtasten *tr* to palpate, to feel out; *tele* to scan.

Abtei *f* abbey; **~lich** *a* abbatial.

Abteil *n* compartment; (*Krankenhaus*) ward; **~en** *tr* to separate; (*durch Wand*) to partition off; (*in Klassen*) to classify; (*in Grade*) to graduate; (*in kleine Teile*) to portion out; **~ung** *f* division, classification; partition; (*Klinik*) ward; *mil* detachment; section, department; **~~sleiter** *m* head of the department; **~~szeichen** *n* mark of division; *gram* hyphen; *typ* dash; *rail* distance (*od* mile) post.

abtelegraphieren *itr* to wire refusal, to cancel by telegram.

abteufen *tr* to sink.

Äbtin, Äbtissin *f* abbess.

Abtönung *f* shade.

abtöten *tr* to kill; (*Fleisch*) to mortify.

Abtrag *m* payment, instal(l)ment; *~ tun* to prejudice, to damage, to injure s. o.; **~en** *irr tr* to carry off, to take away, to remove; (*Tisch*) to clear the table; (*Schuld*) to pay off, to clear off; to pull down, to demolish (a building); to wear out (clothes); *~~ n* demolition; discharge; liquidation.

abträglich *a* injurious; harmful; detrimental.

Abtransport *m* evacuation; transport.

abtreib|en *irr tr* to drive away, to repulse; to jade a horse; *die Leibesfrucht ~~* to procure abortion; *itr* to drift off; **~ung** *f* abortion; **~ungsmittel** *n med* abortifacient.

abtrenn|en *tr* to dissever; to separate; (*Saum*) to rip; (*abreißen*) to rip off (*od* up); **~ung** *f* separation; (*Auftrennen*) unpicking.

abtret|en *irr tr* to tread down; (*abnutzen*) to wear out; (*Ansprüche, Gebiet*) to cede, to transfer, to yield; *itr* (*vom Amt*) to retire, to withdraw, to resign, to abandon; *theat* to go off; **~er** *m* transferrer; (*Matte*) door-mat; **~ung** *f* cession, surrender, transfer; resignation; abdication; **~~surkunde** *f* deed of cession.

Abtritt *m* departure; *theat* exit; (*W. C.*) lavatory; privy, *Am* toilet.

ab|trocknen *tr* to dry up, to wipe off; **~tröpfeln**, **~tropfen** *itr* to trickle down; to drip down; *~~ lassen* to drain, to dry; **~trotzen** *tr* to obtain s. th. from s. o. by obstinacy (*od* persistence); to bully s. th. out of s. o.

abtrudeln *itr aero* to go into a spin; to come down in a spin; (*über den Schwanz*) to go into a tail spin; *sich ~ lassen* to get into a spin.

abtrünnig *a* disloyal, rebellious; apostate; *~ werden* to desert; (*vom Glauben*) to apostatize; *~ machen* to draw off, to alienate; **~e(r)** *m* deserter, renegade; apostate; **~keit** *f* desertion; apostasy.

abtun *irr tr* to put off, to lay aside; (*Mißbrauch*) to abolish, to do away with; (*fertig machen*) to finish off; to settle (an affair), to dispatch (a business).

aburteilen *tr* to decide, to try; *jdn ~* to judge; to condemn; to pass sentence upon; *itr* to criticize severely.

abverdienen *tr* to work off.

abverlangen *tr* to ask s. th. from.

*

abwägen *tr* to balance, to poise; *fig* to weigh; (*erwägen*) to consider carefully.

abwälzen *tr* to roll away, to remove; *von sich ~* to shift from o.'s own shoulders; to throw off.

abwand|eln *tr* (*variieren*) to vary; *gram* to conjugate; to inflect; to decline; **~lung** *f gram* conjugation; inflexion; declension.

abwander|n *itr* to wander away, to migrate from; **~ung** *f* (*vom Land zur Stadt*) wandering, migration; (*Kapital, Besitz*) transfer, exodus.

abwarten *tr* to expect, to wait for; (*ruhig ~*) to wait and see; (*pflegen*) to nurse; *etw ~* to await.

abwärts *adv* down, downwards, aside; *es geht mit ihm ~* he is in declining circumstances; **~bewegung** *f* (*der Preise*) downward trend; **~schalten** *itr mot* (*Getriebe*) to change down; **~transformator** *m el* downwards transformer.

abwasch|en *irr tr* to wash away; (*Geschirr*) to wash up; **~ung** *f* washing, ablution; **~wasser** *n* dish-water, slops *pl*.

Abwässer *n pl* waste water; sewage; **~reinigung** *f* purification of sewage, waste water clarifying; **~n** *tr* to drain; (*Heringe*) to water.

abwechsel|n *itr* to alternate, to vary, to change; *miteinander ~~* to relieve one another, to take turns; **~nd** *a* alternating; *adv* by turns; **~ung** *f* change, alternation, variation; variety; *zur ~~* by way of a change, for a change.

Abweg *m* by-road; wrong way; *fig* devious path; *auf ~e geraten* to get off the right path; to go astray; **~ig** *a* not to the point, irrelevant; misleading.

Abwehr *f* guard, protection, defence; (*Spionage~*) counter-espionage; (*Flieger~*) anti-aircraft defence; **~abteilung** *f* security intelligence branch; **~bereitschaft** *f* preparedness for defence; **~en** *tr* to keep off, to parry; *fig* to avert; **~dienst** *m mil* counter intelligence service; **~maßnahmen** *f pl* meas-

ures of defence; **-mittel** *n* preservative, preventive; means of defence; **-patent** *n* defensive patent; **-schlacht** *f* defensive battle; **-stelle** *f* counter-espionage office; **-streik** *m* defensive strike.
abweich|en *irr itr* (*Richtung*) to deviate; (*Meinung*) to differ from; (*sich unterscheiden*) to vary from; (*Physik*) to decline; (*Wahrheit*) to depart from; (*Weg*) to swerve; **-end** *a* irregular, different; **-ung** *f* deviation, divergence; *-- der Sonne, der Magnetnadel* declination of the sun, of the magnetic needle; *-- von der Regel* deviation from (*od* exception) to a rule.
abweiden *tr* to feed, to graze (on).
abweis|en *irr tr* to refuse; to reject, to send back, to dismiss (a cause), to nonsuit; (*Angriff*) to repel; **-ung** *f* rejection, repulse, dismissal.
abwelken *itr* to fade away.
abwend|en *irr tr* to turn away; (*Hieb*) to parry; to prevent; (*entfremden*) to alienate; *sich -en* to turn from; **-ig** *a*: *-- machen* to alienate, to withdraw; (*Kunden*) to entice away from.
abwerfen *irr tr* to throw, to cast off; (*einbringen*) to yield profit; (*Bomben*) to drop bombs; (*Geweih*) to shed; (*Karte*) to discard.
abwert|en *tr, itr* to devaluate; **-ung** *f* devaluation.
abwesen|d *a* absent; absent-minded, lost in thought; **-de(r)** *m* absent, absentee; **-heit** *f* absence; (*vor Gericht*) non-appearance; contumacy.
abwickel|n *tr* to unroll, to unwind; *fig* to settle, to wind up, to liquidate (a business); **-ung** *f* unwinding; arrangement, settlement; winding up, *Am* windup.
abwimmeln *tr fam* to ward off.
Abwind *m aero* descending current, down-current.
abwinden *irr tr* to unwind, to reel off.
abwinken *itr* to give a sign of refusal, to warn off.
abwirtschaften *itr* to get ruined by bad management; *tr* to ruin, to mismanage.
abwisch|en *tr* to wipe off, to dust; (*Tränen*) to dry; **-tuch** *n* duster; dishcloth.
abwracken *tr* to wreck, to dismantle; to scrap; to break up; to unwrig.
Abwurf *m* throwing down; (*aus Flugzeug*) drop(ping); *sport* goal throw, (*Handball*) throw-off; **-behälter** *m aero* aerial delivery container; jettisonable fuel tank; **-gerät** *n* (*für Bomben*) bomb-release mechanism.
abwürgen *tr* to strangle; to throttle; to kill.
abzahl|en *tr* to discharge, to clear; (*in Raten*) to pay by (*Am* on) instal(l)ments; **-ung** *f* payment, liquidation; *ratenweise --* instal(l)ment; **--sgeschäft** *n* instal(l)ment business; **--skauf** *m* hire purchase, purchase on the instal(l)ment system.
abzähl|en *tr* to count out; *das läßt sich an den Fingern --* that's easy to state; **-ung** *f* counting off.
abzapfen *tr* to draw off, to tap.
abzäumen *tr* to unbridle.
abzäunen *tr* to fence in (*od* off).
abzehren *itr* to consume, to emaciate; *r* to waste away.
Abzehrung *f* emaciation; consumption.
Abzeich|en *n* (*am Anzug, Kleid*) badge; (*Grad-*) badge of rank; stripe; mark, sign; insignia *pl*; **-nen** *tr* to copy, to sketch; to draw; (*mit Sichtvermerk*) to initial; to mark off; (*abhaken*) to tick off; *r* to stand out against; **-nung** *f* sketch, copy.
abzieh|bar *a* deductible; **-bild** *n* transfer-picture; **-en** *irr tr* to draw off, to remove; (*Bett*) to strip; (*Haut*) to skin; to strip off the skin; (*ablenken*) to distract s. o.'s attention from; *chem* to distil(l); (*in Flaschen*) to bottle; (*abhobeln*) to plane off; (*Messer*) to sharpen; (*Rasiermesser*) to strop; *typ* to strike off, to pull off; *phot* to print; (*Hut*) to take off; (*Schlüssel*) to take out; (*Kunden*) to entice away; *math* to subtract; *vom Lohne --* to deduct from wages, to lower wages; (*Handel*) to abate; *itr* to go off, to depart, to retire; (*Rauch*) to disperse; *von der Wache -en* to come off duty, to be relieved; *mit e-r langen Nase -en* to be balked.
Abziehriemen *m* (razor-)strop.
ab|zielen *itr* to aim at, to have in view; **-zirkeln** *tr* to mark out with compasses; *fig* to define precisely.
Abzug *m* departure, retreat; *com* discount; (*vom Lohn*) deduction from wages; *typ* (*Abdruck*) copy; (*Korrekturbogen*) proof; (*Gewehr-*) trigger; *phot* print; *nach - der Kosten* expenses deducted; **-sfähig** *a* deductible; **-sgraben** *m* drain; **-skanal** *m* sewer.
abzüglich *adv* deducting the charges, less charges.
abzupfen *tr* to pluck off, to twitch off.
abzwacken *tr* to pinch off, to squeeze out of.
abzweig|en *tr* to detach, to turn off, to branch off; **-dose** *f* connector box, distributing box; **-klemme** *f* branch terminal; **-ung** *f* branch; (*Eisenbahn*) branching off, branch-line; (*Knotenpunkt*) junction; *el* shunt.
abzwicken *tr* to nip off, to pinch off.
ach! *interj* oh! alas!; *- so!* oh, I see!
Achat *m* agate.
Achse *f* axle, axle-tree; *math* axis; (*Welle*) shaft, spindle; *per - transportieren* to send by car (*od* by waggon); **-nnagel** *m* axle-pin; **-nschnitt** *m* axial section.
Achsel *f* shoulder; *die -n zucken* to shrug o.'s shoulders; *etw auf die leichte - nehmen* to take it easy; *jdn über die - ansehen* to look down upon s. o.; **-band** *n* shoulder-strap; **-bein** *n* shoulder-blade; **-höhle** *f* arm-pit; **-klappe** *f* wing, strap; **-schnur** *f* shoulder-strap; **-träger** *m* time-server; **-zucken** *n* shrug.
acht *a* eight; *alle - Tage* every week; *vor - Tagen* a week ago; *heute über - Tage* this day week.
Acht *f*, **-erklärung** *f* ban(ishment); proscription; *in die - erklären* to outlaw, to ban; (*Obacht*) attention, care; *-geben, -haben* to pay attention to, to attend to; *gib -!* look out! take care! *außer - lassen* to disregard, to neglect; *in - nehmen* to take care of; *sich in - nehmen* to be on o.'s guard, to beware of.
achtbar *a* hono(u)rable, respectable; **-keit** *f* respectability.
acht|e *a* eighth; **-eck** *n* octagon; **-eckig** *a* octagonal; **-el** *n* eighth, eighth part; **-elnote** *f* quaver; **-elpause** *f* quaver rest.
achten *tr* to respect, to esteem; *itr - auf* to take care of, to pay attention to; to attend to; *- auf* (*bemerken*) to be aware of; *nicht - auf* to be heedless of; *- für* to deem, to judge, to consider.
ächten *tr* to outlaw, to proscribe.
acht|ens *adv* in the eighth place; **-er** *m* (*Boot*) the eight; (*Figur*) figure eight; *a mar* aft, after; **-eraus** *adv* astern; **-erbahn** *f* (*auf der Festwiese*) switchback railway, *Am* roller coaster; **-erdeck** *n mar* quarter-deck; **-erlei** *a* eightfold, of eight sorts; **-ern** *adv mar* aft, abaft; **-erschiff** *n* stern; **-ersteven** *m* stern post; **-fach** *a* eightfold; **-jährig** *a* eight years old; **-mal** *adv* eight times; **-monatlich** *a* every eighth month.
acht|los *a* inattentive, careless; **-losigkeit** *f* inattention; **-sam** *a* attentive, careful; **-samkeit** *f* attention, carefulness.
acht|spännig *a* with eight horses; **-stundentag** *m* eight-hour day; **-tägig** *a* of eight days, lasting a week.
Achtung *f* respect, esteem, regard; *interj* attention! *jdm - erweisen* to pay respect to; *jdm - einflößen* to inspire with respect; *aus - vor* out of regard for; **-svoll** *a* respectful; (*Briefschluß*) Yours truly; Truly yours; **-swürdig** *a* respectable, estimable.
Ächtung *f* proscription, outlawing.
achtzehn *a* eighteen; **-te** *a* eighteenth.
achtzig *a* eighty; **-er** *m*, **-erin** *f* octogenarian; **-jährig** *a* eighty years old, octogenary; **-ste** *a* eightieth.
ächzen *itr* to moan, to groan; *- n* groaning.
Acker *m* arable ground, field, land; (*Boden*) soil; (*Maß*) acre; **-bau** *m* tillage, agriculture; farming; **-bauschule** *f* agricultural college; **-bautreibend** *a* agricultural; **-bestellung** *f* tillage; **-boden** *m* arable soil; surface soil; **-gaul** *m* farm-horse; **-gerät** *n* farming-tools *pl*, agricultural implements *pl*; **-gesetz** *n* agrarian law; **-knecht** *m* ploughman, farm labourer, *Am* farm hand; **-land** *n* arable land; **-n** *itr, tr* **to plough, to till**; *fig* **to work laboriously**; **-pferd** *n* farm horse; **-smann** *m* ploughman, tiller, farmer; **-scholle** *f* clod; **-walze** *f* roller.
add|ieren *tr* to add, to sum up; **-iermaschine** *f* adding machine; **-ition** *f* addition.
Adel *m* aristocracy; nobility; (*niederer*) gentry; *von -* of noble birth, of rank; **-ig, adlig** *a* noble, aristocratic; **-ige(r)** *m* nobleman, nobles *pl*; **-n** *tr* to ennoble, to knight; *fig* to exalt; **-sbrief** *m* patent of nobility; **-sstand** *m* nobility, peerage; *in den -- erheben* to raise to the peerage; to knight.
Ader *f* vein; (*Schlag-*) artery; *min* lode; (*Wasser-*) thread of water; *tele* core (of a cable); (*Holz*) streak, grain; (*Verkehr*) arterial road; *zur - lassen* to bleed s. o.; *es ist keine gute - an ihm* there is no good in him.
Aderlaß *m* bleeding.
ädern *tr* to vein.
Adieu *n* (*auch als Gruß*) goodbye, good-by; farewell; *- sagen* to say good-by.
Adjektiv *n* adjective.
Adjutant *m* adjutant; (*e-s Generals*) aide-de-camp; aide, aid; **-ur** *f* adjutancy.
Adler *m* eagle; **-nase** *f* hooked nose, aquiline nose; **-orden** *m* order of the (black *od* red) eagle.
Admiral *m* admiral; **-ität** *f* admiralty; the Admiralty (*in England: Marineministerium, in USA* Navy Department); **-sschiff** *n* flagship.
adopt|ieren *tr* to adopt; **-iv** *a* adoptive; **-ion** *f* adoption.
Adress|ant *m* sender; **-at** *m* addressee; (*von Waren*) consignee.
Adreßbuch *n* directory.

Adress|e *f* address; *per ~~* care of (c/o); **~ennachweis** *m* registry office, agency; **~ieren** *tr* to address; (*Güter*) to consign; *falsch ~~* to misdirect; **~iermaschine** *f* addressing machine; **~zettel** *m* label.

Adria *f*: *das Adriatische Meer* the Adriatic Sea.

Advent *m* Advent; **~szeit** *f* Advent season.

Adverb, **~ium** *n* adverb.

Advokat *m* advocate; barrister; solicitor, attorney; **~engebühr** *f* lawyer's fees *pl*; **~enstand** *m* the Bar, the legal profession; *sich dem ~~ widmen* to become a barrister.

Aero|dynamik *f* aerodynamics *pl*; **~nautik** *f* aeronautics *pl*; **~statik** *f* aerostatics *pl*.

Affe *m* ape, monkey; *mil sl* pack, knapsack; *ein eingebildeter ~* a conceited ass; *e-n ~n haben vulg* to be tipsy; *e-n ~n gefressen haben an* to be very fond of, *Am* to have a crush on; **~nliebe** *f* doting love; **~npinscher** *m* toyterrier, pug; **~nschande** *f fam* scandalous shame; **~nweibchen** *n* she-ape.

Affekt *m* affection, emotion, excitement; **~iert** *a* conceited.

äff|en *tr* to ape, to hoax; **~erei** *f* apishness; mockery.

Afrika *n* Africa; **~ner** *m*, **~nisch** *a* African.

After *m* anus; *fam* backside, posteriors *pl*; **~gelehrsamkeit** *f* pseudo-erudition; **~mieter** *m* second-hand hirer, underlessee, undertenant, subtenant, lodger; **~pächter** *m* under-farmer; **~rede** *f* slander; **~reden** *itr* to slander, to backbite.

Agent *m* agent; **~ur** *f* agency.

Aggregat *n* aggregate; *tech* set, unit; power unit; **~zustand** *m* state of aggregation; condition.

Ägide *f* aegis.

agi|eren *itr* to act; **~tator** *m* agitator; **~tatorisch** *a* inciting, inflammatory; **~tieren** *itr* to agitate; to excite, to stir up.

Agio *n* agio, premium.

Agonie *f* death-struggle.

Agraffe *f* clasp, brooch.

Agr|arier *m* agrarian; **~~tum** *n* landed interest; **~arisch** *a* agrarian; **~arreform** *f* agrarian reform; **~arstaat** *m* agrarian state; **~ikultur** *f* agriculture.

Ägypt|en *n* Egypt; **~er** *m*, **~isch** *a* Egyptian.

ah! *interj* ah! pooh! (*erfüllte Erwartung*) aha; there you see.

Ahle *f* awl; *typ* bodkin.

Ahn *m* ancestor, grandfather; **~en** *pl* ancestry; forefathers *pl*; forebears *pl*; **~ennachweis** *m* proof of ancestry; **~enpaß** *m* ancestry certificate; **~entafel** *f* pedigree, family-chart; genealogical tree; **~frau, ~e, ~in** *f* ancestress; **~herr** *m* ancestor.

ahnd|en *tr* to revenge, to punish; **~ung** *f* revenge, punishment.

ähneln *itr* to look like; to resemble; to bear resemblance to.

ahnen *tr* to anticipate, to have a presentiment of, to forebode, to suspect; (*voraussehen*) to foresee, to guess; (*erkennen*) to realize; *mir ahnt nichts Gutes* my heart misgives me.

ähnlich *a* like, similar; *~ wie* pretty much as; *jdm ~ sehen* to look like s. o.; *~ machen* to assimilate to; *das sieht ihm ~* that is just like him; **~keit** *f* likeness, similarity, analogy.

Ahnung *f* presentiment; misgiving; idea; *er hat keine ~ davon* he has no idea of it; **~slos** *a* unsuspecting; without presentiment; without misgivings *pl*; **~svoll** *a* full of presentiments (*od* presages); ominous.

Ahorn *m* maple-tree.

Ähre *f* ear; *~n lesen* to glean; *in ~n schießen* to form ears; **~nlese** *f* gleaning; **~nleser** *m* gleaner.

Akadem|ie *f* academy, college, university; **~iker** *m* university graduate; **~isch** *a* academic.

Akazie *f* acacia.

akklimatis|ieren *tr* to acclimatize, *Am* to acclimate; **~ierung, ~ation** *f* acclimatization, *Am* acclimation.

Akkord *m mus* accord; chord; (*Vergleich*) settlement, agreement; *auf ~ arbeiten* to work by the job, to work by piece (*od* by contract); **~arbeit** *f* task-work, jobbing; piece work; **~arbeiter** *m* piece worker, bargainman, jobber, contractor; **~eon** *n* accordion; **~ieren** *tr* to agree, to consent to; *itr* to arrange; **~lohn** *m* piece wages *pl*; **~satz** *m* piece-perhour rate, job-rate; rate of composition; **~wesen** *n* time study.

Akkreditiv *n* letter of credit; **~schreiben** *n* credentials *pl*.

Akku(mulator) *m* accumulator; *el* storage battery; **~aufladung** *f* battery charging; **~ladestelle** *f* battery charging plant; **~säure** *f* electrolyte; **~zelle** *f* battery cell.

akkurat *a* (*genau*) accurate, exact; **~esse** *f* accuracy, exactness.

Akkusativ *m* accusative.

Akontozahlung *f* payment on account; (*Abzahlung*) instal(l)ment.

Akrobat *m* acrobat; **~ik** *f* acrobatics *pl*; **~isch** *a* acrobatic.

Akt *m* act, action; *theat* act; *jur* document, (legal) instrument, deed; (*Malerei*) nude; *med* coitus; **~en** *f pl* documents, files, records, registers, reports, papers *pl*, dossier; (*Prozeß~~*) pleadings *pl*; *zu den ~en legen* to file away; **~endeckel** *m* folder; **~enheft** *n* file of deeds; **~enhefter** *m* document-file; **~enklammer** *f* paper-clip; **~enkundig** *a* on (the) record; **~enmappe, ~entasche** *f* portfolio, document wallet; brief-case; **~enmensch** *m* red tapist; **~enschrank** *m* filing cabinet, roll-top-cabinet; **~enständer** *m* pigeon-holes *pl*; **~enstoß** *m* bundle of files; **~enstück** *n* official document; (*e-s Prozesses*) particulars *pl* of a case; **~envermerk** *m* memo, note, summary; **~enzeichen** *n* file number, record number; reference (number); **~modell** *n* nude, life model.

Aktie *f* share, *Am* stock; **~nbörse** *f* stock-exchange; **~ngesellschaft** *f* joint-stock company; **~ninhaber** *m* share-holder, *Am* stockholder; **~nkapital** *n* share capital; (joint-)stock; **~nmehrheit** *f*: *die ~~ besitzen* to hold the controlling interest; **~npaket** *n* parcel of shares.

Aktion *f* action; (*Tätigkeit*) activity; *gemeinsame ~* joint action; **~är** *m* shareholder, *Am* stockholder; **~sprogramm** *n* scheme; **~sradius** *m* radius of action, range.

aktiv *a* active; effective; *mil* (*Soldat*) regular; (*Offizier*) on active service; **~a** *n pl* assets *pl*, *Am* resources *pl*; *~a u. Passiva* assets and liabilities *pl*; **~ieren** *tr* to activate; to realize; **~ierung** *f* activation; **~ität** *f* activity; **~schulden** *f pl* outstanding debts *pl*, assets *pl*.

Aktu|alität *f* actuality; **~ell** *a* topical, timely; present; *~~es Bild* topical picture; *~~e Zeitschrift* topical magazine; *~~ sein* to be timely.

Aktuar *m* actuary, clerk; registrar.

Akust|ik *f* acoustics *pl* (*Lehre vom Schall: mit sing*); **~isch** *a* acoustic(al).

akut *a med* acute; (*vordringlich*) burning, urgent, pressing.

Akzent *m* accent, stress (*auf* on); **~uieren** *tr* to accentuate; to stress.

Akzept *n* acceptance; **~ant** *m* acceptor; **~ieren** *tr* to accept, to pay; (*Handel*) to honour (a bill).

Akzidenz|druck *m typ* job-printing, job-work; **~ien** *n pl* occasional emoluments *pl*.

Alabaster *m* alabaster.

Alarm *m* alarm; *Flieger~* alert, air-raid warning; air-alarm; *blinder ~* false alarm; *~ blasen* to sound the alarm; **~bereitschaft** *f* stand-by; readiness; *in ~~* on the alert; **~glocke** *f* alarm-bell; tocsin; **~ieren** *tr* to alarm; *Am* to alert; **~ierung** *f* alarming; **~zustand** *m* stand-to.

Alaun *m* alum; **~artig, ~haltig** *a* aluminous; **~hütte** *f*, **~werk** *n* alum-works *pl*.

Alban|ien *n* Albania; **~ier** *m* Albanian; **~isch, ~esisch** *a* Albanian.

albern *a* silly, absurd; foolish; *~ itr* to behave foolishly; **~heit** *f* folly, absurdity, silliness.

Album *n* album.

Alchim|ie *f* alchemy; **~ist** *m* alchemist.

Alge *f* sea-weed, alga.

Algebra *f* algebra; **~isch** *a* algebraic.

Aliment *n*, **~e** *pl* alimony.

Alkohol *m* alcohol; liquor; **~artig** *a* alcoholic; **~frei** *a* non-alcoholic; *fam* soft; **~gehalt** *m* alcohol content; **~haltig** *a* alcoholic; **~iker** *m* alcoholic **~isieren** *tr* to alcoholize; **~reich** *a* rich in alcohol; **~schmuggel** *m* bootlegging; **~schmuggler** *m* boot legger.

Alkoven *m* alcove, recess.

all, **~e, ~er, ~es** *a* all, everything; *~es in ~em* on the whole; *~e beide* both of us (you, them); *~e Tage* every day; *~e 2 Tage* every other day; *~e 8 Tage* once a week; *auf ~e Fälle* at all events; *ein für ~emal* once for all; *auf ~e Weise* by all means; *ohne ~en Zweifel* undoubtedly; *dies ~es* all this; *~es, was Sie wollen* anything you like; *vor ~em* above all; *in ~er Frühe* bright and early, very early; *~ n* universe; **~abendlich** *a* every evening; **~bekannt** *a* generally known, notorious; **~e**: *~e sein* to be at an end; *~e werden* to be spent, to disappear: *~e machen* to finish.

Allee *f* avenue.

Allegor|ie *f* allegory; **~isch** *a* allegorical.

allein *a u. adv* alone, single; solitary; only, sole, by o. s.; **~besitz** *m* exclusive possession; **~gespräch** *n* soliloquy, monologue; **~handel** *m* monopoly; **~herrschaft** *f* absolute power; **~ig** *a* only, unique; sole, exclusive; **~mädchen** *n* maid-of-all-work; **~sein** *n* loneliness, solitude; isolation; exclusiveness; **~seligmachend** *a eccl* claiming the monopoly of all means of grace; **~stehend** *a* isolated, detached; (*ledig*) single, unmarried; **~vertretung** *f* exclusive (*od* sole) agency.

allemal *adv* always, every time; *ein für ~* once for all.

allen|falls *adv* if need be; (*höchstens*) at most, at best; *~~ auch* eventually; **~thalben** *adv* everywhere, on every side.

aller|best *a* best of all, very best; **~dings** *adv* surely, certainly, indeed, *Am* sure; **~erst** *adv* first of all; *zu~~* first and foremost; **~gnädigst** *a* most gracious; **~hand** *a* of all kinds, various; **~heiligen** *n* All Saints' Day; **~heiligst** *a* most holy; **~~e(s)** *n* holy of holies; **~lei** *a* various, sundry; *n* medley; **~letzt** *a* last of all; **~liebst** *a* dearest of all, most lovely; **~meist** *a* by far most; *am ~meisten* most of all, chiefly; **~mindest** *a* least; least of all; **~nächst** *a* next of all, the very next; **~neuest** *a* very latest; **~orten, ~orts** *adv* everywhere; **~seelen** *pl* All Souls' Day; **~seits** *adv* on all sides; to all; **~untertänigst** *a* most humble; **~wegen** *adv* everywhere; **~weltskerl** *m* devil of a fellow, smart fellow; **~wenigst** *a* the very least; least of all; **~werteste(r)** *m fam* posterior, backside.

Allerg|ie *f med* allergy; **~isch** *a* allergic; *~~e Krankheit* allergic illness.

alle|samt *adv* all together, in a body, to a man; **~weile** *adv* just now; **~zeit** *adv* at all times, always.

All|gegenwart *f* omnipresence; **~gegenwärtig** *a* omnipresent; **~gemach** *adv* by degrees, gradually; **~gemein** *a* universal, common to all, general; *im ~~en* in general, generally; **~gemeinbefinden** *n* general condition(s *pl*); **~gemeinbildung** *f* general culture; **~gemeinheit** *f* universality, generality; *Pflichten gegen die ~~* duties toward the public; **~gemeinverständlich** *a* adaptable to the popular mind; popular; **~gewalt** *f* supreme power; **~gewaltig** *a* all-powerful; **~gütig** *a* infinitely good; **~heilmittel** *n* cure-all, panacea, universal remedy.

Alli|anz *f* alliance; **~ieren** *tr* to ally, to unite; **~ierte(r)** *m* ally; *die* **~ierten** *m pl* the Allies *pl*; **~ierte Militärregierung** *f* Allied Military Government.

all|jährlich *a* every year, yearly; annual; **~macht** *f* omnipotence, almightiness; **~mächtig** *a* almighty, omnipotent; **~mählich** *a* gradual; *adv* gradually, little by little; by degrees; **~monatlich** *a* monthly, once a month, every month; **~morgendlich** *a* every morning; **~nächtlich** *a* every night.

Allopath *m* allopathist; **~ie** *f* allopathy; **~isch** *a* allopathical.

Allotria *n pl* tomfoolery; *~ treiben* to play the fool.

all|sehend *a* all-seeing; **~seitig** *a* universal; **~~keit** *f* universality; **~stromgerät** *n radio* all-mains set; **~tag** *m* week-day, working-day; **~täglich** *a* daily; (*gewöhnlich*) common, commonplace; trivial; **~~keit** *f* commonness, triviality; **~tagskleid** *n* every-day coat, undress; **~tagsleben** *n* every-day life; **~tagsmensch** *a* commonplace fellow; **~tagsworte** *n pl* household words *pl*; **~überall** *adv* everywhere; **~umfassend** *a* all-embracing; **~vater** *m* Father of all; **~waltend** *a* all-ruling; **~weise** *a* all-wise; **~~** *m* the All-wise; **~weisheit** *f* supreme wisdom; **~wellenempfänger** *m radio* all-wave receiver; **~wetterkarosserie** *f mot* all-weather body; **~wissend** *a* all-knowing, omniscient; **~wissenheit** *f* omniscience; **~wöchentlich** *a* weekly, every week; **~zeit** *adv* always; **~zu** *adv* too, much too; **~zubald** *adv* much too soon; **~zugleich, ~zumal** *adv* all together, all at once; **~zusehr** *adv* too much, overmuch; **~zuviel** *adv* too much; *~~ ist ungesund* too much of a good thing is good for nothing.

Alm *f* mountain pasture.

Almanach *m* almanac, calendar.

Almosen *n* alms *pl*, charity; *ein ~ geben* to give alms, to bestow alms; *um ein ~ bitten* to ask alms; **~amt** *n* almonry; **~büchse** *f*, **~stock** *m* poor-box; **~empfänger** *m* pauper; **~geld** *n* poor-money; **~pfleger** *m* almoner; **~sammlung** *f* collection for the poor.

Aloe *f bot* aloe.

Alp *m*, **~drücken** *n* night-mare.

Alp(e) *f siehe Alm*; **~en** *pl* Alps *pl.*

Alpen|klub *m* Alpine Club; **~pflanze** *f* Alpine plant; **~stock** *m* alpenstock; **~veilchen** *n* cyclamen.

Alpin|ist *m* Alpinist, mountaineer; **~um** *n* rockery, Alpinum.

Alphabet *n* alphabet; **~isch** *a* alphabetic(al); *~~ ordnen* to alphabet.

Älpler *m* native of the Alps.

Alraune *f* mandrake.

als *conj* (*nach Komparativen u.* other, otherwise, else, rather) than; (*nach Verneinungen*) but; (*zu der Zeit, wo*) when; (*in der Eigenschaft*) as; (*ganz so wie*) like; (*dienend*) by way of; *~ daß* = to + *Infinitiv: es ist zu schön, als daß es wahr sein könnte* it is too beautiful to be true; *~ ob, ~ wenn* as if, as though; **~bald** *adv* forthwith, at once, immediately, presently; **~dann** *adv* then, after, thereupon.

also *adv* so, thus; *conj* consequently, therefore.

alt *a* old; aged; ancient; *wie ~ sind Sie?* how old are you? *ich bin 20 Jahre ~* I am twenty years old (of age); *~ werden* to grow old; (*verbraucht*) worn; (*Brot*) stale; *~e Bücher* second-hand books; *~es Eisen* scrap(-iron); *~e Geschichte* ancient history; *das ist e-e ~e Geschichte* that's an old affair; *der ~e Herr* the old man; *~e Sprachen* ancient languages, classics *pl*; *~er Witz* old joke; *aus der ~en Zeit* of yore; *~es Zeug* rubbish; *es bleibt alles beim ~en* everything stands as it was.

Alt *m*, **~stimme** *f* high tenor, counter-tenor; alto (voice).

Altan *m* terrace, balcony.

Altar *m* altar; **~blatt** *n* altar-piece; **~tuch** *n* altar-cloth.

alt|backen *a* stale; **~besitz** *m* old holding; **~bewährt** *a* of long standing; **~deutsch** *a* Old German; **~eingesessen** *a* long established; **~eisen** *n* scrap(-iron); **~e(r)** *m*, **~e** *f* the old one, *fam* the governor, the old woman; **~er** *n* age; *hohes ~er* old age; *im ~er von* at the age of; *vor ~ers* in olden times, in former days; **~ern** *itr* to grow old, to age; to decline, to decay.

Alters|genosse *m* coeval, person of the same age; **~grenze** *f* age limit; **~heim** *n* home for the aged; **~klasse** *f* age group; **~präsident** *m* president by age; **~schwach** *a* age-worn; **~schwäche** *f* decline of life; **~stufe** *f* stage of life; **~versicherung** *f* old-age insurance; **~~skasse** *f* old-age fund; **~versorgung** *f* old-age pension; **~~sgesetz** *n* Old Age and Infirmity Insurance Bill; **~~skasse** *f* provident fund; **~zulage** *f* long-service increase of pay.

Altertum *n* antiquity, the ancients *pl*; **~sforscher** *m*, **~skundige(r)** *m* antiquary, archæologist; **~shändler** *m* dealer in antiquities; **~skunde** *f* archæology.

altertümlich *a* archaic; ancient, antique.

Älteste(r) *m* oldest; eldest; senior.

Alt|gesell *m* foreman; **~gläubig** *a* orthodox.

Altist *m*, **~in** *f* alto singer.

altklug *a* precocious.

ältlich *a* elderly, oldish.

Alt|material *n* salvage, scrap, junk; **~~sammlung** *f* salvage collection; **~meister** *m* past-master; *sport* old champion, old timer; **~modisch** *a* old-fashioned; **~papier** *n* waste paper; **~philolog** *m* classical scholar; **~silber** *n* oxidized silver; **~stadt** *f* old town, city; **~väterisch** *a* antiquated; ancestral, primitive; **~warenhändler** *m* antiquary; second-hand shopkeeper (*od* dealer); **~weibersommer** *m* gossamer, Indian summer.

Aluminium *n* aluminium, *Am* aluminum; **~oxyd** *n* aluminium oxide; **~silikat** *n* aluminic silicate.

Alumnat *n* boarding-school.

am (= *an dem*) *~ 1. November* on November 1st; *Frankfurt ~ Main* F. on the Main; *~ Abend* in the evening; *~ Anfang* at the beginning; *~ Ende* in short; after all; at last; *~ Himmel* in the sky; *~ Hofe* at court; *Gesandter ~ Hofe* ambassador to the court of ...; *~ Sterben* at the point of death; *~ Tage* by day; *~ Tage nach* ... on the day after ...; *~ Ufer* on the shore; *~ besten* best; *~ meisten* most; *~ Leben* alive.

Amalgam *n* amalgam; **~ieren** *tr* to amalgamate; **~ierung** *f* amalgamation.

Amateur *m* amateur; **~photograph** *m* camera fan.

Amazone *f* Amazon.

Amber, Ambra *m* amber(gris).

Amboß *m* anvil; **~stock** *m* anvil-stock.

Ambulanz *f* ambulance; field hospital; **~wagen** *m* ambulance (car).

Ameise *f* ant; (*weiße*) termite; **~nbär** *m* ant-bear; **~nei** *n* ant's egg; **~nhaufen** *m* ant-heap, ant-hill(ock); **~nlöwe** *m* lion-ant; **~nsäure** *f* formic acid.

Amen! amen! *ja u. ~ sagen* to agree (*zu* to).

Amerika *n* America; *Vereinigte Staaten von ~* the United States of America (USA); **~ner** *m*, **~nisch** *a* American; **~nisieren** *tr* to Americanize; **~nismus** *m* Americanism.

Amethyst *m* amethyst.

Amme *f* nurse, wet-nurse; **~nmärchen** *n* nursery tale; cock-and-bull story.

Ammer *f orn* bunting, yellow-hammer.

Ammoniak *n* ammonia; **~dämpfe** *m pl* ammonia vapo(u)rs *pl.*

Amnesie *f* amnesia, loss of memory.

Amnestie *f* amnesty, general pardon; **~ren** *tr* to grant amnesty to, to pardon.

Amöbe *f* am(o)eba; **~nkrankheit** *f* am(o)ebiasis; **~nruhr** *f* am(o)ebic dysentery.

Amok *m* amok, *Am* amuck; *~ laufen* to run amok.

amorph *a* amorphous.

Amortis|ation *f* amortization, redemption; **~ieren** *tr* to redeem, to sink.

Ampel *f* hanging-lamp; (*Blumen~*) hanging flower-pot.

Ampere *n* ampere; **~meter** *n* ampere-meter, ammeter.

Ampfer *m* sorrel, dock.

Amphib|ie *f* amphibium; amphibian; **~isch** *a* amphibian, amphibious; *~~e Kriegführung* amphibious warfare; *~~e Operationen* amphibious operations; *~~er Panzer* (*Schwimmpanzer*) amphibian tank; (*Truppentransporter bei Landungsoperationen*) *Am* alligator, *Am* amtrack; *~~e Streitkräfte* amphibious forces.

Amphitheater *n* amphitheatre.

Ampulle *f* ampoule; (*Fläschchen*) vial (*od* phial).

amputieren *tr* to amputate.

Amsel *f* ouzel, blackbird.

Amt *n* (*öffentliches*) office; (*Behörde*) board, department; (*auf Vertrauen beruhend*) charge; (*Stelle*) place, post; (*Beschäftigung*) employment, function; (*Obrigkeit*) magistracy; (*geistliches*) divine service, ministry; (*Gerichts~*) court, council; (*Auswärtiges ~*) Foreign Office; (*Hoch~*) mass; *tele* exchange; *fig* business, call; (*Pflicht*) official duty; *im ~e sein* to be in office;

ein ~ übernehmen to take office; *sein ~ niederlegen* to resign; *ein ~ ausüben, innehaben* to be in office; *ein öffentliches ~ bekleiden* to hold an office; *jdn des ~es entheben* to oust s. o. from office; *vom ~ zurücktreten* to resign office; *von ~s wegen* ex officio, officially; *sich um ein ~ bewerben* to apply for a post; *ein ~ antreten* to enter upon o.'s duties; *es ist nicht meines ~es* it is no business of mine; **~ieren** *itr* to officiate; **~lich** *a* official; **~los** *a* out of office, private; **~mann** *m* judiciary, bailiff.

Amts|alter *n* seniority in office; **~anmaßung** *f* usurpation of official authority; **~anruf** *m tele* exchange call; **~antritt** *m* entering upon an office; **~arzt** *m* medical officer of health; **~befugnis** *f* competence, authority; **~bereich** *m* jurisdiction; **~bericht** *m* official account; report; **~bezirk** *m* jurisdiction, precinct; **~blatt** *n* official gazette; **~bruder** *m* colleague; **~dauer** *f* term of office, *Am* term; **~diener** *m* beadle, usher; **~eid** *m* official oath; **~enthebung** *f* discharge, dismissal; **~führung** *f* administration; **~geheimnis** *n* official secret; **~genosse** *m* colleague, assistant; **~gericht** *n* district-court; **~gerichtsrat** *m* senior judge in a lower court of justice; **~gewalt** *f* authority; **~haftung** *f* official responsibility; **~handlung** *f* official act; **~kasse** *f* pay office; **~kleid** *n* official gown; **~lokal** *n* office; **~miene** *f* official air; **~pflicht** *f* official duty; **~richter** *m* district-judge; **~schimmel** *m* red tape; **~siegel** *n* official seal; **~sprache** *f* official language; **~stube** *f* office; **~stunden** *f pl* office-hours *pl*; **~tracht** *f* official dress; **~verrichtung** *f* official duty; **~überschreitung** *f* official excess; **~verletzung** *f* misconduct in office; **~verschwiegenheit** *f* official secrecy; **~verwalter, ~verweser** *m* administrator of an office; substitute; **~vormund** *m* public guardian; **~vorstand** *m* head official; **~wohnung** *f* official residence; **~zeichen** *n tele* dial tone; **~zeit** *f* term of office, tenure of office; **~zimmer** *n* bureau, office.

Amulett *n* charm; amulet.

amüs|ant *a* amusing; **~ieren** *tr* to amuse; *sich ~~* to enjoy o. s., to amuse o. s., to have a good time.

*

an *prp* at, on, in, to, against, near, about; *~ seiner Stelle* in his place; *~ der Tür* at the door; *~ der Wand* on the wall; *~ Bord* on board; aboard; *~ der See* by the seaside; *~ der Themse* on the Thames; *bis ~* up to; *ich habe e-e Bitte ~ Sie* I have a favo(u)r to ask; *Mann ~ Mann* man by man; *Brust ~ Brust* breast to breast; *~ seinen Blicken* by his looks; *~ die Wand lehnen* to lean against the wall; *~ die 1000 Leute* about one thousand people; *~ sich, ~ und für sich* in itself; *die Reihe ist ~ mir* it is my turn; *nun geht es ~ die Arbeit* now let us set to work; *es ist ~ der Zeit* the time has come; *es ist ~ dem* it is so; *~ Spesen* to charges; *ein Brief ~ jdn* a letter to s. o.; *von nun ~* henceforth.

Ana|chronismus *m* anachronism; **~log(isch)** *a* analogical, analogous; **~logie** *f* analogy; **~lyse** *f* analysis; (*e-s Stahls*) composition; **~lysieren** *tr* to analyse; **~lytisch** *a* analytic; *~~e Chemie f* analytical chemistry.

Analphabet *m* illiterate: **~entum** *n* illiteracy.

Anäm|ie *f med* an(a)emia; **~isch** *a* (*blutarm*) an(a)emic.

Ananas *f* pine-apple.

Anarch|ie *f* anarchy; **~isch** *a* anarchic(al).

Anatom|ie *f* anatomy; (*Raum*) dissecting-room; **~(iker)** *m* anatomist; **~isch** *a* anatomical.

anbacken *irr itr* to bake gently; to stick.

anbahnen *tr* to open a way to, to bring about, to initiate, to pave the way for; (*bevorstehen*) to be at hand.

anbändeln *itr* to make up to; to flirt with.

Anbau *m* (*Gebäude*) annex, wing, additional building(s *pl*), side-building; (*landwirtschaftlich*) cultivation, culture, tillage; **~en** *tr* to till, to cultivate; (*Korn*) to grow corn; (*an ein Gebäude*) to add (a new wing); **~fläche** *f* arable acreage.

anbe|fehlen *irr tr* to command, to order; **~ginn** *m* beginning, outset; *von ~~* from the outset; **~halten** *irr tr* to keep on.

anbei *adv* annexed, herewith, enclosed, under this cover.

anbeißen *irr itr* to bite at; *fig* to swallow the bait.

anbelangen *imp* to relate to; to concern, to regard; *was mich anbelangt* as to (*od* for) me.

anbellen *tr* to bark at.

anbequemen *tr* to accommodate to; *sich ~* to adapt o. s. to.

anberaumen *tr* to appoint, to fix, to call.

anbet|en *tr* to worship, to adore; **~er** *m*, **~erin** *f* worshipper, lover; **~ung** *f* worship, adoration; **~~swürdig** *a* adorable.

Anbetracht: *in ~* in view of, considering, taking into account.

anbetreffen *irr itr* to concern; *was Sie anbetrifft* as for you, for your part.

anbetteln *tr* to sollicit alms from s.o.

anbiedern: *sich ~ an* (*od mit*) to make friends with; to intrude on; *fam* to chum up with.

anbiegen *irr tr* to bend to.

anbiet|en *irr tr* to offer; *r* to present o. s.; **~ung** *f* offer(ing).

anbinden *irr tr* to tie, to fasten, to bind; *mit jdm ~* to engage in a contest with; *kurz angebunden sein* to be short with, to be pert to.

anblasen *irr tr* to blow, to breathe at; (*anfachen*) to set ablaze; (*Hochofen*) to blow in.

Anblick *m* sight; aspect, view; *beim ersten ~* at first sight; **~en** *tr* to look at, to glance at, to view; *zornig ~~* to frown (at).

anblinz|en, ~eln *tr* to blink at, to wink at; (*angrinsen*) to leer at.

anbohren *tr* to bore, to pierce; (*Faß*) to tap, to broach.

anbrechen *irr tr* to begin, to break, to open; *itr* to break, to dawn; *mit ~dem Tage* at day-break, at dawn; *bei ~der Nacht* at night-fall.

anbrennen *irr tr* to set on fire; (*Zigarre*) to light; *itr* to begin to burn, to catch fire; *~ lassen* to burn; *angebrannt a* burnt.

anbring|en *irr tr* (*festmachen*) to fix to, to apply to; (*Geld*) to place; (*Gründe*) to bring, to put forward; (*ein Wort*) to put in a word; (*absetzen*) to dispose of, to sell; (*Klage*) to enter an action against; to lodge a complaint; (*Schlag*) to bring home, to deal; (*Stoß*) to hit; (*Tochter*) to marry; *jdn ~~* to get a place for.

Anbruch *m* beginning; *min* opening; break, dawn; *~ des Tages* day-break; *~ der Nacht* nightfall.

an|brüllen *tr* to bellow, to roar at, to bawl at; **~brummen** *tr* to grumble at; **~brüten** *tr* to begin to hatch; *angebrütetes Ei* an egg half-hatched.

Anchovis *f* anchovy; **~paste** *f* anchovy paste; **~brötchen** *n* anchovy toast.

An|dacht *f* devotion; *eccl* prayers *pl*; (religious) service; *seine ~~ verrichten* to be at prayers; **~dächtig** *a* devout; devotional, absorbed; pious; (*aufmerksam*) attentive.

andauern *itr* to last, to continue; **~d** *a* continual, continuous, uninterrupted; lasting.

Andenken *n* remembrance; memory; (*Gegenstand*) keepsake; (*Reise*) souvenir; token; *zum ~* in memory of, in remembrance of; *jds ~ feiern* to commemorate.

ander *a* other, different; *einen Tag um den ~en* every other day; *am ~en Morgen* the next morning; *einmal über das ~e* repeatedly, again and again; *eins ums ~e* alternately, by turns; *kein ~er* no one else; *etw ~es* s. th. else; *das ist etw ~es* that is different; *der e-e — der ~e* the one — the other; *nichts ~s als* nothing but; *alles ~e als* anything but; *~e Kleider anziehen* to change o.'s clothes; *eins ins ~e gerechnet* taking things together; *ein ~mal* another time; *~er Ansicht sein* to differ; *unter ~em* among other things; *e-r nach dem ~n* one after the other; one at a time; one by one; *das machen Sie e-m ~n weis!* tell that to the marines! *nichts ~es* nothing else; *~e Saiten aufziehen* to change o.'s tune; *sich e-s ~en besinnen* to change o.'s mind; **~erseits** *adv* on the other hand (*od* side).

ändern *tr* to alter, to change, to modify; *ich kann es nicht ~* I cannot help it; *es ist nicht zu ~* it cannot be helped; *r* to alter, to change.

andern|falls *adv* else, otherwise; **~teils** *adv* on the other hand.

anders *adv* otherwise, differently; *ich kann nicht ~* I cannot help; *wenn ~, wo ~ conj* provided that; *sich ~ besinnen* to think better of it; *~ werden* to change; *ich weiß es ~* I know better; *das ist nun mal nicht ~* that's the way things go; *es war nicht ~ möglich* there was no other way; **~denkend** *a* dissenting; **~~e(r)** *m* dissentient, *Am* dissenter; **~gesinnt** *a* differently minded; **~gläubig** *a* heterodox.

anderseits *adv* on the other hand.

anders|wo *adv* elsewhere; **~woher** *adv* from some other place; **~wohin** *adv* to some other place, elsewhere.

anderthalb *a* one and a half; **~fach** *a* one and a half times; **~jährig** *a* one and a half year old.

Änderung *f* change, alteration; (*geringfügig*) modification.

ander|wärts *adv* in another place; **~weitig** *a* other, further; *adv* elsewhere; in another place (*od* way); at another time.

andeut|en *tr* to indicate, to hint, to give warning of, to intimate; to give to understand; (*raten*) to suggest; **~ung** *f* indication, hint, intimation, suggestion; (*Anspielung*) allusion; **~~sweise** *adv* by way of suggestion.

andicht|en *tr* to ascribe, to attribute falsely to; **~ung** *f* imputation.

andonnern *tr* to thunder at; *wie angedonnert* thunder-struck.

An|drang *m* press, crowd, rush; (*Bank*) run (on a bank); (*Blut*) congestion; **~drängen** *itr* to press (*od* push) on, to crowd against.

andreh|en *tr* to begin to turn; to set going; (*Licht*) to switch on; (*befestigen*)

to tighten; (*Schraube*) to screw on; (*Gas*) to turn on the gas; *mot* to start up; *jdm etw ~~ fig* to palm off upon, to impose upon; **~kurbel** *f mot* (starting) crank.
andringen *irr itr* to push on; (*Feind*) to advance.
androh|en *tr* to menace; *jdm etw ~* to threaten s. o. with; **~ung** *f* menace, threat; *unter ~~* under penalty of, on pain of.
andrücken *tr* to press, to squeeze close to; *aero* to put on speed.
aneifern *tr* to stimulate; to incite, to rouse; to fill with zeal.
aneign|en: *sich etw ~en* to take possession of, to appropriate; to annex; to adopt (opinions); to acquire (knowledge); (*widerrechtlich*) to misappropriate; **~ung** *f* appropriation; usurpation; (*Erwerb*) acquisition.
aneinander *adv* together; to each other, to one another; against one another; **~fügen** *tr* to join together; **~geraten** *irr itr* to fly at each other; **~grenzen** *itr* to be neighbo(u)rs, to bound; **~hängen** *irr itr* to stick together; **~reihen** *tr* to arrange side by side; **~stoßen** *irr itr* to border on; to collide.
Anekdote *f* anecdote.
anekeln *tr* to disgust; *es ekelt mich an* I am disgusted with it.
Anemone *f* anemone, wind-flower.
anempfehl|en *irr tr* to recommend; **~ung** *f* recommendation.
Anerbiet|en *n*, ***~ung*** *f* offer, proposal; tender.
anerkanntermaßen *adv* admittedly, *Am* concededly.
anerkenn|en *irr tr* to acknowledge. to recognize, *Am* to concede; (*loben*) to appreciate; (*Schuld*) to admit; (*Wechsel*) to accept; *nicht ~~* to disavow, to repudiate; **~tnis, ~ung** *f* acknowledg(e)ment, recognition; (*Lob*) approval, appreciation; (*Wechsel*) acceptance; (*Zulassung*) admission; (*Anspruch*) allowance; **~ungsschreiben** *n* letter of approbation; commendation.

*

an|fachen *tr* to fan, to blow into a flame; *fig* to inflame; to stir up; **~fächeln** *tr* to fan.
anfahr|en *irr itr* (*beginnen*) to begin to move; (*bei jdm*) to drive up to; to arrive, to come up in a car; *min* to go to work, to descend; *tr* (*heran*) to carry up; (*zusammenstoßen*) to collide with, to run into; (*Schiff e-n Hafen*) to call at; *jdn ~* to fly at, to rebuke; **~t** *f* driving up; arrival; descent (into a mine); (*Ort zur ~~*) drive, driveway; (*für Schiffe*) landing-place, quay.
Anfall *m* attack, shock; (*Krankheits~*) fit; paroxysm; (*Erbschafts~*) reversion, inheritance; **~en** *irr tr* to attack, to assault, to assail; (*Erbschaft*) to fall to.
anfällig *a* susceptible (*für* to).
Anfang *m* beginning, origin, outset; commencement; (*von Briefen*) opening; (*Wissenschaft*) rudiments *pl*, elements *pl*; *~ Mai* at (*od* in) the beginning of May; *am ~* at the beginning; *für den ~* for the present; *von ~ an* from the outset; *den ~ machen* to begin with, to set about; **~en** *irr tr, itr* to begin, to set about, to start; *von vorn ~en* to begin again, to start again; *ein Gespräch ~en* to engage in a conversation with; *ein Geschäft ~en* to set up in (*od* to start) a business, to establish o.s.; *Streit ~en* to begin to quarrel; *ich weiß nicht, was ich damit ~en soll* I don't know what to do with it; *was fange ich an?* what shall I do?

Anfäng|er *m*, ***~erin*** *f* beginner; **~lich** *a* initial, original; *adv* at first.
anfangs *adv* at first, in (*od* at) the beginning; originally; *gleich ~* at the very outset; **~buchstabe** *m* initial letter; *großer ~~* capital; *kleiner ~~* small letter; **~gehalt** *n*, **~lohn** *m* beginning wages; **~geschwindigkeit** *f phys* initial velocity; initial speed; **~gründe** *m pl* principles, rudiments, elements *pl*; **~punkt** *m* beginning, starting-point; **~spannung** *f el* initial tension; **~zustand** *m* initial state.
anfassen *tr* to touch, to take hold of, to grasp, to seize, to handle; (*helfen*) to lend a hand, to give assistance; *e-e Sache falsch ~ fig* to mismanage s. th., to tackle a problem the wrong way; *jdn ~ fig* (*behandeln*) to treat; *jdn mit Samthandschuhen ~ fig* to treat s. o. gently, *Am* to handle s. o. with kid gloves; *der Stoff faßt sich weich an* the cloth feels soft; *sich ~* to take hands.
anfecht|bar *a* contestable, disputable; **~en** *irr tr* to contest, to dispute; to avoid, to defeat; (*Testament*) to contest a will; (*beunruhigen*) to disturb; to trouble; (*angreifen*) to attack; *eccl* (*versuchen*) to tempt; *jur* to challenge; to appeal against; (*Vertrag*) to rescind, to avoid; (*Meinung*) to oppose; *was ficht dich an?* what is the matter with you? **~ung** *f* contestation, opposition; (*Versuchung*) *eccl* temptation; *jur* avoidance; **~~sklage** *f* action to set aside, action for invalidation (of a contract etc); (*Patentrecht*) interference-proceedings *pl*.
anfeind|en *tr* to persecute with enmity, to show ill-will; **~ung** *f* hostility, enmity.
anfertig|en *tr* to make; to manufacture, to fabricate; (*Liste, Verzeichnis*) to draw up; **~ung** *f* manufacture, fabrication, making.
anfeucht|en *tr* to moisten, to wet (slightly), to damp; **~er** *m* damper; **~ung** *f* moistening; irrigation.
anfeuern *tr* to begin to heat; *fig* to fire, to stimulate, to ginger (up), *Am fam* to spark-plug.
anfleh|en *tr* to implore; (*demütig*) to supplicate; **~ung** *f* imploration; supplication.
an|fliegen *irr itr* to fly against, to come flying; *aero* to land at; to approach; to touch, to call; **~flug** *m* flight; *aero* approach; (*Spur*) touch, tinge, tincture; (*von Röte*) slight blush; (*oberflächliche Kenntnis*) smattering; **~~grundlinie** *f aero* centreline of the runway; **~~weg** *m aero* lane (*od* path) of approach; **~~zeit** *f aero* time of approach.
anforder|n *tr* to demand, to claim, to request; (*bestellen*) to indent (for); **~ung** *f* demand; (*Anspruch*) claim; (*Bedürfnis*) requirement; *hohe ~~en an jdn stellen* to be exacting; *den ~~en genügen* to satisfy requirements.
Anfrag|e *f* inquiry; application; *~e richten* (*an*) to apply to s.o. for information; **~en** *itr* to make inquiry, to ask.
anfressen *irr tr* to nibble at, to gnaw; (*von Säuren*) to corrode.
anfreunden *tr* to make friends with.
anfrieren *irr itr* to freeze on to.
anfüg|en *tr* to join, to enclose, to attach, to annex; **~ung** *f* addition, adjunction.
anfühlen *tr* to feel, to touch; *sich ~* to feel; *~ n: beim ~* in touching.
Anfuhr *f* carriage, conveyance, cartage; supply.
anführ|en *tr* to lead; to command; (*zitieren*) to cite, to quote; (*behaupten*) to allege; (*Beweis, Grund*) to adduce; (*bemerken*) to state; (*plädieren*) to plead; (*täuschen*) to delude; to deceive, to hoax, to cheat, to dupe; **~er** *m* leader, commander, chief; **~ung** *f* direction, lead(ership), command; quotation; **~ungszeichen** *n pl* signs of quotation, inverted commas *pl*.
anfüll|en *tr* to fill up; (*bis zum Übermaß*) to cram; (*wieder*) to replenish, to store; **~ung** *f* filling, cramming.
Angabe *f* declaration; information, instruction; (*bestimmte*) statement; (*nähere*) specification, particulars *pl*, details *pl*; (*Tatsachen*) data *pl*; (*Prahlerei*) showing off; (*Anzeige*) denunciation; *nach seiner ~* according to him.
angaffen *tr* to gape at, to stare at.
angängig *adv* admissible; possible, feasable, practicable.
angeb|en *irr tr* to declare; to make a statement; (*genau*) to specify; (*mitteilen*) to inform, to quote; (*anordnen*) to suggest; (*anzeigen*) to denounce; to inform against; (*vorgeben*) to pretend; (*Wert*) to declare; *den Ton ~en* to give the tune; to lead the fashion; *seinen Namen ~en* to give o.'s name; *Gründe ~en* to allege reasons; *den Kurs ~en* to indicate; *sein Vermögen ~en* to state o.'s fortune; *sein Spiel ~en* to call o.'s game; *itr* (*Kartenspiel*) to deal first; (*Tennis*) to serve; *fam* (*prahlen*) to swagger, to brag, to boast; *geben Sie nicht so an!* don't brag so much! **~er** *m* author; (*Denunziant*) informer; denouncer; (*Prahler*) braggart, swaggerer; **~erei** *f* denunciation.
Angebinde *n* gift, present.
angeblich *a* pretended, supposed; *jur* alleged; *adv* nominally.
ange|boren *a* innate, inborn; inherent; **~bot** *n* offer; *~~ und Nachfrage* offer and demand; (*Börse*) supply and demand; (*bei Auktion*) first bid (*od* offer); (*Zahlungs-, Lieferungsangebot*) tender, *Am* bid; **~bracht** *a* seasonable, suited; *schlecht ~~* ill-suited, out of place; **~bunden** *a: kurz ~~* blunt; **~deihen** *itr: ~~ lassen* to bestow upon, to confer upon; **~denken** *n* remembrance; recollection; **~fressen** *a* (*Metall*) superficially corroded; (*faul*) carious, rotten; **~führt** *a* (*zitiert*) cited; (*erwähnt*) mentioned; (*betrogen*) imposed upon; (*geleitet*) led; **~gossen** *a: wie ~~ sitzen* to fit like a glove; **~griffen** *a* (*beschädigt*) affected; attacked; corroded; (*müde*) exhausted, tired; *~~ aussehen* to look poor; **~heftet** *a* attached; **~heiratet** *a* by marriage; **~heitert** *a* slightly tipsy.
angehen *irr itr* to begin, to open; to catch fire; *~ gegen* to fight against; *das geht nicht an* that won't do; *tr* to address; *mit Bitten ~* to request; to apply to; (*betreffen*) to concern, to regard; *das geht Sie nichts an* that is not to you; *was geht das mich an?* what is that to me? *er geht mich nichts an* he is not related to me; **~d** *a* commencing, beginning, incipient; (*künftig*) future; *prp* concerning, as for.
angehör|en *itr* to belong to, to be related to; (*Kirche*) to be affiliated with; (*Partei*) to be a member of; **~ig** *a* attached to, related to; *meine Angehörigen* my relations *pl* (*od* relatives *od* dependants *pl*); *die nächsten Angehörigen* next of kin; my family.
Angeklagter *m* accused, defendant.
Angel *f* (*Tür~*) hinge; (*Schnur*) angle, hook; (*Fanggerät*) fishing-rod; *aus den ~n heben* to unhinge a door; *fig* to

revolutionize; *aus den* ~*n geraten* to be off the hinges; *zwischen Tür u.* ~ *fig* at the last moment; ~**haken** *m* fishing-hook; ~**leine** *f* line; ~**n** *tr* to angle for; *fig* to fish for; ~**punkt** *m* cardinal point; turning point; *das war der* ~~ *der Frage fig* the question hinged on this very fact; ~**rute** *f* fishing-rod; ~**weit** *adv* wide open.

angelangen *itr* to get to, to arrive at.

Angeld *n* earnest-money.

angelegen *a* important; *sich etw* ~ *sein lassen* to take care of, to take an interest in; ~**heit** *f* concern, affair, matter; *Minister der Auswärtigen* ~~*en* Foreign Minister; (*in England*) Secretary of State for Foreign Affairs, Foreign Secretary; (*in USA*) Secretary of State; ~**tlich** *a* urgent, earnest, pressing; *adv* strongly.

angelernt *a:* ~*er Arbeiter* semi-skilled workman.

ange|loben *tr* to promise, to vow; ~**löbnis** *n* vow, solemn promise.

angemessen *a* suitable, proper, fit; (*Preis*) reasonable, fair; ~**heit** *f* conformity, fitness.

ange|nehm *a* pleasant, agreeable; (*nett*) nice; (*Geruch*) sweet; (*sehr*) ~~! (*Formel beim Vorstellen*) glad to meet you! (*Stimme*) pleasing; ~**nommen** *pp, a* supposing, hypothetical; ~, *daß* let us suppose that; (*bei Wechsel*) accepted; (*adoptiert*) adopted; (*fälschlich*) fictitious, assumed, feigned, false; ~~*er Name* assumed name; (*Dichter*) pseudonym; ~~*es Kind* adoptive child.

Anger *m* meadow, pasture-ground.

ange|sehen *a* esteemed; respected; distinguished; ~**sessen** *a* settled, resident.

Angesicht *n* face, countenance; *von* ~ by sight; *von* ~ *zu* ~ face to face; ~**s** *prp* in view of; considering.

ange|stammt *a* hereditary, innate; ~**stellte** *f*, ~**stellte(r)** *m* employee, *Am auch* employe; clerk; (*technischer*) engineering employee; *die* ~*stellten* the staff; ~*stellter sein bei* to be employed at (*od* in, *Am* with); ~~**nversicherung** *f* employees' insurance; ~**strengt** *a* strained, intense; ~**tan** *pp: dies ist ganz dazu* ~~ there is every likelihood of, it is calculated to; *es ist nicht danach* ~~ it is not very likely, it does not tend to;. ~**trunken** *a* tipsy; ~**wandt** *a* practical; *math* applied; ~**wiesen** *a* depending (*auf* on); ~**wöhnen** *tr* to accustom, to habituate; *sich etw* ~~ to contract (a habit), to get used to, to get in(to) the habit of; ~**wohnheit** *f* habit, custom, use, practice; *aus* ~~ habitually.

Angina *f med* (~ *acuta*) angina acuta; (~ *abscedens*) quinsy; (~ *tonsillaris*) acute tonsillitis.

Angler *m* angler.

angleich|en *irr tr* to assimilate; to approximate; (*Löhne*) to adjust; ~**ung** *f* assimilation.

anglied|ern *tr* to join, to annex; to attach (to); to affiliate; ~**erung** *f* annexation; affiliation.

Angli|st *m* anglicist; English scholar; student of English; ~**stik** *f* study of English philology; ~**zismus** *m* anglicism.

Anglo|-Amerikaner *m* Anglo-American; ~**manie** *f* Anglomania; ~**phile** *m* Anglophile; ~**phobie** *f* Anglophobia.

anglotzen *tr* to gape at, to stare at.

angreifbar *a* attackable, assailable; (*verwundbar*) vulnerable; ~**keit** *f* attackability; effectiveness.

angreif|en *irr tr* to handle, to take hold of; (*feindlich*) to attack, to charge upon; *tätlich* ~~ to assault; (*in Anspruch nehmen*) to touch, to dip into, to draw on (provisions, money); (*etw anfassen*) to set about, to start, to undertake; (*schwächen*) to weaken, to exhaust, to try, to affect (the eyes); *etw. verkehrt* ~*en* to begin at the wrong end; ~**end** *a* fatiguing; aggressive; ~**er** *m* assailant, aggressor, invader.

angrenzen *itr* to border on, to adjoin to; ~**d** *a* adjoining, adjacent, contiguous.

Angriff *m* attack, aggression, assault; (*Luft*~) air-raid; (*Anfang*) undertaking; *in* ~ *nehmen* to begin with, to set about, to tackle; to start; ~ *abfangen* to counter an attack; ~ *abschlagen* to repulse an attack; ~ *im Tiefflug aero* low level attack; *e-n* ~ *machen* to raid, to attack; ~**sboot** *n* assault boat, storm boat, invasion boat; ~**sflug** *m aero* attack mission, sweep; ~**skrieg** *m* invasive war, offensive war, aggressive war, war of aggression; ~**slust** *f* aggressiveness; ~**swaffen** *f pl* weapons *pl* of offence; ~**szeit** *f* zero hour; ~**sziel** *n* target; objective.

angrinsen *tr* to grin at.

Angst *f* anxiety, fear, fright; agony; *sl* funk; *es ist mir angst* I am afraid of; ~ *machen* to alarm, to frighten; ~**geschrei** *n* cry of anguish; ~**hase** *m* anxious person; ~**kauf** *m* scare buying; ~**meier** *m* coward; ~**röhre** *f fam* stove-pipe; ~**schweiß** *m* cold sweat; ~**verkauf** *m* panic sale; ~**voll** *a* anxious, fearful, full of fear.

ängst|igen *tr* to anguish, to strike with fear; *r* to be alarmed at, to fret about s. th.; to be anxious about s. o.; ~**igung** *f* frightening, anguish; ~**lich** *a* anxious, timid; careful; ~**lichkeit** *f* anxiousness; timidity, fearfulness; scrupulousness.

angucken *tr* to peep at, to look at.

anhaben *irr tr* to wear; to have on; *Stiefel* ~ to go in boots; *man kann ihm nichts* ~ there is no getting at (*od* round) him; *das kann mir nichts* ~ that can't do me any harm; *jdm etw* ~ to find s. th. against s. o., to do s. th. to s. o.

anhaften *itr* to be attached to, to adhere to, to stick to.

anhaken *tr* to hook on; (*abstreichen*) to tick off.

Anhalt *m* (*Stütze, Träger*) support; hold; prop; (*Anzeichen*) symptom, indication; (*Schutz*) protection; (*Unterlage, Beweis*) fact, evidence; (~*spunkt*) data *pl*; clue; *e-n* ~ *gewähren* to give a clue to; *ich habe keinen* ~ *dafür, daß* I have no grounds to suppose that; ~**en** *irr tr* to check, to stop, to arrest; *jdn zu etw* ~~ to admonish, to urge s. o. to; to accustom; *itr* (*andauern*) to continue, to last; (*aufhören*) to stop, to discontinue; (*um etw* ~~) to apply for; to sue for, to solicit; (*Heirat*) to propose to; *sich an etw* ~~ to hold to, to cling to; ~**end** *a* continuous, constant, assiduous; ~**spunkt** *m* essential point; clue, criterion.

Anhang *m* appendix, supplement; ~ *e-s Testaments* codicil; (*Gesetz*) amendment, schedule; (*Vertrag*) annex; (*Partei*) followers *pl*, party; adherents *pl*, hangers-on *pl*, ranks *pl*, *Am* column; (*Wechsel*) endorsement; *als* ~ *beifügen* to schedule, to annex; ~**en** *irr itr* to cling to, to be attached to, to stick to, to adhere to.

anhäng|en *tr* to hang on; (*jdm etw aufhängen*) to palm off s. th. upon s. o.; (*jdm etw* ~~) to make insinuations against s. o.; *tele* (*Hörer*) to ring off, to hang up; (*hinzufügen*) to append; to fasten, to annex, to add; ~**er** *m* adherent, follower, partisan, disciple; (*Gepäck*) tag, ticket, tie-on label; (*Schmuck*) locket; (*an Motorrad*) side-car; (*an Auto, Straßenbahn, Fahrrad*) trailer; ~**ig** *a* adhering, cleaving; *jur* pending; *e-n Prozeß* ~~ *machen* to enter a lawsuit, to initiate proceedings against; ~~ *sein* (*vor Gericht*) to be pending; ~**lich** *a* attached to, faithful to; ~**lichkeit** *f* attachment, adherence; fidelity; ~**schloß** *n* padlock; ~**schild** *n* (*am Gepäck*) luggage tag; ~**sel** *n* appendix, appendage; label.

anhauchen *tr* to breathe on; *die Finger* ~ to blow o.'s fingers; (*anherrschen*) to snub; *angehaucht a* inspired by.

anhäuf|en *tr* to pile up, to accumulate; (*sammeln, hamstern*) to hoard up; *sich* ~ to increase; ~**ung** *f* accumulation; aggregation; (*Waren*) hoarding.

anheben *irr tr* to lift up; *itr* to begin.

anheften *tr* to affix to, to attach to; (*mit Reißnagel*) to tack on; (*mit Stecknadel*) to pin to; to sew on.

anheilen *itr* to heal on (*od* up).

anheim|eln *itr* to remind of home; ~**elnd** *a* cosy, snug; ~**fallen** *irr itr* to fall to; ~**stellen** *tr* to leave; to submit to.

anheischig *a: sich* ~ *machen* to promise, to pledge o. s.

anheizen *tr* to kindle a fire, to begin to heat, to heat up.

anherrschen *tr* to snub s. o.

anheuern *tr* to hire.

Anhieb *m: auf* ~ at the first attempt, at the first go-off.

Anhöhe *f* rising ground, height, elevation; hill.

anhören *tr* to listen to, to give an ear to; *sich schlecht* ~ to sound badly.

Anilin *n* aniline.

anim|alisch *a* animal; ~**ieren** *tr* to stimulate; to encourage; to incite; ~**osität** *f* animosity, hatred.

Anis *m* anise; ~**zucker** *m* sugared anise.

ankämpfen *itr* to fight (*gegen* against).

Ankauf *m* purchase, acquisition; ~**en** *tr* to buy, to purchase; *sich* ~*en* to settle at a place; ~**spreis** *m* cost-price; *zum* ~*spreis* at (the first) cost; ~**ssumme** *f* purchase-money.

Anker *m* anchor; *el* armature; (*Seil-, Drahtverankerung*) stay; *vor* ~ *gehen* to (cast) anchor, to moor; *vor* ~ *liegen* to ride at anchor; *den* ~ *lichten* to weigh anchor; *den* ~ *kappen* to cut the cable; *den* ~ *einholen* to heave in the cable; *vor* ~ *treiben* to drag the anchor; ~**boje** *f* anchor-buoy; ~**geld** *n* anchorage; ~**grund** *m* sounding, anchor-hold; ~**mast** *m* (*Luftschiff*) anchor tower, mooring-mast; ~**n** *itr* to (cast) anchor; ~**platz** *m* anchoring-place, berth; ~**seil**, ~**tau** *n* cable; ~**uhr** *f* lever-watch; ~**wicklung** *f el* armature winding; ~**winde** *f* capstan; ~**zeichen** *n* anchor-buoy.

anketten *tr* to chain to.

ankitten *tr* to cement to, to putty.

Anklage *f jur* charge, trial, arraignment; accusation, prosecution; (*öffentliche* ~) bill of indictment; (*Richter-, Ministeranklage*) impeachment; (*Belastung*) charge; (*Anklageschrift*) indictment; ~ *erheben* to bring an accusation against s.o.; to file a charge against s. o.; ~ *vertreten* to prosecute; *unter* ~ *stehen* to be under an accusation; *unter* ~ *stehen wegen* to be on trial for; to be charged with; *unter* ~

stellen wegen to accuse of, to indict for, to charge with; **~bank** *f* (prisoner's) dock; **~n** *tr* to accuse of; (*belasten*) to charge with, to indict for, to put into the dock, to impeach for; **~erhebung** *f* act of indicting; **~punkt** *m* count (of indictment); **~rede** *f* speech for the prosecution; **~schrift** *f* (bill of) indictment; **~zustand** *m: in ~~ versetzen* to indict, to impeach.

Ankläger *m*, ***~in*** *f* accuser, indicter; (*Kläger*) plaintiff; *öffentlicher ~* public prosecutor.

anklammern *tr* to cramp; *r* to cling to.

Anklang *m mus* accord; (*Beifall*) applause, sympathy; (*Billigung*) approbation; (*Ähnlichkeit*) reminiscence; *~ finden* to excite interest; to meet with approval.

ankleben *tr* to glue to, to gum on, to paste on; (*Plakate*) to stick on, *Am* to post (a bill); *itr* to stick to.

ankleid|en *tr u. r* to dress; **~espiegel** *m* dressing-glass, toilet mirror; **~ezimmer** *n* dressing-room; (*Theater*) attiring-room.

ankleistern *tr* to paste on.

anklingeln *tr tele* to ring up, to call, to phone up.

anklingen *irr itr fig* to bear resemblance to, to remind of.

anklopfen *itr* to knock at; *bei jdm ~* to sound s. o. about s. th.

anknipsen *tr* (*Licht*) to switch on.

anknöpfen *tr* to button (on).

anknüpf|en *tr* to knit to, to fasten with a knot; *fig* to begin; to establish; *itr* (*an etw ~~*) to refer to; to resume; *Beziehungen ~~* to establish relations; *ein Gespräch ~~* to enter into conversation; *Unterhandlungen ~~* to enter into negotiations; **~ungspunkt** *m* starting point, connecting link.

ankommen *irr itr* to arrive, to come, to get to; *wohl oder übel ~* to fare well or ill; *unrecht ~* to find o. s. mistaken; *es ~ lassen auf* to take o.'s chance, to run the risk; *es kommt darauf an* it is of importance, it depends; *es kommt mich eine Lust an* I take a fancy to; *es kommt mir schwer an* I find it difficult; *es kommt nur auf Sie an* I leave it to you; *darauf kommt es nicht an* it does not matter; *es kommt nicht auf den Preis an* it's not a matter of price; *darauf kommt es gerade an* this is just the point; **Ankömmling** *m* new-comer, arrival; (*Fremder*) stranger.

ankoppeln *tr* to couple (to *od* together).

ankreiden *tr* to chalk up, to score; *tief angekreidet* deeply in debt; *jdm etw ~* to make s. o. pay for s. th.

ankündig|en *tr* to announce to, to give notice of; to advertise, to publish; **~ung** *f* declaration, announcement; advertisement.

Ankunft *f* arrival; **~sbahnsteig** *m* arrival platform; **~sstation** *f* **terminus;** **~szeit** *f* time of arrival.

ankurbel|n *tr* to crank up; *fig* to boost; to stimulate; **~ung** *f* (*Wirtschaft*) pump priming; reconstruction; **~ungskredit** *m* reconstruction credit.

anlachen, anlächeln *tr* to laugh at; to smile at.

Anlage *f* (*Entwurf, Plan*) plan, draft, outline, sketch, design; arrangement, disposition; (*e-s Gartens*) laying-out; (*Park*) pleasure ground; (*Beilage*) annexed paper, enclosure, the enclosed, the annexed; *laut ~* as annexed; (*Drama*) plot; (*Bau*) construction; (*Geld~*) investment; (*Fabrik~*) plant, installation, works *pl*; (*Steuer~*) tax, duty; (*Neigung*) disposition, tendency, vein; (*Begabung*) gift, talent, ability; **~n** *f pl* grounds *pl*, greens *pl*.

anland|en *itr* to land, to touch at; **~ung** *f* disembarkation.

anlangen *itr* to arrive; *tr* (*betreffen*) to concern, to relate, to regard; *was mich anlangt* as for my part; **~d** *adv* concerning, with regard to.

An|laß *m* occasion, cause, motive, inducement; *~~ geben* to give occasion to, to give rise to; *ohne allen ~~* for no reason at all; *allen ~~ dazu haben* to have every reason for; *aus ~~* on occasion; *es besteht kein ~~* there is no occasion (to); *e-e Gelegenheit zum ~~ nehmen* to take occasion to; *dem ~~ entsprechen* to fit the occasion; **~lassen** *irr tr* (*in Gang setzen*) to set going, to start; (*nicht ausziehen z. B. Jacke*) to keep on; to leave on; *jdn übel ~~* to address s. o. harshly; *sich gut ~~* to promise well; (*Stahl*) to temper, to draw, to anneal; **~lasser** *m* (electric) starter; **~läßlich** *prp* occasionally, on the occasion of.

Anlauf *m* start, run; (*auf Skisprungschanze*) inrun (*od* approach); *aero* (*beim Start*) take-off run; (*Angriff*) onset, attack; dash, rush; *e-n ~ nehmen* to take a run; **~en** *irr tr, itr* to run, to rush upon; (*Schiff*) to touch, to call at, to serve, to put into (a port); *med* to swell; (*Schulden*) to mount up; (*Zinsen*) to accrue; *rot ~en* to blush; (*übel*) to run a bad chance; (*wachsen*) to accumulate, to increase, to rise; (*beschlagen*) to become dim, to tarnish; *Stahl blau ~en lassen* to blue steel; *Motor ~en lassen* to run up, to start; **~hafen** *m* port of call; **~zeit** *f* running-in period.

Anlaut *m* initial sound.

anläuten *tr, itr tele* to ring up, to give a ring, to call (up), to (tele)phone.

anlegen *tr* to put, to lay on (*od* against); *typ* to feed; (*anziehen*) to put on; (*erbauen*) to construct; (*Straße*) to lay out; (*gründen*) to establish, to found; (*Kartei*) to set up; (*Garten*) to lay out; (*bezahlen*) to pay, to spend; *Feuer ~* to set fire to; *Geld ~* to invest money; *Gewehr ~* to take aim at, to aim at; *Ketten ~* to chain, to fetter s. o.; *Hand ~* to set hands to; *Trauer ~* to go into mourning; *es auf etw ~* to aim at s. th., to make it o.'s object; *die letzte Hand ~* to give the finishing touch to; *itr* (*Schiff*) to land, to take berth, to lie alongside; **Anlegebrücke** *f* landing-stage, landing-place, landing, jetty.

anlehnen *tr u. r* to lean against; to recline; (*Tür*) to leave ajar; *fig sich ~ an* (*ein Beispiel*) to follow (the example of).

Anleihe *f* loan; *Staats~* government (*od* public) loan; *langfristige ~* long term loan; *eine ~ lanzieren* to float a loan; *e-e ~ unterbringen* to place a loan; *e-e ~ vermitteln* to negotiate a loan; *e-e ~ zeichnen* to subscribe a loan; *bei jdm eine (kleine) ~ aufnehmen* to borrow money of s. o.; *e-e ~ auflegen* (*od aufnehmen*) to raise a loan; **~ablösung** *f* redemption of a loan; **~geschäft** *n* loan business; **~kapital** *n* loan capital; **~papier** *n* bond; government stock.

anleimen *tr* to glue on.

anleit|en *tr* to guide to, to lead, to direct, to instruct; **~ung** *f* guidance, leading, instruction, direction; key.

anlernen *tr* to train, to teach; to break in; (*Arbeiter*) to train on the job; *angelernter Arbeiter* semi-skilled worker, on-the-job trained worker.

anliefer|n *tr* to supply; **~ung** *f* supply.

anliegen *irr itr* (*angrenzen*) to lie near, to border on; (*Kleider*) to sit close; to fit well; *~ n* interest, request, demand; **~d** *a* adjoining, adjacent; (*Kleider*) tight; (*beiliegend*) enclosed; **Anlieger** *m* (*Nachbar*) neighbo(u)r; (*Fluß*) riverain.

anlock|en *tr* to entice, to attract, to allure; **~ung** *f* allurement, enticement.

anlöten *tr* to solder to.

anlügen *irr tr* to lie to s.o.'s face, to tell s. o. a falsehood.

anmachen *tr* to bind, to attach, to fix, to tie; (*Salat*) to dress; *Feuer ~* to kindle a fire.

anmalen *tr* to paint (over).

Anmarsch *m* approach, advance; **~ieren** *itr* to march on, to advance; **~straße** *f*, **~weg** *m* (road of) approach.

anmaß|en *tr u. r* to assume, to pretend to, to presume, to claim; **~end** *a* arrogant, presumptuous; **~ung** *f* pretention, arrogance; (*widerrechtliche*) assumption; (*Vermessenheit*) presumption; (*Unverschämtheit*) insolence.

anmeld|en *tr* to announce, to give notice of, to report; *sich zu etw ~en* to apply for s. th.; (*Vermögen, Zoll*) to declare; (*Gespräch*) to book, to place; *Konkurs ~en* to file o.'s petition, to present a petition of bankruptey; *Patent ~en* to take out (*od* to apply for) a patent; *sich ~en lassen* to send in o.'s name (*od* card); **~ung** *f* announcement, notification, application; declaration; (*Konkurs*) petition; report, registration; **~~sstelle** *f* registry office; **~~sformular** *n* registration form; (*bei Stellenbewerbung*) form of application.

anmerk|en *tr* to (re)mark, to note; to observe; *sich ~~ lassen* to show, to betray, *fam* to let on; **~ung** *f* note, remark; observation; annotation, foot-note; *Ausgabe mit ~~en* annotated edition; *~~en machen* to comment on; to append notes.

anmessen *irr tr* to (take) measure for; to fit, to adapt.

anmuster|n *tr* to enrol(l), to enlist (soldiers); *mar* to sign on; **~ung** *f* enrol(l)ment, enlistment.

Anmut *f* grace, elegance, sweetness; **~en** *tr* to interest, to please; *seltsam ~~* to seem somewhat curious (*od* strange); **~ig** *a* graceful, charming, gentle.

annageln *tr* to nail on to.

annähen *tr* to sew on to.

annäher|n *r* to approach, to draw near; **~nd** *a* approximat(iv)e, roughly; **~ung** *f* advance, approach; *math* approximation; **~~sgrad** *m* degree of approximation; **~~sweise** *adv* approximately; **~~szünder** *m* proximity fuse.

Annahme *f* acceptance, reception; (*von Kindern, von Meinungen*) adoption; (*e-s Schülers*) admission; (*Gesetz*) passing of a bill, *Am* passage of a law; (*Dienstbote*) engagement; (*Vermutung*) assumption, supposition; *alles spricht für die ~* there is every indication to believe; **~stelle** *f* receiving-office; **~vermerk** *m* acceptance; **~verweigerung** *f* non-acceptance.

Annalen *f pl* annals *pl*, records *pl*.

annehm|bar *a* acceptable, admissible; (*Preis*) reasonable; **~en** *irr tr* to take, to accept; (*Besuch*) to receive, to see; (*Gestalt*) to assume a shape; (*Gesuch*) to admit; (*an Kindes Statt*) to adopt; (*Fall*) to suppose, to take for granted; (*einräumen*) to allow; (*zu-

stimmen) to consent; (*Antrag*) to carry, to adopt; (*Gesetz*) to pass; (*Gewohnheit*) to contract; (*Wechsel*) to accept, to hono(u)r; (*sich zulegen*) to assume; *e-n Auftrag ~en* to undertake an order; *e-e Religion ~en* to embrace a religion; *sich e-r Sache ~en* to take care of; *sich jds ~en* to interest o. s. for; to assist s. o.; *Vernunft ~en* to listen to reason; to stand up for; **~lichkeit** *f* charm, pleasure, convenience, advantage, agreeableness; *~~en des Lebens* comforts of life.

annektieren *tr* to annex.

annieten *tr* to rivet to.

Annonce, **annoncieren** *siehe Anzeige, anzeigen.*

annullier|en *tr* to annul, to quash; to cancel; **~ung** *f* annulment.

Anode *f* anode; **~nbatterie** *f* anode (*od* dry) battery, B battery; **~nkreis** *m* anode-circuit; **~nspannung** *f* anode tension; **~nstrahlen** *m pl* anode rays *pl*; **~nstrom** *m* anode current; **~nverlust** *m* anode loss; **~nwiderstand** *m* plate-resistance.

anöden *tr* to bore.

anonym *a* anonymous.

Anorak *m* (*Windbluse*) anarak, anorak.

anordn|en *tr* to dispose, to direct, to order, to arrange, to regulate; **~ung** *f* direction, disposal, order, arrangement, regulation, instruction; *~~en treffen* to give orders.

anpacken *tr* to lay hold of, to seize, to grasp; (*Arbeit*) to tackle.

anpass|en *tr* to accommodate, to adapt, to fit; (*Anzug*) to try on; *fig* to adjust; *r* to conform to, to adapt o. s. to; **~ung** *f* adaption; adjustment; accommodation; **~~sfähig** *a* adaptable; **~~sschwierigkeiten** *f pl* difficulties of adjustment; **~~svermögen** *n* adaptability.

anpeil|en *tr* to take a bearing; **~ung** *f radio* bearing.

anpflanz|en *tr* to cultivate, to lay out; **~ung** *f* plantation; settlement.

anpflaumen *tr* to pull s. o.'s leg.

anpflöcken *tr* to peg, to pin; to tether (to).

anpicken *tr* to peck.

anpöbeln *tr* to abuse, to vilify.

anpochen *itr* to knock at, to tap.

Anprall *m* bounce, collision; shock, impact; **~en** *itr* to bound against.

anprangern *tr* to pillory.

anpreis|en *irr tr* to praise, to extol, to commend, to recommend strongly; (*Reklame machen für*) to boom, to boost; **~ung** *f* praise, recommendation; (*durch Reklame*) booming, puffing.

Anprob|e *f* fitting-on; **~ieren** *tr* to try on.

anpumpen *tr* to borrow money of s.o., to touch (for money).

anrat|en *itr, tr* to advise, to recommend, to suggest; **~en** *n* recommendation; advice; *auf mein ~~* at my suggestion (*od* advice).

anrauchen *tr* to blow smoke against; (*e-e Zigarre*) to begin to smoke; (*bräunen*) to colo(u)r a pipe; (*neue Pfeife*) to season, to break in (a new pipe).

anrechnen *tr* to charge to s. o.'s account; (*gutschreiben*) to credit; *fig* to impute, to ascribe to; *etw hoch ~* to value greatly, to rate high, to appreciate; *etw zu hoch ~* to overrate, to overcharge; *sich etw zur Ehre ~* to consider it an hono(u)r; *sich etw zum Ruhme ~* to glory in.

Anrecht *n* right, claim, title (to).

Anrede *f* address; (*feierlich*) harangue; (*in Briefen*) salutation; **~n** *tr* to speak to, to address; (*ansprechen*) to accost, to harangue.

anreg|en *tr* to stir, (*stärker*) to stimulate, to incite; (*geistig*) to inspire; (*vorschlagen*) to hint, to suggest; **~end** *a* interesting, exciting, stirring; stimulating; **~ung** *f* stimulation, (*stärker*) excitement; (*Vorschlag*) suggestion, hint, (*erstmalig*) initiative.

anreicher|n *tr* to enrich; to strengthen; to concentrate; (*mit Kohlenstoff*) to carburize; **~ung** *f* enrichment; concentration.

anreiben *irr tr* to rub, to grind.

anreihen *tr* to string, to add; *r* to join; (*anstehen*) to queue up, to form a row, *Am* to line up.

anreiß|en *irr tr* to tear off; to cut into; (*anzeichnen*) to trace, to mark, to draw; **~er** *m* (*Anpreiser*) tout.

Anreiz *m* incitement, stimulus; inducement, edge, spur; **~en** *tr, itr* to incite, to induce; to animate; **~ung** *f* incitement, animation.

anrempeln *tr* to jostle against s. o.

anrennen *irr itr* to run against, to tumble against; *tr mil* to charge, to attack.

anricht|en *tr* (*Mahlzeit*) to prepare, to dress, to serve; (*verursachen*) to cause, to make; (*Schaden*) to do damage; *da haben Sie was Schönes angerichtet* you have made a fine muddle (*od* mess) of it; *es ist angerichtet* dinner is served; **~e(tisch)** *m* dresser, sideboard.

an|rollen *tr, itr* to roll against, to roll along; **~rosten** *itr* to begin to rust, to rust on.

anrüchig *a* disreputable, notorious, ill-famed, infamous.

anrücken *tr* to bring near, to advance; *itr* to approach; **~** *n* approach, advance.

anruf|en *irr tr* (*wegen e-r Sache*) to call on s. o. for s. th.; (*anflehen*) to implore, to invoke; (*ein Schiff*) to hail; *tele* to ring up; *Am auch* to phone; (*ein höheres Gericht*) to appeal to a higher court; (*zum Zeugen*) to call to witness; **Anruf** *m* shout, calling; appeal; *tele* call.

anrühr|en *tr* to touch, to handle; (*Farbe*) to temper; (*Küche*) to mix.

ansäen *tr* to sow.

Ansag|e *f* declaration, announcement; (*Kartenspiel*) bidding; *radio* lead-in, announcement; **~en** *tr* to declare, to announce, to notify; (*Spiel*) *Sie sagen an* it is your turn to call; **~er** *m radio* announcer; **~eraum** *m radio* announcing room.

ansamm|eln *tr* (*Vermögen*) to amass; (*aufhäufen*) to heap up, to pile up; to accumulate; to collect; *sich ~~* to collect, to congregate, to gather; **~lung** *f* collection, accumulation; concentration; congregation; (*von Menschen*) crowd.

ansässig *a* settled, resident, domiciled.

Ansatz *m* added piece; (*Musikinstrument*) lengthening piece, mouthpiece; (*Anfang*) onset, start; (*Anlage*) disposition; (*Rechnung*) arrangement; (*Abschätzung*) valuation, estimation, taxation; (*Niederschlag*) sediment; *aero* (*Flächen~*) wing-root; **~bad** *n chem* initial bath; **~punkt** *m* starting point; foothold, toe-hold; **~rohr** *n* (*Mundstück*) nozzle, mouthpiece; **~stück** *n* attached part.

ansaug|en *tr* to suck in; to take in; **~leitung** *f mot* intake manifold; **~periode** *f mot* suction stroke; **~rohr** *n* suction pipe; **~schalldämpfer** *m mot* intake silencer; **~ventil** *n* inlet (*od* suction) valve.

anschaff|en *tr* to procure, to purchase; to purvey; *r* to supply o. s. with s. th.; **~ung** *f* acquisition, purchase; provisions, supplies *pl*; **~~skosten** *pl* prime cost; **~~spreis** *m* first cost, purchase-price, initial outlay.

anschalten *tr* (*Licht, Radio*) to switch on, to plug in; (*mit Drahtleitung*) to wire up.

anschau|en *tr* to view, to look at, to consider; **~lich** *a* conspicuous, obvious, evident, clear, graphic, vivid; **~lichkeit** *f* distinctness, clearness; **~ung** *f* intuition, view, opinion; (*Vorstellung*) perception, notion, idea; **~~smaterial** *n* illustrative material, (*Filme*) audio-visual aids *pl*; **~~sunterricht** *m* intuitive instruction, object teaching; **~~svermögen** *n* intuitive power; **~~sweise** *f* point of view.

Anschein *m* appearance, probability; *dem ~e nach* to all appearance; *den ~ haben* to seem to be, to have the air of; *sich den ~ geben* to pretend to be, to try to pass for; **~end** *a* apparent, seeming.

anschicken *r* to set about, to begin.

anschieben *irr tr* to shove on; to push against; (*Kegel*) to have the first bowl.

anschielen *tr* to leer at.

anschießen *irr itr* to shoot first, to have the first shot; *chem* to crystallize; *tr* (*verwunden*) to wound; *tech* to join; (*Gewehr ~*) to test a gun.

anschirren *tr* to harness.

Anschlag *m* stroke; (*Musik*) touch; (*Plakat*) poster, placard; bill; (*Notiz, Bekanntmachung*) notice, announcement; (*Plan*) design, plan, project; (*~ auf jds Leben*) attempt (on s. o.'s life); (*Steuer*) assessment; (*Komplott*) plot; (*Gewehr*) present; (*Berechnung*) calculation, estimate; computation; (*Hockey*) bully; *tech* (*Hemmung*) stop, catch, base; *in ~ bringen* to take into account; *e-n ~ machen* to plot against; to have a design upon; **~en** *irr tr* to strike at, to knock at; to ring (the bell); (*an die Wand*) to affix, to fasten, to post; (*Gewehr*) to take aim at; (*abschätzen*) to rate, to value; (*Ton*) to give the key-note; *itr* (*von Hunden*) to bay, to bark; (*wirken*) to operate, to succeed; (*von Arznei*) to take effect; *es schlägt bei ihm an* it agrees with him; *zu hoch ~~* to overestimate; *zu niedrig ~~* to underrate; **~brett** *n*, **~tafel** *f* notice-board, *Am* tack-board, bulletin board; **~säule** *f* advertisement-pillar, *Am* advertising pillar, *Am* pillar post; **~wert** *m* estimated value; **~winkel** *m* (*Tischler*) back square; **~zettel** *m* poster, bill.

anschleichen *irr itr: angeschlichen kommen* to steal near.

anschließen *irr tr* to chain, to fix with a lock; (*anfügen*) to join, to annex, to link; (*verbinden*) to connect; *sich ~* to attach, to join; (*Kleider*) to fit close.

Anschluß *m* (*Einverleibung*) annexation; (*freiwilliger ~*) joining, union; (*Gas~, Wasser~, Netz~*) supply; (*Beitritt zu Bund*) accession, entrance to; (*von Zug u. Telefon*) connection, connexion; *im ~ an* in connection with, with reference to; *den ~ verfehlen* to miss the connection (*od* the connecting train); *~ an e-n Zug haben* to run in connection with another train; *den ~ erreichen* to catch o.'s connection, to make connections; *~ erhalten tele* to get through; *~ suchen* to seek company; **~bahn** *f* *rail* branch (*od* feeder) line; **~bahnhof** *m* railway junction; **~dose** *f el* wall socket, junction-box, contact box; **~flansch** *m* joining flange; **~gleis** *n rail* sidings *pl*; **~kabel** *n el* connection cable; *tele* subscriber's cable; **~klemme** *f* connecting terminal; **~kontakt** *m* connection contact; **~leiter** *m* lead (terminal); **~leitung** *f tele* subscriber's line; **~linie** *f aero* feeder line; **~nummer** *f tele* call number; **~rohr** *n* service pipe; **~schnur** *f* connecting cord, flexible cord, flex, cord; **~station** *f rail* junction; **~stecker, ~stöpsel** *m* plug; **~stück** *n* joining piece; **~zug** *m* corresponding train, connection.

an|schmeicheln *r* to curry favo(u)r with; **~schmieden** *tr* to forge on; (*Verbrecher*) to fetter, to chain up; **~schmiegen** *r* to cling to; to snuggle up (*an* to), to nestle (*an* against); (*passen, eng anliegen*) to fit; to fit in with; **~schmiegsam** *a* pliant, supple; *fig* (*nachgebend*) yielding, compliant; **~schmiegsamkeit** *f* suppleness, pliancy; *fig* compliance; **~schmieren** *tr* to (be)smear, to grease; *fig* to cheat.

anschnall|en *tr* to buckle on; **~gurt** *m* (*im Flugzeug*) safety-belt.

anschnauzen *tr* to blow up; to snub; to bully, *Am* to bawl (out).

an|schneiden *irr tr* to begin to carve; to cut, to begin to cut; to start (cutting); (*Frage*) to broach (*od* to start) a subject; **~schnitt** *m* first cut, outside slice.

anschrauben *tr* to screw to (*od* on).

anschreiben *irr tr* to write down, to put to s.o.'s account; *bei jdm wohl angeschrieben sein* to stand well with s.o.; to be in s.o.'s good books, to be in good with s.o.; *e-e Zeche ~* to score up; *~ lassen* to take on credit.

anschreien *irr tr* to shout at.

Anschrift *f* address; **~endrucker** *m* addressograph.

anschuhen *tr* to shoe.

anschuldig|en *tr* to accuse (of), to charge (with), to incriminate; **~ung** *f* charge, inculpation, incrimination; *falsche ~~* false accusation.

anschüren *tr* to kindle, to stir (up).

anschütten *tr* to heap up against, to fill up.

anschwärz|en *tr* to blacken; *fig* to calumniate, to slander.

anschweißen *tr* to weld on.

anschwell|en *irr itr* to swell; (*nach oben*) to rise, to increase; **~ung** *f* swelling, rising; *med* swelling, tumo(u)r.

anschwemm|en *tr* to wash ashore, to deposit; *angeschwemmtes Land* alluvion; **~ung** *f* wash; (*Land*) alluvion; (*Geröll*) alluvium.

anschwindeln *tr* to swindle; to lie to.

ansehen *irr tr* to look at; (*prüfend*) to consider, to examine; (*sehr genau*) to scan; (*besichtigen*) to go to see, to view; *mit ~* to witness; *etw ~ für* to take, to think for; *~ als* to look upon as, to regard as; *man sieht es ihm an, daß ...* one can see by his face that; *scheel ~* to look askance; *jdn scharf ~* to stare at; *man kann ihm sein Alter nicht ~* he doesn't show his age; *von oben herab ~* to look down on; *sich ~* to see; to take a look at; *sich etw genau ~* to take a good look at; *~ n* appearance; sight, look, aspect; (*Achtung*) consideration, respect, regard, reputation; *ohne ~ der Person* without distinction of s.o.; *dem ~ nach* to judge from appearances; *von ~ kennen* to know by sight; *sich ein ~ geben* to put on airs; *im ~ stehen* to enjoy esteem, to be held in respect.

ansehnlich *a* conspicuous, notable, important; considerable; (*Mittel*) large; **~keit** *f* conspicuousness, importance.

Ansehung *f*: *in ~* in consideration of, in regard of.

anseilen *tr* (*Bergsteigen*) to rope.

ansengen *tr* to singe.

ansetzen *tr* to set on, to join, to fasten; (*annähen*) to sew on; (*auf Rechnung*) to charge in a bill; (*Preise*) to fix; (*schätzen*) to estimate, to tax, to rate; (*Termin*) to set (a date), to appoint, to fix; (*zufügen*) to add (to); *chem* to mix, to prepare; (*Blätter*) to put forth; (*Fleisch*) to put on; (*Fett*) to grow fat; (*Waffe etc aufnehmen*) to take up; (*Verkauf*) to put up; *itr* to make an onset; (*zum Sprung*) to take a run; (*probieren*) to try, to begin.

Ansicht *f* sight, view; *fig* opinion, notion, outlook; (*kritische ~en*) criticisms *pl*; *tech* (*Zeichnung*) drawing, (*Riß*) sectional view; (*von der Vogelperspektive*) bird's eye view; (*im Grundriß*) plan view; *nach meiner ~* in my opinion; *zur ~* on approval; **~ig** *a*: *~~ werden* to get a sight of, to catch sight of; **~skarte** *f* picture (post)card; view card; **~ssache** *f* matter of opinion; **~ssendung** *f* delivery on approval.

ansied|eln *tr* to establish; to colonize, to settle; **~(e)lung** *f* establishment, settlement; colony; **~ler** *m* settler, colonist.

Ansinnen *n* request, desire, demand; *ein ~ stellen* to put a request to; to demand s.th. from s.o.

*

Anspann *m* draught-cattle, team; **~en** *tr* to put to (horse), to harness (*an* to), to hitch up (the horses); (*Feder, Bogen*) to bend, to stretch; *fig* (*Kredit*) to strain, to stretch; (*anstrengen*) to exert, to strain; *alle seine Kräfte ~en* to exert every nerve; **~ung** *f* exertion, strain, tension.

anspeien *irr tr* to spit at.

anspiel|en *itr* to lead (at cards); (*Sport*) to lead off; to play first; *auf etw ~en* to allude to, to hint at; **~ung** *f* hint, reference; allusion.

anspinnen *irr tr* to spin to; *fig* to plot; *e-e Unterhaltung ~* to start a conversation; *r* to begin, to start (secretly); (*Freundschaft*) to spring up.

anspitzen *tr* to point, to sharpen.

ansporn|en *tr* to put spurs to; *fig* to spur (on), to stimulate, to incite; *~ m* spur, incitement, impetus, stimulus.

An|sprache *f* address, speech; **~sprechen** *irr tr* to address, to speak to; *jdn um etw ~* to ask s.o. for s.th.; (*von Bettler*) to solicit; (*gefallen*) to interest s.o.; to please; **~~d** *a* pleasing, engaging, attractive.

an|sprengen *tr* to sprinkle with a liquid; *itr angesprengt kommen* to come up at full gallop; **~springen** *irr tr, itr* to begin to jump; to jump up at; *mot* to start; *angesprungen kommen* to come skipping along.

anspritzen *tr* to (be)sprinkle; (*mit Schmutz*) to splash, to spray.

Anspruch *m* claim, demand, pretension; (*Rechts~*) title; *~ machen auf* to lay claim to; *in ~ nehmen* to claim, to demand, to make use of, to call on; *es nimmt meine Zeit zu sehr in ~* it takes up too much of my time; *e-n ~ aufgeben* to waive a claim, to renounce a claim; *e-n ~ geltend machen* to assert a claim; *~ haben auf* to be entitled to, to have a title to; **~slos** *a* unpretending, unassuming, modest; **~slosigkeit** *f* modesty, unpretentiousness; **~svoll** *a* fastidious; pretentious; (*genau*) exacting; (*übertrieben*) fussy.

anstacheln *tr* to goad on; *fig* to instigate, to spur on, to incite, to stimulate.

Anstalt *f* (*Vorbereitung*) preparation, arrangement; (*Maßnahmen*) measures *pl*; *med* asylum; (*Einrichtung*; *Schule*) institution, establishment; institute, school; *~ zu etw machen* to make preparations for; *~en treffen* to provide for.

Anstand *m* decency, propriety, decorum; (*Bedenken*) hesitation; (*Einwand*) objection; (*Aufschub*) delay; (*Jagd*) stand; *~ nehmen* to hesitate, to pause, to doubt; *auf den ~ gehen* to go (a) shooting; **~sbesuch** *m* formal call; **~sdame** *f* chaperon; **~sgefühl** *n* tact; **~shalber** *adv* for decency's sake, for propriety's sake; **~slos** *adv* without hesitation, without objection; **~swidrig** *a* indecent, improper; unseemly.

anständig *a* decent, proper, respectable; (*Summe*) handsome; **~keit** *f* decency; respectability.

anstarren *tr* to gaze at, to stare at.

anstatt *prp, conj* instead of.

anstaunen *tr* to stare at, to gaze at.

anstechen *irr tr* to prick; (*Faß*) to broach, to tap.

ansteck|en *tr* to stick on; (*mit Nadeln*) to pin on; (*Ring*) to put on; (*Zigarre*) to light, (*Feuer*) to set fire to; (*mit e-r Krankheit*) to infect (with a disease); *angesteckt werden* to catch a disease, to take an infection; **~end** *a* contagious, infectious, catching; *~ende Krankheit* infectious disease; **~ung** *f* contagion, infection; **~ungsstoff** *m* virus, infectious matter.

anstehen *irr itr* (*zögern*) to linger, to hesitate; (*passen*) to become, to fit; (*dauern*) to last, to remain; (*Schlange stehen*) to stand in a queue, to queue (up), *Am* to stand in line, to line up; *~ lassen* to put off, to delay.

ansteigen *irr itr* to mount, to ascend, to rise; to increase.

anstell|en *tr fig* to employ, to appoint, to engage, to hire, to take on; *nicht angestellt sein* to be unemployed; (*Maschine in Gang setzen*) to start; (*Heizung, Radio etc*) to turn on; (*vorbereiten*) to prepare, to arrange, to bring about; (*veranlassen*) to cause; *Betrachtungen ~~* to speculate (*über* on); *Untersuchung ~~* to examine s.th.; (*Versuch*) to make a trial; (*Vergleich*) to draw a comparison; (*Streiche*) to do mischief; *r* to behave, to set about s.th.; *sich ~~ als ob* to pretend, to act as if, to make believe that; (*Schlange stehen*) to queue up for, *Am* to line up for; to stand (*od* wait) in line; *stellen Sie sich nicht so an!* don't make such a fuss! **~ig** *a* able, skil(l)ful, handy; clever; **~ung** *f* employment, appointment; (*Stelle*) place, post, position, employ; *e-e feste ~~* a permanent place.

anstemmen *r* to stem against; *fig* to oppose.

ansteuer|n *tr mar* to head for, to make for; to close; **~ungsfeuer** *n aero* location beacon, landing beacon.

Anstich *m* broaching; (*vom Obst*) worm-bite.

ansticken *tr* to embroider on.

anstieren *tr* to stare at.

anstift|en *tr* to cause, to incite, to plot, to instigate; (*zum Meineid*) to suborn; **~er** *m* author, instigator, plotter; *jur* accessory before the fact, abettor, prime mover; **~ung** *f* incitement, instigation.

anstimmen *tr* to strike up, to intone, to tune up.

Anstoß *m* collision; *fig* impulse; (*Hindernis*) impediment, hesitation; (*Ärgernis*) offence, scandal; (*Fußball*) kick-off; (*Hockey*) bully; *ohne* ~ without hesitation; (*geläufig*) fluently; ~ *erregen* to give offence, to scandalize s. o; ~ *nehmen* to take offence, to be scandalized at s. th.; *Stein des* ~*es* stumbling-block; **~en** *irr tr, itr* to knock, to push on; (*an etw*) to stumble against; to bump against; (*berühren*) to touch; (*leicht* ~~) to nudge; (*Fußball*) to kick-off; (*Eishockey*) to face off; ~~ *bei* to give offence (*Am* offense) to, to offend; (*jdn verletzen*) to hurt s. o., to shock s. o.; to scandalize s. o.; (*zögern*) to hesitate; (*angrenzen*) to adjoin; *mit den Gläsern* ~*en* to touch glasses; *mit der Zunge* ~*en* to lisp; *auf die Gesundheit* ~*en* to drink o.'s health; **~end** *a* contiguous, adjacent.

anstößig *a* offensive, shocking; **~keit** *f* shockingness.

anstreben *tr* to aspire to, to strive for (*od* after).

anstreich|en *irr tr* (*Haus*) to paint; (*tünchen*) to whitewash; (*Fehler*) to underline; (*am Rande des Buches*) to mark; to tick off; **~er** *m* whitewasher, house-painter; **~pinsel** *m* paintbrush.

anstreifen *tr* to graze, to brush against, to touch slightly.

anstreng|en *tr* to exert; to fatigue; *alle Kräfte* ~*en* to strain every nerve; *zu sehr* ~*en* to overwork; *e-n Prozeß* ~*en* to bring in an action against; *sich* ~*en* to exert o. s.; *angestrengte Aufmerksamkeit* close attention; **~~d** *a* hard, strenuous; (*für die Augen*) trying to the eyes; **~ung** *f* exertion, effort; (*große*) strain; (*plötzliche, kurze beim Laufen, Rudern*) spurt.

Anstrich *m* (*das Anstreichen*) painting, colo(u)ring; (*die Farbe selbst*) coat of paint, colo(u)r, varnish; *fig* air, touch; (*Anschein*) appearance; (*geringe Kenntnisse*) smattering; (*Violinspiel*) stroke; *etw e-n neuen* ~ *geben* to give a new colo(u)r to; **~technik** *f* paint practice, coating practice.

anstricken *tr* to knit on (to); to join by knitting; (*Strümpfe*) to foot.

anströmen *itr* to flow towards; *angeströmt kommen* to crowd near, to flock.

anstücke(l)n *tr* to piece (on); to patch; to connect; (*länger machen*) to lengthen.

An|sturm *m* assault, (up)rush, attack, onset; (*Bank*) run; **~stürmen** *itr* to rush against, to (make an) assault upon, to assail, to storm, to charge.

ansuchen *tr: um etw bei jdm* ~ to apply to s. o. for, to sue for, to request; ~ *n* application, suit, request; *auf* ~ at the request, on (the) application of.

Antarkt|is *f* the Antarctic; **~isch** *a* antarctic.

antasten *tr* to touch, to handle; (*verletzen*) to hurt, to question; *ein Recht* ~ to infringe upon a right.

Anteil *m* share, portion, part; dividend, interest; (*Zuteilung*) allotment; *fig* sympathy, interest; ~ *nehmen* to sympathize with; ~ *haben* to participate in; **~ig** *a* proportionate; **~nahme** *f* interest, sympathy; **~schein** *m* share.

antelephonieren *tr* to ring up, to call (up), to give a ring, to (tele)phone.

Antenne *f radio* aerial, antenna, (*für Fernsehsender*) stack; (*Fernsehempfangs*~) dipole aerial; (*Gemeinschafts*~) community antenna; (*Kurzwellen*~) short-wave aerial; (*Rundstrahl*~) omni-directional aerial; (*Richt*~) beam aerial; *eingebaute* ~ built-in antenna; *abgeschirmte* ~ screened aerial; (*Zimmer*~) indoor aerial; (*Hoch*~) outdoor (*od* roof) aerial; (*Netz*~) main aerial; (*Peil*~) direction finder aerial; (*Rahmen*~) frame aerial; (*Schlepp*~) trailing aerial; (*Sende*~) transmitting aerial; **~nableitung** *f* down-lead; **~nabstimmung** *f* aerial (*od* antenna) tuning; **~nanlage** *f* radiating system; **~naufhängung** *f* aerial suspension; **~ndraht** *m* aerial (*od* antenna) wire; (*Litze*) stranded aerial wire; **~nkapazität** *f* antenna capacity; **~nkreis** *m* antenna circuit; **~nleitung** *f* aerial lead; **~nmast** *m* aerial mast, antenna pole; **~nnetz** *n* aerial network; **~nturm** *m* wireless mast; radio tower; **~nzuleitung** *f* down-lead, lead-in.

Anthrazit *m* anthracite, hard coal.

antik *a* antique; **~e** *f* antiquity; **~enkabinett** *n* collection of antiquities.

Antilope *f* antelope.

Antimon *n* antimony; **~artig** *a* antimonial; **~blei** *n* lead-antimony alloy; **~verbindung** *f* antimony compound; **~zinnober** *m* kermisite.

antipath|isch *a* antipathetic; **~ie** *f* antipathy, aversion (*gegen* to).

antippen *tr* to tap.

Antiqu|a *f* Roman type; **~ar** *m* (*Buchhändler*) second-hand bookseller; (*Möbel etc*) dealer in antiques; **~ariat** *n* second-hand bookshop; **~arisch** *a* second-hand.

Antisemit *m* anti-Semite; **~isch** *a* anti-Semitic; **~ismus** *m* anti-Semitism.

Antlitz *n* face, countenance.

antraben *itr* to trot on.

Antrag *m* offer, proposition, proposal; (*Angebot, Offerte*) offer, tender; (*Ansuchen*) application, request, appeal; (*bei Gericht*) petition; (*Anzeige*) relation; (*Vorschlag*) proposal; proposition; (*im Parlament*) motion; *auf* ~ upon application; *e-n* ~ *annehmen* to agree upon a motion; *e-n* ~ *ablehnen* to reject a motion; *e-n* ~ *einreichen bei* to file an application with; *e-n* ~ *einbringen* to move for, to bring forward a motion; *e-n* ~ *durchbringen* to carry a motion; *jdm e-n Heirats*~ *machen* to propose to, to make a proposal to; **~en** *irr tr, itr* to propose; **~sformular** *n* application-form; **~steller** *m* applicant, appellant; (*im Parlament*) mover; (*bei Gericht*) petitioner.

antrauen *tr* to marry to; *angetraut* wedded.

antreffen *irr tr* to meet with, to find.

antreib|en *irr tr* to drive, to push on; (*Schiff*) to propel; *fig* to urge on, to impel; *itr* to drift ashore; **~er** *m* slave-driver, pace-maker; **~e-System** *n* (*bei der Arbeit*) sweating-system, slave-driving system.

antreten *irr tr* to enter (upon an office); to set out on (a journey); *e-e Erbschaft* ~ to take possession of an inheritance; *itr zum Tanz* ~ to take o.'s place (for dancing); *mil zum Appell* ~ to fall in, *Am* to line up for the roll call.

Antrieb *m* impulse, motive; (*treibende Kraft*) drive, moving force, power; *aus eigenem* ~ of o.'s own free will; **~skraft** *f* propulsive power; **~skupplung** *f* driving clutch; **~smittel** *n* (*in Motor*) working fluid; **~smotor** *m* driving motor; **~sriemen** *m* driving-belt; **~swelle** *f* drive shaft.

Antritt *m* beginning; (*Reise*) start, setting out; (*Amt*) entrance upon an office; (*Erbschaft*) taking possession of; (*Regierungs*~) accession; **~sbesuch** *m* first visit; **~srede** *f* inaugural speech; **~srolle** *f* first part; **~svorlesung** *f* inaugural lecture.

antun *irr tr* to put on (clothes); (*Ehre*) to do s. o. hono(u)r; *jdm etw* ~ to do to; to inflict; (*beleidigen*) to insult; (*verletzen*) to injure; *sich etw* ~ to commit suicide; *Schaden* ~ to cause damage (to); to do harm (to); *sich Zwang* ~ to restrain o.s.; *es jdm* ~ to bewitch s.o.; *Gewalt* ~ to do violence to; *sich ein Leid* ~ to lay (violent) hands on o. s.

Antwort *f* answer, reply; *in* ~ *auf* in reply to; *baldige* ~ an early answer; *umgehende* ~ an answer by return of mail; ~ *bezahlt* (*Telegramm*) answer prepaid (*Abk* A. P.); *abschlägige* ~ refusal; *Rede und* ~ *geben* to account for; *keine* ~ *schuldig bleiben* never to be at a loss for an answer; **~en** *itr, tr* to answer, to reply; *drahtlich* ~~ to reply by wire; **~karte** *f* reply card; **~schein** *m* reply-coupon; **~schreiben** *n* answer, reply.

anver|trauen *tr* to confide to, to trust; *sich jdm* ~~ to entrust o. s. to; to confide in, to open o.'s heart to; *jdm etw* ~~ to put s. th. into s.o.'s hands, to commit to the charge of; **~wandt** *a* related to.

anvisieren *tr* to sight (at).

anwachsen *irr itr* to grow to (*od* up), to take root; *fig* (*zunehmen*) to increase; ~ *n* increase.

Anwalt *m* (*allgemein*) lawyer, advocate; *Am* attorney; *schott* writer, law agent; (*plädierend vor Gericht*) barrister; *Am* counsel(l)or; *schott* advocate; (*außerhalb des Gerichts, Parteianwalt*) solicitor; *Am* (private) attorney; (*als Rechtsbeistand des Angeklagten*) counsel (for the defence); *sich e-n* ~ *nehmen* to retain the services of a barrister; *fig* (*Verfechter*) champion, defender; **~schaft** *f* attorneyship, the bar; **~sfirma** *f* solicitor's firm; **~sgebühren** *f pl* attorney's fees, solicitor's costs *pl*; **~stätigkeit** *f* advocacy.

anwand|eln *tr* to come over; to befall; **~lung** *f* fit; (*Neigung*) inclination, impulse; (*geringer Wunsch, der nicht zum Handeln führt*) velleity.

anwärmen *tr* to warm gently.

An|wartschaft *f* expectancy, claim; reversion; **~wärter** *m* expectant, applicant; (*auf Staatsdienst*) candidate, aspirant.

anwehen *tr* to blow upon.

anweis|en *irr tr* (*zuweisen, z. B. Geld*) to assign; to allot; (*Platz im Theater*) to show; (*anleiten*) to instruct, to direct; to order; **~ung** *f* (*Geld*) assignment; (*Zahlungs*~~) cheque, *Am* check, draft; (*Post*~~) money-order; (*Belehrung*) instruction, direction, method.

anwend|bar *a* applicable, available for, practicable; **~barkeit** *f* applicability, practicableness; **~en** *irr tr* to employ; (*Medizin; Gesetz*) to apply; to make use of; *alles* ~*en* to exert o.'s utmost strength; *angewandte Chemie* applied chemistry; **~ung** *f* application; use; **~~sbereich** *m* scope.

anwerb|en *irr tr mil* to enlist, *Am* to draft, to levy, to enrol(l); **~ung** *f* enlistment, levy, recruiting.

anwerfen *irr itr* to throw first; (*Motor*) to set in motion, to start; to crank up; to throw into gear.

Anwesen *n* (real) estate, property, premises *pl*; farm; **~d** *a* present; ~*de ausgenommen* the present company

excepted; *sehr verehrte ~de!* Ladies and Gentlemen! **~heit** *f* presence; **~heitsappell** *m mil* roll call.
anwidern *tr* to disgust.
anwohn|en *itr* to live next, to dwell near; (*e-r Versammlung*) to be present at, to attend (a meeting); **~er** *m* neighbo(u)r.
Anwuchs *m* increase, growth.
Anwurf *m* (*Handball*) throw-off, first throw; (*Verputz*) plastering; (*Rauhputz*) roughcast; *fig* (*Vorwurf*) reproach.
anwurzeln *itr* to take root; *wie angewurzelt fig* as if rooted to the ground.
Anzahl *f* number, quantity; **~en** *tr* to pay a first instal(l)ment; to pay on account; to pay a deposit; **~ung** *f* instal(l)ment, payment on account, part-payment, deposit.
anzapfen *tr* to tap, to pierce casks; *jdn ~* to borrow money of.
Anzeich|en *n* mark; symptom; token; sign; (*Vorbedeutung*) omen, presage, augury, foretoken, foreboding; **~nen** *tr* to mark, to note.
Anzeig|e *f* notice; *com* (*Avis*) advice; (*Bekanntmachung*) announcement; (*bei der Polizei*) information, denunciation; (*in der Presse*) advertisement (*Abk* ad); **~en** *tr* to announce, to inform, to notify, to give notice of, to intimate; (*in der Zeitung*) to advertise; (*bei Gericht*) to file an information against, to inform against, to lodge a complaint against, to denounce; *den Empfang ~en com* to advise the receipt; **~enannahme** *f* advertising office; **~enberechnung** *f* estimating of advertising; **~enblatt** *n* advertising journal; **~enbüro** *n* advertising agency; **~end** *a* indicative, demonstrative; **~enfachmann** *m* ad-man; **~enpreis** *m* ad-rate; **~ensatz** *m* job-work; **~enschreiber** *m* ad-writer; **~entarif** *m* advertisement-rates *pl*; **~enwesen** *n* (*Reklame*) advertising; **~epflichtig** *a* notifiable; to be bound to report; **~er** *m*, **~erin** *f* informer, informant; indicator; (*Zeitung*) advertiser; (*Anzeigetafel bei Spielen*) score-marker; **~ung** (*e-s Diebes etc*) denunciation.
anzettel|n *tr* to plot, to scheme, to instigate, to contrive; **~ung** *f* intrigue, plot.
anzieh|en *irr itr, tr* to draw, to pull on; (*Kleider*) to put on; (*Schraube*) to pull, to tighten, to turn home; (*zitieren*) to quote; *fig* to attract; (*beim Spiel*) to move (first); (*Preise*) to rise; *sich ~en* to dress; **~end** *a* attractive, interesting; **~ung** *f* attraction; **~~skraft** *f* attractive power; (*der Erde*) gravitation; **~~spunkt** *m* centre of attraction.
Anzug *m* approach, entering; *~ des Mannes* suit; (*ganze Bekleidung*) dress, apparel; (*vornehm*) attire; *Gesellschafts~* full dress, evening-dress; *Jagd~* hunting-suit; (*Spiel*) opening move; *im ~e sein* to be approaching, to be brewing, to be coming up, to be in the offing.
anzüglich *a* invective, offensive, satirical; personal; **~keit** *f* invective.
anzünd|en *tr* to light, to kindle; *ein Streichholz ~~* to strike a match; **~er** *m* lighter; (*Gas~*) gas-igniter, gas-lighter.
anzweifeln *tr* to doubt, to contest.
apart *a* singular, odd, uncommon; (*interessant*) interesting, remarkable; charming, *Am* cute.
apathisch *a* apathetic, indifferent.
Apfel *m* apple; *der ~ fällt nicht weit vom Stamm* he is a chip of the old block; *in den sauren ~ beißen* to (have to) swallow a bitter pill; **~auflauf** *m* apple soufflé; **~baum** *m* apple-tree; **~brei** *m*, **~mus** *n* apple-purée; **~gelee** *n* applejelly; **~kern** *m* pip; **~kloß** *m* apple-dumpling; **~kuchen** *m* apple-tart; **~küchle** *n pl*, **~krapfen** *m pl* apple-fritters *pl*; **~pastete** *f* apple-pie; **~most** *m* (new) cider; **~säure** *f* malic acid; **~schale** *f* apple-paring; **~schimmel** *m* dapple-grey horse; **~schnitte** *f* apple-slice; **~sine** *f* orange; **~sinenmus** *n* marmalade; **~sinensaft** *m* orangeade; **~wein** *m* cider.
Apostel *m* apostle; **~amt** *n* apostleship; **~geschichte** *f* Acts *pl* of the Apostles; **apostolisch** *a* apostolical.
Apostroph *m* apostrophe.
Apotheke *f* chemist's (*seltener* apothecary's) shop; pharmacy; *Am* (*nicht nur ~, sondern auch Verkauf von Getränken, Rollfilmen, Speiseeis, Zeitschriften usw*) drug-store; (*Armen~*) dispensary.
Apotheker *m* chemist; pharmacist; *Am* apothecary; druggist (*siehe Apotheke*); **~waren** *f pl* drugs *pl*, druggist's articles *pl*.
Apparat *m* apparatus; (*Vorrichtung*) appliance; *fam* gadget, contraption; (*Einrichtung*) contrivance; (*Werkzeug*) tool, implement, instrument; (*mechanische Anlage*) device; (*Triebwerk, Mechanismus*) mechanism; (*Gerät*) set; unit; (*Photo~*) camera; (*Radio~, Rundfunk~*) (wireless) set, receiver, *Am* radio (set); (*Grammophon~*) gramophone, *Am* phonograph; (*Telefon~*) telephone, *Am* phone; *am ~! tele* speaking! *bleiben Sie am ~! tele* hold the line, please! **~ur** *f* apparatus; outfit, equipment, appliance.
Appell *m mil* roll-call; *fig* (*Anrufung*) appeal; **~ant** *m jur* appellant; party appealing; **~ation** *f* appeal; **~~sgericht** *n* court of appeal; **~ieren** *itr* to appeal to.
Appetit *m* appetite (*auf etw* for s. th.); *fig* (*Wunsch, Verlangen*) desire, longing; craving, *Am fam* yen; *e-n guten* (*od gesunden*) *~ haben* to have a good appetite; *~ bekommen* to get an appetite; *~ machen* to give a good appetite; *den ~ reizen* to stimulate o.'s appetite; *den ~ verlieren* to lose o.'s appetite; **~lich** *a* inviting, delicious; appetizing; *ein ~~er Geruch kam aus der Küche* an appetizing smell came from the kitchen; (*verführerisch, sauber, nett*) tempting, nice; **~losigkeit** *f* want of appetite; **~sbissen, ~shappen** *m* sandwich.
applau|dieren *itr* to applaud; to cheer; to clap o.'s hands; **~s** *m* applause; *das Publikum zum ~~ hinreißen* to bring down the house; *der Schauspieler hatte großen ~~* the actor was loudly applauded.
apportieren *tr* (*Hund*) to retrieve, to fetch.
appret|ieren *tr* (*Stoff*) to dress, to finish; **~ur** *f* dressing, finish; **~~masse** *f* sizing material; **~~mittel** *n* (*Stoff*) finishing liquid; (*Papier*) sizing.
approbier|en *tr* to approve; **~t** *a* certified; duly qualified; *~ter Arzt* doctor, medical practitioner.
Aprikose *f* apricot; **~nbaum** *m* apricot-tree.
April *m* April; *der 1. ~* All Fools' Day; *jdn in den ~ schicken* to send s. o. upon a fool's errand; **~narr** *m* April fool; **~scherz** *m* April-fish.
Aquarell *n* aquarelle; water-colo(u)r (painting); **~ieren** *itr* to paint in water-colo(u)r(s); **~malerei** *f* water-colo(u)r painting.
Äquator *m* equator, line; **~ial** *a* equatorial.
Äquivalent *n* equivalent.
Ar *n* are (*1 a* = $^1/_{100}$ *ha* = *etwa* 120 square yards).
Ära *f* era.
Arab|er *m* Arab, Arabian; **~ien** *n* Arabia; **~isch** *a* Arabian, Arabic.
Arbeit *f* work; labo(u)r; (*mühselige*) toil; (*Plackerei*) drudgery; (*Mühe*) effort, pains *pl*, trouble; *el* (*Energie*) energy; (*geistige*) brain-work; (*Beschäftigung*) employment, job; (*aufgegebene*) task; (*Beschwerde*) trouble; (*schriftliche*) paper, essay; composition; (*bestellte*) order in hand; (*erhabene*) raised work, relief; (*Ausführung e-r ~*) workmanship, piece of work; *e-e gute* (*schlechte*) *~* a fine (bad) piece of work; (*Tätigkeit, Geschäft*) business; (*Hand~*) manual labo(u)r; (*Anstrengung, mil Arbeitsdienst*) fatigue; (*monotone, anstrengende ~*) grind; (*~ außerhalb des Hauses*) out-door work; (*Fabrikat, Fabrikation*) make; (*Schul~, Haus~*) home-work, lesson; (*Putzfrauen~*) char(e), *Am* chore; *bauliche ~en pl* works *pl*; *staatliche* (*öffentliche*) *~en pl* public works *pl*; *laufende ~en pl* routine work; *ohne ~* unemployed, *Am auch* jobless; *gewöhnliche ~* ordinary labo(u)r; *gelernte ~* skilled work; *ungelernte ~* unskilled work; *schwere ~* hard work; *in voller ~* in full swing; *das Recht auf ~* the right to work; *die ~ wiederaufnehmen* to resume work; *~ ausführen* to execute work; *in seiner ~ aufgehen* to put o.'s heart into o.'s work; *in ~ bringen* to put in work; *sich von der ~ drücken* to shirk work; *die ~ einstellen* to strike, to walk out; to stop work; *sich ganz der ~ ergeben fam* to keep o.'s nose to the grind stone; *jdm ~ geben* to give s. o. work (*od* employment); *in ~ geben* (*Auftrag*) to put an order in hand; *an die ~ gehen* to set (*od* to go) to work; *feste ~ haben* to be in good work; *keine ~ haben* to be out of work; *viel ~ haben* to have much to do, to have much work on hand; *von seiner Hände ~ leben* to live by o.'s manual labo(u)r; *~ leisten* to do work; *jdm viel ~ machen* to put s. o. to great inconvenience; *sich an die ~ machen* to get to work, to go about o.'s work, *Am* to get busy; *in ~ nehmen* to take in hand; *die ~ niederlegen* to down tools; *die ~ scheuen* to shirk work; *bei der ~ sein* to be at work; *in ~ sein* (*Sache*) to be in hand; *auf ~ sein* to be out at work; *in ~ stehen* to be employed; *die ~ stockt* the work is at a standstill; *~ suchen* to look for a job; *sich seiner ~ widmen* to apply o. s. to o.'s work; *~ verrichten* to do work; *~ verursachen* to make work; *jdm e-e ~ zuweisen* to set s. o. a task; *um wieviel Uhr gehen Sie morgens zur ~?* what time do you get to (your) work in the morning? *die Dorfbewohner verkaufen ihre ~en* the villagers sell their work; *~ macht das Leben süß* no sweet without sweat; *immer nur ~ u. keine Erholung* all work and no play; **~en** *itr, tr* to work (*an* at), to be at work (*an* on); (*schwer ~~*) to work hard, to labo(u)r, to toil, to drudge; *für jdn ~~* to work for s. o.; *auf etw hin~~* to work away at; (*beschäftigt sein*) to be employed; (*Geschäfte machen mit*) to deal in; *mit jdm* (*geschäftlich*) *~~* to do business with s. o.; *in e-r Firma ~~* to work in a firm; *im Akkord ~~* to work by the piece; *an etw ~~* to be engaged on s. th., to be busy with; (*betreiben, einwirken*

auf) to operate; *(machen, herstellen)* to make, to manufacture, to do; *(Maschine)* to run, to work; to operate; *(funktionieren)* to function; *die Maschine arbeitet gut* the machine works well; *(Teig)* to rise; *(Holz)* to be working; *(Wein etc gären)* to ferment; *Kapital ~~ lassen* to invest; *sich tot ~~* to work o. s. to death; *sich durch den Schnee ~~* to work o.'s way through the snow; *bei welchem Schneider lassen Sie ~~?* who is your tailor? *wer nicht ~~ will, soll auch nicht essen* no mill, no meal; *die ~~den Klassen* the working classes *pl.*

Arbeiter *m* workman, *bes. Am* worker; labo(u)rer; hand; help; *(Erdarbeiter, Schipper)* navvy; *(Fach~)* specialist, skilled worker; *(Hafen~)* dockyard labo(u)rer, docker, *Am* longshoreman; *(Handwerker)* artisan, (handi)craftsman; *(Gattungsbegriff)* labo(u)r; *(in Industrie)* operative; *(Handlanger)* handy-man, *Am* roustabout; *(an Maschine)* operator; *gelernter ~* skilled worker; *(Schwer~)* heavy worker; *(Schwerst~)* heaviest worker; *(schwer, körperlich)* drudge; *ungelernter ~* unskilled worker, hand, help; *angelernter ~* semi-skilled worker, *Am* on-the-job trained worker; *geistiger ~, ~ der Stirn* brain-worker; *seine ~ aussperren* to stand off o.'s workmen, *Am* to lay off o.'s workmen; *seine ~ entlassen* to dismiss o.'s workmen, *fam* to sack *(Am* to fire) o.'s workmen; **~ameise** *f* worker ant; **~angebot** *n* labo(u)r supply; **~annahmestelle** *f* employment office; **~ausschuß** *m* worker's committee; **~ausstand** *m* strike; **~bedarf** *m* man-power requirement; **~bevölkerung** *f* working classes *pl;* **~bewegung** *f* labo(u)r movement; **~einsatz** *m* labo(u)r employment, *Am* man-power management; **~familie** *f* worker's family, working class family; **~frage** *f* labo(u)r-question; **~führer** *m* labo(u)r leader; **~fürsorge** *f* labo(u)r welfare; work relief; **~gewerkschaft** *f* trade-union, trades-union; **~gewinnbeteiligung** *f* profit sharing; **~in** *f* workwoman, working-woman; *(Fabrik~~)* factory-girl, factory-woman; **~klasse** *f* working class; **~kolonne** *f* gang of workmen; **~mangel** *m* shortage of labo(u)r; **~partei** *f (in England)* Labour Party; **~rat** *m* work's council, wage-earner's council; **~schaft** *f* working class(es *pl*); workmen *pl;* *(Belegschaft)* personnel, crew; **~schutz** *m* protection of the working classes; **~siedlung** *f* labo(u)r colony; **~stand** *m* working-class; **~überschuß** *m* labo(u)r surplus; **~unfallgesetz** *n* workmen's compensation act; **~unfallversicherung** *f* workmen's compensation insurance; **~verband** *m* working men's trades-union; **~verein** *m* workmen's union; **~versicherung** *f* workmen's insurance; **~vertreter** *m* labo(u)r representative; **~vertretung** *f* labo(u)r representation; **~viertel** *n* working-class district; **~wohnung** *f* workman's dwelling.

Arbeit|geber *m* employer, master, *Am* boss; *(Betriebsführung)* management; **~~anteil** *m (Sozialbeiträge)* employer's contribution; **~~schaft** *f* employers *pl, Am* management; **~~verband** *m* employer's association; **~nehmer** *m* employee *(Am auch* employe), wage-earner; **~~verband** *m* employee's association; **~~vertretung** *f* employee representation; **~sam** *a (fleißig)* industrious, diligent; *(eifrig, tätig)* busy, active; **~~keit** *f* industry, diligence; activity; **~sparend** *a* labo(u)r-saving; *e-e ~~e Vorrichtung* labo(u)r-saving device.

Arbeits|abkommen *n* labo(u)r convention; **~ablauf** *m* sequence of operation; **~amt** *n* Labour Office, *Am* Labor Exchange; **~angebot** *n* labo(u)r supply, supply of job; **~antritt** *m* taking up of work; **~anweisung** *f* operational instruction; **~anzug** *m* overall(s) fatigue-dress; **~aufsicht** *f* labo(u)r inspection; **~aufwand** *m* expenditure of work; energy; **~ausfall** *m* loss of work caused by absenteeism; **~ausschuß** *m* working committee, advisory committee, study group, *Am* executive committee; **~bedingungen** *f pl* working condition; **~bereich** *m* scope, field of activity; *(e-r Maschine)* range, capacity; **~beschaffung** *f* procurement *(od* provision) of work; **~beschränkung** *f* work curtailment; **~beutel** *m* work-bag; **~buch** *n* workman's passport *(od* pass-book); **~bummelei** *f* shirking in factories; **~dienst** *m* labo(u)r service; *mil* fatigue duty; **~eifer** *m* ardo(u)r for work; **~einheit** *f* unit of work; **~einkommen** *n* earned income; **~einsatz** *m* use of labo(u)r; man-power control; **~einstellung** *f* stoppage of work; *(der Arbeitnehmer)* strike, walk-out, *Am* turn-out; *(der Arbeitgeber)* lock-out, *Am* shut-down; **~entgelt** *n* compensation for work, remuneration; **~erlaubnis** *f* permit to work; **~ersparnis** *f* labo(u)r saving; **~ertrag** *m* produce of labo(u)r; **~fähig** *a* able to work; **~feld** *n* sphere of action, field of activity; **~folge** *f* sequence of operations; **~frieden** *m* industrial peace; **~fürsorge** *f* work relief; **~gang** *m* operation; stage, phase; process; **~gebiet** *n* field of activity; **~gemeinschaft** *f* study group; work-shop group; class-team; working combine; **~genehmigung** *f* work permit; **~gerät** *n* tools *pl,* implements *pl,* utensils *pl;* **~gericht** *n* labo(u)r *(od* industrial) court; **~grube** *f mot* working pit; **~haus** *n* penitentiary, *Am* workhouse; **~hub** *m mot* working *(od* expansion) stroke; **~kamerad** *m* fellow workman; **~kittel** *m* overall(s); **~kommando** *n* service group, *Am* work detail; *mil* fatigue party; **~korb** *m* work-basket; **~kosten** *pl* labo(u)r charges *pl;* **~kraft** *f* working power; worker; **~kräfte** *f pl* labo(u)r *mit sing;* hands *pl;* workmen *pl;* **~lager** *n* labo(u)r camp; **~last** *f* load of work; **~leistung** *f* efficiency of labo(u)r; *(Maschine)* capacity, power; *(Fabrik)* output; **~lenkung** *f* direction of labo(u)r; **~lohn** *m* wages *pl,* pay; **~los** *a* out of work, unemployed; **~lose(r)** *m* unemployed, *Am* jobless; **~losenunterstützung** *f* unemployment compensation *(od* pay *od* relief *od* benefit), dole; *~~ bekommen* to be on the dole; **~~sempfänger** *m* beneficiary of unemployment insurance; **~losenversicherung** *f* unemployment insurance; **~losigkeit** *f* unemployment; **~mann** *m* workman, labo(u)rer; member of labo(u)r service; **~markt** *m* labo(u)r market; **~methode** *f* operating method; **~minister** *m* Minister of Labour, *Am* Secretary of Labo(u)r; **~ministerium** *n* Labo(u)r Ministry; *engl* Labour Department of the Board of Trade, *Am* Department of Labor; **~nachweis** *m* *Am* Labor Exchange; **~paß** *m* labo(u)r passport; **~pause** *f* recess, intermission, interval; **~plan** *m* operation plan, work plan; *(in der Produktion)* production plan; manufacturing schedule; working scheme; **~platz** *m* working place; job; **~prozeß** *m (Verfahren)* working method; manufacturing process; **~raum** *m* workroom; *(Bureau)* office, bureau; **~scheu** *a* work-shy, shirking work, lazy; unwilling to work; *~~ f* aversion to work, laziness, **~schicht** *f* shift (night-shift, *aber* day-turn); **~schutz** *m* safety provisions for workers; **~sperre** *f* lock-out; **~streitigkeit** *f* labo(u)r conflict; **~stunden** *f pl* working hours *pl,* man hours *pl;* **~suchanzeige** *f* job-wanted ad; **~tag** *m* working-day, *Am* workday; **~tagung** *f* labo(u)r conference; **~tier** *n fig* glutton for work; **~unfähig** *a* unfit for work, incapable for work; *(dauernd)* disabled, invalid; **~unterricht** *m (Schule)* learning by doing; **~verdienst** *m* wage-earnings *pl;* **~verfahren** *n* working method; **~verhältnis** *n (berufsrechtlich)* working condition; *(im Betrieb)* labo(u)r condition; **~vermittlung** *f* employment agency; **~vermögen** *n* energy; power; output; **~versäumnis** *f od n* absenteeism; **~verweigerung** *f* refusal to work; **~verwendungsfähig** *a mil* fit for labo(u)r duty only; **~vorgang** *m* operation; procedure; **~weise** *f (e-s Mannes)* practice; *(e-r Maschine)* mode of working, (method of) operation; function; **~wiederaufnahme** *f* resumption of work; **~woche** *f* working week; **~zeit** *f* work(ing) time, working hours *pl;* *(Produktion).* production time; *(Maschinen)* run; **~ ersparnis** *f* saving in time; **~zeug** *n* tools *pl;* **~zimmer** *n* study; studio; **~zwang** *m* compulsory labo(u)r.

Archäolog *m* archaeologist; **~ie** *f* archaeology; **~isch** *a* archaeologic(al).

Arche *f* ark.

Archipel *m* archipelago.

Architekt *m* architect; **~onisch** *a* architectonic; **~ur** *f* architecture.

Archiv *n* archives *pl,* record-office, records *pl;* **~ar** *m* keeper of the archives, archivist, recorder; Master of the Rolls; **~stelle** *f* record-office.

Areal *n* ground, area.

Arena *f* arena; *(Zirkus~)* ring; *(Stierkampf~)* bull-ring.

arg *a* bad, malicious, wicked, evil, mischievous; serious; *fam (sehr)* very, awful; *jdm ~ mitspielen* to deal harshly with s. o.; *ein ~er Fehler* a grave error, a gross mistake; *~ verfahren mit* to be severe with; *~ mißhandeln* to treat cruelly; *das ist zu ~* that's going too far; *~ n* malice, harm; *im ~en liegen* to be far behind, to be in a bad way; *er dachte nichts ~es dabei* he meant no harm by it; *ohne ~* without malice; **~list** *f* craft(iness); **~listig** *a* crafty, cunning; malicious; deceitful; **~los** *a* harmless; innocent; *(ohne Argwohn)* unsuspecting; *(aufrichtig)* candid; *(offen)* frank; **~losigkeit** *f (Unschuld)* innocence; **~willig** *a* ill-willed, malevolent; **~wohn** *m* mistrust, suspicion; *(Besorgnis)* apprehension; *~~ hegen, ~~ schöpfen* to suspect; **~wöhnen** *tr* to suspect; **~wöhnisch** *a* suspicious *(gegen* of); apprehensive; distrustful.

Argentin|ien *n* Argentina, the Argentine (Republic); **~(i)er** *m* Argentine; **~isch** *a* Argentinian, Argentine.

Ärger *m* annoyance, vexation, anger; aggravation, irritation; worry; *aus ~* out of spite; *er hat nichts als ~* he gets nothing but aggravation; *seinen ~ auslassen* to let out o.'s spite; **~lich** *a* vexed, angry; *(Ärger erregend)* annoying, vexating, provoking; *das ist ~~* that is a nuisance; *wie ~~!* how vexing! **~n** *tr* to vex, to annoy, to irritate; *(beleidigt sein)* to take offence;

(*belästigen*) to bother; to pester; to plague; *jdn* ~~ to put s. o.'s back up; *r* to feel vexed at, to be angry at; **~nis** *n* scandal, offence; vexation; ~~ *erregen* to create a scandal; *öffentliches* ~~ *geben* to give public offence.
Arie *f mus* aria; air, song.
Ari|er *m* Aryan; **~sch** *a* Aryan; *nicht* ~~ non-Aryan; **~sieren** *tr* to Aryanize.
Aristokrat *m* aristocrat; **~ie** *f* aristocracy; **~isch** *a* aristocratic.
Arithmet|ik *f* arithmetic; **~isch** *a* arithmetical.
Arkti|s *f* the Arctic; **~sch** *a* arctic, northern; ~~*e Kaltluft* polar air.
arm *a* poor; (*bedürftig*) indigent; (*ohne Geld*) penniless, impecunious, broke; (*in Not*) needy; (*in Bedrängnis*) hard-up; (*mager*) lean; (*von schlechter Qualität*) low grade; ~ *an* poor in, destitute of, void of; ~ *machen* to impoverish; ~ *sein* to be poor; ~ *werden* to become poor; *ein ~er Schlucker* a poor fellow (*od* devil); ~ *wie e-e Kirchenmaus* as poor as a church-mouse; **~e** *m* poor man; *die ~en pl* the poor; **~enanstalt** *f*, **~enhaus** *n* almshouse, workhouse, *Am* poorhouse; **~enkasse** *f* relief fund; poor-box; **~enpflege** *f* poor-relief; **~~r** *m* almoner; **~enrecht** *n jur* poor-law; *unter* ~~ *klagen* to sue in forma pauperis; **~enunterstützung** *f* relief; **~enwesen** *n* charity organization; **~esündergesicht** *n*, **~esündermiene** *f* hang-dog look; **~esünderglocke** *f* bell tolled during an execution; **~selig** *a* poor; (*elend*) miserable, wretched; (*bemitleidenswert*) pitiable; (*schäbig*) shabby; (*erbärmlich*) mean, paltry; **~seligkeit** *f* poorness; misery; shabbiness; wretchedness; paltriness.
Arm *m* arm; (*Fluß~*) tributary; (*Leuchter*) branch; (*Waage*) beam (of scales); (*e-s Rades*) spider; ~ *in* ~ arm in arm; *unter die ~e greifen* to help, to assist; *sich jdm in die ~e werfen* to take refuge with; *jdn in die ~e schließen* to clasp s. o. in o.'s arms; *die ~e in die Seite stemmen* to set o.'s arms akimbo; *jdm in die ~e laufen* to bump into s. o.; **~band** *n* (*Schmuck*) bracelet; (*Band*) wristband; (*Uhr*) watch band, watch strap; **~banduhr** *f* wrist-watch; **~bein** *n anat* humerus; **~beuge** *f* bend of elbow; **~binde** *f* (*Erkennungszeichen*) badge; (*Verband*) sling, bandage; **~blätter** *n pl* (*Schneiderei*) dress-shields *pl*; **~bruch** *m* fracture of the arm; **~brust** *f* cross-bow; **~lehne** *f* arm (of chair), elbow-rest; **~leuchter** *m* chandelier; **~loch** *n* sleeve-hole; **~schiene** *f med* splint; (*Rüstung*) vambrace; **~schlinge** *f* arm sling; **~sessel, ~stuhl** *m* arm-chair, easy chair; **~spange** *f* bracelet; **~voll** *m* (*Menge*) armful.
Armatur *f tech* (*Beschlag*) armature; fittings *pl*; (*Ventile*) valves *pl*, cocks *pl*; (*Verbindungsstücke*) connections *pl*, mountings *pl*; *el* (*Magnet*) armo(u)r; **~enbrett** *n* (*Auto*) dash-board, instrument panel.
Armee *f* army; **~befehl** *m* operation order; **~korps** *n* army corps; **~lieferant** *m* army contractor.
Ärmel *m* sleeve; *aus dem ~ schütteln* to do s. th. off-hand; **~abzeichen** *n* sleeve badge; **~aufschlag** *m* cuff; **~kanal** *m* the Channel; **~loch** *n* sleeve-hole; **~los** *a* sleeveless; **~schoner** *m* sleeve protector, oversleeve.
armier|en *tr* to equip, to arm; (*Kabel*) to armo(u)r; (*Magnet*) to arm; **~ung** *f* equipment, armament; (*Mauerwerk*) reinforcement; (*Schloß*) armature; (*bei Hochspannungskabel*) armo(u)ring.
ärmlich *a* poor; (*elend*) miserable; (*erbärmlich*) mean; (*schäbig*) shabby; (*armselig*) scanty; **~keit** *f* poorness, poverty; misery; (*Schäbigkeit*) shabbiness; meanness.
Armut *f* poverty; (*stärker*) penury, destitution; (*Mangel*) privation, lack; (*Geldmangel*) impecuniosity; (*Knappheit*) scarcity, dearth; deficiency; (*Klemme*) pinch, strait, pass; **~szeugnis** *n*: *sich ein* ~~ *ausstellen* to prove o.'s own incapacity.
Aroma *n* aroma, flavo(u)r; **~tisch** *a* aromatic, spicy.
Arrest *m* arrest, detention, imprisonment, confinement; (*Schul~*) detention; (*Kasernen~*) confinement to barracks; (*Beschlagnahme*) seizure; *in ~ sein* to be under arrest; **~ant** *m* prisoner; **~befehl** *m* arrest-report, (*gerichtlich*) warrant (of arrest); **~lokal** *n*, **~stube** *f* lock-up; guard-room; **~strafe** *f* (sentence of) confinement, detention.
arretieren *tr* to arrest, to take into custody; *tech* to lock, to fix.
Arsch *m vulg* backside, behind, arse, posteriors *pl*; **~backe** *f* buttock.
Arsenal *n* arsenal, armo(u)ry; naval dockyard.
Arsenik *m* arsenic.
Art *f* kind, sort; (*Typ*) type; character, style; (*Rasse, Zucht*) breed, stock, race; species; (*Benehmen*) behavio(u)r; (*Methode*) method; (*Gattung*) description, stripe, kidney, ilk; (*Muster*) example, model, pattern; (*Weise*) manner; (*Beschaffenheit*) nature, quality; (*gewohnheitsmäßige* ~) fashion, mode; *das ist keine* ~ this is bad form; *auf diese* ~ in this way; *die ~ wie* the way (in which); *e-e ~ Federn* a kind of pens; *aus der ~ schlagen* to degenerate; **~en** *itr*: *nach jdm ~en* to take after, to resemble; *gut ~en* to prosper, to succeed; *gut geartet* well-behaved; good-natured; **~eigen** *a* characteristic (*od* peculiar) to race; **~fremd** *a* alien, racially different; **~ung** *f* nature.
Arterie *f* artery; **~nverkalkung** *f* arteriosclerosis.
artesisch *a* Artesian; **~er Brunnen** *m* Artesian well.
artig *a* (*Kinder*) good, well-behaved; (*höflich*) polite; (*hübsch*) pretty; **~keit** *f* good behavio(u)r; (*Höflichkeit*) politeness; *jdm ~~en sagen* to compliment s. o.
Artikel *m gram* article; (*Abschnitt*) part, section; (*Ware*) article, (*einzelne Posten*) item, ware, commodity; (*Zeitungs~*) article, feature; (*kurzer*) news item.
artikulieren *tr* to articulate.
Artillerie *f* artillery; *motorisierte* motorized artillery; **~abteilung** *f* artillery brigade; **~einschlag** *m* shell hit, shell burst; **~feuer** *n* artillery fire, cannonade; **~~leitstand** *m* fire control post; **~flieger** *m* gun spotter; **~flugzeug** *n* artillery spotting aircraft; **~kampf** *m* artillery duel; **~leitstand** *m* command station; **~punkt** *m* trigonometric(al) point; **~schießplatz** *m* artillery range; **~schlepper** *m* prime mover; **~sperrfeuer** *n* artillery barrage; **~vorbereitung** *f* (*Beschuß*) preliminary bombardment; **Artillerist** *m* gunner; artilleryman.
Artischocke *f* artichoke.
Artist *m* circus performer.
Arznei *f* medicine; physic, medicament; (*Drogen*) drugs *pl*; **~ausschlag** *m* drug rash; **~buch** *n* pharmacopeia; **~flasche** *f* dispensing bottle; (*Fläschchen*) small medicine bottle; **~formel** *f* medical prescription; **~gabe** *f* dose; **~glas** *n* phial; **~kästchen** *n*, **~schrank** *m* medicine-chest; **~kraut** *n* medicinal herb; **~kunde, ~kunst, ~wissenschaft** *f* pharmaceutics; **~mittel** *n* medicine; medical supplies *pl*; (*Drogen*) drugs *pl*; (*Heilmittel*) remedies *pl*; **~~lehre** *f* pharmacology; **~~träger** *m* excipient; **~pflanze** *f* medicinal plant; **~trank** *m* potion; **~verordnung** *f* prescription; **~ware** *f* drug.
Arzt *m* physician; (*allgemein*) medical man, doctor (*Abk* medic, doc); (*praktischer* ~) (general) practitioner; (*Fach~*) specialist; (*Wund~*) surgeon.
Ärzt|in *f* lady doctor; **~ekittel** *m* operation overall; **~lich** *a* medical; ~~*e Hilfe* medical assistance; ~~*e Verordnung* medical prescription; ~~*es Zeugnis* medical certificate; *in ~~er Behandlung sein* to be under medical care.
As *n* (*Musik*) A flat; (*Karte*) ace; **~-Dur** *n* A flat major; **~-Moll** *n* A flat minor.
Asbest *m* asbestos; **~faserstoff** *m* asbestos fibre; **~pappe** *f* asbestos board; **~platte** *f* asbestos mat; **~schirm** *m* asbestos screen.
Asche *f* ash, ashes *pl*; *glühende* ~ embers *pl*; (*ausgebrannte Kohlen, verkohltes Holz, Papier*) cinders *pl*; (*Verbrennungsrückstand*) slag; *in ~ legen* to burn down, to lay in ashes; *in Sack u. ~ trauern* to mourn in sackcloth and ashes; **~nbahn** *f* (*sport*) cinder-track, cinder-path; **~nbahnrennen** *n mot* dirt-track racing; **~nbecher, ~r** *m* ash-tray, ash-stand; **~nbestandteil** *m* ash constituent; **~nbrödel** *n* Cinderella; *fig* domestic drudge, scullion; **~ngrube** *f rail* ash-pit; **~nkasten** *m* ash-bin, ash-box, ash-pan; **~nkrug** *m*, **~nurne** *f* cinerary urn; **~nlauge** *f* lye from ashes; **~nsalz** *n* potash; alkali; **~rmittwoch** *m* Ash Wednesday.
asch|fahl *a* ashen, ashy-pale; ~~ *werden* to turn ashen; **~grau** *a* ash-colo(u)red, ash-gray (*od* grey); *das geht ins ~~e fam* that's a stunner.
äsen *itr* to graze, to browse.
Asi|at *m*, **~atisch** *a* Asiatic; **~en** *n* Asia.
Aske|se *f* asceticism; **~t** *m* ascetic; **~tisch** *a* ascetic.
asozial *a* antisocial.
Asphalt *m* asphalt, bitumen; **~ieren** *tr* to asphalt, to pave with asphalt.
Assekur|ant *m* insurer, underwriter; **~anzgesellschaft** *f* insurance-company; **~ieren** *tr* to insure.
Assel *f* wood-louse.
Assessor *m* assessor.
Assimil|ation *f* assimilation; **~~sgrenze** *f* assimilation limit; saturation limit; **~~sprozeß** *m* assimilative process; **~atorisch** *a* assimilatory; **~ierbar** *a* assimilable; **~~keit** *f* assimilability; **~ieren** *tr* to assimilate.
Assist|ent *m* assistant, clerk; **~enzarzt** *m* assistant physician, assistant medical officer, house surgeon, doctor's assistant, intern, **~ieren** *tr* to assist, to help, to succour.
Assozi|ation *f* association; **~~sfasern** *f pl* associative fibres *pl* (*Am* fibers); **~~sfeld** *n* association field; **~ieren** *tr* (*sich*) to associate; *com* to enter into partnership; **~iert** *a med* conjugate; *com* associate, co-operant; (*verbündet*) associated.
Ast *m* bough, branch; (*im Holze*) knag, knot, knob; *anat* (*Nerven, Arterien*) ramus, branch; (*Geometrie*) branch; *sich e-n ~ lachen fam* to split o.'s sides with laughing; **~frei** *a* free of knots; **~ig** *a* full of boughs; (*knorrig*) knotty; **~loch** *n* knot-hole; **~rein** *a* clear of

branches; free of knots; **~werk** *n* branches *pl*, boughs *pl*.

Aster *f* aster.

Asthen|ie *f* asthenia; **~iker** *m* asthenic subject; **~isch** *a* asthenic.

Ästhet|ik *f* (a)esthetics *pl mit sing*; **~iker** *m* (a)esthete; **~isch** *a* (a)esthetic(al).

Asthma *n* asthma, shortness of breath; **~anfall** *m* asthmatic attack; **~tiker** *m* asthmatic; **~tisch** *a* asthmatic(al).

Astro|loge *m* astrologer; (*Sterngukker*) star-gazer; **~logie** *f* astrology; **~logisch** *a* astrologic(al); **~nautik** *f* astronautics; **~nom** *m* astronomer; (*Orter in Flugzeug*) astro-navigator; **~nomie** *f* astronomy; **~nomisch** *a* (*fig unvorstellbar groß*) astronomic(al); *~~e Navigation* (*aero, mar*) celestial navigation; **~photographie** *f* astrophotography; **~physik** *f* astrophysics; **~physiker** *m* astrophysicist.

Äsung *f* pasture, grazing; food.

Asyl *n* asylum, refuge; (*für Geisteskranke, Bewahrungsheim*) asylum, home; *fig* (*Schutzort*) sanctuary; haven (of refuge), harbour; shelter; *~ suchen* to seek sanctuary; *~ für Obdachlose* casual ward; **~recht** *n* right of sanctuary.

Ata|vismus *m* atavism; **~vistisch** *a* atavistic.

Atelier *n* studio.

Atem *m* breath, breathing, respiration; *~ holen* to take breath; *wieder zu ~ kommen* to regain breath; *den ~ anhalten* to hold o.'s breath; *die Bemerkungen waren so erstaunlich, daß er mit angehaltenem ~ zuhörte* the remarks were so astounding that he listened with bated breath; *in e-m ~* with the same breath; *außer ~ kommen* to get out of breath, to lose o.'s breath; *außer ~ sein* to be out of breath, to be panting; *jdn in ~ halten* to keep s. o. on the move; (*keine Entscheidung fällen*) to keep in suspense; **~beklemmung** *f* oppression in breathing; **~beschwerde** *f* difficulty of breathing; **~bewegung** *f* respiratory movement; **~einsatz** *m* (*Gasmaske*) (breathing) drum (of gas-mask); **~gerät** *n* oxygen apparatus; **~geräusch** *n* respiratory sound, breath sound; **~gymnastik** *f* respiratory exercises *pl*; **~holen** *n* breathing; **~lähmung** *f* respiratory paralysis; **~los** breathless, out of breath; **~not** *f* difficulty of breathing; dyspnea; **~pause** *f* breathing-time; (*Entspannung*) breathing-spell; (*Pause*) respite, pause, break, recess, *fam* letup; **~raubend** *a* breath-taking; *fig* exciting; **~störung** *f* disorders *pl* of breathing; **~übung** *f* practice of breathing; **~wege** *m pl* breathing passages *pl*, respiratory tract; **~zug** *m* breath, respiration; *in e-m ~~e* with the same breath; *den letzten ~~ tun fig* (*sterben*) to breathe o.'s last; *bis zum letzten ~~e* to the last breath.

Athe|ismus *m* atheism; **~ist** *m* atheist; **~istisch** *a* atheistical.

Äther *m* ether; *radio* air; **~isch** *a* ethereal; *~~es Öl* volatile (*od* essential) oil.

Äthiop|ien *n* Ethyopia; **~ier** *m*, **~isch** *a* Ethiopian.

Athlet *m* athlete; robust man; **~isch** *a* athletic; *~~e Wettspiele* (*Leichtathletik*) athletic sports *pl*.

Atlant|ik *m* the Atlantic; **~isch** *a* atlantic; *der ~~e Ozean* the Atlantic Ocean.

Atlas *m geog* Atlas; (*Stoff*) satin; (*Kartenwerk*) atlas; *anat* first cervical vertebra, atlas; **~artig** *a* satined, satiny; **~band** *n* satin ribbon; **~kleid** *n* satin dress; **~papier** *n* satin-paper, glazed paper; **atlassen** *a* satin.

atm|en *itr* to breathe; to respire; (*keuchend ~~*) to gasp; (*ein~~*) to inhale; (*aushauchen*) to exhale; *fig* (*zeigen, verraten, bekunden*) to show, to breathe; to manifest; *tief ~~* to draw (*od* to fetch) a deep breath; *wieder ~~ können* to recover o.'s breath; *am Schluß des Rennens ~ete er schwer* he was breathing hard when he finished the race; **~en** *n* breathing, breath; respiration; **~ung** *f* breathing, respiration; *künstliche ~~* artificial respiration; **~~sapparat** *m* respiratory apparatus, respirator; **~~sbeschwerde** *f* asthmatic complaint; **~~sgröße** *f med* vital capacity; **~~sorgan, ~~swerkzeug** *n* respiratory organ; **~~sstoffwechsel** *m* respiratory exchange; **~~szentrum** *n* respiratory centre (*Am* center).

atonal *a mus* atonal; **~ismus** *m* atonalism; **~istisch** *a* atonalistic; **~ität** *f* atonality.

Atmosphär|e *f* atmosphere; **~endruck** *m* atmospheric pressure; **~isch** *a* atmospheric; *~ische Störungen* (*im Rundfunk*) atmospherics *pl*.

*

Atom *n* atom; **~antrieb** *m* atomic propulsion; **~ar** *a* atomic, nuclear; **~auto** *n* atomobile; **~batterie** *f*, **~brenner** *m* atomic pile, nuclear reactor; **~bewegung** *f* atomic motion; **~blitzkrieg** *m* atomic blitz; **~bombe** *f* atom bomb, atomic bomb, A-bomb (= fission bomb); (*mit Wasserstoff*) hydrogen bomb, triton bomb (= fusion bomb); *mit ~~n bombardieren* to atom-bomb; *Bombardierung mit ~~n* atomic bombing; **~~nabwehr** *f* atomic defence; **~~nangriff** *m* atomic attack; (*überraschender*) atomic blitz; **~~nexplosion** *f* atomic explosion, atom-bomb burst; **~~nmonopol** *n* atomic-bomb monopoly; **~~npolitik** *f* atomic-bomb policy; **~~nversuch** *m* atom-bomb test; **~~nvorrat** *m* atomic stockpile, atomic-bomb stockpile; **~brennstoff** *m* atomic fuel; **~energie** *f* atomic energy, nuclear energy; **~~ausschuß** *m* atomic-energy commission; **~~kontrolle** *f* atomic-energy control; **~~werk** *n* atomic-energy plant; **~fabrik** *f* atomic plant, atomic factory; **~forscher** *m* atomic scientist; **~forschung** *f* atomic research; **~gewicht** *n* atomic weight; **~~stafel** *f* table of atomic weights; **~gruppe** *f* group of atoms; **~isch, ~istisch** *a* atomic; **~kern** *m* nucleus of the atom, atomic nucleus; **~~forschung** *f* nuclear research; **~~kettenreaktion** *f* atomic chain reaction; **~~lehre** *f* nucleonics; **~~theorie** *f* nuclear theory of the atom; **~kraft** *f* atomic power, nuclear force; *mit ~~ angetrieben* atomic-powered; *ein mit ~~ angetriebenes Flugzeug* an atomic-powered aircraft; **~~anlage** *f* atomic-power plant; *~~anlage für Schiffsantrieb* atomic-power plant for naval ship propulsion; **~~fabrik** *f*, **~~werk** *n* atomic plant, nuclear power plant; **~krieg** *m* atomic warfare; **~motor** *m*, **~triebwerk** *n* atomic engine; **~physik** *f* atomic physics; **~rakete** *f* atomic rocket; **~säule** *f* atomic pile, nuclear pile; **~spaltung** *f* atomic fission; **~sprengstoff** *m* atomic explosives *pl*; **~staub** *m* (*als Kampfmittel*) atomic dust; **~stoff** *m* atomic material; **~struktur** *f* atomic structure; **~teilchen** *n* atomic particle; **~theorie** *f* atom(ic) theory; **~treibstoff** *m* atomic fuel; **~umwandler** *m* cyclotron; **~umwandlung** *f* transmutation; **~versuchsgelände** *n* atomic testing ground; **~waffe** *f* atomic weapon, nuclear weapon; **~wärme** *f* atomic heat; **~wertigkeit** *f* atomic valence; **~zahl** *f* atomic number; **~zeitalter** *n* atomic age; *Vor~~* pre-atomic age; **~zerfall** *m* atomic disintegration; nuclear fission; decomposition of atoms; **~zertrümmerung** *f* atom-smashing, atom splitting; **~~sanlage** *f* atom-smashing plant; **~~sapparat** *m* atom smasher; cyclotron; **~~sversuch** *m* atom-smashing experiment.

ätsch! *interj* (*Schadenfreude*) it serves you right!

Attent|at *n* assault, attempted murder, attempt on s.o.'s life; murderous attack; *es wurde ein ~~ auf ihn verübt* an attempt was made on his life, he was assassinated; **~äter** *m* assassin, assailant.

Attest *n* attest(ation), certificate; testimonial; *ärztliches ~* medical certificate, *Am* doctor's certificate; *Gesundheits~* health certificate; *ein ~ ausstellen* to grant a certificate; **~ieren** *tr* to testify, to attest, to certify.

Attrappe *f* (*Schaufenster~*) dummy; (*Schaustück, leere Packung etc*) show piece; (*Muster*) sample (for exhibition); (*Versuchsmuster*) experimental model, *Am* mockup; *mot* (*Kühlerverkleidung*) radiator screen, radiator shell; *mil* (*Täuschungsmittel*) dummy; (*Falle*) trap, snare.

Attribut *n* (*Abzeichen, Sinnbild*) symbol, emblem; (*äußeres Zeichen*) attribute; (*Merkmal*) quality, character, characteristic, property; *gram* (*Beifügung*) attribute; **~iv** *a gram* attributive.

atz|en *tr* to feed, to give food; **~ung** *f* feeding; food.

ätz|en *tr* to corrode; to bite (in), to eat (into, away); *med* to cauterize; (*beim Kupferstich*) to etch; **~end** *a* caustic, corrodent; *fig* (*beißend*) biting, caustic, mordant; *~er Stoff mil* vesicant; **~grund** *m* etching-ground; **~kali** *n* caustic potash, hydroxide of potassium; **~kalk** *m* caustic lime, quicklime; **~kraft** *f* corrosiveness; causticity; **~kunst** *f* etching; **~lauge** *f* caustic-soda solution; **~mittel** *n* corrosive; *med* caustic; **~nadel** *f* etching needle, point; **~natron** *n* caustic soda, sodium hydroxide; **~~lauge** *f* caustic-soda solution; **~stoff** *m* corrosive; *med* caustic; **~sublimat** *n* corrosive sublimate; **~ung** *f* corrosion, cauterization; **~wasser** *n* nitric acid, liquid of caustics, caustic solution, aqua fortis; **~wirkung** *f* corrosive action, caustic effect.

au! *interj* oh!

auch *conj, adv* also; too; (*gleichermaßen*) likewise; (*wirklich*) indeed, certainly; (*steigernd*) even; *~ nicht* nor, neither; *~ hier* here too; *ich ~* I too, me too, so do I; *ich ~ nicht* neither do I, me neither; *sowohl als ~* both ... and; *nicht nur ... sondern ~* not only ... but also; *er ist ~ so einer* he is another; *wie dem ~ sei ...* be that as it may; *u. mag er ~ noch so reich sein ...* let him be ever so rich; *was ~* whatever; *wenn ~* though, although, even though, even if, even; *wer ~* whoever; *was es ~ sei* whatever it may be; *wo ~ immer* wheresoever; *~ schon* already; *~ nur* only; *wozu ~?* what is the good of it? *zum Teufel ~!* what the deuce!

Audi|enz *f* audience (*bei* with), interview; access; *um e-e ~ bitten* to request an interview with; *jdm e-e ~ gewähren* to give s. o. a hearing (*od* an audience), to grant an audience to s. o.; *der König gewährte dem Reporter e-e ~* the King granted an audience to the reporter; *bei jdm e-e ~ erhalten* to be admitted to the presence of s. o.; *der Botschafter wurde vom Kaiser in ~ empfangen* the ambassador was received in audience by the Emperor; **~~zimmer** *n* presence-chamber; **~torium** *n* auditory, lecture-room; (*Zuhörer*) audience, hearers *pl*; *ein zahlreiches ~~* a crowd of hearers.

Audion *n* audion; (*Röhre*) detector valve, valve detector, *Am* detector tube; **~empfänger** *m* audion receiver; **~röhre** *f* detector valve; **~verstärker** *m* amplifying detector.

Aue *f* meadow, pasture, green.

Auer|hahn *m* mountain-cock, capercailye; **~henne** *f* mountain-hen; **~ochs** *m* aurochs, bison.

auf *prp* (*auf die Frage wo? mit dat*; *auf die Frage wohin? mit acc*) on, upon; in, into; of; at; by; for; to; about; up, upward, up to; towards; against; *~ den Abend* towards night; *~ Anfrage* on inquiry; *~ e-n Augenblick* for a moment; *~ der Ausstellung* at the exhibition; *~ dem Bahnhof* at the station; *~ der Bank* at (*od* in) the bank; *~ e-n Baum klettern* to climb up a tree; *~ Befehl* upon (*od* by) order; *~ Besuch sein bei* to stay with s. o.; *~ Bestellung* to order; *~ den ersten Blick* at first sight, at a glance; *~ meine Bitte* at my request; *~ dem Bureau* at the office; *~ deutsch* in German; *~ einmal* (all) at once; (*plötzlich*) suddenly; *~ große Entfernung* at a great distance; *~ Ihre Empfehlung hin* on the strength of your recommendation; *~ ewig* for ever; *~ jeden Fall* in any case; *~ keinen Fall* by no means; *~ alle Fälle* at all events; at any rate; *~ der Flöte spielen* to play on the flute; *~ Gas kochen* to cook by gas; *~ seine Gefahr* at his risk; *~ ein Haar* to a hair, to a T; very exactly; *~ dem Hofe* in the courtyard; *~ die Jagd gehen* to be out hunting; *~ immer* for ever; *~ der Karte* in the map; *~ seine Kosten kommen* to recover o.'s expenses; *~ Kredit* on credit; *~ dem Lande* in the country; *~ Leben u. Tod* at the risk of o.'s life; *~ Lebenszeit* for life; *~ dem Markte* in the market-place; *~ die Minute* to a minute; *~ die Post gehen* to go to the post-office; *~ Rechnung* on account; *~ der Reise* in travel(l)ing; *~ Reisen gehen* to go abroad; *~ der Schule* at school; *~ beiden Seiten* on both sides; *~ meiner Seite* on my side; *~ der Stelle* at once, on the spot; *~ der Straße* in the street, *Am* on the street; *~ frischer Tat ertappt* taken red-handed; *~ einige Tage* for some days; *~ Veranlassung von ...* at the suggestion of ...; *~ dem nächsten Weg* by the nearest way; *~ der Welt* in the world; *~ diese Weise* in this manner; *~ Wiedersehen!* Good-by(e)! Au revoir! so long! see you again! *~ mein Wort* upon my word; *jdm ~s Wort glauben* to take s. o.'s word for it; *~ Zeit* on term; at the time; *~ kurze Zeit* for a short time; *bis ~* up to, within; except; till; *alle bis ~ e-n* all but one; *bis ~ weiteres* until further notice; *böse ~ jdn sein* to have a grudge against s. o.; *Einfluß ~* influence over; *~s beste* at best; *~s neue* anew, again; *~s schönste* in the finest manner; *~ 12. Dezember liefern* to supply on the 12th of December; *es geht ~ zwei* it is nearly two o'clock; *es hat nichts ~ sich* it does not matter; it is of no consequence; *es hat viel ~ sich* it is of importance; *adv* up, upwards; open; *~ u. ab* up and down; (*hin u. her*) to and fro; (*vorwärts u. rückwärts*) backward and forward; *das Auf u. Ab des Lebens* the ups and downs of life; *~ u. davon* off and away; *~ u. davon gehen* to run away; *sich ~ u. davon machen* to make off, to be off; *~ sein* to be up, to be not in bed; (*offen stehen*) to be open; *die Türe ist wieder ~* the door is open again; *von Jugend ~* from my youth upwards; *von klein ~* from childhood; *von unten ~ dienen* to serve from the ranks; *conj ~ daß* in order that; *~ daß nicht* lest, for fear that; *interj ~!* (*antreibend*) (get) up! come along! (*ermutigend*) cheer up! go to it! on!

aufarbeit|en *tr* to work up; (*auffrischen*) to renovate; to furbish up; (*vollenden*) to finish, to catch up on s. th; (*Rückstände*) to work off, to clear up arrears; (*Polstersachen*) to upholster; **~ung** *f* (*von Werkzeugen*) dressing; finishing.

aufatmen *itr* to draw a deep breath; to breathe again; to utter a sigh of relief; *fig* to recover.

aufbahr|en *tr* to put upon the bier, to lay out (in state); **~ung** *f* lying-in-state.

Aufbau *m* erection, building (up); (*Montierung*) mounting, assembly; (*e-r Organisation*) set-up; (*Wieder~*) rebuilding, reconstruction; *mot* (*Karosserie*) body; *arch, mar, rail* superstructure; *chem* composition; (*Synthese*) synthesis; (*Struktur*) structure; (*Organisations~*) organization; make-up; (*von Waren*) display; (*e-s Kunstwerkes*) composition; **~en** *tr* to build up, to erect; (*wieder ~~*) to rebuild; to construct; to display; **~end** *a* constructive, constructional; **~lehrgang** *m* training course; **~schule** *f* continuation school; **~ten** *m pl mar* superstructure; *film* set; **~zeit** *f* period of reconstruction.

aufbäumen *r* (*von Pferden*) to rear; to prance; *fig* to rebel.

aufbauschen *tr* to puff up; to swell out; *fig* to exaggerate, to enlarge.

aufbegehren *itr* to remonstrate, to start (up in anger).

aufbehalten *irr tr* (*Hut*) to keep on; (*Augen*) to keep open.

aufbeißen *irr tr* to crack (nuts); to bite open.

aufbekommen *irr tr* (*etw Verschlossenes*) to get open; (*Hausaufgaben in der Schule*) to have a lesson to do, to have (a lesson) set; to get; (*aufessen*) to eat up.

aufbereit|en *tr* to prepare; (*Kohle*) to wash, to clean; (*Erz*) to dress; **~ung** *f* (*Erze*) dressing; (*Kohle*) preparation, reworking; **~~sanlage** *f* dressing-plant, preparation plant; **~~skosten** *pl* dressing-expenses *pl*; **~~sverfahren** *n* processing methods *pl*.

aufbesser|n *tr* to ameliorate, to improve; (*Gehalt*) to increase, to raise; (*Kurse*) to advance, to improve, to move up; **~ung** *f* amelioration, improvement; (*Gehalt*) rise, raising, raise; (*Lohn*) increase.

aufbewahr|en *tr* to keep, to preserve, to store; to lodge for safekeeping; (*Bank*) to deposit; *rail* (*Gepäck*) to book (luggage), *Am* to check (baggage); *als Andenken ~~* to keep as a souvenir; **~ung** *f* preservation, storage; (*Bank*) deposition, safe keeping; **~~sgebühr** *f* (*Eisenbahn*) charge for storage; **~~sort** *m* store-house; (*Lager, Magazin*) warehouse; **~~sraum** *m rail* cloak-room, left luggage office, *Am* check-room; (*für Wertsachen*) receptacle, depository.

aufbieten *irr tr* (*verkünden*) to proclaim; (*zusammenrufen*) to summon up, to call in; (*Truppen*) to raise; (*Brautpaar*) to proclaim (*od* to publish) the banns of; to ask (in church); (*alle Kräfte*) to do o.'s utmost, to strain every nerve.

aufbinden *irr tr* (*öffnen*) to untie, to loosen; (*befestigen*) to bind up, to tie up; (*hinauf~*) to truss up, to turn up; *jdm etw ~* to make s. o. believe, to hoax s. o., to impose on s. o.; *das können Sie e-m andern ~* tell that to the marines; *sich etw ~ lassen* to be taken in, to swallow a lie.

aufblähen *tr* to swell out, to puff up; (*aufblasen*) to blow up; to inflate; (*Segel*) to belly; *r* to elate o. s., to be puffed up, to boast.

aufblasen *irr tr* to blow up, to puff; **aufgeblasen** *a* boastful, bragging, haughty.

aufblättern *tr* (*Buch*) to open; (*Pflanze*) to unfold the leaves, to exfoliate.

aufbleiben *irr itr* to stay up, to sit up; (*offen bleiben*) to be left open, to remain (*od* stay) open; *lang* (*od spät*) *~* to keep late hours.

aufblenden *tr mot* to turn the headlights on; *film* to fade in.

aufblicken *itr* to look up to.

aufblitzen *itr* to flare, to flash up, to flicker.

aufblühen *itr* to blossom; to open, to unfold; *fig* to rise, to increase; to flourish.

aufbocken *tr mot* to jack up.

aufbohren *tr tech* to bore (open).

aufbrauchen *tr* to use up, to consume, to wear up.

aufbrausen *itr* (*Brandung, See*) to surge, to roar; *chem* to effervesce, to fizz; *fig* to fly into a passion; to fire (*od* to flare) up; to get into a rage; **~d** *a* effervescent; *fig* hot-headed, irascible.

aufbrechen *irr tr* to break open, to open, to force a door; *ein Schloß ~* to pick a lock; *itr* (*Wunden*) to burst; (*Knospen*) to open; (*fortgehen*) to set off, to break up, to start; to depart.

aufbrennen *irr tr: ein Zeichen ~* to brand; *jdm eins ~* to shoot at s. o.

aufbringen *irr tr* to bring up, to produce; (*Türe*) to get open; (*Mut*) to summon up; (*Kind*) to bring up; (*Truppen*) to muster up; (*Geld*) to raise; (*Kosten*) to defray; (*Mode*) to bring up, to introduce; to start; *mar* to prize, to capture; *fig* to upset, to irritate; (*herausfordern*) to provoke; (*in Wut*) to infuriate; to put into a passion.

Aufbruch *m* break-up, start, departure, marching off, setting-out; (*Eis~*) breaking-up.

aufbrühen *tr* to scald.

aufbügeln *tr* to iron (again); to press; (*Hut*) to do up.

aufbürd|en *tr* to burden with; *fig* to impose s. th. on s.o.; **~ung** *f* charge; *fig* imputation.

aufdecken *tr* to lay bare; to uncover; (*Tischtuch*) to lay (the cloth); (*Bett*) to turn down the sheets; (*seine Karten ~*) to turn up, to show o.'s hand; *fig* to unveil; *ein Geheimnis ~* to disclose (*od* to reveal a secret); (*Schandtat etc*) to expose.

aufdonnern *r* to smarten o. s. up, to dress up.
aufdrängen *tr* to push open; *jdm etw ~* to force (*od* to urge *od* to obtrude) s. th. on; *sich jdm ~* to intrude on.
aufdrehen *tr* (*Geflecht*) to untwine, to ravel out; to untwist; (*Uhr*) to wind (up); (*Licht*) to switch on; (*Hahn*) to turn on; (*Schraube*) to unscrew; (*sport, loslegen*) to open up, to go up; *fam mot* to step on the gas.
aufdring|en *irr tr* to force, to press on; **~lich** *a* intrusive, obtrusive, importunate; **~lichkeit** *f* obtrusiveness, importunity.
Auf|druck *m* print, imprint; impress; (*Stempel*) stamp; printing; *photographischer ~~* photographic impression; **~drucken** *tr* (*Stempel*) to stamp on; *typ* to print on, to imprint; **~drücken** *tr* to impress; (*öffnen*) to press (*od* to break) open; (*Siegel*) to set a seal to.
aufdunkeln *itr* (*nach Verdunklung*) to light up.
aufeinander *adv* one after another; one on another; one on top of the other; (*gegeneinander*) one against the other; (*nacheinander*) successively; running; at a stretch; **~folge** *f* succession; **~folgen** *itr* to succeed; **~~d** *a* successive, in succession; **~häufen** *tr* to heap up; **~stoßen** *irr itr* to clash together, to collide; (*zufällig*) to meet each other; to hit (up)on.
aufeisen *tr* to break (off) the ice.
Aufenthalt *m* (*vorübergehend*) stay, whereabouts *pl mit sing*; (*dauernder Wohnort*) residence, abode; seat; domicile; (*Zug*) stop(page), halt; *Sie haben 5 Minuten ~ in Stuttgart* you have a five-minute stop in Stuttgart; *wie lange haben wir hier ~?* how long do we stop here? (*Hindernis*) delay, hindrance; **~sbescheinigung** *f* permit (*od* certificate) of residence; **~sdauer** *f* duration of stay; **~sort** *m* abode, residence, domicile, whereabouts *pl mit sing*, location.
aufer|legen *tr* to impose; (*Strafe*) to inflict; *sich Zwang ~~* to force o. s.; **~legung** *f* imposition, infliction; **~stehen** *irr itr* to rise (from the dead); **~stehung** *f* resurrection; **~wecken** *tr* to resuscitate, to raise (from the dead); **~weckung** *f* raising from the dead.
aufessen *irr tr* to consume, to eat up.
auffädeln *tr* to string, to thread.
auffahr|en *irr itr* (*aufsteigen*) to mount; to rise, to ascend; *min* to ascend; (*vorfahren*) to drive up; (*plötzlich*) to rise suddenly, to jump up; to pop up; (*vor Schreck*) to start up; (*Schiff*) to run aground; (*zornig werden*) to fly out; *mot* (*zusammenstoßen*) to collide, to come into collision; to strike against; *tr* to place; to bring up; (*Artillerie*) to place, to park; **~end** *a* violent, hot-headed; (*jähzornig*) irascible; impetuous, hasty; **~t** *f* ascension; (*im Wagen*) driving up; (*Platz zum Auffahren*) drive(-way); **~~srampe** *f* (approach) ramp, platform.
auffallen *irr tr* (*das Knie*) to hurt o.'s knee by falling; *itr* to fall upon; *fig* (*erstaunen, überraschen, befremden*) to astonish, to surprise, to strike; **~d, auffällig** *a* striking, conspicuous, outstanding, remarkable; *~~ gekleidet* showily dressed.
auffang|en *irr tr* (*erhaschen*) to snap up; (*fassen*) to catch (up); to snatch; (*Stöße*) to cushion shocks; to snatch up; (*Hieb*) to parry; (*Regenwasser*) to collect; (*Brief*) to intercept; (*Neuigkeiten*) to fish up news; to pick up; *radio* to intercept, to pick up; **~gebiet** *n* reception area; **~lager** *n* refugee camp, reception centre; **~schale** *f* collecting dish; **~stellung** *f mil* rear position, second line.
auffärben *tr* to dye afresh, to redye; to colo(u)r again; (*auffrischen*) to freshen up, to touch up.
auffass|en *tr* (*mit den Händen*) to pick up, to catch up; (*Masche*) to take up (a stitch); (*begreifen*) to understand, to comprehend; to conceive; to catch on, to grasp; (*erfassen*) to catch; (*e-e Rolle*) to interpret, to grasp; *falsch ~~* to misunderstand; *schwer ~~* to be dull (*od* slow) of apprehension; *anders ~~* to look at s. th. in a different light; **~ung** *f* conception, comprehension; apprehension; (*Auslegung*) interpretation; (*Meinung*) opinion, view; *nach meiner ~~* from my point of view, in my opinion, in my judg(e)ment, to my mind; *falsche ~~* misinterpretation, misunderstanding; **~~sgabe, ~~kraft** *f* perceptive faculty; power of apprehension, intellectual grasp.
auf|finden *irr tr* to find out; to locate, to spot; to trace; (*entdecken*) to discover; to detect; **~fischen** *tr* to fish out; *fig* to pick up; to find.
auf|flackern, ~flammen *itr* to flare up, to flicker up; *chem* to deflagrate; (*entflammen*) to flame up, to burst into flames, to blaze up.
aufflechten *irr tr* to twist up, to untwine; (*Haar*) to undo, to unbraid.
auf|fliegen *irr itr* to fly up; (*Vögel*) to soar; (*Rebhühner*) to whir; (*Flugzeug*) to ascend, to take off; (*Ballon*) to rise, to ascend; (*Türen*) to fly open; (*aufgelöst werden*) to be dissolved; (*in die Luft fliegen*) to explode; (*Mine*) to spring; *~~ lassen* (*in die Luft sprengen*) to blow up; (*Plan, Unternehmen*) to drop; **~flug** *m* flight; ascent.
aufforder|n *tr* to call upon; (*eindringlich*) to urge, to order; (*einladen*) to ask, to invite; to request, to demand; to challenge; (*zum Tanzen*) to ask . . . to dance with one; *er forderte das Mädchen zum Tanze auf* he asked the girl to dance with him; *nicht zum Tanz aufgefordert werden* to get no partner; (*gerichtlich*) to summon; **~ung** *f* call, request; (*Bitte*) invitation; (*gerichtlich*) summons *pl*; (*Einladung*) invitation; (*Herausforderung*) challenge (*an* to).
aufforst|en *tr* to afforest; **~ung** *f* afforestation; reforestation.
auffressen *irr tr* to devour, to eat up; *ich könnte dich* (*vor Liebe*) *~* I could eat you.
auffrisch|en *tr* to refresh, to freshen up, to renew, to brush up, to polish up; to regenerate; (*Bilder*) to retouch; (*Andenken*) to revive the memory of; **~ung** *f* refreshment, revival, regeneration.
aufführ|en *tr* to raise, to erect, to build, to construct; (*die Wache ~en*) to mount guard; (*Theaterstück*) to perform, to represent, to act; (*Menge anführen*) to lead; (*darbieten*) to offer, to present; (*zusammenfassen*) to summarize; (*vor Augen führen*) to bring up; *einzeln ~en* to specify, to itemize; (*Zahlen*) to enumerate; (*auf e-r Liste*) to list, to enter; (*in e-r Tabelle*) to tabulate; (*angeben*) to state; *r* to behave; *sich schlecht ~~* to misbehave; **~ung** *f* erection, construction; *theat* performance; (*von Zahlen*) enumeration, tabulation; representation; (*Betragen*) behavio(u)r, conduct; (*Eintragung*) entry, specification; **~~srecht** *n* (*e-s Schauspiels*) right of performance, acting rights *pl*; **~~szeugnis** *n* certificate of conduct.
auffüllen *tr* to fill up; (*Lücke*) to stop a gap; (*Vorräte etc wieder anfüllen*) to replenish; (*Faß, Flasche*) to cask, to bottle.
Aufgabe *f* (*Telegramm*) handing in, dispatch; (*Gepäck*) booking, *Am* checking; (*Brief*) posting, *Am* mailing; (*Arbeit*) task; duty; assignment; (*Tätigkeit*) business, job; (*Geschäfts~*) shutting down; (*e-s Rätsels*) asking; (*Schul~*) lesson, exercise; problem; homework; (*Lebens~*) mission; (*Denk~*) problem, proposition; (*Endzweck*) scope; (*Verzicht*) giving up, abandonment, resignation; (*Tennis*) service; (*e-r Klage*) waiver; (*von Rechten*) renunciation, release, relinquishment, *~n übernehmen* to take over functions; *e-e ~ ausführen* to perform a task; *er macht es sich zur ~* he makes it his business; *sie ist ihrer ~ nicht gewachsen* she is not equal to her task; *~n übertragen* to confer duties upon; *laut ~* as per advice; **~bahnhof** *m* dispatch point; **~nbereich** *m* functions *pl*; **~ngebiet** *n* field, scope; **~nheft** *n* (*Schulheft*) exercise-book; **~nkreis** *m* tasks *pl*; **~ort** *m* issuing station; **~schein** *m* certificate of delivery; **~station, ~stelle** *f* sending-station; **~stempel** *m* (*Poststempel*) postmark; **~vorrichtung** *f* feeding device; **~zeit** *f* time of dispatch.
aufgabeln *tr fig* to find out, to pick up.
Aufgang *m* (*nach oben führender Gang*) rising; ascent; (*der Gestirne*) rise, rising; (*der Osten*) east; *vom ~ bis zum Niedergang* (*Bibel*) from the rising of the sun unto the going down thereof; (*Anwachsen*) growth, increase; (*Treppe*) staircase, stairs *pl*, steps *pl*, *Am* stairway.
aufgeben *irr tr* (*bestellen, anordnen*) to commission, to order; (*Schulaufgaben*) to give, to assign; (*Hoffnung*) to lose, to give up; (*Telegramm*) to hand in, to deliver, to send; (*Brief*) to post, *Am* to mail; (*Rätsel*) to propose, to ask; (*Plan, Absicht*) to drop, to give up; (*Stadt*) to surrender; (*Vergnügen, Vorteil*) to forgo; (*Gepäck*) to book, to register, *Am* to check; (*verzichten*) to yield up, to quit, to renounce, to waive; (*Amt*) to resign; (*Geist*) to give up *jdm etw ~* to set s. o. a task; *jdn ~* to drop, to have done with.
aufge|blasen *a* puffed up, swelled; inflated; *fig* haughty; **~~heit** *f* haughtiness; **~bot** *n* (public) notice; summons *pl*; (*Ehe*) banns *pl*, asking, *Am* official wedding notice; *dies ist das erste ~~* this is the first time of asking; (*von Truppen*) levy, calling out, conscription, enlistment, *Am* draft; *allgemeines ~~* levée en masse; (*Streitmacht*) body of men; *mit e-m starken ~~ erscheinen* to come out in full force; **~botsverfahren** *n* public citation; **~bracht** *a* angry (*gegen jdn* with, *über etw* at, about); (*wütend*) furious; *sie ist darüber ~~* she is provoked about it; **~donnert** *a* dressed up to the nines (*od* to kill), *Am* dolled up; **~dunsen** *a* bloated, puffed up.
aufgehen *irr itr* (*Gestirne, Teig, Vorhang*) to rise; (*Geschwür*) to break up; (*Saat*) to come up; (*sich öffnen*) to open; (*von Kleidung*) to come undone; *in Rauch ~* to end in smoke; *in Flammen ~* to be consumed in flames; *math* to leave no remainder; (*vereinigt werden mit*) to be merged in; (*gänzlich ~ in*) to be deeply engrossed

in, to be absorbed in; ~ *lassen* to spend money; *gegeneinander* ~ to compensate (each other); *jetzt geht mir ein Licht auf* now I see (*od* understand); *ihm ging das Herz auf bei ihrem Anblick* his heart missed a beat at the mere sight of her.

aufgeklärt *a* enlightened; **~heit** *f* enlightenment.

aufgeknöpft *a fig* (*gesprächig*) communicative.

aufgekratzt *a fig* (*protzig, aufgedonnert*) dressed up, *Am* dolled up; (*vergnügt*) in high spirits.

aufgelaufen *a* (*Fuß*) sore, blistered chafed; (*Zinsen*) accumulated, accrued.

Aufgeld *n* (*Zuschlag*) extra charge, agio, premium; (*Draufgeld*) earnest-money; increase.

aufge|legt *a* disposed, inclined; *~~ sein* to feel like; *gut* (*schlecht*) *~~ sein* to be in a good (bad) humo(u)r; *ich bin heute nicht dazu ~~* I am not in the mood for it today; *com zur Zeichnung ~~* open for subscription; (*Schiff*) laid up; **~räumt** *a fig* in high spirits, cheerful, merry; **~~heit** *f* good humo(u)r, cheerfulness; **~regt** *a* excited; nervous; **~paßt!**, **~schaut!** *interj* look out!; **~sprungen** *a* (*Lippen*) chapped lips; **~weckt** *a* brisk, bright, quick-witted, intelligent, smart, sprightly, clever; **~worfen** *a* turned-up (nose); *~~e Lippen* pouting lips.

auf|gießen *irr tr* to pour upon; (*Tee*) to make, to infuse; **~gliedern** *tr* to split up; **~graben** *irr tr* to dig up; **~greifen** *irr tr* to seize, to pick up; **~guß** *m* infusion; **~~tierchen** *n pl* infusoria *pl*; **~~verfahren** *n* (*Brauerei*) infusion method.

auf|haben *irr tr* (*Hut*) to have on; to wear; (*Laden*) to be open; (*Mund*) to have open; (*zu tun haben*) to have to do; **~hacken** *tr* to hoe up; to hack (*od* to hew) open; (*Straße*) to pick up; to open, to break (the ice); (*von Vögeln*) to peck; **~haken** *tr* to unclasp, to undo, to unhook; **~halsen** *tr* to burden, to saddle with; *fig* to impute.

aufhalten *irr tr* (*offen halten*) to keep open, to hold open; (*hemmen*) to stop, to check; (*hinhalten*) to delay, to detain; *sich ~* to stay; to stop, to reside; *sich mit etw ~* to dwell on; *sich bei jdm ~* to stay with, to live with; *sich über etw ~* to find fault with s. th.

aufhäng|en *tr* to hang up; to suspend; *aero* (*Bomben*) to stow (bombs); *jdm etw ~en* to inflict s. th. on; *sich ~en* to hang o. s.; **~er** *m* (**~eband** *n*) suspensor; (*für Kleider*) loop, hanger; **~ung** *f* hanging; *tech* suspension.

aufhauen *tr* to cut, to hew open.

aufhäuf|en *tr* to pile up, to store up; to heap up, to amass; *sich ~en* to accumulate; **~ung** *f* accumulation; pile.

aufheb|en *irr tr* (*hochheben*) to raise, to hold up, to lift up, to pick up; (*aufbewahren*) to keep, to put by (*od* away), to preserve; *Tafel ~~* to rise from table; (*Patent*) to invalidate; *gut aufgehoben sein* to be in good hands with, to be well looked after; (*abschaffen Gesetze*) to abolish; to repeal; to remove, (*vorübergehend*) to suspend; (*Vertrag*) to annul, to cancel, to defeat, to dissolve; (*Entscheidung*) to disaffirm; (*Klage vor Gericht*) to withdraw (an action); (*Urteil*) to quash; (*Genossenschaft*) to dissolve; (*Belagerung*) to raise; (*Sitzung*) to break up; (*Verlobung*) to break off; (*Bruch*) to reduce; *eins gegen das andere ~~* to neutralize; *sich ~~* to compensate; **~en** *n*, **~ung** *f* (*Abschaffung*) abolition, suspension, repeal, abrogation; (*e-r Versammlung*) breaking-up, dissolution; (*der Ehe*) annulment (of marriage); (*e-r Klage vor Gericht*) nonsuit, withdrawal of an action; (*Urteil*) reversal; (*Vertrag*) rescission, cancellation, annihilation; (*Verordnung*) suspension; (*Sperre*) unblocking; (*Hochheben*) lifting, raising; (*~~ der Hände bei Abstimmung*) show of hands; *~ung der Tafel* rising from table; *viel ~ens von etw machen* to make a great fuss about; *viel ~ens um nichts* much ado about nothing.

aufheften *tr* to fasten, to tie up, to pin up.

aufheiter|n *tr* to brighten, to cheer up; *r* (*Wetter*) to clear up; **~ung** *f* clearing up, enlivening.

aufhelfen *irr tr* to help s. o. up, to lend a hand.

aufhell|en *tr, itr* to brighten; *fig* to enlighten, to elucidate; *sich ~en* to clear up, to become fair; **~er** *m* (*im Filmatelier*) brightener; **~schirm** *m phot* brightening screen; **~ung** *f* clearing up.

aufhetz|en *tr* (*Wild*) to start; *fig* to stir up, to rouse, to incite; to set against; **~er** *m* instigator; **~ung** *f* incitement, instigation, sedition.

aufhissen *tr* to hoist.

aufholen *tr* (*hochwinden*) to fetch up; *mar* to haul up, to hoist up; (*Zeitverlust*) to make up for, to recover.

aufhorchen *itr* to prick up o.'s ears, to listen (to).

aufhören *itr* to leave off, to stop, to quit, to cease, to discontinue; (*allmählich*) to subside; *~ zu arbeiten* to knock off work, to strike; *~ zu zahlen* to suspend payment; *ohne ~* without intermission; *~ mit etw* to have done with; *da hört doch alles auf* that's a pretty pickle, that's the limit, that beats everything; *hör auf damit!* stop it!

aufhüpfen *itr* to jump up, to bound.

aufjagen *tr* to start, to rouse (a deer).

auf|jauchzen, **~*jubeln*** *itr* to shout with joy.

Auf|kauf *m* buying-up, cornering, purchase on speculation, forestalling; **~kaufen** *tr* to buy up; **~käufer** *m* engrosser, wholesale buyer, buying-agent, forestaller; speculator.

aufkeimen *itr* to shoot up, to germinate.

Aufklang *m* beginning; start, onset.

aufklapp|en *tr* to open (a book); to put up the folds of (a table); **~bar** *a* collapsible.

aufklär|en *tr, itr* to clear up; (*unterrichten*) to inform, to instruct; (*erläutern*) to explain, to elucidate; (*Geheimnis*) to clear up, to solve; (*Mißverständnis, Irrtum*) to correct, to set right; *das Wetter hat sich aufgeklärt* the weather has cleared up; *mil* to reconnoitre, to spot, to scout; *jdn über etw ~~* to enlighten; **~er** *m* scout; *mil* (*Flieger*) reconnaissance pilot, (*Flugzeug*) scout plane, reconnaissance plane; **~ung** *f* clearing up; enlightenment; (*sexuelle*) sex-instruction; *mil* reconnaissance, scouting; *~~ im Verband* reconnaissance in force; **~~sabteilung** *f* reconnaissance unit; scouting detachment; **~~sarbeit** *f* campaign of enlightenment; **~~sbomber** *m* scout bomber; **~~sdienst** *m* reconnoitring; **~~sfilm** *m* sex-film; **~~sflug** *m aero* reconnaissance flight; **~~sflugzeug** *n* scout plane, observation plane, reconnaissance plane; **~~sgebiet** *n* reconnaissance area; **~~sraum** *m* reconnaissance sector; **~~sschiff** *n* scout; **~~sspähtrupp** *m* reconnaissance patrol; **~~stätigkeit** *f* reconnaissance activity; **~~szeitalter** *n hist* age of rationalism.

aufklauben *tr* to pick up; to glean.

auf|kleben, **~*kleistern*** *tr* to stick up, to paste on (*od* to); (*Briefmarken*) to affix (*od* to put) stamps on a letter; (*Zettel*) to label, to ticket; **~klebeadresse** *f* gummed label; **~klebezettel** *m* stick-on label, *Am* sticker; **~klinken** *tr* to open, to unlatch; **~klopfen** *tr* to knock open, to crack (nuts); **~knacken** *tr* to crack; **~knöpfen** *tr* to unbutton; **~knüpfen** *tr* to tie up; (*lösen*) to untie, to loosen; (*hängen*) to hang; **~kochen** *tr* to boil again, to warm up; *itr* to boil up; *~~ n* boiling up.

aufkommen *irr itr* to get up; (*wiedergenesen*) to recover; to convalesce; (*gedeihen*) to rise, to prosper; (*entstehen*) to spring up, to come into use; (*Mode*) to come into fashion; (*für Schaden*) to make good; (*für Verluste*) to be liable for (a loss); (*für Kosten*) to pay the expenses; *für etw ~* to be responsible for; *~ gegen jdn* to cope with; *ich kann nicht gegen ihn ~* I can't cope with him, I am no match for him; *gegen etw ~* to contend with; *nicht ~ lassen* to prevent the rise of; *~ n* recovery; introduction; (*Steuer~*) yield; (*e-r Mode*) coming into fashion; (*Verbreitung*) spread; (*Entstehung*) origin, rise; *an seinem ~ wird gezweifelt* his life is despaired of.

auf|kratzen *tr* to scratch open; (*Wolle*) to tease, to card; **~kräuseln** *tr* to curl up, to frizzle; **~krempe(l)n** *tr* to cock (a hat), to turn up (o.'s trousers); **~kriegen** *tr* to get open; (*in der Schule*) to have to do, to have set.

aufkündig|en *tr* to give notice (*od* warning); (*Kapital*) to recall; *jdm die Freundschaft ~en* to break with, to renounce; (*Kauf*) to cancel; (*Genehmigung*) to withdraw; (*Hypothek*) to foreclose; to call in (a mortgage); (*Vertrag*) to revoke, to terminate; (*völkerrechtlich*) to denounce (a treaty); (*Mietsvertrag*) to give notice to quit; *jdm den Gehorsam ~en* to refuse obedience; **~ung** *f* notice, warning; (*von Geld*) recalling; *mil* (*e-s Waffenstillstandes*) termination; *monatliche ~~* a month's warning.

auflachen *itr* to burst out laughing.

auflad|en *irr tr* to lade upon, to load; *aero* (*Motor*) to supercharge, to boost; *jdm etw ~~* to charge with, to burden s. o. with; to saddle with; *el* to charge; *sich etw ~~* to assume s. th.; **~er** *m* loader, packer.

Auflage *f* (*Steuer~*) levy, duty, tax, imposition; *typ* edition; issue, printing; impression; (*Zeitung*) circulation; *neue unveränderte ~* reprint; *neueste ~* latest edition; *vermehrte u. verbesserte ~* revised and enlarged edition; *wie hoch ist die ~?* how many copies have been printed? *tech* (*Stütze*) support, rest; *~* (*beim Schießen*) elbow rest (for shooting); (*obere Schicht*) super-imposed layer; **~fläche** *f* bearing-surface area; **~nhöhe** *f* number to be printed, edition; **~r** *n tech* support; bearing.

auflass|en *irr tr* to leave open; *jur* (*Grundstück*) to convey; to surrender; to cede property to; to abandon (a mine); **~ung** *f* (*von Eigentumsrecht*) transfer of ownership; (*Grundstück*) cession, conveyance.

auflauern *itr* to waylay, to lie in wait for, to wait for.

Auflauf *m* crowd, mob, rush, riot;

(*Speise*) soufflé; **~en** *irr itr* to swell; (*Geld*) to increase, to run up; (*Kapital*) to accumulate; (*Zinsen*) to accrue; *mar* to run aground; *aufgelaufene Zinsen* accumulated interest; *sich die Füße ~en* to get footsore.

auf|leben *itr* to return to life, to revive; **~lecken** *tr* to lick up.

aufleg|en *tr* to put on, to lay on; (*auferlegen*) to impose; (*Geldstrafe*) to fine; (*Strafe*) to inflict; (*Buch*) to publish, to print; (*neu ~~*) to reprint, to republish; (*Anleihe*) to invite subscriptions for a loan; (*Hörer*) *tele* to replace (the receiver); (*Pflaster*) to apply; (*Zeitungen auslegen*) to lay out papers; (*Farbe, Schminke*) to lay on; (*zur Schau*) to exhibit; (*Schiff*) to lay up a ship; *seine Karten ~en* to show o.'s cards; *ein Fäßchen ~en* to broach a cask of beer; (*Tischtuch*) to spread (the cloth); *e-n Eid ~en* to administer an oath to; (*Buße*) to enjoin (a penance upon); *gut* (*schlecht*) *aufgelegt sein* to be in a good (bad) mood; *sich ~en* to lean on o.'s elbows; **~ung** *f* imposition; application; infliction.

auf|lehnen *tr* to lean upon, to rest (up)on; *sich ~~ gegen* to oppose, to rebel against; **~lehnung** *f* opposition, revolt; rebellion; **~leimen** *tr* to glue upon; **~lesen** *irr tr* to gather, to pick up; **~leuchten** *itr* to flash up, to light up; to shine; *ein rotes Licht leuchtete am Instrumentenbrett auf* a red light flashed on the instrument panel; **~liegen** *irr itr* to lie upon; (*zur Besichtigung*) to be on show; (*zum Verkauf*) to be exposed; (*Schiff*) to be laid up; (*jdm zur Last fallen*) to weigh on, to be incumbent on; (*von Zeitungen*) to be kept, to be taken in; *sich ~~* to become bedsore; **~lockern** *tr* to loosen, to relax, to slacken; to aerate; to disaggregate; **~lockerung** *f* loosening; relaxation; (*Verteilung auf größeres Gebiet*) dispersal; **~lodern** *itr* to flash up; to flare up, to blaze up; *fig* to flame up.

auf|lösbar *a* dissolvable; (dis)soluble; *math* solvable; **~lösen** *tr* (*aufmachen*) to loosen, to untie, to undo; (*in Flüssigkeiten*) to dissolve, to melt; to liquefy; *chem* to analyse; (*zerlegen*) to decompose; to disintegrate; *mus* to resolve; *aero* (*Verbandsflug*) to break formation, to peel off; (*Versammlung*) to break up; (*Geschäft*) to dissolve, to wind up; (*Ehe, Gesellschaft*) to dissolve, to liquidate; (*Aufgabe, Rätsel*) to solve; (*Truppen*) to disband; (*Verbindung mit Kirche*) to severe the connection with; (*Brüche*) to reduce; *sich ~~* to dissolve; *sich in Wohlgefallen ~~* to turn out fine; to come to nothing; *sich in Tränen ~~* to melt into tears; **~lösend** *a* dissolvent, diluent; **~löslich** *a chem* soluble.

Auflösung *f* (*in Flüssigkeiten; Versammlung*) dissolution; (*Aufgabe, Rätsel*) solution; (*Truppen*) disbandment; (*Knoten etc*) loosening; (*Zerlegung*) disintegration, decomposition; *chem* analysis; *mus* resolution; (*Geschäfts~*) winding up; (*Konto*) closing, *Am* elimination; (*Tod*) death; (*Ehe*) divorce; **~sfähig** *a* soluble; **~sgeschwindigkeit** *f* velocity of dissolution; **~sgrenze** *f* limit of resolution; **~smittel** *n* solvent, dissolvent; **~svermögen** *n chem* dissolving power; *opt* resolving power; **~swort** *n* (*Rätsel*) solution, answer; **~szeichen** *n mus* natural.

aufmach|en *tr* to open; (*nachdem an der Türe geläutet wurde*) to answer the bell; (*Augen*) to open o.'s eyes; *den Mund ~~* to speak up; (*Kleid*) to undo, to unbutton; (*aufschließen*) to unlock; (*Dampf*) to get up steam; (*Konto*) to open an account; (*Rechnung*) to make up an account; to make out an invoice; (*Flasche*) to uncork (a bottle); (*Nüsse*) to crack (nuts); (*Paket*) to unpack (a parcel); (*Vorhänge, Schirm*) to put up (curtains, an umbrella); *r* to set out for, to make for, to make up; *sich auf u. davon machen* to run away, to be off; **~ung** *f* outward appearance, make-up; (*e-s Buches*) get-up; (*e-r Druckseite*) lay-out; (*als Täuschung*) window-dressing.

auf|malen *tr* to paint on; (*mit Schablonen*) to stencil on; **~marsch** *m* marching-up; *mil* drawing-up; (*Entfaltung der Truppe vor Gefecht*) deployment; **~marschgebiet** *n* deployment zone; **~marschgelände** *n* assembly area; **~marschieren** *itr* to march up, to draw up; to deploy; **~marschplan** *m* operational plan; **~mauern** *tr* to build up (with bricks).

aufmerk|en *itr* (*auf etw*) to attend to s. th., to mind s. th.; (*auf etw, auf jdn*) to listen to; **~sam** *a* attentive, mindful; (*höflich*) polite, attentive (to), regardful; *jdn auf etw ~~ machen* to call (*od* to direct) s. o.'s attention to, to point out s. th. to s. o.; **~samkeit** *f* attention, attentiveness; (*Höflichkeit*) courtesy, politeness; respect; regard; *~~ erweisen* to show (*od* pay) attention to; *die ~~ lenken auf* to call o.'s attention to, to draw s. o.'s attention to.

aufmunter|n *tr* (*aufwecken*) to rouse; to awake; (*ermutigen*) to cheer up, to encourage, to give o.'s spirits a lift; **~nd** *a* encouraging; **~ung** *f* rousing, animation, incitement; encouragement.

*

aufnageln *tr* to nail down (*od* on).

aufnähen *tr* to sew on.

Aufnahme *f* taking up; (*Empfang*) reception; (*Zulassung*) admission, admittance; (*~ an Kindes Statt*) adoption; (*~ e-s Protokolls*) drawing up of the minutes; (*Aufsaugung*) absorption; (*in e-e Liste, Register etc*) enrolment; enlistment; (*Tonaufnahme*) record; making of record; (*Tonaufnahme für Rundfunk*) transcription; (*photographieren*) taking (*od* shooting) pictures; (*die Photographie*) photograph, exposure, shot, snapshot; (*Röntgen~*) radiogram; (*Flugzeug~*) air photo(graph); (*Schallplatten~*) recording; (*tele, Bild~*) television pick-up; (*Anleihe*) raising; (*~ von Beziehungen*) establishment of relations; (*Geld*) taking up, borrowing, loan; (*topographische ~*) measurement, survey; (*geographische ~ e-s Landes*) mapping-out; (*Inventar~*) making-up; (*Lager~*) taking stock; *in ~ kommen* to come into vogue; *~en machen phot* to take photographs, to take pictures; (*Ton~*) to make recordings; **~apparat** *m* (*Film~~*) cine camera, *Am* movie camera; **~bedingungen** *f pl* terms of admission; **~fähig** *a* admissible; (*Markt*) ready, active, broad; **~fähigkeit** *f* capacity for absorbing; (*geistig*) receptivity; **~gebühr** *f* admission-fee; **~gerät** *n phot* camera; **~kasette** *f phot* plate-holder, film-holder, dark-slide; **~leiter** *m* (*Film*) stage manager, director; (*Tonmeister*) recording manager; **~prüfung** *f* examination for admission, entrance examination; **~raum** *m* (*Rundfunk*) studio; **~stellung** *f* rallying position; **~studio** *n* (*Tonfilm*) recording studio; *radio* studio, auditorium; **~vermögen** *n* capacity; **~vorrichtung** *f* (*Ton*) sound recorder; **~wagen** *m radio* recording car (*od* van).

aufnehmen *irr tr* to pick up, to take up; (*wieder ~*) to take up again, to resume; (*einsetzen*) to insert; (*zulassen*) to admit; (*beherbergen*) to accommodate; (*empfangen*) to receive; to take in; (*Hypothek, Anleihe*) to raise; (*Betrieb*) to start operation; (*Markt*) to absorb; (*Masche*) to take up; (*eintragen in Liste*) to list; (*fassen, enthalten*) to hold, to contain; *radio* (*Sendung abhören*) to pick-up, to monitor; (*zeichnen*) to make a design; (*durch Messung*) to survey; (*geographisch*) to map out; (*feststellen*) to register; (*Geld*) to borrow, to take up; (*Inventar*) to make (*od* to draw) an inventory, to take stock ;(*Spur*) to catch; (*photographisch*) to photograph; to take (*od* to shoot) pictures; (*Schallplatte*) to record; (*Ton für Rundfunk*) to transcribe; *den Schaden ~* to assess the damage; (*aufsaugen*) to absorb; *el* to draw; *etw übel ~* to resent, to take s. th. ill, to take in bad part; *für Ernst ~* to take in earnest; *e-e Volkszählung ~* to take a census; *Protokoll ~* to draw up the minutes, to take down the minutes; (*Telegramm*) to take down; (*Diktat*) to take (a dictation); *es mit jdm ~* to cope, to compete with; to be a match for.

aufnorden *tr* to nordicise; to improve the Northern race.

aufnötigen *tr* to press upon, to force upon.

aufopfer|n *tr* to sacrifice; *sich ~n* to sacrifice o. s.; to devote o. s. to; **~ung** *f* sacrifice; devotion.

aufpacken *tr* to pack up, to load on; (*aufbürden*) *fig* to lay on, to impose on; *jdm etw ~* to charge s. o. with s. th.; (*davongehen*) to break off, to depart; (*öffnen*) to unpack.

aufpäppeln *tr* to bring up by hand; (*verzärteln*) to coddle.

aufpass|en *itr* to watch, to look out for; (*aufmerken*) to take care of, to pay attention to, to attend to, to mind; *aufgepaßt!* attention! mind! look out! *jdm ~en* to waylay, to spy; **~er** *m* watcher, supervisor, overseer; spy.

aufpeitschen *tr* (*Nerven*) to stimulate; (*Leidenschaften*) to stir up.

auf|pflanzen *tr* to set up; (*Bajonett*) to fix; *sich ~~ vor jdm* to plant o. s. before s. o.; **~pfropfen** *tr* to graft upon; **~pfropfung** *f* grafting upon; **~platzen** *itr* to burst open; to crack, to split; **~plustern** *r* (*Vögel das Gefieder*) to puff up, to ruffle feathers; *fig* (*prahlen, großtun*) to boast, to give o. s. airs; **~polieren** *tr* to polish up, to rub up; **~prägen** *tr* to impress, to stamp on; (*ein Muster*) *typ* to gauffer; **~prallen** *itr* to rebound; to bounce again; (*auf dem Boden*) to strike; **~probieren** *tr* to try on (a hat); **~protzen** *tr* to limber up; **~pumpen** *tr* to pump up, to inflate (the tire).

Aufputz *m* dress; finery; (*Ausputz*) ornament, trimming; attire; *fam* get-up; **~en** *tr* to adorn; to trim up; (*reinigen*) to clean; to brush up; *r* to make smart, to smarten up; to dress up.

aufquellen *irr itr* to well up; to rise; to swell; *tr* to soak; (*aufkochen*) to parboil.

aufraffen *tr* to rake up, to snatch up; *sich ~* to get up quickly; *fig* to pluck up courage; (*von Kranken*) to recover.

aufragen *itr* to tower up, to rise.

aufräum|en *tr* (*wegschaffen*) to carry off, to remove, to clear away; (*freimachen*) *ein Lager* ~~ to clear (out) a stock; (*Waren*) to sell off, to dispose off; (*ordnen*) to (put in) order; to clear up, to mop up; (*Zimmer*) to tidy up, *Am* to straighten up, to clean up; (*vermindern*) to reduce; *itr* (*mit etw* ~~) to make a clean sweep; **~ung** *f* clearing up, making tidy; **~~sarbeiten** *f pl* (*Trümmerbeseitigung*) clearing of debris; (*Bergungsarbeiten*) salvage work; *mil* (*Ausräuchern feindlicher Truppenreste*) mopping-up; **~~strupp** *m* demolition and clearing squad.

aufrechnen *tr* to count up; (*ausgleichen*) to settle (accounts); *gegeneinander* ~ to balance; to set off against.

aufrecht *a* upright, erect; ~ *gehen* to go upright; ~ *sitzen* to sit up; ~ *stehen* to stand erect; **~erhalten** *tr* (*Ordnung*) to maintain; (*Verbindung, Kontakt*) to keep up; (*Ansicht, Forderung*) to stick to; (*Gebräuche, Urteil, Lehre u. a.*) to uphold; **~(er)haltung** *f* maintenance.

aufreden *tr* (*aufschwatzen*) *jdm etw* ~ to talk s. o. into (buying s. th.).

aufreg|en *tr* to agitate, to excite; to rouse; to incite; to irritate, to disturb; to stir (up), to alarm, to upset; *sich ~en über* to get excited (*od* upset *od* alarmed) about; to work o. s. up; **~ung** *f* trouble, irritation, agitation, excitement; emotion; *in ~~ geraten* to grow excited.

aufreiben *irr tr* to rub sore (*od* open); (*zerstören*) to ruin; *mil* to harass; to wipe out; to destroy; *fig* to exhaust, to worry to death; to wear o. s. out.

aufreihen *tr* to string, to thread.

aufreißen *irr tr* to rend, to rip up, to tear open; (*aufbrechen*) to break up; (*Tür*) to throw open; *die Augen* ~ to stare with o.'s eyes open; to open o.'s eyes wide.

aufreiz|en *tr* to incite, to provoke, to rouse; to stir; *jdn ~~ etw zu tun* to egg s. o. to do s. th.; **~ung** *f* provocation; instigation.

aufricht|en *tr* to set up(right), to erect; (*aufheben, aufstellen*) to lift up, to raise; to put up; *aero* (*nach Sturzflug*) to pull out (of a dive), (*vor der Landung*) to flatten out, to level off; (*unterstützen*) to support, to bear up; (*trösten*) to comfort, to console; *sich ~en* to get up, to rise; (*im Bett*) to sit up; **~ig** *a* sincere, candid, frank, true, honest, upright; straightforward; *mein ~~es Beileid* my sincere condolences; *es tut mir ~~ leid* I am sincerely sorry; *~~ gesagt* frankly; *~~ der Ihrige* (*Ihr sehr ergebener*) yours truly, yours sincerely; **~igkeit** *f* sincerity, cando(u)r, veracity, genuineness.

aufriegeln *tr* to unbar, to unbolt.

Aufriß *m* draught, design, draft; lay-out; (*Skizze*) sketch; (*äußere Ansicht*) elevation, (*Vorderansicht*) front elevation; (*perspektivischer* ~) perspective view.

aufritzen *tr* to slit; to rip (open); (*Haut*) to scratch open, to chap.

aufrollen *tr* to roll up; to coil; *mil* to turn a flank; (*entfalten*) to unroll; *e-e Frage* ~ to broach a question; *itr der Vorhang rollt auf* the curtain rises; *sich* ~ to unfurl; **Aufrollung** *f* convolution, winding up; *mil* flanking movement.

aufrücken *itr* to move up(ward), to rise; *mil* to close the ranks; (*befördert werden*) to be promoted.

Aufruf *m* calling up, call, proclamation; summons *pl*; ~ *an* appeal to; (*Banknoten*) withdrawal; (*Gläubiger*) summoning; **~en** *irr tr* to call up; (*gerichtlich*) to summon, to proclaim; to call on (a pupil); (*Banknoten*) to withdraw from circulation, to call in; *die Namen wurden nach dem Alphabet aufgerufen* the names were called in alphabetical order; *namentlich ~~ mil* to call the roll.

Auf|ruhr *m* riot, uproar, tumult; (*Meuterei*) mutiny, revolt; insurrection; **~rühren** *tr* to stir up; *fig* (*Skandal, alte Geschichte*) to rake up; to bring up; (*Erinnerung*) to revive; (*zum Umsturz*) to incite to rebellion; (*Leidenschaften*) to stir, to inflame; **~rührer** *m* agitator, rioter, ringleader; mutineer, rebel, insurgent; **~~isch** *a* turbulent, mutinous, rebellious, riotous; insurgent; (*Rede*) inflammatory, seditious.

aufrüst|en *tr* to (re)arm; *tech* to assemble, to rig; **~bahn** *f tech* assembly line; **~ung** *f* rearmament.

aufrüttel|n *tr* to shake up; (*aus dem Schlafe*) to rouse; **~ung** *f* rousing.

aufsagen *tr* to recite, to repeat; (*aufkündigen*) to give notice (*od* warning).

aufsammeln *tr* to gather, to pick up; to hoard.

aufsässig *a* refractory, rebellious.

Aufsatz *m* (*oberer Teil*) head-piece, top; (*Tafel~*) centre-piece; (*Abhandlung*) essay, treatise; (*Schule*) composition, paper; (*Zeitungs~*) article; *tech* fixture; *mil* (*Visier*) gun-sight; **~fehler** *m mil* error in range; **~höhe** *f mil* elevation; **~thema** *n* theme; **~winkel** *m mil* tangent elevation.

auf|saugen *tr* to suck up; *chem* to absorb; **~scharren** *tr* to scrape up.

aufschauen *itr* to look up, to lift up o.'s eyes, to take heed; *aufgeschaut!* take care of yourself!

aufscheuchen *tr* to frighten; (*Wild*) to start; to scare (away).

aufscheuern *tr* (*Boden*) to scrub, to scour; (*Haut*) to chafe, to scour off o.'s skin, to gall by scouring.

aufschicht|en *tr* to pile up, to range; to stack; (*in Schichten legen*) to arrange in layers, to stratify; **~ung** *f geol* stratification.

aufschieben *irr tr* to shove open; *fig* to delay, to put off; (*auf Zeitpunkt*) to defer, to postpone; to adjourn; *aufgeschoben ist nicht aufgehoben* omittance is no acquittance.

aufschießen *irr tr* to open (a breach); *itr* to shoot up; (*aufspringen*) to spring up, to leap up; (*groß werden*) to grow tall; *aufgeschossen, lang u. mager* lanky, lean and tall (of limbs).

Aufschlag *m* striking; (*Steuer*) surtax, additional tax; (*Hose*) turn-up; (*am Rock*) lapel, revers; (*am Kleid*) facing; (*e-r Granate*) impact, burst, hit, graze; *sl* dud; (*Ärmel~*) cuff; (*Preis~*) rise; surplus, advance, additional charge, extra cost; (*Tennis*) service; (*bei Versteigerung*) highest bid (at auctions) **~en** *irr itr* (*auftreffen*) to hit, to strike; *aero* (*unfreiwillige Bodenberührung*) to strike ground, to hit the ground, (*aufbumsen*) to pancake; (*Tennis*) to serve; (*Waren*) to rise (in price); *tr* (*aufbrechen*) to break open; (*Zelt, Lager*) to pitch (a camp); (*Gerüst, Bett*) to set up, to put up; (*Buch*) to open; (*Wohnsitz*) to take up (o.'s abode); (*Wort*) to look up (a word); (*Wörterbuch*) to consult; (*Augen*) to open, to cast up o.'s eyes, to look up; (*Preis*) to raise; (*Ärmel*) to tuck up; (*Hose, Hutkrempe*) to turn up; (*Knie*) to cut, to bruise (o.'s knee); **~brand** *m aero* crash-fire; **~etisch** *m* folding-table; **~slinie** *f* service-line; **~zünder** *m* percussion fuse (*Abk* P. fuse), impact fuse (*od* detonator).

Aufschläger *m* (*Tennis*) server.

aufschließen *irr tr* to unlock, to open; *chem* to break up; to disintegrate; to decompose; (*Markt*) to develop, to open up; *fig* (*erklären*) to explain; to disclose; *itr mil* (*die Reihen* ~) to close the ranks; *sich* ~ to unfold; to pour out (o.'s heart).

aufschlitzen *tr* to rip up, to slit open.

Aufschluß *m* (*Erklärung*) disclosure; explication, solution; ~ *geben* to give information about; to give an explanation, to give the particulars of a matter; **~reich** *a* instructive, informative.

aufschmieren *tr* to smear upon, to butter (bread); *fam* to foist s. th.; *itr* to fly open, to spring open.

aufschnallen *tr* to tie on; (*auflösen*) to unbrace; to unbuckle.

aufschnappen *tr* to snap up; (*ein Wort*) to catch a word; to pick up.

aufschneid|en *irr tr* to cut up, to cut open; to unseam; (*Braten*) to carve; *med* to dissect; (*Buch*) to cut the leaves of; *aufgeschnittene Exemplare* copies with cut (*od* trimmed) edges; *itr* (*übertreiben*) to exaggerate, to talk big; (*prahlen*) to brag, to swagger, to boast; **~er** *m* swaggerer, braggart, boaster, story-teller, *Am sl* four-flusher; **~erei** *f* swagger, brag, bragging, boasting; (*Unsinn*) fudge, fabrication, nonsense; (*Übertreibung*) exaggeration.

aufschnellen *itr* to jerk up, to fly up.

Aufschnitt *m: kalter* ~ (slices of) cold meats *pl*, *Am* cold cuts *pl*; **~maschine** *f* (*beim Metzger*) slicing machine.

aufschnüren *tr* to unlace, to untie.

aufschrauben *tr* (*auf etw*) to screw on; (*losschrauben*) to unscrew.

aufschrecken *tr* to rouse, to startle; *itr* to start, to jump.

Aufschrei *m* shriek, scream; *fig* outcry; **~en** *irr itr* to cry out; to shriek, to scream.

auf|schreiben *irr tr* to write down, to record; to put down, to take down, to note, to make a note of; (*belasten*) to charge to s. o.'s account; **~schrift** *f* address, label (on bottles); inscription, epigraph (on monuments); (*auf Schaufenstern, Ladentüren*) sign, name; *ohne ~~* without an address.

Aufschub *m* delay; (*Vertagung*) adjournment; (*auf bestimmte Zeit*) postponement; (~ *der Strafvollstreckung*) stay (of execution); (*e-s Todesurteils*) reprieve; (*für Zahlungen*) respite; deferment; *e-n ~ bewilligen* to grant a respite, to give respite; *ohne* ~ without delay; *die Sache duldet keinen* ~ the matter is most urgent.

aufschürzen *tr* to gird up, to tuck up.

aufschütteln *tr* to shake up; to rouse from sleep.

aufschütt|en *tr* to heap up; to pour on; (*Pulver*) to prime; (*Korn*) to garner; (*Kies*) to metal (the road); (*Erde*) to deposit; (*aufspeichern*) to store up; (*Damm*) to raise, to throw up; **~ung** *f* (*Sand, geologisch*) accumulation, deposit, sediment; (*aufspeichern*) storing, piling up.

aufschwatzen *tr* to talk into buying.

aufschwell|en *irr itr* to swell up; *fig* to enlarge, to increase; **~ung** *f* swelling, protuberance.

auf|schwingen *irr r* to soar up, to rise; *fig* to make o.'s way; **~schwung** *m* swing; (*Turnen*) upward circle, swinging up; (*Phantasie*) flight; (*Seele, Geist*) elevation; (*wirtschaftlich*) sudden growth, rapid development, rise, boom; upswing; (*Antrieb*) stimulus, impulse; (*Fortschritt*) progress; (*Wohlstand*) prosperity; (*Besserung*) improvement, recovery; *e-n neuen ~~ nehmen* to revive.

aufseh|en *itr* to look up; *~~ n* sensation, attention, stir; (*ärgerliches*) scandal; *~~ erregen* to cause (*od* to create) a sensation, to make a stir, to attract attention; *um ~~ zu vermeiden* to avoid notice; **~er** *m* overseer, inspector, surveyor; (*Wärter*) keeper; attendant; (*Stiftung*) custodian; superintendent; (*Gefangenen~~*) jailer, warden; (*im Warenhaus*) shopwalker, *Am* floorwalker.

auf sein *irr itr* to be up; (*Tür*) to be open.

aufsetz|en *tr* to pile up; (*Kegel*) to set up the pins; (*Speisen*) to serve up; (*Hut*) to put on; (*Flicken*) to sew on; *Hörner ~* to cuckold; (*Wasser*) to put the kettle on; *schriftlich ~~* to compose, to draw up; (*entwerfen*) to draft, to make a draft; *aero* (*Maschine bei Landung*) to touch-down; *seinen Kopf ~~* to be obstinate; *ein Gesicht ~~* to put on a face; *e-e Rechnung ~~* to make up an account; *r* to sit upright; *sich gegen etw ~~* to rise against; **~geschwindigkeit** *f aero* touch-down speed; **~punkt** *m aero* touch-down point.

Aufsicht *f* inspection, survey; (*Überwachung*) supervision, control; (*durch Polizei*) surveillance; *staatliche ~* public control; (*Obhut*) guardianship; (*Pflege, Schutz*) care; (*Verantwortung*) charge; (*Draufsicht*) topview; *unter polizeilicher ~ stehen* to be under police-supervision; **~samt** *n* supervisory board, board of control; **~sbeamte(r)** *m* supervisor, superintendent; supervising official; keeper; **~sbehörde** *f* board of control; **~sführender** *m* man who is in charge of; *in ~sführender Eigenschaft* in a supervisory capacity; **~sinstanz** *f* supervisory jurisdiction; supervisory board; **~skomittee** *n* supervising committee; **~smaßnahmen** *f pl* measures of control; **~sorgan** *n* controlling body; **~spersonal** *n* superintending staff, *Am* superintendency staff; **~srat** *m* board of directors.

aufsitzen *irr itr* to sit on (*od* upon); (*nachts*) to sit up; (*von Vögeln*) to perch; (*Schiff*) to run aground; (*auf Pferd*) to mount; *~!* (*Befehl*) mount! *fig* (*in der Klemme sein*) to be in a fix; *~ lassen* to leave in the lurch.

auf|spalten *tr, itr* to cleave, to split, to burst; **~spannen** *tr* to stretch; (*Segel*) to set; (*Schirm, Fächer*) to open, to put up; (*auf Leinwand*) to mount; (*Saite*) to string; **~sparen** *tr* to lay by, to save, to reserve; **~speichern** *tr* to store up; to warehouse; **~speicherung** *f* (*von Energie*) accumulation; (*von Elektrizität*) storage; **~sperren** *tr* (*aufschließen*) to unlock; (*aufmachen*) to open wide; *das Maul ~~* to gape; *Mund und Nase ~~* to be wonder-struck; **~spielen** *tr, itr* to play (to the dance); to strike up; *r* to kick up a dust, to show off; to set up for; **~spießen** *tr* to spit, to pierce, to spear; (*mit der Gabel*) to lift; (*mit den Hörnern*) to gore; (*mit e-m Pfahl*) to impale; **~sprengen** *tr* to break up, to burst open; to blow up; **~springen** *irr itr* to jump up, to bounce; (*Risse bekommen*) to crack; (*Türe*) to fly open; (*Haut*) to chap; **~spritzen** *tr* to sprinkle to; *itr* to splash up; **~sprudeln** *itr* to bubble up; **~sprungbahn** *f* (*beim Skilauf*) alighting ground, landing run; **~spüren** *tr* to spy out, to track s. o. down; to detect, to trace.

aufstacheln *tr* (*antreiben, anspornen*) to goad; *fig* to stimulate, to incite; (*Leidenschaften*) to rouse.

aufstampfen *tr* to stamp o.'s foot, to stamp on the ground.

Auf|stand *m* rebellion, revolt; insurrection; (*Aufruhr*) uproar, riot, tumult; (*Meuterei*) mutiny; **~ständisch** *a* insurgent, rebellious, mutinous. **~ständige(r)** *m* insurgent, rebel, rioter.

aufstapeln *tr* to heap up, to store up, to pile up, to stack up.

aufstechen *irr tr* to prick open; *med* to lance (an abscess).

aufsteck|en *tr* to put upon, to fix, to stick up; (*mit Nadeln*) to pin up; (*Haar*) to do up; (*Vorhänge*) to put up; (*aufgeben, z. B. ein Geschäft*) to giv e up, to abandon; *jdm ein Licht über etw ~~* to enlighten s. o. on s. th.; **~kamm** *m* tucking-comb, dressing-comb; **~schuh** *m* accessory clip.

aufstehen *irr itr* to be open; (*sich erheben*) to get up, to stand up; to recover (from a sickness); (*gegen jdn*) to rise in arms, to revolt, to rebel.

aufsteigen *irr itr* to rise, to mount; (*auf e-n Berg, Ballon*) to ascend; (*auf e-e Leiter*) to climb; (*auf Pferd*) to mount; (*anwachsen*) to increase, to swell; (*Gefühl*) to well up; (*hinaufklettern*) to go up, to climb up; *aero* to take off, to start; to take to the air; to climb; **~d** *a* rising, ascending.

aufstell|en *tr* (*hinstellen*) to put up, to set up, to raise, to erect; (*Falle*) to lay; (*Wachen*) to post; (*bei der Wahl*) to put up s. o. as a candidate, to nominate s. o.; *als Schiedsrichter ~en* to appoint as umpire; (*Truppen*) to activate; to draw up; (*Bilanz*) to draw up, to make up, to prepare; (*Wagen abstellen*) to park; *aero* (*Flugzeug zum Start*) to line-up; (*Lehren*) to start, to lay down; (*Rechnung*) to make up; *e-e Behauptung ~en* to make an assertion; *e-n Grundsatz ~en* to lay down, to set up a principle; *Bedingungen ~en* to make terms (*od* conditions); to stipulate; *Zeugen ~en* to produce (*od* to bring in) witnesses; *e-n Rekord ~en* to establish, to get, to constitute a record; (*montieren*) to fit, to fix, to lay down, to assemble; *sich ~en* to station o. s., to take o.'s post; to place o. s., to post o. s.; to gather, to assemble; *mil* to draw up, to form up; *sich ~~ lassen* (*als Kandidat*) to stand for (Parliament), *Am* to run for (Congress); **~ung** *f* setting up; putting-up; (*Anordnung*) arrangement; (*Darlegung, z. B. Liste von Waren*) statement; (*Tabelle*) table; (*Behauptung*) assertion; (*~~ e-r Mannschaft beim Spiel*) formation, position; (*von Maschinen*) erection, installation, assembly; (*als Kandidat*) nomination; (*zum Verkauf*) display; (*Aufzählung*) inventory; (*Truppen*) drawing-up; (*Liste*) list; (*e-s Zeugen*) producing.

auf|stemmen *tr* to open with a chisel; to force open; to prize open; *r* to lean upon; **~stieg** *m* ascent, *Am meist* ascension; *fig* rise; (*Flugzeug*) take-off; (*sozialer ~~*) advancement; (*am Fahrrad*) (foot)step; **~stöbern** *tr* to rouse; to stir up; (*aufspüren*) to ferret out, to discover; **~stöpseln** *tr* to uncork; **~stören** *tr* to stir up; (*aus der Ruhe*) to rouse, to disturb; **~stoßen** *irr tr* to push open; to fling open; (*auf etw*) to knock against, to struck on s. th.; to occur, to come in s. o.'s way; *itr* (*rülpsen*) *jdm ~~* to belch, to eructate; *mar* to run aground; *fig* to occur to; to stick; **~streben** *itr* to strive (*od* to struggle) upwards, to aspire; **~streichen** *irr tr* to lay on, to spread (butter on bread); **~streifen** *tr* to draw up, to turn up; **~streuen** *tr* to sprinkle upon, to strew upon; **~strich** *m* (*aufs Brot*) spread; (*beim Schreiben*) up-stroke; **~stülpen** *tr* (*Ärmel*) to tuck up, to turn up; (*Hut*) to put on, to clap on (a hat); *aufgestülpte Nase* snub-nose; **~stutzen** *tr* to trim up; to renovate; **~stützen** *tr* to prop up; to support; *sich ~~ auf* to lean on, to rest on.

aufsuch|en *tr* to seek out, to inquire after, to search after (*od* for); *jdn ~en* to go to see, to visit, to look up; **~ung** *f* search.

auf|takeln *tr* to rig up; *~getakelt a* well-rigged, togged up; **~takt** *m mus* up-beat, unaccented beat, anacrusis; *fig*(*Eröffnung, Aufklang*) prelude, preliminaries *pl*; initial phase; **~tanken** *tr aero* to refuel; **~tauchen** *itr* to rise up, to emerge; (*plötzlich erscheinen*) to pop up, to appear; *mar* (*U-Boot*) to break the surface, to surface, to emerge; **~tauen** *tr, itr* to thaw; *fig* to wake up, to thaw out; to melt; **~teilen** *tr* to partition, to apportion, to distribute, *Am* to break down; **~teilung** *f* partition(ing), apportionment, allotment, distribution, *Am* break down; **~~sschlüssel** *m* division key; **~tischen** *tr* to dish up, to serve up; to treat.

Auftrag *m com* (*Bestellung*) order, command; (*Besorgung*) commission; (*Befehl, Pflicht*) charge; (*Ernennung*) appointment, *Am* assignment; (*Weisung*) direction, instruction; *jur* mandate; (*Farben~*) coat; *im ~e von* by order of; *im ~ u. auf Rechnung von* by order and for account of; *im ~, Abk i.A.* by order (of); *e-n ~ erteilen* to give an order; *in ~ nehmen* to book, to reserve; *in e-m besonderen ~* on a mission; *e-n ~ ausführen* to execute a commission; **~en** *tr* to serve up, to dish up; (*Farben*) to lay on, to coat; (*Besorgungen*) to commission; (*Schuhkrem*) to put on the cream; (*Druckerschwärze*) to distribute the printing ink; to roll up; (*prahlen*) to boast, to brag; *jdm etw ~en* to charge; (*übertreiben*) to exaggerate; *dick ~~* to lay it on thick; to put it on thick; (*Grüße ~~*) to ask to give (*od* to convey); *jdm e-e Arbeit ~~* to give s. o. work; (*abnutzen*) to wear out, to use up; **~geber** *m com* (*Besteller*) orderer; commissioner; (*Kunde*) customer; (*Arbeitgeber*) employer; (*Absender*) consignor; *jur* mandator; (*Börse*) principal; **~gemäß** *adv* according to order; *com* as per order; **~sbestand** *m* orders on hand, unfilled orders *pl*; **~sbestätigung** *f* confirmation of a given order; **~sbuch** *n* order book; **~serteilung** *f* conferring of contract; placing of the order; **~sformular** *n* order form, *Am* blank; **~srückstand** *m* backlog of orders; **~szettel** *m* order slip; job ticket; **~walze** *f typ* ink-roller.

auftreiben *irr tr* to drive up; (*ausdehnen*) to blow up; *med* to distend, to swell up; (*aufjagen*) to start, to rouse; (*auffinden*) to hunt up; to obtain, to get hold of; (*die Mittel*) to find the means; (*Geld*) to raise money.

auftrennen *tr* to rip; to unstitch, to undo.

auftreten *irr tr* to tread open, to kick open; *itr* to step on, (*leise*) to tread softly; (*verfahren*) to proceed, to go to work; (*benehmen*) to behave; (*handeln*) to act; *sicher* ~ to act with assurance; (*sich zeigen*) to come forward, to appear; to be found; to break out; (*im Theater*) to perform, to appear (on the scene), to make o.'s appearance, (*zum ersten Mal*) to make o.'s début; (*gegen jdn*) to rise against; (*vor Gericht*) to appear against s. o.; to bring an action against s. o.; *als Zeuge* ~ to appear as witness; ~ *n* way of proceeding; (*Betragen*) bearing, manners *pl*, behavio(u)r; (*Erscheinen*) appearance; (*Vorkommen*) occurrence; (*Ausbruch*) outbreak.

Auftrieb *m* (~ *des Viehs in den Alpen*) driving of cattle into Alpine pasture; *fig* (*Anstoß*) impetus, stimulus; *aero* (*Aufwind beim Segelflug*) up-current, up-draft of the wind; anabatic wind; *phys* lift; buoyancy; *dynamischer* ~ dynamic lift; *thermischer* ~ thermal lift; **~sanzeiger** *m aero* lift indicator; **~sbeiwert** *m* coefficient of lift; **~serhöhung** *f* increase of lift; **~skraft** *f* buoyancy; lift component; **~sverlust** *m* loss of lift.

Auftritt *m* (*Zwischenfall*) incident; (*Auseinandersetzung*) quarrel, argument; (*Erscheinen*) appearance; (*Szene im Theater*) scene; (*Trittbrett*) step; running board; *e-n* ~ *machen* to make (*od* to create) a scene.

auftrocknen *tr*, *itr* to dry up.

auftrumpfen *itr* to boast; to exult.

auftun *irr tr* to open; *r* (*Blumen*) to expand; (*Abgrund*) to yawn; (*Verein*) to get started, to start.

auftürmen *tr* to pile up, to heap up; *r* to tower (up); (*von Schwierigkeiten*) to accumulate.

aufwachen *itr* to awake(n), to wake up; (*plötzlich*) to start up.

aufwachsen *irr itr* to grow up.

aufwall|en *tr* to bubble, to boil up; *fig* to fly into a passion; **~ung** *f* bubbling, swell; *chem* ebullition; *fig* emotion; (*Ausbruch, Anfall*) fit; (*Leidenschaft*) transport; (*Ausbruch*) outburst.

Aufwand *m* expenditure, expense, costs *pl*; (*unnützer*) waste; (*Luxus, Prunk*) luxury, pomp; (*Stimm~*) flow of language; *das ist den* ~ *nicht wert* that isn't worth the effort; *großen* ~ *machen* to live in great style; ~ *von Gelehrsamkeit* display of learning.

aufwärmen *tr* to warm up, to cook up; *fig* to bring up again; *alte Geschichten* ~ to rake up old stories.

Aufwart|efrau *f* (*Putzfrau*) charwoman; **~en** *itr: jdm* ~~ to wait on, to attend on; **~ung** *f* visit; (*Bedienung*) attendance; help; *jdm seine* ~~ *machen* to call upon.

Auf|wärter *m* waiter; attendant; help; **~~in** *f* waitress; **~wärts** *adv* up; upward(s); uphill; *fluß~~* up(stream), *der Dampfer fährt fluß~~* the steamer is going up; *~~! interj* (*Fahrstuhlführer*) going up! **~wärtsbewegung** *f* raising tendency, upward tendency, rise; upswing; **~wärtsflug** *m* climbing flight; **~wärtshaken** *m* (*Boxen*) uppercut, lifting punch; **~wärtstransformator** *m* step-up transformer.

aufwasch|en *irr tr* to wash up; **~küche** *f* scullery; **~schüssel** *f* wash-up basin; **~tisch** *m* wash-up table; **~wasser** *n* dish-water, slop.

auf|wecken *tr* to awake(n), to waken, to wake up; to call up; *fig* to enliven; **~wehen** *tr* to blow up, to blow open; **~weichen** *tr* to wet, to temper (colo(u)rs); to soak; *itr* to grow soft; **~weisen** *irr tr* to show, to present; to exhibit, to produce; to have; *genügende Mittel* ~~ to produce sufficient means; **~wenden** *irr tr* to spend; *unnütz* ~~ to waste; **~wendung** *f* expense; expenditure; *soziale ~wendungen f pl* social disbursements *pl* (*od* expenditure); **~werfen** *irr tr* to cast up, to fling open (a door); (*Graben*) to dig; (*Frage*) to raise a question; *sich* ~ *zu etw* to set up for; **~werten** *tr* to revalorize; **~wertung** *f* revaluation, revalorization; **~wertungsanleihe** *f* stabilization loan; **~wickeln** *tr* to roll up, to turn up (o.'s hair), to wind up; (*loswickeln*) to unfold; to unroll; (*auseinanderwickeln*) to unwrap; (*Taue*) to coil; **~wiegeln** *tr* to stir up, to raise up; (*hetzen*) to instigate, to agitate; to incite; **~wiegelung** *f* instigation; **~wiegen** *irr tr* to outweigh; to compensate for, to make up for; to counterbalance; **~wiegler** *m* agitator, demagog(ue); **~~isch** *a* mutinous; seditious, inflammatory; **~wieglung** *f* instigation, incitement; **~wind** *m aero* up-current, upwind, up-draft, anabatic wind; **~~bö** *f* bump; **~~gebiet** *n aero* upwind region; **~~segelflug** *m* upwind soaring; **~winden** *irr tr* to wind up, to twist; (*aufrollen*) to untwist; (*Last*) to heave, to hoist; (*aufholen*) to haul up; *den Anker* ~~ to weigh the anchor; **~windevorrichtung** *f* hoisting attachment; **~wirbeln** *tr* to whirl up; (*Fenster*) to unbolt; *Staub* ~~ to raise (dust); *fig* to create quite a sensation; **~wischen** *tr* to wipe up; to mop up; (*reinigen*) to clean; **~wühlen** *tr* to root up; to turn up; (*aufgraben*) to dig up; (*Meer*) to lash up; *fig* to agitate; to stir up, to upset; **~wurf** *m* (*Erde*) bank, mound, dam.

aufzähl|en *tr* to enumerate, to detail; (*nennen*) to name; to count up, to reckon up; (*namentlich*) to itemize; (*Geld*) to pay down (money); **~ung** *f* enumeration; counting; **~~sreihe** *f* frequency distribution.

aufzäumen *tr* to bridle; *das Pferd am Schwanz* ~ to put the cart before the horse.

aufzehr|en *tr* to eat up, to consume; to use up; (*erschöpfen*) to exhaust; (*aufsaugen*) to absorb; *fig* to waste, to spend; **~ung** *f* consumption.

aufzeichn|en *tr* to design, to sketch; to draw; (*niederschreiben*) to take down, to write down, to note down; (*in Geschäftsbüchern*) to book, to enter; (*zu Berichten*) to register, to record; **~ung** *f* note; booking; record; **~~en** *f pl* (*e-s Verstorbenen*) papers *pl*.

aufzeigen *tr* (*vorzeigen*) to show; (*als Beweis, ausstellen*) to exhibit.

aufzieh|en *irr tr* to draw up, to open; (*hochziehen, hochheben*) to pull up, to haul up, to hoist, to raise; (*Anker*) to weigh; (*Schleuse*) to open; (*Segel*) to hoist up (the sails); (*Schleife*) to untie; (*Uhr*) to wind up (a watch); (*Schublade*) to open a drawer; (*Kind*) to bring up; (*Vieh*) to breed, to rear; (*Saiten*) to string, to put on; (*Pflanzen*) to cultivate; (*aufkleben, bes. auf Leinwand*) to stretch on, to mount; (*Buchrücken*) to stick; *den Vorhang* ~~ to raise (*od* to draw) the curtain; *gelindere Saiten* ~~ to come down a peg or two; *jdn* ~~ to jeer at, to chaff, to tease, to rally; *itr* (*ankommen*) to march up; (*Gewitter*) to come on, to draw on, to gather; *auf Wache* ~~ to mount guard; (*erscheinen*) to appear; **~er** *m anat* levator muscle; **~karton** *m* mounting board; **~leine** *f aero* (*Fallschirm*) rip-cord.

aufzischen *itr* to fizz.

Aufzucht *f* (*von Vieh*) breeding, rearing.

Aufzug *m* (*Fahrstuhl*) lift, *Am* elevator; (*Flaschen~*) hoist, lift; (*Schräg~*) inclined lift; (*Kran*) crane; *phot* (*Rollfilmkamera, Transportknopf*) winding key; (*für Uhrenwerk*) winder; (*Personen- u. Waren~*) passenger and service lift; (*beim Turnen*) pull-up; (*Küchen~*) *Am* dumb-waiter; (*Weberei*) chain; mounting; (*Umzug*) procession; (*Festspiel, Schauspiel, Parade*) pageant, cavalcade, parade; train; (*Anzug*) show dress, attire, appearance, get-up, outfit; *theat* act; **~hebel** *m phot* (*Verschluß*) setting lever for shutter; **~leine** *f aero* (*Fallschirm*) release-cord, rip-cord; **~schacht** *m* lift-shaft.

auf|zwängen *tr* to press open; **~zwingen** *irr tr* to obtrude, to force upon.

Augapfel *m* eyeball, apple; *fig* (*Liebling*) darling.

Auge *n* eye; (*Kartoffel~*) eye; (*Fett~*) grease drop; (*Knospe*) bud(-eye); (*auf Karten*) pip, point; *ein* ~ *zudrücken* to wink at, to shut o.'s eyes at; *ein* ~ *haben auf* to have an eye upon; *ins* ~ *fassen* to fix o.'s eye upon; *Sand in die ~n streuen* to throw dust in the eyes of; *kein* ~ *zutun* not sleep a wink; *die ~n verbinden* to blindfold; *jdn nicht aus den ~n lassen* to keep o.'s eyes upon; *aus den ~n verlieren* to lose sight of; to lose track of s. o.; *im* ~ *behalten* to keep track of s. th., to keep o.'s eye on s. th.; *ganz* ~ *u. Ohr sein* to be all attention; *mit bloßem* ~ with the naked eye; *unter vier ~n* face to face, in private; *mit e-m blauen* ~ *davonkommen* to have a narrow escape; *in die ~n fallen* to strike (*od* to catch) the eye; *in die ~n fallend* obvious, striking, manifest; (*Sehkraft*) sight; *gute* (*schlechte*) *~n haben* to have a good (bad) sight; *aus den ~n, aus dem Sinn* out of sight, out of mind; (*Ansicht*) view, opinion; *in meinen ~n* in my opinion; *mit anderen ~n ansehen* to take a different view; *ins* ~ *sehen fig* to face; *die ~n gehen mir auf* I begin to see now; *vor ~n führen* to point out, to demonstrate, to visualize; *~n geradeaus! mil* eyes front! *~n rechts!* (*links!*) *mil* eyes right! (left!); *sie tat alles, was sie ihm an den ~n absehen konnte* she anticipated his every wish; *ich sah es ihr an den ~n an, daß sie log* I saw from her face that she was lying; *das paßt wie die Faust aufs* ~ that does not fit at all; *geh' mir aus den ~n* get out of my sight; *mit e-m lachenden u. e-m weinenden* ~ with mingled feelings of joy and sadness; *jdm unter die ~n treten fig* to face s. o.; *jdm schöne ~n machen* to give s. o. the glad eye; *das* ~ *des Gesetzes wacht* the eye of law is ever vigilant; *seine ~n waren größer als sein Magen* his eyes were bigger than his belly.

äugeln *tr* (*okulieren*) to inoculate, to bud; *itr nach jdm* ~ to leer at, to ogle; **äugen** *itr* to look about carefully.

Augen|arzt *m* oculist, eye-doctor; ophthalmologist; **~bad** *n* eyedouche; **~befund** *m med* status of the eye; **~binde** *f* bandage; **~blick** *m* moment, instant; *im* ~~ for the moment; (*im Nu*) in an instant, in a trice; *ein günstiger* ~~ a favo(u)rable moment, a good opportunity; *in dem ~~e wo* at the moment when; **~blicklich** *a* immediate, momentary; instant(aneous); *adv* immediately; for the moment, at present, just now; **~blicksaufnahme** *f phot* snapshot, instantaneous photograph; **~blickswert** *m* momentary value, present value; **~bogen** *m* orbital ridge; **~braue** *f* eyebrow; **~diener** *m* eye-servant; **~entzündung** *f* inflammation of the eye, ophthalmia; **~fällig** *a* conspicuous, evident, obvious; **~farbe** *f* colo(u)r of the eye; **~fehler** *m* visual error; **~flimmern** *n* twitching of eye; **~glas** *n* eye-glass; (*bei Gasmaske*) eyepiece; (*bei Taucher*) lenses *pl*; (*allgemein*) eyewear; **~heilanstalt** *f* ophthalmic hospital; **~heilkunde** *f* ophthalmology; **~höhe** *f*: *in ~höhe* at eye-level; **~höhle** *f* orbit; socket of the eye; **~klappe** *f* patch (over the eye), (*für Pferde*) eye-flap; **~krankheit** *f* disease of the eyes; **~licht** *n* eyesight; **~lid** *n* eyelid; **~maß** *n* eyesight, estimate by the eye; *~~ haben* to have a sure eye; **~merk** *n* point of view, aim, mark; *sein ~~ auf etw gerichtet haben* to aim at; **~mittel** *n* ophthalmic remedy; (*äußerlich*) eye-lotion; **~nerv** *m* eyestring; optic nerve; **~operation** *f* operation on the eye; **~pulver** *n* powder for the eyes; **~salbe** *f* eye-ointment; **~schein** *m* appearance, evidence; (*Besichtigung*) inspection, view; *etw in ~~ nehmen* to take a view of; *das lehrt der ~~* that is evident; **~scheinlich** *a* evident, manifest; **~~keit** *f* obviousness; **~schirm** *m* eye shade; **~spiegel** *m* eye-mirror, ophthalmoscope; **~sprache** *f* language of the eyes; **~star** *m med* cataract; **~stern** *m* pupil; **~täuschung** *f* optic illusion; **~trost** *m bot* eyebright; **~wasser** *n* eyewater, eye-lotion; **~weh** *n* pain in the eye(s); (*Überanstrengung*) eye strain; (*Ermüdung*) eye fatigue; **~weide** *f* delight of the eyes; **~wimper** *f* eyelash; **~wink** *m* twinkle; **~winkel** *m* angle (*od* corner) of the eye; **~zahn** *m* eye-tooth, canine tooth; **~zeuge** *m* eyewitness; **~zittern** *n* mystagmus.

Äuglein *n* little eye; *bot* bud.

August *m* August; (*Name*) Augustus; (*der dumme ~*) clown.

Auktion *f* auction, sale by auction, public sale; *in ~ geben* to put up for auction; **~ator** *m* auctioneer; **~sraum** *m* sale-room.

Aula *f* (great) hall.

Aurikel *f bot* auricula, bear's ear.

aus *prp* 1. from: *~ dem Englischen* from the English; *~ Liebe* from love; *~ guter Quelle* from a good source; *~ den Zeitungen* from the papers; *~ Überzeugung* from conviction, *~ Unwissenheit* from ignorance; *~ Geiz* from avarice; *~ London* from London; 2. of: *~ alter Familie* of ancient family; *werden ~* to become of; *~ Holz* wooden, made of wood; 3. through: *~ Haß* through hatred; *~ Ehrgeiz* through ambition; *~ Höflichkeit* through politeness; *~ dem Fenster* through the window; 4. for: *~ Mangel an* for want of; *~ diesem Grunde* for this reason; *~ Furcht vor* for fear of; 5. in: *~ Gehorsam* in obedience of; *~ Scherz* in jest; 6. out of: *~ Mitleid* out of pity; *~ der Mode* out of fashion; *~ Achtung* out of respect; *~ Liebe für* out of love for; *~ e-m Glase trinken* to drink out of a glass; 7. by: *~ Erfahrung* by experience; *~ freier Hand* by free choice; *ersehen ~* to see by; 8. on: *~ Grundsatz* on principle; *~ bloßem Verdacht* upon mere suspicion; *adv* (*zu Ende, vorüber*) out, over, finished; *die Schule, Kirche ist ~* school, church is over; *~ sein* to be at an end; *~ werden* to end; *es ist ~ mit ihm* he is undone; it is all over with him; *trinke es ~* drink it up; *von Grund ~* thoroughly; *von Haus ~* originally; *weder ein noch ~ wissen* to be at o.'s wits' end; *auf etw ~ sein* to be bent on s. th., to be set upon s. th.; *jahr~, jahrein* year after year; *es ist ~ damit* that's the end of it; *von hier ~* from here; *von mir ~* as far as I am concerned, for my part; *fam* I don't care; *~! interj* (*Ausschalten des Zündmagneten*) switch off!

ausarbeit|en *tr* to work out; (*im einzelnen*) to elaborate; (*Plan, Dokument, Werk*) to prepare; (*schriftlich*) to write, to compose; **~ung** *f* elaboration; (*Vollendung*) perfection, finishing touch; (*schriftliche*) composition, treatise; (*technische ~~*) trimming.

ausart|en *itr* to degenerate; to become rude; to turn rowdy.

aus|ästen *tr* to prune; **~atmen** *tr* to exhale, to breathe out; *itr* to expire.

aus|backen *irr tr* to bake sufficiently; **~baden** *tr* to suffer for; **~baggern** *tr* to drag; to dredge; **~bau** *m* (*Anbau*) outbuilding; (*Erker*) jetty; (*Vergrößerung*) enlargement; (*Vollendung*) perfection, consolidation; (*Fertigbauen*) completion, finishing; (*abbauen*) dismantling; (*innerer Ausbau*) *tech* lining, timbering; walling; **~baufähig** *a* capable of extension **~bauchen** *itr* to belly out; *sich ~~* to bulge; **~bauen** *tr* to improve, to finish, to complete; *fig* to extend, to develop; *tech* to support, to line, to timber; **~bedingen** *irr tr* to stipulate (for); *sich etw ~~* to reserve to o. s.; **~beißen** *irr tr* to bite out; *sich e-n Zahn ~~* to break out a tooth.

ausbesser|n *tr* to mend, to repair; to redress; to darn (stockings); to put in repair (a house); *mar* to refit, to overhaul, to vamp; (*Schuhe*) to patch; (*Bild*) to touch; (*Schriftsatz*) to correct; **~ung** *f* mending, repair; **~~sarbeit** *f* repair work; **~~skosten** *pl* expenses (*od* cost) of repair, repairs *pl*; **~~swerkstatt** *f* repair shop.

ausbeulen *tr* to swell out, to round out, to take the dents (*od* bruises) out of; to beat out; to straighten.

Ausbeut|e *f* profit; yield, produce; gain; (*Ertrag*) output; (*Umsatz*) returns *pl*; (*Ernte*) crop; **~en** *tr* to make the most of; (*ausnützen*) to exploit; (*schinden*) to sweat; *min* to work; (*Boden*) to cultivate, (*übermäßig*) to exhaust; **~er** *m* exploiter, sweater; **~~tum** *n* sweating-system; slave-driving; **~ung** *f* exploitation; **~~ssystem** *n* sweating system.

ausbezahl|en *tr* to pay out; (*vollständig*) to pay in full; *bar ~~* to pay in cash; **~ung** *f* payment; paying off.

ausbiegen *irr tr* to bend outwards, to turn out; *itr* to make way for, to avoid s. o.

ausbieten *irr tr* to offer, to set out (for sale); (*lobend*) to cry up; (*in der Zeitung*) to advertise; *~ n* display of goods.

ausbild|en *tr* to form, to develop; (*geistig*) to educate, to cultivate; (*verbessern*) to improve; (*schulen*) to train; (*Rekruten*) to drill, to train; to instruct; *r* to study for; to perfect o. s.; *ausgebildet* accomplished, trained; **~er** *m* instructor; (*Sport*) trainer, coach; **~ung** *f* accomplishment, development; training, education; **~~sbeihilfe** *f* educational grant; **~~sflug** *m aero* training flight; **~~skurs** *m* course of instruction; **~~slager** *n* training camp; **~~svorschrift** *f* training manual; **~~szeit** *f* period of training.

ausbitten *irr tr* to request s. th., to ask for; *das bitte ich mir aus* I must insist on this.

ausblasen *irr tr* to blow out; (*Hochofen*) to blow off, to stop, to shut down; (*Dampf*) to exhaust; *jdm das Lebenslicht ~* to give a death-blow to; **Ausbläser** *m mil* blind shell.

ausbleiben *irr itr* to stay (away); *die Post blieb aus* the post has not arrived, the mail is overdue; (*vor Gericht*) to fail to appear, to default; *~ n* non-appearance, non-arrival; cessation; *~ der Zahlung* non-payment.

ausbleichen *itr* to fade; to grow pale; *tr* to bleach out.

Aus|blick *m* look-out; *fig* outlook, prospect, view; **~blühen** *tr* to effloresce, to fade, to decay, to wither; **~bluten** *itr* to cease bleeding; to bleed to death; **~blutungsschlacht** *f* battle of attrition; **~bohren** *tr* to bore; to drill out; **~booten** *tr* to boat, to put into boats, to disembark; *fig* (*aus e-m Amt*) to oust; **~borgen** *tr* to lend out, to borrow.

ausbrechen *irr tr* to break out; (*ausspeien*) to vomit; *itr* (*entstehen*) to originate, to arise, to spring; to break out, to come off; *aus dem Gefängnis ~* to break out, to escape from prison; *aero* (*Maschine bei Start od Landung*) to swing off the runway; (*Ringelpietz machen*) to groundloop; (*Steine im Steinbruch*) to quarry out; (*Gewässer*) to overflow; *in Zorn ~* to fly into a rage; *in Tränen ~* to burst into tears; *in ein Gelächter ~* to burst out laughing.

ausbreit|en *tr* to spread out; to extend; (*Arme*) to stretch; to unfold; (*verbreiten*) to promulgate, to propagate, to diffuse; (*ausplaudern*) to divulge; (*entfalten*) to display; (*ausstreuen*) to scatter, to sprinkle; (*allgemein machen*) to universalize; *r* to run out, to spread; to come into use; *sich in Einzelheiten ~~* to go into details, to diffuse into details; **~ung** *f* spreading, extension; promulgation, propagation.

ausbrennen *irr tr* to be consumed by fire, to burn out; (*Wunden*) to cauterize; *itr* to cease burning.

ausbringen *irr tr* to bring out, to take off; *mar* to hoist out (the boat); (*ausbrüten*) to hatch; *e-e Gesundheit ~* to toast, to drink the health of; *~ n* (*Leistung e-r Maschine*) productive capacity, output.

Ausbruch *m* outbreak; (*Vulkan*) eruption; (*Flucht*) escape, flight; (*Zorn~*) explosion, burst; (*Leidenschaft*) outburst; (*Wahnsinn*) fit of madness; (*Freuden~*) ecstasy; *beim ~ von* at the beginning of; *zum ~ kommen* to break out.

ausbrüt|en *tr* to hatch, to brood; (*Pläne*) to contrive; to plot, to hatch; **~ung** *f* brooding; incubation.

Ausbuchtung *f* recess; pocket; bulge; (*Einschnitt*) indentation; *mil* salient.

ausbuddeln *tr* to dig out.

ausbügeln *tr* to iron, to iron out (folds).

Ausbund *m* (*Muster*) pattern; paragon; embodiment; *~ von Gelehrsamkeit* a prodigy of learning; *ein ~ von Schurke* arch-knave.

ausbürger|n *tr* to deprive of citizenship, to denaturalize; **~ung** *f* expatriation.

ausbürsten *tr* to brush thoroughly, to brush out.

aus|dampfen *itr* to evaporate; to

cease steaming; **~dampfung** *f* evaporation; **~dämpfen** *tr* to exhale, to expel by smoke; (*Kleider*) to clean with steam.
Ausdauer *f* endurance, perseverance; steadiness; (*Emsigkeit*) assiduity; (*Zähigkeit*) tenacity, persistence; **~n** *itr* to last to the end; to hold out; **~nd** *a* persistent, patient, persevering; (*geduldig*) enduring; *bot* perennial.
ausdehn|bar *a* expansible, extensible; **~barkeit** *f* expansibility; **~en** *tr* (*räumlich, durch Wärme*) to expand; (*in die Länge, durch Wärme*) to extend; (*vergrößern*) to enlarge; (*verlängern*) to prolong; *fig* to extend; *r* to spread, to extend; **~end** *a* expansive; **ausgedehnt** *a* extensive, wide(spread); *ein ausgedehnter Freundeskreis* a wide circle of friends; **~ung** *f* extension, expansion; extent; (*Vergrößerung*) enlargement; (*Bereich*) range; *math* dimension; *phys* dilatation; **~~svermögen** *n* power of dilatation; expansive force; **~~szahl** *f* co-efficient of expansion.
ausdenken *irr tr* to find out, to invent; *sich ~* to think out (*od* up); (*erfinden*) to invent; (*sich einbilden*) to imagine; *es ist nicht auszudenken* it is unthinkable.
ausdeut|en *tr* to interpret, to expound; **~ung** *f* interpretation, explanation.
ausdienen *itr* to serve o.'s time; *ausgedient haben* to be worn out (clothes); *ausgedienter Soldat* veteran, ex-service man.
ausdörr|en *tr* to dry up; (*Kehle*) to parch; **~ung** *f* parching.
ausdrehen *tr* to turn off (the gas), to put out (a lamp) by turning; to switch off (electric light); *tech* to hollow out.
ausdreschen *tr* to thrash out.
Ausdruck *m* expression, phrase, term; (*einzelnes Wort*) word; *zum ~ bringen* to express; *~ geben, verleihen* to voice; **~en** *tr* to work off, to print at full length; to finish printing; **~slos** *a* expressionless; (*blaß*) blank; (*gedankenleer*) vacant; **~smittel** *n* means of expression; **~svoll** *a* expressive, significant; (*anregend*) suggestive; **~sweise** *f* mode of expression, language.
ausdrück|en *tr* to squeeze out, to wring (clothes); (*Zigarette*) to mushroom, to stub out; *fig* to express, to utter, to give vent (to); *sich ~en* to express o. s.; **~lich** *a* express, explicit; (*streng*) formal, strict; *adv* expressly, explicitly; (*absichtlich*) intentionally.
aus|duften *tr* to exhale, to evaporate; **~dulden** *itr* to endure, to suffer to the end; **~dünsten** *itr* to evaporate; to perspire, to exhale; to sweat out; *bot* to transpire; **~dünstung** *f* evaporation, perspiration, exhalation.
auseinander *adv* asunder, apart, separately; *weit ~* wide apart; **~brechen** *irr tr* to break (asunder); **~bringen** *irr tr* to part; to separate; **~fahren** *irr itr* to start asunder, to separate suddenly; **~fallen** *irr itr* to fall in pieces; **~falten** *tr* to unfold; **~fliegen** *irr itr* to fly asunder; to be scattered; **~gehen** *irr itr* (*sich trennen*) to part; (*Gesellschaft*) to break up; (*Menge*) to disperse; (*Wege*) to branch off; (*Meinungen*) to differ, to be divided; **~~d** *a* divergent; **~halten** *irr tr* to keep apart, to distinguish; **~jagen** *tr* to scatter; **~kommen** *irr itr* to become separated, (*im Gedränge*) to lose sight of one another; **~laufen** *irr itr* to run hither and thither; (*Truppen*) to disband; *math* to diverge; **~legen** *tr* to unfold, to spread out, to take to pieces (a machine); *fig* to explain, to analyse; **~nehmen** *irr tr* to disassemble, to dismantle, to take apart, to take to pieces, to strip; *el* to disconnect; to dismount; **~setzen** *tr* to place asunder; (*erklären*) to make clear, to analyse, to explain; *sich ~~ mit* to come to an understanding with, to come to terms with, to settle a matter with; (*mit den Gläubigern*) to compound with o.'s creditors; **~setzung** *f* (*Erklärung*) explanation, exposition; (*Erörterung*) discussion, dispute; (*endgültige*) *Am fam* showdown; (*Regelung*) settlement, arrangement; (*Trennung*) separation; (*mit Gläubigern*) compound, composition; (*Liquidation*) liquidation; **~treiben** *irr tr* to disperse, to scatter; **~wickeln** *tr* to unwrap, to unroll; **~ziehen** *irr tr* to draw asunder; (*in die Länge*) to lengthen; *itr mil* (*entfalten*) to deploy; to remove into different quarters.
auser|koren *a* chosen, elect, selected; **~lesen** *a* exquisite, choice, picked, select; excellent; **~sehen** *irr tr* to choose, to select, to single out; (*bestimmen*) to destine, to doom; **~wählen** *tr* to (s)elect, to make choice of; *seine* **~wählte** *f* his love, his intended wife.
ausessen *irr tr* to eat up, to empty; *fig* to pay for, to suffer for.
ausfädeln *tr* to unthread, to unravel.
ausfahr|en *irr itr* to drive out, to take a drive; *min* to ascend; *tr* to wear out (the road); (*Fahrgestell*) *aero* to lower; to extend (the undercarriage); *aero* (*Landeklappen*) to extend (flaps); *mar* to put to sea; (*Sehrohr*) to lift; *ausgefahrener Weg* rutty (*od* bumpy) road; *jdn ~~* to take s. o. out for a drive; **~t** *f* (*Ausflug*) drive, ride, excursion; (*Bergwerk*) ascent; (*Torweg*) doorway, gateway, exit; (*e-r Bucht*) opening out; *rail* departure; *mar* outward voyage, passage; (*e-s Hafens*) mouth.
Ausfall *m mil* sally, sortie; (*Haare*) falling-out; (*beim Fechten*) pass, thrust; (*Verlust*) deficit, loss; shortage; (*Ergebnis*) result, issue; (*bei Eisenbearbeitung, allg*) scrap, (*Ausschuß*) waste, (*üblicher, verwendbarer ~*) manufacturing loss; (*Ausbleiben*) omission; (*in der Schlacht*) casualties *pl*, *schwere Ausfälle* heavy casualties; (*Fabrik*) breakdown, stoppage; *el* cutting out of the circuit; (*Röhre*) failure; (*Beschimpfung*) invective; **~bürge** *m* surety; **~bürgschaft** *f* deficit guaranty; **~en** *irr itr* to fall out; (*Zähne*) to come out; to shed (as grain); *mil* to sally forth; (*nicht stattfinden*) to be omitted, not to take place, to be cancelled; (*handlungsunfähig werden*) to be put out of action; *aero mot* to fail, to get out of commission; *die Schule fällt aus* there is no school; (*sich wenden*) to turn, to prove, to result; *gut ~en* to succeed; *schlecht ~en* to turn out ill; (*beim Fechten*) to make pass, to lunge; *~~ n* fall of the hair, depilation; **~end**, **ausfällig** *a* aggressive, insulting; *~end werden* to become personal; **~(s)tor** *n* sally-port; **~stellung** (*Fechten*) *f* lunge; **~straße** *f* arterial road; **~stufe** *f* (*Graben*) sortie step; **~winkel** *m* angle of reflection.
aus|fasern *tr* to ravel out, to untwist; *itr* to unravel; **~fechten** *irr tr* to fight out; *itr* to leave off fighting; **~fegen** *tr* to cleanse, to sweep out; (*Zimmer*) to clean (out); **~feilen** *tr* to file out; *fig* to polish; to file, to elaborate, to give the last finish.
ausfertig|en *tr* to expedite, to dispatch (an order); to draw up, to make out (an account); to execute (a deed); to issue, to make out (a passport); **~ung** *f* drawing up; dispatch; expedition; execution; *in doppelter* **~~** in duplicate; *in dreifacher* **~~** in triplicate; **~~stag** *m* date of issue.
ausfind|en *irr tr* to find out, to discover; **~ig** *a: ~~ machen* to make out, to trace, to locate; (*Person*) to track down.
aus|fischen *tr* to fish out, to empty by fishing; **~flicken** *tr* to mend, to patch, to repair (a house); (*Schuhe*) to cobble; **~fliegen** *irr itr* to leave the nest, to run away; to go on a trip; **~fließen** *irr itr* to flow out; to emanate from; *fig* to issue from.
Aus|flucht *f* elusion, evasion, subterfuge; *Ausflüchte machen* to shuffle, to dodge; *nichts als Ausflüchte* nothing but excuses; **~fluchten** *n tech* alignement; **~flug** *m* flight, flying out; excursion, trip; *e-n ~~ machen* to make an excursion; **~flügler** *m* excursionist; **~flugschneise** *f aero* gate; **~fluß** *m* flowing out; (*von Eiter*) discharge; (*Flußmündung*) mouth; (*trichterförmiger ~*) estuary; (*Öffnung*) outlet; (*Absonderung*) secretion; (*Abfluß*) drainage; (*Wasser*) efflux; (*Gas, Rauch*) escape; *phys* emanation; *fig* expression; (*Ergebnis*) result; **~flußrohr** *n* water-pipe, escape-pipe; (*e-r Dachrinne*) spout.
ausfolgen *tr* to deliver, to hand over.
ausfördern *tr* to get out.
ausforsch|en *tr* to search out, to inquire into s. th.; to explore; (*untersuchen*) to investigate; *jdn ~en* to pump, to sound; **~ung** *f* investigation; *fam* pumping.
ausfragen *irr tr* to interrogate, to question; (*scharf ~*) to cross-examine; (*genau*) to pump, to sound.
ausfransen *tr, itr* to fray out.
ausfräsen *tr* to ream, to mill, to recess, to edge.
ausfressen *irr tr* to eat up, to empty; *chem* to corrode; *etw ~* to do (*od* make) some mischief.
Ausfuhr *f* export, exportation; **~artikel** *m* export goods *pl*; **~bedingungen** *f pl* terms *pl* of export; **~beschränkungen** *f pl* restrictions *pl* on export; **~bestimmungen** *f pl* export regulations *pl*; **~bewilligung** *f* licence to export, export permit; **~güter** *n pl* exports *pl*; **~hafen** *m* shipping port; **~handel** *m* export trade; **~prämie** *f* export premium; bounty; **~rückgang** *m* decline in exports; **~schein** *m* export permit; permit for exportation; **~überschuß** *m* export surplus; **~verbot** *n* ban on export; embargo on exports; **~waren** *f pl* goods for export; exports *pl*; **~ziffern** *f pl* export figures *pl*; **~zoll** *m* duty on exportation; export duty.
ausführ|bar *a* exportable; (*durchführbar*) practicable, feasible, performable; **~~keit** *f* feasibility, practicability; **~en** *tr* to lead out; *com* to export, to ship off; (*Bestellungen, Aufträge, Pläne*) to execute, to carry out, to perform, *Am* to fill; (*genauer darstellen*) to specify, to detail, to explain; (*errichten*) to erect, to construct; *e-m etw ~~* to take s. th. away (secretly) from s. o., to pilfer; **~lich** *a* detailed, full, extensive, full-length, *Am* extended; *adv* in detail, fully; *~~ schreiben*

to write at full length; ~~ *beschreiben* to give full details of; **~lichkeit** *f* ful(l)ness, completeness of detail; **~ung** *f* (*von Aufträgen, Plänen*) execution, performance; (*Bauplan*) design; (*Bau*) construction; (*Type*) type, pattern, model; *com* description, quality; (*Darstellung*) statement; *~~en f pl* representations *pl*, ideas *pl* put forward, statements *pl*; **~~sart** *f* (*Eisenerzeugnisse*) finish, (*Maschinenteile*) type; **~~sbestimmungen** *f pl* regulations *pl*, regulatory statutes *pl*.

ausfüll|en *tr* to fill up (*Am* out); (*Formular*) to fill in the form; (*Zeit*) to occupy, to fill up; (*Platz*) to fill a place; (*jds Stelle*) to supply o.'s place; (*ergänzen*) to complete; (*vollstopfen*) to pad; to stuff; to pack; **~ung** *f* filling in (*od* up); padding; (*mit Schutt*) rubble.

ausfüttern *tr* to line; (*mit Pelz*) to fur.

Ausgabe *f* expense; *Einnahme und ~* receipt and expenditure; (*Auslagen*) outlay, (*Unkosten*) cost; (*Brief~*) delivery, distribution; (*Buch*) edition; (*von Briefmarken*) issue; (*Fahrkarten~*) booking-office, ticket-office; **~nbuch** *n* cash-book; **~stelle** *f* issuing office; *mil* supply point.

Ausgang *m* going out; *Ausgänge* (*Besorgungen*) *machen* to go shopping; (*Öffnung ins Freie*) way out; (*Theater, Bahnhof usw*) exit; *Not~* emergency exit; (*freier Nachmittag*) afternoon-off; day-off; *fig* (*Ergebnis*) result, issue, upshot; (*Schluß*) end, close; *Unglücksfall mit tödlichem ~* fatal accident; **~sbeschränkung** *f* curfew; **~smaterial** *n* original material; **~sprodukt** *n* commencing product; **~spunkt** *m* starting-point, departure; **~sstellung** *f* jumping-off position; **~sstoffe** *m pl tech* basic products *pl*; **~swerkstoff** *m tech* basic material; raw material; **~szoll** *m* export duty.

ausgeb|en *irr tr* to give out, to distribute; (*Befehle, Banknoten, Fahrkarten*) to issue; (*Karten*) to deal cards; (*Geld*) to spend, (*gewählter*) to expend; *sich für etw ~en* to pretend to be; to pose as; *sich ~en* (*an Geld*) to run out of cash; (*abwerfen*) to yield, to bear, to bring in; (*ausreichen*) to suffice; *das gibt nicht aus* it will not do, it is not sufficient; *er muß e-n ~en* the treat is on him.

ausge|bombt *a* bombed out; **~brannt** *a: ~~e Birne* burnout; **~burt** *f* product; offspring; monstrosity; **~dehnt** *a* ample, vast, extensive; **~diente(r)** *m* veteran; ex-service man; (*Beamte*) retired official; **~fahren** *a: e-e ~fahrene Straße* a rutty road; (*routiniert*) well-grooved; **~fallen** *a fig* unusual, odd; queer, strange; *~fallener Motor aero* dead engine; **~feilt** *a* elaborate; **~führt** *pp: wie oben ~~* (*in e-m Brief*) as indicated (*od* outlined) above; **~glichen** *a* balanced; poised; **~~heit** *f* balance; poise; harmony.

ausgehen *irr itr* to go out; (*zu Ende gehen*) to come to an end; (*Feuer*) to go out; (*Haare*) to fall out; (*Vorräte*) to run short; (*Sprit*) *mot* to run out of gas; *die Geduld geht mir aus* I lose all patience; (*Farben*) to fade; *gut* (*schlecht*) *~* to turn out well (badly); (*enden*) to end, to terminate; *der Vorschlag geht von ihm aus* the proposal comes from him; *von dem Grundsatz ~* to start from the principle; *auf etw ~* to aim at, to be bent on; *leer ~* to go away empty; to get nothing; *frei ~* to go free; *ungestraft ~* to come off unpunished; *~* (*von Waren*) to be all sold; *mit jdm ~* to take out s. o., *Am* to step out with s. o.; (*ausstrahlen*) to emanate (from), to originate (from); **Ausgehverbot** *n* curfew.

ausge|lassen *a* (*ungezügelt*) unrestrained, loose, wanton; (*lärmend*) boisterous; (*fröhlich*) frisky, gay, frolicsome; **~~heit** *f* unruliness, exuberance, wantonness; **~leiert** *a* (*Gewinde*) worn out; **~lernt** *a* practised, experienced; **~macht** *a* decided, perfect, settled; *~~er Narr* downright fool; **~mergelt** *a* emaciated; **~nommen** *adv u. conj* except, with the exception of, save; **~prägt** *a* distinct, marked; **~rechnet** *adv* just, exactly; **~schaltet** *a* (*Gerät*) off; **~schlossen** *a* impossible; out of the question; **~schnitten** *a* (*Kleid*) low(-necked); **~sprochen** *fig* marked, decided; **~stalten** *tr* to shape; to elaborate; **~staltung** *f* shaping; (*Anordnung*) arrangement; (*Schmuck*) decoration; **~sucht, ~wählt** *a* exquisite, prime, choice; picked; *besonders ~~* hand-picked; **~tragen** *a* (*Kind*) mature, carried to full time; **~wiesener** *m* expellee; **~wogen** *a* balanced; **~zeichnet** *a* eminent, excellent, first-rate, capital, *Am* bully; *~zeichnet!* fine!; *ganz ~zeichnet! fam* super!

ausgiebig *a* plentiful, abundant, rich; *~en Gebrauch machen von* to make full use of.

ausgieß|en *irr tr* to pour out; (*verschütten*) to spill; to fill up (with lead); **~ung** *f* pouring-out; effusion; *~~ des Heiligen Geistes* descent of the Holy Ghost.

Ausgleich *m* agreement, settlement, arrangement; (*Saldo*) balance; (*Anspruch*) compensation; (*Gleichmachung*) equalization; (*Beilegung, com Berichtigung*) adjustment; (*Schwund~*) *radio* automatic volume control; *zum ~ der Rechnung* in settlement (*od* payment) of your account; (*Tennis*) deuce; (*Sport*) handicap; *el* balance; compensation; **~betrag** *m* compensation, balance; **~düse** *f* compensating jet; **~en** *irr tr* (*gleich machen*) to equal, to equalize, to make even, to level; (*Handel*) to balance, to clear, to settle, to square; (*Differenzen*) to adjust; (*Gläubiger*) to compound; (*Schäden*) to make up, to compensate; (*Streit*) to settle, to make up, to adjust; *r* to come to an agreement; **~getriebe** *n mot* differential (gear); **~ung** *f* level(l)ing, settlement; compensation; liquidation; balance; adjustment; (*Bank*) clearing; (*Vergleich*) compromise; **~ungsbetrag** *m* balancing-amount, amount of balance; **~vorrichtung** *f tech* equalizer.

aus|gleiten *irr*, ***~glitschen*** *itr* to slip; to slide, (*von Fahrzeugen*) to skid.

ausglühen *tr tech* (*Gießtechnik*) to anneal.

ausgrab|en *irr tr* to dig out; (*Leiche*) to exhume; (*alte Bauten, Erde*) to excavate; *fig* to unearth; **~ung** *f* exhumation; **~ungen** *f pl* excavations *pl*.

ausgreifen *irr itr* to step out; **~d** *a fig* far-reaching.

aus|grübeln *tr* to find out, to dive into; **~guck** *m mar* look-out; **~gucken** *itr* to look out.

Ausguß *m* outlet; (*Schnauze an einer Kanne*) spout; (*in der Küche*) sink; (*Gosse*) gutter; **~eimer** *m* slop-pail; **~röhre** *f* drain-pipe.

aus|hacken *tr* to grub up; (*die Augen*) to pick out the eyes; **~haken** *tr* to unhook, to unclasp.

aushalten *irr tr* (*ertragen*) to endure, to suffer; to stand, to bear, to sustain; *el* to carry; (*über sich ergehen lassen*) *Am* to sweat out s. th.; *es ist nicht zum A~* there is no bearing it; *itr* to hold out, to last, to persevere.

aushändig|en *tr* to hand over, to deliver (up); **~ung** *f* surrender, delivery, handing over.

Aushang *m* (*Plakat*) poster, placard; (*Bekanntmachung*) notice; (*von Waren*) display, show; **~en** *irr tr, itr* to hang out, to be exposed for sale.

Aushänge|bogen *m typ* the sheet from the machine, proof-sheet, clean sheet; **~n** *tr* to hang out; (*aushaken*) to unhook; (*eine Tür*) to unhinge; (*Waren*) to make a display of; (*Plakat*) to post, to put up; **~schild** *n* sign(-board).

aus|harren *itr* to hold out; **~hauchen** *tr* to breathe out; to expire; *seine Seele ~~* to breathe o.'s last; **~hauen** *tr* to cut out; (*in Stein*) to carve, to sculpture; (*Wald*) to thin.

ausheb|en *irr tr* to heave off, to lift out, to unhinge (a door); to put out (o.'s arm); (*Truppen*) to enlist, to levy, to enrol, to recruit, to raise; (*e-e Grube*) to dig; (*durch Polizei*) to raid, to mop up; (*Posten*) to capture; **~ung** *f mil* enlistment, *Am auch* draft; recruiting, conscription.

aus|hecken *tr* to hatch; *fig* (*Pläne*) to hatch, to devise, to concoct, to contrive; **~heilen** *itr* to heal thoroughly; **~helfen** *irr itr: jdm ~~* to help out, to aid, to assist; **~hilfe** *f* makeshift; (*Frau*) charwoman; temporary help, aid, assistance; (*Notbehelf*) stopgap; (*Ersatz*) stand-by; (*Reserve*) spare; (*mit Waren*) supply; (*Geld*) accommodation; **~hilfsarbeiter** *m* part-time worker; **~hilfsstellung** *f* temporary post; **~hilfsweise** *adv* by way of a makeshift; **~höhlen** *tr* to hollow out, to excavate; **~höhlung** *f* groove; excavation; **~holen** *itr* to lift up o.'s arm (for striking); *weit ~~* to go (*od* to begin) far back; *tr jdn ~~* to sound, to pump; **~holzen** *tr* to thin, to clear; **~horchen** *tr* to sound, to pump; **~hülsen** *tr* to husk, to shell, to hull; **~hungern** *tr* to famish; to starve out; **~husten** *tr* to cough up, to bring up (by coughing), to expectorate; *itr* to finish coughing.

aus|jäten *tr* to weed out, to root out; **~kämmen** *tr* to comb out; to card; **~kämpfen** *tr* to fight out; **~kaufen** *tr* to buy out; **~kegeln** *tr* to play at ninepins for; **~kehlen** *tr* to channel; to chamfer; **~kehlung** *f* channel; **~kehren** *tr* to sweep out, to clean; **~kehricht** *m* sweepings *pl*; **~keimen** *itr* to germinate, to shoot out; **~keltern** *tr* to press; **~kennen** *irr r fig* to be quite at home in; to be well up in, to be versed in; to know where one is; **~kernen** *tr* to stone; to shell; **~kitten** *tr* to cement; to lute; **~klagen** *tr* to sue for; **~klang** *m* end; **~klatschen** *tr* to condemn a play; *etw ~* to blab out; **~klauben** *tr* to pick out; **~kleben** *tr* to line, to paper; **~kleiden** *tr* to undress, to strip; *mit etw ~~* to line, to coat s. th.; (*mit Weißmetall*) to babbitt; (*schmücken*) to decorate; *r* to undress, to take off o.'s clothes; **~kleidezimmer** *n* dressing-room; **~klingen** *irr itr* to die away (as an echo), to cease to sound; *fig* to end in, to come to an end; **~klinken** *tr* to release, to disengage, to disconnect; **~klinkvorrichtung** *f aero* (*Segelflug*) glider release, tow-cable release; **~klopfen** *tr* to beat out; to clean by beating; (*Kessel*) to scale; (*Rock*) to dust; **~klopfer** *m* (*Person*) beater;

(*Gegenstand*) switch, carpet-beater; **~klügeln** *tr* to puzzle out; to excogitate; **~kneifen** *irr itr* to leave secretly, to run away; to bunk; **~knipsen** *tr* (*Licht*) to switch out; **~knobeln** *tr* to dice (*od* gamble od toss) for; *fig fam* to find out, to puzzle out; **~kochen** *tr* to boil out, to boil thoroughly; (*durch Kochen herausziehen*) to extract by boiling; (*durch Kochen reinigen*) to scald out; *Wäsche* **~~** to clean by boiling; (*Gefäß*) to scald.

aus|kommen *irr itr* to come out; *mit etw* **~~** to have a competence, to manage, to have enough of; *er kommt mit wenig aus* he can do with little; *gerade noch* **~~** to make both ends meet; *mit jdm* **~~** to get on, to get along with; *gut mit jdm* **~~** to agree, to live peaceably with; **~~** *n* livelihood, subsistence; *sein* **~~** *haben* to make a living; *es ist kein* **~~** *mit ihm* there is no getting on with him; **~kömmlich** *a* sufficient; **~körnen** *tr* to pick out the grains; **~kosten** *tr* to taste (*od* to enjoy) thoroughly; **~kramen** *tr* to rummage up, to exhibit; **~kratzen** *tr* to scrape out; *itr fig* to run away, to clear out; to make o.'s getaway, to decamp; **~kratzung** *f med* curettement; **~kriechen** *irr itr* to creep forth; to be hatched; **~kugeln** *tr* to vote by ballot; *sich den Arm* **~~** to dislocate o.'s arm; **~kundschaften** *tr* to explore, to find out; *mil* to scout, to reconnoitre.

Auskunft *f* information; particulars *pl*; intelligence; **~ei** *f* inquiry-office; **~sbeamter** *m* inquiry clerk, inquiry official; *tele* information operator; **~sersuchen** *n* request for information; **~smittel** *n* expedient; resort; **~sperson** *f* informant; reference; **~spflicht** *f* obligation to give information; **~sstelle** *f* information bureau.

auskuppeln *tr* to uncouple; (*Auto*) to declutch; *tech* to disconnect, to ungear.

auslachen *tr* to laugh at, to deride, *Am fam* to give somebody the Bronx cheer; *sich* **~** to laugh to o.'s heart's content.

auslad|en *irr tr* to unload, to discharge; (*Schiff*) to clear, to lighten; (*Truppen aus Schiff*) to disembark, (*aus Zug*) to detrain, (*aus Omnibus*) to debus; (*Gast*) to cancel an invitation; *itr* (*Baukunst*) to jut out; to project; **~~***de Geste* sweeping gesture; **~ebahnhof** *m* goods unloading station; railhead; **~ebahnsteig** *m* unloading platform; **~ehafen** *m* port of discharge; **~ekosten** *pl* unloading-fees *pl*; **~estelle** *f* quay, wharf; unloading place; **~er** *m* unloader, stevedore; (*Schiff*) lighterman; **~ung** *f* unloading, discharge, landing; *arch* projection; *tech* (*Reichweite*) reach, radial range; (*e-s Kranes*) working radius, length of jib, swing; (*e-r Schere*) depth of throat.

Auslage *f* (*Kosten*) expenses *pl*; (*ausgelegtes Geld*) advance, outlay, previous payment; (*Fechtkunst*) position of guard; (*Waren*) display, show; (*Schaufenster*) show (*od* shop)-window (*ausgestellte Waren*) goods exhibited, window goods *pl*; **~n** *anschauen gehen* to go window-shopping; *jdm die* **~n** *erstatten* to reimburse s. o.

Ausland *n* foreign country; *ins, im* **~** abroad; *aus dem* **~** from abroad; **~sanleihe** *f* foreign loan; **~saufenthalt** *m* stay abroad; **~sbrief** *m* foreign letter; **~serzeugnis** *n* foreign product; **~sgeschäft** *n* foreign transaction; **~sgespräch** *n* foreign call; **~shandel** *m* foreign commerce; **~skorrespondent** *m* foreign correspondent; **~skredit** *m* foreign credit; **~smarkt** *m* foreign market; **~snachrichten** *f pl* foreign news *pl*; **~spatent** *n* foreign patent; **~sreise** *f* trip abroad.

Ausländ|er *m*, ***~erin*** *f* foreigner, (*bes. juristisch*) alien; **~isch** *a* foreign, alien; *bot* exotic; *com* outward; **~~***e Bücher* (*in fremder Sprache*) foreign books, (*im Ausland*) books abroad.

auslangen *itr* to suffice; (*ausholen*) to raise o.'s arm.

auslass|en *irr tr* to let out; (*Butter*) to melt; (*Rock*) to let out; (*vergessen*) to omit; (*Wörter*) to leave out; *typ* to make an out; to miss (a date); to skip (a line); (*Dampf*) to exhaust; (*elidieren*) to elide; (*ausmerzen*) to eliminate; (*tilgen*) to delete; (*ausschneiden*) to cut out; *seine Wut an jdm* **~~** to vent o.'s anger on s.o.; *laß mich aus!* leave me alone!; *sich* **~***en* to express o. s. upon; **~hahn** *m* discharge cock; **~ung** *f* omission; (*Äußerung*) expression, remark, utterance; **~ungszeichen** *n* apostrophe; **~ventil** *n mot* exhaust valve.

Auslauf *m* running out; (*von Hühnern*) (grass od hen) run; (*von Schiffen*) sailing; (*beim Skilauf*) outrun *od* finish; *aero* runway; (*bei Landung*) landing run; **~en** *irr itr* to run out, to depart; (*Flüssigkeit*) to run over; (*Gefäße*) to leak (out); *mar* to put (out) to sea, to sail, to set sail to; *aero* to taxi; (*von Farben*) to run (out); (*endigen*) to (come to an) end; (*vorspringen*) to project; (*Serie*) to go out of production; *spitz* **~~** to end in a point; *dünn* **~~** to taper; **~rohr** *n* outlet (*od* discharge) tube; **~spitze** *f* discharge tip.

Ausläufer *m* runner, errand-boy; *bot* runner; (*Berg~*) branch, spur.

auslaug|en *tr* to leach out; **~ung** *f* extraction.

Aus|laut *m* final sound; *im* **~~** when final; **~~en** *itr:* **~~***en auf* to have the final sound, to terminate (in); **~läuten** *tr* to publish by ringing a bell; to ring out; *itr* to cease ringing.

ausleben *r* to enjoy life to the full, to live o.'s life fully.

auslecken *tr* to lick up.

ausleer|en *tr* to empty; (*Briefkasten*) to clear, *Am* to collect mail; (*Glas*) to drink up; (*entwässern*) to drain; (*ausräumen*) to evacuate; (*Darm*) to purge; *das Herz* **~~** *fig* to pour out o.'s heart; **~ung** *f* emptying; (*Briefkasten*) clearing; (*Darm*) evacuation.

ausleg|en *tr* to lay out, to exhibit for sale, to display; (*Zeitschriften*) to lay out, to take in, to keep; (*Geld*) to advance; (*mit Holz*) to inlay, to veneer; (*mit Kacheln*) to tile; (*Kabel*) to lay (out); *mar* to pay out; *fig* (*erklären*) to explain, to comment; (*deuten*) to interpret; *falsch* **~~** to misinterpret; *übel* **~~** to put a bad construction upon; **~er** *m* interpreter, commentator; *mar* outrigger, jib; **~ung** *f* interpretation, comment, exegesis (of the Bible).

ausleih|en *irr tr* to lend (out), *Am* to loan (out); *sich etw* **~~** to borrow s. th. (from); **~er** *m* lender; (*von Pfändern*) pawnbroker.

auslernen *tr* to finish o.'s apprenticeship, to serve o.'s time; *man lernt nie aus* we are never too old to learn.

Auslese *f* choice, selection; (*von Wein*) choice, the choicest wine, superior wine; **~dienstpflicht** *f mil* selective service; **~n** *irr tr* to choose, to pick out; (*ein Buch*) to finish (reading), to read to the end.

auslichten *tr* (*Wald*) to thin (a forest); (*Bäume*) to prune (trees).

ausliefer|n *tr* to deliver (up), to hand over; (*Personen*) to surrender; (*Verbrecher, von e-m Land ins andere*) to extradite; **~ung** *f* delivery; surrender; extradition; **~ungsvertrag** *m* extradition-treaty.

ausliegen *irr itr* to be exhibited; (*Zeitungen*) to be kept, to be taken in.

auslöffeln *tr* to ladle out, to spoon out.

auslösch|en *tr* to quench, to extinguish; (*Licht*) to put out; (*Schrift*) to erase, to efface, to blot out; (*streichen*) to cancel; **~ung** *f* extinguishment, extinction.

auslos|en *tr* to allot; to distribute by lot; (*von Wertpapieren*) to draw by lot; **~ung** *f* allotment, distribution by lot; (*von Wertpapieren*) drawing.

auslös|en *tr* to loosen, to release; (*das Schleppseil e-s Segelflugzeugs*) to release the tow-rope of a glider; *tech* to disengage; (*Wechsel*) to cash; (*Begeisterung*) to arouse, to call forth; to awaken, to kindle; (*verursachen*) to cause; *sich* **~***en* to redeem o. s.; (*Gefangene*) to redeem, to ransom; (*Pfand*) to recover; **~ehebel** *m tech* disengaging lever; coupling lever; **~eknopf** *m* release button; **~er** *m* (*allgemein tech*) release; *phot* trigger; release; *Selbst***~***er m* self-timer, auto timer; *Draht***~***er m* cable (*od* wire) release; (*Röntgenaufnahmen*) switch; (*Segelflug*) release (knob); **~evorrichtung** *f* releasing device; **~ung** *f* redemption; ransom; deliverance; (*einer Uhr*) ratch.

auslüften *tr* to air, to ventilate.

ausmachen *tr* (*Feuer*) to put out; (*Licht*) to switch off; (*herausbekommen*) to figure out; (*ein Ziel*) *mil* to locate; (*Geflügel*) to draw; (*ausfindig machen*) to find out; (*sichten*) to pick up; (*abmachen*) to settle; (*übereinkommen*) to agree upon; (*betragen*) to make up, to come to, to amount to; *was macht das aus?* what of that? *das macht nichts aus!* 'tis no matter! never mind! *würde es Ihnen etw* **~**, *wenn ich rauche?* would you mind my (me) smoking? mind, if I smoke?

ausmahlen *irr tr* (*Mehl*) to extract.

ausmalen *tr* (*Text mit Bildern illustrieren*) to colo(u)r, to illuminate; (*ein Zimmer*) to paint; *fig* to amplify. to depict; *sich* **~** to fancy, to imagine; to picture s. th. to o. s.

Ausmarsch *m* departure; marching-out; **~ieren** *itr* to march out, to depart.

Ausmaß *n* measure(ments *pl*), dimensions *pl*; scale, extent; (*Grad*) degree; (*Verhältnis*) proportion; *in größerem* **~** on a bigger scale; *in solchem* **~** to such an extent.

aus|mauern *tr* to case with stones, to wall up; **~meißeln** *tr* to chisel out; to carve; to chase; **~mergeln** *tr* to emaciate; to enervate; to exhaust; **~***gemergelt a* worn-out, broke; **~merzen** *tr* (*aussondern*) to pick out; (*verwerfen*) to reject, to cast off; (*Namen aus e-r Liste*) to strike out; (*unterdrücken*) to suppress; (*ausschalten*) to eliminate; **~messen** *irr tr* to survey, to measure; to ga(u)ge (a cask); to take the measures of; **~messung** *f* measurement; survey; ga(u)ge; **~misten** *tr* to clear (a stable of dung); **~mitteln** *tr* to find out, to ascertain; **~möblieren** *tr* to furnish; **~münden** *itr* to disembogue, to open into, to flow into; (*Straße*) to lead to; ~**münzen** *tr* to coin, to stamp; ~**mustern** *tr* (*Soldaten*) to discharge (as unfit), to reject; (*auslesen*) to sort (*od* pick) out; (*Waren zurückweisen*) to reject, to discard, to turn off; (*ausmerzen*) to eliminate; to scrap; to overhaul; ~**musterung** *f* discharge; rejection; ~~**sgeld** *n* mustering-out pay; ~~**slehrgang** *m* recruiting course.

Ausnahme *f* exception; *mit* ~ with the exception of, excepting; *ohne* ~ without an exception; *keine Regel ohne* ~ there is no rule without an exception; ~**angebot** *n* exceptional offer; ~**fall** *m* exceptional case; ~**gesetz** *n* exceptional law; ~**zustand** *m* emergency; (*ziviler* ~~) civil state of emergency; *mil* martial law; *den* ~~ *verhängen* to establish (*od* to proclaim) martial law.

ausnahms|los *a* without exception; ~**weise** *adv* exceptionally, by way of exception; for once in a way.

ausnehmen *irr tr* to take out; (*ausweiden*) to embowel, to draw; (*ausschließen*) to except; to exempt, to exclude; *r* to form an exception; (*aussehen*) to look, to show up; *sich gut* ~ to look well; ~**d** *a* exquisite, extraordinary; *adv* exceedingly, exceptionally.

ausnutzen *tr* to profit by, to make the best of; to take advantage of, to use to advantage; *jdn* ~ to utilize; (*ausbeuten, z. B. ein Bergwerk*) to exploit.

auspack|en *tr* to unpack, to uncase; (*Ballen*) to unbale; *fam* (*Neuigkeiten*) to spread out; (*zu reden beginnen*) to begin to talk; to disclose; ~**ung** *f* unpacking.

auspeitsch|en *tr* to whip, to flog; ~**ung** *f* whipping.

auspfänd|en *tr* to distrain on, to seize the goods of a debtor; ~**ung** *f* seizure, execution, distraint.

auspfeifen *irr tr* to hiss, to catcall (a play); to give s. o. the bird; *ausgepfiffen werden* to be condemned.

auspichen *tr* to pitch out; *er ist ausgepicht* he is pot-proof.

ausplätten *tr* to iron (thoroughly).

ausplauder|n *tr* to blab; to blur out; *sich* ~*n* to prattle o.'s fill; ~**er** *m* prattler, telltale.

ausplünder|n *tr* to loot, to plunder, to pillage; ~**ung** *f* plundering, pillage.

aus|polstern *tr* to stuff, to pad, (*mit Watte*) to wad; to upholster; ~**posaunen** *tr* to trumpet forth; (*Waren*) to cry up; (*bekanntmachen*) to blaze, to divulge; ~**prägen** *tr* to coin, to stamp; *fig* to mark distinctly; *r* to show itself; to be visible; *ausgeprägt* pronounced, well marked; ~**pressen** *tr* to squeeze out, to press out, to wring out; (*Geld*) to extort from; (*Seufzer*) to draw; ~**probieren** *tr* to try, to select by trying, to test, to put to the test; (*Wein*) to taste, to sample.

Auspuff *m* exhaust; (*bei Verstäubern*) discharge nozzle; ~**abschirmung** *f aero* exhaust screens *pl*, flame dampers *pl*; ~**flamme** *f aero* exhaust flame; ~**gas** *n* burnt gas; ~**klappe** *f* cut-out; exhaust valve; ~**leitung** *f* exhaust manifold; ~**maschine** *f* non-condensing engine; ~**rohr** *n* exhaust pipe; ~**topf** *m* silencer, *Am* muffler.

auspumpen *tr* to pump out; to exhaust (air).

auspunkten *tr* (*im Boxkampf*) to outpoint, to beat on points.

aus|pusten *tr* to blow out; ~**putz** *m* ornamentation; (*Besatz*) trimming; ~**putzen** *tr* to clean, to polish; to prune (trees); (*schmücken*) to decorate; (*besetzen*) to trim; *sich* ~~ to dress up; ~~ *n* cleaning; decoration.

ausquartier|en *tr* to billet out; to dislodge; ~**ung** *f* billeting out; change of quarters (*od* lodgings).

aus|quetschen *tr* to squeeze out, to crush out; ~**radieren** *tr* to scratch out, to erase; ~**rändern** *tr* to emarginate; ~**rangieren** *tr* to sort out, to cast off; (*Eisenbahn*) to shunt out; ~*rangiert sein fam fig* to be out of date, to be on the shelf, *Am* to be a back number; ~**rauben** *tr* to rob, to plunder, to loot, to pillage; ~**rauchen** *tr* to smoke to the end; ~**räuchern** *tr* to smoke out, to fumigate, to expel by smoke; ~**raufen** *tr* to pluck; *sich die Haare* ~~ to tear o.'s hair out.

ausräum|en *tr* to empty, to evacuate; (*Wohnung*) to remove, to clear; ~**ung** *f* removal, clearing; evacuation.

aus|rechnen *tr* to calculate, to compute, to reckon, to estimate, to add up, *Am* to figure out (*od* up); ~**rechnung** *f* calculation; ~**recken** *tr* to draw out; *sich* ~~ to stretch; ~**rede** *f* evasion, pretence; *faule* ~~*n* lame excuses; ~~*n machen* to shirk the question; ~**reden** *itr* to finish speaking; *jdn* ~~ *lassen* to let s. o. speak out; *tr jdm etw* ~~ to talk s. o. out of, to dissuade from; *sich* ~~ to exculpate o. s., to use evasions; (*sich drücken von*) to wriggle out of; ~**reiben** *irr tr* to rub out, to polish; ~**reichen** *itr* to be sufficient; ~**reifen** *itr* to ripen fully; ~**reise** *f* departure; *mar* sailing, outward voyage; ~**reisegenehmigung** *f* exit permit; ~**reißen** *irr tr* to pull out, to extract; *itr* to break loose, to split, to tear; (*weglaufen*) to decamp, to run away; *mil* to desert; ~**reißer** *m* runaway, deserter, fugitive; ~**reiten** *irr itr* to take a ride, to ride out; *tr* to air a horse; ~**renken** *tr* to disjoint; *sich den Arm* ~~ to dislocate o.'s arm; ~**renkung** *f* spraining, dislocation; ~**richten** *tr* to straighten; *mil* to fall in; to dress (the ranks); (*Auftrag*) to do, to carry out; (*Bestellung*) to deliver, to tell; (*Gruß*) to give o.'s kind regards; (*erlangen*) to obtain, to succeed in; *nichts* ~~ to fail; not to be able to do anything; to labour in vain; *bei jdm etw* ~~ to have great influence with s. o.; ~**richtung** *f* alignment; (*Gleichschaltung*) bringing into line with; ~**ringen** *irr tr* to wring out (linen); *er hat ausgerungen* his struggles are over; ~**ritt** *m* ride, excursion on horseback; ~**roden** *tr* to root out, to clear (land); ~**rollen** *tr* to roll out, to take out of a roll; ~~ *n aero* landing run; ~**rotten** *tr* to root out; to destroy; to extirpate, to eradicate, to exterminate; ~**rottung** *f* uprooting; extirpation; ~**rücken** *itr* to march out, to move out, to decamp; (*ausreißen*) to run away; *tr* (*Schaltkupplung*) to disengage, to throw out; (*bei Kraftfahrzeugen*) to shift; ~**rückvorrichtung** *f* (*bei Maschinen*) shifting device.

Ausruf *m* (out)cry, exclamation; interjection; (*öffentlich*) proclamation; (*der Brautleute*) banns *pl*; (*Versteigerung*) public sale; ~**en** *irr tr, itr* to cry out, to call out, to exclaim; *tr* (*Waren*) to hawk; *zu etw* ~*en* to proclaim; *etw* ~ *lassen* to publish; ~**er** *m* (public) crier, bell-man; showman; proclaimer; auctioneer; ~**ung** *f* outcry, exclamation; proclamation; ~~**swort** *n* interjection; ~~**szeichen** *n* note of exclamation, exclamation mark (*Am* point).

aus|ruhen *itr* to rest, to repose; ~~ *n* rest, repose; ~**rupfen** *tr* to pull out; (*Federn*) to strip a bird of its feathers; (*Gänse*) to pluck geese; (*Haare*) to take out s. o.'s hair; ~**rüsten** *tr* to furnish; to equip; to supply with; *mil* to arm, to equip; *mar* to rig out; to man; *fig* to provide with; (*begaben*) to endow; (*Tuch*) to finish; ~**rüstung** *f* preparation, equipment, outfit (*z. B.* mountaineering outfit *Bergsteiger*~~); *mil* armament, (*e-s Soldaten*) kit; (*zusätzlich*) accessories *pl*; ~~**sgegenstände** *m pl tech* accessories *pl*, fittings *pl*, mountings *pl*; equipment; ~~**skosten** *pl* cost of outfit; ~~**swerkstatt** *f* fitting-out shop; ~**rutschen** *itr* to glide, to slip, to skid.

Aus|saat *f* sowing; (*Saatkorn*) seed-corn; ~**säen** *tr* to sow; *fig* to scatter; to disseminate.

Aussag|e *f* declaration, statement; (*Zeugen*~) evidence; (*unter Verhör bei Gericht*) deposition, testimony; (*eidliche, mündliche*) sworn evidence, sworn deposition; ~*en f pl* (*der Prozeßparteien*) pleadings *pl*; *e-e gerichtliche* ~*e abgeben* to give an evidence; *eidliche* ~*e* affidavit; *gram* predicate; *nach seiner* ~*e* from what he says; ~**en** *tr* to say, to state, to declare; (*gerichtlich*) to give evidence; (*eidlich*) to depose (*od* to attest) on oath; *gram* to predicate; ~**end** *a* predicatory.

aussägen *tr* to saw out.

Aus|satz *m* leprosy; (*der Schafe*) scab; (*beim Billard*) lead; ~**sätzig** *a* leprous; *Spital für* ~~*e* leper-house; ~~**e(r)** *m* leper; ~**saufen** *tr* to drink out.

aussaug|en *tr* to suck out; *fig* to exhaust; ~**er** *m* parasite; *fig* bloodsucker, sponger, extortioner; ~**ung** *f fig* exhaustion; oppression.

aus|schachten *tr* to tunnel, to excavate; *min* to sink; ~**schachtung** *f* excavation; ~**schälen** *tr* to shell, to peel; ~**schalten** *tr* to eliminate; to put out of use; *el* (*Licht*) to turn out (*od* off), to switch off; (*Strom*) to cut out, to break; (*Kupplung*) to throw out, to disengage, to disconnect; ~**schalter** *m* circuit-breaker, cutout; ~**schaltstellung** *f* (*e-s Hebels*) off-position; ~**schaltung** *f* elimination; *el* circuit-breaking, disconnection; ~**schank** *m* (retail-)bar, public bar, pub; (*Tätigkeit*) tapping, serving; (*Genehmigung*) retail-licence; ~**schenker** *m* barman, potman, *Am* bartender; ~**scharren** *tr* to rake out, to dig up; ~**schau** *f*: ~~ *halten nach* to be on the lookout for; to watch for; ~**schauen** *itr* (*aussehen*) to look like, to have an appearance; *es schaut nach Regen aus* it looks like rain; *er schaut wie ein Lehrer aus* he looks like a teacher; *er schaut gut aus* he looks well; *nach jdm* ~~ to look out for; ~**schaufeln** *tr* to scoop out, to shovel out; ~**scheiden** *irr tr* to separate, to eliminate; *chem* to precipitate, to exude, to extract, to eliminate; *med* to secrete; *itr* (*aus Geschäft, Amt*) to retire, to withdraw; ~**scheidung** *f* separation; secretion; retirement; (*Nebenprodukt*) by-product; ~~**skampf** *m* (*Sport*) heat, elimination bout, final; ~~**spiel** *n* try-out; ~**schelten** *irr tr* to scold, to chide, to rebuke; ~**schenken** *tr* to pour out; to put on draught; to (sell by) retail; ~**scheren** *itr mar* to draw out of line; *aero* to peel off; ~**schicken** *tr* to send out, to dispatch; *mil* to detach, to draft off; *nach etw* ~~ to send for; ~**schießen** *irr tr* to shoot out; (*Preis*) to shoot for; (*zurückstellen*) to cast out, to reject; *typ* to impose; *itr* (*Blumen*) to sprout (*od* shoot forth); **~schiffen** *tr* to disembark; **~schiffung** *f* disembarkation, landing; **~~shafen** *m* port of debarkation; **~schimpfen** *tr* to scold; *Am sl* to bawl out; **~schirren** *tr* to unharness; **~schlachten** *tr* (*Tiere*) to cut up; (*Gut*) to parcel out; (*Motorfahrzeuge, Maschinen*) to break up, to take to pieces for use as spare parts, to gut, *Am* to cannibalize; **~schlafen** *irr itr* to sleep o.'s fill; *e-n Rausch ~~* to sleep o. s. sober.

Aus|schlag *m* (*Haut~*) eruption, rash, breaking out, pimples *pl*; (*e-s Zeigers*) deflection; (*Pflanzentrieb*) shoots *pl*, sprouts *pl*; (*e-s Pendels*) amplitude; (*Gutgewicht*) casting weight; (*der Waage*) turn of the scales; *mot* lock; (*Brauerei*) run of wort from the kettle; (*Schaum*) scum, exudation; *den ~~ geben* to turn the scale, to decide the matter (*od* the issue) of s. th.; **~~gebend** *a* decisive; *die ~~gebende Stimme* the casting vote (*od* voice); **~schlagen** *irr tr* to beat, to dash out; to laminate (metals); to jag (leather); to knock out (s. o.'s eye); *mit etw ~~* to line, to trim with; (*ablehnen*) to decline, to reject; to refuse, to deny; *e-m Fasse den Boden ~~* to stave a cask, *fig* that tops everything; *schwarz ~~* to cover with black cloth; *itr* (*hinten*) to kick, to fling out; *bot* to bud, to sprout, to leaf; (*Feuchtigkeit*) to grow moist, to be damp; (*Waage*) to turn; (*ablaufen*) to turn, to prove; *~~ n* refusal; (*Pflanzen*) budding, sprouting; (*Pferd*) kicking.

ausschlämmen *tr* to clear of mud.

ausschleif|en *irr tr* to grind out; (*Zylinder*) to bore; **~ung** *f* grinding out.

ausschließ|en *irr tr* to shut out; to exclude; to bar from; (*Sport*) to disqualify, (*zeitweilig*) to suspend; (*Arbeiter*) to lock out; (*fortjagen*) to expel; *r* to separate o. s.; *ausgeschlossen!* impossible! out of the question! there is no idea of it! **~lich** *a* exclusive; **~ung** *f* exclusion, excommunication; (*Aussperrung von der Arbeit*) lock-out.

aus|schlüpfen *itr* to slip out; *aus dem Ei ~~* to be hatched; **~schlürfen** *tr* to sip up; **~schluß** *m* exclusion, exemption; *mit ~~ der Öffentlichkeit* in private; *unter ~~ der Öffentlichkeit* (*jur*) in camera, at chambers; *Antrag auf ~~ der Öffentlichkeit stellen* to demand the exclusion of the public; *mit ~~ von* with the exception of.

aus|schmelzen *irr tr* to melt out, to dissolve; (*Talg*) to try; (*Erz*) to fuse; **~schmelzung** *f* melting; fusion; **~schmieren** *tr* to smear, to grease; (*mit Pech*) to pitch; **~schmücken** *tr* to decorate, to ornament; (*Kleider*) to trim; *fig* to embroider; (*verschönern*) to embellish; **~schmückung** *f* decoration; *fig* embellishment; **~schnauben** *itr* to recover breath; *tr* to bring up by blowing o.'s nose; *sich ~~* to blow o.'s nose; **~schnaufen** *itr* to get o.'s breath; **~schneiden** *irr tr* to cut out, to carve; (*Ärmel*) to hollow; (*aus Zeitung*) to cut out, *Am* to clip; *med* to extirpate, to excise; (*Bäume*) to lop, to prune; *ausgeschnitten gehen* to wear a low dress, to be low-necked; **~schneidung** *f* cutting out; *med* extirpation; excision.

Ausschnitt *m* cut, opening; cut out; (*e-s Kleides*) low-neck; *Kleid mit spitzem* (*viereckigem*) *Ausschnitt* dress with V-shaped (square) neck; (*Zeitungs~*) cut, press-cutting, *Am* clipping; (*Zeitungs~büro*) press-cutting agency, *Am* clipping bureau; *math* sector; (*Teil, Abschnitt*) section.

aus|schnitzen *tr* to carve; **~schnüffeln** *tr* to smell out; *fig* to pry (into); **~schöpfen** *tr* to ladle out; (*Wasser aus e-m Boot*) to bale (*od* bail) out; (*ausleeren*) to drain off, to empty; to scoop out; *fig* to dry up, to exhaust; **~schrauben** *tr* to screw out, to unscrew.

ausschreib|en *irr tr* (*Brief beenden*) to write to the end, to finish; (*abschreiben*) to copy; (*aus e-m Buch*) to plagiarize, to pilfer from; (*veröffentlichen*) to publish, to call; (*ankündigen*) to proclaim, to announce; (*Rechnung*) to make (*od* to draw) up (an account); (*Wettbewerb*) to invite (competition); (*Versammlung*) to convoke; (*Stelle*) to advertise a vacancy; (*Wahlen*) to issue the writs for an election, (*von Ministern*) to appeal to the country; (*Steuern*) to impose, to lay on; (*festsetzen*) to appoint; *ein Wort ~en* to write in full, to write out; *ganz ~en* to write at full length; (*e-n Konkurs*) to issue a statute in bankruptcy; **~ung** *f* (*e-r Rechnung*) drawing up, abstract, making out; (*des Landtages*) convocation; (*von Steuern*) imposition; (*e-r offenen Stelle*) advertisement of a vacancy; (*Bekanntmachung*) proclamation; (*als Wettbewerb*) prize-competition; submission; tender.

ausschreien *irr tr* to cry (out), to proclaim; (*verschreien*) to defame; (*anpreisen*) to pass off for; *itr* to cease crying; *r* to cry to o.'s heart's content.

ausschreit|en *irr itr* to stride, to pace, to step out; *fig* to go too far, to commit excesses; *tr* to measure with steps; **~ung** *f* (*Ausschweifung*) excess; (*Übertretung, Gesetzverletzung*) transgression; (*Aufruhr*) riot.

Ausschuß *m* (*Abfall*) refuse, waste; (*Schrott*) scrap, waste; (*Kommission*) committee; board; panel; (*Austrittsöffnung der Kugel*) wound of exit; *beratender ~* advisory committee; *ständiger ~* standing committee; *gemischter ~* joint committee; *geschäftsführender ~* managing committee; *an e-n ~ zurückverweisen* to recommit to a committee; *Unter~* subcommittee; *e-m ~ angehören* to sit on a committee; *e-m ~ übergeben* to refer to a committee; (*Wahl~ bes. in USA*) caucus; **~mitglied** *n* member of a board; **~papier** *n* (*äußere Lage*) outsides *pl*; (*Abfall*) waste paper, refuse-paper; maculature; **~sitzung** *f* committee meeting; **~ware** *f* refuse, defective (*od* damaged) goods *pl*, rejects *pl*, throw-outs *pl*.

aus|schütteln *tr* to shake, to shake out; **~schütten** *tr* to pour out; to shower down; (*ausfüllen*) to fill up; (*Dividenden*) to distribute, to pay (dividends); (*sein Herz*) to open (*od* to unburden) o.'s heart to, to unbosom o. s.; *das Kind mit dem Bade ~~* to overshoot the mark, to reject the good with the bad; (*leeren*) to empty; to dip, to dump; to spill; *sich vor Lachen ~~* to roar with laughter.

aus|schwärmen *itr* to swarm out; *mil* to extend; (*fächerartig*) to fan out; **~schwatzen** *tr* to blab out, to spread out; **~schweben** *itr aero* to flatten out, to glide to a landing; to hold off; **~schwefeln** *tr* to fumigate with sulphur, to smoke out.

ausschweif|en *itr* (*im Reden*) to digress; (*liederlich sein*) to lead a dissolute life; **~end** *a* excessive, extravagant; (*liederlich, wüst*) dissipated, dissolute; **~ung** *f* excess, dissolution, debauch(ery).

ausschwenken *tr* to rinse; (*Kran*) to swing out.

ausschwitz|en *tr* to sweat out, to exude; **~ung** *f* exudation.

aussehen *irr itr* to look, to appear; (*nach etw od jdm ausschauen*) to look out for; *nach etw ~* to look important; *es sieht nach Regen aus* it looks like rain; *wie siehst du nur aus?* what a sight you are? *so siehst du aus!* that's what you think! *~ wie* to look like; *wohl ~* to look healthy; *sie sieht gut aus* she is pleasing to the eye; *er sieht fast genau so aus wie du* he looks a lot like you; *wie sieht es aus?* how is it? *die Sache sieht schlimm aus* things are in a bad way; *sich die Augen ~* to look o. s. blind; *~ n* look, air, face, exterior; (*Außenbeschaffenheit*) appearance, finish; *allem ~ nach* to all appearance; *nach dem ~ urteilen* to judge by appearances.

aus sein *irr itr* (*vorbei sein*) to be over; (*Feuer*) to be out; *auf* (*od nach*) *etw ~* to be after.

außen *adv* out, without, outward(s), (on the) outside; (*draußen*) out of doors; *von ~* from without; *nach ~* outward(s); *~ bleiben* to stay out.

aussend|en *irr tr* to send out; (*Strahlen, Radiowellen*) to emit; *radio* (*Programm übermitteln*) to transmit; **~ung** *f* (*Strahlung*) radiation; emission.

Außen|amt *n* Ministry for Foreign Affairs; **~ansicht** *f* exterior; **~antenne** *f* outdoor aerial; **~aufnahme** *f* (*beim Drehen e-s Films*) outdoor shot, exterior shooting; *auf ~aufnahme* on location; **~backenbremse** *f* external cheek brake; **~beamter** *m* outdoor official; **~beleuchtung** *f* outdoor illumination; exterior lighting; **~bezirk** *m* outlying district, outskirts *pl*; **~beschaffenheit** *f tech* surface condition; **~bordmotor** *m* outboard motor; **~dienst** *m* outdoor duty, outdoor service; *mil* duties outside barracks; **~druckkörper** *m* bulge; **~drüse** *f* external gland; **~durchmesser** *m* external (*od* outside *od* outer) diameter; **~flügel** *m* outer wing (section); **~gewässer** *n* extraterritorial waters *pl*; **~gewinde** *n* male screw; **~gitter** *n* outer grid; **~hafen** *m* outer harbo(u)r, outport; **~handel** *m* export trade, foreign trade, imports and exports *pl*, exports *pl*; **~~sbilanz** *f* balance of trade; **~~sförderung** *f* export promotion; **~~smonopol** *n* foreign-trade monopoly; **~~sstelle** *f* foreign-trade department; **~haut** *f* outer skin; outer covering; *anat* epidermis; **~hülle** *f* outside cover; **~landung** *f aero* landing outside an aerodrome, outside landing, off-field landing; **~leiter** *m el* external (*od* outer) conductor; **~leitung** *f el* outer circuit; outdoor line; **~luft** *f* surrounding air, atmosphere; **~maße** *n pl* outside measures *pl*; **~minister** *m* Minister for Foreign Affairs; (*in England*) Secretary of State for Foreign Affairs, (*in USA*) Secretary of State; **~ministerium** *n* Ministry for Foreign Affairs; (*in England*) Foreign Office, (*in USA*) Department of State, State Department; **~politik** *f* foreign policy; foreign affairs *pl*; **~politisch** *a* referring to (*od* concerning) foreign policy, foreign political; **~posten** *m* advanced post; **~seite** *f* surface, outside, outside appearance; **~seiter** *m fig u.*

sport outsider; **~sendung** *f radio* outside broadcast; **~stände** *pl com* outstanding debts (*od* claims, accounts), debts receivable *pl*, arrears *pl*, liabilities *pl*; **~stelle** *f* branch office, sub-office; *radio* outside-station; **~stürmer** *m* (*Fußball*) wing player, wing man; **~temperatur** *f* outdoor temperature; **~wache** *f mil* outlying piquet; **~wand** *f* exterior wall; **~welt** *f* exterior, external world, environment, outer world, visible world; **~werk** *n* advanced work; **~winkel** *m* exterior angle; **~wirtschaft** *f* foreign trade; **~zimmer** *n* outside room.

außer *prp* out of; outside; (*außerhalb, über*) beyond; (*neben*) beside(s); apart from, *Am* aside from; (*noch dazu*) in addition to; (*ausgenommen*) except; *~ Gefahr* out of danger; *~ Übung* out of practice; *~ sich sein* to be beside o. s.; *~ Betrieb* out of gear, out of service, out of order, off; *~ Betrieb setzen* (*Maschinen*) to put out of operation (*od* service *od* action); *~ Gefecht setzen* to knockout; *~ Frage* without question; *~ Zweifel* beyond doubt; *~ sich vor Freude sein* to be frantic with joy; *seien Sie ~ Sorge* be free from care; *~ Kurs setzen* to withdraw from circulation; *~ Betracht lassen* to leave out of consideration; *~ Gebrauch kommen* to go out of fashion, to become obsolete; *~ Atem* out of breath; *~ Dienst* out of employment; *mil* off duty; (*a. D.*) retired; *~ Dienst stellen* (*Schiff*) to put out of commission; *~ Landes* abroad; *~stande sein* to be unable (*od* incapable); *~ der Zeit* out of season; *~ Kraft setzen* to annul, to cancel; *alle ~ e-m* all but one; *~ conj* except, but, save; *~ daß* except that, save that; *~ wenn* unless.

außer|amtlich *a* unofficial, private; **~beruflich** *a* extra-professional; **~dem** *conj u. adv* besides, moreover, over and above; **~dienstlich** *a* unofficial, private; off duty, off-service; outside o.'s official function; **~dienststellung** *f* putting out of commission.

äußere *a* exterior, outer, external; outward; **~(s)** *n* exterior, outside, outward appearance; *Ministerium des Ä~n* Foreign Office, *Am* State Department; *Minister des Ä~n* Minister for Foreign Affairs; Foreign Minister; *engl* Secretary of State for Foreign Affairs, *Am* Secretary of State.

außer|ehelich *a* illegitimate; born out of wedlock; extra-matrimonial; *~~er Geschlechtsverkehr* sexual intercourse (*od* relations) outside marriage; **~europäisch** *a* non-European; **~etatsmäßig** *a* extra-budgetary; **~fahrplanmäßig** *a* not as scheduled; not in accordance with the time-table; **~gerichtlich** *a* extra-judicial; out of court; *~~e Regelung* settlement out of court; *~~e Sachen* non-litigious matters; *gerichtlich u. ~~ vertreten* to represent in judicial proceedings and in all other affairs; *sich ~~ einigen* to settle out of court; **~gewöhnlich** *a* extraordinary, unusual; (*Ausnahme darstellend*) exceptional, special, singular; (*selten*) rare; **~halb** *prp* beyond, without; outside, out of; *~~ der Geschäftsstunden* out of the office hours; *~~ (z. B. der Gesellschaft) stehen* to be out of place; *adv* externally; on the outside; outwardly; *von ~~* from abroad; *ich komme von ~~* I come from out of town; **~kurssetzung** *f* (*Entwertung*) demonetization; withdrawal from circulation.

äußer|lich *a* external; outward; outer; *fig* (*oberflächlich*) superficial; (*scheinbar*) to all appearance, seeming(ly); (*von außen wirkend*) extrinsic; *nur ~~ anzuwenden med* for external application, for external use; *~~es Mittel* local medicament; **~lichkeit** *f* externals *pl*, outward being; exterior; (*Formalität*) formality; (*Oberflächlichkeit*) superficiality; **~~en** *pl* externals *pl*; *bloße ~~en* mere formalities.

äußern *tr* to utter, to express, to show; to manifest, to disclose; (*Urteil*) to pass; (*Gründe vorbringen*) to advance; (*seine Meinung*) to give (*od* to voice) o.'s opinion; *r* (*sich aussprechen*) to express o. s.; (*auftreten, erscheinen*) to appear; (*von Krankheiten*) to make itself felt, to make its appearance; to break out; (*von Dingen*) to show itself.

außerordentlich *a* extraordinary, exceptional, (*ungewöhnlich*) unusual, astonishing, remarkable, uncommon, extreme; *~e Ausgaben* extras *pl*; *~er Professor* assistant professor, university lecturer (*od* reader), associate professor, *Am auch* adjunct professor; *~er Gesandter u. bevollmächtigter Minister* Envoy Extraordinary and Minister Plenipotentiary; **außerplanmäßig** *a* (*Beamter*) supernumerary.

äußerst *a* outermost, *poet* outmost; utmost, uttermost, extreme; (*Preis*) best, highest possible, (*nach unten*) lowest, rockbottom price; (*räumlich*) extreme; (*zeitlich*) last; *adv* extremely, exceedingly; *im ~en Falle* in case of necessity; when the worst comes to the worst; *~es Angebot* lowest offer; *~e Gefahr* utmost peril; *das ~e Ende* the extreme end; *mit ~er Kraft mar* with maximum speed; *in ~er Not* in greatest want; *von ~er Wichtigkeit* of utmost importance; **~e(s)** *n* extremity; the extreme; *sein ~es tun* to do o.'s best, to strain every nerve; *aufs ~e verfolgen* to push o.'s claims to the uttermost; *aufs ~e treiben* to push matters to extremes; to drive to extremities; *aufs ~e gefaßt sein* to be prepared for the worst; *das ~e wagen* to stake o.'s all.

Äußerung *f* (*Kundgebung, Aufzeigung*) manifestation; (*Bemerkung, Rede*) saying, expression, remark, utterance.

aussetzen *tr* to put out; to set out; (*Segel*) to set; (*ein Boot*) to hoist out (a boat); to lower (*od* to launch) a boat; (*im Testament vermachen*) to bequeath; (*Verhandlung*) to suspend; (*Pension*) to settle a pension; (*an unbewohnter Küste*) to maroon; (*Strafvollstreckung*) to suspend (the execution of a sentence); *ein Kind ~* to expose a child; (*an Land setzen*) to land; (*preisgeben*) to expose; *dem Gelächter ~* to turn into ridicule; (*besetzen*) to line with; *typ* to finish composing; (*Belohnung*) to promise, to offer; (*Zahlung*) to suspend; (*e-e Summe*) to appoint, to fix, to settle upon; (*Preis*) to offer; *etw an e-r Sache, an jdm ~* to find fault with; to criticize, to object to; *sie hat nichts daran ausgesetzt* she found nothing wrong with it; *was hast du daran auszusetzen* what objection have you to it; *itr* (*aufhören*) to stop; to intermit; (*unterbrechen*) to interrupt; (*verschieben*) to put off; (*vertagen*) to adjourn, to suspend; (*aufschieben*) to defer, to postpone; (*von Motoren*) to break down; to stall; *fam bes. aero* to konk out; *r* to expose o. s., to make o. s. liable; *sich der Gefahr ~* to run the risk, to take a chance.

Aussetzung *f* (*e-s Kindes*) exposure; (*e-r Pension*) settlement; (*Unterbrechung*) suspension; (*Tadel*) blame, censure; (*Zahlung*) suspension (of payment); (*Aufhören*) intermission; (*Vermächtnis*) bequest; (*Vertagung*) adjournment; (*Strafvollstreckung*) suspension (of the execution); (*e-s Verfahrens*) stay (of an action); (*Verschiebung*) deferment, postponement; (*Puls*) intermittence; (*Stillstand*) stoppage, interruption.

Aussicht *f* view; sight; prospect; look-out; *~ haben auf* to have a view of; *Zimmer mit ~ auf den Fluß* a room overlooking the river; *das Zimmer hat die ~ auf die Straße* the room looks into the street; *fig* (*Aussichten, Zukunft*) outlook for, chance of, prospect of; *in ~ haben* to have in prospect; *in ~ nehmen* to plan, to contemplate, to propose; to view, to consider; *in ~ stellen* to promise, to hold out a prospect of s. th. to s. o.; *es ist keine ~ vorhanden* it is very unlikely that; *gute* (*schlechte*) *~en* good (poor) chances (*od* prospects); *gute ~en haben* to stand fair for.

aussichts|los *a* hopeless; without prospects; **~losigkeit** *f* hopelessness, absence of prospect; **~punkt** *m* watch-point, viewpoint; **~reich**, **~voll** *a* promising, rich in prospect; **~turm** *m* outlook-tower, observation tower; **~wagen** *m* (open) motorcoach, observation-car, char-a-banc, *Am* sight-seeing car, rubberneck-wagon, *rail* vista-dome car.

aus|sieben *tr* to sift out; *fig* (*überprüfen*) to screen; to sift; *radio* to filter (out), to select, to sift; **~sieden** *irr tr* to boil out; **~siedeln** *tr* to evacuate, to transfer; **~siedlung** *f* evacuation, (compulsory) transfer (of population); **~sinnen** *irr tr* to contrive, to devise.

aussöhn|en *tr* to reconcile, to appease; *sich ~en mit* to reconcile to, to get reconciled to, to make peace with, to make it up with; **~ung** *f* reconcilement, reconciliation.

aussonder|n *tr* to separate, to single out; to sort out; (*auswählen*) to select; (*zurückweisen*) to eliminate, to reject; *med* (*absondern*) to secrete, to excrete; **~ung** *f* separation; *med* secretion.

aussortieren *tr* to sort out, to select, to separate, to assort; to classify.

ausspähen *tr* to spy out; *nach etw ~* to look out for s. th.; *mil* to scout, to reconnoitre.

ausspann|en *tr* (*Pferde*) to unharness, to unhitch; (*Kunden*) to entice (away) customers; *tech* (*Werkstück*) to unclamp, to remove, to release; (*ausbreiten*) to extend; (*Seil*) to stretch; (*Netz*) to spread; *itr* (*ausruhen*) to rest, to relax, to take recreation, *Am* to take it easy; **~ung** *f* relaxation, recreation; rest; (*e-s Werkstücks*) stretching of a tool.

ausspar|en *tr* (*Malerei*) to leave space; *tech* to recess; to channel; to notch; to spare; *mil* to by-pass; **~ung** *f* saving (up); *tech* recess, opening; channel; notch.

ausspeien *irr tr* to vomit, to spit (out), to expectorate.

aussperr|en *tr* (*jdn ~en*) to shut out; (*Arbeiter*) to lock out; *typ* to space out; **~ung** *f* (*der Arbeiter*) lock-out.

aus|spielen *tr* to lead, to serve out (the ball); to play to the end; (*gegeneinander*) to play off s. o. against another; *itr* to play first, to lead; *er hat ausgespielt* it is all over with him; *ihr habt ausgespielt!* you've done it! **~spinnen** *irr tr* to spin out; *fig* (*sich weitschweifig auslassen*) to enlarge upon; (*aussinnen*) to think out, to plot; to devise; **~spionieren** *tr* to spy out; **~spotten** *tr: jdn ~~* to mock, to scoff at, to deride; **~sprache** *f* pronunciation, accent; *e-e fremde ~~ haben* to have a foreign accent; (*Gespräch*) (heart-to-heart) talk, discussion; (*Verständigung*) explanation; *mit jdm e-e ~~ haben* to talk the matter fully out with; **~sprechen** *irr tr* to pronounce, (*deutlich*) to articulate; to speak to the end, (*einen Satz*) to finish; *seine Meinung ~~* to express o.'s opinion; (*äußern*) to utter, to declare; (*Urteil*) to pronounce a judg(e)ment, to give a judg(e)ment, to bring in a verdict, to return a verdict; *Todesurteil ~~* to pass sentence of death upon; *itr* to finish speaking; *lassen Sie mich ~~!* let me finish! *sich ~~* to speak o.'s mind; to express o. s. about; to talk over; (*sich das Herz erleichtern*) to unburden o. s.; *~gesprochen a* decided, marked, outspoken; **~spreizen** *tr* to distend, to extend, to stretch apart; (*Beine*) to straddle; *mit ~gespreizten Beinen* astride; **~sprengen** *tr* to sprinkle (water); *fig* (*ein Gerücht*) to spread, to circulate, to set afloat, to divulge; **~spritzen** *tr* to squirt out; *med* to syringe; **~spruch** *m* utterance, saying, opinion; (*Bemerkung*) remark; (*des Gerichts*) judg(e)ment, sentence, finding, decision; (*der Geschworenen*) verdict, finding; (*des Schiedsrichters*) award; *sich dem ~~ des Schiedsrichters unterwerfen* to abide (by) the award; **~sprudeln** *tr* to sputter out; **~spucken** *tr, itr* to spit out; **~spülen** *tr* to clean; to wash out, to flush out; to undermine; *sich den Mund ~~* to rinse out o.'s mouth; **~spüren** *tr* to track (game), to trace; to discover.

ausstaffier|en *tr* to equip, to fit out, to furnish; (*schmücken*) to trim, to dress up, to smarten up, to garnish; **~ung** *f* equipment, outfit; trimming, garnishing.

Aus|stand *m* strike; *im ~e sein* to be on strike; *in den ~~ treten* to go on strike; **~stände** *pl* outstanding debts, claims, arrears *pl*; **~ständig** *a* outstanding, in arrears; (*streikend*) striking, on strike; **~ständige(r)** *m* (*Streiker*) striker; **~stanzen** *tr* to punch out; to cut out, to stamp out.

ausstatt|en *tr* to endow, to fit out, to furnish, to equip, to provide with; (*Tochter*) to portion (off), to furnish *od* to give (a dowry); *~~ mit* to supply with; to bestow upon; (*Buch ~~*) to get up; (*mit Rechten*) to vest s. o. with; *jdn mit allen Vollmachten ~~* to confer full powers upon s. o.; **~ung** *f* (*von Natur*) endowing, equipment, outfit; (*e-r Braut*) dowry, trousseau; portion; (*Aufmachung e-s Buches*) get-up; (*Einrichtung, Zubehör*) fittings *pl*; *theat* scenery; **~ungsstück** *n* spectacular show, transformation-scene; (*Märchenspiel*) fairy-piece, pantomime.

ausstechen *irr tr* (*Auge*) to put out; (*Rasen*) to cut turf; (*Graben*) to dig; *jdn ~* to outdo, to put in the shade, to cut out, to supplant; (*übertreffen*) to outshine, to surpass; (*verdrängen*) to oust.

ausstehen *irr tr* to suffer, to endure, to bear; *ich kann ihn nicht ~* I cannot endure (*od* bear) him, I have an aversion to him; I can't stand him; *itr* (*Geld*) to stand out; *Geld ~ haben* to have money owing; *die Entscheidung steht noch aus* the decision is still pending; *sein Brief steht noch aus* we are still waiting for his letter; **~d** *a* standing out, owing; *~de Schuld* outstanding debt.

aussteig|en *irr itr* to get out, to step out; to alight, *Am* to get off; to step off; (*aus Zug, von Truppe*) to detrain; (*aus Schiff*) to disembark; (*aus dem Flugzeug mit Fallschirm*) to bale out; *Am* to bail out; (*über dem Meer*) to ditch; *Am sl* to kick off; to hit the silk; (*aus dem gelandeten Flugzeug*) to deplane, to disembark; **~en** *n* getting out, disembarkment; **~eplatz** *m* platform; landing-place.

aussteinen *tr* to stone.

ausstell|en *tr* to lay out, to exhibit, to show; to display; (*Wachposten*) to post; (*Pässe*) to issue, to make out; (*Rezept*) to write a prescription; (*Zeugnis*) to issue a certificate; (*Quittung*) to give a receipt; (*Urkunde*) to execute; (*Scheck*) to draw a cheque; (*Wechsel*) to draw (*od* to issue) a bill; (*Rechnungen*) to render accounts; to make out; *etw auszustellen haben* to find fault with; **~er** *m* exhibitor; (*e-s Wechsels*) drawer; **~ung** *f* exhibition, display; show; **fair**; *Am* exposition; (*Tadel*) objection, censure; *~~en machen* to criticize; **~~sdatum** *n* (*e-s Wechsels*) date of issue; **~~shalle** *f* exhibition hall; **~~sort** *m* (*e-s Wechsels*) place of issue; **~~sraum** *m* show-room; display room; **~~sstand** *m* display booth; **~~sstück** *n* exhibit; **~~stag** *m* (*Wechsel*) date.

ausstemmen *tr* to chisel out.

Aussterbeetat *m: auf dem ~ stehen fig* to die out; to be doomed.

aussterben *irr itr* to die out; (*Tiere*) to become extinct; *ausgestorben a* (*Straße etc*) deserted; (*verödet*) desolate(d).

Aussteuer *f* (*e-r Braut*) a bride's outfit of clothes; trousseau; (*Mitgift*) dowry; **~n** *tr* to provide with, to equip; (*e-e Braut*) to furnish (a trousseau); *radio* (*Sender*) to modulate; **~ung** *f* *radio* modulation, tone control; **~versicherung** *f* endowment insurance.

Ausstieg *m* (*Luke*) escape hatch.

aus|stöbern *tr* to search out, to bolt; to stir up; to ferret out; **~stochern** *tr* to pick (o.'s teeth); **~stopfen** *tr* to stuff; (*mit Watte*) to wad; **~stoß** *m* expulsion, ejection; thrust; (*Fechtkunst*) pass; (*Schwimmen*) stroke; (*von Fabrik*) turn-out, output; (*aus dem Heer*) cashierment; dishono(u)rable discharge; **~stoßbeschränkung** *f* output restriction; **~stoßen** *irr tr* to push out, to cast out; (*Auge*) to knock out; (*ausschließen*) to drive out, to expel, to turn out; to eject, to relegate; *gram* to elide, to omit; (*Schrei ~~*) to utter, to ejaculate, to yell; (*Gase, Dampf etc*) to exhaust, to blow off; (*Fabrikerzeugnisse*) to turn out, to manufacture, to produce; *math* to eliminate; (*aus e-m Lande*) to banish, to expatriate, to exile, to expulse; (*Verwünschungen*) to rap out; (*Seufzer*) to fetch a sigh; *itr* (*Fechtkunst*) to make a pass; (*Schwimmen*) to strike out; **~stoßladung** *f* bursting charge; **~stoßrohr** *n* (*Torpedo*) torpedo tube; ejector tube; **~stoßung** *f* expulsion, ejection; elision, suppression; utterance; (*aus dem Heer*) cashiering; (*aus der Kirche*) excommunication; (*Verbannung*) banishment; **~stoßvorrichtung** *f* ejector; **~stoßzahlen** *f pl* output figures *pl*, production figures *pl*; **~stoßziffer** *f* rate of output; **~strahlen** *tr* to radiate; to emit; to emanate; *itr* to emit rays; **~strahlung** *f* radiation, emanation; (*Optik*) emission; **~strahlungsfläche** *f* radiating surface; **~strahlungsvermögen** *n* emissivity, radiating capacity; **~strecken** *tr* to spread out, to extend, to outstretch, to hold out; *sich ~~* (*im Bett*) to stretch (o. s.) out; **~streichen** *irr tr* to obliterate; (*Geschriebenes*) to strike out; to cross out, to erase; (*Falten*) to smooth out, to unplait; **~streuen** *tr* to spread; to scatter; (*Gerüchte*) to disperse; to circulate; **~strömen** *itr* to stream forth (*od* out); to flow out; (*Gas*) to escape; (*Dampf*) to exhaust; (*Licht*) to emanate; **~strömung** *f* outflow; (*von Gasen*) escape; (*Licht*) emanation; (*Wärme*) radiation; **~studieren** *tr* to find out by study, to study thoroughly; *itr* to finish o.'s studies, to take o.'s degree, to graduate; **~suchen** *tr* to search (thoroughly); to select, to pick out, to choose; *~gesucht a* chosen, exquisite, choice.

aus|täfeln *tr* to wainscot, to panel; *~~ n* wainscoting; **~tapezieren** *tr* to hang with tapestry, to paper; **~tausch** *m* exchange; interchange (of products, of ideas); (*Tauschhandel*) barter; **~~bar** *a tech* interchangeable; **~~barkeit** *f* interchangeability; **~~en** *tr* to exchange; (*im Tauschhandel*) to barter; **~~stück** *n* spare part; **~~student** *m* exchange student; **~~werkstoff** *m* substitute, ersatz; **~teilen** *tr* to distribute; (*Fleisch*) to serve out; (*Schläge*) to deal out (blows); (*Befehle*) to give, to issue (orders); (*Spielkarten*) to deal (cards); (*verteilen*) to share, to divide; (*Abendmahl spenden*) to administer the sacrament; **~teiler** *m* distributor; **~teilung** *f* distribution, division; administration.

Auster *f* oyster.

Austern|bank *f* oyster-bed; **~fischer** *m* oyster-dredger; **~händler** *m* oyster-man; **~park** *m* breeding-place of oysters; **~schale** *f* oyster-shell, *Am* shuck; **~zucht** *f* oyster-culture.

aus|tiefen *tr* to deepen; to fathom; **~tilgen** *tr* (*Laster*) to extirpate; (*auslöschen*) to wipe out, to efface; (*ausrotten*) to exterminate, to eradicate; **~tilgung** *f* extirpation; extermination; **~toben** *itr* to leave off raging; (*Sturm*) to abate; *sich ~~* (*Kinder*) to romp; *fig* (*die Hörner ablaufen*) to sow o.'s wild oats; **~tollen** *itr* to leave off being wild; *r* to romp to o.'s heart's content.

Aus|trag *m* end, decision, settlement; issue; *e-n Streit zum ~~ bringen* to settle a dispute; **~tragen** *irr tr* to carry out; (*Briefe*) to deliver; (*ein Kind*) to carry for full term; *fig* (*ausplaudern*) to blab out, to report; to divulge; (*Buchungsposten*) to transfer; (*entscheiden*) to determine; (*Kampf*) to decide; (*Boxkampf*) to stage; *e-e Fußballmeisterschaft wird ausgetragen* (*Am*) a soccer championship is staged; **~treiben** *irr tr* to drive out (*od* off); (*jdn hinauswerfen*) to clean out; (*austreiben, vertreiben*) to oust (*aus* from); (*ausstoßen*) to eject; to expel; (*Teufel*) to exorcize; **~treibung** *f* expulsion; exorcism; **~treten** *irr itr* to step out, to go out; (*aus Kirche*) to secede from (*od* to abandon) a church; (*aus Verein*) to resign from; (*aus Schule*) to leave; (*aus Partei*) to quit, to leave,

Am to bolt; to withdraw; (*Fluß*) to overflow, to break out of the banks; (*Blut*) to extravasate; (*Licht*) to emerge; (*aus Geschäft*) to withdraw (from a business); (*Wasser abschlagen*) to ease o. s.; *tr* to tread out, to trample out (fire); (*Schuhe*) to wear out, to break in (new shoes), to widen (by treading), to stretch; *~~ n siehe Austritt*; **~trimmen** *tr aero* to trim; **~trinken** *irr tr* to empty o.'s glass, to drink off, to finish (a bottle); *rein ~~* to drain off; *trinken Sie aus!* finish your drink! finish your glass! drink up! drink it down! *in e-m Zug ~~* to gulp down, to toss off; *bis auf den letzten Tropfen ~~* to drink to the last drop, to drink to the dregs; **~tritt** *m* stepping out; (*Fluß*) overflow; (*Ausscheiden*) leaving; (*aus Amt*) resignation, retirement; (*aus Verein*) withdrawal; (*aus Firma*) *Am* walkout; (*Öffnung*) outlet, exit, escape, vent, exhaust, issue; (*Licht*) emergence; (*Blut~~*) extravasation; effusion; (*Veranda, Vorplatz*) porch, vestibule; (*Treppenabsatz*) landing; **~~sdüse** *f* outlet nozzle; **~~serklärung** *f* notice of withdrawal (*od* resignation); **~~sgeschwindigkeit** *f* (*Schußwaffe*) muzzle velocity; (*bei Gasen, Dampf etc*) exhaust velocity; **~~sventil** *n* outlet valve; **~~swinkel** *m* angle of emersion (*od* reflection); **~trocknen** *tr* to dry up; (*von Sümpfen*) to drain; to desiccate, to exsiccate; (*Gefäß mit Tuch*) to wipe dry with a cloth; (*Holz*) to season; *itr* to become quite dry; **~trommeln** *tr* to publish by beat of drum, to drum out; *fig* to cry out, to make known; **~trompeten** *tr* to publish by trumpet; *fig* to trumpet forth; **~tröpfeln** *itr* to trickle out; to drop out; **~tüfteln** *tr* to puzzle out; **~tun** *irr tr* to put out; (*streichen*) to efface, to expunge; (*Geld*) to put out money at interest; **~tuschen** *tr* to (paint with Indian) ink, to colo(u)r.

*

ausüb|en *tr* to exercise; (*Beruf*) to practise; (*Gewerbe*) to carry on; (*Druck*) to put (*od* bear) pressure on s. o.; to bring pressure to bear; (*Amt*) to execute; (*Einfluß*) to exert an influence; (*Verbrechen*) to commit (*od* to perpetrate) a crime; *Rache ~en* to take revenge on; **~end** *a* practical; executive; *~ender Arzt* practitioner; *~ende Gewalt* executive power; **~ung** *f* practice, execution, exercise; *in ~~ bringen* to put in(to) practice; *~~ e-s Verbrechens* perpetration of a crime, commission of a crime; *in ~~ seines Berufes* in pursuance of his vocation.

Ausverkauf *m* selling-out, clearance sale, bargain sale; liquidation; *etw im ~ kaufen* to buy s. th. at a clearance sale; **~en** *tr* to sell off (*od* out), to clear (out), to clear off the stock; **~t!** sold out! *theat* Full House! *das Haus ist ausverkauft* all the seats are taken, the house is full (*od* sold out); the theatre is crammed.

aus|wachsen *irr itr* to grow out (*od* up); *bot* to sprout out, to germinate; (*bucklig werden*) to grow hump-backed; *das ist zum A~~* that tires one out of all patience; **~wägen** *tr* to weigh out, to tare; to counterbalance; to calibrate; **~wahl** *f* choosing; choice, selection; (*Warenlager*) assortment; collection; (*Vielfalt*) variety; (*die Besten*) the best; **~~lehrgang** *m* selective course; **~~mannschaft** *f sport* select(ed) (*od* picked) team; **~~prinzip** *n* selection principle (*od* rule); **~~sendung** *f* sending of a selection; assortment; consignment (sent) on approval; **~wählen** *tr* to choose, to cull (out), to select, to pick out; **~walzen** *tr* to roll out (metals).

Auswander|er *m*, ***~erin*** *f* emigrant; **~n** *itr* to emigrate (from... to...); (*Federwild*) to migrate; *tech* (*aus Richtung, von Geschoß etc*) to get out of range; **~ung** *f* emigration; migration; **~~serlaubnis** *f* emigration permit; **~~smesser** *m* (anti-aircraft) range corrector; **~~sstrecke** *f* linear travel of target.

auswärtig *a* outward; (*im Ausland, ausländisch, außerhalb des Landes*) abroad, foreign; external; non-resident; *das A~e Amt* The Foreign Office, Downing Street; *Am* State Department; *der Minister der ~en Angelegenheiten* The Foreign Secretary; *Am* Secretary of State; *~e Angelegenheiten f pl* foreign affairs *pl*; *~es Mitglied* foreign member.

auswärts *adv* outward(s), abroad; (*außerhalb des Wohnsitzes*) away from home; out of doors; *sie kommt von ~* she comes from out of town; *~ schlafen* to sleep out; *~ essen* to dine out; *die Füße ~ setzen* to turn out o.'s toes.

auswasch|en *irr tr* to wash out (*od* away); (*Gläser*) to rinse; (*Wunde*) to bathe; (*Ufer*) to wash away, to undermine; *geol* to erode; **~ung** *f* washing out; *med* ablution; (*Gestein*) erosion.

auswechsel|bar *a* interchangeable, replaceable, removable; exchangeable; renewable; **~n** *tr* to change for; to exchange; to replace; to renew; to reset; to shift; (*mot Reifen*) to change a tyre; **~ung** *f* exchange; *~~ der Gefangenen* exchange of prisoners of war; (*Ersatz*) replacement; (*Erneuerung*) renewal; **~~sfähigkeit** *f* replaceability, facility of replacement.

Ausweg *m* issue; *fig* escape, loophole, way out; expedient; alternative; vent; (*Öffnung*) outlet; *e-n ~ finden* to find a shift; *ein ~ muß gefunden werden* a way out must be found; *ich weiß keinen ~ mehr* I am at my wits' end.

ausweich|en *irr itr* to give way to; to make way for; to duck, to step aside; (*e-m Stoß*) to parry; *fig* to shun, to avoid; to evade; (*sich drücken um*) to dodge; (*e-r Entscheidung*) to side-step (*od* evade) a decision; *rechts ~~, links überholen!* keep to the right, pass on the left! **~end** *a* elusive, shuffling; *~end antworten* to make an evasive answer; **~flugplatz** *m aero* auxiliary landing field; **~geleise** *n* siding(-rail), crossing-rail; turnout track, shunting line; **~hafen** *m aero* alternative aerodrome; alternative base; alternate airfield; (*Nothafen*) emergency airport; **~krankenhaus** *n* auxiliary hospital; **~lager** *n* emergency storehouse; **~manöver** *n mil* (*taktisch*) evading movement; evasive action; withdrawing movement to new position; **~regeln** *f pl aero* air-traffic regulations *pl*; **~station** *f rail* shunting-place, siding; **~stelle** *f* siding, turnout; (*zum Überholen*) passing place; (*Nebenstraße*) by-pass; lay- by; **~stellung** *f mil* alternate position; **~stoff** *m* substitute; ersatz; **~welle** *f radio* alternative wave; (*Radar*) secondary (*od* alternative) frequency; **~werk** *n mil* (*Industrie*) shadow factory; **~ziel** *n mil* alternative target, secondary (*od* alternate) target.

ausweiden *tr* to gut, to eviscerate, to disembowel; (*Geflügel*) to draw.

ausweinen *itr* to cease weeping; *seinen Schmerz ~, sich ~* to relieve o.'s distress by weeping; to weep o.'s fill; *sich die Augen ~* to cry o.'s eyes out.

Aus|weis *m* statement; certificate; proof (of identity); identification; (*Paß*) passport; papers *pl*, permit, pass; (*Personal~~*) identity card; (*Fahrt~~*) voucher, test-certificate; (*Bank~~*) return; (*Dienst~~*) service pass; **~~en** *irr tr* to order-out, to banish, to expel; to turn out; to order to leave; (*zeigen*) to show, to make it evident; (*Ausländer*) to deport; (*aus e-r Wohnung*) to (re-)move; *sich ~~en* to prove o.'s identity; to identify o. s.; **~~karte** *f* identification card; permit; pass; **~~papiere** *n pl* identification papers *pl*; affidavits *pl*, documents *pl*; **~weisung** *f* banishment, expulsion, deportation; **~~sbefehl** *m* deportee warrant, order of expulsion.

aus|weißen *tr* to whitewash; **~weiten** *tr* to widen, to stretch, to enlarge; to expand; to dilate.

auswendig *a* exterior, outside; outward; *fig* (*aus dem Gedächtnis*) by (*od* from) memory, by heart; *~ lernen* to learn by heart; to commit to memory; *~ können* to know by heart.

auswerf|en *irr tr* to throw out, to fling out; to knock out; to eject; (*aussondern*) to reject, to scrap; to shoot; (*Netz*) to cast out; (*Blut*) to spit; (*Schleim etc*) to expectorate; (*Anker*) to cast; (*Feuer*) to vomit, to disgorge (streams of lava); (*Graben*) to cast a trench; (*Handel*) to draw out; *jdm ein Jahrgeld ~~* to settle an annuity on; (*festsetzen*) to fix, to allow, to grant (a sum); **~er** *m tech* ejector, extractor, throw out.

auswert|en *tr* to evaluate, to utilize; to make full use of; (*ausbeuten*) to exploit; (*Meßwerte*) to analyse; (*planen*) to plot; (*auslegen*) to interpret; **~estelle** *f* plotting station; computing station; **~everfahren** *n* plotting method; **~gerät** *n* protractor, reduction instrument; **~ung** *f* evaluation; utilization; analysis, interpretation; (*Lösung*) solution; (*der Lage*) estimate (of the situation), appraisal.

aus|wetzen *tr* to hollow by whetting, to grind off; *e-e Scharte ~~* to make up for; *e-n Schimpf ~~* to revenge an affront; **~wickeln** *tr* to unfold, to unwrap; to unswathe (a child); **~wiegen** *irr tr* to weigh out, to tare; to counterbalance, to balance out; **~winden** *tr* (*Wäsche*) to wring out; **~wintern** *tr* to winter; *itr* to perish in winter; **~wirken** *tr* to work out; (*den Teig*) to knead the dough; (*erlangen*) to procure; (*Begnadigung*) to sue out a pardon; *r* to take effect; to operate; **~wirkung** *f* result, effect; (*Folge*) consequence; (*Rückwirkung*) reflection; **~wischen** *tr* to wipe out; to obliterate, to sponge out; to efface; *jdm eins ~~* to fall foul of s. o. (as a revenge); to deal s. o. a blow; **~wittern** *tr* to weather, to season; *fig* to smell; *itr* to get decomposed by exposure to the air; (*von Salzen*) to effloresce; **~wringen** *tr siehe ~ringen.*

Aus|wuchs *m* growth, protuberance; (*Buckel*) hunch; excrescence; *fig* (*Mißstand*) abuse; (*der Phantasie*) aberration, raving; **~wuchten** *tr* to balance out; to counterbalance; to compensate, to equilibrate; **~wühlen** *tr* to grub up; (*vom Wasser*) to wash away; ~**wurf** *m* throwing out, discharge, ejection, eruption; *med* spitting, sputum; (*Kot*) excrement; (*Schleim*) expectoration; (*Gewebe*~~) tumo(u)r, outgrowth; (*Abfall*) refuse; *fig* outcast, dregs *pl*; ~**würfeln** *tr* to raffle for; ~**wüten** *itr* to leave off raging.

aus|zacken *tr* to indent; to scallop; to notch, to jag; (*sägeartig*) to tooth; to dentate; ~**zahlen** *tr* to pay out (*od* down); (*Arbeiter, Gläubiger*) to pay off; *sich* ~~ to pay; *es zahlt sich nicht aus* it doesn't pay; (*bar*) to pay down in cash, to cash; ~**zahlung** *f* payment; *telegraphische* ~~ telegraphic transfer; ~~**sbescheinigung** *f* certificate of payment; ~~**ssperre** *f* stop-payment order; ~~**sstelle** *f* paying office; ~**zählen** *tr* to count out; (*numerieren*) to enumerate; (*fertig zählen*) to count to the end; (*im Boxkampf*) to count out; (*auspunkten*) to outpoint; ~**zählung** *f* enumeration; ~**zahnen** *itr* to have all o.'s teeth; ~**zanken** *tr* to scold; ~**zapfen** *tr* to draw, to tap out; ~**zehren** *tr* to consume, to exhaust; *itr* to pine away, to waste away; *r* to fall off; ~**zehrung** *f* phthisis; consumption; pulmonary tuberculosis; ~**zeichnen** *tr* (*bezeichnen*) to mark out, to note out; (*Waren*) to price, to ticket, to mark; to label; *fig* to signalize; (*ehren*) to treat with distinction, to hono(u)r; *mit etw* ~~ to award with; *r* to excel; to distinguish o. s.; ~**zeichnung** *f* ticketing; *fig* distinction; (*Orden*) decoration; hono(u)r; *höchste* ~~ top (ranking) hono(u)r; ~**ziehbar** *a* telescopic, extensible, removable; ~**ziehen** *irr tr* to draw out, to pull out; (*Zahn*) to extract, to pull (out); (*Zeichnung*) to ink in; (*mit Tusche*) to trace with India ink; (*Kleider*) to take off; to undress; to strip; (*Handschuhe*) to draw off; (*verlängern*) to extend; *fig* to fleece; *chem* to distil; (*e-n Auszug machen*) to select and abstract; to summarize, to epitomize; (*aus Büchern*) to extract; to make an abstract; (*e e Rechnung*) to make out an account; *die Quadratwurzel* ~~ to extract a square root; *r* to take o.'s clothes off, to undress o. s.; *itr* to march off, to set out, to go forth, to depart; (*ins Feld ziehen*) to take the field; *aus e-m Hause* ~~ to quit a house, to (re)move; ~**zieher** *m tech* extractor; ~**ziehfallschirm** *m* auxiliary parachute; ~**ziehplatte** *f* (pull-out) slide, pull-out shelf; ~**ziehrohr** *n* telescopic tube; ~**ziehsicherung** *f el* pull-out fuse, push-in fuse; ~**ziehtisch** *m* extension-table; ~**ziehtusche** *f* drawing ink; ~**ziehung** *f chem* extraction; ~**ziehvorrichtung** *f* extractor, puller; ~**zimmern** *tr* to line with timber-work; ~**zirkeln** *tr* to measure out with compasses; ~**zischen** *tr* to hiss off; ~**zug** *m* (*Schublade*) drawer, leaf (of an extension-table); (*aus Schrank*) tray; (*Ausmarsch*) marching out, emigration, departure; exodus; (*aus der Wohnung*) remove, removal; *chem* extract, essence; (*e-s Werkes*) abstract, compendium; epitome, summary; (*Sammlung*) digest; (*von neuesten Nachrichten*) news flashes *pl*; (*aus e-r Rechnung*) *com* statement of account; (*Handel*) note, bill; (*Konto*) abstract, statement *od* extract (of account); ~**zugmehl** *n* superfine flour; ~**zugsweise** *adv* by way of abstract, in extracts; in part, partially, in selection; ~**zupfen** *tr* to pluck out; (*Wolle*) to pick; (*Seide*) to unravel.

*

autark *a* self-supporting, self-sufficient; ~**ie** *f* autarky, self-sufficiency; self-supporting country; closed economy.

authentisch *a* authentic(al), genuine.

Auto *n* motor-car, car; *Am auch* auto(mobile); motor vehicle; (*geschlossenes*) sedan, limousine, coupé; (*Sportzweisitzer*) roadster; (*altes*) *Am* jalopy; ~ *fahren* to motor, to drive a car, *Am auch* to auto; ~**antenne** *f* auto radio antenna; ~**ausflug** *m* motor-car trip; ~**ausstellung** *f* motor-show; ~**bahn** *f* motor-highway, motor road; *Am auch* arterial road; autobahn, automobile highway, express highway, cross-country highway; trunk road; ~**benzin** *n* automobile petrol, *Am* automobile gas(oline), motor spirit; ~**bereifung** *f* tyres (*Am* tires) for motor-cars; ~**biographie** *f* autobiography; ~**brille** *f* (motor-) goggles *pl*; ~**bus** *m* (*Omnibus*) (motor-) bus, (omni)bus, *Am* (auto-)bus; motor coach; *einstöckiger* ~~ single-deck bus; *zweistöckiger* ~~ double-deck bus; ~**bushaltestelle** *f* bus stop; ~**buslinie** *f* bus line; ~**dafé** *n* burning of heretics, auto-da-fé, death by fire; ~**didakt** *m* self-taught person; ~**droschke** *f* (*Taxe*) taxi(cab); (motor-)cab; *Am* cab; ~**empfänger** *m radio* car radio receiver, auto radio; ~**fahrer** *m* (*Herrenfahrer*) owner-driver, (*Chauffeur*) driver, chauffeur; *allg* motorist, *Am auch* autoist; ~**fahrt** *f* motor ride, auto ride; ~**falle** *f* (police) trap; ~**flugzeug** *n aero* air car, road-going aircraft; ~**friedhof** *m* junk pile; ~**garage** *f* garage; ~**genapparat** *m* acetylene generator, autogenous welding apparatus; ~**genschweißung** *f* acetylene welding, autogenous welding; ~**giro** *n aero* autogiro, gyroplane; ~**gramm** *n* autograph; ~**graphie** *f* autographical printing; ~**händler** *m* motor-car dealer, *Am* auto(mobile) dealer; ~**hupe** *f* hooter, horn; ~**heber** *m* jack, car lift(er); ~**industrie** *f* motor industry, automobile industry, *Am* automotive industry; ~**kappe** *f* driving helmet, motorist's cap; ~**karte** *f* road map; ~**koffer** *m* motor-car trunk; ~**kolonne** *f* (*Marschkolonne*) motor vehicle column, motor-march column, *Am* (*parademäßig*) motorcade; ~**krat** *m* autocrat; ~**kratie** *f* autocracy; ~**kratisch** *a* autocratic(al); ~**mat** *m* (*automatische Maschine*) automaton, automatic machine; (*Sicherung*) *el* automatic cut-out; *Musik*~~ musical automaton, *Am* juke-box; *Waren*~~ (penny-in-the-)slot-machine; *Speise*~~ food-slot-machine; *Getränke*~~ automatic drink dispenser; ~**matenrestaurant** *n* self-service restaurant; automat, *Am auch* cafeteria; ~**matik** *f radio* (*Abstimmung*) automatic tuning means; ~**matisch** *a* self-acting, automatic; ~**matisierung** *f* automatic control; ~**mobil** *n* passenger car; *siehe Auto*; ~~**anruf** *m* taxicab call; ~~**ausstellung** *f* motor-show; ~~**bau** *m* motor industry, *Am* automotive industry; ~~**ist** *m* motorist; ~~**motor** *m* automobile engine; ~~**wesen** *n* motoring; ~**nom** *a* autonomous; ~**nomie** *f* autonomy, home rule, right of self-government; ~**nummernschild** *n* number plate, licence plate; ~**parkplatz** *m* car park, parking-place, *Am* parking lot; ~**radio** *n* auto radio; ~**reifen** *m* tyre, *Am* tire; ~**rennbahn** *f* racing-track; ~**rennen** *n* motor-race; ~**reparaturwerkstatt** *f* repair (work) shop; ~**ruf** *m* taxicab call; ~**sammelstelle** (*Fahrbereitschaft*) *f* motor-pool; ~**schlepp** *m mot* towing by automobile; *aero* catapulting of gliders by motor-car and cable; ~~**start** *m aero* auto-towed take-off; ~**schlosser** *m* car mechanic; ~**standplatz** *m* taxi-rank, *Am* taxi-stand; ~**start** *m aero* launch by automobile tow; ~**straße** *f* highway, motor-road, autostrade; ~**technik** *f* automobile engineering; ~**typie** *f typ* halftone engraving; ~**verkehr** *m* motor traffic; ~**vermietung** *f* car hiring service; (*für Selbstfahrer*) drive-yourself service; ~**wesen** *n* motoring; ~**zubehör** *n, m* motor-car accessories *pl*.

Autor *m* author, writer; ~**enhonorar** *n* author's royalty; ~**enexemplar** *n* presentation copy; ~**in** *f* authoress; ~**isieren** *tr* to authorize, to empower; ~*isierte Übersetzung* authorized translation; ~*isierte Zeitung* licensed paper; ~**itär** *a* authoritarian; ~**ität** authority; ~~ *über* right over; ~**schaft** *f* authorship.

auweh! *interj* alas! o sad!

Aval *m com* guarantee, *Am* guaranty; ~**ieren** *tr* to guarantee (payment); ~**wechsel** *m* bill given as security.

avancieren *itr* to be promoted.

avis|ieren *tr* to inform, to notify; *jdm e-n Wechsel* ~~ to advise (*od* to inform) s. o. of a bill; ~**o** *m mar* station tender, dispatch boat.

axial *a* axial; ~**druck** *m* axial pressure.

Axt *f* axe, *Am* ax; hatchet; ~**helm** *m* axe-helve, axe-handle; ~**hieb** *m* blow of an axe.

Azalie *f* azalea.

Azetat|seide *f* acetate silk; acetate rayon; ~**zellwolle** *f* spun acetate rayon.

Azetylen *n* acetylene; ~**schweißung** *f siehe Autogenschweißung*.

Azoren *pl* the Azores *pl*.

Azur *m* azure(-colo(u)r); ~**blau** *a* sky-blue; ~**n** *a* azure.

azyklisch *a* acyclic.

B

B *Abk mit* ***B*** *siehe Liste der Abk.*
babbeln *itr* to babble, to prattle.
Baby|ausstattung *f* (*Wäsche*) layette; baby-linen; **~höschen** *n* baby pants *pl.*
Babylon *n* Babylon; **~ier(in), ~isch** *a* Babylonian.
Baccalaur|eat *n* bachelorship; **~eus** *m* Bachelor of Arts (B. A.).
Bacchus *m* Bacchus; **~fest** *n* bacchanals *pl.*
Bach *m* brook, rivulet; stream; *mar, aero sl* (*Meer*) sea, ocean; *Am, auch australisch,* creek; watercourse; *kleine Bäche machen große Flüsse* light gains make a heavy purse; **~binse** *f bot* water bulrush; **~durchlaß** *m* culvert; **~forelle** *f* brook trout; **~krebs** *m* crawfish; **~stelze** *f orn* wagtail; **~weide** *f* water-willow; osier.
Bache *f* wild sow.
Bächlein *n* brooklet, rill, *Am* branch.
Back *f mar* forecastle; (*gemeinsamer Tisch*) mess; (*Schüssel*) bowl; **~bord** *n* port, port side, larboard; **~~** *achteraus* port aft; **~~** *voraus* on the port bow; **~~flak** *f* portside anti-aircraft gun; **~~motor** *m aero* port engine; **~~seite** *f* portside.
Back|apfel *m* biffin; **~birne** *f* baking-pear; **~blech** *n* baking tin.
Backe *f,* ***Backen*** *m* cheek; (*Drechslerei*) coving; (*Einspann~*) wedge grip, jaw; (*Schneide~*) die.
backen *irr tr* to bake; (*in der Pfanne*) to fry; (*Obst*) to dry; (*Ziegel*) to burn; (*zusammen~*) to cake; *neugebacken* new-fangled; ~ *n* baking.
Backen|bart *m* whiskers *pl,* side whiskers *pl, Am fam* sideboard; (*kurzer ~~ bei glattem Kinn*) *Am* sideburns *pl*; **~bein** *n* jawbone, maxillary bone; **~bremse** *f mot* block-brake; **~futter** *n tech* jaw chuck; **~grübchen** *n* dimple in the cheek; **~knochen** *m* cheek-bone; **~streich** *m* box on the ear, slap in the face; **~zahn** *m* molar, grinder.
Bäcker *m* baker; **~ei** *f* bakery; **~geselle** *m* journeyman baker; **~handwerk** *n* baker's trade; **~laden** *m* baker's shop; **~meister** *m* master-baker; **~zunft** *f* bakers' corporation.
Back|fisch *m* fried fish; *fig* flapper; *Am sl* bobby soxer; **~geld** *n* baker's fee; **~haus** *n* bakehouse; **~huhn** *n* fried (*od* roast) chicken; **~mulde** *f* kneading-trough; **~obst** *n* baked (*od* dried) fruit; **~ofen** *m* baker's oven; **~pfanne** *f* frying-pan; **~pflaume** *f* dried plum; (stewed) prune; **~pulver** *n* baking-powder; **~stein** *m* brick; **~~mauer** *f* brick wall; **~~mauerwerk** *n* brickwork; **~~schicht** *f* course of bricks; **~stube** *f* bakehouse; **~trog** *m* kneading-trough, brake; **~ware** *f* baker's wares *pl*; **~werk** *n* pastry.
Bad *n* bath; (*im Freien*) bathe; (*Badezimmer*) bath; (*Färberei*) dip, dye; (*Badeort*) watering-place; seaside-place; spa; *ins ~ reisen* to go to a watering-place (*od* to the seaside); *das Kind mit dem ~e ausschütten* to use no discrimination.
Bade|anstalt *f* bathing-establishment, baths *pl*; *Am* swimming pool; **~anzug** *m* bathing suit, bathing costume, swim(ming) suit; **~arzt** *m* physician at a watering-place; doctor at a spa; **~einrichtung** *f* bathroom installation, bathroom plumbing; **~frau** *f* attendant; **~gast** *m* visitor at a watering-place; **~hose** *f* bathing-drawers *pl* (*od* -shorts *pl*), bathing-pants *pl, Am* (swimming) trunks *pl*; **~kabine** *f* bathing-box, bath-cabin, cubicle, *Am* bathhouse; **~kappe** *f* bathing-cap; **~kur** *f* treatment; course of baths, use of mineral waters; *e-e ~~ machen* to take the waters; **~mantel** *m* bathing-gown; bathing-wrap; bath-robe; **~matte** *f* bathing-mat; **~meister** *m* bath-keeper; bath attendant; (*Schwimmlehrer*) swimming-master, swimming-instructor.
baden *tr* to bath; (*im Freien*) to bathe, to go swimming; *in der Wanne ~* to take a bath.
Bader *m* (*Barbier*) barber.
Bade|ofen *m* geyser, *Am* water-heater; **~ort** *m* watering-place; spa; **~reise** *f* journey to a watering-place; **~schuhe** *m pl* sand-shoes *pl,* bathing slippers *pl*; **~strand** *m* bathing-beach; **~trikot** *n* bathing-tricot; **~tuch** *n* bath-towel, bathing-sheet; **~wanne** *f* bath; (bathing-)tub; **~wäsche** *f* bathing-linen; **~zeit** *f* bathing-hours *pl*; season at watering-places; **~zelle** *f* bathing-cabin; **~zeug** *n* bathing-things *pl*; **~zimmer** *n* bathroom.
baff: *~ sein fam* to be flabbergasted.
Bagage *f* (*Gepäck*) luggage, baggage; *fig* (*Gesindel*) rabble, riffraff.
Bagatell|e *f* trifle, trifling (*od* small) matter; *Am* (*bei Geld*) chicken-feed; **~isieren** to make light of, to minimize (the importance of); **~sachen** *f pl jur* petty cases *pl*; **~schaden** *m* petty damage.
Bagger *m,* **~maschine** *f* dredging-machine, dredge(r); (*Greifer~, Löffel~*) excavator; *min* steam shovel; scoop; **~n** *itr* to dredge.
bähen *tr* (*Brot*) to toast; *med* to foment.
Bahn *f* way, path; course; (*Bahnhof*) station; (*Eisen~*) railway, line, *Am* railroad; (*Zahnrad~*) cog(-wheel) railway, rack railway; (*Seil~*) cable railway; *tech* (*e-s Werkzeugs*) face; (*e-s Hammers*) groove; (*der Säge*) set; (*Schneidwerkzeug*) edge; (*Astronomie*) orbit; (*künstliche Eis~*) rink; (*Kegel~*) bowling-alley; (*Reit~*) riding-school; (*Flug~*) trajectory; (*Tuch~*) breadth; width; (*Fahr~*) road-way; (*Lauf~*) career; (*Renn~*) track; (*Ski~, Rodel~*) run, course; (*Schieß~*) range; (*gedeckte Schieß~*) shooting gallery; (*Schwimm~*) lane; *in geschlossener ~* over a closed circuit; *sich ~ brechen* to push o.'s way through; *auf die schiefe ~ geraten* to slide into evil ways; *mit der ~* by train; by rail; *auf die ~ gehen* to go to the station; *fahren Sie mit der ~ od mit dem Wagen?* do you go by train or by car? **~amtlich** *a* by the railway company; **~anlagen** *f pl* railway buildings *pl,* railway sites *pl,* railway installations *pl,* railway properties *pl*; **~anschluß** *m* rail connection; own siding; **~arbeiter** *m* railway worker; **~bau** *m* railway construction; **~beamte(r)** *m* railway-official; **~betrieb** *m* working of a railway; railway service; **~betriebswerkstatt** *f* railway repair shop; **~brechend** *a* marking a new epoch, epoch-making; pioneering, pioneer; opening the way; **~brecher** *m* pioneer; **~damm** *m* railway embankment; **~durchmesser** *m* diameter of orbit; **~ebene** *f* (*Flugbahn*) trajectory plane; **~eigentum** *n* railway property; **~elektronen** *n pl* orbital electrons *pl.*
bahnen *tr* to make passable; (*Weg*) to open a way; to beat; *fig* to pave the way for, to smooth a way; to prepare the way for; (*erleichtern*) to facilitate; *sich ~* to make o.'s way; to elbow o.'s way; to force o.'s way through.
Bahn|fracht *f* railway carriage, *Am* railroad freight; **~frachtsätze** *m pl* railway rates *pl*; **~frachttarif** *m* railway tariff; **~frei** *a* free on rail, free on board; **~gleis** *n* line, track; **~geschwindigkeit** *f aero* flight-path speed; (*Geschoß*) velocity in trajectory; **~hof** *m* (railway-)station; (*End~~*) terminus; *Am auch* depot, railroad yard; *auf dem ~~* at the station; **~~sbuchhandlung** *f* station bookstand; **~~shalle** *f* station hall, *Am* concourse; **~~skommandantur** *f* office of railway station commandant; **~~straße** *f* station road, *Am* depot street; **~~suhr** *f* station clock; **~~svorsteher** *m* station-master, *Am* station agent; **~~swirtschaft** *f* refreshment-room; **~knotenpunkt** *m* railway junction; **~körper** *m* road, permanent way; bed; **~kreuzung** *f* traverse; *rail* crossing of railway lines; **~krone** *f* crown of road-bed; **~kurve** *f* track curve; **~lagernd** *a* to be kept till called for; **~linie** *f* line; **~netz** *n* railway net (*od* system); **~polizei** *f* railway-police; **~post** *f* railway mail service; **~~wagen** *m* mail-van; **~räumer** *m* cow-catcher; fender; **~schranke** *f* railway-barrier; **~schwelle** *f* sleeper, *Am* tie; **~sperre** *f* platform gate; **~spur** *f* track; **~station** *f* station; **~steig** *m* platform; **~~karte** *f* platform ticket; **~~schaffner** *m* ticket collector, *Am* gateman, gate-keeper; **~~sperre** *f* (platform) barrier, gate; **~~unterführung** *f* platform underpass; **~strecke** *f* line, section of a railway; **~transport** *m* railway transportation; (*Güterverkehr*) goods-traffic; **~überführung** *f* bridge over the railway; overbridge, *Am* undergrade arch crossing; **~übergang** *m* railway-passage, level-crossing; *Am* grade-crossing, railroad crossing; (*bei Gestirn*) orbital transition; **~unterführung** *f* underpass; traffic tunnel; **~verbindung** *f* train connection, railway communication; railway line; **~verkehr** *m* railway-traffic; **~versand** *m* railway dispatch, rail transport; delivery by rail, *Am* shipping by rail; **~~kiste** *f* corrugated board-case for rail; **~wärter** *m* line-keeper, signalman, guard; watchman; lineman; **~~häuschen** *n* line-keeper's lodge; signal-box, block-station.
Bahr|e *f* barrow; (*für Kranke*) litter, stretcher; (*Toten~*) bier; **~tuch** *n* pall.
Bähung *f med* fomentation.
Bai *f* bay; *kleine ~* bight, creek.
Baisse *f* decline, depression, slump, bear market; fall of prices; *auf ~ spekulieren* to bear; **~spekulant** *m* bear; **~spekulation** *f* bear operation, *Am* short sale; **~tendenz** *f* downward tendency, bearish tone.
Bajazzo *m* buffoon.
Bajonett *n* bayonet; *das ~ fällen* to charge with the bayonet; *aufge-*

pflanztes ~ fixed bayonet; **~angriff** *m* charge with the bayonet; **~fassung** *f el* bayonet socket; **~fechten** *n* bayonet exercise; **~griff** *m* bayonet grip; **~stoß** *m* bayonet thrust; **~verbindung** *f*, **~verschluß** *m tech* bayonet joint.

Bake *f* beacon, sea-mark; navigation guide; signal light; (*am Ufer*) land-mark; **~nantenne** *f radio, radar* beam antenna, radio-range aerial; **~ngeld** *n* beaconage; **~ntonne** *f* (beacon) buoy.

Bakelit *n* bakelite.

Bakteri|e *f* bacterium, *pl* bacteria; *fam* germs *pl*, microbes *pl*; **~enfeindlich** *a* bactericidal; **~enforschung** *f* bacteriological research; **~engift** *n* bacterial toxin; **~enhaltig** *a* containing bacteria; **~enkrieg** *m* bacterial warfare; biological warfare; **~entötend** *a* bactericidal; **~enzüchtung** *f* culture of bacteria; **~ologe** *m* bacteriologist; **~ologie** *f* bacteriology.

Balanc|e *f* balance, equilibrium; equipoise; **~ieren** *itr* to balance, to poise; **~ierstange** *f* balance-pole.

bald *adv* soon, shortly, early; (*fast*) almost, nearly; *möglichst* ~ *adv* as soon as possible; ~...~ now...now; sometimes...sometimes; ~ *so*, ~ *so* now one way, now another; *ich wäre* ~ *gefallen* I had nearly fallen; **~ig** *a* quick; early; speedy; **~igst, ~möglichst** *adv* as soon as possible, at your earliest convenience.

Baldachin *m* canopy; *aero* (*Fläche*) centre (*Am* center) section of wing.

Bälde *f*: *in* ~ in a short time, soon.

Balearen *pl* the Balearic Islands *pl*.

Baldrian *m* valerian.

Balg *m* skin; (*der Schlange*) slough; (*Blase*~, *phot*) bellows *pl*; (*e-r Puppe*) body; *fam* (*Kind*) brat, urchin; *die Bälge treten* to blow the organ; **~(*od* Bälge)treter** *m* organ-blower, bellows-treader; **~(en)auszug** *m phot* bellow extension of camera; *sich* **~en** to wrestle; to fight; (*von Kindern*) to romp; **~erei** *f* wrestling scuffle, brawl; romp.

Balken *m* beam; balk, baulk; log; *mar* (*Rundholz*) spar; (*Decken*~) joist; (*Träger*~) girder; (*Waag*~) scale-beam, lever; (*Pfahl*) post; (*Dach*~) rafter; (*Wappen*~) chevron, fesse; (*Violin*~) bass-bar; (~ *des Gehirns*) corpus callosum; *das Wasser hat keine* ~ the sea is not blanked over; **~anker** *m* brace; **~brücke** *f* girder-bridge; **~decke** *f* span ceiling, ceiling of timbers; **~gerüst** *n* scaffolding of girders; **~holm** *m* straight spar; **~holz** *n* square(d) timber; **~kopf** *m* beam-head; *mar* beam-end; **~sperre** *f* timber road block; **~stoß** *m* scarfed joint; **~stütze** *f* prop, stay; **~system** *n* square(d) timber; **~waage** *f* steelyard; **~werk** *n* wood work; timbers *pl*; timber frame work.

Balkon *m* balcony; (*theat: erster Rang*) dress-circle; **~tür** *f* French window.

Ball *m* ball; (*Erd*~) globe; (*Billard*~) billiard-ball; (*Tanz*) ball; dance; dress-ball; (*Masken*~) fancy-ball; (*Übungsball beim Boxen*) punching-ball; (*Eck*~) corner shot; (*Elfmeter*~) penalty kick; (*Flanken*~) flank-kick; (*Flug*~) volley; (*Schmetter*~) smash; (*Schnitt*~) twist-ball; *hoher* ~ (*Tennis*) lob; *lange, flache Bälle pl* long, low volleys *pl*; ~ *spielen* to play at ball; to play at tennis; *den* ~ *anspielen* to serve the ball; *den* ~ *abgeben* to pass the ball; *den* ~ *einwerfen* to throw in the ball; *den* ~ *schneiden* to twist (*od* to cut) the ball; **~anzug** *m* full dress; **~aufnahme** *f phot* bulb exposure; **~auslöser** *m phot* ball release; **~beherrschung** *f* (*Fußball*) ball-control; **~blase** *f* inner tyre of the ball; **~holz** *n* bat; **~hülle** *f* envelope of the ball; **~kleid** *n* evening dress, ball-costume; ball-dress; **~saal** *m* ball-room; **~schläger** *m* (*Kricket*) bat; (*Tennis*) racket; **~schuhe** *m pl* dancing-shoes *pl*; **~sendestation** *f radio* re-broadcast station; **~spiel** *n* game of ball; tennis; **~technik** *f* (*Fußball*) ball-playing cleverness; **~ung** *f* agglomeration; *mil* (*von Truppen*) massing (of troops).

Ballade *f* ballad.

Ballast *m* ballast; *fig* burden, impediment; ~*einnehmen* to ballast; **~schiff** *n* ballast-lighter.

ballen *tr* to form into a ball, to double; (*die Faust*) to clench; *sich* ~ to gather into a ball; to ball; *geballt a* concentrated; *geballte Ladung* pole charge; demolition charge of T. N. T.; ~ *m* bale, pack; (*Hand*~) ball; (*Papier*~, *10 Ries*) ten reams *pl*; (*kleiner* ~) package; **~waren** *f pl* balegoods *pl*; **~weise** *adv* in bales; by the bale.

Ballett *n* ballet; **~meister** *m* ballet-master; **~röckchen** *n* tutu; **~tänzer(in)** *m* (*f*) ballet-dancer; chorus-girl.

Ballist|ik *f* ballistics *pl*; **~isch** *a* ballistic.

Ballon *m* balloon; *Fessel*~ captive balloon; *Frei*~ free balloon; *Stratosphären*~ stratospheric balloon; (*kleiner, lenkbarer* ~) *Am* blimp; (*Glasgefäß, Glas*~) jar, carboy; balloon flask; (*Fußball*) football; **~abweiser** *m* balloon cable fender; antiballoon device; **~aufnahme** *f aero* balloon survey; **~aufstieg** *m* balloon ascent; **~~splatz** *m* balloon tak-off site; **~beobachter** *m* balloon observer; **~beobachtung** *f* balloon observation; **~führer** *m* pilot of the balloon; **~hülle** *f* envelope; **~korb** *m* basket, car, nacelle; **~leinen** *n* balloon linen; **~netz** *n* balloon-net; **~reifen** *m* balloon tyre; **~sender** *m radio* balloon-born transmitter; **~sonde** *f* sounding (*od* registering) balloon; **~sperre** *f* balloon barrage; **~stoff** *m* fabric; **~verfolgung** *f sport* balloon chasing; **~wettfahrt** *f sport* balloon race; **~winde** *f* balloon winch.

Ballo|tage *f* ballot; **~tieren** *tr, itr* to ballot.

Balsam *m bot* balsam; (*biblisch*) balm; **~ieren** *tr* to embalm; **~ine** *f* balsamine; **~isch** *a* balmy; balsamic.

baltisch *a* Baltic; *das Baltische Meer* the Baltic (Sea).

balz|en *itr* to pair; to call; **~zeit** *f* (*Balz*) pairing-time.

Bambus *m*, **~rohr** *n* bamboo; **~stock** *m* bamboo-cane; **~zucker** *m* tabasheer.

Bammel *m fam* (*Angst*) funk; ~ *haben* to be in a funk; **~n** *itr* to dangle.

banal *a* hackneyed, common-place; trite, trifling, trivial; **~ität** *f* banality.

Banane *f* banana; **~nbaum** *m* banana-tree; **~nstecker** *m el* spring (*od* contact) plug, banana plug.

Banaus|e *m* low fellow, philistine; **~isch** *a* narrow-minded.

Band *n* (*pl Bänder*) ribbon, tape; (*Gelenk*~) ligament; (*Binde*) bandage; (*Hut*~) hat-band; (*Schuh*~) shoe-lace; *radio* (*Magnetophon*~) recording tape; (*Faß*~) hoop; (*Reifen*) ring; (*Arm*~) bracelet; *laufendes* ~ continuous-belt conveyer; *am laufenden* ~ (*tech*) on the assembly line; (*Förder*~) conveyer (belt); running belt; (*Felsvorsprung*) ledge; (*pl Bande*) tie, chains *pl*; fetters *pl*; *in* ~*n liegen* to be in irons; *außer Rand u.* ~ beyond control; ~ *m* (*pl Bände*) volume, tome; (*Einband*) binding; cover; **~antenne** *f radio* band (*od* ribbon) aerial, *Am* tape antenna; **~arbeit** *f* moving-belt production; **~artig** *a* ribbon-like; **~aufnahme** *f radio* tape-recording; ~~ *machen, auf* ~ *aufnehmen* to record on tape; **~breite** *f radio* band-width; frequency range; **~~neinstellung** *f radio* frequency-range control; **~~nschalter** *m* band-selector switch; **~~regler** *m* band-width control; **~bremse** *f mot* band brake; *radio* frequency control; **~eisen** *n* hoop-iron, band-iron, strip-iron; **~fabrikation** *f* production-line fabrication; **~fertigung** *f* assembly-line production; **~filter** *n radio* band(-pass) filter; **~förderer** *m* belt conveyer; **~haken** *m* hoop-cramp; tie hook; **~kante** *f* band edge; **~maß** *n* string measure, tape measure, tape line; **~mikrophon** *n radio* ribbon (*od* band) microphone; **~nagel** *m* clamp-nail; **~nudel** *f* ribbon-macaroni, ribbon vermicelli; **~säge** *f* band-saw, ribbon-saw; **~schleife** *f* favo(u)r, knot of ribbons; **~spreizung** *f radio* band spread; **~stahl** *m* strip steel, band steel; **~straße** *f tech* (*Fließband*) assembly-line production; **~stuhl** *m* ribbon-loom; **~waren** *f pl* small wares *pl*, ribbons *pl*; haberdashery; **~weber, ~wirker** *m* ribbon-weaver; **~wurm** *m* tape-worm.

Bandag|e *f* bandage; **~ieren** *tr* to bandage; **~ist** *m* truss-maker.

Bändchen *n* small ribbon; *med* ligament; (*Buch*) small volume.

Bande *f* (*pl Banden*) band, company; bunch; troop; gang; (*im Stoffe*) stripe; (*Billard*) cushion; (*Rand*) edge; **~nbildung** *f* organization of bands; **~nkrieg** *m* guerrilla warfare; **~nmitglied** *n* member of a gang, *Am* gangster; **~nwesen** *n* highway robbery.

bändern *tr* to form into ribbons; (*Stoff*) to stripe, to streak.

Banderole *f* revenue stamp.

bändig|en *tr* to tame; (*Pferd*) to break in; *fig* to subdue; (*unter Kontrolle halten*) to control, to manage, to master; **~er** *m* tamer; **~ung** *f* taming; (*Pferd*) breaking-in; *fig* subduing; checking.

Bandit *m* bandit; (*bewaffneter*) raider, *Am* holdup man, stickup man, high-jacker.

bang|(e) *a* afraid (of), in fear (*vor* of, *um* for); anxious; (*in Sorge*) uneasy; (*in Aufregung*) alarmed; worried, concerned; *jdm* ~*e machen* to make s. o. afraid of; to scare s. o., to frighten s. o.; *es ist mir* ~*e um ihn* I fear for him; *davor ist mir nicht* ~*e* I am not afraid of it; **~emacher** *m* alarmist; panic-monger; **~en** *itr* to be afraid of; to be anxious about; *mir bangt davor* I am afraid of it; *sich* ~~ *um* to be worried about; *nach etw* ~~ (*sich sehnen nach*) to long (*od* yearn) for; **~igkeit** *f* anxiousness, fear.

bänglich *a* rather anxious.

Bank *f* (*pl Bänke*) bench, seat; (*Angeklagten*~) dock; (*Dreh*~) (turning) lathe; (*Hobel*~) carpenter's bench; (*Kirchen*~) pew; (*Sand*~) sand-bank; (*Untiefe*) shoal, shallow; *geol* (*Lager, Schicht*) layer, stratum; bed, stand; (*Schul*~) (school-)bench, form; (*pl Banken*) bank; banking house; *durch die* ~ on an average, without exception; *auf die lange* ~ *schieben* to delay, to put off; ~ *halten* to keep the bank; *die* ~ *sprengen* to break the bank; **~abhebung** *f* withdrawal in cash; **~abschluß** *m* bank returns *pl*, bank statement; **~agio** *n* bank agio; **~aktie** *f* bank-share; **~anweisung** *f* cheque,

Am check; **~auszug** *m* bank-statement; **~aval** *m* banker's guarantee; *Am* banker's guaranty; **~beamte(r)** *m* bank-official, bank-clerk; **~buch** *n* bank book, deposit book; **~dieb** *m* (*durch Unterschlagungen*) embezzler; **~diskont** *m* bank-rate; **~fach** *n* (*Geschäftszweig*) banking (business); (*Aufbewahrungsort*) safe, safe-deposit box; **~fähig** *a* bankable; **~feiertag** *m* bank holiday, *Am* legal holiday; **~filiale** *f* branch bank, bank-agency; **~geschäft** *n* banking firm; **~geschäfte** *n pl* banking transactions *pl*, banking operations *pl*; **~guthaben** *n* bank assets *pl*; bank balance; cash in the bank; **~halter** *m* banker; (*beim Spiel*) keeper of the bank; **~ier** *m* banker; (*großer Finanzmann*) financier; **~konsortium** *n* banking syndicate; **~konto** *n* banking-account, *Am* bank account; checking account; *ein ~~ haben bei* to bank with; **~krach** *m* bank crash; banking failure; **~mäßig** *a* bankable, negotiable, banking; **~nebenstelle** *f* branch bank; **~note** *f* (*als Papiergeld*) soft money; banknote, note, *Am* (bank) bill; **~~numlauf** *m* note circulation, circulation of currency; **~provision** *f* banker's commission; **~satz** *m* bank rate; **~scheck** *m* bank cheque, *Am* bank check; **~überweisung** *f* bank transfer, bank remittance; **~vollmacht** *f* power of attorney valid in a bank; **~wechsel** *m* bank-bill, draft; **~werte** *m pl* negotiable securities *pl*, *Am* bank stocks *pl*; **~wesen** *n* banking; **~zinsen** *m pl* banking interests *pl*.

Bänk|chen *n* small bench; **~elsänger** *m* ballad-singer; minstrel.

Bank(e)rott *m* insolvency, failure, financial crash, bankruptcy; *betrügerischer ~* fraudulent bankruptcy; *~ a* bankrupt; *~ erklären* to declare bankrupt; *~ machen* to go (*od* to turn *od* to become) bankrupt; to fail; to break; *jdn für ~ erklären* (*jur*) to adjudicate s. o. a bankrupt; *sich für ~ erklären* to file o.'s petition in bankruptcy; **~erklärung** *f* declaration of bankruptcy; *jur* adjudication-order; **~eur** *m* bankrupt, defaulter, insolvent firm.

Bankert *m* illegitimate child, bastard.

Bankett *n* banquet.

Bann *m* ban; (*Ächtung*) proscription; (*Kirchenbann*) excommunication; (*kleiner ~*) interdict; *fig* charm, spell; *in den ~ tun* to banish; (*kirchlich*) to excommunicate; *unter dem ~ von etw od jdm stehen* to be under the spell (*od* influence) of; (*stärker*) to be spell-bound (*od* fascinated) by; **~bulle** *f* bull of excommunication; **~en** *tr* to banish, to outlaw; (*kirchlich*) to excommunicate; (*gesellschaftlich*) to taboo; (*politisch*) to boycott; **~fluch, ~strahl** *m* anathema; **~kreis** *m fig* spell, sphere of influence; **~meile** *f* boundary; precinct; **~ware** *f* contraband (goods *pl od* cargo).

Banner *n* banner, ensign, standard, flag; **~träger** *m* standard-bearer.

Bantamgewicht *n* (*Boxkampf*) bantam-weight; **~sringer** *m* bantam-weight wrestler.

•

bar *a* (*ledig*) destitute, devoid of; (*nackt*) bare, naked; (*rein*) pure, mere; *~er Unsinn* sheer nonsense; *gegen ~* for cash; *~es Geld* ready money, cash; *~ bezahlen* to pay (in) cash; **~anschaffung** *f* remittance in cash; **~auslage** *f* actual expense (*od* outlay); cash expenditure; **~bestand** *m* cash in (*od* on) hand, balance in cash; cash reserve; ready money; **~betrag** *m* amount in cash; **~deckung** *f* cash-repayment; cash in hand available for cover; **~einnahme** *f* cash receipts *pl*; **~ertrag** *m* net proceeds *pl*; **~frankierungsmaschine** *f* postage meter machine; **~fuß** *a* barefoot(ed); **~geld** *n* cash, ready money; specie; cash in hand; **~geldlos** *a* cashless; paid by cheque; *~geldloser Zahlungsverkehr* transactions without actual currency; cashless trade; **~geschäft** *n* cash business (*od* transaction); **~häuptig** *a* bare-headed; **~kauf** *m* cash purchase; **~kredit** *m* cash credit; **~lohn** *m* wages in cash; **~preis** *m* cash price; **~schaft** *f* cash property; ready money; **~scheck** *m* open (*od* uncrossed) cheque; cash cheque; **~sendung** *f* cash remittance; (*Goldsendung*) specie consignment; **~vergütung** *f* compensation in cash; **~verkauf** *m* cash sale; **~verkehr** *m* cash trade; **~verlust** *m* clear (*od* net) loss; **~vorschuß** *m* cash advance; **~wert** *m* actual value; cash value; **~zahlung** *f* cash (payment), prompt cash; *nur gegen ~~* terms strictly cash.

Bar *f* tavern, bar; **~dame** *f* bar-maid; **~kellner** *m* bar-keeper, *Am* barman; **~sänger** *m* nightclub-singer, cabaret-singer, *Am fam* torch-singer; **~stuhl** *m* bar-stool.

Bär *m* bear; *der Große ~* the Great (*od* Greater) Bear, *Am* the Big Dipper; *der Kleine ~* the Little (*od* Lesser) Bear; (*Rammklotz*) tup; pile driver, ramblock; rammer; (*e-r Gießpfanne*) skull; *e-m e-n ~en aufbinden* to gammon s.o.; to hoax s. o.; **~beißig** *a* bearish, grumpy, surly; **~enführer** *m* bear-leader; **~enhatz** *f* bear-baiting; **~enhaut** *f* bearskin; **~enwärter** *m* bear-keeper; **~enzwinger** *m* bear-garden, bear-pit; **~in** *f* she-bear.

Baracke *f* barrack; hut, *Am* shack; shanty; **~nbau** *m* barrack construction; **~nlager** *n* hut-camp, hutment; barrack camp (*od* encampment).

Barbar *m* barbarian; **~ei** *f* barbarism; **~isch** *a* barbarous.

Barbarameldung *f mil* (*Artillerie*) meteorological message (*od* report); (*Wetterbericht*) weather report.

Barbe *f* barbel.

Barbier *m* barber; *siehe Friseur*; **~en** *tr* to shave; *über den Löffel ~en* **to lead** s. o. by the nose, to cheat s. o.

Barchent *m* fustian; *feiner ~* dimity; **~macher** *m* fustian-weaver.

Barde *m* bard, minstrel; **~ngesang** *m* bardic song.

Barett *n* biretta, beretta, barret; (*Baskenmütze*) beret; cap.

Bark|asse *f* (motor) launch; **~e** *f* barque; *poet* bark; (*kleine*) barge.

Bärme *f* barm; (*Brauerei*) yeast.

barmherzig *a* merciful, compassionate; *~e Brüder, Schwestern* hospitallers, sisters of charity (*od* mercy); *der ~e Samariter* the good Samaritan; **~keit** *f* mercy, charity, compassion; *~~ üben* to show mercy.

Barock *n* baroque; *a* baroque; *fig* grotesque, odd.

Barometer *n* barometer; *das ~ steigt* the glass is going up; *das ~ fällt* the barometer is falling; **~druck** *m* barometer pressure; **~stand** *m* height of the barometer; barometer reading.

Baron *m* baron; **~esse** *f*, **~in** *f* baroness.

Barre *f* bar; (*Geld*) ingot, bullion; **~n** *m* (*zum Turnen*) parallel bars *pl*.

Barriere *f* barrier; natural obstacle; *rail* gate; (*Geländer*) railing.

Barrikade *f* barricade; *~n bauen* to raise barricades; **~nkampf** *m* barricade-fighting.

Barsch *m* (*Fisch*) perch; *~ a* harsh, gruff; rude, rough; blunt; **~heit** *f* harshness, roughness, rudeness.

Bart *m* beard; (*Schlüssel~*) (key-)bit; (*des Hahnes*) wattle; (*Katze*) whiskers *pl*; (*von Fischen, Pflanzen*) barb, beard; (*Gußnaht*) bur, fash, seam; *sich e-n ~ wachsen lassen* to grow a beard; *sich den ~ abnehmen lassen* to get shaved; *e-m um den ~ gehen* to flatter s. o.; *um des Kaisers ~ streiten* to dispute about trifles; **~flechte** *f* sycosis; barber's itch; *bot* tree-beard, beard moss; **~los** *a* beardless; **~nelke** *f* sweet William.

bärtig *a* bearded; *bot* barbate.

Basalt *m* basalt; whinstone.

Base *f* cousin; *chem* base; *basische Verbindung* basic compound; **~naustausch** *m chem* exchange of bases; **~nbildend** *a* basifying, base-forming; **~nüberschuß** *m* excess base.

Baseballspielplatz *m* baseball park (*od* field), *Am* diamond.

basieren *tr* to base on, to found (up)on; *itr* to be based (*od* founded) (up)on; to rest upon.

Basis *f* base; basis; foundation; (*Säule*) foot; *auf solider ~* on a sane footing; **~entfernungsmesser** *m*, **~gerät** *n* base range finder; **~messung** *f* base measuring; **~projektion** *f* base projection.

Baß *m* bass; **~anhebung** *f radio* bass compensation, bass boosting; **~balken** *m* (*in Saiteninstrument*) bass bar; **~bläser** *m* bassoonist; **~flöte** *f* courtal; **~geige** *f* bass-viol, (violin)cello; (*große*) double-bass, contrabass; **~pfeife** *f* drone-pipe; **~schlüssel** *m* bass-key; **~stimme** *f* bass voice.

baß *adv* (*sehr*) very, exceedingly; *ich war ~ erstaunt, als ich das hörte* I was very surprised when I heard it.

Bassin *n* basin, reservoir, tank; *mar* dock; **~wagen** *m rail* tank car.

Bassist *m* bass singer.

Bast *m* bast; (*bei Flachs*) harl; (*am Hirschgeweih*) velvet, fraying; **~decke** *f* matting; **~faser** *f* bast-fibre; **~hut** *m* chip-hat; **~matte** *f* bast-mat; **~seide** *f* raw silk; **~seil** *n* bast-rope; **~zellulose** *f* cutocellulose.

basta! *interj* stop, enough! *und damit ~!* (and) that's enough!

Bastard *m* bastard.

Bastei *f* bastion.

Bast|elbuch *n* book of amateur construction; **~eln** *tr* to tinker, to rig up; to potter, *Am* to putter; (*e-e Liebhaberei betreiben*) to work at a hobby; **~ler** *m* tinker, dabbler; fan; amateur constructor, handyman; radio amateur; (*Kurzwellen~~*) *Am* ham.

Bataillon *n* battalion; **~sabschnitt** *m* battalion sector; **~sadjutant** *m* battalion adjutant, aide to battalion commander; **~sführer** *m* battalion commander; **~sgefechtsstand** *m* battalion command post, battalion battle H. Q.; **~skommandeur** *m* commander of a battalion, battalion commander; **~sstab** *m* battalion staff; **~sstabsquartier** *n* battalion headquarters *pl*; **~stroß** *m* battalion train; **~sverbandsplatz** *m* battalion aid station.

Batate *f* sweet potato.

Batist *m* cambric.

Batterie *f mil, el* battery; (*Auto~*) accumulator; (*Ersatz~*) spare battery; (*Atom~*) pile; (*Kokerei*) block; (*Anzahl*) set; *e-e ~ laden el* to charge a battery; **~chef** *m* battery commander; **~elektrode** *f* battery electrode; **~element** *n* battery cell; **~empfänger** *m* *radio* battery-operated set, battery receiver; **~entladung** *f el* battery discharge; **~führer** *m mil* battery commander; **~gespeist** *a radio* battery operated; **~glas** *n el* battery jar; **~kasten** *m* battery box (*od* container); **~klemme** *f* battery terminal connection; **~kran** *m mil* gun hoist; **~ladesatz** *m*, **~ladevorrichtung** *f* battery-charger; **~nullpunkt** *m mil* battery's zero point; **~offizier** *m* gun-position officer; battery executive; **~strom** *m el* battery current; **~widerstand** *m el* battery resistance; **~zelle** *f el* battery cell; **~zündung** *f mot* battery (*od* coil) ignition.

Batzen *m* (*Klumpen*) lump; heap.

Bau *m* (*das Bauen*) construction; (*Hoch- u. Tief~*) surface and underground construction; (*Straßen~*) road construction; *im ~* under construction, (*von Schiff*) on the stocks; (*Bauart*) structure; (*Gebäude*) building, edifice; (*Häuserblock*) pile; (*Anpflanzung*) cultivation, culture; (*von Tieren*) burrow, den; (*Berg~*) mining; (*Körper~*) frame, build; (*Organismus*) organism; (*Beschaffenheit*) constitution; (*Gefüge*) make; (*Herstellung*) manufacture, making; **~akademie** *f* architectural academy; **~amt** *n* Board of Works; **~anschlag** *m* builder's estimate; **~arbeiten** *f pl* construction work; **~arbeiter** *m* construction worker; *tele* wireman; **~art** *f* style of building, architecture; *mar* type, class; (*Konstruktion*) construction, design, type, model; *übliche ~~* orthodox design; **~aufseher** *m* inspector; **~aufsicht** *f* construction supervision; *aero* aeronautical inspection; **~aufwand** *m* cost of. construction; **~ausführung** *f* execution of construction; **~ausschreibung** *f* calling for tenders; **~bataillon** *n* construction battalion; **~beschreibung** *f* specification; **~bestandteil** *m* component (part); **~block** *m* building block, housing block; **~en** *tr* to build, to construct; (*errichten*) to erect, to raise; (*anbauen*) to grow, to cultivate, to till; *min* to work; *itr auf jdn ~~* to rely on; **~fach** *n* architecture; building-trade; **~fällig** *a* out of repair, dilapidated, tumble-down, ramshackle, rickety, decaying; **~firma** *f* construction work; **~flucht(linie)** *f* alignment *od* alinement; building line; **~form** *f tech* type of construction; **~führer** *m* manager, overseer; **~führung** *f* building supervision; **~gelände** *n* building-site; **~genehmigung** *f* building-permit; (building-) licence; **~genossenschaft** *f* building society; **~gerät** *n* construction tools *pl*; **~gerüst** *n* scaffold(ing); **~geschäft** *n* building-trade; **~gesuch** *n* application for a building-permit; **~gewerbe** *n* building-trade; **~grube** *f* foundation-trench; **~handwerker** *m* workman in the building-trade; **~herr** *m* builder, owner of the property; **~hof** *m* fitting yard; **~holz** *n* timber, *Am* lumber; **~industrie** *f* building industry; **~ingenieur** *m* constructional (*od* structural) engineer; **~jahr** *n* date when built, year in which constructed; **~kapital** *n* building capital; **~kasten** *m* (*für Kinder*) box of bricks; **~kolonne** *f* gang; construction unit; **~kompanie** *f mil* construction (*od* works) company; **~kosten** *pl* building costs *pl od* expenses *pl*; **~~voranschlag** *m* builder's estimate; **~kredit** *m* building loan; **~kunst** *f* architecture; **~länge** *f* over-all length; **~leitung** *f* works department; supervision of construction; **~lich** *a* architectural; in good repair; *~~e Anordnung* constructional arrangement; **~lichkeit** *f* building; premises *pl*; **~linie** *f* building line; **~los** *n* portion under construction; allotment for construction; **~lustig** *a* fond of building; **~materialien** *n pl* building materials *pl* (*od* supplies *pl*); **~meister** *m* architect, builder; **~muster** *n tech* model; *neuestes ~~* latest model; **~plan** *m* ground-plan; *tech* blueprint, construction plan; (*für ein Gebiet*) development study; **~platz** *m* site, lot, plot, *Am* location; **~polizei** *f* building police; **~reif** *a* developed; **~riß** *m* plan of building; **~sand** *m* building (*od* mortar) sand; **~schule** *f* building school; architect's college; **~schutt** *m* rubbish, rubble; **~sparkasse** *f* building and loan association; **~stahl** *m* engineering (*od* structural) steel; **~stein** *m* brick; **~stelle** *f* building-site; **~stoff** *m* building-material; (*Körper*) nutrient; **~teil** *m* structural part; **~~efabrik** *f* factory for prefabricated components; **~trupp** *m* construction gang (*od* team, unit); **~unternehmer** *m* builder, contractor; **~vorhaben** *n* building project; **~vorrichtung** *f* jig; **~vorschrift** *f* building regulations *pl*; **~weise** *f* construction; **~werk** *n* building; structure; edifice; **~wesen** *n* architecture, building-trade; **~wirtschaft** *f* building economy; **~zaun** *m* hoarding, boarding, planking, paling; **~zeit** *f* time of construction; **~zug** *m* (*Feldbahn*) field railway.

Bauch *m* belly; stomach; (*Unterleib*) abdomen; (*Schmer~*) paunch; (*e-r Geige*) body; (*Schiffs~*) bottom; (*Ausbuchtung*) bulge; (*Flasche*) bulb; (*Segel*) bunt; (*Schwingung*) antinode; **~binde** *f* abdominal bandage, belt; (*Zigarre*) (cigar)band; (*Buchbinde*) (advertising) band, (*Waschzettel*) blurb; **~fell** *n* peritoneum; **~~entzündung** *f* peritonitis; **~grimmen** *n* colic; gripes *pl*; **~gurt** *m* girt; belly-band; **~höhle** *f* abdominal cavity; **~ig** *a* bellied, bulgy, convex; **~laden** *m* vendor's box; **~lage** *f* (*Gymnastik*) lying flat on the belly; **~landung** *f aero* belly landing; **~muskel** *m* abdominal muscle; **~redner** *m* ventriloquist; **~riemen** *m* girt; **~schmerzen** *m pl* belly-ache; **~schneiden** *n* gripes *pl*, colic; **~speicheldrüse** *f* pancreas; **~stück** *n* (*Fleisch*) piece of the belly; *mar* floor-timber; **~typhus** *m* abdominal typhus; enteric fever; **~ung** *f* convexity; (*Schwellung*) inflation, swelling; **~wassersucht** *f* ascites; **~weh** *n* stomach-ache; **~zwicken** *n* gripes *pl*, colic.

Bauer *m* peasant, farmer, (*mit eigenem Besitz*) freeholder; (*Schach*) pawn; (*Karten*) knave; (*Grobian*) boor, churl; yokel; (*Vogel~*) cage.

Bäuer\|in *f* country-woman, farmer's wife; **~isch** *a* rustic; **~lich** *a* rural.

Bauern\|aufstand *m* peasant rising; **~bursche** *m* young peasant; **~dirne** *f* country lass; **~fänger** *m* sharper, crook; (*Karten*) rook; **~fängerei** *f* confidence trick, *Am* confidence game; **~gut** *n* farm, farmstead, *Am auch* ranch; **~haus** *n* farm-house; **~hochzeit** country-wedding; **~hof** *m siehe* **~gut**; **~hütte** *f* cottage; **~knecht** *m* farmer's man; ploughman, *Am* farmer's hand; **~lümmel** *m* country-bumpkin; **~mädchen** *n* country girl; **~regel** *f* peasant lore; weather maxim; **~schaft** *f* peasantry; **~schenke** *f* village inn, country pub; **~schlau** *a* shrewd, canny; **~sprache** *f* country dialect; **~stand** *m* peasantry; **~stolz** *m* upstart-pride; **~tölpel** *m* yokel; **~tracht** *f* rustic dress; **~volk** *n* country people (*od* folk); **~wirtschaft** *f* farm; farmstead; rural economy, agriculture.

Bauers\|frau *f* country-woman, farmer's wife; **~leute** *pl* country people, country-folk; **~mann** *n* countryman, peasant.

Baum *m* tree; (*Nadel~*) conifer; (*Lade~*) derrick, sheers *pl*; (*Mechanik*) bar; (*Wagen~*) shaft; (*Stange, Deichsel*) pole; *mar* boom; (*Hebe~*, *Ketten~*) beam; (*Dreh~*) *mech* arbo(u)r; (*Stall~*) bar; **~allee** *f* avenue of trees; **~bast** *m* inner bark of a tree; **~beobachtung** *f mil* observation from a tree; **~~sstand** *m mil* observation post in a tree; **~blüte** *f* blossom of a tree; *Zeit der ~~* florescence; **~falk** *m* hobby; **~flechte** *f* tree-moss; **~frevel** *m* injury done to trees; **~garten** *m* orchard; **~gipfel** *m*, **~krone** *f* top of a tree; **~grenze** *f* timber-line; **~gruppe** *f* group of trees; **~hacker**, **~läufer** *m* wood-pecker, tree-creeper; **~harz** *n* resin; **~kuchen** *n* pyramid cake; **~lang** *a* (as) tall as a tree; lanky; **~laus** *f* tree-louse; **~leiter** *f* tree-ladder; **~los** *a* treeless; **~marder** *m* baummarten; **~öl** *n* olive-oil; **~pfahl** *m* prop, stay; **~rinde** *f* bark, rind; **~saft** *m* sap; **~säge** *f* tree-saw; pruning (*od* grafting) saw; **~schere** *f* pruning-shears *pl*; **~schlag** *m* foliage; **~schnitt** *m* lopping; **~schule** *f* nursery; **~schwamm** *m* agaric; **~stamm** *m* trunk, stem; **~stark** *a* robust; **~stumpf** *m* stump; **~verhau** *m* abatis, *Am* slashing; **~wachs** *n* mummy, grafting-wax; **~wuchs** *m* growth of trees; **~zucht** *f* arboriculture; nursery; **~züchter** *m* arborist.

baumeln *itr* to dangle, to hang dangling, to bob, to swing.

bäumen *r* to rear, to prance.

Baumwoll\|abfall *m* cotton waste; **~baum** *m* cotton-tree; **~e** *f* cotton; **~en** *a* cotton; **~faden** *m* cotton thread, cotton twine; **~farbstoff** *m* cotton dye; **~garn** *n* cotton yarn, spun-cotton; **~gewebe** *n* cotton fabric, cotton goods *pl*; **~kabel** *n* cotton covered cable; **~pflanzer** *m* cotton grower; **~pflanzung** *f* cotton plantation; **~pfropfen** *m* cotton plug (*od* stopper); **~samen** *m*, **~saat** *f* cotton-seed; **~samt** *m* cotton-velvet; velveteen; **~spinnerei** *f* cotton-mill; **~staude** *f* cotton-plant; **~stoff** *m* cotton-cloth; **~waren** *f pl* cottons *pl*; **~weberei** *f* cotton-manufactory; **~zwirn** *m* cotton thread.

Bausch *m* bolster, pad, wad; *med* compress; *in ~ u. Bogen* on the whole, in the lump; in the bulk; **~ärmel** *m* puffed sleeve; **~en** *itr* to swell, to puff, to bunch; **~ig** *a* puffy, swelled, baggy; **~kauf** *m* purchase in the lump.

Bauten *f pl* buildings *pl*; structures *pl*; *öffentliche ~* public works *pl*.

Bauxit *m* bauxite.

Bayer(in) *m* (*f*) Bavarian; **Bayern** *n* Bavaria; **bayrisch** *a* Bavarian.

Bazill\|us *m* bacillus; germ; **~enkrieg** *m* germ war; biological warfare (*Abk* BW); **~enträger** *m med* carrier.

beabsichtigen *tr* to intend, to design, to propose, to purpose, to aim at, to have in view, to be minded.

beacht\|en *tr* to attend to, to pay attention to; (*gewahren*) to notice, to take notice of; to take care that, to mind that; (*planen*) to plan; (*in Betracht ziehen*) to consider, to take into account, to take into consideration; (*beobachten*) to observe; **~enswert**, **~lich** *a* notable, remarkable, deserving notice, noteworthy; **~ung** *f* consideration, notice, attention; *zur ~~!* notice!

zur gefälligen ~~ for your kind attention; kindly notice; *gebührende* ~~ *schenken* to give due regard to.

Beamt|e(r) *m*, **~in** *f* official, public-servant, civil servant; officer; *Am* office-holder, job-holder; *höhere(r)* ~~ functionary; (*Büro~~*) clerk; **~enabbau** *m* ax(e); **~enbeleidigung** *f* insult to an official; **~enherrschaft** *f* bureaucracy; red-tapism; **~enschaft** *f*, **~entum** *n* civil servants *pl*, civil service.

beängstig|en *tr* to afflict, to alarm, to frighten, to fill with anxiety, to make anxious; **~ung** *f* anxiety, uneasiness.

bean|spruchen *tr* (*Recht*) to claim, to lay claim to; (*etw von jdm*) to demand s. th. from s. o.; (*Aufmerksamkeit*) to engross; (*Eigenschaft*) to pretend (to); (*erfordern*) to require; (*Arbeit, Fleiß, Zeit*) to require, to take; *tech* to stress, to strain; **~spruchung** *f* claim; *tech* (*Ausübung e-r Spannung auf Körper*) stress(ing), strain(ing); (*von Maschinen*) service, condition, load; **~standen** *tr* to object to; (*e-e Wahl*) to contest; (*Vorstellungen machen*) to remonstrate; (*Annahme verweigern*) to refuse acceptance; (*Einwendungen machen*) to demur (*gegen* to); (*sich beklagen*) to complain (*über* of); (*protestieren*) to protest; (*zurechtweisen*) to expostulate; **~standung** *f* objection, protestation; complaint; refusal; (*Einspruch*) protest; (*Einwendung*) remonstration; (*ernste Vorhaltung*) expostulation; ~~*en geltend machen* to bring complaints to notice; **~tragen** *tr* to propose; *parl* to move; to apply for; to file a petition; to make a motion; (*vor Gericht*) to sue out; to solicit.

beantwort|en *tr* to answer, to reply to; **~ung** *f* reply, answer; *in* ~~ *Ihres Schreibens* in reply to your letter.

bearbeit|bar *a* workable; **~~keit** *f* *tech* workability; machinability; **~en** *tr* to work; to cultivate; (*Buch*) to revise; (*Wörterbuch*) to compile; (*Theaterstück*) to adapt; *nach dem Englischen ~et* adapted from the English; (*erledigen*) to handle; (*zurechtmachen*) to dress; (*redigieren*) to edit; (*gestalten*) to fashion; (*sich befassen*) to deal (with); (*behandeln*) to manipulate; *chem* to treat with; to process; *tech* to machine; (*mit Werkzeugen*) to tool; *jdn* ~~ to influence s.o.; to work (up)on s. o.; (*Kunden, Wähler*) to canvass; **~er** *m* author, editor, reviser, adaptor, compiler; **~ung** *f* working; culture; altered edition, revision; (*Theaterstück*) adaptation; (*Musikstück*) arrangement; (*von Personen*) canvassing; *tech* mechanical treatment, (*durch Maschinen*) machining, tooling, (*Zurichtung*) dressing, (*Herstellungsgang*) processing; manufacturing; **~~sgrad** *m* workability; **~~sgüte** *f* workmanship, finish; **~~smethoden** *f pl* manufacturing methods *pl*; **~~splan** *m* operation plan (*od* sheet); **~~svorgang** *m* mechanical process; machining operation; **~~svorschrift** *f* processing prescription; **~~szeit** *f* operating time.

beargwöhnen *tr* to suspect, to be suspicious (of); (*mißtrauen*) to mistrust, to distrust.

beaufsichtig|en *tr* to look after, to control; to supervise; to inspect; to superintend; to keep an eye on; **~ung** *f* supervision, inspection, control; (*Überwachung*) surveillance.

beauftrag|en *tr* to charge with; (*ermächtigen*) to authorize, to commission, to empower; **~te(r)** *m* commissioner; nominee; (*Abgeordneter*) deputy; (*Bevollmächtigter*) proxy, mandatory; authorized agent.

bebändert *a* beribboned.

bebau|bar *a* cultivable; (*Baugelände*) developed; **~en** *tr* (*ein Gelände*) to build on; (*Feld*) to till, to cultivate, to farm; *min* to work; **~ung** *f* (*Feld*) cultivation; (*Gelände*) covering with buildings; **~~splan** *m* zoning-plan, house-building plan.

beben *itr* to shake, (*vor Kälte*) to shiver; (*vor Aufregung*) to dither, to tremble, to quake (with), to quiver; (*Schreck*) to shudder; (*vibrieren*) to quaver, to vibrate, to oscillate; (*schwanken*) to totter, to wobble, *fam* to teeter; **~** *n* shaking; trembling; (*Musik*) tremolo; (*Erd~*) earthquake; **~d** *a* trembling; shivering; (*furchtsam*) tremulous; (*schüchtern*) timid; **~messer** *m* seismograph.

bebildern *tr* to illustrate.

bebrillt *a* bespectacled.

bebrüten *tr* to hatch, to brood.

Becher *m* cup; (*Würfel~*) box; (*Humpen*) beaker; (*Glas mit Fuß*) goblet; (*Bowle, Schale*) bowl; beaker; (*ohne Fuß*) tumbler, mug; (*Aschen~*) ash-tray; (*Eier~*) egg-cup; *bot* cup, calix; (*Bagger*) tipping bucket; **~elevator** *m* bucket elevator; **~förmig** *a* cup-shaped; **~glas** *n* beaker; goblet; chalice; **~kette** *f* conveyer; **~n** *itr* to tipple, to booze; **~rad** *n* bucket wheel; **~transporteur** *m* bucket conveyer; **~werk** *n* bucket-elevator, bucket conveyer.

Becken *n* basin, *Am* bowl; (*Wasch~*) wash-basin; (*Einseif~*) bowl of lather; (*Tauf~*) baptismal basin (*od* font); (*Schwimm~*) (swimming) pool; (*Gegend*) district, region; *min* coal-field; *mus* cymbal; *anat* pelvis.

bedach|en *tr* to roof; **~ung** *f* roofing.

Bedacht *m* consideration, care; (*Überlegung*) deliberation; (*Vorbedacht*) forethought; *mit* ~ considerately, deliberately; *auf etw ~ nehmen* to take s. th. into consideration; **~** *a* thoughtful of, considerate of, mindful of; *auf etw ~ sein* to take care of, to consider a matter, to be intent on; **~sam** *a* considerate; (*vorsichtig*) cautious, prudent; (*umsichtig*) circumspect; **~~keit** *f* considerateness, caution; thoughtfulness.

bedächtig *a* considerate, discreet; (*langsam*) slow; (*überlegt*) deliberate; **~keit** *f* circumspection, caution.

bedanken *r: sich bei jdm ~* to thank s. o., to return thanks to; (*ablehnend*) to refuse; *dafür bedanke ich mich* thank you for nothing.

Bedarf *m* need; lack, want, requirement (*an* of); demand (*an* for); (*Vorrat*) supply; (*Verbrauch*) consumption; *bei ~* if required; *~ haben* to be in need of; *~ decken* to cover (*od* supply) o.'s requirements; *~ befriedigen* to meet the demand; *nach ~* when required; **~sartikel** *m* article of consumption, commodities *pl*; requisites *pl*; utensils *pl*; **~sberechnung** *f* calculation of requirements; **~sdekkung** *f* satisfaction of needs (*od* wants); **~~sschein** *m* purchase voucher; **~sermittlung** *f* determination of requirements; **~sfall** *m* necessity, need; *im ~~e* in case of necessity (*od* need); **~sgegenstand** *m* requirement, requisite, necessary article; **~sgüter** *n pl* necessaries *pl*, requisites *pl*; **~shaltestelle** *f* (*Straßenbahn*) request stop; **~slenkung** *f* consumption control; **~snachweis** *m* purchase permit; **~sschätzung** *f* forecast (*od* estimate) of requirements; **~sträger** *m* consumer, customer; essential user.

bedauer|lich *a* deplorable, regrettable, lamentable; (*unglücklich*) unfortunate; *es ist ~~* it is to be regretted that; **~n** *tr* (*etw ~n*) to regret, to be grieved at; to deplore; to feel sorry; *jdn ~n* to be sorry for, to pity; *ich ~e* (*alltäglich*) (I am) sorry; **~n** *n* pity, compassion, regret; (*Anteilnahme*) sympathy; (*Betrübnis*) sorrow; **~nswert, ~nswürdig** *a* pitiable, deplorable; (*bedauerlich*) regrettable.

bedeck|en *tr* to cover with; (*beschirmen*) to screen; to shelter; (*beschützen*) to protect; (*einhüllen*) to case; to shroud; (*Zucker*) to bottom; *mil* to escort; (*durch Kriegsschiff*) to convoy; (*schützen*) to shelter; *r* to cover o. s.; ~~ *Sie sich!* put on your hat! **~t** *a* (*Himmel*) clouded, overcast; **~~samig** *a* *bot* angiosperm; **~ung** *f* covering, cover; (*Schutz*) protection, safeguard; *mil* escort, (*durch Schiffe*) convoy; **~~sabteilung** *f* *mil* covering party, escort detachment; **~~smannschaft** *f* escort personnel.

bedenk|en *irr tr* to consider, to deliberate on, to reflect on; to think (over); (*beachten*) to mind; (*Sorge tragen*) to care for; *jdn* ~~ to provide (with); (*vererben*) to bequeath; *sich* ~~ to deliberate; *sich anders* ~~ to change o.'s mind; **~en** *n* deliberation, reflection, scruple; hesitation; (*Nachteil*) drawback; ~~ *tragen* to hesitate at; *ohne* ~~ unhesitatingly; **~~los** *a* unscrupulous; **~lich** *a* (*von Personen*) dubious, scrupulous, doubtful, (*von Sachen*) risky; (*Lage*) serious, grave, critical; *es scheint mir* ~~ it strikes me as rather precarious (*od* delicate); **~~keit** *f* doubtfulness, scruple; (*Lage*) critical state, seriousness, gravity; **~zeit** *f* time for reflection; (*Aufschub*) respite.

bedeut|en *tr, itr* to signify, to mean, to stand for; (*wichtig sein*) to be of importance; (*vorbedeuten*) to portend; (*kennzeichnen*) to denote; (*besagen*) to import; (*in sich schließen*) to imply; (*anweisen*) to suggest, to indicate, to inform, to direct; *es hat nichts zu* ~~ it is of no consequence; *was soll das ~~?* what does that mean? *sich ~~ lassen* to be advised; **~end** *a* important, considerable; **~sam** *a* significant; (*imponierend*) imposing; **~ung** *f* signification, sense, meaning; (*Wichtigkeit*) importance; (*tieferer Sinn*) implication; (*Vorbedeutung*) sign, foreboding, presage; *e-e ~~ haben für etw* to have a bearing on s. th.; *nichts von* ~~ nothing to speak of, nothing particular, of little consequence; **~~slos** *a* insignificant, of no account, void of importance; (*ohne Sinn*) meaningless; **~~slosigkeit** *f* insignificance; **~~svoll** *a* significant; (*sinnvoll*) meaning(ful); (*gewichtig*) momentous; (*unheilverkündend*) portentous.

bedien|en *tr* to serve, to attend; to wait on; (*Karten*) to follow suit; *tech* (*Apparate, Maschinen*) to work, to operate; to manipulate, to handle; *sich e-r Sache* ~~ to make use of; to avail o. s. of s. th.; (*bei Tische*) ~~ *Sie sich!* help yourself! **~te(r)** *m* servant, attendant; valet; **~tenseele** *f* flunkey; **~ung** *f* service, attendance; handling, operation, manipulation; (*Dienerschaft*) servants *pl*; (*im Gasthaus*) waitress; **~~sanweisung** *f* instruction book; **~~sfehler** *m* *aero* pilot's error; **~~sgerät** *n radio* main control panel (of radar *od* radio equipment); **~~shebel** *m tech* operating lever; **~~sknopf** *m radio* control knob; **~~smann** *m* (*e-r Maschine*) attendant, operator; **~~smannschaft** *f mil* gunners *pl*, gun team (*od* crew); **~~spersonal** *n tech* operating staff; **~~splan** *m tech* service system; **~~spult** *n* control panel; **~~sschalter** *m* control switch; **~~sstand** *m* operating station; **~~svorrichtung** *f* operation details *pl*; **~~svorschrift** *f* working instruction; directions *pl* for use; **~~szuschlag** *m* extras *pl*; service charge.

beding|en *irr tr* to stipulate, to condition; (*vertraglich*) to agree, to settle; (*voraussetzen, verlangen*) to postulate, to require; (*notwendig machen*) to necessitate; (*in sich schließen*) to involve, to imply; (*beschränken*) to limit, to restrict; **~t** *a* conditional; limited, qualified; (*abhängig*) dependent (on), affected (by); *durch etw ~~ sein* to depend on s. th.; **~theit** *f* limitation; **~ung** *f* condition, agreement; term, stipulation, clause; *unter der ~~, daß* on condition that, provided that; *unter den gegenwärtigen ~~en* under present conditions; *unter keiner ~~* on no account; **~~slos** *a* unconditional; **~~ssatz** *m* conditional clause; **~~sweise** *adv* conditionally.

bedräng|en *tr* to press hard; to oppress; *fig* to afflict; *in bedrängter Lage sein* to be in distress, *fam* to be hard up; **~er** *m* oppressor; **~nis, ~ung** *f* pressure; distress; oppression.

bedroh|en *tr* to menace; to threaten; **~lich** *a* threatening; **~ung** *f* threat, menace.

bedruck|en *tr* to print on (*od* over); **~barkeit** *f* printability.

bedrück|en *tr* to oppress; (*beunruhigen*) to harass; (*Unrecht zufügen*) to wrong; (*verfolgen*) to persecute; (*kränken*) to aggrieve; (*betrüben*) to afflict; (*quälen*) to torment, to torture; **~er** *m* oppressor; **~t** *a* worried; depressed; *~~ sein* to be sad (*od* depressed); **~ung** *f* oppression, pressure.

bedünken *imp: mich bedünkt* I think; it seems to me.

bedürf|en *irr tr* to need, to want, to require; **~nis** *n* want, need, lack, requirement; (*dringendes*) exigency, necessity; **~nisse** *pl* necessaries *pl*; **~nisanstalt** (men's *od* women's) lavatory, public convenience, latrines *pl*; **~nislos** *a* having no wants, frugal; (*bescheiden*) unassuming, unpretentious; **~tig** *a* needy, indigent; *e-r Sache ~~ sein* to be in want of; **~~keit** *f* indigence; necessity, need; **~~keitsprüfung** *f* means test.

Beduine *m* Bedouin.

beduselt *a* tipsy; fuddled.

Beefsteak *n* steak.

beehren *tr* to hono(u)r; (*mit Aufträgen*) to favo(u)r; *ich beehre mich, Ihnen mitzuteilen* I have the hono(u)r to inform you; I beg to inform you.

beeid|(ig)en *tr* to confirm by oath, to declare upon oath, to take oath upon, to make an affidavit; to administer an oath; *jdn ~~* to put s.o. on his oath, to take an oath of; to swear in; **~igt** *a* sworn; *~igte Aussage* sworn evidence; affidavit; *~igter Buchprüfer* chartered accountant; *~igter Übersetzer* sworn translator; **~igung** *f* swearing-in, administration of an oath; confirmation by oath.

beeilen *r* to hasten, to hurry up, to make haste; *beeile dich sl* step on it.

beeindrucken *tr* to impress.

beeinfluss|en *tr* to influence; to affect; (*Abgeordnete*) *Am* to lobby; **~ung** *f* (exertion of) influence.

beeinträchtig|en *tr* to injure ,to wrong; (*schädigen*) to prejudice, to impair; (*von Rechten*) to infringe upon, to encroach upon, to interfere with; **~end** *a* injurious, detrimental; **~t** *a* affected; **~ung** *f* prejudice, wrong, injury; (*Mißstand*) nuisance.

beend|en, ~igen *tr* to end, to finish; to stop, to terminate, to discontinue, to put an end (to), to bring to an end; **~igung** *f* ending, conclusion, close, termination; *~~ des Dienstverhältnisses* cessation of service; *~~ der Kriegsproduktion* shutdown of war industries; *~~ der Luftgefahr* all clear; **~~szeichen** *n* sign-off signal.

beeng|en *tr* to narrow; to cramp; *fig* to restrain; *sich ~t fühlen* to feel oppressed.

beerben *tr* to be o.'s heir (to), to inherit s. th. from s. o., to succeed to s. o.'s property.

beerdig|en *tr* to inter, to bury; **~ung** *f* interment, burial, funeral; **~~sinstitut** *n* undertaker's, *Am* funeral home; **~~skosten** *pl* funeral expenses *pl*; **~~sschein** *m* certificate of death, *Am* burial-permit.

Beere *f* berry; **~nfrüchte** *f pl* soft fruit.

Beet *n* bed; (*Garten~*) border; (*schmales*) ~ platband.

Beete *f* (= *rote Rübe*) beet(-root).

befähig|en *tr* to fit (for), to enable (to); **~t** *a* fit (for); (*begabt*) gifted, talented; *~t sein* to be qualified to (*od* for); **~ung** *f* qualification, capacity; ability; fitness; competence; (*Leistungsfähigkeit*) efficiency; **~~snachweis** *m* certificate of qualification; **~~sprüfung** *f* qualification trial; **~~szeugnis** *n* certificate of capacity (*od* proficiency).

befahr|bar *a* (*Weg*) passable; practicable; (*Fluß*) navigable; **~en** *irr tr* to pass over, to navigate; *ein sehr ~~er Weg* a much frequented road; *Küsten ~~* to sail along the coasts; *e-n Schacht ~~* to descend into a mine.

befallen *irr tr* to befall; to fall on; (*Krankheit*) to strike; to attack; *~ sein von* to suffer from.

befangen *a* confused, shy, self-conscious; (*voreingenommen*) prepossessed; prejudiced; (*parteiisch*) bias(s)ed, partial; (*in Verlegenheit*) embarrassed; *in e-m Irrtum ~ sein* to labo(u)r under a misapprehension (*od* mistake); **~heit** *f* confusion; prejudice; shyness; bias; constraint.

befassen *tr* to touch, to handle; *sich mit etw ~* to occupy o. s. with; to engage in; to interfere in; to meddle o. s. with.

befehd|en *tr* to make war upon; *fig* to show enmity to; **~ung** *f* hostilities *pl*; making war.

Befehl *m* order; command; *auf ~* by order; *bis auf weiteren ~* till further orders; *e-n ~ ausführen* to carry out an order; *~ ausgeführt!* mission accomplished! *zu ~, Herr ...! mil* yes, sir; *mar* ay, ay, sir! *taktischer ~ mil* battle order; *e-n ~ überschreiten* to exceed o.'s orders; **~en** *irr tr* to order, to command, to tell; *~en über* to dispose of; (*anordnen*) to bid; (*anbefehlen*) to commend o. s. to, to commit o. s. to; **~~d** *a* imperative; **~erisch** *a* imperious, dictatorial; **~igen** *tr* to command, to head; *befehligt von* under the command of, led by; **~sausgabe** *f* issuance of orders; **~sbereich** *m* command area, extent of command; **~sbestätigung** *f* confirmatory order; **~sempfänger** *m* runner, orderly; **~serteilung** *f* issuance of orders; **~sform** *f gram* imperative; **~sgemäß** *a* according to order(s); **~sgewalt** *f* authority of command; **~sgruppe** *f* command group; **~shaber** *m* chief; commander; commanding officer, *Abk* C.O.; **~shaberisch** *a* imperious; dictatorial; **~snetz** *n* command (*od* control) net; **~spanzer** *m* command tank; **~ssprache** *f* terminology of orders; **~sstand** *m* command post; **~sturm** *m* (*auf Flugplatz*) *aero* control tower; **~sübermittlung** *f* transmission of orders; **~sübertragung** *f aero* (*Gegensprech*) interaircraft voice (*od* command) communication; **~sverhältnisse** *n pl* chain of command; **~swagen** *m* armo(u)red command vehicle, command car, commander's car; staff car; **~sweg** *m* command channel, chain of command; **~swidrig** *a* contrary to order(s); **~szentrale** *f* control-room.

befestig|en *tr* to fasten to, to fix to; *fig* to strengthen; to confirm; (*Preise*) *sich ~~* to stiffen, to harden; (*nageln*) to nail; (*mit Nadel*) to pin; (*Verhältnis*) to consolidate; (*verschanzen*) to fortify; **~ung** *f* fastening; fixing; *tech* clamping, mounting; (*Festung*) fortification; *fig* consolidation; establishment; **~~sanlagen** *f pl* (field) defences *pl*; entrenchment; *tief gestaffelte ~~* forts *pl* in depth; **~~sklemme** *f el* screw terminal; **~~smittel** *n* fixing agent; **~~sschraube** *f* set screw; **~~szone** *f* entrenchment zone.

befeucht|en *tr* to wet, to moisten; **~ung** *f* wetting, moistening; irrigation; **~~sanlage** *f* moistening apparatus.

Befeuerung *f aero* (*Flugplatz~*) aerodrome lighting; location beacon; (*Strecken~*) beacons *pl*; revolving lights *pl*.

Beffchen *n* clergyman's bands *pl*.

befiedern *tr* to feather.

befind|en *irr itr* (*sich erweisen*) to find; (*beurteilen*) to consider; to think; *sich ~~* to be; *Am* to be located; to feel; *wie ~~ Sie sich?* how are you? *sich in Verlegenheit ~~* to be at a loss; *sich im Irrtum ~~* to be mistaken; **~en** *n* (*gesundheitlich*) (state of) health; (*Meinung*) opinion; *sich nach dem ~~ erkundigen* to inquire after s. o.'s health; **~lich** *a* to be found; present; contained (in).

*

beflaggen *tr* to flag, to deck with flags.

befleck|en to stain, to spot, to soil; to blot; *fig* (*Ruf, Namen*) to stain, to sully; to pollute; (*mit Fett*) to grease; (*durch Schuhmacher*) to heel; **~ung** *f* staining; pollution; defilement; contamination; (*Schuhe*) heeling.

befleißigen: *sich e-r Sache ~* to endeavour; to apply o. s. to s. th.; to exert o. s.; to endeavour, to take pains to; to strive; *sich der Kürze ~* to study brevity.

befliegen *irr tr aero* to fly regularly between; (*e-e Strecke ~*) to fly over a course; to ply (*od* to operate) between; *e-e* (*nicht*) *fahrplanmäßig beflogene Strecke* a(n) (un)scheduled line.

beflissen *a* studious; devoted to, given to; intent upon; **~er** *m* student; **~heit** *f* assiduity; **~tlich** *adv* assiduously; (*absichtlich*) intentionally.

beflügel|n *tr* to wing, to give wings to; to increase the speed of, to lend speed to; *fig* to accelerate, to animate; *Furcht ~te seine Schritte* fear winged his steps; **~t** *a* winged.

befolg|en tr (*Beispiel, Vorschrift, Rat, Regel*) to follow; to comply with; (*Gesetze, Befehle etc*) to obey; to observe; *~e meinen Rat!* take my advice! **~enswert** *a* worth following; **~ung** *f* following, observance (of); (*Durchführung*) carrying out; (*Festhalten an*) adherence (to); *genaue ~~ e-r Anweisung* rigid adherence to an instruction.

beförder|n tr (*allg mit Beförderungsmitteln jeder Art*) to carry; (*laufend ~~, bes. Massengüter*) to convey; (*tragend ~~*) to bear; (*liefern*) to deliver; (*übermitteln, z. B. Funkspruch, Fernspruch*) to transmit; (*Waren, Personen transportieren*) to transport, *Am* to ship; (*mit der Post*) to send by mail; (*übersenden*) to consign; (*Briefe, Waren*) to dispatch, to forward, to convey; (*verschiffen*) to ship; (*beschleunigen*) to hasten; (*begünstigen*) to patronize, to encourage; (*im Range*) to promote; *er wurde befördert* he got his promotion; *er wurde zum Hauptmann befördert* he was promoted to captain; *jdn hinaus~~* to chuck out s. o.; **~ung** *f* forwarding, conveyance, shipment, dispatch, transport(ation); (*im Rang*) advancement, promotion; *~~ nach Dienstalter* promotion by seniority; *~~ auf Grund der Auswahl* promotion by selection; **~~salter** *n* seniority; **~~sanlage** *f* equipment for transportation; **~~sart** *f* mode of transport (*od* conveyance); **~~sbedingungen** *f pl* (*Fracht*) terms of carriage; **~~seignung** *f* qualification; **~~sgebühr** *f* (*Brief*) charges for transmission; **~~skosten** *pl* cost of transport; cost of carriage; charges for conveyance; **~~smittel** *n* means of transport, *Am* means of transportation; vehicle; conveying machinery; **~~smöglichkeit** *f* (*Beruf*) opportunity for advancement; **~~sweg** *m* route.

befracht|en tr (*Wagen*) to load; (*Schiff*) to charter, to freight; **~er** *m* freighter; charterer; *com* consignor; **~ung** *f* freight(ing); *com* loading; *mar* charter(age); **~~smakler** *m* freight-agent; shipping-agent.

befrackt *a* in tails, in tail-coat.

befrag|en tr (*ausfragen*) to question (about); (*verhören*) to interrogate, to query; (*erpressen*) to extort; (*bei Prüfung*) to examine; (*um Rat*) to consult; *sich ~en* to seek information; *auf B~en* in reply to questions; upon inquiry; **~ung** *f* inquiry; (*gerichtliche*) interrogation, interrogatory.

befrei|en tr to deliver from, to set free; to free; (*freilassen*) to release; (*von Sorgen*) to relieve (from); (*erretten*) to redeem, to save (from); (*von Umhüllung*) to unwrap, to strip; (*ein Volk*) to liberate; (*von Verpflichtung*) to exempt; *~t von Beschränkung* exempt from restriction; *~t vom Heeresdienst* exempt from serving in the army, *Am* draft-exempt; (*von Gefahr*) to rescue from; *sich ~~ von* to get rid of; **~er** *m*, **~erin** *f* deliverer; liberator; **~ung** *f* deliverance; liberation; (*Gefangenen~~*) rescue of prisoners; (*Steuer~~*) exemption; (*Freilassung, Auslösung*) release; **~~sgesuch** *n* application for exemption; **~~skampf** *m* struggle for liberation; **~~skrieg** *m* war of liberation; war of independence.

befremd|en tr to appear strange (to); to surprise; to wonder at; (*abstoßen*) to shock, to impress unfavo(u)rably; **~end, ~lich** *a* strange, odd; surprising; **~en** *n*, **~ung** *f* wonder, surprise, astonishment, amazement.

befreund|en: *sich mit jdm ~en* to make friends with s. o.; *sich mit e-m Gedanken ~en* to get familiar with an idea; to become reconciled to an idea; to reconcile o. s. to; **~et** *a* on friendly terms (*mit* with); (*eng*) intimate; *~~ sein* to be friends; *eng ~~ sein* to be on terms of intimacy with s. o.; *die beiden sind eng ~~* these two are close friends.

befried|en tr to pacify; to bring peace to; **~ungspolitik** *f* appeasement policy.

befriedig|en tr to content, to satisfy; *schwer zu ~en* hard to please; (*Hunger*) to appease; (*Gewissen*) to soothe; (*ein Land befrieden*) to pacify; (*Wünsche, Erwartungen*) to answer; (*versehen mit*) to furnish with; (*mit Geld*) to pay off; (*geschlechtlich*) to satisfy sexually; (*beruhigen*) to calm; (*Verlangen*) to gratify; **~end** *a* satisfactory; **~ung** *f* contentment, satisfaction; (*Befriedung e-s Landes*) pacification; (*e-s Gläubigers*) payment; *~~ gewähren, ~~ geben* to give satisfaction; (*Genugtuung, Genuß*) gratification.

befrist|en tr to time, to fix a time; *Am* to deadline; **~et** *a* timed; limited (in time); at a fixed time.

befrucht|en tr to fructify; to fertilize; *mit etw ~~* to impregnate with; *fig* (*anregen*) to stimulate; **~ung** *f* fructification; fertilization; (*Schwängerung*) impregnation; (*künstliche ~~*) artificial insemination; **~~sfähig** *a* capable of impregnation.

Befug|nis *f* right, authority, warrant, powers *pl*; (*Zuständigkeit*) competence; **~t** *a* authorized, entitled; competent, empowered.

befühlen tr to feel, to touch, to handle; (*prüfend*) to examine by touching, *Am* to feel of.

Befund *m* (*von Sachverständigen*) finding(s *pl*), award; (*Zustand*) state, condition; *tech* (*von Abnahmeprüfungen*) test result; data *pl*; (*Bericht*) report; finding; *med* diagnosis; (*Bestand*) inventory; *nach ~* according to circumstances; **~buch** *n* stock book; inventory.

befürcht|en tr to fear, to be afraid of; to apprehend; to be apprehensive of; (*vermuten, argwöhnen*) to suspect; to expect; (*sich Sorge machen*) to worry about; **~ung** *f* fear, apprehension, anxiety.

befürwort|en tr to recommend; to advocate, to stand for; *e-e Bitte ~en* to support a request; **~er** *m* backer; **~ung** *f* recommendation; (*e-r Bitte*) support.

begab|en tr to endow (with); to bestow upon; **~t** *a* endowed with; gifted, talented; **~ung** *f* ability, capacity; endowment, gift; talents *pl*.

begaffen tr to gape at.

begatt|en tr: *sich ~~* to couple; to copulate; **~ung** *f* copulation; (*von Menschen*) cohabitation, sexual intercourse; coitus; **~~sorgan** *n* copulative (*od* generative) organ; **~~strieb** *m* sexual desire; **~~swerkzeug** *n pl* genital apparatus; **~~szeit** *f* time of pairing.

begaunern tr to cheat.

begeb|en irr r to go, to set out (for); to proceed to; (*gewählter*) to betake o. s. to; (*sich ereignen*) to happen; to occur; (*Bibel*) to come to pass; *sich in den Ehestand ~~* to marry; *sich in Gefahr ~~* to expose o. s. to danger; *sich zu Bett ~~* to go to bed; *sich e-r Sache ~~* to resign; to give up, to forgo; (*e-s Rechtes*) to divest o. s. of a right; to waive (a claim); *tr e-n Wechsel ~~* to endorse, to negotiate a bill; **~~heit** *f* occurrence, happening; accident, affair, event; **~ung** *f* negotiation (of a bill); issue.

begegn|en itr (*jdm*) to meet with; (*zus. treffen mit*) to encounter with; (*sich ereignen*) to occur, to happen; (*vorbeugen*) to prevent; (*behandeln*) to treat; (*e-r Gefahr*) to take measures against, *Am* to curb a danger; **~ung** *f* meeting; treatment; interview; (*feindlich*) encounter; (*Empfang*) reception; **~~sgefecht** *n mil* encounter battle; meeting engagement.

begeh|en irr tr to walk (on), to traverse; to pace off, to tread; *tech* to inspect; (*Feste*) to celebrate; (*Fehler*) to make; (*Unrecht*) to do; (*Verbrechen, Tat, Irrtum*) to commit; **~ung** *f* traversing; (*Untersuchung*) inspection; celebration; commission, perpetration.

Begehr, ~en *n* desire, wish; **~en** tr to desire, to wish for; (*dringend verlangen*) to demand, to covet; *wenig ~t* not much in demand; (*im Handel*) *~t sein* to be in request; **~enswert** *a* desirable; **~lich** *a* desirous, covetous of; **~~keit** *f* covetousness, greediness, strong desire for.

begeifern tr to beslaver; *fig* to calumniate, to slander.

begeister|n tr to inspire, to fill with enthusiasm, *Am* to enthuse; *sich ~n* to become enthusiastic (*über* about); to feel inspired by; to be captivated (*für* for), *Am* to fall for; **~t** *a* enthusiastic, elated, ardent, zealous; *~~ reden über* (*od von*) to rave about; *ein ~ter Anhänger e-s Sports etc fam* fan; **~ung** *f* inspiration, enthusiasm; rapture, ardo(u)r, zeal, frenzy.

Begier, ~de *f* longing, desire; appetite; (*Lüsternheit*) covetousness, lust; (*Eifer*) eagerness; **~ig** *a* eager, desirous of, covetous of; *~~ zu erfahren* anxious to know.

begießen irr tr to water; to moisten; (*mit Fett*) to baste; *sich die Nase ~ fig fam* to get drunk; *das müssen wir ~!* that calls for a drink!

Beginn *m* beginning, outset; (*Anfang*) start, *Am* entry; (*Ursprung*) origin; (*Quelle*) source; (*Einführung, Einweihung*) initiation; **~en** *n* beginning; (*Unternehmen*) undertaking; enterprise; *tr, itr irr* to begin, to start; to commence; to originate; to initiate; to undertake.

beglaubig|en tr to attest, to certify; (*amtlich*) to legalize, to authenticate; to verify, to confirm; (*als Gesandter*) to accredit; *ein Dokument ~~ lassen* to have a document legalized; **~t** *a* certified, attested; (*durch Notar*) notarized; (*in Urkunden*) witnessed; *~te Abschrift* certified copy, legalized copy; authentic (*od* attested) copy; **~ung** *f* attestation, authentication, certification; verification, confirmation; (*von Gesandten*) accreditation; (*gerichtliche ~~*) legalization; *zur ~~ dessen* (*jur in Dokumenten*) in witness whereof; **~~sschein** *m* certificate; **~~sschreiben** *n* letter of credence; credentials *pl*.

begleich|en irr tr (*ausgleichen*) to balance; to pay, to settle; **~ung** *f* (*Rechnung*) payment, settlement.

Begleit|adresse *f* declaration form, way-bill, dispatch-note; *Am* pass bill; **~artillerie** *f mil* accompanying artillery; **~batterie** *f mil* accompanying battery; **~brief** *m* covering letter; **~en** tr to accompany; to attend; *mil* to escort, (*von Schiffen*) to convoy; *nach Hause* ~~ to see s. o. home; (*junge Dame in Gesellschaft*) to chaperon; ~**er** *m*, ~**erin** *f* companion, attendant, follower; *mus* accompanist; associate, satellite; partner; (*Helfer*) assistant; ~**erscheinung** *f* symptom, accompanying circumstance; secondary (*od* attendant) phenomenon (*od* action); ~**feuer** *n* accompanying fire; ~**flugzeug** *n aero* escort aircraft, *Am* escorting plane, convoy plane; ~**jäger** *m aero* escort fighter; ~**kommando** *n mil* escort detachment, covering party; ~**mannschaft** *f* escort; ~**panzer(wagen)** *m* accompanying tank; ~**papier** *n* (*Fracht*) bill of lading; ~**schein** *m* pass-bill; ~**schiff** *n* convoy; escort vessel; depot ship; ~**schreiben** *n* letter of transmittal; *com* letter of advice; covering letter; ~**schutz** *m mil* escort; *aero* fighter escort; ~**umstand** *m jur* accessory; ~**umstände** *m pl jur* res gestae; accompanying circumstances *pl*; ~**ung** *f* accompanying, company; (*Gefolge*) retinue, suit; *mil* escort, conduct, (*Schiff*) convoy; *mus* accompaniment; ~**wort** *n* word of explanation; ~**zerstörer** *m mar* destroyer escort vessel, convoying destroyer; ~**zettel** *m* way-bill, bill of lading; supply note; (*e-s Verwundeten für Verbandsplatz*) emergency medical tag; ~**zug** *m mil* accompanying platoon, convoy.

beglücken *tr* to make happy, to bless.

beglückwünsch|en *tr* to congratulate (*zu* on); ~**ung** *f* congratulation.

begnaden *tr* to bless; to favo(u)r (*mit* with).

begnadig|en *tr* to pardon, to amnesty; to reprieve; ~**ung** *f* pardon; amnesty; reprieve; *bedingte* ~~ release on ticket of leave; *Am* release on parole; ~~**sgesuch** *n* petition for mercy (*od* pardon); ~~**srecht** *n* right of granting pardon.

begnüg|en: *sich* ~~ *mit* to content o. s. with, to be satisfied with; to put up with; (*zustimmen*) to acquiesce in; ~**sam** *a* abstemious; moderate.

begönnern *tr* to patronize.

begraben *irr tr* to bury; (*feierlich*) to inter; to entomb; ~ *werden* to be put under ground; *alle Hoffnung* ~ to abandon (*od* to give up) all hopes; *in den Wellen* ~ swallowed (up) in the waves; *das Haus war halb unter Schnee* ~ the house was half buried under snow; *sich auf dem Land* ~ to bury o. s. in the country; *sich in seinen Büchern* ~ to bury o. s. in o.'s books; ~ *werden von der vielen Arbeit* to be snowed under with work; *die Streitaxt* ~ to bury the hatchet; *lassen Sie sich* ~! *fam* go and be hanged! *da liegt der Hund* ~ there is the rub.

Begräbnis *n* burial, funeral; (*Grab*) tomb, sepulchre; ~**feier** *f* funeral, obsequies *pl*; ~**kommando** *n mil* funeral detachment; ~**kosten** *pl* funeral expenses *pl*; ~**platz** *m* burial ground, graveyard, churchyard; cemetery.

begradig|en *tr* (*Kurve*) to smooth; *mil* to level; (*Frontlinie*) to shorten the front line; (*sich zurückziehen*) to retreat; ~**ung** *f mil* (*der Front*) straightening (of the front line).

begreif|en *irr tr* (*befühlen*) to feel, to touch, to handle; (*einschließen*) to include; (*verstehen*) to understand; to comprehend, to grasp, to catch on, to conceive; *ich ~e nicht, wo er bleibt* I can't imagine where he is; *mit darunter begriffen* included; *begriffen sein* to be about (to do); to be; to be engaged in; ~**lich** *a* comprehensible, conceivable; (*natürlich*) natural, evident; *jdm etw ~~ machen* to make s. o. understand s. th.; ~~**erweise** *adv* evidently, obviously, (as a matter) of course, as may be easily understood; naturally.

begrenz|en *tr* to bound; to border; *fig* to confine, to limit; (*einschränken, definieren*) to circumscribe; (*genau festlegen*) to define; to determine; to terminate; (*einengen*) to narrow (down); ~**end** *a* limiting, terminal; ~**t** *a fig* limited, definite; ~**theit** *f* limitation; *fig* narrowness; ~**ung** *f* bordering; bounds *pl*; *fig* limitation, limit, termination, definition; ~~**sanschlag** *m* (back) stop; limiting means; (*verstellbar*) stop dog; ~~**sbake** *f mar, aero* boundary beacon, boundary-marker beacon; ~~**sfläche** *f* area of contact; ~~**shebel** *m* stop lever; ~~**slicht** *n* boundary light; ~~**slinie** *f* boundary line; ~~**sstift** *m mil* (*am M.G.*) traversing stop.

Begriff *m* (*Vorstellung*) idea, notion; (*Intellekt, Verstehen*) understanding, perception; (*Ausdruck*) term; *im ~e sein* to be about to, to be on the point of; to get ready to, *Am fam* to fix; *e-n ~ von etw haben* to have an idea of; *schwer von ~ sein* to be dull of apprehension; to be slow in catching on; (*dumm*) to be stupid; *sich e-n ~ von etw machen* to form an idea of; *sich e-n falschen ~ von etw machen* to get a wrong idea of; *sich keinen ~ von etw machen* to get no idea of; *nach meinen ~en* according to my opinion (*od* judg(e)ment); *das geht über meine ~e* that passes my comprehension; ~**en**: *in etw ~en sein* to be engaged in s. th.; *in Bildung ~en* in formation; *im Bau ~en* in the course of building; in construction, in the process of being constructed; *auf der Rückreise ~en* homeward bound; ~**lich** *a* abstract; notional; theoretic(al); conceivable; ~~ *bestimmen* to fix the notion of; to define; ~**sbestimmung** *f* definition; ~**sbildung** *f* formation of a concept, abstraction; ~**sfach** *n* category; ~**sfassung** *f* formulation of a concept; ~**sgesellung** *f* association of ideas; ~**sklasse** *f* category; ~**smäßig** *a* conform to the idea; ~**sstutzig** *a* puzzle-headed, stupid; dull-witted; (*langsam*) slow; ~**svermögen** *n* apprehension, comprehension, apprehensive faculty (*od* power); ~**sverwirrung** *f* confusion of ideas.

begründ|en *tr* to found, to establish; (*Behauptung*) to base, to prove, to substantiate; to confirm; to justify; to give as a reason for; ~**et** *a* well-founded; established; *nicht* ~~ unfounded; *nicht ~~ sein* to have little foundation; *~~e Rechte jur* vested rights *pl*; *~~er Zweifel* reasonable doubt; *für ~~ halten* (*Anspruch*) to find valid; ~~**heit** *f* validity; ~**er** *m* founder; originator; (*e-r Aktiengesellschaft*) promoter; ~**ung** *f* founding, foundation; establishment; *jur* proof, argument(ation); motivation; reason; *die ~~ geben* to give the reasons; *zur ~~ von* in support of; ~~**sfrist** *f jur* period for giving grounds.

begrüß|en *tr* (*allgemein*) to greet; (*feierlich*) to salute; (*gern sehen*) to welcome; (*anrufen, ansprechen*) to hail; *mil* to hono(u)r; *ich ~e Sie im Namen von...* I greet you on behalf of...; (*dankbar* ~~) to be gratified; ~**ung** *f* greeting, welcome, salutation; salute; ~~**sansprache** *f* words of welcome, *Am* salutatory; ~~**sformel** *f* form of salutation; ~~**srede** *f* welcome speech, *Am* (*zu Beginn des Schuljahres*) salutatory; ~~**sschuß** *m mil, mar* salute.

begucken *tr* to peep at.

begünstig|en *tr* to favo(u)r; (*ermutigen*) to encourage, (*fördern*) to promote, to foster; to support; to patronize; to befriend; *jur* to aid and abet; to act as an accessory after the fact; *den Feind* ~~ to give the enemy aid and comfort; *e-n Gläubiger* ~~ to prefer a creditor; ~**ung** *f* favo(u)r, favo(u)ritism; (*Ermutigung*) encouragement; (*Gönnerschaft*) patronage; *jur* complicity; (*e-s Verbrechens*) abetment, aiding and abetting; (*Bevorzugung*) befriending, preferment; ~~**szoll** *m* preferential tariff.

begutacht|en *tr* to pass an opinion on; to give o.'s judg(e)ment; to report; to give an expert opinion (on); *~en lassen* to submit to an expert; ~**ung** *f* opinion of an expert.

begüt|ert *a* wealthy, rich; well-to-do, well-off; ~**igen** *tr* to appease.

behaar|en: *sich* ~~ to become hairy; ~**t** *a* hairy; (*von Tieren*) hirsute; *bot* pilose (*od* pilous).

behäbig *a* easy, comfortable; (*dick*) corpulent, stout, portly; ~**keit** *f* ease, comfortableness; (*Beleibtheit*) (slight) corpulence; stoutness.

behaftet *a* (*mit Krankheit, Anfällen*) infected with, afflicted with, subject to; (*mit Schulden*) burdened (*od* loaded) with debts.

behag|en *itr u. imp* to suit, to please, to like; *wie behagt es dir?* how do you like it? ~**en** *n* comfort, ease; pleasure, delight; *~~ finden an* to take pleasure in; ~**lich** *a* comfortable; (*traulich*) cosy, snug, at ease; *ich fühle mich* ~~ I feel at ease; ~~**keit** *f* comfortableness; comfort, cosiness, ease.

behalten *irr tr* to keep, to retain; (*im Gedächtnis*) to remember; *recht* ~ to be right in the end; *etw im Auge* ~ to keep in view; *übrig* ~ to have left over; *etw für sich* ~ (*zurückhalten*) to reserve s. th. to o. s.; (*Geheimnis*) to keep s. th. to o. s.; *den Kopf oben* ~ to retain o.'s presence of mind; *das Leben* ~ to remain alive; *die Oberhand* ~ to get the upper hand; (*e-e Zahl beim Addieren*) ~ to carry (a number); *wer hat recht ~?* who was right?

Behält|er *m*, ~***nis*** *n* holder, receptacle, box, bin, case, container; tank, reservoir, vessel; trough; bunker; ~~ *für Brennstoff* fuel tank; ~~ *für Lastabwurf mil aero* container; *Abfall~~* refuse bin, rubbish basket; ~~ *für Sand u. Soda* holder (*od* container) for sand and soda; *Benzin~~* petrol tank, *Am* jerry can; *Wasser~~* water tank, reservoir; *Fisch~~* fishtank; ~**erentlüftung** *f* tank ventilation; ~**erlager** *n* tank farm; ~**erwagen** *m* tank car.

behand|eln *tr* to treat; to handle; to deal with; to manage; (*mit Verstand*) to manipulate; (*e-n Werkstoff*) to process; to work; *schlecht* ~~ to use ill, to ill-treat; (*pfleglich, besonders ärztlich*) to attend; (*Wunden*) to dress; ~**lung** *f* management, handling; manipulation; processing; treatment; medical attendance; therapy; *in ärztlicher ~~ sein* to be under medical treatment; *ambulante* ~~ ambulatory treatment; *bei richtiger* ~~ given reasonable care; *falsche* (*vorschriftswidrige*) ~~ abuse, treatment contrary to regulations; ~~**sart** *f* method of treatment; ~~**smittel** *n* agent; ~~**svorschrift** *f* instruction;

~~sweise *f* method (*od* manner) of treatment; (*Prozeß*) procedure.

Be|hang *m* (*Spitzen~~*) flounce; (*Franse, Saum, Rand*) fringe; (*Drapierung*) drapery; (*Wandbekleidung, Vorhang etc*) hangings *pl*; (*vom Hund*) ears *pl*; **~hängen** *tr* to hang with; (*drapieren*) to drape with.

beharken *tr mil aero sl* to rake with aircraft guns; to fire.

beharr|en *itr* to persist in; to persevere; (*fest bleiben*) to remain firm; (*auf seiner Meinung*) to stand to; to insist on; (*auf e-r Lüge*) to stick to o.'s tale; (*Behauptung*) to maintain o.'s statement; (*auf seinen Grundsätzen*) to adhere firmly to o.'s principles; to stick to o.'s principles; **~lich** *a* constant, steady; persistent, persevering, perseverant; (*hartnäckig*) stubborn, pertinacious; **~~keit, ~ung** *f* constancy, perseverance; persistence; (*Entschlossenheit*) determination; (*Hartnäckigkeit*) tenacity; obstinacy; **~~skraft** *f* inertia; **~~smoment** *n* moment of inertia; **~~spunkt** *m* centre of inertia (*od* mass); **~~svermögen** *n* inertia; **~~szustand** *m* state of inertia, permanence; persistence; (*Gleichgewicht*) state of equilibrium; (*Widerstand e-r Maschine*) resistance; state of resistance; (*gleichmäßiger Zustand*) steady conditions *pl*; regimen.

behauen *tr* to hew; *aus dem Groben ~* to rough-hew; (*mit der Axt*) to trim; (*rechtwinklig*) to square; (*Bauholz*) to chip, to cut; (*e-n Baum*) to lop, to prune.

behaupt|en *tr* to pretend, to uphold; (*bestimmt*) to affirm, to maintain, to assert; (*beanspruchen*) to claim; (*feststellen*) to state; (*sagen*) to say; (*versichern*) to assure; (*vorbringen, anführen*) to allege; (*als Tatsache hinstellen*) to aver; (*erklären*) to declare; (*ein Recht ~~*) to vindicate; (*etw über e-n Gegenstand aussagen*) to predicate; (*beistimmen*) to assent; (*streitend ~~*) to contend; (*zu Unrecht ~~*) to pretend; (*in Abrede stellen*) to disavow; *es wird ~et* it is claimed (*od* asserted *od* reported); *wie können Sie so etw ~~?* how can you say such a th.? *man ~et von ihr, daß* ... she is alleged to ...; *etw steif u. fest ~~* to be positive on, to swear up and down; *das Feld ~~* to gain the day; *sich ~~* to hold o.'s own; (*Preise*) to be steady; to be firm; to keep up; **~ung** *f* assertion, affirmation; (*Feststellung*) statement; (*strittige ~~*) contention; (*unter Beweis zu stellende ~~*) allegation; (*Bekräftigung*) averment; (*Vorschlag*) proposition; (*Anspruch*) claim; *e-e bloße ~~* a mere conjecture.

behaus|en *siehe beherbergen*; **~ung** *f* lodging, habitation, dwelling, abode; domicile; (*Heim*) home; *in meiner ~~* at home.

*

be|heben *irr tr* (*Schwierigkeiten*) to remove; (*e-e Störung*) to repair (the trouble); to correct; (*Hindernis*) to clear away; (*Zweifel*) to dispel; (*Geld*) to draw money; (*Fehler*) to remedy; to eliminate; to put an end to; **~hebung** *f* (*von Mißständen*) adjustment, settling; removal; (*e-r Panne*) servicing; **~heimatet** *a* (*Fahrzeug*) registered at; (*Personen*) domiciled; native; **~heizen** *tr* to heat, to fire; **~heizung** *f* heating, firing.

Behelf *m* (*zur Unterstützung*) expedient, help, resource; (*jur Einwand*) remedy; (*Vorrichtung*) contrivance, appliance; (*Aushilfe*) makeshift, device; **~en** *irr r: sich ~~* to make shift with; to manage (with); to make do; (*mit etw*) to resort (to); *sich ohne etw ~~* to do without; *sich kümmerlich ~~* to live miserably; **~santenne** *f* emergency antenna; makeshift (*od* auxiliary) antenna; **~sartikel** *m* makeshift article; **~sbefestigung** *f mil* field fortification; **~sbetrieb** *m* emergency works *pl*; **~sbrücke** *f* emergency bridge; **~sfähre** *f* emergency (*od* makeshift) ferry; **~sflugplatz** *m* auxiliary landing ground; **~sgerät** *n* auxiliary utensils *pl*; **~sheim** *n* emergency house; makeshift housing, temporary house; **~skonstruktion** *f* makeshift (*od* emergency) construction; **~slandebrücke** *f* makeshift landing stage; **~slieferwagen** *m* auxiliary (*od* temporary) delivery van; **~smäßig** *adv* improvised, auxiliary, makeshift, temporary; by way of an expedient; in the nature of an expedient; provisional; **~smaterial** *n* auxiliary material; **~smittel** *n* expedient; **~sstollen** *m* (*Luftschutz*) emergency underground shelter.

behellig|en *tr* to trouble, to bother, to molest; to importune (*mit* with); **~ung** *f* trouble, molestation, bother; annoyance.

behend|e *a* quick; nimble; agile, smart; (*geschickt*) dexterous; **~igkeit** *f* quickness; dexterity; smartness.

beherberg|en *tr* to lodge, to give) shelter (to); to house, to put up, to take in; to accommodate; to harbo(u)r; to quarter; **~ung** *f* housing, lodging; (*Obdach*) shelter.

beherrsch|en *tr* to reign over, to rule (over), to govern; (*Leidenschaften*) to master, to control; (*beeinflussen*) *Am* to swing; *e-e Sprache ~~* to be master of a language; *sich ~~* to be master of o. s.; to control o. s., to pull o. s. together; (*ein Fach ~~*) to be well acquainted with; (*überragen, Berg*) to look down upon; to command; **~end** *a* commanding; dominating; **~er** *m* ruler, governor, master; **~ung** *f* domination, government, self-control; control; command; (*des Luftraumes*) *aero mil* supremacy (of the air).

beherzig|en *tr* to take to heart, to mind; (*in Betracht ziehen*) to take into consideration, to consider; (*erwägen*) to weigh; **~enswert** *a* noteworthy; **~ung** *f* reflection, consideration.

beherzt *a* courageous, bold-hearted; plucky; **~heit** *f* courage, intrepidity, pluck, daring.

behexen *tr* to bewitch, to enchant.

behilflich *a* helpful; *~ sein* to help.

behinder|n *tr* to hinder, to impede, to hamper, to upset; to obstruct; to restrain, to detain; (*den Gegner im Sport*) to check (the opponent), to charge; **~ung** *f* obstacle; impediment; inhibition; restraint; *sport* body-checking; hindrance.

behorchen *tr* to overhear.

Behörde *f* authority, (*bürgerliche*) (civil) authorities *pl*; board; administrative body; magistrate; (*Orts~*) magistracy, local authorities *pl*; (*Staats~*) government (agency); government(al) agency, governing body; (*zuständige ~*) competent authority; **~napparat** *m* official machinery; **behördlich** *a* official; *~ zugelassen* officially sanctioned, authorized; *~e Vorschriften* public regulations *pl.*

Behuf *m: zu diesem ~e* for this purpose; **~s** *prp* in order to, with a view to, for the purpose of, on behalf of.

behüten *tr* to keep from, to guard, to preserve; *Gott behüte!* God forbid! *behüte!* no! no!

behutsam *a* cautious, careful, wary; *mit etw ~ umgehen* to be on o.'s guards; **~keit** *f* caution, care(fulness).

bei *prp* at, near, by; in, among; with, on; *~ mir (zu Hause)* at home; *~ meinem Onkel (zu Hause)* at my uncle's; *~m Bäcker* at the baker's; *~ der Hand* at hand; *~ der ersten Gelegenheit* at the first opportunity; *~ mir (in der Tasche)* about me; *~ Gott* by God; *~ diesem Wetter* in this weather; *~ guter Gesundheit* in good health; *~ Lebzeiten* in (*od* during) o.'s life-time; *~ Zeiten* in good time, early; *~ Sinnen sein* to be in o.'s right senses; *~ weitem* by far; *~ Tage* by day; *~ Gott schwören* to swear by God; *~ der Hand nehmen* to take by the hand; *~ dieser Gelegenheit* on this occasion; *~ meiner Ankunft* on my arrival; *~ e-m Glase Wein* over a glass of wine; *sehr beliebt ~* very popular with; *~ uns* with us; *Stunden ~* lessons with (*od* from); *bestellen ~* to order of (*od* from); (*Brief*) *~ Braun* c/o Braun; *der deutsche Gesandte ~ den Vereinigten Staaten* the German ambassador to the United States.

beibehalt|en *irr tr* to keep (up), to retain; to maintain; **~ung** *f* retention.

Beiboot *n mar* dinghy.

Beiblatt *n* supplement, extra sheet (*od* edition).

beibringen *irr tr* (*herbei*) to bring forward, to bring by; *jdm etw ~* to suggest s. th. to; to put across; (*Beweise*) to furnish (*od* to exhibit) proof; (*Zeugen, Urkunden*) to produce; (*lehren*) to impart s. th. to, to teach s. o. in s. th.; to make clear; (*Niederlagen*) to inflict on, to administer; to deal.

Beicht|e *f* confession; *~e hören* to confess; *zur ~e gehen* to make confession; to confess (o. s.) to; **~en** *tr* to make confession of; *itr* to confess; **~geheimnis** *n* confessional secret; **~kind** *n* penitent; **~stuhl** *m* confessional; **~vater** *m* father confessor.

beid|armig *a meist sport* with both hands; **~äugig** *a* binocular.

beide *a* the two, both; *e-r von ~n* one of the two; *wir ~* we two, both of us; (*jeder von ~n*) either; *in ~n Fällen* in either case; *keiner von ~n* neither of them; *zu ~n Seiten* on both sides, on either side; **~mal** *adv* both times.

beider|lei *a* both, of both sorts; **~seitig** *a* on both sides; mutual; bilateral; (*gemeinsam*) joint; **~seits** *adv* on both sides; (*wechselseitig*) mutually.

bei|drehen *tr, itr mar* to heave to; to bring to; **~drücken** *tr: das Siegel ~~* to set o.'s seal to; **~einander** *adv* together.

Beifahrer *m mot* (side-car) passenger; second man; driver's mate, assistant driver; (*Soziusfahrer*) pillion rider; auxiliary rider.

Beifall *m* approbation; (*durch Händeklatschen*) applause; (*durch Zuruf*) cheers *pl*; (*Billigung*) approval; (*Zustimmung*) assent; *~ finden* to meet o.'s approval; *~ klatschen* to applaud; **~sbezeigung** *f* mark of applause; **~sruf** *m* cheer; acclaim; **~ssturm** *m* burst of applause.

bei|fällig *a* favo(u)rable; (*zustimmend*) assenting, approving; **~flieger** *m aero* co-pilot; **~folgend** *a* annexed; enclosed; attached; accompanying; **~fügen** *tr* to add, to enclose; to attach; to include; to supplement; **~fügung** *f* addition; notation; *gram* attributive;

~fuß *m bot* mugwort, artemisia; **~gabe** *f* addition, supplement; extra; (*Geschenk*) free gift; **~geben** *irr tr* to add, to attach; *itr klein ~~* to give in; **~geordnete(r)** *m* assistant; **~gericht** *n* side-dish; **~geschmack** *m* aftertaste; peculiar flavo(u)r; taste; tinge; (*auch fig*) smack; *e-n ~~ haben von* to have a spice of; to smack (*von, nach* of); **~gesellen** *tr* to associate (with); **~heft** *n* supplement; **~hilfe** *f* aid, assistance; (*staatliche ~~*) subsidy; subvention; allowance, grant; (*jur bei e-m Verbrechen*) aiding and abetting; **~kommen** *irr itr* to come at; *fig* to come up to; *ihm ist nicht beizukommen* there is no getting at him; (*erlangen*) to reach; (*wagen*) to dare.

Beil *n* hatchet, axe; (*Hack~*) chopper, cleaver.

Beilage *f* addition; annex, appendix; (*Zettel als Reklame*) stuffer; (*Reklame~ e-r Zeitschrift*) inset; (*Zeitungs~*) supplement; insert; (*Brief~*) enclosure; (*Gemüse~*) meat with vegetables.

Beilager *n* nuptials *pl.*

beiläufig *adv* by the way; *a* occasional; incidental, casual; *~ gesagt* in a parenthesis.

beileg|en *tr* to add, to adjoin; to enclose; (*Titel*) to confer (on); (*Streit*) to settle, to put an end to; (*Wert*) to attach value to; (*Eigenschaften*) to attribute; (*Schiff*) to lay by the lee; (*Namen*) to impose upon; *sich etw ~~* to assume; **~escheibe** *f* shim (plate); **~ung** *f* addition, attribution; settlement.

beileibe *adv: ~ nicht!* by no means! on no account whatever!

Beileid *n* condolence; *jdm sein ~ bezeugen* to condole with s. o.; **~sbezeigung** *f* condolence; **~sbrief** *m* letter of condolence; **~skarte** *f* condolatory card.

beiliegen *irr itr* to lie with; *mar* to lie to, to hull to; (*in Brief*) to be enclosed; **~d** *a* enclosed; *~~ sende ich* enclosed please find.

beim *siehe bei dem.*

beimengen *siehe beimischen.*

bei|messen *irr tr* to attribute, to impute; *Glauben ~~* to attach credit to; to believe; *Wert ~~* to attach value to; **~mischen** *tr* to mix to; to admix, to intermix; to intermingle; (*zufügen*) to add; **~mischung** *f* admixture; blend; *mit e-r kleinen ~~ von* dashed with.

Bein *n* leg; (*Knochen*) bone; *jdm ein ~ stellen* to trip s. o. up; *auf die ~e bringen* to raise (an army); *es ging mir durch Mark und ~* it went right through me; *gut auf den ~en sein* to be a good walker; *früh auf den ~en sein* to be early up; *auf die ~e helfen* to set s. o. on o.'s legs; *jdm ~e machen* to make s. o. find o.'s legs; *sich auf die ~e machen* to set out, to start; *sich kein ~ ausreißen* to take o.'s time; not to break o.'s neck over s. th.; **~arbeit** *f sport* foot-work; **~bruch** *m* fracture of a leg; **~chen** *n* ossicle; **~ern** *a* bony; **~fessel** *f* (*beim Ringen*) leg-lock; **~gebrauch** *m sport* foot-work; **~griff** *m* (*beim Ringen*) leg-hold; **~harnisch** *m* cuisses *pl*; **~haus** *n* charnel-house; **~kleid** *n* breeches *pl*, trousers *pl*, slacks *pl*; (*für Frauen*) drawers *pl*, knickers *pl*, panties *pl*, briefs *pl*; **~ling** *m* leg of a stocking; **~prothese** *f* artificial leg; **~schiene** *f med* splint for a broken leg; **~schienen** *f pl* (*beim Hockey*) leg-guards *pl*, pads *pl*; **~stellen** *n* (*beim Ringen*) tripping.

bei|nahe *adv* almost, nearly; *er wäre ~~ gestorben* he was likely to die; *es ist ~~ dasselbe* (*einerlei*) it is much the same thing; **~name** *m* surname; (*spöttischer*) nickname.

bei|ordnen *tr* to adjoin; to coordinate; **~ordnung** *f* coordination; **~packen** *tr* to pack up with; **~pferd** *n* led horse; **~pflichten** *itr* to agree with; to approve of; **~pilot** *m aero* co-pilot; **~rat** *m* adviser; advisory council, advisory body; committee; *örtlicher ~~* local advisory board.

beirren *tr* to mislead; to confuse; (*ablenken von*) to divert from; *sich ~ lassen* to be easily disconcerted; *sich nicht ~ lassen* to stick to o.'s opinion.

bei|sammen *adv* together; *nahe ~~* close by; **~satz** *m* admixture; (*bei Legierung*) alloy; *mit dem ~~, daß* adding that; **~schlaf** *m* cohabitation; **~schläfer** *m* bedfellow; **~~in** *f* concubine; **~schließen** *irr tr* to enclose; **~schluß** *m* (*Sammelsendung von Büchern*) enclosure, delivery (of books), *Am* package; *durch ~~* under cover; **~schreiben** *irr tr* to add a note on the margin, to annotate; **~sein** *n* presence; **~seite** *adv* aside; apart; *~~ legen* (*Geld*) to put by; (*Ware zum Abholen*) to put aside; (*wegwerfen*) to junk; *~~ schieben* to brush aside; *~~ setzen* (*auch fig*) to put aside.

beisetz|en *tr* (*zufügen*) to add, to admix, to alloy; to put to; to put beside; (*Tote*) to inter; (*Segel*) to spread, to unfurl, to make sail; (*alle Segel*) to crowd all the sails; **~ung** *f* burial.

Beisitz *m* assession; **~en** *irr itr* to sit by; **~er** *m* member of a committee; (*Richter*) assistant judge; assessor.

Beispiel *n* example; instance, illustration; *zum ~* for instance; e. g.; *ein ~ geben* to set an example; *ein ~ nehmen an* to take an example from; *ein schlechtes ~* a poor example; *ein warnendes* (*od abschreckendes*) *~* a deterrent example, an awful warning; **~los** *a* unexampled, unheard of, unprecedented, unparalleled; **~sweise** *adv* by way of example, for instance, exemplified.

beispringen *irr itr: jdm ~* to assist; to lend s. o. a hand; to help s. o., to succo(u)r s. o.

beiß|en *irr tr, itr* to bite; (*Pfeffer*) to burn; to be hot; (*Rauch*) to make the eyes water; (*Haut*) to itch; (*Insekt, stechen*) to prick; to sting; (*Wunde*) to smart, to cut; *ins Gras ~~* to bite the dust; *in den sauren Apfel ~~* to swallow the pill; *sich in die Lippen ~~* to bite o.'s lips; **~end** *a* biting; mordant; (*scharf*) acrid, caustic; (*Geschmack*) sharp; pungent; hot; *fig* sarcastic(al); **~erchen** *n* little tooth; **~korb** *m* muzzle, **~zange** *f* pliers *pl*; pincers *pl*, nippers *pl*.

Bei|stand *m* assistance, help; stand-by; *der rechtliche ~~* counsel; (*Sekundant*) second; **~~spakt** *m* pact of mutual assistance; mutual aid pact (*od* treaty); **~stehen** *irr itr* to aid, to stand by, to assist, to help; **~steuer** *f* subsidy, contribution; share; collection; **~steuern** *tr* to contribute (to); **~stimmen** *itr* to agree with, to consent to; **~stimmung** *f* agreement, consent, assent; **~strich** *m* comma.

Bei|trag *m* contribution; (*an Geld*) share; (*Verein*) subscription; fee, *Am* due(s *pl*); **~tragen** *irr tr* to contribute to; (*fördern*) to promote; *itr* to help; **~tragsanteil** *m* share, quota; **~tragspflichtig** *a* liable to contribution; **~treiben** *irr tr* (*Außenstände*) to collect; (*Schulden*) to recover, to collect; (*Abgaben*) to exact; *mil* to requisition; to commandeer; **~treibung** *f* collection; exaction; *mil* requisition; **~treten** *irr itr* to enter into; (*Meinung*) to agree to; to assent to, to accede to; (*e-r Partei etc*) to join (a party); **~tritt** *m* accession, taking part; joining; enrol(l)ment; **~~serklärung** *f* declaration of joining (*od* accession *od* consent).

Bei|wagen *m mot* side-car; (*Anhänger*) trailer coach; **~~maschine** *f* (*Beikrad*) side-car motorcycle; **~weg** *m* by-pass; **~werk** *n* accessories *pl*; **~wohnen** *itr* to be present at, to attend; to witness; (*beischlafen*) to cohabit (with); **~wohnung** *f* presence, attendance; (*Beischlaf*) cohabitation, sexual intercourse; coitus; **~wort** *n gram* adjective; (*schmückendes*) epithet.

Beiz|e *f* (*Gebeiztwerden*) corrosion, maceration; (*Beizmittel*) corrosive; (*Metall*) pickle; *chem* mordant; (*Holz*) stain; *typ* etching acid; *med* caustic; (*Gerberei*) oozing; (*Tabak~*) sauce; (*Jagd*) hawking; **~en** *tr* to corrode; (*Metall*) to pickle; (*Häute*) to tan, to steep in ooze; *med* to cauterize; (*Tischlerei*) to stain; (*schwarz*) to ebonize; (*Jagd*) to hawk; **~end** *a* corrosive, caustic; **~mittel** *n* corrosive; mordant; disinfectant; caustic; **~ung** *f* (*Saat*) seed dressing; disinfection.

beizeiten *adv* early; in (good) time; betimes.

bejah|en *tr* to affirm; to answer in the affirmative; to assent (to); to accept; **~end** *a* affirmative; *im ~~en Falle* if the answer be affirmative; **~ung** *f* affirmation; assertion.

bejahrt *a* aged, advanced in years.

bejammern *tr* to bemoan; to bewail, to lament; **~swert, ~swürdig** *a* lamentable, deplorable.

*

bekämpf|en *tr* to combat; to fight, *Am* to battle; (*Antrag*) to oppose; (*Leidenschaften*) to control, to subdue; **~ung** *f* combat(ing), fight; struggle.

bekannt *a* known; well-known; *~ wegen* noted for; *allgemein ~* notorious; *mit etw ~* (*vertraut*) *sein* to be familiar with; *mit jdm ~ sein* to be acquainted with; *jdn mit jdm ~ machen* to introduce s. o. to s. o.; to have s. o. meet s. o.; *jdn mit etw ~ machen* to acquaint s. o. with; *es wurde ~* it became known; *es ist mir ~* I know that; *er ist mir ~* he is known to me; *es ist ~* it is well known; *ein ~es Gesicht* a familiar face; *~es Gebiet* proven territory; **~e** *f*, **~e(r)** *m* acquaintance; *ein ~er von mir* a friend of mine; **~enkreis** *m* circle; **~ermaßen, ~lich** *adv* as is (well) known; **~geben** *irr*, **~machen** *tr* to make known; to notify, to inform, to disclose; (*öffentlich*) to publish, to make a public notice, to post; (*in Zeitung*) to advertise; (*Gesetze*) to promulgate; **~gabe, ~machung** *f* publication, proclamation; (public) notice; announcement; notification, disclosure; (*Gesetz*) promulgation; (*amtliche ~~*) official notice; (*in der Zeitung*) advertisement; **~schaft** *f* acquaintance; *~~ machen* to form an acquaintance with.

bekehr|en *tr* to convert, to proselyte; *sich ~~* to be converted to; **~te(r)** *m*, **~te** *f* convert; proselyte; **~ung** *f* conversion; **~~seifer** *m* proselytism.

bekenn|en *irr tr* to confess, to acknowledge; (*zugeben*) to admit, to own up; *Farbe ~~ fig* to be frank; (*Kartenspiel*) to follow suit; *nicht ~~* to renounce; *sich schuldig ~~* to plead guilty; *sich zu e-r Religion ~~* to profess a religion; **~er**

m confessor; **~tnis** *n* confession; (*Glaubens~~*) creed; (*zu Konfession, Sekte*) denomination; **~~kirche** *f* (*Deutschland*) Confessional Church; **~~schule** *f* denominational school.

beklag|en *tr* to deplore, to lament; (*bemitleiden*) to pity; *sich ~~ über* to complain of, *Am* to gripe; **~enswert** *a* lamentable, pitiable; **~te(r)** *m*, **~te** *f jur* accused, defendant.

be|klatschen *tr* to applaud; to clap; (*verleumden*) to tell tales of; **~kleben** *tr* to paste over (*od* on), to stick on; (*mit Papier*) to line, to paper; (*Gepäck*) to label; **~klecksen** *tr* to stain, to bespatter; (*mit Tinte*) to blot.

bekleid|en *tr* to clothe, to dress; (*mit Holz ausschlagen*) to wainscot; (*mit Farbe, Isoliermasse*) to cover; to coat; (*bekleiden mit*) to invest with; (*Stellung*) to hold, to occupy (a position); (*Amt*) to fill an office; *mit Tapeten ~~* to paper; *mit Marmor ~~* to line with marble; **~ung** *f* clothing, dress; clothes *pl*; (*Uniform*) uniform; lining; covering; casing; (*Wandbehang*) tapestry; (*Herren~~*) gentlemen's outfit; (*Damen~~*) ladies' clothes; (*Amt*) investiture; tenure; **~~samt** *n* clothing depot; **~~sentgiftung** *f* clothing decontamination; **~~sgegenstände** *m pl* clothes *pl*, clothing; **~~sindustrie** *f* wear industry, clothing-industry; **~~snachweis** *m* clothing account; **~~ssack** *m Am mil* duffel bag; **~~sstücke** *n pl* wearing-apparel, articles of clothing; **~~svorschrift** *f mil* dress regulation; **~~swirtschaft** *f* clothing industry.

bekleistern *tr* to paste over.

beklemm|en *irr tr fig* to oppress; *beklommen a* anxious, uneasy; oppressed (in breathing); **~ung, Beklommenheit** *f* oppression, anguish.

bekohl|en *tr* (*Schiff*) to coal a ship; **~ungsanlage** *f* coaling installation; **~ungshafen** *m* coal bunkering port; **~ungsstation** *f* coaling station.

bekommen *irr tr* to get, to receive; (*durch Bemühung*) to obtain; (*erwerben*) to acquire; (*Krankheiten*) to catch; *Junge ~* to have young ones; *Zähne ~* to cut o.'s teeth; *ich habe Lust ~* I have got a mind; *Hiebe ~* to get a good beating (*od* licking); *es ist nicht zu ~* it is not to be had; *e-n Schilling heraus~* to get a shilling change; *etw wieder ~* to recover; *etw fertig ~* to get s.th. finished; *was ~ Sie?* what do I owe you? *ich habe es geschenkt ~* I had it as a gift; *wir werden Regen ~* we shall have rain; *zu Gesicht ~* to get sight of; *itr* to agree with; *nicht gut ~* to disagree with; *wohl bekomm's!* to your health! **bekömmlich** *a* wholesome, beneficial; digestible.

beköstig|en *tr* to board; to feed; *sich selbst ~~* to feed o. s.; **~ung** *f* board, messing; food.

bekräftig|en *tr* to confirm; to corroborate; to confirm; to emphasize, to strengthen; to aggravate; **~ung** *f* confirmation, corroboration; substantiation, aggravation.

be|kränzen *tr* to wreath; to crown; to decorate (with garland); **~kreuzen** *r* to cross o. s.; **~kreuzigen** *tr* to make the sign of the cross upon; **~kriegen** *tr* to make war upon; **~kritteln** *tr* to criticize, to censure, to carp at; **~kritzeln** *tr* to scrawl upon.

bekümmer|n *tr* to grieve, to distress; (*angehen*) to concern; *über etw ~t sein* to be grieved at; *sich um etw ~~* to trouble o. s. about; *~e dich um dich selbst!* mind your own business! **~nis** *f* grief, pain, sorrow, affliction; **~t** *a* afflicted, grieved, anxious (about).

be|kunden *tr* (*aussagen*) to state; (*dartun*) to show, to manifest; (*eidlich*) to declare upon oath, to depose; **~lächeln** *tr* to smile at; **~lachen** *tr* to laugh at; to deride.

*

belad|en *irr tr* to load, to lade, to freight; *fig* to burden, to charge; *~~ mit* laden with; **~ebühne** *f* loading platform; **~efrist** *f* loading period; **~eplan** *m* loading diagram (*od* table); **~estation** *f* loading station; **~estelle** *f* loading and unloading wharf; **~ezeit** *f* loading time; **~ung** *f* loading, shipping, freighting; (*Last*) load, freight, *mar* cargo.

Belag *m* cover(ing); coat(ing); (*Straße*) surface; (*Platten~*) slab covering of the floor; (*Brücken~*) bridge flooring, plank covering; (*der Zunge*) fur; (*des Spiegels*) foil; (*Zähne*) film; (*Brot*) spread, relish; **~frei** *a* free from coating.

Belager|er *m* besieger; **~n** *tr* to besiege, to lay siege to: **~t** *a* besieged; **~ung** *f* siege; **~~sartillerie** *f* siege-artillery; **~~szustand** *m* state of siege; *den ~~szustand verhängen* to proclaim martial law.

Belang *m* importance; (*Angelegenheit*) concern; (*Interesse*) interest; (*Bedeutung*) meaning; (*Folgerung*) consequence; *von ~* of consequence; *nicht von ~* of no importance (*od* consequence); of no account; **~e** *m pl* interests *pl*; **~en** *tr* (*verfolgen*) to pursue; (*gerichtlich*) to sue at law, to indict for; to take legal steps against s.o.; to file an action against s.o.; to prosecute; (*betreffen*) to concern; *was mich (an)~t* as far as I am concerned, as to me; **~los** *a* unimportant, of no interest, insignificant; **~reich** *a* of consequence, important; (*beträchtlich*) considerable.

belassen *irr tr siehe: lassen*; *es dabei ~* to leave it in a condition; *alles beim alten ~* to leave things as they are.

belast|en *tr* to load, to burden; (*Handel*) to debit; (*Konto*) to charge an account with; (*anklagen*) to accuse (of), to charge (with); (*beschweren*) to weight; (*Hypotheke*) to encumber; *el* to load; *ungleichförmig ~~* to lump-load; (*anstrengen*) to strain, to stress; (*anspannen*) to put tension on; **~et** (*vor Gericht*) incriminated; *minder ~et* less incriminated; *erblich ~et* tainted with a hereditary disease; **~ung** *f* load(ing), burden; (*drückende Last*) *fig* incubus; drag; (*Grundstück*) charge, mortgage, encumbrance; (*Konto*) debit; (*vor Gericht*) incrimination; (*erblich*) hereditary taint; *el, tech* load, strain, stress; (*Kessel*) evaporation; (*Hochofen*) consumption; (*Leistung*) rating; (*Ertrag*) output; (*Ladefähigkeit*) capacitance, loading capacity; (*Extra~~*) handicap; *zulässige ~~* safe load; **~~sanzeige** *f com* debit advice; **~~sfähigkeit** *f* carrying capacity; **~~sgrenze** *f* loading limit; breaking strain; **~~sprobe** *f tech* load test, capacity-test; *fig* crucial test; **~~sschwankungen** *f pl tech* load variations *pl*; **~~szeuge** *m* witness for the prosecution.

belästig|en to molest; (*stören*) to trouble, to bother; (*plagen*) to pester; (*unabsichtlich*) to incommode, to discommode, to inconvenience; (*mit Bitten*) to importune; **~ung** *f* molestation, trouble, vexation; (*Störung*) annoyance.

belaub|en *tr* to cover with leaves; *dicht ~t* leafy; **~ung** *f* foliage.

belauern *tr* to watch; to lie in wait for.

belaufen *irr r: sich ~ auf* to total, to come to, to figure up to, to amount to.

belauschen *tr* to eavesdrop; to overhear; to listen to.

beleb|en *tr* to animate, to enliven; (*neu ~~*) to quicken, to resuscitate; (*aufheitern*) to brighten; (*wieder~~*) to revive, to restore to life; **~end** *a* animating; *~~es Mittel* restorative; **~t** *a* (*Unterhaltung*) lively; (*Geschäft*) brisk, animated; (*geschäftig*) bustling; *~ter Ort* populous place; *~te Straße* crowded (*od* busy) street; **~theit** *f* animation; liveliness; **~ung** *f* (*Wieder~~*) restoring to life; (*Wiederaufleben*) revival; (*Antrieb*) stimulus.

belecken *tr* to lick.

Beleg *m* proof; evidence; (*Unterlage*) voucher; (*Urkunde*) document, deed, record; (*Quittung*) receipt; (*Zitat*) quotation; (*Beispiel*) example, illustration; (*Auflage*) overlay; **~en** *tr* to overlay, to cover; (*mit Dielen*) to floor; (*mit Soldaten*) to quarter, to billet; (*mit Abgaben*) to lay duties on; (*mit Strafe*) to inflict upon, to fine; (*mit Bomben*) to bomb; (*mit Schnellfeuer*) to cover with rapid fire; (*mit Namen*) to give a name; (*Platz*) to reserve, to secure; (*vorherbestellen*) to book; (*Ansichten*) to prove, to substantiate; (*Tiere*) to fecundate; (*Stute*) to cover; (*Kolleg*) to subscribe to (*od* take) a course of lectures; (*mit Beschlag*) to seize; (*Rechnung*) to render an account; (*mit Beweisen*) to verify, to prove; (*mit Beispielen*) to exemplify; *tech* to cover, to overlay, to coat, to line; *können Sie das ~~?* can you furnish proof of that?; **~exemplar** *n* voucher (copy); (*Buch*) author's copy; **~schaft** *f* gang; hands *pl*; personnel, number of employees, staff; *min* shift; **~schein** *m* voucher; **~stelle** *f* quotation; **~stück** *n* tear sheet, *Am* ticket; record; copy; voucher; **~t** *a* overlaid; *~te Stimme* husky voice; *~te Zunge* coated tongue; *~tes Brot* sandwich; (*Platz*) reserved, taken; *tele* busy, engaged; **~ung** *f* (*Spiegel*) tin-plate; covering; *mil* quartering, billeting; (*Abgabe*) imposition; (*Platz*) reservation, booking; (*Strafe*) infliction; *tele* engagement, holding; **~~sdauer** *f tele* holding time.

belehn|en *tr* to invest with a fief; to enfeoff; **~te(r)** *m* vassal; feoffee; **~ung** *f* investiture; enfeoffment.

belehr|en *tr* to teach, to instruct; (*aufklären*) to enlighten; (*beraten*) to advise; *jdn e-s Besseren ~~* to set right; *sich ~~ lassen* to take advice; to listen to reason; **~end** *a* instructive; (*lehrhaft*) didactic; **~ung** *f* instruction, information, advice; (*Berichtigung*) correction; **~~sschießen** *n mil* instruction firing.

beleibt *a* corpulent, fat, stout; **~heit** *f* corpulence.

beleidig|en *tr* to offend, to give offence; (*schwer*) to affront, to insult, to outrage; (*Ohr*) to shock; *sich ~t fühlen* to feel hurt; **~end** *a* injurious; insulting, offensive; **~er** *m* offender; **~ung** *f* offence, injury, outrage, insult; (*Unrecht*) wrong; (*Verleumdung*) slander.

beleihen *tr siehe: belehnen;* (*Handel*) to loan on.

belesen *a* well-read; **~heit** *f* book-learning; reading.

beleucht|en *tr* to light (up); (*festlich*) to illuminate; *fig* to illustrate, to throw light on; (*erklären*) to elucidate;

aero to drop flares; *näher* **~~** to examine; **~ung** *f* lighting; (*festliche* **~~**) illumination *fig* elucidation, illustration; **~~skörper** *m* (light) fittings *pl*, (light) fixture; illuminator; **~~skosten** *pl* lighting charges *pl*; **~~slinse** *f* condensing lens; **~~smesser** *m* lux meter; **~~smittel** *n* illuminant; means of illumination; **~~sschalter** *m* lighting switch; **~~sschirm** *m* reflector; **~~stärke** *f* lighting force; **~~swirkung** *f* illuminating effect.

beleum|det, **~undet** *a: gut* (*schlecht*) **~~** in good (bad) repute.

belfern *itr* to yelp; *fig* to grumble.

Belg|ien *n* Belgium; **~ier** *m*, **~isch** *a* Belgian.

belicht|en *tr phot* to expose (to light); (*bestrahlen*) to irradiate; **~ung** *f* exposure; **~~smesser** *m* photometer, exposure meter; **~~srolle** *f* (*Tonfilm*) sound-recording drum, scanning point, translation point; **~~sspielraum** *m phot* exposure latitude; **~~sstärke** *f* strength of lighting; **~~sstufe** *f* stage of exposure; **~~stabelle** *f* exposure table (*od* scale); **~~szeit** *f* exposure time.

belieb|en *tr* to like; *itr* to please; *wie ~t?* Sir? Madam? *wie es Ihnen ~t* as you like; *wenn es Ihnen ~t* if you please; **~en** *n* will, pleasure, discretion; *nach Ihrem* **~~** as you please; *es steht in Ihrem* **~~** it rests with you; *nach* **~~** at will; **~ig** *a* any, whatever; given; desired; (*wahlfrei*) discretionary, optional; *zu jeder ~~en Zeit* at any time; *von ~~er Größe* of any size; *e-e ~~e Summe* any sum you please; **~t** *a* favo(u)rite, beloved; (*Handel*) in request; (*Mode*) in vogue; *sich ~t machen* to make o. s. popular with; **~theit** *f* popularity, vogue, favo(u)r.

beliefer|n *tr* to furnish, to supply, to provide (with); **~ung** *f* supply, furnishing.

bellen *itr* to bark, to bay.

Belletrist *m* literary man; **~ik** *f* fiction; **~isch** *a* belletristic; *~~e Zeitschriften* literary magazines.

belob|en *tr* to praise, to commend, to make hono(u)rable mention of; **~(ig)ung** *f* praise, citation, commendation; **~~sschreiben** *n* laudatory letter.

belohn|en *tr* to reward, to recompense; (*mit Geld*) to remunerate; (*mit e-m Preis*) to award; *mit Undank* **~~** to serve with ingratitude; **~ung** *f* reward, recompense; (*Geldgeschenk*) gratuity; (*Prämie*) premium; bounty; bonus; (*Preis*) prize; award; *schlechte* **~~** ill-return; *zur* **~~** *für* in requital of.

Belüftung *f* ventilation.

belügen *tr* to (tell a) lie (to).

belustig|en *tr* to amuse, to entertain; to divert; (*ergötzen*) to recreate; **~~d** *a* amusing, entertaining; **~t** *a:* **~~** *über* amused with; **~ung** *f* amusement, entertainment; diversion; recreation.

be|mächtigen *r: sich e-r Sache* **~~** to seize on; to take possession of; (*widerrechtlich*) to usurp s. th.; **~malen** *tr* to paint over, to stain, to colo(u)r; to adorn with paintings; *fam* (*kosmetisch*) to make up; **~mängeln, ~mäkeln** *tr* to find fault with.

bemann|en *tr* to man; **~ung** *f* manning; (*Mannschaft*) crew.

bemäntel|n *tr* to cloak, to cover; to varnish; (*beschönigen*) to palliate; **~ung** *f* cloaking, palliation.

bemast|en *tr* to mast; **~ung** *f* masts *pl*.

bemeistern *tr* to master, to conquer; *sich e-r Sache* **~** to seize on.

bemerk|bar *a* observable, perceptible; noticeable; *sich* **~~** *machen* to make o. s. conspicuous; **~en** *tr* (*merken*) to realize, to perceive; (*mit d. Augen*) to observe; to notice, to note; (*sagen*) to observe, to remark; (*erwähnen*) to mention; (*herausfinden*) to spot; *wie unten bemerkt* as noted below; **~enswert** *a* remarkable, noteworthy, notable, noticeable, conspicuous for; **~lich** *a* observable; (*fühlbar*) sensible; *sich* **~~** *machen* to attract attention; **~ung** *f* observation; remark; (*am Rande*) note, annotation; (*Einwurf*) objection; (*witzige, treffende* **~~**) *Am* wisecrack, smart remark.

bemess|en *irr tr* to measure (out); (*zuteilen*) to proportion, to apportion (to); (*regulieren*) to regulate; (*anpassen*) to adjust; (*Leistung e-s Motors*) to rate; (*abschätzen*) to rate; **~~** *a* dimensioned; exact, symmetrical; **~ung** *f* dimensioning, proportioning; size; rating.

bemitleiden *tr* to pity, to be sorry for; to commiserate; **~swert** *a* pitiable, deplorable.

bemittelt *a* well-to-do; well-off.

bemogeln *tr fam* to cheat, to trick.

bemoost *a* mossy; *fig* old; *~es Haupt* old student; old stager.

bemüh|en *tr* to trouble; *darf ich Sie ~~?* may I trouble you? *r* to take pains, to endeavour, to try (hard); (*um e-e Stelle*) to apply for, to seek; *sich wegen jds* **~~** to try to help; *sich um jdn* **~~** to seek s. o.'s favo(u)r; **~~** *Sie sich nicht* don't trouble, don't bother; *sich um ein Amt* **~~** to strive for an office; **~ung** *f* trouble, care, exertion; (*Anstrengung*) effort, endeavour.

bemüßigt *a: sich* **~** *fühlen* to feel obliged (*od* induced) to; to feel bound to.

bemuster|n *tr* to sample; to send samples; **~ung** *f* sampling.

bemuttern *tr* to mother.

benachbart *a* neighbo(u)ring, adjacent.

benachrichtig|en *tr* to inform (of), to send word (to); (*amtlich*) to notify; *com* to advise (of), to communicate (to), to apprise (of); (*bekanntmachen*) to acquaint (with); *fam* to tip (off); **~ung** *f* information, advice; **~~sgebühr** *f* report charge.

benachteilig|en *tr* to prejudice, to wrong; to handicap; **~t** *a* injured; **~ung** *f* prejudice, wrong, injury, detriment.

be|nagen *tr* to gnaw at; **~namen, ~namsen** *tr* to name, to call.

benebel|n *tr* to cover with mist; to dim; **~t** *a fig* tipsy.

bene|deien *tr* to bless; **~diktiner** *m* Benedictine (monk); **~fiz** *n* benefit; benefice; **~~vorstellung** *f* benefit-play, benefit-night (*od* -performance).

benehmen *irr tr* to take away; to remove; (*berauben*) to deprive; *den Atem* **~** to take away s. o.'s breath; *die Aussicht* **~** to intercept the view; *den Kopf* **~** to make s. o.'s head swim; *sich* **~** to behave o. s., to conduct o. s., to deport o. s., to demean o. s.; (*handeln*) to act; *sie weiß sich nicht zu* **~** she has no manners; *sich albern* **~** to make a fool of o.s.; **~** *n* demeano(u)r, behavio(u)r, conduct; manners *pl*; *sich mit jdm ins* **~** *setzen* to confer with s. o.; *ungehöriges* **~** disorderly conduct.

beneiden *tr* to envy; **~swert** enviable.

benenn|en *irr tr* to call, to name; to denominate; (*e-n Tag festlegen*) to fix a day; *benannte Zahl* concrete number; **~ung** *f* denomination; name, appellation; (*Terminologie*) nomenclature; (*Bezeichnung*) designation; (*Ausdruck*) term; (*Titel*) title.

benetzen *tr* to wet, to moisten, to dabble; (*mit Tau*) to bedew.

Bengel *m fig* rude fellow; *dummer* **~** silly fool; *kleiner* **~** little urchin; (*Knüppel*) club, heavy stick; **~haft** *a* rude.

benommen *a* benumbed, confused.

benötigen *tr* to be in want of; to need, to require; *dringend* **~** to be in urgent want of.

benutz|en *tr* to use, to make use of; (*verwenden*) to employ; (*günstig*) to profit, to take advantage (of), to avail o. s. (of); (*verwerten*) to profit; to utilize; (*Verkehrsmittel*) to take; *jede Gelegenheit* **~~** to avail (o. s.) of every opportunity; **~er** *m* user, employer; **~ung** *f* use, employment; (*Verwertung*) utilization; *zur vorübergehenden* **~~** for temporary use; *mit* **~~** *von* with the help of; **~~sanweisung** *f* use instruction; **~~sgebühr** *f*, **~~srecht** *n* right of user; **~~szwang** *m* compulsory usage.

Benzin *n chem* benzine; *mot* petrol, *Am* gasoline, *fam* gas; **~behälter** *m* container, petrol tank, *Am* jerry can; **~faß** *n* petrol barrel; **~fresser** *m* glutton on petrol; **~hahn** *m* gasoline shut-off (*od* faucet); **~kanister** *m* container, *Am* jerry can; **~leitung** *f* gasoline pipes *pl*; fuel pipe line; **~messer** *m* fuel gauge; **~motor** *m* petrol (*od* gas) engine; **~pumpe** *f* petrol lift, gasoline pump; **~rationierung** *f* gas rationing; **~saugrohr** *n* gasoline suction pipe; **~stand** *m* gasoline level; **~steuer** *f* petrol tax; **~tank** *m* fuel-tank; gasoline tank; **~tankstelle** *f* petrol station, gasoline station; **~transporter** *m* petrol carrier; **~uhr** *f* petrol (*od* gas) gauge, fuel gauge; **~verbrauch** *m* petrol (*od* gas *od* fuel) consumption; **~wagen** *m* petrol car, *Am* gasoline automobile, gasoline wheel tank; **~zapfstelle** *f* filling station, *Am* roadside gasoline pump; **~zuteilung** *f* petrol (*od Am* gasoline) allowance; **Benzol** *n* benzene, benzol(e).

beobacht|en *tr* to watch, to observe; (*scharf*) to scan, to scrutinize; (*überblicken*) to survey, to view; (*betrachten*) to contemplate; (*heimlich*) to shadow; (*festhalten*) to adhere (*an* to); (*Stillschweigen*) to keep (silence); **~er** *m*, **~erin** *f* observer; *mil* observing post; (*Luftspäher*) spotter; (*Betrachter*) spectator, beholder, looker-on, onlooker; (*Augenzeuge*) eyewitness; (*Zuschauer*) bystander; (*beim Kartenspiel*) *Am* kibitzer; (*Radar~~*) radar operator; *aero* observer; observation pilot; **~ung** *f* observation, notice; (*Befolgung*) observance; *tech* (*Ablesen*) the taking of a reading; **~~sabteilung** *f mil* artillery observation battalion, survey battalion (sound and flash); **~~sfehler** *m* error of observation; personal error; **~~sflugzeug** *n* reconnaissance plane; observation plane; **~~sposten** *m* sentinel; observation post; **~~sschlitz** *m* (*Tank*) loop-hole; **~~sstand** *m* observation-post, look-out; **~~sstation** *f med* observation ward; **~~sturm** *m* observation tower.

beorder|n *tr* to order; to command; **~ung** *f* order, command; commission.

be|packen *tr* to load, to charge; **~pflanzen** *tr* to plant; **~pflastern** *tr* (*Wunde*) to plaster over (a wound); (*Straße*) to pave (a street).

bequem *a* convenient, suitable; (*behaglich*) comfortable; *es jdm* **~** *machen* to make s. o. comfortable; *es sich* **~** *machen* to make o. s. comfortable (*od* at home); to take it easy; (*träg*) lazy, indolent, easy-going; (*gleichgültig*) indifferent; **~en**: *sich zu etw ~~* to yield to, to condescend to, to comply (with), to submit (to); **~lichkeit** *f* ease, comfort; convenience; (*Trägheit*) laziness, indolence.

berappen *tr fam* (*bezahlen*) to pay up.

berat|en *irr tr* to counsel; to advise; *schlecht* (*wohl*) *~~ sein* to be ill (well) advised; *r* to confer with; to deliberate; **~~d** *a* advisory; consultative; (*beratschlagend*) deliberative; **~er** *m* counsel(l)or; *technischer ~~* technical adviser; **~schlagen** *itr* to deliberate, to consult; to confer with; **~ung** *f* consultation; conference, deliberation; (*Führung*) guidance; **~~sgegenstand** *m* subject, item; **~~skosten** *pl* consultation fees *pl*; **~~sstelle** *f* advisory board.

beraub|en *tr* to rob of; to deprive of; to despoil of; *jdn e-r Sache ~~* to divest s. o. of; *sich e-r Sache ~~* to deprive o. s. of; **~ung** *f* deprivation, spoliation, robbery; bereavement.

beräuchern *tr* to perfume; *tech* to fumigate; (*mit Weihrauch*) to incense.

berausch|en *tr* to intoxicate, to fuddle; to inebriate; *fig* to enchant; *r* to get drunk; *fig* to become enraptured (with); **~end** *a* intoxicating, heady; **~t** *a* tipsy, drunk; *fig* exalted, elated.

Berberitze *f* barberry.

berechenbar *a* computable, calculable; **~keit** *f* calculability, computability.

berechn|en *tr* to calculate; (*abschätzen*) to estimate, to evaluate; (*ausrechnen*) to compute, to reckon, to figure out; (*zusammenzählen*) to sum up, to total, to add up; (*umrechnen*) *com* to reduce; *jdm etw ~~* to charge s. o. for; **~end** *a* calculating, scheming; (*selbstsüchtig*) selfish, self-interested; **~et** *a fig* intended, premeditated; *wohl ~~* judicious; **~ung** *f* calculation; (*ungefähre ~~*) rough estimate; (*Umrechnung*) conversion, reduction; *ohne ~~* without charge; (*von Maschinenleistungen*) *tech* computation; **~~stafel** *f tech* chart.

berechtig|en *tr* to entitle to, to justify; (*befähigen*) to qualify; (*rechtfertigen*) to warrant; to be justifiable; (*bevorrechten*) to privilege; (*ermächtigen*) to empower, to authorize; **~t** *a* authorized, entitled (to); (*zuständig*) competent; **~ter** *m* licensee; **~ung** *f* authorization; (*Rechtsanspruch*) title, right, claim; (*Vollmacht*) power, warrant, authorization; (*Vorrecht*) privilege, priority; (*Eignung*) qualification; (*Rechtfertigung*) justification; **~~sschein** *m* licence; permit; certificate of priority.

bered|en *tr* to speak of; to talk over; *jdn zu etw ~~* to persuade, to induce to; *sich mit jdm ~~* to deliberate, to consult (with); to confer (with); **~sam, ~t** *a* eloquent; **~samkeit** *f* eloquence.

Bereich *m* reach, extent, domain, district, region, zone, area; *fig* field, compass, sphere, scope; (*z. B. Sende~*) range; *außer dem ~* beyond the reach of; *in dem ~* within the region of, within the scope of; **~ern** *tr* to enrich; to get rich; **~erung** *f* enrichment.

be|reifen *tr* (*Fässer*) to hoop; *mot* to fit with tyres; **~reift** *a* rimy, covered with hoar-frost; (*weiß*) hoary; **~reifung** *f mot* tyres, *Am* tires *pl*; **~reisen** *tr* to journey over; *com* to visit; to frequent (fairs); (*Wahlkreis, Kundschaft*) to canvass.

bereinig|en *tr* to settle; to straighten out, to iron out; **~ung** *f* settlement.

bereit *a* ready, prompt; (*vorbereitet*) prepared; *~ halten* to keep ready; (*Geld*) to tender; *sich ~ halten* to keep o. s. ready, to be prepared; *~ stehen* to keep in readiness; *sich ~ machen* to get ready; **~en** *tr* 1. *irr* to ride over; (*Pferd*) to break in; 2. to prepare, to dress; (*Leder*) to curry; (*verursachen*) to cause, to make; (*herstellen*) to manufacture; *Kummer ~~* to grieve; **~er** *m* riding-master, horse-breaker; **~halten** *irr tr* to hold at the disposal of, to keep on hand; **~s** *adv* already; **~schaft** *f* readiness; (*Polizei~~*) squad; *in ~~ sein* to be ready (*od* at stand-by); (*Alarm~~*) to be on the alert; **~~sbataillon** *n* battalion in support; **~~sdienst** *m* stand-by service; **~stellen** *tr* to keep ready; to prepare; (*Geld*) to provide funds; *mil* to assemble, to place in readiness; (*zurückstellen*) to earmark; (*auf Lager halten*) to hold in readiness; **~stellung** *f mil* final assembly, concentration; (*Geld*) provision of means; (*Rücklage*) provision, reservation; (*Vorbereitung*) preparation; (*Herstellung*) manufacture, making; **~~smittel** *n pl* appropriation fund; **~~sraum** *m* final assembly area; **~ung** *f* preparation, dressing; **~willig** *a* ready, eager; (*dienstfertig*) obliging; **~~keit** *f* readiness, willingness.

berenn|en *irr tr* to assault; **~ung** *f* assault.

bereuen *tr* to repent, to be sorry for to regret.

Berg *m* mountain, hill; (*spitz*) peak; (*vor Eigennamen*) Mount; *über ~ u Tal* over hedge and ditch; *er ist über alle ~e* he is off and away; *zu ~e stehen* to stand on end; *hinter dem ~e halten* to be reserved; to hold back; *über den ~ sein* to be out of the wood (*od* round the corner); *goldene ~e versprechen* to promise wonders; **~ab** *adv* downhill; **~abhang** *m* mountain-slope; **~akademie** *f* mining-school; **~amt** *n* mining-office; **~an, ~auf** *adv* uphill, upwards; **~arbeiter** *m* miner; (*im Kohlenbergwerk*) collier; **~~verband** *m* miner's union; **~bahn** *f* mountain-railway; **~bau** *m* mining(-industry); **~besteigung** *f* climb; **~bewohner** *m* mountaineer, highlander; **~fahrt** *f* mountain trip; (*von Flußschiffen*) up-passage; **~führer** *m* (alpine) guide; **~gegend** *f* mountain-district, highland; **~geist** *m* mountain-sprite, gnome; **~gipfel** *m* mountain-top; **~grat** *m* ridge; **~halde** *f* mountain slope; (*Schutt~*) pit heap; **~harz** *n* bitumen; **~hütte** *f* mountain hut; **~ig** *a* mountainous, hilly; **~kamm** *m* crest; **~kette** *f* chain of mountains, ridge of hills; **~knappe** *m* miner; **~krankheit** *f* mountain sickness; hypobaropathy; **~kristall** *m* rock-crystal; **~kuppe** *f* summit; **~land** *n* mountainous country, highland; **~mann** *m* miner, collier; (*Ingenieur*) mining-engineer; **~männisch** *a* mining; **~meister** *m* surveyor of mines; **~partie** *f* climbing-excursion; **~predigt** *f* Christ's Sermon on the Mount; **~rat** *m* counsellor of mines; **~recht** *n* miners' statutes *pl*; mining-laws *pl*; **~rennen** *n mot* hill-climbing contest; **~rücken** *m* mountain-ridge; **~rutsch, ~sturz** *m* landslip; **~sattel** *m* saddle, dip between two peaks; **~schloß** *n* mountain-castle; **~schlucht** *f* ravine, rift, glen; **~schuhe** *m pl* mountaineering-boots *pl*; **~seil** *n* rope; **~spitze** *f* peak, mountain-top; **~steiger** *m* mountain-climber, mountaineer, (*in den Alpen*) Alpinist; **~~ausrüstung** *f* mountaineering outfit; **~steigerei** *f* mountain climbing, mountaineering; **~steigfähigkeit** *f mot* climbing ability; **~stock** *m* (*Gebirgsmasse*) massive rock; (*langer Stock mit Eisenspitze*) alpenstock; **~straße** *f* mountain road; **~strom** *m* mountain stream, torrent; **~sturz** *m* (*~rutsch*) landslip, *Am* landslide; **~tour** *f* (*~wanderung, ~partie*) mountain tour, alpine tour, climb; **~~ und Talbahn** *f* switchback (-railway), *Am* roller-coaster; **~verwaltung** *f* administration of mines; **~wacht** *f* mountain rescue party; **~wand** *f* steep mountain side; **~wanderung** *f* mountain-tour; **~werk** *n* (*Zeche*) mine, (*Steinkohlengrube*) colliery, (*der Pütt*) pit, (*Schacht*) shaft; **~~sabgabe** *f* (*an Besitzer*) royalty, (*Steuer*) tax (on mines), contribution of mines; **~~saktie** *f* mining share, *Am* mining stock; **~~sarbeiten** *f pl* mining operations *pl*; **~~sgesellschaft** *f* mining company; **~~singenieur** *m* mining engineer; **~~sproduktion** *f* mining produce; **~~sunternehmen** *n* mining concern; **~wesen** *n* mining (-industry), industrial mining; **~wiese** *f* (*Trift*) mountain meadow, alpine meadow; **~wind** *m* mountain wind; **~zinn** *n* mine tin, vein tin, pure tin.

berg|en *irr tr* (*Schiffe, Maschinen*) to salvage; (*schützen*) to save; (*vor Gefahr*) to protect; (*Güter*) to recover; (*Menschen*) to rescue; (*Segel*) to take in, to shorten sail; (*enthalten*) to contain; (*verbergen*) to conceal; (*schirmen*) to shelter; (*abtönen*) to shade; *er ist geborgen* he is safe; **~ung** *f* (*Schiffsfracht, Maschinen*) salvage; (*Strandgüter*) recovery; (*Menschen*) rescue, sheltering, saving; **~~sarbeit** *f* salvage operation; (*Menschen*) rescue work; **~~sdampfer** *m* salvage steamer; **~~sfahrzeug** *n* salvage (*od* recovery) vessel; **~~sgut** *n* salvage (-goods *pl*); **~~skolonne** *f* salvage unit; **~~skosten** *pl* salvage charges *pl*; **~~skran** *m* break-down crane; **~~sprämie** *f*, **~~slohn** *m* salvage money; **~~ssammelstelle** *f* salvage depot; **~~sschiff** *n* salvage vessel; **~~strupp** *m* salvage unit; rescue squad; **~~sverlust** *m* salvage loss.

Bericht *m* report; (*amtlicher*) official report; (*eingehender*) detailed account; full particulars *pl*; (*Auskunft*) information; (*Benachrichtigung*) advice; (*Markt~*) market-report; (*kurzer*) summary; (*Protokoll*) minutes *pl*; (*statistischer*) return; statement; (*Funk~, Hör~*) commentary; *e-n ~ abfassen* to prepare a report; *~ erstatten* to hand in a full statement (of); to give an account (of); *~ einreichen* to submit a report; *laut ~* as advised; (*auf Wechseln*) as per advice; **~en** *tr, itr* to report, to give an account (*od* full particulars); *Am* (*Presseberichter*) to cover; (*amtlich*) to return; (*melden*) to advise; (*unterrichten*) to inform s. o. of s. th.; (*durch Botschaft*) *Am* to message; (*enthüllen*) to reveal, to disclose, to discover; (*verbreiten*) to divulge; (*mitteilen*) to communicate; **~erstatter** *m* (*Presse*) reporter; (*örtlicher*) correspondent; (*Auskunftgeber*) informant; (*Referent*) referee; *radio* commentator; **~erstattung** *f* reporting, making a report; (*Unterrichtung*) information; *Am* (*Presse*) coverage; **~igen** *tr* (*richtigstellen*) to adjust, to amend; (*Rechenfehler*) to rectify; to set right; (*Text*) to emend; (*Schreibfehler*) to correct; (*Irrtum*) to remedy; (*Schulden, Rechnung*) to settle (an account); to pay, to clear, to square; **~igung** *f* (*von Rechenfehlern*) rectification; (*Richtigstellung*) adjustment; (*Verbesserung, Zusatz*) amendment; (*Druckfehler im Buch*) errata; (*Text*) emendation; (*Fehler*) correction; (*Schulden*) settlement; **~~sanzeige** *f* notice of error; **~~sposten** *m com* adjusting entry; **~sjahr** *n* year under report (*od* review); financial year; **~speriode** *f* report-period; **~swoche** *f* week under report (*od* review).

beriechen *irr tr* to sniff at, to nose at.

beriesel|n *tr* to irrigate, to water; (*besprengen*) to spray; **~ung** *f* irrigation; **~~sanlage** *f* irrigation works *pl*; (*Feuerschutz*) sprinkler system; **~~s-kühler** *m* water cooling plant; spray cooler.

beringt *a* covered with rings.

beritten *a* mounted; ~ *machen* to horse.

Berliner|blau *n* Prussian blue; ~ *Pfannkuchen* jelly doughnut.

Berlocke *f* trinket, watch-chain.

Bernstein *m* amber; *schwarzer* ~ jet; **~fang** *m* amber-fishing; **~farbe** *f* amber (-colo(u)r); **~schmuck** *m* amber-ornaments *pl*; **~schnur** *f* string of amber--beads; **~spitze** *f* amber cigar-holder.

bersten *irr itr* to burst, to crack; (*platzen*) to explode, to split; *vor Lachen* ~ to burst with laughing.

berüchtigt *a* notorious, ill-reputed, in bad repute, ill-famed.

berücken *tr* (*verlocken, bezaubern*) to captivate, to fascinate; to charm, to bewitch; (*verleiten*) to inveigle, to induce; *e-e ~de Schönheit* a fascinating beauty.

berücksichtig|en *tr* (*in Betracht ziehen*) to consider, to take into consideration; (*zu seinem Recht kommen lassen*) to regard, to have regard to (*od* for); (*beachten*) to note, to pay attention (to), to mind, to bear in mind; (*einkalkulieren*) to take into account, to allow, to make allowance for; (*Vorzug geben*) to give the preference; *nicht ~~* to take no notice of; **~ung** *f* (*Rücksichtnahme*) regard; consideration; *in ~~, daß* . . . considering that . . .; *mit ~~* considering; *unter ~~* in (*od* with) regard to; with respect to; in consideration of; *unter ~~ der Umstände* under the circumstances; in consideration of the circumstances.

*

Beruf *m* (*innerer*) vocation, call(ing); (*geistige Arbeit*) profession; (*Geschäft*) business; (*Handwerk, Gewerbe*) trade: (*Arbeiter, Angestellte; Beschäftigung, Stelle*) job, occupation; (*Pflichten*) duty; (*Amt*) office, function; (*Wirkungskreis*) sphere; (*Fach*) line; *e-n ~ ergreifen* to enter a profession, to take up (*od* to go in for) a profession; *seinem ~ nachgehen* to attend to o.'s business· *von ~* by profession, by trade; **~en** *irr tr* (*bestellen*) to send for; (*kommen lassen*) to summon; (*Versammlung*) to call; (*Parlament*) to convoke; (*einsetzen, ernennen*) to appoint, to nominate s o.; *sich ~en auf* to refer to s. o., s. th.; (*appellieren*) to appeal to; **~en** *a* (*zuständig*) competent; *~en sein zu* to have a call for; *sich ~en fühlen* to feel called upon (to); **~lich** *a* professional; vocational; *~~e Eignung* qualification; **~sarbeit** *f* professional work; **~sausbildung** *f* professional (*od* vocational) training, professional instruction; **~sbeamter** *m* career civil servant; **~sberatung** *f* vocational guidance; **~~sstelle** *f* vocational guidance (*od* advisory) office; **~seignung** *f* vocational aptitude; **~~s-prüfung** *f* vocational aptitude test; **~sfahrer** *m mot* professional driver; (*sport Radfahrer*) professional (cyclist); **~sgenosse** *m* colleague; **~sgenossenschaft** *f* (*Handwerk*) trade association; (*Einzelhandel*) cooperative association (for retailers); (*Arbeitgeber*) employers' association; (*freie Berufe*) institute of . . .; **~sgliederung** *f* occupational classification; **~sgruppe** *f* trade group; **~skleidung** *f* vocational clothing; overalls *pl*; **~skrankheit** *f* occupation disease; **~skrankenkasse** *f* professional sick fund; **~sleben** *n* professional activity; **~slenkung** *f* vocational guidance; **~smäßig** *a* professional; **~snachwuchslenkung** *f* juvenile vocational guidance; **~sorganisation** *f* trade association; **~spflicht** *f* professional duty; **~sschule** *f* (*Fortbildungsschule*) (day) continuation school; (*Handelsschule*) professional school; (*Gewerbeschule*) vocational school, trade school; (*technische*) technical school; **~ssoldat** *m* professional (soldier); **~ssparte** *f* professional field; **~sspieler** *m* professional, pro; **~sständig** *a* corporate; **~stätig** *a* employed, in occupation; working; **~stätiger** *m* worker, employed person, person engaged in an occupation; **~stätigkeit** *f* professional activity; **~sverband** *m* professional organization; **~sverbrecher** *m* professional criminal; **~svertretung** *f* professional representation, trade union; **~swahl** *f* vocation, choice of a profession.

Berufung *f* (*zu e-m Beruf*) vocation, calling; (*zu e-m Amt*) appointment; (*Einberufung e-s Parlaments etc*) convocation, summoning; (*vor Gericht*) appeal; ~ *einlegen* (*jur*) to appeal (*bei* to, *gegen* against); to lodge an appeal, to make an appeal, to give notice of appeal; *e-r ~ stattgeben* to allow an appeal; *~ verwerfen* to dismiss an appeal; *unter ~ auf* with reference to, referring to; **~sabteilung** *f* appeal division (*od* department); **~sakten** *f pl* appeal papers *pl*; **~sbegründung** *f* arguments and grounds for appeal; confirmation of appeal; **~sbeklagter** *m* appellee, respondent to an appeal, defendant in a court of appeal; **~sfall** *m* precedent; **~sgericht** *n* appellate court, court of appeal; **~~sbarkeit** *f* appellate jurisdiction; **~sinstanz** *f* court of appeal; *zuständig sein als ~~* to have appellate jurisdiction; **~sklage** *f* appeal; **~skläger** *m* appellant, appellor, party appealing, plaintiff in a court of appeal; **~skosten** *pl* costs of (*od* for) appeal; **~srecht** *n* right of appeal; **~sstrafsache** *f* appellate criminal case; **~surteil** *n* sentence of appellate court.

beruh|en *itr* to rest, to be founded (*od* grounded *od* based) on; *auf etw ~~* to depend on; *das ~t auf e-m Irrtum* it is due to (*od* caused by) a mistake; *etw auf sich ~~ lassen* to leave s.th. as it is; to let a matter rest, to let (*od* to leave) a matter alone; **~igen** *tr* to quiet, to soothe, to calm; (*trösten*) to console, to comfort; *sich ~~* to calm (down), to quiet, to set o.'s mind at rest; (*sich fassen*) to compose o. s.; (*Lage etc*) to stabilize; to steady; *sich dabei ~~* to acquiesce in, to comply with, to submit to; *sich ~~chem* to abate; *~~ Sie sich!* take it easy!; **~igung** *f* calming down; (*der Schmerzen*) appeasing; (*Stärkung*) comfort; (*Linderung*) mitigation; (*Stabilisierung*) stabilizing; (*Sicherheit geben*) reassurance, consolation; **~~smittel** *n med* sedative; depressant.

berühmt *a* (*bekannt*) noted, famous; (*gefeiert*) celebrated; (*von Personen*) renowned (*wegen* for); (*hochberühmt*) illustrious; **~heit** *f* (*großer Ruf*) reputation, fame; (*bekannte Person*) famous·person, celebrity; *theat, film* star.

berühr|en *tr* to touch, to finger; to handle; to make contact; to be in contact; (*stark ~~, Schiff auf Grund laufen*) to strike; (*angrenzen*) to border on, to meet; (*nahe angehen*) to concern, to affect; (*erwähnen*) to mention, to allude to; **~ung** *f* touching, touch, contact; *in ~~ kommen* to come in(to) contact with, to get in touch with; *fam* to rub shoulders with; **~~sdauer** *f* time of contact; **~~sebene** *f* tangential plane; **~~sempfindung** *f* perception (*od* sensation) of contact; **~~selektrizität** *f* contact electricity; **~~sfläche** *f* contact surface, area of contact; **~~slinie** *f* tangent; **~~spunkt** *m* point of contact; **~~sreiz** *m* contact stimulus; **~~sschutz** *m* contact safety device; **~~ssicher** *a* (*bei el Geräten*) shockproof.

berußen *tr* to smear with soot, to coat (*od* to cover) with soot, to soot.

besäen *tr* to sow; *fig* to crowd, to stud; to cover; *mit Korn ~* to sow with corn; *mit Sternen besät* (*Himmel*) star-spangled; *mit Bäumen besät* studded with trees.

besag|en *tr* (*inhaltlich angeben*) to say, to purport; (*beweisen*) to prove, to indicate, to attest; (*bedeuten*) to mean, to signify; *das will nichts ~~* that's nothing to speak of; **~t** *a* said, above--mentioned; *~te* (*Person etc*) the same.

besait|en *tr* to string; *zart ~et* sensitive.

Besamung *f* seeding; insemination; propagation.

besänftig|en *tr* to soften (down); (*Leidenschaften*) to assuage; (*mäßigen*) to temper; (*zum Schweigen bringen*) to hush; (*Kummer*) to soothe; (*Zorn*) to mitigate; (*Aufregung*) to allay; (*Unruhe*) to appease, to quiet; *r* to calm down; **~ung** *f* softening; appeasement, appeasing, mitigation.

Besan|mast *m* mizzen-mast; **~segel** *n* mizzen-sail.

Besatz *m* (*Borte*) border; (*Saum*) edge; (*Ausputz, Verbrämung*) trimming; (*Band~*) braid, braiding; (*Spitzen~*) lace; (*Uniformaufschläge*) piping, facings *pl*; *tech* (*Hochofen*) relining; **~artikel** *m* trimmings *pl*; **~streifen** *m* stripe; **~ung** *f* (*e-r Stadt, Garnison*) garrison; (*im Feindesland*) occupying forces *pl*, occupation troops *pl*; (*Schiff, Flugzeug, Panzer*) crew; *fliegende ~~ aero* flight crew, aircrew; **~~samt** *n* occupation office; **~~sarmee** *f* army of occupation; **~~sbehörde** *f* occupying authority; **~~sbereich** *m od n* occupied zone; **~~sdienst** *m* occupational duties *pl*; **~~sheer** *n* army of occupation; **~~shoheit** *f* sovereignty of occupation; **~~skosten** *pl* occupation costs *pl*; *Erhebung von ~~kosten* imposition of occupation costs; **~~smacht** *f* occupying power; **~~smitglied** *n mar, aero* crewman; **~~sstatut** *n* occupation statute; **~~sstreitkräfte** *f pl* forces of occupation, occupying forces *pl*; **~~struppen** *f pl* occupation troops *od* forces *pl*.

besaufen *irr r vulg* to get drunk.

beschädig|en *tr* to damage, to hurt, to injure, to disable; **~t** *a* damaged, injured; (*von Schiffen*) disabled; *~te Ware* spoilt (*od* damaged) goods *pl*; *bomben~t* bomb-damaged; *kriegs~t* war disabled; **~ter** *m* injured person, injured party; **~ung** *f* damage, injury, hurt; (*Havarie von Schiffen*) average.

beschaff|en *tr* (*besorgen*) to procure, to get; (*sich verschaffen*) to obtain; (*erlangen, sichern*) to secure; (*Bedarf decken*) to supply; (*anschaffen*) to provide; (*liefern*) to furnish; *Geld ~~* to find (the) money; **~en** *a* (*geartet*) conditioned, constituted, qualified; *gut* (*schlecht*) *~~* in good (bad) condition; *wie ist es damit ~~?* how does the matter stand? **~~heit** *f* (*Bau*) constitution; (*Eigenart, Zustand*) state, condition; (*Gefüge*) structure; (*Qualität*) quality; (*Art*) character; (*Natur, z. B. des Geländes*) nature; *von guter ~~heit* of a fine quality; *vorzügliche ~~heit* first-rate condition; **~ung** *f* (*Erwerb*) acquisition; (*Besorgung*) procuring, procurement; (*Bedarfsdeckung*) supply, providing; *zur ~~ von* for the supply of; **~~samt** *n* procurement office; **~~skosten** *pl* charges for procurement; **~~sprogramm** *n* procurement program(me); **~~swert** *m* purchase value.

beschäftig|en *tr* (*als Arbeitgeber*) to employ, to give work to ...; (*sich*) to occupy (o. s. *mit* with); *sich ~~ mit* to be engaged in; to work at; *bei jdm ~t sein* to be in the employ of s. o.; **~t** *a* engaged, busy; **~ung** *f* (*allgemein*) occupation, employment; (*Arbeit*) work; (*Geschäft*) business; (*Fach*) line of business; (*Stelle*) job; (*Gewerbe*) trade; (*Beruf*) profession; (*unterhaltende ~~*) entertainment; **~~sart** *f* mode of employment; **~~sbedingungen** *f pl* conditions of employment; **~~sgrad** *m* employment level; degree of activity; **~~slage** *f* labo(u)r market; **~~slos** *a* unemployed; **~~slosigkeit** *f* unemployment; **~~spolitik** *f* employment policy; **~~szwang** *m* compulsory employment.

beschäl|en *tr* (*von Pferden*) to cover, to horse; **~er** *m* stallion.

beschäm|en *tr* to shame, to make ashamed; (*durch Freundlichkeit*) to abash, to embarrass, to confound; **~t** *a* ashamed of; **~ung** *f* humiliation, shame; confusion.

beschatten *tr* to shade, to overshadow; (*unbemerkt verfolgen*) to shadow, *fam* to tail (a suspect).

beschau|en *tr* to look at, to behold; (*prüfen, z. B. Fleisch*) to inspect, to examine; (*durchsuchen*) to search; *fig* to contemplate; **~er** *m* observer; visitor; **~lich** *a* contemplative; **~~keit** *f* contemplativeness; **~ung** *f* contemplation, examination.

Bescheid *m* (*Antwort*) answer, reply; (*Auskunft, Mitteilung*) information, advice; (*gerichtlich*) decision, sentence, decree, judg(e)ment; (*amtlicher*) rescript; (*Anweisung*) instruction, directions *pl*; (*abschlägiger ~*) refusal, negative reply; (*Wissen*) knowledge; *bis auf weiteren ~* till further orders (*od* instructions) *pl*; *~ hinterlassen* to leave word (*bei* with); *~ geben* to send word; *jdm gehörig ~ sagen* to give s. o. a bit of o.'s mind; *~ tun* to drink to the health of; *sie erhielt e-n abschlägigen ~* she was turned down; *wissen Sie darüber ~?* do you know anything about this? *~ wissen* to be acquainted with, to be well informed, to know (how), *Am fam* to be in the know(ing); **~en** *irr tr* (*an e-n Ort kommen lassen*) to call, to appoint; (*vor Gericht zitieren*) to summon; (*benachrichtigen, mitteilen*) to inform; (*unterrichten*) to instruct; (*zuteilen*) to assign, to allot, to apportion s. th. to s. o.; *jdn abschlägig ~~* to refuse s. o., to decline; *sich ~~* (*resignieren*) to resign o. s.; (*zufrieden sein mit*) to be contented with, to acquiesce in; **~en** *a* (*genügsam*) modest; (*Preise*) moderate; (*zurückhaltend*) discreet; (*anspruchslos*) unpretentious, unassuming; **~~heit** *f* (*Genügsamkeit*) modesty; (*Zurückhaltung*) discretion, moderation; (*Anspruchslosigkeit*) unpretentiousness, unassumingness.

bescheinen *irr tr* to light up, to shine upon.

bescheinig|en *tr* to certify, to attest; (*Eingang von Geld quittieren*) to give a receipt for; *es wird hiermit ~t, daß ...* this is to certify that ...; *Ich, Unterzeichneter, ~e hiermit ...* I, the undersigned, do hereby verify ...; *den Empfang e-s Briefes ~~* to acknowledge receipt of a letter; **~er** *m* certifier; **~ung** *f* (*Schreiben*) certificate; (*Bestätigung*) certification; (*Quittung*) receipt, acquittance; (*Bestätigung über Empfangenes*) acknowledg(e)ment; (*Nachweis, Belegschein*) voucher; (*Beglaubigung*) attestation; (*Erklärung*) declaration; (*Vollmacht*) warrant; *~~ ausstellen* to issue a certificate.

besch|eißen *irr tr vulg fig* (*betrügen, übers Ohr hauen*) to cheat; **~issen** *a vulg* (*schmutzig, bedreckt*) soiled, dirty; (*schlecht, unerfreulich*) bad, unsatisfactory; not worth a straw; *er hat mich ~~* he cheated me; **~iß** *m vulg* swindle, fraud.

beschenken *tr* to make a present to, to present (with).

bescher|en *tr* to bestow upon; to give as a Christmas present; (*zumessen*) to mete out to; **~ung** *f* presentation of gifts; *e-e schöne ~~!* a pretty business this! this is a nice mess! *da haben wir die ~~!* there we are! (in a pretty mess); there's the pay-off!

beschick|en *tr* (*Konferenz etc*) to send delegates (*od* deputies) to ...; (*Messe od Märkte*) to forward goods to the markets; to exhibit, to expose; (*Haus*) to put in order; (*Metalle legieren*) to alloy metals; (*Ofen*) to load, to charge, to feed; **~er** *m* (*Aussteller auf Messen*) exhibitor; **~ung** *f* (*e-s Ofens*) loading, charging, feeding, burdening, stocking; *aero, mar* (*bei Kursberechnung*) correction (*od* compensation); radio compass calibration; **~~sanlage** *f tech* charging equipment, feeding installation; **~~smaterial** *n* (*Hochofen*) charge, burden.

beschieß|en *irr tr* to fire upon, to bombard; (*mit Granaten*) to shell; to gun; (*mit Maschinengewehr*) to machine-gun; **~ung** *f* bombardment, shelling, shell fire.

beschiffen *tr* to navigate on.

beschimpf|en *tr* to outrage, to insult, to abuse; to call names; **~ung** *f* insult, abuse, outrage, affront.

beschirm|en *tr* to defend; to protect; to shield, to cover; **~er** *m* protector, defender; **~ung** *f* protection, defence.

beschlafen *irr tr* (*Weib*) to lie with; *fig* (*e-e Sache*) to sleep upon a matter, to take counsel with o.'s pillow.

Beschlag *m* (*tech, Tür etc*) metal-work, mounting, fitting(s *pl*); (*Rückstand*) deposit; (*Schimmel*) mould; (*Feuchtigkeit*) moisture, damp; efflorescence; (*e-s Buches*) clasp; (*e-s Pferdes*) shoe(ing); *jur* seizure, sequestration, attachment; *~ auf etw legen, etw in ~ nehmen* to seize, to impound, to sequester, to levy a distress on, to confiscate; (*Aufmerksamkeit*) to engross; (*Zeit*) to take up; *mit ~ belegen* to arrest; *in ~* under arrest; (*besetzen*) to occupy; *auf ein Schiff ~ legen* to put an embargo on a ship; **~en** *irr tr* to cover with; to fit, to mount; (*Pferd*) to shoe; to calk; *itr* (*anlaufen*) to get tarnished; (*Feuchtigkeit*) to become coated with (*od* to become covered with) moisture; (*Ware*) to sweat; (*von Gläsern*) to fog, to dim; **~en** *a fig* experienced; *gut ~~ sein in* to be well versed in; **~nahme**, **~nehmung** *f* confiscation; (*vorübergehend*) requisition; commandeering; *mar* embargo; *jur* seizure; distraint, attachment; (*Vermögen*) sequestration; *die ~~ aufheben* to derequisition; *der ~~ unterliegen* to be subject to seizure; **~nahmen** *tr jur* to seize, to requisition, to confiscate, to distrain on, to attach; (*requirieren*) to commandeer; **~schmied** *m* blacksmith; **~teile** *n pl* fittings *pl*.

beschleichen *irr tr* to steal in upon (*od* up to); to surprise; (*Wild*) to stalk; *Furcht beschlich mich* fear came over me (*od* seized me).

beschleunig|en *tr* to accelerate, to speed (up), to hasten; to rush; to force; (*durch Vollgasgeben*) *aero* to gun; (*Lieferung, Verkauf*) to expedite; *~t durchführen* to carry out expeditiously; **~er** *m mot* accelerator; **~ung** *f* acceleration; haste, speed, speeding up; **~~sanode** *f* second anode, gun anode; **~~selektrode** *f* accelerator electrode; **~~sfeld** *n* accelerating field; **~~skraft** *f* accelerative force; **~~smesser** *m* accelerometer; **~~smoment** *n* moment of acceleration; **~~spedal** *n mot* accelerator (pedal); **~~spumpe** *f mot* accelerating pump; **~~svermögen** *n mot* acceleration capacity.

beschließ|en *irr tr* (*beendigen*) to end, to finish, to terminate, to conclude, to close; (*sich entscheiden*) to make up o.'s mind; to resolve, to decide, to determine on; (*von Parlamenten*) to vote; (*Antrag*) to carry; *jur* to decree; (*e-r Versammlung*) to take a resolution; *e-e beschlossene Sache* a settled affair; **~er** *m* housekeeper; **~erin** *f* wardrobe-keeper; (lady) housekeeper.

Beschluß *m jur* decision, decree, judg(e)ment; (*Entscheid*) determination; (*e-r Versammlung*) resolution; *Am* result; (*Ende*) close, conclusion; end; *zum ~* finally, in conslusion; *e-n ~ fassen* to resolve; *jur* to take a decision, to decide; (*in e-r Versammlung*) to pass a resolution; to adopt a resolution; **~fähig** *a* to form a quorum; competent to pass a resolution; *~~e Anzahl* (*e-r Versammlung*) a quorum; *nicht ~~ sein* to lack a quorum; **~~keit** *f* quorum; (*Zuständigkeit*) competence; **~fassung** *f* passing of a resolution; coming to a decision.

be|schmieren *tr* to (be)smear, to dirty; (*Brot bestreichen*) to spread on; (*mit Butter*) to butter; (*besudeln*) to scrawl on, to scribble on; **~schmutzen** *tr* (*auch fig*) to soil; to dirty, to foul; to smutch, *Am* to smootch; to sully, to grime; *fig* to blemish.

Beschneid|emaschine *f* (paper) cutting-machine; **~emesser** *n* edging-knife; **~en** *irr tr* to cut, to clip; (*Bücher*) to cut; (*Bäume*) to trim; (*Kind*) to circumcise; (*einschränken*) to curtail, *Am* to curb; (*Verbrauch*) to cut production; (*Preise*) to cut (down);

(*Reben*) to dress; *tech* (*abkanten*) to edge; **~epresse** *f* cutting-press; **~er** *m* (*Buch, Film*) cutter; (*Maschine*) cutting-tool; **~ung** *f* clipping; (*Beschränkung*) reduction, *Am* curb; (*von Kindern*) circumcision.
beschneit *a* snow-covered, snowy.
be|schnüffeln, ~schnuppern *tr* to sniff at; *alles ~~* to put o.'s nose into everything.
beschönig|en *tr* (*schön färben*) to colo(u)r; (*Vergehen, Fehler*) to extenuate, to explain away, to palliate, to excuse; to gloss over; *die Angelegenheit läßt sich nicht ~~* there is no mincing the matter, there is no excuse for the matter; **~end** *a* palliative; **~ung** *f* palliation, excuse, extenuation.
beschottern *tr* (*Straße*) to ballast, to gravel, to metal (a road).
beschränk|en *tr* to limit, to reduce, to restrain, to confine, to restrict, to curtail, *Am* to curb; *sich ~~ auf* to confine o. s. to; **~end** *a* restrictive; **~t** *a* limited, confined; *~t abgabepflichtig* subject to limited taxation; *~te Erbfolge* (*jur*) tail; *~te Geschäftsfähigkeit* limited legal capacity; *~te Haftung* limited liability; *mit ~ter Haftung* limited, *Abk* Ltd.; *in ~ten Verhältnissen leben* to live in straitened circumstances; (*geistig*) *~t* narrow-minded, dull; *~ter Mensch* dullard; **~theit** *f* confinement; limitation; scantiness; narrowness; *fig* dul(l)ness; **~ung** *f* confinement, restriction, limitation; (*Handels~~*) trade barriers *pl*, *Am* trade curb; (*Fabrikations~~*) rationing; *die ~~ aufheben* to lift the ban (on).
beschreib|en *irr tr* to fill with writing; to write upon; *math* (*Kreis etc ~~*) to describe; to draw, to trace; (*Bahn ~~*) *astr* to revolve; (*schildern*) to describe, to depict; **~end** *a* descriptive; **~ung** *f* description, specification; portrayal, characterization; outline; *es geht über alle ~~, es spottet jeder ~~* it beggars all description; *ausführliche ~~* detailed description; *e-r ~~ entsprechen* to answer to a description; *das Landschaftsbild ist über alle ~~ schön* the scenery is beautiful beyond description.
be|schreien *irr tr* (*behexen*) to bewitch; *~~ Sie es nicht!* don't crow over it! **~schreiten** *irr tr* to step over; *den Rechtsweg ~~* to go to law.
beschrift|en *tr* to inscribe; (*etikettieren*) to label; (*mit Titel versehen*) to caption; (*e-e Zeichnung*) to letter a drawing; **~ung** *f* inscription; (*Aufschrift*) lettering; (*e-r Illustration*) caption; (*e-r Münze*) legend.
beschuhen *tr* to shoe, *meist pp* shod.
beschuldig|en *tr* to charge with; to accuse of; to incriminate; **~te(r)** accused; (*Beklagter*) defendant; (*Verbrecher auf der Anklagebank*) prisoner; **~ung** *f* charge, accusation; imputation; *erlogene* (*od falsche*) *~~* trumped-up charge, *Am* frame-up.
beschummeln *tr fam* to bilk; to cheat.
Beschuß *m* (*Prüfung von Schußwaffen*) test firing; proof fire; (*Beschießung*) bombardment; shelling; artillery fire; *unter ~* under artillery fire; **~bild** *n* pattern of proof firing; **~empfindlichkeit** *f* vulnerability to enemy fire; **~ergebnis** *n* firing-test result; **~festigkeit** *f* resistance to gunfire; **~probe** *f* shooting test, bombardment test; **~sicher** *a* bulletproof.
beschütt|en *tr* to throw on, to cover with; (*mit Flüssigkeit*) to pour on; *mit Kies ~~* to gravel; **~ung** *f* gravelling.
beschütz|en *tr* to protect, to shelter; **~er** *m*, **~~in** *f* protector, defender; protectress; **~ung** *f* protection, defence.

*

beschwatzen *tr* to talk s. o. into; *jdn ~* to persuade.
Beschwerde *f* (*Mühe*) pains *pl*, hardship, trouble; (*körperlich*) (bodily) complaints *pl*; (*Alters~n*) infirmities *pl* of age; (*Mißstand*) grievance; unpleasantness; (*Verdruß*) worry; (*Klage*) complaint; (*öffentliche*) remonstrance; (*ständiges Meckern*) *Am sl* gripe, *fam* grouch; *~ erheben, ~ einlegen, ~ führen, ~ vorbringen* to complain (*über* of); *jur* to lodge a complaint (*bei* with); to state a grievance; **~abteilung** *f* appeals department; Board of Appeal; **~begründung** *f* substantiation of complaint; **~buch** *n* complaint-book; **~einrede** *f* rejoinder; **~führer** *m* complainant, complainer; **~führung** *f* statement of grievances; **~gegenstand** *m* matter of complaint; **~gericht** *n* court of appeal; **~grund** *m* grievance; gravamen; **~ordnung** *f* appeal regulation, complaint regulation; **~punkt** *m* grievance, point (*od* subject) of complaint; **~schrift** *f* (written) complaint; remonstrance; petition (for the redress of grievances); appeal papers *pl*, appellatory plaint; **~stelle** *f* complaint section, complaint desk; **~verfahren** *n* procedure for filing a complaint, appeal procedure (*od* action).
beschwer|en *tr* (*belasten*) to charge; to burden; to weight; (*Magen*) to lie heavy on the stomach; (*mit e-r Hypothek ~*) to mortgage; (*belästigen*) to incommode, to molest; *sich ~~ über etw* to complain about; *Am sl* to gripe; *fam* to grouch; **~lich** *a* heavy, hard; troublesome; *jdm ~~ fallen* to importune s. o.; to inconvenience s. o.; to be a burden to s. o.; **~~keit** *f* difficulty; troublesomeness; **~ung** *f* load, loading; burden, burdening; (*Belästigung*) molestation; annoyance, trouble; (*durch Hypothek*) mortgage, encumbrance.
beschwichtig|en *tr* to allay, to quiet; (*beruhigen*) to calm, to appease; (*friedlich stimmen; Hunger, Zorn ~~*) to pacify; (*Streit*) to compose; (*besänftigen*) to soothe; **~ung** *f* allaying.
beschwindeln *tr* (*jdn um etw*) to swindle, to cheat (s.o. out of s.th.); to humbug; (*täuschen*) to hoodwink, to bamboozle; (*betrügen*) *sl* to skin, to fleece.
beschwingt *a* winged, on wings; (*rasch, schnell*) speedy; (*erhebend*) lofty.
beschwipst *a* slightly tipsy; *fam* cock-eyed, fuddled, boozy, groggy, primed.
beschwör|en *irr tr* to swear to; (*Geister*) to raise, to conjure; *jur* to confirm by oath, to take an oath on, to declare on oath; to affirm on oath; to sign an affidavit; *ich bin bereit, meine Aussagen zu ~en* I am prepared to confirm my statements by oath; *jdn etw ~en lassen* to swear s. o. on s. th.; (*bannen*) to exorcize; (*anflehen*) to implore; **~er** *m* exorcist; **~ung** *f* conjuration; exorcism; (*inständiges Bitten*) adjuration, imploring; *jur* confirmation by oath; swearing; **~~sformel** *f* (*Zauberformel*) incantation.
beseel|en *tr* to animate; to inspire; **~ung** *f* animation.
besehen *irr tr* to look at, to view; (*prüfen*) to inspect; *bei Lichte ~* on closer inspection.
beseitig|en *tr* to do away; to set aside; (*Hindernisse*) to remove; (*Streit*) to settle; (*töten*) to kill; *Schwierigkeiten ~~* to do away with, to overcome, to put aside difficulties; *Spannungen ~~* to relieve tensions; to eliminate; (*Störung*) to clear (a fault); *gewaltsam ~~* to subvert; **~ung** *f* removal; elimination, clearing; (*von Streitigkeiten*) settlement.
beseligen *tr* (*glücklich machen*) to make happy; to fill with bliss; *eccl* to beatify, to bless.
Besen *m* broom; *Hand~* hand-brush; *Scheuer~* scrubbing brush; *neue ~ kehren gut* new brooms sweep clean; *fam* (*Dienstmädchen*) skivvy; **~binder** *m* broom-maker; **~reisig** *n* birchen twigs *pl*; **~schrank** *m* broom cabinet; **~stiel** *m* broom-stick.
besessen *a* possessed, demoniac.
be|setzen *tr* (*Kleid*) to trim, to border; (*mit Edelsteinen*) to stud, to set; *mit Diamanten ~setzt* diamond-bestudded; *mil* to occupy; to garrison; (*bemannen*) to man; (*ein Bohrloch ~~*) to tamp (a hole); (*Rollen*) *theat* to cast the parts; (*Amt*) to fill; (*offene Stelle*) to fill up a vacancy; *Stelle e-s Kassiers ist zu ~~* there is a vacancy for a cashier; **~setzt** *a* (*z. B. Straßenbahn*) full up; crowded; *voll ~~* filled (*od* full) to its utmost capacity, *Am* filled (*od* full) to capacity; (*Sitzplatz*) occupied, reserved; *tele* busy, engaged; *Nummer ~~!* number engaged! *Am* line busy! *~~ halten tele* to guard, to hold (the line); *~~es Gebiet mil* occupied territory; **~~zeichen** *n tele* busy (*od* engaged) signal; **~setzung** *f* lacing; *mil* occupation; (*Amts-*) appointment; (*e-r Stelle*) filling (of a post); *mus* complement; *theat* cast; (*Personal~~*) personnel, staff; *sport* nomination, entry; **~~sarmee** *f* army of occupation; **~~szone** *f* zone of occupation.
besichtig|en *tr* to view; (*prüfend*) to examine, to inspect; (*Stadt*) to look around, to see; to survey; to visit; **~ung** *f* view; inspection, visitation; survey; (*von Sehenswürdigkeiten*) sight-seeing; **~~sfahrt** *f* sight-seeing tour; *mil* tour of inspection.
besiedel|n *tr* to settle in, to colonize; to settle; *dicht ~t* densely populated; **~ung** *f* colonization, settlement; **~~sdichtigkeit** *f* density of population.
besiegel|n *tr* to seal; **~ung** *f* decision.
besieg|en *tr* to vanquish, to defeat; to beat; to overcome, to conquer; **~er** *m* conqueror; **~te(r)** *m* defeated foe; **~ung** *f* conquering, conquest.
besingen *irr tr* to sing of; (*preisen*) to celebrate, to praise, to laud.
besinn|en *irr: sich ~~* to remember, to recollect; (*überlegen*) to reflect on s. th., to consider; *sich anders ~~* to change o.'s mind; *sich e-s Besseren ~~* to bethink o. s. better; to think better of; *sich hin u. her ~~* to rack o.'s brains; **~en** *n* reflection, recollection; **~lich** *a* thoughtful; contemplative; **~ung** *f* consideration; (*Vernunft*) reason; (*Erinnerung*) recollection, reflection; (*Bewußtsein*) senses *pl*, consciousness; *die ~~ verlieren* to lose o.'s senses; (*Bewußtsein*) senses *pl*, consciousness; *die ~~ verlieren* to lose o.'s senses; (*Bewußtsein verlieren*) to lose consciousness; *wieder zur ~~ kommen* to recover o.'s senses; **~~slos** *a* senseless, insensible, unconscious; **~~slosigkeit** *f* unconsciousness, insensibility.

Besitz *m* possession; (*Grundvermögen*) property; (*Landbesitz*) (real) estate, realty, real property; (*bewegliche Güter*) personal estate; personality; (*Papiere, Aktien*) holding, holdings *pl*; *rechtmäßiger* (*unrechtmäßiger*) ~ rightful (adverse) possession; *im ~ e-r Sache* in possession of; *im ~ sein von* to be in the possession of; to be possessed of; *~ ergreifen von etw* to take possession of s. th., to take in possession; *in den ~ e-r Sache kommen* (*od gelangen*) to become possessed of s. th., to come into the possession of s. th., to get possession of s. th.; *in ~ nehmen* to take in possession, to possess o.s. of s. th.; *sich in den ~ e-r Sache setzen* to possess o.s. of s. th.; *in anderen ~ übergehen* to change hands; *aus dem ~e vertreiben* to expropriate, to dispossess; *jur* to evict, to oust; (*Briefanfang*) *wir sind im ~e Ihres Schreibens vom* ... we are in receipt of your letter of ...; **~anzeigend** *a gram* possessive; **~ausweis** *m* title-deed; **~dauer** *f* tenure, term; **~en** *irr tr* to possess, to be possessed of; to have; to own; (*innehaben*) to hold; *etw ~~* to be in possession of; *ich ~e* (*fam*) I've got; **~entziehung** *f jur* ejectment; **~entziehungsklage** *f jur* action of ejectment; **~er** *m*, **~erin** *f* possessor, proprietor (proprietress); owner; *unrechtmäßiger ~er* usurper; (*von Wertpapieren etc*) holder; *den ~er wechseln* to change hands, to change owner; **~ergreifung** *f* taking possession of; *jur* seizure, seizin; (*widerrechtlich*) usurpation; (*von Land, unbewohnten Häusern*) squatting; (*Besetzung*) occupation; **~gemeinschaft** *f* joint ownership; **~klage** *f jur* possessory action; **~nahme** *f* taking possession of; occupation; **~posten** *m* assets *pl*; **~recht** *n* tenure; **~stand** *m* possession; *com* assets *pl*; **~steuer** *f* property tax; **~titel** *m* title-deed; **~tum** *n* possession, property; (*Landgut*) estate; **~übertragung** *f* transfer; **~ung** *f* possession, property; *überseeische ~~en* oversea possessions *pl*; **~urkunde** *f* title-deed; **~verteilung** *f* distribution of ownership; **~wechsel** *m* change in ownership; bill receivable **~wert** *m* property-value: **~zeit** *f* term, tenure.

*

besoffen *a vulg* drunk; intoxicated; *fam* tight, boiled, canned, pie-eyed, stewed, fuddled, primed, groggy, spifflicated; *sl* soused, lit, corny, woozy, half-seas-over; **~heit** *f* drunkenness.

besohlen *tr* to sole.

besold|en *tr* to pay, to salary; **~ung** *f* salary, pay; **~~sdienstalter** *n* pay seniority; **~~sordnung** *f* pay regulations *pl*; **~~swesen** *n* pay and allowance administration; **~~szulage** *f* additional pay.

besonder *a* special, particular; (*gesondert*) separate; (*ungewöhnlich*) peculiar; (*hervorragend*) distinctive; (*außergewöhnlich*) exceptional; **~heit** *f* particularity; characteristic; feature; special(i)ty; peculiarity; **~s** *adv* especially; (*getrennt*) separately, apart; (*eigentümlich*) particularly, peculiarly; (*außergewöhnlich*) exceptionally; (*hauptsächlich*) chiefly.

besonnen *a* thoughtful; (*vernünftig, verständig*) sensible; (*zurückhaltend*) discreet; (*wohldurchdacht, überlegt*) considerate; (*vorsichtig*) cautious, prudent; **~heit** *f* thoughtfulness, prudence; circumspection; (*Geistesgegenwart*) presence of mind.

besonnt *a* sunny, sunlit.

besorg|en *tr* (*beschaffen*) to procure; to provide for (*od* s. o. with); to supply with; *jdm etw ~en* to procure s. th. for s. o.; (*organisieren*) to requisition; to scrounge; (*Auftrag*) to attend to; (*tun*) to do; to see to, to get; *~e mir* get me; (*Sorge tragen*) to take care of; to arrange; to manage; (*durchführen*) to execute; *itr* (*Besorgnis hegen*) to apprehend; (*fürchten*) to fear; **~nis** *f* apprehension, fear; *in ~nis geraten* to become alarmed; **~t** *a* anxious, concerned; *~t sein für* to bestow care on; *~t sein um, wegen* to be considerate (*od* apprehensive) of; to be solicitous (about, for, of); *ich bin sehr ~~* I am very worried; **~theit** *f* (*Furcht*) anxiety; (*Unbehagen*) uneasiness; (*Unruhe, Sorge*) concern (*über* about); solicitude (*um* about, for); **~ung** *f* providing; management; care; (*Auftrag*) commission; errand; (*Einkauf*) purchase; *~~en machen* to shop, to go shopping; **~~sgebühren** *f pl* charges *pl*, fees *pl*; commission; **~~szettel** *m* shopping-list.

bespann|en *tr* to put horses to; to harness to; (*Tuch*) to stretch; to span; *aero* (*Tragfläche ~~*) to cover (a wing with fabric); (*Saiteninstrument*) to string (an instrument); **~t** *a* (*mit Pferden*) animal-drawn; horse-drawn; *~~e Kolonne* column of horse-drawn vehicles; **~ung** *f* (pair of) horses; team; (*e-s Saiteninstruments*) stringing; (*Überzug*) covering; (*Stoff~~*) fabric, covering.

be|speien *irr tr* to spit, to vomit on; **~spicken** *tr* to lard; **~spiegeln** *tr* to look at o.s. in a glass; **~spötteln, ~spotten** *tr* to rally, to ridicule.

besprech|en *irr tr* to speak of, to discuss; to talk over; (*Heirat etc*) to arrange; (*Vertragsbedingungen*) to settle; *radio* (*Röhre*) to control; (*Film, Theaterstück*) to criticize; to comment upon; (*Buch*) to review; (*e-e Schallplatte*) to record; (*beschwören*) to conjure; (*verabreden*) to agree upon; *sich ~~* to confer with s. o. about; to put o.'s heads together, *Am* to get together; **~ung** *f* discussion; agreement; review; conference; interview; (*diplomatische*) pourparler; consultation; (*Unterhandlung*) negotiation; (*Beschwörung*) conjuration; (*Kritik*) critique; criticism; *radio* (*Röhre*) voice control; **~~sanlage** *f* sound pickup outfit; **~~sniederschrift** *f* minutes *pl*; **~~sraum** *m* (*Konferenzzimmer*) conference room; *radio* sound studio.

be|sprengen *tr* to (be)sprinkle; (*Straßen*) to water; **~springen** *irr tr* to leap upon; (*Tier*) to cover; **~spritzen** *tr* to sprinkle; (*mit Kot*) to splash; to spatter; (*mit Blut*) to stain with blood; **~spülen** *tr* to wash (against); *mot* (*mit Öl*) to supply with oil; **~spült** *a* watered; wetted.

Bessemer|birne *f* Bessemer converter; **~eisen** *n*, **~stahl** *m* acid Bessemer steel.

besser *a u. adv* better; *desto ~* so much the better; *um so ~* all the better; *etw ~ machen* to better, to improve; *~ sein* to be better; *ich täte ~* I had better; *er konnte nichts B~es tun als* he could not do better than; *sich e-s ~en besinnen* to think better of s. th.; *Wendung zum ~en* a change for the good (*od* the better); *sie ist ~ dran* she is better off; *das Geschäft geht ~* business is improving; *~ werden* to change for the better; *sie hat ~e Tage gesehen* she has seen better days; *Am fam* she is a has-been; **~n** *tr* to better, to improve; to make better; (*aus~~*) to repair; (*Fehler*) to correct; *r* to improve; to get better; to become better; (*sittlich*) to mend; to reform; (*Kranke*) to recover; *das Wetter ~t sich* the weather clears up; **~ung** *f* amelioration; improvement; recovery; (*von Kursen etc*) advance, rise, gain; *gute ~~!* I hope you get well soon! I wish you a speedy recovery! good health to you! *auf dem Weg der ~~ sein* to be on the way to recovery; **~~sanstalt** *f* (*Zwangserziehungsheim*) house of correction, reformatory, remand home, Borstal, *Am* reform, school, workhouse; **~~sfähig** *a* mendable; improvable; **~wisser** *m* prig; *Am fam* smart aleck; **~wisserei** *f* priggishness.

best *a, adv* best, superior; *~en Dank!* many thanks! *aufs ~e* in the best manner possible; *der erste ~e* the first comer; *im ~en Falle* at best; *zu Ihrem ~en* in your interest, for your sake; *nach ~em Wissen* for the best of my knowledge; *in den ~en Jahren* in the prime of life; *auf dem ~en Wege* in a fair way to; *~ens* in the best way; *empfehlen Sie mich ~ens* remember me most kindly to; *ich täte am ~en zu gehen* I had best go; *nicht zum ~en* rather bad; *zum ~en reden* to intercede; *zum ~en geben* to spend; to relate (a story); *zum ~en haben* to gammon; to hoax s. o.; to make a fool of s. o.; to tease, to make fun of; to rag; *fam* to play yo-yo with s. o., to pull s. o.'s leg; *er tat sein Bestes* he did his best; *zum Besten des Volkes* for the benefit of the people.

Bestallung *f* appointment; investiture; **~sbrief** *m*, **~surkunde** *f* commission, diploma, patent.

Bestand *m* duration, continuance, permanence; (*Beharren*) firmness, consistence; (*Zustand*) stability; durability; (*Stärke e-r Einheit*) strength; (*Reserve*) reserve, holding; (*Existenz*) existence; (*eiserner ~*) *mil* iron ration; (*Vorrat*) stock; supply; store; (*greifbarer*) stock on hand; (*Saldo*) balance; (*Warenbestand in der Bilanz*) inventory; (*Forst~*) stand; stock of trees; (*Kassen~*) cash-balance; (*Rest~*) rest, remainder; *~ haben* to continue, to last; **~saufnahme** *f* stock-taking; **~sbewertung** *f* valuation of stocks; **~sbuch** *n* inventory book; **~sliste** *f* record; inventory; **~snachweisung** *f* stock inventory (*od* report); list of stores on charge; **~teil** *m* element, ingredient; component; constituent; (*Einzelteil*) part; *fremder ~~* foreign matter (*od* substance); *mineralische ~~e* mineral matter; *sich in seine ~~e auflösen* to disintegrate; **~sverzeichnis** *n* inventory.

beständig *a* (*unveränderlich, standhaft*) constant; (*ununterbrochen*) continual; (*fortdauernd, stetig*) continuous; (*dauernd, zeitlich*) perpetual; (*stetig*) stable; (*von Personen*) steady; (*Wetter*) settled; (*Farbe*) fast; (*wasser~*) water-proof; (*feuer~*) fire-proof; (*von Baustoffen*) refractory; (*hitze~*) heat-resistant; (*rost~*) rust-resisting, non-corrodible; (*von Stahl*) stainless; **~keit** *f* continuance, duration, constancy; persistence; invariability; continuity; permanence; steadiness; *tech* stability, resistance.

bestärk|en *tr* to fortify, to support; to confirm, to strengthen; **~ung** *f* strengthening, confirmation.

bestätig|en *tr* (*im Amt; Gerücht*) to confirm; (*bekräftigen, erhärten*) to corroberate; (*anerkennen, zugeben, eingestehen*) (*Aussagen*) to verify; (*amtlich*) to attest, to authorize; (*Vertrag*) to ratify, to sanction; (*Empfang*) to acknowledge receipt (of); (*ein Urteil* ~~) to uphold a sentence; (*eidlich*) to declare on oath, to confirm by oath; (*rechtsgültig machen*) to validate; *r* to be confirmed; to prove (true); ~**t** *a* confirmed; verified; *es wird hiermit ~t* this is to certify that; *~ter Abschuß aero sl* confirmed; *~ter Scheck* marked cheque, cheque with bank endorsement, *Am* certified check; ~**ung** *f* confirmation; ratification; sanction; verification; substantiation; corroboration; statement; *~~ beibringen* to produce a statement; (*schriftlich*) certificate; (*~~ e-s Testaments*) probate of a will; *zur ~~ geeignet* confirmable; ~~**sschreiben** *n* letter of confirmation; ~~**surteil** *n jur* confirmatory decision; ~~**svermerk** *m* notice of confirmation.

bestatt|en *tr* to bury, to inter; ~**ung** *f* burial, funeral, interment; ~~**skommando** *n mil* burial detail.

be|stauben *itr* to become (*od* to get) dusty; ~**stäuben** *tr* to dust; to powder; (*von Blüten*) to fructify; to pollinate.

bestech|en *irr tr* to bribe, to corrupt; *fam* to tip; *sich ~~ lassen* to take bribes; *~endes Wesen* engaging manners *pl*; ~**lich** *a* bribable, venal, corruptible; corrupt; ~**lichkeit** *f* venality; ~**ung** *f* corruption; bribery, *Am fam* graft; ~~**sgeld** *n* bribe, *Am sl* slush-fund; ~~**sversuch** *m* attempt at bribery.

Besteck *n med* case of instruments; (*chirurgisches* ~) trousse; (*die Geräte selbst*) set of instruments; (*Eß*~) knife, fork and spoon; cutlery, *Am* silverware; *mar* ship's reckoning, place-reckoning; (*gegißtes* ~) dead reckoning; ~**en** *tr* to stick with, to garnish; (*mit Pflanzen*) to plant.

bestehen *irr itr* to be, to exist; to last; *~ auf* to insist on; *~ aus* to consist of, to be composed of; *~ in* to consist in; *tr* to undergo; (*aushalten*) to resist, to oppose; *ein Examen ~* to pass, *nicht ~* to fail; *e-e Probe ~* to stand a test; (*Abenteuer*) to encounter; *~ n* existence; insistence (on); passing; *seit ~* since its foundation; ~**d** *a* existent; subsisting; *die ~den Gesetze* the established laws; *zu Recht ~d* legal.

bestehlen *irr tr* to rob, to steal from.

besteig|en *irr tr* (*Berg*) to climb, to ascend; (*Pferd*) to mount; (*Thron*) to ascend; (*Schiff*) to (go on) board a ship; *aero* (*Flugzeug*) to enplane; ~**ung** *f* ascent; (*Thron*) accession.

Bestell|bezirk *m* (*Post*) district of delivery; (*Postbote*) round; ~**en** *tr* (*Waren etc*) to order, to give a commission; (*Zeitung*) to subscribe to; (*zu e-m Amt ernennen*) to appoint; (*Plätze etc*) to book, to reserve; *ein Zimmer im Hotel X. ~~* to book a room at the hotel X., *Am* to make reservations at the hotel X., (*schriftlich*) to write for reservations; (*Feld*) to till, to cultivate; (*Briefe zustellen*) to deliver; (*Botengänge*) to do (errands); (*jdm Grüße od Botschaft~~*) to send; to tell, to let know; *jdn zu sich ~~* to send for s. o., to order s o. to come; *sein Haus ~~* to set o.'s house in order; *bestellt sein* to have an appointment; *schlecht* (*übel*) *bestellt sein* to be in bad condition; *es ist schlecht um sie bestellt* she is in a bad way; ~**er** *m* (*Kunde*) customer, client; committer, orderer; (*Käufer*) buyer; (*Überbringer e-s Briefes etc*) deliverer; ~**gang** *m* delivery, errand; ~**geld** *n* (*Post*) fee for postage; ~**liste** *f* want list; ~**nummer** *f* reference number; requisition number; ~**schein** *m* order form; (*bei Lebensmittelkarten*) counterfoil; ~**ung** *f* (*Auftrag*) order; commission; *auf, nach ~~* to order; *~~ neu aufgeben* to renew an order; (*Zeitschrift*) subscription; (*Abrede*) arrangement, engagement; *fam* date; (*Feld*) cultivation; (*Briefe*) delivery; (*Botschaft*) message; (*Ernennung*) appointment; ~~**sabteilung** *f* purchasing department; ~~**surkunde** *f* certificate of appointment; ~**vordruck** *m* order form (*od* sheet); ~**zeit** *f* (*Feldbestellung*) sowing time; ~**zettel** *m* order-form; (*Bibliotheksausleihe*) call slip.

besten|falls *adv* at best; ~**s** *adv* in the best manner, as well as possible; (*Börse*) at best, at the best price; *danke ~~* thank you very much; *ich empfehle mich Ihnen ~~* my best compliments; *er läßt Sie ~~ grüßen* he sends his best regards.

besternt *a* starry; (*Orden*) decorated (with orders).

besteuer|bar *a* taxable, assessable; ~**n** *tr* to impose duties on; to tax; to rate; to assess; ~**ter** *m* tax-payer; ~**ung** *f* taxation, assessment; ~**ungsgrenze** *f* tax immunity limit.

*

besti|alisch *a* bestial, beastly; brutal; ~**e** *f* beast, brute.

bestimm|bar *a* definable, determinable, ascertainable; ~**en** *tr chem* to test for; (*von Gesetzen*) to provide; (*bezeichnen*) to designate; (*zuweisen*) to assign to; (*feststellen*) to ascertain, to determine, to modify; (*entscheiden*) to decide; (*festlegen*) to fix, to set; (*ernennen*) to appoint; (*sagen*) to say; (*ausbedingen*) to stipulate; (*kennzeichnen*) to earmark; (*abschätzen*) to evaluate, to estimate; (*berechnen*) to calculate, to compute; *zu, für etw ~~* to intend, to destine; (*vorschreiben*) to fix, to appoint; (*befehlen*) to settle, to decree; (*bewegen*) to induce s. o. to do s. th., to engage in; *über etw ~~* to dispose of; ~**end** *a* determinative; ~**t** *a* decided, fixed, appointed; distinct, strict; (*fest*) firm; (*unbedingt*) peremptory; (*schicksalsmäßig*) destined; *mar, aero* bound (for); *gram* definite; (*adv*) *ganz ~t!* definite! most decidedly! certainly! *Am* sure! you bet! *~~ wissen* to be positive, to know for sure; ~**theit** *f* decision; determination; certainty; (*Genauigkeit*) precision, exactitude; *mit ~~* positively, for certain; *Am* sure; ~**ung** *f* determination; statement; appointment, disposition; (*amtlich*) regulation, ordinance; *jur* provision; (*Berufung*) vocation; (*Schicksal*) destination, destiny; (*Begriff*) definition; (*nähere ~~en*) particulars *pl*, details *pl*, specifications *pl*; (*e-s Vertrags*) stipulation; (*e-r Krankheit*) diagnosis; *chem* analysis; ~~**sflughafen** *m aero* airport of destination; ~~**sfunkstelle** *f radio* station of destination; ~~**sgleichung** *f* defining equation; definitive equation; ~~**sgröße** *f* defining quantity; ~~**shafen** *m* port of destination; ~~**sland** *n* country of destination; ~~**smethode** *f* method of determination, method of analysis; ~~**sort** *m* destination; ~~**stabelle** *f tech* table, key, schedule; ~~**szweck** *m* designation.

bestirnt *a* starry.

bestmöglich *adv* best possible.

bestoßen *irr tr* to damage by knocking; *tech* to rough-plane.

bestraf|en *tr* to punish, to sentence; to chastise; (*streng*) to castigate; ~**ung** *f* punishment, penalty; reprimand.

bestrahl|en *tr* to beam on, to shine on; to irradiate; to treat with rays; ~**ung** *f* irradiation; *med* ray treatment; exposure to solar radiation, radiation; ~~**slampe** *f* radiation lamp; ~~**szeit** *f* time of exposure.

bestreb|en *r* to take pains, to endeavour; to exert o.s.; ~**en** *n* (*Richtung*) tendency, trend; ~**ung** *f* endeavour, attempt, exertion; aspiration.

bestreichen *irr tr* to spread over, to smear; *mit Butter ~* to (spread) butter; (*mit Artillerie, Fernrohr*) to sweep, to rake.

bestreiten *irr tr* to dispute, to contest, to deny; *die Unkosten ~* to bear (*od* to cover *od* to defray) expenses; *ein Gespräch ~~* to do all the talking; *Bedürfnisse ~~* to supply the means.

bestreuen *tr* to strew; (*mit Mehl*) to dredge, to powder; (*mit Sand*) to sand; (*mit Kiesel*) to gravel.

bestricken *tr* to entangle; *fig* to captivate, to fascinate, to charm, to ensnare; ~**d** *a* charming.

bestück|en *tr* to arm (*od* to furnish) with guns; ~**ung** *f* armament (of a ship); ordnance, guns *pl*.

bestürm|en *tr* to attack, to assail; (*belästigen*) to importune; *mit Bitten ~~* to implore; *die Banken wurden ~t* there was a run on the banks; ~**ung** *f* assault; molestation.

bestürz|en *tr* to perplex, to surprise, to disconcert; ~**t** *a* disconcerted, confounded at; dismayed; puzzled, upset; ~**ung** *f* consternation, confusion, dismay, surprise, alarm.

Besuch *m* visit, call; (*Person*) visitor, company; (*e-s Ortes*) frequentation; (*Anwesenheit*) attendance; *~ haben* to have visitors; *auf ~ kommen* to come to visit; *auf ~ sein* to be for a visit; *e-n ~ machen* to call on, to pay a visit; (*kurzen ~*) to drop in; *er hat ~* he is not alone; ~**en** *tr* to visit, to go (*od* to come) to see; (*Schule*) to attend; ~**er** *m* visitor, caller; (*Gast*) guest; (*Kunde*) customer; (*regelmäßiger*) frequenter; (*Zuhörerschaft*) audience; (*Kino*) picture-goer; *Am* moviegoer; ~**erliste** *f* visiting list, *Am* calling list; ~**skarte** *f* visiting card, calling card; ~**stag** *m* at home day; ~**sstunden** *f pl* visiting hours *pl*, at home; ~**szeit** *f* calling; ~**szimmer** *n* drawing-room, *Am* parlor.

besudeln *tr* to soil, to foul, to dirty; *fig* to contaminate.

betagt *a* aged, elderly; well advanced in years.

betakel|n *tr* to rig, to fit with tackling; ~**ung** *f* rigging.

betast|en *tr* to finger, to touch; ~**ung** *f* feeling, touching, contact; *med* palpation.

betätig|en *tr* (*in Tätigkeit setzen*) to practise, to set in motion; (*Hebel*) to operate; (*dartun, z. B. Eifer*) to manifest, to prove; *sich ~~ bei* to take an active part in; ~**ung** *f* practice, activity; practical proof; (*Teilnahme*) participation; (*e-r Maschine*) manipulation, operation; control; ~~**sknopf** *m* control knob; ~~**sschalter** *m el* trip switch; ~~**svorrichtung** *f* control mechanism.

betäub|en *tr* (*durch Lärm*) to stun, to deafen; (*Gliedmaßen*) to benumb; (*Sinne*) to stupefy; to narcotize; (*abstumpfen*) *fig* to deaden; *med auch* to an(a)esthetize; ~**end** *a* stupefying, narcotic; an(a)esthetic; (*Lärm*) deafening; **~ung** *f* deafening; stupefaction; an(a)esthetization; (*Zustand*) state of insensibility, stupor; (*Starrheit*) torpor; (*Erstarrung*) numbness; (*Narkose*) narcosis; (*örtlich*) local an(a)esthesia; **~ungsmittel** *n* narcotic, an(a)esthetic.

betaut *a* dewy.

Bete *f* beetroot.

beteilig|en *tr* to give a share (in), to make s. o. a partner; *sich ~~* to take part in, to participate in; (*aktiv*) to take an active hand in; **~t** *a* interested (in); *die ~ten pl* the parties concerned; **~ung** *f* participation; share; interest (in); (*Teilhaberschaft*) partnership; (*Zuhörerschaft*) attendance; (*Unterstützung*) support; **~~szahl** *f* quota.

bet|en *tr, itr* to pray, to say o.'s prayers; *vor u. nach Tische ~~* to say grace; *den Rosenkranz ~~* to tell o.'s beads; **~er** *m* worshipper; **~glocke** *f* prayer-bell; **~stuhl** *m* praying-chair; **~tag** *m* day of prayer (*od* thanksgiving).

beteuer|n *tr* to asseverate, to swear; (*behaupten*) to aver; (*feierlich versichern*) to protest; (*verfechten*) to assert; **~ung** *f* protestation; assertion.

betitel|n *tr* to entitle, to name; *r* to be called; **~ung** *f* entitling; title.

Beton *m* concrete; *Eisen~* reinforced concrete, ferro-concrete; *armierter ~* reinforced concrete; *gestampfter ~* rammed concrete; **~bahn** *f* concrete strip; **~bau** *m* concrete building (*od* construction); **~bauwerk** *n* concrete structure; **~bettung** *f* concrete base (*od* foundation *od* bed); **~block** *m* concrete block; **~bombe** *f* concrete bomb; **~brücke** *f* concrete bridge; **~bunker** *m* concrete bunker (*od* pillbox); **~decke** *f* concrete cover; **~fußboden** *m* concrete floor; **~gewölbe** *n* concrete arch; **~ieren** *tr* to (reinforce with) concrete; **~mischmaschine** *f* concrete mixer; **~platte** *f* concrete slab; **~rohr** *n* concrete pipe; **~schicht** *f* layer of concrete; **~sperre** *f* concrete obstacle; **~straße** *f* concrete road; **~unterstand** *m* concrete dugout, concrete shelter; **~werk** *n mil* concrete work (*od* fortification).

beton|en *tr* to accentuate; to stress, to lay stress on; (*nachdrücklich*) to emphasize; **~ung** *f* accentuation, stress; emphasis.

betör|en *tr* to infatuate; (*täuschen*) to delude; *sich von etw ~~ lassen* to be deluded by; **~ung** *f* infatuation, delusion; befooling.

Betracht *m* consideration, regard; *in ~ kommen* to come into question; *in ~ ziehen* to take into consideration; *etw außer ~ lassen* to set aside; *nicht in ~ kommen* to be out of the question; **~en** *tr* to look at; (*ansehen als*) to regard, to consider; (*prüfen*) to examine; (*nachdenken*) to contemplate, to reflect upon; **~er** *m* onlooker, spectator, **~ung** *f* view; consideration; meditation; reflection.

beträchtlich *a* considerable, important; substantial; **~keit** *f* considerableness, importance.

Betrag *m* amount, value; sum, total; *im ~ von* to the amount of, amounting to; *~ erhalten* payment received; **~en** *irr tr* to amount, to come to; (*sich belaufen auf*) to run up to; (*im ganzen*) to total; (*Zeit*) to take; *wieviel beträgt meine Rechnung?* how much is my bill?; *r* to behave (o. s.); **~en** *n* behavio(u)r, conduct,

be|trauen *tr* to entrust s. o. with; **~trauern** *tr* to mourn for, to deplore; **~träufeln** *tr* to sprinkle, to drop upon.

Betreff *m*: *in ~* with regard to, as to; (*im Briefkopf, gleich ~s*) concerning:, subject:, re:; **~en** *irr tr* to befall, to fall upon; (*erwischen*) to surprise, to catch; *auf frischer Tat ~~* to take in the very act; (*angehen*) to concern, to relate to; to pertain to; *was das betrifft* as to that; *an alle, die es betrifft* to whom it may concern; *das betrifft nur mich* that is my business; *was mich betrifft* as for me, concerning me; **~end** *a u. prp* concerning; concerned, in question; respective; *der ~ende Brief* the letter referred to; *der ~ende (zuständige) Beamte* the official concerned; *die ~ende (vorliegende) Sache* the matter in hand (*od* under consideration); *die (der) ~ende (Person)* the person under consideration; *die ~ende Summe* the sum in question.

betreib|en *irr tr* (*Studien*) to pursue, to prosecute; (*Geschäft*) to manage, to carry on a business; to run a business; (*e-e Angelegenheit*) to push forward, to follow up, to urge on; (*auf etw dringen*) to hasten; *auf ~en von* on (*od* at) the instigation of; **~en** *n*, **~ung** *f* (*e-s Berufs*) exercise, carrying on; management; (*e-r Tätigkeit*) pursuit, prosecution.

betreten *irr tr* to tread (up)on; to enter; *a* (*Weg*) beaten, frequented; *fig* embarrassed, puzzled; *~ n*: *~ verboten!* no entrance! no admittance! private road! do not walk on the grass! keep off!

betreu|en *tr* to attend to; to care for; to look after, to take care of; (*beaufsichtigen*) to supervise, to oversee; **~ung** *f* welfare, care of; maintenance; **~ungsstelle** *f* welfare centre.

Betrieb *m* (*Fabrikanlage*) works *pl*, mill, plant, factory; (*Werkstatt*) workshop; (*öffentlicher ~*) public utility; (*Geschäft*) business, undertaking, concern, establishment, firm; (*Eisenbahn*) railway (*Am* railroad) service; (*Gewerbe*) trade; (*Leitung, Führung*) management, administration, running, operation, working; (*Wartung e-r Maschine*) attendance, service; (*~ e-r Maschine*) operation, working, running; driving; (*Herstellungsgang*) manufacture; (*Verkehr*) traffic; *Hoch~* rush time; *im (od in) ~* at work, going, in operation, working; *in vollem ~* in full action; in full swing; *in ~ setzen* to put in(to) operation; to set running, to start; to set to work; to operate; (*Eisenbahnlinie*) to open; *außer ~ sein* to be out of order; to be closed down; *hier ist immer ~* things are always humming; *im Büro war viel ~* we were very busy at the office; *den ~ einstellen* to close, to shut down; *den ~ wiederaufnehmen* to resume activity; to reopen; **~sabteilung** *f* production department; **~sam** *a* active; (*fleißig*) industrious; **~samkeit** *f* activity; industry; **~sanlage** *f* industrial plant; **~sanweisung** *f* operating instruction; **~sausstattung** *f* plant equipment; **~sdauer** *f* (*Arbeitszeit*) working time, working hours *pl*; (*Lebensdauer*) working life; (*e-r Maschine*) service life; **~sdirektor** *m* manager, managing director; work superintendent; **~seinrichtung** *f* plant; **~seinstellung** *f* closing down, shutdown; **~sfähig** *a* in working (*od* running) condition; **~sfähigkeit** *f* working order; **~sfertig** *a* ready for operation (*od* service); **~sführer** *m* general manager, managing director, boss, works manager; **~sführung** *f* plant management; **~sjahr** *n* working year; financial year; **~singenieur** *m* operating (*od* managing *od* manufacturing *od* production) engineer; **~skapital** *n* working capital, stock in trade; **~skosten** *pl* working expenses *pl*, operating expenses *pl* (*od* costs *pl*); **~skrankenkasse** *f* works sickness insurance fund, firm's private health insurance; **~sleiter** *m* (works) manager; **~sleitung** *f* management; **~smaterial** *n* working-stock; (*rollendes ~~ der Bahn*) rolling-stock; **~smittel** *n pl* working stock; operational reserves *pl*; **~sordnung** *f* plant regulations *pl*; **~spersonal** *n* staff; (*Bedienungspersonal*) maintenance personnel; **~srat** *m* factory (*od* workers') council; shop committee; **~ssicher** *a* safe to operate; reliable; fool-proof; dependable; **~~heit** *f* reliability in service; **~sspannung** *f* working voltage; **~sstockung** *f* disturbance of service; **~sstoff** *m mot* (*Treibstoff*) fuel; **~sstörung** *f* stoppage, break-down, shutdown; hitch; interruption of work; **~stechnisch** *a* technical; **~sverhältnisse** *n pl* plant (*od* service) conditions *pl*; **~swirtschaft** *f* industrial economics, industrial administration; **~szeit** *f* working-period; **~szweig** *m* department.

betrinken *irr r* to get drunk.

betroffen *a* affected, struck with; confounded; taken aback, perplexed; **~heit** *f* perplexity, surprise.

betrüb|en *tr* to trouble, to grieve; to afflict; to depress; **~end** *a* grieving; **~nis** *f* affliction, sadness; grief; **~t** *a* afflicted, sad; *~t* (*über*) sorry (for), to be sad on account of s. th.; *ein ~tes Gesicht* a gloomy countenance.

Betrug *m* cheat, fraud, imposture; (*Schwindel*) swindle; (*Täuschung*) deceit, deception; trickery.

betrüg|en *irr tr* to deceive, to cheat; to defraud; to trick (out of); *er ist der Betrogene* he is the dupe; **~er** *m*, **~erin** *f* cheat, swindler, impostor, *fam* sharp(er); rogue; **~erei** *f* fraud, deceit; **~erisch** *a* deceitful, fraudulent; *in ~~er Absicht* with intent to defraud; *~~er Bankerott* fraudulent bankruptcy.

betrunken *a* drunk, intoxicated, tipsy; *in ~em Zustand ein Kraftfahrzeug fahren* driving while under the influence of drink; **~er** *m* drunk (*od* intoxicated *od* tipsy) man; drunkard, soaker, tippler, toper; **~heit** *f* drunkenness.

Bett *n* (*auch Fluß~*) bed; (*Kinder~*) cot; (*Kranken~*) sick-bed; *ein ~ aufschlagen* to put up a bedstead; *am ~* at the bedside; *zu ~ bringen* to put to bed; *das ~ machen* to make the bed; *das ~ überziehen* to put sheets on the bed; *Ober~, Unter~ (in e-r Kabine od im Schlafwagen)* upper berth, lower berth; *zu ~ gehen* to go to bed; *das ~ hüten* to stay in bed; to be confined to bed; **~bezug** *m* bed-linen; **~decke** *f* bed-cover; (*Deckbett*) coverlet; counter-pane; (*wollene*) blanket, *Am* bed-spread; (*gesteppte*) quilt; (*leichte*) bedspread; **~en** *itr* to make a bed; *tr* to put to bed; to give s. o. a bed; *r* to make o.'s bed, to go to bed; *wie man sich bettet, so schläft man* do well and have well; *sie hat sich warm gebettet* she has feathered her nest; **~flasche** *f* (rubber) hot-water bottle; (*Bauch~~*) stomach-warmer; *Am* hot-water bag; **~fuß** *m* foot of the bed; **~genosse** *m*, **~genossin** *f* bedfellow; **~himmel** *m* canopy, tester; **~kissen** *n* pillow; **~lade** *f* bedstead; **~lägerig** *a* bedridden; confined to bed, *Am* bedfast; **~laken** *n* sheet; **~nässen** *n med* enuresis; **~nässer** *m* bed wetter; **~pfosten** *m* bed-post; **~ruhe** *f* bed-

-filling; **~schüssel** *f* bed-pan; **~statt** *f* bed; **~stelle** *f* bedstead; **~(t)uch** *n* sheet; **~überzug** *m* pillow-case, bed-tick; **~ung** *f mil* bedding, (gun-)platform; mounting, base, support; **~vorlage** *f*, **~vorleger** *m* bedside rug; **~wanze** *f* bed-bug; **~wäsche** *f* bed-linen; **~zeug** *n* bed-clothes *pl*, bedding.

Bettel *m* begging, beggary; *fig* (*Plunder*) trash, rubbish; **~arm** *a* wholly destitute, very poor; **~armut** *f* beggarliness, beggary; **~brief** *m* begging-letter; **~bruder** *m* mendicant (friar); professional beggar; **~ei** *f* begging; mendicancy, mendicity; **~haft** *a* beggarly; **~junge** *m* beggar-boy; **~leute** *pl* beggars *pl*; **~mann** *m* beggar; **~mönch** *m* mendicant friar; **~n** *itr* to beg, *Am fam* to panhandle; *um Geld ~n* to beg for money; *~n gehen* to go a-begging; **~n** *n* begging; *sich aufs ~n verlegen* to resort to begging; **~orden** *m* order of mendicant friars; **~sack** *m* beggar's bag; **~stab** *m* beggar's staff; *an den ~~ bringen* to reduce to beggary; *an den ~~ kommen* to become utterly poor (*od* ruined); **~volk** *n* gang of beggars; **~weib** *n* beggar woman; **~wesen** *n* mendicity, beggardom.

Bettler *m*, *~in f* beggar, mendicant; *Am* solicitor; *fam* panhandler; (*Landstreicher*) tramp; *zum ~ machen* to beggar; **~gesindel** *n* beggarly crew.

Beug|e *f sport* bend, bending; *Knie~e* knee-bending; *Rücken~e* back-bend; *Rumpf~e* body-bending; **~en** *tr* to bend, to bow; (*demütigen*) to humiliate, to humble; (*Licht*) to diffract; *gram* to inflect; *das Recht ~en* to bend the law; *r* to stoop, to bow down; to submit to; *gebeugt a* (*vom Unglück*) crushed, dejected; **~er** *m anat* flexor; **~ung** *f* bending, bend, bow; flexion; (*Licht*) diffraction, divergence; (*Verdrehung des Rechts etc*) warping; (*Schleife*) curve; *gram* (*Deklination*) declension, inflexion (*od* inflection).

Beul|e *f* (*Schwellung*) swelling, bump, boil, boss; *med* tumo(u)r; (*Einbeulung an Blech etc*) dent; (*Frost~e*) chilblain; **~enpest** *f* bubonic plague.

beunruhig|en *tr* to disturb, to alarm; to upset, to worry; to harass; **~t** *a* alarmed; **~ung** *f* disquietude, alarm; agitation; trouble, disturbance; uneasiness.

beurkund|en *tr* to verify, to authenticate; to attest, to certify; *unter Eid ~en* to testify on oath; **~et** *a* recorded, registered; **~ung** *f* authentication, verification, certification.

beurlaub|en *tr* to give leave (of absence); *mil auch* to furlough; *r* to take leave of; **~t** *a* (absent) on leave; **~tenstand** *m* reserve status; *Offizier des ~~es* officer commissioned for the duration; **~te(r)** *m* soldier on furlough; **~ung** *f* granting leave; furlough.

beurteil|en *tr* to judge; (*Kunstwerk*) to criticize, to censure; (*Buch*) to review; **~er** *m* judge, critic, reviewer; **~ung** *f* judg(e)ment, censure, review; valuation, estimation; estimate; **~ungskraft** *f*, **~ungsvermögen** *n* judg(e)ment, discernment, critical faculty.

Beute *f* booty, spoil, loot; (*von Tieren u. fig*) prey; (*Opfer*) victim; (*Schiff*) prize; *~ machen* to gain booty; *auf ~ ausgehen* to go out in search of plunder, to go marauding; **~gierig**, **~lustig** *a* eager for plunder, eager for prey; **~gut** *n* captured enemy material; war looty (*od* booty); **~park** *m mil* salvage dump for captured matériel; **~sammelstelle** *f* collecting point for captured matériel; **~zug** *m* raid, plundering expedition.

Beutel *m* bag; (*Geld~*) purse; (*Mehl~*) bolter; (*Tabak~*) tobacco-pouch; *med* sac, pouch; cyst; **~n** *tr* to bolt, to shake; **~ratte** *f* opossum; **~schneider** *m* cutpurse; **~schneiderei** *f* picking pockets; pilfering; swindling; **~tier** *n* marsupial.

Beutler *m* purse-maker, glover.

bevölker|n *tr* to people, to populate; **~t** *a* populated; (*volkreich*) populous; *dicht ~t* densely (*od* thickly) populated; *schwach* (*od dünn*) *~t* sparsely populated; **~ung** *f* (*Bewohner e-s Staates, Stadt etc*) population; (*Einwohner*) inhabitants *pl*; (*zivile*) civilians *pl*; (*die große Masse*) populace; **~~sabnahme** *f* decrease of population; **~~saufbau** *m* structure of the population; **~~saustausch** *m* exchange of population; **~~sbewegung** *f* movement of population; **~~sdichte** *f* density of population; **~~sstand** *m* state of population; **~~sstatistik** *f* demography; population statistics *pl mit sing*; (*Zählung u. Klassifizierung*) census; **~~süberschuß** *m* surplus population; **~~sverschiebung** *f* movement of population; displacement of population; **~~szunahme** *f* increase of population.

bevollmächtig|en *tr* to authorize, (*ermächtigen*) to empower (*zu* to); to invest s. o. with full powers to act; to give s. o. full power to; *jur* to give power of attorney to; (*Gesandter*) to accredit; **~t** *a* authorized; *dazu sind Sie nicht ~t* you are not authorized to do that; (*befugt*) entitled; (*beauftragt*) commissioned; *jur* holding power of attorney; *~ter Gesandter* (*parl*) plenipotentiary; **~te(r)** *m* (*Anwalt*) attorney; (*Mandatar*) mandatory; (*Stellvertreter*) proxy; deputy; (*Beauftragter, Kommissionär*) commissioner; *com* authorized agent, authorized representative; (*bei Konkursverfahren*) trustee, assignee; (*Konkursverwalter*) trustee (*od* assignee) in bankruptcy; (*Gesandter*) plenipotentiary; **~ung** *f* authorization; (*Mandat, Vertretungsauftrag*) mandate; (*Ermächtigung, Befugnis*) warrant, (*Prozeßvollmacht*) warrant of attorney; *jur* (*Generalvollmacht*) power(s) of attorney; (*Auftrag, Instruktion*) commission; *durch ~~* by proxy; (*jur Urkunde*) by power of attorney.

bevor *conj* before, *poet* (*ehe*) ere; *~ nicht* not until; *~ er kam* before he came, prior to his coming; **~munden** *tr* to act as guardian, to hold s. o. in tutelage; to put under the care of a guardian; (*auch fig*) to tutor, to patronize; **~mundete(r)** *m* ward; **~mundung** *f* guardianship; tutelage; **~rechten** *tr* to grant privileges; to give a prior right to, to give priority to; **~rechtigt** *a* privileged, preferential; *~~er Gläubiger* preferential creditor, *Am* preferred creditor; *~~e Forderungen* privileged claims *pl*, preferential (*od* preferred) claims *pl*; **~rechtigung** *f* privilege, monopoly; concession; prerogative; **~schussen** *tr* to advance money on, to lend money on, to grant an advance; **~schussung** *f* advance; **~stehen** *irr itr* to impend over, to lie ahead; to be at hand, to be near, to be approaching; (*unmittelbar drohend*) to be imminent; (*in der Zukunft*) to be in store for; *wer weiß, was ihr noch ~steht* who knows what is still in store for her; *es steht ihr ein Unglück bevor* a misfortune awaits her; **~stehend** *a* approaching, impending; (*unmittelbar*) imminent; *die ~stehende Gefahr* the imminent danger; *der ~stehende Winter* the approaching winter; *die ~stehende Woche* the ensuing (*od* next) week; *die ~stehende Zeit* the time to come; **~teilen** = *übervorteilen*; **~worten** *tr* to preface; **~zugen** *tr* to prefer; (*begünstigen*) to favo(u)r, to show favo(u)ritism; to give preference; (*bevorrechten*) to privilege; **~zugt** *pp u. a* favo(u)red; privileged; (*den Vorzug haben vor jdm*) to be favo(u)red above another; *ausländische Bewerber werden ~zugt* foreign applicants will be given preference; **~zugung** *f* preference (given to s. o.); favo(u)r (shown to s. o.); (*Günstlingswirtschaft*) favo(u)ritism.

bewach|en *tr* to watch (over), to guard; **~ung** *f* watch, guard, custody; (*überwachen im geheimen*) to shadow, to tail; **~ungsfahrzeug** *n* (*auf See*) escort, escort vessel, patrol vessel.

bewachsen *irr itr* to overgrow (with).

bewaffn|en *tr* to arm; to provide with arms, to equip with arms, to furnish with weapons; *fig* to fortify; *sich ~en* to arm o. s. (*mit* with); **~et** *pp u. a* armed; (*ausgerüstet*) equipped, outfitted; *bis an die Zähne ~et* armed to the teeth; *~ete Aufklärung* offensive patrol; *~ete Macht* armed force; *~ete Neutralität* armed neutrality; *mit ~eter Hand* by force of arms, arms in hand; **~ung** *f* (*e-r militärischen Einheit*) arming; (*e-s Kriegsschiffes*) armament; (*die Waffen pl*) arms *pl*; (*Ausrüstung*) equipment; (*e-s Magnets*) armature.

Bewahr|anstalt *f* (*für Kinder*) nursery, kindergarten; **~en** *tr* to keep; *ein Geheimnis ~en* to keep a secret; (*Früchte, Fleisch konservieren*) to preserve; *jdn vor etw ~en* to guard against, to protect (*od* save) from; *Gott ~e!* God forbid! not at all! O dear no! **~er** *m* keeper; **~heiten** *tr* to verify; *sich ~~* to come (*od* prove) true, to turn out to be true; **~heitung** *f* verification; (*jur*) *zur ~~ dessen* in faith whereof; **~ung** *f* (*Behalten*) keeping; (*Bewachung*) custody; (*Schutz*) preservation.

bewähr|en *tr* to prove; (*bestätigen*) to confirm; *sich ~en* to prove true; (*von Personen*) to stand the test; *die Nachricht ~te sich* the news turned out to be true; **~t** *a* tried; approved, experienced; **~ung** *f* proof, trial, test; **~ungsfrist** *f jur* (period of) probation; *~~ gewähren* to grant probation; *~~ bekommen* to be placed on probation.

bewaldet *a* woody, wooded, *Am* timbered.

bewältigen *tr* to overcome; to master; (*Arbeit*) to accomplish, to finish.

bewandert *a* skilled, experienced, versed (*in* in); acquainted with; (*in Sprachen*) proficient in; *gut ~ sein* to be thoroughly conversant (*in* with); to be well up (*in* in); (*literarisch*) well-read.

Bewandtnis *f* condition, state, circumstances *pl*; *damit hat es folgende ~* the state of affairs is as follows; the case is this; *es hat damit e-e ganz andere ~* the case is quite different; *damit hat es e-e eigene ~* it is a peculiar matter, thereby hangs a tale, there is a special reason for that.

bewässer|n *tr* to water, to irrigate; **~ung** *f* watering, irrigation; **~~sanlage** *f* irrigating plant; **~~sprojekt** *n* irrigation project.

beweg|en *(irr) tr* to move; *(aufregen)* to agitate, to stir, to stimulate; *(rühren)* to touch, to excite; *jdn zu etw ~en (veranlassen)* to induce s. o. to do s. th.; to prevail, to influence; to prompt; *(überreden)* to persuade; *was bewog sie dazu?* what made her do it? *bewogen von* actuated by; moved by; *können Sie ihn dazu ~en? (fam)* can you get him to do it? *sich ~en* to stir, to move; to get in motion; *sich weiter ~en* to move on; *sich ~en (von Preisen etc)* to range; *(an der frischen Luft)* to take exercise in the open air; *sich auf und ab ~en (Kolben)* to work up and down; *sich im Kreise od um etw ~en* to revolve round s. th.; **~grund** *m* motive, inducement; **~lich** *a* movable; mobile; *(aktiv)* active, lively; *(veränderlich)* changeable; *(gewandt)* versatile; *(Zunge)* voluble; *(rührend)* moving, stirring; *(bebend)* brisk, agile, sprightly; *(tragbar)* portable; *~~e Funkstelle* mobile radio station; *~~es Geschütz* movable gun; *~~e Habe* movables *pl*; *~~es Mikrophon* portable *(od* following) microphone; *~~es Ziel* moving target; **~lichkeit** *f* mobility, agility; flexibility; *(der Zunge)* volubility; *fam* the gift of the gab; *(Gewandtheit)* versatility; *(Lebhaftigkeit)* sprightliness; *(Behendigkeit)* nimbleness; **~t** *a (Leben)* eventful; *(aufregend)* exciting, troubled; *(gerührt)* touched; *~te Augenblicke* exciting moments; *~te See* rough *(od* heavy *od* agitated) sea; *~te Zeiten* troubled times; stirring times; **~theit** *f (Rührung)* agitation; **~ung** *f* movement, stir; *phys* (com)motion; *(seelisch)* agitation, emotion; *(körperliche)* exercise; *politische ~~* political movement; *in ~~ bringen* to set in motion; to stir up; *in ~~ sein* to be on the move; *fam* to be on the go; *alle Hebel in ~~ setzen* to set every spring in motion; *Himmel u. Hölle in ~~ setzen* to move heaven and earth; *sich ~~ machen* to walk; to take exercise; **~~sachse** *f tech* axis of rotation; **~~sfähigkeit** *f* mobility; **~~sfreiheit** *f* liberty to move; liberty of action; *(Ellenbogenfreiheit)* elbow-room; **~~skraft** *f* motive power; impetus; **~~skrieg** *m* mobile warfare; war of movement; **~~slehre** *f* mechanics *pl mit sing*; **~~slos** *a* motionless; **~~slosigkeit** *f* immobility; **~~s-spiele** *n pl sport* outdoor games *pl*; **~~sunfähig** *a* unable to move; *~~sunfähig schießen (Panzer etc)* to put out of action by gun-fire; **~~svorgang** *m* motional action, phenomenon of motion; **~~svorrichtung** *f* working gear, operating mechanism; **~~szustand** *m* state of motion.

bewehr|en *tr* to arm; *tech* to reinforce, to strengthen, to armo(u)r, to sheath; **~t** *a* armed.

beweibt *a* married, wedded.

beweihräuchern *tr* to cense; *fig (maßlos u. unterwürfig loben)* to extol, to adulate, to flatter, to butter up.

beweinen *tr* to weep for, to deplore; *(betrauern)* to mourn; *(laut beklagen)* to lament, to bewail; to weep over the loss of s. o. *(od* s. th.); **~swert** deplorable, lamentable; *(bemitleidenswert)* pitiable.

Beweis *m* proof; argument; *jur* evidence; *(Beweisstück)* exhibit; *math* demonstration; *(Zeichen)* sign, token; *als ~ dienen* to serve as evidence; *als ~ zulassen* to admit in evidence; *~ erheben (jur)* to hear evidence; *den ~ erbringen* to furnish proof; *den ~ führen* to prove; *(demonstrieren)* to demonstrate; to adduce proof; *den ~ liefern* to produce evidence; to prove; *zum ~ von* in proof of, in support of; *als ~ vorlegen* to tender in evidence; *ausreichender, eindeutiger, schlüssiger, strenger, zwingender ~* sufficient, positive, conclusive, rigorous, cogent evidence; *~e pl* evidence; *sie wurde wegen Mangels an ~en freigesprochen* she was acquitted for lack of evidence; **~auflage** *f jur* injunction to produce proof; **~aufnahme** *f* hearing of witnesses *od* evidence; argumentation; **~bar** provable, demonstrable; **~barkeit** *f* demonstrability: **~beschluß** *m jur* order of the court to produce evidence; interlocutory decision concerning the scope of the evidence; **~en** *irr tr* to prove; *jur* to evidence; *(demonstrieren)* to demonstrate; *(bezeigen)* to show; to manifest; *(feststellen)* to attest, to establish; to give evidence, to furnish evidence; **~ergebnis** *n* result of evidence; **~erhebung** *f* evidence; **~führer** *m* demonstrator; **~führung** *f* reasoning; line of argument; argumentation; demonstration; probation; **~grund** *m* argument, reason; **~kraft** *f* demonstrative power; conclusiveness; *keine ~~ haben* to be inconclusive; **~kräftig** *a* conclusive; convincing; **~last** *f* burden of proof; onus of proof; **~material** *n* evidence, evidenciary material; summary of evidence; *erdrückendes ~~* damning evidence; **~mittel** *n* proof, evidence; voucher; **~satz** *m* theorem; **~schluß** *m* syllogism; **~schrift** *f* exhibit; **~stück** *n* exhibit; (piece of) evidence; (legal) document; (legal) instrument; voucher; **~urkunde** *f* evidence, voucher; evidential value; **~würdigung** *f* weighing of proofs.

bewenden *imp: es dabei ~ lassen* to let s. th. be; *es bei jds Entscheidung ~ lassen* to acquiesce in s. o.'s decision; *~ n: dabei hat es sein ~* there the matter must end *(od* rest); *es hat damit sein eigenes ~* thereby hangs a tale.

bewerb|en *irr r: sich um etw ~~* to apply for, to seek; *sich um e-e Stelle ~~* to apply for a place; *(um den Preis)* to compete for a prize; *(um ein Mädchen)* to court, to woo; *(um Stimmen)* to canvass; **~er** *m* applicant, candidate, *Am* solicitor; *sport* entrant; competitor *(um* for); *(Freier)* suitor, wooer; **~ung** *f* solicitation, application; candidature; *(Wettbewerb)* competition; *(um ein Mädchen)* wooing, courtship; *seine ~ung einreichen* to file *(od* to send in, to present) o.'s application; **~~s-bogen** *m* application blank; **~~frist** *f* tender period; **~~sschreiben** *n* letter of application.

bewerfen *irr tr* to throw upon *(od* at); to pelt; *(mit Bomben)* to bomb, to drop bombs on; *e-e Mauer ~* to rough-cast, to plaster.

bewerkstellig|en *tr* to effect, to bring about, to accomplish; to manage; **~ung** *f* effecting, achievement, accomplishment, execution, performance.

bewert|en *tr* to value, to evaluate, to estimate, to assess; to assign a value to, to weigh(t); to rate *(auf* at); *zu hoch ~en* to overrate; *zu niedrig ~en* to underrate; *sich ~en* to amount to; **~ung** *f* valuation, estimation, assessment; qualification, rating; *(bei Pferderennen)* classification; **~~sgrundlage** *f* basis of valuation; **~~smaßstab** *m* rate of assessment; **~~srichtlinien** *f pl* *(Steuerveranlagung)* assessment principles *pl.*

*

bewillig|en *tr (gewähren)* to grant, to allow; *parl (durch Abstimmung)* to vote; *(zugestehen, einräumen)* to concede; *(einwilligen, zustimmen, genehmigen)* to consent to; to agree to; to approve; **~ung** *f* concession, allowance, grant, consent, permission; licence; **~~sausschuß** *m parl* appropriation committee.

bewillkommn|en *tr* to welcome; **~ung** *f* welcome, kind reception.

bewirken *tr* to effect, to occasion, to cause, to bring about.

bewirt|en *tr* to entertain; to treat; **~schaften** *tr (Gut)* to manage, to administer; *(Acker)* to cultivate; *(Mangelware)* to ration, to control; *~schaftete Güter* rationed goods; **~schaftung** *f* management; (government) control (of commodities), rationing; regulation of scarce supplies; *in ~~ nehmen* to put on the ration list; *von der ~~ freigeben* to take off the ration list; **~~sstelle** *f* control office; **~ung** *f* entertainment, reception, treat; *(im Gasthaus)* attendance; food.

bewitzeln *tr* to ridicule, to chaff; to joke at.

bewohn|bar *a* (in)habitable; **~en** *tr (Stadt)* to inhabit; *(Haus)* to occupy; *(allgemein)* to live in; **~er** *m*, **~erin** *f* inhabitant, resident, *Am* citizen; dweller; inmate; *(von Zimmern)* occupier, lodger.

bewölk|en *tr* to cloud over; *r* to cloud, to become cloudy *(od* overcast); **~t** *a* cloudy; clouded, overcast (with clouds); **~ung** *f* cloudiness, clouding, cloud; **~~sgrad** *m* degree *(od* extent *od* magnitude) of cloudiness; **~~shöhe** *f* ceiling, top limit of visibility; **~~skarte** *f* cloud map.

Bewunder|er *m*, **~~in** *f* admirer; **~n** *tr* to admire *(wegen* for); **~nswürdig** *a* admirable; **~ung** *f* admiration.

Bewurf *m* plastering; coarse *(od* rough) plaster, rough cast.

bewußt *a* aware; known; *es war e-e ~e Lüge* it was a deliberate lie; *sie war sich dessen nicht ~* she didn't realize that; *ich bin mir keiner Schuld ~* I have a clear conscience, I am not conscious of any guilt; *die ~e Sache* the matter in question; *sich e-r Sache ~ sein* to be conscious of; *adv (absichtlich)* deliberately, knowingly; *in ~em und gewolltem Zusammenwirken (jur)* willingly and intentionally in complicity with; **~los** *a* unconscious, insensible; senseless; *~~ werden* to swoon, to faint away; **~losigkeit** *f* unconsciousness; **~sein** *n* consciousness; *in dem ~~* conscious of; *(Überzeugung, Wissen)* knowledge, perception; *das ~~ verlieren* to lose consciousness, to faint.

bezahl|en *tr* to pay; *(Rechnung)* to settle; *(Schulden)* to clear off; *(Auslagen)* to defray; *im voraus ~en* to pay in advance; *bar ~en* to pay cash; *(Wechsel)* to hono(u)r; *nicht ~en* to leave unpaid; **~er** *m* payer, defrayer; **~t** *a* paid, hired; *gut ~~e Arbeit* good paying job; *sich ~~ machen* to pay (for itself), to be lucrative; *das macht sich ~~* that pays well; **~ung** *f* payment, settlement; *(Lohn)* pay; *gegen ~~ von* on payment of; *bei ~~* upon payment.

bezähm|en *tr* to tame; *(zügeln, unterwerfen)* to subdue; to control, to check, to restrain; *sich ~en* to restrain *(od* control) o.s.; **~ung** *f* taming.

bezauber|n *tr* to bewitch; *fig* to charm, to enchant, to fascinate; **~nd** *a* charming, fascinating; enchanting; (*von Frauen*) *Am* glamorous; **~t** *a* enchanted with; **~ung** *f* fascination; spell.

bezechen *r* to get drunk.

bezeichn|en *tr* to mark; (*Waren*) to label, to tag; (*Kennzeichen angeben*) to denote; to designate; to indicate; (*benennen*) to name, to term, to call; **~end** *a* expressive, significant; characteristic (of); **~ung** *f* (*das Bezeichnen*) marking, tagging; (*das Zeichen*) mark, sign, brand; (*Beschreibung*) designation, indication, name, term; nomenclature; notation; (*Symbol*) symbol.

bezeig|en *tr* to show, to express; to manifest; **~ung** *f* show, manifestation.

bezeug|en *tr* to testify, to bear witness to; to attest; (*schriftlich*) to certify; **~ung** *f* testimony, attestation.

bezichtigen *tr* to accuse of, to charge with; *sich selbst* ~ to incriminate o. s., to charge o. s.

bezieh|en *irr tr* (*überziehen*) to cover with; (*Bett*) to put on clean sheets; to change (the bed-linen); (*Ort besetzen*) to occupy, to take possession of; (*Quartier*) to take up quarters; (*Winterquartier*) to get into winter quarters; (*Rationen*) to draw; *mil* (*Stellung*) to occupy; (*Haus*) to move into; (*Schule*) to enter; (*Posten*) to occupy; (*Wache*) to mount guard; (*Instrument*) to string; (*Waren*) to get, to obtain, to procure, to import; (*Zeitung*) to take in; (*Gehalt*) to draw; (*Lohn*) to receive; *ein Lager* ~~ to go into a camp; *r* (*Himmel*) to become cloudy; *sich* ~~ *auf* to refer to, to relate to; to appeal to; *kann ich mich auf ihn* ~~? may I use his name as a reference? *sich* ~*end auf* relative to; **~er** *m* (*Zeitung*) subscriber; (*Kunde*) customer; (*bei Einfuhr*) importer; (*Wechsel*) drawer; (*Aktien*) allottee; **~ung** *f fig* reference (to), connexion, relation; regard, respect; relationship; (*wechselseitige* ~~*en*) correlation; *gespannte* ~~*en* strained relations; *in* ~~ *setzen* to relate to; *in* ~~ *stehen* to be in relation with; *in wechselseitige* ~~ *setzen* to correlate; (*Beziehungen zwischen Arbeitgeber u. Arbeitnehmer*) *Am* industrial relations; *in* ~~ *auf* with regard to; *in jeder* ~~ in every respect; *in dieser* ~~ in this connexion; **~~sweise** *adv* respectively; relatively; as the case may be; or, or else; or rather; **~~swort** *n gram* antecedent.

beziffern *tr* to number, to mark with figures; *sich* ~ to amount to.

Bezirk *m* district; (*Wahl~*) borough; (*e-s Beamten*) circuit; (*Zone, Gebiet*) zone, area; (*eingefriedeter* ~, *Am Grafschafts~*) precinct; (*Grenze*) confines *pl*; **~sausgabe** *f* (*Presse*) local edition; **~sbombe** *f aero mil* large aerial demolition bomb; **~sgericht** *n* district-court; **~skommando** *n* district-command; **~snotariat** *n* district notary; **~spolizei** *f* district constabulary; **~sschulamt** *n* district school inspection; **~ssender** *m radio* regional broadcasting station, regional transmitter; **~sweise** *a* by district.

Bezug *m* covering; cover; case; (*Kissen~*) slip; (*Saiten~*) set of strings; (*Zeitung*) subscription; (*Waren*) purchase, supply; ~ *haben*, ~ *nehmen auf* to relate to; to refer (*auf* to); *es wird* ~ *genommen auf Ihr Schreiben vom* ... reference is made to your letter of ...; ~ *wie oben* subject as above; *in* ~ *auf ihn* (*am Satzanfang*) as for (*od* to) him; *in* ~ *auf* regarding, with regard to; **~nahme** *f* reference; *mit* ~~ *auf* in relation to; *unter* ~~ *auf* referring to; respecting; **~sanweisung** *f* order (for delivery); **~sbedingungen** *f pl* terms of delivery; **~sdauer** *f* duration; **~sgenossenschaft** *f* cooperative purchasing association; **~squelle** *f* source (of supply); **~sschein** *m* supply ticket, order for delivery; (*für Mangelware*) ration ticket, ration card, (ration) coupon; voucher; (individual buying) permit; purchase permit; **~sscheinpflichtig** *a* rationed; **~sspesen** *pl* charges of delivery; petty charges *pl.*

Bezüg|e *m pl* fees *pl*; salary; (*Einkommen*) income; **~lich** *a* relative (to), respecting; *auf etw* ~~ bearing on; referring to.

bezwecken *tr* (*mit Reißnägeln*) to set with pegs; (*beabsichtigen*) to aim at, to intend.

bezweifeln *tr* to doubt (of), to question, to call in question; to query; *e-e Nachricht* ~ to make a question of news; *e-e Aussage* ~ to query a statement; *es ist nicht zu* ~ it is beyond doubt, it is unquestionable.

bezwing|en *irr tr* to master, to conquer; to overcome, to subdue; to reduce; *sich* ~~ to control o. s.; **~er** *m* subduer; **~ung** *f* conquest, subduing.

Bibel *f* Bible; Scripture; **~auslegung** *f* exegesis; **~fest** *a* well-read in the Scriptures; **~gesellschaft** *f* Bible-society; **~spruch** *m* text; scriptural sentence; **~stelle** *f* biblical passage; (*im Gottesdienst*) text, lesson; **~stunde** *f* Bible class, biblical instruction; **~übersetzung** *f* translation of the Bible.

Biber *m* beaver, castor; **~geil** *n* castoreum; **~haar** *n* hair of the beaver; **~hut** *m* castor; **~pelz** *m* beaver (fur); **~schwanz** *m* (*Flachziegel*) flat roofing tile, *Am* plain tile.

Biblio|graph *m* bibliographer; **~graphie** *f* bibliography; **~thek** *f* library; (*öffentliche*) public library; *sich e-e* ~~ *einrichten* to fit up a library; **~thekar** *m* librarian.

biblisch *a* biblical, scriptural; ~*e Geschichte f* sacred history.

Bickbeere *f* bilberry, *Am* huckleberry.

bieder *a* honest, hono(u)rable, loyal, upright; commonplace; **~keit** *f* straightforwardness, loyalty, probity; honesty, respectability; **~mann** *m* hono(u)rable (*od* honest) man, good fellow.

bieg|en *irr tr* to bend; to bow; (*ablenken, umbiegen*) to deflect; (*krümmen, sich wölben*) to camber; (*Licht, el, beugen*) to diffract; (*Strahlen, Wellen, brechen, fig ablenken*) to refract; (*beugen, abbiegen*) to flex; (*Holz*) to wrap, to cast; *gram* to decline, to inflect; (*krümmen, bes. Straße*) to curve; *r* to bend; *um die Ecke* ~~ to turn (*od* round) the corner; *es muß* ~~ *od brechen* they must either yield or succumb; *auf B~~ od Brechen* by hook or by crook; **~sam** *a* pliable, pliant; supple; flexible; *fig* yielding; **~samkeit** *f* pliancy, flexibility; suppleness; **~ung** *f* bending; bent; *tech* bend, deflection; (*Fluß*) winding, (*U-förmig*) *Am* oxbow; (*Weg*) turning, turn, bend; (*Kurve*) curve; (*Beugung, geol Flexur*) flexure; (*Krümmung, Bogenlinie*) curvature; (*Durchbiegung*) sag, sagging; set; **~~sbeanspruchung** *f tech* bending (*od* flexural) stress; **~~sfähig** *a* flexible, pliable, ductile; **~~sfestigkeit** *f* bending strength; tensile strength; **~~svermögen** *n* pliability, flexibility.

Biene *f* bee.

Bienen|fleiß *m* assiduity; **~haus** *n* bee-house, apiary; **~königin** *f* queen-bee; **~korb** *m* beehive; **~orchis** *f bot* bee-orchis; **~schwarm** *m* swarm of bees; **~specht** *m orn* bee-eater; **~stock** *m* beehive; **~vater** *m* bee-master; bee-keeper; hive-owner; **~volk** *n* bee-colony; **~wabe** *f* honeycomb; **~wachs** *n* beeswax; **~weisel** *m* queen-bee; **~zelle** *f* cell (in a beehive); **~zucht** *f* bee-keeping, bee-farming, apiculture; **~züchter** *m* (*Imker*) bee-keeper, bee-master, apiarist.

Bier *n* beer; (*helles*) pale beer, *engl* ale; (*dunkles*) dark beer, *engl* porter, stout; (*Flaschen~*) bottled beer; (*Lager~*) lager (beer); (*in Dosen*) canned beer; (~ *vom Faß*) draught ale; **~bankpolitiker** *m* pothouse politician; **~bankstratege** *m* armchair strategist; **~brauer** *m* brewer; **~~ei** *f* brewery; **~druckapparat** *m* beer-engine; beer-pump; **~eifer** *m* excessive zeal; **~faß** *n* beer-barrel; beer-cask; **~filz** *m* mat; **~garten** *m* popular restaurant; **~glas** *n* beer-glass; **~hahn** *m* tap; **~hefe** *f* yeast; barm; **~kanne** *f* beer-can, ale-pot; pewter; tankard; **~keller** *m* beer-cellar; **~krug** *m* beer-mug, beer-jug; *Am* growler; *Am* stein; **~reise** *f fam* pub-crawl; **~schank** *m* licence for beer; **~schenke, ~stube, ~wirtschaft** *f* public house, *Abk* pub; *Am* (beer) saloon; **~schlegel** *m* beer-mallet, *Am* bung-starter; **~steuer** *f* beer duty; **~wagen** *m* brewer's dray; **~zapfer** *m* tapster.

Biese *f* (*Uniform~*) piping; (*Schnur*) lace, border, cord.

Biest *n* beast; brute.

biet|en *irr, itr tr* to offer, to present; *com* to bid; *mehr* ~~ *als ein anderer* to outbid another person; *jdm die Hand* ~~ to offer o.'s hand to; *Trotz* ~~ to defy; *jdm e-e Gelegenheit* ~~ to afford an opportunity; *es bot sich mir Gelegenheit zu* ... I had a chance to ...; *jdm e-n guten Morgen* ~~ to wish s. o. good morning; *jdm den Rücken* ~~ to turn o.'s back on s. o.; *jdm die Spitze* ~~ to make head against s. o.; to cope with s. o.; *Schach* ~~ to give check to, to check; *Willkommen* ~~ to offer (*Am* to extend) a welcome; *das läßt er sich nicht* ~~ he won't put up with it; he won't stand that; **~ender, ~er** *m* bidder.

Bigam|ie *f* bigamy; **~ist** *m* bigamist.

bigott *a* bigoted; **~erie** *f* bigotry.

Bikini *m* Bikini (suit), two-piece bathing suit.

Bilanz *f* balance, balance sheet, *Am* financial statement, statement of conditions; *die* ~ *ziehen* to strike the balance; *e-e* ~ *frisieren* to fake a balance sheet; *e-e* ~ *aufstellen* to make up (*od* to prepare) a balance sheet; *e-e aktive* (*passive*) ~ a credit (an adverse) balance; **~attest** *n* certificate; **~aufstellung** *f* preparation of the balance sheet; **~auszug** *m* summary of assets and liabilities; **~bogen** *m* balance sheet; **~buch** *n* balance ledger, balance book, statement book; **~ieren** *tr* to balance (accounts); **~prüfer** *m* chartered accountant auditor; **~rechnung** *f* balance account; **~verschleierung** *f* faking of balance (*od* of accounts).

Bild *n* (*allg*) picture; (*Abbild, Ebenbild*) image; (*gemalt*) painting; (*e-s Menschen*) portrait; likeness; (*Stich*) engraving; (*Muster*) pattern; (*in Büchern*) illustration; (*Münz~*) effigy; (*Götzen~*) idol; (*Schilderung*) description; (*Vorstellung*) idea; (~ *auf der Spielkarte*) court-card; (*Redefigur*) metaphor; (*Licht~*) photo; (*Fernseh~*) video; (*Sinn~*) symbol, emblem; (*bildliche Darstellung*) representation; (*Anblick*) sight; (*Gleichnis*) simile; (*Symbol, Vorbild*) figure; (*graphisches ~*) diagram; *hochzeiliges ~ tele* high-definition image (*od* picture); *verschwommenes ~ tele* blurred image; *hartes ~* contrasty picture; *weiches ~* uncontrasty (*od* soft) picture; *lebendes ~* tableau; (*bewegliches ~*) moving (*od* shifting) image (*od* picture); (*stehendes ~*) still picture; *sie ist nicht im ~e* she is not in the know; *ich bin im ~* I see; I understand; *sich ein ~ machen* to picture s. th. to o. s.; *er muß sich erst ein klareres ~ machen* he has to get a clearer picture of it at first; *jetzt bot sich ein anderes ~* the scene changed; *er wurde im ~ verbrannt* he was burnt in effigy; **~abtaster** *m tele* television scanning device, televisor; **~abtastrohr** *n tele* iconoscope, image pickup tube; **~abtastung** *f tele* scanning, analyzing (of the picture), picture scan; **~aufbau** *m tele* picture synthesis; **~aufklärer** *m aero* photo-reconnaissance plane; **~aufklärung** *f aero* photographic reconnaissance; **~aufnahmeröhre** *f* pick-up tube; iconoscope, orthicon; television transmitting tube; **~auswertung** *f mil* interpretation of photographs; **~band** *n* film strip; **~berichter** *m* photo (*od* film) reporter, photo journalist; news photographer, news cameraman; **~detektor** *m* video detector; **~diagramm** *n* pictograph; **~ebene** *f phot* focal plane; **~empfänger** *m* video receiver (*siehe Fernsehempfänger*); **~feld** *n phot* field of vision; **~fenster** *n* picture gate; **~fernschreiber** *m* panoramic teletype; range display writer; **~fernübertragung** *f* picture transmission; **~fläche** *f* picture-sheet, perspective plane; *tele* picture area; *auf der ~~ erscheinen* to come in sight, to appear on the scene; **~flieger** *m* aerial photographer; **~flug** *m* photographic flight; **~folge** *f* time interval between successive photographs; **~format** *n phot* size of print; *tele* size of image, aspect ratio; **~frequenz** *f tele* vision (*od* image *od* picture) frequency, *Am* video frequency; **~funk** *m* wireless (*od* radio) picture transmission; picture telegraphy; television (*siehe Fernsehen*); (*Zeitungsfunk etc*) facsimile broadcast(ing); **~gießer** *m* bronze-founder; **~hauer(in)** sculptor; **~hauerei** *f* sculptor's art; sculpture; **~helligkeit** *f* (*des Fernsehbildes*) brightness of the image; **~hübsch** *a* extremely pretty; **~kanal** *m tele* television channel, *Am* video channel; **~karte** *f* photographic map; relief map; **~kartierung** *f* mapping from photographs; **~lich** *a* figurative, metaphorical; *~~e Darstellung* pictorial representation; **~linie** *f* focal line; *tele* image line; **~mäßig** *a phot* pictorial; **~maßstab** *m* scale (of image, picture *od* photograph); **~meldung** *f mil* photographic report; **~messer** *m phot* view meter; **~meßwesen** *n* photogrammetry; **~modulation** *f tele* image modulation; **~~sfrequenz** *f* picture frequency, *Am* video frequency; **~nachleuchten** *n tele* phosphorescence of picture; **~ner** *m* creator, sculptor; (*Licht~*) pictorial photographer; **~nis** *n* portrait, image; (*auf Münzen*) effigy; **~punkt** *m* spot; picture (*od* scanning) element; video frequency; **~~abtaster** *m tele* analyzer, scanning device; video switch; **~~zahl** *f tele* number of image (*od* picture) elements; **~raster** *m* grating; scanning; *tele* picture raster; **~reihe** *f* strip mosaic; *film* frames *pl*; **~röhre** *f* picture tube, kinescope; *die 12¹/₂ Inch ~~ gibt helle, scharfe, klare Fernsehbilder selbst in beleuchteten Räumen* the 12¹/₂-inch picture tube gives bright, sharp, clear pictures even in lighted rooms; **~rundfunk** *m* television (broadcasting); **~sam** *a* plastic, supple, flexible; (*gelehrig*) docile; **~säule** *f* statue; **~schärfe** *f* contrast, focus; **~schirm** *m* (viewing) screen; projection screen, picture screen; **~schnitzer** *m* (wood-) carver; **~schnitzerei** *f* (wood-) carving; **~schön** *a* of rare beauty; lovely; **~seite** *f* (*Münze*) face, obverse; *fam* head; **~sendeempfangsanlage** *f* radio-picture set; facsimile transceiver set; **~sender** *m* image (*od* video *od* facsimile) transmitter; **~sendung** *f* television (broadcasting); **~stock** *m typ* electro, cut, block; (*am Wegrand*) wayside shrine; **~streifen** *m* film strip, reel of film; record; **~sucher** *m phot* finder; **~telegraphie** *f* picture telegraphy, phototelegraphy; facsimile transmission; **~tongerät** *n phot* sound camera; **~übertragung** *f tele* picture transmission; **~unterschrift** *f* caption; **~verstärker** *m tele* video amplifier; **~wand** *f* projecting screen; **~werfer** *m* projector; (*für Diapositive*) slide projector; (*für Ton- und Stummfilm*) sound and silent projector; **~werk** *n* sculpture; **~wiedergaberöhre** *f* television tube, cathode-ray tube; kinescope; **~winkel** *m* angle of vision; **~wirksam** *a* (*in Photo und Film*) photogenic (*z. B.* she is America's most photogenic girl); (*im Fernsehbild*) telegenic; *nicht ~wirksam* unphotogenic; **~wirkung** *f* pictorial effect; (*plastische*) stereoscopic effect, illusion of depth; **~zähler** *m phot* exposure counter; **~zeile** *f tele* line, picture line, picture strip; **~zerleger** *m tele* scanner, picture analyzer; **~zerlegung** *f tele* scanning, analyzing of picture.

bilden *tr* (*formen, gestalten*) to form, to shape, to fashion; (*kneten*) to mo(u)ld; to model; (*bestehen*) to constitute; to be; (*belehren, unterrichten*) to educate, to cultivate, to civilize; to train; (*ausmachen*) to make up; (*darstellen*) to constitute; (*einrichten*) to organize; (*aufbauen*) to establish, to construct, to found; (*schöpferisch ~*) to create; *sich ~* to form o.s.; to be formed; (*entstehen, entsprechen*) to arise; (*geistig*) to improve o.'s mind; *gebildet a u. pp* educated, cultivated, refined; *ein gebildeter Mensch* an educated person, a cultured man; (*spöttisch*) *Am* a high-brow; **~d** *a* formative, forming; (*belehrend*) instructive; *die ~den Künste pl* the Fine Arts *pl*.

Bilder *n pl von Bild:* **~anbetung** *f* idolatry, image-worship; **~bibel** *f* pictorial Bible; **~bogen** *m* picture-sheet; **~buch** *n* picture-book; **~dienst** *m* photo service; **~fibel** *f* illustrated primer; **~galerie** *f*, **~saal** *m* picture-gallery; **~haken** *m* picture fastener; picture eye; **~handel** *m* trade in pictures (*od* paintings); **~händler** *m* picture-dealer; **~kenner** *m* connoisseur of pictures; **~laden** *m* picture-dealer's shop; **~rahmen** *m* picture-frame; **~rätsel** *n* picture puzzle, rebus; **~reich** *a* rich in pictures; *fig* flowery; figurative; abounding in metaphors; **~sammlung** *f* collection of pictures (*od* paintings); **~schrift** *f* hieroglyphics *pl*, picture writing; (*für Bilddiagramme, Statistiken etc*) pictography; **~sprache** *f* metaphorical language; **~stürmer** *m* image-breaker; iconoclast; **~werk** *n* illustrated work; **~zeitschrift** *f* picture magazine.

Bildung *f* (*allg*) formation; (*Wachstum*) growth; (*Gründung*) foundation, constitution; (*Organisierung*) organization; (*Körper~*) form, shape; (*Gesichts~*) physiognomy; (*Aufbau*) structure; forming; (*Entwicklung*) development; (*Erziehung*) training, education; learning, schooling; (*Kultur*) culture; (*höhere ~*) higher education; accomplishments *pl*; (*Kenntnisse*) information, knowledge; (*gute Sitte*) refinement, polish, good breeding; (*~ neuer Worte*) coinage (of words); *ohne ~* illiterate, ill-bred; *e-e gute ~ genießen* to receive a good education; **~sanstalt, ~sstätte** *f* educational establishment, school; **~sfähig** *a* fit for education; cultivable; **~sgang** *m* course of instruction (*od* education); **~sgrad** *m* degree of culture; mental level of s. o.; *Am* I Q (Intelligence Quotient); **~shunger** *m* thirst for knowledge; **~skraft** *f* formative power; **~smittel** *n* means of instruction; **~strieb** *m* desire for learning; creative power; **~svorgang** *m tech* process of formation; **~swärme** *f tech* heat of formation, enthalpy; **~sweise** *f* manner (*od* mode) of formation.

Billard *n* billiards *pl mit sing*, (*~tisch*) billiard-table; *~ spielen* to play at billiards; **~ball** *m*, **~kugel** *f* billiard-ball; **~markör, ~kellner** *m* billiard-marker; **~queue** *n*, **~stock** *m* billiard-cue; **~saal** *m* billiard-saloon; **~tuch** *n* billiard-cloth; **~zimmer** *n* billiard-room, *Am* pool-room.

Billett *n* (*Eintrittskarte*) ticket; (*Briefchen*) note; *siehe*: *Karte, Fahrkarte.*

billig *a* (*gerecht*) equitable, fair, just, right; (*Preis*) low, cheap, moderate; (*vernünftig*) reasonable; (*wohlfeil*) *Am* popular priced; *~ aber schlecht* cheap and nasty; *das ist nicht mehr als ~* that is no more than fair; *ziemlich ~* rather cheap; *was dem e-n recht ist, ist dem andern ~* what is sauce for the goose is sauce for the gander; **~en** *tr* to approve (of), to consent (to); to sanction, *Am fam* to give the okay; **~erweise** *adv* in fairness; justly; **~keit** *f* equity, justness; (*Preis*) moderateness, cheapness; **~~sanspruch** *m* claim in equity; **~~sgericht** *n* court of equity; **~~sgründe** *m pl* reasons *pl* of fairness; **~~srecht** *n* equity; **~ung** *f* approbation, approval, consent; (*Sanktion, Bestätigung*) sanction.

Billion *f* billion, *Am* trillion.

Bilsenkraut *n* henbane.

bimbam! *interj* ding-dong! *heiliger ~! interj* (*des Erstaunens*) dear me!

bimmeln *itr* to tinkle, to ring.

Bimsstein *m* pumice(-stone).

Binde *f* (*allg*) band; *med* bandage, ligature, dressing; (*Kopf~*) fillet; (*bei Armverletzung*) sling; *den Arm in der ~ tragen*) to carry o.'s arm in a sling; (*Hals~*) tie; (*Arm~ als Abzeichen*) arm-band, armlet; badge; (*Stirn~*) bandeau; (*Damen~*) sanitary towel; (*Leib~*) sash; *er hat sich e-n hinter die ~ gegossen* (*fam*) he took a glass, he has got a few under his belt; *die ~ fiel ihm von den Augen* his eyes were opened; **~balken** *m* girder; tie-beam; **~draht** *m* binding wire, baling wire; **~fähigkeit** *f tech* binding quality, bonding quality; **~garn** *n* twine; **~gewebe** *n anat* connective tissue; **~glied** *n* connecting link; **~haut** *f* conjunctiva; **~hautentzündung** *f* conjunctivitis, pink-eye; **~mäher** *m* mowing-binder; grain binder, harvester and binding machine; **~material** *n* binder; **~mittel** *n tech* binder, bond; (*Bauwesen*) cement; **~strich** *m* hyphen; **~strichler** *m* (*Halbamerikaner*) hyphenated American; **~wort** *n* conjunction, copula; **~zeichen** *n mus* slur, tie, ligature.

binden *irr tr* to bind, to tie, to fasten (to); *ein Buch ~* to bind a book; *mit Stricken ~* to cord; *Heu ~* to bundle hay; *e-n Strauß ~* to make a nosegay; *ein Faß ~* to hoop a cask; *Noten ~* to slur; (*Suppe*) to thicken; *fig* to tie down; *sich gebunden fühlen* to feel bound (to); *jdn ~* (*verpflichten*) to oblige; *itr* (*Farben, Mörtel*) to take; *sich an etw ~* to engage in, to bind o. s.; to commit o. s.; **~d** *a* obligatory; (*Beschluß*) binding (on *od* upon).

Bind|faden *m* string, twine, pack-thread; *es regnet ~faden* it is raining cats and dogs; **~fadenrolle** *f* reel of twine; **~ung** *f* band, tie; *mus* ligature, slur; (*Ski*) binding, strap; *chem* compound; *tech* bond; *fig* obligation, engagement; (*Verpflichtung*) pledge; **~~senergie** *f tech* bond energy; **~~skraft** *f* linkage force; **~~swärme** *f* heat of absorption, heat of combination.

binnen *prp* within; *~ kurzem* shortly, before long; *~ 14 Tagen* within a fortnight; *~ 8 Tagen* in the course of a week, within a week; **~bords** *adv* (*innenbords*) inboard; **~dock** *n* inner dock; **~fischerei** *f* freshwater fishing; **~gewässer** *n* inland water; **~hafen** *m* basin; **~handel** *m* internal trade, home trade, *Am* domestic commerce; **~land** *n* inland; interior; **~länder(in)** inlander; **~ländisch** *a* internal, inland; **~meer** *n* inland sea; **~schiffahrt** *f* inland navigation (*od* water transportation *od* shipping); **~verkehr** *m* inland traffic; **~währung** *f* internal currency; **~wasserstraße** *f* inland waterway; **~zoll** *m* inland duty.

Binom *n* binomial; **~ialreihe** *f* binomial series; **~isch** *a* binomial.

Binse *f* rush; **~nwahrheit** *f* truism, platitude.

Bio|chemie *f* biochemistry; **~chemiker** *m* biochemist; **~chemisch** *a* biochemical; **~graph(in)** *m* (*f*) biographer; **~graphie** *f* biography; **~graphisch** *a* biographical; **~log(e)** *m* biologist; **~logie** *f* biology; **~logisch** *a* biological; *~~ischer Krieg* biological warfare (*Abk* BW); **~physik** *f* biophysics *pl mit sing*; **~se** *f* disaccharid; **~skop** *n* bioscope; **~xyd** *n* bioxide, dioxide.

Birk|e *f* birch-tree; **~en** *a* birch(en); **~enreis** *n* birch-rod; **~ensaft** *m* birch juice; **~enwald** *m* birch-grove; **~hahn** *m* heath-cock, black-cock; **~henne** *f*, **~huhn** *n* heath-hen, moor-hen.

Birma *n* Burma; **~ne, ~in** Burmese; **~nisch** *a* Burmese.

Birn|baum *m* pear-tree; **~e** *f* pear; (*Glüh~*) bulb; (*ausgebrannte*) burnout; *matte ~e* pearl bulb; *tech* converter; *sl* (*Kopf*) *Am sl* bean; *e-e weiche ~e haben sl* to be off o.'s crumpet; **~förmig** *a* pear-shaped; **~most, ~wein** *m* perry.

bis *prp* (*räumlich*) to, as far as; (*zeitlich*) till, until; *2 ~ 3* two or three; *sie ist 2 ~ 3 Tage verreist* she is away for two or three days; *30 ~ 35 Fuß lang* from 30 to 35 feet long; *von ... ~* from ... to; *von Montag ~ einschließlich Freitag* from Monday to Friday inclusive, *Am* from Monday thru Friday; *~* (*spätestens*) by; *~ Ende dieser Woche* by the end of this week; *~ Weihnachten* by Xmas; *~ an* up to; *~ ans Knie* up to the knee; *~ auf* (*ausgenommen*) with the exception of, except for, save; *~ auf bald!* see you soon! *~ aufs Haar* to a T, to a shade, exactly; *alle ~ auf e-n* all but one; *~ auf weiteres* until (*od* till) further notice, for the present, pending further instructions, until further instructions; *~ dahin* by that time, so far; *~ dahin und nicht weiter* you can lead a horse to water but you can't make him drink; *~ heute* up to this day, to date, thus far; *~ hierher* thus far; *~ jetzt* till (*od* until) now, up to now, as yet, hitherto, so far, thus far; *~ jetzt noch nicht* not as yet; *~ morgen!* see you tomorrow! *~ nach* (*örtlich*) to, as far as; *~ wann?* when? how long? *~ wohin?* how far? *~ zu* up to; *~ zum 3. April* up to 3rd April; (*bedingend*) pending; *~ zur Verfallszeit* till due; *~ hinauf* (*zu*) up to; *~ hinab* (*zu*) down to; *conj* till, until; (*nicht eher als*) before; **~her** *adv* hitherto, up to this time, up to now, until now, so far; *wie ~her* as before, as in the past; **~herig** *a* previous, hitherto existing; *die ~herigen Nachrichten* the news received hitherto; **~lang** *adv* as yet, so far; **~weilen** *adv* sometimes; (*gelegentlich*) now and then, occasionally.

Bisam *m* musk; (*Pelz*) musquash; **~apfel** *m* musk-apple; **~katze** *f* civet-cat; **~tier** *n*, **~bock** *m* musk-deer; **~ratte** *f* musk-rat.

Bischof *m* bishop; **bischöflich** *a* episcopal; **~smütze** *f* mitre; **~ssitz** *m* (bishop's) see; **~sstab** *m* crosier; **~swürde** *f* episcopate.

Biskaya *f* Biscay; *Meerbusen* (*od Golf*) *von ~* Bay of Biscay.

Biskuit *m od n* biscuit; (*weicher*) sponge-cake, teacake; *Am* biscuit, cookie, cracker.

Bison *m* bison.

Biß *m* bite; (*Schlangen~*) sting.

bißchen: *ein ~* a little bit; a while; *warten Sie ein ~* wait a while *od* somewhat; *ein ~ länger* a little longer; *kein ~* not a bit.

Biss|en *m* mouthful, bite, tit-bit, morsel; (*eingetaucht*) sop; **~enweise** *adv* bit by bit, in bits; **~ig** *a* biting; (*Hund*) snappish; *fig* cutting; (*scharfzüngig*) acid-tongued; sarcastic; **~igkeit** *f* snappishness, biting severity, sarcasm.

Bistum *n* bishopric, episcopate; diocese.

Bitt|e *f* request; *auf meine ~* at my request; (*dringend*) urgent request, entreaty; (*höflich*) solicitation; (*Gesuch*) petition, application; (*Forderung*) demand; (*demütig, flehend*) supplication; (*Gebet*) prayer; *ich habe e-e ~e an Sie* I have a favo(u)r to ask of you; **~en** *irr tr* to ask s. o. for s. th. (*od* s.th. of s.o.); *jdn um Erlaubnis ~en* to ask leave of s. o.; *jdn her ~en* to ask s. o. to come; *jdn zu Gast ~en* to invite s. o.; (*anflehen*) to implore; (*höflich ersuchen*) to request; (*nachdrücklich*) to beg, to entreat, to pray; *für jdn ~en* to plead for s.o., to intercede for s. o.; *bitte* (*schön od sehr*)*!* please (*mit nachfolgender Bitte*); *wie ~e?* I beg your pardon? *Ich ~ um Verzeihung!* pardon me! I beg your pardon! excuse me! I'm sorry! *Darf ich Sie um Ihren Namen ~en?* may I ask your name? *ich ~e ums Wort!* I beg permission to speak! *Am* may I have the floor? *~e, kommen Sie doch!* (*besonders dringendes Ersuchen*) do come! come and see me, do! *~e bestätigen!* (*im Funkverkehr*) acknowledge! *dürfte ich Sie um das Salz ~en?* may I trouble you for the salt? *wenn ich ~en darf* I would thank you for; *entschuldigen Sie ~e!* sorry! *~e!* (*auf danke schön*) you are (quite) welcome! don't mention it! *~e, das macht nichts!* no trouble! *ich ~e Sie!* (*Ablehnung*) you don't say so! **~gang** *m* procession; **~gesuch, ~schreiben** *n*, **~schrift** *f* petition; **~steller(in)** petitioner, solicitor; **~weise** *adv* by way of request.

bitter *a* bitter; (*Spott*) biting; (*streng*) severe; (*scharf, beißend*) acrimonious; *~er Ernst fig* sad earnest; *~e Wahrheit* plain truth; **~böse** *a* extremely angry; very wicked; **~erde** *f* magnesium oxide; **~feind** *a* very hostile; **~holz** *n* quassia (-wood); **~kalt** *a* bitterly cold; **~keit** *f* bitterness; sarcasm; **~klee** *m* buck-bean; **~lich** *a* bitterish; *adv: ~~ weinen* to cry bitterly; **~mandelöl** *n* oil of bitter almonds; benzaldehyde; **~nis** *f* bitterness; **~salz** *n* sulphate of magnesia; Epsom salt; **~süß** *a* bittersweet; **~wasser** *n* bitter mineral water.

Bitum|en *n* bitumen; **~inös** *a* bituminous; *~inöse Kohle* bituminous coal.

Biwak *n* bivouac; **~ieren** *itr* to camp out, to bivouac.

bizarr *a* (*launenhaft*) bizarre; (*seltsam*) strange. eccentric. odd.

bizon|al *a* bizonal; **~e** *f* Bizone; **~ia, ~ien** *n* Bizonia.

Blachfeld *n* level field, open field, plain.

blaffen *itr* (*kläffen*) to bark.

Blag *n*, ***Blage*** *f dial* brat, urchin, noisy child.

bläh|en *tr* to blow out, to puff up; to inflate; to swell (out); *itr* to cause flatulence; *sich ~~* to swell proudly, to boast of; **~end** *a* flatulent; **~ung** *f* wind, flatulence.

blaken *itr* to smoke.

Blam|age *f* disgrace; shame; **~ieren** *tr* to make s. o. look a fool; to (expose to) ridicule; to compromise; *sich ~~* to make o. s. ridiculous, to make a fool of o. s.

blank *a* bright, shining; (*weiß, hell*) white; (*rein, klar*) clean; (*poliert*) polished; (*glatt*) smooth; (*bloß, nackt*) bare, naked; *~er Unsinn* sheer nonsense; *~er Draht* (*el*) bare wire; *~es Kabel* (*el*) flexible cable, (*nicht armiert*) unarmo(u)red cable; *~e Waffe* cold steel; *~ ziehen* to draw o.'s sword; *ich bin ~ fam* I am penniless, I am dead broke; **~ett** *n* (*völlig unausgefülltes Formular*) blank form; (*französisch*) carte blanche; **~o**: *in ~o* in blank; *~o verkaufen* to bear, *Am* to sell short; **~oakzept** *n* blank acceptance; **~oformular** *n* blank form; **~okredit** *m* blank (*od* unlimited *od* open) credit; **~oscheck** *m* blank cheque, *Am* blankcheck; **~ounterschrift** *f* blank signature; **~ovollmacht** *f* unlimited power(s) (of attorney); **~owechsel** *m* blank bill; **~scheit** *n* busk; **~vers** *m* blank verse.

*

Blas|angriff *m mil* gas attack; **~apparat** *m* blast apparatus; **~arbeit** *f* blasting operation.

Bläschen *n* small bubble, *med* pustule; pimple, small blister.

Blas|e *f* (*Luft~e*) bubble; (*Haut~e*) blister, pustule; *med* vesicle; (*Harn~e*) bladder; (*Destillier~e*) still, boiler; (*im Glas, Eisen etc*) flaw; *~en werfen* to bubble; **~ebalg** *m* (pair of) bellows *pl;* **~ebalgtreter** *m* organ-blower; **~enentzündung** *f* cystitis, inflammation of the bladder; **~engries** *m med* gravel; **~enkatarrh** *m* cystic catarrh; **~enleiden** *n* bladder trouble; **~enstein** *m* urinary calculus; **~enziehend** *a* blistering; vesicant; **~instrument** *n mus* wind-instrument; *Kapelle mit ~instrumenten* brassband; **~musik** *f* brassband; **~rohr** *n tech* blow pipe; (*Schußwaffe*) pea-shooter; **~werk** *n* bellows *pl* (of an organ).

blasen *irr itr, tr* to blow; *mus* to sound; to play; *Alarm ~* to sound an alarm; *zum Angriff ~* to sound the charge; *zum Rückzug ~* to sound the retreat.

Bläser *m* (*von Blasinstrument*) player (on a wind-instrument); *mil* (*Horn~*) bugler; *tech* blower, ventilator.

blasiert *a* blasé, conceited, surfeited.

Blasphemie *f* blasphemy.

blaß *a* pale; *~ werden* to turn pale; *keine ~e Ahnung haben* to have not the faintest idea; **~blau** *a* pale blue; **~grün** *a* pale green; **~rot** *a* pale red.

Blässe *f* paleness, pallidness, pallor.

Blatt *n* (*Buch, Pflanze*) leaf; (*Blumen~*) petal; (*Seite*) page; (*Gras~, Ruder~, Schulter~, Säge~*) blade; (*Papier~*) sheet of paper; (*Zeitung*) (news)paper; journal; (*Tisch~*) board; *vom ~ singen, spielen* to sing offhand (*od* at sight), to play at sight; *das ~ hat sich gewendet* the tables are turned; *kein ~ vor den Mund nehmen* to speak out boldly, to be plain-spoken, not to mince o.'s words, *Am fam* to pull no punches; *das steht auf e-m andern ~* that is another thing; *ein unbeschriebenes ~* a blank page; *er ist ein unbeschriebenes ~ für mich* he is an unknown quantity to me; **~ansatz** *m* stipule; **~feder** *f tech* plate-spring; *mot* leaf-spring; **~förmig** *a* leaf-shaped; **~gold** *n* gold-leaf, leaf-gold; **~grün** *n* chlorophyll; **~halter** *m* (*zum Maschinenschreiben etc*) copy holder; **~laus** *f* plant-louse; **~los** *a* leafless; **~metall** *n* sheet metal; **~pflanze** *f* foliage plant; **~rippe** *f* vein *od* nerve (of the leaf-blade); **~seite** *f* folio, leaf, page; **~silber** *n* silver-leaf; **~stiel** *m* leaf-stalk, petiole; stem; **~vergoldung** *f* leaf-gilding; **~weise** *adv* leaf by leaf; **~werk** *n* foliage; **~winkel** *m* axil.

Blatter *f* blister, pimple; **~n** *f pl* variola, smallpox; **~narbe** *f* pock-mark; **~narbig** *a* marked with smallpox; pock-marked; **~nimpfung** *f* vaccination.

Blätter|gebackene(s) *n* puff-paste; **~ig** *a* leafy; **~los** *a* leafless; **~n** *itr* to turn over the leaves; **~reich** aleafy; **~tabak** *m* tobacco in leaves; **~teig** *m* flaky paste, puff-paste, puff-pastry; **~werk** *n* foliage.

blau *a* blue; *fig* (*betrunken*) tipsy, drunk, *Am* boiled, canned; *trinken bis man ~ ist* to drink till all is blue; *~ vor Kälte* blue with cold; *~ machen* (*fam*) to take a holiday; *~es Blut* (*echter Adel*) blue-blood, aristocracy; *~e Bohne* (*fig*) bullet; *~e Flecken* (*am Körper*) black-and-blue marks; *~er Montag* blue Monday; *~en Montag machen* (*Am fam*) to keep Saint Monday; *jdm ~en Dunst vormachen* to throw dust in s. o.'s eyes, *fam* to bamboozle s.o.; *~ unterlaufene Augen* black eyes; *sein ~es Wunder erleben* to be taken aback with amazement; *mit e-m ~en Auge davonkommen* to have a narrow escape, to be lucky at that, to get off cheaply; *jdn braun und ~ schlagen* to beat s.o. black and blue; *es wurde ihr grün und ~ vor Augen* she turned giddy, she felt quite dizzy; **Blau** *n* (*~e Farbe, Wasch~*) blue (colo(u)r); *ins ~e* (*hinein*) at random; haphazard; *ins ~e hinein reden* (*od hinein schwatzen*) to talk at random; *das ~e vom Himmel herunterlügen* to lie in o.'s throat; *das ~e vom Himmel schwatzen* (*fam*) to talk off a donkey's hind leg; *Fahrt ins ~e* journey into the unknown, mystery tour; **~äugig** *a* blue-eyed; **~bart** *m* (*Frauenmörder*) Bluebeard; **~beere** *f* bilberry, *Am* huckleberry, blueberry; **~blütig** *a* (*adlig*) blue-blooded, aristocratic; **~buch** *n* (*engl Parlamentsdruckschrift*) bluebook; **~en** *itr* to be blue, to turn blue; **~farbe** *f* blue-colo(u)r; **~felche** *f,* **~~n** *m* blue char; **~fuchs** *m* blue fox, arctic fox; **~grau** *a* bluish grey, livid; **~holz** *n* logwood; **~jacke** *f* (*Matrose*) blue-jacket; **~kehlchen** *n orn* blue-breast, blue-throat; **~kraut** *n* (*Rotkohl*) red cabbage; **~kreuzler** *m* (*Temperenzler*) blue-ribbonist; **~meise** *f* blue tit (-mouse), blue-bonnet; **~papier** *n* carbon paper; **~pause** *f* blueprint; **~säure** *f* prussic (*od* hydrocyanic) acid; **~säureverbindung** *f* cyanide; **~schimmel** *m* dapple-grey horse; **~stift** *m* blue pencil; *mit dem ~~ anzeichnen* (*od fig korrigieren, zensieren*) to blue-pencil; **~strumpf** *m* blue-stocking.

Bläu|e *f* blue(ness); (*des Himmels*) sky-blue, azure; (*Waschblau*) washing-blue, *Am* blueing; **~en** *tr* to (dye) blue; *fig* to beat; **~lich** *a* bluish.

Blech *n* (*Grob~*) (heavy) plate; (*Fein~*) (thin) sheet; (*Mittel~*) medium plate (*od* medium sheet); (*Material*) sheet metal; (*Erzeugnis*) metal sheet, steel sheet, iron sheet; (*Karosserie~*) automobile body sheet; (*Kuchen~*) cake tin; (*Schwarz~*) black sheet iron; (*Weiß~*) tin(plate); (*Well~*) corrugated sheet; (*Messing~*) sheet brass, brass plate; (*Blechblättchen*) lamella; lamination of metal; (*Folie*) foil; *gewalztes ~* rolled sheet; *verzinktes ~* galvanized sheet metal; *schußsicheres ~* bulletproof plating; (*Unsinn*) *fig* nonsense, bosh, stuff; *fam* tommy-rot; *red kein ~! fam* don't talk such nonsense! **~abfälle** *m pl* clippings *pl,* plate scrap, sheet scrap; **~arbeit** *f* tinwork, platework; **~bearbeitungsmaschine** *f* plate working machine, metal sheet working machine; **~behälter** *m* metal container; **~belag** *m* plate covering; **~beplankung** *f* metal skin; **~blasinstrument** *n* brass wind instrument; **~büchse, ~dose** *f* tin (box), *Am* can; *in ~dosen* tinned, *Am* canned; **~dosenöffner** *m* tin-opener; *Am* can-opener; **~druck** *m* tin-printing; **~emballage** *f* sheet metal container; tin, box, canister; **~en** *tr, itr* (*bezahlen*) *fam* to pay; to shell (*od* fork) out; *~en müssen* to have to bleed; **~ern** *a* tin; (*im Klang*) tinny; **~erzeugnisse** *n pl* metal plate products *pl;* **~gefäß** *n* tin-vessel; **~geschirr** *n* tinware; **~instrument** *n* brass (instrument); **~kanister** *m* metal container; **~kanne** *f* tin-can; **~kiste** *f* tin case; **~konstruktion** *f* steel-plate construction; **~lehre** *f* metal ga(u)ge; **~löffel** *m* tin spoon; **~marke** *f* tin control plate; **~musik** *f* brass-band; **~schere** *f* plate-shears *pl;* (*mit Rahmen*) guillotine shears *pl;* **~schmied** *m* tinsmith; (*Kesselflicker*) tinker; **~schneidemaschine** *f* shearing machine; **~straße** *f* sheet rolling train, *Am* plate mill train; **~streifen** *m* sheet metal strip; **~verkleidung** *f* sheet metal covering, sheeting; **~walzwerk** *n* plate (rolling) mill; **~ware(n** *pl*) *f* tinware; tin goods *pl.*

blecken *tr: die Zähne ~* to show o.'s teeth (*gegen jdn* at s. o.).

Blei *n* lead; (*~stift*) pencil; (*Lot, Senk~*) plummet; (*Geschoß*) shot; *aus ~* leaden; *gehacktes ~* slugs *pl; es lastet wie ~ auf mir* I feel as heavy as lead; *es liegt mir wie ~ in den Gliedern, meine Füße sind wie ~ fig* my limbs feel like lead; *mit Pulver und ~* with powder and shot; *mit ~ ausgeschlagen* lead-lined; **~abfall** *m* lead waste, *Am* scrap lead; **~abguß** *m* lead cast; **~ader** *f* lead vein; **~akkumulator** *m* lead cell, storage cell, lead-accumulator, lead storage battery; **~arbeiter** *m* plumber; **~barren** *m* lead pig, pig of lead; **~batterie** *f* lead (acid) battery; **~benzin** *n* tetraethyl lead fuel, *Am* lead-doped gasoline; **~bergwerk** *n* lead-mine; **~dach** *n* leads *pl;* leaden roof, *Am* tin roof; **~decker** *m* plumber; **~einfassung** *f* lead-fitting; **~ern** *a* leaden; **~erz** *n* lead ore; **~essig** *m* lead-vinegar; **~farben** *a* lead-colo(u)red, livid; **~gewicht** *n* sinker; *fig* dead weight; **~gießer** *m* plumber; **~gießerei** *f* lead-works *pl;* **~glanz** *m* galena, potter's ore; **~glas** *n* lead glass, crystal glass; **~haltig** *a* plumbiferous; **~hütte** *f* lead-works *pl;* **~kabel** *n* lead-covered cable; **~kugel** *f* leaden bullet; **~legierung** *f* lead-base alloy; **~lot** *n* plumb-line; *mar* plummet; **~platte** *f* lead plate; **~rohr** *n* lead-pipe; **~sammler** *m el* lead acid battery; **~säure** *f* plumbic acid; **~schirm** *m* (*Strahlenschutz*) lead screen; **~schwer** *a* heavy as lead; **~soldat** *m* tin soldier; **~stift** *m* pencil; **~~halter** *m,* **~~hülse** *f* pencil-case; **~~spitzer** *m* pencil sharpener, pencil sharpening machine; **~~zeichnung** *f* pencil drawing; **~vergiftung** *f* lead-poisoning; **~waren** *f pl* leads *pl;* **~wasser** *n* goulard; **~weiß** *n* white lead; **~zucker** *m* sugar of lead.

Blei *m,* ***Blei(h)e*** *f* (*Fisch*) bream.

Bleibe *f* (*Herberge, Obdach*) shelter, lodging; (*Jugendherberge*) youth-hostel; (*Aufenthaltsort, Wohnung*) abode, housing, dwelling, home, residence.

bleiben *irr itr* to stay, to remain; *draußen ~* to stay out; *im Bett ~* to stay in bed; (*verharren ~*) to continue; (*übrig ~*) to be left; (*sterben*) to perish; (*im Krieg*) to fall; *bei etw ~* to persist in, to stick to, to keep to, to adhere to; *ich bleibe bei meiner Ansicht* I stick to my opinion; *sie blieb bei ihrer Meinung* she persisted in her opinion; *liegen ~* not to get up; *fern ~* to keep away; *fest ~, an Ort u. Stelle ~ Am* to stay put; *gesund ~* to remain healthy; *stehen ~* to continue standing; to stop (*bei etw* at); *wo sind wir stehengeblieben?* where did we leave off? *nicht stehen ~!* move on! *sitzen ~* to keep o.'s seat; (*in der Schule nicht mitkommen*) to fail; *sl* to flunk; (*beim Tanzen*) to get no partner; (*als Mädchen ledig bleiben*) to become an old maid; *stecken ~* to stick fast; to break down; *gelassen ~* to keep o.'s temper; *und wo bleibe ich?* where does that leave me? *wo ~* (*was ist los mit*) what about . . .; *wo ist sie geblieben?* what has become of her? *das bleibt unter uns* this is quite between ourselves; this is strictly confidential; that is between you and me; *es bleibt alles beim alten* no change will be made; things go on just as they were; *es bleibt dabei!* agreed! we will leave it at that! *sie bleibt besser, wo sie ist* she is better off where she is; *es bleibt* *mir nichts anderes übrig* I have no other choice; ~ *lassen* to leave (*od* to let) s. th. alone; *lassen Sie das lieber* ~*!* you had better leave that alone! *das lasse ich wohl* ~ I shall do nothing of the kind; ~ *Sie mir vom Halse!* ~ *Sie mir vom Leibe!* stand off! keep your distance! leave me alone! ~ *Sie in der Leitung! tele* hold the line, please! *in Kraft* ~ to remain in force; *am Leben* ~ to survive, to remain alive; *auf dem Platze* ~ to be slain; *bei der Sache* ~ to keep to the point (*od* subject); *bleibt!* (*bei Korrekturen*) let it stand! stet! *sich gleich* ~ to be always the same: **Bleiben** *n* stay; *hier ist meines* ~*s nicht länger* I cannot stay here any longer; ~**d** *a* remaining; abiding; standing; (*Eindrücke*) lasting; (*dauerhaft*) enduring; (*Wohnsitz*) permanent; ~*de Farbe* fast colo(u)r; *keine* ~*de Stätte haben* to have no permanent residence.

*

bleich *a* pale; (*blaß, farblos*) wan, pallid; ~ *werden* to turn pale; (*verblaßt*) faded; (*verblichen*) faint; ~**anstalt** *f* bleachery; ~**e** *f* paleness, wanness; *tech* bleaching- ground; ~**en** *tr* to bleach, to whiten; *itr* to lose colo(u)r; to grow pale, to turn white; to blanch; (*von Farben*) to fade; ~ *n* bleaching; ~**gesicht** *n* paleface; ~**kalk** *m*, ~**pulver** *n* bleaching powder, chloride of lime; ~**mittel** *n* bleaching agent (*od* powder); ~**platz** *m* bleaching-green; ~**sucht** *f* green-sickness, chlorosis; ~**süchtig** *a* chlorotic; maid-pale.

Blend|e *f* (*blindes Fenster etc*) blind; sham; sham door, sham window; blind door, blind window; (*Wandnische*) niche; (*Scheuklappe*) blinker, eye-flap; *mil* blinds *pl*; (*bei Kanonen etc*) mantlet; *min* (*Schwefelerz*) blende, black-jack; *phot* diaphragm, stop; shutter; (*Öffnung*) aperture (stop); orifice; (*Schlitz*) slit; (*Leuchte*) lantern; (*Ausputz an Kleid*) trimming; *bei* ~*e 8* stop-opening of f 8; (*Wandschirm*) (folding) screen; *mar* (*für Luken etc*) deadlights *pl*; ~**en** *tr* (*allg u. fig*) to blind; *fig* to blindfold; (*durch Ausstechen der Augen*) to put out (*od* to gouge out) s. o.'s eyes; (*auch durch Lichtquelle*) to dazzle; (*bezaubern*) to fascinate; (*täuschen*) to deceive; *fam* to hoodwink; (*panzern*) to plate; *itr* to glare; ~*en n* (*der Scheinwerfer*) *mot* headlight glare; ~**end** *a* (*Licht*) glaring; dazzling; (*Redner etc*) brilliant; (*täuschend*) delusive; (*Schönheit*) fascinating; *fam* (*sehr gut*) marvellous; *sie sieht* ~*end aus* she looks fine; ~**eneinstellung** *f phot* diaphragm setting, diaphragm-scale; ~**enöffnung** *f phot* aperture of diaphragm; ~**er** *m* (*Bluffer, Angeber*) bluffer, *Am fam* four-flusher; ~**körper** *m mil* (*Panzerbekämpfung*) frangible-glass smoke grenade; ~**lampe** *f* anti-dazzle lamp; ~**laterne** *f* dark lantern, bull's eye-lantern; ~**leder** *n* (*der Pferde*) blinkers *pl*; ~**rahmen** *m* blind frame; ~**scheibe** *f mot* glare shield; (*für Nebel*) fog disc for lights; ~**schirm** *m* light-screen, reflector; eye-shade; ~**schutzlicht** *n* anti-dazzle lamp; ~**schutzscheibe** *f mot* anti-glare windshield, anti-dazzling screen; *Am* visor; ~**stein** *m* facing brick; ~**ung** *f* blinding, dazzling, dazzlement; ~**werk** *n* (*Sinnestäuschung*) optical illusion, delusion, deception; (*Schwindel*) mockery, false show, eye-wash; (*Bezauberung*) fascination; (*Luftspiegelung, Selbsttäuschung*) mirage.

Blesse *f* (*weißer Stirnfleck*) blaze, white spot; horse (*etc*) with white spot.

Bleuel *m* (*Schlegel zum Wäscheklopfen*) beetle, beater.

bleuen *tr fam* (*schlagen*) to beat.

Blick *m* look; *flüchtiger* ~ glimpse (*auf* at), glance (*auf* at, *in* into, *über* over); *verstohlener* ~ furtive glance; *scharfer* ~ penetrating glance; *sie hat e-n scharfen* ~ she has a sharp eye; *verständnisvoller* ~ knowing look; (*Gesichtsbereich*) view; (*Gesichtssinn*) eye; (*Gold*~, *Silber*~) lightning of gold, silver; *der böse* ~ the evil eye; *sie warf ihm e-n bösen* ~ *zu fam* she gave him a dirty look; *der* ~ *in die Zukunft* forward look; *auf den ersten* ~ at first sight, at first view; *auf e-n* ~ at a glance; *ihr* ~ *fällt auf . . .* her eye lights upon; *e-n* ~ *werfen auf* to glance at, to take a look at, to give a look at, to cast a look at; *jdn mit dem* ~ *durchbohren* to look s.o. through; ~**en** *itr* to glance; to look (*auf, nach* at, into, in); *das läßt tief* ~*en* that speaks volumes; that is very significant; *der Mond* ~*t durch die Wolken* the moon breaks through the clouds; *sich* ~*en lassen* to show o.s., to appear, to put in an appearance; *sie ließ sich nicht* ~*en* she did not show up, she kept out of sight; ~**fang** *m* eye-catcher; ~**feld** *n* field of vision; field of view; *fig* range of vision; ~**feuer** *n* signal light, blue light; signal-fire, flash-light; blinker beacon; ~**linie** *f* line of vision (*od* sight); ~**punkt,** ~**winkel** *m opt* visual point; point of sight; *fig* point of view.

blind *a* blind; (*Metalle, Glas, Spiegel*) tarnished, dull; (*Alarm*) sham, false; (*Fenster, Wand etc*) *tech* blank, dead; ~*er Bombenabwurf* blind bombing; ~*er Eifer* zeal without knowledge; ~*e Gasse* blind alley; ~*er Gehorsam* implicit obedience; ~*e Stelle* (*beim Funkempfang*) blind spot; ~*er Schlag* ineffective blow; ~*er Flansch* blank flange; ~*e Klippe* sunken rocks; ~*er Lärm* false alarm; ~*er Passagier* deadhead; (*auf Schiffen, Flugzeugen*) stowaway; ~*es Werkzeug fig* a mere tool; ~ *auf e-m Auge* blind of one eye, *Am* blind in one eye; ~ *laden mil* to load with a blank cartridge; ~ *schießen* to fire blank cartridges; ~**abwurf** *m aero mil* blind bombing; (*Notwurf*) emergency release; ~**achse** *f* loose axle; ~**darm** *m* blind gut, (vermiform) appendix, caecum; ~**darmentzündung** *f* appendicitis; ~**darmoperation** *f* appendectomy; ~**e(r)** *m, f* blind man, blind woman; (*Kartenspiel*) dummy; ~**ekuh** *f*: ~~ *spielen* to play at blind-man's- buff; ~**enanstalt** *f*, ~**enheim** *n* asylum (*od* home) for the blind; ~**endruck** *m*, ~**enschrift** *f* (printing in) braille, embossed printing for blind; ~**enführerhund** *m* blind-man's dog, *Am* seeing eye dog; ~**enfürsorge** *f* provision for the blind; ~**enschreibmaschine** *f* braille typewriter; ~**fliegen** *irr itr aero* to fly on instruments; ~**flug** *m aero* blind flying, instrument flying; ~~**instrumentierung** *f aero* instrument-flying equipment; ~~**kurve** *f* blind flying bank (*od* curve), blind turn; ~~**landung** *f* instrument landing; ~~**lehrgang** *m* blind flying course; ~~**schule** *f* blind flying school; ~**gänger** *m mil* unexploded bomb *od* shell, blind (shell), *mil sl* dud; ~**geboren** *a* born blind; ~**heit** *f* blindness; *mit* ~~ *geschlagen* struck with blindness; ~**landeeinrichtung** *f aero* blind landing system; radio approach system; ~**landen** *itr* to land on instruments; ~**landeverfahren** *n* method of blind landing; ~**landung** *f* blind landing; ~**lings** *adv* blindly, without consideration, at random; ~**schleiche** *f* slow-worm, blind-worm; ~**schreiben** *n* (*Schreibmaschine*) touch typing.

blink|en *itr* to gleam, to sparkle, to shine; to glitter; to twinkle; (*mit Blinkgerät*) to signal with lamps; ~**er** *m* (*Mann*) lamp-signal(l)er; (*Gerät*) signal lamp; ~**feuer** *n* flashing (*od* intermittent) light, blinker beacon; revolving light (*od* beacon), blinker light; ~**garbe** *f* flash; ~**gerät** *n* blinker-signal equipment, lamp-signal(l)ing apparatus; ~**lampe** *f* flash (*od* blinker) lamp; ~**meldung** *f* blinker message; ~**spruch** *m* blinker-signal message; ~**station** *f* blinker-signal station; ~**trupp** *m* blinker squad; ~**verbindung** *f* signal-lamp communication; ~**zeichen** *n* flashlight signal.

blinzeln *itr* (*mit den Augenlidern*) to blink, to twinkle; (*um Zeichen zu geben*) to wink; ~ *n* blinking.

Blitz *m* lightning; (*einzelner*) flash; *film* statics *pl mit sing*; *der* ~ *schlägt ein* the lightning strikes; *vom* ~ *getroffen werden* to be struck by lightning; *wie vom* ~ *getroffen* thunder-struck; *wie ein geölter* ~ *fam* like greased lightning; *ein* ~ *aus heiterem Himmel fig* a bolt from the blue; ~**ableiter** *m* lightning-conductor; (*Stange*) lightning-rod; (*zur Sicherung elektrischer Anlagen*) lightning-arrester; voltage-discharge gap; *fig fam* (*Sündenbock*) scapegoat (*für* for); ~**artig** *a* lightninglike; ~**blank** *a* shining, very bright; ~**en** *itr* to lighten, to flash; to emit flashes; (*mit Donner*) to fulminate; *es donnert und* ~*t* it is thundering and lightening; (*funkeln*) to sparkle, to glitter; ~**flugzeug** *n* high-speed airplane; ~**gespräch** *n tele* lightning (long distance telephone) call; ~**kerl** *m* (*Hauptkerl*) capital fellow; ~**krieg** *m* lightning war, blitz(krieg); *durch e-n* ~~ *niederwerfen* to blitz; ~~ *mit Atomwaffen* blitz atomic war; ~**leuchte** *f* photo flash, flashgun; ~**licht** *n phot* flash-light; ~~**aufnahme** *f* flash-light photo(graphy); ~~*aufnahmen machen* to take photoflash pictures; ~~**birne** *f* flash bulb; ~~**bombe** *f* flash-light bomb, photo flash bomb; ~~**lampe** *f phot* flash(light) lamp; ~~**pulver** *n* flashlight powder; ~**röhre** *f phot* flash tube; ~**sauber** *a* spruce; shining; (*Mädchen*) very pretty; ~**schlag** *m* thunderclap, lightning stroke; (*Entladung*) lightning-discharge; ~**schnell** *a* as quick as lightning, like lightning; ~**schutzsicherung** *f el* lightning protection fuse; ~**strahl** *m* flash of lightning, thunderbolt; ~**telegramm** *n* lightning telegram; ~**zange** *f* adjustable spanner; ~**zug** *m* flier (*od* flyer), lightning train.

*

bloc: **en** ~ (*com*) in bulk, in the lump.

Block *m* (*Klotz, Notiz*~, ~*strecke rail, Am Häuser*~) block; (*Holz*~) log; (*Schokolade, Seife*) bar; (*Schreib*~) (scratch) pad, scribbling block; (*Parteien*~) *parl* bloc; (*Barren*) ingot, pig; (*Straf*~) stocks *pl*; *gehefteter Buch*~ stitched pack; ~**ade** *f* blockade; *die* ~~ *aufheben* to raise the blockade; *die* ~~ *durchbrechen* to run the blockade; ~**adebrecher** *m* blockade-runner; ~**druck** *m typ* block-printing; ~**en** *itr* (*Boxen*) to counter; ~**flöte** *f* block flute; recorder; ~**haus** *n* (*bes. mil*) blockhouse; log-cabin, log-house, log-

-hut; **~holz** *n* log-timber; **~ig** *a* (*klotzig*) blocky; **~ieren** *tr* to block (up); ***~iertes** Vermögen* blocked property; (*verriegeln*) to lock; (*sperren, z. B. Geld*) to freeze; (*verhindern, vereiteln*) *fig* to stymie; to obstruct; *radio* to jam; *typ* to turn letters; *mil* to blockade; **~kondensator** *m* (*Sperrkondensator*) *radio* block(ing)-condenser; **~mehrheit** *f parl* coalition majority; **~säge** *f* pit-saw; **~schrift** *f* (*Handschrift*) block letters *pl*; *typ* (*fette*) Egyptian type, (*halbfette*) clarendon type; *in ~schrift schreiben* to print in block letters; **~station, ~stelle** *f rail* block station, signal box.

blöd|e *a* (*dumm*) stupid, silly; (*beschränkt*) imbecile; (*schüchtern*) shy, timid; bashful; *fam* (*fadenscheinig*) threadbare, shabby; **~heit** *f* (*Dummheit*) imbecility, stupidity; **~igkeit** *f* (*Schüchternheit*) timidity, shyness; bashfulness; **~sinn** *m* (*Geistesschwäche*) weakness of mind, (*stärker*) idiocy; (*Unsinn, Quatsch bes. beim Reden*) nonsense, trash, rubbish; *interj fam* bosh; *~sinn reden* to talk nonsense; (*Unfug*) nuisance, fun; **~sinnig** *a* (*sehr dumm*) silly; stupid; (*geistig beschränkt*) idiotic; *fam* (*groß, sehr*) very, excessively; *~sinnig teuer* (*fam*) very expensive; *sich ~sinnig freuen* (*fam*) to be mad with joy, to be awfully pleased.

blöken *itr* (*Kuh*) to low, to bellow; (*Schaf*) to bleat.

blond *a* blond(e), fair, light-colo(u)red; *sie hat ~es Haar* she has blond hair; *rötlich~* sandy; *~er Mann* blond; **~e** *f* (*geklöppelte Spitze*) blonde lace; **~ine** *f* a (fair) haired girl, blonde; *Am dim* blondie; (*gefärbte*) a platinum blond girl; *Am fam* a dizzy blonde; **~kopf** *m* fair-haired person; **~lockig** *a* having fair curly hair.

bloß *a* bare, naked; (*nichts als*) mere, simple; *der ~e Gedanke* the mere idea, the very thought; *mit ~en Fäusten* with bare fists; *~er Schwindel* pure swindle; *~e Worte* empty words; *die ~e Erde* the bare ground; *mit ~em Auge* with the naked eye; *auf der ~en Haut* next to the skin; *mit ~em Kopfe* bare-headed; *adv* merely, simply, barely, solely, only; but; *~ um Ihnen zu gefallen* only to please you; *es handelt sich ~ um einige Tage* it is but a question of a few days; **~legen** *tr* to lay bare; *fig* to expose, to unearth; **~stellen** *tr* to expose; *jdn ~stellen* to unmask, to compromise s. o.; *fam* to show up s. o.; *er will mich nur ~stellen* he is just trying to show me up; **~stellung** *f* exposure.

Blöße *f* bareness, nakedness; *sport, fig* weak spot (*od* point); weakness; (*Lichtung im Wald*) glade; *sich e-e ~ geben* to lay o.s. open to attack, to show o.'s weak point; (*sich bloßstellen*) to compromise o.s.; *sich keine ~ geben* to save o.'s face.

blühen *itr* to blossom; (*auch fig*) to flower, to bloom; *fig* to flourish, to prosper, to thrive; *wer weiß, was ihm noch blüht?* who knows what is in store for him? *sein Weizen blüht fam* he is in luck; fortune smiles on him; **~d** *a* blooming, in blossom; *fig* flourishing; (*Aussehen*) rosy; *im ~~sten Alter* in the prime of life.

Blume *f* flower; (*Wein*) bouquet; flavo(u)r; (*Duft*) aroma; (*das Feinste*) flavo(u)r; (*Rede~*) metaphor; (*beim Wild*) tail; *fig* flower, cream; *durch die ~ sprechen* to hint at; to speak in metaphors; *laßt ~n sprechen!* say it with flowers!

Blumen|beet *n* bed of flowers, flower-bed; **~blatt** *n* petal; **~brett** *n* window-box, flower-stand; **~draht** *m* florist's wire; **~duft** *m* fragrance of flowers, perfume of flowers; **~erde** *f* garden-mo(u)ld; **~flor** *m* show of flowers; **~garten** *m* flower-garden; **~gärtner** *m* florist; **~gehänge** *n* festoon, garland; **~griffel** *m* style; **~händler** *m* florist; **~handlung** *f* florist's shop; **~kelch** *m* calix, calyx; **~kenner** *m* florist; **~kohl** *m* cauliflower; **~korb** *m* flower-basket; **~korso** *m* battle of flowers; **~kranz** *m* wreath of flowers; garland; **~krone** *f* corolla; **~laden** *m* flower-shop; **~lese** *f fig* selection, anthology; **~mädchen** *n* flower-girl; **~muster** *n* floral pattern **~reich** *a* bloomy, flowery; **~schnur** *f* festoon; **~sprache** *f* language of flowers; **~staub** *m* pollen; **~ständer** *m* flower-stand; **~stengel, ~stiel** *m* peduncle; flower-stalk; **~stock, ~topf** *m* pot-plant; (*Scherben*) flowerpot; **~strauß** *m* bouquet, nosegay, bunch of flowers; **~tisch** *m* flower-stand; **~topf** *m* flower-pot; (*Pflanze*) flowering pot-plant; **~vase** *f* flower-vase; **~zucht** *f* floriculture; **~zwiebel** *f* bulb.

blumig *a* bloomy, flower-like; flowery.

Bluse *f* blouse; tunic; (*Hemd~*) *Am* waist; shirt blouse; (*Feld~*) *mil* field (*od* battle) jacket; (*Arbeiter~*) smock-frock.

Blut *n* blood; *fig* family, race; parentage, birth; *im ~ liegen fig* to run in the blood; *bis aufs ~* to the quick; *mit kaltem ~e* in cold blood; *wie Milch u. ~ aussehen* to look all lilies and roses; *böses ~ machen* to arouse angry feelings; *es steckt ihm im ~* it runs in his blood; *sein ~ ist in Wallung* his blood is up; *nur ruhig ~!* keep your temper! **~ader** *f* vein; **~andrang** *m* congestion (of blood); rush of blood; **~apfelsine, ~orange** *f* blood orange; **~arm** *a* bloodless; *med* an(a)emic; *fig* extremely poor; **~armut** *f med* an(a)emia; **~auswurf** *m* spitting of blood; **~bad** *n* (*Gemetzel*) slaughter, massacre, carnage, butchery; **~bank** *f* blood bank; **~befleckt** *a* bloodstained; **~blase** *f* blood-blister; **~buche** *f* copper-beech; **~druck** *m* blood-pressure; *zu hoher ~~* (*Hypertonie*) hypertension; **~durst** *m* bloodthirstiness; **~dürstig** *a* bloodthirsty; **~egel** *m* leech; **~en** *itr* to bleed; *fig* to suffer; *fam* (*bezahlen*) to pay (for); *mir ~et das Herz* my heart bleeds; *meine Nase ~et* my nose is bleeding; **~end** *a* bleeding; *mit ~endem Herzen* (*fig*) broken-hearted; **~er** *m* bleeder; **~erguß** *m* effusion of blood; **~erkrankheit** *f* (*Hämophilie*) h(a)emophilia; **~farbstoff** *m* (*roter*) h(a)emoglobin; **~fink** *m orn* bullfinch; **~flecken** *m* blood-stain; **~fluß** *m* h(a)emorrhage; (*weiblich*) monthly courses *pl*, menses *pl*; **~gefäß** *n* blood-vessel; **~gerinnsel** *n* clot of blood; **~gerüst** *n* scaffold; **~geschwür** *n* boil, furuncle, phlegmon; **~gier** *f* bloodthirstiness; **~gierig** *a* bloodthirsty, sanguinary, murderous; **~gruppe** *f* blood-group; *das Gericht erkannte ~gruppenproben nicht an* the court did not accept bloodgrouping tests; **~hochzeit** *f*: *die Pariser ~~* Massacre of St. Bartholomew; **~hund** *m* bloodhound; **~husten** *m med* h(a)emoptysis; **~ig** *a* bloody, blood-stained, blood-covered; *fig* sanguinary; **~jung** *a* very young; **~klumpen** *m*, **~pfropfen** *m* clot of blood; **~körperchen** *n* blood corpuscle; *med* h(a)ematocyte; *weißes ~~* leucocyte; *rotes ~~* erythrocyte; **~kreislauf** *m* circulation of the blood; **~laugensalz** *n* potassium ferrocyanide; **~leer, ~los** *a* bloodless, an(a)emic; **~leere** *f med* isch(a)emia, local an(a)emia; **~mal** *n* red mole; **~mangel** *m* bloodlessness; an(a)emia; **~probe** *f med* blood test; **~rache** *f* vendetta, blood feud; **~reich** *a med* plethoric; **~reinigend** *a* purifying the blood; **~reinigung** *f* purification of the blood; **~rot** *a* blood-red, sanguineous; **~rünstig** *a* bloody; **~sauer** *a* very toilsome; *es sich ~sauer werden lassen* to work like a slave; **~sauger** *m* vampire; *fig* blood-sucker, extortioner; **~schande** *f* incest; **~schänder** *m* incestuous person; **~schänderisch** *a* incestuous; **~schuld** *f* blood-guiltiness; capital crime; **~sfreund** *m* kinsman; **~speien, ~spucken** *n* spitting of blood; **~spender** *m* blood-donor; **~spur** *f* track of blood; **~stillend** *a* blood-stanching; *med* styptic, h(a)emostatic; *~stillendes Mittel med* styptic, h(a)emostat; **~strieme** *f* livid weal; **~stropfen** *m* drop of blood; **~sturz** *m med* h(a)emorrhage; bursting of a blood-vessel; **~sverwandt** *a* related by blood (to), consanguineous; **~sverwandter** *m* blood-relation, relative by blood, kinsman; **~sverwandtschaft** *f* proximity of blood, consanguinity; **~tat** *f* bloody deed; murder; **~übertragung** *f* blood transfusion; **~umlauf** *m* circulation of the blood; **~ung** *f* bleeding; *med* h(a)emorrhage; **~unterlaufen** *a* bloodshot; **~urteil** *n* sentence of death; **~vergießen** *n* bloodshed, slaughter; **~vergiftung** *f* blood-poisoning; sepsis; **~verlust** *m* loss of blood; **~wallungen** *f pl* heats *pl*; **~wasser** *n* lymph, serum; **~wenig** *adv* very little, next to nothing; **~wurst** *f* black-pudding; **~zeuge** *m* martyr.

Blüte *f* blossom, bloom, flower; *fig* prime; heyday; **~nart** *f* kind of species of flower; **~nbecher** *m* cupula; **~nbildung** *f* formation of flowers; **~nblatt** *n* petal; **~ndolde** *f* umbel; **~nfüllung** *f* doubling; **~nkätzchen** *n* catkin; **~nkelch** *m* calyx; **~nknospe** *f* bud; **~nlese** *f* anthology; **~nstand** *m* inflorescence; **~nstaub** *m* pollen; **~nstengel** *m* peduncle; **~zeit** *f* flourishing time, prosperity; (*der Künste*) golden age.

Bö *f* sudden squall, gust; *aero* air-bump; *schwere ~* heavy squall, violent gust; *ausgedehnte ~* line squall; **~enwolke** *f* squall cloud; **~ig** *a* bumpy, squally, gusty; **~~keit** *f* bumpiness; turbulence.

Boa *f* boa.

Bob|(schlitten), Bobsleigh *m* bob (-sleigh), bobsled; *Vierer~* four-seater bobsleigh; **~bahn** *f* bobsleigh course, bob-run; **~fahrer** *m* bob-rider; **~mannschaft** *f* bobsleigh crew.

Bock *m* buck; (*Schaf~*) ram; (*Ziegen~*) he-goat; *fig* (*alter ~*) an old lecher; (*Gestell*) jack, trestle, horse; (*Turnen*) wooden horse, leap-frog; (*Kutsch~*) box; (*Fehler*) blunder, stumble; *spanischer ~* stocks *pl*; *jdn in den ~ spannen* to tie s.o.'s arms and legs together; *e-n ~ schießen* to (make a) blunder; *den ~ zum Gärtner machen* to trust the cat to keep the cream; **~beinig** *a fig* pigheaded; wayward; stubborn; **~bier** *n* bock (beer); **~en** *itr* (*Geruch*) to have a goat-like smell; (*Sprünge machen*) to caper; (*Pferd*) to buck, to capriole, to prance; (*schmollen*) to sulk, to be obstinate; **~ig** *a* (*widerspenstig*) obstinate; (*Pferd*) skittish; *aero* (*Wetter*) bumpy; **~leder** *n* goat's leather; buckskin; **~leiter** *f* double ladder, trestles *pl*; **~shorn** *n*: *jdn ins ~~ jagen* (*fig*) to bully s. o.; to intimidate s. o.; **~springen** *n sport* horse-jumping, horse-vaulting; leap-frog; **~sprung** *m* goat's leap, gambol, capriole; caper; *sport* jump (*od* vault) over the horse; *~sprünge machen* to caper.

Boden *m* (*Erd~*) ground; (*Acker~*) soil; (*Fuß~*) floor; (*Haus~*) loft; (*Dachstube, Bodenkammer*) garret, attic; (*Heu~*) hay-loft; (*Gefäße, Behälter, Meeres~*) bottom; (*Grund und ~*) real estate, land, property; *auf französischem Grund u. ~* on French soil; (*Grundlage*) base, basis, foundation; *auf dem ~* (*Fuß~*) on the floor, (*Dach~*) in the attic; *zu ~* (*Boxen*) to the planks; *jdm ~ abgewinnen* to gain ground upon s.o.; *das schlägt dem Faß den ~ aus* (*fam*) that is the limit; *auf dem ~ der Gesetze bleiben* to keep within the bounds of the law; *der ~ brennt ihm unter den Füßen* the place is getting too hot for him; *zu ~ bringen* to floor s.o., to have s.o. down; *zu ~ gehen* to descend; *dem ~ gleich machen* to raze (*od* level) to the ground; *an ~ gewinnen* to come up ahead; *die Augen zu ~ schlagen* to cast down o.'s eyes; *zu ~ schlagen, zu ~ werfen* to knock s.o. down, *Am* to floor s.o.; *zu ~ sinken* to sink down; *auf den ~ stellen* to ground; *festen ~ verlieren* to lose o.'s footing; *den ~ unter den Füßen verlieren* (*auch fig*) to get out of o.'s depth; *vom ~ freikommen* to become air-borne; *den ~ entrümpeln* (*Luftschutz*) to clear the attic; **~ablagerung** *f* deposit ground, stock pile; **~abstand** *m mot, aero* ground clearance; **~abstandzünder** *m mil* base combination fuse; **~abwehr** *f* ground defences, antiaircraft-artillery defences *pl*; **~angriff** *m aero* ground attack, groundstrafing; *~~e durchführen* to ground-strafe; **~anlage** *f aero* ground installation; air-base service area; **~arbeit** *f* (*Ringen*) *sport* ground work; **~art** *f* type of soil; **~auszug** *m phot* lens extension; **~bearbeitung** *f* cultivation, soil tilling; **~belag** *m* covering of the floor; **~beschaffenheit** *f* condition of the soil; nature of the ground; **~bewegung** *f* earth work; **~bö** *f aero* ground squall, bump; **~bordverkehr** *m aero* ground(-air) communication, air-to-ground radio telephony, communication with aircraft; **~brett** *n mot* floor panel; (*Schreibmaschine*) base board; **~entrümpelung** *f* clearance of attics; **~erhebung** *f* undulation, upheaval, soil elevation, rising, rising ground; **~erschöpfung** *f* soil exhaustion; **~falte** *f* gully, furrow; **~fenster** *n* dormer window; **~fläche** *f* acreage, acres *pl*; (*im Haus*) carpet-area, *Am* floor-space; **~flugleiter** *m aero* ground-control operator; **~fräse** *f* ground mill; **~freiheit** *f mot* ground clearance; **~frost** *m* ground frost, hoarfrost; **~funkdienst** *m* ground radio service, ground W/S service; direction-finding wireless service; **~funkstelle** *f radio* ground radio station; **~geschwindigkeit** *f aero* ground speed; **~gestaltung** *f* terrain features *pl*, formation of ground; **~haftung** *f mot* road traction; **~höhe** *f* ground level, floor level; **~kammer** *f* garret, attic; **~kanzel** *f aero* (*Kampfstand*) ball turret, belly (*od* ventral) turret; **~klappe** *f* drop bottom, bottom gate; **~korrosion** *f* soil corrosion; **~kredit** *m* credit on landed property, credit on real estate; **~kreditanstalt** *f* (land-)mortgage bank, real estate bank; **~los** *a* bottomless; *fig* exceeding, excessive; unheard of; *adv* exceedingly; **~luke** *f* (*Fenster der ~kammer*) garret window; (*kleines Fenster*) skylight, dormer window; *aero* escape hatch; **~markierung** *f* (*Bombenwurf*) *aero mil* target-indicator; **~nähe** *f aero* low altitude, ground level; *in ~~* near the ground; **~nährstoff** *m* soil nutrient; **~navigation** *f aero* pilotage; **~nebel** *m* ground fog; **~neigung** *f* gradient; **~oberfläche** *f* surface; **~organisation** *f aero* ground organization; **~peiler** *m radio* ground direction finder; **~personal** *n*, **~mannschaft** *f* ground personnel, ground-crew, ground-maintenance crew, *Am* groundstaff; **~raum** *m* attic; **~reform** *f* land (*od* agrarian) reform; **~rente** *f* ground-rent; **~satz** *m* sediment, grounds *pl*, dregs *pl*; *chem* residuum, settling; **~schätze** *m pl* treasures of the soil, mineral resources *pl*; **~see** *m* Lake Constance; **~sender** *m* ground station transmitter; **~senkung** *f* declivity; **~sicht** *f aero* (ground) visibility; **~ständig** *a* permanent; native, indigenous; **~station** *f radio* ground-station; **~streitkräfte** *f pl mil* ground forces *pl*; **~thermik** *f* (*Segelflug*) thermic upwash near ground; **~treppe** *f* attic stairs; **~tür** *f* trap-door, door of loft; **~turnen** *n* physical exercises on the floor; **~verdichter** *m* road grader; **~wanne** *f aero* bathtub gunner's pit; **~welle** *f radio* ground (*od* direct) wave; **~wellenempfangszone** *f radio* ground-wave reception zone; **~wetterkarte** *f* ground weather map (*od* chart); **~wind** *m* ground wind.

Bodmerei *f* bottomry.

Bogen *m* (*Biegung, Kurve*) bend, bow; curve; *im ~* in a curve; (*Kreis~*) arc; *arch* arch; (*Waffe*) bow; *den ~ spannen* to bend the bow; (*Papier~*) sheet; *typ* section; (*Geigen~*) bow; *in Bausch und ~* in the lump; **~brücke** *f* viaduct; **~fenster** *n* bay-window; **~förmig** *a* arched, vaulted; curved; **~gang** *m* arch-way, arcade; colonnade; **~lampe** *f* arc-lamp; **~licht** *n* carbon-light; arc light; **~lichtstrahler** *m* high-intensity carbon arc light; **~linie** *f* circular line, curve; **~schießen** *n* archery; **~schluß** *m* keystone, heading stone; **~schütze** *m* archer, bowman; **~sehne** *f* bow-string; *math* chord (of a segment); **~strich** *m mus* bowing (technique); **~weise** *adv* archwise; (*vom Papier*) in sheets; **~weite** *f arch* span, width; **~zahl** *f typ* number of sheets; **~zähler** *m typ* sheet counter.

*

Bohle *f* plank; (*Diele*) thick board; **~n** *tr* to line with planks; **~nbelag** *m* plank bottom; planking; **~nsäge** *f* cleave saw; **~nwand** *f* planking, bulkhead, timbered wall, wall of planks.

Böhm|en *n* Bohemia; **~e** *m* Bohemian; **~isch** *a* Bohemian; *das sind ihm ~ische Dörfer* that is Greek to him.

Bohne *f* bean; *grüne ~n* French beans, *Am* string(-)beans; *Wachs~* wax-bean; *Stangen~* pole-bean; *weiße ~n* haricot beans; (*Kaffee~*) coffee-berry, coffee-bean; *Sau~* broad bean; *blaue ~* (*fig*) bullet; *nicht die ~* (*fig, fam*) *Am* not a hoot; *nicht die ~ wert* (*fig fam*) not worth a straw; **~nkaffee** *m* pure coffee; **~nlied** *n*: *das geht übers ~~* that beats everything; *übers ~~ loben* (*fam*) to praise up to the skies; **~nstange** *f*, **~nstecken** *m* beanpole; *eine lange ~nstange* (*fig, fam*) s.o. as tall as a lamp-post, spindle-shanks *pl mit sing*; **~nstroh** *n* bean-straw; *dumm wie ~~* (*fam*) exceedingly stupid; *grob wie ~~* (*fam*) very coarse, extremely rude.

Bohner *m* rubber, polisher; **~besen** *m* weighted floor polisher; **~lappen** *m* rubbing-cloth; **~maschine** *f* floor polisher; **~n** *tr* to wax, to rub, to polish; **~wachs** *n* rubbing-wax, floor wax (*od* polish).

Bohr|automat *m* automatic boring (*od* drilling) machine; **~bank** *f* boring bench (*od* lathe); **~en** *itr* (*auf~~ auf größeren Lochdurchmesser*) to bore, (*aus dem Vollen*) to drill; (*in Holz nur*) to bore; (*durchbohren*) to pierce; (*durchlöchern*) to punch; (*nach Erdöl*) to drill (*od* sink *od* put down) a well; *in den Grund ~en* to sink, to run aground; to scuttle; **~er** *m* bore(r), drill; (*Nagel~~*) gimlet; (*Preßluft~~*) pneumatic borer; (*Schädel~~*) trephine, perforator; (*Spiral~~*) twist drill; (*Arbeiter*) borer, drilling machine worker; **~gerät** *n* boring (*od* drilling) instrument, (*für Tiefbohrungen*) deep boring tool; **~lehre** *f* (*Schablone*) jig; **~loch** *n* (*aufgebohrt*) borehole, (*aus dem Vollen*) drill-hole; (*bei Holz stets*) borehole; **~maschine** *f* (*zum Aufbohren*) boring machine, (*aus dem Vollen*) drilling machine; (*für Zahnarzt*) drill, burrdrill, dental engine; **~späne** *m pl* borings *pl*; **~turm** *m* (*Öl*) derrick, shaft house; **~ung** *f* boring; (*Motor*) bore; (*Geschütz~~*) calibre; (*Ölsonde*) well; **~wurm** *m* wood fretter, ship's borer (*od* worm).

Boje *f* buoy; *festmachen an e-r ~* to secure to a buoy; *losmachen* (*od loswerfen*) *von e-r ~* to cast off from a buoy.

Boiler *m* (*Warmwassertank*) boiler; (*Heißwasserspeicher*) (storage) water heater, geyser.

Boleine *f* buoy-rope.

Böller *m* small mortar.

Bollwerk *n* bulwark; stronghold.

Bolschew|ik *m* Bolshevik; **~ismus** *m* Bolshevism; **~ist** *m* Bolshevist; *sl* Bolshy; **~istisch** *a* Bolshevik, Bolshevist.

Bolzen *m tech* bolt; (*Zapfen, Stift*) peg, pin; (*Keil*) wedge; (*Plätt~*) heater; (*stehender Balken*) prop, stay; (*für Armbrust*) crossbow bolt, arrow; **~gerade** *a* bolt upright.

Bombard|ement *n* (*Beschießung, bes. auch phys mit Neutronen*) bombardment; **~ieren** *tr* (*beschießen mit Kugeln, Bomben; Neutronen*) to bombard; to bomb; (*mit Artillerie*) to shell; to strafe; **~ierung** *f* bombardment.

Bombast *m* bombast; **~isch** *a* bombastical.

Bombe *f* bomb; *sl* egg; *fig* bombshell, *die Nachricht schlug ein wie e-e ~* the news was like a bombshell; *Brand~* incendiary bomb; *fliegende ~* flying bomb; *~ mit Raketenantrieb* rocket bomb; *Spreng~* explosive bomb; *~n im Reihenwurf* stick of bombs; *~ mit Zeitzünder* delayed-action bomb, time bomb; *~n (ab)werfen* to release bombs; (*auf ein Ziel*) to drop bombs (on a target); (*mit ~n belegen*) to bomb (a town); (*im Notwurf*) to jettison bombs; *ausgebombt* bombed out; *e-n Großangriff mit ~n auf e-e Stadt machen* to blitz a town; **~nabwurf** *m* bombing, bomb dropping, bomb release; (*auf Flächenziele*) area bombing; **~~auftrag** *m* bombing assignment, *Am* bombing mission; **~~gerät** *n* bomb release mechanism; **~~hebel** *m* bomb release lever; **~~kurve** *f* bomb trajectory; **~~vorrichtung** *f* bomb release gear; **~~winkel** *m* range angle; **~~zielgerät** *n* bombsight; **~~zone** *f* bomb release zone; **~nanflug** *m* (*Zielanflug, unmittelbar vor dem Wurf*) bomber run (lining-up period); **~nangriff** *m* bomb(ing) raid, bombing attack, (*Großangriff, bes. auf Städte*) air blitz; **~nattentat** *n* bomb outrage; **~nbeschädigt** *a* bomb damaged, blitzed; **~neinschlag** *m* bomb hit; **~nerfolg** *m* *fam* striking success, *fam* howling success, *Am* smash hit; **~nfest** *a* bomb-proof; *fig* sure and certain; **~nflug** *m* bombing flight; bombing raid; bombing mission; **~nflugbahn** *f* bomb trajectory; **~nflugzeug** *n* (*im Deutschen meist Kampfflugzeug genannt*) bombardment airplane, bombing plane, bomber; **~ngeschädigter** *m* bomb-damaged; **~ngeschäft** *n* *fam* roaring business, a highly profitable business; **~ngeschwader** *n* bombing squadron, bomber wing; **~nkasten** *m*, **~nmagazin** *n*, **~nschacht** *m* bomb container, bomb rack, bomb bay; **~nklappen** *f pl* bomb-bay doors *pl*, bomb doors *pl*; **~nkopf** *m* bomb nose (*od* -tit); **~nladung, ~nlast** *f* bomb load; **~nloch** *n*, **~ntrichter** *m* bomb crater; **~npunktwurf** *m* precision bombing, pinpoint bombing; **~nrakete** *f* rocket bomb; **~nräumtrupp** *m* (*für Blindgänger u. Zeitbomben*) U. X. B. (= unexploded bomb squad); bomb disposal squad; **~nreihenwurf** *m* stick (of bombs); **~nsache** *f* *fam* stunner; **~nschäden** *m pl* air raid damages *pl*; **~nschütze** *m* bombardier, bomb aimer; **~nsicher** *a* bomb-proof; *fig* absolutely certain, dead certain; **~nsplitter** *m* splinter (of a bomb); **~nteppich** *m* (*rollender, zum Üben*) practice-bombing panel; (*zur Flächenzerstörung*) pattern bombing; **~ntiefangriff** *m* low-level bombing attack; **~nträger** *m* bombing plane; **~ntreffer** *m* bomb hit; **~nvisier** *n* bombsight; **~nvolltreffer** *m* direct bomb hit; **~nwagen** *m* bomb cradle; **~nwerfer** *m* (*Attentäter*) bomb thrower, bombtosser; **~nwurf** *m* bombing; (*aus großer Höhe, auf Einzelziele*) high-altitude precision bombing; (*mit Atombomben*) atomic bombing; **~nzielgerät** *n* bomb sight, bomb-aiming device; **~nzerstört** *a* bomb-battered; *e-e durch ~n zerstörte Stadt* a bomb-wrecked town; **~nzünder** *m* (bomb) fuse; **~r** *m* (= *Kampfflugzeug*) bomber; *leichter ~~* light bomber, *mittlerer ~~* medium bomber, *schwerer ~~* heavy bomber, *Düsen~~, Strahl~~* jet bomber; *Jagd~~* (*Jabo*) fighter-bomber; *Nacht~~* night-bomber; *Tag~~* day bomber; **~~besatzung** *f* bomber crew; **~~formation** *f* bomber formation; **~~staffel** *f* bomber flight (*od* squadron); **~~strom** *m* bomber stream; **~~stützpunkt** *m* bomber base; **~~welle** *f* wave of bombing planes.

Bon *m* (*Gutschein*) *com* promisory note; **~bon** *m u. n* bonbon, sweet; (*mit Stäbchen*) lollipop; *Am* (hard) candy; toffy; **~bonladen** *m* sweet shop, *Am* candy-store; **~bonniere** *f* bonbon box; **~d** *m* (*Schuldverschreibung, Wertpapier, (Am) Staatspapier*) bond; **~ifikation** *f* (*Vergütung, Nachlaß*) compensation, allowance; **~ität** *f* (*Güte*) superior quality; (*finanzielle*) solvency; (*Wert*) value; (*Sicherheit*) reliability; (*Güte des Bodens*) quality of the soil; **~itierung** *f* (*Beurteilung der Böden, Güteklassen*) classification of the soil; **~us** *m* (*Zugabe, Vergütung, bes. für entlassene Soldaten*) bonus; (*Gewinnanteil bei Versicherungen*) bonus, *Am* dividend; (*Sonderdividende*) surplus dividend.

Bonz|e *m* (*buddhistischer Priester*) bonze; (*großes „Tier“*) bigwig, *Am* big shot, *fam* big-bug; (*Parteigröße*) party favo(u)rite, *Am* party-boss; **~entum** *n*, **~enwirtschaft**, **~okratie** *f* (*Herrschaft der ~en*) *Am* boss rule.

Boot *n* boat; *großes ~* long-boat; *flaches ~* punt; *kleines ~* skiff, dingey; *leichtes ~* gig; *zusammenlegbares ~* collapsing boat, folding boat; *Renn~* racing boat; *Rettungs~* life-boat; *Riemen~* oar-boat; *Ruder~* rowing boat, *Am* rowboat; *Segel~* sailing-boat, *Am* sail-boat; *~ fahren* to go boating; *ein ~ voll von* a boat-load of; *ein ~ aussetzen* to lower a boat; **~sbauer** *m* boat builder; **~sbesatzung** *f* boat's crew; **~sdeck** *n* boat deck; **~sfahrt** *f* boating; (*mit Ruderboot*) row, (*mit Segelboot*) sail; **~sführer** *m* bargee, boatman; **~shaken** *m* boat-hook, grapnel; **~shaus** *n* boat house; **~shaut** *f aero* skin of the hull, *Am* hull of the boat; **~skörper** *m* hull; **~sleute** *pl* boat's crew; **~smann** *m* boatswain (*Abk* bosun), coxswain (*Abk* coxs'n); **~smotor** *m* motor-boat engine; **~sschuppen** *m* boat-box; **~sschwert** *n* leeboard; **~ssteg** *m* boat-bridge; **~swerft** *f* boat-yard.

Bor *n* boron; **~salbe** *f* boric ointment; **~säure** *f* boric acid; **~ax** *m* borax.

Bord *m* (*Rand*) border, edge, rim, brim; (*das Bücher~*) book-shelf; *mar, aero* board; *an ~ e-s Schiffes* on board a ship, aboard; *an ~ bringen* to put on board; *an ~ gehen* to go on board, to board (a ship); *von ~ gehen* to go on shore; *an ~ sein* to be on board; *~ an ~* (*längsseit*) alongside; *frei an ~* free on board (*Abk* fob); *über ~* overboard; *Mann über ~!* man overboard! *über ~ fallen* to fall over board; *über ~ gehen* to go by the board; *über ~ werfen* to throw over board; (*Ballast etc*) to jettison; **~anlasser** *m aero* cockpit starter; **~aufklärer** *m aero* shipboard reconnaissance plane; **~buch** *n mar* log book; *aero* aircraft log book; **~dienst** *m* service aboard; **~flugzeug** *n* ship-borne aircraft; **~funkanlage** *f aero* aircraft wireless installation; **~funker** *m mar* wireless operator (*od* officer); *aero* air(craft) wireless operator; *Am* radio operator, radio man; **~funkstelle, ~funkstation** *f mar* ship's wireless station; ship radio station; *aero* aircraft set; **~instrumentenbrett** *n aero* dashboard; **~kanone** *f aero* aircraft cannon; **~kino** *n* ship's cinema; **~linie** *f* water-line; **~mechaniker, ~monteur, ~wart** *m* air mechanic (*Abk* A. M.), flight engineer; **~peiler** *m* (ship's) direction finder (*Abk* D. F.); radio compass; **~rakete** *f aero* air-borne rocket; **~rundsuchgerät** *n* air-borne all-round radar search apparatus; **~schütze** *m* air gunner; *~~ des oberen Gefechtsstandes* (*aero*) top turret gunner; **~schwelle** *f*, **~stein** *m* (*Randstein*) edge stone, curb(stone), kerb(stone); **~sprechanlage** *f* interphone system; intercommunication system; (*von ~ zu ~*) interplane phone system; **~station** *f aero* aeroplane W/T, *Am* airplane radio station; *mar* ship radio station; **~telephon** *n aero* interphone; **~verpflegung** *f aero* flight ration; **~verständigungsanlage** *f aero* intercom(munication system); **~waffen** *f pl* armament of an aircraft, aircraft weapons *pl*; *Erdziele mit ~waffen beschießen* to strafe; **~~angriff** *m aero* strafing attack; **~~beschuß** *m* fire from aircraft weapons; **~wand** *f* ship's wall (*od* side); **~~wagen** *m rail* goods wagon, *Am* freight car; **~werkzeug** *mot, aero* tool kit.

Bordell *n* brothel; (*euphemistisch*) house of ill fame, disorderly house; *Am* call-house, love-nest; *ein ~ betreiben* to run a disorderly house; **~viertel** *n* (*e-r Stadt*) red-light district.

***bordier|en*, bördeln** *tr* to border, to edge; to trim, to lace; **~ung** *f* bordering, lacing.

Bordüre *f* edge, edging; border.

Borg *m* borrowing, credit; *auf ~* on credit; *mar* preventer; **~en** *tr, itr* to borrow; (*jdm ausleihen*) to advance, *Am* to loan out; to lend, to give on credit; *~en macht Sorgen* he that goes borrowing, goes sorrowing; **~er** *m* (*Kreditnehmer*) borrower; (*Kreditgeber*) lender.

Borgis *f* (*Schriftgrad*) Bourgeois 9 pts.

Borke *f* bark, rind; (*Kruste*) crust; (*Schorf*) scab; **~nkäfer** *m* bark-beetle.

Born *m* spring, fountain; well; (*Salz*) salt pit; brine.

borniert *a* (*beschränkt*) narrow-minded, stupid.

Börs|e *f* (*Geldbeutel*) purse; *com* (*Geldinstitut od ~engebäude*) stock-exchange, Exchange, *fam* 'Change; (*inoffizielle ~e nach Börsenschluß od Handel mit nicht notierten Werten*) curb market, outside market; *auf der ~e* on the exchange, *fam* on 'Change; *an der ~e gehandelt* (*notiert*) *werden* to be quoted (*Am* listed) at the exchange; *an der ~e zugelassen* listed on stock-exchange; **~enbericht** *m* stock-list, official quotations *pl*, financial news, market-report; **~enblatt** *n* commercial (*od* financial) newspaper; money-market report; **~endrucker, ~entelegraph** *m* ticker; **~enfähig** *a* admitted to the stock exchange, *Am* listed; (*lieferbar*) negotiable; **~engeschäft** *n* exchange transaction (*od* operation); **~enkrach** *m* collapse (*od* crash) of the stock market; **~enkurs** *m* table (*od* rate) of exchange; market price; **~enkurszettel** *m* stock-list; **~enmakler** *m* stock-broker; **~enmanöver** *n* market-rigging, *Am* campaign, demonstration; **~ennotierung, ~ennotiz** *f* quotation; **~enordnung** *f* stock-exchange regulations *pl*; **~enpapiere** *n pl* stocks, shares, securities *pl* quoted (*Am* listed) on the Exchange; **~enpreis** *m* exchange-price, market- price; **~enscheinverkauf** *m* *Am* wash sale; **~enschluß** *m* final hours of trading; trading unit, full lot; **~enschwankungen** *f pl* exchange fluctuations *pl*; **~enschwindler** *m* speculator; **~enspekulant** *m* stock-jobber; **~enspekulation** *f*, **~enspiel** *n* stock-jobbing; **~enspieler** *m* speculator; **~entermingeschäft** *n* time-bargain; **~enumsatzsteuer** *f* stock-exchange tax, *Am* transfer tax; **~enwert** *m* market value; **~enzeitung** *f* financial (*od* commercial) paper; **~enzettel** *m* (money-) market report; **~enzulassung** *f* admission to the stock-exchange; **~ianer** *m* (*~enspieler*) stock-exchange speculator.

Borst|e *f* bristle; *bot* seta; **~enartig** *a* bristly; *bot* setaceous; **~enbesen** *m* hair-broom; **~enpinsel** *m* painter's brush; **~entier, ~envieh** *n hum* hog, pig; **~ig** *a* bristly; *fig* (*verdrießlich*) crusty, grumpy, surly; *~ig werden* (*fam*) to fly into a temper.

Borte *f* border, trimming; (*Besatz*) braid, lace; (*Tresse*) galloon; *mit ~n einfassen* to lace; **~nwirker** *m* lace-maker.

bös|artig *a* malicious, ill-natured; (*auch von Krankheiten*) malignant; virulent; (*von Tieren*) vicious; **~artigkeit** *f* malignity, wickedness, viciousness; ~(e) *a* evil; (*schlimm, schlecht*) bad; (*verrucht*) wicked; (*Zeit*) hard; (*Wunde*) sore; (*zornig, wütend*) angry, *Am* mad; (*garstig*) nasty; *~e Absicht* malice; *~es Blut machen* to create ill-feeling; *sie hat den ~en Blick* she has the evil eye; *ein ~es Fieber* a virulent fever; *ein ~es Gewissen* a bad conscience; *e-e ~e Krankheit* a malignant disease; *ein ~er Ruf* a bad reputation; *ein ~es Tier* a vicious beast; *~es Wetter min* choke damp; *~e Zeiten* hard times; *sie hat e-e ~e Zunge* she has a nasty tongue; *er meinte es nicht ~e* he meant no harm; *~e sein* to be angry (at s.th., with s.o.), *Am* to be mad, to be cross at s.o.; *er ist mir ~e* (*Am*) he is mad at me; *sie wurde sehr ~e* she flew into a passion; *sie sind ~e aufeinander* they are on bad terms with one another; *Gutes mit B~em vergelten* to return evil for good; *gute Miene zum ~en Spiel machen* to make the best of a bad job; **~e** *m* the evil one, the foul fiend, the Devil; **~ewicht** *m* villain, scoundrel; rogue; **~willig** *a* malevolent; *jur* fraudulent, malicious, intentional; *in ~williger Absicht* (*jur*) with malice prepense; *~williges Verlassen von Ehegatten* (*jur*) wilful desertion, malicious abandonment; **~willigkeit** *f* malevolence, malice.

Bosch|horn *n mot* (electric) hooter, *Am* horn, siren; **~magnet** *m* Bosch magneto; **~zündung** *f* Bosch magneto ignition.

Böschung *f* slope; (*Fluß*) embankment.

bos|haft *a* malicious, wicked, spiteful; (*mutwillig*) mischievous, *Am* ugly; **~haftigkeit**, **~heit** *f* malice, wickedness, maliciousness, spite.

Bosn|ien *n* Bosnia; **~ier**, **~iak** *m* Bosniac, Bosnian; **~isch** *a* Bosniac, Bosnian.

boss|eln, ***~ieren*** *tr* to emboss, to mo(u)ld; to model; **~ierer** *m* embosser.

Botan|ik *f* botany; **~iker** *m* botanist; **~isch** *a* botanic(al); **~isieren** *itr* to botanize; **~isiertrommel** *f* plant-box, specimencase, vasculum.

Bote *m* messenger; (*Laufbursche*) errand-boy; (*Fuhrmann*) carrier; *Am* (*bes. Amts~*) page; *reitender ~* estafette, courier; *eigener ~* express messenger; *durch ~n!* by bearer! **~ngang** *m* errand, commission; *~ngänge besorgen* to run (on) errands; **~ngänger** *m* messenger; **~njunge** *m* errand-boy, office-boy; **~nlohn** *m* messenger's fee; (*Fuhrlohn*) porterage.

Botmäßigkeit *f* dominion; jurisdiction; power, rule; *unter seine ~ bringen* to bring under o.'s sway.

Botschaft *f* message, errand; (*Gesandtschaft*) embassy, legation; (*Nachricht*) tidings *pl u. sing*; *gute ~* good news; *e-e ~ übermitteln* to deliver a message; **~er** *m* ambassador; *~~ des Papstes* nuncio; **~erin** *f* ambassadress; **~srat** *m* Council(l)or of Embassy.

Böttcher *m* cooper; **~arbeit** *f* cooperage; **~ei** *f* cooper's workshop.

Bottich *m* coop, tub, vat; (*Brauerei*) tun, tank, vessel.

Bouillon *f* broth, beef-tea; bovril; clear soup; **~würfel** *m* soup cube.

Bovist *m* puff-ball.

Bowle *f* (*Gefäß*) tureen; bowl; (*Getränk*) spiced wine, iced fruit-cup; claret-cup; *e-e ~ brauen* to prepare a punch.

box|en *itr* to box, to fight (with fists); **~er** *m* boxer, pugilist, prize-fighter; *Schwergewichts~er* heavy-weight boxer; **~ermotor** *m* boxer engine; **~handschuh** *m* boxing glove; **~kampf** *m* boxing match, fight; **~regeln** *f pl* prize ring rules *pl*; **~ring** *m* ring; **~schuh** *m* boxing shoe; **~sport** *m* boxing (-sport).

Boykott *m* boycott; **~ieren** *tr* to boycott; (*ausschließen, kaltstellen*) *Am* to freeze out.

*

brach *a* fallow, untilled, unploughed; *~ liegen lassen* to let a field lie fallow; to let go to waste; *fig* to lie idle; **~acker** *m*, **~feld** *n*, **~e** *f* fallow ground; **~en** *itr* to fallow; **~monat** *m* June; **~vogel** *m* curlew; (*kleiner*) dott(e)rel.

Brachialgewalt *f* (*handgreifliche Gewalt*): *mit ~* by open force.

Brack *m* refuse, trash; **~e** *m* (*Hund*) setter; **~gut** *n* refuse of merchandise; trash; **~wasser** *n* brackish water.

Brah|mane, Brahmine *m* Brahman; **~maismus** *m*, **~manentum** *n* Brahmanism; **~manisch** *a* Brahmanic.

Bramarba|s *m* braggart; **~sieren** *itr* to bluster, to swagger, to brag.

Bram|segel *n* topgallant sail; **~stenge** *f* topgallant mast.

Branche *f* (*Fach, Zweig, Abteilung*) *com* branch, line (of business); department; **~kenntnis** *f* knowledge of the trade; **~kundig** *a* experienced in the line; **~nverzeichnis** *n* classified directory.

Brand *m* burning; (*Glut*) blaze; (*Feuersbrunst*) conflagration; (*Feuer~*) fire; (*Verbrennung*) combustion; (*Heizmaterial*) material for heating, fuel; *med* (*Gangrän*) gangrene; *kalter ~* (*med*) mortification; (*im Getreide etc*) blight, blast; *bot* blight, mildew; *com* (*Marke*) brand; (*zur Kennzeichnung von Tieren*) brand; (*starker Durst nach Rausch*) thirst; (*fam Rausch*) intoxication; *e-n ~ anstiften* (*jur*) to commit arson; *e-n ~ anlegen* (*Am*) to set a fire; *in ~ geraten* to catch fire, to take fire; *in ~ setzen* (*od stecken*) to set on fire, to set fire to; *in ~* on fire; **~binde** *f med* bandage for burns (impregnated with bismuth subgallate); **~blase** *f* blister; **~bombe** *f* incendiary bomb; napalm bomb; **~brief** *m* (*dringende Bitte um Hilfe*) urgent letter (asking for money); begging letter; (*Drohbrief*) threatening letter; **~direktor** *m* commander of the fire-brigade; *Am* fireward(en); **~en** *itr* to surge, to (break into) foam; **~er** *m*, **~schiff** *n mar* fire-ship; **~fackel** *f* incendiary torch; *fig* torch of war; **~flasche** *f mil* incendiary bottle, Molotov cocktail; **~flecken** *m* burn, scald; **~fuchs** *m* (*Pferd*) golden bay-horse, sorrel horse; **~geruch** *m* smell of burning, burnt smell; **~geschoß** *n* incendiary bullet; **~glocke** *f* fire-bell; **~granate** *f* incendiary shell; **~ig** *a* (*Geruch*) burnt smell; (*Getreide etc*) blighted, blasted; *med* gangrenous; **~kanister** *m* incendiary canister; **~kasse** *f* fire-insurance office, fire-office; **~leiter** *f* fire-ladder, fire-escape; **~mal** *n* (*Narbe*) brand; *fig* (*Schandmal*) stigma; **~malerei** *f* poker-work, pyrography; **~marken** *tr* (*mit heißem Eisen u. fig*) to brand; *gebrandmarkt sein* to be branded; *fig* to denounce, to stigmatize; **~mauer** *f* fire-wall, fire-proof wall, partition wall; **~munition** *f* incendiary ammunition; **~opfer** *n* burnt offering, holocaust; **~rede** *f* inflammatory address; **~salbe** *f* ointment for burns; **~satz** *m* incendiary composition; **~schaden** *m* damage caused by fire; **~schatzen** *tr* to ravage, to plunder; to lay under contribution; **~schatzung** *f* (war-) contribution; plundering; **~sohle** *f* inner sole; welt; **~stätte**, **~stelle** *f* scene of a fire; **~stifter** *m* (**~in** *f*) incendiary, fire-raiser; *Am fam* fire-bug; **~stiftung** *f* arson, fire-raising; **~tür** *f* fire-proof door; **~ung** *f* surf, surge, breakers *pl*; **~~sboot** *n* surf-boat; **~~swelle** *f* breaker; **~versicherung(sgesellschaft)** *f* fire-insurance (company); **~wache** *f* fire-watch; **~wunde** *f* (*durch trockene Hitze*) burn; (*Verbrühen durch heiße Flüssigkeiten*) scald; **~zeichen** *n* brand.

Branntwein *m* spirits *pl*; *Am* (hard) liquor, schnap(p)s; (*Kognak*) brandy; (*Wacholder*) gin; (*Korn*) whisk(e)y; *~ brennen* to distil(l) spirits; **~blase** *f* alembic, still; **~brenner** *m* distiller; **~brennerei** *f* (brandy) distillery; **~monopol** *n* spirits monopoly; **~nase** *f* bottle-nose; **~schenke** *f* dram-shop, gin-shop, *Am* barroom; **~steuer** *f* tax on spirits; **~waage** *f* alcoholometer.

Brasil|ianer *m*, ***~in*** *f* Brazilian; **~ianisch** *a* Brazilian; **~ien** *n* Brazil; **~holz** *n* brazilwood; **~nuß** *f* Brazil nut.

Brasse *f* brace; **~(n)** *m* (*Fisch*) bream; **~n** *itr mar* to brace.

Brat|apfel *m* baked apple, roasted apple; **~bock** *m* meat rack; **~en** *irr tr* to roast; (*in der Pfanne*) to fry; (*im Ofen*) to bake; (*auf dem Rost*) to grill; (*am offenen Feuer*) to broil; (*am Spieß*) to roast on a spit; *itr* to be roasted; (*an der Sonne*) to be scorched (in the sun); *durchgebraten* well done; *zu wenig, zu stark gebraten* underdone, overdone; **~en** *m* roast (meat); (*Keule*) joint; *den ~en riechen* to smell a rat; **~enbrühe**, **~ensauce** *f* gravy, sauce; **~enfett** *n* dripping; **~enrock** *m* dress-coat; **~enwender** *m* turnspit, roasting-jack; **~fisch** *m* fried fish; **~hering** *m* red-herring, grilled herring; **~huhn** *n* roast(ed) chicken; **~kartoffeln** *f pl* (home-) fried potatoes *pl*; **~pfanne** *f* frying-pan; *Am auch* skillet; **~ofen** *m* frying-oven; **~röhre** *f* oven; **~rost** *m* (*Grill*) grill, gridiron, roaster; **~spieß** *m* spit; **~spill** *n mar* pump windlass; **~wurst** *f* small sausage for frying, fried sausage; *Am* pork sausage.

Bratsch|e *f* viol(a); bass-viol; **~ist** *m* violist, viola player.

***Brau*, Bräu** *m* (*Getränk*) brew, brewage, beer; (*Brauerei*) brewery; **~bottich** *m* brewing-vat, tun; **~en** *tr* (*Bier etc*) to brew; *fig* (*im Schild führen, sich zusammenziehen, im Anzug sein*) to plot, to concoct, to brew (*z. B.* to brew mischief); (*zusammenmischen*) to mix; **~er** *m* brewer; **~erei** *f*, **~haus** *n* brewery, brew-house; (*Lokal*) tavern; **~gerste** *f* brewing barley; **~gewerbe** *n* brewer's trade; **~kessel** *m* coop, copper; **~malz** *n* brewing malt; **~meister** *m* brewmaster, head brewer, master brewer.

Brauch *m* (*Sitte*) custom; (*Herkommen, Geschäfts~, Sprachgebrauch*) usage; *fester ~* common usage; (*Übung*) practice; (*herkömmlicher ~*) observance; (*altbestehender, bes. auch lokaler ~*) prescription; (*Gewohnheit*) habit; **~bar** *a* useful; *tech* usable; fit for use, serviceable, practicable; (*Person*) efficient, handy, apt; **~barkeit** *f* usefulness; practicability; (*Person*) fitness, aptitude; **~en** *tr* (*nötig haben, bedürfen*) to want, to be in want of, to require; *dringend ~en* to need, to be in need of; *~en zu* to want for; *Zeit ~en* to take time; *er braucht nur 2 Stunden, um es zu tun* it will take him only 2 hours to do it; *wir haben alles, was wir ~en* we have all we need; *wie lange wird er* *noch ~en?* how much longer will it take him? *ich ~e Ihnen nicht zu sagen* I need not tell you; *Sie ~en es nur zu sagen* you only need mention it; (*gebrauchen*) to use, to employ, to make use of, to have use for; (*verbrauchen*) to spend, to use up; (*Brennstoff*) to consume; *sie ~en viel Geld* they spend a lot of money; *den Wagen kann ich nicht ~en* I have no use for this car; (*imp*) *es braucht keines Beweises* no proof is required; *es braucht kaum hinzugefügt zu werden* it scarcely needs adding; *es braucht viel Mühe* it takes much trouble; **~tum** *n* custom(s *pl*); *eccl* rite; *com* usance.

Braue *f* eyebrow.

braun *a* brown, dark; (*Pferd*) bay; (*Butter*) fried; *~ machen, ~ werden* to make brown, to get brown; *~ werden* (*von der Sonne*) to become sunburnt, to get a tan, to tan; *Sie sind ~* you are sun-tanned; *~e Schuhe* tan shoes; *~ braten* to brown up; *~ u. blau schlagen* to beat black and blue; *ins ~e gehen* to verge on brown; *~e Butter* fried butter; *Meister ~* (*Bär in der Fabel*) Bruin; **~äugig** *a* brown-eyed; **~bier** *n* brown beer; **~eisenstein** *m* brown iron ore; **~gelb** *a* brownish yellow; **~haarig** *a* brown-haired; **~kehlchen** *n orn* whinchat; **~kohl** *m* broccoli; **~kohle** *f* brown coal; *tech* lignite; **~~nbergwerk** *n* brown coal (*od* lignite) mine; **~~nbrikett** *n* brown coal (*od* lignite) briquette; **~rot** *a* red ochre; **~sche Röhre** *f* (*für Fernsehen*) cathode-ray tube (*Abk* C.R.T.); *Am tele* kinescope; **~schwarz** *a* dark brown; **~stein** *m* manganese (ore).

Bräun|e *f* brownness, *med* angina, quinsy; *häutige ~e* croup; **~en** *tr* (*in Fett*) to brown; (*in der Sonne*) to tan; (*Zucker*) to burn; (*Metall*) to burnish; **~lich** *a* brownish, tawny.

Braus *m* bustle; tumult; *in Saus und ~ leben* to revel and riot.

Braus|e *f* (*Gießkopf e-r Gießkanne*) rose, sprinkling nozzle; *chem* effervescence; fermentation; **~e** *f*, **~ebad** *n* (*Dusche*) shower (-bath), douche, needle-bath; (*Handdusche*) hand spray; **~en** *itr* (*rauschen*, (*aero*) *mit Motorenlärm sausen*) to roar; (*eilen*) to rush; (*summen*) to buzz, to hum; (*in den Ohren*) to sing, to buzz in o.'s ears; (*stürmen*) to storm, to rage; (*toben*) to bluster; (*Orgel*) to peal; (*aufwallen*) *chem* to effervesce; (*aufbrausen*) to fly into a passion; (*sich duschen*) to take a shower-bath, to douche; **~end** *a* (*rauschend*) roaring; (*sprudelnd*) effervescent; (*Jugend*) impetuous, passionate; (*lärmend, Wind*) boisterous; **~ekopf** *m* hot-headed fellow; **~elimonade** *f* fizzy lemonade; **~epulver** *n* effervescent powder; **~~würfel** *m* sparklet.

Braut *f* intended, fiancée; (*am Hochzeitstag*) bride; *sie ist ~* she is engaged; *wer das Glück hat, führt die ~ heim* fortune gains the bride; **~ausstattung** *f* trousseau, wedding-outfit; **~bett** *n* bridal bed; **~führer** *m* best man; **~jungfer** *f* bridesmaid; **~kleid** *n* wedding-dress, bridal gown; **~kranz** *m* bridal garland; **~leute** *pl* bridal pair; (*am Hochzeitstag*) bride and bridegroom; **~nacht** *f* wedding-night; nuptial night; **~paar** *n* bridal pair, engaged couple; (*am Hochzeitstag*) bride and bridegroom; **~schau** *f*: *auf ~~ gehen* to look out for a wife; **~schleier** *m* bride's (*od* wedding) veil; **~stand** *m*, **~zeit** *f* time of engagement; **~vater** *m* bride's father; *den ~~ machen* to give the bride away; **~werbung** *f* match-making.

Bräut|igam *m* intended, fiancé; (*am Hochzeitstag*) bridegroom, *Am* groom; *Freund und Begleiter des ~~s* groomsman; **~lich** *a* bridal, bride-like; nuptial.

brav *a* honest, upright; (*tapfer*) brave, gallant; (*von Kindern*) good, well-behaved; **~o!** *interj* bravo! good! well done! **~oruf** *m* cheers *pl*; shout of bravo.

brech|bar *a* breakable; (*zerbrechlich*) fragile; *opt* refrangible; **~barkeit** *f* (*Zerbrechlichkeit*) fragility, frangibility; *opt* refrangibility; **~bohne** *f* kidney bean; (*grüne*) French bean; **~durchfall** *m med* diarrhoea (*Am* diarrhea) with vomitting; summer-cholera; **~eisen** *n*, **~stange** *f* crow(-bar), handspike; (*kurze*) jemmy, *Am* jimmy; **~en** *irr tr* (*Schweigen, Fasten, Gelübde, Widerstand, Wort, Ketten, Herz etc zerbrechen*) to break; (*Hanf*) to dress; (*grob mahlen*) to crush; (*Früchte, Blumen*) to pluck, to gather; (*Papier*) to fold; (*Licht*) to refract; (*Farben*) to blend; (*Blockade*) to run; (*Steine*) to quarry; (*erbrechen*) to vomit, to throw up; (*Gesetz*) to violate, to break, to infract; *ein Gesetz bricht ein anderes* a law overrides another law; (*Vertrag*) to infringe; (*die Ehe ~en*) to commit adultery; *sein Wort* (*od Versprechen*) *~en* to break o.'s promise; *Bahn ~en* to force a passage; to make way; *seinen Eid ~en* to break o.'s oath; *etw übers Knie ~en* to do s. th. abruptly; *e-n Streit vom Zaun ~en* to pick a quarrel; *das bricht mir das Herz* that breaks my heart; *e-r Flasche den Hals ~en* to crack a bottle; *den Stab ~en über* (*fig*) to condemn s. o. severely; *itr mit jdm ~en* to break with s. o., to have done with s.o.; *die Geduld bricht ihm* his patience is coming to an end; *die Augen ~en ihm* his eyes grow dim; *sich ~en* to break; (*Strahlen*) to be reflected; *die Kälte bricht sich* the cold is abating(*od* getting less severe); (*sich erbrechen*) to vomit, to throw up; *gebrochene Stimme* dying voice, faltering voice; *gebrochen Deutsch sprechen* to speak broken German; **~en** *n* breaking; (*Gesetz*) breach, infraction, violation; (*das Erbrechen*) vomiting; (*Licht*) refraction; **~er** *m* (*Meer*) breaker(s *pl*), heavy seas *pl*; (*Zerbrecher, Gesetz~er*) breaker; (*Maschine*) crusher; pulverizer; (*für Kohle, Erz*) grinding mill; **~koks** *m* crushed coke; **~mittel** *n* emetic, vomitive; *fig* sickener; *er ist ein wahres ~mittel* he is a sickener; **~nuß** *f* vomit-nut; **~reiz** *m* nausea, sickly feeling, heave; (*Erbrechen*)retching; **~ruhr** *f* cholera; **~ung** *f* breaking; (*Strahlen*) refraction; **~~skoeffizient** *m* refraction index; **~~swinkel** *m* refracting angle.

Bregen *m* (*Gehirn*) brains *pl*.

Brei *m* (*Kinderbrei*) pap; (*Haferbrei*) porridge, *Am* mush-porridge; (*weiche Masse, Papier~*) pulp; (*Mus*) mash; *Kartoffel~* mashed potatoes; (*bes. Am Maisbrei*) mush; (*Teig*) paste; *geol* magma; (*Keramik*) slip; *zu ~ zerquetschen* to mash; *zu ~ machen* to pulp; *zu ~ schlagen* (*fam*) to beat into a jelly; *wie die Katze um den heißen ~ herumgehen* to beat about the bush; *viele Köche verderben den ~* many cooks spoil the broth; **~ig** *a* pappy, pulpy; pasty; semifluid; viscous; **~umschlag** *m* poultice; cataplasm.

breit *a* broad, wide; (*ausgestreckt*) flat; (*weit, umfassend*) large; (*ausgedehnt*) extensive, vast, ample; (*weitschweifig*) diffuse; *weit u. ~* far and wide, *Am* high and low; for miles around; *e-n ~en Buckel haben* to take it; *jdn ~schlagen* to persuade, to talk s. o. over; *etw ~treten* to dilate upon, to expatiate on; *sich ~ machen* to take up much room; *fig* to boast, to swagger; **~band** *n radio* wide-band; **~~antenne** *f* broad- (*od* wide-)band antenna; **~~empfänger** *m* wide-band receiver; **~beinig** *a* straddle-legged, straddling; **~e** *f* breadth, width; *geog* latitude; (*Spurweite*) ga(u)ge; (*Schiff*) beam of a vessel; (*Ausdehnung*) extent; (*Geräumigkeit*) spaciousness; (*Weitschweifigkeit*) prolixity, verbosity; diffuseness; **~en** *tr* to spread; to extend; *mar* to brace; (*entfalten*) to unfold; (*breitschlagen*) to flatten; **~~ausdehnung** *f* extension of width; **~~feuer** *n mil* sweeping fire; **~~grad** *m* degree of latitude; **~~kreis** *m* parallel of latitude; **~hacke** *f* mattock; **~krempig** *a* broad-brimmed; **~randig** *a* (*Hut*) broad-brimmed; (*Buch*) with wide margins; **~schult(e)rig** *a* broad-shouldered; **~seite** *f* broadside; **~~geschütz** *n* broadside gun; **~spurig** *a* wide-ga(u)ge; *fig* swaggering; (*Stil*) prolix; **~ung** *f* spread, broadening.

Brems|ausgleich *m* brake equalizer; **~backe** *f* brake shoe, brake block; **~belag** *m* brake lining, brake covering, brake block; *den ~~ erneuern* to reline the brakes; **~berg** *m* braking incline; **~betätigung** *f* brake operation (*od* control); **~~shebel** *m* brake operating lever; **~dauer** *f* braking period; **~e** *f* (*Insekt*) gad-fly, horsefly; (*Nasenknebel des Pferdes*) barnacle; *tech* brake; *Flüssigkeits~e* hydraulic brake; *Luftdruck~e* air brake; *mechanische ~e* cable brake; *Band~e* band brake; *Fuß~e* foot brake; *Hand~e* hand brake; *Not~e* emergency brake; *Vierrad~e* four-wheel brake; *die ~en nachstellen* to adjust the brakes; **~einstellung** *f* brake adjustment; **~en** *tr* to brake, to put on the brake(s), to apply (*od* to pull) the brake(s); *plötzlich scharf ~en* to jam o.'s brakes; to pull up suddenly; (*abbremsen*) to brake the speed; (*anhalten*) to stop, to arrest; (*zurückhalten*) to detain, to hold back, to restrain; (*e-e Bewegung*) to check; to decelerate; **~~futter** *n* brake lining; **~energie** *f* work (*od* energy) of braking; **~er** *m* braker, brakesman, *Am* brakeman; **~erhäuschen** *n rail* brakeman's cabin; **~fallschirm** *m aero* braking parachute; **~fläche** *f* braking area; **~flüssigkeit** *f* brake fluid; **~gestänge** *n* brake linkage, brake rods *pl*; **~hebel** *m* brake(-)lever; **~klappe** *f aero* wing-flap, landing-flap; **~klotz** *m* brake block; *aero* chock, *Am* chock block; **~leistung** *f* brake horse power (*Abk* B.H.P.); **~licht** *n* brake light **~luftschraube** *f aero* brake propeller; **~moment** *n* braking moment; **~nachstellung** *f* brake adjustment; **~pedal** *n* brake pedal; **~schlußlampe** *f* stop and tail lamp; **~schuh** *m* brake shoe, brakehead; **~seil** *n* brake cord; **~spur** *f* brake mark, skid mark; **~stand** *m* brake-testing stand, dynamometer test stand; **~steuerung** *f* brake control; **~strahlung** *f* continuous radiation; **~strecke** *f* stopping distance; **~substanz** *f* (*phys zum Abbremsen der Neutronen im Atombrenner*) moderator; **~trommel** *f* brake drum; **~ung** *f* braking (action); retardation; (*der Elektronen*) deceleration, retardation, (*durch Magnetron*) reflection, deflection; **~vermögen** *n* braking power; **~versuch** *m* braking test; **~vorrichtung** *f* braking device, braking gear; **~weg** *m* stopping distance, brake length; **~widerstand** *m* brake resistance; **~zylinder** *m mot* brake cylinder; (*beim Geschütz*) recoil cylinder.

brenn|bar *a* combustible, (*entzündlich*) inflammable; **~barkeit** *f* combustibility, inflammability; **~dauer** *f* burning-time; *el* lighting hours *pl*; **~ebene** *f opt* focal plane; **~eisen** *n* (*Stempel*) brand-iron, marking-iron; (*für die Haare*) curling-iron(s *pl*), curling-tongs *pl*; *med* cautery; **~en** *irr itr* to burn, to be on fire; (*Haut*) to itch, to burn; (*Augen*) to smart; (*stechen*) to sting; *vor Ungeduld ~en* to burn with impatience; *es brennt!* (*Ruf*) fire! *es brennt in der Stadt* there is a fire in town; *die Arbeit brannte ihr auf den Nägeln* she was terribly pressed with work; *es brannte ihm unter den Sohlen* he wanted to be off; *darauf ~en etw zu tun* to be anxious (*od* to be dying) to do s.th.; *er brannte darauf anzufangen* he was itching to get started; *das Streichholz brennt nicht* the match does not strike; *tr* (*Licht*) to light; (*Haare*) to curl, to wave; (*Ziegel*) to bake; (*Kalk*) to burn; (*Kohle*) to make charcoal; (*Erz*) to calcine; (*Branntwein*) to distil(l); (*Schiff reinbrennen*) to bream; (*Kaffee*) to roast; (*Keramik, Porzellan*) to fire, to bake, to burn; (*zeichnen mit heißem Eisen*) to mark, to brand; (*Wunden ausbrennen*) *med* to cauterize; (*Nesseln*) to sting; (*Pfeffer etc auf der Zunge*) to bite; *sich ~en* to burn o.s.; *fig da ~en Sie sich sehr!* you are greatly mistaken there! **~en** *n* burning; itching; (*Schnaps*) distillation; (*Wunden*) *med* cauterization; **~end** *a* burning, alight; (*Hitze*) scorching; *fig* glowing; fervent; (*Schmerz*) pungent, smarting; (*ätzend*) caustic; (*Liebe*) ardent; (*Verlangen*) eager; (*Frage*) vital, urgent, burning; (*Farbe*) glaring; *~endes Verlangen* eager longing; *die Sonne ist ~end heiß* the sun is scorching; *~end abstürzen* (*aero*) to crash in flames; **~er** *m* (*Gas~~*) (gas) burner, gas jet; (*Schweiß~~*) torch, blowpipe; (*Atom~~*) pile, atomic pile; (*Uran~~*) uranium pile; *den Atom~~ einschalten* to turn on the pile; *den Atom~~ ausschalten* to shut off the pile; *der ~~ lief im September 44 an* the pile went into operation in September 44; (*Schnaps*) distiller; (*Ziegel*) brickmaker; **~erei** *f* (*Schnaps*) distillery, still; **~ermotor** *m* internal combustion engine; **~glas** *n* burning-glass (*od* lens); **~holz** *n* firewood; **~kammer** *f* combustion chamber; **~kraft** *f* intensity of combustion; **~länge** *f* time of burning; setting of fuse; **~material** *n* fuel, firing; **~nessel** *f* (stinging-) nettle; **~ofen** *m* (*Keramik*) kiln; furnace, oven; **~öl** *n* (*Lampe*) lamp-oil; (*Heizöl*) fuel oil; **~punkt** *m fig u. phys* focus, focussing point, focal point; (*Zentrum*) centre, *Am* center; *den ~~ betreffend, im ~~ stehend* focal; **~schere** *f* curling-iron(s *pl*), curling-tongs *pl*; **~schneider** *m* oxy-acetylene cutter; **~spiegel** *m* burning-reflector (*od* -mirror); **~spiritus** *m* spirit; **~stelle** *f* (*Licht*) lighting point; **~stempel** *m* burning (*od* branding) stamp; **~stoff** *m* (*bes. mot, aero*) fuel; gas(oline); (*Material*) combustibles *pl*; *~~ aufnehmen* (*tanken*) to fuel; **~~behälter** *m* fuel tank; *abwerfbarer ~~behälter* (*aero*) droppable fuel tank; **~~düse** *f* fuel jet; **~~einspritzung** *f* fuel injection; **~~pumpe** *f* fuel pump; **~~übernahme** *f* fuelling; **~~verbrauch** *m* fuel consumption; **~~versorgung** *f*, **~~vorrat** *m* fuel supply; **~~zuführung** *f* fuel feed; **~stunde** *f* lighting hour; **~weite** *f opt* focal distance (*od* length); **~wert** *m* fuel value, calorific value; **~zünder** *m* time fuse; pyrotechnic fuse.

brenz|lich, ~lig *a* (*nach Brand riechend*) having a burnt smell, tasting of burning; *fam* (*gefährlich*) precarious; risky, doubtful; *e-e ~lige Angelegenheit* (*od Geschichte*) *fam* a delicate matter; *die Sache wird ~lich fam* the matter is getting critical.

Bresche *f* breach, gap; *e-e ~ schlagen* to clear the way, to thrust forward; *e-e ~ schießen* to batter (*od* make) a breach; *in die ~ springen* to stand in the gap.

bresthaft *a* decrepit.

Bret|agne *f* Brittany; **~one** *m*, **-in** *f* Breton; **~onisch** *a* Breton.

Brett *n* board, plank; (*Bücher~*) shelf; (*Servier~*) tray; (*Schach~*) draught-board; *schwarzes ~* notice board; *mil* bulletin board; *Am* tack board; (*Sprung~*) springboard; *flach wie ein ~* as flat as a pancake; *mit ~ern belegen* to board, to plank, to floor; *ein ~ vor dem Kopfe haben* to be a blockhead; *bei jdm e-n Stein im ~e haben* to be in favo(u)r with; *die ~er pl* stage; *die ~er, die die Welt bedeuten* the boards which typify the world; *das Stück geht über die ~er* the play is acted; (*Skier*) skis, woods *pl*; *die ~er anschnallen* to put on the skis; *auf den ~ern stehen* to be on o.'s skis; (*Ringbretter beim Boxen*) planks *pl*, boards *pl*; *auf die ~er schicken* (*Boxen*) to knock down; **~chen** *n* little (*od* thin) board; **~erbude** *f*, **~erschuppen** *m* booth, shed, (tumbled-down) shanty, *Am* shack; **~erdach** *n* board roof; **~erfußboden** *m* boarded floor; **~ern** *a* boarded, of planks; **~erverschlag** *m*, **~wand** *f* partition (of) boards; **~erwerk** *n* boards *pl*, planking; **~erzaun** *m* wooden fence; boarding (fence); (*für Plakate*) *Am* bill-board; **~l** *n* (*Kabarett*) cabaret, music-hall, kind of variety theatre; **~nagel** *m* nail plank; **~säge** *f* pit-saw, whip-saw; **~schneider** *m* sawyer; **~spiel** *n* (*Damenspiel*) draughts *pl*, *Am* checkers *pl*; **~stein** *m* man (at draughts).

Brevier *n* breviary.

Brezel *f* cracknel; bretzel, *Am* pretzel.

Brief *m* letter; (*kurzer*) note; (*Bibel*) epistle; (*Kurszettel*) for sale; *ein ~ Nadeln* a packet of needles (*od* pins); *eingeschriebener ~* registered letter; *postlagernder ~* letter to be called for; *unbestellbarer ~* dead letter; *unter ~ u. Siegel* under hand and seal; *e-n ~ zur Post geben* (*od aufgeben*) to post a letter, *Am* to mail a letter; *e-n ~ in den Kasten werfen* (*od abschicken*) to drop a letter in the letter-box (*Am* mailbox); *Ihr ~ vom 5. d. M. ist eingelaufen* your letter of the 5th (instant) has been received; *Funk~* radio letter telegram; **~abholung** *f* collection of letters; **~ablage** *f* letter-files *pl*; letter-sorter; **~~fach** *n* letter slot; **~anfang** *m* opening of a letter; **~annahme** *f* reception of letters; **~aufgabe** *f* posting (*Am* mailing) of a letter; **~aufgabestempel** *m* postmark; **~anschrift, ~aufschrift** *f* address; **~ausgabe** *f* postal delivery; **~beschwerer** *m* letter-weight, paper-weight; **~bestellung** *f* delivery of letters; **~beutel** *m Am* mail-bag; letter-bag; **~bogen** *m* sheet of note-paper; **~bote** *m siehe ~träger*; **~buch** *n* letter-book; **~chen** *n* note, billet; **~einwurf** *m* letter-box, *Am* letter-chute; (*Schlitz*) slit; (*Aufschrift am Kasten*) Letters! **~fach** *n* pigeon-hole, letter-rack; **~freund** *m fam Am* pen pal; **~geheimnis** *n* secrecy (*od* privacy) of correspondence, inviolability of letters; **~hülle** *f* envelope; **~hypothek** *f* certificated mortgage; **~kanal** *m* mail chute; **~karte** *f* letter-card; **~kasten** *m* letter-box; (*in Säule*) pillar-box, *Am* mailbox, box; *e-n ~~ leeren* to clear a letter-box; *der ~~ wird fünfmal täglich geleert* (*Am*) mail from this box is collected five times daily; (*in Zeitungen*) Question and Answer Column; **~klammer** *f* letter- (*od* paper-) clip; **~kopf** *m* letter-head, head(ing); **~kurs** *m* offer price, asked price, selling rate; **~lich** *a* written; epistolary; *~licher Verkehr* correspondence; *adv* by letter; **~mappe** *f* writing-case, portfolio, blotter; **~marke** *f* (postage-)stamp; **~~nautomat** *m* postage stamp slot machine; **~~nsammler** *m* stamp-collector, philatelist; **~~nsammlung** *f* stamp-collection; **~öffner** *m* letter-opener, envelope-opener; paper-cutter; **~ordner** *m* (letter-)file, letter-book; **~papier** *n* letter-(*od* writing-)paper, note-paper, *Am* stationery; *dünnes ~~* lightweight stationery; (*Flugpostpapier*) airmail-paper; **~porto** *n* postage; **~post** *f* post, mail; (*im Gegensatz zu Drucksachen etc*) *Am* first class mail (*od* matter); **~schaften** *pl* letters *pl*, papers *pl*; correspondence; **~schreiber** *m* (**-in** *f*) letter- writer; **~schulden** *f pl* arrears of correspondence; **~sperre** *f* stoppage of letters; **~steller** *m* letter-writer; guide for letter-writing; **~stempel** *m* post-mark, letter-mark; **~stil** *m* epistolary style; **~tagebuch** *n* daily mail ledger; **~tasche** *f* letter-case, note-book, notecase, wallet, *Am* billfold; **~taube** *f* carrier-pigeon, homing pigeon, messenger pigeon; **~telegramm** *n* letter telegram, *Am* lettergram, night telegraph letter; **~träger** *m* postman, *Am* mailman, letter-carrier, mail-carrier; **~umschlag** *m* envelope, letter-cover, wrapper, *Am* (*für Urkunden*) jacket; **~verkehr** *m* correspondence; **~waage** *f* letter balance, letter scales *pl*, letter weight, *Am* postage scale; **~wechsel** *m* correspondence; *~~ unterhalten mit jdm* to keep up a correspondence with s. o.; *in ~~ stehen mit* to correspond with s.o.

Bries *n* thymus; sweetbread.

Brigade *f* brigade; **~kommandeur** *m* brigadier, brigadier-general.

Brigant *m* brigand.

Brigg *f* brig.

Brikett *n* briquette, brikette, patent fuel, coal dust brick, *Am* briquet; *Braunkohlen~* brown coal briquette; **~erzeugung** *f* patent fuel manufacturing; **~fabrik** *f* patent fuel plant, briquetting works *pl*.

Brillant *m* brilliant, diamond; **~nadel** *f* diamond neck-tie pin; **~schliff** *m* grinding with facets; **~sucher** *m phot* reflector view finder.

Brille *f* spectacles *pl*; (eye-) glasses *pl*; *e-e ~* a pair of spectacles; (*Schutz~*) goggles *pl*; (*mit doppeltem Brennpunkt für Nah- u. Weitsicht*) bifocals *pl*; (*Klosettsitz*) seat (of a W.C.); **~nbügel** *m* bow of spectacles; **~n(ein)fassung** *f*, **~ngestell** *n* spectacle-frame, spectacle-mount; **~nfutteral** *n* spectacle-case; **~nglas** *n* spectacle glass, lens; **~nmacher** *m* (*Optiker*) optician; **~nschlange** *f* cobra; **~nsteg** *m* bridge, nose saddle; **~ntragend** *a* spectacled; **~nträger** *m* wearer of glasses.

Brimborium *n* fuss, to-do.

bringen *irr tr* (*zu e-m her*) to bring, to fetch; (*von e-m weg, wegtragen, befördern*) to take, to carry, to convey; *jdn nach Hause* ~ to see s.o. home, to escort s.o. home; (*Bescheid*) to bring word; (*Früchte*) to bear fruit; (*Gewinn*) to yield a profit; (*Opfer*) to offer, to make; (*Schaden*) to bring (*od* to cause) injury to s. o.; (*Ständchen*) to serenade s. o.; (*Zinsen*) to bear interest; (*veröffentlichen*) to publish; *in die Garage* ~ to garage, to park; *was bringt Sie her?* what brings you here? *was* ~ *Sie? fam* what's up? *was* ~ *Sie Neues?* what is the news? *die Zeitung hat nichts darüber gebracht* the (news)paper did not say a word about it; *es dahin* ~ (*od fertig* ~ *od zustande* ~ *od zuwege* ~) to manage, to accomplish, to contrive to do, to bring about; *jdn dahin* ~ (*od zu etw* ~) to induce s.o. to; *jdn dazu* ~ *etw zu tun* to make s.o. do s. th., to get s.o. to do s. th.; *es weit* ~ (*od zu etw* ~) to go far, to succeed in a high degree, to make o.'s way, to get somewhere; *jdn* (*od etw*) *beiseite* ~ to put s. o. (*od* s. th.) out of the way; *an den Bettelstab* ~ to reduce to poverty; *an den Mann* ~ to dispose of; (*los*~) to get rid of; (*Tochter*) to find a husband for, to get o.'s daughter (married) off; *an den Tag* (*od ans Licht*) ~ to bring to light; *an sich* ~ to acquire, to obtain; *an den Wind* ~ to bring into the wind; *auf die Beine* ~ to set up, to raise; *auf die Bühne* ~ to put on the stage; *jdn auf den Gedanken* ~ to suggest s.th. to s.o.; *du bringst mich auf den Gedanken* you make me think that; *auf neue Rechnung* ~ to place to a new account; *auf die Seite* ~ to put aside; *ich brachte sie auf meine Seite* I brought her over to my side; *auf die Spur* ~ to put on the track; *aufs Tapet* ~ to bring up; *es auf 90 Jahre* ~ to live to be 90 years old; *jdn aus der Fassung* ~ to disconcert, to upset s.o.; *jdn außer sich* ~ to enrage; *er brachte es bis zum Oberst* he rose to be a Colonel; *in Anwendung* ~ to put into practice; *in Erfahrung* ~ to learn, to get to know; *in Erinnerung* ~ to remind of; *in Gang* ~ to set going, to start; *in e-e peinliche Lage* ~ to put in an embarrassing position; *in Mode* ~ to bring into fashion; *in Ordnung* ~ to arrange, to set in order, *Am* to straighten out s. th.; *in Rechnung* ~ to take into account, to charge s. o. with; *ins reine* ~ to settle; *in ein System* ~ to reduce to a system; *in Verlegenheit* ~ to embarrass; *in Wegfall* ~ to suppress; *mit sich* ~ to bring along with; to bring about; *fig* (*enthalten*) to involve, to entail, to imply; *die Umstände* ~ *es so mit sich* circumstances make it unavoidable; *es übers Herz* ~ to have the heart to; to prevail upon o.s., to get o.s. to; *Unglück über jdn* ~ to bring down misfortune upon s. o.; *jdn um etw* ~ to make s.o. lose s. th., to deprive (of); (*betrügen*) to cheat out of, to defraud; (*berauben*) to rob; *jdn ums Leben* ~ to kill, to murder s.o.; *sich ums Leben* ~ to commit suicide; *um den Verstand* ~ to drive mad; *jdn unter die Erde* ~ to bring down to the grave; *unter die Haube* ~ to find a husband for a girl; *unter die Leute* ~ (*Gerücht*) to spread abroad, to make known, to make public, to circulate; (*Geld*) to spend freely; *von Sinnen* ~ to drive mad; *vor ein Gericht* ~ to go to law with s.o., to bring an action against s. o., to prefer before a court; *zum Abschluß* ~, *zu Ende* ~ to bring s. th. to a close; *zum Äußersten* ~ to provoke to the utmost; *zur Abstimmung* ~ to put (a question) to the vote; *zur Besinnung* ~ to bring s.o. to his senses; *zu Fall* ~ to bring down; (*Mädchen*) to seduce; (*vernichten*) to ruin, to wreck, to upset; *zur Kenntnis* ~ to inform s.o.; *zum Lachen* ~ to make s. o. laugh; *zum Schweigen* ~ to silence; *jdn wieder zu sich* ~ to bring s.o. round (*Am* around); *zur Vernunft* ~ to bring s.o. to reason; *zur Verzweiflung* ~ to drive s.o. to despair; (*Kinder*) *zur Welt* ~ to bring forth, to bear.

Brisanz *f* detonating violence, *Am* brisance; **~bombe** *f* high explosive bomb (*Abk* H. E. bomb); **~granate** *f* high explosive shell (*Abk* H. E. shell); **~munition** *f* high explosive ammunition; **~pulver** *n* high explosive powder; **~sprengstoff** *m* detonating explosive; **~wirkung** *f* (high) explosive effect.

Brise *f* breeze, light wind; *frische* ~ fresh breeze; *steife* ~ gale; *es wehte e-e steife* ~ it blew a gale.

Brit|anniametall *n tech* Brittania metal; **~annien** *n* Britain; *poet* Britannia; *Großbritannien n* Great Britain; **~e** *m hist u. poet* Briton; Englishman; (*angelsächsischer*) Britisher; *Am* (*in Großbritannien ansässiger Engländer*) Britisher; **~in** *f* Briton; Englishwoman; **~isch** *a* British; English; *hist u. poet* Britannic; *Seine Majestät der König von Großbritannien u. Irland* His Britannic Majesty; *~ische Inseln* British Isles; *~isches Kontrollgebiet* British Zone of Control; *~ischer Staatenbund, ~ische Völkerfamilie* British Commonwealth; *~ische Wärmeeinheit* British thermal unit (*Abk* B. T. U.); *~isches Weltreich* British Empire.

Bröck|chen *n* little morsel, crumb; **~(e)lig** *a* crumbly, friable; **~eln** *itr* to crumble, to break into small pieces.

Brocken *m* crumb; (*Stückchen*) scrap; (*Bissen*) morsel; (*Klumpen*) lump; *fig* fragment; (*fam*) *dicke* (*od schwere*) ~ (*Bomben od Geschosse schwerer Geschütze*) heavy bombs; heavy shells; *französische* ~ scraps of French; **~sammlung** *f* collection of junk; **~weise** *adv* bit by bit, piecemeal.

Brod|el, **~em** *m* steam, vapo(u)r, exhalation; **~eln** *itr* to bubble.

Brokat *m* brocade; **~papier** *n* brocade-paper; **~pappe** *f* brocade-board.

Brokkoli *m pl* (*Spargelkohl*) broccoli; (*zu Gemüse*) broccoli sprouts *pl.*

Brom *n* bromine; **~äthyl** *n* ethyl bromide; **~id** *n* bromide of . . .; **~kali** *n* bromide of potassium; **~öldruck** *m phot* bromoil print; **~säure** *f* bromic acid; **~silber** *n* bromide of silver; **~~druck** *m* bromide printing; **~~papier** *n phot* bromide paper; **~wasserstoff** *m* bromide of hydrogen.

Brombeer|e *f* blackberry; **~strauch** *m* bramble, blackberry-bush.

bronch|ial *a* bronchial; **~ialkatarrh** *m* bronchial catarrh; **~ien** *f pl* bronchi *pl*, bronchia *pl*, bronchial tubes *pl*; **~itis** *f* bronchitis.

Bronnen *m poet* spring, well, fountain.

Bronz|e *f* bronze; gun metal; **~efarben** *a* bronze-colo(u)red; **~en** *a* (of) bronze; **~ezeit** *f* Bronze Age; **~ieren** *tr* to bronze.

Brosame *f*, ***Brösel*** *m* crumb.

Brosche *f* brooch, *Am* breast-pin.

Bröschen *n* (*Kalbsmilch*) calf's sweetbread.

brosch|ieren *tr* (*heften*) to bind in paper cover; to sew (*od* to stitch) together; (*Weberei, durchwirken*) to figure; **~iert** *a* stitched, in paper cover(s), in boards; **~üre** *f* stitched book, brochure; booklet, pamphlet, catalog(ue); (*Falt~~*) *Am* folder.

Brot *n* bread; *ein Stück* ~ a piece of bread; *altbackenes* ~ stale bread; *frisches* (*od neubackenes*) ~ new bread; *gesäuertes* ~ leavened bread; *schwarzes* ~ brown (*od* black) bread; *geröstetes* ~ toast; *belegtes* ~ sandwich, *Am* hamburger; *hausbackenes* ~ home-made (*od* household) bread; (*Laib = ganzes* ~) loaf (*pl* loaves); *fig* (*Verdienst, Unterhalt*) livelihood, bread; *das liebe* (*od tägliche*) ~ the daily bread; *sein* ~ *verdienen* to earn o.'s bread (*od* living); (*aurch harte Arbeit*) to work hard for a living; (*ehrlich*) to make an honest living; *er muß sich sein* ~ *selbst verdienen* he has to earn his own living; *sein* ~ *haben* to have a competence (*od* competency); *der Kampf ums liebe* ~ the struggle for life; *jdn um sein* ~ *bringen* to rob (*od* deprive) s. o. of his livelihood; *er kann mehr als* ~ *essen* he is up to a trick (*od* thing) or two; *sich das* ~ *vom Mund absparen* to stint o. s.; *sich ums* ~ *anstellen* to stand in a bread-line; *fremdes* ~ *essen* to serve other people; *auf Wasser u.* ~ *setzen* to put on bread and water; **~arbeit** *f* (*e-s Künstlers*) pot-boiler; **~aufstrich** *m* spread; **~bäcker** *m* baker; **~baum** *m* bread-fruit tree; **~beutel** *m* haversack, field bag, food bag; **~erwerb** *m* (gaining o.'s) livelihood; **~getreide** *n* bread grain; **~herr** *m* master, principal, employer; **~karte** *f* bread ration card; **~korb** *m* bread-basket; *jdm den* ~~ *höher hängen* to keep s. o. short, to make s. o. tighten his belt, to put s. o. upon short allowance; **~krume** *f* crumb of bread; **~lade** *f* bread box, bread drawer; *vulg* mouth; **~laib** *m* loaf (loaves *pl*); **~los** *a* breadless; (*ohne Stellung*) unemployed; *~los werden* to lose o.'s livelihood; (*nicht lohnend*) unprofitable; *~lose Künste* unprofitable arts, idle tricks *pl*; **~mangel** *m* shortage (*od* scarcity) of bread; **~marke** *f* bread ticket, bread coupon; **~nehmer** *m* wage earner, employee; **~neid** *m* professional envy, trade jealousy; **~rinde** *f* crust of bread; **~röster** *m* toasting fork; (*elektrischer*) toaster; **~scheibe, ~schnitte** *f* slice of bread; (*geröstet*) toast; **~schneidemaschine** *f* bread-cutter; **~schrift** *f* body-type, usual printing letters *pl*; **~studium** *n* professional study.

Brötchen *n* (*Semmel*) roll; (*weiches* ~) (soft) bun, *Am* biscuit; *ich esse* ~ *gern* I like rolls.

Bruch *m* breach; (*Unterbrechung*) break(ing); (*Zusammenbruch*) break-down; crack up; (*Knochen~*) fracture (of a bone); (*e-s Gliedes*) breaking (of a limb); (*der Eingeweide*) rupture, hernia; (*e-s Versprechens*) breach of promise; (*der Freundschaft*) breach of friendship; (*Riß*) crack; (*Öffnung*) gap; (*Falte im Papier od Tuch*) fold, crease; *math* fraction; *gewöhnlicher* ~ simple (*od* vulgar) fraction; *echter* ~ proper fraction; (*Vertrag*) *jur* infringement; (*e-s*

Gesetzes) violation, non-observance, breaking (of a law); (*Politik*) rupture, clash; (*Stein~*) quarry; (*Schutt*) debris, rubble; *fam* (*Schund*) trash; *tech* break, rupture, (*Struktur*) structure; (*Versagen e-r Maschine*) failure; (*Absturz*) *aero* crash; (*Schrott*) scrap (iron); (*von zerbrechlichen Waren*) breakage; (*Sumpf*) moor, marsh, fen, swamp, bog; (*Verbruch in e-r Grube*) falling in, downfall; *zu ~ gehen* to break; (*Maschinen*) to fail; *~ machen* (*aero*) to crash; (*beim Landen*) *Am* to crash-land; *in die Brüche gehen* (*fig*) to come to nought; *fam* to go on rocks; *alles ging in die Brüche* everything went to pieces; everything turned out a failure; *e-n Bruch einrichten* (*med*) to set a fracture; **~band** *n* truss, hernia support; **~beanspruchung** *f* breaking strain; **~belastung** *f* breaking load; **~bude** *f fam* dilapidated house, wretched hovel; **~dehnung** *f* elongation; **~fest** *a* break-proof; **~festigkeit** *f* breaking strength; **~fläche** *f* (surface of) fracture; **~frei** *a* free of breakage; **~landen** *itr aero Am* to crash-land; **~landung** *f aero Am* crashlanding; **~last** *f* ultimate strength (*od* load); **~rechnung** *f* fractional arithmetic; fractions *pl*; **~sicher** *a* unbreakable; (*Glas*) shatterproof; **~sicherheit** *f* safety against fracture; **~sicherung** *f* safeguarding (*od* security) against breakage; **~silber** *n* scrap silver; **~spannung** *f* breaking stress (*od* strain); tensile strength; **~stein** *m* quarry-stone, ashlar; **~stelle** *f* spot of rupture (*od* fracture); **~strich** *m* fraction stroke (*od* line), division sign; **~stück** *n* fragment; piece; **~~artig** *a* fragmentary; **~teil** *m* fraction; fractional part; (*e-r Erbschaft*) *jur* portion (of an inneritance); *~teile von Sekunden* split seconds; *im ~teil von Sekunden in Aktion treten* to go into split-second action; **~zahl** *f* fractional number.

brüchig *a* (*zerbrechlich*) fragile; cracked; (*von Metallen*) flawy; (*spröde*) brittle; (*leicht zerbrechlich*) tender; (*rissig*) full of cracks; (*mürbe*) short; (*zerreibbar*) friable; *geol* clastic, fragmental; *~ werden* (*Regenmantel*) to crack; **~keit** *f* (*Sprödigkeit*) brittleness; (*Zerbrechlichkeit*) fragility; *kristalline ~~* cleavable brittleness; (*Bröckeligkeit*) friability.

Brücke *f* (*auch el*) bridge; (*Viadukt*) viaduct; (*Zahn~*) bridge (-work); (*Teppich~*) small rug; *typ* till, shelves *pl*; (*Gymnastik*) backbend; (*Kommando~*) navigating bridge; *schwimmende ~* floating bridge, pontoon bridge, *e-e ~ bauen* to construct (*od* to throw) a bridge, (*über e-n Fluß*) to bridge a river; *e-e ~ sprengen* to blow up a bridge; *die ~n hinter sich abbrechen* to burn o.'s ships (*od* boats) behind one; *er hat alle ~n hinter sich abgebrochen* he has burnt his bridges behind him; **~nbau** *m* bridge-building, bridge construction; **~nbogen** *m* arch (of a bridge); **~nboot** *n* pontoon, *Am* ponton; **~nfähre** *f* ferry bridge; **~nfahrzeug** *n* pontoon-truck; bay section; **~ngeld** *n* bridge-toll, bridge due; **~ngeländer** *n* side rail, parapet; **~njoch** *n* supports *pl* (of a timber-bridge), bridge span; **~nkoffer** *m* (*Auto*) car trunk; **~nkolonne** *f* bridging unit; **~nkopf** *m mil* bridge-head, pier-head; **~nöffnung** *f* bridge opening; **~npfeiler** *m* bridge-pier, bridge-pile; **~nschlag** *m* bridging; **~nsperre** *f* bridge blockade; **~nsteg** *m* foot bridge; **~nwaage** *f* weighing-machine; platform-scale; (*für Wagenlast*) weigh-bridge; **~wache** *f* watch (*od* lookout) on the bridge; **~nweite** *f* span; **~nwiderlager** *n* abutment.

Bruder *m* brother; *pl* brothers; (*in der Kirche und in Ordensgesellschaften*) *pl* brethren; *liebe Brüder!* my brethren! (*Ordens~*) friar; (*Amts~*) colleague; *~ väterlicherseits* brother on the father's side; *~ Lustig* jolly fellow; *das ist es unter Brüdern wert* that's a reasonable price; *gleiche Brüder, gleiche Kappen* share and share alike; **~kind** *n* nephew; niece; **~krieg** *m* fratricidal war; **~kuß** *m* fraternal kiss; **~liebe** *f* brotherly love; *christliche ~~* Christian charity; **~los** *a* brotherless; **~mord** *m*, **~mörder** *m*, **~mörderin** *f*, **~mörderisch** *a* fratricide; **~schaft** *f* fraternity; **~volk** *n* sister nation, *Am* kinsfolk; **~zwist** *m* fraternal strife.

Brüder|chen, ~lein *n* little brother; **~lich** *a* fraternal, brotherly, brotherlike; **~lichkeit** *f* fraternity; **~schaft** *f* brotherhood; (*Genossenschaft*) fraternity, fellowship; (*geistliche*) congregation; *mit jdm ~~ schließen* to fraternize with s.o.; *mit jdm ~~ trinken* to hobnob with; to drink the pledge of brotherhood.

Brüh|e *f* (*Fleisch~*) broth; sauce; (*Braten~*) gravy; (*Flüssigkeit*) soupy liquid; (*Färben*) liquor, bath; (*Leder*) juice, drench, ooze; (*Tabak*) sauce; **~en** *tr* to scald; *die Wäsche ~en* to soak linen (in soda-water); **~heiß, ~warm** *a* scalding (hot), boiling hot; *fig* brand-new, quite fresh; *e-e ~warme Neuigkeit* (*Am*) a red hot news; *sie verbreitete die Nachricht ~warm* (*Am*) she spread the news red hot; **~kessel** *m* scalding-tub; **~würfel** *m* beef-cube.

Brühl *m* marshy place.

Brüll|affe *m* howling monkey, howler; **~en** *itr* (*schreien, heulen*) to howl, to bawl; *das Kind ~t* the child is bawling; (*schimpfen*) to vociferate; (*jammern*) to wail; (*brausen*) to boom; (*donnern*) to thunder; (*dumpf bellen*) to bay; (*Esel*) to bray; (*Löwe*) to roar; (*Ochs*) to bellow; (*Kuh*) to low; (*Kalb*) to bleat; (*Wogen, Wind*) to roar; (*Motoren, Geschütz etc*) to roar; *~en vor Lachen* (*vor Freude*) to roar with laughter (with glee); *Beifall ~en* to cheer vociferously; *der Kerl ist zum ~en! fam* that fellow is a howl! **~frosch** *m* bullfrog; **~ochs** *m* bull.

Brumm|bär, ~bart *m* (*Mensch*) *fam* growler, grumbler, snarler; **~baß** *m* (*der Orgel*) bourdon; (*Streichinstrument*) double-bass; (*Stimme*) bass voice; **~en** *itr* (*summen*) to hum; (*Käfer, Fliegen etc*) to buzz, to drone; *aero* to zoom; *mot* to purr, to drone; (*von Menschen*) to grumble, to snarl, to growl; (*von Tieren*) to growl; *jdm etw aufbrummen* (*fam*) to put s. th. upon s. o.; *seine Strafe ab~* (*im Gefängnis*) to serve o.'s term; *er muß ~en* he is in prison; he must go to prison; *in den Bart ~en* to mutter to o. s.; *er ~te etw in seinen Bart* he muttered s. th. in his beard; *mir ~t der Kopf* (*Schädel*) my head is spinning; **~er** *m* (*Insekt*) blue-bottle (fly); meat fly; (*Käfer*) dung-beetle; (*Mensch*) grumbler, growler; **~fliege** *f* blue-bottle (fly); **~ig** *a* (*verdrießlich*) grumpy, grouchy, grumbling, peevish; **~kreisel** *m* humming-top; **~schädel** *m fig* (*nach Alkoholgenuß*) headache, hang-over; **~ton** *m el, radio* alternating-current hum, hum; **~zeichen** *n tele* buzzer signal.

brünett *a* brownish; brunette; (*Haar*) dark-haired; (*Gesichtsfarbe*) of dark complexion; **~e** *f* (*Mädchen, Frau*) brunette.

Brunft *f* (*Paarungszeit des Wildes*) rut, heat; **~en** *itr* to rut; **~ig** *a* in heat; **~schrei** *m* bell; **~zeit** *f* rutting-season.

brünier|en *tr* (*glänzend machen*) to burnish; (*Metall*) to brown; **~stahl** *m* (*Polierstahl*) burnisher; **~stein** *m* burnishing stone.

Brunnen *m* (*natürliche Quelle*) well, spring; (*künstliche Quelle*) fountain; *artesischer ~* Artesian well; *Gesund~* mineral spring, spa; *e-n ~ bohren* to bore (*od* to sink) a well; *~ trinken* to drink the waters; **~bau** *m* well sinking; **~becken** *n* basin; **~bohrer** *m* well-drill; **~eimer** *m* well-bucket, pail; **~kresse** *f* watercress; **~kur** *f* course (*od* use) of mineral waters, treatment at a spa; *e-e ~~ gebrauchen* to take the waters; **~loch** *n* well-hole, well-pit; **~rand** *m* brim (*od* edge) of a well; **~röhre** *f* water pipe; **~stube** *f* well house; **~vergifter** *m* (*auch fig*) well-poisoner; (*Ränkeschmied, Verleumder*) intriguer, plotter; **~vergiftung** *f* poisoning of a well; *fig* (*politisch*) plotting, backbiting, intrigue; **~wasser** *n* pump-water, well-water.

Brunst *f* (*Paarungszeit der Tiere*) rut, heat; (*geschlechtliche Erregung*) lust, sexual desire; (*Glut, Leidenschaft*) ardour, *Am* ardor; passion; (*Inbrunst*) fervency; **brünstig** *a* (*von Tieren*) in heat; (*geschlechtlich erregt, wollüstig*) lustful, sensual; (*geil*) randy; *fig* (*heiß, innig*) ardent, burning, inflamed; *fam* hot; *ein brünstiges Gebet* a fervent prayer; **~ruf, ~schrei** *m* bell.

brunzen *itr vulg* to make water, to piss.

brüsk *a* blunt, (*kurz angebunden*) brusque; (*barsch*) curt; (*unhöflich*) offhand, impolite; (*mürrisch*) gruff; (*grob*) rude; *sie lehnte ~ ab* she declined bluntly; **~ieren**: *jdn ~~* (*barsch, schroff behandeln*) to snub s. o., to give s. o. a snub.

Brüssel *n* Brussels; *~er Kohl* Brussels sprouts *pl*; *~er Spitzen* Brussels lace.

Brust *f* (*auch fig*) breast; (*Brustkasten*) chest; *anat* thorax, pectus; (*Busen*) breast, bosom; (*von Geflügel*) brisket; (*Hemd~*) shirt front; (*Hochofen*) hearth; *zur ~ gehörend* pectoral, *med* thoracic; *mit bloßer* (*od entblößter*) *~* bare-bosomed; *sie standen ~ an ~* they stood face to face; *~ an ~ Kampf* (*sport*) body-on-body; *jdn an die ~ drücken* to press s. o. to o.'s bosom; *von der ~ entwöhnen* to wean; *e-m Kind die ~ geben* (*od reichen*) to suckle a child, to give suck to a child; (*Kind*) *ohne ~ aufziehen* to dry-nurse a baby; *es auf der ~ haben* to have a cold (*od* pain) in the chest; to suffer from asthma; *komm an meine ~* come to my heart; *er schlug an seine ~* he beat his breast; *jdm die Pistole auf die ~ setzen* to force s. o. at the point of o.'s sword; *aus voller ~* at the top of o.'s voice; *sich in die ~ werfen* to boast, to give o. s. airs; **~beere** *f* (*rote*) jujube; (*schwarze*) sebesten; **~bein** *n anat* breastbone, sternum; (*des Geflügels*) merrythought; **~beklemmung** *f* oppression of the chest; **~beutel** *m* money bag; **~bild** *n* half-length picture (*od* portrait); **~bonbon** *n* cough drops *pl*; **~bräune** *f* angina pectoris; **~drüse** *f* pectoral gland, mammary gland; (*vom Kalb*) sweetbread; **~drüsenentzündung** *f med* mastitis; **~fallschirm** *m* chest pack parachute, *Am* lap pack parachute; **~fell** *n anat* pleura; **~fellentzündung** *f* pleurisy; **~flosse** *f* pectoral fin; **~fernsprecher** *m* portable telephone; **~harnisch** *m* breast-armo(u)r; cuirass; **~höhe** *f* breast-height; **~höhle** *f* thoracic cavity; **~kasten, ~korb** *m* chest, thorax; **~kern** *m* (*Fleischstück*) brisket; **~kind** *n* suckling baby; **~knochen** *m* breastbone; **~krank** *a* suffering from the chest; (*schwindsüchtig*) consumptive; **~krankheit** *f*, **~leiden** *n* chest disease; (*Schwindsucht*) consumption; **~krebs** *m* cancer of mamma; **~latz** *m* (*Mieder*) stomacher; (*der Kinder*) bib; **~leidend** *a* consumptive; **~leier** *f tech* centre bit, crank brace; **~mikrophon** *n* breastplate transmitter; **~mittel** *n* pectoral, expectorant; **~muskel** *m anat* pectoratis major; **~nadel** *f* (*Schmuck*) scarf pin; **~pulver** *n* pectora powder; **~reinigend** *a* expectorant; **~riemen** *m mil* breast strap; (*Pferdegeschirr*) breastplate; **~scheibe** *f mil* half-figure target; **~schild** *n* breastplate; (*Insekten*) thorax; **~schmerz** *m* pain in the chest; **~schwimmen** *n* breast-stroke; **~stimme** *f* natural voice, chest-voice; **~stück** *n* (*Fleisch*) breast, brisket; (*Bild*) half-length portrait; **~tasche** *f* breast pocket; (*innen*) inside pocket; **~tee** *m* pectoral tea; **~ton** *m* chest-note; *im ~~ der Überzeugung* (*fig*) in a voice of deep conviction; **~tuch** *n* neckcloth, wrap, shawl; **~umfang** *m*, **~weite** *f* width of chest; **~verband** *m* chest bandage; **~verletzung** *f* thoracic injury; **~warze** *f* nipple, teat, pap; **~wassersucht** *f* dropsy of the chest, hydrothorax; **~wehr** *f* parapet, breastwork; **~wirbel** *m* thoracic (*od* dorsal) vertebra.

brüst|en *itr: sich ~en* to give o. s. airs, (*mit etw*) to boast of, to glory in s. th.. to plume o.s. on, to brag; ...**~ig** (*in Zssg*) ... chested; **~ung** *f* parapet, breast-wall.

Brut *f* (*Nest mit Jungen*) brood; (*von Fasanen*) nide; (*der Fische*) fry, spawn; (*von Insekten*) eggs *pl*; *fig* (*verächtlich, von Menschen*) set, pack, rabble, spawn; (*Kinder*) brats *pl*; (*das Brüten*) incubation; breeding, **~apparat** *m*, **~maschine** *f*, **~ofen** *m* incubator, hatching-apparatus; **~henne** *f* brood-(*od* sitting-)hen; **~kasten** *m* sitting-box, hatching-box; spawn-hatcher; **~stätte** *f* breeding place; *fig* hotbed.

brutal *a* brutal; *ein ~er Kerl* a brute, a beast; *Am sl* a stiff; **~ität** *f* brutality.

brüt|en *itr, tr* to sit (on eggs); to set; to brood, to hatch, to cover eggs; *die Henne ~et* the hen sets; *fig* (*über etw*) to brood over; *Böses ~en* to hatch (out) mischief; **~ei** *n* egg for hatching.

brutto *a* gross; **~belastung** *f* total load; **~betrag** *m* gross amount; **~einkommen** *n* gross income; **~einnahme** *f* gross receipts *pl*, gross revenue (*od* earnings *pl*); **~ertrag** *m* gross revenue; **~gewicht** *n* gross weight; invoiced weight; **~gewinn** *m* gross profit, gross proceeds *pl*; **~prämie** *f* gross premium; **~preis** *m* gross price; **~registertonne** *f* (*Abk* BRT.) gross register ton; **~tonnengehalt** *m* gross tonnage; **~überschuß** *m* gross surplus; **~umsatz** *m* gross returns *pl*, gross turnover.

bst! *interj* (*Aufforderung zum Schweigen*) hush! hist! be silent! listen!

Bub, ~e *m* (*Junge*) boy, lad; **~e** (*Schurke*) scamp, rogue; knave; (*Kartenspiel*) knave, jack; **~enstreich** *m*, **~enstück** *n* knavish trick; boy's trick; piece of villainy; **~ikopf** *m* bobbed hair, shingled hair; *e-n ~~ schneiden* to bob the hair; **~ikragen** *m* lying-down collar.

Büb|erei *f* knavish trick, knavery, petty villainy; **~in** *f* vixen, hussy, knavish woman; **~isch** *a* roguish, knavish, mischievous; villainous, vile.

*

Buch *n* (*Druckwerk*) book; *ungebundenes ~* book in sheets; (*Band*) volume; *~ in Folio, Quart, Oktav* folio-volume, quarto-volume, octavo-volume; *ein ~ Papier* (*Papiermaß = 24—25 Bogen*) quire; (*vollständiges Kartenspiel*) a pack of cards; (*Blattgold = 25 Blatt*) a book of leaf-gold; *das ~* (*die Bibel*) the Book; *die Bücher der Bibel* the books of the Bible; *~ führen* to keep book; *Am* to keep tab(s) on; *Bücher führen über* to keep records of (*od* on); *ins ~ eintragen* to book, to enter in the books; *wie ein ~ reden* to talk like a book, to talk o.'s head off; *wie es im ~e steht* (*fig*) perfect; complete; *über den Büchern sitzen* to be always poring over o.'s books; *zu ~ stehen* to stand at a price, costprice; *ein ~ verlegen* (*od herausgeben*) to publish (*od* to edit) a book, to bring out a book; **~abschluß** *m com* closing (*od* balancing) of books; **~ausstattung** *f* get-up of a book, finish of a book; **~ausstellung** *f* book exhibition; **~auszug** *m* extract; *com* abstract of account; **~auto** *n Am* bookmobile; **~beschneidemaschine** *f* booktrimmer; **~besprecher** *m* critic, book reviewer; **~besprechung** *f* book review, book reviewing; **~bestand** *m* bookstock; **~binde** *f* (*mit Waschzettel*) *Am* blurb; **~binder** *m* bookbinder, binder; **~binderei** *f* (*Werkstatt*) bookbindery, *Am* bindery; bookbinder's (work) shop, (*Gewerbe*) bookbinding; **~bindereimaschine** *f* bookbindingmachine; **~bindergold** *n* gold-leaf; **~bindergeselle** *m* journeyman bookbinder; **~binderhobel** *m* plough-knife; **~binderleim** *m* bookbinder's glue; **~binderliste** *f* (*e-r Bibliothek*) binding record; **~binderleinwand** *f* bookbinder's calico, cloth; **~binderlohn** *m* bookbinder's wages *pl*; **~binderpresse** *f* binding press; **~block** *m* inner book; **~decke** *f*, **~deckel** *m* book cover; **~drama** *n* closet play; **~druck** *m* printing (of books); **~druckbetrieb** *m* printing plant; **~drucker** *m* printer, pressman; **~druckerei** *f* printing-office, printing works, printing house (*Am* plant); **~~maschine** *f* printing machine; **~druckerfaktor** *m* master-printer; **~druckerkunst** *f* (art of) printing, typography; **~druckerpresse** *f* printing-press, letter-press; **~druckerschwärze** *f* printer's ink; **~druckerschnellpresse** *f* high-speed printing machine; **~druckerstock** *m* head-piece, vignette; **~einband** *m* binding, cover; **~en** *tr* to book, to put down, to record, to post; to enter (in the account), to enter into the books, to make an entry, to carry to account; **~forderung** *f com* book claims *pl*, claim as per accounts, *Am* accounts receivable; **~format** *n* size of a book; **~führer**, **~halter** *m com* book-keeper, accountant; **~führung, ~haltung** *f* book-keeping, accounting; *amerikanische ~~* columnar book-keeping; *doppelte ~~* book-keeping by double entry, *einfache ~~* book-keeping by single entry; **~geld** *com* money of transfer; **~gelehrsamkeit** *f* book-learning, book-lore; **~gemeinschaft** *f* book club; *Am* Book-of-the-month club; **~gewerbe** *n* book-craft, graphic trade; **~gewinn** *m com* book-profit; **~gläubiger** *m* book creditor; **~gold** *n* leaf-gold; **~halter** *m* bookkeeper; (*Haupt~~*) comptroller; **~halterei** *f* book-keeping department; **~haltungsmaschine** *f* book-keeping machine; **~handel** *m* book-trade, bookselling (-trade); *im ~~ erhältlich bei* to be sold by; **~händler** *m* bookseller; (*Sortimenter*) dealer in books; (*Verlags~~, Verleger*) publisher, (*Antiquar*) second-hand bookseller; (*Buch- u. Papierhändler*) stationer; **~händlerbörse** *f* booksellers' exchange, Stationers' Hall; **~händlermesse** *f* booksellers' fair; **~händlerrabatt** *m* booksellers' discount; **~handlung** *f* book-shop, bookseller's shop, *Am* book-store; **~hülle** *f* book jacket, (book-)wrapper; **~hypothek** *f* uncertified mortgage; **~kredit** *m com* book credit; **~leinen** *n* book linen; **~mäßig** *a* according to the books, as shown by the books, as per books; **~laden** *m* book-shop, *Am* book-store; **~macher** *m* book-maker, *fam* bookie; **~papier** *n* (*zum Druck*) plate paper; **~prüfer** *m* (*Bücherrevisor*) auditor, accountant; *vereidigter ~~* chartered accountant, *Am* public accountant; **~prüfung** *f* audit; **~rücken** *m* back of the book; **~saldo** *m* book balance; **~schlager** *m Am* best seller; **~schnitt** *m* (book-) edge; **~schrift** *f* book-face; **~schuld** *f com* book debt, liabilities as per account book; *Am* accounts payable; **~schutzhülle** *f* protective covering for books; **~stabe** *m* letter, character, *typ* type (face); *in ~staben* in words; *~stabe für ~stabe* letter by letter; *die vier ~staben* (*fam*) posterior; *großer ~stabe* capital letter; *kleiner ~stabe* small letter, lower case; *fetter ~stabe* bold face; *nach dem ~staben* literally; *er hält sich an den ~staben des Gesetzes* he sticks to the letter of the law; *auf den ~staben genau erfüllen* to carry out to the letter; *mit lateinischen ~staben* in Latin characters; **~stabenbezeichnung** *f* (*als Signatur e-r Bibliothek*) class mark (consisting of letters); **~stabenform** *f* type mould; **~stabenmensch** *m* pedant; **~stabengieß- u. Setzmaschine** *f* type setting and casting machine; monotype; **~stabenrätsel** *n* anagram, logogriph; **~stabenrechnung** *f* algebra; **~stabenschloß** *n* (*Geheimschloß*) permutation lock, puzzle lock; **~stabensetzmaschine** *f* type setting machine; **~stabieren** *tr* to spell; *falsch ~~* to misspell; **~stabierbuch** *n* spelling-book; **~stabierwettbewerb** *m Am* spelling-bee; **~stäblich** *a* literal, verbal; *adv* to the letter, literally; exactly; *etw ~stäblich nehmen* to take s. th. in its literal meaning; *~stäblich wahr* perfectly true; **~stütze** *f* support, book-rest, bookend; **~titel** *m* title of a book; **~umschlag** *m* (book-)cover; paper cover, *Am* (book-)jacket; **~ung** *f com* booking, posting; (*Posten*) entry; *e-e ~ung berichtigen* to adjust an entry; **~~sbeleg** *m* voucher; **~~sfehler** *m* error in the books; **~~smaschine** *f* booking-machine; **~~sposten** *m* item; **~verkaufsstand** *m* bookstall; **~wert** *m com* book-value; **~wissen** *n* book-learning, book-knowledge; **~zeichen** *n* (*Lesezeichen*) bookmark; (*Eignerzeichen od Standort in e-r Bibliothek*) book-plate; (*Eignerzeichen*) ex libris.

Buch|e *f* (*Baum*) beech, beech-tree; **~ecker, ~eichel, ~el** *f* beech-nut; **~ecköl** *n* beech-nut oil; **~en, büchen** *a* beechen, beech; **~enhain** *m* beech-

-grove; **~enholz** *n* beech-wood; **~enwald** *m* beech-forest; **~esche** *f* silver beech, white-beech; **~fink** *m* chaffinch; **~weizen** *m* buckwheat; **~weizengrütze** *f* barley groats *pl*; buckwheat porridge.

Bücher|abschluß *m com* closing of the books; **~aufzug** *m* book-lift; **~bestellzettel** *m* order form for books; **~bord, ~brett** *n* bookshelf, bookcase, book-stand, *Am* book-rack; *verstellbares ~~* adjustable bookshelf; **~bus** *m Am* bookmobile; **~ei** *f* library; **~einkauf** *m* purchase of books; **~eiregal** *n Am* book stacks *pl*; **~freund** *m* lover of books, bibliophile; **~gestell, ~regal** *n* bookcase, bookshelves *pl*; (*in e-r Bibliothek*) *Am* book stacks *pl*; **~halle** *f* public library; **~halter** *m* book-clamp; **~kenner** *m* bibliographer; **~kunde** *f* bibliography; **~lager, ~magazin** *n* stock of books; (*e-r Bibliothek*) stacks *pl*; **~liebhaber** *m* bibliophile; **~mappe** *f* satchel; **~milbe** *f* book-louse; **~narr** *m* bibliomaniac; **~post** *f* book-post; **~reisender** *m* (*Vertreter*) book travel(l)er, *Am* book-agent; **~revisor** *m* (*Buchprüfer*) accountant, auditor; *vereidigter ~~* chartered accountant, *Am* public accountant; **~sammler** *m* book-collector; book-hunter; **~sammlung** *f* collection of books; library; **~schau** *f* book review; **~schrank** *m* bookcase, *Am* book-rack; **~stand** *m* book-stall; **~stapel** *m* pile of books; **~stütze** *f* bookends *pl*, support, book-rest; **~sucht** *f* bibliomania; **~trödler** *m* stall-keeper; second-hand bookseller, antiquary; **~verleih** *m* lending out of books; **~verleiher** *m* lender of books; owner of a circulating library; **~vertrieb** *m* sale of books; **~verzeichnis** *n* catalogue (*Am* catalog) of books, book-list; **~wart** *m* librarian; **~wurm** *m* bookworm; *sl* swot; **~zettel** *m* form for ordering books.

Buchs(baum) *m* box, box-tree.

Büchse *f* (*Dose*) box, case; (*Rad~*) box; *tech* (*Buchse*) bush(ing), shell, lining; *el* socket, jack; (*Konserven~*) tin, *Am* can; (*Gewehr*) rifle, carbine; gun; (*Gasmasken~*) gas-mask container; *Kleinkaliber~* small-bore rifle; *Luft~* air-gun; *in ~n einmachen* to tin, *Am* to can; **~nfleisch** *n* tinned meat, potted meat, *Am* canned meat; **~ngemüse** *n* tinned vegetables *pl*, *Am* canned vegetables *pl*; **~nkugel** *f* bullet, rifle-ball; **~nlauf** *m* rifle (*od* gun) barrel; **~licht** *n* shooting light; **~nmacher, ~nschmied** *m* gunsmith, gunmaker; *mil* armo(u)rer, warrant ordnance officer; **~nmilch** *f* evaporated milk, tinned milk, *Am* canned milk; **~nobst** *n* tinned fruit, *Am* canned fruit; **~nöffner** *m* tin-opener, *Am* can-opener; **~nschaft** *m* gunstock; **~nschloß** *n* rifle-lock; **~nschuß** *m* gunshot; *e-n ~~ weit* within gunshot; **~nschütze** *m* rifleman.

Bucht *f* bay, bight; (*kleine*) creek; inlet; (*große*) gulf; (*Abteilung im Schweinestall*) box, partition; (*e-s Segels*) belly (of a sail); (*e-r Tauwerksrolle*) bight (of a rope); *sich ~en v* to form a bay; to widen into a bay; **~ig** *a* creeky.

Buckel *m* hump, humpback; (*Rükken*) back; *die ~* (*erhabene Metallverzierung*) boss, stud, knob; (*e-s Schildes*) umbo; (*Schnalle*) buckle; *e-n ~ machen* to stoop; (*sich verbeugen*) to bow low; *die Katze macht e-n ~* the cat puts up her back; *er hat e-n breiten ~* he has a broad back; *du kannst mir den ~ herunterrutschen* (*fam*) go to blazes; *jdm den ~ vollhauen* (*fam*) to give s. o. a thorough thrashing; *es lief mir eiskalt den ~ runter* (*fam*) I felt a cold shiver running down my back; *sich den ~ voll lachen* to split o.'s sides with laughing; **~ig** *a* hump-backed; hunch-backed; **~ige(r)** *m* hump-back.

bück|en *r* to stoop; *sich vor jdm ~~* to bow to; *vor Alter gebückt* bent with age; *gebückt gehen* to go stooping; **~ing, ~ling** *m* (*geräucherter Hering*) bloater, kipper, smoked herring, red herring; **~ling** *m* (*Verbeugung*) bow; (*beim Tanz*) curts(e)y; (*untertänig*) scrape; *e-n ~~ machen* to make a bow.

buddeln *itr fam* to dig; *tr* (*Kartoffeln etc*) to dig up (*od* out).

Buddh|a *m* Buddha; **~ismus** *m* Buddhism; **~ist** *m*, **~istin** *f* Buddhist.

Bude *f* (*Verkaufsstand*) booth, stall, stand; (*Laden*) shop; (*Bretter~*) shed, *Am* shack; (*Studenten~*) *fam* hole, dump, den, digs *pl*; *Leben in die ~ bringen* (*fam*) to make things lively; *Am* to make things hum; *jdm auf die ~ rücken* (*fam*) to come down on s. o.; **~nbesitzer** *m* stall-holder, stall-keeper; **~nzauber** *m*: *e-n ~~ machen* (*fam*) to make a row; to give a noisy party in o.'s den.

Budget *n* (*Haushaltplan*) budget; (annual) estimates *pl*; *das ~ vorlegen* to open the budget; *das ~ betreffend* budgetary; *im ~ vorsehen* to budget for; **~abstrich** *m* budget slicing; **~beratung** *f* debate on the budget; **~kommission** *f* (*Voranschlag*) Committee of Supply, (*Deckung*) Committee of Ways and Means; *Am* (*Beratungsstelle des US-Präsidenten*) Bureau of the Budget; **~kontrolle** *f* budgetary control; **~voranschlag** *m* budget estimates *pl*.

Büffel *m* buffalo; **~leder** *n* buff(skin); **~n** *itr* to toil hard, to grind, *fam* to cram, to swot; *Am* to dig, to plug; **Büffler** *m* plodder, *Am* dig.

Büfett *n* (*Möbel*) sideboard, dresser, buffet; (*Schanktisch, Theke*) bar, *Am* counter; (*Bahnhof~*) buffet; (*Imbißhalle*) snack-bar, *Am* lunch-counter; *ein Glas am ~ trinken* (*fam*) to have a drink at the bar; *kaltes ~* cold cut; Dutch lunch; **~fräulein** *n* bar-maid; **~kellner** *m* barman.

Bug *m* (*Schiffs~*) bow; *aero* nose; (*Biegung*) bend, bow; (*Schulterblatt, Pferd*) shoulder-blade; (*als Fleischstück, beim Rind*) chuck rib, (*beim Hammel und Kalb*) shoulder; **~anker** *m* bow-anchor, bower; **~bewaffnung** *f* front armament; **~fenster** *n* nose window; **~figur** *f* (*Galionsfigur*) figure-head; **~flagge** *f mar* jack; **~kanzel** *f aero* nose compartment, (*MG-Stand*) nose turret; **~lastig** *a aero* nose-heavy; **~MG** *aero* nose gun; **~rad** *n* (*bei Dreiradfahrgestell*) *aero* nose wheel; **~radfahrwerk** *n aero* tricycle undercarriage; *Am* tricycle landing gear; **~röhre** *f* (*Torpedorohr*) bow torpedo tube; **~schütze** *m aero* forward gunner; **~see, ~welle** *f* bow wave; **~sierdampfer** *m* (steam-) tug; **~sieren** *tr* to tow; **~sierlohn** *m*, **~sierkosten** *pl* towage; **~siertau** *n*, **~siertrosse** *f* tow-rope; **~spriet** *n* bowsprit; **~stand** *m* (*Gefechtsstand*) *aero* nose-gun station, *Am* forward gunner's position; **~stück** *n* (*Fleisch*) shoulder-piece; **~welle** *f mar* bow wave; (*e-s Geschosses*) nose wave.

Bügel *m* (*allg tech*) bow; (*Reifen*) hoop; (*Band*) strap; *kardanischer ~* (*für Kompaß*) gimbal; (*Kupplungs~*) *rail* shackle; (*Kleider~*) hanger; (*Steig~*) stirrup; (*Gewehr~*) trigger-guard; (*bei der Straßenbahn*) bow-shaped collector; (*Rahmen~*) frame; (*Kopfhörer*) harness; (*Magnetron*) loop; (*an Eimer od Korb*) handle; (*Nietmaschine*) yoke, bale; **~blech** *n* trim tab; **~bolzen** *m* U bolt; **~brett** *n* ironing-board; **~eisen** *n* (flat-) iron; (*für Schneider*) tailor's goose (*pl* gooses); *elektrisches ~~* electric iron; **~falte** *f* (*in der Hose*) crease; **~los** *a* without stirrups; **~maschine** *f* automatic ironer, ironing machine; **~n** *tr* (*glätten*) to smooth; (*Wäsche*) to iron; (*Kleider*) to press; *geschniegelt und gebügelt* (*fig*) spick-and-span; **~riemen** *m* stirrup-strap; **~schraube** *f* stirrup bolt; **~säge** *f* hacksaw; **~tuch** *n* ironing blanket.

Bügler *m* ironer; (*Kleider~*) presser; **~in** *f* ironing woman, ironer.

Bühl *m* hillock, hill.

Buhl|dirne *f* prostitute, paramour, wanton; **~e** *m u. f poet* love, lover; **~en** *itr poet* to make love to, to woo, to court; to have illicit intercourse with; *um etw ~en* to strive for; *um jds Gunst ~en* to curry favo(u)r with s. o.; **~erei** *f poet* love-making; (*unerlaubter Verkehr*) illicit intercourse with; (*Gefallsucht*) coquetry; **~er** *m* paramour; **~erin** *f* prostitute, wanton, unchaste female; **~erisch** *a* wanton, lewd; amorous; **~schaft** *f* amour, love-affair.

Buhne *f* river-dam, (*Deich*) dike, dam-dike; (*am Meer*) breakwater, groyne; (*Fischzaun*) crawl, pen.

Bühne *f theat* stage; (*die Bretter*) boards *pl*; (*allg das Theater*) theatre, *Am* theater; (*Schauplatz*) scene; (*Gerüst*) scaffold; (*Redner~, Bergwerks~*) platform; *dial* (*Boden, Speicher*) garret, loft, attic; *auf der ~* on the stage; *auf der ~ auftreten* to appear on the stage; *auf die ~ bringen* to produce; to bring on (*od* to) the stage; to stage; *sich auf der ~ halten* (*von Stücken*) to hold the stage; (*Schauspieler*) *an der ~ sein* to be on the stage; *über die ~ gehen* to be put on the stage; *hinter der ~* off the stage, *Am* backstage; **~nangestellter** *m* stage employee; **~nanweisung** *f* stage direction; **~narbeiter** *m* stagehand; **~nausstattung** *f* scenery; décor; scenes *pl*; **~nbearbeitung** *f* adaptation for the stage; **~nbegeistert** *a* stage-struck; **~nbeleuchtung** *f* stage lighting; **~nbild** *n* set stage-picture; background; (*Bilder pl*) scenes *pl*; **~ndekoration** *f* stage decorations *pl*; **~ndichter** *m* playwright, dramatist; **~ndichtung** *f* stage-poetry; **~nerfahrung** *f* stage-craft; **~nfieber** *n* stage-fever; **~ngröße** *f* star of the stage; **~nhorizont** *m* stage horizon, cyclorama; **~nkünstler** *m* (**-in** *f*) player, stage actor (stage actress); **~nleiter** *m* (*Inspizient*) stage-manager; **~nleitung** *f* stage-management; **~nlicht** *n* stage lighting, footlights *pl*, limelight; **~nmaler** *m* scene-painter; **~nscheinwerfer** *m* (*bes. auch für Filmaufnahmen*) *Am* klieglight; **~nsprache** *f* standard speech; **~nstern** *m* star of the stage; **~nstück** *n* stage-play; **~ntanz** *m* ballet; **~nveränderung** *f* scene-shifting; **~nvorhang** *m* curtain; *eiserner ~~* fireproof curtain; **~nwand** *f* (*Kulisse*) side-scene; **~nwesen** *n* theatre-affairs *pl*; **~nwirksam** *a* theatrical; **~nwirkung** *f* stage-effect; **~nzubehör** *n* stage-properties *pl*.

Bukarest *n* Bucharest.

Bukett *n* (*Strauß*) bouquet, nosegay; *kleines* ~ corsage; (*des Weines*) bouquet, aroma, flavo(u)r.
Bulette *f* (*Fleischklößchen*) meat-ball, rissole; Vienna steak, *Am* hamburger.
Bulgar|e *m*, ***~in*** *f* Bulgarian; **~ien** *n* Bulgaria; **~isch** *a* Bulgarian.
Bulk|ladung *f*, ***~waren*** *f pl com* (*Schüttgut*) bulk commodity, bulk cargo.
Bull|auge *n mar* porthole, bull's eye, side scuttle, sidelight; **~dogge** *f* (*Hund*) bulldog; (*Zugmaschine*) (motor) tractor; **~dozer** *m Am* bulldozer; **~e** *m* (*Stier*) bull; **~e** *f* (*Urkunde*) (papal) bull; (*Siegel*) seal; **~enbeißer** *m* bulldog, mastiff; **~enhetze** *f* bull-baiting; **~enhitze** *f* (*fam*) oppressive heat.
bullern *itr* to rumble; (*Feuer im Ofen*) to roar.
Bulletin *n* (*kurzer Tagesbericht*) bulletin.
Bumerang *m* (*Kehrwiederkeule*) boomerang.
Bummel *m* (*Spaziergang*) stroll; *e-n ~ machen* (*umherschlendern*) to go for a stroll; *auf den ~ gehen* (*in Lokalen*) *fam* to go on the spree, to go on a pub crawl, *Am* to make whoopee, to go slumming; **~ei** *f* laziness; dawdling; (*Nachlässigkeit*) negligence, carelessness; **~ig** *a* (*langsam*) slow; (*nachlässig*) careless, unpunctual; (*faul*) lazy, idle; **~ant** *m* shirker, loafer; **~leben** *n* idle life, loafing; dissipated life; **~n** *itr* (*umherschlendern*) to stroll, to take a walk, to lounge about, to loiter, to float around; (*bei der Arbeit*) to loaf; to dawdle; (*in Lokalen*) to go on a pub crawl, to be out on a spree; **~zug** *m* stopping-train, slow train, parliamentary train, *Am* accomodation train, way train; **Bummler** *m* loafer, lounger, revel(l)er, idler, dawdler; *Am f am* bum(mer), scalawag, sluffer.
bums! *interj* bang! bounce! **~en** *itr* to bump, to bang (against); **~landung** *f aero fam* rough landing; **~lokal** *n fam* low-class restaurant, *Am fam* joint.
Buna *m* (*synthetischer Kautschuk*) buna, synthetic rubber; **~reifen** *m* buna tyre.
Bund[1] *m* (*Band, Binde*) band, truss; (*Hosen~*) waistband; *tech* (*Eisen~*) band, brace, tie; (*Wellen~*) collar; (*Bündnis*) alliance; (*Union*) union; (*zeitlich begrenzt, mit bestimmtem Zweck*) coalition; (*von Staaten, Städten; mit zentralistischer Tendenz*) federation, federacy; (*mit größerer Unabhängigkeit der Einzelstaaten*) confederation, confederacy; (*Liga*) league; (*biblisch*) covenant; *~es ..., den ~ betreffend, zum ~ gehörend* federal, federate; *im ~e mit* allied with; *e-n ~ mit jdm schließen* to enter into an alliance with s. o.; *Staaten zu e-m ~ vereinigen* to federalize, to federate; *Deutscher ~* (*hist*) German Confederation; **~esangelegenheit** *f* federal concern; **~esautorität** *f* federal authority; **~esbahn** *f* Federal Railway; **~esbehörde** *f* federal government, federal authorities *pl*; **~eseinheit** *f* federal unity; **~esfahndungsamt** *n Am* Federal Bureau of Investigation (*Abk* F.B.I.); **~esfestung** *f* federal fortress; **~esgenosse** *m* ally, confederate, associate; **~esgenossenschaft** *f* confederacy; **~esgenössisch** *a* federal; **~esgericht** *n* federal court; **~esgesetzgebung** *f* federal legislation; **~esgewalt** *f* federal authority; **~eskanzler** *m hist* chancellor of the Confederation; Chancellor of the Federal Republic of Germany; **~eslade** *f* Ark of the Covenant; **~esmächte** *f pl* federal powers *pl*; **~esmitglied** *n* confederate; **~espräsident** *m* (*Schweiz*) President of the Swiss Confederacy; President of the Federal Republic of Germany; **~esrat** *m* (*Deutschland*) Federal Council; (*Schweiz*) Federal Government; **~esratsverordnung** *f* order (*od* ordinance) of the Federal Council; **~esregierung** *f* federal government; **~esrepublik** *f* federal republic; (*Deutschland*) Federal Republic of Germany; **~esreservebank** *f Am* Federal Reserve Bank; **~esstaat** *m* (con)federation; (*als Einzelstaat*) federal state, confederate state, federated state; *Einzelstaat e-s ~esstaates* member of a federal state; **~esstaatlich** *a* federal; **~estag** *m* (*Deutschland*) Federal Diet; federal assembly, meeting of the confederates; **~estruppen** *f pl* federal troops *pl*; **~esverfassung** *f* federal constitution; **~esvertrag** *m* federal pact; **~esversammlung** *f* federal congress (*od* assembly); (*Deutschland*) Federal Convention.
Bund[2] *n* (*Bündel, als Maß*) bundle; pack, parcel; (*Schlüssel~*) bunch of keys; (*Stroh~*) truss of straw; *ein ~ Flachs* a hank of flax; *ein ~ Heu* a bundle of hay; *ein ~ Radieschen* a bunch of radishes; *ein ~ Reis(ig)* a fag(g)ot; *ein ~ Spargel* a bundle of asparagus; *ein ~ Weintrauben* a bunch of grapes; **~holz** *n* fag(g)ot-sticks *pl* (*od* wood); **~stahl** *m* fag(g)ot steel; **~weise** *a* in bundles, in fag(g)ots.
Bündel *n* bundle, bunch; (*Paket*) packet, parcel; (*Reise~*) luggage; *sein ~ schnüren* to prepare to go, to pack up; *in ~n* by bundles; (*Ruten~*) fasces *pl*; (*Pfeil~*) sheaf of arrows; (*Strahlen~*) pencil; cone; (*Licht~*) beam; (*Papier*) file; **~holz** *n* bundled wood; **~n** *tr* to bundle (up), to bunch (together), to tie up in bundles; **~pfeiler** *m* compound pillar; **~weise** *a* in (*od* by) bundles, in parcels.
bünd|ig *a* (*bindend*) binding; (*rechtsgültig*) valid, lawful; (*verpflichtend*) compulsory; (*beweisend*) conclusive, convincing; (*Stil*) concise, terse; (*genau*) precise; (*abweisend*) curt; *tech* (*fluchtrecht*) flush; *kurz und ~ig* short and to the point; **~igkeit** *f* validity; (*Stil*) conciseness; (*beweiskräftig*) conclusiveness; **~isch** *a* confederate; **~ner**: *das B~ner Land* (*Graubünden*) the Grisons *pl*; **~nis** *n* (*siehe auch*: *Bund*[1]) (*Allianz*) alliance; (*Liga*) league; (*Staatenbund*) confederacy; (*Vertrag*) agreement, covenant; **~nisvertrag** *m* treaty of alliance.
Bunker *m* (*Vorratsbehälter für Kohle, Öl etc*) bunker, coal bunker, oil fuel bunker; (*Getreide~*) silo; (*Behälter, Kasten*) bin; (*Luftschutz*) (air-raid) shelter; *mil* (*betonierter Schutzraum*) bunker, pill-box, concrete dug-out; (*für U-Boote*) pen; **~kehle** *f mil* pill-box gorge; **~kohle** *f mar* bunker coal; **~linie** *f* line of pill-boxes, line of concrete dug-outs; **~n** *tr mar* (*Kohlen*) to coal, to (take) bunker(s); (*Öl*) to fuel; **~stand** *m* concrete emplacement; **~stellung** *f* pill-box position, bunker position; **~turm** *m* (concrete) air-raid shelter tower.
Bunsen|brenner *m* Bunsen burner; **~element** *n* Bunsen cell; **~photometer** *n* grease-spot photometer.
bunt *a* (many-) colo(u)red, colo(u)rful; varicolo(u)red; (*schreiend*) gaudy, glaring; loud; (*heiter*) gay, bright; (*gewürfelt*) checkered; (*gefleckt*) spotted; (*gemustert*) fancy; (*gesprenkelt*) mottled; (*buntscheckig*) motley; (*verschiedenartig od ~farbig*) variegated; (*ungeordnet, durcheinander*) disorderly, topsy-turvy; (*allerlei enthaltend*) mixed; *~er Abend* (*~es Allerlei, ~e Bühne, ~es Programm, ~e Stunde*) *mus, radio* variety program(me), variety show; concert; *radio* musical medley; *~e Blumen* gay flowers; *~es Glas* stained glass; *~e Menge* motley crowd; *~es Treiben* colo(u)rful scene of activity; *~e Reihe machen* to pair off ladies and gentlemen; *~e Weste* loud waistcoat; *das ist mir zu ~!* that's rather too much for me! that's a bit too much! *sie treibt es zu ~!* she is going too far! *es wird immer ~er* confusion is ever growing; *es ging ~ zu* there were fine doings; *alles lag ~ durcheinander* everything was topsy-turvy; *sie ist zu ~ gekleidet* (*fam*) she dresses that you hear her come; *sie trägt wieder ~* she is out of mourning; *sie trägt gern ~* she is fond of gay colo(u)rs; *er ist bekannt wie ein ~er Hund* (*fam*) he is known all over the place; he is known by every dog; **~druck** *m* colo(u)r printing, colo(u)red impression; *lithographischer ~druck* chromolithography; **~färber** *m* dyer, stainer; **~farbig** *a* many-colo(u)red; **~gefiedert** *a* of gay plumage; **~fleckig** *a* spotted; **~gewebe** *n* colo(u)red cloth, dyed cloth; **~heit** *f* gayness of colo(u)rs; **~metall** *n* nonferrous metal; **~papier** *n* colo(u)red paper, fancy paper, (*einseitig*) stained paper; **~sandstein** *m* new red sandstone; *Am* brownstone; **~sandsteingebäude** *n Am* brownstone; **~scheckig** *a* motley; (*Pferd*) piebald; (*Menge*) promiscuous; **~schillernd** *a* opalescent; **~specht** *m* spotted woodpecker; **~stift** *m* (*Farbstift*) colo(u)red pencil, crayon; **~streifig, ~gestreift** *a* streaky; party-colo(u)red, striped; **~weberei** *f* colo(u)r weaving.
Bur *m* Boer; *der* **~enkrieg** *m* the Boer-War.
Bürde *f* (*aufgebürdete Last*) load; (*auch fig Belastung, Kummer, Sorge*) burden; charge; *jdm e-e ~ abnehmen* to relieve s. o. of a burden; *jdm e-e schwere ~ auferlegen* to put a heavy burden on s. o.
Bürette *f* (*Meßglas zur Maßanalyse*) burette, dropping glass.
Burg *f* (*Schloß*) castle; (*Zitadelle*) citadel; (*Feste, Bollwerk*) stronghold; fort; *fig* (*Zuflucht*) refuge; **~flecken** *m* borough; **~frau** *f* lady of the castle; **~fräulein** *n* young lady of the castle; **~friede** *m* party-truce, public peace; (*Schloß*) precincts *pl*; **~graben** *m* castle-moat; **~graf** *m* burggrave; **~herr** *m* lord of the castle; **~verlies** *n* dungeon, keep; **~vogt** *m* castellan, steward; **~warte** *f* castle-tower, watch-tower.
Bürg|e *m* (*bei Gericht*) bail, bailsman, guarantor, guarantee; (*für Geld*) surety; (*Gewährsmann*) warrantor, warranter; (*Referenz*) reference, security; *für jdn ~e sein* to go bail for; *e-n ~en bringen* to offer a bail; to vouch for s. o.; *e-n ~en stellen* to give bail; to grant a surety; to give s. o.'s name as a reference; **~en** *tr* to bail, to go bail for; (*garantieren*) to guarantee; (*einstehen für*) to vouch for s. o. *od* a sum of money, to answer for; to stand security, to give security; to warrant; *mit seinem Wort ~en* to pledge o.'s word on; **~schaft** *f* (*Sicherheitsleistung*) surety, security;

(*Schuldverschreibung*) bond; (*Garantie*) guaranty; sponsorship; *durch ~schaft verpflichten* to bind over; *gegen ~schaft freilassen* to release on bail; *nicht gegen ~schaft freilassen* to refuse bail; *er bewirkte seine Freilassung durch Erstellung e-r ~schaft* he bailed him out; *e-n Häftling gegen ~schaftsleistung freilassen* to admit bail, to allow bail; *~schaft leisten für jdn* to give bail (*Am* bond), to go bail; *e-e ~schaft stellen* to put a guarantee; *~schaft zulassend jur* bailable; **~schaftserklärung** *f* surety warrant, declaration of guarantee; **~schaftsschein** *m* bail-bond; (*in e-r Bibliothek*) guarantor's card; **~schaftssumme** *f* bail; **~schaftsvertrag** *m* contract of warranty; warrant.

Bürger *m*, ***~in*** *f* (*Staats~*) citizen; (*Stadt~*) townsman; freeman; burgher (burgess); (*Patrizier*) patrician; (*Gegensatz Proletarier*) bourgeois; middle-class man; (*nicht adlig*) commoner; (*akademischer ~*) member of a university; (*im Gegensatz zum Militär, Zivilist*) civilian; *Mit~* fellow-citizen; *~ werden* to get the freedom of the city; **~ausschuß** *m* committee of citizens (*od* townsmen); common council; **~brief** *m* certificate of citizenship; act of naturalization; **~eid** *m* citizen's oath, civic oath; **~garde** *f* town-militia; national guard; **~krieg** *m* civil war, intestine war; **~kunde** *f* (*Staatswissenschaft*) civics *pl*; **~lich** *a* civic; civil, civilian; common, middle class; (*Küche*) plain; (*einfach*) simple; *die ~lichen Ehrenrechte* civic rights; *Verlust der ~lichen Ehrenrechte* loss of civic rights; *das ~liche Gesetzbuch* Civil Code, Code of Civil Law; *gut ~liche Küche* plain cooking, *Am* home cooking; *~liche Pflichten* civic duties *pl*; *~licher Rechtsstreit* civil suit, civil case; *~liches Schauspiel* domestic drama; **~meister** *m* mayor; (*von deutschen Städten auch*) burgomaster; *Ober~meister* chief burgomaster; *schott* provost; (*von London*) Lord Mayor; **~meisteramt** *n*, **~meisterei** *f* mayor's office, (*in London*) Mansion House; **~pflicht** *f* citizen's duty, civic duty; **~recht** *n* citizenship; civic rights *pl*; freedom (of a city); *das ~recht erlangen* to be naturalized; **~schaft** *f* community, citizens *pl*; **~sinn** *m* civism, public spirit; patriotism; **~soldat** *m* citizen-soldier; **~stand** *m* middle classes *pl*, citizens *pl*; **~steig** *m* pavement, footpath, *Am* sidewalk; **~tum** *n* (*Gegensatz Proletariat*) bourgeoisie; middle classes *pl*; citizens *pl*; **~versammlung** *f* town-meeting, assembly of the citizens; **~wehr** *f* militia; (*Nationalgarde*) national guard; (*England*) Home Guard.

Burgund *n* Burgundy; **~er** *m*, **~erin** *f* Burgundian; **~errot** *n*, **~er(wein)** *m* Burgundy; **~isch** *a* Burgundian.

burlesk *a* (*possenhaft*) burlesque; **~e** *f theat* (*Posse*) burlesque.

Burnus *m* (*arabisches Mantelgewand od Damenmantel mit Kapuze*) burnoose, burnous(e).

Büro *n* office; bureau; place of business; **~angestellter** *m* clerk, clerical employee, office worker; *Am* white collar worker; *als ~angestellter arbeiten* (*Am*) to clerk; **~arbeit** *f* clerical service; *Am* (*im Gegensatz zu Handarbeit*) white-collar job; **~beamter** *m* official, functionary; **~bedarf** *m* office requirements *pl*, office appliances *pl*, office supplies *pl*; **~bedarfsartikel** *m pl* office requisites *pl*; **~bote, ~diener** *m* office-boy, office-messenger; **~chef** *m* head clerk; **~dienst** *m* clerical and office work; **~direktor** *m* chief clerk; **~hilfe** *f Am* office hand; **~klammer** *f* (paper-) clip; **~krat** *m* bureaucrat, red-tapist; jack in the office; **~kratie** *f* bureaucracy, red tape, officialdom, officialism; **~kratisch** *a* bureaucratic; red tape; **~mäßig** *a* clerical; *~mäßige Arbeit* clerical work; **~möbel** *n pl* office furniture; **~personal** *n* office staff, office clerks *pl*, *Am* office hands *pl*; **~praxis** *f* office routine; **~schalter** *m* counter; **~schluß** *m* closing hour of the office; **~schrank** *m* office cabinet; **~stunden** *f pl* office hours *pl*, *Am* duty hours *pl*; **~vorstand** *m* head clerk, chief clerk.

Bursch\|(e) *m* (*Halbwüchsiger*) lad, boy, chap; youngster, *fam* young shaver; (*Kerl*) fellow, *Am* guy; (*Kamerad*) companion; (*Lehrling*) apprentice; (*Lauf~*) errand-boy; (*Offiziers~*) orderly, attendant, batman; (*Student*) member of a students' association; *ein kluger ~e* a clever fellow; *ein sauberer ~e* (*fig*) a fine chap; **~enherrlichkeit** *f* Old College days; **~enschaft** *f* students' association; **~ikos** *a* jovial, unrestraint; free and easy; studentlike; **Bürschchen, Bürschlein** *n dim* little boy, laddy; *Am* kid; (*Spitzbube*) young rogue.

Burse *f* (*Studentenheim*) student's lodging home, dormitory.

Bürste *f* brush; *Bade~* bath brush; *Draht~* wire brush; *Hut~* hat brush; *Kleider~* clothes brush; *Nagel~* nail brush; *el* (*Kohle od Metall als Kontaktstück*) brush; *tele* wiper; (*Straßen~*) sweeper brush; **~n** *tr*, *itr* to brush; *sich die Zähne ~n* to clean (*od* to brush) o.'s teeth; *sich die Haare ~en* to brush o.'s hair; *~n Sie mich ab* give me a brush; **~nabzug** *m typ* brush-proof; galley-proof; stone-proof; **~nbinder** *m* brush-maker; *saufen wie ein ~nbinder* (*fam*) to drink like a fish; **~nhalter** *m el* brush-holder; **~nrad** *n*, **~nwalze** *f* rotary brush, brush roll; **~nwaren** *f pl* brushware.

Bürzel *m anat* (*Steiß*) coccyx; (*Hintern*) buttock; (*Pferd*) croup; (*Vogel*) rump; (*Schwein*) tail; (*gebratenes Huhn etc*) parson's (*od* pope's)nose.

Bus *m fam* (*Autobus, Omnibus*) bus; **~haltestelle** *f* (*im Linienverkehr*) bus halting place, bus station, bus stop.

Busch *m* (*Gesträuch*) bush; *der feurige ~* (*Bibel*) the burning Bush; (*einzelner Strauch*) shrub; (*kleines Gehölz, Dikkicht*) thicket, copse; (*Wald, Urwald*) wood, virgin forest, backwoods *pl*; (*Büschel von Blättern, Blumen, Haaren*) tuft, bunch; (*Haarschopf*) shock; (*Feder~*) plume; (*Buschen, Besen als Schankzeichen*) brush at a vintner's door; tavern sign; *jdm auf den ~ klopfen* (*fig*) to sound s. o., to feel s. o.'s pulse; *sich* (*seitwärts*) *in die Büsche schlagen* to slip away; *hinter dem ~ halten* to hesitate; **~bohne** *f* bush-bean; **~egge** *f* bush-harrow; **~gras** *n* tussock- grass; **~holz** *n* brushwood, underwood; **~ig** *a* (*mit Gebüsch bedeckt*) bushy, shrubby; (*Haar*) shaggy; **~klepper** *m* (*Strauchdieb*) footpad, *Am* bush-ranger, *Am* bush-whacker; (*in Australien*) highwayman; **~krieg** *m* (*Guerillakrieg*) bush-fighting; **~mann** *m* bush-man; **~messer** *n* (*Art Sichel*) *Am* bush-whacker; **~neger** *m* (*flüchtiger Sklave od dessen Nachkommen in Westindien und Guinea*) maroon; **~obst** *n* bush-fruit; **~werk** *n* brushwood, bushes *pl*, shrubs *pl*, shrubbery, scrub(bery); **~windröschen** *n* wind-plant.

Büschel *n* (*von Haaren*) tuft, wisp; (*Blumen*) bunch; (*von Stroh, Federn*) whisk; (*Schopf der Vögel*) crest; (*Rettiche*) bunch, bundle; (*Blätter, Kirschen*) cluster; (*Reisig*) fag(g)ot; (*Kopfschmuck*) aigrette; (*Bündel, Garbe*) sheaf; (*Federbusch*) plume, aigrette; (*Strahlen~*) bundle, pencil, beam, brush; **~entladung** *f el* brush discharge; **~förmig** *a* bunchy, tufty; **~weise** *adv* in tufts, in bunches, in clusters.

Busen *m* (*Meer~*) bay; (*Golf*) gulf; (*kleinere Bucht*) bight; (*weibliche Brust*) bosom, (*Brüste*) breast; *fig* (*Inneres, Gesinnung*) heart; *im ~ hegen* to cherish in o.'s heart; **~freund** *m*, **~in** *f* (*Herzensfreund*) bosom-friend; crony; **~halter** *m siehe: Büstenhalter;* **~nadel** *f* breast-pin; tie-pin; *Am* stick-pin; scarf-pin; **~tuch** *n* (*Brusttuch*) neckcloth; stomacher; **... busig** (*in Zssg*) bosomed; *vollbusig a* high-bosomed.

Bussard *m orn* buzzard.

Buß\|e *f* penitence; (*Reue*) repentance; (*Genugtuung*) compensation, sanction; (*Sühne*) atonement, amends *pl*; (*Schmerzensgeld*) smart money; (*Geld~*) fine, penalty; (*Reuegeld*) forfeit; *~e tun* to repent, to do penance; (*sühnen*) to atone (*für* for); *~e zahlen* to make amends *pl*; *e-e Geld~e auferlegen* to fine s. o.; *jdm 50 DM ~e auferlegen* to fine s. o. DM 50, to impose a fine of DM 50; *sie wurde zu e-r schweren ~e verurteilt* she was heavily fined; **~fertig** *a* (*reuig*) repentant, penitent; (*zerknirscht*) contrite; **~fertigkeit** *f* (*Reue*) repentance; (*Zerknirschung*) contrition; **~prediger** *m* preacher of penitence; Lenten preacher; **~predigt** *f* penitential sermon; **~psalmen** *m pl* penitential psalms *pl*; **~tag** *m* day of penance; day of humiliation; *~ und Bettag m* day of repentance and prayer; **~übung** *f* exercise of penitence (*od* penance); **~zahlung** *f* fine; **~zelle** *f* penitentiary cell.

büß\|en *tr*, *itr* to repent; (*Buße tun*) to do penance; (*leiden für*) to suffer for; (*sühnen*) to atone for, to pay for; *für etw ~en müssen* to have to pay for; (*mit Geld*) to be fined; *seine Sünden ~en* to atone for o.'s sins; *ein Verbrechen ~en* to expiate a crime; *sie soll es mir ~en!* she shall rue it! *sie haben es bitter ~en müssen* they had to pay for it dearly; *seine Lust ~en* to satisfy o.'s desire, to indulge o.'s passion; **~er** *m*, **~erin** *f* penitent; **~erbank** *f* penitent form, *Am* anxious seat; **~ung** *f* expiation.

Busserl *n dial* (*Kuß*) kiss.

Bussole *f* compass; **~ngehäuse** *n* compass case (*od* housing); **~nrichtkreis** *m* aiming circle.

Büste *f* bust; **~nformer** *m* (*aus Gummi od Zelluloid*) breast pads *pl*; shapelies *pl*, *Am fam* falsies *pl*, gay deceivers *pl*; cheaters *pl*; **~nhalter** *m* brassière, *Abk* bra, bust-bodice, bust-improver, bust-support; *trägerloser ~nhalter* strapless bra; (*Oberteil e-s zweiteiligen Strand~ od Badeanzuges*) halter; **~enhebe** *m* uplift bra(ssière).

Buta\|dien *n chem* (*doppelt ungesättigter Kohlenwasserstoff*) butadiene; **~n** *n chem* (*Butylwasserstoff*) butane; **~nol** *n* butanol, butyl alcohol.

Butenland *n dial* (*Vorland*) outland.

Butt *m* (*Schollenfisch*) flounder; (*Stein~*) turbot; (*Glatt~*) brill.

Bütte, Butte *f* (*Kufe, Wanne*) tub, coop, tough; (*Zuber*) vat, butt, wooden

vessel; (*kleiner Zuber*) kit; (*Kiepe, Trag~*) hod; (*im rheinischen Karneval: Kanzel*) platform; **~npapier** *n* (*handgeschöpftes Papier*) hand-made paper; **~npresse** *f* (*Papierfabrikation*) vat-press.
Buttel *f dial* (*Flasche*) bottle.
Büttel *m fam verächtlich* (*Polizist*) policeman; (*Gerichtsdiener*) bailiff beadle; (*Henker*) hangman; (*verächtlich*) Jack Ketch; (*Gefangenenwärter*) jailer.
Butter *f* butter; *braune ~* fried butter; *frische ~* fresh butter, *Am* sweet butter; *gesalzene ~* salt butter; *ranzige ~* rancid butter; *zerlassene ~* melted butter; *~ zum Kochen* cooking butter; *mit ~ bestreichen* to butter; *~ aufs Brot schmieren* to spread butter on the bread; *alles in ~* (*fam*) all in apple-pie order; *Erdnuß~* peanut butter; *Kakao~* butter of cacao; *Kunst~* butterine; **~ähnlich, ~artig** *a* buttery; *chem* butyric; **~birne** *f* butter-pear, burrel; **~blume** *f* (*Hahnenfuß*) buttercup; (*Dotterblume*) marsh-marigold; (*Löwenzahn*) dandelion; (*allg*) butter and eggs; **~brezel** *f* butter-cracknel; **~brötchen** *n* buttered roll; **~brot** *n* piece (*od* a slice) of bread and butter; (*belegtes*) sandwich; *dürfen wir Sie zu e-m ~brot einladen?* Will you come up for a bite? *für ein ~brot kaufen* (*fast umsonst*) *fam* to buy s. th. for a song; **~brotpapier** *n* greaseproof paper; **~creme** *f* butter-cream; **~büchse, ~dose** *f* (*für den Tisch*) butter-dish; (*mit Schraubverschluß*) butter-box; **~farbe** *f* butter-colo(u)ring; **~faß** *n* butter-tub; (*zum Buttern*) churn; **~fett** *n* butter fat; **~form** *f* butter-mould, butter-stamp, butter-print; **~gebackenes** *n* light pastry; **~gelb** *a* butter-colo(u)red; **~geschäft** *n*, **~handlung** *f* butter shop, dairy; **~händler** *m* butterman, butter-dealer; **~ig** *a* buttery; **~klumpen** *m* butter-ball; **~kühler** *m* butter-cooler; **~maschine** *f* butter churn; **~messer** *n* butter-knife; *~~ m* (*Fettgehaltmesser*) *chem* butyrometer; **~milch** *f* buttermilk; **~n** *tr* to churn; *itr* to turn to butter; **~sauce** *f* melted butter; butter-sauce; **~säure** *f* (*Butyrilsäure*) butyric acid; **~scheibe** *f* (*geformte*) butter-pat; **~schmalz** *n* butter fat; **~schnitte** *f* piece (*od* slice) of bread and butter; **~semmel** *f siehe: Butterbrot;* **~teig** *m* puff-paste, flaky-paste, short paste; **~weck(en)** *m* butter roll, bun; **~weich** *a* as soft as butter.
Buty|l *n chem* butyl; **~lalkohol** *m* butyl alcohol; **~len** *n chem* butylene; **~rin** *n chem* butyrine; **~rometer** *n* (*Fettgehaltmesser*) *chem* butyrometer.
Butzen *m* (*im Obst, im Geschwür*) core; (*am Licht*) snuff; (*Klümpchen*) clump, lump; **~mann** *m* (*Kobold, Schreckgespenst*) bogy(man); **~scheibe** *f* bull's-eye (window-)pane (*od* glass).
Buxe *f dial fam* trousers *pl.*

*

Byzan|tiner *m* Byzantine; **~tinisch** *a* Byzantine; **~tinismus** *m fig* byzantinism; **~z** *n* Byzantium (= Constantinople).

C

Siehe auch unter K, Sch, Z.
C *Abk mit* ***C*** *siehe Liste der Abk.*
Cäcilie *f* (*Vorname*) Cecilia, Cecily, *fam* Cis.
Café *n* (*Lokal*) tea-room, café, coffee-house; **~tier** *m* (*Kaffeehausbesitzer*) proprietor of a café, keeper of a coffee-house.
Calutron *n* (*elektromagnetischer Separator, Zyklotron*) *phys* Calutron (= California University Cyclotron).
Camembert *m* (*Weichkäse*) Camembert cheese.
Canaille *f* (*Gesindel*) rabble, mob, canaille; (*Schurke*) rascal, scoundrel.
Cañon *m* (*tief eingeschnittenes Tal*) canyon, cañon, chasm, gorge.
Caritas *f* charity; **~verband** *m* Catholic Charity Society.
Cäsar *m* Cæsar; **~enherrschaft** *f* Cæsarism, autocracy; **~enwahn(sinn)** *m* Cæsarean madness; **~isch** *a* Cæsarean.
Cell|ist *m* cellist, (violon)cello player; **~o** *n* (violon)cello.
Cellophan *n* cellophane.
Celsius *m* Celsius (thermometer), centigrade (thermometer).
Cembalo *n* harpsichord.
Census *m* (*Volkszählung*) census.
Ces *n mus* C flat.
Cetanzahl, Cetenzahl *f* (*Zündvergleichszahl für Dieselkraftstoff*) *mot* cetane rating, cetene number.
Ceylon *n* Ceylon; *Bewohner von ~* Cingalese; *aus ~* Cingalese; **~kaffee** *m* Ceylon coffee.

*

Chagrinleder *n* (*Narbenleder*) shagreen (leather).
Chaiselongue *f* couch, lounge, divan.
Chamäleon *n zoo u. fig* chameleon; **~artig** *a* chameleonic.
chamois *a* (*rehbraun*) chamois, tan.
Champagner *m* (*Sekt, Schaumwein*) champagne (wine), sparkling wine; *fam* fizz; *herber ~* dry champagne; **~bowle** champagne-cup; **~pfropfen** *m* tampion.
Champignon *m* (*Edelpilz*) champignon, field-agaric, edible (*od* field) mushroom.
Chance *f* (*Aussicht, Glück*) chance; *sie hat ~n* she has good prospects: *jdm e-e ~ geben* (*Am fam*) to give s. o. a break; *die ~n sind gleich* (*sport*) the odds are even; *er hat nicht die mindeste ~ zu gewinnen* (*fam*) he hasn't a show of winning; **~nvoll** *a* (*Börse*) hopeful, promising, offering a fair chance.
chang|eant *a* (*Stoff*) shot-colo(u)red, changeable; (*schillernd*) iridescent; **~ieren** *itr* (*Stoff*) to be shot; (*tauschen*) to change.
Chapeau claque *m* opera-hat.
Chao|s *n* chaos; **~tisch** *a* chaotic.

*

Charakter *m* (*Wesenszug, Merkmal*) character; (*Anlage, Art*) temper, disposition, nature; (*sittlich*) morality; (*Stellung, Rang*) capacity, title, dignity, *mil* (brevet) rank; (*Zeugnis*) character; (*Rolle im Theater*) part; *typ* print, type; letter; (*Energie, Willensstärke*) energy, willpower; (*Qualität*) quality; (*Eigenheit*) peculiarity; **~ähnlichkeit** *f* similarity in character; **~bild** *n* portrait; **~bildung** *f* character-building; **~buchstabe** *m* characteristic letter; **~darsteller** *m theat* character-actor; **~eigenschaft** *f* characteristics *pl*; **~fehler** *m* fault (*od* defect) in s. o.'s character; **~fest** *a* of firm character, steadfast, reliable; of moral strength; **~festigkeit** *f* firmness of character, steadiness, decision of character; **~film** *m* (*mit erstklassiger Besetzung*) feature film; **~isieren** *tr* to characterize; (*beschreiben*) to describe; (*unterstreichen*) to point out; *charakterisierter Major* brevet major; **~isierung** *f* (*Kennzeichnung*) characterization; **~istik** *f* characterization, sketch of a character; (*Schilderung*) description; *tech* characteristic; **~istikum** *n* (*hervorstechende Eigenschaft*) characteristic; **~istisch** *a* characteristic(al) (*für* of), distinctive (*für* of); *~~e Eigenschaft* characteristics *pl*, (*Hauptzug*) feature; **~lich** *adv* morally, in character; **~los** *a* without character, characterless, unprincipled; *~loses Gesicht* face without character; **~losigkeit** *f* want of principles, lack of principles; **~schilderung** *f* characterization, character-sketch; **~schwäche** *f* weakness of character; **~spieler** *m theat* character-actor; **~stärke** *f* strength of character; **~zeichnung** *f* character-drawing; **~zug** *m* (*qualitativ*) characteristic, (*Einzelzug*) trait, (*ausgeprägter Einzelzug*) feature.
Charg|e *f* (military) appointment, office, post; (*Grad*) rank; (*Person*) officer, official, dignitary; (*Hochofenfüllung*) charge; heat; **~ierte(r)** *m* leader of a students' corps.
Charité *f* hospital.
Charlatan *m* (*Marktschreier, Schwindler*) charlatan, quack, impostor; **~erie** *f* charlatanry, charlatanism, quackery.
Charlotte *f* (*Name*) Charlotte, Lottie.
Charm|e *m* (*Anmut, Liebreiz*) grace, charm, fascination, attraction, sweetness; (*Verzauberung*) spell, conjuration; **~ant** *a* (*anmutig, reizend*) charming, fascinating.
Chart|a *f* (*Urkunde, Vertrag*) charter, deed; guarantee of rights; *die ~a der Vereinten Nationen* the United Nations Charter; **~ern** *tr* (*Schiff mieten od befrachten*) *mar* to charter; **~erpartie** *f* (*Fracht- od Mieturkunde*) *mar* charter party;
Chassis *n* (*Fahrgestell*) *mot* frame, chassis; (*Montagegestell bei Apparat und Lautsprecher*) *radio* chassis.
Chauff|eur *m* (*Fahrer*) driver, chauffeur; **~ieren** *tr, itr mot* to drive.
Chauss|ee *f* (*Land-,Kunststraße*) public road, main road; *Am* highway; **~eefloh** *m fam* motor-bike; **~eegraben** *m* ditch (along a public road); **~eewalze** *f* street-roller, road-level(l)er; **~eewärter** *m* roadman, road-mender; **~ieren** *tr* (*beschottern*) to macadamize; (*Straßen anlegen*) to construct roads.

Chauvin|ismus m (*übersteigerte Vaterlandsliebe*) chauvinism, jingoism, exaggerated patriotism; **~ist** m chauvinist, jingo, jingoist; **~istisch** a chauvinistic, jingo(istic).

*

Chef m head, chief; (*Prinzipal*) principal, employer; *Am* boss, governor; *mil* commander; (*Firmenteilhaber*) senior partner; (*Verwalter*) (head) manager; (*Hauptkoch*) chef, head cook; *der ~ des Stabes* the Chief of Staff; **~arzt** m Medical Superintendent; **~ingenieur** m chief engineer; **~konstrukteur** m chief designer; **~pilot** m chief test pilot; **~redakteur** m chief editor; **~sache** f secret.

Chem|ie f chemistry (*ohne Artikel*); *analytische ~* analytic(al) chemistry; *angewandte ~* applied chemistry, practical chemistry; *anorganische ~* inorganic chemistry; *organische ~* organic chemistry; *technische ~* technical chemistry, chemical engineering; nical chemistry, chemical engineering; **~igraph** m process operator; **~igraphie** icals *pl*, (chemical) drugs *pl*; **~ikalisch** a chemical; **~iker** m (*Chemotechniker*) chemical engineer, manufacturing chemist, practical chemist; (analytic) chemist; (*Gerichts~~*) public analyst; (*Pharmazeut*) pharmaceutical chemist; druggist; **~isch** a chemical; *~ischer Aufbau* chemical structure; *~ische Fabrik* chemical plant, chemical works *pl*; *~ische Kampfstoffe* chemical warfare agents; *~ischer Krieg* chemical warfare; *~isches Laboratorium* chemistry laboratory; *~isch reinigen* to dry-clean, to dry-cleanse; *~ische Reinigung* dry cleaning; *~ische Reinigungsanstalt* dry cleaner; *~ische Technologie* chemical engineering; *~ische Verbindung* chemical compound, combination, amalgamation; *~ische Wirkung* chemical action; **~iewerte** m *pl* (*Börse*) chemical stocks *pl*, chemicals *pl*.

Chemo|therapie f *med* chemotherapy, chemotherapeutics *pl*; **~therapeutisch** a *med* chemotherapeutic; **~typie** f *typ* chemitype.

Chesterkäse m Cheshire cheese.

Cherub m cherub, *pl* cherubim *od* cherubs.

Chiff|er, -re f (*Schlüsselbuchstabe*) cipher; (*in Zeitungsannoncen*) box-number; *unter ~er X. X.* under cipher X. X.; **~ernummer** f (*in Zeitungen*) box-number; **~erschlüssel** m cipher code; **~erkunst** f cryptography; **~ertelegramm** n cipher (*od* code) telegram; ciphered message; **~rieren** *tr* (*schlüsseln*) to cipher, to encipher, to code; **~riert** a in ciphers; *~~e Sprache* cipher language; **~riermaschine** f ciphering machine; **~ierung** f enciphermen, coding.

Chil|e n Chili, Chile; **~ene** m Chilean; **~enisch** a Chilean, Chilese; **~esalpeter** m Chile salpetre, nitrate of soda.

Chin|a n China; **~abaum** m Peruvian bark tree; **~arinde** f Peruvian bark, China bark; **~ese** m Chinese (*sing u. pl*), (*abfällig*) Chinaman, *Am sl* chow; **~esisch** a Chinese; *die ~esische Mauer* the Great Wall of China, the Chinese Wall; *~esisches Viertel* (*e-r Stadt*) *Am* Chinatown; **~asilber** n (*Alfenid*) German silver.

Chinin n quinine, quinin, quinia, quinina.

Chiromant m (*Handwahrsager*) chiromancer; **~ie** f (*Handwahrsagerei*) chiromancy, palmistry.

Chirurg m surgeon; **~ie** f surgery; **~isch** a surgical.

Chlor n *chem* chlorine; **~aluminium** n chloride of aluminium (*Am* aluminum); **~äthyl** n ethyl chloride; **~en** *tr* to chlorinate; **~gas** n chloric gas; **~haltig** a chloridic; containing chlorine; **~id** n chloride; **~ig** a chlorous, chloric; **~kalium** n potassium chloride; **~kalk** m chloride of lime, bleaching powder; **~kalzium** n chloride of calcium; **~natrium** n (*Kochsalz*) chloride of sodium, kitchen salt; **~natron** n chloride of soda; **~oform** n chloroform: **~oformieren** *tr* to chloroform; **~ophyll** n (*Blattgrün*) chlorophyll, leafgreen; **~säure** f chloric acid; **~silber** n chloride of silver; **~wasserstoff** m chlorhydric acid; **~zink** n chloride of zinc.

Cholera f cholera; *von der ~ angesteckt werden* to be infected with cholera; **~bazillus** m cholera bacillus; **~epidemie** f cholera epidemic.

Choler|iker m (*Jähzorniger*) person of choleric temper; **~isch** a (*jähzornig*) choleric; (*leicht reizbar*) irascible, hot-tempered, wrathful.

Cholesterin n (*Gallenfett*) cholesterine.

Chor m (*im Drama; Gesang*) chorus; (*Sänger in der Kirche; Hauptaltarraum*) choir, quire; (*Altar*) chancel; *im ~ einfallen* to sing in chorus; *fig* to chime in with; *im ~ singen od sprechen* to chorus; *das ~* (*verächtlich*) crowd, host; **~al** m choral(e), hymn, anthem, sacred song; **~albuch** n hymn-book; **~altar** m high altar; **~amt** n cathedral service; **~dirigent, ~direktor, ~leiter** m conductor (*od* leader) of the chorus, *Am* chorister; (*des Kirchenchors*) choirmaster; **~eographie** f (*Tanzschrift*) chore(o)graphy; **~gang** m aisle; **~gesang** m chorus, choral singing (*od* song); plain chant; **~gestühl** n choir stall; **~hemd** n surplice; (*langes*) alb; (*e-s Bischofs*) rochet; **~herr** m canon, prebendary; **~isch** a choric; **~ist** m chorister; *theat* chorus-singer; (*Kirche*) member of the choir; **~istin** f chorus-girl; **~knabe** m chorister, choir-boy; **~nische** f apsis, apse; **~sänger** m chorister; **~stuhl** m choir-stall; **~us** m chorus; *im ~us* in chorus.

*

Chrestomathie f (*Auswahl, Mustersammlung aus Büchern*) anthology, selection(s *pl*).

Christ m Christian (man, woman); (= *Christus*) Christ; *der Heilige ~* (*Fest*) Christmas; Holy Christ, Christ Child; **~abend** m Christmas-Eve; **~baum** m Christmas tree; **~baumschmuck** m Christmas-tree decorations *pl*; **~baumständer** m stand for the Christmas tree; **~bescherung** f Christmas-presents *pl*; **~dorn** m *bot* Christ's-thorn; **~el** f (*Vorname*) Christina, Christie, Chrissie; **~engemeinde** f Christian community; **~enheit** f Christendom (*ohne Artikel*), the Christian world; **~enpflicht** f Christian duty; **~entum** n Christianity; *zum ~~ bekehren* to christianize; **~enverfolgung** f persecution of the Christians; **~fest** n Christmas, *Abk* X-mas; **~geschenk** n Christmas present; (*für Dienstboten in England*) Christmas-box; **~ian** m (*Vorname*) Christian; **~iane** f (*Vorname*) Christiana; **~iania(schwung)** m (*Schilauf*) Christiania (turn); **~ine** f (*Vorname*) Christina, *fam* Christy; **~kind, ~kindchen, ~kindlein** n Christ-child; the Infant Jesus, *fam* Santa Claus; **~lich** a Christian; *~licher Verein Junger Männer* Young Men's Christian Association (*Abk* Y. M. C. A.); *~liche Wissenschaft* (*Sekte in US*) *Am* Christian Science (*offizieller Name*: Church of Christ, Scientist); *~liche Zeitrechnung* Christian Era; **~messe, ~mette** f Christmas matins *pl*; **~nacht** f Christmas Eve; **~oph** m (*Vorname*) Christopher, *dim fam* Kit; **~tag** m Christmas Day; **~us** m Christ; *vor Christi Geburt* before Christ (*Abk* B. C.); *700 nach ~us* in the year 700 of our Lord (*Abk* A. D.); **~woche** f Christmas week.

Chrom n *chem* chromium, chrome; (*Färberei*) chrome, potassium dichromate; **~at** n (*Salz der ~säure*) chromate; **~atik** f chromatics *pl*; **~atin** n (*färbbarer Zellkernbestandteil*) chromatin; **~atisch** a *opt, mus* chromatic; *~atische Abweichung* (*opt*) chromatic aberration; *~atische Tonleiter* chromatic scale; **~eisen** n chrome iron; **~gelb** n chrome yellow, lemon yellow; **~leder** n chrome leather; **~nickelstahl** m nickel chrome steel; **~olithographie** f (*Buntdruck*) *typ* chromolithography, *Abk* chromo; **~opapier** n chromo paper; **~osom** n (*Kernschleifen, Farbkörper der Zelle*) chromosome; **~osphäre** f chromosphere; **~otypie** f (*mehrfarbiger Buchdruck*) *typ* chromotype; **~säure** f chromic acid; *~saures Salz* chromate; **~stahl** m chromium (*od* chrome) steel.

Chron|ik f (*mittelalterliches Geschichtswerk, Familien~~, Stadt~~, Jahrbuch*) chronicle; (*Bibel*) the Chronicles; *Bücher der ~ika* (Book of) Chronicles; **~isch** a (*langwierig, von Krankheiten etc*) chronic(al); **~ist** m chronicler, annalist; **~ogramm** n (*Zeitinschrift*) chronogram; **~ograph** m (*Zeitschreiber*) chronograph; **~ographie** f chronography; **~ographisch** a chronographic(al); **~olog** m (*Zeitforscher*) chronologist, chronologer; **~ologie** f (*Zeitrechnung, Zeitfolge*) chronology; **~ologisch** a chronologic(al); **~ologisieren** *tr* to chronologize; **~ometer** m (*genauer Zeitmesser*) chronometer, timepiece, timekeeper; **~oskop** n (*Zeitmesser*) chronoscope.

Chrysanthemum n *bot* chrysanthemum.

Chryso|beryll m (*gelbgrüner Edelstein*) chrysoberyl; **~lith** m (*Edelstein, Abart des Olivin*) chrysolite; **~pras** m (*apfelgrüner Edelstein*) chrysoprase.

Cicero(schrift) f (*Schriftgrad, 12 Punkt = 4, 511mm*) pica.

cif *com* (*Abk für:* cost, insurance, freight).

circa (*Abk*: *ungefähr, etwa*) about, roughly, circa (*Abk* c.).

Cirrus(wolke f) m (*Federwolke in großer Höhe*) cirrus (cloud formed of ice particles at high levels).

Cis n *mus* C sharp.

Citrusfrucht f (*Apfelsine, Zitrone, Limone etc*) citrus fruit.

Clearing *com* (*Ausgleich, Verrechnung*) clearing; **~abkommen** n clearing arrangement; **~schulden** f *pl* clearing debts *pl*; **~verkehr** m clearing.

Claque f (*Gesamtheit der bezahlten Beifallsklatscher*) claque; **~ur** m claquer.

Clique f (*Klüngel, Sippschaft*) clique, caucus, coterie, set; **~nwirtschaft** f cliquism, caucusdom.

Clou m (*Glanzpunkt, Hauptzugmittel*) hit, greatest attraction, climax.

Clown m (*Hanswurst*) clown, buffoon; **~komödie** f *theat* slapstick comedy.

Code m (*Telegraphenschlüssel*) cipher code; (*Gesetzbücher*) code, digest.

Coeur n (*Spielkartenfarbe*) hearts *pl*.

Collaborateur m collaborationist.

Comer See *m* Lago di Como, Lake Como.
Compurverschluß *m* (*Objektivverschluß*) *phot* Compur shutter.
Conférencier *m* (*Ansager, Sprecher, Leiter*) announcer, compère, *Am* master of ceremonies, *fam* emcee; *als ~ in einer Veranstaltung tätig sein* (*Am*) to emcee a show; *die Vorführungen wurden durch Rundfunk- und Filmstars angesagt* the shows were emceed by stars of radio and screen; *~* (*Ansager*) *für Schallplattenprogramme* (*radio*) *Am* disc-jockey.
Container *m* (*Behälter für Stückgüter*) container.
contra *jur* versus (*Abk* v.)
Couch *f* (*Liegesofa*) couch, lounge, *Am* davenport.
Couplet *n* (*Liedchen der Kleinkunstbühne*) comic song, music-hall song.
Coupon *m* (*auch*: **Kupon**) (*Abschnitt*) coupon; (*Zinsschein*) dividend warrant; *~s schneiden* to clip coupons; **~bogen** *m* coupon-sheet; **~steuer** *f* tax on coupons.

*

Cour *f* (*Versammlung bei Hof*) levee; (*Flirten*) courting; *die ~ machen* (*od schneiden*) to court a lady; *sie läßt sich gern die ~ machen* she is a great flirt; **~macher** *m* beau, worshipper, admirer, suitor, ladies' man.
Courage *f fam* pluck, plucky spirit.
Courtage *f* (*Maklergebühr*) brokerage, broker's charges *pl*, commission.
Cousin *m* (*Vetter*) (male) cousin; **~e** *f* (*Bäschen*) (female *od* girl) cousin.
Cowboy *m* (*berittener Rinderhirt*) *Am* cowboy; **~fest** *n* (*Wildwestschau*) *Am* rodeo.
Crawl *siehe*: *Kraul.*
Creme *f* cream; **~farben** *a* cream--colo(u)red; **~schnitte** *f* cream-tart, napoleon.
Cumuluswolke *f* cumulus (= a thick piled-up variety of cloud).
Cur|ie *n* (*Maß der radioaktiven Strahlung*) curie (= a unit of mass of radium emanation); **~ium** *n* (*radioaktives Element*) curium.
Cut(away) *m* tails *pl*, *Am* cutaway; (*Herrenschoßrock*) morning coat.
Cutter *m* (*Schnittmeister, Tonschneider*) *film* cutter.
Cyclecar *m mot* cyclecar, quadricycle.
Cyclotron *n siehe*: *Zyklotron.*

D

D *Abk mit* ***D*** *siehe Liste der Abk.*
da *adv* (*örtlich: dort*) there; (*örtlich: hier*) here; *~ und ~* at such and such a place; *hier und ~* here and there, now and then; *~ und dort* here and there; *~ draußen* out there; *~ drinnen* in there; *~ oben, ~ droben* up there; *~ drüben* over there; (*vorhanden, gegenwärtig, anwesend*) *~sein* to be present; *sie ist ~* she is here; (*bei der Hand*) to be at hand; *ist das Buch ~?* is the book available? *es war niemand ~* there was nobody present; *nicht ~sein* to be absent; *wieder ~sein* to have returned, to be back again (*od* once more); *ich bin sogleich wieder ~* I shall be back in a minute; *wer ~?* who is there? *mil* who goes there? *wer ist ~gewesen?* who has been here? who has called? *~ bin ich* here I am; *~ nimm es* here take it, here it is; *fam* here you are; *~ haben Sie es!* there you are! *das Buch ~* that book; *der Mann ~* that man there; *alles schon ~gewesen* there is nothing new under the sun; *~ hört doch alles auf!* that beats everything! (*zeitlich*) then; *siehe ~!* look (there)! *nichts ~!* on no account! (*damals, dann, darauf*) at that time; *von ~ an* from that time, from that moment; since then; *~ erst* then only, only then; (*unter diesen Umständen od Verhältnissen, in dieser Lage*) in such a case; *was war ~ zu machen?* what was to be done in that case? *was läßt sich ~ machen?* what can be done in such a case? *~ conj* (*Tatsache als Grund*) as; *sie kann nicht kommen, ~ sie krank ist* she cannot come as she is ill; (*zeitlich als, zu der Zeit*) as, when, while; *in dem Augenblick, ~* at the moment when; (*weil, bei unbekanntem* (*Grund*) because; (*bei bekanntem* (*Grund*) since; (*in Erwägung, daß*) considering that, owing to; *~ doch, ~ ja, ~ nun einmal* since, now since, since indeed; (*Gegensatz*) *~ aber* but since; *~hingegen* whereas; *~* (*in Zssg*): *~bleiben* to stay (there); *~gegen* contrary to that.
dabei *adv* (*räumlich, örtlich*) near, near by, near at hand, close by; (*bei dem, wovon gerade die Rede ist*) thereby, therewith, by it, with it, through it; (*zugegen*) present, there; *~sein* (*teilnehmen*) to take part in, (*anwesend*) to be present; (*zusehen*) to watch; to witness; *sie war ~* she was one of the party; *ein Schloß und ein Garten ~* a castle with a garden attached to it; *was ist ~?* what does that matter? what difference does it make? (*zeitliche Nähe*) *~sein etw zu tun* (*im Begriff sein*) to be going to do, to be about to do, to be on the point of doing; (*außerdem, überdies*) besides, moreover, as well; (*trotzdem*) yet, notwithstanding, nevertheless; *~ bleiben* to persist in; to stick to; *~ bleibt es!* there's an end of it! there the matter rests! *es bleibt ~!* done! agreed! *ich habe mir nichts Böses ~ gedacht* I did it without meaning any harm; *~stehen* to stand by, to stand near; *es ist ein Haken ~* there is a hitch somewhere; *es kommt nichts ~ heraus* it's of no use; nothing is to be gained by it; *was ist denn weiter ~?* what of that? *das ist der Witz ~!* that is the fun of it!
dableiben *irr itr* (*nicht fortgehen*) to stay (here *od* there), to remain; *~ müssen* (*in der Schule nachsitzen*) to be kept in (at school).
Dach *n* roof; (*e-s Autos*) top, roof; *fig* (*Behausung*) house; *fig fam* (*Kopf*) head; *Am sl* dome; *min* (*hangendes Gestein über dem Abbau*) roof; *das ~ decken* to cover the roof; *ohne ~* roofless; *ohne ein ~ über dem Kopf* houseless; *unter ~ u. Fach* under (cover and) shelter; *er hat eins aufs ~ bekommen* (*fam*) he got a good scolding; *Am fam* he was bawled out; *jdm aufs ~ steigen* (*fam*) to come down upon s. o.; *bei ihm ist gleich Feuer im ~* (*fam*) he is very hot-headed; *ein ~ über dem Kopf haben* to have a roof over o.'s head; *zurückschiebbares ~* (*mot*) sliding roof; **~antenne** *f* overhouse aerial; roof antenna; **~artig** *a* rooflike, roof-shaped; **~aufsatz** *m* skylight; **~balken** *m* roof--tree, beam of the roof; **~belag** *m* roof covering; **~binder** *m* principle truss, bent; **~boden** *m* attic, loft, garret; **~ decken** *itr* to roof; **~decker** *m* roofer; (*Schiefer*) slater; (*Ziegel*) tiler; (*Stroh*) thatcher; **~~arbeiten** *f pl* roof-covering; **~erker** *m*, **~fenster** *n* garret--window, attic-window, dormer window; **~first** *m* ridge (*od* edge *od* top) of a roof; **~garten** *m* roof garden; **~geschoß** *n* attics *pl*, garret floor (*Am* story); loft; **~gesellschaft** *f* holding company, parent company; **~gesims** *n* cornice of a roof; **~giebel** *m* gable; **~kammer** *f* (*Bühnenkammer*) garret, attic, box-room; **~latte** *f* roof lath; **~leiste** *f* (*Autodach*) roof cleat; **~luke** *f* skylight, dormer window; *aero* turret roof door; **~organisation** *f* parent organization; **~pappe** *f* roof(ing)-felt, roofing-paper, tar paper; *Am* prepared roof paper; **~pfanne** *f* flemish (*od* pan) tile; **~platte** *f* (*Ziegel*) tile; (*Blei*) lead; (*Holz*) shingle; (*Schiefer*) slate; **~reiter** *m* ridge turret; **~rinne** *f* gutter, eaves *pl*; (*beim Auto*) cornice; **~schiefer** *m* roof slate; **~schild** *n* (*Reklame*) sky sign; **~schindel** *f* shingle; **~sparren** *m* spar, rafter; **~stube** *f* garret, attic; *bei ihr ist es unterm ~stübchen nicht ganz richtig* (*fig, fam*) she is wrong in her head; **~stuhl** *m* roof-truss, roof supports *pl*, rafters *pl*, (main) couple, roof framework (*od* timbering); **~stuhlbrand** *m* fire in the timbering of the roof; **~traufe** *f* eaves *pl*; **~werbung** *f* (*Reklame*) roof advertisement; **~wohnung** *f* garret; *Am* (*auf dem ebenen Dach e-s Wolkenkratzers*) penthouse; **~ziegel** *m* (roofing) tile.
Dachs *m* badger; *wie ein ~ schlafen* to sleep like a top (*od* a doormouse); **~bau** *m* badger('s) hole, burrow of a badger; **~haarpinsel** *m* badger's hair brush; **~hund, Dackel** *m* badger dog, dachshund; **~jagd** *f* badger-baiting.
dadurch *adv* (*örtlich, dort durch*) through there, that way; (*Grund: durch dieses Mittel*) through that (*od* it), by it, by that, by that means, in that way; (*auf die Frage wodurch?*) hereby, thereby, thus; *was wird sie ~ erreichen?* what will she get by it? *sie ist ~ berühmt* that made her famous; *~, daß* (*in bezug auf Folgendes*) owing to (*od* through) the fact that; by + *Gerundium*: *er rettete sich ~, daß er aus dem Fenster sprang* he saved himself by jumping out of the window.
dafür *adv* for it, for that; (*mit Bezug auf Nachfolgendes*) *~, daß* for + *Ge-*

rundium: *sie wurde ~ bestraft, daß sie gelogen hatte* she was punished for having told a lie; *ich bin ~, daß wir noch e-n Tag warten* I am for waiting another day; (*anstatt*) instead of; (*als Entgelt, Gegenleistung*) in return for, in exchange; (*indessen*) on the contrary; *~ ... aber* but (then); *der Anzug ist teuer, ~ paßt er aber gut* the suit is expensive, but then, it fits well; *teurer, aber ~ besser* dearer, but better in proportion; *ich bin ~ verantwortlich* I'm responsible for it; *er kann nichts ~, daß sie ...* it is not his fault that she ...; *ich kann nichts ~! (ich tat es nicht absichtlich)* I can't help it! *was kann ich ~?* how can I help it? *~ sein* to be in favo(u)r of; (*bei Abstimmungen*) to vote for; *~ sorgen* to see to it; *ich werde Ihnen ~ bürgen* I'll be answerable for it; *ich stehe Ihnen ~* I'll guarantee it; *das D~ u. Dawider* the pros and cons; *~ u. dagegen sprechen* to speak for and against; *sind Sie ~ od dagegen?* are you in favo(u)r of it or are you against it? *es läßt sich vieles ~ u. dawider sagen* much may be said for and against, it has its pros and cons; *~ zahle ich!* (*bei e-r Zeche*) it is my turn to pay, *Am* this is on my side; **~halten** *irr itr* (*der Ansicht sein*) to be of opinion, to think; *D~halten n*: *nach meinem D~halten* in my opinion; *sie hat recht nach meinem D~halten* she is right in my opinion; *~* **stimmen** *itr* to vote in favo(u)r of.

dagegen *adv* against that, against it; *~, daß ...*: *er war ~, daß ich Lehrer wurde* he was against my becoming a teacher; (*im Vergleich*) in comparison with it, compared to it; (*als Gegenleistung*) in exchange; (*im Austausch*) in return; *~ conj* (*aber, indessen*) on the contrary; whereas, whilst; *sie ~ weinte* she, on the contrary, was weeping; (*andererseits*) on the other hand; *~ läßt sich nicht leugnen, daß sie recht hatte* on the other hand there is no denying that she was right; *ich habe nichts ~* I have no objection (to it), I don't mind at all, *Am fam* that's okay with me; *haben Sie etw ~, daß ich eine Zigarette rauche?* do you object to my smoking a cigarette? *haben Sie etw ~, daß ich das Fenster schließe?* would you mind my shutting the window? *wenn Sie nichts ~ haben* if you don't mind; if you have no objection; with your permission; *ich bin ~* I am against it, I am of a contrary (*od* different) opinion; *sie stimmte ~* she voted against it; *das ist nichts ~* that's nothing compared with it; *~ hilft nichts* there is no help for it; there's nothing to be done; *~ gibt es kein Mittel* there is no remedy for it; *5 stimmten für den Antrag u. 3 ~* 5 voted for the motion, and 3 against it; **~halten** *irr tr* to oppose to; to compare with; to contrast.

daheim *adv* (*zu Hause, im Heim*) at home, indoors; (*in der Heimat*) in o.'s own (*od* native) country; *bei mir ~* at my house; *ist Herr Marvin ~?* is Mr. Marvin in? *er wird bald ~ sein* he will be home soon; *bitte, tun Sie, wie wenn Sie ~ wären* please, make yourselves at home; *~ ist es am schönsten* there is no place like home; *Ost od Westen — ~ am besten* east or west, home is best; *in etw ~ sein* (= *in etw bewandert sein*) *fig* to be conversant with, to be versed in s. th.; *das D~* (*das Heim, Haus*) home, house (and hearth).

daher *adv* (*von da*) from that place; from there; *sie kam eben ~* she just came from there; (*aus diesem Grund*) therefore, for that reason, hence; *~ kommt es, daß ...* hence it follows that ...; *~ habe ich den Wagen nicht gekauft* that's why I didn't buy the car; (*also*) so, thus; (*bei Verben der Bewegung*) along; *~kommen* to come along, to draw near; (*Grund*) to result from; *~schleichen* to creep along; *~stolzieren* to come strutting along; *~ conj* (*demgemäß*) accordingly; (*folglich*) consequently; **~um** *adv* thereabouts.

dahin *adv* (*örtlich, dorthin*) there, thither, to that place; (*zeitlich*) *bis ~* until then, by then, by that time, up to that time; (*vorbei, vergangen*) past, over; lost, gone; *für immer ~* dead and gone; *es ist alles ~* it is all lost; *~ sein* to be gone; to be lost; *sie sagte es so ~* she said it at random; *es steht ~* it is uncertain; *meine Meinung geht ~, daß ...* my opinion is that ...; **~aus** *adv* out of there; *~* **bringen** *irr tr* to bring to a certain point; (*jdn bewegen zu*) to induce s. o., to persuade s. o.; to prevail upon s. o.; *es ~ bringen* to bring s. th. about, to succeed with s. th. (*od* in doing); **~ein** *adv* into that place; **~geben** *irr tr* (*aufgeben, opfern*) to abandon, to sacrifice; **~gegen** *adv* on the contrary; *conj* whereas; **~gehen** *irr itr* to walk along; (*Zeit*) to pass; *~* **gehend,** *daß* ... to the effect that ...; **~raffen** *tr* to take away; **~schwinden** *irr itr* to pine away; to fade; **~stellen** *tr*: *~gestellt sein lassen* to leave s. th. undecided, not to go into; **~welken** *itr* to wither.

da|hinten *adv* behind; **~hinter** *adv* behind that (*od* it); beyond; *es steckt etw ~~* there is some secret there; *es steckt nichts ~~* there is nothing in it; **~~kommen** *irr itr* to discover, to find out; **~~machen**: *sich ~~machen* to set to work.

Dalmat|ien *n geog* Dalmatia; **~ier, ~iner** *m* Dalmatian; **~isch** *a* Dalmatian.

damal|ig *a* then, of that time; *der ~~e Gesandte* the then ambassador; **~s** *adv* then, at that time,

Damast *m* damask; **~en** *a* damask.

Damasz|enerklinge *f* Damascus blade; **~ieren** *tr* (*Stoff*) to damask; (*Stahl*) to damascene.

Dämchen *n* little lady; (*Straßendirne*) lady of easy virtue, *fam* street-walker.

Dame *f* lady; (*von Adel*) titled lady; (*im Damespiel*) king; (*im Kartenspiel*) queen; (*beim Tanz*) partner; *Hof~* lady-in-waiting; *die ~ des Hauses* the hostess; *meine ~n u. Herrn!* Ladies and Gentlemen! *die ~ spielen* to play the lady; *sie ist keine feine ~* she is not a lady; *wird die ~ schon bedient?* is somebody waiting on you, Madam? *Für ~n* (*Toilette*) For Ladies; **~brett** *n* draught-board; **~nabteil** *n rail* ladies' compartment; **~nbinde** *f* sanitary towel (*Am* napkin); **~ndoppel** *n* (*Tennis*) the women's doubles *pl*; **~neinzel** *n* (*Tennis*) the women's singles *pl*; **~n(fahr)rad** *n* lady's (*od* woman's) (bi)cycle; **~nhaft** *a* ladylike, **~nhandtasche** *f* lady's handbag; **~nheld** *m* lady's man, lady-killer; **~nhemd** *n* vest; chemise; **~nhut** *m* lady's hat; **~nkleidung** *f* ladies' clothes *pl*, *Am* women's apparel; **~nkonfektion** *f* ladies' ready-made clothes *pl*, *Am* ladies' ready-to-wear; **~nlandung** *f fam aero* nose-over landing, upside-down landing; (*Ballon*) smooth landing; **~nmannschaft** *f sport* women's team; **~nmantel** *m* lady's cloak; **~nnachthemd** *n* lady's night shirt, night-gown; **~nsalon** *m* ladies' room, *Am* ladies parlor; (*beim Friseur*) *Am* beauty parlor; **~nsattel** *m* side-saddle; **~nschirm** *m* lady's umbrella; **~nschlüpfer** *m* (*lang*) drawers *pl*, *fam* panties *pl*, (*kurz*) leg briefs *pl*; **~nschneider** *m* dressmaker, ladies' tailor; **~nstrümpfe** *m pl* ladies' stockings *pl*; nylons *pl* (a pair of nylons); **~nunterkleid** *n* ladies' combination; *Am fam* step-in; **~nunterwäsche** *f* women's underwear; (*elegante*) lingerie; **~nwahl** *f* (*Tanz*) ladie's choice; **~nwelt** *f* the ladies *pl*, the fair sex; **~spiel** *n* (*Brettspiel*) draughts *pl*, *Am* checkers *pl*; *~spiel spielen* to play at draughts. *Am* to play a game of checkers; **~stein** *m* man (at draughts).

Dam|hirsch *m* buck, fallow-deer; **~~kuh** *f* doe; **~wild** *n* fallow-deer.

damit *adv* with it, with that; by it; therewith, thereby; *~ anfangen* to begin by; *was hat das ~ zu tun?* what has that to do with it? *Am fam* what's that got to do with it? *was wollte er ~ sagen?* what did he mean by it? *wie steht es ~?* how do matters stand there? *wir sind ~ einverstanden* we agree to it; *heraus ~!* out with it! *zum Teufel ~!* deuce take it! *Am* bother it! *damit* (*conj*) (*in der Absicht*) (in order) that, in order to (*mit Infinitiv*); so that; *~ nicht* (*conj*) lest, for fear that, in order that ... not.

Däm|lack *m* (*Dummkopf*) fool, simpleton, silly person, fat-head, blockhead; **~lich, ~isch** *a* (*einfältig, dumm*) silly, foolish, stupid; **~lichkeit** *f* silliness, dul(l)ness, stupidity.

Damm *m* (*Erdaufschüttung*) dam; (*Deich*) dike (*auch*: dyke); *rail* embankment; (*Straße*) bank; (*Flußufer*) embankment, *Am* levee; (*Hafen*) pier, jetty, mole; (*Wellenbrecher*) breakwater; (*Fahr~*) roadway, carriage-way, carriage-road, (*durch sumpfiges Gelände*) causeway; (*Hindernis*) *fig* barrier; *anat* (*Mittelfleisch*) perineum; *auf den ~ bringen* to help on o.'s legs; *nicht auf dem ~ sein* not to feel up to the mark; *wieder auf dem ~ sein* to be all right again, *Am* to be up and around again; **~bruch** *m* bursting (*od* rupture) of a dam (*od* dike); breach in a dam; **~erde** *f* mo(u)ld; (*Gießerei*) pit sand; **~grube** *f* (*Glockengießerei*) foundry pit; **~riß** *m anat* rupture of the perineum; **~rutsch** *m* landslip, *Am* landslide; **~weg** *m* causeway.

dämmen *tr* (*Flut*) to dam (in *od* up), to dike in; *Am* (*Fluß*) to levee; *fig* (*zurückhalten*) to restrain, to stop, to check; (*zügeln*) to curb, to bridle; *das Wasser ~* to dam up the water.

dämmer|ig *a* (*Beleuchtung*) dim; dusky, twilight; (*träumerisch*) dreamy; *~ig werden* (*morgens*) to dawn; (*abends*) to dusk, to dusken; **~licht** *n* dim light; (*morgens*) the grey dawn of day; (*abends*) twilight; **~n** *imp* (*morgens*) to dawn; *es ~t* (*morgens*) it dawns, it is getting light, the day breaks; (*abends*) to grow dusk(y), the night sets in; *es ~te ihr* it dawned upon her; *vor sich hin~~* to be semi-conscious; **~schlaf** *m med* twilight-sleep; **~schoppen** *m* sundown; **~stunde** *f* hour of twilight; (*morgens*) dawn; (*abends*) dusk; *in der ~stunde* (*abends*) at nightfall; (*morgens*) at dawning; **~ung** *f* (*morgens*) dawn; (*abends*) dusk, twilight; *bei ~~* (*morgens*) at daybreak (*od* dawning); (*abends*) in the dusk, by twilight; *Götter~~* the twilight of the gods;

~~**seffekt** *m radio* twilight effect, night effect; ~~**sschein** *m* twilight glow; ~~**sstrahlen** *m pl* crepuscular rays *pl*; ~**zustand** *m* semi-conscious state.

Dämon *m* (*böser Geist*) demon; (*weiblicher* ~) demoness; *von e-m* ~ *Besessener m* a demoniac; ~**isch** *a* (*teuflisch*) demoniac(al); (*mit übermenschlichen Kräften*) demonic; ~**englaube** *m* demonism; ~**enlehre** *f* demonology.

Dampf *m* (*Wasser*~) steam; (*im weiteren Sinn*) vapo(u)r; (*Rauch*) smoke; reek; (*Dämpfe*) damp; (*Ausdünstung*) fume, exhalation; ~ *ablassen* to let off steam; ~ *aufmachen* to raise (*od* to get up) steam; *Ab*~ *m* exhaust (*od* waste) steam; *mit Voll*~ *arbeiten* to work at full steam; *Voll*~ *voraus fahren* to go full steam ahead; *Hans* ~ *in allen Gassen* Jack of all trades, *Am* all-rounder, *fam* Handy Andy; ~**artig** *a* vaporous, vapo(u)ry; ~**auslaßröhre** *f* waste (-steam) pipe; ~**antrieb** *m* steam drive; ~**bad** *n* vapo(u)r bath, steam bath; ~**bagger** *m* steam shovel; ~**barkasse** *f* steam-launch; ~**betrieb** *m* steam working (*od* drive); steam power; ~**bildung** *f* formation of vapo(u)r (*od* steam); steam generation; ~**blase** *f* bubble of vapo(u)r (*od* steam); ~**boot** *n*, ~**er** *m*, ~**schiff** *n* steamboat, steamer, steamship; ~**druck** *m* steam pressure, steam tension; ~~**messer** *m* (*Manometer*) steam-ga(u)ge; ~**einlaß** *m* steam inlet; ~**en** *itr* to steam, to emit steam, to give off vapo(u)r; (*rauchen*) to smoke; to reek with; (*schwelen*) to fume; ~**entwicklung** *f* steam generation; evolution of vapo(u)r; ~**er** *m* steamer, steamship; ~~**linie** *f* steamship line; ~**erzeuger** *m* steam generator; ~**förmig** *a* vaporous; ~**gebläse** *n* steam blast; steam blower; ~**heizung** *f* steam heating, central heating; ~**ig** *a* steamy, vapo(u)ry; ~**kessel** *m* boiler; ~**kochtopf** *m* (*Küche*) steam cooker, *Am* pressure cooker; ~**kraft** *f* steam power; ~**kraftwerk** *n* steam power plant; ~**leitung** *f* steam pipe, steam conduct; ~**maschine** *f* steam engine; ~**mühle** *f* steam mill; ~**nudeln** *f pl* stewed paste-balls *pl*; ~**pfeife** *f* steam whistle; ~**pflug** *m* steam plough, *Am* steam plow; ~**rohr** *n*, ~**röhre** *f* steam pipe; ~**roß** *n hum* locomotive; ~**schiffahrt** *f* steam navigation; ~**schlange** *f* steam coil; ~**spritze** *f* steam fire-engine; ~**strahl** *m* steam jet; ~**trockner** *m* steam drier; ~**turbine** *f* steam turbine; ~**überhitzer** *m* steam superheater; ~**ventil** *n* steam valve; ~**verbrauch** *m* steam consumption; ~**wäscherei** *f* steam laundry; ~**walze** *f* steam(-) -roller; ~**winde** *f* steam winch; ~**zuleitung** *f* steam supply.

dämpf|en *tr* to damp (down); *fig* to dampen, to cast a damper on; to calm; (*Speisen*) to stew, to steam; (*Früchte*) to evaporate; (*unterdrücken*) to suppress; (*ersticken*) to smother; (*Farben, Ton*) to subdue; to soften; to deaden; to tone down; (*Geige*) to mute; (*Trommel*) to muffle; (*gegen Geräusche*) to soundproof; to muffle, to damp; (*Feuer*) to quench, to put out; *tele* to attenuate; *mit gedämpfter Stimme sprechen* to speak in a low voice; ~**er** *m* (*auch: fig*) damper; (*Feuer*) extinguisher; (*Atomphysik*) moderator; (*Klavier*) damper; (*Geige*) mute; *radio* (*Lautsprecher*) baffle; (*Schall*~~) *mot* silencer, *Am* muffler; (*Dämpfungsflosse aero*) stabilizer; (*Stoß*~~) shock-absorber; (*Kocher*) steam cooker; ~**ig** *a* steamy, vaporous; (*kurzatmig*) asthmatic; (*von Pferden*) broken-winded; ~**mittel** *n chem* neutralizer (for acids); ~**ung** *f tech u. fig* damping; (*Geräusche*) muffling; (*Licht*) subduing, dimming; (*Stimme*) lowering; (*Speisen*) stewing, steaming; *tele* attenuation; damping; ~~**sfeder** *f* supplementary spring; ~~**sfläche**, ~~**sflosse** *f aero* tail-plane (*Am* horizontal) stabilizer; ~~**smesser** *m tele* decremeter.

danach *adv* (*zeitlich, darauf*) later on; after, thereafter, afterwards; (*in der Folge*) subsequently; (*gemäß*) accordingly; *bald* ~ soon after; *kurz* ~ shortly afterwards; ~ *gingen wir zum Bahnhof* afterwards we went to the station; *ich frage nichts* ~ I do not care for it; *es ist auch* ~ don't ask what it is like; *sie sehnt sich* ~ she is longing for it; *er sieht* ~ *aus* he looks very much like it; *sie will* ~ *handeln* she will act accordingly; *innerhalb von fünf Tagen* ~ within five days thereof.

Dän|e *m*, **Dänin** *f* Dane; ~**emark** *n* Denmark; ~**isch** *a* Danish.

daneben *adv* near it, near by it, by the side of it; next to it; *dicht* ~ hard (*od* close) by; *conj* (*außerdem, überdies*) besides, moreover, at the same time, also; ~**gehen** *irr itr* to miscarry, to go amiss; *fam* to flop; ~**hauen** *irr itr fam* to miss (the mark); ~**schießen** *irr itr* to miss o.'s mark; ~**stehender** *m* by-stander; ~ **wohnen** *itr* to live near by (*od* next door).

danieder, darnieder *adv* down; on the ground; low; ~**liegen** *itr* to be laid up (with); *fig* to be depressed (*od* ruined); to degenerate, to perish.

Dank *m* thanks (*nur pl Konstruktion*); (*Dankbarkeit*) gratitude; (*Lohn, Belohnung*) reward, recompense; (*Anerkennung*) acknowledg(e)ment; *Gott sei* ~! thank God! thank heavens! *herzlichen* ~! hearty thanks! *Tausend* ~! a thousand thanks! thanks a million! (*haben Sie*) *vielen* ~! many thanks! thank you very much (*od* ever so much)! ~ *abstatten* to thank; *mit* ~ *annehmen* to accept gratefully; *jds* ~ *entgegennehmen* to accept s. o.'s thanks; *bitte nehmen Sie meinen wärmsten* ~ *entgegen* pray accept my warmest thanks; ~ *sagen* to thank, to return thanks to s. o.; *jdm zu großem* ~ *verpflichtet sein* to be very much obliged to s. o.; *jdm für etw* ~ *wissen* to be grateful (*od* obliged) to s. o.; *zum* ~ *für* in thanks for; **dank** *prp* owing to; thanks to; ~ *meiner Vorsicht* thanks to my foresight; ~**adresse** *f* vote of thanks; ~**bar** *a* (*mehr äußerlich*) thankful (*für* for); (*dauernd*) grateful; (*jdm verbunden sein*) obliged; *ich war ihr sehr* ~*bar* I was very much obliged to her; *für eine Antwort wäre ich* ~*bar* I should appreciate a reply from you; (*lohnend*) profitable, paying; ~**barkeit** *f* thankfulness, gratitude, gratefulness; ~**brief** *m* letter of thanks; ~**en** *itr* to thank s. o. for; *jdm für etw* ~*en* (*ablehnend*) to decline with thanks; (*e-n Gruß erwidern*) to return a bow; (*verdanken*) to owe to; *seinem guten Stern* ~*en* to thank o.'s lucky stars; *Ihnen im voraus* ~*end* (*Brief*) thanking you in anticipation; ~*e!* thank you, thanks; ~*e schön!* ~*e sehr!* ~*e vielmals!* thank you very much (*od* ever so much); ~*e, gleichfalls!* thanks, the same to you! *nein*, ~*e* no, thank you; *nichts zu* ~*en!* don't mention it! Not at all! ~*end erhalten!* (*auf Quittung*) received with thanks! received! Thank you! ~**enswert** *a* worthy of thanks; deserving thanks; ~**fest** *n Am* Thanksgiving Day (*im Nov. jeden Jahres*); *Essen am* ~~ (*Am*) Thanksgiving dinner; ~**gebet** *n* thanksgiving; *das* ~*gebet sprechen* to give (*od* to return) thanks; ~**gottesdienst** *m* thanksgiving service; ~**opfer** *n* thank-offering; ~**sager** *m* thanksgiver; ~**sagung** *f* expression of thanks, returning thanks; thanksgiving; ~**schreiben** *n* letter of thanks, letter of acknowledg(e)ment.

dann *adv* (*zeitlich*) then, at that time; (*hierauf, sogleich, infolgedessen*) thereupon; (*nachher*) after that, afterwards; (*außerdem*) besides, moreover; (*ferner*) further(more); *u. was* ~? and then what? *was geschah* ~? what happened next? ~ *u. wann* now and then; now and again; ~ *erst* only then; not until then; *selbst* ~ even then; *selbst* ~, *wenn* even if; ~**en** *adv*: *von* ~*en* from that place, thence; *von* ~*en gehen* to go away; to start.

daran, dran *adv* at it, by it; on it, about it; of it, of that; in it, in that; thereon, thereat; thereby; *gut* ~ *sein* to be well off; *nahe* ~ close by, close to; *übel* ~ *sein* to be badly off; *drauf u.* ~ *sein* to be on the point of; *er war drauf u.* ~ *zu gehen* he was on the point of going away; *sie glaubt* ~ she believes in it; *sie mußte* ~ *glauben* she had to pay the price; (*sterben*) she had to die; *es ist nichts* ~ there is nothing in it; it is good for nothing; *er hat nicht* ~ *gedacht* he did not think of it; *Sie sind* ~ (*an der Reihe*) it is your turn; *sie ist nicht schuld* ~ it is not her fault; *was liegt* ~? what does it matter? *die Partei, die* ~ *ist* (*Spiel*) the ins; ~**geben** *irr tr* to give up; ~**gehen** *irr itr* to set to work; *sich* ~**halten** *irr itr* to stick to it; *sich* ~**machen** *itr* to go at it; ~**müssen** *itr* to be obliged to; ~**setzen** *tr* to venture, to risk; to stake; *alles* ~*setzen fam* to go all out to; *sein Leben* ~*setzen* to stake o.'s life on it.

darauf, drauf *adv* (up)on it, on that; thereon, thereupon; (*zeitlich*) later; after (that), afterwards; *den Tag* ~ the next day; *fünf Jahre* ~ five years later; *etw* ~ *geben* to attach importance to; *es kommt* ~ *an* it matters; *sie legt keinen Wert* ~ she doesn't care; *drauf u. dran sein* to be on the point of, to be just about to; *wie kommst du* ~? what makes you think (*od* say) that? ~ *bezüglich* relating thereto; ~**folgend** *a* following; ~**gehen** *irr itr* (*verbraucht werden*) to be consumed, to be spent; ~*gehen lassen* to spend; ~**hin** *adv* after that, thereupon; on the strength of that; ~**kommen** *irr itr* to call to mind, to remember; to hit upon (an idea).

daraus, draus *adv* from this, from that; from there, therefrom; of it, of that; ~ *folgt daß* hence it follows that; ~ *kann ich nicht klug werden* that beats me; ~ *wird nichts!* nothing doing! *es wird nichts* ~ (*werden*) nothing will come of it; *ich mache mir nichts* ~ I do not mind it (*od* that).

darben *itr* to suffer want (of s. th.); to be in want; *sehr* ~ to starve; *jdn* ~ *lassen* to starve s. o.

dar|bieten *irr tr* to offer, to present; to tender; *sich* ~*bieten* to offer o. s.; ~**bietung** *f theat* performance; (*Konzert etc*) entertainment, recital, recitation; (*Warenauslage*) display; (*auf dem Ladentisch*) counter display; *tele, radio* (*Programm*) programme, program; ~**bringen** *irr tr* to bring, to offer, to present; to tender; *ein Opfer* ~~ to make a sacrifice; ~**bringung** *f* offer(ing); presentation.

Dardanellen *pl* the Dardanelles *pl.*

darein, drein *adv* into it (*od* that); therein; *sich* ~**finden,** ~**fügen,** ~**geben,** ~**schicken** to put up with s. th., to submit to; to resign o. s. to; ~**geben** *irr tr* (*obendrein*) to give into the bargain; ~**fahren** *irr itr* to interfere roughly; *sich* ~**mischen** to meddle with; (*störend*) to interfere with; (*als Vermittler*) to intervene, to mediate; ~**reden** *itr* to put in a word, to interrupt s. o.'s speech; ~**schlagen** *irr itr* to strike in, to strike hard; to strike at random; ~**willigen** *itr* to consent (to s. th.).

darin, drin *adv* in it, in that; there, therein; within, inside; ~ *inbegriffen* included, including; ~ *irren Sie sich!* there you are mistaken! *was ist* ~*?* what is inside? *es ist nichts* ~ there is nothing in it; ~**nen** *adv* within, inside.

dar|legen *tr* to lay open; to show, to exhibit; *fig* (*erklären, auseinandersetzen*) to explain, to expose; to interpret; (*erläutern, auslegen*) to expound; (*klarmachen*) to point out; (*enthüllen, entwickeln*) to unfold; (*offenbaren*) to display; (*offen* ~~) to set forth; (*klarlegen, berichten*) to state; (*in e-r Rede*) to make an address; ~**legung** *f* (*Erklärung*) statement, exposition; (*Erläuterung*) explanation; (*endgültige offene* ~~ *der Tatsachen, Absichten etc*) *Am* showdown; ~**leh(e)n** *n* loan (*an, für* to); (*Vorschuß*) advance; *ein* ~~ *aufnehmen* to raise (*od* to take up) a loan; to make a loan; *jdm ein* ~ *geben* to grant a loan; *jdm* (*Geld*) *als* ~ *geben Am* to loan to s. o.; *ein* ~~ *kündigen* to recall a loan; ~**lehnsgeber** *m* lender; ~**lehnskasse** *f* loan bank, loan society; ~**lehnsnehmer** *m* borrower; receiver; ~**leihen** *tr* to lend out; (*Vorschuß*) to advance; *Am* (*Geld*) to loan to s. o.; ~**leiher** *m* (money-) lender.

Darm *m* gut; (*Eingeweide*) intestines *pl*, bowels *pl*; (*Wursthaut*) skin (of a sausage); *blinder* ~ caecum; *dicker* ~ colon; ~**anhang** *m* intestinal appendage; ~**aufblähung** *f* inflation of intestine; ~**bein** *n* ilium; ~**bewegung** *f* peristaltic movement; ~**blutung** *f* intestinal h(a)emorrhage; ~**entleerung** *f* evacuation of intestine; ~**entzündung** *f* inflammation of the intestines, enteritis; ~**fieber** *n* gastric fever; ~**gang** *m* intestinal tube; ~**geschwür** *n* ulcer in the bowels; ~**grimmen** *n* colic; ~**inhalt** *m* intestinal contents *pl*; ~**katarrh** *m* intestinal catarrh; ~**krankheit** *f* bowel (*od* intestinal) complaint; ~**saite** *f* catgut, gut string; ~**verschlingung** *f* twisting (*od* stoppage) of the bowels; ~**verstopfung** *f* constipation; ~**verschluß** *m* intestinal obstruction; ~**wand** *f* intestinal wall.

Darr|e *f* (*das Därren*) kiln-drying; (*Ofen*) drying-stove, kiln; (*Metall*) liquation hearth; (*Kupfer*) smelt; (*Krankheit bei Vögeln*) roup, pip; ~**en** *tr* (*Malz etc*) to kiln-dry; (*Metall*) to liquate, to torrefy; ~**fax** *m* kilnman; ~**malz** *n* kiln-dried malt, cured malt.

darreich|en *tr* to hand, to offer; (*anbieten*) to present; (*überreichen*) to reach forth, to hold forth; (*darbieten*) to tender; (*Sakrament, Medizin*) to administer; ~**ung** *f* presenting, presentation; offering, offer; handing, tender; (*Sakrament, Medizin*) administration.

darstell|bar *a* representable; capable of being prepared; *theat* suitable for the stage; ~**en** *tr* (*vorzeigen*) to exhibit; (*vor Augen führen*) to present; (*anschaulich machen*) to represent; *unrichtig* ~~ to misrepresent; *math* to describe; to construct; *chem* to develop from, to disengage, to liberate; to produce, to prepare to manufacture; to make; *schematisch* ~~ to skeletonize; (*bildlich* ~*en*) to describe; (*schildern*) to give a description (*od* a picture), to picture; *falsch* ~~ to give a false picture; *theat* to perform, to play, to act, (*eine Rolle*) to impersonate; (*Sachverhalt erklären*) to explain; (*im Film, bes. in Hauptrollen*) to feature; (*graphisch*) to plot; to graph, to depict; *e-e Gefahr* ~*en für* to constitute a menace to; ~*ende Geometrie* descriptive geometry; ~**er** *m*, ~**erin** *f* exhibitor, representer; *theat, film* performer, player, actor, actress, (*e-r Rolle*) impersonator; ~**ung** *f* (*Ausstellung*) exhibition, show; (*bildlich*) presentation; (*Kunst*) representation; (*dichterische Gestaltung*) delineation; *tech* process of production; manufacture; *chem* disengagement, liberation; *falsche* ~~ misrepresentation; *theat* performance, acting; (*graphisch*) plotting; diagram, graph; *jur* (*des Tatbestands*) statement of the facts; (*des Tatbestands in der Klage*) brief; *math* construction; ~~**sgabe** *f* descriptive talent; (*Schilderungsgabe*) power of describing; ~~**sverfahren** *n* process of preparation (*od* production); method of obtaining; ~~**sweise** *f* manner of representation; style; *chem* method of preparation.

dar|tun *irr tr* to prove; (*zeigen*) to show; (*anschaulich machen*) to demonstrate; (*klarlegen*) to make evident; (*beweisen*) to substantiate, to evince (s. th., that); ~**über, drüber** *adv* over it; about it, about that; above it; (*mittlerweilen*) meanwhile, in the meantime; (*ehe*) before that; (*hinüber*) across; (*betreffend*) concerning that; ~*über hinaus* beyond; ~*über besteht kein Zweifel* there is no doubt about that; *und* ~*über* and more; *es geht alles drunter u. drüber* all goes topsyturvy; *eine Bescheinigung* ~ *daß* a certificate to the effect that; ~**um** *adv* about it, about that; for it, of it; (*darum herum*) (a)round it, around that; (*deshalb*) that is why, therefore, for that reason; *ich bitte dich* ~*um* I ask you for it; *können Sie sich* ~*um kümmern?* Can you take care of it? *es handelt sich* ~*um* that is the very point in question; *es ist mir nicht* ~*um zu tun* I am not particular about it; ~~**kommen** *irr itr* (*verlieren*) to lose; ~**unter, drunter** *adv* under that, below that; underneath, beneath it; (*unter e-r Anzahl*) among them; in the midst of them; between them; (*weniger*) less; ~*unter verstehen* to mean by it (*od* that); *drunter u. drüber* topsyturvy.

*

das (*Artikel*) the; *prn* who, whom, which, that, those; ~ *bin ich* it is I; that I am; so I am; ~ *sind Neger* those are negroes.

Dasein *n* presence; being; existence; (*Leben*) life; *ein elendes* ~ a miserable existence; *ins* ~ *treten* to spring into existence; ~ *irr itr* to be present; to exist; to be there; *das ist noch nicht dagewesen* that is unprecedented; *ist jemand dagewesen?* has anybody called? ~**sbedingung** *f* condition of existence; ~**sberechtigung** *f* title (*od* right) to existence; ~**skampf** *m* struggle for existence (*od* life).

daselbst *adv* there, in that (very) place.

dasjenige *prn* that.

daß *conj* that; *so* ~ so that; *es sei denn,* ~ unless; ~ *doch* I wish it were, would it were; if only; *nicht* ~ (*nicht als ob*) not that; ~ *nicht conj* lest; *bis* ~ *conj* till.

dasselbe *prn* the same; *das ist genau* ~ it is just the same.

Dat|a, ~***en*** *n pl* (*von Datum*) the facts *pl*; data *pl* (*oft mit sing*), dates *pl*; (*Merkmale*) characteristics *pl*, particulars *pl*; *technische* ~*en* technical data; ~**enschild** *n* (*an e-r Maschine*) rating plate; ~**ieren** *tr* to date; ~*iert sein* to bear date, dated (as of); ~**iv** *m* dative (case); ~**ivobjekt** *n* indirect object; ~**o** *adv* (*bis heute*) of the date; *bis* ~*o* till now, hitherto; ~**oscheck** *m* dated cheque; ~**owechsel** *m* bill after date.

Dattel *f* date; ~**baum** *m*, ~**palme** *f* date-tree, date-palm; ~**kern** *m* date-kernel.

Datum *n* date; *ein Brief vom heutigen* ~ a letter of to-day; *welches* ~ *schreiben wir heute?* which day of the month is it? what is the date to-day? *das* ~ *vom ... tragen* to bear date on; *des gleichen* ~*s* of even (*od* same) date; *ohne* ~ undated, without date; ~ *des Poststempels* postal date, date of the postmark; ~**stempel** *m* dater, date stamp.

Daube *f* stave.

Dauer *f* duration; (*Fortdauer*) continuance, continuity; (*Festigkeit*) durability; (*Zeitspanne*) period, length of time; (*Lebens*~, *Patent etc*) life; *von* ~ *sein* to last; *auf die* ~ in the long run; *für die* ~ for the duration; *für die* ~ *von* for a period of; *von kurzer* ~ of short duration; *von langer* ~ of long standing; ~**anlagen** *f pl com* long term investments *pl*; ~**abstand** *m aero* distance of flying on a beam; ~**apfel** *m* winter apple; ~**beanspruchung** *f* continuous load; fatigue loading; ~**befehl** *m* standing order; ~**belastung** *f* steady (*od* permanent) load; ~**betrieb** *m* continuous operation (*od* working); ~**brandofen,** ~**brenner** *m* slow combustion stove; ~**festigkeit** *f* durability; endurance; fatigue strength; ~**feuer** *n mil* sustained fire; ~**fleisch** *n* preserved meat; ~**flug** *m aero* endurance flight; (*Ohnehaltflug*) non-stop flight; ~~**weltrekord** *m* world flying-endurance record; ~~**wettbewerb** *m* flying-endurance contest; ~**gemüse** *n* dehydrated vegetables *pl*; ~**geschwindigkeit** *f* maintainable speed; ~**haft** *a* durable, lasting; ~*hafter Friede* lasting peace; (*Farben, echt*) fast; (*Leder*) tough; (*Stoff*) long wearing; *er ist* ~*haft* it wears well; ~**haftigkeit** *f* durableness; lasting quality, durability; endurance; (*Festigkeit*) solidity; (*von Stoffen*) wear; ~**karte** *f* (*Abonnement*) season-ticket; ~**lauf** *m sport* endurance run; long-distance race; *tech* endurance test; destruction test; ~**leistung** *f* continuous output, sustained (*od* continuous) power; ~**magnet** *m* permanent magnet; ~**marsch** *m* forced march; ~**milch** *f* sterilized milk; dried milk; condensed milk; ~**n** *itr* to last; to take, to be; to continue; *es wird lange* ~*n* it will take a long time; *es dauert mir zu lange* I can wait no longer; *tr* (*leid tun*) to grieve, to pity; *es dauert mich* I am sorry for it; ~**nd** *a* (*andauernd*) constant, continuous;

lasting, permanent; *kurze Zeit* ~*nd* short-lived; **~pflanze** *f* perennial (plant); **~präparat** *n* permanent preparation; **~probe** *f* endurance test; **~proviant** *m* preserved foods *pl*; **~prozeß** *m* duration process; **~prüfung** *f* endurance (*od* fatigue) test; **~rekord** *m* endurance-record; **~stellung** *f* permanency; permanent job; permanent position; **~störung** *f* continuous interference; **~störsender** *m radio* continuous-wave jammer; **~strom** *m* permanent current; **~tanzwettbewerb** *m* dance endurance contest; dance marathon; *Am sl* walkathon; **~ton** *m* (*Sirene*) continuous blast; continuous tone (*od* sound *od* signal); **~verbindung** *f tele* through connection; **~versuch** *m* endurance test; **~wellen** *f pl* (*Frisur*) permanent waves *pl*, *Abk fam* perms *pl*; *mit* ~*wellen* permanent waved; *sie hat* ~*wellen* she has her hair permed; **~wirkung** *f* lasting effect; **~wurst** *f* hard sausage; **~zustand** *m* steady state.

Daumen *m* thumb; *e-n* ~ *breit* a thumb's breadth; *e-n* ~ *dick* a thumb's thickness; *halten Sie mir den* ~*!* keep your fingers crossed! **~abdruck** *m* thumb-print; **~einschnitt** *m*, **~register** *n* (*Buch*) side index, *Am* thumb index; *mit* ~*register* thumb-indexed; **~lutscher** *m* thumb-sucker; **~nagel** *m* thumbnail; **~rad** *n tech* cam wheel; **~schraube** *f* thumb-screw.

Däumling *m* thumb-stall; *fig* Tom Thumb.

Daune *f* down; eider (-down); **~ndecke** *f* eider-down, quilt.

Daus *n* deuce, ace; *was der* ~*!* what the deuce!

davon *adv* of, about, by it; (*weg*) away, off; *was habe ich* ~*?* what use is it to me? what do I get by it? *das kommt* ~ that's the result of it; **~bleiben** *irr itr* to forbear; to keep off; **~fliegen** *irr itr* to fly away; **~gehen** *irr itr* to go off; **~kommen** *irr itr* to get off; (*mit knapper Not*) to have a narrow escape (*od* a close shave); *sl* to get out by the skin of o.'s teeth; **~laufen** *irr itr* to run away; to turn tail; *Am mil sl* to go A. W. O. L.; **~machen** *r* to slip away; to clear out; to make off; **~schleichen** *irr itr* to sneak off; **~tragen** *irr tr* to carry off; *fig* to obtain; (*Krankheit*) to catch.

davor *adv* in front of (it); of it; before; from it; against it; before that; *ich fürchte mich* ~ I am afraid of it.

dawider *adv* against it; ~ *sein* to resist, to oppose; *dafür und* ~ pro and con; *ich habe nichts* ~ I have no objection.

dazu *adv* to it; *legen Sie es* ~*!* put it to it! (*Zweck*) to that end, for that purpose; *noch* ~ besides; ~ *kommt, daß* add to this that; **~gehören** *itr* to belong to (it); **~gehörig** *a* belonging to; **~kommen** *irr itr* to arrive (unexpectedly), to happen; *nie* ~~ never find time to; *wie kommen Sie* ~*?* how dare you? **~mal** *adv* then, in those days, at that time; **~tun** *irr tr* to add.

dazwischen *adv* between them, among them; in the midst of, amongst; (*manchmal*) between times; **~fahren** *irr itr* to interfere; **~kommen** *irr itr* to come between; to intervene; to prevent; *wenn nichts* ~*kommt* if nothing turns up to prevent; **~kunft** *f* intervention; **~liegend** *a* intermediate; **~treten** *irr itr* to interpose, to intervene.

Debatt|e *f* debate; discussion; *die* ~*e eröffnen* to open the debate; *zur* ~*e stehen* to be at issue; *Schluß der* ~*e beantragen* to move that the debate be closed; **~ieren** *itr* to debate (*über* on); *tr* to discuss (s. th.); *Am* (*ironisch*) to powwow (*über* about); **~ierende(r)** *m* (*Redner*) debater; **~ierklub** *m* debating society (*od* club).

Debet *n* debit; ~ *und Kredit* debtor and creditor; *im* ~ *stehen* to be on the debtor-side; **~posten** *m* debit item; **~saldo** *m* debit balance; balance payable.

Debit *m* sale, market; **~ieren** *tr* to debit, to charge to s. o.'s account; *jds Rechnung* ~*ieren* to charge to s. o.'s account; **~oren** *m pl* debtors *pl*; (*Bilanz*) accounts receivable.

Debüt *n* first appearance, début; **~antin** *f Am* deb(utante); **~ieren** *itr* to make o.'s first appearance (*od* début); (*gesellschaftlich*) to come out; to be presented to society.

Dechant, Dekan *m eccl* dean; (*Universität*) dean of University.

dechiffrieren *tr* to decipher, to decode.

Deck *n mar* deck; bridge; *begehbares* ~ walkable deck; (*Omnibus*) top; *an* ~ *verladen* to ship on deck; *unter* ~ under deck, in the hold; **~abstand** *m aero* distance between wings; **~adresse** *f* accommodation address; **~anruf** *m* code call; **~anstrich** *m* finishing coat; **~aufbauten** *pl mar* superstructure; (*e-s Flugzeugträgers*) island; **~bett** *n* feather bed; (*Decke*) coverlet; **~bewegung** *f mil* covering motion; **~bezeichnung** *f* code name (*od* designation); **~blatt** *n* (*Zigarre*) wrapper, outside leaf; *bot* bract; (*zur Verbesserung e-s Gesetzes etc*) amendment; **~e** *f* cover; (*Bett*) coverlet; (*Stepp*~~) counterpane, quilt, *Am* comforter; (*Woll*~~) blanket, cover; (*Reise*~~) (travel(l)ing-) rug; (*Plane, Verdeck*) hood; awning, tarpaulin; *bot, anat* integument; (*Hülle*) envelope; (*Eis*~) sheet; *min* (*Bergwerk*) roof; (*Bier*) head; (*Geige*) covering board; *mot* cover, tyre, *Am* tire; (*Zimmer*) ceiling; *mit jdm unter e-r* ~*e stecken* to conspire together, *sl* to be in cahoots; *sich nach der* ~*e strecken* to accommodate o. s. to circumstances; to make the best of it; to cut o.'s coat according to o.'s cloth; **~el** *m* lid, cover; (*Kappe*) top, cap; bonnet; (*Wölbung, Dach*) dome; *jeder Topf findet seinen* ~*el* every pot has its lid; (*Buch*) wrapper, cover, board; (*Uhr*) watch-cap; *fam* (*Hut*) hat; **~en** *tr* to cover; (*Ausgaben, Kosten etc*) to cover, to defray the costs; (*Wechsel*) to meet a bill; (*Bedarf*) to meet, to cover; *gedeckt sein* to hold *od* to have (sufficient) security; (*Dach*) to roof; (*mit Schiefer*) to slate; (*mit Stroh*) to thatch; (*mit Ziegeln*) to tile; *den Tisch* ~*en* to set the table, to lay the cloth; *für 6 Personen* ~*en* to lay covers for six persons; *es ist gedeckt!* dinner is served! (*schützen*) to guard from, against; (*Fechten*) to parry, to take up o.'s guard; *sich* ~*en* to protect o. s.; *com* to recover against; to reimburse o. s.; *math* to be equal; to coincide (*mit* with); to be identical; *sich nicht* ~*en* to differ, to diverge; *sich teilweise* ~*en* to overlap; *ein Ziel* ~*en* (*eingabeln*) *mil* to straddle; **~enbeleuchtung** *f* ceiling lighting, ceiling fixtures *pl*; **~engewölbe** *n* arched roof; **~enlampe** *f* ceiling lamp; **~enlicht** *n* (*Oberlicht*) skylight; (*im Auto*) dome light; **~enoberlicht** *n* skylight; **~enprojektor** *m* (*Messung der Wolkenhöhe*) ceiling projector; **~enputz** *m* ceiling plaster; **~enschicht** *f* upper layer; **~enträger** *m* roof beam; **~enventilator** *m* ceiling ventilator; **~farbe** *f* body-colo(u)r; **~geschütz** *n mil* deck gun; **~gewebe** *n anat* epithelial tissue; **~glas** *n* (*Mikroskop*) cover glass; **~hengst** *m* stallion; **~hülle** *f* covering; **~lack** *m* coating varnish; **~ladung** *f* deck cargo; **~landeflugzeug** *n* carrier-borne aeroplane (*Am* airplane); deck-landing plane; **~licht** *n* skylight; **~mantel** *m fig* pretext, cloak; *unter dem* ~~ under cover of, under the guise of; **~name** *m* pseudonym, assumed (*od* cover) name; trade name; alias; **~namenverzeichnis** *n* list of code names; **~offizier** *m* warrant-officer; **~ung** *f* cover(ing); protection; shelter; *mil* cover, shelter, camouflage (*gegen Fliegersicht* from air); *math* equality, congruence; (*im Entfernungsmesser*) stereoscopic contact; *phot* (*Negativ*) density; (*Geld*) reimbursement; margin; (*bei Wechsel*) security; ~~ *haben* to hold security; *ohne* ~~ without funds in hand; *völlige* ~~ ample security; (*des Bedarfs*) supply of needs; *in* ~~ *gehen* to take cover; *zur* ~~ *bringen* to bring to coincidence; *bombensichere, schußsichere, splittersichere* ~~ bombproof, shellproof, splinterproof cover; **~~sfeuer** *n* covering fire; **~~sgraben** *m* shelter trench; **~~sloch** *n mil sl* foxhole; **~~smannschaft** *f* covering troops *pl*; **~~struppen** *f pl* covering force, covering troops *pl*; **~~swinkelmesser** *m mil* angle-of-sight instrument; **~weiß** *n* (*Farbe*) zinc white; **~wort** *n* (*Chiffre*) code word.

dedi|zieren *tr* (*widmen*) to dedicate; (*schenken*) to present (to); **~kation** *f* dedication.

deduzieren *tr* to deduce; to infer.

Defät|ismus *m* (*Miesmacherei*) defeatism; **~ist** *m* (*Miesmacher*) defeatist; **~istisch** *a* defeatist.

defekt *a* defective; ~ *m* defect, deficiency; **~bogen** *m* imperfect sheet; **~buchstabe** *m typ* batter.

defensiv *a* defensive; **~e** *f* defensive; *in der* ~~ on the defensive.

defilier|en *itr mil* to march past, to defile; **~marsch** *m* march past.

defin|ieren *tr* to define; **~ition** *f* definition; **~itiv** *a* definite, final.

Defizit *n* deficiency, deficit; *Am* wantage; *ein* ~ *von 500 $ haben* to be $500 short.

Deform|ation *f* deformation, distortion; change of form; strain, stress; **~ierbar** *a* deformable; **~ierbarkeit** *f* deformability; **~ieren** *tr* to deform; to distort; to strain.

Defraud|ant *m* defrauder; **~ieren** *tr, itr* to defraud, to cheat.

Degen *m* sword; *fig* brave warrior; **~griff** *m* sword-hilt; **~klinge** *f* sword-blade; **~knopf** *m* pomme ; **~quaste** *f* sword-knot; **~scheide** *f* sheath, scabbard; **~stich, ~stoß** *m* thrust with a sword.

Degener|ation *f* degeneration; **~ieren** *itr* to degenerate.

degradieren *tr* to degrade; to reduce to the ranks; to demote.

dehn|bar *a* flexible; (*Metalle*) ductile; elastic; malleable; (*Leder*) extensible; *fig* wide, vague; **~~keit** *f* dilatability, ductility; *fig* vagueness; ambiguity; **~en** *tr* to stretch, to extend; to expand; to lengthen; (*Worte*) to drawl (out); (*Metalle*) to malleate; *r* (*von Personen*) to stretch o. s.; **~ung** *f* stretching, extension; *elastische* ~~ (*tech*) stress, stretch, elongation; *bleibende* ~~ (*tech*) permanent extension; (*durch Erhitzen*) expansion, dilatation; ~~**sfähig** *a* extensible; expansible; ~~**sfähigkeit** *f* elasticity; extensibility, flexibility, expansibility; dilatability; ~~**koeffizient** *m* modulus of extension; ~~**swärme** *f* heat of elastic extension; ~~**szahl** *f* coefficient of expansion (*od* extension).

Deich *m* dike, dyke, dam; embankment, *Am* levee; ~**bruch** *m* breach of a dike; ~**damm** *m* jetty; ~**hauptmann** *m* dike-reeve.

Deichsel *f* shaft, pole, beam, (*Gabel*~) thill; ~**n** *tr fam* (*fertigbringen*) to manage, to wangle.

dein *a* your; yours; *poet* thy, thine; ~**erseits** *adv* on your part; ~**esgleichen** *prn* the like of you, such as you; ~**ethalben,** (*um*) ~**etwillen** *adv* for your sake; on your account; ~**ige,** ~**e** (*der, die, das*) yours; *die Deinigen, die Deinen* your family, your folk.

Dek|ade *f* decade; ~**a(gramm)** *n* 10 gram(me) (2,83 dkg = 1 ounce).

Dekadenz *f* decadence.

Dekan *m* dean.

dekatieren *tr* (*Gewebe*) to hot-press, to steam.

Deklam|ation *f* declamation; ~**ieren** *tr* to declaim, to recite.

Deklar|ation *f* declaration; ~**ieren** *tr* to declare, to enter goods at the custom-house; *haben Sie etw zum ~~?* have you anything to declare? (*Waren*) *zu niedrig* ~~ (*Am*) to underbill.

Deklin|ation *f* inflection, declension; *phys* declination; ~**ieren** *tr* to decline, to inflect.

dekolletiert *a* (*Kleid*) low-cut (*od* (-necked); *sie ist* ~ she wears a low-cut dress (*od* a dress with a low neck-line); (*Dame*) bare-shouldered.

Dekor|ateur *m* (*Schaufenster*) window-dresser; (*Maler*) decorator; painter; (*Polsterer*) upholsterer; ~**ation** *f* decoration; *theat* scenery; ~~**smaler** *m* decorator, painter; *theat* stage-painter, scene-painter; ~**ieren** *tr* to decorate; (*Schaufenster*) to dress a window.

Dekret *n* decree; ~**ieren** *tr* to decree.

delegier|en *tr* to delegate; ~**te(r)** *m* delegate.

delikat *a* delicate, fine; (*wohlschmekkend*) savo(u)ry; *eine ~e Frage* a delicate (*od* ticklish) question; ~**esse** *f* (*Zartheit*) delicacy; (*Leckerei*) daintiness; (*Leckerbissen*) dainty; *Am* delicatessen; ~~**nhandlung** *f* delicatessen shop, Italian warehouse; *Am* delicatessen.

Delikt *n jur* delict, offence, crime.

Delinquent *m* delinquent.

delir|ant *a med* delirious; ~**ieren** *itr* to be delirious; to rave; ~**ium** *n* delirium.

Delkredere *n* delcredere; ~ *übernehmen* to stand delcredere (*od* security).

Delle *f* dent.

Delphin *m* dolphin.

Delta *n* delta; ~**flugzeug** *n* delta-wing (airplane); ~**förmig** *a* deltoid.

dem: *nach ~, was Sie sagen* from what you say; *es ist an* ~ it is the case; *wie ~ auch sein mag* however that may be; *wenn ~ so ist* if that be true; *bei alle~* notwithstanding; ~**entsprechend,** ~**gemäß,** ~**nach,** ~**zufolge** *adv* according to that, accordingly, hence; ~**nächst** *adv* (*nächstens*) next, before long, soon, shortly, in the near future; (*sodann*) after that, thereupon; ~**ungeachtet** *adv* notwithstanding, nevertheless, for all that.

Demagog|(e) *m* demagog(ue); ~**ie** *f* demagogy, demagogism; ~**isch** *a* demagogic(al).

Demarkationslinie *f* demarcation-line.

demaskieren *tr* to unmask.

Dementi *n* (*Ableugnung, Richtigstellung*) denial; ~**ieren** *tr* to deny.

Demission *f* resignation; (*Entlassung*) dismissal; ~**ieren** *itr* to renounce, to resign.

Demobilis|ation *f* demobilization; ~**ieren** *tr* to demobilize, *Abk* to demob.

Demokrat *m* democrat; ~**ie** *f* democracy; ~**isch** *a* democratic; ~**isieren** *tr* to democratize; ~**isierung** *f* democratization.

demolier|en *tr* to demolish; ~**ung** *f* demolition.

demonstra|tiv *a* demonstrative; ~~**pronomen** *n gram* demonstrative pronoun; ~**nt** *m* demonstrator.

demonstrieren *tr, itr* to demonstrate.

Demont|age *f* (*Abbau*) dismantling; removal; demounting; disassembly; ~~**liste** *f* dismantling list; ~**ieren** *tr* to dismantle; to dismount; to strip; (*Maschine zerlegen*) to knock down, to take apart, to break up (*od* down).

demoralisieren *tr* to demoralize.

Demut *f* meekness, humility.

demütig *a* humble, meek; submissive; ~**en** *tr* to humble, to humiliate; ~**ung** *f* humiliation, mortification.

*

denaturier|en *tr* (*vergällen*) to denature, to denaturize; *~ter Alkohol* methylated spirit, *Am* denatured alcohol; ~**ungsmittel** *n* denaturant.

denazifizier|en *tr* (*entnazifizieren*) to denazify; ~**ung** *f* denazification; ~**ungsausschuß** *m* Denazification Board.

dengeln *tr* to sharpen (a scythe).

Denk|art *f* way of thinking; (*Mentalität*) mentality; (*geistige Veranlagung*) disposition; ~**bar** *a* conceivable, imaginable, thinkable; *auf die ~bar einfachste Weise* in the most simple way conceivable; ~**en** *irr tr, itr* (*allgemein*) to think (*an* of, *über* about); (*sinnen*) to cogitate (*über* upon); (*nachdenken*) to reflect (*über* upon); (*logisch ~en*) to reason (*über* about, on); (*sorgfältig und genau erwägen*) to deliberate; (*meinen, glauben*) to suppose, to mean; *Am* to guess, to reckon; (*der Ansicht sein*) to be of the opinion; (*sich erinnern*) to remember; (*sich vorstellen*) to conceive, to imagine, to fancy, to realize, to envisage, to envision; (*in Betracht ziehen*) to consider, to contemplate; *Am* (*planen*) to figure; (*vorhaben, beabsichtigen*) to intend; *ich ~e schon* I think so; I suppose; *was ~en Sie zu tun?* what do you intend to do? *~en Sie an mich!* remember me! *wo ~en Sie hin?* what are you thinking of? *das habe ich mir gedacht* I thought as much; *hin u. her ~en* to turn over in o.'s mind; *das hätte ich nicht von Ihnen gedacht* I am surprised at you; *das gibt mir zu ~en* that sets me thinking; *bei sich ~en* to think to o. s.; *~en Sie sich in ihre Lage* put yourself in her situation; *sich ~en* to fancy; *~e dir!* just imagine! fancy! *das kann ich mir wohl ~en* I can well imagine; *sie denkt nur an sich* she only regards her own interest; *er dachte sich seinen Teil* he kept his own counsel about it; ~**er** *m* thinker; philosopher; ~**faul** *a* disinclined to think; indolent, dull; ~**freiheit** *f* freedom of thought; ~**kraft** *f* intellectual power; ~**lehre** *f* logic; ~**mal** *n* (*Grabmal*) monument, (*Erinnerungsmal*) memorial; ~**malspflege** *f* care and preservation of monuments (*od* works of art); ~**malsschutz** *m* preservation of ancient monuments; ~**münze** *f* commemorative medal; ~**schrift** *f* memoir, memorial; record; address; ~**sportaufgabe** *f* intelligence test; ~**spruch** *m* sentence, maxim; motto; aphorism; ~**ungsart,** ~**art** *f* manner (*od* mode) of thinking; mind; *von vornehmer* ~~ noble-minded; ~**würdig** *a* memorable; (*bemerkenswert*) notable; ~**würdigkeit** *f* memorability, memorableness; (*Memoiren*) memoirs *pl*; (*Erinnerungen*) reminiscences *pl*; ~**zeichen** *n* token of remembrance; keepsake; souvenir; ~**zettel** *m* (*Notiz*) reminder, refresher; memorandum (*Abk* mem *od* memo); (*Strafe*) punishment; *jdm e-n ~~ geben* to give s. o. a lesson.

denn *conj* for; *adv* then; (*als*) than, but; *es sei ~ daß* unless; ~**noch** *adv* yet, still; though, nevertheless, however.

Dentist *m* dentist; (*Techniker*) dental technician.

Denunz|iant *m* informer; denouncer; ~**iation** *f* denunciation; ~**ieren** *tr* to denounce; to inform against s. o.

Depesch|e *f* dispatch; telegram; wire; cable-message; ~**enbote** *m* telegraph-messenger; ~**enbüro** *n* dispatch-agency; ~**ieren** *tr* to wire, to telegraph.

Depon|ent *m* depositor; ~**ieren** *tr* to deposit.

Depositen *pl com* deposits *pl*; ~**bank** *f* deposit bank; ~**kasse** *f* (*Zweigbank*) branch office (of a bank); ~**konto** *n* deposit account.

Depot *n* (*Bank*) deposit; (*Lager*) storehouse, warehouse; depot, dump; ~**schein** *m* deposit slip; ~**schiff** *n* depot ship, storeship; harbour ship; ~**verzeichnis** *n* deposit list.

Depression *f com, phys* depression; *com* slump; ~**sgewölk** *n* depression clouds *pl*; ~**skern** *m* core of depression; ~**szeit** *f com* depression era; ~**szone** *f* zone of negative pressure.

deprimieren *tr* to depress.

Deput|ation *f* deputation; ~**atzahlung** *f* allowance in kind; ~**ieren** *tr* to depute; ~**ierte(r)** *m* deputy.

der (*Artikel*) the; *prn* that, this, he, it; who, which, that; ~**art** *adv* such, in such a manner, of such a kind; so much, to such an extent; ~**artig** *a* of that kind, such, suchlike; ~**einst** *adv* some (future) day, in the future; (*ehemals*) once, in former days; ~**enthalben,** ~**entwegen,** ~**entwillen** *adv* on their account, on whose account; ~**gestalt** *adv* in such a manner; ~~, *daß* so that; ~**gleichen** *a* such(like); *und* ~~ and the like; ~**jenige** *prn:* ~~ *welcher* he that, he who; ~**maßen** *adv* to that degree, in such a manner; ~**selbe, dieselbe, dasselbe** *prn* the same; (*auf Vorhergehendes weisend*) he, she, it; *eben* ~~ the very same; ~**zeit** *adv* at present, now; ~**zeitig** *a* present, actual, for the time being.

derb *a* compact, firm, solid; (*kräftig*) stout, robust; sturdy; (*offen, ohne Umschweife*) blunt; (*grob*) rough; coarse, rude; *min* massive; (*dicht*) dense; ~**heit** *f* solidity; compactness; firmness; sturdiness; (*Grobheit*) bluntness, roughness; coarseness; (*Zote*) obscenity; *~~en pl* hard (*od* rough) words.

Derivat *n* derivative.

Derwisch *m* dervish.
des *Artikel* (*Genitiv m u. n*); **~gleichen** *adv* suchlike, likewise; *com* ditto; **~halb, ~wegen** *adv* therefore, for that reason; that is why; **~ungeachtet** *adv* notwithstanding, for all that, despite all that.
Des *n mus* D flat.
Desert|eur *m* deserter, runaway; **~ieren** *itr* to desert; to run away; *Am mil sl* to go A. W. O. L. (*od* awol = absent without leave).
Desin|fektion *f* disinfection; **~~sanstalt** *f* disinfecting station; **~~smittel** *n* disinfectant; (*bes. für Körpergeruch etc*) deodorant; **~~swasser** *n* disinfecting liquid; **~fizieren** *tr* to disinfect; to deodorize.
Despot *m* (*Gewaltherrscher*) despot; **~isch** *a* despotic; **~ismus** *m* despotism, despotic power (*od* rule).
dessen *prn* whose; of whom, of which. **~thalben, ~twegen, ~twillen** *adv* on that account; on account of which; **~ungeachtet** *adv* nevertheless, for all that.
Dessert *n* dessert.
Destill|ation *f* distillation; **~~sapparat** *m* still; **~~sbenzin** *n* straight-run gasoline; **~~sgefäß** *n* distilling vessel; **~~skokerei** *f* by-product coke-oven plant; **~ieranlageturm** *m* cracking plant; **~ierapparat** *m* distilling apparatus, distilling plant; **~ierblase** *f* distilling vessel, body of a still; retort; (*früher*) alembic; **~ieren** *tr* to distil(l); **~ierer** *m* distiller; **~ierkolben** *m* retort, distilling flask.
desto, ~mehr *adv* the more; **~ weniger** *adv* the less; **~ besser** *adv* (all) the (*od* so much the) better; **~ schlimmer** *adv* the worse.
Detail *n* (*Einzelheit*) detail, particulars *pl*, item; *com* retail; *ins ~ gehen* to enter into particulars; *im ~ verkaufen* to sell by retail; to retail; *alle ~s* full details; **~bericht** *m* detailed statement; **~geschäft** *n*, **~handel** *m* retail firm (*od* enterprise *od* business); retail trade; **~händler, ~list** *m* retailer, shopkeeper; **~konstrukteur** *m* draftsman; **~lieren** *tr* (*aufgliedern*) to specify, to particularize, to detail; *com* to (sell by) retail; **~liert** *a* in detail, with full details; **~preis** *m* retail price; **~zeichnung** *f tech* detail drawing.
Detektiv *m* detective; *Am fam* spotter; *Am fam* sleuth(-hound); *Am sl* dick; **~geschichte** *f* detective story; *Am sl* whodunit.
Detektor *m radio* detector; **~empfänger** *m radio* cristal set, detector receiver; **~nadel** *f* cat's whisker; **~röhre** *f* detector valve, *Am* detector tube.
Deton|ation *f* detonation, bursting; explosion; (*e-r Bombe*) bursting of bomb; **~~sdruck** *m* blast pressure; **~~skapsel** *f* detonating tube (*od* fuse); **~~sladung** *f* detonation charge; **~~swelle** *f* detonation wave; **~ieren** *itr* to detonate, to explode.
Deut *m* doit; *fig* farthing; *keinen ~ wert sein* not to be worth a farthing (*od* a fig); *Am fam* not to be worth a plugged nickel.
deut|eln *itr* to subtilize; to twist (the meaning of); **~en** *tr* to show; to explain, to interpret; *übel ~~* to take ill; *itr ~~ auf* to point at; (*vorankündigen*) to forebode, to be a sign of; *alles ~et darauf hin, daß ...* everything points to the fact that ...; **~lich** *a* clear, distinct; plain; (*lesbar*) legible; *~liche Aussprache* good articulation; **~lichkeit** *f* clearness; plainness; distinctness; **~ung** *f* explanation, interpretation.
Deuteron, Deuton *n* (*Atomphys: Kern des schweren Wasserstoffs*) deuteron.
deutsch *a* German; *Deutsche Demokratische Republik* (*Ostzonenregierung*) German Democratic Republic; *das Deutsche Reich* Germany; *~er Abstammung* of German stock; **~blütig** *a* of German blood; **~e** *n* German, the German language; **~e(r)** *m*, **~e** *f* German; **~feindlich** *a* anti-German; **~freundlich** *a* pro-German; **~land** *n* Germany; **~tum** *n* Germanism; German nationality.
Devalv|ation *f* devaluation, depreciation; **~ieren** *tr* to depreciate, to devalue.
Devise *f* (*Wahlspruch*) device, motto; (*Zahlungsmittel in ausländischer Währung*) *meist pl* **~n** foreign currency, foreign exchanges *pl*, *Am* foreign exchange; **~nbestimmungen** *f pl* currency control regulations *pl*; *die ~~ umgehen* to circumvent the currency control regulations; **~nbewirtschaftung** *f* foreign exchange control; **~ngesetz** *n* foreign exchange (*od* currency) law; **~nknappheit** *f* shortage of foreign currency; **~nkurs** *m* rate of exchange; **~nnotierung** *f* quotation of foreign exchange; **~nschieber** *m* foreign currency smuggler; **~nsperre** *f* exchange embargo; **~nstelle** *f* foreign exchange office; **~nvergehen** *n* violation of currency control regulations; **~nwerte** *m pl* foreign exchange assets *pl*, *Am* foreign security.
devot *a* humble, submissive.
Dextrin *n* starch-gum, dextrin(e).
Dezember *m* December.
dezent *a* (*unaufdringlich*) unobtrusive, plain; discreet(ly polite).
Dezernat *n* department.
Dezigramm (dg) *n* decigram.
dezimal *a* decimal; **~bruch** *m* decimal fraction; **~rechnung** *f* decimal arithmetic; **~waage** *f* decimal balance.
Dezi|meter (dm) *n* decimeter; **~~gebiet** *n* decimeter range; **~~gerät** *n* decimeter apparatus; **~~wellen** *f pl* microwaves *pl*; microrays *pl*; (*Radar*) decimeter wave lengths; **~mieren** *tr* to decimate.
diabolisch *a* diabolic(al).
Dia|dem *n* diadem; **~gnose** *f* diagnosis; *e-e ~~ stellen*, **~gnostizieren** *tr* to diagnose; **~gonal** *a*, **~gonale** *f* diagonal; **~gramm** *n* (*graphische Darstellung*) diagram, graphic representation, *Am* graph; **~kon** *m* deacon; **~konissin** *f* deaconess; Sister of Mercy; **~lekt** *m* dialect; **~~isch** *a* dialectical; **~log** *m* dialog(ue).
Diamant *m* diamond; **~en** *a* diamond; **~ring** *m* diamond-ring; **~schleifer** *m* diamond-cutter; **~schmuck** *m* set of diamonds.
Dia(positiv) *n* (*Stehbild*) glass picture, diapositive; (lantern) slide; tranparency.
Diarium *n* diary, rough-book.
Diarrhöe *f* diarrhœa; *Am* (*meist*) diarrhea.
Diät *f* diet; regimen; *eine strenge ~ einhalten* to keep to a strict diet; **~en** *pl* allowance, salary; **~etisch** *a* dietetic.
dich *prn* you; *r* yourself.
dicht *a* (*undurchdringlich*) tight, dense, impervious; (*fest*) solid, firm; (*Stoff*) thick; (*eng beieinander*) close, compact; *~e Bevölkerung* dense population; *adv* close, closely; *~ daneben* hard by, near by, close to; **~e, ~heit, ~igkeit** *f* density, closeness; compactness, thickness; **~en** *tr mar* (*dicht machen*) to make close, to ca(u)lk; to tighten; (*verfassen*) to compose, to invent; to write poetry; **~er** *m*, **~erin** *f* poet, poetess; **~erisch** *a* poetic(al); **~erling** *m* poetaster; **~halten** *irr tr fig* not to breathe a word, not to let it go further; **~kunst** *f* poetry; **~ung** *f* poetry, poesy; poem; poetical work; (*Prosa*) fiction; *tech* (*Abdichtung, Verschluß*) tightening, seal; (*Packung*) packing; (*von Schiffen*) ca(u)lking; **~~smanschetten** *f pl* gaskets *pl*; **~~sring** *m* packing ring; **~~sscheibe** *f* washer.
dick *a* thick; (*fett*) fat, corpulent; (*beleibt*) stout; (*geschwollen*) swollen; (*umfangreich*) big, bulky, large; (*vielbändig*) voluminous; (*zähflüssig*) viscose; syrupy; *~ u. fett werden* to grow fat; *~e Milch* curdled milk; *~e Freunde* chums; *~e Luft fam* dangerous situation; *ein ~er Brocken mil sl* heavy bomb; *~ tun* to brag; *das ~e Ende kommt nach* the worst is yet to come; **~bäckig** *a* chubby; **~bauch** *m* pot-belly; **~bäuchig** *a* big-bellied, paunchy; **~darm** *m* large intestine; great gut; **~e** *f* thickness, bigness; (*Größe*) size; (*Umfang*) bulkiness; (*e-r Flüssigkeit*) consistency; (*Beleibtheit*) stoutness, corpulence; **~fellig, ~häutig** *a* thick-skinned; **~flüssig** *a* thickly liquid, viscous, viscid; syrupy; **~häuter** *m* pachyderm; **~icht** *n* thicket; **~kopf** *m fig* blockhead; pig-headed fellow; **~köpfig** *a fig* obstinate; stubborn; hardheaded; **~~keit** *f* obstinacy; **~leibig** *a* corpulent; big-bodied; (*Bücher*) voluminous; **~wanst** *m* swag-belly, paunch.
didaktisch *a* didactic.
die *f Artikel; siehe: der*; **~weil** *adv, conj* while, whilst; whereas; because.
Dieb *m* thief, robber; pilferer; *jur* larcenar, larcenist; *fam* lifter; (*Einbrecher*) burglar; *haltet den ~!* stop the thief! **~erei** *f* theft, thieving, pilfering; **~esbande** *f* gang of thieves; **~(e)sgeselle** *m* accomplice; **~(e)sgut** *n* stolen goods *pl*; **~eshöhle** *f* den of thieves, slum; **~eslaterne** *f* dark lantern; **~essicher** *a* burglar-proof; **~essprache** *f* thieves' slang; **~in** *f* female thief; **~isch** *a* thievish; (*Freude*) devilish; *adv* (*sehr*) awfully; **~stahl** *m* theft, robbery; (*kleiner*) pilferage, pilfering; *jur* larceny; *schwerer ~~* aggravated larceny; (*Einbruch*) burglary.
Diel|e *f* board, deal; plank; (*Hausflur*) hall, vestibule; lounge; entrance; *Am* hallway; (*Scheunen~~*) floor; **~en** *tr* to board, to floor.
dien|en *itr* to serve (s. o.); *als etw ~en* to serve as (*od* for); *bei jdm ~en* to be in s. o.'s service; *zu etw ~en* to be of use, to be fit for; *e-m Zweck ~en* to answer (*od* serve) a purpose; *beim Heer ~en* to serve in the Army; *bei e-r Behörde ~en* to serve with an agency; *damit ist mir nicht gedient* that is of no use to me; *fam* that won't do; *womit kann ich Ihnen ~en?* what can I do for you? may I help you? *von der Pike auf ~en* to work up o.'s way from the ranks; to rise from the ranks; *niemand kann zwei Herren ~en* no man can serve two masters; **~end** *a* ancillary (*e-r Sache* to s. th.); **~er** *m* (man-) servant; (*Geistlicher*) minister (of the Gospel); (*Verbeugung*) bow; *stummer ~er* (*Anrichttischchen*) dumb-waiter; **~erin** *f* maid-servant, girl, maid; **~ern** *itr* to bow and scrape; **~erschaft** *f* servants *pl*, domestics *pl*, household staff; **~lich** *a* (*brauchbar*) useful;

serviceable; expedient, fit; (*für die Gesundheit*) wholesome, salutary; *es für ~lich halten* to deem it expedient; *kann ich Ihnen irgendwie ~lich sein?* can I be of any service to you?

Dienst *m* service; (*bei Behörde etc*) duty; (*Funktion*) function; *öffentlicher ~* (*Staats~*) the Civil Service; (*Stellung*) situation, employment, post; (*Verkehrsverbindung*) *rail, mar, aero* service; *außer ~* out of service; (*~frei*) off duty; (*ohne Stellung*) out of employment; (*in Pension*) retired, on half-pay; *im ~* on duty; on active service; *~ haben* to be on duty; *keinen ~ haben* to be off duty; *den ~ antreten* to take up duty; *aus dem ~ entlassen* to dismiss, *Am* to fire; *e-n ~ erweisen* to render service; *e-n ~ leisten* to help, to oblige; *~ an Bord* duty afloat (*od* on board); *~ bei der Fahne* active service; *~ bei der Truppe* field duty; *zum ~ einberufen werden mil* to be called into service; *in Ausübung des ~es* in line of duty; *jdm zu ~en stehen* to be at s. o.'s service; *in ~ stellen* (*mar*) to commission; *außer ~ stellen* (*mar*) to lay up; *~(e) tun* to do service; *in ~ nehmen* to engage s. o., *Am* to hire s. o.; *Unteroffizier vom ~* (*mil*) charge of quarters (*Abk* C Q); **~abteil** *n* service compartment; **~abzeichen** *n* (*der Polizisten*) badge, *Am* shield; **~alter** *n* seniority, years of service; **~altersgrenze** *f* age limit; **~ältester** *m* senior officer; **~anruf** *m* official (*od* service) call; **~anschluß** *m tele* official telephone; **~antritt** *m* installation, taking up o.'s post; **~anweisung** *f* service instructions *pl*; **~anzug** *m mil* (field-)service uniform; **~aufwandsentschädigung** *f* refund for professional expenditure; **~ausrüstung** *f* service equipment; **~bar** *a* subject; (*gefällig*) pleasing; *e-r Sache ~bar sein* to be in service to s. th.; *~barer Geist* factotum; **~barkeit** *f jur* servitude; **~befehl** *m* service order; *e-n ~~ verweigern* to disobey (*od* refuse) an official (*od* service) order; **~beflissen** *a* serviceable; officious; eager to serve, zealous, obliging; **~beflissenheit** *f* serviceableness; zeal; **~bereit** *a* ready for service; **~beschädigung** *f* damage (*od* injury) occurring while in service; **~bescheinigung** *f* certificate of service; **~bezüge** *pl* official income; **~bote** *m* domestic; servant; *Am* help; **~botentreppe** *f* back-stairs *pl*; **~eid** *m* official oath; *mil* oath of enlistment; **~eifer** *m* (professional) zeal; officiousness; **~eifrig** *a* eager to serve, zealous, obliging; (*gefällig*) pleasing, officious; **~eintritt** *m* entry into service; *frühester ~~ 1. Juni* available June 1st at the earliest; **~enthebung, ~entlassung** *f* dismissal (*od* removal *od* dismission *od* discharge) from service (*od* office); *vorläufige ~enthebung* suspension; **~fähig** *a* fit for service; effective; able-bodied (*Abk* A. B.); **~fahrt** *f* official tour; **~fallschirm** *m* service-type parachute; **~fertig** *a* obliging; **~fertigkeit** *f* officiousness; obligingness; **~frei** *a* exempt from service; off duty; **~gebrauch** *m*: *nur für den ~~!* for official use only! *mil* restricted! **~gespräch** *n tele* service call; **~gewalt** *f* authority; **~gewicht** *n* gross (*od* loaded) weight; weight in working order; **~gipfelhöhe** *f aero* service ceiling; **~grad** *m* rank; grade; rating; **~~abzeichen** *n* insignia of rank (*od* grade *od* rating); **~~bezeichnung** *f* rating; **~~herabsetzung** *f* demotion; **~habend** *a* on duty; **~handlung** *f mil* act performed in line of duty; **~herr** *m* employer; master; principal, *Am* boss; **~jahre** *n pl* years spent in service, years of service; **~kompanie** *f* service company; **~kraftwagen** *m* official car; **~last** *f* service load; **~leistung** *f* service; **~leiter** *m* executive head; **~lich** *a* official; in official capacity; **~lohn** *m* (servant's) wages *pl*; **~mädchen** *n* maid-servant, (house-)maid, *Am* (hired) girl; **~mann** *m* porter; messenger, errand-man; **~marke** *f* inland revenue stamp; **~mütze** *f* service cap; **~notiz** *f* service advice; **~ordnung** *f* official regulations *pl*; **~pferd** *n* troop (*od* service) horse; **~pflicht** *f* official duty; *allgemeine ~~* (*mil*) conscription; compulsory military service; **~pflichtige(r)** *m* man liable to serve, *Am* draft registrant, draftee; **~plan** *m* duty roster, service schedule; assignment of hours; timetable; **~prämie** *f* service bonus; **~raum** *m* service room; **~reise** *f* official journey (*od* travel *od* tour); **~sache** *f* official matter, matter of official concern; (*auf Briefumschlag*) On His Majesty's Service; *Am* Official Business; **~schreiben** *n* official correspondence; **~siegel** *n* official seal; **~stelle** *f* office, agency; civil service assignment; administrative department; *mil* headquarters *pl*; (*Regiment*) depot; **~stellung** *f* official function; **~strafordnung** *f* disciplinary rules *pl*; **~stunden** *f pl* office hours, duty hours, business hours *pl*; **~tauglich** *a* fit for service; able-bodied; **~treue** *f* loyalty; **~tuend** *a* on duty, in charge; in attendance; **~untauglich** *a* unfit for active service; disabled; (*altershalber*) superannuated; **~vergehen** *n* disciplinary offence; **~verhältnis** *n* term of employment; **~vernachlässigung** *f* neglect of duty; **~vertrag** *m* contract of employment, service contract; **~vorkommnis** *n* service error (*od* irregularity); **~vorschrift** *f* official service regulations (*od* ordinances) *pl*; **~wagen** *m* official car; **~weg** *m* official channels; *auf dem ~~* through official channels; **~willig** *a* ready to serve; officious; **~wohnung** *f* official residence; **~zeit** *f* time spent in service; enlistment period; *seine ~zeit abdienen* to serve o.'s time; **~zeugnis** *n* character; (service) certificate; reference; **~zulage** *f* allowance for special duty; **~zweig** *m* branch of service.

Dienstag *m* Tuesday.

diesbezüglich *a* referring thereto (*od* to this), relating thereto; corresponding.

Diesel|antrieb *m mot* Diesel propulsion; *mit ~~* Diesel-powered; **~elektrische Lokomotive** *f* Diesel-electric locomotive; **~kraftstoff** *m* Diesel fuel-oil; **~lastwagen** *m* (*fam: Diesel*) Diesel lorry, *Am* Diesel truck; **~lokomotive** *f* Diesel locomotive; **~motor** *m* Diesel-engine, C. I. engine, Diesel power plant; **~motorschiff** *n* Diesel ship; **~öl** *n* Diesel oil; **~omnibus** *m* Diesel omnibus, *Am* Diesel coach; **~triebwagen** *m rail* Diesel rail car; **~zugmaschine** *f* Diesel tractor.

dies|er, **~e, ~es (dies)** *prn* this, these; this one; the latter.

dies|falls *adv* in this case; **~jährig** *a* this year's, of this year; **~mal** *adv* this time, on this occasion; for once; **~seitig** *a* on this side: **~seits** *adv* on this side; **~~** *n* this life; *im ~~* in this life.

diesig *a* misty, hazy; *~es Wetter* haze.

Dietrich *m* skeleton-key, picklock.

diffamier|en *tr* to defame; to vilify, to calumniate, to slander; *Am auch* to smear; **~ung** defamation.

Differ|ential *n* differential; **~~getriebe** *n mot* differential (gear); **~~gleichung** *f* differential equation; **~~rechnung** *f* differential calculus; the calculus; **~enz** *f* difference; balance; (*Überschuß*) surplus; **~enzieren** *tr* to differentiate; **~enziert** *a fig* refined, discriminating; **~ieren** *itr* to differ, to be different.

diffus *a* diffused; scattered; **~ion** *f* diffusion; interfusion; **~~svermögen** *n* diffusivity; diffusibility; **~or** *m* diffuser; delivery space; (*Lader*) vaned diffuser plate.

Dikt|at *n* dictation; (*Befehl*) dictate; *ein ~~ aufnehmen* to take a dictation; *nach ~~* from dictation; **~~aufnahme** *f* (*stenographisch*) taking dictation; take; **~~or** *m* dictator; **~~orisch** *a* dictatorial; **~~ur** *f* dictatorship; **~~zeichen** *n* reference (number); **~ieren** *tr* to dictate; **~iermaschine** *f* (electronic) dictating machine, dictaphone; *Am* voicewriter, voice recorder, dictograph.

dilatorisch *a* dilatory.

Dilettant *m* dilettante, amateur; **~isch** *a* amateurish.

Dill *m* dill.

Dimension *f* dimension; size; **~al** *a* dimensional; **~ieren** *tr* to dimension; **~ierung** *f* dimensioning; sizing, design.

Ding *n* thing, (*Gegenstand*) object, item; (*Angelegenheit*) matter, affair; (*Wesen*) being; *guter ~e sein* to be in high spirits; *vor allen ~en* before all; above all; first of all; *sie nimmt die ~e zu schwer* she takes matters too seriously; *unverrichteter ~e abziehen* to leave without having accomplished anything; *das geht nicht mit rechten ~en zu* there's some hocus-pocus about it; *aller guten ~e sind drei* three is lucky; *das sind mir schöne ~e!* fine doings these! **~en** *irr tr* to hire; to engage; **~fest** *a*: *~~ machen* to seize, to arrest; **~lich** *a jur* real; *~liches Eigentum* real property; *~liches Recht* real right.

dinieren *itr* to dine.

Dinkel *m* spelt.

Diözese *f* diocese.

Diphtherie *f* diphtheria.

Diphthong *m* diphthong.

Diplom *n* diploma, patent; certificate; **~at** *m* diplomatist; *Am* career man; **~atie** *f* diplomacy; **~atisch** *a* diplomatic; *~~es Korps* diplomatic body (*od* corps); *die ~~en Beziehungen wiederaufnehmen* to restore diplomatic relations with; **~ingenieur** *m* graduated (*od* certificated) engineer.

dir *prn Dativ* (to) you; *r* to yourself.

direkt *a* direct; *~e Wagen* through carriages; *~ adv* directly; *Am* right (-away), straight; *~ gegenüber von* straight across from; *~ nach Hause kommen* to come home right away; *~ unmöglich* simply impossible; **~ion** *f* direction; (*Verwaltung*) management; directorate, *Am* directory; (*Vorstand*) board of directors; **~iven** *f pl* instructions *pl*; **~or** *m* (*Schule*) head-master; *Am* principal; (*Geschäft*) manager, director; (*Bank*) governor; *technischer ~~* engineering manager; **~orat** *n* directorship; **~orium** *n* directorate, *Am* directory; board of directors; **~rice** *f* directress; manageress; (*Schule*) head-mistress; *Am* principal (mistress).

Dirig|ent *m mus* leader, conductor; **~~enstab** *m* baton; **~ieren** *tr* to direct; to manage, to rule; *mus* to conduct.

Dirndl *n dial* maid, lass; **~kleid** *n* Bavarian girl's dress, dirndl.
Dirne *f* maid, lass; *feile ~* prostitute, wench; street-walker; **~nunwesen** *n* prostitution.

*

Dis *n mus* D sharp; **~-dur** *n* D-sharp major; **~-moll** *n* D-sharp minor.
Disharm\|onie *f mus u. fig* discord; dissonance; (*Mißhelligkeit*) discordancy; **~onisch** *a mus u. fig* discordant, disharmonious.
Diskant *m mus* treble, soprano; **~schlüssel** *m* treble clef.
Diskont\|(o) *m* discount, bank rate; *Am* rediscount; *e-n ~ gewähren* to allow a discount; *den ~ heraufsetzen* to increase (*od* raise) the discount; *den ~ herabsetzen* to cut (*od* lower) the discount; **~abrechnung** *f* discount note; **~abzug** *m* discount deduction; **~bank** *f* discount bank; **~erhöhung** *f* rise in the bank rate; **~ermäßigung** *f* reduction in the bank rate; **~fähig** *a* discountable; **~ieren** *tr* to discount, to take on discount; **~satz** *m* rate of discount, *Am* rediscount rate.
diskreditieren *tr* to bring disrepute upon.
diskret *a* discreet; (*taktvoll*) tactful; (*zurückhaltend*) reserved; (*behutsam*) cautious; **~ion** *f* secrecy, privacy.
diskriminieren *tr* to discriminate.
Diskus *m sport* discus, disk; *~ werfen* to throw the discus; **~werfer** *m* discus-thrower; discobolus; **~wurf** *m* discus-throwing.
Disku\|ssion *f* discussion, debate; *die Sache ist noch im ~~sstadium* the matter is still in the discussion stage (*od* talk stage); **~~sgegenstand** *m* subject of a discussion; **~~sgrundlage** *f* basis for a discussion; **~~sveranstaltung** *f* discussion meeting, forum; **~tabel** *a* discussible; **~ tieren** *tr, itr* to discuss, to debate (s. th.).
Dis\|pens *m* dispensation, exemption; **~pensieren** *tr* to dispense, to exempt from; **~ponent** *m* manager; **~ponibel** *a* available; **~ponieren** *tr* to dispose (*über* of); to arrange; to plan ahead; **~position** *f* disposal; (*Anordnung*) arrangement; (*Neigung*) disposition; *zur ~~ stellen* (*mil*) to put on half-pay; **~put** *m* disputation; debate; **~putieren** *tr, itr* to dispute (*über* on), to argue (*über* about, *für* for, *gegen* against, *mit* with), to debate (s. th.).
disqualifizieren *tr* to disqualify, to strike off the roll.
Dissertation *f* (*Abhandlung*) dissertation; (*Doktor~*) thesis.
Dissident *m eccl* dissident, dissenter, *Am* dissentient.
Dissonanz *f* dissonance.
Distanz *f* (*Abstand, fig Zurückhaltung*) distance; **~bleche** *n pl mot* shim plates *pl*; **~ieren** *tr* to distance; **~muffe** *f mot* spacer (sleeve); **~ritt** *m* long-distance ride.
Distel *f* thistle; **~fink** *m* goldfinch.
Distichon *n* distich.
Distrikt *m* district.
Disziplin *f* (*Ordnung, Manneszucht*) discipline; (*Wissenszweig, Fach*) branch of knowledge; *~ halten* to keep good discipline; **~argewalt** *f* disciplinary power (*od* control) (*über* over); **~arisch** *a* disciplinary; *~~ belangen* to inflict disciplinary punishment; **~armaßnahmen** *f pl* disciplinary measures *pl*; **~arverfahren** *n* disciplinary action; **~arvergehen** *n* disciplinary offence.
dito *adv* ditto, as aforesaid.
Diva *f* popular performer, star.
divers *a* sundry; **~e(s)** *n* sundries, miscellanies *pl*.
Divid\|end *m*, **~ende** *f* dividend; *e-e ~~e ausschütten* to distribute (*od* to pay) a dividend; *keine ~~e ausschütten* to pass a dividend; **~~enausschüttung** *f* distribution of dividends; **~~enbogen** *m* coupon sheet; **~~enkupon** *m* dividend warrant (*od* coupon); **~ieren** *tr* to divide.
Divis\|ion *f mil* division; *leichte ~~* light (*od* mechanized) division; *schnelle ~~* mobile division; **~~sabschnitt** *m* division combat sector; **~~saufklärungsabteilung** *f* divisional reconnaissance battalion; **~~sbefehl** *m* division combat order; **~~sfeldlazarett** *n* division field hospital; **~~sgefechtsstand** *m* division command post; **~~skommandeur** *m* divisional commander; **~~snachrichtenabteilung** *f* divisional signals battalion, divisional communication section; **~~snachrichtenführer** *m* division signal officer; **~~snachschubführer** *m* O. C. divisional supplies, chief of division supply services; **~~snachschubkolonne** *f* divisional supply column (*od* train); **~~sstab** *m* division headquarters, divisional H. Q. personnel; **~~sstabsquartier** *n* division headquarters; divisional H. Q.; **~~sstreifen** *m* division combat sector; **~~stagesbefehl** *m* division order of the day; **~~sverband** *m* division; **~~sverpflegungsamt** *n* divisional quartermaster office; **~or** *m* divisor.
Divis (*Bindestrich*) *typ* hyphen.
Diwan *m* divan; couch; sofa; settee.
doch *conj u. adv* (*dennoch*) yet; though; nevertheless; (*aber*) but; however; *aber ~* but still; (*nach Verneinung*) yes; oh, yes; *ja ~!* but of course! *nicht ~!* certainly not! don't! *ich habe es ihm ~ gesagt* but I told him so; *hilf mir ~!* do help me! *seien Sie ~ ruhig!* do be quiet! *das ist ~ nicht möglich!* that cannot be possible! *kommen Sie ~ herein!* do come in! *Am* come right in! *das meinen Sie ~ nicht im Ernst?* you don't really mean that? *sie kommt ~?* she is coming, isn't she? *er hat also ~ recht gehabt* so he was right, after all.
Docht *m* wick.
Dock *n mar* dock, dockyard; (*staatlich*) navy yard; *Trocken~* dry-dock, graving-dock; *Schwimm~* floating-dock; *das Schiff muß ins ~* the ship is to be docked; *auf ~ legen* to bring (*od* to put) into dock; **~arbeiter** *m* docker, *Am* dock laborer, longshoreman; **~en** *tr* to dock; **~gebühren** *f pl* dock-dues *pl*, dockage.
Docke *f* (*Puppe*) doll; (*Säule*) baluster; (*Strang*) skein (of yarn); (*Tabak*) bundle; **~n** *tr* to form into a bundle.
Doge *m* doge.
Dogge *f* bulldog; (*dänische*) Great Dane; (*englische*) mastiff.
Dogma *n* dogma; **~tiker** *m* dogmatist; **~tisch** *a* dogmatic.
Dohle *f* jackdaw; (*Kanal*) drain, sewer.
Dohne *f* bird-snare; noose.
Doktor *m* doctor; *Dr. jur* doctor of laws, *Abk* LL. D.; *Dr. med* medical doctor, *Abk* M. D.; *Dr. phil* doctor of philosophy, *Abk* Ph. D.; (*Arzt*) doctor, surgeon, physician, medical man; *Anrede in England meist*: Mr. *od sonstiger Titel, Am immer:* doctor; *den ~ machen* to take the degree of doctor; *er hat eben seinen ~ gemacht* he just got his doctorate **~arbeit** *f* thesis for doctorate; **~at** *n* doctor's degree; **~examen** *n* examination for a doctor's degree; **~würde** *f* doctorate.
Doktrin *f* doctrine.
Dokument *n* document; deed, instrument; voucher; **~arfilm** *m* (*Kultur-, Lehrfilm*) documentary (film); **~arisch** *a* documentary, documental; **~ation** *f* documentation; **~ieren** *tr* to prove (by documentary evidence).
Dolch *m* dagger, dirk; **~stich**, **~stoß** *m* stab with a dagger; stab in the back; **~~legende** *f* stab-in-the-back phrase (*od* legend).
Dolde *f* umbel; **~ntragend** *a bot* umbelliferous.
Dollar *m* dollar; *Am fam* wheel; *Am sl* buck, smacker; *der letzte ~* (*Am fam*) bottom (*od* case) dollar; **~diplomatie** *f* dollar diplomacy.
Dolle *f mar* (*Haltevorrichtung der Ruder*) thole; rowlock, *Am* oarlock.
Dolmetsch\|(er) *m* interpreter; (*Orient*) dragoman; **~en** *tr, itr* to interpret.
Dom *m arch* dome; cathedral; *fig* vault; **~herr** *m* prebendary, canon; **~kapitel** *n* chapter (of a cathedral); **~pfaff** *m orn* bullfinch; **~prediger** *m* pastor of a cathedral; **~probst** *m* provost of a cathedral; **~stift** *n* cathedral-chapter.
Domäne *f* domain, State demesne; crown-land; **~ngut** *n* domain.
Domin\|ante *f* dominant; **~ikaner** *m* Dominican friar; black friar; **~ieren** *itr* to preponderate; to domineer (over).
Domino *m* domino; *~ n* dominoes *pl*; *~ spielen* to play at dominoes; **~stein** *m* domino.
Domizil *n* domicile; (*Wechsel*) indirect bill; **~ieren** *tr* (*e-n Wechsel*) to make payable.
Dompteur *m* tamer, trainer.
Donau *f* Danube; *die Donau betreffend, Donau-* Danubian.
Don Juan *m* (*Verführer*) lady-killer.
Donner *m* thunder; *wie vom ~ gerührt* thunderstruck; (*Geschütz~*) roar (of cannons); **~bö** *f* black squall; **~büchse** *f fam* artillery piece; **~keil** *m* thunderbolt; **~n** *itr imp* to thunder; to roar; **~nd** *a* thunderous; *~~es Gelächter* a peal of laughter; **~schlag** *m* thunderclap; **~stag** *m* Thursday; *Grüner ~~* Maundy Thursday; **~stimme** *f* thundering voice; **~wetter** *n* thunderstorm; *fig* scolding, blowing up; *~~! interj* hang it all! damn it! by Jove!
Doppel *n* (*Duplikat*) duplicate; (*Tennis*) doubles *pl*; **~aderlitze** *f el* double flex, *Am* twin cord; **~adler** *m* two-headed eagle; *Am* (*$ 20 Goldmünze*) double eagle; **~arbeit** *f* duplication of effort; **~armig** *a* two-armed, double-armed; **~atomig** *a* diatomic; **~ausschalter** *m el* double cutout; **~belichtung** *f phot* double exposure; **~bereifung** *f mot* twin-tyres *pl*, *Am* double (*od* dual) tires *pl*; **~bett** *n* twin bed; double-bed; **~bier** *n* double beer, strong beer; **~bild** *n* double-image; (*auf dem Fernsehschirm*) *tele* ghost; **~boden** *m* false bottom; **~decker** *m* biplane; **~deckomnibus** *m* double deck bus; **~deutig** *a* ambiguous; **~düsenvergaser** *m* double-jet carburet(t)or; **~ehe** *f* bigamy; **~fenster** *n* double window; winter window; **~fernglas** *n* field glass, binocular; **~flinte** *f* double-barrel(l)ed gun; **~flugzeug** *n* composite aircraft; **~gänger** *m* doubleganger, double; **~gleis** *n* double-line; **~gleisig** *a* double-railed, double-track(ed); **~griff** *m mus* double stop; **~kinn** *n* double chin; **~kohlensauer** *a* bicarbonate of; **~kopfhörer** *m* double head-phone; **~lauf** *m* double-barrel (of

a gun); **~läufig** *a* double-barrel(l)ed; **~laut** *m* diphthong; **~n** *tr* to double; **~name** *m* compound name; **~polig** *a* bipolar; **~punkt** *m* colon; **~reifen** *m* dual tyre (*Am* tire); **~reihe** *f mil* column of twos; double file; *in ~~ antreten* to fall in, to form column of twos; **~reihig** *a* (*Anzug*) double-breasted; **~röhre** *f* twin valve (*Am* tube); **~rolle** *f aero* double snap roll; **~ruder** *n* twin rudder; **~rumpf** *m aero* twin fuselage; **~schalter** *m el* duplex switch; **~schichtfilm** *m* double-coated film; **~schichtig** *a* two-layered; **~schraube** *f* double threaded screw; **~schraubenschiff** *n* twin screw ship; **~sinn** *m* double meaning; **~sinnig** *a* ambiguous, equivocal; **~sitzer** *m aero* two-seater; **~sohle** *f* clump; **~spat** *m* Iceland spar; **~spiel** *n* double game; **~stecker** *m el* double (*od* two-way) plug, two-way adapter; (*Bananen~~*) U-plug; **~stern** *m mil* double star shell; **~sternmotor** *m aero* two-row radial engine; **~steuerung** *f aero* dual control; **~stiftstecker** *m* two-pin plug; **~stück** *n* duplicate; **~tür** *f* double door; (*Flügeltür*) folding-door; **~verdiener** *m* two-jobman; **~währung** *f* double standard; **~zentner** *m* double centner, two hundredweight, 100 kilograms; quintal (224 lb., *Am* 200 lb.); **~zimmer** *n* (*Zimmer mit Doppelbetten*) two-bed room; **~züngig** *a* double-tongued; **~züngigkeit** double-dealing, deceitfulness.

doppelt *a* double, twofold; *adv* twice, doubly; *~ bezahlen* to pay double the price; *~e Buchführung* book-keeping by double entry.

Dorf *n* village, *Am auch* small town; (*Weiler*) hamlet; **~bewohner** *m* villager; **~gemeinde** *f* rural parish; **~pfarrer** *m* country parson; **~rand** *m* outskirts of a village; **~schenke** *f* village inn; **~schule** *f* village school; **~schulmeister** *m* village schoolmaster; **~schulze** *m* village magistrate.

Dörf|chen *n dim* small village; **~ler** *m* villager; **~lich** *a* rustic.

Dorn *m* thorn; (*Stachel*) prickle; *mot* drift; *bot* spine; (*an Schnalle*) tongue (of a buckle); (*Bolzen, Stift, Eisenspitze*) spike; pin; bolt; punch; (*Dreh~*) mandrel; (*Reibahle*) triblet (*od* tribolet); *er ist mir ein ~ im Auge* he is an eyesore to me; **~busch** *m* thorn-bush; **~enhecke** *f* quickhedge; hedge of thorns; **~enkrone** *f* crown of thorns; **~envoll** *a* thorny; **~röschen** *n* the Sleeping Beauty (in the Wood); **~ig** *a* thorny, spiny.

dörr|en, **dorren** *tr* to dry; to desiccate; (*Holz*) to stove wood; to season wood artificially; *itr* to wither; (*rösten*) to parch; **~fleisch** *n* dried meat; **~gemüse** *n* dried (*od* dehydrated) vegetables *pl*; **~obst** *n* dried fruit; evaporated fruit.

Dorsch *m* cod(fish); codling, torsk; **~lebertran** *m*, **~öl** *n* cod-liver oil.

dort *adv* there; yonder; *von ~* from there; **~her** *adv* from there; thence; **~hin** *adv* thither; there, that way; *bis ~~* as far as there; **~hinauf** *adv* up there; **~hinaus** *adv* out there; **~ig** *a* there; of (at) that place; **~hinten** *adv* yonder; **~herum** *adv* there about; **~zulande** *adv* in that country, over there.

Dose *f* box; (*Konserven~*) tin, *Am* can; (*Steck~*) *el* plug socket; (*Kapsel*) capsule; (*Behälter*) container; **~nbarometer** *n* aneroid barometer; **~nentwicklung** *f phot* tank development; **~nlibelle** *f* level(l)ing indicator; **~nmilch** *f* tinned (*od* canned) milk, (*ungezuckert*) evaporated milk; (*süß*) condensed milk; **~nöffner** *m* tin-opener, *Am* can-opener.

dös|en *itr* to doze; **~ig** *a* sleepy, dull; (*dumm*) stupid, silly.

dosier|en *tr* to dose, to measure out; **~t** *a* in measured quantities; dosed; **~ung** *f* dosage.

Dosis *f* (*pl Dosen*) dose; *zu kleine ~* underdose, *zu große ~* overdose.

Dot|ation *f* dotation; **~ieren** *tr* to endow.

Dotter *m* yolk (of an egg); dodder (of a plant); **~blume** *f* marsh-marigold.

Doz|ent *m* university teacher, lecturer, *Am* assistant professor; **~ieren** *itr* to lecture on; to teach.

*

Drache *m* dragon; *fig* (*Xanthippe*) termagant; *Am sl* battle-axe; (*Papier~*) kite; *einen ~n steigen lassen* to fly a kite; **~naufstieg** *m* kite ascent; **~nballon** *m mil* sausage (*od* kite) balloon; **~nblut** *n* dragon's blood; **~nsaat** *f fig* dragon's teeth; **~ntöter** *m* dragon-slayer.

Drachme *f* drachm; (*Gewicht*) dram.

Dragoner *m* dragoon.

Draht *m* wire; (*el Leiter*) conductor, leader; filament; (*Kabel*) cable; (*Geld*) *fam* cash; *mit ~ befestigen* (*versehen, abgrenzen*) to wire; *Haus mit el Drahtleitungen versehen* to wire; *mit Strom geladener ~* live wire; *eine Sendung über den ~ leiten* (*radio*) to pipe; *zu ~ ausziehen* to wiredraw; *aus ~ geflochten* wire-woven; *aus ~* (*Draht . . .*) wiry; *auf ~ sein fam* to know o.'s stuff, to be efficient, *Am fam* to be on the beam (*od* ball); **~abschneider** *m* wire cutter; **~anschrift** *f* telegraphic address; **~antwort** *f* wire reply, reply by telegram, telegraphic answer; **~anweisung** *f* telegraphic money-order; **~arbeit** *f* (*Filigranarbeit*) filigree; **~auslöser** *m phot* wire-release, cable-release; **~bericht** *m* wire, telegram; **~bürste** *f* wire-brush; **~eisen** *n* wire-drawing plate; **~en** *tr* to telegraph, to wire, (*überseeisch*) to cable; **~funk** *m* wired wireless, wired broadcasting, *Am* wire program distribution; *niederfrequenter ~~* audio frequency wire broadcast; **~~schaltdose** *f* wall socket for wired wireless facilities; **~~sendung** *f* wired radio transmission; **~~system** *n* wire carrier system; **~fußmatte** *f* wire foot mat (*od* scraper); **~gaze** *f* wire gauze; **~geflecht** *n* wire netting; **~gewebe** *n* wire-cloth; **~gitter** *n* wire-grate, *Am* wire grille; **~glas** *n* wire glass, armo(u)red glass; **~~scheibe** *f* wire netting pane; **~haarfox** *m* wire-hair; **~haarig** *a* wire-haired; **~hefter** *m* wire stitcher; **~heftklammer** *f* wire staple; **~ig** *a* wiry; **~korrespondent** *m* (*Presse*) string correspondent; **~lehre** *f tech* wire-ga(u)ge; **~lich** *a* transmitted by wire; **~los** *a* wireless; radio . . .; *~~ gesteuertes Flugzeug* radio controlled plane; drone; *~~ telegraphieren* (*funken*) to wireless; *~~ übermitteltes Telegramm* wireless (*od* radio) telegram; radiogram; *Station für ~~e Telegraphie* wireless station; *~~e Telegraphie* wireless telegraphy (*Abk*: W. T.); *~~e Telephonie* radio telephony; *~~e Verbindung* radio communication; *~~er Empfang* wireless reception; *~~es Fernsehen* television; *~~e Ortsbestimmung* radio direction finding; *~~e Peilung* radio bearing; **~nachricht** *f* telegram; **~nachrichtenbüro** *n* news wire bureau; **~nachrichtendienst** *m Am* wire service; **~netz** *n* (*Schaltung, Leitungen, aero Verspannung*) wiring; wire net; **~öse** *f* staple; **~ring** *m* ring of wire; **~rolle** *f* coil of wire; **~rundfunk** *m* wire broadcasting, broadcast (*od* radio) relay, rediffusion, line radio; **~rundspruch** *m* program transmission over wires; **~saite** *f* wire string; **~schere** *f* wire-shears *pl*, wire-cutters *pl*; **~seil** *n* wire-rope (*od* cable); **~~akrobat,** **~~künstler** *m* wire-walker, wire-dancer; (*auf dem Hochseil*) highwire man; **~~bahn** *f* wire-rope railway; (*Personenschwebebahn*) passenger rope-way; funicular railway; **~~brücke** *f* wire-bridge; **~sieb** *n* wire-sieve (*od* screen); **~speichenrad** *n* wire spoke wheel; **~spule** *f* wire spool, *Am* wire reel; **~stift** *m* wire-tack; **~telegramm** *n* wire message; **~ung** *f* telegram, radiogram; **~verbindung** *f tele* wire communication; wire connection; *el* wiring; **~verhau** *n od m* wire entanglement; **~walzwerk** *n* wire mill; **~wurm** *m* wireworm; **~zange** *f* wire-pliers *pl*; **~zaun** *m* wire fence; **~zieher** *m tech* wire drawer; *fig* wire-puller; *der ~zieher sein* to pull the wires.

Drain|age, Drainierung *f* (*Entwässerung*) drainage, draining; **~ieren** *tr* to drain.

Draisine *f* draisine; *rail* (inspection) troll(e)y.

drakonisch *a* Draconian.

Drall *m tech* twist; pitch (of rifling); (*Luftschrauben*) *aero* torque; (*Elektronen~*) spin (of electrons); (*Torsions~*) torsional force; *phys* moment of momentum; **drall** *a* compact, tight; (*kräftig*) robust; (*von Frauen*) buxom.

Drama *n* drama; **~tiker** *m* dramatist; **~tisch** *a* dramatic; *~~ darstellen* to dramatize; **~tisieren** *tr* to dramatize; **~turg** *m theat* producer; dramaturgist; **~~ie** *f* dramaturgy.

dran = *daran.*

Drang *m* (*Spannung*) stress; (*innerer Antrieb*) urge; (*Andrang, Menge*) throng, crowd; (*Trieb*) impulse; desire; (*Bedrängnis*) oppression, need, urgency; *im ~ der Geschäfte* in the hurry of business; *im ~ der Not* under the stress of circumstances; (*Druck*) pressure.

dräng|eln, **~en** *itr* to press, to throng; to push; to shove; *gedrängt voll* crowded, jammed; *gedrängt sitzen* to sit close together; *herein~en* to crowd in; *sich ~en* to flock, to crowd; *fig* to hurry, to drive; *sich durch das Volk ~en* to force o.'s way through the crowd; *gedrängt schreiben* to write closely together; *fig* to write concisely; *es drängt mich* I burn to; I am eager to; *die Zeit ~t* time presses; **~en** *n* pressing; crowding, jostle; hurry; eagerness.

Drangsal *f* affliction, distress; **~ieren** *tr* to afflict, to oppress; (*plagen*) to torment; to harass; to badger; to vex.

dränieren *siehe: drainieren.*

drapieren *tr* to drape.

drastisch *a* drastic; *fig* strong, powerful.

Drauf|gänger *m* dare-devil, *Am* go-getter; **~gängerisch** *a* spirited, dashing; **~gängertum** *n* daring, audacity; dash; pluck; **~gehen** *irr itr fam* to be ruined, to be lost; (*sterben*) to pass away, to get killed; **~lospfeffern** *tr fam* to let fly, to fire away, to blaze away.

Draufgeld *n* agio; (*Angeld*) earnest-money.

Draufsicht *f* (top) plan view; plan.

draußen *adv* outside; (*im Freien*) out of doors, in the open air; (*in der Fremde*) abroad; *dort* ~ out yonder.

Drechsel|bank *f* turning-lathe; **~n** *tr* to turn.

Drechsler *m* turner; wood-lathe operator; **~ei** *f* turnery; **~meister** *m* master-turner.

Dreck *m* (*Schmutz*) dirt; muck; (*Straßenschmutz*) mire, mud; (*Kot*) filth; (*Exkremente*) excrements *pl*; (*bei Tieren*) dung; (*Kleinigkeit*) trifle, bagatelle; *aero sl* (*Nebel,* ~*wetter*) fog, muggy weather; (*Wolke*) thick cloud; *im* ~ *steckenbleiben* (*Auto*) to stick in the mud, *Am fam* to get stuck in the mud; *in den* ~ *ziehen* to throw dirt at s. o., to drag s. o. in the mud; *das geht dich e-n* ~ *an* (*fam*) that is none of your business; *er hat Geld wie* ~ he is very rich; *im* ~ *sitzen* to be in a nice mess; **~eimer** *m* dust-bin, *Am* ash-can; *engl u. Am* garbage-can; **~fink, ~spatz** *m* dirty fellow; **~ig** *a* dirty, muddy, filthy; **~loch** *n* mud-hole; **~winkel** *m* dirty corner.

Dreh *m fam* (*Drehung, gute Gelegenheit, Trick, Handhabung*) turn; **~achse** *f* axis of revolution, rotation axis; **~automat** *m* automatic lathe; **~bank** *f* (turning-) lathe; **~bar** *a* revolving, rota(to)ry, rotating; *~bar eingesetzt* pivoted; **~bewegung** *f* rotation; **~bleistift** *m* propelling pencil; **~blinkfeuer** *n* rotating beacon; flashing light; **~boden** *m* turntable; **~bohrer** *m* rotary drill; **~bolzen** *m* screw (*od* pivot) bolt; **~brücke** *f* swing-bridge, turning-bridge; **~buch** *n film* (film) script, *Am* movie script; (*mit genauen Szenen- u. Regieanweisungen*) continuity; (motion-picture) scenario; *~bücher für jdn schreiben* to script for; **~~verfasser** *m* scenario writer, script writer, scripter, screen writer (*od* author), continuity writer; **~bühne** *f theat* revolving stage; **~en** *tr* (*drechseln*) to turn, to form on a lathe; (*rotieren*) to rotate; (*zwirnen*) to twist, to twine; *sich ~en* to turn; to rotate, to gyrate, to whirl; (*in Angeln*) to swing; (*auf Zapfen*) to turn upon a pivot; (*herumwirbeln*) to spin; (*um*) to revolve around; *fig* to center around, to be centered around; (*Zigarette, Augen*) to roll; (*Film*) to shoot; *e-e Szene für e-n Film ~en* to shoot a scene for a picture; (*Wind*) to shift, to veer (round), to change; (*Drehorgel*) to grind; (*Schiff*) to tack, to veer; *e-n Griff ~en* to turn (*od* to twist) a handle; *jdm e-e Nase ~en* to lead s. o. by the nose; *es ~t sich darum* the point is whether; *die Frage ~t sich um* the question hinges on; *er ~te mir den Rücken zu* he turned his back on me; *er weiß sich zu ~en u. zu wenden* he is never at a loss for an excuse; **~er** *m* (*an der Drehbank*) turner, lathe-hand; metal-worker; **~farbstift** *m* revolving crayon; **~feder** *f* torsion spring; **~feuer** *n* (*Leuchtturm*) rotary beacon; **~filter** *n* rotary filter; **~flügel** *m* rotating airfoil (*od* wing); **~flügelflugzeug** *n aero* helicopter, gyroplane; rotaplane; **~funkfeuer** *n* rotating radio beacon; omnidirectional radio beacon; **~gelenk** *n* swivel (*od* hinge) joint; **~geschwindigkeit** *f* turning speed, speed of rotation; **~gestell** *n rail* bogie, *Am* truck; **~griff** *m* (*Motorrad*) gas handle, turning handle; control grip; **~knopf** *m* control knob, turning knob; **~kondensator** *m* variable condenser; **~krankheit** *f* staggers *pl*; **~kreuz** *n* (*als Sperre für Fußgänger*) turnstile; **~moment** *n* torque, twisting moment; **~orgel** *f* barrel-organ, hand-organ; **~punkt** *m* centre of motion; turning point; *fig* pivot; **~rahmenantenne** *f* (*Peilrahmen*) rotating loop aerial, rotating loop antenna; **~ring** *m* swivel; (turntable) racer; circular rack; **~rost** *m* revolving grate; **~schalter** *m el* turn switch; **~scheibe** *f* (*Töpfer*) potter's wheel; *rail* turn-plate, *Am* turn-table; *tele* dial; **~~nfluglehrapparat** *m aero* Link trainer; **~~nlafette** *f mil* turn-table gun carriage; **~scheinwerfer** *m* rotating beacon light; **~schieber** *m* rotary slide valve; **~schranke** *f* swing gate; **~spindel** *f* spindle; **~spulinstrument** *n el* moving-coil instrument; **~stabfeder** *f* torsion-bar spring; **~stahl** *m* cutting tool; **~strom** *m el* three-phase current; **~~netz** *n el* three-phase network; **~stuhl** *m* revolving stool, swivel chair; **~tisch** *m tech* rotary (table), revolving platform; (*stummer Diener*) dumb-waiter; **~tür** *f* swivel gate, revolving door, swing door; **~turm** *m mil* (*Schiff, Panzer*) revolving turret; **~ung** *f* turn; (*Rotation*) rotation; (*Umdrehung um*) revolution; (*Torsion*) torsion; **~wähler** *m tele* rotary switch; **~zahl** *f mot* (*Umlaufzahl*) number of revolutions; revolutions per minute (*Abk* r. p. m.); **~zahlbereich** *m mot* range of revolution (per minute); speed range; **~zahlmesser** *m mot* revolution indicator; **~zapfen** *m* trunnion, pivot; gudgeon; turning pin.

drei *a* three; ~ *Schritte vom Leibe!* keep off! *es läßt sich mit ~ Worten sagen* you may put the whole thing in a nutshell; *je ~ und ~* three and three, by threes; *er kann nicht bis ~ zählen* he cannot say boo to a goose; he looks as if butter would not melt in his mouth; **~achser** *m mot* six wheeler; **~achteltakt** *m mus* three-eight time; **~akter** *m* three-act play; **~armig** *a* three-armed; **~atomig** *a* triatomic; **~basisch** *a* tribasic; **~bein** *n* (*Stuhl, Stativ*) tripod; **~beinfahrwerk** *n aero* tricycle landing gear; **~beinig** *a* three-legged; **~blatt** *n* trefoil; **~blättrig** *a* three-leaved; **~blattschraube** *f aero* three-bladed airscrew; **~bund** *m* Triple Alliance; **~decker** *mar m* three-decker; **~drähtig** *a* three-cord; **~eck** *n* triangle; **~eckig** *a* triangular; *ein ~~er Hut* three-cocked hat; **~eckrechner** *m* course and speed calculator, triangulator; **~eckschaltung** *f el* delta connection; **~eckzielen** *n mil* sighting triangle, triangulation; **~einigkeit** *f* Trinity; **~fächer** *m* (*Torpedos*) spread salvo of threes; **~erlei** *a* of three kinds, of three different sorts; **~fach** *a* threefold, treble; *bot* ternate; **~~drehkondensator** *m* three-gang condenser; **~~röhre** *f* three unit (*od* three-purpose) valve (*od* tube); **~~schnur** *f el* triple flexible; **~~stecker** *m* triplug; **~fadenlampe** *f el* three-filament lamp; **~faltigkeit** *f* Trinity; **~farbendruck** *m* three-colo(u)r print; **~farbenfilter** *m phot* tri-colo(u)r filter; **~farbenphotographie** *f* three-colo(u)r photography; **~farbenverfahren** *n* three-colo(u)r (*od* trichromatic) process; **~farbig** *a* three-colo(u)red; tricolo(u)red; **~felderwirtschaft** *f* three-fallowing, three-field system, three-yearly crop rotation system; **~fuß** *m* tripod, trivet; **~ganggetriebe** *n* three-speed gear (*od* transmission); **~gestrichen** *a* thrice accented; **~gitterröhre** *f radio* pentode, three-grid valve (*od* tube); **~gliedrig** *a* three-membered; trinominal; **~holmig** *a aero* with three spars; **~hundert** *a* three hundred; **~~stel** *n* three hundredth part; **~jährig** *a* three-year-old; **~kampf** *m sport* triathlon; **~kantig** *a* three-cornered; **~käsehoch** *m* hop-o'-my-thumb; Tom Thumb; **~klang** *m* triad; **königsfest** *n* Epiphany; Twelfth-night; **~kreiser** *m radio* three-circuit receiver; **~mal** *adv* three times, thrice; **~malig** *a* repeated three times; **~master** *m* ship with three masts; (*Hut*) three-cornered hat; **~monatig** *a* three-months-old; lasting three months; **~monatlich** *a* quarterly; **~motorig** *a aero* trimotor; **~pfünder** *m* three-pounder; **~punktaufhängung** *f* three-point suspension; **~punktlandung** *f aero* three-point landing; **~rad** *n* tricycle; **~radfahrgestell** *n* three-wheeled undercarriage; **~rädrig** *a* tricycle; **~reihig** *a* having three rows; **~röhrenempfänger** *m radio* three-valve receiver; **~ruderer** *m* trireme; **~scharpflug** *m* three-furrow plough (*Am* plow); **~schenkelig** *a* three-legged; **~schiffig** *a* three-bayed; **~seemeilenzone** *f* three-mile limit; **~seitig** *a* trilateral; **~silbig** *a* trisyllabic; **~sitzig** *a* provided with three seats; **~spännig** *a* with a team of three horses; **~sprachig** *a* trilingual; **~sprung** *m sport* hop-skip-and-jump; **~stellig** *a* (*Zahlen*) of three digits; three-figure, to three decimal places; **~stimmig** *a* for three voices; **~stöckig** *a* three-storied; **~stufig** *a* three-stage, with three steps; **~tägig** *a* lasting three days; **~teilig** *a* tripartite, in three parts (*od* sections); **~vierteltakt** *m* triple time; **~-Weg-Hahn** *m mot* three-way tap; **~zack** *m* trident; **~zehn** *a* thirteen; **~zehnte** *a* thirteenth.

dreißig *a* thirty; **~er** *m* person thirty years old; **~fach** *a* thirtyfold; **~jährig** *a* thirty years old; *der Dreißigjährige Krieg* the Thirty Years' War; **~ste** *a* thirtieth; **~stel** *n* thirtieth part.

dreist *a* (*kühn*) bold, courageous; (*frech*) impudent; cheeky; **~igkeit** *f* boldness, courage; impudence.

Drell, Drillich *m* tick(ing), drilling; **~rock** *m* canvas jacket; **~hose** *f* duck trousers *pl*; **~zeug** *n mil* fatigue clothes *pl*.

Dresch|e *f fam* thrashing; **~en** *irr tr* to thresh; (*prügeln*) to thrash; *leeres Stroh ~~* to thrash straw; **~er** *m* thresher; thrasher; **~flegel** *m* flail; **~maschine** *f* threshing-machine; **~tenne** *f* threshing-floor.

Dress|eur *m*, ***Dresseuse*** *f* (*Tierbändiger*) tamer; (*Hunde*) trainer; **~ieren** *tr* to train; (*Pferde*) to break in; **~ur** *f* training; (*Pferde*) breaking-in.

dribbeln *tr, itr* (*Fußball*) to dribble.

Drill *m mil* drill; (*Einübung*) training; (*Schinderei*) *sl* chicken; **~bohrer** *m* (screw) drill; **~en** *tr mil* to drill; to train; *tech* (*verdrehen*) to twist; **~ing** *m* (*Gewehr*) three-barrel(l)ed gun; **~inge** *pl* three produced at a birth; triplet(s *pl*); **~ingsturm** *m mil* triple turret, three-gun turret; **~maschine** *f* (*Reihensämaschine*) drill machine, *Am* drill; **~meister** *m mil* drill-sergeant.

dring|en *irr itr* (*durch etw*) to break through, to get through, to force o.'s way through s. th.; to pierce; to penetrate (*hinein* in, *durch etw* through, *bis zu etw* to s. th.); (*vordringen zu*) to reach, to get to; *in jdn ~en* (*bestürmen*) to urge s. o., to press s. o.; *auf etw ~en* to insist on s. th.; to urge s. th.; *auf Antwort ~en* to press for an answer;

zum Herzen ~*en* to go to the heart; *sich gedrungen fühlen* to feel compelled; **~end, ~lich** *a* urgent, pressing; *~~e Aufforderung* urgent demand; *~~e Gefahr* imminent danger; *ein ~~es Geschäft* a pressing business; *~~es Gespräch* (*tele*) express call; *~~es Staatsgespräch* government priority call; *~~es Telegramm* urgent message; *~~e Meldung* priority message; *~~e Nachfrage* pressure; *~~er Verdacht* strong suspicion; *~~ brauchen* to be in urgent need of; *es ist sehr ~~* it is very urgent; **~lichkeit** *f* urgency, priority; (*Druck der Umstände*) pressure; *bes. ~~ geben* to give high priority to s. th.; *höchste ~~* top priority; **~~santrag** *m* urgent application; *parl* motion of urgency; *es ist der ~~santrag gestellt worden* urgency was moved; **~~serklärung** *f* declaration of urgency; **~~sgrad** *m* degree of priority; **~~sliste** *f* priority list; **~~smeldung** *f* urgent message; **~~sstufe** *f* degree of importance (*od* necessity); **~~szeichen** *n* urgency signal.

drin, drinnen *siehe: darin.*

dritt *a* third; *wir waren zu ~* we were three of us; *durch die ~e Hand* indirectly; **~(t)eil, ~el** *n* a third; **~ens** *adv* thirdly; **~eln** *tr* to divide into three; **~(e)halb** *adv* two and a half; **~letzt** *a* last but two.

droben *adv* above, aloft, up there; on high, in heaven.

Drog|e *f* drug; **~enhändler** *m* wholesale druggist; **~enhandlung** *f* drug business; **~enkunde** *f* pharmacology; **~enwaren** *f pl* drugs *pl*; **~erie** *f* chemist's (shop,) *Am* drugstore; **~ist** *m* druggist.

Droh|brief *m* threatening letter; **~en** *itr* to threaten, to menace; **~end** *a* threatening; (*bevorstehend*) imminent; **~ung** *f* threat, menace; (*tätlich*) assault; *durch ~~* by threats; *durch Gewalt oder ~~* (*jur*) by violence or threats of injury.

Drohne *f* drone; *fig* (*Nichtstuer*) sluggard; **~nschlacht** *f* slaughter of the drones.

dröhnen *itr* (*tönen*) to sound; (*Flugzeug*) to roar; (*Kanone*) to boom; (*Donner*) to roll; (*ferner Donner etc*) to rumble; (*gleichmäßig, summend ~*) to drone; (*Stimme*) to thunder, to boom; (*erzittern*) to shake; to quake.

drollig *a* droll, odd, funny; (*Person*) queer; **~keit** *f* drollery; quaintness.

Dromedar *n* dromedary.

Droschke *f* cab; (*Auto~*) taxi; *eine ~ nehmen* to hire a cab; *mit der ~ fahren* to drive in a cab; **~nhaltestelle** *f* cab-rank, *Am* cab-stand; **~nkutscher** *m* cabman, driver; (*Chauffeur*) taxi driver.

Drossel *f orn* thrush, throstle; (*Sing~*) mavis; *tech* (*Gas~*) throttle; *el* choking coil; **~n** *tr* to throttle; (*Erzeugung*) to cut production; **~spule** *f radio* inductance (coil); **~steuerung** *f* throttle control; **~ung** *f* throttling; curb; **~ventil** *n*, **~klappe** *f* throttle-valve.

drüb|en *adv* yonder; on the other side, over there; **~er** *siehe darüber.*

Druck *m* pressure; (*Flächen~*) compression; (*Gas~*) expansion; (*Belastung*) load; (*Anstoß*) impulse; (*Last*) weight; burden; (*Anforderung, Belastung*) strain; (*Hände~*) squeeze; (*Bedrückung*) oppression; *~ u. Gegendruck* action and reaction; *~ ausüben* to put pressure on; to exert a pressure upon; *fam* to put the screw on; *politischen ~ ausüben* to exert political pressure; (*Buch~*) print; printing; impression; *~ auf Gummi* offset printing; *kleiner ~* small type; *weicher ~* soft impression; *unreiner ~* slur; *schlechter ~* poor print; *in ~ geben* to put in print, to bring out, to send to press, to publish; *in ~ gehen* to go to press; *im ~ sein* (*Buch*) in print, in the press, passing through the press; *~ u. Verlag K., Stuttgart* K., Printers and Publishers, Stuttgart; **~abfall** *m* drop in pressure; **~achse** *f typ* printing shaft; **~änderung** *f* change of pressure; **~anstieg** *m* increase of pressure; **~apparat** *m typ* printing apparatus; (*Tank*) tank apparatus; **~anzug** *m aero* pressure suit; **~ausbreitung** *f* propagation of pressure; **~beanspruchung** *f* pressure load, compression stress; **~behälter** *m* pressure tank; **~belüften** *tr aero* to pressurize; *~belüftete Kabine aero* pressurized cabin; **~belüftung** *f* pressurization; **~berichtigung** *f* correction of the press; **~bewilligung, ~erlaubnis** *f* licence; **~bogen** *m* proof-sheet, printed-sheet; **~buchstabe** *m* block letter; **~dicht** *a* tight; pressurized; **~elektrisch** *a* piezoelectric; **~en** *tr* to print; to publish; *wieder~en* to reprint; *~en lassen* to have s. th. printed; *lügen wie gedruckt* to lie like truth; **~er** *m* printer; **~erei** *f* printing-office, printing-works *pl*, printing-house; **~erlohn** *m* printer's wages *pl*; **~erpresse** *f* (printing-)press; **~erschwärze** *f* printing-ink; **~erzeichen** *n* printer's mark; **~fahne** *f* galley-proof; **~fehler** *m* erratum, misprint, printer's error; **~fehlerteufel** *m* printer's devil; **~fehlerverzeichnis** *n* errata *pl*; **~fertig** *a* ready to go to press; correct; **~festigkeit** *f* compressive strength; **~firma** *f* (*Impressum*) imprint; **~form** *f* (*Rahmen*) printing-block, form; **~genehmigung** *f typ* approval; **~höhe** *f* pressure head (*od* height); **~knopf** *m* (*Klingel, Instrumentenbrett*) push-button, press-button; (*Kleid*) patent-fastener, *fam* popper, *Am* patent (*od* snap) fastener; **~~anlasser** *m* push-button starter; **~~schalter** *m* push-button switch; **~~steuerung** *f* push-button control; **~kosten** *pl* printing expenses *pl*; **~legung** *f* printing, impression; **~leitung** *f* pressure pipe; **~luft** *f* compressed air; **~luftbremse** *f* air-pressure (*od* pneumatic) brake; **~luftanzeiger** *m mot* air-pressure ga(u)ge; **~lufthammer** *m* pneumatic hammer; **~maschine** *f typ* printing-machine; **~messer** *m* pressure ga(u)ge; (*Dampf*) manometer; **~ölbremse** *f* hydraulic brake; **~ort** *m* place of printing; **~papier** *n* printing-paper; **~platte** *f* printing-plate; **~posten** *m* soft job; **~probe** *f* proof, specimen; **~pumpe** *f* forcing-pump, pressure pump; **~punkt** *m* pressure point; *aero* aerodynamic centre; (*Gewehr*) pull-off; *~~ nehmen* (*beim Schießen*) to hold on; *fam* (*sich drücken*) to shirk o.'s duty; **~raster** *m* printer's screen; **~rückgang** *m* depression; **~sache** *f* printed matter, book-post; *Am auch* second (*od* third) class matter; **~schraube** *f aero* pusher airscrew (*od Am* propeller); *Flugzeug mit ~~* pusher plane; **~schrift** *f* (*Veröffentlichung*) publication, print; booklet; *typ* type, letter, print; **~schmierung** *f mot* pressure-feed lubrication; **~stock** *m* cut, electro block, printing-block; **~~abzug** *m* block pull, *Am* engraver's proof; **~~ätzung** *f* block, *Am* engraving; **~tastenabstimmung** *f radio* push-button tuning; **~telegraph** *m* printing telegraph; **~tiegel** *m* platen; **~verfahren** *n* printing method; **~verlust** *m* loss of pressure; **~walze** *f typ* printing-roller; **~waren** *f pl* prints *pl*, printed goods *pl*; **~welle** *f* pressure wave; blast; **~werk** *n typ* printed work; **~zeile** *f* line of print; **~zugschaltung** *f radio* push-pull circuit; **~zylinder** *m* printing cylindre, impression cylindre; pressure cylindre.

Drück|eberger *m* shirker, dodger; slacker; *Am mil* draft-dodger, (*vom Truppendienst*) *sl* goldbricker; **~en** *tr* to press; (*quetschen*) to squeeze; (*kneifen, von Schuhen*) to pinch; (*bedrücken*) to oppress; to lie heavy upon; (*weh tun*) to have pains; (*Preise*) to depress prices, to lower, to bring down; (*Rekord*) to beat; (*Hand*) to shake hands with s. o.; (*Klingel*) to press (the buzzer); *sich ~en* (*um die Pflicht*) to shirk a duty; (*sich davonmachen*) to sneak away; (*vom Truppendienst*) to slacken, to shirk, to crimshank, to funk, *Am sl* to goldbrick; (*von der Schule*) to play hookey; **~end** *a* heavy; (*Hitze*) oppressive; (*Luft*) sultry; **~er** *m* (*Tür*) handle; (*Sicherheitsschloß*) latch-key; (*Gewehr*) trigger.

drucksen *itr fam* to tarry, to hesitate.

Drude *f* witch; **~nfuß** *m* pentagram; *bot* club-moss.

drum *siehe: darum.*

drunt|en *adv* there below; **~er** *siehe: darunter.*

Druse *f* (*Pferdekrankheit*) glanders *pl.*

Drüs|e *f* gland; *geschwollene ~en haben* to have the mumps; (*kleine ~e*) glandule; **~enkrankheit** *f* scrofula, gland disease; **~enschwellung** *f* glandular swelling; **~ig** *a* glandulous.

Dschungel *m od n od f* jungle.

*

du *prn* you; (*bibl.*) thou; *bist du es?* is it you? *auf ~ u. ~ stehen* to be on intimate terms.

Dual(is) *m* dual number; **~ismus** *m* dualism.

Dübel *m* peg, dowel, plug, pin, key.

Dublette *f* doublet; duplicate; (*Jagd*) right-and-left (shot).

duck|en *tr* to bring down; *fig* to humble; *r fig* to stoop; to bow o.'s head; to give in; to knuckle under; **~mäuser** *m* shuffler, dissembler; sneak; (*Feigling*) coward; **~~ei** *f* hypocrisy.

Dudel|ei *f* wretched music; **~n** *itr* to play on the bagpipes; to play badly; *fam* to booze; **~sack** *m* bagpipes *pl*, doodle-sack; **~sackpfeifer** *m* bagpiper.

Duell *n* duel; **~ant** *m* duellist; **~ieren** *r* to fight a duel.

Duett *n* duet(to).

Duft *m* (*Blumen*) fragrance; (*stärker*) perfume; (*Aroma*) aroma; (*Geruch*) odo(u)r, scent; smell; (*Ausdünstung*) exhalation; (*Weihrauch*) incense; (*Wein*) bouquet; **~en** *itr* to exhale fragrance; to scent; to smell; (*nach Kaffee, Tabak etc*) to reek (*nach* of); (*süß*) to smell sweet; **~end** *ppr* fragrant (*nach* with); **~ig** *a* fragrant, odorous, sweet-smelling; (*leicht*) light, airy; **~los** *a* odo(u)rless; inodorous; **~öl** *n* fragrant oil, perfume oil; **~stoff** *m* odorous substance.

Dukaten *m* ducat.

duld|en *tr, itr* to suffer, to endure, to bear; (*zulassen, erlauben*) to allow, to permit, to tolerate, *Am* to stand; *sie ~et keine entgegengesetzte Meinung* she tolerates no contrary opinion; *ich will das nicht länger ~en* I will not stand it any longer; *es ~et keinen Aufschub* it brooks no delay; **~er** *m* sufferer; **~sam**

a tolerant, indulgent; **~~keit, ~ung** *f* tolerance, toleration.

dumm *a* (*stumpfsinnig*) stupid; (*langsam im Begreifen*) dull; slow; *Am fam* dumb; (*einfältig*) simple; (*geistig schwerfällig*) dense; (*albern*) foolish; silly; (*blöd*) idiotical, imbecile; (*unangenehm*) awkward, unpleasant; (*unwissend*) ignorant; (*dünkelhaft, plump*) fatuous; (*verkehrt*) absurd; *e-e ~e Geschichte* an awkward affair; *ein ~er Streich* a foolish trick; *~es Zeug reden* to talk nonsense (*od* humbug); *~es Zeug! interj* rubbish! *es wird mir ganz ~ im Kopf* I feel quite dizzy; *~ wie e-e Gans* as stupid as an owl; *so ~ bin ich nicht* I am not such a fool; *Sie sind gar nicht ~!* you are no fool! *sie ist nicht so ~!* she knows better! *es war sehr ~ von mir* it was very stupid of me; *das ist zu ~* that is too silly for words; *wie ~!* how stupid! *zu ~!* too bad! *~ machen* (*betäuben*) to stupefy; (*betrügen*) to dupe; **~dreist** *a* foolhardy; cheeky; **~dreistigkeit** *f* foolhardiness; **~heit** *f* stupidity, dul(l)ness; (*Handlung*) silly action; *Am* dumbness; (*Fehler*) blunder; **~kopf** *m* blockhead, duffer, simpleton, dunce, mug, flat, fathead; *Am fam* sap(head); jay; sucker; bonehead; dumb-bell; **~stolz** *a* stupidly proud.

dumpf *a* (*Ton*) hollow, dull; (*Donner*) rumbling; (*Luft*) heavy, sultry, (*im Zimmer*) close; (*Wetter*) muggy; (*muffig*) musty; (*stickig*) stuffy; (*feucht*) damp; (*düster*) gloomy; **~ig** *a* mo(u)ldy, musty; (*abgestanden*) stale.

*

Dün|e *f* down; dune; **~enhafer** *m* bent; **~ung** *f* swell, surf.

Dung *m* dung, manure; **~grube** dung-pit, dung-hole.

Düng|emittel *n* dunging-substance, compost; (*künstliches*) (artificial) fertilizer; **~en** *tr* to dung, to manure; to fertilize; *wie oft ~en Sie den Boden?* how often do you fertilize the soil? **~er** *m* dung; compost; (*künstlicher*) artificial manure, fertilizer; **~ererde** *f* garden-mo(u)ld; **~ergrube** *f* dungpit; **~erhaufen** *m* dung-hill; **~erstreuer** *m* manure-spreader; **~ung** *f* dunging, manuring, fertilizing.

dunkel *a* dark, gloomy; (*Farbe*) dark; (*schwärzlich*) dusky; (*düster*) gloomy; (*trübe*) dim; *fig* obscure, vague; *es wird ~* it gets dark, it grows dark; *das dunkle Mittelalter* the dark ages *pl*; *ich erinnere mich ~ sie gesehen zu haben* I vaguely remember having seen her; *~ n* dark(ness); *fig* obscurity; *im ~* in the dark; *ein Sprung ins ~* (*fig*) a leap in the dark; **~blau** *a* dark-blue; **~braun** *a* dark-brown; **~gelb** *a* tawny; **~grau** *a* dark-grey; **~grün** *a* bottle-green; **~heit** *f* dark(ness); gloom; *fig* obscurity; *nach Eintritt der ~~* after dark; **~kammer** *f phot* darkroom; laboratory; **~n** *imp* to darken; (*Farben*) to deepen, to sadden; **~nachtjagd** *f aero mil* night fighting without searchlights; **~rot** *a* dark-red, dim-red; **~suchgerät** *n mil* dark searching instrument.

Dünkel *m* conceit(edness); arrogance; **~haft** *a* conceited; arrogant haughty.

dünken *irr imp* to seem, to appear; *sich ~* to imagine, to fancy o.s.; *sich klug ~* to be wise in o.'s own opinion; *es dünkt mich* methinks; *wie mich dünkt* as it seems to me.

dünn *a* thin; (*schmächtig*) slender, slim; *Am* (*schwach*) slimsy; (*mager*) scrawny; (*Gewebe*) flimsy; (*spärlich*) rare; (*flüssig*) dilute; *~ besiedelt* sparsely settled; *~e Luft* rarefied air; *~es Haar* fine hair; *~ machen* to thin; *sich ~machen* to make o. s. scarce; *~ werden* to grow thin; **~bier** *n* small beer; **~darm** *m* small intestine; **~druckausgabe** *f* India paper edition; **~druckpapier** *n* thin printing paper; **~e, ~heit** *f* thinness, slenderness; (*Flüssigkeit*) weakness; **~gesät** *a* sparsely sown, thinly scattered; *fig* scarce; few and far between; **~flüssig** *a* thinly liquid; watery; fluid; **~schalig** *a* thin-skinned; thin-shelled; **~wandig** *a* thin-walled.

Dunst *m* (*Dampf*) vapo(u)r, steam; (*Ausdünstung*) exhalation; (*Rauch*) smoke, reek; (*Luft*) haze; (*Vogel~*) small shot, dust; (*Schwaden*) fumes *pl*, damps *pl*; (*Feuchtigkeit*) dampness; (*falscher ~*) *fig* smoke, false show; *keinen blassen ~ haben von* not to know the first thing about s. th.; *jdm blauen ~ vormachen* to bamboozle, to humbug s. o.; *in ~ aufgehen, zu ~ werden* to dissolve into thin air; **~bläschen** *n* steam-bubble; **~en** *itr* (*dampfen*) to steam, to fume; (*verdampfen*) to evaporate, to vaporize; (*rauchen*) to smoke, to reek; (*dämpfen*) to steam, to stew; **~haube** *f tech* air dome; **~ig** *a* vaporous, vapo(u)ry; steamy; (*neblig*) foggy, misty; (*feucht*) damp, moist; **~kreis** *m* atmosphere; **~obst** *n* stewed (*od* steamed) fruit; **~schleier** *m* haze.

dünsten *tr, itr* (*dämpfen, schmoren*) to stew, to steam; (*dampfen, rauchen*) to vapo(u)r, to smoke.

Duodez *n* duodecimo; **~band** *m* duodecimo volume; **~fürst** *m* petty prince.

Duplikat *n* duplicate, counterpart.

Düppel *m* window (= metallic strips used to interfere with radar); **~straße** *f* window cloud.

Dur *n mus* major.

Duraluminium *n* duralumin.

durch *prp* (*hindurch, mittendurch*) through, *Am auch* thru; *quer ~* across; (*vermittelst*) by means of; (*wegen*) owing to, because of; (*zeitlich*) during, throughout; *~ die Post* by mail; *~ Zufall* by chance; *adv die ganze Nacht ~* all night long; *~ und ~* completely, thoroughly, *Am auch* thoroly; through and through, out and out; *es ist schon zwei ~* it is past two already; **~ackern** *tr* to plough thoroughly; *fig* to elaborate; **~arbeiten** *tr* to work through; (*ohne Unterbrechung*) to work without intermission; (*Körper*) to train; (*Teig*) to knead; (*Färben*) to pole; *sich ~~* to get through, to make o.'s way; **~ätzen** *tr* to eat through, to corrode; **~aus** *adv* (*vollständig*) completely; (*unbedingt*) absolutely, by all means; *~~ nicht* by no means, not at all, not in the least, not in the very least.

durch'|backen *irr tr* to bake thoroughly; **~'beißen** *irr tr* to bite through; *sich ~~* to get through difficulties; **~'betteln:** *sich ~~* to get o.'s livelihood by begging; **~'beuteln** *tr* (*Mehl*) to bolt; **~'biegen** *irr tr* to break by bending; *r* to sag, to bend; **~'bilden** *tr* to give a thorough education to; to develop fully, to perfect; (*entwerfen*) to design, to construct; *~gebildet pp, a* highly educated; **~'bildung** *f* thorough education; **~'blättern** *od* **~~'** *tr* to turn over; (*Buch*) to skim; **~'bleuen** *tr* to beat soundly; **~'blick** *m* vista, perspective; peep (*od* look) through; **~'blicken** *itr* to look through; *~~ lassen* to give s. o. to understand, to let appear, to give a hint; **~'bohren** *tr* to bore through, to perforate; **~~'** *tr* to pierce, to stab; **~bo'hrend** *ppr* (*Blick*) piercing; (*Schrei*) shrill, piercing; (*Schmerz*) keen; **~bo'hrt** *pp, a* perforate, perforated; **~bo'hrung** *f* perforation, boring through; trepanning; **~'braten** *irr tr* to roast thoroughly; *~gebraten* well done; *nicht ~gebraten* underdone; *nicht ~gebratenes Fleisch* underdone meat, *Am* rare meat; **~'brechen** *irr tr* to break through; *itr* (*Sonne*) to break forth; to force o.'s way; (*Zähne*) to cut through; (*Blätter*) to come out; (*Tränen*) to gush forth; *mil* to cut o.'s way through; (*entweichen*) to escape; to break through; **~bre'chen** *tr* to pierce, to perforate; *mil* to cut o.'s way; (*Blockade*) to run; **~'brennen** *irr itr* to burn through; (*Sicherung*) *el* to fuse, to blow; (*Radioröhre*) to burn out; (*durchgehen*) to run away, to abscond; (*mit e-m Mädchen*) to elope; **~'bringen** *irr tr* to bring through, to put through; (*Geld*) to waste, to dissipate, to squander; (*e-n Kranken*) to bring s. o. round; to pull s. o. through; (*Kinder*) to bring up; (*Gesetz*) to pass; *sich ehrlich ~~* to make an honest living, (*kümmerlich*) to make both ends meet; **~bro'chen** *a* pierced; *~~e Arbeit* (*Näherei*) open work; (*Goldschmied*) filigree-work; **~'bruch** *m* breach, rupture; (*Zähne*) cutting; (*Straße*) piercing; (*e-r Krankheit*) eruption; *mil* break-through; **~~sangriff** *m mil* break-through attack; **~~serfolg** *m* tactical success of break-through; **~~sstelle** *f* point of break-through; **~~sversuch** *m* attempted break-through; **~~tank** *m* heavy tank.

durch|den'ken *irr tr* to think over; *ein wohldurchdachter Plan* a well considered plan; **~'drängen** *tr* to force through; *r* to force o.'s way through the crowd; **~'drehen** *tr* (*Luftschraube*) to pull through, to swing; (*Motor*) to turn over (*od* to crank) an engine; **~'dringen** *irr itr* to get through; (*zum Ziel*) to attain o.'s end; *seine Meinung ist ~gedrungen* his opinion has prevailed; **~~'** *tr* to penetrate, to permeate; (*füllen*) to fill; (*durchsickern*) to percolate; **~~d** *a* penetrating, piercing; (*Stimme*) shrill; (*Verstand*) keen, sharp; *~~de Kälte* biting cold; **~dringung** *f* penetration; *friedliche ~~* peaceful penetration; **~~svermögen** *n* penetrating power; **~'drücken** *tr* to press through; *fig* (*erzwingen*) to enforce; **~duf'ten** *tr* to perfume, to fill with odo(u)r; **~'eilen** *itr*, **~~'** *tr* to hurry, to hasten through.

durch|einander *adv* confusedly, in confusion; disorderly, pell-mell; *sl* snafu; *~~ n* medley, muddle; *Am* snarl; (*Unordnung*) disorder; *fig* confusion; **~~'mengen** *tr* to confound; **~~'schütteln** *tr* to shake thoroughly; **~~'werfen** *irr tr* to mix up, to muddle up.

durch'fahr|en *irr itr*, **~~'** *tr* to pass through, to drive through; (*Schiff*) to sail through; *fig* (*erfüllen*) to go through, to thrill; (*streng ~~*) to be strict with s. o.; to rush through; *unter e-r Brücke ~~* to shoot a bridge; **~t** *f* passing, passage; (*Tor*) gateway; (*Kanal*) channel; (*Durchgang, Straße*) thoroughfare, *Am auch* thorofare; *~~ verboten!* no thoroughfare! **~tsgeld** *n* transit duty; **~tsrecht** *n* right of way, right of passage; **~tssignal** *n rail, mot* green light; **~tszoll** *m* toll, transit-duty.

Durch|fall *m* (*durch Öffnung*) falling through; (*Examen, Wahl*) failure; *theat* (*Mißerfolg*) failure; *fam* flop; *med* diarrhœa, *Am* diarrhea; **~'fallen** *irr itr* (*durch Öffnung*) to fall through; (*Examen*) to fail, to be plucked; *fam* to (be) flunk(ed); (*Wahl*) to be unsuccessful; *theat* to fall flat, to be damned; (*Lotterie*) to get a blank; **~fa'llen** *irr tr* to drop through; **~'faulen** *itr* to rot through (*od* completely).

durch'|fechten *irr tr* to fight through; to battle through; *fig* (*zur Geltung bringen*) to impose (o.'s opinion); to carry (o.'s point); *sich* **~'~** to fight o.'s way; (*bettelnd*) to support o. s. by begging; **~'feilen, ~fei'len** *tr* to file through; *fig* (*e-e Arbeit*) to polish, to give the last finish to; **~feuch'ten** *tr* to soak; to saturate with moisture; **~'finden** *irr: itr sich* **~'~** to find o.'s way through; *fig* to become familiar with; **~flech'ten** *irr tr* to interweave, to intertwine; **~'fliegen** *irr itr,* **~~'** *tr* to fly through; (*e-n Brief*) to hurry over; to skim over; to glance through; **~'fließen** *irr itr,* **~~'** *tr* to flow through; **~'forschen** *itr,* **~~'** *tr* to search through; to investigate, to explore; **~fo'rschung** *f* (thorough) examination; (*Untersuchung*) investigation; (*genaue* **~~**) scrutiny; (*Durchsuchung*) research; (*Land, Gebiet*) exploration; **~'fragen** *tr* to question one after another; *sich* **~'~** to find o.'s way by asking; **~fres'sen** *irr tr* to eat through; to corrode; **~'~** *r* to live upon others; *fig* to struggle through; **~'frieren** *irr itr* to freeze over and over; to be chilled right through; **~fro'ren** *a* frozen through, chilled, benumbed; **~fuhr** *f* passage, transit; **~~hafen** *m* transit port; **~~handel** *m* transit trade; **~~zoll** *m* transit duty; **~führbar** *a* feasible, practicable; **~'führen** *tr* to carry out, to bring about; *tech* (*Werkprüfung*) to conduct; (*vollenden*) to accomplish; to realize, to effect; to implement; *Gesetzgebung* **~~** to enact legislation; *ein Gesetz* **~~** (*durchsetzen*) to enforce; to execute; to carry through; *ein Strafverfahren* **~~** to carry on criminal proceedings; **~führbarkeit** *f* practicability; **~führung** *f* execution, performance; implementation; (*Vollendung*) accomplishment; (*e-s Gesetzes*) law enforcement, complying; *die* **~~** *erzwingen* to enforce a rule; **~führungsverordnung** *f für* carrying-out ordinance; provision for the execution; **~fu'rcht** *a* wrinkled, furrowed.

Durchgabe *f* transmission.

Durchgang *m* (*Durchschreiten*) passing through; (*Tunnel*) crossing; (*Verbindungsgang*) passage, passage-way, alleyway, gateway; *mil* (*Festungsausfalltor*) postern; *com* (*von Waren*) transit; *astr* transit, passing; (*enger* **~~**) defile; **~~** *gesperrt!* closed to traffic! *kein* **~~**! no thoroughfare! no trespassing! private road! **~shandel** *m* transit trade; **~shotel** *n* commercial hotel, *Am* transient hotel; **~slager** *n* transit camp; **~sschein** *m* permit, transit bill; **~sstation** *f* intermediate station; **~sstraße** *f* thoroughfare; **~stransformator** *m radio* by-pass transformer; **~sverbindung** *f tele* through connection; **~sverkehr** *m* through traffic, *Am* thru traffic; *kein* **~~**! no through road! **~svisum** *n* transit visa; **~swagen** *m* corridor-car (riage *od* coach); through carriage; **~szoll** *m* transit duty; **~szug** *m* through (*od* nonstop) train; (*D-Zug*) corridor-train, *Am* vestibule train.

Durch|gänger *m* (*Flüchtling, Durchbrenner*) absconder; (*Pferd*) runaway horse; **~gängig** *a* usual, general; *adv* generally, as a rule; **~'geben** *irr tr* to transmit; **~'gebildet** *a* well-trained.

durch'|gehen *irr itr* to walk, to go, to pass through; to cross; to penetrate, to pierce; (*Pferd*) to bolt; (*fliehen*) to run away, to abscond, to escape, to elope (with a lover); *parl* (*Gesetz*) to pass, to be carried, to be adopted; *jdm etw* **~'~** *lassen* to overlook s. o.'s mistake; *das wird bei ihr nicht* **~'~** that will not go down with her; *das* **~'~** *e-r Gesetzesvorlage* the passing of a bill, *Am* the passage of a bill; **~'~***der Dienst* twenty-four hour service; **~'~***der Zug m* through train; *täglich* **~'~***de Schlafwagenverbindung von u. nach Stuttgart* daily through sleeper service to and from Stuttgart; *tr* (*prüfen*) to examine, to inspect, to review; (*revidieren*) to revise; (*Schuhe*) to wear out; *sich die Füße* **~'~** to walk o.'s feet sore; **~~ds** *adv* generally; throughout; **~gei'stigt** *a* (*Gesicht*) spirited, intelligent; (*Buch*) intellectual; **~'gerben** *tr* to tan thoroughly; *fig* to beat soundly, to curry; **~'gießen** *irr tr* to pour through; (*filtern*) to filter, to strain; **~'glühen** *tr* to make red-hot; **~glü'hen** *tr fig* to inspire; **~'greifen** *irr itr* to put o.'s hand through; *fig* to proceed without ceremony (*od* with vigo(u)r); to act decidedly; **~'greifend** *a* energetic, determined; decisive; **~'~***e Änderung* radical change; **~'~***e Hilfe* effectual help; **~'~***e Maßregeln* sweeping measures; **~'gucken** *itr* to look, to peep through.

durch|halten *irr tr* to hold out (to the end), to stick to s. th., to see s. th. through; *sl* to sweat it out; **~haltevermögen** *n* stamina; **~hang** *m* (*Seil*) sag; (*Senkung*) dip; **~'hau** *m* glade; (*im Walde*) vista; **~'hauen** *irr tr* to hew through, to cut through; (*prügeln*) to beat soundly, to thrash, to flog; *sich* **~~** to force o.'s way through; **~'hecheln** *tr* to hackle thoroughly; *fig* to cut up, to pull to pieces; **~'heizen** *tr, itr* to heat thoroughly; **~'helfen** *irr itr* (*jdm* **~~**) to support, to aid s. o.; *r* to make shift, to get through; **~höh'len** *tr* to hollow out; **~ir'ren** *tr* to wander through; to stray about; **~'jagen** *itr,* **~~'** *tr* to hunt through; to hasten through.

durch|kämp'fen *tr* to fight out; *sich* **~'~** to fight o.'s way; **~'kauen** *tr* to chew through; *fig* to ruminate over; **~'kochen** *tr* to boil thoroughly; **~'kommen** *irr itr* to come through, to get through, to pass through; *fig* to come off; (*genesen*) to recover; to pull through; (*Prüfung*) to pass an examination; (*auskommen*) to subsist, to get along; to manage; *kümmerlich* **~'~** to scrape through; **~'kosten** *tr* to taste one after the other; *fig* to endure; **~kreu'zen** *tr* to cross; *fig* to thwart; **~'kriechen** *irr itr,* **~~'** *tr* to creep through; **~'kühlen** *tr* to cool (*od* to chill) thoroughly; **~'krümmen** *tr* (*Gewehr*) to pull a trigger; **~'laden** *tr mil* to charge a magazine, to load.

Durch'|laß *m* letting through; (*Öffnung*) passage; outlet; opening; (*Sieb*) sieve, filter; (*Brücke*) cut; (*Schleuse*) gate; (*Licht*) transmission; **~~bereich** *m radio* band-pass width of a filter; **~~breite** *f* width of band pass; **~'lassen** *irr tr* to allow to pass, to let through; (*sieben*) to filter, to strain; *fig* to let pass; (*Geräusch; Licht*) to transmit; **~'lässig** *a* permeable; pervious; penetrable; **~'lässigkeit** *f* permeability, perviousness; **~laucht** *f* (Serene) Highness; **~~ig(st)** *a* (most) serene, illustrious; **~lauf** *m* running through; passage; **~'laufen** *irr itr,* **~~'** *tr* to run from one end to the other; (*Flüssigkeit*) to run through; to flow through; (*filtrieren*) to run (*od* to filter) through; (*Gerücht*) to spread, to run all over; (*durchsehen*) to glance over, to run through; to peruse hastily; (*Schuhe*) to wear out; **~le'ben** *tr* to live through, to pass, to experience; *sie hat schönere Tage durchlebt* she has seen better days; **~'lesen** *irr tr* to read over (*od* through); to peruse; (*Buch*) to read from cover to cover; (*flüchtig*) to go over; **~'leuchten** *tr* to light through, to illumine, to illuminate; **~leu'chten** *tr* (*Eier*) to test, *Am* to candle; (*mit Röntgenstrahlen*) to X-ray, to roentgenize, to radio(graph); to fluoroscope; **~leu'chtung** *f* radioscopy, radiogram; **~leu'chtungsschirm** *m* fluoroscopic screen; **~'liegen** *irr r* to get bed-sores, to get sore by lying; **~lo'chen** *tr* (*Karten*) to punch; to perforate, to pierce; **~lö'chern** *tr* to perforate; (*mit Kugeln*) to riddle; (*durchbohren*) to pierce; **~lö'chert** *a* punctured; (*von Kugeln*) riddled with bullets; perforated; (*Schuhe*) holey; **~'lüften, ~lü'ften** *tr* to air, to ventilate; **~lü'ftung** *f* airing, ventilation; **~'lügen** *r* to get off by lying, to help o. s. out by lies.

durch'|machen *tr* to go through, to pass through; to live through; (*erleben*) to experience; (*dulden*) to suffer; *er machte den Krieg durch* he went through the war; *viel* **~~** to have many experiences; **~marsch** *m* march(ing) through; **~'marschieren** *itr* to march through; **~mes'sen** *irr tr* to walk over; to traverse; **~'~** *tr* to measure; **~'messer** *m* diameter; **~'müssen** *itr* to have to pass through; **~mu'stern** *tr* to scan; to inspect closely; to sift carefully; to scrutinize.

durch'|nagen *od* **~~'** *tr* to gnaw through; **~'nähen** *od* **~~'** *tr* to sew through; **~näs'sen** *tr* to soak; to wet through; *ganz* **~näßt** drenched to the skin; **~'nehmen** *irr tr* to go over; *fig* to censure, to lecture.

durch'|pausen *tr* to trace (through); to pounce; **~'peitschen** *tr* to whip through; to whip soundly; *fig* to hurry (*od* rush) through; *parl* (*ein Gesetz*) to rush through a bill; **~'pressen** *tr* to press through; **~'prügeln** *tr* to beat, to cudgel; **~pu'lst** *a* full (of), vibrating (with); **~que'ren** *tr* to cross, to traverse.

durch'|räuchern *tr* to fumigate; to smoke thoroughly; **~'rechnen** *tr* to count over, to figure over, to check; **~'regnen** *itr* to rain through; **~'reiche** *f* (*Küche-Eßzimmer*) hatch; **~'reise** *f* passage; *auf meiner* **~~** on my way through; *er ist auf der* **~'~** he is a transit passenger, *Am* he is a transient; **~'reisen** *itr* to pass (*od* travel) through; **~rei'sen** *tr* (*ein Land*) to traverse, to travel over; **~'reisende(r)** *m* through-passenger, transit passenger, *Am* transient; **~'reisevisum** *n* visé (*Am meist* visa) of transit, transit-visa; **~'reißen** *irr tr* to tear asunder, to rend; **~'reiten** *irr itr,* **~~'** *tr* to ride through; to cross on horseback; *sich* **~'~** to gall, to chafe o. s. by riding; **~'rennen** *irr itr,* **~~'** *tr* to run through; **~'rieseln** *itr,*

~~' *tr* to murmur through; *fig* to thrill; ~'**rosten** *itr* to rust through (*od* completely); ~'**rufen** *irr itr tele* to ring (*od* phone) through; *mil* to pass the word down; ~'**rühren** *tr* to stir up thoroughly; ~'**rütteln** *tr* to shake up, to shake thoroughly.

durch|'sacken *itr aero* to stall, to pancake; ~'**sackgeschwindigkeit** *f aero* stalling speed, critical speed; ~'**sacklandung** *f* pancake landing; ~'**sagen** *tr radio* to announce; ~'**sage** *f radio* announcement, *Am* (*Reklame*~~) spot (announcement); *e-e mit Reklame überladene* ~'~ *mit zuwenig Unterhaltungsprogramm Am* an overcommercialized, underprogrammed spot; ~'**sägen,** ~~' *tr* to saw through; ~'**schalten** *tr tele* (*verbinden*) to put through (a call); (*Kabel*) to jumper; ~'**schauen** *itr* to look through; ~~' to see through s. o. *od* s. th.; *tr* to penetrate; ~**schau'ern** *tr* to thrill (with shuddering); ~'**scheinen** *irr itr* to shine through; ~~**d** *a* transparent; translucent; ~'**scheuern** *tr* to rub through; ~'**schieben** *irr tr* to shove through; ~'**schießen,** ~~' *irr tr* to shoot through; ~~' (*Buch*) to interleave; (*Schriftzeilen*) *typ* to space out, to interline, to lead; ~**schif'fen** *tr* to sail through; ~'**schimmern** *itr* to glitter through; ~'**schlafen** *irr itr* to sleep the night through; ~~' *tr* to sleep away; ~'**schlag** *m* (*Werkzeug*) punch; piercer; (*Öffnung*) opening; (*Schreibmaschinen*~~) (carbon) copy; duplicate; (*Sieb*) screen, sieve; filter, strainer; colander; (*Autoreif*) puncture; *el* puncture; ~'**schlagen** *irr tr* to beat through; (*Erbsen*) to strain; *tech* to punch; (*Wand*) to make an opening in, to pierce; *itr* (*Papier*) to blot; (*Regen*) to wet through; (*Kugel*) to traverse; (*wirken*) to work, to act; *el* to spark; *fig* to have effect; *sich* ~~ to make o.'s way, *Am* to beat o.'s way; *sich mühsam* (*durch die Schuljahre*) *schlagen* to scrape o.'s way (through college); ~~**d** *a* effective; ~'**schlaghammer** *m* drift; ~'**schlagpapier** *n* copy(ing) paper, carbon paper; (*dünnes*) flimsy; ~'**schlagsicher** *a el* puncture proof; ~'**schlagsicherung** *f* puncture cut-out; ~'**schlagskraft** *f* penetrating power; ~'**schlängeln** *itr, r* to wind through; to dodge in and out; ~'**schleichen** *irr itr, r* to steal through; ~'**schlingen** *irr tr* to wind through; ~~' *tr* to entwine, to interlace; ~'**schlüpfen** *itr* to slip through; ~'**schneiden** *irr tr* to cut through; ~~' *tr* to traverse; (*Straßen*) to cross; *r* to intersect.

Durchschnitt *m* cutting through, cut; *math* intersection; profile; (*Querschnitt*) cross-section; *arch* section; *rail* cut; (*Mittelwert*) mean; average; *im* ~~ on an average; *über dem* ~~ above the average; *ungefährer* ~~ rough average; *den* ~~ *nehmen* to strike an average; to average; ~**lich** *a* common; average; *adv* on an average, generally; ~~ *um* at an average of; ~~ *betragend* averaging; ~**salter** *n* average age; ~**sausbringung** *f* average output; ~**sbelastung** *f* average load; ~**sbestimmung** *f* average analysis; ~**seinkommen** *n* average income; ~**sgeschwindigkeit** *f* average speed; *e-e* ~~ *von 600 Meilen pro Stunde erreichen* to average 600 m. p. h.; ~**sleistung** *f* average output; ~**slinie** *f* line of intersection; ~**smaß** *n* average measure; *auf ein* ~~ *abstellen* to equate; ~**smensch** *m* every-day man, Mr. Average Citizen; ~**spreis** *m* average price; ~**ssumme** *f* average (sum); ~**sverbrauch** *m* average consumption; ~**swert** *m* average (*od* mean) value; equated value; ~**szahl** *f* average number, mean; ~**szeichnung** *f* profile, cross-section drawing.

*

Durchschreibe|buch *n* duplicating book; ~**feder** *f* manifold pen; ~**n** *irr tr* to copy, to make a copy; ~**papier** *n* transfer paper; duplicating paper, *fam* flimsy; ~**stift** *m* pencil for making carbon copies.

durch'|schreiten *irr itr,* ~~' *tr* to cross, to walk through; ~'**schrift** *f* (carbon-)copy; ~'**schuß** *m* (*Weberei*) weft; *typ* blank; space line; leads *pl*, white line; margin; slugs *pl*; (~~*blatt*) interleaf; (*Wunde*) a shot through ...; through-and-through wound; ~'**schütteln** *tr* to shake thoroughly; ~'**schwermen** *itr,* ~~' *tr* to spend in revelry; ~'**schwimmen** *irr itr,* ~~' *tr* to swim across; ~'**schwitzen** *tr* to soak with sweat; ~'**segeln** *itr,* ~~' *tr* to sail through; ~'**sehen** *irr tr* to see through; *fig* to revise; to look over; to peruse; (*prüfen*) to examine; to review; ~'**seihen** *tr* to filter; ~'**sein** *irr itr* to be through; (*Prüfung*) to have passed; ~'**setzen** *tr* to effect; to carry through (*od* out); (*mit Gewalt erzwingen*: *Gesetze, Befehle, Ansprüche, Disziplin*) to enforce; *sich* ~'~ to make o.'s way, to succeed; to assert o.s. (successfully); *seinen Willen* ~'~ to carry o.'s point; to have o.'s way; ~**se'tzen** *tr* (*vermischen*) to intersperse, to intermingle, to mix up; ~'**setzung** *f* carrying out, execution; (*mit Gewalt*) enforcement; ~'**sicht** *f* (*Ausblick*) view, vista; *fig* (*Besichtigung*) looking-over, perusal; (*Korrektur*) revision; (*Prüfung*) inspection, checking, examination; *bei* ~~ *der Bücher* in looking over the books; *zur gefälligen* ~~ for your kind inspection; on approval; ~'**sichtig** *a* transparent; *fig* (*klar*) clear, lucid; (*offensichtlich*) obvious; ~**sichtigkeit** *f* transparency; *fig* clearness, lucidity; ~**sichtsbild** *n* lantern slide, diapositive; translucent picture; ~**sichtsschirm** *m* (*Fernseher*) transparent screen; ~**sichtssucher** *m phot* direct-vision view finder, frame finder; ~'**sickern** *itr* to trickle through; to ooze out; (*Nachrichten, Geheimnisse*) to leak out; ~'**sieben** *tr* to sift; to screen; to sieve out; (*mit Schüssen*) to riddle, to pepper; (*Mehl*) to bolt; ~'**sitzen** *irr tr* to wear out by sitting; ~~' to pass sitting; ~'**spalten** *irr tr* to split in two; ~**spie'ßen** *tr* to transfix; ~'**sprechen** *irr tr* to talk over, to discuss; to (tele)phone.

durch'|starten *itr aero* to open up and repeat landing procedure; ~'**stechen,** ~~' *irr tr* to dig through, to pierce through; ~**stecherei** *f* plot, underhand dealings *pl*, intriguing; ~'**stecken** *tr* to stick through; ~**stich** *m* cut, excavation; ~**stö'bern** *tr* to ransack; ~'**stoßen,** ~~' *irr tr* to push (*od* to thrust) through; to stab; *aero* (*Wolkenwand*) to fly through; ~**stoßlandung** *f aero* landing through clouds; ~**stoßverfahren** *n aero* (*bei Schlechtwetter mittels Funk*) penetration method; piercing through clouds; ~**strahlung** *f* radiography, irradiation; penetration by rays; ~'**streichen** *irr tr* to strike out, to cancel; to cross out; ~~' *tr* to ramble through; ~**strei'fen** *tr* to rove through; ~'**strömen** *itr,* ~~' *tr* to stream through; ~'**studieren** *tr* to study thoroughly; ~**su'chen** *tr* to search, to examine closely; ~**suchung** *f* search(ing); (*Polizei*) raid.

durch'|tanzen *tr* to dance away; (*Schuhe*) to wear out by dancing; ~~' *tr* (*Nacht*) to dance the whole night; ~'**tönen** *itr,* ~~' *tr* to sound through; ~'**tragen** *irr tr* to bear through, to carry through; ~**trän'ken** *tr* to saturate, to impregnate; to soak; to bond; ~**trän'kt** *a* saturated, impregnated; ~**träu'men** *tr* to dream away; ~'**treten** *irr itr* to tread through; *tr* to wear holes in; ~**trie'ben** *a* artful, cunning; ~~**heit** *f* cunning, slyness; ~'**triefen,** ~'**tropfen** *itr* to trickle through; ~**tun'neln** *tr* to tunnel; ~'**verbinden** *irr tr* to connect through; *tele* (*Anruf*) to put (*od* to extend) through; ~'**verbindung** *f tele* through connection.

durch|wa'chen *tr* to pass waking; ~'**wachsen** *irr itr* to grow through (an opening); ~~' *a* (*Fleisch*) marbled, (*Speck*) streaked; ~'**wagen** *r* to venture through; ~'**wählen** *itr tele* to dial through; ~'**walken** *tr* to thrash; ~'**wandern** *itr,* ~~' *tr* to wander through; to traverse; ~**wär'men** *tr* to warm through; ~'**waten** *itr,* ~~' *tr* to wade through, to ford; ~**we'ben** *tr* to interweave; ~'**weg** *m* passage; ~~' *adv* without exception, throughout, all; always; ~'**weichen** *tr* to soak thoroughly; *itr* to become soft; ~'**werfen** *irr tr* to cast through, to throw through; ~'**wichsen** *tr* to beat soundly; to spank; ~'**winden** *irr: sich* ~~ to struggle through; ~**win'tern** *itr, tr* to winter; to hibernate; ~**wir'ken** *tr* to interweave; (*durchdringen*) to imbue; (*mit Seide*) to interlace; ~**wüh'len** *tr* to root up; *fig* to ransack; to rummage, to rake over; ~'**wursteln** *r* to muddle through; ~**wür'zen** *tr* to season.

durch'|zählen *tr* to count over; ~'**zeichnen** *tr* to trace; ~'**ziehen** *irr tr* to draw through; to pass through; to drag through; (*Fluß*) to run through; (*Nadel*) to thread; (*durchflechten*) to interlace; *aero* (*aus Sturzflug*) to pull out of a dive; *fig* to censure; *itr* to march through; ~'**zucken** *tr* to flash through; ~**zug** *m* passage; (*Luft*) draught, circulation; (*Träger*) girder; ~~**moment** *n* lugging capacity of an engine; ~~**kraft** *f* pulling power, tractive power; ~'**zwängen,** ~'**zwingen** *irr tr* to force, to squeeze through; *sich* ~~ to force o.'s way through.

dürfen *irr itr* I may, I might, to be permitted, to be allowed; *darf ich fragen?* may I ask? *ich darf nicht* I must not, I am not allowed; *darf man hier rauchen?* are you allowed to smoke here? *darf ich um den nächsten Tango bitten?* may I have the next tango? *man darf wohl erwarten . . .* it is to be expected . . .; *das darfst du nicht vergessen* you must not forget that; *man darf hoffen* it is to be hoped; *ich darf wohl sagen* I dare say; *es dürfte so sein* it is likely to be so; *Sie* ~ *nur befehlen* you have only to command; *wenn ich bitten darf* if you please.

dürftig *a* needy; (*armselig*) mean; (*spärlich*) lean, scanty; (*bedürftig*) indigent; (*schäbig*) shabby; (*erbärmlich*) paltry; (*unzulänglich*) poor, insufficient; ~**keit** *f* neediness; poverty, poorness; want, penury; scantiness; meagreness; indigence; insufficiency.

dürr *a* (*trocken*) dry; (*ausgetrocknet*) parched; arid; (*verwelkt*) withered; (*Holz*) dead; (*Boden*) sterile; barren; poor; (*hager*) meagre; lean, thin; scrawny; *mit ~en Worten* in plain terms; bluntly; **~e** *f* (*Trockenheit*) dryness; (*Unfruchtbarkeit*) barrenness, sterility; (*trockenes Wetter*) drought; (*Magerkeit*) leanness; *fig* (*Reizlosigkeit*) aridity.
Durst *m* thirst (*nach* for); *~ haben* to be thirsty; *seinen ~ löschen* (*od stillen*) to quench o.'s thirst; *~ haben nach fig* to crave for, to long for; **~en, dürsten** *itr* to be thirsty; *~en nach fig* to long for; **~ig** *a* thirsty (of, after); *~~ vor Hitze* dry with heat; **~löschend, ~stillend** *a* thirst-quenching.
Dusch|e *f* (*Brause*) shower(-bath), douche; (*Spritze*) *Frauen~e* feminine syringe; **~bad** *n* shower-bath; (*sich*) **~en** *tr* to take a shower; to douche.
Düse *f* (*zur Zerstäubung etc*) nozzle; (*zur Strahlbildung*) jet; (*Hochofen*) blast pipe; (*e-s Brenners*) head; (*~ des Blasebalges*) tuyère; *Haupt~* (*mot*) high speed nozzle; *Leerlauf~* (*mot*) pilot nozzle; *Staustrahl~* (*aero*) ram jet; *Turbo~* (*aero*) turbojet; **~nantrieb** *m* (*Strahlantrieb*) *aero* jet-propulsion; *mit ~~* jet-propelled; **~nbomber** *m* jet-propelled bomber, jet bomber; **~nflugzeug** *n* (*Strahler, Strahltriebflugzeug*) *aero* jet-propelled aeroplane (*od* aircraft), jet plane, jet; *sich mit der Geschwindigkeit e-s ~~es fortbewegen* to move at jet speed; **~nhalter** *m mot* nozzle holder; **~nhubschrauber** *m aero* jet helicopter; **~njäger** *m aero* (*Maschine*) jet fighter; (*mit 2 Strahlmotoren*) twin-jet fighter; (*Kurzstreckenjäger*) jet interceptor; (*Pilot*) jet pilot; **~nprinzip** *n* (*Strahlantriebsprinzip*) jet principle; **~nrohr** *n* blast pipe; **~ntransporter** *m aero* jet (propelled) transport (plane); **~ntriebwerk** *n* (*Strahltriebwerk*) jet power plant; jet engine; **~nvergaser** *m mot* jet carburet(t)or, spray carburet(t)or; **~nverkehrsflugzeug** *n aero* jet airliner, jet liner.
Dusel *m* giddiness; (*halbe Betäubung*) dizziness; (*Träumerei*) dreaminess; (*Rausch*) stupor; *fam* (*Glück*) windfall, luck; *~ haben* to have a run of luck; **~ei** *f* drowsiness; sleepiness; **~ig** *a* giddy, drowsy, dizzy; dreamy; stupid; dull; **~igkeit** *f* (*Dummheit*) stupidity; **~n** *itr* to be dizzy; (*schläfrig sein*) to be sleepy, to be half asleep, to doze.
Dussel *m fam* (*Dummkopf*) blockhead, dunce, duffer; *Am fam* sucker.
düster *a* dark, gloomy; (*traurig*) sad; (*Farben*) dull; *fig* gloomy; melancholy; dismal; **~heit** *f* darkness, gloominess, gloom; dusk.
Dutzend *n* dozen; *6 ~ Federn* six dozen pens; *~e von Federn* dozens of pens; **~mal** dozens of times; **~mensch** *m* commonplace fellow; **~preis** *m* price by the dozen; **~weise** *adv* by the dozen.
Duz|bruder *m*, **~schwester** *f* very intimate friend; **~en** *tr* to thee-and-thou; *sich mit jdm ~en* to thou each other; *auf ~fuß stehen* to say "du" to.
dwars *a mar* abeam; **~balken** *m* cross-beam; **~linie** *f* loxodromic spiral, rhumb line; in line; *~~ bilden* to form line abreast; *in ~~ angreifen* to attack in line abreast; **~schiffs** *a* athwartship; **~see** *f* athwart (*od* broadside) sea, beam sea; **~wind** *m* cross wind.
Dyn *n phys* (*Krafteinheit*) dyne (= unit of force in the C. G. S. system); **~amik** *f tech* dynamics; *pl mit sing*; **~amisch** *a* dynamic(al); *~~er Lautsprecher radio* moving coil loudspeaker; **~amismus** *m* (*Naturphilosophie*) dynamism; **~amit** *n od m* dynamite; *mit ~~ in die Luft sprengen* to dynamite; **~amitattentäter** *m* dynamiter, dynamitist; **~amitpatrone** *f* dynamite cartridge; **~amo** *m*, **~amomaschine** *f* dynamo generator; (*Lichtmaschine*) *mot* dynamo, *Am* generator; **~amometer** *m* dynamometer.
Dynast|ie *f* dynasty; **~isch** *a* dynastic(al).
Dysenterie *f* (*Ruhr*) dysentery; bloody flux.
D-Zug *m* corridor-train, train with Pullman cars; *Am auch* vestibule-train; express train.

E

E *Abk mit* ***E*** *siehe Liste der Abk.*
Ebbe *f* ebb; *~ u. Flut* high tide and low tide; *fig* ebb and flow; *zur Zeit der ~* at low tide; *es ist ~* the tide is out; it is low water; (*fig fam*) *in seiner Kasse* (*seinem Geldbeutel*) *ist ~* he is hard up, his purse is empty, *Am* he is down to his last cent; **~n** *itr* to ebb; *fig* to decline, to run down; *es* (*od das Meer*) *ebbt* the tide ebbs (*od* is going down).
eben *a* even; level; (*flach*) flat; (*glatt*) smooth; *math* plane; (*Land*) plain; *zu ~er Erde* on the ground-floor; *adv* just; *ich habe ~ gegessen* I have eaten just now; *da kommt er ~* there he comes; (*im Begriff sein*) to be about to; (*genau*) exactly; *das nun ~ nicht* not precisely that; *~ deswegen* for that very reason; *~ erst* only just now, a short time ago; **~bild** *n* image, likeness; picture; *er ist das ~~ seines Vaters* he is the very picture of his father; **~bürtig** *a* equal; equal in birth; of equal birth; **~~keit** *f* equality of birth; **~da, ~daselbst** *adv* at the very same place; ibidem, *Abk* ib; **~derselbe** *prn* the very same; **~deshalb** *adv* for that very reason; **~falls** *adv* likewise, equally, too; **~maß** *n* symmetry; proportion; harmony; due proportion; **~so** *adv* just so; **~sosehr** *adv*, **~soviel** *a* just as much; **~sowenig** *a* just as little; **~so wie** as ... as.
Ebene *f* plain, level ground; *math* plane; **ebnen** *tr* to level, *fig* to smooth.
Ebenholz *n* ebony.
Eber *m* boar; *wilder ~* wild boar; **~esche** *f* rowan-tree, mountain-ash.
Echo *n* echo; *ein ~ geben* to resound; (*Widerhall*) reverberation; **~effekt** *m* doubling effect; **~empfänger** *m* echo receiver; **~laufzeit** *f* echo transmission time; **~lot** *n* sound-device apparatus; sonic depth finder; (*mit Ultraschall*) supersonic echo sounding; *mar* echo-sounder; *aero* sound-ranging altimeter; **~lotung** *f* echo-sounding; (*Radar*) radar (*od* radio) locator; **~sperre** *f* echo suppressor; **~weite** *f* echo area; **~welle** *f* echo wave, reflected wave.
echt *a* (*real, lebenswahr*) real; (*wahrheitsgemäß, getreu, richtig*) true; (*rein*) pure; (*Urkunden, Nachrichten*) authentic; (*rechtmäßig*) lawful, legitimate; (*lauter, unverfälscht*) genuine; (*Farben*) fast; (*Haare*) natural; (*Freund*) staunch; *~es Gold* sterling gold; **~heit** *f* (*e-r Urkunde*) authenticity; *Bescheinigung der ~~* authentication; (*Wahrheit*) genuineness; (*Rechtmäßigkeit*) legitimacy; (*Unterschrift*) identity; (*Reinheit*) purity; (*Farben*) fastness.
Eck *n dial* = *Ecke f*; *über ~* crosswise; **~ball** *m* (*Fußball*) corner (-kick); **~brett** *n* corner-shelf; **~e** *f* corner; (*spitz zulaufend*) angle; (*Kante, Rand*) edge; (*Kurve*) turning, *Am* corner; (*kurze Entfernung*) short distance; (*Winkel*) nook, corner; (*Ende*) end; (*Mauer~e*) quoin; *in die ~e treiben* to corner; *um die ~e* (a)round the corner; *um die ~e biegen* to turn round the corner; *jdn um die ~e bringen* to do away with, to murder; *um die ~e gehen* to perish; *an allen ~en u. Kanten* in every quarter; everywhere; **~ensteher** *m* loafer, *Am* corner-loafer; **~fenster** *n* corner-window; **~grundstück** *n* corner-site, *Am* corner lot; **~haus** *n* corner house; **~ig** *a* angular; (*Hut*) cornered; *~ige Klammer* bracket; *fig* (*unbeholfen*) unpolished, awkward; **~laden** *m* corner-shop; **~pfeiler** *m* corner pillar; **~platz** *m* corner-seat; **~schrank** *m* corner-cupboard; **~stein** *m* corner-stone; (*Prellstein*) curb-stone; (*Grenzstein*) boundary stone; (*Kartenspiel: Karo*) diamond; **~zahn** *m* canine tooth, eye-tooth; (*Hauer*) tusk; **~zimmer** *n* corner-room.
Ecker *f* acorn; (*Karten*) clubs *pl.*
edel *a* (*adlig*) noble, of noble birth; (*vornehm*) gentle; (*~mütig; vom Wein*) generous; (*hochsinnig*) lofty; (*Metall*) precious; (*Pferde*) thorough-bred; (*Körperteil*) vital (parts *od* organs); *ein Edler* person of noble birth; **~dame, ~frau** *f* noblewoman, lady (of noble rank), gentlewoman; titled lady; **~denkend, ~gesinnt, ~herzig** *a* noble-minded, high-thinking; **~fräulein** *n* unmarried lady of noble rank; **~früchte** *f pl* choice fruit; **~gas** *n* rare (*od* inert) gas; **~hirsch** *m* stag; **~kastanie** *f* sweet (*od* edible) chestnut; **~knabe** *m* page; **~leute** *pl* nobility, noblemen *pl*, the gentry; **~mann** *m* nobleman, gentleman; **~metall** *n* precious metal, rare metal; **~mut** *m* magnanimity, noble-mindedness, generosity; **~mütig** *a* magnanimous, generous; **~obst** *n* dessert (*od* choice) fruit; **~stahl** *m* refined steel; **~stein** *m* precious stone; jewel, gem; **~steinschleifer** *m* diamond cutter; **~tanne** *f*

silver fir; **~weiß** *n bot* lion's foot; edelweiss; **~wild** *n* large game, deer.
Edikt *n* edict; proclamation; *ein ~ erlassen* to issue an edict.
Efeu *m* ivy; **~bewachsen** *a* ivy-clad.
Effekt *m* (*Wirkung*) effect; (*Nutz~*) efficiency, effect; *~ machen* to be effective; **~en** *pl* (*Habseligkeiten*) effects *pl*, movables *pl*; (*Wertpapiere*) securities *pl*, stocks *pl*, bonds *pl*; **~enbörse** *f* stock-exchange, stock-market; **~engeschäft** *n* stock-exchange transaction; **~enhändler** *m* stock jobber, *Am* security trader; **~eninhaber** *m* stock-holder, owner of securities; **~enmakler** *m* stock-broker; **~hascherei** *f* seeking after effect; claptrap; (*Prahlerei*) showing-off; **~iv** *a* effective; real, actual; *adv* actually; *~~es Einkommen* real income; *~~er Wert* effective value; *~~er Preis* cash price; **~uieren** *tr* to effectuate; **~voll** *a* effective.
egal *a* equal, the same; alike; *das ist mir ganz ~* it's all the same to me; *sl* I don't give a darn; it makes no difference to me.
Egel *m* leech.
Egge *f* harrow; **~n** *tr, itr* to harrow.
Ego|ismus *m* egoism; **~ist** *m* selfish person, egoist; **~istisch** *a* selfish; egoistic(al); **~zentrisch** *a* egocentric.
ehe *conj* before; until; **~dem** *adv* formerly; **~malig** *a* former, late; *Am* one-time; *~~er Präsident* ex-president; **~mals** *adv* formerly, once; **~r** *adv* (*früher*) earlier, sooner; *je ~~, desto besser* the sooner, the better; (*lieber*) rather; *ich würde ~~ sterben als* I had rather die than; *nicht ~~ bis* not until; **~stens** *adv* as soon as possible, very soon; at the earliest.
Ehe *f* marriage; (*~stand*) matrimony; (*gewählter Ausdruck*) wedlock; *~ aus Liebe* (*Liebesheirat*) love-match; *glückliche ~* happy union; *unglückliche ~* ill-assorted marriage; *rechtsgültige ~* legal marriage; *Kinder aus erster, zweiter ~* children by s.o.'s first, second wife; *wilde ~* concubinage; *e-e ~ schließen* (*od eingehen*) to contract a marriage; **~band, ~bündnis** *n* conjugal tie; **~berater** *m* marriage consultant; **~bett** *n* marriage-bed; **~brechen** *irr itr* to commit adultery; **~brecher** *m*, **-in** *f* adulterer, adulteress; **~brecherisch** *a* adulterous; *in ~~en Beziehungen leben* to live in adultery; **~bruch** *m* adultery; misconduct; *~~ begehen* to commit adultery; to misconduct o. s.; **~fähig** *a* marriageable; **~fähigkeit** *f* marriageability, marriageableness; **~frau** *f* wife, spouse; married woman; **~gatte** *m* husband, spouse; marital partner; **~gattin** *f* wife; **~gemeinschaft** *f* conjugal community; **~glück** *n* conjugal bliss; **~hälfte** *f fam* better half; **~leute** *pl* married people, spouses *pl*; **~lich** *a* conjugal; nuptial; matrimonial; (*von Kindern*) legitimate; *~lich geboren* to be born in wedlock; *unehelich geboren* to be born out of wedlock; *für ~lich erklären* to legitimate; **~lichen** *tr* to marry; **~los** *a* (*ledig*) single, unmarried; **~losigkeit** *f* single life; unmarried state; (*Zölibat*) celibacy; **~mann** *m* husband; *fam* hub, hubby; **~paar** *n* married couple; **~pflicht** *f* conjugal duty; **~ring** *m* wedding ring; **~sache** *f jur* divorce case; **~schänder** *m* adulterer; **~scheidung** *f* divorce; **~scheidungsklage** *f* divorce suit; **~schließung** *f* marriage; contraction of marriage; **~~surkunde** *f* marriage certificate; **~stand** *m* matrimony, wedlock, married life (*od* state); **~stifter** *m*, **-in** *f* match-maker; **~trennung** *f* separation; **~versprechen** *n* promise of marriage; **~vertrag** *m* (*vor der Ehe*) marriage settlement; marriage contract (*od* deed); **~weib** *n* wife, spouse; **~widrigkeit** *f* violation of marriage duties.
ehern *a* brazen, (of) brass; bronzen; *mit ~er Stirn* brazen-faced.
Ehr|abschneider *m* slanderer; **~abschneiderei, ~abschneidung** *f* defamation, slander; **~bar** *a* hono(u)rable, honest, respectable; (*Benehmen*) decent, decorous; **~barkeit** *f* respectability, hono(u)r; decorousness, decency; **~begier(de)** *f* ambition; desire of hono(u)r; **~begierig** *a* ambitious.
Ehre *f* hono(u)r; (*Ruhm*) glory, praise, fame, renown; (*Ruf*) reputation, hono(u)r, prestige; (*Auszeichnung*) distinction; (*Achtung*) esteem, respect; admiration, deference; (*Ehrenverleihung*) hono(u)rs *pl*, dignities *pl*; *auf ~, bei meiner ~* upon my hono(u)r; on my word of hono(u)r; *fam* hono(u)r bright; *Ihr Wort in ~n* with due deference to you; *ihm zu ~n* in his hono(u)r; *seine ~ dareinsetzen zu ..* to make it a point of hono(u)r to; *er steht in großen ~n* he is in great esteem; *in allen ~en* in due hono(u)r; *jdm ~ erweisen* to do hono(u)r to; *jdm die letzte ~ erweisen* to pay the last hono(u)rs to; *jdm die ~ abschneiden* to slander s. o.; *auf ~ halten* to be jealous of o.'s hono(u)r; *in ~n halten* to have s. o. in hono(u)r; *wieder zu ~n bringen* to restore; *kriegerische ~n* hono(u)r of war; *~, wem ~ gebührt* hono(u)r to whom hono(u)r is due.
ehren *tr* to hono(u)r; (*achten*) to respect, to esteem; (*jdm huldigen*) to do (*od* pay *od* render) hommage to s. o.; (*als Anrede in Briefen*) (*sehr*) *geehrter Herr!* (Dear) Sir, *Am* (Dear) Sir:; *sich geehrt fühlen* to feel hono(u)red; **~amt** *n* honorary office (*od* post); post of hono(u)r; dignity; *ein ~~ bekleiden* to be employed in an honorary office; **~amtlich** *a* honorary; in an honorary capacity; unpaid; *~~er Vorsitzender* (*ohne Gehalt*) nonsalaried honorary chairman; **~(begleit)dame** *f* (*Hof*) companion lady of hono(u)r; Lady in waiting; **~bezeigung** *f* reverence; mark of esteem; (*bei Beerdigungen*) burial service; (*Grußpflicht*) *mil* salute, military courtesy; **~bürger** *m* honorary citizen (*od* freeman); *jdn zum ~~ machen* to make s. o. free of a city; **~bürgerrecht** *n* freedom of a city; **~doktor** *m* honorary doctor; **~erklärung** *f* (full) apology; *e-e ~~ abgeben* to apologize; **~gast** *m* guest of hono(u)r; **~gefolge** *n* suit; **~geleit** *n* escort of hono(u)r; **~gericht** *n* court of hono(u)r; **~(grab)mal** *n* war memorial; cenotaph; **~haft** *a* honest; **~halber** *a* for hono(u)r's sake; **~handel** *m* affair of hono(u)r; (*Duell*) duel; **~kleid** *n* ceremonial dress; **~kompanie** *f* hono(u)r-guard company; **~kränkung** *f* affront; defamation; (*schriftlich*) libel; (*mündlich*) verbal slander; insult; injury to reputation; **~legion** *f* Legion of Hono(u)r; **~mal** *n* monument; war memorial, cenotaph; **~mann** *m* hono(u)rable man; man of hono(u)r; **~mitglied** *n* honorary member; **~parade** *f mil* dress parade; **~pforte** *f* triumphal arch; **~platz** *m* position of hono(u)r, place of hono(u)r; **~präsident** *m* honorary president; **~preis** *m* prize; *bot* speedwell; **~punkt** *m* point of hono(u)r; **~rang** *m* honorary rank; **~rat** *m* honorary council, court of hono(u)r; (*Person*) honorary council(l)or; **~räuber** *m* slanderer; **~rechte** *n pl* civil rights, civic rights *pl*; *Verlust der bürgerlichen ~~* loss of civil rights, civic degradation; **~rettung** *f* vindication (of hono(u)r); apology; rehabilitation; **~rührig** *a* defamatory; dishono(u)rable; (*mündlich*) slanderous; (*schriftlich*) libel(l)ous; **~sache** *f* affair of hono(u)r; **~salve** *f* volley; **~schänder** *m* defamer, slanderer; **~schuld** *f* debt of hono(u)r; **~sold** *m* award; **~strafe** *f* degrading punishment; *mil* (*durch Degradierung*) punishment by demotion; (*durch Entlassung*) punishment by dismissal from service; **~titel** *m* title of hono(u)r, honorary title; **~voll** *a* hono(u)rable; respectable; *~~er Abschied* (*mil*) hono(u)rable discharge; **~wache** *f* guard of hono(u)r; **~wert** *a* hono(u)rable, respectable; **~wort** *n* word of hono(u)r; *sein ~~ geben* to give o.'s word of hono(u)r; *auf ~~* upon my hono(u)r; on parole; *sein ~~ geben* to pass o.'s word; *auf ~~ entlassen* (*mil*) to release on parole; **~zeichen** *n* badge of hono(u)r; decoration, medal.
ehr|erbietig *a* respectful; (*rücksichtsvoll, achtungsvoll*) deferential; **~erbietung** *f* (*Respekt*) respect; (*Verehrung*) reverence, veneration; (*Achtung*) deference; *mit der üblichen ~~* with due reverence; *jdm ~~ erweisen* to pay reverence to s. o.; *jdm ~~ zollen* to show (*od* pay) deference to s. o.; *bei aller ~~ vor* with all due deference to; **~furcht** *f* (*Verehrung*) veneration (*vor* of, for); (*Achtung, Scheu*) respect, reverence, awe; *aus ~~ vor* in awe of; *jdm ~~ einflößen* to fill s. o. with awe; to awe; *von ~~ ergriffen* awe-struck; **~fürchtig** *a* reverential; **~furchtsvoll** *a* respectful; **~gefühl** *n* sense of hono(u)r; self-respect; **~geiz** *m* ambition; **~geizig** *a* ambitious; **~lich** *a* honest; (*aufrichtig*) sincere; (*anständig*) fair; (*bieder, redlich, loyal*) loyal; (*treu*) true; *~~ gegen* fair with; *~~ gesagt* to tell the truth; *e-e ~~e Haut* (*fam*) a harmless fellow; *ein ~~es Gesicht* an honest face; *ein ~~er Mann* a man of hono(u)r; *ein ~~er Name* a good (*od* fair) name; *es ~~ meinen* to be sincere about s. th.; *~~ währt am längsten* honesty is the best policy; **~lichkeit** *f* honesty, uprightness; fairness; loyalty, reliability; **~liebe** *f* love of hono(u)r; **~liebend** *a* high-minded, hono(u)r-loving; **~los** *a* dishono(u)rable, infamous; **~losigkeit** *f* dishonesty, infamy; **~sam** *a* honest; respectable; **~samkeit** *f* respectability; **~sucht** *f* (immoderate) ambition; **~süchtig** *a* (very) ambitious; **~ung** *f* hono(u)r (bestowed on s. o.); **~vergessen** *a* base-minded; reprobate; unmindful of hono(u)r; **~verletzend** *a* defamatory; **~verlust** *m* loss of civic rights; **~würden** *f* (*Titel*) Reverence, Reverend, *Abk* Rev.; *Ew. ~~!* Your Reverence! **~würdig** *a* venerable, reverend.
ei! *interj* why! hey! ah! *~ nun!* why! well! how now! *~, ja doch!* why, of course! *~ warum nicht gar!* you don't say so! indeed! *~ was!* nonsense!
Ei *n* egg; *aero sl* (*Bombe*) egg; *anat* ovum; *mit faulen ~ern werfen* to egg; *altes* (*frisches, rohes*) *~* stale (new-laid, raw) egg; *faules ~* rotten egg; *frisches ~* (*im Gegensatz zu ~pulver*) shell egg; *hart* (*weich*) *gekochtes ~* hard-(soft-) boiled egg; *Rühr~er* scrambled eggs, buttered eggs; *Spiegel~er* fried eggs; *verlorene ~er* poached eggs; *Trink~er* fresh eggs; *eingelegte* (*kon-*

servierte) ~*er* preserved eggs, water-glass eggs; *Trocken*~ dried eggs; (*Eipulver*) egg-powder; *Kühlhaus*~*er* cold-storage eggs; ~*er legen* to lay eggs; ~*er kochen* to boil eggs; *ähnlich wie ein* ~ *dem andern* like two peas; *aus dem* ~ *kriechen* to peep out of the shell; *auf* ~*ern gehen* to walk upon hot coals; *jdn wie ein rohes* ~ *behandeln* to handle s. o. very carefully; *Am fam* to handle s. o. with kid gloves; ~*er u. Speck* (*Frühstück*) bacon and eggs; *das* ~ *will klüger sein als die Henne* the egg will be more knowing than the hen; are you trying to teach your grandmother how to suck eggs? *wie aus dem* ~ *gepellt* (*sorgfältig gekleidet*) to look as if one had come out of a bandbox; spick and span; **~austauschstoff** *m* egg substitute; **~dotter** *m u. n* yolk; **~auflauf** *m* puffed omelet(te); **~erbecher** *m* egg-cup; **~erfrucht** *f bot* egg-apple, aubergine, *Am* eggplant; **~erhandgranate** *f* egg-shaped hand-grenade; Mills grenade (*od* bomb); **~erhändler** *m* egg dealer; **~erisolator** *m el* egg insulator; **~erkette** *f el* chain of porcelain insulators; **~erkognak, ~erpunsch** *m* egg nog; egg flip; **~erkuchen** *m* omelet(te), (*süß*) sweet omelet(te); (*Pfannkuchen*) pancake; (*Nachtisch*) doughnuts *pl*; **~erkürbis** *m* vegetable marrow; *Am* squash; **~erlandung** *f aero sl* three-point landing; smooth tail-wheel landing; **~erlöffel** *m* egg-spoon; **~erpflaume** *f* mirabelle-plum; **~ersammelstelle** *f* station for collecting eggs; **~erschale** *f* egg-shell; **~erschläger** *m* (*Schneebesen*) egg-whisk, egg-beater; **~erschnee** *m* whipped white of eggs; **~erspeis** *f dial* scrambled eggs *pl*; **~erspeise** *f* egg-dish; **~erständer** *m* egg-stand; **~erstock** *m anat* ovary; **~ertanz** *m* egg-dance; **~eruhr** *f* egg-glass, egg-timer; **~formbriketts** *pl* egg-shaped briquettes *pl*; **~förmig, ~rund** *a* oval, egg-shaped; **~gelb** *n* (egg-) yolk; **~leiter** *m anat* oviduct; **~pulver** *n* egg-powder; **~weiß** *n* white of an egg; albumen; *chem* albumin; ~~ *schlagen* to whip the whites of eggs; **~weißhaltig** *a* albuminous; containing protein; **~weißstoff** *m* protein; **~zelle** *f* egg-cell, ovum.

Eibe *f* yew.

Eibisch *m* mallow, althea.

Eich|amt *n* gauging-office, *Am* gaging-office; bureau of standards; **~en** *tr* to gauge, *Am* to gage; *radio, tele* to calibrate; to adjust; **~maß** *n* gauge, *Am* gage; standard (measure); **~er, ~meister** *m* gauger; *Am* gager, (*für Gewichte*) sealer; **~stab** *m* ga(u)ging-rod, ga(u)ging-rule; **~ung** *f* ga(u)ging.

Eich|apfel *m* gall-nut, oak-apple; **~e** *f*, **~baum** *m* oak(-tree); **~el** *f* acorn; *anat* glans (glans penis, glans clitoridis); (*Kartenspiel*) clubs *pl*; **~elhäher** *m* jay; **~elmast** *f* mast of acorns; **~en** *a* oaken, (made) of oak; **~enblatt** *n* oak-leaf; **~enbrett** *n* oak plank; **~enkranz** *m* garland of oak-leaves; **~enlaub** *n* oak foliage; oak-leaves *pl*; **~holz** *n* oak-wood, oaken timber; **~horn, ~hörnchen, ~kätzchen** *n* squirrel; *Am* chipmunk, bunny; **~lohe** *f* oak bark; **~wald** *m* oak-forest.

Eid *m* oath; *falscher* ~ false oath, perjury; *e-n* ~ *abnehmen* to administer an oath, to swear in; *e-n* ~ *leisten* (*od schwören*) to take an oath, to swear an oath; *e-n* ~ *brechen* to commit perjury, to perjure o. s.; *von e-m* ~ *entbinden* to release from an oath; *e-n falschen* ~ *schwören* to perjure o. s.; *ich kann e-n* ~ *darauf ablegen* I can swear to it; *unter* ~ *erklären* to affirm under oath; *unter* ~ *aussagen* to give evidence on oath; **~brecher** *m* perjurer; **~bruch** *m* perjury; **~brüchig** *a* perjured, guilty of perjury; forsworn; ~~ *werden* to break o.'s oath; **~brüchige(r)** *m* perjurer; **~esablegung** *f* taking an oath; affidavit; **~esformel** *f* form of (an) oath; *an* **~es Statt** instead of an oath, in lieu of an oath; **~esstattliche Erklärung** (*od Versicherung*) sworn statement; affirmation; affidavit; **~genosse** *m* confederate; **~genossenschaft** *f* confederacy; (*Schweiz*) Swiss Confederation; **~lich** *a* by (*od* upon) oath, under oath, sworn; ~*liche Aussage* sworn deposition, testimony on oath; *jdn* ~*lich vernehmen* to hear (*od* examine) s. o. on oath; **~schwur** *m* oath.

Eidam *m* son-in-law.

Eidechse *f* lizard.

Eider|daunen *f pl* eider-down; **~gans** *f*, **~vogel** *m* eider-duck.

Eifer *m* zeal, eagerness; (*Begeisterung*) ardo(u)r, fervo(u)r; (*Hast*) haste; (*Zorn*) passion; *blinder* ~ *schadet nur* the more haste, the worse speed; **~er** *m* zealot; **~n** *itr* to speak with zeal; *gegen etw* ~~ to declaim against; to inveigh against; ~~ *über* to get angry about; ~~ *um* to vie with s.o. in (doing); **~sucht** *f* jealousy, envy; **~süchtelei** *f* petty jealousy; **~süchtig** *a* jealous; envious (*auf* of).

eifrig *a* zealous, eager for; (*begeistert*) enthusiastic; ~ *bedacht auf* keenly interested in ~ *beschäftigt mit* keenly intent on.

eigen *a* own; (*besonder*) private, separate; (*eigentümlich*) peculiar (to), characteristic (of); particular; (*wählerisch*) choosy, fussy; (*genau*) strict; (*seltsam*) strange, odd, curious, queer; (*innewohnend*) inherent; intrinsic; *auf* ~*e Rechnung* on (*od* for) o.'s own account; *aus* ~*em Antrieb* on o.'s own account; *aus* ~*er Anschauung sprechen* to speak from first-hand knowledge; *das ist mein* ~ that is my own; ~*es Zimmer* private room; *in* ~*er Person* in person; *e-e* ~*e Sache* an awkward business; *er ist sehr* ~ he is very particular; *sein* ~*er Herr sein* to be his own master; *sich etw zu* ~ *machen* to acquire s. th.; (*Gedanken*) to adopt an idea **~art** *f* peculiarity; individuality; feature; **~artig** *a* peculiar; characteristic; (*einzigartig*) singular, unique, original, individual; special; (*sonderbar*) odd, queer, strange; **~artigkeit** *f* peculiarity, **~bedarf** *m* o.'s own needs; internal needs, home needs *pl*; **~belastung** *f* dead load (*od* weight); **~besitz** *m* private estate; **~bewegung** *f* proper motion; **~brötler** *m* crank, eccentric; **~dünkel** *m* self-conceit, presumption; **~frequenz** *f* proper frequency; **~geräusch** *n radio* set noise, background noise; (*Grammophon*) surface noise; **~geschwindigkeit** *f aero* air speed; **~gewicht** *n* dead weight; (*Leergewicht*) weight empty; *com* net weight; **~händig** *a* in (*od* with *od* under) o.'s own hand; private; (*Brief*) autograph; ~~ *ausliefern* to deliver personally; ~~*e Unterschrift* o.'s own signature; ~~ *unterschreiben* to put o.'s own hand and seal to; **~heim** *n* separate home; **~heit** *f* peculiarity; singularity; (*sprachliche*) idiom; (*Abneigung*) idiosyncrasy; **~liebe** *f* self-love; egotism, self-complacency; **~lob** *n* self-praise; ~~ *stinkt* a man must not blow his own trumpet; **~mächtig** *a* arbitrary, without consideration for others; unauthorized; ~~ *handeln* to take the law (*od* things) into o.'s own hand; **~name** *m* proper name, family name, surname; noun; **~nutz** *m* selfishness, self-interest; **~nützig** *a* selfish, self-interested; **~peilung** *f aero, mar* self-bearing; homing (on a beacon); **~s** *adv* expressly, on purpose; especially, particularly; **~schaft** *f* (*Qualität*) quality; (*Merkmal*) property; (*Zug*) trait; (*auszeichnende*) character(istic); attribute; nature; feature; *rechtliche* ~~ legal status; *in seiner* ~~ *als* in his capacity as (*od* of), in his character of; acting as; **~schaftswort** *n gram* adjective; **~sinn** *m* obstinacy, stubbornness; wil(l)fulness; **~sinnig** *a* wil(l)ful; (*rechthaberisch*) obstinate, stubborn; **~ständig** *a* independent; **~tlich** *a* (*wirklich*) real, true, actual; (*wesentlich*) essential; (*genau*) proper, precise; (*wahr, wirklich*) intrinsic; *im* ~~*en Sinn des Wortes* in the literal sense of the word; *adv* (*tatsächlich*) in fact; actually, really; just; indeed; after all; (*genau gesagt*) properly speaking; *Am fam* sort of; **~tum** *n* property (*an* in); possession; *als* ~~ *besitzen* to own; **~tümer** *m* owner, proprietor; **~tümlich** *a* (*zugehörig*) own, proper; (*besonder*) characteristic; specific; (*sonderbar*) peculiar; odd, queer, strange; **~tümlichkeit** *f* peculiarity; (*charakteristisches Merkmal*) feature; characteristic; **~tumsrecht** *n* right of possession; ownership; (*literarisch*) copyright; (*Anspruch*) title; **~tumsübertragung** *f* conveyance of property; **~tumsvorbehalt** *m* property reservation; **~versorgung** *f* self-sufficiency; **~verständigung** *f aero* interphone; intercom(munication); **~wärme** *f* specific heat; body heat; **~willen** *m* self-will, wil(l)fulness; **~willig** *a* self-willed; wilful, *Am* willful; (*eigensinnig*) headstrong.

eign|en *tr* (*gehören*) to own; *sich* ~*en* to suit; to be suited (*od* qualified); to be adapted (*zu* for); *geeignet a* qualified, fit; (*brauchbar*) suitable; *geeignete Maßnahmen* appropriate action; **~er** *m* owner, proprietor; **~ung** *f* (*e-r Person*) qualification, fitness; aptitude; (*berufliche*) professional ability; vocational abilities *pl*; (*Brauchbarkeit*) suitability; (*Verwendbarkeit*) applicability, usability; **~ungsprüfung** *f* aptitude test, ability test, psychological test, *Am* qualification rating.

Eiland *n* island; isle.

Eil|bestellung *f* express delivery; **~bote** *m* special (*od* express) messenger; courier; *durch* ~~*n* by express, by special messenger, by dispatch; (*Aufschrift auf Brief*) Express (Delivery); Special Delivery; ~~ *bezahlt!* express paid! **~brief** *m* express letter; *Am* special delivery; *ein* ~~ *für Frau X.* a special delivery for Mrs. X.; **~briefzustellung** *f* special delivery; **~dampfer** *m* fast steamer; **~e** *f* haste; (*Übereilung*) hurry; rush; (*Geschwindigkeit*) speed; (*rasche Erledigung*) dispatch; *ich habe* ~*e* I am in a hurry; *ich habe große* ~*e* (*fam*) I have precious little time to spare; *es hat keine* ~*e* there is no hurry about it; no rush! *in aller* ~*e* in great haste; *die Sache hat* ~*e* the matter is urgent; ~*e mit Weile* more haste, less speed; **~en** *itr* to hasten, to hurry; to make haste; (*von Sachen*) to be urgent; *sich* ~*en* to hurry; *die Sache* ~*t* (*sehr*) the matter is (very) urgent; (*auf Briefen*) *eilt!*

immediate! no delay! urgent! **~ends** *adv* hastily, in haste, speedily, quickly; **~fertig** *a* hasty, speedy; **~fertigkeit** *f* hastiness; speediness; **~fracht** *f* express goods *pl*, *Am* fast freight; **~gebühr** *f* express fee, *Am* expressage; **~gespräch** *n tele* express call; **~gut** *n* dispatch goods *pl*, express (goods *pl*); *Am* fast freight; railway express; goods shipped on post trains (*od* fast train); *durch ~gut!* by express! by passenger train! *als ~~ befördern* to send (*od* to ship) by express (*od* by mail *od* fast train); **~güterzug** *m* express goods train, fast goods train; **~ig** *a* hasty, fast; (*schnell*) speedy; (*umgehend*) prompt; (*dringend*) urgent, pressing; *es ~~ haben* to be in a hurry; *es ist sehr ~~* it is very urgent; *sehr ~~!* *Am* top urgent! *warum so ~~?* what is the hurry? **~igkeit** *f* haste, hurry; **~igst** *adv* in the greatest haste, in great haste; **~marsch** *m* forced march; **~post** *f* express post (*od* delivery); *Am* special delivery; **~schritt** *m* quick-step; **~triebwagen** *m* expedited Diesel car; **~zug** *m* express (train), fast train; **~zustellung** *f* express delivery; (*Post*) special delivery.

Eimer *m* pail, bucket; **~bagger** *m* ladder dredger.

*

ein, ~e, ~ (*Artikel*) a, an; (*Zahlwort*) one; *prn* one; *e-s Tages* one day; *ein u. derselbe* one and the same; (*irgendeiner*) some one; *~er von beiden* either; *manch ~er* many a one; *~s ums andere Mal* alternately; *mit ~s* suddenly; *um ~s* at one o'clock; *~ für allemal* once and for all; *in ~em fort* continually; *ein* (= *eingeschaltet*) *el* on; *~! aero* (*Ruf zum Einschalten der Zündung beim Anwerfen e-s Flugmotors*) contact! *weder aus noch ~ wissen* to be at o.'s wits' end; *~ u. aus gehen* to frequent; **~ander** *prn* each other, one another; mutually; *auf~~* upon one another; (*zeitlich*) in succession; *bei~~* together; *neben~~* side by side.

Ein|achseranhänger *m mot* two-wheeled trailer; **~achsig** *a* two wheel(ed); **~akter** *m* one-act play; **~aktig** *a* in one act, of one act; **~arbeiten**: *sich ~~ in* to make o. s. acquainted with; to acquaint o. s. with; to familiarize o. s. with; *Am fam* to get into the swing of; *jdn ~~* (*Am*) to train on the job; *~gearbeitete* (*angelernte*) *Angestellte Am* on-the-job-trained employees; **~arbeitungszeit** *f* period of vocational (*od* professional) adjustment; **~armig** *a* one-armed; *~~er Hebel* one-armed lever; **~äschern** *tr* to lay (*od* to burn) to ashes; (*Leichen*) to incinerate, to cremate; **~äscherung** *f* (*Leichen*) incineration, cremation; **~äscherungsofen** *m* incinerator; **~atmen** *tr* to breathe; (*einsaugen*) to inhale; **~atmung** *f* breathing, inhalation; **~atomig** *a* monoatomic; **~ätzen** *tr* to etch (in); **~äugig** *a* one-eyed.

Ein|bahnstraße *f* one-way street, *Am* one-way drive (street); (*Schild*) one-way traffic; **~bahnig** *a* single-track, single-lane; **~balsamieren** *tr* to embalm; **~band** *m* binding; (*Buchdecke*) cover; **~bändig** *a* (in) one volume; **~basisch** *a chem* monobasic; **~bau** *m* (*Gebäude*) interior; *tech* installation, mounting, assembly; **~bauen** *tr* to build in, to install, to fit (in), to fix, to mount; to insert; *~gebautes Bad* built-in bath; **~bauwagenheber** *m mot* built-in jack; **~baum** *m* (*Boot*) dug-out, log-canoe; **~begreifen** *irr tr* to comprise (in); **~begriffen** *a* included, inclusive; **~behalten** *irr tr* to keep back; to withhold, to detain; (*Lohn*) to stop; **~beinig** *a* one-legged; **~bekommen** *irr tr* (*Geld*) to get in; **~berufen** *irr tr* (*Versammlung, parl*) to convoke, to convene, to summon; to call a meeting, to call together (*od* in); *mil* to call up (*od* in *od* out), to call to active duty; *Am* to draft, to induct into military service; **~berufene(r)** *m* conscript, *Am* selectee, inductee, draftee; **~berufung** *f* (*Versammlung*) convocation, call; *mil* calling in (*od* up), call to arms; conscription; *Am* draft call, induction into military service; **~berufungsbefehl** *m* order to join, calling-up order; order to report for active duty; **~berufungskarte** *f Am* notice of induction; **~berufungsort** *m Am* induction station; **~betonieren** *tr* to imbed (*od* to set) in concrete; **~betten** *tr tech* to imbed, to insert; to dam up; **~bettig** *a* single(-bedded); **~bettkabine** *f* single-berth cabine, single-bed cabine; **~beulen** *tr* (*bes. mot*) to dent in; **~beulung** *f* dent; **~biegen** *irr tr* to bend in; *in e-e Straße ~~* to turn into a street.

einbild|en: *sich ~~* (*sich vorstellen*) to imagine (*etw* s. th., *daß jem ist* s. o. to be); (*denken*) to think, to believe; (*wähnen*) to fancy; *sich etw ~~ auf* to pride o. s. on, to plume o. s. on, *fam* to fancy s. th.; *eingebildet sein* to be conceited; *bilden Sie sich ja nicht ein, daß ...* be sure not to fancy that; *sie bildet sich ein, gesehen zu haben* she imagines herself having seen; *sie bildet sich zuviel ein* she thinks too much of herself; *darauf brauchst du dir nichts einzubilden* this is nothing to be proud of; *auf das kann ich mir etw ~~* that is a feather in my cap; **~ung** *f* (*schöpferisch*) imagination; (*Idee*) idea; (*Illusion*) illusion; (*Phantasie, Wahn*) fancy; (*Dünkel*) (self-) conceit, presumption; *nur in der ~~ existierend* only imaginary; *bloße ~~* mere fancy; **~~skraft** *f*, **~~svermögen** *n* power of imagination; imaginative power (*od* faculty); *seiner ~skraft freien Lauf lassen* to give full play to o.'s fancy.

ein|binden *irr tr* to bind; **~blasen** *irr tr* to blow into; to breathe into; *fig* to whisper s. th. to s. o.; (*veranlassen*) to prompt, to suggest privately; *tech* (*unter Druck*) to inject (gas); **~bläser** *m* prompter, secret adviser; **~blattdruck** *m* one-side print; leaflet; offprint; broadsheet; **~blenden** *tr film, tele, radio* (*Ton, Bild*) to fade in; *langsam ~~* (*Manuskriptanweisung*) *radio* to sneak in (*z. B.*: sneak in music); **~blendung** *f* (*e-r Szene etc in die andere*) *film, radio, tele* cross fade; **~bleuen** *tr* to beat into; to inculcate; **~blick** *m* insight; look (into); glance (at); *fig* (*flüchtig*) glimpse; knowledge; *~~ gewähren* to give insight (*in* into); *~~ nehmen* to look (*in etw* into a matter); *~~ in jds Charakter gewinnen* to get an insight into s. o.'s character; **~bohren** *tr* to bore into; *sich ~~* to penetrate (into); **~booten** *tr* to embark; **~bootung** *f* embarkation.

einbrech|en *irr itr, tr* (*ein Loch*) to break (a hole into); (*abreißen*) to pull down; (*aufbrechen*) to break open, to force open; (*zusammenfallen*) to break in, to give way; (*Dieb*) to break (into a house), to commit burglary; *fam* to burglarize, to burgle; (*in ein fremdes Land*) to invade; (*herstürzen*) to rush in; (*einsetzen, z. B. Kälte*) to set in; (*anfangen, beginnen, z. B. Nacht*) to begin; *mit einbrechender Nacht* at nightfall, on the approach of night; **~brecher** *m* burglar, house-breaker; *Am sl* yegg(man), crack(s-man), prowler; **~brecherbande** *f* a gang (*od* band) of burglars.

ein|brennen *irr tr* to burn in; (*heizen*) to heat, to make a fire; (*Glasur*) to bake, to stove; (*Farbe*) to anneal; *med* (*wegätzen*) to cauterize; (*Faß*) to sulfur, to match; (*Brandzeichen*) to brand; **~bringen** *irr tr* (*Antrag*) *parl* to make a motion; (*Gesetzentwurf*) to bring in a bill; (*Gefangene*) to bring in; (*Kapital*) to pay in, to bring in, to invest; (*Ernte*) to gather in; (*Klage*) *jur* to file an action (*gegen* against); (*importieren*) to import; (*in die Ehe*) to bring as a marriage-portion (*od* dowry); (*Ertrag, Zinsen*) to yield, to show profit, to make money; to produce; (*wieder ~~*) to retrieve; (*einholen, aufholen, z. B. verlorene Zeit*) to make up for; (*einführen in*) to insert, to introduce; *typ* to get in, to keep in; **~brocken** *tr* to crumble into; *jdm etw ~~* to do s. o. an ill turn; *sich etw ~~* to get into trouble; **~bruch** *m* burglary; house-breaking; breaking in; (*in ein Land*) invasion; *mil* penetration, raid; break through; *~~ der Dunkelheit* dusk; *bei ~~ der Nacht* at nightfall; **~~sdiebstahl** *m* burglary; **~~sfeuer** *n mil* assault fire; **~~sfront** *f* front of penetration; cold front; **~~ssicher** *a* burglarproof; **~~sversicherung** *f* insurance against burglary; **~~swerkzeug** *n* burglary tools *pl*; **~buchten** *tr fam* to incarcerate; **~buchtung** *f* bay, inlet; (*Gegenstand*) dent; **~buddeln** *tr fam* to dig in; **~bürgern** *tr* to naturalize; *r* to become naturalized; (*Wort*) to gain currency; to come into use; to gain vogue; (*Wurzel fassen*) to take root; **~bürgerung** *f* naturalization; **~buße** *f* loss, damage; **~büßen** *tr* to lose; to suffer a loss; to forfeit.

ein|dämmen *tr* to dam up; *fig* to check, to restrain; **~dampfen** *itr* to evaporate; to boil down; **~decken**: *sich ~~ mit* to lay in a store, to stock up on; (*Dach*) to roof, to cover up; **~decker** *m aero* (*freitragender*) (cantilever) monoplane; **~deutig** *a* unequivocal; plain, clear; **~deutschen** *tr* to Germanize; **~dicken** *tr* to thicken; *chem* to concentrate, to inspissate; **~dorren** *itr* to dry up, to shrink; **~dosen** *tr* to tin, *Am* to can; **~drängen** *r* to intrude o. s. into; **~dringen** *irr itr* to burst in, to penetrate; to press upon; to enter by force; to intrude; *auf jdn ~~* to rush upon s.o.; (*in ein Geheimnis*) to fathom; (*forschend*) to search into; (*mil u. von Flüssigkeiten*) to infiltrate; *in ein Land ~~* to invade a country; *~~ n* irruption, penetration; **~dringlich** *a* impressive; urgent; **~dringling** *m* intruder; gate-crasher; **~dringungsbereich** *m mil, aero* air raid zone; zone of penetration; **~dring(ungs)tiefe** *f aero* radius of action, depth of penetration; **~druck** *m* impression; sensation; effect; *unter dem ~~ stehen, daß* to be under the impression that ...; *~~ machen auf jdn* to impress s. o.; *sie hatte den ~~, als ob* she had the impression that; *etw tun, um ~~ zu machen* to do s. th. for effect; *ein tiefer* (*dauernder*) *~~* a deep (lasting) impression; **~drucken** *tr* to imprint, to impress; **~drücken** *tr* to press in; (*zus.-drücken*) to crush, to squash; (*flach machen*) to flatten; *eingedrückte Nase* flattened nose; **~drucksfähig** *a* impressible; **~druckslos** *a* unimpressive; **~drucksvoll** *a* impressive; **~dünsten** *tr* to stew down; to evaporate down; to concentrate by evaporation; **~dünstapparat** *m* evaporator.

ein|ebnen *tr* to level, to even up, to grade, to flatten; **~ehe** *f* monogamy; **~en** *tr* (= *einigen*) to unite; **~engen** *tr* to compress; to confine; to narrow; to hem in; to concentrate; to limit; (*Fluß*) to embank; (*einzwängen*) to cramp.

einer *siehe*: **ein**; *prn* (some)one, somebody; **~** *m* (*Boot*) skiff; single-sculler; (*Zahl unter 10*) digit; *math* unit; **~lei** *a* one and the same, of one kind; *~~ ob* regardless whether; *es ist mir alles ~~* it is all one to me; *~~ was* no matter what ...; **~lei** *n* sameness, monotony; **~seits, einesteils** *adv* on the one hand.

einernten *tr* to gather in; *fig* to gain.

einexerzieren *tr* to drill thoroughly; to train.

einfach *a* single; (*Kleid*) simple; (*schlicht*) plain, *Am* homely; (*Farbe*) primitive; (*Essen*) frugal; *math* (*Zahl*) prime; (*Bruch*) simple; (*bescheiden*) modest; (*elementar*) elementary, primary; *~~e Fahrkarte* single ticket, *Am* one-way ticket; *~~e Kost* plain fare; *~~er Soldat* private, *Am* enlisted man (*Abk* E M); *~~ unerträglich* simply intolerable; *so etw tut man ~~ nicht* that simply isn't done; **~heit** *f* simplicity, simpleness; *fig* plainness; **~wirkend** *a tech* single-acting.

ein|fädeln *tr* to thread; *fig* to contrive; **~fahren** *irr tr* to carry in, to train (horses) for drawing; to break in; (*ein Auto*) to run in, to break in; *aero* (*Fahrgestell ~~*) to upgear, to retract the undercarriage; *itr* to enter (port); to descend into a mine; (*Zug in den Bahnhof*) to get into the station; to arrive; **~fahr(t)gleis** *n rail* arrival line, *Am* incoming track; **~fahr(t)signal** *n* home (*od* station) signal; **~fahrt** *f* entrance, gateway; way in; (*Torweg*) carriage-entrance; *~!* Entrance! *keine ~!* No Entrance! (*Bergwerk*) descent; (*Hafen~*) entrance, mouth; **~~schleuse** *f mar* entrance lock; **~~speilung** *f* inbound bearing; **~~szeichen** *n* green traffic light, right-of-way signal; **~fall** *m* (*Einsturz*) downfall, fall; (*Zusammenbruch*) collapse; *mil* inroad, invasion; descent; (*guter ~~*) brain-wave, flash of inspiration, *Am fam* brain storm; (*Gedanke*) sudden idea, thought; whim; (*Witz*) a flash of wit, witticism; jest; *Am fam* gag; (*Laune*) fancy, whim; (*Licht*) *phys* incidence; (*Schloß*) *tech* catch, latch; *sie hatte den ~~* it suddenly occurred to her; *wie kommst du auf den ~~?* what gave you the idea? *auf den ~~ kommen* to take it into o.'s head; **~fallen** *irr itr* to fall in, into; (*einstürzen*) to fall down, to collapse; *mus* to join in, to chime in; (*Licht*) to be incident; *min* to dip; *mil* to invade; (*in die Rede*) to strike in; (*zustimmend*) to chime in; (*sich erinnern*) to remember; (*Gedanke*) to come on; (*in den Sinn kommen*) to occur to s. o.; *was fällt Ihnen ein?* what do you mean? *es fällt mir nicht ein, das zu tun* I would not think of doing it; I don't dream of it; *da fällt mir eben ein* it just strikes me; *sich etw ~~ lassen* to think of; **~fallswinkel** *m* angle of incidence; **~falt** *f* innocence; simplicity; stupidity; **~fältig** *a* simple, silly; stupid; **~faltspinsel** *m* simpleton; *Abk fam Am* simp; blockhead, flat(head); *Am fam* sap(head); **~familienhaus** *n* one-family house; self-contained house; villa, bungalow; **~fangen** *irr tr* to catch, to seize; to arrest, to take into custody; (*Elektronen*) to trap, to capture; **~farbig** *a* of one colo(u)r; (*Stoff*) plain; *typ* monochromatic; **~fassen** *tr* to put up, to border, to trim, to edge; to bind; (*in Gold*) to mount; (*einschließen*) to enclose; to trap; (*Edelstein*) to set; **~fassung** *f* (*Kleid*) border; trimming; (*Brunnen*) curb; (*Zaun*) fence; (*Rand*) *typ* border; (*Fenster*) frame; (*Feld*) edging; (*Gemälde*) frame; (*Kleinod*) setting; **~fetten** *tr* to grease, to oil; **~feuchten** *tr* to wet; **~feuern** *itr* to make fire in a stove; **~filtrieren** *itr* to infiltrate; **~filtrierung** *f* infiltration; **~finden** *irr: sich ~~* to be present; to appear; to turn up; to arrive; **~flechten** *irr tr* to interweave; to interlace; (*Haare*) to plait; *fig* to insert; (*Redensart etc*) to interlard (with), to intersperse; to put in; to introduce; **~flicken** *tr* to patch in; **~fliegen** *irr tr aero* to make test flights (with a new airplane); *aero* (*in ein Gebiet*) to enter by air; (*in Feindgebiet*) to penetrate enemy territory by air; **~flieger** *m aero* test pilot; **~fliegerei** *f aero* aircraft-testing; **~fließen** *irr itr* to flow in, into; *~~ lassen* to throw in; *fig* to mention; **~flößen** *tr* to instil(l); to administer; (*eingeben*) to give; *fig* to call forth; to inspire with; **~flößung** *f* instillation, inspiration; **~flug** *m aero* approach; (*Eindringung*) raid, hostile air penetration; **~~erlaubnis** *f aero* permit for entry by air; clearance; **~~meldung** *f aero* approaching report; **~~richtung** *f aero* (*beim Landen*) direction of approach; **~~schneise, ~~zone** *f aero* lane of approach; flying lane, approach track; entrance zone, air corridor; **~~zeichen** *n aero* (*vom Kontrollturm*) come-in signal; (*Funkfeuer*) marker beacon (signal); **~~zeichensender** *m* (*Funkfeuer mit Kennung*) marker transmitter; *Am* radio marker beacon; **~fluß** *m* influx; *fig* influence (*auf* over); power (*auf* over); *~~ haben* to have influence; (*jdn beeinflussen*) to influence s. o.; **~flußbereich** *m* radius of action; **~flußreich** *a* influential; weighty; **~flüstern** *tr* to whisper to; to suggest; **~flüsterung** *f* suggestion; insinuation; (*geheime*) innuendo; **~fordern** *tr* to demand; (*Schulden*) to call in; (*Steuern*) to collect; **~förmig** *a* uniform, monotonous; **~~keit** *f* uniformity, monotony; **~fressen** *irr tr* to swallow; *itr* to eat into; *r* to corrode; *~~ n* corroding; **~friedigen** *tr* to fence; **~friedigung** *f* fence, enclosure; **~frieren** *irr itr* to freeze fast; (*von Guthaben*) to freeze; *eingefroren* frozen up, frost-bound; **~fuchsen** *tr fam* (*eindrillen*) to drill in; **~fügen** *tr* to join; (*Wort*) to insert; *r* to adapt o. s. to; **~fühlen** *r* to feel o. s. (into); to sympathize (with); **~fühlungsvermögen** *n* empathy.

Einfuhr *f* import, importation; **~abgabe** *f* import duty; **~artikel** *m* article of import, imports *pl*; **~bedürfnisse** *n pl* import requirements *pl*; **~beschränkung** *f* import restriction; **~bestimmungen** *f pl* import regulations *pl*; **~bewilligung, ~erlaubnis** *f*, **~schein** *m* import licence (*od* permit); bill of entry; **~geschäft** *n* import transaction; **~hafen** *m* port of entry; **~handel** *m* import trade; **~kontingent** *n* import quota; **~land** *n* importing country; **~sperre** *f* embargo on imports; **~überschuß** *m* adverse balance of trade; **~verbot** *n* import prohibition, *Am* prohibition of importation; **~waren** *f pl* imports *pl*; **~zoll** *m* import duty, entrance duty, customs duty; *Am* duty on importation.

ein|führbar *a* importable, admissible; **~führen** *tr* to bring in; (*zum ersten Mal bringen*) to introduce; (*Waren vom Ausland*) to import; (*jdn vorstellen*) to introduce s. o. to s. o.; (*jdn in Gesellschaft ~~*) to introduce s. o. into a company; (*in ein Amt*) to install; (*Gesetz, Gebrauch*) to establish; (*hereingeleiten*) to usher in, to show in; (*einweihen*) to initiate s. o. in s. th.; (*Mode*) to set (a fashion); (*Maßnahme*) to initiate, to adopt; (*Draht, tech* to lead in; (*einschalten, einrücken*) to insert; (*Werkstück etc zuführen*) to feed into; (*Film*) to thread up; (*Stöpsel*) to plug in; (*einpassen*) to fit in; **~führer** *m* (*Importeur*) importer; **~führung** *f* (*Vorstellung, Einleitung*) introduction; presentation; (*Import*) importation; (*Amt*) installation; (*Einweihung*) initiation, inauguration; (*von Gesetzen etc*) adoption; (*Durchsetzung, Begründung*) establishment; (*Hereinbringen*) entering; (*Einschaltung*) insertion; (*Einspritzung*) injection; (*Drahtzuleitung*) lead-in; **~~sauftrag** *m* initial order; **~~sbrief** *m*, **~~sschreiben** *n* letter of introduction, introduction; recommendatory letter; **~~sdraht** *m* lead-in wire; leadin; drop wire; **~~sfeier** *f* inaugural ceremony; **~~slehrgang** *m* orientation course; **~füllen** *tr* to fill in (*od* up); to pour in; (*in Flaschen*) to bottle; *mot* to refill; **~füllstutzen** *m mot* tank filler (cap); filler plug.

Ein|gabe *f* petition; memorial; application; address; *e-e ~~ machen* to make (*od* to send in *od* to submit *od* to file) a petition; (*Vorlage*) presentation; **~gabeln** *tr, itr mil* to bracket; to straddle; **~gang** *m* entrance; (*Einzug*) entry; *~ verboten!* no entrance! keep out! no admittance! off limits! (*Geld*) payment; *nach ~* on payment (*od* receipt;) (*Einleitung*) introduction; preface; (*Prolog*) prologue; *mus* (*Vorspiel*) overture, prelude; (*Waren*) arrival; (*Schriftstück*) receipt; *~~ finden* to find favo(u)r; *~~ verschaffen* to gain admittance; **~gänge** *m pl com* goods received; **~gangs** *adv* in the beginning; *~~ erwähnt* above-mentioned; **~~sabteilung** *f com* receiving department; **~~sanzeige** *f* notice of arrival; acknowledg(e)ment of receipt; (*Gutschrift*) credit advice; **~~sbestätigung** *f* notice of arrival; confirmation of receipt; **~~sbuch** *n com* book of entries; **~~sflughafen** *m aero* aerodrome of arrival, *Am* airport of entry; **~~shalle** *f* entrance-hall; (*Foyer*) lobby; **~~skreis** *m radio* input circuit; **~~smanifest** *n com* bill of entry; **~~söffnung** *f* entrance; **~~sstollen** *m min* entrance gallery; **~~stransformator** *m* input transformer; **~~stür** *f* entrance-door (*od* -gate); **~~szoll** *m* entrance duty; import duty; **~geben** *irr tr* to give; (*Gesuch*) to present; to hand in, to deliver; (*Medizin*) to administer; *fig* to suggest to; to inspire with; to prompt; **~gebung** *f* inspiration, suggestion.

einge|baut *a* built-in; installed, fitted, mounted; arranged; *~~er Antrieb* built-in drive; *fest ~~e Kanone* (*aero*) fixed cannon; *~~e Antenne* built-in antenna; *~~e Brause* built-in shower; **~bildet** *a* imaginary; fantastical; (*eitel*) conceited; **~boren** *a* native; (*angeboren*) innate; (*Bibel*) only-begotten; **~borene(r)** *m* native; indigen(e); **~dämmt** *a* checked, restrained; **~denk** *a* mindful of; *~~ sein* to remember s. th.; **~fallen** *a* emaciated; (*Wangen*) hollow-cheeked, hollow; (*Augen*) sunk(en); **~fleischt** *a* incarnate; *fig* confirmed; inveterate; dyed-in-the-wool.

eingehen *irr itr* to go in (into), to enter; to arrive; to come in; (*schrumpfen*) to shrink; (*sterben*) to perish, to die; (*aufhören*) to cease; to stop, to come to an end; (*Pflanzen welken*) to wither, to decay; *com Am fam* to fold up; *die Zeitung geht ein* the journal ceases to appear; *~ lassen* to give up, to leave off; *auf etw ~* to agree to s. th., to submit to; *auf etw näher ~* to enter into the particulars of; *tr: e-e Wette ~* to make a bet; *ein Risiko ~* to run a risk; *e-e Verpflichtung ~* to assume an obligation; *e-e Verbindung* (*Heirat etc*) *~* to contract; *auf jds Verlangen ~* to submit to s. o.; *es geht ihr nicht ein* she cannot conceive; **eingehend** *a* detailed, in detail; thorough(ly); full, exhaustive, exact; searching; *eingehend prüfen* to scrutinize; *nicht eingehend* (*von Stoffen*) shrink-proof; *Am auch* sanforized.

einge|legt *a* inlaid; (*von Früchten*) preserved; **~macht** *a* preserved; **~machte(s)** *n* (*Früchte*) preserved fruits *pl*; preserves *pl*; bottled fruit; (*süßes*) conserved confectionary, jam, sweetmeats *pl*; (*in Essig*) pickles *pl*; **~meinden** *tr* to incorporate; **~meindung** *f* incorporation; **~nommen** *a* partial (to); prejudiced (against); prepossessed (in favo(u)r of); (*Kopf*) heavy; (*entzückt*) fond of; *von sich ~~* to be self-conceited; **~~heit** *f* prejudice; **~pflanzt** *a* implanted; **~rostet** *a* rusty; **~rückt** *a* introduced (into); (*Reklameanzeige*) inserted; (*als Soldat*) inducted; (*Maschine*) in gear, engaged; **~sandt** *n* letter to the editor; **~schränkt** *a* restrained, narrow; **~schrieben** *a*: *~~er Brief* registered letter; **~sessene(r)** *m* inhabitant; resident; *alt ~~ Firma* old established firm; **~standenermaßen** *adv* avowedly; **~ständnis** *n* confession, avowal; **~stehen** *irr tr* to confess, to avow; to admit; to own up; **~strichen** *a mus* once-accented; **~tragen** *a* registered; licensed; certified; **~wachsen** *a* incarnated; **~weide** *n u. f pl* bowels, entrails *pl*; entestines *pl*; **~~bruch** *m* hernia; **~~schmerz** *m* gripes *pl*; **~weiht** *a* initiated; in the know; **~weihte(r)** *m* initiate, adept; **~wöhnen** *r* to accustom o. s. to; **~wurzelt** *a* deep-rooted; inveterate; **~zahlt** *a* (*Geld*) paid-in, paid-up; **~zogen** *a* retired, solitary; *mil* called up, *Am* drafted; inducted; *~~es Fahrgestell* retracted undercarriage; retracted landing wheels; **~~heit** *f* retirement.

ein|gießen *irr tr* to pour in, (*Kaffee etc*) to pour out; (*begießen, aufgießen*) to infuse; **~glas** *n* monocle; **~gleisig** *a* single-railed, *Am* single-track; **~gliedern** *tr* to incorporate; to insert; to embody; to make a part of; (*Gebiet*) to annex; to classify; (*wieder ~~*) to repatriate; *sich ~~* to become a member of; **~graben** *irr tr* to dig in; (*begraben*) to bury; (*verbergen*) to hide in the ground; *sich ~~* (*mil*) to entrench o. s.; (*in Stein, ins Gedächtnis*) to engrave; **~gravieren** *tr* to engrave; **~greifdivision** *f* division in reserve; **~greifen** *irr itr tech* (*von Maschinenteilen*) to gear in, to be in gear; to mesh; *tech* to lock; (*Uhr*) to catch; to take hold of; (*in etw*) to interfere with; to intervene in; to meddle with; to take a hand in; to come to the aid of; to join; *in ein Gespräch ~~* to enter in a conversation, to interrupt a conversation; (*in jds Rechte*) to encroach upon; to infringe (up)on; to trespass (on), to invade; *mil* to come into action (*od* operation); **~greifend** *a* energetic; (*wirksam*) effective; *tech* in gear, engaged; **~griff** *m med* operation; (*unblutig*) manipulation, manipulative surgery; *tech* catch, gearing; contact; *im ~~* in gear; *fig* (*Einmischung*) intervention, interference; trespass; (*in ein Recht*) encroachment (on); invasion of; (*Übergriff*) inroad; *~~ in den Erdkampf aero mil* ground strafing, air attack supporting ground attack; *in ~~ stehen* to gear, to mesh, to be in gear, to engage, to mate; **~griffabstimmung** *f* one-knob tuning; **~griffsbereich** *m* zone of contact; **~griffsgetriebe** *n* (*Synchrongetriebe*) meshed gear; **~guß** *m* infusion; (*Gießform*) mo(u)ld; (*Gießloch*) cast.

ein|haken *tr* to hook into; (*befestigen*) to fasten; to pin down; (*Anker*) to catch; (*unterfassen, einhängen*) to take s. o.'s arm; to link arms; **~halt** *m* stop, check; *e-r Sache ~~ tun* to put a stop to; **~halten** *irr tr, itr* to stop, to check, to cease; (*erfüllen*) to observe; *ein Versprechen ~~* to keep an agreement; *seine Zahlungen ~~* to be punctual in paying; (*Bedingungen*) to adhere to; to keep the conditions; (*Vertrag*) to stand to (*od* to abide by) a contract; (*Frist, Termin*) to keep a term; to meet a deadline; *halt ein!* stop there! **~haltung** *f* observance; **~hämmern** *itr* to hammer into; **~handeln** *tr* to purchase, to buy; to barter; **~händig** *a* one-handed, single-handed; **~~en** *tr* to deliver; to hand over; *jur* (*e-e Ladung*) to serve a summons upon s. o.; **~händigung** *f* delivery; **~hängen** *tr* to hang in, to put in; (*Telephonhörer*) to replace, to restore; (*Tür, Fenster*) to put on hinges; **~hauchen** *tr* to inspire with; to instil(l); **~hauen** *tr* to hew in (to); to cut open; (*Loch in Stein*) to sink (a hole in a stone); *itr mil* to charge; to fall upon; to attack; (*essen*) to peg away; to tuck in; **~heften** *tr* to sew in; (*ablegen*) to file; **~hegen** *tr* to fence; **~heimisch** *a* native; home-made; domestic; (*Tiere*) home-bred; *bot* indigenous; (*Krankheit*) endemic; **~heimische(r)** *m* native; *sich als Fremder wie ein ~~ benehmen Am fam* to go native; **~heimsen** *tr* (*aufspeichern*) to garner; *fig* to reap; (*sammeln*) to rake in; **~heirat** *f* marriage into a family (*od* business firm); **~heiraten** *itr* to marry into; **~heit** *f* unity; union; (*Einheitlichkeit*) uniformity; *mil u. math* unit; *Am fam* outfit; *tech* standard; integral part; **~~lich** *a* centralized; uniform; homogeneous; **~~sbauart** *f* standard type; **~~sbelastung** *f* basic load; **~~serzeugnis** *n* standardized production; **~~sfernseher** *m* standard television receiver; **~~sfront** *f* unity front; **~~sführer** *m mil* commander of a unit; **~~sgeschütz** *n* standard gun, dual-purpose gun; **~~sgruppe** *f mil* tactical unit; **~~skleidung** *f* utility clothes *pl*; **~~skurzschrift** *f* standard system of shorthand; **~~sladung** *f phys* unit charge; **~~slokomotive** *f* standard locomotive; **~~smasse** *f phys* unit mass; **~~spartei** *f* unity party; **~~spreis** *m* standard (*od* uniform *od* unit) price; **~~spreisgeschäft** *n* bazaar; five-and-ten store, chain store; dime store, limited price store; **~~sschule** *f* standard school; **~~sstaat** *m* unitary state; **~~starif** *m* uniform tariff; **~~swaffe** *f* standard weapon; dual-purpose weapon; **~~swährung** *f* standard currency; **~~swert** *m* unit value; **~~szeit** *f* standard time; **~heizen** *itr* to heat a stove, to light a fire; *jdm tüchtig ~~* (*fig*) to make it hot for s. o.; **~helfen** *irr itr: jdm ~~* to help in; to prompt; **~hellig** *a* unanimous; **~~keit** *f* unanimity.

einher *adv* along; forth; **~gehen, ~schreiten** *irr itr* to walk (gravely) along.

ein|holen *tr* to collect; to gather; to bring in; *mar* to haul in (*od* down); (*erreichen*) to overtake; to catch up; *ich hole dich ein* I catch you up, *Am* I catch up with you; (*Rat ~~*) to seek; *ärztlichen Rat ~~* to take medical advice; (*Flagge*) to lower (*od* strike) the flag; (*einkaufen*) to shop; *~~ gehen* to go shopping; *Nachricht ~~* to get intelligence; *das Versäumte ~~* to make up for lost time; **~holmbauart** *f aero* single-spar type; **~holmig** *a aero* monospar; **~horn** *n* unicorn; **~hufig** *a* whole-hoofed; soliped; solidungular; **~hüllen** *tr* to wrap up, to envelop in; to enwrap; to encase; to coat; to cover; to sheathe; **~hüllung** *f* envelopment; **~igeln** *r mil* to hedgehog; to take up a position of all-round defence.

einig *a* united; in agreement; unanimous, at one; *~ sein* to agree (together); *~ werden* to come to an agreement; *nicht ~ sein* to differ; **~e** *prn* some; any; a few; several; (*etliche, ein paar*) odd; *Am fam* a couple of; **~emal** *adv* several times; **~en** *tr* to unite; to unify; *r* to agree; to come to terms; **~ermaßen** *adv* to a certain extent; **~keit** *f* union, harmony; concord; agreement; *~~ macht stark* unity is power; **~ung** *f* agreement, union; unification; settlement; understanding; **~~skrieg** *m* war of unification.

ein|impfen *tr* to inoculate; (*impfen*) to vaccinate; *fig* to implant; to instil(l); **~impfung** *f* inoculation; vaccination; **~jagen** *tr: jdm Furcht ~~* to strike s.o. with fear; to frighten, to alarm s. o.; **~jährig** *a* one-year-old; *bot* annual; **E~~Freiwillige(r)** *m* one year's volunteer.

ein|kalkulieren *tr* to take into account; **~kassieren** *tr* (*Geld*) to cash, to collect; (*Schuld, Rechnung*) to call in; **~kassierung** *f* cashing; **~kauf** *m* purchase, buying; *~käufe machen com* to make purchases; (*in der Stadt*) to do shopping; **~kaufen** *tr* to buy, to purchase, to market, to shop; *~~ gehen* to go shopping; *sich in die Lebensversicherung ~~* to insure o. s.; **~käufer** *m* buyer, purchaser; purchasing agent; shopper; **~kaufsabteilung** *f* purchasing department; **~kaufsgenossenschaft** *f* purchasing cooperative; **~kaufsleiter** *m* purchasing manager; **~kaufsliste** *f* (*Stadteinkäufe*) shopping list; **~kaufsnetz** *n* string bag, marketing net; **~kaufspreis** *m* cost price, purchase price; prime cost; *zum*

~~ at cost price; **~kaufstasche** *f* shopping bag; **~kaufsvertreter** *m* purchasing agent; **~kehr** *f* putting up (*od* stopping) at an inn; *fig* contemplation, introspection, self-communion; **~kehren** *itr* to put up, to stop off (at an inn); *bei jdm ~~* to call on s. o.; to stay with s. o.; *bei sich ~~* to commune with o. s.; to feel remorse; *wir sind unterwegs eingekehrt* we stopped for a drink on the way; **~keilen** *tr* to wedge in; **~kellern** *tr* to lay in (a cellar); to cellar; to store in a cellar; **~kerben** *tr* to notch; **~kerkern** *tr* to imprison; to incarcerate; **~kerkerung** *f* incarceration, imprisonment; **~kesseln** *tr* to encircle; to trap; to pocket; **~kesselung** *f* encirclement; **~kitten** *tr* to fix with cement; to putty; **~klagbar** *a jur* actionable; recoverable by law; enforceable in proceedings; **~klagen** *tr* to sue for; to enforce; **~klammern** *tr* to fix with cramp-irons; to cramp; (*Wort*) to bracket; to include (*od* to put) in parentheses; **~klang** *m* accord; harmony; unison; *radio* syntony; consonance; concord; *in ~~ bringen* to reconcile; *in ~~ sein* to agree; *in ~~ stehen* to harmonize with; *nicht in ~~ stehen* to differ from; **~kleben, ~kleistern** *tr* to paste in; **~kleiden** *tr* to clothe; to invest with; to accoutre; to fit out; *eccl* to robe; *chem* to coat; *fig* to give a turn to; **~kleidung** *f* clothing; accoutrement; (*in Worte*) wording; *mil* equipment; **~kleidungsbeihilfe** *f* clothing allowance; **~klemmen** *tr* to squeeze in; to jam; to pinch in; *eingeklemmter Bruch* strangulated hernia; **~klemmung** *f* pinching; *med* strangulation; **~klinken** *tr* to latch; to fall into a notch; to throw in; *aero* to engage (in a catch); **~klopfen** *tr* to knock in; **~knicken** *tr* to break; to fold; to bend in; to turn down; *itr* to bend o.'s knees; **~knopfbedienung** *f radio* single-dial control; **~kochen** *tr* to boil down; to evaporate; to thicken by boiling; (*Marmelade*) to make jam; to preserve; **~kommen** *irr itr* to come in, to enter; *schriftlich ~~* to apply to . . . for; *~~ gegen* to protest against; *~~ n* income, rent; emoluments *pl*; (*Staat*) revenue; *jährliches ~~* annuity; *~~ aus Kapitalvermögen* unearned income; **~~steuer** *f* income-tax; **~~steuererklärung** *f* income-tax return (*od Am* statement); **~~steuerhinterzieher** *m* income-tax dodger; **~~steuerhinterziehung** *f* income-tax evasion; **~kopieren** *tr* to overprint; to double print; **~kreisempfänger, ~kreiser** *m radio* single-circuit receiver; **~kreisen** *tr* to encircle, to surround; **~kreisung** *f* encirclement; **~~spolitik** *f* encircling policy; **~~sschlacht** *f* battle of encirclement; **~~sversuch** *m* attempted encirclement; **~künfte** *f pl* revenue(s *pl*), income; **~kuppeln** *tr* to throw in gear; to clutch, to couple.

*

ein|laden *irr tr* to load (in); to ship; to entrain; to entruck; (*Gäste*) to ask, to invite; **~~d** *a* enticing, attractive; **~ladung** *f* loading; invitation; **~~sschreiben** *n* letter of invitation; **~~sschrift** *f* program(me); **~lage** *f* enclosure, enclosed letter; (*Geld*) share, deposit; (*Spiel*) stake; *theat* inserted song; (*Zigarre*) inside leaves *pl*, filler; (*Zahn*) filling; (*Schuh*) instep-raiser; *phot* dark slide for camera insertion; *mot* (*Reifen~~*) inside tyre protector; (*Füllung*) lining; inlay; charge; **~~sohle** *f* insole; **~lagern** *tr* to store up; to encase; to incorporate; *mil* to quarter; **~lagerung** *f* storage, warehousing; *mil* quartering; (*Einbettung*) embedment; *Am arch* support; **~laß** *m* admission; entrance; inlet; **~~geld** *n* entrance money; **~~karte** *f* admission ticket; **~~ventil** *n mot* intake valve; **~lassen** *irr tr* to let in, to admit; (*einfügen*) to put in, to insert; (*am Kleid*) to nip in; *sich auf, in etw ~~* to engage in, to meddle with; *er läßt sich nicht darauf ein* he won't have anything to do with it, he isn't going in for it; *sich mit jdm ~~* to enter into relations with s. o.; *sich in ein Gespräch ~~* to enter into conversation; **~lauf** *m* (*Briefe*) letters received; (*Ankunft*) arrival; (*für Wasser, Dampf etc*) inlet, influx, intake; (*neuer Motor*) running in, green run; *med* enema; (*Hafen*) entry; **~laufen** *irr itr* to run in, to enter; to arrive, to come in; *sich ~~* (*mot*) to run in; *jdm das Haus ~~* to intrude upon s. o., to pester s. o.; (*Stoff*) to shrink; *nicht einlaufend* (*Stoff*) unshrinkable; shrink-proof; **~laufhafen** *m* port of destination; **~läufig** *a* (*Gewehr*) single-barrel(l)ed; **~läuten** *tr* to ring in; **~leben** *r* to accustom o. s. to; to familiarize o. s. with; to settle down (in); **~legen** *tr* to lay in, to insert, to put in; (*in e-n Brief*) to enclose; (*Extrazug*) to put on; (*e-n Film*) to fill, to load (a camera); to thread up the film; to charge the magazine; *Berufung ~~* to give notice of appeal, to file (*od* lodge) an appeal; to appeal; (*in Essig*) to pickle; (*Fleisch*) to salt; (*Früchte*) to preserve; (*mit Holz*) to inlay; (*Gelder*) to deposit; *Ehre, Schande mit etw ~~* to get hono(u)r, disgrace by; *ein gutes Wort für jdn ~~* to put in a good word for; *Verwahrung ~~* to enter a protest; *Veto ~~* to veto; *eingelegte Arbeit* inlaid work; **~leger** *m* (*Bank*) depositor; (*Geschäft*) investor; (*bei Druckmaschine*) feeder, layer-on; **~legesohle** *f* insole; (cork) sock; cork wedge; **~leiten** *tr* to begin; to introduce; to initiate; to start, to open; to manage; to preface; *mus* to prelude; *jur* to institute a law-suit; *Verhandlungen ~~* to open negotiations; **~~d** *a* introductory; incipient; preliminary; *~~des Gefecht mil* preliminary action; **~leitung** *f* introduction; preface; *mus* prelude; *jur* institution; (*Vorrede*) preamble; **~lenken** *itr* to return; to turn in; (*Rakete*) to guide into path; *fig* to come to terms; to give in; to become more reasonable; *fam* to come down a peg or two; *~~ solange es noch Zeit ist* to go while the going is good; **~lernen** *tr* to learn by heart; *jdm etw ~~* to drill s. th. into s. o.; **~leuchten** *itr* to be evident; **~leuchtend** *a* evident, clear; **~liefern** *tr* to deliver in (*od* up); to take to; to bring back; (*ins Krankenhaus*) *Am* to hospitalize; (*ins Gefängnis*) to commit to prison; **~lieferung** *f* delivery; (*Gefängnis*) commitment to prison; (*Briefe*) posting; (*Effekten*) depositing; **~lieferungsschein** *m* receipt of delivery; (*Einschreiben*) return receipt; **~liegend** *a* enclosed; **~lösen** *tr* to redeem; (*Wechsel*) to take up; to discharge, to retire; (*Gefangene*) to ransom; (*Hypothek*) to dismortgage; (*Pfand*) to redeem a pledge; (*Verpflichtung*) to discharge; **~lösung** *f* discharge; redemption; ransom; **~löten** *tr* to solder in; **~lullen** *tr* to lull to sleep.

ein|machen *tr* to preserve; (*in Zucker*) to preserve with sugar; (*in Essig*) to pickle; (*Fische*) to marinate; (*in Gläser*) to bottle; (*in Büchsen*) to tin, *Am* to can; *eingemacht* preserved, tinned, *Am* canned; **~machglas** *n* preserving jar (*od* bottle); **~machzucker** *m* jamming sugar.

einmal *adv* once, one time; (*ehemals*) once (upon a time); (*in Zukunft*) one day, some time; *auf ~* (all) at once; on a sudden; all of a sudden, suddenly; *ein für allemal* once for all; *~ dies, ~ das* now this, now that; *noch ~* once more, again; *nicht ~* not even, not so much as; *wie es nun ~ ist* such as it is; *ich bin nun ~ so* that is my way; *hör ~!* I say! *~ ist keinmal* once doesn't count; *wenn du sie ~ siehst* if you happen to see her; *sehen Sie ~!* look here! **~eins** *n* multiplication-table; **~ig** *a* done (*od* happening *od* occurring) but once; unique; single, solitary; *~~e Abfindung* lump-sum payment; *e-e ~~e Gelegenheit* a unique chance.

Ein|marsch *m* entry; marching in; **~~ieren** *itr* to march in; **~mauern** *tr* to wall in; to immure; to brick up; to embed; **~mauerung** *f* immuration. embedding; **~mengen, ~mischen** *tr* to mix in; *r* to interfere, to intervene with; **~mischung** *f* meddling, interference; **~mieten** *tr* (*Kartoffeln, Rüben*) to stack up, to pit; to put away; to clamp; to silo; *sich ~~* to take lodgings; **~motorig** *a* single-engined; **~motten** *tr* to mothball; **~mummen** *tr r* to muffle up; **~münden** *itr* to fall into; (*Flüsse*) to discharge into; to flow into; to join; (*Straßen*) to run into; **~mündung** *f* (*Straße*) junction, side-road crossing; (*Fluß*) mouth, estuary; lake basin; **~mütig** *a* united; unanimous; **~~keit** *f* harmony, unanimity.

ein|nähen *tr* to sew in; **~nahme** *f* reception, acceptance, receipt; *mil* taking; (*Land*) conquest; (*Stadt*) capture; (*Geld*) receipts *pl*, proceeds *pl*; (*Einkünfte*) income, revenue, takings *pl*; *theat* (*Kasse*) take; *~nahmen u. Ausgaben* receipts and expenditures; **~nahmebuch** *n* receipt-book; **~nahmequelle** *f* source of revenue; **~nahmeschein** *m* receipt; **~nahmeseite** *f* receipts side; **~nahmeüberschuß** *m* surplus receipts *pl*; **~nebeln** *tr* to smoke, to screen; to smoke-screen; *sich ~~* to put up a smoke screen; **~nehmen** *irr tr med* to take medicine; to take dinner; (*Raum*) to occupy; (*Geld*) to receive; (*Steuern*) to collect; (*Stelle*) to take a place; (*Stelle ausfüllen*) to fill a place; (*e-s andern Stelle*) to succeed to another's place; (*gewinnen*) to charm; to win the heart of s. o.; *für sich ~~* to captivate; *gegen jdn ~~* to prejudice against s. o.; **~~d** *a* engaging, taking; **~nehmer** *m* receiver, collector; **~nicken** *itr* to fall asleep; to nod off; **~nisten** *r* to nestle to, at; *fig* to settle o. s. in a place, to settle down (in).

Ein|öde *f* desert, solitude; **~ölen** *tr* to oil; to grease; **~ordnen** *tr* to arrange in order; (*in Klassen*) to classify; (*Briefe*) to file.

ein|packen *tr* to pack up; (*einwickeln*) to wrap up; *in Kisten ~~* to bale; *in Papier ~~* to paper; *itr fig* to give way; **~passen** *tr tech* to fit in, to trim in; to adapt; to adjust; **~pauken** *tr* to coach, to cram; **~pauker** *m* coach, tutor; *fam* crammer; **~peitscher** *m* (*bei Parteien*) (party) whip; ~**pferchen** *tr* to pen in; *fig* to crowd; ~**pflanzen** *tr* to plant; *fig* to implant; ~**pfropfen** *tr* to cram in; (*Gartenbau*) to engraft; ~**peilen** *tr* to take a radio bearing; ~**pfählen** *tr* to fence with pales, to palisade; ~**pfündig** *a* one-pound; ~**phasig** *a* (*Strom*) single phase, monophase; ~**pökeln** *tr* to salt; to pickle; (*Fleisch*) to cure, to corn; ~**polig** *a el* unipolar, single-pole; ~**prägen** *tr* to impress, to imprint; *fig* to impress (up)on; *sich* ~~ to remember, to note; *das hat sich mir tief eingeprägt* that made a deep impression on me; ~**prägsam** *a* impressive; easily remembered; ~**pressen** *tr* to press in, to squeeze in; ~**probieren** *tr theat* to rehearse; *tech* to fit in; ~**pudern** *tr* to powder; ~**puppen** *r* to change into a chrysalis.

einquartier|en *tr* to quarter, to billet; *r* to take up o.'s quarters; ~**te(r)** *m* billetee; ~**ung** *f* quartering; billeting; (*die Leute*) billeted soldiers *pl*, billetees *pl*, soldiers quartered *pl*; ~~**sschein** *m* billet.

ein|rahmen *tr* to frame; ~**rammen** *tr* to ram in; ~**räuchern** *tr* to smoke; ~**räumen** *tr* to put into a room, to put in order, to furnish, to house; (*abtreten*) to grant, to give up; (*zugeben*) to concede, to admit; *Am auch* to allow; ~**rechnen** *tr* to include; to reckon in; to allow for; (*in Betracht ziehen*) to take into account; ~**rede** *f* contradiction; (*Einwand*) objection; *jur* plea, defence; demurrer; *e-e* ~~ *erheben* to enter (*od* put in) a plea; ~**reden** *tr* to persuade (to), to talk s. o. into s. th.; to urge s. o. to; *sich* ~~ to talk o. s. into; *jdm Mut* ~~ to encourage s. o.; to cheer up s. o.; *itr* (*unterbrechen*) to interrupt; (*widersprechen*) to oppose, to contradict; ~**regnen** *itr* to be caught in a deluge of rain; (*durch Regen festgehalten werden*) ~*geregne sein* to be detained by the rain; ~**regulieren** *tr* to adjust, to regulate; ~**regulierung** *f* adjustment; ~**reiben** *irr tr* to rub (in); ~**reibung** *f* rubbing, friction; ~**reibungsmittel** *n* (*Salbe*) liniment; ~**reichen** *tr* to hand in, to deliver, to file; to send in; to present; *e-n Antrag* ~~ to submit an application; *e-n Bericht* ~~ to file a report; *seine Entlassung* ~~ to tender o.'s resignation; *e-e Klage* ~~ to file (*od* to lodge *od* to bring in) an action; ~**reichung** *f* delivery; ~**reihen** *tr* to range; to class; to classify; to arrange; to insert, to include; to enrol(l); ~**reihig** *a* single; (*Anzug*) single-breasted, single-buttoned; ~**reise** *f* entry; ~**reisebewilligung**, ~**reisegenehmigung**, ~**reiseerlaubnis** *f* entry permit; ~**reißen** *irr tr* (*Haus*) to pull down, to demolish, to tear down; (*demontieren*) to dismantle; *itr fig* to spread, to gain ground, to come into use; to prevail; ~**reiten** *irr tr* (*Pferd*) to break in; ~**renken** *tr* to put in; (*Glied*) to set; *fig* to set right; ~**renkung** *f* reduction; (*Glied*) setting; ~**rennen** *irr tr* to run in; to break open; to force open by running against; *offene Türen* ~~ to force an open door; *e-m das Haus* ~~ to pester s. o.; ~**richten** *tr* to settle; to establish; to institute; to set right; to arrange; (*justieren*) to adjust, to fit; *typ* to lay pages; (*Wohnung*) to furnish, *Am fam* to fix up; (*Schule, Geschäft*) to establish, to set up; (*el Licht, Bad, etc*) to install, to fit (up), to fix; to suit to; (*Gericht*) to set up a tribunal; (*Glied*) *med* to set; *gut* ~*gerichtete Wohnung* comfortable apartment; *sich* ~~ to establish o. s.; (*mit seinen Mitteln*) to plan; *sich auf etw* ~~ to prepare for, to take precautions (against); (*nach den Umständen*) to adapt o. s. to circumstances; ~**richtung** *f* arrangement, setup; management; (*Anlage*) plant, installation; (*Ausstattung*) equipment, outfit; (*Beleuchtung*) installation, fittings *pl*; (*Laden*) fittings *pl*; (*Maschine*) mechanism; (*Möbel*) furniture, furnishings *pl*; (*Vorrichtung*) contrivance, apparatus, device; (*Vorkehrung*) appliance; (*öffentliche* ~~) public utilities *pl*; *typ* (*Justierung*) justification; (*Wirtschaft, Geschäft*) establishment; (*Glied*) *med* setting; ~**richtungsgegenstände** *m pl* fixture, *Am* fixings *pl*; ~**riegeln** *tr* to bolt in; ~**ritzen** *tr* to scratch (in), to engrave; ~**rollen** *tr* to roll up; (*einhüllen*) to wrap up; ~**rosten** *itr* to grow rusty; ~**rücken** *itr* to step into, to march in; *mil* (*Soldat werden*) to join the ranks; to report for active duty; *in jds Stelle* ~~ to succeed s. o.; *tr* (*in Zeitung*) to insert; *tech* to throw into gear; (*Kupplung*) to clutch in; (*Gang*) to shift; (*Zeile*) to indent; ~**rühren** *tr* to stir, to mix (up); (*Eier*) to beat up; (*Mörtel*) to temper.

eins one; (*einig*) on good terms; ~ *werden* to agree, to come to terms; *es läuft auf* ~ *hinaus* it comes to the same thing; *es ist mir alles* ~ it is all the same to me; ~ *ins andere gerechnet* on an average; *es ist* ~ it is one o'clock; ~ *f* (number) one; (*auf Karten, Würfeln*) ace.

ein|sacken *tr* to put into a sack; to sack; to bag; *fig* (*Gewinn*) to pocket; ~**säen** *tr* to sow; ~**salben** *tr* to rub with ointment; to anoint, to embalm; ~**salzen** *tr* to salt; (*Fleisch*) to corn, to cure.

einsam *a* lonely, solitary; lonesome; (*Leben*) retired; ~**keit** *f* loneliness, solitude.

einsamm|eln *tr* (*Ernte*) to gather in; (*Geld*) to collect; (*Obst, Früchte*) to pick; (*Ähren*) to glean; (*Lorbeeren*) to win; to reap; ~**ler** *m* collector; ~**lung** *f* gathering, collection.

einsargen *tr* to coffin.

Ein|satz *m* putting in; (*Einfügung, Kleider*~~) insertion; (*Schachtel, Geschirr, Hochofen*) insert; (*Gefäß*) container; (*Füllmasse*) filling, filler; (*Satz*) nest; (*Koffer*~~) tray; (*Anfang*) start, onset; (*Spiel*) stake, pool; (*Pfand*) pledge; deposit; (*Hemd*) shirt front; (*Kriegs*~~) war activity; (*Arbeits*~~) labo(u)r assignment; *mus* striking in; *mil* engagement, mission, action; *aero* sortie; ~~ *fliegen* to fly a sortie; (*Gestell für Behälter*) tray; (*Verwendung*) use; *durch* ~~ *von amerikanischen Fahrzeugen* by using American vehicles; *bei besonderem* ~~ on active duty; during special commitment; *taktischer* ~~ tactical use; *unter* ~~ *des Lebens* at the risk of o.'s life; *zum* ~~ *bringen* to put into action; to send into action; *im* ~~ in action; ~~**abteilung** *f* operational battalion; ~~**befehl** *m* order to take (*od* to put) into operation; ~~**bereit** *a* ready for use (*od* action); *aero* ready to take off; ~~**bereitschaft** *f* readiness (for action); ~~**besprechung** *f mil* orders conference; *aero* (*Einweisung*) briefing; ~~**flugplatz** *m aero* advance aerodrome (*od* airfield); ~~**hafen** *m aero* (*Heimathafen*) home field; operational aerodrome; ~~**leiter** *m mil* (gunnery) control officer; ~~**ort** *m mil* strategic (*od* tactical) disposition of troops (*od* flight units); ~~**raum** *m mil* operational area; ~~**verpflegung** *f mil* iron rations *pl*; ~**saugen** *tr* to suck in; *fig* to imbibe; ~**säumen** *tr* to hem; ~**schalten** *tr* to insert; (*Licht*) to switch on; (*Rundfunk*) to tune in; to turn on; to switch on; (*Motor*) to turn on; (*Gang*) *mot* to shift (into); *den zweiten Gang* ~~ to shift into second (gear); (*Kupplung*) to clutch in, to throw in (*od* on), to engage; (*Einheit*) *mil* to insert; (*einschieben*) to interpolate; to intercalate; (*einstöpseln*) to plug in; ~**schalthebel** *m* switch lever; ~**schaltstellung** *f* on-position; ~**schaltung** *f* insertion; inserting; interpolation; intercalation; switching on (*od* in); throwing in, engaging; ~**schärfen** *tr* to impress upon; to inculcate; ~**scharren** *tr* to bury, to put into the sand; ~**schätzen** *tr* to assess; to estimate (*auf* at), to appraise; *fam* to size up; ~**schenken** *tr* to fill; to pour out (*od* in); *reinen Wein* ~~ to tell the unvarnished truth; ~**schicken** *tr* to send in; ~**schieben** *irr tr* to shove in; (*zwischen zwei Dinge*) to sandwich in; (*in Schriften*) to interpolate; (*Stecker*) to plug in; (*einfügen*) to insert, (*dazwischenlegen*) to intercalate; ~**schiebsel** *n* interpolation; intercalation; ~**schießen** *irr tr* to batter down; to shoot down; (*Gewehr*) to try, to test; (*Brot in Ofen*) to put in the oven; (*Geld einzahlen*) to pay in, to invest; to deposit; (*beim Weben*) to shoot; *sich* ~~ to practise shooting; (*Artillerie*) to (get the) range; ~**schießpunkt** *m* adjusting (*od* ranging) point; ~**schießziel** *n* registration target; adjustment target; ~**schiffen** *tr* to embark, to ship; ~**schiffung** *f* embarkation, shipping; ~**schlafen** *irr itr* to fall asleep; (*von Gliedern*) to become numb; (*allmählich aufhören*) to abate; to slacken; to drop off, to get out of use; ~~ *lassen* to drop; (*sterben*) to die; ~**schläfern** *tr* to lull to sleep; *fig* to lull into security; (*künstlich*) to narcotize; ~~**d** *a* soporific, narcotic; *fig* somnolent, lulling; ~**schläfrig** *a* single-bedded.

Ein|schlag *m* cover, envelope; (*am Kleid*) fold; (*Gewebe*) woof, weft; (*Granate*) impact; (*Handschlag*) hand-shaking; (*Farbe*) touch, colo(u)ring; ~~**en** *irr tr* to drive in; (*Pflock*) to knock; (*Fenster*) to break; (*einwickeln*) to wrap (up); (*Kleid*) to turn in, to put a tuck in; (*befolgen*) to follow, to adopt; (*Wein*) to sulphur; *e-n Weg* ~~ to take a road; *itr* (*Blitz*) to strike; (*zustimmen*) to consent; (*gelingen*) to succeed; to be successful, to catch on; (*in die Hände*) to shake hands; (*Film, Theaterstück*) to take; (*Waren*) to sell well; *das schlägt nicht in sein Fach* this is not in his line; ~**schlägig** *a* belonging to, relative to; pertinent to; competent; ~~*e Literatur* literature on the subject; ~~*es Beispiel* case in point; ~**schlagpapier** *n* packing paper, wrapping paper; ~**schlagstelle** *f* (*Granate etc*) point of burst; ~**schlagswinkel** *m* angle of impact.

ein|schleichen *irr itr r* to creep in, to steal in; ~**schleppen** *tr* to drag in; (*Ware*) to smuggle in; (*Krankheit*) to bring in, to import.

einschließ|en *irr tr* to lock up; to confine; *mil* to surround, to encircle; (*absperren*) to blockade; (*umfassen*) to embrace; *fig* to include; *jdn ins Gebet* ~~ to remember in o.'s prayer; ~**lich** *a* inclusive, comprising; *von Mittwoch* *bis ~~ Freitag* from Wednesday to Friday inclusive, *Am* from Wednesday thru Friday; **~ung** *f* confinement; blockade.

ein|schlucken *tr* to swallow up; **~schlummern** *itr* to fall asleep; to die; **~schlüpfen** *itr* to glide in; **~schlürfen** *tr* to sip in; **~schluß** *m* inclosure; parenthesis; *mit ~~* inclusive of.

einschmeichel|n *r* to insinuate o. s. into, to ingratiate o. s. with; **~nd** *a* insinuating; taking, winning; **~ung** *f* insinuation.

ein|schmelzen *irr tr* to melt down; **~schmieren** *tr* to smear; to grease; *mot* to lubricate; **~schmuggeln** *tr* to smuggle in; **~schnallen** *tr* to buckle in; **~schnappen** *itr* to catch, to click; to fall in; to snap (in, into); *(verärgert sein) fam* to be peeved (about, at); **~schneiden** *irr tr* to cut in, to carve; *(einkerben)* to notch; **~~d** *a* incisive, decisive; drastic; **~schneien** *itr* to snow up (*od* in *od* under); *der Zug war ~geschneit* the train was snowed under; **~schnitt** *m* incision, cut; *(Vers)* cæsura; *(Erd~~)* cutting; *(Furche, Nute)* groove, kerf, slot; *(Wendepunkt)* turning-point; **~schnüren** *tr* to lace; *(Paket)* to cord; **~schränken** *tr* to confine; *(begrenzen)* to limit; *(stark)* to restrict, to cut down, to curb, to curtail; *r* to retrench, to reduce; to cut down on expenses; **~schränkung** *f* limitation, restriction; retrenchment; curb, curtailment; *ohne ~~* without reservation; *mit (gewissen) ~en* with (certain) reservations; *mit ~~* in a qualified sense; **~schrauben** *tr* to screw in.

Einschreib|ebrief *m* registered letter; **~egebühr** *f* registration fee, *Am* registry fee; **~en** *irr tr* to book, to write in; *sich in ein Buch ~~* to enter o.'s name in a book; *(in die Matrikel)* to matriculate; *(in e-m Verein)* to enrol(l); *e-n Brief ~~ lassen* to have a letter registered; *(in ein Register)* to register; **~ung** *f* entering, registration; matriculation; enrol(l)ment.

ein|schreiten *irr itr* to step in; *jur* to proceed against; to intervene; *(eingreifen)* to interfere; *(Maßnahmen ergreifen)* to take steps; *(plötzlich strafend durch Behörde) Am fam* to crack down; **~schrumpfen** *itr* to shrink up; **~schüchtern** *tr* to intimidate; to frighten; *fam* to bully, *Am fam* to bulldoze, to buffalo; **~schüchterung** *f* intimidation; **~schulen** *tr* to send to school; to train; **~schuß** *m (Wunde)* entry-hole of the bullet; wound of entry; *(Kapital)* capital invested; *(Weberei)* woof, weft; *e-n ~~ feststellen* to register a hit; **~schütten** *tr* to pour in; **~schwärzen** *tr* to blacken; **~schwenken** *itr mil* to wheel round; *tr tech* to swing on, to pivot; **~schwimmerflugzeug** *n* single-float plane; **~schwingen** *tr mar* to turn in; **~segnen** *tr* to consecrate; to confirm; **~segnung** *f* consecration; confirmation; **~sehen** *irr tr* to look into; *(prüfen)* to examine, to investigate; *(Akten)* to have access to files; *(begreifen)* to perceive, to comprehend, to understand, to realize; *etw nicht ~~ wollen* to shut o.'s eyes to; *ein ~~ haben* to be reasonable; **~seifen** *tr* to soap; *(Bart)* to lather; *fig* to dupe, to take in, *Am* to soft-soap; **~seitig** *a* one-sided; *(parteiisch)* partial; *(voreingenommen)* bias(s)ed; *(Nahrung)* unbalanced; *jur* ex parte, unilateral; **~seitigkeit** *f* partiality; bias; one-sidedness; narrowness; **~senden** *irr tr* to send in; to transmit; **~sender** *m* sender; *(Beitrag)* contributor; **~sendung** *f* sending (in), remittance; **~senken** *tr* to let down, to sink in.

einsetz|en *tr* to set in, to place in; *(Brillenglas)* to put in; *(zum Pfande)* to pledge; *(Stoff)* to let in; *(Anzeige)* to insert; *(stiften)* to institute; *(Pflanzen)* to plant; *(verwenden)* to use, to employ; *Zähne ~~* to put in artificial teeth; *in ein Amt ~~* to install in an office; *zum Erben ~~* to constitute o.'s heir; *sein Leben ~~* to stake o.'s life; *sich ~~ für jdn* to stand up for s. o.; to speak up on s. o.'s behalf; *sich für etw ~~* to be engaged in s. th.; *sich voll ~~* to pull o.'s weight; *itr* to set in, to begin; *mus* to strike in; **~ung** *f* institution; installation; appointment.

Einsicht *f* insight; *(Verständnis)* understanding, reason; *(Prüfung)* examination, inspection; *(Urteil)* judg(e)ment; *(Durchsicht)* perusal; *zur ~* for inspection, for perusal; *~ nehmen* to inspect, to peruse; **~ig, ~svoll** *a* sensible; intelligent; well-informed; prudent, judicious; **~nahme** *f*: *zur ~~* on approval; for inspection; **~slos** *a* injudicious.

einsickern *itr* to soak (*in* into); to trickle (in); to infiltrate (*in* into).

Einsied|elei *f* hermitage; solitude, **~ler** *m* hermit; **~lerisch** *a* secluded; solitary.

ein|siegeln *tr* to seal up; **~silbig** *a* monosyllabic; *fig (schweigsam)* taciturn; **~silbigkeit** *f* monosyllabism; *fig (Schweigsamkeit, Wortkargheit)* taciturnity; **~singen** *irr tr* to sing to sleep; *r* to practise singing; **~sinken** *irr itr* to sink down; *(einfallen)* to fall in; **~sitzer** *m* single-seater; **~sitzig** *a* single-seated; **~spannen** *tr* to stretch in a frame; *(Pferde)* to put harness on; **~spänner** *m* one-horse carriage; **~spännig** *a* with one horse; **~sparen** *tr* to gain (money) by economies; to economize; to save (material); to reduce cost; **~sperren** *tr* to lock in; *(Gefängnis)* (to take) to jail, to arrest, to confine, to imprison; **~spielen** *tr (Waage)* to balance (out); *sich ~~ (Person)* to practise well; *(Betrieb)* to function well; *sport* to train; **~spinnen** *irr tr* to spin in; *zoo* to cocoon; *fig sich ~~* to lead a secluded life; to be absorbed (in); **~sprache** *f (siehe: Einspruch)* protest, objection; *~~ erheben* to protest against; *jur* to take exception to; **~sprechen** *irr tr (Mut)* to encourage; *(Trost)* to comfort s. o.; **~sprengen** *tr* to sprinkle; *(aufbrechen)* to burst open; *geol* to intersperse, to disseminate; to interstratify; **~springen** *irr itr (Schloß)* to snap, to catch; *(Ecke)* to re-enter; *(Stoff)* to shrink; *(helfen)* to help out; *für jdn ~~* to step in for s. o.; *(in Klub, Verbindung)* to join; **~spritzen** *tr* to inject; **~spritzdüse** *f mot* injection nozzle; **~spritzpumpe** *f mot* fuel injection pump; **~spritzvergaser** *m* spray, atomizing carburet(t)or; **~spritzung** *f* injection; **~spruch** *m (Einwendung)* objection; *(Protest)* protest; *(Beschwerde)* reclamation; opposition; *~~ erheben* to protest against; *jur* to lodge (*od* file) an objection (*bei* with); to appeal; **~~sfrist** *f* opposition period; **~~srecht** *n* veto; **~spurig** *a* single-track.

einst, **~ens, ~mals** *adv (früher)* one day, once; *(künftig)* some day; **~ig** *a (ehemalig)* former; *(künftig)* future; **~weilen** *adv* in the meantime, meanwhile, for the present; **~weilig** *a* temporary; *jur* interim; provisional, preliminary; *~~e Verfügung jur* (interim) injunction; *(bis zur Verhandlung)* preliminary injunction; *e-e ~~e Verfügung erlassen* to grant an injunction.

ein|stampfen *tr* to stamp in, to ram; *(Schriften)* to pulp; **~stand** *m (festlicher Beginn)* installation; *(Tennis)* deuce; *(Geld)* entrance-fee; footing; **~standspreis** *m* cost price; **~stecken** *tr* to stick in; *(Geld)* to pocket; *(einsperren)* to imprison, to lock up; *(Beleidigung)* to pocket (*od* to put up with) an insult, to swallow, to take; *das Radio ~~* to plug in the radio; **~stecklauf** *m mil* liner; **~steckmagazin** *n* clip; **~stehen** *irr itr: für etw ~~* to answer for; *für jdn ~~* to stand security for; to be responsible for s. o.; **~steigen** *irr itr* to get in(to); *Am (Zug etc)* to get on, to board, to get on board; *~~! interj* take your seats, please! *Am* all aboard! *alles ~~! fam* get in, everybody! *Am* everybody pile in! **~steigluke** *f aero* access hatch; *(Tank)* doorway; **~stellbar** *a* adjustable; *Luftschraube mit ~~en Blättern* adjustable pitch airscrew; **~stellen** *tr* to put in; *(aufhören, unterlassen)* to stop, to leave off; to discontinue, (to bring) to end; *Am* to quit; *(Arbeiter etc)* to engage, to take (on), to employ; *Am* to hire, to put on; *(Rekruten)* to enlist, *Am* to muster in; *(Arbeit)* to strike, to go on strike; to walk out; *(Wagen in die Garage)* to garage; *(in den Brennpunkt bringen)* to focus; *(Fernseher, Radio)* to tune in, to switch on, to dial in; *e-e Rundfunkstation ~~* to tune in on a radio station; *phot* to focus; to screen; *(Fabrikbetrieb)* to shut down; *(Zahlungen)* to stop, to suspend; *(Feuer) mil* to cease; *Feuer ~~!* cease firing! *(justieren) tech* to adjust; to regulate; *(Prozeß) jur* to discontinue (proceedings); to stay a lawsuit; *(Strafverfahren)* to withdraw a charge; *sich ~~ (erscheinen, kommen)* to appear, to come; *(Winter)* to set in; *(anpassen)* to adapt o. s. to; *~~ auf* to standardize against, to make up to; *sich ~~ auf* to be prepared for; **~steller** *m* regulator, thermostat; **~stellig** *a* of one figure; **~stellmarke** *f* reference mark; **~stellraum** *m mot* garage; **~stellscheibe** *f* dial; *phot* focussing screen; **~stellschraube** *f* adjusting screw; *phot* focussing screw; **~stellskala** *f* front scale; **~stellvorrichtung** *f radio* tuning device (of the receiver); **~stellung** *f (Haltung, Ansicht)* attitude, view; *(von Leuten)* engagement; *phot* focussing; *(Zahlungs~~)* suspension (*od* stoppage) of payments; *(Arbeits~~)* strike; *(von Rekruten)* enlistment; *(Verfahren) jur* stay, discontinuance; suspension; *mot* timing; *(Eisenbahnverkehr) Am rail* stoppage; *(Normierung)* standardization; **~stemmen** *tr (Loch)* to chisel out; *(Zapfloch)* to mortise (*od* mortice); *(Arme in die Seite)* to set o.'s arms akimbo; **~sternmotor** *m aero* single row radial engine; **~stich** *m* puncture; *rail* tunnel; **~sticken** *tr* to embroider (in); **~stieg** *m* entrance; *(Berg)* climbing into.

einstimm|en *itr* to chime in; *(teilnehmen)* to join in; *(einwilligen)* to agree with, to consent to; **~ig** *a mus* for one voice; *fig* unanimous; **~igkeit** *f* unanimity; **~ung** *f* agreement.

ein|stöckig *a* one-storied; **~stopfen** *tr* to stuff in; to fill (a pipe); **~stoßen** *irr tr* to push in; (*Tür*) to smash; (*Wand*) to knock down; **~strahlen** *tr* to radiate upon, to irradiate; **~strahlung** *f* irradiation; **~streichen** *irr tr* to rub into; (*Geld*) to take in; to pocket; **~streuen** *tr* to strew in; (*Bemerkungen*) to throw in, to intersperse; **~strömen** *itr* to stream in, to flow in; *fig* to flock (*od* crowd) in; **~strömung** *f* admission, inlet; **~strömungsrohr** *n* inlet pipe (*od* tube), admission pipe; **~strömventil** *n* inlet valve; **~studieren** *tr* to study (well); *theat* to rehearse, to put into rehearsal; **~studierung** *f* study; *theat* rehearsal; **~stufen** *tr* to classify; to grade, to range; (*Steuer*) to rate, to graduate; **~stufig** *a* single-stage; **~stufung** *f* classification; grading; categorization; (*Steuer*) rating, graduation; **~stündig** *a* of one hour's duration; **~stürmen** *itr* to rush in (upon); (*angreifen*) to assail; **~sturz** *m* crash, collapse; falling-in; (*Geologie*) caving-in; (*Bodensenkung*) subsidence; **~stürzen** *itr* (*zusammenfallen*) to fall in, to collapse; to tumble down; (*Decke, Boden, Stollen*) to cave in; *tr* to demolish, to pull down; *sich auf jdn ~~* to assail s. o.; to rush (*auf* upon).

ein|tägig *a* one day old; of one day; ephemeral; **~tagsfliege** *f* day-fly; **~tagsgeschöpf** *n* ephemeral creature; **~tanzen**: *sich ~~* to practise dancing; **~tänzer** *m* a male professional dancing partner; gigolo; **~tänzerin** *f* (*in e-m Tanzlokal*) taxi-dancer; **~tauchen** *tr* to dip in; *itr* to dive; **~tauschen** *tr* to exchange (for); to barter; to swap for; **~teilen** *tr* to divide; (*verteilen*) to distribute; (*anordnen*) to arrange; (*eingruppieren*) to classify; (*in Grade*) to graduate; **~teilung** *f* division, distribution; (*Klassifizierung*) classification; (*Ordnung*) arrangement; (*Thermometer*) scale; **~teilungsgrad** *m* degree; **~tönig** *a* monotonous; **~~keit** *f* monotony; **~topfgericht** *n*, **~topf** *m* single-boiled dish; one-course dish (*od* meal); stew; **~tracht** *f* harmony, unanimity; **~trächtig** *a* unanimous, concordant; **~trag** *m* (*in Buch*) entry; registration; (*Schaden*) prejudice, detriment; *~~ tun* to prejudice s. o.; to be derogatory to s. th.; **~tragen** *irr tr* to carry in; (*in Liste, Buch*) to register, to enter, to list, to record; *eingetragener Kunde* registered customer; *sich ~~ lassen* to register; (*einbringen*) to yield, to bring profit; **~tragung** *f* entry; (*beim Kleinhändler*) registration with retailer; *~~ unter dem Namen des Verfassers* (*Bibliothekskatalog*) author entry; *~~ unter dem Titel* title entry; **~träglich** *a* profitable, lucrative; *~~e Beschäftigung* paid job; remunerative occupation, *Am* gainful occupation; **~träglichkeit** *f* profitableness; productiveness; **~tränken** *tr* to soak, to steep; *es e-m ~~* to make s. o. pay for it; **~träufeln** *tr*, **~tröpfeln** *tr* to infuse by drops, to instil(l); **~treffen** *irr itr* (*ankommen*) to arrive; (*geschehen*) to happen; to come to pass; (*sich verwirklichen*) to come true, to be realized; **~treiben** *irr tr* to drive in; (*Geld*) to call in; (*Schulden*) to recover; (*Steuern*) to collect; **~treibung** *f* driving in; recovery; **~treten** *irr itr* to enter (a house); to come in, to step (*in* into); (*in e-e Firma, ins Heer etc*) to join (a firm, the army); (*Winter, Regen etc*) to set in; (*geschehen*) to happen; (*Ereignis*) to occur; (*Notwendigkeit, Fall*) to arise; *für jdn ~~* to intercede for s. o., to stand up for s. o.; (*für etw*) to advocate s. th., to argue for; *tr* (*aufstoßen*) to kick open (*od* in); *r* to run s. th. into o.'s foot; **~tretendenfalls** *adv* in case of need; should the case arise; **~trichtern** *tr* to pour in with a funnel; *jdm etw ~~* to drive (*od* to drum) s. th. into s. o.'s head; **~trimmen** *tr* to align; **~tritt** *m* entry, entrance; (*Anfang*) beginning, commencement, setting in; (*Optik*) incidence; (*Verein etc*) joining, entering; (*Zulassung*) admission, admittance; *~~ verboten!* no admittance! keep out! *~~ frei!* admission free! **~trittsgeld** *n* (price of) admission, gate-money; (*Gebühr*) entrance fee, *Am* initiation fee; **~trittskarte** *f* admission-ticket; **~trocknen** *itr* to shrink, to dry up; **~tröpfeln** *tr* to drop in, to instil(l); **~trübung** *f* cloudiness, becoming overcast; **~tunken** *tr* to dip in; to sop; **~üben** *tr* to practise, to exercise; to drill; to train.

ein|verleiben *tr* to incorporate; (*einsaugen*) to imbibe; (*angliedern*) to annex; **~verleibung** *f* incorporation; **~vernehmen** *n* understanding; agreement; *in gutem ~~ leben* to be on good terms with; **~verstanden** *a*: *~~ sein* to agree; *ich bin ~~* I am agreeable; *er war mit unseren Plänen ~~* he was agreeable to our plans; *~~! interj* agreed! **~verständnis** *n* accord, understanding, consent; (*mit etw Strafbarem*) connivance, collusion; *in gegenseitigem* (*strafbarem*) *~~ stehen* to connive; to be in conformity with; *sich ins ~~ setzen* to come to an understanding with.

einwachsen *irr itr* to grow (into); *fig* (*einwurzeln*) to become deeply rooted; *tr* (*den Boden ~~*) to apply wax to the floor.

Einwand *m* objection; (*Vorwand*) pretext; *e-n ~ erheben* to raise an objection; *jur* (*Verteidigung*) to put in a plea; **~frei** *a* unobjectionable; indisputable, incontestable; (*fehlerfrei*) faultless; (*tadelfrei*) blameless; *nicht ~frei* objectionable.

Einwander|er *m* immigrant; **~n** *itr* to immigrate; **~ung** *f* immigration.

ein|wärts *adv* inward(s); **~weben** *tr* to weave in; *fig* to interweave; **~wechseln** *tr* to change; (*tauschen*) to give (to get) in exchange; (*umwechseln*) to convert; (*einlösen*) to cash; **~wechslung** *f* exchange, change; changing; **~wecken** *tr* to bottle, to preserve; **~weichen** *tr* to soak; to steep; to macerate; (*Flachs*) to ret; **~weihen** *tr* to inaugurate; to consecrate; *jdn in etw ~~* to initiate into; to let in on (a secret); (*bekannt machen mit*) to acquaint with; (*Kirche*) to consecrate; (*Priester*) to ordain; *e-e Wohnung ~~* to give a house-warming (party); *~geweiht sein* to be in the know; **~weihung** *f* inauguration; consecration; dedication; opening; initiation; **~~sfeier** *f* inaugural ceremony; **~~sfest** *n* (*Haus, Wohnung*) house-warming party; **~~spredigt** *f* inaugural sermon; **~~srede** *f* inaugural address; **~~stag** *m* day of inauguration; **~weisen** *irr tr* to direct; (*Amt*) to install; to introduce; (*in Wohnung*) to allot; *aero mil* (*Besatzung in Flugauftrag*) to brief; **~weiser** *m* guide; traffic-director; **~weisung** *f* installation; introduction; instruction; training; direction; *aero mil* briefing; **~wenden** *tr* to object (*gegen* to); to demur; *jur* to plead; **~wendung** *f* objection; exception; protest; *jur* defence; plea; *~~ en erheben* to make (*od* to raise) objections; to challenge; **~werfen** *irr tr* to throw in; (*Scheiben*) to break; (*Brief*) to post, *Am* to mail; *fig* to object; (*dazwischenwerfen*) *fig* to interject; **~wickeln** *tr* to wrap up; (*einrollen*) to roll up; (*Kind*) to swaddle; *fig* to implicate; **~wickelpapier** *n* wrapping-paper; **~wiegen** *tr* (*~wägen irr*) to weigh and put in; (*Kind*) to rock asleep; *fig* to lull (*in* with); **~willigen** *itr* to consent to; to agree to; **~willigung** *f* consent, agreement; **~wirken** *tr* to weave in; *itr fig* to influence; to impress; to act on; **~wirkung** *f* influence; **~wohner** *m* (*~~in f*) inhabitant; resident; (*Bewohner*) dweller; **~~meldeamt** *n* registration office; **~~schaft** *f* inhabitants *pl*; **~~wehr** *f* citizen guards *pl*; **~~zählung** *f* census; **~wurf** *m* (*Öffnung*) slit, slot; (*Brief*) letter-box; (*Zuführung*) charging, feeding; (*Behälter*) hopper; *fig* objection; *e-n ~~ machen* to object; **~wurzeln** *itr* to take root.

Ein|zahl *f* singular (number); **~zahlen** *tr* to pay in; **~zahlung** *f* payment; (*Bank*) deposit; (*Teil~~*) instal(l)ment; (*Post~~*) postal order; **~~sschein** *m* paying-slip; *Am* deposit slip; **~zäunen** *tr* to fence in; to hedge in; **~zäunung** *f* enclosure; hedge, hedging in; fence; **~zeichnen** *tr* to draw in; to note; to insert; *sich ~~* to enter o.'s name; **~zeichnung** *f* entry; subscription; **~zeilig** *a* one-lined.

Einzel|abteil *n* single compartment; **~anfertigung** *f* single-piece work; **~antrieb** *m mot* separate drive, direct motor drive; **~aufhängung** *f mot* independent suspension; **~aufstellung** *f* itemized schedule; **~ausbildung** *f* individual training; **~ausgabe** *f* (*Buch*) separate edition; **~befehl** *m mil* extract order; **~beratung** *f* individual information; **~betrag** *m* (single) item; **~bildgerät** *n* single-photograph plotting apparatus; **~darstellung** *f* monograph; separate treatise; **~fall** *m* individual case, particular case; **~fertigung** *f* single-part production, *Am* individual construction; **~feuer** *n mil* individual fire, single shots *pl*; **~firma** *f* private firm; **~gabe** *f med* dose; **~gänger** *m* outsider; **~garage** *f* lock-up; **~gesang** *m* solo; **~haft** *f* (*Gefängnis*) solitary confinement; *in ~~ sitzen* to be in solitary confinement; **~handel** *m* retail business, retail trade; **~handelsunternehmen** *n* retail enterprise, retail firm; **~händler** *m* retailer; **~haus** *n* detached house; **~heit** *f* detail, item; *~~en pl* details *pl*, particulars *pl*; *mit allen ~~en* with full details (*od* particulars); *auf ~~en eingehen* to go into details; *betreffs weiterer ~~en* as to further details; **~kampf** *m* single combat; hand-to-hand fight; *aero mil* dog-fight; *sport* individual match; **~krad** *n* solo motorcycle; **~kunde** *m com* retail customer; **~leben** *n* individual life; solitary life; **~leistung** *f* individual performance; **~nummer** *f* (*Zeitung etc*) copy; **~person** *f* individual; **~prokura** *f com* power of procuration; **~schuß** *m* single shot (*od* round); **~schütze** *m* unattached rifleman; **~spiel** *n* (*Tennis*) single; **~stehend** *a* solitary; detached; **~stimme** *f* solo; **~tanz** *m* solo dance; **~teil** *n* component (part), prefabricated parts *pl*; **~unterricht** *m* individual tuition; **~verkauf** *m* sale by retail; (*von Zeitschriften*) sale of single numbers;

~wesen *n* individual; **~wurf** *m* (*Bombe*) dropping of single bomb, single release; **~zeichnung** *f* detail drawing; **~zelle** *f* single cell; (*Haft*) isolation cell; **~ziel** *n mil* point target; **~zimmer** *n* (*Hotel*) single (-bedded) room.

einzellig *a* monocellular; unicellular, single-celled.

einzeln *a* single; (*für sich allein*) individual, isolated; (*abgetrennt*) separate, detached; (*Schuh, Handschuh etc*) odd; *adv* singly, separately; one by one, in detail; *~ angeben* to particularize; *~ aufführen* to specify; *~ verkaufen* to sell by retail; **~e(r)** *m* (*f*) the individual (man *od* woman); *jeder ~e* each and every one; *im ~en* in detail.

einzieh|bar *a* (*eintreibbar*) recoverable, collectible; *aero* retractable; *~~er Antennenmast* retractable aerial mast; *~~es Fahrgestell* retractable landing gear, retractable undercarriage; *~~e Räder* retractable wheels; **~en** *irr tr* (*Kabel*) to draw in, to pull in; (*Faden*) to thread a needle; (*Gebühren, Steuern, Miete*) to collect (*von* from); (*zurückziehen*) to draw back; (*Segel*) to furl (*od* to lower) the sails; (*Flagge*) to strike, to haul down; *aero* (*Fahrgestell*) to retract; (*Antenne*) to wind (*od* to reel) in; (*Wechsel*) to cash, to collect; (*einsaugen*) to suck in; to absorb; (*Papiergeld*) to withdraw; (*Münzen*) to call in; (*Zeile*) *typ* to indent; (*beschlagnahmen*) to seize, to confiscate; *mil* to call up (for duty), to call out, *Am* to draft, to induct; (*Erkundigungen*) to make inquiries, to get (*od* gather) information; *itr* (*hineingehen*) to enter, to march into; (*Wohnung*) to move in(to); to go to live (*bei* with); (*Wasser*) to soak in; **~fahrgestell, ~fahrwerk** *n aero* retractable landing gear, retractable undercarriage; **~ung** *f* drawing in; (*Geld, Steuern*) collection, cashing; (*von Münzen*) withdrawing; (*zum Militär*) induction (into the army), drafting, calling up; (*Beschlagnahme*) confiscation, seizure.

einzig *a* only, sole, single; *der ~e Erbe* the sole heir; (*ohnegleichen*) unique; *~ dastehen* to be unique; *adv: ~ u. allein* simply and solely; entirely; only; **~artig** *a* unique; *e-e ~~e Gelegenheit* a unique chance.

einzuckern *tr* to sugar.

Einzug *m* (*in Raum*) entry, entrance; (*Haus*) move, moving in; (*Geld*) collection; *typ* indention; **~sfest** *n*, **~sschmaus** *m* house-warming (party).

einzwängen *tr* to force in, to squeeze in, to wedge in; *fig* to constrain.

Einzylinder *m* one- (*od* single-) cylinder motor (*od* engine).

Eis *n* ice; (*Speise~, Sahne~, Gefrorenes*) ice-cream, *Am* ice, sundae; (*zwischen zwei Waffeln*) slider; (*in konischer Waffeltüte*) ice-cream cornet, *Am* ice-cream cone; *in, auf ~ kühlen, legen, mit ~ bedecken* to ice; *mit ~ bedeckt* (*od gekühlt*) iced; *zu ~ werden* (*Wasser*) to turn into ice; *vom ~ eingeschlossen* ice-bound, ice-locked; (*Schiff*) an ice-bound vessel; (*Küste, Hafen*) an ice-bound coast, an ice-bound harbo(u)r; *das ~ brechen* (*fig*) to break the ice; *aufs ~ legen* (*zurückstellen*) to put into cold storage; *sich auf dünnes ~ wagen* (*fig: etw Heikles tun*) to skate on thin ice; **~bahn** *f* ice-rink, skating-rink, (*künstliche ~~*) artificial skating-rink; **~bank** *f* field of ice; **~bär** *m* ice-bear, white bear, polar bear; **~bedeckt** *a* ice-covered; **~bein** *n* (*Gericht*) pig's knuckle; pickled pork trotters *pl*; **~berg** *m* (*schwimmender*) iceberg; **~beutel** *m med* rubber bag in which cracked ice is put, ice-bag; (*für Kopf*) ice-cap; **~bildung** *f* ice-formation (*an Flugzeugen* on aircraft); **~blink** *m* iceblink; **~blume** *f* ice-fern; ice-flower, frost-flower; **~bombe** *f* (*aus Speise~*) ice-bomb; ice-pudding; **~brecher** *m* (*Schiff*) ice-breaker; (*an Brücken*) ice-apron, ice-guard; **~decke** *f* ice-sheet; **~diele** *f Am* ice-cream parlo(u)r; **~druck** *m* ice pressure; **~en** *tr* to cut the ice; **~fabrik** *f* ice(-making) plant; **~feld** *n* ice-field; (*Pack~*) ice-pack; **~frei** *a* ice-free; **~fuchs** *m* ice-fox; **~gang** *m* drifting of the ice, breaking up (and floating) of ice; **~gekühlt** *a* ice-cooled; *~~e Flasche* iced bottle; **~glas** *n* frosted glass, crackle glass; **~grau** *a* hoary with age; **~gürtel** *m* (*an der arktischen Küste*) ice-foot, ice-belt; **~händler** *m* ice-dealer, *Am* iceman; (*die drei*) **~heiligen** *m pl* the 11th, 12th and 13th of May; **~hockey** *n* ice-hockey; **~hockeyscheibe** *f* puck; **~ig** *a* icy, frigid; *fig* chilly; **~kaffee** *m* iced coffee; mocha; **~kalt** *a* ice-cold, icy cold; **~kasten** *m* ice-box; **~kegeln** *n sport* curling; **~keller** *m* ice-cellar, ice-house (*od* pit); **~krem** *m* cream ice, *Am* ice-cream; **~kühler** *m* ice-pail; **~lauf** *m sport* skating; **~laufbahn** *f* skating-rink; **~laufen** *irr itr* to skate, to ice-skate; **~läufer** *m* skater; **~laufmeisterschaft** *f* figure-skating championship; **~maschine** *f* refrigerator, freezer, freezing apparatus, ice-machine, ice-maker, (*zur Herstellung von Speise~*) ice-cream freezer; **~meer** *n* polar sea; *nördliches ~~* the Arctic (Ocean); *südliches ~~* the Antarctic (Ocean); **~nadeln** *f pl* (*Meteorologie*) ice needles *pl*; **~pickel** *m* ice-axe; ice-pick; **~pudding** *m* ice-pudding; **~punkt** *m* (*Gefrierpunkt*) freezing point; **~scholle** *f* (*treibende*) ice-floe; flake of ice; **~schrank** *m* (automatic) refrigerator; *Am* icebox; ice-chest, ice-safe; **~segelboot** *n* ice-boat, ice-yacht; **~sport** *m* ice- sports *pl*; **~vogel** *m orn* kingfisher; **~wasser** *n* iced water, *Am* ice water; **~würfel** *m* (*für Getränke etc*) ice-cube; **~zapfen** *m* icicle; **~zeit** *f* glacial period (*od* epoch), ice-age.

Eisen *n* iron; (*Bügel~*) flat-iron; (*Huf~*) horseshoe; (*Werkzeug etc*) iron instrument; iron implement; iron tool; *~ (in Zssg)* iron, ferro-, ferruginous; (*Roh~*) pig (iron); (*Schmiede~*) forging steel; (*Guß~*) cast iron; *altes ~* scrap iron; *weiches ~* soft iron; *T-~* tee-iron, T-iron; *U-~* channel iron, U-iron; *Z-~* Z-iron; *ein Mann von ~* a man of iron; *in ~ (gefesselt)* in iron; *~ entziehen Am* to deironize; *mit ~ beschlagen* to iron; *zum alten ~ werfen* to throw away as useless; to scrap; *Not bricht ~* necessity knows no law; *mehrere ~ im Feuer haben* to have several strings to o.'s bow, to have several irons in the fire; *zu viele ~ im Feuer haben* to have too many irons in the fire; *das ~ schmieden, solange es heiß ist* to strike the iron while it is hot; **~abfälle** *m pl* iron scrap, iron refuse; **~arm** *a* poor in iron; **~artig** *a* iron-like; **~band** *n* iron hoop; **~bau** *m* iron (*od* steel) structure; **~bergwerk** *n* iron-mine, iron-pit; **~beschläge** *m pl* iron-mountings *pl*, iron-fittings *pl*; **~beschlagen, ~bewehrt** *a* iron-bound, iron-clad; **~beton** *m* reinforced (*od* armo(u)red) concrete; **~blech** *n* sheet iron; iron-plate; **~draht** *m* iron wire, steel wire; **~erz** *n* iron-ore; **~erzgrube** *f* iron-ore mine; **~erzlager** *n* iron deposits *pl*; **~farbig** *a* iron-colo(u)red; **~feilspäne** *m pl* iron-filings *pl*; **~fresser** *m fig* bully, braggart, vain boaster; **~gehalt** *m* iron content; **~gießer** *m* iron-founder; **~gießerei** *f* iron-foundry; **~gitter** *n* iron-grate, steel grate; iron bars pl; iron grille; **~gittermast** *m* steel-lattice mast; **~grube** *f* iron-mine, iron-pit; **~guß** *m* (*Werkstück*) iron-casting; (*Werkstoff*) cast iron; **~haltig** *a* ferruginous; **~hammer** *m*, **~hütte**, **~schmiede** *f* iron-forge, iron-mill; **~handel** *m* iron-trade; ironmongery, *Am* hardware trade; **~händler** *m* ironmonger, *Am* dealer in hardware; **~handlung** *f* ironmongery, *Am* hardware store; **~hart** *a* hard as iron; **~hochbau** *m* steel superstructure *pl*; **~hut** *m bot* aconite, monkshood; **~hütte** *f* iron-mill, iron-works *mit pl u. sing*; forge; **~hüttenbesitzer** *m* iron-master; **~industrie** *f* iron-trade; **~konstruktion** *f* iron construction; **~oxyd** *n* ferric oxide, iron-oxide; **~platte** *f* iron plate; (*Panzerung*) armo(u)r plate; **~pulver** *n* iron powder, iron dust; **~rohr** *n* (*gezogen*) iron tube; (*Leitung*) iron pipe; **~rost** *m* iron grate; **~schmied** *m* blacksmith, ironsmith; **~stab** *m* iron bar; **~stange** *f* steel rod; **~träger** *m* steel girder; (*unbearbeitet*) steel beam; **~verbindung** *f* iron compound; **~vitriol** *n* iron vitriol; **~walzwerk** *n* iron-rolling mill; **~waren** *f pl* ironmongery, iron-ware, *Am* hardware; **~warenhandlung** *f* ironmonger's shop, *Am* hardware store; **~werk** *n* iron-works *mit pl u. sing*; iron-forge; **~zeit** *f* iron age.

Eisenbahn *f* railway, train, *Am* railroad; *mit der ~ befördern* to send by rail, *Am* to railroad; *mit der ~ reisen* to travel by rail; *eingleisige ~* single-track railway, *zweigleisige ~* double-track railway; **~abteil** *n* railway-compartment, coupé; **~aktie** *f* railway-share, *Am* railroad stock; **~anlage** *f* railway installation; **~anschluß** *m* railway junction, siding; **~arbeiter** *m* railway-man, gangman, *Am* rail worker; **~aufmarsch** *m mil* assembly by rail, strategic concentration by rail; **~ausbesserungswerk** *n* railway repair shop, *Am* railroad shop; **~bau** *m* railway construction; **~baubataillon** *n mil* railway construction battalion; **~beamte(r)** *m* railway official (*od* clerk), *Am* railroad employee (*od* executive); **~betrieb** *m* railway service; **~betriebskompanie** *f mil* railway operating company; **~betriebsmaterial** *n* rolling-stock; **~damm** *m* embankment, trackway; **~direktion** *f* railway board; **~endstation** *f* railway terminus, *Am* railroad terminal; railhead; **~er** *m* railway-official, railway-man, *Am* railroader, railroadman; **~ergewerkschaft** *f* railway union, *Am* (railroad) brotherhood; **~fähre** *f* train ferry; **~fahrplan** *m* railway time table, *Am* railroad schedule; **~fahrt** *f* railway journey; **~flak** *f* railway anti-aircraft gun, railway A. A. gun; **~geschütz** *n* railway gun; **~gesellschaft** *f* railway-company, *Am* railroad corporation; **~gleis** *n* track; **~haubitze** *f* railway howitzer; **~karte** *f* railway ticket; **~knotenpunkt** *m* railway junction; **~kreuzung** *f* railway crossing; **~kursbuch** *n* railway guide; **~linie** *f* (railway-) line; **~material** *n* (*rollendes*) rolling-stock; **~nachschublinie** *f mil* railway supply line; **~netz** *n* railway network; **~oberbau** *m* railway superstructure; **~panzerzug** *m* armo(u)red train; **~pioniere** *m pl* railway engineers *pl*; **~reisender** *m* rail passenger; **~schaffner** *m* guard, *Am* conductor; **~schiene** *f* rail; **~schranke** *f* railway-gate; **~schwelle** *f* sleeper, *Am* tie; **~signal** *n* railway signal; **~station** *f* railway-station, *Am* depot; **~stellwerk** *n* switch control room; **~strecke** *f* (railway) line, *Am* road; **~tankwagen** *m* tank car; **~tarif** *m* railway tariff, *Am* railroad-rate schedule; **~transport** *m* railway conveyance; *mil* movement by rail; **~transportverkehr** *m* rail transport, *Am* rail freight traffic; **~überführung** *f* railway over-pass; **~übergang** *m* (*schienengleich*) level crossing; **~unglück** *n* railway accident, train disaster; **~unterführung** *f* railway underpass; **~verbindung** *f* communication by rail, connection; **~verkehr** *m* railway traffic; **~verkehrsamt** *n* railway transportation office, *Abk* R T O; **~verwaltung** *f* railway management, railway board; **~wagen** *m* railway-carriage, *Am* railroad car (*od* coach); (*Personen*) passenger coach; (*Schlafwagen*) Pullman (car); (*für Güter*) wag(g)on, truck, *Am* freight-car; (*für Schüttgut*) mineral-wag(g)on, *Am* gondola; **~wärter** *m* linekeeper; **~wegschranke** *f* barrier (*od* gate) of railway; **~zug** *m* (railway) train; *Am* the cars.

eisern *a* iron, made of iron; *fig* strong, durable, hard; inflexible; *~er Bestand* permanent (*od* reserve) fund (*od* stock); *~er Fleiß* unweary zeal (*od* industry); *~e Gesundheit* iron health; *~e Lunge med* iron lung; *~e Ration mil* iron ration, *Am bes.* D ration; *das E~e Tor geog* the Iron Gate(s); *~er Vorhang theat* safety curtain, fireproof curtain; (*zwischen dem russisch kontrollierten Gebiet u. dem Westen*) iron curtain.

eitel *a* conceited; (*nichtig*) vain; useless, futile, hollow; (*weltlich*) frivolous; fallacious; (*lauter, bloß*) mere, nothing but; pure; *~ Gold* pure gold; *das Leben ist nicht ~ Freud* life is not all beer and skittles; *~es Geschwätz* idle talk; *~e Träume* empty dreams; **~keit** *f* vanity, vainness.

Eiter *m* matter, pus; **~beule** *f* abscess, boil; **~ig** *a* purulent; festering; **~n** *itr* to suppurate; to fester; *die Wunde eitert* the wound is festering; **~stock** *m* core of a boil; **~ung** *f* suppuration.

Ekel *m* distaste, aversion; (*mit Brechreiz*) nausea; (*Person*) loathsome person, nasty fellow; *~ erregen* to disgust; **~haft, ~ig** *a* loathsome, disgustful; repulsive, revolting; nasty; **~n** *itr* to sicken, to disgust; *imp es ekelt mich* I am disgusted with; *sich ~n* to be disgusted at, to feel disgusted; to loathe.

Eksta|se *f* ecstasy; **~tisch** *a* ecstatic.

Ekzem *n med* eczema.

Elan *m* (*Schwung*) vitality, vim, verve; dash; pluck; guts *pl*, *Am* pep, zip.

elast|isch *a* elastic; (*beweglich*) mobile; **~izität** *f* elasticity; (*Metall*) ductility; *~~ des Geistes* buoyancy.

Elch *m* elk, *Am* moose.

Elefant *m* elephant; **~enführer** *m* cornac; **~enkrankheit** *f* (*Elefantiasis*) elephantiasis; **~enlaus** *f* (*Frucht des Nierenbaums*) cashew nut; **~enrüssel** *m* trunk; **~enzahn** *m* elephant's tooth (*od* tusk).

eleg|ant *a* elegant; stylish, fashionable, modish; smart, chic; dapper, spruce; *sl* nobby, *Am sl* nifty, snazzy, swank; **~anz** *f* elegance; fashionableness; stylishness.

Eleg|ie *f* elegy; **~isch** *a* elegiac; *fig* melancholy.

elektri|fizieren *tr* to electrify; **~fizierung** *f* electrification; **~ker** *m* (*Installateur*) electrician; (*Elektrotechniker*) electrotechnician, electrical engineer.

elektrisch *a* (*strom- od spannungführend; meist*) electric; (*bei Vokal; zur Kennzeichnung der ~en Eigenschaften u. bei allgemeinen Begriffen*) electrical; *negativ ~* negatively electric; *positiv ~* positively electric; *~ betreiben* to run by electricity; *~ betätigt* electrically operated; *~ verstellbar* electrically controlled; *~e Anlage* electric installation; *~er Antrieb* electric drive; *~e (Schallplatten-)Aufnahme* electrical transcription; *~e Bahn* electric railway; *~e Energie* electrical energy; *~es Feld* electrical field; *~es Heizkissen* electric cushion; *~er Kontakt* electric contact; *~e Kraftübertragung* electric power transmission; *~e Ladung* electric charge; *~es Licht* electric light; *~e Maschine* electrical machine; *~er Ofen* electric furnace; *~er Rasierapparat* electric shaver; *~er Strom* electric current; *~er Stromkreis* electric circuit; *~er Sturm* electric storm; *~e Taschenlampe* electric pocket lamp, electric torch; *~er Unfall* electric accident; *~e Zelle* electric cell; **~e** *f fam* (*Straßenbahn*) *fam* the tram, the electric; electric car, electric tramway; *Am* streetcar, electric trolley, street railway, (*in New York*) surface car.

elektrisier|bar *a* electrifiable; **~en** *tr* (*auch fig*) to electrify; to electrize; **~maschine** *f* electrostatic machine (*od* generator); (*für therapeutische Zwecke*) electrizer; **~ung** *f* electrification; electrization.

Elektrizität *f* electricity; (*Strom*) current, *Am fam* juice; *atmosphärische ~* atmospheric electricity; *Berührungs~* contact electricity; *freie ~* free electricity; *galvanische ~* galvanic electricity; *negative od Harz~* negative *od* resinous electricity; *positive od Glas~* positive *od* vitreous electricity; *Induktions~* induced electricity; *magnetische ~* magnetic electricity; *Reibungs~* frictional electricity, electricity of friction; *Thermo~* thermo (*od* thermal) electricity; *strahlende ~* radiating electricity; **~sentladung** *f* electric discharge; **~sgesellschaft** *f* electric company; **~sladung** *f* electric charge; **~sleiter** *m* electric conductor; **~smenge** *f* quantity of electricity; **~smesser** *m* electrometer; **~smessung** *f* electrometry; **~squelle** *f* source of electricity; **~sversorgung** *f* electric supply; **~swerk** *n* (*Kraftwerk*) power station, electricity works *pl*; (*Maschinenanlage*) power plant; **~szähler** *m* electric supply meter; electricity meter; **~sanzeiger** *m* electroscope.

Elektro|analyse *f* electroanalysis; **~antrieb** *m* electric traction; **~artikel** *m pl*, **~bedarfsartikel** *m pl* electrical supplies *pl* (*od* appliances *pl*); **~biologie** *f* electro-biology; **~bohrer** *m* electric drill; **~chemie** *f* electro-chemistry; **~chemisch** *a* electro-chemical; **~diagnose** *f med* electrodiagnosis; **~dynamik** *f* electrodynamics *pl mit sing*; **~dynamisch** *a* electrodynamic(al); *~~er Lautsprecher* dynamic loud speaker, moving-coil loud speaker; **~dynamometer** *n* electrodynamometer; **~galvanisch** *a* electrogalvanic; **~hängebahn** *f* telpher line; **~herd** *m* electric range, electric cooker; **~induktion** *f* electroinduction; **~industrie** *f* electrical industry; **~ingenieur** *m* electrical engineer; **~installateur** *m* electrician; **~kardiogramm** *n med* electrocardiogram; **~kardiograph** *m med* electrocardiograph; **~karren** *m* electric truck, electric trolley; **~kühlschrank** *m* electric refrigerator; **~lyse** *f* electrolysis; **~lyt** *m* electrolyte; **~lyteisen** *n* electrolytic iron; **~lytgleichrichter** *m* electrolytic rectifier; **~lytisch** *a* electrolytic(al); **~magnet** *m* electromagnet; **~magnetisch** *a* electromagnetic(al); **~magnetismus** *m* electromagnetism; **~mechanik** *f* electromechanics; **~mechaniker** *m* electrician; **~mechanisch** *a* electromechanic(al); **~metallurgie** *f* electrometallurgy; **~meter** *n* electrometer; **~mobil** *n* electromobile, electric motorcar; **~motor** *m* electromotor, (electric) motor; **~motorisch** *a* electromotive; (*angetrieben*) electrically driven; *~~er Antrieb* electric motor drive; *~~e Kraft* (*Abk*: E M K) electromotive force (*Abk*: E. M. F.); **~ofen** *m* electric furnace; **~phor** *m* electrophore, electrophorus; **~plastik** *f* electroplating; **~schweißung** *f* electric welding; **~skop** *n* electroscope; **~stahl** *m* electric steel; **~statik** *f* electrostatics *pl*; **~statisch** *a* electrostatic(al); **~technik** *f* (*Wissenschaft*) electrotechnics, electrotechnology; (*Industrie*) electrical engineering; **~techniker** *m* electrotechnician; electrical engineer; electrician; **~technisch** *a* electrotechnic(al); **~therapeutik, ~therapie** *f med* electrotherapeutics, electrotherapy; electropathy; **~thermisch** *a* electrothermal, electrothermic; **~typie** *f* electrotype, *Abk* electro; **~werkzeug** *n* electric tool.

Elektrode *f* electrode; *negative ~* cathode; *positive ~* anode; *Schweiß~* welding electrode; **~nabstand** *m* electrode spacing.

Elektron *n* (*negatives elektrisches Elementarquantum*) electron; (*Leichtmetallegierung*) electron; *freies ~* free electron; *langsames ~* low-velocity electron; *schnelles ~* high-velocity electron; *kreisendes ~* orbital electron; *positives ~* positive electron, positron; *schweres ~* heavy electron, mesotron, X particle; **~brandbombe** *f* electron incendiary bomb; **~enaufprall** *m* cathodic bombardment; **~enaussendung** *f* electron emission; **~enbahn** *f* electron(ic) path (*od* orbit); **~enbeschießung** *f* electron(ic) bombardment; **~enbild** *n* electron image; **~enbildwerfer** *m* electron image projector; **~enemission** *f* electron emission; **~enentladung** *f* electron discharge; **~enfluß** *m* electron flow; **~engeschwindigkeit** *f* electron velocity; **~enherd** *m* electronic range; **~eningenieur** *m* electronic engineer; **~enkopplung** *f* electronic coupling; **~enküche** *f* electronic kitchen; **~enlinse** *f* electron(ic) lens; **~enmikroskop** *n* electron microscope; **~enoptik** *f* electron optics *pl*; **~enrechenmaschine** *f* electronic computer; **~enröhre** *f* electron(ic) valve, thermionic valve, high-vacuum valve, *Am* electron(ic) tube; **~enröhrengleichrichter** *m* electronic rectifier; **~enschalter** *m* electronic switch; **~enschleuder** *f* electron gun; (*Betatron*) *Am* betatron; **~enstrahl** *m* electron beam, electronic ray;

~enstrahlabtaster *m tele* iconoscope; **~enstrahlerzeuger** *m* electron gun; **~enstrahlung** *f* electronic radiation; **~enstoß** *m* electronic collision (*od* impact); **~enstrom** *m* electronic current; **~entechnik** *f* electronic engineering; **~enübermikroskop** *n* electronic supermicroscope; **~enunterhülle** *f* subshell; **~envervielfacher** *m* electron multiplier; **~enwolke** *f* cloud of electrons; **~ik** *f* (*die Wissenschaft von den Elektronen u. deren Anwendungsgebiete*) electronics *pl mit sing*); **~iker** *m* electronics engineer; **~isch** *a* electronic; **~metall** *n* electron metal; **~volt** *n* (*Abk*: *eV*, *Energiemaß*) electron volt.

Element *n* (*Grundstoff*) element; *el* cell, pile; (*Zelle*) battery; (*Einzelteil*) part, element; *galvanisches* ~ galvanic cell; *nasses* ~ fluid (*od* wet) cell; *Trocken~* dry cell; *in seinem* ~ at home; in his element; **~ar** *a* elementary; first; (*heftig*) elemental, violent; *~are Bedürfnisse* elementary (*od* primary) wants; **~arbuch** *n* primer, elementary book; **~argewalt** *f* elemental power; **~arklasse** *f* junior class (*od* form); **~arlehrer** *m* primary teacher; **~arquantum** *n phys* atomic charge; **~arschule** *f* primary (*od* elementary) school; **~arunterricht** *m* elementary education; **~arwelle** *f radio* elementary wave.

Elen, **~tier** *n* elk

Elend *n* (*Not*) misery, distress, need, destitution; (*Bedrängnis*) affliction; (*Unglück*) wretchedness; (*Armut*) poverty; penury; *ins* ~ *bringen* to reduce s. o. to misery; *ins* ~ *geraten* to sink into poverty; *im größten* ~ *leben* to live in utter misery; ~ *a* miserable, distressful; (*schlecht*) wretched; (*jämmerlich*) pitiful; *sich* ~ *fühlen* to feel wretched (*vor* with), to feel miserable; to feel seedy; *Am fam* to feel mean; ~ *aussehen* to look ill; **~e(r)** *m* wretch; **~iglich** *adv* miserably; wretchedly; **~sgebiet** *n* distressed (*od* special) area; **~sviertel** *n* (*e-r Stadt*) slums *pl*.

Elevator *m* (*Getreide~*) elevator; (*Aufzug*) lift, *Am* elevator; (*Lastenaufzug*) hoist.

Elf *m* goblin; **~e** *f* elf, fairy; **~enkönig** *m* king of the fairies; Oberon; **~enkönigin** *f* queen of fairyland; Titania; **~enreich** *n* fairyland, fairy kingdom; **~enreigen** *m* fairy-dance.

elf *a* eleven; **~fach** *a* elevenfold; **~metermarke** *f* (*Fußball*) penalty spot; **~te** *a* eleventh; **~tel** *n* eleventh part.

Elfenbein *n* ivory; **~drechsler** *m* ivory-turner; **~ern** *a* ivory; ivorylike; **~farbig** *a* ivory-colo(u)red; **~gelb** *n* ivory yellow; **~küste** *f geog* Ivory Coast; **~schwarz** *n* ivory black; **~weiß** *a* ivory-white.

eliminieren *tr* to eliminate.

Elisabeth *f* Elizabeth; **~anisch** *a* Elizabethan.

Elite *f* (*das Auserlesene, die Oberschicht*) the elite, the cream, the pick, the flower, the choice; the best of s. th.; **~einheit** *f mil fam* crack unit; **~truppen** *f pl* picked troops *pl*; *fam* crack troops *pl*.

Elixier *n* elixir.

Ellbogen *m* elbow; *mit den* ~ *stoßen* to elbow; **~freiheit** *f* (*Spielraum*) elbow-room; **~knochen** *m* funny-bone, *Am* crazy-bone.

Elle *f* yard, ell; *anat* ulna; **~nlang** *a* one ell in length; *fig* very long; **~nmaß** *n* ell; **~nweise** *adv* by the ell.

Ellip|se *f* ellipse; *gram* ellipsis; **~tisch** *a* elliptical.

Elmsfeuer *n* St. Elmo's fire; corposant, brush discharge.

Elritze *f* minnow.

Elsaß *n* Alsace; **Elsässer(in)** *m* (*f*) Alsatian; **elsässisch** *a* Alsatian; **~-Lothringen** *n* Alsace-Lorraine.

Else *f* (*Fisch*) shad.

Elster *f* magpie.

elter|lich *a* parental; *~~e Gewalt* parental power (*od* authority); **~n** *pl* parents *pl*; **~nhaus** *n* parental home; **~nliebe** *f* parental love; **~nlos** *a* parentless, orphaned; **~nmörder** *m* parricide; **~nrat** *m* Parents' Council; **~nvereinigung** *f Am* Parents Association; (*mit der Lehrerschaft*) *Am* Parent-Teacher Association (*Abk* P.T.A.).

Email *n*, ***Emaille*** *f* enamel; **~arbeiter** *m* enamel(l)er; **~belag** *m* coating of enamel; **~draht** *m* enamel(l)ed wire; **~farbe** *f* enamel paint (*od* colo(u)r); **~gefäß** *n* enamel(l)ed vessel; **~geschirr** *n* enamel-ware; **~lack** *m* enamel varnish; **~lieren** *tr* to enamel; **~lierofen** *m* enamel(l)ing furnace (*od* kiln); **~lierung** *f* enamel(l)ing; **~schild** *n* enamel sign.

Emanation *f chem* emanation; *Radium~* (*Radon*) radium emanation.

Emanzip|ation *f* emancipation; **~ieren** *tr* to emancipate.

Embargo *n* embargo; *mit* ~ *belegen* to embargo; to lay (*od* put) an embargo on.

Embolie *f* (*Blutaderverstopfung*) *med* embolism.

Embryo *m* embryo(n); fetus; **~logie** *f* embryology; **~nal** *a* embryonal; embryonic; *im ~nalzustand* in embryo.

Emigr|ant *m* refugee; *pol* emigrant; **~ation** *f* emigration; **~ieren** *itr* to emigrate.

Emission *f phys* (*Elektronen*) emission; *thermische* ~ thermionic emission; thermal radiation; *com* issue, issuance; **~sfähigkeit** *f phys* emissivity; **~sgeschwindigkeit** *f phys* velocity of emission; **~skurs** *m com* rate of issue; **~sstrom** *m phys* electronic current; **~svermögen** *n phys* emissive power; **emittieren** *tr phys* to emit; *com* to issue.

Emmentaler *m* (*Käse*) Swiss cheese, Emmental cheese.

Empfang *m* (*von Personen u. durch radio*) reception; (*Willkomm*) welcome; (*von Sachen*) receipt; delivery; *bei* ~ on receipt; (*Waren*) on delivery; *in* ~ *nehmen* to receive; *den* ~ *bescheinigen* (*od bestätigen*) to acknowledge receipt; *nach* ~ after receipt; *auf* ~ *bleiben* (*radio*) to stand by; *drahtloser* ~ wireless reception; *Fern~* long distance reception; **~en** *irr tr* (*erhalten, radio*) to receive; to get; (*abfangen, bes. auch radio*) to intercept; (*annehmen*) to accept; (*willkommen heißen*) to welcome; (*sehen*) to see; *itr* (*Kind*) to conceive; to become pregnant; **~santenne** *f* receiving aerial (*od* antenna); **~sanzeige, ~sbescheinigung, ~sbestätigung** *f com* receipt; acknowledg(e)ment (of receipt); notification of delivery; **~sapparat** *m radio* receiving-set (*od* apparatus); receiver; **~sbereich** *m radio* reception area; **~sbüro** *n* (*im Hotel*) reception office, *Am* hotel desk; **~schef** *m* (*Hotel*) reception-clerk, *Am* room clerk; **~sdame** *f*, **~sherr** *m* (*bei Arzt, Photograph etc*) receptionist; **~sfunkstelle** *f* receiving station; **~sgerät** *n radio* receiving-set; **~sschein** *m* receipt; **~sstärke** *f* receiving intensity; **~sstation** *f* (*Bahnhof*) point of destination; *radio* receiving station; **~sstörung** *f* receiving disturbance; *radio* jammings *pl*; (*atmosphärisch*) statics *pl*, atmospherics *pl*; **~stag** *m* at-home (day); (*bei Hof*) levee; **~strennschärfe** *f* selectivity, *Am* sharp tuning; **~sverhältnisse** *n pl radio* receiving conditions *pl*; **~sverstärker** *m radio* reception amplifier; **~sverteiler** *m* wholesale distributor; **~sversuch** *m* reception test; **~swelle** *f* receiving wave; **~szimmer** *n* reception-room, drawing-room, parlo(u)r, *Am* receiving ward.

Empfäng|er *m* receiver, recipient; (*Waren*) consignee; (*e-s Briefes*) addressee; (*Telegramm*) destinator; (*Wechsel*) acceptor; *radio* (*Apparat*) receiving-set, *Am* radio set; receiver; *tragbarer* ~~ portable; **~erempfindlichkeit** *f radio* receiver sensitivity; **~ergehäuse** *n radio* cabinet; **~erröhre** *f* receiving valve, cut-off tube, *Am* receiving tube; **~lich** *a* susceptible (*für* of); alive (*für* to); responsive (*für* to); sensible; sensitive (*für* to); conceptive; impressionable; **~lichkeit** *f* susceptibility, sensibility, receptivity; **~nis** *f* conception; **~nisverhütend** *a* contraceptive; *~~es Mittel* contraceptive, agent for the prevention of conception; **~nisverhütung** *f* contraception; **~niszeit** *f* period of possible conception.

empfehl|en *irr tr* to (re)commend (to); to advise; *der Arzt empfiehlt e-e Luftveränderung* the doctor advises a change of air; *com* to introduce, to sponsor; (*grüßen*) to remember; *~en Sie mich Ihrer Frau* remember me (*od* give my regards) to Mrs. X. (*fam* your wife); *sich ~en* to recommend o. s. to; to present o.'s compliments to; *ich ~e mich Ihnen* I present my best respects to you; (*verabschieden*) to take leave, to bid farewell to; *fam* (*ohne Abschied, heimlich*) to take French leave, to make a hasty exit; *es empfiehlt sich, daß* it is (re)commendable to, it is advisable to; **~enswert** *a* (re)commendable; **~ung** *f* recommendation; (*Referenz, Zeugnis*) reference; testimonial; (*Grüße*) compliments *pl*; *auf* ~~ on recommendation; *meine ~~ zu Hause!* remember me to all at home! **~ungsbrief** *m*, **~ungsschreiben** *n* letter of recommendation, letter of introduction; reference letter.

empfind|bar *a* perceptible, sensible; **~~keit** *f* perceptibility, sensibleness; **~elei** *f* sentimentality; **~en** *irr tr* to be sensible of; (*fühlen*) to feel; (*erleben*) to experience; **~lich** *a* sensible to, sensitive; (*zart*) delicate; (*leicht verletzt*) touchy; (*reizbar*) irritable; (*schmerzlich*) grievous; (*Kälte*) biting; **~~keit** *f* sensibleness, irritability; touchiness; (*Feingefühl, Empfindungsfähigkeit*) sensitiveness, sensitivity; grievousness; **~sam** *a* sentimental; sensitive; **~~keit** *f* sentimentality; **~ung** *f* feeling; sentiment; sensation; (*Wahrnehmung*) perception; **~~slos** *a* insensible; unfeeling; **~~svermögen** *n* perceptive faculty.

empor *adv* (up)wards, *poet* on high; **~arbeiten** *r* to work o.'s way up; **~blicken** *itr* to look up; **~bringen** *irr tr* to raise; **~e, ~kirche** *f* church-gallery; choir-loft; **~heben** *irr tr* to lift up, to raise; **~kommen** *irr itr* to get up, to rise; **~kömmling** *m* upstart; **~ragen** *itr* to tower, to rise up; **~schauen** *itr* to look up; **~schießen** *irr itr* to gush up; (*wie ein Pilz*) to mushroom up; **~schnellen** *itr* to jerk up; **~schrauben**: *sich* ~~ (*aero*) to soar up, to spiral up;

~schweben *itr* to soar up; **~schwingen** *irr r* to rise aloft; **~steigen** *irr itr* to mount; **~treiben** *irr tr* to drive up (-wards).

empör|en *tr* to raise, to stir up, to revolt, to shock s. o.'s feelings; *sich ~~* to rebel against; (*wütend sein*) to be furious (about); **~end** *a* shocking; **~er** *m* mutineer, rebel, revolter; **~erisch** *a* rebellious, mutinous; **~t** *a* indignant, up in arms, scandalized (*über* at); rebellious; **~ung** *f* rebellion, revolt, insurrection; (*Entrüstung*) indignation.

emsig *a* (*geschäftig*) busy; (*fleißig*) industrious; (*eifrig*) diligent; eager; (*unermüdlich*) assiduous; (*ausdauernd*) sedulous; (*schwerarbeitend*) hard-working; **~keit** *f* assiduity; diligence; industry; eagerness; activity.

End|- *in Zssg*: final, terminal; **~absicht** *f* final design (*od* aim), ultimate design; **~ausbeute** *f* final yield; **~bahnhof** *m* terminus, railhead; *Am* terminal; **~bescheid** *m* definite answer; *jur* final judg(e)ment (*od* sentence *od* decision); **~buchstabe** *m* final letter; **~chen** *n* end, bit; **~e** *n* (*räumlich*) end; (*äußerstes*) extremity; (*unten am Tisch, auf der Seite*) at the bottom; (*zeitlich*) end; (*Geweih~e*) antler; (*Schluß*) close; (*Ausgang*) issue, conclusion, upshot, result; (*Schluß, Abwicklung*) winding-up, *Am* windup; (*Zweck*) purpose, aim, goal; (*Tod*) death; (*dickes ~e von Balken, Baum*) butt; *~e gut, alles gut* all's well that ends well; *am ~e* in the end, after all; in the upshot, in the long run; *zu ~e* over; *der Vortrag ist zu ~e* the lecture is over; *zu dem ~e* to that purpose; *von Anfang bis ~e* from start to finish; (*Buch*) from cover to cover; *zu ~e bringen* to bring to an end, to terminate; *zu ~e gehen* (*Vorräte*) to run short; to come to an end; *ein ~e haben* (*od nehmen*) to come to an end; *letzten ~es* after all; *das dicke ~e kommt nach* the worst is yet to come; *mit seiner Kunst zu ~e sein* to be at o.'s wits' end; *an allen Ecken u. ~en* all over the place; **~en, ~igen** *itr* to finish, to come to an end; *gram* to terminate (*auf* in); to stop, to cease; (*sterben*) to die; *tr* to put an end to, to accomplish; **~ergebnis** *n* final result; **~esunterzeichnete(r)** *m* (the) undersigned; **~flughafen** *m* terminus, *Am* (air) terminal; **~geschwindigkeit** *f* terminal (*od* final) velocity; **~glied** *n* terminal member; **~gültig** *a* definitive, definite, final; for good; **~kampf** *m* *sport* finish, final match; (*Boxen*) closing bout; **~lauf** *m* *sport* final run; **~lich** *a* finite; final, ultimate; *adv* at last, finally, at length; *Sie sollten ~~ wissen* you should know by now; **~los** *a* endless; infinite; boundless; **~losigkeit** *f* endlessness; **~lösung** *f* final solution; **~montage** *f* final assembly; **~produkt** *n* final product, end product; **~punkt** *m* final point, end-point; extreme point; **~reim** *m* end-rhyme; **~resultat** *n* final result, upshot; **~rille** *f* (*Schallplatte*) run-out groove; **~runde** *f* *sport* final; **~silbe** *f* last (*od* final) syllable; **~spannung** *f* *el* final voltage; **~spurt** *m* finish, final spurt; **~station** *f* terminus, *Am* terminal; **~strecke** *f* (*Schiff, Flugzeug*) final leg; **~stück** *n* endpiece; **~summe** *f* total; **~ung** *f* ending, *gram* termination; **~ursache** *f* final cause; **~urteil** *n* final decision, final sentence (*od* judg(e)ment); **~verstärkerröhre** *f* *radio* output valve; **~wert** *m* final value; **~ziel** *n* final objective (*od* aim), ultimate goal; **~zustand** *m* final state (*od* condition); **~zweck** *m* final purpose, eventual objective, goal.

Endivie *f* endive, *Am* chicory.

Energetik *f* energetics *pl mit sing.*

Energie *f* energy; (*Tatkraft*) vigo(u)r, force, power; verve, dash; *fam* punch, *Am fam* go, pep, vim; *~ der Bewegung* kinetic (*od* actual) energy; *~ der Lage* potential energy; *mit ~ füllen* to energize; *die ~(zufuhr) abschalten* to de-energize; *Sende~* transmitting power; *Erhaltung der ~* conservation of energy; *Licht ist e-e Form der ~* light is a form of energy; **~abgabe** *f* release of energy; **~abnahme** *f* decrease in energy; **~änderung** *f* energy change; **~art** *f* form of energy; **~aufspeicherung** *f* energy storage; **~aufwand** *m* energy consumption; expenditure of energy; **~bedarf** *m* demand for energy; **~einheit** *f* (*Erg*) energy unit; **~gleichung** *f* energy equation; **~los** *a* lacking in energy; **~losigkeit** *f* lack (*od* want) of energy; **~quant(um)** *n* energy quantum; **~quelle** *f* source of energy; **~umwandlung** *f* transformation of energy; **~verbrauch** *m* consumption of energy; **~vergeudung** *f* energy dissipation; **~verlust** *m* loss of energy; **~wirtschaft** *f* power industry; power economy; power service; power distribution; **~zufuhr** *f* addition of energy; supply of energy or power.

energisch *a* (*tatkräftig*) energetic(al); vigorous; sharp; *~ machen* to energize.

eng *a* narrow; (*~ sitzend*) tight; (*innig*) close; (*engherzig*) narrow; (*vertraut*) intimate; *dieser Rock ist mir zu ~* the coat pinches me (*od* is too tight for me); *~e Freunde* intimate friends; *~ beieinander sitzen* to sit close together; *~er schreiben* to write closer; *~er machen* to tighten; *im ~eren Sinne* strictly speaking; *der ~ere Ausschuß* select committee; *~ere Wahl* second ballot; short list; **~brüstig** *a* asthmatic; **~~keit** *f* asthma; **~e** *f* narrowness; closeness; tightness; *geog* defile; (*Meerenge; fig Klemme*) straits *pl*; *fig* (*schwierige Lage*) difficulty; *jdn in die ~~ treiben* to urge (*od* to drive) into a corner, to corner; **~herzig** *a* narrow-minded; (*prüde*) strait-laced; **~maschig** *a* close-meshed; **~paß** *m* narrow pass, defile; *com* bottle-neck; **~spaltig** *a* narrow-spaced.

Engag|ement *n* (*Anstellung, bes. theat*) engagement; position; (*Verpflichtung*) engagement, obligation; (*Vertrag*) contract; (*Börse*) commitment; **~ieren** *tr* (*verpflichten*) to engage; (*anstellen*) *jdn ~~ als* to engage s. o. as, to hire, to employ; (*Kapital*) to invest, to lock up; *sich ~~* to engage o. s.; *zum Tanz ~~* to engage for the next dance; *~iert sein* to be engaged; (*beschäftigt sein*) to be busy; *~iertes Kapital* locked-up capital.

Engel *m* angel; (*als Kosewort*) darling, sweetheart; *Sie sind ein ~* you are an angel; *ein ~ flog durchs Zimmer* (*fig*) there was a dead silence in the room; *die ~ im Himmel singen hören* (*fig*) to see stars; *rettender ~* good angel; *Schutz~* guardian angel; *Todes~* angel of death; **~chen** *n* little angel, cherub; **~gleich, ~haft** *a* like an angel; (*himmlisch*) angelic(al); seraphic, celestial; **~hai** *m* angel shark; angel-fish; **~schar** *f* angelic host; **~sgeduld** *f* patience of an angel; **~sgruß** *m* Annunciation, the Angelic Salutation; Angelus, Ave Maria; **~wurz** *f* *bot* angelica; **~szunge** *f* angel's tongue; *mit ~~n reden* to speak with the tongues of angels.

Engerling *m* grub (*od* larva) of the cockchafer.

Eng|land *n* England; **~landfeind** *m* Anglophobe; **~landfeindlich** *a* anti-British; **~landfeindschaft** *f* Anglophobia; **~landfreund** *m* Anglophile; **~landfreundlich** *a* Anglomaniac; **~landfreundschaft** *f* Anglomania; **~länder** *m* Englishman, *Am auch* Britisher; *die ~~* (*als ganzes Volk*) the English; (*einzeln*) Englishmen; *tech* (*Maulschlüssel*) screw-spanner, adjustable spanner, *Am* monkey-wrench, adjustable wrench; **~länderin** *f* Englishwoman, *pl* Englishwomen; **~lisch** *a* English, (*amtlich*) British; *in Zssg* Anglo-; *das E~~e, die ~~e Sprache* English, the English language; *Standard~* the king's (*od* queen's) English; *das ~~e radebrechen* to mishandle (*od* murder) the king's English; *auf ~~* in English; *aus dem ~~en übersetzen* to translate from the English; *ins ~~e übersetzen* to translate into English; *auf gut ~~* in plain English; *sich auf ~~ empfehlen* to take French leave; *~~es Horn* (*mus*) English horn, cor anglais; *~~e Kirche* Anglican Church; (*offiziell*) Church of England; *~~e Krankheit* rickets *pl*; *~~es Pflaster* court-plaster; *~~e Spracheigentümlichkeit* (*Anglizismus*) Anglicism, *Am* Briticism; *~~es Salz* Epsom salt; *~~er Walzer* English waltz; *~~er Gruß* Ave Maria.

engros *adv* wholesale; **~bezug** *m* bulk buying; **~geschäft** *n*, **~handel** *m* wholesale business, wholesale trade; **~firma** *f*, **~haus** *n* wholesale firm; **~händler** *m* wholesale dealer; **~preis** *m* wholesale price, *Am* trade price.

Enkel *m* grandson, grandchild; *die ~* the descendants *pl*; (*Nachwelt*) posterity, succeeding generations *pl*; **~in** *f* granddaughter; **~kind** *n* grandchild.

enorm *a* enormous.

Enquete *f* (*Rundfrage, Untersuchung, Ermittlung*) investigation; (*amtlich*) official inquiry; inquest.

Ensemble *n* ensemble; (*Schauspielertruppe*) entire cast; (*Musikergruppe*) union of soloists; (*Kleidung*) combination of clothing and accessories; (*das Ganze*) the whole; **~spiel** *n* ensemble; **~tänzerin** *f* chorus-girl, *Am* show girl.

ent- *pref in Zssg mit Verben u. Substantiven mit der Bedeutung*: 1. *weg von, weggehen, verschwinden* = dis-, de-, un-, in-, ex-, e-: *z. B. entfernen*; 2. *werden, beginnen, hervorgehen: z. B. entzünden* to inflame; 3. *berauben, wegnehmen, trennen, loslösen: z. B. entschwefeln* to desulfurize.

entart|en *itr* to degenerate; (*verschlechtern*) to deteriorate; **~et** *a* degenerate; debased; (*sittlich verderbt*) depraved; **~ung** *f* degeneration, degeneracy; (*Verderbtheit*) depravation, corruption; (*Verschlechterung*) deterioration.

entäuß|ern *r*: *sich e-r Sache ~~* to part with; to give up; **~erung** *f* abstinence, privation; *jur* alienation.

entbehr|en *tr* to be deprived of, to miss, to lack s. th.; (*sich behelfen ohne*) to do without, to dispense with; (*erübrigen*) to spare; **~lich** *a* superfluous; dispensable; **~~keit** *f* superfluity; **~ung** *f* want, privation.

entbieten *irr tr* to command, to order; *seinen Gruß ~* to send o.'s respects to; (*mitteilen*) to notify, to announce; *zu* *sich* ~ to send for, to summon to o.'s presence.

entbind|en *irr tr* to deliver of; to disengage; to set free; to release; (*Gase*) to evolve; *jdn seines Eides* ~~ to release from an oath; *entbunden werden* to be delivered; **~ung** *f* setting free, release; (*e-r Frau*) accouchement, delivery, confinement; *fig* disengagement; **~~sanstalt** *f* lying-in hospital, maternity hospital; **~~szange** *f* forceps *pl*.

ent|blättern *tr* to strip of leaves; *sich* ~~ to shed (the) leaves; **~blöden**: *sich nicht* ~~ not to be ashamed (of); to have the impudence (to); **~blößen** *tr* to denude; *fig* to strip; (*Schwert*) to draw; *mil* (*Flanke*) to expose; (*Haupt*) to uncover, to bare; (*berauben*) to deprive; **~blößt** *a* bare; destitute of; *~~en Hauptes* bare-headed, uncovered; *von allen Mitteln* ~~ to be destitute of money (*od* funds); **~blößung** *f* denudation; (*von Mitteln*) destitution; **~brennen** *irr itr* to take fire, to blaze up; *fig* to burn (*vor* with); to be inflamed (with); to fly into a passion; *in Liebe* ~~ to fall violently in love; *tr* to kindle.

entdeck|en *tr* to discover; (*Wahrheit*) to find out; (*Verbrechen*) to detect; (*erfinden*) to invent; to discover; (*Geheimnis*) to divulge, to unravel, to reveal; *mil* to spot; (*sein Herz*) to pour out (o.'s heart); (*Quelle, Erz etc*) *Am* to strike; *e-e reiche Quelle* ~~ to strike it rich; *sich* ~~ to make o. s. known; to confide (in); **~er** *m* discoverer; explorer; (*Enthüller*) discloser; **~ung** *f* discovery; (*Erfindung*) invention; (*Enthüllung*) disclosure; **~~sreise** *f* voyage of discovery, expedition.

entdunkeln *tr* to light up; to remove the blackout.

Ente *f* duck; (*Lüge*) fictitious newspaper-report; canard, hoax; *aero* canard, tail first machine; (*junge* ~) duckling; *med* urinal: urino-bottle; **~nbraten** *m* roast duck; **~njagd** *f* duck-shooting; **~nteich** *m* duck-pool; **~rich** *m* drake; (*wilder*) mallard.

ent|ehren *tr* to dishono(u)r; to disgrace; to bring into disrepute; (*entwürdigen*) to degrade; (*schänden*) to ravish, to seduce; to rape, to deflower; *sich* ~~ to disgrace o. s.; **~ehrend** *a* dishono(u)ring, disgraceful; **~ehrung** *f* dishono(u)ring; disgracing; defamation; degradation; (*Schändung*) rape, seduction; defloration; **~eignen** *tr* to expropriate, to dispossess; (*vorläufig*) to sequester, to sequestrate; **~eignung** *f* expropriation; **~~sverfahren** *n* process of expropriation; **~eilen** *itr* to hurry away; to escape; (*Zeit*) to glide away; **~eisen** *tr* (*Windschutzscheibe, Eisschrank, tiefgekühlte Nahrungsmittel*) to defrost; *aero* to de-ice; **~eisung** *f* defrosting; de-icing, ice eliminating; **~eisungsanlage** *f* defroster; de-icer, ice eliminating system; **~erben** *tr* to disinherit; *die ~erbten pl* the disinherited, the outcasts of society; **~erbung** *f* disinheritance.

Enter|beil *n* boarding-axe; **~haken** *m* grappling-iron, boarding-grapnel; **~mannschaft** *f* *mar* boarding party; **~n** *tr* to grapple, to board.

ent|fachen *tr* to kindle, to set ablaze; *fig* to fan; **~fahren** *irr itr* to escape; to slip (out of, from); *das Wort entfuhr ihr* the word escaped her; **~fallen** *irr itr* to fall from; *fig* to escape; *dieses Wort ist mir* ~~ this word has slipped from my memory; this word slipped my mind; *die morgige Vorstellung entfällt* tomorrow's performance does not take place (*od* has been cancel(l)ed); ~~ *auf* (*als Anteil*) to fall to; **~falten** *tr* to unfold; to develop; (*beweisen*) to display; (*ausbreiten*) to expand; (*zeigen*) to exhibit; (*aufrollen*) to unroll; (*Tuch*) to unfurl; *mil* (*Truppen*) to deploy; (*Tätigkeit*) to be active; (*Blumen*) to burst open; (*Fähigkeiten*) to evolve; *sich* ~~ to open; **~faltung** *f* unfolding; (*Entwicklung*) development; (*Prunk, Pomp*) display; (*Bildung*) formation; **~~szeit** *f* *aero* parachute opening(-out) time; **~färben** *tr* to decolo(u)rize; (*bleichen*) to bleach; to make pale; *sich* ~~ to change colo(u)r, to fade; to grow pale; **~färbung** *f* decolo(u)rization; bleaching; change of colo(u)r, growing pale; paleness; **~färbungsmittel** *n* decolo(u)rant, decolo(u)rizer, decolo(u)rizing agent.

entfern|en *tr* to remove (*von* from); to take away; (*beiseite tun*) to put aside; (*Schutt*) to clear away; (*Flecken*) to remove, to take out; (*Namen aus e-r Liste streichen*) to strike out; (*abweichen*) to deviate; (*von der Universität*) to exclude, to expell; *sich* ~~ (*sich zurückziehen*) to retire, to withdraw; to absent o. s. from; (*abreisen*) to depart; (*heimlich*) to abscond; to leave secretly; **~t** *a* (*weggebracht*) removed; (*räumlich, zeitlich*) remote, distant; (*abgelegen*) far (off), far away; out-of-the-way; (*abwesend*) absent; *sich ~t halten von* to keep at a distance; *~te Ähnlichkeit* faint resemblance; *~te Möglichkeit* off chance; *weit ~t daß od zu* (so) far from; *~t verwandt* (*weitläufig*) distantly related; *nicht im ~testen* not in the least; not in the slightest degree; **~ung** *f* (*Abstand*) distance; (*Wegschaffen*) removal; (*vom Amt* from office); (*Abreise*) departure; (*Abwesenheit*) absence; (*Zurückgezogenheit*) retirement; (*Entferntheit*) remoteness, distance; (*Reichweite*) range; *in einiger* ~~ at a distance, at some distance; *auf nächste od kleine* (*große*) ~~ at close (long) range; *auf e-e* ~~ *von* at a range of; (*mil*) *unerlaubte* ~~ *von der Truppe* absence without leave; *die* ~~ *messen* to take the range; ~~ *in gerader Linie* distance in straight line; ~~ *in der Luftlinie* air-line distance; *auf richtige* ~~ *einstellen phot* to focus; *zurückgelegte* ~~ distance run; **~~sänderung** *f* range correction; **~~sermittlung** *f* range determination; **~~sfehler** *m* distance error; range error; **~~smarke** *f* range indicator; **~~smaßstab** *m* telemetric scale; **~~smesser** *m* *phot* (*gekuppelter* coupled; *eingebauter* built-in) rangefinder; (*durch Winkelmessung*) telemeter; (*Mann*) rangetaker; **~~smeßmann** *m* rangefinder operator; **~~smeßstelle** *f*, **~~smeßstand** *m* rangefinder platform; **~~srekord** *m* *aero* long-distance record; **~~sschätzen** *n* range estimation; **~~sskala** *f* *radio* distance scale; *phot* focussing scale; **~~sstellung** *f* range scale; **~~sunterschied** *m* range difference; **~~svorhalt** *m* range lead, range correction; slant.

ent|fesseln *tr* to unchain; to release; to let loose; **~fetten** *tr* to remove fat (*od* oil *od* grease); to ungrease; (*Wolle*) to scour; **~fettung** *f* removal of fat; **~fettungsmittel** *n* *med* remedy for obesity; *chem* scouring (*od* degreasing) agent; **~fettungskur** *f* treatment for obesity; banting-cure; **~flammbar** *a* inflammable; **~flammen** *tr* to set alight; *fig* to inflame, to kindle; to rouse; *itr* (*sich*) to fire up; (*Petroleum etc*) to flash; **~flammend** *a* inflammatory; **~flammungspunkt** *m* flash(ing) point; **~fliegen** *irr itr* to fly away; **~fliehen** *irr itr* to escape, to get off; to flee from, to run away; (*Zeit*) to pass quickly; **~fließen** *irr itr* to flow from; to emanate.

entfremd|en *tr* to alienate; to estrange (from); to provoke the opposition of, *Am* to antagonize; *sich* ~~ to become a stranger; **~ung** *f* estrangement, alienation.

entführ|en *tr* to abduct; to carry off; (*Mädchen*) to elope with; (*Kinder*) to kidnap; **~er** *m* abductor; kidnapper; **~ung** *f* abduction; kidnapping; rape; elopement.

entfuseln *tr chem* to remove fusel oil; to rectify.

entgas|en *tr* to degas, to outgas; to decontaminate; to distil(l); **~ung** *f* degasification; dry distillation; coking; **~~smittel** *n* degassing agent.

entgegen *adv, prp* against, contrary to, opposite; opposed to; in face of; despite of; (*hinzu*) toward(s); *dem Winde* ~ contrary to the wind; *dem Strome* ~ contrary to the stream; **~arbeiten** *itr* to counterwork; to counteract; to thwart; to oppose; to work against; to buck; **~bringen** *irr tr* to carry towards; *fig* to offer, to confer; **~eilen** *itr* to hasten to meet; **~gehen** *irr itr* to go to meet; (*Gefahr*) to face; to encounter; **~gesetzt** *a* opposite, contrary; inverse; opposed; contrasted; *in ~~em Sinne* in contrary direction, on the other hand; *dem Uhrzeiger* ~~ counterclockwise; ~~ *wirkend* antagonistic; *im ~~en Falle* in the contrary case; **~halten** *irr tr* to contrast with; to object; **~handeln** *itr* to act in opposition to, to act against; (*gegen e-e Regel*) to infringe, to contravene; (*jds Plan*) to thwart; **~jubeln** *itr* to greet with shouts of jubilation; **~kommen** *irr itr* to come to meet; *Wünschen* ~~ to meet (*od* anticipate) o.'s wishes; *auf halbem Weg* ~~ to meet halfway; ~~ *n* kindness, courtesy; fair terms *pl*; **~kommend** *a* obliging, conciliating; compliant; kind, helpful; **~laufen** *irr itr* to run to meet; (*Absichten, Plänen*) to oppose; to be repugnant to; **~nahme** *f* reception; **~nehmen** *irr tr* to accept; to receive; **~sehen** *irr itr* to look forward to; to await, to expect; (*Tod*) to look in the face; **~sein** *irr itr* to be opposed to; **~setzen** *tr* to oppose; to contrast; *Widerstand* ~~ to put up opposition; **~stehen** *irr itr* to be opposed; to stand opposite to; **~stellen** *tr* to set against; to oppose; (*vergleichen*) to contrast, to compare; **~strecken** *tr* (*Arme*) to stretch out (o.'s arms); **~stürzen** *itr* to rush to meet; **~treten** *irr itr* to step up to; to advance towards; to stand up to; *fig* to oppose, *Am* to antagonize; (*e-r Gefahr*) to face; to resist; **~wirken** *itr* to thwart, to counteract; to act (*od* to work) against; **~ziehen** *irr itr* to advance (*od* march) towards.

entgegn|en *tr* to return, to reply; to answer; (*scharf od schlagend*) to retort; *Am* to talk back; **~ung** *f* reply; answer; (*scharfe*) retort; counterblast.

ent|gehen *irr itr* (*e-r Gefahr*) to escape (from), to avoid; to get off; (*Nachstellung*) to elude; (*Fehler*) to escape observation (*od* notice); *sich etw* ~~ *lassen* to lose the chance of getting s. th.; to miss s. th.; to slip s. th.;

mit knapper Not e-r Gefahr ~~ to have a narrow escape; *es entging ihr nicht, daß* she was fully aware of, she could not fail to notice; *es ist Ihrer Aufmerksamkeit entgangen, daß* ... it has escaped your notice that ...; *die Gelegenheit* ~~ *lassen* to miss o.'s opportunity; **~geistert** *a* thunderstruck; (*verblüfft*) flabbergasted; **~gelt** *n* (*Lohn*) remuneration; (*Entschädigung*) recompense; (*Vergütung*) compensation; reward; indemnification; (*Gegenwert*) equivalent; (*Vertragsleistung*) consideration; *gegen* ~~ for reward; for a consideration; *ohne* ~~ gratis, gratuitous, free of charge, without charge; **~gelten** *irr tr* to compensate; *fam* to pay for; *fig* (*büßen*) to atone for s. th., to suffer for s. th.; *sie soll es mir* ~~ she shall pay for it; *jdn etw* ~~ *lassen* to make s. o. suffer (*od* pay) for; **~geltlich** *a* for reward, for an equivalent; **~giften** *tr* to detoxicate; (*von Kampfgasen*) to decontaminate; to degas; **~giftung** *f* detoxication; decontamination; **~~sdienst** *m* decontamination (*od* degassing) service; **~~smittel** *n* decontaminating (*od* degassing) agent; **~~station** *f* decontamination station; **~~strupp** *m* decontamination squad; **~gleisen** *itr* to run off the rails, to get off the rails (*od* line), to derail, to be derailed, *Am* to jump the track; *Am* to ditch; ~~ *lassen* to derail; *fig* (*Fehler machen*) to slip, to make a slip; to make a faux pas; **~gleisung** *f* derailment, running off the rails; *fig* slip; **~gleiten** *irr itr* to slip away from; **~gräten** *tr* (*Fische*) to bone.

ent|haaren *tr* to remove hair, to unhair; (*mit Enthaarungsmittel*) to depilate, *Am fam* to de-fuzz; **~haarungsmittel** *n* depilatory; **~halten** *irr tr* to contain; (*fassen*) to hold, to comprise, to include, to embody; ~~ *sein* to be included (*in* in); *sich* ~~ (*von Fall zu Fall*) to refrain from; (*prinzipiell*) to abstain from; (*abstehen von*) to forbear; *ich kann mich des Lachens nicht* ~~ I cannot help laughing; *sich der Stimme* ~~ to refrain from voting; *sich weiterer Schritte* ~~ to refrain from further action; *2 ist in 10 fünfmal* ~~ 2 is contained five times in 10; **~haltsam** *a* abstinent, abstemious; (*mäßig*) moderate; (*im Essen*) frugal; (*im Trinken*) temperate, (*gänzlich*) teetotal; (*geschlechtlich*) continent; **~haltsamkeit** *f* (*Essen, Trinken*) abstinence, abstemiousness; (*Mäßigkeit*) moderation; (*geschlechtlich*) continence; (*im Trinken*) temperance, total abstinence; (*Prinzip der* ~~ *im Trinken*) teetotalism; **~haltung** *f* abstention, forbearance; (*im Essen u. Trinken*) abstinence; **~härten** *tr* to soften; (*Metall*) to anneal; **~härtung** *f* softening; (*Metall*) annealing; **~härtungsmittel** *n* softening agent; **~haupten** *tr* to behead, to decapitate; (*hinrichten*) to execute; **~hauptung** *f* beheading; decapitation; (*Hinrichtung*) execution; **~heben** *irr tr* to relieve of; to exempt from; to free from, to deliver from; to disallow; (*des Amtes*) to dismiss from, to remove from (o.'s office), to oust; (*vorläufig*) to suspend from an office; **~heiligen** *tr* to profane; to desecrate; **~heiligung** *f* profanation; **~hüllen** *tr* (*aufdecken*) to uncover, to unfold; to open up; (*Denkmal*) to unveil; (*entlarven*) to unmask; (*bloßlegen*) to expose; (*offenbaren*) to reveal; *Am* to develop; (*klarlegen*) to disclose; (*Geheimnis*) to divulge, to bring to light; (*wahres Wesen e-r Person od Sache*) *Am* to debunk; (*angebliche od wirkliche Korruptionsfälle* ~~) *Am fam* to muckrake; **~hüllung** *f* uncovering; (*Denkmal*) unveiling; *fig* revealing; (*Offenbarung*) revelation; disclosure; (*erzwungene* ~~ *von Mitteln, Absichten u. Plänen*) *Am* showdown; **~hülsen** *tr* to husk, to peel; (*Erbsen*) to shell; (*Kaffee*) to pulp.

Enthus|iasmus *m* enthusiasm; *in* ~~ *bringen od geraten Am* to enthuse (*über* about); **~iast** *m* enthusiast; *Am* fan (*z. B.*: radio fan, movie fan); **~iastisch** *a* enthusiastic (*über* about, at).

*

ent|ionisieren *tr* to de-ionize; **~jungfern** *tr* to deflower; (*schänden*) to ravish; **~kalken** *tr* to decalcify, to delime; **~keimen** *tr* to degerminate; to disinfect; to destroy bacteria; (*haltbar machen*) to sterilize; to pasteurize; *itr* to germinate; **~kernen** *tr* to stone; **~kleiden** *tr* to unclothe, to strip; *fig* (*berauben*) to divest of; *sich* ~~ to undress; to take off; **~kommen** *irr itr* to escape from, to get off; (*mit knapper Not*) to have a narrow escape (*od* a close shave); *sl* to get out by the skin of o.'s teeth; **~koppeln** *tr radio* to tune out; to neutralize, to balance out; to decouple; **~koppelung** *f radio* tuning out, neutralization; balancing out; decoupling; **~korken** *tr* to uncork; **~kräften** *tr* to weaken; (*widerlegen*) to refute; (*ungültig machen*) to invalidate, to cancel; (*Urteil*) to quash; (*vollständig erschöpfen*) to exhaust, to debilitate; **~ung** *f* enervation, debilitation, exhaustion; (*Abschwächung*) extenuation; (*Urteil, Beweis*) invalidation, quashing; refutation; **~kuppeln** *tr* to uncouple, to disconnect; *mot* to declutch.

Entlade|brücke *f* unloading crane; unloading bridge; **~dauer** *f* time of discharge; **~einrichtung** *f* discharging gear; **~hafen** *m* delivery port; **~hebel** *m* discharge lever; **~kosten** *f pl* discharging expenses *pl*; **~n** *irr tr* (*abladen, ausladen*) to unload; to dump; *phys* to discharge; *fig* (*Zorn*) to pour out o.'s anger; *sich* ~~ to get rid of, to ease o.s. of; (*Gewitter*) to burst, to break; (*Feuerwaffe*) to go off; (*Sprengstoff*) to explode; (*Batterie*) to discharge; **~spannung** *f el* discharge voltage (*od* potential); **~station** *f* discharging station; **~strom** *m el* discharge current; **Entladung** *f* (*Ausladung*) unloading; *el* discharge; (*Explosion*) explosion; (*Ausbruch*) eruption.

entlang *adv* along.

entlarven *tr* to unmask; *fig* to expose.

entlass|en *irr tr allg* to dismiss s. o. (from); *Am fam* to drop; *alle halbtagsbeschäftigten Angestellten wurden* ~~ all part-time employees were dropped; (*wenn ein bes. Grund vorliegt*) to discharge; *wegen Unbotmäßigkeit* ~~ to discharge for insubordination; (*Dienstboten*) to give notice to; (*verabschieden*) to discard; (*vorübergehend* ~~) *Am* to lay off; (*Beamte*) to remove, to dismiss from office; (*pensionieren*) to pension off; (*entheben*) to oust from office; *mil* to discharge (*z. B.* hono(u)rably *od* dishono(u)rably discharged); (*demobilisieren*) to demobilize, *Am auch* to muster out; (*Offiziere*) to put on half-pay (*od* to put on the retired list); (*Truppen*) to disband; (*Mannschaft e-s Schiffes*) to pay off; (*von Schule od Universität*) to send down, *Am* to drop; *jur* (*aus der Haft*) to release; *bedingt* (*auf Parole*) ~~ to release on parole; *auf Bewährung* ~~ to release on probation, to bind over on probation; (*aus e-m Vertrag*) to discharge; *der Richter entließ die Geschworenen* the judge discharged the jury; (*jdn wegjagen, kassieren*) to cashier; (*den Laufpaß geben*) *fam* to sack s. o., *Am fam* to fire, to kick out, to can, to bounce; **~ung** *f* dismissal; discharge; *fristlose* ~~ dismissal without notice, *Am fam* sack(ing), firing, brush-off; (*Entfernung aus dem Amt*) removal; *um seine* ~~ *bitten, seine* ~~ *einreichen* to resign, to tender (*od* to send in *od* to hand in) o.'s resignation; (*vorübergehende* ~~) suspension, *Am* layoff; **~~sgesuch** *n* (offer of) resignation; **~~sjahrgang** *m mil* age class due for discharge; **~~slager** *n* discharge camp, *Am mil* separation center; **~~spapiere** *n pl* discharge papers *pl*, *Am fam* walking-papers *pl*, (walking-) ticket; **~~sschein** *m* certificate of discharge; *fam* (*blauer Brief*) blue envelope; **~~sschreiben** *n* letter of dismissal, notice (of discharge); **~~sstelle** *f mil* demobilization centre, discharge centre; **~~szeugnis** *n* certificate of discharge (*od* dismissal).

entlast|en *tr* to unburden; (*erleichtern*) to relieve s. o. of s. th.; *com* to credit s. o. with; (*vor Gericht*) to exonerate; to clear; to free from; (*verteidigen*) to defend; *~ende Umstände* exonerating circumstances; **~ete(r)** *m* (*politisch*) exonerated person; **~ung** *f* (*Erleichterung*) relief; (*Verbindlichkeit*) discharge; *jur* exoneration; defence; (*Konto*) credit; ~~ *erteilen* to give (*od* grant) a discharge; **~~sangriff** *m mil* diversionary (*od* diverting) attack, attack to relieve pressure; relief attack; **~~sbogen** *m arch* relieving-arch; **~~sstraße** *f* bypass road; **~~sversuch** *m mil* attempt to relieve pressure; **~~szeuge** *m* witness for the defence.

ent|laufen *irr itr* to run away; **~lausen** *tr* to delouse; **~lausung** *f* delousing; **~~sanstalt** *f* delousing station, *Am* delousing center; **~ledigen** to set free, to free from; *sich* ~~ (*Pflicht*) to acquit o. s. of; (*Bürde*) to rid o.s. of; to get rid of; (*Joch*) to shake off; *sich seiner Schuldigkeit* ~~ to perform o.'s duty; to fulfil(l) (*od* to execute) an obligation, to discharge a duty; **~ledigung** *f* deliverance; riddance; execution; acquittance; release; **~leeren** *tr* to empty; to clear; to drain; to discharge; (*Eingeweide*) to eject, to void; *sich* ~~ to relieve o. s.; **~leerung** *f* emptying; ejection, voidance; *med* evacuation; **~legen** *a* distant, remote, far away; out-of-the-way; **~~heit** *f* distance, remoteness; **~lehnen** *tr* to borrow; **~leiben** *r* to commit suicide; **~leihen** *irr tr* to borrow s. th. from s. o.; (*unerlaubt zitieren*) to plagiarize; *fig* (*her-, ableiten*) to derive from; **~leiher** *m* borrower; **~leihung, ~lehnung** *f* borrowing, loan; (*Ableitung*) derivation; (*Abschreiben*) plagiarism; **~loben** (*Verlobung lösen*): *sich* ~~ to disengage o.s., to break off an engagement; **~lobung** *f* disengagement, breaking off an engagement; **~locken** *tr* to draw from; (*Geheimnis*) to elicit, to worm out a secret of s. o.; **~lohnen** *tr* to pay off, to pay for services; to remunerate; *Am* to compensate; (*Arbeiter in Waren* ~~) to truck; **~lohnung** *f* payment, paying off; remuneration, *Am* compensation; **~lüften** *tr* to air, to vent(ilate), to deaerate; *mot* (*Bremsen*) to bleed; **~lüfter** *m* (*Ventilator*) ventilator; (*Stutzen*) (air) vent; **~lüftung** *f* ventilation, airing; **~~srohr** *n mot* vent pipe, breather (pipe); **~~sventil** *n* ventilating valve; **~magnetisieren** *tr* to demagnetize; (*Schiffe gegen magnetische Minen*) to de-Gauss, to degauss; **~mannen** *tr* to castrate; *fig* to emasculate, to unman; to enervate; (*schwächen*) to enfeeble; **~mannung** *f* castration; *fig* emasculation; enervation; **~menscht** *a* (*unmenschlich*) inhuman; (*roh, brutal*) brutish; (*grausam*) cruel; (*barbarisch*) barbarous, savage; **~militarisieren** *tr* to demilitarize; **~militarisierung** *f* demilitarization; **~mündigen** *tr* to put under tutelage, to place under guardianship (*od* control); **~mutigen** *tr* to discourage, to dishearten; *mil* (*Truppen*) to demoralize; **~nahme** *f* taking; (*Strom etc*) drain; extraction; (*Dampf*) bleeding; *com* (*Geld*) drawing, withdrawal; **~nazifizieren** *tr* to denazify; **~nazifizierung** *f* denazification; **~~sausschuß** *m* denazification court *od* panel *od* board; **~nebeln** *tr* to free from mist (*od* fog *od* fume); **~nebelungsanlage** *f aero* fume-dispersion installation; **~nehmen** *irr tr* (*weg~~*) to take (out) from; to remove; (*folgern*) to gather from; (*herleiten*) to infer from, to understand (from), to learn (from *od* by); *sie entnahm aus seinem Brief* ... she gathered from his letter ...; *com* (*Geld*) to draw (*auf* (up)on); (*Konto*) to withdraw; (*aus e-m Buch*) to borrow; (*zitieren aus*) to quote from; **~nerven** *tr* to enervate, to unnerve; to exhaust; **~ölen** *tr* to remove oil from, to unoil, to drain of oil; **~ölt** *a* free of oil.

ent|puppen: *sich ~~* to burst the cocoon; *fig* to turn out to be; **~rahmen** *tr* to skim; to remove the cream from; **~raten** *irr tr, itr* to do without, to dispense with; **~rätseln** *tr* to unriddle; *fig* (*Geheimnis*) to clear up; (*Problem*) to solve; (*Schrift*) to decipher; **~rechten** *tr* to deprive of rights; **~reißen** *irr tr* to tear from; to snatch from; *dem Tode ~~* to save s. o.'s life; **~richten** *tr* to pay, to discharge; (*Dank*) to give; **~ringen** *tr* to wrest from; *sich ~~* to escape; **~rinnen** *irr itr* to run away, to escape; **~rollen** *tr* to unroll; (*Fahne*) to unfurl; (*Bild*) to unfold; **~rücken** *tr* to remove, to snatch away; *fig* to enrapture; *den Blicken entrückt werden* to be wafted out of sight; **~rümpeln** *tr* to clear out; **~rümpelung** *f* clearing of attics; **~rüsten** *tr* (*jdn*) to make angry, to fill with indignation; (*erzürnen*) to provoke, to irritate; *sich ~~* to become angry, to grow indignant; *sie entrüstete sich über ihn* she got angry at him; **~rüstet** *a* angry, in anger; indignant; (*wütend*) in a rage, furious; **~rüstung** *f* indignation; anger; (*Wut*) wrath, rage, fury.

entsag|en *itr* (*aufgeben*) to give up; to turn away from; (*verzichten*) to renounce; (*auf Vorteile verzichten*) to forego; (*Amt, Stellung*) to resign; to demit; (*dem Thron*) to abdicate (the throne), to renounce the throne; (*unter Eid ~~, geloben*) to forswear; (*sich e-r Sache enthalten*) to forbear s. th.; (*etw fliehen, vermeiden*) to eschew; (*Rechte aufgeben, auf etw verzichten*) to waive; (*abtreten, Pläne aufgeben*) to relinquish; **~ung** *f* resignation, renunciation; abdication; abjuration.

Entsatz *m* relief, rescue; (*Hilfstruppe*) succour, relieving army; (*e-r belagerten Stadt*) raising of the siege of a town.

entschädig|en *tr* (*bezahlen*) to pay; (*für Verluste*) to indemnify (*für* for); (*für geleistete Dienste od Mühewaltung*) to compensate (*für* for); (*belohnen*) to remunerate; (*Schadenersatz leisten, etw ersetzen*) to make amends (for s. th. to s. o.); (*gut machen*) to recompense, to repay; (*Unrecht wiedergutmachen*) to repair, to redress; to restitute; (*vergelten*) to requite (*mit* with); (*befriedigen*) to satisfy; (*für Auslagen*) to reimburse (*für* for); *sich ~~* to indemnify o. s. (*für* for); (*Verluste*) to make up, to recover (o.'s losses); **~ung** *f* indemnification, indemnity; remuneration; restitution, reparation, redress; damages *pl*; compensation; reimbursement; amends *pl*; *gegen ~~* for a consideration; *als ~~ leisten od zahlen* to pay by way of remuneration; *~~ verlangen* (*Schadenersatz*) to claim (*od* recover) damages; (*für geleistete Dienste etc*) to demand compensation; (*gerichtlich*) to sue for damages; *~~ zuerkennen* to award compensation; **~~sanspruch** *m* (*für geleistete Arbeit*) right of compensation; (*Schadenersatz*) right of damages; (*Forderung vor Gericht*) claim for compensation, claim for damages; **~~sfestsetzung** *f* determination of compensation; **~~sklage** *f* action for damages; **~~ssumme** *f* (amount of) damages (*od* compensation); indemnity.

entschärf|en *tr* (*scharfe Munition etc*) to render safe; to unprime; to disarm; **~ungskommando** *n* (*für Bomben*) bomb-disposal squad; unexploded bomb squad (*Abk* U. X. B.)

Ent|scheid *m* answer; decision; *siehe*: *Entscheidung*; **~scheiden** *irr tr* (*nach Erwägung des Für u. Wider*) to decide (*über* on); (*Auswahl treffen, festlegen*) to determine; (*Fragen etc zwingend lösen*) to settle; *der Tod ~scheidet alle Probleme* death settles all problems; (*Entschluß fassen*) to resolve, to conclude; to fix; (*durch Gericht, Behörde etc*) to rule; *jur* (*urteilen*) to adjudicate (*über* upon); to hold; to decree; to pass judg(e)ment (for, against); (*durch Schiedsgericht*) to arbitrate, to umpire; *endgültig ~~* to decide finally, *Am* to conclude; *zu jds Gunsten ~~* to decide in s. o.'s favo(u)r; *~~ Sie!* you be the judge! *sich ~~* to decide (*für, gegen, über* for, against, on); to make up o.'s mind, to resolve upon s. th.; (*optieren*) to opt; *es wird sich jetzt ~~* it will be decided now; **~scheidend** *a* (*Zweifel ausschließend*) decisive; (*das Ende betreffend*) final; (*gültig, schlüssig*) conclusive; (*unumstößlich*) peremptory; *die ~~e Frage* the point at issue; *der ~~e Punkt* the crucial point; *die ~~e Stimme* the casting vote; **~scheidung** *f*, **~scheid** *m* decision, determination; *jur* (*Entscheid*) (court) decision; (*Urteil*) (final) judg(e)ment; sentence; adjudication; (*Verfügung*) order; (*e-s Schwurgerichts*) verdict; (*bei Ehescheidung*) decree; (*Schiedsgericht*) award; *gerichtliche ~~* court finding; *gerichtliche ~~ herbeiführen* to go into court; *e-e ~~ bei höherer Instanz* decision in a higher court; *die ~~ liegt bei Herrn X.* decision rests with Mr. X.; *e-e ~~ erzwingen* to force an issue; *e-e ~~ treffen, zu e-r ~~ kommen* to take a decision, to come to a decision; *zur ~~ stellen* to submit to; to bring to a head; **~~sfreiheit** *f* (*Ermessen*) discretion; **~~sgrund** *m* motive; (final) reason; **~~skampf** *m Am* showdown; **~~skern** *m* crux of a decision; **~~slos** *a* indecisive; **~~spunkt** *m* critical point; turning-point; crisis; **~~sschlacht** *f* decisive battle; **~~sspiel** *n* deciding game; final, tie; **~~sstunde** *f* critical hour; **~~svoll** *a* decisive; fatal; **~schieden** *a* (*unzweifelhaft*) decided; (*entschlossen*) determined; resolute; (*fest*) firm; (*bündig, unumstößlich*) peremptory; *adv* decidedly; emphatically; firmly; positively; **~schiedenheit** *f* decision; (*Entschlossenheit*) determination; resoluteness; peremptoriness; (*Festigkeit*) firmness.

ent|schlafen *irr itr* to fall asleep; *fig* to die; to pass away; *die Entschlafenen* the deceased; **~schlagen** *irr: sich e-r Sache ~~* to get rid of; to give up; to dismiss; **~schleiern** *tr* to unveil; *fig* to reveal; **~schließen** *irr: sich ~~* to determine, to resolve; to make up o.'s mind; to intend; *~schlossen sein zu* to be resolved to, *Am* to be bound to; *er hat sich anders ~schlossen* he changed his mind; **~schließung** *f* resolution, decision; **~schlossen** *a* resolute, determined; *kurz ~~* of quick resolve, without hesitation; **~~heit** *f* decision; resoluteness, energy; **~schlummern** *itr* to fall asleep; *fam* to doze off; *fig* to pass away; to die (gently); **~schlüpfen** *itr* to slip away (*aus* from); to escape; *es ist mir so entschlüpft* it just slipped out; **~schluß** *m* decision, resolution; *e-n ~~ fassen* to come to a resolution; to make up o.'s mind; *strategischer ~~* strategic decision; **~~fassung** *f* (formulation of) decision; **~~kraft** *f* power of decision; **~schlüsseln** *tr* to decipher, to decode; **~schlüsselung** *f* decoding, deciphering; breaking a code.

entschuld|bar *a* excusable; (*Verbrechen, Sünde*) venial; **~en** *tr* to release debts; **~igen** *tr* to excuse, to pardon; (*rechtfertigen*) to exculpate; to justify; *sich ~~* to apologize (*bei* to, *wegen* for); to make (*od* offer) an excuse; *ich muß mich ~~* I must apologize; *sie ließ sich ~~* she asked to be excused; *er ~igte sich wegen seiner früheren Rede* he apologized for his former speech; *~~ Sie, bitte!* please, excuse me! I beg your pardon! *~~ Sie, daß ich zu spät komme* excuse me for being late, excuse my being late; *es läßt sich nicht ~~* it admits of no excuse; there is no excuse for it; *zu ~~* excusable; *nicht zu ~~* inexcusable; **~igung** *f* (*um Tadel zu vermeiden*) excuse; (*Abbitte, Bedauern, im Bewußtsein eigener Schuld*) apology; (*Rechtfertigung*) exculpation; (*Einrede*) plea; (*Vorwand*) pretext; (*Bemäntelung*) palliation; (*Ausflucht*) subterfuge; *ich bitte vielmals um ~~* I am awfully sorry; *um ~~ bitten* to beg s. o.'s pardon; *zur ~~* in excuse of; *e-e ~~ vorbringen* to advance an excuse; *dafür gibt es keine ~~* there is no excuse for it; **~~sgrund** *m* excuse, plea; **~~sschreiben** *n* letter of excuse (*od* apology); **~schuldung** *f* disencumberment; regulation of debts, sinking (*od* wiping out) of debts.

ent|schweben *itr* to soar up; **~schwefeln** *tr* to desulphurize, to desulphurate; *Am* to desulfurize, to desulfurate; **~schwinden** *irr itr* to disappear, to vanish; (*aus dem Gedächtnis*) to fade from o.'s memory; (*Töne*) to die away; **~seelt** *a* (*seelenlos*) inanimate; (*tot*) lifeless, dead; **~senden** *irr tr* to send off, to dispatch; **~setzen** *tr* (*in Furcht setzen*) to frighten, to strike with terror; *sich ~~* to be terrified at, to be frightened at; to be shocked (*od* startled *od* horrified *od* aghast); (*Beamten entlassen*) to dismiss (from office); (*vorübergehend*) to suspend; (*absetzen*) to depose; *mil* (*belagerte Stadt*) to relieve (a town), to raise the siege of; *~~ n* (*Furcht, Schrecken*) fright, horror, amazement, alarm; **~setzlich** *a* (*furchtbar*) terrible; (*schrecklich*) dreadful, horrible, horrid; (*scheußlich, ekelhaft*) shocking; atrocious; *fig fam* awful, tremendous; *~~ kalt* awfully cold; **~~keit** *f* frightfulness; terribleness; atrocity; **~setzung** *f* (*Absetzung*) removal, dismissal; deposition; (*zeitweilig*) suspension; *mil* (*e-r belagerten Stadt*) relief; **~seuchen** *tr* to disinfect; **~seuchungsgerät** *n* disinfector; **~sichern** *tr* (*Pistole etc*) to unlock, to release the safety device (*od* safety-catch); (*Bomben*) to make bombs live; (*entschärfen*) *mar* to render innocuous; **~siegeln** *tr* (*öffnen*) to open; to unseal; (*offiziell*) to remove the seal; **~sinken** *irr itr* to sink down, to drop from; *fig* to fail; *der Mut ~sank ihm* his courage failed him; **~sinnen** *irr: sich ~~* to recall, to remember, to recollect; *soviel ich mich ~~ kann* to the best of my remembrance (*od* recollection); **~sittlichen** *tr* to deprave, to demoralize; **~sittlichung** *f* demoralization; depravation, depravity.

ent|spannen *tr* (*nachlassen*) to slacken; to relieve; (*Feder*) to release (a spring); (*Bogen*) to unbend; (*Gewehr*) to uncock; *sich ~~* to relax; (*ausdehnen*) to expand; **~spannung** *f* unbending; removal of stress; *tech* pressure drop; decrease in tension; (*Gelöstheit*) relaxation; (*Ruhe*) rest, repose; (*Zerstreuung*) diversion, amusement, recreation; relieving; easing; *~~ der politischen Lage* détente; **~spinnen** *irr: sich ~~* (*beginnen, anfangen*) to begin; to arise; (*folgen*) to ensue; (*sich entwickeln*) to develop; **~sprechen** *irr itr* (*übereinstimmen, ähnlich sein*) to correspond (to *od* with), to be in accordance with; *math* to satisfy; (*erfüllen, nachkommen*) to comply with, to conform to; (*genügen, befriedigen*) to come up to; to be equivalent to, to be in keeping with; to answer to, to meet, to stand up to; (*passen zu*) to tally (with); to suit; *allen Anforderungen ~~* to answer (*od* meet *od* stand up to) all requirements; *jds Erwartungen ~~* to come up to o.'s expectations, to meet o.'s expectations; *nicht den Tatsachen ~~* not to correspond to the facts, not to be in accordance with the facts; *den Vorschriften ~~* to conform to (*od* to comply with) the provisions; *e-r Bitte ~~* (*nachkommen, erfüllen*) to comply with s. o.'s request; *jds Zweck ~~* to answer s. o.'s purpose; **~sprechend** *a* (*angemessen*) adequate to, appropriate; (*gleichend*) corresponding, matching; (*passend*) suitable, fitting; (*übereinstimmend*) in conformity with (*od* to), in accordance with, according to; corresponding to; *~~e Kleidung* proper clothing; *dem Muster ~~* up to sample, matching the sample; **~sprechung** *f* equivalent, analogy; denotation; (*passendes Seitenstück*) respondency; **~sprießen** *irr itr* to spring up; to sprout; (*abstammen*) to descend (*aus* from); **~springen** *irr itr* (*ausbrechen*) to escape (*aus* from); (*Gefängnis*) to break out (of prison); to run away; (*von Flüssen*) to spring forth, to rise, to have its source; *Am* to head; *der Fluß ~springt in ...* the river has its source in ...; (*herrühren*) to arise (from); (*entstehen*) to originate (in); (*abstammen*) to descend.

ent|staatlichen *tr* (*Kirche*) to disestablish; **~stammen** *itr* to be born of; to descend (from), to spring (from); **~stauben** *tr* to dust (off); **~stehen** *irr itr* to (a)rise (*aus* from); (*anfangen*) to begin, to start; (*herrühren*) to proceed; to result (*aus* from); to ensue (*aus* from); to originate (*aus* in); (*sich bilden*) to come into existence; (*verursachen*) to be caused by; (*geschehen*) to occur, to happen; (*Feuer etc*) to break out; (*Gebühren etc*) to accrue; *im ~~ begriffen* (to be) in the making; nascent; **~stehung** *f* (*Ursprung*) origin; (*Aufstieg, Anfang*) rise; (*Geburt*) birth; (*Bildung*) formation; **~~sgeschichte** *f* (*Bibel*) genesis; **~~sursache** *f* cause; **~~sweise** *f* mode of formation; **~~szeit** *f* date of creation; time of inception; **~~szustand** *m* nascent state; embryonic state; **~steigen** *irr itr* to arise, to emerge (*aus* from); **~steinen** *tr* to stone; **~stellen** *tr* (*verunstalten*) to disfigure, to deface, to deform; (*Züge, Sinn*) to distort; (*verstümmeln*) to mutilate; (*Tatsachen etc*) to misrepresent; (*zurechtmachen, Text*) to garble; (*fälschen*) to falsify; **~stellung** *f* disfigurement; distortion; mutilation; misrepresentation; **~stören** *tr* to clear; to radio-shield, to screen; to eliminate jamming; **~störer** *m* faultsman, repairman; **~stört** *a* interference-free; **~störung** *f radio* interference elimination (*od* suppression); **~~sdienst** *m* radio interference suppression service; **~strömen** *itr* to flow forth (*aus* from); to stream, to issue, to escape (*aus* from); **~sühnen** *tr* to absolve.

enttäusch|en *tr* to disappoint; (*über Irrtum aufklären*) to undeceive; to disabuse; **~t** *a* disappointed; **~ung** *f* disappointment; let-down; (*Ernüchterung*) disillusion, disillusionment (*über* with).

ent|thronen *tr* to dethrone; **~thronung** *f* deposition; **~trümmern** *tr* to remove rubble; **~trümmerung** *f* rubble clearing; **~völkern** *tr* to depopulate; *sich ~~* to decrease in population; **~völkert** *a* depopulated, deserted; **~völkerung** *f* depopulation; **~wachsen** *irr itr* to outgrow; **~waffnen** *tr* to disarm; **~waffnung** *f* disarmament; **~walden** *tr* to deforest; **~warnen** *tr* (*Luftschutz*) to give the all-clear (signal); **~warnung** *f* (*erste, vorläufige ~~*) raiders passed signal; (*nach Fliegeralarm*) all-clear (signal), *Abk* a. c.; (*nach Gasalarm*) cancellation of gas warning; **~wässern** *tr* (*Grund u. Boden*) to drain; to ditch; *chem* (*Wasser entziehen*) to dehydrate; (*austrocknen*) to desiccate; (*rektifizieren*) to rectify; (*sättigen*) to concentrate; **~wässert** *a* drained; *chem* dehydrated; rectified; concentrated; **~wässerung** *f* draining; *chem* desiccation; concentration; (*Kanalisation*) sewerage, canalization; **~~sgraben** *m* draining-ditch; **~~smittel** *n chem* dehydrating agent; **~~srohr** *n* drain pipe; (*Kanalisation*) waste pipe.

entweder *conj*: *~ ... oder* either ... or; *~ oder!* one thing or the other! take it or leave it!

ent|weichen *irr itr* (*Gase etc*) to escape (*aus* from), to leak; (*Gefangener*) to run away, to flee; to escape, to abscond; **~weihen** *tr* to profane, to desecrate; (*schänden*) to pollute, to violate; (*Priester*) to degrade; **~weihung** *f* (*Kirche*) profanation, desecration; (*Schändung*) violation; pollution; **~wenden** *tr* to steal, to pilfer; (*unterschlagen*) to embezzle; (*sich aneignen*) to misappropriate; **~wendung** *f* pilfering, purloining; (*Unterschlagung*) embezzlement; misappropriation; **~werfen** *irr tr* to trace out; (*zeichnerisch*) to design; *Kleider ~~* to design clothes; (*planen*) to plan; to scheme; *e-n Garten ~~* to plan a garden; (*skizzieren, flüchtig zeichnen*) to sketch, to outline, to rough-draw; (*Kurve, Karte*) to plot; (*Vertrag*) to draw up, to draft (a contract); (*Gesetz*) to frame; (*Plan*) to devise, to form; to project, to contrive, to plot; to lay down, to lay out, to lay up; **~werfer** *m* (*Zeichner, Konstrukteur*) designer; (*Planer*) schemer; projector; planner; contriver; **~werten** *tr* (*Preise, Kurse, durch Inflation; abwerten*) to depreciate; to reduce the value; (*Briefmarken*) to cancel, to deface; (*außer Kurs setzen*) to withdraw; *itr* to lose value; **~wertung** *f* (*Abwertung*) depreciation, devaluation; (*durch Stempel*) defacement; (*ungültig machen*) cancellation; (*Außerkurssetzen*) withdrawal, calling in, demonetization; **~~sstempel** *m* (*Briefmarken*) defacing stamp; **~wesen** *tr* to disinfect, to sterilize; to exterminate vermin; to delouse; **~wesung** *f* extermination of vermin; delousing; disinfection.

ent|wickeln *tr* (*auswickeln, enthüllen*) to unroll, to unwrap; (*bilden*) to develop; (*gestalten*) to form; (*fördern*) to advance, to further; to promote the growth of; (*Fähigkeiten*) to evolve; (*Gedanken*) to set forth; (*Gase*) to disengage, to evolve; (*erzeugen*) to generate; *phot* to develop (a film); (*Pläne; erklären*) to explain, to elucidate; (*enthalten*) to unfold, to display; (*zeigen*) to exhibit, to show; *mil* (*entfalten*) to deploy; *seine Pläne e-m Kreis von Zuhörern ~~* to develop o.'s plans to an audience; *der Motor ~wickelt 5 PS* the motor develops 5 horsepowers; *sich ~~* to develop (o. s.); (*heranwachsen*) to grow up; *er ~wickelt sich zu e-m guten Bürger* he is developing into a good citizen; *die Handlung e-s Romans ~wickelt sich* the plot of a novel develops; **~wickler** *m phot* developer; developing bath; (*Erzeuger*) producer; generator; **~wicklung** *f* (*allmähliches Heranwachsen*) develop(e)ment; (*Evolution*) evolution; growth; (*Entfaltung*) unfolding; (*Darlegung von Plänen etc*) explanation; exposition, elucidation, elaboration; (*Gestaltung, Bildung*) formation; *phot* developing; (*von Gasen*) disengagement, generating, generation; (*Theaterstück*) dénouement; catastrophy; *mil* (*Entfaltung von Truppen*) deployment, formation; **~~salter** *n* developmental age; **~~sbad** *n phot* developing liquid, developer; **~~sdose** *f* developing-box (*od* -tank); **~~sfähig** *a* developable, capable of development; **~~sfähigkeit** *f* capacity to develop, developability; **~~sgang** *m* course of development; **~~sgeschichte** *f* history of (the) development; (*Gang*) course of development; **~~skolben** *m chem* generating flask;

~~skrankheit *f* developmental disease; **~~slehre** *f* (theory of) evolution; **~~slinie** *f* line of development; **~~spapier** *n phot* development paper, developing-out paper (*Abk* D. O. P.); **~~speriode** *f* (*Pubertät*) (age of) puberty; **~~srichtung** *f* trend; **~~s-schale** *f phot* developing dish; **~~sstadium** *n*, **~~sstufe** *f* stage of development; **~~stendenz** *f* trend; **~~sverfahren** *n*, **~~svorgang** *m* process of development (*od* evolution); **~~szeit** *f med* time of incubation; **~winden** *irr tr* (*jdm etw*) to wrest (*od* to wring) from; *sich ~~* to disengage o. s. from; **~wirren** *tr* (*lösen, enträtseln*) to unravel; (*herauswinden*) to extricate from; (*befreien*) to disentangle from; **~wirrung** *f* unravel(l)ing; disentanglement; **~wischen** *itr* (*entkommen*) to slip away; to steal away; to escape; *sie ist uns ~wischt* she has given us the slip; **~wöhnen** *tr* to disuse; to disaccustom; (*Kind*) to wean, to ablactate; *sich ~~* to leave off, to break o. s. of, to give up; **~wöhnung** *f* disuse; (*e-s Kindes*) weaning, ablactation; **~wölken** *tr* to uncloud; *sich ~~* to clear up; **~würdigen** *tr* (*entehren, schänden*) to disgrace; (*erniedrigen*) to degrade; (*entweihen, entheiligen*) to profane; **~würdigung** *f* disgrace, degradation; **~wurf** *m* (*Zeichnung, Plan*) design, plan; project; scheme; (*Gesetzes~~*) draft (law *od* bill); (*Blaupause, fig Vorschlag*) blueprint; (*erster ~~, Konzept*) rough copy; *e-n ~~ machen* to make a plan; *im ~~ sein* to be in the planning (*od* blueprint) stage; **~wurzeln** *tr* to uproot, to tear up by the roots; *fig* (*ausrotten*) to eradicate, to extirpate; **~wurzelung** *f* uprootal, unrooting; *fig* eradication.

ent|zaubern *tr* to uncharm, to disenchant; (*der Gloriole berauben*) *Am* to debunk; **~zauberung** *f* disenchantment; **~zerren** *tr phot* to rectify; *el, radio* to correct, to eliminate distortion; **~zerrung** *f phot* rectification; *el, radio* equalization, correction; **~~sgerät** *n phot* rectifier; *el* equalizer; **~ziehen** *irr tr* (*jdm etw*) to withdraw s. th. from s. o.; (*wegnehmen*) to take away, to abstract; (*rauben*) to deprive s. o. of s. th.; to divest of s. th.; *jdm das Vermögen ~~* to divest s. o. of his property; (*Besitz*) to dispossess, to oust; *chem* (*ausscheiden*) to extract; *sich ~~* (*e-r Pflicht*) to shirk, to evade; to shrink from; to shun; to elude; to withdraw from; *sich den Blicken ~~* to flee from the sight; *das ~zieht sich aller Berechnung* it defies all calculation; *die Praxis ~~* to disbar from practice; *sich der Strafverfolgung ~~* to evade justice, to flee from justice; to abscond; *jdm das Wort ~~* to stop speaking; **~ziehung** *f* withdrawal; (*Beraubung*) deprivation; (*von Eigentum*) dispossession; (*Wegnahme*) abstraction; (*Ausscheidung*) extraction; (*Verweigerung*) denial; *jur* (*der Rechte*) ademption; (*des Wahlrechts*) disfranchisement; **~ziehungskur** *f* banting-cure; (*bei Rauschgift*) treatment (for drug-addicts); **~ziffern** *tr* to decipher; (*verschlüsselte Texte*) to decode; (*ausmachen*) to make out; (*lösen*) to solve; *nicht zu ~~* indecipherable; **~zifferung** *f* deciphering; decoding; **~zücken** *tr* (*bezaubern*) to charm; (*begeistern*) *fam* to enthuse, to electrify; to ravish; (*packen*) to thrill; (*erfreuen*) to delight; (*fesseln*) to captivate; (*gefallen*) to please; (*berücken*) to enrapture; (*anlocken*) to allure; (*einnehmen*) to take; (*faszinieren*) to fascinate; (*anziehen*) to attract; **~zückend** *a* delightful; charming, ravishing; enchanting; captivating; alluring; taking; fascinating, bewitching; attractive; **~zückt** *a* delighted (at); excited; *~~ sein über* to be delighted with; **~zückung** *f*, **~zücken** *n* (*Wonne, Ergötzen*) delight; rapture; enchantment; ecstasy; transport; *in ~~ geraten* to fall into ecstasy; **~zündbar** *a* inflammable; combustible; ignitable; **~zündbarkeit** *f* inflammability; **~zünden** *tr* to kindle; to set on fire, to set fire to; to ignite; *fig* to inflame; *med* to irritate, to inflame; *sich ~~* to catch fire; *med* to become inflamed, to be inflamed; **~zündlich** *a* inflammatory; **~zündung** *f* kindling; *tech* ignition; firing; *fig med* inflammation, irritation; *med oft durch angehängtes* -itis: *z. B. Kehlkopf~~* laryngitis; **~~sgemisch** *n* ignition mixture; **~~spunkt** *m* ignition point, burning point.

entzwei *adv* in two; asunder; (*in Stücken*) to pieces, in pieces; (*zerbrochen*) broken; (*zerrissen*) torn; **~brechen** *irr itr* to break in two (*od* asunder); **~en** *tr* to disunite; to divide; (*entfremden*) to estrange, to alienate; *sich ~~* to become estranged; to be at variance; to fall out with one another; (*streiten*) to quarrel; **~gehen** *irr itr* to go to pieces; **~reißen** *irr itr* to tear asunder, to tear to pieces; **~schlagen** *irr tr* to smash; **~schneiden** *irr tr* to cut in two, to cut to pieces; **~sein** *irr itr* to be broken, to be torn; **~t** *a* hostile; at daggers drawn; **~ung** *f* disunion; division; (*Entfremdung*) estrangement; (*Streit*) quarrel; (*Zwist*) dissension.

Enzian *m bot* gentian; (*Likör*) gentian spirit; **~wurzel** *f* gentian root.

Enzyklika *f* (*Rundschreiben des Papstes*) encyclic(al).

Enzyklopäd|ie *f* (en)cyclop(a)edia; **~isch** *a* (en)cyclop(a)edic(al); **~ist** *m* encyclop(a)edist.

*

Epid|emie *f* (*Seuche*) epidemic disease, epidemic; **~emisch** *a* epidemic(al).

Epidiaskop *n* (*Lichtbildapparat*) epidiascope.

Epigone *m* epigonus; (*Nachkomme*) descendant; **~nhaft** *a* epigonous; **~ntum** *n* decadence.

Epigramm *n* (*Sinngedicht*) epigram; **~atiker** *m* epigrammatist; **~atisch** *a* (*kurz u. treffend*) epigrammatic.

Ep|ik *f* epic poetry; **~iker** *m* epic poet; **~isch** *a* epic; **~os** *n* epic poem.

Epikure|er *m* Epicurean; (*Genußmensch*) epicure, glutton, gourmet, gourmand, bon vivant; **~isch** *a* Epicurean; **~ismus** *m* Epicur(ean)ism.

Epil|epsie *f* epilepsy, (*Fallsucht*) falling sickness; **~eptiker** *m* epileptic; **~eptisch** *a* epileptic; *~~e Anfälle* epileptic fits.

Epilog *m* epilog(ue), after-speech.

episkop|al *a* episcopal; **~alkirche** *f* Episcopal Church; **~at** *n* episcopate.

Episod|e *f* episode; **~isch** *a* episodic(al).

Epistel *f* (*Brief*) epistle; (*Sendschreiben des Neuen Testaments*) Epistle; *jdm die ~ lesen* to lecture s. o.; to blow up.

Epithel *n* (*Deckzellenschicht*) epithelium; **~zelle** *f* epithelial cell.

epoch|al *a* epochal; **~e** *f* epoch, era, period; **~emachend** *a* epoch-making, era-making.

Eppich *m bot* (*Sellerie*) celery; celeriac; *poet* (*Efeu*) ivy.

Equilibrist *m* equilibrist; rope-walker.

Equipage *f* equipage, carriage; (*Mannschaft e-s Schiffes*) crew.

equipier|en *tr* (*ausrüsten*) to fit out; (*Schiffe, Heere*) to equip; *sich ~~* to fit out o. s., to equip o. s.; **~ung** *f* equipment, equipage; outfit.

*

er *prn* he; *~ selbst* he himself; *~ ist es* it is he.

erachten *tr* to think, to deem, to hold, to judge, to consider; *wir ~ es für nützlich* we consider it useful; *~ n* opinion; *meines ~s* in my opinion, according to my judg(e)ment, *fam* as I look upon it.

erarbeiten *tr* to gain (*od* get) by working; to obtain by labo(u)r; to earn.

Erb|adel *m* hereditary nobility; **~anlage** *f* gene, hereditary disposition (*od* factor); **~anspruch** *m* claim to an inheritance; **~anteil** *m* hereditary portion; **~bauberechtigte(r)** *m* leaseholder; **~baurecht** *n* leasehold; **~begräbnis** *n* family vault; **~berechtigt** *a* having a hereditary title to; **~berechtigte(r)** *m* devisee; **~e** *m* heir, inheritor; (*von Grundstücken*) devisee; (*e-s Vermächtnisses*) legatee; (*gesetzlicher ~~*) heir at-law; (*Nachfolger*) heir apparent; (*mutmaßlicher ~~*) heir presumptive; *ein ~e antreten* to enter into the heritage of; **~e** *n* inheritance, heritage, (*Legat*) legacy; **~eigen** *a* hereditary; **~en** *tr* to inherit (*von* from), to succeed to, to be heir to; **~engemeinschaft** *f* community of heirs; **~fall** *m* succession; **~fehler** *m* hereditary defect (*od* fault); **~feind** *m* sworn (*od* hereditary) enemy; **~folge** *f* hereditary succession; *gesetzliche ~~* statutory inheritance; **~folgekrieg** *m* war of succession; **~gesund** *a* of healthy stock; **~gut** *n* inheritance; **~hof** *m* hereditary farm; farmer's entail; **~in** *f* heiress; **~krankheit** *f* hereditary disease; **~lasser** *m* testator; legator; *Am auch* decedent; **~lasserin** *f* testatrix; **~lehre** *f* genetics *pl*; **~lich** *a* hereditary; **~lichkeit** *f* heredity, hereditary character; **~masse** *f* estate; assets *pl*; all the hereditary factors; **~onkel** *m* rich uncle; **~pacht** *f* hereditary tenure; **~pächter** *m* hereditary tenant; **~prinz** *m* prince's heir; **~recht** *n* right of succession; law of succession, *Am* law of descent; **~schaft** *f* inheritance, heritage; *e-e ~~ ausschlagen* to renounce an inheritance; *e-e ~~ antreten* to come into an inheritance; **~schaftsgericht** *n* probate court; **~schaftssache** *f jur* will case; **~schaftssteuer** *f* succession duty, estate-duty, legacy duty; **~schleicher** *m* legacy-hunter; **~schleicherei** *f* legacy-hunting; **~stück** *n* heirloom; **~sünde** *f* original sin; **~teil** *m, n* hereditary portion; **~teilung** *f* partition of an inheritance; **~vertrag** *m* agreement (*od* contract) of inheritance; **~zins** *m* ground rent, rent charge.

er|barmen: *sich jds* (*od über jdn*) *~~* to pity, to have pity on, to show mercy to; to commiserate; *daß Gott ~barm!* God have mercy! *fam* good (-ness) gracious! *~~ n* pity, mercy; commiseration; compassion; *es ist zum ~~* it is pitiful; **~~swert, ~~swürdig** *a* pitiable; piteous; deserving pity; **~bärmlich** *a* miserable; pitiable; (*gemein*) mean; pitiful; (*verächtlich*) detestable; **~~keit** *f* misery; (*Gemeinheit*) meanness, baseness; (*Elend,*

Armseligkeit) wretchedness; **~barmungslos** *a* pitiless, merciless; remorseless; ruthless; **~barmungswürdig** *a* pitiable; deserving pity.

erbau|en ***tr*** to build (up), to construct; (*errichten*) to raise; (*Denkmal*) to erect; (*gründen*) to found; *fig* to edify; *sich ~~ an* to be edified by, to be pleased with; **~er** *m* builder, constructor; designer; erector; (*Gründer*) founder; (*Architekt*) architect; **~lich** *a* edifying; devotional; (*ermutigend*) encouraging; (*erfreulich*) gratifying; (*angenehm*) pleasing; **~t** *a fig* (*erfreut*) delighted, elated, excited; **~ung** *f* building, erection, construction; (*Gründung*) foundation; *fig* edification, *Am* (*innere ~~*) uplift; **~ungsbuch** *n* book of devotion, recreational book; **~ungsstunde** *f* hour of devotion.

erbeben *itr* to tremble, to quiver (*vor* with); (*vor Furcht, Erregung, Schwäche*) to shake with (fear, excitement, weakness); to quake.

erbeten *tr* to obtain by o.'s prayers (*od* petition).

er|betteln *tr* to get by begging; **~beuten** *tr* to gain as booty, to capture.

erbieten *irr*: *sich ~~* to offer (o. s.); (*freiwillig*) to volunteer (to do).

erbitten *irr tr* to beg, to request; to ask for; to solicit, to petition for; (*erreichen*) to gain by entreaty; *sich ~~ lassen* to relent, to be moved by entreaties.

erbitter|n *tr* to exasperate; to embitter, to irritate; *erbittert sein auf jdn* to be bitter against s. o.; (*zornig*) to be angry with s. o.; *ein erbitterter Streit* a fierce quarrel; **~ung** *f* animosity, irritation, violent anger; embitterment.

erblassen, erbleichen *itr* to grow pale; to faint; (*sterben*) to die.

er|blicken *tr* to behold; (*bemerken*) to perceive; to lay eyes on; (*entdecken*) to discover, to catch sight of; *das Licht der Welt ~~* to be born; **~blinden** *itr* to grow blind; to be struck with blindness; (*trübe werden*) to dull, to stain, to dim; **~blindet** *a* blind; **~blindung** *f* loss of sight.

er|blühen *itr* to blossom, to bloom; **~borgen** *tr* to borrow; **~bosen** *tr* to exasperate; *sich ~~* to grow angry; **~bötig** *a* willing; *~~ sein* to be willing (*od* ready).

erbrechen *irr tr* to break open; (*Briefe*) to open; *sich ~* to vomit; *~ n* vomition, vomiting.

erbringen *irr tr* to bring forth; *ein Alibi ~* to prove out an alibi; *den Beweis ~* to furnish proof, to produce evidence; to take evidence.

Erbse *f* pea; *grüne ~n* small peas; **~nbrei** *m* pease-pudding; **~nhülse** *f* pea-pod; **~nmehl** *n* pease-meal; **~nsuppe** *f* pea-soup.

Erd|ableitung *f el* earth connection, *Am* ground connection; **~abwehr** *f mil* anti-aircraft defence, ground defence; **~achse** *f* axis of the earth; **~anker** *m* ground anchor; **~anschluß** *m* earth connection, *Am* ground (connection); **~antenne** *f* ground aerial, *Am* ground antenna; buried antenna; **~anziehung** *f* gravitational attraction of the planet, gravity pull; **~apfel** *m* (*Kartoffel*) potato; **~äquator** *m* earth's equator; **~arbeiten** *f pl* earthworks *pl*; digging, excavation work; **~arbeiter** *m* digger, excavator; (*rail, Straßenbau*) navvy, *Am* laborer (on the roads); **~artig** *a* earthy; **~artillerie** *f* field and coast artillery; **~aufklärung** *f mil* ground reconnaissance; **~aufwurf** *m* mound; **~bagger** *m* bulldozer; steam shovel; **~bahn** *f* orbit of the earth; **~ball** *m* (terrestrial) globe; **~batterie** *f mil* ground battery; **~beben** *n* earthquake, *Am* temblor, quake; **~~kunde** *f* (*Seismologie*) seismology; **~~messer** *m* (*Seismograph*) seismometer, seismograph; **~~sicher** *a* earthquake-proof; **~beere** *f* strawberry; **~beereis** *n* strawberry ice-cream (cone); **~beobachtung** *f aero mil* ground observation; **~beschleunigung** *f* acceleration by gravity; **~beschreibung, ~kunde** *f* geography; **~beschuß** *m* anti-aircraft fire, *mil sl* ack-ack fire; **~bewegungen** *f pl* ground level(l)ing; **~bewohner** *m* inhabitant of the world; mortal; **~bildaufnahme** *f* terrestrial survey, ground photograph; **~bildmessung** *f* phototopography; **~boden** *m* the earth; earth's surface; ground, soil; *dem ~~ gleichmachen* to level with (*od* to raze to) the ground; **~bohrung** *f* trial boring; **~damm** *m* embankment, earth bank (*od* dam); **~draht** *m* earth wire, *Am* ground wire; **~drehung** *f* rotation of the earth; **~druck** *m* earth (*od* soil) pressure; thrust; **~e** *f* earth; *Am poet* (God's) footstool; (*Welt*) world; (*Bodenart*) ground, soil, *Am* dirt; *el, radio* (*Erdung*) earth, *Am* ground; *an ~~ legen* to earth, to put to earth, *Am* to ground; *mit ~~ verbinden* to connect to earth, *Am* to ground; *seltene ~~* rare earth; *auf der bloßen ~~ schlafen* to lie on the bare ground; *auf die ~~ fallen* to drop to the ground; *gebrannte ~~* terra cotta; *über der ~~* above ground, overground; *unter der ~~* underground; *zur ~~ gehörig* terrestrial; *zur ebenen ~~* on the ground floor; **~einstellung** *f* (*Radar*) setting; **~en** *a* earthly; terrestrial; **~en** *tr el, radio* to earth, *Am* to ground; **~enbahn** *f* earthly course; **~enbürger** *m* earthly being; **~englück** *n* earthly happiness; **~enleben** *n* life in this world, terrestrial life; **~enwallen** *n poet* earthly pilgrimage; **~erschütterung** *f* earthquake, earth-tremor; **~fahl, ~farbig** *a* earth-colo(u)red, clay-colo(u)red, livid; **~farbe** *f* earth colo(u)r; **~ferne** *f astr* apogee; **~floh** *m* flea-beetle; **~funkstelle** *f* ground signal station; **~gas** *n* natural gas, rockgas; **~geboren** *a* earth-born; (*sterblich*) mortal; **~gegner** *m mil* hostile ground force; **~geist** *m* mountain-goblin; **~geruch** *m* earthy odo(u)r; **~geschoß** *n* ground floor, ground story, *Am* first floor, main floor; **~gürtel** *m* zone; **~halbkugel** *f* hemisphere; **~haltig** *a* earthy; containing earth; **~harz, ~pech** *n* asphalt, bitumen; **~haufen** *m* heap of earth; (*Hügel*) hummock; **~hörnchen** *n* ground-squirrel; **~ig** *a* earthy; **~innere** *n* interior of the earth; **~kabel** *n* underground (*od* buried) cable; **~kampf** *m mil* ground fighting; fighting on land; *in den ~~ eingreifen* to ground strafe; (*mit Raketen*) to rocket; *Eingriff in den ~~* air-to-ground fighting, ground strafing; **~kampftruppe** *f* ground fighting unit; **~karte** *f* (terrestrial) map; **~klemme** *f el* earth terminal, *Am* ground terminal; **~kloß** *m* clod; (*Mensch*) earthling; **~kontakt** *m* grounding contact; **~körper** *m* terrestrial body; **~kreis** *m* sphere; **~krümmung** *f* earth curvature; **~kruste** *f* earth's crust, lithosphere; **~kugel** *f* globe, sphere; **~kunde** *f* geography; **~leiter, ~leitungsdraht** *m el, radio* earth-wire, *Am* ground-wire; **~leitung** *f el, radio* earth connection, *Am* ground connection; **~loch** *n* dug-out; fox-hole; **~magnetfeld** *n* terrestrial magnetic field; **~magnetismus** *m* terrestrial magnetism; **~männlein** *n* leprechaun; **~messer** *m* geodesist; **~miete** *f* earth silo; **~mine** *f mil* ground mine, land mine; **~mineral** *n* earthy mineral; **~mittelpunkt** *m* centre (*Am* center) of the earth; **~nähe** *f astr* perigee; **~nuß** *f bot* peanut, groundnut; **~nußbutter** *f* peanut butter; **~nußöl** *n* peanut oil; **~oberfläche** *f* (earth's) surface; **~öl** *n* petroleum, mineral oil, *Am auch* kerosene; **~ölablagerung** *f* oil deposit; **~ölrückstand** *m* petroleum residue; **~ortung** *f* pilotage; **~pech** *n* mineral pitch; **~peilgerät** *n aero* earth direction finder; **~pol** *m* pole (of the earth); **~reich** *n* earth, ground; **~rinde** *f* earth's crust; **~rutsch** *m* (*auch fig*) landslip, *Am* landslide; **~salz** *n* rock salt; **~schicht** *f* layer, stratum; **~schluß** *m el* earth leakage, *Am* accidental ground; **~scholle** *f* clod (of earth); **~schwere** *f* gravity; *Fliegen mit ~sicht f aero* contact flying; **~spalte** *f* crevice; **~stampfer** *m* (*Ramme*) earth rammer; **~station** *f aero radio* ground station; **~stecker** *m el* ground rod; **~stoß** *m* (earthquake) shock; **~strich** *m* zone, region; **~stufe** *f* terrace; **~sturz** *m* landslip, *Am* landslide; **~teil** *m* continent; part of the world; **~truppen** *f pl* ground troops *pl*, ground forces *pl*; **~umdrehung** *f* (*um eigene Achse*) rotation of the earth; **~umseglung** *f* circumnavigation; **~ung** *f radio* earthing, *Am* grounding; **~ungsschalter** *m radio* earthing switch; **~verbindung** *f el* earth connection, *Am* ground connection; **~vermessung** *f* topographic survey; **~wall** *m* embankment, earth wall, earthwork; mound; **~wärme** *f* temperature of the interior of the earth; **~welle** *f* ground wave; **~werk** *n* earthwork; **~ziel** *n mil* ground target; **~~beschuß** *m mil* firing against ground targets; **~zuleitung** *f* ground lead; **~zunge** *f* neck of land, cape.

er|denken *irr tr* to imagine; to conceive; (*Schlechtes*) to invent; to fabricate; to forge; (*planen*) to plan; to think out; **~denklich** *a* imaginable, possible, conceivable; *sich alle ~~e Mühe geben* to try o.'s utmost; to take all sorts of pains; *alles ~~e für jdn tun* to take all pains imaginable in favo(u)r of s. o.; **~dichten** *tr* to invent, to forge, to fabricate, to feign; **~dichtet** *a* fictitious, fictional; **~dichtung** *f* fiction; invention, fabrication; (*Erzählung*) tale; (*Legende*) legend; **~dolchen** *tr* to stab (with a dagger); **~dreisten:** *sich ~~ zu* to venture, to dare, to have the cheek (to do); to presume; **~dröhnen** *itr* to roar, to resound; **~drosseln** *tr* to strangle; to throttle; **~drücken** *tr* to squeeze to death; (*unterdrücken*) to oppress; (*zermalmen*) to crush; (*zurückdrängen, ersticken*) to stifle; *~~de Übermacht* overwhelming superiority; **~dulden** *tr* (*ertragen*) to endure; (*Tod*) to suffer; (*zulassen*) to tolerate; **~duldung** *f* suffering; enduring; toleration.

ereifer|n: *sich ~~* to grow warm, to get excited; (*wütend werden*) to become angry; to fly into a passion; **~ung** *f* excitement, passion.

ereig|nen: *sich ~~* to happen, to occur; to take place; to come to pass; *fam* to transpire; *Am* to eventuate; **~nis** *n* occurrence, event; incident; phenomenon; action; *einmaliges ~~*

unique (*od* singular *od* nonrecurrent) event; **~nislos** *a* uneventful; **~nisreich** *a* eventful.

ereilen *tr* to overtake, to come up with; to catch up; *fig* to befall suddenly.

Eremit *m* hermit.

ererben *tr* to obtain by inheritance, to inherit (*von* from).

erfahr|en *irr tr* (*hören*) to hear, to learn (*von* from); (*erleben, versuchen*) to experience; to come to know; (*herausbringen*) to find out; (*erleiden*) to suffer; *~~ a* (*geschickt*) expert; (*erprobt*) experienced; (*gereift*) seasoned; (*kundig*) conversant with; (*bewandert*) well versed in; (*gewandt*) skil(l)ful, skilled; **~enheit**, **~ung** *f* experience, practice; skill; knowledge, *Am* know-how; *aus ~ung* by (*od* from) experience; *in ~ung bringen* to learn, to come to know; to ascertain; *aus der ~~ folgernd* a posteriori; *Mangel an ~ung* lack of experience; *gute* (*schlechte*) *~ungen* pleasant (unpleasant) experiences (*mit* with); **~ungsergebnis** *n* empirical result; **~ungsgemäß** *adv* according to experience; **~ungslos** *a* inexperienced; **~ungsmäßig** *a* empirical, known from experience; **~ungssache** *f* matter of experience (*od* practice); **~ungstatsache** *f* matter of experience, practical facts *pl*, empirical data *pl*, experimental data *pl*; **~ungswert** *m* empirical value.

erfassen *tr* (*packen, greifen*) to grasp, to seize; to requisition; to lay hold of; to catch hold of; to pick up; to engage; *fig* (*begreifen*) to conceive, to grasp; to catch on to; (*verstehen*) to understand; to comprehend; (*in e-r Liste*) to register, to record; (*einschließen*) to include.

erfechten *irr tr* to obtain by fighting; *den Sieg ~* to win (*od* gain) the victory.

erfind|en *irr tr* to find out; to invent; to contrive; to devise; (*entdecken*) to discover; (*e-e Geschichte*) to make up (*od* to cook up) a story; (*fälschen*) to fabricate; *er hat das Pulver nicht erfunden* he will not set the Thames on fire; **~er** *m* inventor; contriver; discoverer; *Am* (*Bastler*) gadgeteer; **~ergeist** *m* inventive genius, creative conception; **~erisch** *a* inventive, ingenious; (*klug*) clever; **~ung** *f* invention, device; contrivance; *praktische technische ~~ Am fam* gadget; (*Erdichtung*) fiction; **~~sgabe** *f* inventive faculty, inventiveness; **~~sreich** *a* ingenious; prolific.

erflehen *tr* to implore, to entreat; to beg for; to obtain by entreaty (*od* entreaties).

Erfolg *m* (*glücklicher*) success; *theat, film* hit, go; (*Kassen~*) *Am* box-office; (*Ausgang*) issue; outcome; (*Vollendung, Leistung*) achievement; (*Ergebnis*) result; (*Wirkung*) effect; (*Folge*) consequence; *~ haben* to succeed; to score a success; to achieve a success, *Am auch* to make good; *sich als ~ erweisen* to turn out a success; *keinen ~ haben* to fail; *theat, film* to fall flat; *ohne ~* unavailing, unsuccessful; *alle unsere Bemühungen blieben ohne ~* all our efforts proved unavailing (*od* unsuccessful, fruitless); *das Unternehmen hatte keinen ~* the undertaking has proved unsuccessful; *von ~ gekrönt* crowned with success; *das Theaterstück war ein großer ~* the play was a go, *fam* the play went over big; *die Schauspielerin hatte großen* (*Kassen-*) *~ in ihrem Stück Am* the actress got a big box-office on her show; **~en** *itr* to ensue, to follow, to result from; (*Zahlungen*) to be made; (*stattfinden*) to take place, to occur; *die Antwort ist noch nicht ~t* the answer has not yet arrived, the answer has not yet come to hand; *auf die Sache ist nichts Weiteres ~t* the matter had no further consequences; **~los** *a* vain, unsuccessful, fruitless; ineffective; *adv* without success, in vain; **~losigkeit** *f* unsuccessfulness; uselessness; **~reich** *a* successful; effective; *~~er Mensch* pushing fellow, *Am* go-getter; **~sbilanz** *f com* statement of surplus; **~srechnung** *f com* profit and loss statement; **~versprechend** *a* promising.

erforder|lich *a* necessary, requisite (*für* to, for); required; *~~ sein* to be required; (*unbedingt ~~*) indispensable; *wir wußten nicht, daß ein Zeugnis ~~ war* we did not know that a certificate was required; *das ~~e* (*zur Durchführung*) the wherewithal; **~lichenfalls** *adv* in case of need, if necessary, if need be; **~n** *tr* (*verlangen*) to demand, to require; (*brauchen*) to need; (*notwendig machen*) to necessitate; (*erheischen*) to call for; **~nis** *n* necessity; (*Bedürfnis*) exigency; (*notwendige Bedingung*) requisite (*für* for); (*Voraussetzung*) qualification (*zu* for); (*Bedingung*) condition; **~nisse** *n pl* requirements *pl*; (*des Lebens*) necessaries *pl* (of life); *nach den ~~n der Umstände* according to circumstances.

erforsch|en *tr* (*sich versenken in*) to search into, to dive into; (*Land*) to explore; (*entdecken*) to discover; (*untersuchen*) to investigate; to examine; to research; (*peinlich genau*) to scrutinize; *sich ~~* to examine o. s.; **~er** *m* (*durch Reisen*) explorer; (*Untersuchender*) investigator; searcher; **~ung** *f* (*Prüfung*) inquiry; (*Untersuchung*) investigation; research; (*Entdeckung*) exploration.

er|fragen *tr* to find out by asking (*od* by inquiry); to inquire; (*in Erfahrung bringen, ermitteln*) to ascertain; *ich konnte ihre Adresse nicht ~~* I was not able to ascertain her address; *zu ~~ bei* inquire at, apply to; **~frechen**: *sich ~~* (*sich anmaßen, sich erdreisten*) to presume; (*wagen*) to dare; (*die Frechheit haben*) to have the effrontery (*od* impudence *od* audacity *od* cheek) (*zu* to do); **~freuen** *tr* to gladden; (*Vergnügen machen*) to give pleasure; to rejoice; (*entzücken*) to delight; (*gefallen*) to please, to cheer; (*dankbar begrüßen*) to gratify; to favo(u)r; *das Auge ~~* to relieve the eye; *sich e-r Sache ~~* to enjoy a thing; to rejoice at (*od* in); *sich e-s guten Rufes ~~* to enjoy a good reputation; *sich großer Nachfrage ~~* to be in great demand; *erfreut* pleased (*über* with); glad, delighted (*über* with); **~freulich** *a* delightful; pleasing, pleasant; gratifying; encouraging; favo(u)rable; satisfactory; *e-e ~~e Nachricht* a good news; **~freulicherweise** *adv* fortunately, happily; **~frieren** *irr itr* to freeze to death; to perish with cold, to die of cold; *erfroren a* (*Person*) frozen; (*Glieder, Pflanzen*) frost-bitten; *erfroren sein* to be frozen; killed by frost; **~frierung** *f* (*der Gliedmaßen*) frostbite; **~frischen** *tr* to refresh, to freshen; to cool; *sich ~~* to refresh o. s.; **~frischend** *a* refreshing; cooling; **~frischung** *f* refreshment, recreation; **~~smittel** *n* refreshment; **~~sraum** *m* refreshment room; **~füllen** *tr* (*Aufgaben etc*) to fulfil(l); to perform; *Am oft* to fill; *jur* (*durchführen*) to implement; *math* to satisfy; (*mit Bewunderung*) to fill with admiration; (*Bedingungen*) to comply with the requirements; to fulfil(l) the qualification; (*Bitte*) to comply with, to grant; (*Erwartungen*) to answer o.'s expectations; (*Pflichten*) to do (*od* to perform *od* to carry out) o.'s duty; (*mit Schrekken*) to strike with terror; (*Verbindlichkeiten, Verpflichtungen*) to meet o.'s liability; (*Versprechen*) to keep a promise; (*Vertrag*) to fulfil(l) a contract; (*Vorschriften*) to comply with regulations; (*Zweck*) to accomplish; *sich ~~* to come true; to be realized; *sich nicht ~~* to fail; **~füllung** *f* (*Pflichten etc*) fulfil(l)ment; accomplishment; (*Vertrag*) performance; (*Bedingung, Forderung*) compliance (with); (*Hoffnung*) realization; *in ~~ gehen* to be realized, to come true, to be accomplished; **~~sort** *m* place of fulfil(l)ment (*od* payment); settling-place; (*Bestimmungsort*) destination; **~~spolitik** *f* fulfil(l)ment-policy.

Erg *n phys* (*Einheit der Arbeit*) erg, ergon.

ergänz|en *tr* (*ersetzen*) to supply; to supplement (by, with); (*Wortlaut wiederherstellen*) to restore; (*zufügen*) to add to; (*vervollständigen*) to complete; to integrate; (*Lücken*) to fill up; (*Vorräte auffüllen*) to replenish; (*Verlust, Summe*) to make up; (*vermehren*) to eke (*mit, durch* with); **~end** *a* supplementary (to), complementary; *sich ~~* to serve as supplements; **~ung** *f* (*Vervollständigung*) complement; (*notwendige ~~*) completion; (*Zusatz, Nachtrag*) supplement; supplying; (*Wiederherstellung*) restoration; (*Wiederauffüllen*) replenishment; *~~en f pl* (*Anhang zu e-m Werk*) addenda *pl*; **~~sbataillon** *n mil* reserve battalion; **~~sband** *m* supplement, supplementary volume; **~~sbatterie** *f el* buffer (*od* auxiliary) battery; **~~sbedarf** *m* supplementary supplies *pl*; requirements *pl*; replacement; **~~seinheit** *f mil* division replacement unit; **~~sfarbe** *f* complementary colo(u)r; **~~sheft** *n* supplementary number; **~~smannschaften** *f pl mil* replacements *pl*; replacement crews *pl*; **~~svorrat** *m* reserve stocks *pl*; **~~swerk** *n* supplement; **~~swinkel** *m math* complementary angle.

ergattern *tr fam* (*geschickt verschaffen*) to collar; to obtain; to get hold of; (*Nachrichten*) to hunt up, to pick up.

ergeben *irr tr* (*liefern*) to yield, to produce; (*erweisen*) to prove, to show; (*ausmachen*) to amount to, to make; to accrue; *mil sich ~* to surrender to; (*sich widmen*) to be attached to; to devote o. s. to; (*dem Trunk*) to take to; *sich ~ in* to resign o. s. to, to submit to; to acquiesce in; *sich ~ aus* (*folgen*) to follow from, to result from; *hieraus ergibt sich* hence follows, it follows from this; *es ergibt sich, daß ...* it happens (*od* follows) that ...; *sich auf Gnade od Ungnade ~* to surrender unconditionally; *~ a* devoted, attached to; (*untertänig*) humble; (*gehorsam*) obedient; *dem Laster ~* addicted to; *Ihr ~* (*Briefschluß*) truly yours; **~heit** *f* devotion, attachment; submission; (*Resigniertheit*) resignation; **~st** *a* respectful, obedient; (*Briefschluß*) yours respectfully (*od* faithfully); most truly yours; very truly yours; *ich danke ~st* I am very much obliged.

Ergeb|nis *n* result; (*Ausgang*) issue; (*Ertrag, Ernte*) yield; (*Erträgnis*) output, outcome; (*Folgen*) consequence, conclusion; (*Resultate wissenschaftlicher Arbeiten*) findings *pl* (of studies); *math* (*beim Addieren*) sum, (*beim Subtrahieren*) remainder, (*beim Multiplizieren*) product, (*beim Dividieren*) quotient; *zu keinem ~~ führen* to give (*od* to yield) no result, to prove a failure; **~~los** *a* resultless, without result; futile; **~~reich** *a* positive, bearing results; **~ung** *f mil* surrender; (*in sein Schicksal*) resignation, submission.

ergehen *irr itr* to be published, to be promulgated; (*Gesetz*) to be passed; to come out; *~ lassen* to publish; (*Anordnung, Befehl*) to issue; *Gnade für Recht ~ lassen* to let right give way to mercy; *etw über sich ~ lassen* to suffer patiently; to submit to; to endure, to take; to stand for; *sich ~* to take a walk; *sich im Freien ~* to stroll about; *sich in Hoffnungen ~* to indulge in hopes; *sich in Vermutungen ~* to make guesses; *sich über ein Thema ~* to expatiate on a subject; *sich in Verwünschungen ~* to break out in invectives; *imp* to do, to go; to fare with; *es ist ihm gut* (*schlecht*) *ergangen* it has fared well (ill) with him; he has prospered; *wie ist es Ihnen ergangen während der Reise?* how did you fare during your journey? *wie ist es ihr ergangen?* how did she get on? *wie wird es ihm ~?* what will become of him? *~ n* (*Befinden*) state of health; condition; (*Schicksal*) luck; (*Lebensweise*) way of living.

ergiebig *a* rich, productive; (*von Geschäften*) lucrative, profitable; (*fruchtbar*) fertile; (*ertragreich*) yielding; (*im Überfluß*) abounding, plentiful; **~keit** *f* richness; productiveness; abundance; yield, return; fertility.

ergieß|en *irr tr* to pour out; (*ausstoßen*) to pour forth; (*hineinfließen*) to flow into; to discharge; *sich ~~ in* to fall into; *sich in Lobsprüchen ~~* to break out into praises.

erglänzen *itr* to gleam, to sparkle; to shine forth.

erglühen *tr* to (begin to) glow; to kindle; (*rot werden vor Scham etc*) to colo(u)r; (*vor Liebe*) to be transported with love.

ergötz|en *tr* to please, to amuse; to delight, to divert; (*die Sinne*) to flatter; *sich ~~* to take pleasure (*od* delight) in; to enjoy o. s.; *~~ n* joy, delight; **~lich** *a* delightful, amusing; (*spaßig*) funny, diverting; **~~keit** *f* delight, amusement.

*

ergrauen *itr* to become (*od* to get *od* to turn) gray (*od* grey).

ergreifen *irr tr* to seize, to grasp; to take up; to take possession of, to catch hold; (*rühren*) to touch, to move; *Partei ~* to side with, to take s. o.'s part; *die Gelegenheit ~* to seize the opportunity; *die Flucht ~* to take (to) flight; (*Beruf*) to choose; (*Feder*) to take up the pen; (*Gelegenheit*) to avail o. s. of an opportunity; (*Maßregeln*) to take (*od* adopt) measures (*od* steps); (*Verbrecher*) to arrest, to apprehend; (*Wort*) to begin to speak; (*Feuer*) to reach; (*Krankheit*) to attack, to seize; *auf frischer Tat ~* to take in the very act; **~d** *a* moving, touching; thrilling; **Ergreifung** *f* seizure; capture.

ergriffen *pp, a* struck (*von* with), seized with; (*bewegt*) moved, touched; affected; **~heit** *f* emotion; shock.

ergrimmen *itr* to grow (*od* to get) angry, to grow furious.

ergründ|en *tr* to sound, to fathom; *fig* to explore thoroughly, to get to the bottom of; to ascertain, to discover; (*untersuchen*) to investigate; to find out, to look into, to research; to probe; **~ung** *f* inquiry.

Erguß *m* discharge; outpouring, overflow; *fig* effusion; *med* (*Blut~*) effusion (of blood); extravasation.

erhaben *a* raised, elevated; (*herausragen*) to project; (*Arbeit*) embossed; (*konvex*) convex; *~e Arbeit* relief; *fig* sublime; noble; exalted; dignified; *~ sein über* to be above; **~heit** *f* elevation, eminence; *fig* sublimity.

erhalt|en *irr tr* (*bekommen*) to receive, to get; (*bewahren*) to save, to preserve; (*unterhalten*) to maintain; (*unterstützen*) to support; (*verdienen*) to earn; (*e-n guten Preis*) to secure a good price; *am Leben ~~* to keep alive; *sich ~~ von* to subsist on; *sich* (*selbst*) *~~* to support o. s.; *sich gut ~~* to keep (*od* to wear) well; *gut ~~* in good condition (*od* repair); *schlecht ~~* in bad condition (*od* repair); *~~ bleiben* to be preserved; *nicht zu ~~* (*nicht erhältlich*) not obtainable, not to be had; not available; **~er** *m* preserver; maintainer; supporter; **~ung** *f* preservation; (*Pflege von Maschinen etc*) maintenance; (*von Bauten*) upkeep; *~~ der Energie* conservation of energy; **~~sgesetz** *n* law of conservation; **~~skosten** *f pl* maintenance charge; **~~strieb** *m* instinct of self-preservation; **~~szustand** *m* condition, state of preservation; maintenance standard.

erhältlich *a* obtainable; available, procurable; *im Handel ~* commercially available; *nicht ~* not available, not to be had; not obtainable.

er|handeln *tr* to get by bargaining; (*kaufen*) to purchase, to buy; **~hängen** *r* to hang o. s.; **~härten** *tr* to harden; *fig* to confirm; to prove; to substantiate; to attest; to corroborate; (*eidlich*) to declare on oath; **~haschen** *tr* to catch; to snatch; to seize.

erheb|en *irr tr* to heave up; (*Augen*) to lift up; (*Anspruch*) to claim (s. th., a right); (*Einwand*) to raise (*od* to lodge) an objection; (*Frage*) to start; *jur* (*Feststellungen treffen*) to investigate, to make a legal inquiry; (*Geld*) to raise; to take up; (*Steuern*) to levy (*od* to collect) taxes; (*rühmen*) to extol, to praise; (*zu e-r Würde*) to raise; (*in den Adelsstand*) to ennoble; (*ein Geschrei*) to set up a cry; (*e-e Klage*) to lodge a complaint, to file a charge; to bring an action (*gegen* against); (*ins Quadrat ~~*) to square (a number); (*Protest*) to enter (*od* to raise) a protest; (*Widerspruch*) to object; *sich ~~* (*aufstehen*) to (a)rise, to stand up, to get up; to start up; (*Vogel*) to soar up; (*Frage, Streit*) to arise; (*Wind*) to spring up; (*sich empören*) to rebel against; **~end** *a* elevating, *Am* uplifting; (*eindrucksvoll*) impressive; **~lich** *a* important, considerable; **~~keit** *f* importance; **~ung** *f* elevation; promotion; (*Hügel*) swelling (*od* rising) ground; peak, point; (*Vorsprung*) projection; (*seelische ~~*) exaltation, *Am* uplift; (*Geld*) levying; (*Empörung*) revolt, mutiny; (*e-r Frage*) raising; (*offizielle Befragung*) census, official survey; (*Sondierung*) canvassing; (*Untersuchung*) inquiry; inquest; *~~en anstellen* to make inquiries.

er|heiraten *tr* to acquire by marriage; **~heischen** *tr* to demand, to claim; to require; **~heitern** *tr* to clear up; (*heiter stimmen*) to cheer (up), to exhilarate; (*unterhalten*) to amuse; to enliven; *sich ~~* (*Himmel*) to clear up; (*sich zerstreuen*) to amuse o. s.; **~heiternd** *a* exhilarating, cheering; amusing; **~heiterung** *f* (*Himmel*) clearing up; (*Heiterkeit*) hilarity, cheering; amusement; diversion; **~hellen** *tr* to light up, to enlighten; to illuminate; (*Farben*) to lighten, to brighten; *phot* to expose; *fig* (*Fragen, Probleme etc aufklären*) to clear up, to elucidate; *itr* to become evident (*od* clear); to appear; *daraus ~hellt* hence it appears; **~heucheln** *tr* to obtain by hypocrisy; (*vortäuschen*) to feign, to sham; (*Krankheit*) to simulate; **~hitzen** *tr* to heat, to make hot; (*pasteurisieren*) to pasteurize; *fig* (*Leidenschaften*) to rouse; (*Phantasie*) to fire; (*Mut*) to inflame; *sich ~~* to grow hot; to get hot, to become heated; to heat up; *fig* to grow angry; to fly into a passion; **~hitzung** *f* heating (up); **~~skammer** *f* heating chamber; hearth; **~~swiderstand** *m* heat resistance.

erhoffen *tr* to expect; to hope for.

erhöh|en *tr* to raise; to erect; (*emporheben, moralisch ~~*) to elevate; (*steigern*) to up; (*verstärken, Farbe, Vergnügen*) to heighten; (*Kapital, Wert etc vermehren*) to increase; (*Geschwindigkeit*) to accelerate; (*Preise*) to advance, to raise, to (put) up, *Am* to lift; (*Kredit*) to extend; (*Wert verbessern*) to improve; (*steigern, verstärken*) to intensify; *fig* (*Ruf, Verdienste*) to enhance; (*loben,preisen*) to extol; *fam* to boost; **~ung** *f* elevation; (*Vermehrung*) increase; (*von Löhnen*) rise; (*Gehälter*) raise; (*Wertverbesserung*) improvement; (*Preise*) advance, rise, increase; (*Hügel, Anhöhe*) hill; **~~sfehler** *m* elevation error; **~~sskala** *f* elevation scale; **~~swinkel** *m* angle of elevation; **~~szeichen** *n mus* sharp.

erhol|en: *sich ~~* (*nach e-r Krankheit*) to recover; to recuperate; to gain strength; to get better; (*Markt, Preise*) to recover; (*Börse*) to rally, to pick up; *com* (*nach Zahlungsleistung*) to reimburse o. s. upon; (*sich ausruhen*) to rest, (*entspannen*) to relax; to improve; **~ung** *f* recovery; (*Ruhe*) rest; (*Entspannung*) recreation, relaxation; (*der Preise*) advance; **~~sbedürfnis** *n* need of recovery; **~~sbedürftig** *a* requiring recreation, to be in need of a change, wanting rest; **~~sfähigkeit** *f* recuperative ability; **~~sheim** *n* rest centre, convalescent home; **~~sort** *m* (health) resort; **~~spause** *f* relief period; **~~sreise** *f* pleasure-trip; **~~sstunde** *f* leisure-hour; **~~surlaub** *m* leave, furlough; (*nach Krankheit*) convalescent leave, sick-leave; *Am* vacation; **~~szeit** *f* time of recovery (*od* recuperation).

erhör|en *tr* to hear; (*Bitte*) to grant; **~ung** *f* (*Bitte*) granting; hearing.

Erika *f bot* bell-heather.

erinner|lich *a* present to o.'s mind; *soviel mir ~~ ist* so far as I can recollect; *es ist mir noch ~~* I remember it; **~n** *tr* to remind s. o. of; (*warnen*) to admonish; (*tadeln*) to mention; (*jds Aufmerksamkeit lenken auf*) to draw attention to; to call to mind; to suggest, to observe to; (*dagegen ~~*) to object; *darf ich Sie daran ~~* let me remind you of; *sich ~n* (*nur schwer*) to recollect, (*ohne Anstrengung*) to remember; *wenn ich mich recht ~e* if I remember rightly; *soviel ich mich ~e* as far as I can recollect; **~ung** *f* remembrance, recollection; reminiscence; (*Ermahnung*) admonition; reminder, warning; *in ~~ bringen* to mention, to remind of s. th.; *in ~~ an, zur ~~ an* as a remembrance of, in remembrance of, in memory of; **~~sbild** *n* memory picture; **~~stag** *m* commemoration-day; **~~svermögen** *n* memory; **~~swerbung** *f com* follow-up advertising, *Am* institutional advertising.

erjagen *tr* to get by hunting; *fig* to obtain by great exertion.

er|kalten *itr* to grow cold; *fig* (*Gefühle etc*) to cool down; **~kälten** *tr* to cool, to chill; *sich ~~* to contract a cold, to catch (a) cold; *~kältet sein* to have a cold; **~kältung** *f* cold; chill; catarrh; *e-e ~~ ist im Anzug* a cold is coming on; *sich e-e ~~ zuziehen* to catch (a) cold; **~kämpfen** *tr* to obtain by fighting; **~kaufen** *tr* to purchase, to buy; (*bestechen*) to corrupt, to bribe; *teuer ~~* to pay dearly for.

erkenn|bar *a* discernible, distinguishable, perceptible, recognizable; **~en** *irr tr* to recognize (*an* by); to know; to discern; to perceive, to distinguish; (*einsehen*) to understand; (*Handel*) to credit; (*seine Fehler*) to acknowledge; (*klar sehen*) to realize, to see; *zu ~~ geben* to show, to indicate; *sich zu ~~ geben* to make o. s. known; *sich nicht zu ~~ geben* to keep o.'s incognito; *in e-r Sache ~~* to decide; *jur* to give (*od* to deliver) a judg(e)ment; *für Recht ~~* to adjudge; *auf e-e Geldstrafe ~~* to impose a fine; *für schuldig ~~* to return a verdict of guilty; *sich für schuldig ~~* to plead guilty; *es läßt sich nicht ~~, ob* it is impossible to know whether; *~~ lassen* to reveal, to exhibit; **~tlich** *a* perceivable; (*dankbar*) grateful, thankful; **~~keit** *f* thankfulness; gratitude; **~tnis** *f* perception, understanding; knowledge; (*Begriff, Wahrnehmung*) cognition; *zur ~~ bringen* to make s. o. see; *zur ~~ kommen* to repent; to see (*od* to realize) o.'s mistake; *~~ n jur* decision, finding, sentence, judg(e)ment, verdict (of a court); (*e-s Schiedsgerichts*) award; **~~theorie** *f* theory of cognition; perception theory; **~~vermögen** *n* intellectual power.

Erkennung *f* recognition; **~smarke** *f* identity disk, *Am* identification-tag, *fam* (*Hundemarke*) dog tag; **~swort** *n* watchword, password, parole; **~szeichen** *n* sign of recognition; distinctive mark; distinguishing sign; recognition signals *pl*; *aero* aircraft markings *pl*.

Erker *m* balcony; bay; oriel; **~fenster** *n* bay-window; **~stube** *f* corner-room.

erkiesen *irr tr poet* to choose, to (s)elect.

erklär|bar *a* explainable, explicable; **~en** *tr* (*klar machen, deuten*) to explain; (*darlegen*) to state, to expose; (*Bibel, Gesetz etc auslegen*) to expound; (*erläutern*) to comment upon; (*interpretieren*) to interpret; (*illustrieren*) to illustrate; (*herausbringen*) to elucidate; (*ausführlich beschreiben*) to detail; (*Rechenschaft geben, Gründe angeben*) to account for; *das ~t die Sache* that accounts for it; (*als Zeuge*) to depose; (*öffentlich ~~, bekennen*) to profess; (*kundtun, aussagen, behaupten*) to declare; *Am* to claim; *den Krieg ~~* to declare war on; *für ungültig ~~* to declare void; *für schuldig ~~* to pronounce guilty; *den Belagerungszustand ~~* to proclaim a state of siege; *sich ~~* to declare o. s. (*für, gegen* for, against); to explain to o. s., to account for; **~end** *a* declaratory; illustrative; **~lich** *a* explicable, explainable; (*verständlich*) understandable; (*augenscheinlich*) evident, obvious, apparent; *leicht ~~* easily accounted for; **~t** *a* declared, professed; *~ter Feind* open (*od* sworn) enemy; **~ung** *f* declaration; *e-e ~~ geben* to make a declaration; (*Deutung*) explanation; *zur ~~* in explanation; (*Darlegung*) exposition; (*Auslegung*) interpretation; (*Erläuterung*) elucidation; (*Kommentar*) commentary; (*Illustrierung*) illustration; (*Begriffsbestimmung, Wort~~*) definition; (*Belagerungszustand*) proclamation; *eidesstattliche ~~* affidavit; statutory declaration.

er|klecklich *a* sufficient; (*beträchtlich*) considerable, substantial; **~klettern** *tr*, **~klimmen** *irr tr* to climb up; **~klingen** *irr itr* to sound, to ring; **~koren** *a* select, chosen; **~kranken** *itr* to fall ill; to get sick; to be taken sick; **~krankung** *f* (attack of) illness, sickness; **~kühnen** *r* to venture; to make bold; **~kunden** *tr* to ascertain; (*ausspionieren*) to spy out; *mil* to reconnoitre, to scout; to spot; **~kunder** *m* scout; reconnaissance airplane; **~kundigen**: *sich ~~* to inquire (*nach* after, for); to make inquiries about; *sich nach jds Befinden ~~* to ask for; **~kundigung** *f* inquiry, information; *~~en einziehen* to make inquiries (*bei jdm über etw*) of s. o. on (*od* about) s. th., to gather informations (*über* on); **~kundung** *f* ascertainment, finding out; *mil* scouting, reconnaissance; *gewaltsame ~~* reconnaissance in force; **~~sabteilung** *f mil* reconnoitre detachment; **~~sergebnis** *n* reconnaissance report; **~~sfahrzeug** *n mil* scout (*od* reconnaissance) vehicle; **~~sflieger** *m* air-scout, spotter; **~~sflug** *m* reconnaissance flight; **~~sflugzeug** *n*, **~kunder** *m* reconnaissance aircraft, spotting plane; **~~sspähtrupp** *m* reconnaissance patrol; **~~sstaffel** *f aero* (long-range) reconnaissance squadron; **~~sstreife** *f mil* defensive patrol; **~~strupp** *m* reconnaissance detachment; **~~svorstoß** *m* scouting raid; **~~szug** *m* reconnaissance platoon.

erkünsteln *tr* to affect.

erlahmen *itr* to become lame; (*müde werden*) to get tired; (*nachlassen*) to slacken, to lose o.'s energy.

erlang|en *tr* to reach, to attain; (*erhalten*) to obtain, to get; (*erwerben*) to acquire; **~ung** *f* reaching, acquisition.

Er|laß *m* remission; abatement; (*Verordnung*) proclamation, edict; decree, ordinance; (*e-r Schuld*) release, remission; (*e-r Strafe*) relief; (*Abzug*) deduction; (*von Gesetzen*) issuance (*od* enactment) of laws; *bis zum ~~ allgemeiner Vorschriften* pending the issuance of general regulations; **~lassen** *irr tr* (*Verordnungen*) to issue, to publish, to promulgate; (*Gesetz*) to enact a law; (*Preis*) to yield a reduction; (*Strafe*) to remit; to pardon; *e-e einstweilige Verfügung ~~* to grant an injunction; (*befreien*) to free; (*Schuld*) to remit; (*Rabatt*) to make an allowance, to abate, to deduct; (*Dispensation erteilen*) to dispense from; (*annullieren*) to cancel, to release; **~laßjahr** *n* jubilee; **~lassung** *f* publication; remission; **~läßlich** *a* remissible, dispensable.

erlaub|en *tr* to allow, to permit; (*zugestehen*) to grant; (*dulden*) to tolerate; (*gelten lassen, zugeben*) to admit; *~~ Sie, bitte!* allow me, please! (*dulden*) to suffer; *sich ~~* to take the liberty; (*sich leisten*) to afford; (*sich anmaßen*) to presume; *com* to beg leave, to venture; *was ~~ Sie sich?* how dare you? **~nis** *f* permission, leave; *um ~~ bitten* to beg leave; *jdm ~~ geben* to give s. o. permission, *Am fam* to give s. o. the green light; **~~schein** *m* licence; (*Handel*) permit; **~t** *a* permitted, allowed.

erlaucht *a* illustrious, noble.

erlauschen *tr* to overhear.

erläuter|n *tr* to explain, to clear up; (*veranschaulichen*) to illustrate; (*kommentieren*) to comment (up)on; (*e-e Frage*) to elucidate; **~ung** *f* explanation; illustration; comment; interpretation; note.

Erle *f*, **~nbaum** *m* alder-tree.

erleb|en *tr* to live to see; (*beiwohnen*) to witness; (*erfahren*) to experience; *hat man so etw schon einmal ~t? fam* can you beat that? *der kann was ~~!* he is in for it! **~nis** *n* event, occurrence; adventure; experience.

erledig|en *tr* (*Geschäft*) to settle, to execute, to dispatch; (*durchführen*) to carry through; (*tun*) to do; (*abschließen, beenden*) to wind up (with); (*beim Boxen*) to finish off; (*Zweifel*) to remove; (*Frage*) to answer; *r* to be settled; **~t** *a* settled, finished; *ich bin ganz ~~* I am worn down; I am dead tired; *sie ist für mich ~~* I have finished with her, *Am* I am thru with her; (*Stelle*) vacant; *~te Stelle* vacancy; **~ung** *f* (*Durchführung*) execution, carrying out; (*Vertrag*) completion; (*von Unstimmigkeiten*) settlement; (*von Fragen*) answer; (*e-s Geschäfts*) disposal, dispatch; (*Pflichten*) discharge; *zur ~~ weiterleiten* to forward for compliance.

erlegen *tr* (*Wild*) to kill; (*Geld*) to pay down.

erleichter|n *tr* to lighten, to ease; (*Aufgaben*) to facilitate; (*Herz*) to disburden; to relieve; **~ung** *f* relief, ease; alleviation; (*Aufgabe*) facilitation.

erleiden *irr tr* to suffer; to endure, to bear; (*Verluste, Veränderungen*) to undergo; (*Niederlage*) to sustain.

er|lernen *tr* to learn, to acquire; **~lesen** *irr tr* to select, to choose; *~lesen a* select, exquisite, choice; **~leuchten** *tr* to light up, to illuminate; (*aufklären*) to enlighten; **~leuchtung** *f* illumination; *fig* enlightenment; **~liegen** *irr itr* to succumb to, to sink under; (*e-e Niederlage erleiden*) to be defeated; (*e-r Krankheit*) to die (of); **~listen** *tr* to obtain by artifice.

Erlkönig *m* elf-king, erlking.

erlogen *a* false, untrue; (*erfunden*) fabricated; *das ist ~* that's a lie.

Erlös *m* (net) proceeds, returns *pl*.

erlösch|en *irr itr* to go out; *fig* to die away; (*aufhören*) to expire; to cease; to exist; to die; (*Angebot*) to terminate; (*Versicherung*) to become void; (*Abonnement*) to discontinue; *erloschene Firma* extinct firm; *erloschene Schrift* obliterated writing; **~en** *n* extinction; expiration; termination; (*Vollmacht*) discontinuance, cease

erlös|en *tr* to redeem; to deliver; to release; (*bei Verkauf*) to get; **~er** *m* redeemer; Our Saviour; **~ung** *f* redemption; deliverance.

*

ermächtig|en *tr* to empower, to authorize; *~t sein* to have authority; **~ung** *f* authorization; authority;

(*Vollmacht*) power (of attorney); **~ungsgesetz** *n* enabling act.

ermahn|en *tr* to admonish, to exhort; **~ung** *f* admonition, exhortation.

ermangel|n *itr* to be in want of, to fail; to lack; to be wanting; *es an nichts ~~ lassen* to spare no pains; **~ung** *f* want, absence; *in ~~ dessen* in default of, for want of.

ermannen *r* to take heart.

ermäßig|en *tr* to abate, to reduce; (*Preis*) to mark down, to lower, *Am* to cut down; *zu ermäßigten Preisen* at reduced prices; **~ung** *f* reduction; abatement; (*Steuer*) remission.

ermatt|en *tr* to tire; to weaken; to exhaust; *itr* to faint with, to feel exhausted, to grow tired; *~et von* fatigued with; **~ung** *f* weariness; fatigue; exhaustion; lassitude; **~~sstrategie** *f* strategy of attrition.

ermessen *irr tr* (*abmessen*) to measure; (*schätzen*) to estimate; (*abwägen*) to weigh; (*begreifen*) to conceive, to understand; (*in Betracht ziehen*) to consider; (*prüfen*) to examine; (*beurteilen*) to judge; (*schließen*) to conclude; to infer; *es läßt sich leicht ~* it is easy to understand; *~ n* estimate, opinion; judg(e)ment; (*freies ~*) discretion; *nach meinem ~* according to my judg(e)ment, in my opinion (*od* estimation); *nach freiem ~* at o.'s own discretion; at the pleasure of; *nach bestem ~* to the best of o.'s judg(e)ment; *richterliches ~* judicial discretion.

ermittel|n *tr* to find out; to ascertain, to investigate; to discover; (*identifizieren*) to identify; **~ung** *f* finding out; ascertainment; inquiry; discovery; investigation; (*Analyse*) determination; *~~en anstellen* to institute investigations, to make inquiries (*über* about); **~~sbeamter** *m* investigator; **~~sverfahren** *n* (*Untersuchung*) preliminary investigations *pl*; (*des Gerichts*) legal proceedings *pl*.

ermöglichen *tr* to render possible.

ermord|en *tr* to murder; (*meuchlerisch umbringen*) to assassinate; (*gewaltsam töten*) to slay; (*niedermetzeln*) to slaughter; **~ung** *f* murder; assassination; slaughter.

ermüd|en *tr* to tire out, to weary; *itr* to get tired; **~end** *a* tiresome, wearisome; **~ung** *f* fatigue, lassitude, weariness; (*Erschöpfung*) exhaustion; **~~serscheinung** *f* appearance of fatigue; **~~sfestigkeit** *f* fatigue strength; **~~sgrenze** *f* endurance limit; **~~sstoff** *m* product of fatigue; (*Gift*) fatigue toxin; **~~sversuch** *m* endurance test, fatigue test.

ermunter|n *tr* to awake; *fig* to animate; to enliven; (*aufheitern*) to cheer; (*aufmuntern*) to encourage; to rouse; to urge; **~ung** *f* rousing; animation; encouragement.

ermutig|en *tr* to encourage; **~ung** *f* encouragement.

*

ernähr|en *tr* to nourish, to feed; (*erhalten*) to maintain, to keep; to support; *sich ~~ von* to feed on, to live on; **~end** *a* nourishing, nutritive; **~er** *m* nourisher; maintainer; (*e-r Familie*) bread-winner; **~ung** *f* (*Nahrung*) nourishment, food; *med* nutrition, alimentation; (*Unterhalt*) support, maintenance; *schlechte ~~* malnutrition; **~~samt** *n* Food Office; **~~sbedürfnis** *n* food requirement; **~~skunde** *f* dietetics *pl mit sing*; **~~ssubstanz** *f* food substance; nutrient; **~~sweise** *f* manner of nutrition; feeding habit; **~~swert** *m* nutritive value; **~~szustand** *m* nutritional condition.

ernenn|en *irr tr* to appoint, to nominate; **~ung** *f* appointment, nomination; (*Posten*) *durch ~~ besetzt* filled by appointment, *Am* appointive; **~~surkunde** *f* letter of appointment.

erneu|e(r)n *tr* to renew, to renovate; to repair; (*Bilder*) to restore; (*Farben*) to refresh; *mot* (*Öl*) to change; (*ersetzen, auswechseln*) to replace; (*regenerieren*) to regenerate; (*wieder beginnen*) to revive, to begin again; **~ung** *f* renovation; renewal; revival; replacement; (*Wiederkehr*) repetition; *~~ der Lauffläche* (*Reifen*) retreading; **~t** *a* again, anew.

erniedrig|en *tr* (*Preise etc*) to lower, to reduce; (*herabwürdigen*) to humble, to degrade, to humiliate; *mus* (*Noten*) to flatten; (*Stimme*) to depress; *sich ~~* to humble o. s., to degrade o. s.; (*sich herablassen*) to stoop, to condescend; **~ung** *f* (*von Preisen*) lowering, reduction; (*Herabwürdigung*) humiliation, degradation; **~~szeichen** *n mus* flat.

Ernst *m* earnest(ness); seriousness; sternness; (*Strenge*) severity; (*Würde*) gravity; *im ~* in earnest, *Am fam* no kidding; *ich spreche im ~* I mean business; *jetzt wollen wir einmal ~ reden* (*fam*) now let us talk turkey; *in allem ~e* in good earnest, for good and all; *ist es Ihr ~?* are you in earnest? *das ist nicht Ihr ~* you do not mean to say so; *~ machen mit* to put into practice; *~ a* serious; (*Wesen*) grave; (*streng*) stern; *etw ~ nehmen* to take in earnest; **~fall** *m* event of emergency; actual life; *im ~~* under emergency conditions; **~gemeint, ~haft** *a* earnest, stern; **~haftigkeit** *f* seriousness, gravity; **~lich** *a* serious, earnest; (*eifrig*) ardent, eager.

Ernte *f* harvest; (*Ertrag*) crop; *Rekord~* (*Am*) bumper crop; *~ auf dem Halm* growing crop; **~arbeit** *f* harvesting; **~arbeiter** *m* reaper, harvester; **~aussicht** *f* crop prospect; **~danktag** *m*, **~dankfest** *n Am* Thanksgiving Day; thanksgiving service for the harvest; **~ergebnis** *n* cropping result; *Schätzung der ~~se* estimate of yield; **~ertrag** *m* yield; **~fest** *n* harvest feast; **~helfer** *m* volunteer harvester; **~kranz** *m* harvest wreath; **~maschine** *f* harvester; **~monat** *m* harvest month, August; **~n** *tr, itr* to harvest, to reap, to gather in; *fig* to reap; **~schätzung** *f* yield estimate; **~segen** *m* rich harvest; **~zeit** *f* harvest time.

ernüchter|n *tr* to sober; *fig* to disenchant; to disillusion; **~ung** *f* disenchantment; disillusionment; sobering down.

Erober|er *m* conqueror; **~n** *tr* to conquer, to win; to capture; **~ung** *f* conquest; **~~sdurst** *m* thirst for conquest; **~~skrieg** *m* war of conquest; **~~ssucht** *f* lust of conquest.

erodieren *itr* to erode.

eröffn|en *tr* to open; (*feierlich*) to inaugurate; *Am* to dedicate; *mil* (*Feuer*) to open; (*Geschäft*) to start (*od* to set up) a firm; (*Konto*) to open an account; (*Kredit*) to open a credit; (*Testament*) to probate a will; (*Konkurs*) to institute bankruptcy proceedings; (*anfangen*) to begin; (*erklären*) to publish, to discover, to disclose, to inform; (*förmlich*) to notify; **~ung** *f* opening; inauguration; beginning; (*Mitteilung*) communication, disclosure; **~~sbilanz** *f* initial balance sheet; disclosure; **~~seinakter** *m* curtain-raiser; **~~srede** *f* opening-speech; **~~ssitzung** *f parl* opening session; **~~svorstellung** *f* first night, *Am* opening (night).

erörter|n *tr* to discuss, to debate, to ventilate, to argue; **~ung** *f* discussion, argument.

Erot|ik *f* eroticism; **~isch** *a* erotic; amatory.

Erpel *m* drake.

erpicht *a*: *auf etw ~* intent on; (to be) set on; mad after, (to be) keen on; bent on; *auf das Spiel ~* passionately fond of play.

erpress|en *tr* to extort from; (*Geld*) to blackmail; **~er** *m* extortioner; blackmailer, *Am* racketeer; **~ung** *f* extortion; blackmail; *Am* racket.

erprob|en *tr* to try, to test, to prove; **~t** *a* approved, tried; **~ung** *f* trial, test; **~~sflieger** *m* test pilot; **~~sstelle** *f* testing ground.

erquick|en *tr* to refresh, to comfort; **~end, ~lich** *a* refreshing, comfortable; **~ung** *f* refreshment; comfort.

erraten *irr tr* to find out, to guess; (*lösen*) to solve.

errechnen *tr* to compute, to calculate; to figure out.

erreg|bar *a* irritable, excitable; **~barkeit** *f* irritability, excitability; **~en** *tr* to cause; (*aufregen*) to excite; to stir up; (*reizen*) to provoke; **~end** *a* exciting; stimulating; *~~es Mittel* stimulant; **~er** *m* exciter; exciting cause; instigator; producer; (*wissenschaftlich*) agent; *med* germ; **~~spannung** *f* exciting voltage; **~~strom** *m* exciting current; **~t** *a* excited (*über* with); **~ung** *f* excitement; excitation; **~~sflüssigkeit** *f* exciting fluid; **~~sstadium** *n* stage of excitation.

erreich|bar *a* attainable, available; within reach, get-at-able; **~en** *tr* to reach; (*einholen*) to come up with; (*telephonisch*) to get s. o. on the line; (*stoßen auf*) *Am* to strike; (*erlangen*) to obtain; (*Zug*) to catch, *Am* to make (a train); (*ankommen*) to arrive at; *von e-m Schiebewind unterstützt, ~ten wir London in 13 Stunden* helped by a tail wind, we made London in 13 hours; *seinen Zweck ~~* to gain o.'s end; *ein hohes Alter ~~* to live to a great age.

errett|en *tr* to save, to rescue from; to deliver; **~er** *m* deliverer, rescuer; *eccl* Saviour; **~ung** *f* rescue, deliverance; *eccl* Salvation.

erricht|en *tr* to erect, to build; (*gründen*) to found, to establish; **~ung** *f* erection; establishment, foundation.

erringen *irr tr* to obtain by struggling; (*e-n Erfolg*) to achieve; *den Sieg ~~* to gain the victory; to gain the day; (*Preis*) to carry off; (*vollbringen*) to achieve; *Lorbeeren ~* to capture laurels.

erröten *itr* to blush (*über, vor* at); *~ n* blush(ing).

Errungenschaft *f* acquisition; achievement; attainments *pl*.

Ersatz *m* (*Vergütung*) compensation, indemnity; (*Wiederherstellung*) reparation; (*Ersetzendes*; *Austauschstoff*) substitute; surrogate; (*zusätzlich*) duplicate; reserve, spare; (*Gegenwert*) equivalent; *mil* drafts *pl*, reserve; replacement; *~ leisten* to make restitution for; to make amends; *als ~ für* in exchange (*od* return) for; as a replacement for; **~abteilung** *f mil* replacement detachment; **~anspruch** *m* claim for compensation; **~bataillon** *n* replenishment battalion; replacement training battalion; **~bereifung** *f* spare-tyre equipment; **~beschaffungen**

f pl replacements *pl*; **~brennstoff** *m* substitute fuel; **~dienststelle** *f mil* recruiting centre; **~einheit** *f* reserve unit; replacement training unit; **~elektron** *n* replacing electron; **~fahrer** *m* substitute driver; **~funkstelle** *f* secondary radio station; **~geld** *n* token money; **~glied** *n* artificial limb; **~heer** *n* reserve army; replacement training army; **~kaffee** *m* ersatz coffee; **~kompanie** *f* reserve company; replacement company; **~leder** *n* imitation leather; **~leistung** *f* indemnification, reparation; **~lieferung** *f* substitute, replacement; **~magazin** *n* reserve depot; **~mann** *m* substitute; *film* double, stand-in; *sport* emergency man; **~~schaft** *f mil* fresh draft; replacements *pl*; **~mine** *f* (*Drehbleistift*) refill; **~mittel** *n* substitute; surrogate; ersatz; **~orchester** *n radio* stand-by orchestra; **~pflicht** *f* liability to repair; **~pflichtig** *a* liable for damages; **~programm** *n radio* stand-by program(me); **~rad** *n* spare wheel, stepney; **~reifen** *m* spare tyre, *Am* tire; **~reserve** *f* special reserve, draft registrants *pl*, replacement reservists *pl*; **~spieler** *m sport* emergency man, emergency player; **~teil** *n* spare (part); **~wahl** *f* by-election, *Am* special election; **~wesen** *n* recruiting and replacement administration, draft authorities *pl*; **~zahn** *m* permanent tooth.

er|saufen *irr itr* (*Bergwerk, Schacht*) to become submerged; *fam* (*ertrinken*) to be drowned, to get drowned; **~säufen** *tr* to drown.

erschaff|en *irr tr* to create; to produce; **~er** *m* creator; **~ung** *f* creation.

erschallen *irr itr* to sound, to resound; to ring.

erschauern *itr* to tremble, to shudder, to shiver.

erschein|en *irr itr* to appear; (*vor Gericht*) to attend on the trial; (*kommen*) to show up; (*auftauchen*) to turn up; (*von Büchern*) to be published, to come out; *~~ lassen* to publish, to bring out; *~t demnächst* is going to be published; *soeben erschienen* just come out; *der Angeklagte erschien persönlich vor Gericht* the defendant attended personally in court; *es ~t möglich* it seems possible; *~~ n* appearance; (*vor Gericht*) appearance in court; apparition; publication; **~ung** *f* appearance; *in ~~ treten* to appear; (*Natur~~*) phenomenon; (*Krankheits~~*) symptom; (*Geister~~*) apparition, spectre, vision; *äußere ~~* outward appearance; *das Fest der ~~* Epiphany, Twelfth-night; **~~sform** *f* shape; state; manifestation.

erschieß|en *irr tr* to shoot (dead); *sich ~~* to blow out o.'s brains; **~ung** *f* shooting; *mil* execution; **~~skommando** *n* firing squad.

erschlaff|en *itr* to slacken; *fig* to languish; *tr* to enervate, to slacken; to relax; **~ung** *f* relaxation; *med* atony.

erschlagen *irr tr* to slay, to kill; *vom Blitze ~ werden* to get kill'ed by lightning.

er|schleichen *irr itr* to obtain by tricks, to obtain surreptitiously; to sneak into; **~schleichung** *f* subreption; surreptitious acquisition; **~schlichen** *a* surreptitious; **~schließen** *irr tr* to open; to make accessible; *fig* to infer from; *r* to disclose; **~schmeicheln** *tr* to obtain by flattery; **~schnappen** *tr* to snap up; *fig* to catch up.

erschöpf|en *tr* to drain, to exhaust; *sich ~~* to exhaust o. s.; **~end** *a* exhaustive; depleting; **~t** *a* exhausted; *~~e Batterie el* run-down battery; *meine Geduld ist ~~* my patience is wearied out; **~ung** *f* exhaustion, faintness, weariness; depletion; (*e-r Batterie etc*) running down; **~~szustand** *m* exhaustion.

erschreck|en *tr* to frighten; to terrify, to startle; *irr itr* to be startled by; to be alarmed; *erschrocken* frightened at; terrified; **~lich** *a* frightful, dreadful.

erschütter|n *tr* to shake; (*Gemüt*) to affect deeply, to shock; to unnerve; (*bewegen*) to move; **~ung** *f* shock; (*Gemüts~~*) violent commotion, emotion; *mot* vibration; *tech* concussion, percussion; shake, shaking; **~~sfest** *a* shockproof; **~~sfrei** *a* free from vibration; shockless; **~~ssicher** *a* shakeproof.

erschwer|en *tr* to aggravate; to render difficult, to make more difficult; to complicate; to impede; *~ende Umstände* aggravating circumstances; **~ung** *f* aggravation.

erschwindeln *tr* to get by swindling; to swindle (*od* cheat) out of s. o.

erschwing|en *irr tr* to attain by great efforts; to afford, to manage; **~lich** *a* attainable; within o.'s reach; within o.'s means.

ersehen *irr tr* to see; to learn; to note (*aus* from); *soviel ich ~ kann* as far as I can judge (from it).

ersehnen *tr* to long for.

ersetz|bar, **~lich** *a* reparable; renewable, replaceable; **~en** *tr* to replace, to substitute; (*vertreten*) to fill the place; (*ausgleichen*) to compensate; (*Schaden*) to make good; to make up (for); to compensate for a loss; (*Auslagen*) to reimburse, to refund; **~ung** *f* supplying; reparation; compensation, replacement, renewal.

er|sichtlich *a* evident; obvious; *daraus ist ~~* by this it appears; **~sinnen** *irr tr* to imagine, to devise; to contrive; *Am* to think up; **~spähen** *tr* to espy; to spot; **~sparen** *tr* to spare; to save; to economize; **~sparnis** *f* saving, economy; savings *pl*; **~sprießlich** *a* useful, profitable; beneficial; **~~keit** *f* usefulness; profitableness.

erst *a* first; *fig* foremost, best, prime; leading, superior; *der* (*die, das*) *~e* the first; *fürs ~e* for the present; in the first place, at first; *der* (*die, das*) *~e beste* anyone; anything; the first that comes, the first comer; *aus ~er Hand kaufen* to buy first hand; *in ~er Linie* first of all, primarily; *~e Hilfe* first aid; *im ~en Stock* on the first floor; *zum ~en Mal* for the first time; *zum ~en, zum zweiten, zum dritten!* (*Versteigerung*) going, going, gone! *~ adv* (*zuerst*) at first, first of all; at the outset, at the beginning; only, just; originally; *eben ~, gerade ~* just; *immer ~* always; (*vorher*) before, previously; (*nur, bloß, vor kurzer Zeit*) only; just; no later than; not till; not before; but; *~ vor zwei Tagen* only two days ago; *~ heute morgen* only this morning; *~ gestern* no later than (*od* not till) yesterday, but yesterday; *~ morgen* not till tomorrow; *~ als* only when; *wäre ich ~ dort* if only I was there; (*Steigerung*) *~ recht* all the more; more than ever; *jetzt ~ recht nicht* now less than ever; **~aufführung** *f theat* first-night, première; *Besucher von ~~* first-nighter; **~ausführung** *f tech* prototype; **~ausgabe** *f* first edition; **~ausstattung** *f* initial issue; **~besteigung** *f* (*e-s Berges*) first ascent, first climbing; **~druck** *m* first printing; first edition; (*Wiegendruck*) incunabulum; **~enmal** *adv*: *zum ~~* for the first time; **~ens** *adv* firstly, in the first place; **~ere** *a*: *der erstere ..., der letztere* the former ..., the latter; **~geboren** *a* first-born, eldest; (*Bibel*) first-begotten; **~geburt** *f* first-born child; primogeniture; (*Bibel*) birthright; **~~srecht** *n* birthright, right of primogeniture; **~genannt** *a* first-mentioned, first-named; afore-mentioned, aforesaid; above-mentioned; former; **~klassig** *a* A-1, first-class, first-rate, *Am* exclusive, *Am* banner, *Am* dandy; (*Qualität*) of prime quality, prime, first-chop, of top quality, top-quality; high-grade, outstanding; ace; top-rank; tip-top; *Am* top-notch; (*Wertpapiere*) gilt-edged; *~~e Referenzen* best references; **~lich** *adv* at first, firstly; to begin with; **~ling** *m* first-born; (*bei Tieren*) firstling; *~~e pl* (*bei Früchten*) first-fruits *pl*; first-production; **~~sarbeit** *f* first work; **~~sversuch** *m* first attempt, debut; **~malig, ~mals** *adv* (occurring) for the first time; **~markierer** *m mil aero* initial target marker for night bombing; **~meldung** *f* (*e-r Zeitung gegenüber Konkurrenzblättern*) exclusive news (*od* story), *Am* beat, scoop; **~montage** *f tech* green assembly; **~rangig** *a* of first importance; **~schrift** *f* master copy.

erstarken *itr* to grow strong, to gain strength.

erstarr|en *itr* to stiffen; to grow stiff; (*vor Kälte*) to get chilled; (*Flüssigkeit*) to freeze; (*Metall*) to solidify; (*Fett*) to congeal; (*Zement*) to set; (*vor Schrekken*) to be motionless (*od* paralyzed) with terror; **~t** *a* numb; **~ung** *f* torpidity, numbness, stiffness; (*Metall*) solidification; (*Zement*) setting; hardening; (*durch Kälte*) freezing; (*Fett*) congelation; **~~spunkt** *m* solidification point; freezing point; set point; congealing (*od* coagulation) point.

erstatt|en *tr* to make up to restore; to replace, to return; (*Geld*) to compensate, to refund; to repay; *e-e Gebühr ~~* to rebate a charge; *Bericht ~~* to report (on); **~ung** *f* compensation, restitution; *~~ e-s Berichts* delivery; (*Kosten*) repayment, reimbursement; (*von Steuern*) refunding; **~~spflicht** *f* liability to make restitution.

erstaun|en *tr* to astonish; *itr* to be astonished (*od* surprised) at; *~~ n* astonishment, surprise; amazement; *in ~~ setzen* to astonish, to surprise; **~enswürdig, ~lich** *a* astonishing, surprising, amazing; **~t** *a* surprised, astonished at.

erstechen *irr tr* to stab.

ersteh|en *irr itr* to (a)rise; *tr* to purchase, to buy; to pick up.

ersteig|en *irr tr* to ascend, to scale; to climb, to mount; **~ung** *f* ascent.

ersterben *irr itr* to die away; to expire.

erstick|en *tr, itr* to choke, to suffocate; to smother, to stifle, to asphyxiate; *heiß zum ~~* stiflingly hot; *zum ~~ voll* jammed to suffocation; **~end** *a* (*von Gasen*) asphyxiating; *~~e Kampfgase* asphyxiating gases, lung irritants *pl*; **~ung** *f* suffocation, choking.

er|streben *tr* to strive after (*od* for); to aspire to; **~strecken**: *r* to extend, to stretch to, to reach to; to range, to bear; **~streiten** *irr tr* to obtain by fighting; **~stürmen** *tr* to take by assault; to storm; to take by storm; **~stürmung** *f* assault; storming;

~suchen *tr* to request; ~~ *n* request, demand; *auf ~~ von* on request of; *~~ um Auskunft* information call; *ein ~~ um Gehör einreichen* to file a petition to be heard.

ertappen *tr* to catch; (*überraschen*) to surprise; *auf frischer Tat ~* to seize red-handed, to catch in the very act.

erteilen *tr* to give, to confer on; (*liefern, gewähren*) to furnish; (*verleihen, schenken*) to bestow on; (*zugestehen*) to grant; (*geben, verleihen*) to impart; *Antwort ~* to reply; *Auskunft ~* to give information; *Patent ~* to grant a patent; *Einwilligung ~* to give o.'s consent; *Vollmacht ~* to delegate (*od* to give) authority to s. o.; to empower s. o.; *Auftrag ~* to place (an order); to order, to commission; *Erlaubnis ~* to give permission; *Unterricht ~* to teach, to instruct.

ertönen *itr* to sound, to resound.

ertöten *tr fig* to deaden; to stifle, to smother; *eccl* to mortify; (*Leidenschaften*) to subdue.

Er|trag *m* produce; (*Gewinn*) proceeds *pl*, returns *pl*, profit; *Rein~~* net proceeds *pl*; (*Einkommen*) income, earnings *pl*; revenue; (*Boden*) yield; crops *pl*; **~tragbar** *a* supportable; bearable, tolerable; **~tragbringend** *a* productive; **~tragen** *irr tr* (*aushalten*) to bear, to endure; to stand; (*dulden*) to tolerate; (*leiden*) to suffer; *nicht zu ~~* beyond bearing; **~tragfähig** *a* productive, profitable; **~~keit** *f* productivity, productive capacity; profitableness; **~träglich** *a* supportable; bearable, tolerable, sufferable; **~traglos** *a* unproductive; unprofitable; **~trägnis** *n siehe Ertrag;* **~tragreich** *a* yielding profit; profitable; productive; prosperous; **~trags(be)rechnung** *f* statement of profit and loss; **~tragsteigernd** *a* profit increasing; **~tragswert** *m* value of returns; capitalized value of property; *voraussichtlicher ~~* expectation value.

er|tränken *tr* to drown; **~träumen** *tr* to imagine, to dream of; **~trinken** *irr itr* to get (*od* to be) drowned; *ein Ertrinkender* a drowning man; **~trotzen** *tr* to obtain by pertinacity, to extort (from).

ertüchtig|en *tr* to train; to make fit; (*abhärten*) to harden; **~ung** *f* training; hardening; *körperliche ~~* physical training (*od* drill).

erübrig|en *tr* to save, to spare; to put by; *itr* (*zurückbleiben, übrigbleiben*) to remain; *sich ~~* to be unnecessary; (*überflüssig sein*) to be superfluous; *es ~t sich* it is not necessary.

erwachen *itr* to awake, to wake; (*Tag*) to dawn, to break; (*Gewissen*) to be awakened.

erwachsen *irr itr* to grow up; *fig* to arise, to spring from; *~ a* grown-up; adult; *ein Erwachsener* a grown-up (person), an adult; **~enbildung** *f* adult education.

erwäg|en *irr tr* to weigh; to consider; **~ung** *f* consideration, reflection; *in ~~, daß* considering that; *in ~~ ziehen* to take into consideration, to contemplate.

erwähl|en *tr* to choose; to elect; **~ung** *f* election, creation; choice.

erwähn|en *tr* to mention; **~t** *a* mentioned; **~ung** *f* mention.

erwärm|en *tr* to warm; to heat; *sich ~~ für* to take a lively interest in; **~ung** *f* warming, heating.

erwart|en *tr* (*annehmen*) to expect; (*nichts unternehmen*) to wait for; (*entgegensehen*) to await; (*erhoffen*) to anticipate; **~ung** *f* expectation, anticipation; *in ~~* hoping; **~~en** *f pl* expectations *pl*; **~~svoll** *a* expectant.

erweck|en *tr* to awaken, to rouse; (*Durst*) to excite; (*Hoffnung, Abscheu*) to raise; (*Furcht*) to cause; (*Verdacht*) to arouse; (*vom Tode*) to resuscitate; *wieder ~~* to revive; **~ung** *f* awakening, resuscitation; reviving; *religiöse ~~* revival.

erwehren: *r* to defend o. s. against; to refrain from; to keep off.

erweich|en *tr* to soften; *fig* to touch, to move; **~end** *a* emollient; *fig* moving.

er|weisen *irr tr* (*erzeigen*) to render, to do; (*letzte Ehre*) to pay s. o. the last hono(u)r; (*beweisen*) to prove; *sich ~~* to show o. s.; to turn out to be; **~weislich** *a* provable, demonstrable.

erweiter|n *tr* to widen, to enlarge; to extend; *sich ~~* to grow wider, to get larger; **~t** *a med* (*Pupillen*) dilated; **~ung** *f* enlargement, extension; expansion; widening; (*Ausdehnung*) amplification; (*Vollendung*) completion; (*Ausarbeitung*) elaboration; **~~sbau** *m* annex; **~~sprogramm** *n* expansion program(me).

Erwerb *m* acquisition, gain, profit; living; *von seinem ~e leben* to live by o.'s work; **~en** *tr* to acquire, to gain; to earn; *sein Brot ~~* to earn o.'s bread; *sich um etw Verdienste ~~* to deserve well of; *Eigentum ~~* to acquire the ownership; *Bücher ~~* (*durch Bibliothek*) *Am* to accession; *sich ~~* to earn, to win, to acquire; *sich seinen Lebensunterhalt ~~* to earn a living; *sich Kenntnisse ~~* to acquire knowledge; *sich Freunde ~~* to make friends; *sich jds Achtung ~~* to earn the respect of s. o.; **~er** *m* acquirer; (*Käufer*) purchaser; *jur* transferee; **~sam** *a* (*fleißig*) industrious; **~~keit** *f* industriousness; (*Fleiß*) industry; **~seinkünfte** *pl* professional earnings *pl*; **~sfähig** *a* capable of gaining o.'s living, able to make a living; **~~keit** *f* ability to earn a livelihood; **~sfleiß** *m* industry; **~sgenossenschaft** *f* co-operative society (*od* association); **~slos** *a* (*arbeitslos*) unemployed, out of work; **~~e(r)** *m* unemployed; *die ~~en m pl* the unemployed; **~~enunterstützung** *f* unemployment benefit (*od* relief); *fam* the dole, *Am* unemployment insurance; *~~enunterstützung bekommen* to draw unemployment relief (*od* benefit); to go (*od* to be) on the dole, to get the dole, *Am* to collect unemployment insurance; **~~enversicherung** *f* unemployment insurance; **~slosigkeit** *f* unemployment; **~smittel** *n pl* means of living; subsistence, resources *pl*; **~spreis** *m* purchase price; **~squelle** *f* source of income, means of living; **~ssteuer** *f* profit tax; **~stätig** *a* working; gainfully employed, industrious; **~stätige(r)** *m* gainfully employed person, occupied person; **~stätigkeit** *f* occupation; **~sunfähig** *a* unable to make a living; unfit for work; **~~keit** *f* disablement; (*wegen Krankheit*) sickness disability; **~surkunde** *f* title deed; transfer-deed; **~szweck** *m* profit-making purpose; *zu ~~en* for purpose of profit; **~szweig** *m* line of business; trade; branch of industry (*od* trade); **~ung** *f* acquisition; acquiring; **~~skosten** *f pl* purchase (*od* acquisition) cost (*od* price).

erwider|n *tr* (*entgegnen, antworten*) to say in reply to, to reply, to answer; *jur* to rejoin; (*vergelten*) to return; to retaliate; (*heimzahlen*) to requite; (*Beleidigung zurückgeben; scharf ~~*) to retort; *Am* (*öffentlich entgegnen*) to talk back; (*e-e Gefälligkeit*) to reciprocate; **~ung** *f* reply, answer; return; retort; *fam* back-chat; *jur* rejoinder, replication; **~~sfeuer** *n mil* retaliation fire; counterfire.

erwiesenermaßen *adv* as has been proved.

er|wirken *tr* to bring about; to effect; to achieve; to procure; **~wischen** *tr* (*Dieb*) to catch; *sich ~~ lassen* to get caught; **~wünscht** *a* wished for; desired; (*willkommen*) welcome; (*angenehm*) agreeable; (*wünschenswert*) desirable; **~würgen** *tr* to strangle; to throttle; to choke; (*umbringen*) to slaughter, to kill; **~würgung** *f* strangulation; suffocation; (*Mord*) murder.

Erz *n* (*Gestein*) ore; (*Metall*) metal; brass; bronze; **erz-** *pref* arch-; **~abfälle** *m pl* tailings *pl*; **~ader** *f* mineral vein, lode; **~arm** *a* yielding poor ore; **~artig** *a* metallic; **~aufbereitung** *f* ore dressing; **~betrüger** *m* arch-deceiver; **~bergwerk** *n* ore mine; **~brecher** *m* (*Maschine*) ore-crusher, ore-breaker; **~bischof** *m* archbishop; **~bischöflich** *a* archiepiscopal; **~bistum** *n* archbishopric; **~bösewicht** *m* arrant rogue; **~dieb** *m* arrant thief; **~dumm** *a* hopelessly stupid; **~~kopf** *m* nincompoop; **~en** *a* metal, brazen, bronze; **~engel** *m* archangel; **~faulenzer** *m* very lazy fellow; **~feind** *m* arch-enemy; **~förderung** *f* output of ore; **~gang** *m* mineral vein; **~gauner** *m* arrant swindler; **~gießer** *m* brass-founder; **~grube** *f* mine, pit; **~haltig** *a* containing ore, ore-bearing, metalliferous; **~herzog** *m* archduke; **~~in** *f* archduchess; **~~lich** *a* archducal; **~~tum** *n* archduchy; **~hütte** *f* smelting works *pl*; **~kämmerer** *m* arch-chamberlain; **~ketzer** *m* arch-heretic; **~kunde** *f* metallurgy; **~lager** *n*, **~~stätte** *f* ore deposit; **~lügner** *m* arch-liar, arrant liar; infernal story-teller; **~narr** *m* arrant fool; **~priester** *m* arch-presbyter; **~probe** *f* ore sample; **~schelm** *m* arrant knave; **~spieler** *m* professed gamester; **~spitzbube** *m* arrant rogue; **~stift** *n* archbishopric; **~stufe** *f* lump (*od* piece) of ore; **~trog** *m* buddle; **~vater** *m* patriarch; **~verhüttung** *f* ore-smelting; **~wäscherei** *f* ore-washing plant.

erzähl|en *tr* to tell, to relate; to narrate; (*berichten*) to report; *man ~t sich* people say that; *~~ Sie keine Märchen! fam* don't pull that old stuff! **~end** *a* narrative; epic; **~enswert** *a* worth telling; **~er** *m* narrator, relator, teller of tales; (*Geschichtenerzähler*) story-teller; (*Schriftsteller*) writer; novelist; **~ung** *f* narration, narrative; (*Bericht*) report, account; (*Geschichte*) story, tale; (*Erdichtung*) fiction; (*Geschwätz*) gossip, talk.

erzeigen *tr* to show, to render; (*Gefälligkeit*) to do.

erzeug|en *tr* (*Kinder*) to beget, to procreate; (*fabrizieren*) to manufacture, to produce; (*Dampf, Gas etc*) to generate; (*Landesprodukte*) to grow, to produce, *Am* to raise; (*bilden*) to form; (*Fieber*) to breed; *fig* (*Gefühle hervorbringen*) to engender; *sich ~~* to form; **~er** *m* (*Zeuger*) begetter, progenitor, procreator; father; parent; (*Hersteller*) producer; (*von Waren*) manufacturer; *tech* (*Dampf, Strom etc*) generator; **~~in** *f* mother; **~~preis** *m* producer's price; **~nis** *n* (*des Geistes*) production; (*Natur~~*) produce; *chem etc* product; (*Gewächs*) growth; *deut-*

sches ~~ Made in Germany; of German make, German factory product; (*Fabrikat*) make, fabric; article; (*Ware*) commodity, merchandise, goods *pl*; **~ung** *f* production; (*von Strom, Gas etc*) generation; (*Stahl*) manufacture; (*Herstellung*) making; (*Zeugung*) procreation; begetting; **~~skosten** *pl* prime cost, cost of production; **~~skraft** *f* generative force; productive power; **~~smenge** *f* output; **~~sort** *m* place of production; **~~ssatz** *m* rate of production; **~~sschlacht** *f* struggle for self-sufficiency; **~~ssteigerung** *f* growth in production; **~~svorhaben** *n* production plan.

erzieh|en *irr tr* (*großziehen, auch von Tieren*) to bring up; to raise; (*aufziehen*) to rear; (*geistig* ~~) to educate; (*schulen*) to train; (*züchten; zu guter Lebensart, zu e-m bestimmten Beruf* ~~) to breed; *gut, wohl* (*schlecht*) *erzogen* well- (ill-) bred, well (badly) educated; *fein erzogen* highbred; **~er** *m* educator; (*Hauslehrer*) (private) tutor; (*Pädagoge*) pedagog(ue), (*Schulmann*) education(al)ist; (*Lehrer*) teacher; **~~in** *f* (*Hauslehrerin*) governess; (*Lehrerin*) lady teacher; **~~isch** *a* educational, pedagogic(al); **~ung** *f* (*geistig*) education; (*Lebensart*) breeding; upbringing, rearing (up); *e-e gute* (*schlechte*) ~~ *genossen haben* to have had a good (bad *od* poor) education, to be well (badly) educated; *gemeinsame* ~~ *beider Geschlechter* co-education; **~~sanstalt** *f* school, educational establishment; (*für straffällige Jugendliche*) Borstal institution, reformatory; (*für Fürsorgezöglinge*) remand home, industrial school; *in e-r* ~~*sanstalt unterbringen* to commit to a reformatory; **~~sart** *f* educational method; **~~sbeihilfe** *f* education allowance; **~~skunde, ~~swissenschaft** *f* pedagogics *pl*; **~~smethode** *f* educational method; **~~swesen** *n* educational matters *pl*; educational system; education.

erzielen *tr* (*erreichen*) to obtain, to attain; to arrive at; (*Erfolg*) to achieve; (*Gewinn*) to secure, to realize; (*Preise*) to fetch, to realize; (*hervorbringen*) to produce, to effect; to beget; *e-n Treffer* ~ to score a hit; *sie erzielten 5 Tore* they scored five goals.

erzittern *itr* to shake, to shiver (*vor* at); to tremble.

erzürn|en *tr* to irritate, to enrage, to anger, to make angry; *Am fam* to aggravate; *r* to grow angry; *sich mit jdm* ~~ to quarrel with s. o., to fall out with s. o.; **~t** *a* angry.

erzwingen *irr tr* to force, to enforce; *etw von jdm* ~ to extort s. th. from s. o.; *Liebe läßt sich nicht* ~ love is not to be commanded.

es *prn* it; so; there; *wer ist* ~*?* who is it? *ich bin* ~ it is I, *fam* it is me; *sie sind* ~ it is they; ~ *heißt in der Bibel* it says in the Bible; *ich hab's* I've got it; ~ *regnet* it is raining; ~ *ist kalt* it is cold; *man hat* ~ *mir gesagt* they have told me so; *sie ist reich, ich bin* ~ *auch* she is rich, I am so, too; *ich tat* ~ I did so; *ich glaube* ~ I think so; *gibt* ~ *so was?* is there such a thing? ~ *klopft* there is a knock; *da haben wir* ~*!* there we are! ~ *war einmal* ... once upon a time there was ...; ~ *tut mir leid* I am sorry; *ich weiß* ~ I know; *ich will* ~ *nicht* I won't; ~ *wird getanzt* they are dancing; ~ *lebe der König!* long live the king!

Es *n mus* E flat.

Esche *f* ash; **~nbaum** *m* ash-tree; **~n** *a* ash, ashen.

Esel *m* ass; (*Grautier*) donkey; *männlicher* ~ he-ass, jackass, jack; *Am* burro; *fam* moke, neddy; *Schimpfwort*: ass, jackass, cuddy, duffer, dunce, *Am* mutt; moke; *alter* ~ old fool; *schreien wie ein* ~ to bray; **~chen, ~füllen** *n* colt; **~haft** *a* asinine; *fig* doltish, stupid; **~ei** *f* stupidity; **~in** *f* she-ass, jenny-ass; **~sbrücke** *f* crib, *Am* pony; **~sgeschrei** *n* braying; **~shaut** *f* ass's skin; **~smilch** *f* ass's milk; *bot* creeping hairy spurge; **~sohr** *n* ass's ear; (*im Buch*) dog's ear; **~stritt** *m* kick of an ass; *fig* cowardly revenge; **~treiber** *m* donkey-boy.

Eskadron *f* squad(ron).

Eskimo *m* Eskimo, Esquimau; **~isch** *a* Eskimoan, Esquimauan.

Eskort|e *f* escort, convoy; **~ieren** *tr* to escort; to convoy.

Espe *f* asp, aspen; **~nlaub** *n* aspen leaves *pl*; *er zittert wie* ~ he trembles like an aspen leaf.

eß|bar *a* eatable, edible; ~~*e Pilze* edible mushrooms; **~besteck** *n* tableware; (*Silber*) silver tableware, *Am* flat silver, flat ware; knife, fork and spoon; **~en** *irr tr, itr* to eat, to feed (upon), *mil* to mess, *Am sl bes. mil* to have chow; *zuviel* ~~ to overeat o. s.; *zu Mittag* ~~ to dine, to lunch; *zu Abend* ~~ to have dinner (*od* supper), to sup; *haben Sie schon zu Mittag, Abend gegessen?* have you had your lunch, dinner, supper, yet? *auswärts* ~~ to eat out; *tüchtig* ~~ to eat heartily; *ich esse gern Erdbeeren* I like strawberries; *im Gasthof* ~~ to take o.'s meals at a restaurant; *sich satt* ~~, *sich dick u. rund* ~~ to eat o.'s fill; *wo* ~~ *Sie?* where do you take (*od* have) your meals? **~en** *n* eating, feeding; (*Kost, Verpflegung*) food; (*Mahlzeit*) meal, repast; *mil sl* grub, *Am* chow; (*mittags*) lunch *od* dinner; (*abends*) dinner, (*meist spät abends*) supper; (*in der Kaserne*) mess; *das* ~~ *überschlagen* to dine with Duke Humphrey; *das* ~~ *abtragen* to clear the table; ~~ *fassen mil* to draw (*od* to fetch) o.'s rations; **~~holerschlange** *f Am mil sl* chow line; **~~karte** *f* meal-ticket slip; **~~szeit** *f* dinner-time, eating-time; supper-time, feeding-time; **~~träger** *m* food carrier; **~er** *m* eater; *ein starker* (*schwacher*) ~~ a great (poor) eater; **~gerät** *n Am* dinner pail; **~geschirr** *n* dinner-service; *mil* mess kit; **~gier** *f* gluttony; (*Gefräßigkeit*) voracity; greediness; **~gierig** *a* ravenous, greedy; **~löffel** *m* table-spoon *Abk* tb; *ein* ~~ *voll* a tablespoonful; **~lust** *f* appetite; **~marke** *f* meal ticket; **~saal** *m* dining-room, dining-hall, *Am* eating hall; **~schale** *f* bowl; **~tisch** *m* dining-table; **~waren** *f pl* eatables *pl*, victuals *pl*, provisions *pl*, food-stuff, edibles *pl*, *Am* eats *pl*; **~zimmer** *n* dining-room; (*kleines* ~~) *Am* dinette.

Esse *f* chimney, funnel; chimney-stalk; stack, smokestack; (*Schmiede*) forge; smithy; **~nkehrer** *m* chimney-sweeper, sweep.

Essenz *f* essence.

Essig *m* vinegar; **~älchen** *n* vinegar eel; **~artig** *a* acetous, acetic, vinegar-like; **~äther** *m* acetic ether, ethyl acetate; **~bereitung** *f* vinegar making; **~essenz** *f* vinegar essence; **~ester** *m* acetic ester, ethyl acetate; **~fabrik** *f* vinegar factory; **~flasche** *f*, **~krug** *m* vinegar-cruet, vinegar-bottle; *Öl- u. ~flasche* *f* cruet-stand; **~gurke** *f* pickled cucumber, gherkin; **~sauer** *a* acetic, acetate of; *chem* acetous; **~säure** *f* acetic acid.

Ester *m chem* ester; **~säure** *f* ester acid.

Est|land *n* Estonia; **~e, ~länder** *m* Estonian; **~ländisch, ~nisch** *a* Estonian.

Estrade *f* platform.

Estrich *m* pavement; (plaster-)floor.

etabl|ieren *tr* (*sich*) to establish (o. s.); to settle; to set up in business; to start a business; **~issement** *n* establishment.

Etage *f* stor(e)y, floor; flat; **~nleiter** *m* (*Abteilungsleiter in e-m Kaufhaus*) shopwalker, *Am* floorwalker; aisle-manager, section-manager; **~nwohnung** *f* flat, (*klein, mit Bedienung od Pension*) service-flat, *Am* apartment; **~re** *f* whatnot, stand, shelf, rack.

Etappe *f* (*Teilstrecke e-r Reise*) stage; (*bei Schiff- od Flugzeugreisen*) leg; (*Flugteilstrecke*) hop; *er ist schon in Europa auf der ersten* ~ *e-r Reise um die Welt* he is already in Europe on the first leg of a round-the-world tour; *mil* (*Teilstrecke e-s Marsches*) halting-place, day's march; (*rückwärtiges Gebiet*) line of communications-area, zone of communications; rear area; (*Stützpunkt*) base; **~ngebiet** *n mil* communications zone; **~nlazarett** *n mil* base hospital; stationary hospital (in communications zone); **~nmagazin** *n mil* supply depot in communications zone; **~nort** *m* field base; **~nstraße** *f* rearward road; **~nweise** *a* by stages.

Etat *m* (*Staat*) budget, supplies *pl*; (*Geschäftsabschluß*) balance-sheet; (*Voranschlag des Staats*~) (budget) estimates *pl*; *e-n* ~ *aufstellen* to draw (*od* to make) up the budget; *den* ~ *vorlegen* to introduce the budget; *außer* ~ extra budgetary; **~sberatung** *f* budget debate; **~sjahr** *n* fiscal (*od* financial) year; **~(s)mäßig** *a* budgetary; (*Beamtenstelle*) permanent; **~summe** *f* budget sum; **~stitel** *m* budget item.

etepetete *a fam* finicky, particular.

Eth|ik *f* ethics *pl;* **~isch** *a* ethical; moral.

Ethnograph *m* ethnographer; **~ie** *f* (*Völkerbeschreibung*) ethnography.

Ethnolog|e *m* ethnologist; **~ie** *f* ethnology.

Etikett|e *f* etiquette; ceremonial; (*Schildchen*) label; ticket, *Am* sticker; **~ieren** *tr* to label; **~iermaschine** *f* label(l)ing machine, label(l)er.

etliche *prn* some, several, sundry, a few; ~ *zwanzig* some twenty.

Etui *n* case, box.

etwa *adv* (*ungefähr*) about; nearly, *Am* around; (*vielleicht*) perhaps, by chance; (*falls*) in case; **~ig** *a* possible, eventual.

etwas *prn* something, anything; *ohne* ~ *zu sehen* without seeing anything; *adv* somewhat; a little; ~ *a* some, any; ~ *n*: *ein gewisses* ~ a something; *ein gewisses* ~ *fehlt* it lacks a certain something; *das gewisse* ~ (*Sex Appeal bei Frauen*) *fam* "it", *Am fam* oomph.

Etymolog|ie *f* etymology; **~isch** *a* etymological.

Etzeichen (&) *typ* ampersand.

euch *prn* you.

euer, eure *prn* your; yours.

eure|rseits *adv* on your part; **~sgleichen** *prn* the likes of you; **~thalben, ~twegen** *adv* for your sake, in your behalf; *um* **~twillen** *adv* for your sake; **eurige** *prn* (*der, die, das*) yours.

Eugen|ik *f* eugenics; **~isch** *a* eugenic.

Eule *f* owl; *~n nach Athen tragen* to carry coals to Newcastle; **~nspiegel** *m* Owlglass, Eulenspiegel; **~~ei** *f*, **~~streich** *m* practical joke, tomfoolery, jester's trick, waggery.

Eur|asien *n* Eurasia; **~asisch** *a* Eurasian; **~opa** *n* Europe; **~~-Armee** *f* European Army; **~opäer** *m* European; **~opäisch** *a* European; **~opäisieren** *tr* to Europeanize; **~oparat** *m* Council of Europe.

Euter *n* udder, dug.

Euthanasie *f* (*Gnadentod*) euthanasia; mercy killing.

evakuier|en *tr tech* to exhaust, to empty; (*Personen*) to evacuate; **~te(r)** *m* evacuee; **~ung** *f* evacuation.

evangel|isch *a* evangelical; Protestant; **~ist** *m* evangelist; **~ium** *n* gospel.

Eventu|alität *f* eventuality, contingency; **~ell** *a* (*etwaig*) possible; (*mutmaßlich*) alleged; (*möglich*) potential; *adv* if so; if occasion arises; (*nötigenfalls*) if need be; (*vielleicht*) perhaps, possibly; (*gegebenenfalls*) eventually.

Ewer *m* (fishing-)smack; sculler, lighter; **~führer** *m* lighterman.

ewig *a* eternal; (*Schnee*) perpetual, everlasting; permanent; (*endlos*) endless; (*dauernd*) continual; *ich habe sie ~ nicht gesehen* I haven't seen her in ages; *der ~e Jude* the Wandering Jew; *auf ~* for ever; *dein auf ~* yours for ever; *es ist ~ schade* it is a great pity; **~keit** *f* eternity; perpetuity; *seit e-r ~~* it is ages that; *von ~~ her* from ancient times, from times immemorial; *von ~~ zu ~~* to all eternity; **~lich** *adv* eternally, for ever.

exakt *a* accurate, exact; **~heit** *f* exactness, exactitude.

Exam|en *n* examination, *fam* exam; *im ~~ durchfallen* to fail in an examination; *fam* to be flunked, to be plucked; *ein ~~ machen* to go in for an examination, to take an examination; *im ~~ durchkommen* to pass the examination; **~ensarbeit** *f* paper; thesis; **~inand** *m* examinee; **~inator** *m* examiner; **~inieren** *tr* to examine.

Exege|se *f* exegesis; **~t** *m* commentator.

Exekutive *f* (*Exekutivgewalt*) executive power.

Exempel *n* example, instance; *zum ~* for instance, e. g.; *math* sum, arithmetical problem.

Exemplar *n* copy (of a book); (*Einzelstück*) number, issue; (*Muster*) sample, pattern, model; (*Pflanze*) specimen; **~isch** *a* exemplary.

exerzier|en *tr, itr* to exercise, to drill; to march; **~halle** *f* drill hall; **~ladung** *f* practice charge; **~marsch** *m* practice march, goose step; **~munition** *f* blank (*od* dummy) ammunition, drill ammunition; **~ordnung** *f* drill formation, drill regulation; **~patrone** *f* blank cartridge; **~platz** *m* drill-ground, parade-ground.

Exil *n* exile; **~ieren** *tr* to exile; **~regierung** *f* government in exile.

Exist|enz *f* existence; livelihood; **~~bedingungen** *f pl* conditions of life, living conditions *pl*; **~~berechtigung** *f* right to exist; **~~fähig** *a* capable of existence; **~~minimum** *n* minimum subsistence level; **~~entialismus** *m* existentialism; **~ieren** *itr* to exist; (*leben können*) to live, to subsist.

ex|kommunizieren *tr* to excommunicate; **~matrikulieren** *r* to leave the university, to go down; **~orzieren** *tr* to exorcize.

exotisch *a* exotic.

Exped|ient *m* forwarding (*od* dispatching) clerk; **~ieren** *tr* to dispatch, to forward; **~ition** *f* (*Wegschicken*) dispatching; (*Unternehmen*) expedition, enterprise; (*e-r Zeitung*) office; **~itionskorps** *n mil* expeditionary force.

Experiment *n* experiment; **~alchemie** *f* experimental chemistry; **~alphysik** *f* experimental physics; **~ell** *a* experimental; **~ieren** *itr* to experiment.

Experte *m* expert.

explo|dieren *itr* to explode; **~sibel** *a* explodable; **~sion** *f* explosion; **~~sdruck** *m* explosion pressure; **~~sgefahr** *f* explosion hazard; **~~sgemisch** *n* explosive mixture; **~~smotor** *m* internal combustion engine; **~~spilz** *m* mushroom-shaped explosion; **~~sraum** *m* explosive chamber; **~~ssicher** *a* explosion-proof; **~~stakt** *m* work (*od* explosion) stroke: **~~swelle** *f* wave of explosion; **~~swirkung** *f* effect of explosion; **~siv** *a* explosive; **~sivgeschoß** *n* explosive bullet, bursting projectile; **~sivstoff** *m* explosive.

exponieren *tr* to expose; (*erklären*) to explain, to expound; *sich ~* to expose o. s. to; *fam* to stick o.'s neck out.

Export *m* export(ation); **~abteilung** *f* export department; **~artikel** *m* exports *pl*, export item; **~ausführung** *f* export version; **~eur** *m* exporter; **~genehmigung** *f* export permit; **~geschäft** *n* export trade; (*Einzelabschluß*) export transaction; **~haus** *n* export firm; **~ieren** *tr* to export, to sell abroad; **~kaufmann** *m* export merchant; **~überschuß** *m* export surplus.

express *adv* expressly; *~ n* (*Eilzustellung*) express; *mit ~ schicken* to send by express; *Am* to express (a package *od* merchandise); **~brief** *m* special delivery (letter); **~gut** *n* express luggage, express goods *pl*; **~zug** *m* express (train); **~zustellung** *f* special delivery.

Expression|ismus *m* expressionism; **~ist** *m* expressionist; **~istisch** *a* expressionist(ic).

Extempor|ale *n* exercise in class; extempore; **~ieren** to extemporize, to improvise; to adlib.

extra *adv* extra, special, additional; besides; **~blatt** *n* special edition, *Am* extra; **~fein** *a* superfine; **~ordinarius** *m* reader, (senior) lecturer, *Am* associate professor; **~post** *f* special mail (*od* post); **~wurst** *f*: *fig sie muß immer e-e ~~ gebraten haben* she always has to have something special; **~zug** *m* special train, excursion train.

extrahieren *tr* to extract; to eliminate; to lixiviate.

Extrakt *m* extract, essence.

extrem *a* extreme; exaggerated; *~ n* extreme; *von e-m E~ ins andere fallen* to run into extremes; **~itäten** *f pl* extremities *pl*.

Exzellenz *f* Excellency.

ex|zentrisch *a* eccentric; **~zerpt** *n* extract, epitome; excerpt, excerption; **~zerpieren** *tr* to make excerpts from; **~zeß** *m* excess, outrage.

F

F *Abk mit **F** siehe Liste der Abk*; **~-dur** F major; **~-Schlüssel** *m* F clef; bass clef; *aus dem ff verstehen* to know s. th. thoroughly, to know s. th. inside out.

Fabel *f* (*Tier~*) fable; (*Lüge*) untruth, falsehood; *fig* (*Erdichtung, unglaubliche Geschichte*) tale; fiction; story; legend; (*Gang der Handlung*) plot; **~buch** *n* book of fables; **~dichter** *m* fable-writer; (*Fabulist, Erfinder von Lügen*) fabulist; **~ei** *f* fabulous story; **~haft** *a* (*wunderbar*) fabulous; (*unglaublich*) incredible; (*erstaunlich*) astonishing, amazing; (*großartig, hervorragend*) first-class; *adv* (*ungeheuer*) immensely, enormously; marvellously; **~haftigkeit** *f* fabulousness; **~hans** *m* (*Lügner*) story-teller; **~lehre** *f* mythology; **~n** *itr* (*Lügen erzählen, erfinden*) to tell tales, to tell stories (*über* about); (*schwätzen*) to talk idly; (*Fabel erzählen, fabulieren*) to tell a fable, *poet* to fable; **~tier, ~wesen** *n* fabulous being.

Fabrik *f* (manu)factory; mill (*bes. in Zssg*); (*Werk*) works *pl*; (*Anlage, Anwesen*) establishment, plant, manufacturing plant; **~ant** *m* (*Besitzer*) factory-owner, mill-owner; (*Erzeuger*) manufacturer; (*Hersteller*) maker; **~arbeit** *f* work in a factory, factory work; (*Ware*) manufactured article (*od* goods *pl*); **~arbeiter** *m* factory worker (*od* labo(u)rer); factory hand; (industrial) worker, workman, labo(u)rer; workshop hand; **~at** *n* (*Marke, Fertigung*) make, brand; manufacture; (*Erzeugnis*) product, article; (*Stoff*) (textile) fabric; *dauerhaftes ~~* long wearing fabric; *waschbares ~~* washable fabric; **~ation** *f* manufacture, manufacturing, making; production; fabrication; run; *laufende ~~* course of manufacture; **~~sabfälle** *m pl* broke(s *pl*); (*Papier*) waste; **~~sabteilung** *f* manufacturing department; **~~sanforderung** *f* fabrication requirements *pl*; **~~sanlage** *f* production equipment; **~~sauftrag** *m* job order; **~~sbetrieb** *m* manufacturing plant; **~~sfehler** *m* flaw; factory defect; **~~sfreigabe** *f* admission of manufacturing; **~~sgang** *m* manufacturing process, processing; **~~sgeheimnis** *n* trade secret; **~~skosten** *pl* cost of production; **~~sleiter** *m* superintendent; **~~snummer** *f* serial number, stock number; **~~sprogramm** *n* manufacturing schedule; **~~svorgang** *m* manufacturing operation; **~~szweig** *m* manufacturing branch; **~besitzer** *m* manufacturer; **~betrieb** *m* factory management; (*Anlage*) plant, establishment; **~direktor** *m* plant manager, managing director; superintendent; **~frisch** *a* factory-fresh; **~gebäude** *n* premises of a factory, factory building; **~gegend** *f* industrial quarter; **~mädchen** *n* factory-girl; **~marke** *f* trade-mark; **~mäßig** *a* industrial, by machinery; **~~** *hergestellt* manufactured, factory-made; **~neu** *a* brand-new; **~niederlage** *f* manufacturer's sales branch office; **~nummer** *f* serial number; **~packung** *f* original packing; **~preis** *m* factory price, prime cost; price ex works; **~schornstein** *m* smoke-stack, factory chimney; **~stadt** *f* manufacturing town; **~ware** *f* manufactured goods *pl* (*od* articles); machine-made goods *pl*; **~zeichen** *n* trade-mark; **fabrizieren** *tr* to manufacture; (*herstellen*) to make; (*produzieren*) to produce; *fig* (*Lügen erfinden, etw erdichten*) to fabricate

fabulieren *itr* to invent stories.

Facett\|e *f* facet; **~iert** *a* faceted.

Fach *n* (*Abteil*) compartment, division; (*Schub~*) drawer; (*Bücherbrett*) shelf; *typ* (*im Schriftkasten*) box; (*Füllung e-r Tür*) panel, row; (*in der Wand*) pane; (*Schreibtisch*) pidgeon-hole; (*Ablage~*) filing cabinet; (*Post~*) lock box; (*Schrankabteil*) partition; (*Bank*) safe; *anat* cell; *fig* (*Zweig*) branch; line; field; business; (*Arbeitsgebiet*) department, province; (*Unterrichts~*) subject; *Am* (*Haupt~ e-s Studenten*) major; *als Spezial~ betreiben* to specialize (in, *Am* on); *als Haupt~ studieren Am* to major in; *in welchem ~ ist er?* what is his occupation? *das schlägt nicht in mein ~* that is not in my line; *er versteht sein ~* he knows his business; **~abteilung** *f* special branch; **~arbeit** *f* expert work; **~arbeiter** *m* expert (*od* skilled *od* trained) worker; specialist, technician; craftsman; **~arzt** *m* specialist (*für* in); (*für innere Medizin*) internist; **~ausbildung** *f* special training; professional education; **~ausdruck** *m* technical term; **~ausschuß** *m* professional committee, committee of experts; **~berater** *m* technical adviser, consultant; **~bildung** *f* professional (*od* technical) education; **~bücherei** *f* special library; **~einsatz** *m* vocational employment; **~gebiet** *n* field of work, specialty; **~gelehrte(r)** *m* specialist; **~gemäß** *a* workman-like; **~genosse** *m* professional colleague; **~geschäft** *n* special shop; **~gruppe** *f* section of experts; trade group; **~ingenieur** *m* expert engineer, engineering specialist; **~katalog** *m* special catalogue (*od* catalog); **~kenntnisse** *f pl* special knowledge; **~kräfte** *f pl* skilled labo(u)r; **~kundig** *a* competent, expert; **~lehrer** *m* subject teacher, teacher in a special branch; **~lich** *a* professional, special; functional; **~literatur** *f* technical literature; **~mann** *m* expert, specialist; **~männisch** *a* expert, professional; **~ordnung** *f* classification; **~photograph** *m* professional photographer; **~presse** *f* technical press (*od* literature); **~schaft** *f* vocational union, industrial federation; **~schrifttum** *n* technical literature; **~schule** *f* technical (*od* professional *od* special) school; **~simpeln** *itr fam* to talk (*od* to prattle) shop; **~sprache** *f* technical language, professional terminology; **~studium** *n* professional study; **~trupp** *m* technical troop; specialist squad; **~verband** *m* craft union; **~welt** *f* technical world; **~werk** *n* frame-work, half timbered work; truss; (*Buch*) special work; **~werkhaus** *n* frame(work) house; half-timbered building; **~wissen** *n* expert knowledge; **~wissenschaft** *f* special branch of science; specialty; **~wort** *n* technical term; **~wörterbuch** *n* technical dictionary; **~zeitschrift** *f* special periodical, technical journal; trade-paper.

...fach (*in Zssg*) ... times, ... fold; (*in Zssg*) *z. B. zehnfach* tenfold.

fäche\|ln *itr* to fan; **~r** *m* fan; **~rantenne** *f* fan-shaped aerial; **~raufklärung** *f mil* fanwise reconnaissance; **~rförmig** *a* fan-shaped; *bot* flabelliform; **~~** *ausschwärmen mil* to fan out, to deploy; **~rschuß** *m* (*Torpedos*) spread salvo; **~rturn** *m aero* fan turn.

Facit *n* sum, amount.

Fackel *f* torch, flare; (*Wachs~*) flambeau; *fig* firebrand; **~n** *f pl* (*auf der Sonne*) solar eruption; **~n** *itr* to flare, to blaze; *fig* (*zögern*) to hesitate, to trifle; (*schwindeln*) to fib; to talk nonsense; *ohne lange zu ~n* to make short work; **~schein** *m* torch-light; **~träger** *m* torcher, torch-bearer; **~zug** *m* torch-light procession (*od* parade).

*

Fädchen *n* small thread.

fade *a* unsavoury; stale; tasteless; *fig* (*abgeschmackt*) insipid; (*langweilig*) dull, flat; *ein ~r Mensch* a bore, *Am fam* a boiled (*od* stuffed) shirt; *ein ~r Witz* (*fam*) a corn(e)y joke; *~s Zeug* fiddle-faddle.

Faden *m* thread; twine; (*Maß*) fathom; (*Staub~, el Draht~*) filament; (*Faser*) fibre, *Am* fiber; (*Holz~*) grain; (*Zucker*) string; (*im Okular*) thread hair, web (of a graticule); *keinen guten ~ an jdm lassen* not to have a good word to say for; *der ~ e-r Geschichte* the thread of a story; *ihr Schicksal hängt an e-m dünnen ~* her fate hangs by a thread; *keinen trokkenen ~ am Leibe haben* to be wet to the skin; not to have a dry stitch of clothing on; **~ähnlich, ~artig** *a* threadlike; filamentous; **~heftung** *f* thread-stitching; **~kreuz** *n* spider lines *pl*, crosshairs *pl*; *mil* graticule; **~rolle** *f* reel of thread; cotton reel; **~nudeln** *f pl* vermicelli *pl*; **~scheinig** *a* threadbare, sleazy; (*schäbig*) shabby; **~strahl** *m* (*Elektronen*) thread beam; pencil rays *pl*; **~strich** *m* spider line; **~wurm** *m* nematode; **~ziehend** *a* stringy; ropy.

Fading *n* (*Schwund*) fading; **~ausgleich** *m radio* automatic volume control; **~automatik** *f* automatic volume control; **~effekt** *m* fading effect.

Fadheit *f* dul(l)ness; insipidity.

Fagott *n* bassoon; **~ist** *m* bassoonist.

Fäh *n* fur of minever; *siehe*: *Fehe*.

fähig *a* capable, able; (*qualifiziert*) qualified, fit; *sie ist zu allem ~* she is capable of anything; *ein ~er Kopf* to have a good (*od* clever) mind; **~keit** *f* ability, capability, capacity; qualification; (*Anlagen*) talent, faculty, gift; (*physisch*) fitness.

fahl *a* fallow; (*matt*) faded; (*bleich*) pale; livid; **~gelb** *a* fallow; **~rot** *a* fawn-colo(u)red.

fahnd\|en *itr*: *nach jdm ~* to search for; **~ung** *f* search for criminal (*od* a missing person *od* a fugitive); **~~sbuch** *n* special register of the criminal police; **~~sgesuch** *n* search warrant.

Fahne *f* flag, standard; (*Wimpel*) streamer; (*bes. mil*) colo(u)rs *pl*; banner; *typ* correcting proof, galley; slip; *zur ~ schwören* to swear to o.'s colo(u)rs; *mit fliegenden ~n* with flying colo(u)rs.

Fahnen\|abzug *m typ* slip, galley-proof, proof-sheet; **~eid** *m* oath of enlistment; **~flucht** *f* desertion; **~flüchtig** *a* deserting; **~~e(r)** *m* deserter; **~junker** *m* ensign, colo(u)r-sergeant; officer candidate; (*Reiterei*) cornet; **~kompanie** *f* colo(u)r-guard company; **~schmied** *m* farrier-major; **~stange** *f*, **~stock** *m* flag-staff, *Am* flagpole; **~träger** *m* colo(u)r-bearer; **~wache** *f* standard-guard; colo(u)r guard (*od* sentinel); **~weihe** *f* consecration of the colo(u)rs.

Fähn\|lein *n* pennon; (*Trupp*) squad, troop; **~rich** *m* cadet; officer candidate; *Am* ensign; **~~** *zur See* midshipman.

Fahr\|bahn *f*, ***~damm*** *m* roadway, carriageway, carriage-road, *Am* pavement, driveway; traffic lane; *rail* track(way); **~~decke** *f* road surface; **~bar** *a* passable, movable; practicable; (*schiffbar*) navigable; (*beweglich*) mobile; motor-drawn; portable, movable; **~~keit** *f* portability, movability; **~befehl** *m* driving order; **~bereich** *m mil* radius of action; cruising radius; range of action; operating range; travel(l)ing distance; **~bereit** *a* ready for driving, in running order; **~bereitschaft** *f* motor-pool; **~dienst** *m rail* train-service; **~dienstleiter** *m rail* assistant station-master, *Am* station agent; **~draht** *m el* trolley wire; **~er** *m* driver; *mot auch* chauffeur; (*Rad*) cyclist; **~~flucht** *f* driver's escape, *Am* hit-and-run driving; **~~haus** *n mot* cab; **~~in** *f* woman driver; **~~luke** *f* (*Tank*) driver's access hatchway; **~~optik** *f* (*Tank*) driver's periscope; **~gast** *m* passenger; **~~raum** *m aero* cabin; **~~schiff** *n* passenger-steamer; **~geld** *n* fare; (*Straßenbahn*) tram fare, *Am* car fare; **~geleise** *n* rut; **~gelegenheit** *f* conveyance; (*für Anhalter*) lift; **~geschwindigkeit** *f* driving speed; **~gestell** *n mot* chassis; *aero* undercarriage, *Am* landing gear; *einziehbares ~~* retractable undercarriage; **~ig** *a* fidgety; **~karte** *f rail* ticket; *e-e direkte ~~ lösen bis* to book through to; *einfache ~~* single (*Am* one-way) ticket; **~~nautomat** *m* automatic ticket vending machine; **~~nbeamter** *m* (*Schalterbeamter*) booking-clerk, *Am* ticket-agent; **~~nschalter** *m*, **~~nausgabe** *f* booking-office, *Am* ticket-office (*od* ticket-window); (*für alle Strecken*) joint booking-office, *Am* consolidated ticket-office; **~kolonne** *f mil* transport column; supply train; **~kostenentschädigung** *f* travel allowance; **~lässig** *a* negligent, careless, reckless; **~~keit** *f* negligence, carelessness, recklessness; *grobe ~~keit* gross negligence; *leichte ~~keit* slight negligence; **~lehrer** *m* driving-instructor; **~plan** *m rail* time-table, railway-guide, *Am* (railroad) schedule; **~~mäßig** *a* regular, *Am* (according) to schedule, on schedule; (*rechtzeitig*) (up) to time, *Am* on time; *der Flug von New York nach London soll ~~mäßig 11 Stunden dauern* the crossing from New York to London is scheduled to take 11 hours; **~prahm** *f* barge; tank-landing craft; **~preis** *m* fare; **~~ermäßigung** *f* reduction in fare; **~prüfung** *f mot* driving test; **~rad** *n* bicycle, cycle; *fam* bike, *Am* wheel; **~~anhänger** *m* cycle trailer; **~~motor** *m* bike motor; **~rinne** *f* water-way shipping channel, *mar* fairway; channel passage; (*Straße*) rut; **~schein** *m* ticket;

~schule *f* driving school; **~schüler** *m* learner, *Abk* L; **~straße** *f* highroad, highway; **~stuhl** *m* lift, *Am* elevator; (*für Waren*) hoist; (*Rollstuhl*) wheel chair; *e-e Wohnung ohne ~~ Am fam* a walk-up flat; **~~führer** *m* lift-boy, lift-man, *Am* elevator boy, elevator operator; **~~kabine** *f*, **~~korb** *m* cage, *Am* car; **~t** *f* (*im Wagen*) ride, drive; (*Reise*) trip, journey; (*eilige Reise, Segel~*) run; (*zur See*) voyage, passage, cruise; (*e-s Schiffes*) course, headway; *aero* (= *Geschwindigkeit*) air speed; *~t über Grund aero* ground speed; *in voller ~t* (at) full speed; *~t verlieren* (*Schiff, Flugzeug*) to lose headway; *~t aufnehmen* to gather speed; *~t vermindern* to slacken speed; *halbe ~t mar* half speed; *kleine ~t mar* dead-slow speed; **~~ausweis** *m* ticket; **~~enbuch** *n mot* log-book, trip (record) book; **~~messer** *m aero* airspeed indicator, *Abk* A. S. I.; **~~stufe** *f* rate of speed; **~~richtung** *f* direction of motion; **~~richtungsanzeiger** *m mot* direction indicator; (*mit Lampen*) turn-indicator lights; **~~unterbrechung** *f* break of the journey, *Am* stopover; **~~weg** *m* prescribed route; **~~wind** *m aero* air stream; **~truppen** *f pl* Army Service Corps; horse-drawn supply service; **~unterricht** *m* driving instruction; **~verbot** *n* prohibited to traffic; **~vorschrift** *f* driving regulations *pl*; **~wasser** *n* navigable water, channel; *fig* track, element; *mar* fairway, lane in minefield; *im richtigen ~~ sein Am fam* to be in the groove; **~weg** *m* carriage-way, carriage-road; **~werk** *n aero* undercarriage, *Am* landing gear; **~zeit** *f* running-time; (*Reisedauer*) duration of a journey; **~zeug** *n* vehicle; (*Schiff*) vessel, craft, ship; **~~kolonne** *f mil* motorized column; column of vehicles; **~~verkehr** *m* vehicular traffic.

fahren *irr itr* (*mit e-m Fahrzeug*) to go; (*von Fahrzeugen*) to run; (*im Wagen, auf dem Rad*) to ride; to drive; (*in e-m Schiff*) to sail; (*im Schlitten*) to ride; (*mit der Bahn*) to go by train (*od* rail); (*im Auto*) to motor; (*mit abgestelltem Motor*) *Am* to coast; (*mit dem Omnibus*) to go by bus, to ride in a bus; *hinauf~* to ascend; *hinunter~* to descend; (*reisen*) to travel; *spazieren ~* to go for a drive, to take a drive; *gut, wohl* (*übel*) *~ bei* to fare well (ill) with; to come off well (badly); *was ist in sie ge~?* what has come over her? *fahre wohl!* farewell! *durch etw ~* to pass; *~ über* (*Fluß etc*) to cross; (*Straßenkreuzung*) to pass; *etw ~ lassen* (*aufgeben*) to let go, to give up; to abandon; to pass up; (*ein Wort*) to drop; (*e-e Gelegenheit*) to let slip, to let go by; *~ in betrunkenem Zustand* drunken driving; *rechts ~!* keep right! *um die Ecke ~* to turn round the corner; *der Gedanke fuhr mir durch den Kopf* the thought flashed through my mind; *auf Grund ~* (*Schiff*) to run aground; *aus dem Hafen ~* to clear the port; *in den Hafen ~* to enter (*od* to make) the port; *jdm in die Haare ~* to pull s. o. by the hair; *mit der Hand über das Gesicht ~* to pass o.'s hand over o.'s face; *aus der Haut ~* to burst with impatience; to jump out of o.'s skin; *aus der Hand ~* to slip from o.'s hands; *gen Himmel ~* to ascend to heaven; *zur Hölle ~* to descend to hell; *in die Höhe ~* to start up; (*Ballon, Fahrstuhl etc*) to go up; to ascend; *in die Kleider ~* to slip on o.'s clothes; *tr* (*e-n Wagen lenken*) to drive; (*befördern*) to convey; (*Steine*) to cart; (*Boot*) to row; (*Schiff*) to navigate, to sail (*nach* for); *er kann Auto, Motorrad, rad~* he knows how to drive a car, to ride a motorcycle, a bicycle; *jdn spazieren ~* to take s. o. out for a ride; *sich fest ~* to stick fast; **~d** *ppr, a* going, riding, driving; (*umherschweifend*) vagrant; *~de Habe* movables *pl*; *~der Ritter* knight-errand; *~des Volk* way-faring people, travel(l)ing vagrants *pl*; **~de(r)** *m* vagabond, tramp.

Fähr|e *f* ferry; **~mann** *m* ferryman; **~te** *f* track, trace, trail; scent; *auf falscher ~~* on the wrong track.

Fäkal|düngemittel *n* sewage manure; **~ien** *pl* feces *pl*.

Faksimile *n* facsimile; **~telegraphie** *f* picture telegraphy, phototelegraphy.

fakt|isch *a* effective, real; **~or** *m* manager; *typ* foreman; *math* factor, coefficient, multiplier; submultiple; component part; **~orei** *f* factory; **~otum** *n* factotum; jack-of-all-work; **~um** *n* fact; **~ur** *f* invoice.

Fakult|ät *f* teaching staff, *Am* faculty; **~ativ** *a* optional.

falb *a* fallow; tawny; **~e** *m* dun horse.

Falbel *f* flounce, furbelow.

Falke *m* falcon, hawk; **~nauge** *n* hawk's eye; *fig* eagle eye; **~nbeize**, **~njagd** *f* hawking, falconry; **~nier**, **Falkner** *m* falconer.

Fall *m* fall; (*Sturz*) tumble; (*Herabfall, Senkung*) drop; (*von Preisen, Kursen, Barometer etc*) fall, drop; (*Wasser~*) fall(s *pl*); (*Verfall*) decline, downfall, decay, ruin; (*Unfall*) accident, incident; (*Einnahme e-r Stadt nach e-r Belagerung*) fall (of a city); (*Neigung*) *rail* gradient, slope, incline; (*Zusammenbruch*) failure, *com* bankruptcy; *gram* (*Kasus*) case; (*einzelner Umstand, Vorfall, Rechtsfall, Tatbestand*) case; event; affair; instance; situation; (*Krankheits~*) case; *der Sünden~* the Fall (of man); *Regen~, Schnee~* fall of rain, fall of snow; *der ~ der Blätter* the fall of leaves; *der ~ Meyer gegen Müller* (*jur*) case Meyer versus Müller; *e-n schlimmen ~ tun* to have a bad fall; *zu ~ bringen* (*Regierung*) to overthrow; (*Mädchen*) to seduce; (*jdn zu ~ bringen*) to give s. o. a fall; (*ruinieren*) to ruin; *den ~ setzen* to suppose; *gesetzt den ~, daß* supposing that, assuming that; *der ~ ereignet sich öfters* it frequently happens; *auf alle Fälle gefaßt* prepared for all emergencies, prepared for everything; *wenn der ~ eintritt* if this should take place; *ein schwerer ~* (*Sturz*) a heavy fall; *ein schwieriger ~* a difficult case; *der zur Entscheidung stehende ~* the case at issue; *der vorliegende ~* the case in point; *das ist ganz mein ~* that suits me exactly; *außer im ~e, daß* except if; *für den ~, daß* should the case arise; *im ~, daß, auf den ~, daß* in case that; *im besten ~* at best; *im schlimmsten ~* if worst comes to worst, at the worst; *in manchen Fällen* in some instances; *auf jeden ~* at all events, at all cost; at any rate, in any case, anyhow, *Am* anyway; *auf alle Fälle* in any case; *auf keinen ~* by no means, in no case; on no account; *Knall u. ~* on the spot; *von ~ zu ~* as the case may be; according to its merits; **~bahn** *f* (*Bombe*) trajectory; **~beil** *n* guillotine; **~(benzin)tank** *m mot, aero* gravity tank; **~beschleunigung** *f* (*freie*) gravitational acceleration; (*von Geschossen*) acceleration downward; **~bö** *f aero* air pocket; down gust; **~brücke** *f* draw-bridge; **~geschwindigkeit** *f* velocity of falling bodies; rate of fall; **~gesetz** *n* law of gravity; **~grube** *f* (*auch fig*) pitfall, deadfall; **~hammer** *m tech* drop hammer; pile driver; falling weight; **~höhe** *f* height of fall; **~klappe** *f tele* drop indicator; *aero* escape hatch; **~kraut** *n bot* arnica; **~nest** *n* trap nest; **~obst** *n* windfall(s *pl*); **~reep** *n* ladder-rope; gangway; **~scheibe** *f* falling disk; *phot* drop-shutter; **~schieber** *m* sliding damper; **~schirm** *m* parachute, chute; *Absprung, Abwurf, Ausbildung mit ~~ u. ~~springerabwehr betreffend* para (+ *entsprechendes Substantiv*), *z. B.* paraoperation *Abwehroperation gegen feindliche ~~springer*; paratroop-dropper *Absetzmaschine für ~~truppen*; paraengineer (*mil*) *~~pionier*; *automatischer ~~* automatic parachute; *Auszieh~~* auxiliary (*od* lift off) parachute, *Am* pull off parachute; *Zusammenlegen des ~~s* parachute folding; *Rücken-, Sitz-, Brust~~* back pack, seat pack, lap pack parachute; *mit dem ~~ abspringen* to parachute, to jump (with a parachute); (*bei Gefahr*) to bail out with a parachute; *er sprang mit dem ~~ über der Tschechoslowakei ab* he parachuted into Czechoslovakia; (*Truppen, Ausrüstung etc*) *mit dem ~~ abwerfen* to parachute, to drop; **~~absprung** *m* parachute jump, jump; **~~agent** *m*, **~~saboteur** *m* parasaboteur; **~~anzug** *m* parasuit; **~~bombe** *f* parabomb; **~~fangleine** *f* parachute cord; **~~gurt** *m* parachute harness; **~~jäger** *m* parachutist, parachute rifleman; paratrooper; *Absetzer für ~~jäger* jumpmaster; **~~jägerabteilung** *f* parachute detachment; **~~bataillon** *n* parachute battalion; **~~jägereinheit**, **~~truppe** *f* paratroops *pl*, unit of paratroopers; **~~leuchtbombe** *f* (aircraft) parachute flare; **~~(luft)mine** *f* parachute mine; **~~rakete** *f* parachute rocket signal; **~~reißleine** *f* parachute rip cord; **~~schule** *f* school of parachutists; **~~schützenabzeichen** *n* parachute badge; **~~seide** *f* parachute silk; **~~springer** *m* parachutist, parachute jumper, chutist; **~~springerabwehreinheit** *f* parashoot(er); **~~truppen** *f pl* parachute troops *pl*, paratroops *pl*, airborn troops landing by parachute; **~~truppenabwehr** *f* antiparachutist defence; **~~turm** *m* parachute tower; **~~(verpackungs)sack** *m* parachute pack; **~~wart** *m* parachute rigger; **~strecke** *f* distance of falling; **~strick** *m* snare; *fig* trap; **~stromvergaser** *m* down draft carburet(t)or; **~sucht** *f* epilepsy, falling sickness; **~süchtig** *a* epileptic; **~tafel** *f aero* bomb-trajectory table; **~tank** *m* gravity tank; **~tor** *n*, **~tür** *f* trap door; (*in Tank od Flugzeug*) escape hatch; **~wind** *m* (*Meteorologie*) catabatic wind; **~winkel** *m* angle of descent; **~zeit** *f* time of fall.

Falle *f* trap; (*Schlinge*) snare; (*Grube*) pitfall; *fig* snare; *tech* (*Türriegel*) latch, catch; (*Schleusentor*) sluice; lock gate; *fam* (*Bett*) bed, *sl* sack; *in die ~ gehen* to fall into a trap; *fam* (*ins Bett gehen*) to hit the sack; *in die ~ locken fig* (*umgarnen*) to entice, to inveigle, to ensnare, to lure into a trap; *in der ~ sitzen* to be trapped; *jdm e-e ~ stellen* to lay a snare for s. o.; to set a trap for s. o.; **~nsteller** *m* trapper.

fallen *irr itr* to fall, to drop; (*Preise*) to decline, to fall, to go down;

(*plötzlich* ~) to slump, to tumble; (*Schuß*) to be heard; (*Wasser, Barometer, Nebel, Ebbe*) to fall; (*Wind*) to abate; (*Einfluß*) to wane, to decline; *unter ein Gesetz* ~ to come under a law, to fall within the scope of a law; (*sinken*) to sink, to fall; (*sterben*) to die, to be killed; *im Felde* ~ to be killed in action; *auf die Nase* ~ to fall on o.'s face; *auf die Knie* ~ to kneel down; *um den Hals* ~ to fall on s. o.'s neck; *aus allen Wolken* ~ to be thunderstruck; *mit der Tür ins Haus* ~ to blurt out; *jdm in den Rücken* ~ to attack s. o. from behind; to stab s. o. in the back; *in Ohnmacht* ~ to faint; *in die Augen* ~ to strike the eye; *jdm in die Rede* ~ to interrupt s. o.; *ins Gewicht* ~ to be of great weight; *nicht ins Gewicht* ~ to be of no consequence; *an jdn* ~ to inherit; (*herfallen über*) to fall upon, to rush; *einander in die Haare* ~ to come to blows; *das ist ihr in den Schoß gefallen* it came to her by sheer luck; ~ *lassen* to (let) drop, to discard; *e-e Bemerkung* ~ *lassen* to drop (*od* to make) a remark; *e-e Sache* ~ *lassen* to drop a matter; *ein Wort* ~ *lassen* to throw in a word; *ins Rote* ~ to have a reddish tinge; *schwer* ~ to be troublesome; *es fällt ihm schwer* he finds it hard; *die Arbeit fällt ihm schwer* the work is difficult for him; *der Würfel ist gefallen* the die is cast; *jdm zur Last* ~ to trouble s. o.; *die Aktien* ~ the shares are on the decline; *das Barometer fällt* the barometer is falling; *der Apfel fällt nicht weit vom Stamme* like father, like son; *er ist nicht auf den Kopf gefallen* he is no fool; ~ *n* (*Sturz*) fall; (*Abnehmen*) decline; (*von Preisen*) fall, going down, dropping; depression; (*Abstieg*) descent; (*plötzliches* ~ *der Preise*) break, slump; ~ *u. Steigen* fluctuation.

fäll|en *tr* to fell, to cut down; (*das Bajonett*) to lower; *chem* to precipitate; *ein Urteil* ~~ *jur* to pass sentence; *ein Lot* ~~ to draw a perpendicular; (*Geometrie*) to let fall; **~ig** *a* due; mature; payable; *die Zahlung ist* ~~ the payment is due; *längst* ~~ overdue; *noch nicht* ~~ unmatured; ~~ *werden* to fall due; **~igkeit** *f* falling due; expiration; maturity; **~~stermin** *m* maturity date; **~methode** *f chem* precipitation method; **~mittel** *n chem* precipitant; **~ung** *f* (*e-s Baumes*) felling, cutting; *chem* precipitation; (*e-s Urteils*) *jur* pronunciation.

Fall|iment *n* failure; **~ieren** *itr* to fail; **~it** *m, a* bankrupt.

falls *adv* in case, in the event, provided that; if, if it be that.

falsch *a* (*unecht*) false, *Am fam* phon(e)y; (*irrtümlich*) wrong; (*unrichtig*) incorrect; (*nachgeahmt*) imitated, artificial; mock, sham; (*verfälscht*) adulterated; (*blind*) false, dead, blank; (*betrügerisch*) deceitful; treacherous; (*treulos*) faithless; (*zornig*) angry; (*Banknote*) forged; (*Haar*) false; (*Hartgeld*) base, bad, counterfeit; (*Juwelen*) sham; (*Name*) fictitious, false; (*Spiel*) foul; (*Wechsel*) forged, counterfeit; (*Würfel*) loaded; (*Zähne*) artificial, false; ~ *anwenden* to misapply; ~ *auffassen* to misconceive, to misinterpret, to misconstrue; to misunderstand; ~ *aussprechen* to mispronounce; ~ *berichten* to misinform; ~ *beurteilen* to misjudge; ~ *gehen* (*Uhr*) to go wrong, to be wrong; ~ *schreiben* to mis-spell; ~ *schwören* to commit perjury, to perjure o. s., to swear falsely; ~ *singen* to sing out of tune, *fam* to sing off key; ~ *spielen* (*Karten*) to cheat at play; ~ *sprechen* to speak incorrectly; ~ *verbunden!* sorry, wrong number! ~ *verstehen* to misunderstand, *fam* to get wrong; ~ *sein gegen* to be angry with s. o.; *in ein ~es Licht stellen* to misrepresent; *~e Angabe* false statement, misrepresentation; *~e Anschuldigung* false accusation; *~e Auslegung* misinterpretation; *~er Eid* false oath; *~er Name* false (*od* fictitious) name; pseudonym; *~e Steine* spurious stones *pl*; *~es Spiel fig* foul play; double-dealing, *Am* frame-up; *unter e-m ~en Vorwand* on false pretences; *Falsch m u. n* falsehood, falseness; treachery; guile; *ohne* ~ guileless, pure; **~eid** *m* false oath; **~geld** *n* counterfeit coin; spurious banknote; *Am* bogus money; **~gläubig** *a* heretic; heterodox; **~heit** *f* falsehood, falseness; deceitfulness; (*Unehrlichkeit*) insincerity; doubleness; duplicity; (*Verschlagenheit*) cunning; **~münzer** *m* (false) coiner; forger, *Am* counterfeiter; **~münzerei** *f* counterfeiting, money forging; false coining; **~münzerwerkstatt** *f* coiner's den; **~spieler** *m* card-sharper; cheat.

fälsch|en *tr* to falsify; to forge; (*Rechnung, Bilanz*) to fake, to cook; (*Lebensmittel*) to adulterate; (*Geld*) to counterfeit; **~er** *m* falsifier; forger; (*Lebensmittel*) adulterator; **~lich** *a* false; **~licherweise** *adv* wrongly; falsely; by mistake; **~ung** *f* falsification, fake; (*Geld*) forgery; counterfeiting; (*Verzerrung, Entstellung*) distortion; (*Verunreinigung*) vitiation; (*Betrug, Schwindel*) fraud; (*Lebensmittel*) adulteration; **~~sversuch** *m* attempt at forgery.

*

falt|bar *a* foldable; **~blatt** *n* (*Prospekt*) leaflet, *Am* folder; **~boot** *n* collapsible boat, folding boat, *Am* faltboat, foldboat; **~e** *f* (*allg*) fold; (*Gesichts~*) wrinkle; (*Bügel~*) crease; (*Tuch, Kleid*) plait, pleat; *die ~en glätten* to smooth the folds; *in ~en legen* to fold; to plait, to ruffle; to gather; *die verborgensten ~en des Herzens* the innermost recesses of heart; *~en werfen* to pucker, to crease; *die Stirn in ~en legen* (*od ziehen*) to knit o.'s brows; (*Gewebe*) *in ~en ziehen Am* to shir(r); **~en, fälteln** *tr* (*zusammenlegen*) to fold; (*Stoff*) to pleat, to crease; *die Hände ~en* to join (*od* to clasp, to fold) o.'s hands; **~engebirge** *n* fold mountains *pl*; **~enhemd** *n Am* ruffle-shirt; **~enkleid** *n* plaited dress; **~enlos** *a* without folds; (*ohne Runzeln*) unwrinkled; (*glatt*) smooth; **~enreich** *a* full of folds (*od* creases *od* wrinkles); **~enrock** *m* plaited gown, pleated skirt; **~enwurf** *m* drapery; **~er** *m* (*Schmetterling*) butterfly, lepidopter; **~ig** *a* folded; (*Stirn*) wrinkled; (*Stoff*) pleated, plaited; **~prospekt** *m Am* folder; **~stuhl** *m* folding-chair; **~ung** *f* fold(ing); wrinkling; pleating; doubling; bending.

Falz *m* fold; (*Buchbinder*) guard; (*am Gesimse*) rabbet; (*Zarge*) groove, notch; **~bein** *n* bone-folder, folding-stick, paper-knife; **~en** *tr* to fold (up); (*Buchbinderei*) to sheet; (*Tischlerei*) to rabbet, to rebate, to groove; **~hobel** *m* rabbet-plane; (*Buchbinderei*) book-folder; **~maschine** *f* grooving-machine; (*Buchbinderei*) folding-machine; **~ziegel** *m* grooved tile, gutter tile.

famil|iär *a* familiar; intimate; **~iarität** *f* familiarity (*mit* with); **~ie** *f* family; (*Haushalt*) household; (*Geschlecht*) generation; (*Stamm*) lineage; *Am fam* the folks *pl*; *keine* ~~ *haben* to have no children; *von guter* ~~ *sein* to be of good family; *es liegt in der* ~~ it runs in the family; *das kommt in den besten ~~n vor* accidents will happen in the best regulated families.

Familien|auslese *f* family selection; **~ähnlichkeit** *f* family likeness; **~anschluß** *m*: *mit* ~~ as one of the family; **~anzeige** *f* personal announcement; **~beihilfe** *f* family allowance; **~bad** *n* mixed bathing, promiscuous bathing; **~bande** *pl* family ties *pl*; **~erbstück** *n* heirloom; **~ernährer** *m* supporter of a family; **~fehler** *m* family failing; **~glück** *n* domestic happiness; **~gruft** *f* family vault; **~gut** *n* family estate; **~haupt** *n* head of the family; **~krankheit** *f* hereditary disease; **~kreis** *m* domestic circle; **~leben** *n* family life; **~nachrichten** *f pl* (*Zeitung*) births, deaths, and marriages; **~name** *m* surname, family name, *Am* last name; **~rat** *m* family council; **~stand** *m* personal status; **~stück** *n* heirloom; **~unterhalt** *m* family allowance (*od* relief), *Am* dependency benefits *pl*; **~vater** *m* father of a family; **~zulage** *f* family allowance.

famos *a* famous; (*ausgezeichnet*) splendid, first-rate, capital, *Am* swell.

Fanal *n* torch; *fig* (light) signal.

Fanat|iker *m* fanatic; **~isch** *a* fanatic(al;) **~ismus** *m* fanaticism.

Fanfare *f* flourish of trumpets.

Fang *m* catch, capture; (*das Gefangene*) booty; catch; (*bei Fischen*) draught; (*Fänge e-s Vogels*) talons *pl*, claws *pl*; (*Wildschwein*) tusk; fang; **~arm** *m* tentacle; **~ball** *m* catch-ball; **~eisen** *n* trap; **~en** *irr tr* to catch, to trap; to entrap; to intercept; to capture; to take prisoner; *Feuer* ~~ to take fire; *sich* ~~ to be caught; **~messer** *n* hunting knife; **~strick** *m* noose; **~leine** *f* rope; (*bei Harpune*) harpoon-line; (*Bootstau*) painter; (*Jagd*) leash; (*Fallschirm*) parachute cords *pl*; **~netz** *n* (*gegen U-Boot*) harbo(u)r net, antisubmarine net; **~stoß** *m* parry; **~vorrichtung** *f* (*Bahn*) tray, fender; (*Aufzug*) safety grip; **~zahn** *m* fang, tusk.

Fant *m* coxcomb, fop, puppy; dandy.

Farb|anstrich *m* coat of colo(u)r; painted surface; **~änderung** *f* change in colo(u)r; **~bad** *n* dye bath; **~band** *n* typewriter (*od* colo(u)r *od* inking) ribbon; **~~spule** *f* ribbon spool; **~~wechsel** *m* ink(ing)-ribbon change; **~beständigkeit** *f* fastness of colo(u)r; **~bestimmung** *f* colo(u)r determination; **~buch** *n* colo(u)r book; **~brühe** *f* dye liquor; **~e** *f* (*allg*) colo(u)r; (*wissenschaftlich*) chroma; *typ* ink; (*vorherrschende*) hue; (*dunkle Tönung*) shade; (*helle Tönung*) tint; (*Gesicht*) complexion; (*Färberei*) dye; (*Anstrich*) paint; (*Tinktur*) tincture; (*Kartenspiel*) suit; (*Beize*) stain; (*Farbstoff*) pigment; *~e bedienen, ~e bekennen* to follow suit; to lay o.'s cards on the table; to show o.'s colo(u)rs; *mit der ~e herausrücken fig* to speak o.'s mind; *zuviel ~e auftragen* to lay it on thick; *die ~e wechseln* to change colo(u)rs; *fig* to change sides; *Grund~en* primary colo(u)rs; *Komplementär~en* complementary colo(u)rs; *Misch~en* secondary colo(u)rs; *Prismen~en* prismatic colo(u)rs; **~echt** *a* (of) fast (colo(u)r); fadeless; **~ehaltend** *a* fast, holding colo(u)r; **~enabstufung** *f* colo(u)r gradation; **~enabweichung** *f* chromatic aberration; **~enabzug** *m phot* colo(u)r print; **~(en)aufnahme** *f* colo(u)r shot; *~~n machen* to take colo(u)r pictures; **~enband** *n* spectrum; **~(en)bild** *n* colo(u)r picture; **~enblind** *a* colo(u)r-blind; **~enblindheit** *f* colo(u)r-blindness; **~enbrechung** *f* colo(u)r refraction **~(en)druck** *m* colo(u)r print(ing), chromotypy, lithochromy; (*Bild*) chromotype; **~(en)druckmaschine** *f* colo(u)r printing machine; **~enempfindlich** *a* colo(u)r sensitive; *phot* orthochromatic; **~empfindlichkeit** *f* colo(u)r sensitiveness; **~enempfindung** *f* sense (*od* perception) of colo(u)r; chromatic sensation; **~enerzeugend** *a* chromogenic; **~enerzeuger** *m* chromogenic; **~(en)fehler** *m opt* chromatic defect; **~enfreudig** *a* colo(u)rful; gay; **~(en)gebung** *f* (*Kolorit*) colo(u)ring, colo(u)ration; **~englanz** *m* brilliancy of colo(u)r; **~engrund** *m* ground colo(u)r; **~(en)kasten** *m* paint box, colo(u)r box; **~enkleckser** *m* dauber; **~enlehre** *f* science of colo(u)r, chromatics *pl*; **~enleiter** *f* colo(u)r scale; **~enmischung** *f* colo(u)r mixing (*od* blending); **~(en)photo(graphie)** *f* colo(u)r photo(graphy); **~enpracht** *f* richness in colo(u)r; **~(en)probe** *f* colo(u)r test; dye trial; **~enrand** *m* iris; **~enreich** *a* richly colo(u)red; **~enreichtum** *m* richness in colo(u)r; **~enrein** *a* chromatic pure; **~enreinheit** *f* chromatic purity; **~(en)schattierung** *f* hue, shading; **~enschichtfilm** *m* dye-coated film; **~enschillernd** *a* iridescent; chatoyant; **~enschranke** *f* (*Rassenschranke*) colo(u)r bar, *Am* color-line; **~ensehen** *n* colo(u)r vision; **~ensinn** *m* colo(u)r perception; **~enskala** *f* scale of colo(u)rs; **~enspektrum** *n* (chromatic) spectrum; **~enspiel** *n* play of colo(u)rs; iridescence; **~ensteindruck** *m* chromolithography; **~entube** *f* colo(u)r tube; **~enveränderung** *f* change in colo(u)r, discoloration; **~enverteilung** *f* colo(u)r distribution; **~enwechsel** *m* change in colo(u)r; **~enzerstreuung** *f* colo(u)r (*od* chromatic) dispersion; **~enzufuhrwalze** *f typ* ductor; **~fernsehen** *n* television in natural colo(u)rs, *Am* color(ed) television, color TV; **~fernsehröhre** *f* colo(u)r television tube; **~film** *m* colo(u)r film; (*Kino*) technicolor; (*mit zwei-, dreifacher Emulsion*) bi-pack, tri-pack (film); **~filmverfahren** *n Am* technicolor; **~filmwochenschau** *f* colo(u)r newsreel; **~filter** *n phot* colo(u)r filter, colo(u)r screen; **~gebung** *f* colo(u)ring, colo(u)ration; **~glas** *n* colo(u)red glass; **~holz** *n* dyewood; **~ig** *a* colo(u)red; (*Papier*) stained; *opt* chromatic; **~ige(r)** *m* colo(u)red man; *Am* (*Neger*) colo(u)red gentleman; **~kissen** *n* ink(ing) pad; **~klischee** *n typ* colo(u)r block, *Am* color engraving; **~körper** *m* colo(u)ring body (*od* substance); **~körperchen** *n* pigment granule; **~korrigiert** *a* colo(u)r corrected; **~lack** *m* colo(u)r lake; **~los** *a* colo(u)rless; *opt* achromatic; *fig* indifferent; (*Gesichtsfarbe*) pale; **~losigkeit** *f* colo(u)rlessness; achromatism; **~mine** *f* (*für Farbdrehstift*) colo(u)red lead; **~muster** *n* colo(u)r pattern (*od* sample); **~richtig** *a* orthochromatic, isochromatic; **~rolle** *f* ink(ing) roller, inker; **~saum** *m* colo(u)r fringe; **~scheibe** *f* colo(u)r screen; **~schreiber** *m tele* writing telegraph; **~spritzen** *itr* to spray-paint, to spray-coat; **~spritzpistole** *f* paint spray gun; **~spritzverfahren** *n* spray-gun painting; **~stich** *m phot* predominance of one colo(u)r; **~stift** *m* colo(u)red pencil (*od* crayon); **~stoff** *m* colo(u)ring matter; pigment; stain; (*Technik*) dye(stuff); **~stoffindustrie** *f* dye industry; **~stufe** *f* shade, gradation; **~tiefe** *f* depth of colo(u)r; **~ton** *m* colo(u)r tone, hue, tint; **~tonrichtig** *a phot* orthochromatic, isochromatic; **~topf** *m* paint pot, *typ* ink pot; **~treue** *f* colo(u)r fidelity; **~tuch** *n typ* printing cloth; **~wandel** *m* colo(u)r change; **~wahl** colo(u)r scheme; **~walze** *f* printing roller, composition roller, ink roller; **~waren** *f pl* colo(u)rs *pl*; dyes *pl*; paints *pl*; **~werk** *n typ* inking device; **~wert** *m* colo(u)r value; **~wiedergabe** *f* colo(u)r reproduction; **~zelle** *f* pigment cell.

färb|bar *a* colo(u)rable; stainable; **~ebad** *n* dye bath; **~eflüssigkeit** *f* dying (*od* staining) liquid; **~ekraft** *f* tinting strength; **~emethode** *f* method of dyeing; **~emittel** *n* dye, colo(u)ring agent; **~en** *tr* to colo(u)r, to tinge; (*Stoff*) to dye; (*Glas, Papier, mit Blut*) to stain; (*abtönen*) to tint; *sich ~~* to colo(u)r; (*erröten*) to blush; *sehr gefärbte Darstellung* highly colo(u)red statement; *in der Wolle gefärbt* dyed in grain; *fig* true, staunch; **~end** *ppr* colo(u)ring, staining; **~eprozess** *m* colo(u)ring process, dyeing process; **~er** *m* dyer, stainer; **~erdistel** *f bot* safflower; **~erei** dye-house, dye-works *pl*; dyer's trade; **~errinde** *f* quercitron bark; **~erröte** *f* madder; **~erwaid** *m* woad; **~evermögen** *n* tinting strength, colo(u)ring power; **~stoff** *m* dyestuff; **~ung** *f* colo(u)ring, colo(u)ration; (*Pigmentierung*) pigmentation; (*Farbe*) colo(u)r, tinge; (*Schattierung*) shade; (*Gesicht*) complexion; (*des Schalles*) timbre, sound colo(u)r, tone colo(u)r; **~~smittel** *n* colo(u)ring agent.

Farc|e *f theat* (*Posse*) burlesque, farce; (*Küche*) stuffing; force-meat; **~ieren** *tr* (*füllen*) to stuff.

Farm *f* colonial settlement; (*Gut*) farm, *Am* (*bes. mit Viehzucht, Pferdezucht od Obstplantagen*) ranch; **~er** *m* farmer, *Am auch* rancher, ranchman, ranchero.

Farinzucker *m* powder(ed) sugar.

Farnkraut *n* fern.

Farre *m* bull(ock), young bull.

Färse *f* young cow, heifer.

Fasan *m* pheasant; **~enjäger** *m* hunter of pheasants; **~enwärter** *m* keeper of pheasants; **~erie** *f* pheasantry; **~enhahn** *m* pheasant-cock; **~enhenne** *f* hen-pheasant.

Faschine *f* fascine; **~nmesser** *n* hedge-bill; rifle-sword; **~nwerk** *n* fascine-work.

Fasching *m* carnival.

Fasch|ismus *m* Fascism; **~ist** *m* Fascist; **~istisch** *a* Fascist(ic).

Fasel|ei *f* silly talk; twaddle, drivel; inattention; **~haft, ~ig** *a* silly; **~hans** *m* silly fellow; **~n** *itr* to drivel; to talk foolishly (*od* nonsense).

Faser *f bot, anat* fibre, *Am* fiber; (*Faden*) thread; (*feiner Faden, Draht~*) filament; (*e-s Seiles*) strand; (*Bohnen*) string; (*Holz*) grain; **~ähnlich** *a* fibrous, filamentous; fibrelike; **~gewebe** *n* fibrous tissue; **~gewinnung** *f* production of fibres; **~ig** *a* fibrous, fibred; filamentous; stringy; **~los** *a* fibreless; (*Bohnen*) not stringy; **~n** *itr* (*sich ~~*) to fuzz; to get frayed; (*Papier*) to mottle; to ravel out; **~nackt** *a* stark naked; **~stoff** *m* fibrin, *Am* fiber; **~stoffindustrie** *f* textile industry; **~ung** *f* fuzzing; texture; fibrillation.

Fäserchen *n* fibril; (*Fussel*) fluff.

*

Faß *n* cask, barrel; (*Riesen~*) tun; (*Fäßchen*) keg; drum; (*Butter~*) churn; (*Butte*) butt; (*Zuber, Kübel*) tub; (*Bottich*) vat; (*Braubottich*) keeve; *der Wein schmeckt nach dem Fasse* the wine tastes of the cask; *frisch vom ~* on draught, drawn from the wood; *das schlägt dem ~ den Boden aus* that tops everything; **~band** *n* hoop; **~bier** *n* draught-beer; **~binder** *m* cooper; **~boden** *m* head of a cask; **~daube** *f* stave; *ein Bündel ~~n Am* shook; **~reif** *m* hoop; **~weise** *adv* by barrels, in barrels.

Fassade *f* façade, front (of a building); face; **~nkletterer** *m* cat-burglar, *Am* porch-climber, second story man (*od* worker).

Fäßchen *n* little barrel, firkin, keg.

fassen *tr* to take hold of; (*packen*) to catch; (*ergreifen, begreifen*) to apprehend; to grasp; to seize; (*füllen*) to put in; *mil* (*empfangen*) to receive; *bei der Hand ~* to take by the hand; to seize; (*Edelsteine*) to set; (*andere Dinge*) to mount; (*enthalten*) to contain, to hold; (*begreifen*) to conceive; to understand, to comprehend; *e-n Gedanken ~* to form an idea; *festen Fuß ~* to sink roots; *Wurzel ~* to take roots; *ins Auge ~* to fix o.'s eyes upon; (*planen*) to envisage, to consider; to visualise, *Am* to visualize; *Tritt ~* to fall into step; *e-n Entschluß ~* to take a resolution; *e-n Vorsatz ~* to make up o.'s mind; *sich ~* to recover o.s.; to compose o.s., to calm o. s., to pull o. s. together; *sich ein Herz ~* to take heart, to pluck up courage; *sich zu ~ kriegen* to come to grips; *sich in Geduld ~* to take patience; (*sich ausdrücken*) to express o. s.; *sich kurz ~* to be brief; to make it short; *sich auf etw gefaßt machen* to get ready; *auf etw gefaßt sein* to be ready.

faßlich *a* conceivable, intelligible; easy to understand; **~keit** *f* comprehensibility, obviousness, intelligibility.

Fasson *f* form, shape; design, contour; cut, section; style, way; **~ieren** *tr* to form, to shape, to profile; **~stahl** *m* shaping tool; **~stück** *n* sample.

Fassung *f* (*Edelsteine*) setting, mounting; *fig* composure, poise, self-command; (*schriftlich*) draft(ing); wording, version; (*Stil*) style, diction; (*Verständnis*) comprehension; *el* (*Birnen~*) socket, lamp holder; (*Linsen~*) mounting; *aus der ~ bringen* to perplex, to upset s. o.; *aus der ~ kommen, die ~ verlieren* to lose o.'s self-control (*od* head), to be rattled; *ganz außer ~ sein* to be completely beside o. s.; **~sgabe, ~skraft** *f* perceptive faculty, conception; power of comprehension; **~slos** *a* disconcerted; upset; **~sraum** *m* capacity; **~svermögen** *n* holding (*od* seating *od* loading *od* carrying *od* volumetric) capacity; *fig* (*geistig*) mental capacity; power of comprehension.

fast *adv* almost, nearly; (*um ein Haar*) all but; (*vor Verneinungen*) next to; *~ dasselbe* much the same; *~ nichts* hardly anything; *~ nie* hardly ever.

Fasten *n* fasting, abstinence, Lent; *~ itr* to fast, to abstain from food;

~**predigt** *f* Lent-sermon; ~**speise** *f* lenten food; ~**zeit** *f* Lent, Shrove-tide.
Fastnacht *f* Shrove-tide, (*Dienstag*) Mardi gras, Shrove-Tuesday, carnival; ~**saufzug** *m* masquerade; ~**skostüm** *n* carnival dress; ~**snarr** *m* carnival's buffoon; ~**sschmaus** *m* carnival's banquet.
Fasttag *m* fast-day.
Faszikel *m* (*Bündel, Heft*) bundle, file.
faszinier|en *tr* to fascinate; (*bezaubern*) to charm, to enchant; to enrapture, to captivate; ~*t sein* to be fascinated (*von, durch* by), *Am fam* to be struck up (*von, durch* with); ~**end** *a* fascinating.
fatal *a* (*verhängnisvoll*) fatal, disastrous; (*unglücklich*) unlucky; (*unangenehm*) disagreeable; awkward; (*abscheulich*) odious; ~**ität** *f* misfortune; ~**ismus** *m* fatalism.
Fatum *n* (*Schicksal*) destiny, lot, fate; (*Verhängnis*) fatality.
Fatzke *m* (*Zierbengel*) *fam* fob, dandy; silly person.

*

fauchen *itr* (*Tier*) to spit; (*Maschine*) to hiss, to puff, to whizz.
faul *a* (*Eier, Äpfel etc*) rotten; (*stinkend*) putrid; decomposed; (*von Zähnen*) carious, decayed; (*träge*) lazy, idle, indolent; slothful; (*langsam*) slow; (*minderwertig*) worthless, inferior; *sport* (*unfair*) foul; (*Metall*) brittle; ~*e Fische fig* paltry (*od* lame) excuse; ~*er Friede* hollow peace; ~*es Geschwätz* idle talk; *sich auf die ~e Haut legen* to lead an idle life; *e-e ~e Sache* a shady business; ~*er Witz* bad joke; ~*er Zahler* slow payer; ~*er Zauber* humbug; ~**baum** *m bot* black alder; alder buckthorn; ~**bett** *n* lounge, couch; *fig* inactivity; ~**en** *itr* to rot; to putrefy; to decompose; ~**enzen** *itr* to be lazy, to laze, to lounge; to idle; ~**enzer** *m* lazy fellow, lazy-bones; (*Bummler*) loafer; *fam* slacker, beachcomber, *Am fam* feather merchant; (*Liegestuhl*) deck-chair; ~**enzerei** *f* idling, idleness, laziness; idle life; ~**fieber** *n* putrid fever; *fig* lazy fit; ~**heit** *f* laziness, idleness, sloth; ~**ig** *a* rotten, putrid; ~**pelz** *m* sluggard, do-little; ~**tier** *n zoo* sloth; *fig* lazy fellow.
Fäulnis *f* (*Fäule*) rottenness; putridity; putrefaction; (*Knochenfäule*) caries; *med* sepsis; *in ~ übergehen* to rot; ~**erregend** *a* septic, putrefactive; ~**erreger** *m* putrefactive agent; germ of decomposition; ~**hindernd** *a*, ~**verhütend** *a*, ~**widrig** *a* antiseptic(al).
Faun *m* faun; ~**a** *f* fauna.
Faust *f* fist; *die ~ ballen* to clinch (*od* clench) o.'s fist; *jdn mit der ~ bedrohen* to shake o.'s fist at s. o.; *mit der ~ schlagen* to fight with the fist; to fist; *auf eigene ~* on o.'s own account, *fam* on o.'s own hook; *das paßt wie die ~ aufs Auge* there is neither rhyme nor reason in it; ~**ball** *m* punch-ball; (*für ~~spiel*) fist-ball; ~**dick** *a* as big as a fist; *er hat es ~~ hinter den Ohren* he has cut his eye-teeth; he is a sly rogue; *e-e ~~e Lüge fam* a whopping lie, a whopper; ~**gelenk** *n* wrist joint; ~**groß** *a* the size of a fist; ~**handschuh** *m* mitt(en); ~**kampf** *m* boxing (match); fist fight; fisticuff; prize-fight; ~**kämpfer** *m* (*ohne Handschuhe*) pugilist; (*mit Boxhandschuhen*) boxer; ~**pfand** *n* dead pledge; pawn; ~**recht** *n* club law, fist law; ~**regel** *f* rule of thumb; ~**schlag** *m* blow with the fist; cuff; *pl* fisticuffs *pl*; punch; (*ins Gesicht*) facer; ~**skizze** *f* rough sketch.
Fäust|chen *n* small fist; *sich ins ~~ lachen* to laugh in o.'s sleeve; ~**el** *m* miner's hammer; ~**ling** *m* mitt(en).
Favorit *m* favo(u)rite; (*Günstling*) minion.
Faxe *f* trick, foolery, tomfoolery; ~**nmacher** *m* buffoon, droll, wag.
Fayence *f* fine pottery.
Fazit *n* result, sum total.
Februar *m* February.
Fecht|boden *m* fencing-room; ~**bruder** *m* beggar; ~**degen** *m* foil, rapier; ~**en** *irr itr* to fight; to fence; (*mit den Händen*) to gesticulate; (*von Handwerksburschen*) to beg o.'s way; ~**er** *m* fighter; fencer, swordsman; (*römischer ~*) gladiator; (*Bettler*) beggar; ~**handschuh** *m* fencing-glove; ~**kunst** *f* art of fencing; ~**meister** *m* fencing-master; ~**schule** *f* fencing-school; ~**stunde** *f* fencing-lesson; ~**übung** *f* exercise in fencing.

*

Feder *f* feather; (*Hut~*) plume; *tech* spring; (*Schreib~*) pen; (*Stahl~, Spitze e-r ~*) nib; (*zum Eintauchen*) dipper; (*Füll~*) fountain pen; (*Daunen*) down; (*Uhr~*) watch-spring; (*Gänsekiel*) quill; *die ~n pl fam* (*Bett*): *noch in den ~n liegen* to be still in bed; *sich mit fremden ~n schmücken* to deck o. s. out in (*od* to adorn o. s. with) borrowed plumes; *in die ~ diktieren* to dictate; ~**antrieb** *m* spring action (*od* activation); ~**artig** *a* featherlike; springlike; plumaceous; (*elastisch*) elastic; ~**aufhängung** *f mot* spring suspension; ~**ball** *m* shuttlecock; ~**ballspiel** *n* badminton; ~**barometer** *m, n* aneroid barometer; ~**bein** *n aero* shock absorber leg; telescopic leg; ~**besen** *m* feather-duster; ~**bett** *n* featherbed, *Am* (heavy down) comforter; ~**blatt** *n tech* spring blade; ~**bolzen** *m tech* spring bolt; ~**büchse** *f* pen-case; ~**busch** *m*, ~**büschel** *n* plume, tuft of feathers; (*Vogel*) crest; ~**chen** *n* small feather, featherlet; plumule; ~**förmig** *a* feathery; feather-shaped; ~**fuchser** *m* quill-driver, scribbler, *Am fam* ink slinger, pencil pusher; ~**fuchserei** *f* quill-driving, *Am fam* ink slinging; ~**gehäuse** *n* spring case (*od* box); ~**gewicht** *n* (*Boxer: 118—126 Pfund*) featherweight; ~**halter** *m* penholder; ~**händler** *m* feather-seller; ~**held** *m* quill-driver; ~**hut** *m* hat with feathers; ~**ig** *a* feathery, plumy; ~**kasten** *m* pen-box; ~**kiel** *m*, ~**spule** *f* quill; ~**kissen** *n* feather-pillow; ~**kraft** *f* spring tension, elastic force, resilience, springiness; elasticity; ~**krieg** *m* literary war; ~**leicht** *a* light as a feather; ~**lesen** *n*: *nicht viel ~~s machen* to make short work (of *od* with); ~**matratze** *f* spring-mattress; ~**messer** *n* penknife; ~**n** *itr* to lose feathers, to moult; (*elastisch sein*) to be elastic, to spring; ~**nd** *a* (*elastisch*) springy, elastic; flexible; ~**ring** *m tech* spring washer; ~**spannung** *f* tension of spring, spring tension; *unter ~~* spring-loaded; ~**spitze** *f* nib (of a pen), *Am* pen-point; ~**sporn** *m aero* shock absorbing tail skid; ~**stahl** *m* spring steel; ~**strich** *m* stroke of the pen; ~**ung** *f* springing; resilience; elasticity; springiness; *mot* spring suspension; ~**ventil** *n* spring valve; ~**vieh** *n* poultry; ~**waage** *f* spring balance; ~**werk** *n* spring work; spring motor; ~**wisch** *m* feather-duster; ~**wischer** *m* penwiper; ~**wolke** *f* (*Meteorologie*) cirrus (cloud); ~**zeichnung** *f* pen-and-ink drawing (*od* sketch); ~**zug** *m tech* spring pull; (*mit Schreibfeder*) stroke of the pen.
Fee *f* fairy; ~**nhaft** *a* fairylike; (*wunderbar*) marvel(l)ous; (*magisch*) magic(al); (*prächtig*) gorgeous, magnificent; ~**nkönig(in)** fairy-king, fairy-queen; ~**nkreis** *m* fairy-ring; ~**nland** *n* fairyland; ~**nmärchen** *n* fairy-tale; ~**nreich** *n* fairydom, fairy kingdom; ~**nreigen** *m* fairy-dance; fairy-ring; ~**nstück** *n theat* pantomime; ~**nwelt** *f* fairyland.
Feg|efeuer *n* purgatory; ~**en** *tr* to sweep, to wipe, to clean; to furbish (a sword); (*Korn*) to winnow; *das Gehörn ~~* to rub off (*od* to remove) the velvet; *vor der eigenen Türe ~~* to mind o.'s own business, to sweep before o.'s own door; *itr* (*schnell laufen*) to hasten; to scour along; (*Wind*) to sweep across; ~**er** *m* cleaner, sweeper; (*Stutzer*) gadabout; ~**esand** *m* scouring sand; ~**sel** *n* sweepings *pl*.
Fehde *f* feud; quarrel; war; (*Herausforderung*) challenge; ~**brief** *m* letter of defiance; ~**handschuh** *m* gauntlet; *den ~~ hinwerfen* to throw down the gauntlet; *den ~~ aufnehmen* to accept the challenge.
Feh(e) *f* minever, Siberian squirrel.
fehl *a* amiss; wrong; vain; *adv* in vain, wrongly, erroneously; *~ am Platz sein* to be out of place; *~ m* blemish, blame; fault; ~**anruf** *m tele* lost call; ~**anzeige** *f* negative report, (*bes. mil*) nil return; (*Auskunft*) incorrect (information); (*e-s Wertes*) erroneous declaration (of value); *~~ erforderlich* negative report requested; ~**ball** *m* (*Kricket*) overthrow; ~**bar** *a* fallible; ~**barkeit** *f* fallibility; ~**bestand** *m* deficiency; shortage; ~**betrag** *m* deficit, deficiency; shortage; ~**bitte** *f* vain request; *e-e ~~ tun* to beg in vain, to meet with a refusal; ~**blatt** *n* (*Kartenspiel*) bad card; ~**bogen** *m typ* imperfect sheet; ~**druck** *m typ* misprint; ~**en** *itr* (*irren*) to err; to be (in the) wrong; to do wrong; to commit a fault, to make a mistake; to make a blunder, to pull (*od* to make) a boner; (*nicht da* (*abwesend*) *sein*) to be absent, to be lacking, to be missing; *jur* (*nicht erscheinen*) to make default; *es fehlt ihm an* he is wanting, he lacks, he needs; (*Geld, Lebensmittel*) he is short of; (*fehlschlagen*) to fail; (*nicht treffen*) to miss; (*gegen ein Gesetz etc*) to violate; to offend against; *es an nichts ~~ lassen* to spare no pains or expense; *Sie werden mir sehr ~~* I'll miss you very much; *was ~t Ihnen?* what's the matter with you? (*gesundheitlich*) what ails you? *es ~t ihr immer etw* she is always ailing; *es ~t mir an* I am in need of; *an mir soll es nicht ~~* it shall not be my fault, it shall be no fault of mine; *wo ~t es?* what's the trouble? is anything wrong with you? *es ~t wenig, daß* within a little; *das hat mir gerade noch ge~t!* that's all I needed! *weit ge~t!* far from the mark! you are quite wrong! *es ~t ihr nie an e-r Ausrede* she is never at a loss for an excuse; ~**en** *n* (*nicht vorhanden sein*) absence, lack of; (*Bedürfnis*) want; (*Mangel*) deficiency; ~**entscheid** *m*, ~**entscheidung** *f* misjudg(e)ment; ~**er** *m* (*Charakter*) fault, failing; (*moralische Schwäche*) frailty, foible; (*moralische Verderbtheit*) vice; (*schwache Seite*) weakness; (*Charakterschwäche*) infirmity; (*Mangel*) shortcoming, defect, *Am* trouble; (*Fehlgriff, Schreib~~*) mistake; (*Irrtum*)

error; (*Gebrechen*) failing, ailment; (*Schnitzer*) blunder; (*Makel*) flaw; (*Schandfleck*) blemish; (*Versehen*) mistake, slip; oversight; (*Fehlschuß*) miss; (*in Stromkreis*) trouble; (*e-r Linse*) aberration; (*Dummheit, Ungeschicklichkeit*) gaffe; faux pas; (*grober* ~~, *bei Prüfungen etc*) howler; *fam* boner, bloomer, floater; (*bei Tieren*) vice; *e-n* ~~ *begehen* (*od machen*) to make a mistake; *fam* to put o.'s foot in it; to drop a brick; to blunder; *e-n* ~~ *suchen* to trace a fault; *e-n* ~~ *beseitigen* to remove a fault; *zulässiger* ~~ allowable error; *zufälliger* ~~ accidental error; **~~berichtigung** *f* correction; **~~beseitigung** *f* elimination of errors; removal of faults; **~~eingrenzung** *f* fault location, localizing trouble; **~~frei, ~~los** *a* faultless; *radio* flawless; correct, perfect; sound; **~~grenze** *f* limit (*od* margin) of error; tolerance; **~~haft** *a* faulty; defective, deficient; incorrect; **~~möglichkeit** *f* possibility of error; **~~quelle** *f tech* source of error; **~~taste** *f* (*Fernschreiber*) erasing key; **~~verzeichnis** *n* (list of) errata; **~~voll** *a* faulty, full of mistakes; **~farbe** *f* miscolo(u)r; (*Diamanten, Zigarren*) off shade; (*Kartenspiel*) renounce, off shade; **~~n** *f pl* (*Zigarren*) seconds *pl*; **~geburt** *f* miscarriage, abortion; **~gehen** *irr itr* to go wrong, to miss o.'s way, to go astray; (*Briefe*) to miscarry; *fig* (*mißlingen*) to fail; **~gewicht** *n* short weight; **~greifen** *irr itr* to miss o.'s hold; *fig* to make a mistake (*od* blunder); **~griff** *m* mistake; blunder; error of judg(e)ment; wrong manipulation; **~jahr** *n* bad year, off year, bad harvest; **~kauf** *m* bad bargain; **~leiten** *tr* to misroute; **~leitung** *f* misdirection; **~prognose** *f* false prognosis; **~schießen** *irr itr* to miss in shooting, to miss o.'s aim; *fig* to be mistaken; **~schlag** *m* miss; *fig* failure, disappointment; *sl* washout; (*Baseball*) strike; **~schlagen** *irr itr* to miss o.'s blow; *fig* to fail, to come to nothing, to miscarry; **~schluß** *m* false inference (*od* conclusion); fallacy; paralogism; **~schuß** *m* miss, bad shot; **~start** *m* false start, *Am* wrong start; **~spruch** *m jur* miscarriage of justice; wrong verdict; judicial error; **~treten** *irr itr* to make a false step; to stumble; **~tritt** *m* false step, slip; *fig* fault; error; mistake; slip; faux pas; lapse; **~urteil** *n* misjudg(e)ment; miscarriage of judg(e)ment; **~verbindung** *f tele* wrong connection; **~zünden** *itr mot* to misfire; **~zündung** *f mot* misfiring, misfire.

feien *tr poet* to make proof against; to charm; (*unverwundbar machen*) to make invulnerable; *gefeit gegen Kugeln* bullet-proof; (*Krankheit etc*) immune (*gegen* from, against, to); (*geschützt*) protected (*gegen* against).

Feier *f* (*Ruhe im Gegensatz zu Arbeit*) rest; (*Ferien*) holiday; (*Freisein*) vacation; (*Fest*) celebration; (*Festtag*) festival; *eccl* feast; (*Belustigung, Erholung*) recreation, relaxation; (*Pause*) recess; (*zeremonielle* ~) solemnity; ceremony; (*Gesellschaft*) party; *Am* (*Fest e-s Heiligen, spanische Festlichkeiten*) fiesta; (*im Freien, Gartenfest etc*) fete, fête; *zur* ~ *des Tages* in hono(u)r of the day; **~abend** *m* time of rest, evening leisure; (*Geschäftsschluß*) closing time, *Am* quitting time; (*Aufhören mit der Arbeit*) leaving off work(ing), cessation from work, off-time; *nach* ~~ in spare hours; ~~ *machen* to cease working; to call it a day, to knock off (work), to stop working; **~lich** *a* (*festlich*) festive; (*erhebend*) solemn; (*würdevoll*) dignified; imposing; (*förmlich*) formal, ceremonious; ~~ *begehen* (*ein Fest*) to celebrate; **~lichkeit** *f* solemnity; festivity; (*Pracht*) pomp; *~~en pl* ceremonies *pl*, *Am* exercises *pl*; **~n** *tr* (*Festtag halten*) to keep; (*Fest, Geburtstag etc*) to celebrate; (*gedenken*) to commemorate; (*rühmen, preisen*) to praise, to extol, to hono(u)r; *itr* (*ruhen*) to rest; (*nicht arbeiten*) to be idle; (*streiken*) to strike; (*ohne Arbeit*) to be unemployed; to be absent; (*frei haben*) to have a holiday; to make holiday; to take leisure; **~n** *n* celebration; (*Fernbleiben von der Arbeit*) absenteeism; (*Streik*) strike; **~schicht** *f min* idle shift, play shift; shift lost by absenteeism; *~~en einlegen* to drop shifts; **~stunde** *f* (*Muße*) leisure hour; (*Erholung*) recreation; (*festlich*) festive hour; *eccl* solemnity; **~tag** *m* holiday; *gesetzlicher* ~~ public (*Am* legal) holiday; (*Festtag*) festive day; festival; *eccl* feast; (*im Kalender*) red-letter day.

feig(e) *a* cowardly; (*heimtückisch*) dastardly; (*furchtsam*) frightened; timid, timorous; (*zaghaft*) craven; *sl* funky, yellow; ~ *sein* to be cowardly, *fam* to funk, to show the white feather; **~heit** *f* cowardice, cowardliness; pusillanimity; *fam* funk(iness); (*Furcht*) fear; *fam* white feather; *Am sl* cold feet, yellow streak; **~herzig** *a* faint-hearted; **~herzigkeit** *f* faint-heartedness; **~ling** *m* coward; (*Memme*) dastard; (*Hasenfuß*) poltroon; (*Schleicher*) sneak; (*Bangemacher*) panic-monger; (*Drückeberger*) shirk(er), slacker, *Am fam* quitter.

Feige *f* fig; **~nbaum** *m* fig-tree; **~nblatt** *n* fig-leaf.

feil *a* vendible, to be sold, for sale; *fig* venal, mercenary; *e-e ~e Dirne* prostitute; **~bieten** *irr tr* to put up for sale; **~bietung** *f* offering for sale; **~halten** *irr tr* to have on sale; **~heit** *f* (*Käuflichkeit*) venality; mercenariness; (*Bestechlichkeit*) corruptibility.

Feil|e *f* file; *fig* finish; **~en** *tr* to file; *fig* to polish, to refine; to finish off; **~enhauer** *m* file-cutter; **~späne** *m pl* filings *pl*; **~strich** *m* file cut.

feilsch|en *itr* to cheapen, to barter, to bargain (for); to haggle (about), *Am* (*bes. auch politisch aushandeln*) to dicker; **~en** *n* petty bargaining, bartering, haggling, *Am* dicker(ing); **~er** *m* haggler.

Feim *m*, **~en** *m* stack; rick.

fein *a* (*dünn*) fine; (*zart*) delicate; (*zierlich*) graceful; (*ausgezeichnet*) excellent; (*vornehm*) distinguished, refined; (*elegant*) elegant; (*wohlerzogen*) well-bred; (*schlau*) clever, subtle; (*geschmackvoll*) refined; (*erstklassig*) first-rate, first-class; (*erlesen*) choice; (*rein*) pure, fine; (*Gehör*) sharp; (*Antwort*) shrewd; *nicht* ~ not gentlemanly; *~er Regen* drizzling rain; ~ *heraus sein* (*fam*) to be a lucky fellow; *sich* ~ *machen* (*fam*) to dress up; *das ist ~!* *fam* that's wonderful! *Am* that's swell! *der ~e Ton* good manners; *die ~e Welt* the higher classes; *~e Züge* nice features; **~abstimmknopf** *m* slow motion knob; **~abstimmung** *f radio* sharp (*od* slow) tuning; **~arbeit** *f* precision work; **~bäckerei** *f* confectioner's shop; **~blech** *n* thin plate; **~~walzwerk** *n* sheet rolling mill; **~einsteller** *m* vernier; **~einstellung** *f* fine adjustment; **~eisen** *n* refined iron; light section steel; **~faserig** *a* fine-fibred, fine-grained; **~fühlend** *a* delicate, sensitive; **~fühligkeit** *f* delicacy; **~gehalt** *m* (*Gold-, Silbermünzen*) standard; (*Metall*) fineness; **~gehaltstempel** *m* hall-mark; **~gold** *n* pure (*od* fine *od* refined) gold; **~heit** *f* fineness; (*Benehmen*) politeness, tact; (*Zartheit*) delicacy, grace(-fulness); (*Geschmack*) refinement; (*Kleidung*) elegance; (*Schlauheit*) subtleness, cunning; (*Reinheit*) purity; (*Fernsehbild*) degree of definition of picture; (*Korn*) fineness, grist; size; **~heitsgrad** *m* degree of fineness; **~höhenmesser** *m aero* sensitive (*od* precision) altimeter; **~hörig** *a* quick of hearing; **~kornfilm** *m* fine-grain film; **~körnig** *a* fine-grained; **~kost** *f* delicacy, *Am* delicatessen *pl*; **~kostgeschäft** *n*, **~kostladen** *m* provision dealer, Italian grocer's shop, *Am* delicatessen *pl mit sing*; **~maschig** *a* fine-meshed; **~mechanik** *f* mechanics of precision, precision mechanics; **~mechaniker** *m* precision tool maker; **~mechanisch** *a* fine mechanical; **~meßgerät** *n* precision measuring set; **~porig** *a* fine-pored; **~schmeckend** *a* delicate, savory; **~schmecker** *m* gourmet, gastronomer; epicure; **~seife** *f* toilet soap, fancy soap; **~sinnig** *a* sensitive, delicate; **~sliebchen** *n* sweetheart; **~stellen** *tr* to adjust, to regulate; **~stellschraube** *f* micrometer screw; **~verteilt** *a* finely divided; **~waage** *f* precision balance; **~zeug** *n* (*Papier*) pulp, stuff; **~zucker** *m* refined sugar.

Feind *m*, **~in** *f* enemy; (*unversöhnlicher* ~) foe; (*Widersacher*) opponent; (*Gegner*) adversary; (*Nebenbuhler*) rival; (*Gegenspieler im Kampf*) antagonist; *der böse* ~ (*Teufel*) fiend, the devil, the Evil One; *sich jdn zum* ~ *machen* to make an enemy of s. o.; *feind a*: *jdm* ~ *sein* to be enemy to; **~begünstigung** *f* favo(u)ring the enemy; *jur* giving aid and comfort to the enemy; **~beobachtung** *f* observation of *od* by the enemy; **~berührung** *f* contact with the enemy; **~beschuß** *m* enemy fire; **~besetzt** *a* enemy-occupied; **~besetzung** *f* occupation by the enemy; **~beurteilung** *f* estimate of enemy situation; **~bewegung** *f* enemy movements *pl*; **~druck** *m* enemy pressure; **~einflug** *m aero* penetration by hostile enemy aircraft; **~einsicht** *f* enemy observation; **~einwirkung** *f* enemy action; **~eshand** *f* hand of an enemy; **~esland** *n* hostile territory; **~fahrt** *f mar* operational cruise; war patrol; **~flug** *m aero* operational flight; mission, raid; (*Einsatz*) sortie; **~frei** *a* free from enemy troops, cleared of enemy forces; **~gebiet** *n* enemy territory; **~kräfte** *f pl* enemy forces *pl*; **~lage** *f* situation on the enemy's side; summary of the enemy situation; enemy position; **~lich** *a* hostile (*gegen* to); enemy; inimical; adverse; ~~ *gesinnt* hostile; ill-disposed (*gegen* towards); **~lichkeit** *f* hostility; **~nachrichten** *f pl* informations about the enemy; **~nähe** *f* nearness of the enemy; **~propaganda** *f* enemy propaganda; **~schaft** *f* enmity, hostility (*gegen* to); (*Haß*) hatred; (*Böswilligkeit*) ill-will; **~~lich** *a* hostile; inimical; adverse; **~selig** *a* hostile; malevolent; (*haßerfüllt*) hateful; **~seligkeit** *f* malevolence; (*Haß*) hatred; *die ~~en er-*

öffnen (*einstellen*) to commence (to suspend, to stop) hostilities; *Eröffnung* (*Einstellung*) *der ~~en* outbreak (cessation) of hostilities; **~sicht** *f* enemy observation; **~staat** *m* enemy state; **~tätigkeit** *f* enemy activity; **~truppen** *f pl* enemy troops *pl*; **~vermögen** *n* enemy property; alien property; *Verwalter des ~~s Am* alien property custodian; **~zusammenstoß** *m* collision with the enemy.

feist *a* fat, plump; (*korpulent*) stout, corpulent; obese; **~e, ~igkeit** *f* fatness.

feixen *itr* to grin.

*

Felbel *m, f* velveteen.

Feld *n* field; *flaches ~* plain; (*offenes Land*) open country, open land; (*Schachbrett*) square; (*Wappen*) field, quarter, shield; *arch* (*Türe, Decke, Wand*) panel, compartment; (*Fachwerk*) bay, field; (*Grund, Boden*) ground, soil, land; *mil* (*Kampfgebiet*) (battle) field; *fig* (*Arbeits~*) province, domain; (*Spielraum*) scope, field; (*Tätigkeits~*) sphere, department; *das ~* (*Gesamtheit der Pferde beim Rennen*) the field; *Gesichts~* field of vision; *Gold~* goldfield; *Öl~* oilfield; *Korn~* a field of corn; *Spiel~* (*Fußball, Kricket, Baseball etc*) playground; *elektrisches ~* electric field; *elektrostatisches ~* electrostatic field; *Kraft~* field of force; *magnetisches ~* magnetic field; *auf freiem ~e* in the open fields; *das ~ bebauen* to till the ground; *das ~ behaupten* to hold the field; *das ~ der Ehre* the field of hono(u)r; *jdm freies ~ lassen* to give full scope to s. o.; *im weiten ~ liegen* to be still very uncertain; *ins ~ führen fig* to bring up; *ins ~ rücken* to take the field; to go into the field, to go to the front; *im ~e gefallen* killed in action; *das ~ räumen* to give way; to retire; *aus dem ~ schlagen* to beat off the field; *fig* to defeat, to rout; **~ampfer** *m bot* sheep's sorrel; **~anzug** *m* field uniform; **~apotheke** *f* field dispensary; **~arbeit** *f* field labo(u)r (*od* work); **~arbeiter** *m* field (*od* agricultural) labo(u)rer (*od* hand); **~armee** *f* field army; **~artillerie** *f* field-artillery; **~arzt** *m* army doctor (*od* surgeon *od* physician); **~ausbildung** *f* field training; **~ausrüstung** *f* field equipment (*od* equipage); **~bäcker** *m* army-baker; **~bäckerei** *f* army-bakery; **~bahn** *f* field railway, portable railway; **~bau** *m* agriculture, tillage; **~befestigung** *f* entrenchment, fieldwork; field fortification; **~bett** *n* folding-bed, camp-bed; cot; **~binde** *f* sash, scarf; **~blume** *f* field (*od* wild) flower; **~bluse** *f* service blouse; **~bohne** *f* horse bean; **~dienst** *m* active service; **~~fähig** *a* fit for active service; **~~ordnung** *f* field service regulations *pl*; **~~tauglichkeit** *f* fitness for field service; **~~übung** *f* field practice; field-day; field manoeuvre; **~~vorschrift** *f* field manual; **~einheit** *f mil* field outfit; **~einwärts** *a* across country; **~eisenbahn** *f* field railway; **~~betriebsabteilung** *f mil* field railway operation unit; **~eisenbahner** *m* field railway engineer; **~element** *n tele* field cell; **~erbse** *f bot* common pea; **~fernsprecher** *m* field telephone; **~flasche** *f* canteen, flask, water-bottle; **~flugplatz** *m* flying field; (*vorgeschobener*) advanced airfield; (*Einsatzhafen*) operational airfield; **~frevel** *m* damage done to fields; **~früchte** *f pl* produce of the fields; **~funksprechgerät** *n* field radio set; **~geistliche(r)** *m* army chaplain; *mil sl* Holy Joe; **~gendarm** *m* military policeman; **~gendarmerie** *f* military police (*Abk* M. P.); **~gepäck** *n* baggage; **~gericht** *n* court-martial; provost court; **~geschrei** *n* war-whoop, war-cry; (*Losungswort*) watch-word; **~geschütz** *n* field-piece, field-gun; **~glas** *n* binocular field-glasses *pl*; **~gottesdienst** *m* camp-service; **~grau** *a* field-grey; **~haubitze** *f* field howitzer; **~heer** *n* field forces *pl*, field army; **~herr** *m* commander-in-chief (*Abk* cominch); general; **~herrnkunst** *f* strategy; **~herrnstab** *m* baton; **~hospital** *n* field-hospital, ambulance; **~huhn** *n* partridge; **~hüter** *m* field-guard; **~kessel** *m* field-kettle; **~klappenschrank** *m tele* portable switchboard; **~kriegsgericht** *n* summary court martial; **~küche** *f* field-kitchen, motor-kitchen; **~kümmel** *m bot* (wild) caraway; **~lager** *n* (military) camp; **~lafette** *f* field-carriage; **~lazarett** *n* field-hospital; ambulance; surgical hospital; **~lerche** *f* skylark; **~mark** *f* land mark; (*Markung*) fields *pl* round a village; **~marschall** *m* field-marshal; **~marschmäßig** *a* in marching order; *Am mil sl* in battle dress and full kit; **~maus** *f* field-mouse; **~messen** *n* surveying; **~messer** *m* (land-) surveyor; **~meßkunst** *f* surveying; **~mohn** *m bot* common poppy; **~mütze** *f* field service cap; garrison cap; forage-cap; **~park** *m* (*Nachschublager*) field park; **~post** *f* field post, army postal service; **~postamt** *n* Army Post Office (*Abk* A. P. O.); **~postbrief** *m* letter from the front; **~postnummer** *f* field post number; **~prediger** *m* army-chaplain, field preacher; **~ration** *f* field ration; **~rübe** *f* rape; **~salat** *m* lamb's lettuce; **~schaden** *m* damage done to fields; **~scher** *m hist* army-surgeon; **~schlacht** *f* battle; **~schlange** *f hist* (*Geschütz*) culverin; **~schmiede** *f* army-forge; **~schütz** *m* field guard; **~spannung** *f el* excitation voltage; **~spat** *m* feldspar; **~spule** *f el* field coil; **~stärke** *f* (*magnetische*) field-strength, field intensity; **~stecher** *m* field-glass; **~stein** *m* (*Grenzstein*) land-mark; (*Findling*) rubble stone; **~stiefel** *m* campaign boot, field boot; **~straflager** *n* field disciplinary camp; **~stück** *n hist* field-piece; **~stuhl** *m* folding-chair, camp-stool; **~telegraph** *m* field-telegraph; **~telephon** *n* field-telephone; **~verbandsplatz** *m* field dressing station; **~wache** *f* outpost, field-watch; picket; **~webel** *m* (technical) sergeant; *Ober~~* first sergeant (*Abk* 1st Sgt); *Stabs~~* master sergeant (*Abk* M/Sgt); **~weg** *m* lane, field-path, private road, *Am* dust (*od* dirt) road; **~werkstatt** *f* field workshop; **~werkstattzug** *m* field workshop platoon; **~wetterstelle** *f* field meteorological station, field weather station; **~wicklung** *f* field winding; **~zeichen** *n* military badge, colo(u)rs *pl*; **~zeuglager** *n* ordnance depot; **~zeugmeister** *m* master of the ordnance; quartermaster; **~zug** *m* campaign; expedition; **~zugsplan** *m* plan of operations; **~zulage** *f* field allowance.

Felge *f* (*Rad~*) felly; felloe, rim; (*Acker~*) fallow land; **~nabziehhebel** *m* rim tool; **~nband** *n* rim band, *Am* tire flap; **~nring** *m* tyre locking ring.

Fell *n* (*allg, auch für Haut*) skin; (*bei großen Tieren*: *Pferd, Vieh, Großwild; Verarbeitung zu Schuhleder*) hide; (*bei kleinen Tieren*: *Kalb, Schaf, Ziege etc; Verarbeitung zu Feinlederwaren*) skin; (*Pelz*) fur; coat; (*ungegerbtes ~ von Pelztieren*) pelt; (*Pauken~*) parchment; *das ~ abziehen* to skin; *ein ~ gerben* to tan a hide; *ein dickes ~ haben* to have a thick skin, to be thick-skinned; *jdm das ~ gerben* to give s. o. a sound thrashing, to tan s. o.'s hide; *jdm das ~ über die Ohren ziehen* to flay s. o., to fleece s. o.; **~eisen** *n* knapsack; **~handel** *m* fur-trade; **~händler** *m* dealer in hides; furrier; fell-monger; **~werk** *n* skins *pl*, furs *pl*, peltry; **~zeichnung** *f* coat pattern.

Fels, ~en *m* rock; (*Klippe*) cliff; (*Spitze*) crag; **~block** *m* boulder; block; piece of a rock; **~boden** *m* rock soil; **~enfest** *a* firm as a rock; *~~er Glaube* unwavering faith; **~engebirge** *n* Rocky Mountains *pl*; **~enhuhn** *n orn* stone grouse; **~eninsel** *f* rocky island; **~enkeller** *m* cellar cut out of the rock; **~enriff** *n* reef; **~(en)wand** *f* steep (side of a) rock, wall of rock; **~formation** *f* rock formation; **~geröll** *n* rock debris; **~gestein** *n* rock material (*od* formation); **~glimmer** *m* mica; **~grat** *m* rocky ridge; **~ig** *a* rocky, craggy; rocklike; **~klippe** *f* cliff; **~kluft** *f* cleft, chasm; **~platte** *f* ledge; **~ritze** *f* crevice; **~rücken** *m* ridge; **~rutsch** *m* rock slide; **~schicht** *f* layer (*od* stratum) of rock; **~~ung** *f* stratification of rock; **~spitze** *f* peak, crag; **~sprengung** *f* blasting of rocks; **~strand** *m* rocky shore; **~sturz** *m* fall of rock; **~vorsprung** *m* ledge; **~wand** *f* wall of rock; steep rock; (*Abgrund*) (face of) precipice.

Fem|e *f* (*Freigericht*) vehme; **~gericht** *n* vehmic court.

Fenchel *m* fennel.

Fenn *n* fen, bog, marsh.

Fenster *n* window; (*e-s Gartenbeetes*) glass-frame; (*blindes ~*) mock-window; (*Schiebe~*) sash-window; *Vor~* storm window; *mit ~n versehen* to window; . . . *fenstrig in Zssg*: windowed; **~bank** *f*, **~brett** *n* window-sill, window-bench; **~beschläge** *m pl* window fittings *pl*; **~blei** *n* glazier's lead; **~bogen** *m* window-arch; **~briefhülle** *f* window envelope, outlook envelope; **~brüstung** *f* parapet, ledge; **~chen** *n* small window; (*Ober~*) skylight; **~dichtung** *f* weather strip; **~einfassung** *f* window case; **~flügel** *m* casement; (hinged) window sash; **~gitter** *n* window-grate; lattice; **~jalousie** *f* window blind, Venetian blind; **~kissen** *n* window cushion; **~kitt** *m* putty; **~kreuz** *n* cross-bars *pl* (of a window); **~kurbel** *f mot* window crank; **~laden** *m* shutter, blind, *Am* window-shade; **~leder** *n* chamois (leather); **~los** *a* windowless; **~nische** *f* window-bay; window-recess; embrasure; **~pfeiler** *m* pier; (*Mittelpfosten*) mullion; **~platz** *m* window-seat; **~rahmen** *m* window frame; **~riegel, ~wirbel** *m* sashbolt, window-fastener; **~rose** *f* rose-window; **~scheibe** *f* (window-) pane; **~schirm** *m* window-blind; **~sims** *m* window-sill; **~spiegel** *m* (*Spion*) window-mirror; **~sturz** *m* lintel; **~vertiefung** *f* recess of a window, embrasure; **~vorhang** *m* window curtain; **~werk** *n* windows *pl*; **~wirbel** *m* sash-fastener.

Ferien *f pl* (*Schule, Geschäft*) holidays *pl*, *Am* vacation; (*Hochschule, Gericht*) vacation; *parl* recess; *die großen ~* the long vacation; *~ machen* to take o.'s holidays, *Am* to (take a) vacation; **~kolonie** *f* holiday-camp; **~kurs** *m* vacation course; **~reise** *f* holiday trip; **~zeit** *f* holiday-time.

Ferkel *n* young pig; piglet, pigling; (*Span~*) sucking (*od* suckling) pig, sucker; *fam* dirty person; **~ei** *f* piggishness; **~n** *itr* to farrow, to pig; (*schmutzig sein*) to be dirty; (*schmutzig reden*) to be smutty.

Fermate *f mus* (*Haltezeichen*) pause.

Ferment *n* ferment, enzyme; **~ieren** *tr* to ferment; **~wirkung** *f* fermentation.

fern *a* distant, remote; far, far off, faraway; *e-e ~e Ähnlichkeit* a distant resemblance; *e-r Sache ~ bleiben* to keep aloof from; *das sei ~ von mir!* far be it from me! *von ~* from a distance, from afar, at a distance; *von nah u. ~* from far and near; *es liegt mir ~ zu behaupten* I am far from pretending; **~amt** *n tele* trunk-exchange, *Am* long-distance office (*od* exchange), toll-exchange; *~~ bitte!* trunks! **~anruf** *m* trunk-call, *Am* long-distance call; **~anschluß** *m* trunk-connection, *Am* long-distance connection; **~antrieb** *m* remote control, remote drive; **~anzeige** *f tele* remote indication, remote signalling; **~aufklärer** *m*, **~aufklärungsflugzeug** *n* long-range reconnaissance aircraft (*od* plane), long-distance reconnaissance plane; **~aufklärung** *f* long-distance reconnaissance; strategical reconnaissance; long-range reconnaissance; **~~flugboot** *n* long-range reconnaissance flying boat; **~~flugzeug** *n* long-range reconnaissance plane; **~aufnahme** *f phot* telephotography, telephoto; longshot; **~auslöser** *m phot* automatic release, distance release; **~barometer** *n* telebarometer; **~beben** *n* distant earthquake, (micro)seism; **~bedient, ~betätigt** *a* remote-controlled; (*drahtlos*) radio controlled; **~bedienung** *f* remote control; **~bild** *n* telephoto; **~bleiben** *irr itr* to keep aloof from; *~~ n* (*vom Arbeitsplatz*) absenteeism; **~blick** *m* distant view; **~bomber** *m aero* long-range bomber; **~dienst** *m* (*der Post, im Gegensatz zum Ortsdienst*) out-of-town delivery; **~drehzahlmesser** *m* distance revolution tachometer; **~drucker** *m* teleprinter, teletype apparatus; ticker; **~e** *f* distance, remoteness; *aus der ~~* from a distance, from afar; *aus der ~~ sieht es schön aus* it looks beautiful from the distance; *in der ~~* in the distance, at a distance; *in weiter ~~ liegen* to be still a long way off, to be still looming in the distant future; **~empfang** *m radio, tele* long-range (*od* long-distance) reception; **~er** *a* farther; *nichts lag ihr ~~* nothing was farther from her mind; *adv* further(more); moreover; *~~hin adv* for the future; henceforward; *~~ liefen* (*bei Rennen*) also ran; **~fahrt** *f* long-distance trip; **~flug** *m* long-distance flight; **~funk** *m* long-distance broadcast; transoceanic broadcast; **~funkpeilung** *f* long-range navigation (*Abk* Loran); **~gasleitung** *f* long-distance gas pipe; **~gasversorgung** *f* long-distance gas supply; **~geschütz** *n* long-range gun; **~gespräch** *n* (tele)phone-call (*od* conversation); (*außerhalb der Stadt*) out-of-town call; (*Überland*) trunk-call, *Am* long-distance call; *dringendes ~~* urgent call; (*mit Voranmeldung*) with pre-advice; person to person; *gewöhnliches ~~* routine call; **~gelenkt, ~gesteuert** *a* remote-controlled, guided; (*drahtlos*) controlled by radio signals, radio controlled; *~~e Bombe* remote-controlled bomb; *~~e Flakrakete* guided A A rocket; *~~es führerloses Flugzeug mit Bombenladung* remote-controlled, bomb-laden, pilotless aircraft; **~glas** *n* telescope, field-glass(es *pl*); binoculars *pl*; **~halten** *irr tr* (*jdn von sich*) to keep s. o. at a distance (*od* away); *sich ~~ von* to stand aloof from, to keep clear of; **~heizung** *f* long-distance heating, district heating; **~hörer** *m* telephone receiver, (tele)phone; (*Kopfhörer*) ear-phone; **~jäger** *m aero* long-range fighter; **~kabel** *n* long-distance cable; **~kampfartillerie** *f* long-range artillery; **~kino** *n* film television, telecinematography; **~kompaß** *m* telecompass; **~kurs(us)** *m* correspondence course; **~lastverkehr** *m* long-distance transport traffic; **~lastzug** *m* long-distance transport train; **~leitung** *f tele* trunk-line, *Am* long-distance line, toll-line; *el* (long-distance) transmission line; **~~netz** *n* trunk system; **~lenkboot** *n* distance (*od* remote-) controlled boat; **~lenkflugzeug** *n* tele-controlled aircraft; drone; **~lenkpult** *n* (*für Raketen*) control desk; **~lenkung** *f* remote control; (*drahtlos*) wireless control, *Am* radio control; **~licht** *n mot* bright (*od* driving) light, long-range light; **~liegen** *irr itr* to be far from; **~meldedienst** *m* telecommunications service; **~meldenetz** *n* telecommunication network; **~meldetechnik** *f* telecommunication technique; (*Schwachstromtechnik*) light current engineering, *Am* signal engineering; **~meßgerät** *n* range finder, telemeter; **~mündlich** *a* telephonic, by telephone, over the telephone, *fam* over the phone; **~nachtjagd** *f aero* long-range night interception; **~nachtjäger** *m aero* long-range night-interception plane; **~objektiv** *n* (*Teleobjektiv*) telephoto-lens; **~ortung** *f* (*drahtlos*) radiolocation; **~ost** *m* the Far East; **~photographie** *f* telephoto(graphy); **~punkt** *m* far-point; **~rohr** *n* telescope; **~~büchse** *f* rifle with telescopic sight; **~~lupe** *f* telescopic magnifier; **~~visier** *n* telescopic sight; (*Zielfernrohr*) telescopic rifle sight; **~ruf** *m* (*Rufnummer*) telephone (number); (*Anruf*) (telephone) call; long-distance call; **~rundfunk** *m* long-range broadcasting; **~schalter** *m* remote control switch; **~schaltung** *f* remote control; **~schnellzug** *m* long-distance express train, *Am* limited, express; **~schreibapparat** *m*, **~schreibmaschine** *f*, **~schreiber** *m* teleprinter, telewriter, teletypewriter, teletype (machine); **~schreiben** *irr itr* to teleprint, *Am* to teletype; *~~ n* teleprinter message, teletype message; **~schreiber** *m* (*Person*) telewriter, teletyper; **~schreibnetz** *n* teletype net(work); **~schreibteilnehmer** *m* teletype subscriber; **~schreibvermittlung** *f* teletype exchange; **~schriftlich** *a* by teleprint; **~schuß** *m* shot at long range; **~sicht** *f* prospect, perspective; panorama; visual range; distant visibility, distant view; *beschränkte ~~* limited view; **~sichtig** *a* longsighted; *med* presbyopic.

*

Fernseh|abtaster *m* scanner; **~amateur** *m* television fan, TV fan, *Am meist* video fan, telefan; **~ansager** *m* television announcer, *Am* video announcer; **~antenne** *f* television (*Am* video) antenna; **~apparat** *m* television apparatus, television receiver, television set, TV set, television, televisor; *e-n ~~ aufstellen* to install a television set; *etw im ~~ sehen* to view s. th. on television; *die Zimmer des Hotels sind mit ~~en ausgerüstet* the hotel has television-equipped rooms; *dieser ~~ bringt Ihnen eingebaute Antenne u. automatische Tonregelung — Sie stellen nur das Bild ein u. der Ton ist stets richtig* this television brings you built-in antenna and automatic sound — just tune the picture, sound is right every time; *ein ~~ mit 10-Inch-Bildschirm Am* a TV 10-incher, a 10-inch TV set; **~aufnahme** *f* vision pick-up; *für ~~ sehr gut geeignet* telegenic; *~~ zur späteren Sendung* kinescope recording; **~aufnahmeraum** *m* (*Studio*) television studio, TV studio; **~aufnahmewagen** *m* television reporting van, *Am* television camera truck, video bus, pick up truck; **~auge** *n* television eye; **~band** *n* television (*Am* video) band; **~bearbeitung** *f* (*e-s Stückes*) television version, *Am* video version, televersion; **~berichterstattung** *f* television coverage; **~betrachter, ~teilnehmer** *m* television viewer, viewer, televiewer, *Am* telefan, T-viewer, telescanner; *viele ~~ stellen das Programm nur aus Neugierde ein* many television viewers tune the program(me) in purely out of curiosity; **~bild** *n* television image (*od* picture), telepicture, set image, air picture; *die ~~er werden gesendet* the TV images go on the air; **~bildfläche** *f* field; **~bildschirm** *m* viewing screen, screen; *ein 20-Röhren-Tischmodell mit 4 × 5 Inch großem ~~* a 20-tube table model with a 4-inch by 5-inch screen; **~dienst** *m* television (*Am* video) service; **~drama** *n* television drama; **~drehbuch** *n* television (*od* TV) shooting script; **~einrichtung** *f* television system; **~empfang** *m* television reception; **~empfänger** *m* (*Apparat*) television receiver, television set, teleset, televisor, video receiver; teleview apparatus; (*für Farbfernsehen*) television colo(u)r receiving set; *die Zahl der aufgestellten ~~ hat die 3-Millionengrenze überschritten* the number of television (receiving) sets installed passed the 3 million mark; **~en** *n* television (*Abk* TV), *Am meist* video; *direktes ~~* direct pickup and viewing; *~~ geringer Güte* low-definition television; *~~ hoher Güte* high-definition television; *plastisches ~~* stereoscopic television; *auf das ~~ bezüglich, das ~~ betreffend* televisional, televisionary, *Am* video; *durch ~~ übertragen* to televise, to telecast; *Farb~~* colo(u)r television, television in natural colo(u)rs; *Schwarz-Weiß~~* black-and-white television, monochromatic television; *im ~~ erscheinen* to appear on television; *einige der Filme werden wahrscheinlich bald im ~~ erscheinen* some of the films soon may appear on television; **~en** *irr tr* (*durch Fernsehsender übertragen*) to transmit (*od* to broadcast) by television, to televise, to telecast; *in Paris ist eine ganze Operette durch Fernsehsender übertragen worden* a full operetta has been televised in Paris; **~enthusiast** *m* television fan, TV fan, *Am meist* video fan, telefan; **~er** *m* (*Apparat*) television receiver; *siehe: ~apparat, ~empfänger; ~~-Radio-Plattenspielertruhe f Am* television-radio-phonograph combination; **~fernempfang** *m* long-range television reception; **~film** *m* television motion picture, *Am* telefilm, telemovie, radio movie; **-forscher** *m* television researcher; **-funkturm** *m* television tower; **-gerät** *n* television set; *siehe: -apparat, -empfänger;* **-gesellschaft** *f* television broadcasting station; telecaster, TV broadcaster; **-industrie** *f* television (*Am* video) industry; **-kamera** *f* television (*od* TV) camera, *Am* video camera, *fam* ike (*Abk von* iconoscope); **-kabel** *n* television cable; **-kanal** *m* television (*Am* video) channel; **-kofferempfänger** *m* portable television receiver; **-kommentator** *m* television commentator; **-kunst** *f* television art; **-künstler** *m* television artist; **-kurzakter** *m Am fam* black-out; **-nachrichtenschau** *f* television news show; **-netz** *n* television (*Am* video) network; *sie wird zum ersten Mal vor der Kamera des NBC --es auftreten Am* she will make her television debut on the NBC video network; **-photograph** *m* television photographer; **-programm** *n* television (*od* TV) program(me), television (*od* video) show; television broadcast; *ein -- anschauen* (*od betrachten*) to look at a television broadcast, to teleview; **-publikum** *n* television public; **-reklame** *f* television (*Am* video) advertising; **-revue** *f* television revue; **-röhre** *f* television tube; (*in der Kamera*) pickup tube, image orthicon, camera tube, iconoscope; (*im Empfänger*) viewing tube, picture tube, kinescope; **-rundfunk** *m* television (*Am* video) broadcasting; visual broadcasting; **-schirm** *m* (*am Empfänger*) television screen, telescreen, screen; **-sendeamateur** *m fam* television ham; **-sendegerät** *n* telecasting equipment; **-sender** *m*, **-sendestation** *f* television (broadcasting) transmitter (*od* station), television station, TV station, telestation; *über -- verbreiten* to telecast, to televise; *Aufnahmen zur Übertragung im -- machen* to take pictures for television; *Gastvorstellungen am -- geben* to make guest television appearances; *e-e durch -- übertragene politische Rede* a televised political speech; **-senderaum** *m* television studio; **-senderecht** *n* television right; **-sendung** *f* television transmission, television broadcasting, *Am* telecast; *--en betrachten* to view (*od* to watch) television shows, *Am* to look at video; *Wochenschauen sind zu e-m Hauptbestandteil der --en geworden* newsreels have become a television feature; **-signal** *n* television signal, *Am* video signal; **-technik** *f* television technique; **-techniker** *m* television technician (*od* engineer); **-teilnehmer** *m* television viewer, *Am* video viewer, televiewer, spectator-listener, looker-in; **-teilnehmerkreis** *m* television audience; **-telephon** *n* television telephone, *Am* video telephone; **-theater** *n* (*zur Vorführung übertragener Filme*) *Am* tele-theater; **-übertragung** *f* television transmission; *zur -- geeignet* (*bildwirksam*) telegenic; **-unterhaltung** *f* television (*Am* video) entertainment; **-varieté(programm)** *n* television vaudeville show, *fam* televaudeville, vaudeo; **-verbindung** *f* television connection; **-version** *f* television (*Am* video) version; **-vorführung** *f* television (*Am* video) show; **-welle** *f* television wave, TV wave; **-wellenlänge** *f* television wavelength; **-zeichen** *n* television (*Am* video) signal.

Fernsprech|amt *n* call-office; telephone-exchange, *Am* telephone central office; **-anlage** *f* telephone installation; **-anschluß** *m* telephone-connexion, subscriber's station (*od* line); **-apparat** *m* telephone apparatus (*od* set); (tele)phone; **-aufnahmegerät** *n* (*zur automatischen Aufnahme von Gesprächen*) *Am* telephonograph; **-automat** *m* automatic telephone, taxiphone, coin-box phone, *Am* pay station, coin collector telephone; **-beamte(r)** *m*, **-beamtin** *f* (tele)phone-operator, telephonist; (*Fräulein*) telephone-girl; (*Überwachungsbeamter*) chief operator; **-betrieb** *m* line telephony; telephone operation, *Am* telephone service; **-buch** *n* telephone directory; **-en** *irr itr* to telephone, *fam* to phone, to talk on the phone; **-er** *m* telephone, *fam* phone; *Münz--* taxiphone, coin-box phone, *Am* coin collector telephone; *öffentlicher --* public telephone (*od* station); *Tisch--* table telephone set; *mit Wählscheibe* dial telephone; **-gebühren** *f pl* telephone-fees *pl*, telephone-rates *pl*; **-geheimnis** *n* secrecy of the telephone service; **-hauptanschluß** *m* subscriber's main station; **-kundendienst** *m* customer service, absent subscriber service; **-leitung, -linie** *f* telephone-line; **-nebenstelle** *f* extension (station); **-netz** *n* telephone network; **-nummer** *f* telephone-call number; **-schnur** *f* flexible cord, flex; tensil cord; **-sperre** *f* withdrawal of the telephone service; **-stelle** *f* call-office, telephone-station; *öffentliche --* phone-booth, public call-office; public telephone, telephone box; **-teilnehmer** *m* (telephone-) subscriber; **-teilnehmerverzeichnis** *n* telephone directory; **-verbindung** *f* telephone communication; **-verkehr** *m* telephone-traffic; **-vermittlung** *f* telephone-exchange, *Am* telephone central office; **-verzeichnis** *n* telephone directory; **-weg** *m* telephone-channel; **-wesen** *n* telephony; **-zelle** *f* call-box, telephone-box, *Am* (phone-) booth, call-booth; **-zentrale** *f* (telephone-) exchange, *Am* (telephone-) central.

Fern|spruch *m* telephone message; **-stehen** *irr itr* to be a stranger to; **-stehende(r)** *m* outsider; **-steuerung** *f* distant control, *Am* remote control; (*drahtlos*) radio control, telautomatics *pl*; **-suchgerät** *n* (*Radar*) early-warning radar set; **-thermometer** *n* telethermometer; **-transport** *m* long-haul transport; **-trauung** *f* marriage by proxy; **-trennschalter** *m el* distant circuit breaker; **-unterricht** *m* correspondence course(s *pl*); instruction by correspondence; **-verbindung** *f tele* trunk connection, through connection; (*durch Funk, Telephon, Kabel etc*) telecommunication; **-verkehr** *m mot* long-distance traffic (*od* transport); *tele* long-distance communication; **--sflugzeug** *n* long-range airliner; **--somnibus** *m* long-distance bus; **--sstraße** *f* highway, trunk-road; **-waffe** *f* long-range weapon; **-weh** *n* nostalgia; **-wirkung** *f* distant effect, action at distance; telekinesis; (*durch Strahlung*) radiation effect; (*seelisch*) telepathy; **-zug** *m* long-distance train, main-line train; **-zündung** *f* ignition from a distance.

Ferri|chlorid *n* ferric chloride; **-oxyd** *n* ferric oxide; **-sulfat** *n* ferric sulphate; **-zyankalium** *n* potassium ferricyanide; **-zyanwasserstoff** *m* ferricyanic acid.

Ferro|chlorid *n* ferrous (iron) chloride; **-magnetismus** *m* ferromagnetism; **-zyanid** *n* ferro cyanide; **-zyankalium** *n* potassium ferrocyanide; yellow prussiate of potash.

Ferse *f* heel; *auf den -n folgen* to pursue s. o. closely, to heel s. o.; to be at (on) the heels of s. o.; *jdm auf die -n treten* to step on s. o.'s heels; **-nbein** *n* heel-bone, calcaneum, os calcis; **-nflechse** *f* tendon of Achilles; **-ngeld** *n*: *-- geben* to run away, to take to o.'s heels.

fertig *a* (*bereit*) ready, prepared; (*geschickt*) skilled, skilful; (*gewandt*) dexterous; quick; (*vollendet*) accomplished; (*im Sprechen*) fluent; perfect; (*-gestellt*) finished, done; (*Kleider*) ready-made; *fam* (*ruiniert*) ruined, lost; *fix u. -* quite ready; *es ist alles -* everything is ready; *das Essen ist -* dinner is ready; *sich - machen* to get ready; *machen Sie sich -!* get ready! *-!* (*Kommando*) make ready! *- sein mit etw, mit jdm* to have finished with, *Am* to be thru with; *er ist - mit ihr* he has done (*od* finished) with her, *Am* he is thru with her; *bist du -?* have you finished? *Am* are you thru? *- sein fam* (*vollkommen erledigt sein*) to be done for, *Am* to be washed up, to be all in; (*ruiniert sein*) to be ruined; to be lost; *sie ist mit dem Lesen -* she has done with reading; *mit jdm - werden* to manage s. o., to be able to handle s. o.; *mit etw - werden* to finish s. th., to cope with s. th., *Am* to get away with s. th.; *ohne jdn - werden* to get along without s. o.; *ohne etw - werden* to dispense with; *wir können ohne sie nicht - werden* we cannot do without her; **-bringen** *irr tr* to manage; to accomplish, to bring about; **-eisen** *n* finished iron; **-en** *tr* (*herstellen*) to make, to machine, to manufacture; to process; to finish; to prepare; **-erzeugnis** *n* finished product; **-fabrikat** *n* ready-made article; **-haus** *n* prefabricated house, prefab; *-- aus Metall* prefab in metal; *Hersteller von -häusern* prefabricator; **-keit** *f* (*Geschick*) dexterity, skill; knack; (*Raschheit*) quickness; readiness; (*im Sprechen*) fluency; (*der Zunge*) nimbleness; (*Leichtigkeit*) facility; (*Übung*) practice; *e-e große -- haben in* to be good at; **-machen** *tr* to finish; *typ* to adjust; **-macher** *m* finisher; foreman; *typ* adjuster; **-montage** *f* final assembly; **-produkt** *n* finished product; **-stellen** *tr* to finish, to complete; **-stellung** *f* finish(ing), completion; **-ung** *f* making, fabrication, manufacture, production; yield, output; finish; **--sauftrag** *m* production order; **--sfehler** *m* manufacturing defect; **--shalle** *f* workshop, finishing shop; **--sjahr** *n* year of manufacture; **--sstraße** *f* production line; **--steil** *m* finished part; **--svorbereitung** *f* manufacturing preparation; **--szeit** *f* production time; **-walzwerk** *n* finishing mill; **-waren** *f pl* ready-made (*od* finished) goods *pl*.

Fes *n mus* F flat.

fesch *a* smart, fashionable; stylish; dashing, snappy.

Fessel *f* fetter, chain; irons *pl*; (*Hand-*) shackle; handcuffs *pl*; *jdn in -n legen* to handcuff s. o., to put s. o. in irons; (*Bande*) bond; tie: (*Fesselgelenk*) ankle; (*- des Pferdes*) fetlock, pastern; **-ballon** *m* captive balloon, kite balloon; **-gelenk** *n* fetlock joint; **-los** *a* unfettered, free from chains; **-n** *tr* to fetter, to shackle; *fig* to captivate; (*Blick*) to arrest; (*Aufmerksamkeit in Anspruch nehmen*) to engross; to fascinate; (*Feind*) to retain; to hold; *ans Bett ~n* to confine to o.'s bed; *ans Zimmer ~n* to confine to o.'s room; **~nd** *a* (*packend*) gripping, fascinating; (*interessant*) interesting; (*bezaubernd*) captivating; charming, enchanting, *Am auch* spell-binding; **~ung** *f* chaining up; pinning down; **~~sangriff** *m mil* holding attack.

fest *a* solid; (*fest gemacht*) fast; (*nicht nachgebend*) firm; rigid; hard; compact; (*solide*) secure; (*dauerhaft*) stable; (*gefestigt*) steadfast; (*dick*) massive; (*Schlaf*) sound; (*Schritt; Boden, Grund; Entschluß*) firm; (*Gefäß*) tight; (*Lohn, Gehalt, Preise*) fixed; (*Wohnsitz, Arbeitsstelle*) permanent; (*Abnehmer, Kunde*) steady, regular; (*Überzeugung*) firm, strong, deep; (*Freundschaft*) stanch; (*Blick, Glaube*) steady; (*Gedanke*) strong, fixed; (*unverletzlich, sicher*) proof; (*Geschäft, Handel*) settled; (*Gewebe, Stoff*) close; (*Knoten*) tight; (*stationär*) stationary, fixed; *mil* (*befestigt*) strong, fortified; *auf ~e Rechnung* for firm account; *~es Angebot* firm offer; *~e Kosten* fixed costs; *~er Körper* solid body; *~en Fuß fassen* to gain a firm footing; *~ anziehen* (*Schraube*) to tighten; *~ eingebaut* fixed; *~ überzeugt sein, daß* to be fully convinced that; *~ vornehmen* to make it a point; *~ werden* to consolidate; **~antenne** *f* fixed aerial, fixed antenna; **~backen** *irr itr* to cake together; **~bannen** *tr* to fascinate; **~besoldet** *a* salaried; **~binden** *irr tr* to tie up (*od* fast), to fasten to, to hitch; **~bleiben** *irr tr* to remain firm; to hold on; **~e** *f* stronghold; fortress; citadel; (*Himmels~e*) firmament; **~fahren** *irr itr* to stick fast; (*Schiff*) to run aground; *mot* to stall, to get stuck; *sich ~~* to be stuck; *fig* to be at a deadlock; *die Verhandlungen haben sich festgefahren* discussions came to a deadlock; **~fahrwerk** *n aero* fixed undercarriage; **~fressen**: *sich ~~* to seize; **~gewurzelt** *a* deeply rooted; **~halten** *irr tr* to hold (tight); to arrest; to seize; (*schriftlich*) to write down; (*im Bild*) to portray, to picture; to record photographically; (*im Gefängnis*) to detain; (*anhalten*) to stop; *itr* to hold fast; to keep (*an* to), to stick to, to cling to; *sich ~~* to hold on to, to cling to; **~igen** *tr* to make fast, to make firm; to consolidate; (*stärken*) to strengthen; (*Währung*) to stabilize; **~igkeit** *f* fastness; firmness; steadiness; (*Widerstandsfähigkeit*) strength, solidity; ruggedness; stability; resistance; **~~seigenschaft** *f* mechanical property; **~~sgrad** *m* degree of firmness; **~~sgrenze** *f* limit of stability, breaking strength; **~igung** *f* (*Währung*) stabilization; **~klammern** *tr* to fasten with clamps; to clinch; *sich ~~* to cling to; **~kleben** *tr* to fasten with glue, to glue; *itr* to cleave to, to stick to; **~kraftstoff** *m* solid fuel; **~land** *n* continent, mainland; **~ländisch** *a* continental; **~laufen** *irr: sich ~~* to get stuck, to bog down; to stall; **~legen** *tr* to fix; to pin down; to clamp, to fasten; to lock; (*verankern*) to anchor; *mil* (*Entfernung beim Schießen*) to establish o.'s range; (*planen*) to plot; (*Regeln aufstellen*) to lay down; (*bestimmen*) to determine, to stipulate; to set, *Am* to schedule; *der Abflug ist auf 2 Uhr festgelegt* taking-off is scheduled on 2; (*Geld*) to invest; *sich auf e-e Sache ~~* to undertake to do s. th.; to tie o. s. down; **~legepunkt** *m* (*Artillerie*) reference point; **~legung** *f* fixation; (*Regeln*) laying down; (*Ort*) localization; (*Übereinkommen*) accord, agreement; (*unbeweglich machen*) immobilization; *~~ von Maßstäben* establishment of standards; **~liegen** *irr itr* to be laid up; **~machen** *tr* to fasten, to make fast; to tie up; to fix; (*Luftschiff, Schiff*) to moor; (*Abmachung*) to arrange definitely, to settle; (*Handel*) to conclude; **~meter** *m* (*Holz*) cubic meter; **~nageln** *tr* to nail (fast *od* down); *fig* to prove; **~nahme** *f* apprehension, arrest; capture; **~nehmen** *irr tr* to (put under) arrest, to apprehend; **~punkt** *m* fixed point; **~schnallen** *tr* to buckle; **~schnallvorrichtung** *f aero* safety belt; **~schrauben** *tr* to screw on; **~setzen** *tr* to settle; to appoint; to arrange; (*Tag, Zeit*) to fix a date, *Am* to schedule; *die Sitzung ist festgesetzt auf* the session is scheduled on; (*Preise*) to quote (prices); to fix, to set; (*Bedingungen*) to stipulate (conditions); (*im Gefängnis*) to imprison; *sich ~~* to settle down; to obtain a footing; **~setzung** *f* establishment, appointment; settlement; (*im Gefängnis*) imprisonment; **~sitzen** *irr itr* to sit fast; to fit tightly; (*Schiff*) to be aground (*od* stranded); to settle down; to be stuck; **~stampfen** *tr* to stamp down; to ram; **~stehen** *irr tr* to stand firm (*od* fast); to be steady; to be fixed; *fig* to be certain; **~stehend** *a* stationary; (*konstant*) constant; (*von Gebräuchen*) well-established; (*sicher, gewiß*) certain; **~stellbar** *a* ascertainable, determinable; *tech* fixable, securable; **~stellen** *tr* to establish, to settle; to determine; to state; to fix, to stop; (*herausfinden*) to find (out), to ascertain; (*Personen*) to identify; **~steller** *m* (*Schreibmaschine*) shift lock; **~stellschraube** *f* setscrew; **~stellung** *f* establishment; statement; (*der Personalien*) identification; **~~sklage** *f* action of ascertainment, action for obtaining a declaratory judg(e)ment; **~~surteil** *n* declaratory judg(e)ment; **~wachsen** *irr itr* to grow fast; **~ung** *f* fort(ress); *fliegende ~~ Am* flying fortress; **~~sartillerie** *f* siege-artillery; **~~sbau** *m* fortification, building of fortifications; **~~sgraben** *m* moat; **~~sgürtel** *m* ring of forts; **~~shaft, ~~sstrafe** *f* confinement in a fortress; **~~skrieg** *m* siege war; **~~swall** *m* rampart; **~~swerk** *n* fortification; **~verzinslich** *a* at a fixed rate of interest; fixed interest bearing; **~wert** *m* fixed value; constant; **~zeitgespräch** *n tele* fixed time call, *Am* appointment message; **~ziehen** *irr tr* (*Schraube*) to tighten; to screw down.

Fest *n* (*Feier*) festival; celebration; holiday; (*zeremonielles ~*) solemnity; (*Mahl u. bes. eccl*) feast; (*Gesellschaft*) party; (*Essen*) banquet; (*im Freien, Garten~*) fête, fete; *bewegliches ~* movable feast; *Am* (*Fest e-s Heiligen, spanisches ~*) fiesta; *lärmendes ~* (*fam*) jamboree; *ein ~ begehen* to keep a festival; **~abend** *m* eve of a festival; **~ausschuß** *m* festive committee; **~essen** *n* banquet; public dinner; **~gabe** *f* gift; festive donation, present; **~geber** *m* host; **~gelage** *n* banquet; **~geläute** *n* festive peal of bells; **~halle** *f* banqueting-hall; **~kleid** *n* festive attire; **~lich** *a* festive; (*feierlich*) solemn; *in ~~er Stimmung* in a festive mood; *~~ begehen* to celebrate; **~lichkeit** *f* festivity; **~mahl** *n* banquet; **~ordner** *m* organizer of a fête; **~rede** *f* speech of the day; **~redner** *m* official speaker; **~schrift** *f* anniversary publication; publication in hono(u)r of s. o.; **~spiel** *n* festival (performance); **~tag** *m* festival day, festive day; holiday; *eccl* feast; (*im Kalender*) red-letter day; **~wagen** *m* display vehicle in a parade, *Am* float; **~wiese** *f* amusement park; **~zug** *m* (festive) procession, pageant, parade; cavalcade.

Fetisch *m* fetish.

fett *a* fat; (*Boden*) fertile; (*schmierig*) greasy; (*einträglich*) rich, lucrative; (*brennstoffreich*) rich (gas mixture); *typ* bold type; (*Kohle*) bituminous; *~ machen* to fatten; *~ werden* to grow fat; *~ n* fat; grease; (*Braten~*) dripping; (*Schmalz*) lard; (*für Backwaren*) shortening; *fig* (*Schelte*) scolding; *~ ansetzen* to put on flesh; **~abscheider** *m* grease separator; **~ansatz** *m* corpulence; **~arm** *a* poor in fat; **~auge** *n* drop of grease; eye; **~bestandteil** *m* fatty constituent; **~bauch** *m* fat belly; **~darm** *m anat* rectum; **~druck** *m typ* black (*od* bold-faced) type; clarendon, fat type, heavy-face type; **~en** *tr* (*schmieren*) to oil, to lubricate; **~fleck** *m* spot of grease; **~gas** *n* oil gas; **~gans** *f* penguin; **~gehalt** *m* fat content; **~gewebe** *n* fatty tissue; **~grieben** *f pl* cracklings *pl*; **~haltig** *a* containing fat, fatty; **~heit** *f* fatness; **~ig** *a* fat(ty); (*fleckig*) greasy; (*ölig*) oily, unctuous; **~igkeit** *f* greasiness, fatness; **~kohle** *f* bituminous coal **~leibig** *a* corpulent; **~leibigkeit** *f* corpulence; **~polster** *n* cushion of fat, subcutaneous fatty tissue; **~presse** *f mot* grease gun; **~säure** *f* fatty acid; **~sucht** *f* obesity, fatty degeneration; **~verbindung** *f* fatty compound; **~wanst** *m* fat belly, paunch; **~wanstig** *a* big-bellied.

Fetzen *m* piece; (*Kleider~*) rag; *Am* frazzle; *in ~* in rags; *ein ~ Papier* a scrap of paper; (*Lappen*) rag, tatter; shred.

feucht *a* moist, damp, humid; (*schwül*) muggy; **~en** *tr* to moisten, to damp; *itr* to get moist; **~igkeit** *f* moisture, dampness, humidity; **~~sgehalt** *m* moisture percentage; **~~sgrad** *m* moisture content; **~~smesser** *m* hygrometer; **~kalt** *a* clammy; **~warm** *a* with warm moist temperature.

feudal *a* feudal; (*prächtig, prima*) grand; luxurious; magnificent; opulent; showy, *Am* swell; **~ismus** *m* feudalism; **~recht** *n* feudal law; **~system** *n* feudal system.

Feuer *n* fire; (*Flamme*) flame; (*~sbrunst, Brand*) conflagration; (*Glut*) blaze; (*Herd*) hearth; (*im Freien*) bonfire; (*für Zigarette*) light; *mil* (*Gewehr~*) fire, firing; *aero* (*Flugstrecken~*) airway beacon; *mar* (*Leucht~*) (flashing) light; (*Funk~*) radio beacon, radio beam; radio range; (*Glanz, Funkeln*) brilliance, lustre; (*Begeisterung*) enthusiasm; (*Eifer*) ardo(u)r, vigo(u)r; passion; heat; spirit; (*Inbrunst*) fervo(u)r; (*Rasse, Temperament von Pferden etc*) mettle; *~! ~!* (*Alarm*) fire! fire! (to cry fire); *~! mil* fire! *bengalisches ~* Bengal lights *pl*; *am ~* at the fire; *durch ~ beleuchtet* firelit; *ohne ~* fireless; *~ (an)machen* (*od anzünden*) to make (*od* to light) a fire, *Am fam* to fix a fire; ~ *(aus)löschen* to put out (*od* to extinguish) a fire; *das ~ ist ausgegangen* the fire has gone out; *~ fangen, in ~ geraten* to catch (*od* to take) fire; *fig* to be thrown into a passion; *~ schlagen* to strike a light; *aufs ~ setzen* to put (*od* to set) on fire; *das ~ schüren* to make up the fire; *das ~ unterhalten* to keep up the fire; *das ~ einstellen mil* to cease firing; *~ einstellen!* (*Kommando*) cease firing! *das ~ eröffnen mil* to open fire; *~ geben* (*schießen*) to fire (*auf* at, on, upon); *unter schwerem ~ liegen mil* to be exposed to heavy fire; *unter ~ nehmen mil* to fire at; *unter ~ stehen mil* to be under fire; *das ~ vereinigen mil* to concentrate fire; *das ~ vorverlegen mil* to increase the guns range; *darf ich Sie um ~ bitten?* may I ask you for a light? *fam* got a match, please? *geben Sie mir ~* give me a match, please, *fam* light me; *haben Sie ~?* do you have a light? have you got a light? *~ u. Flamme sein* to be fire and flame (*od* all afire) for; *in ~ u. Flamme geraten* to be enthusiastic about; *fig* to fly into a passion; *mit ~ u. Schwert* with fire and sword; *Öl ins ~ gießen* to pour oil on the fire, to add fuel to the fire; *mit dem ~ spielen fig* to play with fire; *im Wohnzimmer ist ~* (= *ist geheizt*) there is fire in the sitting room; *Kohlen auf das ~ legen* to put coal on the fire; *am ~ kochen* to cook over the fire; *bei langsamem* (*od schwachem*) *~* on a slow fire; *für jdn durchs ~ gehen* to go through fire and water for s. o.; *zwischen zwei ~n stehen* to be between two fires; to be between the devil and the deep sea; *die Kastanien für jdn aus dem ~ holen* to pull the chestnuts out of the fire for s. o.; *gebrannte Kinder fürchten das ~* a burnt child dreads the fire; **~abriegelung** *mil* box-barrage; *~~ schießen mil* to lay down a box-barrage; **~alarm** *m* fire-alarm; **~anbeter** *m* fire-worshipper; **~anzünder** *m* fire-lighter; (*für Kohlen*) coal kindler; **~aufnahme** *f mil* opening fire; **~auftrag** *m mil* fire mission; **~bake** *f mar* light-beacon; **~ball** *m* fire-ball; **~befehl** *m mil* command to open fire, order to fire; fire mission; **~bereich** *m mil* fire-zone, range; **~bereit** *a mil* ready to open fire, ready for action; **~bereitschaft** *f mil* readiness for action; **~beständig** *a* fire-proof; fire-resistive; **~beständigkeit** *f* fire-resistive quality; **~bestattung** *f* cremation; **~blende** *f* fireblende; **~bock** *m* (*Kamin*) fire-dog; **~bohne** *f bot* scarlet runner; **~brand** *m* firebrand; **~büchse** *f tech* fire-box; **~eifer** *m* (glowing) ardo(u)r, fiery zeal; **~eimer** *m* fire-bucket; **~einstellung** *f mil* cessation of fire; **~erlaubnis** *f mil* permission to fire; **~eröffnung** *f mil* opening of fire; **~esse** *f* chimney; (*Schmiede*) forge; **~fangend** *a* inflammable; apt to take fire; **~farben, ~farbig** *a* flame-colo(u)red; **~fest** *a* fire-proof; (*Glas*) heat-resistant; (*unverbrennbar*) incombustible; *~~er Ziegel* firebrick; **~fresser** *m* fire-eater; **~flüssig** *a* molten; **~funke** *m* spark of fire; **~garbe** *f* flash of fire; cone of fire; **~gefährlich** *a* inflammable, combustible; **~gefecht** *n* fire-fight; **~geist** *m* fiery spirit; **~geschwindigkeit** *f mil* rate of fire; **~glocke** *f* alarm-bell; tocsin; *mil* box of artillery fire; **~hahn** *m* fireplug, hydrant; **~haken** *m* (*Schüreisen*) poker; (*der Feuerwehr*) fire-hook; **~herd** *m* fire; hearth, fire-place, fireside; **~hydrant** *m* hydrant, fireplug; **~kampf** *m mil* artillery duel; fire fight; **~kommando** *n* firing command; **~kopf** *m* fiery nature, hotspur; **~kraft** *f* fire-power; **~kugel** *f* fire-ball; **~lärm** *m* cry of fire, fire-alarm; *~~ schlagen* to cry fire; **~leiter** *f* fire-ladder; (*Nottreppe*) fire-escape, *Am* hook-and-ladder; **~leitgerät** *n mil* fire control equipment, (fire control) predictor; **~leitung** *f mil* fire control, range finding; **~~sstand** *m* fire control tower; fire-command post; **~leitverfahren** *n* fire control method; **~lilie** *f bot* orange lily; **~linie** *f* front line; firing line; **~los** *a* fireless; (*glanzlos*) lusterless; **~löschboot** *n* fire-boat, fire-tug; **~löscher** *m* fire-extinguisher; **~löschgerät** *n* fire-fighting equipment; **~löschmannschaft** *f* fire-brigade, firemen *pl*; fire party; **~löschoffizier** *m* fire-prevention officer; **~löschteich** *m* static water tank; **~material** *n* fuel; **~mauer** *f* strong wall; **~meer** *n* sheet of fire; **~melder** *m* fire-call, *Am* fire-alarm (box); (*automatischer*) fire detector; **~n** *itr* (*schießen*) to fire (*auf* at, on, upon); (*heizen*) to make fire, to fuel; to feed; *fig* (*anfeuern, aufreizen*) to inflame; **~nelke** *f bot* scarlet lychnis; **~ordnung** *f* fire-regulations *pl*; **~patsche** *f* (*Luftschutz*) fire swatter; **~pause** *f mil* pause in firing; **~probe** *f* trial by fire; (*Gottesurteil*) fire-ordeal; (*schwere Prüfung*) crucial test, ordeal; *die ~~ bestehen* to stand the test; (*Probealarm*) fire-drill; **~punkt** *m* fire point; (*Optik*) focus; *min* hearth; **~rad** *n* fire-wheel; **~regelung** *f mil* control; **~regen** *m* rain of fire, fiery rain; *mil* rain of steel; **~riegel** *m mil* box-barrage; **~risiko** *n* fire risk; **~rohr** *n* gun; **~rost** *m* (fire-) grate; **~rot** *a* red as fire; red-hot; **~säule** *f* column of flames; **~sbrunst** *f* fire, conflagration; **~schaden** *m* damage by fire; **~schein** *m* glare (*od* gleam) of fire; **~schiff** *n* light-ship; **~schirm** *m mil* fire-screen, fire-guard; **~schlag** *m* heavy artillery fire; short heavy bombardment; rafale, burst of fire; **~schlund** *m* crater; *fig* (*Kanone*) cannon; **~schutz** *m* fire-prevention; *mil* preventive barrage, fire curtain; protective fire; **~schutzmittel** *n* fire-proofing agent; **~schutzpolizei** *f* fire-police; **~schutzschneise** *f Am* fire-break; **~schwamm** *m* female agaric, German tinder; **~sgefahr** *f* danger of fire, fire hazard; (*Gefährlichkeit*) inflammability; **~sicher** *a* fire-proof, fire-resistant (*od* -resisting); **~snot** *f* distress from fire, conflagration; **~speiend** *a* (*vulkanisch*) volcanic; *~~er Berg* volcano; **~sperre** *f* (fire-) barrage; **~spritze** *f* fire-engine; **~stahl** *m* fire-steel; **~stärke** *f mil* volume of fire; **~stätte, ~stelle** *f* fireplace, hearth; scene of a fire; **~stellung** *f mil* fire (*od* firing) position; battery position; (*für Raketen*) launching site; *in ~~* in firing position; **~stein** *m* flint; **~stoß** *m mil* burst of fire; **~strahl** *m* flash of fire; **~taufe** *f* baptism of fire; **~tiefe** *f* depth of fire; **~tod** *m* death by fire; **~ton** *m* fireclay; **~überfall** *m mil* fire attack; strafe; surprise fire; concentration of fire; **~überlegenheit** *f mil* fire superiority; **~ung** *f* (*Heizung*) firing; heating; (*Ofen*) furnace; (*Brennmaterial*) fuel; **~~sanlage** *f* furnace; fireplace; **~~sbedarf** *m* fuel requirement; **~~smaterial** *n* fuel; **~unterstützung** *f mil* fire support; **~vereinigung** *f* concentration of fire; **~vergoldung** *f* hot gilding; **~versicherung** *f* fire-insurance; **~~sanstalt** *f* fire-office; **~~sgesellschaft** *f* fire-insurance company; **~versilberung** *f* hot-dip silver-plating; **~verzinkt** *a* galvanized; **~verzinnt** *a* fire-tinned; **~vorbereitung** *f mil* preparatory fire; **~vorhang** *m* fire screen; curtain of fire; **~wache** *f* fire-watch; (*Beobachter bei Luftangriffen*) fire-watcher; (*Bereitschaft*) fire-station; **~waffe** *f* fire-arm; gun; **~walze** *f mil* rolling barrage, creeping barrage; **~wasser** *n Am hum* fire-water; **~wehr** *f* fire-brigade; *freiwillige ~~* auxiliary fire-brigade, *Am* fire department; **~~auto** *n* (*Motorspritze*) fire-brigade motor car, *Am* fire truck; (*mit Leiter*) hook-and-ladder truck; **~~leiter** *f* fire-ladder; **~~mann** *m* fireman, *Am auch* fire fighter, (*leitender*) fire ward(en); **~welle** *f* fire wave; **~werk** *n* fireworks *pl*; **~werker** *m* fireworker; pyrotechnist; *mil* artificer; gunner; **~werkskörper** *m* fireworks *pl*; **~werkskunst** *f* pyrotechnics *pl*; **~wirkung** *f mil* fire-effect, fire-efficiency; **~zange** *f* (fire-) tongs *pl*; **~zeichen** *n* fire-signal; signal-light; **~zeug** *n* (*Zündhölzer*) match-box; (*mit Benzin*) (cigarette) lighter; **~~füllung** *f* lighter fluid; **~~stein** *m* flint for lighter; **~zug** *m* draught, flue; **~zunder** *m* spunk, touch-wood; **~zusammenfassung** *f* concentrated fire.

feurig *a* fiery; *fig* fervent, ardent; (*Pferd*) spirited; (*Augen*) flashing; (*Rede*) impassioned: inflammatory; (*Wein*) heady.

Fiaker *m* cab, hansom; (*Kutscher*) cabman.

Fiasko *n* failure; *Am parl* landslide; *~ machen* to fail.

Fibel *f* primer, spelling-book; (*Spange*) brooch, clasp.

Fiber *f* fibre (*od* fiber); fiberboard;

Fichte *f* pine(-tree); spruce; **~n** *a* of pine-wood; **~nharz** *n* resin; **~nnadelbad** *n* pine-needles bath; **~nzapfen** *m* pine-cone.

Fideikommiß *m* entail, feoffment.

fidel *a* merry, jovial, jolly.

Fidibus *m* spill.

Fieber *n* fever; (*Temperatur*) temperature; *gelbes ~, hitziges ~* yellow fever, inflammatory fever; *kaltes ~* ague; *das ~ messen* to take the temperature; *das ~ haben* to have a fever; **~anfall** *m* attack of fever; ague-fit; **~erregend** *a* causing fever, febrifacient; **~flecken** *m pl* fever spots *pl*; **~frei, ~los** *a* free from fever; **~frost, ~schauer** *m* chill, feverish shivering; **~haft, ~ig** *a* febrile; *fig* feverish; **~krank** *a* feverish; sick with fever, suffering from fever; **~kurve** *f* temperature curve; **~mittel** *n* febrifuge; **~n** *itr* to be in a fever; to have a temperature; *fig* to rave; **~phantasie** *f* feverish dream; delirium; **~pulver** *n* ague powder; **~rinde** *f* Peruvian bark; quinquina; cinchona bark; **~schauer** *m* ague fit; **~tabelle** *f* temperature-chart; **~thermometer** *n* clinic(al) thermometer; **~vertreibend** *a* febrifuge; **~wahn** *m* delirium; **~zustand** *m* feverishness.

Fied|el *f* fiddle; **~elbogen** *m* fiddlestick; **~eln** *itr* to fiddle; **~ler** *m* fiddler.

Figur *f* figure, shape; (*Karte*) court-card; (*Rede~*) form of speech, figure of speech, rhetorical figure; metaphor; *math* diagram; figure; graph; (*Porzellan~*) statuette, figurine; (*Tanz~*) figure; (*e-s Schiffes*) figure-head; (*Schachspiel*) piece, chessman; *gute ~ machen* to cut a figure; *in ganzer ~*

malen to paint full-length; *e-e komische* ~ a figure of fun; *e-e schlechte* ~ *machen* to make a poor figure; **~entanz** *m* figure-dance; **~enlaufen** *n* (*Eis*) figure-skating; **~ieren** *itr* to figure (*als* as).

figürlich *a* figurative.

Fikt|ion *f* invention; pretence; *jur* fiction; **~iv** *a* fictitious.

Filet *n* netting; (*Fleischstück*) fillet, sirloin; chine; undercut, *Am* tenderloin; ~ *stricken* to net; **~braten** *m* roast fillet; **~nadel** *f* netting-needle; **~strikkerei** *f* net-work.

Filial|e *f* branch(-house); branch establishment; subsidiary; **~bank** *f* branch bank; **~bibliothek** *f* branch library; **~geschäft** *n* branch-establishment; branch-office; (*Kettenladen*) multiple-shop, *Am* chain-store; **~kirche** *f* chapel of ease; **~leiter** *m* branch manager.

Filigran *n*, **~arbeit** *f* filigree.

Film *m* (*Häutchen, Schleier, Schicht, Belag*) film, coat; (thin) coating; *phot phot* film; roll of film; (*Kino~*) cine-(ma)-film, *Am* motion-picture, *fam* moving-picture, movie; (cinema) picture; screen; (*als Gattung, Kino*) the cinema, *Am* the motion-pictures *pl*, the moving-pictures *pl*, the movies *pl*, the pictures *pl*; *die Kinos werden Spitzenfilme vorführen* the cinemas (*od* theaters) will play top pictures; *aktueller* ~ topic; *biographischer* ~ film biography; *Farb~* colo(u)r film, *Am* technicolor; *Groß~*, *Haupt~* full-length film; *Kino~* cine-film; *Kurz~* (film) short; *Lehr~* movie training film; *Normalkino~* (*Material*) bulk film; *plastischer* ~ stereoscopic film; *Sicherheits~* safety film; *positiver* ~ positive film; *Roll~* roll-film; *Schmal~* narrow film; *Spiel~* (*normaler Länge*) feature-length film; feature; *stummer* ~ silent film, silent screen; movie; *Ton~* sound-film, movietone, *Am* sound motion-picture (*od* movie), *fam* talking picture, talkie; *Trick~* trick-film; (*gezeichnet*) film-cartoon, cartoon motion-picture; animated cartoon film; *Schwarz-Weiß* ~ black-and-white film; *unbelichteter* ~ unexposed film, *fam* raw stock; *Zeitlupen~* slow motion film; ~ (*od Kino*) *betreffend* cinematic(al), cine-, filmic, *Am* motion-picture; movie; *beim* ~, *im* ~ on the screen, on the films; *e-n* ~ *drehen* to take a film, to shoot a film (*Am* motion-picture, movie); to film, to screen, to picture; (*herstellen*) to produce a film; *e-n* ~ *einlegen* (*in die Kamera*) to load (*od* to fill) a camera; *e-n* ~ *synchronisieren* to synchronize a film; *e-n* ~ *vorführen* (*od spielen*) to play a film, *Am* to play a picture; *e-n* ~ (*zu*)*schneiden* to cut a film; **~abzug** *m* (*Kopie*) print; **~apparat** *m* film camera, cine-camera, *Am* motion-picture camera, movie camera; **~arbeiter** *m* studio handyman, *Am sl* grip; **~archiv** *n* film archives *pl*; **~atelier** *n* film studio; (*mit aufgebauter Szene*) set; **~aufnahme** *f* (*Vorgang*) shooting (of a film); (*Einzelaufnahme*) film shot, *Am* movie shot, picture; ~~ *durch Mikroskop* cine microphotography; **~aufnahmeleiter** *m* acting director; **~autor** *m* film author, *Am* screen author, screen writer; playwright; **~band** *n* film-strip, reel; **~bar** *a* filmable; **~bearbeitung** *f* (*e-s Romans etc*) film adaption, *Am* screen adaption (of a story, novel etc); **~bericht** *m* screen-record; **~besucher** *m* film-goer, cinema-goer, *Am* movie goer; **~bibliothek** *f* film library; **~bild** *n* motion-picture; (*Einzelbild des Streifens*) frame; **~bildwerfer** *m* film projector, *Am* motion-picture (*od* movie) projector; **~biographie** *f* film biography; **~dichter** *m* film writer, *Am* screen writer; **~diva** *f* film star; **~drama** *n* photo drama; (*Rührstück*) cinemelodrama, film thriller; **~drehbuch** *n* shooting script; **~drehbuchverfasser** *m* scenario writer, *Am sl* scenarist, scriptist; **~ebene** *f* (*im Apparat*) focal plane; **~einakter** *m* (film) short, *Am* movie short, shortie, filler; **~en** (*verfilmen*) *tr*, *itr* to film, to cinematize, *Am* to shoot, to screen, to reel, to picture; to take motion-pictures (of), to photograph with a motion-picture camera; *e-n Roman* ~*en* to film a novel; **~enthusiast** *m*, **~narr** *m* film fan, *Am* motion-picture (*od* movie) fan, *sl* cinemaddict; **~erzeuger** *m* film maker, *Am* movie maker; **~fenster** *n* (*im Apparat*) film gate, picture window; **~führung** *f* (*im Apparat*) film guide; **~gelände** *n* (*mit den Studios etc*) *Am* movie lot; (*bei Außenaufnahmen außerhalb des eigentlichen* ~~*s*) location; **~geräte** *n pl* (*Ausrüstung*) motion-picture equipment; **~gesellschaft** *f* film (*Am* motion-picture *od* movie) company; **~held** *m* film (*Am* movie) hero; **~hersteller** *m* film (*Am* motion-picture *od* movie) producer; **~herstellung** *f* film production; **~idol** *n* film (*Am* movie) idol; **~industrie** *f* the films *pl*, film industry; **~kamera** *f* film camera, cine-camera, *Am* motion-picture (*od* movie) camera; (*für Schmal~*) home movie camera; (*für Roll~*) roll-film camera; **~~mann** *m* (*Kurbler*) cameraman, camera operator; (*bei Wochenschauen*) news-reel camera man; **~~wagen** *m* camera car; **~kassette** *f* (film) cassette, (film) magazine; (*für Filmpack*) film-pack adapter; **~komiker** *m* screen comedian (*od* comic); **~komikerin** *f* screen comedienne; **~kern** *m* (*der Spule*) core; **~kopie** *f* print; (*Musterabzug*) copy; **~kritiker** *m* film (*Am* motion-picture, movie) critic, movie reviewer; **~kunst** *f* cinematics *pl*; **~länge** *f* film length; **~laufbahn** *f* film career, *Am* movie career; **~leinwand** *f* screen, *Am* movie screen, silver screen; **~liebhaber** *m* film fan; **~lustspiel** *n* film comedy, *fam* (film) frolic; **~magazin** *n* (*Trommel*) film magazine; **~magnat** *m* film magnate, *Am* movie magnate, *fam* cinemagnate, cinemogul; **~manuskript** *n* film script; **~operette** *f*, **~singspiel** *n* musical film, *Am* musical motion-picture, movie show, cinemusical, musical; **~pack** *m* filmpack; **~packkassette** *f* film-pack adapter; **~papier** *n* film paper; **~patrone** *f* cartridge; **~preis** *m* (*jährlich vergebene Auszeichnung für gute Leistung*) *Am* oscar, Oscar; **~premiere** *f* film première, *Am* movie première; **~probe** *f* (*für zukünftige Darsteller*) film (*Am* screen) test; *e-e* ~~ *machen* to make a film (*Am* screen) test; **~programm** *n* cinema program(me), cinema show; (*mit e-m Film*) single feature program(me); (*mit zwei Hauptfilmen*) double feature program(me); **~projektionsapparat** *m* film (*Am* motion-picture, movie) projector; **~prüfer** *m* film censor; **~prüfstelle** *f* film censorship office; **~publikum** *n* film (*Am* movie) audience; **~regisseur** *m* film producer, *Am* motion-picture (*od* movie) producer; **~reißer** *m fam* thriller; *Am sl* (*sehr schnell u. mit wenig Kosten hergestellt*) quickie; **~reklame** *f* (*für den* ~) film publicity; (*Werbung auf der Leinwand*) screen advertising; **~schauspieler** *m* film actor, *Am* motion-picture actor, movie actor, screen actor, *sl* cinem-actor, cineman; ~~ *in wichtiger Rolle* *Am* contract player; ~~ *in e-r Nebenrolle* *Am* bit player; **~schauspielerin** *f* film actress, *Am* motion-picture actress, movie actress, screen actress, *sl* cinemactress; **~schichtseite** *f* emulsion side of film; **~schlager** *m* picture hit; **~schneiden** *n* film editing; **~spiel** *n* film play, *Am* photoplay, screen play; **~spule** *f* film spool; (*Kassette*) cartridge; (*mit Streifen*) reel of film; **~spulenkern** *m* spool core; **~star** *m* film star, *Am* motion-picture star, movie star, starlet, movie queen; **~statist** *m* film super, *Am* extra; **~streifen** *m* film-strip; reel; (*mit Einzelbildern*) film slide; **~stück** *n* screen play; **~studio** *n* film (*Am* motion-picture, movie) studio; **~szene** *f* shot; **~theater** *n* cinema, *Am* (motion-)picture theater, picture house, moviehouse; **~titel** *m* film-caption; **~ton(aufnahme)gerät** *n* film recorder; **~tonmeister**, **~tonregisseur** *m* sound engineer; **~tonspur** *f* sound track; **~transport** *m* film transport; film feed; **~transportschlüssel** *m* winding knob; **~trommel** *f* spool-box; film drum; **~untertitel** *m* subtitle, *Am fam* cut-in, leader; **~uraufführung** *f* first release, film première; **~verleih**, **~vertrieb** *m* film distribution (*od* exchange); (*Firma*) film distributors *pl*; **~verleiharchiv** *n* film-rental library; **~vorführapparat** *m*, **~vorführgerät** *n* film projector, cine-projector, *Am* motion-picture (*od* movie) projector; **~vorführer** *m* (film) projectionist, (cinema) operator, *Am fam* booth man; **~vorführung**, **~vorstellung** *f* cinema show, film show, motion-picture exhibition; (*Varieté mit* ~~ *als Beiprogramm*) cine-variety; **~vorschau** *f* (*für Kritiker etc*) preview, prevue; (*Reklame für das nächste Programm e-s Kinos*) trailer; **~welt** *f* film world; filmland, filmdom, *Am fam* movieland; **~wesen** *n* the films *pl*, *Am* the movies *pl*; **~wochenschau** *f* newsreel; **~zensur** *f* film censorship; **~zählwerk** *n* (*in der Kamera*) film counter, meter counter; *Am* footage counter; **~zuschneider** *m* (*Schnittmeister*) (film) cutter; **~zuschneideraum** *m* (film) cutting-room.

Filt|er *m u.* (*tech*) *n* filter; *phot* screen, filter; *el*, *radio* filter, sifter; **~~anlage** *f* filtration plant; **~~element** *n* filter cell; **~~gaze** *f* filter gauze; **~~gefäß** *n* filter(ing) vessel; **~~gerät** *n* filter apparatus; **~~kohle** *f* filter charcoal; **~~masse** *f* (*Brauerei*) pulp, filter mass; **~~mittel** *n* filter material; **~~n** *tr* to filter; **~~papier** *n* filter paper; **~~vorsatz** *m* (*Gasmaske*) air filter; **~rat** *n* filtrate; **~rierapparat** *m* filtering apparatus; **~rierbar** *a* filterable; **~rieren** *tr* to filter, to strain; **~riersack** *m* filter bag, percolator; **~riertrichter** *m* filtering funnel; **~riertuch** *n* filtering cloth; **~rierung** *f* filtration, filtering.

Filz *m* felt; *fam* (*Hut*) felt-hat; *typ* blanket; *bot* tomentum; (*Metall*) slim ore; (*Tadel*) rebuke; (*Geizhals*) miser, sordid niggard, skinflint; **~dichtung** *f* felt packing; **~en** *tr* to felt; (*schelten*) to rebuke; *itr* (*geizen*) to be niggardly (*od* stingy); *sich* ~~ to clot together; **~hut** *m* felt-hat; *Am* (*niedriger, weicher, mit Längskniff*) fedora; (*steifer*) hard hat, bowler, *Am* derby (hat); **~ig** *a* felted, felt-like; (*geizig*) stingy, niggard, sordid: **~igkeit** *f* stinginess; **~laus** *f* crab-louse; **~macher** *m* felt-maker; **~schuh** *m* felt-shoe; (*Pantoffel*) felt slipper; **~sohle** *f* felt-sole.

Fimmel *m* craze.

Finanz|abteilung *f* finance department; fiscal division; **~amt** *n* (inland) revenue-office, tax (*od* fiscal) office; financial department; **~ausgleich** *m* financial compensation; **~ausschuß** *m* finance committee; *parl* Committee of Ways and Means; **~ausweis** *m* financial statement; **~beamte(r)** *m* fiscal officer, clerk of the Treasury; **~bedarf** *m* financial requirement; **~bericht** *m* financial report; **~blatt** *n* financial newspaper; **~en** *f pl* finances *pl*; revenue; **~gebarung** *f* financial policy; **~gesetzgebung** *f* finance legislation; **~iell** *a* financial; *aus ~~en Gründen* for financial reasons; **~ieren** *tr* to finance; (*am Anfang*) to float; **~ierung** *f* financing; (*Anfangs~~*) floating; **~ierungsgesellschaft** *f* finance company; **~jahr** *n* fiscal year; **~kontrolle** *f* budgetary control, finance control; **~kreise** *m pl* financial circles *pl*; **~krise** *f* finance crisis; **~lage** *f* financial state (*od* condition *od* situation); (*persönliche Vermögensverhältnisse*) pecuniary circumstances *pl*; **~mann** *m* financier; **~minister** *m* minister of finances; (*England*) Chancellor of the Exchequer, *Am* Secretary of the Treasury; **~ministerium** *n* ministry of the finance(s); (*England*) (Board of) Exchequer, *Am* Treasury Department; **~politik** *f* financial (*od* fiscal) policy; **~reform** *f* financial reform; **~technisch** *a* fiscal; on the financial side; **~teil** *m* (*Zeitung*) financial page; **~verhältnisse** *n pl* financial conditions *pl*; **~verwaltung** *f* financial administration; (*Steuer*) Board of Inland Revenue; **~welt** *f* finance world; **~wesen** *n* finance(s *pl*); **~wirtschaft** *f* finance economy; **~wissenschaft** *f* science of finances.

Findel|haus *n* foundling-hospital; **~kind** *n* foundling.

find|en *irr tr* to find; (*treffen*) to meet (with); to hit upon; (*entdecken*) to discover; *fig* (*glauben*) to think; to deem; to consider; to judge; *sich in etw ~~* to understand, to comprehend; to accommodate o.s. to, to put up with, to resign o.s. to; *gut od schlecht ~~* to find good or ill; *es wird sich ~~* we shall see; *es wird sich schon alles ~~* it will be all right; *Beifall ~~* to meet with applause; *Fehler ~~ an etw od jdm* to find fault with s.th. *od* s.o.; *e-e Entschuldigung ~~ für* to find an excuse for; *der Richter fand den Häftling schuldig* the judge found the prisoner guilty; *seinen Weg ~~* to find o.'s way; *wie ~~ Sie dieses Buch?* how do you like this book? **~er** *m* finder; *der ~er erhält e-e Belohnung* the finder will be rewarded; **~~lohn** *m* finder's reward; **~ig** *a* clever, sharp, shrewd; **~~keit** *f* sharpness, shrewdness, ingenuity, cleverness; **~ling** *m* foundling; **~~sblock** *m geol* erratic block.

Finger *m* finger; *zoo* toe; *lange ~ haben* to crib, to steal; *durch die ~ sehen* to wink at; *jdm auf die ~ sehen* to have a strict eye upon, to watch s. o. closely; *aus den ~n saugen fig* to invent; *an den ~n hersagen können* to have s. th. at o.'s finger's ends; *sich die ~ verbrennen* to burn o.'s fingers; *sich in den ~ schneiden* to cut o.'s finger; *man kann es an den fünf ~n abzählen* it is obvious; *auf die ~ klopfen* to rap over the knuckles; *die ~ davon lassen* to keep o.'s hands off; *mit ~n weisen auf* to point at; *man kann ihn um den kleinen ~ wickeln* you can twist him (a)round your little finger; **~abdruck** *m* finger-print; *e-n ~~ nehmen von jdm* to take s. o.'s fingerprints, to fingerprint s. o.; **~anschlag** *m* finger-stop; **~breite** *f* digit; **~dick** *a* as thick as a finger; **~druck** *m* pressure of the finger; **~fertig** *a* dext(e)rous; **~fertigkeit** *f* dexterity; **~glied** *n* finger-joint; **~hut** *m* thimble; *bot* foxglove; *ein ~~ voll* a thimbleful; **~ling** *m* finger-stall; **~n** *tr* to touch with the finger; *itr* to finger; **~probe** *f* rule of thumb; **~ring** *m* finger-ring; **~satz** *m mus* fingering; **~spitze** *f* finger-tip; **~spitzengefühl** *n* intuition, instinct, flair; **~zeig** *m* hint, intimation, cue, indication, tip.

fingier|en *tr* to feign, to sham; *itr* to simulate; **~t** *a* fictitious; feigned, dummy.

Fink *m* finch; **~ler** *m* finch-catcher, fowler.

Finn|e *f* (*im Gesicht*) pimple, pustule; acne; (*Schweins~*) measles *pl*; (*Flosse*) fin; **~ig** *a* pimpled; (*von Schweinen*) measly.

Finn|land *n* Finland; **~e, ~länder** *m* Fin(n), Finlander; **~isch** *a* Finnish, Finnic.

finster *a* dark, gloomy, dim; obscure; *fig* sullen. stern, sad, morose; *im ~n* in the dark; *es wird ~* it is getting dark; *~ ansehen* to frown on; *~ aussehen* to look grim; *im Finstern tappen* to grope about in the dark; **~ling** *m* obscurant; **~nis** *f* darkness; gloom; obscurity; dimness; *astr* eclipse.

Finte *f* feint; *fig* trick, fib, artifice.

Firlefanz *m* childish trick, foolery; (*Unsinn*) nonsense; **~erei** *f* fiddle-faddle, trifles *pl*.

Firm|a *f* firm; business; company; (*Name*) style; (commercial) house; establishment; *unter der ~* under the firm of; (*Anschrift*) Messrs.; **~eninhaber** *m* owner of the firm; (*Chef*) principal; **~enstempel** *m* firm stamp; **~enschild** *n* sign-board; commercial sign; (*an Maschine*) maker's name; **~enverzeichnis** *n* trade directory; **~ieren** *tr* to sign; **~ierung** *f* signature.

Firmament *n* firmament, sky.

firm|en *tr* to confirm, to bishop; **~ling** *m* candidate for confirmation; **~ung** *f* confirmation.

Firn *m* névé; last year's snow; perpetual snow; (*Berg*) glacier (-snow), glacier snowfield; **~feld** *n* snowfield.

Firn|is *m* varnish; *japanischer ~~* Japan lacquer; **~issen** *tr* to varnish; **~isser** *m* varnisher.

First *m* ridge (of a roof); *min* back, roof; (*Berg*) mountain ridge, peak, top.

*

Fis *n mus* F sharp.

Fisch *m* fish; (*Sternbild*) Pisces *pl*; *das sind faule ~e* those are subterfuges (*od* lame excuses); *kleine ~e Am fam fig* small potatoes; *gesund wie ein ~ im Wasser* sound as a roach; **~adler** *m* fishing-eagle, *Am* fish-hawk; **~ähnlich** *a* fish-like; **~angel** *f* fishing-hook; **~bein** *n* whalebone; **~blase** *f* fish-bladder; **~brut** *f* fry; **~dampfer** *m* (steam-)trawler; **~en** *tr* to fish; *im Trüben ~~* to fish in troubled waters.

Fischer *m* fisher(man); **~ei** *f* fishing, fishery; **~~hafen** *m* fishing harbo(u)r; **~~schutzboot** *n* fishery protection vessel, fishery patrol boat; **~innung** *f* company of fishermen; **~kahn** *m* fishing-boat; **~netz** *n* fishing-net; **~stechen** *n* mock-seafight of fishermen.

Fisch|fang *m* fishing, fishery; **~gerät** *n* fishing-tackle; **~geruch** *m* fishy smell; **~gräte** *f* fish-bone; **~händler** *m*, **~~in** *f* fishmonger, *Am* fish-dealer; **~kasten** *m* fish-box; **~kelle** *f* (*Vorlegemesser*) fish-slice; **~kessel** *m* fish-kettle; **~kutter** *m* fishing-smack; **~laich** *m* spawn; **~leim** *m* fish-glue; **~logger** *m* lugger, drifter; **~markt** *m* fish-market; **~otter** *m* otter; **~reich** *a* abounding in fish; **~reiher** *m* heron; **~reuse** *f* bownet, weir; **~teich, ~weiher** *m* fish-pond; **~tran** *m* train-oil; **~weib** *n* fish-woman; **~zucht** *f* fish-hatchery; pisciculture; **~zug** *m* draught (of fish), catch, haul.

fisk|alisch *a* fiscal; **~us** *m* exchequer, treasury.

Fission *f phys* (*Spaltung*) fission.

Fistel *f* fistula; **~artig** *a* fistulous; **~stimme** falsetto; *mit ~~ singen* to sing falsetto.

Fittich *m* wing, pinion.

fix *a* firm, solid; (*Idee, Gehalt, Stern*) fixed; (*flink*) quick; *~ u. fertig* quite ready; *machen Sie ein bißchen ~, bitte Am fam* make it snappy, please; *ein ~er Junge* a smart fellow; **~ativ** *n* fixative, fixing-agent; **~geschäft** *n* (*Börse*) transaction on account; **~ierbad** *n* fixing-bath; **~ieren** *tr* to fix; to settle; to fix o.'s eyes upon; **~iermittel** *n* fixative; fixing agent; **~iernatron** *m* sodium thiosulphate; hypo; **~iersalz** *n* fixing salt; **~ierung** *f* fixation; **~stern** *m* fixed star; **~punkt** *m* fixed point; set point; **~um** *n* fixed salary (*od* sum).

flach *a* flat; (*eben*) level, plain; even; (*Land*) open; (*glatt von der See*) smooth; (*nicht tief*) shoal; (*Bild, Photo*) without contrast; (*Kurve*) flat; (*Böschung*) gentle; (*Kiel e-s Bootes*) flat-bottomed; *fig* (*seicht*) shallow; (*oberflächlich*) hasty, superficial; *~ machen* to flatten; *~ werden* to level off, to flatten out; to slope; to become less steep; *die ~e Hand* the palm of the hand; *sich ~ auf den Boden legen* to lie flat on the ground; **~bahn** *f mil* flat trajectory; **~~geschütz** *n* flat trajectory gun; **~bettfelge** *f* flat-base rim; **~brenner** *m* (*Gas*) fishtail burner, flat burner; **~dach** *n* flat roof; **~druck** *m typ* surface printing; lithoprinting; **~druckpresse** *f* flat-bed press; **~fisch** *m* flat fish; **~gedrückt** *a* flattened (down); **~heit** *f* flatness; *fig* shallowness; (*Ausdruck*) platitude; nonsense; **~köpfig** *a* flat-headed; *fig* (*dumm*) dull; **~land** *n* plain, open (*od* flat) country; **~relief** *n* bas-relief; **~rennen** *n* flat race; **~schlag, ~ball** *m* (*Tennis*) drive; **~trudeln** *n aero* flat spin; **~zange** *f* flat nose pliers *pl*.

Fläche *f* (*Flachheit*) flatness; (*Ebene*) plain, level; (*Oberfläche*) surface; (*Gebiet*) area; (*Wasser*) sheet; (*Meer*) expanse; (*Edelstein*) facet; (*Hand*) palm; *math* plane; *aero* (*Flügel, Tragfläche*) wing; **~nausdehnung** *f* square dimension; **~nbelastung** *f aero* wing load(ing); **~nblitz** *m* sheet lightning; **~nbombardierung** *f aero mil* pattern bombing, area bombing; **~nbrand** *m* area conflagration; **~ndrahthindernis** *n* concertina entanglement; **~ndruck** *m* surface pressure; **~nende** *n* wing tip;

~ninhalt *m* superficial contents *pl*, area, superficies; surface area; **~nlastig** *a aero* wingheavy; **~nmaß** *n* square measure; **~nmessung** *f* planimetry; **~nprofil** *n aero* wing profile; **~nrippe** *f aero* wing rib; **~ntreue Projektion** equal area projection; **~nziel** *n aero mil* area target, extensive target.

Flachs *m* flax; **~bau** *m* cultivation of flax; **~blond** *a* flax(en)-haired; **~breche** *f* flax-brake; **~farbig** *a* flaxen; **~feld, ~land** *n* flax-field; **~haar** *n* flaxen hair; **~hechel** *f* flax-comb; **~kopf** *m* flaxen-haired person; **~samen** *m* linseed; **~schwinge** *f* swingle; **~spinnerei** *f* flax-mill.

flackern *itr* (*Feuer*) to flare; (*flattern*) to flutter; (*Licht*) to flicker; (*Stimme*) to quaver, to shake; *~des Licht* flickering (*od* unsteady) light; *~ n* flickering; (*des Fernsehbildes auf dem Bildschirm*) *Am* womp.

Fladen *m* flat cake; (*Kuhmist*) cow-dung.

Flagg|e *f* flag, standard; colo(u)rs *pl*; *die ~ streichen* to strike the flag; *die ~ hissen* (*aufziehen*) to hoist the flag; to run up the flag, to unfurl the flag; *die ~~ halbmast setzen* to fly the flag half-mast, to half-mast the colo(u)rs; *die ~~ niederholen* to lower the colo(u)rs; **~en** *itr* to hoist the flag; to show o.'s flag (*od* colo(u)rs *pl*); *e-e ~ führen* to fly a flag; *die ~ hochhalten* to keep the flag flying; (*beflaggen*) to display flags; *tr mar* to dress (with flags); to deck with flags; **~ensignal** *n* flag-signal; **~enstange** *f*, **~enstock** *m* flag-staff; **~entuch** *n* bunting; **~enwinker** *m* semaphore; **~leine** *f* flag-line; halyard; **~schiff** *n mar, aero* flagship.

Flak *f* (= *Fliegerabwehrkanone*) flak, anti-aircraft gun (*Abk* A. A. gun), anti-aircraft fire, *sl* ack-ack; **~abwehr** *f* anti-aircraft defence; **~alarm** *m* air warning for anti-aircraft artillery units; **~artillerie** *f* anti-aircraft artillery (*Abk* A. A. A.), *sl* ack-ack; **~ausbildung** *f* flak training; **~batterie** *f* anti-aircraft battery; **~bedienung** *f* anti-aircraft gun crew; **~einsatz** *m* anti-aircraft artillery operations; **~feuer** *n* anti-aircraft fire, flak, *sl* ack-ack; **~geschoß** *n* anti-aircraft shell; **~geschütz** *n* anti-aircraft gun; **~einheit** *f* anti-aircraft unit; **~garbe** *f* burst of A. A. fire; **~granate** *f* anti-aircraft shell; **~gürtel** *m* cordon of anti-aircraft fire; **~kampfgruppe** *f* anti-aircraft combat group; **~kommandeur** *m* anti-aircraft artillery commander; **~kommandogerät** *n* anti-aircraft fire director; **~kreuzer** *m* anti-aircraft cruiser, A. A. cruiser; **~leitstand** *m* combination radar optical range finder and director; **~munition** *f* anti-aircraft ammunition; **~posten** *m* anti-aircraft spotter; **~rakete** *f* anti-aircraft rocket; **~raketenwerfer** *m* anti-aircraft rocket launcher (*od* projector); **~regiment** *n* anti-aircraft artillery regiment; **~scheinwerfer** *m* anti-aircraft searchlight; **~schießen** *n* anti-aircraft fire, A. A. fire; **~schiff** *n* flak ship; **~schutz** *m* anti-aircraft protection; **~soldat** *m* anti-aircraft gunner; **~sperre** *f* anti-aircraft barrage, curtain of anti-aircraft fire; **~stellung** *f* anti-aircraft gun emplacement, A. A. station; **~träger** *m* A. A. ship; **~treffer** *m* hit by anti-aircraft fire; **~truppe** *f* anti-aircraft artillery; **~turm** *m* anti-aircraft artillery tower, A. A. tower; **~verband** *m* anti-aircraft artillery unit; **~verteidigung** *f* anti-aircraft defence; **~vierling** *m* four-barrel(l)ed anti-aircraft gun; **~visier** *n* A. A. sight; anti-aircraft backsight; **~volltreffer** *m* direct hit from A. A. fire; **~waffe** *f* anti-aircraft artillery; **~zone** *f* anti-aircraft artillery zone; **~zug** *m rail* flak train.

Flakon *n* small bottle, phial; (*Parfüm*) scent bottle.

Flam|e *m* Fleming; **~in** *f* Flemish woman; **flämisch** *a* Flemish.

Flamingo *m* flamingo.

Flamm|e *f* flame; (*Glut*) blaze; *fig* (*Leidenschaft*) passion; (*alte Liebe*) flame, love, sweetheart; *sie ist e-e alte ~ von mir fam* she is an old flame of mine; **~en** *itr* to flame; to blaze; to flash; to flush; to be in flames; (*lodern*) to flare; (*leuchten*) to sparkle, to shine; *tr* to expose to the flames; (*sengen*) to singe; (*Seidenstoff*) to water, to cloud; to wave; **~enbeständig** *a* flame-proof; **~enbogen** *m* flaming arc, electric arc; **~enbombe** *f* oil bomb; **~end** *a* flaming; flashing; **~enfeuer** *n* glow of flames; **~enlos** *a* flameless; **~enmeer** *n* sea of flames; **~ensicher** *a* flame-proof; **~enstrahl** *m* flame jet; **~~bombe** *f* flame-throwing bomb; **~entod** *m* death by fire; **~enwerfer** *m* flame-thrower (*od* -projector); **~~panzerwagen** *m* flame-throwing tank; **~ig** *a* flamy, flame-like, flaming; (*Stoff*) watered; **~ofen** *m tech* (flaming) furnace; **~punkt** *m* flash point; **~rohrkessel** *m tech* flue boiler.

Flammeri *m* flummery, blancmange.

Fland|ern *n geog* Flanders *pl*; **~risch** *a* Flemish.

Flanell *m* flannel; **~anzug** *m*, **~hose** *f*, **~waschlappen** *m* flannels *pl*.

flanieren *itr* to loiter, to lounge about.

Flanke *f* flank; (*Tennis*) side; (*Turnen*) side-vault; *offene ~* open flank; *die ~ aufrollen* to turn the flank; *die ~ entblößen mil* to expose the flank; *in die ~ fallen* to attack in flank; **~enangriff** *m mil* flank attack; **~nbewegung** *f* flanking movement; **~ndeckung** *f* flank protection; **~neinbruch** *m* flanking penetration; **~nfeuer** *n* flanking fire, enfilade fire; **~nmarsch** *m* flanking march; **~nschutz** *m* flank protection; **~nsicherung** *f* protective flank reconnaissance, flank security; **~nstellung** *f* flanking position.

flankieren *tr* to flank, to outflank; to enfilade.

Flan(t)sche *f tech* flange.

Flaps *m fam* (*Lümmel*) lout, boor; hooligan; bumpkin; **~ig** *a* boorish, loutish; uncouth.

Fläschchen *n* small bottle, phial.

Flasche *f* bottle, flask; (*Arznei~*) vial; phial; (*Gas~*) cylinder; (*geschliffene*) decanter; (*Leidener ~*) Leyden jar; *in ~n füllen* to bottle; *mit der ~ aufziehen* to bring up by hand (*od* on the bottle); *in ~n* bottled; **~nbier** *n* bottled beer; **~nbürste** *f* bottle-brush; **~nfüllerei** *f* bottling plant; **~nfüllmaschine** *f* bottling machine; **~ngestell** *n* bottle-rack; **~ngrün** *a* bottle-green; **~nhals** *m* neck of bottle; **~nkorb** *m* bottle-basket; **~nkürbis** *m bot* bottle-gourd; **~nwein** *m* bottled wine; **~nzug** *m* pulley block, block and tackle.

Flaschner *m* (*Klempner*) plumber, tinner; (*Installateur*) fitter.

flatter|haft, **~ig** *a* unsteady, fickle; **~haftigkeit** *f*, **~sinn** *m* unsteadiness, fickleness; **~mine** *f mil* contact mine; **~n** *itr* to flutter, to flit; (*in der Luft*) to float; *mot* to shimmy, *Am* to wobble; *aero* (*Tragfläche*) to flop; (*Fahne*) to stream, to wave; *fig* to be fickle.

flau *a* (*schwach*) weak; feeble; (*Handel*) slow, dull, flat; (*Getränke*) stale, flat; (*Saison, Wind*) slack; (*Gefühle*) lukewarm, cold; (*Bild*) weak, without contrast; (*verwischt, trübe*) fuzzy; *mir ist ganz ~* I feel queer (*od* faint); **~heit** *f* (*Schwäche*) weakness, faintness; (*Handel*) dul(l)ness, stagnation, slump; (*Getränke*) staleness; (*Gefühle*) coolness; **~macher** *m* alarmist; **~te** *f* (*Windstille*) calm; (*Börse*) dul(l)ness, depression, stagnation.

Flaum *m* down, fluff; fuzz; **~feder** *f* downy feather, downfeather; **~bart** *m* downy beard; **~flocke** *f* fluff; **~ig** *a* downy, fluffy; fuzzy; **~weich** *a* downy.

Flaus, Flausch *m* (*Haar, Wolle*) tuft; (*Stoff*) pilot-cloth.

Flause *f* shift, fib, humbug; *~n machen* to shuffle; **~nmacher** *m* fibber, shuffler; phrase-monger.

*

Flechs|e *f* sinew, tendon; **~ig** *a* sinewy.

Flecht|e *f* (*Haar*) braid, plait, tress, twist; *bot* lichen; *med* herpetic eruption, herpes; tetter; (*Kopf*) ring-worm; **~en** *irr tr* (*Haar*) to braid, to plait; (*Korb*) to plait; (*Kranz*) to wreathe; to bind; **~werk** *n* wickerwork; (*Stuhl~~*) wattle.

Fleck *m* spot; *auf dem ~* on the spot; *vom ~ kommen* to get on, to make headway; *er kam nicht vom ~* he did not get on; (*Makel*) blemish; blur; (*Schuh*) heel; (*Edelstein*) flaw; *fig* blur, blemish; (*Flick~*) patch; (*Schmutz~*) stain, blot; (*Ort*) place; (*blauer ~ etc*) mark; *sie hat das Herz auf dem rechten ~* her heart is in the right place; *nicht vom ~ gehen* not to stir; **~en** *m* (*Schmutz etc*) spot, speck, stain; mark; (*Ort*) market-town, borough; **~en** *tr* to spot; to stain, to mark; *fig* to get on; **~enlos** *a* spotless, pure; **~enreinigung** *f* dry-cleaning; spotting-out; **~fieber** *n* spotted fever; **~ig** *a* spotted, stained; (*gesprenkelt*) speckled; **~schuß** *m* point-blank shot; **~typhus** *m* (spotted) typhus; **~wasser** *n* stain-remover, scouring-water, benzine, (noninflammable) dry-cleaning fluid.

fleddern *tr, itr* (*berauben*) to rob.

Fleder|maus *f* bat; **~wisch** *m* (feather-)duster, whisk.

Flegel *m* flail; (*Tölpel*) churl, boor, lout; roughneck; **~ei** *f* rudeness; churlishness; **~haft** *a* boorish; rude; (*unverschämt*) impertinent; **~jahre** *n pl* cubhood; the salad days; the awkward age; *noch in den ~~n* still in o.'s teens; **~n**: *sich ~~* to behave rudely.

flehen *itr* to implore; to beseech, to entreat (*um* for); *~ n* petition, entreaty, earnest prayer; **~d** *a* supplicant, beseeching; **~tlich** *a* entreating, imploring, beseeching, fervent.

Fleisch *n* flesh; (*Nahrung*) meat; (*Obst*) pulp; *gepökeltes ~* corned beef; *wildes ~* proud flesh; (*am Buchstaben*) *typ* beard; *das eigene ~ u. Blut* o.'s own flesh and blood; *~ ansetzen* to grow fat; *sich ins eigene ~ schneiden* to cut o.'s own coat; *den Weg alles ~es gehen* to go the way of all flesh; **~auswuchs** *m* carnosity, caruncle; **~bank** *f* shambles *pl*, *Am* meat-counter; **~beschau** *f* meat inspection; **~beschauer** *m* inspector of butcher's meat; **~brühe** *f* broth; beef-tea; consommé; clear soup;

~**brühwürfel** *m* bouillon cube; ~**er,** ~**hauer** *m* butcher; ~**ergeselle** *m* butcher's man; ~**erhund** *m* mastiff; ~**erladen** *m* butcher's shop, *Am* meat-market; ~**eslust** *f* carnal desire, lust; ~**extrakt** *m* bovril, extract of meat; ~**farbe** *f* flesh-colo(u)r, carnation; ~**farbig** *a* flesh-colo(u)red; flesh-tinted; nude; ~**fliege** *f* blow-fly; ~**fressend** *a* carnivorous; ~**gewächs** *n* fleshy excrescence; ~**geworden** *a* incarnate; ~**hackmaschine** *f* meat grinder; ~**haken** *m* flesh-hook; ~**ig** *a* fleshy; (*Obst*) pulpy; ~**kammer** *f* larder; ~**klößchen** *n* force-meat; meat-ball; ~**klumpen** *m* mass of flesh; ~**konserven** *f pl* potted meat; tinned (*Am* canned) meat; ~**kost** *f* meat diet; ~**lich** *a* fleshly, carnal; sensual; ~**los** *a* meatless; ~**made** *f* maggot; ~**marke** *f* meat ticket; ~**markt** *m* meat-market; ~**maschine** *f* mincer; ~**pastete** *f* mince-pie; (*kleine*) patty; ~**schnittchen** *n* steak; ~**speise** *f* meat; ~**topf** *m* pot for boiling meat; ~**vergiftung** *f* botulism, ptomaine poisoning; ~**ware** *f* meat, dry-saltery; ~**werdung** *f* incarnation; ~**wolf** *m* mincer; ~**wunde** *f* flesh-wound; soft tissue wound; laceration; ~**wurst** *f* sausage.

Fleiß *m* diligence, assiduity; industry, activity; (*Mühe*) pains *pl*; (*Sorgfalt*) carefulness; *viel ~ verwenden auf* to take great pains with; *ohne ~, kein Preis* no pains, no gains; *mit ~* (*absichtlich*) intentionally, on purpose, purposely; ~**ig** *a* diligent, industrious; hard-working; active; (*Besuche*) frequent; (*sorgfältig*) painstaking; *~~ studieren* to read hard.

flektieren *tr gram* to inflect, to decline.

flennen *itr fam* to whimper, to blub; to whine, to snivel; to cry.

fletschen *tr*: *die Zähne ~* to show o.'s teeth.

Flexion *f gram* inflexion, inflection; ~**s-** (*in Zssg*) inflexional.

flick|en *tr* to mend, to patch, to repair; *Schuhe ~~* to cobble shoes; ~**en** *m* patch; ~**endecke** *f Am* crazy quilt; ~**er** *m* patcher, botcher; ~**erei** *f* patchwork; ~**korb** *m* workbasket; ~**schneider** *m* jobbing-tailor; ~**schuster** *m* cobbler; ~**werk** *n* patchwork; ~**wort** *n* expletive; ~**zeug** *n* (*Nähzeug*) sewing kit; *mot* puncture kit; (puncture) repair outfit.

Flieder *m* elder; (*spanischer*) lilac; ~**beere** *f* elder-berry; ~**blüte** *f* lilac-blossom, elder-blossom; ~**tee** *m* elder(-blossom)tea.

Fliege *f* fly; (*Bärtchen*) imperial; (*Pflaster*) blister; *von ~n beschmutzt* fly-blown; *zwei ~n mit e-r Klappe schlagen* to kill two birds with one stone; ~**ndreck** *m* fly-blow, fly-dirt; ~**nfalle** *f*, ~**nfänger** *m* fly-paper; fly-trap, fly-catcher; ~**nfenster** *n* fly-screen; ~**ngewicht** *n* (*Boxen*) fly-weight; ~**nkopf** *m typ* turned letter; ~**klappe,** ~**klatsche** *f* fly-flap, *Am* fly-swatter; ~**nnetz** *n* fly-net; ~**npapier** *n* fly-paper; ~**npilz,** ~**nschwamm** *m* toadstool, fly agaric; ~**nschrank** *m* meat-safe; ~**nspritze** *f* fly spray gun; ~**nwedel** *m* fly-whisk.

fliegen *irr itr* to fly, to wing; (*Fahne*) to stream; (*eilen*) to fly, to rush; *fam* (*entlassen werden*) *fam* to get the sack, *Am fam* to get fired; *fam* (*durchfallen im Examen*) to flunk (the examination); *in die Luft ~* to blow up, to be blown up, to explode; *in Stücke ~* to burst in pieces; *in die Höhe ~* (*aero od Vogel*) to soar up; *rasch ~* (*aero*) to zoom (up *od* down); *unter 300 m Höhe ~* to fly at zero; *dicht über den Boden ~* to hedgehop; *mit dem Wind ~* to fly with tail wind; *gegen den Wind ~* to fly upwind; *Einsatz ~* to fly a sortie; *sie flogen von Berlin nach London* they flew from B. to L.; *e-e zweimotorige DC-3 flog über die Stadt* a twin-engine DC-3 was winging over the town; *tr* to fly (an airplane, a kite etc); to pilot; ~ *n* flying; (*Luftfahrt*) aviation; (*im Verband*) formation flying; ~**d** *a* flying; *~~es Blatt* fly sheet; *~~e Bombe* (*V 1 u. V2*) flying bomb; winged bomb, *fam* doodle-bug; *~~e Einheit* mobile unit; *mit ~~en Fahnen* with unfurled colo(u)rs; *~~e Festung Am aero* flying fortress; *~~er Fisch* flying fish; *der ~~e Holländer* the Flying Dutchman; *~~es Lazarett* field hospital; *~~es Personal aero* flying personnel, flight echelon; *~~er Start* flying start; *~~e Untertasse* flying saucer.

Flieger *m* flyer, flier; aviator; (*Flugzeugführer*) pilot; (*Soldat der engl u. Am Luftwaffe*) **airman**; (Royal Air Force) aircraftsman; ~**abwehr** *f* anti-aircraft defence, air defence; flak; ~~**feuer** *n* anti-aircraft fire; ~~**geschütz** *n*, ~~**kanone** *f* anti-aircraft gun; ~**abzeichen** *n* (*fliegendes Personal*) *Am* aviation badge, *fam* wings *pl*; ~**alarm** *m* air-raid warning, alert; (*Warnmeldung an Luftschutz*) action warning; ~**angriff** *m* air-raid, air-attack; (*Großangriff*) blitz; ~**aufnahme** *f* aerial (*od* air) photo(graph); ~**benzin** *n* aviation petrol, *Am* aviation gasoline (*od* fuel); ~**beobachtung** *f* aircraft spotting; ~**beschuß** *m* anti-aircraft fire; ~**bild** *n* aerial photograph; ~**bombe** *f* air-bomb, aerial bomb; ~**brille** *f* flying goggles *pl*; ~**dreibein** *n* tripod mounting for anti-aircraft machine-gun; ~**ei** *f* aviation; flying; ~**film** *m phot* aerofilm; ~**führer** *m* air-force commander; ~**geschwader** *n* group; ~**handkamera** *f* aerial portable camera; ~**haube** *f* flying helmet; ~**hauptmann** *m* flight-lieutenant; ~**horst** *m* RAF station, *Am* air-base; service airfield; ~**hotel** *n Am fam* skytel (*Abk von*: sky hotel); ~**in** *f* woman pilot, aviatrix; flying woman; airwoman; ~**jacke** *f* flying jacket; ~**kammer** *f* air camera; ~**karte** *f* air (*od* flight) map; aeronautical chart; ~**kraftstoff** *m* aviation fuel; ~**krankheit** *f* aviator's disease, flier's sickness; ~**leutnant** *m* pilot officer; ~**notsignal** *n* airplane distress signal; ~**personal** *n* flying personnel; ~**offizier** *m* air-force officer; ~**schaden** *m* air-raid damages *pl*: ~~**anspruch** *m* indemnification for air-raid damages; ~**schule** *f* flying school; ~**schutzanzug** *m* flying suit; flying kit; ~**schütze** *m* air gunner; *~~ des oberen Gefechtsstandes* (*im Flugzeug*) upper turret gunner; ~**schutzgraben** *m* anti-aircraft trench; ~**sichtstreifen** *m*, ~**tuch** *n* ground panel; ~**stiefel** *m pl* flying boots *pl*; ~**tauglich** *a* fit for flying; ~**truppe** *f* flying corps, air-force troops *pl*; ~**verband** *m* formation of aircraft; (*für Sondereinsatz*) air task force; ~**warnung** *f* air-raid alarm; ~~**sdienst** *m* air-warning service; ~**wetter** *n fam* unflyable weather; ~**zulage** *f* (*der Löhnung*) flying allowance, flying pay.

*

flieh|en *irr itr* to flee, to run away; *zu jdm ~~* to take refuge with s. o.; *tr* to avoid, to shun, to fly from; ~**ende(r)** *m* fugitive; ~**kraft** *f* centrifugal force; ~~**anlasser** *m aero* inertia starter.

Fliese *f* floor-stone, flag(stone); paving tile; *mit ~n auslegen* to flag, to tile.

Fließ|arbeit *f* assembly-line work, flow production; ~**band** *n* assembly-line; conveyor belt; ~~**fertigung** *f* conveyor belt production; ~~**montage** *f* progressive assembly; ~**en** *irr itr* to flow, to stream, to float; (*Papier*) to blot; *fig* to pass away; *ins Meer ~~* to fall into the sea; ~**end** *a* flowing; *fig* fluent; *~~ sprechen* to speak fluently; *~~ Spanisch können* to be fluent at Spanish; *~~es Wasser* running water; ~**papier** *n* blotting-paper; ~**produktion** *f* serial production.

Flimmer *m* sparkling, glimmer, ~**n** *itr* to glimmer; to glitter; (*Sterne*) to twinkle; (*Filmleinwand*) to flicker; *es ~t mir vor den Augen* sparks are dancing before my eyes.

flink *a* agile, brisk; quick, nimble; *~ wie ein Wiesel* quick like a bunny; *macht ~!* make haste! ~**heit** *f* quickness, nimbleness.

Flinte *f* gun, rifle; musket; (*Schrot~*) shot gun; *die ~ ins Korn werfen* to lose courage, to give up, to throw up the sponge.

Flinten|kolben *m* butt-end of a gun; ~**kugel** *f* musket-ball, bullet; ~**lauf** *m* gun-barrel; ~**schaft** *m* stock of a gun; ~**schloß** *n* lock of a gun; ~**schuß** *m* gunshot.

Flirt *m* flirtation; ~**en** *itr* to flirt; to make love.

Flitter *m* spangle, tinsel; *fig* frippery, gewgaws *pl*; ~**glanz** *m* false lustre; ~**gold** *n* tinsel, leaf-gold; ~**kram** *m* tinsel, finery; ~**n** *itr* to glitter, to twinkle; ~**staat** *m* tawdry finery; ~**wochen** *f pl* honeymoon.

flitzen *itr* to flit (*od* to dash) along.

Flock|e *f* (*Wolle*) flock; (*Schnee*) flake; (*zum Kochen*) *Am* flakes *pl* ; ~**enartig,** ~**ig** *a* flocky, fluffy; (*Schnee*) flaky; ~**seide** *f* flock-silk; ~**wolle** *f* waste-wool.

Floh *m* flea; *jdm e-n ~ ins Ohr setzen* to make s. o. uneasy and suspicious; ~**biß,** ~**stich** *m* flea-bite; **flöhen** *tr* to flea; *r* to catch (o.'s) fleas.

Flor *m* (*Blumen*) bloom(ing); blossom(ing), *fig* flourishing state; (*Trauer~*) crape; *dünner~* gauze; *ein ~ von Damen* a bevy of ladies; ~**binde** *f* crape-band; (*am Hut*) mourning-hatband; ~**ieren** *itr* to flourish, to thrive; ~**schleier** *m* gauze-veil.

Florett *n* foil, floret; ~**band** *n* ferret-ribbon; ~**seide** *f* floss-silk.

Floskel *f* flourish, flowery phrase.

Floß *n* raft, float; ~**brücke** *f* floating bridge; ~**holz** *n* float(ed) timber (*od* wood); ~**sack** *m* rubber boat; **flößen** *tr* to float, to raft; **Flößer** *m* raftsman, rafter, *Am* riverdriver.

Flosse *f* fin; (*Stabilisator*) stabilizing surface; guide, blade.

Flöte *f* flute; pipe; (*langes französisches Weizenbrot*) French bread; (*Kartenspiel*) flush; ~**n** *itr* to play (on) the flute; to whistle; *~n gehen fam* to go to the dogs; to be lost; ~**nbläser** *m* flute-player; ~**nstimme** *f* flute-part; ~**nzug** *m* (*der Orgel*) flute- stop.

flott *a* afloat; floating; swimming, waterborn; (*lustig*) gay; (*schnell*) fast; (*Auftreten*) showy; (*Geschäft*) brisk; (*Kleidung*) smart, stylish; *ein ~es Geschäft* a roaring trade; *~ werden* to get off again; *~ machen* to set a ship afloat again; (*Fahrzeug etc*) to get going again; ~ *leben* to lead a jolly life; to live a free and easy life.

Flotte *f* fleet; (*Marine*) navy; ~**nabkommen** *n* naval agreement; ~**nbasis,** ~**nstation** *f*, ~**nstützpunkt** *m* naval base; ~**nführer** *m* admiral, commodore; ~**nkonferenz** *f* naval conference; ~**nmanöver** *n pl* naval manoeuvres *pl*; ~**nparade,** ~**nschau** *f* naval review; ~**nvorlage** *f parl* navy bill.

Flotille *f* flotilla; squadron; ~**nführer** *m* flotilla leader.

Flöz *n* layer, stratum; (*Kohlen*~) seam; ~**gebirge** *n* sedimentary (= secondary) rocks *pl*.

Fluch *m* (*Verfluchung*) curse, imprecation, *Am fam* cuss; (*Verwünschung*) malediction, execration; *meist eccl* (*Bannfluch, Exkommunikation*) anathema; (*Gotteslästerung*) blasphemy; (*Flucherei*) profanity; (*Schwur, Fluchwort*) oath; (*Fluchwort*) *fam* swear-word, *Am fam* cuss word; *e-n ~ ausstoßen* to utter (*od* to rap out) an oath; *e-n ~ legen auf* to lay a curse upon; ~**beladen** *a* accursed, under a curse; ~**en** *itr* to curse and swear, to swear, *Am fam* to cuss; to use bad (*od* strong) language; *~~ wie ein Türke* (*od Landsknecht*) to swear like a trooper; *jdm ~~* to curse s. o., to call down curses upon s. o.; to swear at s. o.; (*verwünschen*) to execrate s. o.; (*Bannfluch aussprechen*) to pronounce an anathema against; ~**en** *n* swearing, cursing, *Am fam* cussing; ~**er** *m* curser, swearer; (*Lästerer*) blasphemer; ~**würdig** *a* execrable, accursed.

Flucht *f* flight, escape, run; *Am auch* getaway; (*wilde* ~) rout; (*kopflose* ~) stampede; (*Reihe*) range, row; straight line; *tech* (*Spielraum*) scope, room; *Treppen*~ flight of steps; *Zimmer*~ suite of rooms; *in die ~ schlagen* to put to flight; *die ~ ergreifen* to take to flight; to flee; ~**artig** *a* flightlike; (*eilends*) hasty; ~**ebene** *f* vanishing plane; ~**gefahr** *f* risk of escape; ~**linie** *f arch* alignement of houses; building line; *opt* vanishing line; ~**punkt** *m* vanishing point; ~**verdacht** *m* suspicion of escape (*od* flight); ~**versuch** *m* attempt to escape.

flücht|en *itr* to take refuge (*vor* from); to flee, to run away; to escape; to take to flight; (*ausreißen*) *fam* to decamp, *Am fam* to skip; ~**ig** *a* fugitive; (*leichtsinnig*) fickle, inconstant; (*schnell*) hasty, nimble; fleet; (*oberflächlich*) flighty; (*planlos*) desultory; (*rasch überblickend*) cursory; (*Lächeln, Schmerz*) transient; momentary; (*sorglos*) careless; (*seicht*) superficial; (*vorübergehend*) transitory, passing; (*kurzlebig*) ephemeral; short-lived; (*vergänglich*) fleeting; (*schwindend*) evanescent; *chem* volatile; (*e-e Sache gesprächsweise ~~ berühren*) to touch lightly on; *ein ~~er Bekannter* a passing (*od* nodding) acquaintance; ~**igkeit** *f* flightness; carelessness; *chem* volatility; transitoriness; hastiness; ~**ling** *m* fugitive; deserter; refugee; (*Ausbrecher*) escapee; ~~**skommissar** *m* refugee commissioner; ~~**slager** *n* refugee camp; ~~**sorganisation** *f* refugee organization; *Internationale ~~sorganisation* International Refugee Organization (*Abk* IRO).

Flug *m* flight; *aero* flying, flight; (*Vögel*) flock, swarm; (*Rebhühner*) covey; (*Bienen*) swarm; *im ~* in flight, flying, on the wing; *fig* (*eilig*) in haste, in a hurry; *im ~ verstellbar aero* adjustable in flight; *~ um die Welt* round-the-world flight; *~ mit Erdsicht* (*ohne Karte*) contact flight; *~ der Zeit fig* flight of time; *Allein~* (*e-s Flugschülers*) solo (flight); *Autoschlepp~* auto towing; *Blind~* blind flying; *Nacht~* night flight; *Ohnehalt~* non-stop flight; *Schlepp~* airplane towing; *Tag~* day flight; *überzogener ~* stall; *motorloser ~* soaring, gliding; ~**abwehr** *f* anti-aircraft defence; ~**abwehrkanone** *f* anti-aircraft gun (*Abk* A. A. gun), flak; ~**abwehrrakete** *f* anti-aircraft rocket (*Abk* A. A. rocket); ~**asche** *f* flyash, flue ash; ~**bahn** *f math* trajectory; *aero* flight path; (*tatsächliche ~~ über Grund*) track; ~**ball** *m* (*Tennis*) volley; ~**bedingungen** *f pl* flying conditions *pl*; ~**begeistert** *a* air-minded; ~**begeisterung** *f* air-mindedness; ~**benzin** *n* aviation petrol, *Am* aviation gasoline; ~**beratung** *f* meteorological information for aviators; ~**bereich** *m*, ~**weite** *f* range of flight; ~**bereit** *a* ready to fly, in flying condition; ~**besprechung** *f* briefing of flight crews; ~**betrieb** *m* flying operations *pl*; ~**billet** *n*, ~**schein** *m* air-line ticket, air ticket; ~**blatt** *n*, ~**schrift** *f* broadsheet, leaflet; pamphlet; handbill; prospectus; *Am* flier; ~**boot** *n* flying boat; ~**buch** *n* flight log; ~**dauer** *f* duration of flight, endurance; ~**deck** *n* (*Flugzeugträger*) flight deck, landing deck; ~**dienst** *m* air (*od* flying) service; ~**drehfeuer** *n* revolving airway beacon; ~**eigenschaften** *f pl* (*e-r Maschine*) flying qualities *pl*; ~**erfahrung** *f* flying experience; ~**erprobung** *f* flight test; ~**fähig** *a* able to fly; airworthy; ~**feld** *n* flying field, air field; ~**figur** *f* flight manœuvre; ~**form** *f* flight formation; *geöffnete ~~* extended formation; *in Höhe gestaffelte ~~* step formation; ~**fracht** *f* air freight; ~**funk**, ~**funkdienst** *m* wireless (*od* radio) aircraft service; ~**gast** *m* air-passenger; ~**gastraum** *m* passenger cabin; ~**gelände** *n* field licensed for preliminary glider training; flying terrain; ~**geschwader** *n* squadron; ~**geschwindigkeit** *f* flying speed; (*in der umgebenden Luft*) airspeed; (*über Grund*) ground speed; ~**gesellschaft** *f* air-line, airway, carrier; ~**gewicht** *n* flying weight, gross weight, all-up weight, *Am* total weight; ~**hafen** *m* aerodrome, *Am* airdrome; aeroport, *Am* airport; (*Groß~~*) air terminal; (*Horst*) air-base; (*für Wasserflugzeuge*) seadrome, seaplane base; *Ausweich~~* alternate airport; *Eingangs~~* airport of entry; ~~**befeuerung** *f* airport lights *pl*; ~~**bereich** *m* airport area; ~~**betriebskompanie** *f mil* aerodrome maintenance company, *Am* airfield maintenance crew; ~~**bezugspunkt** *m* airport reference point; ~~**drehfeuer** *n* revolving airport beacon; ~~**erkennungszeichen** *n* airport identification sign; ~~**grenze** *f* airport boundary; ~~**kontrollturm** *m* airport traffic control tower; ~~**restaurant** *n* airport restaurant; ~~**(verkehrs)aufsicht** *f* airport (traffic) control; ~~**zone** *f* airport zone; ~**halle** *f* hangar; ~**hallenvorfeld** *n* (*betonierter Teil*) apron; ~**höhe** *f* flying altitude; (*höchste*) ceiling, roof; (*Geschoß*) ordinate of trajectory; ~**horchgerät** *n* sound detection apparatus; ~**ingenieur** *m* aerial engineer; ~**instrumente** *n pl* flight instruments *pl*; ~**kapitän** *m* airplane captain; ~**karte** *f* (*Billet*) air-line ticket; ~**klar** *a* ready to take off; ~**krankheit** *f* air sickness; ~**kunststück** *n Am* (aerial) stunt; *~~e machen Am* to stunt; ~**lehre** *f siehe*: *Aerodynamik;* ~**lehrer** *m* flight instructor; ~**leistung** *f* flight performance; ~**leiter** *m* air traffic controller; ~**leitung** *f* airport traffic control; (*Gebäude*) terminal building; *mil* flying control, *Am* base operations; *Kontrollturm der ~~* airport traffic control tower; ~~**sbeamter** *m* airport-control-tower operator; ~**linie** *f* (*Gesellschaft*) air-line; (*Flugweg*) airline, airway, route; line of flight; ~**liniennetz** *n* air-line system; ~**loch** *n* pigeon-hole; entrance to a hive; ~**maschine** *f* flying machine, aeroplane, *Am* (air) plane; ~**mechanik** *f* mechanics of flight; ~**meldedienst** *m* position (*od* aircraft) reporting service; ~**meldekommando** *n* air observation command; ~**meldenetz** *n* (*bei Feindeinflügen*) air warning net; ~**meldeposten** *m* aircraft observation guard; ~**meldestelle** *f* flight reporting station; ~**meldezentrale** *f* air-raid warning central station; aircraft reporting centre; ~**modell** *n* flying model; model plane; ~**motor** *m* aircraft engine (*od* power plant); ~**navigation,** ~**ortung** *f* air navigation; ~**ordnung** *f* formation; ~**park** *m* air park; ~**plan** *m* time-table; flight plan, *Am* flying schedule; ~**platz** *m* flying field, airfield, aviation field, landing-ground, landing field; ~~**befeuerung** *f* airfield lighting; ~~**leitung** *f* airfield authority; ~~**verkehr** *m* airfield traffic; ~**post** *f* air-post, *Am* air-mail; ~~**brief** *m* air-post letter, *Am* air-mail letter; *durch ~post* by (*od* via) air-post (*Am* air-mail); ~**reichweite** *f* range of flight; ~**richtung** *f* direction of flight; ~**route** *f* flight route; ~**schein** *m* air (travel) ticket;, air-line ticket; *e-n ~~ ins Ausland lösen* to book passage to a foreign country; ~**schiff** *n* flying-boat; ~**schlepp** *m* airplane towing; ~**schneise** *f aero* air-lane; ~**schrauber** *m* autogiro; ~**schrift** *f* pamphlet; ~**schüler** *m* pilot trainee; flying cadet, student flier; ~**sand** *m* quicksand, shifting sand; ~**sicherheit** *f* flying safety; ~**sicherung** *f* air-traffic safety control; ~~**sschiff** *n* air-traffic safety ship; aircraft tender; ~**sport** *m* sport(ing) flying; ~**strecke** *f* airline, airway; flight route; (*Etappe*) leg; (*kurze Etappe*) hop; ~**streckenbefeuerung** *f* airway lighting; ~**strecken(dreh)feuer** *n* (revolving) airway beacon; ~**streckenkarte** *f* airway strip map; ~**streitkräfte** *f pl* air forces *pl*; ~**stunde** *f* flying hour; ~**stützpunkt** *m* air base; *mar* catapult ship; ~**tag** *m* air display; ~**tagebuch** *n* (*Bordbuch*) air log; ~**taxe** *f* taxiplane; ~**technik** *f* aeronautics *pl*, flying technique; aviation; ~**teilstrecke** *f* (*Etappe*) leg; (*kurze*) hop; ~**tüchtig** *a* airworthy; ~**tüchtigkeit** *f* airworthiness; ~**überwachungsinstrumente** *n pl* flying instruments *pl*; ~**unfall** *m* flying accident; ~**unfallversicherung** *f* air insurance; ~**verbot** *n* (*für e-e Maschine*) grounding of an airplane; ~**verkehr** *m* air-traffic, (*regelmäßiger*) air service, plane service; civil aviation; ~**wache** *f* plane spotting post; aircraft lookout station; ~**wachkommando** *n* aircraft observation headquarters, air observation centre; filter centre; ~**weite** *f* flying distance, *Am* range; ~**wesen** *n* aeronautics *pl*, aviation, flying; ~**wettbewerb** *m* flying competition; ~**wetter** *n* (good) flying weather; ~**wetterdienst** *m* aviation weather service, *Am* metereological service; **~woche** *f* flying week; **~widerstand** *m* air drag; **~wissenschaft** *f* aeronautics *pl*; **~zeit** *f* flying time; time of flight; **~zustand** *m* flight attitude; flight position.

Flügel *m* (*Vogel, Haus*) wing; *aero* (*Tragfläche*) wing, plane; (*Profil*) aerofoil, *Am* airfoil; (*Tür*) fold, side, leaf; (*Fenster*) casement; (*Armee*) flank, wing; (*Windmühle*) sail, vane; arm; (*Auto*) mudguard, wing; (*Bombe*) fin; (*Wurfgranate*) vane; (*Rock*) flap; (*Anker*) fluke; (*Piano*) grand piano; (*Miniatur~*) baby grand; *anat* (*Lunge*) lobe, wing; (*Propeller*) blade; *abnehmbarer ~* (*aero*) detachable wing; *freitragender ~* (*aero*) cantilever wing; *pfeilförmiger ~* (*aero*) swept-back wing; *jdm die ~ beschneiden* to clip s. o.'s wings; *die ~ hängen lassen fig* to be downcast; **~abstand** *m aero* wing gap; **~adjutant** *m* aide-de-camp; **~anordnung** *f aero* wing setting; **~anstellwinkel** *m aero* angle of wing setting; **~beplankung, ~bespannung, ~haut** *f aero* wing covering (*od* planking), wing skin; **~bremse** *f aero* wing air brake; **~decke** *f zoo* elytron; **~ende** *n aero* wing tip; **~fenster** *n* French casement; **~fläche** *f aero* wing area (*od* surface); **~förmig** *a* wing-shaped; **~haube** *f mot* helmet; **~hinterkante** *f aero* trailing edge; **~holm** *m aero* wing spar; **~klappe** *f aero* wing flap; **~lahm** *a* broken-winged; *fig* despondent; **~landefackel** *f aero* wing tip flare; **~lastig** *a aero* wingheavy; **~los** *a* wingless, without wings; **~mann** *m* end-man of line; flank man; file-leader, fugleman; **~mine** *f* winged bomb; **~mittelstück** *n aero* wing centre-section; **~mutter** *f* wing nut; **~nase** *f aero* leading edge, wing nose; **~oberseite** *f* upper side of the wing; **~pferd** *n* winged horse; Pegasus; **~profil** *n aero* (wing) profile; **~rad** *n* screw wheel, sail wheel; **~rippe** *f aero* wing rib; **~schlag** *m* flapping (*od* beat) of wings, wing stroke; *fig* flight; **~schraube** *f* thumb-screw; wing screw; **~schwimmer** *m aero* wing tip float; **~spannweite** *f aero* wing-spread, *Am* wingspan; **~spitze** *f aero* wing tip; **~tür** *f* folding-door; **~unterseite** *f aero* underside of the wing; **~verstrebung** *f aero* wing bracing; **~wurzel** *f* wing root; **~zelle** *f* wing cell.

flügge *a* fledged; *noch nicht ~* unfledged; *~ werden fig* to stand on o.'s own feet.

flugs *adv* quickly, at once, instantly.

Flugzeug *n* aeroplane, (*heute meist:*) *Am* airplane, plane; aircraft; flying machine; (*bei großen Maschinen auch*) ship; *ein ~ fliegen* to fly an airplane; *~ abfangen* to pull out the airplane; to flatten out; *~ abschießen* to shoot down an airplane; *aus e-m ~ aussteigen* to deplane; *das ~ dreht in den Wind* the airplane weathercocks; *in ein ~ einsteigen* to emplane; *das ~ rutschte seitlich ab* the plane sideslipped; *~ übersteuern* to overdo the control; *~ überziehen* to stall the plane; *einmotoriges ~* one-engined airplane; *mehrmotoriges ~* multi-engined airplane; *Düsen~, Strahl~* jet plane; *Fracht~* freight airplane; *Ganzmetall~* all metal airplane; *Groß~* airliner; *Land~* land plane; *Langstrecken~* long-range airplane; *Leicht~* light airplane, *Am mil sl* grasshopper; *Muster~* (*erste Ausführung*) prototype; *Nurflügel~* flying wing; all-wing plane; *Post~* mail airplane; *Riesen~* giant airplane; *Sanitäts~* ambulance plane; *Schnellverkehrs~* high speed passenger airplane; *schwanzloses ~* tailless airplane; *Serien~* production airplane; *trudelsicheres ~* non-spinning airplane; *raketengetriebenes Überschall~* supersonic rocket-powered airplane; *überschlagsicheres ~* non-diving airplane; *unüberziehbares ~* non-stalling airplane; *Verkehrs~* passenger airplane; *Versuchs~* test plane; *Wasser~* seaplane; **~abstellplätze** *m pl* parking area; (*befestigt*) hardstandings *pl;* **~absturz** *m* (*ohne Tote od Schwerverletzte*) crack-up; (*mit Toten od Schwerverletzten*) (airplane) crash; (*Maschine völlig zertrümmert*) washout; (*Flugzeugtrümmer*) airplane wreck; *er starb an den Verletzungen e-s ~~es* he died of injuries received in an air crash; **~angriff** *m* plane attack; air-raid; (*Großangriff auf e-e Stadt*) air blitz; **~aufnahme** *f* aerial photograph; aerial view; **~ausstellung** *f* aircraft exhibition; **~bau** *m* aircraft construction; **~bauer** *m* aircraft builder; **~baumuster** *n* airplane model; **~besatzung** *f* flight crew, aircrew; **~bewaffnung** *f* airplane armament; **~bremsen** *f pl* landing brakes *pl*; **~erfassung** *f* airplane recognition; **~erkennungsdienst** *m* aircraft recognition service; **~fabrik** *f* aircraft factory (*od* plant); **~führer** *m* (air) pilot; (*e-r Verkehrsmaschine*) commercial airplane pilot; airline pilot; (*e-r Transportmaschine*) transport pilot; *zweiter ~~* co-pilot, airplane first-officer; (*e-s Düsenjägers*) jet pilot; (*e-r Jagdmaschine*) fighter pilot; (*e-s Bombers*) bomber pilot; **~führerschein** *m* pilot's certificate; pilot's licence; flying licence; **~führerstand** *m* pilot's cockpit; **~gerippe** *n* frame; **~geschwader** *n* wing; (*taktisch*) squadron; **~gruppe** *f* group; **~halle** *f* hangar; **~~nvorfeld** *n* (*betoniert*) apron; **~hallendeck** *n* (*e-s Flugzeugträgers*) hangar deck; **~industrie** *f* aircraft industry; **~kanone** *f* airplane cannon; **~kette** *f* flight; **~kommandant** *m* crew captain, aircraft commander; **~kompaß** *m* air compass; **~konstrukteur** *m* aircraft designer; **~ladung** *f* plane load; **~mechaniker** *m* air(plane) mechanic; *sl* mec; hangar mechanic; *mil* aircraftsman; **~muster** *n* type of aircraft; **~mutterschiff** *n* aircraft-tender; **~ortung** *f* air navigation, avigation; **~personal** *n* aircraft maintenance personnel; **~positionslichter** *n pl* airplane lights *pl*; **~produzent** *m* aircraft manufacturer; **~rampe** *f* (*zum Ein- u. Ausladen*) airplane ramp; **~reparatur** *f* aircraft repair; **~rumpf** *m* fuselage, body, frame; **~schlepp** *m* airplane towing; **~schleuder** *f* catapult; **~~schiff** *n* catapult ship; **~schuppen** *m* (airplane) shed; hangar; **~schwimmer** *m* float; **~sporn** *m* skid; **~staffel** *f* squadron; **~steuergerät** *n* (*automatisches ~~*) gyropilot; **~steuerung** *f* airplane controls *pl*; **~stewardess** *f* air-line stewardess, air-hostess; **~torpedo** *n* airplane torpedo; **~träger** *m* aircraft (*od* airplane) carrier; *Am fam* flattop; *Luftangriff von e-m ~~ aus* carrier-launched air attack; **~treibstoff** *m* aviation fuel; **~trimmung** *f* airplane trim; **~trümmer** *pl* aircraft wreckage; **~unfall** *m* airplane accident; (*siehe: Flugzeugabsturz*); **~überführungsgeschwader** *n* aircraft-ferrying squadron; **~verband** *m* airplane formation; **~versetzung** *f* yaw, drift; **~wart** *m mil* N. C. O. in charge of maintenance crew; aircraft mechanic; **~werk** *n* aircraft plant; **~zelle** *f* airplane frame; **~zubehör** *n* aircraft accessories *pl.*

Fluidum *n* fluid; *fig* atmosphere, tone.

fluktuieren *itr* to fluctuate; (*Bevölkerung*) to float.

Flunder *m od f* flounder.

Flunker|ei *f* fib, sham; **~er** *m* fibber, story-teller; **~n** *itr* to tell fibs; (*aufschneiden*) to brag, to boast.

Fluor *n min* fluorine; **~eszenz** *f* fluorescence; **~~lampe** *f* fluorescent lamp; **~~licht** *n* fluorescent light; **~eszieren** *itr* to fluoresce; **~eszierend** *a* fluorescent.

Flur *f* field, plain; meadow; *~ m* hall, vestibule; **~bereinigung** *f* field clearing; **~buch** *n* terrier, register of lands; **~garderobe** *f* hall-stand; **~name** *m* field-name; **~hüter, ~schütz, ~wächter** *m* field-guard, ranger, keeper; **~schaden** *m* damage done to the fields, damage to crops.

Fluß *m* river; (*Flüßchen*) brook, *Am* creek; (*das Fließen*) flowing; *fig* fluency; (*der Metalle*) fusion; *med* fluxion; catarrh; rheumatism; (*Ausfluß, el, fig*) flux; *geol* fluor spar; (*Seife*) figging; (*Schmelz*) enamel; *weißer ~* whites *pl*; *in ~ kommen* to begin to melt; *fig* to be started; *in ~ bringen* to put into fusion; *fig* to set going; **~ab(wärts)** *adv* down-stream; **~arm** *m* tributary; **~~** *a* lacking rivers; **~auf(wärts)** *adv* up-stream; **~bad** *n* river-bath; **~bett** *n* bed, channel; **~dichte** *f* flux density; **~eisen** *n* low-carbon (*od* ingot) steel; **~gebiet** *n* river basin; **~knie** *n* bend of a river; **~krebs** *m* crayfish; **~lauf** *m* course of a river; **~mündung** *f* mouth of a river; estuary; **~netz** *n* network of rivers; **~pferd** *n* hippopotamus; **~schiffahrt** *f* river-traffic; **~spat** *m* fluor-spar; **~übergang** *m* river crossing; ford, passage; **~ufer** *n* riverside; river-bank; **~wasser** *n* river-water.

flüssig *a* fluid, liquid; (*Handel*) disposable; (*Geld*) ready; (*Metall*) melted; (*Kapital*) available; *~ machen* to liquefy; to melt; (*Geld*) to turn into ready money; *sein Vermögen ~ machen* to realize o.'s property; **~keit** *f* fluid, liquid; (*Getränk*) liquor; (*Zustand*) fluidity; **~~sdruck** *m* hydrostatic pressure; **~~sgemisch** *n* liquid mixture; **~~sgetriebe** *n mot* fluid drive; **~~skompaß** *m* liquid-type compass; **~~smaß** *n* liquid measure; **~~smenge** *f* amount of liquid; **~~smesser** *m* liquid meter; hydrometer; **~~srakete** *f* liquid-fuel rocket; **~~sreibung** *f* fluid friction; **~~sspiegel** *m* surface of a liquid; **~~sstand** *m* level of a liquid; **~~sverlust** *m* loss of liquid; **~~szerstäuber** *m* atomizer; **~werdend** *a* liquescent.

flüster|n *itr* to whisper; **~n** *n* whisper; (*laut, damit es andere hören sollen*) stage-whisper; **~parolen** *f pl*, **~propaganda** *f* whispering campaign.

Flut *f* flood; high water; (*Wogen*) waves, *pl*, billows *pl*; (*Tränen~*) flood of tears; (*Wort~*) flow; outbreak; (*Überschwemmung*) inundation; (*fig große Menge*) deluge; *die ~ steigt* (*fällt*) the tide is coming in (going out); *Ebbe u. ~* tide; **~anker** *m* flood-anchor; **~en** *itr* to flow; to flood, to surge, to swell; (*hin u. her*) to fluctuate; *tr mar* to flood the tanks; **~graben** *m* waste-pit; **~licht** *n el* floodlight, *Am fam* flood; **~lichtwerfer** *m* floodlight projector; **~tor** *n* flood gate; **~ventil** *n mar* flooding valve; **~wechsel** *m* turn of the tide; **~welle** *f* tidal wave; **~zeit** *f* high water.

*

Fock *m*, **~mast** *m* foremast; **~segel** *n* foresail; **~stange** *f* fore-top mast.

Födera|lismus *m* federalism; **~list** *m* federalist; **~listisch** *a* federal; **~tion** *f* federation, confederacy; **~tiv** *a* federative, confederate; **~tivstaat** *m* confederation.

fohlen *itr* to foal; **~** *n* foal; (*Hengst*) colt; (*Stute*) filly.

Föhn *m* föhn, south wind; southerly gale.

Föhre *f* pine, Scotch fir; **~nwald** *m* fir-forest.

Fokus *m phys* focus.

Folg|e *f* succession, series; (*Wirkung*) consequence, result; (*Fortsetzung*) continuation; (*das Nachfolgende*) sequel; set, suit; (*Nachwirkung*) aftermath; *die ~en des Krieges* the aftermath of war; (*Gehorsam*) obedience, compliance; (*Schluß*) conclusion, inference; *in der ~e* for the future; in future, subsequently; *~e leisten* to attend to; to obey; to comply with, (*Einladung*) to accept, (*e-r Aufforderung*) to answer; *zur ~e haben* to entail; to cause; *keine ~en nach sich ziehen* to be immaterial; *e-m Gesuch ~e geben* to grant a petition; *die ~en tragen* to take the consequences; **~eerscheinung** *f* sequence; outcome; corollary; **~en** *itr: jdm ~~* to follow, to succeed; to result from; to obey, to comply with; *es ~t daraus* hence it follows that; *Fortsetzung folgt* to be continued; *auf Regen folgt Sonnenschein* after rain comes sunshine; *jds Beispiel ~en* to follow s. o.'s example; *~en Sie meinem Rat* take my advice; **~end** *a* following; *am folgenden Tage* the following day; *er schreibt folgendes* he writes as follows; **~endermaßen, ~enderweise** *adv* in the following manner, as follows; **~enschwer** *a* weighty, momentous; (*wichtig*) important; (*unheilverkündend*) portentous; **~ereihe** *f* series; set; **~erichtig** *a* consistent, conclusive; logical; **~~keit** *f* consistency; **~ern** *tr, itr* to conclude, to gather, to infer from; **~erung** *f* deduction, conclusion; inference; *die ~~en können Sie selber ziehen* draw your own conclusions; **~esatz** *m* deduction; *gram* consecutive clause; *math* corollary; **~ewidrig** *a* inconsistent, illogical; **~ezeit** *f* time to come; future.

folg|lich *adv* consequently, therefore; hence, thus, so; **~sam** *a* obedient; **~samkeit** *f* docility; obedience.

Foli|ant *m* folio-volume; **~e** *f* foil; film; (*Hintergrund*) back-ground; **~ieren** *tr* to page, to foliate; **~o** *n* folio.

Folter *f* rack, torture; *fig* torment; *auf die ~ spannen* to put to the rack; *fig* to torment; **~bank** *f* rack; **~er, ~knecht** *m* torturer, tormenter; **~kammer** *f* torture-chamber; **~n** *tr* to torture, to torment; **~ung** *f* torture.

Fön *m* (*Haartrockner*) hair-dryer.

Fond *m mot* back seat; (*Grundlage*) foundation; (*Farbe*) ground, bottom; **~s** *m* funds *pl*; capital, stock.

Fontäne *f* fountain.

Fontanelle *f anat* fontanel.

fopp|en *tr* to mock, to rally; to hoax, to fool; to joke; *fam* to pull s. o.'s leg, *Am* to kid; (*necken*) to tease, to chaff; **~erei** *f* chaff; hoax; fooling.

forcier|en *tr* to take by force; to force; *fig* to overdo; **~t** *a* forced.

Förder|anlage *f* hauling plant; conveying equipment; **~band** *n* conveyor, conveying belt; (*endloses*) apron; **~er** *m* (*Gönner*) promoter, furtherer, *Am* sponsor; **~gerüst** *n min* pithead; **~klasse** *f* special class for backward children; **~kohle** *f* pit-coal; **~korb** *m* delivery basket, cage; **~lich** *a* useful; promoting; (*leitend*) *phys* conductive; (*verwendbar*) serviceable; (*schnell*) speedy; **~maschine** *f* hoisting-machine; **~menge** *f* output; **~n** *tr* to further; to advance, to promote; to help; *fig* to prompt, *Am* to sponsor; *zu Tage ~n* to bring to light; (*Erz*) to haul, to dig, to extract; to mine; (*beschleunigen*) to hasten, to accelerate; (*befördern*) to transport, to convey, to forward; (*zuführen*) *tech* to feed; *itr* to advance; to succeed; **~schacht** *m* hoisting shaft; **~seil** *n* hoisting rope; **~turm** *m* winding tower; **~ung** *f* advancement; promotion, furtherance; dispatch; *min* hauling; mining; (*Menge*) output; *betriebliche ~~ Am* in-service training; **~~skurse** *m pl Am* upgrading courses *pl*; **~werk** *n* conveyor (*od* conveyer); elevator, lift; **~wirkung** *f* promoting effect.

forder|n *tr* to ask, to call for, to demand; (*Duell*) to challenge (to); (*gerichtlich*) to summon; (*Preis*) to charge, *Am* to tax; (*beanspruchen*) to claim; (*verlangen*) to require; (*dringend*) to exact; *zu viel ~~* to overcharge; **~ung** *f* demand, claim; challenge; (*behördlich*) requisition; **~~en** *f pl* (*Bücher*) accounts receivable; *~~en geltend machen* to enforce claims.

Forelle *f* trout; **~nbach** *m* trout-stream; **~nfang** *m* trout-fishing; **~nzucht** *f* trout-breeding.

Forke *f* (pitch)fork, manure fork.

Form *f* shape, form, figure; (*von Kleidern*) fashion, cut; (*Muster*) pattern, model; (*Entwurf*) design; (*Schiff*) lines *pl*; (*Seife*) frame; (*Gieß~*) model; mo(u)ld; (*Profil~*) *tech* profile; (*Förmlichkeit*) ceremony, formality, form, usage; *typ* chase; (*Hut~*) block; *gram* voice; *sport* condition; form; (*Buch*) size; (*Schuh~*) last; *in guter ~ sein* to be in good form; to be fit; *unter ~ spielen* to play badly; *in gehöriger ~* in due form; *in aller ~ um Entschuldigung bitten* to make a formal apology; *die ~ wahren* to keep up appearances; *der ~ wegen* for form's sake, pro forma; *sich an die ~en halten* to stand upon ceremony; **~alien** *pl* formalities *pl*; **~alität** *f* formality; **~änderung** *f* change of form; (*Mißbildung*) deformation; **~~sfähigkeit** *f* ductility; plasticity; **~at** *n* size, form; *fig* importance, weight; *Hoch~~* high size; *Quer~~* cross size; **~ation** *f* formation; unit; **~bar** *a* plastic, workable, mo(u)ldable; **~~keit** *f* plasticity; workability; **~beständig** *a* retaining form; **~blatt** *n* blank form; **~eisen** *n* structural (*od* sectional) iron; **~el** *f* form, formula; **~~buch** *n* formulary; **~~wesen** *n* formalities *pl*; **~element** *n* structural element; **~ell** *a* formal; **~en** *tr* to form, to fashion, to shape; to mo(u)ld; **~enlehre** *f* accidence; **~enmensch** *m* formalist, pedant; **~er** *m* mo(u)lder; **~erei** *f* mo(u)lding; mo(u)lding house; **~fehler** *m* informality; irregularity; *jur* flaw; (*gesellschaftlich*) social blunder, offence against etiquette; **~gebung** *f* fashioning, mo(u)lding; **~gerecht** *a* true in form, undistorted; **~ieren** *tr* to form; *mil* to (fall into) line; **~ierung** *f* formation; **~los** *a* formless; unceremonious; *fig* rude; **~losigkeit** *f* shapelessness; formlessness; rudeness; **~sache** *f* formality; *das ist e-e ~~* that's for form's sake; **~sand** *m* mo(u)lding sand; **~schneider** *m* form-cutter, print-cutter; **~ular** *n* form, schedule, *Am* blank; *Fragebogen~~* question form, *Am* question blank; *Telegramm~~* telegraph form, *Am* telegraph blank; *ein ~~ ausfüllen* to fill in a form, *Am* to fill out a blank; **~~buch** *n* precedent-book; **~~sammlung** *f* formulary; **~ulieren** *tr* to formulate; to dress up; to define; **~ulierung** *f* formulation, definition; (*Wortfassung*) wording; **~ung** *f* formation; **~veränderung** *f* change of form; modification; **~verbesserung** *f* improvement of form; **~vollendet** *a* perfect in form; **~zahl** *f* form factor (*od* number).

förmlich *a* formal; in due form; (*feierlich*) ceremonious; (*unmißverständlich*) plain, clear; regular; **~keit** *f* formality; ceremony; forms *pl*.

forsch *a* vigorous, sturdy; (*unternehmend*) dashing, smart, plucky; **~en** *tr* to search, to inquire (after), to investigate; (*wissenschaftlich*) to do research work; **~er** *m* searcher, inquirer; great scholar; scientist; research worker; **~ung** *f* investigation; (*gelehrte*) research; **~~sanstalt** *f* research institute; **~~sarbeit** *f* research work; **~~sgebiet** *n* field of research; **~~sgeist** *m* spirit of research; **~~sreise** *f* exploring expedition; **~~sreisende(r)** *m* explorer.

Forst *m* forest, wood; **~akademie** *f* school of forestry; **~amt** *n* board of woods and forests; forestry-office; **~aufseher** *m* ranger; **~beamte(r)** *m* forest-officer; **~bezirk** *m* forest-district, forest-range; **~frevel** *m* forest offence; **~garten** *m* nursery; **~gesetz, ~recht** *n* forest law; **~haus** *n* forester's house; **~meister** *m* (head) forester; **~revier** *n* forest-district, forest-range; **~schutz** *m* forest protection; **~verwaltung** *f* forest administration; management of woods and forests; **~wesen** *n* forestry; **~wirtschaft** *f* management of forests; forestry; **~wissenschaft** *f* science of forestry.

Förster *m* forester; forest ranger; game-keeper; **~ei** *f* forester's house (*od* office).

*

fort *adv* away; *weit ~* (far) off; (*vorwärts*) forward; on; *~ u. ~* on and on, continually; *in einem ~* continuously; ceaselessly, without interruption; *immer ~* at a stretch; *u. so ~* and so on, and so forth; *ich muß ~* I must be off; *mein Hut ist ~* my hat is gone (*od* lost); *~! ~ mit dir! interj* away with you! get out! *sl* scram! **~an** *adv* from this time, henceforth, for the future; **~arbeiten** *itr* to work on; **~bestand** *m* continuance, duration; *~~ des Staates* national survival; **~bestehen** *irr itr* to continue (to subsist); **~bewegen** *tr* to move on (*od* away); *sich ~~* to move along, to keep moving; **~bewegung** *f* locomotion, progression; **~bilden:** *sich ~~* to keep on studying; **~bildung** *f* advanced training; **~~sschule** *f* continuation school; evening-school, adult-school; **~bleiben** *irr itr* to keep off, to stay away; **~bringen** *irr tr* to move away, to carry away; *sich ~~* to get on (in the world).

Fort|dauer *f* continuance, duration; **~dauern** *itr* to continue, to last; **~~d** *a* continual; **~eilen** *itr* to hasten away.

fort|fahren *irr tr* to drive away, to remove; *itr* (*weg~*) to start, to depart; (*fortsetzen*) to keep on, to continue, to go on; **~fall** *m* cessation, discontinuing; *in ~~ kommen* to cease, to fall away (*od* off); to be abolished; **~fallen** *irr itr* to cease; to fall away (*od* off); to be abolished (*od* omitted); **~fliegen** *irr itr* to fly away; *aero* to take off; **~führen** *irr tr* to lead away; to convey; (*fortsetzen*) to continue; to go on with; (*Geschäft, Krieg*) to carry on; **~führung** *f* conveyance; (*Fortsetzung*) continuation, pursuit.

Fort|gang *m* departure; (*Fortschritt*) progress, success; (*Fortdauer*) continuation; *die Sache hat ihren ~~* it proceeds well; **~gehen** *irr itr* to go away, to withdraw; (*weitergehen*) to continue, to advance; *~~ n* departure; **~geschritten** *a* advanced; **~gesetzt** *a* incessant, continuous.

fort|helfen *irr itr*: *jdm ~~* to help on, to assist; *sich ~~* to support o. s.; **~hin** *adv* henceforth, in future; **~jagen** *tr* to turn away; (*aus der Schule*) to expel; **~kommen** *irr itr* to get away, to escape; *fig* (*gut*) *~~* to prosper, to succeed; *bot* to grow; *~~ n* escape; (*Fortschritt*) advancement, progress; (*Unterhalt, Auskommen*) living, livelihood; **~können** *irr itr* to be able to go on; *ich kann nicht mehr fort* I can't get any farther.

fort|lassen *irr tr* to suffer (*od* to allow) to go, to let off; (*auslassen*) to omit; *nicht ~~* to detain; **~laufen** *irr itr* to run away: (*entkommen*) to escape; (*desertieren*) *mil* to desert; *mar* to run free; (*weiterlaufen*) to continue, to run on, to last; **~~d** *a* continuous, continual; running; current; constant; successive; (*ununterbrochen*) nonintermittent; *~~de Nummer* successive number; **~leben** *itr* to live on; (*überleben*) to survive; *~~ n* (*Überleben*) survival; (*nach dem Tod*) after-life; **~leiten** *tr* to convey, to conduct; to carry off; **~leitung** *f* transfer; conveyance, conduction.

fort|machen *itr* to go on, to make haste; *r* to make off; to run away; **~marschieren** *itr* to march on (*od* off); **~müssen** *irr itr* to be obliged to go.

fort|packen: *sich ~~* to retire, to withdraw; *packt euch fort!* get away! **~pflanzen** *tr phys* to transmit to; to communicate; *r* to propagate; to reproduce; (*Krankheiten*) to spread; (*Tiere*) to multiply; **~pflanzung** *f* propagation; reproduction; *phys* transmission; communication; (*Krankheit*) spread; **~~sfähigkeit** *f* reproductiveness; **~~sgeschwindigkeit** *f* speed of propagation; **~~strieb** *m* reproductive instinct.

fort|reisen *itr* to depart, to leave; **~reißen** *irr tr* to tear away, to draw along; (*Redner*) *jdn ~~* to carry s. o. with one; **~reiten** *irr itr* to ride on, to ride away; **~rennen** *irr itr* to run away (*od* off); **~rollen** *tr* to roll on; **~rücken** *tr* to move away; (*vorwärts*) to advance; *itr* to move along (*od* on); **~satz** *m* continuation; *bot* process; *anat* appendix; **~schaffen** *tr* to carry away, to transport off (*od* away); to remove; to pass off; to get rid off; **~scheren** *r* to cut and run; **~schicken** *tr* to send away, to send off; to dismiss; **~schieben** *irr tr* to shove away; **~schleichen** *irr itr r* to steal away; **~schleppen** *tr* to drag away; *r* to drag o. s. on; **~schreiten** *irr itr* to step forward, to proceed, to advance; *mit der Zeit ~~* to keep up with the times; **~schreitend** *a* progressive; advancing; gradual, linear; **~schritt** *m* progress; (*Besserung*) improvement; proficiency; *~~e machen* to advance; *mil* to gain ground; **~schwemmen** *tr* to wash away; **~schwimmen** *irr itr* to swim away; **~sehnen** *itr* to wish o. s. away; **~senden** *irr tr* to send away (*od* off); **~setzen** *tr* (*wegstellen*) to place farther away; (*fortführen*) to continue, to pursue; **~setzung** *f* continuation, pursuit; (*e-r Geschichte*) sequel; (*e-r Arbeit*) prosecution; *~~ folgt* to be continued; **~stehlen** *irr r* to steal away; **~stoßen** *irr tr* to push away; (*mit dem Fuße*) to kick aside.

fort|tragen *irr tr* to carry away, to carry off; **~treiben** *irr tr* to drive away; *itr* (*im Flusse*) to drift.

fort|währen *itr* to last, to continue; **~~d** *a* continuous, perpetual; constant, incessant; *adv* continually, incessantly; **~weisen** *irr tr* to send away; **~werfen** *irr tr* to throw away; **~wursteln** *itr* to go on muddling, to muddle on.

fortziehen *irr tr* to draw away, to drag away; *itr* to march off; (*wegziehen*) to emigrate; (*Vögel*) to migrate; (*aus der Wohnung*) to remove, to move on; to leave.

Forum *n hist* Forum; (*Gericht*) tribunal; *öffentliches ~* public forum (= judgement of public opinion).

Foto *siehe*: *Photographie.*

Fötus *m anat* f(o)etus.

Fox, Foxterrier *m* (*Hunderasse*) fox terrier, Scotch terrier; *rauhhaariger ~* Aberdeen; *drahthaariger ~* wire-haired fox terrier; *glatthaariger ~* smooth-haired fox terrier.

Foyer *n* (*Theater, Hotel etc*) foyer, entrance-hall, lobby.

Fracht *f* (*Gebühren, Land~*) carriage; *Am auch* freight; rate of freight; (*See*) freight; (*Last, Ladung*) load; (*Schiffsladung*) cargo, shipment; (*Luft~*) air freight; *Hin~* freight out, *Rück~* freight home; *~ berechnen* to charge freight; **~bedingungen** *f pl* terms (*od* conditions) of freight (*od* shipment); **~beförderung** *f* freight service; freight transport; **~brief** *m* freight warrant; (*zu Land*) consignment note, way bill, *Am* bill of lading; (*zu Wasser*) bill of lading, bill of shipping; **~dampfer** *m* cargo-steamer, freighter; **~dokument** *n* shipping document; **~en** *tr* (*Land*) to load; (*See*) to freight, to charter, to ship, to carry, to consign; **~empfänger** *m* consignee; **~er** *m* cargo-steamer, freighter; **~firma** *f* (*Spediteur*) carrier firm; **~flug** *m aero* cargo flight; **~~boot** *n* cargo flying boat; **~~verkehr** *m aero* freight plane service; **~~zeug** *n* air freighter, freight plane, transport plane, freight-carrying airplane; (*Lastensegler*) freight-carrying glider; **~frei** *a* (*Land*) carriage-paid, *Am* prepaid, freight paid; (*See*) freight prepaid; **~führer** *m* carrier; **~geld** *n*, **~lohn** *m* freight(age), freight charges *pl*, carriage, portage, cartage; **~geschäft** *n* freight business, carrying trade; **~gut** *n* goods *pl*, load, cargo, package, *Am* freight; ordinary freight; *als ~~* by goods train, *Am* by freight train; **~handel** *m* carrying-trade; **~kahn** *m* freight boat, tow boat; **~kosten** *pl* freight charges *pl*, freightage, carriage, portage; **~lagerung** *f* cargo (*Am* freight) storage; **~liste** *f* freight list; **~makler** *m* shipping agent; **~raum** *m* shipping capacity, freight capacity; cargo compartment; **~satz,** **~tarif** *m* freight rate(s *pl od* tariff); **~schiff** *n* cargo-ship, cargo-vessel, freighter, trader; **~spedition** *f* freight forwarder; **~stück** *n* package; **~verkehr** *m* goods-traffic, freight-traffic; **~versender** *m* consignor; **~versicherung** *f* freight insurance; **~vertrag** *m* freight contract; (*See*) charter-party; **~vorschuß** *m* account payment on the freight; **~wagen** *m* goods wag(g)on; **~zuschlag** *m* extra (*od* additional) freight (rate); **~zustellung** *f* freight delivery.

Frack *m* dress-coat, dress-suit, *fam* tail-coat; *im ~* in full dress; **~hemd** *n* dress-shirt, evening-shirt.

Frage *f* question, interrogation, inquiry, query; (*Problem*) problem; (*fraglicher Punkt*) doubtful point; (*peinliche Frage*) torture; *~- u. Antwortspiel Am radio* quiz show, quiz program (*Abk* Q and A program); *Ansager e-s ~- u. Antwortspiels Am* quizmaster; *entscheidende ~* crucial question; *die schwierigste ~* the most difficult question, *Am fam* the sixty-four dollar question; *das ist e-e andere ~* that is another question; *e-e ~ aufwerfen* to start a question; *e-e ~ behandeln* (*od erörtern*) to enter into a question; *jdn mit ~n bestürmen* to urge s. o. with questions; *e-e ~ gab die andere* one question arose from another; *die ~ ist nicht berechtigt jur* the question does not arise; *e-e ~ mit „ja" beantworten* to answer a question in the affirmative; *e-e ~ tun, stellen* to ask (*od* to put) a question; *es ist noch die ~* that is still doubtful; *das ist eben die ~* that is just the point (*od* problem *od* question); *die ~ ist ...* the thing is ...; *in ~ stellen* to call in question; to question, to doubt; *in ~ stehen* to be in question; *nicht zur ~ gehören* to be irrelevant to the case; *in ~ kommen* to come into question; *nicht in ~ kommen* to be out of the question; *in ~ kommend* eligible; *die zur Entscheidung stehende ~* the question (*od* fact) at issue; *jdm die ~ vorlegen* to put s. o. to the question; *das ist keine ~* that is beyond question; *ohne ~* unquestionably; undoubtedly; *das ist e-e ~ der Zeit* that's only a matter of time; *indirekte ~* (*gram*) oblique question; *brennende ~* urgent (*od* vital) question; *strittige ~* question at issue; **~bogen** *m* query-sheet; form, questionnaire, *Am* (*bes. politisch*) fragebogen; list of queries; (*bei Examen*) paper; *e-n ~~ ausfüllen* to complete (*od* to fill in) a questionnaire; **~~fälschung** *f* intentionally false replies to the questionnaire, *Am* falsification of fragebogen; **~kasten** *m* (*Zeitung*) answers to correspondents; **~n** *tr* (*allg*) to ask; (*ausfragen*) to question; (*förmlich*) to interrogate; (*um Rat ~~*) to ask for advice; (*Auskunft einholen*) to inquire, to query; (*Arzt*) to consult; (*sich kümmern um*) to care for (*od* about); *nach jdm ~~* to ask for, to inquire about; *jdn nach* (*über, um, wegen*) *~~* to ask s. o. for (after, about) s. th.; *sie fragte nicht nach dem Preis* she didn't ask the price; *nach dem Weg ~~* to ask o.'s way; *sie ging zum Bahnhof, um nach den Zügen zu ~~* she went to the station to ask about the trains; *etw ~~* to ask a question; *es fragt sich, ob* it is a question whether, it is doubtful whether; *sich ~~* to ask o. s., to wonder; *ich frage nichts danach* I don't care a straw about it, *fam* I don't give a hoot about that; *gefragt pp com* in demand; *Kaffee ist sehr gefragt* coffee is very much in demand; **~punkt** *m* matter in question; doubtful point; **~r** *m* questioner; interrogator; **~recht** *n jur* right to cross-examine; **~satz** *m gram* interrogation (*od* interrogative) sentence; **~spiel** *n Am* quiz; **~stellung** *f* formulation of the question; **~wort** *n gram* interrogative; **~zeichen** *n* note (*od* mark) of interrogation, question mark, *Am* interrogation point.

frag|lich *a* (*in Frage stehend*) in question, questionable; *der ~~e Satz* the phrase in question; (*zweifelhaft*) doubtful; (*strittig*) disputable; (*ungewiß*) uncertain; *es ist noch ~~* it is still questionable; **~los** *a* unquestionable, beyond dispute; **~würdig** *a* doubtful, questionable, exciting suspicion.

Fragment *n* fragment; chip; **~arisch** *a* fragmentary.

Fraktion *f* parliamentary group (*od* faction), party; **~ieren** *tr* to fractionate; **~ierung** *f* fractionating, fractionation; **~~sanlage** *f chem* cracking plant; **~sbeschluß** *m* resolution of a party; **~sführer** *m* leader of a party; (*bei Debatten*) whip, *Am* floor leader; **~sgeist** *m* party-spirit.

Fraktur *f typ* Gothic type (*od* letter), German text; black letter; *med* fracture, delayed union; **~schrift** *f* German type, Old English type, Gothic type (*od* character).

frank *a* free, frank; open; *~ u. frei* plainly, openly; **~atur** *f* postage, prepayment; **~(en)** *m* (*Münze*) franc; **~furter Würstchen** *n Am* frankfurter, *fam* franks *pl*; (*heiße, mit Brot*) *Am* hot dogs *pl*; **~ieren** *tr* to prepay, (*mit Marke*) to stamp, to pay the postage; **~iermaschine** *f* postal franking machine, *Am* postage meter (machine), automatic mailing machine; **~iert** *a* post-paid, prepaid, post-free, stamped; (*in Aufschrift* P. P.); *der Brief war nicht genügend ~~* the letter didn't have enough postage; **~ierung** *f* prepayment; **~o** post-paid, prepaid (P. P.); **~tireur** *m* guerilla fighter, franc-tireur.

Frankreich *n* France; *wie Gott in ~ leben* to live in clover.

Franse *f* fringe; *mit ~n besetzen* to fringe.

Franz *m* (*Name*) Frank, Francis; *mil aero sl* (*Beobachter*) observer, navigator; **~iska** *f* (*Name*) Frances.

Franz|band *m* binding in calf; **~branntwein** *m* (French) brandy; **~iskaner** *m* Franciscan monk, Gray friar; **~ose** *m* Frenchman; *die ~~n* (*das Volk*) the French; **~ösin** *f* Frenchwoman; **~ösisch** *a* French.

frapp|ant *a* striking, astonishing; *e-e ~~e Ähnlichkeit* a striking resemblance; **~ieren** *tr* to strike, to impress (strongly), to astonish.

Fräs|arbeit *f* milling work; **~automat** *m* milling automatic; **~e** *f* milling cutter (*od* tool); (*Landwirtschaft*) rotary hoe; **~en** *tr* to mill, to cut; **~er** *m* (milling) cutter; **~maschine** *f* miller, milling-machine.

Fraß *m* eating, food; *sl* grub; (*für Tiere*) feed; (*Weide*) pasture; *med* caries.

fraternisieren *itr* to fraternize.

Fratz *m* (*unartiges Kind*) naughty child; *fam* brat, monkey, little devil.

Fratze *f* grimace; (*Bild*) caricature; *~n schneiden* to make wry faces, to make grimaces; (*häßliches Gesicht*) ugly face; **~ngesicht** *n* apish (*od* ugly) face; **~nhaft** *a* distorted, grotesque; **~nschneider** *m* grimacer.

Frau *f* (*allg weibliches Wesen*) woman; female; *die ~en pl* the women, womanhood; (*Dame*) lady; (*Ehefrau, Gattin*) wife; (*Anrede, Titel*) Mistress X., (*auf Briefen*) *Abk* Mrs. X.; (*Herrin des Hauses*) mistress; *gnädige ~* Madam; (*in Briefen*) *sehr geehrte gnädige ~!* Madam! *sehr verehrte gnädige ~!* Dear Madam! *meine ~* (*gewöhnlich*) my wife, (*förmlicher*) Mrs. X., *fam* my old lady, my Missis; *ist ~ Meier zu Hause?* is Mrs. Meier at home? *Unsere liebe ~* (*eccl*) Our Lady; *alleinstehende ~* single woman; *verheiratete ~* married woman; (*sofort nach der Trauung*) bride; *ohne ~(en)* womanless; *die ~en des* (*eigenen*) *Haushalts* o.'s womenfolk, the womenfolk; *e-e ~ haben* to be married; *~ u. Kinder haben* to have a wife and children; *e-e ~ nehmen* to marry, to get married; *zur ~ nehmen* to take in marriage; *es steckt e-e ~ dahinter* there's a woman in it; *e-e ~ mit Vergangenheit* a woman with a past; *e-e ~ von Welt* a woman of the world; **~chen** *n* little woman; *fam hum* old girl.

Frauen|abteil *n rail* ladies' compartment; **~arzt** *m* specialist for women's diseases, gyn(a)ecologist; **~bekanntschaften** *f pl* women acquaintances *pl*; **~bewegung** *f* women's (*od* feminist) movement; **~dusche** *f* (*Spritze*) feminine syringe; **~feind, ~hasser** *m* woman hater, misogynist; **~enfrage** *f* question of women's rights; **~haar** *n* woman's hair; *bot* maidenhair; **~haft** *a* (*fraulich*) womanlike, womanly; **~heilkunde** *f* gyn(a)ecology; **~hemd** *n* chemise; **~herrschaft** *f* female rule; **~kleid** *n* dress, gown, robe, frock; **~kleidung** *f* ladies' clothes (*od* wear), *Am* women's clothes (*od* wear); **~klinik** *f* women hospital; **~kloster** *n* nunnery; **~krankheit** *f* women's disease; **~putz** *m* woman's finery; **~rechte** *n pl* women's rights *pl*; **~rechtlerin** *f* feminist, (*gewalttätig*) suffragette; **~sleute** *f pl* women, womenfolk(s *pl*); **~sperson** *f*, **~zimmer** *n* female, woman, (*alte Jungfer*) spinster; (*abfällig*) slut; *Am fam* skirt; **~stimmrecht** *n* women's (*od* female) suffrage.

Fräulein *n* young lady; unmarried lady; (*Titel*) Miss; (*~ vom Amt*) *tele* operator, *Am fam* hello-girl; *Ihr ~ Tochter* your daughter; **fraulich** *a* womanly.

frech *a* insolent; (*unverschämt*) impudent; *fam* (*keck*) cheeky, snooty, *Am* fresh; (*trotzig*) bold, saucy; *Am* sassy; (*naseweis*) pert; *mit ~er Stirn* with a brazen face; *~e Antwort Am* back-talk; *seien Sie nicht ~!* don't get fresh! **~heit** *f* insolence, sauciness; impudence; *fam* cheek; *so e-e ~~!* such impudence!

Fregatte *f* frigate; **~nkapitän** *m* commander.

frei *a* free; *~ von* free, exempt (from); *~ von jeder Beschäftigung* off; *~ vom Dienst* off duty; *~ von Furcht* free from fear; *~ von Schulden* clear of debt; (*in Freiheit*) free, at liberty, at large; (*Posten, Amt*) vacant; (*Telephon*) not-busy, vacant; (*Land*) open; (*freisinnig*) liberal; (*freimütig*) free, freespoken; (*offen*) open, plain, candid, frank; (*gratis, kostenlos*) gratuitous, free of expense; (*Brief*) postpaid, prepaid; (*Paket*) carriage-paid; (*unabhängig*) independent, free; (*kühn, frech*) bold, wanton; licentious; (*Eintritt*) free; (*Benehmen*) easy, graceful; (*Stil*) flowing; (*Zimmer, Wohnung*) vacant, empty, unoccupied; (*Zeit*) spare; *Eintritt ~!* admission free! *sind Sie ~?* are you free? *Sie sind ~ zu tun, was Sie wünschen* you are free to do what you like; *Sie brauchen nicht zu bezahlen — es ist ~* you need not pay — it is free; *~ an Bord* free on board (*Abk* f. o. b.); *auf ~em Felde* in the open country; *aus ~er Hand* of o.'s own accord; offhand; (*Zeichnung*) freehand; *unter ~em Himmel* in the open air; *~ Haus* free to the door; *~e Jagd aero* free-lance fighter patrol, fighter sweep; *~ von Kosten* free of charges; *die ~en Künste* the liberal arts; *~e Liebe* free love; *keine ~e Minute haben* not to have a moment to o. s.; *~ ans Schiff* free alongside; *aus ~en Stücken* spontaneously; *jdm ~en Lauf lassen* to give s. o. a full swing; *den Dingen ~en Lauf lassen* to let things take their course; *jdm ~e Hand geben* to give s. o. a free hand; *auf ~en Fuß setzen* to set free; *~er Samstag* off Saturday; *~ ausgehen* to go free; to come clear off; *e-n Tag ~ bekommen* to get a day off; *~e Unterkunft* quarters in kind; *sich ~ bewegen* to move freely; *~ haben* to have a holiday; (*vom Dienst*) to be off duty, *Am* to be off; *sie hat heute abend ~ Am* she is off tonight; *so ~ sein* to take the liberty; to allow o.s.; *darf ich so ~ sein* may I take the liberty; *~ reden, ~ sprechen* (*offen*) to speak openly; (*Redner*) to speak offhand, to speak extemporaneously; *~ umhergehen* to go at large; *~ werden* to get loose; *chem* to become disengaged; *~ heraus* frankly, openly, candidly; bluntly; **~antenne** *f radio* outdoor aerial (*od* antenna), free aerial, free antenna; **~antwort** *f* prepaid answer; **~bad** *n* open air swimming pool; **~ballon** *m* free balloon; **~~führer** *m* balloon pilot; **~betrag** *m* (*bei Steuern*) amount free of tax; (tax) exemption (*od* allowance); **~beuter** *m* pirate, freebooter; **~~ei** *f* piracy, pillage; **~billet** *n siehe Freikarte*; **~bleibend** *adv* (*Preis, Angebot etc*) not binding; without engagement, if unsold; subject to alteration without notice; free offer; **~bord** *n mar* free-board; **~börse** *f* curb market; **~brief** *m* (*Urkunde*) charter; (*Lizenz*) licence, *Am* license; (*Erlaubnis*) permit; (*Vorrecht*) privilege; (*Patent*) patent; **~denker** *m* free-thinker; **~e** *n* (*Feld*) the open field; *im ~en* in the open air; out of doors; *ins ~e gehen* to take a walk; *im ~en übernachten* to camp out; **~en** *tr, itr* to marry; *itr* (*um*) to court, to woo a girl; to make love to a girl; **~er** *m* suitor, wooer; *auf ~ersfüßen gehen* to go courting, *Am* to go sparking, to spark it; **~exemplar** *n* (*für den Buchhändler bei größerer Bestellung*) odd copy; (*für den Autor*) author's (free) copy, presentation copy, gratis copy; complimentary copy; (*zur Werbung*) free copy (*od* specimen); (*zur Besprechung*) press (*od* review) copy; (*Zuschußexemplar*) over copy; **~fallhöhe** *f* height of free fall; **~flug** *m aero* free flight; **~frau** *f*, **~fräulein** *n* baroness; **~gabe** *f* release; (*aus der Konkursmasse*) disclaimer; (*e-r Beschlagnahme*) release; (*e-r Vermögenssperre etc*) unblocking, deblocking; (*von Bewirtschaftung*) decontrol; **~~signal** *n* clear signal; **~geben** *irr tr* (*Personen, Vermögen*) to release; (*Gefangene*) to set free; (*zurückgeben*) to restore, to return, to give back; (*gesperrte Konten*) to deblock; (*Bewirtschaftung*) to decontrol; to take off the ration list; (*Pfandgegenstand*) to release, to replevy; (*Schule*) to give a holiday; (*im Geschäft*) to give time off; (*Straße*) to open (to); (*für Presse*) to release; (*durch Zensur*) to pass; **~gebig** *a* liberal, generous; *~~ mit Geld sein* to be liberal with o.'s money; **~~keit** *f* liberality, munificence, generosity; **~geboren** *a* free-born; **~geist** *m* free-thinker; **~gelassene(r)** *m* freedman; **~gepäck** *n* allowed (*od* not paid for *od* free) luggage; **~gesinnt** *a* liberal; **~gut** *n* freehold; allodium; **~hafen** *m* free port; **~halten** *irr tr* to pay for; to keep free; to treat; **~handel** *m* free trade; *Am* tariff reform; **~händig** *a* free-hand; without support; offhand; *jur* by private contract; *~~ verkaufen* to sell offhand, to sell by private contract; *~~ schießen* to shoot offhand; **~händler** *m* free-trader, *Am* tariff-reformer; **~handzeichnen** *n* free-hand drawing; **~hängend** *a* suspended in air; trailing; **~heit** *f* freedom, liberty; (*Unabhängigkeit*) independence; (*schrankenlose*) licence; (*von Lasten*) immunity, exemption; (*Vorrecht*) privilege; (*Spielraum*) scope; (*dichterische ~~*) poetic(al) licence; (*bürgerliche ~~*) franchise; civil liberty; *persönliche ~~* individual liberty; (*Freizügigkeit*) personal liberty; *~~ der öffentlichen Meinung* freedom of speech and writing; *operative ~~* operational mobility; *politische ~~* political liberty; *Presse~~* freedom of the press; *~~ der Meere* freedom of the seas; *in ~~* at liberty; *sich die ~~ nehmen* to take the liberty (of); *sich ~~en herausnehmen* to take liberties; *in ~~ setzen* to set free, to set at liberty; **~~lich** *a* (*politisch*) liberal; **~~sberaubung** *f jur* deprivation of liberty, unlawful detention, false imprisonment; **~~sbeschränkung** *f* restriction of liberty; **~~sbrief** *m* charter; **~~sdrang** *m* thirst (*od* desire) for liberty (*od* independence); **~~skampf** *m* struggle (*od* fight) for freedom; **~~skrieg** *m* struggle for liberty; (*Unabhängigkeit*) war of independence; **~~sliebe** *f* love of liberty; **~~sliebend** *a* freedom-loving; **~~ssinn** *m* spirit of freedom; **~~sstrafe** *f* imprisonment; **~herr** *m* baron; **~herrin** *f* baroness; **~herrlich** *a* baronial; **~karte** *f* (*Billet*) free (*od* complimentary) ticket; *rail* pass-ticket; *theat* free pass, order; **~korps** *n* corps of volunteers; **~kuvert** *n*, (*heute meist*) **~umschlag** *m* stamped envelope; **~lassen** *irr tr* to set free, to release (from), *Am* to enlarge; (*gegen Kaution ~~*) to release on bail; *jdn gegen e-e Kaution von 100* **$** *~~ Am* to release s. o. under a $ 100 bond; (*bedingt ~~*) to release on probation, to bind over on probation; (*Sklaven*) to emancipate; **~lassung** *f* release; emancipation; **~lauf** *m* free wheel; *~~ mit Rücktrittbremse* free wheel hub with back-pedal brake (*Am* coaster brake); *im ~~ fahren* to freewheel, *Am* to coast; **~~nabe** *f* free-wheel hub; **~legen** *tr* to set free; to lay bare; to expose; **~leitung** *f el* overhead line; **~lich** *adv* certainly, indeed; *ja ~~!* to be sure! yes, of course! **~lichtaufnahme** *f phot* outdoor (*od* exterior) shooting (*od* shot); **~lichtbühne** *f* open-air theatre; (*Am* theater); **~lichtkino** *n* open-air cinema; **~lichtmalerei** *f* plein-air painting; **~lichttheater** *n* open-air theatre; **~los** *n* gratuitous ticket; **~machen** *tr* to set free, to deliver; (*Post*) to prepay, to stamp; (*von Schulden*) to clear (of debts); **~marke** *f* stamp; **~maurer** *m* freemason; **~~ei** *f* freemasonry; **~~loge** *f* freemasons' lodge; **~mut** *m* cando(u)r, sincerity; frankness; **~mütig** *a* frank, candid, open; **~~keit** *f* frankness, openness; **~paß** *m* free pass; **~saß** *m* freeholder, yeoman; **~schar** *f* band of volunteers; irregulars *pl*; **~schärler** *m* volunteer; insurgent; guerrilla; **~schein** *m* licence; **~schule** *f* free school, charity school; **~schüler** *m* free scholar; exhibitioner; **~sinnig** *a* liberal; free-thinking; **~spielen**: *sich ~~* to play o. s. free; **~sprechen** *irr tr* (*von Sünden*) to absolve (*von* from); (*von e-m Verdacht*) to clear; (*entlasten*) to exonerate; *jur* to acquit (of a crime, of a charge), to discharge; **~sprechung** *f* absolution; **~spruch** *m* (*vor Gericht*) acquittal, verdict of not-guilty; **~staat** *m* free state, republic; **~stätte** *f* asylum, sanctuary; refuge; **~stehen** *irr itr* to stand isolated, to stand detached; *es steht Ihnen frei* you are at liberty (*od* free *od* permitted), it is open to you; **~stehend** *a* freestanding, isolated; detached; **~stelle** *f* scholarship, bursary; free place, exhibition; **~stellen** *tr* to leave it to; **~stempelmaschine** *f* postal franking machine, *Am* postage meter (machine); **~stil** *m sport* free style; **~stilringen** *n* catch-as-catch can, all-in; **~stilschwimmen** *n* free-style swimming; **~stoß** *m* (*Fußball*) free kick; **~stück** *n typ* free copy; **~stunde** *f* leisure-hour; play-hour; **~tag** *m* Friday; *Stiller ~~* Good Friday; **~tisch** *m* free board; **~tod** *m* voluntary death; **~tragend** *a* cantilever; *~~e Tragfläche aero* cantilever wing; **~treppe** *f* open stairs *pl*, fliers *pl*, *Am* front stoop; **~übungen** *f pl* gymnastic exercises *pl*; callisthenics *pl*; **~umschlag** *m* stamped envelope; **~werber** *m* match-maker; **~wild** *n* game not preserved; **~willig** *a* voluntary, of o.'s own accord, spontaneous; (*bereitwillig*) willing; *~~ auf sich genommen* self-imposed; *sich ~~ ergeben* to make a voluntary surrender; *~~e Gerichtsbarkeit* voluntary jurisdiction; **~willige(r)** *m* volunteer; **~willigkeit** *f* voluntariness, spontaneity; willingness, free will; **~zeichen** *n tele* free line signal; **~zeit** *f* leisure (*od* spare) time; (*Schulpause*) break; *eccl* camp meeting; **~zeitgestaltung** *f* organization of leisure time; **~zeitlager** *n* holiday camp; **~zügig** *a* free to move; **~zügigkeit** *f* liberty (*od* freedom) to move within the country; freedom of movement.

fremd *a* strange; (*ausländisch*) foreign; (*unbekannt*) unknown; (*nicht dazugehörig*) extraneous; (*unabhängig*) independent; (*aus ~en Ländern*) exotic; *ich bin hier ~* I am a stranger in this place; *~e Pflanzen* exotic plants; *unter e-m ~en Namen* under an assumed name; **~artig** *a* heterogeneous, strange; uncouth, odd; **~~keit** *f* heterogeneousness, singularity; **~befruchtung** *f* cross-fertilization; **~bestandteil** *m* foreign ingredient; **~e** *f* foreign country; *in die ~~ gehen* to go abroad; **~e(r)** *m* stranger; (*Ausländer*) foreigner; **~enbuch** *n* visitors' book; **~enfeindlich** *a* hating aliens, xenophobe; **~enführer** *m* guide; **~enindustrie** *f* tourist industry; **~enlegion** *f* the French Foreign Legion; **~enverkehr** *m* (foreign) visitors, tourist traffic; **~~sbüro** *n* tourist office; visitors' bureau; **~enzimmer** *n* guest-chamber; spare (bed)room; (*im Gasthof*) tourist's room; **~herrschaft** *f* foreign rule; **~körper** *m med* foreign body; **~ländisch** *a* foreign; **~ling** *m* stranger; foreigner; **~peilung** *f radio* position finding; **~rassig, ~stämmig** *a* alien, of different race; **~sprache** *f* foreign language; **~sprachig** *a* foreign-language; **~stoff** *m* foreign substance; **~wort** *n* foreign word.

Frequenz *f* (*Schule*) attendance; (*Zulauf*) crowd; *rail* traffic; *el, radio* frequency; *Bild~* (*tele*) vision frequency; *Fernseh~* video frequency; *Hoch~* high frequency; *Radio~* radio frequency; **~abstand** *m radio* frequency separation; **~band** *n radio* frequency band; (*e-r Station*) service band; **~einstellung** *f radio* (*Grobeinstellung*) frequency selection; **~messer** *m radio* frequency meter; **~modulation** *f radio* frequency modulation; **~~srundfunk** *m* frequency modulation broadcasting (*Abk* F.M. broadcasting); **~zuteilung** *f radio* allocation of frequencies *pl*.

Fresko *n*; **~gemälde** *n* fresco (painting).

fress|en *irr tr* (*Tiere*) to eat; to feed; (*von Menschen*) to devour; (*Rost, Säuren*) to corrode; (*Lager, Kolben*) to seize; *dem Vieh zu ~~ geben* to feed the cattle; *seinen Verdruß in sich hinein~~* to swallow o.'s vexation; *der Neid frißt sie* she is eaten with envy; *um sich ~~* (*Krankheit*) to spread; **~en** *n* eating; (*Tiere*) food; *das war für ihn ein gefundenes ~~* that was nuts for him, *Am* that was right down his alley; **~er** *m* eater, glutton; **~erei** *f* gluttony, treat, *fam* blow-out; **~gier** *f* voracity; **~gierig** *a* gluttonous; voracious; **~napf** *m* trough; **~sack** *m* glutton; **~trog** *m* manger.

Frettchen *n* ferret.

Freude *f* joy; (*Fröhlichkeit*) gladness; (*Erfreutsein*) joyfulness, delectation; (*Entzücken*) delight; (*Vergnügen*) pleasure; (*Wonne*) bliss; (*Lustigkeit*) gaiety; (*Genuß*) enjoyment; (*Glück*) happiness; *vor ~* with joy; *mit ~n* gladly, joyfully; *jdm e-e ~ machen* to give s. o. joy; *jdm die ~ verderben* to spoil s. o.'s pleasure; *herrlich u. in ~n leben* to live in splendid style; *vor ~ außer sich sein* to be mad with joy; *vor ~ weinen* to weep for joy; *seine ~ daran finden* to take pleasure in.

Freuden|bezeigung *f* expression of joy; **~botschaft** *f* glad tidings *pl*; **~fest** *n* jubilee, feast; **~feuer** *n* bonfire; **~geschrei** *n* shouts (*pl*) of joy, acclamation; **~haus** *n* brothel, house of ill fame; **~mädchen** *n* prostitute; **~reich** *a* joyful; **~störer** *m* kill-joy; *fam* wet blanket; **~sturm** *m* transports of joy; **~tag** *m* day of rejoicing, red-letter day; **~tanz** *m* joyful dance; **~taumel** *m* transports (*pl*) of joy.

freud|estrahlend *a* beaming with joy; radiant; **~ig** *a* joyful, joyous; (*froh*) glad; (*heiter*) cheerful; (*erfreut*) pleased; (*strahlend*) beaming; **~igkeit** *f* joyfulness, cheerfulness; **~los** *a* joyless; **~voll** *a* joyful.

freuen *tr* to give pleasure (*od* joy) to; *das freut mich* I am glad of that; *sich ~~* to be pleased with; to be glad of, to rejoice at, to be delighted with; *sich ~ auf* to look forward to; *sich an etw ~* to find pleasure in s. th.; *sich über etw ~* to delight in s. th.; *es freut mich sehr, Sie kennenzulernen* I am very glad to meet you.

Freund *m* friend; (*Bekannter*) acquaintance; (*Kamerad*) pal; *Brief*~ pen-pal; (*e-s Mädchens*) *fam* boy friend; *alter* ~ old friend, *fam* crony, chum; (*Anrede*) old boy, old man; *treuer* ~ staunch friend; *wohlwollender* ~ wellwisher; *dicke* ~*e* (*Knaben*) great chums; fast friends; ~ *sein von etw* to be fond of, to like (to); **~in** *f* (female) friend, *fam* girl friend; **~lich** *a* kind to, friendly; (*leutselig*) affable; (*Wetter*) fair, mild; (*wohlwollend*) benevolent; (*zuvorkommend*) obliging; (*liebenswürdig*) amiable; (*angenehm*) pleasant; ~*er Empfang* friendly welcome; ~*es Zimmer* comfortable room; *seien Sie so* ~~ will you be so kind as to; ~~ *aufnehmen* to receive kindly; **~~keit** *f* friendliness, kindness; (*Höflichkeit*) courteousness, civility; *jdm* ~~*en erweisen* to do s. o. favo(u)rs.

Freundschaft *f* friendship; (*Freundeskreis*) relations *pl*; ~ *schließen mit* to make friends with; **~lich** *a* friendly, amicable; ~~*e Beziehungen* friendly relations; *auf* ~~*em Fuß mit jdm stehen* to be on friendly terms with s. o.; *e-e Sache* ~~ *erledigen* to settle s. th. amicably; **~sbezeigung** *f* mark of friendship; **~sdienst** *m* good offices *pl*.

Frevel *m* crime, outrage; (*Übermut*) wantonness; (*Schändung*) sacrilege; (*Unfug*) mischief; **~haft, ~entlich** *a* sacrilegious; wanton; malicious; wicked; criminal; **~n** *itr* to commit an outrage, to trespass; (*mit Worten*) to blaspheme; **~tat** *f* misdeed, wicked deed; outrage.

Frevler *m* trespasser, malefactor; villain; offender, criminal; blasphemer; **~isch** *a siehe*: *frevelhaft*.

*

Friede *m*, **~n** *m* peace, (*Ruhe*) tranquillity; *im* ~*n* at peace; *in Krieg u.* ~*n* at peace and at war; *den* ~*n bewahren* to keep the peace; *den* ~*n brechen* to break the peace; ~*n um jeden Preis* peace at any price; *ein fauler* ~ a hollow truce; ~*n schließen* to make peace; *laß mich in* ~*n!* leave me alone!

Friedens|abschluß *m* conclusion of peace; **~angebot** *n* peace-offer; **~bedingung** *f* terms (*pl*) of peace, condition of peace; **~brecher** *m* peace-breaker; **~bruch** *m* breach of peace, violation of peace; **~fest** *n* celebration of peace; **~fürst** *m* Prince of Peace; **~konferenz** *f* peace conference; **~miete** *f* pre-war rent; **~partei** *f* peace-party; **~pfeife** *f* calumet, peace-pipe; **~politik** *f* pacific policy; **~preis** *m* pre-war price; **~produktion** *f* peace-time production; **~richter** *m* justice of the peace (*Abk* J. P.), (*als Anrede u. Titel*) squire; **~schluß** *m* conclusion of peace; **~stärke** *f* peace-establishment; **~stifter** *m* peace-maker; **~störer** *m* disturber of peace, peace-breaker; **~verbrauch** *m* peace-time consumption; **~verhandlung** *f* negotiation of peace; **~vertrag** *m* treaty of peace; **~ware** *f* pre-war goods *pl*; **~wirtschaft** *f* peace-time economy; **~zeit** *f* time of peace; *in* ~~*en* in time of peace, in peace-time.

fried|fertig *a* peaceable, pacific; **~~keit** *f* peaceableness; **~hof** *m* churchyard, cemetery; **~lich** *a* peaceable, peaceful; **~liebend** *a* peace-loving; **~los** *a* without peace (*od* rest).

frieren *irr itr, imp* to freeze; *mich friert* I am cold, I feel cold; *mich friert durch Mark u. Bein* I am chilled to the marrow; *es friert mich an den Fingern* my fingers are cold; *es (ge)friert* it freezes; *sich zu Tode* ~ to freeze to death; *der Fluß ist gefroren* the river has frozen.

Fries *m* (*Baukunst*) frieze; (*Zeug*) baize.

Friesel *m*, **~n** *pl med* purples *pl*.

Frikass|ee *n* fricassee; **~ieren** *tr* to cut up.

frisch *a* fresh; (*kühl*) cool, chilly; (*neu*) new; recent; (*munter*) lively, brisk; (*Aussehen*) bright, ruddy; (*erfrischend*) refreshing; (*kräftig*) vigorous; (*lebhaft*) gay; (*Häute*) green; ~ *u. gesund* safe and sound; ~*e Butter* fresh butter, *Am* sweet butter; ~*e Wäsche* clean linen; ~*e Eier* new-laid eggs; (*im Gegensatz zu Eipulver*) shell eggs; *auf* ~*er Tat* in the very act; ~*en Mut fassen* to pluck up courage; *es ist mir noch im* ~*en Andenken* it is fresh in my memory; ~*er werden* to freshen; ~ *gestrichen!* wet paint! *Am* fresh paint! ~ *darauf!* ~ *darauf los!* at it! go ahead! ~ *auf!* look alive! go it! come on! **~arbeit** *f* fining process; **~e** *f* freshness, coolness; briskness; liveliness; brightness; **~en** *tr* to fine; (*Metalle*) to puddle (iron); to revive (copper); to reduce (lead); (*Gummi, Öl*) to reclaim; **~erei** *f* refinery; **~erz** *n* raw ore; **~esse** *f* refining furnace; **~fleisch** *n* fresh meat; **~gebrannt** *a* freshly burned; **~gelöscht** *a* freshly quenched; **~ling** *m* young wild boar; (*Metall*) scoria; **~stahl** *m* natural steel.

Fris|eur *m*, **~euse** *f* (ladies') hairdresser, *Am* barber; **~ieren** *tr* to do (*od* to dress, *Am* to fix) the hair; *sich* ~~ to dress o.'s hair, *Am* to fix o.'s hair; *sich* ~~ *lassen* to have o.'s hair dressed; (*Bericht*) to cook, *fam* to salt; **~iermantel** *m* dressing-jacket; morning-wrapper; (*Damen*) peignoir; **~iersalon** *m* hair-dresser's saloon, *Am* barber shop; (*für Damen*) beauty parlor; **~iertisch** *m* toilet (*od* dressing) table; **~ur** *f* hairdressing, *Am* hair-do.

Frist *f* (*Zeitraum*) (space of) time, period; (*begrenzter Zeitraum*) (set) term, given time, appointed time; (*Termin*) deadline, time limit; (*Zwischenzeit*) interval; (*Zeitpunkt*) moment, date; (*Aufschub*) delay; (*Zahlungsaufschub*) respite; (*Vollstreckungsaufschub*) reprieve; (*Verlängerung*) prolongation, extension; *gesetzliche* ~ limitation of time; *nach Ablauf der* ~ after expiration of the term; *ohne* ~ sine die; *auf kurze* ~ on short terms *pl*; *in (od binnen) kürzester* ~ at a very short notice, in no time, with the minimum delay; *innerhalb Jahres*~ within a year; *zugestandene* ~ time fixed, time allowed; *die* ~ *läuft heute ab* the term expires (*od* is up) today; *e-e* ~ *bestimmen (od setzen)* to fix a time-limit; *e-e* ~ *erbitten* to ask for time; *e-e* ~ *gewähren* to allow (*od* grant) a delay, to give an extension; *com* to give grace; *e-e* ~ *setzen unter Strafandrohung jur* to subpoena; *e-e* ~ *verlängern* to extend the time; *e-e* ~ *verfallen lassen* to let a term expire; *e-e* ~ *wahren (od einhalten)* to observe a term, to meet the deadline, to keep the term; **~en** *tr* (*befristen*) to set a date (*od* term); to delay, to respite; *sein Leben kümmerlich* ~~ to gain a scanty (*od* bare) living; **~gemäß** *a* within specified time; **~gerecht** *a* in time; *nicht* ~~ out of time; **~gesuch** *n* petition for respite; **~gewährung** *f* grant of respite (*od* time); **~los** *a* without notice; ~~ *entlassen* to dismiss without a moment's notice, *Am* to fire without notice; ~~*e Entlassung* dismissal without notice, summary dismissal; **~setzung** *f* fixing of a term (*od* date); **~überschreitung** *f* exceeding of time limit; **~ung** *f* prolongation; **~verlängerung** *f* prolongation of a term, extension (of time); **~versäumnis** *f* default of a term.

Fritter *m* coherer.

frivol *a* frivolous; flippant; **~ität** *f* frivolity.

froh *a* glad, cheerful, joyful; (*glücklich*) happy; (*lustig*) merry; (*in guter Stimmung*) in high spirits; *über etw* ~ *sein* to be glad (of *od* about); *e-r Sache* ~ *werden* to enjoy s. th.; *sie wird ihres Lebens nicht mehr* ~ she doesn't enjoy life any more; **~gelaunt** *a* good-humo(u)red; **~gemut** *a* cheerful; **~locken** *itr* to rejoice at; to exult in (*od* at); **~locken** *n* exultation, triumph; **~sinn** *m* gaiety, cheerfulness.

fröhlich *a* joyous, gay, cheerful, merry; happy; jovial; **~keit** *f* joyousness, gladness, cheerfulness, mirth.

fromm *a* pious, merciful; devout, religious, godly; (*geduldig*) patient; (*Tiere*) tame; *ein* ~*es Leben* a godly life; ~*er Wunsch* wishful thinking, idle (*od* vain) wish; **~en** *itr* to be of use to; to profit; *zu Nutz u. Frommen* for good.

Frömm|elei *f* affected piety; (*Scheinheiligkeit*) sanctimoniousness; (*Heuchelei*) hypocrisy; (*in der Sprache*) cant; (*falscher religiöser Überschwang*) bigotry; **~eln** *itr* to affect piety; **~igkeit** *f* piety, devotion; **~ler** *m* hypocrite, pietist, devotee.

*

Fron|arbeit *f*, **~dienst** *m* compulsory labo(u)r (*od* service); (*nach altem Gesetz*) soc(c)age; *fig* drudgery; **~en** *itr* to do enforced labo(u)r (*od hist* soc(c)age-service); **~leichnam(sfest *n*)** Corpus Christi Day; **~leichnamsprozession** *f* procession on Corpus Christi Day; **~vogt** *m* taskmaster.

frönen *itr*: *s-n Leidenschaften* ~ to be a slave to o.'s passions; *dem Laster* ~ to indulge in vice; *s-n Lüsten* ~ to indulge in sensuality.

Front *f* (*Haus*~) face, front, fore part; *mil* (*vorderste Linie*) first line, front (-line), line of battle; (*Meteorologie*) front; *arktische* ~ arctic front; *breite* ~ wide front; *innere* ~, *Heimat*~ home front; *Volks*~ people's front; *an der* ~ at the front; *waren Sie an der* ~? were you at the front? *an die* ~ *gehen* to go to the front, to go up; *hinter der* ~ behind the line; ~ *machen gegen* to face, to make a stand (against), to front; *die* ~ *wechseln* to change front; *ohne* ~ frontless; **~abschnitt** *m* front sector; **~al** *a* frontal; ~~*er Angriff* frontal attack; **~antrieb** *m mot* front (wheel) drive; **~aufwind** *m* (*Segelflug*) upwash; **~ausgangsstellung** *f* line of departure; **~berichter** *m* front-line reporter; **~böe** *f* line squall; cold-front squall; **~bogen** *m* front arc; **~dienst** *m* service at the front; **~einbuchtung** *f* salient; **~einsatz** *m* combat mission; *aero* combat sortie; **~ensegeln** *n aero* (*Segelflug*) frontal soaring; **~flug** *m* war flight; **~flugspange** *f* war flight badge; **~flugzeug** *n* first-line airplane, combat airplane; **~kämpfer** *m* (first line) combatant, veteran, fighter; **~linie** *f* front-line; **~offizier** *m* front officer, line officer; **~seite** *f* (*Haus*) frontispiece; **~soldat** *m* front(-line) soldier (*od* fighter), combatant; **~urlaub** *m* leave from the front; furlough from the combat zone; **~verband** *m* combat element; support force; **~verkürzung** *f* shortening of the front; **~vorsprung** *m* salient; **~wechsel** *m* change of front; **~zulage** *f* active service allowance; combat pay, front-line pay.

Frosch *m* frog; (*Geigenbogengriff*) nut, frog; (*Straßenbauramme*) detonating rammer; *med* (*Geschwulst unter der Zunge*) ranula; (*Feuerwerk*) cracker; **~hüpfen** *n* (*Spiel*) leap-frog; **~laich** *m* frogspawn; **~perspektive** *f* worm's-eye view; **~schenkel** *m* hind-leg of a frog; **~teich** *m* frog-pond.

Frost *m* frost; (*Kältegefühl*) coldness, chill; (*Fieber~*) fever-shivering; **~beule** *f* chilblain; (*offen*) kibe; **~ig** *a* frosty; chilly; *fig* cold, frigid; **~igkeit** *f* frostiness; frigidity; **~schaden** *m* damage done by frost; **~schutzmittel** *n mot* anti-freeze (mixture); **~schutzscheibe** *f mot* screen defroster, *Am* wind-shield defroster; **~sicher** *a* frost-resistant; **~wetter** *n* frosty weather, *Am* subzero weather.

frösteln *itr* to shiver, to feel chilly; ~ *n* shiver.

frottier|en *tr* to rub; **~handtuch** *n* Turkish towel, rough (*od* bath-) towel, rubber.

Frucht *f* fruit; *eingemachte Früchte* preserves; *kandierte Früchte* crystallized fruits; (*Feld~*) field-produce; (*Getreide*) corn; *med* f(o)etus; (*Erfolg*) result; (*Folge*) consequence; (*Wirkung*) effect; (*Nutzen, Vorteil*) profit, advantage; *~ tragen, ~ bringen* to bear fruit; **~bar** *a* fertile, fecund; fruitful; (*sehr ~~*) prolific; (*Boden*) fat; *fig* fertile, rich; *~~es Jahr* plentiful year; *~~e Phantasie* fertile imagination; **~barkeit** *f* fertility, fruitfulness; fecundity; *fig* richness, copiousness; **~baum** *m* fruit-tree; **~boden** *m bot* receptacle; **~bonbon** *n* boiled sweet, fruit pastille, jujube; **~brand** *m* ergot; **~branntwein** *m* fruit brandy; **~bringend** *a* fruit-bearing, frugiferous; *fig* productive; **~eis** *n* ice-cream, *Am* sundae; **~en** *itr fig* to bear fruit; to be of use; to have effect; **~fleisch** *n* fruit pulp; **~folge** *f* crop rotation; **~gehänge** *n* festoon; **~gelée** *n* fruit-jelly; **~knoten** *m bot* ovary; **~konserve** *f* preserved fruit; **~korb** *m* fruit-basket; **~los** *a* fruitless; **~losigkeit** *f* fruitlessness; **~saft** *m* fruit-juice; **~schale** *f* fruit-dish peel; **~torte** *f* tart, *Am* pie; **~wasser** *n med* fetal fluid; **~wechsel** *m* rotation of crops; **~zucker** *m* fruit sugar, levulose.

frugal *a* frugal.

früh *a* early; *adv* in the morning; (*vorig*) formerly, in former times; *heute ~* this morning; *morgen ~* tomorrow morning; *zu ~* (*adv*) untimely; *~ od spät adv* early or late; *von ~ bis spät* from morning till night; *am ~en Nachmittag* in the early afternoon; *meine Uhr geht zu ~* my watch is too fast; **~apfel** *m* summer (*od* early) apple; **~aufsteher** *m* early riser; **~beet** *n*, **~beetkasten** *m* hotbed; **~birne** *f* summer pear; **~e** *f* early time; *in aller ~e* early in the morning; very early; bright and early; **~er** *a* earlier, sooner; former; *adv* before, formerly; *~er od später* sooner or later; **~este** *a* earliest, first; **~estens** *adv* as early as possible, at the earliest; **~geburt** *f* premature birth; **~gemüse** *n* early vegetables *pl*; **~jahr** *n*, **~ling** *m* spring; **~jahrskostüm** *n* spring suit; **~jahrsmüdigkeit** *f* spring debility; **~jahrsputz** *m* spring house-cleaning; **~lings-** vernal, spring; **~klug** *a* premature, precocious; **~mette** *f* morning service; **~messe** *f* early mass; matins *pl*; **~morgens** *adv* early in the morning; **~obst** *n* early fruit; **~predigt** *f* morning sermon; **~reif** *a* early (-ripe), premature; *~~es Kind* precocious child; **~reife** *f* precocity; **~rot** *n* red morning sky; **~saat** *f* first sowing; **~schoppen** *m* morning pint; **~stück** *n* breakfast; lunch; **~~en** *itr* to breakfast; to lunch; **~zeitig** *a* early, premature; **~zug** *m* early train; morning train; **~zündung** *f mot* pre-ignition, advanced ignition.

Fuchs *m* fox; (*Pferd*) chestnut horse; (*Rotfuchs*) sorrel horse; (*Rotkopf*) red-haired person; (*Goldstück*) yellow boy; (*Billard*) chance-hit; (*Student*) freshman; *ein schlauer ~* a sly blade, a sly old fox; *es ist e-e Gegend, wo sich die Füchse u. Hasen ‚Gute Nacht' sagen* it is far off the beaten track, *Am* it is a way back district; **~balg** *m* fox-skin; **~bau** *m* foxhole, kennel; **~eisen** *n* fox-trap; **~en** *tr* to vex; *sich ~~* to fret, to feel annoyed; **~jagd** *f* fox-hunting; **~rot** *a* sorrel; **~schwanz** *m* foxtail, brush; (*Säge*) pad-saw; **~teufelswild** *a* hornmad, boiling with rage.

Füchsin *f* she-fox, bitch-fox, vixen.

Fuchtel *f* (*Zuchtrute*) rod, whip; *fig* (*Zucht*) severe discipline; *jdn unter der ~ halten* to keep a tight hand over s. o.; *unter jds ~ stehen* to be under s. o.'s thumb; **~n** *itr* (*mit den Händen*) to gesticulate wildly; *tr* (*jdn schlagen*) to thrash s. o.

Fuder *n* (cart) load; (*Faß*) German measure (of wine), fudder, a tun (of wine); **~weise** *adv* by cart-loads.

Fug *m*: *mit ~ u. Recht* with full right, with good cause; justly.

Fuge *f* juncture, joint; (*Falz*) groove; *mus* fugue; *tech* (*Saum*) seam; *aus den ~n sein* to be off the hinges; (*Schlitz*) slit; (*Naht*) suture; *aus den ~n treiben* to knock out of joint; *aus den ~n gehen* to become out of joint; to disjoint; **~n** *tr* to join; (*mit Falz*) to groove; (*Fugen ausstreichen*) to point up (a wall); **~nlos** *a* jointless, seamless.

füg|en *tr* (*zusammensetzen*) to join, to put together; (*verbinden*) to connect, to unite; (*hinzufügen*) to add; (*ordnen, zusammenpassen*) to dispose, to ordain; *sich ~~* (*nachgeben*) to submit to, to bow to; *sich in etw ~~* to comply (*od* to put up) with s. th.; to resign o. s. to, to acquiesce in, to submit (to); (*sich anpassen*) to accommodate o. s. to; *sich in die herrschenden Umstände ~~* to reconcile o. s. to circumstances; *imp* (*geschehen*) *es fügt sich* it happens, it chances; *wie es sich gerade fügt* as occasion demands; **~lich** *a* convenient, easy; just; **~sam** *a* pliant, suitable; submissive; (*Kind*) obedient; **~samkeit** *f* pliancy; **~ung** *f* (*Zusammenpassung*) joining, fitting; (*Zusammentreffen*) coincidence; (*Ergebung*) submission, resignation (to); (*Anordnung*) ordainment; disposal, disposition; (*Schicksal*) fate, dispensation; (*Vorsehung*) providence; *durch göttliche ~~* by divine providence.

fühl|bar *a* (*greifbar*) palpable, tangible, sensible, touchable; (*deutlich*) marked; (*Mangel*) felt; (*geistig*) sensible; (*wahrnehmbar*) perceptible; susceptible; *ein ~~er Verlust* a grievous loss; *e-e ~~e Abnahme* a serious decrease; **~~keit** *f* sensibility, (*geistig*) perceptibility; **~en** *tr* to feel; to touch; to perceive; (*empfinden*) to be sensitive to; (*sinnlich wahrnehmen*) to sense; *Lust zu etw ~~* to be inclined to do s. th.; *jdm den Puls ~~* to feel a person's pulse; *jdm auf den Zahn ~~* to sound, to examine s. o.; *sich getroffen ~~* to feel moved (*od* hit *od* hurt); *sich gewachsen ~~* to feel up to; **~end** *a* sensitive, feeling; **~er** *m* antenna; tentacle; *fig e-n ~~ ausstrecken* to send out a feeler; to feel o.'s way; **~hörner** *m pl* feelers *pl*, horns *pl*; **~los** *a* unfeeling, insensible; **~losigkeit** *f* insensibility; **~ung** *f* touch, contact; *~~ haben mit* to be in touch with, to be in contact with; *in ~~ bleiben* to keep in touch with.

Fuhr|e *f* conveyance, carriage; cart(-ing), carrying, transport; (*Ladung* cart-load, load, *Am* truck-load; **~knecht** *m* carter's man; **~lohn** *m* cartage, carriage, freight; **~mann** *m* carrier, carter, driver, wag(g)oner; **~park** *m* park; **~unternehmen** *n* hauling enterprise, cartage service; **~unternehmer** *m* carrier, *Am* trucking operator; **~werk** *n* carriage, cart, vehicle, wag(g)on; **~wesen** *n* carting, conveyance, carrying-trade.

führen *tr* to lead, to guide; (*feierlich geleiten*) to conduct; (*schützend begleiten*) to escort; to take; to convey; (*in bestimmter Richtung*) to direct; (*steuern*) to steer; to pilot; (*dirigieren, kontrollieren, durchführen*) to handle, to control, to manage, *Am auch* to engineer; *zu Tisch ~* to take in (a lady); (*an den Sitzplatz*) to usher; *wer führt?* who is ahead? *die Straße führt nach ...* the road leads to ...; *das führt zu nichts* that leads us nowhere; (*Waren auf Lager ~*) to carry, to keep; to carry in stock; (*zum Verkauf haben*) to keep, to sell, *Am* to carry; to stock; (*Strom*) to carry; (*Draht*) to run; (*Befehl*) to hold (command); (*kommandieren*) to command; (*Haushalt*) to keep house; to run o.'s house; (*bei sich ~*) to carry about one; *die Feder, den Degen ~* to wield the pen, the sword; *die Geschäfte ~* to manage, to run a business; *e-n Prozeß ~* to carry on a law-suit; (*Strafprozeß*) to try a case; *e-e Beschwerde ~* to lodge a complaint; *im Schilde ~* to have s. th. up o.'s sleeve, to be up to s. th.; *den Beweis ~* to prove; *die Bücher ~* to keep the books; *Krieg ~* to make war on, to wage war with; *e-n Namen ~* to bear a name, to go by; *den Vorsitz ~* to preside; *in Versuchung ~* to lead into temptation; *die Wirtschaft ~* to keep house (*für* for); *zum Munde ~* to raise to o.'s lips; *das Wort ~* to be spokesman; *das große Wort ~* to be always bragging; *e-n Wagen ~* to drive, to operate a car; *ein Flugzeug ~* to pilot a plane; *hinter das Licht ~* to deceive, to dupe; *wohin soll das ~?* what are we coming to? **~d** *a* leading, prominent, *Am* ranking.

Führer *m* leader, conductor; (*für den Weg*) guide; (*Reise~, Buch*) guide (book); *mil* chief, commander; commanding officer; (*Sportmannschaft*) captain; (*Fabrik*) director, manager; (*Rädels~*) (ring-) leader; *mot* (*Fahrzeug*) driver, chauffeur; (*Flugzeug, Schiff*) pilot; (*Lokomotive*) engine-driver, *Am* engineer; (*Boots~*) skipper, master; (*Erzieher*) mentor, tutor; *mus* (*Thema*) motive, theme; **~ausbildung** *f* training of future leaders; **~besprechung** *f* executive meeting; conference; **~eigenschaft** *f* quality of leadership; **~flugzeug** *n* leading airplane of a formation; **~gondel** *f aero* car; **~haus** *n rail*, *mot* driver's cab; **~in** *f* conductress; **~kabine** *f aero* pilot's cabin, pilot's compartment; **~kanzel** *f aero* pilot's cockpit; **~kurs** *m mil* officer training course; **~los** *a* guideless; driverless; *aero* pilotless; *~~es Flugzeug* pilotless plane, *Am* drone; robot plane; **~losigkeit** *f* absence (*od* lack) of leadership; **~prinzip** *n* principle of authoritarian leadership; **~raum** *m aero* pilot's compartment, cockpit, control cabin; **~reserve** *f* reserves to replace fallen officers, officer replacements *pl*; **~schaft** *f* leadership, guidance; command; (*Gesamtheit der ~*) group of leaders, the leaders *pl*; (*Leitung*) direction; **~schein** *m mot* driving licence, *Am* driver's license; *aero* pilot's certificate, *Am* pilot certificate; *aero sl* ticket; **~sitz** *m mot* driver's seat; *aero* pilot's seat, cockpit; (*Panzer*) tankdriver's seat; *verstellbarer ~~* adjustable driver's (*od aero* pilot's) seat; **~stab** *m* command group; **~stand** *m* control cabin, pilot's (*od* driver's) compartment; (*Panzer*) tank commander's position; *rail* cab; **~tum** *n* leadership.

Führung *f* (*Leitung*) leadership, command; guidance, conduct; (*der Geschäfte*) management, direction; control; conduit; (*Verwaltung*) administration; (*Hauptquartier*) *mil* headquarters *pl*, command post; (*Buch~*) keeping (of books); (*Steuerung*) driving, steering; navigation, piloting; *tech* guide, slide; pin guide; pinholder; (*e-s Geschosses*) rotating (*od* driving) band; (*Verhalten*) conduct; personal record; *obere~* (*mil*) higher command; *untere ~* lower command; *die ~ haben* to lead; *~ des Bogens mus* handling of the bow; (*persönliche*) behavio(u)r; *die ~ übernehmen* to take the lead; **~sabteilung** *f mil* tactical group of general-staff sections; **~sattest, ~szeugnis** *n* certificate of (good) conduct; reference; (*für Dienstboten*) character (reference); **~sbahn** *f* (guide)way, track; **~sband** *n* (*Geschoß*) driving (*od* rotating) band; **~sbuch** *n* guidebook; (*persönliche ~*) personal record; **~sgrundsatz** *m* principle of leadership; **~skette** *f aero mil* leading flight; **~skunst** *f* art of leadership; **~sleiste** *f* cam groove; **~snetz** *n mil* command telephone; **~srad** *n* guide wheel; **~srille** *f* (*Schallplatte*) groove (*od* track) of record; **~sring** *m* guide ring; (*Granate*) driving band; **~srolle** *f* guide pulley; **~sschiene** *f* guide-rail, guideway; conductor, track; **~sstab** *m mil* operations staff; **~sstaffel** *f aero mil* leading echelon; **~sstift** *m* guide-pin; **~sstück** *n* guide piece; (*Geschütz*) feed guide; **~swarze** *f* guide lug.

Füll|anlage *f* filling plant; **~anzeige** *f* (*Presse*) stop-gap advertising; **~ansatz** *m* filling sleeve; **~bleistift** *m* propelling pencil, patent lead pencil, filling pencil; eversharp; **~e** *f* (*Vollsein*) ful(l)ness; plenty; (*Vorrat*) store; (*Überfluß*) abundance; (*Verschwendung*) profusion; (*Reichtum*) wealth; (*Körper~~*) plumpness, stoutness; (*des Geistes*) pregnancy; (*gehacktes Fleisch*) forcemeat; *in ~~ vorhanden* abundant, plentiful; *in Hülle u. ~~ haben* to have plenty of; **~en** *tr* to fill; (*eingießen*) to pour in; (*aufladen*) to load; (*stopfen*) to stuff, to cram; *sich ~~* to fill up; *sich den Magen ~~* to fill o.'s stomach; (*wieder ~~*) to replenish; *auf Flaschen ~~* to bottle; *gefüllte Blume* double flower; *gefüllter Truthahn* stuffed turkey; *bis zum letzten Platz gefüllt* crowded; filled to capacity; *e-e Lücke ~~* to stop a gap; **~feder** *f*, **~federhalter** *m* fountain-pen; **~funkspruch** *m radio* dummy radio message; **~gas** *n* (*Ballon*) lifting gas; **~haar** *n* hair for stuffing, wadding; **~horn** *n* horn of plenty; cornucopia; **~klappe** *f* charging door; **~körper** *m* packing material; **~leitung** *f* filling pipe line; **~material** *n* filler, filling material; **~öffnung** *f* fill (*od* charging) hole; **~pulver** *n* powder charge, T. N. T. (= trinitrotoluene); **~rohr** *n* filling pipe; **~sel** *n* stop-gap; (*Küche*) stuffing, farce, farcing; **~station** *f* filling station; **~stopfen** *m* fill plug; **~strich** *m* filling mark; **~stutzen** *m* filler cap; **~trichter** *m* filling funnel; **~ung** *f* filling; (*Küche*) stuffing; (*Flasche*) bottling; (*Granate etc*) charge; (*Tür~~*) panel(ling); (*Zahn~~*) stopping; (*Material*) packing; (*Inhalt*) capacity; (*Luft~~*) inflation; **~~smenge** *f* quantity of filling; **~ventil** *n* fill-up valve; **~vorrichtung** *f* filling device; **~wort** *n* expletive.

Füllen *n* foal; (*Hengst~*) colt; (*Stuten~*) filly.

fummeln *itr* to fumble; (*herum~*) to feel (*od* to grope) about clumsily; to seek awkwardly.

Fund *m* (*Auffindung*) finding; (*gefundene Sache*) find; thing found; *ein wahrer ~* a real find; (*Erfindung, Entdeckung*) discovery; invention; (*Öl~*) strike; *jur* trover; **~büro** *n* lost property office, *Am* lost and found office (*od* department); *rail* lost-luggage office, *Am* lost package office; *auf dem ~~ nachfragen* to inquire at the lost property office; **~gegenstand** *m* article found; **~grube** *f* mine; *fig* rich source, treasury; bonanza; **~ort** *m* source (*od* place) of discovery; **~unterschlagung** *f* illegal detention of s. th. found.

Fundament *n* foundation, basis; (*Grundmauer*) foundation wall, basement; (*Bettung*) bed, seat; (*Grundplatte*) bottom plate, bedplate; **~al** *a* fundamental, basic; **~aushub** *m* excavation; **~ieren** *tr* (*Haus*) to lay the foundation (of); **~ierung** *f* foundation; **~mauer** *f* foundation wall; **~platte** *f* foundation plate; **~stein** *m* foundation stone.

fundier|en *tr* (*begründen*) to found; (*finanziell*) to consolidate; (*Schuld*) to fund; *gut ~t* well-founded; **~ung** *f* founding, foundation; (*finanziell*) backing; (*Schuld*) funding.

fünf *a* five; *~e gerade sein lassen* to stretch a point; *nicht auf ~ zählen können* not to know A from B; *die ~* (*Zahl*) five; (*Würfel*) cinque; **~akter** *m* five-act play; **~armig** *a* five-armed; **~blättrig** *a* five-leaved; **~centstück** *n Am* five-cent piece, nickel; **~eck** *n* pentagon; **~eckig** *a* pentagonal; **~erlei** *a* of five different sorts; **~fach, ~fältig** *a* fivefold, quintuple; **~hundert** *a* five hundred; **~jahresplan** *m* five-year plan; **~jährig** *a* five years old; **~kampf** *m sport* pentathlon; **~mal** *adv* five times; **~polröhre** *f radio* pentode; **~seitig** *a* pentahedral; **~stellig** *a* (*Zahl*) of five digits; **~stöckig** *a* five-storied; **~tausend** *a* five thousand; **~te** *a* fifth; *das ~~ Rad am Wagen sein* to be superfluous; *Karl V.* Charles the Fifth; *~~ Kolonne* fifth column; *Angehöriger der ~~n Kolonne* fifth columnist; **~teilig** *a* having five parts; five-point; **~tel** *n* fifth (part); **~tens** *adv* fifthly, in the fifth place; **~uhrtee** *m* five-o'clock tea; **~wertig** *a* pentavalent.

fünfzehn *a* fifteen; **~te** *a* fifteenth; **~tel** *n* fifteenth part.

fünfzig *a* fifty; **~jährig** *a* fifty years old; **~er** *m* man of fifty (*od* in the fifties); (*Geld*) 50 Pfennig piece, 50 D-Mark note (*Am* bill); **~ste** *a* fiftieth.

fungieren *itr* to function; to act as, to officiate.

Funk *m* wireless, (*heute meist*:) *Am* radio; *siehe auch*: *Rundfunk, Radio, Fernsehen; durch ~ zusprechen* to voicecast; **~abschirmung** *f* (*Zündkerzen*) spark(ing)-plug shield; ignition screening; **~amateur** *m* radio amateur, radio fan, (*Kurzwelle*) *sl* ham; **~anflug** *m* radio landing approach; **~anlage** *f* wireless installation, radio installation, wireless plant, radio plant; **~apparat** *m* wireless set, radio set; **~aufklärung** *f mil* radio intelligence, radio interception; **~ausrüstung** *f* radio equipment; *das Schiff hatte e-e ~~ zur schnellen Nachrichtenübermittlung auf große Entfernung* the ship had electronic equipment for swift and distant communication; **~ausstellung** *f* wireless exhibition, radio show; **~bake** *f* wireless beacon, radio beacon; **~bastler** *m* radio amateur (*od* fan); (*Kurzwellen*) *sl* ham; **~bearbeitung** *f* (*e-s Stückes*) radio adaptation; **~bereitschaft** *f* radio alert; **~berichter** *m* wireless correspondent, radio reporter; **~beschickung** *f* direction finding correction; **~betrieb** *m* wireless service, radio service; *im ~~ sein* to be on the air; **~bild** *n* photoradiogram; **~brief** *m* radio letter telegram; **~dienst** *m* wireless service, radio service; **~e, ~en** *m* spark, sparkle; flash; *fig* (*Stückchen*) bit, particle; *elektrischer ~e* electric spark; *sie hat keinen ~en Anstand im Leibe* there isn't a spark of decency in her; *kein ~en Hoffnung* not the slightest gleam of hope; *~en sprühen* to spark, to emit sparks, to scintillate, to flash; **~einrichtung** *f* wireless installation, radio installation (*od* equipment); **~empfang** *m* wireless reception, radio reception; **~empfänger** *m* wireless receiving set, radio receiver; **~empfangsstelle** *f* wireless receiving station, radio receiving station; **~en** *itr* to wireless, to radio; to broadcast; (*Lichterscheinung*) to spark, to flash; **~~bildung** *f* sparking; **~~entladung** *f* spark discharge; **~~fänger** *m* (*Lokomotive*) spark catcher; **~~sprühend** *a* sparkling, scintillating; **~~telegramm** *n* wireless (*od* radio) message, radiogram; **~~telegraphie** *f* wireless telegraphy; **~~telephon** *n* wireless telephone, radiophone; **~entstört** *a* radio screened; **~entstörung** *f mot* interference suppression; **~er** *m* wireless operator (W/T operator), radio operator; *aero* radioman; *Schiffs~~* ship's radio operator, *fam* sparks; **~ferngesteuert** *a* wireless-controlled, radio-controlled; *~~es führerloses Flugzeug* radio-controlled pilotless plane, *Am* drone; *~~es Schiff Am* drone boat; **~fernschreiber** *m* radio teletyper; **~fernsprecher** *m* radio telephone; (*tragbar*) portable radio telephone set; *der Flugzeugführer sprach über den ~~ mit dem Kontrollturm des Flughafens* the pilot talked by radio telephone with the control tower of the airport; **~fernsprechverbindung** *f* radio telephone circuit; **~fernsteuerung** *f* wireless remote control, radio control; **~feuer** *n* radio beacon; (*mit Kennung*) radio marker beacon; **~frequenz** *f* wireless (*od* radio) frequency; **~freund** *m* wireless amateur, radio enthusiast, radio fan;

~gerät *n* wireless apparatus (*od* set), radio set; **~gespräch** *n* radio conversation; **~gesteuert** *a* radio controlled; **~haus** *n* broadcasting station; **~höhenmesser** *m* radio altimeter; **~horchstelle** *f* radio interception station; **~kanal** *m* radio channel; **~krieg** *m* radio warfare; **~landegerät** *n* radio landing equipment; **~leitsender** *m* radio beacon; **~leitstand** *m* (*Radar*) radar intelligence collation section; **~leitstelle** *f* wireless telegraph controlling station; **~leitstrahl** *m* radio beam; *aero* (*Blindlandung*) glide-path beam, localizer beam; *auf dem ~~ fliegen* to fly the beam; **~liebhaber** *m* wireless amateur; **~linie** *f* wireless circuit, radio line, radio link; **~mast** *m* radio tower; **~meldung** *f* wireless telegram, radio message, radio flash; **~meß** *m*, **~messen** *n*, **~ortung** *f* radiolocation, *Am* radar (= radio detecting and ranging); **~meßgerät** *n* radiolocator, *Am* radar (set); **~~emechaniker** *m* radar mechanic; **~~stellung** *f* radar site; **~meßjagd** *f aero mil* ground controlled interception; **~meßmann** *m* radarman, radar operator; **~meßortungsgerät** *n* radiolocator, *Am* radar (set); **~meßstörsender** *m* radar jammer; **~meßturm** *m* radar station, radar tower; **~nachricht** *f* wireless message, radio message; **~~enprogramm** *n* radio news program(me); **~navigation** *f* radio navigation, Loran (= long range navigation); **~netz** *n* radio network; **~notruf** *m*, **~notsignal** *n* SOS call; **~offizier** *m* wireless officer (*Abk* W. O.); radio officer; **~ortung** *f* radio position finding, radio navigation (*od* bearing); **~panzer(kampfwagen)** *m mil* wireless tank; radio command tank; **~peilen** *tr* to locate with direction finding apparatus; to take bearings; **~peiler** *m* radio direction finder, directional radio; **~peilstation** *f* radio location station, radio direction finder post (*od* station), radio D/F station; **~peilung** *f* wireless bearing, radio bearing, radio direction finding (*Abk* D. F.), radio fix; **~personal** *n* radio station staff; **~raum** *m* wireless room, radio room; **~rufzeichen** *n* radio call signal; **~schatten** *m* dead spot, radio shadow; **~schneise** *f aero* (*Flugplatz*) equisignal track, corridor of approach, radio beacon course; **~schutzkappe** *f mot* radio shielding cap; **~senden** *n* radio transmission; *~~ u. Fernsehsenden über Stratosphärenflugzeug Am* stratovision; **~sendung** *f* radio transmission; **~signal** *n* radio signal; **~sprechen** *irr itr* to radiotelephone, to speak by voice radio; **~sprechgerät** *n* radiophone; *tragbares ~~ Am mil* midget walkie-talkie (*od* handy-talkie); **~sprechweg** *m* radio link; **~spruch** *m* wireless message (*Abk* W/T message), radio message, radiogram; *geschlüsselter ~~* radio code message; *offener ~~* radio message in clear; **~~weg** *m* radio channel; *auf dem ~~weg* by wireless, by radio, via radio; **~station, ~stelle** *f* wireless station, radio station, broadcasting station; *Groß~~* high power radio station; *bewegliche ~~* mobile radio station; **~stille** *f* wireless silence; **~störung** *f* (*als Kampfmaßnahme*) radio jamming; **~strahl** *m* radio beam; **~tagebuch** *n* radio log (book); **~täuschung** *f* wireless (*od* radio) deception; **~technik** *f* wireless technique, radio engineering; **~~er** *m* radio engineer; **~turm** *m* wireless tower (*od* mast), radio tower; **~übertragung** *f* radio relay; **~überwachung** *f* radio monitoring; **~urheberrecht** *n* copyright in broadcasting; **~verbindung** *f* wireless connection, radio connection, radio link, radio communication; radio contact; *das Flugzeug war in ~~ mit dem Kontrollturm des Flughafens* the plane was in radio contact with the control tower of the airport; **~verbot** *n* radio silence; **~verkehr** *m* wireless communication, radio traffic; **~wagen** *m* radio car, radio truck; **~weg** *m* wireless (*od* radio) channel; *auf dem ~~* by wireless, by radio, via radio; **~welle** *f* wireless wave, radio wave; **~wesen** *n* radio engineering (*od* technics); **~wetterstation** *f* radio weather station; **~wettervorhersage** *f* radio weather forecast; **~zeitung** *f* radio magazine.

Fünkchen *n* small spark, scintilla.

funkel|n *itr* to sparkle, to glitter; (*Stern*) to twinkle; *~~ n* sparkling, scintillation; **~nagelneu** *a* bran(d)-new.

Funktion *f* function; action; operation; service; office; *e-e ~ übernehmen* to take charge of a function; *e-e ~ haben* to have a function; *sich in ~ befinden* to exercise a function; *in ~ treten* to function, to serve, to officiate; *e-e ~ betreffend* functional; **~är** *m* functionary; **~ell** *a* functional; **~ieren** *itr* to act, to officiate; to work, to function; to operate, to run, to act; *mein Füllfederhalter ~iert nicht* my fountain-pen doesn't work; **~sprüfung** *f* function test; **~sstörung** *f* functional disorder; **~swert** *m* functional value.

Funzel *f* (*schlecht brennende Lampe*) miserable lamp.

für *prp* (*meist*) for; (*anstatt*) instead of, for; (*als Ersatz*) for, in exchange of; (*zugunsten von*) in favo(u)r of, on behalf of, for the sake of; (*betreffend*) as, as to, as for; (*gegen*) in return for, against; by; to; *ein ~ allemal* once for all; *Interesse ~* interest in; *~s erste* first; *Mann ~ Mann* man by man; *Schritt ~ Schritt* step by step; *e-e Karte ~ das Theater* a ticket to the theatre; *ich ~ meine Person* as for me; *was ~?* what kind of? *es ~ gut halten* to think it advisable; *Mittel ~ Fieber* remedy against fever; *Tag ~ Tag* day after day; *Wort ~ Wort* word for word; *an u. ~ sich* in (*od* of) itself; *~ u. wider* pro and con; *~ sich reden* to speak aside; *adv ~ u. ~* for ever and ever; **~baß** *adv* forward, on, further; **~bitte** *f* intercession; (*Vermittlung*) mediation; (*dringende Bitte*) solicitation; *~~ einlegen* to intercede (*bei* with, *für* for); **~bitter** *m* intercessor, intermediator; **~lieb** *adv* (*heute meist vorlieb*): *mit etw ~~ nehmen* to be satisfied with, to put up with; **~sorge** *f* care; providence; solicitude; (*soziale*) social welfare (work); (*öffentliche*) public assistance; (*Armen~~*) poor relief, private charity; **~~amt** *n* welfare office (*od* centre), *Am* department of welfare; **~~anstalt** *f* reformatory, remand home; **~~einrichtung** *f* social services *pl*; **~~erziehung** *f* child welfare work; trustee education, (*zur Bestrafung*) correctional education; education in a remand home; **~~r, ~~beamter** *m* welfare worker, relief worker, social worker; **~~rin** *f* woman worker for social welfare, woman social worker; **~~tätigkeit** *f* social work; **~~wesen** *n* welfare work; **~sorglich** *a* careful; provident; thoughtful; **~sprache** *f* intercession; (*Vermittlung*) good offices *pl*, mediation; *~~ einlegen* to intercede (*für* for); **~sprecher** *m* intercessor; (*Vermittler*) mediator; (*Anwalt*) advocate; **~wahr** *adv* in truth, truly; indeed, certainly; **~wort** *n gram* pronoun; *das ~~ betreffend* pronominal.

Fur|age *f mil* forage, fodder; **~agieren** *itr* to forage; **~ier** *m* quartermaster sergeant (*Abk* Q. M. Sgt.).

Furche *f* furrow; (*Rinne*) groove; (*Weg*) rut; (*Runzel*) wrinkle; *~n ziehen* to make furrows; **~n** *tr* to furrow, to ridge; to wrinkle; (*pflügen*) to plough, *Am* to plow; **~npflug** *m* ride plough, *Am* ride plow; **~nzieher** *m* ridge plough, *Am* ridge plow.

Furcht *f* fear; (*Angst*) dread, anxiety; (*Befürchtung, Besorgnis*) apprehension; (*Schrecken*) fright; (*Entsetzen*) terror; (*Schauder*) horror; (*Bestürzung*) alarm, (*stärker*) dismay; (*Schüchternheit*) timidity; (*Scheu*) awe; (*Panik, blinde ~*) panic; *aus ~* from fear of; *jdm ~ einflößen* to frighten; *in ~ geraten* to take alarm at; *~ haben* to be afraid of; *bleich vor ~* pale with fear; *~ vor Strafe* fear of punishment; **~bar** *a* fearful, formidable, dreadful; awful, terrible, horrible; *adv fam* (*fürchterlich*) awfully terribly; **~los** *a* fearless, intrepid; **~losigkeit** *f* fearlessness; intrepidity; **~sam** *a* fearful, afraid; (*schüchtern*) timid; (*verzagt*) faint-hearted, chicken-hearted; (*feige*) coward(ly); *fam* funky; **~samkeit** *f* timidity; apprehension; faint-heartedness; (*Feigheit*) cowardice.

fürcht|en *tr* to fear, to dread; to be afraid of; *sich ~~ vor* to be in fear, to be afraid of; *es ist zu ~~* it is to be feared; **~erlich** *a* terrible, horrible; frightful, dreadful; formidable; *adv* awfully, terribly.

Furie *f* (*Mythologie*) Fury; (*böses Weib*) fury, virago, termagant, *Am fam* battle-axe; (*Wut*) fury, rage.

Furnier *n* veneer; **~en** *tr* to veneer; to inlay; **~holz** *n* veneer wood; plywood sheet; **~messer** *n* veneer knife; **~presse** *f* veneer press; **~säge** *f* veneering saw; frame saw; **~ung** *f* veneering, inlaying, inlaid work.

Fürst *m* prince, sovereign; **~bischof** *m* prince bishop; **~engruft** *f* royal burial-vault; **~enstand** *m* princely rank; **~entum** *n* principality; **~in** *f* princess; **~lich** *a* princely, princelike; **~lichkeiten** *f pl* princes *pl*; princely persons *pl*.

Furt *f* ford, passage, crossing.

Furunkel *m* furuncle, boil; **~sucht** *f* (*Furunkulose*) furunculosis.

Furz *m vulg* fart; **~en** *itr* to fart.

Fusel *m* fusel, bad liquor (*od* spirits); **~öl** *n* fusel oil, amylic alcohol.

füsilieren *tr mil* to execute; to shoot (to death).

Fusion *f com, chem* fusion; amalgamation, merger, *Am* consolidation; *die ~ von Wasserstoff in Helium* the fusion of hydrogen into helium; **~ieren** *itr* to amalgamate; to merge (with), *Am* to consolidate; **~spunkt** *m* fusing point; melting point; **~sreaktion** *f* (*Atom phys*) fusion reaction; **~svereinbarung** *f com* agreement of consolidation.

Fuß *m* foot (*pl* feet); (*Stand*) footing; (*Münz~*) standard; (*e-r Säule*) bottom; pedestal, base; (*e-s Glases, e-r Radioröhre etc*) stem, foot; (*Mast*) heel; (*Tisch~, Stuhl~*) leg; *zehn ~ lang* ten feet long; *auf großem ~ leben* to live in grand style; *auf eigenen Füßen stehen* to be on o.'s own; to be independent; *auf dem ~ folgen* to follow hard on; *zu ~* on foot; *vom Kopf* *bis zum ~* from top to toe; *sich den ~ verstauchen* to sprain o.'s ankle; *gut zu ~ sein* to be a good walker; *sie wehrte sich mit Händen u. Füßen dagegen* she fought against it tooth and nail; *stehenden ~es* immediately, instantly; *festen ~ fassen* to get a firm footing; *jdm zu Füßen fallen* to fall at s. o.'s feet; *mit jdm auf gutem ~e stehen* to be on good terms with; *jdn auf freien ~ setzen* to set at liberty, to release; *zu ~ gehen* to walk; **~abblendschalter** *m mot* foot operated dimming switch; **~abstreifer** *m* door-scraper; door-mat; **~abdruck** *m* footprint; **~angel** *f*, **~eisen** *n* caltrop, man-trap; **~anlasser** *m mot* foot starter; kick starter; **~appell** *m mil* foot inspection; **~arzt** *m Am* podiatrist; **~bad** *n* foot-bath; **~ball** *m* football; (association) football, *Am* soccer; (*der Ball*) football, *Am* soccer ball; *Am sl* (*Leder*) pigskin; **~~freund** *m* football devotee, *Am* soccer fan; **~~mannschaft** *f* football team, *Am* soccer team; **~~meisterschaft** *f* football championship, *Am* soccer championship; **~~platz** *m* football field (*od* ground *od* park), *Am* soccer field, *Am fam* gridiron; **~~spieler** *m* footballer, kicker, *Am* soccer player; **~~verband** *m* football association; **~~wettspiel** *n* football match, *Am* soccer match; **~bank** *f* footstool; **~bekleidung** *f* foot-gear, foot-wear; **~betrieb** *m* treadle operation, treadle drive; **~boden** *m* floor, ground; flooring, floor board; **~~belag** *m* floor covering; **~~wachs** *n* floor polish; **~breit** *m*: *jeder ~~* every inch; **~bremse** *f mot* footbrake, pedal-brake, service brake; **~brett** *n mot* footboard, stepboard; **~decke** *f* carpet, mat; **~en** *itr* to foot, to get a footing; to set foot (upon); (*beruhen auf*) to depend (*od* to rely *od* to rest) on; to base, to found (on); **~ende** *n* foot, bottom-end; **~fall** *m* kneeling down, prostration; *e-n ~~ tun* to prostrate o. s.; **~fällig** *a* prostrate on o.'s knees; *jdn ~~ bitten* to supplicate; **~gänger** *m* pedestrian, walker; foot-passenger; (*verkehrswidriger, unvorsichtiger ~~*) *Am sl* jaywalker; **~~furt** *f* (*über verkehrsreiche Straße*) crosswalk for pedestrians; **~gashebel** *m* foot throttle, accelerator pedal; **~gelenk** *n* ankle joint; **~gestell** *n* foot, pedestal; **~gicht** *f* gout, podagra; **~hoch** *a* one foot high; **~knöchel** *m* ankle; **~krank** *a* footsore; **~lappen** *m* foot-bandage; (*Strumpfersatz*) foot-rag; **~latscher** *m mil sl* infantryman, *Am sl* foot-slogger; **~matte** *f* foot-mat; **~note** *f* footnote; **~pfad** *m* footpath; **~pflege** *f* chiropody; (*ärztlich*) podiatry; **~punkt** *m astr* nadir; *math* foot; **~raste** *f mot* foot rest; **~reise** *f* walking-tour; **~sack** *m* foot-muff; **~schaltung** *f mot* foot gear control, foot shifter; **~schemel** *m* footstool; **~sohle** *f* sole of the foot; **~soldat** *m* foot-soldier, infantryman; **~spann** *m* instep; **~spitze** *f* tiptoe, point of the toe; (*Strumpf*) toe; **~spur, ~stapfe** *f* footprint, footmark, footstep; trace, track; *in jds ~stapfen treten* to walk in s. o.'s steps; **~spezialist** *m* podiatrist; **~steig** *m* footpath; pavement; **~steuerung** *f* foot control; **~stütze** *f* footrest; (*im Schuh*) instep-raiser, arch-support; **~tritt** *m* (*Stoß*) kick; (*Bank*) footstool; (*Gang*) step; **~umschalter** *m* floor contact, foot-operated switch; **~volk** *n* foot, infantry; **~wanderung** *f* walking tour; hike; **~wärmer** *m* foot warmer; **~weg** *m* footway, walk; footpath; service walkway; **~wurzel** *f anat* tarsus; **~~knochen** *m anat* tarsal bone; ankle-bone.

Fussel *f fam* fluff.

*

futsch! *interj fam* off! gone! lost! (*kaputt*) spoiled, ruined.

Futter *n* (*Stoff~*) lining; (*Hülle*) case; casing; (*Nahrung*) food; *fam* grub; (*Vieh~*) food, feed, fodder; forage; **~al** *n* case, box; covering; (*Scheide*) sheath; **~almacher** *m* box-maker; **~bank** *f* chopping-bench; **~beutel, ~sack** *m* (*für Tiere*) nose-bag; **~boden** *m* hay-loft; **~gras** *n* greenfodder; **~geld** *n* money paid for keeping an animal; **~kasten** *m* fodder-chest, oat-chest; **~klee** *m* red clover; **~knecht** *m* (h)ostler; **~krippe** *f* (food)trough, manger; **~~njäger** *m* placeman, *Am* spoilsman; **~~nsystem** *n Am* spoils system; **~leinwand** *f* linen for lining; **~n** *tr* (*hum für: essen*) to eat; *fam* to tuck in; *siehe: füttern;* **~napf** *m* food-dish; **~neid** *m fig* professional jealousy; **~schwinge** *f* van; **~seide** *f* silk for lining; **~stoff** *m* lining; **~trog** *m* trough; manger; **~zeug** *n* cloth for lining.

fütter\|n *tr* to feed; to nourish; to give provender; (*mit Pelz*) to fur; (*mit Watte*) to wad; to pad; *tech* to case; (*mit Tuch*) to line; **~ung** *f* feeding, fodder; (*innere Bekleidung*) lining; (*mit Pelz*) furring; (*e-r Mauer*) casing, wainscot(t)ing.

Futur\|(um) *n gram* future (tense); *~~ exactum* second future; **~ismus** *m* futurism; **~istisch** *a* futurist(ic).

G

G *Abk mit **G** siehe Liste der Abk*; **~-dur** G major; **~-moll** G minor; **~-Saite** *f* G string; **~-schlüssel** *m* G clef, treble clef.

Gabe *f* (*Geschenk*) gift, present; (*kleines Geldgeschenk*) gratuity; (*Gefälligkeit*) favo(u)r, boon; (*Schenkung*) largesse, donation; (*Stiftung*) endowment; (*Opfer*) offering; (*Almosen*) alms *mit sing u. pl*; *um e-e milde ~ bitten* to ask for charity; (*Begabung*) gift, talent, endowments *pl*, faculty; (*natürliche*) aptitude; (*Geschick*) knack, bent, turn; (*Dosis*) dose; **~ntisch** *m* table of presents.

Gabel *f* (*zum Essen*) fork; (*Heu*) fork, pitchfork, prong; (*Fahrrad*) fork(s); *mus* tuning-fork, pitch-fork; *tele* cradle, rest; *mil* bracket, straddle; (*Deichsel*) shafts *pl*; (*Geweih*) prong; (*Pflanze*) tendril; (*Baum*) crotch; (*Farbband*) ribbon centre guide; (*Gerüst*) trestle; **~bildung** *f mil* (*Artillerie*) bracketing; **~bissen** *m* snack; titbit; **~förmig** *a* forked, bifurcated, branching off; **~frühstück** *n* lunch(eon); second breakfast; **~führung** *f* fork guide; **~gelenk** *n* fork joint; **~hebel** *m* forked lever; **~hirsch** *m* brocket; **~ig** *a* forked; (*sich*) **~n** to fork, to bifurcate, to branch off; **~stiel** *m* fork-handle; **~stütze** *f* forked support; **~umschalter** *m* hook switch; **~ung** *f* bifurcation, forking, branching off; **~zinken** *m* prong.

gackern, gacksen *itr* (*Henne*) to cluck; (*Gänse*) to cackle, to gaggle; (*plaudern*) to gabble, to chatter; *~ n* cackling; chattering.

Gaffel *f* gaff; **~segel** *n* gaff-sail.

gaff\|en *itr* to gape, to gaze, to stare at; **~er** *m* gaper, idle onlooker, starer.

Gagat *m* jet.

Gage *f* (*Handarbeiter*) wage(s *pl*), pay; (*Gehalt*) salary, stipend; (*Offizier*) pay; (*Vergütung*) fee, honorarium.

gähn\|en *itr* to yawn; to gape; *~ n* yawning; **~krampf** *m* fitof yawning; spasmodic yawning.

Gala *f* gala, pomp, state; *in ~* in full dress; **~kleid** *n* gala-dress; **~uniform** *f* full dress; **~vorstellung** *f* dress-performance.

Galan *m* gallant, spark, lover; paramour.

galant *a* polite, courteous; gallant; *~es Abenteuer* love-affair.

Galanterie *f* courtesy, gallantry; **~arbeit, ~ware** *f* fancy goods *pl*, *Am* notions *pl*; **~~nhändler** *m* dealer in fancy goods.

Galeere *f* galley; **~nsklave, ~nsträfling** *m* galley-slave.

Galerie *f theat* gallery, upper balcony; (gallery) gods; *für die ~ spielen* to play to the gallery, *Am* to play to the grandstand; *sport* bleachers *pl*; (*Bilder*) art gallery; (*Säulenhalle*) portico, colonnade; (*Stollen*) gallery, adit, drift, tunnel, passage.

Galgen *m* gallows *pl mit sing*; gibbet; *film* gallows, boom; *an den ~ kommen* to be hanged; **~dieb, ~strick, ~vogel** *m* gallows-bird; rogue; **~frist** *f* short delay, reprieve, respite; **~gesicht** *n* gallows-face; **~humor** *m* grim humo(u)r.

Galilä\|a *n* Galilee; **~er** *m* Galilean.

Galionsfigur *f* (*an Schiff*) figure-head.

*

Gall\|apfel *m* gall-nut, gall-apple; oak-apple; **~apfelsäure** *f* gallic acid; **~e** *f anat* gall, bile; *tech* (*Gußblase*) honeycomb, flaw, blister; *fig* (*Bitterkeit*) irritation, bitterness; rancour; spleen; *sie spuckt Gift u. ~e* she is fuming; *mir läuft die ~e über* my blood boils; **~enanfall** *m* bilious attack; **~enbitter** *a* bitter as gall; **~enblase** *f* gall-bladder; **~enfieber** *n* biliary fever; **~engang** *m anat* bile-duct; **~enkolik** *f* biliary colic, gall-stone colic; **~enleiden** *n* gall-bladder disease, cholepathia; **~enstein** *m* gall-stone, biliary calculus; **~ensucht** *f* jaundice; **~ig** *a* bilious, biliary; *fig* rancorous; bitter;

irascible; (*Bemerkung*) biting, satirical; **~wespe** *f* gall-fly, gall-wesp.
Gallert *n*, **~e** *f* jelly; gelatin(e); **~artig** *a* gelatinous.
Gall|ien *n* Gaul; **~isch** *a* Gallic, Gaulish.
Galimathias *m* nonsense.
Gallone *f* (4,54 l, *Am* 3,78 l) gallon.
Galopp *m* gallop; (*leichter*) canter; (*Tanz*) galop; *im gestreckten ~* at full speed; *im ~* at a gallop; *es geht mit ihm im ~ abwärts* he is sinking fast; **~ieren** *itr* to gallop (*auf* at); to canter; *~ierender Reiter* galloper; *~ierende Schwindsucht* galloping consumption.
Galoschen *f pl* galoshes *pl*; overshoes *pl*, *Am* rubbers *pl*.
galvan|isch *a* galvanic; **~isieranstalt** *f* electroplating plant; **~isieren** *tr* to galvanize; to electroplate; **~o** *n typ* electrotype, electroplate; **~ometer** *m* galvanometer; **~oplastik** *f* galvanoplastic (art), electroplating; **~otechnik** *f* electroplating, galvanoplastics *pl mit sing*.
Gamsbart *m* goatee beard.
Gamasche *f* gaiter; (*kurz*) spat; (*Reit-*) spatterdash; (*Leder~*) legging; (*Wickel~*) puttee; **~ndienst** *m* pipeclay (service); *fig* empty routine.
Gammastrahlen *m pl* gamma rays *pl*.
Ganef, Ganove *m sl* thief. rogue.
Gang *m* going, walking; (*Spazier~*) stroll, walk; (*von Personen*) gait; (*Geschäfts~*) course; (*Flur*) corridor, aisle; (*Durchgang*) passage; (*Besorgung*) errand; message; (*beim Essen*) course; (*Fortgang*) progress; march; (*Eisenbahnwagen*) corridor, *Am* aisle; *theat* gangway, *Am* aisle; (*Halle*) aisle; (*Steg*) gangway; (*Getriebe~*) *mot* gear, speed; *erster ~* bottom gear, first speed, *Am* low gear; *Gelände~* booster gear; (*Herstellung*) process, course; method of manufacture; (*Maschine*) running; motion; movement; (*Wirkung*) action; *toter ~* lost motion, backlash; *min* dead travel; (*Erz*) lode, vein; (*Arbeits~*) operation, action; play, running; (*Ohr*) labyrinth; *med* passage, canal, duct; (*Schraube*) worm, thread, groove; (*Mühle*) run; (*Fechten*) bout; (*Boxen*) round; *mus* pass; *in vollem ~* in full activity (*od* swing); *in ~ bringen* to set s. th. going, *fam* to start up; *etw ist im ~* s. th. is going on; *in ~, außer ~ setzen* (*Maschine*) to put into, out of operation; (*Getriebe*) to throw in, to throw out; to engage, to disengage; *den zweiten ~ einschalten* to shift into second gear; *im ~ erhalten* to keep going (*od* alive); *~ u. gäbe* customary, usual, current; **~änderung** *f* change in speed; **~anordnung** *f* gear-change diagram; **~art** *f* walk, gait; (*Pferd*) pace; **~bar** *a* (*Weg*) practicable, passable; (*Münze*) current; (*Waren*) saleable, marketable; *nicht mehr ~~* no longer in demand; **~~keit** *f* practicability; (*Maschine*) right motion; (*Münze*) currency; (*Waren*) sal(e)ableness; **~höhe** *f* pitch; **~schalthebel** *m* motion switch lever, *Am* gear shift lever; **~schaltung** *f* speed switching, gear shift; *automatische ~~* automatic gear shift; **~spill** *n* capstan; **~wähler** *m* gear selector; **~wählhebel** *m* gear control hand lever; **~wechsel** *m* change of speed; **~zahl** *f* number of gears.
Gängel|band *n* leading-strings *pl*; *am ~~ führen fig* to lead by the nose; **~n** *tr* to lead by a string.
gängig *a* saleable, marketable; (*gebräuchlich*) current; (*behende*) nimble; (*Hund*) quick-footed.
Gangster *m* gangster, *Am* racketeer; **~tum** *n* racketeering.
Gans *f* goose, *pl* geese; *dumme ~* simpleton.
Gänschen *n* gosling.
Gänse|blume *f* daisy; **~braten** *m* roast goose; **~feder** *f*, **~kiel** *m* goose-quill; **~fett** *n* goose-fat; **~füßchen** *n pl* inverted commas, quotation marks *pl*; **~haut** *f* goose-skin; *fig* goose-flesh, *Am* goose-pimples *pl*; *es überläuft mich eine ~~* my flesh begins to creep; **~klein** *n* (goose-)giblets *pl*; **~leberpastete** *f* goose-liver pie; pâté de foie gras; **~marsch** *m* Indian file, single file; **~nudel** *f* oat-meal ball; **~rich** *m* gander; **~schmalz** *n* goose-dripping; **~wein** *m hum* Adam's ale, water; **~zucht** *f* breeding of geese.
Gant *f* public sale, auction; (*Konkurs*) failure; **~en** *tr* to sell by auction.
ganz *a* all, whole, entire, total; (*ungeteilt*) undivided; (*vollständig*) complete; full; intact; integral; *~ Europa* all Europe, the whole of Europe; *die ~e Zeit* all the time, *Am* all of the time; *~e zehn Tage* full ten days; *den ~en Morgen* all the morning, *Am* all morning; *~e Note* semibreve; *ich bin ~ Ohr* I am all ears; *~ aus Metall* all-metal; *~ unserer Meinung* we quite agree; *~ oder teilweise* in whole or in part; *sie hat nicht so ~ unrecht* she is not so far wrong; *ein ~er Mann* every inch a man; *eine ~e Zahl* a whole number; *adv* quite, wholly, entirely, totally; *es schmeckt ~ gut* it tastes pretty good; *es ist nicht ~ dasselbe* it is not quite the same; *er weiß es ~ genau* he knows it for sure; *~ reizend* quite lovely, *Am* just lovely; *soweit ~ gut* so far, so good; *es ist mir ~ gleich* it is all the same to me; *ich gehe, ~ gleich was er sagt* I am going, no matter what he says; *er hat ~ u. gar recht* he is altogether right; *~ langsam fahren* to drive dead slow; *~ u. gar nicht* not at all; *~ recht* quite right; *~ wenig* very little; *~ wohl* very well; *im ~en* on the whole; *com* wholesale; **~e** *n* whole; (*Gesamtheit*) totality; *aufs ~e gehen* to go all out (for); *Am sl* to go the whole hog; **~automatisch** *a* fully automatic; **~heit** *f* completeness; entirety, totality, wholeness, entireness; **~holzbauweise** *f* all-wood construction; **~leder** *n* (*Buch*) leather-binding, calf; **~leinen** *n* cloth; **~metallbauweise** *f* all-metal construction; **~stahl(wagen)** *m* all-steel (car); **~tagsbeschäftigung** *f* full-time job; **~ton** *m* major second; **~zeitig** *a* on full time.
gänzlich *a* entire, total, whole; *adv* entirely, completely, wholly, totally; in every respect; throughout.
gar *a* (*von Speisen*) cooked through, done; (*fertig*) ready; (*Leder*) dressed; (*Stahl*) refined; (*sogar*) *adv* fully, even; quite, very; *~ nicht* not at all; *es fällt ihm ~ nicht ein, es zu tun* he would not even think of doing it; *er geht fast ~ nicht aus* he hardly ever goes out; *~ nichts* nothing at all; *warum nicht ~!* why indeed! why truly! never! **~aus** *m* ruin, deathblow, finishing stroke; *jdm den ~aus machen* to ruin s. o.; (*töten*) to finish, to dispatch, to do to death; **~küche** *f* cook-shop, eating-house.
Garage *f* garage.
Garant *m* guarantor, guarantee; **~ie** *f* guarantee, guaranty; (*Verkäufer*) warranty; security; *ohne ~~* without obligation; **~ieren** *tr* to guarantee, to pledge, to warrant, to secure; **~ieschein** *m* bond; **~ieversprechen** *n* guarantee contract.
Garbe *f* sheaf; *mil* cone of fire; *in ~n binden* to sheave, to bind into sheaves; **~nbinder** *m* binder; **~nhaufen** *m* pile of sheaves; shock; stack.
Gard|e *f* guard; guards *pl*; **~eregiment** *n* regiment of guards; **~ist** *m* guardsman.
Garderobe *f* (*Kleider*) wardrobe, stock (*od* outfit) of clothes; (*Raum*) dressing (*od* cloak) room, *Am* check(ing)-room; (*Haken*) clothes rack; *den Hut in der ~ ablegen* to leave o.'s hat in the cloak room, *Am* to check o.'s hat; *theat* (*Ankleideraum*) attiring-room; **~nfrau** *f* cloak room attendant, *Am* hat-check girl; **~nmarke** *f* cloak room ticket, *Am* check; **~nständer** *m* coat-stand, hat-stand.
Gardine *f* curtain; (*Vorhang*) blind; hanging(s); *die ~ auf-, zuziehen* to draw the curtain; *hinter schwedischen ~n sein* to be in prison; **~nhalter** *m* curtain-peg; **~npredigt** *f* curtain-lecture; **~nstange** *f* curtain-rod, curtain-rail.
gär|en *irr itr* to ferment; (*aufschäumen*) to effervesce; (*fig*) *es ~t* mischief is brewing; **~bottich** *m* fermenting tub (*od* vat); **~keller** *m* fermenting cellar; **~mittel** *n* ferment; **~ung** *f* fermentation; *fig* (*Erregung*) agitation, tumult, commotion; **~~slehre** *f* zymology; **~~smittel** *n* ferment; (*Hefe*) yeast; **~~sprozeß** *m* process of fermentation; **~~sverfahren** *n* method of fermentation.
Garn *n* yarn; (*Zwirn*) thread; (*Baumwolle*) cotton; (*Strick~*) knitting-yarn; (*Stopf~*) darning-yarn; (*Kamm~*) worsted-yarn; (*Näh~*) sewing thread; (*Netz*) net, toils *pl*; (*Falle*) snare; *ins ~ gehen* to fall into the snare; *ins ~ locken* to decoy, to ensnare, to entrap; *ein ~ spinnen* (*erzählen*) to spin a yarn; **~knäuel** *n* clew (*od* ball) of yarn; **~rolle** *f* yarn reel; reel of thread; **~spinnerei** *f* yarn spinning mill; **~spule** *f* spool, twill; **~winde** *f* yarn-reel.
Garnele *f* shrimp.
garn|ieren *tr* to trim; (*Speisen*) to garnish; (*Salat*) to dress up a salad; **~ison** *f* garrison; *Am* (army) post; *in ~~ liegen* to be quartered in; **~~sdienstfähig, ~~sverwendungsfähig** *a* fit for garrison duty; **~~slazarett** *n* military hospital; **~~sstadt** *f* garrison town; **~itur** *f* (*Besatz*) trimming; (*Satz*) set; (*Ausrüstung*) equipment, outfit; mountings *pl*; (*Zubehör*) fittings *pl*, accessories *pl*.
garstig *a* (*häßlich*) ugly; (*böse*) nasty; (*abstoßend*) repulsive, shocking; (*unangenehm*) unpleasant; (*schmutzig*) dirty, filthy; (*gemein*) mean, indecent; *~es Wetter* foul (*od* nasty) weather; **~keit** *f* ugliness, repulsiveness, meanness.
Garten *m* garden; (*Obst~*) orchard; *Am* (*Gemüse~*) yard; *e-n ~ anlegen* to lay out a garden; **~anlage** *f* laying out a garden; garden-plot; **~arbeit** *f* gardening; **~architekt** *m* landscape-gardener, *Am* landscape architect; **~bau** *m* gardening, horticulture; **~~ausstellung** *f* horticultural show; **~~betrieb** *m* horticultural establishment; market gardening; **~erde** *f* garden-mo(u)ld; **~fest** *n* garden-party, *Am* lawn-fete; **~gerät** *n* garden(ing) tools *pl*; **~gewächs** *n* potherb; **~haus** *n* garden-house, summer-house; **~land** *n* garden plot; **~laube** *f* arbo(u)r, bower; **~messer** *n* pruning-knife; **~schere** *f*

garden-shears *mit pl u. sing*; **~schlauch** *m* garden hose; **~stadt** *f* garden city; **~tür** *f* garden-gate; **~weg** *m* garden path; **~wirtschaft** *f* garden restaurant; **~zaun** *m* garden fence.

Gärtner *m* gardener; **~bursche** *m* under-gardener; **~ei** *f* gardening, horticulture; nursery; (*Ort*) gardener's establishment (*od* shop); (*Handels~~*) market-garden; (*Gemüse~~*) *Am* truck-farm; **~isch** *a* horticultural; **~n** *itr* to do gardening.

Gas *n* gas; (*Lach~*) laughing gas; (*Leucht~*) illuminating gas; (*Brenn~*) fuel (*od* heating) gas; (*Gift~*) poison gas; (*Tränen~*) tear gas; *das ~ andrehen* to light the gas, to turn on the gas; *das ~ abstellen* to turn off (*od* out) the gas; *~ geben* (*mot*) to step on the gas, to open the throttle; *~ wegnehmen* to cut off the gas; *in ~ verwandeln* to gasify; *mit ~ angreifen* to gas; *mit ~ vergiftet werden* to be gassed; *ich koche auf ~* I cook by gas; *Fern~versorgung f* long distance gas supply; **~abblaseverfahren** *n mil* gas-release method; **~abwehr** *f* anti-gas defence; **~~maßnahmen** *f pl* tactical protection against chemical warfare; **~~waffe** *f* gas-defence weapon; **~abzug** *m* gas vent; **~alarm** *m* gas warning; **~angriff** *m* gas-attack; **~anlage** *f* gas-fittings *pl*; **~anstalt** *f* gas-works *pl* (*Am* plant); **~anzünder** *m* gas lighter; **~arm** *a* deficient in gas; *~~es Gemisch* weak mixture; **~artig** *a* gaseous; **~ausbeute** *f* gas output, gas yield; **~ausbildung** *f* gas-defence instruction; **~austritt** *m* gas leakage; **~automat** *m* mechanical gas seller; automatic gas apparatus; **~backofen** *m* gas baking oven; **~ballon** *m mot* gas-bag; **~badeofen** *m* gas geyser, gas stove for bathrooms; **~behälter** *m* gasometer, gas tank; **~beleuchtung** *f* gas lighting; **~bereitschaft** *f mil* gas alert; **~beschädigte(r)** *m mil* gas casualty; **~beschuß** *m mil* gas shell fire; **~blasangriff** *m mil* cloudgas attack; **~bombe** *f* gas bomb; **~brenner** *m* gas-burner, gas-jet; **~dicht** *a* gastight; **~druck** *m* gas pressure; **~entwickler** *m* gas generator; **~erkennungsdienst** *m mil* gas detecting service; **~fabrik** *f* gas works *pl*; **~feuerung** *f* gas firing; **~flamme** *f* gasflame, gas-jet; **~förmig** *a* gaseous, gasiform; **~~keit** *f* gaseity; **~füllung** *f* gas filling; **~gebläse** *n* gas blower; **~gefahr** *f* danger of gas; **~gefüllt** *a* (*Birne*) gas-filled; **~gemisch** *n* gas mixture; *mot* fuel mixed with air; **~geruch** *m* smell of gas; **~geschoß** *n mil* gas-shell; **~gewinnung** *f* gas generation; **~glühlicht** *f* incandescent (gas) light; **~granate** *f* gas-shell; **~hahn** *m* gas-tap, gas-cock; **~hebel** *m mot* accelerator, *Am* gaspedal, *aero* throttle lever; **~heizofen** *m* gas stove; **~heizung** *f* gas heating; **~herd** *m* gas range, gas-kitchener, gas stove; **~installateur** *m* gas-fitter; **~kammer** *f* gas-chamber; **~kampf** *m* chemical warfare; **~~mittel** *n* chemical-warfare material; **~kessel** *m* gasometer, *Am* gas tank; **~kocher** *m* gas-cooker, gas-ring; **~koks** *m* gas coke; **~krank** *a* gas-poisened; gassed; **~krieg** *m* gas war, gas warfare, chemical war(fare); **~lampe** *f* gas lamp; **~laterne** *f* gas street lamp; **~leitung** *f* gas conduit, gas main; gas supply, gas pipes *pl*; **~~srohr** gas pipe; **~licht** *n* gas-light; **~~papier** gaslight paper; **~mann** *m* gas-man; **~maske** *f* gas-helmet, gas-mask, box-respirator; breather; **~messer ~zähler** *m*, gas-meter, gas-counter, tell-tale; **~motor** *m* gas-engine; **~ofen** *m* gas-stove; **~offizier** *m mil* gas officer, chemical-warfare officer; **~öl** *n* oil fuel, gas oil, Diesel fuel; **~olin** *n* gasolene, gasoline, petroleum-ether; **~ometer** *m* gasometer, *Am* gas-tank; **~pedal** *n* accelerator pedal; **~rohr** *n* gas-pipe; **~schleuse** *f* air lock; **~schutz** *m* protection against poisonous gas; gas defence, chemical defence; **~~anzug** *m* gas clothing; **~~gerät** *n* gas-defence equipment; **~~offizier** *m mil* gas officer, chemical-warfare officer; **~~raum** gas-proof-room, anti-gas shelter; **~sicher** *a* gas-proof, gastight; **~spürer** *m mil* gas sentry; (*Gerät*) gas detector apparatus; **~spürfähnchen** *n mil* gassed-area marker; **~spürtrupp** *m* gas detection squad; **~turbine** *f* gas turbine; **~überfall** *m mil* gas attack; surprise gas-shell fire; **~uhr** *f* gas-meter; **~vergiftet** *a* poisoned by gas, gassed; **~vergiftung** *f* gas poisoning, gas contamination; **~versorgung** *f* gas-supply; **~volumen** *n* gas volume, gas capacity; **~warnung** *f* gas warning; **~werfer** *m mil* chemical mortar; **~werk** *n* gas-works *pl*; **~zelle** *f aero* gas-bag; gas-filled photocell; **~zufuhr** *f* gas supply.

Gäßchen *n* lane, alley.

Gasse *f* lane, narrow street, alley, *Am* alleyway; (*Neben~*) byway; (*Personen*) lane, row; *Hans Dampf in allen ~n* busybody; *e-e ~ bilden* to line the streets; **~nbube** *m*, **~junge** *m* street-boy, street-arab, urchin; **~nhauer** *m* street (*od* popular) song, hit.

Gast *m* guest; (*Fremder*) stranger; (*Besucher*) caller, visitor; (*Kunde*) customer, patron; client; (*ständiger*) frequenter; (*ungebetener*) intruder, sponger; *theat* star; *jdn zu ~e bitten* to invite s.o.; *zu ~e sein* to be staying with; *wollen Sie mein ~ sein?* will you dine with me? *Du bist mein ~* you are my guest; it's on me; *Gäste haben* to have guests, to have company; *ich war bei ihm zu ~e* I was a guest at his house; **~bett** *n* spare (*od* guest) bed; **~erei** *f* feast, banquet; **~frei, ~freundlich** *a* hospitable; **~freund** *m* (*Besucher*) guest; (*Wirt*) host; **~~schaft** *f* hospitality; **~geber (in)** *m* (*f*) host, hostess; **~haus** *n* inn, tavern, restaurant, public house, *fam* pub, *Am* saloon; **~~schild** *n* sign of the inn; **~hof** *m* hotel; restaurant; **~hörer** *m* guest student; **~ieren** *itr theat* to star; **~lich** *a* hospitable; **~mahl** *n* feast, banquet; dinner-party; **~professor** *m* guest professor; **~recht** *n* right of hospitality; **~rolle** *f* starring-part; **~spiel** *n* starring (-performance); **~spielreise** *f* starring tour; **~stätte** *f* restaurant; **~~ngewerbe** *n* catering trade; **~~nmarken** *f pl* meal tickets *pl*; **~stube** *f* (*Wirtschaft*) general room; **~tisch** *m* table d'hôte, ordinary; **~vorlesung** *f* guest lecture; **~vorstellung** *f* starring(-performance); **~wirt** *m* innkeeper, landlord, landlady, *Am* saloon-keeper; **~~schaft** *f* inn, hotel, *Am* saloon; **~~sgewerbe** *n* = *~stättengewerbe*; **~zimmer** *n* guest room; (*Hotel*) general room.

Gästebuch *n* visitors' book.

gastrisch *a* gastric.

Gastronom *m* gastronomer; **~isch** *a* gastronomical.

Gatt\|e *m* husband; mate, partner; (*Gemahl*) spouse; consort; *fam* hub, hubby; *die ~en m pl* married couple, man and wife; **~en** *tr* to couple, to unite, to match; to join; *sich ~en* to marry, to take to wife; to copulate; **~enliebe** *f* conjugal love; **~in** *f* wife, spouse, consort; married woman; **~ung** *f* (*Art*) kind, sort, manner, nature; genus; *Am* stripe; *bot* family; *zoo* species; breed; (*Rasse*) race; *gram* gender; (*Bezeichnung*) style, denomination, designation; **~~sbegriff** *m* generic character, specific notion; **~~sname** *m gram* appellative, common noun; (*allg*) generic name.

Gatter *n* railing, lattice, trellis; (*Eisen*) grate, grating; (*Tür*) grille; **~säge** *f* reciprocating (*od* frame) saw; **~tor** *n*, **~tür** *f* grated door, gateway; **~werk** *n* lattice-work.

Gau *m* district, county, province, region.

Gaudium *n* carousal, jovial revelry, *Am sl* jamboree.

Gauk\|elbild *n* (*Einbildung*) illusion; fancy; (*Trugbild*) mirage, phantasm(agoria); (*Gespenst*) phantom, ghost, apparition; (*Wahn*) delusion, **~elei** *f*, **~elspiel, ~elwerk** *n* juggling, juggle, trick, sleight-of-hand, legerdemain, prestidigitation; (*Täuschung*) trick(ery), artifice, deception; **~elhaft** *a* juggling, delusive; (*betrügerisch*) tricky, deceptive; (*verschmitzt*) shifty; **~elkunst** *f* juggler's art, prestidigitation; **~eln** *itr* to juggle; (*Insekt*) to flutter; *tr* (*falsch darstellen*) to misrepresent; (*täuschen*) to deceive, to practise artifice upon; *fam* to do tricks; **~ler** *m* juggler, conjurer, illusionist; (*Betrüger*) trickster, swindler; (*Spaßmacher*) buffoon, clown.

Gaul *m* horse, nag; *alter ~* miserable jade; old crock; *e-m geschenkten ~ sieht man nicht ins Maul* you must not look a gift horse in the mouth.

Gaumen *m* palate, roof of the mouth; *den ~ kitzeln* to be agreeable to the taste; *mir klebt die Zunge am ~* my throat is parched; **~laut** *m* palatal (sound); **~platte** *f* (dental) plate; **~segel** *n* soft palate.

Gauner *m* thief, blackleg, swindler; *sl* crook, trickster; (*Schuft*) rogue, scoundrel; (*Betrüger*) *sl* spiv, shark; cheat; (*Gangster*) racketeer; (*Taschendieb*) pickpocket, cutpurse; **~bande** *f* gang of thieves; **~ei** *f* swindling, cheating, trickery, *Am* skulduggery; (*Unehrlichkeit*) dishonesty; (*Gangstertum*) racketeering; **~n** *itr* to cheat, to swindle; *tr* to trick, to deceive, *fam* to sharp (*um* out of); **~sprache** *f* thieves' cant (*od* slang *od* jargon *od* patter), flash language; **~streich** *m*, **~stück** *n* swindle, trick; (*Betrug*) fraud; (*Streich*) prank; **~tum** *n* riffraff, rabble; (*Abschaum*) scum, ragtag; criminal classes *pl*.

Gaze *f* gauze, (*feine*) gossamer; **~binde** *f* gauze bandage; **~sieb** *n* gauze sieve.

Gazelle *f* gazelle.

Ge\|ächtete(r) *m* outlaw, exile; **~ächze** *n* moaning, groaning; **~ädert** *a* veined; (*Holz*) grained, marbled; **~äst** *n* branches *pl*.

Gebäck, Gebackene(s) *n* pastry, pie crust; (*feines*) fancy cakes *pl*; tea-bread; **~zange** *f* biscuit-tongs *pl*.

Gebälk *n* frame-work, timber (*od* wood) work; (*Balken*) joists *pl*, beams *pl*; (*Säule*) entablature.

geballt *a* concentrated; *~e Ladung* demolition charge (of T. N. T.); pole charge; concentrated charge.

Gebärde *f* gesture, movement; (*Gesichtszug*) feature, mien, air, countenance; (*Aussehen*) look, appearance; (*Benehmen*) demeanour, attitude, carriage; **~n:** *sich ~~* to behave, to conduct o. s., to deport o. s.; **~nspiel** *n* gestures *pl*, gesticulation; mimic action; *theat* (*Pose*) posture, pose; (*stummes Spiel*) byplay, dumb show, pantomime; **~nsprache** *f theat* mimicry; (*Taubstumme*) deaf-and--dumb alphabet, dactylology.

gebaren *r* to behave o. s.; *~ n* demeanour, appearance, behavio(u)r.

Gebär|anstalt *f* lying-in hospital; **~en** *irr tr* to bear, to bring forth, to give birth to; (*Tiere*) to drop; *fig* to produce; *zur Unzeit ~~* to miscarry; *~~ n* bearing; (*Geburt*) birth; **~mutter** *f* womb, *med* uterus; **~schwester** *f* delivery-room nurse.

Ge|bäude *n* building; (*stattliches*) edifice; (*groß, eigenartig gebaut*) structure; (*~komplex*) pile; (*Wohn~*) mansion, dwelling-house; (*Landhaus*) cottage, villa; (*Häuschen*) lodge; (*Herrschaft*) manor house; (*Geschäft*) office(-building), premises *pl*; **~~steuer** *f* house tax; **~bein** *n* bones *pl*; (*Knochengerüst*) skeleton; (*letzte Reste*) remains *pl*; (*Leichnam*) corpse; (*Gliedmaßen*) limbs *pl*; **~~haus** *n* ossuary; **~bell** *n* yelping, barking; (*Kläffen*) yapping; (*Heulen*) howling; (*Hunde*) bay; (*Schelten*) scolding; (*Schreien*) bawling.

geben *irr tr* to give; (*schenken*) to present with, to give away; (*reichen*) to present, to hand over, to turn over; (*gewähren*) to grant, to accord, to award, *Am* to donate (to); (*zuteilen*) to apportion, to allot, to assign; (*Karten*) to deal; (*Tennis*) to serve; *Sie ~* it's your deal; it's your service; *theat* to act, to perform; (*Rolle*) to fill; (*aufgeben*) to give up, to succumb; (*sich ergeben*) to give o. s. up to; (*widmen*) to devote, to addict; (*anbieten*) to offer; *tele* to transmit, to send; (*liefern*) to deliver, to transfer; to furnish, to supply; (*Titel*) to bestow on, to confer s. th. upon s. o.; (*bezahlen*) to pay, to remunerate, to compensate; (*verkaufen*) to sell, to dispose of; (*ausdrücken*) to render, to express, to interpret; (*Ertrag*) to yield; (*Frucht*) to bear, to produce; *von sich ~* (*Ton*) to utter; (*Nahrung*) to vomit, to bring up; (*weggeben*) to part with; (*aussenden*) to emit, *chem* to evolve; *sich ~* (*nachlassen*) to relent; (*Eifer*) to cool; (*Schmerz*) to abate; (*ergeben*) to yield, to surrender, to give in; (*sich ausgeben als*) to pretend to be, to make believe, to simulate, to pass off for; *es gibt* there is, there are; *was gibt es Neues?* what is the news? what's up? *das gibt's nicht!* there's no such thing! *so etw gibt es!* such things do happen! *gibt es heute Regen?* are we going to have rain today? *auf jdn etw ~* to set great store by, to attach value to; *was darf ich Ihnen ~?* what will you have? *was wird heute abend im Theater ge~?* what are they showing at the theatre this evening? *darauf gibt er nichts* he doesn't give a hoot about that; *~ Sie mir Fred! tele* let me have Fred! *ich gebe ihm die Hand* I shake hands with him; *das gibt mir zu denken!* that makes me wonder! *er hat es ihm aber ordentlich ge~* he really let him have it; *sie muß sich damit zufrieden ~* she has to be satisfied with it; *das Stück wurde fünf Monate ge~* the play ran for five months; *ich muß ein gutes Beispiel ~* I must set a good example; *er gab sich große Mühe* he took great pains; *es wird sich schon ~* it'll be all right; *es wird sich ~* it will settle down in course of time; *sich zufrieden ~* to content o. s.; *sich zu erkennen ~* to make o. s. known; *~ ist seliger denn Nehmen* it is more blessed to give than to receive; *gegeben: zur gegebenen Zeit* at a given time; *innerhalb e-r gegebenen Frist* within a given period; *e-e gegebene Größe* a given magnitude; *sind A u. B gegeben, so folgt C* given A and B, C follows; *die Voraussetzungen sind gegeben* the requirements are present; *gegebenenfalls* if need arise; if so; eventually.

Geber *m*, **~in** *f* giver, presenter; (*Stifter*) donor; *tele* transmitting station, transmitter.

Gebet *n* prayer; *sein ~ sprechen* to say o.'s prayers, (*Tischgebet*) to say grace; *ins ~ nehmen* to question closely; *das ~ des Herrn* the Lord's Prayer; **~buch** *n* prayer-book; **~steppich** *m* prayer-rug.

Gebiet *n* territory, district, region; (*Fläche*) area; (*Herrschaft*) dominion; (*Boden*) soil; (*Strecke*) ground; (*Landstrich*) tract; (*Gelände*) terrain; (*Fluß~*) river-basin; *fig* (*Arbeits~*) field, domain, province, sphere, territory, bailiwick; **~en** *irr tr, itr* to command, to order; (*verlangen*) to bid; (*einschärfen*) to enjoin; (*beauftragen*) to instruct, to direct, to charge; (*sagen*) to tell; (*herrschen*) to rule, to govern; *Stillschweigen ~~* to impose silence; (*verfügen über*) to have at o.'s disposal; *den Tränen ~~* to restrain tears; *seinen Leidenschaften ~~* to check o.'s passions; *Ehrfurcht ~~* to command respect; **~er** *m* commander, master, lord, governor, ruler; **~erin** *f* mistress, lady; **~erisch** *a* imperious, dictatorial; commanding, despotic; (*anmaßend*) overbearing; (*entschieden*) peremptory; (*unwiderstehlich*) irresistible; *in e-m ~~en Tone sprechen* to speak peremptorily; **~sbeauftragte(r)** *m* area commissioner.

Ge|bilde *n* creation; (*Erzeugnis*) product; (*Arbeit*) work; *geol* formation; (*Gestalt*) form; (*Phantasie*) vision; (*Bild*) image; (*Weberei*) diaper; **~~t** *a* educated, cultivated, civilized, well--bred, cultured; *die ~~ten* the educated classes; **~bimmel** *n* ringing, tinkle, jingle; **~binde** *n* (*von Garn*) skein; (*Knäuel*) hank; (*Getreide*) sheaf; (*Ziegel*) row; (*Bündel*) bundle; *arch* truss; (*Blumen*) string of flowers; (*Girlande*) festoon; (*Faß*) barrel, cask.

Gebirg|e *n* mountains *pl*; (*Hochland*) highlands *pl*; mountain-chain (*od* range); *min* country, ground, strata; *festes ~e* solid rock; **~ig** *a* mountainous; **~sartillerie** *f* mountain artillery; **~sausläufer** *m* spur; **~sbeschreibung** *f* orography; **~sbewohner** *m* mountaineer; **~seisenbahn** *f* mountain-railway; **~sfaltung** *f* mountain folding; **~sgegend** *f* mountainous region; **~sgrat, ~skamm, ~srücken** *m* mountain ridge; **~sjäger** *m pl mil* mountain troops *pl*; **~sjoch** *n* mountain pass; **~skessel** *m* hollow; **~skette** *f*, **~szug** *m* chain of mountains; **~skunde** *f* orology; **~sland** *n* highland(s *pl*), mountainous country; **~spaß** *m* mountain-pass, defile; **~sschlucht** *f* gorge, (*Hohlweg*) ravine, (*enges Tal*) glen; **~sspalte** *f* pin-crack; **~sstrom** *m* torrent; **~stal** *n* mountain--valley; **~swand** *f* mountain face, rocky shelf; **~szug** *m* = *~skette.*

Ge|biß *n* set of teeth; (*künstliches*) denture; (*Zaum*) bit; **~bläse** *n* (*Blasebalg*) bellows *pl*; *tech* blast, blower; supercharger; (*Hochofen*) airpipe; **~~motor** *m* forced induction engine; blower motor; **~~rad** *n* blower wheel, impeller, *Am* fan-wheel; **~blök** *n* (*der Schafe*) bleating; (*der Rinder*) low(ing); **~blümt** *a* flowered; (*Blumenornament*) floriated; *fig* florid, flowery, ornate; **~blüt** *n* blood, line; (*Abstammung*) descent, lineage; (*Rasse*) race; **~bogen** *a* bent, curved; **~boren** *a, pp* born; (*eingeboren*) native; *ehelich ~~* born in wedlock; *unehelich ~~* born out of wedlock; *~~er Deutscher* German by birth; *~~er Londoner* a native of London; *sie ist e-e ~~e N.* her maiden name is N.; *Frau N., ~~e X* Mrs. N., née X; *~~ werden* to be born; *tot ~~* still-born; *adlig ~~* born of noble blood; *unter e-m glücklichen Stern ~~ sein* to be born under a lucky star, to be born with a silver spoon in o.'s mouth; **~borgen** *a* safe, secured; **~bot** *n* order; law; (*Vorschrift*) precept; ordinance; (*Auktion*) bid(ding); (*Angebot*) offer; (*Erlaß*) decree; *höchstes ~~* highest bid; *ein ~~ machen* to submit a bid; *das erste ~~ machen* to start the bidding; *Not kennt kein ~~* necessity has no law; *die zehn ~~e* the Ten Commandments *pl*, the Decalogue; *jdm zu ~~e stehen* to be at s. o.'s disposal; **~boten** *a* imperative, necessary; **~bräu** *n* brewage; brew(ing); (*Mischung*) mixture; (*Trank*) draught; *med u. verächtlich* concoction.

Gebrauch *m* use; (*Anwendung*) employment; (*Gepflogenheit*) practice; (*Gewohnheit*) custom, habit, usage, ways *pl*; *von etw ~ machen* to make use of; *außer ~ kommen* to fall into disuse, to pass out of use; *im ~* in use; *außer ~ setzen* to invalidate; *heilige Gebräuche pl* sacred rites *pl*; **~en** *tr* to use, to employ, to avail o. s. of; (*benötigen*) to need, to want; *Gewalt ~~* to have recourse to violence; *er ist zu nichts zu ~~* he is good for nothing; *das ist nicht zu ~~* this is of no use; *alle Mittel ~~* to leave no stone unturned; *sich ~~ lassen zu* to lend o. s. to; *~te Kleider* second-hand (*od* worn) clothes; *~tes Auto* reconditioned (*od* rebuilt) car; **~sanweisung** *f* direction for use, instructions *pl*; **~seignung** *f tech* usability, applicability; **~sfertig** *a* ready for use; **~sgegenstand** *m* useful article; requisite; commodity; **~sgraphiker** *m* graphic artist, advertising artist; **~smuster** *n* registered pattern (*od* design); simplified type of patent, sample; **~swert** *m* economic value; **~t** *a* used; (*aus zweiter Hand*) second hand; **~twagenmarkt** *m* used-car market; **~twaren** *f pl* second-hand articles *pl.*

gebräuchlich *a* in use; (*üblich*) customary, wanted, usual; (*gewöhnlich*) ordinary; (*Ausdruck*) current; *nicht mehr ~* out of use, obsolete, antiquated.

Ge|brause *n* roaring, boisterousness; (*Ohren*) ringing; **~brechen** *n* (*Fehler*) want, deficiency; (*körperlich*) defect, infirmity, affliction; *~~ irr: es gebricht mir an Geld* I am short of (*od* in need of) money; **~brechlich** *a* (*schwach*) weak; (*zerbrechlich*) fragile; (*spröde*) brittle; (*wackelig*) rickety; (*kraftlos*) infirm; (*altersschwach*) decrepit; (*hinfällig*) frail; (*Boxen*) groggy; (*saftlos*) sapless; **~~keit** *f* infirmity, frailty; decrepitude; weakness, feebleness; **~brochen** *a* broken, ruined; **~brodel** *n* boiling; **~brüder** *pl* brothers *pl*; *com ~~ Brown* Brown Brothers, *Abk* Bros.; **~brüll** *n* roaring; (*der Kühe*) lowing;

~brumme *n* humming; (*Knurren*) growl(ing); *fig* grumbling.
Gebühr *f* due; (*Pflicht*) duty; (*Schicklichkeit*) decency; (*Geld*) charge, fee, rate; (*Steuer*) tax; *nach ~* according to merit; *über ~* unduly, immoderately; *zu herabgesetzter ~* at a reduced fee; *gegen Zahlung der ~* upon payment of charges; *gesetzliche ~* fee required by law; *e-e ~ erheben* to exact fees; *doppelte ~* double rate; *über die ~* beyond all measure; **~en** *pl* charges *pl*; fee; taxes *pl*; rates *pl*; **~~erlaß** *m* remission of fees; **~~ermäßigung** *f* reduction of charge; **~~festsetzung** *f* rate making; **~~frei** *a* free of charge, exempt from duty; **~~ordnung** *f* scale of fees, tariff; **~~pflichtig** *a* liable to a fee, chargeable, taxable; (*Brief*) postage to be paid; **~~vorschuß** *m* *jur* retainer; **~en** *itr* (*jdm*) to belong to, to be due to; *wie es sich gebührt* as it ought to be; *Ehre, wem Ehre gebührt* hono(u)r to whom hono(u)r is due; **~end, ~lich** *a* fit, proper; seemly; becoming; (*angemessen*) suitable to (*od* for); (*schuldig*) due; **~endermaßen** *adv* properly, duly; (*verdient*) deservedly.
Gebund *n* bunch; (*vom Garn*) skein; **~en** *a* bound, connected; *in ~~er Rede* in verse, metrically; **~~heit** *f* constraint; (*Kürze*) conciseness.
Geburt *f* birth; (*Entbindung*) confinement, delivery, child-bearing; (*Gebären*) parturition; (*Abstammung*) descent, extraction; *fig* rise, origin; *von ~* by birth; *vor Christi ~* before Christ (B. C.); *ein Deutscher von ~* **a** German born; **~enbeschränkung, ~enkontrolle, ~enregelung** *f* birth-control; **~enrückgang** *m* falling birth-rate; **~enüberschuß** *m* excess of births; **~enziffer** *f* birth-rate, natality; **~sadel** *m* inherited nobility; **~sanzeige** *f* notification of a birth; **~sfehler** *m* congenital defect; **~shaus** *n* house at which s. o. was born; **~shelfer** *m* obstetrician, accoucheur; **~~in** *f* midwife; **~shilfe** *f* obstetrics *pl*; **~sjahr** *n* year of birth; **~sjahrgang** *m* age class; **~sort** *m* birth-place, native place; **~sschein** *m* certificate of birth; **~sstadt** *f* native town; **~stag** *m* birthday; **~~sfeier** *f* birthday-party; **~~sgeschenke** *n pl* birthday presents (*od* gifts); **~~skind** *n* birthday celebrant; **~~skuchen** *m* birthday cake; **~~sstrauß** *m* birthday bouquet; **~~stisch** *m* birthday table; **~surkunde** *f* birth certificate; **~swehen** *f pl* (labo(u)r-) pains *pl*, labo(u)r, throes *pl*; *in den ~~ liegen* to be in labo(u)r; **~szange** *f* forceps.
gebürtig *a* native (of), born (in).
Gebüsch *n* bushes *pl*; underbrush; shrubbery; (*Dickicht*) thicket; (*Gehölz*) underwood, coppice, copse.
Geck *m* dandy, swell, beau, coxcomb, *Am fam* dude, mash(er), fop; (*Dummkopf*) fool; **~enhaft** *a* dandyish, foppish.
gedacht *a* imaginary; fictitious; conceived, assumed.
Gedächtnis *n* (*Fähigkeit*) memory; (*Denken*) remembrance, recollection; (*Erinnern*) reminiscence; *zum ~* in remembrance of; *im ~ behalten* to keep in mind; *aus dem ~* by heart, from memory; *jdm etw ins ~ zurückrufen* to remind s. o. of s. th.; *sich ins ~ zurückrufen* to recall to o.'s mind; *prägen Sie das Ihrem ~ ein* commit that to your memory; *es ist meinem ~ entfallen* it has escaped my memory; **~feier** *f* commemoration, memorial day; (*Jahrestag*) anniversary; **~gottesdienst** *m* memorial service; **~hilfe** *f* aid to memory; **~kirche** *f* memorial church; **~kraft** *f* memory; **~kunst** *f* mnemo(tech)nics *pl*; **~rede** *f* commemorative speech (*od* address); **~schwäche** *f* weakness of the memory; **~übung** *f* mnemonic exercise.
gedämpft *a* suppressed; (*Schall*) deadened; damped, deadbeat.
Gedanke *m* thought; (*Absicht*) intention; (*Plan*) design; plan; (*Vorstellung*) idea; (*Begriff*) concept; conception; (*unbestimmte Vorstellung*) notion; (*Eindruck*) impression; (*Ansicht*) opinion; (*Erinnerung*) memory; *~n sind zollfrei* thoughts are free; *mir kam der ~* the thought struck me; *seine ~n nicht beisammen haben* to be absent-minded; *der leitende ~ in* the leading thought of; *e-n ~n fassen* to conceive a thought; *jds ~n lesen* to read s. o.'s thoughts; *der Wunsch ist der Vater des ~ns* the wish is father to the thought; *schlagen Sie sich das aus den ~n* put that out of your head; *es ist gar kein ~ daran, daß* it is quite out of the question that; *sie war in tiefen ~n* she was in a brown study; *seine ~n umreißen* to outline o.'s ideas; *wie kommen Sie auf den ~n?* what gives you that idea? *sie tragen sich mit dem ~n* they are considering; *in ~n sein* to be absorbed in thought; *mit dem ~n umgehen* to intend to do; *auf andere ~n bringen* to divert s. o.'s thoughts; *sich ~n machen* to worry; **~narmut** *f* lack of ideas; **~naustausch** *m* exchange of thoughts; **~nblitz** *m* flash of wit; **~nfolge** *f*, **~ngang** *m* train of thoughts; **~nfreiheit** *f* freedom of thought; **~nleser** *m* thought-reader; **~nlos** *a* thoughtless; *~~ dahinleben* to live in a fool's paradise; **~~igkeit** *f* thoughtlessness; **~nlyrik** *f* philosophical poetry; **~nreich** *a* rich in ideas; **~nschnelle** *f*: *mit ~~* quick as lightning; **~nspäne** *m pl* aphorisms *pl*; **~nstrich** *m* dash; **~nübertragung** *f* thought-transference, telepathy; **~nverbindung, ~nverkettung** *f* association of ideas; **~nvoll** *a* thoughtful; (*sorgenvoll*) full of cares; (*nachdenklich*) pensive; **~nwelt** *f* world of ideas.
gedanklich *a* intellectual, mental.
Ge\|därm *n* bowels *pl*; intestines *pl*, entrails *pl*; (*Kaldaunen*) tripe; **~deck** *n* covering, cover; (*Tisch*) knife and fork; **~deihen** *irr itr* to thrive, to prosper; to do well; (*blühen*) to flourish; (*gelingen*) to succeed; (*vermehren*) to increase, to grow; (*ergeben*) to turn out, to result; *unrecht Gut gedeiht nicht* ill-gotten wealth does not thrive; *die Angelegenheit ist soweit gediehen* the affair has now reached such a point; *wie weit sind die Verhandlungen gediehen?* how far have the negotiations progressed? *dahin ~~* to come to; *~~ n* growth, prosperity; *auf ~deih u. Verderben* for better or for worse; **~deihlich** *a* thriving, prosperous; successful; **~denken** *irr itr: jds ~~* to think of; *e-r Sache ~~* to remember; *tr* (*erwähnen*) to mention; (*ehrend ~~*) to hono(u)r; (*beabsichtigen*) to intend; *ich will es ihm ~~* I will make him remember it; *was gedenken Sie zu tun?* what do you intend to do? *~~ n* memory, recollection; *seit Menschen-~~* within the memory of man; **~denkausgabe** *f* memorial issue; **~denkfeier** *f* commemoration; **~denkmarke** *f* commemorative stamp; **~denkspruch** *m* motto; **~denkstein** *m* memorial (stone); **~denktafel** *f* memorial tablet; **~denktag** *m* remembrance day; anniversary; **~dicht** *n* poem; **~~sammlung** *f* anthology; **~diegen** *a* *min* pure, unmixed, genuine; *fig* (*echt, lauter*) true, solid; (*zuverlässig*) reliable; (*gründlich*) thorough; **~~heit** *f* *min* purity, genuineness; *fig* soundness, solidity, sterling quality; reliability; thoroughness; **~dinge** *n* bargain, contractwork, piecework; *im ~~ arbeiten* to work by the piece; **~dränge** *n* crowd, throng; (*Am Fußball*) scrummage; *fig* (*Notlage*) trouble, embarrassment; **~drängt** *a* narrow; (*Stil*) concise, succinct; *~~ voll* much crowded; *Am* jammed; **~~heit** *f* closeness; (*des Stils*) conciseness, terseness, succinctness; **~drückt** *a pp* depressed; (*Preise*) low; (*schwierig*) difficult; **~~heit** *f* depression; **~drungen** *a* stout, compact; (*genötigt*) compelled; **~~heit** *f* compactness; **~duld** *f* patience; (*Nachsicht*) forbearance, indulgence; (*Ausdauer*) perseverance, endurance; (*Verzicht*) resignation; (*Langmut*) long-suffering, longanimity; *schließlich verlor ich die ~~* finally I lost my patience; *das stellt meine ~~ auf die Probe* that tasks my patience; **~dulden** *r* to have patience; to wait patiently; **~duldig** *a* patient; (*nachsichtig*) forbearing, indulgent; *~~ ertragen* to be patient (of); *Papier ist ~~* paper does not blush; **~duldsfaden** *m*: *ihm riß der ~~* he lost patience; **~duldsprobe** *f* trial of patience; **~duldspiel** *n* puzzle; **~dunsen** *a* sodden; bloated, puffed up.
geerdet *a* earthed, grounded, earth-connected.
Ge\|ehrtes *n com* (*veraltet*); *Ihr ~~ vom* your favo(u)r of; *ich fühle mich ~ehrt* I feel hono(u)red; *sehr ~ehrter Herr!* Dear Sir, My dear Mr. X., *Am* Dear Mr. X.; **~eignet** *a* suitable, fit (*zu* for), appropriate (to, for); *er ist nicht die ~~e Person* he is not the right person; *der ~~e Augenblick* the favo(u)rable moment.
Geest *f* high and dry land.
Ge\|fahr *f* danger; peril; (*Bedrohung*) menace; (*Wagnis*) risk, hazard, jeopardy; *~~ laufen* to run the risk; *auf Ihre ~~* at your risk; *auf die ~~ hin* at the risk of; *es hat keine ~~* there is no risk; *wer sich mutwillig in ~~ begibt, kommt darin um* he who ventures into danger is likely to perish in it; *jdn der ~~ aussetzen* to expose s. o. to danger; *in ~~ bringen* to endanger; *für Rechnung u. ~~ von* for account and risk of; **~~engebiet** *n* danger zone; **~~enherd** *m* danger spot; **~~enmeldung** *f* warning of danger; **~~enpunkt** *m* danger point; **~~enzone** *f* danger area; **~~enzulage** *f* danger pay; **~fährden** *tr* to endanger, to imperil; **~fährlich** *a* dangerous, perilous, risky, hazardous; *fig* critical; *~~ verwundet* heavy wounded; **~~keit** *f* dangerousness; **~fahrlos** *a* safe; without danger; **~fahrlosigkeit** *f* safety, security; **~fahrvoll** *a* dangerous, perilous.
Ge\|fährt *n* vehicle; **~fährte** *m* companion, fellow; (*Kamerad*) comrade; (*Teilhaber*) associate, partner; (*Kollege*) colleague; (*intimer Freund*) chum; **~fälle** *n* (*Abhang*) slope; incline; (*Fluß*) fall; (*Ausgaben*) expenses *pl*; (*Einkünfte*) rents *pl*, income; **~fallen** *irr itr* to please; to like; to suit; *es ~fällt mir* I like it; I am pleased with it; *sich etw ~~ lassen* to put up with s. th., to be pleased with s. th.; to consent to; *das lasse ich mir nicht ~~*

I won't stand it; *es ist schwer, jedermann zu ~~* it's hard to suit everybody; *wie hat ihm der Film ~~?* how did he enjoy the picture? *r* to flatter o. s. with; **~fallen** *n* pleasure; (*Gefälligkeit*) kindness, favo(u)r; *~~ finden an* to take a pleasure in, to take a fancy to; *ich werde dir den ~~ erweisen* I'll do you the favo(u)r; *sie tat es ihm zum ~~* she did it to please him; *jdm e-n ~~ tun* to oblige s. o. with s. th.; *bei Nicht~~ Geld zurück* your money refunded if you are not pleased; **~fallen** *pp, a* killed in action; **~~e(r)** *m* fallen person; *mil die ~~en* the dead, the killed; **~fällig** *a* complaisant to; pleasing, courteous; *wenn es Ihnen ~~ ist* if you please; *was ist Ihnen ~~?* what can I do for you? can I help you? *sie ist immer ~~* she is always obliging; *Ihrer ~~en Antwort entgegensehend com* awaiting (the favo(u)r of) your reply; **~~keit** *f* complaisance, courteousness, kindness, favo(u)r; *aus ~~keit* as a favo(u)r; *jdm e-e ~~keit erweisen* to do s. o. a good turn; *darf ich Sie um e-e ~~keit bitten?* may I ask a favo(u)r of you? **~~keitsakzept** *n*, **~~keitswechsel** *m* accommodation bill; **~~keitslüge** *f* white lie; **~fälligst** *adv* please; **~fallsucht** *f* desire to please; (*weibliche*) coquetry; **~fallsüchtig** *a* coquettish.

gefangen *a: ~nehmen* to take prisoner; (*verhaften*) to arrest, to apprehend; *fig* to captivate; *sich ~ geben* to surrender; *~ halten* to detain; *~ setzen* to imprison; **~e(r)** *m* prisoner, captive; (*Kriegs~~*) prisoner of war, *Abk* P. W.; **~~nanstalt** *f* house of detention; **~~naussage** *f* prisoner's statement; **~~nlager** *n* prison(ers') camp; **~~nsammelstelle** *f* prisoners' collecting point; **~~ntransport** *m* prisoner transport; **~~nvernehmung** *f* interrogation of prisoners; **~~nwagen** *m* prison van, *fam* Black Maria, *Am* patrolwagon; **~nahme, ~nehmung** *f* capture, seizure; **~setzung** *f* arrest; imprisonment; capture; **~schaft** *f* captivity; (*Haft*) custody, imprisonment; confinement; *in ~~ geraten* to be taken prisoner; **~wärter** *m* jailer.

Gefängnis *n* (*Ort*) prison, gaol, jail, cage; *Am* (*Einzelstaat*) state prison; (*Strafe*) imprisonment; *~ bis zu 3 Jahren* imprisonment not more than three years; *im ~ abbüßen* to serve o.'s time; *ins ~ stecken* to put in jail; **~direktor** *m* governor, *Am* warden of a prison; **~haft** *f* detention; **~hof** *m* prison yard; **~ordnung** *f* prison rules *pl*; **~strafe** *f* imprisonment; *zu ~~ verurteilen* to commit to prison; **~verwaltung** *f* penal administration; **~wagen** *m* prison van; Black Maria, *Am* patrol wagon; **~wärter** *m* gaoler, jailer; turnkey; *Am* guard.

Ge|fäß *n* (auch *med*) vessel; receptacle; container; pot; tank; (*Degen*) hilt; **~faßt** *a* prepared for; (*ruhig*) collected, calm; composed; *auf das Schlimmste ~~ sein* to be prepared for the worst; *sich ~~ machen auf* to be ready for.

Gefecht *n* fight, engagement, encounter; (*Treffen*) action; (*Scharmützel*) skirmish; (*Schlacht*) battle; (*Kampf*) combat; *außer ~ setzen* to put out of action; *zum ~ entwickeln* to deploy for action; *hinhaltendes ~* delaying action; containing action; *das ~ abbrechen* to withdraw from action; **~sabschnitt** *m* battle sector; **~saufklärung** *f* close reconnaissance; **~saufstellung** *f* battle disposition; **~sauftrag** *m* combat mission; **~sausbildung** *f* combat training; **~sausfälle** *m pl* combat losses *pl*; **~sbefehl** *m* combat (*od* operation) order; **~sbereich** *m* combat area, zone of action; **~sbereitschaft** *f* readiness for action; *~~ befehlen* (*mar*) to order (*od* sound) general quarters; **~sbericht** *m* combat report; **~sberührung** *f* contact; **~sbreite** *f* combat frontage; **~seinheit** *f* combat unit; **~seinsatz** *m* commitment to action; **~sentwicklung** *f* deployment for action; **~sfahrzeug** *n* combat car; (*gepanzert*) tank; **~sfeld** *n* battlefield; **~sgliederung** *f* tactical grouping; **~shandlung** *f* engagement; operation; **~sklar** *a* cleared for action; **~slage** *f* combat situation, tactical situation (*od* conditions); **~slärm** *m* noise of battle; **~slinie** *f* line of battle; **~smeldung** *f* combat report; **~spause** *f mil* lull; **~sraum** *m* combat area, zone of action; **~ssicherung** *f* combat security; **~sstand** *m* command post; *aero* (*unterer*) ball turret, (*oberer*) top turret; **~sstärke** *f* fighting strength; **~sstreifen** *m* battle zone; zone of action; **~sstätigkeit** *f* combat activity; **~sverlauf** *m* course of action; **~svorposten** *m* combat outpost; **~swert** *m* combat (*od* fighting) value; **~sziel** *n* objective; **~szone** *f* combat zone.

ge|feit *a* invulnerable to; immune (from); proof (against); **~fieder** *n* feathers *pl*; plumage; **~~t** *a* feathered; *bot* pinnate; **~filde** *n* plain; fields *pl*; domain; (*der Seligen*) Elysium; **~flammt** *a* blazing; **~flatter** *n* fluttering; **~flecht** *n* texture; (*aus Holz*) hurdle-work; (*aus Weiden*) wickerwork; *anat* plexus; **~fleckt** *a* speckled; spotted; (*Gesicht*) freckled; (*besudelt*) blotted; **~flissentlich** *a* intentional, premeditated; wilful; *adv* on purpose.

Geflügel *n* birds *pl*, fowls *pl*, poultry; **~farm** *f* poultry farm; **~händler** *m* poulterer; **~t** *a* winged; *~~e Worte* familiar sayings *pl*, household words *pl*; **~zucht** *f* poultry-farming; **~züchter** *m* poultry raiser.

Ge|flunker *n* flummery; bragging; humbug; **~flüster** *n* whispering; **~folge** *n* suite, entourage, train, attendance; followers *pl*; *im ~~ haben* to be attended with; to lead to; **~folgschaft** *f* followers *pl*; (*Fabrik*) personnel; staff; (*Anhänger*) adherents *pl*; (*Schüler*) disciples *pl*; **~folgsmann** *m* follower; (*Lehnsmann*) vassal; retainer; **~fräßig** *a* voracious, greedy, gluttonous; **~~keit** *f* greediness; gluttony; **~freite(r)** *m* lance-corporal, *Am* Private first class, *Abk* Pfc.; *mar* leading seaman; *aero* aircraftman 1; **~frieranlage** *f* freezing plant; **~frierapparat** *m* freezing apparatus, freezer; **~frierbar** *a* congealable; **~frieren** *irr itr* to freeze, to congeal; **~frierfleisch** *n* frozen meat; **~frierpunkt** *m* freezing point; *unter ~~* sub-freezing temperature; *auf dem ~~ stehen* to be at zero; **~frierschrank** *m* (electric) deep-freezer, freezer cabinet; **~frierschutzmittel** *n* antifreeze; **~froren** *a* frozen; **~~e(s)** *n* ice(-cream); *Am* sherbet; **~füge** *n* (*Gewebe*) texture; (*Schicht*) layer, stratum; (*Struktur*) structure, construction, frame; **~~änderung** *f* structural change; **~~los** *a* structureless; **~fügig** *a* pliable flexible; *fig* pliant, docile; **~~keit** *f* pliancy; *fig* docility.

Gefühl *n* feeling; sentiment; (*Bewegung*) emotion; (*Wahrnehmung*) sensation; (*Sinn*) sense; (*Empfindung*) sensibility; (*Tastsinn*) touch; *ich habe das ~* I have a feeling; *für mein ~* to my mind; *~ für Anstand* sense of propriety; *~ der Wärme* sensation of warmth; *sie trägt ihre ~e offen zur Schau* she bears her heart upon her sleeve; *den ~en freien Lauf lassen fig* to let off steam; **~los** *a* unfeeling; senseless of, apathetic; heartless; numb; **~losigkeit** *f* insensibility, senselessness; apathy; **~sausbruch** *m* display of feelings, *Am fam* splurge; **~sduselei** *f* sentimentalism; **~smensch** *m* emotional character, *fam* gushing person; **~swert** *m* emotional value; **~voll** *a* feeling, sensible; sentimental; tender.

gefüllt *a* filled, stuffed; *~e Blume* double flower.

gegebenenfalls *adv* in case.

gegen *prp* (*Richtung*; *in freundlichem Sinn*) towards; (*entgegengesetzt, feindlich*) against; *jur* versus, *Abk* v. *od* vs.; (*im Tausch*) in exchange for; (*Zeit*) about, by, *Am* around; (*entgegen*) contrary to; (*im Vergleich zu*) compared with; *~ bar* for cash; *~ Quittung* on receipt; *es ist gut ~ Kopfweh* it's good for headaches; *ich wette zehn ~ eins, daß* I bet you ten to one that; *~ Kaution entlassen* to release on bail; **~abdruck** *m* counter-impression; counterproof; **~angebot** *n* counter-offer; **~angriff** *m* counter-attack; **~anspruch** *m* counter-claim; **~anstalten** *f pl* counter-measures *pl*, retaliatory measures *pl*; **~antrag** *m* counter-motion, counter-proposal; **~antwort** *f jur* replication; **~auftrag** *m* counter-order; **~ausgleich** *m* counter-balance; **~aussage** *f* counter-evidence; **~bedingung** *f* counter-stipulation; **~befehl** *m* counter-order, countermand; **~beschuldigung** *f* counter-evidence; recrimination; **~besuch** *m* return visit; *e-n ~~ machen* to return a visit; **~bewegung** *f* reaction, *tech* counter-movement; *pol* underground movement; **~beweis** *m* counter-evidence; (*Zeugen*) rebuttal testimony; *e-n ~~ antreten* to put forward a counter-evidence; **~blockade** *f* counter-blockade; **~buch** *n* book of control, memobook; **~buchung** *f* cross-entry, set-off; **~bürge** *m* counter-bail; **~bürgschaft** *f* countersecurity.

Gegend *f* region; (*Himmels~*) part, quarter; *umliegende ~* environs *pl*; (*Gebiet*) district; area; zone; (*Nachbarschaft*) neighbo(u)rhood, section, vicinity; (*Land*) country; *in welcher ~?* where abouts? *aus welcher ~ kommen Sie?* what part of the country do you come from?

Gegen|dampf *m* counter-steam; **~dienst** *m* return service; *e-n ~~ leisten* to return s. o.'s favo(u)r; *zu ~~en gerne bereit* glad to reciprocate; **~druck** *m* reaction, resistance; *tech* back pressure, counter-pressure; **~~turbine** *f* back pressure turbine; **~einander** *adv* against one another; towards each other; head-on; (*~seitig*) reciprocally, mutually; *etw ~~ haben* to be at variance with; *~~ halten* to compare together; *~~ stellen* to confront with one another; **~erklärung** *f* counter-declaration; **~farbe** *f* complementary colo(u)r; contrast of colo(u)rs; **~feuer** *n mil* retaliation fire; **~forderung** *f* counter-claim; **~funkstelle** *f* answering station; repeating station; **~füßler** *m* antipode; **~gabe** *f*, **~geschenk** *n* present in return; *ein ~~ machen* to return a present; **~gewicht** *n* counterweight; counterpoise; *das ~~ halten* to counterbalance; *ungeerdetes ~~* earth screen; **~gift** *n* antidote; antitoxin; **~grund** *m* counter-argument; **~gruß** *m* reciprocal greeting; *mar* return-salute; **~kaiser** *m* rival emperor; **~kandidat** *m* candidate of the opposition; **~klage** *f* countercharge; **~kläger** *m* recriminator; counter-pleader; **~kraft** *f* counteracting force; opposing force; bias; **~kurs** *m* *mar* head away from port, outward course, *aero* flight away from airport; **~läufig** *a* countercurrent; contrarotating; **~leistung** *f* return service, equivalent; counter-performance; *jur* consideration; *als ~~ für* in return for; *ohne ~~* gratuitous; *jur* without valuable consideration; **~licht** *n* false light; *phot* opposite light; *film Am* backlight; **~liebe** *f* mutual love, return of love; *mein Vorschlag fand keine ~~* my proposal met with no support; **~maßnahme, ~maßregel** *f* countermeasure; (*gewaltsam*) reprisal; (*vorbeugend*) preventive measure; *~~n treffen* to counter; **~mine** *f* countermine; **~mittel** *n* (prophylactic) antidote, remedy; **~mutter** *f* lock- (*od* counter-)nut; **~offensive** *f* counter-offensive; **~papst** *m* antipope; **~part** *m* adversary; **~partei** *f* opposite party; (party in) opposition; **~pol** *m* *tech* antipole, reciprocal pole; **~probe** *f* counter-proof; check determination, check test; **~propaganda** *f* counter-propaganda; **~quittung** *f* counter-note; **~rechnung** *f* control account; counterclaim; **~rede** *f* contradiction; (*Antwort*) reply; *jur* counter-plea; **~reformation** *f* counter-reformation; **~revolution** *f* counter-revolution; **~~är** *m* counter-revolutionary; **~satz** *m* contrast, opposite, contrary; (*Hintergrund*) foil; (*Widerspruch*) opposition; (*Ungleichheit*) dissimilarity, unlikeness, disparity; (*Wissenschaft*) antithesis; (*Streitigkeiten*) differences *pl*; *im ~~ zu* contrary to; in opposition to; **~sätzlich** *a* contrary; antithetical; adverse, opposite; **~schlag** *m* counter-blow; **~schrift** *f* refutation; rejoinder; written reply; **~seite** *f* opposite side, reverse; opponent; the other party; **~seitig** *a* mutual, reciprocal; **~~keit** *f* reciprocity; *Abkommen auf ~~keit* mutual agreement; *das beruht auf ~~keit* I feel just the same; *auf der Grundlage der ~~keit* on the basis of reciprocity; **~signal** *n* answering signal, reply; **~spieler** *m* opponent, antagonist; **~spionage** *f* counterespionage, *Am* counterintelligence; **~sprechverkehr** *m* two-way telephone conversation; **~stand** *m* object, item; (*Angelegenheit*) affair; matter; (*als Thema*) topic, subject, theme; *~~ e-s Vertrags* subject-matter of a contract; *zum ~~ haben* to bear upon; **~~slos** *a* to no purpose, fruitless; unnecessary, superfluous; *~~slos machen* to cancel, to abrogate; *~~slos werden* to become obsolete; **~ständlich** *a* objective; (*anschaulich*) graphic; (*deutlich*) perspicuous; **~stelle** *f* *radio* called station; **~stollen** *m* countermine; **~stoß** *m* counter-thrust; (*~rede*) counterblast; *mil* counter-attack; **~strich** *m* stroke against the hair; **~strom** *m* counter-current; **~strömung** *f* eddy; (*Meer*) undertow, underset, *Am* riptide; **~stück** *n* counterpart; match; tally; **~takt** *m* *radio* push-pull; **~teil** *n* contrary; reverse; opposite; antithesis; *ins ~~ verkehren* to negate an effect; *im ~~* on the contrary; *das ~~ ist richtig* the case is quite the reverse; **~teilig** *a* opposite; to the contrary.

gegenüber *adv, prp* opposite to, across from, facing, in front of; (*Vergleich*) as against; over the way; (*Menschen*) face to face; *sich e-r Aufgabe ~ sehen* to be up against a task; *mir ~ ist sie immer höflich* to me she is always polite; *~ n* vis-à-vis, person sitting opposite; **~liegen** *irr itr* to lie opposite, to face; **~~d** *a* opposite; **~stehen** *irr itr* to stand opposite (*od* in front of); to face; **~stellen** *tr* to oppose (to), *jur* to confront with; *fig* to contrast; **~stellung** *f* opposition; contrast; *jur* confrontation; **~treten** *irr itr* to step in front of; *fig* to face.

Gegen|unterschrift *f* counter-signature; **~verschreibung** *f* counter-security; **~versicherung** *f* re-insurance; **~versuch** *m* control experiment; **~vorschlag** *m* counter-proposal; **~vorstellung** *f* remonstrance; **~wart** *f* presence; (*Jetztzeit*) present time; *gram* present tense; **~~swert** *m* actual value; **~wärtig** *a* present; (*tatsächlich*) actual; *adv* at present, nowadays; *~~ sein* to be present; *~~er Preis* current price; **~wehr** *f* defence, resistance; **~wert** *m* equivalent; (*Verkauf*) proceeds *pl*; (*Ausgleich*) balancing entry; *entsprechenden ~~ leisten* to give value for; *entsprechender ~~* valuable consideration; **~~mittel** *n pl* counterpart funds pl; **~wind** *m* head-wind; **~winkel** *m* alternate angle; **~wirkung** *f* reaction; counter-effect; **~zeichnen** *tr* to countersign; (*indossieren*) to back; **~zeuge** *m* counter-witness; **~zug** *m* *fig* countermove; *rail* corresponding train; *e-n ~~ machen* to countermove.

Gegner *m*, **~in** *f* adversary, opponent, rival, antagonist; (*Feind*) enemy, foe; **~isch** *a* adverse, opposing, antagonistic; hostile; of the enemy; **~schaft** *f* antagonism; (*die ~*) opposition; opponents *pl*.

Gehabe *n* behavio(u)r; *sich ~n* to behave (o. s.); *gehab dich wohl!* farewell!

Gehalt *m* (*Inhalt*) contents *pl*; (*Wert*) value, merit; (*Flüssigkeit*) titre, proportion, strength; content; (*Fassungsvermögen*) capacity; (*Münze*) alloy; (*Gold~*) standard; *~ n* salary, emoluments *pl*, pay; *mit vollem ~* on full pay; *festes ~* fixed salary; *auf das ~ angewiesen sein* to be depending on the salary; *~ beziehen* to draw a salary; *von e-m kleinen ~ leben* to live on a small salary; *auskömmliches ~* sufficient income; *das ~ erhöhen* to raise the salary; *~ entsprechend Erfahrung u. Leistung* salary commensurate with experience and ability; **~en** *a* bound, obliged; **~los** *a* empty; (*wertlos*) worthless; **~losigkeit** *f* emptiness; **~reich, ~voll** *a* solid; (*Erz*) rich; (*wertvoll*) of great value; (*Nahrung*) substantial, nutritious; **~sabteilung** *f* pay-roll division; **~sabzug** *m* deduction from the salary, stoppage; **~sangabe** *f* stating salary; (*Liste*) salary data *pl*; **~sanspruch** *m* salary demand, salary expected; **~saufbesserung** *f* increase (*Am* raise) in salary; **~sauszahlung** *f* pay-roll disbursements *pl*; **~seinstufung** *f* salary classification; **~sempfänger** *m* salary earner; salaried worker; **~serhöhung** *f* increase in salary; *um ~~ einkommen* to apply for an increase (*Am* boost) in salary; **~sforderung** *f* salary demand; **~skürzung** *f* salary cut, reduction in pay; **~sliste** *f* pay-roll; **~sstufe** *f* salary group; **~szahlung** *f* payment of salaries; **~szulage** *f* additional pay, bonus.

Ge|hänge *n* slope, declivity; (*Blumen~~*) garland, festoon; (*Ohr~~*) ear-drops *pl*; (*Degen~~*) belt; **~harnischt** *a* harnessed, steel-clad; *fig* angry; sharp; **~hässig** *a* odious; hateful; malicious, spiteful; **~~keit** *f* spitefulness, animosity; malice; **~häuse** *n* box, case; (*Kompaß*) bin(n)acle; (*Obst*) core; *tech* housing, case, shell, cage; *phot* body; (*Seidenraupe*) cocoon; (*Schnekken~~*) shell; **~hege** *n* enclosure, hedge, pen, fence; (*Jagd*) preserve; (*Pferde*) paddock; *jdm ins ~~ kommen* to encroach upon s. o.'s rights.

geheim *a* secret, under-cover; (*verborgen*) concealed, hidden; (*geheimnisvoll*) mysterious; (*unbekannt*) unknown; (*magisch*) occult; (*unerlaubt*) clandestine; (*rätselhaft*) enigmatic; (*vertraulich*) confidential; *streng ~* strictly (*od* top) secret; *~e Volksabstimmung* secret ballot; *etw ~halten* to keep secret; (*in Titeln*) Privy; *e-e ~e Treppe* backstairs; *im ~en* secretly; *streng ~* most secret, *Am* top secret; **~abkommen** *n* secret agreement; **~agent** *m* secret agent, *Am* G-man, under-cover agent; **~befehl** *m* secret order; **~bericht** *m* confidential report, *Am* inside information; **~bund** secret society; **~dienst** *m* secret service; intelligence service; **~fach** *n* secret drawer; private safe; **~haltung** *f* secrecy; privacy; **~~svorschrift** *f* instruction relative to secrecy; **~lehre** *f* esoteric doctrine; **~mittel** *n* secret remedy, arcanum; **~nis** *n* secret, (*nicht ergründbares ~~*) mystery; *ein ~~ verraten* to disclose a secret, *fam* to spill the beans; *er weihte mich in das ~~ ein* he let me into the secret; *er weiß um das ~~* he is in the secret; *ein ~~ vor jdm haben* to conceal s. th. from s. o.; *das ist das ganze ~~* that's the long and the short of it; **~~krämer** *m* mystery-monger; **~~krämerei** *f* mysterious behavio(u)r; **~~voll** *a* secret, mysterious; **~polizei** *f* secret police, *Am* Federal Bureau of Investigation, *Abk* FBI; **~polizist** *m* detective; plain-clothes officer; secret service man, *Am* G-man; **~rat** *m* Privy Councillor; **~schreiber** *m* private secretary; **~schrift** *f* cipher code (words); *Telegramm in ~~* code telegram; **~tinte** *f* sympathetic ink; **~tuerei** *f* secretiveness; mysterious conduct; **~tür** *f* secret door; **~verfügung** *f* secret order; **~vertrag** *m* secret treaty; **~wissenschaft** *f* occult science; **~zeichen** *n* secret sign.

Geheiß *n* order, command; bidding; *auf sein ~* by his order.

geh|en *irr itr* to go; (*zu Fuß*) to walk, to go on foot; (*schreiten*) to tread, to stride; (*schlendern*) to stroll; (*mühselig*) to trudge; (*wandern*) to pad; (*auf Stelzen*) to stump; (*stolz*) to strut; *tech* to go, to work, to operate, to run; (*Waren*) to be selling well; (*Zug*) to leave, to start; (*Schiff*) to be bound for; (*Teig*) to rise; (*Uhr*) to go, to run; (*Wind*) to blow; (*Zeit*) to go by; *zu jdm ~~* to go up to s. o., (*besuchen*) to call upon s. o.; *jdn ~~ lassen* to let s. o. go, (*in Ruhe lassen*) to let (*od* leave) s.o. alone; *sich ~~ lassen* to let o. s. go, to take it easy, to forget o.'s manners; *entgegen ~~* to go to meet s. o.; *in sich ~~* to take stock of s. th; *mit jdm ~~* to accompany s. o.

1. *imp*: *wie ~t es Ihnen?* how are you?

es ~t mir gut I'm well; *es ~t ihm nicht gut* he doesn't feel well; *es ~t um sein Leben* his life is at stake; *es ~t um Tod u. Leben* it's a matter of life and death; *es ~t nichts über* there is nothing better than; *es ~t ins Geld* it runs into a good deal of money; *es ~t mir auch so* I feel the same way; *wenn es nach ihm ~t* if it were upon him; *worum ~t's?* what's it all about? *es ~t auf Mittag* it is getting on to noon; *so ~t es, wenn* that is always the way when; *es ~t gegen ...* it is getting near; *es ~t auf* it will soon be; *es ~t wie der Teufel* (*fam*) it goes like hell; *wohin ~t es hier?* where does this way lead to? *es ~t!* that will do! *danke, es ~t schon* thank you, I can manage very well; *mit ihm ~t es abwärts* he's in a bad way; *es ~t nicht anders* it won't work any other way; *fig* that can't be helped; *mag es ~~, wie es will* come what will; *es ~t mir durch Mark u. Bein* it goes through and through me; *es ~t Sie nichts an!* that's none of your business! *es ~t wie am Schnürchen* it goes like clockwork; *das ~t ein bißchen zu weit* that's going a bit too far; *es ~t alles drunter u. drüber* everything is topsy-turvy.
2. *mit adv od adv Bestimmungen: auf u. ab ~~* to walk to and fro; *aus u. ein ~~* to be going in and out; *auseinander ~~* to separate; *miteinander ~~* to go together; *vor Anker ~~* to cast (*od* drop) anchor; *zur Arbeit ~~* to go to work; *jdm um den Bart ~~* to coax, to flatter s. o.; *zu Ende ~~* to be drawing near its end, (*Sache*) to be coming to an end; *in Erfüllung ~~* to come true; *essen ~~* to have a meal; *e-r Sache auf den Grund ~~* to go to the bottom of s. th.; *zur Hand ~~* to give some help; *zu Herzen ~~* to go to o.'s heart; *das ~t über meinen Horizont* that's beyond me; *durch den Kopf ~~* to pass through the head; *aufs Land ~~* to go into the country; *unter die Leute ~~* to go into society; *rascher ~~* to push on, to go faster; *mit sich zu Rate ~~* to deliberate on, to reflect seriously on; *fam schief ~~* to turn out badly; *schlafen ~~* to go to sleep; *sie ~t mir bis an die Schulter* she comes up to my shoulders; *mit großen Plänen schwanger ~~* to be full of great projects; *in Seide ~~* to wear silk; *um sicher zu ~~, frug ich nochmals* to be on the safe side, I asked again; *spazieren~~* to go for a walk; *vonstatten ~~* to take place; *das Zimmer ~t auf die Straße* the room faces (on) the street; *das Fenster ~t auf die Straße* the window looks into the street; *in gleiche Teile ~~* to be equally divided; *in Stücke ~~* to go to pieces; *meine Uhr ~t nicht* my watch has stopped; *... ~t gut ...* keeps good time; *... ~t zehn Minuten vor ...* is ten minutes fast; *... ~t nach ...* is slow; *verloren~~* to get lost; *~~ Sie voran!* after you! *behutsam zu Werke ~~* to set about cautiously; *zugrunde ~~* to go to ruin; *wie oft ~t 3 in 9?* how many times goes three into nine? **Gehen** *n* going, walking; *das ~~ wird ihm sauer* walking is getting a trouble to him; *das Kommen u. ~~* the going and returning; *die Kommenden u. ~~den, die Aus- u. Eingehenden* the comers and goers; **Sich-gehen-Lassen** *n* self-indulgence; **~er** *m* walker; **~rock** *m* frock-coat; *Am* Prince Albert; **~versuch** *m* attempt of walking; **~weg** *m* pavement, *Am* sidewalk; **~werk** *n* (*Uhr*) clock- (*od* wheel-)work; works *pl*; **~werkzeuge** *n pl* limbs *pl*.

Ge|henk *n* sword-belt; **~henkte(r)** *m* hanged man; **~heuer** *a* secure; *es ist nicht ~~ hier* this place is haunted; *die Sache ist nicht ~~* there's s. th. shaky about it; *es ist mir nicht ~~* I don't feel quite at my ease, *Am* that sounds fishy to me; **~heul** *n* howling; **~hilfe** *m*, **~hilfin** *f* assistant, mate, help; *com* clerk; (*Handwerker~~*) journeyman.

Gehirn *n* brain, brains *pl*; *fig* sense; **~erschütterung** *f* concussion of the brain; **~erweichung** *f* softening of the brain; **~hautentzündung** *f* meningitis; **~schale** *f* skull, brain-pan; **~schlag** *m* apoplexy of the brain; **~trust** *m* brain(s) trust; **~verletzung** *f med* lesion of the brain.

Ge|höft *n* farm-stead, farm premises *pl*; **~hölz** *n* wood, copse; brake, thicket.

Gehör *n* hearing; (*Anhören*) audience; (*Ohr*) ear; *fig* attention; *er hat kein ~* he has no musical ear; *jdm ~ schenken* to listen to; *~ finden* to have (*od* get) a hearing; *ein scharfes ~* a quick ear; *nach dem ~ spielen* to play by ear; **~fehler** *m* defective hearing; **~gang** *m* auditory meatus; **~los** *a* deaf; **~losigkeit** *f* deafness; **~nerv** *m* auditory nerve; **~organ** *n* organ of hearing; **~sinn** *m* (sense of) hearing; **~trommel** *f* drum of the ear, tympanum.

gehorchen *itr* to obey; *tech* to respond.

gehör|en *itr* to belong to; to be necessary for; (*Person*) to find o.'s place, to be included, *Am* to belong in (*od* among); (*Gemeinschaft*) to be affiliated to; (*gebühren*) to be entitled to; *das ~t nicht hierher* that's out of place here; that's beside the point; that's irrelevant; *dazu ~t Zeit* that requires (*od* takes) time; *es ~t Vorsicht dazu* it needs precaution; *er ~t bestraft* he ought to be punished; *er ~t mit dazu* he is one of them; *es ~t sich* it's proper; *das ~t sich nicht* that is not suitable; *so ~t es sich* that's as it should be; **~ig** *a* belonging to; (*schicklich*) fit, suitable; (*nötig*) necessary; (*tüchtig*) good; *nicht zur Sache ~~* irrelevant; *sie bekamen e-e ~~e Tracht Prügel* they got a sound thrashing; *ich hab's ihm ~~ gegeben* I gave him a bit of my mind; *er hat e-e ~~e Achtung vor ihm* he has a healthy respect for him; *in ~~er Form* in due form, duly, properly.

Gehörn *n* horns *pl*, antlers *pl*; **~t** *a* horned, antlered; horny.

gehorsam *a* obedient, submissive; dutiful; obsequious; **~** *m* obedience; duty; **~st** *a* most humble.

Gehr|e *f*, **~ung** (*Zwickel*) gore. gusset; (*Keil*) wedge; (*Tischlerei*) bevel; slope; **~säge** *f* mitre-box saw.

Geier *m* vulture.

Geifer *m* slaver; drivel; spittle; (*Tier*) foam; *fig* anger, rancour; venom; **~n** *itr* to slaver; to drivel; *vor Wut ~~* to be foaming with rage; **~tuch**, **~lätzchen** *n* bib, pinafore, feeder.

Geige *f* violin, fiddle; *die erste ~ spielen* to play first fiddle; **~n** *itr* to play (on) the violin; *fam* to (play the) fiddle; **~nbogen** *m* (violin-)bow; *fam* fiddle-stick; **~nharz** *n* rosin, colophony; **~nkasten** *m* violin-case; **~nmacher** *m* violin-maker; **~nspieler**, **~r** *m* violinist; *fam* fiddler; **~nsaite** *f* violin (*od* fiddle-)string; **~nsteg** *m* bridge of a violin; **~nstrich** *m* stroke on a violin; **~nvirtuose** *m* professional violinist; **~nwirbel** *m* peg of a violin; **~rzähler** *m* Geiger counter.

geil *a* wanton, lustful; voluptuous, lascivious; (*üppig*) luxuriant, rank, exuberant; (*Tier*) hot, ruttish; (*zotig*) smutty, *Am* racy; *~es Fleisch* proud flesh; **~heit** *f* rankness; (*Wollust*) wantonness, lasciviousness.

Geisel *m u. f* hostage; *~n stellen* to give hostages.

Geiß *f* goat; (*Gemse, Reh*) doe; **~blatt** *n* honeysuckle; woodbine; **~bock** *m* billy-goat, he-goat.

Geißel *f* whip, lash; *fig* scourge; **~eln** *tr* to whip, to scourge; to lash, to flog; *eccl* to flagellate; *fig* (*züchtigen*) to chastise; (*kritisieren*) to reprimand, to censure; to criticize severely; **~elung** *f* flagellation, scourging; (*Verurteilung*) condemnation; **~ler** *m* scourger; flagellant.

Geist *m* (*Gegensatz zu Körper*) spirit; (*denkende Kraft*) mind; (*Genius*) genius; (*Verstand*) brains *pl*; intellect; (*Witz*) cleverness; (*Gespenst*) spectre; ghost; (*Kobold*) sprite; *der böse ~* the demon, evil spirit; *der Heilige ~* the Holy Ghost; *ein Mann von ~* a witty man; *ein starker ~* a strong-minded man; *ein kleiner ~* a narrow mind; *den ~ aufgeben* to give up the ghost, to breathe o.'s last; *e-n ~ bannen* to lay a ghost; *den ~ bilden* to cultivate the mind; *wes ~es Kind ist er?* what sort of a man is he? *e-r der größten ~er seiner Zeit* one of the greatest minds of his time; *der ~ ist willig, aber das Fleisch ist schwach* the spirit is willing, but the flesh is weak; *in diesem Hause geht ein ~ um* this house is haunted; *ich werde im ~e bei dir sein* I shall be with you in (the) spirit.

Geister|banner, **~beschwörer** *m* (*Anrufer*) necromancer; (*Austreiber*) exorcist; **~beschwörung** *f* (*Anrufung*) evocation; (*Austreibung*) exorcism; **~bild** *n* ghost image; **~erscheinung** *f* apparition, vision; **~geschichte** *f* ghost-story; **~glaube** *m* belief in ghosts; spiritism; **~haft** *a* ghostly; *fig* ghastly; **~klopfen** *n* spirit rapping; **~n** *itr* to haunt; **~seher** *m* ghost-seer; visionary; **~stunde** *f* ghostly hour; **~welt** *f* spirit-world.

geistes|abwesend *a* absent-minded; abstracted; **~abwesenheit** *f* absence of mind, absent-mindedness; **~anlagen** *f pl* mental faculties *pl*, abilities *pl*; **~anstrengung** *f* mental effort; **~arbeiter** *m* brain-worker; (*Angestellter*) black-coated worker, *Am* white-collar worker; **~bildung** *f* cultivation of the mind; culture; **~blitz** *m* brain-wave, stroke of genius; **~freiheit** *f* liberty of the mind; **~gabe** *f* mental gift; talent; **~gegenwart** *f* presence of mind; **~gestört** *a* insane, mentally deranged; **~~heit** *f* insaneness; craziness; **~größe** *f* greatness of mind; (*Hochherzigkeit*) magnanimity; **~haltung** *f* mentality, intellectual character; mental attitude; **~kraft** *f* power of mind; **~krank** *a* insane; **~~heit** *f* insanity, mental disease; **~leben** *n* spiritual life; **~richtung** *f* intellectual tendency; **~schaffende(r)** *m* mental producer; **~schärfe** *f* sagacity; **~schwach** *a* feeble-minded, idiotic; **~schwäche** *f* feeble-mindedness; imbecility; **~stärke** *f* strength of mind; **~träge** *a* intellectually lazy; **~verfassung** *f* frame of mind; state of mind; **~verwandt** *a* congenial; **~~schaft** *f* congeniality; **~verwirrung** *f* mental derangement; **~wissenschaften** *f pl* human sciences *pl*; the Arts *pl*; **~zustand** *m* state of mind, mental attitude; **~zerrüttung** *f* insanity.

geistig *a* intellectual; mental; (*nicht körperlich*) spiritual; (*alkoholhaltig*) spirituous; *~e Getränke* spirituous liquors, spirits; *~e Arbeit* brain work; *~er Arbeiter* brain worker; *~e Fähigkeiten* intellectual abilities; *das ~e Auge* the mental eye; *~es Eigentum* intellectual (*od* copyright) property; *~ umnachtet* mentally afflicted; **~keit** *f* spirituality; intellectuality; (*Wein*) alcoholic strength.

geistlich *a* spiritual; (*kirchlich*) clerical, ecclesiastical, sacred; (*ordens~*) religious; **~e(r)** *m* (*allgemein*) ecclesiastic, *fam* parson; (*Hochkirche*) clergyman; (*Pfarrer*) rector, vicar; (*katholisch*) priest; (*Sekte*) minister; *~er werden* to take holy orders; **~keit** *f* clergy.

geist|los *a* spiritless; (*langweilig*) dull; (*dumm*) stupid; (*nichtssagend*) trivial, shallow; (*uninteressant*) insipid; **~losigkeit** *f* dul(l)ness; stupidity; want of originality, platitude; **~reich, ~voll** *a* ingenious, bright, clever; witty; **~tötend** *a* soul-killing; dull, monotonous, humdrum, tedious.

Geitau *n* clue-line.

Geiz *m* avarice, greediness; (*Knauserei*) stinginess; (*Genauigkeit*) parsimony; **~en** *itr* to be avaricious of; to be economical with; to economize; (*knausern*) to stint; *nach etw ~~* to aspire to; **~hals, ~kragen** *m* miser, niggard; stingy fellow; skinflint; **~ig** *a* (*sparsam*) parsimonious; (*knauserig*) stingy, niggardly; (*filzig*) miserly; (*habsüchtig*) avaricious.

Ge|jammer *n* lamentation; wailing; **~jauchze** *n* shouting; exultation; **~johle** *n* howling, yelling, hooting.

gekachelt *a* tiled.

Ge|keife *n* scolding and squalling; **~kicher** *n* tittering, giggling, snigger, snicker; **~kläff** *n* (constant) yelping; **~klapper** *n* rattling; **~klatsche** *n* clapping (of hands); *fig* prattle; **~klimper** *n* (*Klavier*) strumming, drumming; (*Münzen*) chinking; **~klingel** *n* tinkling; **~klirr** *n* clank; **~knatter, ~knister** *n* crackling; rustling; **~köpert** *a* twilled; **~körnt** *a* granulated; **~kose** *n* caressing, love-making; **~krach** *n* crash; **~kreisch** *n* screaming, screeching; **~kritzel** *n* scrawl, scribbling; **~kröse** *n* (calf's) pluck; (*Gans*) giblets *pl*; *med* mesentery; **~künstelt** *a* artificial; (*geziert*) affected.

*

Ge|lächter *n* laughing, laughter; (*vergnügtes ~~*) chuckle; (*schallendes ~~*) roar, guffaw; burst (*od* peal *od* shout) of laughter; (*grobes ~~*) horse-laugh; *sich dem ~~ aussetzen* to expose o. s. to ridicule; *ein ~~ erheben* to break out into a laughter; **~lage** *n* banquet, carousal, drinking-bout; **~lähmt** *a* paralyzed.

Gelände *n* ground, tract of land; (*Landstrich*) country; *mil geog* terrain; (*Gegend, Landschaft*) land(scape), topography; territory; (*Gebiet*) area; (*Stück Land*) plot, patch, lot; (*Bau~*) site; *sich dem ~ anpassen* to adapt o. s. to the ground, to camouflage; *~ ausnutzen* to take full use of the ground; *~ behaupten* to stand o.'s ground; *~ verstärken* to reinforce the ground; *ansteigendes ~* rising country; *bedecktes ~* close country; *durchschnittenes ~* intersected country; *ebenes ~* level country; *freies ~* open country; *welliges ~* undulating country; **~abschnitt** *m* area, sector; **~anpassung** *f* adaptation to terrain, blending with the ground; **~antrieb** *m mot* all-wheel drive; **~aufnahme** *f* ground survey; **~ausbildung** *f* field training; **~ausnutzung** *f* utilization of terrain; **~ausschnitt** *m* ground zone; **~auswertung** *f* terrain appreciation; **~beschaffenheit** *f* nature of terrain; **~beurteilung** *f* estimate of terrain; **~bö** *f* ground gust; **~darstellung** *f* cartography; topographical representation; **~dienst** *m* ground defence service; **~einschnitt** *m* coulee; **~entgiftung** *f* ground decontamination; **~erkundung** *f* terrain (*od* ground) reconnaissance; **~erschließung** *f* land development; **~fahrt** *f* cross-country drive; **~fahrzeug** *n* cross-country vehicle; **~falte** *f* fold; **~formen** *f pl* terrain features *pl*; **~gang** *m mot* auxiliary gear; booster gear; **~gängig** *a* having cross-country mobility; **~gestaltung** *f* formation of terrain; terrain features *pl*; **~hindernis** *n* natural obstacle; **~kampfstoff** *m* ground contaminating agent; **~kette** *f mot* track; **~kunde** *f* topography; **~lauf** *m sport* cross-country race; **~orientierung** *f* orientation of terrain, orientation by map; **~punkt** *m* landmark; **~reifen** *m* cross-country tyre, *Am* off-the-road tire; ground-grip tire; **~ritt** *m* point-to-point race; **~senkung** *f* depression of ground; **~skizze** *f* military sketch; **~sport** *m* scouting; field-sports; **~sprung** *m sport* (*Ski*) gelände jump; **~streifen** *m* strip of ground; terrain sector; **~übung** *f* open country (*od* field) exercise; **~unebenheit** *f* roughness of ground; **~wagen** *m* cross-country car; **~welle** *f* undulation of ground, rideau.

Ge|länder *n* railing, balustrade; (*an Treppen*) banisters *pl*; (*aus Stein*) parapet; **~langen** *itr* to arrive at, to come to, to reach; (*Ziel*) to attain; (*erwerben*) to acquire; (*gewinnen*) to win; *zu e-m Vermögen ~~* to make a fortune; *zum Abschluß ~~* to get settled; *zur Ausführung ~~* to become effective; *an e-n Ort ~~* to get to a place; *auf die Nachwelt ~~* to be handed down to posterity; *in andere Hände ~~* to change hands; *~~ lassen* to send, to hand on; **~lärm** *n* continual noise; **~laß** *n* room, space; **~lassen** *a* (*ruhig*) calm, quiet; (*geduldig*) patient; (*gesetzt*) composed; (*beherrscht*) self-possessed; *~~ bleiben* to keep o.'s temper; **~~heit** *f* calm(ness), composure; (*Geduld*) patience; (*Selbstbeherrschung*) self-possession; **~läufig** *a* current, ready; fluent; *~~e Zunge* voluble tongue; *~~e Handschrift* running hand; *er spricht ~~ Englisch* he speaks English fluently; *~~ sein* to be familiar to s. o.; **~~keit** *f* currency, readiness; fluency; (*Zunge*) volubility, glibness; (*Leichtigkeit*) ease; **~launt** *a* disposed, tempered; *gut ~~* good-humo(u)red; *schlecht ~~* ill-humo(u)red, out of temper; **~läut(e)** *n* (*Glockenläuten*) ringing of bells, chime, peal; (*Glockenspiel*) set of bells, peal, chimes *pl*.

gelb *a* yellow; *~e Rübe* carrot, *Am* yellow turnip; *~ werden* to get yellow; **~braun** *a* yellowish brown; **~fieber** *n* yellow fever; **~filter** *n phot* yellow filter; **~gießer** *m* brass-founder; **~kreuz-(gas)** *n* mustard gas; **~lich** *a* yellowish, fallow; **~scheibe** *f* yellow screen; jellow filter; **~schnabel** *m* callow-bird; *fig* greenhorn; **~sucht** *f* jaundice; **~süchtig** *a* jaundiced.

Geld *n* money, *sl* tin, dough; (*Münze*) coin; (*Bargeld*) cash, ready money, (*Kleingeld*) change; (*Papier~*) paper money; (*Kurs*) prices negotiated; *falsches ~* base coin; *fest angelegtes ~* tied up money; *flüssiges ~* ready money; *kurzfristiges ~* money at short notice; *tägliches ~* call money; *überschüssiges ~* surplus money; *verfügbares ~* disposable funds; *ausstehende ~er* outstanding debts; *eingehende ~er* money coming in; *fremde ~er* foreign money; *öffentliche ~er* public funds; *Bewilligung von ~ern* (*parl*) vote of supplies; *~ abheben* to draw money; *~ anlegen* to invest money; *~ aufnehmen* to raise money; *~ ausgeben* to spend money; *~ ausleihen* to lend out money; *~ eintreiben* to collect money; *~ hineinstecken* to invest money; *~ horten* to hoard money; *~ schulden* to owe money; *~ sparen* to save money; *~ vorschießen, ~ vorstrecken* to advance money; *~ zurückerstatten* to refund (*od* reimburse) money; *~ zuschießen* to contribute money; *bei ~e sein* to have plenty of money; *nicht bei ~e sein* to be short of cash; *ganz ohne ~ sein* to be dead-broke; *um sein ~ kommen* to lose o.'s money; *jdn schwer ~ kosten* to be a heavy burden on s. o.'s purse; *nicht mit ~ zu bezahlen* invaluable; *für ~ u. gute Worte* for love and money; *er hat ~ wie Heu* he is rolling in money; *sie hat kein ~ bei sich* she has no money about her; *etw zu ~ machen* to make money of s. th.; *~ bei der Bank aufnehmen* to take up money at the bank; *ins ~ laufen* to run into money; *zu ~ machen* to realize, to convert into money; *sein ~ auf der Bank stehen haben* to have lodged o.'s money with o.'s banker; *mit ~ unterstützen* to subsidize; *er hat ~ in Hülle u. Fülle* he has plenty of money; *er verdient viel ~* he is earning a lot of money; *er muß ~ verdienen* he must make money; *mit ~ läßt sich alles machen* money answers all things; *~ regiert die Welt* money governs the world; *du kannst dein ~ in den Schornstein schreiben* you may whistle for your money; *Hinterlegung von ~ern bei Gericht* lodg(e)ment of funds in court; *~ u. Geldeswert* money and valuables; **~abfindung** *f* (monetary) indemnity; cash settlement, allowance; **~abwertung** *f* devaluation, devalorization; **~angebot** *n* bid; **~angelegenheit** *f* money matter, financial affair; **~anhäufung** *f* accumulation of money; **~anlage** *f* investment of funds; **~anleihe** *f* loan; **~anspruch** *m* claims for money, title to funds; **~anweisung** *f* money order, postal order; **~aristokratie** *f* plutocracy; **~aufnahme** *f* raising of money; **~aufwand** *m* expenditure; **~aufwertung** *f* revaluation of money; **~ausgabe** *f* expenditure, expense, disbursement; **~bedarf** *m* requisite money, *com* money demand; **~bedürfnisse** *n pl* money demands *pl*; **~beihilfe** *f* subsidy; **~beitrag** *m* grant; **~belohnung** *f* remuneration; **~bestand** *m* monetary stock; **~betrag** *m* amount of money; **~beutel** *m* purse; (*Papier~*) wallet, *Am* billfold, pocketbook; money-bag; **~bewilligung** *f* granting of money; **~brief** *m* money letter; **~briefträger** *m* money postman; **~buße** *f* fine; **~eingang** *m* receipts *pl*; **~einlage** *f* deposit; **~einnehmer** *m* collector; **~einwurf** *m* coin-slot; **~einzahlung** *f* payment; **~empfänger** *m* remittee; **~entschädigung** *f* reimbursement; **~entwertung** *f* devaluation (*od* depreciation) of money; inflation; **~erwerb** *m* money-making; **~forderung** *f* money due; **~geber** *m* money lender,

(*Hypotheken*) mortgagee; **~geschäft** *n* money; transaction; **~geschenk** *n* gratuity; (*Trinkgeld*) tip; (*Stiftung*) donation; **~gier** *f* love of money; **~gierig** *a* greedy after money; **~hamsterer** *m* money hoarder; **~heirat** *f* money-match; **~herrschaft** *f* plutocracy; **~hilfe** *f* pecuniary aid; **~hortung** *f* hoarding of money; **~institut** *n* money agency; **~kasse** *f* till, strong-box, (*Registrierkasse*) cash register; **~klemme** *f* pecuniary difficulty; **~knappheit** *f* shortness of money; **~krise** *f* money crisis; **~kurs** *m* money rate; **~leihinstitut** *n* lending-institute; **~leute** *pl* financiers *pl*, moneyed people; **~lich** *a* pecuniary; **~macht** *f* financial power; **~mangel** *m* money scarcity; **~markt** *m* money market; **~mittel** *n pl* funds, means *pl*; **~münze** *f* coin; **~not** *f* tightness of money; **~politik** *f* monetary policy; **~protz** *m* purse-proud person; **~quelle** *f* pecuniary resource; **~reform** *f* monetary reform; **~reserve** *f* money reserve; **~sache** *f* money matter; **~sammlung** *f* collection; **~schein** *m* currency-note; bank-note, *Am* bill; **~schrank** *m* safe, strong-box; **~schrankknacker** *m* safebreaker; **~sendung** *f* remittance in cash; **~sorten** *f pl* coins and notes *pl*; **~spende** *f* contribution; **~strafe** *f* fine; **~stück** *n* coin; **~summe** *f* sum of money; **~system** *n* monetary system; **~überfluß** *m* glut of money, surplus money; **~überhang** *m* excess (*od* surplus) of money; **~überschuß** *m* surplus money; **~überweisung** *f* money transfer, remittance; **~umlauf** *m* circulation of money; **~umtausch** *m* money conversion; **~unterstützung** *f* pecuniary aid; **~verdiener** *m* money-maker; **~verknappung** *f* scarcity of money; **~verlegenheit** *f* financial difficulty; **~verleiher** *m* money-lender; **~verlust** *m* loss of money; **~verschwendung** *f* waste of money; **~vorrat** *m* funds *pl*; **~vorschuß** *m* cash advance; **~währung** *f* currency; **~wechsel** *m* exchange of money; **~wechsler** *m* money changer; **~wert** *m* cash value; **~wesen** *n* financial business; **~wucherer** *m* usurer; **~zahlung** *f* payment.

Gelee *n* jelly.

gelegen *a* (*örtlich*) situated, *Am* located; (*günstig*) opportune; (*passend*) convenient, fit, apt; *~ sein* to lie, to be situated; *jdm daran ~ sein* to be anxious to; *er kam zu ~er Zeit* he came in time; *es kam mir gerade ~* it came just at the right time; *mir ist nichts daran ~* I don't care one way or another; *es ist nichts daran ~* it does not matter; *Sie kommen mir gerade ~* you are just the man I want to see; **~heit** *f* (*Anlaß*) occasion; (*günstige ~~*) opportunity; (*Zufall*) chance; *Am fam* show; (*günstige Aussicht*) opening; *bei erster ~~* at the first opportunity, on the first occasion, at o.'s earliest convenience; *~~ macht Diebe* opportunity makes the thief; *e-e ~~ ergreifen* to seize (*od* profit by) an opportunity; *die ~~ beim Schopfe fassen* to take time by the forelock; *sich e-e ~~ entgehen lassen* to let an opportunity slip; *die ~~ bietet sich* the opportunity presents itself; *die ~~ verpassen* to lose (*od* miss) an opportunity; *jdm die ~~ zu etw geben* to give s. o. the opportunity of s. th.; **~~sarbeit** *f* casual (*od* odd) job, *Am* chore; **~~sarbeiter** *m* casual labo(u)rer, handy man, jobber, pieceworker; **~~sgedicht** *n* occasional poem; **~~sgeschäft** *n* occasional bargain; **~~skauf** *m* bargain; **~~skäufer** *m* outside-buyer; **~~sphotograph** *m* casual cameraman; **~~sverbrecher** *m* accidental criminal; **~tlich** *a* occasional; (*zufällig*) casual, accidental, incidental, chance; *adv* occasionally, on occasion, at o.'s convenience; *Am* once in a while; (*beiläufig*) by the way, by the by.

gelehr|ig *a* docile, teachable; (*klug*) intelligent; **~igkeit** *f* docility, intelligence; **~samkeit** *f* learning, erudition; **~t** *a* learned, erudite; scholarly; **~te(r)** *m* a learned person, scholar.

Geleier *n* monotonous music; *es ist immer das alte ~* it's always the same tune.

Geleise *n* (*Straße*) rut, track; *rail* rails *pl*, line, *Am* track; *fig* routine, beaten track; *im alten ~ bleiben* to keep on the beaten track, to keep in the old rut; *aus dem ~ kommen* to run off the rails; *fig* to be put out; *wieder ins ~ bringen fig* to put right again.

Geleit *n* (*Begleitung*) company; conduct, guidance; *mil* escort; *mar* convoy; (*Begräbnis*) procession; (*Gefolge*) retinue; *freies ~* safe-conduct; *jdm das ~ geben* to accompany, to see s. o. off; **~en** *tr* to accompany, to see s. o. off; *mil, mar* to escort, to convoy; **~fahrzeug** *n* convoy; escort vessel; **~flugzeug** *n* (*Jäger*) escort fighter; **~~träger** *m* escort aircraft carrier; **~kreuzer** *m* convoy cruiser; **~mannschaft** *f* escort personnel, escort crew; **~(s)brief** *m* letter of safe-conduct; permit, pass(port); **~schein** *m* safe-conduct; **~schiff** *n* escort vessel; **~schutz** *m* convoy guard; **~system** *n* convoy system; **~wort** *n* preface, foreword; **~zug** *m mar* convoy; **~~schutz** *m* convoy protection; **~~sicherung** *f* escort of convoy.

Gelenk *n* joint, *anat, bot* articulation; (*Finger~*) knuckle; (*Kettenglied*) link; **~entzündung** *f* arthritis; **~ig** *a* flexible, pliant; (*beweglich*) limber; (*biegsam*) plastic; (*geschmeidig*) pliable; (*gegliedert*) articulate; (*flink*) active, nimble; **~igkeit** *f* pliableness, pliancy, flexibility, suppleness; (*Person*) nimbleness; (*Rührigkeit*) activity; **~kupplung** *f* joint coupling; **~pfanne** *f* socket of a joint; **~rheumatismus** *m* articular rheumatism; **~schmiere** *f* synovia; **~stange** *f* toggle link; **~verrenkung** *f* dislocation of a joint; **~welle** *f* cardan shaft.

Ge|lichter *n* gang, set; riff-raff; *Leute e-s ~~s* the same stamp; **~liebt** *a* loved, dear; **~~e** *m u. f* lover, sweetheart; *e-e frühere ~~* an old flame; **~lind** *a* soft, mild, (*Kälte*) moderate; (*Wetter*) gentle; (*Klima*) bland; (*Schmerz*) slight; (*nachsichtig*) indulgent; (*schonend*) lenient; *~~ gesagt* to put it mildly; *~~ere Saiten aufziehen* to come down a peg or two; **~lingen** *irr itr* to succeed in; to manage, to contrive (to); (*geraten*) to turn out; *es gelingt ihm, es zu tun* he succeeds in doing it; *es gelang ihm nicht, e-e Prüfung zu bestehen* he failed in an examination; *~~ n* success; **~lispel** *n* lisping; (*Geflüster*) whispering; **~lungen** *a, pp* excellent, capital; *wie ist der Kuchen ~~?* how did the cake turn out? *Sie sind aber ~~!* you are funny! *ein ~~er Kerl* a comical fellow.

gellen *itr* to yell, to scream, to squall, to shrill; (*von den Ohren*) to tingle; **~d** *ppr a* yelling, shrill, piercing.

ge|loben *tr* to promise solemnly; to vow; *das Gelobte Land* the Holy Land, the Land of Promise; **~löbnis** *n* solemn promise; (*Gelübde*) vow; (*Versprechen*) pledge.

gelt? *interj* is it not so? *fam* ain't it? truly? *~ a* barren, dry.

gelten *irr itr* (*etw wert sein, kosten*) to be worth; to be of value, to cost; (*gültig sein*) to be valid, to be in force, to be effective, to be in operation; (*betreffen*) to apply to, to concern, to mean; (*Text*) to prevail; (*Münze*) to be current; *etw ~* to have influence, to prevail; *~ für* to be considered as, to pass for; *~ lassen* to approve of s. th.; to admit; to let pass; to let stand; *~d machen* to urge, to assert, to lay stress upon; to bring o.'s influence to bear; (*Rechte*) to maintain; to claim, to put forward; (*Grund*) to plead; *das gilt auch für Sie* that goes for you, too; *das gilt sogar gegenüber* that's true even in regard to; *das gilt nicht!* that doesn't count! *was gilt die Wette?* how much will you bet? *sie gilt viel bei ihm* she stands in high favo(u)r with him; *diese Entschuldigung lasse ich nicht gelten* I won't take that excuse; *viel bei jdm ~* to have great influence with s. o.; *imp*: *es gilt Ihr Leben* your life is at stake; *es gilt mir* it is aimed at me; *es gilt!* agreed! done! *es gilt nicht!* it is not fair play! that's no go! *es gilt als ausgemacht* it's taken for granted; **~dmachung** *f* assertion; (*Klage*) reliance.

Geltung *f* (*Wert*) worth, value; (*Gültigkeit*) validity; (*Münze*) currency; (*Bedeutung*) importance; *~ haben* to be valid; *zur ~ bringen* to make s. th. valid; (*Ansehen*) to assert; (*ausnützen*) to turn to account; *sich ~ verschaffen* to bring o.'s influence to bear; to become important; **~sbedürfnis** *n* desire to show off; **~sbereich** *m* coverage; scope, area; *jur* purview; **~sdauer** *f* duration; **~strieb** *m* desire to dominate.

Gelübde *n* vow, solemn promise; *ein ~ ablegen* (*eccl*) to take a vow.

Gelüst *n* desire; **~en** *itr* to long for, to hanker (after), to feel a strong desire for; *sich ~~ lassen* to covet s. th.

Ge|mach *n* room, apartment; *adv* by degrees, gently; slowly; **~mächlich** *a* soft, slow; comfortable; *adv* slowly; conveniently; *~~ gehen* to amble; *~~ leben* to live at ease; **~~keit** *f* slowness; ease; **~mahl** *m* husband; consort; **~~in** *f* wife; consort; *Frau ~~* Mrs. N.; **~mahnen** *tr* to put in mind; *jdn an etw ~~* to remind s. o. of; *imp*: *es gemahnt an* it seems (as if).

Gemälde *n* picture, painting; portrait; **~ausstellung** *f* exhibition of paintings; **~galerie** *f* picture- (*od* art-) -gallery, *Am* museum; **~händler** *m* picture-dealer; **~sammlung** *f* collection of pictures.

Gemarkung *f* boundary, limit; land-mark; district.

gemäß *a* suitable, conformable (to), appropriate (to, for); *adv, prp* (*entsprechend*) according to, in accordance with, in conformity with, in compliance with; (*zufolge*) in consequence of; *jur* pursuant to, under, subject (to); *~ dem Vertrag* as directed by the contract; **~heit** *f* conformity; **~igt** *a* moderate; *~~e Zone* temperate zone.

Gemäuer *n* masonry; ruins *pl.*

gemein *a* common; (*allgemein*) general; (*verächtlich*) low, base; (*schäbig*) mean; (*öffentlich*) public; (*gewöhnlich*) vulgar; (*roh*) coarse; rank; *das ~e Wohl* the public welfare; *der ~e Haufe* low people; *~e Sache machen mit* to make common cause with; *das ist e-e*

~*e Lüge* that's a dirty lie; *du hast uns e-n ~en Streich gespielt* you played a rotten trick on us; *sie haben nichts miteinander ~* they have nothing in common; ~*er Bruch* vulgar fraction; ~*e Redensarten gebrauchen* to use bad language; ~*er Kerl sl* dirty dog, *Am sl* skunk; **~e(r)** *m* (*Soldat*) private; *Haus der ~en parl* House of Commons; **~e** *n* meanness; **~gefährlich** *a* dangerous to the community; **~geist** *m* public spirit: **~gültig** *a* generally admitted; **~gut** *n* public property; *zum ~~ machen* to popularize; **~heit** *f* vulgarity, meanness, lowness; (*Tat*) rotten (*od* dirty) trick, low act; **~hin, ~iglich** *adv* generally, ordinarily, commonly; **~nutz** *m* common good; public utility; **~nützig** *a* of public utility; charitable; *~~e Einrichtung* welfare organization; *~~er Verein* non-profit making organization; **~platz** *m* commonplace, self-evident truth, platitude, truism, *Am* bromide; **~sam, ~schaftlich** *a* common, joint, in concurrence with; (*gegenseitig*) mutual; (*miteinander*) together; *~säme Sache machen mit jdm* to make common cause with s. o.; *~schaftlich handeln* to act in concert; *auf ~schaftliche Rechnung* on joint account; *~schaftliche Nutznießung* joint use; **~schaft** *f* (*Besitz*) community, joint ownership; *com* partnership; *eccl* communion; (*Beziehung*) connexion; intercourse; *häusliche ~~* common household; *in ~~ mit* together with; **~~sarbeit** *f* team work; **~~sbaden** *n* promiscuous bathing; **~~sbetrieb** *m* joint enterprise; **~~sbewußtsein** *n* solidarity; **~~serziehung** *f* co-education; **~~sgeist** *m*, **~~sgefühl** *n* solidarity, fellowship, community of feelings, party spirit; **~~sschule** *f* co-educational school; **~~ssender** *m radio* chain broadcast station; **~~sspeisung** *f* communal feeding; **~~sverpflegung** *f* common feeding; **~~swerbung** *f* collective (*od* cooperative) advertising; **~schuldner** *m* bankrupt; **~sinn** *m* public spirit; **~verständlich** *a* intelligible to all; popular; *~~ machen* to popularize; **~wesen** *n* public affairs *pl*; community; (*Staat*) commonwealth; **~wohl** *n* public welfare; common weal.

Gemeinde *f* community; (*städtische*) municipality; borough; (*Land~, Pfarr~*) parish; rural community; (*kirchliche*) congregation; (*Sekte*) sect, denomination; (*Zuhörerschaft*) audience; **~anger** *m* common, village green; **~auflagen** *f pl* local rates *pl*; **~beamter** *m* executive officer (of a commune); **~behörde** *f* local authority, municipality; **~betrieb** *m* communal (*od* municipal) undertaking; **~bezirk** *m* parish, borough; district; municipality; **~diener** *m* beadle, parish official; **~eigentum** *n* parish property, common; **~einnahmen** *f pl* local rates *pl*; local revenue; **~finanzen** *f pl* local finance; **~haus** *n* (*Rathaus*) town-hall; *eccl* building for a congregational meeting; **~haushalt** *m* municipal budget; **~mitglied** *n* parishioner; **~ordnung** *f* local code; **~politik** *f* local government policy; **~rat** *m* (*Körperschaft*) city (*od* parish) council; (*Person*) town (*od* parish) council(l)or, *Am* member of the city council, councilman; **~schule** *f* elementary school, council school; **~schwester** *f* visiting nurse; **~steuern** *f pl* rate, local rates *pl*, municipal rates *pl*, *Am* local taxes *pl*; **~unterstützung** *f* poor relief; **~verband** *m* union of local government units; **~verfassung** *f* municipal constitution; **~vermögen** *n* communal property; **~verwaltung** *f* local (*od* municipal) administration; local government; **~vorstand** *m* town-council, board; **~vorsteher** *m* chief magistrate of a small community; (*Stadt*) mayor; **~wahl** *f* municipal election; **~weide** *f* common, village green.

Gemeng|e *n* mixture; mêlée; (*Hand~~*) scuffle; **~teil** *m* constituent; **~sel** *n* medley; hotchpotch.

ge|messen *a* measured; (*bestimmt*) precise, strict; (*Schritt*) slow; (*förmlich*) formal, grave, dignified, stiff; **~messenheit** *f* formality, reserve, gravity; (*Genauigkeit*) precision, strictness; **~metzel** *n* slaughter, bloodshed, massacre, carnage; **~misch** *n* mixture; medley; composition, compound; **~~bildung** *f* mixture formation; **~~regelung** *f* mixture control; **~mischt** *a, pp* mixed; combined; *~~er Verband mil* task force; *~~wirtschaftliches Unternehmen* mixed ownership corporation.

Gemme *f* gem.

Gemse *f* chamois.

Gems|bock *m* chamois-buck; **~jäger** *m* chamois-hunter; **~leder** *n* chamois-leather, shammy.

Gemunkel *n* (*Gerücht*) rumours *pl*; (*Geflüster*) whispers *pl*.

Ge|murmel *n* murmur, murmuring, babble; muttering; **~murre** *n* grumbling, *Am* griping.

Gemüse *n* vegetables *pl*, greens *pl*, *Am* truck; **~bau** *m* cultivation of vegetables; **~garten** *m* kitchen-garden, *Am* truck-farm; **~gärtner** *m* market-gardener, *Am* truck-farmer, trucker; **~händler** *m* greengrocer; **~handlung** *f* greengrocer's shop; **~konserven** *f pl* preserved vegetables *pl*; tinned (*Am* canned) greens *pl*.

Gemüt *n* mind; feeling; heart; soul; temper, nature; temperament, disposition; spirit; *sich etw zu ~e führen* to drink s. th.; **~lich** *a* good-natured, genial, easy-going; (*wohnlich, traulich*) comfortable; snug; cozy (*od* cosy); (*angenehm*) pleasant; *ich mache es mir gerne ~~* I like to take it easy; **~lichkeit** *f* geniality, good nature, sociability; coziness, comfort, snugness; **~los** *a* unfeeling; **~losigkeit** *f* unfeelingness; **~voll** *a* affectionate; full of sentiment.

Gemüts|art, **~beschaffenheit** *f* disposition, temper, character; **~aufwallung** *f* agitation of feeling; **~bewegung** *f* emotion; **~erregung, ~erschütterung** *f* excitement, shock, agitation, fluster; **~krank** *a* diseased in mind; dejected, melancholic; **~krankheit** *f* mental disorder; melancholy; **~leben** *n* internal (*od* affective) life; **~mensch** *m* emotional character, sentimentalist; (*ironisch*) person without feeling; **~roh** *a* rude, brutal; **~rohheit** *f* brutality; **~ruhe** *f* calmness, serenity, composure, equability; peace of mind; **~stimmung, ~verfassung** *f*, **~zustand** *m* attitude (*od* frame *od* state) of mind.

gen *prp* to, towards; *~ Himmel* heavenward(s).

genannt *a* named, aforesaid, said; *eben ~* foregoing; *das oben Genannte* the above.

genau *a* exact, accurate; (*pünktlich*) precise; (*stimmend*) exact; (*ins Einzelne gehend*) minute, detailed; (*haar~*) dead true; (*streng*) strict; (*sparsam*) sparing, parsimonious; *~ rechnen* to reckon correctly, *Am* to reckon straight; *~e Angabe* full information; *ich weiß es ganz ~* I am sure of it; *das ist ~ so gut* that's just as good; *~ so bald* just as soon; *er hält sich ~ an die Vorschriften* he's sticking closely to the regulations; *~er Kostenvoranschlag* exact estimate; *ich weiß ~, daß ...* I know for certain that; *~ um drei Uhr* at three precisely (*od* sharp); *ich habe mir die Sache ~ überlegt* I have carefully considered the matter; *der ~ste Preis* the lowest price; *jdn ~ kennen* to know s. o. well; *man muß es nicht so ~ nehmen* you must not be so particular; *~ genommen* strictly speaking; *Genaueres* further particulars *pl*; **~igkeit** *f* exactness, precision, accuracy, strictness; parsimoniousness; economy; (*in der Wiedergabe*) fidelity; *mit ~~* accurately; **~~sarbeit** *f* precision work; **~~sgrad** *m* degree of accuracy; **~~slandung** *f aero* spot landing; **~~sordnung** *f* order of accuracy.

Gendarm *m* gendarme, rural policeman; **~erie** *f* rural police, constabulary; (*Polizeistation*) police station.

Genealog *m* genealogist; **~ie** *f* genealogy; **~isch** *a* genealogical.

genehm *a* agreeable; (*annehmbar*) acceptable; (*passend*) convenient, suitable; (*willkommen*) welcome; (*genehmigt*) approved of; **~igen** *tr* to assent to, to approve of, *Am* to okay; (*annehmen*) to accept; (*gewähren*) to grant; (*Vertrag*) to ratify; (*Gesetz*) to pass; **~igung** *f* approval, agreement; (*behördliche ~~*) licence (*od* license), permit; (*Erlaubnis*) permission; (*Vertrag*) ratification; (*Ermächtigung*) authorization; *mit ~~* with (the) consent (of), by permit of; *mit freundlicher ~~ durch* by favo(u)r of, *Am* (by) courtesy of; *schriftliche ~~* written approval; *~~ einholen* to secure the approval; *~~ erteilen* to grant the licence; **~~spflichtig** *a* subject to authorization.

geneigt *a* inclined (to), willing; (*wohlwollend*) well-disposed; (*freundlich*) kind; (*ergeben*) prone to, given to, addicted to; (*abschüssig*) sloping, inclined; *~er Leser* gentle reader; *zu etw ~* ready; *jdm ~ sein* to wish s. o. well; **~heit** *f* inclination, readiness; affection, favo(u)r; (*Hang*) tendency.

General *m* general; *kommandierender ~* commander; *aero* air chief marshal; **~admiral** *m* admiral, fleet commander-in-chief; lieutenant admiral general; **~agent** *m* general agent; **~agentur** *f* general agency; **~anwalt** *m jur* sollicitor general; **~arzt** *m* general medical officer; surgeon-general; **~baß** *m* thoroughbass; **~bevollmächtigte(r)** *m* chief representative, general agent; general chargé d'affaires, commissioner; **~direktion** *f* executive board; **~direktor** *m* chief manager, president; **~direktorium** *n* board of directors; **~feldmarschall** *m* field-marshal; **~feldzeugmeister** *m* master-general of the ordnance; **~gouverneur** *m* governor-general; **~inspekteur** *m* inspector-general; **~intendant** *m mil* army commissary general; *theat* head manager; **~isieren** *tr* to generalize; **~issimus** *m* generalissimo; **~ität** *f* generality; body of generals; **~karte** *f* general map; **~kommando** *n* corps headquarters *pl*; command headquarters *pl*; **~kommissar** *m* commissioner-general; **~konsul** *m* consul-general; **~konsulat** *n* consulate-general; **~leutnant** *m* lieutenant-

-general; ~**major** *m* major-general; ~**nenner** *m* lowest common denominator; ~**oberst** *m* colonel general; ~**postmeister** *m* postmaster general; ~**probe** *f* dress-rehearsal; *mus* full rehearsal; ~**quartiermeister** *m* quartermaster general (at G.H.Q.); ~**staatsanwalt** *m* chief public prosecutor, public prosecutor general; ~**stab** *m* general staff; ~**stabschef** *m* chief of general staff; ~**stabskarte** *f* ordnance survey map; military (*od* strategic) map; ~**stabsoffizier** *m* general-staff officer; ~**sekretär** *m* secretary general; ~**streik** *m* general strike; ~**überholung** *f* *mot* general overhaul; ~**unkosten** *pl* general expenses *pl*, overhead charges *pl*; ~**versammlung** *f* general meeting; ~**vertreter** *m* general agent; ~**vollmacht** *f* general (*od* full) power of attorney.

Gene|ration *f* generation; ~**rator** *m* (*Gaserzeuger*) gas-producer; (*Stromerzeuger*) generator; ~**ratorgas** *n* producer (*od* generator) gas; ~**ratorholz** *n* generator fuel; ~**rell** *a* general, universal; ~**risch** *a* generic; ~**rös** *a* generous.

genes|en *irr itr* to recover, to convalesce; to be restored; *e-s Kindes ~~* to give birth to a child; to be delivered of a child; ~**ende(r)** *m* convalescent; ~**ung** *f* recovery, convalescence; ~~**sheim** *n* convalescent home; sanatorium, *Am* sanitorium, health resort; ~~**skompanie** *f* *mil* convalescent company, rehabilitation company; ~~**surlaub** *m* sick leave.

Genf *n* Geneva; *~er See* Lake of Geneva, Lake Leman; *~er Abkommen* Geneva Convention; *~er Rotes Kreuz* Geneva Red Cross.

genial *a* full of genius; ingenious, inspired; highly gifted; ~**ität** *f* genius, extraordinary creative capacity.

Genick *n* nape, neck; *sich das ~ brechen* to break o.'s neck; *er nahm ihn beim ~* he took him by the scruff of the neck; ~**fänger** *m* (*Jagd*) hanger; ~**starre** *f* stiff neck; cerebrospinal meningitis.

Genie *n* genius; (*Person*) man of genius; (*verächtlich*) original; ~**korps** *n* engineers corps; ~**ren** *tr* to trouble, to disturb; to embarrass; to bother; *r* to feel embarrassed; *~~ Sie sich nicht!* make yourself at home! don't be bashful! ~**streich** *m* *hum* foolish deed; cunning trick.

genieß|bar *a* (*Speisen*) eatable; (*Getränke*) drinkable; (*schmackhaft*) palatable; (*angenehm*) enjoyable, agreeable; (*Buch*) readable; *der Wein ist nicht ~~* the wine isn't fit to drink; *er ist heute nicht ~~* he is unbearable today; ~**barkeit** *f* eatableness, drinkability; enjoyment, relish; ~**en** *irr tr* to enjoy, to taste, to relish; to eat, to drink; *nicht zu ~~* not fit to eat *od* drink, unpalatable; (*Menschen*) unbearable; *guten Kredit ~~* to enjoy good credit; *e-e gute Erziehung ~~* to receive a good education; ~**er** *m* gormandizer, glutton.

Genitalien *f pl* genitals *pl*; privy parts *pl*.

Genitiv *m* genitive (*od* possessive) case.

Genius *m* genius; *sein guter ~* his guardian angel.

Genoss|e *m* (*Kamerad*) comrade, companion, mate, *fam* chum, buddy, *Am* bunkie, *sl* pal; (*Amts~~*) colleague; (*Partei~~*) member of a political party; *com* partner, associate; (*Helfershelfer*) accomplice, confederate; ~**enschaft** *f* fellowship, company, association; (*Teilhaberschaft*) partnership; (*Ring*) syndicate; *jur, com* co-operative society; *eingetragene ~~ mit beschränkter Haftpflicht* registered co-operative society with limited liability; ~~**lich** *a* co-operative; ~~**sbank** *f* co-operative bank; ~~**sregister** *n* office of the registrar of companies, *Am* register of co-operatives; ~~**sverband** *m* co-operative union; ~~**swesen** *n* co-operative trading system; ~**in** *f* (female) companion, comrade, mate.

Genoveva *f* Genevieve.

Genre *n* style; genre; ~**bild** *n* genre-painting; ~**maler** *m* genre-painter.

genug *adv* enough, sufficient, sufficing, up to the mark; (*reichlich*) plentiful; *~ davon!* no more of this! *e-r ist ~* one will do; *er hat ~ davon* he is sick of it; *er hat mehr als ~* he has enough and to spare; *~, ich will nicht* in short, I will not; *~ sein* to suffice; ~**tun** *irr itr* (*jdm*) to give satisfaction to s. o., to satisfy s. o.; ~**tuung** *f* satisfaction, reparation; *~~ leisten* to make reparation (*od* amends) for; (*Schadenersatz*) compensation; *sich ~~ verschaffen* to take the law into o.'s own hands; *es gereicht mir zur ~~* it is gratifying to me.

Genüge *f* sufficiency; (*Befriedigung*) satisfaction; (*das Nötige*) the wherewithal; *jdm ~ tun od leisten* to satisfy, to please, *jur* to comply with, to fulfil; *jds Erwartung ~ leisten* to come up to o.'s expectations; *zur ~* enough; sufficiently; ~**n** *itr* to suffice, to satisfy; to be enough; *sich mit etw ~n lassen* to be satisfied with; *den Anforderungen ~~* to meet the requirements; *das genügt* that will do; ~**nd** *a* sufficient, satisfactory; (*Zeugnis*) fair; ~**sam** *a* easily satisfied, frugal; (*bescheiden*) modest; ~**samkeit** *f* moderation, frugality; (*Bescheidenheit*) modesty.

Genus *n* genus; *gram* gender.

Genuß *m* enjoyment, delight, pleasure; (*Nutznießung*) benefit; *jur* use, usufruct; (*Speisen*) eating, drinking, taking; (*Gefallen*) relish; (*Hoch~*) treat; *~ des Abendmahls* partaking of the Lord's Supper; ~**mensch** *m* man of pleasure; epicurean; ~**mittel** *n pl* coffee, tea, cocoa *etc;* (*Lebensmittel*) foodstuffs *pl;* (*Schokolade*) confectionery; ~**reich** *a* delightful; enjoyable; ~**sucht** *f* love of (*od* craving for) pleasures; ~**süchtig** *a* pleasure-seeking.

Geo|däsie *f* geodesy; ~**graph** *m* geographer; ~~**ie** *f* geography; ~~**isch** *a* geographical.

Geolog|(e) *m* geologist; ~**ie** *f* geology; ~**isch** geological.

Geomet|er *m* geometrician; surveyor; ~**rie** *f* geometry; ~**risch** *a* geometric(al); *~~es Zeichnen* lineal drawing.

Geo|physik *f* geophysics *pl*; ~**politik** *f* geopolitics *pl*.

Georgine *f bot* dahlia.

Gepäck *n* luggage; *mil, Am* baggage; *sein ~ aufgeben* to book o.'s luggage, *Am* to check o.'s baggage; ~**abfertigung** *f* dispatch of luggage, *Am* baggage dispatch; (*Büro*) luggage office, cloak-room; ~**annahme** *f* reception of luggage; (*Stelle*) luggage (registration) office; ~**aufbewahrungsstelle**, ~**abgabe** *f* cloak-room, depository for left-luggage, left-luggage office; *Am* check(ing) room; ~**ausgabe** *f* luggage delivery office, *Am* baggage room; ~**auslieferung** *f* luggage delivery; ~**bahnsteig** *m* luggage platform; ~**büro** *n*, ~**halle** *f* luggage-office, *Am* baggage-room; ~**halter** *m* (*Fahrrad*) carrier; ~**marsch** *m* pack march; ~**netz** *n* luggage-rack; ~**raum** *m* luggage-room, *Am* baggage compartment; ~**revision** *f* examination of luggage; ~**schalter** *m* luggage office; ~**schein** *m* (registered) luggage ticket (*od* receipt), *Am* baggage-check; ~**stück** *n* piece of luggage; bag, parcel; ~**träger** *m* porter, *Am* baggage-man, *Am fam* baggage-smasher, redcap; (*Fahrrad*) luggage carrier; ~**troß** *m* *mil* baggage train, baggage convoy; ~**versicherung** *f* registration of luggage; ~**wagen** *m* luggage-van, *Am* baggage-car; ~**zustellung** *f* luggage delivery, *Am* baggage delivery.

ge|panzert *a* armo(u)red, armo(u)r-clad; ~**pfeffert** *a* peppered; ~**pflegt** *a*, *pp* well cared-for; (*Person*) well-groomed; ~**pflogenheit** *f* habit, usage, custom; ~**piepe** *n* puling; ~**plänkel** *n* skirmishing; ~**plapper**, ~**plauder** *n* chatting, babbling; *fam* patter; (*Geschwätz*) tittle-tattle; ~**plärr** *n* bawling; ~**plätscher** *n* splashing; ~**polter** *n* rumbling noise; din; ~**präge** *n* impression; *fig* character; (*Münzen*) coinage; ~**pränge** *n* pomp, splendo(u)r; show; state, pageantry; ~**prassel** *n* rattling; crackling; clatter; ~**quake** *n* croaking.

gerade *a* (*waagrecht*) even; (*geradlinig*) straight; (*unmittelbar*) direct; (*Haltung*) upright, erect; (*aufrichtig*) upright, straight(forward), forthright, aboveboard; sincere, wholehearted, *Am* whole-souled; (*ehrlich*) honest, frank, open, plain; (*Zahl*) even; (*besonders*) particular; *adv* just, exactly, precisely, perfectly; *~ in dem Augenblick* at the very moment; *~ so gut* just as good (well); *~ zur rechten Zeit* in the nick of time; *das hat mir ~ noch gefehlt* that's all I needed; *es ist ~ e-n Monat her* it's a month to a day; *nun tue ich es ~ nicht* now I certainly won't do it; *fünf ~ sein lassen* to stretch a point; *~ umgekehrt* right the other way; *u. ~ du bist an ihn geraten* and you had to be just the one to fall in with him; *da wir ~ von dir sprechen* speaking of you; *der ~ Weg ist der beste* honesty is the best policy; *ich bin ~ dabei* I'm just about; *~ darum* just for that very reason; *nun ~* now more than ever; *ich traf ihn ~* I happened to meet him; *~ f math, rail* straight line; (*Fluß, Weg, Rennbahn*) straight; (*Boxen*) direct hit; *linke ~* jab; ~**aus** *adv* straight on (*od* along *od* ahead); *Augen ~~!* eyes front! ~~**empfänger** *m radio* straight-circuit receiver; ~~**flug** *m* horizontal flight; ~**biegen** *irr tr* to straighten; *fig* to put things straight; ~**halter** *m med* backboard; ~**heraus** *adv* freely, outright, frankly; *~~ gesagt* plainly spoken; ~**so** *adv* just the same; ~**stehen** *irr itr* to stand erect; *~~ für etw* to answer for; ~**(s)wegs** *adv* directly, (*sofort*) immediately, at once; straightway; *fig* straightforwardly; ~**zu** *adv* straight on, directly; *fig* openly, frankly; flatly, candidly; (*wirklich*) sheer, plain; *sie war ~~ ungezogen* she was downright impertinent; *das ist ~~ Wahnsinn* that's sheer madness; *die Ergebnisse sind ~~ überraschend* the results are nothing less than startling; *das ist ~~ fürchterlich* (*fam*) that's positively awful.

Gerad|führung *f tech* guide; ~**heit** *f* straightness; *fig* honesty, uprightness; ~**linig** *a* rectilinear; straight-lined; in direct proportion; ~**linigkeit** *f* straightness; linearity; ~**sinnig** *a* straight forward; ~**zahlig** *a* even-numbered.

Geranium *n bot* geranium.
Gerassel *n* clatter, rattling.
Gerät *n* (*landwirtschaftlich, religiös, primitiv*) implement; (*Handwerkszeug u. fig*) tool; (*kompliziert*) instrument; (*angetrieben*) appliance; (*Haus~*) utensil; (*Fisch~*) tackle; (*Möbel*) furniture; *radio* set; (*Apparat*) apparatus, gear; (*Vorrichtung*) device, gadget; (*Turnen*) apparatus; *mil* stores *pl*; implements *pl*; (*Ausstattung, Ausrüstung*) equipment; fittings *pl*; **~eanordnung** *f* layout of equipment; **~ebrett** *n* instrument board (*od* panel); **~ekammer** *f* store depot, (*Rumpelkammer*) lumber-room; **~ekasten** *m* tool (*od* jockey) box; **~eschalter** *m* plug switch; **~estecker** *m* coupler plug; **~eturnen** *n*, **~übungen** *f pl* heavy gymnastics *pl*; **~ewagen** *m* store wag(g)on, tool and gear truck; **~schaften** *f pl* tools *pl*, implements *pl*, utensils *pl*; **~verwalter** *m* storekeeper.
geraten *irr itr* (*gelangen*) to get (*od* fall) into; to come to, to hit upon; (*ausfallen*) to turn out; (*gelingen*) to succeed; (*treffen*) to meet with; (*gedeihen*) to prosper; *über etw ~* to come across s. th.; *in Entzücken ~* to go into raptures; *in schlechte Gesellschaft ~* to get into bad company; *in Unruhe ~* to become alarmed; *an den Bettelstab ~* to be reduced to poverty; *sie ist nach ihrer Mutter ~* she's just like her mother; *an den Unrechten ~* to catch a Tartar; *auf e-n Gedanken ~* to hit upon an idea; *auf Grund ~* to run aground; *außer sich ~* to lose o.'s temper; to get worked up; *in Schulden ~* to become involved in debts; *in Konkurs ~* to become bankrupt; *in Verlust ~* to get lost; *auf Abwege ~* to get on the wrong track; *in Brand ~* to catch fire; *in Zorn ~* to fly into a passion; *ins Stocken ~* to come to a standstill; *in Streit ~* to fall out with; *aneinander ~, einander in die Haare ~* to come to blows; *in Vergessenheit ~* to fall into oblivion; *~ a* useful, convenient; (*von Kindern*) well brought up; *schlecht ~* ill-bred; (*ratsam*) advisable; (*erfolgreich*) successful; (*geeignet*) proper, fit; (*vorteilhaft*) advantageous; *sein Unternehmen ist nicht gut ~* his undertaking proved a failure; *für ~ halten* to think best.
Ge|ratewohl *n: aufs ~~* at random, at haphazard, at a venture; (*zufällig*) by chance, by accident.
ge|raum *a* ample; long; *~~e Zeit* a long time; *vor ~~er Zeit* long ago; **~räumig** *a* spacious, roomy; **~~keit** *f* spaciousness; roominess; capacity; (*Größe*) size; (*Länge*) length.
Geräusch *n* noise; (*Getöse*) din, racket; (*Lärm*) uproar, pandemonium; (*Geschrei*) hullabaloo; (*Tumult*) bustle; *klopfendes ~* (*mot*) knocking; **~arm** *a* of low noise; noiseless, silent; **~bekämpfung** *f* silencing, *Am* noise abatement; **~dämpfer** *m* silencer, muffler; **~gedämpft** *a* soundproof; **~dämpfung** *f* soundproofing; **~film** *m film* effect film; **~los** *a* noiseless; silent; quiet; **~losigkeit** *f* noiselessness; silence; quietness; **~messer** *m* sound level meter; **~quelle** *f* source of noise; **~spiegel** *m* noise level; **~stärke** *f* noise intensity; **~voll** *a* noisy; ostentatious.
gerb|en *tr* (*zurichten*) to curry, to dress; *rot ~* to tan; *weiß ~* to taw; (*Metall*) to refine; **~er** *m* tanner; **~erei** *f* tannery; tanner's trade; **~erlohe** *f* tan-bark, oak-bark; **~säure** *f* tannic-acid; **~stoff** *m* tannin.
gerecht *a* just; (*rechtschaffen*) righteous; (*geeignet*) fit, suitable; (*billig*) equitable, fair; (*rechtmäßig*) legitimate; *~er Himmel!* good gracious! *der Forderung des Augenblicks ~ werden* to rise to the demand of the moment; *e-e ~e Entscheidung* a square deal; *Verpflichtungen ~ werden* to meet liabilities; *in allen Sätteln ~* well versed; fit for anything; *der Nachfrage ~ werden* to deal with the demand; *jdm ~ werden* to do justice to s.o.; to master; **~igkeit** *f* justice; (*Rechtschaffenheit*) righteousness; (*Billigkeit*) fairness, equitableness; (*Rechtmäßigkeit*) legitimacy; (*Vorrecht*) privilege; prerogative; *~~ walten lassen* to administer justice; *~~ widerfahren lassen* to do one justice; *ausgleichende ~~* poetic justice; **~~sgefühl** *n*, **~~ssinn** *m*, **~~sliebe** *f* feeling of equity; love of justice; **~same** *f* right, privilege, prerogative, title.
Ge|rede *n* talk(ing); (*Gerücht*) report, rumo(u)r; (*Geschwätz*) gossip, tattle, *fam* blab; (*unverständliches ~*) gibberish; *es geht das ~~* there is a rumo(u)r; *ins ~~ bringen* to make the talk of the town; *ins ~~ kommen* to get talked about; **~reichen** *itr: zu etw ~~* to cause s. th.; (*beitragen*) to contribute to s. th.; *zur Ehre ~~* to be a credit to; *es würde mir zur Ehre ~~* I should consider it (as) an hono(u)r; *es würde dir zum Vorteil ~~* it would prove to your advantage; *zum Nachteil ~~* to prove fatal; **~reizt** *a* irritated, angry, fierce (at, against); **~~heit** *f* irritation; **~reuen** *tr* to cause regret to, to repent; *sich ~~ lassen* to repent of; *es gereut mich* I repent (of) it; (*es tut mir leid*) I regret it, I am sorry for it.
Gericht *n* (*Speise*) dish, course; *jur* court (of justice), tribunal; (*Gerichtshof*) court of law (*od* of judicature); (*Anwalt*) bar; (*allg u. fig*) forum; (*Richter*) the judges *pl*; (*Sitzung*) session; (*Rechtsprechung*) jurisdiction; (*Urteil*) judg(e)ment; *das Jüngste ~* the Last Judg(e)ment, Doomsday; *~ erster Instanz* court of first instance; *~ zweiter Instanz* court of appeal, appellate court; *übergeordnetes ~* court of superior authority; *vor ~* in open court; *Anweisung e-s höheren ~es* mandamus; *Anweisung an ein unteres ~* writ; *von ~s wegen* by warrant of the court; *das ~ anrufen* to apply to the court; *vor ein ~ bringen* to bring an action against s. o.; *Berufung an ein ~ einlegen* to appeal to a court (*gegen* against); *vor ~ erscheinen* to appear in court; *vor ~ nicht erscheinen* to be contumacious; *vor ~ gehen* to go to law, to take legal action; *vor ~ kommen wegen* to go on trial before a court on a charge of; *vor ~ laden* to summon; *unter Strafandrohung vor ~ laden* to subpoena; *zu ~ sitzen* to sit in judg(e)ment; *sich dem ~ stellen* to surrender to the court; *vor ~ stellen* to arraign; *sich vor ~ verantworten* to stand o.'s trial; *vor ~ verklagen* to sue, to file a suit; *e-n Fall vor ~ vertreten* to plead a cause; *mit jdm ins ~ gehen* to take s. o. to task, *fam* to haul s. o. over the coals; **~lich** *a* judicial, judiciary; legal; forensic; *~~e Medizin* medical jurisprudence; *~~e Untersuchung* judicial investigation; *~~es Verfahren* legal proceedings; *~~e Verfügung* order (of the court); *~~e Vorladung* summons; *~~ belangen, vorgehen* to sue, to take legal proceedings against; *~~ bestätigen* to attest; *~~ geltend machen* to assert by action.
Gerichts|akten *f pl* court records *pl*; **~arzt** *m* medical examiner; **~assessor** *m* assistant judge; **~barkeit** *f* jurisdiction; *freiwillige ~~* voluntary jurisdiction, non-contentious litigation; **~beamter** *m* law-court official; **~befehl** *m* warrant, writ; **~behörde** *f* court of justice; **~bekannt** *sein* to be of judicial notice; **~beschluß** *m* order of the court; **~bezirk** *m* jurisdiction; circuit; **~bote, ~diener** *m* summoner; usher; **~chemiker** *m* public analyst; **~entscheid** *m* judicial ruling; **~ferien** *pl* recess; **~gebäude** *n* law court, courthouse; **~gebühren** *f pl* law fees *pl*; **~gefängnis** *n* local court prison; **~herr** *m* appointing authority; **~hof** *m* court (of law), tribunal; *oberster ~~* supreme court (of justice); **~kanzlei** *f* court registry; **~kasse** *f* court cashier; **~kosten** *pl* costs *pl* (of the proceedings); law-costs *pl*; **~ordnung** *f* rules of the court; **~referendar** *m* law graduate; **~schranke** *f* bar; **~schreiber** *m* registrar, clerk; **~schreiberei** *f* court office; **~sitzung** *f* hearing of a court; **~stand** *m* jurisdiction, venue; **~stelle** *f* competent court; **~tag** *m* court day; *~~ abhalten* to sit in court; **~termin** *m* trial, law term; **~verfahren** *n* legal procedure; **~verhandlung** *f* judicial hearing; (*Strafverhandlung*) trial; **~vollzieher** *m* (court) bailiff, *Am* sheriff, marshal; **~vorsitzender** *m* president of the court; **~wesen** *n* judicial system.
gerieben *a* cunning; sly; sharp; *ein ~er Kerl* a sly fox; *ein ~er Geschäftsmann* a smart businessman.
gering *a* little, small; (*winzig*) tiny, wee, puny, minute; (*unbedeutend*) unimportant, trifling; (*geringwertig*) inferior, ordinary; (*niedrig*) low, humble, mean; (*ärmlich*) poor, slender; (*geringfügig*) petty; *~er Preis* low price; *~e Ernte* poor crop; *~e Qualität* inferior quality; *~e Kenntnisse* scanty knowledge; *mit ~en Ausnahmen* with but few exceptions; *der Unterschied ist ~* the difference is small; *sich nichts ~es einbilden* to be self-conceited; **~achten** to think little of s. o.; (*verachten*) to despise; **~achtung** *f* disregard, contempt; **~er** *a* inferior, minor, less; *kein ~erer als* no less a person than; **~fügig** *a* insignificant, trifling, petty; (*bedeutungslos*) trivial; (*wirkungslos*) futile; **~~keit** *f* meanness; insignificance; trifle; **~schätzen** *tr* to undervalue; to attach little value to, to slight s. th.; **~schätzig** *a* derogatory, contemptuous, disdainful; **~schätzung** *f* disdain, scorn, neglect, contempt; **~ste** *a* least, slightest; *nicht im ~~sten* not at all, by no means, not in the least; *~~ Geschwindigkeit* minimum speed; *ich habe nicht den ~~n Zweifel* I have not the slightest doubt; *er hat nicht die ~~ Ahnung* he has not the faintest idea; *selbst die ~~n* even the humblest persons; **~wertig** *a* inferior; of inferior quality.
Gerinn|e *n* running, channel, watercourse; **~en** *irr itr* to coagulate; to congeal, to clod; to concrete; *zum ~en bringen* to coagulate, to curdle; **~en** *n* coagulation; **~sel** *n* rill, gill; (*Blut*) clot, coagulated mass; (*Bach*) rivulet.
geriffelt, gerillt *a* fluted, grooved, serrated; corrugated; profiled.
Geripp|e *n* skeleton, carcass; *arch* framework; *aero* air-frame; **~t** *a* ribbed; (*Weberei*) corded; (*kanneliert*) fluted.
gerissen *a* (*schlau*) smart, cunning,

sly, wily; (*gesprungen*) sprung, flawed; (*geplatzt*) split, chinked; (*Leine*) broken.

German|e *m*, **~in** *f* Teuton, German; **~isch** *a* Teutonic, Germanic; **~isieren** *tr* to Germanize; **~ismus** *m* Germanism; **~ist** *m* Germanic scholar, Germanist.

gern *adv* readily, with pleasure, gladly, willingly; *nicht* ~ unwillingly, reluctantly; ~ *tun* to like to do; ~ *geschehen!* don't mention it! *das glaube ich* ~ I can easily believe that; *herzlich* ~ with all my heart; *er sagte* ~ he used to say; *ich möchte* ~ *wissen* I wonder; ~ *haben*, ~ *mögen* to like, to be fond of; *ich möchte* ~ I should like; ~ *gesehen sein* to be welcome; **~egroß** *m* would-be-great; upstart.

Ge|röchel *n* rattling; **~röll** *n* rubble, boulders *pl*.

Gerste *f* barley; **~ngraupen** *pl* peeled barley; **~ngrütze** *f* barley-groats *pl*; **~nkorn** *n* barley-corn; (*am Auge*) sty; **~saft** *m* barley-water, beer; **~nsuppe** *f* barley-soup; **~nzucker** *m* barley--sugar.

Gerte *f* switch, rod, twig.

Geruch *m* smell, scent; (*starker* ~) odo(u)r; (*~sinn*) sense of smelling; *fig* reputation; (*Duft*) fragrance, perfume; (*der Speisen*) savo(u)r; (*des Weins*) bouquet; **~los** *a* scentless; **~losigkeit** *f* scentlessness; **~snerv** *m* olfactory-nerve; **~ssinn** *m* smell, sense of smell(ing); **~svermögen** *n* power of smelling.

Ge|rücht *n* rumo(u)r, report; (*Hörensagen*) hearsay; *Am sl* scuttlebutt; *es geht das* ~~ it is rumo(u)red, the story goes; *ein* ~~ *verbreiten* to set a rumo(u)r afloat; **~~emacher** *m* rumo(u)r monger, tale bearer; **~~weise** *adv* as the rumo(u)r goes; **~ruhen** *itr* to be pleased, to condescend; **~ruhsam** *adv* quietly, peacefully; leisurely; **~rumpel** *n* rumbling; **~rümpel** *n* trash, lumber, junk.

Gerundium *n* gerund.

Ge|rüst *n arch* scaffold(ing); (*Gestell*) trestle; (*Hängewerk*) truss; (*allg Vorrichtung*) platform, stage, frame; *ein* ~~ *aufschlagen* to put up a scaffold; **~~klammer** *f* cramp, dog; **~~stange** *f* scaffolding-pole; **~rüttel** *n* shaking; (*Wagen*) jolting.

*

Ges *n mus* G flat.

Gesalbte(r) *m* Saviour.

gesamt *a* whole, united, entire, total, aggregate, all-round, over-all, general; **~absatz** *m* total sale; **~ansicht** *f* general view; **~arbeiterschaft** *f* entire body of workers; **~arbeitszeit** *f* floor--to-floor time; **~aufkommen** *n* total yield; **~aufstellung** *f* collective statement; **~ausfuhr** *f* total exports *pl*; **~ausgabe** *f typ* complete edition; **~ausgaben** *f pl* total expenses *pl*; **~auslagen** *f pl* total outlay; **~bedarf** *m* total requirement; **~belegschaft** *f* total of employees; **~betrag** *m* total amount, sum total; **~bürgen** *m pl* point guarantors *pl*; **~eigentümer** *m* joint owner; **~einfuhr** *f* total imports *pl*; **~einkommen** *n* aggregate income; **~einnahmen** *f pl*, **~erlös** *m* total receipts *pl*; **~ergebnis** *n* total result; **~ertrag** *m* entire proceeds *pl*; **~fläche** *f* total area; **~flugstrecke** *f aero* maximum range; **~flugzeit** *f aero* total flying time; **~forderung** *f* total claim; **~gebiet** *n* entire territory, whole field; **~gewicht** *n* total weight; **~gewinn** *m* overall profit; **~gläubiger** *m* joint creditor; **~grundschuld** *f* collective charge; **~haftung** *f* joint liability; **~heit** *f* total(ity), the whole; (*Summe*) sum total; **~kapital** *n* joint capital; **~kassenumsatz** *m* total turnover; **~kosten** *pl* total expenses *pl*; **~kriegführung** *f* grand strategy; **~lage** *f* overall situation; **~länge** *f* overall length; **~leistung** *f* total output, *el* total power; **~masse** *f* total estate; **~plan** *m* overall plan; **~produktion** *f* total output; **~prokura** *f* joint procuration; **~schaden** *m* total loss; **~schau** *f* total view; **~schuld** *f* joint and several liability; **~schuldner** *m* joint (and several) debtor; **~stimmenzahl** *f* total votes cast; **~summe** *f* total amount, sum total; **~übersicht** *f* general survey; **~umfang** *m* total volume; **~umsatz** *m* total turnover; **~verantwortlichkeit** *f* collective responsibility; **~vermögen** *n* aggregate property; **~verlust** *m* total loss; **~verpflichtungen** *f pl* total liabilities *pl*; **~wert** *m* total value; **~wohl** *n* public welfare; **~zahl** *f* total number; **~zufuhr** *f* aggregate arrivals *pl*.

Gesandt|e(r) *m* ambassador, envoy; *der päpstliche* ~*e* nuncio; **~in** *f* ambassadress; **~schaft** *f* embassy, legation; **~~sattaché** *m* attaché; **~~spersonal** *n* officials *pl* attached to an embassy.

Gesang *m* song, singing; *eccl* chant, hymn; (*e-r Dichtung*) canto; **~buch** *n* book of songs, hymn-book; **~lehrer** *m* singing-master; **~stimme** *f* vocal part; **~verein** *m* choral society, *Am* glee-club.

Ge|säß *n* seat, backside, bottom, buttocks *pl*; **~~gurt** *m* (*Fallschirm*) leg-loop; **~sause** *n* (*Wellen*) roaring; (*Wind*) whistling; (*Ohren*) singing; **~säusel** *n* murmuring; rustling.

*

Geschäft *n* (*Unternehmen*) transaction; (*Firma*) business, firm, enterprise, concern; (*Angelegenheit*) affair; *Handel*) commerce, trade; (*Risiko*) venture; (*Beschäftigung*) occupation, trade, job; (*Laden*) shop, *Am* store; (*Büro*) office; *com* deal; *ein* ~ *betreiben* to carry on a business; *sich auf ein* ~ *einlassen* to embark upon a business; *ein gutes* ~ *machen* to make a good bargain; *ein* ~ *übernehmen* to take over a business; *ein* ~ *vergrößern* to expand a business; *ein* ~ *zustande bringen* to secure a business; *laufende* ~*e* current business; ~*e abwickeln* to settle o.'s business; *in* ~*en reisen* to travel on business; *ein einträgliches* ~ remunerative business; *im Drange der* ~*e* in the hurry of business; ~*e halber* on business; **~ig** *a* busy, active; (*fleißig*) industrious; (*eifrig*) eager ;(*dienstfertig*) officious; **~~keit** *f* activity, industry; (*Tatkraft*) energy; (*unnötige*) fuss; **~lich** *a* relating to business, commercial; ~~ *betrachtet* from a business point of view; ~~*e Verluste* business losses; ~~ *tätig sein* to be in business; *ich muß ihn* ~~ *sprechen* I have to see him on business; ~~*es Ansehen* business reputation; ~~*e Empfehlung* business reference.

Geschäfts|abschluß *m* conclusion of a business; business transaction; **~adresse** *f* business address; **~angelegenheit** *f* business matter; *in* ~~*en* on business; **~anteil** *m* share in a business, business interest; **~anzeige** *f* business ad(vertisement); **~aufgabe** *f* giving-up of business; retiring from business; (*Liquidierung*) liquidation of business; **~aufschwung** *m* boom; **~aufsicht** *f* legal control; **~aussichten** *f pl* business prospects *pl*; **~bedingungen** *f pl* trade conditions *pl*; **~belebung** *f* recovery; **~bereich** *m* sphere of activity, scope; *jur* jurisdiction; **~bericht** *m* business report; (*Marktbericht*) market report; **~besuch** *m* business call; **~beteiligung** *f* participation in business; **~betrieb** *m* business operations *pl*; (*Ort*) place of business; (*Firma*) commercial enterprise; **~beziehungen** *f pl* business relations *pl*; **~brief** *m* business letter; **~bücher** *n pl* account books *pl*; **~einlage** *f* investment; **~empfehlung** *f* offer of services; **~erfahrung** *f* business experience; **~eröffnung** *f* establishment of a business; **~fähig** *a* legally capable; ~~ *sein* to possess legal capacity; **~fähigkeit** *f* legal capacity; **~flaute** *f* slump; **~frau** *f* business woman; **~freund** *m* correspondent; **~führend** *a* managing, acting; **~führer** *m* manager, superintendent; (*Verein*) secretary; **~führung** *f* conduct of business; **~gang** *m* (*Besorgung*) errand; (*Entwicklung*) course of business; (*Tendenz*) trend of affairs; (*alltäglicher*) office routine; *schlechter* ~~ depression of business; **~gebaren** *n* dealings *pl*, transactions *pl*; business policy; **~gebäude** *n* business premises *pl*; **~gegend** *f* business quarter; (*Läden*) shopping centre; **~geheimnis** *n* business secret; **~gewandt** *a* smart, skilled in business; **~grundlage** *f* business basis; **~gründung** *f* foundation of a business; **~haus** *n* commercial firm; **~inhaber** *m* owner of a firm; **~interesse** *n* business interest; **~jahr** *n* business year; **~kapital** *n* capital; **~kenntnis** *f* experience in business; **~kosten** *pl* costs of management; **~kunde** *m* customer; **~kundig** *a* experienced in business; **~lage** *f* state of business; business outlook; (*Ort*) business quarter; **~leben** *n* business life; **~leiter** *m* manager; **~leitung** *f* management of a firm; **~leute** *pl* businessmen *pl*; (*Stand*) trading class; **~lokal** *n* (*Laden*) shop; (*Büro*) office; **~los** *a* dull, slack, lifeless; **~mann** *m* businessman; (*Laden*) tradesman; **~mäßig** *a* in a businesslike manner; (*mechanisch*) perfunctory; **~methoden** *f pl* business methods (*od* practices) *pl*; **~ordnung** *f parl* standing orders *pl*, (*Tagesordnung*) agenda; (*Büro*) routine orders *pl*; (*Fabrik*) working order; *zur* ~~ *sprechen* to rise to order; **~papiere** *n pl* commercial papers *pl*; **~personal** *n* staff; **~räume** *m pl* business premises *pl*; **~reise** *f* business tour; **~reisende(r)** *m* commercial travel(l)er, *Am* salesman; **~routine** *f* business routine; **~rückgang** *m* business decline; **~schluß** *m* closing time; *nach* ~~ after business hours; **~sitz** *m* place of business; **~spesen** *pl* business expenses *pl*; **~stelle** *f* office; (*untergeordnete*) agency; **~stockung** *f* dul(l)ness of trade; **~stunden** *f pl* office hours *pl*; **~tätigkeit** *f* business activity; **~träger** *m* agent; representative; chargé d'affaires; **~tüchtig** *a* smart; **~übernahme** *f* taking over of business; **~umfang** *m* volume of business; **~umsätze** *m pl* business transactions *pl*; **~unfähig** *a* legally incompetent; **~unfähigkeit** *f* legal incapacity; **~unkosten** *pl* business expenses *pl*; overhead expenses *pl*; **~unterlagen** *f pl* business data *pl*; **~unternehmen** *n* commercial enterprise; **~verbindung** *f* business connection; ~~*en anknüpfen* to open business relations; **~verhältnisse** *n pl* business conditions *pl*; **~verkehr** *m* commercial intercourse; **~verlegung** *f* removal of business; **~viertel** *n* business quarter, shopping district, *Am* business-block; *Am* down town; **~wagen** *m* (*Lieferwagen*) delivery-van; **~welt** *f* business (world); **~zeichen** *n* file number; **~zeit** *f* office hours *pl*; **~zentrum** *n* business centre, (*Läden*) shopping centre; **~zimmer** *n* office, bureau; *mil* orderly room; **~zweig** *m* branch (*od* line) of business; (*besonderer ~~*) speciality.

geschehen *irr itr* to happen, to occur, to chance, to come to pass; (*erledigen*) to be done; (*stattfinden*) to take place; *~ lassen* to allow, to suffer; *nicht ~ lassen* to prevent, to stop; *gern ~!* don't mention it! *was ~ ist, ist ~* what's done is done; *was soll damit ~?* what is to be done with it? ... *so ~ zu* done at ...; *was ist ~?* what's the matter? *das geschieht dir recht* it serves you right; *dein Wille geschehe!* thy will be done! *was soll nun ~?* what shall be done about it? *es ist um ihn ~* he is done for.

Geschehnis *n* event, incident, occurrence, happening; (*Unfall*) accident.

gescheit *a* intelligent, clever, knowing; smart, bright; (*scharfsinnig*) sagacious; (*geschickt*) cunning; *du bist nicht ~!* you must be crazy! *fam* you have bats in the belfry! *ich werde daraus nicht ~* I don't understand it; *sei doch ~* be reasonable; **~heit** *f* intelligence, cleverness, smartness; **~tuer** *m* wiseacre, *Am* wisenheimer.

Geschenk *n* present, gift; (*Schenkung*) donation; (*kleines Geldgeschenk*) gratuity; (*Gabe*) boon; *zum ~ machen* to make a present of s. th.; **~artikel** *m* souvenir, gift; **~~geschäft** *n* gift shop; **~geber** *m* donor; **~nehmer** *m* donee; **~packung** *f* gift box (*od* pack *od* carton).

Geschicht|chen *n* little story, anecdote; **~e** *f* history; (*Erzählung*) story, tale, narrative; (*Angelegenheit*) affair; (*Ereignis*) event; (*persönliche*) story; *biblische ~~* Scripture; *die ~~ des Altertums* Ancient History; *e-e schöne ~~* a pretty mess; *mach keine ~~n!* don't make a fuss! *e-e seltsame ~~* a queer story; *e-e alte ~~* a twice-told tale; *er versucht ~~n zu machen* he tries to make trouble; *die ganze ~~* the whole business; *damit ist e-e ~~ verknüpft* thereby hangs a tale; *~en erzählen* to tell tales; *das ist der Haken an der ~~* that's the great big but; *~~ e-s Falles* case history; **~enbuch** *n* story-book; **~enerzähler** *m* story-teller; **~lich** *a* historical.

Geschichts|auffassung *f*, **~bild** *n* conception of history; **~buch** *n* history-book; **~forscher** *m* historian; **~forschung** *f* historical research; **~kenntnis** *f* knowledge of history; **~klitterung** *f* bias(s)ed account of historical events; **~philosophie** *f* philosophy of history; **~schreiber** *m* historian, (*amtlicher*) historiographer; **~studium** *n* study of history; **~stunde** *f* history lesson; **~tabellen** *f pl* historical tables *pl*; **~unterricht** *m* teaching of history; **~werk** *n* historical work; **~wissenschaft** *f* science of history.

Geschick *n* (*Fähigkeit*) aptitude; (*Geschicklichkeit*) dexterity; skill, facility; (*Schicksal*) destiny, fate, lot; **~lichkeit** *f* skil(l)fulness, ability, aptitude, skill, dexterity; fitness; **~t** *a* skil(l)ful, clever, able; dexterous, deft, handy; *zu allem ~~* up to everything; *zu etw ~~* skilled to.

Geschiebe *n* rubble, boulder, detritus; (*Schieben*) shoving.

geschieden *a* separated; (*Ehe*) divorced; *wir sind ~e Leute* we have done with each other.

Geschirr *n* vessel; (*irdenes*) crockery, earthenware, pottery; (*feuerfestes ~*) heat-proof ovenware; (*Kaffee~*) coffee service; (*Porzellan*) china; (*Küchen~*) kitchen utensils *pl*; (*Tafel~*) plates and dishes; (*Nacht~*) chamber-pot; (*Pferde~*) gear, harness; (*Fuhrwerk*) carriage; *sich ins ~ legen* to launch out; to go at it with a will; **~schrank** *m* china cabinet, (*im Wohnzimmer*) side-board; **~spüler, ~wascher** *m* (automatic) dishwasher; **~tuch** *n* dish towel; tea-cloth.

Geschlecht *n* sex; (*Art*) species; genus; kind; (*Abstammung*) birth; descent; blood; family; race, stock; (*Menschenalter*) generation; *gram* gender; *das schöne ~* the fair sex; **~erfolge** *f* generations *pl*; **~erkunde** *f* genealogy; **~lich** *a* sexual; (*Gattung*) generic.

Geschlechts|akt *m* coitus, copulation; **~beziehungen** *f pl* sexual relations *pl*; **~drüse** *f* genital gland; **~krank** *a* suffering from venereal disease; **~krankheit** *f* venereal disease (*Abk* VD); **~leben** *n* sex life; **~los** *a* sexless; *gram* neuter; *bot* agamous; **~name** *m* surname, family name; **~organ** *n* sexual organ; **~reife** *f* puberty; **~teile** *m pl* genitals *pl*; privates *pl*; **~trieb** *m* sexual desire (*od* libido *od* instinct); *den ~~ reizend* aphrodisiac; **~verkehr** *m* sexual intercourse; **~wort** *n gram* article.

geschliffen *a* (*Glas*) cut; *fig* polished; *mil sl* well-trained.

Ge|schlinge *n* pluck; (*Gedärme e-s Vogels*) ropes *pl*; **~schluchze** *n* convulsive sobbing.

geschlossen *a* (*ganz*) whole, complete; (*gemeinsam*) united; unanimous.

Geschmack *m* taste; (*von Speisen*) savo(u)r, (*angenehmer*) flavo(u)r, relish; *fig* taste, fancy, liking for; *etw nach ~ finden* to find s. th. to o.'s liking; *an etw ~ finden* to relish, to take a fancy to s. th.; *über den ~ läßt sich nicht streiten* there is no accounting for tastes; *jeder nach seinem eigenen ~* everybody to his own liking; *wenig ~ haben an* to have little stomach for; *Geschmäcker sind verschieden* tastes differ; **~los** *a* tasteless; (*fade*) flat, insipid, wishy-washy; *fig* of (in) bad taste; **~losigkeit** *f* tastelessness; flatness; *fig* bad taste; *das ist e-e ~~* that is bad taste; **~sache** *f* matter of taste; **~voll** *a* tasteful, savo(u)ry; (*Kleidung*) stylish, elegant; *~~ gekleidet* dressed in good taste.

Ge|schmeide *n* trinkets *pl*; jewel(le)ry; **~~kästchen** *n* casket, jewel-case; **~schmeidig** *a* pliant, smooth; (*elastisch*) supple, limber, lithe, lissom(e); (*biegsam*) ductile; (*hämmerbar*) malleable; (*einschmeichelnd*) insinuating; *~~ machen* to make supple; **~~keit** *f* pliantness; (*von Metallen*) ductility; (*der Zunge*) volubility of (the) tongue, glibness; **~schmeiß** *n* vermin; *fig* mob, populace, rabble; **~schmetter** *n* (*Trompeten*) flourish; **~schmiere** *n* daub(ing); (*Kritzelei*) scribbling; **~schmorte(s)** *n* stew; **~schnatter** *n* (*Henne, Gänse*) cackling, (*Ente*) quacking, (*Frauen*) chatter(ing); **~schniegelt** *a* smart, trimmed, spruce, dressed-up; *~~ u. gebügelt* spick-and-span; **~schöpf** *n* creature; **~schoß** *n* projectile; (*e-s Geschützes*) shell; (*e-s Gewehrs*) bullet; (*spitziges*) dart; (*ferngelenktes*) guided missile; (*Stockwerk*) stor(e)y, floor, flat; *im ersten ~~* on the first (*Am* second) floor; **~~aufschlag** *m* impact; **~~bahn** *f* trajectory; **~~garbe** *f* cone of fire; **~~hülle** *f* envelope; (*Granate*) case; **~~kammer** *f mar* shell room; **~~kern** *m* core of projectile; **~~wirkung** *f* fire effect; **~schraubt** *a* forced; affected; (*Stil*) stilted; **~schrei** *n* cry; shrieks *pl*; (*Menge*) clamo(u)r; *fig* great noise; fuss; (*Freuden~*) shout; (*Esel*) bray(ing); *ein großes ~~ erheben* to set up a loud cry; *viel ~~ um nichts* much ado about nothing; **~schreibsel** *n* scrawl, scribbling.

Geschütz *n* cannon, gun; piece; *schweres ~* ordnance; *ein ~ auffahren* to bring the gun into action; **~bedienung** *f* gunners *pl*; **~donner** *m* roar of the guns; **~protze** *f* carriage of a gun; **~feuer** *n* gunfire; **~führer** *m* number 1 gunner; **~gießerei** *f* gun foundry; **~instandsetzungswerkstatt** *f* ordnance shop; **~lafette** *f* gun mounting; **~mannschaft** *f* gun crew; **~park** *m* ordnance park; **~rohr** *n* barrel; **~stand** *m* emplacement; **~stellung** *f* gun position; **~turm** *m mar* turret.

Ge|schwader *n* squadron; *aero* group; squadron, wing; **~~flug** *m* flight in formation; formation flying; **~~keil** *m aero* wing wedge formation; **~~kommandeur, ~~kommandant** *m mar, aero* commodore; **~schwätz** *n* idle talk, chatter, gossip, blab, tattle, prattle; (*unaufrichtiges ~~*) *parl Am* buncombe; (*Phrasen*) claptrap; **~schwätzig** *a* talkative, prattling, loquacious, garrulous, voluble; (*einfältiges*) babbling; **~~keit** *f* talkativeness; loquacity, garrulity, garrulousness, volubility, volubleness; **~schweift** *a* arched, curved; (*mit Schwanz*) with a tail; **~schweige** *adv, conj:* *~~ denn* to say nothing of, not to mention; (*noch viel weniger*) much less, let alone, far from.

geschwind *a* quick, swift, speedy, fast, rapid; (*eilig*) hasty; (*schnell u. wirksam*) expeditious; (*flink*) fleet; **~igkeit** *f* quickness, speed; swiftness, rapidity, celerity, velocity, *Am* clip; (*Schwung*) momentum; (*Tempo u. fig*) pace; (*Vorwärtsbewegung*) headway; (*Personen*) haste, hurry; (*rasche Erledigung*) expedition, promptness; (*verhältnismäßige ~~*) rate; *mit e-r ~~ von* at the rate of, at a speed of; *höchste ~~* top (*od* maximum) speed; *mit größter ~~* at full speed; *an ~~ zunehmen* to gather speed; *die ~~ vermindern* to slow down, to decelerate; **~~sabfall** *m* loss of speed; **~~sbeschränkung** *f*, **~~grenze** *f* speed limit; **~~smesser** *m* speedometer, speed ga(u)ge, *aero* airspeed indicator; **~~srekord** *m* speed record; **~schritt** *m* double-quick step.

Geschwirr *n* whirring, buzzing.

Geschwister *pl* brother(s) and sister(s); **~kind** *n* first cousin; **~lich** *a* brotherly, sisterly; **~liebe** *f* brotherly *or* sisterly love; **~paar** *n* brother and sister.

ge|schwollen *a* swollen, tumid; **~schworene(r)** *m* juryman; *die ~schworenen* the jury; **~schworenenbank** *f* jury box; **~schworenengericht** *n* jury, (*periodisch*) assizes *pl*; **~schworenenliste** *f* array, panel; jury-list; **~schwulst** *f* swelling, (*Pustel*) rising; (*Furunkel*) boil; (*Tumor*) tumo(u)r; **~schwür** *n* gathering, sore, ulcer; abscess; boil; **~~ig** *a* ulcerous.

*

Geselchte *n dial* smoked meat.

Gesell|e *m* mate, companion, comrade; (*Kerl*) fellow; (*Handwerk*) helper, journeyman; *Schneider~~* journeyman tailor; **~en** *tr* to associate with, to link together, to join with; *sich ~~ zu* to associate to, to join s. o., to unite; *gleich u. gleich gesellt sich gern* birds of a feather flock together; like will to like; **~enjahr** *n* journeyman's time of service; **~enlohn** *m* journeyman's wages *pl*; **~enstück** *n* journeyman-work; **~ig** *a* social, sociable; (*heiter*) convivial; (*zus. arbeitend*) co-operative; (*umgänglich*) companionable; (*herdenmäßig*) gregarious; (*gastlich*) hospitable; *~~er Mensch Am* good mixer; **~igkeit** *f* sociableness, sociability; social life.

Gesellschaft *f* society, company; (*geladene ~*) party; social gathering; (*Schicht*) set, gang; (*Gruppe*) group, collection, band, *Am* bunch; (*Schauspieler*) troupe; (*Vereinigung*) union; *com* company; untertaking; association; *Am* corporation; (*Aktien~*) joint stock company; *offene Handels~* partnership; *Kommandit~* limited partnership; *~ mit beschränkter Haftpflicht* limited (liability) company (*Abk* Ltd), *Am* incorporated company (*Abk* Inc); *Handels~* trading company; *Angehöriger der guten ~ Am* socialite; *junge Dame, die in die ~ eingeführt wird* deb(utante), *Am* bud; *e-e ~ geben* to give (*Am* to throw) a party; *sich e-r ~ anschließen* to make one of the party; *auf der ~* at the party; *die ganze ~* (*fam*) the whole lot; *ich traf sie manchmal in ~* I sometimes met her socially; *sie ist in die ~ eingeführt* she has come out; *jdm ~ leisten* to keep company with s. o.; to bear s. o. company; *in ~ mit* in company with; *ich befinde mich in guter ~* I am in good company; *viel in ~en gehen* to see much company; *e-e geschlossene ~* a private company; *bürgerliche ~* civil society; *vornehme ~* fashionable society; *~ Jesu* the Society of Jesus; *eingetragene ~* registered (*Am* incorporated) company; *gemeinnützige ~* non-profit making company; *e-e ~ gründen* to promote a company; *jederzeit kündbare ~* partnership at will; *e-e ~ auflösen* to dissolve a partnership, to wind up a company; **~er(in)** *m* (*f*) (lady) companion; *com* partner, associate; *ausscheidender ~~* retiring partner; *stiller ~~* sleeping partner; *tätiger ~* working partner; *er ist ein guter ~~* he is good company; **~lich** *a* social; sociable.

Gesellschafts|abend *m* social evening, party; **~anschluß** *m tele* party line; **~anteil** *m* partner's investment; **~anzug** *m* evening dress; party dress; formal dress; dress uniform; **~dame** *f* lady companion; **~fähig** *a* gentlemanlike; ladylike; **~fahrt, ~reise** *f* conducted tour; **~inseln** *f pl* Society Islands *pl*; **~kapital** *n* (*Grundkapital*) joint stock, *Am* capital stock; **~klatsch** *m* society gossip; **~kleid** *n* evening frock, dinner-gown; party dress; **~kreis** *m* circle of society, circle of acquaintance(s); **~lehre** *f* sociology; **~ordnung** *f* social order; **~raum** *m* banqueting hall; **~reise** *f* conducted tour; **~register** *n* commercial register; **~spiel** *n* round game, party game; **~stück** *n* social drama; **~tanz** *m* society dance; **~vermögen** *n* joint capital; (*AG*) corporate property; (*OHG*) partnership property; **~vertrag** *m* articles (*od* deed) of partnership; social contract; **~wissenschaft** *f* social sciences *pl*; **~zimmer** *n* reception-room, drawing room.

Gesenk *n* socket, pit; *tech* swage; (forging) die; **~arbeit** *f* die work; **~form** *f* die; **~presse** *f* forging press; **~schmiederei** *f* deap forging.

Gesetz *n* law, act; (*Regel, Satzung*) rule; (*Vorschrift, Gebot*) commandment; (*Vorschlag*) bill; *geschriebenes ~* statute; *tech* principle; *auf Grund e-s ~es* under a law, by virtue of a law; *kraft des ~es* on the strength of a law; *ein ~ in Kraft setzen* to enact a law; *ein ~ abändern* to amend a law; *ein ~ annehmen* (*parl*) to pass an act; *ein ~ aufheben* to abrogate (*od* repeal) a law; *ein ~ erlassen* to enact a law; *unter ein ~ fallen* to come under a law; *ein ~ übertreten* to contravene a law; *ein ~ umgehen* to evade (*od* defeat) a law; *ein ~ verletzen, e-m ~ zuwiderhandeln* to violate a law; *das ~ gilt* the law prevails; *zum ~ werden* to pass into a law; *es sich zum ~ machen* to make it a rule; **~antrag** *m* bill; *e-n ~~ stellen* to move a bill; **~auslegung** *f* interpretation of the law; **~blatt** *n* law gazette; **~buch** *n* code, statute-book; **~entwurf** *m* bill, draft law; **~esauslegung** *f* law interpretation; **~esbestimmung** *f* provision of a law; **~eskraft** *f* legal force; *~~ haben* to be enacted; **~eslücke** *f* loophole in the law; **~essammlung** *f* digest (of laws); **~estext** *m* legal text; **~esübertreter** *m* offender; **~esübertretung** *f* transgression (of the law), violation, offence, *Am* offense; **~esvorlage** *f* (draft of a) bill; **~esvorschrift** *f* legal provision; **~gebend** *a* legislative; **~geber** *m* law-giver, legislator; **~gebung** *f* legislature; legislation; **~lich** *a* lawful, rightful, legal, legitimate; statutory; *den ~~en Bedingungen entsprechen* to satisfy the requirements of a law; *~~ geschützt* patented; registered; *~~ vorgeschrieben* required by law; *~~er Erbe* heir at law; *~~es Alter* legal age; *~~er Anspruch* legal claim; *~~es Hindernis* statutory bar; *~~e englische Meile* statute mile; *~~ geschütztes Verfahren* patented procedure; *~~er Vertreter* legal representative; *~~es Zahlungsmittel* legal tender; **~lichkeit** *f* lawfulness, legitimacy; **~los** *a* lawless, illegal; **~losigkeit** *f* lawlessness, illegalness; **~mäßig** *a* lawful, legal; *tech* regular; **~~keit** *f* lawfulness, legality; legitimacy, according to statutes; **~sammlung** *f* body of laws; code; **~tafeln** *f pl* Decalogue; **~widrig** *a* unlawful; **~~keit** *f* unlawfulness.

gesetzt *a* (*ruhig*) quiet, sedate, calm; (*ernst*) grave, serious; (*nüchtern*) sober; (*bescheiden*) modest; *von ~em Alter* of mature age; *~es Wesen* dignified demeano(u)r; *~ den Fall, daß ...* supposed (*od* supposing) that; *~ den Fall, er käme hierher* suppose he should come here; **~heit** *f* sedateness, gravity.

gesichert *a* safe, certain; secured; (*Schraube*) locked.

Gesicht *n* face; (*Miene*) countenance; (*Sehvermögen*) sight; (*Erscheinung*) apparition, vision; (*Sinnestäuschung*) hallucination; (*Aussehen*) aspect, look; appearance; *das steht dir gut zu ~* that is becoming to you; that is suiting you; *jdn zu ~ bekommen* to set eyes upon s. o., to catch sight of; *über das ganze ~ lachen* to be all smiles; *jdm ins ~ sagen* to say to o.'s face; *sie ist ihrer Mutter wie aus dem ~ geschnitten* she's the spitting image of her mother; *er machte ein langes ~* his countenance fell; *er machte ein saures ~* he made a sour face; *ein böses ~ machen* to have an angry look; *das schlägt allen guten Sitten ins ~* that makes light of good manners; *ins ~ sehen* to face; *zweites ~* second sight; *die Sache hat damit ein anderes ~* that puts a different light on the matter; *ins ~ lachen* to laugh in o.'s face; *jdm ein ~ machen* to make mouths at s. o.; *aus dem ~ verlieren* to lose sight of; *~er schneiden* to make faces; **~chen** *n* pretty face.

Gesichts|ausdruck *m*, **~bildung** *f* physiognomy, features *pl*; **~behandlung** *f fam* facial; **~eindruck** *m* visual impression; **~farbe** *f* complexion; **~feld** *n* visual field; field of view; range; visibility; objective (subjective) angular field; **~kreis** *m* (mental) horizon; sphere of activity; *seinen ~~ erweitern* to broaden o.'s mind; *das liegt außerhalb seines ~~es* that's beyond him; *innerhalb des ~~es* within view; **~krem** *m* facial cream; **~linie** *f* visual line; collimation; **~maske** *f* false face; *med* face mask; (*Schutzmaske*) protective mask, face shield; **~massage** *f* facial (massage); **~muskel** *m* facial muscle; **~nerv** *m* facial nerv; (*Sehnerv*) optic nerve; **~operation** *f* (*Kosmetik*) face lifting; **~punkt** *m* point of view, viewpoint, aspect; feature; principle; *phys* point of sight, visual point; **~puder** *m* face-powder; **~rose** *f* erysipelas; **~schärfe** *f* visual acuity; **~schmerz** *m* face-ache; **~seife** *f* toilet (*od* face) soap; **~sinn** *m* vision, (sense of) sight; **~täuschung** *f* optical illusion, hallucination; **~wasser** *n* skin tonic lotion; astringent; **~winkel** *m* optic angle; *med* facial angle; **~zug** *m* lineament, feature.

Gesims *n* mo(u)lding, shelf; (*vorstehender Rand*) ledge; (*Dach*) cornice; (*Fenster*) sill; (*Kamin~*) mantelpiece.

Gesinde *n* domestics *pl*, servants *pl*, household; **~l** *n* rabble, mob, trash, riffraff, ragtag and bobtail, *Am* scalawags *pl*.

ge|sinnt *a* minded, disposed; affected; **~sinnung** *f* mind; way of thinking; (*Auffassung*) opinion; (*Ansicht*) view; (*Glaube*) belief; (*Überzeugung*) conviction; (*Charakteranlage*) disposition; (*Treue*) loyalty; (*fester Glaube*) persuasion; **~~sgenosse** *m* adherent, partisan, follower, supporter; **~~slos** *a* (*wankelmütig*) inconstant; without principles; unprincipled; **~~slosigkeit** *f* lack of character; **~~streu** *a* loyal; **~~streue** *f* loyalty; **~~stüchtig** *a* sta(u)nch, constant, loyal; **~~swechsel** *m* change of mind (*od* opinion); (*politisch*) change of front, reversal of o.'s policy.

ge|sittet *a* (*höflich*) polite, courteous; (*kultiviert*) civilized; *wohl ~~* well-bred; well-mannered; *übel ~~* ill-bred; **~sittung** *f* civilization; (*gutes Benehmen*) good manners *pl*; **~sonnen** *a* inclined, disposed; resolved; **~spann** *n* team, set; (*Ochsen*) yoke; (*Paar*) pair, couple.

gespannt *a* tense, tight; stretched; (*Seil*) taut; (*Gewehrschloß*) cocked; *fig* (*Beziehungen*) strained; (*Lage*) tense; (*Aufmerksamkeit*) intent, close; *~ sein* to be anxious (*od* curious), to wonder; *~e Erwartungen* high-wrought expectations; *~e Aufmerksamkeit* close attention; *mit jdm auf ~em Fuße stehen* to be on bad terms with; **~heit** *f* tightness, tension; (*Aufmerksamkeit*) closeness; (*gespannte Beziehungen*) strained relations *pl*; disagreement with.

Ge|spenst *n* spectre, apparition, ghost, spirit, phantom; *er sieht ~~er* he is seeing things; **~~ergeschichte** *f* ghost-story; **~~erhaft** *a*, **~~ig** *a*, **~~isch** *a* ghostly; ghostlike; **~~erstadt** *f* ghost town; **~~erstunde** *f* midnight hour, ghostly hour; **~sperre** *n* safety catch, ratchet; locking mechanism; *fig* resistance; **~sperrt** *pp, a* blocked up, shut (up); barred; checked; closed, suppressed; *typ* spaced; *~~es Konto com* blocked account; *~~ für Militär* out of bounds, *Am* off limits; **~spiele** *m* playfellow, playmate; **~spielin** *f* playmate; **~spinst** *n* spun yarn, thread; (*Draht~~*) wire netting; (*Tuch*) tissue, textile fabric, web; **~~faser** *f* fibre, *Am* fiber; **~spons** *m* sponse, bridegroom; **~spött** *n* scoffing, mockery, derision, jeer, gibe; *sich zum ~~ machen* to make a fool of o. s.; *sein ~~ mit jdm treiben* to scoff (*od* to mock) s. o.; *zum ~~ dienen* to be the laughing-stock (of).

Gespräch *n* talk, conversation, colloquy; *tele* call; message; connection; (*gelehrtes ~*) discourse; (*Debatte*) discussion; (*Zwie~*) dialog(ue); *sich in ein ~ einlassen* to enter into conversation with; *ein ~ in Gang bringen* to set a conversation going; *das ~ auf e-n Gegenstand bringen* to introduce a subject; *sie war das ~ der ganzen Stadt* she was the talk of the whole town; *dringendes ~* (*tele*) emergency (*od* priority) call; *~ mit Herbeiruf tele Am* messenger call; *~ mit Voranmeldung tele* préavis call, prearranged call; *ein ~ anmelden tele* to book (*od* to file) a call; *ein ~ verlängern* (*über 3 Minuten*) *tele* to extend a call (beyond three minutes); **~ig** *a* talkative, communicative; **~igkeit** *f* affability, talkativeness; **~sabwicklung** *f tele* handling of calls; **~sanmeldung** *f tele* registration of a call; **~sdauer** *f tele* duration of a call; **~sfaden, ~sgegenstand, ~sstoff** *m*, **~sthema** *n* topic of a conversation; subject; **~sform** *f*: *in ~~* in the form of a dialog(ue), interlocutory; **~spartner** *m* interlocutor; **~sweise** *adv* colloquially, by way of conversation; in the course of conversation; **~szeit** *f tele* ticket time.

gespreizt *pp, a* (*auseinanderstehend*) wide apart; *fig* affected, pompous; (*Stil*) stilted; **~heit** *f* affectation, mannerism.

gesprenkelt *a* speckled, mottled.

Gestade *n* (*Meer*) shore; (*flaches Ufer*) beach; (*Fluß*) bank.

Gestalt *f* form; (*Wuchs*) stature; build; (*Figur, Körperbau*) frame; (*äußere ~*) shape; (*Umriß*) figure, contour; (*Schnitt*) fashion; (*Weise*) manner, aspect, kind, fashion; (*in Roman etc*) character; (*Struktur*) configuration; (*Größe*) size, bulk; *tech* design, construction; (*e-r Flugbahn*) curve; (*Psychologie*) *~ annehmen* to take shape; *sich in seiner wahren ~ zeigen* to show o. s. in o.'s true character; *unter beiderlei ~* in both kinds; **~en** *tr* to form, to shape; to mo(u)ld; to arrange; to design; to construct; *r* to take shape, to show, to prove; to turn out; **~er** *m* former, shaper, fashioner; *tech* draftsman, designer, constructor; **~et** *pp, a* formed, shaped; *wohl~~* well-shaped (*od*-shaped); **~los** *a* shapeless, amorphous; (*unkörperlich*) immaterial; **~losigkeit** *f* shapelessness; immateriality; **~ung** *f* formation; *geog* configuration; (*Art*) fashioning, style; (*Zustand*) state; (*Lage*) situation, position; (*Konstruktion*) construction, design, structure; **~~fähig** *a* plastic; **~wandel** *m* metamorphosis.

Gestammel *n* stammering, stuttering.

geständ|ig *a* confessing; *~~ sein* to confess, to plead guilty; **~nis** *n* confession, avowal, acknowledg(e)ment; *ein ~~ erpressen von jdm* to extort an admission from s. o., *Am* to third-degree s. o.; *ein ~~ ablegen* to make a clean breast of s. th..

Gestänge *n* rods *pl*, gear; *rail* track; (*Hirsch*) antlers *pl*; (*Umzäunung*) enclosure of stakes.

Gestank *m* bad smell, stink, stench.

gestatt|en *tr* to permit, to allow; to consent; (*gewähren*) to grant; *r* to take the liberty; *com* to beg to, to venture; *wir ~ uns, Ihnen mitzuteilen* we beg to inform you; *~ Sie* would you mind, permit me; **~ung** *f* permission, consent.

Geste *f* gesture.

ge|stehen *irr tr* to confess; (*anerkennen*) to acknowledge; (*zugeben*) to admit; (*sich ~~*) to own o. s.; (*bekennen*) to avow; *offen gestanden* frankly; *um die Wahrheit zu ~~* to tell the truth; **~stehungskosten** *pl*, **~stehungspreis** *m* production (*od* factory) cost, prime cost; **~stein** *n* stone, mineral; *min* ground, rock; *taubes ~~* barren-ground, refuse rocks *pl*; **~~sbohrer** *m* borer; **~~sgang** *m* streak, lode; dike; **~~shalde** *f* waste heap; **~~skunde** *f* geognosy, mineralogy; **~~smasse** *f* rock; **~~sschichten** *f pl* strata of rocks; **~stell** *n* frame, stand; (*Stütze*) support; (*Vorrichtung*) rack; (*Bock*) trestle, horse; (*Bücher*) shelf, book-stand; (*Brettergerüst*) scaffold; (*Sockel*) pedestal; (*Bett~~*) bedstead; (*Brillen~~*) spectacle-frame; **~stellung** *f* presentation; muster; appearance; **~~saufschub** *m mil* deferment; **~~sbefehl** *m* enlistment order; order to report for duty; order (for recruits) to appear at a muster; induction order; **~~spflicht** *f* liability for appearance before the draft board; **~~spflichtig** *a* bound to appear for military muster.

gestern *adv* yesterday; *~ früh* yesterday morning; *~ abend* last night; *unser gestriges Schreiben* our letter of yesterday; *~ vor acht Tagen* yesterday week.

ge|sternt *a* starred; **~steuert** *a* controlled, guided; steered; synchronized; *~~e Rakete* controlled rocket; *~~es Geschoß* guided missile.

ge|stiefelt *a* booted, in boots; **~stielt** *a* helved; *bot* petiolate, stalked; **~stikulieren** *itr* to gesticulate; **~stirn** *n* star; (*Sternbild*) constellation; **~stirnpeilung** *f* bearing by stars; **~stirnstand** *m* constellation; **~stirnt** *a* starry, starred; **~stöber** *n* shower, snow-drift; storm; **~stotter** *n* stammer(ing), stuttering; **~sträuch** *n* shrubs *pl*, copse; bushes *pl*; shrubbery; **~streift** *a* striped, streaky; **~streng** *a* severe, strict; rigorous; *~~er Herr* Your Worship; **~strichen** *a* painted; *frisch ~~* wet paint; *~~ voll* brimful.

gestrig *a* of yesterday, yesterday's.

Ge|strüpp *n* thicket of shrubs, brushwood, bushes *pl*; underwood; **~stühl** *n* (*Kirche*) pews *pl*; (*Chor*) choir-stalls *pl*; **~stümper** *n* bungling; **~stüt** *n* stud; **~such** *n* request, demand; (*Bewerbung*) application; (*schriftlich*) petition; (*Antrag*) suit; (*Eingabe*) memorial; (*Bittschrift*) supplication; (*dringend*) entreaty; *bei jdm ein ~~ um etw einreichen* to present (*od* file *od* hand in) a petition for s. th.; *mein ~~ wurde abgelehnt* my application was turned down; *ein ~~ gewähren* to grant a request; *~~e in Zeitungen* want ads (*od* advertisements); *Stellen~~e* situations wanted; **~~formular** *n* application form; **~~steller** *m* applicant, petitioner; **~sucht** *a* wanted; (*begehrt*) sought-after, in brisk demand, in favo(u)r; (*umworben*) courted; (*gekünstelt*) artificial; far-fetched, affected; **~~heit** *f* affectation; **~sudel** *n* (*Kleckserei*) daub; (*Schreiben*) scribbling; **~summ(e)** *n* buzzing, hum, whiz(zing).

gesund *a* healthy, sound; (*geistig*) sane; (*zuträglich*) wholesome; (*wohl*) well; (*natürlich*) natural; (*zuträglich*) beneficial; *frisch u. ~* safe and sound; *wieder ~ werden* to get well again, to recover o.'s health; *~er Menschenverstand* common sense, *Am fam* horse sense; *in ~en u. in kranken Tagen* in sickness and in health; *er ist so ~ wie ein Fisch im Wasser* he is as sound as a bell; *er hat ein ~es Aussehen* he looks well; *~ machen* to cure; *~ schreiben* to issue a certificate of good health; *das ist für ihn ganz ~* it serves him right; **~beterei** *f* faith-cure, faith-healing; **~brunnen** *m* mineral spring; **~en** *itr* to be restored to (*od* to regain) health, to recover; **~heit** *f* health(iness); (*Tiere, Sachen, Auffassungen*) soundness; (*geistig*) sanity; (*Heilsamkeit*) wholesomeness; salubrity, salutariness; *wir sind alle bei bester ~~* we are all in the best of health; *vor ~~ strotzen* to be the very picture of health; *~~!* God bless you! *auf Ihre ~~!* your health! *jds ~~ ausbringen* to give (*od* to propose *od* to submit) the toast of s. o.; *er trank auf meine ~~* he drank my health; **~~lich** *a* hygienic, sanitary; **~~samt** *n* Board of Health, Public Health Administration; **~~sappell** *m* physical inspection; **~~sattest** *n*, **~~spaß** *m* certificate of health; **~~sbuch** *n* individual medical record book; **~~szeugnis** *n* certificate of health; **~~sdienst** *m* medical service; *öffentlicher ~~sdienst* public health service; **~~sfördernd** *a* health-giving, salubrious; (*heilsam*) salutary; **~~sfürsorge, ~~spflege** *f* preservation of health; hygiene; sanitation; public health service; **~~sgefährlich, ~~sschädlich** *a* unhealthy, injurious to health; **~~slehre** *f* hygiene; **~~spolizei** *f* sanitary police; *aus ~~srücksichten f pl* for reasons of health; **~~svorschriften** *f pl* sanitary regulations *pl*; **~~swesen** *n* public health; hygiene, sanitation; **~~s(zu)stand** *m* (*e-s Menschen*) physical condition, state of health; (*Stadt*) sanitary (*od* hygienic) conditions.

Ge|täfel *n* wainscot(t)ing, panel-work; panelling; **~tändel** *n* trifling, dallying; flirting; toying; **~tier** *n* animals *pl*, beasts *pl*; **~tigert** *a* spotted like a tiger; **~töse** *n* violent noise, din; (*Meer*) roaring; (*Wind*) howling; (*Aufruhr*) uproar; **~tragen** *a fig* solemn, ceremonious; **~trampel** *n* trampling, clattering; **~tränk** *n* drink, beverage; (*Arznei*) potion; *geistige ~~e* alcoholic liquors *pl*; spirits *pl*; *alkoholfreie ~~e* minerals *pl*, *Am* soft drinks *pl*; **~~esteuer** *f* beverage tax; **~trauen** *r* to dare, to make bold to, to venture.

Getreide *n* corn, *bes. Am* grain; (*genußfertig*) cereals *pl*; *das ~ steht gut* the crop looks promising; **~arten** *f pl* cereals *pl*; **~bau** *m* corn-growing; **~boden** *m* corn-land; (*Speicher*) granary; **~börse** *f* corn exchange; **~brand** *m* smut; **~ernte** *f* corn crop, *Am* grain harvest; **~feld** *n* corn field; **~halm** *m* corn-stalk; **~handel** *m* corn-trade; **~händler** *m* corn factor, *Am* grain broker; **~heber, ~fänger** *m* grain elevator; **~land** *n* corn-growing country; (*Boden*) corn-land; **~mähmaschine** *f* reaping-machine, reaper; **~markt** *m* corn market, *Am* grain market; **~mühle** *f* corn mill; **~pflanzen** *f pl* cereals *pl*; **~reiniger** *m* cereal-seed dresser; **~rost** *m* rust of cereals; **~sack** *m* corn sack; **~schrot** *m od. n* meal; **~schwinge** *f* winnowing machine; **~silo** *m* silo; **~speicher** *m* granary, *Am* grain elevator; **~vorrat** *m* stock of grain.

ge|treu *a* faithful, true, trusty, loyal; *seine ~~en* his faithful followers; *~~e Abschrift* true copy; **~~lich** *adv* faithfully, truly; **~triebe** *n tech* gear, gearing, drive, machine(ry); transmission, mechanism; (*Räderwerk*) wheels *pl*, motion; (*Zahnrad~~*) pinion; (*Triebstock~~*) trundle; (*Leben*) bustle of life; (*Uhr*) springs *pl*, works *pl*; **~~aggregat** *n* gearing-unit; **~~bremse** *f* gear brake; **~~deckel** *m* gear cover; **~~fett** *n* transmission lubricant; **~~gang** *m* stage, speed; **~~gehäuse** *n mot* gear box; **~~los** *a* gearless, ungeared; **~~motor** *m* geared engine; **~~räder** *n pl* gear wheels *pl*; **~~übersetzung** *f* multiplication; **~~umschaltung** *f* gearshift; **~~welle** *f* transmission (*od* gear) shaft; **~trost** *a* confident, in good spirits; **~trösten** *r* to be confident of; to wait patiently; **~tue** *n* idle doings *pl*, fuss; *albernes ~~* silliness; *nutzloses ~~* useless pottering; *was soll das ~~?* what's the good of all? **~tümmel** *n* (*Volksmenge*) crowd; (*Getöse*) bustle; uproar; tumult; hurly-burly; **~tüpfelt** *a* guttate; spotted, sprinkled; **~übt** *a* practised, versed, skilled, experienced; **~~heit** *f* skill, practice; **~vatter** *m*, **~~in** *f* godfather, godmother; *fig* friend; neighbo(u)r, relative, *fam* crony, chum, pal; *~~ Schneider u. Handschuhmacher hum* small tradespeople; *~~ stehen* to stand godfather (*od* godmother) to; **~~schaft** *f* sponsorship; **~viert** *n* square; *ins ~~ bringen* to square.

Getto *n* ghetto.

*

Ge|wächs *n* plant, herb; (*Wein*) vintage; vegetable; (*Wachstum*) growth; growing; *inländisches ~~* home produce; *ausländisches ~~* exotic produce; (*Auswuchs*) ulcer, tumo(u)r; excrescence; protuberance; neoplasm; growth; **~wachsen** *a* grown; sufficiently skilled in; *e-r Sache ~~ sein* to be equal to; *jdm ~~ sein* to be (a) match for s. o.; *er zeigte sich der Lage ~~* he rose to the occasion; *sie ist der Aufgabe nicht ~~* she is not up to the mark; *ich fühle mich dem nicht ~~* I don't feel up to it; *~~er Boden* natural soil, solid ground; **~wächshaus** *n* conservatory, hothouse, greenhouse; **~~pflanze** *f* hothouse plant.

ge|wagt *pp a* hazardous, risky, bold; **~wählt** *a* choice; (*Ausdrücke*) selected; (*vornehm*) select; **~wahr** *a* aware (of); *e-r Sache ~~ werden*, **~wahren** *tr* to become aware of, to catch sight of; **~währ** *f* warrant, guarantee, guaranty; surety; *Am* security; *ohne ~~* without prejudice (*od* engagement); no responsibility is taken (for); *~~ leisten* to warrant, to guarantee, to give security; **~währen** *tr, itr* (*Bitte*) to grant; (*bewilligen*) to afford; (*gestatten*) to allow; (*einräumen*) to accord, to concede, to vouchsafe; *Aufschub ~~* to allow time; *Vorteil ~~* to offer an advantage; *jdn ~~ lassen* to let s. o. do as he likes; *etw ~~ lassen* to let s. th. go on; **~währleisten** *tr* to vouch for, to guarantee; **~währleistung** *f* security; (*des Verkäufers*) warranty, guaranty; **~wahrsam** *m* custody, control; (*strafrechtlich*) detention; (*Haft*) imprisonment; (*Bank*) deposit; *in ~~ halten* to hold in custody; *in ~~ nehmen* to take into custody; to take charge of s. th.; *in sicherem ~~* in safe keeping; **~währsmann** *m* (*Quelle*) informant, authority, source; (*Bürge*) guarantee, warranter, bail(sman); **~währung** *f* granting, concession.

Gewalt *f* (*Macht*) power, might; (*amtlich*) authority, jurisdiction; (*Einfluß*) influence; (*höchste*) sovereignty; (*absolute*) absolutism, despotism; (*Kontrolle*) control, command; (*Herrschaft*) dominion, rule, sway; (*Gewalttätigkeit*) force, violence; (*Zwang*) restraint; *höhere ~* Act of God, Force Majeure; *~ geht vor Recht* might is above right; *er will mit ~ reich werden* he intends to get rich by hook or by crook; *alle ~ geht vom Volk aus* all power originates in the people; *e-m Mädchen ~ antun* to violate a girl; *sich ~ antun* to do violence to o. s.; *mit ~* by force; *mit aller ~* by main force; with all o.'s might; *in der ~ haben* to have command of, to master; *sich in der ~ haben* to have self-control; *etw in seiner ~ haben* to have s. th. in o.'s own hand; **~anmaßung** *f* usurpation of power; **~friede** *m* enforced (*od* dictated) peace; **~haber, ~herrscher** *m* dictator, autocrat, despot, tyrant; **~herrschaft** *f* despotism, tyranny; **~ig** *a* (*mächtig*) mighty, powerful; (*heftig*) vehement; (*sehr groß*) enormous, huge, gigantic, immense, *fam* tremendous; (*Sturm*) furious; (*Stärke*) stupendous; (*Schlag*) stunning; (*Fehler*) egregious; *Sie irren sich ~~* you are badly mistaken; *ein ~~er Unterschied* a vast difference; **~marsch** *m* forced march; **~maßnahme** *f* violent measure; **~mensch** *m* tyrant; (*roh*) brute; **~probe** *f* violent proof; **~sam** *a* violent, forcible; by force, forceful; *~~e Erkundung mil* reconnaissance in force; *~~er Umsturz* violent overthrow; **~~keit** *f* violence, force; **~streich** *m* violent measure, arbitrary act; **~tat** *f* act of violence, outrage; **~tätig** *a* violent, fierce, outrageous, brutal; **~~keit** *f* violence, brutality, outrage.

Ge|wand *n* garment, gown; (*Kleid*) dress, attire; (*Talar*) vestment; **~wandt** *a* (*flink*) agile, nimble, quick; (*klug*) clever; (*geschmeidig*) supple; (*geschickt*) skilled, skil(l)ful, adroit, ingenious; (*ungezwungen*) easy; (*erfahren*) experienced; *~~ sein in* to be good at; *~~ im Rechnen sein* to be quick at figures; **~~heit** *f* agility; quickness, dexterity; cleverness; skill; (*Geläufigkeit*) fluency; **~wärtig** *a*: *e-r Sache ~~ sein* to expect s. th.; **~wärtigen** *tr* to expect, to look forward, to await; (*sich abfinden*) to be resigned (to); (*Strafe*) to be liable to; **~wäsch** *n* chit-chat, idle-talk, twaddle; nonsense; **~wässer** *n* waters, floods *pl*; **~~t** *a* watered, clouded; **~webe** *n* tissue, web; (*Webart*) texture; (*Stoff*) textile, fabric; (*Einschlag*) woof, weft; (*Netzwerk*) netting; *fig* tissue, woof, structure; *nicht eingehendes ~~* pre-shrunk fabric; *durchsichtiges ~~* transparent tissue; **~~lehre** *f med* histology; **~weckt** *a* alert; bright, clever, brisk, lively; **~~heit** *f* liveliness, briskness.

Gewehr *n* gun; (*gezogenes ~*) rifle; (*Waffe*) weapon; (*Feuerwaffen*) (fire-) arms *pl*; *an die ~e!* to arms! *~ ab!* ground arms! *das ~ über!* slope arms! *präsentiert das ~!* present arms! *setzt die ~e zusammen!* pile arms! *Am* stack arms! *mit ~ bei Fuß stehen* to beat the order; *zum ~ greifen* to take up arms; **~abzug** *m* trigger release; **~appell** *m* rifle inspection; **~auflage** *f* parapet; **~feuer** *n* rifle fire; **~führer** *m* machine-gun commander, squad leader; **~geknatter** *n* crackle; **~geschoß** *n* bullet; **~granate** *f* rifle grenade; **~kolben** *m* butt; **~lauf** *m* (gun-)barrel; **~munition** *f* small-arms (*od* rifle) ammunition; **~patrone** *f* cartridge; **~pyramide** *f* pile of arms; **~riemen** *m* rifle-sling; **~schaft** *m* stock; **~schießstand** *m* rifle-range; **~schloß** *n* gun-lock; **~schuß** *m* rifle-shot; **~schütze** *m* rifleman; **~stock** *m* stock; cleaning rod; **~verschluß** *m* breechlock; **~zielfernrohr** *n* telescopic rifle sight; **~zubehör** *n* rifle accessories *pl*.

Geweih *n* horns *pl*; antlers *pl*; **~zacken** *m* prong of antler.

gewellt *a* undulating; wavy.

Gewerbe *n* (*Geschäft*) business; (*Beruf*) vocation, trade, profession, calling; (*Handwerk*) craft; (*Handel*) trade; (*Industrie*) industry; (*Art*) line of business, branch; (*Auftrag*) errand, commission; *ein ~ betreiben* to follow (*od* carry on) a trade; *ein ~ aus etw machen* to make a business of; *er übt das ~ e-s Tischlers aus* he is a joiner by trade; **~aufsicht** *f* trade inspection; **~ausschuß** *m* trade committee; **~ausstellung** *f* industrial exhibition; **~bank** *f* tradesman's bank; **~berechtigung** *f* business licence; **~betrieb** *m* business, factory; (*Werkstatt*) shop; **~ertragssteuer** *f* tax on trade returns; **~erzeugnisse** *n pl* manufactured products *pl*; **~fleiß** *m* industrial activity; **~freiheit** *f* freedom of trade; **~kunde** *f* technology; **~museum** *n* industrial museum; **~ordnung** *f* Industrial Code; industrial legislation; **~schein** *m* trade licence; **~schule** *f* trade (*od* vocational) school; **~steuer** *f* trade tax; excise taxes (*od* duties), *Am* business tax; **~tätig** *a* industrial; **~tätigkeit** *f* industrial activity; **~treibend** *a* industrial, manufacturing; **~treibende(r)** *m* tradesman; (*Fabrikant*) manufacturer; (*Handwerker*) craftsman; **~verein** *m* tradesmen's union; **~zweig** *m* branch of industry, line.

gewerb|lich *a* industrial, trade; professional; **~smäßig** *a* professional; *~~e Unzucht* prostitution; **~stätig** *a* industrial.

Gewerkschaft *f* trade(s)-union, *Am* labor union; **~ler** *m* trade-unionist; **~lich** *a* unionist; *~~ zusammenschließen* to unionize; *~~e Zusammenfassung* trade-unionism; **~sausschuß** *m* trade-union committee; **~sbeiträge** *m pl* union dues *pl*; **~sbund** *m* federation of trade-unions; (*England*) Trade Union Congress (*Abk* T. U. C.); *Am* American Federation of Labor (*Abk* A. F. L.); **~sfeindlich** *a* antiunion; **~sfunktionär** *m* trade union organizer, *Am* labo(u)r union official; **~smitglied** *n* fellow-unionist; **~sekretär** *m* trade union organizer; **~sunterstützung** *f* union benefits *pl*; **~sverband** *m* federation of trade-unions; **~svertreter** *m* union representative; **~zugehörigkeit** *f* union membership.

Ge|wicht *n* weight, *Am* heft; (*Handels~~*) avoirdupois; (*Edelmetall*) troy weight; *Netto~~*, *Brutto~~*, *Eigen~~*, *Lebend~~* net, gross, dead, live weight; (*Wichtigkeit*) gravity, importance; *knappes ~~* short weight; *spezifisches ~~* specific weight (*od* gravity); *Leute von ~~* persons of consequence; *an ~~ verlieren* to lose weight; *geeichtes ~~* standard weight; *~~ verlegen* (*Ski*) to weight; *ins ~~ fallen* to be of great weight, to weigh with; *e-m Wort ~~ beimessen* to give weight to the presence of a word; *auf etw ~~ legen* to lay stress upon; **~~sabgang** *m* deficiency in weight; **~~sabnahme** *f* decrease in weight; **~~sabzug** *m* deduction in weight; **~~sangabe** *f* declaration of weight; **~~sbestimmung** *f* determination of weight; **~~seinheiten** *f pl* units of weight; **~~heber** *m sport* weightlifter; **~~slos** *a* weightless; *fig* without importance; **~~ssatz** *m* set of weights; **~~sunterschied** *m* difference in weight; **~~sverhältnis** *n* proportion in weight; **~~sverlust** *m* loss in weight; **~~sverteilung** *f* distribution of weights; **~~szunahme** *f* increase in weight; **~wichtig** *a* weighty, heavy; *fig* important; *e-e ~~e Persönlichkeit* an influential person; *ein ~~es Wort* a momentous word; **~wiegt** *a* (*erfahren*) experienced, versed, expert; *fam* smart; (*schlau*) shrewd; **~wieher** *n* neighing; **~willt** *a* inclined, willing, disposed, ready; *~~ sein* to intend; **~wimmel** *n* swarm, crowd, throng; **~wimmer** *n* moaning, wailing, whimpering; **~winde** *n* (*Schrauben~~*) thread, worm; (*Blumen~~*) wreath; (*Girlande*) garland, festoon; (*Rolle*) coil; (*Pfad*) winding; (*Ohr*) labyrinth; **~~bohrer** *m* screw-tap; **~~buchse** *f* screw socket; **~~drehbank** *f* threading lathe; **~~gang** *m* thread; **~~lehre** *f* thread pitch ga(u)ge; **~~schneidmaschine** *f* threading machine; **~~steigung** *f* pitch of a screw.

Gewinn *m* (*Vorteil*) profit, advantage, benefit; (*Verdienst*) earnings *pl*; (*gewerblich*) profit, gains *pl*, earnings *pl*; (*Gewinnspanne*) margin; (*Ertrag*) proceeds *pl*; (*Spiel*) winnings *pl*; (*Lotterie*) prize; (*Spekulation*) gain; (*Börse*) premium, advance; *com* return(s *pl*); (*Überschuß*) surplus; *angemessener ~* fair profit; *entgangener ~* profit lost; *erzielter ~* realized profit; *reiner ~* clear profit, net gain; *großer ~* (*fam*) scoop; *~ aus Veräußerungen* sales profit; *wucherischer ~* excess profit; *unehrlicher ~ Am fam* graft; *ein unverhoffter ~* a windfall; *~ abwerfen*, *~ bringen* to yield (*od* leave) a profit; *~ ausschütten* to distribute a surplus; *mit ~ betreiben* to carry on with profit; *~ erzielen* to realize a profit; *mit ~ verkaufen* to sell to advantage; *~ abwerfend* remunerative, paying; **~abführung** *f* surrender of profits; **~abschöpfung** *f* skimming of excess profits; **~anspruch** *m* profit claim; **~anteil** *m* share of profits, dividend; **~ausschüttung** *f* distribution of profits; **~aussichten** *f pl* profit prospects *pl*; **~beteiligung** *f* participation in profits; profit-sharing; **~bringend** *a* profitable, lucrative; *~~ anlegen* to invest advantageously; **~en** *irr tr*, *itr* to win, to gain, to earn; (*erhalten*) to obtain, to receive, to get; (*erwerben*) to acquire; (*Metall*) to extract, to produce, to recover; *chem* to prepare; (*Sympathie, Mitarbeit*) to enlist; (*besser werden*) to improve; *e-n Preis ~~* to win a prize; *ein Vermögen ~~* to gain a fortune; *wie gewonnen, so zerronnen* lightly come, lightly go; *e-n Prozeß ~~* to gain a lawsuit; *jdn lieb~~* to take a liking (*od* fancy) to; *damit ist viel gewonnen* that helps a great deal; *die Oberhand ~~* to get the mastery of; *ich habe ihn für uns gewonnen* I have won him over to our side; *sie gewinnt bei näherer Bekanntschaft* she grows on you as you get to know her; *ich konnte es nicht über mich ~~* I could not make up my mind; I could not bring myself (to); *an Klarheit ~~* to gain in clearness; *wer nicht wagt, der nicht gewinnt* nothing venture, nothing have; **~end** *a*, *ppr* winning, taking; engaging; *ein ~~es Wesen* winning manners; **~er** *m*, **~erin** *f* winner, gainer; *bei den ~~n sein* to be on the winning side, *Am* to get into the bandwagon; **~ler** *m* profiteer; **~liste** *f* list of prizes; **~los** *n* lottery ticket; (*Gewinn*) drawn number; **~nummer** *f* winning number; **~rechnung** *f* account of profit, *Am* income statement; **~reich** *a* profitable, lucrative; **~spanne** *f* profit margin; **~steuer** *f* profits tax; **~sucht** *f* greed (of gain); **~süchtig** *a* greedy (of gain); covetous; **~überschuß** *m* surplus; **~ u. Verlustkonto** *n* profit and loss account; **~ung** *f* winning, gaining; (*Erzeugnisse*) production; (*Erwerbung*) acquirement; (*Erze*) extraction, production; (*Ertrag*) output; **~verteilung** *f* distribution of profits; division of profits; **~vortrag** *m* surplus brought forward; **~ziehung** *f* drawing of prizes.

Ge|winsel *n* whimpering, whining; **~winst** *m* gain; **~wirr(e)** *n* confusion, medley, mass; (*Bestürzung*) maze, jumble; (*Verwicklung*) tangle, *Am* snarl.

gewiß *a* sure, certain, positive; (*festgelegt*) fixed; *ein ~er Herr N.* a certain Mr. N.; *ein ~es Etwas* a something; *adv* certainly, indeed, surely, to be sure, no doubt; *ich bin dessen ~* I am sure of it; *er hat ~ recht* no doubt he's right; *Sie wollten uns ~ überraschen?* you hoped to surprise us, didn't you? *kommen Sie? Aber ~!* are you coming? Why, certainly! *in ~em Sinne hat er recht* in a sense he's right; *~ weißt du, was das ist* I dare say you know what that is; *er wird ~ kommen* he will come without fail; *ich weiß es ~ nicht* I don't know, I am sure; *~! interj* certainly! take it from me! *Am* sure! *sl* you bet! *seiner Sache ~ sein* to be sure of; *so viel ist ~* doubtless; *ganz ~* by all means; *sein ~es haben* to have a fixed income; **~ermaßen** *adv* so to speak; as it were; in a way; to a certain degree; to some extent; **~heit** *f* certainty; surety; (*Klarheit*) evidence; (*genaue Kenntnis*) positive knowledge; (*Beweis*) proof; *sich über etw ~~ verschaffen* to make sure about; **~lich** *adv* certainly, surely.

Gewissen *n* conscience; *nach bestem Wissen u. ~* to the best of o.'s belief; *ein reines ~* a clear conscience; *sein ~ erleichtern* to ease o.'s mind; *ein gutes ~ ist ein sanftes Ruhekissen* a good conscience is a soft pillow; *sein ~ zum Schweigen bringen* to soothe o.'s conscience; *mit ruhigem ~* with a safe conscience; *etw auf dem ~ haben* to have s. th. on o.'s conscience; *sich ein ~ daraus machen* to make it a matter of conscience; *sich ein ~ aus etw machen* to scruple at s. th.; **~haft** *a* conscientious, scrupulous; **~haftigkeit** *f* conscientiousness, scrupulousness; (*ängstliche ~~*) preciseness; **~los** *a* unscrupulous; **~losigkeit** *f* unscrupulousness; **~sangst** *f* pangs of conscience; **~sbisse** *m pl* pricks (*od* twinge) of conscience, remorse, scruple; *von ~~n gepeinigt* stung with remorse; **~sfrage** *f* question of conscience; **~sfreiheit** *f* liberty of conscience; **~skonflikt** *m* conscientious doubt; **~sruhe** *f* peace of conscience; **~ssache** *f* matter of conscience; **~szwang** *m* moral constraint, coercion of conscience; **~szweifel** *m* scruple.

Gewitter *n* thunderstorm, thunder and lightning; *ein ~ liegt in der Luft* thunder is in the air; *es ist ein ~ im Anzug* there is a thunderstorm coming up (*od* gathering); **~bildung** *f* formation of a thunderstorm; **~bö** *f* thunder-squall; **~flug** *m* (*Segelflug*) frontal soaring; **~frontenflug** *m* flight in front of a thunderstorm; **~haft, ~ig** *a* stormy, thundery; **~luft** *f* oppressive air, heavy (*od* sultry) air; **~n** *itr* to thunder; **~neigung** *f* tendency to thunderstorm; **~regen, ~schauer** *m* thunder-shower; thunder plump, deluge; **~schlag** *m* thunder-clap; **~schwanger, ~schwer** *a* thunder-charged; **~schwül** *a* thunderous, sultry, oppressive; **~schwüle** *f* oppressiveness, sultriness; **~störung** *f tele* static, atmospherics *pl*; **~sturm** *m* thunderstorm; **~wolke** *f* thundercloud, cumulo-nimbus cloud.

gewitz(ig)t *a* sharp, shrewd; taught by experience.

Gewoge *n* waving, fluctuation; (*Menschen*) throng, crowd.

gewogen *a* inclined, affectionate; favo(u)rably disposed to; *jdm ~ sein* to show a liking for s.o.; *sich jdn ~ machen* to gain s. o.'s favo(u)r; **~heit** *f* favo(u)r, good-will; *die ~~ haben* to have the kindness to.

gewöhnen *tr* to accustom (*an* to); (*Gewohnheit annehmen*) to habituate; (*bekannt werden*) to familiarize; (*widmen*) to addict; (*abhärten*) to inure (to); (*zähmen*) to domesticate; *gewöhnt sein* to be used to; *r sich an etw ~* to get used to, to get into the habit of, to get accustomed to; to become familiar with; *sich an ein Klima ~* to acclimatize, *Am* to acclimate.

Gewohnheit *f* (*persönliche*) habit; (*Neigung*) habitude, wont; (*Brauch*) practice, usage; (*Herkommen*) custom; (*überliefert*) use; (*Mode*) fashion; *die Macht der ~* the force of habit; *es sich zur ~ machen* to make it a habit; *in die ~ verfallen* to get into the habit; *~ wird zur zweiten Natur* custom is a second nature; *aus ~* by habit; *zur ~ werden* to grow into a habit; *aus der ~ kommen* to get out of practice; **~smäßig** *a* customary; habitual; usual; **~smensch** *m*, *fam* **~stier** *n* creature of habit; **~srecht** *n* prescriptive right, common law; **~ssünde** *f* besetting sin; **~strinker** *m* habitual drunkard; **~sverbrecher** *m* habitual criminal.

ge|wöhnlich *a* (*üblich*) ordinary, usual; (*durchschnittlich*) average; (*nichtssagend*) trivial; (*hergebracht*) customary; (*allgemein*) common, general; (*unfein*) inferior, vulgar; (*gewohnt*) habitual, wonted; (*einfach*) plain; (*geringwertig*) coarse; (*volkstümlich*) popular; *unter ~~en Verhältnissen* under ordinary circumstances; **~~keit** *f* usualness; commonness; **~wohnt** *a* used, accustomed to; usual; (*abgehärtet*) inured (to); *~~es Verfahren* routine processing; **~~ermaßen** *adv* as usual; **~wöhnung** *f* accustoming; use, habit(ude); (*Klima*) acclimatization, *Am* acclimation.

Ge|wölbe *n* vault, arch; (*Kuppel*) dome; (*Laden*) shop, magazine, storehouse; (*Gruft*) family-vault; **~~bogen** *m* arch of a vault; **~~pfeiler** *m* arched buttress; **~~rippe** *f* rib of a vault; **~wölbt** *a, pp* vaulted, arched; domed; *~~e Böschung* convex slope; **~wölk** *n* clouds *pl*; **~wühl** *n* crowd, throng; tumult, turmoil, bustle; *im ~~ der Schlacht* in the thickest of the fight; **~wunden** *a* wound; winding; spiral; coiled; (*gekrümmt*) sinuous; *fig* tortuous; **~würfelt** *a* checked, chequered; **~würm** *n* reptiles *pl*; (*Ungeziefer*) vermin.

Gewürz *n* spice, seasoning, condiment; aromatics *pl*; (*~waren*) grocery-ware; **~essig** *m* aromatic vinegar; **~gurke** *f* pickled cucumber; **~handel** *m* spice trade; **~ig** *a* spiced, spicy, aromatic; **~händler** *m* spice-dealer; grocer; **~laden** *m* spicery; **~nelke** *f* clove; **~reich** *a* spicy, aromatic.

ge|zackt *a* pronged, indented; (*Fels*) jagged; (*Blatt*) serrate(d); **~zähnt** *a* toothed; (*eingekerbt*) notched; *bot* dentate; (*Briefmarken*) perforated; **~zänk** *n* quarrel, dispute; wrangling; squabble; **~zappel** *n* struggling; fidgety ways; **~zeiten** *f pl* tides *pl*; **~~bewegung** *f* tidal impulse; **~~erscheinungen** *f pl* tidal phenomena *pl*; **~~kraftwerk** *n* tidal power plant; **~~strom** *m*, **~~strömung** *f* tidal current(s *pl*); **~~tafel** *f* tide table; **~zelt** *n* tent, pavilion; **~zerre** *n* pulling, dragging; **~zeter** *n* clamo(u)r, screaming; (*Streit*) quarrelling, squabble; **~ziemen** *imp r* to become, to befit; *wie es sich geziemt* as is fitting; **~~d** *a* becoming, due, decent, fit, proper, seemly; **~ziere** *n* affectation; **~ziert** *a* affected, minced; (*gesucht*) studied; (*weit hergeholt*) far-fetched; (*steif*) stiff, prim; (*geckenhaft*) foppish; (*zimperlich*) finical, *Am* finicky; **~ziertheit** *f* affectation; stiffness; primness; foppishness; finicality; **~zirpe** *n* chirping; **~zisch** *n* hissing; **~zischel** *n* whispering; **~zücht** *n* offspring, brood, breed; **~zweig** *n* branches *pl*, boughs *pl*; **~zwitscher** *n* chirping, twitter; **~zwungen** *a* compelled; constrained, compulsory; (*unnatürlich*) unnatural; (*geziert*) affected; (*steif*) stiff, formal; **~~heit** *f* constraint; affectation; formality.

Gicht *f* gout, arthritis; *min* furnace-mouth; **~anfall** *m* attack of the gout; **~artig, ~ig** *a* gouty; **~brüchig** *a* paralytic; *med* gouty; (*gelähmt*) palsied; **~gas** *n* exit gas; **~knoten** *m* gout-stone, *med* chalk-stone; **~krank** *a* gouty; **~schmerzen** *m pl* arthritic pains *pl*.

Giebel *m* gable (-end); (*Zier~*) fronton, pediment; (*Seite*) frontispiece; **~dach** *n* gable(d) roof; **~feld** *n* tympan(um), pediment; **~fenster** *n* gable-window; **~seite** *f* gable-side, frontispiece.

Gier *f* avidity, greed(iness); (*Eifer*) eagerness; **~en** *itr* to long for, to yearn for; *mar* to fall away, to drift from the course; *mar, aero* to yaw; **~fähre** *f* flying ferry, fly bridge; **~ig** *a* greedy of, covetous of.

Gieß|bach *m* torrent; **~en** *irr tr* to pour; (*füllen*) to fill; (*ausschütten*) to shed, to spill; (*schmelzen*) to cast, to found; (*Glas*) to mo(u)ld; (*begießen*) to water; (*Film*) to coat; *es ~t* it is raining cats and dogs; *gegossene Arbeit* cast-work; *Öl ins Feuer ~* to pour oil on the flame; *fig* to add fuel to the fire; *er hat sich e-n hinter die Binde gegossen* (*fam*) he's got a few under his belt; **~er** *m* caster, furnace-man; founder; (*Glas*) ladler, shearer; **~erei, ~hütte** *f* foundry; **~form** *f* casting-mo(u)ld; **~kanne** *f* watering-can, sprinkling can; **~loch** *n* funnel of a furnace; **~löffel** *m tech* casting-ladle; **~ofen** *m* founding-furnace; **~technik** *f* casting practice.

Gift *n* poison; (*Tier~*) venom; (*Ansteckungsstoff*) virus; (*organisch*) toxin(e); (*Bosheit*) malice; *~ u. Galle speien* to vomit o.'s venom; *voll ~ u. Galle* full of rage and malice; *schleichendes ~* slow poison; *darauf kannst du ~ nehmen* you can bet your life on it; **~becher** *m* poisoned cup; **~drüse** *f* venom-gland; **~gas** *n* poison gas; **~hauch** *m* poisonous breath, blight; **~ig** *a* poisonous, venomous, virulent; contagious; toxic; (*boshaft*) malicious, enraged; **~igkeit** *f* poisonousness; (*Bosheit*) malice, malignity, anger; (*Wut*) fury; **~mischer(in)** *m* (*f*) poisoner; **~mischerei** *f* poisoning; **~mord** *m* (murder by) poisoning; **~mörder** *m* poisoner; **~nebel** *m mil* toxic smoke; **~~wolke** *f mil* (toxic) gas cloud; **~pflanze** *f* poisonous plant; **~pille** *f* poisened pill; **~pilz, ~schwamm** *m* poisonous mushroom, toadstool; **~regen** *m aero mil* aerial gas spray; **~~angriff** *m aero mil* spray attack; **~schlange** *f* venomous serpent; poisonous snake; **~schrank** *m* poison-chest; **~spinne** *f* venomous spider; **~stoff** *m* poisonous substance, *med* virus; toxin(e); **~trank** *m* poisoned potion; **~wirkung** *f* poisonous action (*od* effect); **~zahn** *m* venom-tooth, poison-fang.

Gigant *m* giant; **~isch** *a* gigantic, enormous.

Gigerl *m* dandy, beau, fop, swell; *fam* dude.

Gilde *f* guild, corporation, company.

Gimpel *m* bullfinch; *fig* simpleton, stupid, dunce, dolt, imbecile, noodle, *Am sl* sucker; **~ei** *f* foolishness; **~haft** *a* foolish.

Ginster *m* broom, gorse.

Gipfel *m* (*Baum*) top; (*Berg*) summit, peak; (*Höhepunkt*) pinnacle, meridian, apogee; (*Wertskala*) climax; (*Spitze*) apex; (*Vollendung*) acme; (*höchster Stand*) culmination; (*Scheitelpunkt*) zenith; (*Haus*) gable; (*Höhe*) height; *der ~ der Frechheit* the height of impudence; **~höhe** *f aero* ceiling; *höchste erflogene ~~* absolute ceiling; *praktische ~~* service ceiling; **~leistung** *f* record; **~n** *itr* to culminate, to reach o.'s acme; to tower above; **~punkt** *m* highest point, limit; *fig* culminating point, acme, climax; **~ständig** *a bot* apical; **~wert** *m* top (*od* peak) value, maximum.

Gips *m min* gypsum; calcium sulfate; (*gebrannt*) plaster (of Paris); **~abdruck** *m* plaster cast; **~arbeit** *f* plaster work; **~bewurf** *m* coat of plaster; **~brei** *m* plaster of Paris paste; **~brennerei** *f* gypsum burning; **~bruch** *m* gypsum-quarry; **~diele** *f* plaster (of Paris) slab; **~en** *tr* to plaster; **~er** *m* plasterer, stucco-worker; **~figur** *f* plaster-figure; **~figurenhändler** *m* image-seller; **~grube** *f* gypsum-pit; **~haltig** *a* gyps(e)ous; **~mehl** *n* powdered plaster; **~modell** *n* plaster-cast; **~mörtel** *m* plaster, stucco; **~ofen** *m* plaster kiln; **~platte** *f* plaster block; **~verband** *m* plaster dressing; *e-n ~~ anlegen* to put in plaster; *ihr Arm ist in e-m ~~* her arm is in a cast.

Giraffe *f* giraffe.

Gir|ant *m* endorser; **~at** *m* endorsee; **~ierbar** *a* endorsable; **~ieren** *tr* to put in circulation; (*Wechsel*) to endorse (a bill).

Girlande *f* garland, festoon.

Giro *n* endorsement; **~bank** *f* circulation-bank, deposit (*od* transfer) bank; **~konto** *n* deposit's (*od* drawing) account; **~überweisung** *f* bank transfer; **~verbindlichkeiten** *f pl* contingent liabilities *pl*; **~verkehr** *m* clearing(-house) business; transfer bank transaction; **~zentrale** *f* deposit-bank's main office, clearing house.

girren *itr* to coo.

Gis *n mus* G sharp.

Gischt *m* foam, spray; (*Bier*) froth; (*Gärung*) fermentation.

Gitarre *f* guitar.

Gitter *n* (*Gitterwerk, opt*) grating; (*Eisen~*) iron bars *pl*; (*Gatter, Spalier*) trellis, lattice; (*Zaun*) fence; (*Geländer*) railing; *radio* grid; (*Kamin*) fender, grate; (*hölzern u. durchbrochen*) parclose; (*Draht*) wire-netting; **~batterie** *f radio* grid-bias (*od Am* C) battery; **~bett** *n* cot; **~brücke** *f* lattice bridge; **~fenster** *n* lattice-window; barred window; **~förmig** *a* latticed; **~gleichrichter** *m* grid rectifier; **~kondensator** *m* grid condenser; **~konstruktion** *f* lattice work; **~mast** *m* lattice mast; **~modulation** *f radio* grid circuit modulation; **~spannung** *f radio* grid tension; **~steuerung** *f radio* grid control; **~tor** *n* trellised gate; iron gate; **~träger** *m* lattice truss; **~werk** *n* trellis (*od* lattice) work; *arch* twine; **~widerstand** *m radio* grid-leak; **~zaun** *m* fence of trellis work, wire-netting.

Glacéhandschuh *m* kid-glove.

Glanz *m* brightness, brilliancy, shining, glowing, glare; (*strahlend*) radiance, luminosity, luminousness; (*reflektierend*) lustre, *Am* luster; (*Politur*) polish; (*stark*) effulgence; (*heller Schein*) refulgence; (*Stoff*) sheen; (*Oberfläche*) gloss; (*Schimmer*) shimmer; *fig* splendo(u)r; (*Jugend*) boom; (*Ruhm*) glory; (*Gepränge*) show, pomp; (*bezaubernder ~*) glamo(u)r; (*Vornehmheit*) distinction; (*Diamanten*) water; *den ~ verlieren* to tarnish, to fade; **~bürste** *f* polishing brush; **~firniß** *m* glazing varnish; **~garn** *n* glazed yarn; **~gold** *n* burnish gold; (*Keramik*) brilliant gold; **~kattun** *m* glazed calico; **~kohle** *f* glance coal, anthracite, *Am* hard coal; **~leder** *n* patent (*od* lacquered) leather; **~leistung** *f* masterly achievement; record: **~lichter** *n pl* high lights *pl*; **~los** *a* lustreless, dull, dead, mat, dim; **~~igkeit** *f* lusterlessness, dul(l)ness; **~nummer** *f* great attraction; **~papier** *n* glazed paper; **~periode** *f* brightest period; **~presse** *f* glazing-calender; **~punkt** *m* culminating point, climax, acme, great attraction; **~stärke** *f* gloss starch; **~stoff** *m* glazed (*od* glossy) fabric; **~stück** *n theat* draw; **~vergoldung** *f* water gilding; **~voll** *a* splendid, brilliant; **~weiß** *n* brilliant white; **~wichse** *f* shining-blacking, varnish; shoe polish; **~zeit** *f* brightest period.

glänzen *itr* to flash, to gleam, to glance, to glint, to shine; (*funkeln*) to sparkle, to glitter, to glisten, to scintillate, to coruscate; (*schimmern*) to glimmer, to shimmer, to twinkle; (*strahlen*) to radiate; *tr* (*beleuchten*) to illuminate, to brighten, to light up; (*Metall*) to burnish; (*Leder*) to lacquer; (*Schuhe*) to polish, to black; (*Papier*) to glaze; (*polieren*) to gloss, to lustre, *Am* to luster; ~ *in etw* to be brilliant in, to excel in, to be successful in, *Am* to shine in; *seine Hosen* ~ his pants are shiny; *durch Abwesenheit* ~ to be conspicuous by absence; *es ist nicht alles Gold, was glänzt* all is not gold that glitters; *sie will gern* ~ she wishes to show off; *die Schuhe* ~ *nicht* the shoes do not shine; ~ *n* brightness, brilliancy, resplendence, radiance, lustre, refulgence, iridescence; **~d** *a, ppr* bright, brilliant; (*strahlend*) radiant, luminous, lustrous, lucent, effulgent, beaming, lambent; (*poliert*) polished, shiny, sheeny, burnished, glossy; *fig* magnificent, splendid, glorious, resplendent; (*glitzernd*) glittering; *~de Sache od Person Am sl* mustard.

Glas *n* glass; (*Bier~*) tumbler; *volles* ~ bumper; *mattes* ~ cut glass; *gefärbtes* ~ stained glass; *splitterfreies* ~ splinter-proof glass; *splittersicheres* ~ shatterproof glass; *mar* bells *pl*; (*Brille*) spectacles *pl*, (eye-)glasses *pl*; (*Feldstecher*) field glass, binoculars *pl*; ~ *schleifen* to grind glass; *ein* ~ *Marmelade* a jar of preserves; *zu* ~ *werden* (*od machen*) to vitrify; *Glück u.* ~, *wie leicht bricht das* happiness is fragile as glass; *zuviel ins* ~ *gucken* to drink too much; *mit den Gläsern anstoßen* to touch glasses; **~ähnlich** *a* glasslike, glassy; vitreous; **~arbeiter** *m* glass-worker; **~artig** *a* vitreous, glassy; **~auge** *n* glass eye; (*Pferdekrankheit*) wall-eye; **~äugig** *a* wall-eyed; **~ballon** *m* demi-john, carboy; **~bedachung** *f* glass-roofing; **~behälter** *m* sight bowl; **~bild** *n* diapositive; transparency; **~birne** *f* (glass) bulb; **~blase** *f* glass-bubble; blister; fault in glass; **~blasen** *n* glassblowing; **~bläser** *m* glass-blower; **~dach** *n* skylight; **~deckel** *m* glass-cover, glass-top; **~diapositiv** *n phot* lantern slide; **~elektrizität** *f* positive electricity; **~en** *tr mar* to strike (the ship's) bell; **~er** *m* glazier; **~erarbeit** *f* glazier's work; **~erdiamant** *m* glazier's diamond; **~erei** *f* glazier's workshop; **~erhandwerk** *n* glazier's trade; **~erkitt** *m* (glazier's) putty; **~ermeister** *m* master glazier; **~fabrik, ~hütte** *f* glass works *pl*; **~fabrikation** *f* manufacturing of glass; **~faden** *m* glass thread; **~faser** *f* spun glass; **~fenster** *n* glass window; window-pane; **~fertigung** *f* glassmaking; **~fiber** *f* glass-fibre (*Am* -fiber); **~filter** *n* glass-filter; **~flasche** *f* glass-bottle; (*geschliffene*) decanter; **~fluß** *m* paste of glass; vitrification; **~gebrauchsgegenstand** *m* utility glassware; **~gefäß** *n* glass jar; **~geschirr** *n* glass-ware; **~gespinst** *n* glass-fibre (*Am* -fiber), spun glass; **~gießer** *m* shearer; **~glocke** *f* glass bell (*od* shade); (*Lampe*) globe; **~handel** *m* glass-trade; **~händler** *m* dealer in glass; **~hart** *a* brittle; hard like glass; **~haus** *n* glass-house; *wer im* ~~ *sitzt, soll nicht mit Steinen werfen* those who live in glass-houses should not throw stones; **~haut** *f* cellophane; **~hütte** *f* glass-factory; glass works *pl*; **~ieren** *tr* to glaze; (*Malerei*) to varnish; (*Küche*) to frost; to ice; **~ierung** *f* glaze, glazing, glass; (*Küche*) icing, frosting; **~ig** *a* glassy, vitreous; **~kanzel** *f aero* transparent cockpit; **~kasten** *m* glass case; **~kolben** *m chem* flask; *el* glass bulb; **~kugel** *f* glass-ball, glass-sphere; bulb; globe; bunch; **~leinwand** *f* glass cloth; **~maler** *m* glass-painter; **~malerei** *f* glass-painting; stained glass; **~masse** *f* frit, glass-metal; **~ofen** *m* glass-furnace; **~papier** *n* glass paper; **~perle** *f* glass-bead; **~platte** *f* glass-plate; **~röhre** *f* glass-tube; **~sand** *m* vitreous sand; **~scheibe** *f* pane of glass; **~scherbe** *f* broken glass; **~schiebetüre** *f* sliding glass door; **~schleifer** *m* glass-cutter, glass-grinder; **~schleiferei** *f* glass-grinding, glass-cutting; **~schrank** *m* glass-case; **~splitter** *m* glass splinter, fragment; **~stab** *m* glass-rod; stirring rod; **~staub** *m* powdered glass; **~stopfen, ~stöpsel** *m* glass stopper; **~tafel** *f* glass-plate; **~tropfen** *m* glass-drops *pl*, Dutch tears *pl*; **~tür** *f* hall-door; **~ur** *f* glaze, varnish, gloss; (*Kuchen*) icing, frosting; (*Metall, Zahn*) enamel; (*Stoff*) glaze, varnish; **~veranda** *f* glass veranda, *Am* sun parlor; **~vergütung** *f* refining (*od* treating) to optical glass; **~versicherung** *f* plate glass insurance; **~ware** *f* glass-ware; **~weise** *adv* in glasses; **~werk** *n* glass-works *pl*; **~wolle** *f* glass wool.

gläsern *a* glassy, of glass; vitreous.

Glast *m* glare, radiance.

glatt *a* smooth, *Am* slick; (*eben*) even, plane, plain, level, flush; (*kahl*) bare; (*schlüpfrig*) slippery, glib; (*geschmeidig*) sleek, slick, glossy, glabrous; (*poliert*) polished, burnished; (*Aussehen*) blooming, good-looking; (*geradewegs*) plain, downright, outright, flat; (*Worte*) flattering, sweet; *adv* smoothly; (*völlig*) thoroughly, entirely; ~ *anliegen*, ~ *sitzen* to fit close; ~ *streichen* to smooth down; *das ist e-e ~e Lüge* that's an outright lie; *~es Kinn* beardless chin; *~e Stirn* fair forehead; ~ *landen* to land without difficulty; *~es Muster* plain pattern; *~e Oberfläche* smooth surface; ~ *rasieren* to shave close; *~e Ablehnung* flat refusal; *alles ging* ~ everything went smooth(ly); *~es Geschäft* fair business; *~e Worte* smooth (*od* flattering) words; **~eis** *n* glazed frost; slippery ice; **~rasiert** *a* clean-shaven; **~stellen** *tr com* to counterbalance; **~weg** *adv* plainly, bluntly, flatly; ~~ *erzählen* to tell bluntly; **~züngig** *a* smooth-tongued.

Glätt|e *f* smoothness, polish; slipperiness; (*Benehmen*) ease, easiness; politeness; (*Stil*) fluency;; **~en** *tr* to smooth, to sleek; (*Holz*) to plane; (*Metall*) to burnish; (*polieren*) to polish; (*Tuch*) to calender; (*Falten*) to take out; (*Papier*) to glaze; (*Spiegel*) to brighten; **~er** *m* furbisher, grinder, polisher; **~maschine** *f* planing machine; (*Papier*) glazing machine; (*Wolle*) smoothing machine.

Glatz|e *f* baldness, bald head, *Am* bald spot, *sl* shiny poll; *e-e* ~~ *haben* to be bald; **~köpfig** *a* bald-headed.

Glaube, **~n** *m* faith, belief; (*Bekenntnis*) creed; (*Vertrauen*) trust; (*Zuverlässigkeit*) credit; (*Glaubwürdigkeit*) credence; (*Meinung*) opinion; (*Überzeugung*) conviction; (*Gewißheit*) certainty; (*Grundsatz*) doctrine, principle; *sich zu e-m ~n bekennen* to profess a religion; *seinen ~n verleugnen* to abjure o.'s faith; *der* ~ *macht selig* he that believeth shall be saved; *~n schenken* to attach credit to; *Treu u. ~n* good faith; *vom ~n abfallen* to apostatize; **~n** *tr, itr* (*meinen*) to think, to fancy, to hold, *Am fam* to figure; (*für wahr halten*) to believe; (*vermuten*) to suppose, *Am* to guess, to reckon, *fam* to calculate; (*vertrauen auf*) to trust in, to confide in, to give faith (*od* credence) to; (*annehmen*) to consider, to assume; *ich* ~ *es* I think so; *teilweise ~n* to discount; *nicht ~n* to disbelieve; *ich* ~ *schon* I suppose so; *er mußte daran ~n* he had to pay the price; (*sterben*) he has submitted to his fate; *du kannst ihm aufs Wort ~n* you can take his word for it; *glaubst du?* do you think so? *das laß andere ~n* make others believe that; *ich* ~ *wohl, du weißt, was das ist* I dare say you know what that is; *ob du es glaubst od nicht* believe it or not; *es ist kaum zu ~n* it's hardly credible; *jdm ~n* to believe s. o.; *an etw ~n* to believe in s. th.; *an Gott ~n* to believe in God.

Glaubens|abfall *m* apostasy; **~artikel** *m* article of faith; **~bekenntnis** *n* confession of faith, creed; (*politisch*) platform; (*persönlich*) political creed; **~bewegung** *f* religious movement; **~eifer** *m* religious zeal; **~freiheit** *f* religious liberty; **~genosse** *m* fellow-believer, co-religionist; **~lehre** *f* dogma, doctrine of faith; **~meinung** *f* religious opinion; **~punkt, ~satz** *m* doctrine, article of faith; **~sache** *f* matter of faith; **~spaltung** *f* schism; **~streitigkeit** *f* religious controversy; **~streiter** *m* champion of the faith; controversalist; **~vorschrift** *f* religious precept; **~wert, ~würdig** *a* worthy of credit; **~wut** *f* fanaticism; **~zeuge** *m* martyr; **~zwang** *m* intolerance; **~zweifel** *m* scruple (in matters of faith); **~zwist** *m* religious quarrel.

Glaubersalz *n* Glauber's salt, sodium sulphate.

glaub|haft *a* credible, authentic; ~~ *machen* to substantiate, to verify; **~~igkeit** *f* credibility, authenticity; **~~machung** *f* prima facie evidence; *~~machung von Ansprüchen* authentication of claims; **~lich** *a* credible, probable, likely; *es ist kaum* ~~ it's hardly to be believed; **~würdig** *a* credible; (*verbürgt*) authentic; worthy of belief; *ein ~~er Mann* a trustworthy man; *er erfuhr es von ~~er Quelle* he got it from a reliable source; **~~keit** *f* credibility, trustworthiness; credit; authenticity.

gläubig *a* believing, faithful, religious; devout; **~e(r)** *m* believer; follower; *die ~en* the faithful; **~er** *m* creditor; *hypothekarischer* ~~ mortgagee; ~~ *befriedigen* to pay off the claims of creditors; *sich mit ~~n vergleichen* to make an arrangement with creditors; *mit ~~n verhandeln* to negotiate with creditors; ~~ *vertrösten* to put off creditors; **~~forderungen** *f pl* creditors' claims *pl*; **~~nation** *f* creditor nation; **~~versammlung** *f* meeting of creditors; **~keit** *f* confidence, faith.

*

gleich *a* equal; same; (*ähnlich*) like, similar; (*glatt*) even, plain; level; (*direkt, unmittelbar*) direct; *in ~er Weise* likewise; *das sieht ihm* ~ that is just like him; (*gleichbedeutend*) identical, convertible; (*gleichwertig*) equivalent; (*übereinstimmend*) coincident; ~ *machen* to equalize, to level; ~ *sein* to be equal to; *sich immer* ~ *bleiben* to remain always the same; *das ist mir* ~ it is all the same to me; *Gleiches mit Gleichem vergelten* to give measure for measure; ~ *u.* ~ *gesellt sich gern* birds of a feather flock together; *von ~em Alter* of the same age; *das bleibt sich* ~ that's the same; *sie hat genau das ~e gesagt* she said exactly the same thing; *wir sind in der ~en Lage* we are in the same boat; *im ~en Augenblick* at the same moment; *auf ~e Art u. Weise* in like manner; *zu ~en Teilen* in equal parts; *es kommt aufs ~e heraus* it comes to the same thing; *seinesgleichen* his equals; *zu ~er Zeit* at the same time; *der ~e Wert* equivalent; ~ *adv* equally; alike; just; (*sofort*) instantly, at once; immediately; (*direkt*) directly; (*bald*) soon; (*beinahe*) nearly; ~ *zu Anfang* at the very beginning; ~ *darauf* the moment after; *ich komme* ~ (I'm) coming; *ich dachte es* ~ I thought as much; *ich gehe* ~ I'm going right away; *ich bin* ~ *wieder da* I'll be right back; *sie sind* ~ *gut* they are equally good; *wie war doch* ~ *Ihr Name?* What did you say your name was? *es schlägt* ~ *fünf* it's on the stroke of five; ~ *viel, ob es wahr ist* no matter if it be true; ~ *daneben* right beside; *Mädchen u. Knaben in ~er Weise* girls and boys alike; *ich möchte hier* ~ *erwähnen* I may just as well mention here; *habe ich es dir nicht* ~ *gesagt* didn't I tell you so before; ~ *als* as soon as; ~ *als ob* just as if; *wenn~* though; **~achsig** *a* coaxial, equiaxial; **~altrig** *a* of the same age; **~artig** *a* of the same kind, similar, homogeneous; **~~keit** *f* similarity, uniformity; homogeneity; congeniality; **~bedeutend** *a* equivalent (to), tantamount (to); synonymous (with); **~berechtigt** *a* having equal rights, equally entitled to; **~berechtigung** *f* equality of rights; equal status; **~bleibend** *a* always the same; (*unveränderlich*) unchangeable, steady, uniform, even, equable, constant, steadfast; (*konsequent*) consistent; **~denkend** *a* congenial; **~druck** *m* constant (*od* balanced) pressure; **~~gasturbine** *f* constant pressure gas turbine; **~~linie** *f* isobar; **~~turbine** *f* action turbine; **~empfindend** *a* sympathetic, sympathizing; **~en** *irr itr* to be like, to resemble, to look like; (*~kommen*) to equal s.o. *od* s.th.; to be equal (to); *sich* ~~ to match; (*entsprechen*) to correspond (to); *sie gleicht ihrer Mutter* she looks like her mother; **~er** *m* equator; **~ergestalt, ~ermaßen, ~erweise** *adv* in like manner; **~falls** *adv* likewise, too, also, equally; *danke,* ~~*!* thanks, the same to you! **~farbig** *a* of the same colo(u)r; **~förmig** *a* uniform; homogeneous; (*glatt*) smooth; (*ständig*) steady; (*eintönig*) monotonous; ~~ *buchen* to book in conformity; **~~keit** *f* uniformity, conformity; monotony; **~gang** *m*, **~gängigkeit** *f* synchronism, unison; **~geltend** *a* equivalent; **~gerichtet** *a* parallel; *el* rectified, redressed; **~geschaltet** *a* (*politisch*) co-ordinated; **~geschlechtlich** *a* homosexual; **~gesinnt** *a* like-minded, congenial; **~gestellt** *a* co-ordinate; equal; **~gestimmt** *a mus* tuned to the same pitch; *fig* of the same opinion, in accord; **~gewicht** *n* balance, equilibrium, equipoise, poise; (*gespanntes*) tension; *politisches* ~~ balance of power; *seelisches* ~~ composure; *ins* ~~ *bringen* to equilibrate; *aus dem* ~~ *bringen* to unbalance, (*Verlegenheit*) to embarrass s. o.; *das* ~~ *wiederherstellen* to redress the balance; *das* ~~ *bewahren zwischen* to hold the balance between; *das* ~~ *verlieren* to lose o.'s balance; *sich das* ~~ *halten* to be in equilibrium; *im* ~~ in a state of equilibrium; **~~slage** *f* position of equilibrium; **~~slehre** *f* statics *pl*; **~~sstörung** *f* disturbance (*Am* displacement) of equilibrium; **~gültig** *a* indifferent; unconcerned; (*uninteressiert*) incurious, aloof, detached, disinterested; (*apathisch*) apathetic, impassive, phlegmatic; (*kühl*) cool, nonchalant; (*gefühllos*) calluous, unfeeling; *es ist mir alles* ~~ I don't care about anything; *sie ist mir* ~~ she means nothing to me; ~~ *wie du es machst* no matter how you do it; **~~keit** *f* indifference, unconcern, apathy; **~heit** *f* equality; (*Gleichberechtigung*) parity; (*Ebenmaß*) symmetry; (*Geradheit*) evenness; (*Gleichförmigkeit*) monotony, uniformity; (*Gleichwertigkeit*) equivalence, equipollence; (*Identität*) identity; (*Ähnlichkeit*) similarity; (*Gleichartigkeit*) homogeneousness; **~~szeichen** *n math* sign of equality; **~klang** *m mus* accord, unison; (*Übereinstimmung*) consonance; *gram* homonymy; **~kommen** *irr itr*: *jdm* ~~ to equal; to come up to s. o., to match s. o.; *nicht* ~~ to fall short of; **~lauf** *m* synchronism; *radio* ganging; *zum* ~~ *bringen* to synchronize; **~laufend** *a* parallel; synchronous, synchronized; **~läufig** *a* running in the same direction; **~lautend** *a* assonant; consonant; identical; (*Inhalt*) of the same tenor, incidental; *adv* in conformity; *gram* homonymous; ~~ *sein* to tally (with), to correspond (to); *~~e Abschrift* duplicate, true copy; **~machen** *tr* to equalize, to (make) level with (*od* to); to make like; to make uniform; *dem Erdboden* ~~ to raze to the ground; **~macher** *m* equalizer; (*Politik*) level(l)er; **~macherei** *f* level(l)ing mania; **~macherisch** *a* egalitarian; **~maß** *n* proportion, symmetry; **~mäßig** *a* equable, proportionate, symmetrical; uniform, even, equal; regular; constant; smooth; (*ununterbrochen*) steady; *adv* equally, evenly; **~~keit** *f* symmetry; equability; regularity; **~mut** *m* equanimity; (*Ruhe*) calmness; even temper; serenity; **~mütig** *a* calm; even-tempered; **~namig** *a* having (*od* of) the same name; similar, like; homonymous; *math* homologous, correspondent; ~~ *machen* to reduce to the same denominator; **~nis** *n* simile, allegory; (*Bild*) image; (*Vergleich*) comparison; (*Sinnbild*) allegory, parable; (*Metapher*) metaphor, figure of speech; **~~weise** *adv* allegorically, figuratively; by way of comparison; **~richten** *tr el* to rectify; **~richter** *m* rectifier; **~~röhre** *f radio* audion, detector valve (*Am* tube); *el* rectifying valve, *Am* rectifying tube; **~~station** *f* rectifier station; **~richtung** *f* rectification.

gleich|sam *adv* so to say, as it were; **~schalten** *tr* to co-ordinate, to unify; **~schaltung** *f* coordination, unification; bringing into line; **~schenklig** *a* isosceles; **~schritt** *m* cadence march, quick time; **~seitig** *a* equilateral; **~silbig** *a* parisyllabic; **~sinnig** *a* in same direction; **~stehen** *irr itr* to be equal (to); *sport* to equalize; *jdm* ~~ to equal s. o.; **~stellen** *tr* to equalize, to compare; *jdm* ~~ to put on a par (with); **~stellung** *f* equalization, comparison; **~strom** *m* direct (*od* continuous) current, D. C., *Am* d. c.; **~~dynamo** *m* direct current dynamo; **~~empfänger** *m* direct current (operated) receiver; **~~motor** *m* direct current motor; **~~netz** *n* direct current system; **~tun** *irr tr, itr*: *es jdm* ~~ to match s. o.; to compete with s. o.; to rival s.o.; *es jdm* ~~ *wollen* to vie with; **~ung** *f* equation; ~~ *1. Grades* linear equation; *quadratische* ~~ quadratic equation; *kubische* ~~ cubic equation; ~~ *mit mehreren Unbekannten* simultaneous equation; **~viel** *adv* just as much; no matter; **~weit** *a* equidistant; **~wertig** *a* equivalent; **~wie** *adv* even as, just as, as; **~winklig** *a* equiangular; **~wohl** *adv* nevertheless, notwithstanding, yet; however; **~zeitig** *a* simultaneous; (*gleichaltrig*) coeval; (*zeitgenössisch*) contemporary; (*übereinstimmend*) coincident; *adv* at the same time; **~~keit** *f* synchronism; simultaneousness, coincidence.

Gleis *n* = **Geleise**; **~abschnitt** *m* track section; **~abzweigung** *f* branch line; **~anlage** *f* track system; **~anschluß** *m* (own) siding; **~bettung** *f* bedding of track; **~dreieck** *n* triangular junction; **~kette** *f mot* caterpillar track; **~~nantrieb** *m* caterpillar drive; **~~nfahrzeug** *n* track-laying vehicle; **~~panzerfahrzeug** *n* full track armo(u)red vehicle; **~~nschlepper** *m* caterpillar tractor; **~~nzugmaschine** caterpillar tractor, prime mover; **~kontakt** *m* rail contact; **~kreuzung** *f* level crossing; **~kurve** *f* curved spur track, epi; **~los** *a* trackless, railless; **~netz** *n* network of lines; **~verzweigung** *f* railway junction.

Gleisner *m* hypocrite; **~ei** *f* hypocrisy; **~isch** *a* hypocritical, canting, sanctimonious, insincere.

gleißen *itr* to shine, to glisten, to glitter.

Gleit|angriff *m aero mil* gliding attack; **~apparat** *m* airplane glider; **~bahn** *f* slide, shoot; slideway; slips *pl*, slipway; (*Schreibmaschine*) carriage way; **~bombe** *f* glider bomb, *Am sl* glomb; **~boot** *n* gliding-boat, glider; **~en** *irr itr* to glide, to slide, to slip; (*Auto*) to skid; *aero* to glide, to plane; *~ender Preis* sliding price; *~en lassen* (*Hand*) to pass; (*Blick*) to glance over; **~en** *n* sliding; **~fläche** *f* slide face; gliding plane, slip plane; **~flieger** *m aero* glider pilot; airplane glider; **~flug** *m* glide, gliding flight; volplane; **~~geschwindigkeit** *f aero* gliding speed; **~~kurve** *f aero* gliding turn; **~~weite** *f* gliding range; **~~winkel** *m aero* gliding angle; **~~zeug** *n aero* glider; sailplane; **~kufe** *f* landing skid; **~lager** *n* slide bearing; **~landung** *f aero* glide landing; **~laut** *m* glide; **~mittel** *n* lubricant; **~riegel** *m* sliding bolt; **~rolle** *f* trolley; **~schiene** *f* slide rail; (*Schreibmaschine*) carriage rail; **~schritt** *m* (*Tanz*) chassé; **~schuh** *m* guide shoe; gun slide; **~schutz** *m mot* non-skid (tread); **~~kette** *f* non-skid chain; **~~mittel** *n* non-skid device; **~~reifen** *m* non-skid tyre; **~skala** *f* sliding scale; **~verdeck** *n mot* sliding roof; **~verhältnis** *n aero* gliding ratio; **~vermögen** *n aero* gliding quality; **~weg** *m aero* landing (*od* glide) path; **~~bake** *f* glide beam; glide path beacon; **~wendung** *f* slipping turn; **~winkel** *m* gliding angle; **~zahl** *f aero* lift-drag ratio.

Gletscher *m* glacier; snowfield; **~artig** *a* glacial; **~bach** *m* glacier torrent; **~boden** *m* soil formed by glacial action; **~brand** *m* dermatitis, sunburn; **~brille** *f* snow-goggles *pl*; **~bruch** *m*, **~feld** *n* glacier field; **~eis** *n* glacial ice; **~landschaft** *f* glacier landscape; **~mühle** *f* pot-hole; **~periode** *f* glacial period; **~spalte** *f* crevasse; **~tisch** *m* glacier-table; **~tor** *n* glacier mouth; **~wind** *m* glacier breeze; **~zeit** *f* glacial period.

Glied *n* limb; *mil* rank, file; (*Teil*) member; (*Ketten~*) link; (*Gelenk*) joint; *math* term; (*männliches*) penis; *in Reih u. ~* in rank and file; *sie zitterte an allen ~ern* she trembled all over; *ins ~ treten* (*mil*) to fall in; *die ~er recken* to stretch o. s.; *Vettern im dritten ~* third cousins.

Glieder|bau *m* structure, *fam* build; (*Aufbau*) organization; **~füßler** *m* arthropod; **~lahm** *a* palsied; paralytic, paralysed; **~lähmung** *f* palsy, paralysis; **~n** *tr* to joint; to articulate; to arrange (the parts); (*logisch*) to dispose; *mil* to draw up in line; (*Tiefe*) to distribute in depth; (*organisch*) to organize; (*Gruppen*) to group; to classify; *sich ~~* to be composed (of), to be divided (into); **~kette** *f* (open-link) chain; **~puppe** *f* jointed-doll; marionette, puppet; **~reißen** *n*, **~schmerz** *m* pains *pl* in the limbs, shooting pains *pl;* rheumatism; **~tier** *n* arthropod; **~ung** *f* arrangement, logical order, disposition; (*Satz*) construction, structure; (*Einteilung*) classification; (*Aufbau*) organization; *bot, anat* articulation; (*Verband*) affiliation; *mil* formation; **~verrenkung** *f* distortion of the limbs; **~zuckungen** *f pl* convulsions *pl*.

Glied|maßen *pl* limbs *pl*, extremities *pl*; *gesunde ~~ haben* to be sound of limbs; **~weise** *adv* limb by limb, link by link; *mil* in files.

glimm|en *itr* to glow (*od* burn) faintly, to gleam, to glimmer, to smoulder; *~~de Asche* embers *pl*; **~er** *m* glimmer; mica; **~~schiefer** *m* mica-slate; **~lampe** *f* glow (*od* neon) lamp; **~röhre** *f* glow discharge tube; **~stengel** *m* cigar, weed; *fam* fag.

glimpflich *a* gentle; mild; easy, light; indulgent; lenient; *~ davonkommen* to get off with a trifling loss; *mit jdm ~ verfahren* to deal gently with s. o.

glitsch|en *itr* to glide, to slide, to slip; **~(er)ig** *a* slippery.

glitzern *itr* to glisten, to glitter, to flash, to gleam; (*funkeln*) to sparkle, to scintillate, to coruscate; (*Stern*) to twinkle; (*schimmern*) to shimmer, to glimmer.

glob|al *a* global; overall; **~albetrag** *m* global sum; **~alkontingent** *n* wholesale quota of raw materials; **~us** *m* globe.

Glocke *f* bell; (*Glas~*) glass-shade; (*Lampe*) globe; (*Pumpe*) recipient; *bot* cup; (*Uhr*) clock; (*Klingel*) gong; (*Jäger~*) *mil aero* umbrella; *die ~n läuten* to ring the bells; *an die große ~ hängen* to make a great fuss about s. th., to blaze s. th. abroad, to broadcast s. th.; *er weiß, was die ~ geschlagen hat* he knows how the matter stands.

Glocken|blume *f* blue-bell, harebell; campanula; **~boje** *f* bell-buoy; **~förmig** *a* bell-shaped; **~form** *f* bell-mo(u)ld; **~geläute** *n* ringing of bells, chime; **~gießer** *m* bell-founder; **~guß** *m* bell-casting; **~gut** *n* bell-metal; **~hell** *a* clear as a bell; **~isolator** *m* bell-shaped insulator; **~klöppel, ~schwengel** *m* bell-clapper; **~rock** *m* gored skirt; **~schale** *f* gong; **~schlag** *m* stroke of a clock; **~seil** *n* bell-rope; **~speise** *f* bell-metal; **~spiel** *n* chime(s), peal of bells; **~stuhl** *m* belfry; **~turm** *m* bell-tower, steeple; **~zug** *m* bell-pull.

Glöck|lein *n* small bell; **~ner** *m* bell-ringer, sexton.

Glor|ie *f* glory; **~ienschein** *m* glory, halo; aureola; **~ifizieren** *tr* to glorify; **~reich** *a* glorious, illustrious.

Gloss|ar *n* glossary; **~e** *f* gloss; comment; (marginal) note; (*Kritik*) criticism; *über etw ~en machen* to comment upon s. th.; (*tadeln*) to find fault with s. th.; *über alles ~en machen* to sneer at; **~ieren** *tr* to gloss (*od* to comment) upon; (*nörgeln*) to carp at.

Glotz|auge *n* goggle-eye; **~äugig** *a* goggle-eyed, *Am* pop-eyed; **~en** *itr* to stare, to goggle; to gaze, to gape (at).

gluck! *interj* chuck! **~e** *f* clucking hen; **~en** *itr* to cluck; to chuck; **~sen** *itr* (*Wasser*) to gurgle.

Glück *n* (*~sfall*) luck, lucky chance; *er hat viel ~* he has much good luck; *kein ~ haben* to be out of luck; (*das launige ~*) fortune; *sein ~ machen* to make o.'s fortune; (*Erfolg*) success; prosperity; (*inneres ~*) happiness, felicity; (*Geschick*) fate, lot; (*Zufall*) chance, lot; *er wagte es auf gut ~* he took a chance; *du hast ~ gehabt* you were lucky; *ein ~, daß* it's a piece of luck that; *unverhofftes ~ haben* *fam* to strike oil; *Sie können von ~ reden* you can consider yourself lucky; *~ u. Glas, wie leicht bricht das* glass and luck, brittle muck; *mancher hat mehr ~ als Verstand* fortune favo(u)rs fools; *zum ~* fortunately; *~ auf!* good luck! *viel ~!* good luck! (*bei Geburtstag*) many happy returns; *auf gut ~* at a venture; *~ wünschen zu* to congratulate on; *~ zum neuen Jahre wünschen* to wish a happy New Year; *sein ~ machen* to make o.'s fortune; **~bringend** *a* lucky, fortunate, auspicious; **~en** *itr* to turn out well, to work out; to succeed; *es glückt mir* I succeed in (doing s. th.); *es wollte mir nirgends ~~* I failed everywhere; **~lich** *a* lucky, fortunate, happy; (*gedeihlich*) prosperous; (*günstig*) favo(u)rable, auspicious; *~~e Reise!* have a pleasant trip! *sich ~~ schätzen* to count o. s. happy; *~~ vonstatten gehen* to go off well; *alles dem ~~en Zufall überlassen* to commit everything to chance; *er ist ~~ angekommen* he arrived safely; *du ~~er! fam* you happy dog! *dem ~~en schlägt keine Stunde* to the happy time is swift; **~licherweise** *adv* fortunately, luckily; **~selig** *a* blessed, happy; blissful; (*strahlend*) radiant; **~~keit** *f* blessedness, happiness, bliss, felicity.

Glücks|fall *m* lucky chance; stroke of luck, *Am* lucky break; (*unerwartet*) windfall; **~göttin** *f* Fortune; **~güter** *n pl* riches *pl*, earthly possessions *pl*; **~kind** *n* fortune's favo(u)rite; *er ist ein ~~* he is born with a silver spoon in his mouth; **~pfennig** *m* lucky penny; **~pilz** *m fam* lucky fellow, lucky beggar; **~rad** *n* wheel of fortune; **~ritter** *m* fortune-hunter, adventurer; **~sache** *f* matter of chance; **~spiel** *n* game of hazard; **~~automat** *m Am* slot machine; **~stern** *m* lucky star; **~strähne** *f* stroke of luck; lucky strike; **~tag** *m* red-letter day; **~topf** *m* lucky-dip (*od* bag), *Am* grab-bag; **~umstände** *m pl* fortunate circumstances *pl*; **~wurf** *m* lucky throw; **~zufall** *m* lucky chance.

glück|verheißend *a* auspicious, propitious, favo(u)rable; **~wunsch** *m* congratulation, good wishes *pl*; (*zu Festen*) compliments *pl* (of the season); *herzlichen ~~ zum Geburtstag* happy birthday; *herzlichen ~~ zum Neuen Jahr* I wish you a happy New Year; **~~karte** *f* greeting-card; **~~schreiben** *n* letter of congratulation; **~~telegramm** *n* greeting-telegram.

Glüh|birne *f el* (electric) bulb; (*mattiert*) frosted bulb; **~en** *itr* to glow, to be red-hot; *fig* to burn; *vor Eifer ~~* to glow with zeal; *vor Zorn ~~* to burn with anger; *für etw ~~* to be an admirer of; *mir glüht der Kopf* my head burns; *tr* to make red-hot; (*Wein*) to mull; (*ausglühen*) to anneal; (*entzünden*) to ignite; (*durch Brand verzehren*) to calcine; *zu stark ~~* to overheat; **~end** *a* glowing, red-hot; incandescent; *fig* ardent, fervent; *~~e Hitze* tropical heat; *~~e Kohlen* live coals; *auf ~~en Kohlen sitzen* to sit upon thorns, to be on tenterhooks; *~~ heiß* burning hot; *in ~~en Farben schildern* to paint s. th. in glowing colo(u)rs; *~~es Verlangen* burning desire; **~faden** *m* (incandescent) filament; **~heiß** *a* red-hot; **~hitze** *f* red-heat; **~kathode** *f* glowing cathode; **~~nröhre** *f radio* thermionic valve; **~kerze** *f mot* heater plug; **~lampe** *f*, **~licht** *n* incandescent lamp; **~ofen** *m* annealing-furnace; (*Keramik*) hardening-on kiln; **~strumpf** *m* incandescent mantle; **~wein** *m* mulled wine; negus; **~würmchen** *n* glow-worm.

Glut *f* (*Sonne*) blaze; *fig* flame, ardo(u)r, fervo(u)r, passion, fervency; (*Kohle*) live coals *pl*, glowing fire, red-heat; (*Hitze*) heat; *in ~ geraten* to fire (*od* to blaze) up; *die ~ schüren* to stir the fire; **~rot** *a* (as) red as fire.

Glyzerin *n* glycerin(e); **~säure** *f* glyceric acid; **~seife** *f* glycerin(e)-soap, transparent soap.

G. m. b. H. limited (liability) society (*od* company), *Abk* Ltd; *Am* incorporated, *Abk* Inc.

Gnade *f* (*spendende*) grace; (*verzeihende*) mercy, pardon; (*Milde*) clemency; (*Gunst*) favo(u)r; (*Schonung*) quarter; *durch die ~ Gottes* by the grace of God; *um ~ bitten* to plead for mercy; *~ für Recht ergehen lassen* to show mercy; *~ widerfahren lassen* to pardon; *er wurde wieder in ~ angenommen* he was restored to favo(u)r; *um ~ bitten* to ask for mercy; *Euer ~n!* Your Grace! *sich auf ~ u. Ungnade ergeben* to surrender at discretion (*od* unconditionally).

Gnaden|akt *m* act of grace; **~ausschuß** *m* (*für Begnadigungen*) clemency board; (*für Parolegewährung*) parole board; **~bezeigung** *f* favo(u)r, grace; **~bild** *n* miraculous image; **~brot** *n* bread of charity; *das ~~ essen* to live on charity; **~erlaß** *m* act of oblivion, general pardon, amnesty; **~frist** *f* reprieve, respite; *ohne ~~* unreprievable; **~gehalt** *n* allowance; **~geschenk** *n* gratification; **~gesuch** *n* petition of grace (*od* mercy), petition for review (*od* clemency); *ein ~~ einreichen* to file a petition of grace; **~jahr** *n* year of grace; **~lohn** *m* gratuity; **~mittel** *n pl* means of grace; **~ordnung** *f* rules of grace procedure; **~reich** *a* gracious; merciful; **~sache** *f* matter of grace; **~sold** *m* gratuity; **~stoß** *m* death-blow, finishing stroke; knock-out; **~tod** *m* mercy killing, euthanasia; **~wahl** *f* predestination; **~weg** *m* act of grace; *auf dem ~~* (*eccl*) by the grace of God; *jur* on the way of grace, by special grace.

gnädig *a* gracious; (*barmherzig*) merciful (to); (*günstig*) favo(u)rable; (*freundlich*) kind; (*wohlwollend*) benevolent; (*herablassend*) condescending; *Gott sei ihm ~!* the Lord have mercy upon him! *~e Frau* Madam; *~ davonkommen* to get off clear.

Gneis *m* gneiss.

Gnom *m* gnome, sprite, goblin; **~enhaft** *a* gnomish, gnomelike.
Gobelin *m* tapestry, gobelin.
Gockel(hahn) *m* rooster, cock.
Gold *n* gold; *er ist nicht mit ~ zu bezahlen* he is above price; *es ist nicht alles ~, was glänzt* all is not gold that glitters; *Reden ist Silber, Schweigen ist ~* speech is silvern, silence is golden; **~abfluß** *m* drain (*od* efflux) of gold; **~abzüge** *m pl* withdrawals *pl* of gold; **~ader** *f* vein of gold; **~ammer** *f* yellow-bunting; yellow-(h)ammer; **~amsel** *f* oriole; **~anleihe** *f* gold-loan; **~arbeit** *f* goldsmith's work; **~arbeiter** *m* goldsmith; **~barren** *m* bullion, ingot of gold; **~basis** *f* gold basis; **~bestand** *m* gold reserve; **~blättchen** *n* gold-foil; **~blech** *n* gold-foil; **~block** *m* parity union of nations, gold standard; **~borte** *f* gold-lace; **~braun** *a* chestnut; **~brokat** *m* gold brocade; **~buchstabe** *m* gilt letter; **~draht** *m* gold-wire; **~deckung** *f* gold cover; **~doublé** *n* gold plating; **~en** *a* of gold, golden; *~~e Hochzeit* golden-wedding; *~~es Zeitalter* golden age; *den ~~en Mittelweg finden* to find a happy medium; *~e Berge versprechen* to make extravagant promises; **~faden** *m* spun gold; **~farbe** *f* gold-colo(u)r; **~fasan** *m* golden pheasant; **~feder** *f* gold nib, fountain-pen; **~finger** *m* ring-finger; **~fisch** *m* gold-fish; **~~glas** *n* fish-bowl; **~flitter** *m* gold-spangle; **~folie** *f* gold foil; **~fuchs** *m* yellow-dun horse; (*~stück*) yellow-boy; **~führend** *a* auriferous; **~gehalt** *m* alloy, percentage of gold; **~gelb, ~farben** *a* gold-colo(u)red; **~gewicht** *n* troy weight; **~gräber** *m* gold-digger; **~grube** *f* gold-mine; *Am* (*bes. auch fig*) bonanza; **~grund** *m* gold background; **~haltig** *a* gold-bearing; containing gold; auriferous; **~käfer** *m* rose-chafer; **~kind** *n* darling; **~klumpen** *m* lump of gold, nugget; **~körnchen** *n* small grain of gold; **~kurs** *m* gold-rate; **~lack** *m* gold-colo(u)red varnish; (*Blume*) wall-flower; **~legierung** *f* alloy of gold; **~leiste** *f* gilt-cornice; **~macher** *m* alchemist; **~~ei** *f* alchemy; **~mine** *f* gold-mine; **~münze** *f* gold-piece; **~plattiert** *a* gold-plated; **~regen** *m* *bot* laburnum; **~sand** *m* gold-sand; **~schaum** *m* tinsel, leaf-brass; **~scheider** *m* gold-refiner; **~schläger** *m* gold-beater; **~~häutchen** *n* gold-beater's skin; **~schmied** *m* goldsmith; **~schnitt** *m* gilt edge; *mit ~~* gilt-edged; **~standard** *m* gold standard; **~staub** *m* gold dust; **~stickerei** *f* embroidery in gold; **~stück** *n* (*Münze*) gold coin; **~sucher** *m* prospector, gold-digger; **~tresse** *f* gold-lace; **~vorrat** *m* gold holdings *pl*; **~waage** *f* gold-scales *pl*; *alle Worte auf die ~~ legen* to weigh all words well; to be over-particular; **~währung** *f* gold-standard; **~waren** *f pl* jewellery; **~~händler** *m* goldsmith; **~wäsche** *f* gold-washings *pl*; **~wäscher** *m* gold-washer; **~waschrinne** sluice box; **~zufluß** *m* influx of gold.
Golf *m* (*Meeresbucht*) gulf, bay; (*kleine Bucht*) creek; *~ n* (*Spiel*) golf; **~ausrüstung** *f* golfing kit; **~ball** *m* golf ball; **~hindernis** *n* trap; **~hose** *f* plus-fours *pl*; **~junge** *m* caddie; **~platz** *m* (golf-) links *pl*, golf course; **~schläger** *m* golfclub, golf-stick; **~spiel** *n* golf; **~spieler** *m* golfer; **~spielfeld** *n*, **~spielplatz** *m* (golf) course, (golf-) links *pl*; **~strom** *m* Gulf-Stream.

Gondel *f* gondola; (*Luftschiff~*) car; **~führer** *m* gondolier; **~n** *itr* to row about in a boat.
gönn|en *tr* to permit, to grant; not to begrudge; *nicht ~~* to begrudge; *sich ~~* to give (*od* allow) o. s.; *ich ~e ihm das Vergnügen* for my part, let him have his fun; *jdm alles Gute ~~* to wish s. o. all happiness; *nichts Gutes ~~* to wish s. o. ill; *er ~t sich keine Minute Ruhe* he doesn't allow himself a minute's rest; **~er** *m*, **~erin** *f* protector, protectress; patron(-ess), *Am* sponsor; **~erhaft** *a* patronizing; **~ermiene** *f* patronizing air; **~erschaft** *f* patronage, protection, sponsorship, (a)egis.
Göpel *m*, **~werk** *n* whim-gin, horse-gin; winch; capstan.
Gör *n*, **Göre** *f* child; (*verächtlich*) brat.
gordisch *a* Gordian; *den ~en Knoten zerhauen* to cut the Gordian knot.
Gösch *f* *mar* jack.
Gosse *f* gutter, channel, drain; kennel; **~nstein** *m* gutter-stone; (*Küche*) sink.

*

Got|e *m* Goth; **~isch** *a* Gothic; *~~e Schrift* black letter.
Gott *m* God; *der liebe ~* the good God; *~ sei Dank!* thank God! *~ gebe! wollte ~!* God grant it! *um ~es willen!* for God's sake! *~ bewahre* God forbid; *mein ~, was machen Sie denn?* for God's sake, what are you doing? *leider ~es geht es nicht* unfortunately it can't be done; *oh ~!* dear me! *so ~ will* please God; *den lieben ~ e-n guten Mann sein lassen* to let matters slide; *in ~es Namen!* for Heaven's sake! *mit ~es Hilfe* God willing; *du bist wohl ganz von ~ verlassen* you must be completely out of your mind; *von ~es Gnaden* by the Grace of God; *ich schwöre bei ~ dem Allmächtigen* I swear by almighty God; *so wahr mir ~ helfe!* so help me God! **~ähnlich** *a* godlike; **~begnadet** *a* heaven-inspired; **~ergeben** *a* devout, pious.
Götter|bild *n* image of a god; idol; **~bote** *m* messenger of the gods, Mercury; **~dämmerung** *f* twilight of the gods; **~gleich** *a* god-like; **~lehre** *f* mythology; **~mahl** *n* feast for the gods; **~sage** *f* myth; **~sitz** *m* abode of the gods; **~speise** *f* ambrosia; (*Küche*) cream trifle; **~spruch** *m* oracle; **~trank** *m* nectar; **~verehrung** *f* worship of the gods.
Gottes|acker *m* churchyard; cemetery; **~dienst** *m* divine service; **~dienstlich** *a* religious; **~friede** *m* heavenly peace, truce of God; **~furcht** *f* fear of God; **~fürchtig** *a* god-fearing, pious; **~gabe** *f* gift of God; **~gnadentum** *n* divine right; **~gelehrsamkeit, ~gelehrtheit** *f* theology; **~gelehrte(r)** *m* theologian; **~gericht** *n* ordeal; **~glaube** *m* belief in God; **~haus** *n* church, chapel; **~kasten** *m* poor-box; **~lästerer** *m* blasphemer; **~lästerlich** *a* blasphemous; **~lästerung** *f* blasphemy; **~leugner** *m* atheist; **~leugnung** *f* atheism; **~lohn** *m* God's blessing; **~mutter** *f* Blessed Virgin; **~staat** *m* theocracy; **~urteil** *n* ordeal; **~verächter** *m* despiser of God; **~wort** *n* Bible.
gott|gefällig *a* agreeable to God; **~gläubig** *a* believing in God (but rejecting Christianity); **~gleich** *a* godlike; **~heit** *f* deity; divinity; godhead.
Gött|in *f* goddess; **~lich** *a* divine, godlike; (*wunderbar*) marvellous, unique; (*spaßhaft*) funny; *~~e Vorsehung* Divine Providence; **~~keit** *f* divinity, godliness.
gott|lob! *interj* thank God! *fam* thank goodness! **~los** *a* irreligious, impious, godless; (*verrucht*) wicked; **~losenbewegung** *f* anti-religious movement; **~losigkeit** *f* impiety; wickedness, ungodliness; godlessness; **~mensch** *m* God incarnate; **~seibeiuns** *m* the devil, *fam* Old Nick; **~selig** *a* pious, godly; religious; **~~keit** *f* piety, religiousness; **~vergessen** *a* godless, wicked; (*verlassen*) desolate; (*entlegen*) remote; **~verflucht** *a* accursed; ill-fated, detestable; **~verlassen** *a* god-forsaken; **~vertrauen** *n* trust in God; **~voll** *a* inspired by God; *fig* excellent, capital.
Götze *m* idol, false deity.
Götzen|bild *n* idol; **~diener** *m* idolater; **~~in** *f* idolatress; **~dienst** *m* idolatry, idol-worship; **~tempel** *m* temple of an idol, heathen temple.
Gouvern|ante *f* governess; nurse; **~eur** *m* governor; *den ~~ od dessen Amt betreffend Am* gubernatorial.

*

Grab *n* grave; (*gemauert*) tomb; (*Gruft*) sepulchre, *Am* sepulcher; *das Heilige ~* the Holy Sepulchre; *zu ~e tragen* to bury; *am Rande des ~es stehen* to have one foot in the grave; *er ist verschwiegen wie das ~* he's (as) silent as the grave; *jdn zu ~e geleiten* to attend s. o.'s funeral; *am ~* at the grave-side; *ins ~ sinken* to sink into the grave; *sich im ~e umdrehen* to turn in o.'s grave; *sie bringt mich noch ins ~* she'll be the death of me yet; *das ~ des Unbekannten Soldaten* the tomb of the Unknown Soldier; **~en** *m* ditch, *mil* trench; *der vorderste ~en* fire-trench; **~en** *irr tr* to dig, to trench; (*Meißel*) to engrave; (*Stiehel*) to cut; *fig* to impress deeply; (*Kaninchen*) to burrow; **~en** *n* digging, trenching; **~~bagger** *m* trench excavator; **~~böschung** *f* counter-scarp; **~~kampf** *m* trench fighting; **~~krieg** *m* trench warfare; **~~mörser** *m* trench mortar; **~~sohle** *f* trench floor; **~~stellung** *f* trench position; **~~wand** *f* trench wall; **~~wehr** *f* parapet.
Gräber *m* digger; **~funde** *m pl* sepulchral relics *pl*.
Grab|esdunkel *n* darkness of the grave; **~eskirche** *f* church of the Holy Sepulchre; **~esrand** *m* brink (*od* verge) of the grave; **~esruhe, ~esstille** *f* peace of the grave; deathlike silence; **~esschlummer** *m* sleep of death; **~esstimme** *f* sepulchral voice; **~geläute** *n* knell, tolling of bells; **~geleite** *n* procession of mourners; **~gesang** *m* funeral song, dirge; **~gewölbe** *n* vault, tomb; **~hügel** mound, tumulus; (*Hügelgrab*) barrow, cairn; **~kreuz** *n* grave marker; **~legung** *f* burial, interment; **~lied** *n* dirge; **~mal** *n* tomb(stone); monument; **~platte** *f* tombstone; **~rede** *f* funeral sermon (*od* oration); **~scheit** *n* spade; **~schrift** *f* epitaph; **~stätte** *f* grave, tomb, burial-place; **~stein** *m* gravestone; **~stichel** *m* graver, chisel, burin; **~tuch** *n* winding-sheet, shroud; **~urne** *f* funeral urn.
Grad *m* degree, rate; (*Rang*) rank; (*akademischer ~*) degree, *Am* grade; (*Ausmaß*) degree, extent, point; (*Stufe fig*) stage; (*Art, Anordnung*) order; *15 ~ Wärme* (*Kälte*) 15 degrees above (below) zero; *in dem ~e, daß ...* to such an extent that ...; *in höchstem ~e* exceedingly; *bis zu e-m gewissen ~e* up to a certain degree (*od*

point); *in nicht geringem ~e* in no small degree; *e-n akademischen ~ erlangen* to take o.'s degree; *in hohem ~e* in a high degree; *in ~e einteilen* to graduate; **~abzeichen** *n* badge of rank; **~bogen** *m* graduated arc; *math* protractor; **~einteilung** *f* graduation; **~ieren** *tr* to graduate; to refine; **~ierhaus, ~ierwerk** *n* graduation-works *pl*; **~ierung** *f* graduation; **~leiter** *f* graduated scale; **~messer** *m* graduator; **~netz** *n* skeleton map; *aero* grid; **~uiert** *a* graduate; **~weise** *adv* gradually, by degrees; **~zahl** *f* (compass) direction.

Graf *m* earl; (*nicht englisch*) count; **~enkrone** *f* earl's (count's) coronet; **~enstand** *m* earldom; dignity of a count; **~schaft** *f* county, shire.

Gräf|in *f* countess; **~lich** *a* like a count; belonging to a count (od earl).

Gral *m* grail.

Gram *m* grief, sorrow, sadness, affliction; *jdm ~ sein* to bear s. o. grudge, to be cross with s. o.; **~erfüllt** *a* sorrowful, deeply grieved; **~gebeugt** *a* bowed down with grief; **~gefurcht** *a* woe-worn; **~versunken** *a* woe-begone, sunk in grief; **~voll** *a* care-worn, gloomy, sad, sorrowful.

gräm|en *r* to grieve, to pine, to fret, to worry; *sich zu Tode ~~* to pine away; **~lich** *a* sulky, morose, peevish, sullen, ill-humoured, fretful; **~~keit** *f* sulkiness, fretfulness.

Gramm *n* gram(me) (1 g = 15,432 grains; 28,3 g = 1 ounce).

Grammat|ik *f* grammar; **~ikalisch, ~isch** *a* grammatical; **~iker** *m* grammarian.

Grammophon *n* gramophone, *Am* phonograph; (*Plattenspieler*) record player; *Radio~ mit automatischem Plattenspieler* radiogramophone with automatic changer; *Koffer~* portable (gramophone); **~anschluß** *m radio* gramophone (*Am* phonograph) pick-up; **~nadel** *f* gramophone-needle; **~platte** *f* (gramophone, *Am* phonograph) record, disk, disc; *Rundfunksprecher, der ~~nprogramme ansagt Am* disk jockey; **~~narchiv** *n* (*Plattenständer*) record stand; **~schalldose** *f* sound-box; **~tonarm** *m* tone arm.

Gran *n* grain.

Granat *m* (*Edelstein*) garnet; **~apfel** *m* pomegranate; **~e** *f* (*Geschoß*) grenade, shell; **~feuer** *n* shell fire, shelling; **~hülse** *f* shell case; **~kugel** *f* shell; **~loch** *n* shell-crater; **~splitter** *m* shell splinter; **~stein** *m* garnet; **~trichter** *m* crater, shell-hole; **~werfer** *m* trench mortar; **~~nest** *n* mortar pit; **~~zug** *m* mortar platoon.

Grand|e *m* grandee; **~los** *a* grand, sublime.

Granit *m* granite; **~artig** *a* granitic.

Granne *f bot* awn, beard.

granulieren *tr* to granulate.

Graph|ik *f* graphic arts *pl*; **~~er** *m* illustrator, commercial artist; **~isch** *a* graphic; *die ~~en Künste* graphic arts; *Abteilung für ~~e Künste* print division; *~~e Darstellung* plotting, graphic representation, graph; **~it** *m* black-lead, graphite, plumbago; *mit ~~ überziehen* to graphitize; **~~schmelztiegel** *m* graphite crucible; **~~schmierung** *f* graphite lubrication; **~~schwärze** *f* black-lead wash; **~~stift** *m* black-lead pencil; **~~-Uraniumbrenner** *m* graphite uranium pile; **~olog** *m* graphologist; grapho-analist; **~ologie** *f* graphology.

grapsen *itr* to scramble (for), to snatch (at), to grab.

Gras *n* grass; *ins ~ beißen* to bite the dust, to die; *über etw ~ wachsen lassen* to forget s. th.; *er hört das ~ wachsen* he fancies himself exceedingly wise; *mit ~ bewachsen* grass grown; **~affe** *m* young fool; **~artig** *a* gramineous; **~bank** *f* turf-seat; **~boden** *m* lawn, turf; **~butter** *f* may-butter; **~ebene** *f* grassy plain, prairie, savanna; **~en** *itr* to graze; **~fleck** *m* grass-plot; (*in Kleidern*) grass-stain; **~fressend** *a* graminivorous; **~frosch** *m* brown frog; **~grün** *a* grass-green; **~halm** *m* blade of grass, spear, spire; **~hüpfer** *m* grass-hopper; **~ig** *a* grassy; **~land** *n* pasture, meadow; **~mäher** *m*, **~mähmaschine** *f* grass mower, mowing machine; **~mücke** *f orn* hedge-sparrow; **narbe** *f* sward, turf, sod; **~nelke** *f* maiden-pink; **~platz** *m* grass-plot, green, lawn; **~reich** *a* grassy; **~samen**. *m* grass-seed; **~sichel** *f* sickle for cutting grass; **~weide** *f* pasture(-ground); **~wuchs** *m* growth of grass, pasture.

Gräschen *n* small blade of grass.

grassieren *itr med* to rage, to prevail, to spread.

gräßlich *a* terrible, horrible, hideous, ghastly; (*anstößig*) shocking; dire; (*widerlich*) nasty; **~keit** *f* direness, horribleness, atrocity.

Grat *m* edge, ridge, crest; (*scharfe Kante*) *arch* arris; (*~bogen*) *arch* groin; (*feiner ~*) burr; (*Schmiede*) flash; *mil* scoring; (*Leiste*) rabbet.

Grät|e *f* fish-bone; **~ig** *a* full of fish-bones.

Gratifikation *f* gratuity; benefit; bonus; gratification; (*Zulage*) extra pay.

gratis *adv* gratis, free (of charge), gratuitously, *Am* complimentary; (*Zugabe*) into the bargain; *~ u. franko* gratis and post-free; **~beigabe** *f* free supplement; **~exemplar** *n typ* presentation copy.

Grätsche *f* straddling, splits *pl*; **~n** *itr* to straddle, to do the splits.

Gratul|ant *m* congratulator, well-wisher; **~ation** *f* congratulation; **~ieren** *itr* to congratulate (on), to felicitate; *ich gratuliere!* my congratulations! *zum Geburtstag ~~* to wish s. o. many happy returns (of the day).

grau *a* grey; *bes. Am* gray; (*vom Haar auch*) grizzly; grey-haired; (*Vorzeit*) remote, ancient; *seit ~er Vorzeit* from times immemorial; *darüber lasse ich mir keine ~en Haare wachsen* I don't worry about it; *der ~e Markt* the grey market; *~ werden* to grow grey; *das ~e Altertum* remote antiquity; *~ n* grey colo(u)r; *~ in ~ malen* to paint grey in grey; **~bart** *m* grey-beard; **~blau** *a* greyish blue; **~braun** *a* dun; **~brot** *n* rye bread; **~en** *itr* to dawn; *imp* to shudder at, to be afraid, to dread; *es ~t mir davor* I have a horror; **~en** *n* dawning, dawn; *beim ~~ des Tages* at the dawn of day; at day-break; (*Entsetzen*) horror, dread, fear; *von ~~ gepackt* horror-stricken; **~enerregend, ~enhaft, ~envoll** *a* horrid, horrible, horrific; awful, dreadful; terrible, ghastly, gruesome; **~grün** *a* greyish-green; **~guß** *m* grey cast iron; **~haarig** *a* grey-haired; **~kopf** *m* grey-headed person; **~len**: *sich vor jdm ~~* to be afraid of; *tr jdn ~* to caress; **~lich, gräulich** *a* greyish, grizzly; **~markthändler** *m* greymarketeer; **~meliert** *a* sprinkled with grey; grey-mottled; **~pappe** *f* pasteboard, mill board; **~schimmel** *m* grey horse; **~schleier** *m phot* fog; **~tier** *n* ass, donkey; **~wacke** *f* grey-wacke; **~werk** *n* (*Pelz*) miniver.

Graupe *f* peeled grain, groats *pl*, pot barley; **~ln** *f pl* sleet, hailstones *pl*; *~~ imp* to sleet; *es ~lt* sleet is falling; *~~ n* sleeting; **~lschauer** *m* snow-pellet shower; **~lwetter** *n* sleety weather; **~nschleim** *m* gruel; **~nsuppe** *f* barley-broth.

graus *a* awful, dreadful; *~ m* dread, fear, horror; **~am** *a* cruel to; (*wild*) fierce, ferocious, truculent; (*barbarisch*) barbarous, savage; (*unmenschlich*) inhuman; (*erbarmungslos*) merciless, inhuman; *fam fig* excessive, enormous; **~~keit** *f* cruelty, atrocity, ferocity; **~en** *itr* to shudder at; *mir graust* I shudder; *~~ n* awe, horror; **~~erregend, ~ig** *a* awful, fearful, **~lich** *a* dreadful, hideous.

Graveur *m* engraver.

Gravier|anstalt *f* engraver's establishment; **~en** *tr* to engrave; (*belasten bei Gericht*) to aggravate, to charge; **~kunst** *f* art of engraving; **~nadel** *f* (en)graving needle; **~ung** *f* engraving.

Gravit|ation *f* gravitation; **~~sgesetz** *n* law of gravitation; **~ätisch** *a* grave, solemn, ceremonious, *fam* bumptious; **~ieren** *itr* to gravitate (to, towards).

Graz|ie *f* grace, charm; *die drei ~ien* the three Graces; **~iös** *a* graceful; (*reizend*) attractive, charming; (*biegsam*) willowy, supple.

Greif *m* (*in der Fabel*) griffin; **~geier** *m* condor.

Greif|bagger *m* excavator; **~bar** *a* seizable; *com* (*Ware*) available; ready; on (*od* at) hand; *fig* (*deutlich*) tangible, palpable; (*offenkundig*) obvious; **~en** *irr tr* to seize, to grasp; *nach etw ~~* to catch; to snatch at, to get hold of, to reach for, to make a grip at; (*zupacken*) to clutch at; (*Saite*) to touch; (*Note*) to strike; *itr zu den Waffen ~~* to take up arms; *ineinander ~~* to interlock, (*Räder*) to fit (*od* to gear) into each other, *arch* to catch in; *in die Tasche ~~* to put o.'s hand into o.'s pocket; *an die Ehre ~~* to touch o.'s hono(u)r; *völlig aus der Luft gegriffen* mere invention; *die Zahl ist nicht zu hoch gegriffen* the figure isn't too high as an estimate; *nach der Feder ~~* to take up the pen; *zu drastischen Maßnahmen ~~* to resort to drastic measures; *jdm unter die Arme ~~* to lend s. o. a helping hand; *ans Herz ~~* to touch deeply; *in ein Wespennest ~~* to stir a wesp's nest; *fehl ~~, daneben ~~* to miss o.'s hold; *um sich ~~* to spread about, to increase, to gain ground; *mit beiden Händen zu~~* to jump at the chance; **~er** *m* grab, excavator; *mot* cleat; *typ* rapper; *tech* (*Klaue*) claw, catcher, gripper; (*Nähmaschine*) catcher; **~~inhalt** *m* grab capacity; **~~vorrichtung** *f mot* traction device; **~klaue** *f zoo* claw; **~nase** *f tech* whisker; **~werkzeug** *n* gripping device; **~zange** *f* pliers *pl*; **~zirkel** *m* cal(l)ipers *pl*.

grein|en *itr* to blubber, to whimper, to whine; **~er** *m* blubberer; grumbler.

Greis *m* old man; *~ a* grey; hoary; **~enalter** *n* old age; **~enhaft** *a* senile; **~in** *f* old woman.

grell *a* (*Farben*) strong, loud, glaring, gaudy; (*blendend*) dazzling; (*Ton*) shrill, piercing, sharp; (*roh, ungeschminkt*) crude; *fig ~er Unterschied* striking difference; **~heit** *f* shrillness, dazzling brightness; vividness; crudeness.

Grenadier *m* grenadier; rifleman;

~bataillon *n* rifle battalion; **~kompanie** *f* rifle company; **~mütze** *f* busby.

Grenz|auffanglager *n* transient camp; **~aufseher, ~er** *m* custom-house officer, *Am* border patrolman, custom patrol inspector; **~bach** *m* boundary-stream; **~bahnhof** *m* frontier station; **~baum** *m* tree marking a boundary; **~befeuerung** *f aero* boundary lights *pl*; **~berichtigung** *f* rectification of the boundary; frontier adjustment; **~bestimmung** *f* (*Ort*) location; **~bewohner** *m* borderer; **~bezirk** *m* frontier district; **~e** *f* (*Land*) frontier, border(s *pl*); (*Scheidelinie*) boundary; (*Grenzgebiet*) confines *pl*; (*Schranke*) bound, confine; (*Punkt*) term; (*Abgrenzung u. fig*) limit; (*äußerstes Ende*) extreme point; (*Linie*) demarcation line; (*Rand*) edge, verge, skirt; (*obere ~e, Preise, Wolken*) ceiling; (*unterste*) *fam* floor; *alles hat seine ~en* there is a limit to everything; *an der ~e* on the frontier; *ihre Dankbarkeit kannte keine ~en* her gratitude knew no bounds; *seine Geduld hat bald ihre ~e erreicht* he has almost reached the limit of his patience; *~e der Zivilisation Am* border; **~einkommen** *n* marginal revenue; **~en** *itr* (*Land*) to border on; (*in der Nähe sein*) to be adjacent (*od* contiguous) to, to adjoin; *fig* to be next to, to border on, to verge on; *das ~t an Wahnsinn* that borders on insanity; **~enlos** *a* boundless, limitless; unlimited; infinite; *adv* exceedingly; **~enlosigkeit** *f* boundlessness, immensity; infinitude; **~fall** *m* limiting case, critical case; borderline case; **~festsetzung** *f* demarcation, delimitation; **~fläche** *f* boundary surface, contact surface; **~frequenz** *f* cutting-off frequency; **~gänger** *m* black crosser; **~gebiet** border area; **~kontrolle** *f* customs examination; **~krieg** *m* border-war; **~land** *n* border-land; **~lehre** *f tech* limit ga(u)ge; **~linie, ~scheide** *f* boundary line; **~mark** *f* borderland; **~nachbar** *m* neighbo(u)r; **~pfahl** *m* boundary-post; **~regulierung** *f* demarcation; **~riegel** *m* limiting bolt; **~scheidung** *f* demarcation; **~schicht** *f* boundary (*od* marginal) layer; **~schutz** *m* frontier guard, frontier protective force; **~spannung** *f tech* limiting (*od* edge) stress; **~sperre** *f* closing of frontier; **~stadt** frontier-town; **~station** *f* frontier-station; **~stein** *m* boundary-stone (*od* -marker); **~streitigkeit** *f* boundary litigation; **~truppen** *f pl* frontier (*od* border) troops *pl*; **~überflugzone** *f aero* air corridor; **~überschreitung** *f*, **~übertritt** *m* frontier-crossing; **~übertrittsstelle** *f* frontier crossing point; **~verkehr** *m* frontier traffic; frontier trading; **~verletzung** *f* violation of the frontier; **~wache, ~wacht** *f* frontier guard; **~wächter** *m* frontier guard; **~wert** *m* limit; threshold; critical value; limiting value; **~zeichen** *n* landmark; **~zoll** *m* duty, customs *pl*; **~~amt** *n* custom-house; **~~behörde** *f* custom-house authorities *pl*; **~zwischenfall** *m* frontier (*od* border) incident.

Greuel *m* horror; abomination; outrage; *er ist mir ein ~* I detest him; **~märchen** *n*, **~propaganda** *f* slander, calumny; atrocity propaganda; **~tat** *f* atrocity; horrible deed; **greulich** *a* abominable, detestable, horrible; atrocious; (*entsetzlich*) frightful.

Grieben *f pl* greaves *pl*.

Griebs *m* core (of fruits).

Griech|e *m*, **~in** *f* Greek; **~isch** *a* Greek; **~enland** *n* Greece.

Gries|gram *m* croaker, grumbler, grouser, *fam* growler, *Am* grouch; **~grämig** *a* grousing, grumbling; surly, sullen; morose, peevish.

Grieß *m* coarse sand, gravel; (*Graupen~*) grits *pl*, groats *pl*; (*Weizen~*) semolina; farina; **~brei** *m* gruel; **~ig** *a* gravelly; *med* sabulous; **~kohle** *f* slack coal; **~mehl** *n* semolina; **~stein** *m* urinary calculus; **~suppe** *f* semolina soup.

Griff *m* grip, snatch; catch; hold, grasp; *fig* hit, shift; (*Stiel von Messer, Beil, Schirm*) handle; (*Tür*) knob, latch; (*Schublade, Klingel*) pull; (*Henkel*) ear; (*Kunst~*) trick, knack; (*Fingerspitzengefühl bei Stoff, Papier etc*) feel; *mus* touch; *e-n guten ~ tun* to make a good choice; *ein glücklicher ~* a lucky hit; *würgender ~* strangle-hold; *e-n falschen ~ tun* to touch a wrong note; *etw im ~ haben* to be good at; **~bereit** *a* on hand; **~brett** *n* (*Geige*) finger-board; (*Klavier*) key-board; **~el** *m* style, slate-pencil; *bot* style; pistil; **~hebel** *m* hand lever; **~igkeit** *mot* grip, traction; (*des Autoreifens*) tyre (*Am* tire) grip; **~stück** *n* grip, handle; (*Pistole*) stock.

Grille *f* cricket; (*Laune*) freak, whim, crotchet, vagary, caprice, fad; humo(u)r, fancy; *~n fangen* to be low-spirited, to be in low spirits; **~nfänger** *m* whimsical fellow; crank; capricious person; pessimist; **~nhaft** *a* capricious, fanciful, cranky.

Grimasse *f* grimace, wry face; *~n schneiden* to pull faces.

Grimm *m* fury, wrath; anger, rage; **~en** *n* gripes *pl*, colic; **~ig** *a* furious, wrathful, grim; (*übermäßig*) excessive, extreme; *es ist ~~ kalt* it is bitterly cold.

Grind *m* scab, scurf; (*Kopfschorf*) dandruff; (*Räude*) mange; *med* eschar; **~ig** *a* scabby, scurfy; (*räudig*) mangy.

grinsen *itr* to grin; (*einfältig*) to simper; (*schmunzeln*) to smirk; (*höhnisch*) to sneer, to scoff; *~ n* grin; sneer.

Grippe *f* influenza, grippe; *fam* flu(e), *Am* grip.

Grips *m* brains *pl*, intelligence.

grob *a* coarse; (*gewöhnlich*) vulgar; (*ungeschliffen*) gross; (*taktlos*) clumsy; (*stark, dick*) thick; stout; (*sehr grob*) rank; (*schlüpferig*) obscene, ribald; (*verletzend*) rude; (*roh*) rough; (*ungehobelt*) crude; (*unerfahren*) callow; (*unhöflich*) impolite, ill-mannered, uncivil; (*bäurisch*) churlish, uncouth; (*unverarbeitet*) raw; (*Arbeit, Haut*) rough; (*Geschütz*) heavy; (*Lüge*) downright; (*Fehler*) serious, gross, bad; (*Beleidigung*) grievous; (*Undank*) rank; (*ungefähr*) approximate; roughly; *in ~en Zügen* approximately, roughly; *ich bin aus dem Gröbsten heraus* the worst is over; *jdn ~ anfahren* to handle s. o. roughly; **~abstimmung** *f radio* coarse tuning; **~bearbeiten** *tr* to rough-machine; **~blech** *n* thick plate; **~einstellung** *f radio* frequency selection; **~fädig** *a* coarse-threaded; **~fahrlässig** *a* grossly negligent; **~faserig** *a* coarse-fibered; **~heit** *f* coarseness; (*Rohheit*) roughness, rudeness; (*Ungehörigkeit*) impropriety; (*Schlüpfrigkeit*) obscenity; (*Unfeinheit*) grossness; (*Frechheit*) insolence; *jdm ~~en an den Kopf werfen* to be rude to; **~ian** *m* coarse (*od* rude) fellow, boor, brute; (*unverschämt*) insolent fellow; *hum* rough diamond, *Am* a man with the bark on; **~körnig** *a* coarse-grained; **~maschig** *a* coarse-meshed, wide-meshed; **~sand** *m* gravel; **~schlächtig** *a* uncouth, boorish; **~schmied** *m* blacksmith.

gröblich *a* rather coarse; *adv* coarsely; grossly, greatly; *wir haben uns ~ getäuscht* we have been grossly mistaken; *~ beleidigen* to outrage.

grö(h)len *itr* to bawl, to squall; (*kreischen*) to scream.

Groll *m* resentment, rancour; (*Widerwille*) grudge; (*Mißgunst*) ill-will; (*Zorn*) anger; *~ hegen gegen* to bear a grudge against, to be angry with, *Am* to have an edge on s. o.; **~en** *itr* to have a spite against s. o.; to be resentful, to be angry; (*Donner*) to rumble, to peal, to roll; **~end** *a* spiteful; (*boshaft*) malicious; (*feindselig*) malignant; (*bösartig*) pernicious.

Grönland *n* Greenland.

Gros *n* (*Maß*) gross, twelve dozen; *mil* main body; *mar* battle fleet, main force; *en gros* wholesale.

Groschen *m* penny; **~roman** *m* penny dreadful; shilling shocker, dime novel.

groß *a* (*bedeutend*) great; (*räumlich*) large; (*umfangreich, auch fig*) big; (*ausgedehnt*) voluminous; (*riesig*) huge; (*hochgewachsen*) tall; (*Fläche*) vast, extensive; (*geräumig*) spacious; (*sehr groß*) *fam* jumbo; (*ungeheuer*) enormous, immense, gigantic, colossal, mammoth, astronomic(al); (*gewichtig*) heavy; (*großartig*) grand; (*wunderbar*) prodigious; (*erstaunlich*) stupendous; (*hervorragend*) eminent; (*wichtig*) important; (*erwachsen*) grown-up; (*Buchstabe*) capital; (*Hitze*) intense; (*Kälte*) severe; (*Fehler*) bad, serious, big; (*Umweg*) long; *im ~en* on a large scale, in bulk, *com* wholesale; *im ~en* (*u.*) *ganzen* on the whole; *mit ~er Mühe* with great pains; *die ~en Drei* the Big Three; *das ~e Hauptquartier* General Headquarters; *~es Tier sl* big bug, big shot; *mil sl* brass(-hat); *~er Gang* (*mot*) high gear; *~e Kurve aero* gentle bank; *~e Ferien* summer vacation; *der G~e Bär* the Great Bear, *Am* the Dipper; *der G~e Ozean* the Pacific (Ocean); *5 Fuß ~ sein* to be 5 feet high; *das ~e Los* the first prize; *~er Zeiger* hour hand; *~ u. klein* great and small; *~e Augen machen* to stare; *~ anschauen* to look at s. o. wide-eyed; *~ denken* (*von*) to think highly (of); *da geht es ~ her* they live in grand style; *~ herausstellen* (*Presse*) to front-page, to feature, to play up; *beide sind gleich ~* they are both the same size; *~ schreiben* to capitalize; **~abbau** *m* large-scale workings *pl*; **~abnehmer** *m* large customer; **~admiral** *m mar* admiral of the fleet (*Am* navy); **~angelegt** *a* large-scale; **~agrarier, ~bauer** *m* big estate owner; **~angriff** *m* large-scale (*od* major) attack; major offensive operation; **~artig** *a* great, grand; (*hervorragend*) sublime; (*erhaben*) lofty; (*von gewaltigem Ausmaß*) vast; *~~!* splendid! great! (*ausgezeichnet*) excellent, first-rate, *Am* elegant; **~artigkeit** *f* sublimity; vastness; (*Vornehmheit*) grandeur; **~aufnahme** *f film* close-up (shot), *sl* mug shot; **~auftrag** *m* large order; **~bank** *f* big bank; **~-Berlin** *n* Greater-Berlin; **~betrieb** *m* large-scale enterprise; (*Handel*) wholesale trade; **~bomber** *m aero* giant (*od* heavy) bomber; **~britannien** *n* Great Britain; **~britannisch** *a* British; **~buchstabe** *m typ* capital; **~einkauf** *m* bulk purchases *pl*; **~~sgesellschaft** *f* wholesale purchasing company; **~einsatz** *m mil* major commitment, large-scale operation; **~eltern** *pl* grandparents *pl*; **~enkel** *m* great-grandson; **~enkelin** *f* great-granddaughter; **~enteils** *adv* in large part, mostly; **~erzeugung** *f* mass production; **~fabrikation** *f* large-scale manufacture; **~fertigung** *f* mass production; **~feuer** *n* conflagration; **~film** *m Am* super-film; **~finanz** *f* high finance; **~flugboot** *n* big flying boat, *Am* clipper; **~flughafen** *m* air terminal; **~flugzeug** *n* airliner; **~format** *n* large sized paper, large foolscap; **~frachtflugzeug** *n* super-cargo plane, *Am* flying boxcar; sky truck; *durch ~~ befördern* to sky-truck; **~funkstation, ~funkstelle** *f* high-power radio station; **~fürst** *m* (**~~in** *f*) grand duke (duchess); **~grundbesitz** *m* large estates *pl*; landed property; **~~er** *m* landed proprietor, big estate owner; **~handel** *m* wholesale trade; *im ~~* by (*Am* at) wholesale; **~~sgeschäft** *n* wholesale business (*od* firm); **~~sindex** *m* wholesale price level; **~~spreis** *m* wholesale price; **~~srabatt** *m* quantity discount; **~~sspanne** *f* wholesale margin; **~~sunternehmen** *n* wholesale firm; **~~svertreter** *m* wholesale representative; **~händler** *m* wholesale dealer, wholesaler; **~herzig** *a* magnanimous, generous; **~~keit** *f* magnanimity, generosity; **~herzog** *m* (**~~in** *f*) grand duke (duchess); **~~tum** *n* Grand Duchy; **~hirn** *n* cerebrum; **~industrie** *f* heavy industry; **~~ller** *m* captain of industry, *Am fam* tycoon; **~inquisitor** *m* grand-inquisitor; **~jährig** *a* of age; *~~ werden* to come of age; **~jährigkeit** *f* majority; **~kampf** *m* great battle; large-scale fighting; **~~flugzeug** *n aero* superfortress; **~~schiff** *n* capital ship; super-dreadnought; **~~tag** *m* battle-period; **~kapital** *n*, **~kapitalismus** *m* big business, high finance; **~kaufmann** *m* wholesale merchant; **~kaufhaus** (*Lebensmittel*) *Am* super market; **~knecht** *m* (*Bauernhof*) head man; **~köpfig** *a* big-headed; **~kraftwerk** *n* super power station; **~kreis** *m* (*Kugel*) great circle; **~kreuz** *n* grand-cross; **~lautsprecher** *m* giant loudspeaker; power loudspeaker, public address loudspeaker; **~lautsprecheranlage** *f* public address; **~lieferung** *f* bulk delivery; **~macht** *f* great power; **~mächtig** *a* (high and) mighty; **~magd** *f* head maid-servant; **~mama** *f fam* grandma, granny; **~mannssucht** *f* mad ambition, megalomania; **~markt** *m Am* super market; **~mars** *m mar* main top; **~maschig** *a* wide-meshed; **~maul** *n* braggar; **~mäulig** *a* bragging, boastful, swaggering; **~meister** *m* grand-master; **~mut** *m*, **~mütigkeit** *f* magnanimity, generosity; **~mütig** *a* magnanimous, generous; **~mutter** *f* grandmother; *das kannst du deiner ~~ erzählen* tell that to the marines; **~mütterlich** *a* grandmotherly; **~neffe** *m* grandnephew; **~nichte** *f* grandniece; **~oheim, ~onkel** *m* grand-uncle; **~oktav** *n* large octavo; **~orientierung** *f aero* orientation by large landmarks; **~papa** *m* grandpa; **~photo** *n* photomural; **~raum** *m* large area, empire, area of self-sufficiency; **~raumgüterwagen** *m* high capacity bogie wagon, *Am* freight car; **~reihenfertigung** *f* mass production; **~reinemachen** *n* wholesale house-cleaning; (*Frühjahrsputz*) spring cleaning; **~rundfunksender, ~sender** *m* high-power (broadcasting) station; **~schatzmeister** *m* First Lord of the Treasury; **~schlächterei** *f* wholesale butchery, *Am* meat packing plant; **~serienbau** *m* large-scale series production; **~siegelbewahrer** *m* Keeper of the Great Seal; **~sprecher** *m* braggar; **~sprecherei** *f* boasting; **~sprecherisch** *a* bragging, boastful, swaggering; **~spurig** *a* arrogant, haughty, overbearing; **~stadt** *f* large (*od* big) town, (large) city, metropolis; **~städter** *m* inhabitant of a large town; **~stadtgebiet** *n* metropolitan area; **~städtisch** *a* urban, metropolitan; (*Kleidung*) fashionable; **~stadtluft** *f* atmosphere of a big city; **~stadtverkehr** *m* big-city traffic; **~struktur** *f* macrostructure; **~tante** *f* grand-aunt; **~tat** *f* striking deed, exploit; achievement; (*Heldentat*) feat; **~teil** *m* bulk (of); **~tun** *irr itr* to swagger, to brag, *fam* to talk big; (*sich rühmen*) to boast; (*triumphieren*) to crow, to vaunt; **~tuer** *m* braggar; **~unternehmen** *n* large-scale enterprise; **~unternehmer** *m* big industrialist; **~vater** *m* grandfather; *zu ~~s Zeiten Am* in the horse and buggy days; **~~stuhl** *m* easy- (*od* arm-) chair; **~veranstaltung** *f* big event; **~verbraucher** *m* large-scale consumer; **~verkauf** *m* wholesale; **~verkehrsflugzeug** *n* airliner; **~vieh** *n* large cattle; **~versuch** *m* large-scale experiment; **~wirtschaftsraum** *m* economic empire; **~würdenträger** *m* high dignitary; **~ziehen** *irr tr* to bring up, to raise; **~zügig** *a* on a large scale; (*freigebig*) liberal, generous; **~~keit** *f* largeness; (*Freigebigkeit*) generosity; (*Auffassung*) bold conception.

Größ|e *f* (*Umfang, Format, Nummer*) size; (*Umfang, Dicke*) bigness; (*Länge*) tallness; (*Höhe*) height; (*Gestalt*) stature; (*Ausdehnung*) dimensions *pl*; (*Fläche*) area; (*Strecke, auch fig*) extent; (*Weite*) largeness, expanse; (*Wichtigkeit, math, astr*) magnitude; (*Rauminhalt*) volume; (*Masse*) bulk; (*Menge*) quantity; (*Summe*) amount; (*moralisch*) largeness; *fig* magnitude; (*Bedeutung*) greatness; (*Kraft*) force, intensity; (*Berühmtheit*) celebrity, star; (*Rang*) rank; (*Vornehmheit, Erhabenheit*) grandeur; *natürliche ~~* full-scale; full-length; *von mittlerer ~~* middle-sized; *der ~~ nach aufstellen* to line up in order of height; *vereinzelte ~~n* odd sizes, *Am* broken sizes; **~enangabe** *f* statement of size; **~enbeschränkung** *f* size restriction; **~enbestimmung** *f* rating, sizing; **~enfaktor** *m* size factor; variable; **~enklasse** *f* size group; **~enmaß** *n* dimension; **~enordnung** *f* order of magnitude; dimension; **~enordnungsmäßig** *a* according to size; **~enverhältnisse** *n pl* dimensions *pl*, proportions *pl*; **~enwahn** *m* morbid (*od* mad) ambition, *med* megalomania; **~enwahnsinnig** *a* megalomaniac; **~enzusammenstellung** *f* assortment of sizes; **~tenteils** *adv* for the most part, largely; (*hauptsächlich*) chiefly; **~tmaß** *n* maximum size; **~tmöglich** *a* greatest possible; **~twert** *m* maximum value, crest value.

Grossist *m* wholesale trader (*od* dealer), wholesaler.

grotesk *a* grotesque; *~er Stil* grotesque; *~e Zeichnung* grotesque; **~e** *n* grotesque; **~e** *f typ* sanserif.

Grotte *f* grotto.

Grüb|chen *n* dimple; *bot* lacuna; **~elei** *f* musing, brooding, brown study; **~eln** *itr* to brood, to ponder (over); (*nachdenken*) to meditate (on, over), to ruminate (about); (*mühsam*) to rack o.'s brains; *Am* to mull (over); **~ler** *m* (**~~in** *f*) brooding person, ponderer.

Grube *f min* pit, mine; (*Kohlen~*) colliery; (*offene Stein~*) quarry; (*Höhlung*) hole, cavity; *anat* (*Magen~, Herz~*) pit; (*Graben*) ditch; (*Grab*) grave; (*Tiere*) den; (*Fund~*) mine, quarry; *ersoffene ~* drowned mine; *wer andern e-e ~ gräbt, fällt selbst hinein* he who sets a trap for others gets caught himself; *e-e ~ auflassen* to abandon a mine; *e-e ~ unter Wasser setzen* to flood a mine; **~nanteil** *m* share; **~narbeiter** *m* miner, pit worker; **~nbahn** *f* pit railway; **~nbau, ~nbetrieb** *m* underground working; mining; **~nbrand** *m* mine fire; **~nexplosion** *f* colliery explosion; **~ngas** *n* (*Schlagwetter*) fire-damp; mine gas, marsh gas, methane; **~nhalde** *f* burrow; **~nholz** *n* pit-wood; **~nkohle** *f* pit coal; **~nlampe** *f* miner's lamp; **~nlokomotive** *f* mining locomotive; **~nsand** *m* pit sand; **~nschacht** *m* pit (*od* mine) shaft; **~nsohle** *f* mine level; **~nsteiger** *m* mine-captain, overseer; **~nunglück** *n* mine disaster; **~wasser** *n* pit water; **~wetter** *n* mine damp, fire-damp.

Grudekoks *m* coke of brown coal, granular (*od* small) coke from lignite.

Gruft *f* (*Grab*) grave; (*Grabgewölbe*) tomb, vault; (*Grabmal*) mausoleum; (*Kapelle*) crypt; (*Höhle*) cave.

Grummet, Grumt *n* aftermath.

grün *a* green; (*unreif*) unripe; immature; (*frisch*) fresh; (*roh*) raw; (*unerfahren*) inexperienced, new; *~er Junge* greenhorn; *~er Hering* fresh herring; *~er Salat* lettuce; *jdm nicht ~ sein* to bear a grudge against; *~ vor Neid werden* to turn green with envy; *sich ~ u. gelb ärgern* to turn green with vexation; *jdn über den ~en Klee loben* to praise s. o. to the skies; *auf keinen ~en Zweig kommen* not to get on in the world; *am ~en Tisch* at the green table; *vom ~en Tisch aus* only in theory; *~er Tisch* (*Bürokratie*) red tape; **~bewachsen** *a* covered with verdure; **~donnerstag** *m* Maundy-Thursday; **~(e)** *n* green; (*~e Farbe*) greens *pl*, greenness; (*frisches ~*) greenth; (*Pflanzenwuchs*) verdure; *im ~en* amid the verdure; (*auf dem Land*) in country surroundings; *e-e Fahrt ins ~e* a ride into the country; *mit ~ bekleidet* verdurous; **~eisenstein** *m* green iron ore; **~en** *itr* to grow green; *fig* to thrive, to prosper, to flourish; **~fink** *m* greenfinch; **~fläche** *f* green plot, lawn; **~futter** *n* green-fodder; **~gelb** *a* greenish yellow; **~horn** *n* greenhorn; **~kern** *m* green rye; **~kohl** *m* kale; **~kram** *m* greengrocery, green-stuff; **~~laden** *m* greengrocer's shop; **~kreuzkampfstoff** *m* green cross shell filling; poison gas which attacks respiratory organs; **~land** *n* meadows *pl*; **~lich** *a* greenish; **~schnabel** *m* greenhorn, inexperienced person, *Am fam* sucker; **~span** *m* verdigris; **~specht** *m* green woodpecker; **~stein** *m geol* greenstone; **~warenhändler** *m* greengrocer; **~zeug** *n* greens *pl*, green-stuff, herbs *pl*.

Grund *m* (*Unterlage*) ground; (*Boden*) soil;. (*Sockel, Basis, Grundfläche*) basis, base, basement; (*Grundlegung, arch Fundament*) foundation; (*Hintergrund*) background, *theat* backdrop; (*Fläche*) field; (*unterster Teil, Schiffsboden, Fluß, Meer, Talsohle, Fuß e-s Hügels*) bottom; (*Tiefe*) depth; (*Besitz*) landed property, (real) estate; (*Tal*) valley; (*Baustelle*) plot, land; (*Schicht*) couch; (*Bodensatz*) sediment; (*Hefe*) dregs *pl*; *fig* reason, ground(s *pl*); (*Beweisgrund*) argument; (*Ursache*) cause, ground; (*Anlaß*) occasion; (*Beweggrund*) motive, impulse, spring(s *pl*), inducement; (*Anreiz*) incentive, spur; *aus diesen Gründen* on these grounds; *aus welchem ~e?* for what reason? why? *aus dem ~e, daß* on the ground that; *im ~e* at bottom, on the whole, after all; *im ~e genommen* after all; strictly speaking; *von ~ auf* from the beginning, radically; *von ~ aus* thoroughly; *bis auf den ~* (*fig*) to the dregs, to the core; *auf eignem ~ u. Boden* in its own ground; *auf ~ von* on the strength of, on account of, according to, based on; by (*od* in) virtue of, by reason of, pursuant to; under; on the basis of; *ohne triftigen ~* without reasonable excuse; *aus wichtigem ~* with reasonable foundation; *von ~ aus ändern* to change from the ground up; *zwingende Gründe anführen* to clinch an argument; *Gründe angeben* to show cause; *genügenden ~ angeben für* to account for; *auf den ~ gehen* to get to the bottom (*od* to the root) of, to investigate thoroughly; *im ~e genommen* basically (*od* fundamentally) speaking, as a matter of principle; *zu~e gehen* to be ruined, to fail, to perish; *auf ~ geraten* to touch ground; *zu~e legen* to take as a basis, to start out from; *den ~ legen zu* to lay the foundation; *auf dem ~ des Meeres liegen* to lie at the bottom of the sea; *zu~e liegen* to be at the bottom of, to be the basis of (*od* for); *zu~e richten* to ruin; *ein Schiff auf den ~ bohren* to sink a ship; **~abgabe** *f* land tax; **~akkord** *m* fundamental chord; **~ablösung** *f* expropriation; **~anständig** *a* thoroughly honest; **~anstrich** *m* ground (*od* first) coat; **~ausbildung** *f* basic training; **~bedeutung** *f* original meaning; **~bedingung** *f* main condition; **~begriff** *m* fundamental conception, basic idea (*od* principle); **~besitz** *m* landed property, real estate, (*Immobilien*) immovables *pl*; **~~er** *m* land-owner, landed-proprietor; **~bestandteil** *m* elementary constituent, element; (*e-s Gemisches*) base (*od* vehicle) of a mixture; **~brett** *n* baseboard; **~buch** *n* land register, register of landed property; *Am* register of land ownership; **~~amt** *n* land register office; *Am* real estate recording office; **~~eintrag** *m* entry into the land register; **~dienstbarkeit** *f* easement; **~dünung** *f* ground swell; **~ebene** *f* datum plane, datum level; **~ehrlich** *a* thoroughly honest; *~~ sein* to be straight as a die; *Am* to be straight from the ground; **~eigentum** *n* landed property, real estate; **~eigentümer** *m* land-owner, landed-proprietor; **~einheit** *f* fundamental unit; **~eis** *n* ground-ice; **~empfang** *m radio* ground reception; **~erfordernisse** *n pl* basic requisites *pl*; **~erwerb** *m* acquisition of land; **~falsch** *a* radically false (*od* wrong); **~farbe** *f* ground colo(u)r; (*Färben*) bottom colo(u)r; *phys* elementary colo(u)r; **~fehler** *m* radical fault; **~feste** *f* foundation; basis; **~feuchtigkeit** *f* soil moisture; **~figur** *f aero* (*Kunstflug*) basic figure; **~fläche** *f* basal surface, base; area; **~flugmanöver** *n aero* elementary flight manœuvres *pl* (*Am* maneuvers); **~form** *f* primary form; **~~el** *f* fundamental formula; **~gebühr** *f* fixed charge; **~gedanke** *m* fundamental idea; **~gehalt** *n* basic salary, base pay; **~gelehrt** *a* erudite; **~geschwindigkeit** *f* ground speed; **~gesetz** *n* fundamental (*od* basic) law; **~gestein** *n* primitive rock; **~gleichung** *f* basic equation; **~helligkeitsregler** *m tele* background control; **~herr** *m* lord of the manor; **~ieranstrich** *m* prime (*od* priming *od* flat) coat; **~ieren** *tr* (*Maler*) to ground, to prime; (*Papier*) to stain; (*mit Leim*) to size; (*Färben*) to bottom; (*Kattun*) to prepare; **~ierfarbe** *f* priming colo(u)r; **~ierfirnis** *m* filler; **~ierschicht** *f* priming coat; **~industrie** *f* basic industry; **~irrtum** *m* fundamental error; **~kapital** *n* stock, original capital; **~kraft** *f* primary force; **~kreis** *m* base circle; **~kurs** *m* true course, head-on course; **~lack** *m* base lacquer coat; **~lage** *f* groundwork, basis, foundation; (*Begriff*) underlying principle; (*Quellen*) data *pl*; (*Nährboden*) matrix; (*Grund*) ground, base, bottom, foundation; (*Sockel*) basement; (*Fußgestell u. fig*) pedestal; **~~n** *f pl* elements *pl*, rudiments *pl*; *jeder ~~ entbehren* to be without any foundation; *die ~~ abgeben* to supply the foundation; **~lawine** *f* avalanche of earth, *Am* landslide; **~legend** *a* fundamental, basic; **~lehre** *f* theory; **~linie** *f* base (line); ground line; outline; datum line; point of reference; **~lohn** *m* basic wage; base rate; **~los** *a* bottomless, baseless; (*unbegründet*) groundless, unfounded; *~~ entlassen* to dismiss s. o. for no reason; **~losigkeit** *f* unfathomableness; *fig* groundlessness; **~maß** *n* standard of measurement; **~masse** *f* ground-mass; matrix; **~material** *n* ground material, base metal, base material; **~mauer** *f* foundation-wall; **~metall** *n* basic (*od* base) metal; **~mine** *f mil* ground mine; **~nebel** *m* ground fog; **~netz** *n* (*Fischerei*) trawl; **~niveau** *n tele* background level; **~norm** *f* fundamental standard; **~pfeiler** *m* foundation pillar, main support; **~platte** *f* base plate; **~preis** *m* basic price; unit price; **~prinzip** *n* fundamental principle; **~problem** *n* fundamental problem; **~rechnungsarten** *f pl* the first four rules of arithmetic; **~rechte** *n pl* basic rights *pl*; **~regel** *f* basic principle, axiom; **~rente** *f* ground rent; **~richtung** *f mil* (*Artillerie*) base line direction; zero line; **~~slinie** *f mil* base line; **~~spunkt** *m* base point, reference (*od* zero) point; **~riß** *m* ground plan, floor plan; (*Skizze*) outline, sketch; (*Buch*) outline, summary, epitome, abstract; compendium; *im ~~* in plan form; **~~ansicht** *f* plan view; **~~aufnahme** *f* planimetric survey; **~~plan** *m* layout plan; **~satz** *m* principle; tenet, axiom; (*Lebens~~*) maxim; *e-n ~~ aufstellen* to establish a principle; *als ~~ aufstellen* to lay down as principle; *an ~sätzen festhalten* to stick to o.'s principles; *es sich zum ~~ machen* to make it a rule; **~sätzlich** *adv* on principle, as a matter of principle; *a* fundamental, based on principles; **~schicht** *f* fundamental layer; **~schleppnetz** *n* trawl(-net); **~schuld** *f* land charge; **~schule** *f* elementary school, primary school; **~stein** *m* foundation-stone; *fig* cornerstone; *den ~~ legen zu* to lay the foundation-stone of; **~stellung** *f mil* normal position; attention position; **~steuer** *f* land tax; **~stock** *m* basis, foundation; original fund; (*Nährboden*) matrix; **~stoff** *m* element, radical; (*Rohmaterial*) raw material, base; **~strich** *m* (*Schrift*) down-stroke; (*Farbe*) first coat; **~stück** *n* piece (*od* parcel) of land, estate, real estate (*od* property), premises *pl*, lot, plot; (*Bauplatz*) building site, *Am* location; *bebautes ~~* developed real estate; *belastetes ~~* mortgaged property; **~~smakler** *m* real estate agent, *Am* realtor, real estate broker; **~teilchen** *n* fundamental particle; atom; **~thema** *n mus* leading air, leitmotif; **~ton** *m* key-note; fundamental tone; *fig* prevailing mood; *tele* background; **~tugenden** *f pl* cardinal virtues *pl*; **~übel** *n* original evil; **~überholung** *f mot* shop overhaul; **~ursache** *f* primary cause; principal reason; **~verschieden** *a* entirely different; **~wahrheit** *f* fundamental truth; **~wasser** *n* ground-water; **~~spiegel** *m* ground-water level; **~~stand** *m* ground-water level; **~welle** *f* fundamental wave; **~wort** *n* root; **~zahl** *f* cardinal number; unit; base number; **~zins** *m* ground rent; **~zug** *m* leading (*od* main) feature, characteristic(s *pl*).

gründ|en *tr* to found; (*tatsächlich*) to establish; (*ins Werk setzen*) to institute; (*aufbauen*) to organize; (*anfangen*) to start; (*in die Wege leiten*) to set on foot; (*hervorbringen*) to create; *com* to float, to promote, to found, to form; *sich ~~ auf* to rest (*od* to be based) upon; *sich e-n eigenen Hausstand ~~* to set up for o. s.; *fest gegründet* firmly established; **~er** *m* founder, promoter; **~~aktien** *f pl* founders' (*od* primal) shares; **~~mitglied** *n* foundation member, *Am* charter member; **~~zeit** *f* promotion period; *hist* time of wild speculation (1871-73); **~lich** *a* well grounded, thorough, *Am* thoro, thorough-going, profound, solid; (*erschöpfend*) exhaustive; (*vollständig*) complete; (*sorgsam*) careful; (*vollendet*) consummate; (*durchgreifend*) sweeping; (*grundlegend*) fundamental; *etw ~~ verstehen* to be thoroughly versed in; *~~ Bescheid wissen* to know all about it; *jdm ~~ die Meinung sagen* to give s. o. a piece (*od* a bit) of o.'s mind; **~lichkeit** *f* thoroughness, profoundness; (*Genauigkeit*) accuracy; (*Zuverlässigkeit*) solidity; **~ling** *m* groundling, gudgeon; **~ung** *f* foundation, establishment; (*Bildung*) formation; *com* promotion, flo(a)tation; **~~sjahr** *n* year of foundation; **~~skapital** *n* capital stock; **~~surkunde** *f* articles of association *pl*; **~~sversammlung** *f* organization meeting; **~~svertrag** *m* agreement of association.

grunzen *itr* to grunt; *~ n* grunting.

Grupp|e *f* (*zus. gehörende Menschen, Trupp, Abteilung*) group; gang, team; crew, squad; band, set, *Am* out(-fit); (*Haufe*) troop, cluster, flock, herd; (*Schar*) covey (*bes. Rebhühner u. fig*), bevy, (*junge Mädchen*) batch; (*glänzende Gesellschaft*) galaxy; (*Schwarm*) swarm, (*bes. Fische*) shoal; (*Menge*) bunch, stack, lot; (*Aufgebot*) array; (*bes. Vieh*) drove; *mil* squad, section; *aero* (pursuit) squadron, (bombardment) group; (*Heeres~*) commanding staff; (*von U-Booten*) pack; (*Gattung*) class; (*Firmen*) concern, syndicate, trust; (*Bäume*) clump, cluster; *sich e-r ~~ anschließen* to team up with; **~enaufnahme** *f*, **~enbild** *n phot* picture of a group; **~enbildung** *f* formation of groups; **~enführer** *m* section commander; squad leader; section leader; **~engefechtsstand** *m* group command post; **~eninteressen** *n pl* sectional interests *pl;* **~enkeil** *m aero* wing squadron V-flight astern, bombardment-group wedge; pursuit--squadron wedge; **~enkommandeur** *m aero* wing commander; squadron commander; **~enschaltung** *f* series connexion; **~enschlüssel** *m* group key; **~enweise** *adv* in groups; in sections; **~enwinkel** *m aero* wing squadron V astern; group column of squadron V's; **~ieren** *tr* to group, to range; (*zus.stellen*) to compile; (*zus.ziehen*) to concentrate; (*anordnen*) to arrange, to set in order; (*klassifizieren*) to classify; *sich ~~* to form groups; **~ierung** *f* grouping; arrangement; classification; (*Anlage*) *Am* lay-out.

Grus *m* coal-slack.

grusel|ig *a* awful; (*schaudernd*) shuddering; (*grausig*) ghastly; (*unheimlich*) creepy, uncanny; **~n** *imp: mir* (*od mich*) *gruselt* my flesh creeps; *es macht mich ~~* it makes my flesh creep.

Gruß *m* salutation, greeting; *mil* salute; (*in Briefen*) compliments *pl;* regards *pl;* (*vertraulicher*) love; (*Verbeugung*) bow; *herzliche Grüße bestellen* to give o.'s kindest regards to; *mit bestem ~* yours very truly; *mit herzlichem ~* with kindest regards *pl;* *e-n ~ erwidern* to return o.'s salute; **~pflicht** *f* obligation to salute.

grüßen *tr* to greet, to bow to, *Am* to say hello; *mil* to salute; (*Hut abnehmen*) to take off (*od* to touch, to raise) o.'s hat; (*begrüßen*) to hail s. o.; *jdn nicht ~* to cut s. o.; *jdn ~ lassen* to send o.'s compliments (*od* love *od* regards) to; *~ Sie Ihre Mutter von mir* remember me to your mother.

Grütz|e *f*. grits *pl*, groats *pl;* (*Verstand*) brains *pl;* *rote ~~* fruit shape; **~(~)brei** *m* porridge, *Am* mush.

guck|en *itr* to look (curiously); to peep; *gern tief ins Glas ~* to be fond of a drop; *aus dem Fenster ~* to look out of the window; *guck mal!* just take a look! **~fenster** *n* peep-window; **~kasten** *m* raree-show; **~loch** *n* peep--hole, spy-hole.

Guerilla|kämpfer *m* guerrilla; **~krieg** *m* guerilla(-warfare).

Guillotin|e *f* guillotine; **~ieren** *tr* to guillotine.

Gulasch *n* goulash; stewed steak; **~kanone** *f* field-kitchen, *mil sl* cooker.

Gulden *m* florin; (*holländ.*) guilder.

Gülle *f* liquid manure.

gültig *a* (*Münzen*) current, good; (*gesetzlich*) valid, legal; (*zulässig*) admissible; (*Fahrkarte*) available; (*verbindlich*) binding; *in ~er Form* in due form; *~ sein* to be in force, to be good (for), (*Münze*) to be in circulation; *~ bis auf Widerruf* valid until recalled; *~ für* valid for, admitting to, *Am* good for; *~ vom* effective as from; *~ machen* to validate, to render valid; **~keit** *f* currency, validity; availability; legality; **~~sdauer** *f* time of validity.

Gummi *m* (*Klebstoff*) gum, mucilage; (*Leim*) glue; (*Radier~*) eraser, (India-) rubber; (*Kau~*) chewing gum, chicle gum; (*arabischer*) gum arabic; (*elastischer*) rubber; **~abdichtung** *f* rubber joint, washer; **~abfälle** *m pl* scrap rubber; **~abfederung** *f* rubber shock absorber; **~absatz** *m* rubber heel; **~abzugstrockner** *m phot* squeegee; **~artig** *a* gummy, gummous; **~artikel** *m* rubber article (*od* goods *pl*); **~ball** *m* rubber ball; (*Spritze*) rubber syringe; **~band** *n* elastic; (*Binde*) rubber band; **~baum** *m* rubber (*od* gum) tree; **~belag** *m* rubber flooring; **~bereifung** *f* rubber tyres (*Am* tires) *pl;* **~blase** *f* rubber bulb; **~boot** *n* inflatable boat; **~dichtung** *f* rubber gasket; **~druck** *m typ* offset printing; **~einlage** *f* rubber core; **~eren** *tr* to gum; to rubberize; **~erung** *f* gumming; rubberizing, rubber coating; **~erzeugnis** *n* rubber product; **~federung** *f* rubber shock absorber; **~finger** *m* rubber finger stall; **~gutt** *n* gamboge; **~handschuhe** *m pl* rubber gloves *pl;* **~isolierung** *f* rubber insulation; **~kappe** *f* rubber cap; **~knüppel** *m* (rubber) truncheon, *Am* billy; **~lösung** *f mot* gum solution; **~lutscher** *m* rubber teat; **~mantel** *m* waterproof, mackintosh; **~matte** *f* rubber mat; **~motor** *m* rubber motor; **~muffe** *f* rubber sleeve; **~pflaster** *n* rubber patch; **~pfropfen** *m* rubber stopper; **~platte** *f* rubber plate; **~räder** *n pl* rubber wheels *pl;* **~raupe** *f* rubber caterpillar track; **~regenerierung** *f* rubber reclaiming; **~reifen** *m* (India rubber) tyre (*od Am* tire); **~ring** *m* rubber band; **~schlauch** *m* (*Rad*) rubber tube; (*Wasser etc*) rubber hose; **~~boot** *n* rubber dinghi; **~schnur** *f* elastic cord; **~schuhe** *m pl* overshoes *pl*, galoshes *pl*, *Am* rubbers *pl;* **~schwamm** *m* rubber sponge; **~stempel** *m* rubber stamp; **~stiefel** *m pl* rubber boots *pl;* **~stoff** *m* rubberized material; **~stopfen, ~stöpsel** *m* rubber stopper, rubber plug; **~stoßdämpfer** *m* rubber shock absorber; **~strumpf** *m* elastic stocking; **~tier** *n* rubber animal; **~tuch** *n* sheeting rubber, rubber cloth; **~überschuhe** *m pl* rubber overshoes *pl*, rubber galoshes *pl*, *Am* rubbers *pl;* **~überzug** *m* rubber coating; rubber tread; **~unterlage** *f* rubber square; **~walze** *f* rubber roller; **~waren** *f pl* rubber goods *pl;* **~wärmflasche** *f* rubber hot water bottle; **~zelle** *f* padded room; **~zug** *m* elastic.

Gunst *f* favo(u)r; (*Wohlwollen*) good-will; (*moralische Unterstützung*) countenance; (*Freundlichkeit*) kindness; (*Vorliebe*) predilection; (*Parteilichkeit*) partiality; (*Wohlwollen*) grace; (*Vorteil*) advantage; *zu~en von* in favo(u)r of, for the benefit of; *com* to the credit of; *in jds besonderer ~ stehen* to be high in s. o.'s favo(u)r; *e-e ~ gewähren* to grant a favo(u)r; *in jds ~ stehen* to be in s.o.'s good graces; *auf jds ~ angewiesen sein* to depend on s. o. for favo(u)rs; *zu meinen ~en* in my favo(u)r; *sich um jds ~ bewerben* to purchase s. o.'s favo(u)r; *sich bei jdm in ~ setzen* to gain s. o.'s favo(u)r; **~beweis** *m*, **~bezeigung** *f* favo(u)r, act of kindness.

günst|ig *a* favo(u)rable; (*heilsam, z. B. Klima*) benign; (*bequem, zweckdienlich*) convenient; (*glückverkündend*) auspicious; (*geeignet*) propitious (*für* to); (*befriedigend*) satisfactory; (*vielversprechend*) promising; (*nützlich*) profitable; (*vorteilhaft*) advantageous, beneficial; (*wohlwollend*) benevolent; (*freundlich*) kind (to); *bei ~em Wetter* weather permitting; *~es Wetter* fair weather; *im ~~sten Fall* at best, at most; *zu ~~en Bedingungen* on easy terms; **~ling** *m* favo(u)rite, darling; (*verächtlich*) minion; **~~swirtschaft** *f* favo(u)ritism.

Gurgel *f* throat; (*Speiseröhre*) gullet; (*Luftröhre*) wind-pipe; **~n** *itr* to gargle; (*Laut*) to gurgle; **~abschneider** *m* cut--throat; **~n** *n* gargling; **~wasser** *n* gargle.

Gurke *f* cucumber; (*Essig~, Pfeffer~*) gherkin; (*Salz~*) pickled cucumbers *pl;* (*kleine*) gherkin; **~nbeet** *n* cucumber-bed; **~nsalat** *m* cucumber salad; *saure* **~nzeit** *f* slack time; dead season.

gurren *itr* to coo.

Gurt *m* (*Sattel~*) girth; (*Riemen, mil*) belt; (*Gürtel*) girdle; (*Geschirr, Fallschirm*) harness; (*Wehrgehänge*) baldric; (*Lederstreifen*) strap; (*Schärpe*) sash; (*Bett*) stretcher; **~bogen** *m* transverse arch; **~enzuführung** *f* belt feeder; **~füller** *m mil* belt-loading machine; **~förderer** *m* belt conveyor; **~gewölbe** *n* ribbed vault; **~ung** *f tech* boom.

Gürtel *m* girdle, belt; (*Absperrung*) cordon; *geog* zone; (*Festungs~*) ring; (*Taille*) waist; **~rose** *f med* shingles *pl;* **~schloß** *n* clasp of a belt; **~schleife** *f* (*an der Hose*) belt loop; **~tier** *n* armadillo.

gürt|en *tr* to gird; *sich ~ mit* to gird o. s. with; **~ler** *m* brass-founder.

Guß *m tech* casting, founding; (*Druckerei*) fount; (*Regen~*) gush, downpour, torrent, shower of rain; (*Zucker~*) icing, frosting; (*Flüssigkeit*) jet; (*Brauerei*) mash liquor (*od* water); *aus e-m Guß* of one mo(u)ld; *fig* a perfect whole; **~beton** *m* cast concrete; **~blase** *f* flaw in a casting; **~bruch** *m* cast-metal scrap; **~eisen** *n* cast iron, pig iron; **~eisern** *a* cast-iron; **~fehler** *m* casting flaw; **~form** *f* (casting) mo(u)ld; **~naht** *f* burr, seam; **~rohr** *n* cast-iron pipe; **~stahl** *m* cast steel; **~stein** *m* (*Küche*) sink; (*Gosse*) gutter; (*Abfluß*) drain.

gut *a* good; (*gutmütig, menschlich*) good-natured, kind(-hearted), humane; (*gesittet, ordentlich*) well-mannered, orderly, proper; (*aufrichtig, zuverlässig, moralisch gut*) sincere, reliable, honest, virtuous; (*~ aussehend, hübsch, anmutig*) good-looking, fair, graceful, goodly, comely; (*mutig*) brave, courageous, stout-hearted; (*fähig, geeignet, klug*) capable, efficient, qualified, fit, appropriate, adequate; (*günstig*) favo(u)rable, propitious; (*~ erhalten, tadellos*) sound; (*recht, korrekt*) right; (*ausgewählt*) choice, select, picked, exquisite; (*beträchtlich*) considerable, substantial, sizable; *com* (*Scheck*) *Am* eligible; *adv* well; (*ausreichend*) satisfactorily; (*günstig*) favo(u)rably; (*richtig*) rightly; (*ausgezeichnet*) excellently; (*geeignet*) suitably; (*geziemend*) befittingly; (*angemessen*) adequately; (*ganz*) fully, quite; *das ~e* the good; *die ~en* the good (people); *~er Absatz* ready sale; *~es Gewissen* quiet conscience; *~es Wetter* fine weather; *e-e ~e halbe Stunde* a full half-hour; *~e Kenntnisse* fair knowledge; *~es Mutes* in good spirits; *~e Quelle* reliable source; *~e Worte* kind words; *kurz u. ~* in short, to cut it short; *in ~em Glauben* in good faith; *im ~en* in a friendly manner; *zu ~er Letzt* to top it off; finally; *für Geld u. ~e Worte* for love or money; *Ende ~, alles ~* all's well that ends well; *so ~ wie* as good (*od* well) as; *alles ~e!* have a nice time! good luck (to you)! *~e Besserung!* I hope you get well soon! *schon ~!* never mind! *es ist ~!* that will do! all right! *Am* O. K.! *das ist des ~en zuviel!* that's too much of a good thing! *lassen Sie es ~ sein!* never mind! *danke, ~!* thanks, pretty well (*Am* fine)! *~ so!* all right! *für ~ (be)finden* to think proper; *es geht ihm ~* he is getting on well (*fam* nicely); *~ gepflegt* (*Ware*) in high condition; (*Person*) well-groomed, *Am* well-

-healed; ***es ~ haben*** to be well off; ***ich habe bei ihm Geld ~*** he owes me money; ***für ~ halten*** to think fit; ***zu~e halten*** to excuse, to allow for; ***zu~e kommen*** to be benefited by; ***sich e-n ~en Tag machen*** to have an easy time of it, to have a good time; ***wieder ~ machen*** to make up for, to atone; ***Sie haben ~ reden*** it's easy for you to talk; ***es im ~en sagen*** to tell it in a nice way; *für jdn ~ sein* to answer for s. o.; *jdm ~ sein* to love s. o., to like s. o.; ***sind Sie mir wieder ~?*** are we friends again? ***~er Dinge sein*** to be of good cheer; ***~ zu Fuß sein*** to be a good walker; ***~er Hoffnung sein*** to be with child; ***~ bei Kasse sein*** to be flush; ***ein ~er Rechner sein*** to be quick at figures; ***kein ~er Spieler sein*** to be not much of a player; ***wozu ist das ~?*** what's the use of it? ***seien Sie so ~?*** be so kind as to; kindly; may I thank you for? would you be good enough to ...? ***nicht so ~ sein wie*** not to be up to; ***es ist so ~ wie unmöglich*** it is next to impossible; ***mit jdm ~ stehen*** to be on friendly terms with; ***das trifft sich ~*** that's lucky; ***sich etw zu~e tun*** to enjoy on, to pique o.s. on; *das tut gut* that's a comfort; *man tut ~ daran* it is well to; *sich ~ unterhalten* to have a good time, to enjoy o. s.; ***das hat ~e Weile*** there is no hurry about that; ***alles ~e wünschen*** to wish all the luck in the world.

Gut *n* (***Besitz***) property, possession; (***Land***) farm, (landed) estate, (***großes ~***) manor; (***Ware***) goods *pl*, merchandise, wares *pl*, commodities *pl*; (***Vermögen***) assets *pl*; ***Hab u. ~*** goods and chattels *pl*; ***~ u. Blut*** wealth and life; ***herrenloses ~*** derelict; ***unrecht ~ gedeiht nicht*** ill-gotten wealth never thrives; ***das höchste ~*** the greatest good.

Gut|achten *n* expert opinion; (***Auffassung***) judg(e)ment; (***Zeugnis, beeidigte Aussage***) evidence; (***Schiedsspruch***) arbitrator's award; (***Urteil, Meinung***) verdict; (***Ratschlag***) counsel; (***Schätzung***) estimate ***ärztliches ~~*** medical certificate; ***ein ~~ abgeben*** to deliver (*od* render) an opinion; ***ein ~~ einholen*** to take an opinion; **~achter** *m* expert; valuer, assessor; **~~bericht** *m* expert report; **~achtlich** *a* by way of an opinion; **~artig** *a* good-natured; (***Krankheit***) mild, slight, benign; **~~keit** *f* good-nature; (***Krankheit***) mildness; **~bringen** *irr tr com* to credit; **~dünken** *n* opinion, judg(e)ment; ***nach meinem ~~*** in my opinion; ***nach Ihrem ~~*** on your discretion; ***nach ~~*** at pleasure; **~gehend** *a fig* flourishing, thriving; **~gelaunt** *a* in good spirits, in a good temper; **~gemeint** *a* well-meant; **~gesinnt** *a* well-disposed, loyal, friendly; **~gläubig** *a* bona fide, in good faith; (***leichtgläubig***) credulous; **~~keit** *f* good faith; **~haben** *n* credit; (***Konto***) balance in o.'s favo(u)r; (***ausstehende Forderung***) outstanding debts *pl*; (***Vermögen***) assets *pl*; ***kein genügendes ~~*** not sufficient funds *pl*; ***ein ~~ sperren*** to block an account; ***ein ~~ überziehen*** to overdraw an account; **~heißen** *irr tr* to approve (of), to sanction; (***bestätigen***) to confirm; **~herzig** *a* kind-hearted; **~~keit** *f* kindness, kind-heartedness; **~machen** *tr*: ***wieder ~~*** to make amends for, to make up for; **~mütig** *a* good-natured; **~~keit** *f* good nature; **~sagen** *itr*: ***für jdn ~~*** to answer for s. o., to be security (for); **~sbesitzer** *m* landowner; gentleman farmer; **~schein** *m* (***Quittung***) receipt; (***Schuldschein***) bond, promissory note; (***Belegschein***) voucher; (***Bezugsschein***) coupon; (***Unterpfand***) token; **~schreiben** *irr tr* to credit; ***e-m Konto e-n Betrag ~~*** to place an amount to the credit of s. o.; **~schrift** *f* credit(ing); credit item; **~~sanzeige** *f* advice of amount credited, credit note; **~sherrschaft** *f* lord and lady of the manor; **~shof** *m* farm(-yard); estate; **~sverwalter** *m* farm-bailiff; steward, manager of an estate; **~stehen** *irr itr* to answer (***für*** for); **~tat** *f* (***Wohltat***) charity, benefit; (***Freundlichkeit***) kindness; (***Wohltätigkeit***) benefaction; **~tun** *irr itr*: ***jdm etw ~*** to benefit s. o.; (***Arznei***) to prove well; **~willig** *a* voluntary, ready, willing; (***aus freiem Antrieb***) spontaneous; **~~keit** *f* willingness, readiness.

Güt|e *f* goodness; (***Freundlichkeit***) kindness, favo(u)r; (***Vorzüglichkeit***) virtue; (*Vortrefflichkeit*) excellence; (*Wirksamkeit*) efficiency; (***Lesbarkeit***) legibility; (***Klasse***) grade, class; (***Redlichkeit***) rectitude; (***Wert***) worth; (***Ware***) quality; (***Gediegenheit***) solidity; (***Heilsamkeit***) salubrity; (***Echtheit***) soundness; ***du meine ~~!*** my goodness! good Lord (*od* Heavens)! good gracious! ***sich in ~~ einigen*** to settle in a friendly way; ***haben Sie die ~~*** would you be so kind as to, would you be good enough to; ***auf dem Wege der ~~*** by fair means; ***durch die ~~ von*** through the kind offices of; ***erste ~~*** of the first rank, first-rate, first-class; **~~bezeichnung** *f* quality designation; **~~grad** *m* quality; (***Nutzeffekt***) efficiency; **~~vorschrift** *f* standard specifications *pl*; **~~mäßig** *a* in quality; **~chen** *n* small estate; **~ig** *a* (***gutmütig***) good-natured; (***freundlich***) kind, friendly; (***wohltätig***) charitable; (***zuvorkommend***) obliging; (***liebenswürdig***) amiable; (***nachsichtig***) indulgent; ***mit Ihrer ~~en Erlaubnis*** with your kind permission; **~~keit** *f* goodness, kindness; **~lich** *a* amicable, friendly; ***auf ~~em Wege*** amicably, in a friendly way; ***sich ~~ einigen*** to come to a friendly agreement; ***ein ~~er Vergleich*** an amicable settlement; ***sich ~~ tun*** to enjoy o. s., to indulge in.

Güter *n pl* goods *pl*, merchandise, commodities *pl*; (*Verbrauchs~*) consumer goods *pl*; *lebenswichtige ~* essential goods *pl*; *sperrige ~* bulky goods *pl*; *bewegliche* (*unbewegliche*) *~* movables (immovables) *pl*; *~ des täglichen Bedarfs* necessities *pl* of life; **~abfertigung** *f* (***Sendung***) dispatch of goods; (***Stelle***) goods department, *Am* freight office; **~annahmestelle** *f* goods receiving office; **~ausgabe** *f* delivery of goods; (***Stelle***) goods delivery office; **~austausch** *m* exchange of goods; (***Tauschhandel***) barter; **~bahnhof** *m* goods station, *Am* freight yard; **~beförderer** *m* carrier, *Am* freighter, express (agent); **~beförderung** *f* shipping of goods; **~erwerb** *m* acquisition of goods; **~erzeugung** *f* production of goods; **~fernverkehr** *m* long-distance traffic of goods; **~gemeinschaft** *f* joint property; **~kraftverkehr** *m* road haulage; **~laderaum** *m* loading space; **~makler** *m* real-estate agent; **~recht** *n* law of property; **~schuppen** *m* goods shed, *Am* freight shed; **~sendung** *f* consignment of goods; **~speicher** *m* storehouse, *Am* freight house; **~tarif** *m* goods tariff; **~transport** *m* goods traffic; **~trennung** *f* separate property; **~umsatz** *m* turnover of goods; **~verbrauch** *m* consumption of goods; **~verkehr** *m* goods traffic; **~versand** *m* shipment of goods; **~versicherung** *f* cargo insurance; **~verteilung** *f* distribution of goods; **~wagen** *m* (***gedeckt***) covered goods wag(g)on, goods van, *Am* box-car; (***Bordwandwagen***) open goods wag(g)on, lorry, truck; (***Langholzwagen***) timber truck, bogie-car, *Am* flat-car; ***allg*** goods wag(g)on, *Am* freight car; **~zug** *m* goods train, *Am* freight train; **~~lokomotive** *f* goods (*Am* freight) engine.

Guttapercha *f* gutta-percha.

Guttural *m* (***Laut***) guttural (sound).

*

Gymnas|ialbildung *f* classical education; **~ialdirektor** *m* headmaster of a grammar-school; **~iallehrer** *m* master of a grammar-school; **~iast** *m* pupil of a grammar-school; **~ium** *n* grammar-school, college, public-school; *Am etwa* classical high school; (*deutsches*) gymnasium; **~tik** *f* gymnastics *pl*, athletics *pl*; **~tiker** *m* (***Lehrer***) gymnast; **~tisch** *a* gymnastic(al).

Gynäkolog|e *m* (***Frauenarzt***) gyn(a)ecologist; **~ie** *f* (***Frauenheilkunde***) gyn(a)ecology; **~isch** *a* gyn(a)ecologic.

Gyro *m* (***Kreisel(motor)***) gyro; **~kompaß** *m* gyrocompass; **~magnetisch** *a* (***Atomphysik***) gyromagnetic; **~pilot** *m* *aero* (***automatisches Steuergerät***) gyropilot; **~skop** *n* gyroscope; **~skopisch** *a* gyroscopic; ***~~er Horizont*** *aero* gyro horizon.

H

H *Abk mit* ***H*** *siehe Liste der Abk*; *H(mus)* B.
ha! *interj* ha! ah!
Haag *m*: *der* ~ the Hague; *im* ~ at the Hague; *~er Abkommen* Hague Convention; *~er Internationaler Schiedsgerichtshof* International Court of Arbitration at the Hague.
Haar *n* hair; (*einiger Tiere*) wool; (*Pelz*) coat; (*Borste*) bristle; (*am Tuch*) nap; pile; *blondes* ~ (*haben*) (to have) fair hair; *falsches* ~ false hair; *gepflegtes* ~ well-groomed hair; *kurzes* ~ short hair; *langes* ~ long hair; *die ~e auflösen* to let o.'s hair down; *die ~e aufstecken* to put o.'s hair up; *die ~e frisieren* to set o.'s hair; *die ~e kämmen* to comb o.'s hair; *~e lassen* (*müssen*) *fig* to get fleeced; *die ~e machen* to do o.'s hair, *Am* to fix o.'s hair; *die ~e stutzen* to trim the hair; *die ~e verlieren* to lose o.'s hair; *etw an* (*od bei*) *den ~en herbeiziehen* (*od -zerren*) to drag in by the head and shoulders; *jdn an den ~en ziehen* to pull s. o.'s hair; *auf ein ~, aufs ~* to a hair, to a T; exactly; precisely; *um ein ~* within a hair's breadth; narrowly, nearly; *um kein ~ besser* not a whit better; *um ein ~ treffen* to miss by a hair; *man hat ihr kein ~ gekrümmt* they didn't harm a hair on her head; *es ist kein gutes ~ an ihr* she has not a single good quality; *kein gutes ~ an jdm lassen* to cut s. o. up mercilessly, to pick (*od* to pull) s. o. to pieces; *ein ~ in der Suppe* a fly in the ointment; *ein ~ in etw finden* to get disgusted with s. th.; *mir standen die ~e zu Berge* my hair stood on end; *sich in die ~e geraten* to come to blows, *Am* to come to scratch; *sich in den ~en liegen* to be at daggers drawn; *sich die ~e machen* (*od richten*) to dress (*od* to do) o.'s hair, *Am* to fix o.'s hair; *sich die ~e schneiden lassen* to have o.'s hair cut; *sich keine grauen ~e wachsen lassen* not to distress o. s. about s. th.; *sich die ~e waschen* to wash o.'s hair; **~ausfall** *m* loss of hair, fall of the hair; **~band** *n* hair-lace, bow for the hair; **~besen** *m* hair-broom, sweeping brush; **~beutel** *m* hair-bag; bag-wig; **~bleichen** *n* bleaching of hair; **~boden** *m* hair-bed; **~bürste** *f* hair-brush; **~büschel** *n* tuft of hair; **~dünn** *a* hair-thin; **~einlage** *f* hair-pad; **~en** *itr* (*sich ~~*) to shed (*od* to lose) o.'s hair; (*bei Stoff*) to get threadbare; **~entferner** *m*, **~entfernungsmittel** *n* depilatory; **~entfernung** *f* removal of superfluous hair, depilation; **~ersatz** *m* transformation; **~esbreite** *f* hair-breadth; *um ~~* within hair's breadth, by a hair's breadth; *nicht um ~~* not an inch; **~farbe** *f* colo(u)r of hair; **~färbemittel** *n* hair-dye, hair-colo(u)r; **~fein** *a* very fine, hair-like; *fig* subtle; **~feuchtigkeitsmesser** *m* hair hygrometer; **~fixativ** *n* fixature; **~flechte** *f* braid of hair; *med* hair-lichen; **~flechter** *m* hair plaiter; **~fülle** *f* hairiness; **~frisur** *f* head-dress, coiffure, *Am* hairdo; **~gefäß** *n med* capillary (vessel); **~genau** *a* very exact, meticulous, dead true, to a T; **~hemd** *n* hair-shirt; **~ig** *a* hairy, haired; *fam* (*ungeheuerlich*) enormous, stunning; *in Zssg ...ig z. B. weiß~~* white-haired; **~kamm** *m* hair-comb; **~klammer** *f* (*zum Einschieben*) bobby pin, bob pin; **~klauberei** *f* hair-splitting; **~klein** *adv* minutely; every detail; to a hair; **~knoten** *m* top-knot; **~kräusler, ~künstler** *m hum* (*Friseur*) hairdresser, *Am* hair stylist; **~locke** *f* curl, ringlet, lock; **~los** *a* hairless; (*kahl*) bald; **~nadel** *f* hairpin; (*Klammer für kurzgeschnittenes ~*) bob(by) pin; **~nadelkurve** *f mot* hairpin bend (*od* curve); **~nest** *n* chignon; **~netz** *n* hair-net; **~öl** *n* hair-oil; **~pflege** *f* hair care; **~pflegemittel** *n* hair lotion, hair tonic; **~pinsel** *m* hair-brush; **~pomade** *f* pomade; **~puder** *m* hair-powder; **~putz** *m* head-dress; **~röhrchen** *n* capillary tube; **~riß** *m* hairline crack, microflaw; **~salbe** *f* pomade; **~scharf** *a* keen-edged; very sharp; *fig* to a T; very precise; **~scheitel** *m* parting of the hair; **~schere** *f* hair scissors *pl*; **~schleife** *f* bow (*od* ribbon) for the hair; **~schmuck** *m* ornament for the hair; **~schneidemaschine** *f* hair clippers *pl*, hair cutting machine; **~schneiden** *n* hair-cut(ting); **~schneider** *m* hair-cutter, hair-dresser; **~schneidesalon** *m* hair-dressing room; **~schnitt** *m* hair-cut; crop; style of hair-dress; **~schopf** *m* tuft (of hair); (*falscher*) chignon; **~schuppen** *f pl* dandruff; scurf; **~schur** *f* shearing of the hair; **~schweif** *m* (*e-s Kometen*) tail (of a comet); coma; **~schwund** *m* loss of hair; **~seil** *n* seton, rowel; **~sieb** *n* hair-sieve; **~spalter** *m* hair-splitter; pettifogger; **~spalterei** *f* hair-splitting; **~strähne** *f* tuft of hair; **~sträubend** *a* hair-raising, startling, shocking; **~strich** *m* hair-stroke, up-stroke, hairline, serif; **~tonikum** *n* hair tonic; **~tracht** *f* hair-dress; **~trockner** *m* (*Fön, Trockenhaube*) electric hair-dryer; **~tuch** *n* hair-cloth; **~waschen** *n* shampoo(ing); **~waschmittel** *n* shampoo; (*in Tube*) cream shampoo; (*flüssig*) liquid shampoo; **~wasser** *n* hair tonic, hair lotion, hair-wash; **~wickel** *m* (*Lockenwickel*) wave clip; curler; curl clip; (*aus Papier*) curling-paper; **~wuchs** *m* growth of hair; **~wuchsmittel** *n* hair restorer; **~wulst** *m* hair-pad; **~wurzel** *f* root of a hair; **~zange** *f* tweezers *pl*; **~zopf** *m* tress, braid; (*langer*) pigtail.

*

Habann|röhre *f radio* (*Magnetron*) magnetron (tube), ultra-high-frequency tube; **~schwingung** *f* Habann oscillation.
Hab|e *f* (*Eigentum*) property; (*Besitz*) possessions *pl*, goods *pl*; (*persönliche ~e*) belongings *pl*, effects *pl*; (*Vermögen*) fortune; *bewegliche* (*od fahrende*) *~e* (*jur*) movables *pl*, personal estate; *unbewegliche* (*od liegende*) *~e* (*jur*) immovables *pl*, real estate; *~ u. Gut* all o.'s property; goods and chattels *pl*, *fam* bag and baggage; *mit ~ u. Gut* with all o.'s belongings; **~easkorpusakte** *f* (*Staatsgrundgesetz: England 1679, U.S.A. 1787*) Habeas Corpus Act; **~en** *irr tr* to have; (*Besitzverhältnis anzeigend*) to have; *fam* to have got; to be in possession of, to keep, to hold, to own; (*bekommen, ... zu ~~*) to get; *noch zu ~~* still to be had, still for sale; *sie ist noch zu ~~* she is still in the market; *der Wagen ist noch zu ~~* the car is still in the market; *nicht zu ~~* not to be had; *das ist jetzt schwer zu ~~* that's hard to get now; *ich hab's!* I've got it! *zu ~~ bei ...* sold by ...; *acht ~~ auf* to pay attention to; *im Auge ~~* to have in view; *zum besten ~~* to make a fool of; *ein Datum ~~* to bear a date; *Eile ~~* to be in a hurry; *e-e Erkältung ~~* to have a cold; *fertig ~~* to have finished; *jdn zum Freund ~~* to have a friend in s. o.; *Geld ~~* to have some money; *gern ~~* to like, to be fond of; *es gut ~~* to have a fine time; *Geduld ~~* to be patient, to have patience; *Hunger ~~* to be hungry; *lieber ~~* to prefer; *am liebsten ~~* to prefer above all; *e-n Namen ~~* to bear a name; *nötig ~~* to need; to be necessary; *recht ~~* to be right; *Schwierigkeiten ~~* to have difficulties; *unrecht ~~* to be wrong; *Verdacht ~~ auf* to have suspicion against; *e-n Wagen ~~* to have a car; *die Wahl ~~* to have the choice; *Zeit ~~* to have time (*für* for); *keinen Zweifel ~~* to have no doubt; *etw ~~ wollen* (*verlangen*) to ask for; (*wünschen*) to desire, to wish, to want; *so will sie es ~~* that's the way she wants it; *jetzt ~~ wir Winter* it is winter now; *der Juni hat 30 Tage* June has 30 days; *den wievielten ~~ wir heute?* what is the date today? *wir ~~ den 10. Juni* this is the 10th of June; *es zu tun ~~ mit* to have to deal with; *das hat noch nichts zu sagen* there is no need to worry about it; *ihr Vorschlag hat viel für sich* there is much to be said for her suggestion; *sie hat viel von ihrer Mutter* she takes after her mother; *was ~~ Sie?* what's the matter with you? *was ~~ Sie hier zu tun?* what are you doing here? *da hast du es!* there you have it! there you are! *an sich ~~* (*tragen*) to be wearing; *e-n Fehler an sich ~~* to have a fault; *auf sich ~~* to be of consequence; *bei sich ~~* to have about; *etw gegen jdn ~~* to object to s. o.; *es mit jdm ~~* to have relations with s. o.; to have an understanding with s. o.; *unter sich ~~* to be in charge of; *imp: es hat den Anschein* it seems, it appears; *es hat Eile* it is urgent; *es hat keine Eile* there is no hurry; *es hat keine Not* no fear of that; *es hat seine Richtigkeit* it is quite correct, it's a fact; *es hat gute Weile damit* there is plenty of time; it is still a long way off; *r: sich ~~* to behave; (*wichtig tun*) to put on airs; to be fussy, to make a fuss; *es hat nichts auf sich* it is of no consequence; *~~ Sie sich nicht so!* don't make such a fuss! *hat sich was! interj* nonsense! **~en** *n com* credit; credit side, creditors *pl*; *Soll u. ~~* debit and credit, assets and liabilities; *im ~~ buchen* to enter on the credit side; **~enichts** *m* pauper; (*politisch*) have-not; penniless (*od* poor) fellow; **~ensaldo** *m* credit balance; **~enseite** *f* credit side; **~enzinsen** *m pl* interest on credit balance, *Am* interest cost; **~gier** *f* covetousness, greed(iness); (*Geiz*) avarice; **~gierig** *a* covetous, greedy, grasping; avaricious; **~haft** *a*: *e-r Sache ~~ werden* to get possession of ..., to catch hold of; to obtain; (*fangen*) to seize, to catch; **~schaft, ~seligkeit(en** *pl***)** *f* property, goods and chattels *pl*, belongings *pl*, effects *pl*; *mil* kit;

~sucht *f* greediness, avarice, covetousness; **~süchtig** *a* greedy, avaricious.

Haber *m oberdeutsch für: Hafer;* **~feldtreiben** *n* popular lynch justice in Bavaria.

Habicht *m* hawk; *Hühner~* goshawk; **~snase** *f* hook-nose, acquiline nose.

Habilit|ation *f* habilitation, formal admission as an academical lecturer; **~ationsschrift** *f* inaugural dissertation; **~ieren** *r* to acquire the right of holding academical lectures, to habilitate; (*sich niederlassen*) to establish o. s.

Habit *n fam* (*Kleidung, bes. Ordenstracht*) dress, garment; **~us** *m* habitus, habits *pl*, physical appearance; (*Konstitution*) constitution.

Hack|beil *n* chopper, cleaver; **~block** *m* chopping-block; **~brett** *n* chopping-board; **~e** *f* hoe; pick(axe); mattock; **~e** *f*, **~en** *m* (*am Fuß*) heel; *die ~en zusammenklappen mit* to click o.'s heels; **~en** *tr* (*Holz*) to cleave, to chop; (*Fleisch*) to hash, to mince; (*Acker*) to hack, to hoe; (*picken*) to pick, to peck; **~fleisch** *n* minced meat; hash; chopped meat; **~frucht** *f* root crop, *Am* truck crop (potatoes, turnips, and cabbage); **~~bau** *m* cultivation of root crops; **~~ernte** *f* root harvest; **~klotz** *m* butcher's block; **~maschine** *f* (*Fleisch*) meat mincing-machine, mincer, *Am* food (*od* meat) chopper, grinder; (*Schnitzler*) chipper; **~messer** *n* chopping-knife, chopper.

Häcksel *m* chopped straw, chaff; **~maschine** *f* chaff-cutter; **~schneider** *m* straw-chopper, chaff-cutter.

Hader *m* (*Zank*) quarrel, dispute; brawl; *~n pl* (*Lumpen*) (paper) rags *pl*; **~er** *m* quarreller, disputer; **~n** *itr* to quarrel with, to dispute, to argue; to wrangle, to brawl.

Hafen *m* 1. harbo(u)r; port; (*sicherer Ort*) haven; *fig* shelter; (*Flug~*) airport; *e-n ~ anlaufen* to make a port, to call at a port; *aus e-m ~ auslaufen* to clear a port; to leave port; *in e-n ~ einlaufen* to put into port, to enter a port; *e-n ~ sperren* to shut up a port; (*blockieren*) to blockade a port; *in den ~ der Ehe einlaufen* to marry, to get married; 2. (*Topf*) pot; vessel; **~abgaben** *f pl* port charges *pl*, port dues *pl*; **~amt** *n* port authority; **~anker** *m* mooring anchor; moorings *pl*; **~anlagen** *f pl* docks *pl*, harbo(u)r (*od* port) facilities (*od* installations) *pl*; **~arbeiter** *m* longshoreman, dock labo(u)rer, dockyard labo(u)rer, stevedore, docker, lumper; **~aufseher** *m* harbo(u)r-master, berthing-master; **~ausrüstung** *f* port equipment (*od* facilities *pl*); **~bahnhof** *m* maritime railway station; **~barkasse** *f* harbo(u)r launch; **~becken** *n* wet dock, basin; **~behörde** *f* port authority; **~damm** *m* (*Pier, Mole*) jetty, pier, mole; ocean piers *pl*; **~dieb** *m Am fam* wharf-rat; **~einfahrt** *f* entrance into the port; **~einrichtungen** *f pl* port facilities *pl*; **~feuer** *n* harbo(u)r light; **~gebühren** *f pl* harbo(u)r-dues *pl*; **~kai** *f* quay, *Am* wharf; **~lagerhaus** *n* harbo(u)r (*od* dock) warehouse; **~mole** *f* quay; **~mündung** *f* harbo(u)r (*od* port) entrance, harbo(u)r channel; **~schlepper** *m* harbo(u)r tugboat; **~schleuse** *f* harbo(u)r lock; **~sperre** *f* (*für Schiffe*) embargo; (*im Krieg*) blockade; **~stadt** *f* seaport, seaport-town, seatown, port-town; **~überwachung** *f* port control; **~wache** *f* harbo(u)r police; **~zoll** *m* harbo(u)r-dues *pl*; (*Gebühren*) port charges *pl*, anchorage.

Hafer *m* (*Pflanze*) oat; (*Frucht*) oats *pl*; *ihn sticht der ~* he is getting overbold, he is saucy, *Am fam* he feels his oats; **~brei** *m* (oatmeal-) porridge, *Am* (boiled) oatmeal, (*oft auch*) cereal; **~flocken** *f pl* flaked oats *pl*, rolled oats *pl*; **~grütze** *f* groats *pl*, grits *pl*; **~mehl** *n* oatmeal; **~motor** *m hum* (*Pferd*) hay motor, *fam* hay-burner; **~schleim** *m* gruel; **~schleimsuppe** *f* oatmeal soup.

Haff *n* bay, gulf, frith, haff.

Hafner *m* (*Töpfer*) potter.

Haft *f* detention, prison, confinement; imprisonment; custody; arrest; *strenge ~* close confinement; *in ~* in prison, under arrest, in custody; *aus der ~ entlassen* to release; (*gegen Sicherheitsleistung*) to release on bail; *in ~ halten* to detain, to keep in custody; *in ~ nehmen* to put under arrest, to take into custody; **~bar** *a* answerable, responsible (*für* for), liable (*für* for); *~~ machen* to make (*od* to hold) liable (*od* responsible) for; **~barkeit** *f* liability, responsibility; **~befehl** *m* warrant of arrest (*od* apprehension); **~dauer** *f* duration of imprisonment; **~en** *itr* (*an etw kleben*) to cleave; to cling; to adhere (to); *im Gedächtnis ~~* to remain in memory, to stick in o.'s mind; *für etw ~~* (*einstehen*) to answer, to be liable (*od* responsible) for; to be security for; (*garantieren*) to guarantee; **~festigkeit** *f* adhesive strength; **~hohlladung** *f mil* magnetic antitank hollow charge; **~lokal** *n* detention room; **~mine** *f* sticky bomb; **~pflicht** *f* liability, responsibility; *mit beschränkter ~~* with limited liability, limited (*Abk* Ltd); *gegen ~~ versichert sein* to be insured against liability; **~pflichtversicherung** *f* liability insurance, third party insurance; **~sitz** *m tech* stationary (*od* tight) fit; **~ung** *f* liability, responsibility; *tech* adhesion; *chem* adsorption; (*am Erdboden*) stability, low centre (*Am* center) of gravity; *beschränkte ~~* limited; *e-e ~~ übernehmen* to undertake a responsibility; **~verlängerungsbefehl** *m jur* detainer; **~vermögen** *n tech* adhesive power; **~vollzug** *m* imprisonment.

Häftling *m* prisoner.

Hag *m* hedge, enclosure; grove; (*Wiese*) meadow; **~ebuche** *f* hard-beam; hornbeam; **~ebutte** *f* hip, haw; **~~nstrauch** *m* dog-rose; **~edorn** *m* hawthorn.

Hagel *m* hail; sleet; (*Stein~*) shower; (*Schrot*) small shot; *~ von Schlägen* a sound beating; **~bildung** *f* hail formation; **~bö** *f* hail squall; **~dicht** *a* thick as hail; **~korn** *n* hailstone; **~n** *imp* to hail; **~schaden, ~schlag** *m* damage done by hail; **~schauer** *m* hailstorm; **~versicherung** *f* hail-insurance; **~wetter** *n* hailstorm; **~wolken** *f pl* hail clouds *pl*.

hager *a* (*mager*) meagre, *Am* meager, lean; (*abgezehrt*) thin, lean, haggard, emaciated; (*schlank, schmächtig*) slender; (*dürr, knochig*) dry-boned, raw-boned, *Am* scrawny; *~ im Gesicht* lean-faced; **~keit** *f* leanness.

Hagestolz *m* old bachelor.

haha! *interj* (*Lachen*) ho ho! haw-haw!

Häher *m* jay.

Hahn *m* cock, *Am* rooster; (*Gefäß~*) tap, *Am* faucet; (*Sperr~*) stopcock; (*Zapf~*) spigot; *der ~ kräht* the cock crows; *~ im Korbe sein* to be cock of the walk; *den ~ spannen* to cock a gun; *es kräht kein ~ danach* nobody cares a straw about it; **~enfuß** *m bot* crowfoot, goldcup; **~enkamm** *m* cock's comb; *bot* coxcomb; **~enkampf** *m* cock-fight; **~enkampfplatz** *m* cock-pit; **~enschrei** *m* cock-crowing; *mit dem ersten ~~* with the first cock; **~ensporn** *m* cockspur; **~entritt** *m* cock's tread; cock's treadle (in an egg); **~rei** *m* cuckold; *zum ~~ machen* to cuckold; **~reischaft** *f* cuckoldom.

Hähnchen *n* cockerel.

Hai, **~fisch** *m* shark.

Hain *m* grove, wood.

Häkchen *n* little hook crotchet.

Häkel|arbeit *f* crochet-work; **~ei** *f* crochet; **~garn** *n* crochet-cotton; **~muster** *n* crochet-pattern; **~n** *tr* to (work in) crochet; **~nadel** *f* crochet-needle.

Haken *m* hook; (*Spange*) clasp, hasp; (*Klammer*) claw; (*Kleider~*) peg; (*Wand~*) hook, peg; (*beim Abstreichen e-r Liste*) mark, tick; (*beim Boxen*) hook; *linker* (*rechter*) *~* left (right) hook; *e-n ~ versetzen* to hook; *fig* (*Schwierigkeit, Hindernis*) snag, drawback; difficulty; *~ u. Öse* hook and eye; *die Sache hat e-n ~* there's a but in the case, there's a hitch somewhere; *da sitzt der ~!* there is the difficulty! **~en** *itr* to hook on; *sich ~ an* to catch in, to hitch together; **~büchse** *f* arquebuse; **~förmig** *a* hook-like; **~kreuz** *n* swastika; **~nagel** *m* hook-nail; spike; **~nase** *f* hook-nose, aquiline nose; **~schlüssel** *m* pick-lock; **~stock** *m* harping-iron; **~zahn** *m* gullet tooth, hook.

Halali *n* death-haloo, mort, mot; *~ blasen* to sound the death(-haloo); *~!* Tally-ho!

halb *a* half, *in Zssg:* half-, semi-; *adv* half, by halves; *~ so viel* half as much; *nicht ~ so viel* not half so much; *~ u. ~* half and half, *Am* fifty-fifty; *~ umsonst* almost for nothing, *fam* for a mere song; *den ~en Betrag* half the amount; *ein ~es Dutzend* half a dozen, *Am* a half dozen; *es ist ~ eins* it is half past twelve, *Am auch* it is half after twelve, it is twelve thirty; *mit ~em Herzen* half-hearted; *ein ~es Jahr* six months, a half-year; *~e Note mus* minim, *Am* half note; *zum ~en Preis* at half the price; *e-e ~e Stunde* half an hour, *Am* a half hour; *~er Ton mus* semitone; *etw nur ~ tun* to do s. th. by halves; *nur die ~e Wahrheit* a half-truth; *auf ~em Wege* half-way; midway; **~amtlich** *a* semi-official; **~ärmel** *m* half-sleeve; **~atlas** *m* (*Stoff*) satinet(te); **~automat** *m* semi-automatic machine; **~automatisch** *a* semi-automatic, semi-mechanical; **~band** *m* board; **~bildung** *f* superficial education; **~blut** *n* half-cast, half-blood, half-bred (horse); **~bruder** *m* half-brother; **~dunkel** *n* dusk, twilight; half-light; (*Malerei*) clair-obscure, chiaroscuro; **~durchsichtig** *a* semi-transparent; **~edelstein** *m* semi-precious stone; . . . **~en,** . . . **~er** *prp* for, by reason of, on account of; for the sake of; **~erzeugnis, ~fabrikat** *n* semi-finished product, semi-manufactured good, semimanufacture; **~fertig** *a* half-finished; **~fett** *a typ* medium faced; (*Kohle*) semi-bituminous; **~finale** *n* (*Tennis*) semifinal; **~franz(band)** *m* half-binding, half-calf; *in ~~ gebunden* half-bound; **~gar** *a* (*Fleisch*) half-done, underdone, *Am* rare; **~gebildet** *a* half-educated; **~geschwister** *pl* step brothers and sisters *pl*; **~gott** *m* demigod; hero; **~heit** *f* imperfection, incompleteness; half-measure; indecision; **~ieren** *tr* to halve; to cut in half, to divide into halves; to dimidiate; *math* to bisect; **~ierung** *f* halving, bisection; **~~slinie** *f* bisector, bisectrix; **~insel** *f* peninsula; **~jahr** *n* half-year; **~jährig** *a* six months old; **~jährlich** *a* half-yearly, *Am* semiannually ;**~kettenantrieb** *m mot* half-track drive; **~kettenkraftfahrzeug** *n* half-track (motor) vehicle; half-track truck; **~kreis** *m* semicircle; **~kreisförmig** *a* semicircular; **~kugel** *f* hemisphere; **~kugelig** *a* hemispheric(al); **~laut** *a* low; in an undertone; **~lederband** *m* half-leather binding, half-calf; **~leinen** *n* half-linen, half-cloth; **~leinenband** *m* half-cloth; **~mast** *m* half-mast, *Am* half-staff; *auf ~~* at half-mast; **~messer** *m* radius; **~monatlich** *a* fortnightly; semimonthly; **~mond** *m* half-moon; crescent moon; (*Wappen*) crescent; **~~förmig** *a* crescent-shaped; **~nackt** *a* half-naked; **~offen** *a* half-open; (*Tür*) ajar; **~part** *adv* halves; *mit jdm ~~ machen* to go halves with, to make fifty-fifty; **~reif** *a* half-ripe; **~rund** *a* semicircular, half-round; **~schatten** *m* penumbra, half-shadow; **~schlaf** *m* dog-sleep; doze, drowsy sleep; **~schuhe** *m pl* low-shoes *pl*, oxfords *pl*; **~schwergewicht** *n* (*Boxen*) light heavy-weight; **~schwester** *f* half-sister, step-sister; **~seide** *f* silk mixed with cotton, half silk; poplin; **~seiden** *a* half silk and half cotton; **~seite** *f typ* column; **~selbsttätig** *a* semi-automatic(al), semi-mechanical; **~starr** *a aero* semi-rigid; **~stiefel** *m pl* high-lows *pl*, half boots *pl*; **~strümpfe** *m pl* (*Socken*) socks *pl*; half hose; **~stündlich** *a* half-hourly; **~tägig** *a* half-daily; semi-diurnal; **~tagsarbeit** *f* part-time job; *in ruhigen Zeiten werden alle halbtagsbeschäftigten Angestellten entlassen* in off seasons all part-time employees are dropped; **~ton** *m mus* semitone; **~tonbild** *n* (*Autotypie*) half-tone (etching); **~tot** *a* half-dead; **~trauer** *f* half-mourning; **~vokal** *m* semivowel; **~voll** *a* half-full; **~wach** *a* half-awake; **~wegs** *adv* half-way; midway; (*leidlich*) tolerably; **~welt** *f* demi-monde; **~wertzeit** *f phys, chem* half-life (period); half period; **~wissen** *n* superficial knowledge, smattering; **~wisser** *m* smatterer, sciolist; **~wollen** *a* half-woollen; *~~es Zeug* linsey-woolsey; union goods *pl*; **~wüchsig** *a* half-grown, *Am* teen-age; **~~e(r)** *m* juvenile, *Am* teen-ager; **~zeug** *n* semifinished product; **~zeit** *f phys* period of half life, semi-period; *sport* half(-time); *zweite ~~* second time; **~zug** *m mil* half-platoon.

Halde *f* sloping ground, slope; hill-side; (*Schutt~*) waste heap, dump; *min* dump; heap of rocks; dead heap; pit heap; **~enabfall** *m* tailings *pl*; **~enberg** *m* waste tip; **~enbestände** *m pl* dump stocks *pl*; **~envorrat** *m* pit-head supply.

Hälft|e *f* half; moiety; (*Mitte*) middle; *bis zur ~~* (*Mitte*) to the middle; *um die ~~* by half; *um die ~~ teurer* half as dear again; *zur ~~* half of; **~en** *tr* to halve, to bisect, to mottle; **~ig** *a* half; **~ewegs** *adv* half-way.

Halfter *f* (*od m od n*) halter; **~n** *tr* to (tie by the halter; **~riemen** *m* halter-strap.

Hall *m* peal, sound, clang; resonance; **~en** *itr* to (re)sound; to clang, to reverberate.

Halle *f* (*großer Raum*) hall; (*Vorhalle*) vestibule, (*mit Säulen*) porch; (*bedeckter Vorbau*) veranda, *Am* porch; (*Hotel~*) lounge, lobby; (*Markt~*) (market-)hall, bazaar; (*Sport~*) covered court; (*Flugzeug~*) shed, hangar; **~nbad** *n* indoor swimming-bath, *Am* pool; **~neisbahn** *f* indoor ice-rink; **~nsport** *m* indoor sports *pl*; **~ntennis** *n* (*nur in England*) court tennis; **~nvorfeld** *n* (*betonierte Fläche vor Flugzeug~*) apron.

Hallig *f* marsh-islet; holm.

hallo *interj* hallo(o)! hallow! hello! *~?* (*am Telephon*) are you there? *Am* hello? *~ rufen* to halloo (*od* hallow); *~ n fig* (*Getue, Lärm*) fuss, uproar, hubbub; *ein großes ~ machen über* to make a great fuss about s. th.

Halm *m* blade; (*Stengel*) stalk; (*Stroh~*) straw; **~früchte** *f pl* cereals *pl*; **Hälmchen** *n* small blade; *~ziehen* drawing lots with long and short stalks.

Hals *m* neck; (*Kehle*) throat; *e-n rauhen* (*od bösen*) *~ haben* to have a sore throat; *steifer ~* stiff neck; *~ über Kopf* headlong, head over heels; *bis an den ~, bis zum ~e* over head and ears, up to o.'s neck; *vom ~e* off o.'s hands; *aus vollem ~e lachen* to roar with laughter; *aus vollem ~e schreien* to cry at the top of o.'s voice, *Am* to yell at the top of o.'s lungs; *jdm den ~ abschneiden* to cut s. o.'s throat; *bleiben Sie mir damit vom ~e* leave me alone with that, don't bother me with that; *sich den ~ brechen* to break o.'s neck; *jdm den ~ brechen* to break s. o.'s neck, to ruin s. o.; *e-r Flasche den ~ brechen* to crack a bottle; *jdm um den ~ fallen* to embrace s. o.; *jdn beim ~e fassen* to hold s. o. by the throat; *es geht ihm diesmal an den ~* this time it will cost him his head; *es im ~e haben* to have a sore throat; *jdn auf dem ~e haben* to be encumbered with s. o.; *etw auf dem ~e haben* to be troubled with; to be saddled with; *das hängt* (*od wächst*) *mir zum ~e heraus* I am sick and tired of that, I am fed up, I am bored to tears with that, *Am fam* it's coming out of my ears; *das kostet den ~* that will cost his life; *das wird den ~ nicht kosten* that will not be ruinous; *jdm auf dem ~e liegen* to bother s. o.; *etw bis an den ~ satthaben* to be fed up (to the back teeth) with; *sich jdn vom ~e schaffen* to get rid of s. o., to get s. o. off o.'s neck; *bis an den ~ in Schulden stecken* to be in debt up to o.'s ears; *jdm den ~ umdrehen* to wring s. o.'s neck; *sich den ~ verrenken* (*um alles zu sehen*) to crane o.'s neck, *Am sl* to rubberneck; *sich jdm an den ~ werfen* to throw o. s. at s. o.; **~abschneider** *m* cut-throat; *fig* extortioner; **~ader** *f anat* jugular (*od* cervical) vein; **~arterie** *f* carotid artery; **~ausschnitt** *m* neckline, neck; *hoher* (*tiefer*) *~~* high (low) neckline; **~band** *n* necklace, neck ribbon; (*Hund*) collar; **~binde** *f* (neck)tie, cravat; **~bräune** *f med* quinsy, tonsilitis, angina pectoris; **~brechend, ~brecherisch** *a* neck-breaking, breakneck; perilous, risky, dangerous; **~drüse** *f* jugular gland; **~eisen** *n* iron collar; **~entzündung** *f* inflammation of the throat; **~gericht** *n* criminal court; **~kette** *f* neck-chain; **~kragen** *m* collar; cape; (*Pelz*) tippet; **~krankheit** *f* disease of the throat; **~krause** *f* frill, ruff(le); **~mandel** *f anat* tonsil; **~röhre** *f* trachea, windpipe; **~schlagader** *f* carotid artery; **~schlinge** *f* noose; **~schmerzen** *m pl* sore throat; **~schmuck** *m* collar; **~schnur** *f* (*Perlen*) necklace; **~starrig** *a* stiff-necked, stubborn, headstrong, obstinate; **~starrigkeit** *f* obstinacy, stubbornness; **~tuch** *n* neckcloth, (*Schal*) neckerchief, scarf; muffler; (*Wollschal*) comforter; **~vene** *f* jugular vein; **~weh** *n* sore throat; **~weite** *f* size of the neck; **~wirbel** *m* cervical vertebra; **~zäpfchen** *n anat* uvula.

Halt *m* (*Festhalten*) hold; (*Stand*) foothold, footing; (*Anhalten*) stop, halt; standstill; pause; (*Haltestelle*) stopping place; (*Stütze*) support, prop, stay; (*für die Hände*) handhold; *fig* (*Festigkeit, Stetigkeit*) steadiness, firmness; (*Dauerhaftigkeit*) solidity; (*Unterstützung*) support; (*innerer ~*) consistency (of character); *ohne ~* unsteady, unstable; *~machen* to stop, to (make a) halt; to pause, *Am* to stop over (*od* off); *wo machen wir ~?* where are we going to stop? *~! interj* stop! hold! *mil* halt! *~, wer da?* stop (*od* halt), who goes there? *~ adv dial* just, to be sure; I think; *das ist ~ so* that's just the way it is; **~bar** *a* (*was sich aufrechterhalten läßt*) maintainable, tenable; (*stabil*) stable; (*dauerhaft*) durable; (*fest*) firm, solid; lasting; (*Farbe*) fast, permanent; *~~ sein* (*Stoff etc*) to hold up; to keep well; *~~ machen* (*Früchte etc*) to preserve; **~barkeit** *f* stableness, stability; durability, solidity; firmness; endurance; (*Farben*) fastness; *fig* (*Vertretbarkeit*) defensibility; **~barmachung** *f* preservation, conservation; **~efeder** *f* retaining spring; **~egurt** *f* (*Fallschirm*) parachute harness; **~eleine** *f* mooring rope; **~elicht** *n* stop light; **~emast** *m* (*Luftschiff*) mooring-mast; **~en** *irr tr* (*festhalten*) to hold; (*stützen*) to support; (*aufrechterhalten, durchführen*) to maintain; (*zurückhalten*) to retain, to keep, to hold; (*jdn anhalten*) to stop; (*besitzen*) to possess; (*enthalten*) to contain, to hold, to keep; (*beobachten*) to observe; (*bewahren*) to keep; (*Fest etc*) to celebrate; (*Wagen, Pferde*) to keep; *an der Hand ~~* to hold s. o. by the hand; *etw ans Licht ~~* to hold s. th. to the light; *auf Lager ~~* to keep; *viel auf etw ~~* to think a lot of; *viel auf jdn ~~* to make much of; to think very highly of s. o.; *jdn auf dem laufenden ~~* to keep s. o. well informed; to keep s. o. well posted up; *jdn beim Worte ~~* to take s. o. at his word; *jdn frei~~* to treat s. o.; *~~ für* to think, to deem, to esteem; to take for, to take to be; to regard as, to look upon as; *wir ~~ es für ratsam* we deem it advisable; *etw für gut, recht, wahr ~~* to think proper; *wofür ~~ Sie mich?* what do you take me for? *es für nötig ~~* to deem it necessary; *jdn kurz ~~* to keep a strict hand over s. o.; *es mit jdm ~~* to side with, to stick to, to adhere to, to hold with; *was ~~ Sie von ihm?* what do you think of him? *was hält man davon?* what do people think about it? *jdn zum besten ~~* to make fun of s. o.; *zugute ~~* to make allowances for; *die Bank ~~* to keep (the) bank; *seinen Einzug ~~* to make o.'s entry; *e-e Festung ~~* to hold a fortress (*od* place); *das Gleichgewicht ~~* to balance; *Hochzeit ~~* to celebrate o.'s wedding; *Maß ~~* to be moderate; *den Mund ~~* to hold o.'s tongue, to keep quiet, *fam* to be mum, to shut up; *halt den Mund! sl* shut up! *Am sl* pipe down! button your lips! *Ordnung ~~* to keep order; *e-e Predigt ~~* to preach a sermon; *e-e Rede ~~* to deliver a speech; *ein Schläfchen ~~* to take a nap; *Schritt* ~~ to keep pace; *Schule* ~~ to give lessons; to keep school; *e-e Sitzung* ~~ to hold a meeting; *e-e Versammlung* ~~ to hold a meeting; *e-e Vorlesung* ~~ to give a lecture; *Wort* ~~ to keep o.'s word; *im Zaum* ~~ to rein; *fig* to keep a tight hand on, to keep under control; *e-e Zeitung* ~~ to take in a (news)paper, *Am* to subscribe a paper, to get a paper; *itr* (*festsitzen*) to hold; (*haltmachen*) to stop, to halt, to pause; (*mit dem Wagen*) to pull up; (*dauern*) to last, to hold out; (*dauerhaft sein*) to wear well; *der Autobus hält hier* the bus stops here; *das Eis hält nicht* the ice breaks; *an sich* ~~ to master o.'s passions, to contain o. s., to control o. s.; *auf etw zu* ~~ to make straight for; *es mit jdm* ~~ to be on s. o.'s side; *schwer*~~ to be difficult; *sich* ~~ to hold o. s., to maintain o.s.; (*sich betragen*) to behave; (*dauern*) to keep well, to last; (*Preise*) to keep steady; (*Wetter*) to keep up; *sich gerade* ~~ to keep o. s. straight; *sich gut* ~~ to behave well; *sich links* (*rechts*) ~~ to keep to the left (right); *sich warm* ~~ to keep o. s. warm; *sich an etw* ~~ (*sich festhalten*) to take hold of; *fig* to stand to, to stick to; *sich an jdn* ~~ to keep to, to stick to, to stand to; to go to; ~~ *Sie sich an ihn* go to him; **~eplatz** *m* stopping place; (*Taxe*) taxi-rank, *Am* taxi-stand; **~epunkt** *m rail* station, halt, stopping place; (*beim Schießen*) point of aim; (*Kurve*) break; **~er** *m* holder; (*e-s Fahrzeugs, Flugzeugs etc*) legal owner; (*Beschlag*) fixture; fastener; (*Feder*~~) penholder; (*Stütze*) support, hold; (*Griff*) handle; (*verstellbarer* ~) adjustable clamp; **~eschraube** *f* holding screw; **~eseil** *n* holding rope, guy line; **~esignal** *n rail* block-signal, stopping-signal; (*Straßenverkehr*) red light; **~estelle** *f* stop, stopping place, station; stopover; **~etau** *n* mooring cable, guy rope, hauling-down cable; **~evorrichtung** *f* fixture; holding device; **~ezeichen** *n typ* break; (*Verkehr*) stop signal; **~ezeit** *f* halt, pause; **~los** *a* unsteady; without support; unstable; loose; (*pflichtvergessen*) unprincipled; (*unhaltbar*) untenable; **~losigkeit** *f* unsteadiness; instability; absurdity; **~machen** *itr* to stop, to halt; **~station** *f rail* stop, halt; **~ung** *f* (*Einstellung*) attitude; (*Benehmen, Führung*) demeano(u)r, behavio(u)r; (*Körper*~~) carriage, bearing; (*Stellung*) posture; (*Pose*) pose; (*inneres Gleichgewicht*) poise; (*Selbstbeherrschung*) self-control; *feste* ~~ (*Börse*) firmness; *flaue* ~~ (*Markt*) dul(l)ness; *politische* ~~ political bearing (*od* opinion); *sittliche* ~~ moral principles.

Halunke *m* scoundrel, rogue; (*oft scherzhaft*) rascal, scamp, villain knave.

hämisch *a* malicious, spiteful, rancorous; ~*es Lächeln* sardonic smile; sneer.

Hammel *m* wether; (*Fleisch*) mutton; **~braten** *m* roast mutton; **~fleisch** *n* mutton; **~keule** *f* leg of mutton; **~kotelett** *n* mutton-chop; **~sprung** *m parl* division, pairing-off; **~viertel** *n* quarter of mutton.

Hammer *m* hammer; (*Holz*~) mallet, beetle; (*Eisenschmiede*) forge; *unter den* ~ *bringen* to sell by auction; **~schlag** *m* blow (*od* stroke) with a hammer; (*Abfall*) iron-scales *pl*; **~schmied** *m* blacksmith, hammer-smith; **~stiel** *m* handle of a hammer; **~werk** *n* forge; ironworks *pl*.

hämmer|bar *a* malleable; **~~keit** *f* malleability; **~n** *tr, itr* to hammer.

Hämorrhoiden *pl* h(a)emorrhoids *pl*, piles *pl*.

Hampelmann *m* puppet, jumping-jack.

Hamster *m* hamster, (German) marmot; **~er** *m* (food-) hoarder, grabber; **~fahrt** *f* hoarding trip; **~n** *tr* to hoard, to grab; to scour the country-side for food.

Hand *f* hand; (*Schrift*) hand, handwriting; *anat* manus; *Hände pl* (*Arbeitskräfte*) hands *pl*; *die Hände betreffend* manual; *Hände u. Füße pl* extremities *pl*; ~ *u. Fuß haben fig* to hold water; to be to the purpose; *flache* ~ palm; *hohle* ~ the hollow of the hand; *e-e schwielige* ~ a callous palm; *Hände hoch!* hands up! *Am sl* stick them up! *Hände weg!* hands off! ~ *anlegen* (*helfen*) to lend a hand; to set to work upon; ~ *anlegen an etw* to lay hands on s. th.; to put o.'s hand to; ~ *an sich legen* to commit suicide; *die* ~ *ballen* to clench o.'s fist; *jdm die* ~ *bieten* (*od reichen*) to hold out o.'s hand to; (*zu etw*) to offer o.'s help; *jdm die* ~ *drücken* (*pressen*) to squeeze s. o.'s hand, (*beim Gruß*) to shake hands with s. o.; *jdm die* ~ *geben* to give o.'s hand to; (*Gruß*) to shake hands with s. o.; *jdm freie* ~ *geben* to give s. o. a free hand; *kalte Hände haben* to have cold hands; *die* ~ *im Spiel haben* to have a hand in s. th., *fam* to have a finger in the pie; *die* ~ *aufs Herz legen* to lay o.'s hand on o.'s heart; ~ *aufs Herz!* hand on heart! *die letzte* ~ *an etw legen* to give the finishing (*od* last) touch to s. th.; *die Hände in den Schoß legen* to be idle, to do nothing; *es lag in seiner* ~ it was in his hands; *jdm auf die* ~ *sehen* to watch s. o. closely; *die Hände in die Seite stemmen* to set o.'s arms akimbo; *alle Hände voll zu tun haben* to have got a lot of work on o.'s hands; *e-e* ~ *wäscht die andere* one good turn deserves another; *seine Hände in Unschuld waschen* to wash o.'s hands of s. th.; *die Hände über dem Kopf zusammenschlagen* to throw up o.'s arms in astonishment; *an die* ~ *gehen* to aid; (*vorschlagen*) to suggest; *an* ~ *von* with the aid of; on the basis of, by means of; *auf der* ~ *liegen* to be obvious, to be clear, to be evident (*od* patent), to go without saying; *auf Händen tragen* to treat with great care; *aus erster* ~ at first hand; *aus zweiter* ~ second hand, used; *e-e Auskunft aus erster* ~ *erhalten* to get an information at first hand; *aus der* ~ *in den Mund leben* to live from hand to mouth; *aus der* ~ *lassen* to let escape; *bei der* ~ (*zur* ~) at hand; handy; ready; *stets mit e-r Antwort bei der* ~ *sein* to be always ready with an answer; *bei der* ~ *nehmen* to take by the hand; *durch viele Hände gehen* to pass through many hands; *in der* ~ in hand; *die Situation fest in der* ~ *haben* to have the situation well in hand; ~ *in* ~ hand in hand; ~ *in* ~ *arbeiten* to work hand in hand; *in jds* ~ *kommen* to come to hand; *in andere Hände übergehen* to change hands; *ein Spatz in der* ~ *ist besser als e-e Taube auf dem Dach* a bird in the hand is worth two in the bush; *mit der* ~ (*hergestellt*) by hand; *mit eigener* ~ in (*od* under) o.'s own hand; *mit beiden Händen zugreifen* to jump at the opportunity; *sich mit Händen u. Füßen dagegen wehren* to fight against it tooth and nail (*od* with might and main); *ohne die Hände zu rühren* hands down; *unter der* ~ under hand; privately, secretly; *von der* ~ offhand; *von der* ~ *gehen* to work well; *von langer* ~ *vorbereiten* to prepare beforehand; *von der* ~ *weisen* to decline, to reject; *von* ~ *zu* ~ from hand to hand; *vor der* ~ for the present; now; *zu Händen von* (*bei Briefen*) care of (*Abk* c/o), *Am* attention of; *zur* ~ to hand, to o.'s hand; handy; ready; *zur* ~ *sein* to be at hand; *zur rechten* (*linken*) ~ on the right (left) hand (*od* side); **~abzug** *m typ* hand impression; **~anlasser** *m mot* crank starter; **~antrieb** *m* hand drive; *mit* ~~ hand driven; **~apparat** *m tele* handset; **~arbeit** *f* manual work (*od* labo(u)r); handicraft; *pred* handmade, done by hand; (*weibliche*) needle work, *Am* seam; **~arbeitslehrerin** *f* needlework teacher; **~arbeiter** *m* workman, manual labo(u)rer (*od* worker), mechanic; **~atlas** *m* school-atlas; **~auflegen** *n eccl* imposition of hand, laying on of hands; **~ausgabe** *f* pocket-edition; **~ball** *m* (*Spiel*) handball, *Am* fieldball; **~ballen** *m* ball of the thumb, eminence of the hand, *anat* thenar; **~becken** *n* (wash-)hand basin; **~beil** *n* hatchet; **~betrieb** *m* manual operation; **~bewegung** *f* motion, gesticulation; **~bibliothek, ~bücherei** *f* reference library, collection of reference works; **~bohrer** *m* gimlet; **~bohrmaschine** *f* hand-drill; hand-brace; **~breit** *a* of a hand's breadth; **~breite** *f* handbreadth; **~bremse** *f mot* handbrake, emergency brake; **~bremshebel** *m* handbrake lever; **~buch** *n* manual, handbook; book of referenc ; (*Reise*~~) guide; **~druck** *m* block printing, hand printing; **~eisen** *n* handcuff; **~exemplar** *n* copy for o.'s private use, copy in use; **~fallschirm** *m* manually operated parachute; **~fertigkeit** *f* manual skill; (*Geschick*) dexterity; **~fessel** *f* handcuff(s *meist pl*); ~~*n anlegen* to handcuff, to manacle, to put handcuffs on; **~fest** *a* strong, sturdy; robust, stout; **~feuerlöscher** *m* hand fire extinguisher; **~feuerwaffen** *f pl* small arms *pl*; **~fläche** *f* palm (of the hand); **~gashebel** *m mot* throttle lever; **~gebrauch** *m* general use; every-day (*od* daily) use; *zum* ~~ for daily use; **~geld** *n* handsel; earnest (money); (*Vorschuß*) advance; *mil* bounty; **~gelenk** *n* wrist; *etw aus dem* ~~ *erledigen* to do s. th. with o.'s little finger; *das* ~~ *verstauchen* to sprain o.'s wrist; **~gemein** *a* at close quarters; ~~ *werden* to come to blows; **~gemenge** *n* hand-to-hand fight, scuffle, skirmish, fray, *fam* set-to; **~gepäck** *n* small (*od* hand) luggage, *Am* small baggage, grip; *rail* (*Aufbewahrungsraum*) cloak-room, *Am* baggage room; **~gerecht** *a* handy; **~geschmiedet** *a* hand-forged; **~geschöpft** *a* (*Papier*) hand-made; **~gewoben** *a* handwoven; **~granate** *f* hand grenade; **~greiflich** *a* (*fühlbar*) palpable; (*offenbar*) evident, obvious, plain; downright; *ein* ~~*er Spaß* a practical joke; ~~ *werden* to use o.'s hands (*od* fists); ~~**keit** *f* act of violence, assault; **~griff** *m* (hand)grip; (*an Tür, Schirm etc*) handle, knob; (*Tätigkeit, Kniff*) manipulation, knack; *mil* manual exercise; **~habe** *f* handle, hold, grip; *fig* ways *pl*, means *pl*; **~haben** *tr* to handle, to manipulate, to operate; *fig* to manage, to deal with; ~**habung** *f* handling, manipulation, operation; application; ~**harmonika** *f* accordion; ~**hebel** *m* hand lever; ~**karren** *m* hand cart, wheel-barrow, *Am* handbarrow; ~**koffer** *m* suit-case, (travelling) bag, *Am* grip, valise; ~**koloriert** *a* hand-colo(u)red; ~**korb** *m* hand-basket; ~**kurbel** *f mot* starting crank; ~**kuß** *m* kissing s. o.'s hand; ~**lampe** *f* (small) electric portable lamp; inspection lamp; ~**langer** *m* handy-man, helper; jackal; *Am* hand; ~**lesekunst** *f* palmistry; ~**leuchter** *m* candle-stick; ~**lich** *a* handy, wieldy, manageable; ~**mühle** *f* hand-mill; ~**pferd** *n* led horse; pack horse, off-horse; ~**pflege** *f* manicuring; ~**presse** *f* small press; ~**rad** *n* handwheel; ~**ramme** *f* paving ram(mer), hand rammer; ~**reichung** *f* assistance, help; ~**rücken** *m* back of the hand; ~**säge** *f* pad-saw, hand-saw; ~**satz** *m typ* hand composition; ~**schaltung** *f mot* hand-gear control; ~**schelle** *f* handcuff, manacle; ~**schlag** *m* (*Begrüßung*) hand-shake; (*Schlag*) blow with the hand; (*Einschlagen*) offering of the hand; ~**schreiben** *n* confidential letter; autograph; ~**schrift** *f* handwriting, *Am auch* handwrite; (*Buch*) manuscript; (*Unterschrift*) signature; ~~**endeutung** *f* graphology; ~~**lich** *a* written, in writing; in black and white; in longhand; ~**schuh** *m* glove; (*Faust*~~) mitten; (*eiserner*) gauntlet; ~~**fach** *n* (*im Auto*) locker box, *Am* cubby-hole; ~~**leder** *n* glove-leather; ~~**macher** *m* glover; ~~**nummer** *f* glove-size, glove-number; ~**schutz** *m* hand guard; ~**setzer** *m typ* hand compositor; ~**siegel** *n* (private) seal, manual; signet; ~**spiegel** *m* hand-mirror, hand-glass; ~**stand** *m* (straight arm) hand-stand; ~**steuerung** *f* hand gear; ~**streich** *m* surprise (raid); sudden attack; ~**tasche** *f* (hand) bag, *Am* (grip) sack; ~~**ndieb** *m* bag-snatcher; ~**täschchen** *n* vanity bag; ~**teller** *m* palm (of the hand); ~**tuch** *n* towel; ~~**halter** *m* towel-rail (*od* horse *od* bar); ~**umdrehen** *n: im* ~~ in a turn of the hand, in a trice; in a jiffy, in no time; ~**verkauf** *m* retail; ~**voll** *f* handful; ~**wagen** *m* hand cart; ~**waschbecken** *n* hand basin; ~**werk** *n* trade handicraft, craft; *jdm das* ~~ *legen* to put s. o. out of business, *Am* to fix s. o. for good; *ein* ~~ *lernen* to learn a trade; *sein* ~~ *verstehen* to know o.'s business; ~~**er** *m* craftsman, artisan, workman; mechanic; ~~**sbursche** *m* tramp, *Am* hobo; (*früher*) travelling journeyman; ~~**sleute** *m pl* craftsmen *pl*; ~~**smann** *m* craftsman; ~~**smäßig** *a* workmanlike; mechanical; ~~**smeister** *m* master craftsman; ~~**szeug** *n* (small) tools *pl*, hand tools *pl*, implements *pl*; ~~**szunft** *f* corporation, guild; ~**wörterbuch** *n* middle-sized dictionary, pocket dictionary, handy (*od* abridged) dictionary; ~**wurzel** *f* wrist(joint), *anat* carpus; ~**zeichnung** *f* hand drawing, design, draught; (*Skizze*) sketch; ~**zettel** *m* handbill, *Am* dodger.

Händ|chen *n* small (*od* little) hand; ~**edruck** *m* shaking (*od* clasp) of the hands, shake-hands, hand-shake; ~**eklatschen** *n* clapping of hands; applause; ~**eringend** *a* wringing o.'s hands.

Händel *m pl* quarrel(s *pl*), brawl; ~ *suchen* to begin brawls, to pick a quarrel; ~**stifter** *m* breeder of strife; ~**süchtig** *a* quarrelsome.

Handel *m* trade (*mit* in, *nach* with); (*bes. Groß*~ *u. Handelsverkehr*) commerce, traffic; (*Geschäft*) bargain, business, transaction, dealing; (*Handelsmarkt*) market; *im* ~ on the market; *nicht mehr im* ~ (*Ware*) off the market; (*Tausch*~) barter, truck, *fam* swap; *fig* (*Angelegenheit, Geschichte*) affair, matter, business, bargain; (*Rechtssache*) law-suit; (*Streit*~, *Schlägerei, meist pl: Händel*) quarrel, brawl; *Außen*~ export trade; *Binnen*~ home trade, domestic trade; *Groß*~ wholesale trade; *Klein*~ retail trade; *Waren*~ goods trade; *den* ~ *betreffend, zum* ~ *gehörig* commercial; *ein ehrlicher* ~ a square transaction, *Am* a square deal; *ein guter* (*schlechter*) ~ a good (bad) bargain; ~ *u. Gewerbe* commerce and industry; ~ *u. Wandel* trade and traffic; *e-n* ~ *abschließen* to strike (*od* make *od* conclude) a bargain; *in den* ~ *bringen* to put on the market; *der* ~ *liegt darnieder* the trade is depressed; *in den* ~ *kommen* to be put on the market; ~ *treiben* to trade, to carry on trade, to do business (*mit jdm* with s. o.); to traffic; ~**bar** *a* sal(e)able; (*Börse*) negotiable; ~**n** *itr* (*etw tun*) to act, to do; to proceed; (*sich benehmen*) to behave; (*von etw* ~~, *zum Gegenstand haben, behandeln*) to treat of, to deal with, to be about; (~~ *an*) to treat; *sie hat an ihr wie an e-r Schwester gehandelt* she treated her like a sister; *als Bruder an jdm* ~~ to act as a brother to s. o.; (*feilschen*) to haggle, to chaffer, (*um den Preis*) to bargain, to negotiate; (*Handel treiben*) to trade, to buy and sell; to do (*od* transact) business; to traffic, to deal in; *fam* to swap; to market; *an der Börse gehandelt werden* to be quoted; *rechtswidrig* ~~ to act unlawfully; *imp: es handelt sich um* it is a question of ..., the question is ..., it is a matter of ..., it concerns ...; (*in Frage stehen*) to be at stake; *es handelt sich um Ihr Leben* your life is at stake; *worum handelt es sich?* what is the matter? *fam* what's up? what's about? *darum handelt es sich nicht* that is not the issue; ~**n** *n* action; (*Handel treiben*) trade, dealing; ~**nd** *a* acting, active, ~~*e Person theat* actor, character; ~**sabkommen** *n* trade (*od* commercial) agreement; ~*s- u. Zahlungsabkommen* trade and credit agreement; ~**sadreßbuch** *n* trade directory; ~**sakademie** *f* commercial academy, *Am* business school; ~**samt** *n* Board of Trade; ~**sartikel** *m* commodity, article of commerce; ~**sbank** *f* (*für kurzfristige Finanzierung*) commercial bank, (*Remboursbank*) merchant bank, *Am* investment banking house; ~**sbericht** *m* trade report; ~**sbeschränkung** *f* restriction of commerce, trade barrier (*od* curb); ~**sbevollmächtigte(r)** *m* proxy, authorized agent; ~**sbesprechungen** *f pl* commercial negotiations *pl*; ~**sbetrieb** *m* trading business; ~**sbezeichnung** *f* trade designation; ~**sbeziehungen** *f pl* commercial (*od* trade) relations *pl*; *neue* ~~ *anknüpfen* to open new markets; ~**sbilanz** *f* trade balance; ~**sblatt** *n* trade journal; ~**sbrauch** *m* usage; ~**sbrief** *m* commercial letter; ~**sdampfer** *m* merchantman, cargo steamer; ~**seinig** *a:* ~~ *werden* to come to terms; ~**serlaubnis** *f* trade licence (*Am* license); ~**sfirma** *f* trading firm; ~**sflotte** *f* merchant marine, merchant (*od* mercantile) fleet; ~**sfreiheit** *f* freedom of trade; ~**sgängig** *a* commercial, marketable; ~**sgärtnerei** *f* market-garden, *Am* truck-farm; ~**sgärtner** *m* market-gardener, *Am* truck-farmer, trucker; ~**sgeist** *m* commercial spirit; ~**sgenossenschaft** *f* co-operative commercial association; ~**sgericht** *n* commercial court; ~~*lich eintragen* to register legally, *Am* to incorporate; ~~*liche Eintragung* registration, *Am* incorporation; ~**sgesellschaft** *f* trading company, trading concern, joint-stock company, *Am* business corporation; (*offene* ~~) private firm, partnership; ~**sgesetzbuch** *n* commercial code; ~**sgewicht** *n* avoirdupois weight; ~**sgewinn** *m* trading profit; ~**shaus** *n* trading-house, business concern; ~**sherr** *m* principal; ~**shochschule** *f* commercial academy; university of commerce; ~**sindex** *m* business index; ~**skammer** *f* chamber of commerce, *Am* Board of Trade; ~**skorrespondenz** *f* commercial correspondence; ~**skredit** *m* business loan; ~**skrieg** *m* economic war; ~**skrise** *f* commercial crisis; ~**sluftfahrt** *f* air commerce, commercial air service, commercial aviation; ~**sluftfahrtslinie** *f* commercial air line; ~**smann** *m* trader, tradesman, merchant, retailer; (*pl:* ~*sleute* tradesmen *pl*); ~**smarine** *f* merchant (*od* mercantile) marine; ~**smarke** *f* trade-mark; ~**smesse** *f* trade-fair; ~**sminister** *m* Minister of Commerce; *Engl* President of the Board of Trade, *Am* Secretary of Commerce; ~**sministerium** *n* Ministry of Commerce, *Engl* Board of Trade, *Am* Department of Commerce; ~**sname** *m* (*Marke*) trade name; ~**sniederlassung** *f* trading station; ~**splatz** *m* commercial (*od* trading) town; ~**spolitik** *f* trade policy; ~**sprodukt** *n* commercial product; ~**squalität** *f* commercial quality (*od* grade); ~**srecht** *n* commercial law; ~**sregister** *n* commercial (*od* trade) register, register of companies, *Am* official register of trading associations; *im* ~~ *eintragen* to enter in the commercial register, to register, *Am* to incorporate; ~**sreisende(r)** *m* commercial travel(l)er, *Am* traveling salesman, drummer; ~**srichter** *m* commercial judge; ~**sschiff** *n* merchantman, trading vessel; ~**sschiffsraum** *m* merchant tonnage; ~**sschranken** *f pl* trade barriers *pl*; ~**sschule** *f* commercial school, *Am* business school; ~**sseehafen** *m* commercial (*od* trading) seaport; ~**ssorte** *f* market grade, commercial variety; ~**sspanne** *f* trade margin; ~**ssperre** *f* trade embargo; ~**sstadt** *f* commercial town, trading-town; ~**sstand** *m* trading class; ~**sstatistik** *f* commercial (*od* trade) statistics *pl*; ~**steil** *m* (*Zeitung*) trade section; ~**sstörer** *m mar, mil* surface raider; ~**süblich** *a* commercial, prevailing (*od* accepted) in the trade; customary in commerce (*od* trade); ~~*e Qualität* (*od Güte*) commercial grade (*od* quality); ~~*e Toleranz* commercial limit; ~~ *verpackt* packed as usual in trade; ~**sunternehmen** *n* commercial enterprise; ~**sverbindungen** *f pl* commercial relations *pl*, business connections *pl*; ~**sverkehr** *m* commercial intercourse, trading; ~**svertrag** *m* treaty of commerce, commercial treaty; trade agreement; ~**svertreter** *m* commercial (*od* mercantile) agent; ~**swaren** *f pl* commercial articles *pl*; ~**swechsel** *m* commercial bill; ~**sweg** *m* trade route; ~**swert** *m* commercial value; ~**szeichen** *n* trade-mark, trade name; ~**szentrum** *n* commercial centre (*Am* center); ~**szerstörer** *m mar, mil* surface raider; ~**szweig** *m* branch (of trade);

~treibend *a* trading, commercial; **~~e(r)** *m* trader, dealer.

Händler *m* dealer, trader, tradesman; merchant; (*Ladeninhaber*) shopkeeper, *Am* storekeeper; (*Börsen~*) stock jobber.

Handlung *f* (*Betätigung*) action, act; (*Tat*) deed; (*Geschehen im Roman*) story; (*im Drama*) plot; *film* scenario, theme; *Einheit der ~* unity of action; (*Geschäft*) trade, commerce, business; (*Handelshaus*) trading house, firm; business premises *pl*; (*Laden*) shop, *Am* store; *strafbare ~* punishable act, (criminal) offence; (*Verbrechen*) crime; **~sbevollmächtigte(r)** *m* commercial travel(l)er, representative, *Am* traveling salesman, commercial traveler; drummer; **~sfähig** *a* capable of acting; **~sfreiheit** *f* freedom of action; initiative; **~sgehilfe** *m* (*Kontorist*) merchant's clerk; (*Ladenverkäufer*) shop-assistant, *Am* clerk, retail salesman; **~svollmacht** *f* power of attorney; **~sweise, ~sart** *f* course of action, way of acting; method of dealing; procedure, practices *pl*.

hanebüchen *a* (*unerhört*) unheard of; (*absurd*) preposterous.

Hanf *m* hemp; **~acker** *m* hemp-field; **~bereiter** *m* hemp-dresser; **~breche** *f* hemp-brake; **~darre** *f* hemp-kiln; **~dichtung** *f* hemp-packing; **~einlage** *f* hemp-core; **~en** *a* hempen; **~garn** *n* hemp-yarn; **~öl** *n* hemp-oil; **~samen** *m* hemp-seed; **~seil** *n*, **~strick** *m*, **~tau** *n* manila rope, hemp(en) rope.

Hänfling *m* linnet.

Hang *m* declivity, slope; *fig* (*Neigung*) inclination (to), tendency (to); trend; partiality (for); bent, natural disposition; taste (for); propensity; *e-n ~ zu etw haben* to be inclined to; **~aufwind** *m* up-current, anabatic wind; **~bein** *n* swinging leg; **~en** *irr itr* to hang (*an* on, against); to be suspended; (*an jdm od etw*) to be fond of, to be attached to; (*haften, festhängen*) to cling to, to stick to, to adhere to; to catch; to stop, to be stopped; (*noch nicht entschieden*) to be in suspense; (*abhängen von*) to depend upon; *~~ bleiben* to be caught (*an* by, on); *~~ lassen* (*herabbaumeln*) to dangle, to droop; *an e-m Haar* (*od Faden*) *~~* to hang only by a thread; **~mulde** *f* depression on a slope; **~segelflug** *m*, **~segeln** *n aero* slope (*od* ridge *od* hill) soaring; **~start** *m aero* launching of a sailplane with the help of an elastic rope; **~stellung** *f mil* slope position; **~wind** *m aero* (*Aufwind*) anabatic wind, up-current; **~winkel** *m* gradient of slope.

Hangar *m aero* hangar, airplane shed.

Hänge|backe *f* flabby (*od* hanging) cheek; **~bahn** *f rail* suspension-railway (*od* tramway); aerial ropeway; overhead trolley; **~balken** *m arch* mean beam, trussing-piece; **~bank** *f min* mouth of a shaft; **~bauch** *m* paunch, potbelly, pendulous belly; **~boden** *m* hanging floor; loft; **~brücke** *f* suspension-bridge, chain-bridge; **~brust** *f* pendulous breast (*od* mama); **~bügel** *m* suspension link; **~gleiter** *m* hanging glider; **~lager** *n* hanger bearing; **~lampe** *f* hanging (*od* suspended) lamp; **~matte** *f* hammock; *mar* cot; **~motor** *m* inverted engine; **~n** *tr* (*Bilder etc aufhängen*) to hang, to suspend on; (*befestigen*) to fix, to attach; (*Verbrecher*) to hang; *~~ bleiben* to be caught by, to catch; *mot* (*von Ventilen*) to seize, to stick; *das Ventil blieb ~~* the valve sticked open; *~~ lassen* to let drop, to droop; *die Flügel* (*od Fittiche*) *~~ lassen fig* to be downcast (*od* dispirited); *Geld an etw ~~* to waste money on; *den Mantel nach dem Wind ~~* to sail with the wind; *an den Nagel ~~* to hang on a nail; *fig* (*aufgeben*) to give up; *sich ~~* to hang o. s.; *sich an jdn ~~* to be attached to s. o.; to stick to, to cling to; (*an etw*) to set o.'s heart on; *sich an die Strippe ~~ fam* (*telephonieren*) to phone; **~n** *n* hanging; suspension; **~nd** *a* hanging; pendent; suspended; *~~er Motor* inverted engine; *~~es Ventil* (*obengesteuert*) overhead (*od* inverted) valve; **~ohren** *n pl* drooping ears *pl*; **~schloß** *n* padlock; **~weide** *f bot* weeping willow.

Hans *m* (*Vorname*) Jack, John; *fig* fool; *~ Dampf* blusterer, windbag; Jack of all trades; *~ u. Grete* Jack and Gill; *Hänschen n dim* Jackie, Jack, Johnny; **~narr** *m* tomfool; blockhead; **~wurst** *m* buffoon; (*im Zirkus*) clown; (*auf dem Jahrmarkt*) Merry Andrew; **~wurststreich** *m* buffoonery, harlequinade.

Hans|a, Hanse *f* Hanse, Hanseatic League; **~eatisch** *a* Hanseatic; **~estadt** *f* Hanse(atic) town.

hänseln *tr* to chaff, to tease; *fam* to rib.

Hantel *f* dumb-bell.

hantier|en *itr* to manipulate, to handle, to operate; to carry on a business, to manage; **~ung** *f* manipulation, management; handling; (*Handel, Geschäft*) business; trade; employment.

hapern *itr* to be difficult (to manage); to stick; to be wrong, to be amiss; *es hapert mit etw* the affair is at a standstill; there is s. th. wrong; *woran hapert es?* what is amiss?

Häppchen *n* bit, morsel; **Happen** *m* mouthful, morsel, piece; a bite to eat.

Här|chen *n* little hair; **~en** *a* hairy; *sich ~en* to shed the hair.

Hardyscheibe *f mot* dry disk joint, flexible disk.

Häre|sie *f* (*Ketzerei*) heresy; **~tiker** *m* heretic; **~tisch** *a* heretical.

Harfe *f* harp; *~ spielen* to play (on) the harp; **~nantenne** *f* harp antenna, fan antenna; **~nist, Harfner** *m* harper, harpist; **~nspiel** *n* harping.

Harke *f* rake; *jdm zeigen, was e-e ~ ist fig* to tell s. o. what is what; to give s. o. a piece of o.'s mind; **~n** *tr, itr* to rake.

Harlekin *m* harlequin, Jack Pudding; **~streich** *m* drollery.

Harm *m* (*Kummer*) grief, sorrow; (*Kränkung*) harm, insult, wrong; injury; **~los** *a* harmless, innocent; **~losigkeit** *f* harmlessness, innocence.

härmen *r* to grieve about; to worry about, to fret over.

Harmon|ie *f* harmony; (musical) concord; **~ielehre** *f* theory of harmony; **~ieren** *itr* to harmonize; *mit jdm ~~* to agree, to sympathize with s. o.; **~ika** *f* concertina, accordion; **~isch** *a* harmonic, harmonious; **~ium** *n* harmonium.

Harn *m* urine, water; **~(ab)fluß** *m* passing (*od* escape) of urine; (*unwillkürlicher ~~*) incontinence; **~beschwerden** *f pl* urinary troubles *pl*; **~blase** *f* (urinary) bladder; **~drang** *m* strangury; **~en** *itr* to urinate, to pass (*od* make) water, *med* to micturate; **~flasche** *f* urine bottle, urinal; **~gang, ~leiter** *m* ureter; **~glas** *n* urinal; **~grieß** *m* gravel, grit; **~lassen** *n* urination, *med* micturition; **~probe** *f* test for urine; **~röhre** *f* urinary passage, urethra; **~röhrentripper** *m* gonorrhea, gonorrhœa; **~ruhr** *f* diabetes; **~säure** *f* uric acid; **~stoff** *m* urea; **~treibend** *a* diuretic; **~trübung** *f* cloudiness of urine; **~untersuchung** *f* urinary test; examination of urine; **~zwang** *m* strangury.

Harnisch *m* harness, armo(u)r; cuirass; *in ~ geraten* to fly into a passion (*od* rage); *in ~ treiben* to put s. o. into a passion.

Harpun|e *f* harpoon; **~ieren** *tr* to harpoon.

harren *itr* to stay, to await, to wait for; (*hoffen*) to hope for; *~ n* waiting, staying, hope; (*Ausharren*) perseverance.

harsch *a* harsh, stiff, rough; hard; **~schnee** *m* crusted snow.

hart *a* hard; (*fest*) firm; solid; (*gefühllos*) ruthless; (*grausam*) cruel; (*rauh*) rough, harsh; (*streng*) severe; (*schwer*) difficult; *~ an* (*dicht bei*) hard by, close to; *~ am Wege* close to the way; *~ am Wind mar* near the wind; *~ auf ~* it is touch and go; *~ wie ...* as hard as ...; *~es Bild* high-contrast (*od* hard) picture; *~e Eier* hard (-boiled) eggs; *~e Entbehrungen* hard privations; *~es Geld* coins *pl*; hard cash; *~es Holz* firm wood; *ein ~er Kampf* a fierce fight; *e-n ~en Kopf haben* to be stubborn; *~e Landung aero* heavy landing; *ein ~es Los* a hard lot; *jdm e-e ~e Nuß zum Knacken geben* to give s. o. a bone to pick (*od* a hard nut to crack); *ein ~es Schicksal* a cruel fate; *e-n ~en Stand haben* to have a difficult position; *e-e ~e Strafe* a severe punishment; *~es Wasser* hard water; *~e Worte* harsh words *pl*; *~e Züge* (*im Gesicht*) stern features *pl*; *~e Zeiten* hard times *pl*; *es kommt ihn ~ an* he finds it hard; *~ anzufühlen* hard to the touch; *~ arbeiten* to labo(u)r hard, to drudge, to grub; *jdn ~ bedrängen* to press s. o. hard; *~ bedrängt* hard beset; *es wird ~ halten zu ...* it will be no easy matter to ...; *~ machen* to harden, to solidify, to stiffen; *~ werden* to harden, to grow hard; **~blei** *n* hard lead; **~faserplatte** *f* hard board, *Am* molded fiber board; **~futter** *n* oats and grain; **~gefroren** *a* hard frozen; **~gekocht** *a* hard-boiled; **~geld** *n* hard cash, coins *pl*, coined money; **~gelötet** *a* hard-soldered; **~gesotten** *a fig* hardened, inflexible, hard-boiled; **~glas** *n* hard(ened) glass, tempered glass, pyrex (glass); **~gummi** *m* hard rubber; vulcanite, ebonite; **~~gehäuse** *n* hard-rubber case; **~guß** *m* chilled work (*od* casting); **~harz** *n* hardened resin; **~herzig** *a* hard-hearted, hard-boiled; **~herzigkeit** *f* hardheartedness; **~holz** *n* hardwood; **~hörig** *a* dull (*od* hard) of hearing; rather deaf; **~hörigkeit** *f* partial deafness; **~köpfig** *a* headstrong, obstinate; **~leibig** *a* constipated, costive; **~leibigkeit** *f* constipation, costiveness; **~löten** *tr* to braze, to hard-solder; **~mäulig** *a* hard-mouthed; **~metall** *n* hard-metal, hard-pewter; **~näckig** *a* stiff-necked, stubborn, obstinate; (*Krankheit*) chronic; **~näckigkeit** *f* pertinacity, stubbornness; **~post** *f* typewriting paper; **~spiritus** *m* solid alcohol (*od* spirit), *Am* canned fuel.

Härt|e *f* hardness; (*des Gemütes*) roughness, rudeness, cruelty; (*Farbe*) dryness; (*des Schicksals*) severity, hardness; (*e-r Maßnahme*) hardship; (*Strenge*) severity; **~ebad** *n* tempering bath; **~egrad** *m* degree of hardness; (*des Stahls*) temper; **~emittel** *n* hardening agent; **~en** *tr* (*sich*) to harden; to grow hard; (*Eisen*) to caseharden; (*Stahl*) to temper; **~eofen** *m* hardening furnace (*od* stove); **~everfahren** *n* hardening (*od* tempering) process; **~ewert** *m* hardness number; **~ung** *f* hardening, tempering; *Einsatz~~* casehardening; **~~smittel** *n* hardening agent; **~~sverfahren** *n* hardening process; **~~svermögen** *n* hardening capacity.

Harz *n* resin; (*Geigen~*) rosin; **~baum** *m* pinetree; **~en** *tr* to clear from resin, to rub with resin; **~ig** *a* resinous.

Hasardspiel *n* game of hazard (*od* chance), gambling; **~er** *m* gambler.

Hasch|ee *n* (*Hackfleisch*) hash; **~ieren** *tr* to hash.

haschen *tr* to catch, to seize; to snatch s. th.; *itr* (*nach etw* ~) to snatch at s. th.; *fig* to aspire to, to strive for, to aim at; *nach Effekt* ~ to aim at effect; *theat* to play to the gallery, *Am fam* to grandstand; *nach Neuigkeiten* ~ to run after news; *sich* ~ to play at catching.

Häscher *m* bailiff; constable, policeman; catch-pole, myrmidon; guard.

Hase *m* hare, *Am meist* rabbit; *fig* coward; *falscher* ~ meat roll; *e-m ~n das Fell abziehen* to skin a hare; *sehen wie der ~ läuft* to see how the cat jumps; *da liegt der ~ im Pfeffer* that's where the rub comes in; **~nbraten** *m* roast hare; **~nfuß** *m*, **~nherz** *n fig* coward; poltroon; **~jagd** *f* hare-hunting, hare-shooting; **~nklein** *n*, **~npfeffer** *m*, **~nragout** *n* jugged hare, hare-ragout; **~npanier** *n*: *das ~~ ergreifen* to take to o.'s heels; **~nscharte** *f* hare-lip.

Hasel|busch *m* hazel-bush; **~huhn** *n* hazel-hen; **~maus** *f* dormouse; **~nuß** *f* hazel-nut; **~rute** *f* hazel-rod; **~strauch** *m* hazel-tree.

Häsin *f* female hare.

Haspe *f* hasp, hinge; staple; clamp.

Haspel *m od f* (*Garn*) reel; (*Winde*) windlass; (*auf Schiffen*) capstan; winch; **~n** *tr* to reel; *fam* to prattle.

Haß *m* hatred (*gegen jdn* against, to, towards, for s.o.); *poet* hate; (*Erbitterung*) animosity; (*Groll*) grudge; (*Zorn, Verachtung*) spite; (*Feindschaft*) enmity; *aus* ~ out of hatred of, out of spite against; ~ *empfinden gegen* to hate s. o.; *seinen ~ an jdm auslassen* to vent o.'s spite upon s. o.; **~erfüllt** *a* filled with hatred.

hassen *tr* to hate (for); to detest; **~swert** *a* hateful, odious.

häßlich *a* ugly, nasty, hideous, *Am auch* homely; (*Charakter*) wicked, villainous; (*Figur*) deformed; (*Gesicht*) ill-featured; ~ *wie die Nacht* as ugly as sin; **~keit** *f* ugliness; badness.

Hast *f* hurry, haste; precipitation; *in großer* ~ in great haste; **~en** *itr* (*sich*) to hasten; (*eilen*) to hurry, *Am* to hustle; **~ig** *a* hasty, hurried; (*übereilig*) precipitate; *fig* (*Charakter*) fiery, hot-tempered; **~igkeit** *f* hastiness, precipitation.

hätscheln *tr* to fondle, to pamper, to caress; to coddle; to pet.

Hatz *f* hunt, chase.

Hau *m* blow, cut; (*Holzschlag*) place where wood is being felled, felling; **~degen** *m* (*Waffe*) broadsword; (*tapferer Soldat*) brave soldier; warrior; **~e** *f* (*Hacke*) hoe; mattock; pick; *pl fam* (*Hiebe, Prügel*) thrashing, spanking, blows *pl*; *~~ kriegen* to come in for a flogging, to get a good hiding; **~en** *irr tr* (*Bäume*) to hew, to chop, to cut (down); (*fällen*) to fell; (*schlagen*) to strike, to hit; (*prügeln*) to thrash, to spank; (*peitschen*) to whip, to lash; (*ausmeißeln aus Stein, Holz etc*) to carve; *sich ~~* to fight; *um sich ~~* to lay about one; *nach jdm ~~* to strike at; *jdn übers Ohr ~~ fig* to cheat s. o., to take s. o. in, *fam* to gyp s. o.; *über die Schnur ~~* to kick over the traces; *in Stücke ~~* to cut to pieces; **~er** *m* (*Eberzahn*) fang, tusk; **~er** *m*, **Häuer** *m* (*Bergwerk*) hewer, cutter, getter, pick-man; **~klotz** *m* chopping block.

Häubchen *n* little cap.

Haube *f* cap, hood; *hist* coif; (*Schwestern~*) cornet; (*Motor~*) bonnet, *Am* hood, *aero* cowling; (*Propeller~*) airscrew (*Am* propeller) spinner; (*Vogel*) crest, tuft; *arch* dome; *unter die ~ bringen* to marry off; *unter die ~ kommen* to marry, to get married; **~nband** *n* cap-ribbon; **~nente** *f orn* tufted duck; **~nlerche** *f orn* crested lark; **~nstock** *m* milliner's block; **~ntaucher** *m orn* crested diver; **~nverkleidung** *f aero* engine cowling; **~nverschluß** *m mot* bonnet catch, *Am* hood catcher.

Haubitze *f* howitzer.

Hauch *m* breath; (*Atem*) breathing; (*Ausströmen*) exhalation; (*Luft~*) breeze; whiff; puff; (*kalter*) blast; *fig* (*Spur*) trace, touch; (*e-r Farbe*) tinge; *gram* aspiration; **~dünn** *a* filmy; **~en** *itr* to breathe; (*ausströmen*) to exhale; (*blasen*) to blow; *tr* (*ausströmen*) to exhale; (*Duft, Parfüm*) to emit, to spread; (*leise sprechen*) to whisper softly; *gram* to aspirate; **~laut** *m* aspirate; **~zart** *a* filmy, flimsy; delicate.

Haufe, ~n *m* heap; (*gleichmäßig*) pile; (*Zahl*) quantity, great number; (*Menschenmenge*) crowd; (*Masse*) mass; (*Partie, Satz, Menge*) batch; (*Menge, Gesellschaft*) bunch; (*Aufhäufung, Ansammlung*) aggregation, accumulation; *in losen ~n* in bulk; *ein ~n Arbeit* a lot of work; *der große ~, der gemeine ~* the rabble, the multitude, the mob; *über den ~n werfen* to overturn, to upset, to throw aside; to overthrow; **~nweise** *adv* in (*od* by) heaps; in crowds; **~nwolke** *f* cumulus cloud; (*geschichtete ~~*) stratocumulus cloud; **~nwolkenartig** *a* cumuliform; **~nwurf** *m aero* salvo of bombs.

häuf|eln *tr* to form into small heaps, to heap; to earth, to hill (potatoes); **~en** *tr* to heap, to pile up, to accumulate; *sich ~~* to increase; to multiply; to accumulate; **~ig** *a* frequent; (*wiederholt*) repeated; (*in großer Zahl*) numerous; (*reichlich*) abundant; (*üblich*) usual; *adv* often; frequently; **~igkeit** *f* frequency; **~~sfaktor** *m* frequency factor; **~~sverhältnis** *n* abundance ratio; **~lein** *n* small heap; small number; **~ung** *f* heaping; accumulation.

Haupt *n* head; (*Ober~, Führender*) chief, leader; (*im Geschäft*) principal, *Am* boss; (*Stammeshäuptling*) chieftain; *als pref Haupt ...* chief, main, principal, primary, master, *anat* cephalic; *das ~ abschlagen* (*enthaupten*) to behead; *das ~ entblößen* to uncover o.'s head, to take off o.'s hat; *mit entblößtem ~* bare-headed; *aufs ~ schlagen* to rout, to defeat totally; *zu Häupten* at the head of; *gekrönte Häupter* crowned heads; **~absatzgebiet** *n* principal market; **~abschnitt** *m* principal section, chief paragraph; (*Zeit*) most important period; **~absicht** *f* chief design, main object; **~abstimmknopf** *m* main tuning button; **~abteilung** *f* main department; **~achse** *f* main axis; **~aktionär** *m* principal shareholder; **~altar** *m* high altar; **~amt** *n tele* main exchange, *Am* master office; **~amtlich** *a* (*tätig*) (employed) on a full-time basis; **~angriff** *m* main attack, main effort; **~anschluß** *m* main telephone station; **~armee** *f* main army; gross of the army; **~artikel** *m* principal (*od* leading) article; (*Presse*) leader; **~aufgabe** *f* main (*od* chief) task; **~augenmerk** *n* chief aim (*od* attention); *sein ~~ auf etw richten* to direct o.'s special attention to; **~ausgaben** *f pl* principal expenditures *pl*, major expenses *pl*; **~bahn** *f rail* main line, *Am* trunk line; **~bahnhof** *m* central station, main station, (railway-) terminus, *Am* terminal; main railroad station; **~balken** *m* girder, dormant-tree; **~bedeutung** *f* chief importance; **~bedingung** *f* principal condition (*od* requirement); **~begriff** *m* leading idea; **~bedürfnis** *n* chief requirement; **~beobachtungsraum** *m* main observation sector; **~beobachtungsstelle** *f* main observation post; **~beruf** *m* chief occupation; **~bestandteil** *m* chief constituent, principal ingredient; **~beweggrund** *m* leading motive; **~bibliothek** *f* main library; **~~ar** *m* chief librarian; **~blatt** *n* first leaf; **~blickpunkt** *m* principal point of regard; **~blickrichtung** *f* principal line of sight; **~brennpunkt** *m* principal focus; **~buch** *n com* ledger; *das ~~ abschließen* to balance the ledger; **~darsteller** *m theat* topliner, *Am* headliner; **~deck** *n* main deck; **~durchfahrtsstraße** *f* principal thoroughfare, *Am* thru highway; **~eigenschaft** *f* principal quality; **~einbruchsstelle** *f* main point of penetration; **~einfahrt** *f*, **~eingang** *m* main entrance; **~einflugzeichen** *n aero* (*Flugplatz*) inner marker beacon; **~einfuhr** *f* bulk of imports; **~einkommensquelle** *f* principal source of revenue; **~einwand** *m* chief objection; **~erbe** *m* chief heir; *jur* residuary legatee; **~erfordernis** *n* prime (*od* chief) requisite; primary requirement; **~fach** *n* principal subject, chief division; chief line, specialty; (*in der Schule*) *Am* major; *Geschichte als ~~ wählen Am* to major in history, to take history as o.'s major; **~farbe** *f* primary colo(u)r; **~feder** *f* master spring; **~fehler** *m* chief fault; main defect; **~feind** *m* chief enemy; **~feldwebel** *m* sergeant major, *Am* first sergeant; **~feuer** *n aero* principal airway beacon; **~figur** *f* most important figure; **~film** *m* feature film; (*e-s Filmprogramms*) super; **~fluglinie** *f* main line, trunk route; **~fluß** *m* main stream; **~frage** *f* chief (*od* main) question; **~funkfeuer** *n aero radio* main airway radio beacon; **~funkstelle** *f* main wireless station; **~gasleitung** *f* gas main; **~gebäude** *n* main building; **~gedanke** *m* leading idea; **~gericht** *n* (*Essen*) principal dish; **~geschäft** *n* head office, chief house; **~~sführer** *m* chief manager; **~~sstunden** *f pl*, **~~szeit** *f* rush hours *pl*; **~~sviertel** *n* central shopping district, *Am* shopping center; **~gewinn** *m* first prize; (*Vorteil*) main profit; **~grund** *m* principal reason; **~haar** *n* hair of the head; **~hahn** *m* (*Gas, Wasser*) main tap, main cock; **~handelsartikel** *m com* staple; **~inhalt** *m* general contents *pl*; substance; summary; **~kampffeld** *n* main defensive area; **~kampflinie** *f* main battle (*od* defence) line, main fighting line; main line of resistance (*Abk* MLR); **~kasse** *f* central pay office; **~kerl** *m* capital fellow; **~kirche** *f* cathedral; (*der Lehre nach*) mother-church; **~knotenpunkt** *m rail* main junction; **~kräfte** *f pl* main forces *pl*; **~ladung** *f mil* detonator charge; (*Rakete*) primary propelling charge; **~lager** *n* main bearing; **~lehrer** *m* head-master (*od* -teacher); **~leitung** *f el* mains *pl*; (*Gas, Abwasser, Wasser etc*) main pipe, principal pipe (*od* channel for water, gas, sewage etc); **~lesesaal** *m* (*Bibliothek*) main reading room; **~linie** *f* principal line; axis; *rail* main line, *Am* trunk line; **~macht** *f* chief power; *mil* main body, main force; **~mahlzeit** *f* dinner; **~mangel** *m* chief defect; **~mann** *m mil* captain; *aero mil* flight lieutenant; **~masse** *f* bulk, gross, principal mass; *mil* main body; **~mast** *m mar* mainmast; **~menge** *f* bulk; **~merkmal** *n* chief characteristic, characteristic feature; criterion; distinctive (*od* leading) feature; **~messe** *f* great mass; **~mieter** *m* chief tenant (*od* lodger); **~mittel** *n* principal remedy; **~moment** *n* main point; **~nachschubstelle** *f mil* main base of supply; **~nahrungsmittel** *n* chief nutriment (*od* food); staple food; **~nenner** *m math* common denominator; **~nervensystem** *n* central nervous system; **~niederlage** *f com* principal place of business, general (*od* main) office; **~ort** *m* chief place; **~person** *f* principal person, head; (*in der Aktivität*) prime mover; (*theat, Roman etc*) leading (*od* chief) character, hero; *~~ sein* (*fam*) to play the first fiddle; **~post** *f*, **~postamt** *n* General (*Am* Main) Post Office; **~posten** *m* principal item; **~probe** *f theat* dress (*od* full) rehearsal; **~problem** *n* master issue; **~punkt** *m* principal (*od* chief) point; *fig* gist, centre; **~quartier** *n* headquarters *pl* (*Abk* H. Q.); **~quelle** *f* chief source; **~regel** *f* leading rule, general rule; **~richtung** *f* primary course; **~~spunkt** *m* base point, primary aiming point; **~rohr** *n* main (pipe); **~rolle** *f* lead; leading role, star role; *weibliche ~~* feminine lead; leading part (*od* character); *Schauspieler in der ~~* star, *Am auch* headliner; *wer spielt die ~~* (*theat*) who is playing the lead; *die ~~ spielen* to star; (*zus. mit e-m anderen Schauspieler*) to co-star; *film* to feature; *in der ~~ zeigen* to star; *das Stück zeigt Herrn X. in der ~~* the show is starring Mr. X.; **~rollendarsteller** *m* principal performer, star performer; **~sache** *f* great (*od* main) point; chief matter; merits *pl*; gist; main part (*od* thing), most important thing; *das ist die ~~* that's all that matters; *in der ~~* chiefly, mainly, on the whole; *der ~~ nach* in substance; **~sächlich** *a* principal, chief, main, essential; *adv* mainly, in the main, especially; **~saison** *f* peak season; **~satz** *m* main position; axiom, fundamental principle; law; theorem; *gram* principal sentence (*od* clause); *mus* principal theme; **~säule** *f* main column; **~schacht** *m* main shaft; **~schalter** *m el* main switch, line switch; **~schalttafel** *f* main switchboard; **~schlacht** *f* main battle, decisive battle; **~schlagader** *f* aorta; **~schlager** *m* (*e-s Tonfilms etc*) theme-song; **~schlüssel** *m* master-key; **~schriftleiter** *m* chief editor, *Am* city editor; **~schuld** *f* principal fault; **~schuldige(r)** *m jur* principal; major (*od* chief) offender; **~schuldner** *m* principal debtor; **~schutzzone** *f aero* (*Jagdabwehr*) fighter defence area; **~schwierigkeit** *f* main difficulty; **~sender** *m radio* main transmitter; **~sicherung** *f el* main fuse, main cutout; **~signal** *n rail* main (*od* home) signal; *aero* main marker; **~sitz** *m* registered office; head office, principal place of business; **~spaß** *m* capital joke; **~stadt** *f* capital; metropolis; **~städtisch** *a* metropolitan; **~stellung** *f* main position; **~steueramt** *n* general tax office; **~straße** *f* (*in der Stadt*) principal street, *Am* main street; (*Fernverkehr*) main road; arterial road, high road; **~strecke** *f* main line, *Am* trunk line; **~strom** *m* main current; **~~kreis** *m* main circuit; **~stück** *n* principal piece; *eccl* article (of faith), chapter; **~stütze** *f* main support, mainstay; **~stützpunkt** *m* main base; **~summe** *f* sum total; **~tank** *m mot* main fuel tank; **~täter** *m jur* principal (offender); **~tätigkeit** *f* principal duty; **~teil** *m* body, main part; **~titel** *m typ* full title; **~ton** *m gram* principal accent; main stress; *mus* (*auch fig*) keynote; **~träger** *m arch* main girder; *aero* longeron; **~treffen** *n* general fight; **~treffer** *m* (*Lotterie*) first prize, big prize; **~triebfeder** *f* (*auch fig*) mainspring; **~trupp** *m* main force; **~tugend** *f* cardinal virtue; **~tür** *f* main door; **~uhr** *f* (*bei el Uhrennetz*) master clock (*od* watch); **~umstand** *m* leading circumstance; **~unterschied** *m* chief (*od* main) difference; **~ursache** *f* chief cause, principle reason; **~verbandplatz** *m mil* main dressing station; **~verbrechen** *n* capital crime; **~verhandlung** *f jur* (main) trial; hearing; **~verkehrslinie** *f* main line, *Am* trunk line; **~verkehrsstraße** *f* thoroughfare, major (*od* main) road, arterial road; main trunk line; **~verkehrszeit** *f*, **~verkehrsstunden** *f pl* rush hour(s *pl*), crowded hours *pl*; busy hour (*od* period); **~vermittlung** *f* main exchange; **~versammlung** *f* general meeting; **~verteiler** *m* main distributor; **~vertreter** *m* general agent; **~verwaltung** *f* main administration; **~vorkommen** *n* principal occurrence; **~vormarschstraße** *f mil* main road of advance; **~wache** *f* main guard; **~wachtmeister** *m* sergeant-major; master sergeant; **~wasserleitungsrohr** *n* main (pipe); **~welle** *f mot* main shaft; **~wert** *m* chief value; **~widerstandsstellung** *f* main line of resistance; **~windrichtung** *f* prevailing direction of wind; **~wirbel** *m anat* atlas; **~wirkung** *f* chief action (*od* effect); **~wort** *n gram* noun, substantive; **~zahl** *f* cardinal number; **~zeile** *f* (*Schlagzeile*) catch-line, headline; **~zelle** *f* (*Gewebe*) mother cell; **~zeuge** *m* principal witness; **~ziel** *n* primary target; **~zollamt** *n* principal custom-house; **~zug** *m* (*Charakter etc*) chief trait, principal feature; *rail* principal train; **~zuleitung** *f* main inlet; **~zweck** *m* main end, principal aim (*od* object); **~zweig** *m* main branch.

Haus *n* house; (*Herrschafts~*) mansion; (*Herren~ e-s Gutes*) manor; (*Gebäude*) building; (*mit Nebengebäuden*) premises *pl*; (*Wohnung*) habitation, dwelling; (*Wohnsitz*) residence, abode, domicile; (*Heim*) home; (*Familie*) family; (*Fürsten~*) dynasty; (*Hausgemeinschaft, Hausbewohner*) house; (*Haushaltung*) household; (*Geschäfts~*) house, (business) firm, concern; establishment; *parl* (*Beratungshaus, Volksvertretung*) house, *z. B.* the Houses of Parliament, (*Unterhaus*) Lower House, House of Commons; (*Oberhaus*) House of Lords; *Am* (*Volksvertretung, Unterhaus*) House of Representatives; *ein beschlußfähiges ~ bilden parl* to constitute a house; *das ~ ist nicht beschlußfähig! parl* no house! *~* (*bei Namen, z. B. Chile-~*) house, *Am* building; (*Theater*) house, theatre, *Am* theater; (*Zuschauer, Publikum im Theater etc*) audience; *ein volles ~* (*theat*) a full house; *das ~ zu stürmischem Beifall hinreißen theat* to bring down the house; *alleinstehendes ~* detached house; *altes ~* (*fam*) old boy; *fideles ~* jolly fellow; *frei ~* free to the door; *ein offenes ~ haben* to keep open house; *öffentliches ~* public house, house of ill fame, brothel; *~ an ~ mit jdm wohnen* to live next door to s. o.; *aus gutem ~e* of a good family; *jdn aus dem ~ jagen* to turn s. o. out of doors; *außer dem ~e* out of doors; *außer dem ~ essen* to dine out; *in ein ~ einziehen* to move into a house; *jdn ins ~ nehmen* to give house-room to s. o.; *mit der Tür ins ~ fallen fig* to blunder out; *nach ~e* home, homeward; *jdn nach ~e bringen* to see s. o. home; *von ~e aus* originally, from the beginning; natively, by nature; *von ~e* from home; *von ~ zu ~* house-to-house; *von ~ zu ~ gehen* to go from door to door; *zu ~e* at home, in; *zu ~e bleiben* to remain at home, *Am* to remain home; *ist Herr X. zu ~e?* is Mr. X. in? *nicht zu ~e sein* not to be in; *in e-r Sache zu ~e sein* to be quite at home in, to be familiar with; *tun Sie, als ob Sie zu ~e wären* make yourself at home, *Am* make yourself right at home; *das ~ bestellen* to put (*od* set) o.'s house in order; *ein großes ~ führen* to live in great style; *das ~ hüten* to be confined to the house, to keep the house; *jdm das ~ verbieten* to forbid s. o. to enter o.'s house; **~andacht** *f* family devotion (*od* prayers *pl*); **~angestellte** *f*, **~~(r)** *m* (domestic) servant, *Am* houseworker; **~anschluß** *m tele* (*Wohnung*) residence telephone; service line; **~apotheke** *f* family medecine-chest, *Am* first-aid kit; **~arbeit** *f* house-work, indoor work, *Am* (home) chores *pl*; (*Schule*) home work, home lesson; **~arrest** *m* confinement at o.'s house (*od* indoors); *jdn unter ~~ stellen* to put s. o. under house arrest; **~arzt** *m* family doctor; **~arznei** *f* domestic remedy; **~aufgabe** *f* (*Schule*) home-work; **~backen** *a* home-baked, home-made; *fig* plain, prosaic; **~ball** *m* carpet-dance; **~bau** *m* building of a house, *Am* (*Eigenheim*) home construction; **~bedarf** *m* household necessaries *pl*; **~besitzer** *m* house-owner, (*Vermieter*) landlord; **~~in** *f* landlady, house-owner; **~bewohner** *m* inmate; (*Mieter*) lodger, tenant; **~bibliothek** *f* private library; **~boot** *n* house-boat; **~brand** *m* domestic fuel, house coal; **~dach** *n* housetop; **~dame** *f* lady housekeeper; **~diener**, **~bursche** *m* footboy, porter; valet; **~drache** *m* (*böses Weib*) shrew, vixen, scold, termagant, *Am sl* battle-axe; **~eigentümer** *m* owner of a house; **~einfahrt** *f* gateway; **~einweihung** *f* (*Fest*) house-warming; **~en** *itr* to reside, to live, to dwell; (*sparsam*) to live economically; (*übel ~~*) to ravage (everything), to behave badly, to ransack, to play havoc; **~flur** *m* (entrance-)hall, corridor, vestibule, *Am* hallway; **~frau** *f* housewife; lady of the house, mistress; (*Hauswirtin*) landlady; **~~lich** *a* housewifely; **~freund** *m* family friend; **~friede** *m* domestic peace (and security); **~friedensbruch** *m* act of disturbing the domestic peace; unlawful entering another o.'s residence; **~gebrauch** *m* domestic use; **~genosse** *m* inmate, fellow-lodger, house-mate; member of the household; **~gerät** *n* household furniture (*od* utensils *pl*), *Am* house-stuff; **~gespenst** *n* ghost haunting a house; **~gesinde** *n* (domestic) servants *pl*; **~götter** *m pl* household gods *pl*, the Lares and Penates *pl*; **~hahn** *m* (domestic) cock, *Am* rooster; **~halt** *m* housekeeping, household; budget; *den ~~ führen* to run a home; to keep house (*für jdn* for); **~haltartikel** *m pl*, **~haltgeräte** *n pl* household goods *pl* (*od* appliances *pl*); **~halten** *irr itr* to keep house, *Am* to housekeep; (*sparsam*) to husband, to economize, to be economical; *mit seinen Kräften nicht ~~ fig* to burn o.'s candle at both ends; **~hälterin** *f* housekeeper, manager; **~hälterisch** *a* economical; frugal; **~haltsausschuß** *m parl* Committee of Supply; Budget Committee; **~haltsgeld** *n* house-keeping money; **~haltsjahr** *n* fiscal (*od* financial) year; **~haltsplan** *m* budget; *e-n ~~ aufstellen* to budget; **~haltsseife** *f* household soap; **~haltsvoranschlag** *m* estimates *pl*; **~haltswaren** *f pl* household equipment, *Am* domestics *pl*; **~haltung** *f* house-keeping, household; **~haltungsbuch** *n* book of household-expenses *pl*; **~haltungsführung** *f* household management; **~haltungskosten** *pl* household-expenses *pl*; **~haltungsvorstand** *m* head of the household; **~herr** *m* (*Gastgeber*) host, master; (*Hauswirt*) landlord; **~hoch** *a* as high as a house; huge; enormous; *~~ schlagen* to smash utterly, *Am* to blank; **~hofmeister** *m* steward; **~hund** *m* house-dog; **~ieren** *itr* to hawk (about), to peddle (from house to house); to go about peddling; *betteln u. ~~ verboten!* No begging or peddling! **~ierer** *m* hawker, pedlar; **~ierschein** *m* hawker's licence; **~installation** *f el* wiring; (*Gas u. Wasser*) plumbing; **~jacke** *f* house jacket; **~käufer** *m Am* home buyer; **~kleid** *n* house- (*od* home-)dress, undress; dishabille, negligee, morning dress; **~klingel** *f* house bell; **~knecht** *m* (*Gasthof*) boots *pl* mit sing, hostler; (*in e-m Geschäftshaus*) porter; **~kreuz** *n* domestic affliction; *fam* (*böses Weib*) shrew; **~lauch** *m* house-leek; **~lehrer** *m* private tutor; **~lehrerin** *f* governess; **~leinwand** *f* homespun linen; **~macht** *f* dynastic power; **~mädchen** *n*, **~magd** *f* housemaid, maid of all work; **~mannskost** *f* plain fare; commons *pl*; **~meister** *m* (*Mietshaus*) caretaker, porter, *Am* janitor, superintendent; **~miete** *f* house-rent; **~mittel** *n med* household medicine (*od* remedy); **~musik** *f* domestic music; **~mutter** *f* mother of a family; matron; **~mütterlich** *a* motherly; **~nummer** *f* (street) number; **~ordnung** *f* rule of the house; **~pflanze** *f* house plant; **~rat** *m* household stuff (*od* furniture *od* effects *pl*); **~recht** *n* domestic authority; **~rock** *m* house coat; **~sammlung** *f* house collection; **~schere** *f* manicure scissors *pl* (*auch sing*); **~schlachtung** *f* home slaughtering; **~schlüssel** *m* street-door key, latch-key; **~schuh** *m* house shoe, slipper: **~schwalbe** *f* house martin; **~schwamm** *m* dry rot; **~stand** *m* household; *e-n eigenen ~~ gründen* to set up for o. s.; **~suchung** *f* domiciliary visit (by police), raid, house(-to-house) search, *Am* house check; **~suchungsbefehl** *m* search-warrant; **~telephon** *n* private telephone, interphone; telephone extension; **~tier** *n* domestic animal, *Am* (*bes. Vieh, Pferde*) creature; **~tor** *n* gate; **~treppe** *f* inner stairs *pl*; **~türe** *f* street door, front door; **~vater** *m* father of the family; (*in e-r Anstalt*) warden; **~verwalter** *m* steward, *Am* janitor; **~wart** *m* porter; **~wäsche** *f* home-washing; **~wesen** *n* household, domestic concerns *pl*; **~wirt** *m* landlord, householder; **~wirtin** *f* landlady; housewife, housekeeper; **~wirtschaft** *f* housekeeping; domestic science; **~~lich** *a* economical; domestic; **~zeitschrift** *f* (*e-r Firma*) house organ; **~zins** *m* (house-) rent; **~~steuer** *f* rent tax; **~zustellung** *f* house delivery, *Am* door delivery.

Häus|chen *n* small house; maisonette; cottage; *fam* (*Abort, Bedürfnisanstalt*) privy, water-closet; *ganz aus dem ~~ sein* to be quite upset; to be beside o. s.; **~erblock, ~erkomplex** *m* block (of buildings), row of houses; **~erkampf** *m* house-to-house fighting; **~ermakler** *m* estate agent, real estate broker, *Am* realtor; **~erviertel** *n* quarter, *Am* block; **~ler** *m* cottager; **~lich** *a* domestic, household; (*~~ veranlagt*) homekeeping, home-loving; (*sparsam*) thrifty, economic(al); **~lichkeit** *f* home, domestic (*od* family) life; domesticity; economy.

Hausen *m* sturgeon.

Hausse *f com* (*Steigen der Kurse*) rise, advance (of prices), *Am* boom; *Höhepunkt der ~* peak of the boom; *die ~ nimmt ab* the boom is subsiding; **~bewegung** *f* upward movement, upswing of prices; **~markt** *m* boom market; **~spekulant** *m* bull; **~spekulation** *f* bull operation (*od* speculation).

Haut *f allg* skin; (*abgezogen von Tieren, zur Lederverarbeitung*) hide; *rohe ~* raw hide; *gegerbte ~* tanned hide; (*mit Haaren*) coat; (*Pelz*) pelt; (*abgeworfene Schlangenhaut*) slough; (*e-r Frucht*) peel; *bot* membrane; (*bei Flüssigkeit*) film; membrane; (*bei Milch*) cream; *anat* integument, membrane; tunic, pellicle; *äußere ~* epidermis; (*Schiff etc, Beplankung*) planking; (*Metallhaut e-s Flugzeugs*) skin; *durchsichtige ~* cornea; *harte ~* sclerotic coat; *alte, ehrliche ~* (*fam fig*) very nice fellow, good fellow, honest fellow; *die ~ betreffend* cutaneous, dermal, dermatic; *dicke ~* thick skin; *e-e dicke ~ haben* to be thick-skinned; *empfindliche ~* sensitive skin; *mit e-r ~* skinned; *mit ~ u. Haaren* completely, thoroughly; out and out; *nur ~ u. Knochen* nothing but skin and bones; *ohne ~* skinless; *unter die ~* subcutaneous, hypodermic; *mit heiler ~ davonkommen* to escape safely, to escape without a scratch; *aus der ~ fahren fig* to lose o.'s patience, to jump out of o.'s skin; *auf der faulen ~ liegen* to be idle; *naß bis auf die ~* soaked to the skin; *seine ~ zu Markt tragen* to do s. th. at o.'s personal risk; *ich möchte nicht in Ihrer ~ stecken* I wouldn't like to be in your shoes; *sich seiner ~ wehren* to defend o. s.; **~abschürfung** *f* excoriation; **~arzt** *m* dermatologist; **~atmung** *f* cutaneous respiration; **~ätzend** *a* attacking the skin; blister-forming; vesicant; *~~e Kampfstoffe* vesicant gases; **~ausschlag** *m* cutaneous eruption; rash; **~bildung** *f* skin (*od* film) formation; **~blutung** *f* h(a)emorrhage into the cutis; **~bräune** *f* croup; **~bürste** *f* complexion brush; **~ekzem** *n* eczema; **~entgiftungsmittel** *n* skin decontaminant; **~enzündung** *f* skin inflammation, dermatitis; **~farbe** *f* colo(u)r (of the skin); (*Gesicht*) complexion; *braune ~~* tan, *helle ~~* fair complexion; **~farbstoff** *m* pigment of the skin; **~fetzen** *m* scale; **~finne** *f* acne; **~gewebe** *n bot* periderm; *med* dermal tissue; **~gift** *n mil* skin poison, vesicant; **~jucken** *n* itching, *med* pruritis; **~krankheit** *f* cutaneous disease; **~krebs** *m* cancer of the skin; **~krem** *m* skin cream, cold cream; face cream; **~lehre** *f* dermatology; **~pflege** *f* care of the skin, cosmetics *pl*; **~puder** *m* dusting powder; **~reinigend** *a* skin-cleansing; **~reiz** *m*, **~reizung** *f* skin irritation, cutaneous irritant; **~salbe** *f* sebaceous matter; skin ointment; **~schere** *f* manicure scissors *pl*, cuticle scissors *pl*; **~übertragung** *f anat* (*Transplantation*) skin-grafting; **~unreinheit** *f* skin flaw; **~wassersucht** *f med* dropsy; **~zange** *f* (*Nagelpflege*) cuticle nippers *pl*.

Häut|chen *n* thin skin; membrane; (*bei Flüssigkeiten*) film; pellicle; (*dick*) cream; *bot* tunicle; pellicle; cuticle; **~en** *tr* to skin, to flay; *sich ~~* to cast (*od* shed) o.'s skin; *med* to desquamate; (*Schlangen*) to slough; **~ig** *a* skinny, skinned; cutaneous, membranous; dermoid; **~ung** *f* change of the skin, skinning; molting; sloughing; *med* shedding (*od* peeling) of skin; desquamation.

Hautevolee *f* cream of society; *fam* the upper crust.

Hautgout *m* (*Wildgeschmack*) high smell; *~ haben* to smell (*od* taste) high.

Havannazigarre *f* Havana(cigar).

Havarie *f* average, casualty, damage by sea; *~ aufmachen* to draw up the average statement; *~ erleiden* to meet with a casualty; **~agent** *m* average agent, claims agent; **~bericht** *m* damage report; **~bond, ~kontrakt** *m* average bond; **~klausel** *f* average clause.

he! he da! *interj* ha! I say! holla!

Heavisideschicht *f radio* Heaviside layer.

Hebamme *f* midwife.

Heb|ebaum *m* (long) lever; pole; beam; crowbar; **~ebock** *m* jack; **~ebühne** *f mot* car lift; **~eeisen** *n* crowbar; **~efahrzeug** *n mar* salvage vessel; **~el** *m* lever, handle; *den ~~ ansetzen fig* to drive the wedge; *alle ~~ in Bewegung setzen* to leave no stone unturned; **~~antrieb** *m* lever drive; **~~arm** *m* lever arm; **~~kraft, ~~wirkung** *f* leverage; **~~schalter** *m el* lever switch; key; **~~steuerung** *f* lever control; **~~waage** *f* lever (*od* beam) scale; **~~wirkung** *f* lever action, leverage; **~en** *irr tr* (*hochheben*) to lift; (*mit Mühe*) to heave (up); (*hochwinden*) to hoist; (*höher als etw anderes*) to elevate; (*hochbringen*) to raise; (*auflesen*) to pick up; (*hervor~*) to make prominent; (*verbessern*) to improve; *math* to reduce; (*vermehren*) to further; to increase; (*Stimmung*) to exalt, to encourage; *in gehobener Stimmung* in high spirits; *e-n ~~ (fam)* to liquor up, *Am sl* to take in wood; *er hebt gern e-n* he likes his drink now and then; *jdn in den Himmel ~~* to praise s. o. to the skies; (*beseitigen*) to remove, to put an end to; *jdn aus dem Sattel ~~* to unhorse s.o.; *aus der Taufe ~~* to stand godfather, godmother to; *die Form aus der Presse ~~* to take the form out of the press; *r* to rise; (*zunehmen*) to improve, to begin to thrive; (*sich ausgleichen*) to neutralize; *math* to cancel; **~eprahm** *m mar* lifting pontoon; camel; **~er** *m* lever; (*Saug~~*) siphon; (*Stech~~*) pipette; (*Spritze*) syringe; *anat* levator; *mot* (*Wagen~~*) jack; **~erolle** *f* (*Steuerliste*) register of dues and taxes; **~estange** *f* handspike; **~evorrichtung** *f* hoist, hoisting apparatus; lifting device (*od* gear); lifting machine; **~ewerk** *n* hoisting gear, lifting tackle; *rail* car lift; (*für Schiffe*) ship lift; **~ewinde** *f* jack; windlass; **~ezeug** *n* lifting appliance (*od* device), hoisting apparatus; elevator; gin; **~ung** *f* lift(ing); raising; heaving; (*Erhöhung*) elevation; (*Förderung*) promotion, encouragement; improvement; revival; (*Vermehrung*) increase; (*Beseitigung*) removal; (*Silbe*) accented syllable.

Hebrä|er *m* Hebrew; **~isch** *a* Hebrew; the Hebrew language.

Hechel *f* hatchel, hackle; flax-comb; *durch die ~ ziehen* to comb; **~macher** *m* hatcheller; (*Hechler*) *fig* carper, critic; **~n** *tr* to hackle, to comb; *fig* to carp, to criticize, to lash.

Hecht *m* pike, jack; (*ausgewachsener ~*) luce; *~ im Karpfenteich fig* pike in a fish-pond; *ein feiner ~ fig* (*Kerl*) a nice fellow; **~grau** *a* bluish-grey; **~rolle** *f* dive neck-roll; **~sprung** *m* pike dive, header; *Am* jackknife; (*Turnen*) long fly.

Heck *n mar* stern, poop; *mot* rear; *aero* tail; (*Zaun, Koppel*) fence; (*Eingang*) trellisgate; **~antrieb** *m mot* rear drive; **~flagge** *f mar* stern flag; **~gefechtsstand** *m*, **~kanzel** *f aero mil* tail turret; **~geschütz** *n* stern chaser; **~lampe, ~laterne** *f* poop lantern; **~lastig** *a aero* tail-heavy; **~licht** *n aero* tail light; **~ M. G.** *n* (= *Maschinengewehr*) *aero* tail gun; **~motor** *m mot* rear engine (power plant); *Wagen mit ~~* rear engined car; **~pfennig** *m* lucky penny; **~rad** *n mar Am* stern-wheel; *aero* tail wheel; **~~dampfer** *m Am* stern-wheeler; **~rohr** *n* (*Torpedo*) stern tube; **~schütze** *m aero mil* rear gunner, tail gunner, aft gunner, *Am sl* tail end Charlie; **~sporn** *m aero* tail skid; **~stand** *m aero mil* tail turret, *Am sl* conservatory, greenhouse; **~torpedoraum** *m* stern torpedo compartment.

Heck|e[1] *f* hatch; brood; breed; hatching-time; breeding-cage; **~en** *tr, itr* (*ausbrüten*) to hatch, to breed; to produce, to bring forth; *fig* (*aushecken, ersinnen*) to devise, to concoct; **~zeit** *f* breeding-time, pairing-time.

Hecke[2] *f* (*Zaun*) hedge, hedge-row; **~nrose** *f* wild rose, dog rose; **~nschere** *f* hedge clipper; **~nschütze** *m* sniper; **~nspringen** *n aero* (*dicht am Boden fliegen*) flying close to the ground, contour flying, *fam* hedge-hopping, *Am sl* grasscutting, skipping the dew.

heda! *interj* hallo! ho there! nobody there?

Hederich *m* charlock; hedge mustard, field mustard.

Heer *n* army; (*Schar*) host; (*große Menge*) great number, mass, crowd, multitude; *~ u. Flotte* army and navy, the united services *pl*; *stehendes ~* standing army; *in das ~ eintreten* to join the army; *aus dem ~ entlassen* to dismiss from the army; **~bann** *m* levies *pl*, militia; **~esbedarf** *m* army supplies *pl*; **~esbericht** *m* official army communiqué; **~esbestände** *m pl* military stores *pl*; **~esbetreuung** *f* army welfare; **~esbrieftaube** *f* messenger pigeon; **~esdienst** *m* military service; **~~vorschriften** *f pl* army-manual; **~eseinheit** *f* army unit; **~esflak** *f* army A. A. artillery; **~esfliegerkommando** *n* army air co-operation command; **~esführung, ~esleitung** *f* (*oberste ~~*) Supreme Command, Staff; **~esgruppe** *f* army group; **~esjagdflieger** *m* close support fighter; **~eskrankenschwester** *f Am* army nurse; **~esküstenartillerie** *f* army coastal artillery; **~esleitung** *f* army high command; *oberste ~~* supreme army command; **~eslieferant** *m* army contractor, army broker; **~eslieferung** *f* army contract; **~esluftwaffe** *f Am* Army Air Forces *pl*; **~esmacht** *f* military forces *pl*, strength; **~espersonalamt** *n* army personnel branch; **~espostamt** *n* army post office (*Abk* APO); **~esreserven** *f pl* army reserves *pl*; **~essanitätsinspektion** *f* inspectorate of army medical service; **~esstandort** *m* army post; **~esteil** *m* part of an army; **~esverordnungsblatt** *n* army gazette; **~eszeugamt** *n* army ordnance department; **~eszug** *m*, **~fahrt** *f* expedition, march of an army; **~führer** *m* army-leader, general; **~lager** *n* camp; **~säule** *f* column of an army; **~schar** *f eccl* host; *die himmlischen ~~en* the heavenly hosts *pl*; **~schau** *f* review, parade; **~straße** *f* military (*od* strategic) road, highroad.

Hefe *f* yeast, barm; (*Bodensatz*) dregs *pl*; lees *pl*; sediment; (*~ des Volkes*) scum (*od* dregs *pl*); *bis zur ~* to the very dregs; **~nahrung** *f* yeast food; nutriants *pl*; **~(n)gebäck** *n* pastry baked with yeast; **~(n)teig** *m* leavened dough, leaven.

Heft *n* (*Griff*) haft; handle; (*Schwert*) hilt; (*Schreib~*) exercise-book, note-book, copy-book; (*Druck~*) number, part; (*Heftausgabe*) publication in parts (*od* numbers); (*Broschüre*) pamphlet; *das ~ in den Händen haben* to be at the helm, to be master of the situation; **~el** *m* clasp, hook; **~en** *tr* (*befestigen*) to fasten; to fix; to attach; (*feststecken*) to pin; (*ein Buch*) to stitch, to sew; *geheftet a* (*Buch*) in sheets; *geheftetes Buch* stitched book; (*anheften*) to baste, to tack; (*mit Nägeln*) to nail; (*mit Garn*) to stitch; *sich ~~* to stick (to), to cling (to); **~faden** *m* stitching thread, basting thread; **~klammer** *f* (paper) clip, paper-fastener; (*Buchbinderei*) wire stitch, staple; stitching hook; **~lade** *f* sewing-press, sewing-bench; **~maschine** *f* sewing-machine; stitcher; (*Büro*) fastener, staple tacker; **~nadel** *f* stitching-needle; **~pflaster** *n* adhesive plaster (*od* bandage); sticking plaster; courtplaster; **~rand** *m* filing-margin; **~stich** *m* tacking stitch; **~weise** *adv* in parts; **~zwecke** *f* drawing-pin, *Am* thumbtack.

heftig *a* violent; vehement; (*laut*) boisterous; (*stark*) strong, intense; (*stürmisch*) tumultuous; (*Eifer*) fervent; (*Fieber*) high; (*Gewitter*) furious; (*Hunger*) keen (appetite); (*Kopfweh*) splitting; (*Leidenschaft*) violent; (*Liebe*) deep, passionate; (*aufbrausend*) violent, hasty; (*erregbar*) irascible, hot-tempered; (*Wind*) high; (*Regen*) heavy; (*Kälte*) sharp; **~keit** *f* violence, vehemence, intensity.

Heg|emeister *m* gamekeeper; **~en** *tr* (*abschließen*) to fence; (*Wild*) to preserve; (*Pflanzen*) to nurse; (*schützen*) to protect, to preserve; (*pflegen*) to foster, to take care of; to tend; to cherish, to nourish; *fig* (*Gefühle ~~*) to have, to entertain, to nourish, to harbo(u)r, to cherish; *Furcht ~~* to be in fear; *Haß ~~* to have a spite against; *Hoffnung ~~* to entertain hope(s); *Liebe ~~* to bear s. o. love; *Verdacht ~~* to have suspicions; *Wunsch ~~* to have a desire; *Zweifel ~~* to stand in doubt; **~er** *m* gamekeeper, keeper, forester; *fig* cherisher; **~ezeit** *f* close season, *Am* closed season.

Hehl *n* concealment, secrecy; *ohne ~* without secrecy; *kein ~ machen aus* to make no secret of; **~en** *tr* to conceal, to receive stolen goods; to fence; **~er** *m* concealer; (*Diebes~~*) receiver of stolen goods; **~erei** *f* concealment; receiving of stolen goods.

hehr *a* sublime, grand, high.

Heid|e[1] *f* heath; **~eblume** *f* heath-flower; **~egegend** *f* heathy ground; **~ehof** *m* heath farm; **~ekorn** *n* buckwheat; **~ekraut** *n* heath(er); **~elbeere** *f* (*Blaubeere*) bilberry, blueberry, *Am* huckleberry; **~erose** *f*, **~eröschen** *n* wild rose, dog-rose, sweet-briar; **~schnucke** *f* heath-sheep; moorland sheep.

Heid|e[2] *m*, **Heidin** *f* heathen, pagan; (*Bibel*) Gentile; **~enangst** *f* blue funk; **~engeld** *n* lot of money, no end of money; **~enlärm** *m* hullabaloo; **~enmission** *f* foreign mission; **~enspaß** *m* capital fun; **~entum** *n* heathendom, paganism; **~nisch** *a* heathen(ish), pagan.

heikel *a* (*kitzlig, delikat*) delicate, ticklish; (*kritisch*) critical; (*schwierig*) difficult; (*wählerisch, schwer zu befriedigen*) dainty, fastidious; *e-e heikle Frage* a delicate question; *~ sein* to be particular (*od* fussy) (*in bezug auf* about).

Heil *n* welfare; safety; (*Glück*) happiness; *eccl* salvation; (*Segen*) blessedness; *sein ~ versuchen* to try o.'s luck; *sein ~ in der Flucht suchen* to seek safety in flight; *im Jahre des ~s* in the year of grace; *~! interj* hail! good luck! *~ dem Manne, der ...* blessed be he who; *~ a* (*geheilt*) healed; cured; restored; (*unversehrt*) whole, unscathed; uninjured, unhurt; intact; safe and sound; *~ werden* to heal (up); **~and** *m* Saviour, Redeemer; **~anstalt** *f* sanatorium, medical establishment; hospital; nursing home; convalescent home, asylum; **~bad** *n* mineral bath, watering place; spa; **~bar** *a* healable; curable; **~~keit** *f* curableness; **~bringend** *a* salutary, wholesome; **~butt** *m* halibut; **~en** *tr* to cure; *itr* to heal; **~end** *a* curing; **~erfolg** *m* success of treatment; **~froh** *a* overjoyed, delighted; **~gehilfe** *m* barber-surgeon; masseur; **~gerät** *n* therapeutic apparatus; **~gymnastik** *f* remedial exercises *pl*; gymnastics as part of treatment.

heilig *a* holy; sacred; godly, saintly; hallowed; *H~er Abend* Christmas Eve; *~ halten* to hallow, to consider sacred, to observe religiously; *etw ~ versprechen* to promise solemnly; *jdm etw hoch u. ~ versprechen* to give s. o. o.'s solemn promise; *es war ihr ~er Ernst* she was in dead earnest about it; **~e** *f*, **~e(r)** *m* saint; **~en** *tr* to sanctify, to hallow; (*rechtfertigen, gutheißen*) to justify; to sanction; (*~halten*) to keep holy; **~enbild** *n* image of a saint;

~enschein *m* aureole, glory, halo; **~haltung** *f* strict observance; **~keit** *f* holiness, godliness, sacredness, sanctity, saintliness; *~~ der Verträge* sanctity of treaties; **~sprechen** *tr* to canonize, to saint; **~sprechung** *f* canonization; **~tum** *n* sanctuary, shrine; (*Gegenstand*) (holy) relic; **~~sraub** *m* sacrilege; **~~sschänder** *m* sacrilegist; **~ung** *f* sanctification, consecration.

Heil|kraft *f* healing (*od* curative) power; **~kräftig** *a* curative, healing; restorative; **~kraut** *n* medicinal herb; **~kunde** *f* medical science; therapeutics *pl*; **~kundig** *a* skilled in medicine; **~kundige(r)** *m* (*Arzt*) practitioner; **~kunst** *f* medical art; **~los** *a* (*unheilvoll*) fatal, mischievous; (*böse*) wicked, bad; (*schrecklich*) dreadful; **~losigkeit** *f* wickedness, fatalness; **~magnetismus** *m* animal magnetism; **~methode** *f* method of curing; **~mittel** *n* remedy, medicament; drug; cure; **~~lehre** *f* pharmacology; **~pflanze** *f* medicinal plant; **~quelle** *f* mineral spring, medicinal spring; **~sam** *a* wholesome, salutary; *fig* beneficial, good; **~samkeit** *f* wholesomeness, salubrity; **~sarmee** *f* Salvation Army; **~schwindler** *m* quack; **~serum** *n* antitoxic serum, anti-toxin; anti-serum; **~sgeschichte** *f eccl* Life and Sufferings of Christ; **~stätte** *f* sanatorium; **~ung** *f* healing, cure, curing; recovery; **~~sdauer** *f* duration of recovery; **~verfahren** *n* (medical) treatment; mode of treatment; therapy; **~vermögen** *n* healing quality; **~wirkung** *f* curative effect; **~zweck** *m* therapeutic purpose.

Heim *n* home; (*Familie*) family; (*Wohnung*) dwelling; (*Wohnsitz*) domicile; *adv* home; homeward; **~arbeit** *f* outwork, outdoor work; homework; **~arbeiter** *m* outworker, home-worker, outdoor worker; **~at** *f* native land (*od* place *od* country); homeland, home; *in der ~~* at home; *in die ~~ zurückfahren* to return home; **~~erzeugnis** *n* native manufacture; **~~flak** *f* A. A. home-guard; **~~flotte** *f* home fleet; **~~flughafen** *m* home base; **~~front** *f* home front; **~~gebiet** *n* homeland; *mil* zone of the interior; **~~hafen** *m* port of registry, home port; **~~horst** *m aero mil* home base; **~~krieger** *m* armchair soldier; carpet knight; stay-at-home patriot; **~~kriegsgebiet** *n* home defence area; zone of the interior; **~~kunde** *f* local topography; **~~land** *n* native land, homeland; **~~lich** *a* native, home; home-like; **~~los** *a* homeless; outcast; **~~luftschutz** *m* civilian air-raid protection; **~~ort** *m* native place; **~~recht** *n* right of domicile; **~~schein** *m* certificate of citizenship; **~~schlag** *m* (*der Tauben*) pigeon loft; homing loft; **~~schutz** *m* home defence; **~~sinn** *m* homing instinct; **~~staat** *m* country of origin; **~~stadt** *f* home town; **~~urlaub** *m mil* (home) leave; **~begeben**: *sich ~~* to go home; **~begleiten** *tr* to see s. o. home; **~bringen** *irr tr* to see home, to bring home; **~chen** *n* (house) cricket; **~eilen** *itr* to hasten home; **~fahren** *irr itr* to drive home; **~fahrt** *f* return, homeward journey (*od* voyage); **~fall** *m jur* devolution, reversion; **~fallen** *irr itr* to devolve (on), to revert (to); **~fernseher** *m tele* home television set (*od* receiver); **~filmkamera** *f phot* home film (*Am* movie) camera; **~finden** *irr itr* (*sich*) to find o.'s way home; **~führen** *tr* to lead (*od* to take) home; (*repatriieren*) to repatriate; (*Braut*) to marry; **~gang** *m* (*Ableben*) death, decease; **~gehen** *irr itr* to go home; (*sterben*) to decease, to die; **~isch** *a* domestic, homelike; (*eingeboren*) native, indigenous; home-born, home-bred; (*vertraut*) familiar; at home; *~~en Ursprungs* homespun; *~~e Gewässer* home waters; *sich ~~ fühlen* to feel at home; *~~ sein in* to be versed in ...; **~kehr, ~kunft** *f* return, homecoming; **~kehren, ~kommen** *irr itr* to come back, to return home; **~kehrer** *m* returnee, homecomer; repatriated soldier (*od* emigrant); **~kino** *n* home cinema, *Am* home movie; **~lampe** *f phot* reflector lamp; **~leuchten** *tr* to light s. o. home; *fig* to reprove, to give s. o. a piece of o.'s mind, *sl* to tell off, to lick s. o.; **~lich** *a* (*geheim*) secret; (*versteckt*) clandestine, covert, (*verborgen*) hidden, concealed; (*verstohlen*) furtive, stealthy; (*privat*) private; (*heimelig*) snug, comfortable; homelike, *Am* homy; *sich ~~ entfernen* to slip off, to take French leave; *~~ lachen* to laugh in o.'s sleeve; **~lichkeit** *f* secrecy; (*Geheimnis*) secret; (*Verschlossenheit*) closeness; **~lichtuerei** *f* mysterious ways *pl*; **~lichtun** *irr tr* to affect (*od* to put on) a mysterious air; to make a mystery of s. th.; **~reise** *f* homeward journey, *mar* home-voyage; *auf der ~~ befindlich mar* homeward bound; **~schule** *f* boarding school; **~sendung** *f* repatriation; **~stätte** *f* home; (*Siedlung*) home-croft; homestead; *Besitzer e-r ~~* homesteader; **~stättengesetz** *n* homestead law; **~suchen** *tr* (*von Geistern etc*) to haunt; to infest; *eccl* to visit; to afflict, to trouble, to plague; (*strafen*) to punish (for s. th.); **~suchung** *f* visitation; *fig* calamity, affliction, misfortune; trial; **~tücke** *f* malice; **~tückisch** *a* malicious; (*Krankheit*) insidious; mischievous; (*verräterisch*) treacherous; (*hinterlistig*) underhand; **~wärts** *adv* homeward(s); **~weg** *m* way home, return; *auf dem ~~* on the way home; *sich auf den ~~ machen* to set out for home; **~weh** *n* home-sickness; nostalgia; *~~ haben* to be homesick; **~wehr** *f* home guard; **~zahlen** *tr* to pay out, to pay back, to refund; *fig* (*vergelten*) to be revenged on; to get even; to pay s. o. in his own coin; **~ziehen** *irr itr* to go home.

Hein *m*: *Freund ~* Death; **Heinzelmännchen** *n* brownie.

Heirat *f* marriage; (*Partie*) match; (*Vermählung, Hochzeit*) wedding; **~en** *tr* to marry, to wed; *itr* to get married; *wieder ~~* to get married again, to remarry; **~santrag** *m* proposal (*od* offer) of marriage; *jdm e-n ~~ machen* to propose to; **~sanzeige** *f* notice of marriage; announcement of marriage; **~sbüro** *n*, **~svermittlung** *f* marriage agency; **~serlaubnis** *f* marriage licence; **~sfähig** *a* marriageable; *im ~~en Alter* of marriageable age; **~sgut** *n* dowry; portion; **~skandidat** *m* suitor, wooer; **~slustig** *a* eager to marry; **~sstifter** *m* matchmaker; **~surkunde** *f* marriage-lines *pl*, *Am* marriage-certificate; **~sverbot** *n* ban on marriage; **~svermittler** *m* matrimonial agent; **~sversprechen** *n* promise of marriage; *Bruch des ~~* breach of promise; **~svertrag** *m* marriage-contract.

heischen *tr* to demand, to postulate, to require.

heiser *a* hoarse; (*belegt*) husky; *~ werden* to grow hoarse; *~ sein* to be hoarse; to have a sore throat; *sich ~ schreien* to roar o. s. out of breath; **~keit** *f* hoarseness, raucousness.

heiß *a* hot; (*Zone*) torrid; *fig* fervent, passionate; burning, ardent; *mir ist ~* I am hot; *jdm die Hölle ~ machen* to frighten s. o. out of his wits; *~es Blut haben* to be hot-tempered; *kochend ~* boiling hot; *~e Tränen vergießen* to shed hot tears, to weep bitterly; **~blütig** *a* warm-blooded; *fig* hot-tempered; **~~keit** *f* hot temper, passion; **~dampf** *m* superheated steam; **~ersehnt** *a* ardently desired; **~geliebt** *a* ardently loved; **~hunger** *m* ravenous hunger (*od* appetite); **~hungrig** *a* ravenously hungry; **~laufen** *irr itr tech* to (over)heat; to run hot; **~löten** *tr* to hot-solder, to sweat; **~luft** *f* hot air; **~~ballon** *m* hot-air balloon; **~~dusche** *f* hot air apparatus; (*Fön*) electric hair dryer; **~~erhitzer** *m* air heater; **~~strahlantrieb** *m aero* jet propulsion; **~~strahltriebwerk** *n aero* jet propulsion engine; **~mangel** *f* pressure roller; **~sporn** *m* hotspur, *Am* hot-shot; **~wasserbehälter** *m* hot-water container; **~wasserboiler** *m* (*Küche*) geyser, *Am* (hot-) water-heater, boiler; **~wasserheizung** *f* hot-water heating.

heißen *irr tr* to call, to name; (*bedeuten*) to mean, to signify; *jdn etw ~* to bid, to order, to command; *jdn willkommen ~* to (bid s. o.) welcome; *itr* to be called; to mean; *es heißt* it is said, they say; *das heißt* that is to say, that is (*Abk* i. e.); *was soll das ~?* what does it mean? what's the meaning of this? *Am fam* what's the idea? *das will nicht viel ~* that doesn't mean much; *es soll nicht ~, daß* it shall not be said that; *wie ~ Sie?* what is your name? *was heißt das auf Englisch?* what's that in English? what is the English for that? just what do you call that in English? *wie heißt dieser Ort?* what's the name of this place?

heiter *a* serene; (*fröhlich*) cheerful, *Am* chipper; (*Wetter*) bright, fair; *aus ~em Himmel* out of a clear sky; from the blue; *in ~er Stimmung* in gay spirits; *~er werden* to cheer up; **~keit** *f* serenity; cheerfulness, brightness; clearness.

Heiz|apparat *m* heating apparatus, heater; **~bar** *a* easily heated, to be heated; with heating; **~batterie** *f radio* filament battery, *Am* A-battery; **~decke** *f* (*im Bett*) electric blanket; **~draht** *m* heating wire (*od* coil); **~element** *n* heating unit (*od* element); **~en** *tr* to heat, to make a fire; to fire up; *gut geheizt* well heated; *elektrisch geheizter Fliegeranzug* electrically heated suit; **~er** *m* stoker, heater; *rail* fireman; **~faden** *m* heating filament; **~fläche** *f* heating surface; **~gas** *n* fuel gas; **~gitter** *n* heating grid; **~kessel** *m* kettle, boiler; furnace; **~kissen** *n* electric (warming) pad, heating pad (*od* cushion); **~körper** *m* radiator, heater; *elektrischer ~~* electric heater, heating element; **~kraft** *f* calorific power, fuel value, heating power; **~loch** *n* fire door, stokehole; **~material** *n* fuel; **~öl** *n* fuel oil; **~platte** *f* (electric) hot-plate; heating plate; **~raum** *m* furnace room; (*im Ofen*) stoke hole; heating space; **~rohr** *n*, **~röhre** *f* flue; fire (*od* heating) tube; **~schlange** *f* heating coil; **~sonne** *f el* bowl-fire, electric fire; **~spannung** *f radio* filament voltage; **~stoff** *m* fuel; **~strom** *m radio* filament current; **~stromkreis** *m radio* filament circuit; **~ung** *f* (central) heating, *fam* heat; firing; fuel; *die ~~ anstellen* to turn on the radiator (*od* heat); *die ~~ abstellen* to turn off the heat; **~~sanlage** *f* heating system, heating plant; **~wert** *m* heating (*od* calorific) value (*od* power); **~widerstand** *m el* heating resistance; *radio* filament resistance; **~wirkung** *f* heating effect.

Hekt|ar *n* hectare (1 ha *etwa* = 2½ acres); **~o-** hecto, hundred; **~ographieren** *tr* to hectograph; **~oliter** *m* hectolitre (1 hl = 22 (*Am* 26,4) gallons); **~ik** *f* hectic state, consumption, **~isch** *a* hectic(al).

Held *m* hero; (*Vorkämpfer*) champion; *~ des Tages* lion (of the day); **~enfriedhof** *m* military cemetery; **~engedicht** *n* epic (*od* heroic) poem; **~enkeller** *m mil sl* funk-hole, shell-proof shelter; **~enlied** *n* heroic song; **~enmäßig** *a* heroic, hero-like; **~enmut** *m* heroism; **~enmütig, ~enhaft** *a* heroic(al); **~enrolle** *f theat* part of a hero; **~entat** *f* heroic deed, exploit; **~entod** *m* heroic death; death of a hero; death in action; *den ~~ sterben* to die as a hero; **~entum** *n* heroism; **~enverehrung** *f* hero-worship; **~enzeit** *f*, **~enalter** *n* heroic age; **~in** *f* heroine; **~isch** *a* heroic.

helf|en *irr itr* (*jdm ~~*) to help, to support, to assist, to aid; (*nützen*) to be of use, to avail; (*unterstützen*) to succour; *zu etw ~~* to help s. o. to get s. th., to profit; *jdm aus der Not ~~* to relieve s. o.; *sich zu ~~ wissen* never to be at a loss; to know what to do; *sich selbst ~~* to help o. s.; *hilf dir selbst, so hilft dir Gott* God helps those who help themselves; *ich kann mir nicht ~~* I can't help it; *sich nicht zu ~~ wissen* to be at a loss; *was hilft es?* what is the use of it? *es hilft nichts* it is useless; *was wird es ihr schon helfen?* what good will it do her? **~er** *m* helper, aider, assistant; **~erin** *f* woman helper (*od* assistant); (*Schwester*) nurse; **~ershelfer** *m* accessory, accomplice, abettor.

Helikopter *m aero* (*Hubschrauber*) helicopter.

Helio|gravüre *f typ* (*Kupferlichtdruck*) heliography, photogravure, photoengraving; **~therapie** *f* heliotherapy, sun-cure; **~trop** *n bot* heliotrope, cherry pie, turnsole; *min* heliotrope, bloodstone; **~zentrisch** *a* heliocentric(al).

Helium *n* helium; **~entwicklung** *f* production of helium; **~kanalstrahl** *m* helium-canal ray; **~kern** *m* helium nucleus.

hell *a* (*glänzend*) bright; (*leuchtend*) shining; luminous; (*strahlend*) brilliant; (*Farbe*) high, bright; light, fair; (*klar*) clear; distinct; (*laut*) resounding, loud; (*schrill*) shrill; (*durchsichtig*) transparent; (*deutlich*) plain; (*heiter*) serene, clear; *fig* (*einsichtig*) clear-sighted, enlightened; (*verständig, klug*) clear-headed; (*scharfsinnig*) penetrating; (*Augen*) sharp, quick; (*Bier*) pale, light; *ein ~es* a light beer; (*Gelächter*) ringing; (*Glocke*) clear; (*Gesichtsfarbe*) fair; (*Haar*) fair, light; *in ~en Haufen* in large numbers; *der ~e Neid* pure envy; (*Stimme*) clear; (*Tränen*) big, thick; *am ~en Tag* in broad daylight; *~er Verstand* clear head; *~er Wahnsinn* sheer madness; *die ~e Wahrheit* the plain truth; *ein ~er Raum, ein ~es Zimmer* a bright room; *es wird schon ~* the day begins to dawn; **~blau** *a* light blue; **~blond** *a* light, fair; flaxen; **~dunkel** *n* (*Malerei*) clair-obscure; (*Dämmerung*) dusk; **~e** *f* brightness, clearness; (*durchsichtig*) transparency; daylight; **~farbig** *a* light-colo(u)red; (*Haar*) fair; **~gelb** *a* light yellow, straw-colo(u)red; **~grau** *a* light grey; **~grün** *a* light green, pale green; **~hörig** *a* quick (*od* keen) of hearing; **~igkeit** *f* clearness, brightness; (*Fernsehbild*) brilliancy; light (*od* luminous) intensity; **~~sunterschiede** *m pl* variations in the light intensity; tones of brightness; **~~sveränderung** *f* brightness-intensity change; **~~swert** *m* degree of brightness; **~~smesser** *m* luxmeter; **~leuchtend** *a* luminous; **~licht** *a*: *am ~~en Tage* in broad daylight; **~sehen** *n*, **~seherei** *f* clairvoyance; **~seher** *m*, **~~in** *f* clairvoyant; **~sichtig** *a* clear-sighted; clairvoyant; **~tönend** *a* sonorous.

Hellebarde *f* halberd.

Heller *m* farthing; *er hat keinen roten ~* he has not a penny; *auf ~ u. Pfennig bezahlen* to pay to the last farthing.

Helling *f mar* slip, slipway, shipway.

Helm *m* helmet; cap (of an alembic); (*Kuppel*) dome, cupola; *mar* rudder, helm; **~busch** *m* plume of the helmet, crest; **~dach** *n* vaulted roof; **~gitter** *n* visor; **~holz** *n* tiller.

Hemd *n* shirt, (man's) undervest; (*Damen~*) chemise, (woman's) vest; *gestärktes ~* starched shirt, *Am fam* boiled shirt; *bis aufs ~ ausziehen* to strip s. o. naked; *ohne ~* shirtless; **~ärmel** *m* shirt sleeve; **~~diplomatie** *f Am sl* shirt sleeve diplomacy; **~(s)ärmelig** *a* in o.'s shirt sleeves; **~bluse** *f* shirt-blouse, *Am* shirt-waist; **~brust** *f* shirt-front, dicky; **~einsatz** *m* shirt-front; **~enmacher, ~enfabrikant** *m* shirt-maker; **~enstoff** *m* shirting; **~hose** *f* combinations *pl*, *Abk* comb (*eine ~~* a pair of combinations), *Am* union-suit; **~knopf** *m* (shirt-)stud, shirt-button; **~kragen** *m* shirt-collar; **~krause** *f* shirt-frill; **~manschetten** *f pl* (shirt-)cuffs *pl*; **~schoß** *m* shirt-tail.

Hemisphär|e *f* hemisphere; **~isch** *a* hemispherical.

hemm|en *tr* (*Einhalt tun, anhalten*) to stop, to check; to slow up; (*sperren*) to block, to lock; to catch; (*hindern*) to hamper, to hinder; (*durch schwerwiegende Umstände*) to handicap; (*seelisch*) to curb, to restrain, to inhibit; (*verlangsamen*) to slacken; to delay; (*Blut*) to stanch, to stop; **~end** *a* obstructive, cumbersome; *tech* dragging; **~kette** *f* drag-chain, skid; **~nis** *n* check, obstruction; impediment; hindrance, obstacle; handicap; (*Gewicht*) dead weight; **~schuh** *m* brake, drag; skid; **~ung** *f* check, stoppage, restraint; (*seelisch*) restriction, moral scruples *pl*; *med* inhibition; *tech* (*Uhr*) escapement; (*Waffe*) jam, catch, stop(page); **~~slos** *a* unrestraint, unchecked; **~~slosigkeit** *f* impetuosity; **~vorrichtung** *f* brake, braking device.

Hengst *m* stallion, horse; (*Esel*) jackass; **~füllen** *n* colt.

Henkel *m* handle, ear, hook; **~korb** *m* basket with a handle; **~topf** *m* pot with a handle.

henk|en *tr* to hang; **~en** *n* hanging; **~enswert** *a* deserving to be hanged; **~er** *m* hangman, executioner; *fig* tormenter; *jdn dem ~~ übergeben* to deliver s. o. to the hangman; *hol's der ~~!* *interj* damn it! confound it! hang it! **~erbeil** *n* executioner's axe; **~erblock** *m* block; **~ersknecht** *m* hangman's assistant; tormentor; **~ersmahlzeit** *f* last meal; *fig* farewell dinner.

Henne *f* hen; (*junge ~*) pullet; *bot fette ~* orpine.

her *adv* hither, here; from; (*zeitlich*) ago, since; *kommen Sie ~!* come here (to me)! come on! *wo kommen Sie ~?* where do you come from? where are you from? *wo hast du das ~?* where did you get that from? *hin u. ~* to and fro, to and again; over and over again; *von oben ~* from above; *von alters ~* of old, from time immemorial; *von je ~* always; *wie lang ist das ~?* how long ago was that? *es ist schon lange ~* it is long ago; *~ damit!* out with it! hand it over! let's have it! give it up! *hinter jdm ~ sein* to be after s. o.; *nicht weit ~ sein* to be of little value.

herab *adv* down, downwards; *von oben ~* from on high; from above; (*herablassend*) condescendingly; **~baumeln** *itr* to dangle; **~blicken** *itr* to look down (*auf jdn* upon s. o.); **~drücken** *tr* to depress; to press down; (*Preise*) to beat down; to bring down; to force down; **~eilen** *itr* to hasten down; **~fallen** *irr itr* to fall down; **~fahren, ~gehen, ~kommen, ~steigen** *irr itr* to come down; to descend, to dismount, to sink down; **~lassen** *irr tr* to lower, to let down; *sich ~~* (*fig*) to stoop, to condescend, to deign; **~lassend** *a* condescending; **~lassung** *f* condescension; **~mindern** *tr* to diminish, to decrease, to reduce; **~rieseln** *itr* to trickle down; **~schlagen** *irr tr* to beat down; **~sehen** *irr itr* to look down (upon); **~setzen** *tr* to put down; to lower; (*verkürzen*) to curtail; (*in Rang u. Ansehen*) to debase, to degrade; (*Preise*) to reduce; to lower, to cut down; *fig* (*unterschätzen*) to disparage, to cut up, to underrate; **~setzung** *f* degradation; reduction; (*der Geschwindigkeit*) retardation; (*Geringschätzung*) disparagement; **~steigen** *irr itr* to descend (from); **~stoßen** *irr itr aero* to swoop down; to nose down; *auf die Landebahn ~~* to nose down to the runway; **~stürzen** *tr, itr* to tumble down; to push down; to rush down; **~würdigen** *tr* to degrade, to debase; **~würdigung** *f* degradation, abasement; **~ziehen** *irr tr* to draw, to pull down.

Herald|ik *f* heraldry; **~isch** *a* heraldic.

heran *adv* on, near, up to; along(side); *nur ~! immer ~!* come on! **~bilden** *tr* to train, to educate, to bring up; **~bildung** *f* education, training; **~blühen** *itr* to bloom; (*sich entwickeln*) to develop; **~bringen** *irr tr* to bring near; **~drängen:** *sich ~~* to press forward; **~eilen** *itr* to hasten forward (*od* near); **~fahren** *irr itr* to pull in; **~gehen** *irr itr* to go near; **to go (*od* come) up to**; to approach; *an die Arbeit ~~* to set to work; *an etw ~~* to go at, to tackle; **~kommen** *irr itr* to come near, to draw near; to approach to; (*im Vergleich*) to come up to; *etw ~~ lassen* to await s. th.; *die Dinge an sich ~~ lassen* to bide o.'s time; **~machen:** *sich ~~* to edge near, to bustle o.'s way to; *sich an etw ~~* to set to work, to undertake; *sich an jdn ~~* to make up to s. o.; (*an ein Mädchen*) to make a pass at; **~nahen** *itr* to approach, to draw near; (*bevorstehen*) to be imminent; (*drohend*) to threaten; *der Sommer naht ~* summer is coming; *~~ n* approach; **~pirschen:** *sich ~~* to stalk up (to); **~reichen** *itr* to reach up to; **~reifen** *itr* to grow up; to mature, to grow to maturity; **~rücken** *tr* to draw near; (*heranziehen*) to pull up; *itr* to approach, to come on, to advance; *die Zeit rückt ~* the time approaches; **~schleichen** *irr itr* (*sich*) to sneak up to; to steal in upon s. o.; **~treten** *irr itr* to step near, to step up to; *an jdn ~~* to approach s. o.; to accost s. o.; **~wachsen** *irr itr* to grow up; to rise; *das ~~de Geschlecht* the rising generation; **~wagen**: *sich ~~* to venture to approach; **~ziehen** *irr tr* to draw near (*od* on), to pull up; (*interessieren*) to attract, to interest in; (*zu e-r Zahlung etc*) to call upon; (*zitieren, hinweisen auf*) to refer to, to quote; to bring up, to bring into play; (*benutzen*) to use; (*erziehen*) to educate; (*Arzt etc konsultieren*) to consult; *e-n Spezialisten ~~* to call in a specialist; (*beschäftigen zu etw*) to engage in; to employ in.

herauf *adv* up, up here, upwards; up to(ward); (*die Treppe ~*) upstairs; *von unten ~* from below, in rising; *~! interj* come up! **~beschwören** *tr* to conjure up, to evoke; (*herbeiführen*) to bring on, to cause; **~bringen** *irr tr* to bring (*od* take) up; **~fahren** *irr itr* to go (*od* drive) up; **~führen** *tr* to show (*od* lead) up; **~gehen** *irr itr* to go up, to walk up; **~klettern** *itr* to mount up; **~kommen** *irr itr* to come up; to get up; *~~ lassen* to send for; **~setzen** *tr* (*Preise etc*) to raise; **~steigen** *irr itr* to ascend; (*nahen*) to approach; **~ziehen** *irr tr* to draw up; to pull up; *itr* (*Gewitter etc*) to approach, to draw near.

heraus *adv* out, out here; out there; forth; *von innen ~* from within; *von innen ~ heilen* to cure internally (*od* radically); *aus etw ~* from among, out of, from out; *nach vorn ~ wohnen* to occupy the front part of a house; *ein Zimmer nach vorn ~* a front-room; *frei ~, gerade ~, rund ~* downright, plainly, bluntly, flatly; *zum Fenster ~* out of the window; *~! interj* come out! get out! *Wache ~! mil* to arms! *~ damit!* out with it! *~ mit der Sprache!* speak up! *jetzt ist's ~!* now it is out! now the truth has come out; *hier* (*od da*) *~!* this way out! *endlich habe ich es ~* (*bekommen, gelöst*) at last I have found it out; at last I have caught on; at last I have got the knack of it (*Am* the hang of it); **~arbeiten** *tr* to work out; (*formen*) to form; to modulate; (*sorgfältig entwickeln*) to elaborate; (*aus Holz, Stein etc*) to rough-work, to rough-hew; *sich ~~ aus* (*fig*) to get out of s. th.; to extricate o. s. from s. th.; **~beißen** *irr tr* to bite out; *sich ~~* to bite o.'s way out; *fig* to make a credible show; **~bekommen** *irr tr* (*Geld*) to get back (*od* out), to get change; *ich bekomme 3 DM ~* my change comes to three marks; *wieviel haben Sie ~~?* how much change did you get? (*herausfinden*) to find out, to come to know, to become aware of, to get wise to; to arrive at; (*Nagel etc*) to get out; (*Geheimnis*) to worm out, to ferret out; (*Geständnis*) to elicit; (*Rätsel*) to guess; (*Aufgabe*) to solve, to work out; (*erhalten*) to receive; (*gewaltsam ~~*) to force out; (*angelegtes Kapital*) to recover o.'s money; (*entziffern*) to decipher; (*Sinn*) to make (*od* find) out, *Am* to figure out; **~bilden** *tr* to develop; **~bildung** *f* formation, evolution; **~bringen** *irr tr* to bring out, to get out, to take out; (*Buch*) to publish, to edit; to bring out, to put out, to get out; (*Theaterstück*) to stage; (*Rätsel*) to solve; (*erraten*) to find out, to guess; (*entziffern*) to decipher; (*Waren*) to bring out, to turn out; **~drücken** *tr* to press out, to squeeze out; **~eilen** *itr* to rush out, to hurry out; **~fahren** *irr tr* to drive out; *itr* (*von Worten*) to slip out, to slip from o.'s tongue; to rush out; **~finden** *irr tr* to discover; to find out; to trace; to spot; *sich ~~* to find o.'s way out; **~fliegen** *irr itr, tr* (*aero Lufttransport*) to fly out; **~fließen** *irr itr* to flow out, to issue; **~forderer** *m* challenger; **~fordern** *tr* to challenge, to provoke; (*trotzen*) to defy; *die Kritik ~~* to invite criticism; **~fordernd** *a* challenging; (*frech*) provoking; (*trotzend*) defying; (*anmaßend*) arrogant; (*kampflustig*) aggressive; **~forderung** *f* challenge; provocation; **~~skampf** *m* challenge match; **~fühlen** *tr* to feel, to discover, to notice; **~gabe** *f* (*Übergabe*) delivering up, giving up; (*Rückgabe*) giving back, return; restitution; (*Freigabe*) setting free; (*Bücher*) publication, issue; editing, publishing, bringing out; **~geben** *irr tr* to deliver up; to give up; (*zurückerstatten*) to give back, to restore; (*Buch*) to edit, to publish; (*Geld*) to give back; *können Sie mir ~~?* can you give me change? **~geber** *m* (*Verfasser*) editor; (*Verleger*) publisher; **~gehen** *irr itr* to go out of; (*von Flecken*) to vanish; to come out; (*offen sprechen, aus sich ~~*) to speak out freely; **~gießen** *irr tr* to pour out (of); **~greifen** *irr tr* to pick out; to single out; (*auswählen*) to choose; **~gucken** *itr fam* to peep out; **~heben** *irr tr* to lift out; (*betonen*) to set off; (*Nachdruck legen auf*) to lay stress on; *sich ~~* to stand out; **~helfen** *irr itr* to get s. o. out of, to bring off; *aus der Verlegenheit ~~* to draw out of a loss; **~jagen** *tr* to drive out, to expel; to turn out; **~klingeln** *tr* to ring up; **~kommen** *irr itr* to come out (*od* forth); to get out; (*Buch*) to be published (*od* edited *od* issued), to appear; *eben ~gekommen* just out; (*bekannt werden*) to become known; to spread, to transpire, to leak out; *Am* to develop; (*davonkommen*) to come off, to get out of a scrape; (*zur Folge haben*) to result in; (*Lotterie*) to be drawn, to draw a prize; *es kommt auf eins ~* it's all the same; *was wird dabei ~~?* what will come of it? *dabei kommt nichts ~* that leads to nothing; *sie kamen aus dem Weinen nicht ~* they just couldn't stop weeping; **~lassen** *irr tr* to let out; **~laufen** *irr itr* to run out; **~locken** *tr* to entice out; **~machen** *tr* to take out; *sich ~~* (*vorankommen*) to get on; (*erblühen*) to blossom out, to improve; **~nehmen** *irr tr* to take out; to draw out; (*Zahn*) to pull out, to extract; *sich etw ~~* to presume, to venture; *sich zuviel ~~* to make too bold; **~nehmbar** *a* removable; **~platzen** *itr* to pop out; (*lachend*) to burst out, to blurt out; **~pressen** *tr* to press out, to squeeze out; **~putzen** *tr* to dress up, to trick out; to spruce up; to trim, to set off; **~ragen** *itr* to jut out, to stand out; **~reden** *tr* to speak freely; *sich ~~* to make excuses, to hedge off, to try to get off by evasions; **~reißen** *irr tr* to pull out, to extract, to tear out; *fig* to extricate; **~rollen** *itr aero* to taxi (*od* taxy) out; **~rücken** *itr* to march out; *fig* to come out; (*mit der Sprache*) to speak out freely; *tr* (*Geld*) to come down with; to fork out, *Am* to shell out; **~ruf** *m theat* curtain call; **~rufen** *irr tr* to call before the curtain, to call forth; *die Wache ~~* to turn out the guard; **~sagen** *tr* to speak out; *etw frei ~~* to speak freely; **~schaffen** *tr* to transport out, to take out; **~schlagen** *irr tr* (*Geld*) to make a profit, to make money by; *seine Kosten ~~* to cover o.'s expenses; *möglichst viel ~~* to make the most of s.th.; (*aus der Hand*) to knock out; (*Funken*) to strike out (sparks); **~schleichen** *irr tr* (*sich*) to steal out, to sneak out; **~schleppen** *tr* to drag out; **~schleudern** *tr* to throw out, to fling out; (*spritzen*) to spatter; **~schlüpfen** *itr* to slip out; **~schmeißen** *irr tr* to throw out, to cast out; **~springen** *irr itr* to leap (*od* jump) out of; (*mit Fallschirm*) *aero* to bail out; **~spritzen** *tr* to spout out; *fam* to spurt out; **~stecken** *tr* to put out (o.'s tongue), *Am* to stick out (o.'s tongue); **~stellen** *tr* to put out; *schärfer ~~* to bring into sharper focus; *sich ~~* (*sich zeigen*) to turn out, to appear, to come to light, to prove; *sich als richtig ~~* to prove correct; *es stellte sich ~, daß . . .* it turned out that . . .; **~streichen** *irr tr* to play up; to extol, to praise, to puff; **~stürzen** *tr* to throw out; *itr* to fall out; **~suchen** *tr* to choose; **~treiben** *irr tr* to drive out, to beat out; to expel; **~treten** *irr itr* to step (*od* go) out; (*etw zeigen*) to come forward with; *med* to protrude; **~wachsen** *irr itr* to sprout out, to shoot out, to grow out; (*aus den Kleidern*) to outgrow; *das wächst mir zum Hals ~* I am getting sick and tired of that, *fam* I am getting fed up with it; **~wanken** *itr* to stagger out; **~waschen** *irr tr* (*Wäsche*) to wash out; **~wickeln** *tr* to extricate; **~winden** *irr: sich ~~* to extricate o. s., to back out, to wriggle out; **~zahlen** *tr* to pay out; **~ziehen** *irr tr* to draw out, to take out, to pull out; to extract; (*Nagel*) to pull out; (*Pflanze*) to pull up; (*Zahn, Buchzitat*) to extract; *itr* to move out, to march out.

herb *a* (*scharf*) sharp, harsh, acrid, rough; (*sauer*) acid, sour; (*unreif*) crude, raw; (*Wein*) dry; (*Apfel*) tart; *fig* (*bitter*) bitter; (*streng*) austere; harsh; (*sarkastisch*) caustic; **~e, ~heit** *f* acerbity, tartness, bitterness; *fig* harshness.

herbei *adv* here, hither, on, near; **~bringen** *irr tr* to bring forward, to produce; *Beweise ~~* to produce (*od* furnish) evidence; **~eilen** *itr* to approach in haste, to come running; **~führen** *tr* to bring (on); to lead near; *fig* (*verursachen*) to bring about, to cause; (*nach sich ziehen*) to entail, to involve; (*veranlassen*) to induce; *e-n Beschluß ~~* to bring about a resolution; **~holen** *tr* to fetch; **~kommen** *irr itr* to approach, to come on (*od* near); **~lassen** *irr*: *sich zu etw ~~* to condescend (to); **~laufen** *irr itr* to come running along; **~rufen** *irr tr* to call in; (*e-e Taxe*) to call, *Am* to hail; **~schaffen** *tr* to bring near; (*sammeln*) to gather, to collect; (*hervorbringen*) to produce; (*liefern*) to furnish; to get here; (*beschaffen*) to procure; (*finden*) to find; (*Geld*) to raise; **~schleppen** *tr* to drag in; **~strömen** *itr* to flock together; to crowd up; **~stürzen** *itr* to rush in; **~ziehen** *irr tr* to draw in, to drag in; *bei den Haaren ~gezogen* far-fetched.

herbemühen *tr* (*sich*) to trouble to come; to take the trouble to come (here).

Herberg|e *f* (*Obdach*) shelter; lodging; (*Gasthof*) inn; (*Jugend~~*) youth hostel; (*Zuflucht*) refuge; **~en** *tr* to harbour; to shelter; *itr* to lodge; *bei jdm ~~* to lodge with s. o.; **~smutter** *f* hostess; **~svater** *m* host.

her|bestellen *tr* to ask to come, to send for s. o.; to make an appointment with; **~beten** *tr* to say off mechanically; to say over; **~bitten** *irr tr* to invite, to ask to come; **~bringen** *irr tr* to bring here, to bring up.

Herbst *m* autumn; *Am* fall; (*Erntezeit*) harvest-time; (*Wein~*) vintage; **~abend** *m* autumn evening; **~en** *tr* (*Ernte*) to gather in the harvest; (*Trauben*) to gather the grapes; *es herbstet* autumn is drawing near; **~ferien** *pl* autumn holidays *pl*; **~lich** *a* autumnal; *adv* in autumn; **~ling** *m* autumnal fruit; **~monat** *m* September; **~tag** *m* autumnal day; **~wetter** *n* autumnal weather; **~zeitlose** *f* meadow-saffron.

Herd *m* (*Kaminplatz*) hearth, (*offener ~*) fireplace, fireside; *fig* house, home; (*Küchen~*) kitchen-range; kitchen-stove; *min* buddle; *fig* (*Mittelpunkt*) seat, centre; focus; (*Vogel~*) decoy; *e-n eigenen ~ gründen* to set up for o. s.; **~platte** *f* hot plate.

Herde *f* herd; (*Schafe*) flock; (*getriebene ~*) drove, drive; *fig* (*Haufe*) crowd, multitude; **~nbuch** *n* herdbook; **~nmensch** *m* one of the common herd; **~ntier** *n* gregarious animal; **~ntrieb** *m* gregarious instinct; **~nweise** *adv* in herds, in flocks.

herein *adv* in, into; *~! interj* come in! walk in! *Am* come! step in! *hier ~, bitte!* this way in, please! **~bekommen** *irr tr* to get in; to receive; **~bemühen** *tr* to ask s. o. to come in; *sich ~~* to take the trouble of coming in; **~bitten** *irr tr* to invite to come in; **~brechen** *irr itr* to fall, to break in, to set in; to come (up)on; (*Dunkelheit*) to close in; *über jdn ~~* to overtake s. o.; to befall; **~bringen** *irr tr* to bring in; (*Ernte*) to harvest; to gather in; *der Pilot umkreiste den Landeplatz, ehe er die Maschine ~brachte* the pilot circled the field before he brought the plane in; **~fall** *m* bad business; take-in, sell; failure; **~fallen** *irr itr* to fall in: (*betrogen werden*) to be taken in, to fall for; to be (*od* to get) cheated, to be hoaxed (*od* victimized); to be swindled; **~führen** *tr* to show (*od* usher) in; to see in; **~gehen** *irr itr* to enter, to step in; **~holen** *tr* (*Aufträge*) to canvass; **~kommen** *irr itr* to come in(side), to enter; (*unerwartet*) to drop in; **~lassen** *irr tr* to admit; to let in; *laß ihn ~* let him in; **~laufen** *irr itr* to run in; **~legen** *tr* (*jdn ~~*) to let s. o. down; to take s. o. in; to turn s. o. in; to sell s. o. (a pup); *fam* to do; *sl* to pull a fast one; *Am sl* to take s. o. for a ride; **~lotsen** *n aero* piloting-in by ground-air radio communication; **~rufen** *irr tr* to call in; **~schneien** *itr fig fam* (*plötzlich kommen*) to arrive unexpectedly; to turn up, *Am* to blow in; **~steigen** *irr itr* to step in, to get in; **~treten** *irr itr* to step in, to enter; **~ziehen** *irr tr* to draw in.

her|fahren *irr tr* to bring here; *itr* to move along; to come along (in a car); *über jdn ~~* to fall upon, to come upon; (*jdn angreifen*) to set upon; **~fallen** *irr itr*: *über jdn ~~* to fall upon, to come upon; (*jdn angreifen*) to rush in upon, to attack; *über etw ~~* to go at; **~führen** *tr* to lead, to bring here; **~gang** *m* course of events; proceedings, details *pl*; **~geben** *irr tr* to deliver, to let have, to hand over, to give up; *fig* (*gewähren*) to permit, to yield; *sich zu etw ~~* to lend o. s. to, to be a party to; **~gebracht** *a* customary, established; usual, traditional; **~gehen** *irr itr* to go here, to walk along, to proceed; (*über etw ~~*) to fall upon; (*lustig etc zugehen*) to go on, to be going on; (*sich zutragen*) to happen, to come to pass; *so ist es ~gegangen* that's how it happened; *es ging heiß ~* there was hot work; *so geht es in der Welt ~* that's the way of the world; **~gehören** *itr* to belong to the matter **~gehörig** *a* pertinent; to the purpose **~gelaufen** *a*: *ein ~gelaufener Kerl* a vagabond; **~haben** *irr itr* to get from; *wo hast du das ~?* where did you get that from? **~halten** *irr itr* (*ausstrecken*) to hold forth, to tender; (*leiden*) to suffer; to pay; *immer ~~ müssen* to have always to bear the brunt, to be always in for it; **~holen** *tr* to fetch here; *weit ~geholt* far-fetched.

Hering *m* herring; (*Zeltpflock*) tent-pin, tent-peg; *fam* lean person; *geräucherter ~* red herring, smoked herring, bloater; *gesalzener ~* (*leicht geräuchert*) kippered herring, kipper; *frischer* (*od grüner*) *~* fresh (*od* green) herring; *marinierter ~* pickled herring; *zusammengedrängt wie die ~e fig* packed in like sardines; **~sfang** *m*, **~sfischerei** *f* herring-fishing (*od* -fishery); **~sfaß** *n*, **~stonne** *f* herring-keg; **~smilch** *f* herring-milt; **~srogen** *m* soft-roe; **~szug** *m* school of herring.

her|kommen *irr itr* to come near; (*sich nähern*) to come up (*od* on); to approach, to advance; (*abstammen*) to come from, to hail from, to descend, to originate; (*abgeleitet von Worten*) to be derived from; (*herrühren von*) to be caused by; **~kommen** *n* (*Brauch*) custom; usage; practice; routine; tradition; (*Abstammung*) descent; (*Ursprung*) extraction, origin; **~kömmlich** *a* traditional, customary; usual, conventional; **~kunft** *f* (*Abstammung*) descent; (*soziale ~~*) social antecedents *pl;* (*Ursprung*) origin; extraction; (*von Waren*) provenance; (*Ableitung*) derivation; **~~sland** *n* country of origin; **~lassen** *irr tr* to allow to come; **~laufen** *irr itr* to run up; *hinter jdm ~~* to run after s. o.; **~legen** *tr* to lay down here; **~leiern** *tr* to drawl out; to reel off; **~leiten** *tr* to conduct here; *fig* (*ableiten*) to derive (*von* from); (*entwickeln*) to deduce, to infer from; *sich ~~* to date (*von* from); **~locken** *tr* to allure, to entice; **~machen**: *sich ~~ über etw* to set about; (*in Angriff nehmen*) to tackle; (*über jdn*) to fall upon s. o.; (*ausstreichen*) to delete.

Hermelin *m* ermine; ermine-fur.

hermetisch *a* (*adv*) hermetic(ally).

hernach *adv* afterwards, after, hereafter, after this; thereafter; subsequently; *den Tag ~* the day after.

her|nehmen *irr tr* to get from, to take from, to draw; (*schelten*) to lecture; **~nennen** *irr tr* to enumerate, to call over, to name in succession; **~nieder** *adv* down.

Hero|enkult *m* hero-worship; **~enzeitalter** *n* heroic age; **~isch** *a* heroic(al); **~ismus** *m* heroism; **~s** *m* hero, demi-god.

Herold *m* herald; (*Künder*) messenger; (*Ausrufer*) proclaimer; (*Vorbote*) harbinger; **~srock** *m* tabard; **~sstab** *m* herald's staff, wand.

Herr *m* (*im Gegensatz zum Untergebenen, Meister*) master; (*Gebieter*) lord; (*aus höherem Stand*) gentleman; (*Eigentümer*) owner, proprietor; (*Arbeitgeber*) employer, master, *Am* boss; (*Herrscher*) sovereign; (*Gott*) the Lord, Our Lord, the Almighty; *der Tag des ~n* the Lord's day; (*Anrede ohne Name*) sir; *mein ~!* sir! (*Anrede mit Name*) *~ White* Mr. (= Mister) White; (*in der Antwort*) *ja ~ White* yes, sir; *meine ~en!* gentlemen! *meine Damen u. ~en!* Ladies and Gentlemen! (*Für*) *~en* (*Toilette*) Gentlemen, Men('s room); *Ihr ~ Vater* your father; *mil ja, ~ Hauptmann* yes, captain; yes, sir; *~ Hauptmann* (*Anrede*) captain; *~ sein über etw* to have the command of s. th.; *sein eigener ~ sein* to stand on o.'s own feet; *~ über seine Leidenschaften sein* to control o.'s passions; *~ über Leben u. Tod sein* to have power over life and death; *den großen ~n spielen* to lord it; to play the fine gentleman, to do swell; *~ werden* to overcome, to master; *des Feuers ~ werden* to get the fire under; *wie der ~, so der Knecht* like master, like man; *niemand kann zweien ~en dienen* no man can serve two masters; **~enanzug** *m* (gentleman's) suit; **~enartikel** *m pl* gentlemen's outfitting; *Inhaber e-s ~~geschäfts* outfitter, *Am* haberdasher; **~enbekleidung** *f* men's clothing; (*außer Anzug u. Schuhen*) men's wear; **~endoppel** *n* (*Tennis*) men's doubles *pl*; **~eneinzel** *n* men's singles *pl*; **~enessen** *n* (*besonders gutes Essen*) fine dinner; **~enfahrer** *m mot* owner-driver, gentleman driver; **~en(fahr)rad** *n* man's bicycle, *Am* man's bike; **~enfriseur** *m* barber for men; **~engesellschaft** *f*, **~enabend** *m* gentlemen's party, *Am* stag party; **~enhalbschuh** *m* gentleman's walking shoe; **~enhaus** *n* (*Gut*) manor(-house), mansion; (*England, Parlament*) House of Lords; **~enhemd** *n* shirt; **~enleben** *n* high life, gentleman's life; *ein ~~ führen* to lead a gentleman's life; **~enlos** *a* (*ohne Dienstherr*) out of service; (*von Sachen*) without a master; unowned, unclaimed; stray; ownerless; unidentified; (*von Fahrzeugen*) out of control; *~~es Gut* derelict; **~enmensch** *m* master mind; **~enreiter** *m* gentleman rider; **~enschirm** *m* gentleman's umbrella; **~enschnitt** *m* (*bei Damen*) Eton crop; shingled hair; **~ensitz** *m* (*Besitztum*) manor; **~ensocken** *m pl* socks *pl*, half hose; **~entoilette** *f* gentleman's lavatory, men's room; **~enunterhemd** *n* (*mit langem Arm*) long-sleeved vest; **~enunterhose** *f* (*kurz*) drawers *pl*; (*lang*) long pants *pl*; **~envolk** *n* master race; **~enzimmer** *n* study, smoking-room; **~gott** *m* the Lord God; **~in** *f* mistress, lady; **~isch** *a* lordly, domineering; imperious; dictatorial; masterful; **~je!** *interj* Goodness! Gracious! dear me! **~lich** *a* (*großartig*) magnificent; grand; (*stattlich*) stately; (*wunderbar*) wonderful; (*trefflich*) excellent; (*glänzend*) splendid; (*glorreich*) glorious; (*erlesen*) exquisite; **~lichkeit** *f* magnificence, excellence; splendo(u)r, glory; grandeur; **~schaft** *f* dominion; (*persönliche*) rule; (*e-s Fürsten*) reign; (*Regierung*) government; (*Macht*) power, sway; (*Herrschergewalt*) sovereignty; (*Gewaltherrschaft*) tyranny; (*sittliche*) authority; (*Kontrolle*) control; (*Beherrschung*) mastery; (*Befehl*) command (*über* over); (*Herr u. Herrin*) master and mistress; *hohe ~~en* people of (high) rank, distinguished people; (*Ländereien*) territory; manor; estate, domain; *meine ~~en!* (*Anrede*) Ladies and Gentlemen! *sind die ~~en zu Hause?* Are Mr. and Mrs. X at home? **~~lich** *a* belonging to a lord (*od* master); (*erstklassig*) first-class, high class; elegant; **~schen** *itr* to rule, to reign; (*regieren*) to govern; (*vor~~*) to prevail, to be prevalent; (*befehlen*) to command; (*bestehen*) to exist, to reign; to be; (*Krankheit*) to rage; **~~d** *a* (*vor~~*) prevailing, dominant; (*bestimmend*) ruling; (*im Schwang*) in vogue; *die ~~de Klasse* the ruling class; **~scher** *m allg* ruler; (*Fürst*) sovereign; (*Regierender*) governor; **~~gewalt** *f* (sovereign) power, sovereignty; **~~haus** *n*, **~~familie** *f* dynasty, reigning family; **~~miene** *f* commanding air; **~~stab** *m* sceptre, *Am* scepter; **~schsucht, ~schgier** *f* love (*od* fondness *od* thirst) of power, ambition; **~schsüchtig** *a* imperious; (*ehrgeizig*) ambitious; fond of power; (*tyrannisch*) tyrannic(al).

her|reichen *tr* to reach, to hand (to); **~reise** *f* journey hither (*od* here); (*Heimreise*) home-journey, return; **~reisen** *itr* to travel hither; **~richten** *tr* to prepare, to get ready; to set in order, to arrange; (*Holz*) to season; **~rücken** *tr* to draw near; *itr* to advance; to approach; **~rufen** *irr tr* to call hither; **~rühren** *itr* to come from; to arise from; to originate in; to be due to; to be derived from; **~sagen** *tr* to recite, to repeat; **~schaffen** *tr* to bring near (*od* here); to procure, to get; to produce; **~schauen** *itr* to look this way; **~schikken** *tr* to send here; **~schießen** *irr itr* to shoot here; **~schreiben** *irr: sich ~~ von* to come from, to date from; **~sehen** *irr itr* to look here; **~sein** *irr itr* to be (*von* from); **~stammen** *itr* to descend (*von* from); (*sich entwickeln aus*) to develop out of; (*abgeleitet von*) to be derived from; (*Personen*) to be a native of; to hail from; to come from; **~stellbar** *a* capable of being produced; **~stellen** *tr* (*niederlegen*) to put (over) here; (*reparieren*) to repair; (*wieder~~*) to restore; (*Verbindung*) *tele* to establish, to put through; *med* to cure; (*erzeugen, fabrizieren*) to manufacture, to produce, to make; *das Gleichgewicht ~~* to establish the equilibrium; **~steller** *m* (*Erzeuger, Firma*) manufacturer, maker, producer, *Am* concern; **~stellung** *f* (*Erzeugung*) manufacture, production; (*Wieder~~*) restoration; (*nach Krankheit etc*) recovery; **~~sfehler** *m* defect of fabrication; **~~sgang** *m* process (*od* course) of manufacture; **~~skosten** *pl* production costs *pl*; (*Selbstkosten*) prime cost; **~~spreis** *m* price of production; **~~sverfahren** *n* process of manufacture, method of production; **~~svorschrift** *f* prescription, recipe; **~stottern** *tr* to stammer out (*od* forth); **~tragen** *irr tr* to bring here, to carry hither, **~treten** *irr itr* to step near.

herüber *adv* over, across; to this side.

herum *adv* round, about; *um ... ~* around; near; (*bei Drehung*) turning round; (*ungefähr*) about, around; somewhere near; *um 100 Mark ~* about a hundred marks; *um zwei Uhr ~* about two o'clock; *fam* (*vorbei*) over, finished; *da ~* here about; *dort ~* there about(s); *hier ~* here about(s), around here, over here; *irgendwo hier ~* somewhere about here; *rund ~, rings ~* round about, all around; (*hin u. her*) here and there; to and fro; up and down; *immer um jdn ~ sein* to be always about s. o.; *gleich um die Ecke ~* just round the corner; *die Reihe ~* in turn; each one in his turn; *um den Tisch ~* round the table; *in der ganzen Stadt ~* all over the town; *weit ~* far and wide, far and near; **~albern** *itr fam* to fool around; **~balgen:** *sich ~~* to scuffle, to romp; **~bekommen, ~bringen** *irr tr* to get over, to talk over; **~biegen** *irr tr* to bend round; **~bummeln** *itr* to loiter (*od* to loaf *od* to hang) about; **~dirigieren** *tr* to boss around; **~drehen** *tr* to turn (a)round; (*Worte im Mund*) to misconstrue; (*Wind*) to change; *sich ~~* to turn around; (*schnell*) to twirl; **~drücken:** *sich ~~* to hang about (*od* around); (*um die Arbeit*) to shirk o.'s work; to try to get out of all hard work; **~fahren** *irr tr* to take a drive, to drive (to sail, to motor etc) about; *jdn ~~* to take s. o. for a drive, to drive s. o. about; *mit den Händen* (*in der Luft*) *~~* to gesticulate; *itr* to jerk round, to whisk about; **~fingern** *itr* to fumble; **~flattern** *itr* to flutter about; **~fliegen** *irr itr* to fly about; **~fragen** *itr* to ask round; **~führen** *tr* to lead about (*od* round); to show over; to take around; *jdn in der Stadt ~~* to show s. o. around town; *an der Nase ~~* to lead by the nose, to make a fool of s. o.; **~geben** *irr tr* to hand round; to pass; (*Spielkarten*) to deal; **~gehen** *irr itr* to walk about; *es geht mir im Kopf ~* it runs in my mind; *~~ lassen* to hand round, to pass round; *das Gerücht geht ~* a report is about; **~hetzen** *tr* to chase about; **~holen** *tr* to bring round; to fetch over; **~horchen** *itr* to go eavesdropping; (*spionieren*) to spy around; **~hüpfen** *itr* to hop about; **~irren** *itr* to wander around; **~jagen** *tr* to drive about; **~kommen** *irr itr* to come round; to travel about; to get around; (*Gerücht*) to spread about; to become known; *weit ~~* to travel a good deal, to see the world, to get around a lot; *sie ist nicht viel ~gekommen* she hasn't been around much; **~kramen** *itr* to fumble; **~kriechen** *itr* to creep around; **~kriegen** *tr* to talk over, to win round; **~laufen** *irr itr* to run, to stroll about; **~liegen** *irr itr* to be scattered about; **~lungern** *itr* to loaf about, to hang about; **~pfuschen** *itr* to tinker; **~reichen** *tr* to hand round; **~reisen** *itr* to travel about; **~reiten** *irr itr* to ride about; *fig* to harp upon; *auf jdm ~~* to plague s. o.; **~schicken** *tr* to send about; **~schlagen** *irr itr* to wrap around; *sich ~~* to fight; **~schlendern** *itr* to saunter about; **~schleppen** *tr* to drag about; **~schnüffeln** *itr* to sniff about; *Am fam* to snoop about (*od* around); **~schwärmen, ~schweifen, ~streifen** *itr* to roam about; **~spielen** *itr* to play around, to fiddle; **~stehen** *irr itr* (*Sachen*) to stand around; (*Menschen*) to loiter about; *Nicht ~~!* No loitering! **~suchen** *itr* to ferret; **~tappen, ~tasten** *itr* to grope about; **~tragen** *irr tr* to carry round; *fig* to divulge; **~treiben** *irr: sich ~~* to rove about; to loiter about, to hang around; to gallivant around; to gad about; **~wälzen:** *sich ~~* to turn about; **~wandern** *itr* to wander about; **~werfen** *irr tr* to throw about; to turn sharply; **~wickeln** *tr* to wind round, to twist about; **~zanken:** *sich ~~* to quarrel; **~zausen** *tr* to pull about; **~zerren** *tr* to haul about; **~ziehen** *irr tr* to draw about; *itr* to wander about; **~~d** *a* nomadic, strolling; wandering.

herunter *adv* down, downward, off; *von oben ~* from above; *hier ~* down here; *da ~* down there; *gerade ~* straight down; *~! fam 'runter!* down! *~ mit ihm!* down with him! *~ sein* to be run-down, to be down; to be (*od* to feel) low; **~bringen** *irr tr* to bring down; to get down; *fig* to reduce; **~drücken** *tr* to press down, to force down; to reduce, to lower, to minimize; **~gehen** *irr itr* (*von Preisen*) to decline, to fall, to drop; *aero* to descend; *im Gleitflug ~~* to flatten out; **~fallen** *irr itr* to fall down; **~handeln** *tr* (*Preis*) to beat down; **~hauen** *tr: jdm eins ~~* to give s. o. a box on the ear; to box s. o.; **~helfen** *irr itr* to help down; **~holen** *tr* to fetch down; *mil aero* (*abschießen*) to shoot down; **~klappen** *tr* (*Kragen etc*) to turn down; **~kommen** *irr itr* to come down; (*in Verfall geraten*) to decay, to decline, to fall off; to get low; to be pulled down; *~gekommen a* (*gesundheitlich*) worn away, run-down, down-and-out; (*geldlich*) to be hard up; (*schäbig*) shabby, slovenly; down at heel; **~lassen** *irr tr* to let down, to lower; **~machen** *tr fig* to run down, to cut up; to upbraid; **~purzeln** *itr* to fall down; **~putzen** *tr* to reprimand, *Am* to bawl out, to give a bawling out; **~reißen** *irr tr* to pull down; *fig* (*scharf kritisieren*) to pull (*od* to tear) to pieces; to excoriate; **~schalten** *itr mot* (*auf den ersten Gang*) to change down to low gear; **~schlagen** *irr tr* to beat down; **~sehen** *irr itr* to look down; **~setzen** *tr* to put down; (*Preise*) to reduce, to lower; *fig* to disparage; to undervalue, to depreciate; **~werfen** *irr tr* to throw down, to dump; **~wirtschaften** *tr* to run down; **~ziehen** *irr tr* to draw, to pull down.

hervor *adv* forth, forward, out; *unter ... ~* from under ...; **~brechen** *irr itr* to break forth, to issue out; to break through; to rush out; to debouch, to sally forth; **~bringen** *irr tr* to bring forth, to produce; (*erzeugen*) to generate; (*schaffen*) to create; (*verursachen*) to cause; (*Worte äußern*) to utter, to get out; **~bringung** *f* bringing forth, production, creation; **~gehen** *irr itr* to go forth; (*als Sieger etc*) to come off, *Am* to come out; (*entstehen*) to (a)rise; (*sich ergeben*) to result (*od* to follow) from; *daraus geht ~, daß ...* that shows (*od* proves) that ...; hence it follows that ...; *es geht ganz eindeutig daraus ~* it is unequivocally evident; **~heben** *irr tr* to render (*od* make) prominent; to give special prominence to, *Am* to feature; (*betonen*) to stress, to lay stress upon, to emphasize; to accentuate, to underscore; (*herausstreichen*) to show off, to mark out, to highlight; (*Malerei*) to set off; (*im Druck*) *typ* to display; *sich ~~* to be conspicuous; **~hebung** *f* stress, emphasis; **~holen** *tr* to fetch forth; to bring out; **~kommen** *irr itr* to come forth; (*auftauchen*) to appear; (*Gestirne*) to come out (of); **~leuchten** *itr* to shine forth; to be conspicuous; **~locken** *tr* to entice out, to elicit; to educe; to draw out, to lure out, to call forth; **~ragen** *itr* to stand out, to overtop, to be prominent, to project, to jut out (*od* forth); *fam* to stick out; *fig* to excel, to surpass; **~~d** *a* prominent, projecting, salient; *fig* eminent, distinguished; outstanding; remarkable; first-rate; *ein ~~der Autofahrer* a crack driver; **~rufen** *irr tr* to call forth; (*verursachen*) to cause, to evoke, to bring about; (*Bewunderung*) to excite; *phot* (*entwickeln*) to develop; (*Schauspieler*) to encore; to call for; **~springen** *irr itr* to leap forward; **~sprudeln** *itr* to spring forth; *tr* (*Worte*) to sputter out; **~stammeln** *tr* to stammer out; (*stottern*) to stutter forth; **~stechen** *irr itr* to stand out; (*von Farben*) to come out; *fig* to be conspicuous; **~~d** *a* (*auffallend*) striking, conspicuous; **~stehen** *irr itr* to project, to stand out; to be prominent; **~~d** *a* (*herausragend*) salient; (*auffallend*) conspicuous; *~~de Backenknochen* high-cheek bones; **~stürzen** *itr* to rush forth; (*ausbrechen*) to erupt; **~suchen** *tr* to seek out; (*ausgraben*) to dig out; to bring to light; **~treten** *irr itr* to come forward; to step forth; (*auftauchen*) to emerge; (*Augen aus dem Kopf*) to bulge; (*Farben*) to come out; *~~ lassen* to set off; (*gegenüber etw ~~ lassen*) to contrast; *fig* to be distinguished, to be prominent; **~~d** *a* prominent, predominant; bold; (*stark*) articulated; **~tun** *irr: sich ~~* (*auszeichnen*) to distinguish o. s.; **~wagen**: *sich ~~* to dare (*od* to venture) forth; **~zaubern** *tr* to produce by magic; to conjure up; **~ziehen** *irr tr* to draw forth.

her|wärts *adv* hither(ward); this way; **~weg** *m* way here; *auf dem ~~* on the way here.

Herz *n* heart; *in Zssg:* heart-, of the heart, *med* cardiac; (*Gemüt*) mind; (*Seele*) soul; (*Gefühl*) feeling, sympathy; (*Mut*) courage; spirit; *fam* pluck; (*Busen, Brust*) bosom; breast; heart; (*Kern, Innerstes, tech Seele*) core; (*Spielkarten*) hearts *pl mit sing*; (*als Kosewort*) love; dear heart, sweetheart; darling; *fig* (*Mittelpunkt*) centre, *Am* center; central point (*od* part); heart; *Raucher~* smoker's heart; *ein goldenes ~* a kind (*od* generous) heart; *ein hartes* (*gutes*) *~ haben* to be hard-hearted (*od* kind-hearted); *ohne ~* heartless; *ein ~ von Stein* a heart of stone; *ein schwaches ~ haben* to have a weak heart; *sein ~ ausschütten* to unbosom o. s.; *das ~ blutete ihr* her heart bled; *jdm das ~ brechen* to break s. o's heart; *sein ~ erleichtern* to unbosom o. s.; *jds ~ gewinnen* to win the heart of; *das ~ haben zu* to have the heart to; *das ~ fiel ihm in die Hosen fig* his heart went down (in)to his heels; his heart failed him, *fam* he got cold feet; *ihr fing das ~ zu klopfen an* her heart began to pound; *das ~ klopft* the heart is beating; *jdm sein ~ schenken* to give o.'s love, to give o.'s heart to s. o.; *ihr ~ hat gesprochen* she has fallen in love; *~ spielen* (*Kartenspiel*) to play hearts; *wenn dir dein ~ danach steht* if you have a mind to; *sein ~ verlieren* to lose o.'s heart; *krank am ~en sein* to be heart-sick; *das liegt mir am ~en* I have s. th. at heart; *an gebrochenem ~en sterben* to die of a broken heart; *ans ~ drücken* to press to o.'s heart; *ans ~ legen* to urge, to enjoin; to recommend warmly; *ans ~ gewachsen* to be very dear to; *Hand aufs ~!* truly! *fam* hono(u)r bright! cross my heart! *etw auf dem ~en haben* to have s. th. on o.'s mind, to have s. th. at heart; *aus tiefstem ~en* from the depth of o.'s heart; *im ~en der Stadt* in the centre (*Am* center) of the city; *ins ~ schließen* to become fond of, to have a great affection for; *ein Mädchen nach meinem ~en* a girl after my own heart; *ein Mann mit ~* a man of feeling; *etw übers ~ bringen* to have the heart to do s. th.; *ich kann es nicht übers ~ bringen* I haven't got the heart to do it; *ein Kind unterm ~en tragen* to be with child, to be pregnant; *fam* to be in the family way; *mit schwerem ~en* with a heavy heart; *von ~en* (*gern*) with all o.'s heart; most heartily; with the greatest of pleasure; *von ganzem ~en* heartily, cordially; *von ~en* (*lachen*) heartily; *von ~en kommend* hearty; *mir ist ein Stein vom ~en gefallen* a weight is off my mind; *ich kann zu ihm kein ~ fassen* I could not put any confidence in him; *zu ~en gehen* to make o.'s heart thrill; to go to o.'s heart; *sich etw zu ~en nehmen* to take s. th. to heart; *sich ein ~ fassen* to take courage (*od* heart), to pluck up courage; *aus dem ~en, aus dem Sinn* out of sight, out of mind; *ein ~ u. e-e Seele sein* to be hand and glove together; *er hat das ~ am rechten Fleck* his heart is in the right place; *das ~ auf der Zunge haben* to speak o.'s mind freely; **~ader** *f* aorta; coronary vein; **~allerliebst** *a* charming, darling; **~~e** *f*, **~~e(r)** *m* sweetheart; **~beklemmung** *f* oppression of the heart; **~beutel** *m* pericardium; **~~entzündung** *f* pericarditis; **~~höhle** *f* pericardial cavity; **~bewegung** *f* cardiac action; **~blatt** *n* innermost leaflet; unopened leaf bud; *fig* (*~blättchen n*) darling; **~blut** *n* heart's blood; **~bräune** *f* angina pectoris; **~brechend** *a* heart-breaking, moving; **~bube** *m* (*Kartenspiel*) knave of hearts; **~chen** *n* heartlet; (*Kosewort*) love! darling! honey! chicken! **~dame** *f* (*Kartenspiel*) queen of hearts; **~eleid** *n* grief, sorrow; heart-sore; **~en** *tr* to embrace, to hug; to caress; (*küssen*) to kiss; *fam* to neck, to pet; **~ensangelegenheit** *f* love-affair; **~ensangst** *f* heart-ache, anguish; **~enseinfalt** *f* simple-mindedness; **~enserguß** *m* unbosoming; **~ensfreude** *f* great joy; **~ensfreund** *m* bosom-friend, intimate friend; **~ensgut** *a* kindhearted, very kind; **~ensgüte** *f* kindness (of heart), benevolence; **~enslust** *f: nach ~~* to o.'s heart's content; **~ensmeinung** *f* true sentiment; **~enswunsch** *m* heart's desire; **~ergreifend** *a* heart-moving; **~erschütternd** *a* heart-appalling; **~erwärmend** *a* heart-warming; **~erweiterung** *f* dilatation of the heart; **~fehler** *m* heart disease; *med* cardiac defect; **~förmig** *a* heart-shaped; **~gegend** *f* cardiac region; **~geräusch** *n* cardiac murmur; **~gift** *n* cardiac poison; **~grube** *f* pit of the stomach, epigastrium; **~haft** *a* hearty; bold, brave, stout-hearted; *fam* plucky; **~~igkeit** *f* courage, boldness; **~hälfte** *f* half (*od* side) of the heart; **~höhle** *f* cavity of the heart; **~ig** *a* hearty; sweet, lovely; charming, ducky, *Am* cute, cunning; **~innig** *a* hearty, heart-felt; **~inniglich** *adv* heartily; **~insuffizienz** *f* cardiac insufficiency; **~kammer** *f* ventricle (of the heart); **~kirsche** *f* (*weiße*) white-heart (cherry), bigaroon; (*rote*) red-heart; (*schwarze*) black-heart; **~klappe** *f* (cardiac) valve; **~~nfehler** *m* defect of cardiac valve; **~klopfen** *n* palpitation (of the heart); **~krampf** *m* spasm of the heart; **~krank** *a* suffering from the heart; *fig* heart-sick; *~~ sein* to suffer from a heart ailment; **~krankheit** *f* heart's disease; **~kurve** *f* cardioid; (*Kardiogramm*) cardiogram; **~lähmend** *a* paralysing the heart; **~leiden** *n* heart disease; **~leidend** *a* suffering from heart-trouble; **~liebste** *f*, **~liebste(r)** *m* sweetheart; **~lich** *a* affectionate; cordial, hearty; heartfelt; sincere; *adv* very, extremely; *~~e Grüße von meiner Mutter* kind regards from my mother; *~~ gern* with all o.'s heart; readily; **~lichkeit** *f* heartiness; affection; cordiality; **~los** *a* heartless; unfeeling; **~losigkeit** *f* heartlessness, unfeelingness; **~mittel** *n* cardiac remedy; **~muskel** *m* cardiac muscle; **~~entzündung** *f* myocarditis; **~neurose** *f* cardiac neurosis; **~schlag** *m* (*regelmäßiges Schlagen*) heart-beat, heart impulse, palpitation; throb; *med* (*Stillstand des Herzens*) heart failure; cardiac paralysis; *an e-m ~~ sterben* to die of heart failure; **~schwäche** *f* cardiac weakness; **~spitze** *f* apex of the heart; **~stärkend** *a* cordial, cardiac; **~stärkung** *f* cordial; **~stillstand** *m* heart failure; perisystole; **~stück** *n* centre piece; *rail* frog, crossing; **~tätigkeit** *f* action of the heart; **~ton** *m* cardiac sound; **~verfettung** *f* fatty degeneration of the heart; **~vorhof** *m*, **~vorkammer** *f* auricle; **~wand** *f* cardiac wall; **~weh** *n* heartache; *fig* heartfelt grief, affliction; **~zerreißend** *a* heart-rending.

herziehen *irr tr* to draw near; *itr* to go here; to come to live in a place; *~~ über* (*etw od jdn*) to rail at, to speak ill of.

Herzog *m* duke; **~in** *f* duchess; **~lich** *a* ducal; **~tum** *n* duchy; (*Würde*) dukedom.

herzu *adv* here, hither, near; up, up to; towards.

Hess|e *m* Hessian; **~en** *n* Hesse, Hessen; **~isch** *a* Hessian.

Hetäre *f* courtesan.

heterogen *a* (*andersgeartet, ungleichartig*) heterogeneous; **~ität** *f* heterogeneity.

Hetz|e *f* (*Jagd*) hunt(ing); (*Verfolgung*) chase; (*Eile*) haste, hurry, rush; (*Aufreizung*) instigation, agitation; baiting; (*Koppel Hunde*) pack (of hounds); (*Menge*) swarm, host; *dial* (*Österreich*) = *Spaß*; **~en** *tr, itr* (*jagen*) to hunt; to drive; (*Hunde ~~ auf*) to set dogs on (*od* at); to sick on; (*eilen*) to hurry, to rush; (*aufreizen*) to incite, to instigate; to bait; to agitate; (*Leute gegeneinander aufhetzen*) to set at variance; (*verfolgen*) to chase, to pursue; *e-n Hasen ~~* to start a hare; *zu Tode ~~* to run to ground; *mit allen Hunden gehetzt fig* to know the rope; **~er**, **~redner** *m* (*Anstifter, Aufwiegler*) instigator agitator; inciter; baiter; demagog(ue); *Am* rabble rouser; **~erei** *f* incitement; (*Eile, Hast*) hurry; **~erisch** *a* inflammatory; **~feldzug** *m* inflammatory campaign; (*durch Greuelnachrichten*) atrocity campaign; **~hund** *m* (deer-) hound; **~jagd** *f* hunt(ing); (*Eile*) great hurry, rush; **~peitsche** *f* hunting-whip, dog-whip; **~presse** *f* yellow press, jingo paper; inflammatory press; **~rede** *f* inflammatory speech; **~schrift** *f* inflammatory writing; **~zeitung** *f*, **~blatt** *n* rag (newspaper).

Heu *n* hay; *~ einbringen* to bring in the hay; *~ machen* to make hay; *~ wenden* to toss hay; *Geld wie ~ haben* to have lots of money; to have money like dirt; to roll in wealth; to have money to burn; to stink of money; **~bazillus** *m* hay bacillus; **~binder** *m* hay trusser; **~boden** *m* hayloft; **~bündel** *n* bottle (*od* bundle) of hay; **~en** *tr* to make hay; **~er** *m* (*Heumacher*) haymaker; **~ernte** *f* hay harvest, hay-making; **~~maschine** *f* haymaking machine, harvesting machine for hay; **~fieber** *n*, **~schnupfen** *m* hay-fever, pollen-catarrh; **~gabel** *f* pitchfork; **~haufen** *m*, **~miete** *f* haycock, haystack, hayrick; *e-e Stecknadel in e-m ~haufen suchen* to look for a needle in a haystack; **~monat** *m*

July; **~pferd** *n*, **~schrecke** *f* grasshopper; (*Bibel*) locust; **~scheune** *f*, **~schober, ~schuppen, ~stadel** *m* (hay-) barn; hayrick; **~stapler** *m* haystacker; **~wagen** *m* hay-cart; **~wender** *m* hay tedder.

Heuch|elei *f* hypocrisy; (*Verstellung*) simulation; dissimulation; (*Unehrlichkeit*) insincerity, pretence; (*Falschheit*) falsehood, falseness; (*Scheinheiligkeit, Pharisäertum, Muckertum*) pharisaism, cant; bigotry; (*Täuschung, Schein, Schwindel*) sham, double--facedness; (*Betrug*) deceit, imposture; **~eln** *itr* to feign, to dissemble; to simulate; to play the hypocrite; *tr* to simulate, to affect; to feign; **~ler** *m*, **~~in** *f* hypocrite, dissembler; **~lerisch** *a* hypocritical, dissembling, deceitful.

Heuer *f mar* (*Lohn, Gehalt*) pay, hire, wages *pl*; **~baas** *m* crimp; shipping master; **~brief** *m* (*für Schiff*) charter--party; **~n** *tr* (*Matrosen*) to ship, to hire, to engage; (*Schiff*) to charter.

heu|er *adv* this year (*od* season); **~rig** *a* this year's, of this season; current.

Heul|bruder *m* whimperer, whiner; blubberer; sulky person; **~en** *itr* to howl; (*laut*) to scream, to yell; (*Wind*) to moan; to sigh; (*Sturm*) to howl, to roar, to rage; to bellow; (*Eule*) to hoot; (*Hund*) to howl; to yelp; (*Sirene*) to hoot, to screech; (*weinen*) to weep, to cry; (*winseln*) to whimper; (*Kind*) to squall, to brawl, to bawl; (*aus Wut ~~*) to howl with rage; **~erei** *f* howling, whimpering, whining; **~suse** *f fam* cry-baby; **~ton** *m* howling sound; multitone; **~tonne** *f mar* sounding (*od* whistling) buoy.

heut|e *adv* to-day, today, this day; *von ~e an* from this day forward; *~e abend* this evening, to-night, tonight; *~e früh, ~ morgen* this morning; *~e mittag* to-day at twelve o'clock, *Am* today noon; *~e nachmittag* this afternoon; *~e nacht* to-night, tonight; last night; *~e in 8 Tagen, ~e über 8 Tage* this day week, to-day week; *~e über 14 Tage* to-day fortnight; *~e über ein Jahr* a year hence; *~e vor 8 Tagen* a week ago to-day; *~e vormittag* this forenoon; *den wievielten haben wir ~e?* what's the day of the month? *bis ~e* till to-day (*od* this day); *für ~e* for this day; *noch ~e, ~e noch* this very day; *von ~e an* from this date; *~e mir, morgen dir* every one in his turn; **~e** *n* the present time; **~ig** *a* of this day; (*gegenwärtig*) at the present time, present; (*neuzeitlich*) modern; actual; *vom ~~en Tag com* (*Brief*) of this date; **~igentags** *adv* this day, at present; **~zutage** *adv* nowadays; to-day; in these days.

Hex|e *f* witch; hag; vixen; *alte ~~* old hag, hell-cat; **~en** *itr* to practise witchcraft; to work miracles; to conjure; *ich kann doch nicht ~~* I am no magician; **~enbann** *m* spell, charm; **~enbesen** *m* witch's broom; **~enbrut** *f* brood of witches; **~engeschichte** *f* witch-story; **~enkessel** *m fig* (*Durcheinander*) hubbub; **~enkreis** *m* magic circle; fairy ring; **~enkunst** *f* witchcraft; **~enmeister** *m* wizard, magician, sorcerer, conjurer; **~enprozeß** *m* trial for witchcraft; **~enschuß** *m med* lumbago; **~entanz** *m* dance of witches; **~enwerk** *n* witchery; **~erei** *f* witchcraft, magic, sorcery; (*Wirkung*) devil's trick; (*Taschenspielerei*) jugglery.

hie *adv* here; *siehe*: *hier*.

Hieb *m* (*Schlag*) blow; (*starker*) slash; *fam* bat; (*Streich*) stroke; (*Treffer*) hit; (*Schnitt*) cut; (*Wunde*) scar; (*Feilen~*) cut; (*Baum~*) felling; *fig* (*sarkastische Bemerkung*) cut, cutting remark, hit; sarcasm; *auf den ersten ~* at the first try; *~e bekommen* to get a thrashing (*od* licking); **~fest** *a* proof against blows; **~reif** *a* (*Wald*) ripe for the ax(e); **~waffe** *f* slashing weapon; *~~u. Stoßwaffen pl* cut-and-thrust weapons *pl*.

hienieden *adv* here below, in this life, on earth.

hier *adv* here, in this place; (*auf Briefen*) in town, present, *Am* City; *der Mann ~* this gentleman; *weder ~ noch dort* neither here nor there; *~! (Appell)* present! *~ ist es! (beim Überreichen e-s Gegenstandes)* here you are! *~ u. da* here and there, now and then; *~ oben* here above; *~ unten* here below; *von ~ aus* from hence; *~ irren Sie sich* there you are mistaken; *~ ist Frau W.! tele* this is Mrs. W.! *~ bin ich* here I am; **~an** *adv* at this, up here; hereat; after that; hereupon; by that; **~auf** *adv* hereupon, upon this; (*zeitlich*) then; **~aus** *adv* from this; *von ~~* hence; **~bei** *adv* hereat, herein; herewith; enclosed; hereby; **~durch** *adv* by this means, thus, hereby, thereby; (*kraft*) by (virtue of) the present; (*örtlich*) through this, this way; **~ein** *adv* in this, herein; **~für** *adv* for this, for it; **~gegen** *adv* against this; **~her** *adv* hither, here, this way; over here; *~~!* come here! *bis ~~* (*zeitlich*) till now, up to now; so far, thus far; *bis ~~ u. nicht weiter* so far and no farther; *das gehört nicht ~~* that is not pertinent; **~herum** *adv* hereabouts; **~hin** *adv* hither, to this place, this way; **~in** *adv* in this, herein, in it; **~mit** *adv* with this, with it, herewith; **~nach** *adv* after this, after it; hereafter; hereupon; (*demgemäß*) according to this; **~neben** *adv* next door; besides; **~nieden** *adv siehe*: **hienieden**; **~orts** *adv* in this place, here; **~sein** *n* presence; **~selbst** *adv* here, in this place; **~über** *adv* over here, beyond this, about it; (*betreffend*) hereon, on this account; about this; **~um** *adv* about (*od* around) this place; concerning this; **~unter** *adv* under this, beneath this; hereunder; among these; *~~ (verstehen)* by this, by that; **~von** *adv* herefrom, of this; **~zu** *adv* to this, moreover; in addition to this; *~~ kommt noch* to this must be added; **~zulande** *adv* in this country, with us, *Am* on this side of the ocean; **~zwischen** *adv* between these.

Hierarch|ie *f* hierarchy; **~isch** *a* hierarchical.

Hieroglyphe *f* hieroglyph.

hiesig *a* of this place (*od* town *od* country); (*lokal*) local; here; (*einheimisch*) domestic.

Hifthorn *n* hunting- (*od* bugle-)horn.

Hilf|e *f* help; (*Mitwirkung*) aid; co--operation; (*Unterstützung*) support; (*Beistand*) assistance; (*Hilfskraft*) help; stand-by; auxiliary; assistant; (*Rettung*) succour, rescue; help; (*Linderung der Not*) relief; (*Hilfsmittel*) resource; (*Heilmittel*) remedy; (*Abhilfe*) redress; *erste ~e* first aid; *ohne ~e* helpless; *weder Rat noch ~e wissen* to be at o.'s wits' end; *mit Gottes ~e!* with God's help! *zu ~e!* help! help! *jdm seine ~e anbieten* to offer o.'s aid to s. o.; *um ~e bitten* to ask for help; *zu ~e kommen* to come (*od* run) to s. o.'s aid; *~e leisten* to help, to aid, to assist; *etw zu ~e nehmen* to make use of s. th.; *um ~e rufen* to cry for help; **~eleistung** *f* assistance, help; rescue-work; *erste ~~* first aid; **~eruf** *m* cry for help; **~los** *a* helpless, destitute; **~losigkeit** *f* helplessness; **~reich** *a* helpful; charitable; benevolent.

Hilfs|arbeiter *m* assistant; help(er); temporary worker (*od* hand); unskilled worker; (*Beamter*) supernumerary; **~arzt** *m* assistant physician; **~ausschuß** *m* relief committee; **~bedürftig** *a* requiring help, indigent; **~beobachter** *m* assistant observer; **~bereit** *a* eager (*od* ready) to help; **~brücke** *f* auxiliary bridge; **~dienst** *m* auxiliary service; auxiliary A. R. P. service; (*Notdienst*) emergency service, *Am mot* (*bei Autopannen*) wrecker service; **~düse** *f* auxiliary jet; **~fallschirm** *m aero* auxiliary (*od* pilot) parachute; **~flügel** *m aero* auxiliary wing; (*Vorflügel*) slat; **~flugzeugträger** *m* escort (*od* auxiliary) airplane carrier; **~fond** *m* relief fund; **~frequenz** *f radio* auxiliary frequency; **~gelder** *n pl* subsidies *pl*, supplies *pl*; **~größe** *f* auxiliary quantity; **~kasse** *f* relief fund; (*Krankenkasse*) sick-fund; **~kirche** *f* chapel of ease; **~kraft** *f* additional helper, assistant; auxiliary personnel (*od* force), temporary employee; **~kreuzer** *m* auxiliary cruiser; **~kriegsschiff** *n* auxiliary navy vessel; **~lehrer** *m* assistant teacher; tutor; **~linie** *f* (*Geometrie*) auxiliary line; *mus* le(d)ger line; **~maschine** *f* auxiliary machine, donkey engine; **~maßnahme** *f* remedial measure; first-aid measure; relief measure; *~~n treffen* to take first-aid measures; **~mittel** *n* help, resource; (*Heilmittel*) remedy; adjuvant; (*Ausweg, Auskunftsmittel*) expedient, shift; instrument; *letztes ~~* last resort; *die ~~ pl* resources *pl*, means *pl*; aids and appliances *pl*; **~motor** *m* auxiliary motor (*od* engine); **~organisation** *f* relief organization; **~personal** *n* aids *pl*; **~pilot** *m aero* co-pilot; **~polizei** *f* auxiliary police; **~prediger** *m* curate; **~programm** *n* aid program(me); **~quelle** *f fig* resource, expedient; *ohne ~~n* resourceless; **~schiff** *n* auxiliary vessel, tender; armed trawler; **~schule** *f* school for backward children; **~stoff** *m* auxiliary material; **~trupp** *m* repair unit; **~truppen** *f pl* auxiliary troops *pl*; auxiliaries *pl*; replacements *pl*; **~vorrichtung** *f* auxiliary contrivance (*od* implement); **~wagen** *m mot* emergency car, *Am* wrecking car; **~werk** *n* (work of) relief; **~willige(r)** *m* auxiliary volunteer; **~wissenschaft** *f* auxiliary science; **~zeitwort** *n* auxiliary verb; **~zug** *m rail* safety train, relief train.

Himbeer|e *f* raspberry; **~eis** *n* raspberry-ice; **~geist** *m* raspberry brandy; **~saft** *m* raspberry-juice (*od* syrup); **~strauch** *m* raspberry-bush.

Himmel *m* (*der sichtbare ~*) sky; (*Firmament*) firmament, (*manchmal auch*) heavens *pl*; (*in religiösem Sinn*) heaven; (*Paradies*) upper world, paradise; (*Gott*) Heaven, God; (*Klima, Zone, Himmelsstrich*) zone, climate, heaven; (*Decke e-s Himmelbettes*) canopy; tester; *bewölkter ~* cloudy (*od* overcast) sky; *blauer ~* blue sky; *~ u. Hölle* heaven and hell; *der ~ auf Erden* heaven on earth; *am ~* in the sky; *aus heiterem ~* out of the blue; *ums ~s willen* for heaven's sake; *unter freiem ~* under the open sky; *unter freiem ~ schlafen* to sleep in the open air; *zwischen ~ u. Erde* between heaven and earth; ~ *u. Erde in Bewegung setzen* to leave no stone unturned; *der ~ würde nicht einfallen, wenn ...* the sky would not fall if ...; *aus allen ~n fallen* to be cruelly disappointed; *kein Meister ist vom ~ gefallen* no one is born a master; *jdn in den ~ heben* to praise s. o. to the skies; *das Blaue vom ~ herunterlügen* to lie audaciously; *'m siebenten ~ sein* to be in seventh heaven; *beim ~! interj* by Heaven! *dem ~ sei Dank!* thank Heaven! *du lieber ~!* great Heavens! **~an** *adv* (up) to the skies, skyward, heavenwards; **~angst** *f* mortal fear; *~~ a* terribly frightened; *mir wurde ~~* I was terribly frightened, *fam* I was in a blue funk; **~bett** *n* four-poster; **~blau** *a* azure, sky-blue; **~fahrt** *f* Ascension; *Mariä ~~* Assumption; **~~skommando** *n fam* forlorn hope; dangerous mission; **~hoch** *a* sky-high, very high; *adv fig* (*dringend*) urgently; *~~ bitten* to implore very earnestly; **~reich** *n* kingdom of heaven, paradise; **~sbahn** *f* celestial space; **~schreiend** *a* crying to heaven; (*abstoßend*) most atrocious; shameful; **~sgegend, ~srichtung** *f* direction (*od* quarter *od* region) of the heavens; *die vier ~~en* the four points of the compass; **~sgewölbe** *n* vault of heaven; **~skarte** *f* celestial map; **~s-körper** *m* celestial body; **~skreis** *m* celestial sphere; **~skugel** *f* celestial globe; **~skunde** *f* astronomy; **~sleiter** *f* Jacob's ladder; **~sluft** *f* ether; the open air; **~sortung** *f* celestial navigation; **~sraum** *m* celestial space; **~sreklame** *f* sky-writing, *Am* smoke writing; **~srichtung** *f* quarter of the heavens; **~sschlüssel** *n bot* common primrose; **~sschrift** *f aero* (*Reklame*) sky-writing, *Am* smoke writing; **~sstrich** *m* zone, region; climate, clime; latitude; **~swagen** *m astr* Great Bear; **~swölbung** *f* vault of the sky; celestial globe; **~szeichen** *n* celestial sign; **~szelt** *n* vault of heaven; **~wärts** *adv* heavenward(s); **~weit** *a* miles apart; very distant (*od* wide); *~~ verschieden sein* to differ widely; *es ist ein ~~er Unterschied* it makes all the difference in the world.

himmlisch *a* heavenly, celestial; (*göttlich*) divine; *~! interj* lovely! *~er Vater* Our Father in heaven; *~es Wesen* divinity.

hin *adv* there, thither, to; towards; along; over; *oben ~* on the surface; *unten ~* along the ground; *über die ganze Welt ~* all over the world; *nach allen Richtungen ~* in all directions, *nach links ~* to the left; (*vorbei*) away, gone, lost; (*kaputt*) ruined, undone; shot; (*erschöpft*) exhausted, spent; *~ ist ~* gone is gone; lost is lost; *~ u. her* to and fro, backwards and forwards, back and forwards, *Am* back and forth; *darauf ... ~* upon; in consequence of; according to; *auf diese Bedingung hin* (up)on this condition; *auf die Gefahr ~* at the risk; *auf Ihr Wort ~* on your word; *~ sein* to be done for; to be lost; *er ist ~* he is dead; *~ u. wieder* here and there, now and then; *~ u. zurück* there and back; (*Transport*) out and home; *eine Fahrkarte* (*od Flugkarte*) *~ u. zurück* a return-ticket, *Am* a round-trip ticket; *~ u. her bewegen* to move to and fro; *sich ~ u. her bewegen* to move about; *~ u. her fahren* (*od reisen*) to shuttle; *~ u. her gehen* to walk up and down; *~- u. hergehen* to go and come; to reciprocate; *~ u. her laufen* to run backwards and forwards; *~ u. her überlegen* (*od bedenken*) to consider a matter over and over again, to turn over in o.'s mind.

hinab *adv* down; downward(s), down there; *~ mit ihr!* down with her! *hinauf u. ~* up and down; *den Berg ~* down the hill, downhill; *den Strom ~* down the river, downstream; **~bringen** *irr tr* to take (*od* bring) down; **~fahren** *irr itr* to drive (*od* ride, cycle, motor) down; to descend; (*Strom*) to sail (*od* go) down the river; **~fallen** *irr itr* to fall down; **~schleudern** *tr* to precipitate; **~sehen** *irr itr* to look down on; **~spülen** *tr* to wash down; **~steigen** *irr itr* (*Berg*) to climb down; to go down; **~stürzen** *itr* to tumble (*od* fall) down; (*Getränk*) to toss (*od* tip) off; **~wärts** *adv* downward(s).

hinan *adv* up, up to, upward(s); *den Berg ~* uphill; **~steigen** *irr itr* (*Berg*) to ascend, to mount, to climb up.

hinarbeiten *itr* to aim (*auf* at).

hinauf *adv* up, up to; on high; upward(s); *da ~* up there; *~ u. hinab* up and down; *von unten ~* up from below; *die Straße ~* up the street, *Am* upstreet; **~arbeiten**: *sich ~~* (*fig*) to work o.'s way up; **~begeben** *irr: sich ~~* to go up; **~fahren** *irr itr* to drive (*od* ride) up; (*Fluß*) to sail (*od* steam *od* row) up; **~gehen** *irr itr* to go up; (*Treppe*) to go upstairs; (*Preise*) to rise; **~kriechen** *irr itr* to creep (*od* crawl) up; **~setzen** *tr* (*Preise*) to raise; **~steigen** *irr itr* to mount, to ascent; to step up; **~treiben** *irr tr* (*Preise*) to run up; to drive up, *Am* to crowd up; **~ziehen** *irr tr* to pull up; *itr* to go up.

hinaus *adv* out; (*außerhalb*) outside; *~ aus, zu etw ~* out of s. th.; *darüber ~, über etw ~* (*räumlich*) beyond; (*zeitlich*) past; (*übersteigend*) above; *für Monate ~* for months; *da ~* out there; *hier ~* out here; *hinten ~* at the back, in the rear; *sie wohnt nach hinten ~* she is living at the back of the house; *er wohnt nach vorne ~* he is living in front of the house; *oben ~* above out; *über das Grab ~* beyond the grave; *wo soll das ~?* what will that lead to? *sie wußte nicht wo ~* she did not know what to do; she was at her wits' end; *zum Hause ~* out of the house; *zum Fenster ~* out of the window; *zur Tür ~* out through the door, out of doors; *~! interj* out! *Am sl* scram! *~ mit dir!* out with you! *~ mit ihm!* throw him out! **~begleiten** *tr* (*jdn ~~*) to see s. o. out; **~blicken** *itr* to look out; **~dampfen** *itr* to steam out; **~gehen** *irr itr* (*Raum etc verlassen*) to go out, to leave; *nach Süden ~~* to be exposed to the south; *auf etw ~~* (*Zimmer, Fenster etc*) to face, to look out on (*od* into); to open (up)on, to overlook; *über etw ~~* to go beyond; (*übertreffen, übersteigen*) to surpass, to exceed; *fig* (*resultieren, als Ergebnis haben*) to end in, to result in; (*herausstehen*) to jug out; **~jagen** *tr* to turn out, to expel, to chase out; **~kommen** *irr itr* to come out; to amount (to); *auf eins ~~* to come to the same thing; to add up to the same thing; **~laufen** *irr itr* to run out; *fig* to come up (*auf* to), to amount to; *auf dasselbe ~~* to come to the same, to amount to the same thing; *auf nichts ~~* to lead to nothing; **~lehnen**: *sich ~~* to lean out; **~schicken** *tr* to send out; **~schieben** *irr tr* to shove out; (*aufschieben*) to postpone, to put off, to defer, to delay; (*in die Länge ziehen*) to protract; *e-e Frist ~~* to extend the time; **~schießen** *irr itr* (*über das Ziel*) to overshoot the mark; **~schleichen** *irr: sich ~~* to steal away; **~sein** *irr itr* to be past (*od* beyond *od* above) s. th.; not to care for; *darüber ist sie schon ~* she is above such things, she is past that stage now; *über die 19 ~sein* to be out of o.'s teens; **~stellen** *tr* to put out (-side); **~treiben** *irr tr* to drive out, to expel, *Am* to crowd out; **~wagen**: *sich ~~* to venture out; **~werfen** *irr tr* to cast out, to throw out, to expel; (*jdn*) to turn out s. o., to fire s. o., *sl* to chuck out s. o.; (*entlassen*) to dismiss from employment, *Am* to bounce, *Am fam* to fire; (*Geld etc*) *zum Fenster ~~* (*fig*) to throw away; **~werfer** *m* (*in e-m Lokal, e-r Versammlung etc*) *sl* chucker-out, bully, *Am* bouncer; **~wollen** *itr* to want to go (*od* get) out; *fig* (*hinzielen, beabsichtigen*) to drive at, to be driving at, to aim at; *hoch ~~* to aim high; *sie will zu hoch ~* she aims too high; **~ziehen** *irr tr* to drag out, to draw out; (*hinausschieben*) to put off, to prolong; *itr aufs Land ~~* to move out (in)to the country.

Hin|blick *m*: *im* (*od in*) *~~ auf* with regard to, in regard to (*od* of), in view of, with a view to, in consideration of, considering; **~blicken** *itr* (*auf etw*) to look forward to; (*nach etw*) to look (*od* to glance) at; **~bringen** *irr tr* (*transportieren*) to bring, to carry to a place; (*führen*) to lead to, to take there; (*begleiten*) to accompany; (*Zeit*) to pass (away), to spend; (*müßig*) to idle away o.'s time; *sein Leben kümmerlich ~~* to eke out a bare existence; **~brüten** *itr* to brood, to sit brooding; (*schwermütig*) to be in the dumps; *vor sich ~~* to be brooding; *~~ n* brooding; (*schwermütige Stimmung*) gloomy meditation, dumps *pl*; (*stärker*) apathy, lethargy; **~dämmern** *itr* to doze away, to be half asleep, to sleep drowsily; **~denken** *irr itr: wo denkst du hin!* what are you thinking of!

hinder|lich *a* (*im Wege*) in the way; hindering; impeding; obstructive; (*lästig*) cumbersome, troublesome; (*störend*) embarrassing; (*unangenehm*) inconvenient; *~~ sein* to hinder from; (*jdm im Weg stehen*) to stand in s. o.'s way; **~n** *tr* (*aufhalten*) to hinder; (*hemmen*) to hamper, to impede; (*ganz abhalten*) to prevent (*von* from), to stop (*von* from); (*einhalten*) to check; to stop; to bar, to block; (*abhalten, verzögern*) to delay; (*zurückhalten*) to restrain (*an* from); (*verstopfen, fig belasten*) to clog; (*fig fesseln, hemmen*) to trammel, to shackle, *Am* to hog-tie; *das hindert nicht* (*schließt nicht aus*) that does not preclude; **~nis** *n* (*zeitweilig*) hindrance; (*im Weg stehendes ~~*) obstacle; (*Hemmnis*) impediment; (*Verhinderung*) prevention; (*Sperre*) bar, barrier; (*plötzliches ~~*) check; (*Schwierigkeit*) difficulty; (*unerwartetes ~~*) *fig* snag; (*Benachteiligung*) handicap; *gesetzliches ~~* legal impediment; (statutory) bar; estoppel; *jdm ~nisse in den Weg legen* to throw obstacles in s. o.'s way; *~nisse aus dem Weg räumen* to remove all obstacles; *auf ~nisse stoßen* to run into obstacles; *auf ein unerwartetes ~nis stoßen* (*fig*) to run into a snag; *das Haupt~nis war die Zurückhaltung der europäischen Staaten* the chief snag was the reluctance of the European nations; **~~bahn** *f* obstacle course; **~~feuer** *n aero* obstacle (*od* obstruction) light; **~~rennen** *n* obstacle race; (*Pferde*) steeplechase;

(*Hürdenrennen*) hurdle race; **~ung** *f* hindrance; prevention; impediment; obstacle; distortion.

hindeuten *itr* to point (*auf* to *od* at); *fig* to hint, to intimate, to aim (*auf* at); (*anzeigen*) to indicate.

Hindin *f* hind.

Hindu *m* Hindu, Hindoo; **~ismus** *m* Hinduism, Hindooism; **~kusch** *m* (*Gebirge*) Hindu Kush; **~stan** *n* Hindustan, Hindostan; **~stani** *n* (*Sprache*) Hindustani, Hindoostanee.

hindurch *adv* through, *Am auch* thru, throughout; (*über*) across; *durch die Felder ~* across the fields; (*zeitlich*) during; throughout; *das ganze Jahr ~* throughout the year, all the year round; *den ganzen Tag ~* all day (long), all the day; *Jahre ~* for years and years; *mitten ~* right (*od* straight) through; *lange Zeit ~* for a long time; **~arbeiten**: *sich ~~* to make o.'s way through; (*Buch*) to study from beginning to end; **~dringen** *irr itr* to penetrate; to permeate; **~fallen** *irr itr* to fall through, to pass through; **~gehen** *irr itr* to pass through, to transit; **~lassen** *irr tr* to let through, to pass; **~laufen** *irr itr* to pass through; **~leiten** *tr* to lead through, to pass through; **~streichen** *irr itr* to flow through, to pass through; **~strömen** *itr* to flow through, to pass through, to move through; **~ziehen** *irr tr* to pull through, to drag through; to draw through.

hinein *adv* in, into, inside; *in den Tag ~ leben* to lead an easy life; *in den Tag ~ reden* to talk at random; **~arbeiten** *tr* to work in(to); *sich ~~ in* to make o. s. thoroughly acquainted with, to familiarize o. s. with; **~bringen** *irr tr* to take in, to bring in, to get in; **~denken** *irr: sich ~~ in jds Lage* to put o. s. in s. o.'s place; **~dringen** *irr itr* to penetrate into; **~finden** *irr: sich ~~ in* to become familiar with, to understand; **~gehen** *irr itr* to go in(to); (*Platz finden*) to find room; (*fassen*) to hold, to contain; to accommodate; **~legen** *tr* to put in; (*beschwindeln, hereinlegen*) to take in; **~mischen**: *sich ~~ in* to interfere in; **~passen** *tr, itr* to fit, to fit into; **~reden** *itr* to interfere in; *ins Blaue ~~* to talk at random; **~stecken** *tr* to put in(to); (*sein Geld, Vermögen in etw ~~*) to invest o.'s money in; *seine Nase in alles ~~* to stick o.'s nose into everything; **~stehlen** *irr: sich ~~* to sneak in, to steal in; **~tun** *irr tr* to put in(to); to add to; **~wagen**: *sich ~~* to venture (to go) in; **~wollen** *itr* to want to go in; *das wollte mir nicht in den Kopf ~* I couldn't understand it; **~ziehen** *irr tr* to pull in(to); (*in etw verwickeln*) to draw into, to involve in, to implicate; (*einverleiben*) to incorporate; **~zwängen** *tr* to force into.

hin|fahren *irr tr* to drive there; to drive, to convey to (a place); *itr* to go to; (*entlang fahren*) to drive along, to sail along (the coast); (*über etw*) to pass over; *fig* (*sterben*) to die, to pass away; **~fahrt** *f* voyage out; journey (*od* trip) there; *auf der ~~* on the way there; *nur ~~* single, *Am* one way; *~~ u. Rückfahrt rail* round trip; passage (*od* voyage) there and back; **~fallen** *irr itr* to fall (down); *sie ist ~gefallen* she fell; *~~ lassen* to drop; **~fällig** *a* (*schwach*) weak, infirm; (*gebrechlich*) frail, decaying; (*vergänglich*) perishable; (*von Gründen*) shaky, (*unhaltbar*) untenable, (*ungültig*) null and void; (*veraltet*) obsolete; *~~ vor Alter* worn with age; *~~ werden* to fail, to come to nothing; (*Vertrag*) to be cancelled, to be annulled; **~fälligkeit** *f* weakness, infirmity; debility; (*Alter*) decrepitude; (*von Gründen*) shakiness; **~flug** *m aero* outgoing flight; **~fort** *adv* henceforth; (*in Zukunft*) in (the) future, for the future; **~führen** *tr, itr* to take there, to take to; *fig* to lead to; *wo soll das ~~?* where will this lead to? **~gabe** *f* (*Lieferung*) delivery; (*Ergebenheit*) devotedness, devotion; resignation; (*Übergabe*) surrender; **~gang** *m* passage (to); *fig* (*Tod*) decease, death; **~geben** *irr tr* (*weggeben*) to give away; (*aufgeben*) to abandon; (*überlassen*) to give up; (*opfern*) to sacrifice; *sich e-r Sache ~~* to devote o. s. to, to indulge in; *sich ~~* to give o. s. up to; (*sich prostituieren*) to prostitute o. s.; **~gebend** *a* devoted; **~gebung** *f* devotion; surrender; **~~svoll** *a* devoted; **~gegen** *adv* on the other hand; on the contrary; whereas; **~gehen** *irr itr* to go to, to go there; (*vergehen*) to pass (away); *fig* (*über etw ~~*) to pass over s. th.; *etw ~~ lassen* to make allowance for s. th.; to let pass s. th., to overlook s. th.; *~~ u. hergehen tech* to reciprocate; **~halten** *irr tr* to hold out; (*Geld anbieten*) to tender (money); *fig jdn ~~* to put s. o. off; **~~d** *a* holding, delaying; *~~es Gefecht* delaying action; *~~er Widerstand* delaying action; **~hängen** *irr tr* to hang (up); *seinen Mantel ~~* to hang o.'s coat.

hinken *itr* to go lame; to limp; (*humpeln*) to hobble; *fig* to be incomplete; *der Vergleich hinkt* that's a lame (*od* poor) comparison; **~d** *a* lame; *ein ~der Beweis* a lame proof; *der ~de Bote* the lame post.

hin|knien *itr* to kneel down; **~kommen** *irr itr* to come to, to arrive at; to get there; *wo ist mein Geld ~gekommen* what has become of my money; **~langen** *tr, itr* to reach; **~länglich** *a* sufficient, competent, requisite; adequate; *mehr als ~~* enough; **~lassen** *irr tr* to let go to (a place); (*zulassen*) to admit; **~leben** *itr* to live on; *sorglos ~~* to pass o.'s life carelessly; **~legen** *tr* to lay (*od* put) down; *sich ~~* to lie down; (*zu Bett gehen*) to go to bed; **~leiten, ~lenken** *tr* to turn to; to conduct to; *jds Aufmerksamkeit ~lenken auf* to draw s. o.'s attention to; **~nehmen** *irr tr* to take, to accept; to receive; (*sich gefallen lassen, erdulden*) to bear; to suffer; to put up with; **~neigen** *tr, itr* (*sich*) to incline (*od* to lean) to.

hinnen *adv: von ~* from hence, away from here; *von ~ gehen fig* to die.

hin|raffen *tr* to carry off; to snatch away; (*durch Tod*) to cut off; **~reichen** *tr* to hand over; to give; *itr* to be sufficient; to suffice; **~reichend** *a* sufficient; **~reise** *f* journey there; voyage out; *auf der ~~* on the way there; **~reisen** *itr* to go there, to travel to; **~reißen** *irr tr* to tear along, to carry along; *fig* (*entzücken*) to transport, to charm, to ravish; (*bewegen*) to move; (*Leidenschaft*) to carry off; (*Zuhörer im Theater ~~*) to bring down the house; *sich ~~ lassen* to be overcome (*von* with); **~reißend** *a* charming, enchanting, ravishing; **~richten** *tr* to direct toward; (*Verbrecher*) to execute, to put to death; (*enthaupten*) to behead; *el* to electrocute; **~richtung** *f* execution; (*Enthauptung*) beheading; *el* electrocution; **~rotzen** *tr aero sl* to make a crash-landing; **~rücken** *tr, itr* to (re)move there; **~schaffen** *tr* to carry, to convey (*nach* to); to transport (to); **~scheiden** *irr itr* to die, to decease, to pass away; **~schicken** *tr* to send there, to send to; **~schlachten** *tr* to massacre, to butcher, to kill; to murder; **~schlagen** *irr itr* to fall down; **~schleifen, ~schleppen** *tr* to drag along; *sich ~~* to drag on o.'s existence; **~schmeißen** *irr tr fam* to fling down; **~schreiben** *irr tr* (*niederschreiben*) to write down; *nach London ~~* to write to London; **~schwinden** *irr itr* to pass away, to vanish, to dwindle (away), to fade; **~sehen** *irr itr* to look at *od* to(wards); **~setzen** *tr* to put down, to set down; *sich ~~* to sit down, to take a seat; **~sicht** *f* respect, view, regard; (*Erwägung*) consideration; (*Beziehung*) relation; *in jeder ~~* in every respect, on all accounts; *in ~~ auf* with regard to; in regard to, in view of, with respect to; *in dieser ~~* in this regard; **~sichtlich** *a* in respect of, with regard to, concerning; as for; as to; **~siechen** *itr* to pine away; **~sinken** *irr itr* to sink down, to fall; to drop (down); (*zusammenbrechen*) to collapse; **~stellen** *tr* to put down, to place; *fig* to represent; to hold up; **~sterben** *irr itr* to die away; **~strecken** *tr* to stretch out; (*niederschlagen*) to knock down; (*töten*) to kill, to shoot; *sich ~~* to lie down (at full length).

hintan *adv* behind, aside, back, after; **~setzen, ~stellen** *tr* to set aside, to postpone; (*vernachlässigen*) to slight, to neglect, *fig* (*geringschätzen*) to disregard; **~setzung** *f* slighting, neglect, omission, ignoring, forgetting, overlooking, disregard; *unter* (*od mit*) *~~* regardless of.

hinten *adv* behind, after; at the back, in the back; (*im Hintergrund*) in the background; (*ganz ~*) in the rear; *mar* aft; *~ im Buch* at the end of the book; *nach ~* backwards; (*im Schiff*) astern; *nach ~ gehen* to go behind; *nach ~ hin* behind, to the rear; *ein Zimmer nach ~ hinaus* a back-room; *von ~* (*her*) from behind, from the back; *von ~ angreifen* (*od anfallen od überfallen*) to attack from behind, to attack in the rear; *vorn u. ~* in front and behind; *weit ~* far behind, far back; *~ anfügen* to add; *sich ~ anschließen* (*beim Anstehen*) to join in ... the rear; *~ ausschlagen* to kick up o.'s heels; **~nach** *adv* behind; in the rear; (*zeitlich*) afterward(s); subsequently; **~über** *adv* backward(s); upside down.

hinter *prp* behind; back, in back of, at the back of, on the back of, *Am* back of; backwards; after; *~ dem Haus* at the back of the house; *~ den Kulissen theat* backstage; *~ mir* behind me; *~ meinem Rücken* behind my back, unknown to me; without my knowing it; *~ Schloß u. Riegel* under lock and key; *~ etw kommen* to find out, to discover; (*erfassen, verstehen*) to get the knack of s. th., to get into the swim of s. th; *~ etw* (*od jdm*) *her sein* to be after s. th. (*od* s. o.), to run after s. th. (*od* s. o.), to pursue s. th. (*od* s. o.); *~ e-r Sache stecken* to be at the bottom of s. th.; *~ sich bringen* to get over; (*Entfernung*) to cover; *etw ~ sich haben* to have got over s. th., to be through s. th.; *jdn ~ sich haben* to be backed by s. o.; *~ sich lassen* to leave behind, to outdistance; *jdn ~ das Licht führen fig* to deceive (*od* to dupe) s. o.; *sich etw ~ die Ohren schreiben fig* to remember

s. th.; *es* (*faustdick*) ~ *den Ohren haben* to be very cunning, to be a sly one; ~**achsantrieb** *m* rear-axle drive; ~**achse** *f* rear axle; *rail* trailing axle; ~**ansicht** *f* backview, rear view; ~**backe** *f* buttock; ~**bein** *n* hind leg; *sich auf die* ~~*e stellen* (*Pferd*) to rear; *fig* to show o.'s teeth; ~**bliebene** *f*, ~~**(r)** *m* survivor; dependant; dependent; the bereaved; ~**bliebenenfürsorge** *f* dependant's allowance; ~**bliebenenversicherung** *f* survivor's insurance; ~**brin'gen** *irr tr* (*heimlich*) to give notice (*od* information) of s. th.; (*anzeigen*) to inform s. o. of, to denounce, to bring charge against; ~**bringer** *m* informer; tell--tale; (*Denunziant*) denouncer; ~**bringung** *f* information; intelligence; ~**bug** *m* ham; ~**deck** *n mar* (*Achterdeck*) poop, quarter-deck; ~**drein** *adv* behind, after, at the end; (*zeitlich*) too late; ~**e** *a* behind, back, hind; at the back; posterior; ~**e** *m* (*Hinterteil*) hind (part), back (part); behind, backside, posterior; bottom, seat; ~**einander** *adv* one after the other, one after another, one by one; in a row, in succession, in series; successively; *drei Tage* ~~ three days running, three successive days; *dicht* ~~ closely; ~~*gehen* to go in (single) file, *Am* to go in Indian file; ~~*schalten el* to connect in series; ~**einanderschaltung** *f el* serial (*od* series) connection; ~**feder** *f* rear spring; ~**fenster** *n* back (*od* rear) window; ~**flügel** *m arch* back wing; ~**fuß** *m* hind foot, hind leg; ~**gabel** *f* (*Motorrad*) back fork; ~**gebäude** *n* back--building, back premises *pl*; ~**gedanke** *m* (mental) reservation; ulterior motive; *ohne* ~~*n* without reserve (*od* reservation), (*offen*) candidly; ~**ge'hen** *irr tr* (*betrügen, täuschen*) to dupe, to deceive, to fool; to cheat, to impose on, *Am* to double-cross; ~**grund** *m* (*Malerei*) background; rear; *theat* flat scene, background; *im* ~~ in the rear; *im* ~~ *bleiben* to keep in the background; ~**halt** *m* ambush; (*Falle*) trap; *aus dem* ~~ *angreifen* to ambush; *in e-n* ~~ *locken* to draw into an ambush; *im* ~~ *liegen* to lie in ambush; ~**hältig** *a* reserved; (*hinterlistig*) underhand, insidious; sly; malicious; ~**hand** *f* (*Pferd*) hind quarter; (*Kartenspiel*) younger (*mehr als 2 Spieler:* youngest) hand; ~**hang** *m* reverse slope; ~~**stellung** *f mil* reverse-slope position; ~**haupt** *n anat* occiput; ~~**sbein** *n* occipital bone; ~**haus** *n* back (of the) house, back premises *pl*; ~**her** *adv* (*räumlich*) behind, in the rear; (*zeitlich*) after, (*danach*) subsequently, afterward(s); ~~**laufen** *irr itr* to run after; ~**hof** *m* backyard, back court; ~**kante** *f aero* trailing edge (of a wing); ~**kopf** *m* back of head; *anat* occiput; ~**lader** *m* breech-loader; ~**land** *n* interior of a country; inland (area); hinterland; *Am* back-country; ~**lassen** *irr tr* to leave behind; (*testamentarisch*) to bequeath s. th. to s. o.; (*Nachricht etc*) to leave word; ~ *a* (*nachgelassen*) posthumous; ~**lassenschaft** *f* property left, inheritance; *jur* estate; ~**lauf** *m* hind leg; ~**le gen** *tr* to deposit (*bei* with), to place on deposit; to give in trust; ~**leger** *m* depositor; ~**legung** *f* deposition; *gegen* ~~ *von* on deposition of; ~**leib** *m* (*Tiere*) hindquarters *pl*; *anat* back; dorsum; ~**linse** *f phot* back lense; ~**list** *f* artifice; (*Verschlagenheit*) cunning; (*Streich*) trick; (*Betrug*) deceit, fraud; ~**listig** *a* (*verschlagen*) cunning, artful; (*betrügerisch*) deceitful; (*falsch*) false, perfidious; ~**mann** *m mil* rear-rank man; *mar* next astern; *fig* (*Unterstützer*) supporter, backer; (*Drahtzieher*) wire-puller; (*auf Wechseln*) subsequent endorser; ~**n** *m fam* backside, bottom, seat; *auf den* ~~ *fallen* to fall on o.'s bottom; *jdm den* ~~ *voll hauen* to whip s. o.'s backside; ~**rad** *n rail* hind (*od* back) wheel; (*mot, Fahrrad*) rear wheel; ~~**achse** *f mot* back axle; ~~**antrieb** *m mot* rear wheel drive; ~~**aufhängung** *f mot* rear wheel suspension; ~~**bremse** *f* rear wheel brake; ~~**federung** *f* (*Motorrad*) rear wheel springing; ~~**nabe** *f* rear wheel hub; ~~**reifen** *m* back tyre, *Am* back tire; ~**rücks** *adv* from behind; behind o.'s back; *fig* (*verstohlen*) stealthily; treacherously; ~**schiff** *n mar* stern; ~**seite** *f* rear (side); back; ~**sitz** *m mot* backseat, rear seat; ~**st(e)** *a* hindmost, last; ~**steven** *m mar* stern post; ~**teil** *n* back (*od* hind) part; (*Hintern*) backside, bottom; buttocks *pl*; (*Schiff*) stern; ~**treffen** *n* rearguard, reserve; *ins* ~~ *kommen* (*od geraten*) to have to take a backseat, to be handicapped; ~**trei'ben** *irr tr* (*hindern*) to hinder, to prevent; (*vereiteln*) to frustrate, to thwart, to obstruct; to baffle; ~**treibung** *f* hindrance, prevention; (*Vereitelung*) frustration; ~**treppe** *f* backstairs *pl*; ~~**nroman** *m* shilling shocker, *Am* dime novel; ~**tür** *f* back-door; (*Eingang*) back entrance; *fig* escape, loophole; outlet; *sich ein* ~*türchen offen halten* to keep a back--door open; ~**viertel** *n* hind quarter; (*Fleisch*) loin; ~**wäldler** *m* backwoodsman, *Am auch* hillbilly; ~**wärts** *adv* backward(s); behind; ~**zie'hen** *irr tr* (*unterschlagen*) to defraud, to evade, to embezzle; *Steuern* ~~ to defraud the revenues, to evade taxes; ~**ziehung** *f* (*von Steuern*) defraudation, evasion; ~**zimmer** *n* backroom.

hin|tragen *irr tr* to carry there; ~**treten** *irr itr* to step forth; ~**tun** *irr tr* to put, to place; *wo soll ich das Buch* ~~*?* where shall I put the book? *ich weiß nicht, wo ich sie* ~~ *soll* (I have met her before, but) I can't place her.

*

hinüber *adv* over, over there; to the other side; across, beyond; (*Fleisch etc*) high; *er ist* ~ *fig* he is dead and gone; ~**blicken** *itr* to look over to, to look across to; ~**bringen** *irr tr* to bring (*od* to take) over (*od* across); ~**fahren** *irr tr* to carry over, to transport; *itr* to cross, to pass; ~**gehen** *irr itr* to go over, to cross; ~**kommen** *irr itr* to get over; ~**lassen** *irr tr* to let cross over; ~**reichen** *tr* to hand over; ~**schwimmen** *irr itr* to swim over (*od* across); ~**setzen** *tr* to drive over; ~**springen** *irr itr* (*über etw*) to jump over; (*rasch zu jdm gehen*) to run over to; ~**tragen** *irr tr* to carry over (*od* across); ~**werfen** *irr tr* to throw across; ~**wollen** *itr* to want (*od* to wish) to go over; ~**ziehen** *irr tr* to draw over; *itr* to pass over; to move to the other side.

hinunter *adv* down; down there; downwards; *siehe auch: herunter;* (*Berg*) down the hill, downhill; (*Treppe*) downstairs; *die Straße* ~~ down the street; ~**blicken** *itr*, ~**schauen** *itr* to look down (*auf* upon); ~**bringen** *irr tr* to get down; ~**fahren** *irr itr* to go down; ~**fallen** *irr itr* to fall down; ~**gehen** *irr itr* to go down, to walk down, to step down; ~**gießen** *irr tr* to pour down; (*Getränk*) to toss off; ~**schlingen** *irr tr*, ~**schlucken** *tr* to swallow; ~**spülen** *tr* to wash down; ~**werfen** *irr tr* to throw down; *jdn die Treppe* ~~ to kick s. o. downstairs; ~**wärts** *adv* downward(s); ~**'weg** *m* downway; way there.

hinweg' *adv* away, off; ~*! interj* off! ~ *mit dir!* away with you! get away! be gone! ~**begeben** *irr: sich* ~~ to go away; ~**führen** *tr* to lead away; ~**gehen** *irr itr* to go away; *über etw* ~~ to skip s. th.; to pass lightly over s. th.; ~**kommen** *irr itr* (*über etw* ~~) to get over; *er kann nicht darüber* ~~ he can't get over it; ~**raffen** *tr* to cut off; ~**sehen** *irr itr* to see over; to look over s. th.; *fig* (*übersehen*) to overlook; ~**sein** *irr itr* to be above (*od* past) s. th.; *sie ist darüber* ~ she is above such prejudices; *über alle Gefahr* ~~ to be past all danger; ~**setzen**: *sich* ~~ *über* to disregard, to brush aside, to make light of s. th.; ~**streiten** *irr tr* (*hinwegdisputieren*) to argue away (*od* off); ~**zaubern** *tr* to spirit away (*od* off).

Hin|weis *m*, ~**weisung** *f* indication (*auf* to); (*Anspielung*) allusion; hint (*auf* at); (*schriftlicher* ~~) notice; (*Anweisung*) direction; (*Verweis auf*) reference to; (*Rückverweis*) cross reference; ~**weisen** *irr tr* (*jdn* ~~ *auf*) to direct s. o. (to), to refer s. o. (to); (*zeigen*) to show; *itr* (*auf etw* ~~) to point at (*od* to) s. th., to refer to s. th.; to suggest s. th.; to call (*od* draw) s. o.'s attention to; ~**weisend** *a* indicative; *gram* demonstrative; ~**weiskarte** *f* cross-reference card; ~**welken** *itr* to fade away; ~**werfen** *irr tr* to throw down, to fling down; to chuck (it); (*niederschreiben*) to pen, to write down; *ein Wort* ~~ to drop a word; *e-e Bemerkung* ~~ to make (*od* drop) a remark; ~**wieder(um)** *adv* in return; (*zeitlich*) again; (*nochmals*) once more; ~**wollen** *itr* to intend to go to; *ich weiß, wo Sie* ~~ I know what you are driving at; ~**zählen** *tr* to count down; ~**zeigen** *itr* to point at; ~**ziehen** *irr tr* to draw to; *fig* (*anziehen*) to attract; *sich zu jdm* ~*gezogen fühlen* to be attracted by; *sich* ~~ (*zeitlich*) to drag on, to drag out; (*räumlich*) to stretch (*bis nach* to); *itr* (*umziehen nach*) to move to; ~**zielen** *itr* to aim at; to have in view.

hinzu *adv* (*örtlich*) to (the spot), near, there; (*außerdem*) in addition to, moreover, besides; ~**denken** *irr tr* to add in thought; *das übrige können Sie sich* ~~ you may guess the rest; ~**dichten** *tr* to embellish a story, to add with the aid of o.'s imagination; ~**eilen** *itr* to hasten to, to hurry along; ~**fügen** *tr* to add, to subjoin; (*beilegen in Briefen etc*) to enclose; ~**fügung** *f* addition; apposition; *unter* ~~ *von* ... adding ...; ~**gesellen**: *sich* ~~ to join (a company); to associate; ~**kommen** *irr itr* (*herbeikommen*) to come up (to); (*zufällig hinzutreten*) to drop in by chance; (*noch* ~~) to be added; *es kommt noch* ~, *daß* ... add to this, that ...; ~**lassen** *irr tr* to admit; ~**legen** *tr* to add to; ~**rechnen** *tr* to reckon with, to include in; to add; ~**schreiben** *irr*, ~**setzen**, ~**tun** *irr tr* to add to, to annex to; ~**treten** *irr itr* (*herankommen*) to come up (to); to approach; (*sich anschließen*) to join (a company); (*noch dazukommen*) to be added to; (*beitreten*) to accede; *es tritt* ~, *daß* ... it is to be added that ...; ~**wählen** *tr* to elect (*od* to choose) in addition; ~**zählen** *tr* to add to; ~**ziehen** *irr tr* to add, to include; (*zu e-r Gesellschaft*) to draw (in)to; (*zweiten Arzt*) to consult, to call in; *es wurde ein Spezialist ~gezogen* a specialist was called in.

Hiob *m* (*fig Dulder*) Job; **~sbote** *m* bearer of bad news; **~sbotschaft, ~spost** *f* bad news *pl mit sing*; **~sgeduld** *f* patience of Job.

Hippe *f* (*Gartenmesser*) bill-hook, hedging-bill, vine-knife; (*Sense*) scythe; *die ~ des Todes fig* the scythe of death; (*Gebäck*) wafer.

Hirn *n* brain; (*Verstand, Intelligenz*) brains *pl*; **~bohrer** *m* trepan; **~gespinst** *n* chimera, fancy; whim, bogy; **~hautentzündung** *f* meningitis; **~los** *a* brainless; (*zerfahren*) hare-brained; **~säge** *f* crosscut saw; **~schale** *f* cranium, skull; **~schlag** *m* (fit of) apoplexy; **~verbrannt** *a* frantic, crazy; mad; **~verletzte(r)** *m* soldier suffering from brain injury; **~verrückt** *a* crack-brained.

Hirsch *m* stag, hart; deer; *der ~ schreit* (*röhrt*) the stag bells (*od* troats); **~fänger** *m* hanger, cutlass; hunting-knife; **~geweih** *n* attire, antlers *pl*, horns *pl*; **~horn** *n* hartshorn; **~~knopf** *m* buckhorn button; **~~salz** *n chem* carbonate of ammonia; (*Backpulver*) baker's salt; **~jagd** *f* stag-hunt(ing); **~käfer** *m* stag-beetle; **~kalb** *n* fawn, young deer; **~keule** *f* haunch of venison; **~kuh** *f* hind; **~leder** *n* buckskin, deerskin; **~ledern** *a* buckskin, deerskin; **~talg** *m* suet of deer; **~ziemer** *m* saddle of venison; **~zunge** *f* hart's tongue.

Hirse *f* millet; **~brei** *m* millet gruel; **~feld** *n* millet field; **~förmig** *a* miliary; **~korn** *n* millet-grain (*od* -seed); **~mehl** *n* millet-flour.

Hirt *m* herdsman, shepherd; (*Seelen~*) pastor.

Hirten|amt *n* pastorate, parson's office; **~brief** *m* pastoral (letter); **~flöte** *f* Arcadian pipe; Pan pipe; **~gedicht** *a* bucolic, eclogue, idyl; **~hund** *m* shepherd's dog; **~knabe** *m* shepherd-boy; **~leben** *n* pastoral life; **~mädchen** *n* young shepherdess; **~mäßig** *a* pastoral; **~spiel** *n* pastoral; **~stab** *m* shepherd's crook; bishop's crosier; **~tasche** *f* shepherd's purse (*od* pouch); **~volk** *n* pastoral tribe, nomadic nation.

Hirtin *f* shepherdess.

His *n mus* B sharp.

hissen *tr* to hoist (up); **Hißtau** *n* top-rope.

Histor|ie *f* history; story; **~ienmaler** *m* historical painter; **~iker** *m* historian; **~isch** *a* historical.

Hitz|ausschlag *m med* (*Hitzfriesel*) heat rash; **~blatter, ~blase** *f* pimple, blister, pustule; **~drahtinstrument** *n el* hot-wire instrument; **~e** *f* heat, hotness; (*Wetter*) hot weather; *drükkende ~~* oppressive heat; *tropische ~~* tropical (*od* torrid) heat; *zehn Grad ~~* a temperature of ten degrees; *die Zeit der großen ~~* the dogdays *pl*; *~~ ausstrahlen* (*Ofen etc*) to radiate heat; *med* (*Fieber~~*) (the heat of) fever; *fliegende ~~* (*med*) hot fit; *fig* (*Feuer der Leidenschaft*) ardency, ardo(u)r; (*Eifer*) zeal; (*Erregung*) violence; (*Inbrunst*) fervo(u)r; (*Leidenschaft*) passion; (*Wärme*) warmth; (*Jähzorn*) fury; *in der ersten ~~* in the heat of the moment; *in der ~~ der Debatte* in the heat of the debate; *in der ~~ des Gefechts* in the heat of the battle; *in ~~ geraten* to grow hot, to fire up; **~ebeständig** *a* heat-resistant, heat-proof; thermostable; *ein ~~es Glasgefäß* a heat-resistant glass bowl; **~ebeständigkeit** *f* heat resistance; heat-proof quality; **~eeinwirkung** *f* influence of heat; **~eempfindlich** *a* sensitive to heat; **~ehärtung** *f* thermosetting; **~egrad** *m* degree of heat; intensity of heat; **~emesser** *m* pyrometer; **~en** *tr* to heat, to give heat; to make hot; **~eperiode** *f* heat-wave, *Am* hot spell; **~estrahlung** *f* heat radiation; **~ewelle** *f* heat-wave; **~ewirkungsgrad** *m* thermal efficiency; **~ig** *a fig* hot; (*heißblütig*) hot-blooded, hot-headed; (*heftig*) hot-tempered; (*leidenschaftlich*) passionate; (*feurig*) fiery; (*eifrig*) eager; (*jähzornig*) choleric, irascible; (*rasch, schnell*) quick, hasty; acute; (*Wortstreit, Debatte*) sharp, red-hot; (*Angriff*) violent; (*Fieber*) ardent, burning; *~~ werden* to fire up, to lose o.'s temper; **~kopf** *m* hothead, hotspur; spitfire; **~köpfig** *a* hot-headed; **~pickel** *m*, **~pocke** *f* heat rash; **~schlag** *m* heat-stroke, heat-apoplexy.

hm! *interj* hum! ahem!

Hobel *m* plane; (*Schlicht~*) jointer; **~bank** *f* joiner's bench; **~eisen** *n* plane-iron; **~maschine** *f* planing machine, *Am* planer; **~n** *tr* to plane; **~späne** *m pl* chippings *pl*, shavings *pl*, parings *pl*; (*feine*) soft (wood) shavings *pl*, *Am* excelsior.

Hoboe *f* oboe, hautboy; **Hoboist** *m* hautboy(-player), oboist.

*

hoch *a* high; (*groß von Gestalt od Wuchs*) tall; (*von Preisen*) high, dear, steep; *drei ~ fünf math* three to the fifth (power); *fig* (*edel, erhaben, bedeutend*) lofty, noble, sublime; great; (*hervorragend*) eminent; *adv* (*in hohem Grad*) highly, greatly; very (much); in a high degree; *mit hohen Absätzen* high-heeled; *der hohe Adel* the nobility, the peerage; *hohes Alter* old (*od* advanced) age; *ein hohes Alter erreichen* to live to a ripe old age; *in hohem Ansehen stehen* to be highly esteemed; *e-n hohen Begriff von etw haben* to have a high opinion of; *in hoher Blüte* (*Handel etc*) to be very prosperous; *hohe Ehre* great hono(u)r; *e-e hohe Geldstrafe* a heavy fine; *e-e hohe Meinung haben von jdm* to have a high opinion of; *im hohen Norden* in the far North; *die hohe Obrigkeit* the government; *sich aufs hohe Roß setzen* to mount the high horse; *~ zu Roß* on horseback; *hohe Schußfolge* high firing rate; *die hohe See* open sea, offing; *auf hoher See* on the high seas; *hohes Spiel* high playing; *hohe Strafe* severe punishment, heavy penalty; *bei hoher Strafe verboten* prohibited under a severe (*od* heavy) penalty; *~ u. heilig* solemnly; *~ u. heilig versprechen* to make a most solemn promise; *~ u. teuer* faithfully; *~ u. teuer schwören* to swear a solemn oath; *Hände ~!* hands up! *Kopf ~!* head up! *Am* chin up! *fünf Mann ~* five men deep; *5 $ ist zu ~* 5 $ is too much; *das ist ihm zu ~* that is too deep for him; (*verstandesmäßig*) that is beyond him, that is above his understanding; *~ aufhorchen* to be all ears, to listen attentively; *~ anrechnen* to value greatly; *~ gehen* to run high; *es geht ~ her* things are pretty lively; *~ gelegen* elevated; *~ hinaus wollen* to aim high; *wenn es ~ kommt* at (the) most, at the highest; *jdn ~ leben lassen* to toast s. o., to give three cheers for s. o.; *~ lebe der König!* long live the king! *~ zu stehen kommen* to cost dear, to come expensive; *~ steigen* (*Preise*) to run high, to rise; *den Kopf ~ tragen* to carry o.'s head high; *die Nase ~ tragen* to put on airs; **Hoch** *n* toast; cheer; (*Meteorologie*) high (pressure), high pressure area; *ein ~ ausbringen auf jdn* to toast s. o., to cheer s. o.; *ein dreifaches ~ für ...* three cheers for ...; **~achse** *f aero* vertical axis, normal axis; **~achtbar** *a* highly respectable, most hono(u)rable; **~achten, ~schätzen** *tr* to respect, to esteem highly; to make much of; to value; **~achtung** *f* esteem, respect; high regard; *mit vorzüglicher ~~* (*im Brief*) Very respectfully yours ...; **~~svoll** *a* respectful; *adv* with great respects, respectfully; (*in Briefen*) yours faithfully, yours truly, yours sincerely, yours respectfully; **~altar** *m* high altar; **~~stätte** *f* sanctuary; **~amt** *n* high mass; **~angriff** *m aero* high-level (bombing) attack; **~antenne** *f radio* high aerial (*od* antenna), overhead (*od* elevated) aerial, free antenna; **~ätzung** *f* relief etching; **~aufnahme** *f phot* upright picture, upright shot; **~bahn** *f* high-level railway, overhead railway, *Am* elevated railroad (*Abk* El, L); **~bau** *m* surface building, surface engineering; superstructure work, overground works *pl*; (*von Leitungen*) overhead construction; **~begabt** *a* highly endowed (*od* gifted); **~behälter** *m* storage basin, distributing reservoir; **~beinig** *a* long-legged, high-legged; **~berühmt** *a* highly renowned; **~betagt** *a*, **~bejahrt** *a* advanced in years, well on in years, aged; **~betrieb** *m* rush of business, rush (*od* peak) time; intense activity, hustle, bustle; **~bocken** *tr mot* (*Wagen*) to jack up; **~brisant** *a* highly explosive; **~bunker** *m* (*Luftschutz*) tower shelter (A. R. P.); **~burg** *f fig* stronghold; **~decker** *m aero* high-wing monoplane; (*freitragender*) high-wing cantilever plane; **~deutsch** *a* High German; standard German; **~druck** *m* high-pressure; *typ* relief-printing; *mit ~~ arbeiten* to work at high pressure, to run at the highest levels; **~~dampfkessel** *m* high-pressure steam boiler; **~~gebiet** *n* (*Meteorologie*) high-pressure area; high; anticyclone; **~~luftanlage** *f* high-pressure air system; **~~luftflasche** *f* high-pressure air-bottle (*od* air-cylinder); **~~reifen** *m mot* high-pressure tyre (*Am* tire); **~~schmierung** *f* high-pressure lubrication; **~~zentrum** *n* (*Meteorologie*) centre of high barometric pressure, centre of anticyclone; **~ebene** *f* elevated plain; plateau, table-land; **~empfindlich** *a phys* highly sensitive, supersensitive; **~erfreut** *a* overjoyed; greatly pleased; **~erhaben** *a* very lofty; sublime; *~~e Arbeit* high-relief; **~explosiv** *a* (*brisant*) high-explosive (*Abk* H. E.); *~~e Bombe* high-explosive bomb; **~fahrend** *a* haughty; imperious; high-handed; **~fein** *a* superfine; (*erstklassig*) first-rate, A 1, exquisite, tiptop; (*auserlesen*) very choice; **~fieberhaft** *a med* highly feverish; **~finanz** *f* high finance; **~fliegend** *a fig* towering, lofty; high-aimed; ambitious; **~flüchtig** *a chem* highly volatile; **~flut** *f* high-flood, high-tide; *com Am* boom; **~form** *f*: *in ~~ sein* to be topfit, to be in top form; **~format** *n* upright size; **~frequent** *a* high-frequent, of high-frequency; (*vom Schall*) supersonic; *~~er Drahtfunk* wired wireless; **~frequenz** *f* high frequency (*Abk* H. F.), radio frequency; ultra-high frequency (*Abk* U. H. F.); **~~behandlung** *f med* radiothermy, diathermy; **~~drahtsystem** *n radio* wired radio system; **~~drossel** *f*

H. F. choke coil; **~~feld** *n* high-frequency field; **~~heilgerät** *n* short-wave therapeutic apparatus; **~~heizung** *f* electronic heating; **~~kabel** *n* high-frequency cable; **~~spannung** *f* high-frequency voltage; **~~störung** *f* high-frequency noise; **~~stufe** *f* high-frequency stage; **~~technik** *f* radio engineering; **~~telephonie** *f* high-frequency telephony; **~~telegraphie** *f* radio-telegraphy; **~~verstärker** *m* radio-frequency amplifier; **~geachtet** *a* highly esteemed; **~gebirge** *n* high mountain-chain; high mountains *pl*; **~geboren** *a* high-born; (*Titel*) Right Hono(u)rable; **~geehrt** *a* highly hono(u)red; **~gefühl** *n* high feeling; exultation, ecstasy; **~gehen** *irr itr* (*steigen*) to rise, to mount; *fam* (*zornig werden*) to fly into a passion; **~~d** *a* running high; *~~de See* heavy sea; **~gelehrt** *a* very learned; **~genuß** *m* high enjoyment; delight, real treat; **~gericht** *n* place of execution; (*Galgen*) gallows; **~geschätzt** *a* highly praised; **~gesinnt** *a* high-minded; **~gespannt** *a* at high tension; (*groß*) great, high; **~gestellt** *a* high in office, high-ranking; *~~e Persönlichkeit* person of high office; **~gewachsen** *a* high-grown, tall; **~glanz** *m* (*beim Polieren*) high lustre; high-polish; brilliancy; **~~poliert** *a* highly polished; **~gradig** *a* in (*od* to) a high degree; high-grade; *fig* intense, extreme, excessive; **~halten** *irr tr* esteem; to cherish; **~haus** *n* skyscraper; **~heben** *irr tr* to lift up, to hoist; *durch ~~ der Hände* (*bei e-r Wahl*) by show of hands; *mot* (*mit Wagenheber*) to jack up; **~heilig** *a* most holy; **~herzig** *a* noble-minded, high-minded; high-souled; magnanimous; **~~keit** *f* magnanimity; **~kant** *a* end up, edgewise, on edge; **~kirche** *f* (*England*) High Church, Church of England; **~klappbar** *a* tiltable; **~konjunktur** *f* business prosperity, peak season, *Am* boom; **~konzentriert** *a* highly concentrated; **~lage** *f* high altitude; **~land** *n* highland, upland; (*Schottland*) (Scotch) Highlands *pl*; **~länder** *m* Highlander; **~leistung** *f* high capacity, heavy duty; *~leistungs-* (*in Zssg*) high-duty, high-capacity, high-efficiency, heavy-duty, high-power(ed); **~~sbomber** *m* high-performance bomber; **~~sflugzeug** *n* high-performance plane; **~~smaschine** *f* high-duty machine; **~~smotor** *m aero* high-powered engine; **~~sröhre** *f radio* (high-) power tube; **~luftdruckgebiet** *n* high-pressure area; **~meister** *m* grand master; **~modern** *a* up-to-date, modern; **~moor** *n* bog at the top of a mountain; **~mut** *m* haughtiness, loftiness; arrogance, pride; **~mütig** *a* haughty, lofty, arrogant, proud; **~näsig** *a* supercilious, *fam* stuck-up; **~ofen** *m* (blast) furnace; **~~anlage** *f* blast furnace plant; **~ohmwiderstand** *m el* high-ohmic resistance; **~parterre** *n* groundfloor; **~prozentig** *a* of high percentage; *~~er Alkohol* high-proof spirits; **~reißen** *irr tr aero* to pull up the nose of a plane; to zoom; **~relief** *n* alto relievo; **~rot** *a* bright (*od* deep) red, vermilion, crimson; **~ruf** *m* cheer; *donnernde ~~e* ringing cheers *pl*; *drei donnernde ~~e für . . .!* three cheers for . . .! **~saison** *f* peak season; **~schätzen** *tr* to esteem; **~schätzung** *f* esteem, respect; **~schule** *f* academy, university, college, institution of high learning; *~~ für Lehrerbildung* teachers college; *Technische ~~* technical college; technological institute; **~schulführer** *m* calendar, *Am* catalog(ue); **~schullehrer** *m* professor, teacher at a university; **~schwanger** *a* far advanced in pregnancy; **~see** *f* ocean, high sea; deep water; **~~aufklärer** *m*, **~~aufklärungsflugzeug** *n* ocean-going reconnaissance plane; **~~fischer** *m* trawler; **~~fischerei** *f* deep-sea fishery; **~~flotte** *f* deep-sea fleet, sea-going fleet; battle fleet; **~~flugzeug** *n* sea-going aircraft; transatlantic airplane, over-sea-plane; **~~kabel** *n* deep-sea cable; submarine cable; **~~schlepper** *m* ocean-going (*od* sea-going) tug; **~selig** *a* late, deceased; of blessed memory; **~silo** *m* silo; **~sinnig** *a* high-minded; **~sitz** *m* high stand; **~sommer** *m* midsummer; **~spannung** *f* high-tension (*Abk* H.T.), high-voltage (*Abk* H. V.); **~~sblitz** *m phot* (*Elektroblitz*) speedlight, speedflash; stroboflash; electronic (*od* strobe) flash; **~~skabel** *n* high-tension cable; **~~sleitung** *f* high-tension (*od* high-voltage) line, power line; **~~smast** *m* high tension (*od* voltage) pole; **~~snetz** *n* high-tension mains *pl;* **~sprache** *f* standard speech; **~sprung** *m sport* high jump; **~stämmig** *a* high-grown, tall; (*Rosen*) standard; **~stand** *m* (*Ausguck*) lookout post; (*Wasserstand*) high-water mark; *fig* (*Zustand*) fine condition; (*Wohlstand*) prosperity; **~stapelei** *f* swindling; **~stapler** *m* impostor, high-flyer, confidence man (*Abk* con man), fashionable swindler, adventurer, *Am sl* fourflusher; **~stehend** *a* (*im Rang*) high-ranking; *typ* superior; **~strebend** *a* towering; *fig* lofty; **~ton** *m* high pitch; *gram* chief stress; **~~lautsprecher** *m* high-frequency speaker, *Am* tweeter; **~tönend** *a* high-sounding; **~tourig** *a* high speed; **~tourist** *m* mountaineer, alpine climber; **~trabend** *a* high-flown, pompous; (*Rede*) bombastic; high-sounding; **~treiben** *irr tr* (*Preise*) to force up; **~vakuum** *n* high vacuum; **~~röhre** *f* high-vacuum valve, *Am* electron tube; **~verdient** *a* of great merit, highly deserving; **~verrat** *m* high-treason; **~verräter** *m* traitor, person guilty of high-treason; **~~isch** *a* highly treasonable; **~verzinslich** *a* bearing high rates of interest; **~wald** *m* timber forest; high forest; **~wasser** *n* high water, high tide; (*Überschwemmung*) floods *pl*; **~~schaden** *m* flood damage; **~~sicher** *a* flood-proof; **~wertig** *a* of high value; *chem* of high valence; (*erstklassig*) first rate, high-grade, high-quality, *Am* top-grade, top-notch; **~wichtig** *a* highly important; **~wild** *n* big (*od* large) game; red deer; **~willkommen** *a* highly welcome; **~winden** *irr tr* to jack up; **~wirksam** *a* highly active; highly effective; **~wohlgeboren** *a* (*Titel*) Right Hono(u)rable; (*auf Briefen, dem Namen nachgestellt*) Esq.; *Ew. H~~!* Sir! **~würden** *f*: *Ew. H~~!* (*in England nur für katholische Geistliche*) Your Reverence! Your Worship! Reverend Sir! **~würdig** *a* right reverend; **~zeilig** *a tele* (*Bildauflösung*) high-definition; **~ziehen** *irr tr aero* (*Maschine*) to pull (the nose) up; to zoom, to climb.

höchlich *adv* in (*od* to) a high degree, highly, greatly, exceedingly.

höchst *a* highest, greatest; uppermost, topmost; top-flight; extreme; *~-* (*in Zssg*) maximum-, peak-; *adv* extremely, very (much), most; highly, in the highest degree; *aufs ~e* at most; extremely, exceedingly; *~er Gerichtshof* supreme court; *im ~en Grad* to the highest degree; *~e Lust* greatest delight; *in der ~en Not* in greatest distress; *~er Punkt* highest point; *die ~e Überraschung* the greatest surprise; *von ~er Wichtigkeit* of the utmost importance; *es ist ~e Zeit* it is high time; *die ~en Offiziere der Marine* the highest ranking (*Am* top ranking) officers of the navy; *~e Alarmbereitschaft* stand-by, state of preparedness for emergency; **~alter** *n* maximum age; **~angebot** *n* highest tender; **~auftrieb** *m aero* maximum lift; **~beanspruchung** *f* highest stress; **~bedarf** *m* maximum demand; **~belastung** *f* maximum load (*od* duty); **~betrag** *m* maximum amount; limit; **~drehzahl** *f mot* maximum revolutions *pl* (of the engine); **~empfindlich** *a* highly sensitive; **~e(r)** *m* the Almighty; **~eigen**: *in ~~er Person* in person; **~eigenhändig** *a* with o.'s own hands; **~ens** *adv* at (the) most, at best; **~fahrt** *f* full (*od* top) speed; **~fall** *m* maximum case; **~form** *f sport* top form; **~frequenzwellen** *f pl* micro-waves *pl*; **~gebot** *n* highest bid; **~gehalt** *n* maximum salary; **~geldstrafe** *f* maximum fine; **~geschwindigkeit** *f* maximum speed, top speed; *zulässige ~~* speed limit; *Überschreitung der ~~* speeding (over limit); **~gewicht** *n* maximum weight; **~grenze** *f* maximum limit; **~kommandierende(r)** *m* commander-in-chief (*Abk* cominch); **~last** *f* maximum load; **~leistung** *f sport* record; record (*od* top) performance; maximum output; (*e-r Maschine etc*) peak power, maximum power (*od* efficiency *od* capacity); peak load; *die ~~ übertreffen* to beat the record; **~maß** *n* greatest measure; **~möglich** *a* highest possible; **~persönlich** *a* purely personal; **~preis** *m* ceiling price; **~~grenze** *f* price ceiling; **~reichweite** *f* maximum range; **~satz** *m* maximum rate; **~schußweite** *f* maximum range; **~spannung** *f* (*Festigkeit*) maximum stress; **~stand** *m* peak level; *die Bevölkerungszahl der Ver. Staaten erreichte e-n neuen ~~* the population of the United States reached an all-time high; **~wahrscheinlich** *a* most likely, in all probability; as like as not; **~wert** *m* peak (*od* maximum) value; maximum; **~zahl** *f* highest number; **~zulässig** *a* maximum permissible; *~~er Wert* maximum safe value.

Hochzeit *f* marriage; wedding; nuptials *pl*; *~ halten* to celebrate o.'s wedding; *diamantene* (*goldene, silberne*) *~* diamond (golden, silver) wedding; **~er** *m* bridegroom; **~erin** *f* bride; **~lich** *a* nuptial, bridal.

Hochzeits|bitter *m* inviter to a wedding; **~bräuche** *m pl* nuptial rites *pl*; **~essen** *n* wedding breakfast; **~feier** *f* celebration of a wedding; **~fest** *n* wedding (-feast); **~gast** *m* wedding-guest; **~gedicht** *n* nuptial poem; **~geschenk** *n* wedding-gift, wedding-present; **~kleid** *n* wedding-dress, bridal dress; **~kuchen** *m* wedding-cake; **~nacht** *f* wedding-night; **~reise** *f* honeymoon trip, wedding-tour; **~schmaus** *m* wedding-banquet, wedding-dinner; **~tag** *m* wedding-day; (*später*) wedding-anniversary; **~vater** *m* bride's father; **~zug** *m* bridal procession, wedding-party.

Hocke *f* heap of sheaves; (*beim Turnen*) squat; (*aufgestellte Garben*) stook; **~n** *itr* to squat; to crouch; (*auf hohen Stühlen, Stangen*) to perch; *über den*

Büchern ~~ to be poring over o.'s books; *fam* (*lange sitzen bleiben*) to sit tight, to stick to; *sich nieder*~*n* to cower down; ~**r** *m* (*Schemel*) stool; chair without arms; ~**rgrab** *n* prehistoric grave with dead in crouching position.

Höcker *m* (*Auswuchs*) protuberance; knob; bump; (*Buckel*) hump; hunch (-back); *med* gibbosity; *e-n* ~ *haben* to be hunchbacked; ~**hindernis** *n* (concrete) anti-tank obstacle, dragon's teeth; ~**ig** *a* (*buckelig*) hunchbacked; humpy; knobby; (*uneben*) uneven; rugged, rough, ragged; ~**sperre** *f* (*Tanksperre*) anti-tank concrete cone-blocks.

Hoden *m*, **Hode** *f* testicle; ~**bruch** *m* scrotal hernia; ~**entzündung** *f* orchitis; ~**sack** *m fam* purse, *med* scrotum; *in Zssg*: scrotal; ~**wasserbruch** *m med* hydrocele.

Hof *m* yard, court(yard); (*Hinter*~) backyard; (*Meierei*) farm; (*Fürsten*~) court; (*Gasthof*) hotel, inn; *astr* (*Ring um Mond, Sonne*) halo; corona, aureola; *bei* (*od am*) ~*e* at court; *jdm den* ~ *machen* to pay court to s. o., to court s. o.; to flatter s. o.; to make love to; *Am fam* to make passes to, to pitch a woo; ~**arzt** *m* court-physician; ~**begehung** *f* agricultural inspection; ~**brauch** *m* court-etiquette; ~**dame** *f* maid of hono(u)r; lady in waiting; ~**fähig** *a* having the right to appear at court; *fam* presentable; ~**fart** *f* pride, haughtiness; ~**färtig** *a* proud, haughty; ~**fräulein** *n* maid of hono(u)r; ~**gesinde** *n* farm servants *pl*, court servants *pl*; ~**gunst** *f* court favo(u)r; ~**gut** *n* domain, farm; ~**haltung** *f* princely suit; court; *Engl* royal household; ~**halten** *irr itr* to reside; ~**hund** *m* watch-dog, house-dog; ~**ieren** *tr* to court; (*schmeicheln*) to flatter; ~**kreise** *m pl* court; ~**leben** *n* court life; ~**leute** *pl* courtiers *pl*, people at court; ~**lieferant** *m* purveyor to the Court (*Engl* to His Majesty); ~**mann** *m* courtier; ~**marschall** *m* master of the ceremonies; *Engl* Lord Chamberlain; ~**meister** *m* steward; (*Lehrer*) governor, private tutor; ~**narr** *m* court-jester; ~**prediger** *m* court chaplain; ~**rat** *m Engl* Privy Councillor; ~**raum** *m* courtyard; ~**schranze** *f* courtier, flunkey; ~**sitte** *f* court-manners *pl*; etiquette; ~**staat** *m* princely household; (*Kleidung*) court-dress; ~**tor** *n*, ~**türe** *f* (yard-) gate; back-door; ~**trauer** *f* court mourning.

hoff|en *tr, itr* to hope (*auf* for); (*mit Zuversicht*) to trust (*auf* in), to reckon upon, to look forward (*auf* to); (*erwarten*) to expect, to await; *das Beste* ~~ to hope for the best; *auf bessere Tage* ~~ to hope for better days; *ich* ~*e es* I hope so; *es ist sehr zu* ~~ it is much to be hoped; *ich will nicht* ~~, *daß* let me not hope that; ~**entlich** *adv* it is to be hoped; as I hope; I hope so; ~~ *kommt sie* I hope she will come; ~**nung** *f* hope; (*Erwartung*) expectation, anticipation; (*Zuversicht*) trust; *guter* ~~ *sein* to be pregnant, to be expecting a baby, to be expectant, to be in the family way, to be in interesting circumstances; *die* ~~ *aufgeben* to abandon hope; *mit leeren* ~~*en abspeisen* to put off with fair promises; *jdm* ~~*en machen* to hold out hopes to s. o.; *sich* ~~ *machen* to indulge in the hope of, to be in hopes that; to hope for; *keine* ~~ *mehr haben* to be out of hope; *jdm alle* ~~ *nehmen* to put s. o. out of all hope; ~~*en erwecken in jdm* to raise hopes in s. o.; *meine einzige* ~~ *ruht auf ihr* my only hope is in her; *seine* ~~ *setzen auf* to pin (*od* to place *od* to set) o.'s hope on; *geringe* ~~ *setzen auf* to hope against hope that; ~~**slos** *a* hopeless; past (all) hope; unpromising; *e-e* ~~*slose Sache* a hopeless cause; ~~**slosigkeit** *f* hopelessness; ~~**sschimmer** *m* gleam of hope; ~~**sstrahl** *m* ray of hope; ~~**svoll** *a* hopeful, full of hope.

höf|isch *a* courtly, courtier-like; ~**lich** *a* courteous, polite, civil (*gegen* to); (*ritterlich*) gallant; (*verbindlich*) obliging (towards); ~~**keit** *f* politeness, courtesy; ~~**keitsbezeigung** *f* mark of politeness (*od* attention); ~~**keitsformel** *f* polite phrase; ~**ling** *m* courtier.

Höhe *f* height; ~ *über Meeresspiegel* height above sea-level; *aero* (*über Grund*) absolute altitude; *astr, geog, math* altitude; (*geog Breite*) latitude; (*Gipfel*) summit, top, hill; *mus* pitch; *radio* (*Ton*) level of tone; (*Geldbetrag*) amount; rate; (*Preise*) level; dearness; *das ist die* ~! *fam interj* that's the limit! *Am* can you beat it! that takes the cake! *auf der* ~ on the summit; *auf der* ~ *der Situation* equal to the occasion; *auf der* ~ *der Zeit* abreast of o.'s time; *auf der* ~ *sein* to be up to the level, to be up to date; (*gesundheitlich*) to be up to par; *auf gleicher* ~ on a level; *auf der* ~ *von* (*geog Breite*) in the latitude of; *mar* off; *auf* ~ *gehen aero* to climb; *aus der* ~ from on high; *bis zur* ~ *von 5 $* to the amount of $5; *in der* ~ on high, aloft; *in die* ~ up, upwards; *in* (*od auf*) *gleicher* ~ *mit* on the same level with, on a level with; *in* ~ *von* (*Geld*) in the amount of; *in die* ~ *bringen Am* to boost; *in die* ~ *fahren* to start up; *in die* ~ *gehen* (*steigen*) to rise, to climb up; to go up; to soar; (*Preise*) to rise, to go up, to tend upwards, to have an upward tendency; *fig* (*wütend werden*) to become furious; *in die* ~ *heben* to lift up; *in die* ~ *treiben* (*Preise*) to run up prices, to boost prices; (*Kurse*) to bull the market; *in die* ~ *wachsen* to grow up; *sich in die* ~ *arbeiten* to work o. s. up; *sich in die* ~ *richten* to rise, to sit up; ~ *gewinnen aero* to climb; *Am sl* to go upstairs; ~ *verlieren aero* to lose height; ~**nabstand** *m* vertical interval; ~**nangabe** *f* altitude indication; ~**nangriff** *m aero* high-level (bombing) attack; ~**nanzug** *m aero* pressure suit; ~**natmer** *m aero* oxygen breathing mask, high-altitude oxygen apparatus, *Am* respirator; *mit* ~~ *fliegen* to fly on oxygen; ~**nbegrenzung** *f tech* elevating stop; ~**nbomber** *m* high-altitude bomber; ~**nflosse** *f aero* tail plane, *Am* horizontal stabilizer; ~**nflug** *m* (high-) altitude flight; ~**nflugzeug** *n* high-altitude plane; stratoplane; ~**ngashebel** *m*, ~**ndrossel** *f aero* altitude throttle (lever), *Am* altitude gas lever; ~**ngewinn** *m* gain in altitude; ~**nkabine** *f aero* pressurized cabin; ~**nkammer** *f* low-pressure chamber, depression box, *Am* altitude chamber; ~**nkarte** *f* relief map; ~**nklima** *n* mountain climate; ~**nkrankheit** *f* altitude sickness, mountain sickness, air sickness, aeroembolism; (*Höhenschwindel*) height vertigo; ~**nkurort** *m* (*Luftkurort*) high altitude health resort; mountain health resort; ~**nlader** *m aero mot* supercharger, pressurizer, high-level blower; ~**nlage** *f* altitude level; ~**nleitwerk** *n* elevator unit, tail plane and elevator; ~**nlinie** *f* (*Karte, Schichtlinie*) contour (line); ~**nmarke** *f* datum mark; ~**nmesser** *m* height finder; altimeter; hypsometer; (*mit Echolot*) sound-ranging altimeter; (*mit Funkmeß*) radar altimeter; ~**nmessung** *f* measuring of elevations; (*Nivellierung*) levelling; ~**nmotor** *m aero* super-charged (*od* high-altitude) engine; ~**nortung** *f aero* high-altitude navigation; ~**nrauch** *m* peat-smoke; ~**nrekord** *m* height record, altitude record; ~**nrichtfeld** *n* elevation; ~**nrücken** *m* crest of ridge; ~**ruder** *n aero* elevator; (*U-Boot*) hydro gear; ~**nschichtlinie** *f* contour line; ~**nschreiber** *m* barograph, altigraph; recording altimeter; ~**nsonne** *f* mountain sun, Alpine sun; (*künstliche*) sun lamp, ultra-violet lamp, quartz lamp; (*mit Fluoreszenzlampe*) fluorescent sun lamp; (*mit Birne*) bulb type sun lamp; *mit* ~~ *bestrahlen* to ray with a sun lamp; ~**nsonnenbestrahlung** *f med* ray therapy; ~**nstaffelung** *f aero* stepped-up formation; ~**nstellung** *f mil* position on dominant height; ~**nsteuer** *n* elevator (rudder); (*Bedienungshebel*) elevator control; ~**nstrahlen** *m pl* cosmic rays *pl*; ~**nstrahlung** *f* cosmic ray radiation, high-altitude radiation; ~**nstreuung** *f mil* vertical dispersion; ~**nstufe** *f* altitude line; ~**nverlust** *m aero* loss of altitude; ~**nvermessung** *f* altimetry; ~**nweltrekord** *m aero* world record for altitude; ~**nwind** *m* wind at high altitude, upper wind; ~**nwinkel** *m* angle of elevation; ~**nzug** *m* mountain chain, (hill-) range, ridge; ~**punkt** *m* height; (*Gipfel*) peak; summit, crest, top; *astr, fig* zenith; *fig* maximum; culmination, culminating point; crisis; climax; acme; critical point, culminating point; *seinen* ~~ *erreichen* to culminate; (~~ *des Lebens*) heyday of life; *auf dem* ~~ *seiner Macht sein* to be at the peak of o.'s power; *das ist der* ~~! there is nothing to beat it!

Hoheit *f* (*Erhabenheit*) sublimity; grandeur; (*Größe*) greatness; (*Majestät*) majesty; (*Titel*) Highness; *Seine Königliche* ~ His Royal Highness (*Abk* H. R. H.); (*Staats*~) sovereignty; ~**lich** *a* sovereign; ~**sabzeichen** *n aero* airplane markings *pl*; ~**sakt** *m* act of state; ~**sgebiet** *n* territory of a state; ~**sgewässer** *n pl* territorial waters *pl*; ~**sgrenze** *f* three miles limit of territorial waters; ~**srecht** *n* (*Souveränität*) rights of sovereignty; sovereign power, official authority; (*e-s Herrschers*) regalia *pl*; ~**svoll** *a* majestic; ~**zeichen** *n* insignia; emblem of sovereignty; *aero* nationality marking, mark of nationality.

Hohe|lied *n* (*Bibel*) Song of Solomon; ~**priester** *m* high priest; pontiff; ~~**lich** *a* high-priestly; pontifical; ~~**tum** *n* pontificate.

höher *a* higher, superior (to); upper; *fig* loftier; ~ *liegend* more elevated; ~ *geht's nimmer!* there is nothing to beat it! ~*e Bildung* higher education; ~*es Dienstalter* seniority (in rank); ~*e Führung* the higher command; ~*e Gewalt* superior force; Act of God; ~*e Instanz jur* higher court; (*Behörde*) higher authority; ~*e Mathematik* higher mathematics; ~*en Orts* by higher authority; ~*e Schule* secondary school, *Am* high school; ~*e Töchterschule* young ladies' school; ~*e Weisheit* greater wisdom; ~**wertig** *a* of higher value; *chem* of higher valence, multivalent.

hohl *a* hollow; (*konkav*) concave; (*ausgekehlt*) channelled; (*gedämpft klingend*) dull; *fig* (*leer*) empty; (*eitel*) vain; *~e Backen* sunken cheeks; *~e Hand* the hollow of the hand; *~er Kopf fig* a shallow head; *~er Magen* empty stomach; *~e See* a grown sea; *~e Stimme* dull voice; *~er Zahn* hollow (*od* carious *od* decayed) tooth; **~äugig** *a* hollow-eyed; **~bohrer** *m* hollow auger; **~glas** *n* bottle-glass; **~heit** *f* hollowness; *fig* (*Leere*) emptiness, shallowness; **~kehle** *f* hollow groove, channel; **~klinge** *f* hollow blade; **~kopf** *m* numskull, a brainless fellow, dunce, dolt; **~körper** *m* hollow body; **~kugel** *f* hollow sphere, hollow ball; **~ladung** *f mil* hollow charge; **~maß** *n* dry measure, measure of capacity; **~meißel** *m* gouge; **~raum** *m* hollow space; cavity; **~schliff** *m* hollow grinding; **~saum** *m* hemstitch; **~spiegel** *m* concave mirror; reflector; **~steg** *m typ* gutter stick; **~stein** *m* hollow brick; **~wangig** *a* hollow-cheeked; **~weg** *m* (*Engpaß*) narrow pass, defile; (*Schlucht*) gorge; sunken road, lane; **~ziegel** *m* hollow tile, gutter tile; **~zirkel** *m* spherical compasses *pl*; (*Innentaster*) inside cal(l)ipers *pl*; **~zylinder** *m* hollow cylinder.

Höhl|e *f* cavern, (*größere*) cave; (*Loch*) hole; (*Grotte*) grotto; (*Tier~~*) den, hole; kennel; (*Lager*) lair; (*Bude, Verbrecher~~*) den, hole; (*Höhlung*) hollow; *anat* cavity; ventricle; *die ~~ des Löwen* the lion's den; **~en** *tr* to hollow, to excavate; **~enbär** *m* cave-bear; **~enbewohner** *m* cave-dweller, cave-man; **~enwohnung** *f* cave-dwelling; **~ung** *f* excavation, cavity; hollow; (*Loch*) hole.

Hohn *m* (*Geringschätzung*) scorn; (*höhnisches Lachen*) sneer; (*Sarkasmus*) sarcasm; (*Spott*) derision, mockery; ridicule; scoff; (*Beleidigung*) insult; (*Verachtung*) disdain; *ein ~ auf die Menschheit* an insult (*od* disgrace) to mankind; *zum Spott u. ~ werden* to become a laughing-stock; *jdm zum ~* in defiance of s. o.; **~gelächter, ~lachen** *n* scornful laughter; sneer; **~lachen** *itr* to laugh in contempt; to jeer, to deride; **~lächeln** *itr* to sneer (*über* at); **~~d** *a* sneering; **~sprechen** *irr itr* (*trotzen*) to defy; (*verächtlich machen*) to flout; **~~d** *a* defiant; *der Vernunft ~~* to be an insult to reason; *das spricht jeder Beschreibung ~* this defies all description.

höhn|en *tr* to mock; to sneer at; **~isch** *a* scornful, sneering; sarcastic; (*verachtend*) disdainful; (*beleidigend*) insulting; *~~ lachen über* to sneer at; *~~ zurückweisen* to scout; *mit ~~em Blick* with a scornful eye.

Höker *m* (*Krämer*) hawker, coster, costermonger, huckster, hucksterer; street peddler, street vendor; **~ei** *f* huckstering, peddlery; **~frau, ~in** *f*, **~weib** *n* market-woman, basket-woman, huckstress; **~kram** *m*, **~ware** *f* hawker's goods *pl*, huckster's goods *pl*; **~laden** *m* huckst(e)ry: **~n** *itr* to hawk, to huckster, to higgle.

Hokuspokus *m* hocus-pocus, humbug, juggler's trick.

hold *a* (*lieblich, anmutig*) charming, lovely, gracious, sweet; (*zugeneigt*) propitious, favourable, well-disposed, fond of; *ein ~es Lächeln* a sweet smile; *jdm ~ sein* to favour s. o.; *das Glück war ihr ~* fortune favoured her; *das Glück war ihr nicht ~* fortune was against her; **~selig** *a* most charming, most gracious, most lovely; **~seligkeit** *f* loveliness, charm, sweetness.

holen *tr* to fetch; to get; to go for, to come for; *~ lassen* to send for; *sich* (*etw*) *~* (*Krankheit, Tod usw*) to catch, to contract s. th.; *sich e-e Erkältung ~* to catch cold; *sich bei jdm Rat ~* to ask s. o.'s advice, to consult s. o.; *sich bei jdm Trost ~* to seek consolation from s. o.; *Atem ~* to draw breath; *tief Atem ~* to take a deep breath; *da ist nichts zu ~* there is nothing to be gained there; *bei ihr ist nichts zu ~* there is nothing to be got from her; *die Polizei hat ihn geholt* he was arrested by the police; *hol's der Teufel* (*od Henker*)*! interj* confound it! *hol dich der Teufel! interj* go to the devil! *der Teufel soll es ~! interj* hang it!

holla! *interj* holla! hallo!

Holl|and *n* Holland; **~änder** *m* Dutchman; *der Fliegende ~~* the Flying Dutchman, the Phantom Ship; *tech* (*Papierfabrikation*) pulp engine, *Am* beater; **~änderei** *f* Dutch farm, Dutch dairy; **~änderin** *f* Dutchwoman; **~ändisch** *a* Dutch.

Höll|e *f* hell; *fig* hot place, furnace; *Dantes ~e* Dante's Inferno; *in der ~e* in hell; *zur ~e fahren, in die ~e kommen* to go to hell; *fahr* (*od scher dich*) *zur ~e!* go to hell! *jdm die ~e heiß machen* to make it hot for s. o., to give s. o. hell; *jdm das Leben zur ~e machen* to make life hell for s. o.; *Himmel u. ~e in Bewegung setzen* to move heaven and earth; *die ~e ist los* hell is let loose; **~enangst** *f* mortal anxiety; *fam* hellish funk; **~enbrand** *m* brand of hell; *fam* (*Durst*) infernal thirst; **~enbraten** *m* (*schlechter Mensch*) (hell-) rake; **~enbrut** *f* infernal crew; **~enfahrt** *f* (Christ's) descent into hell; **~enfeuer** *n* hellfire; **~enfürst** *m* infernal prince; **~engestank** *m* infernal stench; **~enhund** *m* hellhound; Cerberus; **~enlärm, ~enspektakel** *m* infernal noise, a hell of a noise (*od* row); (*Durcheinander*) pandemonium; *e-n ~enspektakel machen* to kick up a tremendous row; **~enleben** *n* infernal life; **~enmaschine** *f* infernal machine; **~enpein, ~enqual** *f* pains (*od* torments) of hell; *fig* excruciating pain; *~~en ausstehen* to suffer martyrdom; **~enrachen** *m* jaws *pl* of hell; **~enstein** *m* lunar caustic, silver nitrate; **~enstrafe** *f* eternal punishment; **~isch** *a* hellish, infernal; (*teuflisch*) diabolic; *fam* (*sehr groß, riesig*) enormous, excessive, infernal(ly), like hell.

Holm[1] *m* (*Querholz*) beam, transom; (*Barren*) bar; *mar* dockyard; *aero* spar, longeron; longitudinal beam; *durchgehender ~* (*aero*) continuous spar; *Flächen~* wing spar; *Hinter~* rear spar; *Kasten~* box spar; *U-~* channel-section spar; *Vorder~* front spar; *einholmige Fläche* (*aero*) wing of the mono-spar type; **~gurt** *m aero* spar flange, *Am* cap strip.

Holm[2] *m* (*kleine bergige* (*Halb-*)*Insel*) small island, islet, holm; (*kleiner Hügel*) hillock.

holp|ern *itr* (*Wagen etc*) to jolt, to jog; (*dahintrotten*) to jounce along; **~rig** *a* (*Weg*) rough, uneven; rugged; bumpy; (*~~ in der Bewegung, stolpernd*) jouncy, stumbling; *fig* (*Stil*) crabbed, unpolished; *adv ~~ lesen* to stumble in reading.

holterdiepolter *adv* (*Tonwort*) helter-skelter.

Holunder *m bot* (common) elder; *spanischer ~* lilac; **~beere** *f* elderberry; **~blüte** *f* elder blossom, elder flowers *pl*; **~~ntee** *m* elder tea; **~busch, ~strauch** *m* elderberry bush, elder tree; **~mark** *n* elder pith; **~~kugel** *f* pith ball.

Holz *n* wood; (*Bau~ u. Waldbestand*) timber, *Am* lumber; (*Brenn~*) firewood, stove wood; (*Gehölz*) forest, wood, grove; *abgestorbenes ~* dead wood; *gelagertes ~* seasoned wood; *grünes ~, frisches ~* green wood; *Hart~* hard wood; *Kunst~* artificial wood; *schlagbares ~* mature wood; *wurmstichiges ~* worm-eaten wood; *er ist aus gleichem ~ geschnitzt* he is a chip of the old block; **~abfall** *m* wood waste; chips of wood; **~abfuhr** *f* (*Beförderung*) transportation of wood; **~abhieb** *m* wood felling; **~apfel** *m* crab apple, wild apple; **~arbeiter** *m* woodworker; **~arten** *f pl* species *pl* of wood; **~artig, ~ähnlich** *a* ligniform, ligneous, woody, woodlike; **~axt** *f* felling axe, cleaver, wood-feller's axe; **~balken** *m* wood beam, wood frame; **~baracke** *f* wooden hut; **~bau** *m* wooden structure; **~bauweise** *f* wooden construction; **~bearbeitung** *f* wood working, **~~smaschine** *f* wood working machine; **~~sindustrie** *f* woodworking industry, *Am* lumbering industry; **~belag** *m* wood covering; **~bildhauer** *m* wood-carver; **~birne** *f* wild pear; **~blasinstrument** *n* wood-wind instrument; *allg* the wood; **~block** *m* log; **~bock** *m* sawing-trestle, wood-horse; *zoo* tick, capricorn beetle; **~boden** *m* wooden floor; (*für Brennholz*) wood-loft; **~bohrer** *m* auger; **~brei** *m* wood pulp; **~bund, ~bündel** *n* bundle of sticks, fag(g)ot; **~decke** *f* (panel(l)ed) wood ceiling; **~dübel** *m* wood plug; dowel; **~en** *itr* to cut (*od* to fell) wood; to gather wood; *fig* (*prügeln*) to cudgel, to lick; **~erei** *f fam* (*Prügelei*) row; **~essig** *m* wood vinegar; pyroligneous acid; **~fachwerk** *n* timber framework; **~fäller** *m* feller, wood-cutter, *Am* lumberjack, lumberer, lumberman; **~faser** *f* wood fibre, *Am* wood fiber; **~~platte** *f* wood fibre board; **~~stoff** *m* wood fibre pulp, lignin, cellulose; **~fäule** *f* dry rot; **~feuer** *n* wood fire; **~feuerung** *f* combustion of wood; **~fräser** *m* shaper; wood-milling cutter; **~frei** *a* (*Papier*) free from wood pulp; **~frevel** *m* damage to a forest; offence against forest laws; **~gas** *n* wood gas, producer gas; **~gaser** *m mot* wood burner, producer gas driven car; **~gasgenerator** *m* charcoal generator; **~gasmotor** *m* wood-gas engine; **~gehäuse** *n radio etc* wood cabinet; **~geist** *m* wood spirit, methyl alcohol; **~gerippe** *n* frame timber, timber crib; **~gerüst** *n* wooden frame; wood scaffold; **~gestänge** *n* wooden poles *pl*; **~gitter** *n* wooden lattice; **~griff** *m* wooden handle; **~hacker** *m* wood cleaver, wood chopper; **~hammer** *m* mallet; **~~diplomatie** *f* sledge-hammer diplomacy; **~handel** *m* timber trade, *Am* lumber trade; **~händler** *m* dealer in wood, timber-merchant, *Am* lumber-merchant, lumberman; **~hauer** *m* feller, wood-cutter, *Am* lumberjack, lumberer; logger; **~~hütte** *f* logging camp; **~haufen** *m* wood-stack, wood-pile, *Am* wood-rick; **~haus** *n* wooden (*od* timber) house, timber cottage, *Am* frame house, frame cottage; **~hieb** *m* cutting, felling; **~hof** *m* woodyard, timber-yard, *Am* lumberyard; **~ig** *a* woody, ligneous; (*Rettich*) stringy; (*Spargel*) woody, hard; **~imprägnierung** *f* wood impregnation; **~käfer** *m* wood-beetle, wood-bob; **~kasten** *m*,

~kiste *f* wooden box; **~kirsche** *f* wild cherry; **~klotz** *m* block (*od* log) of wood; **~kohle** *f* charcoal; **~konservierung** *f* timber preservation; **~konstruktion** *f* timber construction; **~kopf** *m* (*Schimpfwort*) blockhead, *Am* bonehead; **~lager** *n* woodyard, *Am* lumberyard; **~latte** *f* lath of wood; **~leiste** *f* wood(en) ledge; **~makler** *m* lumber broker; **~maserung** *f* veining of wood; grain of wood; **~masse** *f* wood paste; wood pulp; lignolite; **~mast** *m* pole; wooden mast; **~mehl** *n* wood powder, wood flour (*od* dust); **~modell** *n* wood pattern; **~ofen** *m* wood-burning stove; **~pantinen** *f pl* wooden slippers *pl*, clogs *pl*; **~pflaster** *n* (*Straße*) wooden pavement; **~pflock** *m* hob, peg; **~pfosten** *m* wooden stake; **~platz** *m* timber-yard, *Am* lumber-yard; **~rost** *m* duck-board; **~säge** *f* wood saw; **~säure** *f* pyroligneous acid; **~scheit** *n* log of wood; **~schindel** *f* oak shingle; **~schlag, ~hau** *m* wood-cutting; (*Ort*) clearing (in a forest); **~schleifer** *m* wood pulp grinder; **~~ei** *f* pulp factory; **~schliff** *m* (mechanical) wood pulp; **~schneidekunst** *f* wood engraving, xylography; **~schneider** *m* wood-carver, xylographer; **~schnitt** *m* woodcut, wood engraving; **~schnitzer** *m* wood-carver; **~schnitzerei** *f* wood carving; **~schuh** *m* wooden shoe; (*Pantine*) sabot, clog; **~schuppen** *m* wood-shed; **~schwamm** *m* dry rot, wood fungus; **~späne** *m pl* chips *pl* (of wood); shavings *pl*; *Am* (*weiche*) excelsior; **~splitter** *m* splinter of wood, sliver; **~stange** *f* wooden stick (*od* pole); **~stall** *m* wood shed; **~stich** *m* wood engraving; **~stift, ~nagel** *m* wooden peg; **~stoff** *m* cellulose, wood pulp; lignin, lignone; **~stoß, ~stapel** *m* wood-pile, stack, *Am* wood-rick; (*zur Leichenverbrennung*) funeral pile; **~stuhl** *m* wooden stool, (*niederer*) *Am* cricket; **~stütze** *f* poppet; **~tankstelle** *f* filling station for wood-gas motor vehicles; **~taube** *f* wood-dove (*od* -pigeon), stock-dove; **~teer** *m* wood tar; **~träger** *m* wooden girder; **~tränkung** *f* impregnation of timber; **~turm** *m* wooden tower; **~überreste** *m pl* (*im Wald*) *Am* slash; **~ung** *f* cutting, felling; (*Gehölz*) forest, small wood; **~verkleidung** *f* wood-lining, wood revetment; **~verkohlung** *f* carbonization of wood; **~ vertäfelung** *f* wainscot(t)ing; **~wand** *f* wooden partition; **~weg** *m* cart-track in wood; *auf dem ~~e sein* to be on the wrong tack, to be off the track, to be at fault, *Am* to be way off, to bark up the wrong tree; **~werk** *n* timber-work; frame(-work), wood-work; **~wolle** *f* wood-shavings *pl*, wood-wool, wood fibre, *Am* excelsior; **~wurm** *m* wood worm; death-watch beetle; **~zellstoff** *m* wood pulp, lignocellulose; **~zement** *m* wood cement; **~zucker** *m* wood sugar, xylose.

Hölz|chen *n* small piece of wood; **~ern** *a* made of wood, wooden; *fig* (*linkisch*) clumsy; awkward; (*unbeweglich*) stiff.

homogen *a* homogeneous; uniform; smooth; **~isieren** *tr* to homogenize; **~ität** *f* homogeneousness, homogeneity.

Homonym *n* homonym; **~isch** *a* homonymous.

Homöopath *m* hom(o)eopath(ist); **~ie** *f* hom(o)eopathy; **~isch** *a* hom(o)eopathic.

Homo|sexualität *f* homosexuality; **~sexuell** *a* homosexual; **~sexuelle(r)** *m* homosexual; invert; pervert; *fam* sissy, *Am sl* homie, homo, molly.

Honig *m* honey; **~biene** *f* working-bee; **~kuchen** *m* ginger-bread; **~monat, ~mond** *m* honeymonth, honeymoon; **~scheibe, ~wabe** *f* honeycomb; **~schleuder** *f* honey strainer; **~seim** *m* liquid honey, virgin honey; **~süß** *a* very sweet, honeyed; **~wasser** *n* hydromel; **~zelle** *f* cell in a honeycomb.

Honor|ar *n* fee, honorarium; (*für Autor*) royalty; (*Belohnung*) gratification; (*Entschädigung*) reward, remuneration; **~atioren** *m pl* people of rank, notables *pl*, dignitaries *pl*; **~ieren** *tr* to fee, to pay a fee for; (*Wechsel*) to hono(u)r a bill; *nicht ~~* to dishono(u)r; **~ierung** *f* payment of fees; (*Wechsel*) hono(u)ring.

*

Hopfen *m* hop; (*Brau~*) hops *pl*; *an ihm ist ~ u. Malz verloren* he is lost to shame; he is a hopeless case; he is past hope and amendment; **~bau** *m* hop culture; **~darre** *f* hop-kiln; **~ernte** *f* hop-picking; **~feld** *n*, **~garten** *m* hop-garden, hop-ground; **~stange** *f* hop-pole; *fig* (*langer, dürrer Mensch*) lamp-post.

hopp, hoppla! *interj* hop! hop! hoppla! *interj fam* (*als Entschuldigung*) beg pardon! (*zur Warnung*) look out! go it!

Hops *m* hop, jump; skip; *~ gehen fam* to meet disaster; *mil sl* to go west; **~a!** *interj* hey-day! **~en** *itr* to hop, to skip, to jump; **~er** *m* hop-dance, quick-waltz.

Hör|aufnahme *f radio* sound reception; **~bar** *a* audible; audio; within earshot; (*verständlich*) intelligible; *~~ machen* to render audible; **~barkeit** *f* audibility; intelligibleness; **~~sgrad** *m* audibility factor; **~~sgrenze** *f* limit of audibility; **~bereich** *m* audible (*od* audio) range; range of audibility; (*Sender*) broadcasting range; **~bericht** *m radio* actuality with running commentary; (*Augenzeugenbericht*) eye-witness account; **~bild** *n* sound picture.

horch|en *itr* to listen (*auf* to); to hearken; (*an der Tür etc*) to listen in; (*spionieren*) to spy; *horch! interj* listen! hark! **~dienst** *m* (*Abhördienst*) intercept service; listening service; **~er** *m* listener; (*an der Tür*) eavesdropper; (*Spion*) spy; (*Tonmeßmann*) sound locator; **~gerät** *n*, **~apparat** *m* listening device (*od* apparatus), intercept receiver; sound locator (*od* detector); hydrophone gear; (*Schallmeßgerät gegen U-Boote*) asdic (=anti-submarine detection investigation committee), *Am* sonar (= sound navigation ranging); *ein U-Boot mit dem ~~ feststellen* to locate a submarine by sonar; **~meldung** *f* listening report; **~ortung** *f* sound ranging (*od* location); radio intercept service; **~posten** *m mil* listening post (*od* sentry); **~sappe** *f* listening sap; **~stollen** *m* listening gallery; **~taste** *f tele* listening cam; **~trupp** *m* listening detachment.

Horde *f* horde, tribe; troop, gang; (*Flechtwerk*) hurdle, latticed screen; shelf.

hör|en *tr, itr* to hear; (*hinhören, lauschen*) to listen (*auf* to); *radio* to listen in; *Paris ~~* to listen in to Paris; *mit meinem Radioapparat kann ich Paris ~~* I can get Paris with my radio; (*achtgeben, aufmerksam ~~*) to attend to; *Kolleg ~~* to attend a course of lectures; *die Messe ~~* to attend mass; *auf jdn ~~* to pay attention to s. o.; to follow s. o.'s advice; (*erfahren*) to understand; to learn; (*Gehör schenken*) to give ear (to); (*gehorchen*) to obey; *auf den Namen Mary ~~* to answer to the name of Mary; *hört! hört! interj* hear! hear! *Am* that's right! *beide Seiten ~~* to hear both sides; *soviel man hört* from all account; *~~ Sie auf! interj* stop it! *~~ Sie einmal!* look here! *Am* see here! *Na, ~~ Sie mal! interj* Oh, I say! *~~ Sie zu!* listen! *nichts ~~ wollen* to shut o.'s ears to, to refuse to listen to; *sagen ~~* to hear say; *gut ~~* to hear well; *schwer* (*od schlecht*) *~~* to be hard of hearing; *das läßt sich ~~* that would not be a bad plan; that sounds well; that's the thing; that's something like it; now you are talking; *sich ~~* to hear o. s.; *sie hört sich gerne* she likes to hear herself talk; *das hört sich gut an* that sounds well; *sich ~~ lassen* to make o. s. heard; *von sich ~~ lassen* to give news of o. s.; *ihr verging H~~ u. Sehen* she became quite unconscious; **~ensagen** *n* hearsay; (*Gerücht*) rumo(u)r; *vom ~~* by (*od* from) hearsay; **~er** *m* (*Person*) hearer, auditor; *radio* listener(-in); *pl* audience; (*Universität*) student; (*Gerät*) *tele* telephone receiver, handset; (*Kopfhörer*) ear-phone, headset; *den ~~ abnehmen tele* to take off (*od* to remove) the receiver; *den ~~ anhängen* (*od auflegen*) *tele* to put back the receiver, *Am* to restore the receiver, to hang up; **~~befragung** *f* (*zur Auswertung*) *radio* listener-rating; **~~echo** *n* listener echo; **~~gabel** *f tele* hook (of the receiver); **~~gehäuse** *n tele* receiver case, *Am* receiver shell; **~~kreis** *m*, **~~schaft** *f* hearers *pl*, audience, auditory; (*Universität*) students *pl*; *radio* listening audience; **~~meinungsforschung** *f* listener research; **~fehler** *m* mistake in hearing; mis-apprehension; **~folge** *f radio* (feature) programme, features *pl*; **~frequenz** *f radio* audio- (*od* voice-)frequency; **~gerät** *n* (*für Schwerhörige*) hearing aid; apparatus for the deaf; **~ig** *a* living in bondage, bond; a slave to; **~~keit** *f* bondage, serfdom; **~muschel** *f tele* receiver of telephone, ear-piece; (receiver) cap; **~nerv** *m anat* auditory nerve; **~probe** *f radio* (*für Rundfunkkünstler*) radio audition, tryout; **~rohr** *n* ear-trumpet, *med* stethoscope; **~saal** *m* lecture-room, auditorium; **~~flugzeug** *n mil aero* flying classroom; **~schwelle** *f* threshold of audibility; **~spiel** *n radio* radio play; (*dramatisch*) radio drama, air drama; (*rührseliges ~~*) *Am fam* soap opera; **~sprechschalter** *m* talk-listen switch; **~wacht** *f* listening watch; **~weite** *f* ear-shot; *auf* (*in*) *~~* within hearing (*od* ear-shot); *außer ~~* out of hearing; **~werkzeuge** *n pl* acoustic instruments *pl*.

Horizont *m* horizon; (*~linie*) skyline; *am ~* on the horizon; *künstlicher ~* (*aero* artificial horizon, gyro horizon; *scheinbarer ~* visible (*od* natural *od* apparent) horizon; *wahrer ~* astronomical (*od* real *od* rational) horizon; *fig* sphere of ideas; (*Aussicht*) outlook; *das geht über meinen ~* that's beyond me; that beats me; **~al** *a* horizontal; (*waagrecht*) level; **~~antenne** *f* top antenna, *Am* horizontal antenna; **~~bohrmaschine** *f* horizontal boring machine; **~~bomber** *m* (*im Gegensatz zum Sturzbomber*) bomber for level (*od* precision) bombing; **~~e** *f* horizontal (line); **~~ebene** *f* horizontal plane; **~~flug** *m* horizontal (*od* level) flight; **~~fluggeschwindigkeit** *f* horizontal flying speed; **~~kreis** *m* azimuth circle; **~~linie** *f* base line;

~~projektion *f* horizontal projection; **~~schnitt** *m* horizontal section.

Hormon *n* hormone; **~absonderung** *f* hormonesecretion; **~drüse** *f* hormonal gland; **~haltig** *a* containing hormones.

Horn *n* horn; (*Fühler*) feeler; (*Instrument*) bugle, French horn; (*Hupe*) electric horn, hooter; (*Trink~*) drinking horn; (*Bergspitze*) peak; *jdm Hörner aufsetzen fig* to cuckold; *auf die Hörner aufspießen* to gore; *mit den Hörnern stoßen* to butt, to poke; *in das gleiche ~ stoßen* to agree with s. o.; *ins eigene ~ stoßen fam* to toot o.'s own horn; *den Stier bei den Hörnern fassen* to take the bull by the horns; *sich die Hörner abstoßen* (*od ablaufen*) *fig* to sow o.'s wild oats; **~ähnlich, ~artig** *a* hornlike, horny; corneous; **~bläser** *m* horn-blower, bugler; **~brille** *f* horn spectacles *pl*; **~drechsler** *m* turner in horn; **~eule** *f* horned owl; **~haut** *f* callosity, horny skin, horny layer of epidermis; (*im Auge*) cornea; **~~entzündung** *f med* inflammation of the cornea, keratitis; **~~trübung** *f med* corneal opacity; **~ig** *a* horny, hornlike; **~ist** *m* bugler; **~kluft, ~spalte** *f* cleft in a hoof; **~ochse** *m* (*als Schimpfwort*) blockhead; **~ung** *m* February; **~signal** *n* bugle call; **~vieh** *n* horned cattle; *fam* (*Dummkopf*) blockhead.

Hörn|chen *n* small horn; (*Gebäck*) crescent, French roll, horseshoe roll; **~erblitzableiter** *m* horn-shaped lightning arrester; **~ern** *a* of horn, horny.

Hornisse *f* hornet.

Horoskop *n* horoscope; *ein ~ stellen* to cast a horoscope.

Horst *m* (*Gebüsch*) thicket; (*Gehölz*) cluster of trees, wood; (*Nest*) eyrie; nest; retreat; (*Flieger~*) *aero* airbase; **~en** *itr* to build an eyrie.

Hort *m* treasure; hoard; (*Zufluchtsort*) safe retreat; refuge; (*Schutz*) protection; (*Schützer*) protector; (*Tagesheim für Schulkinder*) day nursery for children of school age; **~en** *tr* (*Geld, Waren etc*) to hoard; **~nerin** *f* nursery-school teacher; **~ung** *f* (*Geld, Waren usw*) hoarding.

Hortensie *f bot* hydrangea.

*

Hose *f* (*lang*) trousers *pl*; (*e-e ~* a pair of trousers), *Am* pants *pl*; (*lange, weite ~, formlos ohne Jacke getragen von Dame od Herrn*) slacks *pl*; *gestreifte ~* striped trousers *pl*; (*kurze Sport- od Sommer~, Shorts*) shorts *pl*; (*zum Sportanzug*) knickerbockers *pl*; (*Flanell~*) flannels *pl*; (*Golf~*) plus-fours *pl*; (*blaue Arbeits~*) dungarees *pl*; (*Unter~*) drawers *pl*, pants *pl*; (*Damenhöschen, Schlupf~*) drawers *pl*, knickers *pl*, briefs *pl*, panties *pl*, step-in; (*Bade~*) bathing-drawers *pl*, *Am* trunks *pl*; *die ~n anhaben fig* to wear the breeches; *das Herz fiel ihm in die ~n fig* his heart went down to his heels; he lost courage; *sich auf die ~n setzen fam* (*eifrig lernen*) to work hard; *das ist Jacke wie ~* (*fam*) it's all the same; *die ~n voll haben fam* to be in a blue funk; **~naufschlag** *m* turn-up; **~nbandorden** *m* Order of the Garter; **~nbein** *n* trousers leg; **~nboje** *f mar* (*Rettungsgerät*) breeches-buoy; **~nbund, ~ngurt** *m* waist-band; **~nklappe** *f*, **~nlatz** *m*, *fam* **~ntürchen** *n* fly, flap; (*mit Reißverschluß*) zipper fly; **~nklammer** *f* (*für Radfahrer*) trouser clip; **~nknopf** *m* trouser button; **~nmatz** *m fam* boy in first trousers; **~nnaht** *f* trouser seam; **~nrock** *m* divided skirt, trouser skirt, culotte(s *pl*); **~nrolle** *f theat* man's part; **~nschlitz** *m* slit (of trousers); **~nstoff** *m* trousering; **~nstrecker** *m* stretcher for trousers; **~ntasche** *f* trousers-pocket; **~nträger** *m* (*pl*) braces *pl*, garters *pl* (*ein Paar ~~* a pair of ...), *Am* suspenders *pl*.

Hospit|al *n* hospital, infirmary; **~ant** *m* temporary auditor of lectures; **~ieren** *itr* to attend college-lectures temporarily.

Hospiz *n* hospice.

Hostie *f* the Host; consecrated wafer; **~ngefäß** *n* pyx; **~nkapsel** *f* tabernacle; **~nteller** *m* paten.

Hotel *n* hotel; *Am* (*für Automobilisten*) motel; *Am* (*für Privatflieger*) skytel; *~ garni* block of service flats, *Am* apartment hotel; **~besitzer, ~ier, ~wirt** *m* hotel-keeper, hotel proprietor, hôtelier; innkeeper; landlord; **~boy, ~page** *m* page (boy), *Am* bellhop, bellboy; **~gewerbe** *n* hotel industry; **~halle** *f* (*Vestibül*) (entrance-)hall, lobby; (*Diele*) lounge; **~portier** *m* hall porter; **~zimmer** *n* hotel room.

hott! *interj* (*Antreiben der Pferde*) gee up! (*nach rechts lenken*) gee! **~ehüh** *n* (*Antreiben der Pferde*) gee up! ho! hoy! (*Pferd in der Kindersprache*) gee-gee.

hu! *interj* hugh! ugh! whoo! whew! *Am* oof!

hü! *interj* (*Antreiben der Pferde*) gee up! go on!

Hub *m* lift, lifting; *mot* (*Kolben~*) stroke; travel; *aufgehender ~* upstroke; **~bewegung** *f* lifting movement (*od* motion); **~geschwindigkeit** *f* lifting (*od* hoisting) speed; **~höhe** *f* hoisting (*od* lifting) height, lift; *mot* (length of) stroke; **~karren, ~wagen** *m* lift truck, industrial truck; jack lift; **~kraft** *f* lifting power (*od* capacity); **~leistung** *f* lifting capacity; **~raum** *m* (*Hubvolumen*) piston displacement; stroke volume; cubic (*od* cylinder) capacity; **~schraube** *f* helicopter screw; **~schrauber** *m* helicopter; *fam* hover plane; rotorplane; *Am sl* eggbeater; *Am sl* (*Truppentransporter*) flying banana; **~weg** *m* height of lift; **~werk** *n* hoisting gear (*od* unit).

hüben *adv* on this (*od* our) side.

hübsch *a* pretty, nice; (*anmutig*) comely; (*reizend*) charming; (*gefällig*) handsome; (*schön*) beautiful; (*lieblich*) lovely; (*sauber*) tidy; (*freundlich*) kind; (*gut aussehend*) good-looking; *nicht ~* unseemly; (*beträchtlich*) handsome, tidy; considerable, fair; *ein ~es Vermögen* a handsome (*od* nice) fortune; *e-e ~e Summe Geld* a tidy sum of money; *e-e ~e Geschichte!* a pretty mess! *das war ~ von ihr* that was very kind of her; *es ist ~ von Ihnen, daß Sie kommen* it is very nice of you to come; *jdm ~ tun* to flatter s. o.; *sei ~ artig!* be nice and good! *ganz ~!* rather pretty! *etw ~ bleiben lassen* to keep clear of s. th.; to take good care not to do s. th.

Hucke *f* back; **~pack** *adv* pick-a-back; **~~flugzeug** *n* pick-a-back plane; composite plane.

Hud|elei *f* bungling; scamped work; (*Schererei*) trouble; **~eln** *tr* to huddle; to scamp; (*jdn quälen u. plagen*) to vex, to torment s. o.; **~ler** *m* huddler.

Huf *m* hoof; **~beschlag** *m* horse-shoeing; **~eisen** *n* horseshoe; **~~förmig** *a* horseshoe-shaped; **~~magnet** *m* horseshoe magnet; **~lattich** *m bot* coltsfoot; **~nagel** *m* hobnail, horseshoe nail; **~schlag** *m* foot-beat; hoof-beat (of a horse); kick; **~schmied** *m* farrier; **~tiere** *n pl* hoofed animals *pl*, ungulate.

Hufe *f* (*Land*) hide.

Hüft|bein *n* hip-bone; ilium; **~e** *f* hip; (*Tier~~*) haunch; **~(en)gegend** *f* region of the hip; **~entasche** *f* hip-pocket; **~former** *m* corset; **~gelenk** *n* hip-joint; **~~pfanne** *f* acetabulum; **~gürtel** *m* suspender-belt; demi-girdle, panty-girdle; **~halter** *m* hip-support; *fam* roll-on; **~lahm** *a* hip-shot; **~nerv** *m* sciatic nerve; **~schlauch** *m* roll-on girdle; **~weh** *n* pain in the hip; sciatica; hip-gout.

Hügel *m* hill; (*kleiner*) hillock; knoll; knob; (*Anhöhe*) elevation, height; **~abhang** *m* hillside; **~ig** *a* hilly; **~kette** *f* range (*od* chain) of hills; **~land** *n* hilly country.

Hugenott *m* Huguenot.

Huhn *n allg* fowl, *Am oft* chicken; (*Henne*) hen; (*Federvieh*) poultry; (*die Hühner auf der Stange*) roost; *junges ~* pullet; chicken; (*bei der Jagd, Reb~*) partridge; *gebratenes ~* roast fowl; *Hühner gackern* chickens cackle; *Hühner halten* to keep fowls; *Hühner locken* to chuck fowl; *ein verrücktes ~ fig fam* a crazy person.

Hühnchen *n* chicken, pullet; (*junger Hahn*) cock-chicken; (*Henne*) hen-chicken); *gebratenes ~* (*Back~*) roast chicken, fried chicken; *mit jdm ein ~ zu pflücken* (*od rupfen*) *haben* to have a bone to pick with s. o., *Am* to have a crow to pick with s. o.

Hühner|auge *n* corn (on the foot); **~~noperateur** *m* chiropodist, corn-cutter; **~~noperation** *f* corn-cutting; **~~npflaster** *n* corn-plaster; **~braten** *m* roast fowl, roast chicken; **~brühe** *f* chicken-broth; **~brust** *f* breast of a fowl, *med* pigeon breast; **~dieb** *m* roost-robber, *Am* chicken thief; **~draht** *m* chicken wire; **~ei** *n* hen's egg; **~eiweiß** *n* white of egg; **~farm** *f* poultry farm, chicken farm; **~geier** *m* kite; **~geschlecht** *n* gallinaceous family; **~habicht** *m orn* goshawk, hen-hawk, chicken-hawk; **~händler** *m* poulterer; **~haus** *n* hen-house; chicken coop; **~hof** *m* poultry yard, fowl-run, *Am* chicken-yard; **~hund** *m* setter, pointer; **~jagd** *f* partridge shooting; **~leiter** *f* hen-roost; small ladder; **~pest** *f* chicken-pest; **~stall** *m* hen-house, chicken coop; **~stange** *f* (hen-) roost, perch; **~stiege** *f fig* break-neck stairs *pl*; **~suppe** *f* chicken-broth, *Am* chicken soup; **~vögel** *m pl* gallinaceous birds *pl*; **~zucht** *f* breeding of poultry, chicken farming; **~züchter** *m* chicken farmer.

hui! *interj* ho! huzza! *in e-m Hui* in a jiffy, in a trice; in a twinkling.

Huld *f* (*Geneigtheit*) grace; (*Gunst*) favo(u)r; (*Güte*) kindness; (*Milde*) clemency; (*Freundlichkeit*) charm; (*Wohlwollen*) benevolence; **~igen** *itr* (*jdm*) to do (*od* to pay) homage to s. o.; (*sich e-r Sache widmen*) to devote o. s. to; (*e-m Laster ~~*) to indulge in; (*e-r Ansicht*) to hold an opinion; **~igung** *f* homage; **~~seid** *m* oath of allegiance; **~reich, ~voll** *a* gracious; (*freundlich*) kind; (*wohlwollend*) benevolent.

Hülle *f* (*Umhüllung*) wrap(per); (*Decke*) cover(ing); (*Schleier*) veil; (*Brief~, Ballon~*) envelope; (*Buch~*) jacket; (*Gehäuse*) case; (*vor den Augen*) bandage; (*Schicht*) layer; (*Scheide*) sheath; (*Kontur, Umriß*) contour; *anat, bot* integument; *die irdische ~, die sterbliche ~* mortal frame, dead body, remains *pl*; (*Kleid*) dress, garment; *die ~ fiel mir von den Augen* the scales fell from my eyes; *in ~ u. Fülle* plenty of, plentiful, in abundance; enough and to spare; *unter der ~ von* under cover of; **~n** *tr* (*einwickeln*) to wrap (up); (*bedecken*) to cover; (*verschleiern*) to veil; *in Dunkel ~~* to veil in obscurity; *in Wolken gehüllt* clouded; *sich in Schweigen ~~* to be wrapped up in silence; **~nelektronen** *n pl phys* shell electrons *pl*; **~nlos** *a* (*unbedeckt*) uncovered, (*unverschleiert*) unveiled; (*offen*) open.

Hülse *f* (*Schalenhaut*) hull; husk; (*Schote*) pod; (*Schale*) shell; *tech* case; shell; cover; sleeve; bush; (*Geschoß*) cartridge case, shell case; (*Dose*) box, case; (*Kapsel*) capsule; (*Patronen~*) case; **~n** *tr* to hull, to shell; **~nartig** *a* leguminous; **~nauswurf** *m mil* ejection of cartridge case; **~nauszieher** *m mil* cartridge case extractor; **~nboden** *m* (*Patrone*) cartridge base; **~nbrücke** *f mil* receiver cover; **~nfänger** *m mil* deflector bag; **~nfrucht** *f* leguminous plant; legume(n); **~nkopf** *m* (*Gewehr*) receiver; cartridge flange; **~nreißer** *m* (stoppage caused by) broken cartridge case; **~nsack** *m* spent-ammunition bag; **~nzieher** *m* extractor; **hülsig** *a* husky; shelly.

human *a* humane; (*leutselig*) affable; (*wohlwollend*) benevolent; **~ismus** *m* humanism; **~ist** *m* humanist; **~istisch** *a* humanistic; *~~e Bildung* classical education; **~itär** *a* humanitarian; **~ität** *f* humaneness; humanity; **~itätsduselei** *f* exaggerated humanitarianism.

Humbug *m* (*Unsinn*) humbug; nonsense; (*Schwindel*) hoax, swindle; hollowness.

Hummel *f* bumble-bee.

Hummer *m* lobster; **~salat** *m* lobster salad; **~schere** *f* claw of a lobster.

Humor *m* comicality; sense of humo(u)r, humo(u)r; (*Stimmung*) mood; *derber ~* robust humo(u)r; *~ haben* to have a sense of humo(u)r; *gar keinen ~ haben* to be wholly deficient in humo(u)r; **~eske** *f* humorous sketch; *mus* humoresque; **~ist** *m* humo(u)rist, comic; humorous person (*od* writer); wag; **~istisch, ~voll** *a* humorous; humo(u)ristic; (*spaßig*) funny, comic; *~~es Blatt* comic paper; **~los** *a* humo(u)rless; devoid of humo(u)r; *~~er Mensch* disgruntled person, *Am fam* sorehead.

humpeln *itr* to hobble, to limp.

Humpen *m* bumper, tankard, *Am* schooner.

Humus *m* humus, vegetable mo(u)ld; **~bildung** *f* humus formation; **~decke** *f* mo(u)ld cover; **~erde** *f* arable land; **~schicht** *f* humus layer; layer of mo(u)ld; **~stoff** *m* humus substance.

Hund *m* dog; (*Jagd~*) hound; *junger ~* puppy, pup; (*Welpe*) whelp; (*Köter*) cur; (*Mischling*) mongrel; (*Kindersprache*) wow-wow; *tech* (*Förderwagen im Bergbau*) truck, dog, hutch, miner's waggon; *fig* (*als Schimpfwort*) scoundrel, rascal, cur; dog; *Am oft* son-of-a-bitch (*Abk* s. o. b.); *toller ~* mad dog; *auf den ~ bringen* to ruin; *auf den ~ kommen* to go to the dogs, to go to pot, to go down in the world; *da liegt der ~ begraben* there's the rub; *er ist vor die ~e gegangen* he is gone to the dogs; *mit allen ~en gehetzt sein* to be up to a thing or two, to be wily; *wie ~ u. Katze leben* to lead a cat-and-dog life; *bekannt wie ein bunter ~* known by old and young, to be known all over the place; *wie ein begossener ~ dastehen* to be down in the mouth; *~e, die bellen, beißen nicht* barking dogs seldom bite; **~eabteil** *n* dog box; **~earbeit** *f fig* hard work, drudgery; **~eausstellung** *f* dog show, *Am* bench show; **~ebiß** *m* dog-bite; **~eführer** *m* dog sentry; **~egattung** *f* dog species; **~egebell** *n* barking of dogs; **~ehalsband** *n* dog-collar; **~ehaus** *n*, **~ehütte** *f*, **~estall** *m* (dog-) kennel, dog-hole, *Am* dog-house; **~ekälte** *f* bitter (*od* sharp) cold; **~ekoppel** *f* dog couple; pack of hounds; **~ekuchen** *m* dog-biscuit; **~eleben** *n* dog's life; *ein ~~ führen* to lead a dog's life; **~eleine** *f* slips *pl*; (*Koppel*) leash; **~eliebhaber** *m* cynophile; **~eloch** *n* dog-kennel; *fig* wretched hole; **~emarke** *f* dog licence disk, *Am* (dog) tag; *mil sl* (*Erkennungsmarke*) identity disk, *Am* dog tag; **~emüde** *a* dog-tired, dog-weary; dead-tired; **~epeitsche** *f* dog-whip; **~erennen** *n* dog race, dog racing; greyhound racing; **~eschlitten** *m* dog sled; **~esohn** *m vulg* (*Schimpfwort*) son-of-a-bitch (*Abk* s. o. b.); **~estaupe** *f* canine distemper; **~esteuer** *f* dog tax; **~etrab** *m* jog-trot; **~ewache** *f mar* dog watch; **~ewetter** *n* dirty (*od* beastly) weather; **~ezucht** *f* breeding of dogs; **~sfott** *m fam* rascal, rogue, cur, scoundrel; **~sfötterei** *f* roguery; **~sföttisch** *a* roguish, rascally; **~sgemein** *a* mean, very low, very vulgar; **~shai** *m* dog shark; **~skohl** *m bot* dog-bane; **~smüde** *a* dead-tired; **~sstern** *m* dog-star, Sirius; **~stage** *m pl* dog-days *pl*, canicular days *pl*; **~stagsferien** *pl* Midsummer holidays *pl*; **~stagshitze** *f* canicular heat; **~swut** *f* hydrophobia, rabies.

hundert *a* hundred; *~ n* hundred; cent; *zu H~en* by (*od* in) hundreds; *5 v. H.* five per cent; **~er** *m* hundred; **~erlei** *a* of a hundred different sorts; of a hundred kinds; **~fach, ~fältig** *a* hundredfold; **~gradig** *a* centigrade; **~jahrfeier** *f* centenary, *Am* centennial; **~jährig** *a* a hundred years old, centenary; centenarian; secular; **~~e(r)** *m* centenarian; **~köpfig** *a* hundred-headed; **~mal** *adv* a hundred times; **~-Meter-Lauf** *m* hundred metres run (*od* dash); 100 metres distance; **~satz** *m* percentage; **~ste** *a* hundredth; *vom ~~n ins Tausendste kommen* to talk on and on; to jump from one subject to another; **~stel** *n* one-hundredth part; per cent; the hundredth; **~stens** *adv* in the hundredth place; **~teilig** *a* centesimal, centigrade; **~weise** *adv* by hundreds.

Hünd|in *f* bitch; **~isch** *a* doggish; *fig* (*kriecherisch*) fawning; cringing; (*schamlos*) shameless; impudent; (*zynisch*) cynical; (*gemein*) vile.

Hüne *m* giant; **~ngestalt** *f* mighty figure; **~ngrab** *n* barrow, cairn; **~nhaft** *a* gigantic; athletic.

Hunger *m* hunger (*nach* after, for); appetite; (*~snot*) famine; *fig* (*Verlangen, Sehnsucht*) violent desire, craving, yearning (*nach* for); *nagender ~* craving hunger; *~ haben* to be hungry, to feel empty; *keinen ~ haben* to have no appetite, not to be hungry; *~s sterben* to starve to death; to die of hunger; *ich sterbe vor ~* I'm dying of hunger; *~ leiden* to starve, to go hungry; *~ verspüren* to feel hungry; *~ stillen* to appease, to satisfy o.'s hunger; *krank sein vor ~* to be ill from hunger; *von ~ geplagt* hunger-bit(ten); *von ~ getrieben* hunger-driven; *von ~ gequält* hunger-stricken; *jdn durch ~ zu etw bringen* to hunger s. o. into s. th.; **~blockade** *f* starvation blockade; **~gebiet** *n* hunger-ridden area; **~ig, hungrig** *a* hungry, starving; *fig* (*begierig nach*) desirous (of); eager (for); to be hungry (for *od* after); *sehr ~~ sein* to be famished; *ich bin ~~* I am hungry; *~~ wie ein Wolf* to be hungry as a wolf (*od* hunter); **~jahr** *n* year of famine; **~krawall** *m* food riot; **~kur** *f med* fasting cure; **~leider** *m* starveling, poor devil; **~lohn** *m* starvation wage; pittance; *zu ~löhnen arbeiten lassen* to sweat; **~marsch** *m* (*der Arbeitslosen*) hunger march; **~n** *itr* (*~ig sein*) to be hungry; to go hungry; *jdn aushungern* to hunger out s. o.; *fig* (*begierig sein nach*) to hunger (after, for); to long (for); **~ödem** *n* nutritional (o)edema (*od* dropsy); **~ration** *f* starvation diet; **~snot** *f* famine; **~streik** *m* hungerstrike; *in den ~~ treten* to hungerstrike; **~~ende(r)** *m* hungerstriker; **~tod** *m* starvation; *den ~~ sterben* to starve; **~tuch** *n*: *am ~~ nagen* to be starving, to starve, to suffer extreme want; **~zustand** *m* fasting condition.

Hunne *m* hun.

Hupe *f mot* (electric) horn, hooter, klaxon, siren; buzzer, **~n** *itr* to hoot, to toot, to honk; to sound o.'s horn; to honk (*od* to blow) o.'s horn; **~nknopf** *m* horn button; **~nsignal, ~nzeichen** *n* hooting signal; honk; *ein ~~ geben* to sound o.'s horn.

hüpfen *itr* to hop; (*springen*) to jump; to skip; *aero* (*Seeflugzeug bei Start u. Wasserung*) to porpoise; (*spielend*) to gambol; *vor Freude ~* to jump with joy; *Seil ~* to skip rope; *das ist gehüpft wie gesprungen fig* that's all the same.

Hürde *f* hurdle; (*Schaf~*) pen, (pin-) fold; (*Pferde~*) corral; **~n** *tr* to pen up, to hurdle, to fence up; **~nlauf** *m* hurdling; **~nläufer** *m* hurdler; **~nrennen** *n* hurdle-race; **~nschlag** *m* foldage; **~nwand, Hürdung** *f* hurdle-work.

Hure *f* whore; prostitute; harlot; (*Gassen~*) street-walker; night-walker; red-light sister; *sie ist e-e ~* she walks the streets; **~n** *itr* to whore; to wench; to fornicate; (*von Frauen*) to prostitute o. s.; **~nbock, ~nhengst** *m* whoremonger, lecher; **~nhaus** *n* (*Bordell*) brothel; whorehouse; house of ill fame; disorderly house; house of call; **~nkind** *n* bastard; **~nleben** *n* prostitution; lewd life; **~npack** *n* lewd rabble; **~nsohn** *m vulg* (*Schimpfwort*) son of a whore, *bes. Am* son-of-a-bitch (*Abk* s. o. b.); **~nviertel** *n* (*e-r Stadt*) red-light district; **~nwirtin** *f* keeper of a brothel; **~r** *m* whoremonger, wencher; fornicator; **~rei** *f* prostitution; whoring; streetwalking; (*Bibel*) fornication; **~risch** *a* whorish, lewd.

hurra! *interj* (hip, hip) hurra(h)! *mit ~ begrüßen, ~ rufen, ~ schreien* to cheer, to shout hurrah; **~patriot** *m* patrioteer, blimpish patriot, jingoist, *Am* jingo; **~~ismus** *m* jingoism, chauvinism; **~~isch** *a* exaggeratedly patriotic, *Am fam* spread-eagle.

hurtig *a* brisk, agile, nimble; (*munter*) lively; (*schnell*) quick, swift, speedy; **~keit** *f* agility; quickness; swiftness; nimbleness.

Husar *m* hussar; **~enmütze** *f* busby; **~entasche** *f* sabretache.

husch! *interj* hush! at once! **~en** *itr* to whisk, to slip away; to scurry.

hüsteln *itr* to cough slightly, to hack.

Husten *m* cough; *den ~ haben* to have a cough; *~ itr* to cough; *fig* (*stark ~*) to bark; **~anfall** *m* fit of coughing;

~bonbon *n* cough-drop; cough lozenge; **~lindernd** *a* cough-allaying; **~mittel** *n* cough remedy; **~reflex** *m* cough reflex; **~reiz** *m* throat irritation; **~stillend** *a* pectoral.

Hut[1] *m* (gentlemen's) hat; (*Damen~*) ladies' hat; (*ohne Rand*) bonnet; toque; *steifer ~* hard hat, bowler, billycock, *Am* derby (hat); (*Filz~*) felt (hat); (*Klapp~*) silk hat, crush hat, *Am* opera hat; (*Haar~*) fur felt hat; (*Trachten~*) Tyrol hat; (*Stroh~*) straw hat; Panama (hat); (*Mode~*) fashion hat; (*weicher ~*) soft hat; (*Homburger*) Homburg hat; (*Pilz*) cap, top; (*Zucker~*) loaf of sugar; (*Wein*) scum; *min* gossan; (*Färben*) layer of spent tanbark; *bot* pileus; *~ ab! interj* hat(s) off! *den ~ abnehmen* to take off o.'s hat; *den ~ aufsetzen* to put on o.'s hat; *den ~ aufhaben* to be covered; *den ~ herumreichen* (*Geld einsammeln*) to pass round the hat; *mir geht der ~ hoch sl* I blow my hat; *mit dem ~ in der Hand* hat in hand; *unter e-n ~ bringen* to reconcile conflicting opinions; **~band** *n* hat-band; **~besatz** *m*, **~garnitur** *f* trimming of a hat; **~borte** *f* hat ribbon; **~bürste** *f* hat-brush; **~fabrik** *f* hat-(manu)factory, hattery; **~feder** *f* plume, feather for a hat; **~filz** *m* hat felt; **~form** *f* shape of a hat; hat block; **~futter** *n* hat-lining; **~geschäft** *n* hattery, hatter's shop; (*für Damenhüte*) milliner's shop; **~händler** *m* hatter; **~kniff** *m* dent; **~kopf** *m* crown; **~krempe** *f* brim (of a hat); *hochgeschlagene ~~* turned-up brim; **~macher** *m* hatter; **~macherin** *f* (*Putzmacherin*) milliner; **~nadel** *f* hat-pin; (*Schmuck*) fancy pin; **~rand** *m* edge of the brim; **~schachtel** *f* hat case, hat-box, bandbox; **~schleife** *f* favo(u)r in a hat; cockade; **~schnur** *f* hat-string; *das geht über die ~~* (*fig*) that tops (*od* beats) everything; that's past a joke; that's about the limit; **~ständer** *m* hat-peg, hat-rack, hat-stand, *Am auch* hat-tree; **~stumpen** *m* hat stump; **~zucker** *m* (cone-shaped) loaf-sugar.

Hut[2] *f* (*Aufsicht*) guard; charge; (*Beachtung, Aufmerksamkeit*) heed; (*Sorge*) care; (*Schutz*) protection; (*Weide*) pasture; *auf der ~ sein* to be on o.'s guard; to be on the lookout; to keep o.'s eyes open; to be careful; *seien Sie auf der ~!* be on your guard!

hüt|en *tr* (*bewachen*) to guard; to watch over; to take care of; (*erhalten*) to keep; (*schützen vor*) to protect against (*od* from); (*Vieh*) to tend cattle, to herd; (*Bett, Zimmer ~~*) to be confined to o.'s bed (*od* room); to keep o.'s bed (*od* room); *das Haus ~~* to keep indoors; *sich ~~ vor* to take care of, to be careful; to beware (of); to be on o.'s guard (against); to guard (against), to watch out for; *~~ Sie sich!* keep off! **~er** *m* guardian; (*Aufseher*) custodian; (*Wärter*) keeper; warden; (*Hirte*) herdsman; **~erin** *f* female guardian.

Hütte *f* hut; (*kleines Häuschen, auch Landhaus*) cottage, cot; (*armselige Behausung*) cabin; (*Berg~*) refuge; (*Schuppen*) shelter, shed, *Am* shack; (*Bruchbude*) *Am sl* shebang; (*Eisen~*) metallurgical plant; forge; foundry; smelting-plant (*od* -house *od* -works *pl*); (iron-) works *pl*; blast-furnace plant; (*Walzwerk*) rolling-mill; **~narbeiter** *m* smelter, founder; foundry worker; **~nbesitzer** *m* proprietor of a foundry; **~nbewohner** *m* cottager; **~nerzeugnis** *n* metallurgical product; **~nindustrie** *f* steel and iron industry; **~nkoks** *m* blast-furnace coke; metallurgical coke; coke-oven coke; by-product coke; **~nkunde** *f* metallurgy; **~nmeister** *m* overseer of a foundry; **~nrauch** *m* (arsenical) fumes *pl*, furnace smoke; white arsenic; **~nrevier** *n* mining district; **~nwerk** *n* metallurgical works *pl*; (*Schmelzerei*) smelting-works *pl*; (*Eisenwerk*) iron-works *pl*; (*Gießerei*) foundry; (*Walzwerk*) rolling-mill; **~nwesen** *n* metallurgy, metallurgical engineering; **~nwirt** *m* (*e-r Berghütte*) hut-keeper; **~nzeche** *f* colliery.

Hutze *f* scoop.

Hutzel *f* (*gedörrtes Obst*) dried apple, dried pear; dried fruit; *fig* (*runzlige Person*) old shrivelled person; **~brot** *n* (*Brot mit eingebackenem Obst*) cake containing dried fruit; **~ig** *a* shrivelled; **~n** *itr* (*ein-, zus. schrumpfen*) to shrivel; **~männchen, ~männlein** *n* (*Kobold*) goblin, brownie, gnome.

•

Hyäne *f* hyena.

Hyazinthe *f bot* hyacinth.

Hydrant *m* hydrant, fire-plug (*Abk* F.P.).

Hydrat *n* hydrate.

Hydraul|ik *f* hydraulics *pl mit sing*; **~isch** *a* hydraulic; *~~e Presse* hydraulic press.

Hydrier|anlage *f* hydrogenation plant; synthetic oil plant; **~en** *tr* to hydrogenate, to hydrogenize; **~ung** *f* hydrogenation; **~~sverfahren** *n* hydrogenation process; **~werk** *n* hydrogenation plant.

Hydro|dynamik *f* hydrodynamics *pl mit sing*; **~elektrisch** *a* hydro-electric; *~~es Kraftwerk* hydro-electric generating station; **~gen** *n* (*Wasserstoff*) hydrogen (*Abk* H.); **~genbombe** *f* hydrogen bomb, H-bomb; **~genisieren** *tr* to hydrogenate; **~graphie** *f* hydrography; **~lyse** *f* hydrolysis; **~meter** *m* hydrometer; **~plan** *m* (*Gleitboot; U-Boot-Tiefensteuer*) hydroplane; **~statik** *f* hydrostatics *pl mit sing*; **~therapie** *f* hydrotherapeutics *pl mit sing*.

Hygiene *f* hygiene, hygienics *pl*; **~ausstellung** *f* health-exhibition.

hygienisch *a* hygienic, sanitary.

Hymne *f* hymn.

Hyperbel *f math* hyperbola; (*Redekunst*) hyperbole.

Hypno|se *f* hypnosis; **~tisch** *a* hypnotic; **~tiseur** *m* hypnotist; **~tisieren** *tr* to hypnotize.

Hypochond|er *m* hypochondriac; **~rie** *f* hypochondria, spleen; **~risch** *a* splenetic, spleenful; hypochondriac(al).

Hypophyse *f* pituitary gland.

Hypotenuse *f* hypotenuse.

Hypothek *f* mortgage; security; (*auf Grundstück*) mortgage on landed property, *Am* real estate mortgage; *Belastung mit e-r ~* hypothecation; *Rückzahlung e-r ~* redemption of a mortgage; *e-e ~ ablösen* to dismortgage; *e-e ~ abtragen* (*od abzahlen*) to pay off a mortgage; *in ~en anlegen* to invest in securities; *e-e ~ aufnehmen* to raise money on mortgage; *mit e-r ~ belasten* to mortgage, to hypothecate; *e-e ~ eintragen* to register a mortgage; *e-e ~ kündigen* (*vom Gläubiger*) to call in a mortgage; (*vom Schuldner*) to give notice of redemption; *e-e ~ löschen* to cancel a mortgage; *e-e ~ für verfallen erklären* to foreclose a mortgage; **~arisch** *a* hypothecary; *adv* on (by) mortgage (security); *~~ belastet* mortgaged, encumbered with mortgages; *~~e Sicherheit* hypothecary security; **~enbank** *f* mortgage bank; **~enbrief** *m* mortgage deed (*Am* note); **~enbuch** *n* register of mortgages; **~eneintragung** *f* registration (*Am* recording) of a mortgage; **~enfrei** *a* free and unencumbered; **~engläubiger** *m* mortgagee; **~enlast** *f* encumbrance; **~enlöschung** *f* cancellation of the entry of a mortgage; **~enpfandbrief** *m* mortgage bond; **~enschein** *m* mortgage certificate (*od* deed); **~enschuld** *f* debt on mortgage; **~enschuldner** *m* mortgagor.

Hypoth|ese *f* hypothesis, supposition; **~etisch** *a* hypothetic(al).

Hyster|ie *f* hysteria; **~isch** *a* hysteric(al); *~~e Anfälle* hysterics *pl*, hysteric fits *pl*; *~~e Anfälle bekommen* to go into hysterics, to have a fit of hysterics.

I

I *Abk mit* ***I*** *siehe Liste der Abk; das Tüpfelchen auf dem ~* the dot on the i; *da fehlt kein Tüpfelchen auf dem ~!* everything is just so! *~ wo!* certainly not! not at all!
iah! *n* (*Esel*) hee-haw; **~en** *itr* to hee--haw, to bray.
Iamb\|e, ~us *m* iambus; **~isch** *a* iambic.
ich *prn* I; *~ selbst* I myself; *~ bin es* it is I, *fam* it is me; *~ Armer!* poor me! *das ~* the I, the self, the ego, *fam* the me; *sein liebes ~* his own dear self; *mein früheres ~* my former self; *mein zweites ~* my second self; **~bewußtsein** *n* consciousness of self; **~sucht** *f* egoism; (*Geltungsbedürfnis*) egotism; (*Selbstsucht*) selfishness; (*Eigenliebe*) self-love; (*Einbildung*) conceit.
Ideal *n* ideal; (*Vorbild*) model; (*Muster*) pattern; (*Beispiel*) example; *er ist das ~ e-s Redners* he is a born orator; *~ a* ideal, perfect; *fam* choice, fine, first-rate; **~bedingung** *f* ideal condition; **~isieren** *tr* to idealize; **~ismus** *m* idealism; **~ist** *m* idealist; **~istisch** *a* idealistic.
Idee *f* idea; (*Begriff*) notion, concept; (*Vorstellung*) conception; (*Gedanke*) thought; (*Eindruck, dunkle Erinnerung*) impression; (*gute ~*) brain-wave; *fam* (*ein wenig, ein bißchen*) a little (bit); *e-e fixe ~* a fixed idea, an obsession; *voller ~n stecken* to be full of ideas; *e-e ~ zu kurz fam* a trifle too short; *e-e ~ dunkler* a shade darker; *e-e großartige ~* a grand idea; *keine blasse ~ von etw haben* to have not the faintest notion of s. th.; *nach seiner ~* in his idea; *keine ~!* certainly not! by no means! **~ll** *a* ideal, imaginary; *~~ konkurrieren jur* to be concurrent with; **~narm** *a* to have no ideas; **~nassoziation, ~nverbindung** *f* association of ideas; **~naustausch** *m* exchange of ideas; **~nfülle** *f*, **~nreichtum** *m* (*Erfindungsgabe*) inventiveness; (*Findigkeit*) resourcefulness; **~nkreis** *m* sphere of ideas; **~nmann** *m* (*Reklame*) ideas man, *Am* visualizer; **~nreich** *a* full of ideas; **~nwelt** *f* world of ideas; (*schöpferische Einbildungskraft*) imagination; (*Denkungsart*) mentality; (*Philosophie*) ideology.
Iden *pl* Ides *pl*.
ident\|ifizieren *tr* to identify; **~ifizierung** *f* identification; **~isch** *a* identical; **~ität** *f* identity; **~itätsnachweis** *m* proof of identity; certificate of origin.
Ideolog\|e *m* ideologist; (*Träumer*) visionary; **~ie** *f* ideology; **~isch** *a* ideological.
Idiom *n* idiom; (*Mundart*) dialect; (*Volkssprache, Jargon*) vernacular; **~atisch** *a* idiomatic(al).
Idiosynkrasie *f* aversion, idiosyncrasy.
Idiot *m* idiot; *Am* moron; **~enanstalt** *f* lunatic asylum; **~ie** *f* idiocy; **~isch** *a* idiotic(al); half-witted, stupid.
Idol *n* idol.
Idyll *n*, **~e** *f* idyl(l); **~isch** *a* idyllic.
Igel *m* hedgehog; (*See~*) urchin; *mil* hedgehog, square of tanks; **~stellung** *f mil* hedgehog defence position; all-around defence position; *tiefgestaffelte ~~en mil* web defence.
Ignor\|ant *m* stupid person; ignoramus; (*Dummkopf*) dunce; **~anz** *f* ignorance; **~ieren** *tr* to ignore, to take no notice of; *jdn ~~* to cut s. o.; (*mißachten*) to slight, to disregard; (*nicht beachten*) to overlook.
ihm *prn dat m, n* (to) him; (*Sache*) (to) it.
ihn *prn acc m* him; (*Sache*) it.
ihnen *prn dat pl* (to) them; *Ihnen* (to) you; *ein Freund von ~* (*Ihnen*) a friend of theirs (yours).
ihr *prn f dat* (to) her; (*Sachen*) (to) it; *pl 2. p* you; *f possessivum* her, (*Sachen*) its, *pl* theirs; (*mehrere Besitzer*) their; *meine u. ~e Anschauungen* my opinions and theirs; (*Anrede*) your; **~er** *prn, a* of her; of it; of them, of their; of you, of your, of yours; *e-s ~er Häuser* a house of yours; (*Briefschluß*) yours (truly); **~erseits** *adv f* on her part; *pl* on their part (*od* turn); (*Anrede*) on your part; **~esgleichen** *a f* her (*pl* their) like, of her (*pl* their) kind; like her (*pl* them); the like of her (*pl* them); *f* her equal(s *pl*); their equal(s); (*Anrede*) (the) like (of) you; **~ethalben, ~etwegen, ~etwillen** *adv f* because of her, for her sake; on her account; *pl* because of them, for their sake; (*Anrede*) because of you, for your sake, on your account; **~ige** *prn possessivum f* hers; *pl* theirs; (*Anrede, Briefschluß*) yours.
illegal *a* illegal; *~ werden* to go underground; **~ität** *f* illegality.
illegitim *a* illegitimate; (*ungesetzlich*) illegal, unlawful; **~ität** *f* illegitimacy.
illoyal *a* disloyal; **~ität** *f* disloyalty.
Illumin\|ation *f* illumination; **~ator** *m* illuminator; **~ieren** *tr* to illuminate; to light up.
Illus\|ion *f* illusion; **~orisch** *a* illusory.
Illustr\|ation *f* illustration; figure; diagram; **~ationsdruck** *m* printing of illustrations; **~ieren** *tr* to illustrate; (*erklären*) to explain; (*anschaulich zeigen*) to demonstrate; (*durch Beispiele belegen*) to exemplify; **~ierte (Zeitung)** *f* (illustrated) paper, picture newspaper; *reich ~iert* heavily illustrated.
Iltis *m* polecat, fitchew, fitchet.
im = *in dem* in the.
imaginär *a* imaginary.
Imbiß *m* short (*od* light) meal; lunch, luncheon; snack; bite; **~halle, ~stube** *f* snack bar, lunchroom, *Am* lunch--counter, luncheonette; *Am sl* dinette, bistro, nookery, one-arm joint.
Imit\|ation *f* imitation; (*Fälschung*) counterfeit; **~ieren** *tr* to imitate; (*nachahmen*) to mimic; (*fälschen*) to counterfeit; (*kopieren*) to copy, to duplicate, to reproduce.
Imker *m* bee-master (*od* -keeper); **~ei** *f* bee-farming (*od* -keeping); apiculture.
immanent *a* immanent, indwelling, inherent.
immateriell *a* immaterial.
Immatrikul\|ation *f* matriculation; **~ieren** *tr* to matriculate, to enrol(l); *sich an e-r Hochschule ~~ lassen* to matriculate (*od* enroll) in a university.
Imme *f* bee.
Immelmannkurve *f aero* Immelmann turn.
immens *a* immense, vast, huge.
immer *adv* always, ever, every time; *Am* all the time; *~ wieder kommen* to keep coming back; *für ~ verlassen* to leave for good; *sie hat es schon ~ gesagt* she said so all along; *auf ~* for ever; *~ größer* bigger and bigger; *~ mehr* more and more; *~ noch* still, as yet; *~ wieder* again and again, over and over again; *noch ~ nicht* not yet; *~ geradeaus!* keep straight ahead! *~ weiter, ~ zu!* keep on! *~ drei* three at a time; *was auch ~* what(so)ever; *wer auch ~* who(so)ever; *wie auch ~* how(so)ever; *wo auch ~* where(so)ever; **~dar** *adv* for ever; for ever and ever, evermore; **~fort** *adv* always, constantly, continually, *Am* all the time, *Am* without letup; **~grün** *a* evergreen; periwinkle; **~hin** *adv* nevertheless, still, in spite of everything, at any rate; **~während** *adv* everlasting; endless; perpetual; **~zu** *adv* permanently, continually; all the time; *nur ~zu!* go on!
Immobilien *f pl* immovables *pl*; (*Grundstücke*) real estate; (*totes Inventar*) dead stock; **~handel** *m* real estate business.
Immortelle *f* everlasting flower.
immun *a* immune (*gegen* from); **~isieren** *tr* to immunize; to render immune; **~isierung** *f* immunization; **~ität** *f* immunity (*gegen* from); *jur* exemption.
Imperativ *m* imperative (mood).
Imperfekt *n* imperfect (*od* past) tense.
Imperialismus *m* imperialism; **~istisch** *a* imperialistic.
imperti\|nent *a* impertinent, insolent, saucy; (*zudringlich*) intrusive; **~nenz** *f* impertinence.
Impf\|arzt *m* vaccinator; inoculator; **~en** *tr* to vaccinate; (*Blattern*) to inoculate; (*Bäume*) to (en)graft, to inoculate; *~~ n*, **~ung** *f* vaccination, inoculation; **~gegner** *m* anti-vaccinationist; **~ling** *m* vaccinated child (man, woman); **~messer** *n* vaccinator; **~nadel** *f* vaccine point; **~pflicht** *f*, **~zwang** *m* compulsory vaccination; **~reis** *n bot* graft; **~schein** *m* certificate of vaccination; **~stoff** *m* vaccine.
Imponderabilien *n pl* imponderable substances *pl*, imponderables *pl*.
imponieren *itr* to impress upon s. o.; (*beeinflussen*) to affect, to influence, to sway; (*beeindrucken*) to touch, to strike; (*täuschen*) to impose upon s. o.; **~d** *a* imposing, impressive; (*stattlich*) stately.
Import *m* import(s *pl*), importation; **~agent** *m* import(ing) agent; **~e** *f* imported Havana cigar; **~eur** *m* importer; **~firma** *f* importing firm; **~geschäft** *n* import business; **~ieren** *tr* to import; **~volumen** *n* volume of imports.
im\|posant *a* imposing; impressive; **~potent** *a* impotent; **~potenz** *f* impotency; **~prägnieren** *tr* to impregnate; (*sättigen*) to saturate; *~prägnierter Regenmantel* waterproof; **~prägniermittel** *n* impregnating agent; **~prägnierung** *f* impregnation; (*Holz*) preservation; **~prägnierverfahren** *n* impregnation process; **~presario** *m* impresario; **~pressionismus** *m* impressionism; **~pressionistisch** *a* impressionistic; impressionary; **~pressum** *n* imprint; **~provisation** *f* improvisation, *Am fam* ad-lib; **~provisieren** *tr* to improvise, to extemporize; *Am fam* to ad-lib; (*be-*

gleiten) *mus* to vamp; to improvise accompaniment; **~puls** *m* impulse; *unter dem ~~ des Augenblicks* on the impulse of the moment; **~~geber** *m* impulse sender, impulse generator; **~~gerät** *n* (*Radar*) pulse modulator; **~~iv** *a* impulsive; *~~iv handeln* to act on impulse; **~~überträger** *m* impulse repeater; **~~zunahme** *f* increase of momentum.

imstande *adv* able; *~ sein* to be able (to), to be in a position; (*fähig sein*) to be capable (of s. th., of doing), *ich fühle mich dazu nicht ~* I don't feel up to it.

*

in *prp* (*räumlich*) in, at; (*Richtung*) into, to; (*zeitlich*) in, during, at; (*innerhalb*) within; *~ kurzem* shortly; *im ersten Stock* on the first floor; *~ der Straße* in (*Am* on) the street; *im Theater* at the theatre; *~ der Schule* at school; *~ die Schule gehen* to go to school; *im vorigen Jahr* last year; *~ der Nacht* at night; during the night; *~ e-r dunklen Nacht* on a dark night; *im Alter von* at the age of; *im Anfang* at the beginning; *~ aller Frühe* at daybreak; *~ ärztlicher Behandlung sein* to be under medical treatment; *~ der Stadt umhergehen* to walk about the town; *~ Geschäften reisen* to travel on business; *~ Verlegenheit sein* to be at a loss; *~ Musik setzen* to set to music; *~ Schutz nehmen* to take under o.'s protection.

inaktiv *a* inactive; (*Offizier*) retired; (*Beamter*) pensioned off.

In|angriffnahme *f* beginning, setting about, attack, start; (*Vorbereitungen*) preliminary operations *pl*; **~spruchnahme** *f* (*Kredit*) availment; (*Kräfte*) strain; (*Anrecht*) claim; laying claim to; (*Bedarf*) requirements *pl*, demands *pl*; (*Zeit, Aufmerksamkeit*) engrossment; *mil* requisition; (*gänzliche ~~*) absorption; **~augenscheinnahme** *f* inspection; **~augurieren** *tr* to inaugurate; **~begriff** *m* (*Wesen*) substance, essence; (*Verkörperung*) embodiment; (*Inhalt*) contents *pl;* (*Gesamtheit*) sum, total(ity); (*Zus.fassung*) abstract, summary, epitome; **~begriffen** *a* included, inclusive of, implied; **~besitznahme** *f* occupation, act of taking possession; **~betriebnahme, ~betriebsetzung** *f* opening, starting; *tech* setting in motion.

In|brunst *f* ardo(u)r, fervo(u)r; **~brünstig** *a* ardent, fervent.

Indanthren *n* indanthrene.

indem *conj* while; whilst; (*Grund*) since, as; because; *adv* meanwhile, in the meantime; *~ er das sagte* (while) saying so; *~ man behandelt* by (*od* on) treating.

Indemnität *f* indemnity.

Inder *m* Indian, Hindoo.

indes, **indessen** *adv* (*zeitlich*) while; meanwhile, in the meantime; (*jedoch*) however; (*noch*) still; (*dennoch*) nevertheless; *conj* nevertheless; for all that; yet; while.

Index *m* index (*pl* indexes, indices); *math* subscript; (*Inhaltsverzeichnis*) table of contents; (*Lebenshaltung*) cost of living; **~strich** *m* index mark, ga(u)ge mark; **~zahl, ~ziffer** *f* index number.

Indianer *m* (Red) Indian, *Am fam* buck; **~geschichte** *f* Red Indian tale; **~häuptling** *m* Red Indian chief; **~stamm** *m* Red Indian tribe.

Ind|ien *n* (East) India; **~ier** *m* Indian, Hindoo.

Indienststellung *f mil* (*Einberufung*) call, draft, calling in; (*Ausrüstung*) arming for active service; *mar, aero* commissioning.

indifferen|t *a* neutral, indifferent; inert; **~zlinie** *f tele* dead line; **~zzone** *f tele* neutral zone.

indigo|blau *a* indigo-blue; **~farbstoff** *m* indigotin.

Indikativ *m gram* indicative (mood).

Indikator *m* indicator; (radioactive) tracer.

indirekt *a* indirect; *~e Beleuchtung* indirect lighting; *~es Feuer mil* indirect (*od* parabolic) fire.

indisch *a* Indian, Hindoo; *~er Flachs* jute; *~er Ozean* Arabian Sea.

indiskret *a* (*taktlos*) tactless; (*neugierig*) inquisitive, prying; indiscreet; **~ion** *f* tactlessness; inquisitiveness; indiscretion, indiscreetness.

individu|alisieren *tr* to individualize; to specify; to particularize; **~alist** *m* individualist; **~alistisch** *a* individualistic; **~alität** *f* individuality; individual characteristics *pl*; character; **~ell** *a* individual; (*eigenständig*) single, separate, particular; **~um** *n* individual; person.

Indi|zienbeweis *m* circumstantial (*od* presumptive) evidence; **~zieren** *tr* to indicate; **~zierung** *f* indication.

*

Indo|china *n* Indo-China; **~chinesisch** *a* Indo-Chinese; **~germane** *m* Indo-European, Aryan; **~germanisch** *a* Indo-European, Indo-Germanic; **~nesien** *n* (Republic of) Indonesia; **~nesisch** *a* Indonesian.

indolent *a* indolent; (*müßig*) idle.

Indoss|ament *n* (in-)endorsement; **~ant** *m* (in-)endorser, endorsor; **~at** *m* (in-)endorsee; **~ierbar** *a* (in-)endorsable; **~ieren** (*Wechsel*) *tr* to (in-)endorse, to back.

Induktion *f* induction; **~sapparat** *m* inductive machine; **~srolle, ~sspule** *f* induction coil; **~sstrom** *m* induction current.

indukt|iv *a* inductive; **~ivität** *f* inductivity; inductance; self-inductance; **~or** *m* inductor; ignition coil; *tele* call crank.

industrial|isieren *tr* to industrialize; **~isierung** *f* industrialization; **~ismus** *m* industrialism.

Industrie *f* industry, manufacturing industry; *Gewerbe u. ~* trade and industry; *chemische ~* chemical industry; *einheimische ~* home industry; *holzverarbeitende ~* timber industry; *lebenswichtige ~* vital industry; *metallverarbeitende ~* metal working industry; *~ der Steine u. Erden* extractive industries; *~- u. Handelskammer* Chamber of Commerce and Industry; **~abwasser** *n* industrial waste water; **~aktien** *f pl* industrial shares *pl*, industrials *pl*; **~anlage** *f* factory, works *pl*, plant; **~arbeiter** *m* industrial worker; **~~schaft** *f* industrial class; **~ausstellung** *f* industrial exhibition; **~bank** *f* industrial bank; **~berater** *m* management consultant; **~betrieb** *m* manufacturing (*od* industrial) plant; **~bezirk** *m* industrial district; **~demontage** *f* dismantling of industries; **~erzeugnis** *n* industrial product; manufacture; **~erzeugnisse** *n pl* manufactured goods *pl*; manufactures *pl*; **~erzeugung** *f* industrial production, industrial output; **~firma** *f* industrial firm; **~flugplatz** *m* factory airfield; **~führer, ~kapitän, ~könig** *m* industrial leader, captain of industry, *Am fam* tycoon; **~gas** *n* industrial gas; **~gebiet** *n* industrial area; **~gegend** *f* industrial region; **~gewerkschaft** *f* trade union; **~kapazität** *f* industrial capacity; **~kapitalismus** *m* industrial capitalism; **~kartell** *n* industrial combine; **~konzern** *m* industrial concern; **~kreise** *m pl* industrial circles *pl*; **~lage** *f* industrial site; **~land** *n* industrial country; **~ll** *a* industrial; **~lle(r)** *m* industrial(ist), manufacturer, producer; (*Umfang*) industrial output...

ineinander *adv* into one another, into each other; **~flechten** *irr tr* to interlace; **~fließen** *irr itr* to flow (*od* run) into one another; (*mischen*) to mix, to mingle; **~fügen** *tr* to fit into one another, to join; **~greifen** *irr itr*, **~wirken** *itr* to work into each other; *tech* to gear, to mesh; (*zus.arbeiten*) to cooperate; **~~** *n* (*Ereignisse*) concatenation, linking together; working into each other; (*Zus.arbeit*) co-operation; **~passen, ~stecken** *tr* to fit together; **~schieben** *irr tr* to telescope; **~weben** *irr tr* to interweave.

Inempfangnahme *f* reception, receiving.

infam *a* infamous; **~ie** *f* infamy.

Infant *m* infante; **~in** *f* infanta.

Infant|erie *f* infantry; **~~angriff** *m* infantry attack; **~~artillerie** *f* accompanying artillery; **~~ausbildung** *f* infantry training; **~~begleitgeschütz** *n* infantry-accompanying gun; **~~division** *f* infantry division; **~~flug** *m aero* contact patrol; **~~geschütz** *n* forward (*od* infantry) gun, close support gun; **~~kampfabzeichen** *n* combat infantryman's badge; **~~kolonne** *f* infantry train; **~~regiment** *n* infantry regiment; **~~schule** *f* infantry school; **~~spitze** *f* infantry point; **~~stellung** *f* infantry position; **~~sturmabzeichen** *n* infantry assault badge; **~erist** *m* infantryman, foot-soldier, *Am fam* G.I., dough-boy.

infantil *a* infantile; **~ismus** *m* infantilism; **~istisch** *a* infantile.

Infektion *f* infection, contamination; **~sherd** *m* focus of infection; **~skrankheit** *f* infectious (*od* communicable) disease.

Infel, Inful *f* mitre.

infiltrieren *tr, itr* to infiltrate.

Inferiorität *f* inferiority; **~skomplex** *m* inferiority complex.

Infinit|esimalrechnung *f* infinitesimal calculus; **~iv** *m* infinitive (mood).

infizier|en *tr* to infect; **~ung** *f* infection.

Inflation *f* inflation; *hemmungslose ~* runaway inflation; **~istisch** *a* inflationary; **~sgefahr** *f* danger of inflation; **~sgewinn** *m* inflation profit; **~sspirale** *f* inflationary spiral; **~szeit** *f* inflation(ary) period.

Influenz *f* electrostatic induction, influence; **~a** *f* influenza, *fam* flu(e).

infolge *prp* in consequence of, owing to; on account of, due to, as a result of; **~dessen** *adv* accordingly, consequently, then, therefore, hence; because of that.

Inform|ation *f* information; (*Nachricht*) news *pl mit sing*; tidings *pl mit sing*; (*Erkundigungen*) advice; inquiry; (*Auskunft*) intelligence; (*vertrauliche Presse~~*) dope; *~~en einholen* to take advice; to make inquiries (*bei jdm über etw* of s. o. on (*od* about) s. th.); **~~sbüro** *n* information bureau, *Am* intelligence office; **~atorisch** *a* informative; **~ieren** *tr* to inform; to acquaint; to notify; to let one know; (*kurz einweisen bes. aero mil*) to brief; *sich ~~* to inform o. s. (*über* of), to make inquiries of s. o. on (*od* about) s. th.; *falsch ~~* to misinform.

infrarot *a* infra-red.

Infus|ionstierchen *n pl*, **~orien** *pl* infusoria *pl*; **~orienerde** *f* infusorial (*od* diatomaceous) earth, kieselguhr.

Ingangsetzung *f* starting, setting to work, putting into service.

Ingebrauchnahme *f* putting into operation (*od* use).

Ingenieur *m* engineer; technical official; technical officer; *leitender ~* chief engineer; **~büro** *n* engineering office; **~wesen** *n* (civil) engineering.

Ingrediens *n*, **Ingredienz** *f* ingredient; component.

Ingrimm *m* concealed rage, anger; (inward) wrath; (*Groll*) spite; **~ig** *a* enraged, fiercely angry; (*wütend*) furious; (*gehässig*) spiteful.

Ingwer *m* ginger; (*gelber*) turmeric; **~bier** *n* ginger beer.

Inhaber *m* possessor; (*Wechsel*) bearer; (*Amt, com*) holder; (*Eigentümer*) proprietor, owner; (*Besitzer*) occupant; (*Geschäft*) principal; (*Grundstück*) tenant; (*Patent*) patentee; (*Meisterschaft*) *sport* title-holder (*od* -defender); *rechtmäßiger ~* legal holder; *~ e-r Aktie* shareholder; *~ e-r Schuldverschreibung* debenture-holder; *~ e-s Herrengarderobengeschäfts* out-fitter; *auf den ~ lauten* to be payable to bearer; **~aktie** *f* bearer share; **~papier** *n* bearer instrument; **~scheck** *m* cheque (*Am* check) to bearer; **~schuldverschreibung** *f* bearer bond; **~wechsel** *m* bearer bill.

inhaft|ieren *tr* to imprison, to arrest, to put in custody; **~nahme, ~ierung** *f* arrest; confinement, imprisonment, detention.

Inhal|ation *f* inhalation; **~~sapparat** *m* inhalator, inhaler; **~ieren** *tr, itr* to inhale, to breathe in.

Inhalt *m* contents *pl*; (*Raummaß*) capacity; holding-power; (*Fläche*) area, extent, space; (*Körper*) volume, content; (*Bedeutung*) meaning, significance, purport; (*tieferer Sinn*) implication; (*Begriffs~*) connotation; (*wesentlicher ~*) substance, essence, subject matter; (*wörtlicher ~*) tenor; (*Zus.fassung*) summary, abstract, epitome; (*Verzeichnis*) index, table of contents; (*Einlage*) *com* enclosure; *des ~s, daß* to the effect that; *seinem ganzen ~ nach* in all its particulars; *zum ~ haben* to purport; **~lich** *a* in substance, in its contents; with regard to the contents; **~sangabe** *f* (*Zus.fassung*) summary, abstract, epitome; (*Verzeichnis*) index, table of contents; (*Zoll*) declaration of contents; **~sanzeiger** *m* level indicator; **~sbestimmung** *f* quadrature; (*Körper*) cubature; **~sleer, ~slos** *a* (*bedeutungslos*) meaningless; (*ohne ~*) empty; **~sreich, ~sschwer, ~svoll** *a* significant, important, momentous; weighty; full of meaning; **~sverzeichnis** *n* table of contents, index.

in|härent *a* inherent; **~hibieren** *tr* to forbid, to prohibit; **~itiale** *f* initial letter; **~itialzündung** *f* priming, primer detonation; initiation.

Initiativ|antrag *m parl* private bill; **~e** *f* initiative; (*Unternehmungsgeist*) enterprise; *die ~~ ergreifen* to take the initiative; *es an ~~ fehlen lassen* to lack initiative; *keine ~~ haben* to have no enterprise; *auf jds ~~ hin* on the initiative of s. o.; *aus eigener ~~* on o.'s own initiative.

Injektion *f* injection, *med auch* shot; **~snadel** *f* (*Kanüle*) hypodermic needle; **~sspritze** *f* (hypodermic) syringe.

injizieren *tr* to inject.

Injurie *f* insult, offence, slander.

Inkasso *n* encashment, cashing, collection; *~ besorgen* to cash, to collect; **~abteilung** *f* collection department; **~auftrag** *m* collection order; **~büro** *n* debt-collecting office; **~gebühr** *f*, **~spesen** *pl* collecting charges *pl*; **~provision** *f* collecting commission; **~vollmacht** *f* collecting power; **~wechsel** *m* bill for collection.

In|klination *f* inclination, dip; **~klusive** *a* inclusive, including; **~kognito** *adv* incognito; **~kommensurabel** *a* incommensurable, incommensurate, disproportionate, inadequate.

inkonsequ|ent *a* inconsistent; contradictory; **~enz** *f* inconsistency; contradiction.

in|korrekt *a* incorrect; **~~heit** *f* incorrectness; **~kraftsetzung** *f*, **~krafttreten** *n* coming into force, taking effect; commencement; *Zeitpunkt der ~~ (des ~~s)* effective date; **~kriminieren** *tr* to incriminate, to charge; **~krustieren** *tr* to incrust; **~kubationszeit** *f* incubation period; **~kunabeln** *f pl* incunabula *pl*; **~kunabelkunde** *f* incunabulogy; **~kurssetzung** *f* (putting into) circulation.

Inland *n* inland; home *od* native country; *im In- u. Ausland* at home and abroad; **~abnehmer** *m* inland customer; **~absatz** *m* home market; **~porto** *n* inland postage, *Am* domestic postage (*od* mail); **~telegramm** *n* inland message; **~sauftrag** *m* home order; **~sbrief** *m* inland letter; **~serzeugnis** *n* domestic article; **~sgeschäft** *n* domestic business; **~shandel** *m* domestic trade; **~sluftverkehrsstrecke** *f* internal air--line; **~smarkt** *m* home market; **~spost** *f* inland mail, *Am* domestic mail; **~spreis** *m* domestic price; **~sprodukte** *n pl* home-produced goods *pl*; **~sschuld** *f* internal debt; **~sverbrauch** *m* home consumption; **~sverkäufe** *m pl* home sales *pl*.

Inländ|er *m*, **~~in** *f* native; **~isch** *a* native, not foreign; home-born, home-bred; national; *Am* domestic; (*Ware*) home-made; (*Verbrauch*) domestic, home; (*Verkehr*) internal; (*Handel*) inland; (*eingeboren*) indigenous.

In|laut *m* medial sound; **~let(t)** *n* bed sacking (*od* tick).

inliegend *a* enclosed, inclosed, attached.

Inmarschsetzung *f* dispatch.

inmitten *prp* in the midst of; amidst, *Am häufiger* amid.

inne *adv* within; *mitten ~* in the midst of; **~haben** *tr* to possess; (*Stelle*) to hold (*od* to fill) a place; (*Rekord*) to hold, to keep; **~halten** *irr tr* (*festhalten an*) to keep to; *itr* (*aufhören*) to stop, to pause; **~werden** *irr itr* to perceive, to become aware of, to learn; **~wohnen** *itr* to be inherent in; **~~d** *a* inherent.

innen *adv* in, within, inside; at home; *nach ~* inward(s); *von ~* from within; *~ u. außen* within and without; **~abmessungen** *f pl* inside dimensions *pl*; **~ansicht** *f* interior view; **~anstrich** *m* interior coating; **~antenne** *f* internal (*od* indoor) aerial (*Am* antenna); **~architekt** *m* interior decorator; **~~ur** *f* interior decoration; **~aufnahme** *f phot* indoor picture (*od* shot); studio shot; **~ausstattung, ~einrichtung** *f* interior decoration (*od* styling *od* equipment); **~dienst** *m* internal service, routine duties *pl*; *mil* garrison duty, barracks duty; indoor service; **~fläche** *f* interior surface; inside, inner side; (*Hand*) palm; **~gewinde** *n tech* female thread; **~leben** *n* inner life; **~leitung** *f* interior wiring, inner circuit; **~minister** *m Engl* Home Secretary; *Am* Secretary of the Interior; (*übrige Länder*) Minister of the Interior; **~~ium** *n Engl* Home Office; *Am* Department of the Interior; (*andere Länder*) Ministry of the Interior; **~politik** *f* domestic (*od* home) policy; **~politisch** *a* domestic, internal; **~raum** *m* interior (*od* inside) room; **~seite** *f* inner side, inside; **~stadt** *f* centre of a town, city; **~steuerlimousine** *f mot* sedan; **~steuerung** *f mot* inside control (*od* drive); **~wandung** *f* inner wall; **~weite** *f* inside diameter; **~welt** *f* internal world; **~winkel** *m math* interior angle.

inner *a* inner, interior, internal; (*innerlich*) inward; (*wesentlich*) intrinsic; *das ~e Auge* the spiritual eye; *~e Angelegenheit* internal affair; *~e Anleihe* domestic loan; *~er Halt* balance, morale; *~e Mission* Home Missions *pl*; *~e Schuld* internal debt; *~er Wert* intrinsic value; **~atomar** *a* intra-atomic; **~eien** *f pl* offals *pl*; **~e(s)** *n* interior, inside; (*Herz*) heart, soul; *Minister des ~n Engl* Home Secretary; *Am* Secretary of the Interior; (*übrige Länder*) Minister of the Interior; **~halb** *prp* within; *adv* within, inside; **~lich** *a* inward, internal, interior; (*geistig*) mental, intrinsic; (*aufrichtig*) sincere; (*tief*) profound; (*herzlich*) hearty; (*tiefempfunden*) heartfelt; (*Gefühl*) deep; *~~ ausgeglichen* internally compensated; *~~ anzuwenden med* for internal use; **~lichkeit** *f* warmth, heartiness; (*Vertraulichkeit*) intimacy; **~molekular** *a* intramolecular; **~politisch** *a* of internal policy; domestic, internal; **~sekretorisch** *a med* endocrine; **~st** *a* in(ner)most; **~ste(s)** the innermost part; *fig* the very heart, intrinsic nature, core; (*Mittelpunkt*) centre, middle, midst; (*Angelpunkt*) hub, omphalos; (*Kern*) nucleus.

innig, ~lich *a* (*herzlich*) heartfelt; (*aufrichtig*) sincere; (*vertraut*) intimate; (*ernstlich*) earnest; (*verständnisvoll*) responsive; (*tief empfunden*) whole-hearted, *Am* whole-souled; (*tief*) deep, profound; **~keit** *f* cordiality, heartiness; (*Glut*) fervo(u)r; (*Vertrautheit*) intimacy.

Innung *f* guild, corporation; **~swesen** *n* guild system.

in|offiziell *a* unofficial; **~okulieren** *tr* to inoculate; **~quisitorisch** *a* inquisitorial.
ins (= *in das*) into that, into it; **~besondere** *adv* in particular, particularly, especially; **~geheim** *adv* secretly, on the sly; **~gemein** *adv* in common, generally, usually; **~gesamt** *adv* altogether, collectively.
Insasse *m* inhabitant, inmate, occupant; (*Fahrgast*) passenger.
Inschrift *f* inscription; (*auf Denkmünzen*) legend; (*Überschrift*) caption; **~enkunde** *f* epigraphy.
Insekt *n* insect, *Am* bug; **~enblütig** *a* entomophilous; **~enfressend** *a* insectivorous; **~enfresser** *m* insectivore, insect-eater; **~engitter** *n* insect screen; **~enkunde, ~enlehre** *f* entomology; **~enkundige(r)** *m* entomologist; *sl* bug-hunter; **~enpulver** *n* insect-powder, insecticide, *Am* pesticide; **~ensammlung** *f* insect collection; **~enstich** *m* sting; **~envertilgungsmittel** *n* insecticide.
Insel *f* island, isle; *künstliche* ~ man-made island; **~bewohner** *m* islander; **~reich** *n* insular country; **~stadt** *f* insular town; **~welt** *f* archipelago.
Inser|at *n* advertisement, insert(ion), *fam* advert, *Am fam* ad; *ein* ~~ *aufgeben* to put an advertisement into a paper; *ohne* ~~ *Am fam* adless; **~atenannahme** *f* advertisement department; **~atenbüro** *n* advertising agency; **~atenteil** *m* advertisement columns *pl*; **~atenwerber** *m* advertising agent (*od Am* solicitor); **~atpreis** *m* advertising rate; **~ent** *m* advertiser; **~ieren** *tr* to advertise (*nach* for), to insert (*in* in); **~tionsgebühren** *pl* advertising charges (*od* fees) *pl*, *Am* ad-rates *pl*.
Insignien *pl* insignia *pl*.
inskribieren *tr* to inscribe; *sich* ~ *lassen* to enter o.'s name.
inso|fern *adv* so far; to that extent; as far as that goes; *conj* as far as, inasmuch as, in so far as, according as; **~weit** *adv* as far as that is concerned, so far as.
insol|vent *a* insolvent; **~venz** *f* insolvency; (*Bankerott*) bankruptcy; (*Zahlungseinstellung*) stoppage (*od* suspension) of payment.
insonderheit *adv* especially.
Insp|ektion *f* inspection; (*Prüfung*) examination; (*Aufsicht*) supervision; **~~sbericht** *m* report of survey; **~~sreise** *f* tour of inspection, inspection trip; **~ektor, ~ekteur** *m* inspector, supervisor, overseer; (*Landwirtschaft*) steward; *rail* station-master; **~izient** *m* inspector; *theat* stage-manager; **~izieren** *tr* to inspect, to oversee, to superintend; (*prüfen*) to examine, to scrutinize, to scan; (*amtlich*) to audit.
Install|ateur *m* (*Klempner*) plumber; (*Monteur*) fitter; (*für Gas*) gas fitter; (*el Licht*) electrician; installer; **~ation** *f* installation; **~~sarbeiten** *f pl* plumbing; **~ieren** *tr* to install, to equip, to put in; (*einführen*) to introduce.
instand|halten *irr tr* to keep up, to keep in good order, to maintain; *tech* to service; **~haltung** *f* maintenance, upkeep; service; **~~sarbeiten** *f pl* maintenance work; **~~skosten** *pl* maintenance charges *pl*, upkeep; **~setzbar** *a* recoverable; **~ setzen** *tr* to enable (*jdn* s. o.); (*reparieren*) to repair, *Am* to fix, to put into shape; (*ausbessern*) to amend; to overhaul; (*reinigen*) to do up; (*flicken*) to mend, to patch; (*Schiff*) to re-float; (*erneuern*) to renew; (*überholen*) to recondition; *wieder* ~~ to restore; **~setzung** *f* repairing, reconditioning; repairs *pl*; **~~sarbeit** *f* repair work; **~~sbedürftig** *a* in need of repair; **~~skosten** *pl* cost of repair; **~~skraftwagen** *m* repair lorry; **~~strupp** *m* repair squad; **~~swerkstätte** *f* repair shop.
inständig *a* urgent, earnest; (*dringend*) pressing, instant; ~ *bitten* to implore, to beseech.
Instanz *f* instance, resort; *in erster* ~ in the first instance; *in der ersten* ~ *zuständig sein* to have original jurisdiction; *höhere* ~ (*jur*) appellate court, (*Verwaltung*) higher authority; *letzte* ~ last resort, final jurisdiction; **~enweg** *m* official channels *pl*; *jur* stages of appeal; *auf dem* ~~ through official channels; **~enzug** *m* sequence of courts.
Instinkt *m* instinct; *aus* ~ by instinct; **~artig, ~iv, ~mäßig** *a* instinctive, on instinct; *~mäßig handeln* to act on instinct.
Institut *n* institute, institution; boarding-school; **~ion** *f* institution; *jur* institutes *pl*.
Instru|ktion *f* instruction; (*Anordnung*) order, direction; (*schriftlich*) brief; **~~sstunde** *f mil* lecture; **~ieren** *tr* to instruct.
Instrument *n* instrument; *tech* (*Werkzeug*) tool, implement; (*Gerät*) appliance, utensil; (*sinnreiche Vorrichtung*) device, *fam* gadget, contrivance, (*verächtlich*) contraption; *jur* instrument, deed; **~albegleitung** *f* accompaniment on a musical instrument; **~almusik** *f* instrumental music; **~ation, ~ierung** *f* instrumentation, orchestration; **~enanordnung** *f* instrument layout; **~enbeleuchtung** *f* lighting of the instruments; dashboard lighting; **~enbrett** *n* dashboard, instrument board (*od* panel); **~enflug** *m aero* instrument flying, blind flying; **~enkunde** *f* knowledge of instruments; **~enmacher** *m* musical-instrument maker; **~enschrank** *m* instrument cupboard; **~ieren** *tr mus* to instrument, to score.
Insulaner *m*, **~in** *f* islander.
Insur|gent *m* insurgent; **~rektion** *f* insurrection.
inszenier|en *tr* to get up, to (put on the) stage; **~ung** *f* staging; get-up.

*

intakt *a* intact, uninjured; (*ganz*) entire; (*unberührt*) untouched.
Intarsie *f* intarsia, marquetry, inlay.
Integr|al *n math* integral; **~alrechnung** *f* integral calculus; **~ieren** *tr* to integrate; *ein* ~~*der Bestandteil* an integrant part; **~ität** *f* integrity.
intell|ektuell *a* intellectual; **~ektuelle(r)** *m* intellectual, *Am* highbrow; **~igent** *a* intelligent; bright, clever; **~igenz** *f* intelligence; (*Denkfähigkeit*) intellect; (*Klugheit*) cleverness, brains *pl*; (*Verständnis*) understanding; (*Personen*) intelligentsia; **~~prüfung** *f* intelligence test.
Intendant *m* intendant, superintendent; *theat* manager; *mil* field officer; commissary; **~ur** *f* board of management; intendancy; *mil* commissariat; Quartermaster General's Department.
Intens|ität *f* intenseness, intensity; **~iv** *a* intense, intensive; **~~brandbombe** *f* high-powered incendiary bomb; **~ivieren** *tr* to intensify; (*antreiben*) to actuate.
interess|ant *a* interesting; (*anziehend*) attractive, alluring, fascinating; **~e** *n* interest (*für* in); (*Anteil*) concern; (*Beachtung*) regard; ~~ *nehmen* to take an interest (*an* in), to be interested (in); ~~ *haben an* to have a concern in; *es liegt in meinem* ~~ it is in my interest; *es liegt im* ~~ *von* it is to the interest of; *das* ~~ *verlieren* to lose interest; *das* ~~ *dreht sich um* the interest turns upon; *das geschieht in deinem* ~~ that is done for your sake; *den* ~~*n schaden* to impair the interests of; *jds* ~~*n vertreten* to look after s.o.'s interests; ~~*n wahren* to protect (*od* to uphold) the interests of s. o.; *von allgemeinem* ~~ of general interest; *nicht miteinander vereinbare* ~~*n* conflicting interests; *in öffentlichem* ~~ *liegen* to benefit public interest; **~~los** *a* uninterested; **~~ngemeinschaft** *f* community of interests; (*Zus.schluß*) combination, combine; pool; syndicate; trust; (*Vertrag*) pooling agreement; **~~ngruppen** *f pl parl* pressure groups *pl*; **~~nsphäre** *f* sphere of interest; **~~nt** *m* person concerned; contracting party; **~~nvertretung** *f* representation of interests; **~ieren** *tr* to interest in, to arouse the interest of; *r* to take an interest (*für* in), to interest o. s., to be interested (in); (*Zuneigung*) to care for s. o.; *es ~iert mich nicht* it has no interest for me; *es wird Sie* ~~ *zu* it will be interesting for you to.
Interferenz *f* interference; **~bild** *n* interference figure.
Interieur *n* (*Malerei*) interior.
inter|imistisch *a* provisional; temporary; transitory; interimistic; **~imsaktie** *f*, **~imsschein** *m* provisional certificate, scrip; **~imsregierung** *f* provisional government; **~imswechsel** *m* bill at interim, provisional bill of exchange.
inter|konfessionell *a* interdenominational; **~kontinental** *a* intercontinental; **~mezzo** *n* intermezzo; (*Zwischenspiel*) interlude; **~mittierend** *a* intermittent.
intern *a* internal; **~at** *n* boarding-school; **~ational** *a* international; **~ationalisieren** *tr* to internationalize; **~ationalismus** *m* internationalism; **~e(r)** *m* boarder; **~ieren** *tr* to intern; **~ierte(r)** *m* internee; **~ierung** *f* internment; **~~slager** *n* internment camp; **~ist** *m* specialist in internal diseases, internal specialist.
Inter|pellation *f parl* interpellation; **~pellieren** *tr* to interpellate; **~polieren** *tr* to interpolate; **~pret** *m* interpreter; **~pretation** *f* interpretation; **~pretieren** *tr* to interpret; (*erklären*) to explain; (*kennzeichnen*) to define; (*näher ausführen*) to comment (upon); (*übersetzen*) to translate; **~punktieren** *tr* to punctuate; **~punktion** *f* punctuation; **~~szeichen** *n* punctuation mark; **~vall** *n mus* interval; **~venieren** *itr* to intervene; to interpose; to interfere; **~vention** *f* intervention; (*Vermittlung*) interposition; (*Fürsprache*) intercession; (*Stützung*) support; **~view** *n* interview; *ein* ~~ *gewähren* to give an interview, *Am* to give out an interview; **~viewen** *tr* to interview; **~zonengrenze** *f* interzonal boundary; **~zonenhandel** *m* interzonal trade; **~zonenpaß** *m* interzonal pass; **~zonenverkehr** *m* interzonal traffic.
Inthronisation *f* enthronement.
intim *a* intimate (with); (*vertraut*) familiar; (*innig*) close; *~er Freund* intimate; **~ität** *f* intimacy, familiarity (with).
intoler|ant *a* intolerant; **~anz** *f* intolerance.

intonieren *tr mus* to intonate, to intone.

intra|atomar *a* intra-atomic; **~nsitiv** *a* intransitive; **~venös** *a med* intravenous.

intrig|ant *a* intriguing; plotting; scheming; **~ant** *m* intriguer, plotter, schemer; (*Schurke*) *theat* villain; **~e** *f* intrigue, plot; cabal; *~en schmieden* to lay plots; **~enspiel** *n Am parl* peanut politics; **~ieren** *itr* to intrigue, to plot; *Am parl* to play peanut politics.

Inumlaufsetzen *n* (*Papiere*) circulation, emission.

Invalid|e *m* invalid, *mil* disabled soldier (*od* sailor); **~enhaus, ~enheim** *n* hospital for disabled soldiers; **~enpension, ~enrente, ~enunterstützung** *f* old-age pension; (*Arbeitsunfähigkeit*) disablement pension, *Am* disability benefit; **~enrentner** *m* old-age pensioner; **~enversicherung** *f* old-age (pension) insurance; **~~sbeitrag** *m* pensions contribution; **~ität** *f* invalidity, disablement, disability; **~~sversicherung** *f* disability insurance.

Invasion *f* invasion.

Invent|ar *n* (*Warenliste*) inventory; (*lebendes*) live stock; (*totes*) dead stock; *~~ aufnehmen* to take stock, to draw up an inventory of; **~~aufnahme** *f* stock-taking; **~~isieren** *tr* to inventory, to draw up an inventory of; to catalog(ue); **~~verzeichnis** *n* stock book (*od* register); **~ur** *f* stock-taking, *Am* inventory; *~~ machen* to take an inventory; **~~ausverkauf** *m* stock-taking sale.

investi|eren *tr* to invest, to place; **~erung** *f* investment, placement; **~tionsbetrag** *m* amount of investment.

inwendig *a* interior, inward, inside, internal.

inwiefern, inwieweit *adv* (in) how far, in what respect, to what extent, in what way.

Inzucht *f* in-breeding.

inzwischen *adv* in the meantime, meanwhile.

Ion *n* ion; **~enbeweglichkeit** *f* ionic mobility; **~enbildung** *f* formation of ions; **~endichte** *f* ionic density; **~engeschwindigkeit** *f* ionic velocity; **~engleichung** *f* ionic equation; **~enreaktion** *f* ionic reaction; **~enreibung** *f* ionic friction; **~enreihe** *f* ionic series; **~enspaltung** *f* ionic cleavage; **~enwanderung** *f* ionic migration; **~isationswärme** *f* heat of ionization; **~isch** *a* ionic; (*Landschaft*) Ionian, Ionic; **~isieren** *tr* to ionize; **~isierung** *f* ionization; **~osphäre** *f* ionosphere.

Iota *n* iota; *nicht ein ~* not the least bit.

ird|en *a* earthen; *~~es Geschirr* earthenware; crockery, *Am* kitchen china; **~isch** *a* terrestrial, earthly; (*weltlich*) worldly, temporal; (*vergänglich*) perishable; (*sterblich*) mortal.

Ir|e *m*, **~in** *f* Irishman, Irishwoman; **~isch** *a* Irish; **~ischer Freistaat** Eire; Irish Free State; **~land** *n* Ireland; **~länder** *pl* (*als Volk*) the Irish; *fam* Paddy.

irgend *prn* (*in bejah. Sätzen*) some, (*in vernein., frag. u. beding. Sätzen*) any; *wenn ich ~ kann* if I possibly can; *~ etwas* something, anything; *~ jemand* somebody, anybody; **~ein, ~~e, ~~r, ~~s** *prn* some(one), any(one); somebody, anybody; **~einmal** *adv* at any time; **~wann** *adv* sometime, at some time or other; **~wie** *adv* somehow (or other), by any means; anyhow; **~wo** *adv* somewhere, some place; anywhere; **~woher** *adv* from somewhere, from anywhere; from some place (or other); **~wohin** *adv* to some place or other, anywhere, somewhere.

Iris *f* iris; **~blende** *f phot* iris diaphragm; **~ieren** *tr* to irisate, to iridize; *itr* to iridesce; **~~d** iridescent; **~ierung** *f* iridescence.

Iron|ie *f* irony; *~~ des Schicksals* irony of fate; **~isch** *a* ironical; **~isieren** *tr* to treat with irony.

irrational *a* irrational; *math* surd; *~e Größe* surd; **~zahl** *f* irrational number, surd.

***irr*, irre** *a* astray, wrong, on the wrong track; (*geistig*) perplexed, confused; (*verrückt*) out of o.'s mind, insane; crazy, mad; *~ werden an* to lose confidence in, to doubt s. o.; *~ e f: in der ~e* astray; *in die ~e führen* to lead astray; (*täuschen*) to deceive; **~e(r)** *m, f* insane person, mad(wo)man, lunatic; **~efahren, ~egehen** *irr itr* to go astray, to lose o.'s way; *fig* to be mistaken; (*Briefe*) to miscarry; **~eführen, ~eleiten** *tr* to lead astray, to mislead, to misguide; (*täuschen*) to deceive, to hoodwink, *sl* to bamboozle; **~~d** *a* misleading; **~emachen** *tr* to confuse, to mix up, to bewilder, to perplex, to puzzle; *sich nicht leicht ~~ lassen* not to be easily put out (*od* perplexed); **~en** *itr* to err; *r* to err, to be mistaken (*in* in s. o., about s. th.), to be wrong; **~~anstalt** *f*, **~~haus** *n* lunatic (*od* insane) asylum, mad-house; **~~arzt** *m* mad-doctor, alienist; **~ereden** *itr* to rave; (*phantasieren*) to be wandering; (*unzus.hängend reden*) to ramble, to talk wildly; **~eseln** *irr itr* (*verwirrt*) to be confused; (*verrückt*) to be crazy, to be out of o.'s wits; *~~ n* madness; insanity, dementia; **~ewerden** *irr itr* to be at a loss, to grow puzzled (by), to become confused; *ich werde an ihm ~e* I cannot make him out; **~fahrt** *f* wandering, vagary; **~gang, ~garten** *m* maze, labyrinth; **~glaube** *m* heresy, false doctrine, heterodoxy; **~gläubig** *a* heretical, heterodox; **~ig** *a* erroneous; (*falsch*) wrong; (*ungenau*) inexact; **~läufer** *m* (*Brief*) letter that has gone to the wrong address; *rail* misrouted railroad car; **~lehre** *f* heresy, false doctrine, heterodoxy; **~lehrer** *m* heretic, false prophet; **~licht** *n* Jack-o'-lantern, Will-o'-the-wisp; **~sinn** *m* madness, insanity, lunacy, mental derangement; **~~ig** *a* crazy, insane; *~~ig werden* to go mad; **~~ige(r)** *m* insane, madman; **~tum** *m* (*schuldhafter ~~*) error; (*Mißverständnis*) mistake; (*Versagen, Versehen*) fault; *~tümer vorbehalten* errors excepted; *sehr im ~~ sein* to be greatly mistaken; *im ~~* in error; *ein oft wiederkehrender ~~* an often recurring error; *e-n ~~ begehen* to make (*od* commit) an error; *auf Grund e-s ~~s* under a mistake; **~tümlich** *a* erroneous, mistaken; wrong; *adv* by mistake; **~ung** *f* error; misunderstanding; **~wahn** *m med* delusion; (*falsche Auffassung*) false belief; (*Aberglaube*) superstition; **~weg** *m* wrong way; *auf e-n ~~ geraten* to go astray, to lose o.'s way; **~wisch** *m* = *~licht*.

irre|gulär *a* irregular; **~levant** *a* irrelevant, unimportant; **~ligiös** *a* irreligious; **~ligiosität** *f* irreligion.

irritieren *tr* (*ärgern*) to irritate, to annoy, to exasperate; (*beirren*) to puzzle, to intrigue.

isabellfarben *a* cream-colo(u)r(ed), light buff.

Ischias *f med* sciatica; gout in the hip.

Isegrim *m* (*Tier*) wolf; (*Mensch*) *fig* grumbler.

Islam *m* Islam(ism); **~itisch** *a* Islamic.

Island *n* Iceland; **isländisch** *a* Icelandic.

Isolation *f* (*Absonderung*) isolation; *tech* insulation; **~ismus** *m* isolationism; **~shülle** *f* insulating covering; **~smaterial** *n*, **~sstoff** *m* insulating material; **~sschicht** *f* insulating layer; **~svermögen** *n* insulating power.

Isolator *m el* insulator.

Isolier|anstrich *m* insulating paint; **~band** *n* insulating tape; **~baracke** *f med* isolation hospital; **~en** *tr* to isolate, to quarantine; *el* to insulate; **~glocke** *f* bell-shaped insulator; **~klemme** *f* insulating clamp; **~masse** *f*, **~material** *n* insulating material; **~schicht** *f* insulating layer; **~stoff** *m* insulating substance; **~ung** *f* isolation, *med* quarantine; *el* insulation; **~zelle** *f* padded cell; cell for solitary confinement.

isomer *a* isomeric.

Isotherme *f* isotherm.

Isotop *n* isotope; **~isch** *a* isotopic.

Israel *n* (*Staat*) Israel; *Bürger od Einwohner von ~* Israeli, *pl* -is; **~isch** *a* Israelite; **~it** *m* (*Jude, Hebräer*) Israelite.

Ist|bestand *m* actual amount (*od* stock); **~stärke** *f* effective force (*od* strength); **~~nachweis** *m* initial return; daily strength report.

Italien *n* Italy; **~isch** *a* Italian; **~er** *m*, **~erin** *f* Italian.

J

J *Abk mit* ***J*** *siehe Liste der Abk.*
ja *adv, Partikel* yes; *zu etw ~ sagen* to consent to; *mit Ja antworten* to answer in the affirmative; (*fürwahr*) indeed; (*gewiß*) certainly, by all means; *parl* ay(e); (*Bibel*) yea, *Am* yea, yep; *~ doch* to be sure; *~ freilich, ~ gewiß, ~ wahrhaftig, ~ wahrlich* yes, indeed; surely, of course; *~ sogar* nay (even); *~ sagen* to consent, to agree; to yes; *zu allem ~ sagen* to say yes to everything; (*Ausruf u. Befehl:*) *ich habe es Ihnen ~ gesagt!* I told you so! *vergiß es ~ nicht!* be sure not to forget! *du siehst ~ so seltsam aus!* you look so funny! *es ist ~ nicht sehr weit!* it really isn't very far! *da sind Sie ~!* well, there you are! *sie ist ~ meine Schwester!* why, she is my sister! *tun Sie es ~ nicht!* don't you dare do it! *Sie wissen ~, daß* ... you know very well that ...; but you know that ...; *das ist ~ e-e schöne Geschichte!* a pretty mess, I am sure! (*hinweisend*) *~, was ich sagen wollte* oh, I was going to tell you; *wenn ~* if so; if this is the case; *sie ist ~ wohl sehr klug, aber* ... she is very clever, to be sure, but ...; *sie konnte ~ nicht kommen* she could not come, could she; **~sager** *m Am* yes-man, stooge; **~wohl** *adv* yes, indeed; to be sure, certainly; **~wort** *n* consent.
Jabo *m* fighter bomber; pursuit bomber; **~angriff** *m* fighter-bomber attack.
Jacht *f* yacht; **~klub** *m* yachting-club.
Jacke *f* jacket; jerkin; (*kurze*) Eton jacket, *Am* roundabout; (*Unter~*) vest; *das ist ~ wie Hose* that's six of one and half a dozen of the other; **~nkleid** *n* lady's suit; **~tt** *n* jacket; short coat.

*

Jagd *f* (*Verfolgung*) chase; pursuit; (*Großwild*) hunt(ing); shooting; (*Hochwild*) deer-hunt, big-game hunting; (*Fuchs~*) fox-hunting; (*Enten*) shooting; (*Kaninchen*) rabbiting; (*Pirsch*) stalking, *Am* hunting, gunning; (*Hetz~*) coursing; (*Wildschwein~*) pigsticking, boar-hunting; (*Schnitzel~*) hare and hounds; *auf die ~ gehen* to go hunting (*od* shooting); *~ machen auf fig* to hunt; to chase; **~abschnitt** *m aero* fighter sector; **~abwehr** *f aero* fighter defence; **~anzug** *m* hunting-suit; **~aufseher** *m* gamekeeper; **~ausflug** *m* hunting trip; **~ausrüstung** *f* hunting outfit; **~bar** *a* chaseable; *~~es Wild* fair game; **~berechtigung** *f*, **~schein** *m*, **~karte** *f* hunting- (*od* shooting-) licence (*Am* license); **~beute** *f* booty; quarry; bag; *~~ machen* to bag; **~bezirk** *m*, **~gebiet**, **~revier** *n* hunting-ground; **~bomber** *m aero* fighterbomber; pursuit bomber; **~einsitzer** *m aero* single-seater fighter; **~fieber** *n Am fam* buck fever; **~flieger** *m aero* fighter pilot; pursuit pilot; (*mit 5 od mehr Abschüssen*) ace; **~~ei** *f aero* fighter aviation; **~~führer** *m* fighter-unit commander; **~~kommando** *n Am* fighter command; **~flinte** *f*, **~gewehr** *n* sporting gun, sporting rifle; (shot) gun; (*für Vögel*) fowling piece; **~flug** *m* fighter patrol, fighter sweep; **~flugzeug** *n aero* fighter (aircraft), interceptor fighter; (*Begleitschutz, Fernjagd*) pursuit (fighter); **~frevel** *m*, **~vergehen** *n* poaching; **~frevler** *m* poacher; **~geleit** *n aero* fighter escort; **~gerecht** *a* huntsman-like; **~geschichte** *f* hunting-story; **~geschwader** *n aero* group of fighter squadrons; pursuit group, fighter wing; **~gesellschaft** *f* hunt; hunting party; **~gesetz** *n* game law; **~gründe** *m pl* hunting-grounds *pl*; **~gruppe** *f aero* fighter group; pursuit group; **~haus** *n*, **~hütte** *f* hunting-box; **~horn** *n* hunting-horn, bugle; **~hund** *m* hound, sporting-dog; (*Vorstehhund*) setter; **~kommando** *n mil* raiding party; **~maschine** *f aero* fighter (*od* interceptor) plane; **~messer** *n* hunting-knife, hanger; **~pächter** *m* game-tenant; **~patrone** *f* sporting (*od* shotgun) cartridge; **~peitsche** *f* hunting-whip; **~pferd** *n* hunter; **~rennen** *n* steeple-chase; **~schlößchen** *n* hunting-lodge; **~schutz** *m aero* fighter escort (*od* protection); *mit ~~* escorted by fighters; **~sperre** *f aero* fighter screen; **~spieß** *m* hunting spear; **~staffel** *f aero* pursuit (*od* fighter) squadron; fighter formation; **~streife** *f aero* fighter sweep; **~tasche** *f* hunting- (*od* game-)bag; **~übungsflugzeug** *n* fighter trainer; **~verband** *m aero* fighter formation; fighter unit, unit of pursuit planes; **~wagen** *m* dog-cart; **~zeit** *f* hunting- (*od* shooting-) season; **~zweisitzer** *m* two-seater fighter (*od* pursuit plane).
jagen *tr* to hunt; (*mit Hunden*) to hound; (*pirschen*) to stalk; (*treiben*) to course, to drive; (*verfolgen*) to chase, to give chase to s. o., to pursue; *fam* to tag, *sl* to tail; (*aufspüren*) to trail; (*hetzen*) to chevy, to chi(v)vy; (*töten*) to kill, to shoot; (*wegjagen*) to send away, to expel, to oust (from); *itr* to hunt, to go hunting (*od* shooting); (*laufen*) to drive at full speed, to rush, to race, to dash, to gallop; *Am* to stave (by); *fig* to hunt (*nach* after), to pursue; *aus dem Hause ~* to turn out of doors, to chase out of the house; *in die Flucht ~* to put to flight; *sich e-e Kugel durch den Kopf ~* to blow out o.'s brains; *zum Teufel ~* to send to the devil; *jdm den Degen durch den Leib ~* to run o.'s sword through s. o.'s body; *ein Witz jagte den andern* a witty remark followed the other.
Jäger *m* hunter, huntsman, sportsman; (*Pirsch~*) stalker; (*Wildhüter*) gamekeeper; (*Förster, Am Forstgehilfe*) ranger; (*Verfolger*) chaser; *mil* rifle(man); *aero* fighter (plane), pursuit plane; interceptor (air-) plane; (*Mann*) fighter pilot; **~bataillon** *n mil* rifle battalion; **~begleitschutz** *m aero* fighter escort; **~ei** *f* hunt(ing). chase; (*Haus*) gamekeeper's lodge; **~in** *f* huntress; **~latein** *n* hunter's yarn; tall stories *pl*; sportsman's slang; **~leitdienst** *m* fighter control service; **~leitoffizier** *m* fighter direction officer (*Abk* F. D. O.), officer commanding fighter control; **~leitverfahren** *n* pursuit guiding method; **~meister** *m* master of the hunt(smen) (*od* chase); **~patrouille** *f aero* fighter patrol, *Am* fighter cruise formation; **~platz** *m* fighter airfield; fighter base; **~schutz** *m aero* fighter escort. fighter protection; *unter ~~* escorted by fighters; **~sprache** *f* hunting terms *pl*.
Jaguar *m* jaguar.
jäh *a* (*steil*) precipitous, steep, abrupt; (*plötzlich*) sudden; (*überraschend*) surprising, startling; (*überstürzt*) precipitous, headlong; (*ungestüm*) impetuous, rash, hasty; (*leidenschaftlich*) passionate; (*unbedacht*) inconsiderate, hasty; (*aufbrausend*) hot-tempered, irascible; *~er Schrecken* panic; **~lings** *adv* suddenly, abruptly; (*kopfüber*) headlong; **~zorn** *m* sudden anger; passionateness; irascibility; (*Wut*) rage, fury; (*Grimm*) wrath; **~zornig** *a* irascible, hot-tempered, choleric; (*hitzig*) passionate, hasty.
Jahr *n* year; twelvemonth; *Kalender~* calendar year; *bürgerliches ~* civil year; *Sonnen~* solar year; *das ~ des Heils* the year of grace; *das laufende ~* the current year; *nächstes* (*vergangenes*) *~* next (last) year; *ein Viertel~* three months; *ein halbes ~* six months; *Dreiviertel~* nine months; *alle ~e* every year; *bei ~en* advanced in years; *einige ~e* a year or two; *~ für ~* year by year; *das ganze ~ hindurch* all the year round; *im ~e* in (the year); *in e-m ~* in a year's time, this day twelvemonth; *in den letzten ~en* of late (*od* recent) years; *in den besten ~en* in the prime of life; *in den neunziger ~en* in the nineties; *im Alter von 10 ~en* at ten years old; *im ~e des Herrn* in the year of our Lord; *ein ~ ins andere gerechnet* one year with another; *in die ~e kommen* to begin to grow old; *mit den ~en* with the years; *nach vielen ~en* after many years; *seit einigen ~en* for some years past; *seit ~ u. Tag* for many years; *über ~ u. Tag* a year and a day; *übers ~* a year hence; *das ganze ~ über* all the year round; *ein ~ ums andere* every year; *viele ~e lang* for many years; *von ~ zu ~* from year to year; *vor e-m ~* a year ago.
jahr|aus *adv: ~~ jahrein* year after year, from year's end to year's end; **~buch** *n* yearbook; almanac; annual register; (*Schulen*) calendar, *Am* catalog(ue); **~bücher** *n pl* annals *pl*; **~elang** *a* (lasting) for years; **~esabonnement** *n* annual subscription; **~esabrechnung** *f*, **~esabschluß** *m* yearly (*od* annual) balance (*od* settlement); **~esanfang** *m* beginning of the year; **~esausweis** *m* annual return (*od Am* statement); **~esbeitrag** *m* annual contribution; **~esbericht** *m* annual report; **~esbilanz** *f* annual balance (sheet); **~esdurchschnitt** *m* annual average; **~eseinkommen** *n* yearly income; **~esertrag** *m* annual proceeds *pl*; **~eserzeugung** *f* annual output; **~esfrist** *f* space of a year; **~esgehalt** *n* annual salary; **~esinventur** *f* annual stock taking; **~eskarte** *f* annual ticket; **~eslauf** *m* course of the year; **~esmiete** *f* rent per annum; **~esmittel** *n* (*Temperatur*) mean annual temperature; **~espensum** *n* annual course, curriculum; **~esproduktion** *f* annual production; **~esprüfung** *f* (*Schule*) final examination; *com* general audit; **~esrate** *f* yearly instal(l)ment; **~esrente** *f* annuity; **~esring** *m bot* annual ring; **~esschluß** *m* year-end, close of the year; **~estag** *m* anniversary; *der hundertste ~~* centenary, *Am* centennial; **~estagung** *f* annual conference, *Am* convention; **~esübersicht** *f* annual return; **~esumsatz** *m* annual

turnover (*od* sale); **~esurlaub** *m* annual vacation; **~esverbrauch** *m* annual (*od* yearly) consumption; **~esverdienst** *m* annual earnings *pl*; **~esversammlung** *f* annual meeting; **~esverzeichnis** *n* annual list; **~eswechsel** *m*, **~eswende** *f* turn of the year; New Year; *mit den besten Wünschen zum ~~* with the compliments of the season: **~eszahl** *f* date, year; **~eszeit** *f* season; *der ~~ entsprechend* seasonable; **~eszeitlich** *a* seasonal; **~fünft** *n* lustrum, quinquennium, period of five years; **~gang** *m* age-group; (*Zeitschrift*) year's set, year of publication, annual publication; volume; (*Wein*) vintage; *mil* class; *mar* crew; **~hundert** *n* century; *ein halbes ~~* half a century; **~hundertelang** *adv* secular; **~hundertfeier** *f* centenary, hundredth anniversary; **~hundertwende** *f* turn of the century; **~markt** *m* fair; **~~sbude** *f* booth, stand; **~~sgeschenk** *n* fairing; **~tausend** *n* millenium; **~~feier** *f* millenary; **~zehnt** *n* decade, space of ten years; **~~elang** *adv* lasting for decades.

jähr|en *r: es ~t sich heute, daß ...* it is a year today (*od* ago) since ...; **~ig** *a* a year old; lasting a year; **~lich** *a* yearly, annual; *e-e ~~e Rente* annuity; *adv* yearly, annually, every year, per annum; *einmal ~~* once a year; **~ling** *m* yearling.

Jakob *m* James; Jacob; *der wahre ~* Cheap-Jack; **~iner** *m* Jacobin; **~~mütze** *f* red (Phrygian) cap; **~sleiter** *f* Jacob's ladder.

Jalousie *f* (Venetian) blind, *Am* window shades *pl*; shutter louver.

Jammer *m* (*Klage*) lamentation; wailing; moaning; (*Elend*) misery, distress; (*Unheil*) calamity; (*Kummer*) sorrow, affliction; (*Verzweiflung*) despair; (*Mitleid*) pity, compassion; (*Katzen~*) seediness, *Am* hangover; *es ist ein ~* it is a pity, it is pitiful; **~bild** *n* picture of wretchedness; **~erregend** *a* pitiable, deplorable; **~geschrei** *n* lamentation; **~gestalt** *f* miserable figure; **~lappen** *m fam* weakling, crock; cry-baby; **~leben** *n* life of misery; **~n** *itr* to lament (*um* for, *über* over), to bewail (*um* for); (*klagen*) to complain, to wail; (*stöhnen*) to moan; *er ~t mich* I pity him, I feel sorry for him; **~n** *n* lamenting, complaining, moaning; **~nd** *a* lamenting, clamorous; (*klagend*) plaintive; (*weinend*) tearful; **~schade** *a: es ist ~~, daß ...* it is a great pity (*od* a thousand pities) that ...; **~tal** *n* vale of tears; **~voll** *a* piteous, deplorable, lamentable.

jämmerlich *a* pitiable; (*mitleiderregend*) piteous; (*kläglich*) lamentable; (*beklagenswert*) woeful; (*traurig*) sad; (*elend*) miserable; (*verächtlich*) contemptible; **~keit** *f* wretchedness; (*Zustand*) pitiable state; (*Elend*) misery.

Janhagel *m* mob, rabble.

Janitschar *m* janizary.

Jänner, Januar *m* January.

Japan *n* Japan; **~er** *m*, **~isch** *a* Japanese, Jap; (*in USA. geboren*) nisei; **~lack** *m* Japan lacquer (*od* varnish); *mit ~~ überzogen* japanned; **~papier** *n* India paper, Japanese paper.

jappen, **japsen** *itr* to gasp; (*keuchen*) to pant.

Jargon *m* jargon, patter.

Jasmin *m* jasmin(e), jessamin(e).

Jaspis *m* jasper.

jäten *tr* to (clear of) weed.

Jauche *f* dung-water; liquid manure; *med* sanies; (*eitriger Ausfluß*) ichor; **~ngrube** *f* cesspool; **~nfaß** *n* tank of liquid manure; **~npumpe** *f* liquid-manure pump.

jauchz|en *itr* to shout with joy; to exult, to rejoice, to triumph, to jubilate; **~~** *n* jubilation, exultation; **~~d** *a* rejoicing, exultant, jubilant, triumphant; (*erhoben*) flushed, elated (with); **~er** *m* loud cheers *pl*, shouts *pl* of joy.

jaulen *itr* to howl.

Jause *f dial* afternoon snack.

Jazz *m* jazz, swing music; (*Negermusik*) ragtime; **~fanatiker** *m* jazz-fiend; **~kapelle** *f* jazzband, jazz orchestra; **~sänger** *m* crooner, jazz singer.

je *adv* ever, always, at any time, at a time; *com* each, apiece; *~ nun! interj* well! well now! *herr~!* dear me! *conj ~ nachdem* according to, in proportion as; *~ nach den Umständen* according to circumstances, as the case may be; *~ ... desto, ~ ... um so* the ... the ...; *~ eher ... ~ besser* the sooner ... the better; *~ nachdem* that depends; *von ~her* at all times; *~ zwei u. zwei* two and two, by twos, two at a time; *für ~ zehn Wörter* for every ten words; **~weilig** *a* for the time being; *nach den ~~en Umständen* according to the particular circumstances; (*gegenwärtig*) actual; (*betreffend*) respective; **~weils** *adv* for the time being; (*bisweilen*) at times; (*gelegentlich*) occasionally; (*hin u. wieder*) now and then, from time to time; (*zu jeder beliebigen Zeit*) at any given time.

jedenfalls *adv* in any case, at all events; most probably; however.

jede|r, ~e, ~es *prn* each, every, any; (*von zweien*) either; *~~ m (f, n)* each one, every one, everybody; *~~, der* whoever; *~~ beliebige* any(body); *ohne ~n Zweifel* without any doubt; *~r einzelne* each and every one; *zu ~r Zeit* at any time.

jed|erlei *adv* of every kind; **~ermann** *prn* everyone, everybody; **~erzeit** *adv* at any time, always; **~esmal** *adv* every time, each time; *~~ wenn conj* whenever; **~~ig** *a* (*tatsächlich*) actual; (*jeweilig*) in each case; (*entsprechend*) respective.

jedoch *adv* however, yet, nevertheless.

jedweder, **jeglicher** *prn* every, each; everyone.

jeher *adv: von ~* at all times; from times immemorial.

Jelängerjelieber *n bot* honeysuckle.

je|mals *adv* ever, at any time; **~mand** *prn* somebody, someone; (*in bedingten Sätzen*) anybody, any one; *sonst ~~, ~~ anders* somebody (*od* anybody) else.

jen|er, ~e, ~es *prn* that, *pl* those; *s* that one, *pl* those ones; (*der erstere*) the former; *dies u. ~es* this and that; **~seitig** *a* opposite, on the other side of; **~seits** *adv* on the other side of, across, beyond; *~~ n* the other world, the life to come; *ein besseres ~~* a brighter world.

Jeremiade *f* Jeremiad, woeful story, lamentation.

Jesuit *m* Jesuit; **~enorden** *m* Society of Jesus, Order of the Jesuits; **~isch** *a* Jesuitic(al).

Jesus *m* Jesus (Christ).

jetzig *a* present, actual; nowadays; (*laufend*) current; (*modern*) modern, fashionable; (*herrschend*) prevailing; *in der ~en Zeit* at the present time; *~e Preise* current prices.

jetzt *adv* now, at present; (*dann*) then; *gerade ~* this very moment; *bis ~* till now, up to now; *~ eben* just now; *von ~ an* henceforth, from this time forth; *für ~* for the present; *gleich ~* at once, instantly; *erst ~* only now; *~ oder nie* now or never; **~zeit** *f* the present day, these days of ours.

Joch *n* yoke; (*Berg~*) mountain-ridge; *arch* cross-beam; (*Tür, Fenster*) transom; (*Boden, Dach*) girder; (*Brükken~*) piles *pl*; *rail* section; *in das ~ spannen* to put to the yoke; *sein ~ abschütteln* to shake off o.'s yoke; *unter das ~ bringen fig* to subjugate; **~bein** *n* cheek-(*od* malar-)bone, zygoma; **~brücke** *f* pile bridge; **~weite** *f* span of the bay.

Jockei *m* jockey.

Jod *n* iodine; **~ammon** *n* ammonium iodide; **~at** *n* iodate; **~haltig** *a* iodiferous; **~id** *n* iodide; **~kali** *n* potassium iodide; **~natrium** *n* sodium iodide; **~oform** *n* iodoform; **~probe** *f* iodine test; **~salbe** *f* iodine ointment; **~säure** *f* iodic acid; **~silber** *n* silver iodide; **~tinktur** *f* tincture of iodine; **~verbindung** *f* iodine compound; **~vergiftung** *f* iodine poisoning.

jod|eln *itr* to yodel;; *Am* to warble; **~ler** *m* yodler; (*Gesang*) yodel, yodle.

Johannis (*~tag, ~fest*) Midsummer Day; **~beere** *f* red currant; **~beersaft** *m* currant-juice; **~brot** *n* carob, St. John's bread; **~feuer** *n* St. John's fire; **~käfer** *m*, **~würmchen** *n* glow-worm; **~kraut** *n* St. John's wort; **~nacht** *f* Midsummer Night.

Johanniter *m* knight of St. John; **~orden** *m* Order of the Knights of Malta.

johlen *itr* to bawl, to boo, to yell, to howl; (*laut schreien*) to cry lustily.

Jolle *f* jolly-boat; yawl; **~nführer** *m* wherry-man.

Jongl|eur *m* juggler, conjurer; (*Betrüger*) trickster, imposter; **~ieren** *itr* to juggle, to use trickery, to play conjuring tricks.

Joppe *f* jacket, jerkin.

Jot *n* letter j; **~a** *n* jot.

Journal *n* journal; (*Tagebuch*) diary; *com* day-book, daily ledger; *mar, aero* log-book; **~ist** *m* journalist, *Am* newspaperman; **~istik** *f* journalism; **~istisch** *a* journalistic.

jovial *a* (*lustig*) jovial, jolly, gay, merry; (*gesellig*) convivial, social, folksy; *~~er Kerl Am bes. pol* back-slapper; **~ität** *f* jollity.

Jubel *m* jubilation; rejoicing; **~feier** *f*, **~fest** *n* jubilee; **~jahr** *n* year of jubilee; *alle ~~e einmal* once in a blue moon; **~n** *itr* to shout with joy, to rejoice; to exult; (*zu~~*) to cheer; **~nd** *a* rejoicing, jubilant, exultant, elated, joyful.

Jubil|ar *m* man who celebrates his jubilee; **~äum** *n* jubilee, anniversary; *ein ~~ feiern* to celebrate a jubilee; **~ieren** *itr = jubeln.*

juch! **~he! ~heißa! juhe!** *interj* hurrah! huzza! hey-day!

Juchten *m* Russia(n) leather.

juchz|en *itr* to shout with joy, to rejoice (*= jauchzen*); **~er** *m* shout of joy.

juck|en *tr* (*sich*) to scratch, to rub; *itr* to itch; **~en** *n*, **~reiz** *m* itching; *med* pruritus; (*Hautjucken*) prurigo; **~end** *a* pruriginous.

Judas Ischariot *m* Judas Iscariot.

Jude *m* Jew; *der Ewige ~* the Wandering Jew; **~nfeind, ~nhasser** *m* anti-Semite, Jew-baiter; **~nfeindschaft** *f* anti-Semitism; **~nfrage** *f* Jewish question; **~nhetze** *f* Jew-baiting; **~nschaft** *f* Jewry, Jewdom; **~nschule** *f* Jewish school; *fig* hullabaloo; (*Tempel*) synagogue; **~nverfolgung** *f* per-

secution of Jews; **~nviertel** *n* Jewish quarter, ghetto.
Jüdin *f* Jewess; **jüdisch** *a* Jewish.
Jugend *f* youth; (*Zeit*) adolescence; (*junge Menschen*) young people, youth; *frühe ~* early childhood; *von ~ an* from o.'s youth; *in meiner ~* when I was a boy (girl); *~ hat keine Tugend* boys will be boys; **~alter** *n* youth, young age; **~amt** *n* youth welfare office; **~arbeit** *f* youth activities (*od* work); **~arrest** *m* juvenile detention; **~bewegung** *f* youth movement; **~blüte** *f* flush (*od* prime) of youth; **~bücherei, ~bibliothek** *f* children's library; **~erinnerung** *f* recollection from o.'s youth; **~ertüchtigung** *f* physical education of youth; **~erziehung** *f* education of youth; **~freund** *m* early friend; school-fellow, *fam* chum, pal; (*Freund der ~*) friend of young people; **~frische, ~kraft** *f* freshness of youth, youthful strength; **~führer** *m* youth leader; **~fürsorge** *f* youth welfare; **~~heim** *n jur* juvenile detention centre; **~gericht** *n jur* Juvenile Court; **~heim** *n*, **~hort** *m* home for the upbringing of the young; **~herberge** *f* youth hostel; **~jahre** *n pl* early years, youthful days *pl*; **~kriminalität** *f* juvenile delinquency; **~lager** *n* youth camp; **~lesesaal** *m* children's reading room; **~lich** *a* youthful, young, juvenile; **~liche(r)** *m* juvenile; adolescent; youth; boy *od* girl; *Am* teen-ager; **~lichkeit** *f* youthfulness, juvenility; **~liebe** *f* (*Person*) old sweetheart; (*Sache*) early love-affair; first love; *hum* calf-love; **~pflege** *f* social work among the young; **~~r** *m* guardian; **~psychologie** *f* adolescent psychology; **~richter** *m* juvenile court judge; **~schönheit** *f* bloom of youth; **~schriften** *f pl* books *pl* for the young; children's books *pl*; **~schriftsteller** *m* writer for the young; **~schutz** *m* protection of the young; **~~gesetz** *n* law for the protection of youth; **~streiche** *m pl*, **~sünden, ~torheiten** *f pl* boyish tricks *pl*, juvenile pranks *pl*; *er hat seine ~torheiten hinter sich* he has sown his wild oats; **~werk** *n* early work; **~wohlfahrt** *f* youth welfare; **~zeit** *f* youth; *in der ~~* in early life; **~~schrift** *f* youth-magazine.
Jugoslaw\|e *m*, ***~in*** *f* Jugoslav; **~ien** *n* Jugoslavia; **~isch** *a* Jugoslav.
Juli *m* July.
jung *a* young, youthful; (*Erbsen*) green; (*Wein*) new; (*Bier*) fresh; (*Gemüse*) new, fresh, early; (*Kupfer*) overpoled; (*vor kurzem*) recent, late; (*Tag, Morgen*) early; *~e Frau* newly-married woman; *~ sein sl* to be a chicken; *~ gewohnt, alt getan* once a use and ever a custom; **~akademikerin** *f* young woman graduate; **~brunnen** *m* fountain of youth; **~e** *m* youth, youngster, boy, lad, kid; (*Lehrling*) apprentice; *dummer ~e* stupid fellow; *grüner ~e* unlicked cub; *alter ~e* dear old chap; *schwerer ~e* professional criminal; *ungezogener ~e* rude boy; **~e(s)** *n* (*Tier*) a young one, a little one; (*Hund*) puppy; (*Raubtier*) cub; (*Elefant*) calf; *~e werfen* = **~en** *itr* to bring forth (*od* to bear) young (ones); (*Hunde*) to pup, to whelp; (*Raubtiere*) to cub; (*Wild*) to fawn; (*Katzen*) to kitten; **~enhaft** *a* boyish; **~~igkeit** *f* boyishness; **~fer** *f* virgin, maid(en); girl; (*Dienerin*) chamber-maid; (*alte ~~*) old maid, spinster; (*Anrede*) Miss; *tech* rammer; *zoo* dragon-fly; *e-e alte ~~ bleiben* to remain an old maid, *fam* to be put on the shelf; **~~nfahrt** *f* maiden trip, maiden voyage; **~~nflug** *m aero* maiden flight; **~~nhäutchen** *n* hymen; **~~nkranz** *m* bridal wreath (*od* garland); **~~nraub** *m* rape; **~~nrede** *f* maiden-speech; **~~nschaft** *f* virginity, maidenhood; *fig* innocence; **~~nstand** *m* maidenhood; **~frau** *f* virgin, maid; *die ~~ von Orleans* the Maid of Orleans; *heilige ~~* Holy Virgin; *die törichten ~~en* the foolish virgins; (*Sternbild*) Virgo; **~~enverein** *m* young women's association; **~fräulich** *a* maidenlike, maiden, virgin; (*unbefleckt*) virginal, immaculate; **~~lichkeit** *f* virginity, maidenhood; **~geselle** *m* bachelor, single man; *eingefleischter ~~* confirmed bachelor; *ewig ~~ bleiben* to live and die a bachelor; **~~nleben** *n* bachelor's life, single life; **~~nstand** *m* bachelorhood; **~~nsteuer** *f* bachelor's tax; **~~nwohnung** *f* bachelor's chambers *pl*; *in e-r ~~nwohnung hausen* to bach; **~gesellin** *f* bachelor girl; **~helfer** *m* young assistant; **~holz** *n* sapwood; young plantation, thicket; **~lehrer** *m* assistant teacher; **~vermählt** *a* newly married; **~vieh** *n* young cattle.
jüng\|er *a* younger, junior; (*Datum*) of a later date; *sie ist 5 Jahre ~~ als ich* she is my junior by five years; *sie sieht ~~ aus, als sie ist* she does not look her age; **~er** *m* disciple, adherer, adherent; follower; **~ling** *m* youth, young man, lad; (*Bürschchen*) stripling; **~~salter** *n* youth, adolescence; **~~sverein** *m* young men's association; **~st** *a* youngest; (*letzte*) last, latest; *der ~ste Tag, das ~ste Gericht* doomsday; the day of the Last Judg(e)ment; *in den ~sten Jahren* of late years; *in der ~sten Zeit* lately, quite recently; *die ~sten Ereignisse* the latest events; *~ adv* recently, newly, lately, of late, the other day; **~stgeboren** *a* youngest (*od* last) born.
Juni *m* June; **~käfer** *m Am* June-bug.
junior *a* junior.
Junker *m* (young) nobleman; country squire; titled landowner; aristocrat; Junker.
Jupiter *m* Jove, Jupiter; **~lampe** *f* sun lamp.
Jura[1] *m* (*der ~*) the Jura Mountains *pl*; **~formation** *f* Jurassic formation; **~kalk** *m* Jura limestone.
Jur\|a[2] *n pl*: *~~ studieren* to study (the) law; **~ist** *m* lawyer; law-student; **~istisch** *a* juridical, legal; *~~e Person* body corporate; legal person (*od* corporation); *~~e Fakultät* faculty of law; *~~er Beistand* counsel; *die ~~e Laufbahn einschlagen* to follow the law; **~isterei, Jurisprudenz** *f* jurisprudence; **~y** *f* jury.

*

just *adv* just, exactly; (*gerade*) only just, just now; **~ieren** *tr* to adjust; *typ* to justify; **~ierschraube** *f* adjusting screw; **~iertisch** *m* adjusting table; **~ierung** *f* adjustment; *typ* justification.
Justiz *f* administration of the law; justice; **~beamte(r)** *m* officer of justice; **~dienst** *m* legal branch; **~gebäude** *n* court-house; **~gewalt** *f* judiciary power; **~inspektor** *m* chief clerk of the court; **~irrtum** *m* mistake of law; **~minister** *m* Minister of Justice, *Am* Attorney General; *Engl* Lord Chancellor; **~~ium** *n* Ministry of Justice, *Am* Department of Justice; **~mord** *m* judicial murder; **~palast** *m* court-house; (*in London*) Law Courts *pl*; **~pflege** *f* administration of justice; **~rat** *m Engl* King's Counsel; **~verwaltung** *f* administration of justice; legal administrative body; **~wesen** *n* law-affairs *pl*.
Jute *f* jute.
Juwel *n* jewel; gem, precious stone; **~en** *n pl* jewel(l)ry, jewels *pl*; **~endiebstahl** *m* jewel-robbery; **~enhandel** *m* jewel(l)er's trade; **~enhändler** *m* jewel(l)er, dealer in precious stones; **~enkästchen** *n* jewel-box; **~enladen** *m* jewel(l)er's shop; **~enschmuck** *m* set of jewels; **~ier** *m* jewel(l)er.
Jux *m* joke; *fam* spree, lark; (*sich*) *e-n ~ machen* to lark.

K

K *Abk mit **K** siehe Liste der Abk.*
Kabale *f* cabal, intrigue.
Kabarett *n* cabaret; night-club; (*Variété*) music hall; (*Programm*) *Am* floor show; **~sänger** *m* cabaret-singer, night-club singer, *Am* torch-singer; **~vorführung** *f Am* floor show.
kabbel\|ig *a* (*Meer*) choppy; **~see** *f* chopping sea.
Kabel *n* cable; wire-rope, cable-rope; *armiertes ~* armo(u)red cable; *blankes ~* bare cable; *unterseeisches ~* submarine cable; **~ader** *f* conductor; **~auftrag** *m* cable order; **~bericht** *m* cable report; **~kanal** *m tele* troughing. cable conduit; **~n** *tr, itr* to cable; **~schnur** *f* flex, *Am* extension-wire; **~schuh** *m* loop-tip terminal; **~telegramm** *n* cablegram; **~trommel** *f* cable reel; **~verlegung** *f* imbedding of cables; (*Meer*) immersion of the cable.
Kabeljau *m* cod(fish).
Kabine *f* cabin; (*Bad*) bathing-box, dressing-room; *Am* bath-house; (*kleiner Raum*) cubicle; (*Abteil*) compartment; (*Fahrstuhl*) cage; *tele* telephone box; *aero, mar* cabin; (*Führersitz*) cockpit; (*Drahtseilbahn*) car, carriage; (*Probierraum*) fitting-room; **~ndach** *n* cabin roof, hood; **~nfenster** *n* cabin window; **~nflugzeug** *n* cabin (transport) plane, airbus; **~nkoffer** *m* cabin trunk.
Kabinett *n* cabinet; closet; (*Museum*) section; **~sbefehl** *m* order in council; **~sfrage** *f* cabinet question; *fig* vital

question; **~skrise** *f* ministerial crisis; **~srat** *m* cabinet council; Privy Council; **~ssitzung** *f* meeting of the cabinet; **~sumbildung** *f* reshuffling of the cabinet.

Kabriolett *n* cab, gig, cabriolet; *mot* cabriolet, *Am* convertible sedan, *Am* convertible; (*Klappverdeck*) convertible cabriolet; (*mit Allwetterverdeck*) all-weather cabriolet; (*falsches ~*) stationary cabriolet.

Kachel *f* Dutch (*od* glazed) tile: **~ofen** *m* stove of Dutch tiles, tiled stove.

Kadaver *m* carcass; (*Leiche*) corpse; **~gehorsam** *m* blind obedience.

Kad|enz *f* cadence; **~er** *m mil* cadre staff; frame.

Kadett *m* cadet; *mar* midshipman; **~enanstalt** *f* military academy, cadet-school; **~enschiff** *n* training-ship.

Käfer *m* beetle, *Am* bug.

Kaff *n sl* poor village.

Kaffee *m* coffee; (*~haus*) café, coffee-house; *~ mit Milch* coffee and milk; *~ verkehrt* milk with a dash of coffee; **~bohne** *f* coffee-bean; **~brenner** *m* coffee-roaster; **~ersatz** *m* coffee substitute; **~(filtrier)maschine** *f* coffee-percolator; coffee-machine; **~geschirr** *n* coffee-service (*od* set); **~haube** *f*, **~wärmer** *m* cosy; **~haus** *n* café, coffee-house, *Am* (*mit Selbstbedienung*) cafeteria; **~kanne** *f* coffee-pot; **~klatsch** *m* gossip at a coffee party; **~kränzchen** *n* ladies' coffee-party; *Am sl* hen party; **~löffel** *m* tea-spoon; **~mühle** *f* coffee-mill; coffee-grinder; **~pflanzung, ~plantage** *f* coffee-plantation; **~röster** *m* coffee-roaster; **~satz** *m* coffee-grounds *pl*; **~service** *n* coffee service; **~strauch** *m* coffee-tree, coffee-plant; **~tasse** *f* coffee-cup.

Käfig *m* cage.

*

kahl *a* bald; (*Landschaft*) barren; bleak, bare; (*Bäume*) stripped of leaves, bare; (*armselig*) poor, empty; (*Wände*) blank, naked; (*Zimmer*) unfurnished; (*Vogel*) unfledged; callow; (*Stoff*) napless; **~geschoren** *a* close-cropped; **~heit** *f* baldness; (*Unfruchtbarkeit*) barrenness; (*Rauheit*) bleakness; **~kopf** *m* baldhead, baldpate; **~köpfig** *a* bald-headed; **~schlag** *m* (*Wald*) clearing, clear felling.

Kahm *m* mo(u)ld; **~ig** *a* stale, mo(u)ldy; (*Wein*) ropy.

Kahn *m* boat; (*Last*) barge, lighter; (*flacher*) punt; (*Baumstamm*) canoe; (*Brücken~*) pontoon; (*kleines Boot*) skiff; *aero sl* transport plane; *~ fahren* to go boating; **~fahrt** *f* boating-trip.

Kai *m* quay, wharf; (*Landungsplatz*) landing-place, pier; (*Fluß*) embankment; **~gebühren** *f pl* pier dues *pl*, pierage, wharfage; **~mauer** *f* jetty wall.

Kaiser *m* emperor; *wo nichts ist, da hat der ~ sein Recht verloren* where naught's to be got, kings lose their scot; *dem ~ geben, was des ~s ist* to render unto Caesar the things which are Caesar's; *um des ~s Bart streiten* to quarrel about trifles; **~haus** *n* imperial family; **~in** *f* empress; **~~ Witwe** *f* Empress Dowager; **~krone** *f* imperial crown; *bot* crown imperial; **~lich** *a* imperial; *seine ~~e Majestät* His Imperial Majesty; **~los** *a* without emperor, interregnum; **~reich** *n* empire; **~schnitt** *m med* Caesarean operation; **~tum** *n* empire; (*Würde*) imperial dignity; **~wahl** *f* election of an emperor; **~würde** *f* imperial dignity.

Kajak *n, m* canoe.

Kajüte *f* cabin; *~ erster Klasse* first-class saloon; **~ntreppe** *f* companion-way.

Kakadu *m* cockatoo.

Kakao *m* cocoa, cacao; *jdn durch den ~ ziehen fam* to kid, to tease, to banter, to jest with; **~bohne** *f* cocoa bean; **~braun** *a* cocoa brown; **~butter** *f* cocoa butter; **~pulver** *n* cocoa powder.

Kakerlak *m* (*Küchenschabe*) cockroach; (*Albino*) albino.

Kaktus *m* cactus.

Kalander *m tech* calender; **~n** *tr, itr* to calender.

Kalauer *m* pun, stale joke.

Kalb *n* calf; **~en** *itr* to calve; **~fell** *n* calfskin; (*Trommel*) drum; (*junges ~~*) *Am* deacon hide; **~fleisch** *n* veal; **~leder** *n* calf(-leather); *in ~~ gebunden* bound in calf; **~sbraten** *m* roast veal; **~sbrust** *f*: *gefüllte ~~* stuffed breast of veal; **~sfuß** *m* calf's foot; **~shaxe** *f* shank of veal; **~skeule** *f*, **~sschlegel** *m* joint (*od* leg) of veal; **~skopf** *m* calf's head; **~skotelett** *n* veal cutlet; **~slende** *f* fillet of veal; **~smagen** *m* rennet, calf's stomach; **~snierenbraten** *m* loin of veal; **~sschnitzel** *n* veal cutlet.

kälbern *itr fig* to frolic; *~ a* of veal.

Kaldaunen *f pl* guts *pl*, tripe; (*Gedärme*) bowels *pl*; intestines *pl*.

Kaleidoskop *n* kaleidoscope.

Kalender *m* calendar; *hundertjähriger ~* perpetual calendar; (*Abreiß~*) sheet-calendar; (*Taschen~*) pocket almanac; **~block** *m* date (*od* calendar) block; tear-off calendar, block-calendar; **~ersatzblock** *m* replacement calendar block; **~jahr** *n* calendar year; **~vierteljahr** *n* calendar quarter.

Kalesche *f* light carriage, chaise.

kalfatern *tr mar* to ca(u)lk.

Kali *n* potash, potassium hydroxide; *kohlensaures ~* carbonate of potash; **~bergwerk** *n* potash mine; **~blau** *a* Prussian blue; **~düngemittel** *n* potash manure, potash fertilizer; **~lauge** *f* potash lye; **~salpeter** *m* saltpeter, potassium nitrate; **~salz** *n* potash salt; **~um** *n* potassium; **~~gehalt** *m* potassium content; **~~haltig** *a* containing potassium; **~~permanganat** *n* potassium permanganate.

Kalib|er *n* (*Feuerwaffen*) calibre, caliber; (*Walze*) grooves *pl*; *fam* sort, kind; **~~maß** *n* calibre-ga(u)ge; **~~ring** *m* bore ga(u)ge; **~rieren** *tr* to size, to calibrate; (*eichen*) to standardize; (*Walze*) to groove.

Kalif *m* caliph.

Kaliforni|en *n* California; **~sch** *a* Californian.

Kaliko *m* calico, *Am* muslin.

Kalk *m* lime, (*~stein*) limestone; *gebrannter ~* quicklime; *gelöschter ~* slaked lime; *mit ~ tünchen* to whitewash; *mit ~ bewerfen* to roughcast; **~ablagerung** *f* lime deposit, calcareous deposit; **~anstrich** *m* whitewash; **~arm** *a* deficient in lime; **~artig** *a* calcareous, limy; **~bewurf** *m* coat of plaster, plastering; **~boden** *m* lime (*od* calcareous) soil; **~brenner** *m* lime-burner; **~brennerei** *f* lime-kiln; **~bruch** *m* limestone quarry; **~brühe** *f* milk of lime; **~ei** *n* waterglass egg; **~en** *tr* to mix with lime, to soak in lime; (*tünchen*) to whitewash; **~düngung** *f* liming; **~erde** *f* lime, calcium oxide; calcareous earth; **~faß** *n* lime-tub; **~gebirge** *n* chalky mountain; **~gehalt** *m* lime content; **~grube** *f* lime-pit; **~haltig** *a* calcareous; containing lime; **~~keit** *f* calcareousness; **~hütte** *f* lime-kiln; **~ig** *a* limy, calcareous; **~mangel** *m* deficiency of lime; **~mergel** *m* lime marl; **~mörtel** *m* lime mortar; **~niederschlag** *m* lime precipitate; **~ofen** *m* lime-kiln; **~salpeter** *m* calcium nitrate; **~sinter** *m* calcareous sinter; **~stein** *m* limestone; **~sulfat** *n* sulfate of lime; **~tropfstein** *m* calcareous dripstone; **~tuff** *m* calcareous tufa; **~tünche** *f* whitewash; **~verbindung** *f* lime compound; **~wasser** *n* limewater; **~werk** *n* lime works *pl*.

Kalkul|ation *f* calculation, computation; *falsche ~~* miscalculation; **~~sbasis** *f* basis for calculation; **~~sfehler** *m* error in calculation, miscalculation; **~~spreis** *m* calculated price; **~ator** *m* calculator; **~ieren** *tr* to calculate, to compute, to reckon.

Kalori|e *f* calorie, calory, heat (*od* thermal) unit; **~engehalt** *m* calorific content; **~meter** *n* calorimeter.

kalt *a* cold; (*kühl*) cool; (*frostig*) chilly, frosty; (*eisig ~*) frigid, freezing; (*gefroren*) gelid; (*arktisch*) arctic; (*Eiszeit*) glacial; *fig* cold; cool; frosty; (*geschlechtlich*) frigid; (*gleichgültig*) indifferent; (*empfindungslos*) insensible; *~er Krieg* cold war; *~er Schweiß* chilly sweat; *~e Küche* cold lunch (*od* meat); *bitter~* bitterly cold; *es überläuft mich ~* (*fam*) I have the shivers; *mir ist ~* I am cold; *das läßt mich ~* that leaves me cold (*od* cool); *~ bleiben* to keep cool (*od* o.'s temper); *~en Blutes handeln* to act in cold blood; *~er Brand* mortification; *~ sein wie e-e Hundeschnauze* to be as cold as a cucumber; *jdm die ~e Schulter zeigen* to give s. o. the cold shoulder; **~blüter** *m zoo* cold-blooded animal; **~blütig** *a* cold-blooded; *fig* cold, cold-blooded; (*gefühllos*) unfeeling; (*unbarmherzig*) ruthless, merciless; *adv* in cold blood, coldly, coolly; (*überlegt*) deliberately; **~~keit** *f* cold-bloodedness; coolness; (*Gefühllosigkeit*) callousness; (*Gleichmut*) equanimity; (*Geistesgegenwart*) presence of mind; **~färben** *n* cold-dyeing; **~guß** *m* spoiled casting; **~hämmern** *tr* to cold-hammer; **~herzig** *a* cold-hearted; indifferent; unkind; **~~keit** *f* cold-heartedness; **~lächelnd** *a* cynical; (*höhnisch*) sneering; **~lagerung** *f* cold storage; **~legen** *tr* (*Hochofen*) to blow out; **~leim** *m* cold glue; *~* **luft** *f* cold air; **~~front** *f* cold front; **~~keil** *m* wedge of cold air; **~machen** *tr* to kill, to murder, to assassinate; *fam* to do for; **~nadeltechnik** *f* drypoint; **~schale** *f* cold soup; **~schnäuzig** *a* impertinent, impudent, saucy; **~stellen** *tr* to keep cold, to put on ice, to put in a cool place, to refrigerate; *fig* to shelve s.o., to side-track s. o., to strip s. o. of his power; **~wasserdusche** *f* cold douche; **~wasserheilanstalt** *f* hydropathic (establishment); **~wasserkur** *f* cold-water treatment.

Kälte *f* cold(ness); (*~gefühl u. fig*) chill; frigidity, frigidness; (*Gleichgültigkeit*) indifference, apathy; (*Frost*) chilliness, frostiness; *~ ertragen* to stand the cold well; *vor ~ zittern* to shiver with cold; *10 Grad ~* ten degrees below zero; *die ~ läßt nach* the cold is breaking up; **~anlage** *f* refrigerating plant; **~beständig** *a* cold-resisting, resistant to cold; (*Frostschutz*) anti-freezing; **~einbruch** *m* sudden inroad of cold weather, *Am* cold snap; **~empfindlich** *a* sensitive to cold; **~erzeugend** *a* frigorific; **~fest** *a* resistant to cold; *~~ machen* to winterize; **~front** *f* (*Wetter*) cold front; **~grad** *m* degree below zero; **~gefühl** *n* sensation of cold; **~maschine** *f* refrigerating machine; (*Eisschrank*) refrigerator;

~mischung *f* freezing mixture; **~mittel** *n* refrigerating agent; **~n** *tr* to chill; **~periode** *f* cold spell; **~probe** *f* cold test; **~punkt** *m* freezing point; **~regler** *m* cryostat: **~rückfall** *m* return of cold weather, *Am* recurrent cold snap; **~schutzmittel** *n mot* anti-freeze; protective agent against cold; **~welle** *f* cold wave.

kalzi|nieren *tr* to calcine; **~um** *n* calcium.

Kambüse *f* caboose.

Kamee *f* cameo.

Kamel *n* camel; **~garn** *n* mohair; **~haar** *n* camel's hair; **~treiber** *m* camel-driver.

Kamelie *f* camel(l)ia.

Kamera *f* camera; (*Klapp~*) folding camera; (*Kasten~*) box camera; (*Spiegelreflex~*) reflex camera; *~ für Farbphotos* colo(u)r camera; *~ für Momentaufnahmen film Am* akeley; **~auszug** *m* camera extension; **~balgen** *m* camera bellows *pl*; **~mann** *m film* cameraman; (*Vorführer*) operator; **~tragtasche** *f* camera carrying case; **~wagen** *m* camera truck; (*bei Szenenaufnahmen*) rotumbulator; *film sl* dolly.

Kamerad *m* comrade, companion, fellow; *fam* chum, *sl* pal, *Am fam* bud(dy); (*Spiel~*) playmate, playfellow; (*Schul~*) schoolmate, schoolfellow, classmate; (*Schlaf~*) bedfellow, roommate, *Am fam* bunkie; **~schaft** *f* fellowship, companionship; **~~lich** *a* friendly, companionable, like a comrade; (*vertraulich*) intimate, familiar, *sl* pally; *adv* friendly, as comrades, in a spirit of camaraderie; **~~sehe** *f* companionate marriage; **~~sgeist** *m* team-spirit; **~~sheim** *n* canteen, service club (canteen).

Kameral|ien *pl*, **~wissenschaft** *f* science of finance.

Kamille *f* camomile.

Kamin *m* (*Schornstein, Berg*) chimney; (*aus Metall*) funnel, smokestack; (*Zimmer*) fireside, fireplace; **~aufsatz** *m* mantelpiece; **~feger** *m* chimney-sweep(er); **~gesims** *n* mantelpiece; **~teppich** *m* hearth-rug; **~vorsetzer** *m* fender.

Kamisol *n* jacket.

Kamm *m* comb; (*Vögel, Welle*) crest; (*Berg*) ridge, crest; (*Schlüssel*) bit; (*Rind*) neck, clod, *Am* chuck; (*Rad*) cog; cam; (*Weberei*) slay, reed; (*Geige*) bridge; *über e-n ~ scheren* to treat all alike; *der ~ schwillt ihm* he bristles up; **~garn** *n* worsted (yarn); **~~gewebe** *n* worsted fabric; **~~spinnerei** *f* worsted-yarn spinning mill; **~~stoff** *m* worsted yarn cloth; **~gras** *n* dog's-tail; **~linie** *f* ridge line; **~muschel** *f* scallop; **~rad** *n* cog wheel; **~stück** *n* (*Fleisch*) neck (-piece); **~wolle** *f* carded wool.

kämmen *tr* to comb; (*Wolle*) to card; *sich ~* to comb o.'s hair.

Kammer *f* (*kleines Zimmer*) small room, closet; (*Schlafraum*) bedroom; (*Behörde*) board, chamber; *parl* chamber; (*Gewehr*) chamber; (*Vorratsraum*) *mil* unit clothing stores *pl*, stockroom; *jur* chamber, panel; (*Herz*) ventricle; (*Dunkel~*) *phot* dark-room; (*Apparat*) camera; (*Abteilung*) compartment; **~auflösung** *f* dissolution of Parliament; **~diener** *m* valet; *königlicher ~~* groom of the (Great) Chamber; **~frau** *f* lady's maid, chambermaid; **~fräulein** *n* maid of hono(u)r; **~gericht** *n* Supreme Court (of Judicature); **~herr** *m* chamberlain, Gentleman of the Bedchamber; **~jäger** *m* rat-catcher, catcher (*od* destroyer) of vermin; **~jungfer** *f*, **~kätzchen** *n*, **~zofe** *f* lady's maid; **~musik** *f* chamber-music; **~sänger** *m* singer at concerts; **~stenograph** *m* parliamentary reporter; **~ton** *m mus* concert-pitch; **~tuch** *n* cambric; **~unteroffizier** *m mil* N. C. O. storeman; supply sergeant; **~warze** *f* bolt lug.

Kämmer|chen *n* closet, cubby (hole); (*Schlafraum*) cubicle; **~ei** *f* board of finances, exchequer; (*städtisch*) office of the city accountant; **~er** *m* (*Hof*) chamberlain; (*Finanz*) treasurer; (*städtisch*) city accountant.

Kämpe *m* champion.

Kampf *m* (*auch fig*) fight; (*bewaffneter ~*) combat; (*Wett~*) contest, match; (*strittiger ~, auch fig*) conflict; (*Schlägerei, mil Geplänkel*) affray; (*Gefecht*) encounter; (*Scharmützel*) skirmish; (*Zus.stoß*) brush; (*Schlacht*) battle, engagement, action, *sl* push; (*Ringen*) struggle (*um* for, *mit* with); (*Runde*) *sport* bout, round; (*Ring~*) wrestling; (*Wettbewerb*) competition; (*Streit*) controversy, variance; (*Hader*) strife; (*Uneinigkeit*) dissension, disagreement; *~ auf Leben u. Tod* life and death struggle; *~ ums Dasein* struggle for life (*od* existence); *~ bis aufs Messer* skin-game, fight to the finish; *~ der Meinungen* conflict of opinions; *ein ~ Mann gegen Mann* a hand to hand fight, a dog-fight; *ein heißer ~* a ding-dong fight; *ein roher ~* a rough and tumble fight; *im ~e fallen* to be killed in action; **~abschnitt** *m* combat sector; **~anlage** *f* fortified battle position; pill-box; **~ansage** *f* challenge (*an* to); **~anweisung** *f* battle directive; **~aufgabe** *f* combat mission, combat task; **~auftrag** *m* combat mission; **~bahn** *f sport* stadium; arena; **~begier(de)** *f* eagerness to fight, combativeness; **~begierig, ~lustig** *a* eager to fight, pugnacious; **~bereit** *a* ready to fight, *mar* cleared for action; *~~ gegenüberstehen* to be at daggers drawn; **~bund** *m* league; **~einheit** *f* combat (*od* fighting) unit; tactical unit; **~einsatz** *m* committing of troops; **~einsitzer** *m aero* single-seater fighter; **~erfahrung** *f* combat experience; **~erprobt** *a* battle-tested (*od* -tried); seasoned; *~~e Truppen* veteran troops *pl*; **~eslust** *f* pugnacity, combativeness; love of fighting; **~fähig** *a* able to fight; in fighting trim; **~fahrzeug** *n* combat vehicle; **~feld, ~gebiet** *n* battlefield, fighting zone, forward area, combat theatre; **~flieger** *m* bomber pilot; **~~ei** *f* bombardment aviation; **~~verband** *m* bombardment formation; **~flugzeug** *n* bomber (aircraft); **~front, ~linie** *f* fire-line; front line, fighting front; **~führung** *f* battle command; **~gas** *n* war (*od* poison) gas; **~geist** *m* fighting spirit; **~gelände** *n* battle terrain; **~gemeinschaft** *f* fighting union; combat team; **~geschwader** *n* bomber (*od* bombardment) wing; **~gewohnt** *a* war-proof; **~gewühl** *n* thick of the fray, turmoil of battle; **~gruppe** *f mil* combat team, combat command; (*selbständige ~~*) task force; **~hahn** *m* fighting cock; (*streitsüchtiger Mensch*) quarrelsome (*od* pugnacious) fellow, wrangler; **~handlung** *f* action; engagement; **~jägerverband** *m* fighter (-plane) formation; **~kraft** *f* fighting power; fighting strength; **~lage** *f* tactical situation; **~linie** *f* line of battle; **~mittel** *n* means *pl* of warfare; **~moral** *f* combat morale; **~nachricht** *f* combat report, combat message; **~natur** *f*: *er ist e-e ~~* he is a quarrelsome fellow; **~platz** *m* battle-field; (*Ring~*) ring; *allg sport* arena; *fig* scene of conflict, lists *pl*; *den ~~ betreten* to enter the lists; **~preis** *m* prize; (*Rennen*) stakes *pl*; **~raum** *m* forward (*od* combat) area; **~rede** *f* fighting speech; (*Schmährede, Brandrede*) philippic (*auf* on); **~richter** *m* umpire, *sport* referee; **~ruf** *m* war-cry, *Am sport* yell; **~schwimmer** *m mil* frogman; **~spiel** *n* prize fight; contest, match, game; (*Turnier*) tournament; **~stand** *m* fortified position, stronghold; *aero* gunner's turret (*od* station); *unterer ~~ (aero) sl* belly bubble; **~stärke** *f* combative force; **~stellung** *f* battle position; **~stoff** *m* poison (*od* war) gas; chemical warfare agent; **~~belegung** *f* covering with gas; **~~bombe** *f* gas bomb; **~~nachweis** *m* detection of gas; **~~verwendung** *f* employment of chemical agents; **~tätigkeit** *f* combat activity; **~truppe** *f* combat element; **~truppen** *f pl* fighting forces *pl*; **~unfähig** *a* out of action, disabled; (*dienstuntauglich*) unfit for active service; *~~ machen* to put out of action, to disable; (*Boxen*) to knock out; **~verband** *m aero* bomber formation; (*Jäger*) fighter formation; *mil* combat team; (*EVG*) groupement; **~verlauf** *m* development of action; **~wagen** *m* tank; combat vehicle; **~~angriff** *m* tank attack; **~~falle** *f* tank trap; **~~geschütz** *n* tank gun; **~~graben** *m* (*Abwehr*) anti-tank ditch; **~~hindernis** *n* tank obstacle; **~~jäger** *m* tank destroyer; **~~landungsschiff** *n* tank-landing craft; **~wert** *m* battle value; fighting quality; combat efficiency; **~wille** *m* will to fight; **~ziel** *n* objective; **~zone** *f* combat (*od* battle) zone.

kämpf|en *itr* (*sich messen*) to contend, to cope (*mit* with); (*körperlich*) to fight; *fig* to conflict, to battle, to war; (*ringen*) to struggle (*um* for); (*streiten*) to quarrel, to wrangle, to altercate, to squabble; (*Widerstand leisten*) to resist, to combat, to withstand; (*konkurrieren*) to compete (with), to vie (with s. o. for s. th.), to rival (in s. th.); (*streben*) to strive (for); *mit dem Tode ~~* to struggle with death; *mit Schwierigkeiten ~~* to contend with difficulties; *mit dem Wind ~~* to beat up against the wind; *mit den Wellen ~~* to buffet the waves; *mit sich selber ~~* to be undecided; **~end** *a* combatant; **~er** *m* fighter, combatant; (*Turnier~*) champion; (*Krieger*) warrior; (*Ringer*) wrestler; (*Boxer*) boxer; *arch* cushion, abutment; *parl* stalwart; **~erisch** *a* pugnacious, warlike.

Kampfer *m* camphor; **~säure** *f* camphoric acid.

kampieren *itr* to camp.

Kanad|a *n* Canada; **~ier** *m*, **~ierin** *f* Canadian; **~isch** *a* Canadian.

Kanal *m* (*natürlich*) channel; (*künstlich*) canal; (*Abzugs~*) pipe, drain, sewer; (*Graben*) ditch; (*Ärmel~*) the Channel; **~arbeiter** *m* navvy; (*Reiniger*) sewer-man; **~inseln** *f pl* Channel Islands *pl*; **~isation** *f* (*im Haus*) drains *pl*; (*Fluß~*) canalization; (*Stadt~*) sewerage; (*Entwässerungsanlage*) drainage; **~isieren** *tr* to canalize; to sewer; to drain; **~netz** *n* sewage system; **~strahl** *m* canal ray, positive ray; diacathode ray.

Kanapee *n* sofa; settee; couch.

Kanarienvogel *m* canary (-bird).

Kandare *f* bridle-bit, curb, bit; *an die ~ nehmen fig* to take in hand (strongly).

Kandelaber *m* chandelier, candelabrum.

Kandid|at *m* candidate; (*aufgestellter*)

nominee; (*Bewerber*) applicant; (*Aspirant*) aspirant; (*auf Probe*) probationer; **~atenliste** *f Am parl* ticket; **~atur** *f* candidature, *Am* candidacy (*um* for); **~ieren** *itr* to be a candidate, *parl* to contest a seat; to stand, *Am* to run (for election).

kand|ieren *tr* to candy; *~ierte Früchte* candied (*od* crystallized) fruits; **~is** *m* sugar-candy; **~iszucker** *m* (sugar-)candy; (*Bonbon*) toffee, taffy.

Kaneel *m* cinnamon.

Kanevas *m* canvas.

Känguruh *n* kangaroo.

Kaninchen *n* rabbit; **~bau** *m* rabbit-burrow; **~gehege** *n* rabbit-warren.

Kanister *m* canister, container; can, jerry can.

Kännchen *n* small can (*od* pot), pannikin, cannikin, *Am* dipper.

Kanne *f* can; (*irdener Krug*) pitcher, jug; (*zylindrisch*) mug; (*Glas mit Deckel*) tankard; (*Krug*) jug; (*Bier~*) pot; **~gießer** *m* pot-house politician, quidnunc; tub-thumber; **~~ei** *f* political twaddle; **~~n** *itr* to talk politics; **~ngießer** *m* pewterer.

kannelier|en *tr* to groove, to channel, to flute; **~ung** *f* canelure, channel(l)ing, fluting; *tech* groove.

Kannibal|e *m*, **~isch** *a* cannibal.

Kannvorschrift *f* discretionary clause.

Kanon *m* canon; **~iker** *m* canon; **~isch** *a* canonical; **~isieren** *tr* to canonize; **~isierung** *f* canonization.

Kanonade *f* cannonade; bombardment.

Kanone *f* gun; piece of ordnance; cannon; *sport* ace, crack, star; *unter aller ~ fam* beneath contempt; **~nboot** *n* gunboat; **~ndonner** *m* thunder of the guns; **~neinsitzer** *m* cannon single-seater; **~nflugzeug** *n* cannon-equipped airplane; **~nfutter** *n* cannon-fodder; **~ngießerei** *f* gun-foundry; **~nkugel** *f* cannon-ball; **~nofen** *m* round iron stove; bomb furnace; **~nrohr** *n* gun-barrel; **~nschlag** *m* exploding charge; (*Feuerwerk*) fire cracker; maroon; **~nschuß** *m* gun-shot; **~nstand** *m aero mil* gun turret.

Kanonier *m* gunner, cannoneer.

Kantate *f* cantata.

Kant|e *f* edge; (*Ecke*) corner; edging; (*Brot~~*) crust (of bread); (*Tuch*) selvage, list; (*Rand*) brim, border; margin; (*Abgrund*) brink, edge; (*Spitzen*) lace; *auf die hohe ~ legen* to put by; **~en** *tr* to edge; (*Stein*) to square; (*mit Rand versehen*) to border, to edge; (*umkippen*) to capsize, to tilt; *nicht ~~!* this side up! **~en** *m* (*Brot*) (top-) crust; **~haken** *m* cant-hook; *jdn beim ~~ fassen* to seize s. o.; **~holz** *n* squared timber; **~ig** *a* angular, edged.

Kantine *f* mess(hall), canteen, (*Marketenderei*) Naafi, *Am* post exchange, (*Abk* PX).

Kanton *m* canton; **~ierung** *f* cantonment; **~ist** *m*: *ein unsicherer ~~* an unreliable fellow.

Kantor *m* precentor; organist; choir-master.

Kanu *n* canoe; *~* **fahren** *n* canoeing.

Kanüle *f med* (*Wundröhrchen*) cannula, tubule.

Kanzel *f* pulpit; *aero* cockpit; (*Bug*) nose; (*Kampfstand*) (gun-) turret; *sl* greenhouse; *vordere untere ~* (*aero*) chin-turret; *von der ~ verkündigen* to proclaim from the pulpit; *sich von der ~ verlesen lassen* to have o.'s banns published; **~beredsamkeit** *f* pulpit-oratory; **~rede** *f* sermon; **~redner** *m* pulpit orator, preacher.

Kanzlei *f* office; chancellery; **~beamte(r)** *m* office-clerk; **~diener** *m* official of a government-office; **~papier** *n* foolscap; **~stil** *m* official style; law-style; **~tinte** *f* record-ink.

Kanzl|er *m* chancellor; **~ist** *m* office-(*od* chancery-)clerk.

Kaolin *n* China clay, kaolin.

Kap *n* cape, promontory; headland.

Kapaun *m* capon.

Kapazität *f* capacity; *fig* eminent scholar, authority; *die ~ ausnutzen* to work to capacity; **~sausnutzung** *f* employment of capacity.

Kapell|e *f* chapel; *mus* band; *tech* cupel; sand bath; **~enofen** *m tech* assay furnace; **~meister** *m* band-master, conductor.

Kaper *f bot* caper; *~ m* (*Seeräuber*) privateer, freebooter, pirate; **~brief** *m* (letter of) marque; **~ei** *f* privateering; **~fahrt** *f* naval raid against enemy merchant shipping; **~n** *tr* to capture, to seize, to catch; **~schiff** *n* privateer.

kapieren *tr fam* to understand, to comprehend, to grasp, to get, to catch on to; to take in.

Kapillargefäß *n* capillary (vessel).

Kapital *n* capital; (*an Bucheinband*) headband; (*Geldmittel*) funds *pl*; (*Grundvermögen*) stock; *~ u. Zins* principal and interest; *angelegtes ~* invested capital; *eingezahltes ~* paid-in capital; *flüssiges ~* available funds *pl*; *freies ~* unemployed capital; *totes ~* dead capital, idle funds *pl*; *verfügbares ~* available funds *pl*; *~ angreifen* to touch the capital; *~ anlegen, hineinstecken* to invest capital; *~ aufbringen* to raise capital; *~ flüssig machen* to realize capital; *~ kündigen* to recall capital; *~ aus etw schlagen* to make capital out of s. th.; *fig* to profit by; **~abfindung** *f* capital indemnification; lump-sum settlement; **~abgabe** *f* capital levy; **~abschöpfung** *f* skimming of capital; **~abwanderung, ~flucht** *f* exodus (*od* flight) of capital; **~anlage, ~einlage** *f* investment; **~anteile** *m pl* shares of stock; **~arm** *a* short of funds; **~bedarf** *m* capital requirement, demand for money; **~beschaffung** *f* raising of capital; **~beteiligung** *f* capital participation; **~bildung** *f* formation of capital; **~erhöhung** *f* increase of capital; **~ertrag** *m* capital yield; **~~ssteuer** *f* capital-profit tax; **~geber** *m* investor; **~ien** *n pl* capital, funds *pl*; **~isieren** *tr* to capitalize; (*Unternehmen*) to finance, to fund; **~ismus** *m* capitalism; **~ist** *m* capitalist; **~istisch** *a* capitalistic; **~knappheit** *f* shortage of capital, stringency of money; **~kräftig** *a* well provided with capital, sound; wealthy; **~mangel** *m* lack of capital; **~markt** *m* money market; **~steuer** *f* capital tax; **~verbrechen** *n* capital crime; **~vermögen** *n* capital asset; **~wertzuwachs** *m* capital increment value; **~zins** *m* interest on capital; **~zufluß** *m* influx of capital.

Kapitän *m* captain, skipper; *~ zur See* captain R. N., *Am* commodore; **~leutnant** *m* lieutenant-commander; naval lieutenant.

Kapitel *n* chapter, head; section; *das ist ein ~ für sich* that's another story; **~überschrift** *f* heading of a chapter.

Kapitell *n arch* capital.

kapitul|ieren *itr* to capitulate; to surrender; (*weiter dienen*) to re-enlist; **~ation** *f* capitulation, surrender; re-enlistment; *bedingungslose ~~* unconditional surrender.

Kaplan *m* chaplain.

Kappe *f* cap; (*Kapuze*) hood; (*der Mönche*) cowl; (*Strumpf*) heel-piece; (*Schuh*) tip, toe-piece, top-piece; (*Mantel*) cape; *arch* (*Haube*) cup, cap, dome; (*Deckel*) top; (*Mauer*) coping; (*Bade~*) bathing cap; *alles auf seine ~ nehmen* to make o.s. responsible for; to answer for; *jedem Narren gefällt seine ~* every one has his hobby; *gleiche Brüder, gleiche ~n* birds of a feather flock together; **~n** *tr* (*abschneiden*) to cut; to sever; (*Bäume*) to lop, to top; (*Hähne*) to capon; to castrate; (*Strumpf*) to heel; (*Schuh*) to tip; **~ngewölbe** *n arch* cellar vault; **~nmacher** *m* cap-maker.

Käppi *n* kepi.

Kapriole *f* capriole; (*Luftsprung*) caper; *~n machen fig* to play tricks.

kaprizieren *r* to take a fancy to s. th.; to stick to.

Kapsel *f* case, box; *bot* capsule; (*Kappe*) cover; cap; (*Guß*) chill, mo(u)ld; *typ* box; (*Keramik*) sagger; (*Spreng~*) detonator; **~blitz** *m phot* flashlight capsule; (*Lampe*) flash-lamp (with flashlight powder); **~förmig** *a* capsular; **~katalog** *m* sheaf catalog(ue).

kaputt *a* (*zerbrochen*) in pieces; broken; (*verdorben*) spoiled; (*zugrunde gerichtet*) ruined; (*von Tieren*) dead; (*übermüdet*) worn out, all in; done-up; (*in Unordnung*) *Am sl* haywire; *~gehen* to get broken; *~machen* to ruin.

Kapuz|e *f* hood; (*Mönch*) cowl; capuchin; **~iner** *m* capuchin (monk); **~~kresse** *f* Indian cress, nasturtium.

*

Karabiner *m* carbine, rifle; (*Haken*) spring (*od* snap) hook; **~haken** *m* spring safety hook.

Karaffe *f* carafe; (*Wein*) decanter.

karambolieren to collide; (*Billard*) to cannon, *Am* to carom.

Karat *n* carat; **~gewicht** *n* troy weight; **~gold** *n* alloyed gold.

Karawan|e *f* caravan; **~enstraße** *f* caravan-route; **~serei** *f* caravansary.

Karbid *n* carbide; **~lampe** *f* carbide lamp.

Karbolsäure *f* carbolic acid; phenol.

Karbonade *f* cutlet, chop.

Karbunkel *m* carbuncle, malignent tumo(u)r; boil.

Kardan|gelenk *n mot* cardan joint; **~getriebe** *n mot* cardan gear; **~welle** *f* cardan shaft.

Kardätsche *f* card; (*Spinnerei*) scribbling-card; (*Pferd*) horse brush, curry-comb; **~n** *tr* (*Wolle*) to card, to comb; (*Tuch*) to teasel; (*Pferd*) to brush, to curry.

Karde *f bot* teasel; *tech* card.

Kardinal *m* cardinal; **~punkte** *m pl* cardinal points *pl*; **~shut** *m* cardinal's hat; **~skollegium** *n* college of cardinals; **~tugenden** *f pl* cardinal virtues *pl*; **~zahl** *f* cardinal number.

Karenz *f* abstinence; **~zeit** *f* waiting time.

Kar|freitag *m* Good Friday; **~woche** *f* Passion (*od* Holy) Week.

Karfunkel *m* carbuncle.

karg *a* (*sparsam*) sparing, thrifty, parsimonious; (*sehr sparsam*) penny-pinching, cheeseparing; (*knauserig*) close (-fisted), tight (-fisted), niggardly, penurious; (*geizig*) miserly, avaricious, stingy, curmudgeonly; (*ärmlich*) poor, scanty; (*erbärmlich*) wretched; (*unfruchtbar*) barren, sterile; **~en** *itr* to be stingy; to be sparing; **~heit** *f* sparingness; parsimony; stinginess, meanness; (*Armut*) poverty, poorness.

kärglich *a* scanty, poor, miserable.

kariert a checked, chequered, Am checkered.

Karik|atur f caricature, Am cartoon; ~~en zeichnen to caricature, Am to cartoon; ~~enserie f Am comic strip, funnies pl; ~~enzeichner, ~~ist m caricaturist, Am cartoonist; ~ieren tr to caricature.

Karl m Charles; ~ der Große Charlemagne, Charlemain.

karmesin a crimson.

Karmin m carmine.

Karneol m carnelian, cornelian.

Karneval m carnival.

Karnies n arch cornice.

Karnickel n rabbit, bunny.

Kärnten n Carinthia.

Karo n square; (Karten) diamonds pl.

Karolinger m Carolingian.

Karosse f state carriage, state coach; ~rie f mot body(-work); ~rieblech n body sheet.

Karotte f carrot.

Karpaten pl Carpathians pl.

Karpfen m carp; ~teich m carp-pond.

Karre f, **Karren** m cart; (wheel-) barrow; die ~ umwerfen to upset the coach; ~n tr to cart; itr to roll a barrow; ~ngaul m cart-horse.

Karree n square.

Karriere f gallop; (Laufbahn) career; ~ machen to get on well in the world.

Kärrner m barrow-man; carter; (Fuhrmann) carrier.

Karst m (Hacke) mattock, hoe; (Berg) naked rock, karst.

Kartätsche f mil case-shot, grape-shot; canister-shot; cartridge.

Kartäuser m Carthusian friar.

Karte f (Land~) map; (See~) chart; (Luftbild~) air survey map, aerophotogrammetric map; (Fahr~, Theater~) ticket; (Post~, Spiel~, Besuchs~) card; (Speise~) bill of fare, menu; ein Spiel ~n a pack of cards, Am a deck of cards; ~n abheben to cut cards; ~n aufdecken to show o.'s hand; ~n geben to deal cards; ~n legen to tell fortunes by the cards; ~ mischen to shuffle the cards; ~n spielen to play at cards; jdm in die ~n sehen to discover s. o.'s design; alles auf e-e ~ setzen to stake everything on one card; zuviel auf e-e ~ setzen to put too many eggs in one basket; ~i f card-index, card catalog(ue); card-file; filing cabinet; ~~karte f filing (od register od index) card; ~~kasten m file cabinet (od drawer); ~nausgabe f booking-office, Am ticket-window; ~nbild n figure on a card; ~nbildanzeiger m (Radar) plan position indicator (Abk PPI); ~nblatt n (single) card; (Landkarte) map sheet; grid sheet; ~~nummer f geographic index number; ~nbrett n map mounting board; ~nbrief m letter-card; ~ndruckerei f map printing office; ~neintragung, ~neinzeichnung f entry on map; ~nentfernung f distance as the crow flies; map range; ~ngitternetz n map grid; ~nhalter m map holder; ~nhaus n fig castle in the air; mar chart house; ~nkunststück n card-trick; ~nkurs m map course; true course; ~nlegerin f fortune-teller; ~nlesen n map reading; ~nmaßstab m map scale; representative fraction; ~nnetz n map grid; ~nperiode f ration period; ~nprojektion f map projection; ~nschalter m ticket-office, Am ticket-window; ~nschlägerin f fortune-teller; ~nskizze f map sketch; ~nspiel n card-playing; (Spiel~n) pack (od Am deck) of cards; game at cards; ~nspieler m card-player; ~nständer m card-rack; ~nstelle f (Lebensmittel) local food ration office; (Land~) map office; ~ntasche f map case; ~ntisch m card table; aero (Leitstelle) filter board; ~nverkauf m sale of tickets; ticket-office; ~nvorverkauf m theat booking; ~nwinkelmesser m protractor; ~nzeichner m cartographer, map designer.

Kartell n cartel, trust, ring, pool; industrial combine; (Konsortium) syndicate; (Großhändlerring) corner; (Verband) combine, combination; (Herausforderung) challenge; ~bruder m member of a confederate students association; ~beziehungen f pl cartel relationship; ~entflechtung f decartelization; ~ierung f cartelization; ~träger m second, ~vertrag m cartel agreement.

Kartoffel f potato, fam spud; ~n in der Schale potatoes in their jackets (od skins); ~n schälen to peel potatoes; dem dümmsten Bauern wachsen die größten ~n fools have fortune; ~bauch m pot-belly; ~branntwein m potato spirits pl; ~brei m mashed potatoes; ~ernte f potato crop; ~käfer m Colorado beetle; ~kloß m potato-ball; ~knödel m potato dumpling; ~mehl n potato flour; ~puffer m potato pancake; ~salat m potato salad; ~schale f skin of a potato, jacket; ~schnaps m potato whisky; ~stärke f potato starch; ~suppe f potato soup.

Kartograph m cartographer; ~isch a cartographic(al); ~~ aufnehmen to map (out).

Kart|on m (Pappe) cardboard; (stark) pasteboard; (Schachtel) cardboard box; (Kunst) cartoon; ~~age f boarding; cardboard (od pasteboard) box; ~~agenfabrik f cardboard factory; ~~ieren tr to bind in boards; ~othek f card index (od file od catalog(ue) od collection).

Kartusch|e f (gun-)cartridge; ~hülse f cartridge case; ~korb m ammunition basket.

Karussell n merry-go-round, roundabout, Am car(r)ousel.

Karzer m prison; lock-up.

Kaschemme f low pub, dive; thieves' den, Am joint; (billiges Absteigequartier) sl doss-house.

kaschieren tr to coat with paper.

Kaschmir m cashmere.

Käse m cheese; ~artig a cheesy, caseous; ~bildung f cheese formation, caseation; ~blatt n (Zeitung) rag; local newspaper; ~brötchen n Am cheeseburger; ~glocke f cheese-(plate) cover; ~händler m cheesemonger; ~kuchen m cheese-cake; ~lab n rennet; ~made f cheese-maggot; ~milbe f cheese-mite; ~n itr to curd(le); ~quark m cheese-curds pl; ~rei f cheese-dairy; ~rinde f rind of cheese; ~säure f lactic acid; ~stoff m casein; ~wasser n whey.

Kasematte f mil casemate.

Kasern|e f barracks pl; (Miets~e) tenement-house; ~enarrest m confinement to barracks; ~enhof m barrack-yard; ~enstube f barrack room; ~ieren tr to barrack, to lodge (od quarter) in barracks.

käsig a cheesy, caseous, curdy; (Gesichtsfarbe) pale.

Kasino n casino; club, mil (officers') mess; ~ordonnanz f mess orderly, Am dining-room orderly; ~vorstand m mess council.

Kaskade f cascade; ~nbombe f aero cascade bomb;„ (Markierung) sky marker, target-marking flare.

Kaskoversicherung f hull insurance; automobile and liability insurance.

Kasperl(e)theater n Punch and Judy show.

Kassa f = Kasse; (Bargeld) cash, ready money; ~buch n cash book; ~geschäft n spot sale, cash business; ~konto n cash account; ~preis m cash price.

Kassation f (Urteil) quashing, cassation, reversal; (Entlassung) dismissal, discharge; cashiering; military degradation; ~sgericht n court of cassation; supreme court of appeal.

Kasse f (Schrank) money (od cash) box, safe; (Zahlstelle) cash (od pay) office; (Theater, Bahnhof) ticket- (od booking- od box-)office, Am ticket window; (Laden) till, desk, counter; (Bank) teller's department; (Bargeld) cash (in hand); (Registrier~) cash register; (Unterstützungs~) relief fund; (Kranken~) sick fund, health-insurance; gegen ~ for cash; netto ~ no discount allowed; gegen sofortige ~ spot cash; gemeinschaftliche ~ joint account; ~ bei Lieferung cash on delivery; nicht bei ~ sein to be short of cash (od hard up); bei ~ sein to be in funds (od flush); zahlen Sie, bitte, an der ~ please pay the cashier; die ~ führen to keep the cash; ~nabschluß m balancing of cash account; ~nanweisung f voucher; ~narzt m panel(-)doctor; ~nbeamter m cashier, (Bank) teller; ~nbericht m cash report; ~nbestand m cash balance; ~nbilanz f cash balance; ~nbote m bank-messenger; ~ndefizit n deficit, Am adverse cash balance; ~ndiebstahl m robbing the till; (Unterschlagung) embezzlement; ~neingänge m pl cash receipts pl; ~neinnahme f cash receipts pl; theat box-office receipt; ~nerfolg m box-office success; ~nführer m treasurer, cashier; ~nführung f cash keeping; ~nkontrolle, ~nprüfung, ~nrevision f cash audit; ~nrevisor m auditor; ~npatient m panel-patient; ~nschalter m bank counter; ~nschein m receipt, bill; docket; treasury bill; ~nschlager m, ~nstück n theat box-office draw (od hit); ~nschrank m safe; ~nsturz m proving cash; counting of cash receipts; ~nüberschuß m cash surplus; ~numsatz m cash turnover; ~nverwaltung f financial administration; ~nwesen n finance accounts pl; ~nzettel m sales slip.

Kasserole f stewpan.

Kass|ette f cash (od strong) box; (Kästchen) casket; arch coffer; phot dark slide, plate-holder; spool chamber; film magazine; film spool; box, film holder; (Decke) coffer, bay; ~~ndecke f coffered ceiling; ~~nfüllung f daylight spool; ~~nrahmen m dark slide carrier; ~~nschieber m shutter of dark slide; ~ieren tr (ungültig machen) to cancel, to annul; (entlassen) to discharge, to dismiss; (ein~) to cash, to collect; (Urteil) to quash, to re, verse, to cancel; ~ier(er) m cashier-treasurer; (Bank) teller; (Kartenverkäufer) ticket-agent, booking clerk.

Kassiber m stiff.

Kastagnette f castanet.

Kastanie f chestnut; eßbare ~n sweet chestnuts; für jdn die ~n aus dem Feuer holen to pull the chestnuts out of the fire for s. o.; ~nbaum m chestnut(-tree); ~nbraun a chestnut (-co-lo(u)red), auburn; ~nwäldchen n chestnut-grove.

Kästchen n casket, little box.

Kast|e f caste; ~engeist m caste feeling; exclusiveness.

kastei|en *tr* to castigate, to chastise; to mortify; **~ung** *f* castigation, mortification.

Kastell *n* (*römisches* ~) Roman fortification; (*befestigtes Schloß*) fort; citadel; **~an** *m* castellan; steward.

Kasten *m* chest, box; (*Behälter*) case, receptacle; (*Truhe*) trunk; (*Brief~*) (letter-)box; (*Kehricht~*) (dust-)bin; (*Kohlen~*) bunker; (*Schrank*) cupboard, wardrobe, closet; (*Werkzeug~*) kit; (*Wagen~*) body; (*Kübel*) vat; (*Einfassung*) collet; *typ* case; (*Violine*) resonance-box; (*Gefängnis*) jail; *alter* ~ (*Haus*) hovel; (*Schiff*) floating coffin; **~drachen** *m* box kite; **~kamera** *f* box camera; **~lautsprecher** *m* cabinet loudspeaker; **~wagen** *m* box cart; *rail* open box car, *Am* lorry; *mot* box-type delivery van.

Kastr|at *m* eunuch; **~ieren** *tr* to castrate, to geld.

Kasuistik *f* casuistry.

Kasus *m* case.

Kata|falk *m* catafalque; **~komben** *f pl* catacombs *pl*.

Katalog *m* catalogue, *Am* catalog(ue), list; *systematischer* ~ classed catalogue; *im* ~ *führen* to keep in a catalogue; **~abteilung** *f* cataloguing department; **~aufnahme** *f* catalogue entry; **~beamter** *m* catalog(u)er; **~isieren** *tr* to catalog(ue); **~karte** *f* catalog(ue) card; **~nummer** *f* catalog(ue) number; **~preis** *m* list price.

Kata|lysator *m* catalyst; **~pult** *m, n* catapult; launching rail; **~~fähig** *a aero* catapultable; **~~flugzeug** *n* catapult plane; **~~ieren** *tr aero* to launch; to catapult off; **~~schiff** *n aero* catapult ship; **~~start** *m aero* catapult start (*od* launching *od* take-off); **~rakt** *m* (*Wasserfall*) cataract, waterfall; (*Augen*) cataract.

Katarrh *m* catarrh, cold.

Kataster *m u. n* land-register; **~amt** *n* land registry office; **~aufnahme** *f* cadastral survey.

Katastroph|e *f* catastrophe; **~al** *a* catastrophic.

Kate *f* (*Hütte*) hut, cottage.

Katech|ese *f eccl* catechizing; **~et** *m* catechist; **~ismus** *m* catechism.

Kateg|orie *f* category; **~orisch** *a* categorical.

Kater *m* male cat, tom-cat; *fig* (*Katzenjammer*) seediness, *Am* hang-over; *e-n* ~ *haben* to feel seedy; *Gestiefelter* ~ Puss-in-Boots.

Katheder *n* lecturing-desk, chair; rostrum; **~blüte** *f* professorial blunder; **~weisheit** *f* professorial wisdom.

Kathedrale *f* cathedral.

Kathode *f* cathode; negative electrode; *lichtelektrische* ~ photo-electric cathode; **~ndichte** *f* cathode density; **~nstrahl** *m* cathode ray; cathodic beam; **~nstrahlenbündel** *n* cathode-ray bundle; **~nstrahlenenergie** *f* energy of cathode rays; **~nstrahlerzeuger** *m* electron gun; **~nstrahloszillograph** *m* cathode-ray oscillograph; **~nstrahlröhre** *f* cathode-ray tube; **~nstrahlung** *f* cathode radiation; **kathodisch** *a* cathodic.

Kathol|ik *m*, **~ikin** *f*, **~isch** *a* (Roman) Catholic; **~izismus** *m* Catholicism.

Kätner *m* cottager.

Kattun *m* calico, cotton; (*bedruckt*) print; (*für Möbel*) chintz; **~druck** *m* calico printing; **~fabrik** *f* calico factory; cotton mill; **~papier** *n* chintz paper; **~presse** *f* calico press.

katz|balgen *r* to scuffle, to fight; **~balgerei** *f* scuffling, wrangle; **~buckeln** *itr* to cringe, to shrink, to bend, to crouch, to stoop; to toady; **~e** *f* cat; *fam* puss(y); (*Pfähle*) *mar* mooring-post; *graubraune* ~~ tabby cat; *schwarz u. gelb gefleckte* ~~ tortoise-shell cat; *neunschwänzige* ~~ cat-o'-nine-tails; (*Geld~~*) purse, pouch; (*Schmeichel~~*) wheedler, coaxer; *falsche* ~~ malicious person; (*Lauf~*) trolley, crab; *bei Nacht sind alle ~en grau* all cats are grey in the dark; *wie die ~~ um den heißen Brei gehen* to beat about the bush; *das ist alles für die ~'!* that's of no use, it's a complete waste; *die ~~ aus dem Sack lassen* to let the cat out of the bag; *die ~~ im Sack kaufen* to buy a pig in a poke; *die ~ läßt das Mausen nicht* cats will catch mice; *wie Hund u. ~~ leben* to lead a cat-and-dog life; **~enartig** *a* catlike, feline; *fig* perfidious; **~enauge** *n* cat's-eye; (*Rückstrahler*) rear (*od* red) reflector; rear light; **~enbuckel** *m* cat's back; *e-n ~~ machen* to arch the back; *fig* to crouch before s. o.; **~endarm** *m* catgut; **~enfreundlich** *a* cringing, servile; **~engeschrei** *n* mewing of cats, caterwaul(ing); **~engold** *n* cat gold, yellow mica; **~enhaft** *a* catlike; (*heimtückisch*) treacherous; **~enjammer** *m* seediness, *Am* hang-over; *e-n ~~ haben* to feel seedy; **~enkraut** *n* cat thyme; (*Minze*) catnip; **~enmusik** *f* caterwauling, infernal row; **~enpfötchen** *n* cat's paw, cat's foot; **~ensprung** *m* cat's leap; *fig* a stone's throw; **~entisch** *m*: *am ~~ essen* to eat at a side-table; **~enwäsche** *f* cat's lick; **~enzunge** *f* cat's tongue.

Kätzchen *n* kitten; *bot* catkin.

Kauderwelsch *n* gibberish; (*Unsinn*) nonsense.

Kau|apparat *m* masticating apparatus; **~bar** *a* masticable; **~bewegung** *f* masticatory movement; **~en** *tr* to chew, to masticate; to bite; (*geräuschvoll*) to munch; *an den Nägeln* ~~ to bite the nails; **~gummi** *m* chewing gum, *Am* gum; **~tabak** *m* chewing tobacco, *Am* chew; **~werkzeuge** *n pl* masticators *pl*.

kauern *itr* (*sich*) to cower, to crouch; to squat.

Kauf *m* purchase, buying, *Am* buy; (*günstiger*) bargain, *Am* a good buy; (*Erwerbung*) acquisition; *e-n* ~ *abschließen* to close (*od* to strike) a bargain; *zum* ~ *anbieten* to offer for sale; *von e-m* ~ *zurücktreten* to cancel a purchase; *mit in den* ~ *nehmen* to put up with; *leichten ~s davonkommen* to come off with a small loss; to get off lightly; ~ *auf Ziel* purchase on terms; ~ *auf feste Rechnung* purchase on account; ~ *gegen bar* cash purchase; **~abneigung** *f Am* sales resistance; **~abschluß** *m* sale; **~anlaß** *m* buying motive; **~anschlag** *m* estimate; **~auftrag** *m* buying order; **~bedingungen** *f pl* conditions *pl* of purchase; **~bereich** *m* shopping area; **~brief** *m* purchase deed; **~en** *tr* to buy, to purchase, to make a purchase (*von* of, from); *jdn* ~~ to bribe s. o., to corrupt by a bribe; *auf Abzahlung* ~~ to buy on the instalment plan; *auf Kredit* ~~ to buy on credit; *auf Rechnung* ~~ to purchase on account; *gegen bar* ~~ to buy for cash; *billig* ~~ to buy cheap; *teuer* ~~ to buy dear; *aus zweiter Hand* ~~ to buy at second hand; *was ich mir dafür kaufe!* that's all rubbish! *den werde ich mir ~~!* I'll let him have it! **~fahrteischiff** *n* merchantman, trader; **~geld** *n* purchase money; **~gesuch** *n* (*Anzeige*) wanted, required; **~halle** *f* baza(a)r; (*Verkaufsraum*) *Am* sale(s)-room; **~haus** *n* stores *pl*, *Am* department store; (*billiges*) sixpenny store, *Am* five-and-ten; **~herr** *m* wholesale merchant; **~interessent** *m* prospective purchaser; **~kraft** *f* purchasing (*od* buying) power; **~~abschöpfung** *f* skimming-off a surplus of purchasing power; **~~lenkung** *f* control of purchasing power; **~~überhang** *m* excess of purchasing power; **~kräftig** *a* able to buy; wealthy, moneyed; **~laden** *m* shop, *Am* store; **~leute** *pl* tradespeople, tradesfolk; **~lust** *f* demand, disposition to buy; **~~ig** *a* eager (*od* keen) to buy; **~~ige(r)** *m* intending purchaser, buyer; **~mann** *m* (*Kleinhändler*) retail-dealer, retailer, shopkeeper, *Am* storekeeper; (*mit offenem Ladengeschäft*) tradesman, dealer, trader; (*Großhändler*) wholesale dealer, merchant; (*Geschäftsmann*) businessman; **~~schaft** *f* commercial world; **~~skreise** *m pl* commercial circles *pl*; **~~sstand** *m* business profession; **~männisch** *a* commercial, mercantile; businesslike; *~~er Angestellter* clerk; *~~e Ausbildung* business training; **~preis** *m*, **~summe** *f* purchase price (*od* money); **~vertrag** *m* contract of sale, sales contract; **~wert** *m* purchase (*od* market) value; **~zwang** *m* obligation to buy; *kein* ~~ free inspection invited.

Käuf|e *m pl* purchases *pl*; (*Ein~~*) shopping; ~~ *besorgen* to go shopping; *bedeutende* ~~ heavy purchases; **~er** *m* buyer, purchaser; (*Bieter*) bidder; (*Kunde*) customer; (*Kurs*) bid, buyers *pl*, money; **~~streik** *m* consumer (*od Am* sales) resistance, buyers' strike; **~lich** *a* (*verkäuflich*) marketable, saleable; (*angeboten*) on (*od* for) sale; purchasable, *fig* (*bestechlich*) corruptible, corrupt, venal; ~~ *erwerben* to acquire by purchase; ~~ *überlassen* to sell; **~~keit** *f* (*Bestechlichkeit*) venality, corruptibility.

Kaulquappe *f* tadpole.

*

kaum *adv* (*mit Mühe*) hardly, with difficulty; (*knapp, bes. bei a*) scarcely; (*gerade noch*) barely, just, just now; just a moment ago; ~ ... *als* no sooner ... than; *ich glaube* ~ I hardly think so.

Kausal|ität *f*, **~zusammenhang** *m* causality.

Kaution *f* security; (*Gericht*) bail; *e-e* ~ *stellen* to give (*od* stand) security; to give (*od* stand) bail for; *gegen* ~ under bond; *nach Hinterlegung e-r* ~ *fliehen* to jump bail, to escape while out on bail; *durch ~serlegung auf freien Fuß bringen jur* to bail out; **~shöhe** *f* amount of security; **~spflichtig** *a* liable to give security.

Kautschuk *m* caoutchouc, India rubber; pure rubber.

Kauz *m* screech-owl; *fig* odd fellow, queer fish.

Kavalier *m* gentleman, cavalier; **~start** *m aero* climbing take-off, quick steep ascent.

Kavaller|ie *f* cavalry, horse; **~ist** *m* horseman; cavalryman, trooper.

Kaviar *m* caviar(e); ~ *fürs Volk* caviar to the general.

Kebsweib *n* concubine.

keck *a* (*kühn*) bold, audacious; (*tapfer*) brave; (*mutig*) plucky, gritty; (*verwegen*) daring, venturous; (*entschlossen*) resolute, determined; (*unerschrocken*) dauntless, undaunted; (*forsch*) dashing; (*frech*) impudent, *fam* cheeky, saucy; **~heit** *f* audacity, boldness, daring; (*Frechheit*) impudence, cool effrontery, *fam* cheek; (*vorlautes Wesen*) pertness.

Kegel *m math* cone; (*Spiel*) ninepins *pl*, skittles *pl*, *Am* bowls *pl*, tenpins *pl mit sing*; *typ* body; *fig* dumpy person; ~ *schieben* to play at ninepins; *mit Kind u.* ~ with bag and baggage, with the whole lot; **~bahn** *f* skittle-alley, *Am* bowling-alley; **~fläche** *f math* conical surface; **~förmig** *a* conical, cone-shaped, coniform; tapered; **~junge** *m* skittle-boy, *Am* pin-boy; **~kugel** *f* skittle-ball; **~mantel** *m math* convex surface of a cone; **~n** *itr* (~ *schieben*) to play at ninepins (*od* skittles); **~rad** *n* bevel wheel, cone wheel; bevel pinion; **~schieber** *m* skittle-player; *tech* bevel slide valve; **~schnitt** *m* conic section; **~spiel** *n* ninepins *pl, Am auch* tenpins *pl mit sing*; **~stumpf** *m* truncated cone; **~ventil** *n* conical valve.

Kehl|ader *f anat* jugular vein; **~deckel** *m* epiglottis; **~e** *f* throat; (*Schlund*) pharinx; (*~kopf*) larynx; (*Luftröhre*) windpipe; (*Speiseröhre*) gullet, o(e)sophagus; *tech* channel, flute, groove; *aus voller ~~ lachen* to shout with laughter; *mir ist die ~~ wie zugeschnürt* a lump is in my throat; *jdm das Messer an die ~~ setzen* to hold a knife to s. o.'s throat; *die Worte blieben mir in der ~~ stecken* the words stuck in my throat; *an der ~~ packen* to seize by the throat; *jdm die ~~ abschneiden* to cut s.o.'s throat; **~en** *tr* to groove, to channel, to flute; **~kopf** *m* larynx; **~~entzündung** *f* laryngitis; **~~mikrophon** *n* throat microphone; **~~spiegel** *m* laryngoscope; **~~telephon** *n* throat phone; **~~verschlußlaut** *m* glottal stop; **~laut** *m* guttural sound; **~leiste** *f arch* ogee, talon, cyma; mo(u)lding; **~stimme** *f* guttural voice; **~ung** *f tech* mo(u)lding; haunch (of a beam); fillet; **~ziegel** *m* gutter-tile.

*

Kehr|aus *m* last dance; (*Aufräumen*) clean-out; (*Umwälzung*) shake-up; **~besen** *m* broom; **~bild** *n phot* film negative; (*Radar*) back-to-back display; **~e** *f* turn(ing), bend; (*Turnen*) flank vault; (*Richtung*) direction; *rail*, *aero* turn (bank), flat bank; loop; **~en** *tr*, *itr* to sweep, to broom; (*abwischen*) to brush; (*abstauben*) to dust; (*zuwenden*) to turn; (*nicht zurückkehren*) *mil aero* to be missing; *r* to pay attention to, to heed, to follow, to mind; *neue Besen ~~ gut* new brooms sweep clean; *kehr vor deiner eigenen Tür!* sweep in front of your own door! *rechtsum kehrt!* right about turn! *das Oberste zuunterst ~~* to turn everything upside down; *alles zum besten ~~* to turn everything to advantage; *in sich gekehrt* retired into o. s.; *sich um nichts ~~* not to care a fig for; **~icht** *m* sweepings *pl*, rubbish, dust; (*Abfall*) garbage, *Am* junk; **~~eimer** *m* dust bin, *Am* ash-can; **~~haufen** *m* dust-heap; **~~schaufel** *f* dust-pan; **~kurve** *f aero* turn; (*hochgezogene ~~*) *aero* Immelmann turn; **~maschine** *f* street sweeper; **~reim** *m* burden, leitmotiv; chorus, refrain; **~schleife** *f* serpentine; **~seite** *f* reverse; (*Stoff*) wrong side; (*Rückseite*) back; (*Münze*) pile,tail; *fig* drawback; *die ~~ des Lebens* the seamy side of life; *jedes Ding hat seine ~~* there is a reverse to every medal; **~tmachen** *itr mil* to face about; (*umkehren*) to turn back; **~twendung** *f* about-face; **~wisch** *m* whisk.

keifen *itr* to scold; (*zanken*) to squabble; (*unaufhörlich tadeln*) to nag; (*lärmend schreien*) to brawl.

Keil *m* wedge; *tech* (*zum Befestigen*) key; (*Schließ~*) cotter; (*Sicherungs~*) forelock; *typ* quoin; *arch* voussoir; (*Nähen*) gore gusset; *aero* V-formation; *hölzerner ~* jack; *auf e-n groben Klotz gehört ein grober ~* rudeness must be met with rudeness; **~artig, ~förmig** *a* wedge--shaped, cuneiform, sphenoid; **~bein** *n anat* wedge-bone; **~e** *f* thrashing; **~en** *tr tech* to wedge, to key; *typ* to quoin; (*verprügeln*) to thrash, to cudgel; (*werben*) to canvass s. o. for s. th.; to win over; (*betrügerisch*) *sl* to rope in; *r* to fight; **~er** *m* wild boar; **~erei** *f* row, beating; fight; **~flosse** *f* vertical tail fin; **~form** *f aero* V-formation; **~hacke** *f* pickax(e); **~kissen** *n* wedge-shaped bolster; **~rahmen** *m* adjustable frame; **~riemen** *m* cone belt; **~schrift** *f* cuneiform characters *pl.*

Keim *m* germ; *bot*, *zoo* bud; (*Schößling*) shoot; (*Frucht~*) embryo; (*Malz~*) sprout; (*Kristall~*) nucleus; *fig* germ, seed; *im ~e ersticken* to nip in the bud; *im ~e vorhanden* seminal, *fig* potential; *~e treiben* to germinate; **~bildung** *f* formation of the germ; **~blatt** *n* seed-leaf, cotyledon; **~drüse** *f* reproductive gland; **~en** *itr* to germ(inate); (*sich zeigen*) to spring up; (*entstehen*) to arise; (*knospen*) to bud, to sprout; **~~d** *a* germinant, nascent; **~fähig** *a* germinable; **~fähigkeit** *f* germinative faculty; **~frei** *a* germ-free, sterile; *~~ machen* to sterilize; (*durch Erhitzen*) to pasteurize; (*desinfizieren*) to disinfect; **~ling** *m* germ, embryo; (*Pflanze*) seedling; **~tilgend** *a* antiseptic; **~tötend** *a* germicidal; *~~es Mittel* germicide; **~träger** *m* (germ-) carrier; **~ung** *f* germination; **~zelle** *f* germ cell.

kein *a* no, not any; *sie ist ~ Kind mehr* she is no longer a child; *~ Wort mehr!* not another word! **~er** *m*, **~e** *f*, **~es** *n* no one, none, nobody, not anybody; *~er von beiden* neither; **~erlei** *a* not of any sort, of no sort, not any; no ... whatever; **~erseits** *adv* on neither side; **~esfalls** *adv* on no account, by no means; **~eswegs** *adv* not at all, not in the least; by no means; **~mal** *adv* not once, never; *einmal ist ~~* once does not count.

Keks *m* biscuit, *Am* cracker, cookie.

Kelch *m* cup, goblet; *bot* calyx; *eccl* chalice, communion-cup; *den ~ der Leiden bis auf die Hefe leeren* to drain the cup of sorrow to the dregs; **~blatt** *n* sepal; **~förmig** *a* cup-shaped; **~glas** *n* cup-shaped glass, tumbler, goblet.

Kelle *f* ladle; (*Schöpflöffel*) scoop; (*Maurer~*) trowel.

Keller *m* cellar, cave; **~assel** *f* wood--louse; **~durchbruch** *m* mouseholing from house to house; **~ei** *f* wine--cellar; cellarage; **~fenster** *n* cellar--window; **~geschoß** *n* underground--story, basement; **~loch** *n* air-hole; wretched underground dwelling; **~meister** *m* butler; (*Kloster*) cellarer; **~wechsel** *m* accomodation bill; **~wohnung** *f* underground dwelling.

Kellner *m*, (**~in** *f*) waiter (waitress); barman, *Am* bartender (barmaid); (*Schiff, Flugzeug*) steward (stewardess).

Kelte *m* Celt, Kelt.

Kelter *f* winepress; **~n** *tr* to press, to tread (grapes).

Kem(e)nate *f* bower.

kenn|bar *a* knowable, distinguishable; (*an Zeichen*) marked; **~buchstabe** *m* indicating letter, identification letter; **~en** *irr tr* to know; to be acquainted with; *nicht ~~* to be unaware of; *sehr wohl ~~* to be fully aware of; *jdn durch u. durch ~~* to know s. o. intimately; *dem Namen nach ~~* to know by name; *nur oberflächlich ~~* to know but slightly; *sich vor Wut nicht mehr ~~* to be quite beside o. s. with rage; *sich gut aus~~* to know the ropes; *Unterschiede ~~* to discriminate; *ich kenne meine Pappenheimer* I know my customers; *etw in- u. auswendig ~~* to know s. th. inside out; **~~lernen** *tr* to become acquainted with, to meet; to get to know, to become familiar (*od* conversant) with; *Sie werden mich noch ~~lernen!* I'll show you! I will make you pay for it! **~er** *m* connoisseur, professional; critical judge; (*Sachverständiger*) expert; (*Autorität*) authority; **~~auge** *n*, **~~blick** *m* glance of a connoisseur; **~~miene** *f* air of a connoisseur; **~feuer** *n* identification beacon; **~karte** *f* identity card; **~~nzwang** *m* compulsory identity passes *pl*; **~nummer** *f* identification number; **~tlich** *a* recognizable; (*unterscheidbar*) distinguishable; (*bezeichnet*) marked; (*bemerkbar*) perceptible; (*deutlich*) clear,distinct; (*in die Augen fallend*) conspicuous; *~~ machen* to mark, to characterize; *sich ~~ machen* to make o. s. known; **~tnis** *f* (*Wissen, Bekanntschaft*) knowledge; (*Auskunft*) information; (*Nachricht*) intelligence; (*Beobachtung*) notice, observation; (*Vorstellung*) notion; (*Bekanntschaft*) acquaintance; (*Erfahrung*) experience; (*Kenntnisbereich*) cognizance; *~tnisse f pl* (*Talente*) attainments *pl*; (*Fertigkeiten*) accomplishments *pl*; (*Wissen*) knowledge; learning; *oberflächliche ~~* smattering; *~~ des Verfahrens* know-how; *jdn in ~~ setzen* to inform s. o. of, to advise, to let know; *~~ nehmen von* to take not(ic)e of; *nehmen Sie zur ~~, daß* . . . I want you to bear in mind that . . .; *~~ erhalten* to hear, to learn, to be informed, to (be given to) understand; *sich von etw ~~ verschaffen* to obtain information about s. th.; *~tnisse vermitteln* to convey knowledge; **~~arm** *a* ignorant; **~~nahme** *f* information, notice, cognizance; *zur ~~nahme* for information; **~~reich** *a* well-informed; (*gelehrt*) learned; (*erfahren*) experienced; (*bewandert*) versed; **~wort** *n* (*Chiffre*) cipher; *mil* password; (*Wahlspruch*) motto; *com* code word; **~zahl** *f* characteristic value (*od* number), coefficient, constant; **~zeichen** *n* sign, token; (*Auszeichnung*) special (*od* distinguishing) mark; (*Abzeichen*) badge; (*Unterscheidung*) characteristic, criterion; (*Anzeichen*) symptom; (*Stempel*) stamp; (*Merkmal*) indication; (*Beschreibung*) specifications *pl*; (*Eigentumszeichen*) ear-mark; *mot* identification mark, registration number, identity plate; **~zeichnen** *tr* to mark, to stamp; to characterize; to ear-mark; to distinguish; **~zeichnung** *f* marking; character; sign, mark; **~~sfarbe** *f* sighting colo(u)r; **~ziffer** *f math* index; characteristic; *com* code number; reference number; (*Schlüssel*) key.

*

kentern *itr* to capsize, to cant, to turn turtle, to heel over; to overturn, to list.

Keramik *f* (*Kunst*) ceramics *pl mit sing*; (*Tonwaren*) pottery, ceramics *pl*.
Kerb|e *f* notch, score, nick, groove, slot; *in die gleiche ~e hauen* to co-operate with s. o.; **~el** *m bot* chervil; **~en** *tr* to notch, to groove, to indent; (*Münze*) to mill; **~holz** *n* notched stick, tally; *etw auf dem ~~ haben* to have s. th. on o.'s score; to have much to answer for; **~messer** *n* notching-knife; **~schnitzerei** *f* chip-carving; **~tier** *n* insect; **~~kunde** *f* entomology.
Kerker *m* gaol, jail, prison; **~haft** *f* imprisonment; **~mauern** *f pl* prison walls *pl*; **~meister** *m* jailer.
Kerl *m* fellow; *fam* chap, beggar, *Am* guy; (*Junge*) lad; (*durchtriebener*) blade; *ein anständiger ~* a decent sort of a fellow; *elender ~* wretch; *ganzer ~* fine fellow, *Am fam* topnotcher, *sl* swell egg; *sie ist ein netter ~* she is a dear; *gemeiner ~* low fellow; *grober ~* churl, rude fellow; *kleiner ~* tot; *pfiffiger ~* sly dog; *schlechter ~* scoundrel, rogue; **~chen** *n* little fellow; (*Gernegroß*) whipper-snapper.
Kern *m* (*Frucht, Getreide, fig*) kernel; (*Getreide*) grain; (*Obst~*) pip; (*Kirsch~*) stone; (*~haus*) core; (*Baum, Salat*) heart; (*Mark, fig*) pith, marrow; *fig* (*Hauptsache*) gist, marrow, heart, pith, core, essence, flower, pick, essential point, root of a matter; (*Seife*) curd; washing soap; (*Kanone*) bore; *tech, el* core; *phys* nucleus (*pl* nuclei); (*Atomkern*) nucleus of the atom; **~abstand** *m* internuclear distance; **~achse** *f* nuclear axis; **~anhäufung** *f* accumulation of nuclei; **~aufbau** *m* nuclear structure, nuclear synthesis; **~bewegung** *f* nuclear motion; **~bombardierung** *f* nuclear bombardment; **~chemie** *f* nuclear chemistry; **~deutsch** *a* thoroughly German; **~durchmesser** *m* nuclear diameter; **~eisen** *n el* core iron; **~elektron** *n* nuclear electron; **~energie** *f* nuclear energy; **~explosion** *f* nuclear explosion; **~fächer** *n pl* basic subjects, *Am* core-curriculum; **~färbung** *f* (*Mikroskopie*) nuclear staining; **~fest** *a* very firm, very solid; **~forscher** *m* nuclear scientist; **~forschung** *f* nuclear research; **~frisch** *a* quite fresh; **~frucht** *f* (seed) fruit, pome; **~gedanke** *m* central thought; **~gehäuse** *n* core; **~gesund** *a* thoroughly sound (*od* healthy); **~haft, ~ig** *a* full of pips; (*Alkohol*) full; (*Leder*) compact; (*kräftig*) vigorous, strong, stout, solid; (*markig*) pithy, kernelly; **~haus** *n* core; **~holz** *n* heart(-)wood; **~igkeit** *f* strength; pithiness; (*Leder*) ful(l)-ness, body; **~isomerie** *f* nuclear isomerism; **~kettenreaktion** *f* nuclear chain reaction; **~körper** *m* nucleolus; **~kräfte** *f pl* nuclear forces *pl*; **~ladung** *f* nuclear charge; *mil* main charge; **~~szahl** *f* atomic number; **~leder** *n* bend leather; **~lehre** *f* nucleonics *pl mit sing*; **~los** *a* without a nucleus, anucleate; **~masse** *f* nuclear substance; **~mehl** *n* best grade of flour, firsts *pl*; **~membran** *f* nuclear membrane; **~munition** *f* armour-piercing ammunition; **~oberfläche** *f* nuclear surface; **~obst** *n* kernel- (*od* stone) fruit; **~physik** *f* nuclear physics *pl mit sing*; **~~er** *m* nuclear physicist; **~problem** *n* root problem; **~punkt** *m* essential (*od* chief) point, nucleus; **~reaktion** *f* nuclear reaction; **~~sbrenner** *m* nuclear reaction pile; **~salz** *n* rock salt; **~schatten** *m* complete (*od* deep) shadow, umbra; **~schuß** *m* point-blank shot; **~schwingung** *f* nuclear vibration; **~segment** *n* nuclear segment; **~seife** *f* curd (*od* grain *od* household) soap; **~spaltung** *f* nuclear fission; **~~sprodukt** *n* fission product; **~spruch** *m* pithy sentence; **~stück** *n* principal item; **~substanz** *f* nuclear substance; **~teilung** *f* nuclear division; nuclear segmentation; **~theorie** *f* nuclear theory; **~truppen** *f pl* picked (*od* choice-)troops *pl*; **~umwandlung** *f* nuclear transformation; **~~sanlage** *f* nuclear reactor; **~verschmelzung** *f* nuclear fusion; **~wolle** *f* prime wool; **~zerfall** *m* nuclear disintegration; **~zertrümmerung** *f* nuclear fission, nuclear disintegration; **~zone** *f* nuclear zone.
Kerze *f* candle; (*dünne*) taper; *mot* sparking plug, *Am* spark plug; **~ngerade** *a* bolt-upright, straight as a dart; **~nleuchter** *n* candlestick; **~nlicht** *n* candle-light; **~nschlüssel** *m mot* spark plug wrench; **~nstärke** *f* candle power.
kess *a fam* smart; cunning.
Kessel *m* kettle; (*Dampf~*) boiler; (*Vertiefung*) hollow; (*großer*) ca(u)ldron; (*Becken*) basin; (*Jagd*) kennel; (*Krater*) crater; (*Tal~*) gorge; (*Landsenke*) depression; (*Weihwasser~*) holy-water vase; *mil*(*Einschließung*) pocket of encircled troops; **~anlage** *f* boiler plant; **~druck** *m* boiler pressure; **~flicker** *m* tinker; **~förmig** *a* kettle-shaped; **~haken** *m* pot-hanger; **~haus** *n* boiler-house; **~pauke** *f* kettledrum; **~schlacht** *f* battle of encirclement; **~schmied** *m* boiler-maker; (*Kupferschmied*) coppersmith; brazier; **~stein** *m* fur, boiler scale; **~~lösemittel** *n* disincrustant; **~treiben** *n* circular beat; (*Treibjagd*) battue; *fig* dragnet raid; **~wagen** *m rail* tank car (*od* wag(g)on); *mot* (fuel) tanker; fuel truck.

*

Kette *f* chain; (*Berg~*) range; (*Folge*) train, series; (*Gewebe*) warp; (*Rebhühner*) covey; *aero* flight; *el* cell, element, circuit; (*Zwang*) bondage; (*Gefangenschaft*) fetters *pl*; (*Sperr~*) cordon; (*Blumen~*) garland, festoon; (*Hals~*) necklet, neck-chain; (*Wagen*) vehicle track; *an die ~ legen* to chain up; *jdn in ~n legen* to put s. o. in irons; **~n** *tr* (*verbinden*) to link, to join, to connect; (*an~~*) to chain; to tie (to); *sich an jdn ~~* to attach o. s. to; **~nantrieb** *m* chain drive; **~nbrief** *m* chain-letter; **~nbruch** *m math* continued fraction; **~nbrücke** *f* suspension-bridge; **~nfahrzeug** *n* track (laying) vehicle; **~nführer** *m aero* flight leader; **~ngelenk, ~nglied** *n* link (*od* member) of a chain; **~ngeschäft** *n* multiple (*Am* chain) store; **~ngetriebe** *n* chain-gear; **~nhandel** *m* chain-trade; black-marketing; **~nhund** *m* watch-dog; *aero* wingman; **~nkasten** *m* gear (*od* chain) case; *mar* chain-locker; **~nkeil** *m aero* wedge; **~nkrad** *n mot* half-track motorcycle; **~nkugel** *f* chain-shot; **~nladen** *m* multiple (*Am* chain) store; **~npanzer** *m* chain-mail; coat of mail; **~nrad** *n* (*Fahrrad*) sprocket wheel; (*Uhr*) chain wheel; **~nraucher** *m* chain-smoker; **~nreaktion** *f* chain reaction; **~~sbrenner** *m* chain-reaction pile; **~nschutz** *m* chain guard; **~nspanner** *m* track-connecting tool; **~nstich** *m* chain (*od* warp) stitch; **~nsträfling** *m* convict confined in chains; **~~e** *m pl Am* chain-gang.
Ketzer *m* heretic; **~ei** *f* heresy; **~gericht** *n* inquisition; **~isch** *a* heretical; **~verbrennung** *f* burning of heretics, auto-da-fé; **~verfolgung** *f* persecution of heretics.
keuch|en *itr* to pant, to gasp; **~husten** *m* whooping-cough.
Keule *f* club, cudgel; (*Knüttel*) bludgeon; *sport* Indian club; (*Mörser~*) pestle; (*Fleisch*) leg, joint; (*Geflügel*) drumstick; (*Frosch, Wild*) hind-leg; (*Radar*) lobe; **~närmel** *m* leg-of-mutton sleeve; **~nförmig** *a* club-shaped, clavate; **~nschlag** *m* blow with a club; *fig* terrible blow; **~nschwingen** *n sport* club-swinging.
keusch *a* chaste, pure; (*bescheiden*) modest; (*tugendhaft*) virtuous; (*unschuldig*) innocent; **~heit** *f* chastity; (*Schamhaftigkeit*) pudicity; (*Reinheit*) purity; (*Unschuld*) innocence; **~~sgelübde** *n* vow of chastity.
Kicher|erbse *f* chickpea; **~n** *itr* to titter, to giggle; (*Erwachsene*) to chuckle, to snigger; *Am* to snicker; **~n** *n* giggle, tittering; chuckle.
Kickstarter *m* kick starter.
Kiebitz *m* pe(e)wit, lapwing; (*Zuschauer*) looker-on, kibitzer.
Kiefer *m* jaw (bone), maxilla; (*von Tieren*) chop; **~** *f* pine, Scotch fir (*od* pine); **~ngehölz** *n* pine-grove; **~knochen** *m anat* jaw-bone; **~nnadel** *f* pine needle; **~nspanner** *m* pine-moth; **~(n)zapfen** *m* pine-cone.
Kiel *m* (*Feder~*) quill; *mar* keel; **~holen** *itr* to careen; (*Strafe*) to keelhaul; **~oben** *adv* bottom up; **~raum** *m* hold; **~wasser** *n* wake, wash, dead-water; **~~strömung** *f* backwash.
Kieme *f* gill; **~natmung** *f* gill breathing.
Kien *m* resinous pine; **~apfel** *m* pine cone; **~fackel** *f* pine(-wood) torch; **~holz** *n* pine(-wood); **~ruß** *m* pine soot; **~span** *m* chip of pine-wood; (*Fackel*) pine-torch.
Kiepe *f* back-basket.
Kies *m* gravel; (*grober*) shingle; (*Schwefel~*) pyrites; **~boden** *m* gravelly soil; **~grube** *f* gravel-pit; **~haltig** *a* pyritiferous, gravelly; **~sand** *m* gravelly sand; **~schicht** *f* layer of gravel; **~weg** *m* gravel-walk.
Kiesel *m*, **~stein** *m* pebble; *min* flint; (*Erde*) silica, silex; **~artig** *a* flinty siliceous; **~erde** *f* silica; **~gur** *m* diatomaceous earth; **~hart** *a* hard as flint; **~ig** *a* siliceous, flinty, pebbly; **~säure** *f* silicic acid; **~stein** *m* pebble gravelstone; flint; **~verbindung** *f* silicate.
Kikeriki cock-a-doodle-doo.
Kilo|(gramm) *n* kilogram(me) (= 2.2046 pounds); **~~kalorie** *f* kilogram(me) calorie (*od* calory); **~~meter** *m* kilogrammetre, -ter (= 7.2334 foot-pounds); **~hertz** *n radio* kilocycle; **~meter** *m* kilometre, -er (= 3280.8 feet); **~~fresser** *m* road-hog; **~~heft** *n rail* mil(e)age ticket; **~~stein** *m* milestone, kilometre stone; **~~zähler** *m mot* mil(e)age recorder, (h)odometer; **~watt** *n* kilowatt; **~~stunde** *f* kilowatt-hour.
Kimm *f* horizon; (*Schiffsbauch*) bilge; **~e** *f* (*Gewehr*) notch of the backsight; (*Rand*) edge, border; (*Vertiefung*) notch; (*Faß*) chime; *~~ u. Korn* ring and bead sights; **~ung** *f* mirage.
Kind *n* child, *fam* kid; (*kleines ~*) baby, babe, tot; (*unmündiges*) infant; (*verächtlich*) brat; *uneheliches ~* child born out of wedlock; *~ der Liebe* illegitimate child; *~ des Todes* dead man; doomed man; *totgeborenes ~* still-born child; *Berliner ~* native of Berlin; *von ~ an* from a child; from infancy; *mit ~ u. Kegel* with bag and baggage; *~ u. Kindeskinder* children and grandchildren; *an ~es Statt annehmen* to adopt; *das ~ mit dem Bad ausschütten*

to kill the goose with the golden egg; *sich wie ein ~ freuen* to be as pleased as Punch; *ein ~ bekommen* to be delivered of a child; *kein ~ mehr bekommen* to be past child-bearing; *kein ~ mehr sein* to be past childhood; *ein ~ erwarten* to be with child, to be in the family way; *ein ~ aus der Taufe heben* to stand sponsor to a child; *das ~ beim rechten Namen nennen* to call a spade a spade; **~bett** *n* childbed, confinement; *ins ~~ kommen* to be brought to bed; **~~fieber** *n* puerperal fever; **~chen** *n* little child, baby, tot.

*

Kinder *n pl* children; *~, gehen wir!* let's go, folks! *aus ~n werden Leute* boys will be men; *gebrannte ~ fürchten das Feuer* a burnt child dreads the fire; *~ u. Narren sagen die Wahrheit* children and fools tell truth; **~arbeit** *f* child labo(u)r; **~ball** *m* children's ball; **~beihilfe** *f* children's allowance; **~bekleidung** *f* kiddies' dress; **~bett** *n* cot, crib; **~betreuung** *f* baby-sitting; **~bewahranstalt** *f* children's home; crèche, *Am* day nursery; **~bibliothek** *f* children's library; **~ei** *f* childishness; (*Streich*) childish trick; (*Kleinigkeit*) trifle; **~~en** *f pl* nonsense; **~ermäßigung** *f* reduction for children; **~erziehung** *f* education of children; **~fahrkarte** *f rail* children's ticket; **~fest** *n* children's party; **~frau** *f* (dry-)nurse; nanny; **~fräulein** *n* nursery-governess; **~freund** *m* friend of children; **~fürsorge** *f* child welfare; **~garten** *m* nursery-school, kindergarten; **~gärtnerin** *f* kindergarten teacher, kindergartner; **~geschrei** *n* crying of children; **~glaube** *m* childish belief; **~gottesdienst** *m* children's service; **~häubchen** *n* child's cap; **~heilstätte** *f* infant asylum, children's hospital; **~hort** *m* nursery-school, kindergarten; **~jahre** *n pl* childhood, infancy; **~klapper** *f* rattle-box; **~kleid** *n* child's dress; **~krankheit** *f* disease of children; *~~en fig Am* teething troubles *pl;* **~krippe** *f* crèche, *Am* day nursery; **~lähmung** *f* infantile paralysis, polio (-myelitis); **~landverschickung** *f* evacuation of children to the country; **~lätzchen** *n* bib, *Am* eating apron; **~lehre** *f* catechization; **~leicht** *a* very easy, fool-proof, child's play, *Am* as easy as falling off a log; **~lieb** *a* fond of children; **~lied** *n* nursery-rhyme; **~los** *a* childless; **~losigkeit** *f* childlessness; (*Unfruchtbarkeit*) barrenness; **~mädchen** *n* nurse(ry)-maid; **~mahlzeit** *f* child's meal; **~märchen** *n* children's tale; **~mehl** *n* infant food; **~mord** *m*, **~mörder** *m* (**-in** *f*) infanticide; **~narr** *m* one who dotes on children; **~possen** *f pl* childish tricks *pl*; **~raub** *m* kidnapping; **~reich** *a* prolific; **~schreck** *m* bogyman; **~schuh** *m* child's shoe; *die ~~e ablegen* to put off childish ways; *noch in den ~~en stecken* to be still in leading strings; **~schule** *f* infant-school; **~schürze** *f* pinafore, child's apron; **~spiel** *n* children's play (*od* game); (*Kleinigkeit*) trifle; **~~platz** *m* children's playground; **~~zeug** *n* children's toys *pl*; **~sprache** *f* children's prattle; **~sterblichkeit** *f* infantile mortality; **~stube** *f* nursery; *ihm fehlt die ~~* he has no manners; **~waage** *f* baby scale; **~wagen** *m* perambulator, *fam* pram, *Am* (baby-)carriage; **~wäsche** *f* baby-linen; **~zeit** *f* childhood; **~zimmer** *n* nursery, *Am* play-room; **~zulage** *f* child(ren's) allowance, dependency allowance for children.

Kindes|alter *n* infancy, child's age; **~annahme** *f* adoption; **~aussetzung** *f* exposure of a child; **~beine** *n pl*: *von ~~n an* from a child, from infancy; **~kind** *n* grandchild; **~kinder** *n pl* children's children; **~liebe** *f* filial love; **~mißhandlung** *f* ill-treatment of a child; **~nöte** *f pl* labo(u)r (of childbirth); *in ~~n sein* to labo(u)r with child; **~pflicht** *f* filial duty.

Kind|heit *f* childhood, infancy, boyhood; **~isch** *a* childish, puerile; (*faselnd*) doting; *~~ werden* to doat, to dote; **~lich** *a* childlike; (*gegenüber den Eltern*) filial; (*unschuldig*) innocent; (*naiv*) simple-minded; **~~keit** *f* childlike nature (*od* simplicity); **~skopf** *m* childish person; (*Dummkopf*) oaf; **~smord** *m* child slaying; **~spech** *n* meconium; **~staufe** *f* christening.

Kine|matograph *m* cinematograph, moving-picture apparatus; **~~isch** *a* cinematographic(al); **~tik** *f* kinetics *pl mit sing.*

Kinkerlitzchen *n pl* knickknacks *pl.*

Kinn *n* chin; *vorstehendes* (*zurücktretendes*) *~* protruding (receding) chin; **~backe** *f* (**~~n** *m*), **~lade** *f* jaw(-bone); *anat* maxilla, mandible; **~bart** *m* imperial; **~haken** *m* (*Boxen*) uppercut; **~kette** *f* (*Pferd*) curb(-chain); **~riemen** *m* chin-strap.

Kino *n* cinema, moving- (*od* motion-) -picture theatre, the pictures *pl*, the screen, picture-house; (*Tonfilm*) talkies *pl*; *Am* movie(-)house, movies *pl*, show; *billiges ~ Am* nickelodeon; *~ für Autofahrer Am* drive-in (motion-picture theater); *ins ~ gehen* to go to the pictures; **~begeistert** *a* movie-struck; **~besuch** *m* motion-picture theatre attendance, *Am* movie attendance, *fam* movie-going; **~~er** *m* cinema-goer; picture-goer, film-goer, *Am* movie-goer; *die ~~er* movie audience; **~enthusiast, ~freund** *m* film- (*od* movie-)fan; **~film** *m* cinema (*od* movie *od* motion-picture) film, cinefilm; **~leinwand** *f* (cinema) screen; **~narr** *m* picture (*od Am* movie)-fiend; **~orgel** *f* cinema organ; **~reklame** *f* cinema publicity, screen advertising; **~stück** *n* photoplay; **~tonverstärker** *m* amplifier for soundfilm recording; **~vorraum** *m* lobby of a moving-picture theatre; **~vorstellung** *f* (cinema-) show, the pictures *pl.*

Kiosk *m* (*Zeitungsstand*) kiosk, *Am* (news)stand.

Kipp|e *f* tilt; edge; brink; (*Schaukelbrett*) seesaw; (*Wendepunkt*) *fig* hinge; (*Zigarren-, Zigarettenstummel*) stub, stump, fag-end, *Am* butt; *auf der ~~* atilt; *fig* on the verge of disaster, (to be) in a critical position; *com* on the brink of ruin; **~(e)lig** *a* tottering, shaky; **~en** *tr* to tilt, to tip (over *od* up); *itr* to tip, to tilt, to dump, to topple over, to upset; to lose o.'s balance; (*nach der Seite*) *aero* to spin; (*nach vorn*) *aero* to stall; **~ensammeln** *n Am* buttsnatching; **~er** *m* tipper, dumper; *mot* tipping truck, tipping wag(g)on; **~hebelschalter** *m* tumbler switch; **~karren** *m* tipcart, dumpcart; **~lore** *f* truck-tipper, tipping car; **~pflug** *m* two-way plough (*od Am* plow); **~schalter** *m* tumbler switch; **~sicherung** *f aero* stabilizer; **~vorrichtung** *f* tipping device; **~wagen** *m* tipper, dump car; tipping truck.

Kirche *f* church; (*Dissidenten*) chapel, preaching house; (*Tempel*) temple; (*Bischofs~*) cath dral; (*Gotteshaus*) house of God; (*Andachtsraum*) sanctuary; (*kirchliche Gemeinschaft*) church; (*Gottesdienst*) divine service; *anglikanische ~* Church of England; *englische Hoch~* High Church (of England); *in der ~* at church; *in die ~* to church.

Kirchen|ältester *m* presbyter; churchwarden, elder; **~bann** *m* excommunication; (*gegen e-n Staat*) interdict; *in den ~~ tun* to excommunicate; **~bau** *m* construction of a church; **~besuch** *m* attendance at church; **~buch** *n* parish register; **~buße** *f* penance; **~chor** *m* (church-)choir; **~dach** *n* roof of the church; **~diener** *m* sexton, sacristan; church officer; **~fahne** *f* banner, gonfanon; **~feindlich** *a* anticlerical; **~fenster** *n* church-window; **~fürst** *m* prince of the church; **~gebet** *n* church-prayer, common prayer; **~gemeinde** *f* parish; **~gesang** *m* (church-)hymn; (*Gemeinde*) congregational singing; **~geschichte** *f* church history; **~gesetz** *n* canon law; **~gestühl** *n* pews *pl*; **~gewänder** *n pl* ministerial garments *pl*; **~glaube** *m* creed; **~glocke** *f* church-bell; **~gut** *n* church property; **~jahr** *n* ecclesiastical year; **~konzert** *n* church-concert; **~lehre** *f* church-doctrine; **~licht** *n* altar-candle; *fig er ist kein ~~ fam* he is no great shakes; he is dull; **~lied** *n* hymn; **~maus** *f*: *sie ist so arm wie e-e ~~* she is as poor as a church-mouse; **~musik** *f* sacred music; **~ordnung** *f* liturgy, church-discipline; **~patron** *m* (*Heiliger*) patron saint; **~rat** *m* consistory, church-committee; (*Person*) ecclesiastical council(l)or; **~raub** *m* sacrilege; **~recht** *n* canon(ical) law; **~~lich** *a* canonical; **~reform** *f* church reform; **~register** *n* parish register; **~schändung** *f* profanation of a church; **~schiff** *n* nave; **~seitenschiff** *n* aisle; **~spaltung** *f* schism; **~staat** *m* Papal State(s *pl*); St. Peter's Patrimony; Pontifical State; **~steuer** *f* church-rate, church tax; **~stuhl** *m* (church-) pew; **~uhr** *f* church-clock; **~vater** *m* Father of the Church; **~väter** *m pl* the Early Fathers *pl*; **~vorsteher** *m* churchwarden; **~zucht** *f* ecclesiastical discipline.

Kirch|gang *m* way to church; church-going; **~gänger** *m* (**~in** *f*) church-goer; **~hof** *m* (*um die Kirche*) churchyard; (*Begräbnisplatz*) cemetery, graveyard, burial-ground; **~~smauer** *f* churchyard wall; **~~sforte** *f* churchyard wicket-gate; **~~sruhe** *f* peace of the churchyard; **~~stor** *n* churchyard gate; **~lein** *n* chapel, small church; **~lich** *a* ecclesiastical, *Am* churchly; (*geistlich*) spiritual; (*religiös*) religious; (*rechtlich*) canonical; (*Geistliche betreffend*) clerical; *~~ gesinnt* devout, religious; *~~e Würdenträger* Lords Spiritual; *~~ getraut* married according to the rites of the church; *~~es Begräbnis* church-burial; **~~keit** *f* religiosity; attachment to the church; **~spiel** *n* parish; **~sprengel** *m* diocese; **~turm** *m* church-tower; (*spitz*) steeple, spire; **~~spolitik** *f* local politics *pl*; **~weih(e)** *f* consecration (*od* dedication) of a church; (*Volksfest*) parish fair, country wake.

Kirmes *f* church-fair, kermis, kermess; country wake.

kirre *a* tame; (*leicht zu behandeln*) tractable; **~n** *tr:* (*~ machen*) to tame, to domesticate; (*ködern*) to bait, to decoy, to allure.

Kirsch|baum *m* cherry-tree; **~branntwein** *m* cherry-brandy; **~e** *f* cherry; *saure ~e* morello; *mit ihm ist nicht gut ~en essen* he is a bad man to monkey with; **~farben** *a* cherry-colo(u)red;

~kern *m* cherry-stone; **~kuchen** *m* cherry-cake; **~rot** *a* cherry-red; **~saft** *m* cherry-juice; **~stiel** *m* cherry-stalk; **~wasser** *n* kirsch.

Kissen *n* cushion; (*Kopf~*) pillow; (*Polster*) bolster; (*Unterlage*) pad; **~bezug, ~überzug** *m* pillow-slip, pillow-case; cushion cover.

Kiste *f* box, chest; packing-case; (*Latten~*) crate; (*Wein~*) case; (*Koffer*) trunk; (*Auto, Flugzeug*) *fam Am* jalopy; **~ndeckel** *m* lid of a box; **~nholz** *n* wood for boxes; **~nverschlag** *m* crate.

Kitsch *m* (*Gemälde*) daub; (*Waren*) trumpery, rubbish, worthless finery, trash; (*Theater, Film*) *Am fam* sob-stuff, twaddle; (*törichtes Gerede*) piffle, *Am sl* hooey, baloney; **~ig** *a* trashy, trumpery, shoddy, showy, gaudy; (*Bilder*) dauby.

Kitt *m* cement, lute, mastic; (*Glaser~*) putty; **~en** *tr* to cement; to putty, to lute; (*leimen*) to glue; **~masse** *f* cementing composition.

Kittel *m* (child's) frock, coat; (*Arbeits~*) smock; overall.

Kitz(e) *n* (*f*) (*Zicklein*) kid; (*Reh*) fawn.

Kitzel *m* tickling, tickle; (*Jucken*) itching; (*Gelüste*) longing, desire; **~ig** *a* ticklish; (*bedenklich*) nice, delicate, difficult; **~n** *tr* to tickle; (*die Sinne*) to gratify; *es kitzelt mich* I feel a tickling; *jdn unter den Sohlen ~~* to tickle the soles of s. o.'s feet; *jdn am Arm ~~* to tickle s. o.'s arm.

Klabautermann *m mar* hobgoblin, bogy(man), evil spirit.

Kladde *f* waste-book; rough copy; (*Tagebuch*) log; day-book.

Kladderadatsch *m* (*Geklirr*) clang, clash; (*Zus.bruch*) catastrophe, ruin.

klaffen *itr* to gape, to yawn; (*sich spalten*) to split; (*Riß*) to crack, to chap; (*Türen*) to be ajar.

kläff|en *itr* to bark, to yelp; (*lärmend äußern*) to clamo(u)r, to brawl; **~er** *m* yelping dog; (*Mensch*) peevish (*od* noisy) person, brawler, wrangler, *Am sl* yap.

Klafter *f* fathom; (*Holz*) cord (wood); **~n** *tr* to fathom; to cord up.

Klag|abweisung *f jur* dismissal of an action; (*Säumnis des Klägers*) non-suit; **~anspruch** *m* claim; **~antrag** *m* application, endorsement of claim; **~bar** *a* actionable, enforceable; *~~ werden gegen jdn* to sue s. o. at law (*wegen* for): **~beantwortung** *f* statement of defence; **~begründung** *f* statement of claim; **~e** *f jur* (legal) action (law)suit, complaint, charge; (*Reklamation*) claim; (*Beschwerde*) complaint, grievance; (*Anklage*) accusation; (*Wehklage*) lament; *~~ u. Wider~~* charge and countercharge; *e-e ~~ abweisen* to dismiss a case; *e-e ~~ anstrengen* (*od einreichen*) to bring an action against, to institute legal proceedings against; *e-e ~~ stützen auf* to found an action upon; *e-e ~~ kostenpflichtig abweisen* to dismiss a claim with costs; **~egeschrei** *n* loud lamentation; **~elaut** *m* plaintive tone; **~elied** *n* dirge, funeral song; lamentation; *ein ~~ anstimmen* to raise a lamentation; **~emauer** *f* wailing wall; **~en** *itr* to complain (*über* of), (*jammern*) to lament; (*weh~~*) to wail; to moan; (*murren*) to grumble, *Am sl* to beef; (*wimmern*) to whimper; *jur* to bring an action against s. o. for s. th., to sue s. o. for, to go to law; *auf Schadenersatz ~~* to sue for damages; *im Armenrecht ~~* to sue in forma pauperis; *auf Scheidung ~~* to file a petition for divorce; *auf Zahlung ~~* to sue for recovery (*von* of); *sein Leid ~~* to pour out o.'s troubles to; *um e-n Verstorbenen ~~* to mourn for; **~eruf** *m* plaintive cry; **~eweib** *n* hired female mourner; **~epunkt** *m jur* count; (*Ursachen*) cause of complaint; **~rücknahme** *f jur* withdrawal of suit; **~schrift** *jur* plaint, writ; declaration; **~zustellung** *f* service of process.

Kläg|er(in) *m* (*f*) *jur* plaintiff, complainant; (*Ehescheidung*) petitioner; *öffentlicher ~~* (public) prosecutor; **~erisch** *a* of the plaintiff; *~erische Partei* complaining party; *der ~erische Anwalt* the counsel for the prosecution; **~lich** *a* (*klagend*) plaintive; (*beklagenswert*) lamentable, deplorable; (*jämmerlich*) wretched, pitiable, poor; **~~keit** *f* wretchedness, deplorableness, pitifulness, poorness; plaintiveness.

klamm *a* close, tight, narrow; (*feuchtkalt*) clammy; (*erstarrt*) numb; (*knapp*) short, scarce; *~ f* ravine, glen.

Klammer *f* (*Krampe*) clamp, cramp, brace, clincher; (*Schnalle*) clasp; (*Niete*) rivet; (*Büro~*) clip; (*Heft~*) staple; (*Wäsche~*) (clothes-)peg, clothes-pin; (*Satzzeichen*) parenthesis, (*eckige*) bracket; *in ~n setzen* to put in parentheses; **~n** *itr* to clamp, to cramp, to clasp; (*befestigen*) to fasten; (*vernieten*) to rivet; *sich ~~ an* to cling to; *sport* to clinch; *sich an e-n Strohhalm ~~* to catch at a straw.

Klamotten *f pl fam* (*Plunder*) trash; (*Habe*) belongings *pl*, *fam* duds *pl*.

Klampe *f* clamp, clasp, cramp; *mar* cleat.

Klampfe *f mus* guitar.

Klang *m* sound; (*der Glocken*) ringing; (*Münze*) ring, chink; (*Geklirr*) clang; (*~art*) tone, note; (*Brausen*) peal; (*Tonfolge*) strains *pl*; *keinen guten ~ haben* to be held in bad repute; *ohne Sang u. ~* unceremoniously; (*heimlich*) secretly, clandestinely; *ein heller* (*dumpfer*) *~* a clear (dull) ring (*od* sound); *schriller ~* discordant note; **~bild** *n* sound pattern; **~~veränderung** *f* change in sound impression; **~blende** *f* tone control; tonalizer; **~farbe** *f* timbre, quality (of a sound), tonality; **~~nregelung** *f radio* tone control; **~fülle** *f* sonority, sound volume; **~getreu** *a* of high fidelity; **~lehre** *f* acoustics *pl mit sing*; **~los** *a* toneless, soundless; (*stumm*) mute; (*dumpf*) hollow; (*nicht betont*) unaccented; **~regler** *m* tone control; **~stufe** *f* interval; **~voll** *a* sonorous, full-sounding; **~welle** *f* sound-wave; **~wirkung** *f* acoustics *pl mit sing*; sound effect.

Klapp|bett *n* folding (*od* camp) bed; **~deckel** *m* spring (*od* hinged) cover; **~e** *f* flap; (*Sperr~~*) trap; (*Deckel*) lid; (*Schieber, mus Dämpfer*) damper; (*Blasinstrument*) key, stop; (*Tisch*) flap, leaf; *tele* annunciator; *tech, bot, zoo* (*Ventil*) valve; (*Briefumschlag*) flap; *fam* (*Bett*) bed; *sl* (*Mund*) mouth, *fam* gab; *zwei Fliegen mit e-r ~~ schlagen* to kill two birds with one stone; **~en** *tr* to clap, to flap, to fold, to tilt; *itr* (*in Ordnung sein*) to click, to work well, to tally; (*zus.~~*) to collapse, to break down, to cave in; *in die Höhe ~~* to tuck up; *es hat alles geklappt* everything clicked; *zum ~~ kommen* to come to the push, to come to fruition; *es klappt nichts* everything is going wrong; **~~betätigung** *f aero* flap-control; **~~schrank** *m tele* switchboard; **~~ventil** *n* clack (*od* flap) valve; **~~verschluß** *m* clack closure; **~flügel** *m aero* folding wing; **~horn** *n mus* key-bugle; **~hut** *m* opera (*od* crush)-hat; **~kamera** *f* folding camera; **~leiter** *f* folding ladder; **~messer** *n* clasp knife, jack-knife; **~pult** *n* folding-desk; **~sitz** *m* flap- (*od* tip-up) seat; **~stuhl** *m* camp stool, folding(-)stool; (*mit Lehne*) folding(-) chair; **~sucher** *m phot* folding finder; **~tisch** *m* folding (*od* flap) table; **~tür** *f* (*Falltür*) trap-door; (*Flügeltür*) folding doors *pl*; **~verdeck** *n mot* collapsible hood, folding hood, folding top.

Klapper *f* rattle; (*Mühle*) clapper; (*Tanz*) castanets *pl*; (*Schnarre*) clapper; **~dürr** *a* (as) lean as a rake; **~frei** *a* rattleproof; **~ig** *a* rattling, clattering; (*mager*) lean, shaky; (*erschöpft*) worn-out; **~kasten** *m* (*Klavier*) tin-kettle; (*Wagen*) rickety wag(g)on, rattletrap, *Am fam* jalopy; **~n** *itr* to rattle; (*Zähne*) to chatter; (*Pantoffeln, Storch*) to clatter; (*Absatz, Mühle*) to clack; **~schlange** *f* rattlesnake, *Am* rattler; **~storch** *m* stork.

Klaps *m* slap, blow, smack; *e-n ~ haben fam* to be balmy; **~en** *tr* to slap.

klar *a* clear; (*hell*) bright; (*deutlich*) distinct; (*durchsichtig*) limpid; *mar* ready; *fig* evident; *~ u. deutlich* plainly, distinctly; *~e Antwort* plain answer; *~ Schiff! mar* clear the deck for action! action stations! *~ zum Tauchen! mar* prepare to submerge! *jdm ~en Wein einschenken* to tell the plain truth (*od* how the matter stands); *sich ~ darüber sein* to realize; *sich ~ sein über* to be clear on; *ich bin mir nicht ~ über* I am hazy about; *nicht im ~en über* uncertain of; **~blickend** *a* clear-sighted; **~heit** *f* clearness; brightness; serenity; purity; distinctness; **~legen, ~stellen** *tr* to clear up; **~machen** *tr* to explain, to make plain to, to bring (*od* drive) home to s. o.; *jdm seinen Standpunkt ~~* to teach s. o. his place; **~meldung** *f* allclear report (*od* signal); **~scheibe** *f mot* de-mister; (*Gasmaske*) anti-dim eyepiece; **~sichtsalbe** *f* antidim compound.

Klär|anlage *f* purification plant; sewerage; **~becken** *n* clearing (*od* settling) basin; **~bottich** *m* settling vat; **~en** *tr* to clear, to clarify, to purify, to defecate; (*reinigen*) to refine; *sich ~~* to clear up, to get clear; (*sich niederschlagen*) to settle; *e-e Frage ~~* to clear up (*od* settle) a question; *damit ist die Sache geklärt* that clears up the matter; **~mittel** *n* clarifier; clarifying agent; **~schlamm** *m* sewage sludge; **~ung** *f* clarification, clearing, clarifying; *fig* elucidation, settling.

Klarinette *f* clarinet.

Klasse *f* class; (*Ordnung, Güte*) order; (*Schiffs~, Dienst~*) rating; (*Stand, Rang*) rank; (*Schule*) form, class, *Am* grade; (*~nzimmer*) classroom, schoolroom; *von derselben ~* of the same type (*od* rank), *Am* in the same class; *erster ~* (*rail*) first class; *der Erste in der ~* the top of his class; *untere, höhere, arbeitende ~n pl* lower, upper, working classes *pl*; *die besitzenden ~n pl* the propertied classes *pl*; *in ~n einteilen* to class(ify); **~nältester** *m* top boy; (*Ordner*) monitor; **~narbeit** *f* classroom-test; **~naufsatz** *m* class-composition; **~nbewußt** *a* class-conscious; **~~sein** *n* class-consciousness; **~nbuch** *n* classbook; (*Tagebuch*) diary; **~ndünkel** *m* caste feeling; class-consciousness; **~neinteilung** *f* classification; **~nerste(r)** *m* (*Schule*) top-boy; **~ngegensatz** *m* class-opposition;

~ngeist *m* caste-feeling; (*Mannschaftsgeist*) teamspirit; **~nhaß** *m* class-hatred; **~njustiz** *f* class-justice; **~nkamerad** *m* classmate; **~nkampf** *m* class-struggle; class-warfare; **~nlehrer** *m* class-teacher, form-master; **~nlektüre** *f* text-book; **~nlotterie** *f* class lottery; **~nspiegel** *m* (*Sitzordnung*) class plan; **~nunterschiede** *m pl* class distinctions *pl*; **~nzimmer** *n* classroom, formroom.

klassi|fizieren *tr* to classify; **~fizierung** *f* classification; **~~splan** *m* classification scheme; **~~svermerk** *m* class-mark; **~ker** *m* classic, standard author; **~sch** *a* classical.

Klatsch *m* (*Schlag*) clap, slap, pop, smack, dab; (*Gerede*) gossip, idle talk, tittle-tattle; (*Lästerung*) scandal; **~base, ~weib** *f* gossip, chatterbox; (*Lästermaul*) scandalmonger; **~e** *f* (*Fliegen~~*) fly-flap; **~en** *itr, tr* (*schlagen*) to clap, to flap, to pop; (*Peitsche*) to smack, to crack; (*Regen*) to splash, to patter; (*plaudern*) to chat; (*plappern*) to prate, to chatter; (*Neuigkeiten*) to gossip; to spread stories; (*üble Nachrede*) to scandalize; *in die Hände ~~* to clap o.'s hands; *Beifall ~~* to applaud; **~erei** *f* gossip; (*Verleumdung*) backbiting, slander; (*Geschwätz*) gabble, *fam* gab; **~haft** *a* gossiping, fond of gossip, chatty, tattling; **~~igkeit** *f* talkativeness; **~maul** *n* telltale, gossip, chatterbox; scandalmonger, talebearer; *den ~mäulern Stoff zum ~en geben* to set the town's tongues wagging; **~mohn** *m*, **~rose** *f* (corn-) poppy; **~naß** *a* sopping (wet); **~nest** *n* nest of gossip; **~sucht** *f* love of gossiping.

klaub|en *tr* to pick (out); (*nörgeln*) to cavil (at, about); (*Worte ~~*) to split hairs; **~erei** *f* hair-splitting.

Klaue *f* (*Pfote*) paw; (*Raubtier*) claw; (*Raubvogel*) talon; (*Huf*) hoof; (*Anker*) fluke; *tech* (*Greifhaken*) clutch, claw, dog; (*schlechte Schrift*) scrawl, poor handwriting; *die ~n des Todes* the jaws of death; **~n** *tr sl* to scrounge, to pilfer, to pinch; **~~kupplung** *f* clutch coupling; **~~seuche** *f*: *Maul-u. ~~seuche* foot-and-mouth disease.

Klause *f* hermitage; (*Zelle*) cell; (*Schlucht*) defile, mountain-pass; **~l** *f* clause, stipulation, proviso.

Klausner *m* hermit, recluse.

Klausur *f* seclusion; (*Prüfungs~*) examination paper; *unter ~~* under supervision.

Klaviatur *f* keyboard, keys *pl*.

Klavier *n* piano; *~ spielen* to play the piano; *am ~* at the piano; *auf dem ~* on the piano; **~abend** *m* piano (forte) recital; **~auszug** *m* piano-score; pianoforte arrangement; **~begleitung** *f* piano-accompaniment; **~konzert** *n* piano-recital; **~lehrer** *m* piano-teacher; **~schule** *f* manual of exercises for the piano; **~sessel** *m* piano-stool; **~spiel** *n* piano-playing; **~spieler(in)** *m* (*f*) piano-player, pianist; **~stimmer** *m* piano-tuner; **~stück** *n* piece of music for the piano; **~stunde** *f* piano-lesson; **~virtuose** *m* virtuoso on the piano; **~vortrag** *m* piano-recital.

Kleb|efalz *m*, **~emarke** *f* adhesive stamp; **~eflugzeug** *n aero mil* shadowing aircraft; **~emittel** *n* adhesive, agglutinant; **~en** *tr* to glue, to paste; (*Marke*) to put, to stick; (*Ohrfeige*) to paste; (*Gummi*) to gum; *itr* (*anhaften*) to stick, to adhere (*an* to); *fig* to cling (*an* to); **~~d** *a* adhesive, adherent, agglutinative; tacky, sticky; **~epflaster** *n* sticking- (*od* adhesive) plaster; (*englisches*) court-plaster; **~er** *m bot* gluten; (*~stoff*) adhesive; (*Mensch*) sticker, gluer; **~(e)rig** *a* sticky, adhesive; (*leimig*) glutinous; (*zähflüssig*) viscid; (*dickflüssig*) ropy; **~~keit** *f* stickiness, viscidity, viscosity; **~erolle** *f*, **~streifen** *m* (roll of) gummed tape, adhesive tape; **~erschicht** *f bot* aleurone layer; **~ezettel** *m* label, *Am* sticker; **~fähig** *a* adhesive; **~kraft** *f* adhesive power; **~kraut** *n* cleavers *pl*; **~mittel** *n*, **~stoff** *m* adhesive (paste), glue; agglutinant, gum, *Am* mucilage; **~wachs** *n* sticking wax.

kleckern *itr* to dribble, to drop (o.'s food).

Klecks *m* blot, blotch, splotch, spot; stain; **~en** *itr* to blot; (*besudeln*) to blotch; (*beflecken*) to blur, to stain; (*schlecht malen*) to daub; (*kritzeln*) to scrawl; **~er** *m* blotter, scribbler; (*Maler*) dauber; **~~ei** *f* scrawling, scribbling; (*Malerei*) daub; **~ig** *a* blotted, splotchy.

Klee *m* clover, trefoil; *weißer ~* shamrock; *spanischer ~* sainfoin; *ewiger ~* alfalfa, lucern; *über den grünen ~ loben* to praise s. th. excessively; **~blatt** *n* clover leaf; *arch* trefoil; (*Irland*) shamrock; *fig* triblet, trio; *ein sauberes ~~* a nice set; **~~förmig** *a* trifoliate; **~feld** *n* field of clover; **~salz** *n* salt of sorrel; **~säure** *f* oxalic acid.

Kleid *n* garment; (*Frauen~, Kinder~*) dress; (*langes Frauen~, Haus~, Talar*) gown; (*loses*) frock; (*Anzug*) suit; (*Kostüm*) costume; (*Kittel, langes Damenjackett*) coat; (*Kleidung*) garb, clothing; (*Tracht*) attire; (*Amts~*) vestment; *bedrucktes ~* printed frock; *buntgemustertes ~* colo(u)rful frock; *fertiges ~* ready-made dress; *festliches ~* festive dress; *sommerliches ~* summer frock; **~en** *tr, r* to clothe (o. s.), to dress (o. s); (*aussehen*) to be becoming to, to look well on, to suit; *sich gut* (*schlecht*) *~~* **to** dress well (badly); *warm* (*leicht*) *gekleidet* warmly (thinly) clad (*od* dressed); *vorteilhaft ~~* to dress to the best advantage; *geschmackvoll ~~* to dress in good taste; *in Worte ~~* to clothe (*od* to couch *od* to express) in words; *jdn von Kopf bis Fuß ~~* to fit s. o. out from head to foot; **~er** *n pl* clothes *pl*; dresses, frocks, garments, gowns *pl*; *sl* togs *pl*; *abgelegte ~~* cast-off clothes *pl*; *gebrauchte ~~* second-hand clothes *pl*; *abgetragene ~~* rags *pl*; *~~ machen Leute* fine feathers make fine birds; **~~ablage** *f* cloak-room, *Am* check-room; **~~aufwand** *m* gorgeous apparel; **~~bügel** *m* clothes (*od* coat) hanger; **~~bürste** *f* clothes-brush; **~~geschäft** *n* clothes establishment; **~~haken** *m* clothes-peg (*od* hook); **~~händler** *m* dealer in clothes; **~~karte** *f* clothing coupon; ration card for clothing; ration-book; **~~kasten, ~~schrank** *m* wardrobe; closet; clothes-press; **~~laden** *m* clothes (*od* apparel) shop; **~~nähen** *n* dressmaking; **~~posamenten** *pl* tailor's trimming; **~~punkt** *m* (*Rationierung*) clothing coupon; **~~puppe** *f* lay figure, dummy; **~~rechen** *m* clothes rack; **~~sack** *m* kit bag; duffel bag: **~~schürze** *f Am* tier; **~~schutz** *m* (*Fahrrad*) skirt-(*od* dress-) guard; **~~ständer** *m* clothes tree; hat and coat stand; **~~stoff** *m* dress-(*od* clothing-)material, tailor's cloth; **~~vorrat** *m* stock of clothes; **~sam** *a* becoming, fitting well; **~ung** *f* clothes *pl*, clothing, costume, dress, wear, garb; *poet* raiment; (*vornehme*) attire; (*von der Stange*) hand-me-downs *pl*, reach-me-downs *pl*; **~~sstück** *n* article of clothing.

Kleie *f* bran; **~nmehl** *n* pollard.

*

klein *a* (*unbedeutend, gering, zärtlich verkleinernd*) little; (*Umfang, Wert, Bedeutung, Anzahl*) small; (*winzig*) diminutive; bantam, wee, tiny, *fam* weeny, teeny; (*sehr ~, unbedeutend*) minute; (*verschwindend ~*) microscopic; (*im ~en*) miniature; (*~ u. hübsch, von e-r Frau*) petite; (*Wuchs*) short; (*zwergenhaft*) dwarfish, midget; (*~lich, geringfügig*) petty, trifling; slight; *Am* picayunish, picayune; (*~lich denkend*) narrow-minded, mean; *mus* minor; (*schwächlich*) puny; (*niedlich*) minikin; (*unbedeutend, alltäglich*) trivial; (*armselig*) paltry; *sl* measly; *groß u. ~* children and grown-ups; high and low; *mein ~er Bruder* my younger brother; *ein ~ bißchen, ein ~ wenig* a tiny (*od* little) bit; *~er Buchstabe* small letter; *~er Fehler* trifling error; *~er Geist* narrow (*od* small) mind; *~es Geld* small coin; *~er Geschäftsmann* petty dealer; *~e Geschichte* short story; *~er Sparer* small investor; *im ~en* on a small scale, in retail; in detail; *von ~ auf* from a child, from infancy; *vor e-r ~en Weile* a little while ago; *~stes Lebewesen* microorganism; *~ anfangen* to start from small beginnings; *~ beigeben* to draw in o.'s horns, to eat humble pie; *~ denken von* not to think highly of; *~ hacken* to cut in pieces;(*Geld*) to squander; *auf e-r ~en Flamme kochen* to cook on a slow fire; *bis in die ~sten Einzelheiten prüfen* to check every minute detail; *kurz u. ~ schlagen* to knock to pieces; *~ schneiden* to cut in pieces; *~ schreiben* to write small; *im ~en sparsam, im großen verschwenderisch* to be pennywise and pound-foolish; *von zwei Übeln wähle das ~ere* of two evils choose the less.

Klein|anzeigen *f pl* classified (*od* small) advertisements *pl*; *Am* want ads *pl* (*od* column); **~arbeit** *f* petty work; finicky detail; **~asien** *n* Asia Minor; **~auto** *n* small car, runabout; *Am sl* flivver; **~bahn** *f* branch-line; light railway; narrow-ga(u)ge railway; **~~hof** *m Am* way-station; **~bauer** *m* small farmer (*od* holder); **~betrieb** *m* small business; *landwirtschaftlicher ~~* small holding; **~bildaufnahme** *f phot* candid photograph; leicograph; **~bildkamera** *f phot* candid (*od* miniature) camera, *fam Am* minicam, *sl* minnie; **~bürger** *m* petit bourgeois, little man, *Am* Babbitt; **~~lich** *a* petty-bourgeois; **~~tum** *n* petty bourgeoisie; **~e(r)** *m* little boy; *~e f* little girl; *~es n* little one, toddler, tot; *die ~en pl* the little ones (*od* kids *pl od* youngsters *pl*); **~flugzeug** *n* baby (aero)plane; light airplane; **~funkapparat** *m* portable radiotelephone set, *Am sl* walkie-talkie; **~funkstelle** *f* portable transmitting station; **~garten** *m* allotment (garden); **~geist** *m* narrow-minded man; **~geld** *n* small coin (*od* change); **~gewerbe** *n* small trade; **~gläubig** *a* of little faith; **~handel** *m* retail trade; *im ~~* by (*Am* at) retail; **~~sgeschäft** *n* retailshop; **~~spreis** *m* retail price; **~händler** *m* retailer, small trader; **~heit** *f* smallness, minuteness, littleness; **~hirn** *n* cerebellum; **~holz** *n* kindling, sticks *pl*, firewood; *~~ machen aero sl* to crash; **~igkeit** *f* petty detail, trifle, bagatelle; (*Geld*) small sum;

(*Mahlzeit*) bite; (*~geld, ~er Lohn*) *Am sl* chicken feed; *um e-e ~~ kaufen* to buy for a mere song; *das ist e-e ~~* that's nothing, *sl* that's a cinch; *sich mit ~~en abgeben* to stand on niceties; **~~skrämer** *m* pettifogger, stickler; **~kaliber** *n* small- (*od* sub-)calibre; **~kaliberbüchse** *f* miniature rifle; **~kind** *n* infant; **~~erbewahranstalt** *f* crèche, day nursery; **~körnig** *a* small- (*od* fine-)grained; **~kraftrad** *n* light motorcycle; **~kram** *m* trifles *pl*, bagatelles *pl*, niceties *pl*; **~krieg** *m* guer(r)illa warfare; **~kriegen** *tr* (*demütigen*) to humble, *fam* to take s. o. down a little; (*Geld*) to squander; **~kunst** *f* floor show; **~~bühne** *f* cabaret; **~landbesitz** *m* small-holding; **~laut** *a* low-spirited, dejected, meek, subdued; *~~ werden fam* to be down, to get very low; *~~ sein fam* to sing small; **~lebewesen** *n* microorganism; **~lich** *a* petty, mean, paltry; (*schikanös*) pettifogging; (*engstirnig*) narrow-minded; *~~er Mensch* pettifogger, fussy fellow; *~~e Haltung* paltry attitude; *~~e Ansichten* narrow outlook; *mit Geld ~~ sein* to grudge expenses; *seien Sie nicht ~~* don't stand on niceties; **~~keit** *f* pettiness, paltriness; **~lichtbildkunst** *f* photomicrography; **~lieferwagen** *m* pickup; **~luftschiff** *n* baby airship, *Am* blimp; **~malerei** *f* miniature painting; **~mut** *m*, **~mütigkeit** *f* despondency; pusillanimity; (*Feigheit*) cowardice; **~mütig** *a* despondent; pusillanimous; (*feig*) coward(ly); **~od** *n* jewel, gem; **~radio** *n* portable radio; **~rentner** *m* pensioner, petty rentier; small investor; **~russe** *m* Little Russian; **~schreibmaschine** *f* portable (typewriter); **~siedler** *m* small-holder; **~sparer** *m* small depositor; **~staat** *m* small state; **~~erei** *f* particularism; **~stadt** *f* small town, *Am auch* tank town; **~städter** *m* provincial; **~städtisch** *a* provincial, homely; **~stkind** *n* baby; **~stmotor** *m* pilot motor; **~stwagen** *m mot* baby car; **~stwert** *m* minimum; **~stwohnung** *f* flatlet; **~unterseeboot** *n* midget submarine; **~verkauf** *m* retail (trade); **~~spreis** *m* retail price; **~vieh** *n* small cattle; **~wagen** *m mot* small car, runabout, *Am mil* bantam, *sl* flivver.

Kleister *m* paste; **~n** *tr*, *itr* to paste, to size (with paste); **~ig** *a* pasty, sticky; (*Brot*) slack-baked; **~pinsel** *m* paste-brush.

Klemm|e *f* (*~schraube*) clamp; (*Klammer*) clip; (*Kneifzange*) tongs *pl*, forceps *sing u. pl*, nippers *pl*; *el* terminal; binding screw; *fig* dilemma, pinch, embarrassing situation, *fam* fix, tight spot; (*Geld*) tightness; *in e-e ~ geraten* to get into a mess; *in e-r schrecklichen ~ sein* to be in a terrible fix, to have not a leg to stand on; *tief in der ~ sitzen* to be deep in the mire, *Am* to stay put; **~en** *tr* to pinch, to squeeze, to jam, to press, to grip, to clamp; *itr* to jam, to squeeze, to skew; (*Tür*) to catch; *sich den Finger ~~* to catch (*od* pinch) o.'s finger; **~enspannung** *f* terminal voltage; **~er** *m* pince-nez, nose glasses *pl*; *tech* pinchcock; **~schraube** *f* binding screw; *el* terminal.

Klempner *m* (*Flaschner, Blechschmied*) tinsmith, tinner, tinman; (*Installateur für Gas, Wasser*) plumber; (*Kupferschmied*) coppersmith; (*Kesselflicker*) tinker; **~ei** *f* (*Flaschnerei*) tinman's workshop.

Klepper *m* nag, hack.

Kleptoman|e *m*, **~in** *f* kleptomaniac; **~ie** *f* kleptomania.

Kler|iker *m* clergyman; **~isei** *f* the parsons *pl*; clerical set; *fig* clique; **~us** *m* clergy.

Klette *f bot* burdock, bur(r); (*Mensch*) bur(r), bore, sticker-on.

Kletter|eisen *n* climbing-iron; **~er** *m* climber; **~n** *itr* to climb, to clamber; (*ansteigen*) to mount, to scale; **~pflanze** *f* creeper; climbing plant; **~rose** *f* rambler; **~seil** *n* climbing-rope; **~stange** *f* climbing pole; **~übung** *f* climbing practice; **~vogel** *m* climber.

Klient *m* client, customer.

Klima *n* climate; *an ein ~ gewöhnen* to acclimatize, *Am* to acclimate; **~anlage** *f* air-conditioning plant (*od* system); airing plant; *mit e-r ~~ versehen* to air-condition; **~krankheit** *f* air-sickness; **~kterium** *n* climacteric; **~tisch** *a* climatic; *~~er Kurort* climatic health-resort.

Klimbim *m fam* humbug, fuss.

klimm|en *itr* to climb; **~zug** *m* (*Turnen*) short-arm stretch.

klimpern *itr* to jingle; (*Klavier*) to strum, *Am* to bang; (*Metall*) to tinkle.

Klinge *f* blade; sword; *über die ~ springen lassen* to put to the sword.

Klingel *f* alarm (*od* door-)bell; (*Summer*) buzzer; **~beutel** *m* alms- (*od* collection-)bag; **~draht** *m* waxed (*od* bell) wire; **~element** *n el* bell ringing cell; **~knopf** *m* bell-button (*od* push); **~leitung** *f* bell-wire; **~n** *itr* to ring (the bell); (*Schelle*) to tinkle, to jingle; *es ~t* the bell rings; *jdm ~~* to ring for s. o.; **~schnur** *f*, **~zug** *m* bell-pull; bell-rope; (*Litze*) bell cord.

klingen *itr* to sound; (*Glocke*) to ring; (*Metall*) to tinkle; (*Glas*) to chink, to clink; (*schrill ~*) to jangle; *mir klingt das Ohr* my ear tingles; *das ~ e-r Glocke* the ding-dong of a bell; *~de Münze* ready money, hard cash; *mit ~dem Spiel* with drums beating, with drums and fifes.

klingklang! ding-dong!

Klinik *f* clinical hospital, nursing home.

Klinke *f* latch; (door) handle; *el* jack, socket-board; **~n** *itr* to press the latch; **~r** *m* clinker.

klipp *adv*: *~ u. klar* clear as daylight, quite evident; *~ u. klar sagen* to tell plump and plain; **~fisch** *m* dried cod; **~ klapp!** *interj* flip-flap! click-clack!

Klippe *f* cliff, rock, crag; reef; **~r** *m* clipper.

klirren *itr* to clink, to clatter, to clash; (*Geschirr*) to clatter; (*Ketten*) to clank; (*Schlüssel*) to jingle; (*Fensterscheiben*) to rattle.

Klisch|ee *n* (printing-)block, cut, cliché, electrotype; **~~abzug** *m* block pull, *Am* engraver's proof; **~~herstellung** *f* cliché manufacturing; **~ieren** *tr typ* to stereotype; to electrotype.

Klistier *n* clyster, enema; **~spritze** *f* enema syringe.

klitsch: *~! klatsch!* slap! **~e** *f* hovel; **~ig** *a* slippery; (*feucht*) soggy, sodden; (*Brot*) slackbaked, doughy; **~naß** *a* sopping wet.

Klo *n* toilet.

Kloake *f* sink, sewer, cesspool, drain; **~nrohr** *n* drainage pipe; **~nwasser** *n* sewage.

Klob|en *m* (*Rolle*) pulley, block; (*Flaschenzug*) tackle; (*Schraubstock*) vice, *Am* vise; (*Kneifzange*) pincers *pl*; (*Holzklotz*) log; (*Mensch*) coarse fellow; **~ig** *a* rude, clumsy; heavy; (*ungeschickt*) awkward.

klopf|en *itr* to knock, to beat; (*sanft*) to tap (*an, auf* at, on); (*Herz*) to throb, to palpitate, to pound; (*Schultern*) to pat; (*Tür*) to knock (*an* at); *mot* to knock; *tr* (*Steine*) to break; (*Nagel*) to drive; *min* to strike; *es klopft* there is a knock at the door; *auf die Finger ~* to rap s. o.'s fingers; *auf den Busch ~* to beat about the bush; **en~** *n* beating, knock, rap; (*Herz*) throbbing, palpitation; (*Puls*) pulsation; *mot* knocking; **~er** *m* (*Tür*) knocker; *tele* decoherer, (*Signalapparat*) sounder; (*Stößel*) beater, mallet; (*Ramme*) beetle; **~fest** *a mot* knockproof, antiknock; anti-pinking; **~~igkeit** *f mot* resistance to knocking, nonpinking, antiknock; **~holz** *n* beater, mallet; **~wert** *m mot* detonating characteristics *pl*, antiknock value; octane number.

Klöppel *m* (*Glocke*) clapper, tongue; (*Spitzen*) (lace-) bobbin; (*Schlegel*) beetle; **~arbeit** *f* bobbin-work; **~kissen** *n* lace-pillow, lace-cushion; **~n** *itr* to make lace; **~spitzen** *f pl* bone-lace.

Klops *m* mincemeat-ball.

Klosett *n* closet, W. C., lavatory, toilet; (*außerhalb des Hauses*) privy; **~deckel** *m* toilet lid; **~muschel** *f* toilet bowl; flush pan; **~papier** *n* toilet-paper; *e-e Rolle ~~* a roll of toilet-paper; **~raum** *m* W. C., toilet, *Am* comfort room.

Kloß *m* (*Erde*) clod, clump, lump; (*Küche*) dumpling; meat ball.

Kloster *n* monastery; (*Frauen~*) convent, nunnery; *ins ~ gehen* (*Frauen*) to take the veil, (*Männer*) to turn monk; **~bruder** *m* friar; **~frau** *f* nun; **~leben** *n* monastic life; **~mauer** *f* convent-wall; **~zelle** *f* monk's (*od* nun's) cell.

klösterlich *a* monastic(al); conventual.

Klotz *m* block; log (of wood); (*Baumstumpf*) stump; (*grober Kerl*) blockhead, dunce; *auf e-n groben ~ gehört ein grober Keil* rudeness must be met with rudeness; **~ig** *a* (*massig*) cloddy; (*schwer*) heavy; (*grob*) rude; *fam* (*sehr viel*) enormous, mighty.

Klub *m* club, association; **~lokal** *n* club-house; **~mitglied** *n* member of a club; **~sessel** *m* leather arm-chair, lounge chair, easy chair.

Klucke *f* sitting hen.

Kluft *f* (*Lücke, fig*) gap; (*Abgrund*) gulf, abyss, chasm; (*Spalte*) cleft, fissure; (*Schlucht*) ravine, gorge; (*Kleidung*) *sl* dress, clothes *pl*.

klug *a* clever, intelligent; (*welt~*) prudent; (*aufgeweckt*) bright; (*verständig*) wise, sensible; (*einsichtsvoll*) judicious; (*begabt*) talented, able, gifted; (*flink, munter*) alert; (*scharfsinnig*) quick-witted; keen, acute; shrewd, sagacious; (*gerissen*) smart; (*erfahren, schlau*) knowing; (*hochbegabt*) brilliant; (*gerieben*) sharp; (*listig*) astute; (*scharfsichtig*) perspicacious; (*verschmitzt, schlau*) cunning; sly; (*erfinderisch*) ingenious; (*geschickt*) adroit, skil(l)ful; *~ werden* to grow wise; *daraus kann ich nicht ~ werden* I cannot make head and tail of it; *durch Schaden wird man ~* bought wit is best; one learns by o.'s mistakes; *aus Ihnen kann ich nicht ~ werden* I cannot figure you out; *ich bin um nichts klüger* I am none the wiser; *der Klügere gibt nach* the wiser head gives in; *das Klügste wäre wohl* it would probably be best; **~heit** *f* (*Verstand*) intelligence, brains *pl*; (*praktische Vernunft*) good sense; (*Einsicht*) prudence, judiciousness; (*Weisheit*) wisdom; (*Scharfsichtigkeit*) sagacity; (*Schlauheit*) shrewdness, cunning; **~tuer**, **~redner** *m* wiseacre, *Am* smart aleck, wisenheimer.

klüglich *adv* wisely, prudently.

Klump|en *m* lump; (*Haufen*) heap; (*Erde*) clod; (*Metall*) ingot; (*Gold*) nugget; (*Masse*) mass; **~fuß** *m* club-foot; **~ig** *a* cloddy.

Klümpchen *n* pat; (*Butter*) dab.

Klüngel *m* clique, snobbish group of people; coterie; **~wirtschaft** *f* party clique, *Am* boss-rule.

Klunker *m* tassel; clod.

Kluppe *f* pincers *pl*, tongs *pl*; die-stock.

Klüse *f* hawse.

Klüver(baum) *m* (jib-)boom.

knabbern *tr, itr* to gnaw, to nibble.

Knabe *m* boy, lad; **~nalter** *n* boyhood; **~nhaft** *a* boyish; **~nkraut** *n bot* orchis; **~nstreich** *m* boyish trick.

Knack, **~s** *m* crack; **~en** *itr* to crack; (*Feuer*) to crackle, to crepitate; (*Schloß*) to click; *tr* to crack; *Nüsse ~~* to crack nuts; *Rätsel ~~* to solve riddles; **~er** *m* cracker; *alter ~~* old fog(e)y, old grumbler; dry old stick; **~laut** *m* glottal stop; **~mandel** *f* shell-almond; **~wurst** *f* saveloy.

Knäckebrot *n* crisp bread.

Knall *m* clap; (*schwacher*) pop; (*Peitsche*) crack, smack; (*Tür*) bang; (*Gewehr*) report, crack; (*Explosion*) detonation; (*Klatschen*) dash; *~! interj* bang! *~ u. Fall* all of a sudden, on the spot; without warning; **~bonbon** *m u. n* cracker; **~büchse** *f* pop-gun; **~dämpfer** *m mil* silencer, *Am* muffler; **~effekt** *m* claptrap, stage effect; **~en** *itr* to crack, to pop, to clap; (*Pfropfen*) to pop; (*explodieren*) to go off, to detonate, to fulminate, to explode; (*Waffe*) to fire; (*Türe*) to bang; *mit der Peitsche ~~* to smack (*od* to crack) the whip; **~erbse** *f* firework cracker; **~gas** *n* oxyhydrogen gas; detonating gas; **~~gebläse** *n* oxy-hydrogen blowpipe; **~quecksilber** *n* fulminating mercury; **~rot** *a fam* bright red, glaring red, scarlet; **~satz** *m mil* detonating composition; **~zündschnur** *f* detonating fuse.

knapp *a* (*spärlich*) scarce, scant; (*unzulänglich*) scanty; (*geringfügig*) exiguous; (*kärglich*) spare; (*dünn, selten*) sparse; (*dürftig*) meagre, *Am* meager; (*Waren*) scanty, scarce; (*eng*) tight, narrow, scrimpy, close; (*kaum ausreichend*) barely sufficient; (*Zeit*) hard; (*beschränkt*) limited; (*Mittel*) stinted; (*Stil*) concise, terse; (*Worte*) brief; (*kurz*) short; *~ bei Kasse* short of cash; *~e Mehrheit* bare majority; *~er Tatsachenbericht* condensed statement of the facts; *sein ~es Auskommen haben* to have barely enough to live upon; *mit ~er Not entkommen* to have a narrow escape; *~ sein* (*Waren*) to be in short supply; *~ werden* to run short (*od* low); *jdn ~ halten* to keep s. o. short; **~e** *m* page; (*Schild~~*) shield bearer; *min* miner; **~heit** *f* (*Mangel*) scarcity, shortage, deficiency; (*Enge*) tightness; narrowness; (*Stil*) conciseness; **~sack** *m* knapsack, wallet; **~schaft** *f* miners' relief association; staff of miners, body of miners; **~~srente** *f* miner's pension.

Knarre *f* rattle; *fig* gun; **~n** *itr* to rattle, to crackle, to creak; (*Türe*) to squeak; (*rasseln*) to jar.

Knaster *m* canaster, tobacco; *fig* old man, grumbler; **~n, knattern** *itr* to crackle, to rattle; (*Motoren*) to roar; (*knistern*) to crepitate.

Knäuel *m u. n* (*Garn*) clew, clue, ball; hank; skein; (*Drahtrolle*) coil; (*Menschen*) crowd, throng, knot; *in ein ~ wickeln* to wind into a ball; **~förmig** *a* convoluted.

Knauf *m* knob, stud; (*Degen~*) pommel; *arch* capital.

knaupeln *itr* to pick, to gnaw.

Knauser *m* niggard, miser, curmudgeon, stingy person; **~ei** *f* niggardliness, stinginess; **~ig** *a* niggardly, mean, stingy (*mit* of), hard-fisted; **~n** *itr* to be a niggard, to be stingy.

knautschen *tr fam* to crease, to crumple, to wrinkle.

Knebel *m* (*Knüttel*) cudgel, short stick; (*Mund~*) gag; *mar, aero* toggle; **~bart** *m* twisted moustache; **~jacke** *f* duffle coat; **~n** *tr* to bind; (*den Mund*) to gag; *fig* (*Presse*) to muzzle; (*unterdrücken*) to suppress; **~presse** *f*, **~verband** *m* tourniquet.

Knecht *m* (*Bauern~*) farm hand; (*Diener*) (man) servant; (*Haus~*) boots *pl mit sing*; (*Unfreier*) bondsman; *tech* trestle horse; jack; *~ Ruprecht* Santa Claus; *wie der Herr, so der ~* like master like man; **~en** *tr* to tyrannize; to enslave; to reduce to servitude; **~isch** *a* servile, slavish; **~schaft** *f* servitude, slavery, bondage; **~ung** *f* enslavement, bondage; servitude.

kneif|en *irr tr* to nip, to pinch; (*drükken*) to squeeze; (*zwicken*) to gripe; *itr* (*sich drücken*) *fam* to dodge, to flinch; **~er** *m* pince-nez; **~zange** *f* pincers *pl*, nippers *pl*; (*kleine*) tweezers *pl*.

Kneipe *f* public house, tavern; dingy pub, *Am* saloon, barrel house (*od* shop), *sl* joint, honky-tonk; *verbotene ~* blind pig (*od* tiger); (*Studenten*) beer party; **~n** *tr* to pinch; *itr* to frequent public houses; (*zechen*) to tipple, to carouse; **~nwirt** *m* bar-keeper, *Am* bar-tender; **~rei** *f* drinking-bout, carousal.

knet|en *tr* to knead; (*Glieder*) to massage; (*Lehm*) to pug; (*drücken, pressen*) to squeeze; **~er** *m* kneader, pug and kneading machine; **~holz** *n* plastic wood; **~maschine** *f* kneading machine; **~masse** *f* plasticine; **~prozeß** *m* kneading process; **~ung** *f* kneading, remo(u)lding.

Knick *m* (*Biegung*) sharp bend; (*Bruch, Kurven~*) break; (*Riß*) crack; (*Winkel*) angle; (*Hecke*) quickset hedge; **~en** *tr* to break, to crack; (*krümmen*) to bend; *tech* to buckle; to break, to burst; (*zus.brechen*) to collapse; *geknickt a* broken-down; *itr* to crack; **~er** *m* niggard; miser; **~erig** *a* niggardly, parsimonious; **~ern** *itr* to be sordid (*od* stingy); **~festigkeit** *f* breaking (*od* bending) strength; (*Metalle*) buckling strength; **~flügel** *m aero* gull-wing; **~stelle** *f* kink, knee; (*e-r Kurve*) break; **~ung** *f* breaking, kink; buckling; **~widerstand** *m* resistance to buckling.

Knick|s *m* curts(e)y, bob; *e-n ~ machen* to drop a curts(e)y; **~sen** *itr* to curts(e)y.

Knie *n* knee; (*Weg*) bend; (*Knick*) *tech* angle; (*~stück*) *tech* elbow; (*Fuge*) joint; *mil* salient; *etw übers ~ brechen* to hurry (*od* slur) s. th. over, to force things; to make short work of; *in die ~e sinken* to go down on o.'s knees; *das ~ beugen vor* to bow the knee to (*od* before); *das ~ aufschlagen* to skin o.'s knee; **~beuge** *f* (*Turnen*) bend of the knee; knee-bending; **~beugung** *f* genuflection; **~(e)n** *itr* to kneel (*vor* to); (*Kirche*) to genuflect; **~fall** *m* prostration: genuflexion; **~fällig** *a* (up)on o.'s knees; **~förmig** *a* knee-shaped, geniculate; **~gelenk** *n* knee-joint; (*Pferd*) stifle; **~~entzündung** *f* gonitis; **~~federung** *f* knee-action suspension; **~hebel** *m* elbow lever, toggle lever; **~holz** *n* knee-timber; dwarf-pine, dwarf-fir; **~hose** *f* (a pair of) breeches *pl*, knicker-bockers *pl*, plus-fours *pl*; shorts *pl*; **~kehle** *f* hollow of the knee; **~kissen** *n* hassock; **~leder** *n* knee-strap; **~riemen** *m* shoemaker's stirrup; **~rohr** *n* elbow tube, bent tube; **~scheibe** *f* knee-pan (*od* cap), patella; **~schützer** *m* kneepads *pl*; **~stand** *m* (*Turnen*) knee-stand; **~strümpfe** *m pl* mid-lengths *pl*; **~stück** *n* (*phot, Malerei*) half-length portrait, *tech* elbow; **~stütz** *m* resting upon the knees; **~tief** *a* knee-deep.

Kniff *m* pinch; *fig* trick, dodge, knack; handy device, helpful hint; shortcut; artifice; (*Falte*) fold; crease; *es ist ein ~ dabei* there is a knack about it; *~en gewachsen sein* to be up to s. o.'s tricks; **~en** *tr* to fold; (*Buch*) to dog's-ear; **~lig** *a* tricky; (*spitzfindig*) subtle, sophistical; (*schwierig*) difficult; (*verwirrend*) puzzling.

knips|en *tr phot* to snap, to take a snapshot of; (*lochen*) to punch; *itr* to snap o.'s fingers; **~er** *m phot* shutter-snapper; **~zange** *f* ticket nippers *pl*.

Knirps *m* little fellow, dwarf, pigmy, hop-o'-my-thumb; (*Schirm*) folding umbrella.

knirschen *itr* to grate; to scroop, to make a rustling sound; (*Schnee*) to crunch; (*mit den Zähnen*) to gnash (*od* to grind) o.'s teeth.

knistern *itr* to crackle; to sizzle, to crack; to crepitate; (*Seide*) to rustle.

knitter|frei *a* crease-resistant (*od* resisting), non-crease; wrinkle resisting; **~ig** *a* creased, crumpled; **~n** *tr* to crease, to crumple, to wrinkle.

*

Knobel|becher *m* dice-box; *mil sl* short wellington; **~n** to play at (*od* to throw) dice (*um* for).

Knoblauch *m* garlic.

Knöchel *m* (*Fuß*) ankle (-joint); (*Hand*) knuckle, joint.

Knochen *m* bone; *naß bis auf die ~* wet to the skin; **~artig** *a* bony; **~asche** *f* bone ash; **~bau** *m* frame; skeleton; **~bildend** *a* bone-forming; **~bruch** *m* fracture; **~dürr** *a* all skin and bone; **~fraß** *m* caries; **~gerüst** *n* skeleton; **~gewebe** *n* bony tissue; **~haut** *f* periosteum; **~kohle** *f* boneblack; animal char; charred bone; **~leim** *m* bone glue, osteocolla; **~mann** *m fam* Death; **~mark** *n* bone marrow; **~masse** *f* osseous material; **~mehl** *n* bone meal (*od* dust); **~öl** *n* bone oil; **~splitter** *m* splinter of a bone; **~trocken** *a* oven-dry; **~wirbel** *m* vertebra.

knöchern, knochig *a* bony, of bone; *med* osseous.

Knödel *m* dumpling.

Knöllchen *n* little knob; (*Klümpchen*) nodule.

Knoll|e *f* lump; *bot* tuber; *anat* tuber(cle); (*Zwiebel*) bulb; **~en** *m* (*Klumpen*) lump, clod; (*Geschwulst*) tumo(u)r; (*kleiner Knoten*) nodule; (*Schwellung*) *anat* tubercle; (*Auswuchs, Höcker, Beule*) protuberance; **~~blätterpilz** *m* death-cup; **~~gewächs** *n bot* tuberiferous (*od* bulbous) plant; **~ig** *a* knobby, cloddy; *bot* bulbous, tuberous.

Knopf *m* button; (*Degen~, Sattel~*) pommel; (*Nadel~*) head; (*Manschetten~*) sleeve-link; (*Kragen~*) collar-stud; (*Klingel~*) bell-button; *bot* bud, knot; *auf den ~ drücken* to press the button; *mit zwei ~reihen* double-breasted; *e-n ~ versetzen* to move over a button; *e-n ~ annähen* to sew on a button; *überzogener ~* covered button; **~loch** *n* buttonhole; **~steuerung** *f* push-button control; **knöpfen** *tr* to button.

knorke *a sl* wonderful, marvel(l)ous.

Knorpel *m* cartilage, gristle; **~haut** *f anat* perichondrium; **~ig** *a* cartilaginous, gristly.

Knorr|en *m* (*Holz*) knot, gnarl; tree stump; (*Ast*) snag; (*Beule*) protuberance; (*Auswuchs*) excrescence; **~ig** *a* knotty, knaggy, gnarly, gnarled; (*kräftig*) vigoro(u)s; (*grob*) coarse.

Knosp|e *f* bud; **~n** *itr* to bud; to sprout; **~ig** *a* budding; full of buds.

Knote *m fam* (*ungebildeter Mensch*) cad.

Knoten *m* knot; *bot, astr* node; (*Knötchen*) *bot* nodule; *anat* (*kleiner*) tubercle; (*Nerven~*) ganglion; *mar* knot; *mar, fig* hitch; (*Tuch, Am Holz*) burl; *fig* difficulty; (*Drama*) plot; *e-n ~ machen* to tie a knot; *e-n ~ lösen* to undo a knot; *fig* to solve a difficulty; (*Drama*) to unravel a plot; *~ tr* to knot; **~punkt** *m* junction; intersection; nodal point; (*bei Linse*) node, nodal point; **~~bahnhof** *m rail* multiple junction; **~stock** *m* knotty stick; **knotig** *a* knotty; *bot* jointed; *fig* rude.

Knöterich *m bot* knot-grass.

Knuff *m* cuff, thump; **~en** *tr* to cuff.

knüllen *tr* to crumple, to crease.

knüpfen *tr* to tie, to knot; (*Freundschaft*) to form; (*Tau*) to bend; (*Knoten*) to tie; (*Netz*) to braid; *e-e Bedingung an etw ~* to add a condition to s. th.; *~ an* to connect with.

Knüppel *m* cudgel, club; (*Polizei~*) truncheon, *Am* club; (*Keule*) bludgeon; *aero* control column, stick; (*Holz*) log, billet; round timber; (*Brötchen*) roll; (*Hindernis*) obstacle; *jdm e-n ~ zwischen die Beine werfen* to put a spoke in s. o.'s wheel; **~damm** *m* corduroy road; **~dick** *a*: *~~ voll fam* crammed full; *es ~~ hinter den Ohren haben* to be a very sly rogue; **~steuerung** *f aero* stick control; **~weg** *m* corduroy road.

knurr|en *itr* to snarl, to growl; *fig* to grumble (*über* at); (*Magen*) to rumble; (*Hund*) to growl, (*heftig*) to snarl; **~ig** *a* growling; grumbling.

knusp|ern *tr* to nibble, to munch, to crunch; **~rig** *a* (*Brötchen*) crisp, short, crackling; (*bröckelig*) friable; (*Mädchen*) good-looking.

Knute *f* knout.

knutschen *tr* to squeeze, to cuddle.

Knüttel *m* cudgel, club; **~vers** *m* doggerel (verse).

koagulieren *tr, itr* to coagulate.

Koalition *f* coalition, *Am* fuse, fusion; **~srecht** *n* freedom of association; **~skrieg** *m* coalition war; **~sregierung** *f* coalition government, *Am* fusion administration.

Kobalt *m* cobalt; **~blau** *n* cobalt blue, smalt; **~glanz** *m* cobaltite; **~grün** *n* cobalt green, cobaltic oxide; **~verbindung** *f* cobaltic compound.

Koben *m* pigsty.

Kober *m* basket, hamper.

Kobold *m* (hob)goblin, sprite; (*in Irland*) leprechaun; (*böser Geist der Flugzeuge*) gremlin, fifinella.

Koch *m* cook; *Chef~* head cook, chef; *Hunger ist der beste ~* hunger is the best sauce; *viele Köche verderben den Brei* too many cooks spoil the broth; **~apfel** *m* cooking-apple; **~apparat** *m* cooking-apparatus; **~becher** *m* beaker; **~beständig** *a* (*Farben*) fast to boiling; (*stabil*) stable on boiling; **~birne** *f* cooking-pear; **~brenner** *m* cooking burner; **~buch** *n* cookery book, *Am* cookbook; **~echt** *a* (*Farbe*) fast to boiling; **~en** *itr* (*Wasser*) to boil, to be cooking; (*leicht*) to simmer; (*sieden*) to wallop; (*langsam*) to stew; *vor Wut ~~* to be boiling with rage; *tr* to cook; (*Wasser, Suppe*) to boil; (*Kaffee*) to make; *sie ~t gut* she is a good cook; *gekochtes Obst* stewed fruit; *zuviel gekocht* overdone; **~en** *n* cooking, cookery; boiling; (*Aufwallung*) ebulition; *im ~~* (*fig*) *Am* aboil; *zum ~~ bringen* to bring to the boil; **~er** *m* cooker; (*Heizplatte*) electric table stove; hot plate; **~gefäß** *n* cooking vessel; **~gerät** *n* boiling (*od* cooking) apparatus; **~gelegenheit** *f* cooking-convenience; **~geschirr** *n* cooking utensils *pl*; pots and pans *pl*; *mil* canteen, mess-tin (*od* -kit); mess gear; **~grube** *f* cooking pit; **~herd** *m* kitchen-range, cooking-stove, *Am* cook-stove; *elektrischer ~~* electric range; **~kessel** *m* (boiling) kettle, boiler; (*groß*) copper, ca(u)ldron; **~kiste** *f* hay box, Norwegian oven (*od* nest); **~kunst** *f* (art of) cooking, cookery; **~löffel** *m* (kitchen-) ladle; **~lösung** *f* boiling agent; **~maschine** *f* cooking-apparatus; **~pfanne** *f* (sauce-) pan; **~platte** *f* cooking (*od* hot) plate; (*el Herd*) cooking surface; **~rezept** *n* recipe; **~salz** *n* kitchen- (*od* common-) salt; **~~lösung** *f* (common-) salt solution; **~schule** *f* school of cookery; **~topf** *m* kitchen pot; saucepan, pot; **~zeit** *f* cooking period; **~zucker** *m* brown sugar; powdered sugar.

Köcher *m* quiver.

Köchin *f* cook.

Kodak *m phot* kodak.

Köder *m* bait, lure; *fig* enticement, attraction; **~n** *tr* to bait, to lure, to decoy.

Kod|ex *m* code; (*Handschrift*) codex; **~ifizieren** *tr* to codify; **~izill** *n* codicil.

Koeffizient *m* coefficient.

Koffein *n* caffeine; **~frei** *a* caffein-free.

Koffer *m* trunk; (*kleinerer*) box; (*Hand~*) portmanteau; (*lederne flache Reisetasche*) suitcase; (*Reisetasche*) (travelling) bag, *Am* grip(sack); (*Wochenend~*) weekend case; *mil sl* shell; bomb; **~apparat** *m*, **~radio** *n* portable (radio) set, portable (battery radio); **~fernseher** *m* portable television receiver; **~gerät** *n* portable set; **~grammophon** *n* portable gramophone; **~kino** *n* portable projector equipment; **~raum** *m mot* trunk compartment, *Am* (luggage) locker; **~träger** *m* (*Netz*) luggage rack; (*Mann*) porter; **~zettel** *m* luggage tag, label.

Kogge *f* cog.

Kognak *m* (French) brandy, cognac; **~bohne** *f* brandy-ball.

Ko|härenz *f* coherence; **~härer** *m* coherer; **~häsion** *f* cohesion; **~~sfestigkeit** *f* cohesion strength; **~~skraft** *f* cohesive force; **~~svermögen** *n* cohesiveness.

Kohl *m* cabbage; *fig* rubbish, twaddle, nonsense, bosh; *fig aufgewärmter ~* raked-up story; **~dampf** *m fam* hunger; *~~ schieben fam* to be hungry; **~garten** *m* kitchen-garden; **~kopf** *m* cabbage(-head); **~meise** *f* great titmouse; **~rabenschwarz** *a* (as) black as coal, jet black; **~rabi** *m* turnip-cabbage, kohlrabi; **~rübe** *f* (Swede) turnip; rutabaga, swede; **~schwarz** *a* coal-black; **~strunk** *m* cabbage-stalk; **~weißling** *m* cabbage-butterfly.

Kohle *f* coal; (*glimmende*) ember; (*glühende ~n*) live coals *pl*; (*Braun~*) brown coal, lignite; (*Holz~*) charcoal; (*Stein~*) hardcoal; *el* carbon; carbon brush, carbon rod; *fette ~* fat coal; *geringwertige ~* poor coal; *feurige ~n auf jds Haupt sammeln* to heap coals of fire on s. o.'s head; *auf glühenden ~n sitzen* to be on pins and needles, to be on tenter-hooks, *Am* to be on the anxious seat; **~beheizt** *a* coal-fired; **~bürste** *f* carbon brush; **~elektrode** *f* carbon electrode; **~mikrophon** *n* carbon microphone; **~n** *tr* (*schwarzbrennen*) to char; (*karbonisieren*) to carbonize, to carburize; to blacken; *itr* to char; *mar* to coal, to bunker; *fam fig* to talk rubbish, to lie.

Kohlen|abbau *m* coal mining, working of coal; **~arbeiter** *m* coal-miner, collier; **~artig** *a* coal-like, carbonaceous; **~asche** *f* coal ash; **~aufbereitung** *f* coal preparation; coal dressing (*od* separation); **~~sanlage** *f* coal-preparation plant; **~becken** *n* coal basin; coal field; (*Pfanne*) brazier; **~bergbau** *m* coal mining; **~bergwerk** *n* coal mine (*od* pit), colliery; **~blende** *f* anthracite; **~brennen** *n* charcoal burning; **~bunker** *m* bunker, coal bin; **~dioxyd** *n* carbon dioxide; **~dunst** *m* vapo(u)r from coals; **~eimer** *m* coal-scuttle; coal-box; **~element** *n el* carbon pile; **~fadenlampe** *f* carbon-filament lamp; **~feuerung** *f* coal furnace; coal firing; **~filter** *n* charcoal filter; **~flöz** *n* layer of coal, coal-seam; **~förderung** *m* coal extraction; coal output; **~füllung** *f* coal charge; **~gas** *n* coal gas; **~gebiet** *n* coal region (*od* district); **~gehalt** *m* percentage of carbon, carbon content; **~gewinnung** *f* digging of coal; **~glut** *f* live coals *pl*; **~grieß**, **~grus** *m* small coal, slack; **~grube** *f* coal mine; coal pit; colliery; **~halde** *f* coal heap; **~haltig** *a* carboniferous, carbonaceous; **~händler** *m* coal merchant; **~handlung** *f* coal-merchant's business; **~herd** *m* coal range; **~hydrat** *n* carbohydrate; **~kasten** *m* coal-box; **~keller** *m* coal cellar; **~knappheit** *f* coal shortage; **~lager** *n* coal-bed (*od* -seam); coal deposit; (*beim Händler*) coal storage, coal yard; **~~platz** *m* coal-storage yard; **~~stätte** *f* coal deposit; **~meiler** *m* charcoal-pile; **~oxyd** *n* carbon monoxide; **~~vergiftung** *f* carbon-monoxide poisoning; **~revier** *n* coal district, coal field; coal-mining district; **~rückstand** *m* carbon residue; **~sack** *m* coal bag; **~sauer** *a* carbonate (of); carbonic; *~~es Wasser* aerated water; *~~es Natron* soda; **~säure** *f* carbonic acid; **~~entwicklung** *f* evolution of carbonic acid; **~~haltig** *a* carbonated; **~schacht** *m* (coal-)pit; shaft; **~schaufel** *f* coal shovel; **~schiff** *n* coal-ship; collier, barge; **~schlacke** *f* cinder, clinker; **~station** *f rail, mar* coaling station; **~staub** *m* coal dust; **~stift** *m* carbon; **~stickstoff** *m* cyanogen; **~stoff** *m* carbon; **~~arm** *a* low-carbon; **~~gehalt** *m* carbon content; **~~haltig** *a* carbonaceous; **~~verbindung** *f* carbon compound; **~teerfarbe** *f* coal-tar colo(u)r; **~träger**, **~trimmer** *m* sweeper, coal passer, trimmer; **~verbrauch** *m* coal consumption; **~vorrat** *m* coal supply; **~wagen** *m* coal truck; *rail* tender; **~wasserstoff** *m* hydrocarbon; **~zeche** *f* coal-pit, colliery; **~zufuhr** *f* coal delivery.

Kohle|papier *n* carbon (paper); **~zeichnung** *f* charcoal drawing.

Köhler *m* charcoal-burner; **~glaube** *m* blind faith.

Koitus *m* coition, coitus.

Koje *f* cabin, berth, bunk, *mar* cot.

Kokain *n* cocaine; *Am sl* snow; **~schieber** *m sl* dope-pedlar; **~süchtig** *a* cocaine-addict; **~vergiftung** *f* cocainism.

Kokarde *f* cockade; badge.

Koker *m* sagger; **~ei** *f* coke works *pl*, coke plant; **~~gas** *n* coke-oven gas.

kokett *a* coquettish; **~erie** *f* coquetry; flirtation; **~ieren** *itr* to flirt, to coquet with.

Kokille *f* ingot mo(u)ld; (*Guß*) chill.

Kokken *f pl* cocci *pl*.

Kokon *m* cocoon.

Kokos, **~baum** *m* coco(a)-nut tree; **~butter** *f* coconut butter; **~faser** *f* coco fibre, coir; **~fett** *n* coconut oil; **~matte** *f* coconut matting; **~nuß** *f* coconut; **~~milch** *f* coconut milk; **~palme** *f* coco palm.

Koks *m* coke; **~ofen** *m* coke-oven.

*

Kolben *m* (*Gewehr~*) butt-end; (*Keule*) club, mace; *bot* spadix, head; (*Maschinen~*) piston; (*große Flasche*) flask; *chem* retort; alembic; (*Löt~*) soldering iron; (*Mais*) *Am* cob; **~antrieb** *m* piston drive; **~boden** *m* piston head (*od* crown); **~bolzen** *m* gudgeon pin, *Am* piston pin; **~förmig** *a* club-like; **~hals** *m* neck of a flask; **~hieb** *m* butt stroke; **~hub** *m* piston stroke; **~motor** *m* reciprocating engine; **~pumpe** *f* piston pump; **~ring** *m* piston ring (*od* packing); **~stange** *f* piston rod.

Kolchose *f* kolkhoze.

Kolibri *m* humming-bird.

Kolik *f* colic; *fam* gripes *pl*.

Kolkrabe *m* common raven.

Kollaborateur *m* collaborator.

kollationieren *tr* (*prüfen*) to check; (*vergleichen*) to collate; to compare carefully.

Kolleg *n* course of lectures; *ein ~ halten* to lecture (*über* on); *ins ~ gehen* to go to a lecture; **~e** *m*, **~in** *f* colleague; **~gelder** *n pl* lecture fees *pl*; **~heft** *n* lecture-notes *pl*; **~ial** *a* collegial; as a good colleague; **~ium** *n* (*Lehrer*) teaching staff, *Am* faculty; (*Behörde*) board, council; (*Lehranstalt*) college.

Kollekt\|e *f* collection; (*Kirchengebet*) collect; **~iv** *a* collective; *~~e Sicherheit* collective security; **~~verhandlungen** *f pl* collective bargaining; **~~vertrag** *m* collective agreement; **~~wirtschaft** *f* collective economy; **~or** *m el* collector, commutator.

Koller *m med* staggers *pl*; *fig* rage; *~ n* (*Kragen*) collar, cape; jerkin; **~n** *itr* (*Stein*) to roll; *tech* to grind and mix; (*Truthahn*) to gobble; *fig* to rage; (*Darm*) to rumble; (*Taube*) to coo.

Kolli *n pl* packages *pl*.

kolli\|dieren *itr* to collide; **~sion** collision.

Kollo *n* bale of goods, parcel.

Kollo\|dium *n* collodion; **~idchemie** *f* colloid chemistry.

Kolloquium *n* colloquy.

Köln *n* Cologne; *~isch Wasser* eau-de-Cologne.

Kolon *n* colon.

kolon\|ial *a* colonial; **~ialminister** *m* colonial minister; *Engl* Secretary of State for the Colonies; Colonial Secretary; **~~ium** *n Engl* Colonial Office; **~ialwaren** *f pl* groceries *pl*; **~~handlung** *f* grocer's shop, *Am* grocery; **~~händler** *m* grocer; **~~laden** *m* grocer's shop, *Am* grocery; **~ie** *f* colony; settlement; **~isieren** *tr* to colonize; **~isation** *f* colonization; **~isator** *m* colonizer; **~ist** *m* colonist, settler, planter.

Kolonnade *f* colonnade.

Kolonne *f* column; convoy; (*Arbeiter~*) gang; *Fünfte ~* fifth column; *Mitglied der Fünften ~* fifth columnist; **~nverkehr** *m* movement of columns.

Kolophonium *n* colophony, rosin.

Koloratur *f mus* grace-note; coloratura, colorature; (*Malerei*) colo(u)ring; **~sängerin** *f* coloratura singer; **~sopran** *m* coloratura soprano.

kolor\|ieren *tr* to colo(u)r; **~it** *n* colo(u)r, colo(u)ring, shade, hue.

Koloß *m* colossus, giant; **kolossal** *a* huge, gigantic; fantastic; *adv* (*sehr groß*) very, extremely; *fam* whopping.

Kolport\|age *f* hawking of books; **~~roman** *m* trashy novel; penny dreadful, shocker; *Am* dime-novel; **~eur** *m* colporteur, pedlar, hawker; **~ieren** *tr* (*Bücher, Gerücht*) to hawk; (*verbreiten*) to spread, to distribute, to sell.

Kolumne *f typ* column; **~ntitel** *m typ* running title, headline.

Kombattant *m* combatant.

Kombin\|ation *f* (*Hemdhose u. fig*) combination; *aero* (*Kombi*) flying suit; **~~sgabe** *f* gift of combining; **~~sgerät** *n* phonograph-radio; television-radio-phonograph; **~~sherd** *m* combination range; **~~sschloß** *n* puzzle (*od* combination) lock; **~~sspiel** *n* combination game; **~~szange** *f* cut(ting)-pliers *pl*; combination pliers *pl*; **~ieren** *tr* to combine; *~ierter Angriff* combined attack; *~ierter Funkschlüssel* combination code.

Kombüse *f mar* galley, caboose.

Komet *m* comet; **~enschweif** *m* tail (*od* train) of a comet.

Komfort *m* luxury; ease; **~abel** *a* comfortable, comfy, easy, snug, cosy; **~wohnung** *f* luxury flat.

Komik *f* comicality, fun; humo(u)r; **~er** *m* comedian, comic (actor); **komisch** *a* comic(al), funny; (*seltsam*) strange.

Komitee *n* committee.

Komma *n* comma; decimal point.

Kommand\|ant, **~eur** *m* commander; commanding officer (*Abk* C. O.); *mar* captain, skipper; **~antur** *f* commander's office; garrison H.-Q.; **~ieren** *tr, itr* to command; to order; (*abstellen*) to detail, to detach *~ierender General* general officer commanding; corps commander; **~itgesellschaft** *f* limited partnership, limited liability company; **~itist** *m* limited partner.

Kommando *n* command; order; (*Stab*) headquarters; command; (*Abteilung*) detachment, detail; (*Sondertruppe*) raiding party, special squad, commando; *Am* ranger; *das ~ führen* to be in command of; *das ~ übernehmen* to take (over) the command; *~ zurück!* (*Befehl*) as you were! **~angriff** *m mil* raid; **~brücke** *f* the bridge, conning-bridge; **~flagge** *f* commander's flag; **~gerät** *n mil* predictor, stereoscopic fire director, data computer, antiaircraft director; **~gewalt** *f* military authority; **~raum** *m* control room; **~sache** *f* confidential military document; **~stab** *m* baton; **~stand** *m* (*U-Boot*) tower; control station; **~stelle** *f* command post; order station; **~truppe** *f* commando; **~turm** *m mar* conning-tower, battery commander's turret; control tower; fighting top; **~wagen** *m Am mil* command car; **~wort** *n* command.

kommen *irr itr* to come (to); (*an~*) to arrive (at); (*zurück~, wieder~*) to return, to come back; (*häufig*) to frequent; (*sich nähern*) to approach, to draw near; (*gelangen*) *fam* to get (to, at); (*bewegt werden*) to go; (*sich ereignen*) to happen, to take place, to occur; (*sich ergeben*) to come out, to arise, to result, to proceed from; *darauf wäre sie nie ge~* that would never have occurred to her; *wie ~ Sie dazu?* what makes you think that? *es komme, wie es wolle* whatever may happen; *wenn es hoch kommt* at the most; *es kommt nichts dabei heraus* nothing will come out of it; *es ist mir zu Ohren ge~* I have been told; *ich komme an die Reihe* it is my turn; (*ich*) *komme gleich!* coming! *aber das Schlimmste kommt noch* but the worst of it is yet to come; *ich komme nicht auf den richtigen Ausdruck* I can't think of the right expression; *wie ~ Sie dazu?* how dare you? *ich bin nicht aus den Kleidern ge~* I didn't get out of my clothes; *das kommt davon!* that's the result! *was kommt nun?* what will be next? *wie kommt es, daß ...* how is it that; *abhanden ~* to get lost; *an die Reihe ~* to have o.'s turn; *an den Unrechten ~* to catch a Tartar; *ans Licht ~, an den Tag ~* to be brought to light; *auf etw ~* (*kosten*) to cost; (*denken*) to think of, to hit upon s. th.; *auf~* (*für*) to be responsible for, to make good; *auf eins heraus~* to be all one; *auf seine Kosten ~* to recover o.'s expenses; *auf seine Rechnung ~* to profit, to benefit (by); *aus den Augen ~* to lose sight of; *davon~* to pull through all right; (*entfliehen*) to escape; *leichten Kaufes davon~* to get off lightly; *mit heiler Haut davon~* to escape unhurt; *mit e-m blauen Auge davon~* to get off with a shaking; *dazu~* (*Zeit haben*) to find time to; (*zufällig*) to happen to come; *dazu kommt noch* add to that, besides; *gegangen ~* to come on foot; *gelaufen ~* to come running; *sehr gelegen ~* to come in very handy; *wie gerufen ~* to come up opportunely; *e-m gleich~* to equal s. o.; *hinter etw ~* to discover; *in Betracht ~* to come into question; *nicht in Betracht ~, nicht in Frage ~* to be out of the question; *in Gang ~* to get into o.'s stride; *in Geldverlegenheit ~* to run short of money, to be hard up; *in Mode ~* to come into fashion; *jdm in die Quere ~* to thwart s. o., to cross (s. o.'s plans); *in den Sinn ~* to remember s. th.; *in schlechte Verhältnisse ~* to fall on hard times; *in Verlegenheit ~* to get into trouble; *jdm ins Gehege ~* to spoil s. o.'s game; (*sich messen mit*) to try conclusions with s. o.; *ins Gerede ~* to be talked of; *jdn ~ lassen* to send for s. o.; *etw ~ lassen* to order; *sich etw zu schulden ~ lassen* to become guilty of; to be to blame for; *jdn* (*nicht*) *zu Wort ~ lassen* to let s. o. get in a word edgewise (to cut s. o. short); *es zum Äußersten ~ lassen* to let matters come to the worst; *gut nach Hause ~* to get home safe(ly); *~ sehen* to foresee, to anticipate; *über jdn ~* to befall; *um etw ~* to lose s. th.; *um Hab u. Gut ~* to lose o.'s possessions; *ums Leben ~* to lose o.'s life; *vom Hundertsten ins Tausendste ~* to talk nineteen to the dozen; *vom Regen in die Traufe ~* to fall from the frying pan into the fire; *zu e-r Entscheidung ~* to come to a decision; *wieder zu Kräften ~* to recover strength; *zu kurz ~* to fall short, to come off a loser; *jdm zu nahe ~* to offend s.o.; *nicht zu Rande ~* to make vain efforts, to fail to accomplish; *zu Schaden ~* to come to grief (over); *zu sich ~* to recover o.'s senses; *jdm teuer zu stehen ~* to cost s. o. dear; *zu spät ~* to be (too) late; *zum Vorschein ~* to turn up, to make

o.'s appearance; *zur Besinnung* ~ to come to o.'s senses; **~d** *pp, a* coming; *~e Woche* next week.
Komment|ar *m* commentary; **~ator** *m* commentator; **~ieren** *tr* to comment (on).
Kommers *m* students' social gathering; drinking-bout; **~buch** *n* book of drinking songs.
kommerz|ialisieren *tr* to commercialize; (*Schuld*) to convert a debt into a negotiable loan; **~iell** *a* commercial; **~ienrat** *m* council(l)or of commerce.
Kommilitone *m* fellow student.
Kommis *m* clerk; salesman.
Kommiß *m* barrack room life; army; **~brot** *n* army-bread, ammunition-bread, barrack bread, *Am* G.I. bread; ration bread; **~stiefel** *m pl* ammunition-boots *pl*, army-boots *pl*.
Kommiss|ar *m* commissary; (*Bevollmächtigter*) commissioner; *Hoch~~* High Commissioner; (*Rußland*) commissar; (*Polizei*) inspector; **~ariat** *n* commissariat; **~arisch** *a* commissarial; provisional; *~~ vernehmen* to examine on commission; **~ion** *f* (*Ausschuß*) committee; (*beauftragte*) commission; (*Auftrag*) order, commission; *gemischte ~~* joint committee; *in ~~* on commission, on consignment; **~~är** *m* commission agent (*Am* merchant); (*Warenempfänger*) consignee; (*Makler*) broker; (*Agent*) factor; **~~sartikel** *m* goods *pl* on consignment; **~~sgebühr** *f* commission; **~~sgeschäft** *n* commission business; **~~slager** *n* commission agency; **~~sverkauf** *m* sale by agent; **~~sweise** *adv* on commission.
Kommode *f* chest of drawers; (*Toilettentisch*) dressing table; *Am* bureau.
kommunal *a* communal, municipal; **~beamte(r)** *m* local (*od* town) official; **~betriebe** *m pl* (public) utilities *pl*; **~politik** *f* municipal policy (*od* politics); **~steuer** *f* local rate; **~verwaltung** *f* municipal administration, *Am* local government.
Kommun|ikant *m* communicant; **~ion** *f* communion; **~iqué** *n* communiqué, official bulletin (*od* statement); **~ismus** *m* communism; *ein mit dem ~~ Sympathisierender Am* fellow travel(l)er; **~ist** *m* communist, *fam* Commie; **~~enhetzer** *Am* red-baiter; **~~isch** *a* communist(ic); *~~ische Partei* Communist Party; *~~ische Internationale* Communistic International, *Abk* Comintern; *~~isches Informationsbüro n* Communistic Information Bureau, *Abk* Cominform; **~izieren** *itr* to communicate.
Kommut|ator *m* commutator; switch; collector (ring); **~ieren** *tr* to commute; *el* to commutate; to reverse; **~ierung** *f* commutation.
Komöd|iant *m* actor; comedian; *fig* hypocrite; **~ie** *f* play; comedy; *fig* farce; *~~ spielen* (*fig*) to sham.
Kompa(g)nie *f* company; *Abk com* Co, *mil* Coy; **~chef, ~führer** *m* company commander· **~geschäft** *n* joint business, partnership.
Kompagnon *m* partner.
Komparativ *m* comparative (degree).
Komparse *m film, theat* super, dumb actor.
Kompaß *m* compass; *nach ~* by compass; **~ablenkung** *f* deviation; **~häuschen** *n* binnacle; **~nadel** *f* compass-needle; **~peilung** *f* compass bearing; **~rose** *f* compass-card; **~strich** *m* point of the compass.
Kompen|dium *n* manual; abridg(e)ment, summary; abstract; **~sation** *f* compensation; **~~sgeschäft** *n* barter trade; **~sieren** *tr* to compensate; *aero* (*Kompaß*) to swing.
kompet|ent *a* authoritative, competent; **~enz** *f* competence; cognizance; *jur* jurisdiction.
Komplet *n* suit of clothes.
kom|plett *a* complete; everything included; **~~ieren** *tr* to (make) complete; **~plex** *m* complex; (*Hemmung*) inhibition; (*Häuser~~*) group of houses; (*Land~~*) plot of real estate.
Kompliment *n* compliment; (*Verbeugung*) bow; (*Knicks*) curts(e)y; *gerne ein ~ hören wollen* to fish for compliments; *keine ~e!* no ceremony! **~ieren** *tr* to compliment.
Kompliz|e *m* accomplice, accessory; **~iert** *a* complicated; intricate.
Komplott *n* plot, conspiracy; *ein ~ schmieden* to form a plot.
kompo|nieren *tr* to compose; **~nist** *m* composer; **~sition** *f* composition; *typ* page make-up, *Am* page lay-out.
Kompositum *n gram* compound (word).
Kompost *m* compost; (*Gartenerde*) garden-mo(u)ld; **~haufen** *m* compost (*od* dung) heap.
Kompott *n* stewed fruit, compote, preserves *pl*; *Am* sauce; **~schüssel** *f* compote dish; **~teller** *n* compote plate.
Kompr|esse *f* compress, bandage; **~essor** *m mot* compressor; supercharger; **~imieren** *tr* to compress.
Kompro|miß *m* compromise; **~mittieren** *tr* to compromise; *r* to compromise o. s.
Komtesse *f* (unmarried) countess.
Komtur *m* commander of an order.
Konden|sator *m* condenser; **~sieren** *tr* to condense; **~smilch** *f* evaporated (*od* tinned) milk; **~sstreifen** *m aero* vapo(u)r- (*od* exhaust) trail; condensation trail, contrail; **~swasser** *n* condensation water.
Konditionalsatz *m* conditional clause.
Konditor *m* pastry-cook, confectioner; **~ei** *f* confectioner's (shop), confectionery, sweetmeat shop; **~waren** *f pl* confectionery, pastries *pl*, tea-bread, cakes *pl*, sweatmeats *pl*.
Kondol|enzbesuch *m* visit of condolence; **~ieren** *itr* to condole (with s. o.), to express o.'s sympathy with.
Konfekt *n* sweetmeats *pl*, sweets *pl*; chocolates *pl*, confectionery; comfit, *Am* candy; **~ion** *f* (manufacture of) ready-made clothes; **~~sabteilung** *f* ready-made (*Am* ready-to-wear) department; **~~sanzug** *m* ready-made (suit); *sl* reach-me-down; **~~sgeschäft** *n* ready-made clothes shop; **~~skleidung** *f* ready-made clothes *pl*, *sl* reach-me-downs *pl*; *Am* ready-to-wear clothes *pl*, store clothes *pl*, *sl* hand-me-downs *pl*; **~~sladen** *m* ready-made (*Am* ready-to-wear) shop.
Konfer|enz *f* conference, meeting; *e-e ~~ abhalten* to hold a meeting; **~~gespräch** *n* conference call; **~~schaltung** *f* conference calling equipment; **~~teilnehmer** *m* member of a conference, *Am* conferee; **~~tisch** *m* conference table; **~~zimmer** *n* conference room; (*Hotel*) commercial room; **~ieren** *itr* to confer, to deliberate (*über* on), to meet for discussion.
Konfession *f* confession; (*Glaube*) creed; (*Glaubensgemeinschaft*) denomination; **~ell** *a* confessional, denominational; **~slos** *a* undenominational, unattached; **~swechsel** *m* change of creed.
Konfirm|and *m* candidate for confirmation; **~ation** *f* confirmation; **~ieren** *tr* to confirm.
konfiszier|en *tr* to confiscate, to seize; **~ung** *f* confiscation.
Konfitüren *f pl* preserves *pl*; confectionery, sweets *pl*; **~laden** *m* sweet-shop; *Am* candy store.
Konflikt *m* conflict.
Konföderation *f* confederation.
kon|form *adv* in conformity with; *~~ gehen* to be in agreement; **~frontieren** *tr* to confront (with).
konfus *a* confused, muddled; *~ machen* to mix up.
Kongreß *m* congress, *Am* convention; **~mitglied** *n Am* congressman, congresswoman.
kongru|ent *a* congruent; **~enz** *f* congruity; **~ieren** *itr* to coincide; to be congruent.
König *m* king; **~in** *f* queen; **~~witwe** *f* queen dowager; **~lich** *a* (*amtlich*) royal; (*wahrhaft ~~*) regal; kinglike; *die ~~en* the Royalists *pl*; **~reich** *n* kingdom, realm; **~sadler** *m* golden eagle; **~skerze** *f bot* mullein; **~skrone** *f* royal crown; *bot* crown-flower; **~smord, ~smörder** *m* regicide; **~swürde** *f* royal dignity; **~tum** *n* royalty; (*Königsherrschaft*) kingship.
konisch *a* conic(al).
Konjug|ation *f* conjugation; **~ieren** *tr* to conjugate.
Konjunkt|ion *f* conjunction; **~iv** *m* subjunctive (mood).
Konjunktur *f com* business-outlook (*od* -prospects *pl*); trade cycle; *günstige ~* favo(u)rable situation (*od* opportunity), *Am* boom; **~bericht** *m* market report; **~forschung** *f* trade research; **~gewinn** *m* market profit; **~lage** *f* market condition; **~schwankung** *f* market vacillation; **~ritter** *m* time-server; *Am* big time operator; (*politisch*) *Am* carpetbagger; **~zusammenbruch** *m* complete slump.
kon|kav *a* concave; **~kret** *a* concrete.
Konkubinat *n* concubinage.
Konkurr|ent *m* competitor, rival, *Am* contestant; **~enz** *f* competition, rivalry; (*Wetteifer*) emulation; (*Widerstand*) opposition; (*Veranstaltung*) *sport* event; (*Personen*) competitors *pl*, rivals *pl*; *außer ~~* not competing; *scharfe ~~* keen competition; *unlautere ~~* unfair competition; *der ~~ die Spitze bieten* to defy competition; *jdm ~~ machen* to compete with s. o.; *sich gegenseitig ~~ machen* to be in competition with each other; **~~ausschreibung** *f* invitation of tenders; **~~erzeugnisse** *n pl* competitor's goods *pl*; **~~fähig** *a* able to compete; (*gangbar*) marketable; (*Preis*) competitive; **~~fähigkeit** *f* competitive position; **~~firma** *f* rival firm; **~~kampf** *m* competitive struggle, trade rivalry; (*auf Leben u. Tod*) cut-throat competition; *sport* event; **~~los** *a* unrival(l)ed, matchless, without competition; exclusive, non-competitive; **~~preis** *m* competitive price; **~~unfähig** *a* unable to compete; **~~unternehmen** *n* rival business concern; **~ieren** *itr* to compete (with).
Konkurs *m* bankruptcy, failure; insolvency; *den ~ anmelden* to declare o. s. a bankrupt; *in ~ geraten* to become bankrupt; **~antrag** *m* petition in bankruptcy; **~erklärung** *f* declaration of insolvency; **~eröffnung** *f* opening of bankruptcy proceedings; **~forderung** *f* claim provable in bankruptcy; **~masse** *f* bankrupt's estate; **~verfahren** *n* bank-

ruptcy proceedings *pl*; *Aufhebung des ~~s* discharge of a bankrupt; **~vergleich** *m* composition; **~verwalter** *m* (*gerichtlich*) receiver in bankruptcy, liquidator; (*Gläubiger*) trustee.
können (*Hilfszeitwort*) *unvollständige Formen*: I can; I could; (*Verneinung*) I cannot, *Am* I can not; I could not; (*Ersatz*) to be able, to be capable, to be in a position (to); (*Annahme, Wahrscheinlichkeit*) I may, (*Verneinung*) I cannot, *Am* I can not; I might; (*Ersatz*) to be likely to, it is possible (*od* likely); (*Erlaubnis*) I may; I might; (*Ersatz*) to be allowed, to be permitted (to); *nicht mehr ~* to be done (up), to be exhausted; *das kann sein* that may be (so); *das kann nicht sein* that is impossible; *ich kann nichts dafür* it is not my fault, I cannot help it; *er kann gehen* he may go; *man kann nur hoffen* it is to be hoped; *er hat es nicht tun ~* he has not been able to do it; *er hätte es tun ~* he could have done it; *ich kann mich irren* I may be mistaken; *ich kann nicht umhin zu lachen* I cannot help but laugh, I cannot help laughing; *tr* (*verstehen*) to know, to understand; *er kann nichts* he doesn't know a thing; *e-e Sprache ~* to know a language; *~ n* (*Fähigkeit*) ability, faculty, power; (*Kenntnisse*) knowledge.
Konnex *m* connection, connexion, relation; (*Zus.hang*) nexus.
Konnossement *n* bill of lading.
konsequ|ent *a* consistent; **~enz** *f* consistency; consequence, result; *~~en ziehen* to draw conclusions.
konserv|ativ *a* conservative; **~atorium** *n* academy of music, *Am* conservatory; **~e** *f* preserve, tinned (*Am* canned) food; **~en** *f pl* tinned (*Am* canned) goods (*od* food); **~~büchse, ~~dose** *f* tin, *Am* can; **~~fabrik** *f* tinning factory, *Am* cannery; (*Fleisch*) *Am* packing-house; **~~industrie** *f* tinning industry; **~ieren** *tr* to preserve, to conserve; **~ierung** *f* preservation; conservation; **~~smittel** *n* preservative; **~~sverfahren** *n* preserving process.
Konsign|ation *f* consignment, consignation; **~ieren** *tr* to consign.
Konsistorium *n* consistory
Konsol|e *f arch* console, bracket; (*Stütze*) support; **~idieren** *tr* to consolidate; **~idierung** *f* consolidation; *~s pl* consolidated funds *pl*, consols *pl*, *Am* consolidated government bonds *pl*.
Konsonant *m* consonant; **~endeutlichkeit** *f* consonant articulation; **~isch** *a* consonantal.
Konsort|en *m pl* associates *pl*; (*Mitschuldige*) accomplices *pl*; **~ium** *n* group, syndicate; association.
konspirieren *itr* to conspire, to plot.
kon|stant *a* constant; **~~e** *f* constant; **~statieren** *tr* to ascertain, to verify; to establish; to state; to confirm; **~sterniert** *a* taken aback; **~stituieren** *tr* to constitute; *~~de Versammlung* constituend assembly; **~stitution** *f* constitution; **~stitutionell** *a* constitutional.
konstru|ierbar *a* constructible; **~ieren** *tr* to construct; (*entwerfen*) to design; *gram* (*zerlegen*) to parse, (*verbinden*) to construe; **~kteur** *m* constructor, designer, designing engineer, *Am* draftsman; **~ktion** *f* construction, design; **~~sbüro** *n* drawing-office; **~~sfehler** *m* error (*od* defect) of construction; faulty design; flaw; **~~szeichnung** *f* shop drawing.
Konsul *m* consul; **~at** *n* consulate; **~ent** *m* counsel, advocate, legal adviser (*od* advisor); **~tieren** *tr* to consult, to ask s. o.'s advice; (*Arzt*) to see the doctor, to take medical advice.
Konsum *m* consumption; **~ent** *m* consumer; **genossenschaft** *f* co-operative society; **~güter** *n pl* consumer goods *pl*; **~ieren** *tr* to consume; **~verein** *m* co-operative society.
Kontakt *m* contact; **~abdruck** *m phot* contact print; **~draht** *m el* contact-wire; **~fläche** *f* surface of contact; **~knopf** *m el* push-button; **~ring** *m* contact-ring; **~rolle** *f* (*Straßenbahn*) trolley; **~schalter** *m el* contact-switch; **~schlüssel** *m* ignition key; **~schnur** *el* flex; **~stecker, ~stöpsel** *m el* (contact) plug; **~stück** *n tech* contact-piece; **~verfahren** *n* contact process.
Konter|admiral *m* rear-admiral; **~bande** *f* contraband; **~fei** *n* portrait, likeness; **~~en** *tr* to portray; **~order** *f* counter-order; **~tanz** *m* square dance, quadrille.
Kontinent *m* continent; **~al** *a* continental; **~~handel** *m* continental trade; **~~klima** *n* continental climate; **~~sperre** *f* continental blockade (*od* system).
Kontingent *n* quota, contingent; allotment; **~ieren** *tr* to fix the quotas; *~ierte Waren* quota goods; **~ierung** *f* quota system; apportionment.
Kontinuität *f* continuity.
Konto *n* account; *gesperrtes ~* blocked account; *laufendes ~* current account, account current; *offenes ~* open account; *überzogenes ~* overdrawn account; *ungedecktes ~* unsecured account; *ein ~ abschließen* to close an account; *e-m ~ belasten* to place to the debit of an account; to debit; *auf ein ~ einzahlen* to pay into an account; *ein ~ eröffnen* to open an account (with); *ein ~ bei e-r Bank haben* to have an account at a bank; *ein ~ überziehen* to overdraw an account; **~auszug** *m* extract (*od* statement) of account; **~bestand, ~stand** *m* balance; **~buch** *n* account book; **~eröffnung** *f* opening of account; **~inhaber** *m* account holder; **~korrent** *n* current account; **~~verbindlichkeiten** *f pl* demand deposit liabilities *pl.*
Kontor *n* office; **~bedarf** *m* office supply; **~ist(in)** *m* (*f*) clerk; **~stuhl** *m* office-stool.
kontra: counter, *jur* versus; *pro u. ~* pro and con; **~baß** *m mus* double bass; **~hent** *m* contracting party; **~hieren** *tr* to contract; *itr* to make a contract; **~punkt** *m mus* counterpoint.
Kontrakt *m* contract, bargain; (*Übereinkommen*) agreement; (*geschriebener ~*) indenture; (*Urkunde*) deed; *e-n ~ abschließen* to enter into a contract; **~bruch** *m* breach of contract; **~lich** *a* stipulated (by contract), contractual; **~widrig** *a* contrary to the contract.
Kontrast *m* contrast; **~ieren** *tr, itr* to contrast.
Kontroll|abschnitt *m* counterfoil; (*Scheck*) stub; **~apparat** *m* control apparatus, controlling device; **~beamter, ~eur** *m* controller; (*Zug, Straßenbahn*) inspector; **~bestimmung** *f* control determination; **~e** *f* control; (*Prüfung*) examination, check(-up); (*Überwachung*) supervision; *unter scharfer ~~ halten* to keep a close watch (*od Am* check) on; **~einrichtung** *f* controlling gear; **~gebiet** *n* area of control; **~ierbar** *a* controllable; **~ieren** *tr* to control, to check, to examine, *Am* to administrate; (*überwachen*) to supervise; (*Bücher*) to audit; (*Richtigkeit*) to verify; (*Fragebogen, Personen*) to screen, *Am fam* to vet; **~karte** *f* (*Uhr*) time card; **~kasse** *f* cash register; **~lampe** *f* pilot lamp; **~marke** *f* ticket, time-keeping check; **~messung** *f* control (*od* check) measurement; **~muster** *n* control (*od* check) sample; **~punkt** *m,* **~stelle** *f* check point; **~rat** *m* control council; *Alliierter ~~* Allied Control Council; **~schein** *m* control ticket; **~stempel** *m* check mark; **~turm** *m aero* airport (traffic) control tower; **~uhr** *f* control-clock, telltale-clock, recording timer; **~vermerk** *m* check mark; **~versuch** *m* control test (*od* experiment); **~zettel** *m* counterfoil, tally, check; **~ziffer** *f* key number.
Kontroverse *f* controversy.
Kontur *f* contour; outline; skyline; **~karte** *f* contour map.
Konus *m* cone.
Konvent *m* convention, gathering, assembly; **~ion** *f* convention; agreement; treaty; **~~alstrafe** *f* penalty for breach (*od* nonfulfillment *od* nonperformance) of contract; demurrage; **~~ell** *a* conventional.
Kon|vergenz *f* convergence; **~vergieren** *itr* to converge; **~~d** *a* convergent; **~versation** *f* conversation; **~~slexikon** *n* encyclop(a)edia; **~vertierbar** *a* convertible; **~vertieren** *tr* to convert; **~vertit** *m* convert; **~vikt** *n* boarding-house for Roman Catholic students; **~volut** *n* set of pamphlets; lot; **~zentration** *f* concentration; **~~slager** *n* concentration camp; **~zentrieren** *tr* to concentrate; **~zentrisch** *a* concentric.
Konzept *n* rough copy, first (*od* rough) draft; (*Skizze*) sketch; *aus dem ~ kommen* to grow confused, to lose the thread to; *aus dem ~ bringen* to put out, to disconcert; **~heft** *n* scribbling-block, scratch-pad; **~papier** *n* scribbling paper.
Konzern *m com* combine, trust, pool.
Konzert *n* concert; *bei* (*od in*) *e-m ~* at a concert; **~agentur, ~direktion** *f* concert management, concert direction; **~besucher** *m* concert-goer; **~flügel** *m* grand piano; **~ieren** *itr* to give a concert; **~meister** *m* conductor; (*erster Geiger*) violinist of the first desk; **~saal** *m* concert-hall; *Am* auditorium; **~sänger(in)** *m* (*f*) public singer.
Konzession *f* concession, licence, *Am* franchise; charter; *e-e ~ erteilen* to grant a licence; **~ieren** *tr* to license; **~inhaber** *m* licensee; concessionary, concessionaire.
Konzil *n* council.
konzipieren *tr* to draft, to plan; (*zeugen*) to conceive.

*

Koordin|atennetz *n* co-ordinate system; **~atenpapier** *n* co-ordinate paper; ruled (*od* graph) paper; **~ieren** *tr* to co-ordinate.
Köper *m* twill.
Kopf *m* head, *fam* pate, noddle; (*oberster Teil*) top; (*Scheitel*) crown; (*Verstand*) brains *pl*; understanding, judg(e)ment, sense; (*kluger Mensch*) talented man; (*Titel*) title, heading; (*Person*) person; (*Pfeife*) bowl; (*Münze*) face side; *~ an ~* closely packed; *auf den ~, pro ~* each, a head, per capita; *aus dem ~* by heart; *Hals über ~* head over heels, headlong; *~ od Schrift* head or tail; *von ~ zu Fuß* from top to toe; *mit bloßem ~* bare-headed; *viele Köpfe, viele Sinne* many men, many minds; *~ hoch!*

keep smiling! *mil* chin up! *über die Köpfe weg* above the heads; *im ~ behalten* to remember; *nicht auf den ~ gefallen sein* to be no fool; *sich e-e Sache durch den ~ gehen lassen* to think it over; *den ~ hängen lassen* to be (so) down in the mouth; *jdm im ~ herumgehen* to run in s. o.'s head; *sich e-e Kugel durch den ~ jagen* to blow o.s' brains out; *jdm seinen ~ lassen* to give s. o. his head; *sich etw aus dem ~ schlagen* to dismiss s. th. from o.'s mind; *nicht richtig im ~ sein* to be crazy, *Am* to be out of o.'s head (*od* mind); *sich in den ~ setzen* to take into o.'s head; *bis über den ~ in Schulden stecken* to be up to o.'s ears in debt; *in den ~ steigen* to go to o.'s head; *ich weiß nicht, wo mir der ~ steht* I don't know whether I'm coming or going; *auf den ~ stellen* to turn upside down (*od* topsy-turvy); *vor den ~ stoßen* to hurt, to offend; to antagonize; *den Nagel auf den ~ treffen* to hit the nail on the head; *jdm den ~ verdrehen* to turn s.o.'s head; *den ~ verlieren* to lose o.'s head; *über den ~ wachsen* to be too much for; *e-m den ~ waschen* to give s. o. a dressing-down; *sich den ~ zerbrechen* to rack o.'s brains (over); *auf den ~ zusagen* to tell s. o. to his face.

Kopf|arbeit *f* brain work; **~~er** *m* brain worker, *Am* white-collar worker; **~bahnhof** *m* terminal station, terminus, *Am* terminal, railhead; **~ball** *m* *sport* heading; **~bedeckung** *f* head-covering (*od* gear); **~ende** *n* head (of a bed); **~geld** *n* (*Währungsreform*) quota per capita; (*Steuer*) poll-tax; (*Belohnung*) head money; **~grippe** *f* encephalitis; **~haar** *n* hair (of the head); **~hänger** *m* pessimist, spiritless person; (*Duckmäuser*) sneak, hypocrite; **~~ei** *f* pessimism; sneaking, hypocrisy; **~haut** *f* scalp; **~hörer** *m tele, radio* head-phone (*od* receiver), ear-phone, *Am sl* muffs *pl*; **~kissen** *n* pillow; **~~bezug** *m* pillow-case (*od* slip); **~lastig** *a aero* noseheavy; **~laus** *f* head-louse; **~leiste** *f typ* head-piece; **~linie** *f* headline, *Am* by-line; **~los** *a* headless, acephalous; *fig* confused; out of o.'s wits; (*töricht*) silly; *~~ werden* to lose o.'s head; *~~ machen* to upset s. o., to throw into confusion; *~~ herumrennen* to run around like chickens with their heads cut off; **~losigkeit** *f fig* thoughtlessness; stupidity; **~nicken** *n* nod; **~nuß** *f* blow on the head; **~putz** *m* head-dress; **~rechnen** *n* mental arithmetic (*od* computation); **~salat** *m* garden (*od* head *od* cabbage) lettuce; **~scheu** *a* (*Pferd*) restive; (*Mensch*) shy, timid; *jdn ~~ machen* to intimidate; **~schmerz** *m*, **~weh** *n* headache; *~~en verursachend fam* headachy; *rasende ~~en haben* to have a splitting headache; **~schuppen** *f pl* dandruff; scurf; **~schuß** *m* shot in the head; **~schütteln** *n* shaking of o.'s head; **~schützer** *m* head-protector; **~sprung** *m* header; **~stand** *m sport* head-stand; *aero* nose-over, landing on the nose; *e-n ~~ machen aero* to nose over; **~steinpflaster** *n* cobbled pavement; **~steuer** *f* poll-tax; **~stimme** *f* falsetto; **~stück** *n* head-piece, header; **~sturz** *m aero* nose-dive; crash; **~tuch** *n* kerchief, scarf, head-shawl; **~über** *adv* headlong, head foremost; *~~, ~unter* pell-mell; **~verbrauch** *m* consumption per capita; **~wand** *f* end wall; **~wäsche** *f* shampooing; **~wunde** *f* wound in the head; **~zahl** *f* number of persons; **~zeile** *f* headline, *Am* by-line; **~zerbrechen** *n* racking of the brain, cogitation, rumination; *ohne viel ~~* without much pondering; **~zünder** *m* nose fuse.

Köpf|chen *n* small head; *bot* capitulum; **~en** *tr* to behead; (*Bäume*) to poll, to lop.

Kopie *f* copy; carbon copy; *phot* print, photoprint; (*Zweitschrift*) duplicate; (*Abschrift*) transcript; (*Nachbildung*) facsimile; reproduction; (*Nachahmung*) imitation; **~ranstalt** *f* printing shop; **~rapparat** *m* copying apparatus; mimeograph; **~rautomat** *m* automatic printing machine; **~rbuch** *n* copying-book; **~ren** *tr* to copy; to transcribe; to mimeograph; to trace, to make a tracing; *phot* to print; *zu dunkel ~~* to overprint; **~rpapier** *n* printing-paper; sensitive paper; copying paper; **~rpresse** *f* copying-press; **~rrahmen** *m* printing-frame; **~rstift** *m* copying-pencil; indelible pencil; **~rtinte** *f* copying ink; **~werk** *n* printing shop, printing studio.

Kopist *m* copyist; scribe.

Koppel *n mil* belt; *~ f* (*Hunde*) pack, leash; couple; (*Pferde*) string; (*Gehege*) enclosure; (*Pferdeweide*) paddock; **~kurs** *m* dead reckoning; **~n** *tr* (*Pferde*) to string; (*Hunde*) to leash, to couple; (*einzäunen*) to enclose, to fence in; (*verbinden*) to link; *radio* to couple; **~navigation** *f aero* flying (*od* avigation) by dead reckoning; **~ung** *f* coupling; (*Kreise*) *radio* hook-up; **~~sspule** *f radio* coupling-coil; **~~sverkauf** *m* conditional sale, tie-in sale.

kopulieren *tr* to couple, to pair; to unite; to marry.

*

Koralle *f* coral; **~nbank** *f* coral-reef; **~nfischer** *m* coral-diver (*od* fisher); **~nhalsband** *n* coral neck-lace; **~ntier** *n* coral.

Koran *m* Koran.

Korb *m* basket; (*Pack~, Eß~*) hamper; (*großer*) crate; *min* corf, cage; (*Bienen~*) hive; (*Papier~*) waste-paper basket; (*Fische*) creel; (*Binsen~*) frail; (*Trag~ für Tiere*) pannier; *fig* refusal, denial; rebuff; *Hahn im ~ sein* to be cock of the walk; *e-n ~ geben* to turn s. o. down; *e-n ~ bekommen* to meet with a refusal; **~ball** *m* basket-ball; **~blütler** *m pl* composite flowers *pl*; **~flasche** *f* carboy; demijohn; **~flechter** *m* basket-maker; **~flechterei** *f* basketry, osier-goods manufacture; **~möbel** *n pl* wicker-furniture; osier-furniture; **~sessel** *m* basket (*od* wicker) chair; **~voll** *m* basketful; **~wagen** *m* basket-carriage; **~weide** *f bot* osier, wicker.

Kord *m* (*gerippter Stoff*) corduroy; **~el** *f* cord, string; twine; pack-thread; groove; **~hosen** *f pl* a pair of corduroys; **~ieren** *tr tech* to knurl.

Korinthe *f* currant.

Kork *m* cork; (*Pfropfen*) cork stopper; **~baum** *m* cork-tree; **~eiche** *f* cork-oak; **~en** *tr* to cork; *~~ a* (of) cork; corky; *~~ m* cork stopper; **~isolation** *f* cork insulation; **~schicht** *f* periderm; **~sohle** *f* cork-sole; **~weste** *f* cork-jacket; **~zieher** *m* corkscrew; *aero* corkscrew spin, spiral.

Korn *n* grain; (*Getreide*) corn; (*Gewehr*) sight; bead; (*Münzen*) standard, alloy; (*Schnaps*) type of brandy; *aufs ~ nehmen* to aim at; *die Flinte ins ~ werfen* to give up, to throw up the sponge; *von altem Schrot u. ~* of the good old stamp; **~ähre** *f* ear of corn; **~bau** *m* growing of corn; **~beschaffenheit** *f* character of grain; **~bildung** *f* grain formation; granulation; crystallization; **~blume** *f* corn-flower; **~boden** *m*, **~kammer** *f* granary; **~branntwein**, **~schnaps** *m* grain spirits *pl*, whisky; **~feinheit** *f phot* fineness of grain; **~garbe** *f* sheaf; **~handel** *m* corn-trade; **~käfer** *m* grain weevil; **~kammer** *f* granary; **~rade** *f bot* cockle, corn-campion; **~schwinge** *f* corn-fan, winnowing-sieve; **~sieb** *n* grain-sieve.

Kornelkirsche *f* cornel-tree.

körn|en *tr* to granulate; (*Leder*) to grain; **~er** *m tech* ga(u)ge point, punch mark; **~ig** *a* granular.

Kornett *m* cornet, standard-bearer; *~ n mus* cornet.

Korona *f* corona; *el* corona discharge; brush discharge.

Körper *m* body; *phys* substance, compound; (*fester ~ math*) solid; (*Schiffs~*) hull; *am ganzen ~ zittern* to tremble all over; **~bau** *m* structure of the body, build; anatomy; **~behindert** *a* impeded; physically impaired; **~beschaffenheit** *f* constitution; **~chen** *n* corpuscle, particle; **~farbe** *f* body colo(u)r; pigment; **~flüssigkeit** *f* body fluid; **~fülle** *f* corpulence; **~gegend** *f* region of the body; **~geruch** *m* body odo(u)r; **~gewicht** *n* weight; **~größe** *f* stature; **~haltung** *f* bearing, attitude, deportment; **~höhle** *f* cavity of the body; **~inhalt** *m* volume; **~kraft** *f* physical strength; **~lich** *a* bodily; corporeal; material; physical; **~los** *a* bodiless, immaterial, incorporeal; **~maß** *n* cubic measure; **~pflege** *f* hygiene, beauty culture; **~~mittel** *n* cosmetic; **~puder** *m* talcum powder; **~schaft** *f* corporation; body; body corporate; **~~ssteuer** *f* corporation income tax; **~schulung** *f* physical training, physical culture; **~schwäche** *f* bodily weakness; **~stärke** *f* physical strength; **~strafe** *f* corporal punishment; **~teil** *m* part of the body; **~~chen** *n* particle; molecule; **~übung** *f* physical exercise, gymnastics *pl*; **~verletzung** *f* bodily injury; **~wärme** *f* body heat; **~welt** *f* material world.

Korporal *m* corporal; **~schaft** *f* section; squad.

Korp|s *n mil* corps; body; **~~geist** *m* team-spirit, group spirit; morale; esprit de corps; **~ulent** *a* corpulent, fat; **~ulenz** *f* corpulence; **~us** *f typ* long primer.

korrekt *a* correct; **~heit** *f* correctness; **~ionsanstalt** *f* remand home; **~ionsfaktor** *m* correction factor; **~ionsglied** *n* corrective term; **~or** *m typ* proof-reader, press-corrector; **~ur** *f* correction; *typ* proof(-sheet); *zweite ~~* revise; *druckfertige ~~* press proof; *~~ lesen* to read the proofs; **~~abzug**, **~~bogen** *m* proof sheet; **~~fahne** *f* slip proof; **~~zeichen** *n* correction.

Korrespond|ent *m* correspondent; **~enz** *f* correspondence; **~~büro** *n* news agency; pressagency; **~ieren** *itr* to correspond (with s. o., to s. th.).

Korridor *m* corridor, passage; (*Hausflur*) hall.

korrigieren *tr* to correct; *typ* to read the proofs; (*zum zweiten Mal*) to revise; (*bessern*) to mend.

Korrosion *f* corrosion; rusting; **~sbeständig** *a* corrosion-resistant, rust-resisting; stainless; **~sschutz** *m* rust protection, protection against corrosion.

kor|rumpieren *tr* to corrupt; **~ruption** *f* corruption; (*Bestechung*) bribery; (*Unehrlichkeit*) dishonesty; *parl Am* log-rolling; **~~sschnüffler** *m Am* muckracker.

Korsar *m* corsair, pirate.

Kors|e *m*, **~in** *f*, **~isch** *a* Corsican.
Korsett *n* corselette, *Am* all-in-one; **~stange** *f* busk, bone.
Koryphäe *f* celebrity, star.
Korvette *f* sloop (of war), corvette; **~nkapitän** *m* lieutenant commander.
Kosak *m* Cossack; **~enstiefel** *m pl* Russian boots *pl*.
koscher *a* pure, kosher.
kose|n *itr* to make love; *tr* to caress, to fondle; **~name** *m* pet name.
Kosinus *m* cosine.
Kosm|etik *f*, **~isch** *a* cosmetic; **~~er** *m* cosmetician, beauty operator; **~~laden** *m Am* beauty parlo(u)r.
kosm|isch *a* cosmic; **~opolit** *m*, **~~isch** *a* cosmopolitan; **~os** *m* universe.
Kost *f* food; (*Lebensmittel*) victuals *pl*; (*Nahrung*) diet; (*Speise*) fare; (*Bewirtung*) cheer; (*Beköstigung, Pension*) board; (*Lebensunterhalt*) living; *magere ~* meagre fare, *med* low diet; *reichliche ~* full diet; *fleischlose ~* vegetarian diet; *in ~ sein bei* to board with; *jdn in ~ nehmen* to board s. o.; *~ u. Wohnung* board and residence; *leichte ~ fig* slight fare; **~frei** *a* with free board; **~gänger** *m* boarder; **~geld** *n* board; board-wages *pl*; **~probe** *f* dainty morsel; **~verächter** *m*: *kein ~~ sein* to enjoy o.'s food.
kost|bar *a* precious, valuable; (*kostspielig*) costly; expensive; (*prächtig*) sumptuous; **~barkeit** *f* expensiveness, preciousness; object of value; **~spielig** *a* costly, expensive; (*prächtig*) sumptuous; **~~keit** *f* costliness; sumptuousness.
Kosten *pl* (*Preis*) cost(s *pl*), price; (*Gebühren*) charges *pl*; (*Unkosten*) expenses *pl*; (*Ausgaben*) expenditure; (*Auslagen*) outlay; *auf ~ von* at the expense of; *laufende ~* standing charges; *die ~ bestreiten* to defray the expenses; *die ~ tragen* to pay the expenses; *~ veranschlagen* to appraise the cost; *~ zurückerstatten* to refund the expenses; *mit ~ verbunden sein* to involve charges; *sich in ~ stürzen* to go to great expense; *auf seine ~ kommen* to recover expenses, to be breaking even; *fig* to get o.'s money's worth; *keine ~ scheuen* to spare no expense; **~anschlag** *m* estimate, tender; **~aufstellung** *f* statement of costs, cost sheet; **~aufwand** *m* expenditure; **~berechnung** *f* calculation of expenses; **~beteiligung** *f* sharing of costs; **~ersparnis** *f* saving of expenses; **~feststellung** *f* cost-finding; **~frage** *f* question of costs; **~frei, ~los** *a* free, free-of-charge; for nothing; **~höhe** *f* amount of costs; **~pflichtig** *a* liable for the costs; *~~ abweisen* to dismiss with costs; **~preis** *m* cost price; **~punkt** *m* expenses *pl*; **~rechnung** *f* bill, calculation, estimate; **~stelle** *f* accounting department; **~voranschlag** *m* estimate; **~vorschuß** *m* expenses advanced.
kosten *tr* (*Geld*) to cost; (*erfordern*) to require, to take; (*versuchen*) to try, to taste; (*schlürfen*) to sip; *koste es, was es wolle* cost what it may; at any cost; *Zeit u. Mühe ~* to take time and trouble; *es sich viele Mühe ~ lassen* to take much pains about it; *wieviel kostet es?* how much is it? what's the price?
köstlich *a* delicious, delightful, tasty; (*wertvoll*) valuable, precious; (*hervorragend*) excellent; (*erlesen*) exquisite, choice; (*reizend*) charming; (*prächtig*) magnificent.
Kostüm *n* costume; coat and skirt; suit; dress; fancy dress; **~fest** *n* fancy dress ball; **~ieren** *tr* to dress up, to disguise; to dress; **~probe** *f* dress rehearsal.
Kot *m* (*Schmutz*) mud, muck; (*Dreck*) dirt, filth; (*Schlamm*) mire; (*Matsch*) sludge; (*menschlicher*) f(a)eces *pl*, excrements *pl*; (*tierisch*) droppings *pl*; *in den ~ ziehen* to drag in the mud; *im ~e wälzen* to wallow in the mire; **~abgang** *m* defecation; **~blech** *n*, **~flügel** *m* mud-guard, wing, *Am* fender; **~geruch** *m* fecal odo(u)r; **~ig** *a* dirty, muddy.
Kotau *m* kotow.
Kotelett *n* (*Kalb*) cutlet; (*Schwein, Hammel*) chop; **~en** *pl* side whiskers *pl*.
Köter *m* cur, dog.
kotzen *itr sl* to vomit; *mot* to splutter, to sputter.

*

Krabb|e *f* crab; (*Garnele*) shrimp; (*Kind*) brat; **~eln** *itr* (*kriechen*) to crawl, to creep; (*sich winden*) to wriggle; (*jucken*) to tickle, to itch; *tr* to scratch, to tickle, to cause a creeping sensation.
Krach *m* crash, crack, slam; (*Lärm*) noise, din; (*Streit*) quarrel, row, blow-up; *sl* rumpus; (*Szene*) scene; (*Zus.bruch*) crash, smash, break-down; (*Donner*) roar; *mit Ach u. ~* with difficulty, only just; **~en** *itr* to crack, to crash; (*Feuer*) to crackle; (*bersten*) to burst; (*donnern*) to roar; *com* to collapse; (*Tür*) to bang; **~mandel** *f* soft-shelled almond.
krächzen *itr* to croak; to caw; *e-e ~de Stimme* a hoarse voice.
Krack|ung *f* (*Ölraffinerie*) cracking (oil); **~~sanlage** *f* cracking plant; **~verfahren** *n* cracking process.
Krad *n mil* (= *Kraftrad*) motor-cycle (*Abk* mobike, *mil* M. C.); **~fahrer** *m* motor-cyclist; **~mantel** *m* motor-cyclist's overcoat; **~melder** *m mil* motor-cycle despatch rider; **~schütze** *m mil* motor-cyclist; motorcycle rifleman; **~~bataillon** *n mil* M. C. battalion; **~~nzug** *m mil* M. C. platoon; **~späher** *m* motorcycle scout; **~spitze** *f* motorcycle point of advance guard.
kraft *prp* by virtue of, on the strength of.
Kraft *f* (*Widerstands~, ~quelle*) strength; (*Stärke*) force; (*Schwung*) vim; (*Macht, tech, fig*) power; potency; (*Rüstigkeit*) vigo(u)r; (*Wirksamkeit*) efficacy; (*seelische, geistige ~*) faculty; (*Fähigkeit*) ability; (*Tat~, phys Energie*) energy; (*sehr große, übernatürliche ~*) might; (*Stütze, fig*) arm; (*Person, Arbeiter*) person; worker, professional; labo(u)r *mit sing*; *außer ~ setzen* to annul, to abrogate; *zeitweilig außer ~ setzen* to suspend; *in ~ sein* to be in force; *in ~ treten* to come into force, to take effect, to go into effect; *wieder in ~ setzen* to revive; *mit allen Kräften* with all o.'s might; *nach besten Kräften* to the best of o.'s ability; *das geht über meine Kräfte* that's too much for me; *wieder zu Kräften kommen* to regain o.'s strength; **~anlage** *f* (electric) power plant (*od* station); **~anstrengung** *f*, **~aufwand** *m* exertion, effort; expenditure of force; **~ausdruck** *m* strong language; **~bedarf** *m* power demand; **~betrieb** *m* power installation; **~brot** *n* fortified bread; **~brühe** *f* clear soup, beef-tea; strong broth; **~droschke** *f* taxi; **~einheit** *f* unit of force; **~ersparnis** *f* economy of force; energy saving, power saving; **~fahrabteilung** *f mil* motor transport detachment; **~fahrer** *m* driver; motorist; **~fahrkampftruppe** *f mil* mechanized combat force; **~fahrpark** *m* motor park; **~fahrpersonal** *n* motor transport personnel; **~fahrschau** *f* automobile show (*od* exhibition); **~fahrspritze** *f* (*Feuerwehr*) motor-pump; **~fahrzeug** *n* motor vehicle; **~~bau** *m* automotive engineering; **~~reparaturwerkstatt** *f* motor vehicle repair shop; **~~steuer** *f* motor vehicle tax; **~feld** *n phys* field of force; **~futter** *n* concentrated feed; **~gefühl** *n* feeling of strength; **~lastwagen** *m* motor lorry, *Am* motor truck; **~linie** *f* line of force; **~los** *a* powerless, forceless; (*schwach*) weak, feeble; **~losigkeit** *f* lack of strength (*od* vigo(u)r); (*Schwäche*) debility; *fig* washiness; **~mensch** *m* tough; **~messer** *m* dynamometer; **~probe** *f* trial of strength, *Am fam* showdown; **~quelle** *f* source of power; **~rad** *n* motor bicycle (*Abk* mobike); motor-cycle; **~radfahrer** *m* motor-cyclist; **~reserve** *f* power reserve; **~säge** *f* power saw; **~schlepper** *m* tractor; **~stoff** *m* liquid fuel; petrol; **~~anlage** *f* fuel supply; **~~behälter** *m* fuel tank; **~~gemisch** *n* fuel mixture; **~~leitung** *f* fuel pipe; **~~verbrauch** *m* fuel consumption; **~strom** *m* electric power; **~strotzend** *a* vigorous; **~stück** *n* stunt; **~übertragung** *f* power transmission; **~voll** *a* vigorous, powerful; pithy; (*sehnig*) sinewy; (*tatkräftig*) energetic, full of force; **~wagen** *m* motor car (*od* vehicle), automobile; (*Last~~*) motor lorry, *Am* truck; **~~fahrer** *m* driver; **~~kolonne** *f mil* mechanized supply column; **~~park** *m* motor pool; fleet of motor cars; **~~staffel** *f mil* motor transport echelon; **~~transport** *m* motor transport; **~~werkstatt** *f* garage; **~~werkstattzug** *m mil* mobile repair shop; **~werk** *n*, **~zentrale** *f* power station, power plant; **~wirkung** *f* effect, action (of a force); **~zugmaschine** *f* motor-tractor.
Kräft|eersparnis *f* economy of manpower; **~everfall** *m* loss of strength; **~everlagerung** *f* shifting of forces; **~ezersplitterung** *f* scattering of forces (*od* power); **~ig** *a* strong, robust, *Am* husky; (*mächtig*) powerful; (*energisch*) vigorous; (*wirksam*) forcible; (*nahrhaft*) nourishing, substantial; **~~en** *tr* to strengthen; (*stärken*) to invigorate; (*erfrischen*) to refresh, to restore; (*abhärten*) to harden, to steel; **~~ung** *f* strengthening.
Kragen *m* collar; (*Umhang*) cape; *beim ~ nehmen* to collar, to seize by the collar; *das kann ihm den ~ kosten* that may cost him his head; **~knopf** *m* collar-stud, *Am* collar-button; **~spiegel** *m mil* facing, collar patch; collar insignia; tab; **~weite** *f* collar size.
Kragstein *m* corbel.
Krähe|e *f* crow, rook; *sl* (*Flugzeug*) aircraft; **~en** *itr* to crow; *es kräht kein Hahn danach* nobody troubles about it. *Am* nobody gives a hoot about that; **~~füße** *m pl* (*Schrift*) scrawl; (*Runzeln*) crow's feet; **~~nest** *n* rookery; **~winkel** *n* Gotham.
Krakeel *m* quarrel; brawl, squabble; **~en** *itr* to quarrel, to brawl; (*Spektakel machen*) to kick up a row; **~er** *m* brawler, rowdy.
Kralle *f* claw; (*Vögel*) talon; **~n** *itr* (*sich ~~*) to claw.
Kram *m* retail trade; (*Waren*) small wares *pl*, retail goods *pl*; (*Gegenstände*) things *pl*; (*Plunder*) trash, stuff, rubbish; (*Angelegenheit*) business, affair; *das paßt mir nicht in den ~* that doesn't suit my purpose; **~en** *itr* to

rummage; **~laden** *m* small shop; haberdasher's shop.

Krämer *m* shopkeeper; small tradesman; (*Kolonialwarenhändler*) grocer; **~geist** *m*, **~seele** *f* mercenary spirit, petty spirit.

Krammetsvogel *m* fieldfare.

Krampe *f* cramp(-iron); staple.

Krampf *m* cramp, *med* spasm, convulsion; (*plötzlicher Anfall*) fit(s *pl*); **~ader** *f* varicose vein, varix; **~artig**, **~haft** *a* convulsive; spasmodic; (*verzweifelt*) desperate, frantic; **~en** *tr* (*sich*) to contract; to clench; **~lindernd**, **~stillend** *a* antispasmodic; sedative.

Kran *m* crane; (*mit Dreharm*) derrick; (*Aufzug*) hoist; **~arm** *m* crane jib; **~führer** *m* craneman, *Am* crane operator; **~ich** *m orn* crane.

krank *a* sick, ill, diseased; (*unwohl*) unwell; (*leidend*) suffering, ailing; (*schwach*) weak; ill (*nur prädikativ*); *~ darniederliegen* to be lying ill; *~ werden* to fall ill, *Am* to be taken sick; *~ schreiben* to certify as ill; to put on the sick-list; ***sich*** *~ melden* to go (*od* to report) sick; *sich ~ lachen* to split o.'s sides (with laughter), *Am* to laugh o.s. sick; **~e** *m* patient, sick person; (*Fall*) case; *die ~en pl* the ill, *Am* the sick; **~en** *itr* to be ill (with), to suffer (from); (*fehlen*) to lack; **~enabteilung** *f* sick-ward; **~enabtransport** *m* evacuation of sick; **~enauto** *n* motor ambulance; **~enbahre** *f* litter, stretcher; **~enbesuch** *m* visit to a patient; **~enbett** *n*, **~enlager** *n* sick-bed; *ans ~~ gefesselt* confined to bed, bedridden; *am ~~* at the bedside; **~enblatt** *n* medical record; **~enbuch** *n* patients' book; **~enfürsorge** *f* assistance to the sick; **~engeld** *n* sick-benefit; sick-pay; **~engeschichte** *f* medical history; **~enhaus** *n* hospital; *in ein ~~ schaffen* (*od einliefern*) to put in a hospital, *Am* to hospitalize; *Überführung in ein ~~* hospitalization; *in ein ~~ aufnehmen* to admit to a hospital; **~enkasse** *f* health insurance, sick fund, medical plan; **~~narzt** *m* panel doctor; **~enkost** *f* sick diet; **~enpflege** *f* nursing; **~~r** *m* male nurse; **~~rin** *f* nurse; **~enrevier** *n mil* sick barrack, sick-bay; **~ensaal** *m* sick-room, ward, infirmary; *mil* sick-bay; **~ensammelstelle** *f mil* collecting station for casualties; **~enschein** *m* medical certificate; **~enschwester** *f* nurse; **~enstube** *f* sick-bay, sickroom; **~enstuhl** *m* invalid (*od* bath) chair; **~entrage** *f* stretcher, litter; **~enträger** *m* ambulance man, stretcher-bearer; **~entransportwagen** *m* ambulance truck; **~enuntersuchung** *f* examination of the sick; **~enversicherung** *f* health insurance; **~enwagen** *m* (motor) ambulance; **~enwärter** *m* male nurse; hospital attendant, orderly; **~enzimmer** *n* sick-room; **~enzug** *m* ambulance train; **~haft** *a* morbid, pathological; irregular, abnormal; **~heit** *f* illness, sickness; (*bestimmte*) disease; *ansteckende ~~* contagious disease; (*organische*) malady; (*Leiden*) ailment; (*Unwohlsein*) indisposition; (*Beschwerde*) complaint; (*Erkrankung*) affection; *e-e ~~ durchmachen* to go through an illness; *sich e-e ~~ zuziehen* to fall ill, to contract (*od* develop) a disease; **~~sausbruch** *m* outbreak of disease; **~~säußerung** *f* manifestation of disease; **~~sbericht** *m* bulletin, doctor's report; **~~sbild** *n* aspect of a disease; **~~serreger** *m* excitant of disease; **~~sfall** *m* case; **~~shalber** *adv* owing to illness; **~~sherd** *m* seat of disease; **~~skeim** *m* disease germ; **~~sträger** *m* carrier; **~~sübertragung** *f* transference of disease; **~~surlaub** *m* sick-leave; **~~sverhütung** *f* preventive health care; prophylaxis; **~~sverlauf** *m* course of disease; **~~svortäuschung** *f* malingering; **~~szeichen** *n* (*subjektiv*) symptom, (*objektiv*) sign.

kränk|eln *itr* to be in poor health, to be sickly; **~en** *tr* to vex, to hurt; (*beleidigen*) to offend; *r* to feel hurt; to worry; to fret; **~lich** *a* sickly, in poor health; ailing; **~~keit** *f* sickliness, weak state of health; **~ung** *f* insult, offence; mortification.

Kranz *m* garland, wreath; (*Licht~*) corona; (*Einfassung*) border, ring; (*Rad~*) rim, ring; **~binder** *m* garland maker; **~gesims** *n* cornice; **~jungfer** *f* bridesmaid; **~spende** *f* funeral wreath.

Kränz|chen *n* small wreath; *fig* coffee party; ladies' meeting; club, (social) circle, private circle, private party, *Am* bee; **~en** *tr* to adorn; to crown, to wreathe.

Krapfen *m* fritter.

Krapp *m* madder.

kraß *a* crass, gross, sharp; (*Lüge*) big; (*Widerspruch*) striking.

Krater *m* crater; **~bildung** *f* crater formation; **~fläche** *f* crater area; **~öffnung** *f* vent in the crater.

Kratz|bürste *f* scrubbing-brush; *fig* cross-patch; **~bürstig** *a* cross, irritable; (*mürrisch*) gruff; **~e** *f* scraper; rabble; scrapings *pl*; **~eisen** *n* (door) scraper; **~en** *tr* to scrape, to scratch; (*Wolle*) to card; (*Metall*) to rabble; *itr* to scratch, to grate; (*Geschmack*) to be harsh; (*schreiben*) to scrawl; **~~d** *a* harsh; (*Geschmack*) irritating; **~er** *m* scraper, scratcher; (*Schramme*) scratch; **~fuß** *m* (awkward) curts(e)y, clumsy bow; **~geräusch** *n el*, *radio* contact noise; crackling; **~wunde** *f* scratch.

Krätz|e *f* itch; *med* scabies; *tech* waste; **~er** *m* wretched wine; **~ig** *a* itchy; (*Hund*) mangy.

krauen *tr* to scratch softly.

kraulen *tr* to rub gently; *itr* to crawl.

kraus *a* crisp, curly, curled, crinkled, kinky; (*Stoff*) ruffled, nappy; *die Stirne ~ ziehen* to knit o.'s brow; **~e** *f* ruffle, frill(ing), **~haarig** *a* curly-haired; **~kopf** *m* curly head.

kräuseln *tr* to curl; to crisp; to crimp; (*plissieren*) to goffer; (*Wasser, Federn*) to ruffle; (*fälteln*) to frill; *r* (*Wasser*) to ripple; (*Rauch*) to wreathe.

Kraut *n* herb; plant; (*Kohl*) cabbage; (*Unkraut*) weed; (*Rüben*) top; *ins ~ schießen* to run into leaves; *wie ~ u. Rüben durcheinander* a terrible mess, higgledy-piggledy, jumbled; **~acker** *m* cabbage-field; **~artig** *a* herbaceous; **~en** *tr* to weed; **~garten** *m* kitchen-garden; **~junker** *m* country-squire; country-bumpkin; **~kopf** *m* head of a cabbage.

Kräuter|buch *n* herbal; **~essig** *m* aromatic vinegar; **~fressend** *a* herbivorous; **~käse** *m* green cheese; **~kunde** *f* botany; **~salbe** *f* herbal salve; **~salz** *n* vegetable salt; **~sammlung** *f* herbarium; **~suppe** *f* julienne; **~tee** *m* herb tea, infusion of herbs; **~wein** *m* medicated wine.

Krawall *m* riot, uproar, row; (*Lärm*) noise; *fam* rumpus.

Krawatte *f* cravat, (neck-)tie; **~n** *f pl* neckwear; **~~halter** *m* tie-clip; **~~nadel** *f* scarf-pin, *Am* tie-pin.

kraxeln *itr fam* to clamber up, to climb.

Kreatur *f* creature.

Krebs *m* crayfish, crawfish; (*Taschen~*) crab; (*See~*) spring lobster; *astr* Cancer; *med* cancer; ulcer, carcinoma; **~artig** *a* crustaceous, crablike; *med* cancerous; cancer-like; **~bildung** *f* canceration; **~erreger** *m* carcinogen; **~forschung** *f* cancer research; **~gang** *m* backward movement; *den ~~ gehen* to go backward; *fig* to make a retrograde movement; **~geschwulst** *f* cancerous swelling, tumo(u)r; **~geschwür** *n* cancer, carcinoma; **~gewebe** *n* cancer tissue; **~ig** *a* cancerous; **~rot** *a* red as a lobster; **~schaden** *m* cancerous sore; *fig* deep-seated evil, canker; **~schere** *f* claw of a crayfish; **~suppe** *f* crayfish-soup.

Kredenz *f* sideboard; **~en** *tr* to present, to serve, to offer.

Kredit *m* (*Anleihe*) credit, loan; (*Vorschuß*) advance; (*Ruf*) reputation; (*Vertrauen*) trust, *auf ~* on credit, *fam* on tick; *kurzfristiger ~* short-term credit; *langfristiger ~* long-term credit; *~ aufnehmen* to raise a loan; *~ einräumen* to grant a credit; *auf ~ geben* to give on trust; *jdm ~ geben in Höhe von* to give s.o. credit for; *~ haben* to enjoy credit; *auf ~ kaufen* to buy on credit; *e-n ~ eröffnen* to open a credit with s.o.; **~abkommen** *n* credit arrangement; **~anspannung** *f* credit strain; **~anstalt** *f* loan (*od* credit) bank; **~begrenzung** *f* credit line; **~brief** *m* letter of credit; **~einräumung** *f* allowance of credit; **~einschränkung** *f* credit restriction; **~fähig** *a* sound, solvent; **~~keit** *f* financial soundness; **~geber** *m* creditor; **~genossenschaft** *f* mutual loan society; **~grenze** *f* limit of credit; **~ieren** *tr* to credit; (*stunden*) to give on credit; **~inanspruchnahme** *f* credit use; **~iv** *n* credentials *pl*; full power; **~knappheit** *f* credit stringency; **~markt** *m* money market; **~orenkonto** *n* accounts *pl* payable; **~nehmer** *m* borrower, beneficiary; **~seite** *f* creditor; **~würdig** *a* sound, safe, trustworthy, reliable; **~~keit** *f Am* credit rating.

Kreide *f* chalk; (*Malerei*) crayon; *tief in der ~ sitzen* to be deeply in debt; *bunte ~* colo(u)red chalk; **~artig** *a* chalky, cretaceous; **~bleich** *a* dead-white; **~fels** *m* chalky rock; **~formation** *f* cretaceous formation; **~haltig** *a* containing chalk, cretaceous; **~papier** *n* enamel(l)ed paper; **~strich** *m* chalk-line; **~weiß** *a* (as) white as a sheet; **~zeichnung** *f* chalk-drawing.

Kreis *m* circle; ring; (*Wirkungs~*) sphere; (*Um~*) compass; (*~bahn, Strom~*) circuit; (*Lebens~*) span of life; (*Zone*) zone; (*Gebiet*) district; *astr* orbit; (*Reichweite*) range; (*Freundes~*) set, round; (*Bekannte*) circle; (*Bevölkerung*) group, walk of life; (*abgeschlossener ~*) coterie, clique; *sich im ~e drehen* to rotate, to spin round; *im ~ herumsitzen* to sit around in a circle; *e-n ~ beschreiben* to describe a circle; *in Parlaments~en* in Parliamentary quarters; *in weiten ~en der Bevölkerung* in wide sections of the population; *in zuständigen ~en* in competent quarters; **~abschnitt** *m* segment; **~arzt** *m* district medical officer; **~ausschnitt** *m* sector; **~bahn** *f* circular path, orbit; **~bewegung** *f* rotation, rotary (*od* circular) motion; revolution; *bot* circumnutation; **~bogen** *m* arc of a circle; *arch* circular arch; **~el** *m* spinning top; gyroscope, gyro; **~~bewegung** *f* gyroscopic motion; **~~elektron** *n* spinning electron; **~~horizont** *m* artificial horizon; **~~kompaß** *m* gyro-compass; **~~lader** *m* centrifugal supercharger; ~~n *itr* to spin like a top, to revolve, to whirl round; ~~**pumpe** *f* centrifugal pump; ~~**rad** *n* impeller, rotor; turbine; ~**en** *itr* to revolve, to turn round in a circle, to circle, to circulate; (*umlaufen*) to rotate; (*Raubvogel*) to hover; ~**fläche** *f* circular area; *aero* airscrew disc; ~**förmig** *a* circular, round; ~**gericht** *n* district (*od* county) court; ~**kegel** *m* circular cone; ~**korn** *n* ring-and--bead sight; ~**lauf** *m* circulation, circular course, circuit; (*Umlauf*) rotation, revolution; (*Periode*) cycle; (*Jahreszeiten*) succession; *anat* (*großer* ~~) systemic (*od* greater) circulation, (*kleiner* ~~) pulmonic (*od* lesser) circulation; ~~**störung** *f med* circulatory disturbance; ~**linie** *f* circular line, circumference; ~**ordnung** *f* district regulation; ~**rund** *a* circular; ~**säge** *f* circular saw, *Am* buzz saw; ~**stadt** *f* county town; ~**tag** *m* District Council; ~**umfang** *m* circumference, periphery; ~**verkehr** *m* roundabout traffic, gyratory system of traffic.

kreischen *itr* to shriek, to scream.

kreiß|en *itr* to be in (child-)labo(u)r; ~~ *n* labo(u)r; ~~**de** *f* woman in labo(u)r; ~**saal** *m* delivery room, lying-in room.

Krematorium *n* crematorium, *Am* crematory.

Krempe *f* brim; ~**l** *m* rubbish, stuff; (*Wolle*) card; ~**ln** *tr* to card; (*Baumwolle*) to willow.

krepieren *itr* (*Tiere*) to die; *mil* to burst; to explode, to detonate.

Krepp(flor) *m* crape; ~**papier** *n* crêpe paper; ~**sohle** *f* crêpe sole.

Kresse *f bot* cress.

Krethi und Plethi rag-tag and bobtail; Tom, Dick and Harry.

Kreuz *n* cross; (*Karte*) club; (*Musik*) sharp; (*Pferde*) croup; (*Lende*) loins *pl*; *typ* obelisk; *anat* small of o.'s back, (*Hinterteil*) rump; *fig* (*Kummer*) affliction, grief, sorrow; *das* ~ *schlagen* to cross o. s.; *ans* ~ *schlagen* to nail to the cross; *zu* ~*e kriechen* to eat humble pie, to sing small; ~ *u. quer* in all directions, all over, criss-cross; *übers* ~ crosswise; *mir tut das* ~ *weh* my back aches; ~**abnahme** *f* descent from the cross; deposition; ~**band** *n* (postal) wrapper; *unter* ~~ *schicken* to send by book-post; ~**bein** *n* sacrum; ~**brav** *a* thoroughly honest; ~**donnerwetter!** *interj* confound it! the deuce! ~**dorn** *m* buckthorn; ~**en** *tr* to cross; (*überschreiten*) to traverse; (*Tiere, Pflanzen*) to interbreed, to hybridize; *itr* to cross; *mar* to cruise; *r* to cross, to intersect; ~**er** *m* cruiser; ~**erverband** *m* cruiser squadron; ~**erhöhung** *f* elevation of the cross; ~**esstamm** *m* the Holy Rood; ~**estod** *m* death on the cross; ~**eszeichen** *n* (sign of the) cross; seal; ~**fahrer** *m*, ~**ritter** *m* crusader; ~**feuer** *n* cross-fire; ~**fidel** *a* merry as a cricket; ~**förmig** *a* cross-shaped, cruciform, cruciate; ~**gang** *m arch* cloister; ~**gelenkkupplung** *f* universal joint; ~**gewölbe** *n arch* cross vault; ~**igen** *tr* to crucify; *fig* to mortify; ~**igung** *f* crucifixion; ~**kopf** *m* cross-head; ~**lahm** *a* broken-backed; ~~ *sein* to have backache; ~**otter** *f* adder, common viper; ~**schiff** *n arch* cross aisle, transept; ~**schmerzen** *m pl* lumbago; pains *pl* in the loins; ~**schnabel** *m* crossbill; ~**spinne** *f* cross-spider, garden spider; ~**stich** *m* cross-stitch; ~**unglücklich** *a* despondent, downcast; ~**ung** *f* crossing, intersection; (*Übergang*) crosswalk; (*Tiere, Pflanzen*) cross-breed(ing), hybridization; (*Rasse*) hybrid; mongrel; ~~**spunkt** *m* intersection; ~**vergnügt** *a* fit as a fiddle; ~**verhör** *n* cross-examination; *ins* ~~ *nehmen* to cross--examine, *Am fam* to grill; ~**verweisung** *f* cross reference; ~**weg** *m* cross--road(s *pl*), crossing; *eccl* way of the cross; ~**weise** *adv* crosswise, crossways; ~**worträtsel** *n* crossword puzzle; ~**zug** *m* crusade.

kribbeln *itr* to crawl, to swarm; (*jucken*) to itch, to tickle.

Kricket *n* cricket; ~**platz** *m* cricket--field (*od* ground); ~**schlagholz** *n* bat, willow.

kriech|en *irr tr* to creep, to crawl; (*aus dem Ei*) to hatch; *fig* to fawn (on s. o.), to cringe (before s. o.), to toady; *auf dem Boden* ~~ (*vor*) to grovel (before, to s. o.); ~~**d** *a fig* obsequious, sneaking; ~**er** *m fig* sneak(er), toad-eater, toady; (*Schmeichler*) sycophant, flatterer; ~~**ei** *f* slavishness, cringing, servility; ~~**isch** *a* fawning, slavish; (*niedrig*) mean, base; ~**pflanze** *f* creeper, trailer; ~**tier** *n* reptile.

Krieg *m* war; *fig* (*Kampf, Streit*) warfare; ~ *bis aufs Messer* war to the knife; *im* ~ at war; in war-time; *kalter* ~ cold war; *im* ~ *sein* (*mit*) to be at war (with); ~ *anfangen* (*mit*) to go to war (with); ~ *führen* to carry on (*od* make) war (with), to wage war (on); *e-n* ~ *provozieren* to provoke a war; ~**en** *tr fam* (*bekommen*) to get, to obtain; (~ *führen*) to wage war (on); ~**er** *m* warrior, soldier; ~~**denkmal** *n* war-memorial; ~~**gräber** *n pl* war--graves *pl*; ~~**isch** *a* warlike, martial; ~~*isch gesinnt* war-minded; ~~**verein** *m* military veterans' society; ~~**witwe** *f* war-widow; ~**führend** *a* belligerent; ~**führung** *f* conduct of war; warfare; (*Strategie*) strategy.

Kriegs|ächtung *f* outlawing of war; ~**akademie**, ~**schule** *f* military academy; staff-college; ~**anleihe** *f* war--loan; ~**artikel** *m pl* articles *pl* of war; ~**ausbruch** *m* outbreak of war; ~**ausweitung** *f* extension (*od* spread) of war; ~**auszeichnung** *f* war decoration; ~**bedarf** *m* military stores *pl*; ammunition; ~**beil** *n* war-hatchet; ~**bemalung** *f Am* war-paint; ~**bereit** *a* ready for war; ~~**schaft** *f* readiness for war; ~**bericht** *m* war communiqué; ~**berichter(statter)** *m* war correspondent (*od* reporter); ~**beschädigt** *a* disabled on active service; ~~**e(r)** *m* disabled ex-serviceman; ~**beschädigung** *f* line-of-duty ailment; ~**beseitigung** *f* elimination of war; ~**besoldung** *f* war pay; ~**beute** *f* war booty, loot, spoils *pl* of war; ~**blinde(r)** *m* war--blinded man; *die* ~~**n** the war--blinded; ~**braut** *f* war-bride; ~**dienst** *m* military service; ~~**verweigerer** *m* conscientious objector, *fam* conchy; ~**drohung** *f* war threatening; ~**ende** *n* end of war; ~**entschädigung** *f* war indemnity; ~**erfahrung** *f* war experience; ~**erklärung** *f* declaration of war; ~**fall** *m* case of war; ~**flagge** *f* war flag; *mar* ensign; ~**flotte** *f* navy, naval force; ~**flugzeug** *n* military aircraft; combat plane, warplane; ~**freiwillige(r)** *m* volunteer; ~**fuß** *m* war-footing; ~**gebiet** *n* war zone; *Am* theater of war; ~**(ge)brauch** *m* custom of war; ~**gefangene(r)** *m* prisoner of war (*Abk* P.O.W.); ~**gefangenschaft** *f* war captivity; *in* ~~ *sein* to be a prisoner of war; ~**gerät** *n* war material; ~**gericht** *n* court-martial; ~~**srat** *m* Judge Advocate; ~**geschichte** *f* military history; ~**geschrei** *n* war-cry; *Am* (*Indianer*) whoop; ~**gesetz** *n* military law; ~**getümmel** *n* din of battle; ~**gewinnler** *m* war-profiteer; ~**gewölk** *n* war-cloud; ~**glück** *n* military success; fortune of war; ~**gott** *m* war-god; ~**grab** *n* war--grave; ~**gräberausschuß** *m*, ~**gräberfürsorge** *f* War-Graves Commission; ~**hafen** *m* naval port; ~**handlung** *f* hostile action; ~**handwerk** *n* military profession; ~**heer** *n* army; ~**held** *m* hero of war; ~**herr** *m* supreme commander; war lord; ~**hetze** *f* war-mongering; ~~**r**, ~**treiber** *m* war-monger; ~**hinterbliebene** *pl* surviving dependants of service-men; ~**industrie** *f* war industry; ~**kamerad** *m* fellow-soldier, *Am fam* army buddy; ~**kasse** *f* war--chest; ~**kind** *n* war baby; ~**kosten** *pl* war-expenses *pl*; ~**kunst** *f* art of war; strategy; tactics *pl*; ~**lasten** *f pl* war load; ~**lazarett** *n* base hospital; ~**lied** *n* war-song; ~**list** *f* stratagem; ~**lustig** *a* bellicose, eager for war; ~**macht** *f* military forces *pl*; ~**marine** *f* navy; ~**mäßig** *a* warlike; ~**material** *n* war material (*od* matériel); ~**minister** *m* minister of war; *Engl* Secretary of State for War, *Am* Secretary of War; ~~**ium** *n* War Office; *Am* War Department, *Am fam* Pentagon; ~**müde** *a* war--worn; ~**notwendigkeit** *f* military necessity; ~**objekt** *n* war objective; ~**philosophie** *f* philosophy of war; ~**pfad** *m Am* war-path; ~**pflicht** *f* military duty; ~**plan** *m* war plan; ~**potential** *n* military resources *pl*; national war preparedness; ~**rangliste** *f* army directory; ~**rat** *m* council of war; ~**recht** *n* martial law; ~**ruf** *m* war-cry; ~**ruhm** *m* military glory; ~**rüstung** *f* armament; ~**schäden** *m pl* war damages *pl*; ~**schauplatz** *m* theatre (*od* seat) of war ~**schiff** *n* battleship, warship; ~**schuld** *f* war guilt; ~~**en** *f pl* war-debts *pl*; ~~**lüge** *f* war guilt lie; ~~**verschreibung** *f* war-bond; ~**schule** *f* officer aspirants training school; ~**sitte** *f* custom of war; ~**spiel** *n* war game, *Am* map maneuver; ~**stammrolle** *f* unit roster; ~**stand** *m* war footing; ~**stark** *a* on a war-footing; ~**stärke** *f* war strength; ~**steuer** *f* war-tax; contribution; ~**tanz** *m Am* war-dance; ~**teilnehmer** *m* combatant; (*nach Ende*) ex-soldier (*od* -serviceman), *Am* war - vet(eran); ~**trauung** *f* war-wedding; ~**tüchtig** *a* fit for war; ~**verbrecher** *m* war criminal; ~~**prozeß** *m* war crimes trial; ~**verletzte(r)** *m* disabled ex--soldier, *Am* disabled veteran; ~**versehrt** *a* disabled on active service; ~~**enrente** *f* physical-disability benefit; ~**verwendungsfähig** *a* fit for active (military) service; ~**volk** *n* forces, troops *pl*; ~**vorbereitungen** *f pl* preparations *pl* for war; ~**wichtig** *a* of military importance; ~~*e Ziele* military targets; ~**wirtschaft** *f* wartime economy; ~**wissenschaft** *f* military science; ~**zeit** *f* war-time; ~**ziel** *n*, ~**zweck** *m* war aim; ~**zucht** *f* military discipline; ~**zug** *m* military expedition; ~**zulage** *f* allowance for service in the field; ~**zustand** *m* state of war.

krimin|al *a* criminal; ~~**abteilung** *f* criminal investigation department (*Abk.* CID); ~~**beamter** *m* detective, (*in Zivil*) plain-clothes man; ~~**ität** *f* criminality; ~~**polizei** *f* criminal investigation department; *Am* plain-clothes police; detective force; ~~**roman** *m* detective novel, *Am fam* whodunit; ~~**reißer** *m* shocker, *Am* thriller; ~**ell** *a* criminal.

Krimmer *m* krimmer; imitation astrakhan.
Krimskram *m* knickknacks *pl;* pleasing trifle; trinket.
Kringel *m* ring; cracknel.
Krinoline *f* crinoline; hoop skirt.
Krippe *f* crib, manger; (*Kinder~*) crèche; **~nspiel** *n* nativity play.
Krise, Krisis *f* crisis, *pl* -ses; *com* depression; (*Höhepunkt*) acme; **~nfest** *a* panic-proof; **~nunterstützung** *f* emergency unemployment relief; **~nzeit** *f* time of crisis; **~ln** *itr*: *es kriselt* a crisis is approaching.
Kristall *m* crystal; **~bildung** *f* crystallization; (*Zucker*) granulation; **~detektor** *m radio* crystal detector; **~eis** *n* crystal ice; **~en** *a* of crystal; **~flasche** *f* decanter; **~förmig** *a* crystalloid; **~glas** *n* crystal; **~hell, ~klar** *a* crystal-clear, transparent; **~inisch** *a* crystalline; **~isieren** *tr, itr* to crystallize; **~(l)inse** *f anat* crystalline lens; **~waren** *f pl* (crystal) glassware; **~zucker** *m* refined sugar in crystals.
Krit\|ik *f* criticism; (*Besprechung*) critique, review; *unter aller ~~* beneath contempt; **~ikaster** *m* carper; **~iker** *m* critic; reviewer; **~iklos** *a* uncritical, undiscriminating; **~iklosigkeit** *f* lack of discrimination; **~iksucht** *f* fault-finding; **~isch** *a* critical; *~~ besprechen* to review; *~~ prüfen* to scan; **~isieren** *tr* to criticize, to find fault (with); to review, to comment (upon); (*tadeln*) to censure; *scharf ~~* to clapperclaw, to revile, to criticize spitefully.
kritt\|eln *tr* to find fault (with); to carp (*über* at); (*nörgeln*) to cavil; (*sich in den Haaren liegen*) to wrangle; **~ler** *m* fault-finder, carping critic, caviller.
Kritzel\|ei *f* scrawl, scribble; **~ig** *a* scrawling; (*unleserlich*) illegible; **~n** *tr, itr* to scrawl, to scribble; to scratch (on).
Kroki *n mil* sketch map; rough sketch; croquis.
Krokodil *n* crocodile; **~tränen** *pl* crocodile tears *pl.*
Krokus *m* crocus, saffron.
Kron\|anwalt *m* attorney-general; **~e** *f* crown; (*Adel*) coronet; (*Baum*) top; (*Zahn*) cap, crown; *bot* corolla; *astr, anat, bot* corona; (*Kranz*) wreath; (*Gipfel, Kamm*) crest; *das setzt der Sache die ~~ auf* that puts the lid on it; *was ist ihm in die ~~ gefahren?* what's the matter with him? *etw in der ~~ haben* to have had a little too much; **~erbe** *m* heir to the crown; **~güter** *n pl* crown-lands *pl;* **~insignien** *pl* regalia *pl;* **~juwelen** *n pl* crown-jewels *pl;* **~leuchter** *m* chandelier, lustre; *el* electrolier; **~prinz** *m* crown prince; *Engl* Prince of Wales; **~~essin** *f* crown-princess; *Engl* Princess Royal; **~rat** *m Engl* Privy Council; **~zeuge** *m* King's evidence; chief witness, *Am* States' evidence.
krön\|en *tr* to crown; **~ung** *f* coronation; crowning.
Kropf *m* crop; (*Krankheit*) goitre; **~ig** *a* goitrous; **~taube** *f* pouter (pigeon).
kröpf\|en to bend at right angles; **~ung** *f arch* corner mo(u)lding; *tele* bend.
Kröte *f* toad, paddock; *fig* brat.
Krück\|e *f* crutch; *tech* rake, rabble; **~stock** *m* hooked stick.
Krug *m* jug; (*Metall~*) can; (*Trinkbecher*) mug; (*Wasser~*) pitcher; (*Bier~, Seidel*) tankard; (*Wirtshaus*) inn, tavern.
Kruke *f* stone-bottle (*od* -jar).
Krülltabak *m* curled tobacco, shag.
Krume *f* crumb; (*Acker~*) mo(u)ld, topsoil.
Krümel *m* tit-bit; (*Krume*) crumb; **~ig** *a* crumbling, crummy; **~n** *itr* to crumble.
krumm *a* crooked; (*gekrümmt*) curved; (*verkrümmt*) distorted; (*schief, verkehrt*) awry; (*verbogen*) twisted; (*verzogen*) warped; (*gewölbt*) arched; (*unehrlich*) fraudulent, sneaking; *~e Wege fig* crooked ways; *~e Nase* hooked nose; *~e Linie* curved line; *etw ~ nehmen* to resent s. th., to take s. th. amiss of s. o.; *~ sitzen* to cower; **~beinig** *a* bandy-legged, knock-kneed; **~darm** *m anat* ileum; **~holz** *n* crooked timber; (*Baum*) dwarf mountain pine; **~linig** *a math* curvilinear; **~säbel** *m* scimitar; **~stab** *m* crozier.
krümm\|en *tr* to crook, to bend; *sich ~~* to grow crooked; (*Fluß*) to wind; (*vor Schmerzen*) to writhe with pain; *fig* to cringe; *sich ~~ vor Lachen* to split with laughter; **~ung** *f* bend, curve, turn, sinuosity; (*Weg, Fluß*) winding; *med* (*Verzerrung*) contortion; (*Rückgrat*) curvature; (*Zustand*) crookedness; *aero* camber.
Kruppe *f* crupper.
Krüppel *m* cripple; *zum ~ machen* to cripple; **~haft, ~ig** *a* crippled; (*verstümmelt*) maimed; (*mißgestaltet*) deformed; (*verkümmert*) stunted.
Krust\|e *f* crust; *med* scurf; (*Küche*) crackling; **~enartig** *a* crustlike, crustaceous; **~enbildung** *f* crust formation, incrustation; **~entier** *n* crustacean; **~ig** *a* crusty; crustaceous.
Kruzifix *n* crucifix.
Krypt\|a *f* crypt; **~ogamisch** *a* cryptogamian.
Kübel *m* tub; (*Eimer*) pail, bucket; (*Bottich*) vat; *min* skip; *mil* (*Wagen*) (open) cross country car, *Am* jeep; **~sitz** *m mot* bucket seat; **~wagen** *m* cross country car, reconnaissance car, bucket car, skip, *Am* jeep.
Kubik\|-, kubisch *a* cubic; **~fuß** *m* cubic foot; **~inhalt** *m* cubic contents *pl;* **~maß** *n* cubic measure; **~wurzel** *f* cube-root; **~zahl** *f* cube; **~zentimeter** *m* cubic centimeter.
Kubus *m* cube.
Küche *f* kitchen; (*Kochen*) cookery, cooking, cuisine; (*Spül~*) scullery; *mar* galley; *kalte ~* cold meat(s *pl*); *bürgerliche ~* plain (*od* home) cooking; *kleine ~* kitchenette; **~nabfälle** *m pl* garbage, waste; **~nabfallschlucker** *m* automatic waste-disposer; **~nanrichte** *f* (kitchen)dresser; **~nbulle** *m mil sl* cook, mess sergeant; **~nchef, ~nmeister** *m* chef, head cook; **~ndienst** *m mil sl* kitchen police; **~neinrichtung** *f* kitchen-fittings *pl;* **~ngarten** *m* kitchen-garden; **~ngeruch** *m* skillet smell; **~ngeschirr** *n* kitchen-utensils *pl;* kitchenware; **~nherd** *m* kitchen grate, kitchen range; **~njunge** *m* kitchen-boy; **~nlatein** *n* dog-Latin; **~npersonal** *n* kitchen personnel, cuisine; **~nsalz** *n* common salt; **~nschabe** *f* cockroach; **~nschelle** *f bot* pasque flower; **~nschrank** *m* larder, (kitchen-)cupboard; **~ntisch** *m* kitchen-table; (*Anrichte*) dresser; **~nunteroffizier** *m* mess sergeant; **~nzettel** *m* menu, bill of fare.
Kuchen *m* tart; (*Torte*) (French) cake; (*~stück*) cake; (*Feingebäck*) pastry; **~bäcker** *m* pastry-cook; **~blech** *n* baking tin; (*rundes*) griddle; **~form** *f* cake-tin, cake-mo(u)ld; **~teig** *m* cake-dough, paste.
Küchlein *n* chicken.
Kücken *n* chick(en); (*junges Mädchen*) flapper, *Am* chicken.
Kuckuck *m* cuckoo; *zum ~!* bother it! hang it! darn it! **~sblume** *f* ragged robin; **~sei** *n* cuckoo's egg; **~sruf** *m* cuckoo call (*od* note); **~suhr** *f* cuckoo-clock.
Kufe *f* vat, tun, tub; (*Schlitten~*) skid, runner, *Am* bob.
Küfer *m* cooper; (*Kellermeister*) cellar-man; **~ei** *f* cooperage.
Kugel *f* ball; *sport* shot; (*Erd~*) globe; *math* sphere; (*Geschoß*) ball; (*Flinten~*) bullet; (*Wahl~*) ballot; *med* head (of a bone); *sich e-e ~ durch den Kopf jagen* to blow out o.'s brains **~abschnitt** *m math* spherical segment; **~ähnlich** *a* spheroidal; ball-like; **~blitz** *m* ball-lightning; **~durchmesser** *m* diameter of a sphere; **~fang** *m* butts *pl;* **~fest** *a* bullet- (*od* shot-)proof; **~fläche** *f* spherical surface; **~form** *f* spherical form; (*Gußform*) bullet mo(u)ld; **~förmig** *a* globular; spherical; **~gelenk** *n* ball-and-socket joint; *med* socket (-joint); **~gestalt** *f* spherical form; **~lager** *n* ball-bearing; **~n** *tr, itr* to roll; to form into a ball; *sich ~n* to roll; *es war zum ~n* I nearly split with laughing; **~regen** *m* shower of bullets; **~rund** *a* round as a ball; **~schreiber** *m* ball pen, ball-point pen; **~sicher** *a* bullet-proof; **~stoßen** *n* putting the weight, *Am* shot put(ting); **~ventil** *n* ball valve.
Kuh *f* cow; (*Färse*) heifer; *frischmelkende ~* dairy-cow, cow in milk; *blinde ~* blind-man's-buff; **~brücke** *f mar* orlop; **~euter** *n* cow's udder; **~fladen** *m* cow-dung; **~handel** *m fig* lobbying, *Am* horse-trading, *Am* log-rolling; **~haut** *f* cow-hide; *das geht auf keine ~~ fam* that beats everything; **~hirt** *m* cowherd, *Am* cowpuncher; **~milch** *f* cow's milk; **~pocken** *pl* cow-pox, **~~impfung** *f* vaccination; **~reigen** *m* Alpine cowherd's tune; **~stall** *m* byre, cowshed, *Am* cow barn.
kühl *a* cool, chilly; (*frisch*) fresh; *fig* cool, reserved, cold; *jdn ~ empfangen* to receive s. o. coolly; *jdn ~ behandeln* to turn the cold shoulder on s. o.; **~anlage** *f* cooling (*od* refrigerating) plant, cold-storage plant; **~apparat** *m* cooling apparatus; refrigerator; **~e** *f* coolness; (*Frische*) freshness; *fig* coldness; **~en** *tr, itr* to cool; (*auffrischen*) to refresh; (*Wind*) to freshen; *tech* to refrigerate; to chill; (*Glas*) to anneal; (*Zorn*) to vent (o.'s anger on); (*~ werden*) to grow cool; *r* to get cool; **~er** *m mot* radiator; (*Anlage*) refrigerator; condenser; cooler; **~~figur** *f* radiator mascot; **~~haube** *f* radiator muff, bonnet; **~~klappen** *f pl* radiator flaps *pl;* gills *pl;* **~~mantel** *m* condenser (*od* cooler) jacket; **~~(schutz)gitter** *n* radiator stone protector; **~~schutzmittel** *n* radiator anti-freeze substance; **~~verkleidung** *f* radiator shell, grille; **~flüssigkeit** *f mot* cooling liquid, coolant; **~haus** *n* cold-storage depot; **~kammer** *f* cooling chamber; **~maschine** *f* refrigerating machine; **~mittel** *n* refrigerant; **~ofen** *m* annealing oven; **~raum** *m* cooling chamber; cold-storage chamber; **~rippe** *f mot, tech* radiator-fin, gill; cooling-rib; **~rohr** *n* cooling tube; condenser tube; **~schiff** *n* (*Brauerei*) cooling back, cooler; *mar* cold-storage ship; refrigerator ship; **~schlange** *f* cooling coil; **~schrank** *m* refrigerator; cooling cabinet; *im ~~ aufbewahren* to keep under refrigeration; **~stoff** *m* coolant; **~ung** *f* cooling, refrigeration; freshness; **~wagen** *m* refrigerator wag(g)on (*od Am* car); (*Lastwagen*) refrigerator lorry (*od* truck), *fam*

reefer; **~wasser** *n* cooling water; lead water; **~wirkung** *f* cooling effect.

kühn *a* bold; (*verwegen*) daring; (*furchtlos*) fearless; (*vermessen*) audacious; (*tollkühn*) foolhardy; (*keck*) forward; (*forsch*) dashing; (*gewählt*) hardy; **~heit** *f* boldness, daring, audacity.

kul|ant *a* obliging, fair; **~anz** *f* fair dealing.

Kuli *m* coolie.

kulinarisch *a* culinary.

Kulisse *f* side-scene, wing; movable scene; corridor; *was geht hinter den ~n vor?* what's going on backstage? *hinter den ~n geführte Verhandlungen* backstage negotiations; **~nmaler** *m* scene-painter; **~nreißer** *m Am sl* ham actor; **~nschieber** *m* scene-shifter.

Kulmin|ation *f* culmination; **~~spunkt** *m* culminating point; **~ieren** *tr* to culminate.

Kult *m* cult; worship; **~gemeinschaft** *f* religious association; **~ivierbar** *a* civilizable; **~ivieren** *tr* (*bebauen*) to cultivate, to till; (*sorgfältig*) to culture; (*geistig entwickeln*) to cultivate; to culture; (*in die ~ur einführen*) to civilize; (*verbessern*) to improve; **~iviert** *a* cultivated; *fig* cultured; *zu sehr ~~* sophisticated; **~stätte** *f* place of worship; **~ur** *f* (*geistige*) culture; (*fortgeschrittene soziale Entwicklung*) civilization; (*als Ergebnis*) cultivation; (*Boden, Bienen, Fische, Bakterien*) culture; (*Urbarmachung*) cultivation; plantation; tilling; growing; **~~arbeit** *f* cultural work; **~~aufgabe** *f* problem of civilization; **~~austausch** *m* cultural exchange; **~~ell** *a* cultural; **~~fähig** *a* (*Boden*) arable, tillable; **~~feindlich** *a* hostile to civilization; **~~film** *m* educational (*od* instructional *od* documentary) film; **~~frage** *f* question of civilization; **~~gebiet** *n* civilized region; **~~geschichte** *f* history of civilization; **~~geschichtlich** *a* with relation to the history of civilization; **~~land** *n* cultivated (*od* tilled) land; **~~landschaft** *f* cultivated land; **~~los** *a* uncivilized; barbarous; savage; **~~mensch** *m* civilized human being; **~~methode** *f* method of culture; **~~politisch** *a* politico-cultural; **~~propaganda** *f* propaganda for civilization; **~~schicht** *f* culture stratum; **~~staat** *m* civilized state; **~~stufe** *f* stage of civilization; **~~volk** *n* civilized nation (*od* race *od* people); **~~zentrum** *n* cultural centre; **~~zweck** *m* cultural purpose; **~us** *m* cult; religious; worship **~~minister** *m* Minister of Education (and Public Worship); **~~ministerium** *n* Ministry of Education (and Public Worship).

Kümmel *m* caraway (-seed); (*römischer*) cumin; (*Branntwein*) kümmel.

Kummer *m* grief, sorrow, affliction; (*Unruhe*) trouble; (*Elend*) distress; (*Verdruß*) worry; *jdm viel ~ bereiten* to cause s. o. a lot of grieve; *das ist mein geringster ~* that is the least of my troubles; **~voll** *a* sorrowful, grievous; afflicted.

kümmer|lich *a* miserable, wretched; (*armselig*) poor, scanty, measly; **~ling** *m* miserable creature; **~n** *tr* to grieve, to worry, to trouble; (*betreffen*) to concern, to regard; *ich kümmere mich nicht darum* I don't care about it; that's no business of mine; *was kümmert Sie das?* what is this to you? *r* (*sorgen*) to care (for), to take care (of), to tend (to), to look (after); (*achtgeben*) to pay attention (to); (*erledigen*) to attend (to); (*sich befassen*) to mind; (*sich ängstigen*) to worry; (*besorgt sein um*) to care (about); *~~ Sie sich um Ihre eigenen Angelegenheiten!* mind your own business! **~nis** *f* affliction; grief, anxiety.

Kum(me)t *n* (horse-)collar.

Kumpan *m* fellow, companion, pal.

Kumpel *m min* pitman, coal digger; (*Freund*) comrade, mate, pal, *Am fam* buddy.

Kumulus *m* cumulus cloud; **~bildung** *f* cumulus formation; **~wolke** *f* cumulus cloud.

kund *a* known; public; *~ u. zu wissen ...* take notice that; **~bar** *a* known, manifest; notorious; **~e** *f* (*Nachricht*) information, news *pl mit sing*, tidings *pl mit sing u. pl*; (*Wissenschaft*) science; **~e** *m*, **~in** *f* customer, (*für Dienstleistung*) client; *fam* patron; *med* patient; (*bei der Werbung*) account; (*Arzt*) patient; (*voraussichtlicher*) prospect, prospective customer; (*Landstreicher*) tramp; *ein böser ~~* a nasty customer; *als ~~ häufig einkaufen* to patronize; **~endienst** *m* (customer) service; **~enfang** *m* touting; **~enkreis** *m* customers *pl*, clients *pl*; **~enliste** *f* list of customers; **~enwerbung** *f* canvassing of customers; **~geben, ~machen, ~tun** *irr tr* to notify, to inform, to make known; to manifest, to declare; to publish; **~gebung** *f* manifestation, demonstration; rally; (*Veröffentlichung*) publication; (*Erklärung*) declaration; **~ig** *a* well-informed; (*bekannt*) acquainted (*mit* with); (*erfahren*) experienced, skil(l)ful, expert, learned; **~machung** *f* publication; (*Anzeige*) notification; **~schaft** *f* customers *pl*, clients *pl*; (*Gesamtheit*) patronage, custom, clientele; (*als Wert*) goodwill; (*Nachricht*) information, intelligence; *die ~~ übernehmen* to acquire the goodwill; *die ~~ erhalten* to retain the custom; *e-e große ~~* a run of customers; **~~en** *tr* to reconnoitre; **~~er** *m* scout; (*Spion*) spy; explorer; (*Sendbote*) emissary.

künd|bar *a* recallable; (*Anleihe*) redeemable; *jederzeit ~~* at call; **~en** *tr* to make known, to announce; **~igen** *tr, itr* (*Wohnung, Arbeit*) to give notice (*od* warning) of; (*Vertrag*) to revoke, to cancel; (*Geld*) to call in; **~igung** *f* notice, warning; (*Geld*) calling in; (*Vertrag*) cancellation; *mit monatlicher ~~* subject to a month's notice; *wöchentliche ~~* seven day's notice; **~~sfrist** *f* term to give notice; period of notice; **~~srecht** *n* (*Vertrag*) cancellation privilege; **~~stermin** *m* last day for giving notice; cancellation date.

künftig *a* future; next; (*bevorstehend*) imminent; **~hin** *adv* henceforth; for the (*od* in) future.

Kunst *f* art; (*Geschicklichkeit*) skill; (*Kniff*) trick, knack; (*Wasser~*) waterworks *pl*; (*schwarze ~*) black art; (*freie Künste*) liberal arts *pl*; (*schöne Künste*) fine arts *pl*; *die bildenden Künste* the plastic arts *pl*; *das ist keine ~* that's easy; *mit seiner ~ zu Ende sein* to be at o.'s wits' end; **~akademie** *f* academy of arts; **~anstalt** *f typ* fine art printers *pl*; **~ausdruck** *m* technical term; **~ausstellung** *f* art exhibition; **~bauten** *pl rail* constructive works *pl*; artificial works *pl*; **~begeisterung** *f* devotion to fine arts; **~beilage** *f* artistic supplement; **~blatt** *n* (art-)print; **~butter** *f* artificial butter; (oleo) margarine; **~druckpapier** *n* art (*od* coated *od* enamelled) paper; **~dünger** *m* artificial manure, fertilizer; **~eis** *n* artificial ice; **~faser** *f* artificial (*od* synthetic) fibre; **~fehler** *m* technical error; **~fertig** *a* skil(l)ful, skilled; **~~keit** *f* technical skill, artistic skill; **~fett** *n* artificial fat (*od* grease); **~fleiß** *m* industry; **~fliegen** *n* stunt flying; aerobatics *pl mit sing*; **~flieger** *m aero* stunter; aerobatic pilot; **~flug** *m aero* stunt-flight; aerobatic flight, aerobatics *pl mit sing*; *~~ im Verband* aerobatics in formation; **~~figur** *f* stunt flying figure; **~~meister** *m* aerobatic champion; **~~vorführung** *f* aerobatic display; (*Wettbewerb*) aerobatic contest; **~freund** *m* amateur, dilettante; (*reicher*) maecenas; **~gärtner** *m* horticulturist; **~gärtnerei** *f* horticulture; nursery; **~gegenstand** *m* object of art (*od* virtu); **~gemäß, ~gerecht** *a* correct, skil(l)ful, workman-like; **~geschichte** *f* history of art; **~geschichtlich** *a* pertaining to the history of art; **~gewerbe** *n* arts and crafts *pl*, applied (*od* useful) art; **~~schule** *f* polytechnic school; school of arts and crafts; **~griff** *m* trick, dodge, knack; device; artifice; **~handel** *m* fine art trade; **~händler** art dealer; **~handlung** *f* fine-art repository; **~handwerk** *n* arts and crafts *pl*; **~handwerker** *m* artisan, craftsman; **~harz** *n* synthetic resin; plastic; synthetic plastic material; **~honig** *m* artificial honey; **~kenner** *m* connoisseur; **~kniff** *m* trick, dodge; knack; **~kritiker** *m* art-critic; **~lauf** *m* (*Eis*) figure skating; **~leder** *n* artificial (*od* imitation) leather, leatheroid; **~liebhaber** *m* amateur, dilettante; **~los** *a* artless; natural, simple; unskilled; **~maler** *m* painter; **~mittel** *n* artificial means *mit pl u. sing*; **~pause** *f* pause for effect; awkward pause; **~produkt** *n* artificial product; **~reich, ~voll** *a* artistic; ingenious; **~reiter** *m* circus-rider; **~richter** *m* critic; **~sammlung** *f* collection of works of art; **~schlosser** *m* art metal worker; **~schreiner, ~tischler** *m* cabinet-maker; **~seide** *f* artificial silk, rayon; **~~verarbeitung** *f* rayon processing; **~sinnig** *a* art-loving; **~spinnfaser** *f* synthetic fibre; **~sprache** *f* (*Fachsprache*) technical language; (*künstlich*) artificial language; **~stein** *m* artificial stone; **~stickerei** *f* art needlework; **~stoff** *m* synthetic material, artificial substance, plastics *pl*; **~~gehäuse** *n* plastic case; **~stopferei** *f* invisible mending; **~stück** *n* feat, trick, *Am* stunt; **~verein** *m* art-union; **~verlag** *m* art publishers *pl*; **~verstand** *m* taste for objects of art, virtu; **~verständige(r)** *m* expert; connoisseur; **~werk** *n* work of art; **~wissenschaft** *f* science of art; aesthetics *pl mit sing*; **~wolle** *f* artificial wool; shoddy; **~wort** *n* technical term; **~zweig** *m* branch of art.

Künst|elei *f* affectation; (*Malerei*) mannerism; **~eln** *itr, tr* to over-refine, to subtilize; *gekünstelt a* elaborate; affected; **~ler** *m*, **~lerin** *f* artist; **~~isch** *a* artistic, artist-like; **~~name** *m* stage-name; **~~tum** *n* artistic gift; genius; **~lich** *a* artificial; synthetic; (*nachgemacht*) imitated; (*Haar*) false; (*sinnreich*) artful, ingenious.

kunterbunt *a* higgledy-piggledy, topsy-turvy; (*farbig*) party-colo(u)red.

Kupee *n rail* compartment; *mot* coupé.

Kupfer *n* copper; **~bergwerk** *n* copper-mine; **~blech** *n* sheet copper, copper foil; **~draht** *m* copper wire; **~druck** *m* copper-plate; **~farben** *a* copper-colo(u)red; **~geld** *n* coppers *pl*; **~haltig** *a* containing copper, cupriferous; **~n** *a*

copper(y); **~oxyd** *n* cupric oxide; **~platte** *f* copper plate; **~schmied** *m* coppersmith; **~stecher** *m* copper-plate engraver; **~stich** *m* copper engraving; **~tiefdruck** *m* copper-plate printing; photogravure; **~überzug** *m* copper coating; **~verhüttung** *f* copper smelting; **~vitriol** *n* blue vitriol, copper sulfate
kupieren *tr* (*Schwanz*) to dock.
Kuppe *f* knoll, dome; rounded hilltop; (*Nagel~*) head.
Kuppel *f* cupola, dome; **~artig** *a* dome-shaped; **~dach** *n* dome-shaped roof; **~ei** *f* matchmaking; *jur* pandering, procuring, pimping; **~n** *itr, tr* to make a match; *jur* to pander, to pimp, to procure; *tr* to couple, to unite; *mot* to clutch; *tech* to engage, to connect; (*Färberei*) to develop; *radio* to couple; **~ung** *f* *tech* (*Wellen~~*) coupling; joint; (*Schalt~~*) *mot* clutch; *die ~~ einrücken* to let in the clutch; *die ~~ ausschalten* to throw out the clutch, to disengage the clutch; **~~spedal** *n* clutch pedal; **~~sstecker** *m* *el* adapter plug.
Kuppler *m*, **~in** *f* matchmaker; pander.
Kur *f* cure, treatment, course of treatment; *sich e-r ~ unterziehen* to go through a cure; *jdn in die ~ nehmen* to put s. o. through the paces; *jdm die ~ machen* to make love (to); **~abgabe, ~taxe** *f* tax de sejour; **~arzt** *m* physician at a watering-place; **~fürst** *m* elector; **~~entum** *n* electorate; **~~lich** *a* electoral; **~gast** *m* visitor; patient (at a health resort); **~haus** *n* pump room, casino, spa hotel; **~ie** *f* curia; **~ier** *m* courier, express; **~~en** *tr* to cure; (*mit Medizin*) to physic; **~liste** *f* list of visitors; **~ort** *m* watering-place, health-resort, spa; *klimatischer ~~* mountain-resort; **~pfalz** *f* the Palatinate; **~pfuscher** *m* quack; **~~ei** *f* quackery.
Kurant *n* currency.
Küraß *m* cuirass, breastplate; **~ier** *m* cuirassier.
Kur|atel *f* guardianship, trusteeship; *unter ~~ stehen* to be in ward; **~ator** *m* curator, trustee, guardian; **~atorium** *n* board of curators.
Kurbel *f* crank; handle; winch; *mot* (*Anlaß~*) starting-handle; **~ei** *f* *aero sl* dog-fight; **~gehäuse** *n* crank-case (of an engine); **~kasten** *m* *mot* crank-case; *phot* film camera; **~n** *tr* *mot* to crank; *phot* to reel off; **~stange** *f* connecting rod; **~welle** *f* crank-shaft; **~wellenlager** *n* crank-shaft bearing.
Kürbis *m* pumpkin; gourd; **~kern** *m* pumpkin (*od* gourd) seed.
küren *tr* to choose, to elect.
kurios *a* strange, odd; **~ität** *f* rare object, a curiosity.
Kurrentschrift *f* running hand.
Kurs *m* *mar* course; (*Peilung*) bearing; (*Weg, Richtung*) tack; (*Lauf, Tendenz*) tend; *aero* heading; *com* rate of exchange; (*Lehrkurs*) course; (*Umlauf*) circulation; currency; (*Wertpapiere*) value, quotation; (*Preis*) price; *vom ~ abkommen mar, aero* to yaw; to deviate from course; *~ nehmen nach* to set course for; *den ~ ändern* to alter the course; *fig* to haul; *ohne ~ (com)* not quoted; *zum ~ von* at the exchange of; *amtlicher ~* official rate; *im ~ fallen* to fall, to go down; *in ~ setzen* to set in circulation; *außer ~ setzen* to call in; *im ~ steigen* to go up, to rise, to improve; *e-n ~ nehmen* to take a course; to shape a course; *hoch im ~ stehen* to be at a premium; **~abweichung** *f* variation of course; **~bericht** *m* market quotation; **~buch** *n* time-table, Bradshaw, *Am* railroad guide, folder; **~geber** *m* course control, *aero* heading selector; auto-pilot control; **~geld** *n* fees *pl*; **~gewinn** *m* exchange profit; **~ieren** *itr* to circulate, to be current; **~kreisel** *m* directional gyro; **~makler** *m* stock-broker; **~notierung** *f* exchange quotation; **~orisch** *a* cursory, hasty; superficial; **~rückgang** *m* decline in prices; **~schwankungen** *f pl* exchange fluctuations *pl*; **~stabilität** *f* *aero* yaw stability; **~stand** *m* price level, level of rates; **~steuerung** *f* *aero* auto(matic) pilot, gyropilot; **~sturz** *m* fall in prices, slump; **~teilnehmer** *m* trainee **~us** *m* course; **~verlust** *m* loss on exchange; **~wagen** *m* through coach; **~weiser** *m* *aero* radio beacon; **~wert** *m* exchange value; **~zeiger** *m* course indicator; **~zettel** *m* stock-exchange list.
Kürschner *m* furrier; **~ei** *f* furrier's trade; **~ware** *f* furs and skins *pl*.
kursiv *a* italic; **~schrift** *f* italics *pl*; *in ~~ drucken* to italicize.
Kurve *f* curve; (*Biegung*) bend, turn; *Achtung, ~!* Caution, curve! *scharfe ~!* sharp turn! *gezogene ~ (aero)* climbing turn; *senkrechte ~ (aero)* vertical turn; *steile ~ (aero)* steep turn; ground loop; *leichte ~ (aero)* gentle turn; flat turn; **~n** *itr aero* to turn; **~nast** *m* branch of a curve; **~nblatt** *n* graph; **~nflug** *m* *aero* turn; **~ngleitflug** *m* *aero* spiral (gliding) descent; **~nkampf** *m* *aero* dog-fight; **~nlage** *f* *aero* bank; **~nlagenmesser** *m* turn and bank indicator; **~nlicht** *n* *mot* sidelamp; **~nradius** *m* radius of turn; **~nschneiden** *n* cut corner.
kurz *a* short; (*bündig*) brief, short; (*Worte*) laconic; (*zus.gefaßt*) summary; (*Stil*) concise; (*gedrängt*) succinct; (*Welle*) choppy; (*schroff*) abrupt; *adv* in short, shortly, briefly; *binnen ~em* within a short time; *in ~em* shortly, soon; *seit ~em* a short time; *über ~ od lang* sooner or later; *vor ~em* recently, the other day; *vor ~er Zeit* a little while ago, lately; *~e Zeit nachher* shortly after; *~ u. gut* in short, to make a long story short; *~ u. bündig* short and to the point; *~ vor ...* short of ...; *~ angebunden sein* to be curt; *~ u. klein schlagen* to smash to bits, to break to pieces; *jdn ~ halten* to keep s. o. short; *es ~ ausdrücken* to put it briefly (*od* in a nutshell); *zu ~ kommen* to come off badly; *~ treten! interj* mark time! *sich ~ fassen* to make it short; *den kürzeren ziehen* to get the worst of it, to be the loser; *kürzer machen* to shorten; **~akter** *m* short act; *tele sl* black out; **~arbeit** *f* partial layout; short-time work; **~~er** *m* short-time worker; **~~erunterstützung** *f* benefit for short-time workers; **~armig** *a* short-armed; **~atmig** *a* short-winded; **~~keit** *f* shortness of breath; **~beinig** *a* short-legged; **~beschreibung** *f* précis; **~biographie** *f* profile; **~dauernd** *a* short, transient; **~erhand** *adv* without hesitation; on the spot; briefly; **~film** *m* two reeler, film short, *Am* (movie) short, quickie; **~form** *f* abbreviation; **~fristig** *a* short-dated (*od* -termed); **~gefaßt** *a* concise, brief, compendious; **~geschichte** *f* short story; **~geschoren** *a* closely shorn; **~haarig** *a* short-haired; (*Wolle*) short-stapled; **~lebig** *a* short-lived; **~nachricht** *f* brief account (*od* statement), *Am* bulletin; **~schließen** *tr irr* to short, to short-circuit; **~schluß** *m* *el* short circuit; **~schrift** *f* shorthand; **~sichtig** *a* short-sighted; **~~keit** *f* short-sightedness; **~signal** *n* short-code signal; **~streckenjäger** *m* interceptor; **~streckenläufer** *m* sprinter; **~um** *adv* in short; **~waren** *f pl* haberdashery; trimmings *pl*; *Am* dry goods *pl*, notions *pl*; **~~händler** *m* haberdasher; **~~geschäft** *n* haberdasher's, *Am* dry-goods store; **~weg** *adv* offhand, abruptly; **~weil** *f* amusement, pastime; **~~ig** *a* amusing, entertaining, diverting; **~welle** *f* short-wave; *auf ~~* in the short-wave meter band; *über ~~ senden* to operate via short-wave (from); **~~namateur** *m* short-wave amateur, *sl* ham; **~~nansprache** *f* short-wave talk; **~~nabhörstation** *f* short-wave listening post; **~~nband** *n* short-wave band; **~~nbereich** *m* short-wave range; **~~ndiathermie** *f* radiothermy; **~~nempfang** *m* short-wave reception; **~~nempfänger** *m* short-wave receiver; **~~nfunk** *m* short-wave broadcasting; **~~nsender** *m* short-wave transmitter; **~~nübertragung** *f* short-wave transmission; **~~nverbindung** *f* short-wave communication; **~wort** *n* curtailed word; (*aus Anfangsbuchstaben*) acronym.
Kürz|e *f* shortness, brevity; *in aller ~~* as briefly as possible; **~en** *tr* to shorten; (*ab~~*) to abridge; (*verringern*) to reduce, to cut (down); (*stark*) to slash; *math* to simplify; **~lich** *adv* lately, of late, recently, not long ago; **~ung** *f* shortening; (*Ab~~*) abbreviation; (*Verminderung*) reduction, cut; slash; (*Abzug*) deduction.
kuschen *itr* (*Hund*) to lie down; *fig* to crouch.
Kusin *m*, **Kusine** *f* cousin.
Kuß *m* kiss; *e-n ~ geben* to kiss; **~echt** *a* kiss-proof; **~hand** *f* blown kiss.
küssen *tr* to kiss, *sl* to neck.
Küste *f* coast, shore; (*Strand*) beach; *an der ~* on shore; *die ~ entlang* along the coast; *an der ~ entlangfahren* to coast; **~nartillerie** *f* coast defence artillery; **~nbefestigungen** *f pl* coast-defences *pl*; **~nbewohner** *m* dweller on the coast; **~ndampfer** *m* coasting-vessel, coaster; **~nfunkdienst** *m* coastal radio service; **~ngebiet** *n* coastal area; **~ngewässer** *n pl* coastal zone; **~nhandel** *m* coasting-trade; **~nland** *n* littoral; **~nschiffahrt** *f* coasting; **~nstadt** *f* coastal town, sea-side town; **~nstrich** *m* coast-line; **~nverteidigung** *f* coast-defence; **~nwache** *f* coast guard (station); **~nwachboot** *n* coastal patrol vessel; **~nziel** *n* coastal target.
Küster *m* sacristan, sexton, verger.
Kutsch|bock *m* coachman's seat **~e** *f* carriage; coach, cab; **~enschlag** *m* coach-door; **~entritt** *m* foot-board; **~er** *m* driver, coachman, *fam* cabby; **~ieren** *itr* to drive; **~kasten** *m* coach-body; **~pferd** *n* coach-horse.
Kutte *f* cowl.
Kutteln *f pl* tripe.
Kutter *m* cutter.
Kuvert *n* envelope; wrapper; (*Gedeck*) cover; **~ieren** *tr* to put in an envelope.
Kux *m* *min* mining share.
Kybernetik *f* cybernetics *mit sing.*

L

L *Abk mit* **L** *siehe Liste der Abk.*
Lab *n* rennet; **~kraut** *n bot* bedstraw; galium; **~magen** *m* rennet bag.
Laban *m* (*Bibel*) Laban; *langer* ~ (*fig*) daddy-longlegs.
labbern *tr, itr* (*schlürfen*) to lap; (*lecken*) to lick.
labbrig *a* (*fad*) tasteless, insipid.
Lab\|e *f* (*Erfrischung*) refreshment; (*Stärkung*) tonic, cordial; *fig* (*Trost*) comfort; **~eflasche** *f* bottle of cordial, canteen; **~en** *tr* (*erfrischen*) to refresh (o. s.); (*beleben*) to revive; (*ergötzen*) to enjoy; (*trösten, stärken*) to comfort; **~end** *a* (*erfrischend*) refreshing; (*tröstend*) comforting; (*köstlich*) delicious; enjoyable; **~sal** *n* refreshment; (*Trost*) comfort; **~trank, ~trunk** *m* refreshing draught; **~ung** *f* refreshment.
lab\|ial *a* (*Phonetik*) labial; **~iallaut** *m* labial sound; **~iodental** *a* labio-dental.
labil *a* (*schwankend*) unstable; (*bes. von Gefühlen*) labile; (*veränderlich*) variable.
Labor *n fam* (=*Laboratorium*) laboratory, *Am fam* lab; **~ant** *m*, **~antin** *f* laboratory assistant (*od* helper), *Am* lab assistant; assistant chemist; **~arbeiter** *m* laboratory man; **~atorium** *n* laboratory, *Am fam* lab; **~ieren** *itr* to do laboratory work; *fam* (*leiden an*) to labo(u)r (*an* under), to suffer (*an* from, by), to be afflicted (*an* with); **~versuch** *m* laboratory test (*od* experiment).
Labyrinth *n* labyrinth, maze.
Lache[1] *f* (*Pfütze*) puddle, pool; plash; (*Sumpf*) bog.
Lach\|e[2] *f* (*Gelächter*) laugh, laughter; **~en** *n* laugh, laughing, laughter; *brüllen vor* ~~ to roar with laughter; *ein ~~ hervorrufen* to raise a laugh; *in ~~ ausbrechen* to burst into laughter; *das ist nicht zum* ~~ that's no laughing matter; *erzwungenes* ~~ forced laugh; *das ~~ verbeißen* to choke o.'s laughter; *unter* ~~ laughingly; *ein schmutziges* (*od dreckiges*) ~~ a dirty (*od* ugly) laugh; **~en** *itr* to laugh (*über* at); *über Schwierigkeiten* ~~ to laugh at difficulties; *jds Befürchtungen hinweg*~~ to laugh away s. o.'s fears; *heimlich in sich hinein* ~~ to chuckle; *laut* ~~ to roar with laughter, to give a good laugh; *plötzlich laut* ~~ to break into a laugh; *leise vor sich hin* ~~ to titter; *höhnisch* ~~ to sneer; *aus vollem Halse* ~~ to laugh heartily; to burst out laughing; *jdm ins Gesicht* ~~ to laugh in s. o.'s face; *er hat gut* ~~ he can afford to laugh; *das Glück lacht ihm* fortune smiles upon him; *ihm lacht das Herz im Leibe* his heart leaps for joy; *sich ins Fäustchen* ~~ to laugh in o.'s sleeve; *sich* (*halb*) *tot* ~~, *sich krank* ~~ to die with laughing, to split o.'s sides with laughing; *worüber* ~~ *Sie?* what are you laughing at? *wer zuletzt lacht, lacht am besten* he laughs best who laughs last; **~end** *a* laughing; smiling; ~~ *über etw hinweggehen* to laugh s. th. off; *~~e Erben* joyful heirs *pl*; *~~er Himmel* a bright sky; *ein ~~es Gesicht* a laughing face; **~er** *m* laugher; *die ~~ auf seiner Seite haben* to have the laugh on o.'s side; **~gas** *n* laughing gas, nitrous oxide; **~haft** *a* laughable, ridiculous; **~krampf, ~anfall** *m* fit of laughter; hysterical laughing; **~lust** *f* inclination to laugh; **~lustig** *a* fond of laughing; **~muskel** *m* risible muscle; **~taube** *f* ring-dove; **~zwang** *m* irresistible impulse to laugh.
lächl\|eln *itr* to smile (*über* at); (*süßlich* ~~) to smirk; (*höhnisch* ~~) to sneer; *albern* ~~ to simper, to snigger; *das Glück hat ihm immer zugelächelt* Fortune has always smiled (up)on him; *worüber ~~ Sie?* what are you smiling at? *über das ganze Gesicht* ~~ to be all smiles; ~~ *n* smile; **~erlich** *a* laughable, ridiculous; (*komisch*) comic(al); (*spaßig*) funny; (*unbedeutend*) derisive, derisory; ~~ *machen* to ridicule, *fam* to guy, *Am fam* to josh; *sich ~~ machen* to make a fool of o. s.; *machen Sie sich nicht* ~~ don't be ridiculous; *er wurde ~~ gemacht* he was held up to ridicule; *etw ins ~~e ziehen* to make a joke of s. th., to make fun of; **~erlichkeit** *f* ridicule; absurdity; *jdn* (*od etw*) *der ~~ preisgeben* to hold up s. o. (*od* s. th.) to ridicule; **~ern** *itr: es ~ert mich* it makes me laugh.
Lachs *m* salmon; **~fang** *m* salmon-fishing; **~farbe** *f* salmon-colo(u)r; **~farbig** *a* salmon-colo(u)red; **~forelle** *f* salmon trout; **~rot** *a* salmon pink; **~schinken** *m* (fillet of) smoked ham; **~schnitte** *f* fillet of salmon; (*~schnittchen*) salmon scollop.
Lack *m* (*Harz~, Gummi~*) (gum) lac; (*auf Ölbasis*) varnish; (*auf Zellulosebasis*) lacquer; (*Email~*) enamel varnish; (*Japan~*) japan (varnish); (*Nitrozellulose~*) nitrocellulose lacquer; (*Überzugs~*) finishing (varnish); **~anstrich** *m* coat of lacquer; **~arbeit** *f* lacquer, japan; **~farbe** *f* (*Trockenfarbe*) lake (colo(u)r); (*Öl~*) paint; (*Email*) enamel; **~farbig** *a* lake-colo(u)red; **~firnis** *m* lac varnish; **~harz** *n* gum-lac; **~ieren** *tr* to varnish, to lacquer; to dope; to japan; *fig* to cheat, to take in, *sl* to dope; **~ierer** *m* varnisher, lacquerer; **~ierung** *f* enamel finish; paintwork; **~~lack** *m* lac dye, lac-lake; **~lasurfarbe** *f* transparent varnish colo(u)r; **~leder** *n* patent (*od* varnished) leather, japanned leather; **~mus** *m* litmus; **~~lösung** *f* litmus solution; **~~papier** *n* litmus paper; **~~tinktur** *f* litmus tincture; **~schuh, ~stiefel** *m* patent leather boot; pump; dress shoe; **~überzug** *m* coat of lacquer; **~waren** *f pl* lacquered goods *pl*.
Lactoflavin *n* (= *Vitamin B 2*) riboflavin.
Lade *f* (*Kasten*) box, case; trunk, chest; (*Schub~*) drawer; (*Heft~*) sewing-frame.
Lade\|aggregat *n el* charging set, battery charger; **~anlage** *f* loading (*od* filling) plant; **~baum** *m* derrick, jib, *Am* cargo boom; **~brücke** *f* loading bridge (*od* gangway); **~bühne** *f* loading stage, loading platform; **~damm** *m* jetty; landing stage; **~dichte** *f el* charge density; **~druck** *m aero mot* boost pressure; **~~anzeiger** *m aero mot* boost pressure ga(u)ge; **~dynamo** *m* battery charging generator; **~fähigkeit** *f el* rate of charge; (*Wagen, Schiff*) loading capacity, net capacity; *mar* tonnage (of a ship); burden; **~fläche** *f* loading area; **~frist** *f mar* loading days *pl*; time for loading; **~gebühren** *f pl* loading expenses *pl*; **~gewicht** *n* service weight; *mar* deadweight tonnage; **~gleichrichter** *m el* charging rectifier; **~gleis** *n* loading siding (*od* track); **~griff** *m mil* (*Gewehr*) loading movement; **~gurt** *f mil* cartridge belt; **~hafen** *m* port of loading; **~hemmung** *f mil* (*e-r Feuerwaffe*) jam; stoppage; **~kai** *m* wharf (*pl* wharves); **~kanonier** *m* gun-loader; **~kapazität** *f* loading capacity; charging capacity; **~klappe** *f mot* tail board, *Am* tail gate; **~kontrollampe** *f mot* (*für Akku*) charging control lamp; warning light; **~kran** *m* loading crane; **~linie** *f* load line, Plimsoll line (*od* mark); **~liste** *f* loading bill, way bill; **~luftkühler** *m aero mot* intercooler; **~luke** *f* (cargo) hatch; **~manifest** *n mar* manifest (of the cargo on board).
laden[1] *irr tr* (*Gäste einladen*) to invite; *zu Tisch* ~ to ask s.o. to dinner; (*vorladen*) to summon, to call, to cite; *als Zeuge* ~ to summon (*od* to call) as a witness.
laden[2] *irr tr* (*mit Fracht beladen*) to load; to freight; (*in Schiff*) to ship; *el* to charge; (*Feuerwaffe*) to load, to charge; *auf sich* ~ to burden o. s. with; *blind* ~ to load with a blank cartridge; *scharf* ~ to load with a ball; *er hat schwer geladen fig fam* he is half-seas over, *Am* he's got a load on; *geladen sein fig fam* to be mad; to be furious at s. o.
Laden[3] *m* (*Kauf~*) shop, *Am* store, (*mit Selbstbedienung*) self-service store; *e-n ~ aufmachen* to set up shop; *den ~ schließen* (*sich aus dem Geschäft zurückziehen*) to shut up shop; (*Fenster~*) shutter; **~angestellte(r)** *m* shop assistant; **~auslage** *f* store display; **~besitzer** *m* shopkeeper, *Am* store-keeper, store-owner; **~dieb** *m* shop-lifter; **~diebstahl** *m* shoplifting; **~diener** *m* shopman; **~einbrecher** *m* smash-and-grab raider; **~einbruch** *m* smash-and-grab raid; **~einrichtung** *f* shop fittings *pl*, *Am* store fixtures *pl*; **~fenster** *n* shop window, store window; **~front** *f* store front; **~geschäft** *n* shop; **~glocke** *f* shop-bell; **~hüter** *m* unsaleable article, dud stock, drug; white elephant, *Am auch* sticker; **~inhaber** *m* shopkeeper; **~kasse** *f* till, cash-desk; **~mädchen** *n* shop girl; **~miete** *f* shop rent; **~preis** *m* selling price, retail price; (*Buch*) publishing price; **~schild** *n* shopsign; **~schluß** *m* closing-time, shop closing; **~schwengel** *m* counter-jumper; **~straße** *f* shopping centre; **~tisch** *m* (sales) counter, desk; *Auslage auf dem* ~~ counter display; **~verkaufszeiten** *f pl* shop hours *pl*; **~viertel, ~zentrum** *n* shopping centre, *Am* shopping center.
Lade\|platz *m* loading place; *mar* loading berth, wharf; *rail* goods-platform; **~pumpe** *f mot* charging pump; **~r** *m* (*Mann*) loader, packer; *mot* supercharger, blower; **~rampe** *f* loading ramp; **~raum** *m* loading space, hold; (*e-r Waffe*) chamber; **~schütze** *m mil* loader; **~schein** *m* bill of lading; **~spannung** *f el* charging voltage; **~station** *f el* charging station; **~stelle** *f* loading point; **~stock** *m* ramrod, rammer; **~streifen** *m mil* cartridge belt; magazine clip, cartridge clip; (charger) strip; **~strom** *m el* charg-

ing current; **~trommel** *f* cartridge drum; **~vermögen** *n mar* deadweight capacity; **~vorrichtung** *f* feeding mechanism; *el* charging equipment; **~winde** *f* windlass.

lädieren *tr* (*beschädigen*) to injure, to damage; (*verletzen*) to hurt.

Ladung[1] *f* (*vor Gericht*) summons, citation; (*unter Strafandrohung*) subpoena; *jdm e-e ~ zustellen* to serve the summons on s. o.

Ladung[2] *f* (*Beladung*) load, loading; (*Fracht*) freight, cargo; shipment; (*beim Sprengen*) shot; (*e-s Geschosses*) explosive charge; (*e-r Waffe*) charge; *el* (electric) charge; *statische ~* static (charge); *geballte ~* concentrated charge; *gestreckte ~* distributed charge; *~ einnehmen* (*Schiff*) to take in cargo; **~sdichte** *f* density of charge; **~sraum** *m* (ship's) hold; **~sträger** *m radio* charge-carrier; **~sverzeichnis** *n* (ship's) manifest; **~swolke** *f el* charge cloud.

Lafette *f* gun-carriage; gun mount (-ing); **~nschwanz** *m* trail.

Laffe *m* fop, puppy.

Lage *f* situation; place; position; (*Haltung*) attitude, posture; (*räumliche ~ e-s Gegenstandes*) site; (*örtliche ~*) location; (*Anblick*) aspect; (*Schicksal, Los*) fate, lot; (*Zustand*) state, condition; (*Umstände*) circumstances *pl*; (*Klemme*) predicament, plight, straits *pl*; (*Farben~*) coat(ing); (*Schicht*) layer; bed; stratum; deposit; (*Papier*) quire; *mil* (*strategische ~*) strategic position; *mil* (*Schuß~*) points of impact; *mil mar* (*Breitseite*) broadside; *mil* (*Artillerie*) salvo; *mus* pitch; compass; (*Fecht~*) guard; (*Bier*) round; *e-e ~ ausgeben* to pay a round; *die ~ der Dinge* state of affairs; *bei der gegenwärtigen ~ der Dinge* as matters stand at present; *jds ungünstige ~ ausnützen* to take s. o. at a disadvantage, *Am* to get the drop on s. o; *das ändert die ~* that puts a new face on things; *die ~ des Marktes* the condition (*od* state) of the market; *in der ~ sein* to be in a position (to); to be able, to be prepared; *nicht in der ~ sein* to be unable; *bedrängte ~* embarrassment, distressed condition; *finanzielle ~* financial status; *e-e gespannte ~* a tense situation; *in e-r mißlichen ~ sein* to be in a predicament; *rechtliche ~* legal status; *wirtschaftliche ~* economic situation; *versetzen Sie sich in meine ~* put yourself in my place; **~bericht** *m* situation report; informational report; summary of the situation; **~berichtigung** *f* rectification of position; **~bestimmung** *f* localization; **~beurteilung** *f* estimate of the situation; **~beziehung** *f* relative position; **~festigkeit** *f* stability; **~nkarte** *f mil* situation map; **~nweise** *a* in layers; **~plan** *m* general plan; lay-out; plan (of a site).

Lager *n* (*Lagerstatt*) couch; (*Bett*) bed; (*e-s Tieres*) lair; *mil* (*Feld~*) camp, encampment; (*Vorrats~*) depot; (*Munitions~*) dump; (*Geologie*) layer, stratum; deposit; (*Waren~*) warehouse, storehouse; (*Fässer*) stand; (*Vorrat*) stock(s *pl*), supply, store; (*Bodensatz*) dregs *pl*; *tech* bearing; support; *fig* (*Partei, Seite*) party, side; *das ~ abbrechen* to strike (*od* to break) camp; *das ~ auffüllen* to restock, to replenish o.'s stocks; *das ~ aufschlagen* to pitch o.'s camp; *ab ~* ex warehouse; *auf (dem) ~ haben* (*od halten*) to have on hand, to have in stock; *auf ~ nehmen* (*od legen*) to put in store; *feindliches ~* hostile camp; *im feindlichen ~* on the side of the enemy; *fertig auf ~* ready-made; **~aufnahme** *f* (*Inventur*) stock-taking, inventory; **~aufseher** *m* warehouse-keeper; storekeeper; **~bestand** *m* stock, inventory; **~bier** *n* lager (beer); **~bock** *m* bearing stand, floor stand (*od* frame); pedestal; **~buch** *n* store-book, stock-book; **~buchse** *f tech* bearing bush(ing); **~butter** *f* cold-storage butter; **~deckel** *m tech* bearing cap; **~entnahme** *f* withdrawal from stock; **~faß** *n* storage cask; **~fett** *n* mineral jelly; **~feuer** *n* camp-fire; **~gebühr** *f*, **~geld** *n*, **~miete** *f*, **~zins** *m* warehouse-rent, storage; **~gehäuse** *n tech* bearing case, bearing housing; **~halter** *m* warehouseman; **~haltung** *f* stock-keeping; **~~skosten** *pl* storage; **~haus** *n* warehouse, storehouse; store; **~~gesellschaft** *f* storage company, warehouse company; **~~kosten** *pl* warehouse costs *pl*; **~hof** *m* storage yard; **~hütte** *f* barrack, camphut; **~ist** *m* warehouse-clerk; **~keller** *m* storage cellar; **~kontrolle** *f* stock control; **~kosten** *pl* storage costs *pl*, warehousing costs *pl*; **~leitung** *f* camp authorities *pl*; **~liste** *f* stock list; **~meister** *m* storekeeper; **~metall** *n* bearing metal, bushing metal; babbitt (metal); **~möglichkeiten** *f pl* storage facilities *pl*; **~n** *tr* to lay (down); *com* to store, to warehouse; (*ablagern, Holz, Wein etc*) to season; *tech* (*betten*) to support, to bed; *itr* to lay; to be warehoused, to be stored; *mil* to encamp; *fig* to brood over; (*sich*) *~~* to lie down, to camp, (*im Freien*) to camp out; (*ruhen*) to rest, to repose; (*von Tieren*) to couch; **~ort** *m* camp site; **~platz** *m* resting place, camp site; (*für Waren*) storage place, depot; dump; **~prozeß** *m* storage process; **~raum** *m* (store-) depot; storeroom, warehouse; **~schale** *f* bearing bush, bearing brass; bearing shell; bearing lining; **~schein** *m* warehouse receipt; warrant; **~schuppen** *m* store shed, storage shed; **~statt, ~stätte, ~stelle** *f* resting-place, camp site; couch; bed; (*Geologie*) deposit; **~ung** *f* (*Aufbewahrung*) storage, warehousing; packing; *tech* (*Bettung*) bedding, support; bearing; suspension; (*Geologie*) stratification; (*Stein*) grain; (*Kristall*) orientation; **~~smöglichkeit** *f* storage capacity, storage facilities *pl*; **~verwalter** *m* storekeeper; warehouseman; **~vorrat** *m* stock; **~wache** *f* camp watch, camp guard.

Lagune *f* lagoon.

lahm *a* lame; paralysed; crippled; (*schwach*) weak; impotent; poor; feeble; *an e-m Bein ~* lame of one leg; *ein ~es Bein haben* to have a lame leg; *vollständig ~ sein* to be dead lame; *e-e ~e Entschuldigung* a poor excuse; *e-e ~e Geschichte* a lame story; **~en** *itr* to be lame; to walk lame; (*hinken*) to limp; **~heit** *f* lameness; **~legen** *tr* to paralyse, *Am* to paralyze; (*ruinieren*) to ruin; to cripple; (*zum Stocken bringen*) to bring to a standstill; to neutralize; *der Krieg legt den Handel ~* war paralyses trade; *der Verkehr war ~gelegt* traffic was paralysed; **~legung** *f* paralysation, paralysing; crippling; neutralization; stoppage.

lähm|en *tr* to paralyse, *Am* to paralyze; to lame, to make lame; *fig* to hamstring; to disable; to hinder; to cripple; to stop; *gelähmt sein* to be paralysed; *gelähmt vor Schrecken* paralysed with fear; *seit Jahren gelähmt* paralysed for years; *~ender Einfluß* palsy; **~ung** *f* paralysis; paralysation; (*Lahmheit*) lameness; *med* (*Schlagfluß*) palsy; **~~serscheinung** *f* symptom of paralysis.

Laib *m* loaf.

Laich *m* spawn; **~en** *itr* to spawn.

Laie *m* layman; *fig* uninitiated person; novice, outsider; amateur; **~nbruder** *m* lay brother; **~nhaft** *a* amateurish; lay; **~nhelferin** *f* volunteer nurse; **~nschwester** *f* lay sister; **~nstand** *m* laity; **~npriester** *m* lay priest; **~nrichter** *m* lay judge.

Lakai *m* lackey, footman; **~enhaft** *a* lackey-like; servile; **~enseele** *f* flunkey.

Lake *f* brine, pickle.

Laken *n* sheet; (*Toten~*) pall, shroud.

lakonisch *a* laconic.

Lakritze *f* licorice, liquorice; **~nsaft** *m* liquorice juice, extract of licorice; **~nstange** *f* stick of liquorice.

lallen *itr* (*aus Furcht, Verlegenheit etc*) to stammer; (*wegen Sprachfehler; stottern*) to stutter; (*plappern*) to babble; (*hervorsprudeln, überstürzt sprechen*) to sputter.

Lama[1] *n zoo* llama; **~wolle** *f* l(l)ama (-wool).

Lama[2] *m* (*Buddhapriester*) lama; **~ismus** *m* Lamaism.

Lamelle *f* (*dünnes Blättchen*) lamel(la); *el* bar, lamina (*pl* laminae); *tech* plate, disk; *phot* (*Irisblende*) leaf, blade; *bot* gill; (*dünne Schicht*) layer, segment; **~nkörperchen** *n* lamellate corpuscle; **~nkühler** *m mot* sheet metal radiator; **~nkupplung** *f mot* plate-clutch, disk-clutch; **~nmagnet** *m* lamellar (*od* laminated) magnet; **~nrohr** *n* gilled tube; **~nsicherung** *f el* laminated fuse, strip fuse; **lamellieren, laminieren** *tr* to laminate.

lament|ieren *itr* to lament (*über* over, *um* for); (*klagen*) to wail; **~o** *n* lamentation; wail(ing).

Lametta *f* silver tinsel; (*Engelshaar als Christbaumschmuck*) angels' hair.

Lamm *n* lamb; **~braten** *m* roast lamb; **~en** *itr* to cast lambs, to ewe; **~fell** *n* lambskin; **~fleisch** *n* lamb; **~fromm** *a* gentle (as a lamb), lamblike; **~sgeduld** *f* Job's patience.

Lämm|chen *n* (*Lämmlein*) little lamb, lambkin; **~ergeier** *m* lammergeyer; **~erwolke** *f* cirrus.

Lampe *f* lamp; **~nanzünder** *m* lamp-lighter; **~ndocht** *m* lampwick; **~nfaden** *m* lighting filament; **~nfassung** *f* lamp-socket, lamp fitting; **~nfieber** *n theat* stage-fright; **~nglocke** *f* lamp-globe; **~nlicht** *n* lamp light; **~nruß** *m* lampblack; **~nschirm** *m* lamp-shade; **~nschwarz** *n* lampblack; **~nzylinder** *m* lamp-chimney.

Lampion *m* Chinese lantern, Japanese lantern.

*

lancier|en *tr* (*in Gang bringen, starten*) to launch; (*Anleihe*) to float; (*jdn od etw fördern*) to promote; (*werfen*) to push; **~rohr** *n* (*für Torpedo*) torpedo tube.

Land *n* (*im Gegensatz zu Wasser*) land; (*Fest~*) mainland, continent; (*Ackerland*) soil, ground; earth; (*im Gegensatz zur Stadt*) country; (*Gebiet*) region, territory; state, land; *fig* realm; *bebautes ~* (*Acker*) ploughed land; *ein Stück ~* a plot of ground; *das Gelobte ~* the Land of Promise; *das Heilige ~* the Holy Land; *~ sichten* to make (the) land; *sich dicht am ~e halten mar* to hug the land; *an ~ gehen* to go ashore; to land; *ans ~ bringen* to bring to shore; (*Fisch*) to land; *ans ~ kommen* to get on shore; *auf dem ~e* in the country; *auf dem ~e wohnen* to live in the country; *aufs ~ gehen* to go into the country; *aufs ~ ziehen* to move to the country; *außer ~es gehen* to go abroad; *zu ~e* by land; *bei uns zu ~* with us; **~abflug** *m aero* land take-off; **~adel** *m* provincial nobility; (*niederer ~~*) landed gentry; **~arbeit** *f* agricultural labo(u)r; **~arbeiter** *m* farm labo(u)rer; (*Hilfsarbeiter*) farm help, farm hand; **~armee** *f* land forces *pl*; **~arzt** *m* country doctor; **~auer** *m* (*Kutsche*) landau; **~aulette** *f mot* landaulet, *Am* town coupé; **~aus**: *~aus, ~ein* far afield; **~bau** *m* agriculture; farming; **~bauer** *m* farmer; **~baugenossenschaft** *f* agricultural co-operative; **~besitz** *m* land, landed property (*od* estate); **~besitzer** *m* landowner, landholder, land proprietor; **~bevölkerung** *f* rural population; **~bewohner** *m* countryman; s. o. living in the country; **~briefträger** *m* rural postman, *Am* rural carrier; **~eanweisung** *f aero* (*der Flugleitung*) landing instruction; **~eauslauf** *m aero* landing run; **~ebahn** *f aero* landing runway (*od* strip); airstrip, flight strip; landing surface; **~ebahnbeleuchtung** *f* landing area floodlight; **~ebake** *f aero radio* landing (*od* homing) radio beacon; **~ebakenstrahl** *m* landing beam; **~ebakenverfahren** *n* blind landing method; **~ebremse** *f aero* (*an der Maschine*) air brake; **~edeck** *n* (*Flugzeugträger*) landing deck, *Am* flight deck; **~edelmann** *m* (country-) squire; **~eeinrichtungen** *f pl* (*e-s Flugplatzes*) landing facilities *pl*; **~efackel** *f aero* landing flare, (*an den Flügelenden*) wing-tip flare; **~efeuer** *n aero* landing light; airport beacon; landmark beacon; **~egeschwindigkeit** *f aero* landing speed; **~ehilfe** *f aero* landing device; **~eigentum** *n* landed property; **~eigentümer** *m* landowner, landed proprietor; **~einwärts** *adv* inland, up-country; **~eklappe** *f aero* (landing) flap; air brake; **~eklappenbedienung** *f aero* flap control; **~ekopf** *m mil* beach-head, bridgehead; **~ekreuz** *n aero* landing T; **~eleitlinie** *f*, **~eleitstrahl** *m aero* glide path, landing path; landing beam; **~elicht** *n aero* (*am Flugzeug*) landing light, landing lamp; (*Leuchtpfad*) landing direction light; approach light; (*Fackel*) flare for night-flying; **~emeldung** *f aero* arrival message, landing report; **~en** *tr, itr* to land; *mar* (*Schiff anlegen*) to reach port, to dock; (*Truppen etc*) to disembark, to go (*od* to put) ashore; *e-n Kinnhaken ~~* to land an uppercut; *im Gefängnis ~~* to land in jail; *aero* to land, to alight; to make landfall; *auf dem Wasser ~~* to alight on water; *aero* (*niedergehen*) to touch down; *wenn Sie auf dem Londoner Flughafen ~~, sind Sie nur noch 45 Minuten vom Trafalgar Square* you're only 45 minutes from Trafalgar Square when you touch down at London Airport; *glücklich ~~* (*aero*) to make a safe landing; **~enge** *f* isthmus; **~entschädigung** *f* territorial compensation; **~epeilstrahl** *m aero radio* landing beam; **~epeilverfahren** *n aero* air track system of instrument landing; **~episte** *f aero siehe: Landebahn;* **~eplatz** *m mar* quai; *aero* (*ohne weitere Landeeinrichtungen*) landing ground; **~epunkt** *m* landing spot; **~erad** *n* landing wheel; **~erichtung** *f aero* direction of landing; **~erziehungsheim** *n* boarding-school in the country; **~esangehörigkeit** *f* nationality; citizenship; **~esaufnahme** *f* ordnance survey; topographical mapping; **~esausschuß** *m* executive committee; **~esbeschreibung** *f* topography; **~esbrauch** *m* national custom; **~escheinwerfer** *m aero* landing searchlight; landing floodlight; **~eseigen** *a* state-owned; **~eserzeugnis** *n* home produce, agricultural product; **~esfarben** *f pl* national colo(u)rs *pl*; **~esfürst, ~esherr** *m* sovereign, ruler; **~eshoheit** *f* sovereignty; **~esgrenze** *f* frontier; **~eskind** *n* native; **~eskirche** *f* national church; *Engl* established church; **~esobrigkeit** *f* supreme authority; government; **~espolizei** *f* state police, state troopers *pl*; **~esregierung** *f* government (of a country); provincial (*od* regional) government; **~esschuld** *f* national debt; **~essprache** *f* vernacular (tongue); **~esteg** *m* landing ramp; **~estelle** *f* landing spot; **~estoß** *m aero* bump; **~estracht** *f* national costume; **~estrauer** *f* public mourning; **~estreifen** *m aero* landing strip; **~esüblich** *a* usual (*od* customary) in a country; **~esvater** *m* sovereign; **~esvermessung** *f* surveying the land; **~esvermessungsnetz** *n* triangulation network; **~esverrat** *m* high treason; quislingism; **~esverräter** *m* traitor (to his country); quisling, quisler; **~esverteidigung** *f* defence of the country, national (*od* home) defence; (*zivile*) civil defence; **~esverwaltung** *f* administration of a district (*od* province); **~esverweisung** *f* banishment; expulsion; exile; **~esverweser** *m* governor; viceroy; **~eswährung** *f* standard currency; **~e-T** *n aero* landing T; **~everbot** *n* landing restriction; **~eweg** *m aero* landing path; **~ewinkel** *m aero* landing angle; **~ezeichen** *n* landing-signal; (*Leuchtzeichen*) luminous ground mark; **~ezone** *f* landing area; **~ezonenbeleuchtung** *f* landing area floodlight; **~fahrzeug** *n* land vehicle; **~flucht** *f* migration from the country (to the town), rural exodus; *Am* off-the-farm movement; **~flüchtig** *a* fugitive; exiled; **~flugplatz** *m* airport; **~flugzeug** *n* landplane; **~fremd** *a* foreign; **~friede** *m* public peace; **~funkstelle** *f* ground station; land (radio) station; **~gang** *m mar* shore liberty; **~geistliche(r)** *m* country clergyman; **~gemeinde** *f* village community, country parish; **~gericht** *n* district court, county court; **~graf** *m* landgrave; **~gräfin** *f* landgravine; **~gut** *n* estate; country-seat; manor; **~haus** *n* country--house, villa; (*kleineres*) cottage, chalet; **~heer** *n* land-force(s *pl*); army; **~innere** *n* inland, interior; **~jäger** *m* rural policeman, *Am* rural constable; **~junker** *m* (country-) squire; **~karte** *f* map; **~kreis** *m* rural district; **~krieg** *m* land warfare; **~~sordnung** *f* rules of land warfare; **~kundig** *a* notorious; **~kutsche** *f* stagecoach; **~läufig** *a* customary, ordinary; current; **~leben** *n* country life; **~leute** *pl* country-people *pl*, farmers *pl*, peasants *pl*; **~macht** *f* land power; (*Heer*) army, land-forces *pl*; **~mädchen** *n* country girl; **~makler** *m* estate-agent, *Am* realtor; **~mann** *m* countryman, farmer, peasant; villager; **~marke** *f mar* landmark; *aero* airway ground mark, *Am* field marker; **~maschine** *f* agricultural machine; **~messer** *m* (land-) surveyor; **~mine** *f mil* land-mine; **~nebel** *m* land (*od* country) fog; **~pächter** *m* farmer tenant, *Am* (*~~, der seine Pacht mit Erträgnissen bezahlt*) sharecropper; **~partie** *f* (rural) excursion, picnic; **~peilstation** *f aero radio* land direction finding station; **~pfarrei** *f* country-parsonage; **~pfarrer** *m* country parson; **~plage** *f* scourge; *fig* public calamity; *e-e wahre ~~* quite a nuisance; **~planke** *f* gangplank; **~pomeranze** *f* country girl; **~rat** *m etwa:* district president, district magistrate; **~ratte** *f* landlubber; **~räuber** *m* (*in Irland*) landgrabber, *Am* land-shark; **~recht** *n* common law; **~regen** *m* persistent rain; **~reise** *f* journey; **~richter** *m* county court judge; **~rücken** *m* ridge of hills; **~schaft** *f* (*Gebiet*) province, district, state; country; (*phot, Malerei*) landscape, scenery; **~schaftlich** *a* provincial; rural; scenic; relating to landscape; **~schaftsbild** *n* landscape; scene; (*Umgegend*) surroundings *pl*; **~schaftsgärtner** *m* landscape gardener, *Am* landscape architect; **~schaftslinse** *f phot* landscape lens; **~scheide** *f* boundary; **~schulheim** *n* boarding-school in the country; **~see** *m* (inland) lake; **~~, See- u. Luftoperation** *f* (*kombiniert*) triphibious operation; **~ser** *m fam* common soldier, private, infantryman, *Am* doughboy, GI Joe, *sl* trooper; **~seuche** *f* epidemic; **~sichtung** *f mar* landfall; **~sitz** *m* country-seat; **~sknecht** *m* (*Söldner*) mercenary; foot-soldier; **~smann** *m* fellow-countryman; (*aus der gleichen Stadt*) fellow townsman; compatriot; *was für ein ~~ sind Sie?* what is your native country? what nationality are you? **~spitze** *f* cape; promontory; **~stadt** *f* provincial town, *Am* (*Kleinstadt*) tank town; **~stände** *m pl* States *pl*; **~straße** *f* highroad, highway; overland route; **~straßenschreck** *m hum mot* road-hog; **~streicher** *m* tramp, vagabond, vagrant, landlo(u)per, *Am sl* hobo, crook; **~streicherei** *f* vagrancy; **~streitkräfte** *f pl* ground forces *pl*; surface forces *pl*; **~strich** *m* (*Gegend*) region, tract of land; (*Gebiet*) district; climate; **~sturm** *m* veteran reserve; *Engl* Territorial Reserve; **~tag** *m* diet; legislature; **~tagsabgeordnete(r)** *m* deputy (*od* member) of the diet; **~transport** *m* overland transport; **~truppen** *f pl* landforces *pl*, ground troops *pl*; **~ung** *f mar, aero* landing; *aero* alighting, landfall; (*Ausschiffung*) disembarkation, debarkation; *bei der ~~ aufsetzen aero* to touch-down; *zur ~~ anschweben* to come in for a landing; *amphibische ~~* amphibious landing; *Bums~~* rough landing; *Blind~~* blind landing; *Dreipunkt~~* three-point landing; *Not~~* forced landing; *Zweipunkt~~* two-point landing; *~~ im Gleitflug* glide landing; *~~ mit Rückenwind* down-wind landing; *~~ mit Seitenwind* cross-wind landing; *~~ mit stehendem Propeller* (*fam stehender Schraube od Latte*) dead (stick) landing; **~~sabteilung** *f* landing (*od* beach) party; **~~sboot** *n mil* landing craft (*Abk* LC); landing barge; assault craft; **~~sbrücke** *f*, **~~ssteg** *m* jetty, pier, landing-stage; **~~sfahrzeug** *n* landing craft; **~~sfunkfeuer** *n* landing beacon; **~~sgebiet** *n* landing area; **~~sgestell** *n* landing gear; **~~skai** *m* landing quay; **~~skorps** *n* landing detachment; **~~slicht** *n* landing light; **~~smannschaft** *f aero* ground crew; **~~smast** *m* (*Luftschiff*) mooring-mast; **~~splatz** *m* landing-place; quay, pier; *aero* landing ground; **~~spunkt** *m* (*Aufsetzpunkt*) touch-down point; **~~srauchzeichen** *n aero* landing smoke signal; **~~sscheinwerfer** *m* landing searchlight, landing projector; landing floodlight; **~~sschiff** *n* landing ship; **~~sstoß** *m aero* landing shock; bump; **~~ssturmboot** *n* landing assault craft; **~~struppen** *f pl* landing (*od* beach) troops *pl*; **~~sunternehmen** *n* invasion (*od* landing) operation; **~urlaub** *m* shore liberty (*od* leave); **~vermessung** *f* land-survey(ing); **~verschickung** *f* evacuation to the country; **~vogt** *m* governor (of a district); bailiff; **~volk** *n* country-people *pl*, peasants *pl*; **~wacht** *f* rural police, special rural constabulary; **~wärts** *adv* landward; **~-Wasser-Panzer** *m* amphibian tank; **~weg** *m* overland route; *auf dem ~~* by land; **~wehr** *f* militia; landwehr; *Engl* Territorial Reserve; **~wein** *m* home-grown wine; **~wind** *m* off-shore wind, land-breeze; **~wirt** *m* farmer; agriculturist; landlord; **~wirtschaft** *f* agriculture, farming; **~~lich** *a* agricultural; *~~liche Maschinen* agricultural machines, *Am* farm machinery; *~~liche Vereinigung* agricultural association, *Am* grange; **~~sbank** *f* agricultural bank, *Am* land bank; **~~sministerium** *n* *Engl* Board of Agriculture, *Am* Department of Agriculture; **~~sschule** *f* agricultural school; **~zeitung** *f* rural daily; **~zunge** *f* neck (*od* tongue) of land; spit of land.

Länd|erei *f* landed property; lands *pl*; estates *pl*; **~erkunde** *f* geography; **~errat** *m* Council of States; (German) State Co-ordinating Agency; **~ler** *m* (*Tanz*) slow waltz; **~lich** *a* rural; rustic; countrylike.

lang *a* long; (*groß von Menschen*) tall; *10 Meter ~* ten meters long, ten meters in length; *adv 2 Jahre ~* for two years; *wochen~* for weeks; *die ganze Woche ~* all the week through; *~e Finger machen fig* to be long-fingered; to pilfer, to steal; *ein ~es Gesicht machen* to pull a long face; to look very much disappointed; *e-n ~en Hals machen* to crane forward; *sein Leben ~* all his life; *den lieben ~en Tag* the livelong day; *etw ~ u. breit erklären* to explain s. th. in detail; *die Zeit wird ihr ~e* time hangs heavy on her hands; *auf die ~e Bank schieben* to put off; *auf ~e Sicht* at long term (*od* sight); (*Wechsel*) long-dated; *auf ~e Zeit* for a long time; *in nicht zu ~er Zeit* in good season; before long; *seit ~er Zeit* long ago; *vor ~er Zeit* long ago; **~atmig** *a* long-breathed; *fig* long-winded; lengthy; **~baum** *m* perch; **~beinig** *a* long-legged; **~(e)weile** *f* boredom, weariness; tediousness; **~finger** *m* thief, pickpocket; **~format** *n* oblong size; **~fristig** *a* long-dated, long-termed; **~gestreckt** *a* extended, elongated, oblong; **~holz** *n* timber; planks *pl*; **~jährig** *a* of long standing; **~lauf** *m* (*Schi*) langlauf, long-distance skiing; **~läufer** *m* (*Schi*) long-distance ski runner; **~lebig** *a* long-lived; **~lebigkeit** *f* longevity; **~mut** *f* long-suffering; longanimity; forbearance; patience; **~mütig** *a* long-suffering; forbearing; patient; **~ohr** *n* (*Esel*) long-ear; jackass; **~sam** *a* slow; (*Motorenlauf*) idling; (*zögernd*) tardy; *fig* (*geistig*) dull; *~~ fahren* to drive slowly; *~~er werden* to slow down; *mot* (*auf Warnschild*) slow down! **~samflug** *m* *aero* slow flight, stalling flight; **~samkeit** *f* slowness; *fig* dullness; **~schiff** *n* nave; **~schläfer** *m* late riser; **~sichtig** *a* long-sighted; **~spielplatte** *f* (*Schallplatte*) long playing record (*Abk* LP record); **~strecken** ... (*in Zssg*) long-distance, long-range; **~~angriff** *m aero* long-distance attack; **~~bomber** *m aero* long-range bomber; (*mit Düsenmotoren*) long-range jet bomber; **~~flug** *m* long-distance flight; **~~flugzeug** *n* long-range (*od* long--distance) airplane; **~~jäger** *m aero* long-range fighter; **~~lauf** *m sport* long--distance race; **~~läufer** *m* long-distance runner; stayer; **~vorschub** *m tech* longitudinal feed; **~weilen** *tr* to bore; to tire; *sich ~~* to feel (*od* to be) bored; *sich zu Tode ~~* to be bored to death; *gelangweilt sein von* (*fam*) to be fed up with; **~weilig** *a* boring, tedious; (*Person*) dull; (*ermüdend*) tiresome; *~~e Person* bore, *Am fam* boiled (*od* stuffed) shirt; **~welle** *f radio* long--wave; **~~nbereich** *m* long-wave band; **~~nempfänger** *m radio* long--wave receiver; **~~nsender** *m radio* long-wave transmitter; **~wellig** *a* long--waved; *in Zssg* long-wave ...; **~wierig** *a* of long duration; protracted; lengthy; tedious, wearisome; lingering; *e-e ~~e Geschichte!* a tedious business! **~wierigkeit** *f* wearisomeness.

lang|(e) *adv* long; a long while; *~e her* long ago, a long time ago; *~e hin* a long time yet; *noch ~e nicht* far from; *sie ist noch ~e nicht fertig* she is far from being ready; *so ~e als* as long as; *über kurz od ~* sooner or later; *~ machen* to be long in doing; *sind Sie schon ~e hier?* have you been here long?

Läng|e *f* length; (*Gestalt*) tallness; (*Größe*) size; (*Dauer*) duration; *gram* (*Quantität*) quantity; *astr, geog, math* longitude; *~e über alles* overall (*od* total) length; *~en haben* (*Gedicht usw*) to have tedious passages; *auf die ~e* in the long run; *der ~e nach* lengthwise; at full length, longitudinal; *in die ~e ziehen* to prolong, to draw out; to elongate; to drag on (*od* out); *sich in die ~e ziehen* to lengthen out; **~enausdehnung** *f* linear expansion; **~endurchschnitt** *m* longitudinal section; **~eneinheit** *f* unit of length; **~engrad** *m* degree of longitude; **~enmaß** *n* linear measure; **~er** *a* longer; *je ~~, je lieber* the longer, the better; *immer ~~* longer and longer; *schon ~~* for some time; *~~e Zeit* for a considerable time; *es wird ~~e Zeit dauern* it will take some time; **~lich** *a* longish; oblong; **~lichrund** *a* oval: elliptical.

langen *tr* (*ergreifen, packen*) to grasp; to seize; (*herunternehmen*) to take down; (*geben*) to hand, to give; *jdm e-e* (*Ohrfeige*) *~* to box s. o.'s ears; *itr* (*genügen*) to suffice, to be enough; *nach etw ~* to reach for; *es wird nicht weit ~* it won't go far; *~ Sie zu!* (*bei Tisch*) help yourself! *mit dem Geld ~* to last with the money; *in die Tasche ~* to put o.'s hand in o.'s pocket.

längs *adv* along, alongside of; **~achse** *f* longitudinal axis; **~ebene** *f* longitudinal plane; **~neigungsmesser** *m aero* inclinometer; **~profil** *n* longitudinal stiffener; **~schiff** *a* fore and aft; **~schnitt** *m* longitudinal section; **~schott** *n* longitudinal bulkhead; **~seits** *a* alongside; **~stabilität** *f aero* longitudinal stability, lateral stability; **~streuung** *f mil* longitudinal dispersion.

längst *adv* for a long time, long ago; *a* longest; *schon ~* long ago, for a long time; *noch ~ nicht* not nearly; *am ~en* the longest; **~ens** *adv* at the latest; at the most.

Lanz|e *f* lance, spear; *für jdn e-e ~~ brechen* (*od einlegen*) to stand up for s. o.; **~ette** *f* lancet; **~~nförmig** *a* lanceolate; **~ierrohr** *n* (*Torpedo*) launching tube.

Lappalie *f* trifle.

Lapp|e *m* Laplander; **~land** *n* Lapland; **~länder** *m* Laplander.

Lapp|en *m* (*Lumpen*) rag; (*Tuch~~*) cloth; (*Wisch~~*) duster; (*Flick~~*) patch; (*Fetzen*) shred; (*Ohr~~*) flap; *anat, bot* lobe; *durch die ~~ gehen fam* to run away, to escape; **~enartig, ~ig** *a* ragged; (*schlaff*) flabby; *anat, bot* lobed, lobate; **~ung** *f* serration.

läpp|ern *itr* to sip, to lap; *sich zusammen~~* to run up; to accumulate; to come in driblets; **~isch** *a* (*dumm*) silly, foolish; (*kindisch*) childish.

Lärche *f* larch.

Larifari *n* nonsense; *interj ~!* rubbish!

Lärm *m* noise; (*anhaltender ~*) din; (*Tumult*) uproar; (*Radau*) row; (*Durcheinander*) hubbub, pandemonium; (*Spektakel*) racket; (*Geschrei*) hullabaloo, clamo(u)r; (*Stimmengewirr*) babel; *blinder ~* false alarm; *was bedeutet der ~?* what's that noise? *~ schlagen* to give (*od* to beat *od* to sound) the alarm; *fam* (*Krach schlagen*) to kick up a row; *viel ~ machen* to make a great bustle; *viel ~ um nichts* much ado about nothing; a great fuss about nothing; **~bekämpfung** *f* noise abatement, combating of noise; **~en** *itr* to make a noise, to be noisy; *fam* to kick up a row; (*schreien*) to shout; **~end** *a* noisy; (*tobend*) uproarious; riotous; **~ig** *a* noisy, loud; clamorous; **~pfeife** *f* alarm whistle; **~signal** *n* sound signal.

Larve *f* mask; (*Gesicht*) face; (*Puppe*) grub, larva.

lasch *a* flabby, limp; **~heit** *f* flabbiness; laxity.

Lasche *f* (*Klappe*) flap; (*Zwickel*) gusset; (*Schuh~*) tongue (of shoe); *rail* fish-plate, *Am* joint bar; *tech* joint; shackle; (*Holzarbeit*) groove; *arch* strip.

lassen *irr tr, itr* (*zulassen, erlauben*) to let, to allow, to permit, to yield; (*dulden*) to suffer; (*befehlen*) to order, to command; (*veranlassen*) to get, to make, to have ... (done); to cause; (*zurücklassen, hinterlassen, überlassen*) to leave, to abandon, to part with, to let go; (*unterlassen*) to abstain from, to desist from, to refrain from; (*verlieren*) to lose; *~ Sie das!* leave it alone! don't bother! *laß!* don't! stop it! *~ Sie nur!* never mind! *~ Sie das Licht brennen!* keep the light burning! *~ Sie es niemals darauf ankommen!* never take a chance! *außer acht ~* to disregard; *Blut ~* to let blood; *die Hände von etw ~* to keep off o.'s hands; *sein Leben ~* to sacrifice o.'s life (*für* for), to lose o.'s life; *jdn in Ruhe* (*od zufrieden*) *~* to let s. o. alone; *aus dem Spiele ~* to leave out of the question; *Wasser ~* to make water, to urinate; *Zeit ~* to give time; *sich Zeit ~* to take o.'s time; *die Zügel schießen ~* to slacken the reigns; *drucken ~* to have printed; *fallen ~* to drop, to let drop; *es fehlen ~* to be wanting (*an* in); *holen ~* to send for; *kommen ~* to send for, to ask to come; *leben u. leben ~* to live and let live; *sich malen ~* to sit for o.'s portrait; *sich machen ~* to have made, to have done; *etw auf Bestellung machen ~* to have s. th. made to order; *sich rasieren ~* to get a shave; *mit sich reden ~* to be reasonable, to listen to reason; *sich raten ~* to listen to advice; *rufen ~* to call, to send for;

sagen ~ to send word; *ich habe mir sagen* ~ I have been told; *sich sagen* ~ to take advice; *sehen* ~ to show; *sich nicht sehen* ~ to keep out of sight; *etw tun* ~ to have s. th. done; *von etw* ~ to renounce; *sich e-n Bart wachsen* ~ to grow a beard; *warten* ~ to keep waiting; *das läßt sich denken* that may easily be imagined; I should think so; *es beim alten* ~ to stick to the old ways; *es läßt sich nicht leugnen* there is no denying the fact, it cannot be denied; *das läßt sich tun* that can be done; *das muß man ihr* ~ you have to grant her that; *darüber ließe sich reden* that's a thing to be considered; ~ *n* (*Benehmen*) behavio(u)r, conduct; *das Tun u.* ~ commissions and omissions.

lässig *a* lazy, idle; indolent; (*sorglos, nachlässig*) careless, negligent; **~keit** *f* laziness, indolence.

läßlich *a* (*verzeihlich*) pardonable; (*Sünde*) venial.

Lasso *m od n* lasso.

Last *f* (*Ladung, Belastung*) load; (*Fracht*) cargo, freight; (*Ladefähigkeit*) tonnage; (*Bürde*) burden; (*Gewicht*) weight, charge; *fig* encumbrance; (*Mühe*) trouble; *~en pl* (*Steuern*) taxes *pl*; *Nutz~* useful load; *öffentliche ~en* public charges; *zahlende* ~ pay load; *zu ~en von* to the debit of; for account of; *die Auslagen gehen zu meinen ~en* I am to be charged with the expenses; *jdm zur* ~ *fallen* to be a burden to; *jdm zur* ~ *legen* to charge s. o. with s. th.; *die zur* ~ *gelegte Tat* the alleged charge; *jdm e-n Betrag zu ~en schreiben* to debit an amount to s. o.; **~anhänger** *m mot* trailer; **~arm** *m* load arm; leverage of load; **~auto** *n* (motor) lorry, van, *Am* (motor) truck; **~dampfer** *m* cargo boat, freight ship, freighter; **~en** *itr* to weigh (*auf* upon, on), to press heavily upon; *fig* to be a heavy burden to; *die ganze Verantwortung lastet auf ihr* the whole responsibility rests on her; **~enaufzug** *m* goods lift, goods elevator, hoist, *Am* freight elevator; **~enausgleich** *m* equalization of burdens; **~enfallschirm** *m aero* cargo parachute; **~enfrei** *a* tax-free, free of tax; free from charges; **~ensegler** *m aero* freight(-carrying) glider, cargo-transport glider, cargo glider, troop-carrying glider; *ein mehrmotoriges Flugzeug kann zwei od drei ~~ gleichzeitig schleppen* a multi-motored airplane can pull two or three cargo gliders simultaneously; **~enseglerschleppzug** *m aero* aerial train; **~er** *m siehe*: *Lastkraftwagen*; **~flugzeug** *n* freight-carrying plane, freight airplane, cargo plane, transport plane; **~gebühr** *f* tonnage; **~gewicht** *n* loading weight; **~hebemagnet** *m* lifting magnet; **~igkeit** *f* tonnage; trimming; **~kahn** *m* lighter, barge; **~(kraft)wagen** *m* (*Abk* LKW) motor lorry, van, *Am* (motor *od* cargo) truck; *leichter ~~* light truck; *mittlerer ~~* medium duty truck; *schwerer ~~* heavy duty truck; **~~anhänger** *m* trailer; **~~fahrer** *m* lorry driver, *Am* truck driver; **~~kolonne** *f* convoy of lorries; **~pferd** *n* pack-horse; **~schlepper** *m* cargo trailer; **~schrift** *f com* (*Anzeige*) debit note; (*Buchung*) debit entry, debit item; **~tier** *n* pack animal, beast of burden; **~träger** *m* porter; **~verteilung** *f* load distribution; load rating; **~vieh** *n* beasts of burden; **~wagen** *m* cart, truck, lorry, van, wag(g)on; freight car; **~~fernverkehr** *m* long distance motor traffic; **~~transport** *m* road goods transport, *Am* highway transportation, motor truck transportation; **~zug** *m mot* road train, train of loaded motor lorries; tractor train; truck with trailer.

Laster *n* vice; (*Verderbtheit*) wickedness; (*Verworfenheit*) depravity; **~haft** *a* vicious; wicked; **~haftigkeit** *f* viciousness; wickedness; depravation; **~höhle** *f* den of iniquity; **~leben** *n* vicious life.

Läster|er *m* slanderer; (*Gottes~*) blasphemer; **~lich** *a* slanderous; scandalous; **~maul** *n* (*Person*) scandalmonger; slanderer; scold; **~n** *tr* to slander; to calumniate; (*Gott ~~*) to blaspheme; **~sucht** *f* calumnious disposition; **~süchtig** *a* slanderous, scandalmongering; **~ung** *f* calumny; slander; defamation; (*Gottes~~*) blasphemy; **~zunge** *f* slanderous tongue; (*Person*) slanderer, scandalmonger.

lästig *a* troublesome, irksome; burdensome; nasty; (*unangenehm*) disagreeable; (*unbequem, beschwerlich*) inconvenient; (*verdrießlich*) tedious, annoying; *jdm* ~ *fallen* to bore s. o.; *~er Ausländer* undesirable alien; *~er Mensch* nuisance; **~keit** *f* burdensomeness; troublesomeness; irksomeness; inconvenience.

Lasur *f* azure; ultramarine; lapis lazuli; **~blau** *n* azure, sky-blue; **~farbe** *f* azure, ultramarine; **~farben** *a* azure, sky-blue; **~lack** *m* transparent varnish; **~stein** *m* (lapis) lazuli.

Lat|ein *n* Latin; *mit seinem ~~ zu Ende sein fig* to be at a nonplus; to be at o.'s wits' end; **~einamerika** *n* Latin America; **~einer** *m* Latinist; **~einisch** *a* Latin; *~~e Buchstaben typ* Roman letters *pl*; **~einschule** *f* high school; **~inisieren** *tr* to latinize; **~inismus** *m* Latinism.

Latenz *f* latency; (*Inkubation*) incubation; **~stadium** *n* latent stage; **~zeit** *f* latent period.

Laterne *f* lantern; (*Lampe*) lamp; (*Straßen~*) street-lamp, *Am* street light; (*Blend~*) dark lantern; **~nanzünder** *m* lamplighter; **~nförmig** *a* lantern-shaped; **~npfahl** *m* lamp-post; *an e-m ~~* (*auf*)*hängen* to string up to a lamp-post; *jdm e-n Wink mit dem ~~ geben fig* to give s. o. a broad hint, to give s. o. the straight tip.

Latrine *f* latrine; **~ngerücht** *n*, **~nparole** *f fam* (*bes. mil sl*) rumo(u)r, gossip, latrine gossip, latrine rumo(u)r, *Am parl* cloakroom gossip, *Am sl* scuttlebutt, *mil* galley news, galley yarn.

Latsch|e[1] *f* (*Schuh*) old, downtrodden slipper; **~en** *itr* to shuffle along; to waddle; to slouch; **~er** *m* shuffler; *Fuß~~* foot-slogger; **~erei** *f* foot-slogging; **~ig** *a* shuffling; (*schlampig*) slovenly; (*träge*) sluggish, drowsy.

Latsche[2] *f bot* dwarf-pine; **~nkiefer** *f* dwarf-pine, knee-pine; **~nöl** *n* templin oil.

Latte *f* lath, batten, (*kleine* ~) slat; *aero sl* (*Propeller*) stick, screw, *Am* prop(eller): (*Hochsprung*) bar; *Landung mit stehender* ~ (*aero*) a dead-stick landing; *aus ~n bestehend* lathen; *lange* ~ *hum* (*Mensch*) lanky fellow, May-pole; *mager wie e-e* ~ thin as a lath; **~nkiste** *f* crate; **~nrost** *m* lath floor; **~nsteg** *m* ladder bridge; **~nverschlag** *m* lattice(d) partition; **~nwerk** *n* lath-work; trellis-work; **~nzaun** *m* lattice (*od* lath) fence, wooden fence; paling; railing.

Lattich *m* lettuce.

Latwerge *f* electuary.

Latz *m* (*Geifer~*) bib; (*Hosen~*) flap; (*Schürzen~*) pinafore; (*Blusen~*) stomacher.

lau *a* tepid; lukewarm; (*mild*) mild; *fig* indifferent; half-hearted; (*flau*) dull; *~es Wetter* mild weather; ~ *werden* to cool down, to slacken in o.'s zeal; **~heit, ~igkeit** *f* (*auch fig*) lukewarmness, tepidity; *fig* indifference; indolence; **~warm** *a* lukewarm, tepid.

Laub *n* foliage, leaves *pl*; **~abfall** *m* leaf fall; **~artig** *a* foliaceous; **~baum** *m* tree with leaves, deciduous tree, broad-leaved tree; **~dach** *n* leafy canopy, leaf ceiling; **~frosch** *m* tree-frog; **~holz** *n* deciduous (*od* foliage) trees *pl*; **~hüttenfest** *n* Feast of Tabernacles; **~krone** *f* leaf crown; **~reich** *a* leafy; **~säge** *f* fret-saw; **~wald** *m* deciduous forest; broadleaf wood; **~wechsel** *m* change of foliage; **~werk** *n* foliage.

Laube *f* arbo(u)r, summer-house, garden house; arcade; *poet* bower; **~ngang** *m* arcade; pergola; **~ngärtner** *m* small allotment holder; **~nkolonie** *f* allotment gardens *pl*, garden lots *pl*.

Lauch *m* leek.

Lauer *f* look-out; watch; (*Hinterhalt*) ambush, lurking-place; *auf der* ~ on the look-out; *auf der* ~ *liegen* (*od sein*) to lie in wait; **~n** *itr* (*versteckt liegen*) to lurk, to be on the watch, to lie in wait for; *~~ auf* to wait for; **~stellung** *f* observation post; ambush.

Lauf *m* course; pace; (*Motor*) run, running; operation; (*Wett~*) race; (*Gewehr~*) barrel; (*Treppe*) flight; (*von Tieren*) leg, foot; (*Fortbewegung*) progress; (*Reichweite*) range, course; (*Wasser*) current, flow; (*Gestirne, Bahn*) track, path; (*Bewegung*) motion; action; *mus* run; roulade; *fig* scope, play, course; *der* ~ *der Dinge* the way things go; *freien* ~ *lassen* to give free play to; *seinen Gefühlen freien* ~ *lassen* to vent o.'s feelings; *im ~e von* in the course of; *im vollen ~e* at top speed; in full swing; *im ~e der Zeit* in course of time; **~bahn** *f* (*Bahn*) course; (*Beruf*) career; *mot* (*Reifen*) tread of tyre (*od* tire); *aero* runway; (*Rennen*) race-course; *astr* orbit; *mil* (*Torpedo*) torpedo track (*od* wake); *die militärische ~~ einschlagen* to follow (*od* to enter) a military career; **~bahnabzeichen** *n mil* specialist's insignia; **~band** *n* leading-strings *pl*; **~brett** *n* running board; **~brücke** *f* (*Steg*) foot-bridge; plank bridge; *mar* gangway; (*auf dem Schiff*) fore-and-aft bridge; **~bursche, ~junge** *m* errand boy, office boy; **~decke** *f mot* (*Reifen*) tyre casing, *Am* tire casing; **~en** *irr itr* to run; to walk; *fam* to go; to move; (*Maschine*) to go, to work, to play; (*erstrecken*) to extend, to stretch, to run; (*fließen*) to flow; (*Gefäß*) to leak, to run out; (*Zeit vergehen*) to pass, to go by, to go on; *sich heiß ~~* to run hot; *leer ~~* (*Motor*) to idle; *~~ lassen* to let go; to let slide; (*Gefangene*) to release; *laß sie ~~* let her go; *es läuft auf das gleiche hinaus* it comes to the same thing; *jdm in die Arme ~~* to bump into; *Gefahr ~~* to run the risk; *unter dem Namen ~~* to go under the name; *den Motor sehr schnell ~~ lassen* to race the engine; **~end** *a* running; current, present; (*folgend*) consecutive; *~~e Arbeiten pl* routine work; ~~e *Ausgaben pl* current expenses *pl*, *Am* operating costs *pl*; ~~es *Band* assembly line; (*Förderband*) conveyor belt; ~~es *Jahr* present year; ~~er *Kommentar* running commentary; ~~es *Konto* current account; ~~en *Monats* instant (*Abk* inst.); ~~e *Nummer* serial number; consecutive number; *auf dem* ~~en *bleiben* to be well up in, to be au courant of; *auf dem* ~~en *halten* to keep posted (*über* on); to keep currently informed; *sich auf dem* ~~en *halten* to keep abreast of; *auf dem* ~~en *sein* to be up to date; **~erei** *f* running about (*od* around); **~feuer** *n* surface fire; running-fire; *fig* wildfire; *die Nachricht verbreitete sich wie ein* ~~ the news spread like wildfire; **~fläche** *f* (*Reifen*) tread; (*Lager*) journal; bearing surface; **~geschwindigkeit** *f* speed in running; **~gewicht** *n* sliding weight; **~graben** *m mil* communication trench; sap; approaches *pl*; **~katze** *f* crane crab (*od* carriage); overhead tackle; **~kette** *f* track; **~kran** *m* travel(l)ing (*od* overhead) crane; **~kunde** *m* irregular customer; **~kundschaft** *f* passing trade; **~mantel** *m* (*Gewehr*) barrel casing; **~masche** *f* (*im Strumpf*) ladder, slipped stitch, *Am* run, runner; **~nummer** *f* order number; **~paß** *m* notice, dismissal, sack; *Am fam* walking-papers *pl*, walking-ticket; *den* ~~ *bekommen sl* to get the sack; *jdm den* ~~ *geben* to dismiss s. o., *Am* to give s. o. the gate, to fire s. o.; **~planke** *f* gangway; **~rad** *n* bogie wheel; *aero* landing wheel; **~richtung** *f* direction of motion; **~rolle** *f* roller, runner; (*Panzer*) bogie wheel; **~schiene** *f* guide rail, track; **~schritt** *m* sling-trot, double-quick; *im* ~~ at the double; **~sohle** *f* (*Schuh*) outsole; **~steg** *m* foot bridge; **~werk** *n* working gear, mechanism; **~zeit** *f* (*Brief, Telegramm etc*) transmission time; duration; (*Wechsel*) currency term; *sport* time; (*Tiere*) rutting season; **~zettel** *m* circular letter; interoffice slip; control tag; tracer.

Läufer *m* (*Person*) runner; (*Treppen~*) stair-carpet; (*in der Wohnung*) carpet strip; (*grober ~*) drugget; (*Tisch~*) table runner; (*Schachspiel*) bishop; (*Fußballspiel*) half (-back); (*junges Schwein*) young pig, sucker; *mus* run; roulade; *tech* (*Rotor*) rotor; (*Schieber*) slider; *arch* stretcher, bonder.

läufig *a* (*von Tieren*) in heat, ruttish.

Lauge *f* lye; (*Wasch~*) buck; leach; solution; lixivium; electrolyte; **~n** *tr* (*Wäsche*) to buck; (*auslaugen*) to leach; to lye, to steep (in lye); *chem* to lixiviate; **~nartig** *a* alkaline; lixivial; **~nasche** *f* alkaline ashes *pl*; potash; **~nbehälter** *m* leaching vat (*od* tank); **~nbeständig** *a* alkali-resistant; **~nlösung** *f* leach solution; **~nsalz** *n* alkaline salt; **~verfahren** *n* leaching method; lixiviation process.

Laune *f* fancy; (*Grille*) whim, whimsey; crotchet; (*Unberechenbarkeit*) vagary; (*Einfall*) freak; (*Schrulle*) caprice, vagary; (*Stimmung*) temper, mood, frame of mind; humo(u)r, spirit; *~n haben* to be full of whims; to be changeable; *jdm die ~ verderben* to set s. o. out of heart; *in guter ~ sein* to be in good temper, to be in high spirits; *die gute ~ verlieren* to lose o.'s temper; *bei schlechter ~ sein* to be out of temper; *nicht in der ~ sein etw zu tun* not to be in the vein to do s. th.; **~nhaft** *a* capricious; whimsical; (*sprunghaft*) vagarious, fitful; **~nhaftigkeit** *f* capriciousness, moodiness; **~ig** *a* humorous; (*komisch, lustig*) funny, droll; comical; (*witzig*) witty; **~isch** *a* moody; variable, changeable; fickle; wayward; splenic; ill-humo(u)red.

Laus *f* louse, *pl* lice; *Läuse sind Krankheitsträger* lice are disease carriers; *sich e-e ~ in den Pelz setzen* to saddle o. s. with a troublesome thing; *jdm Läuse in den Pelz setzen* to play s. o. a dirty trick; *e-e ~ ist ihm über die Leber gelaufen* he is out of temper; **~bube, ~ebengel, ~ejunge** *m* young scamp, little rogue; blackguard; **~bubenstreich** *m* boy's trick; (*Gaunerstreich*) knavery, villainous act; **~en** *tr* to delouse, to rid of lice; *sich ~~* to louse o. s.; **~ig** *a* lousy; *fig* (*schmutzig*) filthy, dirty; (*geizig*) mean, stingy; (*verächtlich*) wretched; (*lumpig*) paltry, beggarly; *fam* (*sehr*) very; *~~ schwer* very difficult.

lausch|en *itr* to listen (*auf* to); (*horchen*) to harken; (*an der Türe*) to listen at the door, to eavesdrop; (*abhören*) to intercept; **~er** *m* listener, eavesdropper; peeping Tom; **~gerät** *n mil* listening equipment, intercept set; **~ig** *a* (*gemütlich*) cosy, snug; pleasant; (*ruhig*) quiet.

Läusepulver *n* insect-powder; insecticide.

Laut *m* sound; tone, note; *e-n ~ von sich geben* to utter a sound; *~ geben* (*Hund*) to give tongue, to bay; *~ a* loud; (*klar*) clear; (*hörbar*) audible; (*lärmend*) noisy; (*schallend*) ringing; *~ adv* aloud, loud(ly); *~er!* (*als Aufforderung an Redner*) speak up! *Am* louder! *mit ~er Stimme* at the top of o.'s voice; *~ lesen* to read aloud; *~ vorlesen* to read out; *~ sprechen* to speak up; *~ verkünden* to proclaim; *~ werden* to become audible; *fig* to become public (*od* known), to get about; *~ werden lassen* (*verraten*) to betray; *~es Gelächter* roars of laughter; *~ prp* (*gemäß*) in accordance with, according to; in conformity with; *com* as per; (*kraft*) by virtue of; under; *~ Befehl* by order, as ordered; *~ Bericht* as per advice, as per statement; *~ Rechnung* as per account; *~ Verfügung* as directed, according to order; **~angleichung** *f* assimilation of sounds; **~bar** *a* notorious, public, known; (*hörbar*) audible; **~bezeichnung** *f* phonetic transcription; **~e** *f mus* lute; **~en** *itr* to sound; (*sagen*) to say; (*Inhalt e-s Schreibens etc*) to run, to read, to purport; to be worded; *wie folgt ~~* to run as follows, to be worded as follows; *~~ auf* (*zahlbar an*) to be payable to; (*ausgefertigt auf*) to be issued to; *auf den Inhaber ~~* to be payable to bearer; *an Order ~~* to be payable (*od* issued) to order; *das Urteil lautet auf* the judg(e)ment has been passed to the effect that, the judg(e)ment results in; **~enmacher** *m* lute-maker; **~enschläger** *m* lute-player; **~erzeugung** *f* sound production; **~gesetz** *n* phonetic law; **~heit** *f* loudness, audibility; **~ieren** *tr* to read phonetically; **~lehre** *f* phonetics; phonology; **~lich** *a* phonetic; **~los** *a* silent; soundless; mute; hushed; (*geräuschlos*) noiseless; **~losigkeit** *f* silence; hush; **~malerei** *f* onomatopœia; **~schrift** *f* phonetic transcription, phonetic script, phonetic spelling; **~sprecher** *m radio* loudspeaker, speaker, *Am sl* squawk (*od* voice) box; (*elektro-*)*dynamischer ~~* dynamic speaker, coil-driven (*od* moving-coil) speaker; *Konus~~* cone speaker; *permanent dynamischer ~~* permanent magnet speaker; *Trichter~~* horn-type speaker; *Groß~~* high power loudspeaker; *zweiter ~~* (*radio*) extension-loudspeaker; **~~gehäuse** *n* speaker case; **~~membran** *f* moving cone; diaphragm; **~~röhre** *f* (*Endröhre*) power valve (*Am* tube), loudspeaker valve (*Am* tube); **~~trichter** *m* horn; funnel; **~~übertragungsanlage** *f* public address system, speaker system; **~~wagen** *m* loudspeaker van, *Am* loudspeaker truck, sound truck; **~stärke** *f* sound intensity; loudness; *radio* volume; signal strength; **~~anzeiger, ~~messer** *m* volume indicator; **~~regler** *m* volume control(ler); gain control; **~~regelung** *f* (*automatischer Schwundausgleich*) automatic volume control (*Abk* A. V. C.); **~~umfang** *m* volume range; **~tafel** *f* sound chart; **~verschiebung** *f* sound-shifting; Grimm's law; **~verstärker** *m radio* volume (*od* sound) amplifier; **~verstärkung** *f* amplification of sound; **~verzerrung** *f* sound distortion; **~wandel** *m* sound change; **~wirkung** *f* sound effect; **~zeichen** *n* phonetic symbol.

läut|en *tr, itr* to ring; *es ~et* the bell rings; (*laut*) to peal; to sound; (*langsam feierlich*) to toll; *die Begräbnisglocke läutete feierlich* the funeral bell tolled solemnly; (*bimmeln e-s Glöckchens*) to tinkle; *ich habe etw davon ~~ hören fam* I have heard a rumo(u)r thereof; I have heard s. th. to that effect; **~werk** *n* sounder; ringing device (*od* apparatus); (alarm-) bell.

lauter *a* (*rein*) pure; (*hell*) limpid; (*durchsichtig*) transparent; (*klar*) clear; (*aufrichtig, offen*) candid, true; (*echt*) genuine; honest; (*unvermischt*) unmixed, unalloyed; *~es Gold* pure gold; *~e Wahrheit* plain truth; *~er Wein* pure wine; *adv* (*nichts als*) nothing but; sheer, mere; rank; only; *~ Freunde* friends, all of them; *~ Lügen!* nothing but lies! **~keit** *f* pureness; clearness; limpidity; genuineness; integrity.

läuter|n *tr* to clear; to purify; to purge; (*raffinieren*) to refine; (*filtrieren*) to filter; (*klären*) to clarify; (*Flüssigkeiten*) to rectify; **~ung** *f* refining; purification; rectification; clarification; **~~smittel** *n* purifying agent; **~~sprozeß** *m* refining process.

Lava *f* lava; **~strom** *m* torrent of lava.

Lavendel *m* lavender.

lavieren *itr* to veer; to tack (about); *fig* to shift.

Lawine *f* avalanche; snow-slip; **~nartig** *a* like an avalanche; **~ngefahr** *f* danger from snow-slips.

lax *a* lax, loose; (*Sitten*) licentious; **~heit** *f* laxity; **~ieren** *tr* to purge; to take an aperient; **~iermittel** *n med* laxative, purge, aperient.

Lazarett *n mil* military hospital; infirmary; (*Feld~*) field-hospital; ambulance; *mar* sick-bay; **~apotheke** *f* dispensary; **~aufnahme, ~einlieferung** *f* *Am* hospitalization; **~flagge** *f* flag of protection; **~gehilfe** *m* dresser; **~schiff** *n* hospital-ship; **~wagen** *m* ambulance; **~zug** *m* hospital-train, ambulance-train.

Lebe|hoch *n* cheer, cheers *pl*; cheering; (*beim Trinken*) toast; *ein ~~ ausbringen auf jdn* to drink to s. o.'s health; to propose s. o.'s health; **~mann** *m* man about town, loose liver; bon vivant, *Am sl* playboy; **~männisch** *a* epicurean; **~n** *n* life; (*Dasein, Existenz*) existence; (*Sein*) being; (*Lebhaftigkeit*) animation, liveliness; stir; activity; (*Lebenskraft*) vitality; (*Un-*

terhalt) subsistence; living; livelihood; bread; *das nackte* ~~ bare life; *ein bequemes* (*elendes*) ~~ *führen* to lead an easy (wretched) life; *mein ganzes* ~~ *hindurch* all my life(time); *am* ~~ *bleiben* to survive; *am* ~~ *sein* to be alive; *ist sie noch am* ~~*?* is she still alive? *auf* ~~ *u. Tod* at the risk of o.'s life; a matter of life and death; *sich das* ~~ *nehmen* to commit suicide; *sie nahm sich das* ~~ she took her (own) life; *Kampf auf* ~~ *u. Tod* life-and-death struggle; *etw für sein* ~~ *gern tun* to be very fond of doing s. th.; *nur einmal im* ~~ only once in a lifetime; *ins* ~~ *rufen* to start, to originate; to call into existence; *Kinder ins* ~~ *setzen* to give birth to children; *e-m Kind das* ~~ *schenken* to give birth to; *mit dem* ~~ *davonkommen* to save o.'s life; *nach dem* ~~ from life; *nach dem* ~~ *trachten* to attempt s. o.'s life; *ums* ~~ *bringen* to kill; *ums* ~~ *kommen* to lose o.'s life; to die, to perish; **~n** *itr* to live, to be alive; (*existieren*) to exist; (*wohnen*) to live, to dwell, to reside; to stay; ~~ *von* to live by, to subsist on; (*sich nähren von*) to feed on; *auf großem Fuß* ~~ to live in great style; ~~ *u.* ~~ *lassen* live and let live; *hoch* ~~ *lassen* to cheer; to drink the health of, to toast s. o.'s health; *wie er leibt u. lebt* his very image; *über seine Verhältnisse* ~~ to live beyond o.'s income; *entsprechend seinen Verhältnissen* ~~ to live within o.'s income; *genug zu* ~~ *haben* to have enough to live on; *zurückgezogen* ~~ to lead a retired life; *so wahr wir* ~~*!* upon our lives! *es läßt sich gut* ~~ *hier* it is good living here; *es lebe der König!* long live the King! **~nd** *a* living; live; alive; ~~*e Bilder* tableaux vivants; ~~*e Fische* live fish; ~~*e Hecke* quickset hedge; ~~*es Inventar* live-stock; ~~*e Sprachen* modern languages; **~ndgewicht** *n* live weight; **~ndig** *a* living, alive; lively, vivid; quick; ~~*e Farben* bright colo(u)rs; ~~*e Kraft* kinetic energy; **~ndigkeit** *f* liveliness, quickness; animation; vivacity.

Lebens|abend *m* old age, evening of life; **~abriß** *m* biographical sketch; **~abschnitt** *m* period of life; **~ader, ~linie** *f fig* life line; life string; *die* ~~ *e-s Volkes abschneiden* to sever the life line of a nation; **~anschauung** *f* view of life; **~aussicht** *f* prospects *pl* of life; (*Versicherung*) life expectancy; **~art** *f* way (*od* manner) of living; *fig* (*Benehmen*) behavio(u)r; manners *pl*, good breeding; **~aufgabe** *f* life work; vital task; **~äußerung** *f* sign (*od* manifestation) of life; **~bahn** *f* life; (*Laufbahn*) career; **~bedingungen** *f pl* living conditions *pl*; essential conditions for life; **~bedrohend** *a* threatening life; **~bedürfnisse** *n pl* necessaries of life; **~bejahend** *a* optimistic; virile; **~beruf** *m* vocation; profession; **~beschreibung** *f* biography; life (history); **~bezirk** *m* life zone; **~bild** *n* biographical sketch; **~dauer** *f* duration of life; life span; (*Dauerhaftigkeit*) durability; ~~ *e-s Autoreifens* tyre life; ~~ *e-s Geschützes* (accuracy) life; ~~ *e-r Maschine* service life; *jur auf* ~~ for life; *voraussichtliche* ~~ expectation of life; **~drang** *m* vital instinct; **~einstellung** *f* outlook on life; **~ende** *n* end of life; *bis an mein* ~~ until my last breath; **~erfahren** *a* experienced in life; **~erfahrung** *f* experience of life; personal experience; **~erhaltung** *f* preservation of life; **~erhaltungstrieb** *m* life-preserving instinct; instinct of self-preservation; **~erscheinung** *f* biological phenomenon; **~faden** *m* thread of life, life-strings *pl*; **~fähig** *a* capable of living; full of vitality, to have vitality; *med* viable; **~fähigkeit** *f* capacity for living; vitality; *med* viability; **~form** *f* form of life; **~frage** *f* vital question; **~freude** *f* joy of life; **~fremd** *a* unfitted for life; **~führung** *f* manner of living; **~funktion** *f* vital function; **~gefahr** *f* danger to life; *unter* ~~ at the risk (*od* peril) of o.'s life; (*auf Warnschildern*) *Vorsicht!* ~~*!* Caution! Danger! **~gefährlich** *a* perilous; highly dangerous (to life); (*Krankheit*) dangerous; **~gefährte** *m* partner for life; life's companion; husband, wife; **~gehalt** *m* living essence; **~geister** *m pl* animal (*od* vital) spirits *pl*; **~gemeinschaft** *f* partnership for life; *eheliche* ~~ conjugal community; **~genuß** *m* enjoyment of life; **~geschichte** *f* life history, biography; **~gewohnheit** *f* habit; **~glück** *n* happiness of o.'s life; **~größe** *f* life-size; *in* ~~ in full length, life-size(d); **~haltung** *f* standard of life (*od* living); **~~sindex** *m* cost of living index, *Am* cost of living figure; **~~skosten** *pl* cost of living; living expenses *pl*; **~kampf** *m* struggle for existence; **~keim** *m* vital germ; **~klugheit** *f* worldly wisdom; **~kraft** *f* vigo(u)r; vital energy (*od* power *od* force); *med* vitality; **~kräftig** *a* vigorous, strong; **~lage** *f* position in life; situation; emergency; *in jeder* ~~ in every emergency; **~länglich** *a* lifelong; for life, perpetual; ~~*es Mitglied* life member; ~~*e Rente* life annuity; *zu* ~~*em Zuchthaus verurteilen* to sentence to hard labour for life; **~lauf** *m* life, career; (*geschriebener*) curriculum vitae; record; life story; history of life; personal record; course of life; (*bei Bewerbungen*) personal background; (*Lebensgeschichte*) biography; **~lehre** *f* biology; **~licht** *n* lamp of life; *jdm das* ~~ *ausblasen* to do away with s. o.; **~los** *n* lot; **~lust** *f* love of life; **~lustig** *a* fond of life; cheerful; gay, merry; jovial; **~mittel** *n pl* food; provisions *pl*, victuals *pl*; (*Einkäufe etc im Laden*) groceries *pl*; (*Eßwaren*) eatables *pl*; ~~ *kaufen, beschaffen, beibringen* to cater (for); **~~amt** *n* food office; **~~behälter** *m aero mil* (*zum Abwurf*) container for food; **~~geschäft** *n*, **~~laden** *m* grocer's shop, food shop, provisions shop, *Am* grocery (store), food store; **~~händler** *m* provision dealer; **~~karte** *f* food ration card; **~~knappheit** *f* food shortage; **~~lieferant** *m* caterer; **~~marke** *f* (*Kartenabschnitt*) food ration coupon (*od* ticket); **~~paket** *n* food package; **~~ration** *f* food ration; **~~untersuchung** *f* food research; **~~verarbeitung** *f* processing of food products; **~~versorgung** *f* food supply; **~~zuteilungsperiode** *f* ration period; **~~zwangswirtschaft** *f* food rationing; **~müde** *a* tired (*od* weary) of life; **~mut** *m* vital energy; **~nähe** *f* closeness to life; **~nerv** *m fig* mainspring **~ordnung** *f* rule of life; *med* diet, regimen; **~prinzip** *n* vital principle; **~prozeß** *m* vital process; **~raum** *m* living space, lebensraum; **~regel** *f* maxim; **~rente** *f* (life-) annuity; pension for life; **~retter** *m* life-saver; (*Rettungsschwimmer*) member of the Royal Human Society, *Am* life-guard, life-saver; (*Apparat*) life-saving apparatus, (*Sauerstoffatmer*) oxygen breathing apparatus; **~schwäche** *f* debility; **~standard** *m* living standard; **~stellung** *f* social position (*od* status); permanent post; appointment for life; **~strafe** *f* capital punishment; *bei* ~~ on pain of death; **~trieb** *m* vital instinct, vital impulse; **~überdruß** *m* disgust of life; **~überdrüssig** *a* sick (*od* weary) of life; **~unterhalt** *m* living, maintenance, subsistence; (*durch Verdienst*) livelihood; *sich seinen* ~~ *verdienen* to earn o.'s living; ~~ *gewähren* to give sustenance; **~verhältnis** *n* condition of life; **~versicherung** *f* life-assurance, assurance, *bes. Am* life-insurance; *e-e* ~~ *abschließen* to effect a life-insurance; **~~sgesellschaft** *f* life-assurance company, life-insurance company; **~~sprämie** *f* life-insurance premium; **~voll** *a* full of life; **~wahr** *a* true to life; lifelike; (*Bild, Photo*) speaking; **~wahrscheinlichkeit** *f* expectation (*od* expectancy) of life; **~wandel** *m* life, conduct; morals *pl*; *schlechter* ~~ disorderly life; *e-n unsittlichen* ~~ *führen* to lead an immoral life; **~wärme** *f* vital warmth; **~weise** *f* way of living; mode of life; (*Gewohnheit*) habit; **~weisheit** *f* worldly wisdom; practical philosophy; **~wert** *a* worth living; **~wichtig** *a* vital, vitally important, of vital importance; essential; ~~*e Industrie* key industry; ~~*e Verbindungslinie fig* life-line; **~wirklich** *a* actual; **~zeichen** *n* sign of life; **~zeit** *f* lifetime; age, life; *auf* ~~ for life; *Zuchthäusler auf* ~~ lifer; *einmaliger Beitrag* (*für Abonnement etc*) *auf* ~~ life-subscription; **~zweck** *m* aim in life; **~ziel** *n* aim in *od* end of life; **~zyklus** *m* life cycle.

Leber *f* liver; hepar; *in Zssg* hepatic; *von der* ~ *weg reden* to speak frankly, to speak o.'s mind; *was ist ihm über die* ~ *gelaufen? fam* what has bitten him? **~absceß** *m* liver abscess; **~(an)-schwellung** *f* swelling (*od* enlargement) of liver; **~blasengang, ~gallengang** *m* bile duct, hepatocystic duct; **~blümchen** *n* liverwort, hepatica; **~entzündung** *f* inflammation of the liver, hepatitis; **~fleck(en)** *m* liver-spot; *med* chloasma; (*Muttermal*) mole; (*Sommersprosse*) freckle; **~gegend** *f* hepatic region; **~haken** *m* (*Boxen*) liver hook; **~knödel** *m* faggot; **~krank** *a* having a diseased liver; **~kranke(r)** *m* patient with liver disease; **~krankheit** *f*, **~leiden** *n* liver complaint; *med* hepatic disease; **~mittel** *n* liver remedy; **~pastete** *f* goose-liver pie; **~schmerz** *m* hepatic pain; **~tran** *m* cod-liver oil; **~wurst** *f* liver sausage, *Am* liverwurst.

Leb|ewesen *n* living being; living creature; organism; *kleinstes* ~~ micro-organism; **~ewohl** *n* farewell; good-by(e); adieu; *jdm* ~~ *sagen* to bid s.o. farewell; **~haft** *a* lively, vivacious; (*rasch*) brisk; (*lustig*) gay, cheerful; (*munter*) vivid; bright; spirited; *Am* chipper; (*Geschäft*) active; ~~*e Farben* bright colo(u)rs; ~~*er Handel* brisk trade; ~~*e Phantasie* vivid imagination; *e-e* ~~*e Straße* a frequented street; ~~*er Verkehr* heavy traffic; ~~ *empfinden* to be keenly alive to; **~haftigkeit** *f* liveliness; life; vivacity; briskness; quickness; **~kuchen** *m* ginger-bread; **~los** *a* lifeless; (*unbeseelt, com flau*) inanimate; (*ruhig*) quiet; (*Handel, Börse*) dull, flat, inactive; inanimate; (*träge*) heavy; **~losigkeit** *f* lifelessness; dullness; **~tag** *m* day of life; *mein* ~~ (in) all my life; **~zeiten** *f pl* lifetime, life; *zu* ~~ in the lifetime; while alive; *zu seinen* ~~ in his lifetime.

lechzen *itr* (*Durst haben*) to be thirsty; to be parched (with thirst); *fig* (*sich sehnen nach*) to languish (for); to long (for); *nach Blut* ~ to thirst for blood.

Leck *n* leak; leakage, leaking; *ein ~ haben* to leak, to be leaky; *~ a* leaky; leaking; *~ sein* to leak, to have sprung a leak; to make water; *~ werden* to spring a leak; **~age** *f* leakage; **~en**[1] *itr* to leak, to run; to drip out; to trickle out; **~sicher** *a aero* (*Benzintank*) self-sealing; **~verlust** *m* leakage loss.

leck|en[2] *tr* to lick; *jds Speichel ~~* to fawn upon s. o.; **~er** *a* delicate, dainty; (*Geschmack*) tasty; (*köstlich*) delicious; (*hübsch*) nice; (*wählerisch*) fastidious; **~erbissen** *m* delicacy, titbit; choice morsel; **~erei** *f* delicacy; dainty, daintiness; appetizer; **~erhaft** *a* dainty, lickerish; **~erhaftigkeit** *f* daintiness; **~ermaul** *n fig* sweet tooth.

*

Leder *n* leather; (*weiches*) skin; kid; (*Fußball*) leather; *in ~ gebunden* (*Buch*) bound in calf; (*Ganz~*) full bound; (*Halb~*) half-bound; *jdm das ~ gerben* to thrash s. o.; *vom ~ ziehen* to draw o.'s sword; *zäh wie ~* tough as leather; leathery; **~abfall** *m* leather waste; **~ähnlich, ~artig** *a* leathery, leatherlike; **~artikel** *m pl* leather goods *pl*; **~band** *m* (*Buch*) leather binding (in calf); **~bereiter** *m* currier; **~bereitung** *f* leather-dressing; **~beutel** *m* leather bag; **~braun** *a* leather-brown; **~einband** *m* binding in calf; **~einfassung** *f* leather binding; **~ersatz** *m* artificial leather; **~etui** *n* leather case; **~fett** *n* dubbing; **~gamaschen** *f pl* leggings *pl*, leather gaiters *pl*, *mil* spats *pl*; **~farbe** *f* leather colo(u)r; **~gelb** *a* buff; **~gürtel** *m* leather belt; *mil* (*Offizierskoppel mit Schulterriemen*) Sam Browne (belt); **~handel** *m* leather trade; **~händler** *m* leather dealer; **~handschuh** *m* leather (*od* skin) glove; **~haut** *f anat* true skin, corium, cutis; **~hose** *f* leather shorts *pl;* **~imitation** *f* leatherette, leatheroid; **~koffer** *m* leather trunk; **~luxuswaren** *f pl* leather luxury products *pl*; **~n** *a* leathern, of leather, leathery; *fig* (*langweilig*) dull, silly; (*steif*) stiff; (*zäh*) tough; **~riemen** *m* leather strap; eather belt; (*Abziehriemen des Friseurs*) razor-strap; **~schuh** *m* leather shoe; **~schürze** *f* leather-apron; **~tasche** *f* leather case (*od* bag); **~überzug** *m* leather cover; **~waren** *f pl* leather goods *pl*; **~werk** *n* leather work; **~zäh** *a* tough as leather; **~zeug** *n* leather straps *pl*; *mil* leathers *pl*, straps and belts *pl*.

ledig *a* (*unverheiratet*) unmarried, single; (*unbesetzt*) vacant; empty; open; (*e-r Sache*) free from; exempt from; **~ensteuer** *f* bachelor's tax; **~keit** *f* celibacy; **~lich** *adv* merely, only, solely, purely and simply; quite.

Lee *f mar* lee, leeside; *nach ~ zu* leeward; **~bord** *n* larboard; **~brassen** *f pl* lee-braces *pl*; **~küste** *f* lee-shore; **~segel** *n* studding sail; **~seite** *f* leeside; (*e-s Hanges*) leeside slope, leeward slope.

leer *a* empty; (*Stellung*) vacant, open; (*Wohnung usw unbesetzt*) unoccupied, vacant; (*unbeschrieben*) blank; (*müßig*) idle, unfounded; (*eitel*) vain; (*arm an*) void of, bare of; *~e Ausrede, ~e Entschuldigung* lame (*od* sham) excuse; *~e Drohung* empty threat; *~es Gerede* idle talk; *~es Gerücht* unfounded rumo(u)r; *mit ~en Händen* empty-handed; *~e Stelle* vacant place, vacant situation; *~e Versprechungen* empty promises; *~es Zimmer* a free room; *~ ausgehen* to go away empty-handed, to be left out in the cold; *~es Stroh dreschen* to flog a dead horse; *~ machen* to empty, to void; *~e Worte machen* to beat the air; **~darm** *m anat* jejunum; **~e** *f* emptiness, void(ness); vacancy; *phys* (*luftleerer Raum*) vacuum; *~~ im Magen* feeling of emptiness; *fig* emptiness, hollowness; vainness; **~en** *tr* to empty, to void; (*räumen*) to evacuate, to clear; (*bis zur Neige*) to drain; *ein Glas ~~* to finish (off) a glass; *den Briefkasten ~~* to clear the letter-box, to collect the letters; *Am* to collect the mail; **~fracht** *f* dead freight; **~gang** *m* lost motion; idle motion; *mot* neutral (*od* idler) gear; **~gewicht** *n* dead weight, weight empty; **~gut** *n com* (returned) empties *pl*; **~lauf** *m tech* idle (*od* lost) motion; *mot* idling (speed), ticking-over of engine, running idle; (*Gang*) idler (*od* neutral) gear; (*Ganghebelstellung*) neutral (position of gears); *fig* (*Zeit, Kräfte*) waste; *auf ~~ schalten* to shift to neutral, to put it in neutral; *im ~~ fahren Am* to coast; *im ~~ laufen lassen* to allow to tick over; **~~düse** *f mot* idler jet, slow running jet; pilot jet; **~~schraube** *f* idler adjusting screw; **~laufen** *irr itr mot* to (run) idle; to tick over; *~~ lassen* to allow to tick over; **~laufvorrichtung** *f* idling device; **~packung** *f* (*Schaupackung*) dummy; mannequin; **~stehend** *a* (*Wohnung usw*) vacant, unoccupied; empty; **~taste** *f* (*Schreibmaschine*) space bar; **~ung** *f* clearing, emptying; (*Räumung*) evacuation, clearance.

Lefze *f* (*e-s Tieres*) lip.

legal *a* legal; **~isieren** *tr* to legalize, to authenticate; to authorize; **~isierung** *f* legalization, authentication; **~ität** *f* legality; authenticity.

Legat *m* (*päpstlicher Gesandter*) legate; *~ n* (*Vermächtnis*) legacy, bequest; *jur* devise; **~atar** *m* legatee; (*Grundbesitz*) devisee; **~ion** *f* legation; **~ionsrat** *m* legation council(l)or, council(l)or to an embassy; **~ionssekretär** *m* secretary to an embassy.

Lege|henne *f* laying-hen; **~zeit** *f* laying-time.

legen *tr* to put, to lay; (*an e-n bestimmten Platz*) to place; *beiseite ~* to reserve, to put aside; (*sparen*) to lay by; (*verwerfen*) to discard; *Eier ~* to lay eggs; *Erbsen, Bohnen ~* to plant, to sow; *jdm das Handwerk ~* to put a stop to s. o.'s practices; *Karten ~* to tell fortunes by the cards; *Nachdruck ~ auf* to attach importance to; *etw schriftlich nieder~* to put s. th. in writing; to put on record; *jdm etw nahe~* to suggest s. th. to s. o.; *Schlingen ~* (*fig*) to put snares to s. o.; *Wert ~ auf* to lay great stress on s. th.; to attach much value to s. th.; *etw aus der Hand ~* to lay s. th. aside; *Hand an etw ~* to take s. th. in hand; *ans Herz ~* to conjure; *jdm etw ans Herz ~* to impress s. th. on s. o.; *an die Kette ~* to chain up; *an die Luft ~* to expose to the air; *auf Zinsen ~* to invest; *in Asche ~* to reduce to ashes; *in Ketten ~* to put in chains; *in die Kurve ~* (*aero*) to bank a plane; *in Trümmer ~* to reduce to ruins; *in den Weg ~* to obstruct, to hinder s. o.; *zur Last ~* to impute; *sich ~* to lie down; (*aufhören*) to abate, to calm down; (*nachlassen*) to cease; (*Fieber*) to go down, to drop; *sich auf e-e Sache ~* to apply o. s. to; *sich ins Mittel ~* to interfere, to interpose; *sich vor Anker ~* to cast anchor; *sich zu Bett ~* to go to bed.

Legende *f* legend.

legier|en *tr* to alloy; (*Küche*) to thicken; **~ung** *f* alloy; alloying; alloy metal; composition; **~~bestandteil** *m* alloying constituent; **~~sstahl** *m* alloy steel.

Legion *f* legion; **~är** *m* legionary.

Legis|lative *f* legislative power, legislative body; **~latur** *f* legislature; legislative assembly; **~~periode** *f* legislative period.

legitim *a* legitimate; lawful; **~ation** *f* legitimation; proof of identity; **~ationspapier** *n* paper of identification; (*Kennkarte*) identity-card; **~ieren** *tr* to legitimate; *sich ~~* to prove o.'s identity; **~ität** *f* legitimacy.

Leh(e)n *n* fief; feudal tenure; **~seid** *m* oath of allegiance; oath of fealty; **~sherr** *m* feudal lord; liege lord; **~smann** *m* vassal; **~spflicht** *f* feudal duty; **~srecht** *n* feudal law; **~sträger** *m* feofee; **~swesen** *n* feudality.

Lehm *m* loam; (*Ton*) clay; mud; **~boden** *m* clay soil (*od* ground); *arch* earthen floor; **~form** *f* loam mo(u)ld; **~formerei** *f* loam-mo(u)lding shop; **~grube** *f* clay-pit; loam-pit; **~ig** *a* clayey, loamy; muddy; **~mergel** *m* loamy marl; **~wand** *f* mud-wall; **~ziegel** *m* sun-dried brick, clay brick, loam brick.

Lehn|e *f* (*Stütze*) support, rest; prop; (*e-s Stuhles*) back (of a chair); (*Geländer*) (hand-) rail, railing; (*Abhang*) declivity, slope; **~en** *tr, itr* to lean (against); to rest (upon); *sich ~~* to lean; to recline; to lie back; *nicht aus dem Fenster ~~!* don't lean out of the window! **~sessel, ~stuhl** *m* arm-chair, elbowchair, easy chair.

Lehn|satz *m gram* lemma, *pl* lemmata; **~wort** *n gram* loan-word, a word borrowed from another language, borrowed word.

Lehr|amt *n* teacher's profession, teacher's post; (*Schule*) mastership; (*Universität*) professorship; **~amtskandidat** *m* probationer; **~anstalt** *f* educational establishment; school, college, academy; *höhere ~~* secondary school, *Am* high school; **~art, ~methode** *f* method of teaching; **~auftrag** *m* invitation to lecture on a subject; **~bar** *a* teachable; **~begriff** *m* system; **~beruf** *m* teaching profession; **~bogen** *m arch* centre; **~brief** *m* certificate of apprenticeship; indentures *pl*; **~buch** *n* (*Textbuch*) text-book; (*Handbuch*) manual; (*Abriß*) compendium; (*für Elementarunterricht*) primer; **~bursche** *m* apprentice; **~fach** *n* (*als Beruf*) teaching profession; (*Gegenstand*) branch of learning, branch of study; teaching-line; subject; **~fähigkeit** *f* capacity for teaching; **~film** *m* educational film; training film, instructional film; documentary film; *Unterricht durch ~~* audio-visual instruction; **~freiheit** *f* freedom of instruction; **~gang** *m* course of instruction; curriculum; *e-n ~~ besuchen* to take a course; **~gangsleiter** *m* instructor; director of training; **~gebäude** *n* system (of instruction); **~gedicht** *n* didactic poem; **~gegenstand** *m* subject of instruction; **~geld** *n* premium (for apprenticeship); *~~ zahlen fig* to pay dear for o.'s experience; **~gruppe** *f* training group; *mil* tactical operational unit; **~haft** *a* didactic; **~herr** *m* master, employer, *Am* boss; **~jahre** *n pl* years of apprenticeship; **~junge** *m* apprentice; **~körper** *m* teaching staff; (*Universität*) staff, professorate, *Am* faculty; **~kraft** *f* qualified teacher; **~kursus** *m* course of study; **~ling** *m* apprentice; **~lingsausbildung** *f* apprenticeship; **~mädchen** *n* girl apprentice;

~meinung *f eccl* dogma, tenet; **~meister** *m* teacher, instructor; (*Handwerker*) master; **~methode** *f* method of teaching; **~mittel** *n pl* means (*od* material) of instruction; appliances for teaching; apparatus; **~personal** *n* teaching staff; **~plan** *m* (school) curriculum; course (*od* plan) of instruction; (e-r *Klasse(nstufe)* syllabus; **~reich** *a* instructive; **~saal** *m* lecture-room, class-room; (*Hörsaal*) auditory; **~satz** *m* doctrine, rule; *math* theorem, proposition; (*Grundsatz*) maxim; *eccl* dogma, tenet; **~schau** *f* educational exhibition; **~spruch** *m* sentence; maxim; axiom; **~stand** *m* teaching-profession; **~stelle** *f* apprenticeship; **~stoff** *m* subject (*od* matter) of teaching; **~stuhl** *m* (professor's) chair; **~stunde** *f* lesson, lecture; **~tätigkeit** *f* educational work; **~truppe** *f mil* experimental unit; **~vertrag** *m* indentures *pl*; articles of apprenticeship; **~weise** *f* method of instruction; **~zeit** *f* (term of) apprenticeship; time of learning; *seine ~~ durchmachen* to serve o.'s apprenticeship; *während seiner ~~* during the time of his articles; **~zeugnis** *n* apprentice's certificate; graduation certificate.

Lehre *f* lesson, instruction; (*Warnung*) warning, hint, lesson; (*Nutzanwendung*) moral; (*theoretische ~*) doctrine, dogma; theory; science; (*praktische*) advice, rule; (*Vorschrift*) precept; (*beim Handwerk*) apprenticeship; (*das Leben*) teaching; *tech* (*Meßlehre*) gauge, *Am* gage; size, pattern, calibre, caliber; (*Form*) model, mould, *Am* mold; (*Bohr~*) jig; *arch* (*Bau~*) centering; *seine ~ absolvieren* to serve o.'s articles; *in die ~ geben* to apprentice to; *in die ~ gehen* to serve o.'s apprenticeship, to work as an apprentice; *in die ~ tun* to bind apprentice (to); *jdm e-e gute ~ geben* to teach s. o. a good lesson; *das soll ihr e-e ~ sein* it shall be a warning to her; **~n** *tr* to teach, to instruct; (*öffentlich*) to profess; (*beweisen*) to prove, to show; *die Zeit wird es ~~* time will show; **~nhaltig** *a* according (*od* true *od* accurate) to ga(u)ge.

Lehrer *m allg* teacher, instructor; (*an Grundschulen*) schoolmaster; (*an höheren Schulen*) master; (*Grundschul~*) primary teacher; (*höhere Schule*) secondary teacher; (*Studienrat*) assistant master; (*Hochschule*) professor; lecturer; (*Haus~*) tutor; **~bildungsanstalt** *f* training college for teachers; **~in** *f* (female *od* lady) teacher, governess, school-mistress, *Am* schoolma'am, *fam* schoolmarm; **~kollegium** *n* staff (of teachers); (*an Hochschulen*) faculty; **~konferenz** *f* meeting of masters; **~schaft** *f* body of teachers, staff of school; **~seminar** *n* training college for teachers; *Am* teachers' college; **~zimmer** *n* common room; staff room.

Leib *m* body; frame; (*Unterleib*) belly, abdomen; (*Mutter~*) womb; (*Oberkörper, Taille*) waist; (*Gestalt*) shape, figure; (*Rumpf*) trunk; *der ~ des Herrn eccl* the Bread, host; *am ganzen ~e* all over; *am ganzen ~e zittern* to tremble all over; *an ~ u. Seele* in body and mind; *wohl bei ~e* stout, corpulent; *bei ~e nicht!* by no means! on no account! not for my life! *bei lebendigem ~e* while alive; *mit ~ u. Seele* with heart and soul; *ihm lacht das Herz im ~e* his heart leaps up within him; *vom ~e bleiben* to keep off, to stand off; *bleiben Sie mir damit vom ~e!* don't bother me with that! *jdm zu ~e gehen* (*od rücken*) to attack s. o.; **~arzt** *m* physician (*od* surgeon) in ordinary; private (*od* personal) physician; **~binde** *f* scarf; sash; body belt, abdominal belt; *med* body bandage, body pad; **~chen** *n* bodice, corset; vest; **~eigen** *a* in bondage, villain; in thrall; **~eigene(r)** *m* bondman, serf; thrall; **~eigenschaft** *f* bondage, serfdom; **~garde, ~wache** *f* body guard; **~gericht** *n*, **~speise** *f* favo(u)rite dish; **~grimmen** *n* colic, gripes *pl*; **~gurt** *m* belt; *mil* (*mit Schulterriemen*) Sam Browne belt; **~haft, ~haftig** *a* (*verkörpert*) embodied, incarnate; (*personifiziert*) personified; (*sprechend*) speaking; (*echt*) living, real, true; *adv* personally; *der ~~e Teufel* the devil incarnate; **~lich** *a* corporeal, bodily; (*materiell*) material; somatic; in person; *sein ~~er Sohn* his own son; *~~es Wohlbefinden* material well-being; **~rente** *f* (life-) annuity; **~riemen** *m* (garrison) belt; **~schmerzen** *m pl*, **~schneiden, ~weh** *n* stomach-ache, colic, gripes *pl*; **~wäsche** *f* underwear; (body-) linen; **~ung** *f arch* intrados, soffit; **~~sdruck** *m* bearing pressure.

leib|en: *wie er ~t u. lebt* his very self, the very image of.

Leibes|beschaffenheit *f* constitution of body; **~erbe** *m* legitimate heir; descendant; offspring; **~erben** *m pl* issue; **~erziehung** *f* physical training (*Abk* P. T.); **~frucht** *f* foetus, fetus, embryo; offspring; **~größe** *f* stature, size; **~höhle** *f anat* body cavity; **~kraft** *f* physical strength; *aus ~kräften* with might and main, with all o.'s might; *er schrie aus ~kräften* he shouted at the top of his voice; **~nahrung** *f* nourishment, food; **~strafe** *f* corporal punishment; **~übung** *f* (bodily) exercise; **~~en** *f pl* gymnastics *pl*, physical jerks *pl*; **~umfang** *m* corpulence.

Leichdorn *m* corn.

Leiche *f* dead body, corpse; cadaver; (*verächtlich, Tier~*) carcass; (*Begräbnis*) funeral; *typ* out, omission, word omitted; *über ~n gehen fig* to stop at nothing; *e-e wandelnde ~* (*fig*) a living skeleton; *er ist e-e ~!* he is a dead man!

leichen|artig *a* cadaverous; **~ausgrabung** *f* exhumation; disinterment; **~begängnis** *n* funeral, burial; **~beschauer** *m* coroner; **~bestatter** *m* undertaker, *Am* mortician, funeral director; **~bestattung** *f* funeral; **~bitter** *m* inviter to a funeral; **~bittermiene** *f* woebegone countenance (*od* look); **~blaß** *a* pale as death; **~buch** *n* register of deaths and burials; **~(er)öffnung** *f* (coroner's) inquest; *med* postmortem examination, autopsy; **~farbe** *f* cadaverous hue; **~feier** *f* obsequies *pl*; **~frau** *f* layer-out; **~finger** *m* dead finger; *mil sl* tracer bullet; **~fledderer** *m* one who robs dead soldiers of valuables; **~gedicht** *n* funeral poem, epitaph; **~geruch** *m* cadaverous smell; **~gerüst** *n* catafalque; **~gift** *n* ptomaine; **~halle** *f* dead-house; mortuary; **~haus** *n* house of mourning; (*auf dem Friedhof*) mortuary chapel; **~hemd** *n* shroud; **~musik** *f* funeral music; **~predigt, ~rede** *f* funeral sermon; **~räuber** *m* body-snatcher; **~schänder** *m* desecrator of dead bodies; **~schändung** *f* desecration of dead bodies or of cemeteries; rape of a dead body; vampirism, necrophilism; **~schau** *f* inquest (on a dead body); *med* autopsy, necroscopy; **~schauhaus** *n* morgue; **~schmaus** *m* funeral repast; **~starre** *f* rigidity of death; rigor mortis; **~stein** *m* tombstone; **~träger** *m* (pall) bearer; **~tuch** *n* shroud, pall; **~verbrennung** *f* cremation; **~verbrennungsanstalt** *f* crematorium; **~verbrennungsofen** *m* crematorium furnace; **~vergiftung** *f* poisoning by ptomaines; **~wache** *f* death watch; **~wachs** *n* adipocere; **~wagen** *m* hearse; **~zug** *m* funeral procession.

Leichnam *m* dead body, remains *pl*; corpse.

leicht *a* light; (*~ zu machen*) easy; (*gering*) slight; (*unbedeutend*) insignificant, trifling, little; (*dünn*) thin; (*gewandt*) facile; (*vom Tabak*) mild; (*leichtfertig*) careless, reckless; frivolous; *adv* lightly, easily; *~ beschädigt* slightly damaged; *~ entzündlich* highly inflammable; *~ zu erlangen* easy to get; *~ zugänglich* of easy access: *das fällt ihr nicht ~* that's not easy for her; *etw ~ nehmen, etw auf die ~e Schulter nehmen* to make light of s. th., to take it easy; *alles zu ~ nehmen* to take everything too easy; *es sich ~ machen* to take it easy; *das ist ~ möglich* that is quite possible; *das ist nicht so ~, wie es aussieht* that is not so easy as it looks; *es ist ihm ein ~es* it comes easy to him; *es könnte ~ sein, daß* it is quite possible that; *~e Arbeit* easy work; *~er Bomber* (*od Kampfflugzeug*) light bomber; *~e Erkältung* a slight cold; *~e Flawaffen* light A.A.; *~er Irrtum* a slight error; *~er Kreuzer* light cruiser; *~e Seestreitkräfte* light naval forces; *~er Sieg* walk-over; *~es Spiel haben* to have an easy task; *~er Tank* (*od Panzer*) light tank, cruiser tank; *~e Steuerbarkeit* ease of handling; *~er Unfall* minor accident; *~e Wartung* ease of maintenance; *~e Wunde* flesh wound; **~athlet** *m* athlete; **~athletik** *f* (light) athletics *pl*, games *pl*, track and field sports *pl*; **~athletikmannschaft** *f* track team; **~bau** *m tech* light construction; **~~platte** *f* plastic material; **~~weise** *f* lightweight construction; **~benzin** *n* light petrol, *Am* light benzine, gasoline; **~bewaffnet** *a* light-armed; **~begreiflich** *a* plain, popular; **~beschwingt** *a* light-winged; *ein ~~es Lustspiel* a lightweight comedy; **~beweglich** *a* very mobile, easily movable; **~blütig** *a* sanguine; **~er** *m mar* lighter, barge; **~faßlich** *a* popular, plain; easily understood; **~fertig** *a* light; (*mutwillig*) wanton; (*unbeständig*) fickle; (*frivol*) frivolous; loose; flippant; (*oberflächlich*) superficial; shallow; (*gedankenlos*) thoughtless; light- (*od* giddy-) headed; (*von der Ausdrucksweise*) free, risky; **~fertigkeit** *f* levity; wantonness; frivolity; thoughtlessness; looseness; **~flüchtig** *a* readily (*od* highly) volatile; **~flugzeug** *n* light (air)plane; **~flüssig** *a* easily fusible, easily liquefiable; mobile; **~flüssigkeit** *f* easy fusibility; fluidity; mobility; **~fuß** *m* gay young spark, happy-go-lucky fellow, light-minded person; **~füßig** *a* light-footed, nimble; **~gepanzert** *a* thinly (*od* lightly) armo(u)red; **~gewicht** *n* (*Boxen*) lightweight; **~gläubig** *a* credulous; (*einfältig*) gullible; **~gläubigkeit** *f* credulity; (*aus Einfalt*) gullibility; **~herzig** *a* light-hearted; cheerful; **~hin** *adv* lightly, casually; carelessly; **~igkeit** *f* (*Gewicht*) lightness; *fig* (*Mühelosigkeit*) ease, readiness; facility; **~kraftrad** *n* light motorcycle; **~kranke(r)** *m* ambulatory (*od* minor) case; **~lebig** *a* easy-going; light-hearted; happy-go-lucky; **~legierung** *f* lightweight alloy; **~lich**

adv easily, lightly; **~löslich** *a* easily soluble; **~matrose** *m* ordinary seaman; **~metall** *n* light metal; light alloy; **~öl** *n* light oil; **~schmelzbar** *a* easily fusible; **~siedend** *a* low-boiling; **~sinn** *m* levity; (*mangelnder Ernst*) frivolity; (*Sorglosigkeit*) carelessness; (*Unbedachtsamkeit*) recklessness; imprudence; (*Gedankenlosigkeit*) thoughtlessness; **~sinnig** *a* light-headed, light-minded; irresponsible; reckless, careless; thoughtless; frivolous; *mit seinem Geld ~~ umgehen* to be careless with o.'s money; *~~er Mensch* scatterbrain(s); **~verdaulich** *a* easily digestible; **~verderblich** *a* perishable; corruptible; *~~e Waren* perishables *pl*; **~verwundet** *a* slightly wounded (*od* injured), walking wounded; **~verwundete(r)** *m mil* minor casualty; slightly wounded; **~~nsammelplatz** *m* walking wounded collecting post.

leid[1] *adv*: *es tut (od ist) mir ~, daß* ... I regret that ...; *das tut mir ~!* I am sorry (about it)! I am sorry for it! *es tut mir sehr ~!* I am greatly distressed about it! *es tut mir ~ um sie, sie tut mir ~* I am sorry for her; *jetzt tut es ihm sehr ~* now he feels very bad about it; *es ist mir ~ geworden* I have changed my mind about it; I am sick of it.

Leid[2] *n* (*Sorge, Betrübnis*) sorrow, grief; (*Schmerz*) pain; (*Bedauern*) regret; (*Schaden*) harm, hurt; (*Unrecht*) injury, wrong; (*Unglück*) misfortune; (*Trauer*) mourning; *jdm sein ~ klagen* to pour o.'s troubles out to s. o.; *~ tragen* to mourn; *jdm etw zu~e tun* to hurt s. o., to harm s. o., to wrong s. o.; *sich ein ~ antun* to commit suicide, to lay hands upon o. s.; *sie tat es mir zu~e* she did it to vex me; *niemand zuliebe, niemand zu~e* impartially, without respect of persons; *in Freud u. ~* for better, for worse; *auf Freud' folgt ~* after sunshine comes rain; *Freude u. ~ mit jdm teilen* to share o.'s joys and sorrows with s. o.; **~erfüllt** *a* woebegone; **~tragende(r)** *m* mourner; *er ist der ~~* he is the chief mourner; he suffers by it; **~voll** *a* sorrowful; **~wesen** *n* regret, sorrow; affliction; *zu meinem ~~* to my regret (*od* sorrow); *zu meinem ~~ muß ich sagen* I am sorry to say.

Leideform *f gram* passive voice.

leiden *irr tr* to suffer; (*zulassen*) to permit, to allow; to admit; (*ertragen, dulden*) to tolerate; to stand, to bear; to endure; (*gern haben*) *~ können, gern ~ mögen* to like, to like a lot; (*erfahren*) to undergo, to experience; *viel zu ~ haben* to have a hard time; *ich kann ihn nicht ~* I can't stand him; *Not ~* to be in want; *Schaden ~* to suffer damage; *e-n Verlust ~* to sustain a loss; *itr an etw ~* to suffer from; to be subject to; to complain of; *woran leidet er?* what is his complaint? what is the matter with him? *~ n* suffering; (*Krankheit*) complaint; ailment, disease; malady; indisposition; (*Kummer*) affliction, distress; (*Schmerz*) pain; (*Unglück*) misfortune; (*Widerwärtigkeit*) trouble; *das ~ Christi* the passion of Christ; **~d** *a* suffering; (*kränklich*) ailing, sickly; *gram* passive; **~schaft** *f* passion; (*Gemütsbewegung*) emotion; (*Wut, Zorn*) rage; *von ~~ besessen* passion-ridden; *in ~~ geraten* to fly (*od* get) into a passion; *ein Ausbruch der ~~* a burst of passion; *Lesen ist ihre ~~* reading is a passion with her; **~schaftlich** *a* passionate; with a passion; (*begierig*) eager; (*begeistert*) enthusiastic; (*heftig*) vehement; (*glühend*) ardent; *~~ lieben* to be passionately fond of; **~schaftlichkeit** *f* passionateness; vehemence; impulsiveness; **~schaftslos** *a* dispassionate; passionless; apathic; **~sgefährte** *m* fellow sufferer; **~sgeschichte** *f* story of woe; *eccl* Christ's passion; **~skelch** *m* cup of sorrow; bitter cup; **~sweg** *m* way of the Cross.

leid|er *adv* unfortunately; to my (our *etc*) regret; I am sorry to say; *~~ sehe ich, daß* ... I am sorry to see that ...; *~~ muß ich gehen* I am afraid I have to go; *~~! interj* alas! what a pity! *~~ läßt sich das nicht machen* unfortunately that can't be done; **~ig** *a* tiresome; (*unangenehm*) unpleasant, disagreeable, troublesome; nasty; (*schlimm*) fatal; evil, unfortunate; (*schrecklich*) dismal; (*bedauerlich*) pitiful; **~lich** *a* (*erträglich*) tolerable; (*mittelmäßig*) moderate, middling, mediocre; reasonable; passable, (pretty) fair; *es geht ihr ~~* she is so-so; *ein ~~er Preis* a pretty fair price; *~~ davonkommen* to get off pretty well.

Leier *f* lyre; *tech* (*Brust~*) (crank-) brace; (*Kurbel*) crank, winch; *es ist immer die alte ~* it's always the same old story; **~kasten** *m* barrel-organ, hurdy-gurdy; **~kastenlied** *n* street song, street ballad; **~(kasten)-mann** *m* organ-grinder; hurdy-gurdy man; **~n** *itr* tc grind a barrel-organ; *tech* to turn a crank (*od* winch); *fig* (*beim Sprechen*) to drawl; *immer dasselbe ~~* to keep harping on the same string.

Leih|amt *n* loan office; (*Leihhaus*) pawnshop; **~bibliothek, ~bücherei** *f* circulating (*od* lending) library, *Am auch* rental library; **~en** *irr tr* to lend; (*Geld*) to loan, to lend, *Am* to advance, to loan; (*verleihen*) to hire out; *etw von jdm ~~* (*mieten*) to hire s. th. of s. o.; (*entleihen, borgen*) to borrow (*von* of *od* from); *sich etw ~~* to borrow s. th.; *Geld auf Zinsen aus~~* to lend money at interest; *jdm Gehör ~~* to give ear to s. o.; **~er** *m* (*Verleiher*) lender; (*Entleiher*) borrower; **~frist** *f* loan period; **~gabe** *f* loan; **~gebühr** *f* lending fee; **~haus** *n* pawn-shop, pawnbroker's shop, *Am oft* loan office; *aufs ~~ bringen* to pawn, to put in pawn; *aus dem ~~ holen* to redeem from pawn; **~schein** *m* pawnticket; (*Bücherei*) slip; **~~ u. Pachtgesetz** *n Am* Lend-Lease Act; *auf dem ~~ u. Pachtwege liefern Am* to lend-lease; **~vertrag** *m* contract of loan; **~weise** *adv* as a loan, by way of a loan; (*gegen Miete*) on hire.

Leim *m* glue; (*Papier, Wand, Stoff*) size; (*Vogel~*) lime; *auf den ~ gehen* (*od kriechen*) *fig* to fall for, to fall into a trap, to take the bait; *aus dem ~ gehen* (*auseinanderfallen*) to fall apart, to fall to pieces; *jdn auf den ~ führen fig* to decoy s. o.; **~artig** *a* gluelike; gelatinous; **~en** *tr* to lime, to glue; (*Papier*) to size; *fig* (*hereinlegen*) to take a person in; to cheat s. o.; *geleimt werden* to go into the trap; **~farbe** *f* limewater-colo(u)r; (*Malerei*) distemper; **~ig** *a* gluey; glutinous; **~pinsel** *m* glue-brush; **~rute** *f* lime-twig; **~sieder** *m* glue-boiler; *fig* slow-coach; **~stange** *f* lime-stick; **~topf** *m* glue-pot; **~wasser** *n* glue-water.

Lein *m* (*auf dem Felde*) linseed; (*Flachs*) flax; linen; **~acker** *m* flaxfield; **~bau** *m* cultivation of flax; **~e** *f* (*Wäsche*) line; (*Tau*) rope; (*Schnur*) cord; (*Hunde~~*) (dog's) lead; leash; **~en** *a* linen, made of linen; *Halb~~* **half** linen; (*Farbe*) flaxen; **~en** *n* **linen,** linen goods *pl*; *in ~~ gebunden* bound in cloth; **~enband** *n* tape; *~~ m* (*Buch*) cloth (binding); **~enfaden** *m* linen thread; **~engarn** *n* linen yarn; **~engewebe** *n* linen texture; **~enware** *f* linen (goods *pl*); **~(en)weber** *m* linen-weaver; **~(en)weberei** *f* manufacture of linen; (*Fabrik*) linen factory; **~(en)zeug** *n* linen (goods *pl*); **~kuchen** *m* oilcake; **~öl** *n* linseed oil; **~pfad** *m* towing-path, track-road; **~saat** *f*, **~samen** *m* linseed, flax-seed; **~tuch** *n* linen (cloth); (*Bettuch*) (bed) sheet; **~wand** *f* linen; (*für Zelte, zum Bemalen*) canvas; (*für Bücher*) book-cloth; (*Kino*) (movie) screen; *auf die ~~ bringen* to bring to the screen; *in ~~ gebunden* (*Buch*) bound in cloth; **~~handel** *m* linen-trade; **~~händler** *m* linen-draper; **~~schuhe** *m pl* canvas shoes *pl*.

leise *a* (*nicht laut*) low; (*schwach*) weak, faint; (*sacht, zart*) soft, gentle; delicate; (*leicht*) light, slight; imperceptible; *bitte, ~!* Please, don't make any noise! *die ~ste Ahnung* the slightest (*od* faintest) suspicion; *ein ~s Gehör haben* to be sharp of hearing; *~r Schlaf* light sleep, *fam* cat's sleep; *e-n ~n Schlaf haben* to sleep lightly, to be a light sleeper; *mit ~r Stimme* in a low (*od* soft) voice, in an undertone; *ich hatte nicht den ~sten Zweifel* I had not the shadow of a doubt; *~ berühren* to touch lightly; (*erwähnen*) to mention s. th.; *~ sprechen* to speak low, to speak in a low voice; *~ stellen* (*radio*) to tune down; **~treter** *m fig* sneak, eavesdropper, *Am* pussyfooter; **~treterisch** *a* submissive, sneaking, *Am* pussyfooting.

Leiste *f* (*Tischlerei*) ledge, ridge; rabbet, reglet; beading; (*Zimmerei*) strip, slat; *arch* fillet; (*Buchbinderei*) border, edge; (*Tuch*) list, selvage; *typ* head-piece, border; *anat* groin; **~nbeuge** *f* flexure of the groin; **~nbeule** *f med* bubo; **~nbruch** *m* inguinal (*od* groin) rupture; inguinal hernia; **~ndrüse** *f* inguinal gland; **~ngegend** *f* inguinal region; **~ngrube** *f* inguinal fossa; **~nhobel** *m tech* fillet plane.

leisten *tr* (*tun*) to do; (*arbeiten*) to work; (*liefern*) to afford, to provide; (*ausführen*) to carry out, to execute; to perform; (*durchführen*) to effect; to realize; (*erfüllen*) to fulfil(l); to accomplish; *sich etw ~* to treat o. s. to; (*Streich*) *fam* to be up to some doings; *es sich ~ können* to be able to afford; *jdm Beistand ~* to give assistance to, to aid; *für jdn Bürgschaft ~* to give bail (for); *e-n Dienst ~* to render a service; *e-n Eid ~* to take an oath; (*Amtseid*) to be sworn in; *Folge ~* to comply with; to attend to; (*e-r Einladung*) to accept; to follow; (*e-m Befehl*) to obey; *jdm Gehorsam ~* to be obedient to s. o.; *Genüge ~* to satisfy; *jdm Genugtuung ~* to give s. o. satisfaction; *jdm Gesellschaft ~* to keep s. o. company; *Großes ~* to achieve great things; *Sicherheit ~* to furnish a surety; to give security; *Verzicht ~* to renounce s. th.; *Vorschub ~* to uphold; to promote; *Vorschuß ~* to advance money on; *Widerstand ~* to offer resistance; *Zahlung ~* to make (a) payment, to pay.

Leisten *m* (*Schuh~*) last; (*zum Füllen*) boot-tree; block; *über den ~ schlagen* to (put upon the) last; *alles über e-n ~ schlagen fig* to treat all alike.

Leistung *f* (*Arbeits~*) work (done); (*Fähigkeit*) ability; efficiency; (*Durch-*

führung) performance, accomplishment; (*Dienst*) service; (*Ausführung*) execution; (*Kunst~*) achievement; (*Tat*) feat; (*Errungenschaft, Kenntnisse*) attainment; (*Ergebnis*) result; (*Eides~*) taking of an oath; (*Geldzahlung*) payment; (*Natural~*) payment in kind; (*Verbindlichkeit*) obligation; (*Versicherung*) benefit; *tech* (*Wirkungsgrad*) efficiency; effect; (*Erzeugung*) production; (*Abgabe, Ausstoß*) output; (*Kraft*) power; (*Leistungsfähigkeit*) capacity, performance; *ausgestrahlte ~* (*radio*) radiated power; **~sabfall** *m* loss of power; **~sabgabe** *f* power output; **~sabzeichen** *n* badge of performance; **~sangabe** *f* performance characteristic; **~sanreiz** *m* incentive; **~sbelastung** *f* power load(ing); **~sberechnung** *f* capacity rating; **~sbereich** *m* range (of action); **~sbericht** *m* efficiency report; **~sbild** *n* (*e-r Maschine*) indicator diagram; **~sbuch** *n* efficiency book; **~seinheit** *f* unit of energy (*od* power); **~seinstufung** *f* rating; **~sfähig** *a* able, capable; fit; serviceable; (*tüchtig*) efficient; (*produktiv*) productive; (*finanziell*) solvent; **~sfähigkeit** *f* ability, capacity for work; ability to perform; efficiency; (*Kraft*) power; (*Ausstoß*) productive power; *com* (*Zahlungsfähigkeit*) solvency; **~sfaktor** *m* power factor; **~sformel** *f* efficiency formula; **~sgewicht** *n* weight per horsepower; **~skampf** *m* proficiency drive; **~skarte** *f* output record card; **~skurve** *f* performance graph; **~slohn** *m* piece work; **~smesser** *m* wattmeter; output meter; **~sprüfung** *f* efficiency test; **~srechnung** *f* calculation of performance; **~sschwach** *a* inefficient; (*Sender*) low-powered; **~sschild** *n* rating plate; **~ssegelflugzeug** *n aero* performance-type glider; performance sail plane; **~sstark** *a* efficient; (*Sender*) high-powered; **~ssteigerung** *f* increased output; **~sunfähig** *a* inefficient; **~sverbrauch** *m* power consumption; **~sverstärker** *m* power amplifier; **~szahlen** *f pl* performance figures *pl*; **~szulage** *f* efficiency bonus (*od* premium), proficiency pay.

Leit|artikel *m* leading article, leader, *Am* editorial; **~artikelschreiber, ~artikler** *m* leader writer, *Am* editorial writer; **~barkeit** *f* ductibility; conductibility; (*Beweglichkeit*) versatility; **~blech** *n* deflector; fin; **~en** *tr* (*führen*) to lead; (*lenken*) to guide, to direct, to pilot; to handle; (*steuern*) to steer; (*befehligen*) to head; (*beaufsichtigen*) to oversee, to control; (*verwalten*) to administer, *Am* to administrate; *phys, el* to conduct, to lead; (*fortpflanzen*) to convey; (*Unternehmen*) to direct, to manage; (*Geschäft*) to conduct, *Am* to run, to operate (a business); (*Staat*) to govern, to rule; (*Versammlung*) to preside over (a meeting), to be in the chair; *sich ~~ lassen* to be docile; **~end** *a* (*führend*) leading; (*Stellung*) executive; (*anweisend*) directive; *el* conductive; *gut ~~* highly-conductive; *nicht ~~* non-conductive; *~~er Ingenieur* chief engineer; *die ~~en Kreise* the governing classes; *in ~~er Stellung* in managerial capacity; in a key position; *~~er Angestellter* executive; *~~e Schicht el* conducting layer (*od* stratum); **~er**[1] *m* (*Führer*) leader; (*Dirigent*) conductor; (*Chef*) principal; head; chief; boss; (*Geschäftsführer*) manager; director; (*Schule*) headmaster, *Am* principal; *phys, el* conductor; **~faden** *m* clue; key; (*Handbuch*) textbook, manual, guide, compendium; introduction; **~fähig** *a* conducting; conductive; **~fossilien** *pl* index fossils *pl*, key (*od* leading) fossils *pl*; **~frequenz** *f radio* directing frequency, pilot wave; **~funkstelle** *f* directing station; **~gedanke** *m* key-note; main thought; **~hammel** *m* bell-wether; *den ~~ spielen* to bellwether; **~hund** *m* line-hound; **~karte** *f* guide-card; **~linie** *f* directrix; **~motiv** *n* leitmotiv; **~rad** *n* guide wheel; **~rolle** *f* guide pulley; **~satz** *m* guiding principle; thesis; **~schiene** *f* directrix; live rail; **~seil** *n* guide-rope; leash; **~sender** *m* regional broadcasting station; **~spindeldrehbank** *f* engine lathe; **~stand** *m mil* command post; **~station** *f radio* control radio station; **~stern** *m* pole-star; *fig* guiding star; **~strahl** *m* (*Radiusvektor*) radius vector; *radio aero* (localizer) beam; glide path; equisignal radio range zone; *auf dem ~~ bleiben* to stay on the beam; **~~sender** *m* radio-range beacon; landing beacon; **~tier** *n* leader; **~vermerk** *m* (*Brief*) indication; **~vermögen** *n* conductibility, conductivity; **~vorrichtung** *f* guiding device; **~werk** *n aero* tail unit, controls *pl*, *Am* empennage; **~~fläche** *f aero* tail surface; **~wert** *m el* (electric) conductance.

Leiter[2] *f* ladder; (*e-s Wagens*) rack; (*Tonleiter*) gamut; (*Stufenleiter*) scale; *e-e ~ besteigen* to climb a ladder; **~baum** *m* beam; **~förmig** *a* ladder--shaped; **~sprosse** *f* ladder-rung; **~stange** *f* pole, ladder wood; **~wagen** *m* rack-wag(g)on, cart (with sparred frame).

Leitung *f* (*Führung*) direction; conduct; guidance; (*Aufsicht, Kontrolle*) control, command; charge, care; (*Verwaltung*) management; *anat* (*Kanal, Röhre*) duct; *el* (*Stromkreis*) circuit; (*Draht~*) wire, lead; conductor; *tele* line; (*Kabel*) cable; (*Hauptstrom~*) mains *pl*; (*Rohr~*) conduit; duct; tube; pipe; piping, tubing; (*Gashaupt~*) main; (*Wasser~*) tap; *~ besetzt! interj tele* the line is engaged! *Am* the line is busy! *die ~ übernehmen* to take over (control); *schlechte ~* mismanagement; *e-e lange ~ haben fig fam* to be slow in catching on; **~sabzweigung** *f el* branching of a conductor; **~sanschluß** *m el* branch circuit connection; **~sdraht** *m* conducting wire, conductor; line wire; *mit elektrischen ~sdrähten versehen* to wire; **~sende** *n el* terminal; **~sfähig** *a* conductive; **~sfähigkeit** *f* conductibility; conductivity; conductive capacity; **~shahn** *m* water-tap, *Am auch* faucet; **~smast** *m* pole; **~snetz** *n* supply network, distributing network; **~srohr** *n*, **~sröhre** *f* conduit (-pipe), conducting pipe (*od* tube); *chem* delivery tube; (*Gas*) main; **~sschnur** *f el* cord, flexible cord; flex; lead; **~sspannung** *f* voltage of the line; **~sstörung** *f* defect in line; **~sstrom** *m* conduction current; **~svermögen** *n* conductivity; **~swasser** *n* tap water, hydrant water; **~swiderstand** *m* line resistance.

Lekt|ion *f* (*Lehrstunde, Aufgabe*) lesson; (*scharfe Belehrung*) rebuke; *jdm e-e ~~ erteilen* (*od geben*) to give s. o. a lecture (*od* scolding); **~or** *m* (*Universität*) lecturer; teacher, tutor; (*in e-m Verlag*) reader; **~orat** *n* lectorship; **~üre** *f* reading; books *pl*, literature.

Lemur *m* (*Geist Verstorbener*) lemures *pl*; (*Geister*) ghosts *pl*, spirits *pl*; *zoo* maki.

Lende *f* loin, loins *pl*; (*Hüfte*) hip, haunch; (*Oberschenkel*) thigh; **~nbraten** *m* roast loin; (*vom Rind*) roast sirloin, *Am* porterhouse, porterhouse steak; **~ngegend** *f* lumbar region; **~nlahm** *a* hip-shot, lame in the hip; *~~ sein* to be done up; **~nschnitte** *f* rump-steak; **~nschurz** *m* loin cloth; **~nstück** *n* (*Fleisch*) loin, undercut, fillet, *Am* (fillet) tenderloin; **~nweh** *n* lumbago; **~nwirbel** *m* lumbar vertebra.

Lenk|achse *f mot* steering axle; **~bar** *a* (*steuerbar*) steerable, dirigible; guidable; *fig* (*umgänglich*) manageable, tractable; *~~er Ballon* steerable balloon; *~~es Luftschiff* dirigible (airship); *~~er Torpedo* dirigible torpedo; **~en** *tr* (*führen*) to lead; (*regieren*) to govern; to rule; to direct; (*Fahrzeuge, Pferde*) to drive; (*steuern*) to steer; *mar, aero* to pilot; (*leiten*) to guide; (*verwalten*) to manage; (*kontrollieren*) to control; (*wenden*) to turn, to bend; *sich ~~ lassen* to be docile (*od* manageable); *jds Aufmerksamkeit ~~ auf* to call s. o.'s attention to; *den Blick auf etw ~~* to turn o.'s eyes to; *das Gespräch auf etw ~~* to turn the conversation upon; *seine Schritte ~~ nach* to turn to, to go; *der Mensch denkt, Gott lenkt* man proposes, God disposes; **~er** *m* manager, disposer; governor; *aero* pilot; *tech* (*Leitvorrichtung*) guide; (*Lenkstange beim Fahrrad, Motorrad*) handle-bar; **~~griff** *m* (*Motorrad*) handle-bar grip; **~hebel** *m mot* steering lever; **~luftschiff** *n aero* dirigible (airship); **~rad** *n mot* (*Steuerrad*) steering wheel; **~~schaltung** *f* steering--column gear control; **~sam** *a* guidable; (*nachgiebig*) tractable; (*biegsam*) flexible, pliable; **~samkeit** *f* manageableness; obedience; flexibility; **~säule** *f mot* steering column; **~schenkel** *m mot* steering knuckle; **~schnecke** *f mot* steering worm; **~schubstange** *f mot* steering rod; **~stange** *f* steering gear, connecting rod, link; (*Motorrad, Fahrrad*) handle-bar(s *pl*); **~ung** *f* (*Leitung, Führung*) guidance; governing; *mot* (*Steuerung*) steering; (*Wirtschafts~~*) control; **~~sbetätigung** *f mot* steering control; **~vorrichtung** *f* steering gear, guiding device; **~zapfen** *m mot* steering pivot.

Lenz *m* spring; *fig* (*des Lebens*) prime (of life); **~monat** *m* March.

lenz|en *tr, itr mar* (*leerpumpen*) to pump (the bilges), to free a ship; (*U-Boot*) to blow tanks; (*vor dem Wind*) to scud; **~pumpe** *f* b lge pump.

Leopard *m* leopard.

Lepra *f* leprosy; **~kranke(r)** *m* leper.

Lerche *f* lark; **~nfang** *m* catching of larks; **~nstrich** *m* passage of larks.

lern|bar *a* learnable; **~begier(de)** *f* desire of learning, eagerness to learn; love of study; **~begierig** *a* desirous of learning, eager to learn; studious; **~eifer** *m* application; **~en** *tr* to learn; (*studieren*) to study; (*in der Lehre sein*) to serve o.'s apprenticeship; *er lernt das Schreinerhandwerk* he learns to become a joiner; *auswendig ~~* to learn by heart; *sehr gut ~~* to be quick to learn; *kennen ~~* to get to know; to make the acquaintance of, to become acquainted with; (*jdn*) *näher kennen ~~* to become familiar with s. o.; (*etw*) to familiarize o. s. with; *lesen ~~* to learn to read; *sie lernt das Schreiben* she learns how to write; *man lernt nie aus* one lives and learns; *gelernt a* skilled, trained; by trade; *gelernter Arbeiter* skilled worker; *er ist gelernter Mechaniker* he is a mechanic

by trade; *das muß man gelernt haben* there is an art to it; **~~de(r)** *m* (*Lehrling*) apprentice; (*Schüler*) pupil, scholar; learner; (*Student*) student.
Les|art *f* reading; manner of reading; (*Version*) version; *gewöhnliche ~~* ordinary version; *verschiedene ~arten pl* variants *pl*; **~bar** *a* (*leserlich*) legible; (*entzifferbar*) decipherable; (*lesenswert*) readable, worth reading; **~barkeit** *f* legibility; readableness; readability.
Lese *f* (*Wein~*) vintage; (*Früchte etc*) gathering; (*Ähren*) gleaning.
Lese|abstand *m* reading distance; **~brille** *f* reading glasses *pl*; **~buch** *n* reading-book, reader; (*Fibel*) primer; (*Anthologie*) anthology, chrestomathy; **~früchte** *f pl* selections *pl*; (*Sammlung*) chrestomathy; **~glas** *n* reading glass; **~halle** *f* reading-room; news room; **~hunger** *m* hunger for reading; **~hungrig** *a* hungry for reading; **~kränzchen** *n* reading-circle; **~lampe** *f* reading-lamp; floor lamp; **~lupe** *f* reading lens; **~lustig** *a* fond of reading; **~n** *irr tr* (*Früchte, Holz, Trauben etc*) to gather; (*Ähren*) to glean; (*auslesen, auswählen*) to select, to pick (up); to cull; (*Bücher*) to read; (*Kolleg*) to lecture (*über* on), to give lectures; *die Messe ~~* to say mass; *Korrektur ~~* to read a proof; *zweite Korrektur ~~* to revise; *e-n Schriftsteller ~~* to interpret; to recite an author; *sich ~~* to read; *das Buch liest sich gut* the book reads well; *es liest sich wie ein Roman* it reads like a novel; **~n** *n* gathering; reading; lecturing; **~nswert** *a* worth reading; **~probe** *f theat* rehearsal; **~pult** *n* lectern, reading-desk; **~r** *m*, **~rin** *f* (*Buch*) reader; (*Sammler*) gatherer; (*Ähren*) gleaner; **~ranalyse** *f* (*Reklame*) readership analysis; **~ratte** *f fig* bookworm; **~rkarte** *f* (*Bibliothek*) reader's card, borrower's card; **~rkreis** *m* circle of readers; **~rlich** *a* legible; **~rschaft** *f* readers *pl*; **~rstamm** *m* stock of regular readers; **~rzuschrift** *f* (*Zeitung*) letter to the editor; **~saal** *m* reading-room; news room; (*mit Tageszeitungen*) newspaper room; (*für Kinder*) children's reading-room; **~stoff** *m* reading (matter); **~stunde** *f* reading lesson; **~übung** *f* reading exercise; **~zeichen** *n* (*Buch*) bookmark; **~zeit** (*Weinberg*) vintage; **~zimmer** *n* reading-room; **~zirkel** *m* reading-circle.
Lesung *f* reading; *~ e-s Gesetzentwurfes parl* reading of a bill.
letal *a* (*tödlich*) fatal, mortal, lethal.
Letharg|ie *f* (*Betäubung, Trägheit*) lethargy; **~isch** *a* lethargic(al).
Lett|e *m*, ***~in*** *f* Latvian; **~land** *n* Latvia; **~isch** *a* Latvian.
Letten *m* loam, potter's clay.
Letter *f* letter, character; *typ* (printing-)type; **~kasten** *m typ* lower case; **~länge** *f typ* height-to-paper; **~ngießmaschine** *f* composing machine; **~ngut**, **~nmetall** *n typ* type metal; **~nsetzmaschine** *f* monotype.
Lettner *m arch* rood-loft.
letzen *tr* to refresh; *r* to relish, to enjoy.
letzt *a* last; (*abschließend, endgültig*) ultimate; (*äußerst*) extreme; (*spätest*) latest; (*unterst*) lowest; *bis auf den ~en Mann* to the last man; *die Vergnügungslokale waren bis auf den ~en Platz besetzt* the places of entertainment were crowded to the doors; *zu guter ~* finally; to sum up; in the end; as a fitting conclusion; last not least, *Am fam* to top it off; *sein ~es hergeben* to do o.'s utmost; *~er Ausweg* last resource; *im ~en Grunde*, *~en Endes* in the last analysis; after all; *jdm die ~e Ehre erweisen* to attend s. o.'s funeral; *auf dem ~en Loch pfeifen* to be upon o.'s last legs; *~en Monats com* ultimo (*Abk* ult.), of last month; *~en Montag* last Monday; *~e Meldungen, ~e Nachrichten* (*Presse*) late news *pl*, stop-press news *pl*; *~e Nummer* (*e-r periodischen Veröffentlichung*) current issue; *~e Ölung eccl* extreme unction; *~e Runde sport* final round; *~er Schliff* master touch; *~er Versuch* last effort; last resource; last trial; *~er Wille* (last) will; *~e Woche* last (*od* previous) week; *das ~e Wort* the last word; *in den ~en Zügen liegen* to be at the last gasp; to be dying; *in ~er Zeit* of late, lately; recently; **~angeführt** *a* last-quoted; **~ens**, **~lich** *adv* lately, of late; recently; **~ere(r)** *a* (the) latter; **~erwähnt** *a* last-mentioned; **~genannt** *a* last-named; latter; **~hin** *adv* lastly, in the last analysis; (*kürzlich*) lately, the other day; **~jährig** *a* of last year; **~willig** *a* testamentary; *~~e Verfügung* testamentary disposition.
Leu *m poet* lion.
Leucht|bakterien *n pl* photogenic bacteria *pl*; **~boje**, **~feuerboje** *f* light buoy; **~bombe** *f phot* flash bomb; *aero mil* (parachute) flare, flare bomb; *e-e ~~ setzen* to drop a flare; **~brenner** *m* illuminating burner; **~dichte** *f* luminous density; **~draht** *m* filament; **~e** *f* (*Licht*) light; *fig* shining light, star; (*Lampe*) lamp; (*Laterne*) lantern; (*Beleuchtungskörper*) lighting fitting; *e-e ~~ der Wissenschaft* a luminary of science; **~elektron** *n* emitting electron; photoelectron; **~en** *itr* to light, to give light, to emit light; (*glänzen*) to shine; (*erleuchten, aufhellen*) to illuminate; (*Meer*) to phosphoresce; (*strahlen*) to beam, to radiate; to gleam; (*glühen*) to glow; to burn; (*glänzen, funkeln*) *bes. auch fig* to coruscate; *jdm ~~* to light s. o.; *sein Licht ~~ lassen* to let o.'s light shine; **~en** *n* shining; (*Meer*) phosphorescence; *fig* (*Glanz, Funkeln*) coruscation; (*Erleuchtung*) illumination; (*Glühen*) glow; **~end** *a* bright; luminous; shining; lustrous; *mit ~~en Augen* with shining eyes; **~er** *m* (*Kerzen~~*) candlestick; (*Kron~~*) lustre; chandelier; (*Arm~~*) bracket; (*Wand~~*) branch; **~erscheinung** *f* luminous phenomenon; **~fackel** *f* flare; **~faden** *m* filament; **~fadenkreuz** *n mil* illuminated sight; **~fähig** *a* capable of luminescence; **~fallschirmbombe** *f aero mil* parachute flare; **~farbe** *f* luminous paint (*od* colo(u)r); **~feuer** *n* beacon, beacon lamp, beacon light; light fire; *aero* flare; **~gas** *n* gas (for lighting); coal gas, illuminating gas; **~~erzeugung** *f* production of illuminating gas; **~~vergiftung** *f* illuminating gas poisoning; **~geschoß** *n* star shell; **~käfer** *m* glow-worm, fire-fly, *Am auch* lightning bug; **~kompaß** *m* illuminated (*od* luminous-dial) compass; **~korn** *n* (*an Gewehr, M.G.*) illuminated (fore-) sight; **~körper** *m* (*Lampe*) lamp; **~kraft** *f* illuminating power, luminosity; *~~ der Farben* luminous power of colo(u)r; **~kugel**, **~patrone** *f* Very light; signal rocket; flare (*od* signal) cartridge; **~masse** *f* luminous mass; luminescent (*od* phosphorescent) substance; **~material** *n* illuminating medium (*od* material); **~mittel** *n* illuminant; **~munition** *f* signal cartridge; **~öl** *n* paraffin, *Am* kerosene; **~pfad** *m aero* flare path; landing direction lights *pl*, runway lights *pl*; **~pistole** *f* Very (light) pistol, signal pistol; **~punkt** *m* flash point, luminous spot; **~quarz** *m* glow crystal, luminous quartz; **~rahmen** *m tele* television screen; **~rakete** *f* light rocket, light flare; *aero* landing (signal) rocket; *mil* Very light; **~reklame** *f* (*Transparent*) translight; **~röhre** *f* vacuum tube (lamp); illuminating tube, neon tube, fluorescent tube; luminous-discharge lamp (*od* tube), soffit lamp; **~satz** *m mil* tracer composition; flare composition; **~schiff** *n mar* lightship; **~schild** *n* light sign; illuminated sign; **~schirm** *m* (*tele, Röntgenoskopie*) fluorescent screen; *tele* television screen; cathode-ray screen; **~schuß** *m* tracer round; **~skala** *f radio* illuminated dial; **~spur** *f* tracer (fire); **~~geschoß** *n* tracer bullet; **~~granate** *f* tracer shell; **~~munition** *f* tracer ammunition; **~stab** *m el* flash-light, torch; **~stärke** *f* brightness; **~stofflampe** *f* fluorescent lamp; **~tonne** *f mar* light-buoy; **~turm** *m* lighthouse; **~~wächter** *m* lighthouse-keeper; **~uhr** *f* luminous clock, luminous watch; **~verbot** *n* blackout; illumination prohibition; **~vermögen** *n* illuminating power; **~visier** *n mil* luminous sight; **~zeichen** *n* flare signal; **~zifferblatt** *n* luminous dial.
leugn|en *tr* to deny; (*abstreiten*) to contest; (*verneinen*) to disavow; (*widersprechen*) to contradict; (*nicht anerkennen*) to disown; *jur* (*Tatsachen, Behauptungen bestreiten*) to traverse; *nicht zu ~~* undeniable; *es kann nicht geleugnet werden* it cannot be denied, it is not to be denied; *entschieden ~~* to deny flatly; **~en** *n* denial; disavowal; negation; **~er** *m* denier.
Leuk|ämie *f* leuk(a)emia; **~oplast** *n* adhesive, adhesive tape (*od* plaster); **~ozyten** *pl* (*weiße Blutkörperchen*) white blood corpuscles *pl*; **~ozytose** *f med* leucocytosis.
Leumund *m* reputation, repute; character; name; renown; *guter ~* good (*od* high) reputation, good name; *schlechter ~* ill fame, bad name, bad reputation; **~szeugnis** *n* certificate of good conduct (*od* character); testimonial.
Leut|e *pl* people; persons *pl*; folks *pl*; public, the world; (*Dienerschaft*) servants *pl*; (*Arbeitskräfte*) hands *pl*, men *pl*; *mil* men *pl*, the rank and file, *Am* enlisted men (*Abk* E.M.); *meine ~~* (*Dienerschaft*) my servants; (*die Familie zu Hause*) my folks, folks at home; *unter die ~~ bringen* to spread about; *seine ~~ kennen* to know who's who, to know o.'s customers; *unter die ~~ kommen* (*bekannt werden*) to become known; (*in Gesellschaft gehen*) to go into society; *was werden die ~~ dazu sagen?* what will people say? **~eschinder** *m* (*gegen Arbeiter*) sweater, slavedriver; **~selig** *a* affable; (*herablassend*) condescending; **~seligkeit** *f* affability.
Leutnant *m* (*Heer*) second lieutenant; (*Flieger~*) pilot officer; (*Marine*) *~ zur See* sub-lieutenant; **~sstelle** *f* lieutenancy.
Levante *f* the Levant.
Levit *m* levite; *jdm die ~en lesen* to lecture s. o.
Levkoje *f bot* stock, gillyflower.
lexik|alisch *a* lexical; **~ograph** *m* lexicographer; **~ographisch** *a* lexicographic(al); **~on** *n* (*Wörterbuch*) dic-

tionary; (*Konversations~~*) encyclop(a)edia; **~onband** *m* (*Einband*) limp leather binding; **~onformat** *n* large octavo.

Libelle *f* dragon-fly, *fam* darning needle; *tech* (*Wasserwaage*) (water) level, spirit level; **~naufsatz** *m* (*Geschütz*) clinometer sight.

liberal *a* liberal; **~isierung** *f* liberalization; **~ismus** *m* liberalism; **~istisch** *a* liberalistic; **~ität** *f* liberality.

Licht *n* light; (*Beleuchtung*) illumination; lighting; (*Kerze*) candle; (*Helligkeit*) brightness; (*Öffnung*) opening; (*Diamant*) lustre, lights *pl*; (*Auge des Wildes*) eye; *elektrisches ~* electric light; *~er u. Schatten* (*Malerei*) lights and shadows; *ans ~ bringen* to bring to light, to bring forth; *an das ~ halten* to hold to the light; *ans ~ treten* to become known; *jdm aus dem ~e gehen* to stand out of s. o.'s light; *bei ~* by light, by day; *bei ~e betrachtet* looked at closely; *hinters ~ führen* to dupe, to cheat, to deceive s. o.; to impose upon s. o.; *sich im ~e stehen* to stand in o.'s own light; *ins rechte ~ setzen* to show in its true colo(u)rs *pl*; *in ein schiefes ~ stellen* to place in a wrong light; to misrepresent; *jdm ein ~ aufstecken* to open s. o.'s light; *~ anmachen*, *~ einschalten* to put on (*od* to switch on *od* to turn on) the light; *~ ausschalten* to switch off (*od* to turn off) the light; *das ~ der Welt erblicken* to come into the world, to be born; *plötzlich ging ihm ein ~ auf* suddenly he began to see clearly, suddenly he saw the light, suddenly it began to dawn on him; *das ~ scheuen* to shun publicity; *~ werfen auf* to throw a light on; *ein schlechtes ~ werfen auf* to reflect upon; *er ist kein großes ~ fig* he is no great light; *~ a* (*hell*) light; bright; shining; (*leuchtend*) luminous; (*durchsichtig*) clear; (*dünn, spärlich*) thin, sparse; *~e Augenblicke* lucid intervals; *~er Durchmesser* inside diameter; *~e Farben* light colo(u)rs; *~e Höhe* clearance; *~er Tag* broad daylight; *~e Stelle* (*im Wald*) open space; **~abgabe** *f* emission of light; **~abschluß** *m* exclusion of light; *unter ~~* in the absence of light; **~absorption** *f* light absorption; **~abstufung** *f* gradation of light; **~aggregat** *n* lighting set; **~anlage** *f* lighting plant; lighting system; **~anlasser** *m mot* generator-starter; **~anschlußdose** *f el* light socket; **~antenne** *f radio* light antenna, *Am* mains aerial; **~ausbeute** *f* light efficiency; **~ausstrahlung** *f* radiation of light; **~bad** *n med* insolation; **~batteriezündung** *f mot* dynamo-battery-ignition unit; **~beständig** *a* fast to light, stable in (*od* to) light; photostable; **~beugung** *f* refraction of light; **~bild** *n* photograph, photo; (*Schnappschuß*) snapshot; (*Diapositiv*) (lantern-) slide; **~~apparat** *m* projector; **~~aufnahme** *f* photography, photo(graph); **~~auswertung** *f* photogrammetry; *mil* interpretation of aerial photograph; **~~erkundung** *f* photographic reconnaissance; **~~gerät** *n* photographic apparatus; **~~ervortrag** *m* lantern-slide lecture; **~~lich** *a* photographic; **~~ner** *m* photographer; **~~nerei**, **~~kunst** *f* photography; **~blau** *a* light (*od* pale) blue; **~blende** *f* diaphragm, light stop; **~blick** *m fig* ray (*od* spark) of hope; **~blitz** *m* flash of light; scintillation; **~blond** *a* fair; **~bogen** *m* arc; **~~schweißung** *f tech* arc welding; **~braun** *a* light brown; **~brechend** *a* refracting, refractive; dioptric(al); **~brechung** *f* refraction of light; **~~svermögen** *n* refractive power, refractivity; **~bündel** *n* pencil of light (*od* rays); **~chemisch** *a* photochemic(al); **~dicht** *a* light-proof, light-tight; **~druck** *m typ* phototype, photogravure; photographic printing; **~durchlässig** *a* transmitting light, translucent; **~durchlässigkeit** *f* transparency, permeability; **~echt** *a* fast (*od* resistant) to light; fadeless, nonfading, sunfast; **~echtheit** *f* fastness to light; **~effekt** *m* luminous effect; **~einfall** *m* incidence of light; **~einwirkung** *f* effect (*od* action) of light; **~elektrisch** *a* photoelectric; **~empfindlich** *a* sensitive to light; sensitized; light-sensitive, photosensitive; *~~ machen* to (photo)sensitize; *~~es Papier* photographic paper; *~~e Platte* sensitized plate; *~~e Zelle* photo(electric) cell; **~empfindlichkeit** *f* sensitivity; *phot* speed; **~empfindung** *f* sensation of light; **~erglanz** *m* brightness; brilliance, brilliancy, lustre, *Am* luster; **~erloh** *a* blazing, all ablaze, in full blaze; **~erscheinung** *f* luminous phenomenon; light effect; **~faden** *m* (electric) filament; **~farben** *a* light-colo(u)red; **~farbendruck** *m* photomechanical colo(u)r printing; **~filter** *n* colo(u)r filter; **~fleck** *m* light spot; **~fortpflanzung** *f* transmission of light; **~geschwindigkeit** *f* velocity of light; **~hof** *m arch* well, inner court; *astr, phot* halo; (*Bildung e-s ~~s*) halation; **~hoffrei** *a phot* anti-halo; **~kabel** *n* electric lighting cable; **~kegel** *m* cone of light; luminous cone; (*Scheinwerfer*) beam of searchlight; **~kranz** *m* (*Sonne*) corona; **~lehre** *f* optics *pl*, science of light; **~leitung** *f* lighting circuit; (lighting) mains *pl*; **~maschine** *f mot* dynamo, *Am* generator; **~mast** *m* lamp pole; **~meß** *f eccl* Candlemas; **~meßbatterie** *f mil* flash-ranging battery; **~messer** *m* photometer; **~meßtrupp** *m mil* flash-spotting troop, flash-ranging section; **~messung** *f* photometry; *mil* flash-ranging; **~netz** *n* mains *pl*; **~netzantenne** *f radio* light (*od* socket) antenna, *Am* mains aerial; **~pause** *f* blueprint, calking; photographic tracing; **~pauspapier** *n* blueprint paper, calking paper; printing paper; **~punkt** *m* luminous spot (*od* point); **~quant** *n* photon; light quantum; **~quelle** *f* source of light; **~reflektierend** *a* light-reflecting; **~reflexion** *f* reflection of light; **~reiz** *m* sensation of light; **~reklame** *f* sky-sign; illuminated advertisement; neon advertisement; **~schacht** *m* light-shaft; *phot* (*Reflexkamera*) focussing hood; **~schalter** *m el* light(ing) (*od* installation) switch; **~schein** *m* gleam (of light); shine; **~scheu** *a* shunning the light; *fig* shunning publicity; afraid of light, aphotic; **~schirm** *m* screen; (lamp-) shade; **~schwach** *a* of low light intensity **~seite** *f fig* bright side; **~signal** *n* light signal; flash signal; (*Verkehr*) traffic light; **~spielhaus**, **~spieltheater** *n* cinema, picture-house, *Am* motion (*od* moving) picture theater, *Am* moving pictures *pl*, *Am* movies *pl*; *ein ~~ betreiben* to operate a cinema; **~spielhausreklame**, **~spielhauswerbung** *f* cinema advertising, film advertising, *Am* moving-picture advertising; **~sprechgerät** *n* infra-red telephone; **~stark** *a* of high intensity; *~~es Objektiv* fast objective, high-speed objective; **~stärke** *f* intensity of light; *phot* (*Objektiv*) speed, rapidity; (*e-r Birne*) wattage; **~steckdose** *f* light (wall) socket; **~steindruck** *m* photolithography; **~strahl** *m* ray of light, light ray, beam of light; luminous ray; **~strahlabtastung** *f tele* flying-spot television; **~strahlung** *f* light radiation; **~streifen** *m* light beam; **~strom** *m* current for lighting; **~teilchen** *n* particle of light; **~tonaufnahme** *f film* photographic sound-film recording; **~tonverfahren** *n* (*Tonfilm*) sound-on-film system; **~umflossen** *a* bathed in light, radiant; **~undurchlässig** *a* light-proof, light-tight; opaque (to light); **~unempfindlich** *a* insensitive (*od* not sensitive) to light; **~voll** *a* light; luminous, lucid; **~weite** *f tech* clearance; **~welle** *f* light wave; **~werbung** *f* light advertising; **~wirkung** *f* action (*od* effect) of light; **~zeichen** *n* light signal; lamp signal; **~zelle** *f* visual cell; photo(electric) cell; **~zentrale** *f* light and power station; **~zerstreuung** *f* dispersion of light.

licht|en *tr* (*Wald*) to clear; (*Haar, Reihen*) to thin out; (*öffnen*) to open; (*Anker*) to weigh (anchor); to lighten (a ship); *sich ~~* to get thin, to grow thinner; (*heller werden*) to grow brighter; to clear up; **~ung** *f* (*im Wald*) clearing, glade, vista; opening; (*spärlich werden*) thinning.

Lichter *m mar* lighter, barge.

Lid *n* eyelid; **~bindehaut** *f* conjunctiva of the eye; **~rand** *m* margin of the eyelid; **~drüse** *f* tarsal gland.

lieb *a* (*teuer*) dear; (*geliebt*) beloved; (*angenehm*) agreeable, pleasant; (*nett*) nice; (*liebenswürdig*) kind; (*gut*) good; *jdn ~ haben* to like, to be fond of, to love; (*liebkosen*) to caress; *es ist mir ~* I am pleased (*od* glad); *es wäre mir ~* I should like; I would appreciate it, if ...; *den ~en langen Tag* the live-long day; *seine ~e Not haben* to have no end of trouble (*mit* with); *um des ~en Friedens willen* for peace' sake; *du ~er Himmel! interj* Good Heavens! *du ~e Zeit! interj* Dear me! Good Gracious! **~äugeln** *itr* to ogle (*mit jdm od etw* s. o. *od* s. th.); to make eyes at; to flirt (*mit* with); **~chen** *n* sweetheart, darling, love; **~e** *f* love (*zu jdm* of, for, to, towards s. o., *zu etw* of, for s. th.); (*christliche ~~*) charity; (*Zuneigung*) affection; *Kind der ~~* love-child; *~~ macht blind* love is blind; *aus ~~ zu* for love of; *mir zuliebe* for my sake; **~ediener** *m* time-server, toady; **~edienerei** *f* servility, time-serving; obsequiousness, cringing; flattery, cajolery, *Am fam* taffy; **~elei** *f* flirtation, amour; **~eln** *itr* to flirt, to make love; **~en** *tr* to love, to like; to be fond of; (*hegen*) to cherish; *itr* to be in love; **~enswert** *a* worthy of love; **~enswürdig** *a* amiable, lovable; (*freundlich*) kind; **~enswürdigkeit** *f* amiability, kindness; **~er** *a* (*Komparativ*) dearer; more agreeable; *adv* rather; (*eher*) sooner; better; *je länger, je ~~* the longer, the better; *~~ als* in preference to; *~~ haben* to prefer, to like better; *ich möchte ~~* ... I had rather ...; *du sollst es ~~ lassen* you had rather leave it; **~esabenteuer** *n* love-adventure, intrigue; **~esangelegenheit** *f* love-affair; **~esantrag** *m* love-suit; proposal; **~esapfel** *m* tomato; **~esband** *n* band of love, love-tie; **~esblick** *m* loving glance; ogle; **~esbote** *m* messenger of love; **~esbotschaft** *f* love-message; (*am 14. Februar*) valentine; **~esbrief** *m* love-

-letter; **~esbriefchen** *n* billet-doux; **~esdienst** *m* good turn; kind office, (act of) kindness; *jdm e-n ~~ erweisen* to do s. o. a good turn; **~eserklärung** *f* declaration of love; proposal; *e-e ~~ machen* to declare o.'s love; **~esgabe** *f* gift; *pl* (*für Soldaten*) comforts *pl*; Red Cross parcels *pl*; **~~npaket** *n* gift parcel, care parcel, *Am* gift package; **~esgedicht** *n* love-poem; **~esgenuß** *m* enjoyment of love; **~esgeschichte** *f* love-story, romance; **~esgeständnis** *n* confession of love; **~esgott** *m* Cupid, Eros, Amor; **~esgöttin** *f* Venus; **~eshandel** *m* love-affair, intrigue; **~esheirat** *f* love-match; **~eskrank** *a* love-sick; **~eskummer** *m* lover's grief; **~eslied** *n* love-song; **~esmühe** *f*: *verlorene ~~* Love's Labo(u)r's lost; **~espaar** *n* couple (of lovers), lovers *pl*; **~espfand** *n* love-token; *fig* (*Kind*) child, pledge of love; **~esrausch** *m* transport of love; **~estoll** *a* mad with love, madly in love; **~estrank** *m* love-potion; **~estrunken** *a* intoxicated with love; **~esverhältnis** *n* love-affair; (*flüchtiges Verhältnis*) liaison; **~eswerbung** *f* courtship; **~eswerk** *n* work of charity; **~eszauber** *m* love-spell; **~eszeichen** *n* love-token; **~evoll** *a* loving; affectionate; kind, tender; **~gewinnen** *irr tr* to grow fond of; to take a fancy to, *Am* to take a shine to; **~haben** *tr* to love, to like; to be fond of; **~haber** *m* lover, sweetheart; beau, *Am* spark; (*Kenner*) fancier; (*Kunst*) amateur, dilettante; *com* (*Käufer*) buyer; (*Enthusiast*) *Am* fan; *theat erster ~~* leading actor; *jugendlicher ~~* juvenile lead; **~~ausgabe** *f* (*Buch*) edition de luxe; **~~ei** *f* fancy; fondness, liking; partiality; (*Steckenpferd*) hobby; *aus ~~ei* for amusement's sake; **~~photograph** *m* amateur, *Am* camera fan; **~~preis** *m* fancy price; **~~rolle** *f* *theat* role of lover; **~~theater** *n* private theatricals *pl*; **~~wert** *m* sentimental value; **~kosen** *tr* to caress, to fondle; to hug, to pet; (*Kind*) to cuddle, to dandle; *Am fam* (*umarmen*) to neck; **~kosung** *f* caress, petting, fondling; **~lich** *a* (*anmutig*) lovely; (*süß*) sweet; (*reizend*) charming; (*köstlich*) delightful; (*Wein*) smooth; **~lichkeit** *f* loveliness; charm, sweetness; (*Anmut*) grace; **~ling** *m* favo(u)rite; *fam* darling; (*Anrede*) *fam* honey; (*Tier*) pet; **~~saufenthalt** *m* (*von Tieren*) *Am* stamping ground; **~~sbeschäftigung** *f* favo(u)rite occupation; **~~sgericht** *n* favo(u)rite dish; **~~swunsch** *m* wish of o.'s heart; **~los** *a* unkind; loveless; **~losigkeit** *f* unkindness; **~reich** *a* kind, amiable, loving; **~reiz** *m* charm, grace; attraction; sweetness; **~reizend** *a* charming; graceful; (*anziehend*) attractive; **~schaft** *f* love-affair; intrigue; amour; **~st** *a* dearest, favo(u)rite; *am ~~en haben* to like best; *sie habe ich am ~~en* I like her best of all; *das habe ich am ~~en* I like it best so; *meine ~~e Beschäftigung* my favo(u)rite pastime; **~ste** *f*, **~ste(r)** *m* dearest, beloved; love, sweetheart, darling; **~wert** *a* dearly beloved.

Lied *n* song; (*Schlager*) hit (song); (*Weise*) tune; air; melody; (*Trink~, Tafel~*) glee; (*lustiges ~*) carol; (*Rundgesang*) catch; (*Kirchen~*) hymn; *das ist ein anderes ~* that's another story; *es ist immer das alte ~* it's always the same old story; *davon kann ich auch ein ~ singen* I could tell you a thing or two about that myself; *das ist das Ende vom ~e* that's the end of the matter; **~chen** *n* ditty; **~erabend** *m* concert (of songs); **~erbuch** *n* song-book; *eccl* book of hymns; **~erdichter** *m* lyric(al) poet; song-writer; **~ersammlung** *f* collection of songs; **~ertafel** *f* choral union.

liederlich *a* (*schlampig*) slovenly; (*ohne Sorgfalt*) careless; (*unordentlich*) disorderly; (*Lebenswandel*) loose; immoral, debauched, dissolute; **~keit** *f* slovenliness; carelessness; (*Lebenswandel*) debauchery, loose conduct.

Liefer|ant *m* purveyor; supplier; (*nach Vertrag*) contractor; (*Beschaffer*) furnisher; (*Lebensmittel*) caterer; (*Versorger*) provider; (*Hersteller, Fabrikant*) manufacturer; (*Vertreiber, Verteiler*) distributor; **~bar** *a* deliverable; (*greifbar*) available (for delivery); (*sofort*) loco spot; to be delivered; (*verkäuflich*) sal(e)able, marketable; *nicht ~~* unavailable; **~barkeit** *f* availability; **~bedingungen** *f pl* terms of delivery; **~bote** *m* delivery man; **~datum** *n* delivery date; **~firma** *f* contracting firm, supplying firm; **~frist** *f* term (*od* date) of delivery; **~hafen** *m* delivery port; **~menge** *f* quantity delivered; **~n** *tr* (*ausliefern*) to deliver; (*beschaffen*) to furnish; (*versorgen*) to supply; (*Ertrag, Ernte*) to yield; to produce; (*verschaffen*) to provide; (*gewähren*) to afford; (*übergeben*) to (sur)render; *e-e Schlacht ~~* to give battle; *zu ~~ an* to be delivered to; *geliefert sein fam* to be done for; **~schein** *m* bill of delivery, delivery note; receipt; **~spesen** *pl* delivery charges *pl*; **~ung** *f* (*Auslieferung*) delivery; (*Beschaffung*) furnishing; providing; (*Versorgung*) provision, supply(ing); (*für die Wehrmacht*) issue; (*in Teilen; Buch*) part, number; *in ~~en* (*Buch etc*) in parts, in numbers; *Bezahlung bei ~~, zahlbar bei ~~* cash on delivery; *sofortige ~~* prompt delivery, spot delivery; *~~ frei Haus* delivered free at residence; **~~sangebot** *n* tender; offer; **~~sbedingungen** *f pl* terms of delivery; delivery requirements *pl* (*od* specifications *pl*); specifications of sale; **~~skontrakt, ~~svertrag** *m* supply contract; **~~sverzögerung** *f* delay in delivery; **~~sweise** *adv* (*in Einzellieferungen*) in parts, in issues, in numbers; **~~swerk** *n* (*Buch*) serial; **~vertrag** *m* contract for future delivery; **~wagen** *m mot* delivery van, speed wag(g)on, *Am* (motor) delivery truck, *Am* (*kleiner, schneller*) pickup; **~zettel** *m* supply note; **~zeit** *f* time (*od* date) of delivery, term of delivery.

Liege *f* (*Chaiselongue*) couch, divan; **~deck** *n* (*Schiff, Großflugzeug*) lounge deck; **~geld** *n mar* demurrage; **~krippe** *f* day nursery; **~kur** *f* rest cure; **~n** *irr itr* to lie; to be lying; to rest; (*an Orten gelegen sein*) to be situated, to be placed, *Am* to be located; (*sich befinden*) to be, to stand; (*in Garnison ~~*) to be billeted, to be quartered; *hier liegt...* (*Grabinschrift*) here lies...; *die Fenster ~~ nach Norden* the windows face north; *am Herzen ~~* to be of interest for; *auf dem Rücken ~~* to be lying on o.'s back; *krank im Bett ~~* to be sick in bed; *im Sterben ~~* to be at the point of death; *im Streite ~~* to have a dispute; *jdm in den Ohren ~~* to din into s. o.'s ears; *in den letzten Zügen ~~* to be breathing o.'s last; *vor Anker ~~* to lie at anchor; *zugrunde ~~* to underlie; *an wem liegt es?* whose fault is it? *es liegt an ihm* it is his fault; *soviel an mir liegt* as far as lies in my power, as far as I am concerned; *es liegt auf der Hand* it is obvious, it is plain; *es liegt bei ihm* it rests with him; *es liegt daran, daß ...* the reason is that ...; *es liegt mir daran* it is of great consequence to me, I am anxious to, I am interested in the matter, *fam* I care a lot, it means a lot to me; *das liegt daran, daß* this is due to the fact that; *es liegt nichts daran* it is of no consequence; *es liegt viel* (*wenig*) *daran* it matters much (little); *ihr lag nichts daran* she didn't care for it; *es liegt nahe* it suggests itself, it is natural; *das liegt mir nicht* that is not in my line, I don't take to it, I am not built that way; *wie liegt die Sache?* what is the situation? *wie die Sachen jetzt ~~* as matters now stand; **~nbleiben** *irr itr* (*im Bett*) to stay (*od* to remain) in bed, to keep o.'s bed; (*Briefe*) not to be sent off; (*Waren, unverkäuflich*) to be unsal(e)able, to remain unsold; (*stecken bleiben, Zug, Auto etc*) to break down; (*aufgeschoben werden*) to lie over; (*unerledigt bleiben*) to stand over; **~nd** *a* lying; situated; horizontal; (*hingestreckt*) prostrate, recumbent; prone; *~~e Güter* landed property, immovables *pl*; **~nlassen** *irr tr* to let lie; (*zurücklassen*) to leave (behind); (*absichtlich*) to give up; (*Arbeit*) to leave off; (*herum~~*) to leave lying around; *jdn links ~~* to cut s. o.; *laß das liegen!* leave that alone! **~nschaften** *f pl* (*Grundstücke*) landed property, real estate, immovables *pl*; **~platz** *m mar* berth; **~statt** *f* (*Lagerstatt, Bett*) bunk; **~stuhl** *m* deck-chair, *fam* loafer; **~stütz** *m* (*Freiübungen*) frontleaning rest on ground; **~tage** *m pl mar* laydays *pl*; **~zeit** *f* laydays *pl*, running days *pl*; quarantine.

Lift *m* (*Fahrstuhl*) lift, *Am* elevator; **~boy, ~junge** *m* lift-boy, buttons *pl mit sing*, *Am* elevator boy.

Liga *f* league; **~meisterschaft** *f* (*Baseball*) league pennant; **~spiel** *n sport* league-match; **~~e** *n pl* series *pl*; **~spieler** *m sport* leaguer.

Ligatur *f typ, med* ligature.

Lignin *n* lignin; **~haltig** *a* containing lignin; **~reich** *a* rich in lignin.

Liguster *m bot* privet.

liiert *a* united; allied.

Likör *m* liqueur, cordial.

lila, **~farbig** *a* lilac, pale violet, lavender.

Lilie *f* lily; (*im Wappen*) fleur-de-lis; *tech* plug; **~nartig** *a* liliaceous.

Liliputaner *m* Lilliputian.

Limonade *f* lemonade; (*Zitronen~*) lemon-squash.

Limone *f bot* citron, cedrat; (*süße*) lime; (*saure*) lemon.

Limousine *f mot* limousine, saloon-car, *Am* sedan; (*mit Schiebedach*) sunshine limousine, sliding-roof limousine; (*viertürige*) fourdoor (*fam* fordor) sedan; (*zweitürige*) coach, *Am* tudor sedan; *die ~ hatte ein deutsches Nummernschild* the sedan was bearing a German licence plate.

lind *a* soft, gentle; mild, smooth; **~ern** *tr* (*weich machen*) to soften; (*erleichtern*) to relieve; to alleviate; to allay; (*mäßigen*) to mitigate; (*erleichtern*) to ease; (*mildern*) to soothe; *jur* (*Strafe*) to commute; **~erung** *f* mitigation; softening; alleviation, palliation; relief; **~~smittel** *n* soothing remedy, anodyne; lenitive, palliative.

Linde *f* lime-tree, linden-tree; **~nbast** *m* linden-bast; **~nblüte** *f* lime-tree blossom; **~nblütentee** *m* lime-blossom-tea.

Lindwurm *m* dragon.
Line|al *n* ruler, rule; straightedge; **~ar** *a* linear.
Linie *f* line; (*Reihe*) line-up; (*Abstammung*) descent, lineage, ancestry; branch of a family; *die ~* (*Äquator*) the line, equator; (*Zeile*) line; (*Straßenbahn*) number; *fahren Sie mit ~ zehn!* take number ten! *tele, rail* (*Gleis, Strecke*) line; route; *mil* (*Front*) line; *typ* (*Setzlinie*) composing rule; *aufsteigende, absteigende, direkte, männliche, weibliche ~* ascending, descending, direct, male, female line; *auf der ganzen ~* all along the line; *auf gleicher ~ mit* on a level with; *in erster ~* in the first place, first and foremost, first of all, above all; primarily; *in e-r ~ stehen* to stand in line; *in letzter ~* in the last analysis, finally; *die ~ des geringsten Widerstandes* the line of least resistance; *~n ziehen* to draw lines; **~nblatt** *n* sheet with guide-lines (*od* ink-lines); underlines *pl*; **~nförmig** *a* linear; **~npapier** *n* ruled paper; **~nrichter** *m sport* line-umpire, linesman; **~nschiff** *n* battleship, ship of the line; dreadnought; **~ntreu** *a* following (*od* true to) the party line; **~ntruppen** *f pl* troops of the line, regulars *pl*; **~ren, liniieren** *tr* to rule, to draw a line.
link *a* left; (*Tuchseite*) wrong side; (*beim Reittier*) near; (*Wappenkunde*) sinister; (*Münze*) reverse; *~e Seite* left hand; *mein ~er Nebenmann* my left-hand man; *~er Hand, zur ~en* on (*od* to) the left; *~er Zügel* near rein; *sie ist heute mit dem ~en Fuß zuerst aufgestanden fig* she got up on the wrong side of the bed to-day; **~e** *f* (*Hand*) left hand; (*Seite*) left (side); *parl* opposition, parties of the left; (*Boxen, die gerade ~~*) jab; **~e(r)** *m* (*Boxen*) left; **~erhand** *adv* on the left; **~isch** *a* (*ungeschickt*) awkward, clumsy, left-handed; *~~es Wesen* awkwardness; **~s** *adv* left; (*auf der Linken*) on the left, (*nach, zur Linken*) to the left; *~~ sein* to be left-handed; *~~ liegen lassen* to cold-shoulder, to give s. o. the cold shoulder, to ignore s. o. completely; *~~ um! mil* left about! *Augen ~!* eyes left! *~~ von* to the left of; *von ~~* from the left; **~saußen(stürmer)** *m* outside left, *Am* left wing, left outside; **~sdrehend** *a* rotating counterclockwise; *chem* levorotatory; **~sgerichtete (r)** *m parl* left-winger; **~sgewinde** *n* left-hand thread; **~shänder** *m* left-hander, *Am bes. sport* southpaw; **~shändig** *a* left-handed, *Am* southpaw; **~släufig** *a* counterclockwise; **~sradikal** *a* leftist; **~sradikale(r)** *m parl* leftist; **~sschraube** *f* left-handed screw; **~sstricken** *itr* to purl; **~swerfe(r)** *m Am* (*Baseball*) southpaw.
Linnen *n* linen.
Linol|eum *n* lino(leum); **~schnitt** *m* lino cut.
Linotype|setzmaschine *f typ* linotype (machine), type setter; **~setzer** *m* linotype operator.
Linse *f bot* lentil; *opt* lens, *phot* (*Objektiv*) objective; (*~ im Auge*) crystalline lens; **~nartig** *a* lenticular, lens-shaped; **~ndurchmesser** *m* lens diameter; **~nfassung** *f* lens mount; **~nförmig** *a* lentiform, lenticular; **~ngericht** *n* dish of lentils, (*Bibel*) red pottage; *für ein ~~ verkaufen fig* to sell for a mess of pottage; **~ngroß** *a* lentil-sized; **~nsuppe** *f* lentil soup; **~nsystem** *n opt* system of lenses, lens combination; **~ntrübung** *f med* opacity of lens.
Lippe *f* lip; *anat* labium, border, edge; *bot* label(lum); *sich auf die ~n beißen* to gnaw o.'s lips; *an jds ~n hängen fig* to hang on s. o.'s words; **~nartig** *a* liplike; **~nbekenntnis** *n* lip-service; **~nblütler** *m pl bot* labiate plants *pl*, Labiatae; **~nförmig** *a* labiate; **~nlaut** *m gram* labial (sound); **~nstift** *m* lip-stick; *sie nahm ihren ~~ aus der Handtasche u. schminkte ihre ~n* she was getting her lipstick out of her bag and did her lips; **~~halter** *m* lip-stick holder; **~~hülse** *f* lip-stick case.
liquid *a* (*flüssig*) liquid; *com* (*zahlungsfähig*) solvent; (*Forderung offen*) unpaid; (*zahlbar*) payable; (*fällig*) due; *~es Geld* ready money; **~ation** *f* liquidation; (*Abwicklung*) winding up, *Am* windup; (*Abrechnung*) settlement; (*Realisierung*) realization; (*Honorar*) charge, fee; *~~ der laufenden Geschäfte* winding up of pending affairs; *in ~~ treten* to wind up; to go into liquidation; *in ~~* in liquidation; **~ator** *m* liquidator, receiver; **~ieren** *tr* to liquidate, to go into liquidation, to wind up; to realize; (*Honorar*) to charge; (*töten, umbringen*) to liquidate; **~ierung** *f* liquidation, winding up; **~ität** *f* liquidity; solvency.
lispeln *itr, tr* to lisp; (*flüstern*) to whisper.
Lissabon *n* Lisbon.
List *f* (*Schlauheit, Verschlagenheit*) cunning, craft, artfulness; (*Trick, Kunstgriff*) ruse, trick, underhand; (*Kriegslist*) stratagem; (*Vorwand*) pretence, *Am* pretense; (*Ausrede*) subterfuge; *zu e-r ~ greifen* to resort to a ruse; **~ig** *a* (*verschlagen*) cunning; (*hinterlistig*) crafty; (*schlau*) sly; astute; **~igerweise** *adv* craftily, cunningly.
Liste *f* list; (*Register*) register, roll, *bes. Am* roster; (*Katalog*) catalogue, *Am* catalog; (*Geschworene*) panel; (*Inventarverzeichnis*) inventory; (*Aufzählung*) specification; (*Tabelle*) table (synopsis); schedule; *e-e ~ aufstellen* to draw up a list; *in e-e ~ eintragen* to put down, to (en)list; to enrol(l); to register; *Schwarze ~* Black List; *auf die schwarze ~ setzen* to blacklist; **~nförmig** *a* in tabular form; *~~ zusammenstellen* to tabulate; **~npreis** *m* list price, catalog(ue) price; **~nwahl** *f parl* election by ticket.
Litanei *f* litany; *fig* long-winded story; *die alte ~* the same old story.
Litau|en *n* Lithuania; **~er** *m* Lithuanian; **~isch** *a* Lithuanian.
Liter *n* litre, *Am* liter (1 l = $1^3/_4$ pints); **~weise** *adv* by litres.
liter|arisch *a* literary; **~at** *m* man of letters, writer; **~atur** *f* literature; **~~geschichte** *f* history of literature.
Litfaßsäule *f* (*Reklame*) advertisement pillar, hoarding, *Am* billboard.
Lithograph *m* lithographer; **~ie** *f* lithography, lithographic print; **~ieren** *tr* to lithograph; **~isch** *a* lithographic; *~ische Anstalt* lithographic printing-establishment.
Liturgie *f* lithurgy.
Litze *f* lace, string, cord, braid; (*Uniform*) braiding; *el* strand, flex(ible); **~ndraht** *m* stranded wire, litzendraht wire.
Livland *n* Livonia; **Livländer** *m* Livonian; **livländisch** *a* Livonian.
Livree *f* livery; **~bediente(r)** *m* livery servant, footman.
Lizenz *f* permit; licence, *Am* license; poetic licence; *in ~* under licence; **~abgaben** *f pl* licence fees *pl*; **~bau** *m* construction under licence; **~geber** *m* licenser; **~gebühr** *f* licence fee; royalty; **~inhaber, ~träger** *m* licensee; **~pflichtig** *a* subject to licence arrangements; **~vergebung** *f* issuance of licence.
Lob *n* praise; (*Empfehlung*) commendation; (*Ruhm*) fame; (*Beifall*) approval, applause; *Gott ~ u. Dank!* thank God! *über alles ~ erhaben* above all praise; **~en** *tr* to praise; (*empfehlen*) to commend; (*übertrieben ~~*) to extol; **~end** *a* laudative, commendatory; *jdn ~~ erwähnen* to speak in high terms of s. o.; **~enswert** *a* praiseworthy; **~eserhebung** *f* high praise, encomium; **~gedicht** *n* laudatory poem; **~gesang** *m* hymn; song of praise; **~hudelei** *f* fulsome praise, base flattery; **~hudeln** *tr, itr* to praise in fulsome terms; **~hudler** *m* sycophant, servile flatterer; **~lied** *n* hymn; **~preisen** *irr tr* to praise, to extol; **~preisung** *f* praise; **~rede** *f* eulogy; panegyric, encomium; **~redner** *m* eulogist, panegyrist; **~singen** *irr tr* to sing praises; **~spruch** *m* eulogy.
löblich *a* laudable, praiseworthy, commendable.
Loch *n* hole; (*Öffnung*) aperture; (*Lochung, Durchbohrung*) perforation; (*Höhlung*) hollow, cave; cavity; (*Lükke*) gap; (*Billard*) pocket; (*~ im Luftreifen*) puncture; (*im Käse*) eye; (*schlechte Wohnung*) dirty hole; *fam* (*Gefängnis*) prison, jail, *sl* squod; (*Luft~*) air-pocket, air-hole; *auf dem letzten ~ pfeifen fig fam* to be on o.'s last legs; **~abstand** *m film* perforation pitch; **~ball** *m sport* pinball; **~blende** *f phot* diaphragm; **~bohrer** *m* auger; **~breite** *f* band width, transmission range; **~eisen** *n* (hollow) punch; **~en** *tr* to perforate, to pierce; to punch; **~er** *m* (file-) punch; perforator; **~karte** *f* perforated card; **~säge** *f* compass saw, pad saw; **~streifen** *m* perforated tape (*od* slip); **~ung** *f* perforation, boring, punching; **~zange** *f* punch pliers *pl*.
Löchelchen *n* small hole.
löcherig *a* full of holes, porous.
Lock|e *f* (*Haar~~*) curl, lock; (*Ringel*) ringlet; **~en** *tr* (*kräuseln*) (*sich*) to curl; **~enhaar** *n* curly hair; **~enkopf** *m* curly head; **~enwickel** *m* (*Metall*) curler; (*Papier*) curl-paper; **~ig** *a* curly, curled.
Lock|artikel *m* (*im Laden*) show article, catcher, *Am* loss leader; **~en** *tr* to allure, to lure; (*versuchen*) to tempt; (*durch List*) to decoy; (*anlocken*) to entice; (*ködern*) to bait; (*Henne*) to cluck; (*anziehen*) to attract; *an sich ~~* to entice; **~ente** *f* decoy-duck; **~mittel** *n* bait(ing); allurement; inducement; **~pfeife** *f* decoy-whistle, bird-call; **~ruf** *m* (*Vogel*) call; **~speise** *f* lure; bait; **~spitzel** *m* agent provocateur, *Am* stool-pigeon; **~ung** *f* attraction, alluring; (*Verleitung*) enticement; (*Versuchung*) temptation; **~vogel** *m* decoy-bird; *fig* allurer, enticer; decoy.
locker *a* loose; (*nicht straff*) slack; (*Boden*) light, loose; (*Brot*) spongy; (*Lebenswandel*) loose, lax, dissolute; frivolous; *~ machen* to loosen; *~ lassen* to let go, to budge; *nicht ~ lassen* to insist upon; *~ werden* to get loose; **~n** *tr* to loosen, to slacken; *fig* (*entspannen*) to relax; (*Sitten*) to demoralize; (*Boden*) to break up; **~ung** *f* loosening; disintegration.
Loden *m* coarse woollen cloth.
lodern *itr* (*Feuer, Flamme*) to blaze, to flare, to flame; *fig* to burn, to glow.
Löffel *m* spoon; (*Schöpf~*) ladle; (*Hasenohr*) ear; (*e-s Baggers*) bucket; (*Schöpfeimer*) bailer; *mit dem ~ füt-*

tern (*od aufziehen*) to spoon-feed; *die Weisheit mit ~n gefressen haben* to know all the answers; **~bagger** *m* (crane-) navvy, *Am* steam-shovel, shovel dredger; **~kraut** *n bot* scurvy-grass; **~n** *itr, tr* to eat with a spoon, to ladle out; to sup; *tech* to bail; **~stiel** *m* spoon handle; **~voll** *m* spoonful; **~weise** *adv* by spoonfuls.

Log *n mar* log; **~buch** *n* log-book; **~ger** *m mar* lugger; (*bewaffneter*) drifter.

Logarith|mentafel *f* logarithm table; **~misch** *a* logarithmic; **~mus** *m* logarithm (*Abk* log).

Loge *f theat* box; (*Freimaurerei*) lodge; **~nbruder** *m* brother mason; **~nkarte** *f theat* box-ticket; **~nmeister** *m* master of a lodge; **~nschließer** *m theat* attendant.

Log|ierbesuch *m* guests *pl*, visitors *pl*; **~ieren** *itr* (*wohnen*) to stay, to lodge (*bei* with s. o.), *Am* to room; *tr* to lodge; to accommodate; **~ierzimmer** *n* guest room; **~is** *n* lodgings *pl*; *mar* crew space; mess deck; *Kost u. ~~* board and lodging; **~isherr** *m* lodger, subrenter, *Am* roomer.

Log|ik *f* logic; **~iker** *m* logician; **~isch** *a* logic(al); **~ischerweise** *adv* logically.

Loh|beize *f* tanning; **~brühe** *f* ooze; **~e** *f* tanning-bark; (*Flamme*) flame; **~en** *tr* to tan; *itr* (*von der Flamme*) to blaze up, to flare up; **~farben** *a* tawny; **~gerber** *m* tanner; **~gerberei** *f* tannery; **~grube** *f* tan-pit; **~kuchen** *m* tan-turf; **~mühle** *f* tan-mill.

Lohn *m* (*Wochenlohn*) wages *pl*; (*Monatslohn, Gehalt*) salary; (*Bezahlung*) pay, payment; (*Belohnung*) reward, gratification; (*Vergütung*) compensation; (*Miete*) hire; *gleicher ~* equal pay; *üblicher ~* going wages; *viel ~* high wages; *wenig ~* low wages; *den ~ drücken* to undercut wages; **~abbau** *m* cut in wages (*od* pay), reduction of wages; **~abkommen** *n* wages agreement; **~abzug** *m* deduction from wages; **~angleichung** *f* wage adjustment; **~arbeiter** *m* (paid *od* common) workman, labo(u)rer, *Am* wage worker, day worker; jobber; **~aufbesserung** *f* wage increase, wage rise, *Am* raise, wage hike, pay boost; **~ausfall** *m* wage loss; **~buchhalter** *m* timekeeper; **~büro** *n* pay-office, pay roll office; **~diener** *m* hired servant, extra help; **~drückerei** *f* sweating; **~empfänger** *m* wage-earner; *allg pl* wage-earning population; **~en** *tr* (*belohnen*) to reward, to compensate, to recompense, to remunerate; (*bezahlen*) to pay; (*wert sein*) to be worth (while); *mit Undank ~~* to repay with ingratitude; *Gott lohne es dir!* God bless you for it! *es lohnt sich* (*der Mühe*) it is worth while; *es lohnt sich nicht* it doesn't answer, it doesn't pay; **~end** *a* profitable, paying; (*vorteilhaft*) advantageous; (*einträglich*) lucrative; **~erhöhung** *f* wage increase, wage rise, *Am* wage raise, wage hike, pay boost; **~forderung** *f* wage claim; **~gruppe** *f* pay scale; **~herabsetzung** *f* pay reduction; **~höhen** *f pl* wage levels (*Am* ceilings; **~kampf** *m* labo(u)r conflict; **~klasse** *f* wage group; **~kosten** *pl* labo(u)r cost; **~kürzung** *f* wage cut; **~kutscher** *m* cabman; **~liste** *f*, **~zettel** *m* pay-list, pay-sheet, *Am* pay roll; **~pfändung** *f* wage garnishment; **~politik** *f* wage policy; **~-Preis-Spirale** *f* wage-price spiral; **~sätze** *m pl* rates of pay; **~skala** *f* salary scale, scale of wages; **~steuer** *f* wage tax; **~stillhalteabkommen** *n* wage truce; **~stopp** *m* wage peg, wage ceiling, wage freeze; **~stunde** *f* wage hour; **~tag** *m* pay-day; **~tarif** *m* wage scale, rate of pay; **~tüte** *f* pay envelope; **~verhandlungen** *f pl* wage negotiations *pl*; collective bargaining; **~zahlung** *f* payment of wages; **~zuschlag** *m* bonus, extra pay.

löhn|en *tr, itr* to pay wages; *mil* to pay; **~ung** *f* payment, pay; **~~sappell** *m mil* pay-parade (*od* -call); **~~sstelle** *f* cash service; **~~stag** *m* pay-day.

lokal *a* local; suburban; *~ n* locality; place; (*Raum*) room; (*Wirtschaft*) restaurant, pub, inn, *Am* saloon; place to eat (*od* drink); (*Geschäfts~*) business premises *pl*; office; (*Laden*) shop, *Am* store; **~anästhesie** *f med* local anesth(a)esia; **~bahn** *f* local railway; **~behörden** *f pl* local authorities *pl*; **~bericht** *m* local report; **~berichter** *m* local reporter; **~blatt** *n* local paper; **~e(s)** *n* local news *pl mit sing*; **~farbe** *f* local colo(u)r; natural colo(u)r; **~größe** *f* local bigwig, *Am* local big noise; **~isieren** *tr* to localize; **~ität** *f* locality; **~kenntnisse** *pl* local knowledge; **~nachrichten** *f* local news *pl mit sing*; **~patriotismus** *m* local patriotism; **~posse** *f* village farce, local farce; **~presse** *f* local papers *pl*; **~redaktion** *f* local newsroom; **~schriftleiter** *m* local editor, *Am* city editor; **~sendung** *f radio* spot broadcasting; **~verkehr** *m* local traffic, short-haul traffic; **~zug** *m* local train, stopping train, *Am* way train, local.

loko *adv com* (*am Ort*) on the spot; *~ Stuttgart* to be delivered at St., free Stuttgart; **~markt** *m* local market; **~preis** *m* spot price; **~rechnung** *f* loco invoice; **~waren** *f pl* spots *pl*, spotgoods *pl*.

Lokomotiv|e, kurz Lok *f* locomotive, (locomotive) engine, *Am* engine; **~führer** *m* engine driver, *Am* engineer; (*e-r el Lok*) motorman; **~heizer** *m* stoker, fireman; **~schuppen** *m* engine shed, running shed, *Am* round-house; **~wechsel** *m* change of engine.

Lokus *m fam* lavatory, W. C.

Lombard|bank *f* loan-bank; **~darlehen** *n* collateral loan; **~fähig** *a* acceptable as collateral; **~ieren** *tr* to make a loan on securities, goods etc, to lend on securities, *Am* to hypothecate securities; **~zinsfuß** *m* bank rate for loans, *Am* lending rate.

Looping *m aero* (*Überschlag*) looping, loop; (*nach oben*) inside loop; (*nach unten*) outside loop.

Londoner *m* Londoner; *ein richtiger ~* a cockney.

Lorbeer *m* laurel, bay; *auf seinen ~en ausruhen fig* to rest on o.'s laurels; *~en ernten* to win laurels, to gain laurels; *mit ~ geschmückt* laurel(l)ed, crowned with laurel; **~baum** *m* laurel; **~blatt** *n* bay leaf, laurel leaf; **~kranz** *m* laurel crown; **~kraut** *n* spurge laurel.

Lore *f rail* lorry, truck; open goods wag(g)on.

Lorindüse *f aero* (*L-Triebwerk, Strahltriebwerk*) athodyd (= aero-thermo-dynamic duct); *Am* ramjet.

Los *n* (*Anteil, Partie Waren*) lot, share, portion, parcel; (*Grundstück*) plot, lot; (*Schicksal*) destiny, fate, chance; (*Anleihe*) lottery bond; (*Lotterie~*) lottery ticket; *Doppel~* twin ticket; *etw durch das ~ entscheiden* to decide s. th. by casting lots, to ballot for s. th.; *das große ~* the first prize, *Am* the jackpot; *das große ~ gewinnen* to win the first prize, *Am* to hit the jackpot; *das ~ ziehen* to draw (*od* to cast) lots (*um* for); **~nummer** *f* (lottery) number; **~ziehung** *f* (lottery) drawing.

los *a, adv* (*nicht fest*) loose, slack; (*frei*) free; flowing; (*abgetrennt*) off, detached; *der Hund ist ~* the dog is loose; *~ von* free from; *etw ~ haben* to be thoroughly versed in; *jdn, etw ~ sein* to be rid of s. o., s. th.; *ich bin ihn ~* I am rid of him; *er wurde seine Schulden ~* he cleared himself of his debts; *hier ist der Teufel ~* hell broke loose here, it is hell let loose; *als ob nichts ~ wäre* as if nothing had happened; *was ist hier ~?* what's the matter? what's the trouble? what's going on? what's up? *Am fam* what's cooking? *es ist nichts ~* nothing doing; *hier ist viel ~* there's plenty going on here; *es ist etw ~* s. th. is on, *Am* s. th. is up; *es ist nicht viel ~ mit ihm* he's not up to much, there isn't much to him; *los! interj* go on! go ahead! shoot! fire away! begin! (*Tennis*) play! *auf die Plätze! ~!* take your marks! go *Eins, zwei, drei ~!* One, two three, go!

los|arbeiten *itr* to work away (at); *sich ~~* to extricate o. s.; **~binden** *irr tr* to untie, to loosen; **~brechen** *irr tr* to break off; *itr* to break out, to burst out; **~bröckeln** *tr, itr* to crumble off; **~drücken** *tr, itr* (*Gewehr*) to fire, to fire off; **~eisen** *tr* to free; **~essen** *irr itr: darauf ~~* to tuck in; **~fahren** *irr itr* (*abfahren*) to depart; *auf jdn ~~* (*fig*) to fly out at, to fall upon s. o.; **~feuern** *tr* to fire (off); **~geben** *irr tr* to release, to set free; **~gehen** *irr itr* to come off; (*sich lösen*) to loosen, to become loose; (*Gewehr*) to go off; (*anfangen*) to begin, to start; *auf jdn* (*od etw*) *~~* to attack, to go at s. o. (*od* s. th.); **~haken** *tr* to unhook; **~kaufen** *tr* to redeem, to ransom, to buy off; **~ketten** *tr* to unchain; **~knüpfen** *tr* to untie; **~kommen** *irr itr* to come off, to get away; *aero* to get off, to rise; *von jdm ~~* to get rid of s. o.; **~koppeln** *tr* to unleash; **~kuppeln** *tr* to uncouple, to disconnect, to throw out of gear; **~lassen** *irr tr* to let go, to let loose; to let off; to set free; (*e-n Gefangenen*) to release; (*Hund*) to set (*auf jdn* on), to unleash (*auf* upon); *laß mich los!* let me alone! let me go! **~legen** *itr fam* (*anfangen*) to begin, to start; *legen Sie los!* start in! **~lösen** *tr* to loosen, to detach, to untie; *sich ~~* to come off, to disengage o. s.; *sich von jdm ~~* to get rid of; (*vom Feind*) to disengage o. s. from; **~machen** *tr* to unfasten, to make loose; to release, to free; *mar* (*ablegen*) to unmoor, to cast off; *sich von jdm ~~* to shake s. o. off; **~platzen** *itr* to burst off, to explode; *fig* to burst out (laughing); to blurt out; **~reißen** *irr tr* to tear off; (*trennen*) to separate; **~sagen**: *sich ~~ von etw* to renounce s. th.; to give up s. th.; to part from; **~sagung** *f* renunciation; **~schießen** *irr tr* to fire off, to fire away; *itr* (*mit e-r Geschichte*) to start, to begin; (*auf jdn*) to make a rush upon, to rush at, to flash at; *schießen Sie ~!* Fire away! Shoot! **~schlagen** *irr tr* (*wegschlagen*) to knock off; (*verkaufen um jeden Preis*) to sell off at any price; (*bei e-r Auktion*) to knock down; *itr* (*Krieg*) to begin war, to open the attack, to strike; (*auf jdn*) to attack s. o.; **~schnallen** *tr* to unbuckle; *sich ~~* to undo o.'s belt; **~schrauben** *tr* to unscrew, to screw off; **~schwirren** *itr aero* (*beim Start*) to zip off; **~sprechen** *irr tr* to absolve, to acquit; to (declare) free; **~sprechung** *f* absolution; **~sprengen** *tr* to blast off, *Am* to dynamite; **~springen** *irr itr* to spring upon, to rush upon, to fly at; **~stürmen** *itr* to rush at, to rush forth; **~stürzen** *itr*: *auf jdn ~~* to dart upon, to dash at; **~trennen** *tr* to undo, to separate, to unsew; (*wegreißen*) to rip off; to sever, to detach; to tear apart; **~werden** *irr tr* to get rid of; **~werfen** *irr tr mar* to unmoor, to cast off; **~wickeln** *tr* to unwind, to disentangle; **~winden** *irr tr* to untwist; **~ziehen** *irr itr* to set out, to pull away; to march (*auf etw* against); *fig gegen* (*od über*) *jdn ~~* to inveigh against, to rail at.

lösbar *a chem* soluble; *math* dissoluble, resolvable; **~keit** *f* (dis)solubility.

Lösch|anlage *f mar* loading (*od* unloading) plant; (*Kalk*) lime slaking plant; (*Koks*) coke quenching plant; **~blatt** *n* blotting-paper; **~eimer** *m* fire bucket; **~dienst** *m* fire-fighting service; **~en** *tr* (*Feuer*) to extinguish; (*Licht*) to put out; (*Durst stillen*) to quench; (*Kohle*) to damp, to quench; (*Kalk*) to slake (lime); (*auswischen*) to blot out; (*streichen, tilgen*) to efface, to erase; (*annulieren*) to cancel; (*Forderung*) to liquidate (a debt); (*Hypothek*) to release (a mortgage), to cancel; (*Schiff entladen*) to unload, to discharge, to lighten; **~er** *m* (*Tinten~~*) blotter; (*Feuer~~*) extinguisher; (*Auslader*) unloader, discharger; (*Arbeiter*) docker, *Am* longshoreman; **~gerät** *n* fire-fighting apparatus; (fire-) extinguisher; **~hafen** *m mar* port of discharge; **~kalk** *m* quick (*od* slack *od* slaked) lime; **~mannschaft** *f* fire-brigade, firemen *pl*; **~papier** *n* blotting-paper; **~taste** *f* cancel (*od* clearing) key; **~trupp** *m* (*Feuerwehr*) fire-fighting party; **~ung** *f* (*Feuer*) extinction; (*Streichung, Tilgung*) annulment; cancellation, cancel(l)ing; (*e-r Firma*) dissolution, extinction; (*Hypothek*) cancellation; (*Schiffsladung*) unloading, discharging; landing; **~wasser** *n* water for fire fighting; **~zeit** *f* (*Entladezeit*) running days for discharging.

lose *a* (*nicht angebunden*) loose; (*frei*) free; (*locker*) slack; (*beweglich*) mov(e)able; (*unverbunden*) incoherent, disconnected; (*unverpackte Waren*) unpacked, unpackaged; in bulk; *fig* (*Benehmen, Moral*) lax, bad; light-hearted; frivolous; dissolute; *~ Formation* loose formation; *~s Haar* loose (*od* flowing *od* dishevelled) hair; *e-e ~ Hand haben* to be always ready to strike; *~ Ladung* bulk; *~s Mädchen* wanton girl; *~s Maul, ~r Mund, ~s Mundwerk, ~ Zunge* loose (*od* sharp *od* malicious) tongue; *~ Reden pl* idle words *pl*, foolish speech; *~r Vogel* wag; *~r Zahn* loose tooth; **~blattform** *f* book form, tumble form, loose-leaf form.

Lös|egeld *n* ransom; **~en** *tr* (*losmachen*) to loose(n), to untie; to undo; *sich ~~* to (get) loose, to loosen; (*abtrennen*) to detach, to sever; (*einlösen*) to redeem; *chem* to dissolve; (*Glieder*) to relax; (*Pfand*) to redeem (a pledge); (*Eintrittskarte, Fahrkarte, Flugkarte etc*) to buy (*od* to take) a ticket, (*im voraus*) to book; (*Geld einnehmen*) to receive, to make money (out) of; to realize; (*Schuß*) to fire, to discharge; (*Problem*) to solve; (*Frage*) to answer; (*Schwierigkeit*) to settle; (*Beziehungen*) to break off, to give up, to solve; (*Vertrag*) to end, to annul; to cancel; (*Rätsel*) to solve, to guess, to answer; (*Versprechen*) to fulfil o.'s promise; **~end** *a* dissolving; *med* solvent, expectorant, purgative; **~lich** *a* soluble; **~lichkeit** *f* solubility; **~ung** *f* loosening; solving; discharge; *fig, chem* solution; **~~sfähigkeit** *f* dissolving capacity; **~~smittel** *n med* solvent; **~~svermögen** *n* dissolving power.

los|en *itr* to draw (*od* to cast) lots (*um* for); **~ung** *f* (*Losungswort*) password, watchword, parole; countersign; *fig* rallying cry; (*beim Wild*) droppings *pl* ; dung, excrement.

Lot *n* (*Bleigewicht mit Schnur*) plummet, lead, plumb-line; *math* perpendicular; (*Lötmetall*) solder; (*Gewicht*) half an ounce, 10 gram(mes); *ein ~ fällen* to draw a perpendicular line; *im ~* right by the plummet, on end; perpendicular; **~achse** *f aero* vertical axis; **~en** *itr, tr tech* to plumb; *mar* to sound, to take soundings, to lead; **~gerät** *n mar* sounding apparatus; **~leine** *f* plumb line; **~recht** *a* perpendicular; vertical; **~rechte** *f* vertical line; **~ung** *f* plumbing; *mar* sounding.

Löt|apparat *m* soldering apparatus; **~bar** *a* solderable; **~blei** *n* lead solder; **~en** *tr* to solder; **~flußmittel** *n* soldering flux; **~klemme** *f* soldering terminal, tag; **~kolben** *m* soldering iron; **~lampe** *f* soldering lamp, *Am* blowtorch; **~rohr** *n* blow-pipe; **~stelle** *f* soldering point; soldering seam; **~wasser** *n* soldering fluid; **~zinn** *n* soldering tin.

Lothring|en *n* Lorraine; **~er** *m* Lothringian; **~isch** *a* Lothringian.

Lotse *m* pilot; *den ~n aussetzen* to drop the pilot; **~n** *tr* to pilot; **~nboot** *n* pilot-cutter; pilot-boat; **~ndienst** *m* pilot service; **~nflagge** *f* pilot flag; **~ngebühr** *f*, **~ngeld** *n* pilotage.

Lotter|bett *n* couch, lounge; **~bube** *m* rascal, vagrant; **~ig** *a* (*schlampig*) slovenly; *fig* (*liederlich*) dissolute; **~leben** *n* dissolute life.

Lotterie *f* lottery; *in der ~ spielen* to play in the lottery, to buy a lottery ticket; **~einnehmer** *m* lottery office keeper, collector; **~geschäft** *n* lottery office; **~gewinn** *m* prize; **~los** *n* lottery ticket; **~ziehung** *f* lottery drawing.

Lotto, **~spiel** *n* lot(t)o.

Lotus *m* lotus, lote.

Löwe *m* lion; *astr* Leo, the Lion; **~nanteil** *m* lion's share; **~nbändiger** *m* lion-tamer; **~ngrube** *f* lion's den; **~nhaut** *f* lion's skin; **~jagd** *f* lion hunting; **~nmaul** *n bot* snapdragon; **~zahn** *m bot* dandelion; **Löwin** *f* lioness.

loyal *a* loyal, faithful; **~ist** *m* loyalist; **~ität** *f* loyalty, allegiance; **~itätseid** *m* oath of allegiance.

Luchs *m* lynx; **~augen** *n pl* lynx-eyes *pl*; **~äugig** *a* lynx-eyed.

Lücke *f* gap; (*wissenschaftlich*) lacuna; (*Öffnung, Loch*) hole, opening; (*Bresche*) breach; (*Unterbrechung*) break; (*Kluft*) chasm; (*Auslassung*) omission; (*leere Stelle*) blank; void; (*Mangel*) deficiency; defect; (*Spalte, Zwischenraum*) interstice; *auf ~ stehend* staggered; *e-e ~ ausfüllen* to fill (up) a gap; to supply a want; *e-e ~ schließen fig* to step into the breach; **~nbüßer** *m* stop-gap; (*Strohmann*) dummy; (*Aushilfe*) stand-in; make-shift; **~nhaft** *a* full of gaps; (*unvollständig*) incomplete; defective; *fig* fragmentary; **~nlos** *a* (*vollständig*) complete; (*ununterbrochen*) unbroken, uninterrupted; (*ganz und gar*) consistent.

Luder *n* (*Aas*) carrion; *fam* (*Hure*) wretch, hussy; (*Schimpfwort*) beast; **~jan** *m* rake; **~leben** *n* dissolute life.

Lue|s *f med* (*Syphilis*) lues, syphilis, *fam* pox; **~tiker** *m* luetic, syphilitic; **~tisch** *a* luetic, syphilitic.

*

Luft *f* air; (*Windhauch*) breeze; (*Atem*) breath; (*Atmosphäre*) atmosphere; *tech* (*Spiel*) play, clearance; *in der freien ~* in the open air; *in der ~* (*schwebend*), *durch die ~* airborne; *dicke ~* (*mil sl*) heavy shelling; *flüssige ~* liquid air; *leichter als ~* lighter-than-air; *die ~ ist rein fig* the coast is clear; *er hat keine ~* he is short of breath; *sie kann keine ~ kriegen* she can't breathe; *für mich ist er ~* he doesn't exist as far as I am concerned; *an die ~ bringen* to air; *der ~ aussetzen* to air; *in die ~ fliegen* to be blown up; *aus der ~ greifen* (*erfinden*) to invent; *aus der ~ gegriffen* unfounded, invented; pure imagination; *in der ~ hängen fig* to be undecided as yet; *es liegt etw in der ~* s. th. is in the air; *sich ~ machen, seinem Herzen ~ machen* to give vent to o.'s feelings; *an die ~ setzen* to throw out, to turn out; to give s. o. the air; *frische ~ schöpfen* to take the air, to draw breath; *in die ~ sprengen* to blow up; *an der ~ trocknen* to air-dry; *drei Jagdflugzeuge stießen in der ~ zusammen* three fighter planes collided in mid-air; **~abkommen** *n* air convention (*od* pact); **~abscheider** *m* (*Entlüfter*) air separator; **~abschluß** *m* exclusion of air; hermetic (*od* air) seal; **~abwehr** *f* air defence; anti-aircraft (defence); **~~geschütz** *n*, **~~kanone** *f* anti-aircraft gun; **~~stelle** *f* air defence department; **~abzug** *m* air exhaust; **~akrobat** *m* (*Zirkus*) circus aerialist; **~akrobatie** *f aero* air stunting; **~aktivität** *f* air operations *pl*, general air activities *pl*; **~alarm** *m* air-raid alarm; **~amt** *n* Air Board; Air Ministry; **~angriff** *m* air-raid, air-attack, air strike, air assault; (*sehr schwerer*) air blitz; *durch schwere ~~e zerstören* to blitz; **~ansaugstutzen** *m* air intake, air horn; **~ansicht** *f* aerial view; **~antenne** *f radio* overhead aerial; **~armada** *f* air fleet, air armada, *Am* airmada; **~artig** *a* aeriform, gaseous; **~attaché** *m* air attaché; **~aufklärung** *f* air (*od* aerial) reconnaissance; (*aus großer Höhe*) high-altitude reconnaissance; **~aufnahme** *f* aerial (*od* air) photograph, aerial view; airplane picture; air survey; mosaic; **~aufsicht** *f* air police (service), airtraffic control; **~~sstelle** *f* bureau of airtraffic supervision; **~auftrieb** *m* air buoyancy; **~austritt** *m* air exhaust; **~bad** *n* air bath; **~ballon** *m* air-balloon; **~basis** *f* base of operations, airbase; **~beobachtung** *f* aerial observation; **~bereifung** *f* pneumatic tyres *pl*; **~beschuß** *m* fire from aircraft; **~bewegung** *f* flow of air; **~bild** *n* air photo(graph), aerophoto, aerial photograph, *Am* air (*od* aerial) view; (*zur Landvermessung*) aerial survey photograph; (*Schrägaufnahme*) oblique air photograph; (*Senkrechtaufnahme*) vertical air photograph; *fig* (*Vision*) vision; **~~aufklärung** *f* photographic reconnaissance; **~~ausrüstung** *f* aerial photographic equipment; **~~auswertung** *f* plotting (*od* restitution) from air photographs; **~~gerät** *n*, **~~kamera** *f* air camera, aerial camera; **~~karte** *f* aerial mosaic; air photographic map; **~~vermessung** *f* air survey, aerial mapping; **~blase** *f* (air) bubble; air pocket; *anat* vesicle; **~bö** *f* gust; **~bombe** *f* air bomb; **~bremse** *f aero* (*mit Klappen*) air brake; (*mit Druckluft*) pneumatic (*Am* air) brake; **~brennstoffgemisch** *n* fuel-air mixture; **~brücke** *f* air lift; *über e-e ~~ befördern* to airlift; **~dicht** *a* air-tight, air-proof; hermetic(al); *~~e Kabine* sealed cabin; **~dichte** *f* air density; **~dienst** *m* air service; **~division** *f mil* air division; **~druck** *m* atmospheric pressure; (*Stoß u. Sog bei Explosion*) blast; **~~bremse** *f* pneumatic (*Am* air) brake, compressed-air brake; **~~messer** *m* barometer; **~~prüfer** *m mot* air pressure gauge, tyre gauge, *Am* tire gage; **~~pumpe** *f* pneumatic pump, air compressor; **~~wirkung** *f* effect of air pressure; **~düse** *f* air jet, air nozzle; **~einsatz** *m aero mil* air action, air activity; **~eintrittsöffnung** *f* air intake; **~elektrizität** *f* atmospheric electricity; **~erkundung** *f aero mil* air reconnaissance; **~erscheinung** *f* atmospheric phenomenon; **~fährdienst** *m* ferry service; **~fahrer** *m* airman; **~fahrt** *f* aviation, aeronautics *pl*; air navigation; **~~ausstellung** *f* aviation exhibition; **~~feuer** *n* airway beacon; **~~forschung** *f* aerial research; **~~geschichte** *f* aviation history; **~~gesellschaft** *f* airways company; **~~industrie** *f* aircraft industry; **~~linie** *f* (*Gesellschaft*) air-line, air-carrier; **~~medizin** *f* aeronautical medical science; aeromedicine; **~~minister** *m* air minister; **~~ministerium** *n* Air Ministry; **~~netz** *n* air net; **~~sachverständige(r)** *m* aviation expert; **~~straße** *f* airway, airlane; **~~technik** *f* aero engineering, *Am* aerotechnics *pl*; **~fahrzeug(e** *pl***)** *n* aircraft; (*schwerer als Luft*) aerodyne; (*leichter als Luft*) aerostat; *mit ~~ befördern* to fly; **~feuchtigkeit** *f* atmospheric humidity; atmospheric moisture; **~~smesser** *m* hygrometer; **~filter** *n* air cleaner, air filter; **~flotte** *f* air fleet; air farce; (*starke*) air armada, *Am* airmada; **~förmig** *a* gaseous, aeriform; **~fracht** *f* air cargo, air freight, airborne freight; **~~dienst** *m* air delivery service; **~~er** *m* air freighter; **~gaskrieg** *m mil* chemical war from the air; **~gefahr** *f* air(-raid) danger; **~gefecht** *n* aerial combat; **~gekühlt** *a mot* air-cooled; **~geräusche** *n pl radio* atmospherics *pl*; **~geschwindigkeit** *f* air speed; **~gewehr** *n* air gun; **~hafen** *m* aerodrome, *Am* airport, airdrome; **~hahn** *m* air cock; **~härtestahl** *m* air hardening steel; **~heer** *n* army of the air; **~heizung** *f* hot-air heating; **~herrschaft** *f* air supremacy, command (*od* control *od* mastery) of the air; air domination; **~hoheit** *f* sovereignty of the air; **~horchdienst** *m aero mil* air (-defence) listening service; **~hülle** *f* atmosphere; **~hutze** *f*, **~stutzen** *m* airscoop; **~ig** *a* airy, aerial; (*windig*) breezy; (*dünn*) thin, flimsy; **~igkeit** *f* airiness; **~infanterie** *f* airborne infantry, air infantry; **~kammer** *f* air box; **~kampf** *m* aerial combat, air fight, air battle; **~kanal** *m* air flue; **~kissen** *n* air-cushion; **~klappe** *f* air valve; *aero* air flap; **~kobold** *m aero sl* gremlin, aerial pixy; **~kontrolle** *f* air control; **~konvention** *f* air convention; **~korridor** *m* air corridor; **~krank** *a* airsick; **~krankheit** *f* airsickness; **~kreislauf** *m* air circuit; **~krieg** *m* air war, war in the air; aerial warfare; **~kühlung** *f* air cooling; **~kurort** *m* health resort; **~kursbuch** *n* air timetable; **~kutscher** *m fam* pilot; **~lage** *f aero mil* tactical air situation; **~~meldung** *f* report on enemy air activity; **~landebrückenkopf** *m* airhead; **~landedivision** *f* airborne division (*Abk* A. B. Division); **~landeinfanterie** *f* airborne infantry; **~landetruppen** *f pl* airborne troops *pl*, airborne forces *pl*, *Am auch* sky troops *pl*; *~~ absetzen* to land airborne troops; **~landeübung** *f* airborne exercise; **~landeunternehmen** *n* airborne operation; **~landung** *f* airborne landing; **~leer** *a* void of air, exhausted, vacuous; *~~er Raum* vacuum; air exhaustion; **~leiter** *m radio* aerial, antenna; **~linie** *f* (*direkte Verbindung*) bee-line, *Am auch* air line; (*Flugverkehr*) air-line, airway; *in der ~~* as the crow flies; **~linienentfernung** *f* air line distance, crow-fly distance; **~loch** *n* air-hole; *aero* air-pocket; **~macht** *f* air power, air strength; **~mangel** *m* deficiency of air, lack of air; **~manöver** *n* air manœuvre; **~marschall** *m* Air Marshal; **~masse** *f* (*Meteorologie*) air mass; **~mast** *m* (*U-Boot*) breathing mast, schnorkel; **~meer** *n* atmosphere; **~meile** *f* air mile; **~meldedienst** *m* aircraft reporting service; **~meldequadrat** *n* aerial reference square; **~mine** *f* aerial mine, parachute mine; **~minenabwurf** *m* mining from the air; **~nachrichtentruppe** *f* air signals unit; air-force signal corps; **~navigation** *f* air navigation, avigation; **~not** *f aero mil* aircraft (*od* airman) in distress; **~offensive** *f* air offensive; **~öffnung** *f* air bleed; **~operation** *f* air operation; **~ortung** *f* aerial (*od* air) navigation; **~parade** *f* aerial review; **~park** *m aero mil* air(craft) park, air depot; **~photobrief** *m* (*Mikroaufnahmen*) airgraph, *Am* V-mail; **~planquadrat** *n* aerial reference square; **~politik** *f* air politics, aeropolitics; **~polizei** *f* air police; **~polster** *n* air cushion; **~post** *f* air mail; (*Pakete*) air parcel post; **~~aufnahme** *f* (*im Flug*) air mail pickup; **~~ausgabe** *f* air mail edition; **~~brief** *m* air mail letter; **~~dienst** *m* air mail service; **~~marke** *f* air mail stamp; **~~strecke** *f* air mail route; **~~verkehr** *m* air mails *pl*; **~presser** *m tech* air compressor; **~pumpe** *f* pneumatic pump, air pump; tyre pump; **~rakete** *f* (*zur Panzerbekämpfung aus der ~*) *Am* anti-tank aircraft rocket (*Abk* ATAR), *mil sl* ram; **~raum** *m* atmosphere; air space; **~regelklappe** *f* gill; **~reifen** *m* tyre, *Am* tire; **~reiniger** *m mot* air cleaner, *Am* filter; **~reinigungsanlage** *f* air-conditioning plant; **~reise** *f* air travel, air journey; flight, voyage by air; **~reisende(r)** *m* air travel(l)er; **~recht** *n* air law; **~reklame** *f* sky advertisement; **~rennen** *n* air race, Aerial Derby; **~riese** *m* (*Riesenflugzeug*) sky giant; **~röhre** *f* air tube, air pipe; *anat* windpipe; trachea; **~~nentzündung** *f* bronchitis; **~route** *f* airway, airlane, skyway; **~rüstung** *f* air armament; **~sack** *m* (*Flugplatz*) wind-sleeve, wind-sack, wind direction indicator; **~schacht** *m* air shaft; **~schaukel** *f* swing-boat; **~schicht** *f* stratum, atmospheric layer, air layer; **~schiff** *n* airship, dirigible; (*kleines, unstarres*) blimp; **~schiffahrt** *f* aerial (*od* air) navigation, aeronautics; **~schiffhalle** *f* airship shed, *Am* dock; *ein Luftschiff in die ~~ bringen* to dock; **~schirm** *m aero mil* (air) umbrella; **~schlacht** *f* air battle; *die ~~ um England* the air battle of Britain; **~schlange** *f* paper streamer; **~schlauch** *m mot* inner tube, (air) tube; **~schleppzug** *m* air train, sky train; **~schleuse** *f* air lock; **~schloß** *n* castle in the air, air castle; **~schraube** *f* airscrew, *Am* propeller (*Abk* prop); **~~nbremse** *f* airscrew brake; **~~nnabe** *f* airscrew spinner; **~~nsteigung** *f* airscrew pitch; **~~nstrahl** *m* slipstream; **~~nwelle** *f* airscrew shaft; **~~nzug** *m* airscrew thrust; **~schutz** *m* (*ziviler*) passive air defence; air-raid precautions *pl* (*Abk* A.R.P.); air-raid protection; Civil Defence Service; **~~bunker** *m* concrete air-raid shelter; **~~deckungsgraben** *m* air-raid trench; **~~keller** *m* bomb-proof cellar, air-raid shelter (A.R.P. shelter); **~~leiter** *m* chief (air) warden; **~~maßnahmen** *f pl* air-raid precautions *pl*; **~~raum** *m* air-raid shelter, A.R.P. shelter; **~~rauminsasse** *m* shelterer; **~~schulung** *f* anti air-raid drill; **~~sirene** *f* air-raid siren; **~~stollen** *m* subterranean air-raid trench; **~~übung** *f* A.R.P. drill; **~~warndienst** *m* air-raid warning system; **~~wart** *m* air (-raid) warden, A.R.P. warden; **~schwimmblase** *f* air bladder; **~schwingung** *f* vibration of air; **~sog** *m aero* wake; **~sicherung** *f* (*für Erdtruppe*) air umbrella; **~späher** *m* (airplane) spotter, air-raid spotter, air guard, air sentry; **~spediteur** *m* air carrier; **~sperre** *f* prohibited flying area; air barrage; A. A. defences *pl*; balloon barrage; **~sperrballon** *m* barrage balloon; **~sperrgebiet** *n* air space reservation; aerial security zone; prohibited flying zone; **~spiegelung** *f* fata morgana, mirage; **~sport** *m* aerial sport; **~sprung** *m* caper, somersault; **~steward** *m* flight steward; **~stewardess** *f* flight (*od* airline) stewardess; **~störungen** *f pl radio* statics *pl*, atmospheric disturbances *pl*, atmospherics *pl*; **~stoß** *m* blast, gust of air; **~strahl** *m* air stream; air draft, air jet; **~strahltriebwerk** *n* (*IL-Triebwerk*) intermittent impulse duct, *Am* pulsojet, pulse jet; **~strategie** *f* aerial strategy; **~strecke** *f* air route, airway; **~~nnetz** *n* network of air routes; **~streitkräfte** *f pl* air forces *pl*; **~streitmacht** *f* air-force; air armada; **~strom** *m* air current, air stream; air blast; **~stützpunkt** *m aero mil* air-base; **~taktik** *f* aerial tactics *pl*; **~tanken** *n aero* aerial refuel(l)ing; **~taufe** *f aero* first flight, maiden flight; **~taxe** *f* air taxi, taxiplane; **~temperatur** *f* air temperature; **~torpedo** *m* aerial torpedo; **~transport** *m* airtransport, air conveyance, air transportation; **~~dienst** *m* airtransport service; **~trocken** *a* air-dried, air-dry; **~tüchtig** *a* airworthy; **~tüchtigkeit** *f* airworthiness; **~überfall** *m* air raid; **~überlegenheit** *f* air superiority, air supremacy; **~unterdruck** *m* air depression; **~unterstützung** *f* air support; **~ventil** *n* air valve; **~veränderung** *f* change of air; **~verdichter** *m* air compressor; **~verflüssigungsanlage** *f* liquid air plant; air liquefying plant; **~verfrachtung** *f* air shipment; **~verkehr** *m* airtraffic, airtransport, air commerce; *das Zeitalter des ~~s* the air age; **~~sbestimmungen** *f pl* airtraffic rules *pl*; **~~sgesellschaft** *f* air-line operating company; **~~skontrolle** *f* airtraffic control; **~~slinie** *f* air-line, airway, air-route; **~~snetz** *n* air-line system; **~~sstrecke** *f* airway, airlane; **~~sweg** *m* airway, airlane; **~verteidigung** *f* air (*od* aerial) defence; **~waffe** *f* air-force; German Air Force; **~~narzt** *m* flight surgeon; **~~nbefehlshaber** *m* air commander; **~~ndienstvorschrift** *f Engl* Air Publication; **~~neinheit** *f* air unit; **~~neinsatz** *m* (*e-r Maschine*) sortie, mission; **~~noperation** *f* air-force operation; **~~nstützpunkt** *m* air-force base; **~warndienst** *m* (*ziviler*) civilian air-raid ground-observer-service; **~warnsystem** *n* air-raid warning system; **~warnung** *f* air-raid warning, alert; **~warnzentrale** *f* plotting-room; **~wechsel** *m* change of air; **~weg** *m* *aero* air-route, airway, airlane; *anat* respiratory tract; *auf dem ~~* by air, airborne; *auf dem ~~ befördert* air-shipped, airborne; *auf dem ~~ versorgen* to supply by air; **~werbung** *f* aerial advertising; **~widerstand** *m phys* air resistance; *aero mil* air opposition; **~wirbel** *m* vortex, whirl; **~zelle** *f* air cell; **~ziegel** *m* air-dried brick; **~ziel** *n mil* aerial target; **~zufuhr** *f* air supply; **~zug** *m* draught, *Am* draft, current of air; (*Sog*) airflow; **~zustelldienst** *m* air delivery service; **~zwischenraum** *m* air gap.

Lüft|chen *n* breeze, (breath of) air; zephyr; **~en** *tr* to air, to ventilate, to aerate; to weather; (*heben*) to lift, to raise; (*enthüllen*) to reveal, to disclose; **~er** *m* ventilator; **~ung** *f* airing, ventilation, aeration; (*Hebung*) lifting; (*Enthüllung*) disclosing; **~~sflügel** *m* (*im Autofenster*) ventilating wing; **~~srohr** *n* ventilation shaft.

*

Lug *m siehe: Lüge*; *~ u. Trug* lies and frauds.

Lüg|e *f* lie, untruth, falsehood; (*Not~~*) fib; *e-e gewaltige ~~* a big lie, *fam* a thumper, a tough one, *Am fam* a whopper; *jdn ~en strafen* to give s. o. the lie, *Am* to belie; **~en** *irr itr* to lie, to tell a lie, to tell stories; (*flunkern*) to fib; *~~ wie gedruckt* to lie like truth, to lie like the devil; **~endetektor** *m* lie detector; **~engewebe** *f* tissue of lies; **~engeschichte** *f* yarn; *e-e ~~ zusammenbrauen* to cook up a yarn; **~enhaft** *a* lying, mendacious; untrue; (*trügerisch*) deceitful; false; **~enmaul** *n* impudent liar; *(stärker)* habitual liar; **~ner** *m*, **~nerin** *f* lier, story-teller; **~nerisch** *a* lying, untrue; false, deceitful.

lugen *itr* to look out, to peep.

Luke *f* (*Dach~*) dormer-window, garret-window; skylight; (*auf Schiffen*) hatch(way), (*kleine ~*) scuttle; (*Flugzeugeinstieg*) *mil* hatch; (*Panzer*) doorway; (*Falltür*) trap-door; **~ndekkel** *m* lid; shutter; hatch-cover.

lullen *itr* to lull (to sleep).

Lümmel *m* lout, boor, hooligan; bumpkin; **~haft** *a* loutish, boorish; **~n** *itr*: *sich ~~* to slouch.

Lump *m* ragamuffin; (*vom Charakter*) rascal, dirty fellow; scamp, blackguard; **~en** *itr: sich nicht ~~ lassen* to come down handsomely; **~en** *m* (*Lappen*) rag, tatter, clout; (*wertloser Plunder*) rubbish, trash; **~enbrei** *m* (*Papier*) pulp; **~engeld** *n* trifling sum; *für ein ~~* dog-cheap, dirt-cheap, for a mere song; **~engesindel, ~enpack** *n* riff-raff, low rabble, rag-tag and bobtail; **~enhändler** *m* ragman; **~enhund, ~enkerl** *m* rascal, scamp, blackguard; **~ensammler** *m* rag-picker; **~enwolf** *m tech* rag-tearing machine, devil; **~erei** *f* shabby trick; (*Kleinigkeit*) trifle; **~ig** *a* (*zerlumpt*) ragged; *fig* (*schäbig*) shabby; (*unbedeutend*) trifling.

Lünette *f tech* stay; *arch* (*über der Tür*) fan-light, *Am* transon.

Lunge *f* (*Flügel*) lung, lungs *pl*; (*von geschlachteten Tieren*) lights *pl*;; *Lungen-* (*in Zssg*) pulmonary; **~narterie** *f* pulmonary artery; **~nbläschen** *n* lung vesicle; **~nentzündung** *f* pneumonia; **~nflügel** *m* lobe of the lung, pulmonary lobe; **~ngeschwür** *n* ulcer in the lungs; **~ngift** *n* lung-irritant; **~nheilstätte** *f* tubercular sanatorium, *Am* tubercular sanitarium; **~nkrank** *a* consumptive; **~nkranke(r)** *m* tubercular person, consumptive, *fam* lunger; **~nkrankheit** *f* pulmonary disease; **~nleidend** *a* suffering from the lungs; **~nschützer** *m* respirator; **~nschwindsucht** *f* (pulmonary) consumption, tuberculosis, phthisis; **~nschwindsüchtig** *a* consumptive, phthisic(al); **~nspitze** *f* apex of the lung; **~ntuberkel** *f* lung tubercle; **~ntuberkulose** *f* tuberculosis (of the lungs).

lungern *itr* to loiter, to idle, to loll about; *herum~ verboten!* no loitering!

Lunte *f* slow match, match cord; (*Schwanz des Fuchses*) fox's brush; *~ riechen* to smell a rat, to take the alarm.

Lupe *f opt* magnifying-glass; magnifying-lens; magnifier; (*Taschen~*) pocket-lens; *unter die ~ nehmen* to examine under a magnifying glass; *fig* to scrutinize, to examine closely.

Lupine *f bot* lupine.

Lurch *m zoo* batrachian; **~e** *m pl* batrachia *pl*.

Lust *f* (*Vergnügen*) pleasure; (*Freude*) joy, delight; amusement, mirth; (*Neigung*) mind, disposition, inclination; (*Verlangen*) desire; (*sinnliche ~*) lust; *mit ~ u. Liebe* with heart and soul; *seine ~ an etw haben* to take a delight in s. th.; *~ haben zu* to have a mind to, to feel like doing s. th.; *große ~ haben zu* to have a good mind to; *wenig ~ haben zu* not to be keen about; *ich habe keine ~ dazu* I do not care for it, I have no stomach for it; *alle ~ an etw verlieren* to lose all interest in; *jdm ~ machen zu* to give s. o. a desire for; **~barkeit** *f* festivity, diversion; amusement; *~~en f pl* revels *pl*; (*öffentliche*) public entertainments *pl*; **~~ssteuer** *f* entertainment tax, amusement tax, *Am* admission tax; **~empfindung** *f* pleasant sensation; **~fahrt** *f* pleasure-trip, excursion, *Am* joy-ride; **~garten** *m* pleasure garden; **~häuschen** *n* summer house; **~ig** *a* gay, merry, joyous, *Am* chipper; (*von Natur*) jovial, jolly; cheerful; (*erheiternd*) amusing, funny; *in ~~er Stimmung* in a gay mood; *sich über jdn ~~ machen* to make fun of s. o., *Am* to guy s. o.; **~igkeit** *f* merriment, fun; mirth; gaiety; cheer; **~los** *a* without desire; *com* (*Markt, Börse*) inactive, dull, flat, slackening; **~losigkeit** *f* dul(l)ness, flatness; **~mord** *m* murder and rape, rape-slaying; **~schloß** *n* pleasure seat; **~seuche** *f* syphilis, venereal disease (*Abk* V.D.); **~spiel** *n* comedy; **~wandeln** *itr* to take a walk, to stroll about.

Lüster *m* (*Glanz*) lustre; (*Kronleuchter*) chandelier.

lüst|ern *a* (*gierig*) longing (*nach* for), desirous (*nach* of), eager (*nach* after), greedy (*nach* for); (*sinnlich*) lascivious, lustful, lewd; **~ernheit** *f* (*Begierde*) greediness; (*Sinnlichkeit*) lasciviousness; **~ling** *m* voluptuary, sensualist; debauchee, libertine.

Luther|aner *m* Lutheran; **~isch** *a* Lutheran.

lutsch|en *tr, itr* to suck; **~er** *m* (*Lutschgummi*) dummy.

Lutter *m* (*Vorlauf*) singlings *pl*, low wine; **~n** *tr* to distil(l) low wine.

Luv *f* weather-side, luff; **~en** *itr* to luff; **~gierig** *a* weatherly; **~küste** *f* weather-shore; **~seite** *f* weather-side; **~wärts** *adv* to windward; **~winkel** *m* drift-angle.

luxuriös *a* luxurious; (*prächtig*) sumptuous; magnificent; (*teuer*) costly, rich.

Luxus *m* luxury; sumptuousness, splendo(u)r, extravagance; superabundance; **~abzug** *m typ* fine paper copy; **~artikel** *m* luxury article, luxury (*od* fancy) goods *pl*, fancy items *pl*; **~ausführung** *f* deluxe model; **~ausgabe** *f* library edition, edition de luxe; **~einband** *m* rich binding; **~kajüte** *f* stateroom; **~modell** *n* luxury model; **~steuer** *f* luxury tax; **~waren** *f pl* luxury articles *pl*, fancy goods *pl*; **~zug** *m rail* Pullman-car express, train de luxe.

Luzerne *f bot* (*Kleeart*) lucerne, *Am* alfalfa.

*

Lymph|bahn *f* lymph tract; **~bildung** *f* formation of lymph; **~drüse** *f* lymphatic gland; **~e** *f* lymph, vaccine; **~gefäß** *n* lymphatic vessel; **~knoten** *m* lymphatic ganglion; **~körperchen** *n* leucocyte, lymph corpuscle; **~strom** *m* lymphatic current.

lynch|en *tr* to lynch; **~justiz** *f* lynch-law, mob-law.

Lyr|a *f* lyre; **~ik** *f* lyric poetry; **~iker** *m* lyric poet; **~isch** *a* lyric(al).

Lyzeum *n* girl's secondary school.

M

M *Abk mit* ***M*** *siehe Liste der Abk.*
Mäander *m* (*Zierband*) meander; (*Flußwindung*) meandering stream.
Maar *n* crater (lake).
Maas *f* (*Fluß*) (River) Meuse.
Maat *m* mate; petty officer.
Mach|art *f* make; (*Mode*) fashion; (*Stil*) style; (*Form*) shape; (*Art*) description, kind, sort; brand; **~e** *f* making; (*Aufmachung*) make-up; (*Schein*) pretence, show; (*Täuschung*) humbug; (*Schönfärberei*) window-dressing; *in der ~~ haben* to have in hand; **~enschaften** *f pl* machinations *pl*; **~er** *m* (*Hersteller*) maker, manufacturer; **~erlohn** *m* charge for making; cost of production; (*Schneider*) tailor's wages *pl*; **~werk** *n* bungle, clumsy piece of work.
machen *tr* to make; (*herstellen*) to manufacture; (*bewirken*) to produce, to effect, to procure; (*tun, verrichten*) to do, to perform; (*verursachen*) to cause, to occasion, to induce, to bring about; (*errichten*) to erect, to build, to form, to construct; (*erschaffen*) to create; (*ernennen*) to appoint s. o. s. th.; (*in e-n Zustand versetzen*) to render; (*kosten*) to come to, to amount to; (*in Ordnung bringen*) to tidy, to put to rights, to make up; (*Geschäfte*) to deal, to trade; *sich ~* (*zustande kommen*) to come about, to happen, to appear; (*vorankommen*) to get on, to do well; *sich aus dem Staube ~* to make off; *sich aus e-r Sache etw ~* to attach importance to a matter; *sich die Haare ~* to dress o.'s hair; *sich an etw ~* to apply o. s. to; to begin on, to set about, to start work upon; *sich nichts daraus ~* not to care about s. th.; *sich auf den Weg ~* to set out, to depart; *sich mit etw bekannt ~* to familiarize o. s. with s. th.; *sich viel ~ aus* to care much about; *ängstlich ~* to alarm, to frighten s. o.; *bekannt ~* to publish; to proclaim; to introduce to s. o.; *durstig ~* to cause thirst; *fähig ~* to enable; *fertig ~* to get ready; *fett ~* to fatten; *fröhlich ~* to cheer up; *glatt ~* to smooth, to polish; *jdn glücklich ~* to render s. o. happy; *naß ~* to wet; *es jdm recht ~* to suit everybody; *sauber ~* to clean; *schüchtern ~* to intimidate; *traurig ~* to afflict; *ungültig ~* to invalidate; *zornig ~* to exasperate, to enrage; *zunichte ~* to annihilate, to annul; *Anspruch auf etw ~* to lay claim to s. th.; *Anstrengungen ~* to make efforts; *Aufhebens ~* to make fuss about; *e-n Ausflug ~* to make an excursion; *Besuch ~* to pay a visit; *ein Ende ~* to put an end (to); *Ehre ~* to do hono(u)r; *Erfahrungen ~* to gain experiences; *e-e Eroberung ~* to make a conquest; *e-n Fehler ~* to make a mistake; *Feuer ~* to kindle a fire; *Freude ~* to give pleasure; *Fortschritte ~* to make progress; *Hoffnung ~* to give hope; *Holz ~* to chop wood; *Licht ~* to switch on a light; to light a candle; *Platz ~* to make room, to give way; *Spaß ~* to joke; (*sich freuen an*) to get fun out of; *Schritte ~* (*fig*) to take steps; *Schwierigkeiten ~* to make difficulties; *Umstände ~* to cause trouble; *Verdruß ~* to cause vexation; *e-n Vorschlag ~* to make a proposal; *Zugeständnisse ~* to make concessions; *etw ~ lassen* to have s. th. made, to order s. th.; *das läßt sich ~* that's feasible; *lassen Sie ihn nur ~!* leave him alone for that! *das macht nichts!* that does not matter! never mind! *Am* no matter! *so mach' doch!* do be quick! *mach' fix!* hurry up! look alive! *fam* buck up! *nichts zu ~!* nothing doing! *was ~ Sie?* how do you do? how are you? what are you up to? what are you about? *mach, daß du fortkommst!* get out of here! *Am sl* scram!
Macht *f* power; (*Kraft*) force; (*Tatkraft*) energy; (*Stärke*) strength; arm; (*übermenschliche Kraft*) might; *poet* puissance; (*Einfluß*) influence; control; (*~befugnis*) authority; (*bewaffnete ~*) army, forces *pl*; *an der ~* in power; *mit aller ~* with might and main: *~ der Gewohnheit* force of habit; *~ des Schicksals* force of destiny; *das steht nicht in seiner ~* that's beyond his power; *~ geht vor Recht* might goes before right; *die kriegführenden Mächte* the belligerent powers; **~befugnis** *f* competency, authority; **~bereich** *m* sphere of influence; *jur* jurisdiction; **~ergreifung, ~übernahme** *f* assumption (*od* seizure) of power; **~fülle** *f* authority; **~gebot** *n* authoritative order; **~gier** *f* greed of power; **~haber** *m* ruler; lord; dictator; **~haberisch** *a* despotic; **~kampf** *m* struggle for power; **~los** *a* powerless; **~~igkeit** *f* powerlessness; weakness; **~politik** *f* power-politics; policy of the strong hand; **~probe** *f* trial of strength; **~spruch** *m*, **~wort** *n* command, peremptory order; **~stellung** *f* political power, strong position; **~streben** *n* (*Staat*) imperialism; **~vollkommenheit** *f* authority; *aus eigener ~~* on o.'s own authority.
mächtig *a* powerful, mighty, strong; potent; *min* thick, wide; high; *fam* (*sehr, groß*) very, very much, extremely; enormously, *Am* mighty; (*riesig*) huge, immense; *~ sein* to be master of; *e-r Sprache ~ sein* to know a language perfectly; **~keit** *f* mightiness; *min* thickness.
Machzahl *f aero* Mach number.
Mädchen, Mädel *n* girl; (*gewählter*) maid(en); (*Mädel*) lass, *Am sl* baby, babe, gal, peach; (*Dienst~*) servant(-girl), maid(-servant), girl; *~ für alles* general servant; **~haft** *a* girlish, maidenly; **~handel** *m* white slave traffic; **~kammer** *f* servant's room; **~name** *m* girl's name; (*e-r Frau*) maiden-name; **~raub** *m* rape; **~räuber** *m* ravisher; **~schule** *f* girls' school; (*höhere*) high school for girls; ladies' college; **~zimmer** *n* maid's room.
Mad|e *f* maggot, mite; grub; **~enschraube** *f* grub screw, headless screw; **~ig** *a* maggoty, full of mites; (*Früchte*) worm-eaten.
Madonna *f eccl* the Holy Virgin, the Madonna.
Magazin *n* magazine, depot, store, storeroom, warehouse, storehouse; (*Gewehr*) magazine; (*Zeitschrift*) magazine, periodical, review; **~gehäuse** *n* (*Gewehr*) magazine chamber; **~halter** *m* (*Gewehr*) magazine holder (*od* catch); **~verwalter** *m* store-keeper.
Magd *f* servant, maid(-servant); **~tum** *n* virginity.
Mägdlein *n* little maid, little girl.
Magen *m* stomach; *fam* tummy; (*Tier~*) maw; *verdorbener ~* disordered (*od* upset) stomach; *mit leerem ~ zu Bett gehen* to go to bed on an empty stomach; **~beschwerden** *f pl* indigestion; gastric trouble (*od* disorder); **~bitter** *m* bitters *pl*; **~brennen** *n* heartburn, pyrosis; **~darmkatarrh** *m* gastro-intestinal catarrh; **~drücken** *n* pain in the stomach; **~fieber** *n* gastric fever; **~geschwür** *n* gastric ulcer; **~grube** *f* pit of the stomach; **~knurren** *n* intestinal rumbling; **~krampf** *m* spasm in the stomach; gastrospasm; **~krank** *a* dispeptic; **~krankheit** *f* disorder of the stomach; **~krebs** *m* cancer in the stomach; **~leiden** *n* stomach-complaint; gastropathy; **~saft** *m* gastric juice; **~säure** *f* gastric acid; **~schmerzen** *m pl*, **~weh** *n* stomach-ache; **~stärkend** *a* stomachic; **~stärkung** *f* stomach-cordial; **~tropfen** *m pl* stomach drops *pl*, stomachic (*od* digestive) tonic; **~überfüllung** *f* overloading of the stomach, surfeit; **~verstimmung** *f* gastric disorder, stomach upset; **~wand** *f* gastric wall.
mager *a* thin, lean; (*unzulänglich*) scanty; (*schlank, gering*) slender; (*sparsam*) frugal; (*knochig*) *Am* scrawny; (*dürftig*) meagre, poor; (*Boden*) barren; *~ werden* to emaciate; **~keit** *f* meagreness, leanness; *fig* barrenness; poorness; **~kohle** *f* semi-bituminous coal; **~milch** *f* skim(med) milk; **~~pulver** *n* dried skim milk.
Mag|ie *f* magic; **~ier** *m* magician; **~isch** *a* magic(al); *~~es Auge radio* electron-ray tube, magic eye, cathode-ray tuning indicator.
Magister *m* master; school-master, tutor; *~ der freien Künste* master of arts (M.A.).
Magistrat *m* town council; borough council; **~sperson** *f* town council(l)or; **~ur** *f* town council(l)orship.
Magma *n* magma, ground mass.
Magnat *m* magnate, *Am* tycoon, baron.
Magnesi|a *f* magnesia; **~um** *n* magnesium; **~~fackel** *f* magnesium flare (*od* torch); **~~haltig** *a* containing magnesium; **~~licht** *n* magnesium light; **~~pulver** *n* magnesium powder.
Magnet *m* magnet, magneto (*Abk* mag); *künstlicher ~, natürlicher ~, permanenter ~* artificial magnet, natural magnet, permanent magnet; **~anker** *m el* pole armature; magnet keeper; **~ausschalter** *m* field break switch; **~band** *n* magnetic tape; **~eisen** *n* magnetic iron; **~feld** *n* magnetic field; **~~röhre** *f* magnetron; **~induktor** *m* magneto generator; **~isch** *a* magnetic; *~~e Mine* magnetic mine; **~iseur** *m* magnetist, mesmerist; **~isieren** *tr* to magnetise, *Am* to magnetize; **~ismus** *m* magnetism; **~lautsprecher** *m radio* magnetic loudspeaker; **~nadel** *f* magnetic needle; **~ophon, ~tongerät** *n* magnetic tape recorder, (*tragbar*) portable tape recording apparatus; battery-powered minitape machine; (*mit Drahtspule*) wire recorder; **~ophonbandaufnahme** *f* tape-recording; **~ron** *n* magnetron; **~spule** *f* magnetic coil; **~stahl** *m* magnet steel; **~stein** *m* magnetite; **~tonverfahren** *n* magnetic sound-recording method; **~wicklung** *f*

field winding (*od* coil), magnet coil; **~zünder** *m* magneto; **~zündung** *f* magneto (-electric) ignition.

Mahagoni(holz) *n* mahogany (wood).

Mahd *f* mowing; (*Schwaden*) swath; (*Heuernte*) hay harvest (*od* crop); *zweite ~* second mowing.

Mäh|binder *m* reaper and binder; **~drescher** *m* combined harvester, *Am* combine; harvester thresher; **~en** *tr* to mow, to cut; to reap; **~er** *m* mower, reaper; harvester, haymaker; **~maschine** *f* mowing-machine; reaping-machine, reaper, (*Rasen~~*) mower.

Mahl *n* meal, repast; (*Fest~*) banquet, feast; repast; **~en** *tr* (*Korn*) to grind, to mill; (*zermalmen*) to crush; (*sehr fein*) to pulverize; (*Papier*) to beat; *wer zuerst kommt, mahlt zuerst* first come, first served; **~gang** *m* set of millstones; **~korn** *n* grist; **~stein** *m* millstone; **~strom** *m mar* maelstrom; **~zahn** *m* molar (tooth); **~zeit** *f* meal, repast, *Am* feed.

Mahn|brief *m com* letter requesting payment, request to pay, reminder, dunning letter, *Am* collection letter; tickler; **~en** *tr* (*erinnern*) to remind of; (*er~~*) to admonish, to exhort; (*heftig*) to dun; (*auffordern*) to urge, to demand; (*warnen*) to warn; *zur Vorsicht ~~* to tell to be careful; **~er** *m* admonisher; (*ungestümer ~~*) dun; **~mal** *n* memorial (-stone); **~ung** *f com* reminder, (*dringend*) dunning; (*Er~~*) admonition; (*Warnung*) warning; **~verfahren** *n* dunning proceedings *pl*; **~zettel** *m* reminder, demand (*od* prompt) note, *Am* tickler.

Mähne *f* mane.

Mähre *f* mare; (*schlechtes Pferd*) jade.

Mähr|en *n* Moravia; **~isch** *a* Moravian.

Mai *m* May; *der erste ~* May-day; **~baum** *m* birch; may-pole; **~feier** *f pol* May-day demonstration; **~glöckchen** *n bot* lily of the valley; **~käfer** *m* cockchafer, May-bug.

Maid *f* maid(en).

Mai|land *n* Milan; **~länder** *m* Milanese; **~ländisch** *a* Milanese.

Mainz *n* Mayence.

Mais *m* maize, *Am* Indian corn, corn; *~ rösten Am* to pop; **~feld** *n* maize-field, *Am* corn-field; **~flocke** *f Am* cornflake; **~kolben** *m* corn-cob; **~mehl** *n* Indian meal, *Am* corn meal; **~~brei** *m Am* mush; **~pfannkuchen** *m Am* corn-dodger, corn-cracker. **~schnaps** *m Am* corn-juice.

Maisch|bottich *m* mash-tub; **~e** *f* mash; **~en** *tr* to mash, to mix; **~kessel** *m* mash copper; **~kolonne** *f* beer still; **~würze** *f* mash wort.

Majestät *f* majesty; **~isch** *a* majestic; **~sbeleidigung** *f* lese-majesty.

Major *m* major; *aero* squadron leader; **~an** *m bot* marjoram; **~at** *n* (right of) primogeniture; (*Gut*) entail; **~enn** *a* of (full) age; **~~ität** *f* majority; **~isieren** *tr* to beat by a majority of votes; **~ität** *f* majority.

Majuskel *f* capital letter.

Makel *m* stain, spot, blot; *fig* blemish, fault; **~los** *a* spotless, stainless; *fig* faultless, immaculate.

Mäk|elei *f* carping, fault-finding, censoriousness, *Am* griping; (*wählerisches Wesen*) daintiness; **~elig** *a* fault-finding, censorious; (*wählerisch*) fastidious; (*leckerhaft*) dainty; **~eln** *itr, tr* to find fault with, to carp at, to cavil at (*od* about), *Am fam* to gripe; to pick at; **~ler** *m* fault-finder, cavil(l)er, *Am fam* griper.

Makkaroni *pl* mac(c)aroni.

Makler *m* broker, jobber; **~gebühr** *f* brokerage; **~geschäft** *n* broker's business.

Makrele *f* mackerel.

Makrone *f* macaroon.

Makul|atur *f* waste-paper; **~ieren** *tr* (*Papier*) to (re)pulp; (*Druck*) to print waste.

Mal *n* (*Zeichen*) sign, mark, token; (*Fleck*) spot, stain; stigma; (*Mutter~*) mole; (*Wund~*) scar; (*Grenz~*) boundary; *sport* goal, base; (*Ablauf*) start; base, tee; (*Erinnerungs~*) monument; (*Wahrzeichen*) landmark; (*Zeit*) time; turn; *~ adv* once; just; *dieses* (*e-e*) *~* for once; *ein für alle~* once and for all; *mit e-m ~* all of a sudden, suddenly; *zum ersten ~* for the first time; *ein ums andere ~* alternately, by turns; *besuchen Sie uns doch ~!* come and see us sometime! *denk dir ~!* just imagine! *sieh ~ her!* now look here! *2 mal 5 ist* (*od macht*) *10* twice five are (*od* make) ten; *5 mal 4 ist* (*od macht*) *20* five times four are (*od* make) twenty; **~nehmen** *irr tr* to multiply.

malaiisch *a* Malayan.

Malaria *f* malaria; **~fieber** *n* malarial fever, ague; **~gegend** *f* malarial district; **~kranke(r)** *m* malaria patient; **~kur** *f* malarial therapy, malarialization.

mal|en *tr, itr* to paint; (*porträtieren*) to portray; (*bildlich darstellen*) to represent; (*zeichnen*) to draw; (*skizzieren*) to sketch, to delineate; *nach der Natur ~~* to paint from nature; *sich ~~ lassen* to sit for o.'s portrait, to have o.'s portrait painted; **~er** *m* painter, artist; **~~atelier** *n* painter's studio; **~~ei** *f* painting; (*Gemälde*) picture; **~~farbe** *f* painter's colo(u)r; **~~isch** *a* picturesque; pictorial; artistic; **~~leinwand** *f* canvas; **~kasten** *m* paint-box.

Malteserkreuz *n* Maltese cross.

Malv|e *f* mallow; **~en** *a* mauve.

Malz *n* malt; **~bier** *n* malt beer; **~bonbon** *n* cough lozenge; **~bottich** *m* malt vat; **~darre** *f* malt kiln; **~en** *tr* to malt; **~extrakt** *m* malt extract; **~kaffee** *m* malt coffee; **~schrot** *n* bruised malt; **~schroterei** *f* malt-bruising plant; **~tenne** *f* malt-floor; **~zucker** *m* malt sugar, maltose.

Mälzer *m* maltman; maltster; **~ei** *f* malting, malthouse.

Mama *f* mamma, ma, *fam* mummy, *Am* mom.

Mammon *m* mammon, pelf.

Mammut *n* mammoth.

Mamsell *f* miss; (*Haushälterin*) house-keeper; (*Kellnerin*) waitress.

man *prn* one, we, you, they, people; *~ hat mir gesagt* I was told; *~ sagt so* so they say; *~ munkelt schon lange davon* it's been rumo(u)red for some time.

manch|(er, ~e, ~es) *prn* many a, many a one (*od* person, man); **~e** *pl* some; **~erlei** *a* diverse, different, various; **~es** *a* many a thing, many things *pl*; **~mal** *adv* sometimes, now and again, once in a while.

Manchester *m* (*Stoff, Samt*) velveteen, Manchester velvet; fustian.

Mand|ant *m* mandator; client; customer; **~at** *n* mandate; authorization; (*Anwalt*) brief; (*Behörde*) writ; *parl* seat; *sein ~~ niederlegen* to resign o.'s seat; **~~ar** *m* mandatary, **~~sgebiet** *n* mandated territory; **~~smacht** *f* mandatory power.

Mandarine *f bot* mandarin, tangerine (orange).

Mandel *f* (*Frucht*) almond; (*Drüse*) tonsil; (*Getreidepuppe*) stook; (*Maß*) number of fifteen; (*Garbenhaufen*) shock; stook; *gebrannte ~n* sugared almonds; **~baum** *m* almond-tree; **~blüte** *f* almond blossom; **~drüse** *f* tonsil; **~entzündung** *f* tonsillitis; (*Bräune*) quinsy; **~förmig** *a* almond-shaped, amygdaloid; **~kern** *m* almond kernel.

Mandoline *f* mandolin(e).

Mandrill *m* (*Affenart*) mandrel.

Mandschurei *f* Manchuria.

Manege *f* (circus) ring; arena; riding--school.

Mangan *n* manganese; **~eisen** *n* ferromanganese; **~erz** *n* manganese ore; **~haltig** *a* manganiferous; **~it** *m* manganite; **~sauer** *a* manganate of; **~säure** *f* manganic acid; **~stahl** *m* manganese steel.

Mange(l) *f* mangle, rolling-press, calender; **~brett** *n* mangling-board; **~n** *tr* to mangle; **~holz** *n* calender--roller.

Mangel *m* want (*an* of), need; (*Knappheit*) shortness, deficiency, dearth (of); (*Fehlen*) lack, absence; (*Fehler*) fault, defect, flaw, shortcoming; (*Nachteil*) drawback; (*Armut*) poverty; *an etw ~ haben* (*od leiden*) to be in want of; *aus ~ an, mangels* for want of; **~beruf** *m* critical occupation; **~erscheinung** *f med* deficiency symptom; **~haft** *a* (*fehlerhaft*) faulty, defective; (*unbefriedigend*) unsatisfactory, poor; (*unzureichend*) inadequate; (*unvollständig*) incomplete; **~haftigkeit** *f* defectiveness; faultiness; deficiency; imperfection; **~krankheit** *f* deficiency disease, disease of malnutrition; illness due to vitamin deficiency *od* malnutrition; **~material** *n* deficiency materials *pl;* **~n** *itr imp* to be wanting; to want; to fail, to lack; *es mangelt mir an* I am in want of, I am short of; **~s** *prp* in default of; **~waren** *f pl* goods *pl* in short supply, scarce goods *pl*, short commodities *pl*.

Mangold *m bot* beet.

Mani|e *f* mania; **~sch** *a* manic; *~~-depressives Irresein* manic depressive insanity.

Manier *f* manner, habit, fashion, way; (*Betragen*) deportment; (*Stil*) style; **~en** *pl* manners *pl* (polite, engaging, etc); **~iert** *a* mannered, affected; **~~heit** *f* mannerism; **~lich** *a* mannerly, polite; civil; **~lichkeit** *f* civility, politeness.

Manifest *n* manifest(o); **~ieren** *tr* to manifest, to declare.

Maniküre *f* (*Hand- u. Nagelpflege*) manicure; (*Person*) manicurist; **~n** *tr* to manicure.

Manko *n* defect, deficiency; (*Fehlbetrag*) deficit.

Mann *m* man; (*Gatte*) husband; (*Soldat*) soldier, man; *der gemeine ~* the common people; the man in the street, *Am* Mr. Citizen; *~ für ~* man for man; *~ gegen ~* hand to hand; *ein ~, ein Wort* an honest man is as good as his word; *seinen ~ stellen* to stand up to it like a man; *Waren an den ~ bringen* to dispose of goods; *wenn Not am ~ ist* if the worst comes to the worst; *der ~ auf der Straße* the man in the street; *~s genug sein* to be a match for it; *ein gemachter ~* a made man; *so viel auf den ~* so much a head; *mit ~ u. Maus sinken* to sink with all hands on board; *an den rechten ~ kommen* to come to the right man; **~bar** *a* marriageable, pubescent, virile; (*Mädchen*) nubile; **~~keit** *f* manhood, womanhood; puberty, virility;

~esalter *n* manhood; ~eskraft *f* manly vigo(u)r, virility; ~esschwäche *f* impotence; ~esstamm *m* male line; ~eswort *n* word of a man; ~(e)szucht *f* discipline; ~haft *a* manly; ~~igkeit *f* manliness; ~heit *f* virility, manhood; ~loch *n tech* manhole; ~sbild *n* male; ~schaft *f* personnel; gang; body of men; force; *mil* (enlisted) men *pl*, ranks *pl*; (*Schiff*) crew; *sport* team; ~~sdienstgrade *m pl* the rank and file soldiers *pl*; ~~sersatz *m mil* troop replacements *pl*; ~~sführer *m sport* captain; ~~sgeist *m* team spirit; ~~sräume *m pl* living quarters *pl*; ~~srennen *n sport* team race; ~~stransportwagen *m mil* (armo(u)red) troop-transport car (*od* troop carrier); ~~sunterkünfte *f pl* barracks *pl*; ~shoch *a* as tall as a man; ~shöhe *f* man's height; ~sleute *pl*, ~svolk *n* men-folk; ~stoll *a* nymphomaniac, mad about men; ~~heit *f* nymphomania; ~weib *n* virago, mannish woman; amazon.

Männ|chen *n* little man; (*Tiere*) male; (*Vögel*) cock; *aero* (*Kunstflugfigur*) vertical stall, whipstall; tail slide; ~~ *machen* to sit up and beg; ~~ *zeichnen* to doodle; ~er *m pl* men; ~~gesangverein *m* men's glee club; ~~kleidung *f* men's clothing; ~~welt *f* male sex; ~lich *a* male, masculine; (*mannhaft*) manly; ~~keit *f* manliness, manhood.

mannig|fach, ~faltig *a* manifold, various; ~faltigkeit *f* variety, multiplicity.

Manometer *n* pressure ga(u)ge.

Manöv|er *n* manœuvre, *Am meist* maneuver; (*List*) trick; (*Truppenübungen*) field-practice, manœuvres *pl*; ~erbombe *f* dummy bomb; ~~gelände *n* manœuvre area; ~rieren *tr* to manœuvre; (*Schiff*) to handle; ~rierfähigkeit *f* manœuvrability; ~rierunfähig *a* out of control; disabled.

Mansarde *f* garret, attic; top floor, mansard; ~ndach *n* mansard roof; ~nfenster *n* dormer-window, attic-window; ~nwohnung *f* lodgings on the top floor; ~nzimmer *n* attic, top room.

mansch|en *itr* (*planschen*) to paddle, to dabble; to splash about; (*mischen*) to mix (up); ~erei *f* paddling; dabbling; (*Mischung*) mixture, muddle; mess.

Manschette *f* cuff; *tech* collar; packing ring; ~n *haben fam* to funk; to be afraid (*vor* of); ~nknöpfe *m pl* sleeve-links *pl*.

Mantel *m* cloak, coat; (*loser* ~ *ohne Ärmel*) mantle; (*Winter*~) overcoat, greatcoat; *tech* jacket, case, casing, shell; (*Muffe*) sleeve; *math* convex surface; (*Reifen*) outer cover; *com* bond (without the coupon sheet); *fig* mantle; *den* ~ *nach dem Winde hängen* to set o.'s sails to the wind; to trim o.'s sails according to the wind; ~aufschlag *m* lapel; ~blech *n* shell plate; ~geschoß *n* metallic cartridge; ~kragen *m* coat collar; ~manschette *f* (*beim Reifen*) blowout patch; ~riemen *m* cloak strap; ~sack *m* valise, portmanteau; ~tarif *m* skeleton agreement; ~vertrag *m* omnibus agreement.

Mantille *f* mantilla.

Manu|al *n* note-book; field book, manual; (*Musik*) keyboard; ~ell *a* manual; ~~*er Fallschirm* manually operated parachute; ~faktur *f* (*Erzeugnis*) manufacture; (*Fabrik*) factory; ~~waren *f pl* manufactured goods, dry goods *pl*; ~skript *n* manuscript; *typ* copy; (*Film*~~, *Drehbuch*) script, scenario; *als* ~~ *gedruckt* privately printed; ~~abteilung *f radio Am* script department.

Mappe *f* (*Akten*~) portfolio; brief-case; document case; leather wrapper; (*Schreib*~) writing-case; folder; (*Schul*~) schoolbag, satchel; (*Sammel*~) file.

Mär(e) *f* report, tale; story; news *pl mit sing*, tidings *pl*.

Märchen *n* fairy-tale; *fig* story; (*Lüge*) fib; ~buch *n* book of fairy-tales; ~haft *a* fabulous, legendary; *fig* fictitious; ~land *n* wonderland, dreamland.

Marder *m* marten; ~pelz *m* marten-skin.

Margarete *f* Margaret, Margery, Marjory.

Margarine *f* margarine.

Marg(u)erite *f bot* marguerite.

Maria *f* Mary, May.

Marien|bild *n* image of the Virgin Mary; ~fest *n* Lady Day; ~glas *n* mica, selenite; ~käfer *m* lady-bird, *Am* lady-bug; ~kirche *f* Our Lady's church; ~kult *m* Mariolatry.

Marine *f* marine; (*Schiffswesen*) shipping; (*Kriegs*~) navy; Royal Navy (*Abk* R. N.), *Am* U. S. Navy (*Abk* U. S. N.); ~akademie *f* naval academy; ~artillerie *f* naval artillery; ~attaché *m* Naval Attaché; ~aufklärer *m aero* naval reconnaissance plane; ~blau *a* navy; marine-blue; ~flak *f* naval A. A. artillery; navy anti-aircraft; ~flieger *m* naval aviator; naval aviation pilot; ~flugstützpunkt *m* naval air base; ~flugwesen *n* Fleet Air Arm; naval aviation; ~flugzeug *n* seaplane; naval plane; navy aircraft; ~funkstelle *f* naval radio station; ~infanterie *f* marines *pl*; ~ingenieur *m* Engineer sub-lieutenant (N); naval engineer, naval engineer officer; ~lazarett *n* navy hospital; ~leitung *f* Naval Command Staff; *Am* Navy Department; ~luftschiff *n* naval airship; ~minister *m Engl* First Lord of the Admiralty; *Am* Secretary of the Navy; ~ministerium *n Engl* Admiralty; *Am* Navy Department; ~offizier *m* naval officer; ~politik *f* naval policy; ~reserve *f* naval reserve; ~sanitätswesen *n* naval medical service; ~schule *f* naval training school, ~soldat *m* marine; ~station *f* naval base; ~streitkräfte, ~truppen *f pl* marines *pl*; *Am* marine corps; ~werft *f* naval (dock)yard; ~zahlmeister *m* paymaster (N), (N) accountant officer.

marinieren *tr* to marinate, to pickle.

Marionette *f* marionette, (wire-) puppet; ~nregierung *f* puppet government; ~nspieler *m* wire-puller; ~ntheater *n* puppet-show; puppet theatre.

Mark *n anat* marrow, medulla; *bot* pith, pulp; (*Kern, Innerstes*) core; (*Wesen*) essence; ~ *f* (*Grenzgebiet*) frontier, boundary, marches *pl*; (*Geldstück*) mark; *ins* ~ *treffen* to cut to the quick; *das geht mir durch* ~ *u. Bein* that thrills me to the marrow; ~ant *a* characteristic; (*in die Augen fallend*) striking; (*gut bezeichnet*) (well-)(-)marked; ~erschütternd *a* blood-curdling; ~graf *m* margrave; ~gräfin *f* margravine; ~ig *a* marrowy, pithy; strong, vigorous; ~klößchen *n pl* (*Küche*) marrow-balls *pl*; ~knochen *m* marrow-bone; ~stein *m* boundary-stone; *fig* land-mark, milestone; ~ung *f* village bounds *pl*.

Marke *f* (*Zeichen*) mark, sign, token; designation; (*Signal, Bake*) beacon; mark; (*Kennziffer*) index; (*Handels*~) trade-mark; (*Waren*~) brand, sort, description; grade, kind; (*Qualität*) quality; (*Type*) type; (*Auto, radio etc*) make; (*Kontroll*~) check, ticket; (*Brief*~) stamp; (*Spiel*~) counter, chip; (*Wein*) growth, vintage; (*Rationierung*) ration ticket, coupon; ~nalbum *n* stamp album; ~nartikel *m* trade-marked goods *pl*, branded articles *pl*; ~nbezeichnung *f* trade-mark, brand; ~nerzeugnisse *n pl* branded commodities *pl*; ~nfrei *a* non-rationed, coupon-free; ~nname *m* trade-name; ~npflichtig *a* rationed; ~nschutzgesetz *n* Trade Marks' Registration Act; ~nware *f* proprietary article.

Marketender *m* sutler; ~in *f* canteen-woman; ~ei *f* canteen, military (*od* naval *od* air force) stores *pl*; *Engl* Naafi (= Navy, Army, Air Force Institutes), *Am* post exchange (*Abk* PX); ~waren *f pl* goods *pl* in an army canteen.

markier|en *tr* to mark; (*mit Zeichen versehen*) to sign; (*bezeichnen*) to indicate; (*mit Kennzeichen versehen*) to earmark; (*kennzeichnen als*) to label, to stamp (*als* as); (*Waren*) to brand; (*ausersehen*) to designate; (*genau abgrenzen, definieren*) to define; (*umreißen*) to outline; (*Fahrrinne, Flugweg bezeichnen*) to beacon; (*hervorheben, betonen*) to stress, to accentuate; (*Atom kenntlich machen*) to tag; *fig* (*simulieren, vortäuschen*) to simulate, *fam* to put on; ~ung *f* marking; designation; delimination; beaconing, signal(l)ing; ~~sbake *f* marker beacon; ~~sscheibe *f* disk marker; ~~ssender *m aero radio* marker beacon; ~~sstrich *m* mark; ~~svorrichtung *f* marker; *film* notcher.

Markise *f* awning, blind.

Markt *m* market; (*Absatz*~) outlet; (*Ort*) market-place; (*Geschäft*) business, trade; (*Jahr*~) fair; *aufnahmefähiger* ~ broad market; *heimischer* ~ home (*od* domestic) market; *schwarzer* ~ black market; *auf den* ~ *bringen* to put on the market, to put out; *auf den* ~ *kommen* to come on the market; ~analyse *f* market investigation; ~beobachtung *f* market inquiry; ~bericht *m* market report; (*Börse*) quotation; ~bude *f* booth, stall; ~en *itr* to bargain (*um* for) to haggle; ~fähig *a* sal(e)able, marketable; ~flecken *m* small market-town; ~forschung *f* market(ing) research; ~gängig *a* current, marketable; ~gefüge *n* market structure; ~halle *f* market hall, covered market, indoor market; ~korb *m* market basket; ~krämer *m* stall keeper; ~lage *f* state of the market, market condition; ~ordnung *f* market regulations *pl*; ~platz *m* market-place; ~preis *m* market-price; *heutiger* ~~ current price; ~sachverständiger *m* marketing expert; ~schreier *m* (*Ausrufer*) market crier, booster, puffer; (*Quacksalber*) quack, mountebank; (*billiger Jakob*) Cheap Jack; ~~ei *f* quackery, puffing, *Am* ballyhoo; ~~isch *a* showy, charlatan; ~schwankung *f* fluctuation of the market; ~stand *m* market stand; ~tag *m* market-day; ~tasche *f* market-(ing-)bag, shopping bag; portfolio, briefcase; ~weib *n* market woman; ~wert *m* current value.

Markus *m* (*Name*) Mark.

Marmelade *f* jam; (*Apfelsinen*~) marmalade.

Marmor *m* marble; ~artig *a* marmoraceous; ~bruch *m* marble-quarry; ~ieren *tr* to marble, to vein; ~n *a* (of) marble; ~platte *f* marble-slab; ~säule *f* marble-column; ~**stein** *m* marble-stone; ~**treppe** *f* marble stairs *pl*.

marod|e *a* knocked-up, weary, exhausted, tired; ill; ~**eur** *m* marauder; ~**ieren** *itr* to pillage.

Marokk|aner *m* inhabitant of Morocco; ~**anisch** *a* Moroccan; ~**o** *n* Morocco.

Marone *f* sweet (*od* edible) chestnut.

Maroquin *n* marocco.

Marotte *f* fancy, caprice, whim; (*Steckenpferd*) hobby, fad.

Mar|quis *m* marquis; ~**quise** *f* marchioness.

Mars *m mar* top; ~**rahe** *f* topsail-yard; ~**segel** *n* topsail; ~**stange** *f* topmast.

Marsch *m* march; hike, tramp; ~ *f* (*Land*) marsh, fen; ~*!* march! ~ ~*!* double! ~ *ohne Tritt* route step; *auf dem* ~ en route, marching; *in* ~ *setzen* to move, to start; *jdm den* ~ *blasen fig* to give s. o. a piece of o.'s mind; ~**abstand** *m* distance between march units; ~**bataillon** *n* battalion in waiting, *Am* marching battalion; ~**bauer** *m* fen land farmer, marshman; ~**befehl** *m* march orders *pl*; ~**bereit** *a* ready to move; ~**boden** *m* marshy soil; ~**breite** *f* width of marching column; ~**disziplin** *f* march discipline; ~**fähig** *a* able to march; ~**gepäck** *n* baggage, full pack; ~**geschwindigkeit** *f* rate of marching, *aero, mar* cruising speed; ~**gliederung** *f* march formation; ~**ieren** *itr* to march; ~~ *lassen* to march; ~**ig** *a* marshy; ~**kolonne** *f* route column; ~**kompaß** *m* prismatic (*od* lensatic) compass; ~**krank** *a* unable to march, footsore; ~**leistung** *f* marching performance; ~**mäßig** *a* in marching order; ~**ordnung** *f* order of march; ~~*!* break step! ~**pause** *f* rest on the march; ~**richtung** *f* direction of march; ~**sicherung** *f* protection on the march; ~**spitze** *f* head of column; ~**stiefel** *m* lace boot; ~**tag** *m* day of march; ~**tempo** *n* rate of marching, ~**tiefe** *f* depth of a marching column; ~**verpflegung** *f* supply on the march; ~**ziel** *n* destination, march objective; ~**zucht** *f* march discipline.

Marschall *m* marshal; ~**stab** *m* marshal's baton.

Marstall *m* royal stud, royal stables *pl*.

Marter *f* torment, pang; (*Folter*) torture; ~**n** *tr* to torment; (*foltern*) to rack, to torture; ~**pfahl** *m* stake; ~**tod** *m* martyr's death; death by torture; ~**voll** *a* excruciating; ~**werkzeug** *n* instrument of torture.

Martha *f* (*Name*) Martha; Patty, Matty.

martialisch *a* martial.

Martin|i, ~***stag*** *m* Martinmas; ~**sgans** *f* Martinmas goose; ~**verfahren** *n* Martin process, open-hearth process.

Märtyrer *m* martyr; ~**tum, Martyrium** *n* martyrdom.

Marxis|mus *m* Marxism, ~**t** *m*, ~**tisch** *a* Marxian.

März *m* March.

Marzipan *n od m* marchpane, marzipan.

Masch|e *f* (*Strick~*) stitch; (*Netz~*) mesh; (*Schleife*) bow; (*Trick*) *fam* trick, scheme, cunning device; ~**endraht** *m* chicken (*od* screen) wire; ~**enfest** *a* (*Strumpf*) ladderproof; ~**enwerk** *n* network; ~**ig** *a* meshed, meshy netted; reticulated.

Maschine *f* machine, engine; (*Gerät*) implement, appliance, contrivance; (*Apparat*) machinery, apparatus; (*Dresch~*) thrashing-machine; (*Näh~*) sewing-machine; (*Schreib~*) type-writer; (*Dampf~*) steam-engine; (*Flug~*) aeroplane, aircraft, airplane, plane; (*Auto*) car; *mit* ~*n bearbeiten* to machine; *auf der* ~ *schreiben* to type (-write); ~**ll** *a* mechanical; ~~*e Bearbeitung* machining; ~**nanlage** *f* plant; ~**nantrieb** *m* machine drive; ~**nbau** *m* engine building; ~~**er** *m* machine builder; mechanical engineer; ~**nfabrik** *f* machine factory, engine works *pl*; ~**nfett** *n* lubricant; ~**nflak** *f mil* quick-firing A.A. gun; ~**ngarn** *n* machine-spun yarn, twist; ~**ngewehr** *n* machine gun; (*leichtes*) Bren gun; *mit* ~~ *beschießen* to machinegun; *aero* to strafe; ~~**bedienung** *f* machine-gun crew; ~~**bock** *m* machine-gun support; ~~**drehkranz** *m* rotating gun ring; ~~**nest** *n* pill-box; ~~**salve** *f* burst of machine-gun fire; ~~**schlitten** *m* machine-gun sleigh mount; ~~**schütze** *m* gunner; ~~**stand** *m* emplacement cupola, machine-gun post; *aero* turret; ~~**wagen** *m* machine-gun cart; ~~**zielfernrohr** *n* machine-gun telescopic sight; ~~**zug** *m mil* M.G. platoon; ~**nhaus** *n* power house; ~**nkanone** *f* shell gun; automatic cannon; pom-pom; ~**nleistung** *f* mechanical power; ~**nmäßig** *a* machinelike, mechanical; ~**nmeister** *m* machinist; engine-driver; *theat* stage mechanic; ~**nmensch** *m* robot; ~**nöl** *n* machine (*od* lubricating) oil; ~**npistole** *f* submachine gun, tommy gun; sten gun; *Am sl* burp gun; ~~**nschütze** *m* tommy gunner; ~**nraum** *m* engine room; ~**nsatz** *m* generating plant; *typ* machine composition; ~**nschaden** *m* engine trouble; ~**nschlosser** *m* engine fitter; ~**nschmiere** *f* lubricating grease; ~**nschreiben** *irr itr* to type(-write); *blindes* ~~ touch typing; ~**nschreiber** *m*, ~~**in** *f* typist; ~**nschrift** *f* typescript; ~**nsender** *m* automatic transmitter; machine transmitter; ~**nsetzer** *m typ* operator, machine compositor; ~**nsockel** *m* engine base; ~**ntelegraph** *m* automatic (*od* machine) telegraph; ~**nwaffe** *f* automatic fire-arm; ~**nzeitalter** *n* Machine Age; ~**rie** *f* machinery; *Am* gadgetry.

Maschinist *m* machinist; engine driver; engineer; mechanic; mechanical engineer.

Maser *f* spot, speckle, mark; (*Holz*) vein, knot; ~**holz** *n* curled (*od* veined) wood; ~**ig** *a* speckled; veined; ~**n** *pl* measles *pl*, rubeola; ~**n** *tr* to vein, to grain; ~**ung** *f* speckling, graining, veining; periodical flame effect.

Mask|e *f* mask; (*Verkleidung*) disguise; (*Fechten*) visor, face-guard; *theat* make-up; (*Tarnung*) camouflage; *film* face shield mat; ~**enball** *m* masked ball; fancy dress ball; ~**enkleid** *n* fancy dress; ~**enverleih** *m* hire of theatrical properties *pl*; ~**erade** *f* masquerade; ~**ieren** *tr* to mask, to disguise; to camouflage; to conceal, to cover; ~~ *r* to put on a mask; ~**iert** *a* in disguise.

Maskulinum *n* masculine (noun).

Maß *n* measure; (*Größe*) size; (*Ausdehnung*) extent, dimension; (*Normal~*) standard; ga(u)ge; (*höchstes* ~) ceiling; (*Eben~*) proportion; (*Verhältnis~*) index, rate, scale; (*Grad*) degree; (*Gattung, Art*) manner; (*Messung*) measurement; (*Schranken*) bounds *pl*, limit; (*Bier*) litre; *mus* bar, time; (*Vers*) metre, measure; (*Mäßigung*) moderation, decorum, propriety; *nach* ~ *machen* to make to order; ~ *nehmen* to take measure for, to take the measurement of; *nach* ~ *gemacht* made (*od* tailored) to measure, bespoke, *Am* custom-made; *das* ~ *vollmachen* to fill the cup to the brim; ~ *halten* to be moderate; *in hohem* ~*e* in a high degree; *über alle* ~*en* exceedingly, excessively; beyond measure; *in großem* ~*e* on a large scale; *in gewissem* ~*e* in a measure; *in dem* ~*e wie* in (the same) measure as; *in dem* ~*e, daß* to such a degree that; ~**abteilung** *f* bespoke department; ~**analyse** *f* volumetric analysis; ~**anzug** *m* bespoke suit, *Am* custom suit; ~**arbeit** *f* made to measure; ~**einheit** *f* unit of measure; ~**gabe** *f* measure, proportion; *nach* ~~ *von* according to; in proportion to; *mit der* ~~, *daß* provided that; ~**gebend,** ~**geblich** *a* authoritative, standard, decisive, conclusive; (*zuverläßlich*) reliable; ~~*e Stelle* competent office; ~~ *sein* to prevail; to set the standards of; to take the lead in; *seine Ansicht ist für mich nicht* ~~ I don't go by his opinion; ~**gefäß** *n* measuring vessel; ~**gerecht** *a* true to size; ~**halten** *irr itr* to observe moderation; to keep within limits; ~**kleidung** *f* clothes *pl* made to measure, *Am* custom clothes *pl*; ~**krug** *m* tankard, mug; ~**lieb(chen)** *n bot* daisy; ~**los** *a* (*unmäßig*) immoderate; (*grenzenlos*) boundless; (*übertrieben*) exorbitant, excessive; (*überspannt*) extravagant; ~~**igkeit** *f* want of moderation; recklessness; extravagance; ~**nahme,** ~**regel** *f* measure, step; (*Hilfsmittel*) expedient; (*durchgreifende*) ~~*n treffen* to take (sweeping) measures; *geeignete* ~~*n ergreifen* to take suitable action; ~~*n zur Absatzsteigerung* sales promotion; ~**regeln** *tr* to inflict disciplinary punishment on; (*tadeln*) to reprimand; ~**regelung** *f* disciplinary punishment; reprimand; ~**schneider** *m* bespoke tailor, *Am* custom tailor; ~~**ei** *f* tailoring to measure; ~**stab** *m* (*Meterstab*) yard measure, ruler; measure, rule; (*Karten*) scale; *tech* ga(u)ge; *fig* standard; (*Prüfstein*) criterion; *in großartigem* ~~ on a gigantic scale; *in verkleinertem* ~~ scaled down, on a reduced scale; *natürlicher* ~~ plain scale; full size; *e-n* ~~ *anlegen an* to apply a standard to; ~~**gerecht** *a* in correct scale; ~**stäblich** *a* according to scale; (*natürliche Größe*) full size; ~**stiefel** *m pl* boots *pl* made to measure, *Am* custom-made boots *pl*; ~**system** *n* system of measurement; ~**verhältnisse** *n pl* dimensions *pl*; ~**voll** *a* moderate; ~**werk** *n arch* tracery; ~**zahl** *f* unit of measurement.

Mass|age *f* massage; ~**eur** *m* masseur; ~**euse** *f* masseuse; ~**ieren** *tr* to massage; (*Truppen*) to mass.

Masse *f* mass; (*Haupt~*) bulk; (*Klumpen*) lump; (*Anhäufung*) *math* aggregate; (*körperliche* ~) substance; material mass; (*Menge*) quantity; lots *pl* (of), a great deal (of); (*Haufen*) heap(s *pl*); pile; (*Menschen*) the masses *pl*, the crowd, the multitude, the people; (*Gedränge*) crowd, drove; throng; *jur* (*Vermögen*) assets *pl*, property; (*Erb~, Konkurs~*) estate; (*Gießerei*) dry sand; (*Keramik*) paste; (*Papier*) pulp; *el* (*Erdung*) ground, earth; (*Material*) material; (*Partie, Satz, Stoß*) batch; *die breite* ~ the rank and file *pl*; *in großen* ~*n* in large numbers, in droves; *in* ~*n produzieren* to mass-produce; *e-e* ~*e Geld* lots of money; *kritische* ~ (*phys*) critical mass; ~**nabsatz** *m* wholesale (selling); ~**nabwurf** *m aero* salvo bombing; ~**nanfertigung** *f* mass production; ~**nangriff** *m* massed attack, massive raid; **~nanziehung** *f* gravitation; **~narbeitseinstellung** *f* general strike; **~narbeitslosigkeit** *f* mass unemployment; **~nartikel** *m* wholesale article, articles made in bulk; **~naufgebot** *n* general levy; **~naufmarsch** *m* mass rally; **~n-ausgleich** *m aero* weight balance; **~naussperrung** *f* general lock-out; **~nbeförderung** *f* transport in bulk; **~nbefragung** *f Am* public opinion poll; **~ndemonstration** *f* mass demonstration; **~nentlassungen** *f pl* mass dismissals *pl*; **~nerzeugung, ~nfabrikation, ~nherstellung, ~nproduktion** *f* mass production, production in bulk; **~nfallschirmabsprung** *m mil* mass-jump; **~nflucht** *f* mass-flight; **~ngrab** *n* common grave; **~ngüter** *n pl* bulk articles *pl*; **~nhaft** *a* in large quantities, wholesale; numerous; **~nkundgebung** *f* mass-meeting, *Am* rally; **~nmoment** *n phys* moment of inertia; **~nmord** *m* general massacre; butchery; **~npsychologie** *f* mass psychology; **~npsychose** *f* mass psychosis; **~nquartier** *n* billets *pl* for large numbers; **~nstreik** *m* general strike; **~nsuggestion** *f* mass suggestion; **~nteilchen** *n phys* corpuscle; **~nträgheit** *f* mass moment of inertia; **~nverbrauch** *m* consumption in bulk; **~nverhaftungen** *f pl* wholesale arrests *pl*; **~nversammlung** *f* mass-meeting, *Am* rally; **~nwanderung** *f* mass movement; **~nweise** *adv* in large numbers, wholesale; **~nwirkung** *f* mass action; **~nzerstörung** *f* mass destruction; **~verwalter** *m jur* Official Receiver.

Masseleisen *n* pig iron.

mass|ig *a* bulky, voluminous; solid; **~iv** *a* massive, solid.

mäßig *a* temperate, moderate, *Am* conservative; (*nüchtern*) sober; (*enthaltsam*) frugal; (*Preis*) moderate, reasonable; (*mittel~*) middling; (*Schule*) poor, mediocre; (*Gesundheit*) fair; **~en** *tr* to moderate; (*mildern*) to mitigate, to soften, to assuage; (*beschränken*) to restrain, to curb, to check; (*Geschwindigkeit*) to slacken; (*Preis, Stolz, Steuer*) to abate; *~~ r* to moderate o. s., to restrain o. s., to control o. s., to calm o. s.; *gemäßigte Zone* temperate zone; **~keit** *f* moderation, frugality; (*Trinken, Gefühlsäußerung*) temperance; **~keitsverein** *m* temperance society; **~ung** *f* moderation; self-control; restraint.

Mast *m* mast; (*Stange*) pole; (*freitragender ~*) pylon; *aero* mooring mast, tower; *~ f* mast; (*Futter*) pig's food, beech nuts *pl*, acorns *pl*; **~baum** *m* (*seemännisch nur: Mast*) mast; *vordere(r) ~~* fore-mast; *hintere(r) ~~* mizzen-mast; **~darm** *m* rectum; **~hühnchen** *n* fat pullet; **~ochs** *m* fattened ox; **~kalb** *n* fatted calf; **~korb** *m* crow's nest, masthead; **~kur** *f* fattening diet; **~schwein** *n* fattened hog; **~spitze** *f* top of pole, masthead; **~vieh** *n* fattened cattle.

mästen *tr* to feed, to fat; (*~ r*) to fatten

Mastix *m* mastic.

*

Mater *f* matrix, *fam* mat.

Material *n* material; (*Stoff*) *fig* substance; (*Gerät*) implements *pl*, apparatus; (*Vorrat*) stores *pl*, stock; (*Arbeits~*) stock-in-trade; (*rollendes ~*) *rail* rolling-stock; (*Ausrüstung*) matériel equipment, requisites *pl*, fittings *pl*; (*Börse*) offerings *pl*; **~ien** *n pl* materials *pl*; (*~waren*) groceries *pl*; **~beanspruchung** *f* stress; **~bearbeitung** *f* processing of material; **~bedarf** *m* consumption of material; **~beschaffenheit** *f* quality (*od* condition) of material; **~beschaffung** *f* procurement; **~eigenschaft** *f* property of material; **~einkäufe** *m pl* material purchases *pl*; **~ersparnis** *f* economy of materials; **~fehler** *m* defect of material; fault (*od* flaw) in material; **~isieren** *tr* to materialize; **~ismus** *m* materialism; **~ist** *m* materialist; **~~isch** *a* materialistic; **~knappheit** *f* stringency of materials: **~kontrolle** *f* testing of material; **~kosten** *pl* cost of material; **~krieg** *m* war of materials; **~lager** *n mil* dump; **~preis** *m* price of material; **~prüfung** *f* testing of materials; **~sammelstelle** *f* salvage dump; **~schaden** *m* fault (*od* flaw) in material; **~schlacht** *f* battle of machinery; **~schuppen** *m* store shed; **~verbrauch** *m* consumption of materials; **~waren** *f pl* groceries *pl*, colonial produce, *Am* drugs *pl*; **~~handlung** *f* grocer's shop, *Am* grocery; **~~händler** *m* grocer.

Materie *f* matter, stuff; (*Gegenstand*) subject; (*Eiter*) matter; **~ll** *a* material; materialistic; (*geldlich*) financial.

Mathemat|ik *f* mathematics *pl mit sing* (*Abk* maths); **~iker** *m* mathematician; **~isch** *a* mathematical.

Mathilde *f* Matilda, Tilda.

Matjeshering *m* white herring.

Matratze *f* mattress.

Mätresse *f* (kept) mistress.

Matrikel *f* register, roll.

Matrize *f* matrix; (*Stempel*) die; (*Schablone*) stencil; (*Negativ*) master negative; **~nschreiben** *n* stencil cutting.

Matrone *f* matron.

Matrose *m* sailor; (*Dienstgrad*) ordinary seaman; **~nanzug** *m* sailor suit; **~nbluse** *f* sailor blouse; **~njacke** *f* reefer-jacket, pea-jacket; **~nkragen** *m* sailor collar; **~nlied** *n* sailor's song; **~schenke** *f* sailor's inn.

Matsch *m* (*breiweiche Masse*) squash, pulp; (*Schlamm*) mud; sludge, slush; (*Kot*) mire; (*Kartenspiel*) capot; **~en** *itr* to squash; to capot; **~ig** *a* squashy; muddy, slushy; pulpy.

matt *a* (*glanzlos*) mat(t), dull, lustreless, unpolished; (*dumpf*) dead, dull-sounding, muffled; (*körperlich*) tired, weak, faint, feeble, exhausted, flabby; (*Augen*) dim; (*Glas*) ground; (*Farbe*) dull; (*Licht*) soft; (*Stimme*) faint; (*Metall*) pasty, tarnished; *com* dull, lifeless, slackening, stagnant; (*Gold*) dead; (*Silber*) frosted; (*Kugel*) spent; (*Schach*) mate (at chess); (*geschmacklos*) dull, insipid; (*flau*) flat; (*Witz*) pointless; *~ setzen* to (check-)mate; **~anstrich** *m* lustreless paint; **~eisen** *n* white pig iron; **~farbe** *f* deadening colo(u)r; **~gelb** *a* pale-yellow, cream; **~geschliffen** *a* ground, frosted; **~glanz** *m* dull finish; **~glas** *n* ground (*od* frosted) glass; **~glasur** *f* (*Keramik*) mat glaze; **~gold** *n* dead gold; **~heit, ~igkeit** *f* tiredness; debility, feebleness, faintness; exhaustion; *com* flatness, dul(l)ness; **~ieren** *tr* to tarnish, to dull, to deaden; to give a mat surface to; (*Glas*) to grind; **~kohle** *f* dull coal; **~scheibe** *f* ground-glass plate, focusing screen; **~schleifen** *irr tr* to grind, to frost; **~vergoldung** *f* dead-gilding; **~weiß** *a* dull white.

Matte *f* (*Wiese*) meadow; *poet* mead; (*Decke*) mat.

Matthäus *m* Matthew; Mat; **~evangelium** *n* Gospel according to St. Matthew.

Matze(n) *f* (*m*) unleavened bread.

Mätzchen *n* tricks *pl*; *~ machen* to play the fool; to be fussy.

Mauer *f* wall; **~absatz** *m* offset; **~anschlag** *m* poster; **~assel** *f* wood-louse; **~blümchen** *n* wall-flower; **~brecher** *m* battering-ram; **~brüstung** *f* cornice; **~kalk** *m* mortar; **~kranz** *m* mural crown; **~n** *tr* to build, to make a wall; *itr* (*Kartenspiel*) not to risk anything; **~pfeffer** *m bot* stone-crop; **~schwalbe** *f* black martin, swift; **~stein** *m* (building) stone; (building) brick; **~werk** *n* stonework, masonry.

Mauke *f med* malanders *pl*.

Maul *n* mouth; (*Schnauze*) muzzle; (*Schweine~*) snout; *ein böses ~* malicious tongue; *er hat immer das große ~* he always talks big; *das ~ nicht auftun* not to open o.'s lips; *er ist nicht aufs ~ gefallen* he is not tongue-tied; he is always ready with an answer; *ein ~ machen* to pout; *halt's ~!* hold your tongue! shut up! *e-m geschenkten Gaul guckt man nicht ins ~* don't look a gift horse in the mouth; **~affe** *m* gaper; *~affen feil halten* to stand gaping about; **~beerbaum** *m* mulberry-tree; **~beere** *f* mulberry; **~en** *itr* to hang the lip; to pout; (*schmollen*) to be sulky; **~esel** *m*, **~eselin** *f* mule; (*kleiner ~~*) hinny; **~eseltreiber** *m* muleteer; **~faul** *a* too lazy to speak, taciturn; **~fäule** *f med* flaps *pl*; **~held** *m* big-talker, braggart; **~korb** *m* muzzle; **~schelle** *f* slap (in the face), box on the ear; **~sperre** *f* lock-jaw; **~tier** *n* mule; **~trommel** *f* Jew's harp; **~~ u. Klauenseuche** *f* foot (*Am* hoof) and mouth disease; **~weite** *f tech* opening, clearance; (*Magnet*) interpolar distance; **~werk** *n* gift of the gab; **~wurf** *m* mole; **~~sfalle** *f* mole-trap; **~~shaufen, ~~shügel** *m* molehill, moleheap.

Maur|e *m* Moor; **~isch** *a* Moorish.

Maurer *m* bricklayer, mason; **~arbeit** *f* brickwork; **~geselle** *m* journeyman mason; **~handwerk** *n* masonry, bricklaying; **~kelle** *f* trowel; **~meister** *m* master mason; **~pinsel** *m* whitewash-brush; **~polier** *m* head mason, bricklayer's foreman.

Maus *f* mouse (*pl* mice); **~efalle** *f* mousetrap; *fig* deathtrap; **~eloch** *n* mouse-hole; **~en** *itr* to catch mice; *tr* (*stehlen*) *fam* to pilfer, to pinch, to scrounge, to lift; **~etot** *a* stone-dead; as dead as a door nail; **~grau** *a* mouse-grey; **~ig** *a*: *sich ~~ machen* (*fam*) to show off, to put on airs.

mauscheln *itr* to talk sheeny.

Mäuschen *n* little mouse; *fig* my darling; **~still** *adv* quiet as a mouse, stock-still.

Mäuse|bussard *m* common buzzard; **~dreck** *m* mouse dung; **~fraß** *m* damage done by mice; **~gift** *n* ratsbane; **~loch** *n* mouse-hole.

Mauser *f* moulting, mewing; **~n** *r* to moult.

Maut *f* toll, customs *pl*; **~ner** *m* custom-house officer.

maximal *a* maximum, maximal; **~betrag** *m* maximum amount; **~gewicht** *n* maximum weight; **~leistung** *f* maximum output; *el* maximum effect; **~lohn** *m* maximum wage; **~preis** *m* maximum price, ceiling; **~tarif** *m* maximum tariff; **~wert** *m* maximum value.

Maxime *f* maxim.

Maximum *n* maximum; (*Kurve*) peak.

Mazedon|ien *n* Macedonia; **~ier** *m*, **~isch** *a* Macedonian.

Mayonnaise *f* mayonnaise (sauce).

Mäzen *m* Maecenas.

Mechan|ik *f* mechanics *pl mit sing*; mechanism; **~iker** *m* mechanic(ian), engineer, fitter; *aero* aircraftman; **~isch** *a* mechanical; **~isieren** *tr* to mechanize; **~isierung** *f* mechanization; **~ismus** *m* mechanism.

Mecker|er *m* grumbler, carper, *sl* grouser, *Am* griper; **~n** *itr* to bleat; (*nörgeln*) to carp (*über* at); (*murren, schimpfen*) *fam* to grumble, to grouse, to nag, *Am* to gripe, to beef, to kick.

Medaill|e *f* medal; **~on** *n* medallion; (*Schmuck*) locket.

Medikament *n* medicament, remedy.

Medizin *f* (*Arznei*) medicine, physic; (*Wissenschaft*) science of medicine; **~alrat** *m* public health officer; **~ball** *m* medicine-ball; **~er** *m* physician, medical man; medical student; **~isch** *a* medicinal; (*ärztlich*) medical; **~mann** *m* medicine man; medico, (*Eskimo*) angekok.

Meer *n* sea; (*Welt~*) ocean; (*hohe See*) main, high sea; (*Ufer*) seashore; *am ~* on the seashore, at the seaside; *über das ~ fahren* to cross the sea; *übers ~* oversea(s); *an das ~ gehen* to go to the seaside; *auf dem ~* at sea; *auf dem offenen ~* in the open sea, on the high seas; **~busen** *m* gulf, bay; **~enge** *f* straits *pl*, channel; **~esarm** *m* arm (*od* branch) of the sea; **~esboden, ~esgrund** *m* sea-bottom; **~esbrandung** *f* surf (of the sea); **~esbucht** *f* bay, bight; **~eshöhe** *f* sea-level; **~eskunde** *f* oceanography; **~esküste** *f* sea-coast; **~esleuchten** *n* phosphorescence of the sea; **~esspiegel** *m* sea-level, surface of sea; **~esstille** *f* calmness of the sea; **~esstrand** *m* beach, sea-boarder; **~esströmung** *f* current of the sea; **~estiefe** *f* depth of the sea; **~eswoge** *f* billow; **~gott** *m* sea-god; **~grün** *a* sea green; **~kalb** *n* sea-calf; **~katze** *f* long-tailed monkey; **~mädchen** *n* mermaid, siren; **~rettich** *m* horse-radish; **~salz** *n* sea salt; **~schaum** *m* sea foam; meerschaum; **~schlamm** *m* sea ooze; **~schwein** *n* porpoise; **~~chen** *n* guinea-pig; **~ungeheuer** *n* sea monster.

Megahertz *n* megacycle per second.

Megaphon *n* megaphone, speaking trumpet.

Megäre *f* termagant; vixen.

*

Mehl *n* flour; (*grobes*) meal; (*Staub*) dust, powder; *mit ~ bestreuen* to flour; **~beutel** *m* bolter; **~brei** *m* meal-pap; **~ig** *a* farinaceous, floury, mealy; **~kleister** *m* paste; **~kloß** *m* flour-dumpling; **~sack** *m* flour-bag; **~sieb** *n* bolter; sifter; flour-sieve; **~speise** *f* farinaceous food; (*süß*) pudding; **~suppe** *f* gruel; **~wurm** *m* meal-worm; **~zucker** *m* ground (*od* powdered) sugar.

mehr *adv* more; *immer ~* more and more; *nicht ~* no more, no longer; *~ od weniger* more or less; *um so ~* so much the more; *je ~, desto ~* the more, the more; *~ als* more than; upwards (of), *Am* rising (of); *nie ~* never again; *nur ~* only, nothing but; *es war nichts* (*niemand*) *~ da* nothing (nobody) was left; *er will kein Wort ~ davon hören* he doesn't want to hear another word about it; *es ist nicht ~ als billig* it's only fair; *was noch ~?* what else? *~ n* (*Überschuß*) surplus, excess; (*Mehrheit*) majority; (*Vermehrung*) increase; *com* over; **~achsantrieb** *m* multi-axle drive; **~achser** *m* multi-axle vehicle; **~arbeit** *f* overtime (work); **~atomig** *a phys* polyatomic; **~aufwand** *m*, **~ausgabe(n)** *f* (*pl*) additional expenditure; **~bändig** *a* in several volumes; **~bedarf** *m* excess demand; additional requirements *pl*; **~belastung** *f* surplus load; overload; **~bestand** *m* excess stock; **~betrag** *m* surplus; **~deutig** *a* ambiguous; **~~keit** *f* ambiguity; equivocation; **~einkommen** *n* surplus income; **~einnahmen** *f pl* additional receipts *pl*; **~en** *tr* to augment, to increase; *sich ~~* to multiply, to grow; **~er** *m* augmenter, enlarger; **~ere** *a* several; diverse, sundry; **~eres** *a* several things *pl*; sundries *pl*; **~erlei** *a* various, divers(e); **~erlös, ~ertrag** *m* surplus; **~fach** *a* manifold, several; several times; (*wiederholt*) repeated(ly); (*vielfach*) multiple, multiplex; **~~betrieb** *m tele* multiplex operation; **~~bild** *n tele* multiple image; **~~leitung** *f tele* multiple line; **~~röhre** *f radio* multiple valve, *Am* multiple-unit tube; **~~schaltung** *f el* multiple connection; **~~stecker** *m el* multiple plug; **~familienhaus** *n* multiple family dwelling; **~farbendruck** *m* multicolo(u)r print(ing); **~farbig** *a* polychromatic; **~~keit** *f* polychromatism; polychromy; **~forderung** *f* increased demand; **~förderung** *f* increased delivery; **~frontenkrieg** *m* war on several fronts; **~gängig** *a* multiple; **~gebot** *n* overbid; **~gepäck** *n* excess luggage **~gewicht** *n* overweight, surplus weight; excess weight, advantage; **~gitterröhre** *f radio* multiple-grid valve, *Am* multigrid tube; **~gleisig** *a* witch several tracks; **~gliederig** *a* having several members; multimesh, multisection; **~heit** *f* majority; plurality; multiplicity; *absolute* (*einfache*) *~~* absolute (simple) majority; *Zweidrittel~~* twothirds majority; *überwältigende ~~* overwhelming odds *pl*; *mit zwei Stimmen ~~* by a majority of two; **~~sabstimmung, ~~swahl** *f* majority vote; **~~sbeschluß** *m* majority decision; *durch ~~sbeschluß* by a majority of votes; *Am* by a plurality (of votes); **~jährig** *a* several years old; of several years; **~kanalfernsehen** *n* multichannel television; **~kanonenjäger** *m aero* multicannon fighter plane; **~kantig** *a* many-sided; **~kernig** *a phys* polynuclear; **~kosten** *pl* additional expense; **~kreisempfänger, ~kreiser** *m radio* multi (-tuned) circuit receiver; **~ladegewehr** *n*, **~lader** *m* magazine weapon, magazine (*od* repeating) rifle; **~leistung** *f* increased efficiency; surplus production; **~lochschlüssel** *m* combination wrench; **~malig** *a* repeated, reiterated; **~mals** *adv* several times, again and again; **~motorig** *a* multi-engine(d); **~phasenstrom** *m el* polyphase current; **~polig** *a el* multipolar; **~porto** *n* additional postage, surcharge; **~preis** *m* surplus price; extra (charge), increase in price; **~schichtig** *a* many-layered, multilayered; **~seitig** *a* with many sides, polygonal; **~silbig** *a* polysyllabic; **~sitzer** *m* multi-seater; **~sprachig** *a* polyglot; **~stimmig** *a* arranged for several voices; (*Lied*) part (song); **~stufig** *a el* multistage; **~stündig** *a* lasting for hours, of several hours' duration; **~tägig** *a* of several days' duration; **~teilig** *a tech* multisectional; **~ung** *f* increase, multiplication; **~umsatz** *m* increased turnover; **~verbrauch** *m* additional consumption; **~wert** *m* surplus value; (*Wertzuwachs*) increment value; **~~ig** *a chem* multivalent, polyvalent; **~zahl** *f* majority, most of; *gram* plural; *die große ~~* the great majority; the bulk; **~zweck** *m* general purpose, dual purpose, multiple purpose; **~~flugzeug** *n* multipurpose aircraft; **~~waffe** *f* dual (*od* multiple) purpose arm.

meiden *tr* to avoid, to shun.

Meier *m* dairy-farmer; (*Verwalter*) steward; **~ei** *f*, **~hof** *m* (dairy-)farm.

Meile *f* mile; league; *englische ~* British mile, statute mile; *nautische ~* nautical mile; **~ngeld** *n Am* mileage; **~nstein** *m* milestone; **~nstiefel** *m pl* seven-leagued boots *pl*; **~nweit** *adv* for miles; very far.

Meiler *m* charcoal-kiln (*od* -pile).

mein, ~e, ~ *prn* my; **~er** *m*, **~e** *f*, **~es** *n* mine; *ich für ~ Teil* as to me, as far as I am concerned; *~es Wissens* so far as I know; *ich war ~er nicht mehr mächtig* I had lost control over myself; *~e Damen u. Herrn!* Ladies and Gentlemen! *das ist nicht dein Buch, sondern ~es* that isn't your book, it's mine; *Mein u. Dein* mine and thine; **~erseits** *adv* for my part, as far as I am concerned; **~esgleichen** *prn* my equals *pl*, people like me, such as I; **~esteils** *adv* on my part; **~ethalben, ~etwegen** *adv* for my part, as for me, as far as I am concerned; (*wegen mir*) on my account; because of me; for my sake; (*ich habe nichts dagegen*) I have no objection; I don't care; as you like; I don't mind; *mach' dir ~~ keine Sorgen* don't worry about me; **~etwillen** *adv* for my sake; **~ig** *a, prn* my, mine;**~~e** *m* (*f, n*) mine; **~~en** *pl* my people; *ich habe das ~~e getan* I have done my duty.

Meineid *m* perjury; *e-n ~ leisten* to commit perjury; *zum ~ verleiten* to suborn to perjury; **~ig** *a* perjured; **~~er** *m* perjurer.

mein|en *tr, itr* (*denken, glauben*) to think, to believe, to be of (the) opinion; *Am* to reckon; *Am* to guess; *Am* to allow; (*äußern*) to say; (*vermuten*) to suppose; (*anspielen*) to refer to; (*sagen wollen*) to mean, to intend; *wie ~~ Sie das?* what do you mean by that? *jdn ~~* to speak of; *es gut mit jdm ~~* to have good intentions towards s. o.; *ich ~e es gut* I mean well; *das will ich ~~!* I quite believe it! *wie ~~ Sie?* what did you say? I beg your pardon? **~ung** *f* opinion, idea, view; (*Auffassung*) meaning; (*Absicht*) intention; *meiner ~~ nach* to my mind, in my opinion (*od* judg(e)ment), *Am* I reckon; *ich bin der ~~, daß* I am of opinion that; *seine ~~ äußern dürfen über* to have o.'s say in; *über etw anderer ~~ sein als jem* to disagree with s. o. about s. th.; *anderer ~~ sein* to dissent; *verschiedener ~~ sein* to differ; *derselben ~~ sein* to agree (with); *jdm seine ~~ sagen* to give s. o. a bit of o.'s mind; (*heftig*) to bawl s. o. out; *öffentliche ~~* public opinion; *vorgefaßte ~~* prejudice; *herrschende ~~* prevailing opinion; *abweichende ~~* dissenting opinion; **~~säußerung** *f* statement of opinion; expression of opinion; **~~saustausch** *m* interchange of views; discussion; **~~sbefragung** *f Am* (public) opinion poll; **~~sbildung** *f* formation of opinion; **~~s forscher** *m* expert on public opinion polls, *Am* pollster; **~~sforschung** *f* public opinion research; *Am* polls *pl*; **~~sfreiheit** *f* freedom of speech and writing; **~~sverschiedenheit** *f* difference of opinion; misunderstanding; disagreement; dissent.

Meise *f* titmouse.

Meißel *m* chisel; (*Arbeitsstahl*) tool; **~n** *tr, itr* to chisel, to carve; to sculpture.

meist *a* most; *die ~en a* most; *pl* most people; *am ~en* most (*od* more than all); *die ~e Zeit* most of the time; **~begünstigt** *a* most-favo(u)red; **~begünstigung** *f* (*Zoll*) preference; **~~s-klausel** *f* most-favo(u)red nation clause; **~bietend** *a* offering most; *~~ verkaufen* to sell to the highest bidder; to sell by auction; **~bietende(r)** *m* highest bidder; **~ens, ~enteils** *adv* for the most part; mostly; **~gebot** *n* best offer, highest bid.

Meister *m* master; (*Industrie*) foreman; chief operator; *Am* boss; *sport* champion; *seinen ~ finden* to meet o.'s match; *Übung macht den ~* practice makes perfect; **~haft, ~lich** *a* masterly; **~in** *f* mistress; *sport* (woman) champion; **~n** *tr* to master, to overcome; to control; (*tadeln*) to find fault with; **~prüfung** *f* examination for the title of master; **~sänger, ~singer,** *m* mastersinger; **~schaft** *f* mastery; mastership; *sport* championship; **~schuß** *m* best shot; **~streich** *m* master-stroke; **~stück, ~werk** *n* master-piece.

Melanchol|ie *f* melancholy; **~iker** *m* hypochondriac; **~isch** *a* melancholy; sad, gloomy; pensive; *~~ sein fam* to be in the blues.

Melasse *f* molasses *pl*; treacle.

Meld|eamt *n* registration office; *tele* record office, *Am* recording board; **~ebogen** *m* registration form; **~eblock** *m* message pad; **~edienst** *m* warning service; **~efahrer** *m* messenger; *mil* dispatch-rider; **~efahrzeug** *n* messenger vehicle; **~egänger** *m* messenger, runner; **~ehund** *m* messenger dog; **~ekopf** *m* message centre, *Am* message center; **~elampe** *f* alarm lamp; signal lamp; telltale lamp; **~eläufer** *m* runner; **~eliste** *f sport* list of entries; **~en** *tr* (*ankündigen*) to announce to; to let know; to give notice; (*benachrichtigen*) to inform, to advise; (*erwähnen*) to mention; *mil* to report; (*hinweisen*) to call attention to, to point out; (*amtlich*) to notify; *sich ~~* to report (to); to present o. s.; (*Stellung*) to apply for; (*antworten auf*) to answer; (*Prüfung*) to enter o.'s name for; (*Polizei*) to report (to), to register (with); *sich ~~ lassen* to send in o.'s name; *sich freiwillig ~~* to volunteer; to enlist; *sich krank ~~* to go sick; **~enetz** *n aero* spotting system; **~epflicht** *f* obligation to report o. s.; obligatory reporting; **~~ig** *a* notifiable, declarable; subject to registration; **~equadrat** *n* reference square (of map); **~er** *m mil* orderly; messenger, runner; dispatch-rider; **~ereiter** *m* dispatch-rider; **~esammelstelle** *f mil* report centre; **~eschein** *m* registration form; **~eschluß** *m sport* closing date for entries; **~estelle** *f* local reporting office; control office; **~etasche** *f* message bag; **~eweg** *m* messenger route; **~ewurfgranate** *f mil* message bomb; **~ezettel** *m* registration form; **~ung** *f* (*Ankündigung*) announcement, news *pl mit sing*; (*Mitteilung*) advice, information, notification, message, notice; (*dienstlich*) report; (*Bewerbung*) application; *sport* entry; *seine ~~ zurückziehen sport* to scratch.

meliert *a* mottled, mixed, speckled, blended; *~es Papier* granite paper; *grau~* greying.

meliorieren *tr* to ameliorate.

Melisse *f bot* balm-mint.

Melk|eimer, **~kübel** *m* milking-pail, milking-tub; **~en** *irr tr* to milk; (*aussaugen*) to drain; **~er** *m* milker; **~kuh** *f* milk cow; **~schemel** *m* milking-stool.

Melo|die *f* (Weise) tune; (*liedhafte ~~*) air; (*gefällige Tonfolge*) melody: **~dienreigen** *m* melody roundup; **~disch** *a* tuneful, melodious; **~drama** *n* melodrama.

Melone *f* melon; (*Hut*) bowler, *Am* derby.

Meltau *m* mildew, blight; *von ~ befallen* blighted; **~befall** *m bot* blight infection.

Membran|(e) *f* membrane: *tele* diaphragm; **~pumpe** *f* diaphragm pump, surge pump; **~schwingung** *f* diaphragm oscillation.

Memme *f* coward; craven; poltroon.

Menagerie *f* menagery.

Mem|oiren *n pl* memoirs *pl*; personal reminiscences *pl*; **~orieren** *tr* to memorize, to learn by heart.

Meng|e *f* quantity, *Am* grist; (*Bestand, Masse*) amount; (*Volumen*) volume; (*Teil von*) portion (of); (*Zahl*) great (*od* large) number, scores *pl*; *math* aggregate, set; (*sehr viele*) a lot of, lots *pl* of, a great many, a great deal of; (*Überfluß*) abundance; (*Unzahl*) host; (*Menschen~~*) crowd, multitude, throng; (*Massen*) the masses *pl*; (*Andrang*) press, crush; (*Pöbel*) mob; (*Horde*) horde, swarm; (*Kinder*) troop; (*Mädchen*) bevy; (*schöne Frauen*) galaxy; (*Verbrecher*) gang; (*Fische*) band; school; (*Wölfe*) pack; (*Rebhühner*) covey; *in ~en* in abundance, plenty of, (*Menschen, Tiere*) in crowds; *nach der ~~* quantitative; **~en** *tr* to mix, to blend; *sich ~~* to mix, to mingle; (*sich einmischen*) to meddle, to interfere (with); **~enbestimmung** *f* quantitative determination; quantitative analysis; **~enbezeichnung** *f* designation of quantity; **~eneinheit** *f* unit of quantity; **~eneinkauf** *m* bulk buying; **~enfertigung** *f* mass production; **~enmäßig** *a* quantitative, by volume; **~ennachlaß** *m* quantity rebate; **~enuntersuchung** *f* quantitative examination; **~enverhältnis** *n* quantitative relation, proportion; **~enverlust** *m* loss of volume; **~futter** *n* mash; **~gestein** *n* conglomerate; **~sel** *n* mingle-mangle, mixture, hotchpotch.

Mennig *m*, **~e** *f* minium, red lead.

Meniskus *m opt, anat* meniscus.

Mensch *m* human being, man; (*Einzelwesen*) individual, person; (*Sterblicher*) mortal; *~ n vulg* hussy, wench; *die ~en* people; mankind; *jeder ~* everybody, everyone; *der ~ denkt, Gott lenkt* man proposes, God disposes; *ein lieber ~* a dear fellow; *es erschien kein ~* not a soul came; *er ist auch nur ein ~* he's only human; *so sind die ~en* such is the way of the world; *e-e Menge ~en* a great many people; **~enaffe** *m* anthropoid ape; **~enähnlich** *a* manlike; anthropoid; **~enalter** *n* generation, age; **~enart** *f* race of men; human nature; **~enblut** *n* human blood; **~enfeind** *m* misanthropist; **~~lich** *a* misanthropic; **~enfleisch** *n* human flesh; **~enfresser** *m* cannibal; **~~ei** *f* cannibalism; **~enfreund** *m* philanthropist; **~~lich** *a* philanthropic; **~~lichkeit** *f* philanthropy; affability; benevolence; **~enführung** *f* personal management; control of public opinion; **~enfurcht** *f* fear of men; **~engedenken** *n*: *seit ~~* within the memory of man, from time immemorial; **~engeschlecht** *n* mankind; human race; **~engestalt** *f* human shape; **~engewühl** *n* crowd of people, throng; **~enhaar** *n* human hair; **~enhand** *f* hand of man; **~enhaß** *m* hatred of mankind; **~enherz** *n* human heart; **~enkenner** *m* judge of human nature; **~enkenntnis** *f* knowledge of human nature; **~enkunde** *f* anthropology; **~enleben** *n* human life; *~~ waren nicht zu beklagen* there were no lives lost; *~~ gefährden* to endanger human life; *Verluste an ~~* (*mil*) casualties *pl*; **~enleer** *a* deserted, devoid of people, uninhabited; unfrequented; **~enliebe** *f* philanthropy; human kindness; charity; **~enlos** *n* fate of men; human destiny, lot; **~enmaterial** *n* manpower; **~enmauer** *f* throng; **~enmenge** *f* crowd, multitude, throng; mob; **~enmöglich** *a* humanly possible, within the power of man; *wenn es ~~ ist* if it can be managed, if there is the slightest chance; **~enmord** *m* homicide; murder; **~enmörder** *m* murderer; **~enopfer** *n* human sacrifice; **~enpflicht** *f* human duty; **~enraub** *m* kidnapping; **~enräuber** *m* kidnapper; **~enrecht** *n* right of man; natural law; **~~sprogramm** *n Am* civil rights program; **~enscheu** *a* unsociable, shy; *~~ f* shyness, unsociableness; **~enschinder** *m* oppressor; extortioner; slave-driver; **~~ei** *f* extortion; **~enschlag** *m* race of men; **~enseele** *f* human soul; *keine ~~* not a living soul; **~enskind** *n*: *~~!* man alive! **~ensohn** *m* the Son of Man; **~enstimme** *f* human voice; **~enverächter** *m* despiser of mankind; **~enverstand** *m* (*gesunder ~~*) common sense, *Am* horse sense; human understanding; **~enwerk** *n* work of man; **~enwürde** *f* dignity of man; **~enwürdig** *a* worthy of a human being; **~heit** *f* human race, mankind; humanity; **~lich** *a* human; *fig* (*human*) humane; *~~e Arbeitsstunden* man-hours *pl*; **~~keit** *f* human nature, humanity; humaneness; *Verbrechen gegen die ~~keit* crime against humanity; **~werdung** *f* incarnation.

Menstru|ation *f med* menstruation; catamenia; **~~sbeschwerde** *f* painful menstruation, menstrual molimen; **~ieren** *itr* to menstruate.

Mensur *f* students' duel; *chem* measuring vessel; graduated vessel; graduate; *mus* measure; scale; **~glas** *n* measuring (*od* graduated) glass.

Mentalität *f* mentality.

Menuett *n* minuet.

Mergel *m* marl; **~artig** *a* marly; **~boden** *m* marly soil; **~erde** *f* earthy marl; **~grube** *f* marl-pit; **~n** *itr* to (manure with) marl.

Meridian *m* meridian; **~bogen** *m* arc of the meridian; **~ebene** *f* meridian plane; **meridional** *a* meridional.

merk|bar *a* perceptible, noticeable; (*im Gedächtnis*) retainable; (*offensichtlich*) evident; **~blatt** *n* leaflet; pamphlet; specification; memorandum; instructional pamphlet; **~buch** *n* note-book, memo(randum) book, *Am* tickler; **~en** *tr* (*sehen*) to notice, to perceive, to observe, to note; (*gewahr sein*) to be aware (of), *Am* to be knowing (to); (*schreiben*) to mark, to note down, to jot down; (*argwöhnen*) to suspect; (*fühlen*) to feel, to be sensitive to; (*auf etw kommen*) to hit upon; *~~ r* to bear in mind; to retain; (*sich erinnern*) to remember, to keep track (of); (*achtgeben*) to pay attention to; to heed; *sich etw ~~ lassen* to let on s. th.; to betray; *sich nichts ~~ lassen* to appear to know nothing; to conceal; *~~ Sie sich meine Worte!* mark my words! *Am* get this straight! *man merkt ihm sein Alter nicht an* he does not look his age; *das werde ich mir ~~* that shall be a lesson to me; *er ließ mich ~~, daß* he gave me to understand that; ~lich a perceptible, appreciable; (sichtlich) evident; (beträchtlich) considerable; ein ~~er Unterschied a marked difference; ~mal n characteristic; (Erkennungszeichen) mark of identification; (charakteristische Eigenschaft) attribute; (Zeichen) mark, sign, token; (Kennzeichen) indication; (Kennziffer) index; (Nebenbedeutung) connotation; (bes. ~~e pl) peculiarities pl, Am marks pl; (geistiges ~~) criterion; (Grundzug) feature; ~~sträger m biol gene; ~punkt m (im Gelände) landmark; (Bezugpunkt) reference point, index point; ~würdig a (seltsam) strange, curious; (bemerkenswert) noteworthy, remarkable, (besonders) peculiar; ~~erweise adv strange to say; strangely enough; ~~keit f strangeness; (Besonderheit) peculiarity; (Gegenstand) curiosity; (Sehenswürdigkeit) sight(s pl); ~zeichen n characteristic; mark; guide mark; distinctive mark; sign; ~zettel m data card.

Merkur m Mercury.

meschugge a vulg crazy; ~ sein to be off o.'s chump, to be crazy.

Mesner m sexton, sacristan.

Mesopotamien n Mesopotamia.

Mesotron n phys mesotron; meson.

Meß|amt n celebration of mass; tech measuring office; (Ausstellungsamt) office of the fair; ~analyse f volumetric analysis; ~apparat m measuring apparatus; ~band n tape measure; ~bar a measurable; ~beobachtung f ranging; ~bereich m measuring range; ~bild n scale drawing; ~~verfahren n photogrammetry; ~brücke f el measuring bridge, Wheatstone's bridge; ~buch n missal, mass-book; ~diener m acolyte; ~e f eccl mass; (Markt) fair; market; (Offiziers~~) mess; ~~ lesen to say mass; ~~amt n office of the fair; ~~bericht m report of the fair; ~~besucher m visitor of a fair; ~~ordnung f fair regulations pl; ~~stand m booth, stall; ~en irr tr to measure; (Land) to survey; (prüfen) to test; to check; (Höhe, Tiefe loten) to sound; (Zeit) to time; (Temperatur) to take the temperature; (eichen) to calibrate; (mit Meßapparat) to meter; (mit Lehren) to caliper; to ga(u)ge; (enthalten) to contain; ~~ r to compete (with), to compare (with), to cope (with), to match s. o., to rival s. o. in s. th., to come up to s. o.; to try o.'s strength (with); sich nicht ~~ können mit to be no match (for), to be not equal (to); mit Blicken ~~ to eye, to take stock of, to cast an appraising glance (at); ~ergebnis n result of measurement; ~fehler m error in measurement; ~flasche f measuring bottle; ~flug m aero (Probeflug) test flight; (Geländevermessung) photogrammetric flight; ~funk m siehe: Funkmeß; ~gefäß n measuring vessel; ~genauigkeit f accuracy of measurement; ~gerät n measuring apparatus (od tool); ~gewand n vestment; chasuble; ~glas n measuring glass, graduated glass vessel; ~heber m measuring pipet(te); ~hemd n alb; ~instrument n measuring instrument; ~kelch m eccl chalice; chem measuring cup; ~latte f surveyor's rod; ~leine f measuring line; ~mann m mil range taker; radar operator; ~marke f measuring mark; pylon; stake; ~methode f testing method; measuring method; ~objekt n mil target; ~opfer n (sacrifice of the) mass; ~stange f measuring staff; ~stelle f control point; plotting centre; ~strich m indicating line; ~sucher m phot view and range finder; ~technik f testing technique, technique of measurement; ~tisch m surveyor's table; el test desk; ~tischblatt n ordnance survey map; plane-table survey; ~trupp m survey section; tele testing crew; ranging (od measuring) section; ~ung f measuring, measurement, mensuration; (Prüfung) test, testing; ~verfahren n process of measurement; tele testing method; ~wein m sacramental wine; ~werkzeug n measuring instrument, measuring tool; ~wert m measurement result, test result, test value; datum; pl test data pl, ~ziffer f index number; ~zylinder m measuring cylinder.

Messer n knife; (Dolch) dagger; med scalpel; ein Kampf bis aufs ~ a fight to the finish; auf des ~s Schneide on the razor's edge; jdm das ~ an die Kehle setzen to put a knife to s. o.'s throat; Krieg bis aufs ~ war to the knife; ~bänkchen n knife-rest; ~flug m vertical sideslip; ~förmig a knife-shaped; ~griff m knife-handle; ~held m cut-throat; ~klinge f blade of a knife; ~rücken m back of a knife; ~scheide f case of a knife; ~schleifer m knife-grinder; ~schmied m cutler; ~schneide f knife-edge; ~spitze f point of a knife; ~stecher m cut-throat; ~stecherei f knife-battle; ~stich m stab (with a knife).

Messias m Messiah.

Messing n (yellow) brass; ~blech n brass plate, sheet-brass; ~draht n brass wire; ~en a brazen, (made of) brass; ~farben a brass-colo(u)red; ~fassung f brass mounting; ~gießer m brass founder; ~rohr n brass tube; ~schild n brass plate.

Mestize m mestizo.

Met m mead.

Metall n metal; aus ~ metallic; edles ~ noble metal; unedles ~ base metal; ~abfall m metal waste (od scrap); ~arbeiter m metal worker; ~artig a (sub)metallic; ~asche f metallic ashes pl; ~band n metal tape, metallic ribbon; ~baukasten m metal architectural box; ~bauweise f metal construction; ~bearbeitung f metal working; ~beplankung f metal covering; ~blech n sheet metal, metal plate; ~en a made of metal, metallic; brazen; ~fadenlampe f metallic-filament lamp; tungsten lamp; ~flugzeug n metal plane; ~geld n specie, hard cash; ~glanz m metallic lustre; ~isch a (of) metal; metallic, metalline; ~kunde f science of metals; metallography; ~(l)egierung f metallic alloy; ~(l)uftschraube f aero metal airscrew; ~ograph m metallographer; ~ographie f metallography; ~oxyd n metallic oxyd; ~platte f metal plate; sheet metal; ~ring m metal ring; ~rohr n, ~röhre f metal tube (od pipe); ~schere f plate shears pl; ~schildchen n metal label; ~sieb n metallic screen; ~spritzverfahren n metallization; ~überzug m metall(ic) coating; ~urg(e) m metallurgist; ~urgie f metallurgy; ~verarbeitung f metal processing; ~verbindung f metallic compound; ~vergiftung f metal poisoning; ~vorrat m (Bank) bullion reserve; ~währung f metallic standard; ~waren f pl (metal) hardware.

Meta|morphose f metamorphosis; ~pher f metaphor; ~phorisch a metaphorical, figurative; ~physik f metaphysics pl (od mit sing); ~physisch a metaphysical; ~verbindung f meta compound od derivative.

Meteor n meteor; ~eisen n meteoric iron; ~ologe m meteorologist, fam weatherman, Am mil meteorology officer; ~ologie f meteorology; ~ologisch a meteorological; ~~e Station weather bureau; ~schwarm m meteoric shower, host of meteors; ~staub m meteoric dust; ~stein m meteoric stone, aerolite, meteorolite.

Meter n (m) metre, Am meter (1 m = 39.37 inches); ~maß n metre rule (od stick); tape-measure, pocket rule; metric measure; ~sekunde f metres per second; ~wellen f pl radio (UKW) ultra short waves pl, very short waves pl; ~zähler m film Am film-footage counter.

Method|e f method; ~ik f methodology; ~isch a methodical; ~ist m methodist.

Methyl|alkohol m methyl alcohol; ~äther m methyl ether; ~verbindung f methyl compound; ~wasserstoff m methyl hydride, methane.

Metr|ik f prosody; versification; metrics pl; ~isch a metric(al); ~~es Gewinde metric thread; ~~es Maßsystem metric system; ~um n metre.

Metropole f metropolis.

Metteur m typ maker-up; clicker; foreman in the composing room.

Mette f matins pl.

Mettwurst f German sausage.

Metze f (Dirne) strumpet, prostitute.

Metz|elei f slaughter; butchery; massacre; ~eln tr to slaughter; to butcher, to massacre; ~elsuppe f sausage soup; pudding broth; ~ger m butcher; ~~ei f butcher's shop, Am meat-market; ~~junge m butcher-boy.

Meuchel|mord m assassination; ~mörder m assassin; ~mörderisch murderous; treacherous; ~n tr to assassinate; ~lings adv treacherously, insidiously.

Meute f pack of hounds.

Meuter|ei f mutiny, sedition; ~er m mutineer; ~isch a mutinous; ~n itr to mutiny.

Mexik|aner m, ~anerin f, ~anisch a Mexican; ~o n Mexico.

miauen itr to mew; to caterwaul.

mich prn me; (reflexiv) myself.

Michael m (Name) Michael; Micky; Mike.

Michaelis|fest n, ~tag m Michaelmas.

Mieder n bodice; (B. H.) bra(ssière).

Mief m (muffige Luft) fam frowst, fetid air; fug.

Miene f (Aussehen) air; (Gesicht) countenance, face; (Mienenspiel) mien; (Züge) feature; (Äußeres, Aussehen) look, aspect; entschlossene ~ air of decision; e-e finstere ~ machen to frown; e-e freundliche ~ machen to look pleasant; überlegene ~ air of superiority; keine ~ verziehen not to bat an eye; ohne e-e ~ zu verziehen without moving a muscle; ~ machen to pretend, to make believe; gute ~ zum bösen Spiel machen to make the best of a bad job; to grin and to bear it; ~nspiel n play of features; changing expressions pl; pantomime; mimicry.

mies a fam miserable, disagreeable; ~macher m alarmist, croaker, grumbler, Am crank; calamity howler; ~muschel f (sea) mussel.

Miet|e f (Entgelt) rent; hire; (~sverhältnis) lease; (Schober) stack, rick; (Garben~~) shock; (Kartoffel~~) potato clamp (od pit); zoo mite; zur ~~ wohnen to live in lodgings, to be a tenant; rückständige ~~ arrears pl of rent; ~aufkündigung f notice to quit;

~ausfall *m* renting failure; **~auto** *n* taxi(cab); **~dauer** *f* period of lease; **~einkommen** *n* rental; **~einnehmer** *m* rent collector; **~en** *tr* (*Haus, Wohnung*) to rent; (*Sachen, Menschen*) to hire; (*Grund u. Boden*) to lease, to take on lease; *mar* to charter; **~entschädigung** *f* allowance for house rent; **~er** *m* tenant, lodger, *jur* lessee, *Am* renter; (*Einzelzimmer*) *Am* roomer; (*Grundstück*) leaseholder; *mar* charterer; **~~schutz** *m* protection of tenants; **~~schutzgesetz** *n* law on the protection of tenants; **~erhöhung** *f* increase in rent; **~ertrag** *m* rental; **~flugzeug** *n* taxiplane; **~frei** *a* rent-free; **~gebühr** *f* rental fee; **~haus** *n* block of flats, tenement house, house with flats to let, *Am* apartment-house; **~höchstpreise** *m pl* rent ceilings *pl*; **~kaserne** *f* tenement house, *fam* rookery; **~ling** *m* mercenary, hireling; **~preis** *m* rent; **~stallung** *f* livery stable, *Am* boarding stable; **~steigerung** *f* increase in rent; **~summe** *f* rental; **~verhältnis** *n* tenancy; **~vertrag** *m* lease; **~wagen** *m* hired vehicle, *Am* hack; **~weise** *adv* on hire; **~wert** *m* rental value; **~wohnung** *f* lodging(s *pl*), flat, tenement, *Am* apartment; **~zins** *m* rent; **~zuschlag** *m* rent allowance.

Mieze *f* pussy(-cat); puss.

Migräne *f med* sick headache; migraine, megrim.

Mikro|be *f* microbe; **~bisch** *a* microbial; **~brief** *m* airgraph; **~chemie** *f* microchemistry; **~film** *m* microfilm; (*für Bücher*) bibliofilm; *auf ~~ aufnehmen* to microfilm; **~~brief** *m* airgraph (letter), *Am* V-mail letter; **~kosmos** *m* microcosm; **~meter** *m* micrometer; **~~schraube** *f* micrometer ga(u)ge (*od* screw); **~n** *n* micron; **~organismus** *m* microorganism; **~(phon)** *n* microphone, transmitter, *fam* mike, mic; (*Aufnahme~~*) *radio* pick-up transmitter; (*Kehlkopf~~*) laryngophone; *elektromagnetisches ~~ mit Eisenanker* moving-iron microphone; *gerichtetes ~~* beam (*od* directional) microphone; *über das ~(~) gehen* to come off the air, to pass through the mike; **~~galgen** *m* microphone boom; **~~geräusch** *n* side tone, transmitter noise; **~~kapsel** *f* microphone capsule, transmitter inset; **~~verstärker** *m* speech amplifier; **~photographie** *f* microphotography; **~skop** *n* microscope; **~~ieren** *tr* to examine with the microscope; **~~isch** *a* microscopic(al); **~strahlen** *m pl* micro-rays *pl*; **~tom** *n* microtome; **~waage** *f* microbalance; **~wellen** *f pl* microwaves *pl*.

Milb|e *f* mite; **~ig** *a* mity.

Milch *f* milk; (*Fisch~*) milt, soft roe; *dicke od saure ~* curdled milk; *die ~ entrahmen* to skim the milk; **~bart** *m* downy beard; *fig* milksop; greenhorn; **~brei** *m* milk-pap; **~brot** *n* French roll; **~brötchen** *n* (*mit Rosinen*) bun; **~bruder** *m* foster-brother; **~drüse** *f* mammary gland, lacteal gland; **~eimer** *m* milk-pail; **~en** *itr* to (give) milk; **~fälschung** *f* adulteration of milk; **~fieber** *n* milk-fever; **~frau** *f*, **~mädchen** *n* milkwoman, milkmaid; **~gebiß** *n* milk dentition, set of milk-teeth; **~geschäft** *n* dairy; **~gesicht** *n* baby face; **~glas** *n* opalescent (*od* frosty) glass; **~halle** *f* milk-bar; dairy lunch room; **~händler** *m* milkman; **~ig** *a* milky; **~~e** *Flüssigkeit* emulsion; **~kanne** *f* milk-can; **~kuh** *f* milch cow; **~kühler** *m* milk cooler; **~kur** *f* milk-cure; **~laden** *m* creamery; **~mann** *m* milkman; **~(n)er** *m* (*Fisch*) milter; **~pantscher** *m* adulterator of milk; **~produkt** *n* dairy product; **~pulver** *n* powdered (*od* evaporated) milk; **~rahm** *m* cream; **~reis** *m* milk-rice; **~säure** *f* lactic acid; **~schorf** *m* milk-scall (*od* -crust); crusta lactea; **~schwester** *f* foster-sister; **~speise** *f* milk-food (*od*-diet); **~straße** *f astr* Milky Way, galaxy; **~suppe** *f* milk-soup; **~topf** *m* milk-pot; **~tuch** *n* strainer; **~wirtschaft** *f* dairy; **~zahn** *m* milk-tooth; **~zentrifuge** *f* cream separator; **~zucker** *m* sugar of milk, lactose.

mild *a* mild; (*gütig*) kind, gentle, tender; (*weich, mürbe*) mellow; (*leicht*) light, soft; (*nachsichtig*) indulgent (to), lenient, tolerant, merciful, forbearing; (*gering*) slight; (*zart*) delicate, dainty; (*edelmütig*) generous; (*wohltätig*) charitable (to); (*fromm*) pious; *~e Stiftung* pious foundation; *~e gesagt* to put it mildly; **~e** *f* mildness, gentleness; indulgence; **~ern** *tr* to mitigate, to alleviate, to assuage; (*Schmerz*) to soften, to ease, to relieve, to soothe; (*versüßen*) to sweeten; (*mäßigen*) to moderate; (*abschwächen*) to temper; (*beschönigen*) to extenuate; (*Ausdruck*) to qualify; (*Säure*) to correct; *jur* to mitigate; **~~d** *a med* mitigant, lenitive; *~~de Umstände* extenuating circumstances; **~erung** *f* mitigation, moderation; *chem* correction; **~~sgrund** *m* extenuating reason; mitigating cause; **~herzig** *a* tenderhearted, charitable; **~~keit** *f* goodheartedness; **~tätig** *a* charitable; **~~keit** *f* charitableness, charity.

Milieu *n* environment, surroundings *pl*, background, sphere, society; (*Lokalfarbe*) local colo(u)r.

Militär *n* military, soldiery, army; (*~dienst*) service; *~ m* military man, soldier; *zum ~ gehen* to join the army; *zum ~ einberufen* (*od ausgehoben*) *werden* to be drafted (*od* conscripted); to be inducted (into the army); **~ähnlich** *a* para-military; **~anwärter** *m* soldier entitled to civil employment; **~arzt** *m* Medical Officer (M.O.), military *od* army surgeon; **~attaché** *m* military attaché; **~behörden** *f pl* military authorities *pl*; **~bündnis** *n* military alliance; **~dienst** *m* (active) service; **~~tauglich** *a* fit for service; **~~verweigerer** *m* conscientious objector; **~diktatur** *f* military dictatorship; **~fahrschein** *m* military warrant; **~flugplatz** *m* military airfield; **~flugzeug** *n* military aircraft; **~friedhof** *m* military cemetry; **~gefängnis** *n* stockade, military prison; **~geistliche(r)** *m* army chaplain; padre; **~gericht** *n* (*einfaches*) summary military court; (*mittleres*) intermediate military court; (*oberes*) general military court; (*internationales*) International Military Tribunal; **~~sbarkeit** *f* military jurisdiction; **~gesetzbuch** *n* military code; **~gouverneur** *m* military governor; **~hospital** *n* military hospital; **~intendantur** *f* commissariat; **~isch** *a* military; martial; soldierlike; *~~e Formen* military courtesy; *~~es Ziel aero* strategic target; **~lazarett** *n* military hospital; **~luftfahrt** *f* military aviation; **~macht** *f* military power; **~marsch** *m* military march; **~maß** *n* standard measure; **~mission** *f* military mission; **~musik** *f* military music; (*Kapelle*) military band; **~person** *f* military man; **~pfarrer** *m* (military) chaplain; **~pflicht** *f* liability to serve in the army, compulsory military service; **~~ig** *a* liable to military service; **~polizei** *f* military police (*Abk* M.P.); **~polizist** *m* military policeman (*Abk* M.P.), *fam* red cap; **~regierung** *f* miltary government; **~strafgesetzbuch** *n* Military Criminal Code, *Am* Penal Military Code; **~transport** *m* military transportation; **~verwaltung** *f* military (*od* army) administration; military government; **~vorlage** *f parl* armybill; **~zeit** *f* service with the colo(u)rs; **~zensur** *f* military censorship.

Militarismus *m* militarism.

Miliz *f* militia; **~soldat** *m* militiaman.

Mill|ennium *n* millenary; **~iardär** *m* multi-millionaire; **~iarde** *f* milliard, a thousand millions, *Am* billion; **~imeter** *n* millimetre (1 mm = $^1/_{25}$ inch), *Am* millimeter; **~~papier** *n* graph paper; **~ion** *f* million; **~ionär** *m* millionaire; **~ionste** *a* millionth.

Milz *f* spleen, milt; **~brand** *m* inflammation of the milt; (*bei Tieren*) anthrax; **~drüse** *f* spleen; **~erkrankung** *f* splenopathy; **~sucht** *f med* hypochondriasis, spleen; **~süchtig** *a* splenetic.

Mim|e *m* actor; (*komische Rolle*) mime, mimic; **~en** *tr theat* to mime; (*heucheln*) to pretend, to feign; **~ik** *f* miming; mimic art; **~isch** *a* mimic.

Mimose *f* mimosa.

*

minder *a* less, lesser; (*kleiner*) smaller; (*niederer*) lower; (*geringer*) inferior; minor; *mehr od ~* more or less; *~ gut* inferior; *nicht mehr, nicht ~* neither more nor less; **~bedarf** *m* reduced demand; **~begabt** *a* subnormal; **~belastet** *a* less incriminated; **~belastete(r)** *m* lesser offender; **~bemittelt** *a* of moderate means; **~betrag** *m* deficit, cash short; **~bewertung** *f* undervaluation; **~einnahmen** *f pl* smaller receipts *pl*; **~ertrag** *m* reduced yield, decreased yield; **~gebot** *n* lower bid; **~gewicht** *n* underweight, short weight; **~heit** *f* minority; *in der ~~ sein* to be in the minority; **~~enfrage** *f* question of minorities; **~~enführer** *m parl* minority leader; **~~enrecht** *n* right of minorities; right of the minority; **~~enschutz** *m* protection of minorities; **~jährig** *a* under age, minor; *~~ sein* to be a minor; **~~e(r)** *m* minor, person under age; **~~keit** *f* minority; **~n** *tr* to diminish, to lessen, to decrease; (*herabsetzen*) to abate, to reduce, to lower; (*Wert*) to depreciate; **~umsatz** *m* reduction in turnover, falling-off in sales; **~ung** *f* decrease, diminution; (*Herabsetzung*) reduction, abatement; (*Wert*) depreciation; **~wert** *m* lesser value; inferiority; **~wertig** *a* inferior, of inferior quality; (*Waren*) off-grade, sub-standard; (*billig*) cheap; *chem* of lower valence; **~~keit** *f* inferiority, inferior quality; *chem* lower valence; **~~keitsgefühl** *n*, **~~keitskomplex** *m* inferiority complex; (*Hemmung*) inhibition; **~zahl** *f* minority.

mindest *a* least; (*klein*) smallest; (*niedrig*) lowest; *attr* minimum; *nicht im ~en* not in the least, not at all, by no means; *zum ~en* at least; **~alter** *n* minimum age; **~anforderung** *f* minimum requirement; **~arbeitszeit** *f* minimum working hours *pl*; **~auflage** *f* (*Zeitung*) minimum circulation; (*Bücher*) minimum edition; **~bedarf** *m* minimum demand; **~betrag** *m* minimum amount; **~einlage** *f* (*Bank*) minimum deposit; **~ens** *adv* at least; **~gebot** *n* lowest bid; **~gehalt** *n* minimum salary; **~lohn** *m* minimum wage; **~maß** *n* minimum; *auf das ~~ zurückführen* to minimize; **~preis** *m* minimum price, *fam* floor; **~programm** *n* minimum program(me); **~tarif** *m* minimum scale; **~unterstützung** *f* minimum benefit; **~verdienst** *m* minimum pay; **~versorgung** *f* minimum supply; **~wert** *m* least (*od* minimum) value.

Mine *f* mine; (*Bleistift~*) lead; (*Ersatz~*) refill; *auf e-e ~ laufen* to hit a mine; *~n schärfen* to fuse mines; **~nabteilung** *f* mine-laying detachment; **~nabweiser** *m* paravane; **~nbombe** *f* (heavy) high-explosive bomb (*Abk* H.E.bomb); **~nfalle** *f Am* booby trap; **~nfeld** *n* mine-field; **~nflugzeug** *n* mine-carrying aircraft; **~ngang** *m* gallery, tunnel; **~ngasse** *f* gap (*od* lane) in mine-field; **~nleger** *m* mine-layer; **~~-U-Boot** *n* mine-laying submarine; **~nräumboot** *n* mine-sweeper; **~nräumung** *f* mine clearance; **~nsperre** *f* mine barrier; **~nsucher** *m*, **~nsuchboot** *n* mine-locating craft; mine-sweeper; **~nsuchgerät** *n* mine detector; **~ntrichter** *m* mine crater; **~nverseucht** *a* mined; *~~es Gebiet* mine-infested area, mined zone; **~nwerfer** *m* (trench) mortar; mine-thrower.

Mineral *n* mineral; **~bad** *n* mineral bath; **~bestandteil** *m* mineral constituent; **~brunnen** *m* mineral spring (*od* well); **~fett** *n* mineral fat (*od* grease); vaseline; petroleum jelly; **~ien** *pl* minerals *pl*; **~isch** *a* mineral; **~og(e)** *m* mineralogist; **~ogie** *f* mineralogy; **~ogisch** *a* mineralogical; **~öl** *n* mineral oil; petroleum; **~quelle** *f* mineral spring; **~reich** *n* mineral kingdom; **~salz** *n* mineral salt; **~schmiermittel** *n* mineral lubricant; **~stoff** *m* mineral substance; **~~gehalt** *m* mineral content; **~vorkommen** *n* mineral occurrence; **~wasser** *n* mineral water, soda water, minerals *pl*, *Am* soft drinks *pl*; **~~ausschank** *m* soda counter, soda fountain.

Miniatur *f*, **~gemälde** *n* miniature; **~flügel** *m mus* baby grand; **~maler** *m* miniature-painter.

minier|en *tr* to (under)mine; to sap; **~er** *m* miner, sapper.

Minimal|betrag *m* lowest amount; **~gewicht** *n* lowest weight; **~satz** *m* minimum rate; **~wert** *m* minimum value.

Minimum *n* minimum.

Minister *m* minister; *Engl* Secretary of State, *Am* Secretary; *~ des Äußern Engl* the Secretary of State for Foreign Affairs, the Foreign Secretary, *Am* State Secretary, Secretary of State; *~ des Innern Engl* the Secretary of State for Home Affairs; **~ialdirektor** *m* assistant secretary in a government department; **~ialdirigent** *m* junior assistant secretary in a government department; **~ialerlaß** *m* ministerial order; **~ialrat** *m* principal in a government department; **~iell** *a* ministerial; **~ium** *n* ministry; *Engl* Office, *Am* Department; *~~ des Äußeren Engl* Foreign Office, *Am* State Department; *~~ des Inneren Engl* Home Office; **~präsident** *m* Prime Minister, Premier; **~rat** *m* Cabinet Council.

Minne *f hist* love; **~sänger** *m* minstrel, minne-singer.

minor|enn *a* minor, under age; **~ität** *f* minority; nonage.

minus *adv* minus, less; *zehn ~ vier gibt sechs* ten minus four are six; *~ n* deficit; deficiency; shortage; **~ader**, **~leitung** *f el* minus wire; **~betrag** *m* deficit; **~kel** *f* minuscule; **~leitung** *f* negative lead; **~pol** *m* negative element; **~zeichen** *n* minus sign.

Minute *f hist* minute; *in der ~* per minute; *auf die ~ kommen* to come right on the dot, to arrive on time; **~nlang** *adv* for (several) minutes; **~nzeiger** *m* minute-hand.

minutiös *a* minute.

Minze *f bot* mint.

mir *prn* me, to me; myself; *~ nichts dir nichts* without any more ado, unceremoniously; *ich wasche ~ die Hände* I wash my hands; *~ ist schlecht* I feel sick, I'm sick at my stomach; *von ~ aus* so far as I'm concerned; *wie du ~, so ich dir* tit for tat.

Mirabelle *f* small yellow plum.

Mirakel *n* miracle.

Misch|apparat *m* mixing apparatus, mixer; **~barkeit** *f* miscibility; **~becher** *m* shaker; **~bottich** *m* mixing tub; **~ehe** *f* mixed marriage; **~einrichtung** *f radio* (*Studio*) mixer, mixing unit; **~en** *tr* (*vermischen*) to mix, to mingle; (*Tabak, Kaffee*) to blend; (*Metalle*) to alloy; (*Karten*) to shuffle; (*Würfel*) to shake; (*verfälschen*) to adulterate; (*kreuzen*) to cross; (*vermengen*) to jumble, to mix up; (*Metall*) to alloy, to fettle; (*Getränk verdünnen, Farben*) to temper; (*zusammensetzen*) to compound; (*verschmelzen*) to merge; (*vereinigen*) to unite, to combine; *~~ r* to mix (*unter* with), to mingle (with); (*mitmachen*) to join (in); (*sich einmischen*) to interfere (with), to have a hand (in), to meddle (with), to mix (in); **~er** *m* mixer; **~farbe** *f* mixed colo(u)r; **~~n** *a* of mixed colo(u)r; **~futter** *n* mixed provender; **~gerät** *n radio* mixer, mixing unit; **~hahn** *m* mixing faucet; **~ling** *m* hybrid, cross(breed), mongrel; (*Menschen*) half-breed, half-caste; mestizo; mulatto; **~masch** *m* hotchpotch, medley; **~maschine** *f* mixing machine; **~pult** *n radio* mixer; fader; control desk; **~rasse** *f* mongrel race; **~röhre** *f radio* converter (tube), mixer valve; **~ung** *f* mixture; (*Tabak, Tee*) blend; (*Verbindung*) composition, combination, compound; (*Verfälschung*) adulteration; **~~sbestandteil** *m* ingredient of a mixture; **~~sfähig** *a* miscible; **~~sverhältnis** *n* ratio of components, mixing proportion; **~~swärme** *f* heat of mixing; **~volk** *n* mixed race; **~wald** *m* mixed forest.

Mispel *f* medlar.

miß|achten *tr* to slight, to despise; (*vernachlässigen*) to disregard, to neglect; **~achtung** *f* disregard, neglect, disdain; *~~ des Gerichts* contempt of court; **~behagen** *n* dislike, displeasure, discomfort; *v imp* to displease; **~bilden** *tr* to misshape; **~bildung** *f* deformity; disfigurement; malformation; **~billigen** *tr* to disapprove (of); **~billigung** *f* disapproval, disapprobation; **~brauch** *m* misuse; abuse; improper use; **~brauchen** *tr* to misuse; (*absichtlich*) to abuse; (*ausnützen*) to take advantage (of); (*mißhandeln*) to outrage; (*Namen Gottes*) to take in vain; (*Vertrauen*) to betray; **~bräuchlich** *a* improper; **~deuten** *tr* to misinterpret, to misconstrue; **~deutung** *f* misinterpretation; **~en** *tr* to miss, to want; (*entbehren*) to do without, to dispense (with); **~erfolg** *m* failure; unsuccess, nonsuccess; (*Unwirksamkeit*) inefficacy; fiasco; *fam* fizzle, flop, *sl* washout; **~ernte** *f* bad harvest, crop failure.

Misse|tat *f* misdeed; (*Verbrechen*) crime; **~täter** *m* evil-doer, offender; (*Verbrecher*) culprit; criminal, felon.

miß|fallen *irr itr* to displease; *~~ n* displeasure, dislike; **~fällig** *a* displeasing; (*ungünstig*) unfavo(u)rable; (*geringschätzig*) disparaging; (*unangenehm*) disagreeable; (*anstößig*) shocking; **~farben**, **~farbig** *a* discolo(u)red; inharmonious in colo(u)r; **~geburt** *f* monster, deformity; (*Fehlgeburt*) miscarriage, abortion; **~gelaunt** *a* ill-humo(u)red, sulky; **~geschick** *n* bad luck, misfortune, disaster; **~gestalt** *f* deformity; (*Ungeheuer*) monster; **~~et** *a* deformed, misshapen; **~gestimmt** *a* bad-tempered; (*niedergeschlagen*) dejected; **~glücken** *itr* to fail; *es ist ihm ~glückt.* he has not succeeded; **~gönnen** *tr* to envy, to grudge; **~griff** *m* mistake, blunder, *Am* break; **~gunst** *f* envy; ill will; jealousy; **~günstig** *a* envious, jealous (of), grudging; **~handeln** *tr* to maltreat, to ill-treat, to mistreat; (*schmähen*) to abuse; **~handlung** *f* maltreatment, cruelty; (*tätliche Beleidigung*) *jur* assault and battery; **~heirat** *f* misalliance; **~hellig** *a* discordant; dissentient, disagreeing; **~~keit** *f* dissonance; misunderstanding, discord, dissension.

Mission *f* mission; *innere ~* home mission; **~ar** *m* missionary; **~sgesellschaft** *f* missionary society.

Miß|jahr *n* bad year, bad harvest; **~klang** *m* dissonance; **~kredit** *m* discredit; *in ~~ bringen* to discredit, to bring into ill repute, *Am fam* to get s. o. in wrong (with); **~lich** *a* awkward; (*gefährlich*) dangerous; (*ungelegen*) embarrassing; (*unsicher*) precarious; (*unglücklich*) unfortunate; (*bedenklich*) critical; **~lichkeit** *f* awkwardness; danger; difficulty; **~liebig** *a* unpopular; *sich ~~ machen bei jdm* to incur the displeasure of s. o.; **~lingen** *irr itr* to fail; *~~ n* failure; **~mut** *m* displeasure, ill-humo(u)r; **~mutig** *a* ill-humo(u)red, sullenly discontented, sulky, morose, ill-tempered, *Am fam* grouchy; **~raten** *irr itr* to fail, to turn out badly; *~~ a* (*Kind*) ill-bred, naughty; **~stand** *m* grievance; (*Mißbrauch*) abuse; (*Ungehörigkeit*) impropriety; (*Zustand*) sorry (*od* deplorable) state of affairs; (*Ungelegenheit*) inconvenience, nuisance; *~stände beseitigen* to remedy abuses; **~stimmen** *tr* to upset, to put out of temper; **~stimmung** *f* discord, dissension; ill-humo(u)r; **~ton** *m* dissonance, false tone, discord; **~tönend** *a* out of tune, discordant; **~trauen** *itr* to distrust; *~~ n* distrust, mistrust (*gegen* of, *in* in); (*Verdacht*) suspicion; (*Befürchtung*) apprehension (*über* at); (*Zweifel*) doubt, disbelief (in); **~~santrag** *m* motion of 'no confidence'; **~~svotum** *n* vote of 'no-confidence'; **~trauisch** *a* distrustful; suspicious; **~vergnügen** *n* displeasure; **~vergnügt** *a* dissatisfied, discontented; **~verhältnis** *n* disproportion; incongruity; **~verständlich** *a* misleading; **~verständnis** *n* misunderstanding; (*leichter Streit*) dissension, *fam* breeze, tiff; **~verstehen** *irr tr* to misunderstand, *Am* to get s.o. wrong; (*verkennen*) to mistake; **~wachs** *m* bad harvest; **~weisung** *f* (*Kompaß*) aberration, variation; **~wirtschaft** *f* maladministration, mismanagement; (*widerrechtliche Verwendung*) misappropriation, misapplication.

Mist *m* dung, manure; (*Tiere*) droppings *pl*; *mar* fog; (*Schmutz*) dirt; *fig fam* trash, rubbish, junk; **~beet** *n* hotbed; **~~fenster** *n* garden-frame; **~en** *itr, tr* to manure, to dung; (*Stall*) to clean; **~fink** *m* dirty (*fig* nasty) person; **~fuhre** *f* load of manure; **~gabel** *f* dung-fork, pitchfork; **~grube** *f* dung-hole; **~haufen** *m* dung-hill, manure heap; **~jauche** *f* liquid manure; **~käfer** *m* dor, dung-beetle; **~pfütze** *f* puddle, plash; **~wagen** *m* dung-cart.

Mistel *f bot* mistletoe.

*

mit *prp* with, by, at, upon; *~ aller Macht* with all o.'s might; *~ offenen Armen* with open arms; *~ der Post* by post; *~ e-m Wort* in a word; *~ e-m Schlag* at a blow; *~ e-m Mal* all at once, all of a sudden; *~ Muße* at leisure; *~ Namen* by name; *~ heutigem Tage* from this day (forth); *~ vier Jahren* at the age of four; *~ dem Auto* by car; *~ Bleistift* in pencil; *~ der Zeit* in time; *komm ~!* come along! *~ nichten* by no means; *adv* (*auch, ebenso*) also, likewise, as well; *das gehört ~ dazu* that belongs to it also; *~ dabei sein* to be of the party; **~angeklagter** *m* co-defendant; **~arbeit** *f* collaboration, cooperation; (*Unterstützung*) assistance; **~~en** *itr* to collaborate, to cooperate; (*beitragen*) to contribute (*zu* to); (*Zeitung*) to be on the staff (of); **~~er** *m* fellow-labo(u)rer, co-worker; collaborator; (*Zeitung*) contributor, correspondent, *Am* (*unabhängig*) free lance; **~~erstab** *m* staff; **~begründer** *m* foundation-member, *Am* charter-member; **~bekommen** *irr tr* to get at the same time; to receive when leaving; (*Mitgift*) to get as dowry; **~benutzen** *tr* to use in common; **~benutzer** *m* joint user; **~benutzungsrecht** *n* joint usufruct; **~besitz** *m* joint property; **~~er** *m* joint proprietor; **~bestimmen** *tr* to be a contributory determinant; **~bestimmungsrecht** *n* right of contribution; (*der Arbeiterschaft*) co-determination law, co-rule in plant; **~beteiligt** *a* partaking, concerned; *~~ sein an* to be interested in; **~bewerben** *irr r* to compete (*um* for); **~bewerber** *m* competitor; **~bewohner** *m* (*Mieter*) fellow-lodger; coinhabitant; associate; **~bezahlen** *tr, itr* to pay o.'s share; to pay for s. o.; **~bringen** *irr tr* to bring (a present); (*nach sich ziehen*) to bring along with; **~bringsel** *n* present, souvenir; **~bruder** *m* brother; fellow, comrade; **~bürge** *m* co-surety; **~bürger** *m*, **~~in** *f* fellow-citizen; **~eigentümer** *m* joint proprietor; part owner; **~einander** *adv* together; jointly; *alle ~~* one and all; *gut ~~ auskommen* to get along well; **~empfinden** *irr tr* to feel for, to sympathize with; *~~ n* sympathy, fellow-feeling; **~erbe** *m* coheir; **~essen** *irr tr, itr* to eat with, to dine with; **~esser** *m* (*Haut*) blackhead, grub; comedo, acne punctata; **~fahren** *irr itr* to ride with; (*anhalten*) to hitchhike; *~~ lassen* to give s. o. a lift; **~fühlen** *tr* to feel for, to sympathize with; **~~d** *a* sympathetic; **~führen** *tr* to carry along with; **~geben** *irr tr* to give along with, to bestow upon; **~gefangene(r)** *m* fellow-prisoner; **~gefühl** *n* sympathy; **~gehen** *irr itr* to accompany, to go along; *~~ heißen fam* to steal; **~genießen** *irr tr fam* to enjoy with others; **~genommen** *a* worn-out, run-down; **~gift** *f* dowry, portion; **~~jäger** *m* fortune-hunter; **~glied** *n* member, fellow; *eingeschriebenes ~~* enrollee; *beitragzahlendes ~~* due-paying member; **~~erliste** *f*, **~~verzeichnis** *n* list of members; **~~erversammlung** *f* meeting of all members; **~~sbeitrag** *m* subscription, *Am* dues *pl*; **~~schaft** *f* membership; **~~skarte** *f* membership-card; **~halten** *irr itr* to take part (in); to hold conjointly with; *tr* (*Zeitung*) to take in together with others; **~helfen** *irr itr* to assist in; **~helfer** *m* helper, assistant; **~herausgeber** *m* co-editor; **~hilfe** *f* assistance; **~hin** *adv* therefore, consequently; **~hördienst** *m* radio-monitoring service; **~hören** *tr tele* to listen (in), to monitor; (*widerrechtlich*) to tap the telephone wire; (*zufällig*) to overhear; **~inbegriffen** *adv* including; **~inhaber** *m* copartner; **~kämpfer** *m* fellow-combatant; fellow-soldier; **~kläger** *m* co-plaintiff; **~klingen** *irr itr* to resonate; **~kommen** *irr itr* to come along with; *fig* to be able to follow, to keep up with; (*im Auto*) to catch a ride; *ich bin nicht ganz ~gekommen* I didn't catch what you said; *ich komme nicht mehr ~* that beats me; **~können** *irr itr* to be able to go, to come along with; **~kriegführend** *a* cobelligerent; **~lachen** *itr* to laugh with the others; **~laufen** *irr itr* to run with, to pass with the rest; **~läufer** *m* (*e-r Partei*) nominal member, follower; (*Anhänger*) hanger-on; (*Sympathisierender*) *Am* fellow travel(l)er; (*Opportunist*) time-server, trimmer; **~laut** *m* consonant.

Mitleid *n* pity, compassion; (*Mitgefühl*) sympathy; (*Gnade*) mercy; *~ mit jdm haben* to have pity on; **~en** *irr itr* to sympathize; **~enschaft** *f*: *in ~~ ziehen* to affect, to involve; **~ig** *a* pitiful, compassionate; **~sbezeigung** *f* condolence; **~(s)los** *a* pitiless, ruthless; **~(s)voll** *a* compassionate.

mit|lesen *irr tr* to read conjointly; to control; (*Zeitung*) to be a joint subscriber to (a paper); **~machen** *tr, itr* to join in, to take part in, to be in on, *Am fam* to chip in; (*Mode*) to follow; (*leiden*) to go through; **~marschieren** *itr* to march along with; **~mensch** *m* fellow-creature; **~nahme** *f* carrying, taking; **~nehmen** *irr tr* to take along with, to take s. o. to; (*im Auto*) to give s. o. a lift; (*erschöpfen*) to wear out, to exhaust; to weaken; (*in Mitleidenschaft ziehen*) to affect; *jdn arg ~~* to treat harshly; to criticize severely; **~nehmer** *m tech* catch; cam; nose clutch; gripper; **~nichten** *adv* by no means, not at all; **~pilot** *m aero* copilot; **~rechnen** *tr* to include in the account; **~reden** *itr* to put in a word; to join in conversation; *ich habe auch ein Wort ~zureden* I have also a word to say; *Sie haben hier nichts ~zureden* you have no say in this matter; **~regent** *m* coregent; **~reisen** *itr* to travel along with; **~~de(r)** *m* fellow-travel(l)er; **~reißen** *irr tr* to drag along; *fig* to carry (with), to sweep along; **~reiten** *irr itr* to ride along with; **~samt** *adv* together with; **~schicken** *tr* to send s. th. with s. o.; to enclose; **~schleppen** *tr* to drag along; **~schreiben** *irr tr* to take down, to jot down; to note down; **~schuld** *f* participation in guilt, complicity; **~schuldig** *a* accessory (to); implicated (in); **~~e(r)** *m, f* accomplice; **~schuldner** *m* joint debtor; **~schüler** *m* schoolfellow; fellow pupil; **~~in** *f Am fam* coed; **~schwingen** *irr itr* to resonate; to covibrate; **~schwingung** *f* resonance; covibration; **~senden** *irr tr* to send along; to enclose; **~spielen** *itr* to play, to join in with; *mus* to accompany; *jdm übel ~~* to play s. o. a nasty trick; *nicht mehr ~~* to cut out; **~spieler** *m* partner; *theat* supporting player; (*Spielgefährte*) playfellow; **~sprechen** *irr tr, itr* to join in; to come into consideration.

Mittag *m* midday, noon; (*Süden*) south; (*Essen*) dinner, lunch; *gegen ~* towards noon; *freier ~* (*von der Arbeit*) afternoon-off; *zu ~ essen* to dine, to have dinner; **~brot, ~essen** *n* (early) dinner, lunch; **~s** *adv* at noon; at lunch-time; **~(~)ausgabe** *f* noon edition; **~(~)gesellschaft** *f* company to luncheon; **~(~)glokke** *f* noon-bell; **~(~)glut, ~(~)hitze** *f* midday heat; **~(~)kreis** *m* meridian; **~(~)linie** *f* meridian line; **~(~)mahl(zeit)** *n* (*f*) midday meal; **~(~)pause** *f* lunch hour; **~(~)ruhe** *f*, **~(~)schlaf** *m* siesta, after-dinner nap; **~(~)sonne** *f* midday sun; **~(~)stunde** *f* noon; **~(~)tisch** *m* table; lunch, dinner; **~(~)zeit** *f* noontide; lunch- (*od* dinner-) time.

mittäglich *a* noonday, midday; (*südlich*) meridional, southern.

mit|tanzen *itr* to join in a dance; **~tänzer** *m* partner; **~täter** *m* accomplice, accessory; joint offender; **~~schaft** *f* complicity; **~tätig** *a*: *~~ sein, siehe mitarbeiten.*

Mitte *f* middle; (*Punkt*) centre, *Am* center; (*unter e-r Menge*) midst; (*Mittel*) *math* mean; medium; *~ der Straße* crown; *gegen ~ des Monats* around the middle of the month; *~ Vierzig* in the middle forties; *die goldene ~* the golden mean; *aus ihrer ~* from among them; *in die ~ nehmen* to take between; *in der ~* amidst, in the middle.

mitteil|en *tr* to inform (*jdm etw* s. o. of s. th.), to impart, to intimate, to pass on; *fam* to let s. o. know, to send s. o. word, to tell about; *com* to advise; (*amtlich*) to notify, to communicate; *ich erlaube mir, Ihnen mitzuteilen* I beg to inform you; *~~ r* to unbosom o. s.; **~sam** *a* communicative; **~~keit** *f* communicativeness; **~ung** *f* communication, information; message, report; (*amtlich*) notification, notice; communiqué; *com* advice, notice; *vertrauliche ~~* confidential communication.

Mittel *n* means *pl u. sing*; (*Abhilfe*) expedient; (*Notbehelf*) shift; (*Heil~*) remedy; (*Geld~*) funds *pl*, means *pl*, property; (*letzter Ausweg*; *Geld~*) resource(s *pl*); (*Durchschnitt*) average; *math* mean; *phys* medium; (*Vorrichtung*) device; *chem* (*Mischung*) compound, agent; (*Vorräte*) (expendable) supply; *jur* (*Maßnahme*) measure; *widerrechtliches ~* illegal measure; *er ist ohne ~* he is penniless; *die ~ besitzen zu* to be in a position (to); *sich ins ~ legen* to mediate, to interpose, to intervene; *meine ~ erlauben es mir nicht* I cannot afford it; *er ist entschlossen, sein Ziel mit allen ~n zu erreichen* he is determined to go to any length; *ihre eigenen ~* their own resources; *~ u. Wege* ways and means; *der Zweck heiligt die ~* the end justifies the means; *zu den letzten ~n greifen* to take extreme measures; **~alter** *n* Middle Ages *pl*; **~~lich** *a* medi(a)eval; **~amerika** *n* Central America; **~asien** *n* Central Asia; **~bar** *a* indirect, mediate; **~~keit** *f* indirectness; **~bau** *m* frontage; **~blende** *f phot* middle diaphragm; **~deck** *n mar* middle deck; **~deutschland** *n* Central Germany; **~ding** *n* intermediate thing, something between; compromise; cross; **~ebene** *f phot* (*Objektiv*) central plane of the lens; **~ernte** *f* average crop; **~europa** *n* Central Europe; **~europäisch** *a* Central European; **~fein** *a* good medium, middling; **~finger** *m* middle finger; **~fußknochen** *m* metatarsal bone; **~gang** *m* central walk; gangway; *rail* corridor, gangway, *Am* aisle; **~gebirge** *n* secondary chain of mountains; hills *pl*; **~gewicht**

n middle weight; **~glied** *n* middle limb; *fig* intermediate stage; *anat* middle phalanx; **~groß** *a* of medium size, medium-sized; **~hand** *f* metacarpus; **~hochdeutsch** *a* Middle High German; **~kurs** *m* (*Börse*) middle-price; **~lage** *f* neutral position; central position; *mus* (*Stimme*) tenor; **~ländisch** *a*: *das ~~e Meer* the Mediterranean (Sea); **~latein** *n* Medi(a)eval Latin; **~lauf** *m* middle course; **~läufer** *m sport* centre halfback, *Am* center half; **~linie** *f* equator; axis; centre line; (*Tennis*) half-court centre line, centre service line; (*Fußball*) centre line; **~los** *a* without means, destitute; **~~igkeit** *f* destitution, lack of means; **~mächte** *f pl* Central European Powers *pl*; **~maß** *n* average; (*Größe*) middling size; *math* mean; **~mäßig** *a* middling, mediocre, poor; (*durchschnittlich*) average; (*Absatz*) moderate; **~~keit** *f* mediocrity; **~meer** *n* the Mediterranean (Sea); **~ohr** *n* middle ear; tympanum; **~~entzündung** *f* inflammation of the middle ear; mastoiditis; **~partei** *f* moderate party; **~~ler** *m* centrist; **~punkt** *m* centre, *Am* center; central point, focus; *~~ der Stadt* heart of the town; *~~ des Luftverkehrs* air hub; **~s** *adv* by means of; through; by; **~schiene** *f* central rail; **~schiff** *n* middle aisle; **~schule** *f* lower grade secondary school (in Germany); **~smann** *m*, **~sperson** *f* mediator, go-between; (*Unparteiischer*) *sport* umpire; *com* middleman; **~sorte** *f* medium quality; **~spieler** *m* centre, *Am* center; **~st** *adv* by means of; **~stand** *m* middle classes *pl*, *Am* white collar section of population; **~stellung** *f* mid-position; **~stimme** *f* tenor; baritone; middle parts *pl*; **~streckenlauf** *m* half-long distance race; **~stück** *n* middle piece, central portion; **~stufe** *f* (*Schule*) intermediate grades *pl*; **~stürmer** *m sport* centre forward; **~ton** *m mus* mediant; **~wand** *f* partition wall; **~weg** *m* middle course; mean, compromise; *e-n ~~ einschlagen* to adopt a middle course; **~welle** *f radio* medium wave; **~~nbereich** *m* medium wave band; **~~nempfänger** *m radio* medium wave receiver; **~~nsender** *m radio* medium wave transmitter; **~wert** *m* mean (value), average; **~wort** *n* participle; **~zeit** *f* mean time.

mitten *adv* in the middle of, amidst, in the centre of; *~ in, auf, unter* in the midst of; *~ durch* right across; right through, through the middle; *~ drinne* in the very centre; midway; *~ entzwei* broken in two; *~ am Tage* in broad daylight; *~ im Winter* in the depth of winter.

Mitter|nacht *f* midnight; (*Himmelsgegend*) north; **~~sschicht** *f* graveyard shift; **~nächtlich** *a* midnight; northern.

Mittfasten *pl* Mid-Lent.

mittler *a* middle, inner, central; (*durchschnittlich*) medium, average; (*mittelmäßig*) mediocre, middling; *math* mean, middle; (*Zeit, Temperatur*) mean; (*dazwischen*) intermediate; *von ~em Alter* middle-aged; *~ m* mediator, intercessor; third party; **~amt** *n* mediatorship; **~weile** *adv* meanwhile, (in the) meantime.

mit|tragen *irr tr* to carry (with others); (*Verlust*) to share; **~trinken** *irr itr* to drink with others; **~tun** *irr itr* to join in doing; to help.

mitt|schiffs *adv* amidships; **~sommer** *m* midsummer; **~woch** *m* Wednesday.

mitunter *adv* now and then, sometimes, once in a while, occasionally; **~schreiben** *irr tr, itr* to add o.'s signature; (*gegenzeichnen*) to countersign; **~schrift** *f* joint-signature; **~zeichnete(r)** *m* co-signatory.

Mit|verfasser *m* joint author; **~verschulden** *n jur* contributory negligence; **~verschworene(r)** *m* fellow-conspirator; **~vormund** *m* joint guardian; **~welt** *f* the present generation; our contemporaries *pl*; **~wirken** *itr* to co-operate (*bei* in), to contribute; (*teilnehmen*) to take part (in); **~~de(r)** *m mus* player; (*Schauspieler*) actor, member (of the cast); **~wirkung** *f* co-operation, participation; assistance; **~wissen** *n* (joint) knowledge, cognizance; *ohne mein ~~* without my knowledge, unknown to me; **~wisser** *m jur* accessory; (*Vertrauter*) confidant; **~~schaft** *f* complicity; collusion; **~zählen** *tr* to include in the account; *itr* to be included (in the account); **~ziehen** *irr tr* to drag along; *itr* to march along with.

Mix|becher *m* cocktail-shaker, *Am sl* jigger; **~er** *m* bartender; **~tur** *f* mixture.

Möbel *n* piece of furniture; *pl* furniture; **~ausstattung** *f* furniture; **~einrichtung** *f* furniture; **~expeditionsfirma** *f* removal contractor's firm, removal contract firm; **~fabrik** *f* furniture works *pl*; **~geschäft** *n* furnishing house; **~händler** *m* furniture-dealer; **~politur** *f* furniture polish; **~spediteur** *m* furniture remover; removal contractor; **~speicher** *m* furniture repository; **~stück** *n* piece of furniture; **~tischler** *m* cabinet-maker; **~transportgeschäft** *n* firm of furniture-removers; **~wagen** *m* furniture (*od* removal) van, pantechnicon, *Am* furniture truck.

mobil *a* (*beweglich*) movable; (*flink*) nimble, quick, active; *mil* mobile; **~iar** *n* furniture, movables *pl*; **~iarvermögen** *n* personal property; **~ien** *pl* movables *pl*; **~isieren** *tr* to mobilize; **~machung** *f* (*Abk* **Mob**) mobilization; **~~sbefehl** *m* mobilization order; **~~splan** *m* plan of mobilization; **~~stag** *m* mobilization day (*Abk* M-day).

möblier|en *tr* to furnish; *~tes Zimmer* furnished room; **~ung** *f* furnishing.

Mode *f* fashion, mode; vogue; (*Brauch*) custom, use; *in der ~* in fashion, in vogue; *nach der ~* fashionably; *neueste ~* latest fashion, new look; *nach der neuesten ~* up-to-date in style; *in ~ bringen* to bring into fashion; *~ sein* to be the fashion; *die ~ mitmachen* to follow the fashion; *aus der ~ kommen* to grow out of fashion; **~artikel** *m pl*, **~waren** *f pl* novelties *pl*, fancy goods *pl*; **~dame** *f* lady of fashion; **~farbe** *f* fashion colo(u)r; **~geschäft** *n* draper's shop; millinery; **~haus** *n* fashion house; **~linie** *f* fashion line; **~narr** *m* dandy, fop, beau, fashion-monger; **~(n)schau** *f* fashion show, mannequin parade; **~salon** *m* fashion house; **~schriftsteller** *m* popular writer; **~vorschau** *f* fashion preview; **~welt** *f* fashionable world; **~werkstätte** *f*, **~salon** *m* fashion house; **~wort** *n* vogue-word; **~zeichner** *m*, **~~in** *f* dress designer; **~zeichnung** *f* fashion pattern; **~zeitung** *f* fashion magazine.

Modell *n* model; pattern, design; type; (*Muster, Form*) mo(u)ld; *tech* (*Nachbildung*) mock-up; *~ stehen* to pose for an artist; **~flugzeug** *n* model aircraft; **~~wettbewerb** *m* model aircraft contest; **~ierbogen** *m* cutting-out model; **~ieren** *tr, itr* to model, to shape, to mo(u)ld, to fashion; **~ierer** *m* model(l)er; **~ierklasse** *f* class for model(l)ing; **~iermasse** *f* model(l)ing clay; **~tischler** *m* pattern-maker.

modeln *tr* to mo(u)ld; to model; to modulate; (*ändern*) to change.

Moder *m* mo(u)ld; putridity, decay; **~duft, ~geruch** *m* musty smell, smell of decay; **~ig** *a* mo(u)ldy, musty; **~n** *itr* to mo(u)lder, to rot, to putrefy; to decay.

modern *a* modern, fashionable, up-to-date, in the latest style (*od* fashion); (*ironisch*) new-fangled, *Am* (*ausgezeichnet*) elegant, *Am* (*fortschrittlich*) streamlined; *~ eingerichtet* with all the modern facilities, *Am* with all the improvements; **~isieren** *tr* to modernize, to bring up to date, *Am* to streamline; **~isierung** *f* modernization, *Am* streamlining.

modifizieren *tr* to modify, to alter; to tone down.

modi|sch *a* fashionable, modish, stylish; *~sche Einzelheit* fashion detail; *~sche Wirkung* fashion effect; *~sche Fußbekleidung* fashion footwear; **~stin** *f* milliner.

Modu|lation *f* modulation; control; *verzerrungsfreie ~~* linear modulation; *~~ der Stimme* inflection of voice; **~~sfrequenz** *f* modulating frequency; **~~sstrom** *m* modulating current; **~~ston** *m* note of modulation; **~~swelle** *f* wave of modulation; **~lator** *m* modulator; **~~röhre** *f* modulator valve (*Am* tube); **~lieren** *tr* to modulate; *~lierte ungedämpfte Welle* (*radio*) modulated continuous wave; **~s** *m* mode; method; *gram* mood.

Mogel|ei *f fam* cheating; trickery; **~n** *itr* to cheat; to trick; *sl* to wangle.

mögen *irr tr* (*gern haben*) to like, to care for, to be fond of; (*wünschen*) to wish; (*Erlaubnis*) to let; *aux* may, might; *ich möchte* I should like to; *lieber ~* to prefer, to like better; *ich möchte lieber* I would rather; *das mag sein* that may be so; *nicht ~* to dislike; *ich möchte nicht* I don't want to, I should not like to; *was möchten Sie?* what do you want? *ich mag nicht* I do not want to, I do not like to; *wie dem auch sein mag* be that as it may; *was ich auch tun mag* no matter what I do; *er möchte sofort zu mir kommen* ask him to come and see me immediately; *sie mochte zwanzig Jahre alt sein* she looked about twenty years old.

möglich *a* possible; (*durchführbar*) practicable, feasable; (*möglich*) likely; eventual; *es ist ihm nicht ~* he can't possibly; *so schnell wie ~* as quickly as possible; *alles ~e* all sorts of things; everything possible; *das ist wohl ~* that may be; *nicht ~!* it can't be! you don't say so! well I never! *so wenig wie ~* the least possible; as few ... as possible; as little as can be; **~enfalls, ~erweise** *adv* if possible, possibly; perhaps; **~keit** *f* possibility, eventuality, chance; (*Durchführbarkeit*) practicability, feasibility; (*mögliche Kraft*) potentiality; *nach ~~* as far as possible; **~st** *a, adv: sein ~~es tun* to do o.'s utmost; *~~ schnell* as quickly as possible.

Mohammedan|er *m*, **~erin** *f* Mohammedan; **~isch** *a* Mohammedan.

Mohn *m* poppy; **~kapsel** *f* poppy capsule; **~öl** *n* poppy-seed oil; **~saft** *m* poppy-juice, opium; **~samen** *m* poppy-seed.

Mohr *m* Moor, negro, darky; **~enwäsche** *f fig* vindication; **~in** *f* negress.

Möhre, Mohrrübe *f* carrot.
Moiré *m* moiré; tabby; watered silk.
mokieren *r* to sneer (*über* at).
Mokka(kaffee) *m* mocha, Mocha (coffee).
Molch *m* newt.
Mole *f* mole, pier, jetty; dam (of a harbo(u)r; **~nkopf** *m* pier head.
Molekel, Molekül *n* molecule; **~adhäsion** *f* molecule adhesion.
molekular *a* molecular; **~abstoßung** *f* molecular repulsion; **~anziehung** *f* molecular attraction; **~bewegung** *f* molecular motion; **~brechung** *f* molecular refraction; **~drehung** *f* molecular rotation; **~druck** *m* molecular pressure; **~gewicht** *n* molecular weight; **~größe** *f* molecular magnitude; **~reibung** *f* molecular friction; **~verbindung** *f* molecular compound.
Molk\|e *f* whey; **~erei** *f* dairy.
Moll *n mus* minor; **~ig** *a* comfortable, snug; (*rundlich*) rounded, soft; **~ton** *m mus* minor key; **~uske** *f* mollusc.
Molybdän *n* molybdenum; **~eisen** *n* ferromolybdenum.
Moment *m* moment, instant; **~** *n tech* momentum; (*Anlaß*) motive, reason; (*Antrieb*) impulse, impetus; (*Faktor*) factor; *e-n ~!* wait a moment! half a moment! one moment! *das ist der richtige ~* now is the time; **~an** *a* momentary; instantaneous; right now, right this moment, at the moment; for the present; **~aufnahme** *f*, **~bild** *n* instantaneous photograph, snapshot, candid photograph; **~klemme** *f* instantaneous clamp; **~um** *n* momentum; **~verschluß** *m phot* instantaneous shutter.
Monade *f* monad.
Monarch *m* monarch; **~ie** *f* monarchy; **~isch** *a* monarchical; **~ist** *m* monarchist.
Monat *m* month; *wieviel verdient er pro ~?* how much does he make a month? **~elang** *adv* for months, of months' duration; lasting a month (*od* months); **~lich** *a* monthly; **~sabschluß** *m* monthly balance; **~sausweis** *m* monthly return; **~sbericht** *m* monthly report; **~sbinde** *f med* sanitary towel; **~sfluß** *m* menstruation, period; menses *pl*; **~sfrist** *f*: *binnen ~~* within a month; **~sgehalt** *n*, **~slohn** *m* monthly salary (*od* pay *od* wage); **~sheft** *n* monthly part (*od* number); **~skarte** *f* monthly season-ticket, *Am* commutation(-ticket); **~sname** *m* name of a month; **~srate** *f* monthly instal(l)ment; **~sschrift** *f* monthly magazine; monthly (publication); **~sverdienst** *m* monthly profit; **~swechsel** *m* one month's bill; **~(s)weise** *adv* by the month; **~szeitung** *f* monthly paper (*od* review); monthly magazine.
Mönch *m* monk, friar; **~isch** *a* monkish, monastic; **~skloster** *n* monastery; **~skutte** *f* monk's frock; **~sleben** *n* monastic life; **~sorden** *m* religious order; **~sschrift** *f typ* black letter; **~(s)tum** *n* monasticism; **~szelle** *f* friar's cell.
Mond *m* moon; *astr* satellite; *poet* month; *der ~ scheint* the moon is shining; *halber ~* crescent; *voller ~* full moon; *zunehmender ~* increasing moon; *abnehmender ~* wanting moon; **~aufgang** *m* moonrise; **~bahn** *f* moon's orbit; **~finsternis** *f* eclipse of the moon; **~förmig** *a* crescent-shaped; lunate; **~gebirge** *n* mountains of the moon; **~halo** *n* lunar halo; **~hell** *a* moonlit; **~hof** *m* halo round the moon; lunar aurora; **~jahr** *n* lunar year; **~kalb** *n* moon-calf; moler; *fig* ugly person; dolt; **~nacht** *f* moonlight night; **~phasen** *f pl* phases of the moon; **~scheibe** *f* disk of the moon; **~schein** *m*, **~licht** *n* moonlight; **~sichel** *f* crescent, sickle-moon; **~stein** *m* moonstone; selenite; **~sucht** *f* somnambulism; **~süchtig** *a* moonstruck, lunatic; **~viertel** *n* quarter of the moon; **~wechsel** *m* change of the moon.
Moneten *pl fam* money, tin, *Am sl* dough, jack, spondulics *pl*, gingerbread.
monieren *tr* (*kritisieren*) to find fault with; to censure, to criticize; (*erinnern, mahnen*) to remind.
Mono\|gamie *f* monogamy; **~gramm** *n* monogram; **~graphie** *f* monograph; **~kel** *n* monocle; **~kultur** *f* monoculture; **~lith** *m* monolith; **~log** *m* monologue, soliloquy; **~mane** *m* monomaniac; **~manie** *f* monomania; **~pol** *n* monopoly (*auf* of, *Am* on); **~~erzeugnis** *n* proprietary article; **~~isieren** *tr* to monopolize; **~~stellung** *f* exclusive control, monopoly; **~theismus** *m* monotheism; **~theist** *m* monotheist; **~ton** *a* monotonous; **~~ie** *f* monotony.
Mongol\|ei *f*: *die ~* Mongolia; **~isch** *a* Mongolian.
Monstranz *f* monstrance.
monstr\|ös *a* monstrous; **~um** *n* monster; freak.
Monsun *m* monsoon.
Montag *m* Monday; *blauer ~* Saint Monday, blue (*od* idle) Monday; **~s** *adv* every Monday, on Mondays.
Mont\|age *f* setting up, fitting; erection; assembling; production line; **~~band** *n*, **~~rampe** *f* assembly line; **~~gestell** *n* jig; (*fahrbar*) dolly; **~~gruppe** *f* assembly; **~~halle** *f* assembly shop; **~~haus** *n* prefabricated house; **~~hebel** *m mot* tyre lever; **~~luke** *f* building-hatch; **~~werk** *n* assembly plant; **~eur** *m tech* fitter; *mot* mechanic, mechanician; *el* electrician; *aero* rigger; **~~anzug** *m* overall; **~ieren** *tr tech* to mount; (*errichten*) to set up, to erect; (*zus.setzen*) to assemble; (*einrichten*) to instal(l); (*einstellen*) to adjust; (*ausrüsten*) to equip; **~ierhebel** *m* tyre (*od* tire) lever; **~ierung** *f* mounting, fitting up; erecting, setting up; **~ur** *f* uniform.
Montan\|aktie *f* mining share; **~industrie** *f* mining industry; **~markt** *m* mining market.
Moor *n* moor, fen, bog, marsh, swamp; **~bad** *n* mud-bath; **~boden** *m* marshy soil; **~huhn** *n* moor-hen; **~ig** *a* moory, fenny, boggy, marshy.
Moos *n* moss; (*Geld*) *sl* tin, cash; *Am sl* dough; **~bedeckt** *a* moss-grown; **~flechte** *f* lichen; **~ig** *a* mossy; **~rose** *f* moss rose.
Mop *m* mop; **~pen** *tr* to mop; **~s** *m* pug; **~sen** *tr sl* to pinch; *r* to be bored.

*

Moral *f* (*sittliche Lehre*) moral; (*sittliche Grundsätze*) morals *pl*; (*Sittlichkeit*) morality; (*Zucht*) morale; **~inonkel** *m fam* wowser; **~insauer** *a* Pecksniffian; **~isch** *a* moral; **~isieren** *itr* to moralize; **~ist** *m* moralist; **~ität** *f* morality; **~pauke, ~predigt** *f* (moral) lecture.
Moräne *f* moraine.
Morast *m* morass, fen, marsh, bog; (*Kot*) mire, dirt; **~ig** *a* moory, boggy, marshy; (*kotig*) miry.
Moratorium *n* moratorium, respite.
Morchel *f* morel.
Mord *m* (*vorsätzlich*) murder; (*Totschlag*) manslaughter; (*Tötung*) homicide; *einfacher ~* second-degree murder; *schwerer ~* first-degree murder; *e-n ~ begehen* to commit a murder; *wegen ~es verurteilen* to convict of murder; *es gab ~ u. Totschlag* it ended in bloodshed; **~anschlag** *m* murderous attack; **~brenner** *m* incendiary; **~bube, ~geselle** *m* assassin; cutthroat; **~en** *tr* to murder, to kill; **~~** *n* murder; massacre; **~geschichte** *f* tale of murder; **~geschrei** *n* cry of murder; **~gier** *f* bloodthirstiness; **~~ig, ~lustig** *a* bloodthirsty; **~io** *interj*: *Zeter u. ~~ schreien* to cry murder; **~kommission** *f* homicide squad; **~sgeschichte** *f* cock-and-bull story; **~sglück** *n* stupendous luck; **~skerl** *m* devil of a fellow; stunner; **~slüge** *f* corker, cracker; **~smäßig** *a* awful, terrible; terrific; **~sradau, ~sspektakel** *m* fearful din, hullabaloo; **~tat** *f* murder(ous deed); **~versuch** *m* attempt at murder; **~waffe** *f* murderous weapon.
Mörder *m* murderer; assassin; **~grube** *f*: *aus seinem Herzen keine ~~ machen* to be very outspoken; **~in** *f* murderess; **~isch** *a* murderous; (*Klima*) deadly; **~lich** *a* murderous; *fig* enormous, violent; terrible.
Morgen *m* morning; (*Tagesanbruch*) dawn, daybreak; (*Vormittag*) forenoon; (*Osten*) East; (*Feldmaß*) acre; *am ~, des ~s* in the morning; *guten ~!* good morning! **~** *adv* tomorrow, *~ in acht Tagen* a week from tomorrow; *~ früh* tomorrow morning; *~ abend* tomorrow evening; *heute ~* this morning; **~andacht** *f* morning prayers *pl*; **~ausgabe** *f* morning edition; **~blatt** *n* morning paper; **~dämmerung** *f*, **~grauen** *n* daybreak, dawn; *in der ~~* in the early twilight; **~dlich** *a* (in the) morning, matutinal; **~frische, ~kühle** *f* morning freshness; **~gabe** *f* dowry; bridegroom's gift to bride; **~gebet** *n* morning prayer; **~gruß** *m* morning salute; **~gymnastik** *f* morning gymnastics *pl*; **~kaffee** *m* morning coffee; **~kleid** *n* morning gown; **~land** *n* Orient, East, Levant; **~länder** *m* Oriental; **~ländisch** *a* oriental, eastern; **~luft** *f* morning air, morning breeze; *~~ wittern* to scent an advantage; **~nebel** *m* morning fog; **~post** *f* first mail; morning post; **~rock** *m* dressing gown; *Am* bath-robe; house gown, negligée, wrapper; (*Männer*) house coat; **~rot** *n*, **~röte** *f* dawn; *poet* aurora; **~s** *adv* in the morning; *früh ~s* early in the morning; **~seite** *f* eastern side; **~sonne** *f* morning sun; **~ständchen** *n* morning music; **~stern** *m* morning star, Venus; **~stille** *f* calmness in the morning; **~stunde** *f* morning hour; **~tau** *m* morning dew; **~wind** *m* morning breeze; (*Ostwind*) east wind; **~zeitung** *f* morning paper, *Am fam* A.M.
morgig *a* of tomorrow; *der ~e Tag* tomorrow.
Morphi\|nismus *m* morphiomania; **~nist, ~umsüchtiger** *m* morphiomaniac, morphine addict; **~um** *n* morphine, morphia; **~~spritze** *f* morphia injection; (*Instrument*) syringe for injecting morphia.
morsch *a* rotten, decayed; (*zerbrechlich*) friable, frail; (*spröde*) brittle; *~es Eis* soft ice.
Morse\|alphabet *n* Morse alphabet; **~apparat** *m* Morse printer; **~n** *itr* to morse, *sl* to pounder brass; **~punkt** *m* dot; **~schreiber** *m* Morse printer; (*Farbschreiber*) (Morse) inker; **~schrift** *f* Morse code; **~streifen** *m* Morse slip; **~strich** *m* dash; **~taste** *f* Morse key; **~zeichen** *n* Morse signal.
Mörser *m* mortar; *mil* mortar; heavy howitzer; **~keule** *f* pestle.
Mörtel *m* mortar; (*zum Bewurf*) plaster, cement; *mit ~ bewerfen* to plaster, (*grob*) to rough-cast; **~bewurf**

m plaster; **~kelle** *f* trowel; **~maschine** *f* pugging mill; **~trog** *m* hod.
Mosaik *n od f* mosaic(-work); **~fußboden** *m* tesselated pavement.
Moschee *f* mosque.
Moschus *m* musk; **~ochs** *m* musk-ox; **~tier** *n* musk-deer.
Moses *m* Moses; *die 5 Bücher Mosis* the Pentateuch.
Moskito *m* (tropic) mosquito; **~netz** *n* mosquito-net.
Moslem *m* Moslem, Moslim.
Most *m* must, new wine, grape juice; (*Apfel~*) cider; (*Birnen~*) perry; **~rich** *m* mustard.
Mot|ette *f* motet; **~ion** *f* motion; **~iv** *n* motive; (*Gegenstand*) subject; (*Malerei, mus*) motif, theme; **~~ieren** *tr* to motivate, to give reasons (for); **~~ierung** *f* motivation.
Motor *m el* motor; (*Verbrennungsmaschine*) engine; (*Verbund~*) compound motor; (*Zweitakt~*) two-stroke engine; (*Verbrennungs~*) combustion engine; *attr* power-driven; *den ~ anwerfen* (*od anlassen*) to start the engine; *den ~ abbremsen* to run up the engine; *den ~ abdrosseln* to close the throttle; *den ~ abstellen* to stop the engine; *den ~ auseinandernehmen* to dismantle the engine; *den ~ anwärmen* to warm up the engine; *den ~ überholen* to overhaul the engine; *mit abgestelltem ~* engine off; *mit laufendem ~* engine in (*od* on); *der ~ setzt aus* (*springt nicht an*) the motor is cutting out (does not pick up); *der ~ läuft einwandfrei* the engine runs faultlessly; *den ~ voll beanspruchen* to run the engine all out; **~anlaßschalter** *m* motor-starting switch; **~anlasser** *m* starter; **~aufhängung** *f* motor mounting bracket; *aero* engine supports *pl*; **~ausfall, ~defekt** *m*, **~panne** *f* engine failure (*od* trouble); **~barkasse** *f mar* motor launch; **~bock** *m* engine bracket; **~boot** *n* motor-boat; (*Schnellboot*) speed-boat; **~drehmoment** *n* engine torque; **~drehzahlmesser** *m aero* engine speed indicator, *Am* tachometer; **~einbau** *m* engine mounting; **~enanlage** *f* power-plant; **~engeräusch** *n* noise of engines; **~engondel** *f aero* engine support bay, nacelle; **~enhalle** *f* engine shop; **~enlärm** *m* noise of engines; **~enschlosser** *m* mechanic; **~fahrzeug** *n* motor vehicle; **~flugzeug** *n* power plane; **~gehäuse** *n* engine crank case; *el* motor casing; **~generator** *m* motor generator; **~getriebe** *n* engine gear (*od* drive); **~haube** *f* bonnet, *Am* hood; *aero* engine cowling (*od* hood); **~isieren** *tr* to motorize, *mil* to mechanize; **~isiert** *a* mobile; flying; motorized; **~isierung** *f* motorization; **~kühler** *m* radiator; **~lager** *n* engine bearing; **~leistung** *f* motor output (*od* performance), engine power; **~pak** *f mil* self-propelled anti-tank artillery; **~pflug** *m* motor (-driven) plough, tractor plough; **~prüfstand** *m* engine-test stand; **~prüfung** *f* engine test; **~pumpe** *f* motor-driven pump, power pump; **~rad** *n* motor-cycle; (*leichtes*) motor bike; *~~ fahren* to ride on a motor-cycle; *~~ mit Beiwagen* motor-cycle with side-car; **~~anzug** *m* cycling-suit, *Am* wheel suit; **~~fahrer** *m* motorcyclist; **~~rennen** *n* cycle-race; **~roller** *m* motor scooter; **~säge** *f* power saw; **~schaden** *m* engine trouble; **~schiff** *n* motor ship; **~schlepper** *m* traction engine; **~schlitten** *m* aerosled; snowmobile; **~segler** *m* motor glider; **~sport** *m* motoring; **~spritze** *f* fire engine; **~störung** *f* engine failure (*od* trouble), break down of the engine; **~träger** *m* engine mounting; **~triebwagen** *m* rail motor-car; **~überholung** *f* engine overhaul (-ing); **~verkleidung** *f aero* engine cowling (*od* fairing); **~vorbau** *m* engine mounting; **~wagen** *m* motor car; **~welle** *f* motor shaft, main shaft; **~winde** *f* motor winch.
Motte *f* moth; **~nfraß** *m* damage done by moths; **~nkugel** *f* mothball; **~npulver** *n* insect-powder, insecticide; **~nzerfressen** *a* moth-eaten.
Motto *n* motto.
moussieren *itr* to sparkle, to effervesce; **~d** *a* sparkling.
Möwe *f* sea-gull, mew.
Muck|e *f* whim, caprice; **~en, ~sen** *itr* to grumble, to be sulky; *er darf nicht ~~* he dare not say a word; (*sich rühren*) to stir; **~er** *m* hypocrite, bigot; **~~ei** *f*, **~~tum** *n* bigotry, cant.
Mücke *f* gnat, midge; (*Fliege*) fly; (*Stech~*) mosquito; *aus e-r ~ e-n Elefanten machen* to make a mountain out of a molehill, *sl* to make the devil of a fuss; **~nstich** *m* gnat-bite, midge-bite.
müd|e *a* tired, weary; (*abgespannt*) fatigued; (*kraftlos*) languid; (*erschöpft*) exhausted, worn-out; (*genug haben*) sick of; *~~ werden* to tire, to get tired; *sie ist zum Umfallen ~~* she's so tired she's ready to drop; **~igkeit** *f* weariness, fatigue, lassitude.
Muff *m* muff; (*Geruch*) mo(u)ldy smell; **~e** *f tech* coupling-box; sleeve, socket, pipe-connector; **~el** *f tech* muffle; (*Mund*) snout; **~~** *m* sulky person; **~ig** *a* sullen; sulky; (*Geruch*) fusty, musty, mo(u)ldy; (*Luft*) close.
muh! moo! **~en** *itr* to low.
Müh|e *f* trouble, pains *pl*; (*Ermüdung*) fatigue; (*Unbequemlichkeit*) inconvenience; (*Schwierigkeit*) difficulty; (*Verdruß*) annoyance, bother; (*Anstrengung*) effort, exertion, labo(u)r, toil; *nicht der ~~ wert* not worth while, not worth the trouble; *mit leichter ~~* easily; *verlorene ~~* a waste of effort; *mit ~~ u. Not* barely, only just, with difficulty; *sich ~~ geben* to take pains; *~~ machen* to give trouble; *keine ~~ scheuen* to grudge no pains; **~~los** *a* easy, effortless, without trouble; **~~losigkeit** *f* ease, easiness, facility; **~~n** *r* to take pains (about), to trouble o. s.; **~~voll** *a* laborious, difficult, irksome; **~~waltung** *f* care, trouble, pains *pl*; efforts *pl*; *für seine ~~waltung* for the trouble he has taken; **~sal** *f* (*n*) trouble, toil; (*Ungemach*) hardship; (*Elend*) misery; (*Not*) distress; **~sam, ~selig** *a* troublesome; (*ermüdend*) tiresome; (*schwierig*) difficult; (*verworren*) intricate; (*schwer*) hard; **~seligkeit** *f* hardship, toil(someness).
Mühl|bach *m* mill-brook; **~e** *f* mill windmill; *das ist Wasser auf seine ~~* that's grist to his mill; **~graben** *m* mill-race; **~rad** *n* mill wheel; **~stein** *m* millstone.
Muhme *f* aunt, niece; female cousin.
Mulatte *m*, **-in** *f* mulatto.
Mulde *f* tray, trough; (*im Gelände*) hollow, depression, valley; **~nförmig** *a* trough-shaped; **~nkippwagen** *m* dump-type hopper truck.
Mull *m* mull, muslin; **~binde** *f* (gauze) bandage.
Müll *m* dust, refuse, rubbish, garbage; **~abfuhr** *f* removal of refuse; sanitation service; **~abholer** *m* dustman, *Am* ash-man; **~eimer, ~kasten** *m* dust-bin, *Am* ash-can; **~er** *m* miller; **~~in** *f* miller's wife; **~grube** *f* refuse pit; **~haufen** *m* rubbish-heap; **~kutscher** *m* dustman, *Am* ash-man; **~platz** *m* refuse tip, *Am* dump; **~schaufel** *f* dust-pan; **~schlucker** *m* (kitchen) waste-disposer; **~verbrennungsofen** *m* destructor, *Am* incinerator; **~wagen** *m* dust-cart, *Am* ash-cart, garbage truck, dirt wag(g)on.
mulmig *fam a* rotten, worm-eaten; *fig* precarious.
Multipl|ikation *f* multiplication; **~ikator** *m* multiplier; **~izieren** *tr* to multiply (by).
Mumi|e *f* mummy; **~fizieren** *tr* to mummify.
Mummelgreis *m* old fogey.
Mummenschanz *m*, **Mummerei** *f* mummery, masquerade.
Mumpitz *m sl* nonsense, bosh, stuff.
Mumps *m* (*Ziegenpeter*) mumps *pl*.
Münchhausiade *f* cock-and-bull story.
Mund *m* mouth; (*Öffnung*) opening; *tech* muzzle, vent, orifice; *~ u. Nase aufsperren* to stand staring and gaping; *den ~ halten* to hold o.'s tongue, *fam* to shut up, *sl* to dry up; *reinen ~ halten* to keep a secret; *von der Hand in den ~ leben* to live from hand to mouth; *den ~ voll nehmen* to brag, to talk big; *jdm das Wort aus dem ~ nehmen* to take the words right out of s. o.'s mouth; *sich den ~ verbrennen* to put o.'s foot in it; *kein Blatt vor den ~ nehmen* not to mince (any) words; *nach dem ~ reden* to flatter; *nicht auf den ~ gefallen sein* to have a ready tongue; *über den ~ fahren* to cut short; *im ~e führen* to talk constantly about; *jdm den ~ wässerig machen* to make s. o.'s mouth water; *halten Sie den ~!* hold your tongue! keep quiet! *fam* shut up! **~art** *f* dialect; **~~lich** *a* dialectical, provincial; **~en** *itr* to be appetizing, to taste good; **~faul** *a* tongue-tied; (*schweigsam*) taciturn; **~fäule** *f* thrush; stomatitis; **~gerecht** *a*: *jdm etw ~~ machen* to make s. th. palatable for s. o.; **~geruch** *m* bad breath; **~harmonika** *f* mouth-organ; **~höhle** *f* oral cavity; **~klemme, ~sperre** *f* lockjaw; **~koch** *m* cook to a person of rank; **~pflege** *f* care of the mouth; oral hygiene; **~raub** *m* theft of comestibles; **~schenk** *m* cup-bearer; **~stellung** *f* position of the mouth; **~stück** *n* mouthpiece; (*Zigarette*) tip; *mit ~~* tipped; **~tot** *a*: *jdn ~~ machen* to (reduce to) silence; *parl* to gag s. o.; **~tuch** *n* (table-) napkin; **~voll** *m* mouthful; **~vorrat** *m* victuals *pl*, provisions *pl*; **~wasser** *n* gargle, mouth-wash; **~werk** *n*: *ein gutes ~~ haben* to have the gift of the gab (*od* a glib tongue); **~winkel** *m* corner of the mouth.
Münd|el *n* ward; minor; **~~geld** *n* trust-money; **~~sicher** *a* gilt-edged; **~en** *itr* to flow into; (*Straße, Fluß*) to run into; **~ig** *a* of age; *~~ werden* to come of age; **~~keit** *f* majority, full age; **~lich** *a* oral; (*Antwort, Botschaft*) verbal, personal; *adv* by word of mouth; *~~e Vernehmung jur* parole evidence; **~~keit** *f jur* oral proceedings *pl*; **~ung** *f* mouth; (*Meeresbucht*) estuary; (*Röhre*) outlet, aperture, orifice; *rail* terminus; (*Gewehr*) muzzle; **~~sbremse** *f* muzzle-brake; **~~sfeuer** *n* gun flash; **~~sgebiet** *n* delta; **~~sweite** *f* (*Kanone*) calibre.
Munition *f* ammunition, munition, *mil sl* ammo; **~ieren** *tr mar* to receive

ammunition; **~saufzug** *m mar* ammunition-hoist; **~sausgabestelle** *f* ammunition-distribution point; **~sbestand** *m* ammunition to hand; **~sergänzung** *f* replenishment of ammunition supplies; **~sdepot, ~lager** *n* ammunition dump; **~sfabrik** *f* ammunition factory; **~skammer** *f mar* shell room; **~skasten** *m* ammunition-box; **~skolonne** *f* ammunition column; **~smangel** *m* lack of ammunition; **~snachschub** *m* ammunition supply; **~sverbrauch** *m* expenditure of ammunition; **~svorrat** *m* (supply of) ammunition; **~swagen** *m* ammunition-car.

munkeln *itr* to whisper about; *man munkelt* there is a rumo(u)r.

Münster *n* minster, cathedral.

munter *a* brisk, lively; (*wach*) awake; (*lustig*) cheerful, merry, jolly; (*gesund*) healthy; *~!* cheer up! *gesund u. ~* safe and sound; **~keit** *f* vigilance, briskness, sprightliness, liveliness.

Münz|e *f* coin; (*~stätte*) mint; (*Kleingeld*) change; (*Denk~~*) medal; *bot* mint; *Worte für bare ~~ nehmen* to take words at their face value; *jdm mit gleicher ~~ heimzahlen* to pay s. o. out in his own coin; **~einheit** *f* monetary unit; **~einwurf** *m* coin slot; **~en** *tr* to coin, to mint, to stamp; *auf etw gemünzt sein* to be aimed at; **~fälscher** *m* (false) coiner, forger; **~fälschung** *f* forging of coin; **~fernsprecher** *m* coin-box telephone, public call-office, telephone-box; **~fuß** *m* standard; **~gehalt** *m* fineness, standard of alloy; **~gesetz** *n* Coinage Act; **~kabinett** *n*, **~sammlung** *f* collection of coins; **~kenner** *m* numismatist; **~kunde** *f* numismatics *pl*; **~meister** *m* mint-master; **~recht** *n* right of coinage; **~sammlung** *f* collection of coins, numismatic collection; **~sorte** *f* species of money; **~stempel** *m* stamp for coining, die; **~umlauf** *m* monetary circulation; **~verschlechterung** *f* debasement of coin(age); **~wesen** *n* monetary system; **~zähler** *m* slot-meter; **~zeichen** *n* mint-mark, coiner's mark; **~zusatz** *m* alloy.

mürbe *a* (*reif*) ripe, mellow; (*Küche*) well-cooked; (*zart*) tender; (*Teig*) short, crisp; (*brüchig*) brittle, friable; *fig* worn-down, unnerved; weary, demoralized, down and out; *jdn ~ machen* to curb s. o., to break s. o.'s spirit, *mil* to soften up; *~ werden* to give in; **~kuchen** *m* shortcake; **~teig** *m* shortbread, (short) pastry.

Murmel *m* toy marble; **~n** *itr* to murmur, to mumble, to mutter; **~n** *n* murmur; **~tier** *n* marmot, *Am* woodchuck; *wie ein ~~ schlafen* to sleep like a top (*od* like a dormouse).

murr|en *itr* to grumble, to growl, to grouse, *Am* to grouch; **~kopf** *m* grumbler; grouch.

mürrisch *a* gloomy; (*schlecht gelaunt*) cross; (*unzufrieden*) discontented; surly, sullen, morose.

Mus *n* pap; purée; (*Früchte*) jam, stewed fruit; (*Apfelsinen*) marmalade.

Muschel *f* cockle; (*Tier mit Schale*) mussel; (*Schale*) shell; conch; *tele* ear-piece; (*Ohr*) auricle, external ear; **~bank** *f* shell-bank; **~erde** *f geol* crag; **~glas** *n* globular lens; **~haltig** *a* shelly; **~kalk** *m* shell-lime; **~schale** *f* mussel-shell; **~tier** *n* mollusk, shell-fish; **~werk** *n* shell-work.

Muse *f* Muse; **~nalmanach** *m* almanac of the Muses; **~nsohn** *m* poet; university student.

Museum *n* museum.

Musik *f* music; band of musicians; *in ~ setzen* to set to music; **~alien** *pl* music; **~~handlung** *f* music-shop; **~akademie** *f* academy of music; **~alisch** *a* musical; **~ant** *m* musician; **~apparat** *m* musical apparatus; **~automat** *m* coin operated gram(m)ophone, *Am* juke-box; **~begleitung** *f* accompaniment by music; **~direktor, ~meister** *m* director of music, bandmaster; **~drama** *n* opera; **~er** *m* musician, bandsman; **~fest** *n* musical festival; **~folge** *f* musical program(me); **~hochschule** *f* conservatoire, *Am* conservatory; **~instrument** *n* musical instrument; **~kapelle** *f*, **~korps** *n* band; **~lehrer** *m* music-master; **~meister** *m* bandmaster, *Am* bandleader; **~liebend** *a* music-loving; **~pavillon** *m* bandstand; **~schrank** *m* radiogram(ophone); **~schule** *f* music school; **~stimme** *f* part; **~stück** *n* piece of music; **~stunde** *f* music-lesson; **~truhe** *f* radiogram(ophone); **~us** *m* musician; **~verein** *m* musical society; **~verlag** *m* music publishing house; **~wissenschaft** *f* musicology; **~zimmer** *n* music room.

musizieren *itr* to play; to have music; to make music.

Muskat *m* nutmeg; **~blüte** *f* mace; **~eller, ~wein** *m* muscatel; **~ellerbirne** *f* musk-pear; **~ellertraube** *f* muscadine grape; **~enbaum** *m* nutmeg-tree; **~enblume, ~enblüte** *f* mace; **~nuß** *f* nutmeg.

Muskel *m* muscle; **~band** *n* ligament; **~faser** *f* muscular fibre; **~gewebe** *n* muscular tissue; **~kater** *m* stiffness and soreness; **~kraft** *f* muscular strength; **~schwund** *m* muscular atrophy; **~zerrung** *f* sprained muscle.

Musket|e *f* musket; **~ier** *m* musketeer.

Muskul|atur *f* muscular system; **~ös** *a* muscular, brawny; (*sehnig*) sinewy.

Muß *n* necessity; *es ist ein ~* it is a must.

Muße *f* leisure; (*Freizeit*) spare time; (*Bequemlichkeit*) ease; *wenn Sie einmal ~ haben* at your leisure; *mit ~* at leisure; **~stunde** *f* leisure-hour; *in ~~n* during o.'s spare hours.

Musselin *m* muslin, organdie.

müssen *itr* to have to, to be obliged (*od* forced *od* compelled) to, to be made, to be bound; *ich muß* I must; *er muß fort sein* I suppose he is gone; *er muß immer zu spät kommen* he never fails to be late; *ich muß lachen, wenn ...* I cannot help laughing when ...; *es tut mir leid, sagen zu ~* I am sorry to say; *das muß erst noch kommen* that is yet to come; *ich müßte* I ought to; *es müßte jetzt fertig sein* it ought to be ready by now; *er hätte um 9 Uhr in London sein müssen* he ought to have been in London by nine o'clock; *du hättest mir das vorher sagen müssen* you ought to have told me that before; *diese Arbeit müßte sofort erledigt werden* this work ought to be done at once; *er müßte krank sein* unless he is ill.

müßig *a* idle, unemployed; (*überflüssig*) superfluous; *~es Geschwätz* idle (*od* useless) talk; *~ gehen* to be idle; (*bummeln*) to saunter; **~gang** *m* idleness, laziness, *~~ ist aller Laster Anfang* idleness is the root of all evil; **~gänger** *m* idler, loafer; **~gängerisch** *a* idle, idling.

Muster *n* model, specimen; (*Vorbild*) example, exemplar, paragon; (*Maßstab*) standard; (*Typ*) type; (*Zeichnung*) design, pattern; (*Probe*) pattern, sample; *als ~ ohne Wert* by sample post; **~anstalt** *f* model school; **~beispiel** *n* example; **~betrieb** *m* model factory; **~buch** *n* book of patterns, sample book; **~exemplar** *n* sample copy; type specimen; **~gatte** *m* model husband; **~getreu** *a* equal to sample; **~gültig, ~haft** *a* model, exemplary, perfect; standard, classical; **~gut** *n* model farm; **~karte** *f* pattern card, sample book; **~klammer** *f* paper-fastener; **~knabe** *m* prig, model boy; **~koffer** *m* box of samples, sample-bag; **~lager** *n* sample stock; **~messe** *f* sample fair; **~n** *tr* (*prüfen*) to examine, to eye; (*Soldaten*) to muster; (*Truppen*) to review, to inspect; (*Stoffe*) to figure, to pattern; (*Papier*) to emboss; (*Farbe*) to bring to shade; *gemustert a* figured, fancy; **~rolle** *f mil* muster-roll; **~sammlung** *f* collection of samples; **~schüler** *m* pattern-pupil; **~schutz** *m* trade-mark, registered pattern; **~~recht** *n* copyright on design; **~stück** *n* model, pattern, specimen; **~ung** *f* examination; (*Soldat*) muster; (*Truppen*) inspection, review; **~zeichner** *m* draftsman, designer; **~zeichnung** *f* design.

Mut *m* courage, spirit; (*Herz*) heart; (*Schneid*) pluck, *Am sl* sand; (*Seelenstärke*) fortitude; (*Charakterfestigkeit*) grit, backbone; (*Temperament*) mettle; (*Entschlossenheit*) resolution; (*Zähigkeit*) tenacity; (*Widerstandsfähigkeit*) endurance, *sl* guts *pl*; (*Stimmung*) humo(u)r, mood; *jdm ~ machen* to encourage s. o.; *~ fassen* to take courage; *den ~ sinken lassen* to lose courage; *den ~ nicht sinken lassen* (*od nicht verlieren*) to keep up o.'s courage, to bear up; *jdm den ~ nehmen* to discourage s. o.; *gutes ~es sein* to be of good cheer; *mir ist zu~e* I feel; *ihm sank der ~* his heart failed him; **~ieren** *itr* (*Stimme*) to break; **~ig** *a* courageous, brave, spirited; **~los** *a* discouraged, despondent; **~losigkeit** *f* despondency, discouragement; **~maßen** *tr* to guess, to suppose, to surmise, to conjecture; **~maßlich** *a* presumable, probable, supposed conjectural; (*Erbe*) presumptive; **~maßung** *f* conjecture, supposition, surmise; (*Verdacht*) suspicion; **~wille** *m* wantonness, mischievousness; (*Ausgelassenheit*) playfulness, frolicsomeness; (*Scherzhaftigkeit*) sportiveness; (*Übermut*) devilry; **~willig** *a* (*boshaft*) mischievous, wanton, roguish; (*ausgelassen*) sportive, frolicsome, playful, *fam* rollicky; (*lustig*) frisky; (*verschmitzt*) tricksy; (*schelmisch*) waggy.

Mütchen *n*: *sein ~ an jdm kühlen* to vent o.'s anger (on).

Mutter *f* mother; (*Gebär~*) matrix, uterus; (*~tier*) dam; *tech* nut, female screw; *werdende u. stillende Mütter* expectant and nursing mothers; *sich ~ fühlen* to feel o. s. with child; *die ~ Gottes* Our Blessed Lady, the Virgin Mary; *bei ~ Grün schlafen* to sleep in the open air; **~boden** *m*, **~erde** *f* native soil; (*Biologie*) parent tissue; (*Garten*) garden mo(u)ld; **~brust** *f* mother's breast; **~freude** *f* maternal joy; **~fürsorge** *f* maternity care; **~gefühl** *n* motherly feeling; **~gesellschaft** *f com* parent company; **~gestein** *n* gangue, matrix; **~gewebe** *n* mother tissue, matrix; **~gottes** *f* the Virgin; **~~bild** *n* image of the Holy Virgin; **~harz** *n* galbanum; **~haus** *n fig* parent house; *com* chief office, central firm; **~herz** *n* maternal heart; **~kalb** *n* heifer calf; **~kind** *n* spoilt child; (*Liebling*) pet;

~kirche *f* mother church; **~korn** *n* ergot; **~kraut** *n* feverfew; **~kuchen** *m* placenta; **~land** *n* mother-country; **~lauge** *f* mother liquor; **~leib** *m* womb; *vom ~~e an* from birth; **~liebe** *f* motherly love; **~los** *a* motherless; **~mal** *n* birth-mark, mole; **~milch** *f* mother's milk; *mit der ~~ einsaugen* to imbibe from the earliest infancy; **~mord, ~mörder** *m* matricide; **~mund** *m anat* os uteri; **~pech** *n med* meconium; **~pferd** *n* mare; **~pflicht** *f* maternal duty; **~recht** *n jur* matriarchy; **~schaf** *n* ewe; **~schaft** *f* motherhood, maternity; **~schiff** *n aero* mother-ship; **~schlüssel** *m* nut wrench, spanner; **~schmerz** *m* grief of a mother; **~schoß** *m* mother's lap; **~schraube** *f* female screw; **~schutz** *m* protection of motherhood, **~schwein** *n* sow; **~seelenallein** *pred a, adv fam* all alone; **~söhnchen** *n* mother's pet, *fam* milksop; **~sprache** *f* mother tongue; **~stelle** *f: ~~ vertreten* to be like a mother to children; **~tag** *m* Mother's Day; **~teil** *m* maternal inheritance; **~tier** *n* brood animal; **~witz** *m* mother-wit, common sense; **~zelle** *f* mother (*od* parent) cell.

*

Mütter|beratungsstelle *f* maternity centre; **~chen** *n* little mother; (*altes*) granny, little old woman; **~lich** *a* motherly, maternal; **~~erseits** *adv* on the mother's side; **~~keit** *f* motherliness.

Mutti *f* Mummy.

Mutung *f min* claim, demand, concession.

Mütze *f* cap; (*Haube*) bonnet; **~nmacher** *m* cap-maker; **~nschirm** *m* shade of a cap, peak.

*

Myriade *f* myriad.

Myrrhe *f* myrrh.

Myrte *f* myrtle; **~nkranz** *m* myrtle-wreath.

Myst|erien *pl* mysteries *pl*; **~eriös** *a* mysterious; **~erium** *n* mystery; **~ifizieren** *tr* to mystify; **~ik** *f* mysticism; **~iker** *m* mystic; **~isch** *a* mystic(al).

Myth|e *f* myth, fable; **~isch** *a* mythical; **~ologie** *f* mythology; **~ologisch** *a* mythological; **~us** *m* myth.

N

N *Abk mit* ***N*** *siehe Liste der Abk.*

na! *interj* why! well! now! *~ also!* then! *~ nu!* well I never! *~ warte!* just you wait! *~ wenn schon!* so what!

Nabe *f* (*Rad~*) nave; hub; (*der Schiffsschraube*) boss; **~nabzieher** *m* hub drawer; **~nmutter** *f* nut plate; **~nstern** *m* hub spider.

Nabel *m* navel; umbilicus; **~binde** *f* umbilical bandage (*od* binder); **~bruch** *m* omphalocele. umbilical hernia; **~schnur** *f* umbilical cord, navel-string.

Nabob *m* nabob.

nach *prp, adv* (*Richtung*) to, toward(s), for; *ich fahre ~* I'm going to; *gehen Sie ~ links!* go to the left! *der Zug ~ London* the train for London; *die Häuser liegen ~ dem Süden* the houses face towards the south; (*Reihenfolge, Zeit*) after, past, on; behind; *e-r ~ dem andern* one after another, one by one; one at a time; *~ dem Essen* after dinner; *ein Viertel ~ fünf* a quarter past five (*Am* after five); *~ Empfang* on receipt; *~ Ankunft* on arrival; *er kam ~ mir* he was behind me; (*Art u. Weise, gemäß*) according to, as regards, from, by, in, of, to, like; *allem Anschein ~* according to all appearances; *der Größe ~* according to size; *~ der Natur malen* to paint from nature; *urteilen ~* to judge from; *~ dem, was sie sagt* from what she says; *dem Namen ~ kennen* to know by name; *~ Gewicht* by the weight; *ihrem Gesicht ~* to judge by her face; *~ meiner Uhr* by my watch; *meiner Meinung ~* in my opinion; *aller Wahrscheinlichkeit ~* in all probability; *~ Essig schmecken* to taste of vinegar; *auf der Suche ~* in search of; *~ meinem Geschmack* to my taste; *~ bestem Wissen u. Gewisser* to the best of o.'s knowledge and belief; *es sieht ~ Regen aus* it looks like rain; *~ Hause* home; *~ oben* upstairs; *~ u. ~* gradually, little by little, by degrees; bit by bit; *~ wie vor* still, as usual, as (much as) ever; *er ist ~ wie vor derselben Meinung* he's still of the same opinion.

nachäffen *tr* to ape, to mimic.

nachahm|en *tr* to imitate, to copy; to duplicate; (*nachäffen*) to mimic, to ape; (*verfälschen*) to counterfeit; to adulterate; (*nacheifern*) to emulate; **~enswert** *a* worth imitating; worthy of imitation; **~er** *m* imitator; **~ung** *f* imitation; (*Fälschung*) forgery, counterfeit; (*Wetteifer*) emulation; **~~strieb** *m* imitative instinct.

Nacharbeit *f* maintenance, repair; refinishing operation; overhauling of the work; **~en** *tr* to touch up, to finish up; to refinish, to dress; to recondition; (*Muster*) to work from a model; to copy; (*Zeit nachholen*) to make up for lost time.

Nachbar *m*, **~in** *f* neighbo(u)r; *mil* (*anschließende Einheit*) adjacent unit; **~division** *f mil* division on the flank; **~gebiet** *n* adjacent domains; **~haus** *n* neighbo(u)ring house; *im ~~* next door; **~lich** *a* neighbo(u)rly; **~schaft** *f* neighbo(u)rhood; vicinity; **~verband** *m mil* adjacent formation, flank formation.

Nachbehandlung *f* after-treatment; re-treatment; curing.

nachbekommen *irr tr* to receive in addition; to obtain afterwards.

nachbessern *tr* to improve upon, to mend, to touch up.

nachbestell|en *tr* to order subsequently (*od* later); to order a fresh supply, to reorder; to order some more; to repeat an order; **~ung** *f* additional (*od* second) order.

nachbet|en *tr, itr fig* to repeat mechanically, to echo; to parrot; **~er** *m* parrot; thoughtless repeater.

Nachbewilligung *f* subsequent grant, supplementary allowance.

nachbezahl|en *tr* to pay afterwards, to pay the rest; **~ung** *f* subsequent payment.

Nachbild *f* copy, counterfeit; imitation; replica; facsimile; (*Psychologie*) after-image; **~en** *tr* to copy; to imitate; to reproduce; to simulate; to counterfeit; **~ung** *f* replica; copy, imitation; *tech* mock-up; *mil* (*Geschütz, Panzer*) dummy gun, dummy tank.

nach|bleiben *irr itr* to remain behind, to be left; (*nachhinken*) to lag; (*Schule*) to be kept in; **~blicken** *itr* to look (*od* to gaze) after; **~blüte** *f* second blossoming; aftergrowth; **~blutung** *f* secondary haemorrhage; **~brennen** *irr itr* to smolder; to burn again; *~ n tech* afterburning; late combustion; **~brenner** *m mil* hang-fire shell (*od* cartridge); *aero* afterburner; **~bringen** *irr tr* to bring after; **~datieren** *tr* to postdate.

nachdem *adv* afterwards, after that; *je ~* according as; *conj* after, when; *je ~ das Wetter ist* depending on the weather; *je ~* it depends; *je ~ es sich trifft* according to circumstances.

nachdenk|en *irr itr* to meditate (on), to think (over, about), to reflect (on); to ponder (*über* on *od* over); *Am* to mull over; *~~ n* reflection, meditation; (*Grübelei*) brown study; **~lich** *a* reflecting, meditative, thoughtful; pensive.

Nach|dichtung *f* free version; paraphrase; (*Nachahmung*) imitation; **~drängen** *itr* to press after, to crowd after; to push after; *~~ n* (*Verfolgung des Gegners*) pursuit; pressure; **~dringen** *irr itr* to pursue (after).

Nach|druck *m* (*Tatkraft*) energy, vigo(u)r; (*Ton*) stress, emphasis; (*Gewicht*) weight; (*Bücher*) reprint(ing), reproduction; (*unerlaubt*) piracy; pirated edition; (*Fälschung*) counterfeiting; *~~ legen* (*auf*) to lay stress (upon), to stress; to emphasize; *mit ~~ arbeiten* to work with vigo(u)r; *~~ verboten* all rights reserved; **~~en** *tr* to reprint; (*unerlaubt*) to pirate; **~~srecht** *n* copyright; **~~svoll, ~drücklich** *a, adv* energetic, strong; (*betont*) emphatic; (*eindringlich*) forcible.

nachdunkeln *itr* to deepen, to darken (subsequently); to become darker; (*Färberei*) to sadden.

Nach|eiferer *m* emulator; **~eifern** *itr* to emulate; **~eiferung** *f* emulation.

nach|eilen *itr* to hasten after; (*nachhinken*) to lag; to run slow; **~eilung** *f* lag, lagging; trail (behind); retardation; **~einander** *adv* one after another; successively; in turn, by turns; **~empfinden** *irr itr, tr* to sympathize (with); to enter into s. o.'s feelings; to feel for.

Nachen *m* boat, skiff; (*flacher ~*) sculler, punt; (*Barke*) barge.

Nach|ernte *f* second crop; aftermath, after-harvest, gleaning; **~ernten** *itr* to glean; **~erzählen** *tr* to repeat; to paraphrase; *dem Englischen nacherzählt* adapted from the English; **~erzeugnis** *n* afterproduct; **~exerzieren** *itr* to have an extra drill; to do extra drill; **~fahr** *m* descendant; **~fahren** *irr itr* to drive after; to go after; to follow; **~färben** *tr* to colo(u)r (*od* dye) again; **~fassen** *itr fig* to insist on; to intervene; *mil* (*beim Essen*) to get a second helping; *com* to dun; **~feier** *f* later (*od* extra) celebration.

Nachfolge *f* succession; ~ *Christi* Imitation of Christ; **~n** *itr* to follow; to succeed s. o.; **~~d** *a* following, subsequent; consecutive, continuous; **~r** *m* follower; (*Amt*) successor.

nach|fordern *tr* to claim subsequently; (*zusätzlich*) to demand (*od* to charge) extra; **~forderung** *f* afterclaim; extra charge; **~forschen** *itr* to search (for), to investigate s. th.; (*untersuchen*) to inquire (into); **~forschung** *f* research, investigation, scrutiny; query; search.

Nachfrage *f* (*Erkundigung*) inquiry; *com* demand, call; requirements *pl*; (*starke* ~) craze; *das Gesetz von Angebot u.* ~ the law of supply and demand; **~n** *itr* (*verlangen*) to ask for, to inquire for (*od* after); to demand; (*nachforschen*) to inquire about.

Nachfrist *f* time extension; respite.

nach|fühlen *itr* to feel for (*od* with s. o.); to sympathize (with); **~füllen** *tr* to fill up, to replenish; to refill; to top up; (*Betriebsstoff*) to refuel; **~geahmt** *a* imitated; feigned; counterfeit.

nach|geben *irr itr* to give in, to yield to, to comply with, *Am fam* to cave in; *fam* to back down; (*Sache*) to give way; (*Kurse*) to decline, to slacken; (*nachsichtig sein*) to indulge s. o.; *e-m nichts* ~~ to be in no way inferior to s. o.; to be second to none; **~geboren** *a* posthumous; **~gebühr** *f* excess postage, surcharge, *Am* postage dues; **~geburt** *f* afterbirth, placenta; **~gehen** *irr itr* to follow; (*Geschäften*) to attend to, to pursue; (*Sache*) to investigate, to inquire (into), to look (into); (*Gerücht*) to follow up; (*Spur*) to trace; (*Vergnügen*) to be out (for); (*sich widmen*) to be addicted to; (*Uhr*) to be slow; to lose (time); **~gelassen** *a* posthumous; **~gemacht** *a* imitated; false; bogus; (*künstlich*) artificial; **~geordnet** *a* subordinate; **~gerade** *adv* by now, by this time; after all; (*allmählich*) gradually; **~geschmack** *m* aftertaste; **~gewiesenermaßen** *adv* as has been proved.

nachgiebig *a* yielding; (*verbindlich*) obliging; (*nachsichtig*) indulgent; (*bequem*) easy-going; (*Börse*) soft, declining; yielding; (*biegsam, elastisch*) flexible, ductile; elastic; pliable; **~keit** *f* yieldingness, compliance; (*Gefügigkeit*) tractability; (*Nachsicht*) indulgence; (*Börse*) softness; **~gießen** *irr tr* to refill, to replenish; to add more; **~glühen** *tr, itr* to glow again; *tech* to anneal, to re-anneal; to temper; to draw.

nach|graben *irr itr* to dig for; **~grübeln** *itr* to speculate (*über* on), to reflect (on), to muse (on), to ponder (over).

Nachhall *m* echo; resonance; **~en** *itr* to echo, to resound.

nach|haltig *a* lasting, enduring; protracted; durable; (*dauernd*) permanent; (*ausdauernd*) persevering; (*wirksam*) effective; (*hartnäckig*) persistent; **~hangen, ~hängen** *itr* to follow; to give way to; to be addicted; *seinen Gedanken* ~~ to muse; to indulge o.'s fancies; (*örtlich*) to be behind, to come after; to lag; **~helfen** *irr itr* to help; to lend s. o. a helping hand; to assist; (*Kunst*) to retouch; **~her** *adv* afterwards, after; (*später*) later; *bis ~~! interj* so long! see you later! **~herbst** *m* end of autumn; late autumn; **~herig** *a* subsequent, later, posterior; **~hilfe** *f* assistance; help, aid; (*Schule*) coaching; **~~stunde** *f* (*für Schüler*) private lesson; *jdm ~~stunden geben* to coach s. o.; **~hinken** *itr* to lag behind; **~holbedarf** *m* suppressed (*Am* pent-up) demand; **~holen** *itr, tr* to make good; to make up for; to recover; (*Unterrichtsstunde*) to take later; (*örtlich*) to fetch afterwards, to bring up; **~hut** *f* rear(-guard); **~~gefecht** *m* rear-guard action.

nachjagen *itr* to chase; to pursue, *Am* to gun (for).

Nach|klang *m* resonance; echo; *fig* reminiscence; (*Wirkung*) after-effect; **~klingen** *irr itr* to linger in the ear; to resound, to echo; **~kommando** *n* rear-guard detachment.

Nachkomme *m* descendant, offspring; **~n** *irr itr* to come after; to come later; (*Schritt halten*) to keep up (with); *fig* to perform; to comply with; to fulfil; *seinem Versprechen ~n* to keep o.'s promise; *seinen Verbindlichkeiten ~n* to meet o.'s engagements; **~nschaft** *f* descendants *pl*, posterity, issue.

Nachkömmling *m* descendant.

Nach|kriegs ... post-war ...; *Am* postwar; **~~handel** *m* post-war trade; **~~jahre** *n pl* post-war years *pl*; **~~luftverkehr** *m* post-war air transport; **~~zeit** *f* post-war period; **~kur** *f* rest after treatment; **~laden** *irr tr* to recharge.

Nach|laß *m* (*der Strafe*) remission; (*Erbe*) estate, assets *pl*, inheritance; (*Preis*) statement, allowance, deduction, reduction; discount; ~~ *gewähren* to allow a statement; **~~gericht** *n* probate-(*Am* surrogate-)court; **~~steuer** *f* legacy duty; **~~verwalter** *m* executor; **~lassen** *irr tr* to leave (behind); (*Preise*) to reduce; to make a reduction in the price; (*Strafe*) to remit; (*Metall*) to temper, to anneal; *itr* (*entspannen*) to slacken, to release; (*vermindern*) to diminish, to grow less; (*aufhören*) to cease, to stop, *fam* to let up; (*Kälte*) to abate; (*Wind*) to calm; (*Preise*) to drop, to decline, to yield; (*Arbeit*) to slow down, *fam* to let up; **~lassenschaft** *f* estate; inheritance; **~lässig** *a* negligent, neglectful; careless; (*Sprache, Stil, Kleidung*) slipshod, sloppy; **~~keit** *f* negligence, carelessness, idleness; **~laufen** *irr itr* to run after; *tech* to lag; to go behind; **~leben** *itr* to live up to, to observe; ~~ *n* after-life; **~legen** *tr* (*Ofen*) to make up the fire, to put on more ...; **~lernen** *tr* to learn after; **~lese** *f* gleaning; (*literarisch*) supplement; **~lesen** *irr itr, tr* to glean; (*in einem Buche*) to read (again); (*e-e Stelle im Buche*) to look up (a passage); **~leuchten** *itr* to phosphoresce; to shine afterward; ~~ *n* phosphorescence, afterglow; **~liefern** *tr* to deliver subsequently (*od* later); to complete; **~lieferung** *f* subsequent delivery; **~lösen** *tr, itr* (*Fahrkarten*) to pay the additional fare; to buy a ticket en route; to take a supplementary ticket; **~lösebüro** *n* excess-fare office; **~machen** *tr* to imitate; (*betrügerisch*) to counterfeit; (*parodieren*) to mimic; (*ein zweites Exemplar herstellen*) to duplicate; (*kopieren*) to copy; *das soll mir jd ~~!* I'd like to see anybody else do that! **~malen** *tr* to copy; **~malig** *a* subsequent; **~mals** *adv* afterwards; subsequently; **~messen** *irr tr* to control; to measure; to re-check; to check the dimension; **~mittag** *m* afternoon, *Abk* p. m. (post meridiem); *heute* ~~ this afternoon; **~~s** *adv* in the afternoon, *Am* afternoons; **~~skleid** *n* afternoon dress, tea-gown; **~~sschläfchen** *n* afternoon nap; **~~svorstellung** *f* matinee.

Nach|nahme *f* cash (*Am* collect) on delivery (*Abk* C. O. D.); *durch ~~ erheben* to cash (*Am* to collect) on delivery; *per ~~ schicken* to send C. O. D.; **~~betrag** *m* amount to be collected on delivery; **~~gebühr** *f* C. O. D. fees *pl*; **~~paket** *n* C. O. D. parcel; **~~telegramm** *n* collect message; **~name** *m* surname, last name; **~nehmen** *irr tr* to collect (*od* to cash) on delivery.

nach|plappern *tr* to repeat mechanically; to parrot; **~porto** *n* additional charge, postage due, surcharge; excess postage; **~prüfen** *tr* to (re-)examine, to check; to inspect; to control; (*erproben*) to test; (*Richtigkeit*) to verify, to make sure; **~prüfung** *f* checking, revision; testing; inspection; control; verification; *jur* (*Entscheidung*) review.

nach|rechnen *tr* to examine; to check (*Am* upon), to audit, to go over the figures; to recompute; **~rede** *f* epilog(ue); (*üble*) slander; (*Gerede*) gossip; **~reden** *tr, itr* (*wiederholen*) to repeat; (*Übles*) to slander, to speak ill (of s. o.); (*Gutes*) to speak well (of s. o.).

Nachricht *f* news *pl mit sing;* (*Büchersprache*) tidings *pl*; (*Auskunft*) information; (*wichtige, mil*) intelligence; (*Meldung, com*) advice(s *pl*); (*Bericht*) report, account; (*Notiz*) notice; (*Wink*) intimation; (*Telegramm~*) flash; (*Funk*) radio message; *e-e* ~ a piece of news; *vermischte ~en* miscellanies *pl*; *letzte ~en* last (*od* last-minute) news, stop-press; ~ *geben* to send word, to let know; (*unterrichten*) to inform; (*mitteilen*) to advise; (*amtlich*) to notify; *~en einziehen* to make inquiries; **~enabteilung** *f mil* intelligence department (*od* division); communication (*od* signals) section; communication (*od* signal) battalion; **~enamt** *n* news department; **~enagentur** *f*, **~enbüro** *n* news (*od* press) agency, *Am* wire service; **~enaufklärung** *f* signal intelligence; **~enberichterstatter** *m* newsman, *Am* newscaster; **~enbeschaffung** *f* procurement of information; **~enbeurteilung** *f* evaluation of information; **~endienst** *m* the news (service); *mil* intelligence service; signals *pl*; signal corps; **~enfernsehsendung** *f* news telecast; **~enflugzeug** *n* communications plane; **~enführer** *m* chief signals officer; commander of a signal(l)ing unit; **~engeheimnis** *n* secrecy of correspondence; **~engerät** *n* signal equipment; **~enhelferin** *f mil* signal-communication woman auxiliary; **~enjäger** *m* (*Presse*) newshound; **~enkommentator** *m* news analyst; **~enkompanie** *f* signal company; **~enkontrollamt** *n* office of information control; **~enkontrollvorschrift** *f* information control regulation; **~enleiter** *m radio* news director; **~enmaterial** *n* news material, copy; **~enmittel** *n* channel of communication; *mil* signals equipment; **~ennetz** *n* communication network; **~enoffizier** *m* signals (*od* communications) officer; intelligence officer; **~enpark** *m mil* signal-supply depot; **~enschlager** *m* (*Presse*) exclusive story, *Am* scoop, beat; **~ensendung** *f radio* newscast; **~ensperre** *f* news blackout;

news ban; **~ensprecher** *m* newscaster, news announcer; **~enstelle** *f* message (*od* information) centre; **~entechnik** *f* telecommunication technique; science of communications; **~entruppe** *f mil* signals, *Am* signal corps; **~enübermittlung** *f* transmission of intelligence (*od* communications); **~enverbindung** *f* channel of communication; **~enverkehr** *m* signal-communication traffic; **~enweg** *m* signal-communication channel; **~enwesen** *n* communication service; **~enzeitschrift** *f Am* news magazine; **~enzentrale** *f*, **~enzentrum** *n* news-centre; message centre, *Am* message center; **~enzug** *m* signal section; communications platoon.

nach|rücken *itr* to move up; (*folgen*) to follow; (*vorrücken*) to move forward, to advance; *mil* to march after; **~ruf** *m* obituary (notice); **~ruhm** *m* posthumous fame; **~rühmen** *tr* to say in praise of; to say to s. o.'s credit.

nach|sagen *tr* to repeat mechanically; to speak of, to say of; *das würde er sich nicht ~~ lassen* he wouldn't let anybody say that about him; **~saison** *f* off-season; **~satz** *m* postscript; *gram* final clause; minor proposition (*od* term); **~schauen** *itr* to look after; **~schicken** *tr* to send after; (*Briefe*) to forward; **~schlagen** *irr tr* to consult (a book); to look up a word (in a book); *itr* to take after; **~schlagewerk** *n* reference book; **~schleichen** *irr itr* to sneak after; **~schleppen** *tr* to drag (*od* trail) after; (*Boot, Wagen*) to tow; **~schlüssel** *m* (*Hauptschlüssel*) master-key; (*Dietrich*) picklock, skeleton-key; **~schmecken** *itr* to taste of; to leave a taste of; **~schreiben** *irr tr* to copy, to write down; to write from dictation; **~schrift** *f* (*Brief*) postscript (*Abk* P. S.); (*Abschrift*) copy, transcript; (*Diktat*) dictation; (*Notizen*) notes *pl*; **~schub** *m mil* reinforcements *pl*, reserves *pl*; (*Verpflegung*) supply; bringing up of supplies; **~~abwurf** *m* dropping of supplies (from aircraft); **~~bataillon** *n* supply battalion; **~~bewegung** *f* movement of supplies; **~~bombe** *f* airplane-dropped supply canister; **~~dienst** *m* service of supply; **~~fahrzeug** *n* supply vehicle; **~~führer** *m* quartermaster general; **~~geleit** *n* supply convoy; **~~kolonne** *f* supply column (*od* train); **~~lager** *n* supply dump; **~~linie** *f* axis of supply; supply line; line of communication; **~~offizier** *m* supply officer; **~~park** *m* supply dump (*od* depot); **~~straße** *f* supply route; line of communication; **~~stützpunkt** *m* supply base, supply centre (*Am* center); **~~transport** *m* transport of supplies; **~~truppe** *f* supply troops *pl*; **~~umschlagstelle** *f* supply point; **~~verkehr** *m* supply traffic; **~~weg** *m* supply road, supply route; **~~wesen** *n* supply services *pl*.

nach|sehen *irr itr, tr: jdm ~~* to gaze after; (*sorgen*) to look after; *etw ~~* to check, to revise, to examine; (*Rechnungsbücher*) to audit; (*Wörterbuch*) to look up, to consult; (*Maschinen*) to overhaul; (*gehen u. sehen*) to go and see, to see (whether); (*nachsichtig sein*) to be lenient (with); (*entschuldigen*) to excuse, to overlook, to condone; *das ~~ haben* to go empty-handed, to have o.'s trouble for nothing, to be left out in the cold; **~senden** *irr tr* to send after; (*Briefe*) to forward, to redirect; *bitte ~~!* please forward (to)! *nicht ~~!* not to be forwarded! **~setzen** *itr* (*verfolgen*) to hunt after, to pursue; *tr* (*geringer achten*) to think less of.

Nachsicht *f* forbearance, indulgence; leniency; (*Prüfung*) inspection; *com* respite; *~ haben mit* to have patience with; **~ig, ~svoll** *a* forbearing, indulgent, lenient.

Nach|silbe *f* suffix; **~sinnen** *irr itr* to muse, to reflect (on), to meditate (on); **~sitzen** *irr itr* to be kept in; *~~ lassen* to keep in; **~sommer** *m* Indian summer, late summer; **~spannen** *tr* to re-tighten; **~spähen** *itr* to spy after; to investigate; **~speise** *f* sweet; dessert; **~spiel** *n theat* afterpiece; epilog(ue); *mus* postlude, voluntary; *fig* sequel; **~sprechen** *irr tr* to repeat; **~sprengen** *itr* to gallop after s. o.; **~springen** *irr itr* to jump after s. o.; **~spülen** *tr* to rinse out; to flush again; **~spüren** *itr* to track, to trace s. o.; *fig* to investigate.

nächst *a* (*Entfernung*) nearest, shortest, closest; (*Reihenfolge*) next, following; *die ~en Angehörigen* next of kin; *~en Montag* on Monday next; *~en Monat* next month, proximo; *~er Tage* one of these days; in the next few days; *prp* next to, next after; **~beste** *a* second best; **~dem** *adv* thereupon, shortly; (*bald*) soon; **~e(r)** *m* fellow creature; neighbo(u)r; **~enliebe** *f* charity; love for o.'s fellow men; **~ens** *adv* very soon, shortly; one of these days; (*~es Mal*) next time; **~folgend** *a* following, next; **~liegend** *a* nearest (at hand); **~~e** *n* the obvious thing; **~verwandt** *a* next of kin.

nach|stehen *irr itr* to be behind s. o.; to be inferior to; (*Platz machen*) to make way for; **~~d** *adv* hereafter; following; mentioned (*od* described) below; as under; **~stellbar** *a tech* regulable; adjustable; **~stellen** *tr* to place behind; (*Uhr*) to put back; (*Schraube*) to regulate; to adjust; to reset; *itr jdm ~~* to lay snares, to waylay; (*verfolgen*) to pursue; **~stellung** *f* pursuit, persecution; (*Hinterhalt*) ambush, snare; *tech* adjustment; **~stellvorrichtung** *f tech* adjusting device; **~stenographieren** *tr* to take down in shorthand; **~steuer** *f* additional tax; **~stoßen** *irr itr* to push forward, to pursue; to thrust after; **~strömung** *f* wake.

nach|streben *itr* to strive for (*od* after), to aspire (to); *jdm ~~* to emulate; **~stürzen** *itr* to rush after; **~suchen** *itr* to search after; *tr* (*anfragen*) to apply for; **~~de(r)** *m* applicant; **~suchung** *f* search; (*Bewerbung, Forderung*) request, application, petition; (*Untersuchung*) inquiry; **~tanken** *itr* to refuel.

Nacht *f* night; (*Dunkelheit*) darkness; *bei ~, des ~s, in der ~* at night; *bei ~ u. Nebel* under cover of the night; *mit einbrechender ~* at nightfall; *e-s ~s* in a night; *in tiefster ~* in the middle of the night; *die ganze ~ hindurch* all night (long); *in e-r dunklen ~* on a dark night; *über ~* over night; during the night; *heute ~* to-night; (*vergangene*) last night; *Tausend u. e-e ~* Arabian nights *pl*; *über ~ bleiben* to stay the night, to stop at; *bei ~ arbeiten* to work by night; *zu ~ essen* to sup; *die ~ zum Tage machen* to turn night into day; *jdm gute ~ wünschen* to wish (*od* bid) s. o. good night; *es wird ~* it's growing dark; **~angriff** *m* night raid, night attack; **~arbeit** *f* night-work; **~asyl** *n* night-shelter; **~aufklärung** *f mil* nigh) reconnaissance; **~aufnahme** *f* night photograph; **~ausgabe** *f* (*Zeitung*) extra special; **~befeuerung** *f aero* night beacon lighting; **~blindheit** *f* night-blindness; **~bombenangriff** *m aero mil* night-bombing attack; **~bomber** *m aero mil* night-bomber; **~dienst** *m* night-duty; **~essen** *n* supper; **~eule** *f* screech-owl; **~falter** *m* moth; **~flug** *m aero* night-flight; **~~ausbildung** *f* night flying instruction; **~~ausrüstung** *f* night flying equipment; **~~karte** *f aero* night flying chart; **~frost** *m* night-frost; **~gebet** *n* evening prayer; **~gebühr** *f* night rate; **~gefecht** *n mil* night operation; night engagement, night combat; **~geschirr** *n*, **~topf** *m* chamber-pot; **~gewand** *n* night-dress; **~gleiche** *f* equinox; **~glocke** *f* night-bell; **~hemd** *n* nightdress (*od* -gown), *Am* night robe; (*Männer*) nightshirt; **~jagd** *f aero* night interception, night fighting; night pursuit flight; **~~gebiet** *n* night fighter area; **~~geschwader** *n* wing of night fighters; **~~radargerät** *n* night fighter detection apparatus; **~jäger** *m aero mil* night fighter (airplane); **~~sperre** *f aero* night fighter patrol; **~klub** *m* night club, *Am sl* honky-tonk; **~lager** *n* night-quarters *pl*, night's lodging; **~landung** *f* night landing; **~leben** *n* night life; **~leuchtend** *a* luminous, illuminated; **~licht** *n* night-light; **~lokal** *n* night-club, *fam* night-spot; **~luft** *f* night-air; **~~kampf** *m* night fighting; **~~postdienst** *m* night airmail service; **~~verkehr** *m* night air traffic; **~mahl** *n* supper; **~mahr** *m* nightmare; **~musik** *f* serenade; **~mütze** *f* night-cap; (*schläferiger Mensch*) sleepy-head, dullard; **~portier** *m* night-porter; **~quartier** *n* night-quarters *pl*; **~ruf** *m tele* night call; **~ruhe** *f* night-rest; **~s** at (*od* by) night, *Am* nights; *bis 2 Uhr ~~* till two in the morning; **~schatten** *m* nightshade; **~~gewächse** *n pl* solanaceae *pl*; **~schicht** *f* nightshift; **~schlafend** *a: bei ~~er Zeit* when everyone is asleep; **~schmetterling** *m* moth; **~schriftleiter** *m* night editor; **~schwärmer** *m fig* night-revel(l)er; (*liederlicher Mensch*) rake; **~seite** *f fig* seamy side; **~sicht** *f* night vision; **~start** *m aero* night take-off; **~stunde** *f* night-hour; *späte ~~n* small hours; **~tarif** *m* night tariff; **~tisch** *m* bedside table; **~topf** *m* chamber-pot; **~übung** *f mil* night operation; **~vogel** *m* night-bird; **~vorstellung** *f* night performance; **~wache** *f* night-watch, vigil; **~wächter** *m* night-watchman; **~wandeln** *itr* to walk in o.'s sleep; **~wandler** *m* sleep-walker, somnambulist; **~~isch** *a: mit ~~ischer Sicherheit* with absolute certainty (*od* infallibility); **~zeit** *f* night-time; *zur ~~* at night; **~zeug** *n* night-clothes *pl*; **~zug** *m* night-train.

Nachteil *m* disadvantage, *fam* let-down; (*Schaden*) detriment, prejudice; (*Verlust*) loss; (*Schädigung*) injury; *jur* damage; (*Kehrseite*) drawback; *im ~ sein* to be at a disadvantage; *ohne ~ (jur)* without prejudice (to); *zum ~ von* to the prejudice (of); *jdm zum ~ gereichen* to be detrimental to s. o.; *mit ~ verkaufen com* to sell at a loss; **~ig** *a* disadvantageous, detrimental, prejudicial, derogatory; disparaging; (*ungünstig*) unfavo(u)rable; *~~ behandeln* to discriminate against s. o.

nächt|elang *adv* for whole nights; **~igen** *itr* to spend the night; **~lich** *a* nightly; nocturnal; **~~erweile** *adv* at night-time.

Nachtigall *f* nightingale; **~enschlag** *m* nightingale's song.

Nachtisch *m* (*Früchte*) dessert; (*süßer*) sweet course, *Am* dessert.

nach|tönen *itr* to resound; to echo; **~trab** *m* rear(-guard); **~trachten** *itr* to aspire to; **~trag** *m* supplement, addition; addendum; (*zu e-m Brief*) postscript; *jur* (*zu Testament*) codicil; **~tragen** *irr tr* to carry after; (*zufügen*) to add to; *fig jdm etw ~~* to bear a grudge against; (*Bücher*) to bring up to date; **~trägerisch** *a* vindictive, resentful; **~träglich** *a* supplementary, additional; *adv* further, by way of addition; (*zeitlich*) later; **~tragszahlung** *f* additional payment; payment after a certain date; **~treten** *irr itr* to step after, to follow closely; **~treter** *m* hanger-on; follower; adherent; **~trieb** *m* after-drift; after-shoots *pl*; **~trupp** *m* rear-guard; **~tun** *irr tr: jdm etw ~~* to copy s. o., to imitate s. o.; **~untersuchung** *f* check, check-up; **~urlaub** *m* additional leave; **~verbrennung** *f* after-burning; **~verlangen** *tr* (*bestellen*) to order additionally; (*verlangen*) to claim afterwards; **~verzollung** *f* post entry.

nach|wachsen *irr itr* to grow later; to grow again; **~wägen** *irr tr* to weigh over; **~wahl** *f* by-election, *Am* special election; **~wehen** *f pl* after-pains *pl*; after-effects *pl*; *fig* painful consequences *pl*; **~weinen** *itr* to deplore s. o.; to mourn, to bewail; **~weis** *m* proof, evidence; indication; (*Referenz*) reference, information; (*Unterlage*) record, list; direction; (*Feststellung*) statement; (*Amt*) agency; *den ~ führen* to prove, to demonstrate; **~~bar** *a* demonstrable; detectable; traceable; evident; **~weisen** *irr tr* to point out, to refer to, to prove, to establish; to demonstrate; (*ausweisen*) to identify; (*ermitteln*) to detect; (*Arbeit*) to get for s. o.; (*Behauptung, Anspruch*) to substantiate; **~weislich** *adv* demonstrable, evident, authentic; **~weisung** *f* proof; detection; indication; (*Feststellung*) identification; statement; (*Liste*) list, record, account; (*Stärke~~*) strength report; (*Material~~*) stock report; **~welt** *f* posterity; **~werfen** *irr tr* to throw s. th. after s. o.; **~winter** *m* second winter; **~wirken** *itr* to have an after-effect; to be felt afterwards; **~wirkung** *f* after-effect; **~wirkzeit** *f* hangover time; **~wort** *n* epilog(ue); **~wuchs** *m* after-growth; after-crop; *fig* the rising generation; new blood, junior set; supply of personnel; (*Theater*) newcomer; **~~sorgen** *f pl* worry about new blood.

nach|zahlen *tr* to pay in addition; **~zahlung** *f* additional payment; **~zählen** *tr* to count over again; **~zeichnen** *tr* to draw from a model; to copy; **~ziehen** *irr tr* to draw after; to drag along; (*Striche*) to trace; (*Augenbrauen*) to pencil; (*Schraube*) to screw up, to tighten; *itr* to march after; to follow; **~zotteln** *itr* to trot after; **~zügler** *m* straggler; camp follower; **~zündung** *f* *mot* retarded ignition.

Nacken *m* nape of the neck, neck; **~schlag** *m* blow from behind; *fig* drawback, disaster.

nackt, nackend *a* (*Mensch*) naked, nude; *Am fam* in the raw; (*Körperteile, Erde, Mauer, Tatsachen*) bare; (*Malerei*) nude; (*Wahrheit, Worte*) plain; (*Vogel*) unfledged, callow; *~e Frankfurter* skinless Frankfurter; *~es Chassis* stripped chassis; *jdn ~ ausziehen* to strip s. o. naked; **~badeverein** *m* nudist bathing society; **~heit** *f* nakedness, nudity; bareness; (*Kahlheit*) baldness; **~klub** *m* nudist club; **~kultur** *f* nudism; **~samig** *a bot* gymnospermal; **~tänzerin** *f Am* strip-teaser.

Nadel *f* (*Steck~, Haar~*) pin; (*Näh~*) needle; (*Zeiger*) hand, pointer; *ich sitze wie auf ~n* I'm on pins and needles; **~abweichung** *f* magnetic declination; **~arbeit** *f* needlework; **~ausschlag** *m* deflection of the needle, needle throw; **~baum** *m* conifer; **~büchse** *f* needle-case; **~förmig** *a* needle-shaped, needlelike, acicular; **~geld** *n* pin-money; **~geräusch** *n* needle scratch; **~hölzer** *n pl* conifers *pl*; **~kissen** *n* pincushion; **~kopf** *m* pin-head; **~lager** *n mot* needle bearings *pl*; **~öhr** *n* eye of a needle; **~stich** *m* prick; stitch; *fig* pin-prick; **~wald** *m* coniferous forest.

Nadir *m* nadir; **~distanz** *f* nadir distance, tilt; **~punkt** *m* plumb point.

Nagel *m* nail; (*großer*) spike; (*hölzerner*) peg; (*Zier~*) stud; (*Stift*) tack; *den ~ auf den Kopf treffen* to hit the nail on the head; *an den ~ hängen* (*fig*) to give up, to do away with; *keinen ~ breit* not an inch; *an den Nägeln kauen* to bite o.'s nails; *auf den Nägeln brennen* to be urgent; **~bohrer** *m* gimlet; **~bürste** *f* nail-brush; **~feile** *f* nail file; **~geschwür** *n* withlow; **~kopf** *m* head of a nail; **~lack** *m* nail polish; **~n** *tr* to nail; to spike; **~neu** *a* bran(d)-new; **~probe** *f tech* nail test; *die ~~ machen* to thumb o.'s glass; **~pflege** *f* manicure; **~schere** *f* nail scissors *pl*; **~zange** *f* nail puller.

nag|en *itr, tr* to gnaw; (*knabbern*) to nibble (*an* at); (*zerfressen*) to corrode; (*Boden*) to erode, to eat into; *fig* to prey (up)on, to rankle in o.'s mind; *am Hungertuch ~* to be starving; *nichts zu ~ u. zu beißen haben* not to have a morsel to eat; *an e-m Knochen ~~* to pick a bone; **~end** *a* gnawing; (*Tiere*) rodent; *~~er Hunger* ravenous appetite; **~er** *m*, **~etier** *n* rodent, gnawing animal.

*

nah, nahe *a* near, close (to); local; short range; (*bevorstehend*) imminent, approaching; *adv* near, nearly; (*dicht bei*) close (to); *~e daran sein* to be about (to), to be on the point (to, of); *jdm zu ~e treten* to hurt s. o.'s feelings, to offend; **~abwehrjäger** *m* interceptor fighter; **~angriff** *m* close range attack; **~aufklärung** *f* close patrol reconnaissance; **~~sflugzeug** *n* observation airplane; **~aufnahme** *f film* close-up; **~beben** *n* neighbo(u)ring earthquake; **~beobachtung** *f* close-range observation; **~ebei** *adv* close (to); **~egehen** *irr itr* to affect, to grieve; **~einstellung** *f phot* short-range focus; **~ekommen** *irr itr* to draw (*od* come) near, to approach; (*erreichen*) to get at; **~elegen** *tr* to urge (upon), to suggest; **~eliegen** *irr itr* to lie near, to border (on), to be adjacent; *fig* to be obvious, to suggest itself; **~~d** *a* near at hand; *fig* obvious, manifest; **~empfang** *m radio* short-distance reception; **~en** *itr* (*sich*) to approach, to draw near, to come up (to); **~estehen** *irr itr* to be closely connected with; **~etreten** *irr itr: jdm zu ~* to hurt s. o.'s feelings; **~ezu** *adv* almost, nearly; **~kampf** *m mil* close combat; hand-to-hand fighting; (*Boxen*) clinch; **~~artillerie** *f* close-support artillery; **~~fliegerverband** *m* formation of close-support airplanes; **~~spange** *f* close-combat clasp; **~~waffe** *f* close-combat weapon; **~verkehr** *m* local traffic; *mot* short-haul traffic; *tele* junction (*od* toll) service, short distance traffic; **~~samt** *n tele* toll exchange; **~verteidigung** *f* close defence; **~werfer** *m mil* short-range flame thrower; **~wirkung** *f* close (*od* proximity) effect.

Nähe *f* vicinity; nearness; proximity; neighbo(u)rhood; *in unmittelbarer ~* close by near at hand; *in der, ~* not far off, adjacent, neigh-bo(u)ring, *Am* nearby; *aus der ~* from close up; **~r** *a* nearer; (*kürzer*) shorter; (*unmittelbar*) more direct; (*genauer*) further, more detailed; (*vertrauter*) more intimate, closer; *etw ~~ ausführen* to elaborate (up)on: **~re(s)** *n* details *pl*, particulars *pl*; *~~ bei ...* apply to ...; **~rn** *tr* to place near, to bring near; *r* to approach, to draw (*od* get) near; **~~d** *a*: *sich ~~d* oncoming; **~rung** *f* approach, approximation; **~~sformel** *f* approximation formula; **~~slösung** *f* approximate solution; **~~sverfahren** *n* approximation method; **~~sweise** *adv* approximately; **~~swert** *m* approximate value.

Näh|arbeit *f* needlework, sewing; **~en** *tr, itr* to sew, to stitch; *med* to suture; **~erei** *f* needlework, sewing; **~erin** *f* needlewoman, seamstress; **~garn** *n* sewing-cotton; **~kästchen** *n* sewing box; **~kissen** *n* sewing-cushion; **~korb** *m* work-basket; **~kränzchen** *n Am* quilting-bee; **~maschine** *f* sewing-machine; **~nadel** *f* sewing needle; **~seide** *f* sewing-silk; **~tisch** *m* sewing-table; **~zeug** *n* sewing kit, housewife.

Nähr|boden *m chem* nutrient medium, culture medium; fertile soil; **~brühe** *f* nutrient broth; **~en** *tr* to feed, to nourish, to nurture; (*Mutter*) to nurse, to suckle; *fig* to cherish, to foster, to nourish; *itr* to be nourishing; *r* to live (on), to feed (on); to maintain o. s.; *sich kümmerlich ~* to scrape up a miserable living; **~~d** *a* nourishing, nutritious, nutritive, nutrient; **~flüssigkeit** *f* nutritive liquid; **~hefe** *f* nutrient yeast; **~kraft** *f* nutritive power; **~mittel** *n* food nutriment; (*aus Mehl*) flour products *pl*; cereal-based processed foodstuffs *pl*; **~präparat** *n* food preparation, patent food; **~stand** *m* the peasants *pl*; **~stoff** *m* nutritive substance; (*Nahrungsmittel*) foodstuff; **~wert** *m* nutritive value.

nahr|haft *a* nourishing, nutritious, nutritive; (*Mahlzeit*) substantial; (*Boden*) fertile, productive; *com* lucrative; profitable; **~ung** *f* nourishment, food; (*Kost*) diet; (*Tiere, fam für Menschen*) feed; (*Unterhalt*) livelihood, maintenance, subsistence, sustenance; **~~saufnahme** *f* absorption of food; **~~sbedarf** *m* food requirement; **~~sfreiheit** *f* food autarky; **~~smangel** *m* scarcity of provisions; **~~smittel** *n pl* food, foodstuffs *pl*, victuals *pl*; *hochwertige ~~smittel* concentrated (*od* vitaminized) food; **~~smittelchemiker** *m* food chemist; **~~smitteleinfuhr** *f* food import; **~~smittelfälschung** *f* adulteration of food; **~~smittelkürzungen** *f pl* food cuts *pl*; **~~ssorgen** *f pl* cares of subsistence, struggle for livelihood; **~~sstoff** *m* nutritive substance.

Naht *f* seam; *med, bot* suture; *tech* joint; weld; lap, edge; *schlecht ausgeführte ~* pucker; *überwendliche ~* overcast; *versetzte ~* staggered seam; *wulstlose ~* ridgeless seam; **~los** *a* weldless, seamless, jointless; *~~es Rohr* seamless tube; **~schweißung** *f* seam welding; **~stelle** *f mil* boundary (position) between units.

naiv *a* naive, natural, artless, simple; **~ität** *f* ingenuousness, simplicity, naivety.

Name *m* name; (*Vor~*) Christian (*od* first) name; (*Bei~*) surname; (*Ruf*) name, reputation; (*Benennung*) appellation; *im ~* on behalf of; *die ~n verlesen* to call over the names, to call the roll; *das Kind beim rechten ~n nennen* to call a spade a spade; *mit vollem ~n unterschreiben* to sign in full; *dem ~n nach* by name; *unter dem ~n* under the pretext; **~ngebung** *f* christening; naming; (*Terminologie*) nomenclature; **~nliste** *f* list of names, roll; (*Ärzte, Geschworene, Rechtsanwälte*) panel; **~nlos** *a* nameless, anonymous; (*unaussprechlich*) inexpressible, unutterable; *adv* (*äußerst*) utterly; **~~igkeit** *f* namelessness, anonymousness; **~nregister, ~nverzeichnis** *n* name index; (*Verfasser*) author index; list of names; **~ns** *prp* named, by name of; (*im Auftrag von*) in the name of, on behalf of; **~nsaufruf** *m* roll-call; **~nschild** *n* name plate; **~nsfest** *n*, **~nstag** *m* nameday, Saint's day; **~nsunterschrift** *f* signature; **~nsvetter** *m* namesake; **~nszug** *m* signature; (*Schnörkel*) flourish; **~ntlich** *a* named, by name; *~~e Abstimmung* voting by call; *adv* (*besonders*) especially, particularly; *~~ sagen* to tell specifically.

namhaft *a* (*bekannt*) renowned, well-known; (*beträchtlich*) considerable, appreciable; *~ machen* to (mention by) name, to specify.

nämlich *a* same, identical; *adv* namely, and that is; that is to say (*Abk* i. e., viz.); of course.

nanu! *interj* well, well! come, come!

Napf *m* bowl, pan, basin; **~kuchen** *m* pound-cake; **Näpfchen** *n* little basin.

Naphtha *n* naphtha; raw petroleum; **~lin** *n* naphthalene.

Narb|e *f* scar; *med* cicatrice; (*Leder*) grain; *bot* stigma; (*Mangel*) defect, flaw; **~nbildung** *f tech* pitting; **~ig** *a* scarred, cicatrized; (*Leder*) grained.

Nark|ose *f* narcosis; *med* an(a)esthesia; **~otisch** *a* narcotic; an(a)esthetic; **~otisieren** *tr* to narcotize; to an(a)esthetize.

Narr *m* fool, simpleton; buffoon; jester; *Am fam* sucker; *jdn zum ~en halten* to make a fool of s. o., to pull s. o.'s leg, *Am sl* to kid s. o.; *e-n ~en fressen an* to take a great fancy to; *sei kein ~!* don't be foolish! *Am* be yourself! **~en** *tr* to fool; **~enhaus** *n* madhouse, lunatic asylum; **~enkappe** *f* fool's cap; **~enpossen** *f pl* foolery, buffoonery; **~enseil** *n*: *jdn am ~~ führen* to make a fool of s. o.; *fam* to pull the wool over s. o.'s eyes; **~ensicher** *a* fool-proof; **~enstreich** *m* foolish trick; **~etei** *f* tomfoolery; **~heit** *f* foolishness; folly.

Närr|in *f* fool, foolish woman; **~isch** *a* foolish, mad; (*sonderbar*) strange, odd.

Narzisse *f* narcissus; *gelbe ~* daffodil.

Nasal(laut) *m* nasal sound.

nasch|en *tr, itr* to nibble, to eat titbits; (*verstohlen*) to eat sweets on the sly; *gern ~~* to have a sweet tooth; **~haft** *a* dainty-mouthed; sweet-toothed; **~~igkeit** *f* love of titbits, daintiness; **~maul** *n* sweet-tooth; **~werk** *n* dainties *pl*, delicacies *pl*, sweets *pl*.

Näscher *m* sweet-tooth; **~eien** *f pl* dainties, sweets, lollipops; titbits *pl*.

Nas|e *f* nose; (*Geruch*) scent; (*Schnauze*) snout; *fig* (*Verweis*) rebuke; (*Vorsprung*) beak, lug, tappet; (*Ausguß*) spout, nozzle; *der ~e nach gehen* to follow o.'s nose; *e-e ~e drehen* to make a fool of; *jdm e-e lange ~e machen sl* to cock a snook at s. o.; *seine ~e in anderer Leute Angelegenheiten stecken* to stick o.'s nose into other people's business; *jdn an der ~e herumführen* to lead s. o. by the nose, to give s. o. the run-around; *auf der ~e liegen fig* to be ill; *die Tür vor der ~e zuschlagen* to slam the door in o.'s face; *jdm etw unter die ~e reiben* to bring s. th. home to s. o., to rub it in; *die ~e rümpfen* (*über*) to turn up o.'s nose (at); to look down o.'s nose (at); *der Zug fuhr mir vor der ~e weg* I missed the train by a hair; *sich die ~~ putzen* to blow o.'s nose; *e-e gute ~~ haben für* (*fig*) to have a flair for; *die ~~ voll haben von* to be fed up with; **~enbein** *n* nasal bone; **~enbluten** *m* nose-bleeding, nosebleed; **~enflügel** *m* side of the nose; **~enlänge** *f sport: um e-e ~~ schlagen* to nose out; **~enloch** *n* nostril; **~enrücken** *m* bridge of the nose; **~enscheidewand** *f anat* column of the nose; **~enschleimhaut** *f anat* pituitary membrane; **~enspitze** *f* tip of the nose; **~ensteg** *m* (*Brille*) nosepiece; bridge of a nose; **~enstüber** *m* snubbing, fillip; **~eweis** *a* cheeky, saucy, *Am* fresh; **~~heit** *f* sauciness, pertness; **~führen** *tr* to dupe, to hoax, to bamboozle; **~horn** *n* rhinoceros.

näseln *itr* to speak through the nose, to nasalize; to snuffle; *~ n* nasal twang; **~d** *a* nasal.

naß *a* wet; (*feucht*) humid, moist; (*Kleider*) drenched; *~ bis auf die Haut* wet to the skin; *~ werden* to get wet, to get soaked; *~ n* liquid; **~kalt** *a* dampish, chilly and cold, raw.

Nassauer *m* Nassovian; (*Schmarotzer*) sponger, *Am sl* chiseler, dead beat.

Nässe *f* wetness; moisture, humidity; **~n** *tr* to wet; to moisten.

Nation *f* nation; *verbündete ~en* Allied Nations; **~al** *a* national; **~~bewußtsein, ~~gefühl** *n* nationalism, patriotism; **~~charakter** *m* national character; **~~eigentum** *n* national property; **~~farben** *f pl* national colo(u)rs *pl*; **~~flagge** *f* national flag; (*England*) the Union Jack, *Am* Stars and Stripes *pl*; **~~hymne** *f* national anthem; **~~isieren** *tr* to nationalize; **~~isierung** *f* nationalization; **~~ist** *m* nationalist; **~~ität** *f* nationality; **~~ökonomie** *f* political economy; **~~schuld** *f* national debt; **~~sozialismus** *m* National Socialism; **~~vermögen** *n* national property; **~~versammlung** *f* national assembly.

Natrium *n chem* sodium.

Natron *n chem* soda, sodium hydroxide; (*doppel*)*kohlensaures ~* (bi-)carbonate of soda; **~haltig** *a* containing soda; **~lauge** *f* soda lye; **~salpeter** *m* soda saltpeter; **~salz** *n* soda salt; **~seife** *f* soda soap.

Natter *f* adder, viper.

Natur *f* nature; (*Körperbeschaffenheit*) constitution; (*Veranlagung*) temper(ament), disposition; (*geistig u. körperlich*) make-up; (*Charakter*) character; *von ~* by nature; inherent; *nach der ~ zeichnen* to draw from nature; *e-e starke ~* a strong constitution; *in ~* in kind; *das geht mir wider die ~* that goes against my grain; **~alien** *pl* natural produce; (*Naturgeschichte*) natural history specimens *pl*; **~~kabinett** *n*, **~~sammlung** *f* natural history collection; **~alisation** *f* naturalization; **~alisieren** *tr* to naturalize; **~alismus** *m* naturalism; **~alleistung** *f* payment in kind; **~alverpflegung** *f* food supplies in kind, rations in kind; **~alwert** *m* value in kind; **~alwirtschaft** *f* barter; **~anlage** *f* disposition; character; temper(ament); **~beobachtung** *f* observation of nature; **~beschreibung** *f* description of nature; **~bursche** *m* child of nature; **~ell** *n* nature, disposition, temper; **~ereignis** *n*, **~erscheinung** *f* natural phenomenon; **~erzeugnis** *n* produce; natural product; **~farben** *a* of natural colo(u)r, nature-shade; (*Leder*) fair; **~forscher** *m* scientist; physicist; **~forschung** *f* scientific research; **~freund** *m* lover of nature; **~gabe** *f* gift of nature; **~gefühl** *n* feeling for nature; **~gemäß** *a* natural, according to nature; *adv* naturally; **~geschichte** *f* natural history; **~gesetz** *n* law of nature, natural law; **~getreu** *a* life-like, true to nature; full-scale, full-size; **~gummi** *m* natural rubber; **~heilkunde** *f* nature cure; **~heilkundige(r)** *m* nature-cure practitioner; **~kraft** *f* natural force; **~lehre** *f* natural science (*od* philosophy); physics *pl mit sing*; **~mensch** *m* natural man; **~notwendig** *a* necessity; **~produkt** *n* natural product, native substance; **~recht** *n* natural right; **~reich** *n* kingdom (*od* domain) of nature; **~schutzgebiet** *n* national preserved area, preserve; national park; **~spiel** *n* freak of nature; **~stoff** *m* natural substance; **~treue** *f* faithfulness, fidelity; realistic properties *pl*; **~trieb** *m* instinct; **~volk** *n* primitive race; **~wahr** *a* life-like, true to nature; **~widrig** *a* unnatural, abnormal; **~wissenschaft** *f* natural science; **~~ler** *m* scientist; **~~lich** *a* pertaining to natural science; scientific; **~wüchsig** *a* natural, original; (*offen heraus*) blunt; **~wunder** *n* prodigy; **~zustand** *m* natural state.

natürlich *a* natural; (*echt*) genuine, unaffected; (*angeboren*) innate; (*ungekünstelt*) artless; *~e Größe* full-scale, actual size; *adv* of course, certainly; **~keit** *f* naturalness; simplicity; *~~ der Wiedergabe* faithfulness (*od* realism) of reproduction.

Naut|ik *f* nautics, nautical science; navigation; **~isch** *a* nautical.

Navig|ationsraum *m* chart-room; **~ator** *m aero* navigator; **~ieren** *tr* to navigate.

Nazi|(st) *m* Nazi; **~feindlich** *a* anti-Nazi; **~freundlich** *a* pro-Nazi; **~smus** *m* Nazism; **~stisch** *a* Nazi.

Nebel *m* fog; (*weniger dick*) mist; (*ganz dünn*) haze; (*leichter Regen*) drizzle; (*mit Rauch gemischt*) smog; (*künstlich*) smoke-screen; (*Schleier*) *fig* veil, mist; *astr* nebula; **~abblasgerät** *n* smoke-filled chemical cylinder; **~apparat** *m* atomizer, sprayer; **~artig** *a* mist-like, misty, foggy; **~bank** *f* fog-bank; **~bildung** *f* formation of fog; **~bombe** *f mil* smoke-ball (*od* -bomb); **~decke** *f* smoke blanket (*od* screen); **~dunst** *m* mist; **~entwicklung** *f* generation of smoke; **~fleck** *m astr* nebula; **~gerät** *n* smoke equipment; **~granate** *f* smoke shell; **~haft** *a* misty, foggy, hazy, dim; *fig* hazy, nebulous; **~horn** *n* fog-horn; **~ig** *a* foggy, misty, *Am* smoky; **~kammer** *f* cloud chamber; **~kasten** *m* smoke box; **~kerze** *f* smoke candle; **~krähe** *f* hooded crow; **~landung** *f* fog (*od* instrument) landing; **~n** *itr* to be foggy; to lay down smoke; **~regen** *m* drizzle; **~scheibe** *f* de-mister; **~scheinwerfer** *m mot* fog lamp; **~schleier**

m veil of mist; *mil* smoke-screen; **~schwaden** *m* damp fog; **~streif** *m* misty cloud; **~tropfen** *m* fog particle (*od* drop); **~wand** *f aero, mar* smoke-screen; **~werfer** *m mil* smoke mortar; (*Do-Werfer*) multiple rocket launcher; *sl* Moaning Minnie; **~wetter** *n* foggy weather; **~wolke** *f* stratus cloud; **~zone** *f mil* smoke-screened area.

neben *prp, adv* (*örtlich*) beside, by the side of; next to; (*nahe*) close to; (*unter*) among; (*dazu*) in addition to, besides; **~abrede** *f* collateral agreement; **~abschnitt** *m mil* adjoining sector; **~absicht** *f* secondary objective; **~amt** *n* subsidiary office; **~~lich** *a* part-time; **~an** *adv* next door, close by; **~anlage** *f* additional plant, annex; **~anschluß** *m tele* extension; **~antrieb** *m* auxiliary drive; **~arbeit** *f* spare-time work, extra work; **~ausgaben** *f pl* incidentals *pl*; **~ausgang** *m* side-door; **~bahn** *f rail* branch-line, local line; **~bedeutung** *f* secondary meaning; connotation; **~bedingung** *f* secondary condition; **~begriff** *m* subordinate notion; **~bei** *adv* by the way, incidentally; (*außerdem*) besides, moreover, *Am* on the side; *~~ bemerkt* by the way, incidentally; **~beruf** *m*, **~beschäftigung** *f* additional occupation; sideline, out-side job; avocation; **~bestandteil** *m* secondary ingredient; **~bestimmung** *f* incidental provision; **~betrieb** *m* subsidiary business; branch business; **~bezüge** *m pl* perquisites *pl*; **~buhler** *m*, **~~in** *f* rival; **~~schaft** *f* rivalry; **~einander** *adv* side by side, abreast, next to each other; **~~bestehen** *n* simultaneous existence; **~~schalten** *tr el* to connect in parallel; **~~schaltung** *f* parallel (*od* multiple) connection; **~~stellung** *f* juxtaposition; **~eingang** *m* side entrance; **~einkommen** *n*, **~einkünfte** *pl*, **~einnahmen** *f pl* additional income, casual earnings *pl*, perquisites *pl*; **~ergebnis** *n* by-product; **~fach** *n* subsidiary subject, *Am* minor; **~fluß** *m* tributary, affluent; **~gasse** *f* by-street, by-lane; **~gebäude** *n* adjacent building, outhouse; annex(e); **~gebühren** *f pl* incidental charges *pl*; **~gedanke** *m* secondary thought; **~gelaß** *n*, **~kammer** *f* adjoining room, box-room; **~geleise** *n* (railway) siding, *Am* side-track; *auf ein ~~ schieben* (*Am*) to side-track; **~geräusch** *n tele* crackling, hissing; *radio* atmospherics *pl*, strays *pl*; **~gericht** *n* side-dish, entremets *pl*; **~geschmack** *m* after taste, tang; **~gewinn** *m* incidental profit; **~handlung** *f* underplot, by-play; **~haus** *n* adjoining building; **~her, ~hin** *adv* by the side of, along with; (*nebenbei*) by the way; **~hode** *f anat* epididymis; **~klage** *f* incidental action; **~kläger** *m* co-plaintiff; **~kosten** *pl* extras *pl*, incidental expenses *pl*; **~liegend** *a* adjacent; **~linie** *f* collateral line; *rail* branch line; **~mann** *m* next man; (*rechts*) right-hand man; **~mensch** *m* fellow creature; **~niere** *f* adrenal gland, suprarenal capsule; **~person** *f theat* subordinate figure; **~postamt** *n* branch post-office; **~produkt** *n* by-product; **~programm** *n film* supporting program(me); **~punkt** *m* accessory point; **~rolle** *f* subordinate part; **~sache** *f* matter of secondary importance, subordinate (*od* minor) matter; **~sächlich** *a* unimportant, incidental; **~satz** *m gram* subordinate clause; **~schluß** *m* shunt; **~sender** *m radio* relay station; outlet (*od* affiliated) station; **~sitzer** *m* seat mate; **~sonne** *f* parhelion; **~spesen** *pl* incidentals *pl*, extras *pl*; **~stehend** *a* annexed, marginal; alongside; *~~e Abbildung* opposite illustration; *adv* on the margin; **~stelle** *f tele* extension; (*Vertretung*) agency; (*Bank*) branch; **~straße** *f* by-street; minor road; **~strecke** *f rail* branch-line; **~teil** *m* accessory part; **~titel** *m* sub-title; **~tür** *f* side-door; **~umstand** *m* minor (*od* accessory) detail; **~unkosten** *pl* extras *pl*, incidentals *pl*; **~ursache** secondary (*od* incidental) cause; **~verdienst** *m* incidental earnings *pl*, perquisites *pl*; **~weg** *m* by-way; **~winkel** *m* adjacent angle; **~wirkung** *f* secondary effect; **~zimmer** *n* next room; **~zweck** *m* secondary objective; **~zweig** *m* lateral branch.

nebst *prp* together with, including.

neck|en *tr* to tease, to banter, to chaff; *Am sl* to kid; **~erei** *f* teasing, banter, raillery; chaff; **~isch** *a* teasing, (*komisch, drollig*) queer, funny, comical, droll; playful.

Neffe *m* nephew.

negativ *a* negative; *~ n phot* negative; *dichtes* (*flaues, hartes*) *~* (*phot*) dense (faint, hard) negative; **~bild** *n* negative picture; **~druckstock** *m typ* negative (plate).

Neger *m* negro, *Am* colored gentleman, *fam* buck; (*verächtlich*) nigger; **~amme** *f* black nurse; colo(u)red female nurse, *Am dial* mammy; **~in** *f* negress; **~musik** *f* syncopated music; **~kind** *n* piccaninny; **~schweiß** *m mil sl* coffee; **~sklave** *m* black slave.

negieren *tr* to deny; to answer in the negative.

Negligé *n* undress, dishabille, negligee; (*Morgenkleid*) morning-gown; *im ~ sein* to be in dishabille.

*

nehmen *irr tr* to take (*etw von jdm* s. th. from s. o.); (*heraus~*) to take out; (*weg~*) to take away; (*fortbewegen*) to move; (*zurück~*) to take back; (*ergreifen*) to seize, to lay hold of; (*an~*) to accept; (*erhalten*) to receive, to get; (*kaufen*) to buy; (*in Besitz ~*) to appropriate; (*gefangen ~*) to capture; (*Hindernis*) to take, to clear; (*Graben*) to leap over; (*Eintrittskarte*) to book; (*unrechtmäßig*) to arrogate s. th. to o. s.; *Abschied ~* to say good-by(e); to take leave; *sich in acht ~* to be careful (*vor* of); *in Anspruch ~* to lay claim (to); *unter Feuer ~* to shell, to fire upon; to strafe; *alles in allem genommen* all things considered; *Anstoß ~* to object; *auf sich ~* to take s. th. upon o. s.; *kein Blatt vor den Mund ~* to give s. o. a piece of o.'s mind; *ein Ende ~* to come to an end; *es auf sich ~* to take it upon o. s.; *es sich nicht ~ lassen* to insist on; *es genau ~* to be very particular; to be pedantic; *sich etw zu Herzen ~* to lay s. th. to heart; *sich das Leben ~* to commit suicide; *leicht ~* to treat lightly; *den Mund voll ~* to talk big; *~ wir den Fall* let us suppose; *Partei ~* to take sides, to side with; *Platz ~* to have (*od* take) a seat; *Schaden ~* to suffer damage; *streng* (*od genau*) *genommen* strictly speaking; *Urlaub ~* to get leave of absence; *wie man's nimmt!* that depends! *jdn beim Wort ~* to take s. o. at his word; *zu sich ~* (*Nahrung*) to eat, to have s. th., to take nourishment; (*Person*) to take in, to take to o.'s home.

Nehmer *m* taker; (*Käufer*) buyer, purchaser; (*Kurs*) bid, money.

Nehrung *f* narrow tongue of land; coastal beach belt.

Neid *m* envy (*auf jdn* of s. o.; *über etw* at (*od* of) s. th.); (*Mißgunst*) grudge; (*Eifersucht*) jealousy; *grün werden vor ~* to be green with envy; *vor ~ vergehen* to be eaten up with envy; *bei jdm ~ erregen* to excite s. o.'s envy; *aus ~* out of envy; *aus ~ sagen sie so abscheuliche Sachen über mich* they say such scandalous things about me out of envy; *aus ~ gegen* from envy of; **~en** *itr* to envy s. o. s. th.; **~er, ~hammel** *m* grudger, envious person; dog in the manger; **~erfüllt** *a* full of envy, filled with envy; **~isch** *a* envious; jealous (of); grudging; **~los** *a* unenvious, ungrudging.

Neig|e *f* decline, wane; (*Abhang*) slope; (*Überbleibsel*) remnant; (*im Glase*) heel-tap; *bis zur ~~ leeren* to drink to the dregs; *auf die ~~ gehen* to be on the decline, *com* to run short; **~en** *tr* to incline, to bend; (*senken*) to lower; (*kippen*) to tilt; *itr* to incline (to), to tend (to), to be disposed (to), to be susceptible (to); *r* (*Ebene*) to slope, to dip, to slant; (*Person*) to bend, to incline, to lean; (*sich ver~*) to bow; (*zu Ende gehen*) to draw (to a close); (*Neigung zeigen*) to tend (to); *geneigt sein* to be inclined (to); **~ung** *f* (*Lage*) incline, declivity, inclination; (*Abhang*) slope; *rail* gradient, *Am* grade; (*Magnetnadel*) dip; (*Zuneigung*) inclination, liking (for); (*Vorliebe*) preference; (*Geschmack für*) taste (for); (*Hang*) disposition (to), tendency (towards), (*zum Schlechten*) proneness (to); **~~sebene** *f* inclined plane; **~~sehe** *f* love match; **~~sgrad** *m* obliquity; **~~slinie** *f* gradient; **~~smesser** *m* clinometer; *aero* inclinometer; **~~swinkel** *m* angle of incidence; angle of inclination.

nein *adv* no, *Am* I guess not, *Am sl* nope; *~, so was!* well, I never! *~ u. abermals ~!* a thousand times no! *parl* (*Neinstimme*) no; the Noes *pl*; *das ~ überwiegt parl* the Noes have it; *zwei Ja gegen fünf ~* two Ayes to five Noes; *mit ~ antworten* to answer in the negative; *~ sagen* to deny, to refuse.

Nekrolog *m* necrology; obituary notice.

Nektar *m* nectar.

Nelke *f* pink, carnation; (*Gewürz*) clove.

nenn|bar *a* mentionable; **~belastung** *f tech* nominal load; **~en** *irr tr* to name, to call; (*erwähnen*) to mention by name, to speak of; (*benennen*) to term; *sich ~~* to be called; **~enswert** *a* worth mentioning; **~er** *m* denominator; **~geld** *n sport* entry-fee; **~leistung** *f* rated (*od* nominal) power; normal output, normal efficiency; **~ung** *f* (*mit Namen, Ernennung*) naming; nomination; *sport* entry; **~~sliste** *f sport* entries *pl*, list of competitors; **~~sschluß** *m sport* close of entries; **~wert** *m* nominal value; *zum ~~* at par; **~wort** *n* noun.

Neon|licht *n* neon light; **~leuchtschild** *n* neon sign; **~röhre** *f* neon tube.

neppen *tr sl* to fleece.

Nerv *m* nerve; *auf die ~en gehen* to get on o.'s nerves, to be a strain on s. o.'s nerves; to drive s. o. mad; **~enanfall** *m* nervous attack; **~enarzt** *m med* neurologist; **~enaufreibend** *a* nerve-racking; **~enberuhigend** *a* nervine; **~enbündel** *n* bundle of nerves; **~enenden** *n pl* (*Zahn*) nerve pulp; **~enentzündung** *f* neuritis; **~enfasern** *f pl* nerve fibre; **~enfieber** *n* nervous (*od* typhoid) fever; **~enheilanstalt** *f* clinic for nervous diseases; mental hospital; **~enheilkunde** *f* neurology; **~enkitzel** *m* titillation of the nerves; **~enknoten** *m* (nerve) ganglion; **~enkrank** *a* neurotic, neurasthenic; neuropathic; **~~heit** *f* nervous disease; neurosis; neuropathy; **~enkrieg** *m* war of nerves; **~enkunde** *f* neurology; **~enleiden** *n* nervous complaint; **~~d** *a* neuropathic; **~enreiz** *m* nerve stimulus; **~enschmerz** *m* neuralgia; **~enschock** *m* nervous attack (*od* shock); **~enschwäche** *f* nervous debility, neurasthenia; **~enstärkend** *a* tonic; nervine; **~enstrang** *m* nerve-cord; **~ensystem** *n* nervous system; **~enüberreizung** *f* nervous irritation; **~enzelle** *f* nerve-cell; **~enzerrüttung** *f* shattering of the nerves; **~enzusammenbruch** *m* nervous breakdown; **~ig** *a* nervous; (*kräftig*) sinewy, pithy; **~ös** *a* nervous, nervy, *Am* goosey; **~~** *sein* to be jumpy (*od* jittery *od* highly strung); to have the jitters, to be on edge; **~osität** *f* nervousness, nervosity, *sl* jitters *pl*.

Nerz *m zoo* mink, Chinese weasel.

Nessel *f* nettle; (*Taub~*) dead nettle; (*Gras*) China grass; (*Gewebe*) nettle cloth; *sich in die ~n setzen* to get into hot water; **~fieber** *n* nettle-rash, urticaria; **~tuch** *n* muslin; unbleached calico.

Nest *n* nest; (*Horst*) aerie; *fam* bed; *fam* (*Kleinstadt*) hole; small provincial town; (*Knoten in Haartracht*) chignon; *mil* (*Stellung*) emplacement; (*Schützen~*) group of foxholes; **~häkchen, ~küken** *n* nestling; nest-chicken; *fig* pet, baby.

Nestel *f* lace; (*Schuh~*) boot-laces *pl*, *Am* shoe-strings *pl*; **~n** *itr* to lace up, to fasten.

nett *a* neat, fair, pretty; (*freundlich*) nice; (*niedlich*) dainty, dinky, *Am* cunning, cute; **~igkeit** *f* properness; neatness, prettiness, kindness.

netto *adv* net, clear; **~betrag** *m* net amount; **~einnahme** *f* net receipts *pl*; **~ertrag** *m* net proceeds *pl*; net yield; **~lohn** *m* take-home pay; **~gewicht** *n* net weight; **~gewinn** *m* net gain, clear profits *pl*; **~preis** *m* net price; **~verdienst** *m* net income.

Netz *n* net, netting; (*Anlage*) *rail*, *radio* network, system; *tele* area; *el* mains *pl*, grid; power supply; *opt* (*Faden~*) reticle; (*~werk*) reticulation; (*Kartengitter*) graticule; (*Gitter*) grate; (*Gepäck~*) rack; *aero* air-net; (*Adern, Nerven, fig*) plexus; *med* (*Darm*) omentum; (*Jagd*) toils *pl*; (*Falle*) snare, trap; (*Gaze*) gauze; *jdm ein ~ stellen* to lay a snare for s. o.; *ins ~ gehen* to go into the net; **~ähnlich** *a* netlike, reticular; **~anode** *f radio* grid terminal; B-battery eliminator; **~anschluß** *m* mains (*od* network) supply, connexion to mains; **(~)~empfänger** *m radio* mains operated receiver; **~~gerät** *n* power supply unit; **~antenne** *f radio* mains aerial; **~artig** *a* reticular; **~auge** *n* compound eye; **~ausfall** *m el* mains failure; **~ausschalter** *m* mains switch, mains cutout; **~betrieb** *m* mains power supply; **~brummen** *n radio* hum; **~drossel** *f* hum eliminator coil; **~en** *tr* to wet, to moisten, to sprinkle; **~filter** *n radio* hum eliminator; **~flügler** *m pl* neuroptera *pl*; **~förmig** *a* net-shaped; netlike; reticular; **~gerät** *n* power-supply unit; power pack; **~gespeist** *a* mains-fed; **~haut** *f* retina; **~~entzündung** *f* retinitis; **~gerät** *n radio* mains set; **~hemd** *n* cellular shirt; **~karte** *f rail* area season ticket; **~sicherung** *f* mains fuse; **~spannung** *f* mains (*od* line) voltage; **~spiel** *n* (*Tennis*) net-play; **~stecker** *m* power-supply plug; **~strom** *m* mains current; **~werk** *n* network.

neu *a* new; (*frisch*) fresh; (*modern*) modern; (*kürzlich*) recent; (*~artig*) novel; *adv aufs ~e, von ~em* anew, afresh, again; *wieder ~ anfangen* to start all over again; *~ere Sprachen* modern languages; *~e Kartoffeln* young potatoes; *die ~(e)ste Mode* the latest style; *~este Nachrichten* latest news; *~e n* novelty, new thing; *was gibt es ~es?* what's the news? *Am* what's new? *das ist mir nichts ~es* that's no news to me; **~ankömmling** *m* new-comer, arrival; **~anlage** *f* new installation; **~anschaffung** *f* new purchase, recent acquisition; **~artig** *a* novel; unorthodox; **~auflage** *f* new edition; **~ausgabe** *f* republication; (*~druck*) reprint; **~backen** *a* newly baked; just made; **~bau** *m* new building, reconstruction; **~bearbeitung** *f* revised edition, revision; **~bekehrte(r)** *m* neophyte, novice; **~belebung** *f* revival; **~besetzung** (*Stelle*) filling (of vacancies); **~bildung** *f* new formation (*od* growth); *med* neoplasm; **~druck** *m* reprint; **~einstellung** *f* replacement; **~einstudierung** *f* new staging; **~einstufung** *f* reclassification; **~erdings** *adv* recently, newly, lately; **~erer** *m* innovator; **~erlich** *a* late, recent; repeated, renewed; **~erscheinung** *f* (*Buch*) new book; **~erung** *f* innovation; novelty, newness; (*Mode*) latest fashion; (*Wort*) neologism; **~~ssucht** *f* passion for innovation; **~~ssüchtig** *a* fond of innovations; **~estens** *adv* lately, of late, recently; **~fundland** *n* Newfoundland; **~gebacken** *a* newly baked; just made; **~geboren** *a* new-born; **~gestalten** *tr* to reorganize, *Am fam* to revamp; **~gestaltung** *f* reorganization; modification; **~gier(de)** *f* curiosity, curiousness, inquisitiveness; **~gierig** *a* curious, inquisitive (*auf* after, about, of, into); **~~** *sein* to be curious, *Am sl* to rubberneck, to snoop; **~~** *sein ob* to wonder if (*od* whether); **~gierige(r)** *m* inquisitive (*od* prying) person, *fam* nosy parker, *Am sl* rubberneck; **~gründung** *f* new establishment; **~gruppierung** *f* realignment; **~heidentum** *n* neopaganism; **~heidnisch** *a* neopagan; **~heit** *f* novelty; newness; **~hochdeutsch** *a* Modern High German; **~igkeit** *f* (a piece of) news; **~~skrämer** *m* news-monger; **~inszenierung** *f* new mise-en-scene; **~jahr** *n* New Year; *jdm zu ~~ gratulieren* to wish s. o. a happy New Year; **~~sabend** *m* New Year's Eve; **~~sgeschenk** *n* New Year's gift; **~~s(glück)wünsche** *m* good wishes for a happy New Year; **~konstruktion** *f* redesign; reconstruction; **~land** *n fig* virgin territory; **~lich** *adv* the other day, recently; **~ling** *m* beginner, novice, neophyte, tiro; green hand, *fam* greenhorn, *Am sl* tenderfoot, sucker; **~modisch** *a* fashionable; newfashioned, newfangled; **~mond** *m* new moon; **~ordnung** *f* reorganization; **~orientierung** *f* reorientation; readjustment; **~philologe, ~sprachler** *m* student (*od* teacher) of modern languages; **~regelung** *f* rearangement, new set-up; **~reiche(r)** *m* wealthy parvenu; **~schnee** *m* new(-fallen) snow; **~seeland** *n* New Zealand; **~silber** *n* German silver, argentan; **~vermählt** *a* newly married; *die ~~en* a newly wedded couple, *Am* the newly weds *pl*; **~verteilung** *f* redistribution; **~wahl** *f* (*Wiederwahl*) re-election; **~wert** *m* value (as) new; **~zeit** *f* modern times *pl*; **~~lich** *a* modern; up-to-date.

neun nine; **~auge** *n* river-lamprey; **~eck** *n* nonagon; **~erlei** *a* of nine different sorts; **~fach** *a* ninefold; **~jährig** *a* nine years old; **~malkluge(r)** *m* wiseacre, *Am* weisenheimer; **~t** *a* ninth; **~tel** *n* ninth, ninth part; **~zehn** nineteen; **~zehnte** *a* nineteenth; **~zig** ninety.

Neur|algie *f* neuralgia; **~algisch** *a* neuralgic; **~algismus** *m* psychalgia; **~asthenie** *f* neurasthenia; **~astheniker** *m* neurastheni(a)c; **~asthenisch** *a* neurasthenic; **~ose** *f* neurosis.

neutr|al *a* neutral; (*unparteiisch*) impartial; (*indifferent*) indifferent; *~~e Flagge* neutral colo(u)rs; *~~ bleiben* to remain neutral; to stand aloof; **~alisieren** *tr* to neutralize; **~alität** *f* neutrality; *bewaffnete ~~* armed neutrality; **~~sabzeichen** *n* badge of neutrals; **~ino** *n phys* neutrino; **~~emission** *f* neutrino emission; **~on** *n phys* neutron; *langsame ~~en* slow neutrons; *schnelle ~~en* fast neutrons; **~um** *n* neuter.

nicht *adv* not; *~ doch!* certainly not! *~ einmal* not even; *durchaus ~, ganz u. gar ~* not at all, by no means; *~ ganz* fractional; *~ mehr* no longer; *noch ~* not yet; *ich auch ~* nor I either; *~ wahr?* isn't it? *mit~en* not at all; *zu~e machen* to annihilate; (*zugrunde richten*) to ruin, to destroy; (*unwirksam machen*) to undo; (*vereiteln*) to frustrate; *~ daß ich wüßte* not that I know of; **~achtung** *f* disregard, disrespect; **~amtlich** *a* unofficial; **~anerkennung** *f* non-acknowledg(e)ment; (*Vertrag*) repudiation; **~angriffspakt** *m* pact of non-aggression; **~annahme** *f* non-acceptance; **~anwesenheit** *f jur* non-attendance; absence; **~arier** *m*, **~arisch** *a* non-Aryan; **~beachtung, ~befolgung, ~beobachtung** *f* non-observance, neglect; **~berechtigt** *a* not entitled; **~bezahlung** *f* non-payment; **~eingeweihte(r)** *m* uninformed person, uninitiated person; **~einhaltung** *f* non-compliance (*von* with); **~einlösung** *f* non-payment; **~einmischung** *f* non-intervention; **~eintreffen** *n* non-arrival; **~eisenmetall** *n* non-ferrous metal; **~erfüllung** *f* non-fufil(l)ment, non-execution; non-performance; default; (*Lieferung*) non-delivery; **~erscheinen** *n jur* non-appearance, contumacy; contempt; default; (*zum Dienst*) non-attendance; **~fachmann** *m* non-professional; inexperienced hand; **~gewünschte(s)** *n*: *~~ bitte durchstreichen* delete which is undesired; **~ig** *a jur* null, void; (*rechtsungültig*) invalid; (*eitel*) vain, empty; (*nichtssagend*) futile, idle; (*vergänglich*) transitory; (*wirkungslos*) ineffectual; (*wertlos*) of no worth, nil; (*Entschuldigung*) hollow; (*Vorwand*) flimsy; *null u. ~~* null and void; *für ~~ erklären* to annul, to declare null and void, to cancel; **~~keit** *f* nullity, invalidity; (*Eitelkeit*) vanity; (*Wertlosigkeit*) worthlessness; nonentity; (*Unzulänglichkeit*) futility, flimsiness; **~~keiten** *f pl* trifles *pl*; **~~keitsbeschwerde** *f jur* plea of nullity; **~~keitserklärung** *f* annulment, cancellation, nullification; **~~keitsklage** *f jur* action for cancellation, suit for annulment; **~~keitsverfahren** *n* invalidation suit; **~kämpfer,**

~kombattant *m* non-combatant; civilian; protected person; **~leitend** *a* non-conductive; non-conducting; **~leiter** *m el* non-conductor; **~leuchtend** *a* non-luminous; **~lieferung** *f* failure to deliver; **~magnetisch** *a* non-magnetic; **~metallisch** *a* non-metallic; **~militär** *m* civilian; **~mitglied** *n* non-member; **~öffentlich** *a* closed; (*privat*) private; *jur* in camera; **~periodisch** *a* aperiodic; **~raucher** *m* non-smoker; **~~abteil** *n* non-smoking compartment; **~rostend** *a* rust-proof, non-rusting; stainless; non-corroding; *~~er Stahl* stainless (*od* rust-proof) steel; **~schwimmer** *m* non-swimmer; **~sein** *n* non-existence; **~splitternd** *a* non-splintering; **~staatlich** *a* private, particular; **~ständig** *a* non-permanent; temporary; transitory; transient; **~übereinstimmung** *f* discordance, disagreement; (*Mißverhältnis*) incongruity; **~übertragbar** *a* non-transferable; *com* non-negotiable; **~umkehrbar** *a* non-reversible, irreversible; **~verantwortlich** *a* irresponsible; **~vorhanden** *a* null, nil; **~vorhandensein** *n* absence, lack; **~wissen** *n* ignorance; **~wollen** *n* unwillingness; **~zahlung** *f* default (*e-r Schuld* on a debt); non-payment; *bei ~~* (*jur*) in default of payment; **~zerfallbarkeit** *f* (*Atomphys*) non-fissionability; non-disintegrability; **~zulassung** *f* non-admission; **~zutreffende(s)**: *~~ ist zu streichen* strike out words not applicable.

Nichte *f* niece.

nichts *adv* nothing, not anything, naught; *~ als* nothing but; *ganz u. gar ~* nothing at all; *~ mehr* nothing more; *um ~* for nothing; *~ anderes* nothing else; *~ weniger als* anything but; *mir ~, dir ~* quite coolly, bold as brass; *~ u. wieder ~* absolutely nothing; *es macht ~* it doesn't matter; *~ zu machen!* nothing doing! *~ dergleichen* nothing of the kind; *soviel wie ~* next to nothing; *wenn es weiter ~ ist!* if that's all there is to it! *das hat ~ zu bedeuten* this is of no consequence; *er bringt's zu ~* he won't get anywhere; *es ist ~ an der Sache* there is no trick in it; *~ n* nothing; (*Geringfügigkeit*) trifle; (*Nichtigkeit*) nothingness; (*unbedeutender Mensch*) nonentity; *ein ~* a mere shadow, a (mere) nothing; **~ahnend** *a* unsuspecting, without misgiving; **~destoweniger** *adv* nevertheless, notwithstanding, in spite of all that; **~könner** *m* ignorant person, ignoramus, *fam* duffer; **~nutz** *m* good-for-nothing, ne'er-do-well; **~~ig** *a* useless, worthless; **~sagend** *a* meaningless, insignificant; (*farblos*) colo(u)rless; (*fad*) flat, dull, insipid; (*Ausdruck*) trite, hackneyed; **~tuer** *m* idler; **~tuerei** *f*, **~tun** *n* idling; (*Muße*) leisure; (*Erholung*) relaxation; **~würdig** *a* vile, base, infamous; **~~keit** *f* vileness, baseness.

Nickel *n* nickel; **~beschlag** *m* nickel trimmings *pl*; **~chromstahl** *m* chrome-nickel steel; **~eisen** *n* nickel iron, ferronickel; **~legierung** *f* nickel alloy; **~überzug** *m* nickel plating; **~verbindung** *f* nickelous compound.

nick|en *itr* to nod; (*schlafen*) to nap, to snooze; **~erchen** *n* snooze, nap, doze.

nie *adv* never, at no time; *fast ~* hardly ever; *jetzt oder ~* now or never.

nieder *a* low; mean, base; (*Wert*) inferior; *adv* down; *auf u. ~* up and down; **~beugen** *tr* to bend down; *fig* to depress; **~brechen** *irr tr* to break down; **~brennen** *irr tr, itr* to burn down; **~bücken** *r* to stoop; **~deutsch** Low German; **~druck** *m* low pressure; **~drücken** *tr* to weigh down; *fig* to depress; (*bedrücken*) to oppress; **~druckgebiet** *n* low-pressure area; **~druckreifen** *m* low-pressure tyre; **~drückung** *f* oppression, depression; **~fahren** *irr itr* to come down, to descend; **~fallen** *irr itr* to fall down; **~frequenz** *f* low frequency; **~~schaltung** *f radio* audio-frequency circuit; **~~strom** *m* low-frequency current; **~führung** *f* (*der Antenne*) down-lead; **~gang** *m* descent, decline; (*Sonne*) sunset; (*in e-m Schiff*) companionway, companion ladder; **~gehen** *irr itr* to go down, to set; (*Regen*) to fall; *aero* to alight; **~geschlagen** *a* dejected, cast down, downhearted, depressed; *fam* blue; **~~heit** *f* depression, dejection; **~halten** *irr tr* to suppress; to keep down; to paralyse, *Am* to paralyze; to immobilize; (*Erdtruppen durch Fliegerbeschuß*) to pin down; **~hauen** *irr tr* to cut down; **~holen** *tr* to lower; **~holz** *n* underwood; **~kämpfen** *tr* to overpower; to reduce; to put out of action; (*feindliches Feuer*) to silence; **~kämpfung** *f* destruction; reduction; putting out of action; **~knien** *itr* to kneel down; **~kommen** *irr itr* to lie in, to be confined; **~kunft** *f* lying-in, confinement.

Nieder|lage *f mil* defeat; (*Magazin*) warehouse, depot; *com* agency, branch; **~lande** *n pl* the Netherlands *pl*; **~ländisch** *a* Dutch; **~lassen** *irr tr* to let down, to lower; *r* (*sich setzen*) to sit down, to take a seat; (*sich festsetzen*) to establish o. s., to settle; (*absteigen, landen*) to alight; to touch down; **~lassung** *f* settling; settlement, colony; *com* branch, establishment; **~legen** *tr* to lay down, to deposit; (*Krone*) to abdicate; (*Amt*) to resign; (*Geschäft*) to retire (from); (*Waffen*) to lay down; (*Arbeit*) to stop, to knock off, to walk out, to strike; *r* to lie down; (*schlafen gehen*) to go to bed; **~legung** *f* laying down; abdication, resignation; (*Arbeit*) strike.

nieder|machen, **~metzeln** *tr* to cut down; to wipe out; to kill, to slay, to massacre; **~metzelung** *f* massacre, slaughter; **~reißen** *irr tr* to pull down, to demolish; **~rennen** *irr tr* to run down; **~schießen** *irr tr* to shoot down; *itr* to rush down; **~schlag** *m chem* precipitate, precipitation; (*Feuchtigkeit*) precipitation; (*Regen*) rain(fall); (*Ablagerung*) sediment, deposit; (*Schlag*) knock-out; (*Ergebnis*) result, outcome; **~schlagen** *irr tr* to knock down, to fell; (*Augen*) to cast down; (*unterdrücken*) to suppress, to hush up; *jur* to quash; (*Unkosten*) to cancel; *chem* to precipitate; *fig* to discourage, to dishearten; **~~d** *a* depressing, dejecting; *chem* precipitant; **~schlagsarm** *a* poor in precipitate; of light precipitation; (*trocken*) dry; **~schlagsgebiet** *n* encatchment area; **~schlagsmenge** *f* amount of precipitate; **~schlagung** *f chem* settling; precipitation; depositing, deposition; (*e-s Aufstandes*) suppression; (*von Schulden od Steuern*) cancellation; *jur* quashing; **~schmettern** *tr* to dash to the ground; *fig* to overwhelm, to crush; **~~d** *a* shattering; **~schreiben** *irr tr* to write down; **~schreien** *irr tr* to shout down; **~schrift** *f* writing-down; notes *pl*; manuscript; (*Protokoll*) record, report; **~setzen** *irr tr* to set down; *r* to sit down; **~sinken** *irr itr* to sink down, to drop; **~spannung** *f* (*Gas*) low pressure; *el* low tension (*od* voltage); **~stechen** *irr tr* to stab; **~steigen** *irr itr* to descend; **~stoßen** *irr tr* to knock down; **~strecken** *tr* to knock down; to cut down; **~stürzen** *itr* to tumble down; **~tracht** *f* meanness, baseness; **~trächtig** *a* low, mean, abject, dirty, base, rotten; **~~keit** *f* abjectness, baseness; (*Tat*) villainy, base act; **~treten** *irr tr* to trample down; **~ung** *f* lowland; (*Grasland, Sumpf*) marsh; (*Ebene*) plain, flat; **~wärts** *adv* downward(s); **~wasser** *n* low water level; **~werfen** *irr tr* to throw down; (*unterdrükken*) to crush, to suppress; (*überwältigen*) to overwhelm; *r* to prostrate o. s.; **~wild** *n* small game; **~ziehen** *irr tr* to pull (*od* draw) down.

niedlich *a* nice, neat; delicate; (*hübsch*) pretty, dainty, *fam* sweet, *Am* cute.

Niednagel *m* agnail, hangnail.

niedrig *a* low; *fig* (*gemein*) base, mean; (*Qualität, Wert*) inferior; (*Preis*) cheap, low; (*mäßig*) moderate; (*Stand*) humble; *~ gesinnt* vulgar-minded; *~er hängen* to debunk; **~keit** *f* lowness; *fig* meanness; humbleness; **~wasser** *n* low tide, low water.

*

niemals *adv* never, at no time; *~ u. nimmer* never more; *fast ~* hardly ever.

niemand *prn* nobody, no one, not ... anybody; *~ anders* nobody else; *~ als er* nobody but he; **~sland** *n* no-man's land.

Niere *f* kidney; (*Klümpchen*) nodule, concretion; **~n** *f pl* reins *pl*; loins *pl*; **~nbraten** *m* roast loin of veal; **~ndrüse** *f* renal gland; **~nentzündung** *f* nephritis; **~nförmig** *a* kidney-shaped, reniform; **~ngries** *m* renal gravel; **~nkrankheit** *f*, **~nleiden** *n* disease of the kidneys, nephritic disease; **~nstein** *m* kidney stone; nephrolith; renal calculus.

niesel|n *itr* to drizzle; to mizzle; **~regen** *m* drizzle.

nies|en *itr* to sneeze; **~kraut** *n bot* sneezewort; **~wurz** *f bot* hellebore.

Nieß|brauch *m* usufruct; benefit; **~braucher, ~nutzer** *m* usufructuary.

Niet *n* (*Stift*) rivet, pin; *~ u. nagelfest* clinched and riveted, nailed fast; **~e** *f* (*Lotterie*) blank; *fig* (*Person*) flop, wash-out, failure; **~en** *tr* to rivet; **~er** *m* riveter; **~kolonne** *f* riveting gang; **~nagel** *m* rivet(ing-nail); **~senkkopf** *m* countersunk rivet head; **~ung** *f* riveting.

Nihil|ismus *m* nihilism; **~ist** *m* nihilist; **~~isch** *a* nihilistic.

Nikola(u)s *m* Nicholas; *Sankt ~* Santa Claus.

Nikotin *n* nicotine; **~frei** *a* free from nicotine, nicotine-free; **~gehalt** *m* nicotine content; **~haltig** *a* containing nicotine; **~säure** *f* nicotinic acid; **~vergiftung** *f* nicotine-poisoning.

Nil *m* the Nile; **~pferd** *n* hippopotamus.

Nimbus *m* nimbus; *fig* prestige.

nimmer, **~mehr** *adv* never, nevermore; (*ganz u. gar nicht*) by no means, on no account; **~satt** *a* insatiable; *~~ m* glutton; *Am* grab-all; **~wiedersehn** *n: auf ~~* farewell for ever.

Nippel *m* nipple.

nipp|en *itr* to sip; **~sachen** *f pl* (k)nick-(k)nacks *pl*, trinkets *pl*, gimcrack, *Am* pretties *pl*.

nirgend(s), **~wo** *adv* nowhere, not ... anywhere.

Nische *f* niche; (*im Zimmer*) alcove.

Niß *m*, **Nisse** *f* nit.

nist|en *itr* to (build a) nest; *fig* to nestle; **~gewohnheit** *f* nesting-habit;

~kasten *m* nesting-box; **~platz** *m* breeding-place.

Nitrat *n chem* nitrate.

Nitr|ierapparat *m* nitrating apparatus; **~ieren** *tr* to nitrate, to nitrify; **~ierung** *f* nitration; (*Eisen*) nitridation; **~obenzol** *n* nitrobenzene; **~ofarbstoff** *m* nitro dye; **~oglyzerin** *n* nitroglycerine; **~otoluol** *n* nitrotoluene; **~ozellulose** *f* nitrocellulose rayon, nitro-rayon.

Niv|eau *n* level; standard; (*Oberfläche*) surface; **~~fläche** *f* level surface; **~~linie** *f* grade (*od* potential) line; **~~übergang** *m rail* level crossing; grade crossing; **~ellieren** *tr* to level, to grade; **~ellierinstrument** *n* level(l)ing instrument; **~ellierung** *f* level(l)ing (process); **~ellierungstraktor** *m* bulldozer; **~ellierwaage** *f* spirit-level.

Nix *m* nick, water-sprite, water-elf; **~e** *f* water-nymph.

nobel *a* noble; distinguished; generous; (*freigebig*) free-handed, munificent; (*elegant*) elegant, stylish; **~preis** *m* Nobel prize; **~~träger** *m* Nobel prize winner.

noch *adv* (*Dauer u. bei Steigerung*) still; (*bei Zahlwort*) more; (*bei Verneinung*) yet; (*dazu*) in addition, besides; *~ einmal* once more; *~ nicht* not yet; *~ nichts* nothing yet; *~ einmal soviel* as much again, twice as much; *~ immer* still; *~ nie* never (before), not ... ever; *~ dazu* in addition, into the bargain; *~ ein* another; *~ etwas* something (*od* anything) else; *~ so* ever so; *~ heute* this very day; even to this day; *~ gestern* only yesterday; *~ jetzt* even now; *~ etwas?* anything else? *weder ... ~* neither ... nor; *sie wollte ~ bleiben* she wanted to stay longer; *ich habe nur ~ zwei Bücher* I have only two books left; **~ mal** *adv* (once) again, once more; *~ ~ soviel* twice as much; **~malig** *a* repeated; **~mals** *adv* again, once more.

Nocke *f* dumpling.

Nocken *m tech* cam; lifter; **~antrieb** *m* cam drive; **~hebel** *m* cam lever; **~scheibe** *f* cam plate; **~steuerung** *f* cam steering, cam gear; **~welle** *f* camshaft.

nöl|en *tr fam* to dawdle; **~peter** *m* slow-coach.

Nomad|e *m* nomad; **~entum** *n* nomadism; **~isch** *a* nomadic.

Nomenklatur *f* nomenclature.

Nomin|alwert *m* nominal value; **~ativ** *m* nominative; **~ell** *a* nominal; **~ieren** *tr* to nominate.

Nonius *m* vernier; **~einteilung** *f* vernier scale.

Nonne *f* nun; **~nkloster** *n* nunnery; convent.

Noppe *f* nap; burl; **~n** *tr* to burl, to nap; to pick; **~nmuster** *n* nap pattern.

Nord, **~en** *m* north; *poet* north wind; **~amerika** *n* North America; **~atlantikpakt** *m* North Atlantic Treaty; **~en** *tr: e-e Karte ~~* to orient a map; **~isch, nördlich** *a* northern, northerly; arctic; (*skandinavisch*) Norse, Nordic; (*Sprachen*) Teutonic; *Nördliches Eismeer* Arctic Ocean; **~länder** *m* northener; **~licht** *n* aurora borealis, northern lights *pl*; **~ost(en)** *m* north-east, *Abk* N. E.; **~östlich** *a* north-east(ern); **~pol** *m* North Pole, Arctic Pole; **~polarkreis** *m* Arctic Circle; **~polfahrt** *f* arctic expedition; **~see** *f* North Sea, German Ocean; **~stern** *m* pole-star; **~wärts** *adv* northward; **~west(en)** *m* north-west, *Abk* N. W.; **~westlich** *a* north-wester(ly); **~wind** *m* north-wind.

Nörg|elei *f* nagging, grumbling; fault-finding; **~eln** *itr* to grumble, to growl, to nag, to grouse, *Am* to gripe, to beef, to grouch, to kick; **~ler** *m* grumbler, fault-finder; *Am fam* (*Quengler*) crank, (*Pedant*) stickler.

Norm *f* standard, rule; standard specifications *pl*; (*Maß*) measure, yardstick; *~en festsetzen* to standardize; **~al** *a* normal; (*Maß, Gewicht*) standard; (*üblich*) regular; **~~arbeitstag** *m* standard working day; **~~ausrüstung** *f* standard equipment; **~~film** *m* normal film; **~~geschwindigkeit** *f* normal (*od* proper) speed; **~~gewicht** *n* standard weight; **~~größe** *f* normal size; standard size; **~~isieren** *tr* to normalize, to standardize; **~~maß** *n* standard measure; **~~-Null** *f* sea-level; **~~spur** *f* standard ga(u)ge; **~~uhr** *f* standard clock; **~~verbraucher** *m* normal consumer; **~~zeit** *f* mean time; standard time; **~~zustand** *m* normal condition; **~blatt** *n* specifications *pl*; **~en** *tr* to standardize; **~enaufstellung** *f* laying down of standard rules; **~entsprechend** *a* normal, standard; **~ieren** *tr* to standardize, to ga(u)ge; (*regulieren*) to regulate; **~ierung, ~ung** *f* standardization; normalization.

Norweg|en *n* Norway; **~er** *m*, **~erin** *f*, **~isch** *a* Norwegian.

*

Not *f* (*Mangel, Elend*) want, need, pinch; (*dringende~*) exigency, neediness; (*Zwang*) necessity; (*Unglück*) distress, affliction, adversity; (*Schwierigkeit*) difficulty, trouble; extremity; (*Gefahr*) danger; emergency; (*mißliche Lage*) predicament; (*Sorge*) grief; sorrow; (*Lage*) plight; *ohne ~* needlessly, without real cause; *im Fall der ~* in case of need, in an emergency; *zur ~* in (*od* at) a pinch, if need be; *mit knapper ~ davonkommen* to have a narrow escape (*od* close shave), *Am* to have a close call; *die liebe ~ haben mit* to have a hard time with; *~ macht erfinderisch* necessity is the mother of invention; *in großer ~ sein* to be very hard up; *~ kennt kein Gebot* necessity knows no law; *aus der ~ e-e Tugend machen* to make a virtue of necessity; *~ tun* to be necessary; *~ leiden* to suffer want; *fam in der ~ frißt der Teufel Fliegen* beggars can't be choosers; *in Nöten sein* to be hard pressed; **~anker** *m* sheet-anchor; **~antenne** *f* emergency aerial; **~ausgang** *m* emergency exit; **~ausstieg** *m* emergency hatch; **~behelf** *m* makeshift; (*Ausweg*) expedient; (*Lückenbüßer*) stopgap; **~beleuchtung** *f* emergency illumination; **~bremse** *f* emergency brake; **~brücke** *f* temporary bridge; **~durft** *f* necessity, pressing need; *die ~~ verrichten* to relieve nature; **~dürftig** *a* scanty; (*bedürftig*) poor, necessitous, needy; (*behelfsmäßig*) makeshift; *~~ ausbessern* to make a rough and ready repair; **~fall** *m* case of emergency; *im ~~* in an emergency; *für den ~~* if need be; **~gedrungen** *a* compulsory, forced; *adv* needs; **~geld** *n* emergency money; **~gemeinschaft** *f* (research) aid society, cooperative aid council; **~ groschen** *m* nest-egg; **~hafen** *m* harbo(u)r of refuge; emergency port; **~hilfe** *f* emergency service; *technische ~~* organization for the maintenance of supplies, *Abk* O. M. S.; **~lage** *f* distress, calamity; (*Geld*) embarrassment; **~lager** *n* shake-down; **~landen** *itr aero* to make a forced landing, to be forced down; **~landung** *f aero* forced (*od* emergency) landing; **~leidend** *a* suffering, distressed; (*arm*) poor, needy; (*Wechsel*) dishono(u)red; (*Fälligkeit*) overdue; **~leine** *f* communication-cord, *Am* emergency cord; **~lüge** *f* white lie; fib; **~maßnahme** *f* emergency measure; **~opfer** *n* emergency property tax; **~pfennig** *m* savings *pl*, nest-egg; *sich e-n ~~ aufsparen* to put money by for a rainy day; **~ruf, ~schrei** *m* cry of distress; emergency call; **~schlachtung** *f* emergency slaughter; **~signal** *n* signal of distress; *mar* distress-gun; *aero* Mayday, *mar* SOS; **~sitz** *m mot* dickey-seat, spare-seat, *Am* rumble-seat; **~stand** *m* urgency, state of distress; destitution; critical state, emergency; **~~sarbeiten** *f pl* relief works *pl*; **~~sgebiet** *n* distressed area; **~~smaßnahmen** *f pl* emergency measures *pl*; **~taufe** *f* private baptism; **~verband** *m med* temporary dressing, first field dressing; **~~päckchen** *n* first-aid packet; **~~tasche** *f* first-aid pouch; **~verkauf** *m* emergency sale; **~verordnung** *f* emergency decree; **~wassern** *itr* to make a forced landing on water; *sl* to go into the drink; to ditch a plane; **~wehr** *f* self-defence; **~wendig** *a* necessary (*für* to, for; *daß* for s. o. to do); (*dringend*) urgent; (*unentbehrlich*) indispensable, requisite; **~~keit** *f* necessity; urgency; **~wohnung** *f* makeshift quarter; **~wurf** *m aero* emergency (salvo) release; *Bomben im ~~ abwerfen aero* to jettison bombs; **~zeichen** *n* distress signal; **~zucht** *f* rape; **~züchtigen** *tr* to rape, to assault; **~zug** *m aero* jettison lever.

Nota *f* (*Rechnung*) bill, invoice; memorandum.

Notar *m* notary; *öffentlicher ~* notary public; **~iat** *n* notary's office; **~~sgebühren** *f pl* notarial fees *pl*; **~iell** *a* notarial, attested by a notary; *~~ bescheinigen* to attest, to certify.

Note *f* (*Geld*) banknote; *parl* note; (*Rechnung*) bill, memorandum; (*Schule*) mark, report; *mus* note; *ganze ~* semi-breve, *Am* whole note; *halbe ~* minim, *Am* half note; *viertel ~* crotchet, *Am* quarter note; *achtel ~* quaver, *Am* eighth note; *sechzehntel ~* semi-quaver, *Am* sixteenth note; *nach ~n singen* to sing at sight; *bringen Sie Ihre ~n mit* bring your music along; *nach ~n fig* thoroughly, downright, properly; **~nausgabe** *f* issue of bank-notes; **~nbank** *f* issuing bank; **~nblatt** *n* sheet of music; **~ndeckung** *f* note cover; **~ndruck** *m mus* music printing; (*Banknote*) printing of notes; **~nhalter** *m*, **~npult** *n*, **~nständer** *m* music-stand; **~nlinie** *f* line of the staff; **~npapier** *n* music paper; **~npresse** *f* printing-press (for notes); **~nsystem** *n mus* staff; **~numlauf** *m* circulation of notes; **~nwechsel** *m* exchange of notes.

notier|en *tr* to note (down), to make a memo(randum) of, to make a note of; (*schnell*) to take down, to jot down; (*bemerken*) to notice, to observe; (*Liste*) to record, to enter in; (*Börse*) to quote (at), to state; **~ung** *f* (*Börse*) quotation; (*Eintragung*) entry; (*Notiz*) note; noting.

nötig *a* necessary; needful; requisite; *~ haben* to need, to want; *das ~e* the wherewithal; **~en** *tr* to compel, to urge, to press; *sich ~en lassen* to need pressing; *ich habe das nicht ~!* I don't have to stand for that! **~enfalls** *adv* in case of need, if need be; **~ung** *f* com-

pulsion, forcing; (*Essen*) pressing; (*Zwang*) constraint; *jur* duress.
Notiz *f* (*Zeitung*) notice, (news) item; (*Vermerk*) note, memo(randum), jottings *pl*; ~ *nehmen* to take notice (of), to pay attention (to); **~block** *m* (note-) pad, jotter; scribbling-block, *Am* scratch-pad; **~buch** *n* note-book, memo-book.
notorisch *a* notorious; evident; publicly known.
Nougat *m* nougat, almond cake.
Novell|e *f* short story, short novel, novelette; (*Gesetz*) supplementary law; **~ist** *m* novelist.
November *m* November
Nov|ität *f* novelty; (*Buch*) new publication; **~ize** *m u. f* novice; **~iziat** *n* novitiate.
Nu *n* moment; *im* ~ in a twinkling, in an instant, in no time, in a flash, in a jiffy; *~! interj* now! well!
Nuance *f* shade.
nüchtern *a* empty, fasting; (*vernünftig*) clear-headed, sensible; (*geistlos*) jejune, dull, insipid, dry; (*mäßig*) sober; *fig* matter-of-fact; (*geschmacklos*) flat; (*prosaisch*) prosaic; (*besonnen*) calm; *noch ~ sein* not to have breakfasted; **~heit** *f* sobriety; temperance; *fig* prosiness, jejuneness, dullness.
Nudel *f* macaroni; (*Faden~n*) vermicelli; *Am* (*flache ~*) noodle; **~brett** *n* vermicelli-board; **~holz** *n* rolling-pin; **~n** *tr* to cram with food; **~suppe** *f* vermicelli-soup.
Nukle|arkern *m phys* nucleus; **~arphysik** *f* nuclear physics *pl mit sing*; **~on** *n* nucleon; **~us** *m* nucleus.
null *a* nil, null; (*Tennis*) love; null; *~ u. nichtig* null and void; *für ~ u. nichtig erklären* to annul; *~ f* (*Ziffer*) naught, cipher; (*auf Skalen*) zero; *tele* o; *fig* a mere cipher; **~einstellung** *f* zero adjustment; **~(l)eiter** *m* neutral wire, zero conductor; **~punkt** *m* zero, freezing-point; **~spannung** *f* zero voltage; **~stellung** *f* zero (*od* off) position; **~strich** *m* zero mark; **~zeit** *f mil* zero-hour, zero-time.
numer|ieren *tr* to number; *com* to ticket; *~ierter Platz* reserved seat; **~isch** *a* numerical.
Numismatik *f* numismatics *pl.*
Nummer *f* number, *Abk* No., no.; *pl* Nos., nos.; (*Größe*) size; (*Zeitung*) copy, issue, number, part; (*Lotterie*) ticket; (*Sport*) event; *tele* line, number; (*Programm*) item, turn; *e-e große ~ spielen* to be influential; *e-e gute ~ haben* to be well-thought of; *laufende ~* lot (*od* serial) number; *e-e ~ wählen* (*tele*) to dial a number; **~nbezeichnung** *f* numbering; **~nfolge** *f* numerical order; **~nscheibe** *f tele* dial; **~schild** *n mot* number (*od* licence) plate.
nun *adv* now, at present; *interj* well! *~ also* why then; well then; *von ~ an* henceforth; *~ u. nimmermehr* never; *was ~?* what next? **~mehr** *adv* now, by this time; **~mehrig** *a* present, actual.
Nunt|iatur *f* nunciature; **~ius** *m* nuncio.
nur *adv* only, solely, alone; (*ausgenommen*) except, but; (*eben*) just; (*nichts als*) nothing but; (*möglicherweise*) possibly; (*weiter nichts als*) merely; *conj* but; *wenn ~* provided that; *nicht ~ ... sondern auch* not only ... but also; *wer ~ immer* whoever; *wenn ~* if only; *~ zu! interj* go on! *~ noch* still; *er weiß ~ zu gut* he knows well enough; **~flügeldüsenjäger** *m aero* flying-wing jet fighter; **~flügelflugzeug** *n aero* tailless airplane; flying wing; (*mit Düsenantrieb*) jet-propelled flying wing.
Nuß *f* nut; walnut; *fig* a hard task; *e-e ~ aufzuknacken geben* to give s. o. a nut to crack; **~baum** *m* (wal)nut-tree; **~baumholz** *n* walnut; **~braun** *a* nut-brown; (*Augen*) hazel; (*Haar*) auburn; **~kern** *m* kernel; **~knacker** *m* nut-cracker; **~kohle** *f* nut coal, nuts *pl*; **~schale** *f* nut-shell.
nuscheln *itr fam* to slur, *Am* to mouth the words.
Nüster *f* nostril.
Nute *f* rabbet, key-bed, groove, slot.
Nutriafell *n* nutria.
nutschen *tr, itr* to suck.
nutz,|nütze *a* (*nur prädikativ*) useful; *zu nichts ~ sein* to be of no use; to be good for nothing; *sich etw zunutze machen* to avail o. s. of s. th.; to profit by s. th.; to turn s. th. to advantage; *zu ~ u. Frommen* for the good (of); **~anwendung** *f* moral (*od* practical) application; utilization, (*Lehre*) useful lesson; **~bar** *a* useful; profitable; utilizable, realizable; (*wirksam*) effective; (*gültig*) available; *~~ machen* to utilize, to employ, to turn to account, to make useful; **~barkeit** *f* usefulness, profitableness; **~barmachung** *f* utilization; **~bringend** *a* profitable, productive, advantageous; *etw ~~ anwenden* to turn s. th. to good account; **~effekt** *m* useful effect, efficiency; effective power; **~en** *m* (*Gebrauch*) use; (*Vorteil*) profit, gain, advantage, benefit; (*Nützlichkeit*) utility, usefulness; (*Ertrag*) yield, return, proceeds *pl*; *zum ~~ von* for the benefit of; *großen ~~ ziehen aus* to derive great benefit from; *~~ abwerfen* to yield profit; *von geringem ~~* of little avail; *wirtschaftlicher ~~* commercial efficiency; *von ~~ sein* to be of service; *~~ bringen* to be an advantage, to yield a profit, to bring grist to the mill; **~~, nützen** *tr* (*gebrauchen*) to make use (of), to use, to utilize; *itr* to be of use, to be profitable, to do good; (*dienen für*) to serve for; (*vorteilhaft sein*) to be of advantage, to be of benefit; *e-e Gelegenheit ~~* to avail o. s. of an opportunity; *es nützt nichts* it's no use; **~fahrzeug** *n* commercial vehicle; **~fläche** *f* useful area, effective area; (*Landwirtschaft*) agricultural acreage; **~garten** *m* kitchen-garden; **~holz** *n* timber, *Am* lumber; **~kraft** *f* effective power; **~last** *f* loading capacity, working (*od* pay *od* commercial) load, live load; **~leistung** *f* useful output, effective force, efficiency; *mot* brake horsepower; **~los** *a* useless, futile, *Am* footless; unprofitable, of no utility; **~~igkeit** *f* uselessness, futility; **~nießen** *tr* to have the usufruct (of); **~nießer** *m* usufructuary; profiteer; beneficiary; **~nießung** *f* usufruct; **~spannung** *f el* useful voltage; **~tier** *n* useful animal; **~ung** *f* (*Ertrag*) produce, yield; (*Einkommen*) revenue; (*Gebrauch*) use, using; utilization, exploitation; **~~sdauer** *f* useful (*od* service) life; **~~srecht** *n* right of usufruct; **~vieh** *n* domestic cattle; **~wert** *m* useful (*od* economic) value; **~wirkung** *f* useful effect, efficiency.
nützlich *a* useful, of use; profitable, advantageous, expedient; serviceable; **~keit** *f* usefulness, utility; advantage.
Nylonstrümpfe *m pl* nylon stockings *pl*, nylons *pl.*
Nymphe *f* nymph.

O

O *Abk mit* ***O*** *siehe Liste der Abk.*
O, o *n* (the letter) O, o; *o! interj* oh! ah! *~ ja* oh yes; indeed; *~ nein* oh no, not at all; *~ weh!* oh dear! alas! **~-Beine** *n pl* bandy legs *pl*, bow-legs *pl*; **~-beinig** *a* bandy-legged.
Oase *f* oasis.
ob *conj* whether, (I wonder) if; *als ~* as if, as though; *nicht als ~* not that; *na u. ~!* rather, I should say so! *prp* (*oberhalb*) above, over, beyond; (*wegen*) on account of.
Obacht *f* attention, care, heed; *~ geben* to pay attention (to), to take care (of); *~!* take care! look out! beware!
Obdach *n* shelter; lodging; **~los** *a* homeless, roofless; *~~ werden* to be made homeless; **~~enasyl** *n* casual ward; **~~e(r)** *m, f* homeless person, casual.
Obduktion *f* post-mortem examination.
oben *adv* above; (*in der Höhe*) up; (*hoch oben*) aloft, on high; (*die Treppe hinauf*) upstairs; (*auf der Oberfläche*) on the surface; *~ auf* on (the) top of, (*Buchseite*) at the top of; *von ~ bis unten* from top to bottom, (*Person*) from head to toe, up and down; *dort ~* up there; *nach ~* upwards; (*im Haus*) upstairs; *wie ~* the same as above; *wie ~ erwähnt* (as) mentioned above; *von ~ herab fig* haughtily; **~an** *adv* at the top; in the first place; **~auf** *adv* on the top of, on top; on the surface; uppermost; *~~ sein fig* to be in great form; **~drein** *adv* over and above; into the bargain, in addition; **~erwähnt, ~genannt** *a* aforementioned, aforesaid, above-mentioned; **~gesteuert** *a mot* overhead; *~~er Motor* valve-in-head engine; *~~e Ventile* overhead valves *pl*; **~hin** *adv* superficially, perfunctorily.
ober *a* upper, higher, superior; supreme; senior; leading; *die ~en Zehntausend* the upper ten (thousand); *~ m* (head-) waiter; **~amtmann** *m* high bailiff; **~arm** *m* upper arm; **~arzt** *m* head physician; senior physician; chief doctor; **~aufseher** *m* supervisor, superintendent; **~aufsicht** *f* superintendence; **~bau** *m arch* work above

ground; (*Brücke*) superstructure; *rail* permanent way, roadbed; *Straße mit festem ~~* surfaced road; **~befehl** *m* chief command; high command; supreme command; **~befehlshaber** *m* commander-in-chief (*Abk* cominch): **~begriff** *m* superimposed concept; **~beleuchter** *m film* chief electrician; top-light controller; **~bett** *n* coverlet, feather-bed, (heavy down) comforter; **~bürgermeister** *m* Lord Mayor; **~deck** *n* upper deck; **~e** *n* top; **~e(r)** *m* chief, head; superior; **~feldwebel** *m* sergeant-major, *Am* first sergeant; **~fläche** *f* surface; area; *unter der ~~ fig* behind the scenes; *an die ~~ kommen mar* to surface; **~~nbehandlung** *f* surface treatment; **~~ngeschwindigkeit** *f* (*U-Boot*) surface speed; **~~ngestalt** *f* shape of surface; **~~ngestaltung** *f* topography; **~~nwelle** *f radio* surface (*od* direct) wave; **~~nzustand** *m* finish; **~flächlich** *a* superficial; shallow, slight; cursory; **~flügel** *m* upper wing; **~förster** *m* head forester; **~gärig** *a* top-fermenting; **~gefreite(r)** *m mil* corporal; **~geschoß** *n* upper story; **~gewalt** *f* supremacy; **~halb** *adv* above; **~hand** *f* upper hand; *die ~~ gewinnen* to get the better of s. o., to carry the day, *Am* to get the best of; **~haupt** *n* head, chief; sovereign; leader; **~haus** *n* House of Lords; **~hemd** *n* upper (*od* white *od* day) shirt; **~~einsatz** *m* shirt-front, *Am* bosom; **~herrschaft** *f* supremacy; **~hofmeister** *m* Lord High Steward; **~in** *f* Mother Superior; (*Krankenhaus*) hospital matron; **~irdisch** *a* overground, surface, above ground; *el* overhead; **~jägermeister** *m* Master of the Buck-hounds; **~kellner** *m* head-waiter; **~kiefer** *m* upper jaw; **~kirchenrat** *m* High Consistory; **~klassen** *f pl* upper (*od* higher) classes *pl*; (*Schule*) top forms, *Am* senior classes *pl*; **~kleid** *n* upper garment; **~kommando** *n* supreme command; **~körper** *m* upper part of the body; **~landesgericht** *n* Provincial Court of Appeal; **~längen** *f pl* ascenders *pl*; **~lastig** *a* top-heavy; **~lauf** *m* upper course; **~leder** *n* uppers *pl*; **~lehrer** *m* senior assistant master; **~leitung** *f* direction; *el* overhead system; **~~somnibus** *m* trolley bus, trackless trolley car; **~leutnant** *m* (first) lieutenant; **~licht** *n* skylight, fanlight; **~lippe** *f* upper lip; **~maat** *m* petty officer; **~meister** *m* head foreman; **~postamt** *n* General Post Office; **~postmeister** *m* postmaster general; **~priester** *m* high priest; **~prima** *f* Upper VI; **~quartiermeister** *mil* quarter-master general; **~rechnungskammer** *f* audit-office; **~richter** *m* chief justice; **~schenkel** *m* (upper) thigh; **~schicht** *f fig* upper classes *pl*; **~schlächtig** *a* overshot; **~schlesien** *n* Upper Silesia; **~schule** *f* Secondary School; **~schwester** *f* senior sister, *Am* head (*od* chief) nurse; **~schwingung** *f* overtone, harmonic vibration; *harmonische ~~* harmonic; **~seite** *f* upper side; **~st** *a* uppermost, upmost, topmost, top; chief, principal; first, head; *fig* supreme; *Am* top-flight, top-grade, top-notch; *das Unterste zu ~~ kehren* to turn (things) topsy-turvy; *zu ~~* uppermost; *~~e Heeresleitung* General Headquarters *pl*; **~st** *m* colonel; **~~leutnant** *m* lieutenant-colonel; **~stabsarzt** *m* major (medical); *mar* staff-surgeon; **~staatsanwalt** *m* attorney-general; **~steiger** *m* foreman of the mine; **~steuermann** *m* first mate; **~stimme** *f* treble, soprano; **~stübchen** *n* attic, garret, toproom; *er ist nicht ganz richtig im ~~* (*fig*) he is not right in the upper storey; **~studiendirektor** *m* head-master, *Am* principal; **~stufe** *f* senior class, seniors *pl*; **~tasse** *f* cup; **~wasser** *n* (*Schleuse*) upper water; (*Mühle*) overshot water; *~~ haben fig* to have the upper hand; **~welt** *f* upper world; **~zollamt** *n* general custom-office.

obgleich *conj* although, though, *Am* altho.

Obhut *f* protection, care; custody; (*Verwahrung*) keeping; *in ~ nehmen* to take care (*od* charge) of.

obig *a* above-mentioned, above, aforesaid, foregoing.

Objekt *n* object; **~glas** *n* (*Mikroskop*) slide, mount; **~halter** *m* specimen holder; **~iv** *a* objective, unbiased, impartial; **~iv** *n* lens; object glass, objective; **~~deckel** *m* lens cover; **~~fassung** *f* lens mount, objective mount; **~~linse** *f* objective lens; **~~öffnung** *f* lens aperture; **~~ring** *m* lens ring (*od* adapter); **~~satz** *m* set of lenses; lens combination; **~~träger** *m* lens carrier; microscope slide; **~~verschluß** *m* instantaneous shutter; **~ivität** *f* objectivity; impartiality.

Oblate *f* wafer; *eccl* host.

obliegen *irr itr* to apply o. s. to; *jdm ~* to be incumbent upon s. o.; **~heit** *f* duty, obligation.

obligat *a* necessary, indispensable; **~ion** *f* bond; obligation; **~~sinhaber** *m* bondholder; **~~sschuldner** *m* bond debtor; **~orisch** *a* compulsory, obligatory, mandatory.

Obmann *m* chairman; (*Betrieb*) shop-steward; (*Schiedsmann*) umpire; (*Sprecher*) spokesman; (*der Geschworenen*) foreman (of a jury).

Obo|e *f* hautboy, oboe; **~ist** *m* oboe player.

Obrigkeit *f* magistrate; authorities *pl*; government; **~lich** *a* magisterial, official; government(al); *adv* by authority; **~~sstaat** *m* authoritarian state.

obschon = *obgleich*.

Observatorium *n* observatory.

obsiegen *itr* to prevail, to overcome; to triumph over; to be victorious, to get the better of; to carry the day.

Obsorge *f* care (*über* of); (*Aufsicht*) supervision; inspection.

Obst *n* fruit; **~bau** *m* fruit-growing; **~baum** *m* fruit-tree; **~~schädlinge** *m pl* fruit tree pests *pl*; **~ernte** *f* fruit-crop; **~garten** *m* orchard; **~händler** *m* fruiterer, *Am* fruit-seller (*od* -dealer); **~handlung** *f* fruiterer's (shop); *Am* fruit-store; **~kelter** *f* fruit-press; **~kern** *m* stone, kernel; (*kleiner*) pip; **~korb** *m* basket of fruit; **~messer** *n* fruit-knife; **~pflücker** *m* fruit-gatherer; **~salat** *m* fruit-salad; **~schale** *f* fruit-dish; **~stand** *m* *Am* fruit-stand; **~torte** *f* tart, *Am* fruit pie; **~wein** *m* cider, fruit-wine; **~zucht** *f* fruit-growing; **~züchter** *m* fruit-grower.

Obstruktion *f* blocking; *parl* obstruction; (*gewerkschaftliche Arbeits~*) ca'canny; *med* constipation; **~srede** *f*, **~redner** *m Am parl* filibuster.

obszön *a* obscene; filthy, smutty; **~ität** *f* obscenity; (*Zote*) smutty joke.

Obus *m* trolley-bus.

obwalten *itr* to exist; to prevail; *unter den ~den Umständen* under the circumstances, as matters stand.

obwohl = *obgleich*.

Ochs|e *m* ox, bull(ock); (*junger ~*) steer; *fig* duffer, blockhead; **~en** *itr* to cram, to fag, *sl* to swot; **~enauge** *n* fried egg; **~enfleisch** *n* beef; **~engespann** *n* ox-team; **~enhaut** *f* ox-hide; **~enschwanz** *m* ox-tail; **~~suppe** *f* ox-tail soup; **~enziemer** *m* horse-whip; **~enzunge** *f* ox-tongue.

Ocker *m* ochre.

Ode *f* ode.

öd|e *a* empty, bleak, bare; (*unbewohnt*) uninhabited, desolate, desert(ed), unfrequented; (*unbebaut*) waste; (*langweilig*) dull, dreary; **~e** *f* waste, desert, solitude; (*Langweiligkeit*) dul(l)ness, tedium, tediousness; **~land** *n* fallow land.

Odem *m poet* breath.

Ödem *n* (o)edema.

oder *conj* or; *~ aber* or else, or instead; *~ auch* or rather; *entweder — ~* either — or; (*sonst*) otherwise.

Odyssee *f* Odyssey.

Ofen *m* stove; (*Back~*) oven; (*Brenn~*) kiln; (*Hoch~*) furnace; **~bank** *f* bench by the stove; **~heizung** *f* furnace heat; **~hocker** *m* stay-at-home; **~kachel** *f* Dutch tile; **~klappe** *f* damper; **~lack** *m* stove varnish; **~loch** *n* oven-hole; **~putzer** *m* chimney-sweeper; **~rohr** *n* stove-pipe; *mil* (*Raketenpanzerabwehrwaffe*) (portable) anti-tank rocket launcher, *Am* (Big) Bazooka; **~röhre** *f* stove-pipe; (*zum Abstellen*) recess; **~schirm** *m* (fire-)screen; **~setzer** *m* stove-fitter.

offen *a* open; (*Stelle*) vacant; free; (*öffentlich*) public; *fig* frank, sincere; candid; outspoken; (*offenbar, offensichtlich*) overt; *~ gesagt, ~ gestanden* to be honest, to tell the truth, frankly; *e-e ~e Antwort Am* a straight answer; *~e Flanke* exposed flank; *~e Rechnung* current account; *~e Handelsgesellschaft* private firm; *~e Stadt* unfortified town; *~es Sportflugzeug* open sports airplane; *~e Sprache* plain language; uncoded (*od* open) language; *~e Stelle* vacancy; *~er Güterwagen* railway-truck, *Am* gondola car; *auf ~er Strecke* on the road; *auf ~er See* on the open sea; *~ erklären* to declare frankly; *~es Geheimnis* public secret; *~er Wechsel* blank cheque; **~bar** *a* obvious, manifest, evident; **~baren** *tr* to disclose, to manifest, to reveal (to); **~barung** *f* manifestation; (*Enthüllung*) revelation, disclosure; *die ~~ Johannis* Revelation of St. John; **~~seid** *m* oath of manifestation; **~heit** *f* openness, frankness, cando(u)r; **~herzig** *a* open-hearted, frank, sincere, candid; **~~keit** *f* sincerity, frankness; **~kundig** *a* notorious, public; well-known; obvious, evident; *~~e Lüge* downright lie; **~sichtlich** *a* obvious, apparent, evident, manifest; **~stehen** *irr itr* to stand open; (*Rechnung*) to remain unpaid; (*gestattet sein*) to be allowed, to be at liberty (to); **~~d** *a* open; (*Rechnung*) outstanding, unsettled.

offensiv *a*, **~e** *f* offensive; *die ~e ergreifen* to take the offensive.

öffentlich *a* public; open; *~e Anleihe* public loan; *~e Bedürfnisanstalt* public convenience, *Am* public comfort station; *~e Betriebe* public utilities *pl*; *~e Bibliothek* public library; *~e Fernsprechstelle* public telephone; *~es Interesse* common interest; *~e Meinung* public opinion; *Befragung der ~en Meinung Am* opinion poll; *~er Sammelschutzraum* public air-raid shelter; *~er Verkehr* public use, public correspondence; *~e Versammlung* open meeting; *~es Wohl* public welfare; *~ be-*

kanntgeben to make public; (*amtlich*) to promulgate, to proclaim; *in die ~e Hand überführen* to nationalize; *im Brennpunkt des ~en Lebens stehen* to be in the public eye; **~keit** *f* public; publicity; *der ~~ unterbreiten* to give publicity (to s. th.); *unter Ausschluß der ~~ tagen* to meet behind closed doors (*od jur* in camera); *in aller ~~* in public; *an die ~~ gelangen* to become known; *vor die ~~ bringen* to bring before the public; **~rechtlich** *a* under public law.

offer|ieren *tr* to offer; **~te** *f* offer; tender; bid; *e-e ~~ einreichen* to submit an offer.

offiziell *a* official.

Offizier *m* (commissioned) officer; *~ des Beurlaubtenstandes* reserve officer; *~ vom Dienst* officer on duty; *wachthabender ~* officer of the guard; *zum ~ ernannt werden* to be commissioned; **~anwärter** *m* candidate for a commission; **~ausbildung** *f* officers' training; **~korps** *n* body of officers; **~sbursche** *m* batman, orderly; **~skasino** *n* officers' mess; *mar* (*Messe*) ward-room; **~spatent** *n* commission.

Offiz|in *f* workshop; dispensary; laboratory; chemist's shop; printing-house; **~iös** *a* semi-official.

öffn|en *tr, r* to open (*aufschließen*) to unlock, (*mit Dietrich*) to pick; (*Flasche*) to uncork; (*Siegel, Lippen*) to unseal; (*Körper*) to dissect; (*Fallschirm*) to release, to open (a parachute); **~ung** *f* opening, aperture; (*Loch*) hole; (*Lücke*) gap; (*Schlitz*) slot, slit; (*Sack, Röhre*) mouth; orifice; (*Durchgang*) passage; (*Ausgang*) outlet; **~~szeiten** *f pl* hours *pl* of opening.

Offset|druck *m* offset printing; **~walze** *f* offset roller.

oft, **~mals** *adv* often, frequently; *je öfter . . . desto* the more ... the; **~malig** *a* frequent, repeated, reiterated; **öfters** *adv* (quite) often, frequently.

oh! *interj* oh! o! dear me!

Oh(ei)m *m* uncle.

ohne *prp* without, excepted; (*tadelnd*) devoid of; (*abgesehen von*) but for; except; (*frei von*) devoid of; destitute of, lacking; (*außerhalb*) out of; *~ Bedeutung* without importance; of no consequence; *~ allen Einfluß* devoid of all influence; *~ Gewähr* without engagement; *~ Sie* but for you; *~ Stellung* unemployed, out of work; *~ weiteres* without more ado; right off; *so ~ weiteres geht das nicht* it doesn't work that easily; *die Sache ist nicht ~* there is some truth in it; it is by no means bad; *sei ~ Sorge* don't worry; *conj ~ daß er es weiß* without his knowing it; **~dies, ~hin** *adv* apart from this, besides; anyhow, anyway, all the same; **~gleichen** *a* unequalled; **~haltflug** *m* nonstop flight.

Ohn|macht *f* (*Bewußtlosigkeit*) faint, swoon, unconsciousness; *med* syncope; *aero* blackout; (*Machtlosigkeit*) powerlessness; (*Schwäche*) weakness, impotence; *in ~ fallen* to faint (*vor* from); **~mächtig** *a* in a faint, unconscious; (*hilflos*) helpless, powerless; (*schwach*) weak; *~~ werden* to faint; **~machtsanfall** *m* fainting-fit.

Ohr *n* ear; *fig* hearing; *ganz ~ sein* to be all ears; *auf dem linken ~ taub sein* to be deaf in the left ear; *jdn übers ~ hauen* to cheat s. o., to take in s. o., *sl* to gyp s. o.; *bis über die ~en in Schulden stecken* to be up to o.'s ears in debt; *jdm in den ~en liegen* to pester s. o., to importune s. o.; *die ~en steif halten* to keep up o.'s courage; *die ~en spitzen* to prick up o.'s ears; *es geht zum e-n ~ hinein u. zum anderen heraus* it goes in one ear and out the other; **~enarzt** *m* ear specialist, otologist; aurist; **~enbeichte** *f* auricular confession; **~enbetäubend** *a* ear-deafening; **~enbläser** *m* telltale, scandalmonger; **~bläserei** *f* scandal, slander; **~enentzündung** *f* inflammation of the ear; **~enklingen** *n* ringing in the ears; **~enleiden** *n* disease of the ear; **~ensausen** *n* buzzing in the ears; *med* tinnitus; **~enschmalz** *n* ear-wax; **~enschmaus** *m* musical treat; **~enschmerz** *m*, **~enweh** *n* ear-ache; **~enschützer** *m* ear-flap, *Am* ear-muff; **~enspeicheldrüse** *f med* parotid gland; **~enspiegel** *m* auriscope, otoscope; **~enzerreißend** *a* ear-splitting; **~enverschlußwatte** *f* ear-plug; **~enzeuge** *m* auricular (*od* ear-) witness; **~feige** *f* box on the ear, slap on the face; *jdm e-e ~~ geben*, **~feigen** *tr* to box s. o.'s ears, to slap s. o.'s face; **~förmig** *a* auriform; **~gehänge** *n* ear-drop; **~läppchen** *n* lobe of the ear; **~muschel** *f* concha, external ear, auricle; *tele* (*Hörermuschel*) ear-piece, cap; **~ring** *m* ear-ring; **~schnecke** *f anat* cochlea; **~trompete** *f anat* eustachian tube; **~wurm** *m* earwig.

Öhr *n* (*Nadel~*) eye; (*in Stoffen, Segeln*) eyelet.

Okkultismus *m* occultism.

Ökonom *m* economist; (*Landwirt*) farmer; (*Verwalter*) manager, housekeeper; steward; **~ie** *f* agriculture; economy; economics; housekeeping; **~isch** *a* economical.

Okt|aeder *m* octahedron; **~ant** *m* octant; **~anzahl** *f* octane value (*od* rating), anti-knock value; octane number; **~avband** *m* octavo (volume); **~ave** *f mus* octave; **~ett** *n* octet.

Oktober *m* October.

Okul|ar *n* eye-piece; ocular; **~~linse** *f* ocular lens; **~~öffnung** *f* pin-hole; **~ieren** *tr* to graft, to bud, to inoculate; **~iermesser** *n* budding-knife.

Okzident *m* occident.

Öl *n* oil; (*Schmier~*) machine (*od* engine *od* lubrication) oil; (*Speise~*) salad oil; *~ ins Feuer gießen fig* to throw oil on the fire, to add fuel to the fire; *in ~ malen* to paint in oils; **~ablaß** *m* oil drain; **~ablaßhahn** *m* oil-drain valve; **~abscheider** *m* oil separator; **~anstrich** *m* coat of oil-painting; **~bad** *n* oil bath; **~baum** *m* olive tree; *falscher ~~* oleaster; **~behälter** *m* oil container; *mot* oil tank; **~berg** *m eccl* Mount of Olives; **~bild** *n* oil-painting; **~bohrung** *f* oil well; **~brenner** *m* oil burner; **~dicht** *a* oil -tight; **~druck** *m* (*Bild*) oleograph; chromo (lithograph); *phot* oil printing; *tech* oil pressure; **~~bremse** *f* oil brake; hydraulic brake; **~~messer** *m* oil pressure ga(u)ge; **~~schmierung** *f* oil pressure lubrication; **~einfüllstutzen** *m mot* oil filler cap (*od* tube); **~en** *tr* to oil; (*salben*) to anoint; *tech* to lubricate; **~er** *m tech* oiler, oil cup, lubricator; **~farbe** *f* oil paint; oil colo(u)r; **~farbendruck** *m* oleograph(y); **~faß** *n* oil barrel; **~feld** *n* oil-field; **~feuerung** *f* oil-burning; **~film** *m* oil-film; layer of oil; **~filter** *m* oil-filter, *Am* strainer, screen; **~fläschchen** *n* oil cruet; **~fleck** *m* oilstain; **~frei** *a* barren of oil; **~fresser** *m tech* oil hog; **~getränkt** *a* oil-impregnated; **~gewinnung** *f* oil production; **~haltig** *a* containing oil, oleiferous; **~handel** *m* oil trade; **~ig** *a* oily, oleaginous; unctuous; **~igkeit** *f* oiliness; **~kanne** *f*, **~kanister** *m* oil-can; **~kohle** *f* oil carbon; *von ~~ befreien* to decarbonize; **~kuchen** *m* oil-cake; **~kühler** *m* oil cooler; **~lack** *m* oil varnish; **~lagerstätte** *f* oil pool; **~lampe** *f* oil-lamp; **~leitung** *f* (*Erdölfeld*) pipeline; *mot* oil-pipes *pl*; oil lead, oil feed; **~malerei** *f* painting in oil, oil painting; **~meßstab** *m mot* oil dipper, *Am* oil level ga(u)ge; **~motor** *m* oil engine; **~mühle** *f* oil-mill; **~nebel** *m mot* oil mist; **~papier** *n* oil-paper; **~presse** *f* oil-press; **~pumpe** *f mot* oil pump; **~quelle** *f* oil-spring; **~raffinerie** *f* oil refinery; **~rohr** *n* oil-pipe; **~rückstand** *m* oil residue; **~sardine** *f* sardine; **~schalter** *m el* oil-switch; **~schiefer** *m* oil shale; **~schlägerei** *f* oil-press; **~schmierung** *f* oil lubrication; **~sieb** *n* oil filter screen; **~sperre** *f* oil embargo; **~spritze** *f* oil-gun; **~stand** *m* oil-level; **~~anzeiger** *m* oil-ga(u)ge; **~stoßdämpfer** *m* oil shock-absorber; **~tuch** *n* oilskin; **~umlauf** *m mot* oil circulation; **~ung** *f* oiling; (*Salbung*) anointment; *tech* (*Schmierung*) lubrication; *Letzte ~~* extreme unction; **~verbrauch** *m* oil consumption; **~verdünnung** *f* oil dilution; **~wanne** *f mot* sump, *Am* oil-pan; **~wechsel** *m* oil changing; **~zeug** *n* oilcloth; **~zuführung** *f* oil feed; **~zweig** *m* olive branch.

Olive *f* olive; **~nbaum** *m* olive-tree; **~nfarben** *a* olive (-colo(u)red); **~nförmig** *a* olivary; **~ngrün** *a* olive-green (*od* -drab); **~nöl** *n* olive-oil.

Olymp *m* Olympus; **~iade** *f* Olympiad; **~isch** *a* Olympian, Olympic; *die ~~en Spiele* the Olympic Games *pl.*

Omelette *f* omelet.

Omen *n* omen; **ominös** *a* ominous.

Omnibus *m* (omni)bus, motorbus, motor coach; *mit dem ~ fahren* to ride (*od* take) a bus, to go by bus; **~fahrer** *m* bus driver; **~haltestelle** *f* bus stop; **~halteplatz** *m* bus zone; **~linie** *f* coach line, bus line; **~park** *m* bus fleet; **~schaffner** *m* bus conductor; **~verkehr** *m* bus service.

ondulieren *tr* (*Haare*) to wave.

Onkel *m* uncle.

Opal *m* opal; **~isieren** *itr* to opalesce; **~~d** *a* opalescent.

Oper *f* opera; (*Gebäude*) opera-house; *e-e ~ aufführen* to give (*od* to perform) an opera; *in die ~ gehen* to go to the opera; **~ette** *f* operetta, musical comedy; **~nglas** *n* opera-glass; **~nhaus** *n* opera-house; **~nmusik** *f* operatic music; **~nsänger** *m*, **~~in** *f* opera-singer; **~nstar** *m* opera star; **~ntext** *m* libretto, book.

Oper|ateur *m* operator, operating surgeon; **~ation** *f* operation; *sich e-r ~~ unterziehen* to submit to an operation; **~~sabteilung** *f mil* operations section; **~~sbasis** *f mil* base of operation; **~~sbefehl** *m mil* combat order; **~~sgebiet** *n mil* theatre of operations; **~~smantel** *m* gown for surgeon; operating apron; **~~snarbe** *f* postoperative scar; **~~splan** *m mil* operations plan; **~~sradius** *m* operating radius; **~~ssaal** *m med* operation theatre, surgery room; **~~stisch** *m* operating (*od* surgical) table; **~~sverfahren** *n* method of operation; **~~sziel** *n mil* tactical objective; **~ativ** *a* operative; *mil* operational, strategic; **~~es Ziel** *mil* object of operations; **~ieren** *tr, itr* to operate on s. o.; *jdn ~~* to perform an operation on; *sich ~~ lassen* to be operated (on), to undergo an operation.

Opfer *n* sacrifice; (*Gabe*) offering; (*Geopfertes*) victim, martyr; *ein ~*

bringen to make a sacrifice; *kein* ~ *scheuen* to shrink from no sacrifice; *ein* ~ *werden* to fall a victim; **~altar** *m* sacrificial altar; **~becken** *n* altar-basin; **~büchse** *f* offering box; **~flamme** *f* sacrificial flame; **~freudig** *a* self-sacrificing; **~gabe** *f* offering; **~gebet** *n* offertory; **~geld** *n* money-offering; **~kasten** *m* poor-box; **~lamm** *n* sacrificial lamb; *fig* victim; **~n** *tr* to sacrifice; (*Tiere*) to immolate; **~priester** *m* sacrificer; **~stätte** *f* place of sacrifice; **~stock** *m* poor-box; **~tag** *m* flag-day; **~tier** *n* victim; **~tod** *m* sacrifice of o.'s life; **~ung** *f* sacrifice; sacrificing; immolation; **~willig** *a* willing (*od* ready) to make sacrifices.

Opium *n* opium.

oppo|nieren *itr* to oppose; **~sition** *f* opposition; *der* ~~ *angehören parl* to be in opposition; **~~sführer** *m parl* opposition leader.

optieren *tr* to choose; to decide in favour of.

Opti|k *f* optics *pl*; *phot* lens system; **~ker** *m* optician, *Am auch* optometrist; **~~gewerbe** *n* optometry; **~sch** *a* optic(al).

Optim|ismus *m* optimism; **~ist** *m* optimist; **~istisch** *a* optimistic.

Orakel *n*, **~spruch** *m* oracle; **~haft** *a* oracular; **~n** *itr* to speak in riddles.

Orange *f* orange; **~farben** *a* orange; **~nschale** *f* orange-peel; **~nschnitz** *m* orange quarter; **~erie** *f* orangery.

Orang-Utan *m* orang-outang.

Oratorium *n* oratorio.

Orchester *n* orchestra; band; **~raum** *m theat* orchestra pit; **~sessel** *m theat* orchestra stalls, *Am* orchestra (seat).

Orchidee *f* orchid.

Orden *m* order; (*Zeichen*) decoration; badge; (*Denkmünze*) medal; **~sband** *n* ribbon of an order; medal ribbon; **~sbruder** *m* member of an order; friar. monk; **~sburg** *f* castle of order; **~sgeistliche(r)** *m* ecclesiastic; regular; **~sgelübde** *n* vow, profession; **~skleid** *n* monastic garb (*od* habit); **~sregel** *f* statute(s *pl*) of an order; **~sschnalle** *f* suspension-brooch; **~sschwester** *f* sister; nun; **~sstern** *m* plaque; **~sverleihung** *f* conferring (of) an order; **~szeichen** *n* badge, order.

ordentlich *a* tidy, orderly; (*anständig*) decent, steady; (*regelmäßig*) regular; (*tüchtig, gehörig*) sound, pretty large, considerable, downright; (*achtbar*) respectable; *~er Professor* university professor; professor in ordinary; **~keit** *f* regularity, orderliness; respectability.

Order *f* order, command; *an die* ~ *von com* to the order of.

ordin|är *a* ordinary, common; low, vulgar; **~arius** *m* professor in ordinary; **~ärpreis** *m* sale price, net price; **~ate** *f* ordinate; **~ation** *f* ordination; **~ieren** *tr* to ordain; to invest; *ordiniert werden* to take orders.

ordn|en *tr* to put in order; (*zurecht machen, sauber machen*) to tidy; (*der Ordnung nach aufstellen*) to classify, to arrange; to settle; (*aussortieren*) to sift, to sort; (*regeln*) to regulate; (*Briefe etc*) to file; *sich die Haare* ~~ to dress o.'s hair; **~er** *m* organizer; (*Schule*) prefect, monitor; (*Akten*) filer, file, *Am* press; (*Briefe*) sorter; **~ung** *f* order; (*Sauberkeit*) tidiness; (*Anordnung*) arrangement, classification, class; disposition, form; degree; (*Aufstellung in Linie*) line-up; *mil* (*Schlachtordnung*) array; (*Pünktlichkeit*) accuracy; *math* order; (*Regelung*) regulation; *alles in* ~~*!* all right! *Am* okay! okeh! O. K! *in guter* ~~ shipshape, in good order, well arranged; *in* ~~ *befinden* to be in order; *etw in* ~~ *bringen* to put s. th. in order, to straighten s. th. out, *Am* to fix s. th.; (*regeln*) to settle a matter; *wieder in* ~~ *bringen* to adjust; *in* ~~ *finden* to think s. th. quite right; *in* ~~ *halten* to keep in order; *zur* ~~ *rufen* to call to order; *zur* ~~ *zurückkehren* to return to law and order; *geöffnete* ~~ (*mil*) extended order; *geschlossene* ~~ (*mil*) close order; **~~sdienst** *m* security police force; **~~sgemäß**, **~~smäßig** *a* orderly, regular; according to order; **~~sgrad** *m* degree of order; **~~snummer** *f* shelf number; **~~spolizei** *f* uniformed regular police; constabulary; **~~sruf** *m* call to order; **~~sstrafe** *f* disciplinary penalty; (*Geld*) fine; **~~swidrig** *a* against order, contrary to orders; (*unregelmäßig*) irregular; (*ungesetzlich*) illegal; **~~swort** *n* (*Bibliothek*) entry word, heading; **~~szahl** *f* ordinal number.

Ordonnanz *f* (*Verordnung*) ordinance; *mil* orderly; **~offizier** *m* special-missions staff officer; administrative officer; assistant adjutant.

Organ *n* (*Körper*) organ; (*Stimme*) voice; (*Zeitung*) journal, periodical; (*Amt,Stelle*) agency, part, organ; agent; **~die** *m* (*Stoff*) organdy; fine muslin; **~isation** *f* organization; **~~sstab** *m* organizational staff; **~isator** *m* organizer; **~~isch** *a* organizing; **~isch** *a* organic; **~isieren** *tr* to organize; (*stehlen*) *sl* to scrounge; to lift, *Am* to liberate; *~isierter Arbeiter* unionist; **~ismus** *m* organism; **~ist** *m* organist.

Orgel *f* organ; **~bauer** *m* organ-builder; **~konzert** *n* organ-recital; **~n** *itr* to play the organ; *fam* to strum; to grind (*od* to play) a barrel-organ; **~pfeife** *f* organ-pipe; **~spieler** *m* organist; **~werk** *n* works (*pl*) of an organ.

Orgie *f* orgy; *~n feiern* to celebrate orgies.

Orient *m* Orient; Levant; **~ale** *m*, **~alisch** *a* Oriental, Eastern; **~ieren** *tr* to orientate, to locate; (*informieren*) to inform, to set right, to instruct; *r* to take o.'s bearings about; to take a bearing; to fix (*od* to find) a position; *sich nicht mehr* ~~ *können* to have lost o.'s bearings, *fam* to be all at sea; *~iert sein über* to be acquainted (*od* familiar) with; **~ierung** *f* information; orientation; direction; survey; (*Neigung*) trend, inclination; *die* ~~ *verlieren* to become lost, to lose o.'s bearings; **~~sfeuer** *n aero* route beacon; **~~slinie** *f* orienting line; **~~spunkt** *m* check point.

Origin|al *n* original; *a* original; **~~aufnahmen** *f pl radio* spot pickups *pl*; **~~ersatzteil** *m mot* factory-engineered part; **~~modell** *n* master pattern; **~~negativ** *n phot* master negative; **~alität** *f* originality; **~ell** *a* original.

Orkan *m* hurricane, typhoon; **~artig** *a*: *~~er Sturm* heavy storm.

Ornament *n* ornament, decoration; dressings *pl*; **~ik** *f* ornamentation.

Ornat *m* (official) robes *pl*, vestments *pl*.

Ort *m* (*Stelle, Punkt*) spot; (*Platz*) place; site; locus; (*Punkt*) point; (*Stelle*) position; (*Gemeinde, Dorf*) village; (*Gegend*) region; (*Örtlichkeit*) locality; *min* termination; *am* ~ *wohnend* resident; *an* ~ *u. Stelle* on the spot; in the site; in situ; ~ *der Handlung* scene of action; *von* ~ *zu* ~ from place to place; *ein gewisser* ~ the WC; *höheren* ~*s* at high quarters; *ein abgelegener* ~ a remote spot, *Am fam* a one-horse town; **~en** *itr* to orientate; *aero* to locate; (*franzen*) to navigate; **~er** *m aero* navigator; (*Radar*) observer; **~~raum** *m* navigator's department; **~samt** *n tele* local exchange, *Am* local central office; **~sangabe** *f* indication of a place; address; **~sanruf** *m tele* local call; **~sansässig** *a* resident (in the locality); indigenous, local; **~sansässige(r)** *m* resident; **~sanwesend** *a* present; **~sbeben** *n* local earthquake; **~sbehörde** *f* local authorities *pl*; **~sbeschaffenheit** *f* nature of a place; **~sbeschreibung** *f* topography; **~sbesichtigung** *f* local inspection; **~sbestimmung** *f* localization; position finding; position fixing; orientation; *radio* bearing; **~sbezirk** *m* local area; **~sbiwak** *n* close billet; **~schaft** *f* place; village; **~sempfang** *m radio* local reception; **~sfernsprechnetz** *n* local exchange area; **~sfest** *a* fixed; stationary; static; *~~e Flak* fixed anti-aircraft artillery, static A.A.; **~sfeststellung** *f* fix; (*durch Radio*) radio fix; **~sgebiet** *n* local area; **~sgebrauch** *m* local custom; **~sgedächtnis** *n* sense of direction; (*Tiere*) homing instinct; **~sgefecht** *n mil* combat in towns; **~sgespräch** *n tele* local call, *Am* local message; **~sgruppe** *f* local branch; **~skenntnis** *f* local knowledge, knowledge of a place; **~skommandant** *m* town major; local commandant; commander of army post; **~skommandantur** *f* town headquarters; army post command (in war zone); **~skrankenkasse** *f* local sick insurance (*od* fund); **~skundig** *a* acquainted with the locality; familiar with the area; **~slandung** *f aero* spot landing; **~slazarett** *n* local hospital; **~smißweisung** *f* local declination; **~sname** *m* place-name; **~snetz** *n tele* local telephone network, *Am* local plant; **~spolizei** *f* local police; **~spostbezirk** *m* town postal district; **~sruf** *m tele* local call; **~ssender** *m radio* local transmitter (*od* radio station); **~ssinn** *m* local sense, bump of locality; **~steilnehmer** *m* local subscriber; **~üblich** *a* customary in a place; **~sunterkunft** *f mil* billet(s *pl*); **~sveränderung** *f* change of place; **~sverbindung** *f tele* local connection; **~sverkehr** *m* local traffic; **~sverzeichnis** *n* list of places; **~svorsteher** *m* mayor, (village) magistrate; **~szeit** *f* local time; **~szulage** *f* local bonus; **~szustellung** (*Post*) local delivery; **~ung** *f* orientation, location, bearing, position finding; navigation; **~~sbake** *f* localizer transmitter; localizer beacon; **~~sgerät** *n* localizer, position finder; **~~spunkt** *aero* reference point; *mar* landmark; **~~sverfahren** *n* method of orientation.

ortho|dox *a* orthodox; **~doxie** *f* orthodoxy; **~graphie** *f* orthography; **~graphisch** *a* orthographic(al); **~pädie** *f* orthop(a)edics *pl*, orthop(a)edy; **~pädisch** *a* orthop(a)edic.

örtlich *a* local; **~keit** *f* locality.

Öse *f* (*Ring*) loop; ear; ring; (*Haken*) eye; (*Schuh*) eyelet; **~nbolzen** *m* eyebolt; **~nhaken** *m* eyehook; **~nzange** *f* eyelet pliers *pl*.

Ost *m* east; (*Wind*) Eastwind; **~afrika** *n* East Africa; **~asien** *n* Eastern Asia; **~deutschland** *n* Eastern Germany; **~en** *m* east, Orient; *der Nahe* (*Ferne*) ~~ the Near (Far) East; **~feldzug** *m* eastern campaign; **~flüchtling** *m* Eastern refugee; **~flügel** *m* east wing; **~front** *f* eastern front; **~gote**

m Ostrogoth; **~indien** *n* India, the East-Indies; **~see** *f* the Baltic (Sea); **~wärts** *adv* eastward(s); **~wind** *m* east wind; **~zone** *f* (*Deutschland*) Eastern zone.
ostentativ *a* ostentatious.
Oster|abend *m* Easter eve; **~ei** *n* Easter egg; **~fest** *n*, **~n** *pl* Easter; (*jüdisch*) Passover; **~fladen** *m* Easter cake; **~hase** *m* Easter-bunny, Easter-rabbit; **~lamm** *n* paschal lamb; **~messe** *f* Easter-fair.
Öst|(er)reich *n* Austria; **~~er** *m*, **~~in** *f*, **~~isch** *a* Austrian; **~erlich** *a* of Easter; paschal; **~lich** *a* eastern, easterly, oriental.
Osz|illation *f* oscillation; **~illator** *m* oscillator, generator; **~illieren** *itr* to oscillate; **~illograph** *m* oscillograph.

*

Otter *f* adder, viper; **~** *m* (*Fisch~*) otter; **~ngezücht** *n* generation of vipers.
Otto|motor *m* internal-reciprocating combustion engine; Otto carburettor engine; spark-ignition engine.
Ouvertüre *f* overture.
oval *a* oval.
Oxhoft *n* hogshead.
Oxyd *n* oxide; **~ation** *f* oxidation; **~~svorgang** *m* oxidation process; **~~swirkung** *f* oxidizing action; **~ieren** *itr*, *tr* to oxidize; **~ierung** *f* oxidation, oxygenation; **~reich** *a* rich in oxide; **~ul** *n* suboxide.
Ozean *m* ocean; *der Große* (*od Stille*) **~** the Pacific; *der Atlantische* **~** the Atlantic; **~dampfer** *m* liner; **~flug** *m* trans-Atlantic flight; **~isch** *a* oceanic.
Ozon *n* ozone.

P

P *Abk mit* **P** *siehe Liste der Abk.*
Paar *n* pair; couple; (*Tiere*) brace; *ein ~ Ochsen* a yoke of oxen; *zu ~en treiben* to put to flight, to rout; *~ a: ein ~* a few, some; a couple of; several; *vor ein ~ Tagen* a few days ago; *ein ~ Zeilen* a line or two; *schreiben Sie mir ein ~ Zeilen* drop me a line; *~ od un~* odd or even; **~en** *tr* to pair; to couple, to copulate; to match, to mate; *fig* (*vereinigen*) to join; *r* to pair, to couple; **~ig** *a* in pairs; **~laufen** *n* (*Schlittschuh*) couple-skating; **~mal** *adv: ein ~~* several times, a couple of (*od* a few) times; **~ung** *f* pairing, mating; copulation; **~~szeit** *f* rutting season; **~weise** *adv* in couples, by pairs, two by two.
Pacht *f* lease, tenure; rent; (*Leih~*) lend-lease; *in ~ geben* to let (out) on lease; *in ~ nehmen* to take on lease; **~brief** *m* lease; **~en** *tr* to (take on) lease, to rent, to farm; (*für sich beanspruchen*) *fam* to monopolize; **~ertrag** *m* rental; **~frei** *a* rent-free; **~geld** *n* (farm-)rent; **~gut** *n* farm, tenement, leasehold estate; **~land** *n* leasehold-land; **~~ u. Leihvertrag** *m* *Am* Lend-Lease Act; **~ung** *f* taking on lease, farming; (*das Gepachtete*) leasehold, tenement; **~vertrag** *m* lease; **~weise** *adv* on lease; **~zins** *m* rent.
Pächter *m* (*Land*) landholder, tenant, farmer; (*Mieter*) lessee; *jur* leaseholder.
Pack *m* pack; (*Ballen*) bale; (*Bündel*) bundle; (*Paket*) packet, parcel; (*Gesindel*) rabble; *mit Sack u. ~* with bag and baggage; **~eis** *n* pack ice; **~en** *tr* (*festhalten*) to seize, to grasp; (*einpacken*) to pack (up), *Am* to package; (*weg~~*) to stow away; *fig* (*ergreifen*) to affect, to thrill; to hold; *r* (*sich davonmachen*) to clear out, to bundle off; *den Stier bei den Hörnern ~~* to take the bull by the horns; **~~d** *a* fascinating, thrilling, absorbing; **~er** *m* packer; *mar* stevedore; **~esel** *m* sumpter-mule, pack-ass; *fig* drudge; **~garn** *n* pack-thread, twine; **~korb** *m* crate, hamper; **~leinwand** *f* packing cloth, bagging; burlap; **~material** *n* packing material; **~papier** *n* packing (*od* wrapping) paper, brown paper; (*starkes ~~*) kraft; **~pferd** *n* pack horse; **~raum** *m* packing (*od* shipping) room; *mar* stowage; **~sack** *m mil Am* duffle bag; **~sattel** *m* pack-saddle; **~schnur** *f* pack thread; **~tasche** *f* saddlebag; **~träger** *m* porter; (*Fahrrad*) carrier; **~ung** *f* packing, wrapper; package, box; *med* (cold-) pack; cold compress; *tech* oil retainer ring, gasket, packing; *e-e ~~ Zigaretten* a packet of cigarettes; **~wagen** *m* luggage van, *Am* baggage car; *mil* baggage-waggon; **~zettel** *m* packing slip.
Päckchen *n* small parcel, packet, *Am* package; (*Zigaretten*) pack; (*Banknoten*) *Am* wad.

*

Pädagoge *m* education(al)ist; (*Schulmeister, Pedant*) pedagog(ue); **~ik** *f* pedagogy; **~isch** *a* pedagogic(al), educational.
Paddel|boot *n* canoe, paddling-boat; **~n** *itr* to canoe, to paddle.
paff! *interj* bang! **~en** *itr* (*rauchen*) to whiff; (*drauflosschießen*) to pop.
Page *m* page; (*Hotel*) buttons, *Am* bellboy; *jdn durch e-n ~n suchen lassen* *Am* to page; **~nkopf** *m* bobbed hair.
paginier|en *tr* to page, to paginate; **~ung** *f* pagination.
pah! *interj* pooh! pshaw!
Pair *m* peer; **~swürde** *f* peerage.
Pak *f* anti-tank gun; tank destroyer (*Abk* TD); **~führer** *m* antitank-gun commander; **~zug** *m* antitank platoon.
Paket *n* parcel, packet, package; *ein ~ aufgeben* to mail a package; **~adresse** *f* despatch-note; **~annahme** *f* parcels-receiving office, *Am* parcel-post window; **~ausgabe** *f* parcel-delivery; **~beförderung** *f* carriage of parcels; **~boot** *n* mail-boat; **~karte** *f* parcel form, *Am* parcel-post mailing form; **~post** *f* parcel post.
Pakt *m* pact, agreement; **~ieren** *itr* to agree (on); to come to terms.
paläolithisch *a* paleolithic.
Palast *m* palace; **~artig** *a* palatial; **~dame** *f* lady-in-waiting.
Palästin|a *n* Palestine; **~ensisch** *a* Palestinian.
Paletot *m* overcoat, greatcoat.
Palette *f* palet(te).
Palisade *f* palisade; **~nzaun** *m* stockade.
Palisanderholz *n* rosewood.
Palm|baum *m*, **~e** *f* palm-tree; **~kätzchen** *n* catkin; **~öl** *n* palm-oil; **~sonntag** *m* Palm Sunday; **~wedel** *m* palm-branch.
Pamphlet *n* (*Flugblatt*) pamphlet; (*Schmähschrift*) lampoon; **~ist** *m* lampoonist.
pan|amerikanisch *a* Pan-American; *~~er Kongreß* Pan-American Congress; *~~e Union* Pan-American Union; **~europa** *n* Pan-Europe.
Paneel *n* panel; wainscot.
Panier *m* banner; **~en** *tr* to dress with egg and bread-crumbs.
Pan|ik *f* panic, stampede; **~isch** *a* panic; *fam* panicky.
Panne *f* motor trouble; break-down; (*Reifen~*) puncture, flat; *fig* hitch, mischance; mishap; *e-e ~ haben* to have a break-down; to break down; (*Reifen*) to have a blowout (*od* flat tyre).
Panoptikum *n* panopticon, waxworks *pl*.
panschen, pantschen *tr* (*vermischen*) to mix, to adulterate; (*plantschen*) to splash (about), to dabble.
Pansen *m* (*Magen*) rumen, paunch.
Panslavismus *m* Panslavism.
Panthei|smus *m* pantheism; **~st** *m*, **~stisch** *a* pantheist.
Panther *m* panther.
Pantine *f* clog, patten.
Pantoffel *m* slipper; (*offene*) mule; scuff; *in ~n sein* to be in slippers; *unter dem ~ stehen* to be henpecked; **~held** *m* henpecked husband.
Pantomim|e *f* pantomime, dumb show; **~isch** *a* pantomimic.
Panzer *m* (*Rüstung*) coat of mail, armo(u)r; armo(u)r-plate; (*Harnisch*) cuirass; *mil* (*Kampfwagen*) tank; *Begleit~* accompanying tank; *leichter ~* light tank; *mittlerer ~* medium tank; *schwerer ~* heavy tank; *e-n ~ abschießen* to knock out a tank; *~ greifen ein* tanks go into action; **~abschuß** *m* tank kill; **~abwehr** *f* anti-tank defence, tank-blocking defence; **~~büchse** *f* anti-tank rifle, (*Ofenrohr*) bazooka; **~~kanone** *f* anti-tank gun; **~~mine** *f* anti-tank mine; **~~waffe** *f* anti-tank weapon; **~ansammlung** *f* tank concentration; **~antenne** *f* tank aerial; **~aufbau** *m* tank body; **~aufklärungsabteilung** *f* armo(u)red reconnaissance battalion; **~befehlswagen** *m* commander's tank; **~begleitwagen** *m* armo(u)red observation-tank; **~besatzung** *f* tank crew; **~brechend** *a* tank-busting, armo(u)r piercing; **~brigade** *f* tank brigade; **~dekkungsloch** *n* anti-tank-fire trench, slit trench; **~division** *f* armo(u)red division; **~drehturm** *m* turret; **~einheit** *f* armo(u)red unit; **~faust** *f* anti-tank bomb, *Am* bazooka; **~formation** *f* tank formation; **~flugzeug** *n* armo(u)red plane; **~funker** *m* tank wireless operator; **~funkwagen** *m* armo(u)red radio vehicle; **~gefecht** *n* armo(u)red combat; **~geschoß** *n* armo(u)r-piercing shell (*od* bullet); **~gewölbe** *n* (*Bank*) strong-room, vault;

~glas *n* bullet-proof glass; **~graben** *m* anti-tank ditch, tank-trap; **~granate** *f* armo(u)r-piercing shell; **~handschuh** *m* gauntlet; **~hemd** *n* coat of mail; **~hindernis** *n* tank obstacle; **~jäger** *m pl* anti-tank troops *pl*, tankkiller team; (*Fahrzeug*) tank chaser; **~kabel** *n* armo(u)red cable; **~(kampf)wagen** *m* tank; armo(u)red car; **~knacker** *m* tank buster; **~korps** *n* armo(u)red corps; **~kräfte** *f pl* tank forces *pl*, armo(u)red forces *pl*; **~kreuzer** *m* battle-cruiser, pocket-battleship; **~kuppel** *f* armo(u)red cupola; turret of tank; **~landungsboot** *n* tank landing craft; **~mine** *f* anti-tank mine; **~n** *tr* to armo(u)r; (*Schiff*) to plate; (*bewaffnen*) to arm; *r* to arm o. s., to put on armo(u)r; **~platte** *f* armo(u)r plate; **~regiment** *n* tank (*od* armo(u)red regiment; **~schiff** *n* armo(u)red ship, capital ship; **~schlacht** *f* tank battle; **~schrank** *m* safe, strongbox; **~schreck** *m* (*Raketenwerfer*) *Am* bazooka; **~schütze** *m* private in a tank unit; tank gunner; **~spähtrupp** *m* armo(u)red reconnaissance unit; **~spähwagen** *m* armo(u)red (scouting) car; **~sperre** *f* anti-tank obstacle; **~sprenggranate** *f* armo(u)r piercing shell; **~truppe** *f* tank corps; **~truppen** *f pl* armo(u)red troops *pl*; **~turm** *m* armo(u)red turret, gun-turret, tank turret; **~ung** *f* armo(u)r-plating; plate lining; **~vorstoß** *m* armo(u)red thrust; **~waffe** *f* tank force; **~wagen** *m* armo(u)red car; **~wart** *m* tank mechanic; **~werk** *n* armo(u)red fort; **~weste** *f* armo(u)r; **~wrack** *n* wrecked tank; **~zerstörer** *m* combat car; **~zerstörtrupp** *m* tank-killer team; **~zug** *m* armo(u)red train.

Päonie *f bot* peony.

Papa *m* papa; *fam* dad(dy), pop.

Papagei *m* parrot; **~enkrankheit** *f* psittacosis.

Papier *n* paper, **~e** *pl com* securities *pl*, stocks *pl*; (*Aktie*) shares *pl*; (*Wechsel*) bill; (*Urkunde*) documents *pl*; (*Ausweis*) identity papers *pl*; *holzhaltiges ~* ligneous paper; *holzfreies ~* paper free from cellulose; *geripptes, geschöpftes ~* laid, handmade paper; *liniiertes ~* ruled paper; *ein Bogen ~* a sheet of paper; *zu ~ bringen* to write down, to put on paper; *in ~ einwickeln* to wrap up in paper; **~abfall** *m* paper waste; **~abfälle** *m pl* waste-paper; **~bogen** *m* sheet of paper; **~brei** *m* paper pulp; **~en** *a* (of) paper; *fig* imaginary; **~fabrik, ~mühle** *f* paper factory (*od* mill); **~~ation** *f* manufacture of paper; **~geld** *n* paper money, *Am fam* greenbacks *pl*, fiat money, (*verächtlich*) rag; (*Geldschein*) note, *Am* bill; **~~tasche** *f* note-book, *Am* bill-book; **~handel** *m* paper trade; stationery; **~händler** *m* stationer; **~handlung** *f* stationer's shop, *Am* stationary; **~korb** *m* waste-paper basket, *Am* wastebasket; **~krieg** *m* red tape, paper work; **~laterne** *f* Chinese lantern, **~manschette** *f* cover to hide flower-pot; **~maché** *n* papier-maché; **~rolle** *f* paper roll, web of paper; **~~nhalter** *m* tape roll holder; **~sack** *m* paper bag; **~schlange** *f* paper streamer; **~schnitzel** *n pl* scrap of paper; **~serviette** *f* paper napkin; **~streifen** *m* paper strip; **~tüte** *f* paper-bag; **~umschlag** *m* paper wrapping; **~währung** *f* paper currency; **~waren** *f pl* stationery; **~zeichen** *n* watermark.

Papist *m* papist; **~isch** *a* papistic, popish.

Papp *m* (*Brei*) pap; (*Kleister*) paste; **~arbeit** *f* pasteboard work; **~band** *m* pasteboard-binding, (book) in boards; **~deckel** *m* pasteboard; **~e** *f* pasteboard; (*Karton*) cardboard; (*Brei, Kleister*) paste; *das ist nicht von ~!* *fam* that's nothing to sneeze at! *er ist nicht von ~* (*fam*) he's not made of sugar; **~en** *tr, itr* to paste, to stick; **~~stiel** *m fig* trifle; *für e-n ~~stiel fig* for a song; **~erlapapp!** *interj* fiddlesticks! nonsense! rubbish! **~ig** *a* sticky; pasty, doughy; **~karton** *m*, **~schachtel** *f* paperboard box, carton; **~schnee** *m* pasty snow.

Pappel *f* poplar; **~weide** *f* black poplar.

päppeln *tr* to feed; (*verzärteln*) to coddle.

Paprika *m bot* capsicum; (*Gewürz*) paprika; red pepper.

Papst *m* pope; **~krone** *f*, **~mütze** *f* tiara; **~tum** *n* Papacy; (*verächtlich*) Popery; **~würde** *f* papal dignity.

päpstlich *a* papal, pontifical; (*verächtlich*) popish.

Parabel *f* parable; *math* parabola.

Parade *f* parade, show; *mil* review; (*Abwehr*) parry, ward; *e-e ~ abnehmen mil* to hold a review; **~marsch** *m* march past; **~pferd** *n* parade-horse; *fig* show-boy; **~platz** *m* parade-ground; **~schritt** *m* drill-step, goose-step; **~uniform** *f* full-dress uniform, gala uniform.

paradieren *itr* to parade, to make a show.

Para|dies *n* paradise; **~~apfel** *m* tomato; **~~vogel** *m* bird of paradise; **~diesisch** *a* paradisiac(al), *fig* heavenly, delightful; **~digma** *n* paradigm, model; **~dox** *a* paradoxical; **~doxon** *n* paradox.

Paraffin *n* white wax; paraffin wax; **~kerze** *f* paraffin candle.

Paragraph *m* section; paragraph; (*Zeichen*) section-mark; **~enreiter** *m* litigious (*od* pettifogging) person; **~enzeichen** *n* section-mark.

parallel *a* parallel; **~e** *f* parallel; **~ogramm** *n* parallelogram; **~schalten** *tr* to connect in parallel, to shunt, to tee together; **~schaltung** *f el* connection in parallel, shunt connection.

Paraly|se *f* paresis, palsy; (*auch fig*) paralysis; **~sieren** *tr* to paralyse; **~tiker** *m*, **~tisch** *a* paralytic.

Para|nuß *f* Brazil-nut; **~phe** *f* paraph, flourish; **~phieren** *tr* to paraph, to sign with a flourish; **~phrase** *f* paraphrase, lengthy commentary; **~sit** *m* parasite; **~~isch** *a* parasitic(al); **~~jäger** *m aero* parasite jet fighter; **~typhus** *m* paratyphoid fever.

Parenthese *f* parenthesis.

Parforce|jagd *f* hunting on horseback; **~ritt** *m* steeple-chase.

Parfüm *n* perfume, scent; **~erie** *f* perfumery; **~flasche** *f* scent-bottle; **~ieren** *tr* to perfume, to scent; *r* to use perfumes, to scent o. s.; **~zerstäuber** *m* scent-spray, *Am* atomizer.

pari *adv* at par; *über, unter ~* above, below par; **~kurs** *m* par of exchange; **~tät** *f* parity, equality; **~~isch** *a* proportional, pro rata, at par, on an equal footing; in equal numbers.

Paria *m* pariah.

parieren *tr* (*Stoß*) to parry, to ward (off); (*Pferd*) to rein in; *itr* (*gehorchen*) to obey.

Paris|er *m*, **~~in** *f* Parisian; **~ienne** *f typ* ruby, *Am* agate.

Park *m* park; grounds *pl*; (*Lager*) depot, dump, distributing point; **~anlagen** *f pl* park; **~aufseher** *m* park-keeper; **~en** *tr, itr mot* to park; *~~ verboten!* no parking! **~platz** *m* parking place (*od* lot *od* space), car park; (*Wohnwagen*) trailer park; **~verbot** *n* "no parking".

Parkett *n* inlaid floor, parquet(ry); *theat* stalls *pl*, *Am* parquet; **~boden** *m* inlaid (*od* parquet) floor; **~ieren** *tr* to parquet; **~platz** *m* stall; **~wachs** *n* floor wax.

Parlament *n* parliament; *das ~ auflösen* to dissolve parliament; *das ~ einberufen* to convene parliament; *e-n Sitz im ~ haben* to hold a seat in Parliament; *ins ~ gewählt werden* to enter (*od* to go into) Parliament; **~är** *m* bearer of a flag of truce; **~~flagge** *f* flag of truce; **~arier** *m* parliamentarian; **~arisch** *a* parliamentary; **~ieren** *itr* to parley, to negotiate; **~sbeschluß** *m* vote of parliament; **~sdauer** *f* session; **~sferien** *pl* recess(ing); **~sgebäude** *n* the Houses of Parliament; parliament building, *Am* Statehouse; **~sschluß** *m* prorogation of parliament; **~ssitzung** *f* sitting of parliament; **~sverhandlung** *f* parliamentary debate (*od* proceedings *pl*).

Parnaß *m* Parnassus.

Parodie *f* parody; **~ren** *tr* to parody.

Parole *f* watchword, password, parole; *pol* slogan.

Partei *f* party; (*Parteiung*) faction; (*Haus*) tenant; *jur* side; *~ ergreifen* to take sides, to side with; *~ nehmen für* to take o.'s. part; *e-r ~ beitreten* to join a party; *in e-r Sache ~ sein* to be biased in a matter; *nicht beteiligte ~* third party; *schuldige ~* party in fault; *vertragschließende ~* contracting party; *herrschende ~* party in power; **~abzeichen** *n* party badge; **~anwärter** *m* provisional party member, candidate; **~ausschuß** *m* steering committee of a party; **~außenseiter** *m Am* maverick, dissenter; **~bonze** *m* party-boss, *Am* caucuser; **~buch** *n* party-book, membership card of a party; **~direktive** *f* party line; **~disziplin** *f* party-discipline; *~~ halten* to follow the party line; **~führer** *m* party-leader; **~gänger** *m* partisan; *ein strammer ~~* a steadfast partisan, *Am* a stalwart; **~genosse** *m* member of a party; party-comrade; **~gliederung** *f* party organization; **~grundsatz** *m* article of the platform of a political party, *Am* plank; **~isch, ~lich** *a* partial, biased; one-sided; unfair; **~lichkeit** *f* partiality; **~kandidat** *m* party nominee; **~kongreß** *m* party-conference, *Am* party convention; **~klüngel** *m* party machine, *Am* caucus; **~leitung** *f* party leadership; **~los** *m* impartial, neutral; *parl* independent, non-party; **~~er** *m Am* fence-man; **~~igkeit** *f* impartiality, neutrality; **~mitglied** *n* party member; **~nahme** *f* partisanship; **~organisation** *f* party organization, *Am* machine; **~programm** *n* party-programme, *Am* platform, party ticket, plank; **~tag** *m* party rally; **~ung** *f* division into parties; **~versammlung** *f* party meeting; caucus; **~zugehörigkeit** *f* party affiliation.

Parterre *n* ground- (*od* first *od* main) floor, *Am* first-floor; *theat* pit, *Am* orchestra (circle); *im ~ wohnen* to live on the ground-floor; *erstes ~* stalls *pl*; **~loge** *f* pit-box.

Partie *f* (*Land~*) excursion; (*Gesellschaft*) party; (*Spiel*) game; (*Tennis*) set; (*Heirat*) match; (*Waren*) lot, parcel; (*als Teil eines Ganzen*) part; *e-e gute ~ machen* to marry a fortune; *sie ist e-e gute ~* she's a good catch;

~ll *a* partial; *adv* part(ial)ly; not entirely; **~ware** *f* job-goods *pl.*
Partikel *f* particle.
Partikular|ismus *m* particularism; **~istisch** *a* particularistic.
Partisan *m* partisan; **~enbewegung** *f* partisan movement.
Part|itur *f* score; **~izip** *n* participle; **~ner** *m* partner; **~~schaft** *f* partnership.
Parze *f* Fatal Sister; *die ~n* the Fates *pl.*
Parzell|e *f* parcel; allotment; plot, *Am* lot; **~ieren** *tr* to parcel out; to divide into lots.
Parzival *m* Percival.
Pasch *m* doublet(s *pl*); **~a** *m* pasha; **~en** *tr, itr* to throw doublets; (*Waren*) to smuggle; **~er** *m* smuggler.
Paspel *m u. f* edging, piping; **~ieren** *tr* to edge with piping.
Paß *m* pass; (*Durchgang*) passage; (*enger Durchgang*) defile; (*Reisepaß*) passport; (*Gangart*) amble; *zu ~e kommen* to serve o.'s. turn; **~amt** *n*, **~büro** *n*, **~stelle** *f* passport-office; **~bild** *n* passport photograph; **~gang** *m* amble; **~gänger** *m* ambling horse; **~kontrolle** *f* examination of passports, passport inspection; **~zwang** *m* compulsory passport system.
Passagier *m* passenger; fare; *blinder ~* dead-head, *mar* stowaway; **~dampfer** *m* passenger steamer; **~flugdienst** *m* air passenger service; **~flugzeug** *n* airliner, passenger airplane; (*mit Düsenmotoren*) jet liner; **~gut** *n* passenger's luggage (*Am* baggage).
Passah *n*, **~fest** *n* Passover.
Passant *m* passer-by; (*Durchreisender*) travel(l)er, *Am* transient.
Passatwind *m* trade-wind.
passen *itr* to fit s.o., to suit; (*geziemen*) to become; (*an rechter Stelle sein*) to be to the purpose; (*Spiel*) to pass; (*warten auf*) to wait for; *zueinander ~* to be well matched; to harmonize; *schlecht ~* to misfit; *genau ~* (*fig*) to dovetail (*zu* into); *r* to be proper, to be seemly; *es paßt mir nicht* it doesn't suit me; *wenn es dir nicht paßt* if you don't like it; *zu e-r Farbe ~* to match a colo(u)r; *der Hut paßt nicht zum Anzug* the hat doesn't go with the suit; *sie ~ nicht zueinander* they are not suited for each other; *sobald es Ihnen paßt* at your earliest convenience; **~d** *a* fit, convenient, suitable; (*treffend*) appropriate, apt; (*kleidsam*) becoming; *e-e dazu ~de Krawatte* a tie to match; *~d machen* to condition; *für ~~ halten* to think proper.
Passepartout *m* (*Hauptschlüssel*) master-key; (*Dauerkarte*) free admission ticket; (*Rahmen*) mount.
passier|bar *a* passable, practicable; **~en** *tr, itr* (*vorbeigehen*) to pass; (*hindurchgehen*) to go through; to cross; (*Küche*) to sieve; (*sich ereignen*) to happen, to occur, to take place; **~schein** *m* permit, pass.
Passion *f* passion; fondness, craze, love; (*Steckenpferd*) hobby; **~iert** *a* passionate, ardent; impassioned; **~swoche** *f* passion week.
passiv *a* passive; *~ n* passive voice; *~er Widerstand* (*der Arbeiterschaft*) ca' canny; **~a, ~en** *pl* liabilities *pl*, debts *pl*; **~ität** *f* passivity; **~seite** *f* left side (of the ledger), liabilities *pl.*
Paste *f* paste.
Pastell *n* pastel; **~farbe** *f* crayon; **~stift** *m* crayon-pencil.
Pastete *f* (meat-, *Am* pot-) pie; pastry; **~nbäcker** *m* pastry-cook.
pasteurisieren *tr* to pasteurize.
Pastille *f* lozenge.
Pastor *m* pastor, vicar; minister.
Pat|e *m* godfather; *~~ f* godmother; (*Förderer*) sponsor; *~~ stehen* to stand godfather (to); to stand sponsor; **~enkind** *n* godchild; **~enstelle** *f* sponsorship; *bei e-m Kinde ~~ vertreten* to act as godfather (*od* godmother) to a child; **~in** *f* godmother.
Patent *n* (letters) patent, licence; *mil* commission; *ein ~ anmelden* to apply for a patent; *angemeldetes ~* pending patent; *ein ~ verletzen* to infringe a patent; *~ a* regular, splendid; **~amt** *n* patent office; **~anmeldung** *f* application for a patent, *Am* caveat; **~anwalt** *m* patent agent, patent solicitor; **~erteilung** *f* patent grant, issue of letters patent; **~fähig** *a* patentable; **~gebühr** *f* patent fee; **~ieren** *tr* to (grant a) patent (to); *~~ lassen* to take out a patent; **~iert** *a* patented; **~inhaber**, **~träger** *m* patentee; **~lösung** *f* pat solution; **~recht** *n* patent right; patent law; **~schrift** *f* patent specification; **~schutz** *m* protection by patent; **~verletzung** *f* patent infringement; **~verschluß** *m* patent stopper, snap-fastener.
Pater *m* father; **~noster** *n* paternoster, the Lord's Prayer; **~~aufzug** *m* paternoster (*od* continuous) lift, hoist; **~~schöpfwerk** *n* paternoster bailing work; **~~werk** *n* bucketchain.
pathetisch *a* (*feierlich*) solemn; elevated, lofty; pathetic; **Pathos** *n* pathos.
Patholog|e *m* pathologist; **~isch** *a* pathological.
Patient *m* (male, female) patient; *stationärer ~* in-patient.
patinieren *tr* to patinate.
Patriarch *m* patriarch; **~alisch** *a* patriarchal.
Patriot *m* patriot; **~isch** *a* patriotic; **~ismus** *m* patriotism.
Patrize *f* top die, punch, slamp.
Patrizier *m* patrician.
Patron *m* patron; protector, *mar* skipper; *ein lustiger ~* a jolly fellow; *ein unangenehmer ~ Am* a tough customer; **~at** *n* patronage; **~in** *f* patroness.
Patrone *f* (*Modell*) model, pattern; *mil* cartridge, *Am* shell; *scharfe ~* ball cartridge; **~nauswerfer** *m* ejector; **~ngurt** *m* cartridge belt; **~nhülse** *f* cartridge case; **~ntasche** *f* cartridge pouch.
Patrouill|e *f* patrol; **~ieren** *itr* to patrol.
patsch! *interj* swash! **~e** *f* (*Hand*) hand; (*Pfütze*) plash; *fig* fix; awkward position; *in der ~~ sitzen* to be in a fix, to be in hot water; *in e-e ~~ geraten* to step into a puddle; *jdn in der ~~ lassen* to leave s. o. in the lurch; **~en** *itr* (*spritzen*) to splash; (*schlagen*) to slap, to smack; **~hand** *f* (tiny) hand; **~naß** *a* soaked to the skin, soaking wet.
patzig *a* saucy, impertinent; rude.
Pauk|e *f* timbal, kettledrum; *fam* lecture, dressing-down; *anat* tympanum; *mit ~n u. Trompeten* with drums beating and trumpets sounding; **~en** *itr* to beat the kettledrum; (*büffeln*) *fam* to swot, to cram; *r* to fight a duel; **~enschlag** *m* beat of the kettledrum; **~enwirbel** *m* roll of the kettledrum; **~er** *m* kettledrummer; (*Lehrer*) crammer; coach; **~~ei** *f* cramming, grinding; (*Zweikampf*) duel; (*Schlägerei*) fight, row.
pausbackig *a* chubby-faced.
Pauschal|betrag *m* global (*od* flat) sum; **~gebühr** *f* lump sum, flat rate; **~preis** *m* flat rate (price), all-in price; **~summe** *f* lump sum; **~tarif** *m* flat-rate tariff.
Paus|e *f* pause, stop; *theat* interval, *Am* intermission; (*Schule*) interval, break, *Am* recess; (*Nachlassen*) lull; *mus* rest; (*Zeichnung*) tracing; traced design; *e-e ~~ einlegen* to pause; *in ~~n* intermittently; **~en** *tr* to trace, to pounce; **~~los** *a* uninterrupted, without pause; **~~zeichen** *n radio* interval, call sign, interval tune, chime, signature, theme; **~ieren** *itr* to pause; **~papier** *n* tracing paper.
Pavian *m* baboon.
Pavillon *m* pavilion.
Pazifis|mus *m* pacifism; **~t** *m* pacifist, advocate of peace.
Pech *n* pitch; cobbler's wax; *fig* bad luck, ill-luck, mishap, mischance, *Am* tough luck, hard luck; *fam* hoodoo; **~artig** *a* pitchy, pitchlike, bituminous; **~blende** *f* pitchblende; **~draht** *m* shoemaker's thread, pitched thread; **~fackel** *f* torch; **~kiefer** *f* pitch pine; **~kohle** *f* pitch coal; **~schwarz** *a* pitch-black; **~strähne** *f* run of ill-luck; **~uran** *n* pitchblende; **~vogel** *m* unlucky person.
Pedal *n* pedal.
Pedant *m* pedant; **~erie** *f* pedantry; **~isch** *a* pedantic, meticulous.
Pedell *m* beadle; (*Schule*) janitor, porter.
Pegel *m* water-ga(u)ge, tide-ga(u)ge; **~stand** *m* water-mark.
Peil|anlage *f aero* direction finder installation; *mar* sounding device; **~antenne** *f* direction finder aerial; **~bake** *f* radio beacon; **~empfänger** *m* directional receiver, direction finder; radio range receiver; **~en** *tr mar* to sound; to ga(u)ge; (*Land*) to take bearings; to take a fix; *sich ~~ lassen* to get WS-bearings; **~er** *m* direction finder; bearer; **~feld** *n* bearing field; *aero* radio range (of an airfield); **~funk** *m* directional radio; **~~er** *m* direction finder operator; **~~empfänger** *m* direction finder, radio-location instrument; **~~sender** *m* radio beacon; **~~station** *f* directional finding station; **~gerät** *n* homing device, wireless direction finder; D/F apparatus; **~grenze** *f* bearing limit; **~karte** *f* great circle map; **~kompaß** *m* bearing-compass; **~linie** *f* line of bearing; **~lot** *n* sounding lead; **~rahmen** *m* direction finding loop, loop antenna; aerial loop; *Abk* D/F-loop; **~sendestation** *f* directional finding station; radio D/F station; **~station** *f* radio range station; directional wireless receiving station; **~stelle** *f* main D/F station; **~strahl** *m* radio bearing beam, beacon course; bearing ray; **~ung** *f mar* sounding, measuring; (*Land*) taking the bearings; *aero* direction-finding; bearings by wireless; radio direction finding, radio bearing; *e-e ~~ vornehmen* to take bearings with direction finder; *~~ erhalten* to receive bearings by wireless; **~zeichen** *n aero* directional signal; directional finding signal.
Pein *f* pain; torture, agony; **~igen** *tr* to torment, to harass; *fig* to distress; **~iger** *m* tormentor; **~lich** *a* (*unangenehm*) embarrassing, painful; (*genau*) scrupulous, meticulous; *jur* capital, penal; *es ist mir sehr ~~, etw zu tun* I hate to do s. th.; **~~keit** *f* painfulness; scrupulousness, exactness, carefulness.
Peitsche *f* whip, scourge, lash; **~n** *tr* to whip, to flog, to lash; *ein Gesetz durch das Parlament ~~* to rush a bill

through the House; **~nhieb** *m* lash, cut with the whip; **~nknall** *m* whip crack; **~nschnur** *f* thong (*od* lash) of a whip; **~nstiel** *m* whip-stick.
pekuniär *a* pecuniary.
Pelerine *f* cape, pelerine.
Pelikan *m* pelican.
Pell|e *f* skin, peel; **~kartoffeln** *f pl* potatoes in their skins (*or* jackets).
Pelz *m* pelt; (*zubereitet*) fur; (*Fell*) skin, hide; (*Mantel*) fur coat; *jdm auf den ~ rücken* to importune s. o.; *mit ~ füttern* to line with fur; **~besatz** *m* fur trimming; **~besetzt, ~gefüttert** *a* trimmed with fur; fur-lined; **~futter** *n* fur lining; **~geschäft** *n* fur shop; **~handel** *m* fur-trade; **~händler** *m* furrier; **~handschuh** *m* furred glove; **~jäger** *m Am* (fur) trapper; **~kragen** *m* fur cape, fur collar; **~mantel** *m* fur coat; **~mütze** *f* fur cap; **~tiere** *n pl* fur-bearing animals *pl*; **~tierzucht** *f* fur farming; **~waren** *f pl*, **~werk** *n* furriery, furs *pl*, skins *pl*, peltry; **~weste** *f* fur waistcoat.
Pendel *n* pendulum; **~betrieb, ~verkehr** *m aero, rail* shuttle-service (*od* traffic); *Zug im ~~* shuttle-train; *Flugzeug im ~~* shuttle-plane; **~bewegung** *f* movement of pendulum; gyratory movement; **~gleichrichter** *m el* vibrating rectifier; **~n** *itr* to oscillate, to swing, to vibrate, to undulate; **~rahmen** *m* cradle frame; **~säge** *f* pendulum saw; **~schwingung** *f* oscillation, swing; **~tür** *f* swinging-door; **~uhr** *f* pendulum clock; **~zug** *m* shuttle-train.
Pendler *m* commuter
Penn|al *n* (secondary) school; **~äler** *m* schoolboy; **~bruder** *m sl* tramp; *Am sl* bum; **~e** *f* (*Herberge*) doss-house; *sl* (*Schule*) (secondary) school; **~en** *itr fam* to sleep.
Pension *f* (*Ruhegehalt*) pension; *mil* retired pay; *mit ~ verabschiedet* pensioned off; (*Hotel*) boarding-house; (*Schule*) boarding-school; *billige ~* doss-house, *Am* flophouse; *in ~ sein* to board (*bei* with); (*pensioniert*) to be retired; **~är** *m* pensioner; boarder; **~at** *n* boarding-school; **~ieren** *tr* to pension (off); *mil* to put on half pay; **~sberechtigt** *a* entitled to a pension; **~skasse** *f* pensionary fund; **~spreis** *m* (*für Hotel*) charge for boarding; board.
Pensum *n* task, lesson.
Pentagramm *n* pentacle.
per *prp* by, per; *~ Adresse* care of, *Abk* c/o; *~ Post* by post; **~fekt** *a* perfect, accomplished; (*Vertrag*) concluded; *~~ n* perfect tense; **~fid** *a* perfidious, insidious; **~~ie** *f* perfidy; **~forieren** *tr* to perforate.
Pergament *n* parchment; vellum; **~papier** *n* vellum-paper.
Period|e *f* (*Zeitabschnitt*) period; *geol* age; *gram* phrase, period; *mus* period; *med* menstruation, monthly courses *pl*; *el* cycle; period, phase; *parl* duration of a session; **~isch** *a* periodic(al); *~er Dezimalbruch* recurring decimal; *~~ erscheinende Zeitschrift* periodical; *~~ wiederkehren* to cycle.
Peripherie *f* periphery; circumference; (*Stadt*) outskirts *pl*.
Perl|e *f* pearl; (*künstlich*) bead; *fig* gem; (*Wasser~~*) bubble; **~en** *itr* to sparkle; to effervesce; to form bubbles; **~enfischer** *m* pearl-fisher; **~enkette, ~enschnur** *f* pearl necklet, string of pearls; **~farben** *a* pearl-coloured; **~grau** *a* pearl-gray; **~huhn** *n* guinea-fowl; **~muschel** *f* pearl-oyster; **~mutter** *f* mother-of-pearl; **~schrift** *f typ* pearl.
perman|ent *a* permanent; **~enz** *f* permanence.
Per|pendikel *m, n math* perpendicular; (*Pendel*) pendulum; **~petuum mobile** *n* perpetual motion; **~plex** *a* dum(b)-founded; **~ron** *m* platform; **~senning** *f* tarpaulin.
Pers|er *m* Persian; **~ianer** *m* (*Pelz*) Persian lamb; (*Mantel*) Persian lamb coat; **~isch** *a* Persian; **~ien** *n* Persia.
Person *f* person; (*Persönlichkeit*) personage, great person, somebody; *theat* character, role, part; *jur* juridical person, corporation; (*Einzelwesen*) individual; fellow; *in ~* in person, personally; *ich für meine ~* I for my part; **~al** *n* (*Angestellten*) staff, personnel, employees *pl*; officials *pl*; (*Dienerschaft*) servants, attendants *pl*; *fliegendes ~* air crews *pl*; *mit ~~ versehen* to staff; *nicht genügend mit ~~ versehen* understaffed; **~~abbau** *m* reduction of staff; **~~abteilung** *f* staff department, personnel division (*od* department); **~~akte** *f* personnel file, personnel records *pl*; **~~angaben** *f pl* personal data *pl*; **~~ausweis** *m* identity card; identification papers *pl*; **~~beschreibung** *f* description of a person; **~~bestand** *m* number of personnel; **~~büro** *n* personnel office; **~~chef** *m* personnel (*od* staff) manager; **~~daten** *pl* personal data *pl*; **~~ien** *pl* particulars *pl* about a person; identification of s. o.; **~~politik** *f* personnel policy; **~~pronomen** *n* personal pronoun; **~~union** *f* personal union; **~enaufnahme** *f phot* portrait; **~enaufzug** *m* passenger-lift; **~enbahnhof** *m* passenger-station; **~enbeförderung** *f* conveyance of passengers; **~endampfer** *m* passenger-boat; **~en- u. Güterverkehr** *m* passengers and goods traffic; **~en(kraft)wagen** *m* passenger car, passenger vehicle; motor-car; **~enluftverkehr** *m* passenger flying; air passenger service; **~enschaden** *m* personal damage; **~enstand** *m* (personal) status; **~enverkehr** *m* passenger traffic; **~enverzeichnis** *n* register of persons; *theat* dramatis personae; **~enwagen** *m rail* passenger-carriage, *Am* coach, (*erster Klasse*) first class (*od* parlor) car; *mot* passenger car, motor-car; **~enzug** *m* passenger (*od* local) train, parliamentary train, *Am* accommodation train; **~ifizieren** *tr* to personify; to impersonate.
persönlich *a* personal; *adv* personally, in person; *~! (Brief)* private! **~keit** *f* personality, individuality, personal character; (*bedeutender Mensch*) great person, personage.
Perspektiv|e *f* perspective; *fig* prospect, chance; **~isch** *a* perspective.
Peru *n* Peru; **~aner** *m*, **anisch** *a* Peruvian; **~balsam** *m* Peruvian balsam.
Perücke *f* (peri)wig; **~nmacher** *m* wig-maker.
pervers *a* perverse; **~ität** *f* perversity.
Pessimis|mus *m* pessimism; **~t** *m* pessimist, *Am fam* calamity howler; **~tisch** *a* pessimistic.
Pest, ~ilenz *f* pestilence; (*Landplage*) plague; (*Epidemie*) epidemic; **~artig** *a* pestilential; **~beule** *f* plague-boil; *fig* plague-spot; **~hauch** *m* pestilential masma; **~krank** *a* infected with the plague.
Peter *m* Peter; **~spfennig** *m* Rome-scot, Peter's-penny; **~silie** *f* parsley.
Petit(schrift) *f typ* brevier.
Petroleum *n* oil; paraffin; petroleum; *Am* (mineral) oil; kerosene; **~gesellschaft** *f* petroleum (*Am* oil) company; **~haltig** *a* containing petroleum; **~heizung** *f* heating with petroleum; **~kocher** *m* petroleum-stove; **~lampe** *f* oil-lamp, *Am* kerosene lamp; **~quelle** *f* oil-well; **~rückstand** *m* masut.
Petschaft *n* seal, signet.
Petz *m* (*Bär*) Bruin; **~e** *f* bitch; **~en** *itr* to inform, to tell tales.
Pfad *m* path; **~finder** *m* Boy-Scout; *aero mil* pathfinder (plane); **~~in** *f* Girl-Scout; (Girl-Guide); *Am auch* campfire girl; **~los** *a* pathless.
Pfaffe *m* priest; parson; **~ntum** *n* clericalism.
pfäffisch *a* priestlike; priest-ridden.
Pfahl *m* stake; (*Stange*) pole; (*Pfosten*) post; (*Stütz~*) prop; (*Grund~*) pile; (*Pflock*) picket; (*Zaun*) pale; (*Schand~*) pillory; *e-n ~ einrammen* to drive a pile; *zwischen meinen vier Pfählen* on my own ground, in my own house; **~bau** *m* pile-work; **~bauten** *m pl* lake-dwellings *pl*; **~bürger** *m* citizen; (*verächtlich*) Philistine; **~dorf** *n* lake-village; **~jochbrücke** *f* pile bridge; **~muschel** *f* pile-worm; **~rost** *m* pile-support; **~werk** *n* paling, pile-work; palisade; **~wurzel** *f* tap-root; **~zaun** *m* paling, stockade.
pfählen *tr* to fasten with stakes; to prop; (*Strafe*) to impale.
Pfalz *f* imperial palace; *geog* the Palatinate; **~graf** *m* Count Palatine.
Pfand *n* pawn; pledge; (*Hinterlegung*) deposit; (*Unterpfand*) gage; (*Bürgschaft*) security; (*Hypothek*) mortgage; (*Spiel*) forfeit; *zum ~e (ein)setzen* to pawn; to pledge; *auf Pfänder leihen* to lend upon pawn; *ein ~ einlösen* to redeem a pledge; **~brief** *m* mortgage (bond); **~darlehen** *n* loan on security; **~geschäft, ~haus** *n* pawnshop, pawn office, *Am* loan-office; **~gläubiger** *m* mortgagee; lienholder; **~hinterlegung** *f* deposit; **~inhaber** *m* pawnee, mortgagee; **~leiher** *m* pawnbroker; **~recht** *n* lien; **~schein** *m* pawn ticket; **~schuld** *f* mortgage debt; **~~ner** *m* mortgagor; **~verschreibung** *f* mortgage deed.
pfänd|bar *a* distrainable; attachable, seizable; **~en** *tr* to seize, to distrain, to take in pledge; (*beschlagnahmen*) to impound; **~erspiel** *n* game of forfeits; **~ung** *f* seizure, distraint; *~~ beantragen* to sue for a distraint; **~~sbefehl** *m* distress-warrant; **~~sbeschluß** *m* order of attachment; **~~sverfahren** *n* attachment proceedings *pl*.
Pfann|e *f* pan; (*Siede~*) copper, boiler; (*Brat~*) baking-tin; *anat* socket, acetabulum; (*Ziegel*) pantile; *tech* bearing, bush(ing); seat; socket; (*Gieß~*) (casting) ladle; **~enflicker** *m* tinker; **~enstiel** *m* pan-handle; **~kuchen** *m* pancake; *Berliner ~~* doughnut.
Pfarr|amt *n* ministry, curacy, rectory; **~bezirk** *m* parish; **~dorf** *n* parochial village; **~e, ~ei** *f* parsonage, vicarage; **~er** *m* clergyman; parson; (*engl. Staatskirche*) rector, vicar, curate; (*Dissidenten u. Am*) minister, pastor; (*katholisch*) priest; **~gemeinde** *f* parish; **~haus** *n* rectory, vicarage; parsonage; **~kirche** *f* parish church.
Pfau *m* peacock; **~enauge** *n* peacock-butterfly; **~enfeder** *f* peacock's feather; **~henne** *f* peahen; **~enrad** *n* peacock's fan.
Pfeffer *m* pepper; *da liegt der Hase im ~* there's the rub; that's where the hitch comes in; **~büchse** *f* pepper-box; **~gurke** *f* gherkin; **~kuchen** *m* gingerbread; **~minze** *f* peppermint; **~korn** *n* peppercorn; **~n** *itr* to pepper; *sl* (*werfen*)

to throw; *gepfefferter Preis* exorbitant price; **~nuß** *f* ginger-nut, *Am* ginger-snap; **~streuer** *m* peppershaker.

Pfeife *f* whistle; (*Tabaks~, Boots~*) pipe; (*Quer~*) fife; (*kurze*) cutty; *nach jds ~ tanzen* to dance to s. o.'s. tune; *e-e ~ stopfen* to fill a pipe; **~n** *itr irr* to whistle, to blow a whistle; to pipe; (*Wind, radio*) to howl; *tele* (*Verstärker*) to sing; (*Mäuse*) to squeak; *auf etw ~~* not to care a straw for; not to give a hoot about; *e-m Hund ~~* to whistle to o.'s dog; *auf dem letzten Loch ~~* to be on o.'s last legs; **~ndeckel** *m* pipe-lid; **~nkopf** *m* pipe-bowl; **~nrohr** *n* pipe-tube; **~ntopf** *m* whistling kettle; **~nstopfer** *m* pipe-stopper; **~r** *m* whistler; *mus* fife-player piper.

Pfeil *m* arrow, (*Wurf~*) dart; *poet* shaft; **~en** *tr aero* to sweep-back; **~flügel** *m aero* sweepback wing; **~form** *f aero* sweepback; **~förmig** *a* arrowshaped; *aero* backswept; **~gerade** *a* straight as an arrow; **~gift** *n* arrow-poison; **~schnell** *a* swift as an arrow; **~schütze** *m* archer; **~spitze** *f* arrowhead; **~stellung** *f aero* sweepback; **~verzahnung** *f tech* herringbone gearing; **~winkel** *m aero* angle of sweepback.

Pfeiler *m* pillar; (*Brücke*) pier; (*Pfosten*) prop, post; **~bogen** *m arch* pier-arch; **~brücke** *f* bridge resting on piers.

Pfennig *m fig* penny; **~fuchser** *m* miser, *fam* pinch-penny; **~~ei** *f* stinginess.

Pferch *m* fold, pen; **~en** *tr* to fold.

Pferd *n* horse; (*Stute*) mare; (*Mähre*) jade; *nicht zugerittenes ~* (*Am*) bronco; (*Turnen*) vaulting horse; long horse; pommelled (*od* wooden) horse; *zu ~e* on horseback; *sich aufs hohe ~ setzen fig* to ride the high horse, *Am* to be high-hat; *keine zehn ~e bringen mich dahin* a team of wild horses couldn't drag me there; *mit frischen ~en versehen* to remount; **~ebespannt** *a* horse-drawn; **~ebremse** *f* horse-fly, cleg; **~edecke** *f* saddle-cloth; **~efahrzeug** *n* horse-drawn vehicle; **~efleisch** *n* horse-flesh; **~efuß** *m* (*Teufel*) cloven foot; **~efutter** *n* horse's fodder; **~egeschirr** *n* harness; **~egetrappel** *n* trot of a horse; **~ehändler** *m* horse dealer, *Am* horse trader; **~ehindernisrennen** *n* steeplechase horse race; **~eknecht** *m* groom, ostler; **~ekoppel** *f* paddock; **~ekraft** *f* horse-power (*Abk* HP); **~elänge** *f* length (of a horse); **~emist** *m* horse-dung; **~erennbahn** *f* race-course, *Am* race-track; **~erennen** *n* horse-race (*od* -racing); (*mit Hindernissen*) steeplechase; **~eschwemme** *f* horse-pond; **~estall** *m* stable; **~estärke** *f* metric horsepower; **~ezucht** *f* horse-breeding; **~ezüchter** *m* breeder of horses.

Pfiff *m* whistle; *fig* trick; **~erling** *m bot* chanterelle; *fig* trifle; *keinen ~~ wert* not worth a fig; *ich würde keinen ~~ darum geben* I wouldn't give a straw for it; **~ig** *a* cunning, sly; **~~keit** *f* cunningness, artfulness; **~ikus** *m* sly fellow.

Pfingst|abend *m* Whitsun-eve; **~en** *pl*, **~fest** *n* Whitsuntide; **~montag** *m* Whit-Monday; **~rose** *f* peony; **~sonntag** *m* Whitsunday, Pentecost; **~woche** *f* Whitsun-week.

Pfirsich *m* peach; **~blüte** *f* peach blossom; **~bowle** *f* peach-cup; **~eis** *n* pêche Melba; **~kern** *m* peach-stone *Am* peach pit.

Pflanz|e *f* plant **~en** *tr* to plant, to set, to lay out; **~~asche** *f* plant ashes *pl*; **~~butter** *m* vegetable butter; **~~decke** *f* covering of vegetation; **~~dünger** *m* plant food; **~~eiweiß** *n* vegetable albumin; vegetable protein; **~~erde** *f* vegetable mo(u)ld, humus; **~~erzeugnis** *n* plant (*od* vegetable) product; **~~faser** *f* vegetable fibre (*Am* fiber); **~~faserstoff** *m* vegetable fibrin; cellulose; **~~fett** *n* vegetable fat; **~~fressend** *a* herbivorous; **~~gattung** *f* genus of plant; **~~kost** *f* vegetable diet; **~~kunde, ~~lehre** *f* botany; **~~leben** *n* vegetable life; plant life; **~~öl** *n* vegetable oil; **~~reich** *n* vegetable kingdom; flora; **~~saft** *m* vegetable juice, sap; **~~sammlung** *f* herbarium; **~~schädling** *m* (plant) pest; **~~schutzmittel** *n* plant protective; **~~wachstum** *n* plant growth, vegetation; **~~zelle** *f* plant cell; **~~zellstoff** *m* cellulose; **~~zucht** *f* plant breeding; **~er** *m* planter; (*Siedler*) settler, colonist; **~lich** *a* vegetable; **~reis** *n* scion; **~schule** *f* nursery; **~stätte** *f* settlement; *fig* hotbed, source; **~ung** *f* plantation; (*Niederlassung*) settlement.

Pflaster *n* (*Straße*) pavement; (*Wund~*) plaster; *englisches ~* court-plaster; (*Heft~*) adhesive (plaster); *ein teueres ~ fig* an expensive place; *ein holperiges ~* a bumpy pavement; **~er** *m* paver; **~n** *tr* to pave; to plaster; **~stein** *m* paving-stone; paving brick, road stone; **~treter** *m* idler, lounger, loafer, loiterer; **~ung** *f* paving.

Pflaume *f* plum; (*getrocknete ~*) prune; **~nbaum** *m* plum-tree; **~nkern** *m* plum-stone; **~nmus** *n* plum-jam.

Pfleg|e *f* (*Körper*) care; (*Kranke*) nursing; (*Kind*) rearing; (*Verwaltung*) administration; (*Kunst, Garten*) cultivation; *tech* (*von Maschinen, Autos, Flugzeugen etc*) maintenance work, maintenance; routine repair work; *in ~~ nehmen* to take charge of; *in ~~ geben* to put out to be nursed; **~ebefohlene(r)** *m* charge; (*Mündel*) ward; **~eeltern** *pl* foster-parents *pl*; **~eheim** *n* nursing home; convalescent home; **~ekind** *n* foster-child; **~emutter** *f* fostermother; **~en** *tr* to take care of, to care for, to attend to, to tend; (*Haar, Äußeres*) to groom; (*Kranken*) to nurse; (*Kind*) to foster, to rear, to bring up; (*liebevoll*) to cherish, to foster; (*Kunst*) to cultivate; (*aufrechterhalten*) to entertain; *tech* to maintain; *itr* (*gewohnt sein*) to be accustomed to, to be used to, to be in the habit of; *r* to take care of o. s.; (*verzärteln*) to pamper o. s.; *er pflegte es oft zu sagen* he often used to say so; *manchmal pflegte er ihm e-n Streich zu spielen* sometimes he would play a joke on him; **~er** *m*, **~erin** *f* nurse; *jur* (*Vormund*) guardian; (*Verwalter*) curator; (*Eigentum*) trustee; **~evater** *m* foster-father; **~lich** *a* careful; **~ling** *m* foster-child; (*Pflegebefohlener*) charge; (*Mündel*) ward; **~schaft** *f jur* guardianship; tutelage; (*Vermögensverwaltung*) trust.

Pflicht *f* duty, moral obligation; (*Zwang*) compulsion, constraint, restraint; (*Verantwortung*) responsibility, accountability, answerability; (*Verpflichtung*) obligation, engagement; (*Amt*) office; *seinen ~en obliegen* to attend to o.'s duty; *es obliegt ihm die ~* he is in duty bound to; *seine ~ verletzen* to fail in o.'s duty; **~arbeit** *f* compulsory work; **~beitrag** *m* contingent; quota; **~bewußt** *a* conscious of o.'s duty; **~eifer** *m* zeal; **~eifrig** *a* zealous in o.'s duties; **~enkreis** *m* sphere of responsibility; responsibilities *pl*; **~erfüllung** *f* performance of a duty; **~exemplar** *n* deposit copy; **~fach** *n* (*Schule*) compulsory subject matter; core; **~gefühl** *n* sense of duty; **~gemäß** *a* dutiful, conformable to duty; as in duty bound; **~getreu** *a* dutiful, conscientious; **~jahr** *n* compulsory domestic service for girls; **~~mädchen** *n* girl enrolled in compulsory domestic service; **~landung** *f aero* compulsory landing; **~schuldig** *a* as in duty bound; obligatory; **~teil** *m* compulsory (*od* legitimate) portion, lawful share; **~treu** *a* conscientious, dutiful; **~treue** *f* devotion to o.'s duty; fidelity; dutifulness; **~vergessen** *a* delinquent, undutiful, disloyal, *Am* derelict; **~~heit** *f* disloyalty, dereliction, delinquency; **~verletzung** *f* neglect of duty; violation of duty; **~versäumnis** *n, f* shortcoming; **~wert** *m* contract value; specification value; **~widrig** *a* undutiful, contrary to duty.

Pflock *m* peg; plug, pin; (*Pfahl*) picket, stake.

pflöcken *tr* to peg, to plug.

pflücken *tr* to pick, to pluck; (*sammeln*) to gather.

Pflug *m* plough, *Am* plow; scraper; **~eisen** *n* co(u)lter; **~schar** *f* ploughshare; **~~bein** *anat* vomer.

pflüg|en to plough, *Am* to plow; to till; **~er** *m* ploughman.

Pförtchen *n* little door, little gate.

Pforte *f* door, gate, entrance; portal; (*Öffnung*) opening; *mar* port(-hole); (*äußere Öffnung*) orifice; *die ~n der Ewigkeit* the portals of eternity.

Pförtner *m* porter, door-keeper; *Am* doorman; (*Hausmeister*) janitor; *anat* pylorus; **~wohnung** *f* (porter's) lodge.

Pfosten *m* post; (*Tür*) jamb; (*Pfahl*) pale, stake; (*Mittelpfosten an Fenstern*) mullion; (*Bohle*) plank.

Pfote *f* paw.

Pfriem *m*, **~e** *f* awl; (*Punze, Dorn*) punch(eon); *typ* bodkin.

Pfropf|(en) *m* (*Stöpsel*) stopper, cork; (*Holz*) plug; (*Watte~*) wad; (*~reis*) graft; *med* thrombus, embolus; (*Blut~*) clot (of blood); (*Tampon*) tampon; **~en** *tr* to cork; to stopper; (*stopfen*) to cram (into), to stuff (full of); (*Obstbäume*) to graft; (*Rosen*) to bud, to inoculate; *gepfropft voll* crammed full, jammed; **~enzieher** *m* corkscrew; **~messer** *n* grafting-knife; **~reis** *n* graft, scion; **~säge** *f* pruning (*od* grafting) saw.

Pfründ|e *f eccl* prebend, living; benefice; *fig* sinecure; **~ner** *m* prebendary; beneficiary, incumbent.

Pfuhl *m* pool; (*Pfütze*) puddle; slough.

Pfühl *n* bolster, pillow; cushion.

pfui! *interj* fie! for shame! pooh! phovey! phew!

Pfund *n* pound (*Abk* lb, *pl* lbs); *~ Sterling* pound (sterling), *Abk* £; **~gewicht** *n* pound-weight; **~ig** *a fam* (*erstklassig*) swell; **~leder** *n* sole leather; **~ssache** *f fam* whopper; **~weise** *adv* by the pound.

pfusch|en *itr* to botch, to bungle; to blunder; (*nachlässig ausführen*) to scamp, to do sloppy work; *in etw ~~* to meddle with, to dabble in; **~er** *m* bungler, botcher; (*Kur~~*) quack; *Am sl* boondoggler, slouch; **~erei, ~arbeit** *f* bungling; scamped work.

Pfütze *f* puddle; (*Tümpel*) pool; (*schlammig*) wallow, mud hole, slough.

Phänomen *n* phenomenon; **~al** *a* phenomenal.

Phant|asie *f* imagination, fancy;

(*schöpferische Kraft*) inventive faculty; (*Träumerei*) reverie; daydream; (*Wahnvorstellung*) chim(a)era, fantastic vision; *mus* fantasia, fantasy; (*Fieber*) ravings *pl*; **~~gebilde** *n* creation of the imagination; **~~reich, ~voll** *a* fanciful; imaginative; **~~ren** *itr med* to be delirious, to ramble, to rave; (*sich ausdenken*) to indulge o.'s imagination, to daydream, to imagine; *mus* to improvise; **~ast** *m* fantast, visionary, dreamer; **~~erei** *f* wild fancy, fantasy, queer illusion; **~~isch** *a* fantastic(al); fanciful; (*großartig*) excellent, first-rate; *Am sl* swell; **~om** *n* phantom. vision.

Pharisä|er *m* Pharisee; self-righteous person; **~~tum** *n* pharisaism; **~isch** *a* pharisaic(al), hypocritical.

Pharma|kologie *f* pharmacology; **~zeut** *m* pharmaceutist, pharmacist; chemist, *Am* druggist; **~~isch** *a* pharmaceutical.

Phase *f el* phase; (*Stadium*) stage; (*Epoche*) epoch; **~nänderung** *f* phase change; **~nausgleich** *m* phase correction; **~ngleichheit** *f* phase balance (*od* coincidence); **~nmesser** *m* phase indicator; **~nschwankung** *f* phase variations *pl*; **~nschwund** *m* phase fading; **~nspannung** *f* star voltage; phase voltage; **~nverschiebung** *f* phase displacement; **~nverzögerung** *f* phase lagging; **~nzahl** *f* number of phases.

Philanthrop *m* philanthropist; **~isch** *a* philanthropic.

Philist|er *m* Philistine; **~erhaft, ~rös** *a* narrow-minded; **~erhaftigkeit** *f* narrow-mindedness.

Philolog *m* philologist; **~ie** *f* philology; **~isch** *a* philological.

Philosoph *m* philosopher; **~ie** *f* philosophy; **~ieren** *itr* to philosophize; **~isch** *a* philosophical.

Phiole *f* phial.

Phlegma *n* phlegm, dul(l)ness, sluggishness; coolness; **~tiker** *m* phlegmatic person; **~tisch** *a* phlegmatic.

Phonet|ik *f* phonetics *pl*; **~isch** *a* phonetic.

Phönix *m* phenix.

Phönizier *m* Phoenician.

Phonotruhe *f* radiogram, *Am* radio-phonograph.

Phosgen *n* phosgene, carbonyl chloride.

Phosphat *n* phosphate; **~dünger** *m* phosphate fertilizer.

Phosphor *m* phosphorus; **~brandbombe** *f*, **~kanister** *m* phosphorus incendiary bomb; **~eszieren** *itr* to phosphoresce; **~eszierend** *a* phosphorescent; **~ig** *a* phosphorous; **~munition** *f* tracer ammunition; **~säure** *f* phosphoric acid; **~vergiftung** *f* phosphorus poisoning; **~wasserstoff** *m* hydrogen phosphoride, phosphorus hybride.

Photo|album *n* photo album; **~apparat** *m* camera; (*Kleinbild*) miniature camera; **~ausrüstung** *f* photo equipment (*od* outfit); **~bericht** *m* camera chronicle; **~chemie** *f* photochemistry; **~chromie** *f* photochromy; **~dienst** *m* photo finishing service; **~elektrisch** *a* photo-electric; *~~er Belichtungsmesser* photo-electric exposure meter; **~gen** *a* photogenic; **~gewehr** *n* camera gun; **~grammetrie** *f* photographic surveying, photogrammetry; **~graph** *m* photog(rapher), cameraman; **~~enapparat** *m* camera; **~graphie** *f* (*Kunst*) photography; (*Bild*) picture, photo(-graph); (*Momentaufnahme*) snapshot; (*Bild ohne Bewegung*) still; *aero* photogram; **~~ren** *tr* to (take a) photograph, *Am* to take a picture; *sich ~~ren lassen* to have o.'s photo(graph) taken; (*sich stellen*) to pose for a photopraph; *zum ~~ren hervorragend geeignet* photogenic; **~~rgesicht** *n* photogenic face; **~graphisch** *a* photographic; *~~es Atelier* photographic studio; **~gravüre** *f* photo-engraving; **~händler** *m* photo-dealer; **~kopie** *f* photographic copy, photoprint; **~~ren** *tr* to photostat; **~lampe** *f* photoflood lamp; **~lithographie** *f* photolithography; **~meter** *n* photometer; **~metrie** *f* photometric recording, photometry; **~metrisch** *a* photometric; **~modell** *n* model; cover girl; **~montage** *f* photographic layout; photomontage; **~reportage** *f* photographic reportage; **~typie** *f* collotype; phototypy; **~wettbewerb** *m* photo (-graphic) contest; **~zelle** *f* photoelectric cell.

Phrase *f* phrase; trite remark, cliché, *Am fam* bromide; *~n dreschen* to spin fine-sounding sentences; **~ndrescher** *m* phrase-monger; would-be fine speaker; **~~ei** *f* claptrap; **~nhaft** *a* bombastic, grandiloquent; **~ologie** *f* phraseology.

Physik *f* physics *pl mit sing*; natural philosophy; **~alisch** *a* physical; **~er** *m* physicist; **~um** *n med* preliminary examination (*Abk* prelim).

Physio|gnomie *f* physiognomy; **~logie** *f* physiology; **~logisch** *a* physiological.

physisch *a* physical; material, bodily.

Pian|ino *n* cottage piano; upright piano; **~ist** *m* pianist; **~o(forte)** *n* piano(forte).

pichen *tr* to pitch; (*Schuhmacher*) to wax.

Pick *m fam* grudge; **~e** *f* pickax(e).

Pickel *m* (*im Gesicht*) pimple; (*Eis~*) pickax(e); **~flöte** *f* piccolo; **~haube** *f* spiked helmet; **~hering** *m* pickled herring, bloater; **~ig** *a* pimply.

picken *itr* to peck, to pick.

Picknick *n* picnic, *Am* basket dinner (*od* lunch); **~koffer** *m Am* outing kit.

pieken *tr fam* to prick; (*Insekt*) to sting.

piep|en, ~sen *itr* (*Vögel*) to cheep, to peep, to chirp; (*zirpen*) to chirrup; (*Mäuse*) to squeak; **~matz** *m* dicky-bird

Pier *m, f* pier, jetty, mole; *am ~ anlegen* to secure to a pier.

piesacken *tr fam* to torment; to pester, to molest, to annoy, to dun, to bully.

Piet|ät *f* piety; reverence; regard; **~~los** *a* irreverent; **~~voll** *a* reverent; **~ismus** *m* pietism; cant; **~ist** *m* pietist.

piff paff! *interj* flick!

Pigment *n* pigment; **~bildung** *f* pigment formation; **~ieren** *tr* to pigment; **~papier** *n* carbon paper.

Pik *n* (*Karten*) spade(s *pl*); *~m* (*Groll*) grudge; (*Berg*) peak; **~ant** *a* piquant; *fig* spicy; *~~es Vorgericht* appetizer; *~~e Nachspeise* savoury; **~~erie** *f* spicy story; **~e** *f* pike; *von der ~e auf dienen* to rise from the ranks; **~ee** *m* piqué; **~fein** *a* smart. tiptop, slap-up, dressed-up, *sl* classy; **~ieren** *tr bot* to prick out; **~iert** *a* offended; irritated, vexed; **~kolo** *m* boy waiter, *Am* bell-hop; **~~flöte** *f* piccolo.

Pikrinsäure *f* picric acid.

Pile *f* (*Atombrenner*) atomic pile; nuclear reactor; **~gitter** *n phys* lattice.

Pilger *m* pilgrim; **~fahrt** *f* pilgrimage; **~n** *itr* to go on a pilgrimage, to wander; **~schaft** *f* pilgrimage; **~stab** *m* pilgrim's staff.

Pille *f* pill; **~nschachtel** *f* pill box.

Pilot *m* pilot; *~ e-r Verkehrsmaschine* airline pilot; *automatischer ~* automatic pilot, *fam* George; **~ballon** *m* sounding (*od* registering *od* pilot) balloon.

Pilz *m* fungus; (*eßbarer*) mushroom; *giftiger ~* toadstool; (*Rauchsäule*) smoke column after explosion; *wie ~e aus der Erde schießen* to pop up like mushrooms; **~förmig** *a* fungiform; **~isolator** *m* mushroom (*od* umbrella) insulator; **~kunde** *f* mycology; **~lautsprecher** *m* mushroom loud-speaker; **~tötend** *a* fungicidal; **~vergiftung** *f* poisoning by mushrooms.

pimpelig *a* sickly; soft; flabby; effeminate; whining.

Pimpf *m* (*Junge*) cub.

Pinasse *f* pinnace.

Pinguin *m* penguin.

Pinie *f* stone-pine.

pinkeln *itr vulg* to piddle, to make water.

Pinne *f* peg, pin; *mar* tiller; (*Hammer*) peen; (*Zapfen*) pivot, tenon.

Pinscher *m* terrier.

Pinsel *m* brush; (*Maler~*) paint-brush; (*feiner*) (hair-)pencil; (*Einfalts~*) noodle, simpleton, dunce; **~ei** *f* daub(ing); **~führung** *f* touch; **~n** *itr, tr* to paint; (*schmieren*) to daub; **~stiel** *m* pencil-stick; **~strich** *m* stroke of the brush.

Pinzette *f* tweezers *pl* (*eine ~* a pair of tweezers); pincette.

Pionier *m* pioneer; sapper, engineer; (*Bahnbrecher*) *Am* trail-blazer; **~arbeit** *f* spade-work, pioneer work; **~bataillon** *n* pioneer battalion, *Am* combat-engineer battalion; **~park** *m* pioneer park, *Am* combat-engineer equipment dump; **~truppe** *f* engineers, *Am* engineer corps.

Pips *m med* pip.

Pirat *m* pirate; **~erie** *f*, **~entum** *n* piracy.

Pirol *m* yellow thrush, oriole.

Pirsch *f* hunting, deer-stalking; **~en** *itr* to hunt, to stalk deer.

pissen *itr vulg* to make water, to piss.

Pistazie *f* pistachio.

Piste *f* beaten track; *aero* runway.

Pistole *f* pistol, *Am* gun, automatic, shooter; *wie aus der ~ geschossen* like a bolt from the blue; *antworten wie aus der ~ geschossen* to answer quick as a flash; *gesicherte ~* pistol with safety on; **~ngriff** *m* butt-end of a pistol; **~nschuß** *m* pistol-shot; **~ntasche** *f* holster.

*

plack|en *tr* to plague; (*sich mühen*) to drudge, to toil; **~erei** *f* drudgery.

pläd|ieren *itr* to plead; to argue; **~oyer** *n* pleading; address, speech.

Plage *f* plague, torment, vexation; worry; (*Mißstand*) nuisance; *Am fam* worriment; **~geist** *m* plague, tormentor; bore; **~n** *tr* to plague, to pester, to harass; (*belästigen*) to bother; (*bedrücken*) to grind; (*quälen*) to haunt; *r* to drudge, to slave, to grub; (*sich abmühen*) to struggle, to plod, to trouble o. s. (*mit* with).

Plagiat *n* plagiarism; *ein ~ begehen* to plagiarize; **~or** *m*.plagiarist.

Plakat *n* placard, bill, poster; *ein ~ ankleben* to post a bill, to placard; *~ ankleben verboten!* stick no bills! **~ankleber** *m* billposter, billsticker; **~anschlag** *m* bill-posting (*od* sticking), placarding; **~fläche** *f* hoarding, *Am* billboard; **~ieren** *tr* to stick (*od* post) bills; **~künstler, ~zeichner** *m* poster artist, designer; **~reklame** *f* poster

advertising; **~säule** *f* advertisement pillar; **~träger** *m* sandwich-man.
Plakette *f* plaque; badge.
Plan *m* plan; (*Absicht*) intention; design; (*Vorhaben*) project, scheme; (*Anschlag*) plot; (*Entwurf*) draft; (*Anlage*) layout; (*Blaupause*) blueprint; (*Landkarte*) map; (*Stunden~, Fahr~*) time-table, schedule; (*graphische Darstellung*) diagram; (*Ebene*) plain, *math* plane; (*Malerei*) ground; ~ *a* (*eben*) level, flat; *e-n ~ durchführen* to follow out a plan; *e-n ~ entwerfen* to make a plan; *e-n ~ fassen* to think out a plan; *auf dem ~ erscheinen* to turn up; **~e** *f* awning; tarpaulin; cover; **~en** *tr, itr* to plan, to project, to scheme; (*ausarbeiten*) to map out; (*festlegen*) to lay-out, to arrange; to schedule; **~feuer** *n mil* barrage fire; directed map fire; **~film** *m phot* flat film; **~gemäß, ~mäßig** *a* according to plan (*od* schedule); systematic, methodical; **~ieren** *tr* to plane, to smooth, to level, to planish; (*Papier*) to size; **~ierraupe** *f* caterpillar, grader; **~~n-schlepper** *m* angledozer; **~imetrie** *f* planimetry; **~konkav** *a* plano-concave; **~konvex** *a* plano-convex; **~los** *a* without a fixed plan, aimless; desultory; at random; **~losigkeit** *f* lack of plan; **~pause** *f* map tracing; **~quadrat** *n* map square; **~schießen** *n* calculated firing; **~spiegel** *m* plane mirror; **~stelle** *f* permanent established post; **~übergang** *m rail* level crossing; **~ung** *f* planning, plan; *nicht über die ~~ hinausgehen* not to go beyond the planning stage; *in ~~ sein* to be in the design stage; **~voll** *a* methodical, systematic; carefully planned; **~wagen** *m* covered wag(g)on; **~wirtschaft** *f* planned economy, economic planning; **~zeiger** *m* coordinate scale.
Pläneschmied *m* schemer.
Planet *m* planet; asteroid; **~arium** *n* planetarium, orrery; **~engetriebe** *n mot* epicyclic gear; (*Tank*) planet drive; **~ensystem** *n* planetary system.
Planke *f* plank, board.
Plänkel|ei *f* skirmishing; **~n** *itr* to skirmish.
Plantage *f* plantation.
Plankton *n* plankton; **~netz** *n* dredge, plankton net.
Plan(t)sch|becken *n* paddling-pool; **~en** *itr* to splash, to dabble, to paddle.
Plapper|ei *f* babbling; **~maul** *n* chatterbox; **~n** *itr* to prattle, to babble, to chatter; to patter.
plärren *itr* to blubber; (*schlecht singen*) to bawl.
Plasti|k *f* plastic art; (*Bildwerk*) sculpture; *med* plastic; **~sch** *a* plastic.
Plastilin *n* plasticine.

*

Platane *f* plane-tree, *Am* sycamore, button-ball (*od* -wood).
Platin *n* platinum; **~blond** *a* platinum-blonde; **~draht** *m* platinum wire; **~erz** *n* platinum ore; **~haltig** *a* platiniferous.
plätschern *itr* to splash, to dabble; (*Bach*) to ripple, to murmur.
platt *a* (*eben*) flat, level; (*abgeschmackt*) insipid, silly, vapid; (*gewöhnlich*) low, vulgar; (*überrascht*) dum(b)founded, bewildered, confused; **~deutsch** *a* Low German; **~e** *f* plate; (*Metall*) sheet; (*Tisch*) top; leaf; (*Stein*) flag; (*Felsen*) ledge, slab; (*Hochebene*) plateau, table-land, upland; *phot* plate; (*Lichtbild~~*) slide; (*Grammophon*) record, dis(k); (*Tablett*) tray, salver; (*Gericht*) dish; (*Fleisch*) platter; (*Kopf*) bald head; *dünne ~~* lamina; *kalte ~~* cold meat(s *pl*); *lichtempfindliche ~~* sensitized plate; **~enabnützung** *f* record wear; **~enabzug** *m* stereotyped proof; **~endrehung** *f* revolution of gramophone turntable; **~endruck** *m* printing from plates; **~engeräusch** *n radio* surface noise; **~enkassette** *f* plate magazine; **~enkondensator** *m* plate condenser; **~enrille** *f* groove (of record); **~enspieler** *m* record player; *radio* turntable; *Radio mit eingebautem ~~* record-player radio; radiogram, *Am* radio-phonograph; **~enteller** *m* turntable (of gramophone); **~enwechsler** *m* automatic record changer; **~erdings** *adv* absolutely, decidedly; **~form** *f* platform; *aero* tarmac; **~~redner** *m Am fam* soap-boxer; **~~wagen** *m rail* platform car; *Am* flat car, **~fuß** *m* flat-foot; *mot* puncture, blow-out; *~~ haben mot* to get a flat tire; **~~einlage** *f* arch-support, foot-easer, pad; **~füßig** *a* flat-footed; **~heit** *f* flatness, staleness; (*unbedeutende Redensart*) platitude, triteness, dul(l)ness, *Am fam* bromide; **~ieren** *tr* to plate.
Plätt|brett *n* ironing-board; **~eisen** *n* (smoothing-)iron, flatiron; **~en** *tr* to iron, to press; (*Fliesen*) to flag; **~erin** *f* ironer; **~stahl** *m* heater; **~wäsche** *f* linen (to be ironed).
Platz *m* place, spot; (*Örtlichkeit*) locality; (*Raum*) space, room; (*öffentlicher*) square; circus, (*Sitz*) seat; (*Stellung*) position; (*Halte~*) stand; (*Bau~*) site; (*Anker~*) berth; *sport* ground; (*Tennis*) court; (*Festung*) fortress, stronghold; *~ nehmen* to take a seat, to sit down, *Am* to have a seat; *~ machen* to make room (for); (*weggehen*) to give way to; *~ greifen* to gain ground; *am ~e sein* to be opportune; *Plätze bestellen theat* to book seats; *rail* to book for, *Am* to make a reservation; *mar* to book a passage; *wieder an seinen ~ tun* to put back; *immer auf dem ~e sein* to be on the alert; *am ~e com* in town; *alle Plätze sind besetzt* all the seats are taken; *bis auf den letzten ~ gefüllt* crowded to capacity; **~agent** *m com* local agent; **~angst** *f* agoraphobia; **~anweiser(in)** *m* (*f*) usher(ette); **~bedarf** *m com* local requirements *pl*; **~befeuerung** *f aero* airdrome light(ing); **~en** *itr* (*bersten*) to burst; to explode; (*zerreißen*) to split; (*Glas*) to crack; (*Reifen*) to burst, *Am* to blow out; *vor Neugierde ~~* to burst with curiosity; *e-e Naht ist geplatzt* a seam is open; **~karte** *f* ticket for reserved seat, *Am* (train) reservation; **~kommandant** *m* town major; **~mangel** *m* lack of space; **~nummer** *f* (*Bücherei*) shelf number; **~patrone** *f* blank cartridge; **~raubend** *a* encumbering; **~regen** *m* downpour, heavy shower, pelting rain; **~runde** *f* circuit of the airdrome: *e-e ~~ fliegen* to circle the field; **~spesen** *pl com* local expenses *pl*; **~wechsel** *m* change of place; migration; *com* local bill.
Plätzchen *n* little place; (*Gebäck*) fancy cake, biscuit, *Am* cookie; (*knusperig*) wacker.
Plauder|ei *f* chat, small talk; (*Klatsch*) gossip(ing); *radio* broadcast talk; **~er** *m* conversationalist; talker, speaker; (*Schwätzer*) chatterbox; **~n** *itr* to chat, to gossip; to talk; *aus der Schule ~~* to tell tales; **~stimmung** *f* chatting mood; **~ton** *m* conversational tone.
plauz! *interj* bang!
Pleb|ejer *m* plebeian; **~s** *m, f* mob, rabble.
Pleite *f* bankruptcy, smash, failure, flop; *a* bankrupt, *fam* broke, *Am* bust; *~ machen fam* to go broke (*od* bust).
Plenarsitzung *f*, ***Plenum*** *n* plenary meeting.
Pleuel|stange *f tech* connecting-rod; **~welle** *f* crankshaft.
Plexiglas *n* lucite; safety glass.
Plinse *f* pancake.
Pliss|ee *n* pleating; **~ieren** *tr* to pleat.
Plomb|e *f* lead seal; (*Zahn*) filling, plug, stopping; **~ieren** *tr* to lead; (*Zähne*) to plug, to fill, to stop.
Plötze *f* (*Fisch*) roach.
plötzlich *a* sudden; *adv* suddenly, all of a sudden; **~keit** *f* suddenness.
Pluderhosen *f pl* wide breeches *pl*, plus-fours *pl*.
Plumeau *n* feather-bed.
plump *a* (*ungeschickt*) awkward; (*unfein*) coarse; (*taktlos*) crude, tactless; (*untersetzt*) dumpy; (*unbeholfen*) unwieldy, clumsy; (*ungestaltet*) shapeless; (*schwerfällig*) heavy; **~heit** *f* clumsiness; coarseness; **~s!** *interj* plump! **~sen** *itr* to (fall with a heavy) plump, to plop.
Plunder *m* lumber, trash, rubbish, *Am* junk.
Plünder|er *m* plunderer; **~n** *tr, itr* to plunder, to pillage, to loot, to rifle; (*Orte*) to sack; (*durchsuchen*) to ransack; **~ung** *f* plundering, pillage, sack, looting.
Plural *m* plural.
plus *adv* plus; **~leitung** *f* plus wire; **~pol** *m* positive element; **~quamperfekt** *n* pluperfect; **~zeichen** *n* plus sign.
Plüsch *m* plush, *Am* shag.
Pluton|brenner *m* Plutonium pile; **~ium** *n chem* plutonium.
Pneumat|ik *m* pneumatic tyre; **~isch** *a* pneumatic.
Pöbel *n* mob, rabble, populace; **~haft** *a* low, vulgar; **~herrschaft** *f* mob rule.
poch|en *itr* (*Türe*) to knock (*an* at); (*Herz*) to pound, to beat, to throb, to palpitate; (*leicht*) to rap; (*stampfen*) to stamp; *auf etw ~~* (*fig*) to boast of, to brag; *tr* (*zerstoßen*) to pound, to stamp; **~~** *n* knocking; throbbing, palpitation; **~gestein** *n min* stamp rock; **~werk** *n* stamp mill.
Pocke *f* pock; *die ~n pl* smallpox; **~nimpfung** *f* vaccination; **~nnarbe** *f* pock-mark; **~nnarbig** *a* pock-marked.
Podest *n* landing; stage.
Podium *n* rostrum, platform.
Poesie *f* poetry.
Poet *m* poet; **~ik** *f* poetics *pl*; **~isch** *a* poetic(al).
Point|e *f* punch line; *fig* (*Witz*) witticism; *Am* (*Kernpunkt*) nub; (*Schärfe*) pungency, sharpness; **~iert** *a* pointed, sharp, captious.
Pokal *m* goblet, (drinking-)cup; *sport* (challenge-)cup; **~spiel** *n sport* cup-tie.
Pökel *m* brine, pickle; **~faß** *n* pickling tub; **~fleisch** *n* salt meat; **~hering** *m* pickled herring; **~n** *tr* to salt, to pickle.
Pokereinsatz *m* ante.
pokulieren *itr* to carouse, to drink.
Pol *m* pole; *el* (*auch*) terminal; *positiver* (*negativer*) *~* positive (negative) pole; *gleichnamige ~e* like (*od* similar) poles; **~ar** *a* polar, arctic; **~~eis** *n* polar ice; **~~forscher** *m* polar explorer; **~~fuchs** *m* artic fox; **~~gürtel** *m* frigid zone; **~~hund** *m* Eskimo dog, husky; **~~isation** *f* polarization; **~~isieren** *tr* to polarize; **~~ität** *f* polarity; **~~kreis** *m* arctic circle; **~~licht** *n* northern lights *pl*, aurora borealis; **~~luft** *f* polar air; **~~meer** *n* arctic ocean; **~~stern** *m* Pole-star; **~~strom** *m* artic current; **~~zone** *f* arctic zone; **~ende** *f* electrode;

~höhe *f* latitude; **~klemme** *f* pole terminal; connection clamp; **~papier** *n el* pole paper; **~schuh** *m el* pole shoe; **~stärke** *f el* strength of pole; **~wechsel** *m el* reversal of poles; **~wender** *m* current reverser.

Pol\|e *m* Pole; **~en** *n* Poland; **~in** Polish woman; **~nisch** *a* Polish.

Polemi\|k *f* polemics *pl*, controversy; **~sch** *a* polemic; **~sieren** *itr* to carry on a controversy.

Police *f* policy, (*Lebensversicherung*) life policy; *e-e ~ ausstellen* to issue a policy.

Poli\|er *m* foreman; **~eren** *tr* to polish, to burnish; **~erer** *m* polisher; **~erflüssigkeit** *f* polishing liquid; **~ermasse** *f* polishing paste; **~ermittel** *n* polishing agent; **~erscheibe** *f* polishing wheel; **~erwachs** *n* polishing wax; **~tur** *f* polish(ing); shellac varnish.

Poliklinik *f* policlinic; department of a hospital at which outpatients are treated; dispensary.

Polit\|ik *f* politics *pl*; (*praktische ~~*) policy; **~iker** *m* politician, statesman, policymaker, (*verächtlich*) pettifogging politician, *Am* politico, peanut politician; **~isch** *a* political; *~~er Standpunkt* platform; **~isieren** *itr* to talk politics; (*kannegießern*) to dabble in politics; *tr* to make political-minded.

Polizei *f* police; **~aufgebot** *n* body of policemen; **~aufsicht** *f* police supervision; *unter ~~* on ticket of leave; **~beamte(r)** *m* police officer; constable; **~behörde** *f* police-authorities *pl*; **~bericht** *m* charge sheet, *Am* police blotter; **~büro** *n* police-station; **~direktor** *m* chief constable, *Am* chief of police; **~funk** *m* police radio; **~gefängnis** *n* police jail; **~gewahrsam** *m* lock-up; **~hund** *m* police-dog; **~knüppel** *m* truncheon, *Am* club, espantoon, billy; nightstick; **~kommissar** *m* inspector of police; **~lich** *a* police, of the police; *Rauchen ~~ verboten!* No smoking! By order of the police; *auf ~~es Verlangen vorzeigen* to show upon request by the police; **~präsident** *m* Chief Constable; **~präsidium** *n* police president's office; (*London*) Scotland Yard; **~revier** *n* police station; **~richter** *m* police-magistrate, *Am* police-court judge; **~staat** *m* police state; **~spitzel** *m* police spy, *sl* nark; **~streife** *f* police raid; patrol; **~~nwagen** *m* squad (*od* prowl) car; **~stunde** *f* closing hour, legal closing time; (*Sperrstunde*) curfew; **~trupp** *m* body of police, *Am* platoon of police; **~überwachung** *f* police surveillance; **~verordnung** *f* police regulation; **~wache** *f* police station, *Am* station-house; **~wachtmeister** *m* police-inspector; **~widrig** *a* contrary to police regulations.

Polizist *m* policeman, constable, *fam* bobby, *sl* cop; (*Geheim~*) detective, *Am* plain-clothes man, *sl* dick.

Polo *n* polo; **~feld** *n* polo ground; **~hemd** *n Am fam* T-shirt.

Polster *n* (*Polsterung*) stuffing; (*Wattierung*) pad(ding); (*Kissen*) cushion, pillow; bolster; (*Füllung*) wadding; **~klasse** *f rail* upholstered class; **~möbel** *n pl* upholstery; upholstered furniture (*nur mit sing*); **~n** *tr* to stuff, to wad, to pad, to bolster; to upholster; to cushion; to line; **~sessel, ~stuhl** *m* easy chair; **~ung** *f* upholstery, stuffing, padding.

Polter\|abend *m* wedding eve; **~er** *m* blusterer; **~geist** *m* goblin; **~n** *itr* to rattle; (*zanken*) to bluster, to scold; (*rumpeln*) to rumble.

Polygamie *f* polygamy.

polym\|er *a* polymeric; **~erie** *f* polymerization, polymerism; **~erisation** *f* polymerization; **~erisieren** *tr* to polymerize.

Polyp *m* polyp; *med* polypus.

Polytechnik *f* polytechnics *pl*; **~um** *n* technical college.

Pomad\|e *f* pomade; **~ig** *a fig fam* phlegmatic.

Pomeranze *f* orange.

Pommes frites *pl* chip, *Am* French fried potatoes, *fam* French fries *pl*.

Pomp *m* pomp; **~haft, ~ös** *a* pompous.

Ponton *n* pontoon; **~brücke** *f* pontoon (*od* boat) bridge; **~kran** *m* floating crane; **~wagen** *m* pontoon carrier; **~zug** *m* pontoon platoon.

Popanz *m* bugbear, bog(e)y, *Am* bugaboo; (*Vogelscheuche*) scarecrow.

Popelin *m* poplin, *Am* broadcloth.

Popo *m fam* posteriors *pl*, behind, backside.

popul\|är *a* popular; **~arisieren** *tr* to popularize; **~arität** *f* popularity.

Por\|e *f* pore; **~ös** *a* porous; **~osität** *f* porosity.

Porphyr *m* porphyry.

Porree *m bot* leek.

Portal *n* portal; porch; front gate; (*e-s Krans*) gantry; **~kran** *m* gantry (*od* portal) crane.

Porte\|feuille *n* portfolio; **~monnaie** *n* purse.

Portier *m* doorkeeper, porter, *Am* doorman.

Portion *f* portion; (*das Aufgetragene*) helping; (*Eis*) dish; (*Fisch*) order; (*Tee*) pot; *mil* ration; *zwei ~en Kaffee* coffee for two; *eiserne ~* iron ration.

Porto *n* postage; (*Paket*) carriage; **~auslagen** *f pl* postage expenses *pl*; **~frei** *a* postage paid, post-free, carriage paid, prepaid, postpaid; **~gebühren** *f pl* postal rates *pl*; **~kasse** *f* petty cash; **~kosten** *pl* postal expenses *pl*; **~pflichtig** *a* subject to postage, liable to postage fee; **~satz** *m* rate of postage; **~zuschlag** *m* surcharge.

Portrait *n* portrait, likeness, picture; **~ieren** *tr* to portray; **~maler** *m* portrait-painter.

Portug\|al *n* Portugal; **~iese** *m*, **~iesisch** *a* Portuguese.

Porzellan *n* china; (*dünnes ~*) porcelain; *Meißner ~* Dresden china; **~artig** *a* porcelain, porcellanic; **~brennerei** *f* porcelain manufactory; **~erde** *f* porcelain clay, kaolin; **~fabrikation** *f* porcelain manufacture; **~geschirr** *n* china table-plate; **~handlung** *f* china-shop; **~malerei** *f* painting on china; **~schrank** *m* show-case; **~service** *n* set of china.

*

Posamentier *m* lace-maker, trimming- (*od* loop-) maker; haberdasher; **~waren** *f pl* lace-work, trimmings *pl*; haberdashery.

Posaune *f* trombone, *fig* trumpet; **~n** *itr* to play the trombone; *fig* to proclaim aloud, to trumpet; **~nbläser** *m* (*Posaunist*) trombonist.

Pos\|e *f* (*Haltung*) pose; attitude; posture; (*Angabe*) showing off; affectation; posing; (*Feder*) quill; **~ieren** *itr* to pose, to strike an attitude; **~ition** *f* position; **~~sanzeiger** *m* position indicator; **~~skrieg** *m* position warfare; **~~slampe** *f* navigation light; position light; **~~slichter** *n pl* navigation lights *pl*; aerial lights *pl*, identification lights *pl*, *Am* position lights *pl*; **~~smeldung** *f aero* position report; **~itiv** *n* positive (picture); *~~ a* positive; **~itron** *n* positron; **~itur** *f* posture; *sich in ~~ setzen* to square o.'s shoulders; (*angeben*) to show off, to put on trimmings, to put on side.

Poss\|e *f theat* farce; (*Clown*) antic; (*Spaß*) jest; **~en** *m* (*Unfug*) practical joke, trick; *~en reißen* to play a trick on, to play pranks on; **~enhaft** *a* funny, droll, farcical; **~enreißer** *m* jester, buffoon; **~enspiel** *n theat* farce; *fig* nonsense; **~ierlich** *a* droll, funny; (*sonderbar*) queer, odd, quaint.

Post *f* post, mail; (*Zustellung*) delivery; (*Gebäude*) post office; (*Eil~*) express post, *Am* special delivery; (*Luft~*) airmail; *mit der ersten ~* by the first delivery; *mit gewöhnlicher ~* by surface mail; *mit umgehender ~* by return of post; *~ abfertigen* to dispatch the mail; *e-n Brief auf die ~ geben* to post a letter; *Am* to mail a letter; **~alisch** *a* postal; **~amt** *n* post office; **~annahmestempel** *m* date stamp; **~anschrift** *f* mailing address; **~anstalt** *f* post office; **~antwortschein** *m* reply coupon; **~anweisung** *f* money order (*Abk* M. O.); postal order (*Abk* P. O.); *telegraphische ~~* money telegram; **~auftrag** *m* postal collection order; **~auto** *n* post-van, *Am* mail car; (*Omnibus*) motorbus; *Am* mail bus; **~beamte(r)** *m* post-office clerk; **~bezirk** *m* postal district; **~bezug** *m* order through the post-office, *Am* mail-order; **~bezugspreis** *m* postal subscription rate; **~bote** *m* postman, *Am* letter-carrier, mailman; **~dienst** *m* postal (*Am* mail) service; **~direktor** *m* postmaster; **~direktion** *f* general post office; **~einlieferungsschein** *m* post-office receipt; **~fach** *n* post-office box (*Abk* P. O. box); **~~nummer** *f* box number; **~flieger** *m* airmail pilot; **~flug** *m* mail flight; **~flugzeug** *n* mail carrier aircraft; postal plane, mail plane; **~gebäude** *n* post office; **~geheimnis** *n* sanctity of the mail, secrecy of the postal service; **~gebühren** *f pl* postal rates *pl*; **~gut** *n* mail; **~horn** *n* postilion's horn; **~karte** *f* postcard, *Am* (*mit aufgedruckter Marke*) postal card; (*Ansichts~~*) picture postcard, *Am* illustrated postal card; *~~ mit Antwortkarte* reply postal card; **~kasten** *m* post-box, letter-box, *Am* mailbox; **~kutsche** *f* stage-coach, mail; *Zeit der ~~* (*Am*) horse-and-buggy days; **~lagernd** *a* to be called for, poste restante, *Am* (in care of) general delivery; **~leitzahl** *f* postal number; **~liste** *f* mailing list; **~meister** *m* postmaster; **~nachnahme** *f* cash on delivery (*Abk* C.O.D.); *Am* collect on delivery; **~nachnahmesendung** *f* collect on delivery mail; **~paket** *n* postal packet, *Am* parcel post package; **~~adresse** *f* dispatch note; **~sachen** *f pl* mails *pl*; **~sack** *m* mail bag; **~schalter** *m* (post office) counter (*od* window); **~scheck** *m* postal cheque (*Am* check); **~~amt** *n* postal cheque office; **~schiff** *n* mail boat, packet boat; **~schließfach** *n* post-office box, *Abk* P. O. box; pigeon hole; **~sparguthaben** *n* postal savings *pl*; **~sparkasse** *f* post-office savings bank; **~sparkassenbuch** *n* post-office savings book; **~sperre** *f* interruption of postal services; **~station** *f* post station; **~stempel** *m* postmark, *Am* mail stamp; **~tarif** *m* postal rates *pl*; **~überwachungsstelle** *f* postal censor's office; **~überweisung** *f* letter payment; **~verbindung** *f* mail service; **~verkehr** *m* postal communication; **~versandfähig** *a* mailable; **~versandhaus**

n Am mail order house; **~wagen** *m* mail coach; *Am* mail car; **~wendend** *a* by return of post; posthaste; *Am* by return mail; **~wertzeichen** *n* (postage) stamp; **~wurfsendung** *f* printed matters and mixed consignment; direct mail; **~zug** *m* mail train; **~zustellung** *f* delivery.

Postament *n* pedestal, base.

Posten *m* (*Ort*) post, place; station; (*Anstellung*) position, job; (*Aufstellung*) item; sum; (*Eintragung*) entry; (*Ware*) lot, amount, quantity; parcel, shipment; (*Streik~*) picket; *mil* sentry, sentinel, guard; outpost; picket; *~ vor Gewehr* arms sentry; *~ ablösen* to relieve sentries; *~ aufstellen* to post a sentry, to post a guard; *auf ~ stehen* to be on guard; *nicht ganz auf dem ~ sein* not to be quite up to par; *e-n ~ neu besetzen* to fill a vacancy; **~jäger** *m* place-hunter, *Am* job hunter; **~kette**, **~linie** *f mil* outpost line; **~stehen** *n* sentry (*od* guard) duty; **~weise** *adv* by items; *~~ aufführen* to itemize.

postieren *tr* to post, to place.

Potenti|al *n* potential; potential function; **~~abfall** *m* fall of potential; **~~differenz** *f* potential difference; **~~gleichung** *f* potential equation; **~~wert** *m* potential value; **~ell** *a* potential.

Potenz *f* power; exponent; **~ieren** *tr math* to raise to a higher power.

Potpourri *n mus* (musical) selection, medley; potpourri.

Pott|asche *f* potash; **~wal** *m* sperm whale.

potztausend! *interj* good gracious!

poussieren *itr* to flirt.

*

Pracht *f* pomp, state, splendo(u)r; luxury; **~ausgabe** *f* édition de luxe; large paper edition; **~einband** *m* rich binding; **~kerl** *m* stunner, cracker-jack, sport; **~liebend** *a* ostentatious; fond of show; **~stück** *n* superb specimen; **~voll** *a* splendid, magnificent, gorgeous.

prächtig *a* pompous, magnificent, gorgeous, splendid; great, fine.

Prädikat *n* predicate; (*Titel*) title; (*Schule*) marks *pl*; **~snomen** *n gram* complement.

Präg|e *f* stamp; (*Gesenk*) swage; **~eanstalt** *f* mint; **~edruck** *m* relief print; **~eform** *f* matrix, mo(u)ld; **~emaschine** *f* coining machine; embossing machine; **~en** *tr* to stamp; (*Münzen*) to coin; *fig* to impress on; **~eort** *m* mint; **~estempel** *m* die; matrix; **~ung** *f* (*Münze, Wörter*) coinage; (*Gestaltung*) shaping.

prägnan|t *a* (*genau*) precise, exact; (*bedeutungsvoll*) suggestive, meaningful; **~z** *f* terseness.

prähistorisch *a* prehistoric.

prahl|en *itr* to boast of, to brag; to talk big; to show off; **~er** *m* boaster; **~erei** *f* bragging, braggadocio, vapo(u)rings *pl*; **~erisch** *a* boastful, bragging, vapo(u)ring, *Am* hot air; spread-eagle; (*prunkhaft*) ostentatious; **~hans** *m* braggart, boaster, show-off braggadocio, *Am sl* ritzer; **~sucht** *f* boastfulness.

Prahm *m* barge, flat-bottomed boat, lighter, *Am* flatboat.

Prakti|k *f* practice; trick; **~kant** *m* probationer; practitioner; **~ker** *m* practical man; expert; **~kum** *n* practical course; **~kus** *m* old hand, old stager; **~sch** *a* practical, useful; (*geschickt*) clever, handy; (*erfahren*) experienced; *~~er Arzt* general practitioner, *Abk* G. P.; **~zieren** *itr* to practise, *Am* to practice.

Prälat *m* prelate.

Präliminar|frieden *m* preliminary peace; **~ien** *n pl* preliminaries *pl*.

Praline *f* chocolate almonds *pl*; chocolate cream; (*kandierte Nuß*) praline.

prall *a* (*Backen*) chubby; (*feist*) plump; (*rund u. voll*) stout, well-rounded; (*straff*) tight, tense; (*Seil*) taut; (*Sonne*) blazing; *~ m* rebound; collision; **~en** *itr* to bound (*gegen* against); to rebound; to bounce; to be reflected; (*zusammen~~*) to rush together; (*aufeinander~~*) to meet violently; (*Sonne*) to shine dazzlingly.

Präludium *n* prelude.

Prämi|e *f* premium; (*Preis*) prize, award; (*Dividende*) bonus; (*Anreiz*) bounty; (*Versicherung*) premium; **~eneinziehung** *f* collection of premium; **~enerhöhung** *f* increase of premium; **~enfrei** *a* free of premium; **~engeschäft** *n* option (business), *Am* trading in privileges; **~engewährung** *f* bonus issue; **~enhöhe** *f* amount of premium; **~enmarke** *f* premium voucher; **~enrate** *f* premium rate; **~enreserve** *f* premium reserve; **~ieren** *tr* to award a prize to.

prang|en *itr* to glitter, to shine; to make a show; **~er** *m* pillory.

Pranke, Pratze *f* claw, paw.

pränumerando *adv* in advance.

Präpar|at *n med, chem* preparation; (*Mikroskop*) slide; **~ierbesteck** *n* dissecting case; **~ieren** *tr* to prepare; to dissect; **~iernadel** *f* dissecting needle.

Präposition *f* preposition; **~al** *a* prepositional.

Prärie *f* prairie.

Präsen|s *n gram* present (tense); **~t** *n* present, gift **~~ieren** *tr* to present, to offer; **~~ierteller** *m* tray, salver; **~zbibliothek** *f* reference library; **~zstärke** *f* effectives *pl*.

Präsid|ent *m* president; chairman; (*Am Kongreß*) Speaker; *Amtszeit des ~~en* presidential term; **~~enwahl** *f* presidential election; **~ieren** *itr* to preside; **~ium** *n* presidency, chair.

prasseln *itr* (*Feuer*) to crackle; (*Regen*) to patter.

prass|en *itr* to feast, to carouse; (*schwelgen*) to revel; **~er** *m* glutton; spendthrift; **~erei** *f* gluttony, debauchery; feasting; revelry.

Prätendent *m* pretender.

Präteritum *n* preterite, past tense.

Präventivkrieg *m* preventive war.

Praxis *f* practice; (*Raum*) consulting-room(s), surgery, *Am* doctor's office.

Präzedenzfall *m* precedent, test case.

präz|is *a* precise; punctual; **~isieren** *tr* to render precise, to define; **~ision** *f* precision; accuracy; **~~sarbeit** *f* precision work; **~~sbombenabwurf** *m* precision (*od* pin-point) bombing; **~~sinstrument** *n* precision instrument; **~~skleinbildkamera** *f* precision miniature camera; **~~swaage** *f* precision balance; **~~swerkzeug** *n* precision tool.

*

predig|en *itr, tr* to preach; **~er** *m* preacher, minister, clergyman; **~t** *f* sermon; *fig* lecture; *e-e ~~ halten* to deliver a lecture.

Preis *m* (*Kosten*) price, cost; (*Wert*) value; (*Kurs*) rate; (*Wettbewerb*) prize; (*Bedingungen*) terms *pl*; (*Gebühr*) fee; (*Fahrgeld*) fare; (*Lob*) praise, glory; *um jeden ~* at any price (*od* cost); *um keinen ~* not for all the world; not for anything; *zum ~e von* at the price of; *äußerster ~* lowest price, *Am* rock-bottom price; *plötzliches Fallen der ~e* slump; *niedrig im ~* low priced; *ermäßigter ~* reduced price; *„feste ~e"* "no reductions"; *reelle ~e* fair prices; *sinkende ~e* declining prices; *steigende ~e* rising prices; *~e erzielen* to fetch prices; *im ~ herabsetzen* to mark down; *unter dem ~ losschlagen* to let go under price; to sell under the value; *~e in die Höhe treiben* to send up prices, to jump prices; **~abbau** *m* reduction of prices; **~abschlag** *m* decrease in price; **~abzug** *m* rebate, discount; **~änderung** *f* price change; **~angabe** *f* quotation of prices; **~angebot** *n* offer; **~anstieg** *m* rise in prices; **~aufgabe** *f* subject for a prize-essay; **~aufschlag** *m* (*Zuschlag*) extra charge; **~ausschreiben** *n* (prize-)competition; **~auszeichnung** *f* shop mark; **~behörde** *f* price control authority; **~berechnung** *f* costing; **~beschränkung** *f* price control; **~bestimmend** *a* price-determining; **~bestimmungen** *f pl* price provisions *pl*; **~bewegung** *f* movement of prices; **~bewerber** *m* competitor, *Am* contestant; **~bildung** *f* price fixing; **~drückerei** *f* close bargaining; **~en** *irr tr* to praise; to glorify, to extol; **~entwicklung** *f* price development; **~erhöhung** *f* rise in prices, price increase; **~ermäßigung** *f* price cut; **~festsetzung** *f* price fixing; **~frage** *f* (*Wettbewerb*) subject for prize competition; **~gabe** *f* surrender, abandonment; **~geben** *irr tr* to surrender, to give up; (*opfern*) to sacrifice; (*aussetzen*) to expose; (*enthüllen*) to reveal; **~gebunden** *a* price-controlled; **~gefüge** *n* structure of prices; **~gericht** *n* jury; **~gestaltung** *f* price formation; **~grenze** *f* price limit, ceiling; **~herabsetzung** *f* price reduction, cut; **~index** *m* price level, index number; **~krönen** *tr* to award a prize to; **~lage** *f* price range; **~liste** *f* price-list, price-current, rate-book; prospectus; **~nachlaß** *m* abatement, reduction; **~niveau** *n* price level; **~notierung** *f* quotation; **~politik** *f* price policy; **~prüfung** *f* verification of prices; **~~samt** *n* price control office; **~richter** *m* arbiter, umpire; **~rückgang** *m* price recession; **~schere** *f* divergence; **~schild** *n* price tag; **~schießen** *n* shooting competition; **~schleuderei** *f* undercutting of prices; **~schraube** *f* price spiral; **~schrift** *f* prize-essay; **~schwankungen** *f pl* fluctuations *pl* in prices; **~senkung** *f* price-cut; **~spanne** *f* price margin; **~spirale** *f* price spiraling; **~stabilisierung** *f* stabilization of prices; **~stand** *m* level of prices; **~steigerung** *f* advance in prices, rise, *Am* raise; **~stopp** *m* price stop; **~~verordnung** *f* price pegging regulation; **~sturz** *m* price slump, fall in prices; (*Börse*) *Am* break; **~stützung** *f* price support; **~träger** *m* prize-winner; **~treiberei** *f* forcing up of prices; **~überhöhung** *f* excessive prices *pl*; **~überwachung** *f* price control; **~~sstelle** *f* price control office; **~unterbietung** *f* price dumping; **~unterschied** *m* difference in prices; **~veränderung** *f* change in prices; **~vereinbarung** *f* price agreement; **~verteilung** *f* distribution of prizes; **~verzeichnis** *n* price list (*od* current); **~wert** *a* cheap, reasonable; (*lobenswert*) praiseworthy; **~zuschlag** *m* extra charge, markup.

Preiselbeere *f* cranberry.

Prell|bock *m* buffer-stop; **~en** *tr* to toss; to make rebound; *fig* to cheat, to take in, to swindle; (*Haut*) to contuse; **~erei** *f* fraud, swindle;

~**schuß** *m* ricochet-bullet; ~**stein** *m* kerb(-stone); ~**ung** *f med* contusion.

Premiere *f* first night; ~**nbesucher** *m* first-nighter.

Presbyterium *n* presbitery.

Press|e *f typ* press; (*Zeitungswesen*) journalism; *tech* press; (*Spinnerei*) clasp; (*Schule*) crammer; ~~**agent** *m* press agent; ~~**amt** *n* public relations office; ~~**ausweis** *m* press card; ~~**büro** *n* news agency; ~~**bericht** *m* cover story; ~~**chef** *m* press chief; ~~**dienst** *m* press service; ~~**fehde** *f* press feud; ~~**feldzug** *m* press campaign, stunt; ~~**freiheit** *f* freedom of the press; ~~**gesetz** *n* press law; ~~**kamera** *f* press camera; ~~**konferenz** *f* press conference; ~~**mitteilung** *f* hand-out; press-release; ~~**n** *tr* to press, to squeeze; (*drängen*) to urge; (*formen*) to mo(u)ld; ~~**notiz** *f* newspaper notice; ~~**photograph** *m* press photographer; ~~**stelle** *f* public relations office; ~~**stimme** *f* press comment, review; ~~**telegramm** *n* news (*od* press) message, flimsy; ~~**tribüne** *f* press gallery; ~~**vergehen** *n* offence against the press laws; ~~**zensur** *f* press curb (*od* censorship); ~**filter** *n* press filter; ~**form** *f* matrix, mo(u)ld; ~**futter** *n* press mo(u)ld; ~**gehäuse** *n* plastic cabinet; ~**guß** *m* pressure casting; ~~**stück** *n* die pressing; ~**hefe** *f* pressed yeast; ~**ieren** *itr* to be urgent; *es ~iert nicht* there is no hurry; ~**kohle** *f* pressed (char)coal; briquetted coal; briquette; patent fuel; ~**kopf** *m* headcheese; ~**luft** *f* compressed air; ~~**antrieb** *m* drive by compressed air; ~~**behälter** *m* compressed air tank; ~~**bohrer** *m* air (*od* pneumatic) drill; ~~**flasche** *f* compressed air cylindre; ~~**hammer** *m* air hammer, rock drill; ~**masse** *f* mo(u)lded plastic; plastic material; synthetic; plastic; ~**most** *m* must; ~**stoff** *m* pressed material; plastic material; mo(u)lded plastics; fictile material; ~**stroh** *n* baled straw; ~**stücke** *n pl* pressings *pl*; ~**ung** *f* pressure, compression; ~**verfahren** *n* pressing process.

Preuß|e *m*, ~**in** *f*, ~**isch** *a* Prussian.

prickeln *itr* to prick(le); (*jucken*) to itch; ~**d** *a fig* spicy, piquant.

Priem *m* quid (of tabacco).

Priester *m* priest; ~**amt** *n* priesthood; ~**herrschaft** *f* hierarchy; ~**in** *f* priestess; ~**lich** *a* priestly, sacerdotal; ~**rock** *m* cassock; ~**schaft** *f* clergy; ~**tum** *n* priesthood; ~**weihe** *f* ordination of a priest.

Prima *f* (*Schule*) highest class, (*in England*) sixth form; ~ *a* first class, first rate; *Am* top notch, *Am* A one, *sl* swell; *das ist ~ Zeug* that's good stuff; ~**ner** *m* sixth-form boy; ~**s** *m* primate; ~**t** *n* primacy; ~**wechsel** *m* first bill of exchange.

primär *a* primary; protogenic; ~**abstimmung** *f radio* preselector means; ~**elektron** *n* primary electron; ~**empfänger** *m radio* primary receiver; ~**schaltung** *f* primary circuit; ~**spannung** *f* primary voltage; ~**wicklung** *f* primary winding.

Primel *f* primrose, primula, cowslip.

prim|itiv *a* primitive; ~~**ität** *f* primitiveness; ~**us** *m* head-boy; ~**zahl** *f* prime number.

Prinz *m* prince; ~**essin** *f* princess; ~**gemahl** *m* prince consort; ~**lich** *a* princely.

Prinzip *n* principle; *im ~* as a matter of principle, on principle; ~**al** *m* principal, head; employer; ~**iell** *adv* on principle; in principle; ~**ienrede** *f pol Am* keynote speech; ~**ienreiter** *m* stickler for principles, pedant; ~**ienstreit** *m* dispute about principles.

Prior *m* prior; ~**in** *f* prioress; ~**ität** *f* priority; ~~**saktien** *f pl* preference shares *pl*; ~~**sanspruch** *m* priority claim; ~~**srecht** *n* priority right.

Prise *f* (*Schnupftabak*) pinch; *mar* prize; ~**ngerichtshof** *m* prize court; ~**nkommando** *n* prize crew; ~**nmannschaft** *f* boarding-party; ~**nordnung** *f* regulations governing prizes; ~**nrecht** *n* right of capture; law governing prizes.

Prism|a *n* prism; ~**enfläche** *f* prism face; ~**enförmig** *a* prismatic; ~**englas** *n* prism glass; prismatic telescope; ~**ensucher** *m* prism(atic) finder (*od* seeker).

Pritsche *f* iron bed, plank bed; (*Harlekin*) wooden sword.

privat *a* private; ~**anschrift** *f* home address; ~**aufführung** *f* preview; ~**auskunft** *f* exclusive information; ~**dozent** *m* university lecturer; ~**eigentum** *n* private property; ~**einkommen** *n* personal income; ~**fernsprechleitung** *f* private wire; ~**flieger** *m* private pilot; ~**fliegerei** *f* civilian flying; ~**flugzeug** *n* private plane; ~**gebrauch** *m* private use; ~**gespräch** *n* private conversation; *tele* private call; ~**im** *adv* privately; ~**initiative** *f* private enterprise; ~**interessen** *n pl* interests *pl* as individual; ~~ *verfolgen Am* to have an ax(e) to grind; ~**isieren** *itr* to live on o.'s means; ~**kapital** *n* private capital; ~~**ismus** *m* private capitalism; ~**klinik** *f* nursing-home, *Am* private hospital; ~**korrespondenz** *f* private correspondence; ~**leben** *n* private life; ~**meinung** *f* individual opinion; ~**patient** *m* pay(ing) patient; ~**person** *f* private person; ~**recht** *n* civil law; ~**sache** *f* private matter; ~**schreiben** *n* confidential letter; ~**schule** *f* private school; ~**sekretär** *m* private secretary; ~**sender** *m radio* commercial station; ~**stunde** *f* private lesson; ~**telegramm** *n* private message; ~**unternehmen** *n* private enterprise; ~**unterricht** *m* private teaching (*od* tuition); ~**vermögen** *n* private property; personal means *pl*; ~**vorstellung** *f* invitation performance; ~**weg** *m* drive, *Am* driveway; ~**wirtschaft** *f* private industry, free business (*od* economy); ~**wohnung** *f* private dwelling.

Privileg *n* privilege; ~**ieren** *tr* to privilege; *e-e ~ierte Kaste* a privileged caste.

probat *a* proved, tried; excellent.

Probe *f* experiment, trial; (*An~*) fitting; (*Versuch*) test; (*Metall-, Erz~*) assay; (*Muster*) pattern; (*Nachprüfung*) check; (*Waren~*) sample, specimen; (*Beweis*) proof; (*Prüfung*) probation; *theat* rehearsal; *zur ~* on trial; on probation; *auf die ~ stellen* to (put to the) test; *e-e ~ ablegen* to give proof of; *die Geduld auf e-e harte ~ stellen* to be a heavy strain on o.'s patience, to try o.'s patience too far; *e-e ~ machen* to (make a) check; ~**abdruck**, ~**abzug** *m* proof; ~**abstimmung** *f* straw-vote; ~**alarm** *m* test alert; ~**aufnahme** *f* test picture; trial shot; *film* screen test; ~~*n machen von jdm* to screen-test s. o.; ~**auftrag** *m* trial order; ~**band** *m* dummy; ~**bogen** *m typ* proof sheet; ~**ehe** *f* companion marriage; ~**n** *tr, itr* to try; to check, to test; to sample; *theat* to rehearse; ~**exemplar** *n* specimen copy; ~**fahrt** *f* test drive; trial run; ~**flug** *m aero* trial (*od* test) flight; *fam* test hop; ~**jahr** *n* year of probation; ~**lauf** *m tech, fig* trial, trial run, test run; green run; running-in test; *Am sl* dry run; ~**nahme** *f* sampling, testing; test portion; ~**nummer** *f* specimen copy (*od* number); ~**schuß** *m* trial shot; ~**seite** *f* specimen page; ~**sendung** *f* sample sent on approval; ~**stück** *n* specimen, pattern, sample; ~**weise** *adv* on approval, on trial; ~**zeit** *f* time of probation, probationary period; qualifying period.

Probier|dame *f* mannequin; ~**en** *tr* (*versuchen*) to try, to attempt, to essay; (*an~~*) to try on, to be fitted for; to make the trial of, to test, to prove, to try out; (*Metalle*) to assay; (*Küche*) to taste; ~**gefäß** *n* testing vessel; ~**glas** *n* test tube; ~**nadel** *f* touch needle; ~**waage** *f* assay balance.

Problem *n* problem; *fig* problem, puzzle; *ein ~ lösen* to solve a problem; *sich mit e-m ~ auseinandersetzen* to get down to a problem; ~**atisch** *a* problematic; ~**atik** *f* problems *pl*; ~**stellung** *f* posing the problem.

Produkt *n* (*Erzeugnis*) product, production;(*Naturerzeugnisse*) produce *mit sing*; (*Ergebnis*) result; (*Waren*) goods *pl*, commodities *pl*; ~**enbörse** *f* produce exchange; ~**enhandel** *m* trade in produce; ~**enhändler** *m* dealer in produce; ~**enmarkt** *m* produce market; ~**ion** *f* production, producing; (*Menge*) output, yield; ~~ *am laufenden Band* assembly line production; ~~ *drosseln* to curb the production; ~~**sanlagen** *f pl* productive facilities *pl*; ~~**sapparat** *m* productive apparatus; ~~**sausfall** *m* falling off in production; ~~**sausweitung** *f* expansion of production; ~~**sbedingungen** *f pl* manufacturing conditions *pl*; ~~**sbeschränkung** *f* curtailing of production, output restriction; (*zur Verhinderung der Arbeitslosigkeit*) featherbedding; (*künstlich durch Arbeiter*) ca'canny; ~~**serfahrung** *f* production experience, *Am* industrial know-how; ~~**serhöhung** *f* increase in production; ~~**sgang** *m* production process; ~~**sgebiet** *n* production area; (*Zweig*) production line; ~~**sgemeinschaft** *f* production pool; ~~**sgüter** *n pl* production goods *pl*; ~~**skapazität** *f* productive capacity; ~~**skosten** *pl* production costs *pl*; ~~**sleiter** *m* plant manager; *film* production chief, producer; ~~**sleistung** *f* production capacity; ~~**smenge** *f* output (in volume); ~~**smethode** *f* manufacturing method, process; ~~**smittel** *n pl* means *pl* of production; ~~**smöglichkeit** *f* potential production; ~~**splan** *m* production schedule; ~~**sprogramm** *n* manufacturing program; ~~**srückgang** *m* falling production, production drop; ~~**sstand** *m* level of production; ~~**sstätte** *f* manufacturing plant; ~~**ssteigerung** *f* increase in production; ~~**sumfang** *m* volume of production; ~~**sverfahren** *n* manufacturing technique; ~~**sziffer** *f* production record; ~~**szweig** *m* branch of production; ~**iv** *a* productive; ~~**ität** *f* productivity.

Produz|ent *m* producer, manufacturer; grower; ~**ieren** *tr* to produce; *r* to show off, to exhibit.

profan *a* profane; ~**ieren** *tr* to profane; ~**ierung** *f* profanation.

Profess|ion *f* profession; (*Handwerk*) trade, vocation; ~**or** *m* (*Universität*) *Engl* reader, lecturer, professor, *Am* (assistant) instructor, assistant (*od* associate *od* adjunct) professor, full professor; (*Am* professor *auch für Erzieher, Kapellmeister, Tanzlehrer usw.*); **~ur** *f* professorship.

Profil *n* profile; section; cross-section; *aero* aerofoil profile, wing profile; *im ~ darstellen* to draw in profile, to represent the profile of, to profile; *sich im ~ abzeichnen* to stand out in profile; **~dicke** *f* profile thickness; **~draht** *m* streamline wire; **~eisen** *n* sectional (*od* structural) iron; **~hinterkante** *f aero* trailing edge; **~ieren** *tr* to set up profiles; to draw profiles; **~iert** *a* sidefaced, profiled; **~ierung** *f aero* fairing; **~stahl** *m* structural steel; **~widerstand** *m aero* profile drag.

Profit *m* profit, gain, proceeds *pl*; **~ieren** *itr* to profit, to gain (by); **~jäger, ~macher** *m* profiteer.

Proformarechnung *f* pro forma invoice.

Prognose *f* forecast; *med* prognosis.

Programm *n* program(me); (*Rennen*) card; (*Schul~*) annual report, prospectus; *theat* program(me), playbill; (*Tagesordnung*) order paper, *Am* calendar; (*Partei~*) platform, political statement; (*Plan*) schedule; *~ auf Schallplatten* recorded program(me); **~füller** *m radio* filler; **~gesellschaft** *f Am radio* program producing service; **~leiter** *m radio* network program supervisor; **~musik** *f* program(me) music; **~punkt** *m* item.

Prohibit|ion *f* prohibition; *die ~~ einführen Am* to go dry; *für die ~~ stimmen Am* to vote dry; *Anhänger der ~~* (*Am*) prohibitionist; **~iv** *a* prohibitive, prohibitory; **~~zoll** *m* prohibition duty.

Projekt *n* project, scheme; **~ieren** *tr* to project, to plan, to scheme; **~ion** *f math* projection; (*Bild*) projected image; **~~sapparat** *m* projector; **~~sbirne** *f* projection bulb; **~~sfläche** *f*, **~~sschirm** *m* screen; **~~slampe** *f* projector filament lamp.

projizieren *tr* to project, to make projection of.

Proklam|ation *f* proclamation; **~ieren** *tr* to proclaim.

Prokur|a *f* procuration; proxy; *per ~~* by proxy (*Abk* per pro., p. p.); **~ist** *m* head-clerk, authorized manager.

Prolet *m* proletarian; **~ariat** *n* proletariat(e); *geistiges ~~* (*Am*) white-collar proletariat; **~arier** *m* proletarian; **~ariertum** *n* proletarianism; **~arisch** *a* proletarian; **~arisieren** *tr* to proletarianize; **~arisierung** *f* proletarianization.

Prolog *m* prologue.

Prolong|ation *f* prolongation; continuation; **~ieren** *tr* to prolong; (*Wechsel*) to renew.

Promen|ade *f* promenade, *Am* avenue; (*Spaziergang*) walk; **~~ndeck** *n* promenade deck; walk; **~ieren** *itr* to take a walk.

prominent *a* prominent, important, leading, well-known; conspicuous, noticeable; **~er** *m* prominent person; (*Gesellschaft*) *Am* socialite.

Promo|tion *f* graduation; **~vieren** *tr* to confer a degree; *itr* to graduate (at, *Am* from), to take a degree.

prompt *a* prompt, quick, ready.

Pronomen *n* pronoun.

Propag|anda *f* propaganda; publicity; *com Am* plug; *aufreizende ~~* inflammatory propaganda; *aufdringliche ~~* blatant advertising, *Am* ballyhoo; **~~ballon** *m* propaganda balloon; **~~feldzug** *m* propaganda campaign (*Am* drive); **~~krieg** *m* propaganda war; political warfare, *Am* psychological warfare; **~~leiter** *m* press agent; **~~methoden** *f pl* propaganda methods *pl*; **~~ministerium** *n* Ministry of Information; **~~stück** *n Am* stunt; **~andist** *m* propagator; **~andistisch** *a* propagandist; (*agitatorisch*) agitprop; **~ieren** *tr* to propagate, to propagandize, to spread; *com Am* to plug; *itr* to carry on a propaganda.

Propeller *m* air-screw, *Am* propeller; **~bremse** *f* propeller brake; **~enteiser** *m* propeller anti-icer; **~flügel** *m aero* blade, *mar* fan; **~geräusch** *n* propeller noise; **~nabe** *f aero* airscrew boss; **~~nverkleidung** *f* nose spinner; **~schub** *m* propeller thrust; **~strom, ~wind** *m* slipstream, *Am fam* prop blast; **~turbine(nluftstrahltriebwerk** *n*) *f* (*Abk: PTL*) propeller turbine; airscrew gas turbine, turboprop; jetprop, propjet.

Prophe|t *m* prophet; *der ~~ gilt nichts in seinem Vaterland* no man is a prophet in his own country; **~~ie, ~zeiung** *f* prophecy; **~~in** *f* prophetess; **~~isch** *a* prophetic; **~zeien** *tr* to prophesy; to foretell.

Proportion *f* proportion; **~al** *a* proportional; *umgekehrt ~~* inversely proportional; **~iert** *a* proportionate; well proportioned.

Propst *m* provost.

Prosa *f* prose; **~iker, ~ist** *m* prose-writer; **~isch** *a* prosaic; commonplace.

Proselyt *m* proselyte.

pros(i)t! *interj* cheers! here's to you! your health! (*beim Niesen*) God bless you! *~ Neujahr!* a happy New Year to you!

Prospekt *m* (*Aussicht*) prospect; (*Anzeige*) prospectus, hand-bill.

prostitu|ieren *tr* to prostitute; **~ierte** *f* prostitute, street-walker, whore, harlot, strumpet, *Am* slut; **~tion** *f* prostitution, street-walking.

Proszeniumsloge *f* stage-box.

*

prote|gieren *tr* to patronize; to encourage; **~ktieren** *tr* (*Reifen*) to retread, to rubberize; **~ktion** *f* protection, *Am* pull; **~~swirtschaft** *f* protectionism; **~ktorat** *n* protectorate; patronage, auspices *pl*.

Protest *m* protest; *mit ~* under protest; *~ einlegen* to enter a protest, to protest; **~ant** *m*, **~antisch** *a* Protestant; **~~ismus** *m* Protestantism; **~ieren** *itr* to protest, to make a formal declaration (against); **~versammlung** *f* meeting of protest, *Am* indignation-meeting.

Prothese *f* artificial limb.

Protokoll *n* minutes *pl*; (*Urkunde*) record; (*Verzeichnis*) register; *~ führen* to keep the minutes; *zu ~ nehmen* to take down; to record officially; *zu ~ geben* to make a deposition (*od* statement); *nicht für das ~ bestimmt* (*Am*) off the record; **~arisch** *a* upon records; in the minutes; **~buch** *n* minute-book, *Am* blotter; **~chef** *m* Marshal of the Diplomatic Corps, chef de protocol; **~führer** *m* keeper of the minutes; (*amtlich*) recording clerk; (*Registrator*) registrar; **~ieren** *tr* to keep the minutes, to draft the report; (*eintragen*) to enter, to record; (*registrieren*) to register.

Proton *n* proton; **~enwanderung** *f* movement of the proton.

Protz *m* purse-proud person; snob, *Am* swell, shoddy; **~en** *itr* to put on airs, to show off; to be purse-proud; **~entum** *n*, **~erei** *f* snobbism, snobbery; **~ig** *a* snobbish, purse-proud.

Protze *f* limber.

Prov|enienz *f* origin, source, provenance; **~iant** *m* provisions *pl*, victuals *pl*, supplies *pl*, stores *pl*; **~~amt** *n mil* supply depot, food-office; **~~kolonne** *f mil* supply column; **~~lager** *n* supply dump; **~~meister** *m mar* purser; steward; **~~schiff** *n* supply ship; **~~zug** *m* supply train.

Provinz *f* province; *er kommt aus der ~* (*Am fam*) he's from the sticks; **~ial, ~iell** *a* provincial; **~blatt** *n* local paper; **~ler** *m* provincial, countrified person; **~stadt** *f* provincial town.

Provis|ion *f* commission; (*Makler*) brokerage; (*Prozentsatz*) percentage; **~~sreisender** *m* travel(l)ing agent; **~~sweise** *adv* on commission; **~orisch** *a* temporary, provisional; **~orium** *n* provisional arrangement.

Provo|kation *f* provocation; **~zieren** *tr* to provoke; to challenge.

Prozedur *f* procedure; proceeding.

Prozent *n* per cent; **~satz** *m* percentage; **~ual** *a* expressed as percentage; *~~er Anteil* percentage.

Prozeß *m* (*bürgerl. Rechtsstreit*) lawsuit, action, legal proceedings *pl*; (*Vorgang*) process; (*Gerichtsverfahren*) trial, case; (*Rechtsstreit*) litigation; *tech* process; *etw od jdn e-m ~ unterwerfen* to process; *gegen jdn e-n ~ anstrengen* to bring an action against s. o., to institute legal proceedings against s. o., to sue s. o.; *in e-n ~ verwickelt sein* to be involved in a lawsuit; *kurzen ~ machen mit* to make short work of, to dispose of in short order; **~akten** *f pl* minutes *pl*; files *pl*; (*des Anwalts*) brief; **~führer** *m* litigant; **~führung** *f* conduct of case; **~gegenstand** *m* matter in dispute; **~gegner** *m* opposing party; **~ieren** *itr* to go to law with; to carry on a lawsuit; **~ion** *f* procession; **~kosten** *pl* law costs *pl*; **~ladung** *f* writ of summons; **~ordnung** *f* rules *pl* of the court; **~partei** *f* party to an action; **~recht** *n* adjective law; **~vollmacht** *f* power of attorney.

prüde *a* prudish; **~rie** *f* prudery.

Prüf|abzug *m* proof; **~apparat** *m* testing apparatus; **~bar** *a* capable of being tested; **~bedingung** *f* condition of testing; **~belastung** *f tech* ultimate strength; **~einrichtung** *f* testing outfit; **~en** *tr* to examine; (*durch Fragespiel*) *Am* to quiz; (*erproben*) to try, to test; (*besichtigen, mustern*) to inspect; to survey; (*nach~~*) to check (up), to review; to verify; (*erweisen*) to prove; (*durch Erprobung ausführen*) to give s. o. a trial; (*genau*) to investigate, to scan, to scrutinize, *Am* to canvass; (*Konten, Bücher*) to audit; (*Papiere*) to vet, *Am* to screen; (*Erz*) to assay; (*gründlich durchsehen*) *tech* to overhaul; (*sondieren*) to explore; (*flüchtig*) *Am fam* to give s. o. the once-over; (*überlegen*) to ponder; (*abwägen*) to weigh; (*kosten*) to taste; (*heimsuchen*) to afflict, to plague, to trouble; *~~ r* to examine o.'s conscience; to study (*od* to search) o. s.; *geprüfter Lehrer* licensed teacher; **~er** *m* examiner; *com* auditor; (*Nach~~*) checker; (*Besichtigender*) inspector; (*Wahl~~*) scrutineer, *Am* canvasser; **~ergebnis** *n* test result; **~feld** *n* proving ground, test field; **~gerät** *n* testing apparatus; **~ling** *m* examinee, applicant for an examination; *tech* test piece; **~stand** *m mot* test house; **~~versuch** *m mot* bench test, *Am* block test; **~stein** *m* touchstone; test; **~ung** *f* examination, *fam* exam; (*Fragespiel*) *Am* quiz;

(*Nachforschung*) investigation; (*Erprobung*) testing; (*Bewährung*) proof; (*eingehende Untersuchung*) scrutiny, *Am* canvass, checkup; (*gründliche Durchsicht*) perusal, *tech* overhauling; (*flüchtige ~~*) *Am fam* once-over; (*Besichtigung*) inspection; survey; (*Erz*) assay; (*Stimme*) audition; (*Heimsuchung*) trial, affliction; (*Versuchung*) temptation; (*schwere ~~*) *fig* ordeal; *sich e-r ~~ unterziehen* to undergo an examination; *e-e ~~ bestehen* to pass an examination; *bei e-r ~~ durchfallen* to fail, to be rejected, *fam* to be plucked; **~~sanstalt** *f* testing laboratory; **~~sarbeit** *f* examination paper; **~~saufgabe** *f* subject for an examination; paper; **~~sausschuß** *m* board of examiners; (*Sachen*) review board; **~~sbericht** *m* report on an examination; test instruction; survey; **~~sergebnis** *n* result of examination; **~~sgebühren** *f pl* examination fees *pl*; **~~skandidat** *m* examinee; **~~skommission** *f* board of examiners; **~~sschein** *m*, **~~szeugnis** *n* certificate; **~~sversuch** *m* trial; **~~svorschrift** *f* test specification; **~verfahren** *n* testing method; **~zeichen** *n* test mark.

Prügel *m* stick, cudgel; (*Tracht ~*) thrashing, *fam* a good licking; **~ei** *f* row, fight, brawl, *Am* free-for-all; **~knabe** *m* scapegoat; *Am sl* stooge; **~n** *tr* to thrash, to beat; *r* to fight; **~strafe** *f* corporal punishment.

Prunk *m* splendo(u)r, show; **~bett** *n* bed of state; **~en** *itr* to parade, to show off, to make a show of; *mit etw ~~* to boast of s. th.; **~gemach** *n* state room; **~haft** *a* ostentatious, showy; **~los** *a* unostentatious, plain; **~süchtig** *a* ostentatious; **~voll** *a* splendid, gorgeous.

prusten *itr* to snort; (*lachen*) to burst out (laughing).

Psalm *m* psalm; **~buch** *n* psalter; **~ist** *m* psalmist.

Psalter *m* (*Instrument*) psaltery; (*Psalmbuch*) psalter.

Pseudonym *n* pseudonym, fictitious name; *~ a* pseudonymous, fictitious.

pst! *interj* hush! stop!

Psych|iater *m* psychiatrist, alienist; **~iatrie** *f* psychiatry; **~isch** *a* psychic (-al); **~oanalyse** *f* psycho-analysis; **~ologe** *m* psychologist; **~ologisch** *a* psychological; **~opath** *m* psychopath; **~ose** *f* psychosis; **~otherapie** *f* psychotherapy.

Pubertät *f* puberty.

Publi|kum *n* public; *das große ~~* the public at large; (*Zuhörerschaft*) audience; **~zieren** *tr* to publish; **~zist** *m* publicist, writer; press agent; **~zistik** *f* journalism.

puddel|n *itr* to puddle; **~roheisen** *n* forge pig; **~verfahren** *n* puddling process; **~werk** *n* puddling works *pl.*

Pudding *m* pudding; (*Apfel*) charlotte; (*gerollter*) roly-poly; (*mit Wasser gekocht*) jelly; (*mit Milch*) blanc-mange; **~form** *f* pudding-basin.

Pudel *m* poodle; *des ~s Kern* the gist of the whole matter; *wie ein begossener ~ dastehen* to stand dumbfounded; **~naß** *a* drenched, sopping.

Puder *m* (toilet) powder; **~dose** *f* powder-box; (*für die Handtasche*) vanity-box, *Am* compact; **~kaffee** *m* instant coffee; **~mantel** *m* peignoir; **~n** *tr* to powder; **~quaste** *f* powder-puff; **~unterlage** *f* foundation cream, day cream; **~zucker** *m* powder(ed) sugar.

Puff *m* (*Stoß*) push, thump; (*leichter ~*) nudge; (*Schlag*) blow; (*Knall*) bang, report, pop, crash; *vulg* brothel; *interj* puff! bang! **~ärmel** *m* puffed sleeve; **~en** *tr* to push, to nudge, to thump; (*wiederholt*) to pummel; *itr* (*Gewehr*) to shoot, to pop; (*Lokomotive*) to puff; **~er** *m rail* buffer, *Am* bumper; (*Kartoffel~*) potato-cake; **~~staat** *m* buffer state; **~~wirkung** *f* buffer action; **~~ung** *f* cushioning, buffering; **~otter** *f* puff-adder; **~spiel** *n* backgammon.

Pulk *m mil* unit; collection; group (of planes, mechanized vehicles etc).

Pulle *f* (*Flasche*) *fam* bottle; *mil sl mot* throttle; **~n** *itr mar* to pull, to row.

Pullover *m* pull-over, slip-on sweater; jumper; cardigan; *fam* sweat shirt.

Puls *m* pulse; **~ader** *f* artery; (*große*) aorta; **~ieren** *itr* to pulsate; *fig* to pulse, to throb; **~schlag** *m* pulse beat; pulsation; **~wärmer** *m* woolen wristlet; **~zahl** *f* pulse rate.

Pult *n* desk.

Pulver *n* powder; (*Schieß~*) gun-powder; *das ~ nicht erfunden haben* to be no mental giant; *er ist keinen Schuß ~ wert* he's not worth powder and shot; **~artig, ~ig** *a* powdery; **~fabrik** *f* powder factory; **~faß** *n* powder keg; **~isierbar** *a* pulverable; **~isieren** *tr* to powder, to pulverize; **~ladung** *f* powder charge; **~magazin** *n* powder magazine; **~schnee** *m* powdery snow; **~treibladung** *f* propelling powder charge.

Pump *m* credit; *auf ~ nehmen* to buy on tick; **~e** *f* pump; **~en** *tr* to pump; (*borgen*) to take on tick; (*leihweise geben*) to give on tick; *von jdm ~~* to touch s. o. for; **~~floß** *n* pump float; **~~hub** *m* pump lift; **~~schwengel** *m* pump-handle; **~ernickel** *m* Westphalian rye-bread; **~hosen** *f pl* wide knickerbockers, plus-fours *pl*; **~station** *f* water-station; **~werk** *n* pumping-work.

Punkt *m* point; *typ* full stop, *Am* period; (*i-Punkt, tele*) dot; (*Ort*) spot, place; *Am* (*Parteiprogramm*) plank; (*Bericht*) item, point; (*Vertrag*) clause, term; (*Gesprächsgegenstand*) subject, matter, topic; (*Kleiderkarte*) coupon, point; (*Kartenspiel*) pip; *~ 10 Uhr* on the stroke of ten, at ten sharp; *auf den toten ~ gelangen* (*fig*) to come to a dead-lock; *e-n wunden ~ berühren* to touch a sore spot; *nach ~en verlieren* to lose on points; *bis zu e-m gewissen ~* to a certain extent; *in allen ~en* in every respect; *die wesentlichen ~e* (*jur*) the merits *pl*; *~ für ~* point by point; in detail; *ein strittiger ~* a point at issue; *der springende ~* the salient point; **~feuer** *n* converging fire; **~förmig** *a* punctiform; in lumps; cratershaped; **~ieren** *tr* (*mit ~en versehen*) to punctuate, to point; (*tüpfeln*) to dot; *med* to tap, to puncture; (*Kupferstecher*) to stipple; *~ierte Linie* dotted line; **~iernadel** *f med* puncturing-needle; **~ionsflüssigkeit** *f med* puncture exudate; **~muster** *n* (*Kleid*) polka dot; **~reihe** *f* row of dots, series of points; **~richter** *m sport* referee, umpire; **~roller** *m* massage roller; **~schweißung** *f* spot welding; **~sieg** *m* winning on points; **~~er** *m* winner on points; **~um** *n* full stop; end; *damit ~~!* there's an end of it! **~ur** *f med* puncture; **~weise** *adv* point-for-point, point-by-point; **~wertung** *f* classification by points; **~zahl** *f sport* score; **~ziel** *n mil* pin-point target.

pünktlich *a* punctual, prompt, in (*od* to, on) time, at the right time, *Am sl* on the nose; (*genau*) accurate, exact; **~keit** *f* punctuality.

Punsch *m* punch; **~bowle** *f* punch-bowl, negus; **~essenz** *f* punch-extract; **~löffel** *m* punch-ladle.

Punze *f* punch; **~n** *tr* to punch.

Pupille *f* pupil; **~nabstand** *m* distance between the pupils; **~nerweiterung** *f* dilation of the pupil, mydriasis.

Püppchen *n* little doll; (*kleines Mädchen*) *fam* moppet; (*Liebling*) darling.

Puppe *f* (*Kinderspielzeug*) doll; (*häßliche ~*) golliwog; (*Draht~*) puppet; (*Kleiderpuppe, fig Strohmann*) dummy; *zoo* chrysalis, pupa; (*Seidenspinner*) cocoon; **~ngesicht** *n* doll's features *pl*; **~nhaus** *n* doll's house; **~nspiel** *n* puppet-show; **~ntheater** *n* Punch-and-Judy show; **~nwagen** *m* doll's pram, doll carriage.

pur *a* pure, sheer; **~gieren** *tr, itr* to purge; **~giermittel** *n* purgative.

Puritan|er *m* Puritan; **~ertum** *n* Puritanism; **~isch** *a* Puritan.

Purpur *m* purple; **~n, ~rot** *a* purple-(-coloured).

Purzel|baum *m* somersault; **~n** *itr* to tumble down.

Puste *f fam* breath; **~n** *itr* to puff; to blow.

Pustel *f* pustule, pimple; (*kleine Blase*) bubble, bleb; **~ausschlag** *m med* pustular eruption; **~flechte** *f med* impetigo.

Pute *f* turkey-hen; **~r** *m* turkey-cock; **~rrot** *a* scarlet.

Putsch *m* uprising; insurrection; revolt; riot; **~en** *itr* to riot; *tr* (*auf~*) to goad on; **~ist** *m* rebel, insurgent; rioter.

Putz *m* (*Staat, Kleid*) dress, finery, *fam* get-up; (*Besatz*) trimming; (*Zierat*) ornaments *pl*; (*Modewaren*) millinery; (*Ver~*) rough-cast; plaster, parget; **~(baum)wolle** *f* cotton waste; **~bürste** *f* (polishing-)brush; **~en** *tr* (*reinigen*) to clean, to cleanse, to polish; *chem* to dry-clean; (*scheuern*) to scour, to mop, to scrub; (*fegen*) to sweep; (*abwischen*) to wipe; (*Nase*) to blow, to wipe; (*Zähne*) to brush; (*Schuhe*) to polish, to black, *Am* to shine; (*Metall*) to burnish; (*Pferd*) to groom; (*Baum*) to lop; (*Geflügel, Gemüse*) to pick; (*kleiden*) to dress; (*garnieren*) to trim; (*schmücken*) to adorn; to decorate; (*ver~~*) to roughcast; to plaster; *r* to dress up, to smarten; **~er** *m* cleaner; *mil* batman; **~frau** *f* char-woman, *Am* scrubwoman; **~geschäft** *n* millinery, milliner's shop; **~ig** *a fam* funny, droll; **~lappen** *m* duster, flannel, polishing cloth; mop, cleaning rag, scouring cloth; **~leder** *n* chamois (leather); **~macherin** *f* milliner; **~mittel** *n* cleaning material; cleanser, detergent; **~pulver** *n* polishing powder; whiting; **~sand** *m* burnishing sand; **~sucht** *f* love of dress; **~süchtig** *a* fond of finery; **~tisch** *m* dressing table; **~tuch** *n* cloth for cleaning; **~waren** *pl* millinery; **~wolle** *f* cotton waste; rags *pl*; **~zeug** *n* cleaning utensils *pl*; *~~ u. Nähzeug mil* field kit.

Pygmäe *m* pygmy.

Pyjama *m* pyjamas *pl*, *Am* pajamas *pl.*

Pyramide *f* pyramid; (*Gewehr~*) stack; **~nförmig** *a* pyramidal.

Pyrenä|en *pl* Pyrenees *pl*; **~isch** *a* Pyrenean; *~~e Halbinsel* Iberian Peninsula.

Pyrotechni|k *f* pyrotechnics *pl*; **~~er** *m* pyrotechnist; **~sch** *a*: *~~e Waren* fireworks *pl.*

pythagoreisch *a* Pythagorean.

Q

Q Abk mit Q siehe Liste der Abk.
quabbel|ig *a* flabby, wobbly; (*Moorboden*) quaky, quaggy; (*glitschig*) gelatinous; (*zitterig*) quivering; (*fleischig*) puddy, plumy; **~n** *itr* to be flabby; to shake (like jelly); to wobble; (*Boden*) to be quaky; (*Wangen, Muskeln etc*) to be flaccid.
Quack|elei *f* (*Plunder*) trash, rubbish; (*Unentschlossenheit*) irresolution, wavering; (*Rederei*) silly talk; **~eln** *itr* to shilly-shally; **~salber** *m* quack; (*Marktschreier*) mountebank; **~~arznei** *f* quack medicine; **~~ei** *f* quackery; **~~n** *itr* to doctor, to (play the) quack; to experiment on.
Quader *m* square stone; ashlar; block; **~mauerwerk** *n* ashlar facing; **~sandstein** *m* freestone; **~stein** *m* square stone; ashlar; **~verkleidung** *f* dressed-stone facing, ashlar facing.
Quadrant *m* quadrant; leg; **~enfläche** *f* quadrant plate; **~zirkel** *m* quadrant compass.
Quadrat *n* square; *ins ~ erheben* to square; **~fuß** *m* square foot; **~isch** *a* quadratic, square; **~kilometer** *n* square kilometre (1 qkm = 0.38 square mile); **~meter** *n* square metre (1 qm = 10.76 square feet); **~netz** *n* square grid (*od* net), grid net; **~ur** *f* quadrature; **~wurzel** *f* square root; *die ~~ ziehen* to extract square root; **~zahl** *f* square number; **~zentimeter** *n* square centimetre (1 qcm = 0.155 square inch).
quadr|ieren *tr* to square; to raise to second power; **~ille** *f* quadrille; **~illion** *f* quadrillion.
quak! *interj* croak! **~en** *itr* (*Ente*) to quack; (*Frosch*) to croak.
quäk|en *itr* to squeak; **~er** *m* member of the Society of Friends; quaker; **~~bund** *m* Society of Friends.
Qual *f* pain, torment, torture; (*Seelen~*) grief, agony; (*stechender Schmerz*) pang; **~voll** *a* very painful, agonizing; full of anguish; distressing.
quäl|en *tr* to pain, to torment; (*foltern*) to torture; (*kränken*) to grieve; (*necken*) to tease; (*belästigen*) to bother, to pester; (*ärgern*) to annoy, to worry, to harrass; (*langweilen*) to bore; *r* (*abarbeiten*) to toil hard, to drudge; (*durchkämpfen*) to struggle, **~end** *a* very painful; tormenting; (*stärker*) agonizing; (*Schmerz*) excruciating; (*nervenaufreibend*) harrowing, distressing; vexing; **~er** *m* tormentor (*od* -er); (*langweiliger Mensch*) bore; **~~ei** *f* tormenting; torture; (*durch Necken*) teasing; (*Zudringlichkeit mit Bitten*) importunity, importuning; (*Ärger*) annoyance, pestering, worry, *Am* worriment; (*schwere Arbeit*) drudgery; **~geist** *m* nuisance, plague.
Qual|ifikation *f* qualification; capacity; ability; **~ifizieren** *tr* to qualify; *r* to be fit for; **~ität** *f* quality, rate, grade; class; (*Art*) kind; (*Sorte*) sort, type; (*Marke*) description, mark, brand; *erster ~~* of prime quality; first-rate, topnotch; *schlechte ~~* poor quality; **~~sarbeit** *f* work of high quality; **~~sbestimmung** *f* quality grading; **~~sbezeichnung** *f* quality description; **~~serzeugnis** *n* high quality product; **~~sstahl** *m* high-grade steel; **~~sverbesserung** *f* improvement in quality; **~~sverschlechterung** *f* deterioration in quality; **~~svorsprung** *m* qualitative advantage; **~~sware** *f* article of superior quality; high-class article; **~itativ** *a* qualitative, in quality.
Qualle *f* jelly-fish, medusa.
Qualm *m* dense smoke; (*Dampf*) vapo(u)r, steam; (*Dunst*) fume; **~en** *itr* to smoke; to emit thick smoke; **~ig** *a* smoky.
Quant|en *n pl* energy elements in atoms; **~enausbeute** *f* quantum efficiency; **~ensprung** *m* quantum transition (*od* jump); **~entheorie** *f* quantum theory; **~enzahl** *f* quantum number; **~ität** *f* quantity; (*große Zahl*) bulk; (*Masse*) amount; **~~sbestimmung** *f* quantitative determination; **~~sbeschränkung** *f* limitation on the quantity; **~itativ** *a* quantitative; **~um** *n* quantum, quantity, amount; (*Anteil*) portion, share, quota.
Quappe *f* eel-pout; (*des Frosches*) tadpole.
Quarantäne *f* quarantine; *unter ~ stellen* to quarantine; **~flagge** *f* yellow flag; **~hafen** *m* quarantine port.
Quark *m* curd(s *pl*); *fig* rubbish, trifle; **~käse** *m* whey-cheese, cottage cheese.
Quart *n* quart; *typ* quarto; *mus* fourth; (*Fechten*) carte; **~a** *f* third form; **~al** *n* quarter (of a year); (*Termin*) quarter-day; (*Zeitraum*) term; **~~sabrechnung** *f* quarterly statement of accounts; **~~srechnung** *f* quarterly bill; **~~sweise** *adv* quarterly, every three months; **~~zahlung** *f* quarterly payment; **~aner** *m* third-form boy; **~är** *n* quaternary; **~band** *m* quarto volume; **~e** *f* quart; *mus* fourth; (*Fechten*) carte; **~ett** *n* quartet(te); **~format** *n typ* quarto.
Quartier *n* (*Stadtteil*) quarter; district; (*Wohnung*) lodging(s *pl*); *mil* quarters, billets *pl*; *in ~ legen* to billet upon; *im ~ liegen bei jdm* to be quartered (*od* billeted) upon s. o.; **~amt** *n* quartering (*od* billeting) office; **~macher** *m* billeting officer; **~meister** *m* quartermaster; **~zettel** *m* billet, billeting paper (*od* slip).
Quarz *m* quartz; **~artig** *a* quartzous, quartzose; **~faden** *m* quartz filament; **~gesteuert** *a* crystal-controlled; **~glas** *n* quartz glass; **~gleichrichter** *m* crystal rectifier; **~haltig** *a* quartziferous; **~lampe** *f med* quartz lamp; **~steuerung** *f* crystal control; quartz control.
quasi *adv* as it were.
quasseln *itr fam* to talk nonsense (*od sl* rot).
Quaste *f* tassel, tuft; (*Pinsel*) brush.
Quatsch *m* nonsense, foolish talk; *fam* bosh, *Am fam* poppycock, *sl* applesauce, baloney, bunk; **~en** *itr* to talk nonsense (*od* bosh), to twaddle; **~kopf** *m* twaddler.

*

Quecke *f* couch-grass, quick-grass.
Quecksilber *n* mercury, quicksilver; **~artig** *a* mercurial; **~barometer** *n* mercury barometer; **~dampflampe** *f* mercury-vapo(u)r lamp; **~gleichrichter** *m* mercury rectifier; **~lampe** *f* mercury lamp; **~legierung** *f* mercury alloy, amalgam; **~n** *a* mercury, mercurial; **~oxyd** *n* mercuric oxyd; **~präparat** *n* mercurial preparation; **~salbe** *f* mercurial ointment; **~säule** *f* column of mercury; (*Luftdruck*) barometric pressure; **~stand** *m* mercury level; **~vergiftung** *f* mercury poisoning.
Quell *m* spring; **~bach** *m* river source; **~e** *f* spring; (*Ursprung*) source; (*Öl*) well; (*Springquell, Behälter*) fountain; *fig* origin; *aus erster ~~* first hand information; *es aus guter ~~ wissen* to have it on good authority (*od* from a good source); *e-e ~~ fassen* to confine a spring; **~en** *irr itr* (*herausströmen*) to gush, to well; (*sprudeln*) to spring; (*fließen*) to flow (from); (*hervorkommen*) to arise; (*aufschwellen*) to swell, to expand; (*einweichen*) to soak, to steep, to imbibe moisture; *fig* to arise, to originate, to spring (from); *tr* to soak; **~~angabe** *f* mention of sources used; **~~forschung** *f* critical investigation, original research work; **~~mäßig** *a* authentic; on good authority; **~fassung** *f* capture of spring, well shaft; **~gebiet** *n* headwaters *pl*; **~niveau** *n* spring horizon; **~salz** *n* spring salt; **~schicht** *f* swelling layer; **~sole** *f* spring brine; **~ung** *f* swelling; (*Geschwulst*) tumefaction; (*Einweichen*) soaking; **~wasser** *n* spring water, well water.
Quendel *m bot* wild thyme.
Queng|elei *f* grumbling; nagging, whining; fault-finding; **~(e)lig** *a* grumbling; cranky; **~eln** *itr* to grumble; to nag; to whine; to jangle; *Am* to gripe; **~ler** *m* grumbler; griper; crank.
Quentchen *n* dram; *fig* trifle.
quer *a* cross, transverse, transversal; diagonal; (*schräg*) slanting, oblique; (*seitlich*) lateral; *adv* crosswise, crossway, across; obliquely; *kreuz u. ~* criss-cross, all over, in all directions; *~ gehen fig* to go wrong; **~ab** *adv* abreast (of), athwart; off; **~achse** *f* transverse axis; lateral axis; roll axis; **~aufnahme** horizontal picture; **~arm** *m* branch rod; crossarm; **~balken** *m* crossbeam; **~beet** *adv: ~~ fahren fam* to drive cross-country; **~bewegung** *f* transverse movement; **~binder** *m* bow tie; **~durch** *adv* right across; **~e** *f* transverse direction; (*Breite*) breadth; *der ~~ nach* crosswise, athwart; *jdm in die ~~ kommen* to thwart (*od* to cross) s. o.'s plans; to interfere; **~en** *tr* to cross; to traverse; **~falte** *f* transverse fold; **~faser** *f* cross grain; **~feder** *f* transverse spring; **~feldein** *adv* across country; cross-country; **~festigkeit** *f* lateral strength; **~feuer** *n mil* enfilading fire; **~flöte** *f* German flute; **~format** *n* broadsheet; **~gang** *m* alleyway; *min* traverse; **~gestreift** *a* transversely striated; **~kopf** *m* queer fellow; crank; **~köpfig** *a* wrong-headed; **~lage** *f aero* bank; *med* cross-birth; **~laufend** *a* transversal, transverse; **~leiste** *f* cross-piece; **~leitung** *f* cross-line; **~moment** *n aero* rolling moment; **~neigung** *f aero* bank, turn; banking turn; **~~sgrad** *m aero* degree of bank; **~~smesser** *m aero* bank and turn indicator; **~nute** *f* transverse slot; **~pfeife** *f* fife; **~profil** *n* cross section; **~rahmen** *m* cross frame; **~reihe** *f* cross-row; **~richtung** *f* cross direction; **~riegel** *m* transom, traverse; girder, beam; **~ring** *m* transverse ring; **~ruder** *n aero* aileron; wing flap; *~~ geben* to apply bank; **~~ausschlag** *m* aileron

deflection, movement of the aileron; **~~hebel** *m* aileron lever; **~~trimmung** *f* aileron trimming; **~schiene** *f* crossbar; **~schiff** *n* transept; **~~s** *adv* athwartships; **~schläger** *m mil* ricochet; **~schnitt** *m* cross-section, cross cut; profile; *med* transverse incision; **~~ansicht** *f* cross-sectional view; **~~ebene** *f* plane of cross section; **~schott** *n mar* transverse bulkhead; **~schub** *m* lateral thrust; **~spalte** *f* transverse fissure; **~spant** *m* bulkhead; **~stabilität** *f aero* lateral (*od* latent) stability; **~steuer** *n aero* aileron control; **~~ung** *f aero* lateral control; **~straße** *f* cross-road, side road; *zwei* **~~n** *entfernt wohnen* to live two blocks from here; **~strich** *m* crossline; (*Gedankenstrich*) dash; (*Federstrich*) stroke; **~summe** *f* total of the digits of a number; **~tal** *n* transversal valley; **~träger** *m* traverse; **~treiberei** *f* intrigue; **~über** *adv* (right) across; **~verbindung** *f* lateral (*od* direct) communication; **~wand** *f* transverse wall; **~weg** *m* by-road, cross-road, cross-country road; **~welle** *f* transverse shaft.

Querul|ant *m* querulous person, grumbler, *Am* griper; **~ieren** *itr* to be querulous, to grumble, *Am* to gripe.

Quetsch|e *f* pinch; presser; squeezer; *min* crusher; (*kleines Unternehmen*) small shop; **~en** *tr* to press, to squash, to smash; to squeeze; to pinch; (*zerdrücken*) to crush, to quash; *med* to bruise, to crush, to contuse; **~falte** *f* inverted pleat; **~kartoffeln** *f pl* mashed potatoes *pl*; **~kommode** *f fam* accordion; **~ung, ~wunde** *f* contusion, bruise; contused wound.

*

quick *a* lively, brisk; **~born** *m poet* fountain of rejuvenescence; **~en** *tr tech* to amalgamate; **~sand** *m* quicksand.

quieken *itr* to squeak, to squeal.

quietsch|en *itr* to squeak, to scream, to squeal; (*Tür*) to creak; **~vergnügt** *a* gay as a lark; merry as a grig; fit as a fiddle.

Quinta *f* second form; **~ner** *m* second-form boy; **~e** *f* quinte; *mus* fifth; **~essenz** *f* quintessence, *Am sl* low-down; **~ett** *n* quintet.

Quirl *m* twirling-stick, whisk, beater; *bot* whorl, verticil; **~en** *tr* to twirl; (*Eier*) to whisk, to beat up; **~förmig** *a bot* verticillate.

quitt *a* quits, even, square; (*frei*) free, rid; **~** *sein mit* to be quits with, *Am* to be about an even treat; (*nichts mehr zu tun haben*) to be through; **~ieren** *tr* to (give a) receipt (for), to mark paid, to acknowledge receipt of; (*verlassen*) to quit, to abandon, to leave; **~ung** *f* receipt, acknowledg(e)ment; *gegen* **~~** on receipt; *e-e* **~~** *ausstellen* to give a receipt; **~~sbuch** *n* receipt book; **~~sformular** *n* receipt form; **~~sstempel** *m* receipt stamp.

Quitte *f* quince; (*Baum*) quince-tree; **~ngelb** *a* (as) yellow as a quince; **~nmus** *n* quince preserve.

Quot|e *f* quota; (*Anteil*) share, portion; *anteilsmäßige* **~~** pro rate share; **~ient** *m* quotient; **~ieren** *tr* to quote.

R

R *Abk mit* ***R*** *siehe Liste der Abk.*

Rabatt *m com* (trade) discount, allowance, rebate (*auf* on), abatement, deduction; *bei Barzahlung* **~** *geben* to allow discount for cash; *wieviel* **~** *geben Sie?* what discount is there? *10%* **~** *bekommen* to get a ten per cent discount; **~** *gewähren* to grant (*od* to allow) discount (*od* rebate *od* deduction); **~ieren** *tr* to discount, to abate; **~marke** *f* discount ticket.

Rabatte *f* (*Gartenbeet*) bed, border; (*Schneiderei*) facing.

Rabbin|er *m* rabbi; **~isch** *a* rabbinical.

Rabe *m* raven; *weißer* **~** (*fig*) rare bird; rarity; *stehlen wie ein* **~** to steal like a magpie; **~naas** *n* carrion; **~neltern** *pl* unnatural parents *pl*; **~nmutter** *f* unnatural mother; **~nschwarz** *a* raven-black; **~nstein** *m* place of execution; **~nvater** *m* unnatural father.

rabiat *a* (*aufgebracht, zornig*) rabid, raving, furious.

Rabulist *m* pettifogger; **~erei** *f* pettifoggery; **~isch** *a* pettifogging.

*

Rach|e *f* revenge, vengeance; **~~** *nehmen an* to take revenge on; *nach* **~~** *schreien* to cry for vengeance; **~eakt** *m* act of vengeance; **~edurst** *m* thirst of (*od* for) revenge; **~egöttin** *f* avenging goddess; **~eschnaubend** *a* breathing vengeance; **~eschwur** *m* oath to revenge o. s.; **~gier, ~sucht** *f* thirst for revenge; vindictiveness; revengefulness; **~gierig, ~süchtig** *a* revengeful; (*nachtragend*) vindictive.

räch|en *tr* to avenge, to revenge; *sich* **~~** to take revenge on; to revenge o. s. on; *sie rächte sich an ihm* (*Am fam*) she got it back on him; *es wird sich an ihm* **~~** it will come home to him; **~er** *m*, **~erin** *f* avenger, revenger.

Rachen *m* throat, *anat* pharynx, fauces *pl*; (*Mundhöhle*) oral cavity; (*Maul*) mouth, jaws *pl*; *fig* (*Schlund*) abyss, jaws *pl*; **~abstrich** *m* throat swab; **~bräune** *f med* diphtheria, angina faucium; **~entzündung** *f* pharingitis; **~höhle** *f* pharynx, pharyngeal cavity; **~katarrh** *m* cold in the throat, pharyngitis.

Rachit|is *f* rickets *pl*; **~isch** *a* rickety.

Racker *m* rascal, roguey; (*Mädchen*) minx.

Rad *n* wheel; (*Rolle*) trundle; (*Spinn~*) spinning-wheel; (*Fahr~*) (bi)cycle, machine, *fam* bike; (*Glücks~*) wheel of fortune; (*ein*) **~** *schlagen* to turn somersaults (*od* cartwheels), *Am* to turn handsprings; (*Pfau*) to spread the tail; *aufs* **~** *flechten* to break on the wheel; *das fünfte* **~** *am Wagen sein fig* to be superfluous; *unter die Räder kommen fig* to go to the dogs; **~abzieher** *m* wheel remover (*od* puller); **~achse** *f* axle-tree; **~antrieb** *m* wheel drive; **~bremse** *f* hub-brake; **~dampfer** *m* paddle-steamer, *Am* side-wheeler; **~durchmesser** *m* wheel diameter; **~eln** *itr*, **~fahren** *irr itr* to cycle, to ride a bicycle, to bike; to pedal; **~fahrer, ~ler** *m* cyclist, bicycle rider, *Am* cycler; **~fahrweg** *m* cycle track; **~felge** *f* felloe, felly; **~förmig** *a* wheel-shaped; **~gabel** *f* wheel fork; **~gestell** *n tech* wheel frame; *rail* bogie, *Am* truck; **~kappe** *f mot* wheel cap, hub cap; **~kasten** *m* wheelcase; (*Dampfer*) paddle-box; **~kranz** *m* rim; **~lichtmaschine** *f* bicycle dynamo; **~nabe** *f* nave, hub; **~reifen** *m* tyre, *Am* tire; **~rennbahn** *f* cycling track; **~rennen** *n* cycle race; **~schaufel** *f* (*Wasserrad*) sweep; paddle-board; **~scheibe** *f* wheel disk; **~schuh** *m* brake, skid; **~speiche** *f* spoke; **~sport** *m* cycling; **~spur** *f* rut, wheel track; **~stand** *m mot* wheel-base; **~sturz** *m mot* camber of wheels; **~verkleidung** *f* wheel casing, streamlining of the wheel; **~welle** *f* wheel-shaft; **~zahn** *m* cog (of a wheel); **~zapfen** *m* spindle, pivot; **~zugmaschine** *f* wheeled traction vehicle.

Radar *n* (*Funkmessen*) *mil Am* radar; *ein mit* **~** *ausgerüsteter Düsenjäger* a radar-equipped jet fighter; **~abwehrgerät** *n* anti-radar detection device; **~abwehrnetz** *n* defence radar network; **~apparat** *m* radar set; **~bombe** *f* radar bomb; **~bombenzieleinrichtung** *f* radar bomb sight; **~einrichtung** *f* radar installation; **~feuerleitung** *f* (*der Flak*) radar fire control (for anti-aircraft guns); *Flak mit* **~~** radar directed anti-aircraft gun; *Flakfeuer mit* **~~** radar controlled anti-aircraft fire; **~flugzeug** *n* radar plane; **~flugzeugwarnnetz** *n* radar aircraft warning network; **~gerät** *n* radar (-set), radar device; *was ist im* **~~** *zu sehen?* what is on the radar? *mit dem* **~~** *erfaßtes Flugzeug* an aircraft picked up by radar; *Superfestungen bombardierten mit Hilfe des* **~~s** *Brükken u. Flakbatterien* Superforts radar bombed bridges and flak batteries; **~gesteuert** *a* radar-guided; **~~e** *Bombe* radar-guided bomb; **~~e** *Rakete* radar-guided rocket; **~höhenmesser** *m aero* radar altimeter; **~leuchtschirm** *m* radar screen; **~mann** *m* (*Funkmeßmann*) radar man, *Am sl* Mickey; **~navigationsgerät** *n* plan-position indicator (*Abk* P.P.I.); **~navigation** *f aero* (*Luftnavigation*) oboe; (*Fernnavigation*) loran; **~netz** *n* radar network; **~offizier** *m* radar officer; **~ortungsgerät** *n* radar-detection device; **~reichweite** *f* radar range; **~schirm** *m* radar screen, *Am* radar scope; **~sicher** *a* radarproof; **~station** *f* radar station; (*Küstenstation*) shore-based radar station; *e-e feindliche* **~~** *ausfindig machen* to locate an enemy radar station; *die* **~~** *faßte den Bomber* the radar station picked up the bomber; **~steuerung** *f* (*von Geschossen*) radar guiding (of missiles); **~suchantenne** *f* radar search antenna; **~techniker** *m* radar operator; **~visier** *n aero, mil* radar sight; *Kanone mit* **~~** radar sighted cannon; **~wagen** *m aero Am* GCA radar truck; **~warnnetz** *n* radar warning network; **~warnschirm** *m* radar warning screen; **~warnstation** *f* (*Flugmeldestation*) radar warning station; **~zeichen** *n* (*auf dem Beobachtungsschirm*) radar trace; blip; **~zielballon** *m* radar target balloon.

Radau *m fam* noise, row, racket; riot; rumpus; hubbub; (*Kinder*) *sl* rag; *~ machen* to kick up a row; **~bruder, ~macher** *m* rowdy, rioter; **~komödie** *f theat* slapstick comedy; **~lustig** *a* quarrelsome, cantankerous, *Am* rambunctious.

Rade *f bot* cockle.

radebrechen *itr, tr* to stammer and stutter; to jabber; to murder (*od* to mangle) a language; *das Englische ~* to speak broken English; to mangle the King's English.

Rädelsführer *m* ringleader.

räder|n *tr* (*Verbrecher*) to break (up)on the wheel; (*martern*) to torture; *wie gerädert sein* to be quite knocked up; **~werk** *n* gearing, wheels *pl*; (*Uhr*) clock-work.

Radial|ebene *f* radial plane; **~fräser** *m* radial-milling cutter; **~geschwindigkeit** *f* radial velocity; **~motor** *m* radial engine; **~turbine** *f* radial-flow turbine.

radier|en *tr, itr* (*mit Gummi*) to rub out, to erase; (*in Kupfer*) to etch; **~er** *m* etcher; (*Gummi*) india-rubber; **~gummi** *m* (india-) rubber, *Am* eraser; **~kunst** *f* etching; **~messer** *n* eraser, penknife; **~nadel** *f* pointer, etching-needle; **~ung** *f* (*Bild*) etching; (*Radieren*) erasure.

Radieschen *n bot* radish; *mil* signal flare, illuminating flare.

radikal *a* radical; **~e(r)** *m* radical; extremist; **~isieren** *tr* to radicalize; **~ismus** *m* radicalism.

Radio *n* wireless, broadcast, *Am meist* radio; *siehe auch: Funk, Rundfunk*; (*Apparat*) wireless set, radio set, radio; *~ für Wechselstrom, Gleichstrom od Batterie* radio playing on AC, DC or battery; *~ mit Münzeinwurf* coin-operated radio; *ich habe es im ~ gehört* I have heard it on the radio; *im ~ sprechen* to speak over the radio; *das ~ abstellen* to turn off the radio; *das ~ einstellen* to tune in the radio; *~ hören* to listen (in), to listen to the wireless; **~aktiv** *a* radioactive; *~~ machen* to make radioactive, to activate; *~~es Isotop* radioactive isotope; *~~e Kriegführung* radioactive warfare; *~~es Produkt* metabolon; *~~er Spurenfinder* radioactive tracer; *~~er Staub* radioactive dust, radioactive cloud; *~~es Teilchen* radioactive particle; *~~e Teilchen entströmen den Kernreaktionen, die im Zyklotron in Gang gesetzt wurden* radioactive particles emanate from the nuclear reactions set up within the cyclotron; *~~e Umwandlung* radioactive transformation; *~~e Vergiftung* radioactive poisoning; *~~e Waffen* radioactive weapons; **~aktivität** *f* radioactivity; *induzierte ~~* induced radioactivity; *künstliche ~~* artificial radioactivity; *das Zyklotron ist zum Schutz gegen ~~ durch Betonwände abgeschirmt* the cyclotron is shielded against radioactivity by concrete walls; **~amateur, ~bastler** *m* broadcast amateur, radio amateur, amateur radio operator, *sl* (radio) ham; **~anlage** *f* radio installation; **~apparat** *m* wireless set, radio set, radio, radio receiver, radio apparatus; **~ausrüstung** *f* radio equipment; **~bastler** *m* home constructor; **~biologe** *m* radiobiologist; **~darbietung** *f* radio broadcast; **~durchsage** *f* spot announcement; **~empfang** *m* broadcast (*od* radio) reception; **~empfänger** *m* wireless receiving set, radio receiving set, radio set, (radio) receiver; **~gehäuse** *n* receiver cabinet; **~geschäft** *n* radio shop, *Am* radio store; **~goniometer** *m* (*Funkpeiler*) radiogoniometer; **~gramm** *n* wireless message, radiogram; **~grammophon** *n* (*Kombination*) radio gramophone (*Abk* radiogram), *Am* radio phonograph combination, phono-combination; **~hochfrequenz** *f* radio high frequency; **~händler** *m* radio dealer; **~hörer** *m* broadcast (*od* radio) listener; **~indikator** *m* (*Isotop*) tracer; **~industrie** *f* radio industry; **~inserent** *m* radio advertiser, *Am* sponsor; **~isotop** *n* radioisotope; **~kanal** *m* (*Frequenz*) radio channel; **~loge** *m* radiologist; **~logie** *f* radiology; **~logisch** *a* radiological; *~~e Kriegführung* radiological warfare; **~kommentator** *m* radio commentator, *Am* (*bei e-m Sendenetz*) network commentator; **~mechaniker** *m* radio mechanic, radio repairman, radio technician, radio trouble shooter, *Am* radiotrician; **~meter** *n* (*Strahlungsmesser*) radiometer; **~peilgerät** *n* radio direction-finder; **~peilrahmen** *m* radio loop; **~phonie** *f* radiophony; **~plattenspieler** *m* record-player radio, *Am* radio phonograph; **~reklame** *f* radio advertising; **~röhre** *f* wireless valve, *Am* (radio) tube; **~schaltung** *f* radio circuit; **~schlager** *m* radio hit (song); **~sender** *m*, **~station** *f* broadcasting station, transmitter, (radio) station; **~sendung** *f* radio transmission, broadcast; **~sonde** *f* radiosonde, radiometeorograph; **~studio** *n* radio studio; **~technik** *f* radiotechnology; **~techniker** *m* radio technician (*od* engineer); **~telegramm** *n* radio telegram, radiogram; **~telegraphie** *f* radio telegraphy; **~telephon** *n* radio telephone; (*tragbar*) *Am* walkie-talkie, handie-talkie; **~telephonie** *f* radio telephony; **~truhe** *f* (*mit Plattenspielerschrank*) radio console; **~übertragung** *f* broadcast transmission; **~wellen** *f pl* broadcast waves *pl*, radio waves *pl*, airwaves *pl*; **~werbesendung** *f* (*Reklamesendung*) radio advertising; **~zeitung** *f* radio newspaper.

Radium *n* radium; **~behälter** *m* radiode; **~behandlung, ~therapie** *f* radiumtherapy, Curie-therapy; **~emanation** *f* (*Radon*) radium emanation, radon; *Einheit der ~~* curie; **~strahlen** *m pl* radium rays *pl*; **~strahlung** *f* radium radiation; **~zerfall** *m* disintegration of radium; **~zerfallsreihen** *f pl* radium disintegration series *pl*.

Radius *m* radius; **~vektor** *m* radius vector.

Radscha *m* Raja(h).

raff|en *tr* to snatch up; to pick up; to carry off; *ein Kleid ~~* to tie up a dress, to gather up; **~gier** *f* rapacity; **~gierig** *a* rapacious.

Raffin|ade *f* refined sugar; **~ement** *n fig* refinement; **~erie** *f* refinery; **~ieren** *tr* to refine; **~iert** *a* refined; *fig* cunning, shrewd, clever; **~~heit** *f* cunning; *fig* craftiness.

ragen *itr* to tower, to tower up; to project, to be prominent.

Ragout *n* stew, hash, ragout, hotchpotch.

Rahe *f* yard; *große ~* main yard; **~segel** *n* yard-sail.

Rahm *m* cream; *Schlag~* whipped cream; *den ~ abschöpfen* (*auch fig*) to take off the cream, to skim the milk; **~bonbon** *n* toffee, *Am* taffy; **~eis** *n* ice cream; **~käse** *f* cream cheese; **~kelle** *f* cream skimmer; **~löffel** *m* cream spoon; **~torte** *f* cream tart.

Rahmen *m* frame; (*Gestell*) rack; (*Mitnehmer*) *tech* carrier; (*Bilder~*) picture-frame; (*Fenster~*) window-frame; (*Stick~*) tambour; (*Schuh~*) welt; (*Einfassung*) edge; *fig* limit, compass; (*Bereich*) scope; (*Ort u. Handlung*) setting; surroundings *pl*, milieu; *in engem ~* within a close compass, within narrow bounds; *~ tr* (*ab~*) to skim, to cream off; (*ein~*) to frame; **~antenne** *f* frame (*od* loop) aerial, *Am* loop antenna, coil antenna; **~empfang** *m radio* loop reception; **~empfänger** *m* loop receiver; **~erzählung** *f* framework story; **~peiler** *m* loop direction finder; **~stickerei** *f* frame-embroidery, tambour-work; **~sucher** *m phot* direct vision finder.

Rain *m* balk, head-land, ridge; edge.

raisonieren *itr* to argue; (*schelten*) to grumble.

Rakete *f* rocket; (*Signal~*) sky-rocket; *fliegende ~* flying rocket; *~ mit rasanter Flugbahn* high-velocity (anti-tank) rocket (*Abk* HVATR); *panzerbrechende ~* armo(u)r-piercing rocket; *radargesteuerte ~* radar-guided rocket; *zweistufige ~* two-stage rocket; *mit ~n ausgerüsteter Düsenjäger* rocket-bearing jet fighter; *e-e ~ abfeuern* to launch (*od* to shoot) a rocket; *mit ~n beschießen* to rocket; *die feindlichen Truppen wurden mit Bomben belegt u. mit Bordwaffen u. ~n beschossen* the enemy troops were bombed, strafed and rocketed; **~nabschuß** *m* rocket launching; **~~basis** *f* rocket launching site; (*Bettung*) rocket launching platform; **~nangriff** *m* rocket attack; (*aus der Luft*) aerial rocket attack; **~nantrieb** *m* rocket propulsion, rocket drive, rocket power; *mit ~~* rocket-driven, rocket-propelled, rocket-powered; **~nbatterie** *f* rocket battery; **~nbombe** *f* rocket bomb, rocket-driven bomb; V-2 rocket bomb; **~nflugzeug** *n* rocket plane, rocket-propelled airplane; jet-rocket plane; **~nforschung** *f* rocket research; **~ngeschoß** *n* rocket projectile; **~ngeschütz** *n* rocket gun; **~ngranate** *f* rocket shell; **~njäger** *m aero* rocket fighter plane; **~nmotor** *m* (*Abk R-Trieb*) rocket engine, rocket motor, *Am* rocket, rocketjet; **~nsatz** *m* rocket composition; **~nsignal** *n* rocket signal; **~nsperrfeuer** *n* rocket barrage; **~nstart** *m* rocket-assisted take-off; **~ntechnik** *f* rocket technique; **~nversuchsgelände** *n* rocket testing ground; **~nvortrieb** *m* rocket propulsion; **~nwerfer** *m* rocket launcher; rocket projector; (*Stalinorgel*) multiple rocket launcher; (*Ofenrohr, Panzerschreck*) *Am* bazooka; (*Kanone*) recoilless gun.

Rakett *n* racket.

Ramm|bär, ~b(l)ock *m* rammer, ram; **~e** *f* rammer, paving-beetle; pile-driver; **~eln** *itr* to buck; to ram; to rut; **~en** *tr* to ram, to beat down; (*Beton*) to tamp; to drive in; **~ler** *m* buck; male hare, buck-hare.

Rampe *f* ramp, ascent; drive; slope; *rail* platform; *mar* landing-place; *theat* apron; **~nlicht** *n* foot-lights *pl*

ramponieren *tr* to damage, to bash, to spoil.

Ramsch *m* junk, job lot; rubbish; *im ~* in the lump, in lots; **~händler** *m* junk-dealer; **~verkauf** *m* rummage-sale, jumble sale; **~waren** *f pl* job lots *pl*, *Am* broken lots *pl*.

Rand *m* edge, brink; (*Saum*) border; (*um runde Gegenstände, Hut, Tasse* *usw.*) rim, brim; *voll bis an den* ~ full to the brim; brimful; (*Buch*) margin; (*Wunde*) lip; (*Spitze*) tip; (*Borte*) skirt; (*Grenze*) boundary; (*Umkreis*) periphery; *math* collar; *äußerer* (*innerer*) ~ outer (inner) surface; *vorspringender* ~ shoulder, ledge; *vorstehender* ~ flange; *am ~e des Verderbens* on the verge of ruin; *außer ~ u. Band* out of bounds, *Am sl* whoopee: *das versteht sich am ~e* that is a matter of course; *nicht zu ~e kommen* to make vain efforts; **~auslösung** *f* marginal release; **~aussparung** *f* setting-aside margin; **~bemerkung** *f* marginal note; **~fassung** *f* rim; **~feuerpatrone** *f* rim-fire cartridge; **~glosse** *f* commentation, side note; **~gebiet** *n* fringeland; **~leiste** *f* cornice, rubbing strip; **~los** *a* (*von Augengläsern*) rimless; **~noten** *f pl* marginal data *pl*; **~staat** *m* border state; **~stein** *m* curbstone; **~steller** *m* (*Schreibmaschine*) margin stop; **~tief** *n* secondary depression; **~verzierung** *f* marginal adornment.

rändern, rändeln *tr* to border, to rim; (*Münzen*) to mill.

Ranft *m* crust; *auch* = *Rand.*

Rang *m* rank, order; (*Stellung*) position; (*Wert, Qualität*) class, rate, quality; *theat erster* ~ dress circle, *Am* first balcony; *zweiter* ~ upper circle; *ersten ~es* first-rate, first-class; *den ~ ablaufen* to outdo, to outrun, to get the better of, *fam* to steal a march on s. o.; **~abzeichen** *n* badge of rank; **~älteste(r)** *m* senior officer; **~liste** *f* ranking list, *mil* Army List; **~ordnung** *f* order of precedence; **~stufe** *f* order, rank; degree; **~verlust** *m* loss of rank, degradation.

Range *f* young scamp, romp; (*Mädchen*) tomboy.

Rangier|bahnhof *m* shunting-station, marshalling-yard, *Am* switching yard, railroad yard; **~en** *tr* to arrange; to classify; *rail* to shunt, *Am* to switch; *itr* to be classed; to rank; *über jdm ~~* (*Am*) to rank s.o.; **~er** *m* shunter, *Am* switchman; **~gleis** *n* siding, *Am* switching track; **~lokomotive, ~maschine** *f* shunting-engine, *Am* switcher.

rank *a* slim, slender; **~e** *f* tendril, string; (*Rebe*) (vine-) shoot; branch; **~en** *itr* (*sich*) to climb, to creep; **~engewächs** *n* creeper, climber; **~enwerk** *n bot* tendrils *pl*; *arch* ornament; (*Blumenornament*) fleuron.

Ränke *f pl* intrigues *pl*, tricks *pl*, machinations *pl*; (*Anschläge*) plots *pl*; ~ *schmieden* to intrigue; to plot, to scheme; **~schmied** *m* intriguer, schemer, plotter; *parl* wire puller; **~süchtig, ~voll** *a* full of tricks, plotting, scheming, tricky.

Ranunkel *f* ranunculus.

Ränzel *n*, **Ranzen** *m* knapsack; (*Schulmappe*) satchel, school-bag.

ranzig *a* rancid; spoilt, rank.

Rapier *n* rapier, foil.

Rappe *m* black horse; *auf Schusters ~n* to go on Shanks' pony.

Rappel *m* madness; *e-n ~ haben* to be crazy, to be cracked; **~ig** *a* excited, crazy, mad; **~kopf** *m* crazy person; **~köpfisch** *a* hot-headed; **~n** *itr* to rattle; (*Geräusch machen*) to make a rattling noise; *bei ihm rappelt's* he is mad.

Raps *m*, **~saat** *f* rape-seed.

Rapunzel *m* rampion.

rar *a* rare, scarce; (*vorzüglich*) exquisite; *sich ~ machen* to make o. s. scarce; *machen Sie sich nicht so ~!* don't be such a stranger! **~ität** *f* rarity, curiosity; (*für Sammler*) collector's item; **~itätenhandlung** *f* curiosity--shop; **~itätenkabinett** *n* cabinet of curios; rare-show.

rasan|t *a mil* (*von Flugbahn*) sweeping, rasant, flat trajectory; *~tes Feuer* flat trajectory fire; *~te Flakartillerie* flat trajectory A.A.; **~z** *f* flat trajectory; *~~ der Flugbahn* flatness of trajectory.

rasch *a* speedy, swift, quick, hasty; *Am fam* (*unverzüglich*) pronto; *machen Sie ~!* be quick! hurry up! *Am fam* make it snappy! **~heit** *f* quickness, swiftness, haste.

rascheln *itr* to rustle.

rase|n *itr* to rage; (*irre sein*) to rave; (*toll, verrückt*) to be mad; to be frantic; (*vorwärtsstürmen*) to rush; *sl* to stave; to race; (*mit dem Wagen*) to speed; to scorch; (*eilen*) to blow, *Am* to breeze; **~nd** *a* raging, furious; *med* delirious; mad; (*sehr schnell*) splitting, tearing; *~nd machen* to drive one mad, to enrage s. o.; *~nd werden* to go mad; *~nd verliebt* desperately in love; *~nde Kopfschmerzen haben* to have a splitting headache; **~nde(r)** *m* (*Verrückter*) madman, maniac; **~rei** *f* raving, rage, fury; (*Wahnsinn*) madness; (*mit dem Wagen*) speeding, scorching, reckless driving.

Rasen *m* grass; (*Grasplatz*) lawn; (*Rasendecke*) turf, sod; **~bank** *f* turf-seat; **~mähmaschine** *f*, **~mäher** *m* lawn-mower; **~platz** *m* grass-plot, lawn; **~sprenger** *m* lawn-sprinkler.

Rasier|apparat *m* safety-razor; **~en** *tr* to shave; *sich ~~ lassen* to get shaved; **~klinge** *f* (razor-)blade; **~krem** *m* shaving-cream; **~messer** *n* razor; **~pinsel** *m* shaving brush; **~schale** *f* shaving mug; **~seife** *f* shaving soap; **~wasser** *n* after-shave lotion; **~zeug** *n* shaving-things, *pl*, *Am* shaving kit.

Raspel *f* rasp; **~n** *tr* to rasp; *Süßholz ~n* to flirt; **~späne** *pl* raspings *pl.*

Rass|e *f* race; (*von Tieren*) breed; stock; (*Blut*) blood; **~enabsonderung** *f* race segregation; apartheid; **~enbewußtsein** *n* racialism; **~enforschung** *f* racial research; **~enfrage** *f* question of racial prejudice; **~enhaß** *m* race hatred; **~enhochzucht** *f* pure breeding; **~enhygiene** *f* eugenics *pl*; **~enkampf** *m* racial conflict; **~enkreuzung** *f* cross-breeding; **~enkunde** *f* science of race; **~enmischung** *f* miscegenation; racial mixture, *Am* amalgamation; **~enreinheit** *f* racial purity; **~enverwandt** *a* related to a race; **~ig** *a* (*rein~~*) thoroughbred; (*vom Wein, gut gebaut von Person*) racy; **~isch** *a* racial.

Rassel *f* rattle; **~geräusch** *n med* rhonchus, râle, rattling; **~n** *itr* to rattle, to rustle, to clatter; *mit Ketten ~n* to clank o.'s chains.

Rast *f* rest, repose; resting; (*Erholung*) recreation; *mil* halt; *tech* notch, groove, device for stopping; *ohne* ~ restless; ~ *machen* to take a rest; to make a halt; **~en** *itr* to rest, to repose; *mil* to halt; (*Tennis*) to be a bye; **~los** *a* restless; (*unermüdlich*) indefatigable; **~~igkeit** *f* restlessness; **~ort** *m* resting place; **~vorrichtung** *f* click-stop device; **~tag** *m* day of rest.

Raster *m phot, typ* screen; *tele* scanning; *tech* ratcheting; **~bild** *n* scanning-pattern image; **~blende** *f* scanning device, diaphragm; **~fläche** *f* scanning pattern; **~schirm** *m* mosaic screen; **~ung** *f* definition of a picture, lenticulation; **~zahl** *f* number of picture elements.

Rasur *f* (*auf Papier*) erasure; (*Bart*) shave; *e-e glatte ~* a clean shave.

Rat *m* advice, counsel; (*Beratung*) consultation; (*Überlegung*) deliberation; (*Ausweg*) means *pl*, expedient, remedy; (*Versammlung*) council, board; (*Beschluß*) decree; (*Ratschluß*) decision; (*Person*) council(l)or, alderman; (*Ratgeber*) adviser; (*Rechtsberater*) legal adviser; *um ~ fragen* to ask advice, to consult; *sich bei jdm ~ holen* to ask s. o.'s advice; *jdm ~ geben* to advise s. o.; *mit ~ u. Tat* by word and deed; *~ schaffen* to find ways and means, to manage, to devise means; *keinen ~ wissen* to be at o.'s wits' end; *zu ~e ziehen* to consult; **~en** *irr itr* to advise, to give advice; to counsel; (*erraten*) to guess, to solve; *sich nicht zu ~~ wissen* not to know what to do; *raten Sie mal!* give a guess! **~geber** *m* adviser; **~haus** *n* town hall, *Am* city hall; **~los** *a* helpless, at a loss; *~~ sein* to make neither head nor tail of s. th.; **~losigkeit** *f* helplessness; perplexity; **~sam** *a* (*rätlich*) advisable; (*förderlich*) expedient; (*nützlich*) useful; (*klug*) prudent; *für ~~ halten* to believe advisable; *nicht ~~* inadvisable; *ein guter* **~schlag** a good piece (*od* bit) of advice; **~schläge** *m pl* advice, counsel; **~schlagen** *itr* to deliberate; to consult; **~schluß** *m* decree; resolution, decision; **~sdiener** *m* beadle, summoner; **~sherr** *m* town-council(l)or; senator; alderman; **~skeller** *m* town-hall cellar (restaurant), *Am* rathskeller; **~ssaal** *m* council chamber; **~sschreiber** *m* town clerk; **~ssitzung** *f* meeting of a council; **~sstube** *f* council-chamber; **~sversammlung** *f* council board.

Rate *f* instal(l)ment; *in ~n* by instalments; **~nkauf** *m* hire purchase; **~nweise** *a* by instalments; **~nzahlung** *f* payment by instalments, time payment; **~~splan** *m* hire purchase system, instalment plan, time payment plan.

Räte|republik *f*, **~rußland** *n* Soviet Republic, Soviet Russia.

Ratifi|kation *f* ratification; **~zieren** *tr* to ratify.

Ration *f* ration; *eiserne ~* iron ration; (*Portion, Anteil*) allowance, portion, share; *jdn auf halbe ~ setzen* to put s. o. on half rations; *in ~en zuteilen* to dole out; **~ieren** *tr* to ration; *~ierter Zucker* rationed sugar; **~ierung** *f* rationing; (*Punktsystem*) points scheme; *~~ von Mangelwaren* rationing of scarce commodities; *die ~~ aufheben* to deration; **~~svorschriften** *f pl* rationing regulations *pl*; **~skürzung** *f* ration cut.

ration|al *a* rational; **~alismus** *m* rationalism; **~alisierung** *f* rationalization; **~alistisch** *a* rationalist(ic); **~ell** *a* rational, reasonable, expedient; (*systematisch*) systematic; (*sparsam*) economical.

rätlich *a* advisable; (*fördersam*) expedient; (*heilsam*) wholesome; (*nützlich*) useful.

Ratsch|e *f* ratchet (drill); rattle; **~er** *m mil sl* (*Ratschbum*) whiz bang.

Rätsel *n* (*~ zur Lösung*) riddle; (*verwirrendes ~*) puzzle; (*Geheimnis*) enigma; (*Mysterium*) mystery; (*Problem*) problem; (*Scherzfrage*) conundrum; (*Fragespiel*) quiz; (*Bilder ~*) rebus; *das ist mir ein ~* that's a puzzle to me; it puzzles me; *sie ist mir ein ~* she is a riddle to me; I don't know what to make of her; *des ~s Lösung* the solution (*od* answer) of the riddle; **~frage** *f* puzzling question; **~haft** *a* mysterious; enigmatic(al); puzzling.

Ratte *f*, ***Ratz*** *m* rat; *wie ein Ratz schlafen* to sleep like a dormouse; *~n fangen* to rat; **~nfalle** *f* rat-trap; **~nfänger** *m* (*Mann*) rat-catcher; (*Hund*) ratter; *der ~~ von Hameln* the Pied Piper of Hamelin; **~ngift** *n* rat-poison; **~nkahl, ratzekahl** *a* quite bare; **~nkönig** *m fig* tangle; **~nloch** *n* rat-hole; **~nschwanz** *m* rat-tail; *fig* (*umfangreiche Aktenansammlung*) rattailed file.

rattern *itr* to rattle, to clatter, to chatter, to rumble.

*

Raub *m* (*Räuberei*) robbery, robbing; rapine; (*Straßen~*) highway robbery, *Am* hi(gh)jacking; (*Plünderung*) plundering, pillaging; (*Beute, bes. von Tieren*) prey; (*Kriegsbeute*) loot; (*Seeräuberei; fig unerlaubter Nachdruck*) piracy; (*Geraubtes*) booty; (*Siegesbeute*) spoils *pl*; (*Entführung von Personen*) kidnap(p)ing, abduction; *auf ~ ausgehen* to go plundering; (*von Tieren*) to go on the prowl, to prowl about; *ein ~ der Flammen werden* to be destroyed by fire; **~anfall** *m* predatory (*od* armed) attack; raid; **~bau** *m* (*Boden*) exhausting the soil, overcropping, robber farming; (*Wald*) destructive lumbering; (*Bergwerk*) robbing (of) a mine; unmethodical working of a mine; (*Ausbeutung*) ruinous (*od* wasteful *od* ruthless) exploitation; *~~ treiben* to exhaust; (*ruinieren*) to ruin; **~en** *tr* to rob (*jdm etw* s. o. of s. th.); (*jdn berauben*) to deprive of s. th.; (*plündern*) to plunder; (*wegnehmen*) to take by force; (*stehlen*) to steal; (*Person entführen*) to kidnap; to abduct; (*Ehre*) to defame; *itr* to commit robberies; **~fisch** *m* fish of prey; **~gesindel** *n* band of robbers; gang of thieves; **~gier, ~sucht** *f* rapacity; **~gierig, ~süchtig** *a* rapacious; **~gut** *n* stolen goods *pl*; **~krieg** *m* predatory war; **~lust** *f* lust of booty; **~mord** *m* murder with robbery; **~mörder** *m* robber who commits murder; **~nest** *n* haunt of robbers; **~ritter** *m* robber-knight; **~schiff** *n* pirate ship, privateer; **~staat** *m* piratical state; **~tier** *n* beast of prey; **~überfall** *m* predatory (*od* armed) attack; foray, *Am* holdup; (*Straßenraub*) hi(gh)jacking; **~vogel** *m* bird of prey; **~wirtschaft** *f* ruinous exploitation; **~zeug** *n* (*Jagd*) vermin; **~zug** *m* (*Überfall*) raid; (*Streifzug*) incursion; (*Plünderung*) depredation.

Räuber *m* robber; raider; *Am* holdup man, stickup man; (*Straßen~*) highwayman, brigand, *Am* hi(gh)jacker; (*Dieb*) thief; *~ u. Gendarm spielen* (*Kinder*) to play "cop-and-robber"; **~bande** *f* band of robbers, gang of thieves; **~ei** *f* robbery; plunder; depredation; **~geschichte** *f* tale of robbery; (*unglaublich*) cock-and-bull story; **~hauptmann** *m* robber chief, captain of robbers; **~höhle** *f* den of thieves; **~isch** *a* rapacious; predaceous, predatory; **~n** *itr* to go robbing, to commit robberies.

Rauch *m* smoke; (*Mischung von ~ u. Nebel*) smog (= smoke and fog); *poet* haze; (*Dampf*) steam, vapo(u)r; (*Ruß*) soot; (*Dunst*) fume; (*starker Dunst*) reek; *in ~ aufgehen* to end in smoke, to be consumed by fire; *fig* to come to nothing; **~abzugskanal** *m* flue; **~altar** *m* incense-altar; **~bahngeschoß** *n* tracer shell; **~belästigung** *f* smoke nuisance; **~bildung** *f* formation of smoke; **~bombe** *f* smoke-bomb; **~dicht** *a* smoke-tight, smoke-proof; **~en** *itr, tr* to smoke; (*dampfen, dunsten*) to reek; (*räuchern, duften*) to fume; **~en** *n* smoking; *~~ verboten!* no smoking! **~entwicklung** *f* smoke development; **~entwickler, ~erzeuger** *m* smoke generator; **~er** *m* smoker; *Nicht~~* non-smoker; **~erabteil** *n rail* smoking compartment, *Am* smoker; smoking car; **~erkarte** *f* (*Rationierung*) smoker's ration card; **~fahne** *f* smoke trail, exhaust trail; smoke streamer; **~fang** *m* chimney, flue; **~faß** *n* censer; **~fleisch** *n* smoked meat; **~frei** *a* smokeless, free of smoke; **~gas** *n* flue gas; fumes *pl*; **~geschoß** *n mil* smoke shell; **~geschwärzt** *a* smoke-stained; **~glas** *n* tinted (*od* smoked) glass; **~ig** *a* smoky; **~los** *a* smokeless; **~meldekapsel** *f mil* message-container with smoke signal; **~meldepatrone** *f mil* smoke indicator; smoke-signal cartridge; **~ofen** *m aero* (*Flugplatz*) small stove for emitting smoke on an aerodrome; smudge fire; **~patrone** *f* smoke cartridge; smoke-signal cartridge; **~plage** *f* smoke nuisance; **~satz** *m* smoke mixture; **~säule** *f* column of smoke; **~schirm, ~(schutz)schleier** *m* (*künstlicher ~~*) smoke-screen; *mit e-m ~~ einhüllen* (*einnebeln*) to smokescreen; **~schrift** *f* (*Himmelsschrift*) sky writing; **~schwach** *a* (*Pulver*) smokeless; **~schwaden** *m pl* wisps of smoke; **~schwarz** *a* black as soot; **~signal** *n* smoke signal; **~tabak** *m* tobacco; **~topas** *m* smoky topas; **~vergiftung** *f* smoke inhalation; **~verzehrer** *m* smoke consumer; **~vorhang** *m* smoke curtain; **~wand** *f mil* smoke-screen; **~waren** *f pl* (*Tabak*) tobacco, cigars, cigarettes etc; tobacco and tobacco products; (*Rauchwerk, Pelzwerk*) furs *pl*, peltry; **~wolke** *f* smoke cloud; **~zeichen** *n* smoke signal; **~zimmer** *n* smoking-room.

Räucher|essenz *f* aromatic essence; **~essig** *m* aromatic vinegar; **~erig** *a* smoky; reeking; **~faß** *n* censer; **~hering** *m* kipper, *Am* smoked herring; **~kammer** *f* smoking chamber, smoke room; *Am* smokehouse; **~kerze** *f* fumigating candle (*od* pastille); **~mittel** *n* fumigant; **~n** *tr* (*Fleisch*) to smoke; (*Fisch*) to cure; (*Raum aus~~*) to fumigate; *eccl* to burn incense; (*parfümieren*) to perfume, to scent; **~papier** *n* fumigating paper; **~pulver** *n* fumigating powder; **~ung** *f* fumigation; smoking; incense burning.

Räud|e *f* (*bei Hunden*) mange; scab; **~ig** *a* mangy, scabby, scabbed; *~~es Schaf fig* black sheep.

Rauf|bold *m* bully, ruffian, brawler, *Am* rowdy, tough; **~en** *tr, itr* (*aus~*) to pull, to pluck, to tear; *sich mit jdm ~~* to scuffle, to fight, to tussle (with s. o. for); **~erei** *f* scuffle, brawl, row, fight, tussle; **~lust** *f* pugnacity; **~lustig** *a* pugnacious, quarrelsome.

Raufe *f* rack.

rauh *a* rough; (*uneben*) uneven; rugged; unpolished; (*Hals*) sore (throat); raw; (*Haut*) raw; (*Stimme*) hoarse, coarse; (*heiser*) raucous; (*Sitten*) coarse; rude; (*Behandlung*) harsh; (*Boden*) sterile, desert; (*Ton*) harsh; (*Land*) wild; (*Klima, Wetter*) raw, inclement, rough, bleak; (*Winter*) severe; (*streng*) rigorous; *aus dem ~en arbeiten* to rough-hew; *~ behandeln* to manhandle; *in ~en Mengen* in a large quantity; *die ~e Wirklichkeit* the hard facts *pl*; **~bein** *n fig* rough diamond, *Am sl* rough-neck; **~beinig** *a* caddish; **~en** *tr* to roughen; (*Tuch*) to tease, to dress; to nap; **~futter** *n* coarse food; roughage; **~haarig** *a* shaggy, hirsute; (*Hund*) wire-haired; **~heit** *f* roughness; (*Wetter*) inclemency; rigo(u)r; (*Stimme*) hoarseness; (*Sitten*) coarseness, harshness; rudeness; **~reif** *m* hoar-frost, white frost; rime; **~~bildung** *f* frozen fog formation.

Raum *m* (*Platz*) place; (*offener ~*) space; (*umschlossener ~*) room; (*ausgedehnter ~*) expanse; (*Räumlichkeit*) locality, room, accomodation, compartment; (*Ausdehnung*) expansion; (*Schiffs~*) hold; (*luftleerer ~*) vacuum, void, empty space; (*Gebiet*) area, zone; territory; district, neighbourhood; (*Zwischen~*) play, clearance, space; (*Fassungsvermögen*) capacity, volume; *fig* (*Spiel~*) scope, opportunity; clearance; *wenig ~ beanspruchend* small in bulk; *viel ~ beanspruchend* (*von Waren etc*) bulky; *bestrichener ~* (*mil*) danger zone; *gedeckter ~* (*mil*) safety zone; dead space; *~ geben* to give way to; to indulge in; *e-r Bitte ~ geben* to comply with a request; *Hoffnungen ~ geben* to indulge in hopes; *~ gewähren* (*Unterkunft*) to accomodate; **~akustik** *f* room (*od* architectural) acoustics *pl*; **~änderung** *f* change of volume; **~aufteilung** *f* floor plan; **~bedarf** *m* space required; **~bestimmung** *f* determination of volume; **~bild** *n phot* stereoscopic picture; (*Schaubild*) space diagram; panoramic picture; **~~entfernungsmesser** *m* stereoscopic range finder; **~~vorführung** *f* stereoscopic picture projection; **~chemie** *f* stereochemistry; **~dichte** *f* density by volume; volumetric density; **~effekt** *m* plastic effect; **~einheit** *f* unit of space (*od* volume); **~ersparnis** *f* space saving; **~fahrt** *f* (*Welt~~*) space-travel; **~flug** *m aero* astronautics *pl mit sing*; **~gefühl** *n* (*beim Sehen*) space feeling; **~gehalt, ~inhalt** *m* volume, capacity; **~geometrie** *f* solid geometry; **~gewicht** *n* volumetric weight; bulk density; **~gewinn** *m* gaining of ground; progress; **~gitter** *n* (*Atomphysik*) atomic structure; space grid; **~heizung** *f* room heaters *pl*; **~höhe** *f* headroom; **~inhalt** *m* volume; cubic content, capacity; **~integral** *n* space integral; **~kunst** *f* interior decoration; **~ladegitter** *n* space-charge grid; **~ladung** *f* space charge; **~lehre** *f* geometry; science of space; **~los** *a* spaceless, roomless; **~luftschiff** *n* stratosphere airship; **~luftschiffahrt** *f* astronautics *pl mit sing*; **~mangel** *m* lack of room (*od* space); space restriction; **~marke** *f* space mark; spatial mark; **~maß** *n* measure of capacity; dimensions *pl*, volume; **~menge** *f* volume, contents *pl*; area; surface; **~meßbilder** *n pl* stereoscopic pictures *pl*; **~messung** *f* stereometry; **~meter** *m* cubic metre; **~schiff** *n aero* space ship; **~schiffahrt** *f* astronautics *pl mit sing*; interplanetary aviation; **~sinn** *m* space perception; **~strahl** *m* space ray; **~strahler** *m* direction beam; **~strahlung** *f* space radiation; **~teil** *m* part by volume; **~telegraphie** *f* space telegraphy; **~tonwirkung** *f* stereophonic sound effect; **~verhältnis** *n* proportion by volume; **~wärme** *f* room temperature; **~welle** *f radio* sky (*od* indirect) wave; **~wirkung** *f* stereoscopic effect; (*vom Ton*) stereophonic effect.

räum|en *tr* to clear (away), to remove; *das Feld* ~~ to quit the field; (*Wohnung, Zimmer*) to vacate; to clear; (*Warenlager*) to clear (off); (*säubern*) to clean; *mil* (*evakuieren*) to evacuate, to leave (a place); *aus dem Wege* ~~ to kill; **~er, ~pflug** *m* (*Straßenbau*) bulldozer; (*Erd~~*) scraper; **~lich** *a* relating to space; spatial; three-dimensional, volumetric; steric; stereoscopic; spacious; **~lichkeit** *f* (*Geräumigkeit*) spaciousness, roominess, space; (*Raum*) locality; room; (*e-s Hauses*) conveniences *pl*, accomodation (*Am* -s *pl*); **~ung** *f* removal, removing; clearing; (*e-r Wohnung*) quitting; *mil* (*Evakuierung*) evacuation; *zur* ~~ *zwingen* to turn out, to eject; **~~s(aus)verkauf** *m* clearance sale; **~~sbefehl** *m jur* eviction notice; **~~sgebiet** *n mil* evacuation area; **~~sklage** *f* action of ejectment; **~~strupp** *m* demolition squad (*od* party); **~werkzeug** *n tech* scraping tools *pl*.

raunen *itr, tr* to whisper.

raunzen *itr fam* (*meckern*) to grumble, to grouse, *Am* to gripe, to beef.

Raupe *f* caterpillar; *tech* caterpillar-track; tractor; **~nantrieb** *m* caterpillar drive, *Am* track-laying drive; **~nfahrzeug** *n* full-track vehicle; caterpillar car, *Am* tracklaying craft; **~nfraß** *m* damage done by caterpillars; **~ngängig** *a* caterpillar-tracked; **~nkette** *f* caterpillar-track; **~nkrad** *n* motor-cycle tractor; **~nleim** *m* insect lime; **~nlesen** *n* clearing of caterpillars; **~nplanierer** *m* calfdozer; caterpillar grader; **~nplanierpflug** *m* push dozer; **~nrad** *n* caterpillar wheel; **~nschere** *f* gardener's shears *pl*; **~nschlepper** *m* caterpillar (tractor), tracklaying tractor; crawler tractor.

Rausch *m* intoxication, drunkenness; tipsiness; *fig* frenzy; transport; ecstasy; *e-n* ~ *haben* to be drunk; *sich e-n* ~ *antrinken* to get drunk; *seinen* ~ *ausschlafen* to sleep o. s. sober; **~gift** *n* narcotic (drug), *Am sl* dope; **~~handel** *m* drug trade, drug-trafficking; **~~schieber** *m Am* dope pedlar; **~~sucht** *f* drug addiction; **~~süchtige(r)** *m* (drug)addict; *Am* dope addict; **~gold** *n* tinsel; leaf-gold.

rauschen *itr* to rush; to gurgle; to murmur; *radio* (*der Röhren*) to whistle, to rustle; (*Wind, Blätter*) to roar; (*Stoffe*) to rustle; ~ *n* roaring, rushing; **~d** *a* rustling; (*Bach*) murmuring; (*Beifall*) ringing.

räuspern *r* to clear o.'s throat.

Rausschmeißer *m fam* chucker-out, *Am* bouncer.

Raute *f bot* rue; *math* rhomb; rhomboid; (*Wappenkunde*) diamond, lozenge; **~nförmig** *a* rhombic; lozenge-shaped; diamond-shaped; **~nkranz** *m* lozenged wreath.

Razzia *f* (*Polizei~*) (police-)raid, dragnet raid, *Am* police round-up; shake-up; swoop, sweep; check-up; (*übliche Kontrolle*) routine check; *e-e* ~ *durchführen* (*od halten od machen*) to make a raid, to raid.

Reag|ens *n* reagent; **~enzglas** *n chem* test-tube; **~~kultur** *f* culture in test-tube; **~enzpapier** *n* test-paper, litmus paper; **~enzröhrchen** *n* test-tube; **~ieren** *itr* to react (*auf* upon).

Reaktion *f* reaction; **~är** *a* reactionary; ~~ *m* reactionary, diehard; *Am* standpatter; **~santrieb** *m aero* jet propulsion; reaction propulsion; **~sbremse** *f* moderator; **~sfähigkeit** *f* power of reacting; **~sgeschwindigkeit** *f* reaction velocity; **~skette** *f* series of reactions; **~smittel** *n* reaction agent, reagent; **~smoment** *n* moment of reaction; **~smotor** *m* reaction motor; **~sverlauf** *m* course of reaction; **~swärme** *f* heat of reaction; **~szeit** *f* reaction time.

Reaktor *m phys* (*Atombrenner*) reactor.

real *a* real; **~ien** *pl* real facts *pl*; realities *pl*, knowledge of the exact and historical sciences; **~isieren** *tr* to perform, to realize; to turn (*od* to convert) into money; **~ismus** *m* realism; **~ist** *m* realist; **~istisch** *a* realistic; **~ität** *f* reality; *jd, der den* ~~*en des Lebens entflieht* escapist; **~katalog** *m* subject catalog(ue); **~lexikon** *n* encyclop(a)edia; **~lohn** *m* real wages *pl*; **~politik** *f* realist politics *pl od sing*.

Reb|e *f* vine; (*Wein~~*) grape; (*Ranke*) tendril; **~ensaft** *m* grape-juice, wine; **~huhn** *n* partridge; **~laus** *f* phylloxera; **~stock** *m* vine.

Rebell *m* rebel, mutineer; **~ieren** *itr* to rebel, to mutiny, to revolt; **~ion** *f* rebellion, mutiny; **~isch** *a* rebellious, mutinous.

Rechen *m* rake; ~ *tr* to rake.

Rechen|aufgabe *f* sum, (arithmetical) problem; **~brett** *n* abacus; **~buch** *n* sumbook, arithmetic-book; **~fehler** *m* arithmetical error; mistake; miscalculation; **~kunst** *f* arithmetic; **~lehrer** *m* arithmetic teacher; **~maschine** *f* calculating machine; electronic computer, electronic calculator; **~meister** *m* arithmetician; **~pfennig** *m* counter, marker; **~probe** *f* check calculation; **~schaft** *f* account; ~~ *geben* (*od ablegen*) to render an account of; to account for, to answer for; *zur* ~~ *ziehen* to call to account for; **~~sbericht** *m* statement of account; report; **~schieber** *m* slide rule; **~stunde** *f* arithmetic lesson; **~tabelle** *f* ready reckoner; **~tafel** *f* slate.

rechn|en *tr* to reckon; (*berechnen*) to calculate; (*abschätzen*) to estimate; to rate; to value; (~~ *zu*) to class with; to rank amongst; (*zus.*~~) to figure; to do sums; to compute; *itr* (*zählen*) to count; *im Kopfe* ~~ to reckon mentally; *dazu* ~~ to add; *mit dazu gerechnet* including, inclusive of; *eins ins andere gerechnet* taking one thing with the other; *auf jdn* ~~ to count upon, to reckon, to depend, to rely on; *sich etw zur Ehre* ~~ to consider it an hono(u)r; **~en** *n* arithmetic, calculation; calculus; **~er** *m* reckoner, arithmetician; (*Rechnungsführer*) accountant; (*Berechner*) calculator; computer; **~erisch** *a* arithmetic, mathematical; analytically; by computation; (*berechnet*) calculated; ~~*er Wert* book value; **~ung** *f* calculation, reckoning, sum; (*Aufstellung*) bill; account; (*Ware*) invoice; *meine* ~~ *bitte!* my bill (*Am* check), please! *auf seine* ~~ on his account; *laut* ~~ as per account; *auf* ~~ *kaufen* to buy on credit; ~~ *ablegen* to render an account of; *e-e* ~~ *bezahlen* to settle an account; *in* ~~ *bringen* to bring to s. o.'s account; *die* ~~ *ohne den Wirt machen* to reckon without o.'s host; *den Umständen* ~~ *tragen* to accommodate o. s. to circumstances.

Rechnungs|ablegung *f* rendering of accounts; **~abschluß** *m com* balancing of accounts; **~auszug** *m com* statement of account; **~beleg** *m* voucher; **~betrag** *m* amount total; **~führer** *m* accountant, book-keeper; **~führung** *f* accountancy, keeping of accounts; **~jahr** *n* account year; (*staatlich*) financial (*od* fiscal) year; **~legung** *f* submitting (*od* making) an accounting; **~prüfer** *m* auditor; **~stelle** *f* account section; **~vorlage** *f* submission of accounts; **~wesen** *n* accounting, accountancy.

recht *a* (*Gegensatz: links*) right, right-handed; (*richtig*) accurate, correct; (*geeignet, passend*) proper, fitting, befitting, suitable; (*schuldig*) due; (*wirklich*) real; (*echt*) genuine; (*gerecht*) just; (*schuldig*) due; (*gesetzlich*) lawful, legitimate; (*angenehm*) agreeable; (*gehörig*) thorough; (*tüchtig*) solid, sound; *adv* right(ly), well; (*wirklich*) really, quite; (*wichtig*) correctly; (*sehr*) very; much; pretty; *~e Hand* right hand; *die ~e Hand des Direktors* the director's right-hand man; *der ~e Mann* the right man; *am ~en Ort* in the proper place; *~e Seite* the right side; *~er Winkel* right angle; *zur ~en Zeit* in due time, at the right time; in the nick of time; *~ behalten* to be right in the end; *~ geben* to agree with; *es geschieht ihr ~* it serves her right; *~ haben* to be right; *an den ~en kommen* to meet o.'s match; *es jdm ~ machen* to suit, to please s. o.; *man kann es nicht allen ~ machen* you can't please everybody; *nach dem ~en sehen* to see to things; *~ tun* to do right, to do what is right; *das ist nicht ~ von dir* you are wrong there; *mir ist es ~* I don't object (*od* mind), I agree, that's all right with me; *nicht mit ~en Dingen zugehen* there is witchcraft in it; I suspect foul play; *das ist ~ u. billig* it is fair; *~ u. schlecht* fairly good; not bad; *ganz ~!* just so! quite! quite so!; *so ist's recht!* all right! *Am* okay! okeh! O.K.! *schon ~!* never mind! *erst ~* all the more, just; more than ever; *erst ~ nicht* less than ever, certainly not; *~ gern* with pleasure, most willingly, gladly; *~ gut* quite well; *es ist ~ schade* it is a great pity; *was dem e-n ~ ist, ist dem andern billig* what's sauce for the gander is sauce for the goose.

Recht *n* right; (*Gerechtigkeit*) justice; (*Vorrecht*) privilege; (*Anspruch*) claim (on), title, right (to); (*Gewalt*) power; (*Gesetz*) law; (*Rechtspflege*) administration of justice; (*Rechtsverhandlung*) legal proceedings *pl*; (*Rechtsordnung*) legal procedure; *Doktor der ~e* Doctor of Laws (*Abk* LL. D.); *Doktor beider ~e* Doctor of Civil and Canon Law; *die ~e studieren* to study law; *~ sprechen* to administer justice; *bürgerliches ~* civil law; *gemeines ~* common law; *öffentliches ~* public law; *internationales ~* international law; *wohlerworbenes ~* well established right; *das ~ haben* to have the right; *das ~ zu klagen u. verklagt zu werden* the capacity to sue and to be sued; *alle ~e vorbehalten* all rights reserved; *für ~ erkennen* to decide; *mit ~* rightly, justly, with reason; *mit vollem ~, mit Fug u. ~* for good reasons; *ohne ~* unjustly; *im ~ sein* to be within o.'s right; *mit ~ sagen* to be correct in saying; *von ~s wegen* by right(s), de jure, according to law; by virtue of law; *zu ~ bestehen* to be valid; **~e** *f* (*Hand*) right hand; the right-hand side; *parl* the right; *die äußerste* ~~ the extreme right, the rightest; **~eck** *n* rectangle; **~eckig** *a* rectangular; square; **~en** *itr* (*bestreiten*) to contest, to dispute; to plead; to litigate; **~ens** *adv* by law, legally;

~er Hand *adv* on the right-hand side; **~fertigen** *tr* to justify, to defend, to vindicate, to account for; *sich ~~* to clear o. s., to exculpate o. s.; **~fertigung** *f* justification, vindication; defence, *Am* defense; exoneration; **~~sgrund** *m* plea; excuse; **~gläubig** *a* orthodox; **~~keit** *f* orthodoxy; **~haber** *m* quarrelsome person; dogmatic person; **~haberisch** *a* dogmatic(al); positive; (*hartnäckig*) obstinate; **~lich** *a* just; lawful, legitimate, in law, legal; (*~~ denkend, anständig*) fair, just; honest, upright; *ohne ~~en Grund* without a sufficient legal ground; **~lichkeit** *f* integrity, honesty; (*Gesetzmäßigkeit*) lawfulness, legality; **~linig** *a* rectilinear; **~los** *a* illegal; without rights; (*vogelfrei*) outlawed; **~~igkeit** *f* unlawfulness,illegality; outlawry; **~mäßig** *a* lawful, legal; rightful; according to law; *als ~~ bestätigen* to legalize; *für ~~ erklären* to legitimate; *~~er Eigentümer* rightful owner; **~~keit** *f* legality; lawfulness; rightfulness; legitimacy; (*e-r Handlung*) validity; **~schaffen** *a* honest, just, upright, true; *adv* very; exceedingly; righteously; **~~heit** *f* honesty, probity; **~schreibung** *f* orthography, spelling; **~sprechung** *f* administration of justice; jurisdiction; **~weisend** *a* (*Magnetnadel*) true; **~winklig** *a* right-angled, square, rectangular; **~zeitig** *a* opportune, seasonable; *adv* in due time, in due course, in (good) time; *Am* on time; (*pünktlich*) punctually.

rechts *adv* on the right, (*nach ~*) to the right; (*Wappenkunde*) dexter; *~ oben in der Ecke* in the right-hand (top) corner; *schauen Sie nach ~* look to your right; *sich nach ~ wenden* to turn (*od* to keep) to the right; *zweite Straße ~* second turn to your right; **~angelegenheit** *f* legal matter (*od* affair); **~anspruch** *m* legal claim, (legitimate) title; **~anwalt** *m* lawyer, solicitor; (*plädierender*) counsel, barrister, *Am* attorney-at-law, counsel(l)or-at-law; **~~schaft** *f* bar; *in die ~~schaft aufnehmen* to call (*Am* admit) to the bar; **~~skammer** *f* General Council of the Bar, *Am* Bar Association; **~anwendung** *f* application of the law; **~ausdruck** *m* legal term; **~außen(stürmer)** *m sport* outside right, *Am* right winger, right wing; **~befugnis** *f* competence; **~beistand** *m* counsel, *Am* legal adviser; **~beratungsstelle** *f* legal advisory board; **~betreuung(sstelle)** *f* (office for) legal aid; **~beugung** *f* miscarriage of justice, perversion of justice, defeating the ends of justice; **~bruch** *m* infringement of the law; **~deutung** *f* legal interpretation; **~drall** *m tech mil* clockwise rifling; (*Kabel*) right-hand twist; **~drehend** *a* clockwise, right-hand; dextrorotatory; **~drehung** *f* clockwise rotation; **~einwand** *m* demurrer, plea, objection; (*Einspruch*) protest; remonstrance; *e-n ~~ erheben* to put in a plea, to raise on objection; **~fähigkeit** *f* legal capacity; **~fall** *m* law case, case in court, suit; **~form** *f* legal form; **~frage** *f* legal question; point in law; (*strittige ~~*) issue (of law); **~gang** *m* legal procedure; practice; course of law; *tech* (*Schraube*) right-handed action; **~gängig** *a tech* right-handed; **~gelehrsamkeit** *f* jurisprudence; **~gelehrte(r)** *m* jurist, lawyer; **~geschäft** *n* law business, legal transaction; **~gewinde** *n* right-hand thread; **~grund** *m* legal argument (*od* ground *od* title); **~~satz** *m* principle of law; **~gültig** *a* legal, valid (in law); final; **~gutachten** *n* legal expert opinion, counsel's opinion; **~handel** *m* lawsuit; (legal) action; cause; **~händer** *m* (*Baseball*) right-hander; **~hilfe** *f* legal assistance; legal aid; **~innen (-stürmer)** *m sport* inside right; **~irrtum** *m* mistake in law; **~konsulent** *m* lay adviser; **~kraft** *f* legal force; **~kräftig** *a* legal, valid; legally binding; final; **~kurve** *f* right turn; right-hand curve; **~lage** *f* legal status, legal situation; **~lenkung, ~steuerung** *f mot* right-hand drive; **~mittel** *n* legal remedy; right of appeal; legal (means of) redress; **~nachfolger** *m* assign, legal successor; **~nachteil** *m* prejudice; **~notwehr** *f* legally recognized self-defence; **~person, ~persönlichkeit** *f* body corporate, legal personality; **~pflege** *f* administration of justice; **~pfleger** *m* judicial administrator; **~radikal** *a parl* rightest; **~radikale(r)** *m parl* rightest; **~sache** *f* legal affair, lawsuit; **~sprache** *f* legal terminology; **~spruch** *m* (*der Geschworenen*) verdict; (*Strafsache*) sentence; (*Zivilsache*) judg(e)ment; decision; (*Schiedsgericht*) award; **~staat** *m* constitutional state; **~stellung** *f* legal status; **~streit** *m* lawsuit, legal contest; litigation (*gegen* versus); **~titel** *m* legal title; **~um!** *adv mil* right turn! **~ungültig** *a* illegal, invalid; **~verbindlich** *a* legally binding; *~~e Unterschrift* legal signature; **~verdreher** *m* pettifogger, pettifogging lawyer; **~verfahren** *n* legal procedure; **~verkehr** *m mot* right-hand drive; **~verletzung** *f* trespass; infringement; **~weg** *m* course of law; *den ~~ beschreiten* to take legal steps, to go to law; **~wesen** *n* judicial system; **~widrig** *a* illegal; **~~keit** *f* illegality; **~wirksam** *a* effective; *~~ machen* to validate; **~wissenschaft** *f* jurisprudence; law.

Reck *n* (*Turngerät*) horizontal bar; **~e** *m* valiant hero, warrior; giant; **~en** *tr* to stretch, to extend, to rack; *sich ~~* to stretch o. s.; *die Glieder ~~* to stretch o.'s limbs; *den Hals ~~* to crane o.'s neck (*nach* at); **~spannung** *f* tensile stress.

Redakt|eur *m* (*Schriftleiter*) editor; *Chef~~* editor-in-chief; *zweiter ~~* sub-editor, *Am* copy-reader; **~eurstelle** *f* editorship; **~ion** *f* (*Stab*) editors *pl*, editorial staff; (*Büro*) editor's office, editorial premises *pl*; (*Abfassung*) editing, wording; **~ionell** *a* editorial; **~ionsschluß** *m* copy dead-line.

Rede *f* talk; (*Vortrag*) speech; (*Ansprache*) address; (*Erörterung*) discourse; (*Unterhaltung*) conversation; (*feierliche ~*) oration; (*Äußerung*) utterance; (*Predigt*) allocution, sermon; (*Sprache, Redeweise*) language; (*Gerücht*) rumo(u)r; *die Gabe der ~* the gift of speech, *fam* the gift of the gab; *e-e ~ halten* to make a speech; *e-e ~ schwingen* to speechify; *jdm in die ~ fallen* to interrupt s. o.; to cut s. o. short; *~ stehen* to account for, to answer for; *zur ~ stellen* to call s. o. to account; *in ~ stehen* to be under discussion; *es geht die ~* people say that, it is rumo(u)red that, there is a talk of; *nicht der ~ wert* not worth mentioning; *jdn mit leeren ~n abspeisen* to put s. o. off with mere words; *ihren ~n nach* according to what she says; *davon kann keine ~ sein* that's out of the question; *davon ist nicht die ~* that's not the point; *wovon ist die ~?* what is the matter? what are you talking of (*od* about)? what's it all about? **~fluß** *m* flow of words, fluency of speech; (*Wortreichtum*) volubility; **~freiheit** *f* freedom of speech; **~gewandt** *a* eloquent, fluent, glib; **~~heit** *f* faculty of speech, eloquence; **~kunst** *f* rhetoric; **~n** *itr, tr* to speak (*mit jdm* with *od* to s. o.); (*zwanglos*) to talk; (*sich unterhalten*) to converse (*mit* with, *über* on); (*erörtern*) to discuss; (*begeistert ~~ über*) to rave about; (*e-e Rede halten*) to make a speech; (*vor Gericht*) to plead; *offen ~~* to speak out; *~~ Sie deutsch!* speak out! *nicht zu ~~ von* to say nothing of; *nicht mit sich ~~ lassen* not to listen to reason; *sie läßt mit sich ~~* you can talk with her; *von sich ~~ machen* to cause a stir; *sie hat nichts zu ~~* she has no say; *~~ ist Silber, schweigen ist Gold* the less said, the better; **~nsart** *f* locution; (*treffende ~~*) phrase; (*Ausdruck*) expression; (*Spracheigentümlichkeit*) idiom; (*aus Höflichkeit*) compliment; (*Ausrede*) empty phrase; (*Sprichwort*) proverb; *bloße ~~en* mere words, empty talk; *billige ~~* catch-word; **~rei** *f* (*kindliche ~~*) prattle; (*leeres Gerede*) empty talk; (*müßige ~~*) palaver; (*lange ~~*) tirade; (*Unsinn*) rubbish; **~schwall** *m* burst of eloquence; **~teil** *m* part of speech; **~übung** *f* exercise in speaking; **~weise** *f* manner of speech (*od* speaking); style; **~wendung** *f* (*Ausdruck*) expression; (*Spracheigentümlichkeit*) idiom, idiomatic expression; (*Satz*) phrase.

redigieren *tr* to edit; to revise.

redlich *a* honest, just, *fam* square; (*billig*) fair; (*aufrecht*) upright; (*aufrichtig*) candid; **~keit** *f* honesty; probity, integrity; uprightness; (*Offenheit*) cando(u)r.

Redner *m* speaker, orator; speechmaker; (*Kanzel~*) preacher, (*eifernder Kanzel~*) tub-thumper; (*politischer ~*) platform speaker; (*Volks~, Wahl~*) stump-orator, stump-speaker, *Am sl* soap-box orator, *Am* (*faszinierender ~*) spell-binder; **~bühne** *f* platform; tribune; floor; (*improvisierte*) *Am* soap-box; *die ~~ besteigen* to take the floor; **~gabe** *f* oratorical gift, power (*od* gift) of speech; **~isch** *a* oratorical, rhetorical; **~stuhl** *m* chair.

Redoute *f mil* redoubt; (*Maskenball*) masquerade.

redselig *a* talkative; (*langweilig*) garrulous; (*unaufhörlich*) loquacious; (*zungenfertig*) voluble; *er ist sehr ~* he has the gift of the gab; **~keit** *f* talkativeness; garrulity; loquacity; volubility.

Redu|ktion *f* reduction; **~ktionsgetriebe** *n* reduction gear; **~ktionsmittel** *n* reducer, reducing agent; **~zierbar** *a* reducible; **~zieren** *tr* to reduce to; to decrease; to lower, to step down; (*Mannschaften*) to cut, to diminish; **~zierung** *f* reduction; **~zierventil** *n* reducing valve.

Reede *f* roadstead; **~r** *m* shipowner; **~rei** *f* (*Schiffahrtslinie*) shipping (-line); shipping-firm, shipping company, *Am* steamship company; (*Schiffsausrüstung*) fitting out (of a merchantman).

reell *a* (*Firma*) solid; (*anständig*) respectable, reputable, sincere; honest; (*Ware*) good; (*Angebot*) real; (*Preis*) fair, *fam* square; *~ bedient werden* to get good value for o.'s money; **~ität** *f* (*Firma*) solidity; (*Anständigkeit*) respectability; honorability.

Reep *n* rope.

Refer|at *n* (*Bericht*) report; (*Vortrag*) talk, lecture; **~endar** *m* junior barrister, law graduate in the preparatory service; **~ent** *m* official adviser, referee; reporter, reviewer; speaker; **~enz** *f* reference; information; **~ieren** *tr, itr* to report (*über* upon); (*in e-m Vortrag*) to lecture (*über* on).

Reff *n* dosser; *mar* reef; **~en** *tr* to reef.

Reflekt|ant *m* intending purchaser, prospective customer (*od* buyer); **~ieren** *tr* (*Licht, Wärme zurückstrahlen*) to reflect; *itr* (*nachdenken*) to reflect (*über* upon s. th.), to consider; *auf etw* **~~** to look out for s. th., to have o.'s eye on; to think of buying s. th.; **~or** *m* (*Scheinwerfer*) reflector, projector.

Reflex *m* reflex; *phys* false flash; **~bahn** *f* reflex tract; **~bewegung** *f* reflex action; **~ebene** *f* plane of reflection; **~ion** *f* reflexion; *phys* reflection; **~iv** *a* reflective; (*Pronomen*) reflexive; **~kamera** *f phot* reflex camera; **~visier** *n* (*Revi*) *aero mil* reflector sight.

Reform *f* reform; **~bestrebungen** *f pl* reformatory efforts *pl*; **~ation** *f* reformation; **~ator** *m* reformer; **~atorisch** *a* reformatory; **~haus** *n* health food store; **~ieren** *tr* to reform; **~ierte(r)** *m* Calvinist; member of the Reformed Church; **~maßnahmen** *f pl* reformatory measures *pl*.

Refrain *m* burden, refrain; chorus; *den ~ mitsingen* to join in the chorus.

Refrakt|ion *f phys* refraction; **~ionsmesser** *m* refractometer; **~ionswinkel** *m* angle of refraction; **~or** *m opt* refractor, refracting telescope.

Regal *n* (*Gestell*) shelf, stack; (*Scheidewand*) partition; (*Bücher~*) (book-)-shelves *pl*; *typ* stand; **~ieren** *tr* to regale, to treat (*mit* on).

Regatta *f* regatta, boat-race.

rege *a* (*geistig*) active; (*flink*) agile; (*lebhaft*) brisk, lively; (*beweglich*) nimble, alert; (*fleißig*) industrious; busy; (*wach, munter*) alert, wide--awake; *~ machen* to stir up; to excite; *~ werden* to be stirred up.

Regel *f* rule; (*Vorschrift*) regulation, precept; (*Grundsatz*) principle; (*Norm*) standard; *med* menses *pl*, menstruation; *die Ausnahme bestätigt die ~* the exception proves the rule; *in der ~* as a rule, generally; **~ausführung** *f* standard design, *Am* conventional design (*od* type); **~bar** *a* regulable, adjustable; **~belastung** *f* normal load; **~detri** *f* rule of three; **~los** *a* irregular; informal; chaotic; haphazard, random; **~mäßig** *a* regular, normal; ordinary; clockwise; periodical; *~~e Prüfung* routine test; **~~keit** *f* regularity; **~n** *tr* to regulate, to arrange; to put in order; to settle; to control, to direct; **~recht** *a* regular; correct; proper; *ein ~~er Schwindler* a regular swindler; *e-e ~~e Schlacht* a pitched battle; **~schaltung** *f* control circuit; **~stellung** *f* normal position; **~ung** *f* control; regulation; adjustment; settlement; arrangement; **~widrig** *a* contrary to rule; abnormal; *sport* foul; **~~keit** *f* irregularity; foulness; abnormality, abnormity; *e-e ~~keit begehen sport* to commit a foul.

regen *r* to stir, to move, to rouse, to budge; (*Gefühle*) to take rise, to rise, to stir.

Regen *m* rain; (*Sprüh~*) drizzle, drizzling rain; (*Schauer*) shower, scud; (*Guß*) rainstorm; (*Platz~*) downpour; (*Wolkenbruch*) cloud burst; (*~flut*) deluge; (*Niederschläge*) precipitation; *starker ~* heavy rain, pelting rain; *ein ~ von Blumen, Granaten, Schlägen fig* a rain of flowers, shells, blows; *aus dem ~ in die Traufe kommen* to fall out of the frying-pan into the fire, to get from bad to worse; *es sieht nach ~ aus* it looks like rain; *auf ~ folgt Sonnenschein* after rain comes sunshine (*od* fair weather); **~arm** *a* dry, rainless; **~bach** *m* torrent; **~bekleidung** *f* rainwear; **~bö** *f* squall; **~bogen** *m* rainbow; **~~farben** *f pl* colo(u)rs of the rainbow, prismatic colo(u)rs *pl*; **~~farbig** *a* rainbow colo(u)red, iridescent; **~~haut** *f anat* iris; **~dach** *n* penthouse; **~decke** *f* tarpaulin; **~dicht** *a* rain-proof, waterproof; **~fall** *m* rainfall (*pl* rains *pl*); **~faß** *n* water-butt; **~fest** *a* waterproof; **~flut** *f* flood of rain, deluge; **~gewölk** *n* rain-clouds *pl*, nimbus; **~grau** *a* gray with rain; **~guß** *m* shower, downpour, *fam* drencher, *Am fam* gully-washer; **~haut** *f* oilskin coat; **~höhe** *f* depth of rainfall; **~jahr** *n* rainy year; **~luft** *f* rainy air; **~macher** *m* rain-maker; **~mantel** *m* waterproof, rainproof, mackintosh (*Abk* mac), trenchcoat, *Am* raincoat; **~menge** *f* amount of rain; **~messer** *m* rain-ga(u)ge, pluviometer; **~monat** *m* rainy month; **~periode** *f Am* rain(y)-spell; **~pfeifer** *m orn* plover; **~pfütze** *f* puddle; **~reich** *a* rainy, having a heavy rainfall; **~schatten** *m* rain shadow, rainless side; **~schauer** *m* shower of rain, flurry; **~schirm** *m* umbrella; **~~ständer** *m* umbrella-stand; **~sturm** *m* rain-storm; **~tag** *m* rainy day; **~tonne** *f* water-butt; **~tropfen** *m* drop of rain, raindrop; **~wasser** *n* rain-water; **~wetter** *n* rainy weather; **~wolke** *f* rain-cloud; **~wurm** *m* earth-worm, *Am* angle-worm; **~zeit** *f* rainy season; (*Tropen*) monsoon.

Regene|ration *f* regeneration; **~ratgummi** *m* regenerated (*od* reclaimed) rubber; **~rator** *m* regenerator; **~rieren** *tr* to regenerate; **~rierung** *f* regeneration, reclaiming, recovery.

Regent *m* (*Stellvertreter*) regent; (*Herrscher*) ruler, sovereign; governor; **~in** *f* (female) regent; **~schaft** *f* regency, regentship.

Reg|ie *f* (*Verwaltung*) administration, management; (*Monopol*) state (*od* public) monopoly; *theat, film* production, direction, stage-management, staging; **~ieanweisung** *f* stage direction; **~ieassistent** *m film* assistant director; **~iekosten** *pl* overhead expenses *pl*; **~iepult** *n radio* control (*od* mixing) desk; mixer, mixing table; console, fader; **~ieraum** *m radio* control room; **~iezelle** *f radio* control cell; **~isseur** *m theat* stage-manager; *film, radio* producer, production man, director.

regier|en *itr* (*herrschen*) to reign; (*diktatorisch beherrschen*) to rule; (*den Staat leiten*) to govern; *schlecht ~~* to misgovern; *tr* (*herrschen*) to reign (*über* over); (*willkürlich, zeitweilig*) to rule (*über* over); (*verfassungsmäßig*) to govern; (*lenken*) to guide; to conduct, to manage; to direct; to handle; (*regeln*) to regulate; *sich selbst ~~* to control o. s.; *gram* to govern; **~ung** *f* government (*Engl mit sing, Am mit pl*), *Am* administration; cabinet; rule; (*~~szeit*) reign; (*Lenkung*) direction; (*Militär~~*) Military Government; *namens der ~~* on behalf of the government; *zur ~~ gelangen* (*Kabinett*) to come into power; *unter der ~~ von* (*Fürst*) in the reign of; **~~sanleihe** *f* government loan; **~~santritt** *m* accession (to the throne); **~~sapparat** *m* government machine; **~~sbeamte(r)** *m* (government) official; civil servant, *Am* governmental officer, department clerk; **~~sbefehl** *m* government order; **~~sbehörde** *f* governmental agency; **~~sbezirk** *m* administrative district; **~~sbildung** *f* forming of a cabinet; **~~sblatt** *n* official gazette; government paper; **~~sfeindlich** *a* oppositional; belonging to the opposition; *die ~~en Parteien* the opposition; **~~sform** *f* form of government; **~~sfreundlich** *a* governmental; **~~sgewalt** *f* supreme (*od* sovereign) power, supreme authority; **~~skreise** *m pl* governmental circles *pl*; **~~smaßnahme** *f* government measure, *Am* administration measure; **~~spartei** *f* party in power; the ins *pl*; **~~spolitik** *f* government's policy; **~~spresse** *f* government-controlled press; **~~ssekretär** *m* secretary to the government; Secretary of State; **~~ssitz** *m* seat of government; **~~sstelle** *f* government agency; **~~ssystem** *n* system of government, political system; **~~svorlage** *f* government bill; **~~swechsel** *m* change of government; **~~szeit** *f* reign.

Regime *n* (*Regierungsform*) regime, prevailing governmental (*od* social) system; (*Diät, Lebensordnung*) regimen.

Regiment *n* rule, government; command; *das ~ haben* to command; *sie führt das ~* she wears the breeches, *Am* she wears the pants; *mil* (*Truppeneinheit*) regiment; *das ~ betreffend* regimental; *bei e-m ~ dienen* to serve with a regiment; *bei welchem ~ waren Sie?* what regiment were you in? **~sabzeichen** *n* numeral; **~sadjutant** *m* adjutant of a regiment; **~sarzt** *m* regimental medical officer; **~sbefehl** *m* regimental order; **~schef** *m* colonel-in-chief; honorary colonel; **~skommandeur** *m* commander of a regiment; **~smusik, ~skapelle** *f* regimental band; **~snachrichtenoffizier** *m* regimental communications officer; **~snachrichtenzug** *m* regimental communications platoon; **~sschreiber** *m* staff sergeant; **~sstab** *m* regimental staff; **~stambour** *m* drum-major; **~suniform** *f* regimentals *pl*.

Region *f* region, district; *die höheren ~en* the upper regions; *in höheren ~en schweben fig* to be absent-minded; **~al** *a* (*örtlich*) regional.

Regist|er *n* (*Liste, Verzeichnis*) record, list; (*Namens~~*) register; (*Familien~~*) family record; (*Inhaltsverzeichnis*) index, table of contents; (*Katalog*) catalogue, *Am* catalog; *mus* (*Orgel*) (organ-) stop; *typ* register; *tele* sender; *ein ~~ führen* to maintain a register; *alle ~~ ziehen fig* to call all hands; *in ein ~~ eintragen* to enter in a register; to register, to record; **~ertonne** *f* register(ed) ton; **~rator** *m* registrar, recorder; (*Akten*) filing clerk; **~ratur** *f* registry; (*Amt*) registrar's office; record-office; **~rierapparat** *m* recorder, recording apparatus; **~rierballon** *m* (*Pilotballon*) sounding balloon, pilot balloon; **~rieren** *tr* to register; to record; (*eintragen*) to enter; (*in den Akten*) to file; to index; **~riergerät** *n* (*Schallmeß*) chronograph; **~rierkasse** *f* cash register, recording counter; **~rierpapier** *n* record paper, recording chart; **~rierung** *f* registration; entering; recording; **~~sausweis** *m* registration card; **~riervorrichtung** *f* recorder, recording mechanism.

Regl|er *m el* control(ler); (*Widerstand*) rheostat; regulator; (*Kraftmaschinen*) governor; *automatischer ~~* automatic regulator; **~~getriebe** *n* governor gearing; **~~leitung** *f* pilot wire; **~~pult** *n* control desk; **~~welle** *f* governing shaft; **~~widerstand** *m* rheostat; **~ung** *f* (*Einstellung*) timing; adjustment, control, regulation.

regn|en *itr* to rain; (*sprühen*) to drizzle; (*tröpfeln*) to sprinkle, to trickle; to spit; (*gießen*) to pour; *es regnet* it rains; *es regnet in Strömen* it pours in torrents, *fam* it rains cats and dogs; **~er** *m* (*Garten~~*) sprinkler; **~erisch** *a* rainy.

Regreß *m* recourse; (*Schaden~*) recovery (of damage); **~pflichtig** *a* liable to recourse.

regsam *a* (*Geist*) active; (*Denken*) nimble; (*Bewegung*) agile; (*energisch*) brisk; quick, active; **~keit** *f* quickness, activity; nimbleness, briskness.

regul|är *a* regular; *~~er Preis* regular price; *~~e Truppen* regulars *pl*; **~ativ** *n* regulation, rule; **~ator** *m* governor; regulator: **~ierapparat** *m* regulating gear; **~ierbar** *a* controllable, adjustable; **~ierbrett** *n* adjuster board; **~ieren** *tr* to regulate, to govern; to adjust; (*Rechnung*) to settle; **~iergewicht** *n* governor weight; **~ierhebel** *m* choke arm; **~ierschraube** *f* adjusting screw: **~ierung** *f* regulation; adjustment: (*e-r Rechnung etc*) settlement; **~iervorrichtung** *f* regulating device; **~ierwiderstand** *m el* adjustable resistance, rheostat.

Regung *f* movement, moving, motion; stirring; *fig* (*Gemüts~*) emotion; (*Erregung*) agitation; (*heftige ~*) excitement; (*Stimmung*) affection; (*Antrieb. Anwandlung*) impulse; **~slos** *a* motionless; **~slosigkeit** *f* motionlessness; inertia.

Reh *n*, **~bock** *m* roe, roebuck; (*weiblich*) doe; **~braten** *m* roast venison; **~farben** *a* fawn-colo(u)red; **~fell** *n* doe-skin; **~kalb** *n* fawn; **~keule** *f* haunch (*od* leg) of venison; **~lendenbraten** *m* loin of venison; **~leder** *n* doeskin; **~posten** *m* buck-shot; **~rücken** *m*, **~ziemer** *m* back of a roe; **~wild** *n* roe deer.

rehabilitier|en *tr* to rehabilitate; **~ung** *f* rehabilitation.

*

Reib|ahle *f* broach; **~e** *f*, **~eisen** *n* grater, rasp; **~echt** *a* fast to rubbing; **~ekeule** *f* pestle; **~elappen** *m* rubber; **~en** *tr* to rub; to grate (bread); (*Farben*) to grind; to pulverize; (*Reibung erzeugen*) to cause friction; *wund ~~* to chafe (skin), to gall; (*durchscheuern*) to fret; *sich an jdm ~~* to provoke s. o.; to be at variance with; to vex, to irritate; to annoy; *sich die Hände ~~* to rub o.'s hands; *die Tränen aus den Augen ~~* to wipe the tears from o.'s eyes; *ich rieb es ihr unter die Nase* I rubbed it into her, I cast it into her teeth; **~er** *m* rubber, grater; **~erei** *f* friction; (*Zusammenstoß*) collision; conflict, clash; **~estein** *m* grinding-stone; **~elaut** *m* (*Phonetik*) fricative; **~festigkeit** *f* resistance to abrasion, chafing resistance; **~fläche** *f* striking (*od* rough) surface; rubbing surface; **~ung** *f tech* friction; rubbing, grating; *fig* difficulty, friction, clash, collision; **~~selektrizität** *f* frictional electricity; **~~sfläche** *f fig* source of irritation; **~~skoeffizient** *m*, **~~szahl** *f* coefficient of friction, frictional index; **~~slos** *a* frictionless; (*glatt*) smooth; **~~sverlust** *m* friction load (*od* loss); **~~sversuch** *m* shear test; **~~swärme** *f* friction heat; **~~swiderstand** *m* frictional resistance; **~wunde** *f* gall; **~zündhölzchen** *n* friction match.

Reich *n* (*Kaiser~*, *~ allgemein*) empire; (*König~*, *~ Gottes, Natur~*) kingdom; *Pflanzen~* vegetable kingdom; *Stein~* mineral kingdom; *Tier~* animal kingdom; *Deutsches ~* (*hist*) the German Reich; (*Staatsverband*) commonwealth; (*staatsrechtlicher Ausdruck u. bildlich*) realm; **~sadler** *m* German Eagle; **~sangehörige(r), ~sdeutsche(r)** *m* German national; **~sanleihe** *f* government loan; **~sapfel** *m* mound, orb; **~sautobahn** *f* autobahn, State arterial motor-road; **~sbahn** *f* German Railways *pl*; **~sfarben** *f pl*, **~sflagge** *f* national colo(u)rs *pl* (*od* flag); **~sgebiet** *n* territory of the Reich; **~sgericht** *n* Supreme Court of Justice; **~shauptstadt** *f* capital of Germany; **~sinnenminister** *m* home secretary; **~skanzlei** *f* Chancery of the Reich; State Chancery; **~skanzler** *m* Chancellor of the Reich, State Chancellor; **~skleinodien** *n pl* crown jewels *pl*; **~smarine** *f* German navy; **~~amt** *n* admiralty; **~smark** *f* reichsmark; **~spost** *f* German State Post; **~ssender** *m* German radio station, Government station; **~sstraße** *f* national highway; **~~nverkehrsordnung** *f* German highway traffic regulations *pl*; **~sverfassung** *f* constitution of the German Reich; **~swehr** *f hist* the 100,000-man army; **~swetterdienst** *m* meteorological service of Germany.

reich *a* rich (*an* in); (*wohlhabend*) wealthy, well off; opulent; (*reichlich*) copious; abundant; ample; *~ bebildert* (*Zeitschrift*) profusely illustrated; *in ~em Maße* amply, copiously; *e-e ~e Auswahl* a wide selection; *~ werden* to become rich; **~e(r)** *m* rich man; *die ~en pl* the rich, the wealthy classes; **~haltig** *a* rich; (*überreich*) copious; (*voll*) full; (*umfassend*) comprehensive; ample; (*mehr als genug*) abundant; (*gut ausreichend*) plentiful; **~haltigkeit** *f* richness; (*Überfluß*) abundance; (*Fülle*) fullness; (*Abwechslung*) variety; **~lich** *a* ample; (*Versorgung*) bountiful; (*Ertrag*) plenteous; (*Überfluß*) profuse, exuberant; (*mehr als genug*) enough and to spare; *mit etw ~~ versehen sein* to have plenty of s. th.; *e-e ~~e Mahlzeit* a hearty meal; *adv* (*ziemlich*) rather, fairly, *Am fam* plenty; *pred fam* flush, *Am fam* plenty; **~tum** *m* (*Wohlstand*) wealth (*an* of), riches *pl*; (*Vermögen*) fortune; (*Überfluß*) abundance; opulence; (*Mannigfaltigkeit*) variety; *im ~~ schwimmen* to roll in riches.

reich|en *tr* (*geben*) to hand, to pass; to reach; to offer, to present; *itr* (*aus~~*) to do, to go, to last; (*Lebensmittel*) to suffice, to hold out; (*sich erstrecken*) to stretch (*bis* to); *das reicht!* that will do! *er kann ihm das Wasser nicht ~~* he is not fit to hold a candle to him; *sich die Hände ~~* to join hands; **~weite** *f* reach; (*Artillerie, aero, mar*) range; (*Bereich*) radius; radius of influence; (*Aktionsradius*) radius of action; (*e-s Senders*) *radio* transmission range, coverage of a radio station; *außer ~~* out of reach, out of range; *in*(*nerhalb*) *der ~~* within reaching distance, within range; *große ~~* long range; *in der ~~ übertreffen* to outrange.

reif *a* (*Früchte, Alter*) ripe; *fig* (*innerlich fest*) mature; ripe; (*mürbe*) mellow; (*entwickelt*) fully developed; (*fertig*) ready; *~ werden* to ripen, to grow ripe; *~ für* fit for; *das ~e Alter* ripe old age; **~e** *f* ripeness; *fig* maturity; (*Geeignetheit zu*) fitness for; (*geschlechtliche ~~*) puberty; **~en** *tr* to ripen; to mature; *itr* to ripen, to grow ripe; *der Jüngling reift zum Manne* the youth ripens into manhood; *e-n Plan ~~ lassen* to mature a plan; **~eprüfung** *f* (*Schule*) leaving-examination; **~ezeit** *f* age of maturity; **~ezeugnis** *n* (*Schule*) leaving-certificate; **~lich** *a* mature; thorough, careful; *nach ~~er Überlegung* after thorough consideration; upon second thought; *etw ~~ überlegen* to think over thoroughly; **~ung** *f* maturing; **~~sdauer** *f* time for ripening.

Reif[1] *m* (*Rauh~*) hoar-frost, white frost; frozen fog; *poet* rime; *mit ~ bedecken* to rime; **~bildung** *f* frozen-fog formation; **~en** *imp: es reift* there is a hoar-frost.

Reif[2] *m* (*Faß~*) hoop; (*Ring*) ring; circlet; collar; **~förmig** *a* hoop-shaped; **~rock** *m* crinoline.

Reifen *m* (*Spielzeug, Faß~*) hoop; (*Ring*) ring; (*Schmuck~*) circlet, bracelet; (*Fahrrad, Auto*) tyre,pneumatic, *Am* tire; *Ersatz~* spare tyre; *die ~ aufpumpen* to inflate the tyres; *e-n ~ aufmontieren* to fit a tyre; *e-n ~ abmontieren* to remove a tyre; *~ wechseln* to change tyres; **~druck** *m mot* tyre pressure; **~druckmesser** *m mot* tyre gauge, *Am* tire gage; **~flickzeug** *n* tyre repair kit; **~gewebe** *n mot* tyre cord, fabric, *Am* tire canvas; tire flap; **~mantel** *m* outer cover, tyre cover; casing; **~montagehebel** *m* tyre lever; **~panne** *f*, **~schaden** *m mot* (tyre) puncture, *Am* blowout, flat (tire); *~~ haben* to suffer a puncture, *Am* to have a blowout (*od* flat); **~profil** *n* tread; **~pumpe** *f* tyre pump; **~reparatur** *f* tyre repair; **~schlauch** *m* tyre tube; **~spur** *f* tyre track; **~vulkanisierung** *f* tyre vulcanizing, tyre repairing; **~wand** *f* tyre wall; **~wulst** *f* tyre rim; bead of tyre.

Reigen *m* round dance; *den ~ eröffnen* to lead the dance, to open the ball.

Reihe *f* (*hintereinander*) file, (*nebeneinander*) rank; (*e-e Linie*) row (of houses); range (of hills); *fig* series (of accidents); set (of books, of swindlers); (*Sitzreihe*) tier; *math* series; progression; (*Folge*) succession; sequence; suit; rotation; *typ* (*Spalte*) column; *arithmetische ~* arithmetical progression; *geometrische ~* geometrical progression; *unendliche ~* infinite series; *in e-r ~* in a row, in a line; *der ~ nach adv* in turn, by turns; *in Reih u. Glied* in rank and file; *in ~ marschieren* to march in file; *wer ist an der ~?* whose turn is it? *du mußt warten, bis du an die ~ kommst* you must await your turn; *ich bin an der ~* it is my turn; it is up to me; *in e-r ~ mit* in range with; *außer der ~* out of turn; *in e-e ~ stellen* to draw up; *in ~ schalten el* to connect (*od* to join) in series; *in ~ geschaltet el* series connected, serially connected; **~n** *tr* to put in a row; to file; to rank; (*in e-r Linie*) to range, to arrange (in a line); (*Perlen auf~~*) to string; **~nabwurf** *m aero mil* (*von Bomben*) dropping of a stick of bombs; salvo; **~~gerät** *n* automatic bomb-release mechanism; **~narbeit** *f* repetition work; **~naufnahme** *f* serial survey; **~nbau** *m* series production; **~nbild** *n aero phot* aerial mosaic; **~~kamera** *f aero phot* aerial mapping camera; automatic (aerial) camera; serial camera; mosaic camera; **~nbö** *f* (*Meteorologie*) line squall; **~nfertigung, ~nherstellung** *f* serial production;

mass production, assembly-line production; **~nfeuer** *n* bursts of fire; **~nflug** *m* line formation; **~nfolge** *f* succession, turn; (*gleichmäßig, logisch*) sequence; (*Ordnung*) order; arrangement; (*Serie*) series; (*unmittelbare* **~~**) consecutiveness; *alphabetische* **~~** alphabetic order; *der* **~~** *nach* in sequence, in succession; **~~** *der Wichtigkeit* order of merit; **~ngroßfertigung** *f* large-scale production; **~nhäuser** *n pl* terraced houses *pl*; **~nhäuserbau** *m* ribbon-building; **~nmotor** *m mot* in-line engine; **~nnummer** *f* serial number; **~nschaltung** *f el* series connection (*od* arrangement); series circuit; **~nweise** *adv* in rows; **~~** *ordnen* to file; **~nwurf** *m aero mil* stick bombing; **reihum** *adv* in turns, by turns.

Reiher *m* heron, hern; egret; **~beize** *f* hawking of herons; **~busch** *m* aigrette; **~feder** *f* heron's feather, aigrette; **~horst** *m* heronry.

Reim *m* rhyme; **~en** *tr* to rhyme; *sich* **~~** to rhyme (*auf* to, with); *fig* to agree (with); **~er** *m*, **~schmied** *m* rhymer, rhymester; **~erei** *f* rhyming, verse-making; **~silbe** *f* rhyming syllable.

rein *a* (*sauber*) clean; (*ordentlich*) neat, tidy, proper; (*klar, hell*) clear; (*unvermischt, unschuldig*) pure; (*echt*) genuine; (*Alkohol*) absolute; (*Metall*) unalloyed; (*Flüssigkeiten unverfälscht*) undiluted; (*keusch, edel*) chaste; (*Gewinn, Verdienst*) net; *fig* (*völlig, absolut*) sheer; mere; *adv* quite, entirely; downright; **~** *unmöglich* quite impossible; *die Luft ist* **~** (*fig*) the coast is clear; *chemisch* **~** chemically pure; **~***e Aussprache* correct pronunciation; **~***er Bogen Papier* blank sheet of paper; **~***es Gewissen* clear conscience; **~***e Lüge* downright lie, plain lie; **~***en Mund halten* to hold o.'s tongue, to keep a secret, to keep mum; **~***e Seide* pure silk; **~***e Sprache* clear voice; **~***en Tisch machen* to make a clean sweep; **~***er Ton* pure (*od* simple) tone; *aus* **~***em Trotz* out of sheer obstinacy; **~***er Unsinn* sheer nonsense; *die* **~***e Wahrheit* plain truth; **~***e Wäsche* clean linen; **~***en Wein einschenken* not to mince matters, to tell the plain truth; **~***er Zufall* the merest accident; **~***e machen* to turn out a room; *ins* **~***e bringen* to settle; *ins* **~***e schreiben* to make a fair copy of; **~ausfuhr** *f* net export; **~druck** *m typ* clean proof; **~einkommen** *n* net income; **~ertrag** *m* net proceeds *pl*, clear gain, net yield, net profit, net revenue; **~fall** *m* let-down, failure, frost; *fam* flop; *sl* sell; **~gewicht** *n* net weight; **~gewinn** *m* net profit; **~heit** *f* cleanness; cleanliness; clearness; purity; pureness; (*Tonwiedergabe*) fidelity (of reproduction); **~igen** *tr* to clean, *Am meist* to cleanse; (*chem* **~~**) to dryclean; (*waschen*) to wash; (*desinfizieren*) to disinfect; *fig* (*Blut, Seele, Sprache, chem*) to purify; (*von Sünden, Eingeweide, Partei*) to purge; (*Metall, Öl, Stil*) to refine; (*Flüssigkeiten*) to clarify; **~igend** *a* cleansing; *med* abluent, detergent; **~igung** *f* cleaning; washing; (*Abscheidung*) separation; (*Läuterung*) purification; purging; *monatliche* **~~** menstruation, menses *pl*; *in der* **~~** (*Kleidungsstück*) at the cleaner's; *zur* **~~** *geben* to send to the cleaner's; **~~sanstalt** *f chem* dry cleaner; **~~smittel** *n* cleaner, detergent, *Am* cleansing agent; *med* (*Abführmittel*) purgative, aperient; **~~sprozeß** *m* purification process; refining process; **~kultur** *f* pure culture, bacilli culture; **~lich** *a* clean(ly); (*Kleidung*) neat; (*Zimmer*) tidy; (*deutlich*) distinct, clean cut; **~~keit** *f* cleanliness; (*Kleidung*) neatness, tidiness; **~machefrau** *f* charwoman, cleaning woman, *Am* scrubwoman; **~machen** *tr* to clean; **~rassig** *a* (*Pferde*) thoroughbred; (*Hunde*) pure-bred; **~schrift** *f* fair copy, final copy; **~seiden** *a* all-silk; **~ton** *m radio* single-frequency tone; **~waschen**: *sich* **~~** (*fig*) to clear o. s., to justify o. s., to exculpate o. s., to whitewash o. s.; **~weg** *adv* flatly; **~zucht** *f* pure culture.

Reis[1] *m* rice; **~auflauf** *m* rice pudding; **~brei** *m* boiled rice; **~feld** *n* rice ground, rice field; paddy; **~mehl** *n* rice flour; **~puder** *m* rice powder; **~suppe** *f* rice soup.

Reis[2] *n* twig, sprig; (*Ableger, Pfropf***~**) scion; (*Zweig*) bough; (*Feueranmachholz*) brushwood, small fire-wood; **~bund, ~bündel** *n* fag(g)ot; fascine **~holz, ~ig** *n* brushwood, twigs *pl* **~igfeuer** *n Am* smudge.

Reise *f* (*mit festem Ziel*) journey; (*auf längere Zeit*) travel(s *pl*); (*kurze*) trip; (*Ausflug*) excursion; (*Vergnügungs***~**) pleasure trip, tour; (*See, Flugzeug*) voyage; (*Überfahrt*) passage; (*Forschungs***~**) expedition; **~** *ins Ausland* journey abroad; **~** *um die Welt* trip round the world; *Hin***~** out journey, *Rück***~** return journey; *e-e* **~** *antreten* to go upon a journey; *e-e* **~** *machen* to make (*od* to take) a journey, to take a trip; *auf die* **~** *schicken* to launch; *auf* **~***n sein* to be travel(l)ing; *jdm glückliche* **~** *wünschen* to bid s. o. god-speed; *Glückliche* **~***!* a pleasant journey to you! have a nice trip! *er unternahm e-e* **~** *zu den Musikfestspielen in Salzburg* he took a trip to the music festivals at Salzburg; *wohin geht die***~***?* where are you going to? **~abenteuer** *n* (traveller's) adventure; **~andenken** *n* travel(l)ing souvenir; **~anzug** *m* travel(l)ing suit; travel(l)ing costume; **~artikel** *m* travel(l)ing article; **~ausweis** *m* travel document; **~apotheke** *f* portable medicine-chest; **~bericht** *m* report of a journey; **~beschreibung** *f* (*Buch*) (book of) travels *pl*; **~büro** *n* tourist office, tourist agency, travel bureau, travel agency, travel agent; *rail* railway travel office; *Am* tourist bureau; **~decke** *f* travel(l)ing rug; **~erinnerungen** *f pl* travel(l)ing reminiscences *pl*; **~fertig** *a* ready to start; *sich* **~~** *machen* to make ready to start; **~film** *m* travelog(ue) film; **~flug** *m aero* cruise; **~~zeug** *n* touring aircraft; **~führer** *m* (*Mann*) guide; (*Buch*) guide-book; **~gefährte** *m* fellow-travel(l)er, travel(l)ing companion; (*Bahn, Schiff*) fellow-passenger; **~geld** *n* travel(l)ing money; **~genehmigung** *f* travel permit; **~gepäck** *n* luggage, *Am* baggage; **~~versicherung** *f* luggage insurance; **~geschwindigkeit** *f* cruising speed; **~gesellschaft** *f* travel(l)ing party; **~handbuch** *n* guide-book; **~kleid** *n* travel(l)ing dress; **~koffer** *m* suitcase, box, (*großer*) trunk, portmanteau, *Am* valise; **~kosten** *pl* travel(l)ing expenses *pl*; **~~vergütung** *f Am* mileage; **~lustig** *a* fond of travel(l)ing; **~mantel** *m* travel top coat; **~marsch** *m mil* route-march; cross-country march; **~n** *itr* to travel, to go (*nach* to), to journey; (*ab***~~**) to start, to leave, to set out; (*wandern, zu Fuß* **~~**) to tramp, to hike; (*mit Anhalter*) to hitch-hike, *sie ist viel gereist* she has travel(l)ed a lot (*od* a great deal); *weit gereist* travel(l)ed; *gern* **~~** to be fond of travel(l)ing; *für e-e Firma* **~~** to travel for a firm; *mit der Eisenbahn* **~~** to go by rail; *über Stuttgart* **~~** to go via (*od* by way of) Stuttgart; *zum Vergnügen* **~~** to travel for pleasure; *Am fam* to go places; **~nde(r)** *m* travel(l)er; passenger, tourist; (*Handels***~~**) *com* commercial travel(l)er, *Am* traveling salesman; **~necessaire** *n* dressing-case; **~paß** *m* passport; **~plan** *m* travel arrangement, itinerary; **~route** *f* route; **~scheck** *m* travel(l)er's cheque; **~schreibmaschine** *f* portable (typewriter); **~spesen** *pl* travel(l)ing charges *pl*; **~tag** *m* travel(l)ing-day; **~tasche** *f* travel(l)ing bag, travel(l)er's hand-bag, *Am* grip(sack); **~unterbrechung** *f* break of journey, *Am* stopover; **~verkehr** *m* tourist traffic; **~verpflegung** *f* travel ration; **~wagen** *m* tourist car; **~ziel** *n* destination.

Reisig(e)r *m hist* horseman; horse-soldier; trooper warrior.

Reiß|aus *n, m fam*: **~** *nehmen* to take to o.'s heels; to decamp; **~blei** *n* black-lead, graphite; **~brett** *n* drawing-board; **~en** *irr tr* to tear; (*ziehen*) to pull; (*zerren*) to drag; (*weg***~~**) to snatch, to plunk; (*zer***~~**) to tear; (*entzwei***~~**) to rend; to rip; (*fort***~~**) to tear away, to tear off; *an sich* **~~** to snatch up, to seize hold of, to grasp; (*Geschäftszweig, Unterhaltung*) to monopolize; (*auseinander***~~**) *tr, itr* to split, to snap, to break; to burst; *sich* **~~** (*ritzen*) to scratch o.s.; to get scratched; *sich ein Loch* **~~** to tear o.'s clothes; *ich habe mir ein Loch in die Hose gerissen* I tore a hole in my trousers; *sich um etw* **~~** to fight for (*od* over), to scramble for; *die Geduld riß mir* I lost patience; *in Fetzen* **~~** to tear to shreds; *in Stücke* **~~** to tear to pieces; *wenn alle Stricke* **~~** if all resources fail; if the worst comes to the worst; *Witze* **~~** to crack jokes; *Zoten* **~~** to talk smut; **~en** *n med* rheumatism, rheumatics *pl*, rheumatic pains *pl*; **~end** *a* (*rasch, schnell*) rapid; (*ungestüm*) turbulent, impetuous; (*Tiere*) rapacious; (*raubgierig*) ravenous; (*Fluß*) torrential; (*Schmerz*) violent, acute, sharp; **~~er** *Absatz* rapid sale; **~~er** *Strom* torrent; **~~***e Fortschritte machen* to make rapid progress; **~er** *m theat* thriller, box-office success (*Abk* B.O. success); **~feder** *f* drawing-pen; **~festigkeit** *f* resistance to tearing, tensile strength; **~kohle** *f* charcoal-crayon; **~leine** *f aero* (*Fallschirm*) rip cord, release line; (*zwischen Fallschirm u. Flugzeug*) static line; (*Ballon*) gas release cord; **~nagel** *m*, **~zwecke** *f* drawing-pin, *Am* thumbtack; **~schiene** *f* T-square, tee-square; **~verschluß** *m* zip-fastener, pull-fastener, slide-fastener, fastener, zipper, zipper closure; (*verdeckter* **~~**) sunken zip fastener; *e-n* **~~** *öffnen* to unzip; *mit e-m* **~~** *schließen* to zip in; *Lederetui mit* **~~** leather case with zipper closure; **~~beutel** *m* zipper pouch; **~~glied** *n* zip-fastener link; **~~tasche** *f* zipper case; **~zeug** *n* mathematical (*od* drawing) instruments *pl*; **~widerstand** *m* breaking strain; **~wolle** *f* re-used wool; **~zahn** *m* canine tooth; **~zirkel** *m* drawing-compass(es *pl*).

Reit|bahn *f* riding-school, manege, circus; **~en** *irr itr, tr* to ride, to go on horseback; *Schritt* ~~ to pace; *Trab* ~~ to trot; *Galopp* ~~ to gallop; *auf Schusters Rappen* ~~ to ride on Shanks' mare; *auf e-r Sache herum*~~ to harp on the same subject; *sich wund* ~~ to gall o. s. in riding; ~**en** *n* riding, equitation; ~**end** *a* riding, mounted, on horseback; ~~*e Artillerie* horse-artillery; ~**er** *m* rider, horseman; (*Polizist, Kavallerist*) trooper; (*Kartei*) tab; (*Schreibmaschine*) tabulator stop; *spanische* ~~ turn-pikes; *mil leichte* ~~ *pl* light horse; ~~**ei** *f* cavalry, horse, horsemen *pl*; ~~**gefecht** *n* engagement of horsemen; ~~**in** *f* horsewoman; ~~**regiment** *n* regiment of cavalry; ~~**smann** *m* horseman; ~~**statue** *f* equestrian statue; ~**gerte** *f* riding-whip; ~**gurt** *m* riding-girth; ~**hose** *f* riding-breeches *pl*; ~**kissen** *n* pillion; ~**kleid** *n* riding-habit; ~**knecht** *m* groom; ~**kunst** *f* art of riding; horsemanship; ~**peitsche** *f* riding-whip; jockey stick; ~**pferd** *n* riding-horse, saddle-horse; mount; ~**rock** *m* riding-coat; ~**schule** *f* riding-school; ~**sport** *m* equestrian sport; ~**stall** *m* stable for saddle-horse; riding-stable; ~**stiefel** *m* riding-boots, top-boots; ~**stunde** *f* riding-lesson; ~**weg** *m* riding-path, bridle-path; ~**zeug** *n* riding-equipage, riding-things *pl*.

Reiz *m* charm; (*Anziehung*) attraction; attractiveness; (*Zauber*) fascination; (*Verlockung*) enticement; (*Anreiz*) stimulus, incentive; (*Antrieb*) impulse, impulsion, impetus; *der* ~ *der Neuheit* the charm of novelty; (*Erregung*) irritation; ~**bar** *a* sensitive, irritable, *Am* sore (*über* about); (*nervös*) nervous; ~**barkeit** *f* susceptibility, irritability; ~**en** *tr* (*Haut, Zorn*) to irritate; (*auf*~) to egg (on), to excite, to stir up; to instigate, to incite; (*anregen*) to stimulate; (*verlocken*) to charm, to entice, to (al)lure; *den Appetit* ~~ to whet o.'s appetite; *durch Neckerei* ~~ to provoke; ~**end** *a* charming; fascinating; enticing, enchanting; sweet, *Am fam* cute; *das ist ja* ~~*!* that's just dandy! ~**fähig** *a* irritable; ~**gas** *n mil* irritant gas; ~**gift** *n* irritant poison; ~**kerze** *f mil* irritant smoke candle; ~**leitung** *f* conduction of stimuli; ~**los** *a* charmless; unattractive; ~**losigkeit** *f* unattractiveness; ~**mittel** *n* incentive, stimulus; *med* stimulant; ~**schwelle** *f* threshold of stimulation (*od* sensation); ~**stoff** *m* (*anregend*) stimulating substance; (*irritierend*) irritant (substance); ~**ung** *f* irritation; (*Auf*~~) incitation, incitement; (*Herausforderung*) provocation; (*Verlockung*) enticement; ~**voll** *a* charming, attractive, alluring, glamorous; *ein* ~~*es Mädchen* an attractive girl, *Am* a glamorous girl, a glamo(u)r girl; ~**wirkung** *f* irritating effect.

rekeln, räkeln: *sich* ~ to loll about, to wriggle.

Reklam|ation *f* (*Rückforderung*) claiming back; (*Einwand*) protest; (*Klage*) complaint; ~**ieren** *tr, itr* to reclaim; (*protestieren*) to protest; to object; to complain; (*freistellen vom Militär etc*) to apply for exemption from military service; to exempt from; to request deferment; (*sich beklagen*) to make complaints (about).

Reklame *f* (*Propaganda*) propaganda; (*bezahlte Werbung*) advertising, advert(isement); *Am fam* ad; publicity; puffing; (*nachdrückliche Reklame od Propaganda*) *Am* boost; (*Stimmungsmache*) *Am* boom; (*lärmende, sensationelle* ~) *Am* high-pressure advertising; *Am* blurb(ing), plug(ging); *sl* ballyhoo; (*im Rundfunk*) air plug; commercial; spot; ~ *macht sich bezahlt* it pays to advertise; ~ *machen* to advertise; (*übertrieben anpreisen*) to puff s. th., *Am* to boost; (*intensiv u. ständig*) *Am* to plug; ~**abteilung** *f* advertisement (*Am* advertising) department; ~**artikel** *m* advertising article; ~**beleuchtung** *f* advertisement illumination; ~**broschüre** *f* advertising leaflet; ~**büro** *n* advertising agency; ~**chef**, ~**leiter** *m* advertising manager; ~**diapositiv** *n* (*Kinoreklame*) advertising slide, cinema slide; ~**durchsage** *f radio* credit, *Am* radio plug; ~**fachmann** *m* advertising expert, *Am* adman; (*Verkaufs*~~) sales promotion expert; ~**feldzug** *m* advertising campaign; ~**film** *m* advertising film, publicity film; ~**fläche** *f* advertising space; (*Hauswand etc*) boarding(s *pl*), *Am* billboard; ~**flug** *m* advertising flight; ~~**zeug** *n* advertising airplane; ~**funk** *m* (*Werbefunk*) radio advertising, broadcast advertising; ~**künstler** *m* advertising artist; ~**macher** *m Am* booster; ~**mann** *m* advertising man; ~**material** *n* advertising material, promotion matter; ~**säule** *f* (*Litfaßsäule*) advertisement pillar; ~**seite** *f* (*Zeitung etc*) advertising page; ~**schild** *n* advertisement sign, signboard; (*auf Hausdächern*) sky sign; ~**schönheit** *f* model, *Am* cover girl; pin-up (girl); ~**sendereihe** *f Am radio* commercial series; ~**sendung** *f Am radio, tele* commercial; (*kurzer Text im Unterhaltungsprogramm*) credit; spot; commercial; ~**sprecher** *m Am radio* plugger; ~**tafel** *f* signboard; ~**treibende(r)** *m* advertiser; ~**trick** *m* promotional stunt; ~**zeichner** *m* advertising designer; ~**zeichnung** *f* advertising drawing (*od* design); ~**zettel** *m* handbill, *Am* dodger; *fam* throwaway; flier.

rekognoszier|en *tr mil* to reconnoitre; ~**ung** *f* reconnoitring; reconnaissance, *mil oft* recce.

rekonstruieren *tr* to reconstruct.

Rekonvales|zent *m* convalescent; ~**zenz** *f* convalescence.

Rekord *m* record; *Welt*~ world's record; *amtliche Anerkennung e-s* ~*s* homologation of a record; *e-n* ~ *anerkennen* to recognize (*od* to acknowledge), (*angreifen* to attack, *aufstellen* to set up, to establish, *brechen* to break, *drücken* to lower, *halten* to hold, *innehaben* to hold, *schlagen* to beat, *verbessern* to improve) a record; ~**besuch** *m* record attendance; ~**brecher** *m* record breaker, record smasher; ~**ernte** *f* record crop, bumper crop; ~**flieger** *m* record flier; ~**flug** *m* record breaking flight; ~**halter**, ~**inhaber** *m* record holder; ~**lauf** *m* record run; ~**preis** *m* record price; ~**tiefstand** *m* (*von Preisen*) record low; ~**versuch** *m* attempt to beat a record; ~**zeit** *f* record time.

Rekrut *m* recruit, conscript; *fam* rookie, rooky; ~**enaushebung** *f* recruitment, enlistment, conscription; ~**enjahrgang** *m* annual contingent of recruits; class; ~**ieren** *tr* to recruit; *sich* ~~ to be recruited (*aus* from); ~**ierung** *f* recruiting; ~~**sbehörde** *f* recruiting service, *Am* draft board.

rektifizier|en *tr* to rectify; to adjust; ~**ung** *f* rectification.

Rektor *m* (*Universität*) chancellor, *Am* (University *od* college) president; (*Schule*) headmaster, *Am* principal; ~**at** *n* office of chancellor, *Am* office of (university *od* college) president; headmastership.

Rekurs *m* appeal; recourse; regress.

Relais *n el* relay; ~**schaltung** *f* relay connection; ~**sender** *m radio* relay station; rebroadcast transmitter; ~**steuerung** *f* relay control.

relativ *a* relative; (*sich beziehend auf*) relating (to); ~**ität** *f* relativity; ~**itätstheorie** *f* theory of relativity.

relegieren *tr* (*Schule*) to exclude, to expell, to send down; (*Universität*) to rusticate.

Relief *n* relief; embossment; *Hoch*~ high relief; *Flach*~ low relief; ~**bild** *n* ghost image; ~**druck** *m typ* printing in relievo; ~**karte** *f* embossed map; relief map; ~**schreiber** *m* embosser.

Religion *f* religion; (*Glaube*) faith; (*Bekenntnis*) confession; creed; denomination, *Am* religious preference; (*Schulfach*) scripture; ~**sbekenntnis** *n* confession of faith; profession; ~**sbrauch** *m* rite, ceremony; ~**sfreiheit** *f* religious liberty; freedom of worship; ~**sgemeinschaft** *f* religious community; ~**sgenosse** *m* coreligionist; ~**sgeschichte** *f* history of religion; ~**sgesellschaft** *f* religious association (*od* society); ~**slehre** *f* religious instruction; ~**slos** *a* irreligious; ~**sspaltung** *f* schism; ~**sstreit** *m* religious controversy.

religiös *a* religious; (*fromm*) pious; **Religiosität** *f* religiousness.

Reling *f* (*Schiff*) rail.

Reliquie *f* relic; ~**nschrein** *m* reliquary; shrine.

remilitarisier|en *tr* to remilitarize; ~**ung** *f* remilitarization.

Remise *f* coach-house; shed.

Remitt|enden *f pl* (*Buchhandel*) remainders *pl*, books to be returned; ~**ieren** *tr* to remit; to return; ~**ierung** *f* remittance.

Remont|e *f* remount; ~**ierung** *f* supply of horses for the cavalry; ~**epferd** *n* remount; ~**ereiter** *m* rough-rider.

Rem(o)uladensauce *f* salad-cream.

Rempel|ei *f* jostling; rumpus; ~**n** *itr* to jostle; *sport* to barge; to bump together.

Ren *n* (*Rentier*) reindeer.

Renaissance *f* renaissance.

Rendezvous *n* rendez-vous, tryst; (place appointed for a) meeting, *Am fam* date; *mit jdm ein* ~ *haben* to have an appointment with s. o., *Am fam* to have a date with s. o.; *mit jdm ein* ~ *verabreden* to make an appointment to meet s. o., *Am fam* to make a date; ~**partner** *m Am fam* date, datee, date-up, meetee.

Renegat *m* renegade.

Renette *f* (*Apfelsorte*) rennet.

reniten|t *a* (*widerspenstig, widersetzlich*) refractory, obstinate; ~**z** *f* refractoriness.

Renn|bahn *f* race-course, *Am* race track; (*Aschenbahn*) cinder track; (*Wagen*~~) *mot* track; *Am mot* speedway; (*Pferde*) turf; ~~**gerade** *f* straightaway; ~~**besucher** *m* racegoer; turfgoer; ~**boot** *n* race-boat, racing shell, racer, *Am* speedboat; ~**en** *irr itr* to run; (*wett*~~) to race; to run a race; (*vorwärtsstürzen*) to dash; to rush (along); (*anrennen an*) to bump against; (*zusammen*~~) to collide, to clash; *mit dem Kopf gegen die Wand* ~~ to run o.'s head against the wall; *in sein Verderben* ~~ to rush headlong into destruction; *tr* (*sich fest*~~) to get stuck; (*über*~~) to run over (*od* down), to knock down in running;

den Degen durch den Leib ~~ to run s. o. through; **~en** *n* run(ning), rush; (*Wett~~*) race, course; *flaches* ~~ flat race; *mit Hindernissen* steeple-chase; *totes* ~~ dead heat; (*Einzel~~*) heat; *das* ~~ *machen* to make the race; **~er** *m* runner; race horse; **~fahrer** *m* (*Fahrrad*) racing cyclist; *mot* racing motorist; race driver, racer; **~~lager** *n*, **~~boxe** *f* pit; **~flugzeug** *n* racing plane, racer; **~jacht** *f* racing yacht; **~mannschaft** *f* race-crew; **~maschine** *f* *mot* racing machine; **~pferd** *n* race horse, racer; flyer; **~platz** *m* track; (*Pferde~~*) race-course; **~reiter** *m* jockey, race rider; **~saison** *f* racing season; **~schuhe** *f* spike *pl*; **~sport** *m* (*Pferde*) turf; **~stall** *m* (racing) stable; **~strecke** *f* course, race track; distance to be run; **~wagen** *m* racing car, racer; **~ziel** *n* winning post.

Renomm|ee *n* (*Ruf*) reputation; (*Ansehen*) fame, renown; (*Name*) name; **~ieren** *itr* to boast, to swagger, to brag; **~iert** *a* (*berühmt*) highly reputed; (*bekannt wegen*) well-known (for); **~ist** *m* bully; bragger, boaster; big talker.

renovier|en *tr* to renovate; to renew; (*reparieren*) to repair, to do up; (*Zimmer etc*) to redecorate; **~ung** *f* renovation; redecoration.

rent|abel *a* profitable, lucrative; productive; paying; **~abilität** *f* profitableness, lucrativeness; profits *pl*; earning capacity; productiveness; **~~sgrenze** *f* margin of profitableness, break-even point; **~~srechnung** *f* calculation of profit; **~amt** *n* revenue office; **~e** *f* (*Alters~~*) (old age) pension; (*Pacht*) rent; (*jährliche*) annuity; (*Einkünfte*) (unearned) income; revenue; (*Ertrag*) profit; (*Unterstützung*) benefit; **~enbank** *f* annuity office; **~enbrief** *m* annuity bond; **~enempfänger** *m* annuitant; **~enschuld** *f* mortgage debt; **~ier, ~ner** *m* (old age) pensioner; rentier; annuitant; man of private means, person of independent means; **~ieren**: *sich* ~~ to pay; to yield profit; to be profitable; to profit; to be worth while; *sich gerade* ~~ to break even.

reorganisier|en *tr* to reorganize; **~ung** *f* reorganization.

*

Reparation *f* reparation; *~en leisten* to pay reparations; **~sabgabe** *f* reparation levy; **~sforderung** *f* reparation claims *pl*; **~skommission** *f* reparation commission; **~skonto** *n* reparation account; **~sleistung** *f* reparation delivery; **~spflichtig** *a* liable to pay reparations; **~szahlung** *f* reparation payment.

Reparatur *f* repair; recondition; (*Ausbessern*) mending; *größere* ~ major repair; *kleine* ~ minor repair; *in* ~ under repair; *in* ~ *geben* to get repaired; **~anlagen** *f pl* repair facilities *pl*; **~bedürftig** *a* in need (*od* in want) of repair; out of repair; **~betrieb** *m* repair shop; **~dienst** *m* repair service; **~fähig** *a* mendable; repairable; **~grube** *f* repair pit, inspection pit; **~kasten** *m* repair box, repair kit; **~kosten** *pl* (cost of) repairs *pl*; **~wagen** *m mot* trouble car, *Am* wrecking car; **~werkstatt** *f* repair shop; maintenance depot; *mot* motor-car repair shop, *Am* garage, service station.

reparieren *tr* to repair; (*ausbessern*) to mend.

repatriier|en *tr* to repatriate; **~ung** *f* repatriation.

Repertoire *n theat* stock (of plays), repertory; repertoire; *ein reiches* ~ *haben* to have a large selection of plays; **~stück** *n* stock-play.

repetier|en *tr* to repeat; **~gewehr** *n* magazine rifle; **~uhr** *f* repeater.

Replik *f* (*Entgegnung*) reply, retort; (*Kopie e-s Kunstwerkes*) replica.

Report *m com* (*Börse*) contango; **~age** *f radio* (running) commentary, news-reporting work; (*Augenzeugenbericht*) eyewitness account; on-the-spot report; **~~film** *m* newsreel, topical film; **~er** *m* (*Presse*) reporter, correspondent, *Am auch* leg man.

Repräsent|ant *m* representative; **~antenhaus** *n Am* House of Representatives; **~ation** *f* representation; **~ativ** *a* representative; **~ieren** *tr* to represent; (*etw vorstellen*) to cut a fine figure.

Repressalien *f pl* reprisals *pl*; (*Vergeltung*) retaliation; ~ *anwenden gegen* to make reprisals on.

Reprodu|ktion *f* reproduction; rendering; **~~skraft** *f* reproductive power; **~zieren** *tr* to render; to reproduce.

Reptil *n* reptile.

Republik *f* republic; **~aner** *m* republican; **~anisch** *a* republican.

requi|rieren *tr mil* to requisition, to commandeer; **~siten** *n pl* requisites *pl*; *theat* properties *pl*; props *pl*; **~sition** *f mil* requisition.

Reseda *f bot* mignonette.

Reserv|e *f* reserve; *in* ~~ in store; *stille ~~n com* undisclosed reserves *pl*; *~~n ansammeln* to accumulate reserves; *die ~~n einberufen mil* to call up the reserves; *auf die ~~n zurückgreifen* to fall back on o.'s reserves; **~eapparat** *m* stand-by equipment; **~ebehälter** *m* reserve tank; **~efonds** *m* reserve fund; **~elager** *m* reserve stock; **~enummer** *f* unallotted number; **~eoffizier** *m* reserve officer, officer in the reserve; **~erad** *n mot* spare wheel; **~eteile** *n pl* spare parts *pl*, spares *pl*; **~etruppen** *pl* reserves *pl*, reserve forces *pl*; **~ieren** *tr* to reserve; (*zurückstellen*) to set aside; (*Zimmer etc belegen*) to book in advance, *Am* to make reservations; **~iert** *a* reserved; (*Börse*) inactive; **~ierung** *f* reservation; **~ist** *m* reservist; **~oir** *n* tank, pool, reservoir.

Resid|enz *f* (*Wohnort*) residence; (*Hauptstadt*) capital; (*Fürstensitz*) seat (of the court); **~ieren** *itr* to reside.

Resign|ation *f* resignation; **~ieren** *itr* to resign.

resolut *a* (*entschlossen*) resolute; determined.

Resonanz *f* echo, resonance; **~boden** *m* sounding-board.

Respekt *m* respect, regard; **~abel, ~ierlich** *a* respectable; **~ieren** *tr* to respect, to hono(u)r; **~ive** *adv* respectively; **~los** *a* without respect; irreverent; **~sperson** *f* person held in respect; (*angesehene*) nobility; **~voll** *a* respectful; **~widrig** *a* disrespectful.

Ressort *n* department; province, sphere; *das gehört nicht zu meinem* ~ that's out of my line.

Rest *m* rest, (*auch math*) remainder; (*Stoff~*) remnant; (*Überrest*) remains *pl*, relic; (*Rückstand*) residue, *chem* residuum; (*Überschuß*) balance, surplus; (*Zahlungs~*) arrears *pl*; *jdm den* ~ *geben* to give s. o. the finishing stroke; *das gab ihr den* ~ that finished her; **~auflage** *f* remainders *pl* (of an edition); **~bestand** *m* remainder; *chem* residue; **~betrag** *m* remainder, balance; **~e(r)** *pl* (*Stoffe*) remnants *pl*, adds and ends *pl*; **~etag** *m* remnant day; **~kaufgeld** *n* balance of purchase price; **~kommando** *n mil* reserve detachment; **~lager** *n* stock of remnants; **~lich** *a* remaining, left over; *chem* residual; **~los** *a* complete, without a rest; *adv* entirely, completely, thoroughly; **~posten** *m* remaining stock; **~schulden** *f pl* remaining debts *pl*; ~~ *bezahlen Am* to ante up; **~summe** *f* remainder, remaining amount; **~zahlung** *f* payment of balance; final payment.

Restant *m* person in arrears; *~en pl* arrears *pl*; odd lots *pl*.

Restaur|ant *n* (*Gasthaus*) restaurant; grill room; dining-rooms *pl*; tavern; **~ateur** *m* (*Wiederhersteller*) restorer; (*Gastwirt*) restaurant keeper; **~ation** *f* (*Wiederherstellung*) restoration; (*Gasthaus*) restaurant; (*Bahnhofs~~*) refreshment-room; **~ieren** *tr* (*wiederherstellen*) to restore; to repair; *sich* ~~ to take refreshments.

Result|at *n* (*Ergebnis*) result; (*Wirkung*) effect; outcome; upshot; *sport* score; **~atlos** *a* without result; fruitless; useless; **~ieren** *itr* to result (*aus* from).

Retorte *f* retort.

rett|en *tr* to save; to rescue; (*befreien*) to deliver, to release; *seine Ehre* ~ to vindicate o.'s hono(u)r; *~e sich wer kann!* every man for himself! **~er** *m* deliverer, saver; (*Heiland*) Saviour, Redeemer.

Rettich *m* radish.

Rettung *f* (*aus Gefahr, von etw Bösem etc*) rescue; (*Einbringung, Bergung*) salvage; (*Befreiung*) deliverance, release; (*Entkommen*) escape; (*Hilfe*) help; (*Strandgut*) *Am* wrecking; (*Seelenheil*) redemption; (*Erlösung*) salvation; **~sanker** *m* sheet-anchor; **~sanstalt** *f* station of the Humane Society; **~sarbeit** *f* rescue operation; **~sboje** *f* life-buoy; rescue-buoy; **~sboot** *n* life-boat; *aero* (*abwerfbar für Flugzeug*) parachute boat; **~sdienst** *m* life-guard service; **~sfahrzeug** *n* life-saving boat, *Am* lifeboat; **~sfloß** *n* raft; **~sgürtel** *m* life-belt; **~skolonne** *f* rescue squad; **~sleine** *f* life-line; **~sleiter** *f* fire-escape; **~slos** *a* irrecoverable, irretrievable; remediless, irremediable, past help; **~sluke** *f* escape hatch; **~smannschaft** *f* rescue party, rescue team; **~smedaille** *f* life-saving medal; **~smittel** *n* remedy; **~sring** *m* life-belt, life-preserver; **~sstation** *f* first-aid post; **~struppe** *f* rescue brigade (*od* squad); salvage troop; **~sversuch** *m* attempt at rescue; **~swerk** *n* rescue work.

retuschieren *tr* to retouch; to touch up.

Reu|e *f* (*Bedauern*) regret; (*Schuldgefühl*) penitence, repentance; (*Selbstvorwürfe*) compunction, (*tiefes Schuldgefühl*) contrition, (*quälendes Schuldgefühl*) remorse; **~en** *imp* to repent, to be sorry for; *es ~t mich* I repent of it, I am sorry for it; **~evoll, ~ig** *a* repentant; **~geld** *n* smart money, forfeit, forfeiture; **~mütig** *a* repentant, penitant; contrite, remorseful.

Reuse *f* eel-basket, eel-pot; wicker-trap; **~nantenne** *f* cage antenna.

reuten *tr* (*ausroden, fig ausrotten*) to root out.

Revanch|e *f* revenge; satisfaction; **~epartie** *f*, **~espiel** *n* return-match; **~ieren**: *sich* ~~ *für* to take o.'s revenge; to return a favo(u)r.

Reverenz *f* reverence, bow; curt(e)sy.

Revers *m* bond; (*Münzen*) reverse; (*Erklärung*) declaration; (*Rockaufschlag*) lapel.

revidieren *tr* to revise, to examine; to check; *com* to audit.

Revier *n* district, quarter, environs

pl; preserve, hunting-ground; (*Polizei*) beat; (*Postbote*) round, walk; *mil* sick quarters; *mar* sick bay; **~dienst** *m* hospital orderly duty; light (military) duty; **~förster** *m* quarter-ranger; **~kranke** *m pl* men sick in quarters; **~stunde** *f mil* sick parade (*Am* call).

Revision *f* revision, revisal; *com* auditing; *jur* (*Rechtsmittel*) appeal; (*Wiederaufnahme*) rehearing, new trial; *~ einlegen* to lodge an appeal, to give notice of an appeal; *e-r ~ stattgeben* to allow an appeal; *e-e ~ verwerfen* to dismiss an appeal; **~sbogen** *m typ* revise.

Revisor *m typ* reviser; *com* examiner of accounts, auditor.

Revolt|e *f* revolt, rising, insurrection; **~ieren** *itr* to revolt, to rise.

Revol|ution *f* revolution; **~~är** *a, m* revolutionary; **~~ieren** *tr* to revolutionize; **~ver** *m* revolver, *Am* gun; **~~drehbank** *f* capstan lathe; **~~kopf** *m* turret-head; *phot* lens turret; **~~schießerei** *f Am* gunfight; **~~trommel** *f* cartridge cylinder.

revozieren *itr, tr* to recall, to revoke.

Revue *f theat* revue; musical show; *mil* (*Truppen*) review; (*Zeitschrift*) periodical, review; *~ passieren lassen* to pass in review; **~girl** *n*, **~tänzerin** *f* chorus-girl, show girl.

Reyon *m* filament rayon.

Rezens|ent *m* critic, reviewer; **~ieren** *tr* to review, to criticize; **~ion** *f* criticism; critique, review; **~ionsexemplar** *n* reviewer's copy, press copy.

Rezept *n med* prescription, recipe; (*Koch~*) receipt, recipe; **~raum** *m* formula room.

rezi|prok *a* reciprocal; **~tativ** *n* recitative; **~tator** *m* reciter; **~tieren** *tr, itr* to recite.

Rhabarber *m* rhubarb.

Rhapsodie *f* rhapsody.

Rhein *m* Rhine; **~fall** *m* falls *pl* of the Rhine; **~wein** *m* hock, *Am* Rhine wine.

Rhetor|ik *f* rhetoric; **~isch** *a* rhetorical.

rheumat|isch *a* rheumatic; **~ismus** *m* rheumatism.

Rhinozeros *n* rhinoceros.

Rhombus *m* rhomb(us).

rhythm|isch *a* rhythmical; **~us** *m* rhythm.

Richt|antenne *f radio* directional aerial, *Am* directional antenna; (*Netz*) directional aerial array; **~aufsatz** *m mil* gun sight; **~balken** *m* traverse beam; **~baum** *m* pulley-beam; **~bake** *f* landmark; **~beil** *n* executioner's axe; **~blei** *n* plumb-line, plummet; **~block** *m* executioner's block; **~en** *tr* (*lenken*) to direct; to turn; to guide; (*zielen*) to point; to aim, to level (*auf* at); (*in Ordnung bringen*) to arrange; to put in order, to adjust, to set straight, *Am* to fix; (*reparieren*) to repair; (*zubereiten, vorbereiten*) to prepare; (*Bleche*) to straighten; (*herrichten*) to dress; (*errichten*) to erect; (*hoch~~*) to raise; (*Frage an jdn ~~*) to address; *mil* (*ausrichten*) to dress (in a line); (*hinrichten auf dem Richtplatz*) to execute; (*Richter*) to judge, to pass sentence (on); *sich ~~* (*mil*) to align o. s.; *sich auf etw ~~* to keep o. s. ready for s. th.; *sich ~~ nach* to conform to; to comply with; to depend on; to go by; to act in harmony with, to act according to; to be guided by; *gram* to agree with; *der Preis richtet sich nach* the price is determined by; *die Segel nach dem Wind ~~* to trim the sails to the wind; *das richtet sich ganz nach den Umständen* that will depend entirely on the circumstances; *das Zeitwort richtet sich nach dem Hauptwort* the verb agrees with the noun; *ich richte mich ganz nach Ihnen* I'll leave it entirely up to you; *in die Höhe ~~* to raise; *zugrunde ~~* to ruin; **~fernrohr** *n mil* telescope sight; dial sight; **~fest** *n* builder's treat; **~funkbake** *f*, **~funkfeuer** *n aero radio* directional radio beacon, radio beam; **~gerät** *n mil* laying gear; **~kanonier** *m mil* (gun-) layer; **~kreis** *m mil* director, aiming circle; **~~zahl** *f* director reading; **~linien** *f pl* (general) directions *pl*, instructions *pl*; guiding-principle; rule; policy; *math* axis; guide-line; **~lot** *n* plumb-line; **~maß** *n* standard, gauge, *Am* gage; **~platz** *m*, **~stätte** *f* place of execution; **~preis** *m* standard price; **~punkt** *m* aiming point; base; **~~verfahren** *n mil* indirect laying; **~satz** *m* guiding rate; **~scheit** *n* level, rule(r); straight-edge; **~schnur** *f tech* plumb-line, chalk line; *fig* guiding-principle, rule (of conduct), precept; model; **~schütze** *f* gunner, layer; **~schwert** *n* executioner's sword; **~sendung** *f radio* beam transmission; **~strahler** *m radio* beam wireless; (*Antenne*) directional aerial, beam aerial, *Am* directional antenna; *mit ~~ senden* to beam; *Sendung mit ~~* beam transmission; *ein Programm mit ~~ nach Deutschland* a programme beamed at Germany; **~~system** *n radio* beam system; **~ung** *f* direction; (*Ansicht, Meinung, Tendenz*) trend, tendency; (*Wolken, Gedanken*) drift; *mil* alignment; (*Weg, Kurs*) course, line, route; (*auf e-n bestimmten Punkt zu*) bearing, orientation; setting; *in gerader ~~* straight on, straight ahead; *nach allen ~~en* in all directions; *in der ~~ des Uhrzeigers* clockwise; *aus der ~~* out of line, skew; *in e-r ~~* one-way; *die ~~ verlieren* to lose o.'s bearing (*od* way); **~~sänderung** *f* change of direction; **~~sanzeiger** *m mot* direction (*od* turn) indicator, trafficator; **~~sempfang** *m radio* directional receiving; **~~skreisel** *m* directional gyro; **~~slos** *a* directionless; **~~spfeil** *m* directional marker; **~~spunkt** *m* bearing point; **~~sumkehr** *f* reversal; **~~sweiser** *m* signpost, pointer; *radio* radio beacon; *aero* (*mit Nordmarkierung*) directional marker; **~waage** *f* level; **~wert** *m* approximate value; standard value; determining factor: **~zahl** *f* coefficient.

Richter *m* judge; (*Friedens~*) justice of peace (*Abk* J.P.); (*Polizei~*) magistrate; (*Schieds~*) arbiter; *sport* umpire, referee; *~ sein* to sit on the bench, to be judge; *vor den ~ bringen* to bring to justice; **~amt** *n* judicature; judicial function; office of a judge; **~kollegium** *n* bench; **~lich** *a* judicial; *~~e Funktion* judicial function; *~~e Gewalt ausüben* to exercise judicial functions; to be armed with judicial powers; *~~e Unabhängigkeit* judicial independence; **~spruch** *m* (*Zivilprozeß*) judg(e)ment, decision; (*Strafprozeß*) sentence; (*Schiedsgericht*) award; (*Geschworenengericht*) verdict; **~stand** *m* judges *pl*; bench; judicature, *Am* judiciary; **~stuhl** *m* seat of a judge; *fig* tribunal; bar.

richtig *a* right; correct, proper; appropriate; (*genau*) exact, accurate; (*angemessen*) adequate; (*geeignet*) suitable, fit; (*gerecht*) just, fair; (*gehörig*) due; (*Urteil*) sound; (*regelrecht*) regular; (*echt*) real, genuine; true, true-born; *~! interj* just so! sure enough! quite right! behold! all right! *~, da ist er!* sure enough, there he is! *sein ~er Name* his real name; *sitzt mein Hut ~?* is my hat on straight? *es geht nicht ~ damit zu* there is s. th. wrong about it; *die Uhr geht nicht ~* the watch does not go right; *~ machen* to adjust, to settle; *das ist nicht ~* that's not as it should be; *das ~e* the real thing, the genuine article, *Am* the goods, *Am sl* the real McCoy; **~gehend** *a* (*Uhr*) keeping good time; (*regulär*) real, regular; **~keit** *f* rightness, correctness; justness; accuracy; fairness; exactness; *es hat seine ~~* that is all right, it is quite correct; it is a fact; **~stellen** *tr* (*berichtigen*) to put right, to set right; to rectify, to correct; **~stellung** *f* rectification.

Ricke *f* doe.

rie|chen *irr tr, itr* to smell; (*wittern*) to scent; (*stinken*) to stink; (*ausfindig machen*) to detect; (*schnuppern, Gefahr ~*) to sniff (danger); *nach etw ~* to smell of; *an etw ~* to smell at; *gut ~* to smell good, to have a pleasant smell, *schlecht ~* to smell bad, to have an unpleasant smell; *angebrannt* (*od brenzlich*) *~* to smell burnt; *stark ~* to smell high (*od* strong); *aus dem Munde ~* to have an unpleasant breath; *ich kann ihn nicht ~* I cannot bear the sight of him, I can't stand him; *den Braten ~, Lunte ~* to smell a rat; *das konnte ich doch nicht ~?* how could I know? **~cher** *m* nose; *e-n guten ~~ haben* to have a fine nose; **~fläschchen** *n* smelling-bottle; **~nerv** *m* olfactory nerve; **~organ** *n* olfactory organ; **~probe** *f* smelling test; **~salz** *n* smelling salt; **~stoff** *m* scent, perfume; odoriferous substance; **~werkzeuge** *n pl* olfactory organs *pl*.

Ried *n* (*Schilf, Rohr*) reed; (*Sumpfland*) marsh; **~gras** *n* reed-grass, sedge.

Riefe *f* flute; groove; channel; chamfer; **~ln, ~n** *tr* to chamfer, to channel, to groove; to flute.

Riege *f* section.

Riegel *m* rail; (*Schloß~*) bolt; (*Fenster~*) bar; (*Seife*) bar; (*Kleider~*) peg; *arch* girder, lintel, tie-beam; *mil* flank-group (*od* bolt) position; *e-n ~ vorschieben* (*jdm*) to put a spoke in s. o.'s wheel; *e-r Sache e-n ~ vorschieben* to check (*od* to prevent) s. th., to put a stop to s. th.; **~bau** *m* half-timber construction; **~n** *tr* to bolt up, to bar; **~stellung** *f mil* bolt position, switch line.

Riemen *m* (*Leder~*) strap; (*dünner*) thong; (*Treib~*) belt; (*Streich~*) razor strap, strop; (*Schuh~*) bootlace; (*Schulter~*) shoulder strap; (*Gürtel~*) brace; belt; (*Gewehr~*) sling; (*Brett*) fillet; (*Ruder*) oar; *die ~ beinehmen* to ship oars; *mit ~ peitschen* to lash; **~antrieb** *m* belt drive; **~ausrücker** *m* belt shifter; **~durchhang** *m* sag of a belt; **~leder** *n* belting; **~lochzange** *f* belt punch; **~parkett** *n* herring-bone parquetry; **~scheibe** *f* pulley; **~zeug** *n* harness, (leather) straps *pl*.

Ries *n* (*Papier*) ream (of paper).

Ries|e *m* giant; *nach Adam ~~* (*fig*) according to Gunter; **~enerfolg** *m* smash hit; *e-n ~~ haben* to score a hit; **~engroß, ~enhaft, ~ig** *a* gigantic; huge, vast, immense; colossal; *fam* whacking, whopping; *adv* (*sehr*) terribly; **~enbomber** *m aero* superbomber; **~enluftreifen** *m mot* giant air tyre; **~enrad** *n Am* Ferris wheel; **~enschlange** *f* boa constrictor; **~enschritte** *m pl* gigantic strides *pl*; *~~ machen* to go at a tremendous pace; **~enschwindel** *m fam* whopper; **~enschwung** *m sport* gigantic swing; **~enslalom** *m* giant slalom; **~enstärke** *f* gigantic power; **~entanne** *f* (*kalifornische*) mammoth--tree, sequoia; **~in** *f* giantess.

Riesel|felder *n pl* irrigated fields *pl*, sewage farm, sewage(-fields *pl*); **~n** *itr* to ripple, to gush; to trickle; to percolate; to run; to purl; *film* to swarm; *imp* to drizzle; *es rieselt* it drizzles; **~regen** *m* drizzling rain, drizzle; **~turm** *m* trickling tower; **~wasser** *n* irrigation water; trickling water.

Riff *n* reef; (*Sandbank*) sand-bank, shelf; (*Korallen~*) coral reef.

Riffel *f* flax-comb; **~blech** *n* checker(ed) plate; **~glas** *n* frosted (*od* ribbed) glass; **~n** *tr* to flute, to chamfer, to channel; (*Flachs*) to ripple; **~ung** *f* corrugation, groove, knurl.

rigolen *tr* to turn up the ground, to trench-plough.

rigoros *a* rigorous; (*streng*) strict; stern; rigid; stringent.

Rille *f tech* (*Schallplatte etc*) groove; *arch* flute, chamfer; (*Ackerbau*) small furrow; (*Saat~*) drill; **~n** *tr tech* to groove; *arch* to chamfer; (*Ackerbau*) to drill; **~npflug** *m* drill plough, *Am* drill plow; **~nsaat** *f* sowing in rills.

Rimesse *f com* remittance.

Rind *n* neat; (*Ochse*) ox; bullock; (*Kuh*) cow; (*Färse*) heifer; *allg* head of cattle; **~er** *pl* cattle; beeves *pl*; **~erbouillon** *f* beef broth; **~erbraten** *m* roast beef, roast of beef; **~erfett** *n* beef suet; **~erfillet** *n* fillet of beef; **~erherde** *f* herd of cattle; **~erhirt** *m* neat--herd, *Am* cow-boy, *Am* cow-puncher, *Am* buckaroo; **~erkraftfleisch** *n* corned beef; **~erpest** *f* rinderpest, cattle-plague; **~ertalg** *m* beef tallow; **~erzucht** *f* cattle breeding; **~erzunge** *f* beef tongue; **~fleisch** *n* beef; **~~brühe** *f* beef broth, beef-tea; **~skeule** *f* round of beef; **~sleder** *n* neat's leather, cow--hide; **~~n** *a* cow-hide; **~slendenstück** *n* rump-steak, *Am* tenderloin; **~srückenstück** *n* sirloin of beef; **~sschnitte** *f* beef-steak; **~szunge** *f* ox-tongue; **~vieh** *n* (horned) cattle; *fig* (*als Schimpfwort*) duffer, block-head.

Rinde *f* (*Käse, Apfel*) rind; (*Baum*) bark; (*Brot*) crust; *anat* (*Gehirn*) cortex.

Ring *m* (*Reif, Finger~ etc*) ring; (*Kettenglied*) link; (*Kreis*) circle, circlet; (*um Gestirne*) halo; (*Box~*) ring; (*Öhr, Öse*) loop, hoop; (*Draht~*) coil; *arch* collar; (*Dichtungs~*) washer; *fig* (*Gesellschaft*) clique, society; gang; *com* trust, ring; pool, *Am* combine; (*Aufkäufer~*) corner; *e-n ~ bilden com* to pool; (*beim Einkauf*) to corner the market; *in den ~ steigen* (*Boxen*) to climb into the ring; *die ~e wechseln* to exchange rings; *e-n ~ tragen* to wear a ring; **~bahn** *f* circular railway; **~bildung** *f chem* ring formation; **~fallschirm** *m aero* annular parachute; **~finger** *m* ring--finger; **~förmig** *a* ring-shaped; annular; cyclic; *~~e Sonnenfinsternis* annular eclipse; **~haube** *f aero mot* cowl-ingring; **~kästchen** *n* ring-case; **~mauer** *f hist* city wall; circular wall; **~richter** *m* umpire, referee; **~sendung** *f radio* hook-up; **~skala** *f* dial scale; **~straße** *f* boulevard; **~tausch** *m* barter ring; **~tennis** *n* deck-tennis; **~verbindung** *f chem* ring compound; **~wall** *m* rampart.

Ringel *m*, **~chen** *n* small ring, ringlet, circlet; (*Locke*) curl; **~blume** *f* marigold; **~haar** *n* curled hair; **~locke** *f* ringlet; **~n** *tr* to ring; *r* to curl; to coil; **~natter** *f* ring-snake; **~reigen, ~reihen** *m* round dance; **~pietz** *m aero sl* ground loop; **~taube** *f* ring-dove.

ring|en *irr itr* to wrestle (*mit* with); (*kämpfen*) to struggle (against, for, with), to fight for; (*streben nach, sich mühen um*) to strive (after *od* for), to make efforts (to get s. th.); *tr* (*winden*) to ring; (*herauswinden*) to wrest, to wrench (s. th. from s. o.); *die Hände ~* to wring o.'s hands; *mit dem Tode ~~* to be in the last agonies; *nach Atem ~~* to gasp for breath; **~er** *m* wrestler; **~kampf** *m* wrestling match; **~kämpfer** *m* wrestler.

rings *adv* (a)round; **~herum, ~umher** *adv* around, all round, all around; round about.

Rinn|e *f* groove; (*Strombett*) channel; (*Fahr~*) canal; (*Erdfurche*) furrow; (*Leitung*) duct, conduit; (*Gosse*) gutter; (*Gleitbahn*) chute; **~en** *irr itr* to run, to flow; (*von Fässern*) to leak; (*tröpfeln*) to trickle, to drip; **~sal** *n* channel, watercourse; streamlet; bed (of a river); (*kleiner Bach*) rill, *Am* run; **~stein** *m* (*in Küche*) sink; (*Dach~~*) gutter; (*Straße*) curbstone; (*unterirdisch*) culvert, drain-pipe.

Ripp|chen *n* cutlet; **~e** *f* (*Mensch, Schiff, aero*) rib; (*Schokolade*) bar; *arch* groin; (*Flosse*) fin; (*Flügel*) *tech* vane; (*Furche*) corrugation; (*Berg*) buttress; (*Heizrohr*) ribbed heating pipe; **~en** *tr* to rib; *arch* to groin; **~enatmung** *f* costal breathing; **~enbogen** *m anat* costal arch; **~enfell** *n* (costal) pleura; **~~entzündung** *f* pleurisy; pleuritis; **~enrohrkühler** *m* flanged--tube radiator; **~enschmerz** *m* costal pain; **~enstoß** *m* nudge (*od* thrust) in the ribs; *jdm e-n ~~ versetzen* to nudge s. o.; **~enstück** *n* rib-piece; **~enspeer** *m* (smoked) ribs of pork.

Rips *m* (*Stoff*) rep.

Risiko *n* risk; *ein ~ übernehmen* to incur a risk.

risk|ant *a* risky, perilous; **~ieren** *tr* to risk (o.'s life); to run the risk of.

Rispe *f bot* panicle.

Riß *m* (*Kleider, Stoff*) tear, rent; (*Sprung*) crack, flaw, chink; (*Spalt*) cleft, crevice, split; (*Haut*) chaps *pl*; (*Spaltung*) fissure; *geol* crevasse; (*Leck*) leakage; (*Loch*) hole; (*Lücke*) gap; (*Bruch*) fracture, breakage; (*Kratzer*) scratch; (*Wunde*) laceration; (*Plan, Zeichnung*) design, plan, sketch, drawing, draft; *Grund~* ground plan; *Auf~* front elevation; *Seiten~* side elevation; (*Uneinigkeit*) breach; *eccl* schism; **~wunde** *f* lacerated wound.

rissig *a* full of rents; full of crevices; (*gespalten*) split; fissured; (*fehlerhaft*) faulty; (*Haut*) cracked; (*Boden*) chappy, chinky; flawed; *~ werden* to get brittle; to crack.

Rist *m* (*des Fußes*) instep; (*Hand*) wrist; back of the hand; (*Pferd*) withers *pl* (of a horse).

Ritt *m* ride (on horseback); (*Gallop*) short gallop; sprint; *e-n ~ machen* to take a ride, to go on horseback; **~lings** *adv* astride, astraddle (*auf* of); **~meister** *m* captain (of cavalry).

Ritter *m* knight; (*Kavalier*) cavalier; (*Kämpfer*) champion; *fahrender ~* knight-errand; *~ des Hosenbandordens* Knight of the Garter (*Abk* K. G.); *zum ~ schlagen* to knight, to dub s. o. a knight; *arme ~* (*Speise*) fritters *pl*; **~burg** *f* knight's castle; **~gut** *n* manor; **~~sbesitzer** *m* lord (owner) of a manor; **~kreuz** *n mil* (*Deutschland*) Knight's Cross (of the Iron Cross); **~~träger** *m* bearer of the Knight's Insignia of the Iron Cross; **~lich** *a* knightly; *fig* chivalrous; **~~keit** *f* chivalry, gallantry; **~orden** *m* order of knighthood; **~roman** *m* romance of chivalry; **~schaft** *f* knighthood; **~schlag** *m* knighting, accolade; dubbing; *den ~~ erhalten* to be dubbed a knight; **~sitz** *m* knightly residence; **~sporn** *m bot* larkspur; delphinium; **~stand** *m* knighthood; **~tum** *n* chivalry; **~zeit** *f* age of chivalry.

Rit|ual *n*, **~uell** *a* ritual; **~us** *m* rite.

Ritz *m*, **~e** *f* chink, cleft; (*Spalt*) fissure; (*Spalte*) cranny; crevice; gap; rift; (*Sprung*) crack; (*Schlitz*) slit; (*Schürfung*) abrasion; (*Schramme*) scratch; **~en** *tr* (*sich*) to graze (o. s.), to scratch (o. s.); *tech* (*Glas ~~*) to cut; (*schneiden*) to carve; **~ig** *a* crannied; scratched; **~rot** *a* high (*od* fiery) red, scarlet; **~wunde** *f* scratch wound.

Ritzel *n tech* pinion; driver; **~welle** *f* pinion shaft.

Rival|e *m* rival; **~isieren** *itr* to rival; to compete, to be in competition with; (*wetteifern*) to emulate; **~ität** *f* rivalry; (*Wettbewerb*) competition; (*Wetteifer*) emulation.

Rizinusöl *n* castor oil.

*

Robbe *f* sea-calf, seal; **~n** *itr mil* (*robbenartig kriechen*) to creep, to crawl, to glide along; **~nfang** *m* seal hunting; sealing; **~nfänger** *m* sealer, seal hunter; **~ntran** *m* seal oil.

Robber *m* (*Whist*) rubber.

Robe *f* robe, gown.

Robot *m* robot; **~bombe** *f* robot bomb; flying bomb, buzz bomb; V-1; rocket bomb, *Am* robomb; **~~flugzeug** *n* robot bomb plane; **~en** *itr hist* to do compulsory service (*od* statute labo(u)r); **~er** *m* robot; mechanical man, (speaking) automaton; **~gleitbombe** *f* (television controlled) robot glider--bomb, *Am* glomb; **~pilot** *m*, **~steuerung** *f aero* automatic pilot; robot.

robust *a* robust; stout, strong; hard, sturdy; *hum* robustious; (*Stil, Humor, Geist*) vigorous, sane, not inclined to subtlety; **~heit** *f* robustness; brutality.

röcheln *itr* to rattle (in o.'s throat).

Roche(n) *m* ray.

rochieren *itr* (*Schach*) to castle o.'s king.

Rock *m* (*Jacke*) coat, jacket; (*Frauen~*) skirt; (*Amts~*) robe, gown; *Schlaf~* dressing-gown; **~aufschlag** *m* facing; **~falte** *f* pleat of a dress; **~futter** *n* lining of a coat; **~schoß** *m* coat-tail; **~zipfel** *m* lappet; **Röckchen** *n* little coat; (*für Kinder*) child's frock; (*Schottenröckchen*) kilt; (*e-r Ballett-tänzerin*) tutu.

Rocken *m* distaff.

Rodel *m* toboggan; (*um liegend zu fahren*) skeleton; (*mit Steuerung*) bobsleigh; luge; **~bahn** *f* toboggan--run (*od* -slide), tobogganing course; **~fahrt, ~partie** *f* toboggan-ride; **~n** *itr* to toboggan; to sledge, to sled; to coast; to luge; **~n** *n* tobogganing, sledding; **~schlitten** *m* toboggan.

rod|en *tr, itr* to root out, to grub up; to stub up; (*Wald*) to clear; (*urbar machen*) to make arable; **~ung** *f* cleared woodland.

Rogen *m* (hard) roe, spawn; **~er** *m* spawner.

Roggen *m* rye; **~brot** *n* rye-bread; **~feld** *n* rye field; **~mehl** *n* rye flour; **~saatgut** *n* rye seed; **~stärke** *f* rye starch; **~stengelbrand** *m* stripe smut of rye; **~stroh** *n* rye straw; **~vollkornschrot** *n* coarse rye flour.

roh *a* (*unverarbeitet, unbearbeitet, unfertig*) raw; crude; unwrought; in native state; (*Zucker, Öl, Metalle*) crude; (*unfertiges Buch*) in sheets; *fig* (*Personen, Sitten etc*) rough, rude; gross; (*derb*) coarse; (*barsch*) gruff; (*grob*) uncouth; (*wild*) savage, ferocious; (*gewöhnlich*) vulgar; (*gemein*) obscene; (*ungebildet*) uncivilized; (*brutal*) brutal; *jdn wie ein ~es Ei behandeln fig* to handle s. o. with kid gloves; *~er Betrag* gross amount; *~es Fleisch* raw flesh (*od* meat); *~e Gewalt* brute force; *~er Mensch* brute; *~er Stein* unhewn stone; *in ~en Zügen darlegen* to outline roughly; **~bau** *m* rough brickwork, *im ~~ fertig* finished in the rough; **~baumwolle** *f* raw cotton; cotton wool; **~benzol** *n* crude benzene; (*od* benzol); **~bilanz** *f* trial balance; **~blende** *f* raw blende, crude glance; **~diamant** *m* rough diamond; **~einkünfte** *pl* gross revenue; **~einnahme** *f* gross receipts *pl*; **~eisen** *n* pig-iron; **~eit** *f* rawness, raw state; crudity, crudeness; *fig* (*Sitten etc*) rudeness, roughness; brutality; **~entwurf** *m* rough drawing; **~ertrag** *m* gross receipts *pl* (*od* proceeds *pl*); gross yield; total revenue; **~erz** *n* raw ore; **~erzeugnis** *n* raw product; **~faser** *f* crude fiber; **~film** *m* raw (*od* blank) film, *Am* motion picture raw stock; **~frucht** *f* unprocessed produce; **~garn** *n* unbleached yarn; **~gewicht** *n* gross weight; **~gewinn** *m* gross profit; **~gummi** *m* crude (*od* raw) rubber; **~guß** *m* pig-iron casting; **~haut** *f* rawhide; **~kost** *f* uncooked vegetarian food; **~köstler** *m* vegetarian, fruitarian; **~kupfer** *n* crude copper, pig-copper; **~leder** *n* untanned leather; **~ling** *m* brute, ruffian, *Am* thug; *tech* (*Rohblock für Presse*) slug; (*Gießerei~~*) casting; (*geschmiedet*) blank; **~material** *n* raw material, primary material; **~metall** *n* crude metal; **~öl** *n* crude (*od* rock) oil; crude petroleum; naphta; **~ölmotor** *m* crude oil engine; **~produkt** *n* raw product; **~seide** *f* raw silk; **~stahl** *m* natural steel; **~stoff** *m* raw material; **~~bewirtschaftung** *f* control of raw material supplies; **~~knappheit** *f* raw material shortage; **~~mangel** *m* scarcity of raw materials; **~wolle** *f* raw wool; **~zucker** *m* raw (*od* unrefined) sugar; (*Rohrzucker*) cane sugar; **~zustand** *m* raw state.

*

Rohr *n* (*Schilf~*) reed; (*Bambus~*) cane; (*indisches ~*) bamboo; (*Ofen~*) flue; (*Bratenröhre*) oven; (*Kanal*) duct, channel; (*Gewehrlauf*) barrel; (*Röhren aus Gußeisen*) pipe; (*Röhren aus Stahl od Metall*) tube; (*Messing~*) tubing; *biegsames ~* flexible tube; **~abschnitt** *m* pipe section; **~abzweigung** *f* branch piece; **~ammer** *f orn* reed-bunting, reed-sparrow; **~anschluß** *m* pipe connection, pipe joint; **~armaturen** *f pl* tube fittings *pl*; **~bremse** *f mil* buffer (brake), recoil brake; **~bruch** *m* pipe burst; **~dach** *n* reed-thatch; **~dommel** *f orn* bittern; **~flansch** *m* pipe flange; **~flöte, ~pfeife** *f* reed-pipe; **~förmig** *a* tubular; **~geflecht** *n* basketwork, wickerwork; **~gewinde** *n* pipe thread; **~krepierer** *m mil* burst in the bore; **~leger** *m* pipe fitter; (*Installateur*) plumber; **~leitung** *f* main, conduit; *Am* pipe line, piping, tubing; **~matte** *f* reed matt; **~mündung** *f* (*Kanone*) muzzle; barrel muzzle; **~netz** *n* pipes *pl*, conduit; **~plattenkoffer** *m* rush plate trunk; **~post** *f* pneumatic post, tube post; **~rahmen** *m* tubular frame; **~rücklauf** *m mil* gun (*od* barrel) recoil; **~~bremse** *f mil* recoil brake, buffer; **~sänger** *m orn* reed-warbler; **~schelle** *f* pipe support, pipe hanger; **~schilf** *n* common reed; **~schlange** *f* coil, spiral tube; **~spatz** *m orn* reed-sparrow; *schimpfen wie ein ~~* (*fam*) to scold like a fishwife; to swear like a trooper; **~stiefel** *m* high-boot, Wellington, *Am* boot; **~stock** *m* cane, bamboo; **~stuhl** *m* cane (-bottomed) chair, basket chair; **~verbindung** *f* tube (*od* pipe) joint (*od* connection); **~wandung** *f* wall (of a pipe); **~waren** *f pl* reed goods *pl*; **~weite** *f* bore, internal diameter (*Abk* i. d.); **~zange** *f* pipe-wrench; **~zucker** *m* cane sugar; *chem* saccharose, sucrose.

Röhr|e *f* tube; (*Leitungs~~*) conduit; pipe; (*Gas, Wasser etc*) main; (*Kamin*) funnel; (*Braten~~*) oven; *anat* duct; channel; (*Röhrchen*) tubule, cannula; capillary tube; (*Fuchsbau*) entrance; (*Tunnel*) shaft, tunnel; (*Gießkannen~~*) spout; (*Ausguß~~, Röhrenöffnung*) nozzle; *radio* valve, *Am* tube; *Braunsche ~~* cathode ray tube; *Elektronen~~* electronic valve, *Am* electron tube; *Ersatz~~* spare valve, *Am* spare tube; *Neon~~* neon tube; *Radio~~* wireless valve; *Am* radio tube; *Sende~~* sending valve, *Am* transmitting tube; *Speise~~* gullet, oesophagus; **~enabschirmung** *f radio* valve shield, *Am* tube shield; **~enapparat** *m radio* valve set, valve receiver; **~enausfall** *m radio* valve failure; **~enartig** *a* tubular, tube-like; *med* fistular; **~enbauweise** *f tech* tubular construction; **~enbestückung** *f* tube line-up; **~enblitz** *m* (**~gerät** *n*) electronic flash (unit), *Am* strobe flash (unit); **~encharakteristik** *f* valve characteristic; **~endetektor** *m radio* valve detector, audion, *Am* vacuum tube detector; **~enempfänger** *m radio* valve (*Am* tube) receiver, valve set; *Acht~~* eight-valve receiver; **~enfassung** *f radio* valve holder, valve socket; **~enfernleitung** *f* pipe line; **~enförmig** *a* tubular; **~engeschwür** *n med* fistula; **~engleichrichter** *m el* valve rectifier, *Am* vacuum tube rectifier; **~enheizung** *f radio* valve (*od* tube) heating; **~enkabel** *n* conduit cable; **~enkennlinie** *f* valve (*od* tube) characteristic; *Am* radio tube performance chart; **~enklammer** *f* tube clamp; **~enknochen** *m* tubular bone; long hollow bone, medullated bone; **~enkühler** *m* tubular cooler; pipe radiator; **~enleistung** *f radio* valve output; **~enlibelle** *f tech* air (*od* spirit) level, tube level; **~enleitung** *f* conduit-pipes *pl*; piping, pipe line; (*Netz*) main; *mit ~~en versehen* to fit with pipes, *Am* to pipe; **~ennudeln** *f pl* macaroni *pl*; **~enofen** *m* tube furnace; **~enprüfgerät** *n radio* valve tester, *Am* tube tester; **~enpilz, ~enschwamm** *m bot* boletus; **~enrauschen** *n* valve (*Am* tube) noise; valve rustle, *Am* tube hiss; **~ensatz** *m* valve set; **~ensender** *m radio* valve (*od* radio) transmitter; **~ensockel** *m* valve socket, *Am* tube holder (*od* base); **~enstraße** *f* tube rolling train; (*Walzwerk*) tube mill; **~enträger** *m tech* tube support; **~enverbindung** *f* pipe joint (*od* fitting); **~enverstärker** *m radio* valve amplifier, *Am* vacuum tube amplifier; **~enwalzwerk** *n* tube rolling mill; **~enwerk** *n* tubing, piping; **~enzwischensockel** *m radio* valve adapter.

rö(h)ren *itr* (*Hirsch*) to bell, to bellow.

Röhricht *n* reeds *pl*, reed-bank, *Am* cane-brake.

Rokoko *n* rococo.

Roll|aden *m* roller blind, roll(ing) shutter; *Am* shade; **~bahn** *f aero* (*Flugplatz*) rolling track, taxi track, taxi strip, taxi way; (*Startbahn*) runway; (*befestigte ~~*) paved runway; (*zementierte ~~*) concrete pavement, tarmac (runway); (*vor den Hallen*) apron; (*Ringstraße um den Platz*) perimeter track; (*Autobahn*) arterial road, trunk road; *tech* (*Fabrik*) roller conveyor; *rail* rail track; (*Elektronenbahn*) cycloidal path (of electrons); **~bandmaß** *n* spring-tape measure; roll tape measure; **~bar** *a* rollable; **~bein** *n anat* trochlea; **~bett** *n* truckle-bed; **~bewegung** *f* (*Schlingern*) rolling motion; **~brücke** *f* swing bridge; **~dach** *n mot* sliding roof, sunshine roof; **~e** *f* (*Walze*) roll, roller; (*Zylinder*) cylinder; (*Film~~, Geld~~, Tabak~~, Papier~~*) roll; (*beim Turnen*) roll; (*Flaschenzug*) pulley; block; (*Spule*) reel, spool; (*Tau*) coil; (*Faden*) reel; bobbin; (*unter Möbeln*) castor, *Am* caster; (*Liste*) list, register, rolls *pl*; (*Spirale*) *arch* scroll; (*Mangel*) mangle; calender; *theat* part, rôle, (*heute meist*) role; *anat* trochlea; *aero* (*Kunstflug*) roll; *~~ links* roll to the left; *~~ rechts* roll to the right; *ungesteuerte ~~* horizontal spiral; *halbe ~~* half roll; *auf ~~n laufen* to run upon rolls; *~~n drehen aero* to roll (an aircraft); *aus der ~~ fallen fig* to misbehave; to forget o. s.; *in e-m Stück die Haupt~~ spielen* to star in a play, to feature in a play; *ein Film mit X. in der führenden ~~* a film featuring X.; *e-e ~~ spielen* to play a part; *fig e-e große* (*armselige*) *~~ spielen* to cut a great (poor) figure; *die erste ~~ spielen fig* to play first fiddle; *Geld spielt keine ~~* money is no object; *das spielt keine ~~* that does not matter, that makes no difference; *spielt keine ~~!* never mind! *Am* forget about it! *bei diesem Verkehrsunfall spielte der Alkohol e-e ~~* the alcohol was a factor in this traffic accident; **~en** *tr* to roll; (*auf~~*) to roll up; (*auf Rädern*) to wheel; (*Wäsche*) to mangle; (*Tuchweberei*) to calender; *sich ~~* to roll o. s.; (*Film*) to curl; (*sich wälzen*) to trundle; *das „R" ~~* to roll o.'s r's; *itr* to roll; (*Sturm, Geschütze*) to roar; (*Donner*) to rumble; (*Fahrzeug*) to roll, to run on wheels; *mar, aero* (*schlingern*) to roll; *aero* (*auf dem Boden*) to taxi; (*sich wälzen*) to roll (*von* from, *in* into); *ins ~~ kommen* to get under way, *Am* to start the ball rolling; *~~der Angriff mil* relay attack, attack in waves, incessant attack; *~~der Luftangriff* rolling attack; massed air attack; *~~des Material rail* rolling stock, *mot* vehicle park; *in ~~den Wellen* in waves; **~enartig** *a* cylindrical; **~enbesetzung** *f theat* cast; **~enfach** *n theat* department, kind of character; **~enfenster** *f phot* roller film gate; **~enförmig** *a* roll-shaped; cylindrical; **~engelagert** *a* mounted on roller bearings; **~enkreis** *m aero* (*Kunstflug*) gyroscopic roll; **~enlager** *n tech* roller bearing; **~enpapier** *n* paper in reels, endless paper; **~enquetscher** *m phot* roller squeegee; **~enstromabnehmer** *m* trolley; **~entabak** *m* tobacco in rolls, roll tobacco; **~enzug** *m tech* block and tackle; pulley block; **~er** *m* (*Spielzeug*) scooter; (*Motor~~*) motor scooter; (*Möbel~~*) castor, *Am* caster; (*Kana-

rien~~) canary; (*Meereswoge*) roller, rolling sea; (*Wäsche*) mangler; (*Tuch*) calenderer; **~erlaubnis** *f aero* (*vom Kontrollturm*) taxi clearance; **~feld** *n aero* movement (*od* manoeuvring) area; tarmac; **~~ringstraße** *f aero* perimeter (track); **~film** *m* roll-film; **~~apparat** *m*, **~~kamera** *f* roll-film camera; **~~kassette** *f* (roll-film) cassette; (*Patrone*) cartridge; (*Magazin*) magazine; **~fuhrdienst** *m* carrier service; **~fuhrmann** *m* carter; **~fuhrunternehmer** *m* carrier's business; railway carting agent; **~geld** *n* cartage, carriage, truckage, transport charges *pl*, *Am* drayage; **~gelenk** *n* pivot joint; **~genehmigung** *f aero* permit to taxi aircraft; **~gerste** *f bot* winter barley; **~gut** *n* rolled material; *rail* carted goods *pl*; **~handtuch** *n* roll towel, rollertowel; **~holz** *n* rolling-pin; **~jalousie** *f* roller blind; hinged curtain; **~kommando** *n* raiding squad; **~kragen** *m* turtle neck collar; **~kran** *m* travel(l)ing crane; **~kutscher** *m* carter, carrier; **~(l)aden** *m* roller blind; revolving shutter; **~(l)eiter** *f* sliding ladder; **~mops** *m* pickled herring; **~ordnung** *f aero* tarmac control; **~pult** *n* roll-top desk; **~schein** *m aero* permit to taxi aircraft; **~schiene** *f* rail; **~schinken** *m* rolled ham; **~schrank** *m* roll-fronted cabinet; **~schuh** *m* roller skate; *~~ laufen* to rollerskate; **~~bahn** *f* roller-skating rink; **~~läufer** *m* roller skater; **~~sport** *m* skating on roller skates; **~sitz** *m* (*Ruderboot*) sliding seat; **~sperrfeuer** *n mil* (*Feuerwalze*) creeping barrage; **~straße** *f aero* taxi-track, taxiway; perimeter track; **~strecke** *f aero* rolling distance, run: runway; **~~nstreifen** *m aero* taxi-ing strip; **~stuhl** *m* wheel-chair, Bath-chair; **~treppe** *f* moving stair(case), *Am* escalator; **~tür** *f* sash-door; **~verband** *m med* roller bandage; **~verdeck** *n* sliding roof; **~vorhang** *m* roller blind; **~wagen** *m* truck, lorry; dray; low waggon, trolley; **~weg** *m aero* taxiway; take-off strip; **~~ feuer** *n aero* taxiway lights *pl*; **~werk** *n aero* undercarriage, *Am* landing gear; **~widerstand** *m* rolling friction, resistance to rolling; *mot* road resistance; *aero* drag when taxi-ing.

Roman *m* novel; (work of) fiction; *kurzer ~* novelette; (*Ritter~*) romance; *e-n ~ in Fortsetzungen erscheinen lassen* to serialize; **~dichter, ~schreiber, ~schriftsteller** *m* novel-writer, novelist; **~en** *m pl* Romance (*od* Neo-Latin) peoples *pl*; **~folge** *f* serial (story); **~haft** *a* romantic, fictitious, novelistic; **~held** *m* hero of a romance (*od* novel); **~isch** *a* Romanic; *~~e Sprachen* Romance languages *pl*; **~leser** *m* novel reader; **~literatur** *f* fiction; **~tik** *f* romanticism; **~tiker** *m* romanticist; **~tisch** *a* romantic; **~ze** *f* romance; ballad.

Röm|er *m* Roman; (*Pokal*) large wine-glass; **~isch** *a* Roman.

Rommé *n* (*Kartenspiel*) rummy.

*

Rond|e *f* round; circle; disk; ronde; **~ell** *n* round garden-bed; **~engang** *m mil* rounds *pl*; **~o** *n* roundelay.

röntgen *tr* to X-ray, to radiograph, to roentgenise; *~ n* (*Einheit*) roentgen; **~analyse** *f* X-ray analysis; **~anlage** *f* X-ray equipment; X-ray plant; **~apparat** *m* X-ray apparatus; **~arzt** *m* radiologist; **~aufnahme** *f*, **~bild** *n* X-ray photograph, radiograph, radiogram, roentgenogram, roentgen-photo; skiagraph; **~bestrahlung** *f* radiotherapy; **~diagnostik** *f* radio diagnostics *pl*; **~dosismeter** *m* X-ray dosimeter; **~durchleuchtung** *f* X-ray examination, radioscopy; **~film** *m* X-ray film; **~isieren** *tr* to X-ray, to roentgenise; **~lehre** *f* radiology; science of X-rays; **~metallographie** *f* radiometallography; **~ologe** *m* roentgenologist, radiologist; **~reihenuntersuchung** *f* mass radiography; **~röhre** *f* X-ray tube; **~schwester** *f* X-ray nurse; **~spezialist** *m* X-ray specialist; **~strahlen** *m pl* X-rays *pl*, roentgen rays *pl*; *Hautentzündung durch ~~* actinodermatitis; *mit ~~ durchleuchten* to X-ray; **~strahlung** *f* X-radiation; **~therapie** *f* X-ray therapy, X-ray treatment, roentgenotherapy, radio therapeutics *pl*; **~untersuchung** *f* X-ray test; X-ray examination, radiographic inspection, radiography.

Rosa *n*, **~farbig** *a* rose-colo(u)red; roseate, pink.

rösch *a* crusty; brittle, roasted, coarse.

Röschen *n* little rose.

Rose *f* rose; *wilde ~* wild brier; wild rose; (*Hunds~*) eglantine; *med* erysipelas; (*Kompaß*) compass card.

Rosen|busch *m* rose-bush; **~duft** *m* scent of roses; **~essig** *m* rose-vinegar; **~garten** *m*, **~hecke** *f* rose-garden, rose-hedge; rosery; **~knospe** *f* rose-bud; **~kohl** *m* Brussels sprouts *pl*; **~kranz** *m* garland of roses; (*katholisch*) rosary; *den ~~ beten* to tell o.'s beads; **~monat** *m* month of roses, June; **~montag** *m* last Monday before Lent; **~öl** *n* attar of roses; **~rot** *a* rose-colo(u)red; **~stock** *m* rose-bush; **~strauß** *m* bunch of roses; **~wasser** *n* rose-water; **~züchter** *m* grower of roses.

Rosette *f arch* rosette; (*Verzierung*) (silk) rosette; *bot* rosette of leaves; (*Fenster*) rose window.

rosig *a* rosy, roseate; rose-colo(u)red; *~e Aussichten* (*fig*) rosy prospects; *~e Ansichten* roseate views; *die Lage sieht nicht sehr ~ aus* things don't look too rosy; *in der ~sten Laune* in the happiest mood.

Rosine *f* raisin, sultana; (*kleine*) currant; (*große*) plum.

Rosmarin *m* rosemary.

Roß *n* horse; *poet* steed; **~arzt** *m* veterinarian; veterinary surgeon, farrier; **~bändiger** *m* horse-tamer; **~haar** *n* horsehair; **~händler, ~kamm, ~täuscher** *m* horse-dealer; **~käfer** *m* dung-beetle; **~kamm** *m* curry-comb; **~kastanie** *f* horse-chestnut; **~kur** *f* drastic treatment; **~schlächter** *m* knacker; **~schweif** *m* horse-tail.

Rösselsprung *m* knight's move; (*Rätsel*) problem on the knight's move.

Rost[1] *m* (*auf Eisen*) rust; *bot* (*Brand*) rust; (*Getreide*) wheat rust, corn smut; (*Meltau*) mildew, blight; *~ ansetzen* to put on rust; *~ abkratzen* to scrape off the rust; *von ~ zerfressen* rust-eaten; *vom ~ befallen bot* mildewed; **~beständig** *a* rust-resisting, rustproof; rustless; **~bildung** *f* rust formation, corrugation, staining; **~braun** *a* rusty brown; **~en** *itr* to rust; to get rusty; to corrode, to oxidize; **~entfernung** *f* rust removal; **~farben** *a* rust-colo(u)red; **~fleck(en)** *m* iron-mo(u)ld, rust stain; **~fleckig** *a* iron-mo(u)lded, rust-stained, rust-spotted; **~frei** *a* rustproof; (*Stahl*) stainless; *~~er Stahl* stainless steel; **~~heit** *f* immunity to corrosion; **~gefahr** *f* danger of rusting; **~gelb** *a* rusty yellow; **~ig** *a* rusty, corroded; **~narbe** *f* corrosion pit; **~pilz** *m bot* rust; **~schicht** *f* layer of rust; **~schutz** *m* rust prevention; **~~farbe** *f* rust (-proof) colo(u)r (*od* coating), anti-corrosive paint; **~~mittel** *n* rust preventing agent, rust preventive.

Rost[2] *m* (*Brat~*) roaster; gridiron, grill; (*Feuer~*) grate; (*Gitter~*) grill grate; (*Pfahl~*) pile-work; pile-grating; *auf dem ~ braten* to grill; **~braten** *m* roast beef, roast meat; (roast) joint; **~feuerung** *f* grate firing, grate fire; **~fläche** *f* grate-surface; **~fleisch** *n* grilled meat.

Röst|e *f* grill, (*Pfanne*) roaster; (*Flachs~~*) steeping; **~en** *tr* (*Fleisch*) to broil, to grill, to roast; (*Brot*) to toast; (*Kaffee*) to roast; (*Korn*) to parch; (*Mais*) *Am* to pop (corn); **~kartoffeln** *f pl* roast potatoes *pl;* **~mais** *m Am* pop-corn; **~produkt** *n* product of roasting; roasted (*od* calcined) product; **~ung** *f* roasting, roast; calcination; **~verfahren** *n* roasting process; calcining method.

rot *a* red; (*frisch*) ruddy; (*~braun*) auburn; (*Beefsteak nicht durchgebraten*) rare; (*~haarig*) rufous; *~ färben* to dye red; *~ werden* to redden, to blush, to colo(u)r, to crimson, to flush; *brennend ~* scarlet; *leuchtend ~* sparkling red; *ich habe es mir ~ im Kalender angestrichen* I've marked it in red on my calendar; *heute ~, morgen tot* here today, gone tomorrow; *~ wie ein gesottener Krebs* red as a boiled lobster; *~ n* red; redness; (*Kartenspiel*) red suit; red point; (*Schminke*) rouge; *~ auftragen* to rouge; *zu stark ~ aufgetragen* over-rouged; *helles ~* crimson, bright red; **~auge** *n* roach; **~bäckig** *a* red-cheeked, rosy-cheeked; ruddy; cherry-cheeked; **~bart** *m* red-beard; **~blond** *a* auburn; **~braun** *a* reddish brown; red-brown; bay; **~buche** *f* red beech, copperbeech; **~dorn** *m bot* pink hawthorn; **~eiche** *f* red oak; **~eisen** *n* hematite iron; **~empfindlich** *a phot* red-sensitive; **~fink** *m* chaffinch; **~fleckig** *a* red-spotted; **~fuchs** *m* (*Pferd*) sorrel horse, bay horse; **~gelb** *a* orange (-colo(u)red); **~gerber** *m* tanner; **~gießer** *m* brazier; **~glühend, ~heiß** *a* red-hot; **~glut** *f* red heat; **~haarig** *a* red-haired, red-headed; **~haut** *f* redskin; **~hirsch** *m* red deer, stag; **~käppchen** *n* (Little) Red Riding Hood; **~kehlchen** *n* robin (redbreast); **~kohl** *m* red cabbage; **~kopf** *m* redhead; carroty person; **~köpfig** *a* red-haired, red-headed; **~lauf** *m* erysipelas; (*bei Schweinen*) red murrain; **~nasig** *a* red-nosed; **~schimmel** *m* roan horse; **~schwänzchen** *n orn* redstart; **~spon** *m* claret; **~stift** *m* red pencil, red crayon; **~tanne** *f* spruce, red fir; **~wangig** *a* red-cheeked; **~wein** *m* red wine; claret; **~~bowle** *f* claret-cup; **~welsch** *n* thieves' cant (*od* slang), thieves' Latin; gibberish; **~wild** *n* red deer, venison; **~wurst** *f* red sausage, black pudding.

Röt|e *f* red, redness; (*Erröten*) blush; (*Gesichtsfarbe*) red complexion; **~el** *m* ruddle, red chalk, red ochre; **~eln** *pl med* German measles *pl*; **~en** *tr* to redden, to colo(u)r red; *sich ~~* to flush, to get red; *die Sonne rötete den Himmel* the sun flushed the sky; **~lich** *a* reddish; ruddy.

Rotation *f* rotation, revolution; **~sbewegung** *f* rotary motion; **~sdruck** *m* rotary machine printing; **~~maschine** *f* rotary printing press; (*schnelle*) rotary;

~sgeschwindigkeit *f* velocity (*od* speed) of rotation; **~svermögen** *n* rotatory power; **rotieren** *itr* to rotate; to revolve.

Rotor *m* rotor; rotator; armature; **~flügel** *m aero* rotor blade; **~flugzeug** *n* rotor plane.

Rotte *f* (*Menge*) crowd; (*Pöbel*) mob, rabble; (*Bande*) gang, band; troop; (*Herde Tiere*) flock, pack; *mil* file; *aero mil* group of two aircraft.

rotten *r* to band together, to flock together; to gang; to form into troops; **~feuer** *n* volley; **~führer** *m mil* N.C.O.; (*bei der Arbeit*) foreman; **~weise** *adv* in files; in gangs, in troops.

Rotz *m* mucus; *fam* snot; (*der Pferde*) glanders *pl*; **~ig** snotty; (*Pferd*) glandered; **~nase** *f* snotty nose; running nose; *fig* saucy boy, snotty fellow, brat; *e-e ~~ haben* to snivel.

Roulade *f* Swiss roll.

Roul|eau *n* sun-blind, roller-blind; (window) shade; **~ette** *f* roulette; *tech* ring-roll mill.

Routin|e *f* routine, practice; **~iert** *a* experienced, versed; trained.

Rowdy *m* hooligan, *Am* thug.

Rüb|e *f* rape; *gelbe ~~* carrot; *rote ~~* beet(root); *weiße ~~* turnip; **~enacker** *m*, **~enland** *n* turnip-field; **~enzucker** *m* beet-sugar; **~öl** *n* rape-oil; **~samen** *m*, **~saat** *f*, **~sen** *m* rapeseed.

Rubel *m* rouble.

Rubin *m* ruby.

Rubri|k *f* rubric; (*Spalte*) column; (*Überschrift*) heading, title; **~zieren** *tr* (*in Spalten*) to arrange in columns; to tabulate; (*mit Überschrift versehen*) to head.

ruch|bar *a* notorious; *~~ werden* to become known; **~barkeit** *f* notoriousness; **~los** *a* profligate, reprobate; nefarious; wicked; impious; **~losigkeit** *f* profligateness; (*Tat*) wicked act.

Ruck *m* (*Stoß*) push, jerk, start; shove; *Am sl* yank; (*von Fahrzeugen*) jolt; (*ziehen*) pull, wrench; *auf e-n ~* at one go; *e-n ~ geben* to give a start; *sich e-n ~ geben* to pull o. s. together; **~artig** *a* jerky; **~sack** *m* knapsack, rucksack; **~weise** *adv* by jerks, by fits and starts; in snatches.

Rück|ansicht *f* back view, rear view; **~anspruch** *m* counter-claim; **~antwort**, **~äußerung** *f* reply, answer; **~~karte** *f* reply coupon, reply card; **~bewegung** *f* retrograde movement; *tech* return stroke; **~bezüglich** *a* reflexive; **~bildung** *f* involution; regeneration; regression; retrogressive metamorphosis; **~blenden** *tr film* to flashback; **~blendung** *f* cut-back, flashback; **~blick** *m* retrospect, backward glance, glance back; (*Übersicht über Vergangenes*) survey; *e-n ~~ werfen auf* to cast a retrospective glance at; **~~spiegel** *m mot* rear view (*od* driving) mirror, rear vision; **~datieren** *tr* to antedate; **~datierung** *f* dating back; (*Nach~~*) antedating; **~erinnerung** *f* reminiscence, recollection; **~erstatten** *tr* to refund, to repay, to reimburse; **~erstattung** *f* repayment, refund, restitution; **~~sanspruch** *m* restitution claim; **~fahrkarte** *f* return-ticket, *Am* round-trip ticket; **~fahrt** *f* return journey, return trip; **~fall** *m* (*in ein Verbrechen*)recidivism, relapse; (*Heimfall*) reversion; *med* relapse; **~~fieber** *n* relapsing fever; **~fällig** *a* recidivous, relapsing; revertible; *~~ werden* to backslide, to relapse; **~fällige(r)** *m* backslider, recidivist; **~fenster** *n mot* rear window, backlight; **~forderung** *f* claim; reclamation; **~fracht** *f* return (*od* home) freight; **~frage** *f* query, further inquiry; check-back; **~~n** *itr* to request; **~flug** *m aero* return (*od* homeward) flight; **~fluß** *m* reflux; **~führen** *tr* (*in die Heimat*) to repatriate; *tech* to lead back, to pass back; **~führung** *f* repatriation; **~gabe** *f* return; redelivery; restoration; reinstatement; **~gang** *m* retrogression; return movement; (*Preise*) drop, decline; (*Erzeugung*) decrease, falling-off, downward movement; (*Verminderung*) reduction; (*Kurse*) recession; **~gängig** *a* retrograde, retrogressive; dropping, declining; *~~ machen* (*Auftrag*) to countermand, to cancel; (*abbrechen*) to break off; (*Vertrag*) to annul; (*widerrufen*) to revoke; (*aufheben*) to rescind, to quash; **~gängigmachung** *f* cancellation; **~gewähren** *tr* to return, to restore; **~gewinnen** *irr tr* to recover, to salvage; **~gewinnung** *f* reclamation; recovery; (*Energie*) recuperation; (*Neubildung*) regeneration; **~gliedern** *tr* to reintegrate; **~grat** *n* backbone, spine; vertebral column; **~~los** *a fig* spineless, lacking backbone; **~~(s)verkrümmung** *f* curvature of the spine; (*seitliche*) scoliosis; **~greifend** *a* retrogressive; **~griff** *m* recourse; **~halt** *m* support, stay; (*Reserve*) reserve; *e-n ~~ haben in* to be backed (up) by; **~haltlos** *a* unreserved, without reserve; (*offen*) frank, openly, plainly; **~handschlag** *m* (*Tennis*) back-hand (stroke); **~hut** *f* covering force; **~kauf** *m* buying back, repurchase; redemption; **~~srecht** *n* right of redemption; **~~swert** *m* repurchase value, surrender value; **~kehr**, **~kunft** *f* return, returning; *fig* (*Wiederaufstieg*) *Am* come-back; **~kehrer** *m* returnee; **~kehrpunkt** *m math, tele* cusp; **~koppeln** *itr radio* to couple back, to feed back; **~kopplung** *f radio* reaction (-coupling), feed-back; **~kreuzung** *f* (*Rassen*) backcrossing; **~ladung** *f* return cargo; **~lage** *f* reserve fund, reserves *pl*, savings *pl*; **~lauf** *m* return movement; reversing stroke; *mil* gun recoil; **~~bremse** *f mil* recoil buffer; **~läufer** *m* (*Brief*) dead letter; **~läufig** *a* retrograde, recurrent; (*Preise*) dropping; **~leitung** *f* return line; **~licht** *n mot* rear light, rear lamp; **~lieferung** *f* redelivery; **~~sschein** *m* return slip, return bill; **~lings** *adv* backward(s), from behind; **~marsch** *m* march back (*od* home); *mar* return voyage; (*Rückzug*) retreat; **~nahme** *f* taking back; (*Angebot*) revocation; (*Anklage, Berufung*) withdrawal; (*Gesetz*) repeal; **~porto** *n* return postage; **~prall** *m* recoil, rebound; repercussion; **~reise** *f* return (journey), journey home; *auf der ~~* homeward bound; **~ruf** *m tele* recall; **~schau** *f* retrospect; review; **~schlag** *m* back-stroke; (*Flamme*) backfire; (*Waffe*) recoil; *fig* (*Rückgang*) reverse, check, setback; recession; reaction; repercussion; reverberation; (*Rückbildung*) atavism; **~~ventil** *n* back pressure valve; **~schluß** *m* conclusion, inference; *e-n ~~ ziehen* to draw a conclusion from, to infer from; **~schreitend** *a* retrogressive, retrograde; **~schritt** *m* stepback, backward movement; *fig* retrogression, falling-off, relapse; (*Reaktion*) reaction; **~~lich** *a* reactionary; **~seite** *f* back; wrong side; (*Kehrseite*) reverse; (*Münze*) tail; *auf die ~~ schreiben* to endorse; **~senden** *irr tr* to send back, to return; **~sendung** *f* return, redelivery; **~setzlampe** *f mot* reversing lamp, back-up light; **~sicht**, **~sichtnahme** *f* regard, consideration, respect; motive; *mit ~~ auf* in (*od* with) respect to, in (*od* with) regard to, because of, in the light of; *ohne ~~ auf* irrespective of, regardless of; *auf etw ~~ nehmen* to pay regard to; to allow for; **~sichtslos** *a* inconsiderate, without consideration; regardless (of); relentless; unfeeling; (*entschlossen*) determined, at all costs; ruthless; reckless; *~~es Fahren mot* reckless driving; **~sichtslosigkeit** *f* regardlessness; **~sichtsvoll** *a* considerate, regardful (*gegen* of); **~sitz** *m* back-seat; *mot* reserve seat, dickey, *Am* rumble seat; **~spiel** *n* return match; **~sprache** *f* discussion, consultation; conference; conferment; *~~ nehmen* to talk over, to discuss, to confer (*mit* with); **~stand** *m* (*Schuld*) arrears *pl*; *chem* residue; (*Satz*) sediment; (*Rest*) remainder; (*Lieferung, Aufträge etc*) backlog; (*Abfall*) waste; *Lohn~~* arrears of pay, *Am* back pay; *Miets~~* arrears of rent, *Am* back rent; *im ~~* in arrears, behindhand; *im ~~ sein mit* to be behind with; *seine Miete ist 3 Monate im ~~* his rent is 3 months in arrears; *~stände eintreiben* to collect outstanding debts, to recover debts; **~ständig** *a* (*Zahlung*) in arrears, behind; (*Geld*) outstanding; (*Raten*) overdue, delinquent; *fig* (*altmodisch*) old-fashioned, not up-to-date; backward; obsolete; *~~ sein* (*fam*) to be a back number; **~~keit** *f* backwardness; **~stellen** *tr* to reset, to replace; **~stelltaste** *f* resetting key; **~stellung** *f* reserve; *tech* release, replacement; **~stoß** *m* repulsion; (*Schub*) thrust; (*e-r Waffe*) recoil; **~~antrieb** *m aero* jet propulsion, reaction propulsion; **~~dämpfer** *m* muzzle brake; **~~flugzeug** *n* jet plane, jet propelled plane; **~~jäger** *m aero* jet fighter; **~~los** *a* recoilless; **~~motor** *m* jet (propulsion) engine; **~~triebwerk** *n* jet engine, jet; **~strahlen** *tr* to reflect; **~strahler** *m* rear reflector; (*Katzenauge*) cat's eye; **~~lampe** *f* back-reflecting lamp; **~streumantel** *m* (*Atombombe*) tamper, reflector; **~strom** *m* return current; **~taste** *f* (*Schreibmaschine*) back spacer; resetting key; **~trift** *f aero* trail; lag; **~tritt** *m* (*vom Amt*) resignation, retirement; (*Rückzug*) retreat; (*vom Vertrag*) rescission; withdrawal; *seinen ~~ einreichen* to submit (*od* to tender) o.'s resignation, *Am* to file o.'s resignation; **~~bremse** *f* back-pedal(ling) brake; **~~salter** *n* retirement age; **~übersetzung** *f* retranslation; **~umschlag** *m* return envelope; **~vergütung** *f* reimbursement; refunding; repayment; (*Rabatt*) rebate; **~verlegung** *f* retardation; (*örtlich*) removal backward; **~versicherung** *f* reinsurance; counter-insurance; **~verweisung** *f* recommitment; (*Vorinstanz*) remittal; **~wand** *f* back wall, rear wall; **~wanderer** *m* returning emigrant; **~wärtig** *a* rear, rearward; behind the lines; *~~es Armeegebiet* line of communications area; *~~er Dienst* service behind the lines; *~~e Verbindung* rear communication; **~wärts** *adv* backward(s), back; *~~ fahren* to back up, to reverse; *~~ gehen fig* to decline; to fall off; **~~bewegung** *f* backward movement; (*Geschäft*) decline; **~~gang** *m mot* reverse (gear); **~wechsel** *m* re-exchange; **~weg** *m* way back, return route; return; **~wirken** *itr* to react; **~wirkend** *a* retroactive; (*Gesetze, Steuern*) retrospective; *~~es Gesetz* ex post facto law; *mit ~~er Kraft* retroactively; **~wirkung** *f* reaction (*auf* on), (*Gesetze*) retrospectiveness; (*Auswirkung*) repercussion; *radio* feed-back, reaction; **~zahlbar** *a* repayable; **~zahlen** *tr* to repay, to refund; (*Anleihe*) to redeem; **~zahlung** *f* repayment, reimbursement; refund; (*Anleihen*) redemption; **~zug** *m* withdrawal; retreat; return; *begrenzter ~~* (*mil*) limited withdrawal; *zum ~~ blasen* to sound the retreat; **~~sgefecht** *n* running fight; **~~srichtung** *f* line of retreat; **~zündung** *f* backfire; *radio* backlash.

rücken *tr* (*fort~*) to (re)move; to transfer; (*stoßen*) to push; (*schieben*) to shove, to shift; *itr* to move away; (*Platz machen*) to move over, to make room; *mil* to march; *aneinander~* to come closer (*od* together); *näher ~* to approach, to draw near; *höher ~* to rise; *weiter ~* to proceed; to advance; *ins Feld ~* to take the field; *jdm zu Leibe ~* to press s. o. hard.

Rücken *m* back; (*Rückseite*) rear; *anat* dorsum, tergum; (*Nasen~*) bridge; (*Buch~*) back; (*Rückenstück Fleisch, Fisch*) chine; saddle; (*Berg~*) ridge; *mil* rear; *am ~ befindlich* dorsal; *hinter jds ~* behind s. o.'s back; *im ~* in the rear; *in den ~ fallen* to attack in the rear, to stab in the back; *mit dem ~ gegeneinander, ~ gegen ~* back to back; *den ~ beugen* to bend o.'s back; to stoop; *fig* to cringe; *sich den ~ decken* to keep on the safe side; *auf den ~ fallen* to fall on o.'s back; *fig* to be taken aback; *den ~ kehren* to turn o.'s back (upon); *e-n krummen ~ machen* to stoop (from age); *fig* to cringe, to fawn; **~deckung** *f* rear cover, protection for the rear; (*Festung*) parados; *fig* backing; **~fallschirm** *m aero* back-pack parachute, back type parachute; **~flosse** *f* dorsal fine; **~flug** *m aero* inverted flying, upside-down flying, flying on the back; **~lage** *f* lying on the back; upside-down position; **~lehne** *f* (*Stuhl*) back (-rest); (*Bett*) bedrest; **~leiden** *n* spinal affection; **~mark** *n* spinal cord (*od* marrow); **~~sanästhesie** *f med* spinal anesthesia; **~~slähmung** *f med* spinal paralysis; **~~schwindsucht** *f* spinal consumption; **~naht** *f* back seam; **~schild** *n* (*Schildkröte*) back-shell, turtleback; (*Buch*) book label; **~schmerz** *m* back-ache; **~schwimmen** *n* backstroke; **~titel** *m* (*Buch*) lettering; **~trage** *f* back-basket; *tele* pack, portable reel; **~wind** *m* (*Schiebewind*) tail wind, following wind, *Am auch* rear-on wind; *mit ~~ fliegen* to fly down wind, *Am* to fly with the wind in the tail; **~wirbel** *m anat* dorsal vertebra.

*

Rüde *m* male dog (*od* fox *od* wolf); large hound; *~ a* rude, coarse, brutal.

Rudel *n* (*Hunde, Wölfe*) pack; (*Kinder*) troop; (*Schafe, Ziegen*) flock; (*Hirsche*) herd; *mar mil* pack (of submarines), wolfpack; **~weise** *adv* in herds, in troops; in gangs.

Ruder *n* oar; (*Steuer~*) rudder, helm; (*Heck~*) scull; *aero* rudder; control surface; *fig ans ~ kommen* to come into power; *am ~ sein* to be at the helm, to be at the head of affairs; to be in power; **~bank** *f* seat for a rower, *mar* thwart; **~blatt** *n* blade of an oar; **~boot** *n* rowing-boat; *Am* row boat; sculler; (*kleines*) dinghy, **~er** *m* oarsman, rower; **~fläche** *f* control surface; **~klampe** *f* rowlock; **~klub** *m* rowing club; **~n** *itr* to row, to pull; to go for a row; **~pinne** *f* tiller; **~regatta** *f* boat race, regatta; **~schlag** *m* stroke of the oar; **~stange** *f* oar; (*zum Staken*) punt-pole; **~volk** *n* crew of rowers.

Ruf *m* call; (*Schrei*) cry, shout, *Am* (*beim Sport*) yell; (*Telephon*) call; ring; (*Berufung*) calling, vocation; (*Ernennung*) appointment, summons; (*Nachrede*) character, reputation, repute, fame; *com* standing, credit; *er hat e-n ausgezeichneten ~* he bears an excellent character; *in gutem ~ stehen* to be in high repute; *in schlechtem ~ stehen* to be in bad repute, to have a bad reputation; *ein Mann mit schlechtem ~* a man of ill repute; **~en** *irr tr* to call, to summon, to hail; *itr* (*schreien*) to cry, to shout, to bawl; *um Hilfe ~* to cry for help; *ins Gedächtnis ~* to call to mind; *~~ lassen* to send for; *wie gerufen kommen* to come at the right moment; **~name** *m* name ordinarily used, Christian name, *Am* first name; **~nummer** *f* telephone (call-)number, call number; **~weite** *f*: *in ~~* within call, within earshot; **~welle** *f radio* calling wave; **~zeichen** *n radio* call signal, call letter.

Rüffel *m* (*Verweis*) reprimand, rebuke; (*scharfer Vorwurf*) upbraiding; (*Schelten*) scolding, *fam* wigging **~n** *tr* to reprimand; to rebuke; (*Unzufriedenheit*) to chide; to upbraid; to scold, to rate.

Rüge *f* (*leichter Tadel*) blame, censure, reproof; (*Ermahnung*) admonishment; (*Rüffel*) reprimand; **~n** *tr* to blame, to find fault with; to reprove; (*ermahnen*) to admonish; (*kritisieren*) to animadvert (on); to censure.

Ruhe *f* quiet, quietude; (*Seelen~*) calm, calmness; (*geistig*) tranquillity; (*Ende der Arbeit*) rest; (*Ausruhen*) repose; (*Gefaßtheit*) composure; (*Erholung*) repose, rest; (*Frieden*) peace; (*Stille*) silence; stillness; *fig* sleep; *in ~ lassen* to let alone; *sich zur ~ begeben* to go to rest, to retire; *sich zur ~ setzen* to retire from business; *zur ~ bringen* to calm, to silence, to still; to hush (a rumo(u)r); *immer mit der ~! fam* take it easy! *~!* mum! **~bank** *f* bench; **~bett** *n* couch, sofa; **~gehalt** *n* pension, retiring allowance, retirement pay, *Am* retired pay; **~~sempfänger** *m* pensionary; **~kissen** *n* pillow; **~lage** *f* resting (*od* equilibrium) position; *sich in ~~ befinden* to be at rest; **~los** *a* restless; **~~igkeit** *f* restlessness; **~n** *itr* to rest; to sleep; (*aufhören*) to cease working; (*Recht*) to fall into abeyance, to be suspended; (*beruhen auf*) to be based on, to rest on; *hier ruht* here lies; *ich wünsche wohl zu ~~* I wish you a good night's rest; **~~d** *a* resting; inoperative; *tech* static, constant, latent; **~pause** *f* pause; (*ruhige Zeit*) lull; **~platz** *m* resting-place; **~punkt** *m* resting-point; *mus* pause; (*Totpunkt*) dead-centre; **~stand** *m* state of repose; retirement; *in ~~ versetzen* to superannuate, to pension off; **~stätte** *f* place of rest; *fig letzte ~~* last home, grave; **~stellung** *f tech* unoperated position, normal position; *mil* stand at ease position; **~störer** *m* disturber of the peace; rioter, brawler; **~störung** *f* breach of peace, disturbance, riot; disorderly conduct; **~tag** *m* day of rest; **~zeit** *f* time of rest, leisure; **~zustand** *m* state of rest.

ruhig *a* (*Seele, See, Wetter*) calm; (*geräuschlos*) quiet, silent; (*bewegungslos*) silent, still; (*innerlich ~*) tranquil; (*heiter*) serene; (*gefaßt*) composed; (*friedlich*) peaceful; (*kaltblütig*) cool; (*Farbe*) sober; *~ adv* safely; *~er Gang* smoothness of action.

Ruhm *m* glory; (*Berühmtsein*) fame, renown; **~bedeckt** *a* covered with glory; **~begier(de)** *f* thirst for glory, love of fame; ambition; **~begierig** *a* eager for glory; ambitious; **~los** *a* inglorious; **~redig** *a* vainglorious; boastful; **~~keit** *f* vainglory, boasting; **~reich** *a* glorious; **~sucht** *f* passion for glory; **~süchtig** *a* ambitious; **~voll** *a* glorious; famous; **~würdig** *a* praiseworthy.

rühm|en *tr* (*loben*) to praise, to laud; (*preisen*) to eulogize, to extol; (*verherrlichen*) to glorify; *r* to boast of, to brag about; **~enswert** *a* praiseworthy; **~lich** *a* glorious; hono(u)rable.

Ruhr *f* dysentery.

Rühr|ei *n* scrambled eggs; **~en** *tr* to stir, to move; to agitate; to beat (the drum); (*innerlich*) to affect, to touch; *itr an etw ~~* to touch; *vom Blitze, vom Schlage gerührt werden* to be thunder-struck, to be struck by apoplexy; *nicht daran ~~!* let sleeping dogs lie! *r* to stir o. s.; to budge; *das rührt mich nicht* that makes no impression on me; *rührt euch!* stand at ease! **~end** *a* touching, affecting, moving, pathetic; **~ig** *a* active, agile, nimble, *fam* go-ahead; **~~keit** *f* activity, nimbleness; **~löffel** *m* (pot-) ladle; **~selig** *a* sentimental, lachrymose; emotional; **~stück** *n theat* melodrama, *Am* sobstuff; **~ung** *f* emotion.

*

Ruin *m* ruin, decay; (*Untergang*) downfall; **~e** *f* ruins *pl*; a ruin; *fig* wreck; **~ieren** *tr* to ruin, to bring to ruin; (*Kleider*) to spoil; (*zerstören*) to destroy.

Rülps *m* belch; **~en** *itr* to belch.

Rum *m* rum.

Rumän|e *m*, **~in** *f* Rumanian; **~ien** *n* Rumania; **~isch** *a* Rumanian.

Rummel *m* (*Plunder*) trash, rubbish, lumber, old things *pl*; (*Lärm*) racket, noise; hubbub; activity; rush; (*Jahrmarkts~*) revel; (*Tumult*) row; *im ~* (*com*) in the lump; *fam den ~ verstehen* to be up to snuff, to know what's what; **~ei** *f* rumbling noise; **~platz** *m* place of amusement, amusement park (*od* fair), *Am* midway.

Rumor *m* noise, bustle; **~en** *itr* to make a noise, to bustle.

Rumpel|kammer *f* lumber-room; **~kasten** *m* lumber-box; *fig* (*Kutsche*) rattletrap; **~n** *itr* to rumble, to rattle; (*Wagen*) to jolt.

Rumpf *m* (*Körper, Leib*) body, trunk; (*Torso*) torso; (*Baumstumpf*) stump (of a tree); (*e-s Schiffes*) hull, shell, carcass; *aero* (*e-s Flugzeuges*) fuselage, body; (*Flugboot*) hull; (*Atom*) core, kernel; *mit ~ u. Stumpf ausrotten fig* to extirpate root and branch; **~bespannung** *f aero* fuselage-covering fabric; **~beuge** *f* (*Turnen*) trunk bending; **~ende** *n aero* end (*od* tail) of fuselage; **~gliedmaßen** *n pl* body legs *pl*; **~holm** *m aero* longeron; **~kanzel** *f aero* rear cockpit; **~lastig** *a aero* tail-heavy; **~parlament** *n hist* Rump Parliament; **~spitze** *f aero* nose of fuselage.

rümpfen *tr: die Nase ~* to turn up o.'s nose at; (*über etw*) to sneer at s. th.

Rumpsteak *n* rump(-steak), *Am* sirloin, porterhouse steak.

rund *a* round; (*kreis~*) circular; (*abgerundet*) rotund; *bot* rotundate; (*kugel-*

förmig) globular, spherical; (*walzenförmig*) cylindrical; (*plump, dick*) plump; ~ *u. dick fam* roly-poly; (*länglich*) oval; *fig* plain, frank; *ein ~es Nein* a plain "No"; (*etwa*) about, approximately, around; *ein ~es Dutzend* a good round dozen; *~es Gesicht* full face; *~e Klammer* round (*od* curved) bracket, parenthesis; *~e Summe* round sum; *in ~en Zahlen* in round numbers (*od* figures); ~ *abschlagen* to refuse flatly; ~ *machen* to round; (*abrunden*) to round out; *etw ~ heraus sagen* to state s. th. in plain terms; **~backig** *a* round-cheeked; chubby; **~bahn** *f rail* circular line, *Am* (*Ringbahn der Straßenbahn*) belt line; **~bau** *m* circular building; (*mit Kuppeldach*) rotunda; **~beet** *n* circular bed; **~biegen** *irr tr* to bend; **~bild** *n* panorama (photo); **~blick** *m* panorama, view round; **~~aufsatz** *m* panoramic sight; **~~fernrohr** *n* panoramic telescope; **~bogen** *m arch* Roman arch; round arch; **~~fenster** *n* round-headed window; **~~stil** *m* round style; **~brenner** *m tech* annular (*od* ring) burner; **~e** *f* round; (*Kreis*) circle; (*Polizei*) beat, round; (*Boxen*) round; (*Baseball*) inning; (*Rennsport*) lap, circuit; (*Bier*) round; (*Tafel~~*) party, set; *mil* patrol; *die ~~ machen* to make the rounds, to go o.'s rounds; *in die ~~* around; **~eisen** *n* round iron, *Am* rod iron; **~en** *tr* (*sich*) to round (o. s.), (*vervollständigen*) to round out, to round off, to finish; (*rund machen*) to make round; *abgerundet* well-rounded; **~erhaben** *a* convex; **~erlaß** *m* circular; **~erneuern** *tr* to retread; to rerubber; to cap; **~erneuerung** *f mot* (*Reifen*) retread; **~fahrt** *f* round trip; drive round; circular tour; (*mit Auto etc*) sight-seeing tour; **~~wagen** *m mot* sight-seeing car; **~feile** *f* round file; **~fenster** *n* circular window; **~flug** *m aero* circuit (flight), local flight; (*Platzrunde e-s Flugschülers*) go-round; **~frage** *f* inquiry, questionnaire; **~gang** *m* round; circuit; (*Spaziergang*) stroll; **~gemälde** *n* panorama, panoramic view; **~gesang** *m* glee; roundelay; (*Kanon*) round, catch; **~gespräch** *n* round-table conference; *tele* conference call; **~heit** *f* roundness, sphericity; **~heraus** *adv* plainly, roundly, flatly, in plain terms; **~herum** *adv* round about, all around; **~holz** *n* round timber, log timber, round wood; **~lauf** *m* (*Turngerät*) giant-stride; **~lich** *a* round, roundish; (*dick*) plump; **~naht** *f* circumferential seam; **~reise** *f* circular tour, *Am* round-trip; **~~billet** *n*, **~~(fahr)karte** *f* circular ticket, *Am* round-trip ticket; tourist-ticket; **~schau** *f* panorama; (*Zeitung*) review; **~schiffchen** *n* (*Nähmaschine*) circular shuttle; **~schreiben** *n* circular (letter); (*Papst*) encyclical letter; *~~ richten an* to circularize, *Am* to circulate; **~schrift** *f* round-hand; **~skala** *f* circular dial; **~spruch** *m radio* broadcasting; radiophony; **~stab** *m* rod, round pole; **~stahl** *m* round steel; **~strahler** *m radio* omnidirectional aerial (*Am* antenna); **~strecke** *f* circuit; **~stuhl** *m* circular knitting machine; **~tempel** *m* circular temple; **~um** *adv* round about, all around; **~~verteidigung** *f mil* allround defence; **~ung** *f* roundness; rounding; (*Kurve*) curve; **~verkehr** *m* round-about traffic, gyratory system (of traffic); **~weg** *adv* roundly, plainly, flatly, bluntly; *jdm etw ~~ abschlagen* to give s. o. a flat refusal; **~zange** *f* round nose pliers *pl*

Rundfunk *m* (*siehe auch*: *Funk . . . u. Radio . . .*) broadcast, wireless, *Am meist* radio; radio (broad)casting; *am ~* on the radio, on the air; (*e-e Frage etc*) *am ~ diskutieren* to discuss on the air; *am ~ gastieren* to star on the radio; *am ~ sprechen* to go on the air, to be on the air; *er weigerte sich, am ~ zu sprechen* he refused to go on the air; *durch ~ verbreiten* to broadcast; *durch den ~ mit der Welt in Verbindung bleiben* to keep in radio touch with the world; *Verbreitung durch den ~* radiocasting; *für den ~ besonders geeignet* (*Stimme, Stück etc*) radiogenic; *im ~* on the radio, on the air, in radio; *im ~ auftreten* to make a radio appearance, to be on the air; *~ hören* to listen to, to listen-in; *etw im ~ hören* to get s.th. on the air, to hear s. th. over the air; *das kam im ~* this was broadcast, this was announced over the wireless; *über den ~* on the radio; *über den ~ sprechen* to speak over the radio, to go on the radio; **~abhörstelle** *f* listening post; **~ansager** *m* wireless (*Am* radio) announcer; (*bei Schallplattensendungen*) *Am* disk jockey; **~ansprache** *f* radio address; **~apparat** *m* wireless set, radio set; **~aufnahmeraum** *m* studio; **~auslandskorrespondent** *m* radio foreign correspondent; **~ausrüstung** *f* wireless receiving equipment; **~berater** *m* radio adviser; **~bericht** *m* radio report, (*von Ort u. Stelle*) live radio report; running-commentary (*über* on); **~berichter** *m* radio reporter; **~berichterstattung** *f* radio coverage; *direkte ~~ über den Krieg in Korea* direct radio coverage of the Korean war; **~darbietung** *f* wireless (*Am* radio) program(me), *Am* radio show; **~en** *tr, itr* to broadcast; **~empfang** *m* broadcast (*od* radio) reception; **~empfänger** *m* wireless set, broadcast receiver, radio receiver, radio set; *~~ mit Plattenspieler* radiogram(ophone); **~empfangsstelle** *f* broadcast receiving station; **~entstörungsdienst** *m* radio interference suppression service; **~frequenzband** *n* broadcast band; **~gebühr** *f* charge for wireless; **~gesellschaft** *f* broadcasting company, *Am* radio corporation; **~gottesdienst** *m* radio chapel; **~händler** *m* radio dealer; **~hörer** *m* listener, listener-in; **~~kreis** *m*, **~~schaft** *f* listening audience, radio audience; **~industrie** *f* wireless industry, radio industry; **~künstler** *m* radio artist; **~leitung** *f tech* (*Draht*) broadcast circuit, music (*od* program) circuit; **~liebling** *m* radio favo(u)rite; **~manuskript** *n* radio script; **~mikrophon** *n* radio microphone, *Am fam* mike; **~nachrichten** *f pl* news bulletin, news broadcast, radio news; *~~ hören* to catch the newscast; **~nachrichtenredaktion** *f* radio newsroom; **~nachrichtensendung** *f* newscast; (*von Ort u. Stelle*) live newscast; **~netz** *n* radio network; **~programm** *n* broadcast (*od* radio) program(me), (radio) show; (*ohne Reklameteil*) sustaining program; **~rede** *f* radio address; **~regisseur** *m* radio producer; **~reich** *n Am hum* radiodom; **~reklame** *f* radio advertising; **~~sendung** *f Am* commercial; **~röhre** *f* wireless valve, *Am* radio tube; **~sender** *m* wireless (*od* broadcast) transmitter, broadcasting station (*od* transmitter *od* sender), radio station; **~senderaum** *m* (broadcasting) studio; **~sendung** *f* radio broadcast(ing); (*unter Mitwirkung des Publikums*) *Am* audience participation program; *~~ einstellen* to go off the air; **~sprecher** *m* radio announcer, reporter; broadcaster; **~station** *f* broadcasting station; *~~ im Betrieb* on the air, *außer Betrieb* off the air; *e-e ~~ einstellen* (*im Empfänger*) to tune in a station; **~störungen** *f pl* atmospherics *pl*; **~technik** *f* wireless (*Am* radio) engineering; (*vom Studio aus*) broadcasting technique; **~~er** *m* radio engineer; **~teilnehmer** *m* (broadcast) listener, owner of a wireless set; **~übertragung** *f* broadcast transmission; broadcast relaying, wireless relay(ing); program transmission; re-broadcast; **~vortrag** *m* radio talk; **~welle** *f* broadcast wave; medium-frequency wave; air wave; **~~nlänge** *f* wavelength; **~werbung** *f* radio advertising.

Rune *f* rune; runic letter; **~nartig** *a* runic; **~nschrift** *f* runic writing, runic character(s *pl*); **~nstab** *m* runic wand; **~nstein** *m* runic inscription.

Runge *f* stake, standard, stanchion; **~nwagen** *m rail* platform car, *Am* flat-car.

Runkelrübe *f* beet, *pl Engl* beetroots *pl*, *Am* beets *pl*.

Runse *f* rivulet, rill; gully.

Runzel *f* (*Hautfalte*) wrinkle; (*um den Mund*) pucker; (*um die Augen*) crows' feet; *~n bekommen, ~ig werden* to get wrinkles; **~ig** *a* wrinkled, puckered; (*schrumpelig*) shrivelled; *~~ werden* to wrinkel; (*im Alter*) to shrivel; **~n** *tr* (*sich*) to wrinkle; to fold; to crease; to shrivel, to pucker; *die Brauen ~~* to knit o.'s brows; *die Stirn ~~* to frown.

*

Rüpel *m* lubber, lout; coarse fellow; **~ei** *f* rudeness, insolence; **~haft** *a* insolent; unmannerly; rude, brutal.

rupfen *tr* (*Geflügel*) to pluck; (*ausreißen*) to pull out; *fig* (*betrügen*) to fleece, to cheat; *mit jdm ein Hühnchen zu ~ haben fig* to have a bone to pick with s. o.; *~ m* (*Sackleinwand*) Hessian sack cloth; canvas.

Rupie *f* rupee.

ruppig *a* (*grob, unfreundlich*) rough, rude, brutal, coarse; (*schäbig*) shabby; (*zerlumpt*) ragged; (*armselig*) poor; (*knauserig*) close-fisted, niggardly, mean.

Ruprecht *m*: *Knecht ~* Santa Claus; Father Christmas.

Rüsche *f* (*Mode*) ruche, frilling.

ruschel|ig *a* overhasty; **~n** *itr* (*flüchtig arbeiten*) to work carelessly.

Ruß *m* soot; (*Kien~*) lamp-black; **~ablagerung** *f* deposit of soot; **~en** *itr* to smoke; (*rußig färben*) to smut, to blacken; **~fleck** *m* smut; **~flocke** *f*, **~teilchen** *n* soot flake; sooty particle; **~ig** *a* sooty; *sich ~~ machen* to blacken o. s. with soot; **~schicht** *f* layer of soot; **~tau** *m* sooty mo(u)ld.

Russ|e *m*, **~in** *f* Russian; **~isch** *a* Russian; **Rußland** *n* Russia.

Rüssel *m* (*Schweins~*) snout; (*Elefant*) trunk; (*Schnauze*) muzzle; (*Insekten*) proboscis; **~förmig** *a* trunk-shaped; **~käfer** *m* weevil; **~tier** *n* proboscidian.

Rüst|baum *m* scaffolding-pole, trestle; **~brett** *n* scaffolding plank; **~e** *f* roost, rest; *zur ~~ gehen* (*Geflügel*) to roost, to perch; (*Sonne*) to set; **~en** *tr* (*vorbereiten*) to prepare; (*ausrüsten*) to fit out, to rig out; to equip, to furnish; (*aufrüsten*) to arm, to mobilize; *zum Krieg ~~* to arm, to prepare for war; to mobilize; *gut gerüstet* in fighting condition; *itr* (*sich*) to get ready, to prepare (*zu* for); **~gewicht** *n aero* structural (*od* construction) weight; (gross) tare weight; **~halle** *f* assembling room; erecting shop; **~ig** *a* (*kräftig*) strong, vigorous; robust; (*munter*) alert; (*rührig*) active; *er ist noch ~~* he bears his years well; **~igkeit** *f* vigo(u)r; robustness; activity; **~kammer** *f* armo(u)ry, arsenal; **~ung** *f* (*das Rüsten*) preparation(s *pl*) (*zu* for); (*Ausrüstung*) equipment (*zu* for); (*Bewaffnung*) arming; armament; mobilization; (*Geräte*) implements *pl*; (*Harnisch*) armour, coat of mail; *arch* scaffolding; **~~samt** *n* ordnance department; **~~sanlage** *f*, **~~sbetrieb** *m* armament factory, war factory, munition works *pl*, *Am auch* armory; **~~sanleihe** *f* armament credit; **~~sarbeiter** *m* munition worker; **~~sauftrag** *m* war contract; **~~sausgabe** *f* armament expenditure; **~~sbeschränkung** *f* limitation of armaments; **~~sfabrik** *f* war factory; **~~sfertigung** *f* war production; **~~sindustrie**, **~~swirtschaft** *f* armament industry; war industry; **~~smaterial** *n* armament; **~~spolitik** *f* armament policies *pl*; **~~sstand** *m* state of preparedness; **~~swerk** *n* armament works *pl*, war factory; **~~swettlauf** *m* armament race; **~~szentrum** *n* war production centre; **~zeug** *n* (*Werkzeug*) tools *pl*, set of tools; implements *pl*; *fig* (*Kenntnisse, Wissen*) knowledge; capacities *pl*.

Rüster *f* (*Baum*) elm.

*

Rute *f* rod; (*Gerte*) switch; (*Zweig*) twig, switch; *Wünschel~* divining-rod; *zoo, anat* penis; (*Tierschwanz*) tail; (*Fuchs*) brush; *die ~ geben* to whip; **~nbündel** *n* bundle of rods; fag(g)ot; (*Liktoren*) fasces *pl*; **~ngänger** *m* dowser, water-finder; **~nschlag** *m* stroke with a rod; lash.

Rutsch *m* glide, slide; *Erd~* landslip, *Am* landslide; *ein ~ nach fam* a short trip to; **~bahn** *f* slide, slide-way; chute; (*im Schwimmbad*) water-chute; (*Kinderspielplatz*) playground slide, chute; (*Rummelplatz*) toboggan slide, the slip; *Am* chute-the-chutes; (*Achterbahn*) switch-back (railway), *Am* roller-coaster; *auf der ~~ fahren* to go on the switch-back; **~e** *f tech* chute; slide (-way); **~en** *itr* (*gleiten*) to glide, to slide; *mot* to skid; (*aus~~, ausgleiten*) to slip; (*Erdreich*) to give way, to crumble; (*auf dem Stuhl*) to fidget about; *aero* (*slipen, seitlich ~~*) to side-slip; **~ig** *a* (*Straße*) slippery; **~partie** *f* slide; (*Ausflug*) short excursion; **~sicher** *a* non-skid; **~tuch** *n* (*Feuerwehr*) (fire-) chute, fire-escape, canvas chute.

rütteln *tr, itr* (*durchschütteln*) to shake up; (*stoßen*) to jog; (*hin u. her ~*) to rock; (*Wagen, durch schlechte Straße*) to jolt; *aus dem Schlaf ~* to shake s. o. out of his sleep; *an etw ~ fig* (*Verfassung, Grundlagen etc*) to try to upset, to undermine; *daran kann nicht gerüttelt werden* that's a well-established fact; *ein gerütteltes Maß voll fig* a full (*od* good) measure.

S

S *Abk mit* **S** *siehe Liste der Abk.*

Saal *m* large room, assembly room; hall.

Saargebiet *n* Saar (Basin) Territory.

Saat *f* (*das Säen, die Aussaat*) sowing; (*das Ausgesäte*) seed; (*Getreide auf dem Halm*) green (*od* standing) corn, green-crops *pl*; *die ~ der Zwietracht fig* the seed of discord; *die ~ bestellen* to sow; *die ~ steht schön* the crops are promising, the crops look well; **~beet** *n* seedbed; **~beizmittel** *n* seed disinfectant; **~bestellung** *f* sowing; **~enstand** *m* state of crops; condition of the crops; **~feld** *n* cornfield, seed-field; **~getreide** *n* cereal seed; **~gut, ~korn** *n* seedcorn; **~kartoffel** *f* seed-potato; **~krähe** *f orn* rook; **~schnellkäfer** *m* spring (*od* click) beetle; **~schule** *f* (*für Pflanzen*) nursery; **~wechsel** *m* rotation of crops; **~zeit** *f* seedtime, sowing(-time).

*

Sabbat *m* Sabbath; **~jahr** *n* sabbatic(al) year; **~lich** *a* sabbatic(al); **~schänder** *m* Sabbath breaker; **~schändung** *f* Sabbath breaking.

Sabber|ei *f* slavering, slobbering; *fig* (*Geschwätz*) drivel; **~n** *itr* to slaver, to slobber, to drivel; *Am* to drool; *fig* (*schwatzen, quatschen*) to twaddle; **~tuch, ~lätzchen** *n* (*für Kinder*) bib.

Säbel *m* sabre, *Am* saber; (*Schwert*) sword; *kurzer ~* cutlas; *krummer ~* scimitar; **~beine** *n pl* bow-legs *pl*, bandy legs *pl*; **~beinig** *a* bow-legged, bandy-legged; **~hieb** *m* sword-cut, sabre-cut; **~klinge** *f* sword-blade; **~n** *tr, itr* to (cut with a) sabre; **~rasseln** *n* rattling the sabre; *mit dem ~ ~* to rattle the sabre; *~~der Militarist* sword-rattling militarist.

Sabot|age *f* sabotage; **~ageakt** *m* act of sabotage; **~agetruppe** *f mil* commando (troup), *Am* rangers *pl*; *Angehöriger dieser Spezialtruppe* commando(man), *Am* ranger; **~eur** *m* saboteur; **~ieren** *tr* to sabotage.

Sacharin *n* saccharin(e).

Sach|angabe *f* statement of facts; information, particulars *pl*; **~bearbeiter** *m* referee; expert; professional; compiler; **~beschädigung** *f* damage to property; **~dienlich** *a* relevant, pertinent; appropriate; (*nützlich*) useful; **~e** *f* (*Gegenstand*) thing, object; (*Angelegenheit*) affair; (*geplante ~~*) proposition; (*Geschäft*) business; matter; (*persönliche Angelegenheit*) concern; (*Fall*) case; *jur* case; cause; suit; (*Tat~~*) fact; (*Punkt*) point; (*Ur~~*) cause; (*Geschehnis*) event; occurrance; (*Umstand*) circumstance; *com* (*Artikel*) article; **~en** *pl* (*Habseligkeiten*) things *pl*, chattels *pl*; (*Güter*) goods *pl*; (*Kleider*) clothes *pl*; *abgetragene ~en* old clothes; (*Gepäck*) luggage, belongings *pl*; (*Möbel*) furniture; *fremde ~en* property of another; *meine sieben ~en* all my belongings, my bag and baggage; *e-e abgekartete ~~* a got-up affair, *Am* a put-up job; *e-e gute ~~* (*com*) a good proposition; *e-e heikle ~~* a delicate point; *die ganze ~~* the whole thing; *die vorliegende ~~* the subject in hand, the subject under discussion, the matter in question; *e-e ~~ für sich* a matter apart; *in ~en X. gegen Y. jur* in the case of X. versus Y.; re X. versus Y.; *die ~~ steht schlecht* matters look bad; *das ist e-e ganz andere ~~* that's an entirely different thing; *das ist nicht meine ~~* that's no business of mine; *das ist Ihre ~~* that's your affair, that is your look-out, it's up to you; *das sind ja nette ~en!* that's a nice mess! *lassen Sie die ~~ auf sich beruhen* let the matter rest; *zur ~~ gehörig* relevant; *nicht zur ~~ gehörig* irrelevant; *zur ~~!* to the point! to the business! *parl* Question! *zur ~~ sprechen* to speak to the point; *sich e-r ~~ annehmen* to take a matter in hand; to take charge of; *bei der ~~ bleiben* to stick to the point; *e-e ~~ drehen fam* to wangle; *e-r ~~ aus dem Wege gehen* to avoid s. th.; *zur ~~ kommen* to come to the point, to get down to details, to get down to business, *Am* to get down to brass-tacks; *e-e ~~ laufen lassen* to let things slide; *gemeinsame ~~ machen* to make common cause (*mit* with); *seine ~~ gut* (*schlecht*) *machen* to acquit o. s. well (ill); *bei der ~~ sein* to be intent on; *nicht bei der ~~ sein* to pay no attention to; *seiner ~~ sicher sein* to be sure of o.'s point; *für e-e gute ~~ sterben* to die for a good cause; *seine ~~ verstehen* to be an expert in; *seine ~~ vorbringen* to present o.'s case; **~gebiet** *n* subject; department of knowledge; **~gemäß** *a* appropriate, pertinent, proper; *adv* in a suitable manner; **~katalog** *m* subject catalog(ue); **~kenner** *m* expert; (*Kunst*) connoisseur; **~kenntnis** *f* expert knowledge, experience; practical experience, special knowledge; competence; **~kunde** *f* expert knowledge; **~kundig** *a* experienced, expert, versed; competent; (*beruflich*) skilled; trained in a profession; **~~e(r)** *m* expert; (*Kunst*) connoisseur; **~lage** *f* state of affairs, factual situation; (*Umstand*) circumstance; **~leistung** *f* payment in kind, performance in kind; **~lich** *a* (*treffend*) to the point, pertinent; (*bestimmt*) real, positive; (*gegenständlich*) objective; (*tatsächlich*) factual, material; real; essential; technical; (*unparteiisch*) impartial, impersonal; unbiassed; (*von Personen*) matter-of-fact; (*Architektur*) practical; *~~ bleiben* to stick to the facts; **~lichkeit** *f* reality, objectivity; realism; *die neue ~~* the new practicality; **~register** *n* (subject) index, table of contents; **~schaden** *m* damage to property; property damage; material damage; **~~ersatz** *m* compensation (*od* indemnity) for property damage; **~verhalt** *m* state of affairs, facts of a case; circumstances (of a case); factual situation; **~vermögen** *n* tangible property; **~verständig** *a* experienced, versed; **~verständige(r)** *m* expert, authority; specialist; **~verständigengutachten** *n* expert's opinion; **~verzeichnis** *n* subject index; **~walter** *m* advocate; legal adviser; attorney, counsel; caretaker; **~wert** *m* real (*od* actual) value; **~~e** *m pl* goods of material value; **~wörterbuch** *n* encyclop(a)edia; **~zuwendung** *f* (*Sachbezüge*) payment in kind.

sächlich *a* neuter.

Sachs|e *m* Saxon; **~en** *n* Saxony; **sächsisch** *a* Saxon.

sacht(e) *a* light, gentle; (*langsam*) slow; *adv* (*vorsichtig*) gingerly; (*Ausruf*) gently! take time! *~! ~!* come, come!

Sack *m* bag, sack; (*Tasche*) pocket; pouch; *e-n ~ voll Neuigkeiten* a budget of news; *mit ~ u. Pack* with bag and baggage; *jdn in den ~ stecken* to nonplus s. o.; *die Katze im ~ kaufen* to buy a pig in a poke; *wie ein ~ schlafen* to sleep like a top; **~artig** *a* baggy; **~bahnhof** *m* dead-end station.

Säck|chen *n* little bag; **~el** *m* purse; **~elmeister** *m* bursar, treasurer.

sack|en *tr* to sack, to fill; to put into sacks; *itr r* (*sich setzen*) to settle, to give way; to sink, to sag; **~flug** *m aero* stalled flight, stalling flight; **~~geschwindigkeit** *f* stalling speed; **~~landung** *f* stall landing; **~garn** *n* sack-thread, twine; **~gasse** *f* blind alley; cul-de-sac, dead end (street); *fig* dilemma; stalemate, *Am* sidetrack; impasse; *in e-e ~~ gelangen* to reach an impasse; *ein Weg aus der ~~* a way out of the impasse; **~hüpfen** *n* sack-race; **~landung** *f aero* stalled landing; pancake landing; **~leinwand** *f* sacking, sackcloth; **~pfeife** *f* bagpipe; **~träger** *m* porter, sack-heaver; *fig* ass; **~tuch** *n* sacking; (*Schnupftuch*) pocket-handkerchief; **~zucker** *m* sugar in bags.

Sadis|t *m* sadist; **~mus** *m* sadism; **~tisch** *a* sadistic.

Sä(e)|mann *m* sower; **~maschine** *f* sowing-machine, drill-plough; **~n** *tr* to sow; *dünn gesät fig* sparse (population); *Zwietracht ~* to sow discord; **~tuch** *n* seed-bag; **~zeit** *f* sowing-time.

Saffian *m* morocco, Spanish leather; **~fabrikant** *m* morocco-dresser.

Safran *m* saffron; **~gelb** *a* saffron yellow, saffron.

Saft *m* (*Obst~*) juice; (*Pflanzen~*) sap; (*Flüssigkeit*) fluid; (*Fleisch~*) gravy; (*Säfte des Körpers*) humo(u)rs of the body; *ohne ~ u. Kraft* stale, insipid; **~grün** *a* sap-green; **~ig** *a* sappy, juicy, succulent; *fig* lush; spicy; **~los** *a* sapless; juiceless; *fig* insipid.

Sage *f* legend, myth; (*Überlieferung*) tradition; tale; *es geht die ~* the story goes; **~nhaft** *a* mythical, legendary, fabulous; (*überliefert*) traditional; **~nkreis** *m* legendary cycle.

Säge *f* saw; **~artig** *a* sawlike; (*gezackt*) serrated; **~blatt** *n* saw-blade; **~bock** *m* sawing-trestle, jack, sawhorse, *Am* sawbuck; **~fisch** *m* sawfish; **~mehl** *n*, **~späne** *m pl* sawdust; **~mühle** *f* sawmill; **~r** *m* sawer, sawyer; **~werk** *n* sawmill; **~zahn** *m* saw tooth; **~~artig** *a* saw-toothed.

sagen *tr* to say; (*mitteilen*) to tell; (*sprechen*) to speak; (*befehlen*) to command; (*bedeuten*) to mean, to signify; *sagen wir . . .* suppose, say . . .; *sozu~* so to say, as it were; *auswendig ~* to say by heart; *~ lassen* to send word; *sie läßt sich nichts ~* she will not listen to reason; *er hat sich ~ lassen, daß* he has been told that; *die Meinung ~* to give s. o. a piece of o.'s mind; *das brauchen Sie mir gerade noch zu ~!* you're telling me! *nichts zu ~ haben* to have no say in; *es hat nichts zu ~* it is no matter, it does not matter, never mind; *gesagt, getan* no sooner said than done; *was soll man dazu ~?* it is incredible; *was wollen Sie damit ~?* what are you driving at? what are you alluding to (*od* aiming at)? *nebenbei gesagt* by the way; by the by; *wie gesagt* as I said before; *unter uns gesagt* between you and me; *was Sie nicht ~!* (*ironisch*) *Am sl* sez you! *laß dir das gesagt sein* let it be a warning to you; *jdm gute Nacht ~* to bid s. o. good night.

Sago *m* sago; *weißer ~* tapioca.

Sahne *f* cream; *die ~ abschöpfen* to skim the cream off; **~bonbon** *n* toffee, toffy, *Am* taffy; **~neis** *n* cream-ice, *Am* ice-cream; **~nkäse** *m* cream-cheese; **~ntorte** *f* cream-tart.

Saison *f* season; *stille* (*od tote*) *~* dead season, off-season, dull time; *außerhalb der ~* in the off-season; *Hoch~* height of the season; **~arbeit** *f* seasonal work; **~arbeiter** *m* seasonal worker; **~artikel** *m* seasonal article; **~ausverkauf** *m* clearance sale, seasonal sale; **~einfluß** *m* seasonal influence; **~schwankungen** *f pl* seasonal fluctuations *pl*; **~tarif** *m* seasonal tariff.

Saite *f* string, chord; *mit ~n bespannen* to string an instrument; *die richtige ~ anschlagen* to strike a responsive chord; *die ~n zu hoch spannen* to strain the strings too high; *gelindere ~n aufziehen* to come down a peg or two; **~ninstrument** *n* stringed instrument; **~nspiel** *n* string music.

Sakko *m* lounge jacket; **~anzug** *m* lounge suit, *Am* business suit.

Sakrament *n* sacrament; *das ~ des Altars* the Lord's Supper, the Eucharist; *das ~ spenden* to administer the sacrament; **~lich** *a* sacramental.

Sakrist|an *m* sacristan, sexton; **~ei** *f* vestry; sacristy.

säkularis|ieren *tr* to secularize; **~ierung** *f* secularization.

Salamander *m* salamander.

Salami *f* (*Wurst*) salame (sausage).

Salat *m* salad; (*Pflanze*) lettuce; **~öl** *n* salad-oil; **~schüssel** *f* salad-dish.

Salbader *m* idle prattler, twaddler; (*Quacksalber*) quack; **~ei** *f* idle talk, twaddle; **~n** *itr* to twaddle.

Sal|band *n*, **~leiste** *f* list, selvedge, selvage; *geol* gouge.

Salb|e *f* ointment, unguent, salve, liniment; (*Pomade*) pomade; **~ei** *m od f* (garden-)sage; **~en** *tr* to anoint; *poet* to salve; **~ung** *f* anointing; *fig* unction; **~~svoll** *a* unctuous, pathetic.

sald|ieren *tr* to balance, to clear; to settle, to square; **~o** *m* balance; *den ~o ziehen* to strike the balance; **~okonto** *n* current account book; **~ovortrag** *m* balance forward.

Saline *f* salt-pit, saline, salt-works *pl*.

Salizylsäure *f* salicylic acid.

Salm *m* salmon.

Salmiak *m* sal ammoniac, ammonium chloride; **~element** *n el* sal ammoniac cell; **~geist** *m* liquid (*od* aqueous) ammonia; **~salz** *n* sal ammoniac; ammonium chloride.

Salon *m* drawing-room; *Am* parlor; (*auf Schiffen*) saloon; **~bolschewik** *m* drawing-room Bolshevist, *Am* parlor Red, pink; **~fähig** *a* presentable; **~flieger** *m* arm-chair pilot; **~held**, **~löwe** *m* ladies' man, carpet-knight, *Am* lounge-lizard; **~wagen** *m rail* Pullman coach, saloon carriage, *Am* parlor-car, *Am* chair-car.

salopp *a* slovenly.

Salpeter *m* saltpetre, *Am* saltpeter, nitre, *Am* niter, sodium nitrate; **~artig** *a* nitrous; **~bildung** *f* nitrification; **~erde** *f* nitrous earth; **~grube**, **~hütte** *f* saltpetre works *pl*; **~ig** *a* nitrous; **~sauer** *a* nitrate of, nitric; *~~es Natron* sodium nitrate; *~~es Salz* nitrate; *~~e Tonerde* aluminium (*Am* aluminum) nitrate; **~säure** *f* nitric acid; **~siederei** *f* saltpetre-manufactory.

Salto *m* somersault; (*~ mortale*) breakneck leap.

Salut *m* salute (of guns), rifle salute; *ein ~ von 12 Schuß* a twelve-gun salute; *~ schießen* to fire a salute; **~ieren** *tr, itr* to salute.

Salv|e *f* volley; burst; (*Geschütz~*) salvo; (*ein Schuß aus jedem Rohr*) round; (*Ehren~*) salute; *e-e ~~ abgeben* to fire a volley; *mar* to deliver a broadside; to fire a salute; **~engeschütz** *n* salvo gun; multiple rocket launcher; **~ieren** *tr* to save.

Salz *n* salt; *in ~ legen* to salt away, to salt down; **~artig** *a* saline; **~bad** *n* salt bath; **~bergwerk** *n* salt-mine; **~brühe** *f* brine, souse; **~brunnen** *m* saline spring; **~en** *tr* to salt, to season (with salt); to pickle; *zu stark ge~~* salted too much; *ge~~e Preise* exorbitant prices; **~faß** *n* salt-box; **~fäßchen**, **~näpfchen** *n* salt-cellar; **~fleisch** *n* corned (*od* salt) meat; **~gurke** *f* pickled cucumber; **~haltig** *a* saliferous; **~handel** *m* salt-trade; **~händler** *m* saltman, salter; **~hering** *m* pickled (*od* salted) herring; **~ig** *a* salty, briny; (*gesalzen*) salted; (*Wasser*) brackish; **~igkeit** *f* saltness; **~korn** *n* grain of salt; **~lake** *f* pickle, souse; brine; **~lecke** *f* salt lick; **~niederschlag** *m* saline deposit; **~säure** *f* hydrochloric acid; **~see** *m* salt-lake; **~sieder** *m* salt-maker; **~siederei** *f* salt-works *pl*; **~sole** *f* salt-spring; **~steuer** *f* salt-duty, salt-tax; **~streuer** *m* salt shaker; **~wasser** *n* salt-water; brine; **~werk** *n* saltery, salt-works *pl*; (*zur Meersalzgewinnung durch Verdunsten*) saltern.

Samariter *m* Samaritan; *der barmherzige ~* the good Samaritan.

Samen, Same *m* seed; (*der Tiere*) sperm; (*der Fische*) spawn; (*vom Menschen*) semen; (*Nachkommenschaft*) posterity; *in ~ schießen* to run to seed; **~behälter** *m* seed-vessel; **~bildung** *f* seed formation; **~drüse** *f* spermatic gland; testicle; **~faden** *m* spermatozoid; **~flüssigkeit** *f* seminal fluid; **~gang** *m* spermatic duct; **~gehäuse** *n* core, pericarp, seedcase; **~händler** *m* seed merchant; **~hülle** *f* episperm; perisperm; **~kapsel** *f* seed-pod; capsule; **~korn** *n* grain of seed; **~staub** *m* pollen; **~tierchen** *n* spermatozoon; **~tragend** *a* seed-bearing; **~zelle** *f* seminal cell; spermatozoon; **~zwiebel** *f* seed bulb.

Sämerei(en) *f* (*pl*) seeds *pl*.

sämisch *a* chamois-dressed; **~leder** *n* wash-leather, chamois leather; **~gerber** *m* chamois-dresser.

Sammel|anschluß *m tele* collective numbers *pl*; private branch exchange (line); **~~teilnehmer** *m tele* subscriber with several lines; **~bahnhof** *m* central terminus; railway (*od Am* railroad) collecting point; **~band** *m* (omnibus) volume; (*gesammelte Werke*) collected works *pl*; **~batterie** *f el* storage battery, accumulator; **~becken** *n* (*Behälter*) reservoir, basin, cistern; sump; receiver; collecting tank, storage tank; storage bin; **~begriff** *m*, **~bezeichnung** *f* collective name;

~**bogen** *m* recapitulation sheet; ~**büchse** *f* collecting box, charity box; ~**buchung** *f* compound entry; ~**fahrschein** *m rail* ticket for group of travel(l)ers; ~**gebiet** *n* (*für Wasser*) water gathering ground; catchment basin; ~**gefäß** *n* collecting vessel; receiver, reservoir; ~**gespräch** *n tele* conference call, round call; ~~**seinrichtung** *f* conference calling equipment; ~~**verbindung** *f* conference call connection; ~**gut** *n* (*Spedition*) mixed consignment, bulk goods *pl*; ~**heizung** *f* central heating; ~**konto** *n* general account; ~**ladung** *f* collective consignment (*od* shipment), groupage; collective truck, *Am* consolidated (*od* combined) carload; ~**lager** *n* collecting point (*od* camp), central camp; ~**lazarett** *n mil* collecting hospital; ~**leitung** *f tele* collecting line, omnibus circuit; ~**linse** *f* convex (*od* converging) lens; focussing lens; ~**liste** *f* register; ~**n** *tr* (*ein~*) to gather; (*für e-n bestimmten Zweck, Münzen, Briefmarken etc*) to collect; (*anhäufen*) to accumulate; (*aufhäufen*) to amass; to treasure up; to store up, to stock, to heap up; (*auflesen*) to pick (up); (*ernten*) to harvest; *mil* to concentrate, (*wieder~~*) to rally; (*in e-m Brennpunkt*) to focus; (*Abonnenten, Inserate ~~*) to canvass for subscribers (*od* ads); (*aus verschiedenen Schriften*) to compile; (*Neuigkeiten ~~*) to pick up news; (*Kenntnisse*) to acquire; *für die Armen ~~* to make (*od* to raise) a collection for the poor, *fam* to send round the hat for the poor; *sich ~~* to gather, to assemble; (*in e-m Punkt*) to converge; (*zu Scharen*) to flock together; (*wieder ~~*) to rally; *fig* (*sich fassen*) to compose o. s., to recover o. s.; to collect o.'s thought; (*sich zusammenreißen*) to pull o. s. together; ~**name** *m* general (*od* collective) term; collective noun; ~**nummer** *f tele* collective number; directory number; ~**paß** *m* collective passport; ~**platz** *m* meeting place, collecting place; assembly point; place of appointment; *mil* rallying point, rendezvous; collecting station; (*Ansammlung*) assemblage, gathering; (*Depot*) depot, dump; ~**punkt** *m opt* (*Brennpunkt*) focal point; (*Treffpunkt*) meeting place, rallying point; ~**referat** *n* collective review; ~**ruf** *m mil* (*Signal*) assembly; *radio* general call; *tele* collective call, general call; *fig* (*Wahlspruch, Losung, Schlagwort*) rallying cry, slogan; ~**schiene** *f el* bus-bar, omnibus bar, distributing bar; ~**schutz** *m* public protection, collective protection; ~~**raum** *m* (*Luftschutz*) public air-raid shelter; ~**sendung** *f* collective shipment; ~**spiegel** *m* concave mirror; ~**stelle** *f* central depot, collecting centre; collecting point; salvage dump; ~**surium** *n* medley, jumble; *fam* (*Durcheinander*) mess, hodge-podge; ~**transport** *m* collective transport; ~**unterkunft** *f* collective quarters *pl*; ~**verbindung** *f tele* conference circuit; ~**werk** *n* compilation; ~**wort** *n* collective noun.

Samml|er *m* gatherer; collector; (*Zusammensteller aus verschiedenen Werken*) compiler; *el* accumulator, secondary cell, storage cell; ~~**batterie** *f* accumulator, *Am* (storage-) battery; ~~**kasten** *m* battery crate, *Am* battery box (*od* case); ~~**kraftwagen** *m* battery car; ~~**zelle** *f* accumulator cell, *Am* storage cell; secondary cell; ~**ung** *f* collection; accumulation; set; *ausgewählte ~~* choice collection; (*Zusammenscharen*) rally (*um* round); (*für Arme*) subscription; *mil* assembly; (*Blütenlese, Auswahl*) selection; (*Gedichts~~*) anthology; chrestomathy; (*Gesetzes~~*) body of law; *fig* (*innere Fassung*) composure; (*Konzentration*) concentration.

Samowar *m* samovar.

Samstag *m* Saturday; (*des*) *~s* on Saturdays.

samt *prp* together with; along with; including; *adv*: *~ u. sonders* all together, each and all, one and all, jointly and severally.

Samt *m* velvet; (*für Hüte*) velure; *baumwollener ~* velveteen, cotton-velvet; *in ~ u. Seide* in silk and satin; ~**artig** *a* velvet, velvety, velvet-like; ~**band** *n* velvet ribbon; ~**en** *a* velvety; ~**fabrik** *f* velvet factory; ~**glanz** *m* velvet gloss; ~**handschuh** *m* velvet glove; *jdn mit ~~en anfassen fig* to touch s. o. with kid gloves on; ~**kleid** *n* velvet dress; ~**pfötchen** *n*: *~~ machen fig* to put on velvet gloves; ~**schwarz** *a* velvet black; ~**weber** *m* velvet maker; ~**weich** *a* velvety, soft as velvet; ~**weste** *f* velvet waistcoat.

sämtlich *a* (*vollständig*) whole, complete; *~e Werke Shakespeare's* Shakespeare's complete works; *adv* (*alle*) all, all together, all of them; to a man.

Samum *m* simoom.

Sanatorium *n* sanatorium, health resort, *Am* sanitarium.

Sand *m* sand; (*grober ~*) grit; (*ganz feiner ~*) quick-sand, shifting sand; fine-grain sand; (*Kies*) gravel; *auf ~ bauen fig* to build on the sands, to plough the sand(s); *auf ~ geraten* to ground; *im ~ verlaufen fig* to come to nothing, to peter out; *mit ~ bestreuen* to sand; *jdm ~ in die Augen streuen fig* to throw dust in s. o.'s eyes; *wie ~ am Meer* as the sand of the sea; ~**ablagerung** *f* deposition of sand; ~**anschwemmung** *f* encroachment by sand; ~**artig** *a* sandlike, sandy; arenaceous; ~**aufbereitung** *f* sand preparation; ~~**sanlage** *f* sand-preparing plant; ~**bad** *n chem* sand bath; ~**bank** *f* sandbank, sand bar; layer of sand, arenaceous deposit; sands *pl*; shoal, shallowness, shallows *pl*; *auf e-e ~~ geraten mar* to strike the sands; ~**blatt** *n* (*Zigarre*) shrub; ~**boden** *m* sandy soil; ~**büchse** *f*, ~**faß** *n* sand box; ~**düne** *f* sand dune; ~**ebene** *f* sandy plain; ~**en** *tr* to sand, to gravel; ~**farben** *a* sand-colo(u)red; ~**floh** *m* sand flea, sand hopper; ~**form** *f* sand mo(u)ld; ~~**erei** *f* sand mo(u)lding; ~**gebirge** *f* sandy mountains *pl*; ~**gebläse** *n tech* sandblast; ~**gegend** *f* sandy region, *Am* sandbowl; ~**gewächse** *n pl* arenarious plants *pl*; ~**glimmer** *m* mica; ~**gras** *n* sand grass (*od* reed); ~**gries** *m* coarse sand, gravel; ~**grube** *f* sandpit, gravel pit; ~**hafer** *m* lyme grass; ~**haltig** *a* arenaceous; ~**hase** *m mil sl* infantryman; ~**haufen** *m* heap of sand; ~**hose** *f* gyrating column of sand; sand spout; ~**hügel** *m* sandhill; ~**huhn** *n bot* sand grouse; ~**ig** *a* sandy; sabulous; arenaceous; (*kiesig*) gritty; *~~e Beschaffenheit* grittiness; ~**kasten** *m* sand box; sand model; ~**korn** *n* grain of sand; ~**kraut** *n bot* sandwort; ~**mann** *m* sandman; ~**mergel** *m* sandy marl; ~**papier** *n* sandpaper; *mit ~~ (ab)schleifen* to sand, to sandpaper; ~**rücken** *m* sand ridge; hogback; ~**sack** *m* sandbag, ballast sack; *mit e-m ~~ niederschlagen Am* to sandbag; ~~**barrikade** *f* sandbag barricade; ~~**bekleidung** *f* sandbag revetment; ~**schicht** *f* layer of sand; ~**stein** *m* sandstone, freestone, *Am* (*zum Bauen*) brownstone; *geol* gritstone; *bunter ~~* new-red sandstone; ~~**bruch** *m* sandstone quarry; ~~**gebäude** *n Am* brownstone; ~~**mauerwerk** *n* sandstone walling; ~**strahl** *m* sandblast; sand jet; ~~**en** *tr* to sandblast; ~~**gebläse** *n* sandblast, sandblasting equipment; ~**streuer** *m* sander; ~**sturm** *m* sandstorm, duststorm; ~~**gebiet** *n Am* (*im Westen der USA*) dust bowl; ~**torte** *f* sponge-cake, Madeira cake; ~**uhr** *f* sandglass, hourglass; ~**weg** *m* sandy road; ~**wüste** *f* sands *pl*, sandy desert; ~**zucker** *m* raw ground sugar, brown sugar.

Sandale *f* sandal.

Sandelholz *n* sandalwood.

sanforisieren *tr Am* to sanforize.

sanft *a* soft; (*zart*) tender, delicate; (*mild*) mild; (*~mütig*) meek; (*lieblich*) sweet; (*glatt*) smooth; (*ruhig*) quiet, calm; (*leicht*) gentle; slight; (*Tod*) peaceful; *~er Abhang* easy gradient; *e-s ~en Todes sterben* to die an easy death; *~ wie ein Lamm* gentle as a lamb; *~ lächeln* to smile gently; *ruhe ~!* rest in peace! *~er Zwang* non-violent coercion; ~**heit** *f* softness; smoothness; mildness; gentleness; ~**mut** *f* gentleness, sweetness; meekness; placidness, placidity; ~**mütig** *a* gentle, placid; meek, mild.

Sänfte *f* sedan-chair, litter; ~**nträger** *m* sedan-chair man.

Sang *m* song; singing; *mit ~ u. Klang* with ringing bells; *ohne ~ u. Klang* with muffled drums; *fig* quietly, silently, unceremoniously; ~**bar** *a* singable; melodious; ~**esfroh** *a* fond of singing.

Sänger *m* singer; (*Vogel*) songster; (*Minne~*) minstrel; *poet* (*Dichter*) poet; (*Volkslied-, Schlagersänger*) crooner; (*Chor~*) choir-boy; ~**fest** *n* choral festival, singing festival; ~**in** *f* songstress, singer, opera-singer.

Sanguin|iker *m* sanguine person; ~**isch** *a* sanguine.

sanier|en *tr* to restore; to reorganize, to reconstruct; (*Finanzen e-s Geschäftes*) to put on a sound basis; to stabilize: to relieve; (*heilen*) to cure, to restore to health; (*Gebiet etc*) to improve the sanitary conditions of; ~**ung** *f* renovation; (financial) reorganization, reconstruction; stabilization; *med* sanitation; (*Wiederherstellung*) restoration; ~~**splan** *m* reorganization plan, reconstruction plan; ~~**sstation** *f med* (*zur Schutzbehandlung gegen Geschlechtskrankheit*) prophylactic station.

sanitä|r *a* sanitary, hygienic; ~**t** *f* sanitation, hygiene; health; ~**ter** *m* ambulance man, first-aid man, sanitary man; *mil* medical orderly, hospital orderly, stretcher-bearer, *Am* corpsman.

Sanitäts|artikel *m pl* sanitary articles *pl*; ~**ausrüstung** *f* medical equipment; ~**auto** *n* (motor) ambulance; ~**bedarf** *m* medical supply requirement; ~**behörde** *f* Board of Health; health commission; ~**bericht** *m* medical report; ~**dienst** *m* medical service; Army Medical Corps, *Am* Medical Department; ~**einrichtung** *f* medical installation; ~**flugzeug** *n* ambulance plane; ~**großflugzeug** *n* air-borne ambulance; ~**hund** *m* first-aid dog, ambulance dog; ~**kasten** *m* medicine chest, surgical chest; first-aid box (*od* kit); ~**kolonne** *f* ambulance column; **~korps** *n* Army Medical Corps (*Abk* A.M.C.), *Am* Medical Department (*Abk* M.D.); **~kraftwagen** *m* motor ambulance, ambulance, ambulance van, *mil* field ambulance; **~~abteilung** *f mil* motor-ambulance section; **~maßregel** *f* sanitary measure; **~offizier** *m* medical officer; public health officer, sanitary inspector, *Am sl* medic; **~park** *m* medical depot; **~personal** *n* medical personnel; **~polizei** *f* sanitary police, sanitary inspectors *pl*; **~soldat** *m* medical (*od* hospital) orderly; soldier in the A.M.C., *Am* corpsman; **~tasche** *f* first-aid outfit; **~wache** *f* sanitary station, first-aid post (*od* station); **~wagen** *m* (motor) ambulance; **~waren** *f pl* sanitary articles *pl*; **~wesen** *n* sanitation, sanitary matters *pl*; medical service, medical branch (*Abk* M.B.); hygiene; **~zug** *m rail* (*Lazarettzug*) ambulance (*od* hospital) train.

Sanka *m* (= *Sanitätskraftwagen*) *mil* field ambulance, motor ambulance.

Sankt *a* (*Abk St.*) Saint (*Abk* St.); **~ Elmsfeuer** *n* Saint Elmo's fire; **~ Nikolaus** *m* Santa Claus.

Sankt|ion *f* (*Billigung*) sanction; (*Zwangsmaßnahme*) sanction, compulsory measures *pl*; **~ionieren** *tr* to sanction; **~ionistisch** *a* sanctionist; **~uarium** *n* (*Heiligtum*) sanctuary.

Saphir *m* sapphire; **~spat** *m* cyanite.

Sappe *f* sap (trench).

sapperlot! sapperment! zounds! the deuce! the dickens! deuced! by Jove! *Am* Gee whiz!

Sard|elle *f* sardelle, anchovy; **~ine** *f* sardine; pilchard; *~~n gefüllt* stuffed sardines; *~~n in Öl* sardines in oil; **~~nbrötchen** *n* sardine sandwich; **~~nöl** *n* sardine oil; **~inien** *n* Sardinia; **~isch** *a* Sardinian.

sardonisch *a* sardonic; *~es Lachen* sardonic laugh.

Sarg *m* coffin, *Am auch* casket; **~deckel** *m* coffin-lid; **~tuch** *n* pall.

Sarkas|mus *m* sarcasm; mordacity; (*Bemerkung*) sarcastic remark, hit; **~tisch** *a* sarcastic, biting, slashing; (*ironish*) ironical.

Sarkophag *m* sarcophagus.

Satan *m* (*Teufel*) Satan, devil, fiend; **~isch** *a* satanic, devilish; fiendish, diabolic, infernal; **~sbraten** *m* devil's brood; **~skerl** *m* devil of a fellow.

Satellit *m* satellite; **~enstaat** *m* satellite state.

Satin *m* satin; (*Baumwoll~*) sateen; **~ieren** *tr* to satin, to glaze; (*Papier*) to calender, to glaze; **~papier** *n* glazed paper, atlas; **~weiß** *a* satin white.

Satir|e *f* satire; **~iker** *m* satirist; **~isch** *a* satiric(al).

satt *a* satisfied, full; satiated; (*Farbe*) saturated; (*intensiv, leuchtend*) rich, dark, deep; *fig* (*überdrüssig*) weary of, tired of, sick of; *ich bin ~* I have had enough; *sind Sie ~?* are you full? *ein ~er Bauch* a full stomach; *ein ~es Grün* a dark green; *etw ~ bekommen* (*fam kriegen*) to get tired (*od* sick) of; *etw ~ haben* to have had enough of, to be sick of, *fam* to be fed up with; *e-r Sache ~ werden* to get tired of; *sich ~ essen* to eat o.'s fill (*an* of); *sich ~ trinken* to drink o.'s fill (*an* of); *ich kann mich nicht ~ sehen* I cannot take my eyes off; **~heit** *f* satiety; (*Farben*) richness, deepness; **~sam** *a* sufficient; *adv* enough; sufficiently.

Satte *f* bowl, dish; milk-pan.

Sattel *m* saddle; *fam* pigskin; (*Nasen~, Geigen~*) bridge; (*Berg~*) ridge; pass; *typ* gallows *pl*; *in allen Sätteln gerecht* to be good at everything, to be fit for anything; *aus dem ~ heben* to dismount, to unhorse; *fig* to supersede, to supplant; **~baum, ~bogen** *m* saddle-tree, saddle-bow; **~dach** *n* saddle roof, ridged roof; **~decke** *f* saddle-cloth; **~fest** *a* firm in the saddle; to have a good seat; *fig* to be well versed in s. th., to be well up in, to be quite firm in; **~gurt** *m* belly-band, girth; *Am* cinch; **~kissen** *n* panel, pillion, pad; **~knecht** *m* groom; **~knopf** *m* pommel; **~n** *tr* to saddle; **~pferd** *n* saddle-horse; riding-horse; near horse; **~platz** *m* paddock; **~schlepper** *m mot* articulated six-wheeler, saddle tractor, tractor lorry, *Am* semitrailer (truck), truck tractor; **~~anhänger** *m* semitrailer; **~tasche** *f* saddle-bag; **~trunk** *m* stirrup-cup; **~zeug** *n* saddle and harness.

sättig|en *tr* (*befriedigen*) to satisfy, to fill, to satiate; *poet* to sate; *tech, chem* to saturate; (*durchdringen*) to impregnate; *jdn ~~* to appease s. o.'s hunger; **~end** *a* nourishing, satisfying; **~ung** *f* (*Hunger*) appeasing; satiation, satiety; (*Befriedigung*) satisfaction; *chem, tech* saturation; impregnation; neutralisation; **~~sdruck** *m* saturation pressure; **~~sfähig** *a* capable of saturation; **~~sgefühl** *n* sense of satiation; **~~sgrad** *m* degree of saturation; **~~spunkt** *m* saturation point.

Sattler *m* saddler; harness-maker; **~ei** *f* saddlery, saddler's trade; saddler's workshop; **~meister** *m* master harness-maker.

saturieren *tr* to saturate; to carbonate.

Satz *m* (*Sprung*) leap, bound; jump; (*Boden~*) dregs *pl*, lees *pl*; (*Kaffee*) grounds *pl*, sediment; *mus* movement; (*Druck*) composition; matter; copy; setting; (*Tennis*) set; (*Spiel, Wette*) stake; (*Rede~*) sentence, phrase, clause, period; *einfacher ~* simple sentence; *zusammengesetzter ~* compound sentence; *Haupt~* main clause, principal clause; (*beigeordneter*) co-ordinate main clause; *Neben~* subordinate clause; *hauptwörtlicher ~* substantive clause; *Umstands~* adverbial clause; *verkürzter ~* phrase; *Infinitiv~* infinitive phrase; (*Garnitur*) assortment; set; (*Fischbrut*) young fry; (*Junge*) nest; (*Behauptung*) proposition; thesis; (*Lehr~*) tenet; (*Leit~*) axiom, theorem, maxim; *math* problem; *com* fixed sum; (*Tarif*) rate; (*Betrag*) amount; (*Gebühr*) fee; (*Preis, Wert*) price, rate; *in ~ geben typ* to give to the printer; *den ~ stehen lassen typ* to keep up; *zum ~ von com* at the rate of; *höchster ~ (com)* maximum rate; **~anordnung** *f typ* graphical arrangement; **~aussage** *f gram* predicate; **~bau** *m gram* construction; **~bild** *n typ* setting; **~fehler** *m* typographical error, misprint, printing mistake; **~gefüge** *n* complex sentence; **~kosten** *pl* costs of composition; **~laus** *f typ* imperfection; **~lehre** *f gram* syntax; **~regal** *n typ* composing frame; **~spiegel** *m typ* face, type area; (*Zeitung*) dummy; **~ung** *f* (fixed) rule, regulation, ordinance; (*von Körperschaften*) by-law(s *pl*); statute(s *pl*); (*städtische*) *Am* city-ordinance; (*Gesetz*) law; (*Vereine, Gesellschaften etc*) article(s *pl*) of association; **~~sänderung** *f* alteration of the statutes; **~~smäßig** *a* statutory; **~weise** *adv* by leaps; intermittent; sentence by sentence; **~zeichen** *n gram* punctuation mark; **~~setzung** *f* punctuation.

Sau *f* sow, hog; (*Jagd*) wild boar; *fig* dirty fellow; *vulg* slut; *fam* (*Glück*) luck; *fam* (*Tintenklecks*) blot of ink; splotch; *tech* (*Eisen*) sow; (*Darre*) drying kiln; *wilde ~* wild sow; *zur ~ machen mil sl* to smash up; **~arbeit** *f fam* drudgery, very hard (*od* disgusting) work; **~bohne** *f bot* broad bean, horse bean, fodder bean, soybean; **~borste** *f* hog's bristle; **~dumm** *a fam* very (*od* awfully) stupid; **~fraß** *m* hogwash; *fam* bad food; **~grob** *a fam* very rude, rude as a boor; **~hatz, ~jagd** *f* boar hunt; **~hirt** *m* swine-herd; **~igeln** *itr fam* to talk obscenely; **~kerl** *m fam* dirty fellow, beast; swine; **~koben** *m* hog-sty, *Am* hog-pen; **~leben** *n fam* beastly life; **~mäßig** *a fam* beastly, filthy; **~mensch** *n vulg* slut, wench; **~pech** *n fam* rotten luck; **~stall** *m* hog-sty, pigsty, *Am* hog-pen; *fam* piggery, nasty mess, maladministration; **~wetter** *n fam* beastly weather; **~wirtschaft** *f fam* filthy mess, maladministration; **~wohl** *a fam* awfully jolly, top-hole, cheerful as a sand-boy.

sauber *a* clean; (*nett*) neat, tidy, *fam* natty; (*hübsch*) pretty, snug; (*gut gearbeitet*) accurate, workmanlike; (*ironisch*) nice, pretty, fine; *e-e ~e Bescherung* a fine (*od* pretty *od* nice) mess; *e-e ~e Geschichte* a nice kettle of fish; *ein ~es Früchtchen* a promising young rascal; *peinlich ~* spick and span; *~ machen* to clean (up); **~keit** *f* cleanness, neatness; prettiness.

säuber|lich *a* clean, neat; (*anständig*) proper, decent; **~n** *tr* to clear; to clean, to cleanse; *ein Zimmer ~~* to turn out; *mil* (*ein Gebiet von Feindtruppen ~~*) to mop up; (*Polizei*) to comb out; *fig* (*von schlechten Elementen befreien, z. B. Partei*) to purge; (*Buch von Anstößigkeiten*) to expurgate; **~ung** *f* cleaning; clearing; clearance; *mil* mopping-up; (*Polizei*) comb-out; **~~saktion** *f mil* mopping-up action; (*innerhalb e-r Partei*) purge; **~~strupp** *m mil* mopping-up party; **~~sunternehmen** *n mil* mopping-up operation.

Sauc|e *f* sauce; (*Braten~*) gravy; **~iere** *f* sauce-boat.

sauer *a* sour, acid; (*herb*) tart; *fig* troublesome; hard; (*mürrisch*) surly, morose, sulky; peevish, sour; *~es Gesicht* vinegar-face; *~ werden* to sour; to get (*od* to go *od* to grow *od* to turn) sour; (*Milch*) to turn; *~e Gurke* pickled cucumber; *~e Milch* curdled milk; *die Milch ist ~ geworden* the milk has turned; **~ampfer** *m* sorrel; **~braten** *m* beef steeped in vinegar and roasted, *Am* sauerbraten; **~brunnen** *m* acidulous spring (*od* mineral) water; **~kirsche** *f* morello cherry; **~klee** *m* wood-sorrel; **~kohl** *m*, **~kraut** *n* sauerkraut, pickled cabbage; **~milch** *f* curdled milk; **~quelle** *f* acidulous (*od* aerated) spring; **~salz** *n* acid salt; **~stoff** *m* oxygen; **~~anreicherung** *f* enriching with oxygen; **~~apparat** *m* oxygen apparatus; **~~arm** *a* poor in oxygen; **~~flasche** *f* oxygen cylinder (*od* bottle); **~~gehalt** *m* oxygen content; **~~gemisch** *n* oxygen mixture; **~~gerät** *n* oxygen (breathing) apparatus; **~~haltig** *a* containing oxygen; **~~ion** *n* anion; **~~mangel** *m* oxygen deficiency; (*in großer Höhe*) anoxia; **~~maske** *f* (*Höhenatmer*) oxygen mask; **~~schutzgerät** *n* oxygen respirator; **~~vorrat** *m* oxygen supply; **~~zuführung**

f oxygen feed; **~süß** *a* sour-sweet; *fig* half-cross; **~teig** *m* leaven; **~topf** *m fig* morose fellow, sourtop; **~töpfisch** *a* peevish, sour, cross; sullen; morose, fretful; crabbed; **~wasser** *n* sour water, acidulous (*od* sparkling) water; **~werden** *n* souring, acetification.

säuer|lich *a* sourish; acidulous, acidulated; **~ling** *m* mineral spring charged with carbon dioxide; **~n** *tr* to sour; (*Teig*) to leaven; *itr* to acidulate, to acidify; to turn sour.

Sauf|abend *m* drinking bout, *sl* drunken spree, binge; **~aus, ~bold** *m* drunkard; **~en** *irr tr* to drink; *itr fam* to drink hard; to carouse, to booze, to tipple, to swill, to swig; *jdn unter den Tisch ~~* to drink s.o. under the table; *sich voll ~~* to get drunk, *fam* to fuddle o. s., to swill o. s. drunk; **~erei** *f*, **~gelage** *n*, **~gesellschaft** *f* drinking bout, *sl* drunken spree, binge, soak, *Am* bender.

Säufer *m* drunkard, inebriate, alcoholic, dipsomaniac, sot, toper, tosspot, tippler, soak, revel(l)er; **~nase** *f* drunkard's nose, grog-blossom; **~wahnsinn** *m* delirium tremens, alcoholic insanity; *fam* jumps *pl*, blue-devils *pl*.

Säug|amme *f* wet-nurse; **~en** *tr* to suckle, to give suck; to lactate; to nurse; **~en** *n* suckling; **~er** *m* mammal; **~etier** *n* mammal; **~ling** *m* infant, baby, suckling babe, suckling; **~~sausstattung** *f* layette; **~~sfürsorge** *f* infant welfare work; **~~sheim** *n* crèche, baby nursery; **~~ssterblichkeit** *f* infant mortality; **~~swäsche** *f* baby linen.

saug|en *itr*, *tr* to suck; (*auf~~*) to absorb; (*in sich ~~*) to imbibe; *aus den Fingern ~en* to invent, to trump up; *~~ n* sucking, suction; **~er** *m* sucker; (*e-r Flasche*) nipple; *tech* suction apparatus; exhauster; **~fähig** *a* absorbent; absorptive; **~fähigkeit** *f* absorptive capacity; **~festigkeit** *f* suction strength; **~flasche** *f* feeding (*od* sucking) bottle; **~glas** *n* breast pump; **~heber** *m* siphon; pipette; **~hub** *m* suction (*od* induction *od* admission *od* intake) stroke; **~kolben** *m* (*Pumpe*) valve piston; **~kreis** *m radio* suction circuit; wave trap; **~luft** *f* indraft; vacuum; **~näpfchen** *n* suction cup; **~papier** *n* absorbent paper; **~propfen** *m* rubber teat, dummy; **~pumpe** *f* suction pump; **~rohr** *n* induction pipe; **~rüssel** *m* proboscis; sucker, siphon; **~ventil** *n* suction valve; **~welle** *f* surge; **~wirkung** *f* sucking, suction, sucking action, suction effect.

säuisch *a* piggish; *fig* obscene.

Säule *f* (*Pfeiler*) pillar; *arch* (*mit bestimmtem Stil*) column; (*Bild~*) statue; (*Pfosten*) post; *el* pile; dry battery; *Atom~* atomic pile; *Rauch~* column of smoke; *Uran~* uranium pile; *galvanische ~* galvanic pile; *thermoelektrische ~* thermo-electric battery; *mit ~n versehen* columnated; **~nartig, ~nförmig** *a* columnar; **~nfuß** *m* pedestal, base; **~ngang** *m* colonnade; arcade; perystile; **~nhalle** *f* (*mit Säulen im Innern*) pillared hall; (*außen*) portico, porch, gallery; **~nheilige(r)** *m* stylite, pillarist; **~nhof** *m* peristyle; **~nknauf** *m* capital; **~nordnung** *f* order; **~nplatte** *f* plinth; (*Deckplatte*) abacus; **~nreihe** *f* row of columns; **~nschaft** *m* shaft (of a column); **~ntempel** *m* perystilar temple; **~nvorbau** *m* portico; **~nwerk** *n* colonnade.

Saum *m* (*Näh~*) seam, hem; (*Rand, Einfassung*) edge, border; margin; strip; (*e-r Stadt*) outskirts *pl*; (*Franse*) fringe; (*Salband*) selvage, list; *Wald~* borders (*pl*) of a forest; **~esel** *m* sumpter mule; **~pfad** *m* mule track; **~pferd** *n* pack-horse; **~sattel** *m* pack-saddle; **~tier** *n* sumpter mule; beast of burden.

säumen[1] *tr* (*einfassen, Näherei*) to hem, to seam; (*verbrämen*) to border, to edge; to skirt; to list; (*Schuhe*) to welt; *tech* (*Brett*) to square a plank.

säum|en[2] *itr* (*hinausschieben*) to delay; to linger; (*zaudern*) to hesitate, to tarry; **~ig** *a* (*langsam*) slow; (*hinausschiebend*) dilatory; (*zögernd*) tardy, hesitating; (*lässig*) negligent, careless; slack; *~~er Zahler* slow payer; defaulter; **~nis** *f* delay; **~~zuschlag** *m* extra charge for overdue payment.

saumselig *a* tardy; dilatory; negligent; **~~keit** *f* tardiness, dilatoriness; negligence.

Säure *f* sourness; acidity, acidness; (*Herbheit*) tartness; *chem* acid; *fig* (*Stimmung*) sourness, acrimony; **~anzug** *m* acid-proof clothing; **~artig** *a* acidlike; **~äther** *m* ester; **~ballon** *m* acid carboy; **~batterie** *f* lead-acid battery; **~behälter** *m* acid container; **~beständig, ~fest** *a* acid-resisting, acid-proof; **~bildend** *a* acid-forming; **~bildner** *m* acidifier; **~bildung** *f* acid formation, acidification; **~dichte** *f* specific gravity of acid; **~flasche** *f* acid bottle; **~frei** *a* free from acid; **~haltig** *a* containing acid, acidiferous; **~löslich** *a* acid-soluble; **~prüfer** *m* (*Batterie*) battery hydrometer; **~reich** *a* rich in acid; **~wirkung** *f* action of acids.

Sauregurkenzeit *f* silly season, slack season, dead (*od* dull) season.

Saurier *m* saurian.

Saus *m* storm; whistle; rush; whiz; *in ~ u. Braus leben* to riot, to revel; *ein Leben in ~ u. Braus* riotous life.

säuseln *itr* to rustle; to whisper; *~ n* rustling.

sausen *itr* to rush, to dash; (*Wind*) to whistle; to sough; to bluster; to blow hard; (*Geschoß*) to buzz; to whistle; (*zischen, rasen*) to whiz(z); *~ n* rush and roar; (*in den Ohren*) humming (*od* singing) in the ears.

*

Savanne *f* savanna(h).

Savoyen *n* Savoy.

Saxophon *n* saxophone.

Schab|e *f tech* shaving-tool; *zoo* blackbeetle, cockroach; **~(e)fleisch** *n* scraped meat; **~eisen** *n* scraper; planing (*od* shaving) knife; **~en** *tr* to scrape, to shave; (*abscheuern*) to scour; (*wegschälen*) to pare; (*ab~~, reiben*) to chafe, to grate; to rub; to abrade; **~er** *m* scraper; **~kunst** *f* mezzotint; **~messer** *n* scraping-knife.

Schabernack *m* monkey-trick, *Am sl* monkeyshine; prank, frolic; trick; practical joke; foolish jokes *pl*; *fam* lark; *jdm e-n ~ spielen* to have a lark with, to play a practical joke on, to play a prank on.

schäbig *a* shabby; *fam* seedy; worn (-out); *fig* mean; (*geizig*) stingy, sordid; dowdy; *Am fam* tacky; **~keit** *f* shabbiness; *fig* meanness.

Schablone *f* stencil; (*Bohr~*) jig; (*Guß~*) template; (*Arbeits~*) routine; (*Exemplar, Modell, Muster*) exemplar, model, pattern; **~nhaft** *a* mechanical; *fig* conventional, stereotyped; *~~e Arbeit* routine work; **~nwesen** *n* routine.

Schabracke *f* caparison, saddle-cloth.

Schabsel *n* scrapings *pl*, shavings *pl*.

Schach *n* chess; *~ bieten* to check; to put the king in check; *fig* to defy; *~ dem König!* check! *~ spielen* to play at chess; *im ~ halten* to keep in check; **~aufgabe** *f* chess-problem; **~brett** *n* chess-board; **~~artig** *a* tesselated; **~feld** *n* square; **~figur** *f* chessman; *fig* (political) figurehead; **~förmig** *a* chequered, tesselated; staggered; *Am* checkerboardlike; **~matt** *a* (check-) mate; *fig* (*erledigt*) exhausted, weary, knocked out; **~meisterschaft** *f* chess-championship; **~partie** *f*, **~spiel** *n* game of chess; **~spieler** *m* chess-player; **~stein** *m* chessman; **~turnier** *n* chess-tournament; **~zug** *m* move (at chess); *fig* dexterous move, clever dodge.

Schacher *m*, **~ei** *f* low trade, chaffering, bargaining; haggling; *parl* jobbery; **~er** *m* haggler; **~n** *itr* to haggle, to barter, to bargain, to chaffer; *Am* to dicker.

Schächer *m* robber; (*Bibel*) thief; *armer ~* poor fellow.

Schacht *m* shaft, pit; (*Kohlen~*) colliery, coal-pit; (*Einsteig~*) manhole; (*Schlucht*) gorge; (*Graben*) ditch; (*Höhlung*) cavity; (*Ofen~*) fire-room; tunnel; **~abteufung** *f* shaft sinking; **~anlage** *f* mine; shaft plant; **~arbeiter** *m* pitman; **~betrieb** *m* shaft-mining; **~deckel** *m* (*Straßenkanalisation*) manhole cover; **~förderung** *f* shaft hauling; **~mündung** *f* pit mouth; **~ofen** *m* shaft furnace; **~öffnung** *f* pit mouth.

Schachtel *f* box; case, tin; *alte ~* (*fig*) old maid, *fam* old frump; **~halm** *m* horse-tail, shavegrass; **~satz** *m* involved period.

schächt|en *tr* to kill according to Jewish rites; **~er** *m* Jewish butcher.

schade *a*: *es ist ~* it is a pity, it is to be regretted; *es ist sehr ~* it is a great pity; *es ist ewig ~, daß* ... it is a thousand pities that ...; *es ist ~ darum* it is too bad about that; *es ist ~ um ihn* it is a pity for him, it is too bad about him; he is greatly to be pitied; *sie ist zu ~ dafür* she is too good for it; *schade, daß Sie nicht kommen konnten* too bad that you couldn't come; *wie ~!* what a pity!

Schädel *m anat* skull, cranium; *Toten~* death's head; *jdn den ~ einschlagen* to knock out s.o.'s brains; **~band** *n* cranial ligament; **~basis** *f* base of the skull; **~~fraktur** *f* fracture of the skull base; **~bohrer** *m med* threphine, (*früher*) trepan, cranial perforator; **~bruch** *m* fracture of the skull; **~dach** *n* vault of the cranium; **~decke** *f* scalp, skullcap; **~fuge** *f* cranial suture; **~haut** *f* pericranium; **~höhle** *f* cavity of the cranium; **~hohlraum** *m* skull cavity; **~index** *m* index of the cranium; **~knochen** *m* cranium, skull bone; **~lehre** *f* phrenology; **~messer** *m* craniometer; **~naht** *f* cranial suture; **~stätte** *f* Calvary; Golgatha; **~wölbung** *f* vault of the cranium; **~wunde** *f* cranial wound.

Schaden *m* (*seltener: Schade m*) damage (*durch* by); (*Verlust*) loss; (*Nachteil*) detriment; (*Mangel, Fehler*) defect; (*Beschädigung*) injury; (*Nachteil*) disadvantage, détriment; (*Unrecht*) harm; (*Verletzung*) hurt; (*Gebrechen*) infirmity; (*Kriegsschaden*) enemy action; (*Übel*) evil; wrong; *durch ~ wird man klug* you learn from your mistakes; *niemand kam zu ~* no one was injured; *unerheblicher ~* negligible damage; *ohne ~*

without loss; *zum ~ von* to the prejudice of; *zu meinem ~* to my detriment; *es ist kein ~ angerichtet worden* there is no harm done; *~ bringen* to cause damage, to damage; to harm; *e-n ~ decken* to cover a loss; *e-n ~ ermitteln* to assess a damage; *e-n ~ ersetzen* to repair a loss; *für den ~ haften* to stand to the loss; *zu ~ kommen* to come to grief; *~ leiden* to suffer damages; *~ nehmen* to come to grief; *den ~ tragen* to bear the loss; *mit ~ verkaufen* to sell at a loss; *~ zufügen* to inflict losses; (*jdm*) *fam* to give s. o. the black eye; **schaden** *itr* (*beschädigen, Schaden zufügen*) to damage; (*weh tun*) to harm, to do harm; (*verletzen, Abbruch tun*) to hurt, to injure, to be injurious to; (*benachteiligen*) to prejudice; *es schadet nichts* it doesn't matter! no matter! that's nothing! never mind! *das wird ihr nichts ~* that will not hurt her, it won't do her any harm; *das schadet ihm nichts* (*geschieht ihm recht*) it serves him right; *es könnte nicht ~* (*etw zu tun*) it would not be amiss to ..., there would be no harm in ...; *wem schadet das?* who's the worse for it? *was schadet das?* what does it matter? *e-r Sache ~* to cause damage to; *ein Versuch kann nichts ~* there is no harm in trying; *seinem guten Ruf ~* to compromise o.'s reputation; *sich selbst ~* to stand in o.'s own light; to discredit o. s.; **~ersatz** *m* compensation, damages *pl*; indemnification, indemnity; amends *pl mit sing*; (*Wiedergutmachung*) reparation; redress, relief; *~~ beanspruchen* to claim damages; *auf ~~ klagen* to sue for damages; *~~ leisten* to pay damages (*od* compensation); to make amends for; to indemnify; to make reparation for; **~~anspruch** *m* claim for damages (*od* compensation); **~~klage** *f* action for damages; suit in damages; **~~leistung** *f* indemnification; **~~pflicht** *f* liability for damages; **~~pflichtig** *a* liable for damages; **~feuer** *n* destructive fire; **~freude** *f* malicious joy, schadenfreude; **~froh** *a* malicious, mischievous, enjoying another's misfortune; **~regulierung** *f* adjustment of damages; **~schätzung** *f* damage assessment; **~sfall** *m* case of loss; **~versicherung** *f* insurance against damages.

schad|haft *a* damaged; (*Material*) defective, faulty; (*Zähne*) carious; (*baufällig*) dilapidated; **~~igkeit** *f* damaged state; **~los** *a* indemnified; harmless; innocent; *~~ halten* to make up for, to make good, to indemnify for; *sich ~~ halten* to recoup o. s. for; **~~haltung** *f* indemnification; compensation, damages *pl*; recourse.

schäd|igen *tr* to damage, to harm, to wrong; (*benachteiligen*) to prejudice; (*verletzen*) to hurt, to injure; *der geschädigte Teil jur* the aggrieved party; **~igung** *f* damage, harm; (*Nachteil*) detriment, injury, prejudice; **~lich** *a* harmful, hurtful; (*verderblich*) noxious; (*nachteilig*) detrimental, injurious; prejudicial (*für* to); (*bösartig*) pernicious; (*giftig*) poisonous; (*gefährlich*) dangerous; (*schlecht*) bad; (*ungesund*) unhealthy; (*von Speisen etc*) unwholesome; *~~er Einfluß* bad influence (*auf* on); *~~e Nachwirkung* harmful after-effect; **~~keit** *f* noxiousness, harm(fulness); injuriousness; hurtfulness; perniciousness; unwholesomeness; **~ling** *m* (*Mensch*) noxious (*od* vile) person; (*für die Allgemeinheit*) common enemy; (*Ungeziefer, Unkraut*) parasite; vermin, pest; destructive insect, destructive weed; **~~sbekämpfung** *f* pest control.

Schaf *s* sheep; (*Mutter~*) ewe; *fig* simpleton, stupid, sheep's head; *das schwarze ~ der Familie* the black sheep of the family; *ein räudiges ~* a mangy sheep; *fig* a black sheep; **~artig** *a* sheepish, sheep-like, sheepy; **~blattern** *f pl* chicken-pox, sheep-pox; varicella; **~bock** *m* ram; **~darmsaite** *f* catgut; **~fell** *n* sheepskin; (*mit der Wolle*) fleece; **~fleisch** *n* mutton; **~garbe** *f bot* yarrow, milfoil; **~haut** *f* sheepskin; *anat* amnion; **~herde** *f* flock of sheep; **~hirt** *m* shepherd; **~hürde** *f* sheepfold, sheepcot(e), pen; **~käse** *m* cheese from ewe's milk, ewe-cheese; **~leder** *n* sheep's leather, sheepskin; **~mäßig** *a* sheepish; **~milch** *f* ewe's milk; **~pelz** *m* sheepskin coat, fleece; *Wolf im ~~* the wolf in sheep's clothing; **~pferch** *m* sheepfold, sheepcot(e), coop; **~pocken** *f pl* sheep-pox, ovinia; **~schere** *f* sheep shears *pl*; **~schur** *f* sheep-shearing, slip; **~sdämlich** *a* very stupid, sheepish; **~skopf** *m* sheep's head; *fig* (*Dummkopf*) blockhead, duffer; **~stall** *m* sheep-fold; **~stand** *m* stock of sheep; **~trift, ~weide** *f* sheep-walk, sheep-run; **~wolle** *f* sheep's wool; **~zecke** *f* (*Laus*) sheep-tick; **~zucht** *f* sheep-breeding; **~züchter** *m* sheep breeder, sheep master, sheep grower; wool grower.

Schäf|chen *n* little sheep; lamb(kin); (*~~wolken*) *f pl* cirrus clouds *pl*, mackerel sky, fleecy clouds *pl*; mare's tails *pl*; *sein ~~ ins trockene bringen, sein ~~ scheren* to feather o.'s nest; *sein ~~ im trockenen haben* to be out of the wood; **~er** *m* shepherd; **~erei** *f* sheep farm, sheep ranch; **~ergedicht** *n* pastoral, idyll; **~erhund** *m* sheep dog, shepherd's dog; (*schottischer ~~*) collie, colly; *deutscher ~~* Alsatian (wolf-hound); *der ~~ hütet die Schafe* the sheep dog tends the sheep; **~erhütte** *f* shepherd's cot; **~erin** *f* shepherdess; **~erlied** *n* pastoral song; **~erkarren** *m* shepherd's cart; **~erpfeife** *f* shepherd's pipe; **~erspiel** *n* pastoral play; **~erstab** *m* shepherd's crook; **~erstündchen** *n*, **~erstunde** *f* lover's hour; **~ertasche** *f* shepherd's scrip.

schaffen[1] *irr* (*schuf, geschaffen*) *tr, itr* (*er~*) to create; (*hervorbringen*) to produce, to bring forth, to call forth; to make; to originate; *e-e Rolle ~ theat* to create a role; *wie geschaffen sein für etw* to be born for s. th., to be cut out for s. th., to be made for; **~d** *a* creative; productive; constructive.

schaffen[2] *tr, itr* (*schaffte, geschafft*) (*arbeiten*) to work, to make, to do; to act, to perform; to be busy; (*erreichen*) to accomplish; (*be~, ver~*) to provide, to procure; (*her~, liefern*) to supply s. th. to; to supply s. o. with; to furnish; to bring; (*fort~*) to convey, to remove; to transfer; *vom Halse ~* to get rid of; *Hilfe ~* to procure assistance; *Linderung ~* to soothe, to relieve, to bring relief; *Rat ~* to know what to do; *etw auf die Seite ~* to put aside; (*unterschlagen*) to embezzle; *beiseite ~* to remove; (*töten*) to kill; *aus dem Weg ~* to get out of the way; *jdm zu ~ machen* to cause (*od* to give) trouble; *sich zu ~ machen* to be busy with; to tinker at s. th., to potter about; *ich habe nichts damit zu ~* I have nothing to do with it; that's no business of mine; I wash my hands of it; that is no concern of mine; *ich schaffte es* I made it, I managed it; **~d** *a* working.

Schaffens|drang *m* creative impulse; **~kraft** *f* creative power; **~lustig** *a* creative; *in ~~er Stimmung* in a creative mood.

Schaffner *m* steward, manager, administrator; *rail* guard, *Am* (railroad) conductor; (*für Fahrkarten*) ticket collector, ticket taker; (*Straßenbahn~, Omnibus~*) conductor; **~in** *f* (*Straßenbahn, Bus*) conductress, *fam* clippie; (*Haushälterin*) housekeeper.

Schaffung *f* creation; production.

Schafott *n* scaffold; *das ~ besteigen* to mount the scaffold.

Schaft *m* (*Fahnen~*) stick; (*Flinten~*) (gun)stock; (*Lanzen~*) shaft; (*Werkzeug~*) shank; (*Säulen~*) shaft; (*Säge~*) handle; (*Stiefel~*) leg; (*Baum~*) trunk; (*Blumen~*) stalk, stem; **~stiefel** *m* knee-boot, high-boot, top-boot, Wellington-(boot), *Am* boot.

schäften *tr* to furnish with a stock, a handle, etc; to stock (a gun); to leg (boots).

Schah *m* shah.

Schakal *m* jackal.

Schäker *m* fun-maker, joker, jester, wag; **~ei** *f* fun, joke; **~n** *itr* to joke; (*mit Damen*) to dally, to flirt.

Schal *m* shawl; scarf; muffler; (*wollener ~*) comforter; **~brett** *n* outside plank, slab.

schal *a* (*abgestanden*) stale; (*geschmacklos*) insipid; *fig* flat.

Schälchen *n* small bowl, small cup.

Schal|e *f* (*Eier~~, Nuß~~, Schildkröten~~*) shell; (*Frucht~~*) paring; (*abgeschälte ~~*) peel; (*Kartoffel~~*) skin; (*Hülse*) husk, hull; (*Eichel*) cap; (*Schote*) pod, cod; (*Rinde*) bark, rind; (*Kruste*) crust; (*Muschel*) valve, *Am* shuck; (*Messer~~*) scale, plate; (*Buchdeckel*) cover; (*Lager~~*) *tech* bush(ing), brass; *fam* (*Anzug*) rig, togs *pl*; *fig* (*äußere ~~*) outside, cover; (*Oberfläche*) surface; (*Waag~~*) scale; (*Trink~~*) bowl; (*Gefäß*) dish, vessel; saucer; (*Tasse*) cup; *chem* basin, tray, capsule; *~~ des Zorns* vial of wrath; *sich in ~e werfen sl* to doll up; *kalte ~~* cold fruit; **~enbau** *m* monocoque (*od* shell) construction; **~enbretter** *n pl* form boards *pl*; **~eneisen** *n* sow iron; **~enentwicklung** *f phot* dish development; **~enform** *f* shell form; **~enförmig** *a* bowl-shaped; like a shell; (*in Schichten*) in layers; **~enfrucht** *f*, **~enobst** *n* shell fruit; (*Gräsersamen*) caryopsis; **~engehäuse** *n* shell; **~enguß** *m tech* chill casting; **~engußform** *f* chill; **~enkreuz** *n aero* (*Windmesser*) cup anemometer, *Am* cross arms *pl*; **~enrumpf** *m aero* shell body, monocoque fuselage; **~holz** *n* pit timber; **~ig** *a* covered with a shell (*od* skin); scaly; shelly, shelled; lamellated; **~tier** *n* crustacean (*pl* crustacea); **~~versteinerung** *f* fossil shell.

schäl|en *tr* (*Äpfel*) to pare; (*Orangen*) to peel; (*Kartoffeln*) to skin, to peel, to pare; (*Baumrinde*) to bark; (*Mandeln*) to blanch; (*Eier*) to remove the shell; (*Nüsse*) to peel; (*Mais*) to husk; *sich ~~* (*Haut*) to peel (off), to skin; to blister; (*Schlangen*) to cast the skin, to slough; (*Rinde*) to shed the bark; (*abschuppen*) to scale off; *geschälte Kartoffeln* potatoes with their jackets off; **~eisen** *n* peeler; sheller; husker; barker; **~hengst** *m* stallion; **~holz** *n* peeled wood; **~messer** *n* paring (*od* peeling) knife; **~pflug** *m* paring-plough (*Am* plow); **~ung** *f* peeling.

Schalk *m* knave, rogue; (*Spaßvogel*) wag; **~haft** *a* wanton, roguish; waggish; **~~igkeit** *f*, **~heit** *f* waggery, waggishness; roguery; **-snarr** *m* buffoon.

Schall *m* sound; (*Klang*) ring; (*Dröhnen von Glocken etc*) peal; (*Klangfülle*) resonance; (*Lärm*) noise; (*Echo*) echo; *- dämpfen* to muffle; **-abstrahlung** *f* sound radiation (*od* projection); **-aufnahme** *f* sound recording, electrical recording; **-aufnahmegerät** *n* sound recording instrument; **-ausbreitung** *f* propagation of sound; **-boden** *m* sounding board; **-brechung** *f* refraction of sound; **-dämpfend** *a* sound deadening, sound absorbing; **-dämpfer** *m* sound absorber; *mot* silencer, *Am* muffler; (*Klavier*) soft pedal; (*bei Tonaufnahme*) *film* gobo; **-dämpfung** *f* silencing, soundproofing; sound insulation; **-dicht** *a* sound-proof; *-- machen* to soundproof; *ein --er Raum* a sound-proof room; **-dose** *f* sound-box; *el* (*Grammophon*) pick-up; playback reproducer; **-druck** *m* sound pressure; **-durchlässigkeit** *f* sound permeability; **-empfänger** *m* sound receiver; **-en** *itr* to sound, to resound; to peal; *--der Donner* peal of thunder; *--des Gelächter* burst (*od* peal) of laughter, guffaw; *--der Schlag* bang; **-erzeuger** *m* sound generator; **-geschwindigkeit** *f* velocity of sound, speed of sound; *mit -- fliegen aero* to fly at the speed of sound; **--sgrenze** *f* speed of sound barrier; **-gesteuert** *a* autosonic; **-isolierung** *f* sound insulation, soundproofing, silencing; **-(l)ehre** *f* acoustics *pl*; **-(l)och** *n* (*Geige*) sound hole; (*Glockenturm*) louvre window; aperture; **-meßbatterie** *f mil* sound-ranging troup; **-meßgerät** *n mil* sound ranging instrument; (*U-Bootsortung*) asdic; sonar; **-meßtrupp** *m mil* soundranging section; **-messung** *f*, **-meßverfahren** *n* sound ranging; **-mine** *f mil* acoustic mine; **-ortung** *f* sound location; **-platte** *f* (gramophone) record, *Am* phonograph record, disk, disc; *Langspiel--* long playing record; *normale --* standard record; *--n abspielen* to play (back) records; *--n aufnehmen* to record; *--n auf Wachs aufnehmen* to wax; **--naufnahme** *f* disk recording, *radio* transcription; **--naufnahmegerät** *n* recording equipment; recorder; **--naufnahmetisch** *m radio* recording turntable; **--ngeräusch** *n* record (*od* surface) noise; **--nmusik** *f* recorded (*od* canned) music; **--nprogramm** *n* recorded program(me); *Ansager bei --nprogramm radio Am* disk jockey; **--nübertragung** *f radio* transmission of records *pl*; **--nverstärker** *m* pick-up amplifier; **-quelle** *f* sound generator (*od* source); **-schwingung** *f* sound vibration; **-stärkemesser** *m radio* sound meter, volume meter; **-tarnung** *f mil* sound screening; **-trichter** *m* bell-mouth, mouthpiece; (*Lautsprecher*) (sound) horn, trumpet; projection; (*Sprachrohr*) megaphone; **-- u. Lichtmeßstelle** *f mil* sound and light range-finding; **-wand** *f* (*Lautsprecher*) baffle (-board); sounding board, sound panel; **-welle** *f* sound wave; **-wiedergabe** *f* sound reproduction; **-zeichen** *n* sound signal.

Schalmei *f* shawm; **-glocke** *f* sheep gong; **-wecker** *m* gong bell.

Schalotte *f bot* shal(l)ot, spring onion *Am* scallion.

Schalt|ader *f el* cross-connecting wire; **-anlage** *f* switch gear; **-anordnung** *f* circuit diagram; **-apparat** *m* switch apparatus; controlling apparatus; controller; **-ausrüstung** *f* control equipment; **-bild** *n* wiring diagram, circuit diagram; (*Schema*) skeleton; **-brett** *n el* switchboard; electrical control panel; *mot* instrument panel, dashboard; **-dose** *f* switch box; **-einrichtung** *f* switching equipment; **-en** *tr* (*regieren*) to rule, to command; to deal (*mit* with); *-- u. walten* to be master over, to manage; *-- u. walten lassen* to give s. o. full power; *el* to switch (*ein* on, *aus* off, out); *ein--* to insert; *um--* to switch over; *hintereinander--* to connect in series; *nebeneinander--* to connect in parallel; *zusammen--* to join up; (*Maschine*) to operate, to control; (*Motor*) to start; *mot* (*Getriebe*) to change (gears), to shift (gears); to control; *radio* (*Apparat ein--*) to tune in; **-er** *m el* switch-key; circuit breaker; *tech* controller; (*Fenster*) sliding window, shutter; *rail, theat* booking-office, *Am* ticket-office (window); (*Bank*) window; (*Post*) counter; **--beamte(r)** *m* booking clerk, *Am* ticket agent; (*Post*) post-office official; **--dienst** *m* counter service; **--halle** *f rail* passenger hall, entrance hall; **-getriebe** *f mot* change-over gear; gearbox; **-hebel** *m* switch (lever), contact lever; control lever; *mot* gear-lever, *Am* gearshift (lever); **-jahr** *n* leap year; **-kupplung** *f* shifting coupling, clutch; **-plan** *m* circuit diagram, wiring diagram (*od* scheme); **-pult** *n tele, radio* control desk, switch desk; **-rad** *n* control gear, indexing gear; **-raum** *m* switch room; **-schema** *n* wiring diagram (*od* scheme), connections *pl*; **-schlüssel** *m mot* (*Zündschlüssel*) ignition key; **-schrank** *m* switch cabinet; **-skizze** *f* circuit diagram; **-stellung** *f* "on" position of switch; **-stöpsel** *m* plug; **-stufe** *f* switch step; **-tafel** *f* switchboard; *mot* instrument board; *aero* dashboard; **-tag** *m* intercalary day; **-ung** *f* (gear) control; shifting, gear-change; (*Schreibmaschine*) escapement; *el* connection, connection lay-out; circuit arrangement; *radio* hookup; *-- an der Lenkradsäule mot* steering-column gear control; **--sanordnung** *f* switching arrangement; **--splan** *m* switch system; **-vorgang** *m* switching operation; shifting operation; **-werk** *n* switch cabinet; control mechanism; feed mechanism; *film* film feed; **-zeichen** *n* legend, list of symbols.

Schaluppe *f* sloop, jolly-boat.

Scham *f* shame, chastity; (*Schande*) disgrace; (*Geschlechtsteile*) privy parts *pl*, genitals *pl*, pudenda *pl*; *männliche -* penis; *weibliche -* vulva, pudendum; *er hatte alle - verloren* he was lost to all shame; *bar aller -* to be past shame; *vor - erröten* to colo(u)r up with shame, to blush with shame; *vor - vergehen* to die with shame; **-bein** *n anat* pubic (*od* share) bone, pubis; **--bogen** *m anat* arch of the pubis; **--fuge** *f anat* pubic symphysis; **-berg, -hügel** *m anat* pubes, mons veneris; **-bogen** *m anat* pubic arch; **-fuge** *f* pubic symphysis; **-gang** *m anat* vagina; **-gefühl** *n* sense of shame; *gegen das -- verstoßen* to shock s. o.'s modesty; **-gegend** *f* pubic region; **-haar** *n* pubic hair; **-haft** *a* modest, bashful; chaste; **--igkeit** *f* bashfulness, modesty, chastity; **-leiste** *f* groin, perineum; **-lippe** *f* labium, *pl* labia; **-los** *a* shameless; (*unverschämt*) impudent; (*unzüchtig*) indecent; (*zynisch*) cynical; **--igkeit** *f* shamelessness; impudence; cynicism; **-rot** *a* blushing (with shame), red; *-- werden* to blush; to colo(u)r up; **-röte** *f* blush(ing); **-teile** *m pl* genitals *pl*, privy parts *pl*, pudenda *pl*.

schämen: *sich -* to be ashamed (*über* of), to feel ashamed (*über* of); *Sie sollten sich -* you ought to be ashamed of yourself; *sie schämte sich, ihm unter die Augen zu treten* she was ashamed to face him; *schäme dich!* for shame! shame on you! *beschämt* ashamed, abashed by, shamefaced.

Schamotte *f* fire-clay; **-ziegel** *m* fire-brick.

Schampun *n* shampoo; **-ieren** *tr* to shampoo.

schand|bar *a* shameful, disgraceful; ignominious, infamous; **-bube** *m* scoundrel, villain; **-e** *f* (*Schmach*) shame; (*Entehrung*) dishono(u)r; (*Entwürdigung*) disgrace; (*Verlust der Wertschätzung*) discredit; (*öffentliche -*) ignominy; (*Schmach*) infamy; *zu-en machen* to frustrate, to baffle, to balk, to foil, to thwart; *-e über jdn bringen* to bring dishono(u)r on; *zu-en werden* (*Pläne*) to miscarry, to founder; to come to nought; *ein Pferd zu-en reiten* to founder a horse; *Armut ist keine -e* poverty is not a shame; **-fleck** *m* stain, blemish; **-gebot** *n com* underbidding; **-geld** *n* money got by infamy; disgraceful price; *für ein -- verkaufen* to sell for a song; **-mal** *n* stigma, brand; **-maul** *n* evil tongue, backbiter, slanderer; (*Xanthippe*) *Am sl* battle-ax(e); **-pfahl** *m*, **-säule** *f* pillory; **-preis** *m* scandalous (*od* ridiculous) price; **-schrift** *f* lampoon; **-tat** *f* crime; misdeed; shameful action.

schänd|en *tr* to disgrace, to dishono(u)r; (*Mädchen*) to rape, to ravish; (*entheiligen*) to profane; (*besudeln*) to soil; (*verunstalten*) to disfigure; (*verderben*) to spoil; (*beschimpfen*) to insult; **-er** *m* defamer; violator; ravisher; **-lich** *a* shameful; (*niederträchtig*) infamous; (*gemein*) scurrilous; (*entehrend*) disgraceful; *adv fam* (*sehr*) immensely, extremely; awfully; *e-e --e Rede* an opprobrious speech; *das ist --!* it's too bad! **--keit** *f* shamefulness, disgraceful act; infamy; **-ung** *f* (*Entstellung*) spoiling, disfiguring; (*Entweihung*) profanation, desecration, sacrilege; (*Vergewaltigung*) violation, rape, ravishment.

schanghaien *tr* (*gewaltsam heuern, entführen*) to shanghai.

Schank *m* retail of alcoholic liquors; tap-room; **-erlaubnis, -gerechtigkeit** *f* publican's licence; **-stätte** *f* public house, licensed premises *pl*; **-wirt** *m* publican; **-wirtschaft** *f* public house, tavern, *sl* pub, *Am* saloon.

Schanker *m med* chancre; chancroid; **schankrös** *a* chancroidal.

Schanz|arbeiten *f pl* entrenchments *pl*; **-arbeiter, -er** *m* pioneer, sapper; **-e** *f* entrenchment; field-work, redoubt; *mar* quarter-deck; *sein Leben in die - schlagen* to risk o.'s life; to fling away o.'s life; **-en** *itr* to dig, to entrench; *fam* to drudge, to toil; **-entisch** *m* (*Ski*) ski-jumping platform; **-gerät** *n* entrenching tools *pl*; **-gräber** *m* pioneer; sapper; **-korb** *m* gabion; **-pfahl** *m* palisade; **-zeug** *n* pioneering-implements *pl*; entrenching tools *pl*.

Schar *f* (*Kinder*) troop, host; (*Gänse, Ziegen*) flock; (*Fische*) shoal; (*Tauben*) flight; (*Mädchen, Rehe, Wachteln*) bevy; (*Rebhühner*) covey; (*Wölfe, Hunde*) pack; (*Männer*) posse; (*Pflug-*) ploughshare; **-bock** *m med* scurvy; **-en** *r* to collect, to assemble; to flock (together); **~enweise** *adv* in troops, in bands; **~führer** *m mil* platoon leader; **~wache** *f* watch.

Scharade *f* charade.

Schären *f pl* rocky islets *pl*.

scharf *a* (*schneidend*) sharp; keen; (*spitz*) acute, pointed; (*Munition*) live; *Übungsangriff mit ~en Bomben* a practice-raid with live bombs; (*beißend*) shrewd, caustic; (*rauh, herb*) harsh; (*streng*) severe; (*genau*) strict, exact; (*Ton*) piercing, shrill; (*~gefaßt*) sharply defined; *phot* well-focus(s)ed; (*Pfeffer*) hot; (*Antwort*) cutting; (*Ohr*) quick; *~e Luft* sharp (*od* keen) air; *~e Kurve* sharp turning (*od* bend); *~er Verweis* severe rebuke; *~e Kritik* caustic criticism; *~ Ausschau halten* to keep a sharp look-out; *~ im Auge behalten* to keep a sharp eye on; *~ aufpassen* to keep close watch; *~e Brille* strong glasses; *~e Züge* sharp features; *~ ansehen* to fix o.'s glances upon; *~ einstellen* to bring into clear focus; *~ schießen* to shoot with balls (*od* bullets); *~ beschlagen* to rough-shoe; *~ betonen* to accent strongly; *~ sehen* (*hören*) to have a sharp eye (quick ear); *~ machen* (*Mine*) to activate; (*Handgranate*) to prime; *~ reiten* to ride quickly; *~ sein* (*fam*) to be keen (*auf* on); **~abstimmung** *f radio* sharp tuning; (*automatische ~~*) automatic frequency control (*Abk* A. F. C.); **~blick** *m* quick eye; piercing look, penetrating glance; acuteness; insight; **~blickend** *a* clear-sighted; **~einstellung** *f opt* focusing; **~kantig** *a* sharp-edged; square; **~macher** *m fig* fire-brand, demagogue, agitator; **~richter** *m* hangman, executioner; *fam* Jack Ketch; **~schießen** *n mil* firing with live rounds; **~schmeckend** *a* acrid, pungent; tart; **~schuß** *m mil* shot with ball; **~schütze** *m mil* marksman, sharpshooter; sniper; **~sicht** *f* keenness of sight; perspicacity; **~sichtig** *a* clear-sighted, keen-sighted; *fig* penetrating, discerning; **~sichtigkeit** *f* quick-sightedness; penetration; **~sinn** *m*, **~sinnigkeit** *f* sagacity, acumen; acuteness; ingenuity; **~sinnig** *a* (*weise*) sagacious, ingenious; (*klug*) clever; penetrating; (*schlau*) shrewd; (*urteilsfähig*) discerning.

Schärfe *f* sharpness; acuteness; *fig* (*Verstandes~*) shrewdness; (*Strenge*) severity; (*Bitterkeit*) acrimony; (*Schroffheit*) asperity; (*Verbitterung*) acerbity; (*Herbheit*) tartness; **~n** *tr* to sharpen, to whet; (*zuspitzen*) to point; *fig* (*ver~*) to heighten, to aggravate; to intensify; **~ntiefe** *f phot* depth of focus; **~~nring** *m* (*od* **~skala** *f*) depth-of-field ring (*od* scale).

Schärfung *f* sharpening.

Scharlach *m*, **~farbe** *f* scarlet; (*Krankheit*) scarlet fever; **~fieber** *n* scarlet fever; **~rot** *n* scarlet-red.

Scharlatan *m* charlatan; (*Kurpfuscher*) quack; **~erie** *f* quackery.

scharmant *a* (*reizend*) charming; nice; fascinating.

Scharmützel *n* skirmish; **~n** *itr* to skirmish.

Scharnier *n* hinge; joint; **~gelenk** *n* hinge-joint; **~stift** *m* hinge pin.

Schärpe *f* scarf, sash.

Scharre *f* scraper, raker; **~n** *itr* to scrape, to scratch; (*Pferd*) to paw.

Schart|e *f* (*Porzellan*) nick; (*Kerbe*) notch; (*Riß*) fissure; crack; (*Lücke*) gap; (*Schieß~~*) loop-hole, embrasure; (*Einschnitt*) indentation, dent, dint; *e-e ~e bekommen* to become dented; *e-e ~e auswetzen* to make amends for, to make reparation for; to repair a fault (*od* damage); **~eke** *f* old book, trashy volume; **~ig** *a* jagged, notched; (*gezahnt*) crenated, indented; *~~ werden* to gape.

scharwenzeln *itr* to toady; to fawn upon; to dance attendance on.

Schatten *m* (*sonnengeschützt*) shade; (*Schlag~, fig*) shadow; (*Verstorbener*) phantom, (departed) spirit; *itr* to shade, to cast a shadow; *im ~ sitzen* to sit in the shade; *in den ~ gehen* to go into the shade; *die Sonne wirft ~* the sun casts shadows; *beschatten* to shadow, to cast a shadow; (*schützen*) to shade (eyes); *in den ~ stellen* to overshadow; to throw into the shade, to take the shine out of a person; *er ist nur noch ein ~* he is reduced to a shadow; *sie folgt ihm wie ein ~* she follows him like a shadow; *er war nur noch ein ~ seiner selbst* he was the shadow of his former self; **~bild** *n* silhouette; **~boxen** *n sport* shadow boxing; **~fabrik** *f*, **~werk** *n* shadow factory; **~gestalt** *f* phantom, phantasm; *pl* shades *pl*; **~haft** *a* shadowy; **~könig** *m* mock king; **~licht** *n* half-light; chiaroscuro; **~linie** *f* outline; **~los** *a* shadowless, shadeless; **~reich** *n* (*Unterwelt*) realm of shades. Hades; **~riß** *m* silhouette, outline; **~seite** *f* shady side, dark side; *fig* seamy side, draw-back; **~spiel** *n* shadow play; (Chinese) shades *pl*; *fig* phantasmagoria.

schatt|ieren *tr* to shade, to shadow out; (*schraffieren*) to hatch; (*abtönen*) to tint; **~ierung** *f* shading; (*Farbton*) shade, tint; (*Schraffierung*) hatching; **~~sverfahren** *n* variable-density recording method; **~ig** *a* shadowy, shady.

Schatulle *f* cash box; privy purse (of a prince).

Schatz *m* treasure; (*Reichtümer*) riches *pl*; wealth; (*Vorrat*) store; *fig* sweetheart, darling, *fam* deary, *Am* cutie; *mein ~* my love; **~amt** *n* treasury, Exchequer, Board of Exchequer, *Am* Treasury, Treasury Department; **~anleihe** treasury loan; **~anweisung** *f* exchequer bill, treasury bill (*od* bond), *Am* treasury certificate; **~gräber** *m* digger for (hidden) treasure(s); **~kammer** *f* public treasury; Exchequer, *Am* Treasury; *fig* (*Vorratskammer, Ansammlung*) storehouse; **~meister** *m* (*Verein*) treasurer, secretary; Chancellor of the Exchequer, *Am* Secretary of the Treasury; **~schein, ~wechsel** *m* treasury bill; **~sekretär** *m Am* Secretary of the Treasury; **~ung** *f* (*Abgabezwang*) levy, taxation.

schätz|bar *a* valuable, estimable; **~en** *tr: jdn ~en* (*anerkennen*) to regard; (*ehren*) to respect; (*hochachten*) to esteem; *etw ~en* to estimate, to value, to appreciate; to prize; (*einschätzen*) to appraise, to fix the value, to rate, to reckon; *sich glücklich ~en* to be delighted to; *sich zur Ehre ~en* to think it an hono(u)r; *zu ~en wissen* to appreciate; **~enswert** *a* estimable, appreciable; **~er** *m* valuer; appraiser; (*Steuer*) assessor; (*beeidigter ~~*) licensed valuer, sworn appraiser; **~ung** *f* (*Sachwert*) valuation, estimate; *jur* taxation; (*Berechnung*) calculation, computation; (*Steuer~~*) assessment, rating, *Am* assessed valuation; (*Versicherung*) appraisal; (*Voranschlag*) estimates *pl*; (*Urteil*) estimation; (*Hochschätzung*) esteem; **~~sfehler** *m* error in estimation; **~~sweise** *adv* approximately, roughly; **~~swert** *m* estimated value; (*Steuer*) assessed value; (*Versicherung*) appraised value.

Schau *f* (*Ausstellung, Schaustellung*) show, exhibition; (*Aussicht*) view; (*Anblick*) sight; perception; (*Nach~*) inspection; (*innerliche ~*) vision; (*zur Besichtigung*) inspection, survey; *mil* (*Besichtigung*) review; *zur ~ stellen* to exhibit, to display; to lay out for inspection; *zur ~ tragen* to display; to parade, to sport; to show off; to boast of; **~begierig** *a* eager to see; **~bild** *n* (pictorial) diagram, chart, graph; figure, perspective view; exhibit; **~brot** *n* (*Bibel*) shewbread; **~bude** *f* (*Jahrmarkt*) (show-)booth; **~~nbesitzer** *m* showman; **~bühne** *f* stage, theatre, *Am* theater; **~en** *tr* to see; to view; (*erblicken*) to behold; (*beobachten*) to observe; (*prüfen*) to examine; *itr* to look (at), to gaze (upon); *schau, schau!* look at that! *weder rechts noch links ~en* to look neither right nor left; **~fenster** *n* shop-window, *Am* show-window, store window; *im ~~ ausstellen* to display in the window; *die ~~ ansehen Am* to go window-shopping; **~~auslage** *f* window display; **~~beleuchtung** *f* show-window illumination; **~~dekorateur, ~~gestalter** *m* window dresser, **~~dekoration** *f* window dressing (*od* trimming); **~~einbruch** *m* smash-and-grab raid; **~~plakat** *n* showcard, window card; **~~plünderung** *f* broken-window looting; **~~reklame** *f* window display advertising; **~~wettbewerb** *m* window display competition; **~fliegen** *n aero* stunt-flying; **~flug** *m aero* exhibition flight; **~gefecht** *n* shamfight; **~gepränge** *n* pageantry; **~gerüst** *n* (*für Zuschauer*) platform; (*Tribüne*) grand-stand; (*Bühne*) stage; **~glas** *n* ga(u)ge (*od* level) glass; inspection glass; (*für Proben*) sample glass; display glass; **~haus** *n* mortuary; **~hörerschaft** *f* aural and visual audience; **~kampf** *m* (*Boxen*) exhibition match; **~kasten** *m* display case; show case; **~linie** *f* (*Diagramm*) curve, line; **~loch** *n* peephole, spyhole; **~lustig** *a* curious; **~lustige(r)** *m* onlooker, sightseer, *Am* rubberneck; **~modell** *n aero* (*aus Holz, in großem Maßstab*) mock-up; **~münze** *f* medal (-lion); **~packung** *f* dummy; mannequin; **~platz** *m* scene; stage, theatre; (*Kriegs~~*) theatre of war, seat of war; *vom ~~ abtreten fig* to go off the scene; **~prozeß** *m* show trial; **~spiel** *n* (*Stück*) play, drama; (*Anblick*) spectacle, sight; (*Szene*) scene; **~~dichter** *m* playwright, dramatist; **~~dichtung** *f* drama; **~~direktor** *m theat* manager; **~~er** *m* actor, player; **~~erin** *f* actress; **~~erisch** *a* stagey, theatrical; histrionic; **~~ern** *itr* to act, to play; *fig* (*schwindeln*) to sham; **~~haus** *n* playhouse, theatre, *Am* theater; **~~kunst** *f* dramatic art; **~steller** *m* (*Jahrmarkt*) showman; **~stellung** *f* exhibition; show; pageant; **~stück** *n* show-piece; (*Muster*) specimen; **~tafel** *f* diagram, chart, graph; **~turnen** *n* gymnastic display; athletic events *pl*; **~zeichen** *n* signal; visual signal; optical signal.

Schauder *m* shudder(ing), shiver; *fig* horror; (*Schrecken*) terror; (*Furcht*) fright; **~erregend** *a* horrific; **~haft, ~voll** *a* horrible, shocking; atrocious; awful, terrible; **~n** *itr* to shudder, to shiver (at), to tremble; *mir ~t* I shudder; *der bloße Gedanke daran macht mich ~~* the mere thought of it makes me shudder:

sich ~~d abwenden to shudder away; *es macht mich ~n* it makes my flesh creep.

Schauer *m* (*Schauder*) shudder; chill; *med* (*Anfall*) access; fit, attack; *fig* (*Anwandlung*) fit; thrill; (*Schrecken*) terror; (*Scheu*) awe, tremor; (*Regen*) shower of rain; downpour; *einzelne Regen~* scattered showers; (*Schuppen*) shed; shelter; **~drama** *n* thriller; **~film** *m* *Am* movie thriller; **~ig, ~lich, ~voll** *a* dreadful; horrible; **~leute** *pl* dockers *pl*; stevedores *pl*, *Am* longshoremen *pl*; **~n** *siehe*: *schaudern*; **~roman** *m* thriller, penny-dreadful, shilling shocker, *Am* dime novel.

Schaufel *f* shovel; (*kleine ~*) scoop; *Mehl~* flour scoop; (*Turbine*) blade; vane; turbine bucket; (*Rad~, Ruder~*) paddle; (*Anker~*) fluke; **~geweih** *n* palmed antlers *pl*; **~n** *tr, itr* to shovel; **~rad** *n* paddle-wheel; **~stiel** *m* handle of a shovel.

Schaukel *f* swing; **~bewegung** *f* rocking (*od* tilting) motion; **~brett** *n* seesaw; **~n** *tr, itr* to swing; to rock; to move to and fro; to oscillate; *wir werden das Kind schon ~~* (*fig fam*) we will swing it somehow; *itr mil* to roll; *r* to swing, to rock, to seesaw; **~pferd** *n* rocking-horse; **~politik** *f* seesaw policy; **~stuhl** *m* rocking-chair, *Am* rocker.

Schaum *m* foam; (*auf Getränken*) froth; (*auf Bier*) head; *med* (*Geifer*) slaver, spume; (*Meeres~*) spray, foam; (*Schaumgebackenes*) meringues *pl*; (*Milch~, Ab~*) scum; (*Seifen~*) lather; *fig* bubble; *zu ~ schlagen* (*Eiweiß*) to whip, to whisk; to beat up; *zu ~ werden fig* to end up in smoke; **~ähnlich, ~artig** *a* foamlike, foamy; frothy; **~bedeckt** *a* foam-covered; foamy; **~bildung** *f* formation of foam (*od* froth); **~blase** *f* bubble; **~feuerlöscher** *m* foam fire extinguisher; **~gebäck** *n* meringues *pl*; **~gold** *n* imitation (*od* Dutch) gold; tinsel; **~gummi** *m* foam(ed) rubber; **~~matratze** *f* foam rubber mattress; **~haube** *f* (*Bier*) head; **~ig** *a* frothy, foamy; **~kelle** *f*, **~löffel** *m* skimming ladle, skimmer; **~kraut** *n bot* cardamine; **~krone** *f* (*Woge*) white crest (*od* cap), white horses *pl*; **~los** *a* foamless, frothless; **~löschgerät** *n* foam fire extinguishing apparatus, foam-spray(er); **~perle** *f* bead; **~schläger** *m* (*Gerät*) whipper, egg-beater; *fig* (*Prahler*) windbag, gas-bag, empty talker, braggart, swaggerer, swashbuckler; **~schlägerei** *f fig* swashbuckling; **~seife** *f* lathering soap; **~wein** *m* sparkling wine, champagne; **~zucker** *m* meringue.

schäumen *itr* to foam, to froth; (*Wein*) to sparkle; (*Seife*) to lather; (*brausen*) to effervesce; to fizzle; (*Bier*) to foam; (*Meer*) to churn, to foam; (*aus Wut*) to fume; to boil (with rage); *die Seife schäumt gut* the soap lathers well; **~d** *a* foamy.

schaurig *a* horrible, dreadful.

Scheck *m* cheque, *Am* check; *Blanko~* blank cheque; *Post~* postal cheque; *Reise~* travel(l)er's cheque; *Verrechnungs~* negotiable cheque; *e-n ~ ausstellen* to draw a cheque; *e-n ~ einlösen* to cash a cheque; *e-n ~ sperren* to stop a cheque; *gefälschter ~* forged cheque, *sl* stumer-cheque, *Am* rubber check; *unausgefüllter ~* blank cheque; *ungedeckter ~* uncovered cheque; **~abschnitt** *m* counterfoil, *Am* check stub; **~aussteller** *m* drawer of cheque; **~buch** *n* cheque book; **~fälscher** *m* cheque forger, *Am* fake check customer; **~fälschung** *f* forgery of a cheque; **~formular** *n* cheque-form, *Am* blank check; **~heft** *n* cheque book; **~konto** *n* cheque account; **~verkehr** *m* cheque transactions *pl*; **~zahlung** *f* payment by cheque.

Scheck|e *f* piebald (*od* dappled) horse; **~ig** *a* piebald, spotted, dappled.

scheel *a* squint-eyed; *fig* jealous, envious; *~ ansehen* to look askance at; **~sucht** *f* envy; **~süchtig** *a* envious.

Scheffel *m* bushel; *sein Licht unter den ~ stellen* to hide o.'s light under a bushel; **~n** *tr fig* (*Geld*) to heap up, to amass; *itr* to yield abundantly; **~weise** *adv* by bushels.

Scheibe *f* disc, disk; (*Riemen~*) pulley; (*Unterlag~ aus Gummi, Leder, Metall*) washer; (*dünnes Plättchen*) lamella; *tele* (*Wähl~*) dial; (*Dichtungs~*) gasket; (*Mond~*) orb; (*Schieß~*) target; (*Töpfer~*) potter's wheel; (*Glas~*) pane, square; (*Brot~*) slice, cut; (*Honig~*) honeycomb; **~nförmig** *a* disk-like; **~ngardine** *f* short curtain; **~nglas** *n* plate-glass, window-glass; **~nhonig** *m* honey in the comb; **~nkupplung** *f mot* plate clutch; **~nrad** *n mot* disk (*od* disc) wheel; **~nschießen** *n* target shooting (*od* practice); **~nschlepper** *m aero mil* target-towing aircraft; **~nschütze** *m* marksman; **~nstand** *m* butts *pl*; rifle (*od* shooting) range; **~nweise** *adv* in slices; **~nwischer** *m* (wind-)screen wiper, *fam* wiper, *Am* windshield wiper.

Scheid|e *f* (*Grenze, Trennungslinie*) border, boundary; limit; line of demarcation; parting; separation; (*Wasser~~*) (water) divide; (*Schwert~~*) sheath; scabbard; *anat* vagina; **~eanstalt** *f* parting work, refinery; **~eblick** *m* parting look; **~ebrief** *m* farewell letter; *jur* (*bei Scheidung*) bill of divorce; **~egruß** *m* last farewell, adieus *pl*; **~ekunst** *f* assaying; chemical analysis; **~elinie** *f* line of demarcation; party line, boundary line; **~emauer** *f* partition-wall; **~emünze** *f* (*Kleingeld*) small coin, change; **~estunde** *f* hour of parting; (*Todesstunde*) hour of death; **~everfahren** *n* refining method, separation method; **~ewand** *f* partition, dividing-wall; barrier; **~ewasser** *n* nitric acid, aqua fortis, aqua regia; **~eweg** *m* (*Gabel*) forked way, parting of the ways; (*Kreuzweg*) cross-road; *fig* moment of decision; *am ~~ sein* to be at the cross-roads; **~ung** *f* separation, parting; *chem* analyzing; decomposing; extraction; (*Abtrennung*) sorting; severing; picking; (*Absonderung, Aufspaltung*) segregation; *jur* (*Ehe~*) divorce; (*Trennung*) separation; *auf ~ klagen* to sue for divorce; *der ~~ widersprechen* to oppose the divorce; **~~sgrund** *m* ground (*od* cause) for divorce; **~~sklage** *f* petition for divorce, divorce suit; **~~sprozeß** *m* divorce suit; **~~surteil** *n* divorce judg(e)ment; (*vorläufiges*) decree nisi (of divorce); (*endgültiges*) decree absolute (of divorce).

scheiden *irr tr* to separate, to part; (*trennen*) to sort (*von* from); to divide (*von* from); (*auseinandertrennen*) to sever; *chem* to analyse; to refine; (*zersetzen, zerlegen*) to decompose; (*isolieren*) to isolate; (*Ehe*) to divorce; *von Tisch u. Bett ~* to separate from bed and board; *sich ~ lassen* to seek a divorce (*von* from); to sue s. o. for divorce; to get a divorce; to obtain a divorce; *geschieden sein* to be divorced; *wir sind geschiedene Leute* we are through for good; *die Spreu vom Weizen ~* to winnow wheat; *itr* (*abreisen*) to depart, to leave; (*zurückziehen*) to retire, to retreat, to withdraw; *sie schieden als Freunde* they parted as friends; *hier ~ sich die Wege* here the roads part; *Scheiden tut weh* partings are grievous; **~d** *a* parting.

Schein *m* shine; (*Licht*) light; (*Schimmer*) gleam, glitter, glimmer; luster; glow; (*Aussehen*) air, look; (*Glanz*) brightness, brilliancy, brilliance, radiance, splendo(u)r; (*Strahl*) flash; (*An~*) appearance, pretence, semblance, show; (*Heiligen~*) halo, *fig* glory; (*Erscheinung*) appearance; (*Wahrscheinlichkeit*) likelihood; (*Vorwand*) pretext, colo(u)r; (*Quittung*) acquittance, receipt; (*Bescheinigung*) certificate, ticket, attestation; (*Bank-*) bank-note, *Am* bill; (*Schuld~*) bond; *zum ~e* for the sake of appearance; *der äußere ~* appearances *pl*, show, outside, face; *dem ~e nach, anscheinend* apparently; *den ~ wahren* to keep up appearances, to save appearances; *den ~ geben, als ob* to pretend to; *der ~ trügt* appearances are deceiving; *des falschen ~s entkleiden Am* to debunk; *urteile nicht nach dem ~* never judge by appearances; *Schein . . .* (*in Zssg*): sham . . ., mock . . ., dummy . . ., *Am* phony . . .; **~angriff** *m* sham attack, feint, feigned attack, mock assault; **~argument** *n* spurious argument; **~auktion** *f* mock auction; **~bar** *a* (*anscheinend*) apparent, seeming; (*vorgeblich*) make-believe; (*wahrscheinlich*) likely, plausible; **~bewegung** *f* apparent movement; **~beweis** *m* sham proof; **~bild** *n* illusion; phantom, mockery; **~blüte** *f* apparent prosperity, sham boom; **~christ** *m* lip-Christian; **~ehe** *f* fictitious marriage; mock marriage; **~en** *irr itr* to shine; (*den Anschein haben*) to appear; to seem; *es scheint mir* it appears to me that; *ins Gesicht ~en* to shine into o.'s face; *mir scheint* it seems to me; *wie es scheint* as it seems; **~friede** *m* sham peace, hollow peace, *Am* phony peace; **~funkspruch** *m radio mil* dummy message; **~gebot** *n* sham bid, *Am* straw bid; **~gefecht** *n* sham fight, *Am* sham battle; **~geschäft** *n* dummy transaction; **~gold** *n* imitation gold; **~grund** *m* fictitious reason; sophism; (*Vorwand*) pretext, pretence, *Am* pretense; **~heilig** *a* sanctimonious; hypocritical; **~~e(r)** *m* hypocrite; **~~keit** *f* sanctimony; hypocrisy; cant; **~horizont** *m* visual horizon; **~kauf** *m* sham purchase; **~konjunktur** *f Am* sham boom; **~krieg** *m* sham war, *Am* phony war; **~luftkrieg** *m* sham air war; **~platz** *m aero mil* decoy airdrome; dummy airfield; **~stellung** *f mil* dummy position; **~tod** *m* apparent death, suspended animation; trance; **~tot** *a* seemingly dead; **~vertrag** *m* fictitious (*od* sham) contract; **~werfer** *m* reflector, projector; flashlight; floodlight; *mil* search-light; *theat* spot-light; *film Am* klieglight; *mot* headlight, headlamp; *mit ~~n anstrahlen* to floodlight, *Am* to klieglight; **~~flugzeug** *n aero mil* searchlight plane; **~~kegel, ~~strahl** *m* search-light beam; **~~lampe** *f* projector lamp; **~widerstand** *m el* impedance.

Scheiße *f vulg* shit; **~n** *itr* to shit.

Scheit *n* log, billet, piece of wood.

Scheitel *m* summit; apex; top; crown (of the head); (*Haar~*) parting; **~abstand** *m* zenith distance; **~bein** *n* *anat* parietal bone; **~bogen, ~kreis** *m* azimuth; **~linie** *f* vertical line; **~n** *tr* to part (o.'s hair); **~punkt** *m math* vertex, angular point; *astr* zenith; *fig* summit; **~recht** *a* vertical; **~winkel** *m* vertical angle.

Scheiter|haufen *m* funeral pile; pyre; (*für lebenden Menschen*) stake; *auf dem ~~ sterben* to die at the stake; **~n** *itr* to be wrecked, to be lost; *fig* to fail, to miscarry; *~~ n* shipwreck; *fig* failure, miscarriage.

Schellack *m* shellac.

Schelle *f* (hand-)bell; (*Fesseln*) manacles *pl*; handcuffs *pl*; *fam* (*Ohrfeige*) box on the ear; *tech* (*Rohr~*) **clamp**; clip; clamping ring; **~n** *n* diamonds (at cards); **~n** *tr, itr* to ring the bell for, to tinkle; **~nbaum** *m* crescent; **~ngeläute** *n* tinkling of bells, sleigh-bells *pl*; **~nkappe** *f* fool's cap with bells.

Schell|fisch *m* haddock; **~kraut** *n* celandine.

Schelm *m* rogue; knave, villain; *der arme ~!* the poor fellow! *ein ~, der Böses dabei denkt!* honni soit qui mal y pense! **~enroman** *m* picaresque; **~enstreich** *m* roguish trick; prank; **~erei** *f* roguery; (*Schurkerei*) knavery, villainy; **~isch** *a* roguish; knavish; sly, waggish.

Schelt|e *f* reprimand, scolding; *~~ bekommen* to be scolded; **~en** *irr tr* to chide for, to scold at; to objurgate; *fam* to blow up; (*tadeln*) to rebuke; (*schimpfen*) to revile, to abuse; *itr* to inveigh against; **~wort** *n* reproachful term, invective, abusive word.

Schema *n* order; form; arrangement: (*Muster*) model, pattern; (*Plan*) schedule, scheme; diagram, sketch; **~tisch** *a* schematic, diagrammatic; mechanical; in accordance with a certain plan (*od* pattern); *~~e Zeichnung* skeleton sketch; **~tisieren** *tr* to schematize; to standardize; (*skizzieren*) to sketch; **~tismus** *m* schematism; (*in der Verwaltung*) red tape.

Schemel *m* (foot)stool.

Schemen *m* phantom; shadow; delusion; **~haft** *a* shadowy; unreal.

Schenk *m* (*Mund~*) cup-bearer; (*Wirt*) publican, ale-house keeper; **~e** *f* ale-house, public house, *sl* pub; inn, tavern, beer house, roadhouse, *Am* saloon, bar.

Schenkel *m* (*Ober~*) thigh; (*Unter~*) shank; (*Zirkel*) foot; (*Winkel*) side; (*Bein, Dreieck*) leg; **~bruch** *m* fracture of the thigh(-bone); **~druck** *m* (*Reiter*) pressure of the leg; calf pressure; **~gegend** *f* crural region.

schenken *tr* to give, to make a present of; (*erlassen*) to pardon; (*Schuld, Strafe*) to remit; (*übermachen*) to endow, *Am* to donate; (*ein~*) to pour out; (*e-e Schenke führen*) to retail, to keep an ale-house; *jdm das Leben ~* to pardon; *mil* to give quarter; *Glauben ~* to put faith in, to have faith in, to place confidence in; to trust.

Schenk|er, ~geber *m* giver, donor; **~gerechtigkeit** *f* licence for retailing beer, etc; **~mädchen** *n* barmaid; **~stube** *f* tap-room; *Am* bar, saloon; **~tisch** *m* bar, sideboard; **~ung** *f* donation, gift; **~~surkunde** *f* deed of gift; **~wirt** *m* inn-keeper, publican, landlord; **~wirtschaft** *f* public house, *sl* pub; inn, tavern, ale-house, *Am* saloon, bar.

scheppern *itr fam* (*klappern*) to rattle; to clatter; (*klirren*) to jingle; to clank.

Scherbe *f*, ***~n*** *m* (*Bruchstücke e-s Topfes*) pot-sherd; (*Splitter*) fragment; broken piece (*od* bit) of glass, china etc; (*Blumen~*) flowerpot; (*Topf*) crock; *chem* cupel; *hum* (*Monokel*) monocle; *mar* scarf; *in ~n gehen* to go to pieces; *~n pl* (*Überreste*) remains *pl mit sing*; **~ngericht** *n* ostracism.

Scher|e *f* (a pair of) scissors *pl*; *große ~e* shears *pl*; shafts *pl* (of a carriage); (*Krebs~~*) claw; nipper, chela; (*Schaf~~*) sheep-shears *pl*; (*Draht~~*) wire-cutter; (*Blech~~*) plate-shears *pl*; (*Haarschneidmaschine*) clippers *pl*; **~en** *reg u. irr tr* (*Bart*) to shave (*od* to trim) s. o.'s beard; (*Haare*) to cut s. o.'s hair; (*Schafe*) to shear; (*Hecke*) to clip, to cut; (*Baum*) to poll, to lop; (*Rasen*) to mow (the lawn); (*abschnippeln*) to snip; *mar* (*vom Kurs abweichen*) to shear; *aero* to yaw; *glatt geschoren* close-shaved, close-cropped; (*jdn betrügen*) *fig* to fleece s. o.; *sich um etw ~~* to trouble o. s. about; *das schert mich nicht* I don't mind it; *sich ~~* to go away; to be off; *scher dich zum Henker!* get you gone! go to the devil! **~enfernrohr** *n mil* stereo-telescope; scissor telescope; periscope; **~enschleifer** *m* knife-grinder; **~enschmied** *m* cutler; **~enschnitt** *m* silhouette; **~er** *m* shearer, barber; **~erei** *f* trouble, vexation, annoyance, nuisance, bother; *jdm viel ~~ machen* to give s. o. much trouble, to lead s. o. a pretty dance; **~maschine** *f* shearing-machine; **~messer** *n* shearing knife; (*Rasiermesser*) razor; **~winkel** *m aero* angle of yaw(ing); **~wolle** *f* shearings *pl*.

Scherflein *n* mite; *sein ~ zu etw beitragen* to contribute o.'s share to; to do o.'s bit.

Scherge *m* (*Soldat*) myrmidon; (*Gerichtsdiener*) bailiff; (*Büttel*) beadle; (*Henker*) hangman, executioner.

Scherz *m* (*Scherzwort, Spaß*) joke; (*andere angreifend*) jest; (*Unterhaltung*) fun; sport; (*witziger Einfall*) quip, witticism; (*scherzhafte Antwort*) *fam* wisecrack, crack; (*plumper Witz, Ulk*) *fam* gag; wit; (*Erheiterung*) pleasantry; (*Stichelei, Spott*) jibe, gibe; (*Schäkerei, Neckerei*) badinage; *aus ~, im ~e* in jest, for fun; *~ treiben mit* to make merry with; to make fun of; *im ~ od im Ernst* in jest or in earnest; *als ~ auffassen* to treat as a joke; *e-n ~ machen* to crack a joke; *im ~ reden* to be jesting; *sie verstehen keinen ~* they don't understand a joke; *e-n ~ zu weit treiben* to carry a joke too far; *~ beiseite!* joking apart! **~artikel** *m pl* (*Karneval*) tricks *pl*, comic articles *pl*, puzzles *pl*; **~en** *itr* to jest, to joke, to make fun (of), to have fun (with); to trifle (with); *Sie ~~!* you can't be serious! *Am* you are kidding! *damit läßt sich nicht ~~* this is no joking matter; *mit ihr ist nicht zu ~~* she is not to be trifled with; *er läßt nicht mit sich ~~* he is not a man to be trifled with, he is not in the mood for trifling; **~frage** *f* jocular question; **~gedicht** *n* comic poem; **~haft** *a* (*scherzliebend*) playful, jocose, jocular; (*humorvoll*) humorous; (*witzig*) facetious; (*drollig*) droll; (*komisch*) comical; (*spaßig*) funny; (*lustig*) merry, sportive; **~macher** *m* joker, humorist; **~name** *m* nickname; **~rätsel** *n* conundrum; **~weise** *adv* jestingly, for fun; **~wort** *n* joke, facetious word; witticism.

scheu *a* shy; (*zaghaft*) timid; faint-hearted; (*schüchtern*) bashful, coy; (*menschen~*) unsociable; self-conscious; (*zurückhaltend*) reserved; (*Pferd*) shying, skittish; *~es Wesen* skittishness; *ein ~es Lächeln* a shy smile; *~ machen* to frighten, to start; *~ werden* to take fright at, to shy at; *~es Pferd* shyer, jibber; *~ f* shyness, timidity; *~ haben etw zu tun* to dread doing s. th.; *~ vor* aversion to; *ohne ~* without the least fear; *heilige ~* awe; **~klappe** *f*, **~leder** *n* (*Pferd*) blinker, *Am* blinder.

Scheuche *f* scarecrow; (*Schreckbild*) bogy, bugbear; **~n** *tr* to scare, to frighten away; (*Tiere, Vögel*) to shoo away; to drive away by crying "shoo".

scheuen *tr* to avoid, to shun, to dread; to shrink from; (*fürchten*) to fear, to be afraid of; *keine Mühe ~* to spare no pains; *ohne die Kosten zu ~* regardless of expenses; *sie hat keine Kosten gescheut* she spared no expense; *itr* to shy, to take fright at, to be frightened; *sich ~ vor* to be shy of; to be afraid of; (*zögern*) to be reluctant to; *sich vor nichts ~* to stick at nothing.

Scheuer *f* barn, shed.

Scheuer|bürste *f* scrubbing-brush, *Am* scrub-brush; **~faß** *n* washing-tub; **~festigkeit** *f* abrasion resistance; **~frau, ~magd** *f* charwoman, *Am* scrubwoman; **~lappen, ~wisch** *m* scouring cloth; (*Schrubber*) swab; mob; **~leiste** *f* skirting-board; **~mittel** *n* scouring agent; **~n** *tr* to scour, to scrub; (*Haut*) to rub, to chafe; *wund ~~* to rub the skin off; **~pulver** *n* scouring powder; **~sand** *m* scouring-sand; **~wunde** *f* chafe, chafing.

Scheune *f* barn, shed, hayflot; granary; **~ndrescher** *m* thresher; *essen wie ein ~~* to eat like a lumberjack (*od* farmer).

Scheusal *n* monster; *ein wahres ~* a perfect fright.

scheußlich *a* hideous, ugly; abominable, horrid; awful, terrible, horrible; shocking; *~es Wetter* awful weather; **~keit** *f* atrocity, horror.

Schi, Ski *m* ski; *die ~er anschnallen* to put (*od* to adjust) the skis; *~ fahren, ~ laufen* to ski; *~ heil!* ski heil! **~abfahrtslauf** *m* down-run; **~anzug** *m* ski(ing) suit; **~aufzug** *m* ski-lift, chair-lift, *Am auch* skimobile; **~ausrüstung** *f* ski(ing) equipment; **~bindung** *f* ski-binding; **~bluse** *f* anorak, anarak; **~fahrer** *m* skier; *begeisterter ~~* ski fan; **~gebiet** *n* ski-field; **~gelände** *n* skiing ground; **~grätenschritt** *m* herring-bone skiing step; **~handschuhe** *m pl* ski-mitts *pl*; **~haserl** *n* snow bunny; **~hose** *f* ski-pants *pl*; **~hütte** *f* ski(ing) hut; **~ jacke** *f* ski-jacket; **~jöring** *n* skijöring; **~klub** *m* skiing club; **~kurs** *m* ski lessons *pl*. skiing courses *pl*; **~langlauf** *m* long distance skiing; cross-country race; **~lauf** *m*, **~laufen** *n* skiing; **~läufer** *m* skier, ski-runner; **~lehrer** *m* ski-coach, skiing trainer; **~mütze** *f* ski-cap; **~rucksack** *m* ski-pack; **~säugling** *m* beginner; **~spitze** *f* ski-tip; **~sport** *m* skiing; **~springen** *n* ski-jumping; **~sprungschanze** *f* ski-jump; **~stadion** *n* skiing stadium; **~stiefel** *m pl* ski-boots *pl*; **~stock** *m* ski-pole, ski-stick; **~tour** *f* ski-tour; **~wachs** *n* ski-waxing; **~wetter** *n* skiing weather; **~wettkampf** *m* skiing contest, ski competition.

Schicht *f* (*Lage, Sand~, Staub~ etc*) layer; *geol* (*Gesteins~*) stratum, *pl* strata; (*Kruste, Lage*) layer, bed; *min* roof, floor; (*Mauer~, Stein~*) course (of bricks), range, row; (*Zone*) zone; *phot* emulsion, coating; (*Bodensatz*) sediment; (*Haufen, Stapel*) pile; (*auf Flüssigkeiten*) film; (*Farb~*) coat; (*dünne ~*) coating; (*Hochofen*) charge; (*Menge, Papier~,*

Gieß~) batch; (*Arbeitsgruppe*) gang; (*Arbeitsauftrag*) task; (*zeitliche Arbeits~*) shift; turn; spell; (*Pause in der Arbeitszeit*) rest, off-time, break, pause; *fig* (*Gesellschafts~*) (social) class; rank; *pl* social strata; *die oberen ~en* the upper ten (thousand), the upper crust; *Leute aus allen ~en* people from all walks of life; *in ~en arbeiten* to work in shifts; *in ~en* in layers; *~ machen* to stop working, to knock off; *Nacht~* night-shift; *Tag~* day-turn; **~arbeit** *f* shift-work; **~arbeiter** *m* day-worker, shift-worker; **~ebene** *f* plane of stratification; **~en** *tr* (*in Schichten legen*) to arrange (*od* to put) in layers (*od* beds); (*ordnen*) to set in order; (*auf~~*) to pile up; to put in piles; (*ansammeln*) to accumulate; (*Hochofen beschicken*) to charge; *geol* to stratify, to bed; (*Holz*) to stack; *mar* (*Ladung*) to stow; (*in Klassen einteilen*) to classify; **~enaufbau** *m* stratification; **~enbau** *m* stratified structure; **~englas** *n* laminated glass; **~enkonstruktion** *f* sandwich construction; **~enstörung** *f geol* dislocation of strata; **~enweise** *adv* in layers, in strata; **~folge** *f* series (*od* sequence) of strata; **~gefüge** *n* lamellar strata; **~gestein** *n* stratified rocks *pl*, sedimentary rock; **~holz** *n* stacked wood; cordwood; **~linie** *f* (*Landkarte*) contour line; **~lohn** *m* shift wage; **~meister** *m* overseer (of miners), foreman; **~seite** *f phot* film side, emulsion side; **~träger** *m phot* emulsion carrier; **~ung** *f* arrangement in layers; striation, lamination; piling up; *geol* stratification; **~wasser** *n* ground water; **~wechsel** *m* change of shift; **~weise** *adv* in layers, stratified; **~wolke** *f* (*niedere ~~*) stratus, *pl* strati; (*höhere ~~*) cirro-stratus; (*noch höher*) alto-stratus; **~zahn** *m* milk tooth.

Schick *m* (*Gewandtheit, Geschick, Kunstkniff*) skill, dexterity, fitness; (*in der Kleidung*) elegance; (*Geschmack*) taste, tact; stylishness, smartness; *~ haben für* to have a knack of; (*in Kleidung*) to be stylishly dressed; *~ a* chic, elegant; stylish; fashionable, smart, swell, *Am* swank.

schicken *tr* to send, to dispatch; (*Brief*) to mail, to post; (*Güter*) to convey; (*Geld*) to remit; *nach jdm ~* to send for; *in den April ~* to make an April-fool of; *auf die Reise ~* to launch; *auf den Weg ~* to route; *r* (*geschehen*) to come to pass, to happen; (*geziemen*) to suit; to behove, *Am* to behoove; *es schickt sich nicht* it does not become; *e-s schickt sich nicht für alle* the same thing will not do for all; *sich in etw ~* to put up with; (*sich fügen*) to comply with, to be resigned to; to accommodate o. s. to, to yield to; *sich in die Zeit ~* to go with the times.

schicklich *a* becoming, decent, convenient, suitable; **~keit** *f* propriety; (*Anständigkeit*) decency, (*Anstand*) decorum; **~~sgefühl** *n* sense of propriety, tact.

Schicksal *n* fate; (*Lebensbestimmung*) destiny; (*Los*) lot; (*Glück*) fortune; *trauriges ~* sad lot; *unabwendbares ~* fatality; *wechselndes ~* the ups and downs of life, the vicissitudes of life; *sein ~ ist besiegelt* his fate is sealed; *jdn seinem ~ überlassen* to leave s. o. to his fate; *niemand entrinnt seinem ~* no one can avoid his destiny; **~sdeuter** *m* interpreter of destiny; **~sfügung** *f* divine ordinance; **~sgang, ~sweg** *m* march of destiny; **~sgefährte** *m* companion, fellow-sufferer; **~sgemeinschaft** *f* community of fate; **~sglaube** *m* fatalism; **~sgöttinnen** *f pl* the Fates *pl;* **~slinie** *f* (*in der Hand*) fatal line; **~sprüfung** *f* trial, ordeal; **~sschlag** *m* heavy (*od* fatal) blow, stroke of fate; reverse; **~sschwestern** *f pl* weird sisters *pl*; **~stücke** *f* malice of destiny.

Schickung *f* Providence; divine will, divine guidance, divine care; dispensation; (*Heimsuchung*) affliction.

*

Schieb|eblende *f* sliding diaphragm; **~ebühne** *f* movable (*od* sliding) platform, traverser; **~edach** *n mot* sliding roof, sunshine roof; **~edruck** *m* separation pressure; **~efenster** *n* sash-window, slide window; **~(e)karren** *m* wheelbarrow, *Am* pushcart; **~ekupplung** *f* sliding coupling; **~elandung** *f* cross wind landing; **~elineal** *n* sliding rule; **~en** *irr tr* (*stoßend ~~*) to push; (*mit größerer Kraftanstrengung*) to shove; (*gleitend ~~*) to slide (*in* into); (*bewegen*) to move; (*vorwärtstreiben*) to thrust. to propel; *aero* (*Abdrängen aus Flugrichtung durch Seitenwind*) to crab; *beiseite ~~* to move off, to turn aside; *sich ineinander ~~* to telescope: *nach außen ~~* to squash, to skid; *itr fig* (*Schiebergeschäfte machen*) to profiteer, to racketeer, to wangle; (*unredlich verfahren*) to shift; *das Brot in den Ofen ~~* to put bread into the oven; *Kegel ~~* to play at nine-pins, *Am* to play at tenpins; *in den Mund ~~* to put into o.'s mouth; *in die Tasche ~~* to put into o.'s pocket; *etw auf die lange Bank ~~* to put off, to defer, to postpone; to adjourn; *die Schuld auf jdn ~~* to lay the blame on s. o; *jdm etw in die Schuhe ~~* to put s. th. to s. o.'s account; **~er** *m tech* pusher; slider; extractor; shovel; corrector; (*Halsband etc*) slide; (*Riegel*) bolt; *fig* (*Betrüger*) profiteer, racketeer; (*Schwarzmarkthändler*) black-marketeer; underground operator; loafer, spiv, *Am* grafter, *Am* spoilsman; **~erdruckregler** *m* regulating feed valve; **~ergeschäft** *n* racket, profiteering-job; **~ermotor** *m mot* sleeve valve engine; **~ersteuerung** *f* slide valve gear; **~ertum** *n* racketeering, profiteering; **~erventil** *n* gate valve; **~erwiderstand** *m* slide rheostat; **~esitz** *m* close sliding fit; *mot* sliding seat; **~etür** *f* sliding door; **~ewand** *f* sliding partition; **~ewind** *m aero* (*Rückenwind*) tail wind; **~kasten** *m* drawer, till; **~lehre** *f* slide gauge, *Am* slide ga(u)ge; **~ung** *f* pushing, shoving; *fig* (*betrügerische Machenschaften*) profiteering, foul play; backstairs politics *pl*; sharp practices *pl*; *Am parl* spoils *pl*; tricks *pl*; manoeuvres *pl*, *Am* maneuvers *pl*; underhand-dealings *pl*; illegal transaction.

Schieds|gericht *n* court of arbitration, court of awards; arbitration board; (*Wettbewerb*) committee of judges; *Streitigkeiten durch ein ~~ entscheiden* to settle disputes by arbitration; *an ein ~~ verweisen* to refer to arbitration; *e-e Entscheidung durch ein ~~ vereinbaren* to agree to submit to arbitration; **~~sbarkeit** *f* arbitrary jurisdiction; **~~shof** *m* court of arbitration; *Ständiger Internationaler ~~shof* Permanent Court of International Justice; **~~sklausel** *f* arbitration clause; **~gutachten** *n* arbitrator's award; advisory opinion; **~parteien** *f pl* parties to arbitration; **~richter** *m* arbitrator; moderator; (*Sport*) umpire; (*Fußball, Boxen*) referee; (*Wettkämpfe*) judge; **~richterlich** *a* arbitral, by private arbitration; *adv* by arbitration, by umpire; **~spruch** *m* (*Urteil*) arbitration, award; (arbitral) decision; *e-n ~~ fällen* to make an award, to arbitrate; *sich e-m ~~ unterwerfen* to submit to an award; **~verfahren** *n* (procedure of) arbitration; **~vertrag** *m* agreement to go to arbitration; treaty of submission to arbitration.

schief *a* (*schräg*) oblique; (*geneigt*) inclined; (*abfallend*) sloping; slant(ing); (*nach e-r Seite hängend, einseitig*) lopsided; (*krumm*) crooked; twisted; (*Gesicht*) wry; *fig* (*falsch, verkehrt*) false, wrong; biassed; (*verzerrt*) distorted; perverse; *adv* askew, askance; slantwise; awry; obliquely; *~e Ansicht* distorted view; *~e Ebene* gradient, *math* inclined plane; *auf die ~e Ebene kommen* to go off the straight path; *~e Lage fig* predicament, quandary, plight; *in e-r ~en Lage sein* to be in an awkward position; *ein ~es Licht werfen auf jdn* to put s. o. in a bad light; *~er Winkel* oblique angle; *jdn ~ ansehen* to frown upon s. o., to look cross at s. o.; *~ blicken* (*schielen*) to squint; *~ gehen fig* (*mißlingen*) to go wrong, to go awry; to turn out badly; *die Sache ging ~* the plan miscarried; *~ geladen fam* (*betrunken*) half-seas over; *~ gewickelt sein fig fam* to be wrong; *~ liegen* to be on the wrong side; **~äugig** *a* squint-eyed; **~blatt** *n bot* begonia; **~e** *f* obliqueness, obliquity; (*Krummheit*) crookedness, wryness; *fig* (*Verschrobenheit*) crookedness; perversity; warp; (*Neigung*) slope, inclination; slant; declivity; inclined plane; **~hals** *m* wry-neck; **~liegend** *a* inclined; oblique; **~mäulig** *a* wry-mouthed; **~treten** *irr tr: die Absätze ~~* to tread o.'s boots down at the heels; **~winklig** *a* oblique-angled; **~wuchs** *m med* scoliosis.

Schiefer *m* slate; (*Gestein*) schist; *mit ~ decken* to slate; **~ähnlich, ~artig** *a* slatelike, slaty; schistous; **~bedachung** *f* slating; **~blau** *a* slate-blue; **~boden** *m* slaty soil; **~brecher** *m* slate-cutter; **~bruch** *m* slate-pit, slate-quarry; **~dach** *n* slate roof; **~decker** *m* slater; **~farbe** *f* slate colo(u)r; **~grau** *a* slate-grey, slate-colo(u)red; **~haltig** *a* containing slate, slaty; schistous; **~ig** *a* slaty; **~n** *itr r* to come off in scales, to scale off; to exfoliate; **~öl** *n* schist oil; **~platte** *f* slab of slate; **~stein** *m* lithographic stone; **~stift** *m* slate-pencil; **~tafel** *f* school-slate; **~ton** *m* slate clay, shale; **~ung** *f* scaling off, exfoliation.

schiel|en *itr* to squint; *nach etw ~en* to leer at; **~~** *n med* strabismus, squinting; **~äugig** *a* cross-eyed, *Am* cockeyed; *fam* swivel-eyed; **~end** *a* squinting; **~er** *m* squinter.

Schienbein *n* shin(-bone), tibia; shank; **~schützer** *m sport* shin-pad, shin-guard.

Schiene *f* (*Rad*) iron band; *tech* bar; (*Chirurgie*) splint; *rail* rail; (*Schienenstrang, Geleise*) track; *aus den ~n kommen* to run off the rails, to get off the rails; to derail, to be derailed; **~n** *tr med* to splint, to put in splints, to apply a splint; to plate (a fracture); (*Schlitten*) to shoe; (*Rad*) to tire; **~nbahn** *f* rail line; (*Straßenbahn*) tramway, *Am* streetcar; *rail* railway, *Am* railroad; **~nbruch** *m* breaking of rails; **~nfahrzeug** *n* rail vehicle; rail car; **~ngleis** *n* track; **~nkreuzung** *f* crossing; **~nlasche** *f* fish plate, *Am* joint bar; **~nleger** *m* plate-layer, *Am* tracklayer; **~nnetz** *n* railway system, *Am* railroad system; **~n(omni)bus** *m* rail bus; **~nprofil** *n* rail section; **~nräumer** *m* sweeper, track-clearer, rail-guard, *Am* cow-catcher; **~nstoß** *m* rail joint; jolt; **~nstrang** *m* line of rails, metals *pl*; *rail* track(s *pl*); **~nübergang** *m rail* (*schienengleicher Übergang*) level crossing, *Am* grade crossing, crossing at grade; **~nüberhöhung** *f* cant of rails; **~nwalzwerk** *n* rail rolling mill; **~nweg** *m* railway line; **~nweite** *f* (railway) gauge, *Am auch* (railroad) gage.

schier *a* (*rein*) pure, sheer; *adv* (*beinahe, fast*) nearly, almost.

Schierling *m* hemlock; **~sbecher** *m* poisoned cup.

Schieß|ausbildung *f* musketry-training; rifle practice; (*Artillerie*) gunnery-training; **~auszeichnung** *f* shooting badge, marksman's badge; **~bahn** *f* range, shooting-ground; **~baumwolle** *f* gun-cotton; **~bedarf** *m* ammunition; **~buch** *n* score-book; **~bude** *f* shooting-gallery; **~en** *irr tr, itr* to shoot (*auf, nach* at), to fire (*auf, nach* at), to discharge (an arrow); (*sprengen*) to blow up, to blast; (*Flüssigkeit*) to gush, to spout, to squirt, to jet; (*Raubvogel*) to swoop down, to pounce on; (*Pflanzen*) to spring (up), to shoot up, *Am* (*wie Pilze*) to mushroom up; (*schnelle Bewegung*) to rush, to dash, to spurt, to shoot along, to dart along, to pounce into (room), to tear along; (*Gedanke*) to flash; *ein Gedanke schoß mir durch den Kopf* an idea flashed through my mind; *nicht ~en!* don't shoot! *vorbei ~en* to miss in shooting; *~en Sie los!* fire up! *~en lassen* to let fly; *blind ~en* to shoot with blank cartridge; *scharf ~en* to shoot with powder and ball; *e-n Bock ~en fig* to make a blunder, *Am* to pull a boner; *tot ~en* to kill; *gut ~en* to be a good shot; *aus dem Hinterhalt ~en* to snipe; *sich e-e Kugel in den Kopf ~en* to blow out o.'s brains; *die Zügel ~en lassen* to give the rein to; *ins Kraut ~en* to shoot, to sprout; *in Ähren ~en* to shoot into ears; *in Samen ~en* to run to seed; *ein Tor ~~* (*Fußball*) to score a goal; *r* to fight a duel with; **~en** *n* shooting; (*Wett~~*) rifle-match; *~~ mit Erdbeobachtung mil* ground-observed fire; *~~ mit Karte* map firing; *das ist zum ~en! fam* that beats cockfighting! *Am* that's a scream! *Am* that's a riot! **~eisen** *n hum Am* shooting iron; **~erei** *f* gunfight; **~ergebnis** *n* effect of firing; **~gestell** *n* (fork) rest; **~gewehr** *n* gun; **~grundlage** *f*, **~unterlagen** *f pl* firing data *pl*; **~hund** *m* (*Jagd*) pointer; *aufpassen wie ein ~~* (*fam*) to watch like a lynx; **~krieg** *m* shooting war, hot war; **~lehre** *f* ballistics *pl mit sing*; **~lehrer** *m* musketry instructor; **~plan** *m* fire-control map; **~platz** *m* practice ground; (calibration) range, artillery range; **~prügel** *m fam* fire-arm, *Am* shooting iron; **~pulver** *n* gunpowder; **~scharte** *f* loophole, embrasure; (*Schlitz*) (fire-)slit; **~scheibe** *f* (practice) target; **~sport** *m* rifle shooting; **~stand** *m* shooting-gallery, shooting-range; *mil* rifle-range, gun-testing pit, butts *pl*; **~übung** *f* shooting (*od* rifle) practice; (*Artillerie*) artillery practice; **~verfahren** *n* shooting process; **~vorschrift** *f* regulations for gunnery (*od* musketry); **~zeit** *f* (*Jagd*) shooting season.

Schiff *n* ship, (*für große seegehende ~e*) vessel; (*für jeden Schifftyp u. kollektiv*) craft; (*für kleine, offene ~e*) boat; *poet* argosy; *typ* galley; (*Wasser~ im Herd*) boiler; (*Kirchen~*) nave; (*Weber~*) shuttle; *zu ~e gehen* to go on board, to embark, to take ship for; *an Bord des ~es* on board ship, on board of the ship; on shipboard; *~ in Seenot* ship in distress; *einfahrendes, ausfahrendes ~* home-bound ship, outward-bound ship; *ein ~ festmachen* to moor a ship *das ~ verlassen* to abandon ship *klar ~* decks cleared for action; **~bar** *a* navigable; *nicht ~~* unnavigable; *~~ machen* to canalize; **~barkeit** *f* navigability; **~barmachung** *f* canalization; **~bau** *m* ship-building; **~bauer** *m* ship-builder, naval architect; **~baukunst** *f* naval architecture; **~bruch** *m* shipwreck; *~~ erleiden* to be shipwrecked; **~brüchig** *a* shipwrecked; **~~ige(r)** *m* castaway; **~brücke** *f* pontoon bridge, floating bridge; (*Teil des ~es*) bridge; **~chen** *n* little ship, small boat; *mil sl* (*Kopfbedeckung*) forage-cap; (*Weber~~*) shuttle; *typ* composing galley; **~en** *itr* (*ein~~, ver~~*) to ship; (*fahren, steuern*) to navigate, to cross the sea; (*Urin lassen*) to make water.

Schiffer *m* (*allg für das gesamte Schiffspersonal*) mariner; (*gelernter Seemann*) seaman, sailor; (*Schiffsführer*) ship-master, master mariner; (*Schiffsführer e-s Fischereibootes od kleinen Handelsschiffes*) skipper; (*Pilot e-s Küstenschiffes*) boatman; (*Kahnführer*) bargee; **~ausdruck** *m* nautical term; **~klavier** *n* accordion, concertina; squiffer; **~knoten** *m* sailor's knot; **~lied** *n* sea-song; **~lohn** *m* sailor's wages *pl*; **~patent** *n* (*für große Fahrt*) master's certificate; (*für kleine Fahrt*) mate's certificate; **~sprache** *f* nautical language; **~stechen** *n* regatta; sham-fight between boats.

Schiff|(f)ahrer *m* navigator; sailor, seaman; **~(f)ahrt** *f* navigation, voyage; **~~samt** *n* Shipping Board; **~~sausschuß** *m* maritime commission; **~~sgesellschaft** *f* shipping company; **~~skanal** *m* ship-canal; **~~skunde** *f* navigation; **~~slinie** *f* shipping line; steamship line; **~~spool** *m* shipping pool; **~~ssperre** *f* embargo; **~~sstraße** *f* navigation route, ship(ping) lane; **~~sstreik** *m* shipping strike; **~~sweg** *m* ship lane; route; **~~szeichen** *n* nautical sign; **~~treibend** *a* (*Volk*) seafaring; **~schaukel** *f* swingboat.

Schiffs|agent *m* ship's agent; **~angelegenheiten** *f pl* shipping-concerns *pl*; **~anlegeplatz** *m* landing-place; pier, dock, *Am* slip; **~artillerie** *f* naval artillery; **~arzt** *m* ship's doctor, ship's surgeon, medical officer; **~bauch** *m* hold (of a ship); **~befrachtung** *f* ship's freight; **~bergung** *f* salvage service; **~besatzung** *f* (ship's) crew; **~beute** *f* prize; **~boden** *m* ship's bottom; **~boot** *m* long-boat; **~breite** *f* beam of a boat; **~brücke** *f* pontoon bridge; **~bug** *m* bow; **~flagge** *f* flag; **~fracht, ~miete** *f* freight; **~frachtbrief** *m* bill of lading; **~funker** *m* ship's radio operator; **~funkstelle** *f* ship station; (*Sender*) ship transmitter; **~gerippe** *n* carcass of a ship; **~geschütz** *n* armament; **~haken** *m* grapple; **~heck** *n* stern; poop; **~hebewerk** *n* ship-lifting device; **~helling** *f* slipway; **~herr, ~eigner** *m* ship-owner; **~journal** *n* log(-book); **~junge** *m* cabin-boy; **~kapitän** *m* captain; **~karte** *f* passenger ticket; **~kiel** *m* keel; **~klasse** *f* rating; **~koch** *m* ship's cook; **~körper** *m* hull; **~küche** *f* caboose, galley; **~ladung** *f* cargo, freight; (*Last*) shipload; **~länge** *f* over-all length of a ship; **~laterne** *f* ship's lantern; poop-lantern; **~lauf** *m* course; **~lazarett** *n* sickbay, ship's hospital; **~leiter** *f* ship ladder, safety ladder; **~liegeplatz** *m* loading berth; **~luke** *f* hatch; **~makler** *m* ship-broker; **~mannschaft** *f* crew; **~motor** *m* marine engine; **~nachrichten** *f pl* shipping-intelligence; **~ortung** *f* position finding, dead reckoning; **~papiere** *n pl* ship's papers *pl*; **~patron** *m* skipper, patron; **~raum** *m* hold (of a ship), tonnage; shipping space; *Mangel an ~~* deficiency of tonnage; **~reeder** *m* owner of a ship; **~rumpf** *m* hull (of a ship); **~schnabel** *m* prow, beak; **~schraube** *f* propeller, screw; **~tagebuch** *n* log(-book); **~tau** *n* rope, hawser; **~taufe** *f* naming of a ship; **~teer** *m* pitch and tar; **~tiefe** *f* depth of a ship; **~treppe** *f* ship's ladder; **~verband** *m* group of vessels; **~verfrachter, ~vermieter** *m* charterer, freighter; **~volk** *n* crew; **~wache** *f* ship's watch; look-out; **~werft** *f* shipyard, ship-building yard; (*Marinewerft*) dock-yard, naval-yard, *Am* navy yard; **~winde** *f* (spill) capstan; (*Ladewinde*) winch; (*Ankerwinde*) windlass; **~wrack** *n* shipwreck; **~ziel** *n* ship as target for bombers; **~zimmermann** *m* (*an Bord*) ship carpenter; (*bei e-r Werft*) ship-wright; **~zoll** *m* freightage; **~zwieback** *m* ship-biscuit.

Schikan|e *f* chicane, chicanery, unfair (*od* sharp) practices *pl*, annoyance, vexation; (*Rafinesse, Vorteil*) frills *pl*, refinements *pl*; *mit allen ~~n ausgestattet* with all the frills; **~ieren** *tr* to annoy, to vex, to irritate, to torment; **~ös** *a* (*kleinlich*) pettifogging, vexatious.

Schild *m* shield; (*kleiner, runder*) buckler; (*Wappen~*) scutcheon, escutcheon, bearings *pl*, coat of arms; (*Schutz*) shield; *auf den ~ erheben* to raise on the shield; *fig* to choose as leader; *etw im ~e führen* to be up to s. th.; *~ n* signboard; shop-board; (*Büro~ e-s Arztes, Rechtsanwalts etc*) *Am* shingle; (*Anschlagtafel*) notice-board; (*Tür~*) door-plate; (*Straßen~*) name-plate; (*Wegweiser*) sign-post; (*Ausweis*) identification plate; (*Abzeichen*) badge; (*Flaschen~, Waren~*) label, ticket, *Am* sticker; (*Mützen~*) shade, peak; (*Kopf~, Brust~ bei Insekten*) scutum, scute; (*Schildkröte*) shell, carapace; (*Schildlaus*) scale; (*Brustgefieder beim Rebhahn*) shield; (*Auerhahn*) white spot; (*Stirnfleck bei Pferd u. Rind*) star; **~bürger** *m fig* Gothamite, dunce; **~~streich** *m* silly blunder; folly; **~chen** *n* (*Etiquette*) label, *Am* sticker; **~drüse** *f* thyroid gland; **~~nentzündung** *f med* thyroiditis, strumitis; **~~nextrakt** *m* thyroid solution; **~~nstörung** *f* disturbance of the thyroid gland; **~erhaus** *n* sentry-box; **~ermaler** *m* sign-painter; **~ern** *tr* (*anschaulich mit Worten darstellen*) to depict; (*umreißen*) to sketch; (*entwerfen*) to portray; (*zeichnen*) to draw; (*beschreiben*) to describe; (*erzählen*) to relate; (*farbig malen*) to paint, to colo(u)r; **~erung** *f* (*mit Worten*) description; relation; representation; picture; **~knappe, ~träger** *m* shield-bearer, squire; **~kröte** *f* (*See~~*) turtle; (*Land~~*) tortoise; **~~nschale** *f* carapace, shell; **~~nsuppe** *f* turtle-soup; (*falsche*) mock turtle-soup; **~patt** *n* tortoiseshell; **~~kamm** *m* shell-comb; **~wache** *f* sentry, sentinel; guard; ~~ *stehen* to be on guard; **~zapfen** *m* trunnion, gudgeon.

Schilf *n* reed; (*Binse*) rush; **~gras** *n* sedge; **~ig** *a* reedy, sedgy; **~matte** *f* rush-mat; **~rohr** *n* reed(s *pl*), cane.

Schiller *m* splendo(u)r, lustre, *Am* luster, play of colo(u)rs; iridescence; (*Wein*) wine from red and white grapes mixed; **~farbe** *f* changeable colo(u)r, iridescent colo(u)r; **~glanz** *m* iridescent lustre; **~ig** *a* iridescent, opalescent; **~n** *itr* to opalesce, to iridesce, to exhibit a play of colo(u)rs, to change colo(u)rs; **~nd** *a* iridescent, opalescent; (*Stoffe*) shot; **~seide** *f* shot-silk; **~wein** *m* wine from red and white grapes mixed.

Schilling *m* shilling, *fam* bob.

Schimäre *f* chimera.

Schimmel *m* (*Nahrungsmittel*) mo(u)ld; (*Leder, Papier*) mildew, mustiness; (*Pferd*) grey (*od* white) horse; **~artig** *a* mo(u)ldlike, mo(u)ldy; **~geruch** *m* mo(u)ldy smell; **~ig** *a* mo(u)ldy, musty, mildewed; **~n** *itr* to mo(u)ld, to get mo(u)ldy; **~pilz** *m* mo(u)ld fungus, vine mildew; oidium; **~pilzkultur** *f* culture of mo(u)ld.

Schimmer *m* gleam, glimmer, glitter; (*Schmelz, Duft*) bloom; *ich habe keinen ~* (*fig*) I have not the faintest notion; I have no inkling of s. th.; **~n** *itr* to gleam, to glitter, to shine, to glimmer, to glisten; **~nd** *a* glittery, resplendent.

Schimpanse *m* chimpanzee.

Schimpf *m* abuse, insult, affront; (*Schande*) disgrace; **~en** *tr* to abuse, to revile; *itr* to scold, to grumble (*über* at); to inveigh (*auf* against); *fam* to gripe, to kick, to knock; **~erei** *f* reviling; (*wüste ~~*) billingsgate; blackguarding; **~lich** *a* (*beleidigend*) insulting; (*entehrend*) disgraceful, dishono(u)rable, scandalous; outrageous; (*schändlich*) ignominious; **~name** *m* nickname; **~wort** *n* invective; term of abuse.

Schind|aas *n* carrion; **~anger** *m* knacker's yard; **~grube** *f* carrion-pit.

Schindel *f* shingle, clapboard; wooden tile; **~dach** *n* shingle roof; **~n** *tr* to shingle, to clapboard, to roof with shingles.

schind|en *irr tr* to flay, to skin; *fig* (*jdn bedrängen, bedrücken*) to oppress, to harass; to squeeze, to torment; (*Arbeitskräfte ausnützen*) to sweat, to grind, to exploit; (*ohne zu bezahlen, heraus~~*) to do on the cheap, to try to get for nothing; *sich ~~* to work hard, to toil hard; to slave, to drudge; to toil and moil, to work like a nigger; **~er** *m* (*Henker*) hangman; (*Abdecker*) knacker, flayer; (*Quäler*) skinner; *fig* (*Erpresser*) extortioner; (*Bedrücker*) oppressor; (*Wucherer*) shaver; (*Leute~~*) sweater; **~erei** *f fig* (*mühselige Arbeit*) hard labo(u)r; (*Plackerei*) drudgery; grind; (*Ausnützen der Arbeitskräfte*) sweating; (*Bedrückung*) extortion; **~erkarren** *m* knacker's cart; **~erknecht** *m* knacker's servant; **~luder** *n* (*Aas*) carrion; *fig fam* (*Luder*) wretch, hussy; beast; *mit jdm ~~ treiben* to make cruel sport of s. o., to play fast and loose with s. o.; to treat s. o. badly; **~mähre** *f* worn-out horse, jade, *Am sl* skate.

Schinken *m* ham; *fig hum* (*Schmöker*) old book; *~ mit Ei* ham and eggs; **~brötchen** *n* ham sandwich, ham-roll.

Schinn *m* scurf, dandruff.

Schippe *f* spade; (*Schaufel*) shovel; (*kleine*) scoop; (*Kartenspiel*) spades *pl*; **~n** *tr itr* (*schaufeln*) to shovel; *Schnee ~~* to shovel snow; **~r** *m* shovel(l)er; *mil* sapper.

Schirm *m* (*Regen~*) umbrella; (*Sonnen~*) parasol, sunshade; (*Wind~, Ofen~, Licht~*) screen; (*Lampen~*) shade; (*Mützen~*) peak; visor; (*Projektions~*) screen; (*Luftabschirmung durch Jagdflugzeuge*) air umbrella; (*Schild, Schutz*) shelter, protection; shield; *Leucht~* luminescent screen; *Fall~* parachute, chute; **~antenne** *f radio* umbrella aerial (*od* antenna); **~bild** *n* image on screen; **~dach** *n* shed, penthouse; (*Markise*) awning; **~eindecker** *m aero* parasol; **~en** *tr* to screen, to shield, to shelter, to shade; (*verteidigen, beschützen*) to defend, to protect (*gegen* against), to guard, to safeguard; **~förmig** *a* umbrella-shaped; **~futteral** *n* umbrella-case; **~gestell** *n* umbrella-frame; **~gitter** *n radio* screen-grid; **~~röhre** *f* screen-grid valve, *Am* screen-grid tube; **~glucke** *f* (*Brutmaschine*) brooder; **~griff** *m* handle, crook; **~herr, ~er** *m* protector, patron; **~herrschaft** *f* protectorate, patronage; auspices *pl*; aegis; **~isolator** *m el* umbrella insulator; **~mütze** *f* peaked cap; **~rippe** *f* rib of an umbrella; **~ständer** *m* umbrella-stand, hall-stand; **~ung** *f el* screening, shielding; **~wand** *f* screen (-ing wall); **~wirkung** *f* screening effect; **~zwinge** *f* umbrella-tip.

Schirokko *m* sirocco.

schirr|en *tr* to harness; **~macher** *m* cartwright; **~meister** *m* headman, foreman; *mil* supply sergeant.

Schisma *n* schism; **~tiker** *m*, **~tisch** *a* schismatic.

Schiß *m vulg* shit; *fig fam* (*Angst*) blue funk; *~ haben* to be in a blue funk.

schizo|id *a* schizoid; **~phren** *a* schizophrenic; **~phrenie** *f* schizophrenia.

*

schlabber|ig *a* lapping; slabbering; prating, talkative; **~n** *itr* (*schlürfen*) to lick up, to lap; (*geifern*) to slabber, to slaver, to drool, to slobber; (*plappern*) to babble, to prattle.

Schlacht *f* battle; (*Treffen*) engagement; (*Gefecht*) action; (*Kampf*) fight, combat; *e-e ~ zwischen Heeren* a battle between armies; *die ~ bei ...* the battle of ...; *die ~ um England* the battle of Britain; *in die ~ gehen* to go into action; *e-e ~ schlagen* to fight a battle; *e-e ~ liefern* to give battle; *die ~ gewinnen* to carry the day, to win the day; *e-e regelrechte ~* a pitched battle; *der Stärkste gewinnt nicht immer die ~* the battle is not always to the strong; **~bank** *f* shambles *pl*; slaughter-house; *zur ~~ führen* to slaughter; **~beil** *n* butcher's axe; *hist* (*Streitaxt*) pole-axe; **~bomber** *m* ground-attack bomber; **~en** *tr* to kill, to slaughter; (*hinschlachten*) to butcher; (*massakrieren*) to massacre; **~enbummler** *m* hanger-on, camp-follower; **~englück** *n* fortune of war; **~enlenker** *m* (*Feldherr*) strategist; (*Gott*) God of hosts; **~enmaler** *m* battle-painter; **~entscheidung** *f* decision through battle; **~erfolg** *m* success in battle; **~feld** *n* battle field, battle-ground; *auf dem ~~ von ...* on the field of ...; **~fleisch** *n* butcher's meat; **~flieger** *m* close-support fighter; (*Mann*) combat pilot; **~~bombe** *f* anti-personnel bomb; **~~verband** *m* battle-plane unit; ground-attack unit; **~flotte** *f* battle fleet; **~flugzeug** *n aero mil* ground-attack airplane, assault plane; ground-strafing plane, fighter-bomber; **~front** *f* battle front; **~gesang** *m* battle-song; **~geschrei** *n* battle-cry; **~geschwader** *n mar* battle squadron; **~gewicht** *n* dead weight; **~gewühl** *n* din of battle; thick of the fight; **~haus** *n*, **~hof** *m* slaughter-house; *Am* (*Viehhof*) stock-yard; meat-packing plant; **~kreuzer** *m* battle-cruiser; **~linie** *f* line of battle; **~messer** *n* butcher's knife; **~opfer** *n* sacrifice; *fig* victim; **~ordnung** *f* battle-array; order of battle; *in ~~ aufstellen* to array for battle; **~plan** *m* plan of action; (*od* operations); **~reif** *a* (*Schwein*) ready for slaughtering; **~reihe** *f* line of battle; **~roß** *n hist* battle-horse, war-horse, charger; **~ruf** *m* war-cry, battle-cry; **~schiff** *n* battleship, capital ship, *sl* battlewagon; **~~sverband** *m* battleship force; **~steuer** *f* duty on butcher's meat; **~tag** *m* (*Schweineschlachten*) slaughtering-day; (*Kampftag*) day of battle; **~ung** *f* killing, slaughter(ing); **~vieh** *n* slaughter cattle, fat stock; **~viehmarkt** *m* cattle market.

Schlächter *m* butcher; **~ei** *f* (*Laden*) butcher's shop, *Am* meat market; *fig* (*Metzelei*) slaughter, butchery; **~geselle** *m* journeyman butcher.

Schlack|e *f* (*Metall*) dross, slag, cinder, scoria; (*Stein~*) clinker; (*heiße Kohle*) cinder, (*Asche*) cinders *pl*; *fig* (*Hefe, nutzlose Reste, Abschaum*) dregs *pl*, sediment, scum; waste matter; **~en** *itr* to slag, to clinker; to form slag; **~enartig** *a* slaggy, drossy; **~enbeton** *m* slag concrete; **~enbildend** *a* slag-forming; **~enbildung** *f* formation of slag; scorification; **~enfrei** *a* slagless; **~engrube** *f* cinder pit, slag pit; **~enhalde** *f* slag (*od* cinder) dump; **~enwolle** *f* slag wool; mineral wool; **~enzement** *m* slag cement; **~enzuschlag** *m* slag addition; **~ig** *a* drossy, slaggy; scoriaceous; *~iges Wetter fam* sloppy weather; **~wurst** *f* German sausage.

Schlaf *m* sleep; *der erste, erfrischende ~* (*vor Mitternacht*) beauty sleep; *ein 5stündiger ~* a 5 hours sleep; *sehr tiefer ~* a dead sleep; *der ewige ~* o.'s last sleep; *ohne ~* sleepless; *im ~e* in my sleep; *in tiefen ~ fallen* to fall into a profound sleep; *in tiefem ~e liegen* to be fast asleep; *fam* to sleep like a top; *in ~ sinken* to drop off to sleep; *ein Kind in den ~ singen* to lull a baby to sleep; *im ~ reden* to talk in o.'s sleep; *im ~ wandeln* to walk in o.'s sleep; *e-n ~ tun* to sleep a sleep; *seinen letzten ~ tun* to sleep o.'s last; *e-n festen* (*od tiefen*) *~ haben* to be a sound sleeper; *e-n leichten ~ haben* to be a light sleeper; **~abteil** *n rail* sleeping-compartment, *Am* sleeping-section, sleeper; **~anzug** *m* pyjamas *pl*, sleeping-suit, *Am* pajamas *pl*; **~bursche** *m* night-lodger; **~decke** *f* blanket; **~en** *irr itr* to sleep, to be asleep; *fam* to roost; *gut* (*schlecht*) *~~* to sleep well (badly); *über etw ~~* to sleep on s. th.; *wir wollen darüber ~~* let's sleep on it; *den Schlaf des Gerechten ~~* to sleep the sleep of the just; *den ganzen Morgen durch~~* to sleep away the morning; *~~ Sie wohl!* good night! sleep well! *sie konnte nicht ~~* she hardly slept a wink; *~~ gehen, sich ~~ legen* to go to bed; to retire; (*Kindersprache*) to go bye bye; *vor dem Schlafengehen* before going to bed; *laß die Sache ~~!* drop that affair! *der Fuß schläft mir* my leg is asleep; *wie ein Murmeltier ~~* to sleep like a top; *Kopfschmerzen aus~~* to sleep off a headache; *volle 12 Stunden ~~* to sleep the clock round; *im Haus* (*außer dem*

Haus) ~~ to sleep in (out); *unter freiem Himmel* ~~ to sleep in the open air; *sich* ~*end stellen* to sham sleep; **~enszeit** *f* bedtime; **~flugzeug** *n aero* sleeper plane; **~gänger** *m* lodger; **~geld** *n* pay for a night's lodging; *fam* doss money; **~gelegenheit** *f* sleeping accommodation; *jdm* ~~ *bieten* to provide sleeping accommodation for; to accommodate s. o., *Am* to sleep s. o.; *der Raum hat* ~~ *für 3 Personen* the room accommodates 3 persons, *Am* the room sleeps 3 persons; **~gemach** *n* bedroom; **~gesell** *m* bedfellow; **~kabine** *f* sleeping cabin; **~kammer** *f* bedroom; **~koje** *f rail, aero* sleeping berth; (*für Matrosen*) bunk; **~krankheit** *f* sleeping-sickness; **~lähmung** *f med* sleep-palsy; **~lied** *n* lullaby; **~los** *a* sleepless, wakeful; ~~*e Nacht* bad night; **~losigkeit** *f* sleeplessness; *med* insomnia; **~mittel** *n* soporific, somnifacient; **sleeping tablet**; (*Narkotikum*) narcotic; opiate, drug; **~mütze** *f* nightcap; *fig* sleepy person, sleepy-head; **~mützig** *a* sleepy, drowsy; (*langsam*) slow; **~ratze** *f* dormouse; *fig* sound sleeper; **~raum** *m* sleeping accommodation; **~rock** *m* dressing-gown, morning-gown, robe; sleep coat; house coat; wrap(p)er; **~saal** *m* dorm(itory); **~sack** *m* sleeping-bag; **~sofa** *n* couch; **~stätte, ~stelle** *f* sleeping-place, night's lodging; **~störung** *f med* disorder of sleep; somnipathy; **~stube** *f* bedroom, bedchamber, *Am auch* sleeping-room; **~sucht** *f* somnolency; *med* morbid sleepiness, lethargy; sopor; hypersomnia; **~tablette** *f* sleeping pill; (*od* tablet); **~trunk** *m* sleeping-draught; (*Gläschen vor dem Schlafengehen*) *fam* nightcap; **~trunken** *a* very drowsy; overcome with sleep; sleep-drunken; **~trunkenheit** *f* drowsiness; **~wagen** *m* sleeping-car(riage), *Am* sleeping-car, sleeper, Pullman; *fliegender* ~~ *aero* sleeper plane; **~wandeln** *itr* to walk in o.'s sleep; **~wandler** *m* sleep-walker, somnambulist; **~wandlerisch** *a* sleep-walking; **~zimmer** *n* bedroom, *Am* sleeping-room.

Schläf|chen *n* doze, nap, slumber forty winks *pl*, snooze, drowse; (*Nickerchen im Sitzen*) *Am* cat nap; *ein* ~~ *machen* to nap, to doze, to snooze, to take a nap, to have o.'s forty winks *pl*; **~e** *f* temple; **~enbein** *n* temporal bone; **~er** *m*, **~erin** *f* sleeper; **~ern** *imp* to feel sleepy; *es schläfert mich* I feel drowsy (*od* sleepy); **~rig** *a* drowsy, sleepy; ~~ *machen* to make sleepy; *fig* (*faul*) humdrum; (*langsam*) slow; **~rigkeit** *f* sleepiness; drowsiness.

schlaff *a* (*schlapp*) slack, loose; (*welk, matt*) flabby; (*weich*) soft; *fig* (*Grundsätze*) lax; (*kraftlos*) weak, limp; yielding; (*verweichlicht*) effeminate; (*lauwarm*) lukewarm; (*träge*) indolent; (*tatenlos*) inactive; ~ *machen*, ~ *werden* to slacken; **~heit** *f* slackness; looseness, limpness; *fig* (*Trägheit*) indolence; (*Laxheit*) laxity.

Schlafittchen *n*: *jdn am* ~ *nehmen* to collar s. o., to take s. o. by the collar.

Schlag *m* blow; (*mit flacher Hand*) slap; stroke, knock; (*kurzer* ~) rap; (*mit dem Finger*) fillip, flip; (*leichter* ~) flick, flap; (*klatschender* ~) smack; tap, dab; (*heftiger* ~) whack, slog; sledge-hammer blow, *Am* soak; *Am* slug; (~ *ins Gesicht*) slap, facer; (~ *hinter die Ohren*) box on the ear, clout on the ear; (*mit dem Schnabel*) peck; (*Krach*) bang; (*Faust*~) cuff, lick; (*Boxen*) punch, blow, cut; (*harter* ~) stinger; (*Treffer*) hit; (*entscheidender* ~) finisher; (*Nieder*~) knock-out (blow), *Am sl* sockdolager; *e-n* ~ *landen* to land a blow; (*Krachen, Explosion*) crash; (*Ein*~) impact; (*e-r Schallplatte, e-r Welle*) wobble; (*Herz*~) beating, throb, pulsation; (*Uhr*~) beat, stroke; (*vom Pferde*) kick; (~*fluß*) apoplexy; *el* shock; (*Donner*) peal, clap; (*der Vögel*) warbling; (*Holz*~) wood-cutting, felling, cut; (*Feld*) field; (*Wagen*~) carriage-door; (*Tauben*~) pigeon-loft, dove-cot; (*Art*) kind, sort, stamp, race; breed (of horses); *mit dem* ~*e acht* on (*od* at) the stroke of eight, at 8 o'clock sharp; *ohne e-n* ~ *zu tun* without striking a blow; ~ *auf* ~ in rapid succession, blow upon blow; *mit e-m* ~ at (one) blow; at (one) stroke; (*mit e-m Krach*) with a bang; *ein entscheidender* ~ a decisive blow; *ein dumpfer* ~ a thump; *ein vernichtender* ~ a destructive blow; *ein* ~ *ins Wasser* a vain attempt; *wie vom* ~ *gerührt fam* pole-axed; *vom richtigen* ~ of the right sort; *Leute seines* ~*es* the like of him; *das ist ein harter* ~ *für sie fig* that's a hard blow for her; *zwei Fliegen auf e-n* ~ (*fig*) two birds with one stone; *mich rührt der* ~! *fam* I'll drop dead! *e-n* ~ *erhalten* to receive a shock; *jdm e-n* ~ *versetzen* to deal s. o. a blow; *Schläge bekommen* to get a thrashing; **~ader** *f* artery, aorta; **~anfall** *m* stroke (of apoplexy), apoplectic fit; *e-n* ~~ *bekommen* to have a stroke; **~artig** *a* sudden, prompt, surprise; (*heftig*) violent; (*rasch nacheinander*) in rapid succession; **~ball** *m* rounders *pl*; **~bar** *a* (*Holz*) fit for cutting; **~baum** *m* turnpike; toll-bar; (*Pferdestall*) kick wall; **~bereit** *a* ready to strike; **~besen** *m* egg-whisk, egg-beater; **~bolzen** *m* (*Gewehr*) striker; firing-pin; **~~feder** *f* main spring; **firing-pin spring, striker spring**; **~~mutter** *f* striker nut; **~~spitze** *f* **point of firing-pin**; **~empfindlichkeit** *f* sensitiveness to percussion; **~en** *irr tr* (*mit der Hand od e-m Stock etc e-n Schlag versetzen*) to strike; (*heftig u. wiederholt bearbeiten*) to beat; (*treffen*) to hit; (*hauen*) to knock, to slog, *Am fam* to slug; (*mit der offenen Hand, ins Gesicht* ~~) to slap; (*mit der Faust*) to punch; (*knuffen, puffen*) to cuff; (*prügeln*) to thrash, to lick; (*Fliegen tot*~~) to swat; (*Ohrfeige geben*) to box, to clout; (*leicht* ~~) to dab, to tap; (*besiegen*) to defeat, to beat; (*übertreffen*) *Am* to whip, *Am* to skin; *Am fam* (*im Spiel*) to skunk; *zu Boden* ~~ to knock down; *entzwei* ~~ to smash, to dash to pieces; *in die Flucht* ~~ to put to flight; *den Takt* ~~ to beat the time; *Alarm* ~~ to sound the alarm; *die Augen zur Erde* ~~ to look down, to cast down o.'s eyes; *mit Blindheit* ~~ to smite with blindness; *in Fesseln* ~~ to put in irons; *Öl* ~~ to press oil; *in Papier* ~~ to wrap up in paper; *die Zinsen zum Kapital* ~~ to add the interest to the capital; *Holz* ~~ to fell, to cut (wood); *Wurzel* ~~ to take root; *ans Kreuz* ~~ to crucify; *e-n Kreis* ~~ to describe a circle; *e-e Brücke* ~~ to bridge; to build (*od* to extend *od* to make) a bridge; *sich etw aus dem Sinn* ~~ to banish s. th. from o.'s mind; ~~ *Sie es sich aus dem Kopf* forget about it! *e-n Purzelbaum* ~~ to turn a somersault; *sein Gewissen schlug* his conscience smote him; *itr* to beat; (*Pferd*) to kick; (*Blitz*) to strike; (*Herz*) to throb, to beat, to palpitate, to flutter; (*Vogel*) to warble; (*Uhr*) to strike; (*Glocke*) to ring; (*Räder*) to be out of true; (*Segel*) to flap; *aus der Art* ~~ to degenerate; *fig nach jdm* ~~ to take after; *das schlägt nicht in mein Fach* that is not in my line; *r* (*handgemein werden*) to come to blows, to close with s. o., to come to close quarters, to engage at close quarters, to grapple with; (*fechten*) to fence, to fight; to fight a duel; (*Faustkampf*) to engage in boxing with, to box; *sich zu jdm* ~~ to join, to side with; **~en** *n* striking, knocking, beating; (*Pferd*) kicking; (*Herz*) pulsation; (*Brücke*) building, construction; (*Holz*) felling; (*Wogen*) shock etc; **~end** *a fig* (*treffend*) striking; (*eindrucksvoll*) impressive; (*offenkundig*) manifest; (*schwerwiegend*) pregnant; (*überzeugend*) convincing; (*beweisend*) conclusive, demonstrative; (*entscheidend*) decisive; (*unwiderlegbar*) irrefutable; (*zündend*) flashing; ~~*e Antwort* pertinent reply, *fam* squelch(er); ~~*es Argument* cogent argument, irrefutable argument; ~~*er Beweis* convincing proof; ~~*e Wetter* (*Bergwerk*) firedamp, fiery vapo(u)rs, mine-gas; **~er** *m* (~~*melodie*) song-hit, hit-tune; musical hit; *theat, film* success, draw, hit; (*Publikumserfolg*) smash hit, hit show, *fam* go-over; (*Kassen*~~) box-office draw, *Am sl* B. O. attraction; (*bei Besprechungen in der Presse*) topliner, *Am* headliner; (*Buch*~~ *des Jahres*) *Am* best-seller; (*Verkaufs*~~) *com* hit; **~~komponist** *m* song writer, *Am sl* tunesmith; **~~melodie** *f* song-hit, hit-tune; **~~preis** *m com* rock-bottom price; **~~sänger** *m* jazz singer, swing singer, *Am bes. radio* crooner, croonie; **~fertig** *a* ready for action (*od* fight *od* battle); (*in Antworten*) ready-witted, quick at repartee; ~~*e Antwort* ready answer, repartee; **~~keit** *f* readiness for battle; ready wit, quickness of repartee; peak of preparedness, acuteness; **~festigkeit** *f* impact resistance; resistance to shock; **~flügler** *m* ornithopter; **~fluß** *m* stroke, apoplectic fit; apoplexy; **~gold** *n* leaf-gold; **~holz** *n* (*Schlegel*) mallet; beetle; (*Baseball, Kricket*) bat; (*Golf*) club; (*Holz im Wald*) regular fellings *pl*; **~instrument** *n* percussion instrument; **~kraft** *f* striking power, hitting power; striking force; *mil* fighting efficiency; **~kräftig** *a* efficient; strong; *fig* (*Beweis*) conclusive; (*überzeugend*) persuasive; **~leine** *f* chalk-line; **~licht** *n* (*auch fig*) strong light; glare; direct light; ~~*er aufsetzen fig* to highlight; *ein* ~~ *werfen auf fig* to shed a strong light on; **~loch** *n* (*Straße*) (road) hole, pothole; **~löcher!** (*Warnschild*) bumps! **~lot** *n tech* hard solder, spelters *pl*; **~mal** *n* (*Baseball*) *Am* home plate; **~mann** *m* (*Ruderer*) stroke; **~mannschaft** *f* (*Baseball*) team at bat; **~mühle** *f tech* hammer mill; **~netz** *n* (*Ballspiel*) racket; (*Vogelfang*) clap-net; (*Fischfang*) seine; **~obers** *n* (*in Österreich*), **~rahm** *m* whipped cream; **~partei** *f* (*Baseball*) home team; **~probe** *f tech* impact test; **~regen** *m* pouring rain; **~ring** *m* (*Waffe*) knuckle-duster; (*Glocke*) rim; (*für Zither*) plectrum; **~sahne** *f* whipped cream; **~schatten** *m* cast-shadow; **~seite** *f mar* list; lop-side; ~~ *haben mar* to list; *fam* (*betrunken*) to be half-seas-over; ~~ *bekommen mar* to heel over; *mit* ~~ *liegenbleiben* to remain in a listing condition; *ein Schiff mit schwerer* ~~ a ship listing heavily; **~sieb** *n* precipitating sieve; vibrating screen; **~stift**

m firing-pin; detonating rod; **~uhr** *f* striking clock; (*Taschenuhr*) repeater; **~wechsel** *m* (*Boxen*) change of blows; **~weite** *f* striking distance; effective range; *el* spark distance; **~welle** *f* (*See*) camber; breaker; **~werk** *n* (*Uhr*) striking apparatus; (*Ramme*) rammer; **~wetter** *n pl* (*Bergwerk*) firedamp; **~~sicher** *a* gasproof, flame proof; **~widerstand** *m tech* impact resistance; **~wort** *n* slogan, catchcry, catch-phrase; watchword; (*Katalog*) subject; **~~e** *n pl* (*Phrasendrescherei*) claptrap; **~~katalog** *m* (*Bibliothek*) alphabetical subject catalog(ue); **~~register** *n* subject index; **~wunde** *f med* contused wound; **~zeile** *f* (*in der Zeitung*) title line, head(ing); headline, catchline, *Am* caption, *Am* (*über 2 u. mehr Spalten*) spread, spreadhead, *Am* (*4-8 spaltig über die ganze Zeitungsbreite*) streamer, *Am* banner, banner head, flag, *Am* (*sensationelle ~~*) screamer; *Am* (*mit übergroßen Buchstaben*) scarehead; *Am* (*Überschrift unter e-r großen ~~*) ribbon, hanger; *Am* (*nur mit großen Buchstaben*) all-cap; *der Artikel hat e-e ~~* the article carries a headline; **~~nstil** *m* headlinese; **~zeug** *n* percussion instrument, drums *pl*; **~zünder** *m* (*Granate*) percussion fuse; (*Sprengladung*) percussion igniter; **~zündung** *f* percussion priming.

*

Schläger *m* beater, hitter, striker; (*Raufbold*) swashbuckler, *Am sl* slugger, thug; (*Pferd*) kicker; (*Baseball, Mann*) batsman; (*Kricket, Mann*) batter, swiper; (*Fechtwaffe*) rapier, sword; (*Tennis~~*) racket; (*Kricket~~*) cricket-bat; (*Baseballschlagholz*) bat; (*Golf*) golf club; (*Polo*) mallet; (*Federball*) battledore; (*Singvogel*) warbler; (*Schnee~*) egg-whisker, egg-beater; **~ei** *f* fight, fighting, battery; tussle, scuffle; (*mit viel Geschrei u. Lärm*) brawl, row; fracas; *fam* set-to; *parl* mêlée; (*unter Schülern*) rumpus; *fam* scrap; (*allgemein*) free fight, *Am* free-for-all; *Am sl* shindy; *e-e ~~ anfangen fam* to kick up a row; *es kam zu e-r ~~* it came to blows; **~träger** *m* (*Golfjunge*) caddy.

Schlaks *m* gangling fellow; **~ig** *a* gangling, gangly, lanky; gawky.

Schlamassel *n fam* (*mißliche Lage*) dilemma, difficulty, quandary, emergency; scrape, predicament; *Am sl* fix, jam, mess, stew, hot water; (*Durcheinander*) *Am fam* mix-up, pretty pickle, nice go; pretty muddle, hell of a fix; *im ~ sein* (*od sitzen od stecken*) *fam* to be in hot water, to be in the soup, to be on the spot, *Am fam* to be in for it, to be hard up, to be stuck fast, to have a tough time.

Schlamm *m* mud, slime, sludge, ooze; (*Pfütze*) mire; (*sandig*) silt; (*Rückstand*) sediment; *fig* mire; *im ~ stecken bleiben* to stick in the mud, *Am fam* to get stuck in the mud; **~ablagerung** *f* deposition of mud; **~artig** *a* muddy, slimy; **~bad** *n* mud-bath; **~bedeckt** *a* covered with mud; **~beißer** *m* (*Fisch*) mud-fish; **~boden** *m* muddy soil; **~grube** *f* sink; **~ig** *a* muddy; miry; sludgy; slimy; oozy; **~kratze** *f* mud scraper; **~loch** *n* mud-hole; **~periode** *f* mud season; **~pfütze** *f* pool, bog; puddle; **~ringkampf** *m sport* mud match; **~schicht** *f* slime layer; **~vulkan** *m* mud volcano; **~wasser** *n* muddy water.

schlämm|en *tr* (*reinigen*) to clean, to cleanse; (*waschen*) to wash; (*Kalk*) to purify; (*Metall*) to buddle; *chem* to elutriate, to levigate; **~erei** *f tech* washing plant; **~faß** *n* washing tank; **~kohle** *f* washed coal; **~kreide** *f* whiting, washed (*od* precipitated) chalk; **~verfahren** *n* washing process; *chem* elutriating process; **~ung** *f* washing; sedimentation; elutriating; levigating.

Schlamp|e *f* (*unordentliche Frau*) slut, slattern, dowdy, *fam* draggle-tail; *fam* trapes, traipse; (*Schlumpe*) trallop; slummock; (*Vogelscheuche*) frump; (*Dirne*) drab; **~er** *m* sloven; **~erei** *f* (*Unordnung*) disorder, untidiness, slovenliness; (*Durcheinander*) mess, *Am* muss; (*Wirrwarr*) muddle; (*Nachlässigkeit*) negligence, carelessness; **~ig** *a* (*nachlässig, unordentlich*) untidy; unkempt; slatternly; draggle-tailed; *fam* slouchy; (*liederlich*) *fam* sloppy; (*Arbeit, Tätigkeit*) slipshod; slovenly (workmanship); (*altmodisch, verkommen*) frumpish; (*schmutzig*) frowzy, dirty; (*unelegant, nachlässig*) dowdy, negligent; (*zerzaust*) blowsy, blowzed.

Schlange *f* snake, serpent; (*als Schimpfwort*) viper; *fam* (*wartende Personen*) queue, *Am* waiting line; *~ stehen* to queue up, to stand in queue, *Am* to stand in a waiting line, *Am* to line up; *tech* (*Kühl~ etc*) coil; worm; (*Wasserschlauch*) hose; *astr* Serpent; *e-e giftige ~* a poisonous snake; **~nähnlich** *a* snaky; **~nanbeter** *m* snake-worshipper; **~nartig** *a* snake-like, serpentine; **~nbeschwörer** *m* snake charmer; **~nbiß** *m* snake-bite; **~nbohrer** *m* screw bit; spiral drill; **~nbrut** *f fig* generation of vipers; **~ngift** *n* snake venom; **~nhaut** *f* snake skin; **~nkühler** *m tech* spiral (*od* coil) condenser; **~nkurve** *f* serpentine; **~nleder** *n* snake leather; **~nlinie** *f* wavy line, serpentine (line); *typ* waved rule; **~nlinig** *a* serpentine; sinuous; **~nmensch** *m* (*Zirkus*) contortionist; **~nröhre** *f tech* winding pipe, spiral pipe, worm, (spiral) coil; **~nstab** *m* snaky wand; **~ntanz** *m* serpentine dance; snake dance; **~nweg** *m* winding road; **~nwindung** *f* winding, sinuosity; *fig* meandering; **~nzüngig** *a fig* back-biting; of venomous tongue.

schlängeln *itr* (*sich*) to wind (*fort, heraus* out, *hinein* in); (*Fluß, Straße*) to meander; (*sich biegen u. drehen*) to twist; (*sich krümmen*) to squirm, to crinkle; (*hin u. her*) to wriggle; (*sich zus. rollen*) to coil; (*sich schlingen um*) to twine (*um* round, about); (*Flammen*) to bicker, to flicker; *sich durch~* to thread o.'s way through, *fam* to corkscrew o.'s way through; *sich heraus~* (*aus e-r üblen Lage*) to wriggle out of; *fig* (*sich schleichen*) to sneak, to glide; to creep; *sich an jdn heran~ fig* (*jds Vertrauen erschleichen*) to wriggle up to s. o.; to worm o.'s way into s. o.'s confidence, to wind o.'s way into s. o.'s affections; *~ n* winding; twisting; *tech* spiral motion, tailing (*od* rocking) motion.

schlank *a* (*Wuchs*) slender, slim, svelte; *~ gebaut* of slim build; (*groß*) tall; (*dünn*) thin, lean; (*zerbrechlich*) *Am fam* slimsy; (*zart, fein*) delicate, fine, graceful; slight; *die ~e Linie* the slender waistline, the slimming line; *im ~en Trabe* at a fast trot; *~ wie e-e Tanne* slim as a young sapling; *~ machen* (*Kleidung*) to slenderize, to slim; *~ werden* to slim, to get slim; **~heit** *f* slenderness; (*Wuchs*) slimness, tallness; (*Zartheit*) slightness; thinness; (*Feinheit*) gracility, fineness; **~~sgrad** *m* slenderness ratio; **~~skur** *f*: *e-e ~~skur machen* to (be on a) diet; to slenderize; **~~sverhältnis** *n* ratio of slenderness, fineness ratio; **~machend** *a* slimming; **~weg** *a* (*rundweg*) roundly, flatly; (*schlechtweg*) downright, right-away, readily, straightaway; *~~ ablehnen* to refuse flatly.

schlapp *a* (*schlaff*) slack; (*matt, hängend*) flabby; (*weich, schwach, kraftlos*) limp; *fig* (*ohne Schwung*) lax; (*träge*) indolent; (*Haltung*) weak-kneed; spineless; (*müde*) tired, *Am fam* (to feel) washed-out; *~ machen fam* (*versagen*) to break down, *Am* to be a quitter; (*in Ohnmacht fallen*) to collapse, to faint, to swoon; **~e** *f* (*Rückschlag*) reverse, check, rebuff; (*Verschlechterung*) set-back; (*Schlag, Unglück*) blow; *mil* (*Niederlage*) defeat; (*Verlust*) loss; *e-e ~~ erleiden* to meet with a check (*od* reverse), to come off a loser; **~en** *m pl* (*Pantoffeln*) slippers *pl*; **~en** *itr* (*lose herunterhängen*) to hang loose, to flap; (*schlurfend od schleppend gehen*) to shuffle; *tr, itr* (*schlürfend trinken*) to lap, to lick up; **~ern** *tr, itr* (*schlürfend trinken*) to lap, to lick up; *fam* (*schwätzen*) to prattle, to babble; **~heit** *f* slackness; floppiness; laxity; (*Trägheit*) indolence; (*Schwäche*) weakness; **~hut** *m* slouch(ed) hat; **~ig** *a* slack, limp; **~macher** *m* slacker, *Am* quitter; **~ohr** *n* flop-ear; *pl* lob ears *pl*; **~schwanz** *m* (*energieloser Mensch*) flabby person, molly-coddle; (*Weichling*) weakling, flop, milksop; *Am fam* big sissy, *Am* softie, *Am* doughface, jellyfish; (*Drückeberger*) shirker, slacker; (*Feigling*) coward, *Am fam* funkie, pussyfoot; **~seil** *n* (*Zirkus*) slack rope; **~werden** *n* slackening.

Schlaraffen|land *n* Utopia, land of milk and honey; lubberland; lotus-land; Cockaigne; Shangrila; **~leben** *n* life of idleness and luxury.

schlau *a* (*verschlagen*) sly, tricky, canny, shrewd, *Am* wise; *fam* cute; (*klug*) clever; (*geschickt*) cunning; crafty; (*wendig, verschmitzt*) artful; smart, sharp; (*listig*) wily, foxy; (*intelligent*) intelligent, quick-witted; ingenious; (*argwöhnisch*) *Am fam* cag(e)y; (*diplomatisch*) diplomatic, scheming; (*hinterhältig, heuchlerisch*) shifty, double-faced, deceitful, crooked, stealthy; *ein ~er Kerl* a foxy fellow, *Am fam* a sly dog; *ein ~er alter Fuchs* a sly old stager; *sie ist nicht gerade ~* she won't set the Thames on fire; *können Sie daraus ~ werden?* can you make anything out of this? **~berger, ~kopf, ~meier** *m* cunning (*od* foxy) fellow; artful dodger; slyboots *pl mit sing*; *Am fam* wise guy; **~heit, ~igkeit** *f* (*Verschlagenheit*) slyness; shrewdness; (*Listigkeit*) cunning; (*Wendigkeit*) craftiness; (*Gewandheit*) artfulness; smartness.

Schlauch *m* (*Wein~, Öl~*) skin, leather-tube; (*Röhre aus Metall od Gummi*) metal tube, rubber tube; *biegsamer ~* flexible tube (*od* pipe); (*Feuerwehr~*) hose; (*Auto~, Fahrrad~*) inner tube, air tube; *~ u. Mantel* inner tube and cover; *fig* (*Säufer, Schlemmer*) drunkard; *fig* (*Eselsbrücke für Schülerübersetzungen etc*) *sl* crib, *Am sl* pony; **~anschluß** *m* hose coupling; **~artig, ~förmig** *a* tube-like, hose-shaped; **~boot** *n* rubber boat, rubber dinghy; inflatable boat, *Am* pneumatic boat; **~en** *tr* (*Brauerei*) to hose; *fig fam* (*scharf hernehmen bes. mil*) to drill brutally; (*überanstrengen, schikanieren*) to torment, to annoy, to irritate; to strain; **~endstück** *n* lance; **~gewinde** *n* union-joint; **~klemme** *f* tube clamp; **~leitung** *f* hose line; **~los** *a* tubeless; *~~er Autoreifen* tubeless tyre (*Am* tire); **~rolle** *f* hose reel; **~stutzen** *m* nozzle; **~ventil** *n mot* tyre valve; **~verbindung** *f* hose connection.

Schläue *f* slyness, cunning.

Schlaufe *f* loop; runner; noose, running noose.

schlecht *a* (*nicht gut*) bad; (*böse*) evil; (*Laune, Charakter, Wille*) ill; (*niederträchtig, schlimm*) wicked, vicious; villainous; (*übel, widerlich, garstig*) nasty; (*erbärmlich, eklig*) wretched; (*gemein*) mean, low, base; vile; (*verworfen*) reprobate, corrupt; depraved; (*lasterhaft*) profligate; immoral, unmoral, amoral; (*unartig von Kindern*) naughty; (*wertlos*) worthless; useless; (*verdorben von Waren*) spoiled, rotten; (*geringwertig, ungenügend*) poor, *Am fam* bum; inferior; *~er Absatz com* poor sale; *~e Augen* bad eyes; *~e Aussichten* bad outlook, poor prospect; *~e Einnahmen* poor receipts; *~e Entschuldigung* bad excuse; *~es Geld* base coin, bad money; *~es Geschäft* bad bargain; *~e Gesundheit* poor health; *~e Kleidung* poor dress; *~e Laune* ill humour; *~e Luft* foul air; *~er Mensch* a wicked man; *~e Papiere com* dubious stocks *pl*; *~e Qualität* inferior quality; *~er Ruf* bad reputation; *~e Sicht* poor visibility; *ein ~er Trost* poor comfort; *in ~er Verfassung* in poor condition; *in ~en Verhältnissen leben* to live in straitened circumstances, to be hard up; *~e Waren* inferior goods *pl*; *~es Wetter* nasty (*od* bad *od* adverse) weather; *~e Zeiten* hard times; *billig u. ~* cheap and nasty; *~ u. recht* somehow; after a fashion; *e-e Prüfung ~ u. recht bestehen* to scrape through an examination; *hier riecht es ~* there's a bad smell here; *er kann das Geld ~ aufbringen* he can ill afford the money; *~ behandeln* to ill-treat; *~ beschaffen* ill-conditioned; *~ bezahlt sein* to be paid badly, *Am fam* to be paid peanuts; *~ zusammenpassend* ill-matched; *mir ist ~, ich fühle mich ~* I feel ill, *fam* I feel pretty shaky, *Am* I feel sick; *es geht mir ~* (*geldlich*) I am bad off; I am hard up; *~ auf jdn zu sprechen sein* not to speak well of s.o.; *jdn ~ machen* to speak ill of s.o.; *etw ~ machen* to run s. th. down; *~er machen* to make worse; *~ werden* to deteriorate, to go bad; (*verderben*) to turn sour; to spoil; *~er werden* to go from bad to worse, to change for the worse; *das ist kein ~er Gedanke* that's not a bad idea; *nicht ~!* not so bad! *~ adv* badly, ill, poorly; *das ~e* the worst, the bad side; *jdm ~es nachsagen* to speak ill of s.o.; **~erdings** *adv* absolutely, utterly; decidedly; by all means; *~~ unmöglich* utterly impossible; **~gebaut** *a* jerry-built; **~gelaunt** *a* in a bad temper, ill-humo(u)red; **~gesinnt** *a* evil-minded; **~hin, ~weg** *adv* plainly, simply; quite, positively; absolutely; **~igkeit** *f* badness; (*Niederträchtigkeit*) vileness, baseness; (*Bosheit*) wickedness; (*Gemeinheit*) meanness; (*Verworfenheit, Verderbtheit*) depravity; (*e-r Tat*) base action, sly (*od* mean) trick; (*von Waren*) inferiority; (*Wertlosigkeit*) worthlessness; **~wetter** *n* bad weather; **~~flug** *m* flying in dirty weather; **~~landeanlage** *f aero* bad-visibility landing aid; **~~landeausrüstung** *f aero* bad-weather aerodrome approach equipment; **~~landung** *f aero* bad-weather landing.

schleck|en *tr* to lick; *itr* to like sweets; **~er** *m*, **~ermaul** *n* sweet tooth, dainty person; **~erei** *f* sweetmeat; sweetie; candy; sweets *pl*; **~erhaft** *a* sweet-toothed; lickerish; dainty.

Schlegel *m* (*Holzhammer*) wooden hammer; (*leichter Holz~, sport Schläger*) mallet; (*schwerer Holz~*) beetle, maul; (*Hutmacher~*) beater; (*Prügel*) club; (*Schmiede~*) sledge(-hammer); (*Fäustel*) striking hammer; (*Trommel~*) drum-stick; (*Gong~*) gongstick; (*Kalbs~*) leg.

schlegeln *itr fam* to kick, to struggle, to sprawl.

Schleh|dorn *m* blackthorn, sloe tree; **~e** *f* sloe; wild plum.

Schlei *m*, **~e** *f* (*Fisch*) tench.

schleich|en *irr itr* (*kriechen*) to creep, to crawl; (*gleiten*) to glide; (*im Dunkeln herum~~*) to prowl about; (*verstohlen*) to sneak, to slink; to steal; *Am sl* to gumshoe; (*lauernd*) to skulk; (*Zeit etc*) to drag, to creep; *sich davon~~* to steal away, to sneak off, *sich hinein~~* to slip in; *sich vom Schiff ~~* to steal from the ship; **~end** *a* creeping; sneaking; (*heimlich*) furtive; *med* lingering, slow; *~~es Fieber* slow fever; *~~es Gift* slow (*od* lingering) poison; *~~e Krankheit* lingering illness; **~er** *m* creeper, crawler; *fig* sneak, skulker; (*Heuchler*) hypocrite; (*Leisetreter*) *Am sl* gumshoe man; (*bes. politisch*) pussyfoot(er); **~erei** *f* sneaking, creeping; *fig* underhand dealing; **~gut** *n* smuggled goods *pl*, contraband (goods *pl*); **~handel** *m* illicit trade, illegal trafficking; underhand dealing; (*Schwarzhandel*) black-market(ing) (*mit* in); (*Schmuggel*) contraband (trade), smuggling; (*mit Alkohol*) bootlegging; **~händler** *m* underhand dealer; (*Schwarzhändler*) black-markete(e)r; (*Schmuggler*) smuggler; **~ströme** *m pl el* vagabond currents *pl*; **~ware** *f* contraband (goods *pl*); **~weg** *m* secret (*od* hidden) path; *fig* underhand (*od* secret *od* crooked *od* indirect) means *pl*; crooked (*od* secret) way; *auf ~~en* indirectly.

Schleier *m* veil; (*Gaze*) gauze; *ein Nebel~* (*fig*) a veil of mist; (*Rauch~*) screen; *mil* smoke-screen; (*vor den Augen*) film; *phot* fog, haze, mist; (*Braut~*) bridal veil; (*Trübung; Verworrenheit*) turbidity; *den ~ fallen lassen* to drop the veil; *der ~ fiel ihr von den Augen fig* the scales fell from her eyes; *den ~ lüften* to raise the veil; *unter dem ~ der Vaterlandsliebe* under the veil of patriotism; *den ~ nehmen* (*Nonne*) to take the veil; *e-n ~ über etw werfen fig* to cast (*od* to draw *od* to throw) a veil over s. th.; **~eule** *f* barn-owl; **~flor** *m* crape; **~förmig** *a* veil-like; **~haft** *a* veil-like; *fig* (*verhüllt*) veiled; (*rätselhaft*) enigmatic, mysterious; (*unverständlich*) incomprehensible; (*verschwommen*) hazy; (*dunkel*) dark; (*unerklärlich*) inexplicable; *das ist mir ~~* (*fig*) I don't know what to make of it; **~ig** *a* (*bes. phot*) foggy, fogged, hazy, misty; **~los** *a* veilless; unveiled; **~n** *tr* to veil; *phot* to fog, to cloud; **~schwärzung** *f phot* fog density; **~tanz** *m* skirt-dance; **~tuch** *n* lawn; *com* veiling; (*Spitzen~~*) mantilla; **~wolke** *f* cirro-stratus cloud.

Schleif|arbeit *f* grinding operation; grinding work; **~automat** *m* automatic grinder; **~bahn** *f* slide; **~bock** *m* wheel stand, *Am* grinder; **~bürste** *f el* brush; **~e** *f* (*Schleifbahn*) slide; (*Rutsche*) chute; (*schlittenartiges Gestell*) sled, sledge; drag; (*Knoten*) (slip-) knot, sliding knot; kink; bight; (*Schlinge*) loop, noose; snare; (*Band~~*) bow; (*Fahnen~~, Kranz~~*) streamer; (*Kopf~~*) topknot, fillet; (*Wegkurve*) bend, curve, horseshoe curve; sweep; *aero* (*senkrechter Schleifenflug*) loop, looping; (*Schleifenlinie*) loop-line; **~en**[1] *tr* (*schleifte, geschleift*) (*schleppen*) to drag, to pull along; (*nachschleifen*) to draggle; (*Mantel, Kleid, Schleppe etc*) to trail along; (*Häuser etc niederreißen*) to demolish; *mil* (*Festung*) to raze (a fort); to dismantle; *mus* (*Töne*) to slur; *itr* (*schlittern*) to slide; (*rutschen*) to skid; (*gleiten*) to glide; (*Tanz*) to scrape; **~en**[2] *irr tr* (*schliff, geschliffen*) (*glätten, schärfen*) to grind; (*Werkzeuge schärfen*) to sharpen, to whet; to edge; (*feinschleifen*) to smooth; (*polieren*) to polish; (*abschleifen*) to abrade; (*Holz*) to sand; (*Edelsteine*) to cut; (*Rasiermesser*) to set; *jdn ~~ fig fam bes. mil* to put s.o. through his paces, to drill brutally; *matt ~~* to frost, to rough; **~enantenne** *f* (*Peilrahmen*) loop aerial, *Am* loop antenna; **~enbahn** *f math* lemniscate; **~enbildung** *f* looping; **~enflug** *m aero* loop, U-turn; loop manœuvre (*Am* maneuver); *~~ in Achterflug* figure-eight; *e-n ~~ machen* to loop (the loop); **~enförmig** *a* loop-shaped; **~enkurve, ~enlinie** *f math* lemniscate; **~enrückenflug** *m aero* inverted loop; **~er** *m* (*Scheren~~*) grinder; (*Diamant~~, Glas~~*) cutter; (*Polierer*) polisher; *mus* slurred note; *tech* slip ring; **~erei** *f* grinding shop; grinding works *pl*, grinder's trade; grindery; (*Papier~~*) pulp manufacture; **~feder** *f* sliding spring; wiper; **~glas** *n* cut glass; **~kontakt** *m* sliding contact; **~lack** *m* grinding-paste, high-gloss painting, body varnish, enamel varnish; **~~möbel** *n pl* enamelled furniture; **~leinen** *n* abrasive cloth; **~maschine** *f* grinding machine, *Am* grinder; **~material, ~mittel** *n* abrasive; **~papier** *n* sand paper, emery paper; **~pulver** *n* grinding (*od* polishing *od* abrasive) powder; **~rad** *n* polishing (*od* grinding) wheel; **~riemen** *m* (*Rasiermesser*) razor-strop; **~ring** *m el* collector ring; **~scheibe** *f* grinding disk; **~schritt** *m* (*Tanz*) sliding step; **~sporn** *m aero* tail skid; **~stein** *m* grindstone, whetstone, hone(stone); sharpening stone; oilstone; **~stoff** *m* (*Holzschliff*) ground (*od* paper) pulp; **~ung** *f* (*Zerstörung*) demolition; *mil* (*von Festungswerken*) razing; dismantling; (*Neigung*) slope; **~vorrichtung** *f* grinding (*od* honing) device; **~weg** *m* road slide; **~werkzeug** *n* grinding tool.

Schleim *m* slime; *med* mucus, phlegm; *bot* mucilage; **~absonderung** *f* mucous secretion; (*Fluß*) blennorrh(o)ea; **~auswurf** *m* mucous expectoration; **~beutel** *m anat* mucous bag, synovial bursa; **~~entzündung** *f med* bursitis; **~bildend** *a* slime-forming; **~drüse** *f* mucous gland; **~en** *tr* (*Zucker*) to scum; (*Fische*) to clean, to purge; **~fieber** *n* mucous fever, typhoid fever; **~fluß** *m* blennorrh(o)ea; **~haut** *f* mucous membrane; **~~gewebe** *n* tissue of mucous membrane; **~ig** *a* slimy, mucous; viscous; **~~keit** *f* sliminess; **~lösend** *a* dissolving mucous; **~pfropf** *m* mucous plug; **~suppe** *f* (thick) gruel; **~tier** *n* mollusk (*od* mollusc).

Schleiß|e *f* (*langer Span*) splint, splinter; **~en** *irr tr* (*spalten, Späne abreißen*) to split; to tear; (*Federkiele*) to strip (quills); *itr* (*abnutzen*) to wear out; **~wirkung** *f* wearing action.

Schlemm *m* (*Kartenspiel*) slam.

Schlemm|boden *m* diluvial soil; **~en** *itr* (*festen*) to feast; to revel; (*trinken*) to carouse, to guzzle; (*üppig essen*) to gormandize; to gorge; to eat greedily; *tech* to saturate (with water); **~er** *m* glutton; gormand; gourmet; *fam* gorger, stuffer; crammer; **~erei** *f* feasting; gluttony; gormandizing; carousing; revelry; **~erhaft** *a* gluttonous, gormandizing; (*üppig*) plentiful; abundant; luxuriant; **~erleben** *n* gluttonous life; debauched life; **~ermahl** *n* luxurious banquet; **~kreide** *f* *tech* prepared chalk; carbonate of lime.

Schlempe *f* (*Destillationsrückstand*) distiller's wash; vinasse; slop; (*Futterbrei*) sloppy food for cattle.

schlend|ern *itr* (*bummeln*) to stroll; to saunter; to lounge; (*herumlungern*) to loiter; **~rian** *m* (*Bürokratie*) routine; slow course; jog-trot; beaten track; *Am fam* go-as-you-please; *am alten ~~ festhalten* to tread the beaten path.

schlenkern *itr, tr* (*mit den Füßen baumeln*) to dangle; (*mit den Armen*) to swing; (*schleudern*) to sling; to fling; (*im Gehen*) to shamble; to shuffle along.

Schlepp|antenne *f aero radio* trailing aerial, *Am* trailing antenna, drag antenna; **~dampfer** *m* steam-tug, tug(boat), tow-boat; **~dienst** *m* car tow; **~e** *f* (*Schwanz*) trail; (*Kleider~~*) train; **~en** *tr* (*schwer tragen*) to lug, to carry, *Am fam* to tote; (*schleifen, hinter sich herziehen*) to trail; to drag along; (*nachschleifen*) to draggle; (*ziehen, zerren*) to haul, to pull along; (*hochziehen*) to heave up; *com* (*Kunden*) to tout; *mar, aero* to tow, to tug; *e-n Lastensegler ~~* to tow a glider; *jdn vor Gericht ~~* to haul s.o to court; *sich ~~* to drag o.s. along; *sich mit etw ~~* to be encumbered with; **~end** *a* dragging; (*Stil*) heavy; (*Gang*) shuffling; (*Sprache*) drawling; (*langsam*) slow; (*schwerfällig*) cumbersome; (*flau, schwach*) languid; (*langwierig, lästig, ermüdend*) tedious; **~enkleid** *n* dress with train; **~enträger** *m* trainbearer; **~er** *m* dragger; *mot* (*Traktor*) tractor, prime mover; (*für Landwirtschaft*) farm tractor, agrimotor; *mar* tug(boat); (*Lastkahn*) tender, lighter; *com* (*Kunden~~*) tout(er); (*Helfershelfer*) bonnet; *min* (*Gruben~~*) hauler, haulier; **~erführer** *m* (*Traktorführer*) tractor driver; **~flug** *m* towed flight; glider towing; **~flugzeug** *n* tow plane, glider, tug for glider; (*Lastensegler*) (tow) glider; **~kahn** *m* towed boat, lighter, barge; **~lohn** *m* *mar* towage; **~lift** *m* drag-lift; **~netz** *n* drag-net, dredge, trammel; (*Hochsee~~*) trawling-net; **~~fischer** *m* trawler; **~~fischerei** *f* trawling; **~säbel** *m* cavalry-sabre, *fam* dangler; **~sack** *m aero* (*für Flackübungsschießen*) towed sleeve target; **~scheibe** *f aero mil* towed target; **~schiff** *n* tug(-boat); **~schiffahrt** *f* towing; **~segel** *n aero* drift sail; landing apron; **~seil** *n* towing cable, tow-rope; *das ~~ ausklinken* to release the towing cable; **~start** *m aero* tow take-off, towed start; **~tau** *n* tow-rope; towing cable; tow, tow-line, towing hawser; *ins ~~ nehmen* to (take in) tow, to tug; **~wagen** *m* tow car; **~winde** *f* tow winch; **~zug** *m mar* train (*od* string) of barges; convoy; *aero* air (*od* sky) train; *mot* truck train, truck with trailer.

Schles|ien *n* Silesia; **~ier** *m*, **~isch** *a* Silesian; **~wig** *n* Slesvig.

Schleuder *f* (*Stein~*) sling, *Am* slingshot; *aero* (*Flugzeug~*) catapult; *tech* (*Zentrifuge*) centrifugal (machine), centrifuge; extractor; (*Milch~*) cream separator; **~anlage** *f aero* catapult; **~artikel** *m com* catchpenny article; **~ausfuhr** *f* dumping; **~ei** *f com* underselling, undercutting; **~er** *m* (*Werfer*) slinger; *com* underseller; **~flug** *m* *aero* catapult flight; **~flugzeug** *n* catapult (air)plane; **~gebläse** *n* centrifugal air pump; **~geschäft** *n* undercutting business; **~guß** *m* centrifugally cast (iron); **~honig** *m* strained (*od* extracted) honey; **~kraft** *f* centrifugal force; **~maschine** *f* (*Zentrifuge*) centrifugal (machine); extractor; separator; **~n** *tr* (*werfen, stoßen*) to throw; to hurl; to dart; to toss; to pitch; (*mit Schleuder*) to sling; (*Flüssigkeiten*) to centrifuge; to whizz; *aero* to start by catapult; *den Bannstrahl ~~* (*eccl*) to anathematize; *itr com* (*unterbieten*) to undersell, to sell under cost-price; to spoil prices; *mot* (*rutschen*) to skid, to slip, to side-slip; *~~ in der Kurve* skidding on a curve; (*sich drehen*) to spin; (*Schiff*) to roll, to lurch; *aero* (*mit Katapult*) to catapult; **~preis** *m* underprice; cut rate; ruinous price, ridiculously low price; *zu ~~en* dirt-cheap; *Verkauf zu ~~en* (*im Ausland*) dumping; **~sitz** *m aero* pilot ejector seat; **~start** *m aero* catapult take-off; **~trommel** *f* centrifugal drum; **~vorrichtung** *f aero* catapult launching gear; **~waffe** *f* missile; **~waren** *f pl* bargain articles *pl*, catchpenny articles *pl*.

schleunig *a* (*schnell*) speedy, hasty; quick; (*sofort*) prompt, immediate; ready; *adv* in all haste; (*sofort*) immediately, promptly; at once; **~keit** *f* speed, quickness; promptness; **~st** *adv* as quickly as possible; as speedily as possible; in all haste; forthwith, *Am* right away.

Schleuse *f* sluice; sluiceway; (*Kanal~*) lock; (*Abzugsgraben*) sewer, gully hole; drain; *bewegliche ~* hydraulic elevator; **~ngeld** *n* sluice-dues *pl*, lock-charges *pl*; **~nkammer** *f* lock (*od* sluice) chamber; **~nmeister, ~nwärter** *m* lock-keeper; **~nschütz, ~ntor** *n* flood-gate, lock-gate, sluice-gate; draw-gate; **~~flügel** *m* leaf of sluice-gate; **~nsohle** *f* lock floor; **~nwärter** *m* lock-keeper.

Schlich *m* (*Kunstkniff*) trick; artifice, *fam* dodge; (*Umweg*) secret way; by-way; *~e pl* (*Ränke*) intrigues *pl*; *hinter jds ~e kommen* to be up to s. o.'s tricks.

schlicht *a* (*einfach*) plain; simple; homely; straightforward; (*glatt*) sleek, smooth; even; fine; (*bescheiden*) modest, unpretentious; *~er Abschied* dismissal; *~ feilen* to file smooth; *~es Haar* smooth hair; *~er Mann* a straightforward man; **~beil** *n* chip-ax(e); **~bohrer** *m tech* finishing bit, polisher; **~en** *tr* (*glätten*) to smooth, to polish; *tech* (*ebnen*) to plane, to level; to make even, to make level; to finish; (*Gießerei*) to blackwash; (*Tuch, Wolle*) to dress, to size; *fig* (*Fragen, Streitigkeiten, Differenzen, Gegensätze etc ausgleichen, ordnen, entscheiden*) to adjust, to arrange; to make up; to put right (*od* straight); to compose; (*schiedsgerichtlich*) to arbitrate, to reconcile, to compromise; *e-n Streit* (*od e-e Auseinandersetzung*) *~~* to settle a dispute; (*schiedsgerichtlich*) to settle by arbitration; **~er** *m* arbitrator; (*Vermittler*) mediator; **~feile** *f* fine file; **~heit** *f* (*Einfachheit*) plainness, simplicity; (*Bescheidenheit*) modesty; **~hobel** *m* smoothing-plane; **~messer** *n* plane knife; **~ung** *f* (*Streitigkeiten*) settlement; mediation, arbitration; arrangement; accommodation; **~~samt** *n* conciliation board; mediation (*od* arbitration) board; **~~sausschuß** *m* arbitration (*od* mediation) committee; **~~sstelle** *f* (*bei Lohnstreitigkeiten etc*) fact-finding board.

Schlick *m* slime, mud, ooze; silt; slay; **~bad** *n* mud bath; **~bank** *f* mudbank; **~grund** *m* mud bottom.

schliefen *irr itr* (*kriechen*) to slip; to creep.

schliefig *a* (*Brot*) doughy, slack-baked.

Schliere *f* streak, schliere; **~naufnahme** *f* schlieren photograph; **~nzone** *f* dead zone.

Schließ|bolzen *m* cotter pin; eyebolt and key; **~e** *f* (*Schloß*) forelock; (*Einhakvorrichtung*) fastening, pin, peg, catch, latch, cotter; (*Buch~~*) (book-) clasp; **~en** *irr tr, itr* (*Buch, Fenster, Türe etc zumachen*) to shut; to close, (*einsperren*) to shut up; (*mit Schlüssel*) to lock; *doppelt ~~* (*Schloß*) to double-lock; (*verriegeln*) to bolt; (*beenden*) to finish, to end, to bring to an end; to stop; to close; to terminate; to wind up (*mit* with); (*Debatte*) *parl* to closure, *Am* to cloture; *aus etw ~~* (*folgern*) to conclude from s. th.; to infer from; to deduce; to gather from; to draw an inference (*od* conclusion) from; (*urteilen*) to judge by; to reason; *kurz ~~* (*el*) to ground; (*passen, sitzen von Kleidern*) to fit (well); *die Augen ~~* to shut (*od* to close) o.'s eyes; *den Betrieb ~~* to shut down; to close down; *die Bücher ~~* (*com*) to balance the books; *ein Bündnis ~~* to form an alliance; *e-e Freundschaft ~~* to form a friendship; *Frieden ~~* to make peace; *ein Geschäft* (*od e-n Handel*) *~~* to strike a bargain; *e-e Heirat ~~* to contract a marriage; *e-e Klammer ~~* to close a bracket; *e-n Kompromiß ~~* to reach a compromise; *ein Konto ~~* to close an account; *e-n Kreis ~~* to form a circle; *die Reihen ~~* to close the ranks; *e-e Rede ~~* to finish (*od* to conclude) a speech; *e-n Stromkreis ~~* to close (*od* to make *od* to complete) a circuit; *e-n Vergleich ~~* to come to an agreement (*od* to terms); *die Verhandlung ~~* (*bei Gericht*) to close the court; *e-n Vertrag ~~* to make a contract, to conclude a treaty; *e-e Versammlung ~~* to break up a meeting; *e-e Wette ~~* to make a bet; *der Schlüssel schließt nicht* the key doesn't work; *die Schule schloß heute* to-day the school broke up; *ans Herz ~~* to press to o.'s heart; *jdn ins Herz ~~* (*fig*) to take a liking to, to take s. o. into o.'s heart; *in die Arme ~~* to embrace, to clasp in o.'s arms; *etw in den Schrank ~~* to lock s. th. up in the cupboard; *in Ketten ~~* to fetter; *sich ~~* to shut, to close; *sich e-r Tatsache ver~~* to shut o.'s eyes to a fact; *sich ~~ an* to join to; *er schließt sich meinen Grüßen an* he joins with me in kind regards; *in sich ~~* (*enthalten*) to comprise, to include; to comprehend; (*bedeuten, besagen*) to imply; (*umfassen*) to involve; *ein geschlossenes Ganzes* a compact whole; *e-e geschlossene Gesellschaft* a private party; a club; *in geschlossenen Reihen* close-banded; *mil* in serried ranks; *e-e geschlossene Veranda* an enclosed porch; *geschlossen für etw sein* to go solid for; *hinter geschlossenen Türen* with closed doors; *jur* with exclusion of the public; in camera; **~ende(r)** *m* (*bei Akten*) file closer; **~er** *m* (*Pförtner*) doorkeeper, (*Gefängniswärter*) jailer, turnkey; (*Schlußvorrichtung*) *anat* constrictor,sphincter; adductor; *el* (*Kontakt*) contact; **~erin** *f* (*Wirtschafterin*) housekeeper; stewardess; **~fach** *n* (*Post*) post-office box, post-box (*Abk* P.O. Box); (*Bank*) safe; locker; **~feder** *f* breech-closing spring; (*Pistole*) safety-grip spring; **~haken** *m* lock hook; catch; hasp; **~kontakt** *m el* closing contact; **~korb** *m* hamper (with lock); **~lich** *a* last, eventual; conclusive; (*endgültig*) final, ultimate, definitive; *adv* finally, eventually; after all; in the long run; in conclusion, in the upshot; at last, at length; *~~ u. endlich* when all is said and done; **~muskel** *m anat* sphincter, constrictor; adductor; **~ung** *f* (*Schließen*) closing, close; shutting; (*Ende*) end; (*Schluß*) conclusion; (*Betriebseinstellung*) shut-down; (*Geschäftschluß*) closing-time; (*~~ e-r Versammlung*) breaking-up; *el* (*Kontakt*) make; (*Stromkreis*) closing; *~~ der Debatte parl* closure, *Am* cloture; (*zeitweilig*) suspension; **~~sdraht** *m* connecting wire; **~vorrichtung** *f* closing device; **~zeit** *f* (*Laden, Büro etc*) closing-time.

Schliff *m* (*Diamant, Glas*) cut; *tech* (*Schärfe, Schärfung*) sharpening; grind, grinding; polishing; (*Fläche*) ground section; surface; slide; (*Glätte der Oberfläche*) polish, finish, smoothness; *fig* (*Lebensart*) refined (*od* good) manners *pl*; *mil* (*Drill*) hard drill, rigid training; *den letzten ~ geben tech* to touch up; *fig* to put the finishing touch to; **~fläche** *f* polished section; **~stopfen** *m* ground-in stopper.

schlimm *a* (*schlecht*) bad; (*übel*) ill; (*böse*) evil, wicked; (*wund*) sore; (*beunruhigend*) serious, grave; (*nichtsnutzig*) naughty; (*traurig*) sad; (*fatal*) fatal; (*unangenehm*) disagreeable, unpleasant; annoying; (*durchtrieben*) cunning; (*krank, unwohl*) unwell, sick; (*gefährlich, ernst; eklig, garstig*) nasty; *das ist ~* this is bad; *das ist ~ für ihn* that is hard (lines) on him, *Am* that is tough on him; *es sieht ~ aus* it looks bad; *es steht ~ um ihn* he is in a bad way; *es war nicht so ~* it was not so bad; *ein ~es Ende nehmen* to turn out badly; *e-e ~e Geschichte* a sad tale; *e-e ~e Hand haben* to have a sore hand; *e-n ~en Husten haben* to have a bad cough; *e-e ~e Krankheit* a serious illness; *ein ~er Kerl* a nasty fellow; *das ist e-e ~e Kurve für e-n großen Wagen* that's a nasty corner for a big car; *e-e ~e Lage* a serious situation; **~er** *a* worse; *immer ~~* worse and worse; *um so ~~!* all the worse! *es regnete ~~ als je* it was raining worse than ever; *etw ~~ machen* to aggravate s. th.; *~~ werden* to deteriorate, to go from bad to worse; *am ~sten* (*Superlativ*) the worst; *machen Sie sich aufs ~ste gefaßt* be prepared for the worst; *wenn das ~ste eintrifft* should the worst befall; *alles von der ~sten Seite ansehen* to look at the dark side of everything; **~stenfalls** *adv* if the worst comes to the worst; at (the) worst; in the worst case.

Schling|e *f* (*Schleife, Öse*) loop, noose; (*Draht~~*) coil; curl; *med* (*Binde*) sling; *bot* tendril; (*zum Fangen*) snare; gin; wire; *fig* (*Falle für jdn*) trap, snare; *in e-e ~~ legen* (*Arm etc*) to sling; *~~n bilden* to curl; *sich aus der ~~ ziehen fig* to get out of a difficulty, to come off safe; *jdm e-e ~~ legen fig* to set a trap for s. o.; *in die ~~ gehen* to fall into the snare; **~el** *m* rascal, bad egg; (*Junge*) naughty boy; *fauler ~~* lazybones; *kleiner ~~* urchin; **~en[1]** *irr tr* (*binden*) to tie; (*winden*) to twist; to (en)twine; (*Pflanzen*) to creep, to climb; *sich um etw ~~* to wind, to coil; to turn; to twine round, to sling round; *um den Hals ~~* (*Schal*) to wrap round the neck; *ineinander ~~* to intertwist; (*Arme kreuzen*) to cross; **~en[2]** *irr tr, itr* (*hinunter~~*) to gulp, to swallow; to gorge; (*verschlingen*) to devour; **~enleger** *m* snarer; **~erbewegung** *f* rolling; **~erkiel** *m* bilge keel; **~ern** *itr* (*Schiff*) to roll, to lurch; **~ertank** *m mar* anti-rolling tank; **~gewächs** *n*, **~pflanze** *f* climbing plant; climber; creeper; twining plant.

Schlips *m* (*Krawatte*) cravat, tie, *Am* necktie; (*Halsbinde, Halstuch*) scarf; *sich auf den ~ getreten fühlen fig fam* to be offended, to be scandalized; **~nadel** *f* scarf-pin, *Am* tie pin; **~träger** *m mil sl* (*Zivilist*) civilian, *Am sl* civvy, cit.

Schlitt|en *m* sledge, *Am* sled; (*Rodel~~*) toboggan; (*Pferde~~*) sleigh; *leichter Pferde~~* light sleigh, *Am* cutter; *tech* (*Gleitwagen, Gleitvorrichtung*) sliding carriage; (*Schreibmaschine*) carriage; slide; craddle; saddle; (*Säge~~*) chariot; *aero* (*Kufen*) skid; *aero sl* (*alte Kiste*) *sl* jalopy; *auf ~~ befördern* (*od fahren*) to sledge, to sleigh, *Am* to sled; *~~ fahren* to go in a sledge, to ride (*od* to drive) in a sleigh; (*rodeln*) to toboggan, *Am* to coast; **~enbahn** *f* sledge-road, sledging-course; slide; **~enfahren** *n* sleigh riding; **~enfahrt** *f* sledge-ride, drive in a sledge; **~enführung** *f tech* slide conveyer; **~enhund** *m* sled dog; **~enkufen** *f pl* sledge runners *pl*, sleigh runners *pl*; *aero* skid runners *pl*; **~enpartie** *f* sledging-party, sleighing (-party); **~ensport** *m* sledging; **~ern** *itr* to slide; (*Auto*) to skid; *hinein ~~ fig* to bungle into (war); to skid into (a situation); **~schuh** *m* (ice-) skate; *ein Paar ~~e* a pair of skates; *~~ laufen* to ice-skate; *kannst du ~~ laufen?* do you know how to (ice-)skate? **~~bahn** *f* ice-rink, skating-ground, skating -rink; **~~läufer** *m* skater; **~~schlüssel** *m* skate key.

Schlitz *m* slit; (*Spalt*) cleft, rift; split; slash; (*Riß*) fissure; *anat* (*Öffnung*) aperture; (*längliches Loch*) slotted hole; (*Einwurf an Automat etc*) slot; (*Entlüftungs~*) vent; (*Kerbe*) notch; (*Nute, Auskehlung*) groove; *mot* (*Zylinder*) port; *aero* (*am Flügel*) slot; *Seh~* observation slit, sight; **~auge** *n* slit eye (*pl* slits *pl*); Mongolian eye; **~äugig** *a* almond-eyed; slit-eyed; **~blende** *f* slit stop; slotted diaphragm; **~brenner** *m* (bats)wing burner; slit burner; **~en** *tr* to slit, to split; to cleave; to slash, to slot; to rip; to crack; **~flügel** *m aero* (*Spaltflügel*) slotted wing; **~förmig** *a* slitlike; **~messer** *n* slitting knife; **~verschluß** *m phot* focal-plane shutter; slit-type shutter.

schlohweiß *a* snow-white; white as sloe-blossoms.

Schloß *n* (*Burg*) castle; (*Palast*) palace; (*Herrschaftshaus*) manor-house; country-seat; *tech* (*Gewehr~, Tür~*) lock; (*Vorhänge~*) padlock; (*Riegel~*) bolt; *aero* (*Bomben~*) bomb release; (*Buch~*) clasp; (*Halsband~*) snap, hasp, clasp; (*Muschel~*) hinge; *unter ~ u. Riegel halten* to keep under lock and key; *hinter ~ u. Riegel setzen* to take in custody; *hinter ~ u. Riegel sitzen* to be locked up (in prison); *jdm ein ~ vor den Mund legen fig* to close s. o.'s mouth; *der Schlüssel steckt im ~* the key is in the door; **~aufseher** *m* castellan, custodian; **~blech** *n tech* lock (*od* main) plate; **~feder** *f tech* spring of a lock; **~freiheit** *f* precincts *pl* of a castle; **~garten** *m* palace-garden; **~graben** *m* moat; **~herr** *m* lord of a castle; **~hof** *m* castle-yard, court-yard; **~hund** *m*: *heulen wie ein ~~* (*fig*) to cry o.'s eyes out; to shed hot tears; **~platz** *m* palace-yard; **~riegel** *m tech* bolt of a lock; **~tor** *n* castle-gate; **~turm** *m* castle-tower; **~verwalter, ~vogt** *m* castellan; **~wache** *f* castle guard, palace guard; **~zuhaltung** *f tech* lock hasp.

Schloße *f* hail-stone; sleet; pellet of hail; **~n** *pl* hail; *imp* to hail.

Schlosser *m* (*Bau~*) locksmith; (*Maschinen~*) mechanic, fitter; machinist; (*Metaller*) metal worker; (*Werkzeug~*) tool maker; (*Auto~*) garageman; **~arbeit** *f* locksmith's work; **~ei** *f* locksmith's (work)shop; fitting shop; **~handwerk** *n* locksmith's trade; **~meister** *m* master locksmith; **~n** *itr* (*basteln*) to tinker; to hammer at; **~werkstatt, ~werkstätte** *f* locksmith's workshop.

Schlot *m* (*Esse, Schornstein*) chimney; (*Feuerzug*) flue; (*Fabrik~*) smoke-stack; (*Abzugsrohr; Vulkanöffnung*) vent; *rail, mar* funnel; *fig fam* (*ungebildeter, unfeiner Kerl*) lout, boor, *Am sl* duffer, geezer, stiff; *rauchen wie ein ~* to smoke like a chimney; **~baron, ~junker** *m fam* industrial magnate, *Am sl* tycoon; **~kehrer** *m* chimney-sweep, sweep, sweeper.

schlott|(e)rig *a* (*lose*) loose; (*herabhängend*) dangling; (*wackelig*) shaky; wobbly; tottery; (*schlaff*) flabby; *fig* (*nachlässig*) negligent; (*liederlich*) slovenly; *~~ gehen* to totter along; *~~e Knie* knocking (*od* shaky) knees; **~ern** *itr* (*Kleider etc*) to hang (*od* to fit) loosely; (*baumeln*) to dangle, to flap; (*wackeln*) to wobble; (*torkeln*) to totter; (*zittern*) to tremble, to shake; (*mit den Knien*) to knock together; *~~ vor Angst* to tremble with fear.

Schlucht *f* gorge, (*tiefe ~*) glen; gully, *Am* (*tiefe Bergbach~*) gulch; *Am* (*Erosions~*) canon, canyon; (*Hohlweg*) ravine; (*Abgrund*) abyss; *fig* gulf; **~wald** *m* canyon forest.

schluchzen *itr* (*weinen*) to sob; to snivel; (*den Schlucken haben*) to hiccup; *~ n* sobbing, sobs *pl*.

Schluck *m* draught, gulp; (*Mundvoll*) mouthful; sup, sip; *ein ~ Wasser* a drink; **~auf** *m* hiccup(s *pl*), hiccough(s *pl*); **~beschwerden** *f pl* difficulty of swallowing, *med* dysphagia; **~en** *tr, itr* to swallow; to gulp (down); to gorge; (*absorbieren*) to absorb; (*aufsaugen*) to suck up; *fig* (*Beleidigung etc*) to stomach; **~en** *m* hiccup(s *pl*), hiccough(s *pl*); *den ~~ haben* to hiccup; **~er** *m*: *armer ~~* poor devil, poor wretch; **~ung** *f* absorption; **~weise** *adv* by draughts, by gulps, by mouthfuls.

Schlummer *m* slumber; (*leichter ~*) doze, drowse; *fam* (*Nickerchen*) snooze, nap; **~lied** *n* lullaby; craddlesong; **~n** *itr* to slumber, to doze; *fam* to snooze, to nap; *fig* to be latent, to lie dormant; **~nd** *a* slumbering, dozing; *fam* snoozing, napping; *fig* dormant; **~rolle** *f* round pillow, bolster cushion (for the neck); **~trank** *m* nightcap.

Schlump|e *f* slut, sloven, slattern; **~ig** *a* slovenly.

Schlund *m* (*Kehle, Gurgel*) throat; *anat* (*Halsöffnung*) gorge, gullet, pharynx; (*Speiseröhre*) esophagus (*pl* esophagi); (*Abgrund*) abyss, chasm; gulf; (*Vulkankrater*) crater; *fig* (*Öffnung, Kanonen~*) mouth; **~bogen** *m anat* pharyngeal arch; **~gewölbe** *n anat* vault (*od* fornix) of the pharynx; **~röhre** *f anat* esophagus, esophageal tube; **~sonde** *f* stomach tube.

Schlupf *m tech* (*toter Gang*) slippage, backlash; *aero* (*Propeller*) slip; **~hose** *f* knickers *pl*, *Am* bloomers *pl*; **~jacke** *f* sweater; **~loch** *n* loophole; hiding place, refuge; **~wespe** *f bot* ichneumon; **~winkel** *m* hiding-place; lurking-place; refuge; haunt; recess, retreat.

schlüpf|en *itr* to slip; (*rutschen*) to slide; (*gleiten*) to glide, to steal; *in die* (*aus den*) *Kleider(n)* ~~ to slip on (*od* off) o.'s clothes; *der Fisch ~te mir durch die Finger* the fish slipped through my fingers; *er ~te vorbei ohne gesehen zu werden* he slipped past without being seen; **~er** *m* (*Damen~~*) (a pair of) knickers *pl*, *Am* (*mit Beinansatz u. Gummibandansatz*) bloomers *pl*; (*nur Beinansatz*) panties *pl*, (*weite Form*) step-in; (*kurzer, leichter Sommer~~*) leg panties *pl*, (leg) briefs *pl*; (*Mantel*) raglan; **~ergürtel** *m* (*mit Strumpfhalter*) *Am* panty-girdle; **~e(r)ig** *a* slippery; oily; *fig* (*pikant*) piquant; (*unanständig*) indecent; (*obszön*) racy, obscene, lascivious; **~rigkeit** *f* slipperiness; oiliness; lubricity; *fig* obscenity.

schlurfen, schlurren *itr* (*schleppend gehen*) to shuffle along; to scuffle along; to walk with dragging gait.

schlürfen *tr* to sip; to sup up; (*gierig trinken, bes. von Tieren*) to lap; to drink in; (*Pumpe*) to suck air.

Schluß *m* (*Ende, Halt*) end; close; termination; finish, stop; (*Ablauf*) expiration; (*Ergebnis, Abschluß, Folgerung*) issue, upshot; outcome, result; (*Ende, Abwicklung*) winding-up, *Am* windup; (*Schließung*) shutting, closing; (*Folgerung*) conclusion, concluding; deduction; inference; (*logische Folgerung*) syllogism; (*Entscheid*) decision; *el* (*Kurz~*) short circuit; *~! tele* that's all! finished! *parl* the debate is closed! time! *~ damit!* stop it! finish! that's enough of that! *fam* cut it out! *~ der Debatte parl* closing; (*auf Antrag*) (to move the) closure, *Am* cloture; *~ folgt* to be concluded; *~ der Redaktion* before going to press; *~ der Vorstellung* end of the performance; *am ~* at the end (of); *zum ~* in conclusion; in the end, finally; to finish up; *bis zum ~* to the last; *zum ~ bringen* to bring to a close; *zu dem ~ kommen* to come to the conclusion; *zu e-m ~ gelangen* (*od kommen*) to arrive at a conclusion; (*plötzlich*) to jump at a conclusion; *e-n ~ aus etw ziehen* to conclude, to infer; to draw a conclusion (*od* interference) from; *~ machen* to put an end to; (*bei der Arbeit*) to knock off; to quit; **~abrechnung** *f* final settlement (*od* balance); **~akt** *m* last act; **~antrag** *m* final conclusion; *parl* motion for closure; **~bemerkung** *f* final (*od* concluding) remark; final observation; **~bericht** *m* final report; **~bestimmung** *f* concluding clause (*od* provision); **~bilanz** *f* final balance sheet; **~effekt** *m* upshot; **~ergebnis** *n* final result, final issue; upshot; **~examen** *n* final examination, *Am* end terms *pl*, final exams *pl*, finals *pl*; **~feier** *f* (*Schule*) speech-day, prize-day, *Am* graduation exercises *pl*, *Am* commencement; **~folge, ~folgerung** *f* inference, reasoning; conclusion, deduction; argument; *~folgerungen ziehen* to argue; to put two and two together; **~formel** *f* close; closing-phrase; (*Brief*) complimentary ending; **~inventur** *f* annual stock-taking; **~kurve** *f* end curve; (*Rennbahn*) home turn; **~lauf** *m* (*Baseball*) final run; **~läufer, ~mann** *m* (*Staffel*) last runner; **~leiste** *f typ* tail-piece; **~licht** *n mot* tail-light, tail lamp; *mar* stern-light; **~linie** *f typ* dash; **~meldung** *f* final report; **~notierung** *f* (*Börse*) final (*od* closing) quotation; **~pfiff** *m sport* final whistle; **~protokoll** *n* final protocol; **~prüfung** *f* (*Schule*) final examination, *Am* end terms *pl*, final exams *pl*, finals *pl*; **~punkt** *m gram* full stop; (*Abschluß*) last item; **~rechnung** *f* account of settlement, final balance (*od* account); **~rede** *f* final address; concluding speech; (*Nachwort*) epilogue; **~reim** *m* end-rhyme; (*Refrain*) burden; **~rennen** *n sport* final heat; last event; **~runde** *f sport* final round, final; *Teilnehmer der ~~* finalist; *in die ~~ kommen* to get into the final; **~satz** *m* concluding sentence, conclusion; final proposition; (*Philosophie*) consequent; *mus* finale; (*Tennis*) final set; **~schein** *m com* contract note; sales certificate; **~sitzung** *f* final meeting; closing session; **~spiel** *n* final game; **~stand** *m sport* final score; **~stein** *m* keystone; corner-stone; **~termin** *m* final hearing; **~verkauf** *m* seasonal sale; **~vignette** *f* tail-piece; **~wort** *n* last word; (*Zusammenfassung*) summary; **~zahlung** *f* final payment; **~zeichen** *n* final signal; *gram* (*Punkt*) full stop; **~zeile** *f typ* catch-line; **~zettel** *m* sale-note.

Schlüssel *m* (*Tür~*) key; *falscher ~* skeleton key, picklock; (*Schrauben~*) spanner, *Am* wrench; *mus* clef; *Baß~* bass clef; *Violin~* violin clef; *el* (*Schalter*) switch; *fig* (*Verteilungsquote*) quota; *fig* (*Chiffrier~, Geheim~*) code, cipher; *fig* (*zum Geheimnis*) clue; *ohne ~* keyless; **~bart** *m* (key-) bit; **~bein** *n* collar-bone, clavicle; **~blatt** *n* (*zum Chiffrieren*) enciphering sheet, code sheet; **~blech** *n* key-plate; **~blume** *f* (*gelbe ~~*) cowslip; (*helle ~~*) primrose; **~brett** *n* key-board, key-shelf; **~buchstabe** *m* cipher; **~bund** *m* bunch of keys; **~fertig** *a* ready for immediate occupation; *ein ~~es Haus* a new house ready for moving in; **~gewalt** *f* power of the keys; **~gruppe** *f* (*beim Chiffrieren*) code group; **~industrie** *f* key industry; **~loch** *n* keyhole; *durchs ~~ gucken* to spy through the keyhole; **~punkt** *m* key point; **~ring** *m* key-ring; **~roman** *m* roman à clef; novel with a key; **~stellung** *f* key position, key post; (*Beamter in ~~*) key official; **~text** *m* (*beim Chiffrieren*) cipher text; **~unterlage** *f* encoding and decoding chart; **~wort** *n* (*beim Chiffrieren*) code-word; key-word; **~zahl** *f* (*Quote*) ratio of distribution; quota.

schlüssel|n *tr* (*chiffrieren*) to encode, to code, to encipher, to cipher; **~ung** *f* (en)coding, enciphering; cryptographing.

schlüssig *a* resolved, determined; sure; (*logisch*) logical; *~er Beweis* conclusive proof (*od* evidence); *nicht ~* (*Beweis*) inconclusive; *sich ~ sein* to be determined, to have made up o.'s mind; *sich ~ werden* to make up o.'s mind (*über* about); to decide.

Schmach *f* (*Beschimpfung*) insult; (*Schimpf*) ignominy; (*Unehre*) disgrace; (*Beschimpfung, gröbliche Beleidigung*) outrage; (*Demütigung*) humiliation; **~bedeckt** *a* covered with shame; **~voll** *a* (*unehrenhaft*) disgraceful; (*demütigend*) humiliating; (*schmählich, schimpflich*) ignominious.

schmacht|en *itr* to languish (*vor* with, from); *vor Durst ~~* to be parched with thirst; (*nach etw ~~*) to languish for, to yearn after, to pine for (*od* after), to long for; *~~ lassen* to tantalize; **~end** *a* languishing; *~~e Augen werfen* to cast sheep's eyes; *ein ~~er Blick* a languishing glance; **~lappen** *m* lovesick swain; **~locke** *f* lovelock; earlock; **~riemen** *m fam* truss, belt (to contract the stomach); *den ~~ enger schnallen fam* to tighten o.'s belt.

schmächtig *a* (*schlank*) slim, lanky; slender; *fam* skimpy; (*mager*) lean; (*dünn*) thin; (*schwach, zart*) delicate; slight; *ein ~es Mädchen* a slip of a girl; **~keit** *f* slimness, slenderness; leanness; (*zarte Gesundheit*) delicate health.

schmackhaft *a* (*appetitanregend*) savoury, appetizing; tasty; palatable; (*lecker*) delicious, dainty; *~ machen* (*Speisen würzen*) to season; *jdm etw ~ machen fig* to talk s. o. into s. th.; (*nach dem Mund reden*) to flatter; **~igkeit** *f* savouriness, savour; taste; palatableness.

Schmäh|brief *m* defamatory letter; **~en** *tr* (*beschimpfen*) to abuse; (*losziehen gegen*) to revile; (*durch üble Nachrede*) to slander; to speak ill of; (*beleidigen*) to insult; (*Geheiligtes ~~*) to blaspheme; **~lich** *a* (*schändlich*) scandalous; (*schimpflich*) ignominious; disgraceful; (*demütigend*) humiliating; *fig* (*sehr, groß*) awful; **~rede** *f* abuse; diatribe; calumny; backbiting; **~schrift** *f* libel; (*Flugblatt*) lampoon; **~sucht** *f* love of slander (*od* scandal); **~süchtig** *a* (*verleumderisch*) slanderous; (*beleidigend*) insulting; **~ung** *f* (*Beschimpfung*) invective; abuse; (*Beleidigung*) defamation, slander; **~wort** *n* invective; abusive word.

schmal *a* (*eng*) narrow; (*schlank*) slender, slim; (*dünn*) thin; (*klein*) small; (*kurz*) short; *fig* (*knapp*) scanty; (*arm*) poor; (*mager*) meagre; *~e Bissen essen* to be in straitened circumstances; *auf ~e Kost setzen* to keep s. o. on short commons; *~es Einkommen* scanty income; *ein ~es Gesicht* a thin face; *~e Schrift typ* lean type; **~bäckig** *a* hollow-cheeked; **~blätterig** *a bot* narrow-leaved; stenopetalous; **~brüstig** *a* narrow-chested; **~film** *m* substandard film, narrow film; 8 mm film; **~~kamera** *f* narrow film camera, *Am* amateur movie camera; **~geiß** *f* one year old roe; **~hans** *m* starveling; niggard; *hier ist ~~ Küchenmeister* they are on short commons; **~heit** *f* narrowness; *fig* scantiness; **~kante** *f* narrow edge; **~randig** *a* narrow-brimmed; **~schultrig** *a* slender built; **~seite** *f* narrow side; **~spur** *f* narrow ga(u)ge; **~~bahn** *f* narrow ga(u)ge railway; **~spurig** *a* narrow-ga(u)ge(d); **~tier** *n* hind in her second year; **~vieh** *n* (*Schafe, Ziegen, Schweine*) small cattle; **~wangig** *a* hollow-cheeked.

schmälen *tr, itr* (*auszanken*) to scold; (*schelten*) to chide; (*heruntermachen*) to abuse; (*beschimpfen*) to insult; (*kritisieren*) to criticize.

schmäler|n *tr* to narrow; (*Geldbetrag, Einnahmen, Ausgaben etc beschneiden*) to curtail; (*verkürzen*) to shorten, to cut down; (*beeinträchtigen*) to impair; (*vermindern, verringern*) to lessen; to diminish; (*Ansehen, Ruf etc herabsetzen*) to belittle; to detract (from); (*Rechte ~~*) to encroach upon; to derogate; **~ung** *f* curtailment; diminution; lessening; derogation; impairment; encroachment; detraction; infringement.

Schmalz *n* (*Schweine~*) lard; (melted) fat; (*Schmierfett*) grease; (*Braten~*) dripping; (*Talg*) tallow, suet; (*Ohren~*) ear-wax, cerumen; *fig* sentimentalism; (*Pathos, Salbung*) unction; **~artig** *a* lardy, lardaceous; **~birne** *f* butter-pear; **~brot** *n* slice of bread and dripping; **~butter** *f* melted butter; **~en, schmälzen** *tr* (*Kochkunst*) to lard, to butter; to put dripping (*od* lard) into; *weder gesalzen noch geschmalzen* without fat or salt; *fig* (*fad*) flat; tasteless; **~faß** *n* lard tub; **~gebakkene(s)** *n Am* cruller, doughnut; **~ig** *a* lardy, lardaceous; (*fettig*) fatty; (*schmierig*) greasy; *fig* (*sentimental*) sentimental, pathetic; (*salbungsvoll*) unctuous; *mus* (*Schlager*) corn(e)y, *Am* schmaltzy; sweet; **~kuchen** *m* fritter, lard-cake, dripping cake; **~pfanne** *f* frying-pan; **~stulle** *f* bread and dripping.

schmarotz|en *itr* (*Mensch*) to sponge (*bei* on); *bot, zoo* to live as a parasite; **~er** *m fig* (*Mensch*) sponger, sponge; *Am sl* (dead) beat; (*Kriecher, Schmeichler*) sycophant, fawner, truckler; *bot, zoo* parasite; **~erei** *f* sponging; parasitism; **~erisch** *a* sponging; spongy; (*kriecherisch*) sycophantic; *bot, zoo* parasitic(al); **~erleben** *n* parasitic life; **~erpflanze** *f* parasitic(al) plant; **~ertier** *n* animal parasite; **~ertum** *n* sponging; parasitism.

Schmarr|e *f* slash; (*Narbe*) cicatrice, scar (in the face); **~en** *m* (*Mehlspeise*) gratin; kind of omelette; (*Kitsch, Schund, Machwerk*) trash; rubbish; shocker; (*Bagatelle*) worthless object; nothingness; **~ig** *a* scarry.

Schmatz *m* hearty kiss, smack, smacker; **~en** *tr* to smack, to kiss; to give a hearty kiss; *itr* (*mit den Lippen ~~*) to smack o.'s lips.

schmauchen *tr, itr* to (enjoy a) smoke; (*Pfeife*) to puff at a pipe.

Schmaus *m* feast, banquet; treat; *Ohren~* musical treat; **~en** *itr* to feast (*von* upon), to banquet; to eat heartily; **~erei** *f* feasting, banquet; *fam* tuck-in, tuck-out.

schmeck|en *tr* (*kosten*) to taste, to try; to sample; to smack; (*genießen*) to enjoy, to relish; *itr* to savo(u)r (*nach* of); to taste (*nach* of); to smack (*nach* of); *dieser Wein ~t mir* I enjoy (*od* like) this wine; *angenehm ~~* to taste nice; *gut* (*schlecht*) *~~* to taste good (nasty); *sauer ~~* to taste acid; *ich bin erkältet u. kann nichts ~~* I have a cold and cannot taste anything; *wie ~t es?* how do you like it? are you enjoying it? *es ~t mir nicht* I don't like it; *nach etw ~~* to taste of; to have a spice of; *nach nichts ~~* to have no taste whatever, to taste of nothing; *nach mehr ~~* to taste like more; *die Medizin ~t nach Schwefel* the medicine smacks of sulphur; *die Suppe ~t zu sehr nach Zwiebeln* the soup tastes too much of onions; *es sich gut ~~ lassen* to relish, to eat with relish, to enjoy; *laß ihn mal die Peitsche ~~* give him a taste of the whip; *ich kann ihn nicht ~~* (*fam*) I don't like him.

Schmeich|elei *f* flattery; (*Kompliment*) compliment; (*niedrige, kriecherische ~~*) adulation, fawning, wheedling; (*Schönrederei*) coaxing; (*Liebkosung*) cajolery; (*falsche ~~*) *fam* blarney, *sl* soft soap, softsawder, *Am sl* apple sauce, taffy; *jdm durch ~~ etw abgewinnen* to coax s. th. out of s. o., to wheedle s. th. out of s. o.; **~elhaft** *a* flattering; (*kriecherisch*) adulatory; **~elkatze** *f*, **~elkätzchen** *n fig* wheedler; cajoler; **~eln** *itr* to flatter (*jdm* s. o.); (*Komplimente machen*) to compliment; (*überreden zu*) to wheedle (into doing), to gush over; to coax; (*kriecherisch*) to fawn upon, to truckle, to adulate; (*einseifen*) *sl* to soft-soap, to softsawder; (*liebkosen*) to caress, to fondle; to cajole; *sich mit Hoffnungen ~~* to flatter o. s. with hopes; *sich geschmeichelt fühlen* to feel flattered; *diese Aufnahme schmeichelt dir nicht* this photo does not flatter you; **~elname** *m* pet name; **~elnd, ~lerisch** *a* flattering; complimentary; (*kriecherisch*) adulatory; **~elrede** *f* flattering speech; **~elwort** *n* flattering word; **~ler** *m*, **~lerin** *f* flatterer; (*Kriecher*) adulator, adulatress; cringer; wheedler; coax(er); sycophant; (*Speichellecker*) lick-spittle, hanger-on, flunkey; tufthunter; toady, toadeater; truckler; bootlicker; **~lerisch** *a* flattering; complimentary; (*glatt*) smooth; (*kriecherisch*) fawning; wheedling; adulatory; (*salbungsvoll*) unctuous, oily; *fam* buttery; (*einschmeichelnd*) caressing, coaxing.

schmeiß|en *irr tr fam* to throw, to fling; to hurl; to cast; (*Türe*) to slam; *fam* (*herauswerfen*) to chuck (out); *itr* (*schlagen, stoßen*) to smite, to strike, to kick; *e-e Sache ~~* (*fam*) to manage s. th. successfully, *Am* to run the show; *er wird es ~~* he will pull through; *mit Geld um sich ~~* to throw away o.'s money; *e-e Flasche Wein ~~* (*fam*) (*ausgeben*) to stand a bottle of wine; **~fliege** *f* bluebottle, meatfly, blowfly.

Schmelz *m* (*Email, Zahn~*) enamel; (*Glanz, Glasur*) glaze; (*Metall*) blue powder; *fig* (*~ der Jugend*) bloom; (*der Stimme*) mellowness; melodious ring; (*von Tönen*) sweetness; **~anlage** *f* melting plant, foundry; **~arbeit** *f* enamel, enamel(l)ing (process); (*Erz etc*) smelting process; **~~er** *m* enamel(l)er; (*Erz*) (s)melter, founder; **~artig** *a* enamellike; **~bad** *n* melting (*od* molten) bath; (*beim Schweißen*) pool; **~bar** *a* meltable; fusible; *schwer ~~* refractory; **~~keit** *f* fusibility; **~butter** *f* melted butter; **~draht** *m el* fuse (*od* fusible) wire; **~e, ~ung** *f* (*Schnee~~*) melting; melt; (*Verflüssigung*) liquefaction; **~e** *f* (*Schmelzerei*) smelting works *pl*, foundry; (*Masse*) fused mass; **~en** *irr tr* to melt; (*Erz*) to smelt, to fuse; *itr* (*auflösen*) to dissolve; (*flüssig werden*) to liquefy, to become liquid; *fig* (*weich werden*) to soften; (*schwinden*) to diminish, to melt away; *geschmolzene Butter* melted butter; **~end** *a* melting; *fig* (*Stimme*) mellow; (*Töne*) sweet, melodious; (*schmachtend*) languishing; (*rührend*) moving; **~er** *m* melter, smelter, founder; **~erei** *f* foundry, smeltery; **~erz** *n* smelting ore; **~farbe** *f* enamel colo(u)r, vitrifiable colo(u)r; **~fluß** *m* fused mass, melt; **~flüssig** *a* molten; fusible; **~glasur** *f* enamel; **~grad** *m* fusing (*od* melting) point; **~gut** *n* melting charge (*od* stock); **~herd** *m* furnace hearth; **~hitze** *f* melting heat; **~hütte** *f* foundry, smelting works *pl*; **~kessel** *m* melting pot; **~ofen** *m* smelting-furnace; melting-oven; (blast-) furnace; **~prozeß** *m* melting (*od* smelting) process; **~pulver** *n* flux; **~punkt** *m* melting (*od* fusing) point, fusion point; **~sicherung** *f el* fuse, fuse cut-out; safety fuse; **~stahl** *m* natural (*od* German) steel; **~tiegel** *m* crucible, melting pot; **~ung** *f* fusion, melt(ing), smelting; heat; **~verfahren** *n* melting process; **~wärme** *f* heat of fusion; **~wasser** *n* melted snow and ice; **~werk** *n* foundry, smeltery; **~zone** *f* (s)melting zone; fusion zone.

Schmer *m* fat, grease; (*Talg*) suet; **~bauch** *m* paunch; big belly, pot-belly, *fam* corporation, *Am fam* false front, bay window, front porch, hangover, jelly belly; **~fluß** *m med* seborrh(o)ea oleosa.

Schmerle *f* (*Fisch*) loach, groundling.

Schmerz *m allg* pain; (*andauernder ~, Weh*) ache; (*brennender ~*) smart; (*plötzlicher ~*) pang; (*krampfartiger, ziehender ~*) throe; (*reißender, stechender ~*) twinge; (*stechender ~*) stitch; lancination; (*Krankheit*) ailment; (*seelischer ~, Kummer*) sorrow, grief; affliction; heart-ache; (*höchster ~, Pein, Seelenqual*) agony; anguish; (*Trübsal*) distress; (*Leiden, Dulden*) suffering; (*Qual, Marter*) torment, torture; *poet* (*Jammer, Leid*) woe; (*Anfall von ~en*) paroxysm; *mit ~en erwarten* to wait impatiently; *~en haben* to be ailing; to be in great pain; *haben Sie ~en?* do you feel any pain? does it hurt? *~en verursachen* to pain, to afflict; *vor ~ zusammenzucken* to wince; *mit ~en vernehmen* to regret to hear; *geteilter ~ ist halber ~* company in distress makes trouble less; **~anfall** *m* attack of pain; pang; **~äußerung** *f* manifestation of pain; **~bekämpfung** *f* fighting (*od* alleviation) of pain; **~betäubend** *a* pain-deadening; analgesic, narcotic; **~betäubung** *f* analgesia; **~empfindlich** *a* sensitive to pain; **~~keit** *f* sensitiveness to pain; **~empfindung** *f* sensation of pain; **~en** *tr* to pain; (*Wunde etc*) to cause pain, to give pain; (*weh tun*) to hurt; (*betrüben, seelisch ~~*) to grieve; to wound; to afflict; *es schmerzt mich* it pains me, it grieves me; I am sorry to hear; I feel sorry; *es schmerzt mich sehr fig* I feel it very deeply; *mein Ohr schmerzt* (*mich*) my ear aches; *itr* (*körperlich*) to ache, to smart; to be painful; **~ensgeld** *n* smart-money; (*Entschädigung*) compensation; *jur* (*Reugeld*) forfeit; **~enskind** *n* child of sorrow; **~enslager** *n* bed of suffering (*od* pain); sick-bed; **~ensmutter** *f eccl* Our Lady of Dolours; **~ensreich** *a* deeply afflicted; woeful; woebegone; **~ensschrei** *m* cry of pain; **~erfüllt** *a* deeply afflicted; **~erregend** *a* causing pain; **~frei** *a* free of (*od* from) pain, painless; **~gefühl** *n* feeling of pain, painful sensation; **~grenze** *f* threshold of feeling (*od* pain); **~haft** *a* painful; smarting, aching; sore; (*betrüblich*) grievous; afflicting; distressing; **~~igkeit** *f* grievousness, painfulness; **~lich** *a* (*seelisch*) painful, grievous; (*traurig*) sad, grievous; *es ist ~~ zu sehen* it is distressing to see; *~~ entbehren* to miss sadly; *ein ~er Verlust* a severe loss; **~lindernd** *a* alleviating (*od* deadening *od* relieving) pain; pain-stilling; *med* anodyne, analgesic, antalgic; (*besänftigend*) soothing; lenitive; **~linderung** *f* alleviation, relief; **~los** *a* painless; *med* indolent; **~~igkeit** *f* painlessness; *med* analgesia; **~schwelle** *f* threshold of feeling; **~sinn** *m* pain sense; **~stillend** *a* alleviating (*od* deadening *od* assuaging) pain; pain-stilling; *med* anodyne, analgesic, antalgic; *~~es Mittel* anodyne, analgetic; *fam* pain-killer; **~unempfindlich** *a* analgesic; **~voll** *a* painful; grievous; bitter.

Schmetter|ball *m* (*Tennis*) smash ball, cannon ball; **~ling** *m* butterfly; *~~e pl* lepidoptera; **~~sblütler** *m* papilionaceous plant; **~~snetz** *n* butterfly-net; **~~ssammlung** *f* butterfly-collection; **~~sstil** *m* (*Schwimmen*) butterfly-style; **~n** *itr* (*Trompeten*) to blare, to clang, to bray; (*von Vögeln*) to warble; (*Donner*) to thunder; to peal; (*schallen*) to ring, to resound; *tr* (*zu Boden ~~*) to throw down, to floor, to knockdown; to dash; to crash; (*in Stücke*) to smash, to dash (to pieces); (*Tennis*) to smash; *e-n ~~* (*fam*) to wet o.'s beak; **~schlag** *m* (*Tennis*) (overhead) smash.

Schmied *m* smith; (*Grob~*) blacksmith; (*Huf~*) farrier; **~bar** *a* malleable, forgeable; of smithing quality; capable of being wrought; *~~es Eisen* malleable iron, wrought iron; **~~keit** *f* forgeability, malleability, forging quality; **~e** *f* smithy, forge; smith's-shop, *Am* smith-shop; **~eamboß** *m* smith's anvil; **~earbeit** *f* forging; metal work; **~eeisen** *n* wrought iron; malleable iron; forging steel, low-carbon steel; **~eeisern** *a* wrought-iron, wrought; **~eesse** *f* forge; **~efeuer** *n* forge fire; **~ehammer** *m* forging hammer, sledge hammer; **~ekohle** *f* forge (*od* smithy) coal; **~en** *tr* to forge; to smith; to fuse; (*hammern*) to hammer; *im Gesenk ~~* to drop forge, to drop stamp; *fig* (*ersinnen*) to frame, to devise, to construct; to plan; (*Pläne*) to hatch, to lay, to concoct, to scheme (plans); (*anzetteln*) to breed, to concoct; to forge; to fabricate; *Verse ~~* to versify; *Waffen ~~ gegen* to furnish arms against; *das Eisen ~~* to strike the iron; *in Ketten ~~* to enchain; *Ränke ~~* to plot; **~epresse** *f* forging press, drop hammer; **~erohling** *m* rough stamping; **~estahl** *m* wrought (*od* forged) steel; **~estück** *n* forging; **~ewaren** *f pl* forgings *pl*, hardware; **~ewerkstatt** *f* forge, smithy; **~ewerkzeug** *n* forging tool; **~ezange** *f* blacksmith's tongs *pl*.

Schmieg|e *f* bevel, carpenter's folding-scale; **~en** *itr* to bend, to bevel; *sich* (*an*)*~~* to press close (to), to creep close (to); (*eng*) to nestle (against), to snuggle, to cuddle; to cling (to); (*umklammern*) to twine (round); **~sam** *a* pliant, flexible, supple; *fig* submissive; **~samkeit** *f* pliancy, pliability; flexibility.

Schmier|behälter *m* grease-box; **~buch** *n* waste-book; **~büchse** *f* grease-box; (*Ölkanne*) oil-can, oil-cup; **~e** *f* smear; (*Salbe*) ointment, salve; (*Schmiermittel*) grease, lubricant; (*Fett*) fat; (*Talg*) tallow; suet; (*Wagen~~*) axle grease; (*Schmutz*) slush; *theat* (*Bumslokal*) *fam* gaff, low music-hall; (*schlechte Wanderbühne*) troop of strolling players; (*Aufstrich*) spread; (*Butter*) butter; *~~ stehen sl* to be look-out man; **~en** *tr* to smear; (*mit Öl*) to oil, to lubricate; (*mit Fett*) to grease; (*mit Salbe einreiben*) to anoint, to smear; *typ* (*verschwommen drucken*) to slur; *jdm e-e ~~ fam* (*Ohrfeige geben*) to box s. o.'s ears; *jdn ~~ fam* (*bestechen*) to bribe s. o., to grease s. o.'s hand (*od* palm); *itr* (*sudeln, schlecht schreiben*) to scrawl, to scribble; (*schlecht malen*) to daub; *wie geschmiert fam* in a jiffy, like greased lightning; **~enkomödiant**, **~enschauspieler** *m* strolling player, barnstormer, *Am sl* ham actor; **~er** *m* greaser; (*Sudler*) scrawler, scribbler; (*schlechter Maler*) dauber; **~erei** *f* smearing, greasing; (*Sudelei*) scrawl; (*schlechte Malerei*) daub; **~esteher** *m sl* look-out man; **~fink** *m* dirty fellow; **~geld(er)** *n* (*pl*) palm-oil, palm grease; bribe; *Am sl* fixing money, (golden) grease; hush(money); (*bes. politisch*) slush(-fund), pork barrel; **~ig** *a* smeary; greasy; (*ölig*) oily; (*schmutzig*) dirty, smudgy, filthy; *fig* mean; sordid; (*Geschäfte*) fishy; **~~keit** *f* (*Papier*) wetness; *fig* sliminess, unctuousness; **~käse** *m* soft cheese, cream cheese, *Am* cottage cheese; **~lappen** *m* rag (for smearing); *fig* dirty fellow; **~maxe** *m* *Am aero sl* grease monkey; **~mittel** *n* lubricant, grease; *med* liniment; (*Öl*) lubricating oil; (*Fett*) lubricating grease; **~nippel** *m* grease nipple; **~öl** *n* lubricating oil, *Am* lube (oil); **~pistole**, **~presse** *f* grease gun; **~plan** *m*, **~schema** *n* lubrication chart (*od* diagram); **~salbe** *f* soft salve, ointment; **~seife** *f* green (*od* brown) soap, soft soap; **~stelle** *f* oiling point, oil-hole; lubricating point; **~stoff** *m* lubricant; (*Salbe*) ointment; **~~behälter** *m* oil tank; **grease sump**; **~ung** *f* lubrication, oiling; **~vorrichtung** *f* lubricating device; lubricator; **~wirkung** *f* lubricating action.

Schmink|dose *f* rouge-pot; **~e** *f* (grease-) paint, face-paint, *Am fam* grease, smear; (*allg*) make-up; (*rote ~~*) rouge; (*weiße ~~*) flake white, pearl white; (*für Zirkusclown*) clown white, *Am sl* muck; *fig* varnish, gloss; *~~ auflegen* to paint the face, to lay on paint (*od* rouge), to rouge; to make up; *die ~~ abwaschen* (*sich abschminken*) to wash off the paint; *theat* to take off o.'s make-up; **~en** *tr* (*sich*) to paint the face; to lay on paint; to rouge; to make up, *Am fam* to fresh up, to mug up, to touch up, to put on the war paint; *die Lippen ~~* to put on the lipstick; *zu stark geschminkt* overrouged; **~mittel** *n* cosmetic, grease-paint; **~pflästerchen** *n* beauty-patch; **~rot** *n* rouge; **~stift** *m* (*Lippenstift*) lipstick; **~topf** *m* rouge-pot, grease-pot; **~unterlage** *f* base; **~wasser** *n* skin tonic.

Schmirgel *m* emery; abrasive powder; **~leinen** *n*, **~leinwand** *f* emery cloth; **~n** *tr* to polish with emery; to rub (*od* to grind) with emery; to emery; **~papier** *n* emery paper; **~scheibe** *f* emery wheel; **~tuch** *n* emery cloth.

Schmiß *m* (*Hieb*) dash, stroke, blow; (*Eleganz*) smartness; (*Narbe*) cut; lash; (*Studenten~*) duel(l)ing-scar; (*Schneid*) go, dash, verve, *Am sl* pep, vim; punch; **schmissig** *a fam* dashing, pushing; smart; full of go, *Am* full of pep (*od* vim).

Schmitz *m* lash, cut (with a whip); **~e** *f* cracker, whip-lash.

Schmock *m* (*Schreiberling*) cheap (*od* hack) journalist, *Am fam* ink-slinger; quill-driver; knight of the pen; phrase-monger.

Schmöker *m* (*altes Buch*) old book; (*Groschenroman*) light novel, yellow-back; thrashy book; **~n** *itr* (*in Buchladen, Bibliothek*) to browse; (*lesen*) to pore over a book.

schmoll|en *itr* to pout, to be in the pouts, to be sulky, to sulk; **~en** *n* pouting, sulking; **~winkel** *m* sulking-corner.

Schmor|braten *m* stewed steak; **~en** *tr* to stew; *itr* to be suffocated with heat; **~pfanne** *f* stew(ing)-pan; **~stelle** *f el* spot of arcing; **~topf** *m* stew-pot.

Schmu *m fam* unfair gain; *~ machen* to swindle; to cheat.

Schmuck *m* (*Zier*) ornament; (*Dekoration*) decoration; (*Geschmeide*) trinket(s *pl*); (*Putz*) attire; finery; (*Ausschmückung*) trimmings *pl*; (*Juwelen*) jewels *pl*, jewel(le)ry; *~ a* (*hübsch*) handsome, pretty; (*Mädchen*) nice, *Am* cute; (*elegant*) smart; (*nett*) dapper; (*sauber*) neat, natty; tidy; (*gut angezogen*) trim; (*geschniegelt*) spruce; **~arbeit** *f* jewel(le)ry; fancy work; **~blatt(telegramm)** *n* greetings-telegram; **~feder** *f* fancy feather, plume; **~gegenstände** *m pl* jewels *pl*, trinkets *pl*; **~kästchen** *n* jewel-case, jewel-box; (*sauberes Haus*) a jewel (*od* gem) of a house; **~laden** *m* jewel(l)er's shop; **~los** *a* unadorned; (*einfach*) plain, simple; (*nackt, bar*) nude; **~~igkeit** *f* plainness; (*Strenge*) severity; **~nadel** *f* breast-pin; **~sachen** *f pl* jewels *pl*, trinkets *pl*; **~stück** *n* piece of jewel(le)ry; **~waren** *f pl* jewel(le)ry.

schmücken *tr* to adorn, to decorate; to deck (out); to trim; (*verzieren*) to ornament; (*aus~*) to embellish; (*kleiden*) to attire.

Schmuddel *m* sloven (*od* slipshod) person; **~ei** *f* slovenly work, slush; **~ig** *a* (*unsauber*) untidy, dirty; filthy; (*aufgeweicht*) slushy, sloppy; **~wetter** *n* dirty weather.

Schmugg|el *m*, **~elei** *f* smuggling; **~eln** *tr*, *itr* to smuggle, *Am* (*Alkohol*) to bootleg; **~elware** *f* smuggled goods *pl*, contraband; **~ler** *m* smuggler, *Am* (*Alkohol*) bootlegger; **~lerschiff** *n* smuggling-boat.

schmunzeln *itr* to smile, to smirk; to grin; *~ n* broad smile; smirk.

Schmus *m sl* (*Gerede*) prattle, cheap talk; (*Schmeichelei*) soft soap; (*Gewinn*) bargain, broker's commission; **~en** *itr* (*viel reden*) to prattle; (*schön tun*) to fawn, to soft-soap; (*verraten*) to betray; (*schäkern, liebkosen*) *fam* to spoon, *Am fam* to neck; **~er** *m* coaxer; (*Liebster*) lover, sweetheart; (*Vermittler*) go-between; match-maker; **~erei** *f* (*Schäkerei*) *Am fam* petting party, necking party.

Schmutz *m* dirt; (*Dreck*) filth; (*Straßen~*) mud, slush; (*Fleck*) smudge; (*Ruß*) grime; (*Mist, Dreck*) muck; *fig* (*Zote*) smut, filthiness; **~ärmel** *m* protecting sleeves; **~blatt** *n* fly-leaf; **~blech** *n* mudguard; **~bogen** *m typ* spoilt-sheet; **~bürste** *f* scrubbing-brush; **~en** *itr* to soil, to smudge; *tr* (*be~~*) to dirty; to smudge, to smutch, to begrime; **~erei** *f* *fig* (*Zote*) obscenity; **~fänger** *m* mudguard; **~fink** *m fam* dirty fellow; **~fleck** *m* stain, spot; smear, smutch, smudge; blotch; **~ig** *a* (*dreckig*) muddy, dirty; soiled; (*sehr ~~*) filthy; (*unsauber*) unclean; (*schmierig*) greasy; (*aufgeweicht*) sloppy, slushy; *fig* (*geizig*) sordid; (*schäbig*) shabby; (*gemein*) mean, low; (*zotig*) obscene, smutty; *~~ machen*, *~~ werden* to soil, to dirty; **~igkeit** *f* dirtiness; **~konkurrenz** *f com* unfair competition; **~lappen** *m* dirty rag; clout; *fig* dirty fellow; **~liese** *f* slut, sloven; **~literatur** *f* pornography; **~presse** *f* gutter press; **~titel** *m typ* half-title, fly-title; bastard title; **~wasser** *n* dirty water; (*Abwasser*) sewage.

Schnabel *m* (*Vogel*) neb, nib; (*kleiner ~*) bill; (*e-s Raubvogels*) beak; *fam* (*Mund*) mouth; (*Schiffs~*) prow; nose; (*e-r Kanne*) spout; (*Ausguß*) nozzle; *er spricht wie ihm der ~ gewachsen ist* he does not mince his words; he speaks plain English; *halt den ~!* hold your tongue! *Am* shut up! **~förmig** *a* beak-shaped, beaklike; **~hieb** *m* dab (with the beak); **~schuhe** *m pl* pointed shoes *pl*; **~tasse** *f* feeding cup; **~tier** *n* duck-bill, platypus.

schnäbeln *r* (*Vögel*) to bill; (*Liebende*) to bill and coo.

Schnack *m* talk, chit-chat; gossip, chatter; **~en** *tr*, *itr* to talk, to chat(ter); to gossip; to babble, to prattle.

Schnake *f* midge, gnat, cranefly; mosquito; *fam* (*Schnurre, Witz*) merry tale; jest, joke; **~nstich** *m* midge-bite.

Schnalle *f* (*Schuh*) buckle; (*Gürtel*) clasp; (*Tür~*) latch; (*Schnäpper, Klinke*) catch; *fam* (*Hure*) prostitute, harlot, whore; strumpet; **~n** *tr* to buckle; to fasten; to strap (up); *länger ~~* to lengthen; *kürzer ~~* to shorten; *seinen Gürtel enger ~~* to tighten o.'s belt; *sich e-n Gürtel um den Bauch ~~* to strap a belt round o.'s waist; **~ndorn** *m* tongue (*od* pin) of a buckle; **~nschuh** *m* shoe with buckles.

schnalz|en *itr* (*mit der Zunge*) to click (*od* to smack) o.'s tongue; (*mit den Fingern*) to snap o.'s fingers; (*mit e-r Peitsche*) to crack a whip; **~laut** *m* (*Phonetik*) clicking sound.

schnapp! *interj* snap! bang! **~en** *tr* (*ergreifen, erwischen*) to grab s. th.; *jdn ~~* to get hold of s. o., to arrest s. o.; *itr nach etw ~~* to snap at, to snatch at; *der Hund ~te nach mir* the dog snapped at me; *nach dem Köder ~~* to snap at bait; *nach Luft ~~* to pant for breath, to gasp for air; *in die Höhe ~~* to tip up; (*Schloß zu~~*) to catch; *ins Schloß ~~* to snap shut; (*Feder, Taschenmesser*) to snap to; **~er** *m* catcher, latch; safety bolt; **~feder** *f* catch spring; **~hahn** *m* highwayman; **~messer** *n* clasp-knife, jack-knife; **~ring** *m* snap-ring; **~sack** *m* knapsack; **~schalter** *m* snap-switch; **~schloß** *n* spring-lock; **~schuß** *m phot* snapshot; candid photograph; **~~einstellung** *f* zone focus(s)ing; **~stativ** *n* self-locking tripod.

Schnäpper *m med* (blood) lancet; (*Fallklinke*) catch, snap; (*Tür~*) latch; (*Billardspiel*) side-hit; **~schloß** *n* spring-bolt lock.

Schnaps *m* (*Branntwein*) spirits *pl*, strong liquor (*od* drink), *Am* hard liquor; (*Wacholder~*) gin, schnapps; (*Korn~*) whisky; (*Weinbrand*) brandy; (*Likör*) liqueur; *ein Gläschen* (*od e-n Schluck*) *~* dram (of strong liquor); *~ trinken* to tipple; **~brenner** *m* distiller; **~brennerei** *f* distillery; **~bruder** *m* dram-drinker; tippler; **~bude, ~kneipe** *f* dram-shop, gin-shop; *Am* gin-mill; **~en** *itr fam* to tipple; **~flasche** *f* brandy-flask, bottle of brandy; bottle of whisk(e)y; **~glas** *n* gin-glass; **~idee** *f fam* silly idea; **~laden** *m* gin-shop; **~nase** *f* gin-and-water nose; copper-nose; **~trinker** *m* tippler; gin-drinker; **~schenke** *f* dram-shop, gin-shop; (*feine*) gin-palace.

schnarch|en *itr* to snore; (*schnauben bes. von Tieren*) to snort; **~en** *n* snoring, snorting; **~er** *m* snorer; snorter; **~ventil** *n tech* snifting valve, breather.

Schnarr|e *f* (*Knarre*) rattle; (*Summer*) buzzer; *orn* (*Drossel*) missel-thrush; (*Wachtelkönig*) corncrake; **~en** *itr* (*knarren*) to rattle; (*Musikinstrumente etc*) to vibrate; to grate; to jar; (*Säge, Summer*) to buzz; (*Insekten*) to stridulate; (*summen*) to hum; (*schnurren*) to whir; (*kratzen, raspeln*) to rasp; (*beim Sprechen näseln*) to (speak with a) twang; to speak in the throat; (*das r rollen*) to roll o.'s r's; to burr; (*brummen*) to growl, to snarl; *mit ~ender Stimme sprechen* to speak with a strong twang; **~summer** *m el* buzzer; **~ton** *m* rattling sound, jarring sound; **~wecker** *m* buzzer alarm; **~werk** *n* (*Orgel*) reed-stops *pl*.

Schnatter|ei *f* cackling; (*Geschwätz*) chattering, gabbling; **~er** *m* chatterer; chatterbox; **~haft** *a* chattering; chatty; **~gans, ~liese** *f fam* chatterbox, chatterbag; **~n** *itr* (*Gänse, Enten*) to cackle; (*durcheinanderschwatzen*) to chatter, to gabble; to prattle; *vor Kälte ~~* to shiver with cold; *er ~te mit den Zähnen* his teeth chattered.

schnauben *itr, tr* (*bes. von Pferd*) to snort; (*von Menschen*) to puff, to blow; (*keuchen*) to pant; *sich ~, sich die Nase ~* to blow o.'s nose; (*nach*) *Rache ~* to breath vengeance, to pant for revenge; *vor Wut ~* to fret and fume; to foam with rage.

schnauf|en *itr* to wheeze, to breathe hard (*od* heavily), to blow; (*keuchen*) to pant; **~er** *m fam* (*Atemzug*) breath.

Schnauz|bart *m* moustache; **~bärtig** *a* with a moustache; **~e** *f* (*Tier~~*) snout, muzzle; *tech* (*Tülle, Düse*) nozzle; (*Ausguß, Mund*) mouth; (*Kanne*) spout, beak; (*Topf*) lip; (*Dachrinne*) spout; gargoyle; (*Spitze, bes. Flugzeugspitze*) nose; *fig vulg* (*Mund*) jaw; mug; *halt die ~~! vulg* shut up! hold your jaw! *e-e große ~~ haben vulg* to have the gift of the gab; *nach ~~ fliegen aero sl* to fly by guesswork; **~en** *itr fam* to shout (at), to jaw; **~er** *m* (*Hund*) schnauzer, wire-haired terrier; **~ig** *a fig* rude.

Schnecke *f* (*Garten~*) snail, (*nackte ~*) slug; *anat* (*Ohr*) cochlea; (*Mädchenfrisur*) earphones *pl*; *arch* (*Säulen~*) volute; scroll; helix; (*in Uhr*) fusee; *tech* (*endlose Schraube*)(endless) screw; (*Transport~*) screw conveyer; *math* helix; (*Getriebe*) worm(-gear); (*Spirale, Schneckenlinie*) spiral; spire; *langsam wie e-e ~* slow as a snail; **~nantrieb** *m* worm drive; **~nartig** *a* snail-like; *tech* helical, helicoid; **~nförderer** *m* worm (*od* screw) conveyer; **~nförmig** *a* spiral; helical; helicoid; winding; **~nfraß** *m* damage done by snails; **~ngang** *m fig* (*langsamer Gang*) snail's pace; *tech* spiral walk; winding alley; (*Bohrer*) auger; *anat* (*Ohr*) canal of cochlea; **~ngehäuse** *n tech* worm-gear housing, worm casing; **~nhaus** *n* snail-shell; *anat* (*Ohr*) bony cochlea; **~ngetriebe** *n* worm-gear(ing); **~ngewinde** *n* helix, worm thread; **~nlinie** *f* spiral line; helix; **~nmuschel** *f* conch; **~npost** *f* snail's post, slowcoach; *mit der ~~* at a snail's pace; **~nrad** *n tech* worm gear, worm wheel, spiral wheel; **~nschale** *f* snail shell; **~nspirale** *f* elongated spiral; **~nstein** *m* conchite; **~ntempo** *n fig* snail's pace; *im ~~* (*fig*) at a snail's pace; **~ntrieb** *m tech* worm (-gear) drive; **~ntreppe** *f* winding stairs *pl*; *anat* (*Ohr*) scala of cochlea; **~nwindung** *f* spiral; *arch* volution.

Schnee *m* snow; *~ u. Regen gemischt* sleet; (*Eier~*) whip of milk and eggs; *nasser ~* wet snow; *trockener ~* dry snow; *Pulver~* powdery snow; *der ewige ~* the eternal snows *pl*; *mit ~ bedeckt* covered with snow; *in ~ begraben* snowed up (*od* under); *vom ~ eingeschlossen* snow-bound; **~ammer** *f orn* snow-bunting; **~artig** *a* snow-like; **~auto** *n* (*Arktik*) *Am* snowmobile; **~ball** *m* snowball; *bot* guelder rose, viburnum; **~~en** *itr* to form a snowball; to throw a snowball; (*sich*) to snowball (one another); **~~system** *n com* (*Hydrasystem*) snowball system; **~~schlacht** *f* snowball fight; **~bedeckt** *a* snow-covered, snow-blanketed; snowy; (*Gebirge*) snow-topped, snow-capped, snow-clad, snow-crested; **~beere** *f bot* snowberry; **~belastung** *f* snow load; **~berg** *m* snow hill; **~besen** *m* (egg-) whisk, egg-beater; **~blind** *a* snow-blind; **~blindheit** *f* snow-blindness; **~blink** *m* snow-blink; **~brille** *f* (a pair of) snow-goggles *pl*; **~brett** *n* snow slab; **~bruch** *m* snow break; **~decke** *f* blanket of snow; fall of snow; **~dichte** *f* density of snow; **~druck** *m* crushing by snow; **~eule** *f orn* snowy owl; **~fall** *m* snowfall; snows *pl*; **~fanggitter** *n* snow fence; **~feld** *n* snowfield; **~fink** *m orn* snowbird, snowfinch; **~fläche** *f* snowfield; **~flocke** *f* snowflake; **~frei** *a* free of snow; **~galerie** *f rail* snowshed; **~gans** *f orn* snow-goose; **~gebirge** *n* snow mountains *pl*; **~gestöber** *n* snow-drift, snow-squall; driving snow, *Am* snow flurry; (*starkes*) snow-storm; **~gitter** *n* snow guard; **~glöckchen** *n bot* snowdrop; **~grat** *m* snow ridge; **~grenze** *f* (perpetual) snow line, snow limit; **~hase** *m* Alpine hare; **~häschen** *n fig fam* pretty girl skier; **~haufen** *m* heap of snow; **~hemd** *n* parka; (*Anorak*) anarak; **~huhn** *n* white-grouse, snow-grouse; ptarmigan; **~hütte** *f* (*Eskimohütte*) igloo; **~ig** *a* snowy, snow-white; (*schneebedeckt*) snow-covered; **~kette** *f mot* non-skid chain, snow (*od* tyre) chain; **~könig** *m* snow-man; *sich freuen wie ein ~~* to be happy as a king; **~kristall** *m* snow crystal; **~kufen** *f pl aero* skis *pl*, landing skids *pl*; snow runners *pl*; **~~fahrwerk** *n aero* ski undercarriage, ski landing gear; **~kuppe** *f* snowy peak; **~landung** *f* snow landing; **~last** *f* snow load; **~lawine** *f* avalanche; **~los** *a* snowless; **~luft** *f* snowy air; **~mann** *m* snow-man; **~mantel** *m* (*der Landschaft*) white coat of snow; *mil* (*Tarnmantel*) white coat; **~massen** *f pl* snows *pl*, snowbank; **~matsch** *m* (snow) sludge, snow-broth; **~messer** *m* (*Metereologie*) snow ga(u)ge; **~pfad** *m* snow track; **~pflug** *m* snow-plough, *Am* snowplow; **~~bogen** *m* (*Skifahren*) double stem; **~pudding** *f* snow pudding; **~regen** *m* sleet; **~region** *f* snow zone (*od* region); **~roller** *m* snow roller; **~schauer** *m* snow shower, *Am* snow flurry; **~schaufel** *f* snow shovel; **~schaum** *m* whip of milk and eggs; **~schippe** *f* snow shovel; **~schipper** *m* snow-sweeper (*od*-shoveller); **~schläger** *m* whisk, wire whip, egg-beater; **~schleuder** *f* rotary snow-plough (*Am* snowplow); **~schmelze** *f* snow break; **~schuh** *m* (*Überschuh*) snow boot; (*Schneeteller*) snowshoe; (*Ski*) ski; *~~ laufen* (*mit Schneetellern*) to travel on snowshoes, to snowshoe; (*mit Skiern*) to go skiing, to ski; **~~lauf** *m* (*Ski*) skiing; **~~läufer** *m* (*Ski*) skier; (*mit Schneetellern*) snowshoer; **~~torlauf** *m* slalom; **~stern** *m* snow crystal; **~stiefel** *m* snow boot; **~sturm** *m* snow-storm, *Am* blizzard; **~sturz** *m* snow-slide, snowslip; **~tarnhemd** *n* camouflage ski-smock; **~teller** *m* (*Skistock*) disk; **~treiben** *n* snow-drift, heavy snowfall; *Am* (*Sturm*) blizzard; **~verhältnisse** *n pl* snow conditions *pl*; *wie sind die ~~?* how is the snow? **~verweht** *a* snow-bound; hemmed in by snow; **~verwehung** *f* snowdrift, accumulation of snow; **~wächte** *f* snow cornice, snowdrift; **~wasser** *n* snow water, slush; **~wehe** *f* snow cornice, snowdrift; snow-wreath; **~weiß** *a* snow-white; snowy; white as snow; *mit ~~en Haaren* snow-haired; **~wetter** *n* snowy weather; snow-storm; **~wind** *m* snow wind; **~wittchen** *n* Little Snow White; **~wolke** *f* snow cloud; **~zeit** *f* snowy season.

Schneid *m, f* (*Schärfe*) sharpness; (*Energie*) energy; (*Mut*) pluck; *fam* go, *fam* guts *pl*; (*Eleganz*) smartness, dash; *keinen ~ haben* to have no guts; **~apparat** *m* cutter; **~backe** *f tech* (cutting) die, bolt die; **~bohrer** *m* tap; **~brenner** *m tech* cutting torch, flame cutter; blowpipe; **~dose** *f* gramophone recorder; **~maschine** *f* cutter, slicer; **~ig** *a* (*scharf*) sharp-edged; cutting; *fig* (*energisch*) energetic; keen; (*entschlossen*) resolute, determined; (*mutig*) plucky, spirited; (*elegant*) smart, stylish; dashing, *Am* nifty; **~igkeit** *f fig* (*Energie*) energy; (*Mut*) pluck; *fam* go, *fam* guts *pl*; (*Entschlossenheit*) resolution, determination; (*Eleganz*) dash; smartness, stylishness.

Schneide *f* (*Schärfe, Kante*) edge; (*e-s Werkzeuges*) cutting edge; cutter; (*Hobel*) blade; (*Beil*) bevel; (*Hackmaschine*) tooth; (*Bohrer*) bit; (*Waagebalken*) knife edge; *fig* hit; *auf des Messers ~ stehen fig* to be on the razor's edge; *mit e-r scharfen ~* keen-edged; **~apparat** *m* cutter; **~bank** *f* chopping-bench; **~bohnen** *f pl* French beans *pl*, string-beans *pl*; **~brett** *n* cutting- (*od* carving-)board, trencher; **~eisen** *n* chopping-knife; *tech* die; plate; **~holz** *n* timber for sawing; **~kante** *f* (cutting) edge; **~maschine** *f* cutting-machine; cutter; (*für Häcksel*) chaff-cutter; **~messer** *n* cutting knife; **~mühle** *f* saw mill; **~stahl** *m* cutting tool, cutter; **~waren** *f pl* cutlery; **~werkzeug** *n* cutting tool; **~zahn** *m* incisor; (*Raubtiere*) scissor tooth.

schneiden *irr tr* to cut; *in Stücke ~* to cut to pieces; (*Bäume, Äste*) to prune, to lop (off), to trim; to pare; (*Gras*) to mow; (*Holz*) to cut up, to chop; (*sägen*) to saw; (*Brot, das Haar*) to cut; *sich die Haare ~ lassen* to have o.'s hair cut; (*Fleisch, Braten*) to carve; (*Finger, Nägel*) to pare, to clip, to cut; (*Getreide*) to reap, to cut; (*in Holz ~*) to carve in; (*Ball bei Tennis etc*) to cut, to twist; *klein ~* to cut up, to mince; to hash; (*übervorteilen, betrügen*) to cheat, to fleece; to overcharge; (*Stoff etc zu~*) to cut; (*Wellen pflügen*) to cleave (the waves); (*Rückzug ab~*) to cut off (retreat); (*zer~*) to slash; (*auf~*) to slash open; (*kastrieren*) to castrate, to geld; *zurecht~* to trim; *Gesichter ~* to make (*od* to pull) faces (*od* grimaces); *med* (*operieren*) to operate on s. o.; *jdn ~* (*die kalte Schulter zeigen*) *fig* to cut s. o.; *sich ~* (*mit e-m Werkzeug*) to cut o. s.; (*sich in den Finger ~*) to cut o.'s finger; *math* (*von Linien*) to intersect; *fig* (*sich täuschen*) to be mistaken, to be disappointed; *sich ins eigene Fleisch ~* to cut o.'s own throat; *durchs Herz* (*od die Seele*) *~ fig* to cut to the quick; **~d** *a* (*scharf*) cutting; sharp; (*Kälte*) pinching, nipping; (*durchdringend*) piercing; (*Wind*) cutting, keen; *fig* (*Verstand*) keen, penetrating; (*Blick*) withering; (*beißend*) sarcastic; (*Hohn*) biting, *Am* nippy.

Schneider *m* (*Kleidermacher*) tailor; *tech* (*Werkzeug*) cutter, cutting nippers *pl*; *tech* (*Mann*) cutter, carver; *Herren~* gentlemen's tailor; *Damen~* ladies' tailor; *fig* (*Schwächling*) weakling; *bei welchem ~ lassen Sie arbeiten?* who is your tailor? *vom ~ angefertigt* tailor-made; **~anzug** *m* tailored suit; **~arbeit** *f* tailor's work; **~ei** *f* tailoring; tailor's business; (*Damen~~*) dress making, couture; **~geselle** *m* journeyman tailor; **~handwerk** *n* tailor's trade; **~in** *f* **ladies' tailor; dressmaker,** tailoress; **~kleid** *n* tailor-made dress; **~kostüm** *n* tailor-made (suit); **~kreide** *f* tailor's chalk; **~lehrling** *m* tailor's apprentice; **~lohn** *m* tailor's wages *pl*; **~meister** *m* master tailor; **~n** *itr* to make clothes, to do dressmaking; to do tailoring, to tailor; *tr* to make; **~puppe** *f* dummy; **~rechnung** *f* tailor's bill; **~seele** *f fig* coward; **~werkstatt** *f* tailor's shop, *Am* tailor shop; **~zunft** *f* guild of tailors.

schneien *imp* to snow; *es schneit* it snows, it is snowing; *jdm ins Haus ~ fig* to drop in suddenly.

Schneise *f* (*Wald*) vista, aisle; forest path; ride; *aero* (*Flug~*) flying lane; corridor, gate; (*Anflug~*) approach path; (*Anfluggrundlinie*) centreline of the runway; (*Funk~*) radio-beacon course; equisignal track (*od* sector).

*

schnell *a* (*vom bewegenden Objekt, wie z. B. Auto, Zug, Flugzeug etc*) fast; (*in bezug auf die Geschwindigkeit des Objekts*) rapid; (*rasch ohne bes. Anstrengung*) swift; *poet* fleet; (*geschwind, lebhaft, schnellwirkend*) quick; (*schleunigst, unverzüglich*) speedy; (*hastig*) hasty; (*rasch u. präzis mit e-r festen Absicht*) expeditious; (*plötzlich*) sudden; (*beweglich, bereit*) prompt; (*Verkauf*) brisk; *~ wie der Blitz* as quick as lightning; *nicht so ~!* gently! easy! *so ~ als möglich* as fast as possible; *immer ~er* faster and faster; *mach ~!* be quick! make haste! hurry up! *Am sl* make it snappy! *~ auffassen* to be quick of apprehension; *~ leben* to live fast; *~ fahren* to drive fast, *Am* to step on it; *~ lernen* to be quick at learning; *~ rechnen können* to be quick at figures; *~er werden* to accelerate, to speed up; *~ wirkend* quick acting; *~e Besserung* speedy recovery; *~e Division* motorized division; *in ~er Folge* in rapid succession; *~er Fortschritt* rapid progress; *~er Entschluß* prompt decision; *~e Erwiderung* prompt reply; *~e Rolle aero* snap (*od* flick) roll; *mit ~em Schritt* at a rapid pace; *~e Truppen* mechanized troops, motorized troops, mobile troops; *~er Umsatz* quick returns *pl*; **~ablaß** *m aero* quick-release; **~amt** *n tele* toll exchange, multi-exchange system, *Am* multi-office exchange; **~arbeitsstahl** *m* high-speed steel tool; **~bahn** *f* high-speed railway; (*für Autos*) superhighway, autobahn; **~binder** *m* quick-setting cement; **~bleiche** *f* chemical (*od* quick) bleaching; **~bohrer** *m* speed drill; **~bomber** *m* high-speed bomber; **~boot** *n* speed-boat, *mil* motor-torpedo boat (*Abk* MTB); motor assault boat; mosquito boat; E-boat, S-boat, PT-boat; **~brücke** *f mil* portable footbridge; **~dampfer** *m* fast steamer; greyhound; **~drehlegierung** *f* high-speed alloy; **~e** *f* speed, velocity, swiftness; (*Strömung*) rapid; **~einstellhebel** *m* quick-adjusting lever; **~en** *tr* to snip; (*Feder*) to snap; (*ab~~*) to let fly; (*mit dem Finger ~~*) to fillip; (*mit Schwung bewegen*) to flick; (*schleudern*) to dart; (*werfen, rucken*) to jerk, to toss; to fling; *fig* (*prellen, betrügen*) to cheat, to bamboozle; *itr* (*fort~~*) to spring; to fly off; (*in die Höhe*) to tip up; to kick up; (*schnappen*) to snap; to jerk; **~entwicklung** *f* high-speed development; **~fahren** *n mot* (*Verkehr*) speeding; **~fahrer** *m mot* speeder; **~färbung** *f* quick staining; **~feuer** *n mil* heavy fire, rapid fire, quick fire; **~~geschütz** *n* quick-firing gun, *Am* rapid-fire gun; **~~waffe** *f* automatic weapon; **~flug** *m* high-speed flight; **~~zeug** *n* high-speed aircraft; **~flüssig** *a* easily fusible, readily meltable; **~füßig** *a* swift(-footed), nimble; **~~keit** *f* nimbleness; **~gang** *m mot* high speed; (*Schongang*) overdrive; **~~getriebe** *n* high-speed gear; overdrive transmission; **~gaststätte** *f Am* quick-service restaurant, *Am* eat-and-run lunch-counter; **~gericht** *n* (*Speise*) hurry-up stew; *jur* summary court; **~hefter** *m* folder, letter file; **~igkeit** *f* swiftness; rapidity; quickness; fastness; promptness; (*Eile, Hast*) haste, hurry; (*Geschwindigkeit*) speed; (*Gang*) rate; *tech* velocity, celerity; (*Strömung*) drift; **~käfer** *m* click beetle; **~kampfflugzeug** *n* pursuit plane; **~kochtopf** *m* pressure cooker; **~kurs** *m* accelerated course; **~(l)adekanone** *f* quick-firing gun; **~(l)astwagen** *m* fast delivery van, *Am* fast truck, speed truck; **~(l)auf** *m* **run, race;** (*Eis~~*) **speed-skating; ~(l)aufend** *a* **high**-speed, rapid; *~~er Motor* high-speed engine; **~(l)äufer** *m* runner, racer; speedster; (*Eis~~*) speed-skater; (*Maschine*) high-speed engine; **~(l)ebig** *a* (*Zeit*) swiftly moving; (*Lebensspanne*) rapidly completing the life cycle; **~methode** *f* rapid method; shortcut; **~photographie** *f* instantaneous photography; (*Bild*) snapshot; **~post** *f* express-mail; *hist* diligence; **~presse** *f typ* steam-press; mechanical press; high-speed printing-machine; **~schlepper** *m mar* speed-tug; **~schrift** *f* shorthand, stenography; **~schritt** *m mil* quick march; **~schuß** *m typ* rush; **~segler** *m* fast sailer, *Am* clipper; **~siederkurs** *m fig fam* lightning course, *Am* snap course; **~stahl** *m* high-speed (tool) steel; **~tauchen** *n* (*U-Boot*) crash dive; *itr* to crash-dive; **~telegraph** *m* high-speed telegraph; **~triebwagen** *m* high-speed rail coach; express Diesel car; **~trocknend** *a* quick-drying, siccative; **~verfahren** *n tech* high-speed processing, rapid process; *jur* summary jurisdiction; **~verkehr** *m* high-speed traffic; express traffic; **~~sflugzeug** *n* high-speed commercial airplane; express airliner; **~waage** *f* steelyard; **~zeichner** *m* (*Varieté*) lightning artist; **~zug** *m* express (train); fast train; *Am auch* flyer; **~~slokomotive** *f* express engine; **~zünder** *m* quick match; quick fuse; **~züngig** *a* voluble, fluent; **~~keit** *f* volubility.

Schnepfe *f orn* snipe, woodcock; *vulg* (*Straßendirne*) street-walker; **~nstrich** *m* flight of snipe; *fig vulg* street-walking.

Schneppe *f* spout, nozzle, snout, lip; (*e-r Haube*) peak; *vulg* (*Straßendirne*) street-walker.

schneuzen *r* to blow o.'s nose.

Schnickschnack *m* tittle-tattle.

schniegeln *tr* to dress up; to smarten; to groom; *sich ~* to make o. s. smart; *geschniegelt u. gebügelt* spick and span.

Schniepel *m fam* (*Geck*) dandy, fop; (*Frack*) dress-coat.

Schnipfel *m* chip, bit; scrap; trim; shred; **~n** *tr* to cut up; to chip; to carve.

Schnippchen *n*: *jdm ein ~ schlagen fig fam* to play a trick on s. o., to outwit s. o., to do s. o.

Schnipp|el, ~sel *m*, *n* bit, chip, scrap, shred; **~eln, ~seln** *tr* to shred, to snip, to cut up; **~en** *tr, itr* (*mit den Fingern*) to snap (o.'s fingers); (*mit der Schere*) to click (the scissors); **~isch** *a* snappish; (*frech, aufreizend*) saucy, pert; snubby; (*unverschämt*) impertinent, *Am* snippy; *~~ antworten* to snub at, to snap at s. o.; *~~ behandeln* to snub, to rebuff.

Schnitt *m* (*Längs~, Durch~*) cut, profile; (*Arbeitsvorgang*) cutting; (*Stück, Scheibe*) slice; (*Machart der Kleidung*) fashion, style; (*Muster~*) pattern; (*Buch~*) edge (of a book); (*Gesichts~*) contour; shape; *med* (*Operation*) operation, (*Einschnitt*) incision, cut; (*Amputation*) amputation; (*Durchschneidung, Kreuzung, Schneidepunkt*) intersection; *math* (*Zeichnung*) section, sectional view; (*Quer~*) cross-section; (*Kegel~*) conic section; *typ* (*e-r Schrift*) cut; (*Linoleum*) lino-cut; (*Holz~*) woodcut, wood stock, wood block, wood engraving; *film* cutting and editing; (*Ernte*) crop, harvest, reaping; (*Scheibe Fleisch*) slice, cut; piece; (*Kerbe*) notch, kerf; (*Spalt, Schlitz*) slit, cut; *fig* (*Gewinn*) profit, gain; interest; *der goldene ~* medial section; *nach dem neuesten ~* after the latest fashion; **~ansicht** *f tech* sectional view; **~ball** *m* (*Tennis*) cut; **~blumen** *f pl* cut flowers *pl*; **~bohne** *f* French bean, *Am* stringbean; **~breite** *f* cutting width; (*Säge*) saw cut, kerf; **~brenner** *m* slit (*od* batswing) burner; **~chen** *n* little cut; (*Scheibe*) small slice; **~darstellung** *f* transverse section; **~e** *f* (*Scheibe*) slice, cut; *e-e ~~ Brot* a slice of bread; (*belegtes Brot*) sandwich; (*von Ochsenfleisch*) steak; chop; (*von Speck*) rasher; **~ebene** *f* sectional plane; cutting plane; **~er** *m*, **~erin** *f* reaper, mower; harvester; **~färbung** *f* section staining; **~film** *m* cut film; **~fläche** *f* section; sectional area; cut surface; **~handel** *m* haberdashery; **~händler** *m* haberdasher; **~holz** *n* sawed timber; **~ig** *a* smart; racy; (*Auto etc*) streamlined; **~kante** *f* cutting edge; **~kopie** *f* edited print; **~kurve** *f* **intersecting curve**; **~länge** *f* **length** of a cut; (*Papier*) chop; **~lauch** *m bot* chive(s *pl*); **~leistung** *f* cutting efficiency; **~ling** *m bot* cutting; **~linie** *f* cutting line; secant; intersecting line; profile line; **~meister** *m film* cutter; **~messer** *n* cutting knife; drawknife; **~modell** *n* cut-away model; **~muster** *n* paper pattern, dress model; form; **~präparat** *n* section preparation; **~probe** *f* test by cutting; **~punkt** *m* (*von Linien*) point of intersection; (*Winkel*) vertex; (*Kreuzung*) intersection; **~salat** *m* small lettuce; **~(t)iefe** *f* depth of cut; **~waren** *f pl* (*Kurzwaren*) haberdashery, *Am* dry-goods *pl*; mercery; drapery; (*Holzwaren*) sawn timber; **~~geschäft** *n* drapery, (*Seide*) mercery, *Am* dry-goods business, dry-goods store; **~~handel** *m* mercer's trade; **~~händler** *m* draper; (*Seide*) mercer; **~weise** *a* in cuts, in slices; **~werkzeug** *n* cutting tool; **~winkel** *m* cutting angle; **~wunde** *f* cut; incised wound; (*tiefe*) gash; **~zeichnung** *f* cross-sectional view (*od* drawing), sectional drawing; cut-away drawing; picture, view; figure; **~zeit** *f* time of cutting.

Schnitz *m* (*kleines Stück, Scheibe*) cut, chip; chop; slice; **~arbeit** *f* (wood-) carving; **~bank** *f* carving bench; (*Küfer*) cooper's bench; **~el** *n* chip; slice; (*Kartoffel*) shred, chip; (*Abfall*) *pl* parings *pl*, (*Holz~~*) *pl* shavings *pl*; (*Papier~~*) scrap; (*Rüben~~*) beet slices *pl*; (*Filet~~*) fillet; (*Kalbs~~, Wiener ~~*) veal cutlet, *Am auch* schnitzel; **~elei** *f* carving; **~eljagd** *f* paper-chase; hare and hounds; **~elmaschine** *f* slicer, shredding machine; **~elmesser** *n* chopper, slicing knife; **~eln** *tr, itr* to cut, to cut up; (*in Stückchen*) to chip, to shred; to whittle; (*Bohnen*) to slice; **~en** *tr* to carve; to sculpture, to cut (in wood); to whittle; **~er** *m* (*Arbeiter*) cutter, carver; (*Werkzeug*) paring tool, knife; *fig* (*Fehler*) blunder, bloomer; (*grober ~~*) howler, *Am* boner; **~erei** *f* (wood-) carving, carved work; **~holz** *n* wood for carving; **~messer** *n* carving knife; **~werk** *n* carved work.

schnodd(e)rig *a* (*vorlaut*) cheeky, pert; (*unverschämt*) insolent; **~keit** *f* cheekiness, pertness; insolence.

schnöde *a* (*geringschätzig*) **disdainful**, contemptuous, scornful; (*beleidigend*) outrageous, insulting; (*verächtlich*) mean, base; (*niederträchtig*) vile; (*schändlich*) disgraceful, shameful; *~r Gewinn* vile profit; *~r Mammon* filthy lucre; *~r Undank* black ingratitude; *jdn ~ behandeln* to treat s.o. with scorn and contempt.

Schnorchel *m mil mar* (*U-Boot*) schnorkel, snorkel, breathing mast, air funnel, air intake; **~unterseeboot** *n* snorkel-equipped U-boat, snorkel submarine.

Schnörkel *m arch* scroll, ornament; (*Unterschrift*) flourish, paraph; *~ machen fig* to flourish; **~ei** *f* scroll-work, **~haft** *a* (*Schrift*) flourishy; full of flourishes; overloaded with ornaments; *fig* (*launisch*) capricious; **~kram** *m fig* red tape; officialism; **~n** *itr* (*beim Schreiben*) to make flourishes; *arch* to adorn with scrolls.

schnorr|en *itr fam* to cadge (*um* for), to sponge; to go begging; *Am sl* to bum; **~er** *m fam* cadger; *armer ~~* poor devil.

schnüff|eln *itr* to sniff, to snuffle, to smell; *fig* to act the spy, to pry, to prowl, *Am fam* to snoop (about *od* around); **~ler** *m* snuffer, sniffer; *fig* (*Spion*) spy; *Am fam* snoop, snooper; **~lerisch** *a fig* prying, spying, *Am fam* snoopy.

schnull|en *itr* to suck; **~er** *m* (*Lutscher für Säugling*) (rubber) teat, comforter, soother, dummy.

Schnupf|en *m* cold (in the head); *med* (nasal) catarrh; common cold; (acute) rhinitis, coryza; upper respiratory infection; *vulg* (*Tripper*) gonorrh(o)ea; *den ~en haben* to have a cold; *den ~en bekommen* to catch cold; *sich e-n ~en holen* to get (*od* to catch) (a) cold; **~en** *itr* (*mit Tabak*) to take snuff; *tr* to snuff; **~enartig** *a* catarrhal; **~enfieber** *n* catarrhal fever; **~tabak** *m* snuff; *e-e Prise ~~* a pinch of snuff; **~~(s)dose** *f* snuff-box; **~tuch** *n* (pocket-) handkerchief.

Schnuppe *f* (*e-r Kerze*) snuff (of a candle); (*Stern~*) shooting star; *das ist mir ~* (*fam*) it's all the same to me; I don't care tuppence; *fam* I don't care a damn.

schnuppern *itr* (= *schnüffeln*) to sniff, to snuffle; to nose (after, for); to smell out.

Schnur *f* string, cord; line; (*Am meist*) twine; *el* (*Leitungs~*) flexible cord, flex; (*Einfaß~; zum Schnüren*) lace; (*Besatzlitze*) tape; (*Band*) trim, band; *el* (*Glühfaden*) filament; (*Akten~*) file; *anat* (*Nabel~*) umbilical cord; (*Perlen~*) string of pearls; *mit Schnüren besetzen* to border; *nach der ~* by the line; regularly; *über die ~ hauen fig* to kick over the traces; **~antrieb** *m* string drive; **~besatz** *m* braid-trimming, piping; **~gerade** *adv* straight (as a die); *in ~~r Linie* in a straight line, in a bee-line, as the crow flies; **~lauf** *m tech* groove wheel; **~leiste** *f* lashing wedge; **~leitung** *f* cord line; **~litze** *f* strand; **~rolle** *f* cord pulley; **~stracks** *adv* (*direkt*) directly, straight; right away; point-blank; diametrically; (*sofort*) immediately, on the spot, at once; forthwith; *~~ entgegengesetzt* diametrically opposed; *~~ losgehen auf* to make a bee-line for; *~~ nach Hause gehen* to go straight home; **~wurm** *m* ribbon worm.

Schnür|band *n* (*für Korsett*) (stay-) lace; **~boden** *m theat* gridiron; *mar* (sail) loft; **~chen** *n* little string; *wie am ~~* like clock-work; *wie am ~~* (*auswendig*) *können* to have at o.'s fingers' ends; **~en** *tr* to lace; (*befestigen*) to fasten with a lace; (*binden*) to string, to cord; to strap; to tighten; to tie up, to tie with cord (*od* string); (*zus. ziehen*) to constrict; *sein Bündel ~~* to pack up; *sich ~~* to tight-lace, to wear stays; **~leib** *m* corset; **~loch** *n* eyelet; **~nadel** *f* bodkin; **~riemen, ~senkel** *m* boot-lace, shoe-lace, *Am* shoestring; **~schuhe, ~stiefel** *m pl* lace-shoes *pl*; lace boots *pl*, lace-up boots *pl*; **~stock** *m* (*Webstuhl*) upper roller; **~ung** *f* tying-up, cording.

Schnurr|bart *m* m(o)ustache; *e-n ~~ haben* (*od tragen*) to wear a m(o)ustache; *sich e-n ~~ wachsen lassen* to grow a m(o)ustache; **~bärtig** *a* moustached; **~e** *f* (*Holzklapper*) rattle; (*Kreisel*) humming top; *fig* (*Posse*) farce; (*lustige Erzählung*) funny story; (*Witz*) jest, joke; quip; **~en** *itr* (*Rad, Saite*) to whir, to hum; (*Insekten*) to hum, to buzz, to drone; (*Holzklapper*) to rattle; (*Katze*) to purr; *fam* (*betteln, schmarotzen*) to go begging, to sponge, *fam* to cadge (*um* for); **~haare** *n pl* cat's whiskers *pl*; **~ig** *a* (*witzig*) funny, droll; (*komisch*) comical; (*seltsam, wunderlich*) queer, odd; *ein ~~er Kauz fam* an odd fish.

Schnute *f* snout, nose; *fam* (*Mund*) mouth; *e-e ~ machen fam* to pout.

Schober *m* heap; (*Heumiete*) stack; rick (of hay); (*Heuscheune, Holzschuppen*) barn; pile (of wood); **~n** *tr* to stack (hay); to pile (wood).

Schock[1] *n* threescore; *ein halbes ~* thirty; **~weise** *adv* by threescores.

Schock[2] *m med* shock; *Nerven~* nervous shock; *~ durch Granatexplosion mil* shell-shock, *Am* battle fatigue; **~behandlung** *f med* shock therapy, shock treatment; (*durch el Schläge*) electroshock therapy; **~organ** *n* shock organ.

schofel *a* (*erbärmlich*) miserable; mean; (*armselig*) paltry; (*garstig*) nasty; (*schäbig*) shabby; (*geizig*) stingy, miserly.

Schöffe *m* juror, lay assessor; juryman; **~ngericht** *n* lay assessors court.

Schokolade *f* chocolate; *gefüllte ~* chocolate cream; *flüssige ~* chocolate syrup; **~nauflauf** *m* soufflé of chocolate; **~nbraun** *a* chocolate (colo(u)red), chocolate brown; **~neis** *n* chocolate ice-cream, *Am* sundae; **~nfarbe** *f* chocolate colo(u)r; **~nfarben, ~nfarbig** *a* chocolate (colo(u)red), chocolate brown; **~ngeschäft** *n* sweet-shop, *sl* tuck-shop, *Am* candy store; **~nkanne** *f* chocolate pot; **~nplätzchen** *n* chocolate drop; **~npudding** *m* chocolate pudding; **~nriegel** *m* chocolate bar; **~ntafel** *f* slab (*od* cake) of chocolate; (*Riegel*) chocolate bar.

Schol|ar *m* scholar, pupil; **~astik** *f* scholasticism; **~astiker** *m* scholastic; **~astisch** *a* scholastical.

Scholle[1] *f* (*Fisch*) plaice; flounder; sole.

Scholl|e[2] *f* (*Erd~~*) glebe; (*Klumpen*) clod; (*Rasenstück*) sod; (*Schicht*) stratum, layer; (*Eis~~*) flake, floe, lump of ice; *heimatliche ~~* (*fig*) native soil; native country; home; *an die ~~ gefesselt* to be bound to the soil; **~enbrecher** *m* clod crusher; **~engebirge** *n* mountains formed by plateau-forming movements; **~ig** *a* cloddy; lumpy; (*schwer*) heavy.

schon *adv* (*zeitlich*) already; (*in Fragen, Zweifel ausdrückend*) yet; as early as; so far; since; by this time; as yet; (*bloß*) the very, the bare; (*sogar*) even; (*sicherlich*) certainly, surely; no doubt; after all; it is true; indeed; *es ist ~ 2 Uhr* it's already two o'clock; *es ist ~ dunkel* it is already dark; *er hat es ihr ~ zweimal gesagt* he told her twice already; *~ 5 Jahre* these five years; *ich komme ~!* (I am) coming! *ist er ~ gekommen?* has he come yet? *müssen Sie ~ gehen?* need you go yet? (*sind Sie*) *~ zurück?* (What! are you) back already? *~ am folgenden Tag* the very next day; *~ um 5 Uhr* as early as five o'clock; *~ im Jahre 1938* as early as 1938; as long ago as 1938; *~ im 15. Jahrhundert* as far back as the 15th century; *er lebt ~ seit 10 Jahren in Paris* he has been living in P. for 10 years; *er ist ~ 60 Jahre alt* he is 60 years old; *werden Sie ~ bedient?* are you being attended to? *~ von Anfang an* from the very outset; *~ früher* before now; before this; *~ gestern* as early as yesterday; *~ heute* this very day; *~ immer* always; *~ jetzt* now; *~ lange, ~ längst* long ago; for a long time (past); *es ist ~ lange her, daß ...* it is a long time since ...; *wie lange ist sie ~ hier?* how long has she been here? *~ oft* often; *~ wieder* again; *da ist sie ~ wieder* there she is again; *was gibt es ~ wieder?* what is it again? *er wollte ~ weitergehen* he was about to go; *sind Sie ~ in Berlin gewesen?* (*kürzlich*) have you been in B. yet? (*jemals*) have you ever been in B.? *es wird ~ besser werden* it will soon be better; *es wird ~ gehen* surely it will turn out all right; *ich verstehe ~!* Oh, I see! *er weiß ~ warum!* he knows why, all right! *~ gut!* all right! that will do! *Am* O.K.! okay! okeh! *~ recht* I have no objection; *es wird sich ~ machen* it will come all right in the end; *ich werde es ~ machen* I'll see to it; *das wird ~ gehen* this will do, I am sure; *das ist ~ richtig, aber ...* that's very true, but ...; that's all very well, but...; *wenn ~ conj* although; *wenn sie doch ~ ginge!* if only she would go! *wenn sie doch ~ käme!* if she would only come! *wenn ~* even so; *nun* (*od na*) *wenn ~!* so what! well, what of it! *wenn ~, denn ~* come what may; *sie mußte ~ zugeben* she could not help admitting; *ich war ~ sehr froh zu hören ...* I was indeed very glad to hear ...; *~ der Anblick* the very sight (of); *~ der Gedanke* the very idea, the mere thought; *~ der Name* the bare name; *~ deswegen* if it were only for this reason; *~ wegen, ~ weil* just because; if it were only because.

schön *a* (*vollendet ~, vollkommen in jeder Hinsicht*) beautiful; (*lieblich, entzückend*) lovely; (*makellos, rein, frisch*) fair; (*gut proportioniert, formschön, ansehnlich*) handsome; (*hübsch, nett*) nice; trim; (*ebenmäßig, hübsch, graziös*) pretty; bonny; (*gut aussehend, physisch anziehend*) comely; good-looking; (*elegant*) elegant, exquisite; (*auserlesen*) choice, select; (*erstklassig*) excellent; (*prächtig*) splendid, resplendent; glorious; superb; (*edel; stattlich*) noble; lofty; grand; (*beträchtlich*) considerable, great; (*gut*) good; (*anziehend*) attractive; (*bezaubernd*) bewitching; (*reizend, betörend*) charming, glamerous; (*hum, poet, Zeitungssprache*) beauteous, pulchritudinous; (*fein, schöngebaut, groß*) fine; *ein ~er Anfang* a nice beginning; *das ist e-e ~e Art u. Weise, e-n Freund zu behandeln* that's a fine way to treat a friend; *e-e ~e Bescherung* a nice mess; *Sie sind mir ein ~er Bruder!* you are a fine fellow! *ein ~er Charakterzug* a noble trait; *~en Dank!* thanks! *ein ~es Durcheinander* a nice mess; *e-e ~e Gelegenheit* a favo(u)rable opportunity; *das ist e-e ~e Geschichte!* pretty story this! a fine business! *ein ~es Gesicht* a fair face; *das ~e Geschlecht* the fair sex; *ein ~es Geschenk* a handsome present; *e-n ~en Gruß an Ihre Schwester* best regards to your sister; *e-e ~e Handschrift* a fair handwriting; *die ~en Künste* the fine arts; *die ~e Literatur* belles-lettres *pl*; literature; *e-e ~e Menge von* a large quantity of; *e-s ~en Morgens* one fine morning; *~e Qualität* excellent quality; *das sind mir ~e Sachen!* pretty things indeed! *e-e ~e Seele* a fair soul; *e-e ~e Summe Geld* a handsome sum of money; *e-s ~en Tages* one fine day; one day; *e-e ~e Tracht Prügel* a good (*od* sound) thrashing; *e-e ~e Überraschung!* a nice mess! *ein ~es Vermögen* a handsome fortune; *~e Versprechungen* fair promises; *die ~e Welt* the fashionable (*od* elegant) world; *~es Wetter* fine weather, *Am u. mar* fair weather; *es wird ~es Wetter sein* it's going to be fine; *~e Worte* fair words; *das klingt alles recht ~ u. gut* that's all very fine, but ...; *Sie haben ~ lachen* it's very easy for you to laugh; it's all very well for you to laugh; *das ist nicht ~ von ihr* that's not nice of her; *wir sind ~ dran* we are in a nice fix; *er ist ~ heraus* he is well off; *bleiben Sie ~ sitzen!* don't move! don't stir! *er wird sich ~ wundern* he will be greatly surprised; *~ in der Patsche sitzen* to be in a nice fix; *das Barometer steht auf ~* the barometer stands at fair; *~ bleiben* (*Wetter*) to keep fair; *sie haben mich ~ erschreckt* you have frightened me out of my wits; you gave me quite a start; *~ machen* to embellish, to clean up; (*Hund*) to beg; *sich ~ machen* to smarten o. s. up; to titivate; to rig o. s. out; *~ schmecken* to have a pleasant taste; *~ tun* to flirt, to coquet; (*mit jdm* with s. o.); *sich ~ warm halten* to keep o. s. nice and warm; *bitte ~!* if you please! *danke ~!* thank you! *na, ~!* very well! all right! certainly! *das wäre noch ~er!* certainly not! that's all we need! that would beat everything! **~druck** *m typ* first form, blank paper; primer; **~e** *n* the beautiful; *Sie werden was ~es von mir denken* you will have a nice opinion of me; *Sie haben etw ~es angerichtet* you have made a fine mess of it; **~e** *f poet* (*Person*) beautiful woman; beauty; belle; sweetheart; **~färben** *tr* (*beschönigen*) to palliate, to gloss over; **~färber** *m fig* optimist; **~färberei** *f fig* colo(u)ring, heightening; embellishment; optimism; **~geist** *m* wit; bel esprit; (*Ästhet*) aesthete; **~~erei** *f* witticism; (pretension to) wit; literary affectation; **~~ig** *a* aesthetic(al); (*literarisch*) literary; **~heit** *f* beauty; handsomeness; prettiness; nobleness; fineness; perfection; (*schöne Frau*) beautiful woman, beauty; professional (*od* society) beauty; **~~sbedürfnis** *n* longing for beauty; **~~sfehler** *m* corporal defect; flaw; disfigurement; **~~sfleck** *m* patch; **~~sgefühl** *n* sense of beauty; taste; **~~skönigin** *f* beauty queen; *die ~~ von Deutschland* Miss Germany; *die ~~ von Europa* Miss Europe; **~~skonkurrenz** *f*, **~~swettbewerb** *m* beauty contest; **~~slehre** *f* aesthetics *pl mit sing*; **~~slinie** *f* line of beauty; **~~smittel** *n* cosmetic; **~~spflästerchen** *n* patch; **~~spflege** *f* beauty treatment; (*Kosmetik*) cosmetology; **~~ssalon** *m* beauty parlo(u)r, beauty shop; **~~ssinn** *m* sense of beauty; taste; **~~swasser** *n* beauty wash, lotion; **~redner** *m* speechifier, spout; rhetorician; **~~ei** *f* fine talking; speechifying; **~~isch** *a* rhetorical; **~schreibekunst** *f*, **~schreiben** *n* calligraphy; **~schreiber** *m* calligraphist; **~schrift** *f* calligraphy; **~tuer** *m* flirt, gallant; (*Schmeichler*) flatterer; **~~ei** *f* flirtation, coquetting; (*Geziertheit*) affectation; (*Schmeichelei*) flattery; **~tun** *irr itr* (*schmeicheln*) to flatter, to fawn upon; (*sich zieren*) to be affected; (*flirten*) to flirt; to coquet; **~wetterpilot** *m aero fam* fair-weather pilot.

schon|en *tr* (*verschonen*) to spare; (*einsparen*) to save; to economize; to manage; to husband; (*sorgfältig behandeln*) to take care of; (*schützen*) to protect; (*erhalten*) to preserve; (*Eigentum, Rechte, Gefühle etc respektieren*) to respect; *sich ~~* to look after o. s.; to take care of o. s.; to mind o.'s health; *jdn ~~* (*gut behandeln*) to treat s. o. with consideration (*od* indulgence); (*Leben*) to spare s. o.'s life; *seine Augen ~~* to save o.'s eyes; *seine Gesundheit nicht ~~* to be regardless of o.'s health; *seine Kleider ~~* to take care of o.'s clothes; *seine Kräfte ~~* to spare o.'s strength; *jds Gefühle ~~* to have regard for s. o.'s feelings; **~end** *a* careful; (*rücksichtsvoll*) full of consideration, considerate; indulgent; forbearing; *e-e Nachricht ~~ beibringen* to break a news to s. o.; **~er** *m* (*Schutzdecke*) protector; (*Möbeldeckchen*) antimacassar; *mar* (*Schiff*) schooner; **~gang** *m mot* overdrive; **~~getriebe** *n* high-speed gear; **~ung** *f* sparing; (*Nachsicht*) regard, consideration, indulgence; forbearance; (*sorgliche Behandlung*) careful treatment; taking care of; (*Erbarmen, Gnade*) mercy; (*Wald*) nursery; young forest plantation; (*Gehege für Wild*) preserve; **~~slos** *a* (*ohne Gnade*) merciless; unsparing; (*erbarmungslos*) pitiless; relentless; unrelenting; **~~slosigkeit** *f* relentlessness; **~~svoll** *a* considerate, forbearing; indulgent; full of consideration; **~zeit** *f* close season, *Am* closed season.

Schopf *m* (*Kopfwirbel*) crown; top; (*Haar~*) bob, tuft; (*Stirn~ des Pferdes*) forelock; (*Vogel~, Feder~*) crest; *jdn beim ~ haben* to have a firm grip of

s. o.; *die Gelegenheit beim ~e fassen fig* to seize (on) the opportunity, to take time by the forelock.

Schöpf|bohrer *m* auger; **~bütte** *f* (*Papierfabrikation*) pulp vat; **~brunnen** *m* draw-well; **~eimer** *m* (bailing) bucket; **~en** *tr* (*Wasser etc*) to draw; (*aus~~*) to scoop (*aus* out of, from); to bail; to ladle out; to dip out; *aus etw ~~* (*fig*) to borrow from; to get; to obtain; *aus dem vollen ~~* to give from o.'s plenty; **~er** *m* (*Erschaffer*) creator; (*Hersteller*) maker; (*Urheber*) originator; (*Gott*) the Creator; (*Autor*) author; (*Komponist*) composer; (*Maler*) painter; (*Bildhauer*) sculptor; (*Erbauer*) constructor; (*Wasser~~*) drawer; dipper; bailer; **~~geist** *m* creative spirit; **~~isch** *a* creative; ingenious; productive; **~~kraft** *f* creative power; **~gefäß** *n* scoop; **~kelle** *f* scoop; **~löffel** *m* ladle; bailer; skimmer; strainer; **~papier** *n* (*Bütten*) hand-made paper; **~rad** *n* bucket-wheel; **~ung** *f* creation; making; production; (*Werk*) work; (*Geistesprodukt*) conception, brain-child; (*Weltall*) the universe; (*Natur*) nature; *die Herren der ~~* the lords of creation; **~~sgeschichte** *f* Genesis; **~~stag** *m* day of creation; **~~swerk** *n* work of creation; **~werk** *n* (*Paternoster*) bucket elevator; (*Wasserbau*) water-engine.

Schoppen *m* (*kleiner Trunk, z. B. Dämmer~, Früh~*) early-evening glass of beer; morning pint; (*Flüssigkeitsmaß* $\frac{1}{4}$—$\frac{1}{2}$ *l*) a quart; pint; half a bottle; *ein ~ Bier* a pint (*od* glass) of beer; **~weise** *adv* by the pint.

Schöps *m* wether; *fig* simpleton; **~enfleisch** *n* mutton; **~enkeule** *f* leg of mutton.

schoren *itr* to dig, to dig up, to turn up.

Schorf *m med* (*Kopfgrind*) scurf; (*Wund~*) eschar, crust; scab, slough; (*Kopf~*) dandruff; **~bildung** *f* sloughing; **~ig** *a* scabby; scurfy.

Schorle *n, f,* ***~morle*** *n* wine mixed with mineral water (*od* soda-water).

Schornstein *m* chimney; (*Dampfer, Lok etc*) funnel; (*Fabrik~*) (smoke-) stack; (*Rauchfang, Feuerzug*) flue; *e-e Schuld in den ~ schreiben fig* to write off a debt; to drop a claim; *rauchen wie ein ~* to smoke like a chimney; **~aufsatz** *m* chimney top; (*aus Blech*) chimney cowl; **~brand** *m* chimney on fire; **~deckel** *m* cover of the chimney; **~feger** *m* (chimney-) sweep; **~rohr** *n* smoke-pipe; **~schieber** *m* chimney damper; **~zug** *m* chimney (*od* stack *od* flue) draught (*od* draft).

Schoß[1] *m* (*pl Schosse*) *bot* shoot, sprout, sprig.

Schoß[2] *m* (*pl Schöße*) lap; (*Mutterleib*) womb; (*Rock~*) (coat-)tail, flap, skirt; *fig* middle, centre; *fig* bosom; womb; *in Abrahams ~ sein fig* to be in Abrahams bosom; to be well off; *auf den ~ nehmen* (*Kind*) to take on o.'s lap (*od* knees); *auf dem ~ halten* to hold on o.'s knees; *auf jds ~ sitzen* to sit on s. o.'s lap; *ihm fiel alles in den ~* (*fig*) everything fell right into his lap; everything came to him over night; *die Hände in den ~ legen fig* to cross o.'s arms; to fold o.'s hands; to rest upon o.'s oars, to remain idle; *sie legt gern die Hände in den ~* (*fig*) she is very fond of doing nothing; *im ~e der Familie* in the bosom of the family; *das ruht im ~e der Götter* that lies on the knees of the gods; *im ~e des Glückes sitzen* to sit in fortune's lap; *im ~e der Kirche* within the pale of the church; *im ~e der Zukunft* in the womb of time; **~bein** *n anat* os pubis; **~fuge** *f anat* pubic symphysis, symphysis of pubis; **~hund** *m*, **~hündchen** *n* lap-dog; pet; **~kind** *n* pet, darling; **~kissenfallschirm** *m aero* lap-pack parachute; **~knochen** *m anat* pubis.

Schößling *m* (off-)shoot, sprig.

Schote[1] *f bot* pod, cod, husk, shell; **~n** *f pl* (*Kochkunst*) green peas *pl*; **~nförmig** *a* pod-shaped; **~ngemüse, ~ngewächs** *n*, **~npflanze** *f* leguminous plant.

Schote[2] *f mar* (*Tau*) sheet.

Schott *n*, **~e** *f mar* bulkhead; *wasserdichtes ~* watertight bulkhead; (*Trennwand, Abteil*) partition, separation; compartment; **~wand** *f* bulkhead partition; fire wall.

Schott|e *m* Scot, Scotsman; *die ~en pl* the Scotch; **~in** *f* Scotchwoman; **~isch** *a* Scottish, Scotch; **~land** *n* Scotland; **~länder** *m* Scot, Scotsman.

Schotter *m* (*Straßenbau*) road-metal, macadam; (*Kies etc*) gravel, broken stone, *Am* crushed rock; *rail* ballast; **~bank** *f* gravel bank; **~belag** *m* metalling; *rail* ballasting; **~boden** *m* gravelly soil; **~decke** *f* road metal surface; **~n** *tr* to metal; to macadamize; to gravel; **~straße** *f* metalled road; macadam(ized) road; gravel road; **~werk** *n* road metal plant; *rail* ballast works *pl*.

schraff|ieren *tr* to hatch, to hachure; (*schattieren*) to shade; to line; **~iert** *a* hatched; shaded; section lined; **~ierung, ~ur** *f* hatching, hachure; shading.

schräg *a* oblique; cross; (*geneigt*) inclined, sloping, slanting; (*quer laufend*) diagonal, transversal; (*Stoff, Kleider*) bias; (*schief, nach e-r Seite hängend*) lopsided; *~ abschneiden* to cut diagonally; *~ abfallend, ~ geneigt* sloping, slanting; inclined; *~ gegenüber* nearly opposite; across (*von* from); *sie wohnt ~ gegenüber von mir* she lives diagonally across from me; *~ nach links unten* towards the left bottom corner; *~ nach links oben* toward the left top corner; *den Hut ~ aufsetzen* to cock o.'s hat; *~e Musik sl* hot music, hot jazz; **~ansicht** *f* three-quarter view; **~ansteigend** *a* upward-sloping; **~aufnahme** *f* oblique photograph; *aero* (*Luftbild*) oblique air photograph; **~aufzug** *m* inclined hoist; inclined elevator; **~bahn** *f* inclined track; **~e, ~heit** *f* obliquity; (*Neigung*) slope, slant, inclination; *tech* bevel; **~ebene** *f* slant plane; **~en** *tr* to bevel; **~feuer** *n mil* flanking (*od* oblique) fire; enfilade; **~fläche** *f* slope; slant; (*Schneidwerkzeug*) bezel; **~kante** *f* chamfer, bezel; **~lage** *f* sloping position; *aero* angle of bank, angle of roll; **~~anzeiger** *m aero* bank indicator; **~liegend** *a* oblique; **~linie** *f* diagonal; **~schnitt** *m* diagonal cut; **~schrift** *f typ* (*Kursivdruck*) italics *pl*; (*Handschrift*) sloping handwriting; **~steg** *m typ* inclined quoin; **~stellbar** *a* inclinable; **~stellen** *tr* to incline, to tilt; **~streifen** *m* oblique marking; **~strich** *m* diagonal streak; **~über** *adv* nearly opposite; across.

Schragen *m* (*Gerüst*) trestle; (*Fleischer~*) stall; (*Bahre*) bier; (*Rollbett*) truckle(-bed).

Schramm|e *f* (*leichte Wunde*) slight wound; (*Kratzwunde*) scratch; (*Abschürfung*) abrasion; graze; (*Schnitt*) slash; (*Narbe*) scar; cicatrice; (*auf Politur*) scratch; **~en** *tr* (*kratzen*) to scratch; (*streifen*) to graze; (*ritzen, furchen*) to scar; **~ig** *a* scratched; scarred.

Schrammel|n *pl: Wiener ~~* (*mus*) popular Viennese band (accordion, violin and guitar); **~musik** *f* popular Viennese music, played by a Viennese band.

Schrank *m* (*Kleider~*) wardrobe; (*Spind*) locker; (*Bücher~*) bookcase; (*Küchen~, Geschirr~*) cupboard, *Am* closet; (*Kunst~ mit Schubfächern*) cabinet; (*Geld~*) safe; (*Wäsche~*) press; (*Büffet*) sideboard; (*Gehäuse*) case; *tele* (*Vermittlungs~*) switchboard; **~empfänger** *m radio* (*Truhe*) console receiver; **~fach** *n* compartment; partition; (*Bank*) safe; (*für Ablage*) pigeon-hole; **~koffer** *m* wardrobe trunk.

Schranke *f* (*Schlagbaum*) bar; barrier; (*Zaun*) enclosure; fence, fencing-in; (*Gitter*) rail(ing); (*Gerichts~*) bar; (*Zoll~*) toll-bar; *hist* turnpike; (*Eisenbahn~*) railway gate; barrier; *fig* (*Grenze*) bound(s *pl*), limit; **~n** *f pl* (*Kampfplatz*) lists *pl*; *sich in ~n halten* to keep within bounds; (*sich zurückhalten*) to restrain o. s.; *in den ~n bleiben* to keep within bounds; *jdn in die ~n fordern* to challenge s. o.; *in die ~n treten fig* to enter the lists; to challenge comparison; *e-e ~ setzen* to set bounds, to limit; *innerhalb der gesetzlichen ~n* within the pale of the law; *die ~n überschreiten* to go beyond bounds; *jdn vor die ~n des Gerichts rufen* to call s. o. before the bars of justice; *jdn in seine ~n weisen* to put s. o. in his proper place; **~nlos** *a* boundless, limitless; (*übertrieben*) unbounded; exaggerated; **~~igkeit** *f* boundlessness; *fig* licence; (*Übertreibung*) exaggeration; **~nstange** *f* railing bar; **~nwärter** *m* gate-keeper, gate-man, gate-tender; signalman, *Am* watchman, flagman.

schränk|en *tr* to put across, to cross; (*Säge*) to set the teeth; **~ung** *f aero* (*positive, negative ~~*) washout, washin.

Schranne *f* corn-exchange; (*Fleischbank*) shambles *pl mit sing*.

Schranze *f* servile courtier, parasite; toady.

Schrapnell *n* shrapnel.

schrap(p)|en *tr, itr* to scrape; **~er** *m* (*Werkzeug*) scraper.

Schrat(t) *m* (*zottiger Waldgeist*) faun, satyr.

Schraub|e *f* (*ohne Mutter, Holz~~*) screw; (*mit Mutter*) bolt; (*Schnecke, ~~ ohne Ende*) worm; *aero* (*Propeller*) air-screw, *Am* propeller; *mar* (*Schiffs~~*) screw-propeller, screw; *alte ~~* (*fig*) *fam* old woman; old spinster; *~~ ohne Ende* endless screw; (*Schnecke*) worm; *versenkte ~~* countersunk screw; *e-e ~~ anziehen* to tighten the screw; *die ~~ anziehen fig* to put on the screw; *bei ihr ist e-e ~~ los fig* she has a screw loose; *das ist e-e ~~ ohne Ende fig* it's a vicious circle; **~en** *tr, itr* to screw; (*drehen*) to turn, to twist; (*sich winden*) to wind; (*in Spiralen*) to spiral; *seine Forderungen herab~~* to lower (*od* to scale down) o.'s demands; *die Preise in die Höhe ~~* to run up the prices, to force (*od* to send) up the prices; *geschraubt fig* (*Stil, Sprechweise*) affected; strained; stilted; unnatural; **~~artig** *a* helical; helicoidal; spiral; **~~bakterie** *f* spirillum; **~~bohrer** *m* screw tap; auger bit; twist drill; **~~bolzen** *m* (screw) bolt; **~~dampfer** *m* screw-steamer; **~~drehbank** *f* screw-cutting lathe; **~~drehmoment** *n aero* torque; **~~druck** *m aero* screw (*Am* propeller) thrust; **~~fassung** *f el* screwed holder; screw base; **~~feder** *f* coil spring, helical (*od* spiral) spring; **~~fläche** *f* helicoidal surface; **~~flügel** *m aero* air-screw (*Am* propeller) blade; **~~flugzeug** *n* helicopter, rotating-wing aircraft, *Am sl* egg-beater; (*Drehflügler*) autogiro; **~~förderer** *m* screw conveyer; **~~förmig** *a* screw-shaped; helical, helicoidal; spiral; twisted; **~~gang** *m* screw thread; **~~getriebe** *n* worm gear; **~~gewinde** *n* (screw) thread, worm (of a screw); **~~klemme** *f* screw clamp; **~~kopf** *m* screw head; bolt head; **~~kreis** *m aero* air-screw (*Am* propeller) disk; **~~lehre** *f* micrometer; **~~linie** *f* spiral (line); helix; **~~loch** *n* screw hole; **~~mutter** *f* nut; female screw; **~~schlüssel** *m* (screw) spanner; wrench; *Am* (*Universal~~*) monkey-wrench; **~~spindel** *f* spindle; **~~strahl, ~~strom** *m aero* slip stream; **~~verbindung** *f* screw joint; screw connection; **~~windung** *f* turn of a screw; spiral turn; **~~zieher** *m* screw driver; **~~zug** *m aero* thrust; **~~zwinge** *f* (screw) clamp; **~klemme** *f* screw terminal; **~stock** *m* vice, *Am* vise; *in den ~~ spannen* to vice; **~verschluß** *m* threaded cock; screw plug.

Schreber|garten *m* allotment (garden); **~gärtner** *m* small allotment holder.

Schreck *m siehe*: *~en m*; **~bewegung** *f* repulsive movement; **~bild** *n* terrific vision; fright; bugbear; scarecrow; (*für Kinder*) bogy; (*böser Traum*) nightmare; **~en** *m* (*heftiger ~~*) terror; (*plötzlicher ~~*) fright; (*jäher ~~*) scare; (*Furcht*) fear; (*Angst*) dread; (*Abscheu, Schauder*) horror; (*Entsetzen*) dismay; (*Panik*) panic; (*Bestürzun g*) consternation; (*Befürchtung*) alarm, apprehension; (*Erregung, Unruhe*) trepidation; *die ~~ des Krieges* (*Todes*) the horrors of war (death); *der ~~ liegt mir in allen Gliedern* I am frightened to death; *außer sich sein vor ~~, vor ~~ fast vergehen* to be frightened out of o.'s wits; *e-n ~~ bekommen* to be frightened; *jdm e-n ~~ einjagen* to give s. o. a (dreadful) scare; to alarm s. o., to frighten s. o.; *sich von seinem ~~ erholen* to recover from fright; *von ~~ ergriffen* horror-stricken, horror-struck; panic-stricken, panic-struck; *vor ~~ bleich werden* to turn pale with fear; *vor ~~ davonlaufen* to run away in a fright; *mit ~~ bemerken* to note with apprehension; *mit dem bloßen ~~ davonkommen* to get off with the fright; *mit ~~ erfüllen, ~~ einflößen* to fill with dismay; **~en** *tr* to frighten; to scare; (*stärker*) to terrify; (*aufregen*) to alarm; to upset; (*einschüchtern*) to intimidate; (*auf~~*) to startle; *tech* (*ab~~ in Wasser*) to chill; to pour cold water on; **~~sbleich** *a* pale (*od* livid) with terror; **~~sbotschaft, ~~skunde, ~~snachricht** *f* alarming news, terrible news, scare news; **~~sherrschaft** *f* reign of terror; terrorism; **~~snacht** *f* dreadful night; **~~ssystem** *n* terrorism; **~~stat** *f* atrocious deed; **~~szeit** *f* terrorism; **~gespenst** *n* terrible vision; phantom of fright; bugbear; nightmare; *Am* bugaboo; (*Popanz*) scarecrow; (*Kinderschreck*) bogy; *das ~~ des Krieges* the horrors of war; **~haft** *a* (*ängstlich*) easily frightened; fearful; (*schüchtern*) timid, timorous; (*nervös*) nervous; **~~igkeit** *f* fearfulness; timidity; nervousness; **~ladung** *f mil* booby-trap, booby-mine; anti-personnel bomb; **~lähmung** *f med* paralysis from fright; **~lich** *a* (*furchtbar*) terrible, frightful; (*entsetzlich*) awful, dreadful; (*grausig*) horrible; (*riesig, ungeheuerlich*) tremendous, formidable; *adv* frightfully, terribly, dreadfully; extremely; *~~ unangenehm* painful, unpleasant; *fam* cruel, *Am* fierce; *~~ langweilig* awfully boring; *ein ~~er Mensch* a perfect horror; **~lichkeit** *f* terribleness; horror; atrocity; **~mittel** *n* scare; scarecrow; **~neurose** *f med* fright neurosis; **~nis** *n* horror, fright; horrid thing; **~reaktion** *f* reaction provoked by violent fright; **~schuß** *m* shot fired in the air; alarm-shot; *fig* (*falscher Alarm*) false alarm; scare; *e-n ~~ abfeuern* (*od abgeben*) to fire in the air; **~~pistole** *f* booby pistol; **~sekunde** *f* reaction time; *Weg in der ~~* reaction distance; **~wirkung** *f* effect of fright; nervous trouble.

Schrei *m* cry; (*lauter*) shout; (*gellend*) yell; (*kreischend*) shriek, scream, screech; (*klagend*) wail; (*Gebrüll*) roar; (*Geheul*) howl; *Freuden~* whoop of joy; *Hahnen~* crow(ing); *Hilfe~* cry for help; *Kriegsge~* whoop, war-cry, battle-cry; *ein ~ der Entrüstung* an outcry of indignation; *der letzte ~ fig* (*Mode etc*) the newest fashion, le dernier cri; *Am fam* the newest wrinkle; *e-n ~ ausstoßen* to utter a cry; to shout, to scream, to yell.

Schreib|apparat *m* writing mechanism; **~arbeit** *f* clerical work, office work, desk work; **~art** *f* (*Stil*) style; manner (*od* method) of writing; (*Orthographie*) spelling; **~bedarf** *m* writing materials *pl*; stationary; **~block** *m* (writing-) pad, note-pad; **~empfänger** *m* (*Fernschreiber*) teletype (receiver); recording receiver; **~en** *irr tr, itr* to write; (*buchstabieren*) to spell; (*registrieren*) to register; (*mit der Schreibmaschine*) to type; (*auf~~*) to mark, to put down, to note; (*ab~~*) to copy; *com* (*abbuchen*) to write off; (*aus~~*) to write out; (*mitteilen*) to inform; *tech* (*aufzeichnen durch Instrumente*) to record; *noch einmal ~~* to rewrite; *~~ lernen* to learn to write; *schlecht ~~* to write badly; to scrawl; *ein Wort richtig ~~* to spell a word correctly; *ein Wort falsch ~~* to misspell a word; *seinen Namen unter etw ~~* to put o.'s name to; to sign s. th.; *sich etw hinter die Ohren ~~* to note s. th.; *sie gab ihm sage u. ~e eine Mark* she gave him precisely one mark; *Noten ~~* to copy music; *auf Konzept ~~* to (make a) draft, to make a rough copy of; *ins reine ~~* to make a fair (*od* final) copy of; *jdm auf die Rechnung ~~* to put down to s. o.'s account; *jdm etw zugute ~~* to place to s. o.'s credit; *mit der Schreibmaschine ~~* to typewrite, to type; to tap on the typewriter; *Kurzschrift ~~* to write shorthand; *für e-e Zeitung ~~* to write for a paper; *jdm ein paar Zeilen ~~* to drop s. o. a line; *wie schreibt sich dieses Wort?* how do you spell this word? *wie ~~ Sie sich?* how do you spell your name? *~~ Sie!* (*bei Diktat*) take a letter! **~en** *n* (*Schriftstück; Tätigkeit*) writing; (*Brief*) letter; (*kurzer Brief*) note; *com* favo(u)r; (*Mitteilung*) communication; (*amtliches ~~, Erlaß*) writ; *diplomatisches ~~* note; *eccl* epistle; **~end** *a* writing; (*Meßgerät*) recording; **~er** *m* writer; (*Büroangestellter*) clerk, clerical worker; (*Ab~~*) copyist; (*Sekretär*) secretary; (*Kopist, abfällig: Schriftsteller*) scribe; *der ~~ dieses Briefes* the undersigned; *tech* (*Registrierapparat*) recorder, recording apparatus; **~erei** *f* writing; clerical (*od* office) work; (*Korrespondenz*) correspondence; (*Schmiererei*) scribbling; **~erling** *m*, **~erseele** *f* quill-driver, ink-slinger; **~erstelle** *f* clerk's place; **~faul** *a* lazy about writing; **~feder** *f* (*Stahlfeder*) pen; nib; stylus; (*Gänse~~*) quill; **~fehler** *m* slip of the pen; error in writing, misspelling; clerical error (*od* mistake); typographic error; **~fertigkeit** *f* penmanship; **~fläche** *f* writing surface; **~freudig** *a* fond of writing; **~freund** *m* pen pal; **~gebühr** *f* copying fee(s *pl*); **~gerät** *n tech* recording instrument; recorder; **~griffel** *m* style; **~heft** *n* writing-book; exercise-book; copy-book; **~kräfte** *f pl* clerical staff; **~krampf** *m* writer's cramp; cramp in the hand; **~kunst** *f* penmanship; **~künstler** *m* writing-master; **~mappe** *f* portfolio; blotter; writing-case; writing kit; **~maschine** *f* typewriter; *~~ schreiben* to type, to typewrite; *mit der ~~ geschrieben* typewritten, typed; **~~nfarbband** *n* typewriter ribbon (*od* tape); **~~nfräulein** *n* typist; **~~ngummi** *m* typewriter eraser; **~~nmanuskript** *n* typewritten copy, typescript; **~~nschrift** *f* typescript; **~~nschreiber** *m*, **-in** *f* typist; typewriter; **~~nwalze** *f* platen, roller; **~materialien** *n pl* writing materials *pl*, stationary; **~papier** *n* writing-paper, note paper; **~pult** *n* (writing) desk, bureau; writing shelf; **~schrift** *f typ* script (type); (*Handschrift*) handwriting; **~spitze** *f* nib; **~stift** *m* pencil, crayon; stylus, style; engraving tool; **~stube** *f* office; *mil* orderly room; **~stunde** *f* writing-lesson; **~tafel** *f* note-book; (*Schiefertafel*) slate; (*Wandtafel*) blackboard; **~tinte** *f* writing ink; **~tisch** *m* writing-table; desk; bureau; **~~lampe** *f* desk lamp; **~~sessel** *m* desk arm-chair; **~~stratege** *m* arm-chair strategist; swivelchair strategist; **~~flieger** *m* arm-chair pilot; **~trommel** *f* recording drum; **~ung** *f* (*Orthographie*) spelling; *falsche ~~* misspelling; **~unterlage** *f* blotting-pad, writing-pad; **~vorlage** *f* copy; **~waren** *f pl* writing materials *pl*, stationary; **~~geschäft** *n*, **~~handlung** *f* stationary, *Am* stationary store; **~~händler** *m* stationer; **~weise** *f* (*Stil*) style; (*Orthographie*) spelling; **~zeug** *n* inkstand, pen and ink; **~zimmer** *n* writing room.

schrei|en *irr itr, tr* to cry (*nach* for); (*ausrufen*) to cry out, to call out; (*laut ~~*) to shout; (*kreischend ~~*) to scream, to shriek; (*gellend ~~*) to yell, *Am* to yip; (*lärmend ~~*) to bawl; (*heulen*) to howl; (*weinen*) to weep; (*Kind*) to squall; to whimper; (*knarren*) to creak; (*zusammen ~~*) to clamo(u)r; (*im Chor*) to chorus; *itr* (*Hirsch*) to bell; (*Esel*) to bray; (*Schwein*) to squeak; (*Eule*) to hoot, to screech; *~~ vor Vergnügen* (*Schmerz, Zorn*) to shout with delight (pain, anger); *aus Leibeskräften ~~, aus vollem Halse ~~* to shout at the top of o.'s voice (*od* lungs); *jdm in die Ohren ~~* to bawl into s. o.'s ears; *sich heiser ~~* to shout o. s. hoarse; *sich tot ~~* to scream o.'s lungs out; *um Hilfe ~~* to call (out) for help; *nach Brot ~~* tc clamo(u)r for bred; *nach Rache ~~* to cry out for revenge; *nach jdm ~~* (*heranrufen*) to shout for s. o. to come; *vor Lachen ~~* to roar with laughter; *es ~t zum Himmel* it is crying to Heaven; **~en** *n* crying; shouting; screaming; (*vom Zinn*) crackling (sound); *es ist zum ~~* that's screamingly funny; **~end** *a* clamorous; (*schrill*) shrill; (*himmelschreiend*) crying; (*offenkundig*) flagrant; (*ungeheuerlich*) monstrous; (*Farben*) gaudy, glaring, loud; *ein ~~es Unrecht* a flagrant injustice; **~er** *m* crier; bawler, brawler; *fig* (*Unzufriedener*) clamo(u)rer; (*Hetzer*) agitator, baiter; rioter; **~erei** *f* bawling; clamo(u)r; **~hals** *m* bawler; (*Kind*) cry-baby, squalling child; noisy brat; **~krampf** *m* crying fit.

Schrein *m* (*Reliquien ~*) shrine; (*Toten~*) coffin, *Am* casket; *poet* (*Schrank*) cupboard, press; (*Lade, Truhe, Kasten*) coffer, case; box; chest; cabinet; **~er** *m* joiner; (*Tischler*) cabinet-maker; (*Zimmerer*) carpenter; **~erarbeit** *f* joiner's work; joinery; **~erei** *f* joiner's workshop; **~ergeselle** *m* journeyman joiner; **~ern** *itr* to do joiner's work.

schreiten *irr itr* to step; (*ab~*) to pace; (*mit langen Schritten*) to stride; (*stolzieren*) to stalk, to strut; *im Zimmer auf u. ab~* to pace up and down the room; *an etw vorüber~* to pass by s. th.; *vorwärts~* to advance; *weiter ~* to proceed; *ans Werk ~, zu etw ~* to set about (*od* to work); to proceed to do s. th.; *zur Abstimmung ~* to come to the vote; *zum Äußersten ~* to take extreme measures.

Schrift *f* writing; (*Hand~*) handwriting; (*~zeichen*) character, letter; (*Druck~*) type; print; script; (*Art der Druck~*) fo(u)nt, cast; (*Aktenstück, ~stück*) paper, document, deed; (*Urkunde*) record; (*Veröffentlichung*) publication; (*~werk*) work; (*kleine ~*) pamphlet; (*Buch*) book; (*~ auf Münzen*) legend; *Kopf od ~?* heads or tails? *die Heilige ~* the Holy Scriptures *pl*, the Bible; *Schillers sämtliche ~en* Schiller's whole works (*od* collected works); *deutsche ~* (*Fraktur*) Gothic (*od* German) script; *fette ~* bold type; *magere ~* light type; *mittlere ~* medium-sized type; *kleine ~* small type; *schmale ~* compressed type; *Latein~* (*Antiqua*) roman type; *kursiv ~* italics *pl*; *Monats~* monthly; *Vierteljahres~* quarterly; *Wochen~* weekly; **~absatz** *m* paragraph; **~art** *f* kind of type; **~auslegung** *f eccl* exegesis; **~bild** *n typ* face; setting; **~deutsch** *n* literary German; **~führer** *m* clerk; protocolist; writing chairman; (*Verein, Partei etc*) secretary; **~gelehrte(r)** *m* (*Bibel*) scribe; **~gießer** *m* type-founder; **~gießerei** *f* type-foundry; **~gießmaschine** *f* type-casting machine; **~grad** *m* size of letters, size of type; **~guß** *m* type casting; **~kasten** *m* type-case; **~kegel** *m* body, fo(u)nt; depth of letter; **~leiter** *m* sub-editor, *Am* copy reader (*od* writer), editor; **~leitung** *f* editorship; editorial staff, editors *pl*; newspaper office; **~lich** *a* written, in writing; *adv* by letter; *~~er Befehl* letter order; *~~er Beweis, ~~e Unterlagen* written evidence; *~~e Erklärung* written statement; *~~ bestätigen* to confirm in writing; *~~ niederlegen* to put into writing; *~~ wiedergeben* to transcribe; *f* **~linie** *typ* alignment (of type); **~material** *n typ* stock of types; (*Unterlagen*) literature; references *pl*; bibliography; **~metall** *n* type metal; **~probe** *f* (*Handschrift*) specimen of (hand)writing; *typ* specimen of type; **~sachverständige(r)** *m* expert on handwriting; **~satz** *m typ* type; composition; matter; (*Darlegung, Bericht*) memorial, writ; *jur* pleadings *pl*, brief; **~setzer** *m* compositor; typesetter; typo(grapher); **~sprache** *f* written (*od* literary) language; **~steller** *m* author; writer; **~~ei** *f* literary carreer; writing; **~~in** *f* authoress; writer; **~~n** *itr* to write; to do literary work; **~~name** *m* pen-name; **~stück** *n* paper, document; piece of writing; brief; **~tum** *n* literature; (*bibliographisch*) documentation; bibliography; source material; **~~sangabe** *f*, **~~shinweis** *m* reference to literature; **~~sverzeichnis** *n* bibliography; bibliographic list; **~verkehr** *m* correspondence; **~walter** *m* editor; **~wart** *m* (*Verein*) secretary; **~wechsel** *m* exchange of letters; correspondence; **~zeichen** *n* character; letter; signal; **~zeug** *n typ* type metal; **~zug** *m* (written) character; (*Schnörkel*) flourish, handwriting.

schrill *a* shrill; grating; screaming; (*durchdringend*) piercing; *e-e ~e Stimme* a shrill voice; *ein ~er Schrei* a piercing (*od* shrill) cry; **~en** *itr* **to utter a shrill sound, to sound shrilly**; (*Glocke etc*) to ring shrilly; (*Heimchen*) to chirp.

Schrippe *f* French roll.

Schritt *m* step; (*langer ~*) stride; (*Tempo*) pace; (*Gang*) walk, gait; (*e-r Hose*) crotch; *fig* (*Maßnahme*) step, move, measure: *~ für ~* step by step; (*allmählich*) gradual(ly); *bei jedem ~* at every step; *auf ~ u. Tritt* (*überall*) everywhere; (*immer*) all the time; *jdm auf ~ u. Tritt folgen* to dog s. o.'s (foot-) steps; to shadow s. o.; *~ halten mit* to keep pace (*od* step) with; to keep up with; *fig* to keep abreast with; *nicht mit der Zeit ~ halten* to be out of step with the times; *aus dem ~ kommen* to get out of step; *e-n großen ~ zum Erfolg tun fig* to make a long step towards success; *jdn am ~ erkennen* to know s. o. by his steps; *sie konnte keinen ~ weiter gehen* she couldn't walk a step further; *den ersten ~ tun fig* to take the initiative; *~e unternehmen* to take steps, to take action; *was ist der nächste ~?* what's the next step? *~ fahren! mot* slow down! dead slow! *Am* drive slow! **~macher** *m* pace-maker; pacer; **~wechsel** *m* change of step; **~weise** *a* step by step; by steps; (*allmählich*) gradual(ly); **~weite** *f* step width; interval; length of stride; **~zähler** *m* pedometer.

schroff *a* (*steil*) steep; (*jäh*) precipitous; (*zerklüftet*) rugged; (*abschüssig*) abrupt; *fig* (*rauh*) rough; surly; (*roh*) rude; uncouth; (*grob*) gruff; (*barsch*) harsh; (*kurz, grob*) blunt; (*gerade, offen*) straightforward; (*plötzlich, glatt ablehnend*) abrupt; brusque; (*streng*) severe; rigid; *er hat e-e ~e Art* he has a brusque way about him; *gegen jdn ~ sein* to be abrupt with s. o.; *~e Ablehnung* flat refusal; *~e Äußerung* harsh utterance; *~er Widerspruch* downright contradiction; **~heit** *f* (*Steilheit*) steepness; (*Jäheit*) precipitousness; (*Zerklüftung*) ruggedness; *fig* (*rauhes Wesen*) roughness; ruggedness; (*Barschheit*) harshness; (*Grobheit*) bluntness; gruffness.

schröpf|en *tr med* **to cup; to bleed;** *jdn ~~ fig* **to fleece s. o.;** *fam* **to milk s. o.;** **~kopf** *m* cupping glass; **~messer** *n* scarifier, cupping instrument.

Schrot *m, n* (*Stück, Abschnitt*) piece, cut; scrap, waste; (*Kugelkörner*) small shot; slug; (*Rehposten*) buckshot; (*grob gemahlenes Getreide*) crushed grain, bruised grain; coarse-ground corn; (*Hafer~*) groats *pl*; (*Münzfeingehalt*) weight of coin, due weight; value; *von altem ~ u. Korn* of the old stamp, of the good old type, of the old block; of sterling probity; **~axt** *f* wood-cutter's axe; **~brot** *n* whole-meal bread; **~büchse, ~flinte** *f* shotgun, fowling-piece; **~en** *tr* (*grob mahlen*) to granulate, to grind small; to crush; (*Korn*) to rough-grind, (*Malz*) to bruise; (*Metall*) to chisel; (*Fässer*) to lower, to roll down; *mar* to parbuckle; **~feile** *f tech* trimming file; **~hobel** *m* jack plane; **~kleie** *f* coarse brand of groats; **~korn** *n* groats *pl*; bruised corn; **~kugel** *f* pellet; **~leiter** *f* cart-ladder; **~mehl** *n* coarse meal, groats *pl*, grits *pl*; **~meißel** *m tech* scrap chisel, scraper; **~mühle** *f* bruising mill; **~säge** *f* great saw, pit-saw; crosscut saw; **~schuß** *m* shot with small shot.

Schrott *m* (*Abfalleisen*) scrap (iron); scrap metal; **~berg** *m* pile of scrap; **~en** *tr* to scrap; **~entfall** *m* waste material; manufacturing loss; **~händler** *m* scrap dealer; **~haufen** *m* scrap pile; **~lager** *n* scrap yard; scrap-stock yard; **~platz** *m* scrap yard; **~wert** *m* scrap value.

schrubb|en *tr* to scrub; *mar* to swab; **~er** *m* scrubber; scrubbing-brush.

Schrull|e *f fam* (*Grille, Laune*) fad, whim; crotchet; freak, odd fancy; (*Manie*) mania; spleen; caprice; vagary; **~enhaft, ~ig** *a* whimsical.

Schrump|el *f* (*Runzel*) wrinkle; (*alte Frau*) withered old woman; **~(e)lig** *a* crumpled, creased; (*verschrumpelt*) wrinkled, shrivelled; **~eln** *itr* to shrivel; to shrink.

schrumpf|en *itr* (*sich runzeln*) to shrivel; (*sich zus.ziehen*) to contract; to shrink; (*sich vermindern, verringern*) to diminish; *med* to atrophy; **~en** *n* shrinkage; **~grenze** *f* shrinkage limit; **~niere** *f* atrophy of the kidney; **~sitz** *m* shrink fit; **~ung** *f* shrinking, shrinkage; **shrivelling; contraction;** *med* **stricture;** **~~sprozeß** *m* shrinkage; **~~sriß** *m* contraction strain; **~versuch** *m* shrinkage test.

Schrund *m*, **Schrunde** *f* (*Riß, Spalte*) cleft, crack; chink; crevice; **~ig** *a* cracked, chapped.

Schub *m* (*Stoß*) push, shove; *tech* (*Scherkraft*) shear(ing); (*Vorschub*) thrust; (*Kegel~*) throw (at ninepins), set of ninepins; (*Brotein~*; *~ Briefe, Leute, Ernennungen etc*) batch; (*Haufen*) heap; crowd; (*Zwangsbeförderung von Landstreichern u. Unerwünschten*) compulsory conveyance of tramps or undesirables (by police); (*Ausbruch*) outburst, onset; relapse; **~bewegung** *f* drift; **~düse** *f* propelling nozzle; *aero* jet; **~fach** *n* drawer; (*Briefe etc*) pigeon-hole; **~fenster** *n* sash-window; **~festigkeit** *f* shear(ing) strength; **~karre** *f*, **~karren** *m* wheel-(barrow), *Am* pushcart, hand truck; **~kasten** *m*, **~lade** *f* drawer; chest of drawers; **~~fach** *n* drawer section; **~kraft** *f* pushing force; **~lehre** *f* (*Meßwerkzeug*) slide ga(u)ge, slide rule; sliding cal(l)ipers *pl*; vernier cal(l)iper; **~leistung** *f* thrust; **~riegel** *m* push-bolt, sliding-bolt; sash-bolt; **~s** *m fam* push, shove; **~sen** *tr, itr* to shove, to push; **~stange** *f tech* connecting-rod; *mot* (*Lenkung*) drag rod; **~ventil** *n* slide valve; **~weise** *adv* (*in Grüppchen*) by shoves; in batches; by thrusts; (*allmählich*) gradually.

schüchtern *a* (*scheu*) shy; (*verschämt*) bashful; (*zaghaft*) timid; backward;

(*furchtsam*) timorous; (*nervös*) nervous; (*bescheiden*) modest; (*scheu, spröde*) coy; (*zögernd*) hesitating; (*unsicher, mißtrauisch*) diffident; (*kleinmütig, verzagt*) pusillanimous; (*vorsichtig*) cautious; wary; (*zurückhaltend, zimperlich*) mealy-mouthed; **~heit** *f* shyness, bashfulness, timidity.

Schuft *m* scoundrel, rascal; scamp; knave; blackguard; *Am fam* heel; highbinder; *sl* skunk(-skin); *sl* mucker; **~en** *itr* to drudge, to toil; to slave; to fag, to plod; **~erei** *f fam* drudgery, hard work; **~ig** *a* base; (*gemein*) mean; vile; (*niederträchtig*) abject, rascally; knavish; **~igkeit** *f* baseness.

Schuh *m* shoe; (*Stiefel*) boot; (*altes Längenmaß*) foot; *jdm etw in die ~e schieben fig* to lay a fault at s. o.'s door; to put the blame on s. o.; *Am* to pass the buck to s. o.; *ich möchte nicht in seinen ~en stecken fig* I should not like to be in his shoes; *wo drückt der ~? fig* where does the shoe pinch? *die ~e putzen* to black (*od* to clean) the boots, *Am* to shine the shoes; *~putzen gefällig? Am* shine, Sir? **~abkratzer** *m* door-scraper; **~absatz** *m* heel; **~anzieher** *m* shoehorn, shoe-lift; **~band** *n* **~nestel** *m* bootlace, *Am* shoe-string; **~bürste** *f* shoe-brush, blacking-brush; **~draht** *m* wax-end, shoemaker's thread; **~fabrik** *f* boot-factory; **~flicker** *m* cobbler; **~größe** *f*, **~maß** *n* size; **~krem** *m*, **~pasta** *f* shoe-cream, (shoe-) polish; **~laden** *m* boot-shop; *Am* shoe store, shoe saloon; **~leder** *n* shoe-leather; **~leisten** *m* last; **~löffel** *m* shoehorn; **~macher** *m* shoemaker, boot-maker; **~~meister** *m* master shoemaker; **~plattler** *m* Bavarian folk-dance; **~putzer** *m* shoeblack; *Am* shoe-shiner; boot-black; *jdn wie e-n ~~ behandeln* to treat s. o. like dirt; **~putzladen** *m Am* shoe-shine parlor; **~putzmittel** *n* shoe-polish; **~putzzeug** *n* shoe-shine kit; **~riemen** *m* bootlace, shoe-lace, *Am* shoe-string; **~schmiere** *f* dubbing, grease; **~schnalle** *f* shoe-buckle; **~schrank** *m* shoe cabinet; **~sohle** *f* sole (of a shoe); **~spanner** *m* boot-tree; **~spitze** *f* shoe-tip, point of a shoe; **~waren** *f pl* boots and shoes *pl*; **~werk** *n* footwear, footgear; boots and shoes *pl*; **~wichse** *f* (boot-)polish; shoe-polish; shoeblacking; *Am* shoe shine; **~zeug** *n* footwear; **~zwecke** *f* shoe-tack; (*aus Holz*) shoe-peg.

Schul|amt *n* (*Lehramt*) teacher's post; (*lokale Aufsichtsbehörde der Volksschulen*) school board; (*Ministerium*) Board of Education; **~anstalt** *f* school; educational establishment; **~arbeit, ~aufgabe** *f* (*Hausaufgabe*) task, lesson; home-work, *Am* (*Aufsatz*) theme; *seine ~~n machen* to do o.'s lessons; **~arrest** *m* detention (at school); **~arzt** *m* school doctor; **~atlas** *m* school atlas; **~aufsatz** *m* composition written in school; *Am* theme; **~aufseher** *m* school inspector; **~aufsicht** *f* school inspection; **~ausflug** *m* pupil excursion; **~ausgabe** *f* school edition; **~ausschuß** *m* school committee; **~bank** *f* (school) form, bench; *auf der ~~ sitzen* to be a boy at school; **~bedarf** *m* school requisites *pl*; **~behörde** *f* (*lokal*) school board; (*staatlich*) Board of Education; **~beispiel** *n fig* test; case; typical example; case in point; **~besuch** *m* attendance at school; **~betrieb** *m* training; **~bezirk** *m* school district; **~bibliothek** *f* school library; **~bildung** *f* education; school learning, schooling; *höhere ~~* secondary education; *e-e gute ~~* a thorough schooling; **~bube** *m* schoolboy; **~buch** *n* school book, class book; (*Leitfaden*) text book, reader; manual; **~diener** *m* porter; janitor; attendant; **~dienst** *m* teaching profession; **~direktor** *m* headmaster, *Am* principal; **~~in** *f* headmistress; **~e** *f* school; educational establishment; (*Gebäude*) school, school house; (*Unterricht*) schooling; teaching; (*Kursus*) course; (*Fertigkeit*) routine; (*die Schüler*) school; the boys and girls (of a school); (*Lehrsystem, Richtung*) school (of thought); doctrine; (*Akademie*) academy; *Kinder~~* infant school; *Volks~~* elementary school; (*öffentliche*) board school; *heute*: (*Unterstufe*) junior school, (*Oberstufe*) senior school; (*Vorschule für exklusive Privat~~*) primary school; *Am* public school; elementary (*od* grade) school; *höhere ~~* (*staatlich*) modern secondary school; (*exklusive Privat~~*) public school; *Am* high (*od* secondary) school, (*mit Unter- u. Oberstufe*) junior high school, senior high school; undergraduate (*od* junior) college; *Latein~~* (*entsprechend Gymnasium*) grammar school; *Hoch~~* university, *Am* university, college, (post)graduate school; *Abend~~* evening (*od* night) school; *Fach~~* professional school; *Fortbildungs~~* continuation school; *Internats~~* boarding school; (*ohne Pensionat*) day school; *konfessionelle ~~* denominational school, confessional school; *Knaben~~* boys' school; *Mädchen~~* girls' school; *Knaben- u. Mädchen~~* mixed school, *Am* co-educational school; *Simultan~~* school for children of different confession; *Volkshoch~~* University Extension; *Hohe ~~ reiten* to put a horse through his paces; *von der ~~ abgehen* to leave school; *e-e ~~ besuchen* to attend a school; *welche ~~ besucht er?* what school does he attend? *zur ~~ gehen* to go to school; to be at school; *~~ halten* to keep school; to teach a class; *~~ machen fig* to find followers (*od* adherents); to form a precedent; *die ~~ schwänzen* to stay away from school; to play truant, *Am* to play hooky; to cut school; *aus der ~~ schwatzen fam* to peach; *fig* to tell tales out of school; *auf der ~~, in der ~~* at school; *heute ist keine ~~* there is no school to-day; *die ~~ ist aus* school is over; *durch e-e harte ~~ gehen fig* to go through the mill; **~en** *tr* to train, to teach, to school; **~entlassen** *a* having left school; **~entlassung** *f* school leaving, *Am* graduation (*von* from); **~~salter** *n* school leaving age; **~~sfeier** *f* speech day, *Am* prom (= promotion); **~~szeugnis** *n* leaving certificate; **~erziehung** *f* school education; **~feier** *f* school festival; speech day; **~ferien** *pl* school holidays *pl*; *Am* vacations *pl*; **~film** *m* educational film; **~flug** *m aero* training flight; school flying; **~~zeug** *n* training aircraft, training plane; trainer; (*für Grundausbildung*) primary trainer; **~form** *f* kind of school; **~frei** *a* having a holiday; *~~er Tag* holiday, (*Nachmittag*) half-holiday; **~freund** *m* school friend, *fam* chum; **~fuchs** *m* pedant; **~fuchserei** *f* pedantry; **~funk** *m* school radio; educational broadcasting; **~gebäude** *n* school house; school; school building; school premises *pl*; **~gefechtsschießen** *n* combat practice firing; **~gelände** *n* school grounds, *Am* campus; **~geld** *n* (school) fee(s *pl*); schooling; tuition; terms *pl*; **~gelehrte(r)** *m* bookish man, scholar; **~gelehrsamkeit** *f* book-learning; **~gemeinde** *f* community of pupils of one school; **~gerecht** *a* methodical; **~gesundheitspflege** *f* school hygiene; **~gleiter** *m aero* (*Segelflug*) (elementary) training glider; **~haus** *n* school, school house, school building; school premises *pl*; *Am* (*e-r kleinen Landgemeinde*) the little red schoolhouse; **~heft** *n* exercise book; **~helfer** *m* emergency trained teacher; **~hof** *m* playground, schoolyard; *Am* (*Schulgrundstück*) campus; **~inspektor** *m* school inspector; **~isch** *a* referring to schools; **~jahr** *n* scholastic year, school year; **~~e** *n pl* school days *pl*; **~jugend** *f* school children *pl*, schoolboys and girls *pl*; **~junge, ~knabe** *m* schoolboy; **~kamerad** *m* schoolmate, schoolfellow, *fam* chum; **~kenntnisse** *f pl* knowledge acquired at school; **~kind** *n* school child; **~kino** *n* school cinema; **~klasse** *f* form, *Am* class, grade; *die unteren ~~n* the lower school; *die oberen ~~n* the upper (*od* senior) school; **~kreide** *f* blackboard chalk; **~küche** *f* school kitchen; **~lehrer** *m* schoolmaster, teacher; **~~in** *f* schoolmistress, lady-teacher, *Am fam* (*oft hum*) school-ma'am, school-marm; **~leiter** *m* headmaster, *Am* principal; **~mädchen** *n* schoolgirl, schoolmaid; **~mann** *m* pedagogue; education(al)ist; teacher; **~mappe** *f* schoolbag, satchel; **~meister** *m* schoolmaster, teacher; *sl* (*Eton*) beak; **~~ei** *f* pedantism; **~~lich** *a* pedantic; schoolmasterly; **~~n** *tr* (*lehren*) to teach; to play the schoolmaster; (*kritisieren*) to censure; **~omnibus** *m* school bus; **~orchester** *n* school band; **~ordnung** *f* school regulations *pl*; school discipline; **~pferd** *n* trained horse; **~pflicht** *f* compulsory school attendance; **~pflichtig** *a* of school age; bound to attend school; schoolable; *~~es Alter* compulsory school age; **~prüfung** *f* school examination; **~ranzen** *m* schoolbag, satchel; **~rat** *m* (*Behörde*) Board of Education; (*Titel*) inspector of schools; supervisor; **~reform** *f* reform of the educational system (*od* school system); **~reiten** *n* acrobatic riding; **~reiter** *m*, **~~in** *f* manege rider; **~roman** *m* school-story; **~sachen** *f pl* school requisites *pl*; **~schießen** *n mil* practice fire; **~schiff** *n* training ship; **~schluß** *m* break-up; **~schwänzen** *n* truancy, *Am* hooky; **~sender** *m* educational station; **~sparkasse** *f* school savings bank; **~speisung** *f* school (relief) meal(s), *Am* school lunch; **~stube** *f* class room, schoolroom; **~stunde** *f* lesson, period; **~system** *n* school (*od* scholastic) system; **~tafel** *f* (*Wandtafel*) blackboard; (*Schiefertafel*) (school) slate; **~tag** *m* schoolday; **~tasche** *f* schoolbag, satchel; **~übung** *f* school exercise; theme; **~ung** *f* schooling; education; training; practice; *pol* indoctrination; *sich durch ~~ gewöhnen an* to school o. s. to; **~~samt** *n* schooling office; **~~sfähig** *a* schoolable; **~~skursus, ~~slehrgang** *m* training course, orientation course; refresher course; **~~slager** *n* training camp; **~~swoche** *f* one week's course of instruction; **~~szentrum** *n* training centre; **~unterricht** *m* school teaching, schooling; school instruction; school (*ohne Artikel*); *im ~~* in school; **~verfassung** *f* statutes *pl*, regulations *pl* (of a school); **~versäumnis** *n* non-attendance; **~verwaltung** *f* school administration; **~vorstand, ~vorsteher** *m* headmaster, *Am* principal; **~wanderung** *f* school excursion; **~weg** *m* way to school;

~weisheit *f* school learning; **~wesen** *n* system of education; educational matters *pl*, school affairs *pl*; public instruction; **~wörterbuch** *n* school dictionary; **~zeit** *f* school time, school days *pl*; **~zeugnis** *n* school record; **~zimmer** *n* class room; (*Privatschulraum*) school room; **~zucht** *f* school discipline; **~zwang** *m* compulsory (school) education.

Schuld *f* (*Geld~*) debt, sum due; *~en pl* debts *pl*; (*Verbindlichkeiten*) liabilities *pl*; (*Forderung*) claim; (*Verpflichtung*) obligation; (*Verschuldung*) indebtedness; (*sittliche ~, strafrechtliches Vergehen*) guilt; offence; delinquency; fault; (*Sünde*) sin; (*Fehler*) fault; (*Verantwortung*) blame; (*Ursache*) motive, cause; *Gesamt~* collective guilt; *drückende ~en* heavy debts; *öffentliche ~* public debt; *rückständige ~* overdue debt; *ungetilgte ~* uncrossed debt; *unkündbare ~* funded debt; *e-e ~ abtragen* to pay off a debt; *mit ~en belastet* encumbered with debts; *in ~en geraten* to run (*od* to fall) into debt; *~en haben* to have debts; *fam* to be in the red; *keine ~en haben* to be in the black; *~en eintreiben* to collect (*od* to recover) debts; *~en tilgen* to pay off debts; *~ haben* (*~ig sein*) to be guilty; (*verantwortlich sein*) to be responsible; *in jds ~ stehen* to be in s. o.'s debt, to be under an obligation to s. o.; *die ~ tragen* to bear all the blame; *e-e ~ zugeben* to plead guilty; *jdm e-e ~ zuschieben, auf jdn die ~ schieben* to lay the blame on s. o.; *er ist ~ daran* it is his fault; he is to blame for it; *wer ist ~?* who's to blame? *wessen ~ ist das?* whose fault is it? *sich etw zu ~en kommen lassen* to be guilty of; *vergib uns unsere ~(en)* forgive us our trespasses; **~abzahlung** *f* liquidation of debts; **~anerkenntnis** *n* acknowledg(e)ment of debt; IOU (= I owe you); **~ausspruch** *m jur* (*Strafrecht*) verdict of guilt; **~bekenntnis** *n* admission of guilt; **~beladen** *a* laden with crime; **~beweis** *m* proof of guilt; **~bewußt** *a* conscious of guilt; **~bewußtsein** *n* consciousness of guilt; **~brief** *m* bond; obligation; promissory note; **~buch** *n* account book; ledger; **~en** *tr* to owe (*jdm etw* s. o. s. th.); to be indebted to; *jdm e-e Summe ~~* to be indebted to s. o. for the sum of; **~enfrei** *a* free from debt; (*dinglich*) unencumbered; **~enhalber** *adv* owing to debts; **~enlast** *f* burden of debt, liabilities *pl*; (*dingliche ~~*) encumbrance; **~enmacher** *m* contractor of debts; **~entilgung** *f* amortization of debt, liquidation of debt; **~erlaß** *m* remission of debt; **~frage** *f* question of guilt; **~gefängnis** *n* debtor's prison; **~haft** *f* imprisonment for debt; *~~ a* guilty; culpable; **~haftung** *f* liability for debt; **~ig** *a* (*strafbar*) guilty (of); (*gebührend*) due; (*Geld*) owing; indebted; (*zu bezahlen*) due, unpaid; (*verpflichtet*) bound, obliged; *sich ~~ bekennen* to plead guilty; *für ~~ befinden jur* to rule guilty; *~~ sein* to be guilty of; *~~ sprechen jur* to find guilty; *jdm etw ~~ sein* to owe s. o. (a sum); *jdm Dank ~~ sein für* to be obliged to s. o. for; to be indebted to s. o. for; *keine Antwort ~~ bleiben* never to be at a loss for an answer, to give as good as one gets; *was bin ich Ihnen ~~?* how much do I owe you? **~ige(r)** *m* culprit; (*Geld*) debtor; *jur* guilty party; *wie wir vergeben unsern ~~n* as we forgive them that trespass against us; **~igerkennung** *f jur* conviction; **~igkeit** *f* (*Pflicht*) duty; (*Verpflichtung*) obligation; *seine ~~ tun* to do o.'s part, *fam* to keep o.'s end; *es ist meine verdammte Pflicht u. ~~ . . .* it is my damned duty to . . .; **~los** *a* innocent, not guilty; guiltless; faultless; **~losigkeit** *f* innocence, guiltlessness; **~ner** *m*, **~in** *f* debtor; (*Hypothek*) mortgager; **~~land** *n* debtor nation; **~posten** *m com* debit item; **~schein** *m* promissory note; I. O. U. (= I owe you); bond; *Am* debenture; note of hand; **~spruch** *m jur* verdict of guilty; finding of guilty; **~umwandlung** *f* conversion of debts; **~verpflichtung** *f* liability; obligation; **~verschreibung** *f* promissory note; I. O. U.; bond; debenture stock; *Am* debenture (bond); **~versprechen** *n* promise to pay.

Schüler *m* pupil; schoolboy; *fam* (*Elementar~*) scholar; *Am* (*Oberschule*) (high-school) student; (*e-s Lehrganges*) trainee; (*Jünger*) disciple, follower; *fig* (*Anfänger, Neuling*) novice, tyro; *ehemaliger ~ e-r Schule* old boy; *Entlaß~* school-leaver; *ein fahrender ~* an itinerant scholar; **~arbeit** *f* task, exercise; tyro's work; **~austausch** *m* exchange of pupils; **~ausschuß** *m* student council; **~ball, ~tanz** *m* college (*od* school) dance, *Am* prom(enade); **~bibliothek** *f* school library; **~haft** *a* boy-like; (*unreif*) immature, inexperienced; (*ungeschickt*) blundering; bungling; **~heim** *n* hostel; boarding school; **~in** *f* schoolgirl, schoolmaid; pupil; **~selbstverwaltung** *f Am* government organization (*Abk* G.O.); **~speisung** *f* school relief meal(s), *Am* school lunch; **~sprache** *f* school slang; **~streich** *m* schoolboy's prank; **~tanzabend** *m* class-dance, *Am fam* prom.

Schulter *f* shoulder; *anat* humerus; *~ an ~* shoulder to shoulder; (*dichtgedrängt*) closely packed; *breite ~n haben* to have a broad back; *etw auf die leichte ~ nehmen* to make light of; *jdm die kalte ~ zeigen* to turn the cold shoulder on s. o.; to give s. o. the cold shoulder; *mit der ~ zucken* to shrug o.'s shoulder; *Wasser auf beiden ~n tragen fig* to blow hot and cold; *mit bloßen ~n* bare-shouldered; *mit gebeugten ~n* stoop-shouldered; **~band** *n anat* ligament of shoulder joint; **~bein** *n anat* shoulder-bone; humerus; **~blatt** *n* shoulder blade, scapula; **~breite** *f* breadth of the shoulders; **~decker** *m aero* mid-wing monoplane; high-wing monoplane; **~gegend** *f* scapular region; **~gelenk** *n* shoulder joint; **~frei** *a* (*Kleid*) strapless, off-the-shoulder (frock); **~höhe** *f anat* acromion; **~klappe** *f mil* (*Mannschaft*) shoulder-strap; **~n** *tr* to shoulder; **~polster** *n* shoulder pad; **~punkt** *m* shoulder point; **~riemen** *m mil* shoulder belt, crossbelt; **~stück** *n mil* (*Offiziers~~*) shoulder-strap; epaulet; *tech* (*bei M.G.*) shoulder piece; **~stütze** *f mil* (*bei M.G.*) support; **~verrenkung** *f* dislocation of the shoulder; **~wehr** *f* breastwork, traverse.

Schultheiß, Schulze *m* village mayor.

schummeln *itr fam* to cheat.

Schummer *m* (*Dämmerung*) twilight, dusk; **~ig** *a* dusky; **~n** *itr, tr* to become dusky; to dawn; (*Karten*) to shade; **~ung** *f* (*bei Karten*) hatching, hachures *pl*.

Schund *m* trash; (*Abfall*) refuse, waste; rubbish, junk; garbage; (*Tuch*) shoddy; **~artikel** *m* catchpenny article; **~literatur** *f* trashy literature; **~preis** *m* vile price; **~roman** *m* penny-dreadful, shilling shocker; pot-boiler; *Am* dime-novel; **~~verfasser** *m* pot-boiler; **~waren** *f pl* trashy (*od* low-class) goods *pl*; slop-made goods *pl*; shoddy wares *pl*.

schunkeln *itr* (*schaukeln*) to seesaw; (*sich wiegen*) to move to and fro; to rock.

Schupf, Schupp *m* (*Stoß*) shove, push; **~en, schup(p)sen** *tr* (*stoßen*) to shove, to push.

Schupo *f* (= *Schutzpolizei*) police (-force); *~ m* (= *Schutzpolizist*) policeman, constable; *fam* Bobby, *Am* cop.

Schüppe *f* (= *Schippe*) shovel, scoop; (*Kartenspiel*) spades *pl*.

Schupp|e *f zoo* scale, scute; (*Haut*) flake, scale; (*Kopf~en*) scurf, dandruff; *bot* squama; *die ~en fallen ihm von den Augen fig* the scales fall from his eyes; *es fiel ihm wie ~en von den Augen fig* his eyes were opened; **~en** *tr* to (un)scale; to scrape; *sich ~~* to peel off; **~~artig** *a* scaly; squamous; **~~nbildung** *f* flaking; **~~neidechse** *f* scaly lizard; **~~nfisch** *m* scaly fish; **~~nflechte** *f med* psoriasis; **~~nflügler** *m pl* lepidopters *pl*; **~~nförmig** *a* scaly; (*wie Dachziegel*) imbricated; **~~ngrind** *m med* dandruff, scurf of scalp; **~~nhaut** *f*, **~~nkleid** *n* scaly skin; **~~nkrankheit** *f med* lichthyosis; **~~npanzer** *m hist* coat of mail; **~~ntier** *n* scaly animal; *zoo* ant-eater; **~ig** *a* scaly, scaled; flaky; squamous; *bot* scaly foliated; (*dachziegelartig*) imbricated.

Schuppen *m* shed, hut; shelter; *Am* shack; (*Scheune, Am auch Vieh~*) barn; (*Vorrats~*) warehouse; (*Wagen~*) coach-house; (*Auto~*) garage; (*Flugzeug~*) hangar; (*Lokomotiv~*) engine-house, *Am* roundhouse.

Schur *f* shearing; (*Wolle*) fleece; (*Hecke etc*) clipping; cropping; *fig fam* (*Quälerei, Neckerei*) trouble, vexation.

Schür|eisen *n* poker, fire-iron; rake, stoker; **~en** *tr* (*Feuer im Ofen*) to poke (the fire); to stir (up), to stoke; to rake; to rabble; *fig* (*Streit, Zwietracht*) to incite, to fan, to stir up; **~er** *m* (*Heizer*) stoker; poker; *fig* (*Aufrührer*) fomenter; inciter; **~haken** *m* poker, fire-hook; **~loch** *n* fire-hole; door; poke-hole, stirring hole.

Schurf *m min* (*Grubenloch*) digging, searching; trial pit; opening; (*Schramme*) scratch, abrasion; **~bohrung** *f* (*Öl*) *Am* wildcat; **~grube** *f* test pit; **~loch** *n min* prospect hole; **~schacht** *m* exploration shaft.

Schürf|arbeit *f min* prospecting work; **~befugnis** *f* authority to prospect; **~en** *tr* (*schrammen, kratzen*) to scratch; to cut; to scrape; *min* to prospect (*nach* for); to explore; to search; to dig; *tief ~end fig* thorough; **~er** *m min* prospector; searcher; **~ung** *f* (*Schramme, Hautab~~*) scratch, abrasion, scraping; *min* prospecting, digging, search; **~wunde** *f* abrasion; flesh-wound.

Schurigel|ei *f fam* vexation; **~n** *tr fam* to vex, to trouble; to nag; to plague; to worry.

Schurk|e *m* villain, rascal, rogue; scoundrel, *Am fam* tough, hoodlum, hooligan, highbinder; **~enstreich** *m*, **~erei** *f* villainy, rascality; dirty trick, *Am* skulduggery; **~isch** *a* rascally.

Schurre *f* slide, chute; runway; **~n** *itr* to glide along; to slide down; to rush down.

Schurz *m* apron; (*Lenden~*) kilt; *arch* chimney mantel; **~fell** *n* leather apron.

Schürze *f* apron; (*Kinder~*) pinafore; *fam fig* female, petticoat, wench; *sich e-e ~ umbinden* to put on an apron; *jeder ~ nachlaufen* to run after every petticoat; **~n** *tr* to tuck up, (*hochheben*) to pick up; (*knüpfen*) to tie; *den Knoten ~n fig* to entangle the plot; **~nband** *n* apron-string; **~njäger** *m* girlchaser, skirtchaser, *sl* mash(er), *Am sl* wolf, chickchaser, knave of hearts, playboy.

Schuß *m* (*mit e-r Waffe*) shot; (*Knall*) report; blast; (*Sprengladung*) charge; (*Salve, Ladung*) round; (*Schußwunde*) gunshot wound, bullet wound; (*Fußball, Tor~*) shot (for goal); *bot* (*Trieb, Schößling*) sprout, shoot; (*Weberei*) weft, woof; filling; (*Bäckerei*) batch (of bread); (*Schilaufen, Schußfahrt*) schuss; (*Schwung, rasche Bewegung*) rapid motion (*od* movement), rush; (*Hoch-, Aufschießen*) shooting; (*kleine Menge e-r Flüssigkeit zum Zugießen*) (a) dash (of); *ein ~ Wein* a dash of wine; *die Lehre vom ~* (*mil*) ballistics *pl mit sing*; *blinder ~* blank firing; *direkter ~* aimed (*od* direct) shot; *im direkten ~* point-blank; *scharfer ~* shot with ball; *in vollem ~* in full swing; *weit vom ~* wide of the mark; far from the danger zone; *~ ins Blaue* random shot; shot in the air; *~ ins Schwarze* (shot into the) bull's eye; *er ist keinen ~ Pulver wert fig* he is not worth his salt; *Am fam* he isn't worth a shot, to fire a round; *es fiel ein ~* a shot was fired; *in ~ bringen* to bring into working order; *in ~ kommen* to rush along; (*in Ordnung bringen*) to get into working order; *vor den ~ kommen* (*Jagd*) to come within shot; *nicht jeder ~ trifft* not every shot tells; *im ~ sein* (*im Gang sein*) to be in full swing; *im Schusse* at full speed; **~abstand** *m* shooting distance; **~bahn** *f* trajectory; **~beobachtung** *f* spotting; **~bereich** *m* effective range; zone of fire; *im ~~* within range; **~bereit** *a* ready to fire; **~ebene** *f* firing plane; **~elemente** *n pl* firing data *pl*; **~entfernung** *f* range; **~faden** *m* (*Weberei*) weft, shoot; warp thread; **~fahrt** *f* (*Schilauf*) schuss, schussing; *in ~~ abfahren* to schuss; *in ~~ den Hang hinabfahren* to schuss down the slope; *~~ üben* to practice schussing; **~feld** *n* field of fire; range; *das ~~ freimachen* to clear the field of fire; **~fertig** *a* ready to fire; ready for action; **~fest** *a* bullet-proof, shell-proof; **~folge** *f* rate of fire; **~freudig** *a* (*schießlustig*) eager to shoot; *mil sl* trigger-happy; **~garbe** *f* cone of range; **~gerecht** *a* (*Jagd*) sportsmanlike; (*Pferd*) trained to stand fire; **~höhe** *f* maximum vertical ceiling; **~kanal** *m med* (*Wunde*) track of gunshot wound; path of projectile; **~leistung** *f* gun efficiency, firing efficiency; **~linie** *f* line of fire, firing line (*od* zone); line of sight; **~loch** *n* shot-hole; **~öffnung** *f* bullet hole; **~richtung** *f* direction of fire; line of fire; **~sicher** *a* bullet-proof, shot-proof; shell-proof; *~~e Deckung* shell-proof cover; *~~er Betriebstofftank aero* self-sealing fuel tank, bullet-proof fuel tank; leak-proof (*od* fuel-tight) tank; **~tafel** *f* range (*od* firing) table; **~verbesserung** *f* shooting correction; **~verletzung** *f* gunshot injury; gunshot wound; **~waffe** *f* fire-arm; *~~n f pl* fire-arms *pl*, small arms *pl*; **~wechsel** *m* exchange of shots *pl*; **~weise** *adv* by jerks; **~weite** *f* (shooting) range; *außer ~~* out of range; *in* (*od innerhalb*) *~~* within range; **~werte** *m pl* firing data *pl*; **~winkel** *m* angle of firing; departure; **~wirkung** *f* fire (*od* firing) effect; **~wunde** *f* gunshot wound, bullet wound; **~zahl** *f* number of rounds; **~zeichen** *n* hit mark.

Schussel *f fam* (*fahriger Mensch*) fussy person; **~ig** *a fam* fussy; *Am sl* jittery; **~n** *itr fam* to haste, to walk in flurried haste.

Schüssel *f* dish; (*Suppen~*) tureen; (*flache*) platter; (*Schale*) pan; (*Napf*) bowl; basin; (*Gericht*) dish (of); plate (of); bowl (of); *e-e ~ Fleisch* a dish of meat; *e-e ~ Milch* a bowl of milk; **~brett** *n* plate-drainer; **~förmig** *a* dish-shaped; bowl-shaped; **~flechte** *f bot* leaf-lichen; **~gestell** *n* plate-rack; **~schrank** *m* dresser; **~wärmer** *m* dish-warmer.

Schusser *m* marble, taw.

Schuster *m* shoemaker; (*Flick~*) cobbler; *auf ~s Rappen* on Shanks' pony, on foot; *~, bleib bei deinem Leisten* cobbler stick to your last; **~ahle** *f* awl; **~arbeit** *f* shoemaking; **~brust** *f med* funnel breast; **~draht** *m* twine; **~junge** *m* shoemaker's apprentice; **~kneif** *m* paring-knife; **~n** *tr* to make shoes; to cobble; **~pech** *n* cobbler's wax; **~werkstatt** *f* shoemaker's workshop.

Schute *f mar* lighter, barge.

Schutt *m* (*Abfall, Kehrricht*) rubbish, refuse, garbage; waste; sweeping; (*Trümmer*) rubble, debris, ruins *pl*; *~ abladen* to deposit rubble; *~ abladen verboten!* No trash! *~ wegräumen* to clear rubble, to work at rubble clearing; *in ~ u. Asche legen* to lay in ruins and ashes; **~abladeplatz** *m* refuse dump; trash dump; garbage dump; city dump; *Am* (public) dumping ground; **~ablagerung** *f* accumulation of debris; (*geologisch*) detrital deposit; **~aufräumung** *f* rubble clearance (*od* clearing); **~~skommando** *n* rubble and debris detail; **~halde** *f min* (*Gehänge*) scree; talus; slope covered with rock debris; **~haufen** *m* rubbish (*od* dust) heap; dump; rubble heap; *in e-n ~~ verwandeln* to lay in ruins; **~karren** *m* dust-cart; **~kegel** *m* debris cone; talus fan; **~ramme** *f* bulldozer.

Schütt|beton *m* heaped (*od* poured) concrete; **~boden** *m* (*für Getreide*) corn-loft, granary; **~damm** *m* earth bank; embankment; **~e** *f* (*Bündel Stroh etc*) bundle, truss; *aero* (*für Brandbomben*) container, frame (for incendiary bombs); **~elapparat** *m* shaker; **~elbewegung** *f* shaking motion; **~elflasche** *f* emulsion test flask; shaker; **~elfrost** *m* shivering (*od* cold) fit; the shivers *pl*; (shaking) chill; rigor; **~elkrampf** *m* shaking spasm; **~eln** *tr* to shake; (*stark*) to toss, to churn, to rock; (*hin u. her*) to agitate, to vibrate, to oscillate; (*Wagen*) to jostle, to jog, to joggle; (*Pferd*) to jounce; *sich ~~* to tremble, to shiver; *jdm die Hand ~~* to shake hands with s. o., to shake s. o.'s hand; *mit dem Kopf ~~* to shake o.'s head; (*wackeln*) to wag o.'s head; *aus dem Ärmel ~~* (*fig*) to shake s. th. out of o.'s sleeve; to extemporize; to produce offhand; *die Faust ~~* to shake o.'s fist; *den Staub von den Füßen ~~* (*fig*) to shake off the dust from o.'s feet; *vor Gebrauch ~~!* shake before using! **~elreim** *m* spoonerism; limerick; **~elrost** *m* shaking grate; **~elrutsche** *f* shaking shoot; shaking trough; **~elsieb** *n* shaking sieve (*od* screen); grizzly; **~elverfahren** *n* vibration method; **~elvorrichtung** *f* shaking gear; **~en** *tr, itr* to shed, to cast; (*Korn*) to shoot; (*aufhäufen*) to heap (up); (*werfen*) to throw; (*verteilen*) to distribute; (*gießen*) to pour (out); (*ver~~*) to spill; (*auffüllen*) to fill, to charge; *es schüttet* (*Regen*) it pours down; it is pouring with rain; **~er** *a* (*dünn*) thin, sparse; thinly scattered; **~ergebiet** *n* (*geol*) region of disturbance; **~ern** *itr* to shake, to tremble, to be shaken; **~gewicht** *n* bulk weight; bulk density; **~gut** *n* bulk (*od* loose) material; bulk goods *pl*; **~~wagen** *m rail* hopper car; **~kasten** *m aero* (*für Bomben*) cluster box (for dropping bombs); *~~weise abwerfen* (*Bomben*) to drop in clusters; **~klappe** *f* chute trap; **~ladung** *f* shipment in bulk; **~rinne** *f* chute; **~stein** *m* rubble; (*Küchenausguß*) sink; **~trichter** *m* discharge funnel; **~ung** *f* (*Auf~~*) fill; pouring; (*Schotterung*) ballast(ing); **~vorrichtung** *f* charging apparatus; **~wurf** *m aero* (*mit Bomben*) salvo release.

Schutz *m* protection (*gegen* from); (*Verteidigung*) defence, *Am* defense; (*Schirm*) screen, shield; guard; (*Obdach*) shelter, refuge; (*Deckung*) cover; (*Schutzgeleit*) safeguard; (*Sorge*) care, keeping; *tech* (*Wärme~*) isolation, insolation; *~ u. Schild* help and shield; *~~ u. Trutzbündnis* offensive and defensive alliance; *im ~ der Nacht* under cover of night; *~ vor Regen suchen* to take shelter from the rain; *unter dem ~ von* under the aegis of; *~ gewähren* to harbo(u)r, to give protection; to grant asylum; *in ~ nehmen* to take under o.'s protection; to defend, to come to s. o.'s defence; to vindicate (*gegen* against); *~ suchen* to take shelter (*bei* with, *vor* from), to **take refuge with** s. o.; *~ u. Zuflucht suchen* to seek sanctuary in; **~anstrich** *m* (*gegen Rost*) protective coat(ing); *mil* (*zur Tarnung*) camouflage; *mar* baffle paint, dazzle paint; **~anzug** *m* protective clothes *pl*; (*Fallschirmjäger*) protective uniform; **~ärmel** *m* sleeve protector; **~befohlene** *f*, **~~(r)** *m* charge; protégé(e *f*); ward; client; **~blatt** *n* (*Buch*) fly-leaf; **~blattern** *pl* cow-pox; **~blech** *n* guard; *mot* mudguard; wing; *Am* fender; **~brief** *m* (letter of) safe-conduct; **~brille** *f* (a pair of) protective goggles *pl*; protective glasses *pl*; safety goggles *pl*; **~bügel** *m* bow-wing skid; **~bündnis** *n* defensive alliance; **~dach** *n* protective roof; shed, shelter; penthouse; (*an Baugerüst*) rigger; **~decke** *f* cover(ing); **~deckel** *m* cover; dust cap; carton; **~engel** *m* guardian angel; **~erdung** *f el* protector ground; **~färbung** *f zoo, orn* protective colo(u)ring; **~frist** *f* term of copyright; **~gatter** *n* (*Wehr*) flood-gate; (*Gitter*) barrier; **~gebiet** *n* protectorate; *Am* (*Reservat*) reservation; *~~e pl* dependencies *pl*; *Natur~~* nature reserves *pl*; **~geist** *m* (tutelary) genius; **~geländer** *n* guard rail, parapet; **~geleit** *n* safe-conduct; escort; *mar* convoy; *aero* air cover; **~gitter** *n* (barrier) guard; *mot* (radiator) grille; *radio* screen grid; **~glas** *n* protective glass; **~glocke** *f* globe; *aero mil* fighter umbrella; **~gott** *m* tutelary god; **~gürtel** *m* protective belt, defence belt; **~hafen** *m* harbo(u)r of refuge; **~haft** *f* protective custody; preventive arrest (*od* detention); **~haube** *f* cover; *mot* bonnet; *aero* cockpit cover; **~heilige** *f*, **~~(r)** *m* patron saint; **~helm** *m* protective helmet; **~herr** *m* protector; patron; **~~in** *f* protrectress; patroness; **~herrschaft** *f* protectorate; **~hülle** *f* sheath;

protective covering; (*Decke*) tarpaulin; (*Kabel*) casing; (*Buch*) cardboard case; **~hütte** *f* shelter hut; refuge; **~impfung** *f* protective inoculation; **~insel** *f* (*Straßenverkehr*) street island; refuge; **~kappe** *f* protecting cap; **~karton** *m* case; cardboard box; **~kleidung** *f* protecting clothes *pl*; **~leiste** *f* protection strip; **~los** *a* unprotected; defenceless; **~macht** *f* protecting power; **~mann** *m* policeman, constable, *Am* patrolman; *fam* bobby, *Am* cop; **~~schaft** *f* police, constabulary; **~marke** *f* trade-mark; *eingetragene ~~* registered trade-mark; **~maßregel** *f* protective measure, preventive measure; **~mauer** *f* screen wall; bulwark; **~mittel** *n* preservative (*gegen* against), preventive (*gegen* of); prophylactic; **~patron** *m* patron saint; **~pocken** *f* cow-pox; **~~impfung** *f* vaccination; **~polizei** *f* protecting police; (municipal) police; constabulary; *Am* city police force; **~präparat** *n* preservative; **~raum** *m* (*LS-Raum*) air-raid shelter; (*gegen Atombomben*) atomic bomb shelter; *unterirdischer ~~* underground shelter; *den ~~ aufsuchen* to go to shelter; **~rechte** *n pl* patent rights *pl*, trade-mark rights *pl*; **~scheibe** *f mot* windscreen, *Am* windshield; **~schicht** *f* protective layer; safety film; **~schild** *m* protective shield; blast screen; **~staffel** *f aero* protection flight, *Am* home-defense squadron; **~truppe** *f* colonial force; force guarding occupied territory; **~überzug** *m* protective coating (*od* film); **~umschlag** *m* (*Buch*) wrapper; jacket; dust cover; **~verband** *m* protective dressing; **~vereinigung** *f* protective association; **~verkleidung** *f* protective covering; **~vorrichtung** *f* safety device; **~wache** *f* escort, safeguard; **~waffe** *f* defensive weapon; **~wand** *f* protective screen; *mil* rampart; **~wehr** *f* fence; *mil* bulwark, defence (work); (*Wasserbau*) lock-weir; sluice; **~wirkung** *f* protective effect; **~zoll** *m* protective duty, *Am* protective tariff; **~zöllner** *m* protectionist; **~zollsystem** *n* protective system; **~zone** *f* protective zone; (*gegen Versteppung in USA.*) shelter-belt.

Schütz *n el* (*Relais*) relay; contactor; **~e** *f* (*Falle*) flood-gate; (*Schleusen~~*) sash gate; sluice-board; (*Weberschiffchen*) shuttle.

Schütz\|e *m* shot, marksman; (*Bogen~~*) archer; (*Jäger*) huntsman; *mil* rifleman; private; (*Scharf~~*) sharpshooter; (*M.G.~~*) machine-gunner; *astr* Sagittarius, the Archer; **~en** *tr* to protect (*gegen* against); (*verteidigen*) to defend (*gegen* against); (*behüten*) to guard; (*bewahren*) to preserve (*vor* from); (*schirmen*) to screen, to shield; (*sichern*) to secure; (*gegen Witterungseinflüsse etc*) to shelter; *sich ~~ gegen* to protect o. s. from, to guard o. s. against; *Gott ~e dich!* God protect you! **~end** *a* protective; preservative; prohibitory; tutelary; **~enfest** *n* shooting-match; **~enfeuer** *n mil* independent fire, rifle fire; **~engefecht** *n mil* skirmish; **~engilde** *f* rifle-corps, rifle-association; **~engraben** *m mil* trench; dugout; **~~geschütz** *n* trench gun; **~~krieg** *m* trench warfare; **~~spiegel** *m* trench periscope; **~engruppe** *f mil* section of riflemen; **~enhaus** *n* club-house of a rifle club; **~enkette** *f mil* skirmishees *pl*, skirmish line; **~enkompanie** *f* infantry company, rifle company; **~enkönig** *m* champion shot; **~enlinie** *f* firing line, skirmish line; line of riflemen in extended order; **~enloch** *n mil* foxhole; rifle-pit; **~enmine** *f mil* anti-personnel mine; **~enmulde** *f mil* skirmisher's trench; **~ennest** *n mil* group of entrenched riflemen; **~enpanzerwagen** *m mil* armo(u)red troop-carrier; **~enreihe** *f mil* file of riflemen; **~enschleier** *m mil* infantry screen; covering party; **~enschnur** *f mil* markmanship fourragère; **~enzug** *m mil* rifle platoon; **~ling** *m* charge; protégé(e *f*).

schwabb\|eln *itr* (*schwanken*) to wabble, to wobble; (*überfließen*) to slop over; *fam* (*schwätzen*) to twaddle, to babble; *tech* (*polieren*) to buff; **~elig** *a* shaky, wobbly; **~elscheibe** *f* buffing wheel, buff.

Schwabber *m* mop, swab; **~n** *itr* to swab; to try with a mop.

Schwabe *m* Swabian; **~** *f fam* (*Küchenschabe*) cockroach; **~n, ~nland** *n* Swabia; **~nalter** *n* the age of forty; years of wisdom; **~nstreich** *m* tomfoolery; trick.

schwäb\|eln *itr* to speak in Swabian dialect; **~in** *f* Swabian; **~isch** *a* Swabian; *die ~~e Alb* the Swabian Alb; *das ~~e Meer* the Lake of Constance.

schwach *a* (*körperlich*) weak; (*zart*) delicate; tender; debile; (*geistig*) imbecile; (*kraftlos*) feeble; feckless; (*hinfällig*) infirm; (*altersschwach*) decrepit; (*zer-, gebrechlich*) frail; (*unzureichend*) scanty; sparse; (*machtlos*) powerless; (*dünn*) thin; slender; (*armselig*) meagre, *Am* meager, poor; (*wenig, jung*) little, small; (*gering*) slight; light; ineffective; *com* (*flau*) weak; dull; (*leicht, matt, kraftlos*) faint; (*Ton, Licht*) faint; *~e Ähnlichkeit* remote resemblance; *~e Augen* weak (*od* poor) eyes; *~er Augenblick* moment of weakness; *~ auf den Beinen sein* to be shaky; *~er Beweis* poor argument; *~es Bier* small beer; *sich gegen jds Bitten ~ zeigen* to yield to s. o.'s entreaties; *e-e ~e Entschuldigung* a lame excuse; *~es Gedächtnis* bad (*od* poor) memory; *ein ~es Gedicht* a poor piece of poetry; *~e Hoffnung* faint hope; *e-e ~e Kurve* a gentle turn; *~es Licht* dim light; *ein ~er Magen* a weak stomach; *~er Puls* low pulse; *~e Seite* (*charakterlich*) a foible; *fig* weak point; *e-e ~e Stunde* the frailty of a moment, an unguarded moment; *ein ~er Trost* a poor consolation; *ein ~er Versuch* a feeble (*od* mild) attempt; *~es Zeitwort* weak verb; *mir wird ~, ich fühle mich ~* I feel faint; I feel low; *es wurde ihr ~* she fainted; *~ (od schwächer) werden* to get weak; (*Kräfte*) to decline, to decay; to fail; (*Ton*) to die away; **~heit** *f* (*allgemein*) weakness; (*sittlich*) frailty; (*Kraftlosigkeit*) feebleness; **~herzig** *a* faint-hearted; **~kopf** *m* dunce, blockhead; simpleton; imbecile; *fam* flat, *Am fam* saphead, sap; **~köpfig** *a* dull, silly; imbecile; weak-headed; **~matikus** *m* weakling; **~motorig** *a* low-powered; **~sichtig** *a* weak-eyed; dimsighted; amblyoptic; **~~keit** *f* amblyopia; **~sinn** *m* feeblemindedness, weakness of mind; **~sinnig** *a* weak-minded, feeble-minded; imbecile; *Am* moron; **~~e(r)** *m* half wit, feeble-minded person, *Am* moron, ament; **~~keit** *f* weak-mindedness; dementia; **~strom** *m el* weak current; low-tension current, low-voltage current; **~~technik** *f* light-current engineering; communication art, *Am* signal engineering.

Schwäch\|e *f* weakness; feebleness; (*Geistes~*) imbecility; (*Gebrechen*) infirmity; debility; invalidity; (*Impotenz*) impotence, impotency; (*des Charakters*) foible; failing; weakness; weak points *pl*; (*Fehlerhaftigkeit*) defectiveness; (*Dünnheit*) thinness; slenderness; slightness; (*Ton, Licht*) faintness; *das ist e-e ~~ von ihr* that is her weak side; **~en** *tr* (*körperlich*) to weaken; (*entkräften*) to debilitate; to enfeeble; to enervate; (*vermindern, verringern*) to lessen, to diminish; to attenuate; (*mildern*) to tone down; (*schädigen*) to impair; (*abstumpfen*) to blunt; (*Ton*) to mute; (*Licht*) to absorb; **~lich** *a* weak, feeble; (*zart*) delicate; (*kränklich*) infirm; sickly; **~~keit** *f* infirmity; feebleness; delicacy; **~ling** *m* weakling; mollycoddle, *Am fam* sissy, sis; **~ung** *f* weakening; (*Verminderung*) attenuation.

Schwaden *m* (*Heu- od Getreide~*) swath (of mowed corn *od* grass); (*Dunst*) damp, vapo(u)r; *min* (*Feuer~*) fire-damp; (*erstickende*) choke-damp; (*Gas~*) gas cloud; (*Rauch~*) cloud of smoke; layer of smoke; (*Rauchschleier*) smoke-screen; **~rechen** *m* (*Heurechen*) side rake; **~schießen** *n mil* (*Gaskrieg*) surprise gas attack.

schwadern *itr fam* to prate, to prattle.

Schwadron *f* squadron; **~eur** *m* talker; gas-bag; swaggerer; **~ieren** *itr* to talk much at random; to jaw.

schwafeln *itr fam* to talk nonsense.

Schwager *m* brother-in-law; *fam* (*Postkutscher*) postillion.

Schwäger\|in *f* sister-in-law; **~schaft** *f* affinity (*od* relations) by marriage.

Schwalbe *f* swallow; *e-e ~ macht noch keinen Sommer* one swallow doesn't make a summer; **~nnest** *n* swallow's nest; *aero* (*M.G.-Stand*) blister; gun turret; **~~bildung** *f* honeycomb formation; **~nschwanz** *m* (*Schmetterling*) swallow-tail; (*Frack*) dress-coat; *Am* swallowtail; (*Tischlerei*) dovetail; **~~förmig** *a* dovetailed; **~~lafette** *f mil* split-trail; **~~verbindung** *f* dovetail joint; dovetailing; **~nwurz** *f bot* milk-plant.

schwalchen *itr* to smo(u)lder.

Schwall *m* swell, crowd, flood; deluge; *ein ~ von Worten fig* a torrent of words; *ein ~ von Fragen fig* a deluge of questions.

Schwamm *m* sponge; (*Pilz*) mushroom; (*Feuer~*) German tinder; (*Schimmelpilz*) fungus; *med* (*Wucherung*) spongy (*od* fungating) growth; fungus; (*Haus~*) dry rot; *~ d(a)rüber!* done with it! wipe it out! *Am* let's forget about it! *fam* skip it! **~artig** *a* sponge-like; spongy; **~fischerei** *f* sponge-fishery; **~gummi** *m* sponge rubber; foamed latex; **~ig** *a* spongy; fungous; fungoid; (*Holz*) rotten, decayed; (*porös*) porous; (*aufgedunsen*) bloated; **~~keit** *f* sponginess; fungosity; **~seife** *f* porous soap.

Schwan *m* swan; (*junger ~*) cygnet; **~engesang** *m fig* swan song; death song; last poem; **~enhals** *m* swan-neck; *tech* goose-neck; **~enhalsförmig** *a* S-shaped; **~enteich** *m* swannery.

schwan\|en *imp: mir ~t, daß ...* I have the presentiment that ...; *mir ~t nichts Gutes* my mind misgives me; *mir ~t etw!* now, I understand!

Schwang *m* swing, vogue; *in ~ kommen* to become the fashion; *im ~e sein* to be in vogue, to prevail.

schwanger *a* pregnant, expectant, enceinte, gravid, *Am* expecting; (*um-*

schreibend) with child; in the family way; in interesting circumstances; *hoch~* far advanced in pregnancy; *mit etw ~ gehen fig* to hatch with s. th.; *mit großen Plänen ~ gehen fig* to labo(u)r with great projects; **~e** *f* pregnant woman; woman with child; **~schaft** *f* pregnancy; gestation, gravidity; being with child; *~~ verhütendes Mittel* contraceptive; **~~sende** *n* term; **~~snarbe** *f* stria after pregnancy; striations of pregnancy; **~~sunterbrechung** *f* interruption of pregnancy; artificial abortion; **~~sverhinderung, ~~sverhütung** *f* contraception, prevention of pregnancy.

Schwänger|er *m* begetter, father; **~n** *tr* to make pregnant; to get with child; (*befruchten*) to impregnate, to fecundate; *chem* to saturate; to impregnate; **~ung** *f* getting with child; impregnation; fecundation; *chem* saturation; **~~sklage** *f jur* charge of affiliation.

Schwank *m* prank; hoax; trick; good joke, jest, drollery; (*kurze, lustige Anekdote*) short anecdote; merry (*od* funny) tale; *theat* farce; **~macher** *m* joker, jester.

schwank *a* (*biegsam wie z. B. Rohr*) pliable, flexible; supple; pliant; (*schwach, dünn, schlank*) slender; slim; *fig* (*unsicher, wankend*) unsteady, wavering; uncertain; **~en** *itr* (*wanken*) to stagger; (*torkeln, wackeln*) to totter; (*taumeln*) to reel; (*wellenartig*) to undulate; (*schwingen, pendeln*) to oscillate; (*vibrieren*) to vibrate; (*zittern*) to shake; to tremble; to flutter; (*hin u. her schwingen, wackeln*) to vacillate; (*neigen, biegen, wiegen*) to sway; (*schaukeln*) to rock; (*schlingern, stoßen*) to toss, to be tossed; (*rollen*) to roll; (*stampfen*) to pitch; (*gieren*) to yaw; *com* (*auf u. ab von Preisen, Kursen etc*) to fluctuate; (*sich ändern*) to vary, to change; (*Flamme*) to flicker; *fig* (*zögern, zaudern*) to waver, to falter; to hesitate; to vacillate; to be irresolute; to shilly-shally, *Am* to back and fill; *zwischen zwei Parteien ~~* to seesaw, *Am* to sit on the fence; **~en** *n* staggering; undulation; oscillation, oscillating motion; shaking, rocking; fluttering; (*Preise, Kurse*) fluctuation; *fig* (*Zaudern, Zögern*) hesitation; vacillation; inconstancy; fickleness; **~end** *a* tottering, staggering; wavering; (*unsicher*) uncertain, unsteady; (*unbestimmt*) vague; unsettled; (*Preise, Kurse*) fluctuating; unsettled; (*wankelmütig*) fickle; unprincipled; undecided; vacillating; *~~er Charakter* waverer; *e-e ~~e Haltung einnehmen* to play a waiting game, *Am* to sit on the fence; **~ung** *f* (*Preise, Kurse*) fluctuation; *phys* oscillation; vibration; undulation; (*Schiff*) rolling; lurching; pitching; (*Erdachse*) nutation; *fig* irresolution; vacillation.

Schwanz *m* (*Tier~*) tail; *aero* tail, *Am* empennage; (*Kometenschweif, Noten~*) tail; (*Ende*) end; tip; (*Anhang, Gefolge*) train; (*Reihe*) file; *Lafetten~*) trail; (*Fuchs*) brush; (*Wolf*) stern; *vulg* (*Penis*) penis, *vulg* cock; *über den ~ abtrudeln* to tailspin; *den ~ abschneiden* to cut off the tail; *den ~ zwischen die Beine nehmen fig vulg* to turn tail; to run off; to sneak away; *den ~ hochnehmen aero* to get the tail up; *den ~ e-s Pferdes stutzen* to dock a horse; *mit dem ~ wedeln, mit dem ~ wippen* to wag o.'s tail; **~bein** *n anat* tailbone; **~blech** *n* tail spade; **~ende** *n* tip of the tail; *aero* tail end; **~feder** *f* tail feather; **~fläche** *f aero* tail surface; *Am* empennage; **~flosse** *f* tail fin; **~gesteuert** *a aero* tail-controlled; **~kufe** *f aero* tailskid; **~landung** *f aero* tail landing; **~last** *f aero* tail load; **~lastig** *a aero* tail-heavy; **~leitwerk** *n aero* tail unit, *Am* empennage; **~los** *a* tailless; *~~es Flugzeug* (*Nurflügelflugzeug*) tailless airplane; **~rad** *n aero* tail wheel; **~riemen** *m* crupper; **~säge** *f* bow-saw, whip-saw; **~sporn** *m aero* tailskid; **~steuer** *n aero* rudder; **~stück** *n* (*Fisch*) tail piece; (*Ochsenfleisch*) rump; (*Geschützlafette*) trail; **~wirbel** *m anat* caudal vertebra.

schwänz|eln *itr* to wag o.'s tail; (*Mensch*) to waddle; to strut; *fig* (*schmeicheln*) to wheedle; to fawn upon; **~elpfennig** *m* unlawful profit; **~en** *tr* to provide with a tail; to affix a tail to; *die Schule ~~* to stay away from school, to shirk; *fam* to play truant, to skip classes, *Am* to play hooky; *e-e Stunde ~~* to cut a lesson, to skip a lesson; *Vorlesung ~~* to cut a lecture; *itr* to idle about.

Schwapp *m* flap, slap; *interj* slap! dash! **~eln** *itr* to wobble; *tr* to spill, to spill over, to slop over.

Schwär *m*, **~e** *f* abscess, ulcer; boil; **~en** *n* ulcer; **~en** *itr* to suppurate, to ulcerate, to fester.

Schwarm *m* (*Bienen~, Fliegen~*) swarm; (*Vögel, Wespen*) flight; flock; (*Fische*) shoal; (*Rebhühner*) covey; (*Wachtel*) bevy; (*Herde, Rudel von Tieren*) flock; herd; (*Menge Menschen*) throng; crowd; troop; multitude; (*Haufen, Gruppe*) cluster; (*Trupp Kinder*) troop; *ein ~ Mädchen* a bunch of girls; *mil* (*Schützenlinie*) swarm of skirmishers; *aero mil* section of 5 aircraft; flight of several planes in formation; *fig* (*Liebhaberei, Gegenstand der Liebhaberei*) ideal; fancy; *fam* craze; *fam* **flirt**; **idol**; hero; *sie ist mein ~, ich habe e-n ~ für sie* I adore her; she is my idol; she is my flirt; I have a crush on her; I am gone on her; **~bildung** *f* clustering; **~geist** *m* (*Eiferer, unruhiger Geist*) enthusiast; fanatic; gusher; **~linie** *f mil* extended order; **~weise** *adv* in swarms; in throngs; in crowds.

schwärm|en *itr* (*Bienen*) to swarm; to buzz round; (*umher~*) to rove about; to gad about; to wander; to migrate; to stray; *mil* (*aus~~*) to skirmish; to extend into skirmishing line; (*prassen*) to riot about, to revel; (*träumen, phantasieren*) to daydream; to be lost in daydreams; *~~ für* to be enthusiastic about, *Am* to enthuse about; to be smitten with; to have a crush on, to be gone on; to be crazy about; (*überschwenglich reden*) to gush; (*verehren*) to adore; (*begeistert reden*) to rave (*über* about, *von* of); to gush about; *für die Bühne ~~* to be stage-struck; **~en** *n* swarming; (*Prassen*) rioting; revelry; (*Begeisterung*) enthusiasm; (*Träumer*) daydreaming; revery, *Am* reverie; **~er** *m* (*Prasser*) rioter; reveller; (*Herumstreicher*) rover, wanderer; (*Träumer, Phantast*) visionary; dreamer, daydreamer; (*Enthusiast*) enthusiast; addict (*z. B.* radio addict); (*Liebhaber*) lover, flirt; *eccl* (*Fanatiker*) fanatic; (*Abendschmetterling*) hawk-moth; sphinx-moth; (*Feuerwerk*) (fire) cracker; squib; **~erei** *f* (*Phantasterei*) fancy; (*Träumerei*) daydreaming; *eccl* (*Fanatismus*) fanaticism; (*Prasserei*) revelry; (*Begeisterung*) enthusiasm; zeal; (*Überschwenglichkeit*) ecstasy; gush; (*Ergebenheit*) devotion (*für* to); **~erisch** *a* fanciful, fantastic(al); visionary; (*begeistert*) enthusiastic; (*fanatisch*) fanatic(al); (*überspannt*) eccentric, gushing, gushy; *~~ verehren* to adore s. th.; **~zeit** *f* (*der Bienen*) swarming time.

Schwart|e *f* rind, skin; (*Speck~*) rind of bacon; (*Schweinebraten~*) crackling; (*Schalbrett, ~nbrett*) slab, plank; (*äußere Hülle, Kruste*) covering, crust; *fam* (*altes Buch*) old book; *daß die ~n knacken fig fam* vigorously; **~nbrett** *n* boarding; bolster; **~nmagen** *m* (*Wurst*) collared pork (head); **~ig** *a* thick-skinned.

schwarz *a* black; (*dunkelhäutig, sonnverbrannt*) swarthy; (*sehr ~*) of the deepest dye; (*Wappenkunde*) sable; (*tinten~*) inky; (*ebenholz~*) ebony; (*Gesichtsfarbe*) sunburnt; tanned; tawny; (*geschwärzt*) blackened; (*kohl~*) coal-black; jet(-black); (*rußig*) sooty; smutty; (*Brot*) brown; *fig* (*dunkel*) dark, dusky; (*düster*) gloomy; dismal; (*niedrig, gemein*) wicked, base; *in ~* in black; in mourning; *~ n* black; blackness; (*Wappenkunde*) sable; *mit ~en Augenbrauen* black-browed; *~e Blattern med* smallpox; *~es Brett* black board; notice board; bulletin board; *Am* tack board, billboard; *~e Börse* black bourse; sidewalk exchange; bucket shop; *der ~e Erdteil* Africa; *~e Gedanken* gloomy thoughts; *~en Gedanken nachhängen* to be in a melancholy mood; *~er Kaffee* black (*od* strong) coffee (without milk); *die ~e Kunst* (*Magie*) necromancy; black art; *~e Kugel* (*bei Wahl*) blackball; *~e Liste* blacklist; *auf die ~e Liste setzen* to put on the blacklist, to blacklist; to boycott; *auf der ~en Liste stehen* to be blacklisted; *der ~e Mann* (black) bog(e)y; *das ~e Meer* the Black Sea; *~er Markt* blackmarket; *~ wie die Nacht fam* pitch-dark; *~er Rand an Fingernagel fam* mourning border; *~e Seele fig* black soul; *~er Star med* amaurosis; *~er Tag* black-letter day; *~er Tod* (*Pest*) Black Death; bubonic plague; *e-e ~e Tat* an atrocious crime; a black deed; *~er Undank* black ingratitude; *~e Wäsche fig* dirty linen; *bei jdm ~ angeschrieben sein* to be in s. o.'s black books; *sich ~ ärgern* to burst with spite; *sich alles ~ ausmalen fig* to take a gloomy view of things; *etw ~ ausmalen fig* to give a gloomy view of s. th.; *~ färben* to dye black; *~ importieren* to smuggle in; *sich ~ kleiden* to dress in black; *~ gekleidet sein* to be dressed in black, to wear black; *~ machen* to blacken; *sich ~ machen* to blacken o. s.; to smudge o. s.; *er ist nicht so ~, wie er gemalt wird* he is less black than he is painted; *~ tragen* to wear a black dress; *~sehen fig* to look on the dark side of everything; to be a pessimist; to be afraid; to be gloomy; to take a dim view of; *immer alles ~sehen fig* to see always the dark side of things; to see everything in a bad light; *etw ~ auf weiß haben* to have in black and white; (*gedruckt*) in print; *~ u. weiß gestreift* black and white; *~ u. weiß nicht unterscheiden können* not to know black from white; *~ werden* to blacken; to turn black; *es wird mir ~ vor den Augen* my head begins to swim; *~ gebrannter Whisky* illicitly distilled whisky, *Am fam* moonshine whisky; *~es Brot* brown bread; **~amsel** *f orn* blackbird; **~arbeit** *f* illicit work, blackleg work; non-union labo(u)r; **~äugig** *a* dark-eyed; **~beere** *f* bilberry; **~birke** *f* river birch; **~blau** *a* very dark blue; **~blech** *n* black iron plate; black sheet; **~~tafel** *f* sheet-iron plate; **~blei** *n* black lead; graphite; **~braun** *a* very dark-brown; swarthy; tawny; sunburnt; black-faced; **~brenner** *m* illicit distiller, *Am fam* moonshiner; **~~ei** *f* illicit distillery; **~brot** *n* brown bread; (*Roggenbrot*) (black) rye bread; **~brüchig** *a* black short; **~dorn** *m bot* black thorn; sloe; **~drossel** *f orn* blackbird; **~druck** *m* printing in black; **~e(r)** *m*, **~e** *f* (*Neger, Negerin*) black, negro; blackamoor; colo(u)red (gentle)man; African; *Am fam* dark(e)y; black fellow; (*abfällig*) nigger; Jim Crow; buck nigger; (*Negerin*) colo(u)red woman; negress; *Am fam* black mama; shady lady; (*Amme*) mammy; (*alte Negerin*) duntie; *der ~e* the Devil, old Nick; **~e** *n* black colo(u)r; *ins ~~ spielen* to have a blackish tint; *ins ~~ treffen* to hit the bull's eye; **~erde** *f* black soil; **~farbig** *a* black-colo(u)red; **~färbung** *f* blackening; **~fahren** *itr* to take (*od* to go for) a joy-ride; **~fahrer** *m* joy-rider; (*ohne Fahrschein in Verkehrsmittel*) faredodger; **~fahrt** *f* joy-ride; *e-e ~~ machen* to joy-ride; **~gänger** *m* (*Grenzgänger*) illegal border crosser; **~gelb** *a* very dark yellow; tawny yellow; **~grau** *a* dark grey; **~gestreift** *a* with black stripes; **~handel** *m* blackmarket (-ing), illicit trading; blackmarketeering; *~~ treiben* to carry on illicit trade; to blackmarketeer; **~händler** *m* blackmarketeer, blackmarket dealer; spiv; (*~~ mit Eintrittskarten*) (ticket) scalper; **~holz** *n* blackwood; **~hören** *n* use of an unlicensed wireless set; **~hörer** *m* pirate listener, listener-in (without a licence); clandestine radio listener; **~kauf** *m* illicit purchase; **~kittel** *m* (*Wildschwein*) wild boar; **~kunst** *f* (*Magie*) necromancy; **~künstler** *m* (*Magier*) necromancer, magician; **~markt** *m* black market; **~~händler** *m* black marketeer; blackmarket operator; **~mehl** *n* dark-colo(u)red (rye) flour; low-grade flour; **~pulver** *n* black powder; **~rock** *m* (*abfällig für Priester*) black-coat; *fam* crow; **~rot** *a* dark red; **~schlachten** *n*, **~schlachtung** *f* illegal (*od* illicit) slaughtering of cattle; **~seher** *m* pessimist; scaremonger; *Am* alarmist; *Am fam* calamity howler; **~~ei** *f* pessimism; **~sender** *m* unlicensed transmitter; secret radio station; clandestine (*od* underground) radio transmitter; **~specht** *m orn* black woodpecker; **~weiß** *a* black-and-white; **~~bild** *n* black-and-white picture; **~~fernsehen** *n* black-and-white television; **~~film** *m* black-and-white film; **~~künstler** *m* black-and-white artist; **~~zeichnung** *f* black-and-white drawing; **~wald** *m* Black Forest; **~wasserfieber** *n* blackwater fever; **~wert** *m tele* black-level value; **~wild** *n* wild boars *pl*; (*Birkhühner*) black game; black grouse; **~wurz, ~wurzel** *f bot* viper's grass; scorzonera; comfrey.

Schwärz|e *f* blackness; (*Hautfarbe*) swarthiness; *typ* (*Drucker~~*) printer's ink; *~~ auftragen typ* to (beat the) ink; (*Farbe, Wichse*) black; black dye; blacking; (*Gießerei*) black wash; blackening; *fig* (*Abscheulichkeit, Niedertracht, Bosheit*) atrociousness; heinousness; baseness, meanness; (*Dunkelheit*) darkness; **~en** *tr* to black(en); to make black; *sich ~~* to make o. s. black, to grow black; *fig* (*schlecht machen, verleumden*) to defame; to slander; (*verfinstern*) to darken; to obscure; *typ* to ink; (*Gießerei*) to blackwash; **~lich** *a* blackish, darkish; (*Haut*) swarthy; tawny; *ins ~~e spielen* to incline to black; **~rolle** *f typ* ink roller; **~ung** *f* blackening; *phot* density (of negative); **~~sabstufung** *f phot* density graduation; **~~sbereich** *m phot* density range; **~~sdichte** *f* density.

Schwatz *m* chat, talk; blab; *fam* powwow; **~base, ~liese** *f*, **~maul** *n* tattler, prattler; gossip; chatterbox; *sl* chatterbug; **~en, schwätzen** *itr* (*viel u. unnütz reden*) to talk (glibly); to pour forth; to prate, to chatter, to tattle; to twaddle, to prattle; to blab; to jabber; to gossip; *Am* to chipper, *sl* to yap; to talk nonsense; *ins Blaue hinein ~~* to talk at random; **~haft** *a* talkative; loquacious; garrulous; voluble; effusive; glib; **~~igkeit** *f* loquacity; talkativeness; garrulity; gush; slush; effusiveness; **~sucht** *f* love of gossip; verbosity; *fam* gift of the gab.

Schwätzer *m* talker, chatterer, twaddler; babbler, drivel(l)er, gossip; chatterbox; parrot, jay, *fam* windbag, *Am fam* blatherskite, yap; *sl parl* slangwhanger; **~ei** *f* tattling, gossiping; prattle.

*

Schweb|e *f* suspense; suspension; *in der ~~* undecided; trembling in the balance; *in der ~~ hängen* to be in suspense; to hang; *in der ~~ lassen* to keep in suspense; *in der ~~ sein* to be undecided; *jur* to be pending; **~ebahn** *f* suspension railway, *Am* suspended railroad; (*Drahtseilbahn*) cableway, aerial railway; **~ebaum** *m* (*Turnen*) balancing form; **~efähigkeit** *f* suspension power, floating power; *aero* soaring quality; **~efähre** *f* aerial ferry; **~eflug** *m* (*z. B. Hubschrauber*) hovering; **~eleistung** *f aero* soaring performance; **~en** *itr* to be suspended, to be poised; (*hängen*) to hang; (*in der Luft*) to float (in the air); (*auf der Stelle in der Luft*) to hover; (*nach oben ~~*) to soar; (*hin u. her*) to wave; (*gleiten*) to glide; (*schwimmen*) to swim; *fig* (*noch unentschieden*) to be undecided; *jur* to be pending; *die Sache schwebt noch* the matter is still pending; *vor Augen ~~* to wave (*od* to be) before o.'s eyes; *zwischen Furcht u. Hoffnung ~~* to waver between hope and fear; *in Gefahr ~~* to be in danger; *sie schwebt in Lebensgefahr* her life is in danger; *es schwebt etw in der Luft* there is s. th. in the air; *in Ungewißheit ~~* to be kept in suspense; *auf der Zunge ~~* to have on the tip of o.'s tongue; *das Wort schwebt mir auf der Zunge* the word is on the tip of my tongue; **~end** *a* suspended; hanging; in suspension; *jur* pending; (*in der Luft*) floating, hovering, soaring; *~~e Betonung* level stress; *~~e Frage* pending question; *~~e Schuld* floating debt; *~~er Schritt* elastic step; **~estoffe** *m pl* suspended substance (*od* matter); **~eteilchen** *n* suspended particle; **~stoffilter** *n* filter for suspended substance; mechanical filter; **~ung** *f radio* (*Interferenz*) beat; surge; **~~sempfang** *m radio* beat reception, heterodyne reception; **~~sempfänger** *m* heterodyne receiver; **~~stheorie** *f* beat theory; **~~ston** *m* beat note.

Schwed|e *m*, **~in** *f* Swede; Swedish woman; *alter ~~: fig fam* (*Anrede*) old man! old boy! **~en** *n* Sweden; **~isch** *a* Swedish.

Schwefel *m* sulphur, *Am* sulfur; (*Bibel u. in einigen Verbindungen*) brimstone; **~arm** *a* poor in sulphur; **~artig** *a* sulphur(e)ous; **~äther** *m* sulphuric ether; **~bad** *n* sulphur bath; **~bande** *f fam* band of vagrants; set of rascals; **~blüte** *f* flowers of sulphur; **~bromür** *n* sulphur monobromide; **~erz** *n* sulphur ore; **~faden** *m* sulphured wick; **~farbe** *f* sulphur colo(u)r; **~farbstoff** *m* sulphur dye; **~gehalt** *m* sulphur content; **~gelb** *a* sulphur yellow; **~geruch** *m* sulphur odo(u)r; **~grube** *f* sulphur pit (*od* mine); **~haltig** *a* containing sulphur; sulphur(e)ous; **~holz, ~hölzchen** *n* sulphur match; **~hütte** *f* sulphur refinery; **~ig** *a* sulphur(e)ous; *~~e Säure* sulphur(e)ous acid; **~kammer** *f* sulphur (chamber) stove; **~kies** *m* (iron) pyrites *pl*; **~kohle** *f* high-sulphur coal; **~kohlenstoff** *m* carbon disulphide; **~n** *tr* to sulphurate, to sulphurize; to vulcanize; to dip in brimstone; (*ein Faß*) to match a cask; **~natrium** *n* sodium sulphide; **~niederschlag** *m* precipitate of sulphur; **~quelle** *f* sulphur spring; **~salz** *n* sulphur salt; sulphate; **~sauer** *a* sulphate of; *~~er Kalk* calcium sulphate; **~säure** *f* sulphuric acid; **~~ballon** *m* (*Gefäß*) carboy, demijohn; **~~fabrik** *f* sulphuric acid plant; **~silber** *n* silver sulphide; **~stange** *f* sulphur roll; **~ung** *f* sulphuration; sulphuring; fumigation; sulphur treatment; **~verbindung** *f* sulphur compound; **~wasser** *n* sulphur water; **~wasserstoff** *m* hydrogen sulphide, sulphuretted hydrogen; **~werk** *n* sulphur refinery; **~zink** *n* zinc sulphide; **~zinn** *n* tin sulphide; **schweflig** *a* sulphur(e)ous.

Schweif *m* (*Schwanz*) tail; *fig* (*Gefolge, Schleppe*) train; **~en** *itr* to rove, to wander about; to stroll; to ramble; to roam, to range; *den Blick ~~ lassen* to let o.'s eye travel; *in die Ferne ~~* to stray far away; *tr* to curve; **~säge** fret saw; **~stern** *m* comet; **~ung** *f* curve; sweep; curving, sweeping; (*e-r Glocke*) swell (of a bell); **~wedeln** *itr* to wag the tail; *fig* (*schmeicheln*) to wheedle; to fawn (*vor* upon); to toady; to cajole; **~wedler** *m fig* (*Speichellecker*) toady, fawner.

Schweig|egeld *n* hush-money; **~en** *itr* to keep silence; to be silent; to be quiet; *ganz zu ~~ von* to say nothing of, not to speak of; let alone; (*den Mund halten*) to hold o.'s tongue; *fam* to be mum; (*aufhören*) to cease; *tr* to hush up; *die Sache wurde totgeschwiegen* the affair was hushed up; *~~ Sie!* be quiet! hush! silence! (*grob*) shut up! *~~ wie das Grab* to be as silent as the grave; *zum ~~ bringen* to hush; to calm, to quiet; to pacify; *mil* to silence; **~en** *n* silence; *Reden ist Silber, ~~ ist Gold* speaking is silver, silence is gold; *jdm ~~ auferlegen* to impose silence upon s. o.; **~end** *a* silent; tacit; *sich ~~ verhalten* to keep silence; to hold o.'s tongue; *~~ darüber hinweggehen* to pass s. th. over in silence; *~~ zuhören* to listen in silence; **~epflicht** *f* obligation to be silent (*über* about); (*beruflich*) professional discretion; **~er** *m* taciturn person; **~ezone** *f* shadow region; **~sam** *a* silent, quiet; taciturn; (*zurückhaltend*) reserved; (*verschwiegen*) discreet; **~~keit** *f* taciturnity; discretion.

Schwein *n* pig; *Am meist* hog; (*pl*) swine; (*Fleisch*) pork; *fam* (*Glück*) good luck; lucky hit; *fig* (*Schimpfwort*) dirty person; *wildes ~* wild boar;

~ haben fig fam to have luck, to be in luck, to be lucky; to strike oil; to come off with flying colo(u)rs; to be a lucky dog; **~eborsten** *f pl* hog's bristles *pl*; **~ebraten** *m* roast pork; **~efett** *n* pork-fat, hog-fat; lard; **~efieber** *n* hog fever; **~efleisch** *n* pork; **~efraß** *m* food for pigs; *fig (schlechtes Essen)* filthy grub; **~egalopp** *m fam* lively trott; **~ehals** *m* thick neck; **~ehirt** *m* swineherd; **~ehund** *m (Schimpfwort)* filthy swine; **~ekoben** *m* pigsty; *Am* hog-pen; **~emarkt** *m* hog-market; **~emast** *f* mast for swine; **~emäster** *m* pig-breeder; *Am* hog-raiser, hog-grower; **~epest** *f* swine-fever; **~erei** *f* piggery; *(Unordnung)* mess; *(Schmutz)* dirtiness, filthyness; *(schmutziges Geschäft, gemeine Handlung)* rotten business; dirty trick; dirty thing; **~erne(s)** *n* pork; **~erotlauf** *m* swine erysipelas; **~eschlächter** *m* pork-butcher; **~~ei** *f* pork-butcher's shop; **~eschmalz** *n* hog's lard; **~eschmer** *m* lard; **~eseuche** *f* swine plague; **~estall** *m* pigsty, *Am* hog-pen; **~etreiber** *m* swineherd; **~etrog** *m* pig's trough; **~ewirtschaft** *f fig* dirty mess; **~ezucht** *f* pig-breeding, *Am* hog-growing; **~ezüchter** *m* pig-breeder, *Am* hog-raiser, hog-grower; **~igel** *m* hedgehog; *fig* dirty fellow, *fam* sweep; **~igelei** *f (Zote)* obscenity; filthiness; **~igeln** *itr* to behave in a beastly way; *(Zoten reißen)* to make obscene remarks; **~isch** *a* swinish, piggish; hoggish; *(schmutzig)* dirty; *(zotig)* obscene; **~sblase** *f* pig's bladder; **~sfisch** *m* porpoise, dolphin; **~sfilet** *n* pork fillet; **~sfüße** *m pl* pig's trotters *pl*; **~sjagd** *f* boar-hunt; **~skeule** *f* leg of pork; haunch of a wild boar; **~skopf** *m* hog's head; boar's head; **~skotelett** *n* pork chop; **~sleder** *n* pigskin, hogskin; **~~band** *m* pigskin volume; **~~n** *a* of pigskin; **~srippchen** *n* salted pork chop; **~srücken** *m* pig's back; **~srüssel** *m* pig's snout; **~swurst** *f* pork sausage.

Schweiß *m* sweat; perspiration, transpiration; *(Feuchtigkeitsniederschlag)* moisture, steam; *(Ausschwitzung)* exudation; *fig (Mühe)* toil(ing); hard labo(u)r; drudgery; sweat; *der ~ rann ihm von der Stirne* the sweat was running down his forehead; *der ~ stand ihm auf der Stirne* drops of perspiration stood on his forehead; *in ~ gebadet* wet with perspiration; *in ~ kommen* to get into a perspiration; *im ~e seines Angesichts fig* in the sweat of his brow; *es klebt viel ~ daran, es hat viel ~ gekostet* it has cost a good deal of hard toil; **~absonderung** *f* perspiration, sweating, sudation, transpiration; **~apparat** *m tech* welding apparatus *(od* machine); **~arbeit** *f tech* welding; **~ausbruch** *m* sweating attack, sweats *pl*; **~automat** *m tech* automatic welding machine; **~bar** *a tech* weldable; **~~keit** *f tech* weldability, weldableness; **~bedeckt** *a* covered with perspiration; **~bläschen** *n pl med* sudamina, miliaria; **~blätter** *n pl (im Kleid etc)* dress-preservers *pl*, dress-shields *pl*; **~bogen** *m tech* welding arc; **~brenner** *m tech* welding torch; blowpipe; cutting-off burner; **~brille** *f tech* welding goggles *pl*; **~draht** *m tech* welding rod; **~drüse** *f anat* sweat gland; sudoriferous gland; **~echt** *a (Stoffe)* fast to perspiration; **~elektrode** *f* welding electrode; **~en** *tr tech* to weld; *(Gießerei)* to fuse; *itr (vom Wild)* to bleed; *(Faß, Gefäß)* to leak; **~er** *m tech* welder; welding operator; **~erei** *f tech* welding plant, welding operation; **~fehler** *m tech* defect in welding; **~fieber** *n med* sweating fever, sweating sickness; miliary fever; **~fleck** *m* sweat spot; **~flüssigkeit** *f med* sweat; **~friesel** *m med* sudamina; miliaria; **~fuchs** *m (Pferd)* sorrel (horse); **~fuß** *m* sweaty *(od* perspiring) foot; **~geruch** *m* smell of perspiration; body odo(u)r *(Abk* b. o.); **~hund** *m* bloodhound; sleuthhound; **~ig** *a* sweaty; perspiring; covered with perspiration; *(feucht)* moist; *(Jagd)* bloody; **~leder** *n (im Hut)* hat leather, sweat leather; **~lichtbogen** *m tech* welding arc; **~mittel** *n med* sudorific, diaphoretic; *tech* (welding) flux; **~naht** *f tech* weld(ed) seam; weld; **~ofen** *m tech* welding furnace; **~perle** *f* drop of sweat; *tech* globule; **~pore** *f* sweat pore; **~prozeß** *m* welding process; **~punkt** *m tech* welding point *(od* spot); **~stahl** *m* wrought *od* weld steel; **~stelle** *f* weld; shut; welded joint; **~technik** *f tech* welding technique; **~treibend** *a med* sudorific, diaphoretic; hidrotic; *~~es Mittel* sudorific; **~triefend** *a* sweating, wet with perspiration; **~tropfen** *m* bead of perspiration, drop of sweat; **~tuch** *n (Bibel)* sudarium; **~ung** *f tech* welding, weld; *autogene ~~* autogenous welding; oxyacetylene welding; *elektrische ~~* electrowelding, arc welding; **~verbindung** *f tech* welded joint; **~wolle** *f* greasy wool; wool containing suint.

Schweiz *f* Switzerland; *poet* Helvetia; **~er** *m* Swiss; *(Meier)* cowkeeper; *(Melker)* dairyman; milker; *(Türsteher)* porter; *(Mitglied der päpstlichen Garde)* member of the Papal body-guard; switzer; *die ~er Eidgenossenschaft* Swiss *(od* Helvetic) Confederacy *(od* Confederation); **~erdegen** *m typ* compositor and printer; **~erdeutsch** *a* Swiss German; **~erei** *f* dairy; **~ergarde** *f* Papal body-guard; Swiss guards *pl*; **~erhaus** *n* Swiss cottage; chalet; **~erin** *f* Swiss (woman *od* girl); **~erisch** *a* Swiss; Helvetic; of the Swiss; of Switzerland; **~er Käse** *m* Swiss cheese; Gruyère; **~erland** *n* Switzerland; **~ervolk** *n* the Swiss, the Swiss people.

*

Schwel|anlage *f* low-temperature carbonizing plant; **~en** *itr* to smo(u)lder; to burn slowly, to burn by a slow fire; *tech* to carbonize (at a low temperature); *(Teer)* to distil(l); *~~de Trümmer* smo(u)ldering ruins; **~gas** *n* gas from low-temperature distillation; carbonization gas; incompletely burned gas; **~kohle** *f* high-bituminous lignite coal; coal for distilling; **~koks** *m* low-temperature (carbonization) coke; **~teer** *m* tar from low-temperature carbonization; **~ung** *f* smo(u)ldering, slow burning; low-temperature carbonization; **~werk** *n* carbonizing plant.

schwelg|en *itr (gut essen, feiern)* to feast; to carouse; *(zechen, schmausen)* to revel in; *(üppig leben, sich ergehen in)* to luxuriate (in), to indulge (in); *in etw ~~ (fig)* to take delight in, to enjoy s. th.; to wallow in; *im Überfluß ~~* to live in luxurious abundance; **~er** *m (Genießer)* epicure, sybarite; *(im Essen u. Trinken)* glutton, revel(l)er, carouser; *(zügelloser Mensch)* debauchee; **~erei** *f (Schmauserei)* revelry, feasting; gluttony; *(Wohlleben, Üppigkeit)* luxury; *(Ausschweifung)* debauchery; orgy; **~erisch** *a* revel(l)ing; riotous; gluttonous; *(ausschweifend, üppig)* luxurious; orgiastic; sybaritic; *(wollüstig)* voluptuous; debauched; *(Mahl)* opulent.

Schwell|e *f (Tür~~)* sill; *(steinerne)* doorstep; *(auch fig u. psychologisch)* threshold; *(Zimmerei)* beam; girder; joist; *(Querbalken)* crossbar; *(Sims)* ledge; *(Architrav)* architrave; *(Eisenbahn~~)* sleeper, *Am* tie; *(Furt)* ford; *(Schwellenwert)* threshold value; *fig (Anfang, Eingang)* brink, verge, door; threshold; *an der ~~ des Greisenalters* on the verge of old age; *an der ~~ des Lebens* in the dawn of life; *an der ~~ des Todes* on the brink of the grave; *jds ~~ überschreiten* to cross s. o.'s threshold; *das Land ist an der ~~ des Ruins (Wohlstandes)* the country is on the threshold of ruin (prosperity); **~en** *irr tr, itr (an~~)* to swell; *(dick werden)* to belly, to grow fat; *(auf~~)* to bloat; *(aufblasen)* to inflate; *(sich ausdehnen)* to distend; *(Wasser)* to rise; *(von Wogen)* to heave; *fig (ansteigen)* to increase; to grow (bigger *od* thicker); *geschwollene Beine* swollen legs; *geschwollene Mandeln* swollen tonsils; *er spielt den Geschwollenen fig* he suffers from swelled head; *der Wind schwillt die Segel* the wind is filling the sails; *ihm schwillt der Kamm fig* his crest is rising; he is puffed up with pride; **~end** *a (Brüste)* swelling; heaving; *(Segel)* bellying; *(Lager)* springy; **~enfeuer** *n aero* threshold lights *pl*; **~enreiz** *m* threshold excitation; **~enwert** *m* threshold value; stimulus threshold; *phot* exposure factor; **~er** *m (Orgel)* swell; **~gewebe** *n anat* erectile tissue, cavernous tissue; **~körper** *m anat* corpus cavernosum; **~rost** *m* frame-grate; grating (of the foundation); timber platform.

Schwemm|e *f* watering-place, horse-pond; *(Schankraum, Kneipe, billiger Laden)* slap-bang (shop); grab joint; slop kitchen; dive; *ein Pferd in die ~~ reiten* to take a horse to water; **~en** *tr* to wash up *(od* off); to rinse; *(Vieh)* to water; *(anschwemmen)* to deposit; *(Holz)* to float; **~kanalisation** *f* sewerage; **~land** *n* alluvium, alluvial land; delta soil; brook deposit; **~~boden** *m* alluvial soil; **~mulde** *f* alluvial basin; **~sand** *m* drift(ing) sand; **~stein** *m* pumice stone; porous brick; **~wasser** *n* wash *(od* flushing) water.

Schwengel *m (Glocken~)* clapper; *(Pumpen~)* handle; *(Wagen~)* swing-bar; *(Dreschflegel)* swingle; *(Waage)* balance lever.

Schwenk|achse *f* swivel axis; **~antrieb** *m* pivot drive; **~arm** *m* swivel arm; **~~lafette** *f mil* swivel gunmount; **~aufnahme** *f phot* oscillating exposure; **~bar** *a* swivel-mounted; traversable, swingable; manœuvrable, orientable; revolving, rotable; sluable; **~bereich** *m* field of traverse; **~bewegung** *f* swing; **~bühne** *f* swinging platform; **~en** *tr (schwingen)* to swing; *(Stock)* to brandish; *(Fahne etc)* to flourish; *(Tuch, Hut)* to wave; *(schütteln)* to toss, to shake; *(Glas spülen)* to rinse; *itr mil* to wheel; *(drehen)* to turn (around); *(seitwärts drehen, Geschütz richten)* to traverse; *(herumdrehen)* to slew, to slue; *(auf e-m Zapfen drehen)* to swivel; *(sich drehen)* to pivot *(um* on, round); *(in Gelenk drehen)* to fulcrum; *(rund herum, rotieren)* to rotate; to revolve; *(kippen)* to tilt; *fig (Gesinnung ändern)* to change (sides); *links schwenkt — marsch!* left wheel — march! **~er** *m* tailed coat; **~getriebe** *n* turning gear; **~hebel** *m* rocking lever; **~kartoffeln** *f pl* pommes sautées *pl*; **~kran** *m* swinging crane;

-lafette *f* swivel gunmount; flexible gunmount; **-rad** *n* swivel wheel; **-radius** *m* turning radius; **-ung** *f* swinging, turning movement; turn; *mil* wheeling; evolution; (*Seitwärtsdrehung*) traversing; *fig* (*in der Gesinnung*) change (of mind); **--spunkt** *m* pivot; **-vorrichtung** *f* swinging device.

schwer *a* (*von Gewicht*) heavy; (*-wiegend*) weighty; *fam* hefty; (*drückend, lästig*) oppressive; burdensome; (*schwierig*) difficult, hard: arduous; complicated; tough; stiff; (*Verbrechen*) grave; (*-fällig*) clumsy; ponderous; cumbersome; (*Wunde, Krankheit*) serious; (*Strafe*) severe; (*Fehler*) gross, bad; (*Wein, Zigarre*) strong; (*Nahrungsmittel*) heavy; (*- verdaulich*) indigestable; (*grausam*) cruel; (*ermüdend*) fatiguing; (*schlimm*) bad, grievous; sad; *da hast du dich aber - getäuscht* you are seriously mistaken there; *der Kopf ist mir -* (*fig*) I am muddled; *das ist drei Pfund -* that weighs three pounds; *es wird mir sehr -* it is very painful to me; *das -ste liegt jetzt hinter uns* now we are out of the wood; *-e Arbeit* hard work; *-e Artillerie* medium artillery; *-e Aufgabe* hard task; *math* difficult problem; *-e Bewaffnung* heavy armament; *-e Bö* heavy squall; *-er Boden* heavy (*od* rich) soil; *-er Bomber* heavy bomber; *-er Duft* heavy scent; *-e Dünung* heavy swell; *-es Elektron* heavy electron; *-e Entbindung* difficult birth; *-er Fehler* gross mistake; blunder; *-es Feuer mil* heavy fire; *-e Frage* difficult question; poser; *-e Funkstelle mil* large radio station; *ein -es Gehör haben* to be hard of hearing; *das kostet -es Geld* that costs much (*od* a lot of) money; *-es Geld verdienen* to make big money; *-es Geld zahlen* to pay a stiff price; *-es Geschütz mil* heavy ordnance; *mit -em Herzen* with a heavy heart; *-er Irrtum* grave (*od* serious) error; *-er Junge* (*Verbrecher*) thug, *Am sl* tough(ie); *-er Kampf* hard struggle; *-e Kompanie mil* heavy-weapons company; *-er Kreuzer* heavy cruiser; *-e Lungenentzündung* severe case of pneumonia; *-er Panzer* heavy tank; *ein -er Schlag fig* a hard blow; *-e See* a heavy sea; *-e Seide* heavy silk; *-e Speise* indigestable food; *-er Unfall* serious accident; *-es Verbrechen* grave crime; *-er Verlust* severe loss; *-e Wahl* hard choice; *-es Wasser* heavy water, heavy hydrogen, deuterium; *-er Wein* full-bodied wine, strong wine; *-e Zeiten* hard times; *-e Zigarre* strong cigar; *-e Zunge* slow tongue; *sich - ärgern* to be greatly vexed; *- angeschlagen mil* badly mauled; *- atmen* to breathe heavily; *jdn - beleidigen* to offend s. o. grievously; *- zu befriedigen* hard to please; *- bestrafen* to punish severely; *für etw - büßen müssen* to have to pay dearly for s. th.; *- begreifen*, *- von Begriff sein* to be rather slow (of comprehension); to be slow-witted; *- darnieder liegen* to be dangerously ill; *- drücken* to weigh heavily; *- fallen* to be difficult; *es fällt mir sehr -* I find it very hard; *das fällt ihr -* that is hard for her; *- ins Gewicht fallen* to tell heavily, to weigh heavily; *- halten* to be difficult; to be attended with great difficulty; *- hören* to be hard of hearing; *- im Magen liegen* hard to digest; to lie heavy on o.'s stomach; *jdm das Herz - machen* to grieve s. o.; *etw - nehmen* to take s. th. to heart; *nimm es nicht so -* take it easy; *- beschädigt* badly damaged; *- betrunken* dead drunk; *- bewaffnet* heavy armed; *- erhältlich* hard-to-get; *- gekränkt* deeply offended; *- verkäuflich* difficult to sell; *- verletzt* badly wounded; disabled; **-arbeit** *f* heavy labo(u)r (*od* work); **-arbeiter** *m* manual labo(u)rer; heavy worker (*od* labo(u)rer); **--zulage** *f* (*bei Rationierung*) supplementary rations for heavy workers; bonus for heavy worker; **-athletik** *f* heavy athletics *pl mit sing*; **-atmig** *a* short of breath; asthmatic; **--keit** *f* shortness of breath; **-beladen** *a* heavily laden; **-benzin** *n* heavy benzine; **-benzol** *n* heavy benzol; **-beschädigte(r)** *m* seriously injured person; seriously disabled; **-bewaffnet** *a* heavily armed; **-blütig** *a* thick-blooded; *fig* melancholic; **-brennbar** *a* slow-burning; **-e** *f* (*Gewicht*) weight, heaviness; (*Wein*) body, strength; (*e-s Verbrechens*) gravity; seriousness; (*Strafe*) severity; *fig* hardness, difficulty; (*Bedeutung*) significance; meaning; *phys* (*Schwerkraft*) gravity; **--beschleunigung** *f* acceleration due to gravity; **--feld** *n* field of gravity; **-enöter** *m fam* fast young man; gay Lothario; **-erziehbar**: *--es Kind* problem child; **-fällig** *a* heavy; (*geistig*) dull, slow; (*träge*) slack; (*linkisch*) clumsy; awkward; (*Stil*) long-winded, ponderous; (*- zu handhaben*) unwieldy, cumbersome; **--keit** *f* heaviness; clumsiness; dullness; **-flüchtig** *a chem* not volatile; **-flüssig** *a* viscous heavy; **-gewicht** *n* heavy-weight; *fig* (*Nachdruck*) chief stress; emphasis; **--ler** *m* (*Boxer*) heavy-weight; **--smeisterschaft** *f* heavy-weight championship; **-hörig** *a* hard of hearing; (*taub*) deaf; **--keit** *f* defective hearing; deafness; **-industrie** *f* heavy industry; **-kraft** *f* (force of) gravity; gravitational force; **--anlasser** *m aero* inertia starter; **--beschleunigung** *f* gravity acceleration; **--feld** *n* gravitational field; **--wirkung** *f* influence of gravity; **--zentrum** *n* centre of gravity; **-krank** *a* dangerously ill; **-kriegsbeschädigte(r)** *m* heavily disabled (soldier); crippled soldier; **-lastwagen** *m* heavy duty truck; **-lich** *a* (*kaum*) hardly; scarcely; (*unter Schwierigkeiten*) with difficulty; **-löslich** *a chem* difficultly soluble; **-metall** *n* heavy metal; **-mut** *f*, **-mütigkeit** *f* melancholy; (*Traurigkeit*) sadness; (*Niedergeschlagenheit*) depression; **-mütig** *a* melancholy; (*traurig*) sad; sorrowful, mournful; (*niedergeschlagen*) depressed; **-öl** *n* heavy oil, crude oil; Diesel oil; **--motor** *m* heavy-oil engine; **-punkt** *m* centre of gravity; centre of mass; *fig* (*Hauptpunkt*) main point, crucial (*od* focal) point; (*der Macht*) concentration (of power); **--bildung** *f mil* formation of streng point; massed concentration of weapons; **--division** *f* division carrying out the main attack; **-spat** *m* heavy spar; baryte(s *pl*); **-verbrecher** *m* criminal, gangster; thug; **-verdient** *a* hard-earned; **-verständlich** *a* difficult to understand; abstruse; **-verwundet** *a* severely wounded; **--e(r)** *m* stretcher case; **-wiegend** *a* heavy, weighty; *fig* grave, serious.

Schwert *n* sword; (*am Schiffskiel*) centre-board, lee (-board); drop-keel; *das - ziehen* to draw o.'s sword; *mit Feuer u. - ausrotten* to exterminate with fire and sword; *sich ins - stürzen* to rush on o.'s sword; **-adel** *m* military nobility; **-ertanz** *m* sword dance; **-feger** *m* sword-cutler, blade-smith; **-fisch** *m* sword-fish; **-förmig** *a* sword-like, sword-shaped; **-fortsatz** *m anat* ensiform process; **-griff** *m* sword-hilt; **-lilie** *f* iris; **-streich** *m* sword-stroke; *ohne --* without striking a blow.

Schwester *f* sister; (*Kindersprache*) sissy, *Am* sis; *barmherzige -* sister of mercy; (*Kloster-*) nun; *- Oberin* Sister Superior; (*Kranken-*) nurse; **-chen** *n* dear little sister; **-firma** *f* affiliated firm; **-kind** *n* sister's child; (*Neffe*) nephew; (*Nichte*) niece; **-lich** *a* sisterly; **-liebe** *f* sisterly love; **-nhelferin** *f* junior nurse, nurse's aid; **-npaar** *n* couple of sisters; **-schaft** *f* sisterhood; sorority; **-sohn** *m* nephew; **-tochter** *f* niece; **-waffe** *f mil* related arm.

Schwibbogen *m* archway, flying-buttress.

Schwieger|eltern *pl* parents-in-law; **-mutter** *f* mother-in-law; **-sohn** *m* son-in-law; **-tochter** *f* daughter-in-law; **-vater** *m* father-in-law.

Schwiel|e *f* callosity; weal, wale; *med* callus; (*Strieme*) welt; (*Verhärtung*) induration; **-ig** *a* callous, horny; indurated; weal-like; marked with wales.

schwierig *a* difficult, hard; (*schwer löslich*) tough, intricate; (*heikel*) delicate, ticklish; (*kompliziert*) complicated; (*mißlich*) trying; (*verwickelt*) knotty; (*schwer zu behandeln*) difficult to deal with; (*eigen*) particular; fastidious; (*anstrengend*) exacting; *-e Arbeit* difficult piece of work; *-er Fall* hard case; *e-e -e Frage* a difficult question; poser; *Am fam* a sixty-four dollar question; *ein -er Handel* a hard bargain, *Am* a tight bargain; *in e-r -en Lage sein* to be in a difficult situation (*od* in a dilemma *od fam* in a fix); *-e Umstände* difficult (*od* trying) circumstances; *-e Sache* hard matter; *-e Verhältnisse* trying circumstances; *-e Zeit* crucial period; *es ist -, mit ihm auszukommen* he's a rather difficult person to get on with; *über den -sten Teil e-r Sache hinweg sein* to be over the hump; *der -ste Teil e-r Flugstrecke aero* hump; most difficult part of a flight; **-keit** *f* difficulty; crux; (*plötzliche --*) facer; (*Hindernis*) obstacle, obstruction, hitch; (*Einwand*) objection; (*Härte*) hardness; (*Engpaß*) bottleneck; *ohne --en* without a hitch; *jdm --en bereiten* to put difficulties in s. o.'s way; *--en bieten* to present difficulties; *da liegt die --* there's the rub; *e-e -- beseitigen* to remove (*od* to overcome) a difficulty; to sweep away a difficulty; *mit --en zu kämpfen haben* to labo(u)r under difficulties; *auf --en stoßen* to encounter (*od* to meet with) difficulties; to hit a snag; *alle --en überwinden* to overcome all difficulties, *Am* to make the grade; *jem, der alle --en aus dem Weg räumt Am fam* trouble-shooter.

Schwimm|anstalt *f* swimming-baths *pl*; *Am* (*Hallenbad*) natatorium; **-anzug** *m* bathing suit, swim suit; **-auftrieb** *m* buoyancy; **-bagger** *m* (floating) dredge(r); **-bad** *n* swimming-bath; (swimming) pool; **-(bade)seife** *f* floating bath soap; **-bahn** *f* lane; **-bassin**, **-becken** *n* pool; **-blase** *f* (*Fisch*) air-bladder, sound; (*zum -en lernen*) water-wings *pl*; **-brücke** *f* floating bridge; **-dock** *n mar* floating dock; **-en** *irr itr* to swim; (*von Sachen*) to float, to drift; *in Tränen --* to be bathed in tears; to overflow with tears; *in Blut --* to swim in blood; *fig* (*in Geld etc*) to roll; to welter; *sie schwimmt in Geld* she is rolling in money; *an Land* ~~ to swim ashore; *mit dem Strom* ~~ (*fig*) to swim with the tide (*od* current); *gegen den Strom* ~~ to strive against the current; *auf dem Rücken* ~~ to swim on o.'s back; *mir schwimmt es vor den Augen* my brain swims; ~**end** *a* swimming; floating; *mar* afloat; ~~*er Tank* amphibious tank; ~~*der Flugstützpunkt* floating airbase; ~**er** *m* (*Mann*) swimmer; (*tech, aero, mot, Angel*) float; ~~**flugzeug** *n* float plane, seaplane; ~~**stummel** *m aero* sponsor; ~~**wagen** *m aero* beaching carriage; ~**fähig** *a* able to swim; floatable; ~~**keit** *f* buoyancy; ~**fahrzeug** *n mil* amphibian; ~**fest** *n* swimming contest (*od* match); ~**flosse** *f* fin; ~**fuß** *m* webbed foot; ~**gürtel** *m* life-belt, water-wings *pl*; ~**haut** *f* web; ~**holz** *n* submerged wood; ~**hose** *f* bathing-drawers *pl*, bathing-trunks *pl*; ~**kampfwagen** *m* amphibious tank; ~**körper** *m* float; ~**kraft** *f* buoyancy; ~**kran** *m* floating crane; ~**kunst** *f* (art of) swimming; natation; ~**lehrer** *m* swimming-master; ~**panzer(wagen)** *m* amphibious tank; *Am* alligator, *sl* beetle boat; *Am* (*für Mannschaftstransport*) amtrac (= troop carrying amphibious tractor); ~**sand** *m* quicksand, shifting sand; ~**schule** *f* swimming school; ~**sport** *m* swimming; ~**stein** *m* floatstone; ~**stoß** *m* stroke; ~**vogel** *m* web-footed bird; ~**wagen** *m mil* amphibious truck, D.U.K.W.S., *sl* duck; ~**werk** *n aero* float landing gear; floatation gear; float undercarriage; ~**weste** *f* life jacket, air jacket; life-belt (*od*-preserver); life-saving jacket, *Am sl aero* Mae West.

Schwind|el *m* vertigo; giddiness; dizziness; *fig* (*Täuschung*) swindle; cheat; humbug, hoax; bubble; trick, shuffle; (*Betrug, Schwindelei*) fraud; imposture; racket; *Am* (*Machenschaft*) frame-up; (*Quatsch, Unsinn*) twaddle, *sl* bunk, *Am sl* buncombe; *ausgemachter* ~~ downright swindle, *Am* out-and-out swindle; *der ganze* ~~ (*fig*) the whole lot; *es ist alles* ~~ the whole thing is a plant; *auf jds* ~~ *hereinfallen* to be taken in by s.o.'s tricks; ~~**anfall** *m* fit of dizziness, *Am* dizzy spell; ~~**bank** *f* bogus bank; ~~**ei** *f* swindle; *sl* sell; cheat; take-in; trick; (*Betrug*) fraud; ~~*eien verüben* to prey upon the public; ~~**erregend** *a* vertiginous; causing giddiness; ~~**firma** *f* bogus firm, long firm; ~~**frei** *a* free from giddiness; not liable to giddiness; ~~**gefühl** *n* vertigo; feeling of giddiness; ~~**geschäft** *n* swindle; *Am sl* skin-game; (*Firma*) bogus company; *Am* wild cat company; ~~**geschichte** *f* made-up story; ~~**haft** *a* (*Preis etc*) very high, extravagant; (*betrügerisch*) cheating, swindling; fraudulent; deceptive; bogus; ~**(e)lig** *a* giddy; dizzy; *mir ist* ~~ I am (*od* feel) dizzy; *mir wird* ~~ my head swims; *das macht mich* ~~ it makes me giddy; ~**eln** *itr* to swindle; (*flunkern*) to humbug, to hoax; to fake, *fam* to fib; (*betrügen*) to cheat; *Am sl* to chisel; *fam* to diddle; *imp es schwindelt mir* I feel giddy; my head swims; ~**elpreis** *m* cheating price; ~**elunternehmen** *n com* bogus enterprise; ~**ler** *m* swindler; diddler; cheat; charlatan; (*Betrüger*) impostor; *Am fam* fraud, shark, bunco steerer; fake; ~**lerisch** *a* (*betrügerisch*) swindling; humbugging; sham; fraudulent.

schwind|en *irr itr* (*weniger werden*) to dwindle; to decrease; to grow less; (*verschwinden*) to disappear; (*plötzlich*) to vanish; (*abnehmen*) to waste; (*schrumpfen*) to shrink, to contract; (*verfallen*) to decline; (*welken*) to wither; to lose in weight (*od* measure); *radio* to fade (away); ~**erscheinung** *f radio* fading effect; ~**sucht** *f* consumption; phthisis; pulmonary tuberculosis; ~**süchtig** *a* consumptive; phthisical; hectic; ~~**e(r)** *m* consumptive; ~**ung** *f* shrinkage; contraction.

Schwing|achse *f mot* independent axle; oscillating axle; ~**bewegung** *f* vibratory movement; ~**e** *f* (*Getreide*) winnow; (*Wanne*) fan; (*Flachs*) swingle; (*Flügel*) wing; *poet* pinion; ~**en** *irr tr* to swing; (*Peitsche*) to flourish; (*Speer*) to brandish; (*Fahne, Tuch*) to wave; (*Korn*) to winnow, to fan; (*Flachs*) to swingle; (*Szepter*) to rule; *itr* (*Pendel*) to swing; (*schwanken*) to sway; (*schwimmen*) to float; (*vibrieren*) to vibrate; (*rasch hin u. her*) to oscillate; (*wellenartig*) to undulate; *sich* ~~ to swing o.s.; (*springen*) to leap; to vault; to jump; (*in die Luft*) to soar; to ascend; *sich aufs Pferd* ~~ to vault on horseback; *sich auf den Thron* ~~ to take possession of (*od* to usurp) the throne; *das Tanzbein* ~~ to dance, *fam* to hop; ~**enflug** *m* flapping flight; ~**enflugzeug** *n* ornithopter; flapping-wing machine; ~**er** *m* (*Boxen*) swing; *Am sl* haymaker; *radio* oscillator; ~**hebel** *m tech* rocking lever; balancer; ~**kreis** *m* resonant (*od* oscillatory) circuit; ~**röhre** *f radio* oscillating tube; ~**ung** *f* swinging; *phys* oscillation; vibration; wave; undulation; (*Zyklus*) cycle; *in* ~~ *kommen* to begin to vibrate; *in* ~~ *setzen* to cause to vibrate; to set in oscillating motion; ~~**sdämpfer** *m* vibration damper; ~~**sdauer** *f* period of vibration; time of oscillation; ~~**sebene** *f* plane of vibration; ~~**skreis** *m* oscillation circuit; tuned circuit; ~~**sweite** *f* amplitude (of vibration); ~~**szahl** *f* vibration number; vibration frequency (*od* rate); ~~**szeit** *f* time of vibration.

Schwipp|schwager *m* brother of a brother-in-law; ~**schwägerin** *f* sister of a sister-in-law.

Schwips *m fam* (*kleiner Rausch*): *e-n* ~ *haben* to be tipsy; to be half-seas-over; (*leichter Schlag*) smack.

schwirren *itr* (*sausen, pfeifen*) to whiz(z), to whistle; (*Pfeil*) to whir; (*Käfer, aero*) to buzz; (*summen*) to hum; (*Gerüchte*) to fly; to spread.

Schwitz|bad *n* vapo(u)r-bath; Turkish bath; ~**en** *itr* to perspire; to sweat; *stark* ~~ to be in a strong perspiration; *am ganzen Körper* ~~ to perspire all over; *hinter seinen Büchern* ~~ to toil over o.'s books; *tr* (*Kochkunst*) to fry lightly in butter; *Blut* ~~ (*fig*) to be in extreme anxiety; ~**kasten** *m* sweating-box; (*beim Ringen*) headlock; ~**kur** *f* treatment by sweating; sweating-cure; ~**mittel** *n* sudorific; diaphoretic; ~**stube** *f* sweating-room; ~**wasser** *n tech* sweat; steam.

Schwof *m vulg* (*Tanz*) public dance; hop; ~**en** *itr vulg* to hop; to dance.

schwören *irr tr, itr* to swear; (*Eid*) to take an oath; *hoch u. heilig* ~ to swear solemnly; *falsch* ~ to commit perjury, to perjure o.s.; to forswear o.s.; *jdn* ~ *lassen* to swear s.o. in; to administer an oath to s.o.; to put s.o. on his oath; *Rache* ~ to vow vengeance; *Treue* ~ to swear (the oath of) allegiance; *bei Gott* ~ to swear by God; *ich könnte* ~, *daß* ... I could take my oath that ..., I could swear that ...; ~ *auf* to have absolute confidence in, *fam* to swear by.

schwül *a* sultry, close; (*drückend*) oppressive, sweltering hot; muggy; sticky; *fig* langurous; *es ist furchtbar* ~ it's awfully sultry; *vulg* (*schwul*) homosexual; *ein* ~*er Bruder vulg* molly, sweet homo; ~**e** *f* sultriness, close air.

Schwulität *f fam* trouble; (*Furcht, Angst*) fear; *fam* funk; *in* ~*en sein fam* to be in a fix; *jdn in* ~*en bringen* to get s.o. in trouble.

Schwulst *m* (*im Stil*) bombast; turgidity; (*Rede*) inflated speech.

schwülstig *a* (*Stil, Rede*) inflated, bombastic, turgid; ~**keit** *f* turgidity, bombastic style.

schwummerig *a fam* benumbed; *mir ist* ~ (*fam*) I feel pretty shaky.

Schwund *m* (*Schwinden*) disappearance; consuming; wasting away; decay; dwindling; (*Schrumpfung*) shrinkage; (*Auslaufen*) leakage; (*Haar*~) falling off; *med* atrophy; *gram* (~ *der Endung*) loss; (*Abfall*) dropping; *radio* fading; ~**ausgleich** *m radio* anti-fading device; (automatic) volume (*od* gain) control; ~**erscheinung** *f radio* fading; *med* atrophy; ~**periode** *f radio* fading period; ~**regler** *m radio* automatic volume control circuit; ~**zone** *f radio* wipe-out area.

Schwung *m* swing; (*Sprung*) vault; bound; (*Aufschwung*) rising; *fig* motion; (*Lebhaftigkeit*) verve, animation; (*Eifer*) ardo(u)r; (*Tatkraft*) impetus, vitality; vim; energy; *fam* punch; dash; go; *Am* zip, pep; (*Geistes*~) buoyancy; (*Phantasie*) flight; (*edler* ~) noble diction, lofty strain; ~ *der Rede* emphasis; *in* ~ *bringen* to set in motion; to set going; to activate; to energize; to start; to accelerate; *im* ~ *sein* to be in full swing; ~ *bekommen* to gather momentum; *in* ~ *kommen* to get into o.'s stride; ~**brett** *n* spring-board; ~**feder** *f* pen-feather; pinion; ~**haft** *a* swinging, lofty, sublime; (*Geschäft*) flourishing; (*Handel*) lively, roaring, brisk; (*Rede*) emphatic; ~**kraft** *f* centrifugal power; *fig* buoyancy, elasticity; verve, energy, liveliness; *Am* zip, pep; ~~**anlasser** *m* inertia starter; ~**los** *a* dull; vapid; spiritless; ~**masse** *f* gyrating mass; ~**moment** *n* moment of inertia; ~**rad** *n* flywheel; ~**voll** *a* full of enthusiasm, spirited; animated energetic; full of fire; ~~*e Rede* stirring speech.

Schwur *m* oath; swearing; (*Gelübde*) vow; *e-n* ~ *leisten* to take an oath; ~**finger** *m* middle finger; ~**formel** *f* wording of an oath; ~**gericht** *n* (court of) assizes *pl*; jury; ~~**sverfahren** *n* trial by jury; ~**zeuge** *m* sworn witness.

Sech *n* co(u)lter.

sechs *a* six; ~**eck** *n* hexagon; ~**eckig** *a* hexagonal; ~**ender** *m* stag with six points; ~**erlei** *a* of six sorts; ~**fach** *a* sixfold; ~**jährig** *a* six-year-old; sexennial; ~**mal** *adv* six times; ~**monatig** *a* lasting six months; ~**monatlich** *a adv* every sixth month, half-yearly; ~**motorig** *a aero* six-engined; ~**pfünder** *m* six-pounder; ~**seitig** *a* hexagonal; ~**spännig** *a* with six horses; ~**stellig** *a* of six digits; ~**stündig** *a* of six hours; ~**tagerennen** *n* six-day bike racing, six-day (cycling) race; ~**te** *a* sixth; ~**tehalb** *a* six and a half; ~**tel** *n* sixth part; ~**tens** *adv* in the sixth place, sixthly.

sechzehn *a* sixteen; ~**ender** *m* stag with sixteen points; ~**te** *a* sixteenth; ~**tel** *n* sixteenth part; ~~ *Note mus* sixteenth note; semiquaver.

sechzig *a* sixty; *fam* threescore; **~er** *m* **~erin** *f* sexagenarian; *in den ~er Jahren* in the sixties; *er ist in den ~en* he is over sixty; he is on the shady side of sixty; he is in the sixties; **~jährig** *a* sixty-year old; aged sixty; **~ste** *a* sixtieth; **~stel** *n* sixtieth part.

Sedez *n*, **~band** *m*, **~format** *n* (a volume) in 16mo.

Sediment *n* sediment; **~är** *a* sedimentary; **~gestein** *n* sedimentary rocks *pl*; **~ierung** *f* sedimentation.

See[1] *m* lake; *schott* loch; (*Teich*) pond.

See[2] *f* (*Weltmeer*) sea; (*Ozean*) ocean; (*Woge, Welle*) wave, sea; *das Boot nahm e-e ~ über* the boat shipped a sea; *freie ~* high sea, the high seas; *glatte ~* smooth (*od* calm) sea; *kabbelige ~* chopping sea; surf; *kurze ~* short sea; *offene ~* open sea; the open; main; *rauhe ~* rough sea; *ruhige ~* calm sea; *schwere ~* heavy sea, rough sea; *stürmische ~* stormy (*od* rough) sea; *auf ~ sein* to be at sea; *auf hoher ~* on the high (*od* open) seas; *er wurde auf ~ bestattet* he was buried at sea; *an der ~* by the seaside, at the seaside, *Am* at the beach; *Ferien an der ~* holidays by the sea; *an die ~ gehen* to go to the seaside, *Am* to go to the beach, to go to the seashore; *in ~ sein* to be in open water; *in ~ gehen, in ~ stechen* to put (out) to sea; to stand (*od* to steer) out to sea; (*Segelschiff*) to set sail; *über ~* overseas; beyond (*od* across) the sea(s); *zur ~* at sea; *zur ~ fahren* (*Beruf*) to follow the sea; *zur ~ gehen* to go to sea; *Kapitän zur ~* captain; *der Handel zur ~* maritime commerce; **~aal** *m* sea-eel; **~ablagerung** *f* sea-deposit; **~abrüstung** *f* naval disarmament; **~adler** *m* (white-tailed) sea-eagle; **~alpen** *f pl* Maritime Alps *pl*; **~amt** *n jur* admiralty court; maritime court; **~anemone** *f zoo* sea-anemone; **~arsenal** *n* naval dockyard; **~aufklärer** *m aero* (naval) patrol plane; **~bad** *n* (*Ort*) seaside resort (*od* place), watering-place; seashore resort; resort town; (*Bad in der ~*) bath in the sea; sea-bath; **~bär** *m zoo* sea-bear; *alter ~~* (*fig fam*) old sailor, old mariner; sea-dog, water-rat, old salt; **~barke** *f* (*Fisch*) plain surmullet; **~barsch** *m* (*Fisch*) bass; sea-perch; **~bataillon** *n* marines *pl*; **~beben** *n* seaquake; **~beschädigt** *a* damaged at sea; sea damaged; **~brasse(n)** *m* (*Fisch*) sea-bream; **~beute** *f* prize; **~brise** *f* sea-breeze; **~dampfer** *m* ocean liner; sea-going steamer; **~dienst** *m* naval service; sea-duty; **~elefant** *m zoo* sea-elephant; **~fähig** *a* seaworthy; **~~keit** *f* sea worthiness; **~fahrend** *a* seafaring; (*die ~ befahrend*) sea-going; *~~es Volk* seafaring nation; **~fahrer** *m* seafaring man, sailor, mariner; navigator; *poet* seafarer; **~fahrt** *f* (sea-) voyage; cruise; navigation; **~fest** *a* (*Schiff*) seaworthy; (*Passagier*) not subject to seasickness; to be a good sailor; *nicht ~~* to be a bad sailor; *~~ werden* to find (*od* to get) o.'s sea-legs; **~festung** *f* fortified naval base; **~feuer** *n* sea-lights *pl*; **~fisch** *m* salt-water fish; sea-fish; **~~erei** *f* maritime fishing; deep-sea fishing; **~flieger** *m* naval flier; **~~ei** *f* naval aviation; **~flughafen** *m*, **~flugstation** *f* seaplane station (*od* base); seadrome; (*ohne bes. Landeeinrichtung*) seaplane anchorage; **~flugzeug** *n* seaplane, hydroplane; float plane; naval plane; **~~mutterschiff** *n* seaplane tender; **~~stützpunkt** *m* seaplane base; **~~träger** *m* seaplane carrier; seaplane tender; **~fracht** *f* (sea)freight, *Am auch* ocean freight; **~~brief** *m* bill of lading (*Abk* B./L.); **~funk** *m radio* marine radio; **~~dienst** *m* marine radio service; **~~stelle** *f* marine radio service station; (*auf Schiff*) ship radio station; **~gang** *m* (motion of the) sea; **~gefahr** *f com* sea-risk; **~gefecht** *n* naval battle, naval action; naval combat; sea-fight; **~geltung** *f* sea-power; mastery of the sea; prestige at sea, naval prestige; **~gemälde** *n* sea-piece, seascape; **~geschichte** *f* sea-story; yarn; **~gesetz** *n* maritime law; **~gras** *n* (*Tang*) seaweed, green alga; (*zum Polstern*) sea-grass; **~grün** *a* marine green; **~gurke** *f zoo* sea-cucumber; **~hafen** *m* seaport; maritime port; harbo(u)r; (*Stadt*) seaport(town); **~handbuch** *n* sea annual; **~handel** *m* maritime trade; sea trade; sea-borne trade; **~held** *m* naval hero; **~herrschaft** *f* naval supremacy; command of the sea; **~höhe** *f* altitude (*od* height) above sea level; **~hund** *m zoo* seal; **~~sfell** *n* sealskin; **~igel** *m zoo* sea-urchin; **~jungfer**, **~jungfrau** *f* mermaid; siren; **~kabel** *n* (sub)marine cable; ocean cable; **~kadett** *m* naval cadet; *früher* midshipman; **~kalb** *n* sea-calf; **~kampfflugzeug** *n*, **~kampfmaschine** *f* seaplane fighter; naval fighter plane; **~karte** *f* (sea-) chart; nautical map; **~klar** *a* ready to put to sea; ready to sail; **~klima** *n* maritime climate; **~konferenz** *f* naval conference; **~kräfte** *f pl* sea-forces *pl*; **~krank** *a* seasick; *leicht ~~ werden* to be a bad sailor; *nicht ~~ werden* to be a good sailor; **~~heit** *f* seasickness; **~krebs** *m* (*Hummer*) lobster; **~krieg** *m* naval war; naval warfare; **~~führung** *f* (conduct of) naval warfare; **~~soperation** *f* naval operation; **~~srecht** *n* law of naval warfare; **~~sstrategie** *f* naval strategy; **~kuh** *f zoo* (*Walroß*) sea-cow; **~küste** *f* sea-coast; seashore, seaboard; seaside, *Am* beach; **~lachs** *m* salmon; **~leute** *pl* seamen *pl*, sailors *pl*; marines *pl*; **~lord** *m Engl* Sea Lord; **~lotse** *m* sea-pilot; **~löwe** *m zoo* sea-lion; **~luft** *f* sea-air; **~~hafen** *m aero* seadrome; **~~streitkräfte** *f pl* navy air-force; **~macht** *f* naval (*od* maritime) power; sea-power; **~mann** *m* (*pl ~leute*) seaman; (*Matrose*) sailor; mariner; **~~sausdruck** *m* sea-term; **~männisch** *a* seamanlike, sailor-like; (*nautisch*); nautical; **~maschine** *f aero* seaplane; **~mäßig** *a* suitable for shipment; seaworthy; *~~e Verpackung* seaworthy packing; **~meile** *f* (*= 1,852 km*) nautical mile; sea-mile; knot; **~mine** *f* sea-mine; **~möve** *f* (sea-) gull; seamew; **~muschel** *f* sea-shell; **~not** *f* distress (at sea); **~~dienst** *m* air-sea rescue; sea rescue service; **~~flugzeug** *n* sea rescue aircraft; **~~frequenz** *n aero* distress frequency; **~~ruf** *m* distress call; **~~welle** *f* distress wave-length; **~nplatte** *f* flat country covered with lakes; **~offizier** *m* naval officer; **~otter** *m, f zoo* sea-otter; **~pferdchen** *n* sea-horse; **~pflanze** *f* sea-plant; **~ratte** *f fig* old salt; **~raub** *m* piracy; **~räuber** *m* pirate; corsair; raider; sea-rover; *du alter~~! interj fam* you old son of a gun! **~~flagge** *f* black flag, black jack; **~~ei** *f* piracy; **~~isch** *a* piratical; **~~schiff** *n* pirate (ship); **~recht** *n jur* maritime law; maritime right; (*Kriegsrecht*) law of naval warfare; **~reise** *f* (sea-)voyage; cruise; **~roman** *m* sea-novel; **~rose** *f bot* water-lily; **~route** *f* sea-route, *Am* sea-road; **~rüstung** *f* naval armament; **~salz** *n* sea-salt; **~sand** *m* sea-sand; **~schaden** *m* loss suffered at sea; average; damage to a ship (*od* cargo); **~schiff** *n* sea-ship; sea-going ship; **~schiffahrt** *f* sea-navigation; **~schiffsreederei** *f* ocean shipping company; **~schlacht** *f* naval battle (*od* engagement); **~schlange** *f* sea-serpent; **~schlick** *m* sea-ooze; **~schwalbe** *f orn* seaswallow; tern; **~sieg** *m* naval victory; **~soldat** *m* marine; *Am sl* leatherneck; **~sprache** *f* nautical language; **~stadt** *f* maritime town; seaport; coast town; seaside town; **~stern** *m zoo* starfish; **~strand** *m* seaside, beach; **~strategie** *f* naval strategy; **~streitkräfte** *f pl* naval forces *pl*; **~stück** *n* (*Malerei*) seascape, sea-piece; **~stuka** *m aero* naval dive-bomber; **~stützpunkt** *m* naval-base; **~sturm** *m* storm at sea; **~taktik** *f* naval tactics *pl*; **~tang** *m bot* seaweed; brown alga; **~tonne** *f* buoy; **~transport** *m* seatransport; naval transport; shipment by steamer; **~treffen** *n* sea-fight; **~truppen** *f pl* marines *pl*; **~tüchtig** *a* (*Schiff*) seaworthy; **~~keit** *f* seaworthiness; **~ungeheuer** *n* sea-monster; **~untüchtig** *a* unseaworthy; **~verbindungslinie** *f* life-line; **~verkehr** *m* maritime (*od* ocean) traffic; sea-borne traffic; **~versicherung** *f* marine insurance; **~~sgesellschaft** *f* marine insurance company; **~vogel** *m* sea-bird, sea-fowl; **~volk** *n* maritime nation; **~walze** *f zoo* sea-cucumber; **~warte** *f* naval observatory; **~wärts** *adv* seaward; **~wasser** *n* salt-water, sea-water; *poet* brine; **~weg** *m* sea-route, *Am* sea-road; *auf dem ~~* by sea; per sea; sea-borne; **~wesen** *n* naval affairs *pl*, navy; nautics *pl*; *auf das ~~ bezüglich* nautical; **~wind** *m* sea-wind; sea-breeze; **~wissenschaft** *f* nautical science; **~wurf** *m* jettison; (*Gegenstand*) jetsam; **~zeichen** *n* sea-mark; **~zunge** *f* (*Fisch*) sole.

Seel|e *f* soul; (*Gesinnung, Gemüt*) mind; (*Geist*) spirit; (*menschliches Wesen*) human being, individual; (*das Wesentliche*) heart; *tech* (*Geschützinneres*) calibre, *Am* caliber, bore; *tech* (*Kabel~~, Drahtseil~~*) core; (*Spiralbohrer~~*) stem; (*Hochofen~~*) shaft; *600 ~en* (*= Einwohner*) 600 souls; *die ~~ des Unternehmens* the very soul of the enterprise; *die ~~ der Gesellschaft* the life and soul of the company; *e-e gute ~~* a good fellow; a good soul; *die ~~ aushauchen* to draw o.'s last breath; *jdm etw auf die ~~ binden* to lay strong injunctions upon; to enjoin solemnly; *auf der ~~ brennen* to prey on o.'s mind; *das liegt mir auf der ~~* that weighs heavily upon me; *aus voller ~~* with all o.'s heart; *von ganzer ~~* candidly; *aus tiefster ~~* from my soul; *jdm aus der ~~ sprechen* to guess s. o.'s thoughts; *Sie haben mir aus der ~~ gesprochen!* you said it! *bei meiner ~~!* (up)on my soul! by my soul! *es war keine ~~ zu sehen* there wasn't a soul to be seen; *ein Herz u. e-e ~~ sein* to be of one heart and mind; *sich in der ~~ schämen* to be deeply ashamed (of); **~enachse** *f tech* axis of the bore; **~enadel** *m* nobility of soul; nobleness of mind; **~enamt** *n* requiem, office for the dead; **~enanalyse** *f* psychoanalysis; **~enangst** *f* anguish of soul; agony of fear; mental agony; mortal fright; **~endrama** *n* psychological drama; **~endurchmesser** *m tech* bore; calibre, *Am* caliber; **~enfang** *m* fishery of souls; proselytism; **~enforscher** *m* psychologist; **~enfriede** *m* peace of mind; **~enfroh** *a* extremely (*od* very *od* heartily) glad; **~engefährtin** *f* soul mate; **~engröße** *f* magnanimity; greatness of mind; **~engüte** *f* kindness (of heart); **~enheil** *n* salvation; spiritual welfare; **~~kunde** *f* psychiatry; **~enhirt** *m* pastor; **~enkampf** *m* mental strife (*od* struggle); **~enkraft** *f* strength of mind; (*Fähigkeit*) mental faculty; **~enkrankheit** *f* mental disease; **~enkunde** *f* psychology; **~enleben** *n* mental life; spiritual life; psychic life; life of the soul; **~enlehre** *f* psychology; **~enleiden** *n* mental suffering; **~enlos** *a* soulless; (*ohne Leben*) lifeless; inanimate; **~enmesse** *f* mass for the dead; requiem; **~ennot** *f* distress of mind; **~enpein, ~enqual** *f* agony of mind; mental agony; anguish of soul; **~enreinheit** *f* purity of soul; **~enruhe** *f* calmness; composure; tranquillity of mind, peace of mind; placidity; **~enstärke** *f* fortitude; **~enstörung** *f* mental disturbance; **~entätigkeit** *f* inner activity; **~envergnügt** *a* very (*od* thoroughly) happy; enraptured; **~enverkäufer** *m* kidnapper; (*Werber*) crimp; (*Schiff*) cranky boat; cockle-shell; **~enverwandtschaft** *f* congeniality; mental affinity; **~envoll** *a* (*gefühlvoll, bewegt*) soulful; (*zärtlich*) tender; (*sentimental*) sentimental; **~enwanderung** *f* transmigration of souls; metempsychosis; **~enwärmer** *m fam* comforter; **~enzustand** *m* psychic condition; **~isch** *a* psychic; (*geistig*) mental; of the mind; spiritual; (*Gefühl betreffend*) emotional; *~~e Schmerzen* mental anguish; *~~e Wirkung* moral effect; *das ~~e* spirituality; **~sorge** *f* ministerial work; ministry; **~sorger** *m* minister; clergyman; pastor.

Segel *n* sail; *mar* (*die ~ pl*) canvas; *anat* (*Gaumen*) velum; (*Herzklappe*) segment; *unter ~* (*mar*) under canvas; *unter ~ gehen* to set sail; *mit vollen ~n* under press of sail; (to fly) under full sails; *die ~ aufziehen* to hoist the sails; *alle ~ beisetzen* to crowd all sail; *die ~ streichen* to strike sail; *fig* to submit to; *den Wind aus den ~n nehmen* to take the winds out of the sails (of); to blanket; **~anweisungen** *f pl* sailing directions *pl*; **~artig** *a* sail-like; **~boot** *n* sailing-boat; *Am* sail-boat; *sport* yacht; **~~sport** *m* yachting; **~fertig, ~klar** *a* ready to sail, ready for sea; *sich ~~ machen* to get under sail; **~fliegen** *n* gliding, soaring; sailplaning, sail flying; motorless flight; **~flieger** *m* glider, soarer; soaring pilot, sailplane pilot; (*bes. bei Lastensegler*) glider pilot; **~~ei** *f* gliding, sailing, soaring; motorless flying; **~~lager** *n* gliding camp; **~~schein** *m* soaring certificate; **~flug** *m* glide; gliding flight; glider flying; soaring flight, sailing flight; motorless flight; *Schulung im ~~* training in glider flying; **~~dauerrekord** *m* gliding-duration record; **~~entfernungsrekord** *m* gliding-distance record; **~~gelände** *n*, **~~platz** *m* gliding field; soaring site; **~~modell** *n* model sailplane; **~~wettbewerb** *m* gliding contest; **~flugzeug** *n* (*Gleiter*) glider; (*zur Schulung*) primary glider; (*Leistungs~~*) secondary glider; (*Hochleistungs~~*) performance-type glider; sailplane; (*Lastensegler für Transport u. Truppenbeförderung*) cargo-transport glider; freight glider; troop and cargo glider; troop-carrying glider, cargo-carrying glider; (*Motorsegler*) auxiliary sailplane; underpowered motor glider; (*für Kunstflug*) aerobatic sailplane; *mit e-m ~~ fliegen* to soar, to glide; to sailplane; **~~anhänger** *m* (*für Landtransport*) trailer for sailplane; **~~bau** *m* sailplane construction; **~~führer** *m* sailplane pilot; glider pilot; **~~muster** *n* type of sailplane; **~~schlepp** *m* glider-towing; **~fläche** *f* area of sails; **~karte** *f* sailing chart; **~klasse** *f* (*bei Rennbooten*) rating; **~klub** *m* yachting club; **~kunstflug** *m* glider aerobatics *pl mit sing*; **~leinwand** *f* (*Persenning*) canvas; sail cloth; duck; **~macher** *m* sail-maker; **~n** *itr* to sail; to yacht; to go for a sail; *aero* to soar; to glide; to carry out a soaring flight; *gegen den Wind ~~* to make way against a head wind; *unter falscher Flagge ~~* (*auch fig*) to sail under false colo(u)rs; *vor dem Wind ~~* to sail right before the wind; *geschwind ~n* to carry a press of sail; *in den Grund ~n* to sink; *um ein Vorgebirge herum ~n* to double a cape; *mit vollem Winde ~n* to sail whole wind, to run before the wind; *eine Küste entlang ~n* to coast along; **~regatta** *f* sailing race; regatta; **~schiff** *n* sailing ship; sailing vessel; sailing barge; **~schlitten** *m* ice-yacht; **~sport** *m* yachting; **~stange** *f* (sail-) yard; **~stellung** *f aero* (*der Luftschraube*) feathered position of airscrew; *in ~~ bringen* to feather; **~tau** *n* cable; **~tuch** *n* canvas, sail-cloth; duck; **~~hülle** *f* canvas cover, tarpaulin; **~~plane** *f* tarpaulin; **~~schuhe** *f* (*Turnschuhe*) gymnasium shoes, *Am sl* sneakers *pl*; **~~stoff** *m* sail-cloth; canvas; **~vogel** *m* soaring bird; **~werk** *n* sails *pl*; **~wettfahrt** *f* sailing race; regatta; yachting race; **~wind** *m* fair wind for sailing; **~yacht** *f* yacht; **Segler** *m* (*Sport~*) yachtsman; (*Schiff*) sailing vessel; sailer; *aero* sailplane, glider; *siehe*: *Segelflugzeug*.

Segen *m* blessing; *eccl* benediction; (*Wonne*) bliss; (*Erfolg, Glück*) luck; (*Danksagung vor u. nach dem Essen*) grace; (*Gebet*) prayer(s *pl*); (*Kreuzeszeichen*) sign of the cross; (*Beschwörungsformel*) spell; (*reicher Ertrag*) benefit. abundance; yield; produce; (*Wohltat*) boon; *ein wahrer ~* a godsend to s. o.; *meinen ~ haben Sie* you have my blessing; *den ~ geben* to give o.'s blessing; *zum ~ von* for the benefit of; *das bringt keinen ~* that brings no luck; **~erteilung** *f eccl* benediction; **~spendend** *a fig* beneficial; fertile; benedictory; **~sreich** *a* blessed, blissful; **~sspruch, ~swunsch** *m* benediction, blessing, kind wishes *pl*.

Segment *n* segment; section; sector; **~förmig** *a* segmental; **~ring** *m* segmented ring; **~schaltung** *f* segment shift.

segn|en *tr* to bless, to make the sign of the cross; *das Zeitliche ~en* to die; to depart this life; *gesegnet mit etw* to be blessed (*od* endowed) with; *in gesegneten Umständen* with child, pregnant; **~ung** *f* blessing, benediction.

Seh|achse *f* axis of vision; **~en** *irr tr, itr allg* to see; (*schauen, anschauen, anblicken, erblicken*) to look; (*erfassen*) to behold; (*wahrnehmen*) to perceive; (*ansehen*) to regard; (*betrachten*) to view; (*beobachten*) to watch, to observe; (*bemerken*) to notice, to note; (*erspähen*) to espy, to descry; (*unterscheiden*) to discern; *ähnlich ~~* to resemble; *das sieht ihm ähnlich* that is just like him; *scharf ~~* to be sharp-sighted; *flüchtig ~~* to get only a glimpse of; *gern ~~* to like; *ungern ~~* to dislike; *ich habe es selbst gesehen* I saw it myself; *ich schaute hin, sah aber nichts* I looked but saw nothing; *sie hat schon bessere Zeiten gesehen* she has seen better times; *gern bei jdm gesehen sein* to be a welcome guest; *hat man je so etw gesehen?* did you ever see the like of it? *Am fam* can you beat it? *das wird man erst ~~* that remains to be seen; *wir werden schon ~~* we'll see; *wir werden ja ~~* time will tell; *weder rechts noch links ~~* to look neither right nor left; *jdn nicht ~~ wollen* to cut s. o.; *daraus ist zu ~~* hence it appears; *wenn ich recht sehe* if my eyes do not deceive me; *ich sah es ihn tun* I saw him do it; *er allein sah die Wahrheit* he was the only one who saw the truth; *gut ~~* to have good eyes; *schlecht ~~* to have a bad eyesight; *aus dem Fenster ~~* to look out of the window; *ich kann nicht aus den Augen ~~* I cannot open my eyes; *das Haus sieht auf die Straße* the house looks into (*od* faces) the street; *auf etw ~~* to look at; to take care of; *nach etw ~~* to look for, to look about (*od* round) for, to look out for; *jdm auf die Finger ~~* to watch s. o. narrowly (*od* closely); *man muß ihm auf die Finger ~~* he needs close watching; (*sorgen für*) to look after; to take care of; *~~ lassen* to show, to display; to let be seen; *sich ~~ lassen* to present o. s.; to put in an appearance; to show up; *sich nicht ~~ lassen* to keep out of sight; *sie kann sich ~~ lassen* she need not be ashamed of herself; *lassen Sie mich ~~!* let me see! *lassen Sie sich nie wieder ~~!* don't let me see you again! *durch die Finger ~~* to connive; *zur Erde ~~* to cast down o.'s eyes; *in die Sonne ~~* to look into the sun; *jdm ins Herz ~~* to see in s. o.'s heart; *in der Zeitung ~~* to read in the paper; *in die Zukunft ~~* to see into the future; *nach dem Rechten ~~* to see that everything is in order; *~~ Sie!* see! look! *~~ Sie, da geht er!* look! there he goes; *~~ Sie mal!* look here! *sieh mal an! interj* I say! indeed! dear me! *siehe oben* see above; *siehe unten* see below; **~en** *n* seeing, looking, sight, eyesight; vision; *indirektes ~~* indirect vision, peripheral vision; *natürliches ~~* natural vision; *räumliches ~~* stereoscopic vision; *ich kenne sie nur vom ~~* I know her only by sight; **~enswert** *a* worth seeing; (*merkwürdig*) curious; (*bemerkenswert*) remarkable; **~enswürdigkeit** *f* object of interest, *pl* sights *pl*; (*Merkwürdigkeit*) curiosity; (*Schau*) show; spectacle; *die ~~en e-r Stadt ansehen* to see all the sights of a town; to do a place, *Am fam* to see the elephant; *jem, der ~~en aufsucht* sight-seer; **~er** *m* seer, prophet; **~~blick** *m* prophetic look; **~~gabe** *f* gift of prophecy (*od* of second sight); **~erin** *f* prophetess; **~erisch** *a* prophetic; **~fehler** *m* visual defect; **~feld** *n* field of vision; **~funktion** *f* visual function; **~hilfsmittel** *n* aid to vision; **~hügel** *m anat* optic thalamus; **~~hirn** *n anat* interbrain; **~klappe** *f* observation port; **~kraft** *f* visual faculty (*od* power); (eye)sight; vision; **~kreis** *m* (circle of the) horizon; circle of vision; **~lappen** *m* optic lobe; **~leistung** *f* visual power (*od* capacity); **~linie** *f* line of vision (*od* sight); axis; visual line; **~loch** *n anat* pupil; optic foramen; **~nerv** *m* optic nerve; **~organ** *n* organ of sight (*od* vision); **~probe** *f* vision test; **~prüfung** *f* testing of vision; **~purpur** *m anat* visual purple;

~**reiz** *m* visual stimulus; ~**rohr** *n* (*U-Boot*) periscope; telescope; ~**schärfe** *f* sharpness of vision; visual acuity; acuteness of vision focus; ~**schlitz** *m* (*Panzer*) observation slit, look-out slit (*od* hole); peephole; sight; visor; diopter; ~**schwäche** *f* weakness of vision; *med* amblyopia; ~**sphäre** *f* visual area; ~**störung** *f* visual disorder (*od* disturbance); dyspopia; ~**strahl** *m* visual ray; ~~**ung** *f* optic radiation; ~**tiefe** *f* depth of focus (*od* field); ~**vermögen** *n* faculty of sight (*od* vision), power of vision; ~**vorgang** *m* process of sight; ~**weite** *f* range of sight; visual range; (*Gesichtskreis*) ken; *in* ~~ within sight; ~**werkzeug** *n* organ of sight; ~**winkel** *m* visual (*od* viewing) angle; ~**zelle** *f* *anat* visual cell; ~**zentrum** *n* visual centre, *Am* visual center.

Sehn|e *f anat* tendon; (*Flechse; auch fig*) sinew; (*Bogen*~~) string; *math* chord; ~**enausbreitung** *f med* aponeurosis; ~**enband** *n anat* ligament; ~**endurchschneidung** *f anat* tenotomy; ~**enebene** *f math* chordal surface; ~**enentzündung** *f* inflammation of tendon; ~**enreflex** *m med* tendon reflex; ~**enscheide** *f anat* sheat of tendon; ~~**nentzündung** *f* tendovaginitis; ~**enschnitt** *m math* tangential cut; ~**enzerrung** *f* wrenching of a tendon; ~**ig** *a* sinewy; tendinous; (*Fleisch*) stringy; (*von Person*) strong, muscular, sinewy.

sehn|en: *sich nach etw* ~~ to long for; (*stärker*) to yearn for; (*heftig*) to crave for; (*schmachten nach*) to languish for; *sich nach jdm* ~~ to long for s. o.; *ich ~e mich danach, meine Mutter wiederzusehen* I am longing to see my mother again; ~**en** *n* longing; yearning; ardent desire; (*Heimweh*) nostalgia (*nach* for); ~**lich** *a* longing; (*glühend*) ardent; (*leidenschaftlich*) passionate; ~**sucht** *f* longing; yearning; (*Wunsch*) desire; (*heißer Wunsch*) ardent desire; (*Ungeduld*) impatience; (*Trachten, Streben*) aspiration (*nach* for, after); ~**süchtig,** ~**suchtsvoll** *a* longing, yearning; (*glühend*) ardent; (*leidenschaftlich*) passionate; (*ungeduldig*) impatient.

sehr *adv* very, much (*nur beim Verb*), greatly; *fam* jolly; *fam* awfully; *Am fam* real (*z. B.* a real good time); (*höchst*) most; *ich bedaure es* ~ I regret it very much; *bitte* ~ you are (quite) welcome; *danke* ~ thank you very much; *jdn* ~ *lieben* to be very fond of s. o.; *es hat ihm* ~ *gefallen* he liked it very much; he was very pleased with it; ~ *gern* most willingly; ~ *viel* (*vor Steigerung*) much; (*vor Hauptwort*) a great deal of, plenty of, a lot of; ever so much; ~ *viele* a great many; *so* ~ so much; *so* ~ *wie* as much as; *wie* ~ *auch* however much; *zu* ~ too much.

Seich *m*, ~**e** *f vulg* (*Harn*) urine, piss; *fam* (*Gerede, Gewäsch*) idle talk, tittle-tattle; platitude; (*Gesöff*) swill, slip-slop; ~**en** *itr vulg* to urinate; to make water; (*schwätzen*) to prattle, to tattle.

seicht *a* (*flach, nicht tief*) shallow, flat; *fig* superficial; (*armselig*) poor; (*fade*) insipid; (*Bemerkung*) banal, trivial; (*Gerede*) frivolous; *ein ~er Geist* a shallow mind; ~**igkeit** *f* shallowness; *fig* superficiality; insipidity; frivolousness.

Seid|e *f* silk; *chinesische* ~~ China silk; *echte* ~~ (*Natur*~~) natural silk; *reine* ~~ real silk; *rohe* ~~ (*Roh*~~) raw silk; *wilde* ~~ wild silk; *gezwirnte* ~~ thrown silk; *Näh*~~ sewing silk; *Kunst*~~ artificial silk, rayon; *Stick*~~ embroidery silk; *mit* ~~ *umsponnen* silk-covered; *e-e Spule* ~~ (*Nähfaden*) a reel of silk, *Am* a spool of silk; *in Samt u.* ~~ (*fig*) in purple and fine linen, in silks and satins; *keine* ~~ *bei etw spinnen* to gain nothing by s. th.; ~**en** *a* silk; silken; ~**enabfälle** *m pl* waste silk; ~**enähnlich** *a* silk-like; ~**enarbeiter** *m* silk-weaver; ~**enartig** *a* silky; ~~*er Glanz* silky sheen; silking; ~**enatlas** *m* (silk-) satin; ~**enband** *n* silk ribbon, silk band; ~**enbau** *m* silk culture; sericulture; rearing of silk-worms; ~**enbaumwolle** *f* silk-cotton; ~**enbesetzt** *a* (*plattiert*) silk plated; ~**enbespannung** *f* silk covering; ~**enernte** *f* yield of cocoons; ~**enerzeugnis** *n* silk produce; ~**enfabrik** *f* silk factory, silk mill; ~**enfaden** *m* silk thread; *an e-m* ~~ *hängen* to hang by a silk thread; ~**enfallschirm** *m* silk parachute; ~**enfaserstoff** *m* fibroin; ~**enflor** *m* silk gauze; ~**engarn** *n* silk yarn; ~**engespinst** *n* cocoon of the silkworm; ~**engewebe** *n* silk fabric; silk cloth; silk weave; ~**englanz** *m* silky lustre (*od* gloss); ~**englänzend** *a* silky; ~**enhaar** *n* silky hair; ~**enhaarig** *a* silken-haired; ~**enhandel** *m* silk-trade; mercery; ~**enhändler** *m* dealer in silk; (silk-) mercer; ~**enindustrie** *f* silk industry; ~**enkultur** *f* silk culture; ~**enpapier** *n* tissue paper; ~**enraupe** *f* silkworm; ~~**nzucht** *f* rearing of silkworms; ~**ensamt** *m* silk velvet; ~**enspinner** *m* (*Schmetterling*) (mulberry) silk-moth; *tech* (*Weber*) silk-spinner; ~~**ei** *f* silk factory, silk mill, silk spinnery; ~**enspitze** *f* broad silk lace; blonde lace; ~**enspule** *f* silk reel, silk winder; ~**enstickerei** *f* silk embroidery; ~**enstoff** *m* silk cloth, silk fabric; ~**enstrümpfe** *m pl* silk stockings *pl*; (*dünne*) sheer stockings *pl*; sheers *pl*, rayons *pl*; ~**enstrumpfwaren** *f pl* hosiery of silk; ~**enwaren** *f pl* silk-goods *pl*; silks *pl*; ~**enweich** *a* silky; soft as silk; ~**enwurm** *m* silkworm; ~**enzeug** *n* silk stuff; ~**enzucht** *f* silk-worm breeding, sericulture; ~**enzüchter** *m* silk-grower; sericulturist; ~~**ei** *f* breeding of silkworms; ~**enzwirn** *m* silk twist; ~**ig** *a* silky; ~~*e Faser* silky fibre; ~~*e Wolle* silky wool; ~~*er Glanz* silky lustre (*od* gloss).

Seidel *n* (*Bier*~) mug; (*Maß* = $\frac{1}{2}$ *l*) pint; ~**bast** *m bot* daphne; mezereon.

Seif|e *f* soap; *geol* (*Ablagerung*) deposit; stratum; *Schmier*~~ soft soap; *ein Stück* ~~ a cake of soap; *ein Riegel* ~~ a bar of soap; ~~ *sieden* to make soap; ~**en** *tr* to soap; (*einseifen*) to lather; (*scheuern*) to scour; (*waschen*) to wash; ~**enartig** *a* soapy; saponaceous; ~**enbad** *n* soap bath; ~**enbaum** *m bot* soapbark tree; quillai; ~**enbereitung** *f* soapmaking; ~**enblase** *f* soap-bubble; ~~**n** *machen* to blow soap-bubbles; ~**enbrühe** *f* soap-suds *pl*; ~**enbüchse** *f* soap-box; ~**enersatz** *m* soap substitute; ~**enfabrik** *f* soap factory; ~**enflocken** *f pl* soap-flakes *pl*; *e-e Packung* ~~ a package of soap-flakes; ~**enkiste** *f* soap-box; ~~**nredner** *m Am* soap-box orator; ~~**nrennen** *n* soap-box racing (*od* derby); ~**enkugel** *f* wash-ball; ~**enlauge,** ~**enlösung** *f* soap solution, soap-suds *pl*; ~**ennäpfchen** *n* soap dish; ~**enpulver** *n* soap powder; ~**enriegel** *m* bar of soap; ~**enschabsel** *n* soap scrabs *pl*; ~**enschale** *f* soap dish; ~**enschmiere** *f* soap stuff; ~**ensieder** *m* soap boiler; *es geht mir ein* ~~ *auf fig* I begin to see clear; it dawns upon me; ~~**ei** *f* soap works *pl*; ~**enspäne** *m pl* soap shavings *pl*; ~**enstein** *m* soap-stone; ~**enstück** *n* cake of soap; ~**enwasser** *n* soap water, soapy water; suds *pl*; ~**enzäpfchen** *n* suppository; ~**ig** *a* soapy; saponaceous; (*Kartoffeln*) waxy.

Seiger *m* hour-glass, clock; ~ *a min* perpendicular; ~**hütte** *f* refining-house; ~**n** *tr* to refine, to liquate; to segregate; (*aus Zinn heraus*~~) to sweat out; ~**schacht** *m min* perpendicular shaft.

Seih|e *f*, ~**er** *m* strainer, filter(ing-vessel), colander; (*Rückstand*) dregs *pl*; residue; ~**en** *tr* to strain, to filter; ~**papier** *n* filter paper; ~**sack** *m* filtering bag; ~**trichter** *m* filtering-funnel; colander; ~**tuch** *n* straining-cloth.

Seil *n* cord, rope; line; loop; strand; (*Kabel*) cable; cable-wire rope; cable rope; ~**anker** *m* stay wire; ~**antrieb** *m* cable (*od* rope) drive; ~**bahn** *f* (*Luft*~~) rope railway, ropeway; cableway, *Am* cable railroad; (*Stand*~~) funicular (railway), *Am* cable car; ~**draht** *m* rope wire; ~**en** *tr* to fasten with rope; *an*~~ to rope together; ~**er** *m* cord-maker, rope-maker; ~**erbahn** *f* rope-walk; ~**erei** *f* ropery; ~**erhandwerk** *n* rope-making; ~**erware** *f* rope-yarn, cordage; ~**litze** *f* strand of cable; ~**post** *f* rope post; pickup system; ~**rolle** *f* rope pulley; ~**scheibe** *f* pulley; ~**schlinge** *f* loop of rope; chain loop; ~**schwebebahn** *f* cable railway; ~**seele** *f* core; ~**sperre** *f aero* barrage cable; ~**springen** *n* skipping (the rope); ~**start** *m aero* towed take-off; ~**tänzer** *m* rope-dancer; tight-rope walker; ~**trommel** *f* cable drum; ~**verbindung** *f* splice; ~**werk** *n* cordage; ~**winde** *f* rope winch, cable winch; ~**ziehen** *n sport* (*auch fig*) rope-pulling, tug of war; ~**zug** *m* tackle-line, tow-line.

Seim *m* (*Honig*~) honey; *bot* mucilage; viscous fluid; ~**ig** *a* mucilaginous; viscous.

sein *irr itr* to be, to exist, to live, to take place; *es ist* it is, there is, there are; *durstig, hungrig* ~ to be thirsty, hungry; *was ist Ihnen?* what's the matter with you? *ihm ist übel* he feels sick; *es ist mir kalt* I feel cold; *es sei denn, daß* except, unless; *es ist mir, als wenn* I feel as if; *nicht mehr* ~ to be no more; *ich bin es* it is I, *fam* it is me; *wenn ich Sie wäre, würde ich zu Hause bleiben* if I were you, I would stay home; *im Begriffe* ~ to be going to; *wenn dem so ist* if it is so; if that be so, if that be the case; *es sei!* let it be so!; *sei dem, wie ihm wolle* be that as it may; *seien Sie vorsichtig!* be careful! *sei es, daß ..., od daß* whether — or; *wie dem auch* ~ *mag* as it may be, however that may be; *das mag* ~ that may be; *etw* ~ *lassen* to let, to leave alone; *lassen Sie es lieber* ~ better leave it alone; *lassen Sie das* ~*!* stop it! drop it! skip it! *zwei mal fünf ist zehn* two times five equals ten; ~ *n* being, existence; (*Wesenheit*) entity.

sein *prn* his, its; her; one's; of him, of it; *das ~e* his property; *die ~en* his people; o.'s people; ~**erseits** *adv* for his part, as for him; on his side; as far as he is concerned; ~**erzeit** *adv* in due course; in due time; one day; (*früher*) formerly; in those days; in its time; ~**esgleichen** *prn* his like; o.'s equals; people such as he; people like him; *jdn wie* ~~ *behandeln* to treat s. o. like o.'s equal; *er hat nicht* ~~ there is no one like him; **~ethalben, ~etwegen, um ~etwillen** *adv* for his sake, in his behalf; on his account; (*was ihn angeht*) as far as he is concerned; *sie hat es ~~ getan* she did it because of him; **~ige** *prn* his, its; *das Seinige* his property, his own; o.'s property; his due, his share; his part, o.'s part; his duty; *das ~~ tun* to do o.'s utmost; to do o.'s part; *die Seinigen* his family, his relations, his relatives, his people; his friends; his folks.

seis|misch *a* seismic; **~mograph** *m* seismograph, seismometer; geophone; **~mologisch** *a* seismologic(al); **~moskop** *n* seismoscope.

*

seit *prp* since, for; *schon ~ 3 Jahren* these three years; *~ alters* time out of mind; *~ einiger Zeit* for some time past; *~ jener Zeit* since that time; *~ kurzem* of late, lately; *~ langem* for a long while; *~ neuestem* (*neuerdings*) lately; *~ wann* (*von wann an?*) since when; (*wie lange?*) how long; **~dem** *conj* since; *adv* since that time, since then, from that time; ever since; **~her** *adv* since then; up to now; till now.

Seite *f allg* side; (*Flanke*) flank; (*Richtung*) direction; (*Druck~*) page; (*Speck~*) flitch; (*Partei*) party, side; *math* (*Gleichung*) member; (*Rück~*) reverse; (*e-s Körpers*) face; *fig* (*Gesichtspunkt*) aspect; (*Quelle*) source; *obere ~* upperside; *untere ~* underside; *hintere ~* back; *vordere ~* front; *schwache ~* foible; weakness; weak point; *bei~* apart, aside; out of the way; *abseitig* out-of-the-way; *Scherz bei~* joking apart; *jedes Ding hat zwei ~n* there are two sides to every shield; *~ an ~* side by side; *mar* alongside; *an jds ~ sitzen* to sit next to; *an die ~ stellen* to compare; *auf die ~* aside, away; *auf allen ~n* in all directions; on all sides; *auf beiden ~n* on either side, on both sides; *auf meiner ~* on my side; *auf der e-n ~* on the one side; *fig* on the one hand; *etw auf der ersten ~ der Zeitung bringen Am* to front-page s. th.; *auf die ~ bringen* (*od schaffen*) to put aside; (*heimlich*) to make away with; *auf seine ~ bringen* to bring over to o.'s side; *etw auf die ~ legen* to put aside; *auf der ~ liegen* to lie on o.'s side; *auf die ~ nehmen* to take aside; *sich auf jds ~ stellen* to side with s.o.; *auf jds ~ stehen* to take s.o.'s part; *auf die ~ treten* (*od gehen*) to step aside; *auf jds ~ treten* to side with s.o.; *in die ~ gestemmt* (*Hände*) akimbo; *Stiche in der ~* stitches in o.'s side; *nach allen ~n* in all directions; *von ~n* on the part of; *von dieser ~* from that quarter; *von meiner ~* on my part; *von der ~ adv* askance; *von der ~ ansehen* to look askance at; *alles von der guten ~ ansehen* to look at the bright side of everything; *von der ~ angreifen mil* to attack in the flank; *etw von seiner besten ~ nehmen* to look at the bright sight of things; *sich vor Lachen die ~n halten* to split o.'s sides with laughing; *zur ~* by the side; *mir zur ~* by my side; beside me; *jdm zur ~ stehen fig* to stand by s.o.; to help, to assist s.o.

Seiten|abrutschanzeiger *m aero* side-slip indicator; **~abstand** *m* interval; **~abweichung** *f* (*Geschoß*) deviation (from trajectory); drift; deflection error; **~achse** *f* lateral axis; **~allee** *f* by-walk; **~angriff** *m mil* flank attack; **~ansicht** *f* side-view; side-elevation; lateral view; (*Profil*) profile; **~anzeiger** *m* register, index; **~arm** *m* side branch; lateral arm; **~aufriß** *m* side-elevation, lateral elevation; **~bahn** *f* branch-line; **~band** *n radio* side band; **~bewegung** *f* lateral motion; *mar, aero* yawing; (*plötzliches Abschwenken*) swerve; **~bezeichnung** *f* pagination; **~bezirk** *m* lateral area; **~blatt** *n* side-leaf; **~blick** *m* side-glance; side-look; **~deckung** *f mil* flank guard; flank security; **~druck** *m* side pressure; side force; **~drucker** *m typ* page printer; **~eingang** *m* side-entrance; **~empfänger** *m radio* azimuth receiver; **~erbe** *m* collateral heir; **~falz** *m* groove; **~fehler** *m* lateral error; **~fenster** *n* side-window; **~fläche** *f* side-face, lateral surface; flat side; facet; **~flosse** *f aero* (vertical) fin; tail fin; **~flügel** *m* side-aisle, side-wing; **~gang** *m* side-way, slip; *rail* corridor **~gebäude** *n* wing (of a building); **~geleise** *n rail* sidetrack; siding; *auf ein ~~ schicken fig* to side-track; **~gespräch** *n theat* aside; **~gewehr** *n mil* bayonet; side-arm; **~gleitflug** *m aero* sideslip; **~griff** *m* side handle; **~hieb** *m* side-cut; *fig* (*Anspielung*) home-thrust; dig; **~kanal** *m* lateral channel; **~kante** *f* lateral edge; **~kipper** *m* side-tip car; **~kraft** *f* component force; **~lampe** *f* side lamp; **~lang** *a* filling pages; voluminous; **~länge** *f* lateral length; **~lehne** *f* side-rail; (*Stuhl*) arm; **~leitwerk** *n aero* rudder; *doppeltes ~~* twin rudder; **~linie** *f* collateral line; branch-line (of a railway); **~loge** *f* side-box; **~moräne** *f* lateral moraine; **~öffnung** *f* side opening; **~ortung** *f aero* directional avigation; **~panzer** *m* side armo(u)r; **~pfad** *m* bypath; **~planke** *f* side-plank; **~platz** *m* side-seat; **~richtfeld** *n* field of fire; field of traverse; **~richtung** *f* side direction, deflection; **~riß** *m* side-elevation; profile; **~ruder** *n aero* side rudder; *~~ geben aero* to move the rudder over; **~rutsch** *m aero* sideslip; **~schiff** *n arch* aisle; **~schnitt** *m anat* lateral incision; **~schritt** *m* side-step; **~schub** *m* side thrust; **~schutz** *m* flank protection; **~schwimmen** *n* side-stroke; **~sicherung** *f mil* flank protection; **~sprung** *m* side-leap; caper; double; *fig* escapade; *e-n ~~ machen fig* to make an escapade; **~stabilität** *f* directional stability; **~stechen** *n* stitches (*pl*) in the side; **~steuer** *n aero* rudder (pedal); rudder bar; *~~ geben* to put on rudder; **~strahlung** *f* stray radiation; **~straße** *f* side-street; **~stück** *n* side-piece; *fig* counterpart; pendant; companion picture (to); **~tasche** *f* side-pocket; **~teil** *m* side-part; **~tal** *n* side-valley; transverse valley; **~teilkreis** *m* azimuth scale; **~driftwinkel** *m* drift angle; **~tür** *f* side-door; **~verhältnis** *n* picture ratio; aspect ratio; **~verschiebung** *f* lateral deflection, lateral deviation; **~versetzung** *f* sidewise displacement; **~vorhalt** *m* lateral lead; **~~swinkel** *m* lateral angular lead of target; **~verwandte(r)** *m* collateral relation; **~verzierung** *f* (*am Strumpf*) clock; **~wagen** *m* side-car; *Motorrad mit ~~* combination; **~wand** *f* side-wall; **~wechsel** *m sport* change of ends; **~weg** *m* by-way, sideway; **~wendung** *f* turning aside; **~wind** *m* cross-wind, side-wind; *Landung mit ~~* (*aero*) cross-wind landing; **~winkel** *m* angle of yaw; bearing; **~zahl** *f* number of pages folio; number of a page.

seit|ens *adv* in behalf of; on the part of; on the side of; **~lich** *a* lateral; *fig* collateral; *adv* at the side; *~~ abrutschen aero* to fall off; to sideslip; *~~es Gleiten* skidding; **~wärts** *adv* sideways; sideward(s); aside; on one side; laterally; *~~ geneigt* slanting; sloping.

Sekante *f* secant.

Sekret *n* secretion, secreta *pl*; secreted material; **~ion** *f* secretion; **~~fördernd** *a* secretomatory; **~~hemmend** *a* secretoinhibitory; **~orisch** *a* secretory; **~stoff** *m* secreted substance.

Sekret|är *m* secretary, clerk; (*Möbelstück*) writing-table; bureau; **~ärin** *f* (lady) secretary; **~ariat** *n* secretary's office; secretariate.

Sekt *m* champagne; dry wine; **~kellerei** *f* champagne-cellar.

Sekt|e *f* sect; **~ierer** *m* sectarian; **~ion** *f* section; *med* dissection, post-mortem (examination); autopsy; **~~sbefund** *m* findings of a post-mortem examination; necropsy finding; **~~ssaal** *m med* dissecting room; **~~sschnitt** *m* incision for necropsy; **~or** *m* sector; gate; *der amerikanische ~~ von Berlin* the United States sector of Berlin; **~~angriff** *m* sector attack; **~~enverschluß** *m phot* segment shutter.

Sekund|a *f* (*England*) fifth form; **~aner** *m* fifth-form boy; **~ant** *m* second; **~är** *a* secondary; subordinate; **~~bahn** *f* branch-line; **~~batterie** *f* accumulator battery; storage cell; **~~elektron** *n* secondary electron; **~~empfang** *m radio* secondary reception; **~~strom** *m* induced current; **~e** *f* second; *im Bruchteil e-r ~~* in a split second; **~enbruchteil** *m* split second; **~enuhr** *f* watch with a seconds-hand; **~~zeiger** *m* second(s)-hand; *Am* secondhand; **~ieren** *itr* to second; to accompany; **~ogenitur** *f* right of the younger son.

selb|ander *prn* we two; **~ige** *prn* (*der die, das*) (the) same; selfsame.

selber, selbst *prn* self; in person; personally; (*sogar*) even; *ich ~* I myself; *~ kommen* to come personally; *das versteht sich von ~* that goes without saying; *von ~* voluntarily; of o.'s own accord; (*automatisch*) automatically; (*spontan*) spontaneously; *selbst wenn* even if, even though.

selbst|abdichtend *a aero* (*Tank*) self-sealing; **~achtung** *f* self-esteem, self-respect; **~anlasser** *m* self-starter; automatic starter; **~annäherungsgerät** *n* homing device; **~anschluß** *m* automatic telephone; (*Apparat*) dial telephone; **~ansteckung** *f* self-infection; **~auslöser** *m phot* self-timer; auto(matic) release; **~bedarf** *m* personal requirement; **~bedienungsladen** *m Am* super market; **~befleckung** *f* onanism; self-abuse; **~befruchtung** *f* self-fertilization; **~beherrschung** *f* self-control; self-command; **~beobachtung** *f* self-observation; introspection; **~bekenntnis** *n* voluntary confession; **~beköstigung** *f* boarding o.s.; **~beschämung** *f* self-abasement; **~bestäubung** *f bot* self-pollination; **~bestimmung** *f* self-determination; self-government; **~~srecht** *n* right of self-determination; **~betrug** *m* self-deception; **~bewußt** *a* (*seelisch*) self-conscious; (*sicher im Benehmen*) self-assertive; (*mit Vertrauen auf sich selbst*) self-confident; self-sure; (*stolz*) proud; (*eingebildet*) conceited; **~~sein** *n* self-consciousness; self-assurance; self-assertion; self-conceit; **~binder** *m* (*Krawatte*) open-end tie; (*Erntegerät*) self-binder; **~biographie** *f* autobiography; **~einschätzung** *f* self-assessment; **~entsagung** *f* self-denial; **~entzündung** *f* spontaneous ignition; self-ignition; **~erhaltung** *f* self-preservation; **~erhitzung** *f* self-

-heating; **~erkenntnis** *f* knowledge of o. s.; **~erregend** *a* self-exciting; **~fahrartillerie** *f* self-propelled artillery; **~fahrer** *m mot* (*Person*) owner-driver; (*Stuhl*) self-propelling chair; *Wagenvermietung für ~~* (*Am*) drive-yourself service; **~~wagen** *m* self-drive car; **~fahrgeschütz** *n* self-propelled gun; **~fahrlafette** *f* self-propelled artillery mount (*od* gun); **~füller** *m* self-filling fountain pen; **~gebacken** *a* home-made; **~gebraut** *a* home-brew; **~gefällig** *a* self-satisfied; self-sufficient; complacent; **~~keit** *f* (self-) complacency; **~gefühl** *n* consciousness; self-reliance; self-respect; self-confidence; self-esteem; amour-propre; **~gerecht** *a* self-righteous; **~gespräch** *n* soliloquy; monologue; **~gezogen, ~gezüchtet** *a* home-grown, home-bred; **~herrlich** *a* autocratic; **~herrschaft** *f* self-control; *pol* autonomy; (*Autokratie*) autocracy; **~herrscher** *m* autocrat; **~hilfe** *f* self-help; self-defence; (*Luftschutz*) passive air-defence; **~induktion** *f el* self-induction; **~isch** *a* selfish; ego(t)istic; **~kosten** *pl* cost of production; factory cost; net cost; **~~berechnung** *f* calculation of production cost; **~~preis** *m* cost price; prime cost, *Am* flat cost; **~ladegewehr** *n* automatic rifle; **~ladepistole** *f* automatic pistol; self-loading pistol; **~lader** *m* automatic weapon; automatic; **~ladevorrichtung** *f* automatic loader; **~laut(er)** *m* vowel; **~leuchtend** *a* self-illuminating; luminous; **~liebe** *f* self-love; **~los** *a* unselfish; altruistic; disinterested; **~~igkeit** *f* unselfishness; **~mord** *m* suicide; *~~ begehen* to commit suicide, *fam* to suicide; **~mörder** *m* suicide; **~~flugzeug** *n* suicide plane; (*in Japan*) kamikaze; **~mörderisch** *a* suicidal; **~mordversuch** *m* suicidal attempt; **~quälerisch** *a* self-tormenting; **~redend** *a* self-evident; (*augenscheinlich*) obvious; *das ist ~~* that is a matter of course; **~regelnd** *a* self-regulating; **~regierung** *f* autonomy; **~schreiber** *m* (automatic) recorder; **~schuß** *m* spring-gun; **~schutz** *m* self-protection; self-defence; **~sicher** *a* self-confident; **~~heit** *f* self-confidence; aplomb; **~steuer** *n*, **~~ung** *f* automatic control; **~steuergerät** *n aero* automatic pilot, robot pilot, gyro pilot; *aero sl* George; *allg* automatic control apparatus; **~sucht** *f* selfishness, ego(t)ism; **~süchtig** *a* selfish, ego(t)istic(al); *fam* mean; **~tätig** *a* spontaneous; *tech* automatic, self-acting; *~~er Schwundregler radio* automatic volume control; **~täuschung** *f* self-delusion; **~teilung** *f* fission; **~tragend** *a* self-supporting; **~überheblich** *a* overweening; **~überhebung** *f* presumption, self-conceit; **~überwindung** *f* self-victory; **~übung** *f* practice; **~unterbrecher** *m* automatic interrupter; buzzer; **~unterricht** *m* self-instruction; **~verlag** *m*: *im ~~* published by the author; **~verleugnung** *f* self-denial, self-abnegation; **~vernichtung** *f* self-destruction; **~versenkung** *f* (*von Schiffen*) scuttling; **~versorger** *m* self-supplier; self-supporter; small farmer; **~versorgung** *f* self-sufficiency; **~verständlich** *a* self-evident; obvious; natural; *adv* of course; *es ist ~~* it goes without saying; **~~keit** *f* matter of course; foregone conclusion; **~verstümmelung** *f* self-mutilation; self-inflicted wounds *pl*; **~verteidigung** *f* self-defence; **~vertrauen** *n* self-reliance; self-confidence; **~verwaltung** *f* autonomy; self-government; self-management; home rule; **~wähler** *m tele* dial (set telephone); **~zersetzung** *f* spontaneous decomposition; **~zucht** *f* self-discipline; **~zufrieden** *a* self-satisfied; complacent; **~~heit** *f* self-content; **~zünder** *m* automatic lighter; self-igniter; *chem* pyrophorus; **~zündung** *f* spontaneous ignition; compression ignition; **~zweck** *m* end in itself.

selbständig *a* independent; self-supporting, self-contained; autonomous; *sich ~~ machen* to set up for o. s.; **~~keit** *f* independence; self-sufficiency; autonomy.

selch|en *tr* to smoke; **~er** *m* butcher; **~fleisch** *n* smoked meat.

Selekt|ion *f* selection; elimination; **~iv** *a radio* (*abstimmscharf*) selective; *nicht ~~* non-selective; **~ivität** *radio* selectivity.

Selen *n* selenium; **~eisen** *n* ferrous selenide; **~haltig** *a* seleniferous; **~it** *n min* selenite; **~metall** *n* (metallic) selenide; **~verbindung** *f* selenium compound; **~zelle** *f* selenium (*od* selenious) cell.

selig *a* blessed, happy; blissful; (*verstorben*) deceased, late; *fam* (*betrunken*) tipsy; *meine ~e Mutter* my late mother; *~en Angedenkens* of blessed memory; *~sprechen* to beatify, to canonize; *~ machen* to save; *~ werden* to attain salvation, to be saved; *die ~en* the departed; **~keit** *f* salvation, felicity; happiness, bliss; **~macher** *m* Saviour; **~preisung** *f* (*Bibel*) Beatitude; **~sprechung** *f* beatification.

Sellerie *m od f* celery; celeriac; **~salat** *m* celery salad.

selt|en *a* rare; (*knapp*) scarce; (*ungewöhnlich*) unusual; (*merkwürdig*) curious; (*außerordentlich*) singular; exceptional; *adv* seldom, rarely; *~~es Exemplar* (*e-s Buches*) scarce copy; *ein ~~er Vogel fig fam* a white crow; *höchst ~ ~* hardly ever; *fam* once in a blue moon; **~enheit** *f* rarity; scarcity; rareness; curiosity; **~~tswert** *m* rarity value; **~sam** *a* strange; (*eigentümlich*) singular; (*sonderbar*) odd, queer; rum; (*merkwürdig*) curious; **~samkeit** *f* strangeness; singularity; oddness, oddity; peculiarity.

Selters|flasche *f* a bottle of seltzer; **~wasser** *n* seltzer; soda-water.

Semester *n* semester, half-year; session; term; *im ~ anwesend* in attendance, *Am* on the campus; **~schluß** *m* close of the term.

Semikolon *n* semicolon.

Seminar *n* seminar, training-college (for teachers); (*Priester~*) seminary; **~ist** *m* seminarist; pupil of a training-college.

Semit *m* Semite; **~isch** *a* Semitic.

Semmel *f* roll; (*runde, flache*) muffin; *wie warme ~n abgehen* to sell rapidly; to go off like hot cakes; **~blond** *a* flaxen-haired.

Senat *m* senate; **~or** *m* senator; **~orisch** *a* senatorial; **~sausschuß** *m* senatorial committee, senate committee; **~sbeschluß** *m* decree of the senate; **~swürde** *f* senatorship.

Send|bote *m* messenger; envoy; **~brief** *m* circular letter; epistle; missive; **~eantenne** *f radio* transmitting aerial (*od* antenna); **~eapparat** *m* transmitting set; **~ebereich** *m* broadcasting area; **~ebühne** *f* stage in the broadcasting studio; **~eeinrichtung** *f* transmission equipment; **~efolge** *f* broadcasting program(me); **~egesellschaft** *f* broadcasting company; **~eleistung** *f* sending power; output; *große* (*kleine*) *~~* high-power (low-power) output; **~eleiter** *m* (broadcasting) producer; **~emanuskript** *n Am* continuity; **~en** *irr* (*sandte, gesandt*) *tr* (*schicken*) to send; *nach jdm ~~* to send for; (*übersenden*) to forward; *radio* (*sendete, gesendet*) to transmit, to broadcast; to radio; to go on the air; to air a program(me); to put a program(me) on the air; (*Fernsehsender*) to take to the air; *die Fernsehstationen ~~ nur 4 Stunden täglich* TV stations telecast only four hours a day; **~eprogramm** *n* broad- casting (*od* radio) program(me); **~er** *m radio* sender; transmitter; broadcasting station; sending station; (*tragbarer*) portable transmitter; **~eranlage** transmitter station; **~erantenne** *f* transmitter aerial; **~eraum** *m* (broadcasting) studio; **~ereichweite** *f* transmission range; **~erempfänger** *m* transceiver; **~ergruppe** *f*, **~ernetz** *n* network; broadcasting chain; **~erleistung** *f* power of a transmitter; **~eröhre** *f* transmitter valve (*Am* tube); **~espiel** *n* radio play; broadcasting-studio performance; **~estärke** *f* transmitting power; **~estation** *f* transmitter; transmitting station; sending station; radio station; *e-e ~~ eröffnen* to open a station; **~estelle** *f* broadcasting station; (*Nebenstelle e-s Senders*) outlet station; affiliated station; **~eturm** *m* transmission tower; **~ezeichen** *n* call-sign; **~ezeit** *f radio* air time; station time; **~ling** *m* emissary; messenger; **~schreiben** *n* letter; **~ung** *f* sending; *com* shipment, consignment; *fig* (*Mission*) mission; *radio* transmission; broadcast; *mit der ~~ beginnen* to go on the air; *mit der ~~ aufhören* to go off the air; *kommerzielle Sendung Am* sponsored program; *~~ ohne Reklame Am* sustaining program(me); *~~ von Nachrichten* newscasting.

Senf *m* mustard; *fam e-n langen ~ machen* to enlarge on; *seinen ~ dazu geben* to put in o.'s word; **~fabrikant** *m* mustard-maker; **~gas** *n* mustard gas; **~gefäß** *n*, **~topf** *m* mustard-pot; **~gurke** *f* cucumber pickled with mustard; **~korn** *n* grain of mustard seed; **~pflaster** *n*, **~umschlag** *m* mustard plaster.

Seng|e *f fam* sound thrashing; *~~ beziehen* to get licked; **~en** *tr* to singe, to scorch; to burn; (*dörren*) to parch; (*Schwein*) to scald; *itr* to catch fire; *~~ u. brennen* to burn and ravage, to lay waste; **~erig** *a* burnt; *hier wird es ~~* (*fam*) it is rather hot quarters here.

Senior *m* senior, chairman.

Senk|blei *n* plummet, sounding-lead; **~brunnen** *m* sunk well; **~e** *f geog* valley; trough; dip; crevasse; depression; shallow subsidence; **~el** *m* lace; **~en** *tr* to sink, to lower, to let down; *ins Grab ~en* to entomb; *die Augen ~en* to cast down (o.'s eyes); *den Kopf ~en* to bow o.'s head; *r* to settle; to sink; to go down; to subside; (*Mauer*) to sag; (*sich neigen*) to dip, to slope; **~er** *m* sinker; *bot* layer; **~fuß** *m* flat foot; **~~einlage** *f* arch-support, instep-raiser; **~grube** *f* cesspool, sink-hole; **~kasten** *m* (sunk) caisson; **~körper** *m* sinker; bob; **~leine** *f* fathom-line; **~nadel** *f* probe; **~niet** *m* flush rivet; countersunk rivet; **~rebe** *f* layer of vine; **~recht** *a math* perpendicular, vertical, right; at right angle to; *~~es Hochreißen aero* zooming up; *~~e Kurve aero* vertical turn; *~~er Sturzflug aero* vertical dive; **~~aufnahme** *f aero* vertical air photograph; **~~aufstieg** *m aero* direct take-off; **~~e** *f* perpendicular line; plumb (line); vertical; normal; **~reis** *n* layer; **~ung** *f* sinking; (*Vertiefung*) depression; (*Nei-*

gung) inclination; (*Lohn, Preise*) reduction, cut; (*Abhang*) slope, declivity, dip; (*Mauer*) sag; (*Vers*) unaccented syllable; *mus* thesis; **~waage** *f* areometer.
Senn|e *f* herd of cattle; cheese-dairy; **~(er)** *m* Alpine herdsman; **~erin** *f* dairymaid (in the Alps); **~hütte** *f* Alpine dairy, chalet.
Sensal *m* broker.
Sennesblätter *n pl* senna leaves *pl*.
Sensation *f* sensation; thrill; shocker; (*Presse*) *sl* scoop; **~ell** *a* sensational; thrilling; *sl Am* (*schaurig*) blood-and-thunder; **~sblatt** *n* sensational newspaper, *Am* yellow journal; **~smeldung, ~snachricht** *f* sensational news *pl mit sing*, *Am* scoop; beat; **~spresse** *f* sensational press, *Am* yellow press; **~sroman** *m* penny-dreadful, thriller; *Am* dime novel; **~ssucht** *f* sensationalism.
Sense *f* scythe; **~nmann** *m* scytheman, mower; *fig* Death; **~nschmied** *m* scythe-smith.
sensib|el *a* sensitive; sensible; sensory; **~ilität** *f* sensibility; feeling; sensitiveness.
Sentenz *f* maxim; aphorism; **~lös** *a* sententious.
sentimental *a* sentimental, *fam* soft; **~ität** *f* sentimentality; sentimentalism.

*

separat *a* separate; **~ausgabe** *f* special edition; **~eingang** *m* separate entrance; **~ismus** *m* separatism; **~ist** *m* separatist; **~konto** *n* separate (*od* special) account; **~zimmer** *n* separate chamber; **~vertrag** *m* special agreement.
Sepia *f* (*Fisch*) cuttle-fish; (*Farbe*) sepia; **~papier** *n phot* sepia paper; brown print paper; **~ton** *m phot* sepia tone; **~zeichnung** *f* sepia drawing.
Sep|sis *f* sepsis, septicemia; **~tisch** *a* septic.
Sept|ember *m* September; **~ett** *n* septet(te).
Sequest|er *n* sequestration; **~rieren** *tr* to sequestrate.
Serail *n* seraglio.
Seraph (*pl* **~im**) *m* seraph.
Serb|e *m* Serbian; **~ien** *n* Serbia; **~isch** *a* Serbian.
Serenade *f* serenade.
Sergeant *m* sergeant.
Serie *f* (*Reihe*) series; line; (*Ausgabe, Folge*) issue; (*von Zeitschriften, Büchern, Karten, Werkzeugen etc*) set; *nach ~n geordnet* serial; *in ~e liegend* in series; **~narbeit** *f* repetition work; **~nartikel** *m* mass produced article; **~nbau** *m* building in series; series production; serial construction; production line; **~nfabrikation, ~nherstellung** *f* series production, quantity production; mass production; serial manufacture; **~nfertigung** *f* quantity production; manufacturing in series; **~nflugzeug** *n* production aircraft, *Am* stock aircraft; **~nlos** *n* serial lottery ticket; **~nmäßig** *a* standard, regular, in series; *~~e Ausrüstung* standard equipment; *~~ herstellen* to produce in quantity, to mass produce; **~nnummer** *f* serial number; **~nproduktion** *f* mass production; **~nreife** *f tech* production stage; **~nschalter** *m* multicircuit switch; **~nschaltung** *f el* series connexion, connexion in series; **~nteil** *m* duplicate piece; **~nwagen** *m mot* standard type car, *Am* stock car; **~nweise** *a* = *~nmäßig*; **~nwerk** *n* serial; **~nwicklung** *f el* series winding.
seriös *a* serious; (*zuverlässig*) reliable; responsible.
Sero|loge *m* serologist; **~logie** *f* serology; **~logisch** *a* serologic(al); **~reaktion** *f* seroreaction; **~therapie** *f* serum therapy.
Serpentin *m min* serpentine; ophite; **~e** *f* (*Schlangenlinie*) serpentine line; (*Straßenkehre*) turn, bend; (*gewundene Straße*) winding road; **~stein** *m* serpentine-stone.
Serum *n* serum; blood serum; **~artig** *a* serous; **~diagnose** *f* serodiagnosis; **~therapie** *f* serum therapy, serotherapy.
Serv|ice *n* service, set (of plates); **~ierbrett** *n* tray; **~ieren** *tr,itr* (*den Tisch decken*) to serve, to lay the cloth; (*bedienen*) to wait (at table); *es ist ~iert!* dinner is served! **~iertisch** *m* sideboard; **~ierwagen** *m* dumb-waiter; dinner-wagon; **~iette** *f* (table-) napkin; serviette; **~~nring** *m* napkin-ring; **~il** *a* servile, obsequious; **~itut** *f jur* servitude, easement.
Servo|bremse *f* servo (-assisted) brake; **~motor** *m* servo-motor; auxiliary engine; **~ruder** *n aero* servo flap; **~steuerung** *f* servo control.
Servus! *interj fam* hello! so long!
Sessel *m* easy-chair; arm-chair; **~lift** *m*, **~seilbahn** *f* chair-lift.
seßhaft *a* settled; established; stationary; (*ansässig*) resident; sedentary; *mil* (*Kampfstoff*) persistent; **~igkeit** *f* settledness; stationariness; residency; persistency.

*

Setz|art *f mus* composition; **~bett** *n tech* settling tank; **~bottich** *m tech* settling vat; **~brett** *n typ* composing board; *chem* settling bottom; **~eier** *n pl* (*Spiegeleier*) fried eggs *pl*; (*verlorene*) poached eggs *pl*; **~eisen** *n* (*Schmiede*) cutter, smithing chisel; **~en** *tr* (*hinstellen*) to set; (*plazieren*) to place; (*legen*) to put; (*Frist etc festlegen*) to fix; (*aufhäufen*) to stack, to pile; (*Denkmal*) to erect (a monument to); to put up; (*Baum*) to plant; *mus, typ* to compose; to set up in type; (*Junge*) to breed; (*von Fischen*) to spawn; (*Geld beim Spiel*) to stake; (*beim Pokerspiel*) to ante up; *alles daran ~~* to risk everything; to leave no stone unturned; to do all in o.'s power; *den Fall ~~* to put the case; to suppose; *gesetzt den Fall, daß* ... suppose ...; *ein Ende ~~* to put an end to; *jdm e-e Frist ~~* to fix a term to s. o.; *zur festgesetzten Stunde* at the appointed hour; *an den Mund ~~* to put to o.'s lips; *an die Luft ~~* to kick s. o. out; to turn s. o. out; *fam* to give s. o. the gate; *an Stelle von ... ~~* to substitute for ...; *auf Grund ~~* (*Schiff*) to run (a ship) aground; *den Hut auf den Kopf ~~* to put o.'s hat on; *alles auf e-e Karte ~~* to stake everything on one card; *fam* to put all eggs into one basket; *auf jds Rechnung ~~* to charge (*od* to place) to s. o.'s account; *aufs Spiel ~~* to venture, to risk; *auf die Seite ~~* to put s. th. aside; *auf die Straße ~~* to turn out into the street; *seine Hoffnung ~~ auf* to pin (*od* to pitch) o.'s hope(s) to; *große Hoffnungen auf etw ~~* to set o.'s hopes high on; *Vertrauen auf jdn ~~* to trust in s. o.; *außer Kraft ~~* (*Gesetz*) to invalidate; to abrogate; to repeal; to rescind; *in Bewegung ~~* to set in motion, to set going; *Himmel u. Hölle in Bewegung ~~* to leave no stone unturned; *in Erstaunen ~~* to astonish, to surprise; *in Freiheit ~~* to set at liberty, to set free, to liberate; *in Furcht* (*od in Angst*) *~~* to put in fear; (*erschrecken*) to frighten; *in Gang ~~* to set in motion; to set going; *in Noten ~~* to set to music; to compose; *für Klavier ~~* to score for the piano; *instand ~~* to repair; *seinen Stolz in etw ~~* to take a pride in s. th.; *in Szene ~~* (*theat*) (*inszenieren*) to stage; to mount (a play); *in Verlegenheit ~~* to embarrass, to puzzle; *in die Welt ~~* (*Kinder*) to put into the world; to give birth to; *ins Werk ~~* to set on foot; to execute; *in die Zeitung ~~* to put into the paper; *unter Druck ~~* to put pressure on; *seinen Namen unter etw ~~* to put o.'s name to; *unter Wasser ~~* to submerge; *vor die Tür ~~* to turn s. o. out; *zur Rede ~~* to call to account; *itr* (*schnell laufen*) to run; (*hüpfen*) to leap (*über* over); to vault; (*über e-n Fluß*) to cross (*od* to pass) a river; (*bei Wette*) to bet on; to back; *es wird Hiebe ~~* it will end in a fight; it will come to blows; you will catch it; *an Land ~~* to land, to disembark; *über e-n Graben ~~* to take a ditch; *sich ~~* to sit down; (*Platz nehmen*) to take a seat, *Am* to have a seat; (*von Vögeln*) to perch; *sich zu jdm ~~* to sit down beside s. o.; *chem* (*Flüssigkeiten*) to subside; to precipitate; to be deposited; to settle; to clarify; *~~ Sie sich!* sit down! be seated! take your seat! *Am* have a seat! (*sich senken*) to sink; *sich an die Arbeit ~~* to set to work; *sich an jds Platz ~~* to put o. s. in s. o.'s place; (*verdrängen*) to supersede s. o.; *sich auf e-e Bank ~~* to sit down on a bench; *sich gegen etw ~~* to object to s. th.; *sich in Bewegung ~~* to get in motion; *sich bei jdm in Gunst ~~* to ingratiate o. s. with; to start up; to stir; *sich etw in den Kopf ~~* to take (*od* to get) it into o.'s head; (*sich fest entschließen*) to have o.'s mind set on; *sich in ein gutes Licht ~~* to put o. s. in good light; *sich in Verbindung ~~ mit* to get in touch with; to contact; *sich zu Pferd ~~* to mount on horseback; *sich zur Ruhe ~~* to retire, to withdraw; *sich zu Tisch ~~* to sit down to table, to sit down to dinner; *sich zur Wehr ~~* to defend o. s.; **~er** *m typ* compositor; *Am* type setter; typo(grapher); **~erei** *f typ* compositor's room; composing room; case-department; **~erlehrling** *m typ* printer's devil; **~ersaal** *m* composing room; **~fehler** *m* typographical error; printer's error; misprint; erratum (*pl* errata); **~hammer** *m* (*Schmiede*) sledge hammer; **~hase** *m* (*Häsin*) doe hare; female hare; **~kasten** *m typ* letter-case; (type-) case; (*Trog*) hutch; (*für Kohlen*) jigger; **~ling** *m* layer; slip; (*Fisch*) fry; **~linie** *f typ* reglet; composing- (*od* setting-) rule; **~maschine** *f typ* type-setting machine; composing-machine; (*für Einzelbuchstaben*) monotype; (*Zeilen~~*) linotype; **~rahmen** *m typ* composing frame; **~rebe** *f* layer of vine; **~regal** *n typ* letter (*od* type) shelf; composing frame; **~reis** *n* slip; shoot; **~schiff** *n typ* (composing) galley; **~teich** *m* store-pond; **~tisch** *m typ* composing table; **~~ und Gießmaschine** *f* linotype (machine); **~waage** *f* (field) level; **~werkzeug** *n typ* composing tool; **~zeit** *f* (*bei Tieren*) breeding time; (*von Fischen*) spawning-time.
Seuche *f* epidemic; infectious disease, contagious disease; contagion; plague, pestilence; *e-e Seuche ist ausgebrochen* an epidemic broke out; **~nartig** *a* epidemic, endemic; contagious; **~nbekämpfung** *f* control of epidemics; **~nfest** *a* immune; **~ngesetz** *n* law relating to contagious diseases *pl*; **~nhaft** *a* epidemic; **~nherd** *m* centre (*Am* center)

of contagion; **~nlazarett** *n* hospital for infectious diseases.

seufz|en *itr* to sigh (*vor* with, for; *über* at); to fetch (*od* to heave) a deep sigh; to groan; *~end* with a sigh; *~end äußern* to sigh out; *jdm die Ohren voll ~* to be always dinning into s.o.'s ears; **~er** *m* sigh, groan; *e-n ~~ ausstoßen* to heave a sigh; to utter a groan; *seinen letzten ~~ aushauchen* to draw o.'s last breath; **~erbrücke** *f* (*in Venedig*) Bridge of Sighs.

Sext|a *f* sixth class; (*England*) first form; **~aner** *m* sixth-form boy, first-form boy; **~ant** *m* sextant; **~ett** *n* sestet, sextet(te).

sexual, sexuell *a* sexual; *auf das Sexuelle bezüglich sl* sexy; **~empfindung** *f* sexuality; **~forscher** *m* sexologist; **~hormon** *n* sex hormone; **~hygiene** *f* sex hygiene; **~ität** *f* sexuality; **~wissenschaft** *f* sexology; **~zelle** *f* germ cell.

Sezession *f* secession; **~skrieg** *m* war of secession.

Sezier|besteck *n* post-mortem case; **~en** *tr anat* to dissect; *fam* to cut up; *fig* to analyse; **~messer** *n* dissecting-knife; (*kleines*) scalpel; **~saal** *m* dissecting room; **~tisch** *m* dissecting table; **~ung** *f* dissection.

Shampoo *n* shampoo; **~nieren** *tr* (*Haare waschen*) to shampoo.

Siam *n* Siam; Thailand; **~ese** *m*, **~esin** *f* Siamese; **~esisch** *a* Siamese; *die ~~en Zwillinge* the Siamese twins.

Sibir|ien *n* Siberia; **~ier** *m* Siberian, native of Siberia; **~isch** *a* Siberian.

sich *prn* himself, herself, itself; themselves; yourself, yourselves; oneself; one another, each other; *an ~* in itself; *sie hat viele Fehler an ~* she has many faults; *an u. für ~* in itself; considered by itself; *außer ~ sein* to be beside o. s.; *es hat nichts auf ~* it is of no consequence; it does not matter; *das spricht für ~ selbst* that speaks for itself; *das ist e-e Sache für ~* that is a matter by itself; that is another story; *wieder zu ~ kommen* to come to; to recover consciousness; *das Ding an ~* the thing in itself; *sie haben ~ sehr gern* they are very fond of each other.

Sichel *f* sickle; (*Mond~*) crescent; *anat* falx; **~förmig** *a* sickle-shaped; *anat* falciform; **~n** *tr* to cut with the sickle; to reap.

*

sicher *a* (*vor Gefahr*) safe, (*aus gutem Grund*) secure; (*gewiß*) sure; certain; (*positiv*) positive; (*fest*) firm; steady; (*bestimmt*) definite; (*zuverlässig*) reliable; trusty; trustworthy; (*wahr*) true; (*zuversichtlich*) confident; (*sorglos*) over-confident; *e-e ~e Anlage* a safe investment; *~es Benehmen* self-possessed behavio(u)r; *ein ~er Beweis* a sure proof; *~es Geleit* safe-conduct; *e-e ~e Hand* a steady hand; *~e Nachrichten* reliable news, reliable information; *ein ~er Posten* a safe job; *e-e ~e Sache Am sl* a cinch; *der ~e Tod* certain death; *aus ~er Hand* (*od Quelle*) on good authority; *in ~em Gewahrsam* in safe keeping; *in ~er Hut* in safe keeping; *~ vor Gefahr* secure from danger; *~ gehen* to be (*od* to keep) on the safe side; to make quite sure; *seiner Sache ~ sein* to be certain of s. th.; *vor etw ~ sein* to be safe from s. th.; *um ~ zu gehen* in order to be on the safe side; *~stellen* to put in safe keeping; *Geld ~stellen* to tie up money; *sich ~ stellen* to secure o. s.; *~ schießen* to be a dead shot; *~ wissen* to know for certain; *sie wird ~ kommen* she is sure to come; *absolut ~* infallible, *Am* sure-fire; *das ist so ~ wie nur was* that is as sure as anything; *aber ~!* take it from me! *Am sl* you bet! *~!* certainly! *Am* sure! **~heit** *f* (*vor Gefahr*) safety; margin of safety; *öffentliche ~~* public safety; (*auch com*) security; secureness; (*Gewißheit*) certainty; positiveness; (*Auftreten, Überzeugung*) assurance; (*Zuverlässigkeit*) trustworthiness; reliability; (*Vertrauen*) confidence; (*Garantie*) guarantee, *Am* guaranty; (*Bürgschaft*) bail; (*Deckung*) cover; (*Pfand*) pledge; (*Festigkeit*) firmness; steadiness; *kollektive ~~* collective security; *die ~~ gefährden* to endanger the security; *~~ leisten* to give (*od* to offer) security; *jur* to go bail, *Am* to raise bond; *die ~~ wiederfinden* to regain confidence; *in ~~ bringen* to secure; to get out of danger; to place in safety; *sich in ~~ bringen* to make for safety; *sich* (*jdn*) *in ~~ wiegen* to lull o. s. (s. o.) into security; *man kann mit ~~ behaupten* it is safe to say; **~~sabstand** *m* safety zone; **~~ausschuß** *m* committee of public safety; **~~sbeanspruchung** *f* safety stress; **~~sbehörde** *f* security board; **~~sbolzen** *m* safety bolt; **~~sbremse** *f* safety (*od* emergency) brake; **~~sbrennstoff** *m* safety fuel; **~~sdienst** *m* security service; (*Luftschutz*) air-raid precautions service; **~~sdraht** *m* safety wire; **~~sfaktor** *m* factor of safety; **~~sfarbe** *f* safety paint; **~~sfonds** *m com* guarantee fund; reserve fund; **~~sgerät** *n* safety equipment (*od* device); emergency outfit; **~~sglas** *n* safety glass; (*Auto*) non-shatterable glass; **~~sgrad** *m* margin of safety; **~~sgurt, ~~sgürtel** *m aero* safety belt; **~~shaken** *m* safety hook; **~~shalber** *adv* for safety; **~~shöhe** *f aero* safety level; **~~skette** *f* (*an Tür*) door-chain; guard-chain; (*Armband*) safety-chain; **~~sklausel** *f* safe-guard; **~~skoeffizient** *m* factor of safety; **~~slampe** *f* safety-lamp; *min* davy; **~~sleistung** *f* security; *jur* bail; **~~sleiter** *f* safety ladder; **~~smaßnahme** *f* safety precaution; **~~smaßregel** *f* safety measure; security-measure; safety-first measure; **~~smutter** *f* lock nut; **~~snadel** *f* safety pin; **~~spakt** *m* security pact; *Nordatlantischer ~~spakt* North Atlantic Security Pact; **~~spaß** *m* safe conduct; **~~spfand** *n* pledge; **~~spolizei** *f* security police; **~~srasierapparat** *m* safety razor; **~~srat** *m* (United Nations) Security Council; **~~sreserve** *f* investment reserve; **~~sriegel** *m* safety catch; **~~sschacht** *m* escape shaft; **~~sschloß** *n* safety-lock; **~~sschlüssel** *m* patent key; **~~sspielraum** *m* margin of safety; **~~ssprengstoff** *m* safety explosive; **~~sstift** *m* shearing pin; **~~sstreichholz** *n* safety match; **~~s- u. Hilfsdienst** *m* (*Abk SHD*) air-raid protection service; **~~svorrichtung** *f* safety device (*od* appliance); **~~svorschriften** *f pl* safety rules *pl*, safety code; **~~szahl** *f* factor of safety; **~~szone** *f* security zone; **~~szünder** *m* safety fuse; **~~szündholz** *n* safety-match; **~~szündschnur** *f* safety fuse; **~lich** *a* surely; certainly; *~~!* certainly! *Am* sure! *Am* you bet! *Am* sure thing! *Am* I guess that's so! (*ohne Zweifel*) without doubt; undoubtedly; **~n** *tr* to secure; (*schützen*) to protect; to guard; to check; to cover; (*befestigen*) to fasten; (*gewährleisten*) to guarantee; (*in Sicherheit bringen*) to safeguard; (*Gewehr*) to set (*od* to place) at 'safe'; (*blockieren*) to block; *sich gegen etw ~~* to make sure against s. th.; **~stellen** *tr* to guaranty, to give security; **~stellung** *f* safeguarding; (*durch Deckung*) cover; (*durch Garantie*) guarantee, guaranty; (*Kredit*) securing; **~ung** *f* securing; protection; guarantee; *tech* safety mechanism; *el* fuse, fuze; cut-out; *mil* protection; (*gegen Erdgegner*) ground defence; (*gegen Luftgegner*) anti-aircraft protection; (*an Schußwaffe*) safety-catch, safety-bolt; **~~sabstand** *m mil* march interval; **~~sfahrzeug** *n mar* escort vessel; **~~sflügel** *m* safety stirrup; (*bei Waffe*) safety catch; (*strategisch*) protective flank (*od* wing); **~~shaken** *m* quick-release hook; **~~shebel** *m* safety lever; safety catch; **~~skappe** *f* (*Munition*) safety-cap; **~~skasten** *m* fuse-box; **~~spanzer** *m* covering tank; **~~sregiment** *n mil* defence regiment; **~~sriegel** *m* safety catch; **~~srücklage** *f* reserve fund; **~~sschalter** *m* safety switch; **~~sschiff** *n aero* (*Seenotschiff*) sea-plane rescue boat; *mar* coastal defence ship; escort vessel; picket boad; **~~sschraube** *f* safety screw; **~~sstöpsel** *m* safety plug; **~~sstreitkräfte** *f pl mil* security forces *pl*; *mar* escort craft; coastal defence units; **~~struppen** *f pl* security forces *pl*; **~~szone** *f* security zone.

Sicht *f* sight; (*Aus~*) view; outlook; (*Sichtigkeit*) visibility; (*Klarheit*) clearness; transparency; *~ nach vorn* forward view; *~ nach hinten* rear view; *gute ~* good visibility, good view; *schlechte ~* poor visibility; *auf ~* at sight; *auf lange ~* at long date; long-term; *ein Plan auf lange ~* a long-range plan; *auf kurze ~* short-dated; at short date; short-term; *Wirkung auf weite ~* long-range effect; *bei ~* at sight; *auf 8 Tage ~* seven days after sight; *drei Tage nach ~* three days after sight; *außer ~ kommen* to disappear from sight; *außer ~ sein* to be out of sight; *in ~ kommen* to come in sight; *in ~ bleiben* to keep in sight; **~bar, ~lich** *a* visible, perceptible; visual; (*offenbar*) evident; apparent, obvious; *~bar werden* to appear; **~barkeit** *f* visibleness; visibility; **~barmachung** *f* visualization; **~bereich** *m* zone of visibility; **~deckung** *f* sight defilade; **~en** *tr mar* (*sehen*) to sight; (*erblicken*) to catch sight of; (*durchsieben*) to sift; (*Getreide, Mehl*) to winnow, to bolt; *fig* (*prüfen*) to examine; (*aussuchen*) to sort out, to sift; to screen; (*trennen*) to separate; (*ordnen, einteilen*) to classify; to grade; **~feld** *n* field of vision; **~ig** *a* clear; **~igkeit** *f* visibility; clearness; transparency; **~meßgerät** *n* visibility meter; **~schutz** *m* camouflage; **~ung** *f* sighting; observation; (*Trennung, Aussortierung*) sifting; sorting; separation; testing; **~verbindlichkeit** *f com* sight bill; **~verhältnisse** *n pl* visibility; **~vermerk** *m* visé, visa; **~wechsel** *m* sight bill; bill payable at sight; **~weite** *f* range of sight; sighting distance, visual range; line of sight; **~winkel** *m* viewing angle, angle of sight; **~zeichen** *n* (ground) signal; sign.

Sicker|kanal *m* drainage culvert; **~loch** *n* drainage pit; **~n** *itr* to trickle, to ooze (out), to drop; to percolate; to leak; to seep; **~schacht** *m* seepage shaft; **~ung** *f* trickling; percolation; seepage; **~wasser** *n* leakage water; percolating waters *pl*; *arch* ground water.

sie *prn* she, her; it; they, them; *sie sind es* it is they; **Sie** you; *gehen Sie!* go!

Sieb *n* sieve; (*Durchschlag*) strainer; colander; (*grobes* ~) riddle; sifter; (*Sand*~) screen; (*Mehl*~) bolter; (*Draht*~) mesh; *radio* filter; eliminator; network; *ein Gedächtnis wie ein* ~ a bad memory; **~artig** *a* sieve-like; **~bein** *n anat* ethmoid bone; cribriform bone; **~en** *tr* to sieve; to sift; to strain; to riddle; *radio* to filter; *fig* (*heraussuchen*) to screen; to pick out; to select; to weed; **~feinheit** *f* mesh size; **~kette** *f radio* band-pass filter; **~kreis** *m radio* selective circuit; sifter; **~macher** *m* sieve-maker; **~mehl** *n* sifted flour; **~platte** *f anat* sieve-plate; **~tuch** *n* bolting-cloth; **~ung** *f* screening; sifting; sorting; *radio* filtration; filtering.

sieben *a* seven; *böse* ~ *fig* (*Xanthippe*) termagant; shrew; *Am* battle-ax; **~blättrig** *a bot* seven-leaved; heptaphyllous; **~bürgen** *n geog* Transylvania; **~eckig** *a* heptagonal; **~erlei** *a* of seven different sorts; **~fach** *a* sevenfold; **~gestirn** *n* Pleiades *pl*; **~hundert** *a* seven hundred; **~jährig** *a* septennial; seven-year-old; *der S~~e Krieg* the Seven Years' War; **~mal** *adv* seven times; **~~ig** *a* seven times repeated; **~meilenstiefel** *m pl* seven-league boots *pl*; **~monatskind** *n* seven months' child; **~sachen** *f pl* bag and baggage; belongings *pl*; goods and chattels *pl*; **~schläfer** *m* lazybones; *zoo* dormouse; **~tägig** *a* lasting seven days; seven days old; **~te, siebte** *a* seventh; **~tehalb** *a* seven and a half; **~tel, siebtel** *n* seventh part; **~tens** *adv* in the seventh place.

siebzehn *a* seventeen; **~te** *a*, **~tel** *n* seventeenth; **~tens** *adv* in the seventeenth place.

siebzig *a* seventy; **~er** *m* septuagenarian; **~jährig** *a* seventy-year-old; **~ste** *a* seventieth.

siech *a* sickly, infirm, ailing; invalid; **~bett** *n* sick-bed; **~en** *itr* to be sickly, to languish, to pine away; **~enhaus** *n* infirmary, hospital for incurables; **~tum** *n* long illness; invalidhood; languishing state.

Siede|grad *m* boiling-point; **~grenze** *f* boiling range; **~haus** *n* boiling-house; **~heiß** *a* seething-hot; piping hot; scalding hot; **~hitze** *f* boiling-heat; **~kessel** *m* boiler; **~en** *irr tr, itr* to seethe, to boil, (*gelind*) to simmer; **~nd** *a* boiling; **~punkt** *m* boiling-point; **~rohr** *n* boiling-tube; boiler pipe; **~~kessel** *m* water-tube boiler; **~rei** *f* refinery; boilery; **~salz** *n* (common) salt; **~verlauf** *m* boiling progress.

sied|eln *itr* to settle; to homestead; to colonize; **~ler** *m* settler; homesteader; colonist; **~~stelle** *f* settler's holding; homestead; **~~stolz** *m fam hum* home-grown tobacco; **~lung** *f* settlement; colony; housing estates *pl*; housing project; (*Vorstadt*) garden city; colony **~~sgesellschaft** *f* building-society.

•

Sieg *m* victory; triumph; (*Eroberung*) conquest; *leichter* ~ (*fam*) walkover, walkaway; *entscheidender* ~ *Am sport* clean sweep; conquest; *den* ~ *davontragen* to gain the victory, to win the day; *fam* to bring home the bacon; **~en** *itr* to win, to conquer; to be victorious; to win the day; **~er** *m* victor; conqueror; *sport* (prize-) winner; *zweiter* ~~ runner-up; **~~kranz** *m* conqueror's crown; **~~staat** *m* victor nation; **~esbewußt, ~esgewiß** *a* confident of victory; **~esdenkmal** *n* monument of victory; **~esfreude** *f* triumphal joy; **~esgöttin** *f* Victory; **~esjubel** *m* triumphal jubilation; **~espforte** *f* triumphal arch; **~espreis** *m* reward of victory; **~essäule** *f* trimphal column; **~estrunken** *a* elated (*od* flushed *od* intoxicated) with victory; **~eszeichen** *n* trophy; (*Weltkrieg II*) V-sign; **~eszug** *m* triumphal march; (*e-r Laufbahn*) victorious career; **~haft** *a* triumphant; **~reich** *a* victorious.

Siegel *n* seal, signet; *unter dem* ~ *der Verschwiegenheit* in strict confidence; *Brief u.* ~ sign and seal; *ein Buch mit sieben* ~*n* a book sealed with seven seals; *fig* a profound mystery; **~abdruck** *m* impress (of a seal); **~bewahrer** *m* keeper of the seal; Lord Privy Seal; **~erde** *f* Lemnian earth; **~lack** *m* sealing-wax; *e-e Stange* ~~ a stick of sealing-wax; **~n** *tr* to seal; to affix a seal; **~ring** *m* signet-ring.

Siel *n* sluice; (*Abzugsgraben*) sewer; culvert; **~anlage** *f* sewer system; **~e** *f* belt; horse-collar; harness; breast-piece (of a harness); *in den* ~*en sterben* to die in harness.

Sigel *n* (*Kurzschrift*) grammologue; (*Abkürzung*) abbreviation.

Signal *n* signal; (*Zeichen*) sign; indicator; *mil* (*Horn*~) bugle-call; ~ *geben mot* to honk o.'s horn; *das* ~ *zum Angriff blasen* to sound a charge; **~anlage** *f* signal(l)ing system; **~apparat** *m* signal(l)ing-apparatus; **~bombe** *f mil* signal flare; **~buch** *n* signal book; code of signals; **~ement** *n* personal description; **~feuer** *n* signal-light, beacon; **~flagge** *f* signal-flag; Blue Peter; pennant; **~gast** *m mar* signaller; **~geschoß** *n* star shell; **~glocke** *f* warning bell; **~horn** *n* signal horn; bugle; **~hupe** *f* klaxon; (*Sirene*) siren; **~isieren** *tr* to signal; *Am rail* to flag; **~lampe** *f* signal lamp; indicating lamp; warning light; **~laterne** *f* signal lamp; danger light; **~leine** *f* signal cord; communication-cord; bell-rope; **~leuchte** *f* signal flare; **~mast** *m* signal mast; semaphore; **~pfeife** *f* signal whistle; **~rakete** *f* signal rocket; **~scheibe** *f* signal(l)ing-disk; **~stange** *f* semaphore; *mar* perch; **~tafel** *f* signal code table; **~wärter** *m* signal man; **~wesen** *n* signal system; **~zeichen** *n* signal.

Sign|atarmächte *f pl* signatory powers *pl*; **~atur** *f* (*Unterschrift*) signature; (*Zeichen, Charakteristikum*) sign, mark; characteristic; brand; (*auf Karten*) conventional sign; (*Buch*~~) class-mark; **~et** *n* (*Verlag, Druckerei*) publisher's mark, printer's mark; **~ieren** *tr* to brand, to mark, to sign; to label; to stamp; to designate; **~um** *n* brand; mark; designation.

Silbe *f* syllable; *keine* ~ *sagen* not to utter a syllable, not to breathe a word; *er versteht keine* ~ *davon* he cannot make head or tail of it; **~nmaß** *n* quantity, metre; **~nmessung** *f* prosody; **~nrätsel** *n* charade; **~nstecher** *m* word-catcher, hair-splitter; **~~ei** *f* hair-splitting; **~ntrennung** *f* syllabication; **~nweise** *adv* in syllables.

Silber *n* silver; (*~zeug*) plate; *Am* silverware; (*Neu*~) German silver; ~ *in Barren* silver in ingots; bar silver; bullion; **~arbeit** *f* silver-work, plate; **~arbeiter** *m* silversmith; **~arm** *a* poor in silver; **~artig** *a* silvery; **~barren** *m* silver bar (*od* ingot); **~blatt** *n* silver foil; **~blick** *m* brightening of silver; **~chlorid** *n* silver chloride; **~draht** *m* silver wire; **~elektrolyse** *f* electrolytic silver refining; **~farbig** *a* silver-colo(u)red; **~fuchs** *m* silver-fox; **~gehalt** *m* silver content; standard; **~geld** *n*, **~münze** *f* silver money; silver coin; **~geschirr** *n* plate; *Am* silverware; **~haltig** *a* argentiferous; **~hell** *a* silvery; **~klang** *m* silvery sound; **~ling** *m* piece of silver; silverling; **~locke** *f* silvery lock; **~lot** *n* silver solder; **~n** *a* silver; ~*ne Hochzeit* silver wedding; **~nitrat** *n* silver nitrate; **~papier** *n* silver foil; silver paper; **~pappel** *f* white poplar; **~plattierung** *f* silver-plating; **~schmied** *m* silversmith; **~schrank** *m* plate-chest; **~stift** *m* silverpoint; **~streifen** *m fig* silver lining; **~tanne** *f* silver fir; **~ton** *m* silvery sound; **~währung** *f* silver standard; **~waren** *f pl* silver goods *pl*; *Am* silverware *pl*; **~zeug** *n* silverplate, *Am* silver.

Silhouette *f* silhouette.

Silikat *n* silicate.

Silizium *n* silicon.

Silo *m* silo; storage bin; (*Getreide*) grain elevator.

Silvester, **~abend** *m* New Year's Eve.

Simili(stein) *m* artificial stone.

simpel *a* (*einfach*) simple, plain; (*dumm*) stupid; ~ *m* simpleton; *Am fam* simp.

Sims *m od n* (*Brett*) shelf; (*Fenster*~) windowboard, sill-board; (*vorspringender Rand*) *arch* cornice, ledge, mo(u)lding; (*Kamin*~) mantelpiece.

Simul|ant *m* sham patient; malingerer; **~ieren** *itr, tr* to malinger, to sham; to simulate, to feign; *e-e Krankheit* ~~ to sham illness; **~tan** *a* simultaneous; **~~kirche** *f* undenominational church; **~~schule** *f* undenominational school; **~~spiel** *n* (*Schach*) simultaneous chess-playing; **~~verbindung** *f tele* composited circuit.

Sinekure *f* cushy job, *Am sl* soft snap.

Sinfonie *f* symphony; **~orchester** *n* symphony orchestra.

Sing|akademie *f* singing-academy; **~bar** *a* fit to be sung; **~chor** *m* choir; **~drossel** *f orn* song-thrush; **~en** *irr tr, itr* to sing; (*leise*) to hum; to croon; (*Vögel*) to warble; to carol; *vom Blatt* ~~ to sing at sight; *mehrstimmig* ~~ to sing in parts; *nach Noten* ~~ to sing from notes; *falsch* ~~ to sing out of tune; *ein Lied davon* ~~ *können fig* to know from experience; *immer dasselbe Lied* ~~ (*fig*) to be always harping on the same string; *zu hoch* ~~ to sing too high, to sing sharp; *zu tief* ~~ to sing too low, to sing flat; *in den Schlaf* ~~ to sing (*od* to lull) to sleep; *jds Lob* ~~ to sing s. o.'s praises; **~en** *n* singing, chanting; ~~ *vom Blatt* sight-singing; **~oper** *f* grand opera; **~sang** *m* sing-song; (*Aussprache*) twang; **~spiel** *n* operetta, musical comedy; vaudeville; **~~film** *m* musical; musical film; **~~halle** *f* music-hall; **~stimme** *f* vocal part; **~stunde** *f* singing-lesson; **~vogel** *m* singing-bird, songster, warbler; **~weise** *f* melody, tune.

Singular *m* singular.

sink|en *irr itr allg* to sink; (*fallen, bes. der Preise*) to fall, to drop; to abate; (*Schiff*) to sink; to go down; to founder; (*plötzlich* ~~, *stürzen*) to slump; to tumble; (*hängen lassen*) to droop; (*sacken, fallen*) to sag; (*zurückweichen*) to recede; (*nachgeben*) to give way; to yield; (*sich vermindern*) to decrease; (*abnehmen*) to decline; *chem* to precipitate; *aero* to lose flying speed; **~en** *n* sinking; (*Preise*) decline, slump; depression; *auf den Boden* ~~ to sink on (*od* to) the ground; *auf die Knie* ~~ to drop to o.'s knees; *jdm in die Arme* ~~ to fall into s. o.'s arms; *ins Grab* ~~ to sink into the grave; *in Ohnmacht* ~~ to faint away; *in Schlaf* ~~ to fall asleep; to nod off; *sein Stern ist im ~~* his star is in the descendant; *im Wert ~~* to decline in value; *~~ lassen* to lower; to sink; *den Mut ~~ lassen* to lose courage, to lose heart; *seine Stimme ~~ lassen* to lower o.'s voice; *wie tief ist sie gesunken!* what has become of her! **~geschwindigkeit** *f* velocity of descent; sinking speed; **~körper** *m* sinker; **~sicher** *a* unsinkable; **~stoff** *m* sediment; deposit; settlings *pl.*

Sinn *m* sense; (*Fähigkeit, Talent*) faculty; (*~esorgan*) sense, organ of perception; (*Neigung*) disposition; inclination, tendency; (*Verstand*) intellect, mind; understanding; (*Bewußtsein*) consciousness; (*Wunsch*) wish; desire; (*Gedanke*) idea, thought; (*Meinung*) opinion; (*Ansicht*) view; (*Geschmack*) taste; (*Gemütsart*) feeling; temper; temperament; disposition; (*Vorliebe*) liking; (*Herz, Seele*) heart; soul; (*Wille*) will; (*Bedeutung*) import, meaning; purport; interpretation; construction; *die fünf ~e* the five senses *pl*; *seine fünf ~e beisammen haben* to be in o.'s senses, *fam* to be all there; *ohne ~ u. Verstand* without rhyme or reason; having neither rhyme nor reason; *aus den Augen, aus dem ~* out of sight, out of mind; *sich etw aus dem ~ schlagen* to put s. th. out of o.'s mind; to dismiss s. th. from o.'s mind; *das will mir nicht aus dem ~* I cannot take my mind off it; *bei ~en sein* to be in o.'s senses; *nicht bei ~en sein* to have lost o.'s senses; *im ~e des § 2* within the meaning of section 2; *im ~e des Uhrzeigers* clockwise; *im übertragenen ~* in the figurative sense; *im wahrsten ~e des Wortes* in the fullest sense of the word; *etw im ~ haben* to intend; to take into o.'s head; *etw anderes im ~ haben* to have s. th. else in mind; *was hat sie nur im ~?* what's she up to? *in jds ~ handeln* to act to s. o.'s mind; *in gewissem ~* in a way, in a sense; *das kommt ihr nicht in den ~* that does not occur to her; *von ~en sein* to be out of o.'s mind; *~ haben für* to have a feeling for; *~ haben für Kleider* to be clothes-minded; *das hat keinen ~* there is no sense in it (*od* to that); there is no point in that; *da steckt kein ~ drin* it simply doesn't make sense; *das ist nicht nach meinem ~* that is not to my liking; **~bild** *n* emblem, symbol; allegory; **~~lich** *a* emblematic, symbolic(al); **~en** *irr itr* (*überdenken*) to think (over); to meditate; to reflect; (*erwägen*) to consider; (*spekulieren*) to speculate (*über* upon); (*grübeln*) to ruminate, to brood (*über* on); *~~ auf* (*Pläne machen*) to plan, to plot; to scheme; *auf Unheil ~~* to plot mischief; *auf Rache ~~* to meditate revenge; *gesonnen sein* to be inclined, to purpose, to mean; to have a mind to; **~en** *n* meditation; reflection; consideration; speculation; (*Träumerei*) revery, *Am* reverie; *in ~~ versunken* to be lost in meditation, *fam* to be in a brown study; **~end** *a* pensive; meditative; reflective; thoughtful; **~enfreude** *f*, **~engenuß** *m*, **~enlust** *f* sensual pleasure; sensuality, voluptuousness; **~enmensch** *m* sensualist; **~entstellend** *a* distorting the meaning, garbling; **~enrausch** *m* intoxication of the senses; **~enreiz** *m* sensuality; **~enwelt** *f* material (*od* external) world; **~esänderung** *f* change of mind; change of heart; **~esart** *f* character; disposition; temper; **~eseindruck** *m* sensory impression; **~esempfindung** *f* sensory perception; **~esnerv** *m* sensory nerve; **~esorgan** *n* sense organ; **~esreiz** *m* stimulus; **~esstörung** *f* mental derangement; delusion; **~estaumel** *m* (*sexuell*) orgasm; **~estäuschung** *f* hallucination, illusion; vision; **~eswahrnehmung** *f* apperception; **~eswerkzeuge** *n pl* sense organs *pl*; **~eszentrum** *n* sensory centre; **~fällig** *a* obvious; **~gedicht** *n* epigram; **~gemäß** *a* analogous; equivalent; rational; logical; **~getreu** *a* faithful; **~ig** *a* (*verständig*) sensible; (*überlegt*) thoughtful; (*sinnreich*) ingenious; (*zart*) pretty; (*voll Geschmack*) tasteful; (*zweckmäßig*) appropriate; **~~keit** *f* sensibleness; thoughtfulness; **~lich** *a* (*wahrnehmbar*) sensible; (*auf die Sinne bezüglich*) sensuous; (*stofflich*) material; (*den Sinnengenuß betreffend*) sensual; (*fleischlich*) carnal; fleshly; voluptuous; *~~e Liebe* sensual love; *ein ~er Mensch* a sensualist; *die ~~e Welt* the material world; **~lichkeit** *f* sensuousness; sensuality; **~los** *a* senseless; (*absurd, verrückt*) absurd; mad; foolish; (*bedeutungslos*) meaningless; *~~ betrunken* dead drunk; *es ist einfach ~~* it just doesn't make sense; **~losigkeit** *f* senselessness; foolishness; absurdity; **~reich** *a* (*klug ersonnen*) ingenious; (*klug*) clever, intelligent; (*geistreich*) witty; **~spruch** *m* epigram; maxim; sentence, device, motto; **~störend** *a* misleading; **~verständlichkeit** *f* intelligibility; **~verwandt** *a* synonymous; *~~es Wort* synonym; **~verwandtschaft** *f* synonymity; **~voll** *a* (*zweckmäßig*) convenient; (*bedeutungsvoll*) significant, meaningful; (*klug*) intelligent, clever; ingenious; logical; **~widrig** *a* absurd; senseless.

Sinologe *m* sinologist.

sintemal *conj* since, whereas.

Sinter *m* dross of iron; agglomerate; **~erzeugnis** *n* sinter cake; **~kohle** *f* sinter coal; **~n** *tr* to sinter, to cake; to trickle, to drop; to slag; **~ofen** *m* sintering furnace; **~ung** *f* sintering; vitrification; agglomeration.

Sintflut *f* flood, deluge; (*Bibel*) the Flood; Deluge.

Sinus *m math* sine; sinus; **~funktion** *f* sine function; **~kurve** *f* sine curve; sinusoid; **~winkel** *m* sine of angle.

Siphon *m* siphon.

Sipp|e, **~schaft** *f* kin, kinship, kindred; (*die Verwandten*) relatives *pl*; (*Stamm*) tribe; (*ironisch*) set, lot, clique; *die ganze ~~* the whole clan; every mother's son of them; *mit der ganzen ~~* with kith and kin; **~enforschung** *f* genealogical research; **~enherkunft** *f* origin of tribe.

Sirene *f* (*Meerweib, Verführerin, Tonzeichen*) siren; (*Hupe*) hooter; *die ~ heult* the siren is wailing; **~nhaft** *a* siren-like; **~ngeheul** *n* hooting of sirens.

Sirup *m* (*Zuckersaft*) treacle, *Am* molasses *pl mit sing*; (*Fruchtsaft mit Zucker*) sirup, syrup.

sistier|en *tr* to inhibit, to stop; *jdn ~~* to arrest s. o.; **~ung** *f* inhibition, nonsuit.

Sitt|e *f* custom; (*Brauch*) usage; (*Lebensgewohnheit*) habit; (*Mode*) fashion; (*Praxis*) practice, etiquette; *die ~en pl* (*Sittlichkeit*) morals *pl*; manners *pl*; *gute ~en* good habits; *schlechte ~en* bad habits; loose morals; *das ist hier nicht ~~* that's not the custom here; *es ist ~~, daß ...* it is customary to; *die ~en u. Gebräuche e-s Landes* manners and customs of a country; **~enbild**, **~engemälde** *n* picture of manners (*od* morals); **~engeschichte** *f* history of manners and morals; **~engesetz** *n* moral law, moral code; **~enlehre** *f* ethics *pl mit sing*; moral philosophy; **~enlehrer** *m* moralist; **~enlos** *a* immoral, dissolute, profligate; wicked; **~~igkeit** *f* immorality, profligacy; **~npolizei** *f* control of prostitutes; **~enpredigt** *f* moralizing sermon; **~enrein** *a* pure, chaste; **~~heit** *f* chastity; **~enrichter** *m* censor; moralizer; Mrs. Grundy, *Am sl* wowzer; **~enspruch** *m* maxim; **~enstreng** *a* austere; puritanical; **~~e** *f* austerity; **~enverderbnis** *f* corruption of morals, demoralization; **~enverfall** *m* moral decay; depravity; **~enzeugnis** *n* certificate of (good) conduct; **~ig** *a* modest; chaste; well-bred; well-behaved; **~lich** *a* moral, pure; **~lichkeit** *f* morality, morals *pl*; **~~sverbrechen** *n* indecent assault; **~sam** *a* modest, decent, virtuous; **~~keit** *f* modesty, decency.

Sittich *m* parakeet; parrot.

Situation *f* (*Zustand der Dinge*) situation, state of affairs; (*örtlich*) site; (*Stellung*) position; *er rettete die ~* he saved the situation; *Herr der ~ sein* to be master of the situation; *sie war der ~ nicht gewachsen* she was not equal to the situation (*od* occasion); **~splan** *m arch* site plan; *mil* ground plan; plot of situation; **~sskizze** *f* layout plan.

situiert *a*: *gut ~* wealthy, well-to-do, well-off.

Sitz *m* seat; chair; (*Wohnsitz*) residence; domicile; dwelling-place; lodg(e)ment; (*von Kleidern*) fit; (*Platz*) spot, place; locus; (*Bischofs~*) see; (*Beifahrer~*) pillion; *tech* (*Ventil~ etc*) seat; (*Passung*) fit; *~ und Stimme haben* to have seat and vote; *verstellbarer ~* adjustable seat; *auf e-n ~* at one sitting; *mit dem ~ in Berlin* with the place of business and legal seat in Berlin; **~anordnung** *f* seating arrangement; **~arbeit** *f* sedentary work; **~art** *f tech* kind of fit; **~bad** *n* hip-bath, sitz-bath; **~bank** *f* sofa seat; **~bein** *n anat* ischium; **~bereitschaft** *f aero* readiness to start; **~brett** *n* seat; **~en** *irr itr* to sit, to be seated; (*von Vögeln*) to perch; (*auf Eiern*) to hatch; (*Hieb*) to go home; to hit home; (*Sitzung abhalten*) to hold a meeting; (*wohnen*) to live, to dwell; (*von Kleidern*) to fit; (*dem Maler*) to sit to a painter; *fam* to be in prison, to be confined; to be imprisoned; *fam* to do time; *müßig ~~* to sit idle; *teuer ~~* to pay a high rent; *jdm auf der Pelle ~~* (*fam*) to be at s. o.'s heels; *auf dem trockenen ~~* to be left high and dry; (*kein Geld haben*) to be out of cash; to be in low water; *auf Dornen ~~* to sit on thorns; *bei jdm ~~* to sit beside s. o., to sit by s. o.'s side; *fest ~~* to stick fast; to adhere; *ein Schiff sitzt fest* a ship is aground; *bei Tisch ~~* to sit at table; *er hat e-n ~~* (*fam*) he is a little high; *in der Klemme ~~* to be in great distress; *im Peche ~~* to have misfortune; *über e-r Arbeit ~~* to be occupied with; *über den Büchern ~~* to sit over o.'s books; *über jdn zu Gericht ~~* to sit in judg(e)ment on; *etw auf sich ~~ lassen* to put up with; to pocket; *diese Beleidigung lasse ich nicht auf mir ~~* I am not going to take that insult; **~enbleiben** *irr itr* (*nicht aufstehen*) to keep o.'s seat, to remain seated; (*beim Tanzen*) to get no partner; to be a wallflower; (*bei der Heirat*) to remain unmarried (*od* a spinster); (*in der Schule*) not to get o.'s remove; to be kept (*od* left) back; **~end** *a* sitting; seated; *~~e Lebensweise* sedentary life; *in ~~er Stellung* in a sitting position; **~enlassen** *irr tr* (*verlassen*) to leave; to desert; to abandon; (*bei Verabredung*) to leave in the lurch; (*im Stich lassen*) to let s. o. down; to throw s. o. over; *Am sl* to walk out on s. o.; (*Mädchen*) to jilt a girl, *fam* to leave a girl high and dry; *Am* to bilk a girl; **~fallschirm** *m aero* seat-type parachute, *sl* chair chute; **~fläche** *f* seat(ing); **~fleisch, ~leder** *n* sedentariness; (*Ausdauer*) perseverance; steadiness; *~~ haben* to be persevering; *er hat kein ~~* (*keine Ausdauer*) he does not stick to his work; (*aufgeregt*) he is fidgety; **~gelegenheit** *f* seat(s *pl*); seating accommodation; **~kissen** *n* (seat) cushion; **~krieg** *m fam* phon(e)y war; **~knochen, ~knorren** *m anat* tuberosity of the ischium; **~platz** *m* seat; (*Fassungsraum*) seating capacity; *das Theater hat 1000 ~plätze* the theatre has a seating capacity of 1000; **~polster** *n* upholstery; **~raum** *m* (*Auto*) seat-room; *aero* cabin; **~reihe** *f theat* tier; row (of seats); **~riemen** *m* seat strap; **~stange** *f* perch; **~streik** *m* sit-down strike; sit-down; stay-in strike; **~ung** *f* (*Einzel~~*) sitting; (*Versammlung*) meeting; (*Zeitdauer*) session; *e-e ~~ aufheben, eröffnen, halten, vertagen, schließen* to break up, to open, to hold, to adjourn, to close a meeting; *das Parlament hat die ~~ beendet* Parliament has risen; **~~sbericht** *m*, **~~sprotokoll** *n* minutes *pl* (of proceedings); proceedings *pl*; report (of session); treatise; **~~speriode** *f* session; *jur* term; **~~ssaal** *m*, **~~szimmer** *n* session-room; *parl* chamber; *Am* hall; floor; **~~szeit** *f* session; *Am* (*Kongreß*) term; **~verstellung** *f* seat adjustment; **~vorrichtung** *f* riding attachment; **~welle** *f* (*Turnen*) seat circle; **~zahl** *f* seating capacity.

Sizili|aner *m* Sicilian; **~anisch** *a* Sicilian; **~en** *n* Sicily; **~er** *m* Sicilian; **~sch** *a* Sicilian.

Skabiose *f bot* scabious.

Skal|a *f* scale; *mus auch* gamut; *anat* scala; (*Einteilung*) graduation, measure, division; *tele, radio* dial; *gleitende ~~* sliding scale; **~enablesung** *f* scale reading; **~enbeleuchtung** *f* dial light; **~eneinteilung** *f* graduation (of scale); **~enscheibe** *f* dial, scale disk.

Skalde *m* scald.

Skalp *m* scalp; **~ell** *n med* scalpel; **~ieren** *tr* to scalp.

Skandal *m* scandal; (*Lärm*) row; noise; riot; *Am* ruckus; *~ machen* to kick up a row, *Am sl* to whoop it up; *es ist ein ~, wie sie sich benimmt* it's a disgrace the way she acts; **~chronik** *f* chronicle of scandal; **~ieren** *itr* to kick up a row; **~ös** *a* scandalous; (*empörend*) shocking; revolting; **~geschichte** *f* scandal; **~presse** *f* gutter press.

skandieren *tr* (*Verse*) to scan.

Skandinav|ien *n* Scandinavia; **~ier** *m*, **~isch** *a* Scandinavian.

Skat *m* skat; **~spieler** *m* skat player.

Skelett *n* skeleton; *zum ~ abgemagert* nothing but skin and bones.

Skep|sis *f* doubt, scepticism; **~tiker** *m* sceptic; **~tisch** *a* sceptic, sceptical.

Ski *m siehe Schi.*

Skizz|e *f* sketch; (*Entwurf*) draft; drawing; outline; (*Karten~*) sketch-map; **~enbuch** *n* sketchbook; **~enhaft** *a* sketchy; **~ieren** *tr* to sketch, to rough-draw, to touch off; to outline; to delineate.

Sklav|e *m* slave; (*Leibeigener*) serf; *poet* thrall; **~enarbeit** *f* slave-work; *fig* drudgery; *~~ verrichten* to slave; **~enbefreiungsbewegung** *f Am hist* abolitionism; **~enhalter** *m* slave-owner; **~enhandel** *m* slave-trade; **~enhändler** *m* slave-trader; **~erei** *f* slavery; servitude, serfdom, bondage, thral(l)dom; *Gegner der ~~* (*Am*) abolitionist; **~isch** *a* slavish; servile, abject.

Skonto *m, n com* discount.

Skorbut *m* scurvy.

Skorpion *m* scorpion.

Skribent *m* (*Schreiberling*) scribe; quill-driver, ink-slinger.

Skrof|eln *f pl med* scrofula; **~ulös** *a* scrofulous.

Skrup|el *m* scruple; *sich ~~ machen* to scruple; **~ellos** *a* unscrupulous; **~ellosigkeit** *f* unscrupulousness; **~ulös** *a* scrupulous.

Skulptur *f* sculpture.

Skunk *m* skunk.

skurril *a* farcical.

Slaw|e *m* Slav; **~isch** *a* Slavonic; **~entum** *n* Slavdom.

Slip *m aero* slip; sideslip; *mar* slipway.

Slowak|ei *f* Slovakia; **~isch** *a* Slovak Slovakian.

Slowenien *n* Slovenia.

Slum *m* slum; depressed area; **~wohnung** *f* slum dwelling.

Smaragd *m*, **~en** *a* emerald; **~grün** *a* emerald (green).

Smoking *m* dinner-jacket; *Am* tuxedo, *fam* tux.

so *adv* so, thus; such; in that manner; *bald ~, bald ~* now he says one thing, then another; *~!* quite right!; *Ach ~!* Oh, I see! So that's it! *Na ~ was!* Of all things! the idea! what do you know! *~ hören Sie doch!* Now, do listen! *~?* Is that so? really? indeed? *wie ~?* how that? *~ od ~* by hook or by crook; this way or that way; *~ u. ~ oft* ever so many times; *~ daß* so that; *~ sehr, daß* to such a degree that; *~ . . . wie* as . . . as; *nicht ~ . . . wie* not so . . . as; *um ~ besser* all the better; *noch einmal ~ viel* twice as much; *soso* tolerably well; *~ conj* therefore, then, so; *~ reich er auch sei* however rich he may be; **~bald** *conj* as soon as.

Sock|e *f* sock; *sich auf die ~en machen* to take to o.'s heels; **~el** *m* socle, base, pedestal; **~enhalter** *m* (sock-) suspender, *Am* garter.

Soda *f* soda; **~wasser** *n* soda-water; *Am* seltzer; **~~ausschank** *m Am* soda fountain.

so|dann *conj* then; afterwards; *~ daß conj* so that.

Sodbrennen *n* heartburn, pyrosis.

so|eben *adv* just, this minute; **~fern** *conj* so far, as far as; *insofern* in as much as.

Sofa *n* sofa; couch, divan, *Am* davenport; (*kleines ~*) settee; **~ecke** *f* sofa-corner; **~kissen** *n* sofa-cushion; **~lehne** *f* back of a sofa; **~schoner** *m* antimacassar.

Soff *m* drinking; drunkenness.

Söff|el, **~er** *m* drinker, drunkard; *vulg* tippler.

Soffitten *f pl theat* flies *pl*; **~lampe** *f* tubular lamp; strip lamp; scaffold lamp.

so|fort *adv* immediately, at once; *Am* right now, right off; right away; *Am fam* instanter, just; *~~!* coming! **~~entscheid** *m* on-the-spot decision; **~~hilfe** *f* emergency relief aid, *Am* stop-gap aid; **~~ig** *a* immediate; instantaneous; **~~programm** *n* on-the-spot action; **~gar** *adv* even; **~genannt** *a* so-called; (*sich selbst so nennend*) would-be, pretended; **~gleich** *adv* at once.

Sog *m* (*Explosions~*) suction; (*Wasser*) undertow, wash, wake; **~pumpe** *f* vacuum pump.

Sohl|e *f* sole; *min* bottom, floor; (*Tal~*) level; bottom; **~en** *itr* to sole; (*lügen*) to lie; **~engänger** *m* plantigrade; **~enleder** *n* sole-leather.

Sohn *m* son; *der verlorene ~* the prodigal son; **Söhnchen** *n* little son; *fam* sonny, sonnie.

Soiree *f* evening party, soirée.

solang(e) *adv* as long as, so long as; *conj* whilst; *~ nicht* till, until.

Solawechsel *m* bill of exchange; promissory note.

Solbad *n* salt-water bath, salt-water springs *pl*; brine bath.

solch|er, **~e, ~es** *prn* such, so; **~ergestalt** *adv* in such a manner, to such a degree; **~erlei** *a* of such a kind, such-(like); **~ermaßen, ~erweise** *adv* in such a way.

Sold *m* pay; *fig* wages *pl*; *in ~ nehmen* to take in pay; **~buch** *n mil* pay-book; individual pay record.

Soldat *m* soldier; *ausgedienter ~* ex-service-man; *freiwilliger ~* volunteer; *~en spielen* to play at soldiers; *gemeiner ~* private; *alter ~* veteran; *entlassener ~* ex-soldier, *Am* veteran; *die ~en* (*Mannschaften*) the rank and file, *Am* enlisted men; *der Unbekannte ~* the Unknown Warrior; **~enbund** *m Am* veteran's organization; **~enheim** *n* soldier's home, *Am* service club; **~enkost** *f* soldier's fare; **~enrock** *m* uniform, regimentals *pl*; **~enstand** *m* military profession; **~entum** *n* soldiery; **~eska** *f* rabble of soldiers; **~isch** soldierlike, military; martial.

Söld|ling, **~ner** *m* mercenary, hireling; **~nerheer** *n* mercenary army.

Sol|e *f* salt-water, brine; **~ei** *f* egg boiled in salt-water.

solid|arisch *a* joint; unanimous; responsible; *sich mit jdm ~~ erklären* to declare o.'s solidarity with; **~arität** *f* solidarity; **~(e)** *a* solid; (*stark*) strong; substantial; (*gesund*) sound; (*Preis*) reasonable, fair; (*gründlich*) thorough; (*angesehen*) respectable; trustworthy; (*zuverlässig*) reliable; (*sicher*) safe; **~ität** *f* solidity; steadiness, honesty; respectability.

Sol|ist *m* soloist; solo-singer; solo-player; **~itär** *m* brilliant.

Soll *n com* debit, debit side; debtor; requirement, required value; (*Lieferung*) quota; target (figure); *~ u. Haben* debit and credit; *ins ~ eintragen, im ~ verbuchen* to debit, to enter on the debit side; **~ausgaben** *f pl* estimated expenditures *pl*; **~bestand** *m* nominal balance; *mil* required strength; **~betrag** *m* nominal amount; **~bruchstelle** *f tech* predetermined breaking point; **~einnahme** *f* estimated (*od* supposed) receipt; supposed returns (*od* proceeds) *pl*; **~frequenz** *f radio* assigned frequency; **~höhe** *f aero* designed height; **~kurs** *m mar, aero* chartered course, prescribed course; **~menge** *f* theoretical quantity; **~posten** *m* debit item; **~saldo** *n* debit balance; **~seite** *f* debit side; *auf der ~~ verbuchen* to debit; **~stärke** *f* authorized strength (and equipment); **~wert** *m* theoretical (*od* desired) value; face value; **~zinsen** *m pl* debit interest.

sollen *itr* shall, should; ought; to be to; to be bound to; to have to; must; to be told; to be ordered; (*angeblich*) to be supposed to; (*Gerücht*) to be said; *er soll tot sein* he is said to be dead; *du sollst nicht töten* thou shalt not kill; *was soll das heißen?* what does that mean? *was soll ich tun?* what am I to do? *man sollte meinen* one would think; *sollte er es vergessen haben?* can he have forgotten it? *sollte das möglich sein?* can this be possible? *Jungen sollten gehorchen* boys ought to obey; *man sollte sie bestrafen* she ought to be punished; *das hätten Sie nicht glauben ~* you shouldn't have believed it; you ought not to have believed it; *sie weiß nicht, was sie tun soll* she doesn't know what to do; she doesn't know what she is supposed to do; *die Abreise soll heute stattfinden* the departure is to take place to-day; *wenn ich sterben sollte* if I come to die.

Söller *m* loft; platform; balcony.

Solo *n* solo; **~flug** *m aero* solo flight; **~geiger** *m* solo violinist; **~gesang** *m* solo singing; **~partie** *f* solo part; **~sänger** *m* solo singer; **~stimme** *f* solo part; **~stück** *n* solo; **~tänzer** *m*, **~~in** *f* first dancer, principal dancer.

solvent *a* solvent, able to pay; financially sound.

somit *adv* consequently, so.

Sommer *m* summer; *im ~* in (the) summer; during (the) summer; *Nach~* Indian summer; *e-e Schwalbe macht noch keinen ~* one swallow makes not a spring; **~abend** *m* summer evening; **~aufenthalt** *m* summer-residence; **~fäden** *m pl* gossamer; air-threads *pl*; **~fahrplan, ~flugplan** *m* summer timetable; **~ferien** *f pl* summer vacation; **~flecken** *m pl* freckles *pl*; **~frische** *f* health resort; place in the country; *in die ~~ fahren* to go to the country; **~frischler** *m* summer visitor, holiday-maker; **~frucht** *f* summer fruit; **~gast** *m* summer visitor; **~gerste** *f* spring barley; **~getreide** *n*, **~saat** *f* summer corn; **~gewitter** *n* summer thunderstorm; **~halbjahr** *n* summer term; **~häuschen** *n* (*einstöckig*) bungalow; summerhouse, *Am* cottage; **~holz** *n* summer wood; **~hitze** *f* heat of summer; **~kartoffel** *f* early potato; **~kleidung** *f* summer dress; **~laden** *m* Venitian blind; **~lich** *a* summer-like, summery; **~mode** *f* summer fashion; **~n** *itr, imp es sommert* summer is drawing near; *tr* (*sömmern*) to expose to the sun, to bask; (*Vieh*) to summer; *tech* (*Reifenprofil*) to tecalemite; (*Ziegel*) to season; **~nachtstraum** *m* Midsummer Night's Dream; **~pflanze** *f* summer plant; **~saat** *f* summer seed; **~schlaf** *m* estivation; **~seite** *f* sunny side, south-side; **~semester** *n* summer half, summer session; **~sonnenwende** *f* summer-solstice; **~sprossen** *f pl* freckles *pl*; **~sprossig** *a* freckled; **~theater** *n* open-air theatre; **~überzieher** *m* dust-coat; **~ung** *f* (*Reifen*) tecalemiting; **~weg** *m* summer road, seasonal road; dust road, soft road; **~wohnung** *f* summer-residence, *Am* cottage; **~zeit** *f* summer season; (*zum Lichtsparen*) summer time, *Am* daylight-saving time; **~zeug** *n* summer-clothes *pl*.

sonach *adv* consequently; so.

Sonate *f* sonata.

Sond\|e *f med* probe, sound; *mar* plummet; (*Meteorologie*) weather-forecasting equipment; radiosonde; **~ierangriff** *m mil* probe; **~ierballon** *m* sounding balloon; **~ieren** *tr, itr* to probe; *mar* to sound; *fig* to feel o.'s way; to explore the ground; *jdn ~~* to pump s. o.

sonder *prp* without; (*spezial*) special; (*getrennt*) separate; **~(ab)druck** *m* reprint, separate (re-)print; offprint; (*Auszug*) extract; **~abkommen** *n* special agreement; **~absicht** *f* ulterior motive; mental reservation; **~angebot** *n* special offer; bargain; **~antrieb** *m tech* special drive; accessory drive; **~aufbau** *m mot* special body; **~auftrag** *m* special mission; **~ausführung** *f* special design; **~ausgabe** *f* (*Extrablatt*) special edition; (*Buch*) separate edition; (*geldlich*) extraordinary expenses *pl*; extras *pl*; **~ausschuß** *m* special committee; (*kleiner*) select committee; **~ausweis** *m* special pass; **~bar** *a* (*seltsam, fremd*) strange; odd; queer; *fam* (*komisch*) funny; (*eigentümlich*) singular; peculiar; (*außerordentlich*; *ungewöhnlich*) extraordinary; (*interessant*) interesting; *was ist daran ~~?* what's strange about it? *mir ist so ~~* I feel very queer; **~barerweise** *adv* strange to say; **~barkeit** *f* strangeness; oddity; singularity; peculiarity; **~bauart** *f tech* special type; **~beauftragte(r)** *m* special representative; trouble shooter; **~beilage** *f* supplement; (*Zeitung*) inset; **~bericht** *m* special report; **~~erstatter** *m* special (correspondent); **~bestellung** *f* special order; **~bestrebung** *f* particularism; separatism; **~bevollmächtigte(r)** *m* plenipotentiary; **~bote** *m* special messenger; **~bund** *m* separate league; **~bündler** *m* separatist; **~dienst** *m* special service; **~ermäßigung** *f* special price reduction; **~erzeugnis** *n* special(i)ty; **~fach** *n* special line; speciality; **~fall** *m* special (*od* exceptional case); **~flug** *m* extra flight; **~~zeug** *n* special-type plane; **~fonds** *m* special purposes fund; **~formation** *f pl* special auxiliary troops *pl*; **~friede** *m* separate peace; **~funkspruch** *m* special radio message; **~gebiet** *n* special line; special(i)ty; **~gelüste** *n pl* particular desires *pl*; **~gericht** *n* special tribunal; special court; **~gesandte(r)** *m* special envoy; **~geschwader** *n aero* special task force; **~gesetz** *n* special law; **~gesetzgebung** *f* special legislation; **~gleichen** *adv* unequalled; unique, matchless; incomparable; unparallelled; **~interesse(n)** *n* (*pl*) special interest; private interest; particular interest; **~konto** *n* separate account; **~kosten** *pl* extraordinary costs *pl*; extra charges *pl*; **~lich** *a* particular, special, remarkable; *nicht ~~* not specially; not much; **~ling** *m* (*Original*) original, odd person, strange fellow, crank; **~meldung** *f* special announcement; **~n**[1] *tr* (*abtrennen*) to separate, to sever, to segregate; to part; (*einteilen, auswählen*) to sort out; to assort, to classify; to grade; to size; **~n**[2] *conj* but; *nicht nur . . . ~ auch* not only . . . but; **~nummer** *f* special number; special edition; **~posten** *m* separate item; **~preis** *m* special price; **~rabatt** *m* extra discount; **~recht** *n* privilege; priority; **~regelung** *f* separate settlement; **~s** *adv*: *samt u. ~~* each and all; all together; **~sitzung** *f parl* special session; *zu e-r ~~ zusammentreten* to meet in special session; **~stahl** *m* special (*od* alloy) steel; **~stellung** *f* exceptional position; **~steuer** *f* special duty; **~ung** *f* separation; sifting; **~verband** *m mil* task force; **~verkauf** *m* bargain sale; **~vermögen** *n* private fortune; **~vertrag** *m* special agreement; **~vorführung** *f* special performance; **~wagen** *m* special car; **~zug** *m rail* special train, extra train; special; **~zulage** *f* special bonus; **~zuschlag** *m* extra charge; **~zuteilung** *f* special allotment; extra rations *pl*; **~zweck** *m* special purpose.

Sonett *n* sonnet.

Sonnabend *m* Saturday; *~s* on a Saturday; (*immer ~s*) on Saturdays.

Sonne *f* sun; (*Bogenlicht für Film*) sun arc, *Am* klieg light; *in der ~ liegen* to bask in the sun; *jdm in der ~ stehen* to stand in s. o.'s light; *unter der ~* on earth, in the world; *die ~ scheint* the sun shines; *es geschieht nichts Neues unter der ~* there is no new thing under the sun.

sonnen *tr* to expose to the sun's rays; to sun, to air; *sich ~* to bask; to sun o. s.; **~anbeter** *m* sun-worshipper; **~aufgang** *m* sunrise; *Am dial* sunup; *bei ~~* at sunrise; **~bad** *n* sun bath; **~bahn** *f* ecliptic; orbit of the sun; **~ball** *m* orb of the sun; **~beschienen** *a* sunlit; **~bestrahlung** *f* solar radiation; exposure to sunlight; **~blende** *f phot* lens shade; (*Schild bei mot etc*) sun visor; **~blume** *f* sunflower; **~brand** *m* burning heat of the sun; (*der Haut*) sunburn; **~bräune** *f* (*Haut*) sunburn, *Am* (sun) tan; **~brille** *f* sun glasses *pl*; sun blinkers *pl*; **~dach** *n* (*vor Fenstern*) sun-blind; *mar* awning; *mot* sunshine roof; **~ferne** *f* aphelion; **~finsternis** *f* eclipse of the sun; **~fleck** *m* sun spot, solar spot; **~förmig** *a astr* solar; **~gebräunt** *a* sunburnt; (sun-) tanned; **~geflecht** *n anat* solar plexus; **~glanz** *m* splendo(u)r of the sun; **~glut** *f* blaze of the sun; **~gott** *m* sungod; Helios; **~haft** *a* sun-like; radiant; akin to the sun; **~hell** *a siehe ~klar*; **~helligkeit** *f* brightness of the sun; **~hitze** *f* heat of the sun; solar heat; **~hof** *m* solar corona; **~höhe** *f astr* sun's altitude; **~hut** *m* sun-hat; **~jahr** *n* solar year; **~käfer** *m* lady-bird; **~klar** *a* clear, sun-bright; sunny; (*offensichtlich*) evident, clear as daylight; **~kraft** *f* heat of the sun; **~lauf** *m astr* course of the sun; **~licht** *n* sunlight; **~los** *a* sunless; without sunshine; **~messer** *m* heliometer; **~monat** *m* solar month; **~nähe** *f* perihelion; **~scheibe** *f* disk of the sun; **~schein** *m* sunshine; *auf Regen folgt ~~* after rain comes fair weather; **~schirm** *m* sunshade, parasol; **~schutz** *m* sunshade; **~~brille** *f* sun glasses *pl*; **~segel** *n mar* awning; **~seite** *f* sunny side; **~stand** *m* (*Höhe*) altitude (*od* position) of the sun; (*Wendepunkt*) solstitial point; **~stäubchen** *n* mote; **~stich** *m* sunstroke; **~strahl** *m* sunbeam; **~~ung** *f* solar (*od* sun's) radiation; **~~ungsmesser** *m* solarimeter, actinometer; **~system** *n* solar system; **~tag** *m* (*voll Sonne*) sunny day; *fig* day of happiness; *astr* solar day; **~überflutet** *a* sun-drenched; **~uhr** *f*, **~weiser** *m* sundial; **~untergang** *m* sunset; *Am* sundown; **~verbrannt** *a* sunburnt; tanned; **~vorhang** *m* sunshade; **~wärme** *f* solar heat; **~wende** *f* solstice; **~wendfeuer** *n* St. John's fire; **~zeit** *f* solar time; **~zelt** *n* awning.

sonnig *a* sunny.

Sonn\|tag *m* Sunday; **~tägig** *a* dominical; **~täglich** *a* Sunday; (*jeden ~~*) every Sunday; *~~ gekleidet* dressed in o.'s Sunday best.

Sonntags\|anzug *m* Sunday best; Sunday clothes *pl*, *Am* go-to-meeting clothes *pl*; **~ausflügler** *m* week-ender; **~ausgabe** *f* Sunday issue; **~beilage** *f* Sunday supplement; **~fahrer** *m* Sunday driver, *Am sl* road hog; **~fahrkarte** *f* week-end ticket; **~jäger** *m* amateur sportsman; **~kind** *n* Sunday-child; *ein ~~ sein* to be born under a lucky star; to be born with a silver spoon in o.'s mouth; **~kleid** *n* Sunday-dress; **~predigt** *f* dominical sermon; **~ruhe** *f* Sunday rest; Sabbath rest; **~reiter** *m* unskilful rider; **~schule** *f* Sunday-school; **~staat** *m* Sunday-clothes *pl*.

sonor *a* sonorous.

sonst *adv* (*im andern Fall*) otherwise, else; (*außerdem*) besides; in other respect; (*überdies*) moreover; (*gewöhnlich, üblicherweise*) as a rule; usual(ly); (*ehemals*) formerly; at any other time; ~ *etw* anything else; ~ *nichts* nothing else; ~ *nirgends* nowhere else; ~ *jem* anybody else; *wenn es ~ nichts ist* if that is all; *wie ~* as usual; **~ig** *a* other; remaining; former; **~wo** *adv* elsewhere; **~woher** *adv* from some other place; **~wohin** *adv* to another place, somewhere else.

Sophis|ma *n*, ***~mus*** *m* sophism; **~t** *m* sophist; quibbler; **~terei** *f* sophistry; special pleading; quibbling; **~tisch** *a* sophistic(al).

Sopran *m mus* soprano; (*Diskant*) treble; **~istin** *f*, **~sänger** *m*, **~sängerin** *f* soprano (singer), sopranist; **~schlüssel** *m* treble clef.

*

Sorg|e *f* (*Kummer*) sorrow; (*Leid*) grief; anguish; distress; (*Unruhe*) uneasiness; (*Angst*) anxiety; (*Befürchtung*) apprehension; fear; perturbation; alarm; (*tiefe Beunruhigung, Interesse*) concern; (*quälende ~e*) worry, (*meist pl* worries); (*Fürsorge, Sorgfalt*) care; (*liebevolle*) solicitude; (*Ungelegenheit*) trouble; (*Problem*) problem; *schwere ~e* grave concern; *keine ~e!* don't worry! *Kummer u. ~en* sorrow and trouble; *das ist meine geringste ~e* that is the least of my cares; *~en haben, in ~en leben* to be in trouble; *jdm ~en machen* to worry s. o.; to cause trouble to s. o.; to give s. o. much anxiety (*od* concern); *sich ~en machen* (*über, um*) to worry about, to fret about; to be concerned about; to be uneasy in o.'s mind about; *sich keine ~en machen* to be free from care; not to trouble o. s. about, not to bother about; *sich mehr ~en machen über ... als ...* to lose more sleep over ... than ...; *in ~e sein* to be anxious; to fear; to be afraid lest; *in großer ~e sein um* to be in great anxiety about; *außer ~e sein* to be at ease, to be unconcerned; *laß das meine ~e sein* leave that to me; *~e tragen für* to take care of (*od* for); to see to; to attend to; to look after; to take charge of; to cater for; to care for; (*Vorsorge treffen*) to make provision for; *es jds ~e überlassen* to commit s. th. to s. o.'s charge; **~en** *itr* (*~e tragen, sich kümmern um*) to take care (*für* of *od* for); (*fürsorgen*) to make provision for; to provide for; to fend for; (*dafür ~en, daß*) to attend to, to see to (*od* after); (*um Nahrung etc*) to cater for; (*Verantwortung übernehmen*) to take charge of; *sich ~en* (*fürchten*) to be anxious; to be uneasy; to fear; to be apprehensive; (*sich quälend ~en*) to worry; *sich ~en* (*um, wegen*) to be concerned about; to trouble o. s. about; (*sich härmen*) to grieve (*über* at, over, *um* for); *bitte ~en Sie dafür, daß ...* please, see that ...; it is your duty to see that; *dafür werde ich ~en* leave that to me; *dafür ist gesorgt* that has been seen to; **~enbrecher** *m* banisher of care; **~enfalte** *f* wrinkle of care; **~enfrei** *a* (*ohne ~en*) carefree; exempt (*od* free) from care; (*ungestört*) untroubled; (*bequem*) easy; **~enkind** *n* (*charakterlich*) problem child; (*gesundheitlich*) delicate child; **~enlast** *f* load of care; **~enlos** *a siehe: ~enfrei*; **~enschwer** *a siehe*: *~envoll*; **~enstuhl** *m* easy chair, arm chair; **~envoll** *a* full of cares; (*von ~en gequält*) careworn; worried; (*mit Furcht erfüllt*) apprehensive; anxious; uneasy; **~falt, ~fältigkeit** *f* care; carefulness; heedfulness; (*liebevolle ~~*) solicitude; (*Genauigkeit*) accuracy; exactness; (*Pünktlichkeit*) painstaking; precision; (*Aufmerksamkeit*) attention; (*Überlegung*) thoughtfulness; *viel ~~ verwenden auf* to put a lot of care into s. th.; **~fältig** *a* careful; heedful; (*aufmerksam*) attentive; (*fleißig*) diligent; (*genau*) accurate; precise; exact; (*pünktlich*) painstaking; (*übertrieben ~~*) punctilious; scrupulous; meticulous; (*behutsam*) chary; (*überlegt*) deliberate; *~~ untersuchen* to scan; **~lich** *a* careful; anxious; solicitous; **~los** *a* carefree; (*unachtsam*) careless; reckless; heedless; (*leichtfertig*) lighthearted; (*gedankenlos*) thoughtless; (*unbekümmert*) unconcerned (*über* about); happy-go--lucky; (*nachlässig*) negligent; (*gleichgültig*) indifferent; (*vertrauensselig*) too trusting; *ein ~~es Leben* a carefree life; **~~igkeit** *f* carelessness; recklessness; (*Leichtsinn*) lightheartedness; (*Gedankenlosigkeit*) thoughtlessness; (*Nachlässigkeit*) negligence; (*Gleichgültigkeit*) indifference; (*Unbekümmertheit*) unconcern; **~sam** *a* careful, heedful; particular; (*vorsichtig*) cautious; **~~keit** *f* carefulness; (*Vorsicht*) caution.

Sort|e *f* (*Art*) sort; kind; description; (*Gattung*) species; variety; *Am* (*Charakter*) stripe; (*Klasse*) class; grade; rank; (*Güte, Qualität*) quality; (*Marke*) mark; (*bes. von Zigarren, Zigaretten, Markenartikeln*) brand; (*Wolle*) break; (*Typ*) type; *von allen ~en* of all sorts, of every description; *erste ~e* best quality; A 1; *gangbarste ~e* leading species, current description; *geringere ~e* inferior quality; **~en, ~ieren** *tr* (*aus~~*) to sort (out); to assort; (*anordnen*) to arrange; (*klassifizieren*) to classify; (*nach Qualität abstufen*) to grade; (*nach Größe*) to size; (*trennen*) to separate, to sift; (*auslesen*) to pick; (*Wolle*) to break; **~enzettel** *m* (*Börse*) bill of specie; **~iermaschine** *f* sorting machine; sizing apparatus; separator; **~ierung** *f* sorting; assortment; assorting; (*Trennung*) separation, sifting; (*Klassifizierung*) classification; (*nach Größe*) sizing; (*nach Qualität*) grading; **~iment** *n* (*Auswahl*) assortment; collection; (*Satz*) set; (*Buchhandel*) retail book-trade; (*Buchladen*) book-shop; **~~er, ~~sbuchhändler** *m* bookseller; **~~sbuchhandlung** *f* bookseller's shop.

Soße *f* (= *Sauce*) sauce; (*Braten~*) gravy.

Souffl|eur *m*, ***~euse*** *f* prompter; **~eurkasten** *m* prompt-box; **~ierbuch** *n* prompt-book; **~ieren** *itr* to prompt.

Souterrain *n* basement; (*Erdgeschoß*) ground-floor; (*Keller*) cellar.

Souverän *m*, *~ a* sovereign; **~ität** *f* sovereignty.

so|viel *adv* so much; *~ conj* as far as, so far as; as much as; *~~ wie* fully, as much as, *Am auch* all of; **~weit** *conj* as far as; **~wenig** *conj* as little as; **~wie** *conj* as; as well as; as soon as; just as; also; **~wieso** *adv* anyhow; in any case; **~wohl** *conj*: *~~ ... als auch* as well ... as; both ... and

Sowjet *m* (*Rat*) Soviet; *der Oberste ~* the Supreme Soviet; *die ~ Militärverwaltung* the Soviet Military Administration; *unter dem Einfluß der ~s* Soviet sponsored, Soviet-oriented; **~armist** *m* Soviet soldier; red soldier; **~feindlich** *a* anti-soviet; **~isch** *a* soviet(ist); **~isierung** *f* sovietization; **~kongreß** *m* Union Congress of Soviets; **~macht** *f* Soviet Power; **~republik** *f* Soviet Republic; (*amtlich*) Russian Socialist Federated Soviet Republic; **~rußland** *n* Soviet Russia; (*amtlich*) Union of Soviet Socialist Republics; **~system** *n* sovietism; **~stern** *m* Soviet star; **~union** *f* Soviet Union; (*amtlich*) Union of Soviet Socialist Republics (*Abk* U.S.S.R.).

sozial *a* social; public; *~e Fürsorge, ~e Wohlfahrt* social welfare (work); *die ~en Verhältnisse* social conditions; **~abgaben** *f pl* social charges *pl* (*od* contributions *pl*); **~amt** *n* social welfare office; **~beamte(r)** *m* (social) welfare worker; **~beiträge** *m pl* social insurance contributions *pl*; **~demokrat** *m* social democrat; **~demokratie** *f* social democracy; **~demokratisch** *a* social--democratic; *~~e Partei (in Deutschland SPD)* Social-Democratic Party; **~fürsorge** *f* welfare work; **~~r** *m*, **~~rin** *f* social welfare worker; **~gesetzgebung** *f* social legislation; **~isieren** *tr* (*Industrie*) to socialize, to communize, (*England*) to nationalize; **~isierung** *f* nationalization; socialization; **~ismus** *m* socialism; **~ist** *m* socialist; **~istisch** *a* socialist(ic); *~~e Einheitspartei* Socialist Unity Party; **~lasten** *f pl* social (security) expenditure; social costs *pl*; **~lohn** *m* social wages *pl;* **~politik** *f* social politics; **~~er** *m* social thinker; **~politisch** *a* socio-political; sociological; **~produkt** *n* gross national product (*Abk* GNP); total product: national income (per capita); **~psychologie** *f* social psychology; **~rentner** *m* old-age pensioner; annuitant; **~versicherung** *f* social insurance; **~~samt** *n* *Am* Social Security Board; **~~sbeitrag** *m* premium for social insurance; pay--roll taxes *pl;* **~~sgesetz** *n* Social Insurance Act, *Am* Social Security Act; **~wissenschaft** *f* sociology; **~~lich** *a* sociological; **~zulage** *f*, **~zuwendungen** *f pl* benefits *pl*, family bonus.

Soziolog *m* sociologist; **~ie** *f* sociology; **~isch** *a* sociological.

Sozius *m* partner; *mot* pillion rider; **~sitz** *m mot* pillion seat; *auf dem ~~ mitfahren* to ride pillion.

sozusagen *adv* so to speak; as it were.

Spachtel *m, f* (*Werkzeug*) spatula; (*Messer*) putty knife; (*Maler~*) scraper; smoother; (*Kitt*) primer, filler; priming material; knifing glaze; **~kitt** *m* filler, primer; **~n** *tr* to make smooth; to scrape; to prime; *itr fam* (*essen*) to tuck in; **~messer** *n* putty knife; **~ung** *f* knifing the filler.

Spagat *m* (*Bindfaden*) binding thread; string; twine.

Späh|dienst *m mil* scouting service; **~en** *itr* (*spionieren*) to spy; (*kundschaften*) to reconnoitre, to scout; to patrol; (*aus Neugier*) to pry into; (*verstohlen*) to peer; (*hinsehen, beobachten*) to look out (for); to be on the lookout; to observe, to watch; (*suchen*) to search; (*erforschen*) to explore; **~er** *m* (*Spion*) spy; (*Kundschafter*) scout; (*Beobachtender*) look-out; **~~auge** *n* keen eye; **~~blick** *m* searching glance; **~flugzeug** *n* patrol airplane; **~trupp** *m mil* patrol; scouting party, scouting squad; **~~tätigkeit** *f*, **~~unternehmen** *n mil* patrol activity; **~wagen** *m mil* reconnaissance car; (*Panzer*) armo(u)red scouting car, *Am* scout car.

Spalier *n* (*am Haus*) trellis, espalier; (*von Leuten*) lane; avenue; line (of people); *~ bilden mil* to form a lane; *am ~ ziehen* to train; **~baum** *m* wall tree; trained fruit tree; **~bildung** *f* lining the street; **~förmig** *a* trellised; **~obst** *n* wall fruit; **~trauben** *f pl* wall grapes *pl*; **~wuchs** *m* espalier growth.

Spalt *m*, **~e** *f* cleft; crevice; fissure; (*Riß*) crack; chap; split; rent; (*Schlitz*) slit; slot; (*Lücke*) gap; (*Ritze*) chink; (*Öffnung*) opening; aperture; clearance; (*Erdkluft*) chasm; *fig* gulf; chasm; **~bar** *a* cleavable; divisible; fissile; *phys* (*Atom*) fissionable; *nicht ~~* nonfissionable; *~~er Stoff* fissionable material; **~barkeit** *f* cleavability; cleavage; **~bildung** *f* fissure formation; **~blende** *f phot* slit diaphragm; **~breite** *f* width of slit; **~bruch** *m anat* fissure; **~e** *f typ* column; (*Gletscher~~*) crevasse; (*Einschnitt*) incision; *die ~en füllen typ* to fill the columns; **~en** *tr* to split (up); to cleave; to fissure; (*Holz ~~*) to chop, to cleave (wood); (*schlitzen*) to slit; (*Risse bekommen*) to crack; (*aufreißen*) to rend; to rift; (*teilen*) to divide; *chem* to decompose; to ferment; *Haare ~~* to split hairs; *sich gabelförmig ~~* to bifurcate; *die Partei hat sich ge~~* the party has split; *die Meinungen sind ge~~* opinions are divided; *ein Uraniumatom kann durch Beschuß mit e-m Neutronenstrom ge~~ werden* a uranium atom can be made to split under the bombardment of a stream of neutrons; **~enbreite** *f typ* width of column; **~enweise** *adv* in columns; **~fläche** *f* cleavage face; plane of cleavage; **~flügel** *m aero* slot (*od* slotted) wing; wing-tip slot; **~fuß** *m* split foot; **~füßig** *a* cleft-footed; **~hilfsflügel** *m aero* split flap; **~holz** *n* firewood, sticks *pl*; **~hufer** *m pl* ruminants *pl*; **~ig** *a* fissured; cracked; *typ* columned; **~keil** *m* wedge; **~klappe** *f aero* slotted flap; **~leder** *n* skiver; **~pilz** *m* fission-fungus; **produkt** *n* split product; *chem* product of separation; *phys* (*Atom*) fission product; **~ung** *f* cleaving, cleavage; split; splitting; cracking; (*Atom*) fission; (*Trennung*) separation; segregation; *chem* decomposition; *fig* (*Uneinigkeit*) disunion; dissension; (*der Meinungen*) division; (*Bruch*) rupture; disruption; (*e-r Partei*) split, *Am* break; *eccl* (*Kirchen~~*) schism; *~~ des Uran 235* fission (*od* splitting) of U-235; *~~ ist nur bei den schwersten Elementen möglich* fission can be produced only in the heaviest elements; **~~sbombe** *f* fission bomb; **~~senergie** *f* energy of splitting; **~~sprodukt** *n* fission product; **~~sprozeß** *m phys* fission process; *im ~~sprozeß wird ein Atomkern gespalten u. ein Teil seiner Bindungsenergie freigemacht* in the process of fission an atomic nucleus is split and some of its binding force released; **~sversuch** *m* cleavage (*od* splitting) test.

Span *m* (*Holz~*) chip; (*Splitter*) splinter; (*Späne pl*) shavings *pl*, parings *pl*; (*Abfall*) shreds *pl*; (*Metall~*) turning; cutting; **~abhebend** *a tech* cutting, machining; **~ferkel** *n* sucking pig; porkling; sucker; **~grün** *n* verdigris; **~holz** *n* chips *pl*; **~korb** *m* wood-shaving basket, chip basket; **~schachtel** *f* chip box; **~trocken** *a* bone-dry.

spänen *tr* (*Tiere*) to wean; (*Parkett*) to clean.

Spange *f* (*an Buch*) clasp; (*Schnalle*) buckle; slip; (*Brosche*) brooch; (*Stoffstreifen*) strap; (*Verschluß*) bar; (*Arm~*) bracelet; **~nschuh** *m* buckled shoe; strap shoe.

Span|ien *n* Spain; **~ier** *m*, **~ierin** *f* Spaniard; **~isch** *a* Spanish; *~~e Wand* folding-screen; *das kommt mir ~~ vor fig* that's all Greek to me.

Spann *m* (*Fußrist*) instep.

Spann|draht *m aero* cross-bracing wire; **~e** *f* span; (*Zeit~~*) short space (of time); span; (*kurze Entfernung*) short distance; interval; (*Reichweite*) range; *com* (*Verdienst~~, Preis~~*) margin; **~en** *tr* (*strecken*) to stretch; (*straffen*) to strain; (*an~~*) to (put under) stress; to make tense; (*Schraube*) to tighten; (*fest~~*) to clamp; to hold; to brace; (*Feder*) to subject to tension; (*aufziehen*) to wind up; (*Bogen*) to bend; (*Flinte*) to cock; (*überbrücken*) to span; (*Gewölbe*) to vault; to arch; (*Pferd an Wagen*) to put to, to harness; (*in Schraubstock*) to put into a vice; (*Saiten*) to tighten; to screw up; *phot* (*Verschluß*) to set (the shutter); (*auf~~*) to put up; *auf die Folter ~~* to put to the rack; *fig* to keep in painful suspense; to keep on tenter-hooks; *Forderungen zu hoch ~~* to ask too much; *zu hochgespannt* overstrained; (*übertrieben*) exaggerated; *auf etw ~~, auf etw gespannt sein* to be anxious to; to be curious; *jds Erwartungen hoch ~~* to work up s. o.'s expectations to a high pitch; *er hörte gespannt zu* he listened intently; *mit jdm auf gespanntem Fuß leben* to be on bad terms with; *itr* (*drücken*) to pinch; to pull; (*zu eng sein*) to be too tight; (*Kleider*) to fit tightly; *fig* (*aufpassen*) to listen eagerly (to); to attend (to); to excite; *sich ~~* to stretch, to arch; **~en** *n* gripping; clamping; chucking; tightening; holding; stretching; **~end** *a* (*anliegend*) tight; *fig* (*interessant*) deeply interesting; (*aufregend*) exciting, thrilling; (*fesselnd*) fascinating; absorbing; (*packend*) gripping; (*ergreifend*) moving; **~er** *m anat* tensor; (*Schuhleisten*) boot-tree; last; *tech* vise, vice; chuck; (*Schmetterling*) butterfly; **~feder** *f* tension (*od* cocking) spring; **~futter** *n tech* chuck; **~haken** *m* tenter-hook; **~hebel** *m* cocking lever; bolt lever; **~kette** *f* drag-chain; **~kraft** *f* tension; (*Elastizität*) elasticity; extensibility; *tech* clamping power; **~kräftig** *a* (*elastisch*) elastic; **~muskel** *m anat* tensor; **~mutter** *f* spring nut; **~(n)agel** *m* peg; large nail; **~rahmen** *m* (*Tuch*) tenter (-frame); **~riemen** *m* tightening belt; knee-strap; **~säge** *f* frame saw; **~schloß** *n* turnbuckle; tightener; tension lock; **~seil** *n* bracing wire; shackle; guy rope; **~ung** *f tech, el, fig* tension; *tech* strain; (*elastische ~~*) stress; (*Gas~~*) pressure; *el* voltage; potential; *unter ~~* (*setzen*) (to make) alive; *innere ~~* internal stress; *fig* (*Aufmerksamkeit*) close attention; (*Intensität*) intensity; (*Erwartung*) expectation; (*Ungewißheit*) suspense; (*Aufregung*) excitement; (*Angst*) anxiety; *in größter ~~ bleiben fig* to remain on tenter-hooks; (*gespannte Beziehungen*) strained relations; **~~sabfall** *m* voltage drop; **~~sfeder** *f* tension spring; **~~sgefälle** *n el* voltage drop; potential drop; **~~slos** *a el* (*stromlos*) dead; **~~smesser** *m el* voltmeter; **~~sreihe** *f el* contact series; **~~steiler** *m radio* potentiometer; **~~sunterschied** *m* potential difference; **~vorrichtung** *f* chuck; stretching device; **~weite** *f* spread; (*Flügel~~*) span; *Am* wingspread; (*Brücke*) span width; span length; (*Reichweite*) range.

Spant *m mar, aero* rib; frame, former; timber; **~ring** *m* former, frame.

Spar|bank *f* savings-bank; **~brenner** *m* pilot burner; **~buch** *n* deposits book; pass book; **~büchse** *f* money-box; **~einlage** *f* savings deposit; **~einleger** *m* savings bank depositor; **~en** *tr, itr* to save; (*sparsam verwenden*) to economize, to spare; (*Ausgaben einschränken*) to cut down expenses; (*Geld zurücklegen*) to lay (*od* to put) by money; to save up; *seine Kräfte ~~* to reserve o.'s forces; *seine Worte ~~* to spare o.'s words; *Benzin u. Öl ~~* to save on gas and oil; **~er** *m* saver; **~feldzug** *m* economy drive; **~geld** *n*, **~groschen** *m pl* savings *pl*; **~guthaben** *n* savings-account, *Am* savings-bank account; **~herd** *m* economical kitchen-range; kitchener; **~kasse** *f* savings-bank; **~~nbuch** *n* savings-bank book; **~konto** *n* savings-account, *Am* savings-bank account; **~maßnahme** *f* measure of economy; **~pfennig** *m* savings *pl*, nest-egg; money for a rainy day; **~plan** *m* (*England*) austerity plan; **~programm** *n* (*England*) austerity program; **~~ u. Darlehenskasse** *f* savings and credit bank; **~sam** *a* economical, saving; thrifty; (*genügsam*) frugal; *~~ mit Lob* chary of praise; *~~ umgehen* to use s. th. sparingly; to economize on; **~~keit** *f* economy; thriftiness; thrift; (*Einfachheit*) frugality; (*übertriebene ~~*) parsimony; **~stoff** *m* high-priority material; **~zwang** *m* compulsory saving.

Spargel *m bot* asparagus; *mar sl* periscope; *~ stechen* to cut asparagus; **~beet** *n* asparagus bed; **~kohl** *m* broccoli; **~messer** *n*, **~stecher** *m* asparagus knife; **~zeit** *f* asparagus season.

spärlich *a* (*knapp*) scanty; (*selten*) scarce, rare; (*mager*) meagre; (*dürftig*) poor; (*einfach*) frugal; (*dünn*) thin; (*zerstreut*) sparse; (*schwach*) faint; (*gering*) little; (*mäßig*) moderate; *~ bevölkert* sparsely populated; *~er Gewinn* meagre profit; *~es Haar* thin hair: *~e Nachrichten* meagre news; *~ vorhanden* scarce; **~keit** *f* scantiness; rarity, rareness; scarcity; sparseness; frugality; poorness.

Sparren *m* spar, rafter; *fam e-n ~ zuviel haben* to have a screw loose; to be cracked; **~werk** *n* rafters *pl*.

Spaß *m* jest, joke; fun, sport; play; (*Zeitvertreib*) amusement; pastime; (*handgreiflicher ~, Unfug*) horse-play; *zum ~, aus ~* in jest, for fun; *~ beiseite!* joking aside! *Am* this is no dream! no kidding! *nur zum ~* just for the fun of it; *schlechter ~* bad joke; *lassen Sie Ihre dummen Späße!* none of your silly jokes! *viel ~!* enjoy yourself! have a good time! *ich habe nur ~ gemacht* I was only joking; *es machte ihr ~* she enjoyed it, it amused her, *Am fam* she got a kick out of that; *~ muß sein* a joke never comes amiss; *jdm den ~ verderben* to spoil s.o.'s sport; *~ verstehen* to take a joke; *darin versteht sie keinen ~* she won't stand joking about that; *an etw ~ haben* to enjoy s. th.; **~en** *itr* to jest, to joke; to sport, to make fun; *er läßt nicht mit sich ~en* he is not to be joked with; *damit ist nicht zu ~~* that is no joking matter; **~eshalber** *adv* for fun; **~haft**, **~ig** *a* jocose, joking, jocular; amusing; odd; sportive, droll, funny, ludicrous; **~macher**, **~vogel** *m* jester, wag; buffoon; **~verderber** *m* spoil-sport, kill-joy, *Am* wet blanket.

Spat *m min* (*Feld~*) spar; (*Pferdekrankheit*) spavin; **~artig** *a min* spathic; **~eisenstein** *m* siderite; **~stein** *m* specular stone, selenite.

spät *a* late; (*verspätet*) belated; (*unpünktlich*) slow; (*~ eintretend*) backward; (*zögernd*) tardy; (*nachfolgend*) subsequent; ~ *aufstehen* to get up late; ~ *kommen* to be late, *Am* to be tardy; *wie ~ ist es?* what time is it? *es ist schon ~* it is late; *es wird schon ~* it is getting late; *am ~en Nachmittag* late in the afternoon; ~ *am Tage* late in the day; *die ~e Jahreszeit* the advanced season; *früh u. ~* morning and night; *von früh bis ~* from morning till night; *zu ~* too late; *zu ~ gehen (Uhr)* to be slow; *zu ~ kommen* to be late; to be behind time; *zu ~ in die Schule kommen* to be late for school; **~er** *a, Komparativ* later; afterwards; later on; hereafter; after that; subsequently; *früher od ~~* sooner or later; *e-e Woche ~~* a week after; *in ~~en Jahren* in after-life; *~~e Geschlechter* future generations; *in ~~en Zeiten* in later times; *in der ~~en Zukunft* in the remote future; **~erhin** *adv* later on; **~estens** *adv* at the latest; not later than; *um 5 Uhr ~~* at 5 o'clock at the latest; **~frost** *m* late frost; **~frucht** *f* late fruit; **~geburt** *f* late confinement; late birth; **~gotik** *f* latest Gothic style; perpendicular style; **~herbst** *m* late autumn, *Am* fall of the year; **~heu** *n* aftermath; **~jahr** *n* autumn, *Am* fall; **~ling** *m (Früchte)* late fruit; *(Vieh)* lamb *etc* born late in the season; *(Mensch)* late-come child; **~nachmittag** *m* late afternoon; **~obst** *n* late fruit; **~sommer** *m* latter part of summer, late summer; Indian summer; **~zündung** *f mot* retarded ignition, sparking retard.

Spatel *m siehe Spachtel.*

Spaten *m* spade; **~stich** *m* cut with a spade; *den ersten ~~ tun* to turn the first sod.

spationieren *tr typ* to space.

Spatz *m* sparrow; *das pfeifen die ~ von den Dächern fig* that is the talk of the town; the story is in every o.'s mouth.

spazier|en *irr itr* to take a walk; to stroll; to walk about; **~enfahren** *irr itr* to go for a drive, to take a drive; **~enführen** *itr* to take out for a walk, to take for a stroll; **~engehen** *irr itr* to go for a walk; **~enreiten** *irr itr* to take a ride, to go for a ride; **~fahrt** *f* drive; *(in Schiff)* sail; row; **~gang** *m* walk, stroll; promenade; **~gänger** *m* walker, stroller; promenader; **~ritt** *m* ride; **~stock** *m* walking-stick; cane; **~weg** *m* walk.

Specht *m* woodpecker.

Speck *m (Schweine~)* bacon; *(Fett, Fettansatz)* grease; *(Schmalz)* lard; dripping; *(Walfisch~)* blubber; *typ* fat; *geräucherter ~* smoked bacon; *mit ~ fängt man Mäuse* good bait catches fine fish; *im ~ sitzen* to live in clover; **~artig** *a* fatty; lardaceous; **~bauch, ~wanst** *m* paunch, belly; *fam* corporation; **~eier** *n pl* ham and eggs; **~hals** *m* fat neck; **~ig** *a* very fat; lardy; *(schmutzig)* greasy, dirty; **~scheibe, ~schnitte** *f*, **~streifen** *m* rasher of bacon; **~schwarte** *f* sward, rind of bacon; **~seite** *f* flitch of bacon; *die Wurst nach der ~~ werfen* to give a sprat to catch a herring; **~stein** *m* steatite, soapstone.

sped|ieren *tr* to dispatch; to ship; to send off, to forward; **~iteur** *m* carrier, forwarding agent; shipping agent, freight forwarder; carter; *Am* shipper; expressagency, expressman; *(Möbel~~)* furniture remover; **~ition** *f* forwarding, carrying, shipping, *Am* expressing, shipment; forwarding agency; **~~sauftrag** *m* dispatch order; *Am* shipping order; **~~sgebühren** *pl* forwarding charges *pl*, *Am* shipping charges *pl*; **~~sgeschäft** *n* forwarding agency; carrier's business; *(Möbel)* furniture removal business; *Am* express company; **~~sgüter** *n pl* freight; **~~shandel** *m* forwarding trade; **~~sprovision** *f* forwarding commission.

Speer *m (Waffe)* spear; *sport* javelin; *(Lanze)* lance; **~förmig** *a* spear-shaped; *bot* lanceolate; lanciform; **~spitze** *f* spearhead; **~stechen** *n* spearing; **~werfen** *n sport* throwing the javelin.

Speiche *f* spoke; *anat* radius.

Speichel *m* spittle; saliva; **~absonderung** *f* salivation; discharge of saliva; **~drüse** *f* salivary gland; **~fluß** *m* flow of saliva; salivation; **~flüssigkeit** *f* saliva; **~gang** *m* salivary duct; **~lecker** *m* toady, sycophant, bootlick(er), fawner; toadeater; cringer; **~~ei** *f* adulation; **~röhre** *f* salivary duct.

Speicher *m (Korn~)* granary; silo, *Am* elevator; *(Waren~)* warehouse, storehouse; storeroom, storage place; *(Möbel~)* depository, *Am* storage warehouse; *(Boden~)* loft; attic; *(Wasser~)* reservoir; *(Druckwasser)* hydraulic accumulator; *el (Akku)* storage battery; *(Kriegs~)* magazine; depot; **~batterie** *f el* storage battery; **~becken** *n* reservoir; storage basin; **~gebühren** *f pl* warehouse rates *pl*, storage; **~kraftwerk** *n* storage power station; **~n** *tr* to store, to warehouse; to store up; to lay up; to accumulate; *(aufstapeln)* to stockpile; *fig* to treasure up; to hoard; **~ung** *f* storage; storing (up); accumulation.

spei|en *irr itr, tr (spucken)* to spit; *(sich erbrechen)* to vomit; *(Feuer ~~)* to belch; *Gift u. Galle ~~* to vent o.'s spleen; *Wasser ~~ (aus Rohr)* to discharge water; **~er** *m (Wasser~~)* gargoyle; **~gatt** *n mar* scupper; **~napf** *m* spittoon, *Am* cuspidor; **~tüte** *f aero* sanitary paper bag.

Speierling *m* service-berry; **~sbaum** *m* service-tree.

Speiler *m* skewer.

Speise *f* food, nourishment; *(Mahl)* meal; *(Gericht)* dish; *(Kost)* fare; *(Süß~)* pudding; sweet; *(Eßwaren)* eatables *pl*; *~n auftragen* to serve up s. th.; *~ u. Trank* meat and drink; *die ~n abtragen* to clear the table; *(Glocken~)* metal; speiss; *(Mörtel)* mortar; **~anstalt** *f* eating-house; restaurant; **~aufzug** *m* dinner-lift; service-lift; *Am* dumbwaiter; **~brei** *m* chyme; **~eis** *n* ice-cream; **~fett** *n* fat for cooking, cooking fat; nutrient *(od* edible) fat; **~haus** *n* eating-house, dining-rooms *pl*; **~kammer** *f* larder, pantry; **~karte** *f* bill of fare; *Am meist* menu; *Herr Ober, bitte die ~~* waiter, may I have the menu, please; **~leitung** *f tech* feeder, feed line; **~n** *itr* to eat; *(im Gasthaus)* to take o.'s meals; *zu Mittag ~n* to dine; *zu Abend ~n* to sup; *wohl zu ~n!* good appetite; *tr (beköstigen)* to board; to feed; to entertain; to give to eat; *(versorgen)* to supply; *tech* to charge, to load; to energize; **~nfolge** *f* menu; **~nische** *f* dining alcove, *Am* dinette; **~öl** *n* sweet-oil, salad-oil; **~pumpe** *f tech* feed-pump; **~r** *m* feeder; **~rest** *m* food particle; **~~e** *m pl* leftovers *pl*; **~restaurant** *n* restaurant, *Am (kleines)* diner; **~rohr** *n tech* feed pipe, supply pipe *(od* tube); **~röhre** *f anat* gullet, œsophagus; **~saal** *m*, **~zimmer** *n* dining-room; *(in Klöstern)* refectory; *(Saal)* dining-hall; banqueting-hall; *(Schiff)* dining-saloon; *(Offiziere)* mess-room; **~saft** *m* chyle; **~salz** *n* common salt; **~schrank** *m* larder, meat-safe; *Am* safe; **~sirup** *m* table sirup; **~tisch** *m* dinner-table, dining-table; **~wagen** *m* dining-car, restaurant-car, *Am* diner; **~walze** *f tech* feeding roll(er); **~wärmer** *m (auf dem Tisch)* meat warmer, *Am* chafing-dish; **~wasser** *n tech* feed water; **~~pumpe** *f tech* feed-water pump; **~~vorwärmer** *m tech* feed-water preheater; **~wirt** *m* keeper of dining-rooms; **~~schaft** *f* eating-house, restaurant; **~zettel** *m* bill of fare, *Am meist* menu; **~zimmer** *n* dining-room; **~zucker** *m* table sugar, brown sugar; **~zwiebel** *f* onion.

Speisung *f* eating; feeding; boarding; *tech* supply, feed; input; *el* excitation; *~ der 5000 (Bibel)* feeding of the five thousand.

Spektakel *m* noise, uproar; *(Radau)* row, shindy; racket; *e-n großen ~ machen über* to make a great fuss about . . .; **~macher** *m* rowdy; **~stück** *n* show-piece; sensational play.

Spektr|alanalyse *f* spectrum analysis; spectroscopic analysis; **~alanalytisch** *a* spectroscopic; spectrometric; **~alapparat** *m* spectroscope; spectroscopic apparatus; **~alaufnahme** *f* spectrograph; **~albeobachtung** *f* spectroscopic observation; **~alfarbe** *f* spectral colo(u)r; **~allinie** *f* spectrum *(od* spectral) line; **~altafel** *f* spectral chart; **~ogramm** *n* spectrogram; **~oskop** *n* spectroscope; **~oskopie** *f* spectroscopy; **~um** *n* spectrum; irization, iridescence.

Spekul|ant *m* speculator; gambler, adventurer; *Am sl* wild catter; **~ation** *f* speculation, venture, gamble, *fam* spec; *(in kleinem Umfang)* flutter; *sich auf e-e ~~ einlassen* to embark *(od* to take part) in a speculation; *auf ~~ kaufen* to buy on spec; **~~sartikel** *m* speculative article; **~~sgeschäft** *n* speculative transaction, gamble; **~~sgewinn** *m* speculative profit; **~~spapiere** *n pl* speculative investments *pl*, *Am* fancy stocks *pl*; **~ativ** *a* speculative; **~ieren** *itr* to speculate (on); to venture; to operate; *auf Baisse ~~* to sell bear, *Am* to sell short; *auf Hausse ~~* to bull.

spellen *tr* to split, to cleave.

Spelt, Spelz *m* spelt; **~e** *f bot* beard (of ears); awn; glume; **~ig** *a* glumaceous.

Spelunke *f* den, low gin-shop, *Am fam* dive; *Am sl* joint, honky-tonk, dump, slapbang, slophouse.

Spend|e *f (Gabe)* gift; *(Geschenk)* present; *(Beitrag)* contribution; *(Stiftung)* donation; *(Almosen)* charity, alms; dole; **~en** *tr (geben)* to give, to bestow; *(verteilen)* to dispense; to administer; *(beitragen)* to contribute (to); *(Almosen)* to distribute; *(Lob)* to bestow (praise on s. o.); *(Abendmahl)* to administer; *jdm Trost ~~* to comfort s. o.; **~er** *m (Geber)* giver; *(Stifter)* donor; *(Austeiler)* distributor; *(Wohltäter)* benefactor; *(Beitragzahlender)* contributor; **~ieren** *tr* to pay for; to spend liberally; to lavish; to stand; *jdm etw ~~* to treat s. o. to s. th.; **~ung** *f* distribution; *(Sakrament)* administration.

Spengler *m (Klempner, Flaschner)* tinman, tin-smith; *(Installateur)* plumber; *(Karosserieflaschner)* sheet-metal worker.

Sper|ber *m* sparrow-hawk; **~ling** *m* sparrow.

Sperma *n* sperm; semen; **~kern** *m* sperm nucleus; **~tozoon** *n* spermatozoon, spermatozoid, male generative cell.

sperr|angelweit *adv:* **~~** *offen* wide open; gaping; **~ballon** *m mil aero* barrage balloon, *Am sl* flying elephant; **~~haltetau** *n mil* barrage balloon cable; **~baum** *m* bar, barrier; (*Schlagbaum*) turnpike; **~blockierung** *f* blocking; **~bolzen** *m* strain bolt; **~boot** *n* barrage vessel; **~brecher** *m* barrage breaker; anti-boom ship; **~damm** *m* dam; **~depot** *n com* blocked deposit; **~drachen** *m mil aero* barrage kite; **~druck** *m typ* spaced type; italics *pl*; **~e** *f* shutting, closing; close; closure; stoppage; *tech* click; catch; stop; lock; (*Absperrung*) block; (*Straßen~~*) barricade, *Am* blockade; (*Bahnhof~~*) barrier, *Am* gate; *mil* barrage; (*Stacheldraht~~*) entanglement; (*Hindernis*) obstacle; (*Einfuhr~~*) embargo; (*Hafen~~*) blockade; *mar* (*Gesundheits~~*) quarantine; (*Konto~~, Geld~~ etc*) blocking; freezing; (*Beschlagnahme*) *jur* seizure; attachment; *radio* rejector; wave trap; suppressor; (*Rad~~*) drag; (*Eingangs~~*) gate; *fig* (*Hinderung*) impediment; prohibition; obstruction; ban; *Schaffner etc an der ~~* ticket collector, *Am* gateman, gatekeeper; *~~ fliegen aero mil* to fly on defensive patrol; *~~ verhängen* to block; to closure; to ban; **~en** *tr* (*schließen*) to shut, to close; to shut up; (*Licht, Gas ~~*) to cut off, to shut off; (*anhalten*) to stop; to arrest; to detain; (*verschließen*) to lock, to lock up; (*Hafen*) to lock; (*Straße*) to block; (*ausschließen*) to exclude; to lock out, to block; (*hemmen*) to hinder, to hamper; to obstruct; (*blockieren*) to blockade; to barricade; (*unterbrechen*) to interrupt; (*Warenverkehr*) to lay on, to embargo; (*durch Polizei etc ab~~*) to cordon off; (*bewachen*) to guard; (*isolieren*) to isolate, to insulate; (*abdämmen*) to dam; (*sichern*) to secure; (*unterdrücken*) to suppress; *sport* (*Spieler ~~*) to disqualify; (*abhalten von*) to debar from; (*auseinanderspreizen*) to spread asunder; (*Beine*) to straddle; to sprawl out; *typ* to space (out); (*Scheck stornieren*) to stop; *ins Gefängnis ~~* to put in prison; to lock up; (*Preise, Löhne, Gelder etc ~~*) to block, to stop, to freeze; *die Regierung sperrte alle offenen Stellen* the government froze all vacancies; *sich ~~* to resist; to refuse; to struggle; (*zaudern*) to hang back; *Straße gesperrt!* road closed! **~fahrzeug** *n mil* boom working vessel; **~feder** *f* click (*od* retaining) spring; trigging-spring; **~feld** *n mil* obstacle field; blocked zone; **~feuer** *n mil* curtain fire, barrage (fire); counter barrage, preventive barrage, defensive fire; (*Flak~~*) box barrage; *~~ legen* to lay down a barrage; **~~raum** *m mil* barrage area; **~~streifen** *m* barrage lane; **~~walze** *f mil* moving barrage; **~filter** *n radio* rejector circuit; stopper circuit; suppression filter; **~flieger** *m aero* patrol aircraft; (*Jäger*) interceptor; **~flug** *m aero* interception flight; barrage flight; **~fort** *n mil* outer fort; **~frist** *f* period of disallowance (*od* interdiction); **~gebiet** *n* forbidden (*od* prohibited *od* restricted) area; barred zone; danger zone; mined zone; (*Blockade*) blockade zone; (*für Truppen etc*) out of bounds! Off limits! **~geld** *n* entrance money; **~gürtel** *m mil* fortified lines *pl*; **~gut** *n* (*~güter n pl*) bulky goods *pl*, *Am* bulk freight; **~guthaben** *n* blocked account; **~hahn** *n* stopcock; **~haken** *m* catch; click; hatch; pawl; (*für Schloß*) skeleton key; **~hebel** *m* ratchet lever; locked lever; check lever; pawl; **~höhe** *f mil* barrage height; **~holz** *n* plywood; **~~beplankung** *f* plywood covering; **~~platte** *f* plywood plate; **~~rumpf** *m aero* plywood fuselage; **~jäger** *m aero* interceptor; **~ig** *a* wide spreading; wide open; spread; (*massig*) bulky; unwieldy; (*lose*) loose; *~~es Gut* (*Fracht*) bulky goods *pl*, *Am* bulk freight; **~kabel** *n mil* barrage cable; **~kegel** *m* click, pawl; trigger; pin; **~kette** *f* drag (*od* curb) chain; *radio* low-pass filter; **~klinke** *f* safety-catch; lock pawl; ratchet; **~kommando** *n mil* barrage command; **~kondensator** *m* blocking condenser; **~konto** *n com* blocked account; **~kreis** *m radio* filter circuit; stopper circuit; rejector circuit; suppression filter; wave trap; **~linie** *f mil* fortified line; **~mark** *f* blocked mark; **~mauer** *f* dam; **~(r)ad** *n* ratchet wheel; cogwheel; **~(r)aste** *f* stop notch; **~(r)aum** *m mil* barrage area; **~(r)iegel** *m* lock bolt; *mil* line barrage; **~(r)ing** *m* locking ring; retainer ring; **~schalter** *m* holding key; **~schicht** *f* barrier layer; insulating layer; **~schiene** *f* lock bar; **~sitz** *m theat* stall; reserved seat; *Am* orchestra (seat); **~stift** *m* pin, click; **~stück** *n* stop; **~stunde** *f* closing hour; closing time; *mil* curfew; (*von Abenddämmerung bis Morgengrauen*) dusk-to-dawn curfew; **~trupp** *m mil* blocking party; **~ung** *f* barricading; blocking; barring; stoppage; (*Waren*) embargo; *mar* (*Hafen*) blockade; (*e-s Telephonanschlusses*) suspension; (*Absperrung*) interception; (*Unterdrückung*) suppression; **~ventil** *n* stop valve; **~vorrichtung** *f* locking device; catch; stop; lock; **~waffe** *f mil* mine; **~zeit** *f* closing time; **~zoll** *m* prohibitive duty; **~zone** *f* prohibited area.

Spesen *f pl* (*Auslagen*) charges *pl*, expenses *pl*; (*Kosten*) costs *pl*; (*Gebühren*) fees *pl*; *kleine ~* petty expenses; **~ersatz** *m* reimbursement of charges; **~frei** *a* free of charges; **~nachnahme** *f* reimbursement for expenses.

Spezerei *f* spice; grocery; **~en** *pl*, **~ware** *f* spices *pl*.

Spezi *m fam* (*Busenfreund*) bosom-friend; crony.

Spezial|arzt, ~ist *m* specialist; *~ist sein in* to specialize in; **~aufbau** *m mot* special body; **~bibliothek** *f* special library; **~boot** *n mil mar* motor gunboat; **~bericht** *m* special report; particulars *pl*; **~fach** *n* special line; speciality; **~fall** *m* special case; **~flugzeug** *n* special aircraft; **~gebiet** *n* special subject; special department; **~geschäft** *n* one-line shop; *Am* specialty store; **~ien** *f pl* particulars *pl*, details *pl*; **~isieren** *itr* to specialize; *sich in Geschichte ~~* to specialize in history, *Am* to major in history; **~isierung** *f* specialization; **~ität** *f* speciality; special branch; special line; **~katalog** *m* catalogue of a special library; **~merkmal** *n* special characteristic; **~stahl** *m* special steel; **~truppen** *f pl* special-service troops *pl*; **~zweck** *m* special purpose.

spez|iell *a* special, specific; particular; **~ies** *f* species; *die vier ~~* the four first rules (of arithmetic); (*Heilmittel*) drugs *pl*; (*Kräuter*) herbs *pl*; (*Muster*) samples *pl*; **~ifisch** *a* specific; *~~es Gewicht* specific gravity; **~ifizieren** *tr* to specify, to particularize; *Am* to itemize; **~ifizierung** *f* specification; **~imen** *n* specimen.

Sphär|e *f* sphere; **~isch** *a* spherical; *~~e Abweichung* spherical aberration; *~~e Navigation* spherical flying; *~~e Trigonometrie* spherical trigonometry; **~oid** *n* spheroid; **~okristall** *m* spherocrystal.

Sphinx *f* sphinx; **~gesicht** *n Am* poker face; *sl* dead-pan (face).

Spick|aal *m* smoked eel; **~en** *tr* to lard, to smoke; (*Person*) to bribe; *den Beutel ~en* to fill o.'s purse; **~gans** *f* smoked goose; **~nadel** *f* larding-pin.

Spiegel *m* looking-glass, mirror; (*Wasser~*) surface; (*Meeres~*) level; (*glatte Oberfläche*) polished surface; reflecting surface; (*Reflektor*) reflector; *med* speculum; (*bei Pferden*) dapple; (*bei Rot- u. Rehwild*) escutcheon; (*Schießscheibe*) bull's eye; (*Kragen~*) tab; facing; (*Heck e-s Schiffes*) stern, buttock; (*Edelsteinschliff*) table; (*e-r Tür*) panel; *com* (*oberste Schicht*) face, top layer; *typ* (*Satz~*) type area; *fig* (*Muster*) model; pattern; example; **~ablesung** *f* reading by mirror (*od* reflection); **~belag** *m* tinfoil; **~bild** *n* reflected image; (*Luftspiegelung*) mirage; **~bildlich** *a* homologous; specular; **~blank** *a* spick and span; shining; bright as a mirror; **~ei** *n* fried egg; **~fabrik** *f* looking-glass manufacture; **~fechter** *m* dissembler; juggler; **~fechterei** *f* mock-fight, dissimulation; humbug; **~fernrohr** *n* telescope; **~fläche** *f* smooth surface; reflector surface; mirror; **~folie** *f* tinfoil; **~glas** *n* plate-glass; **~glatt** *a* as smooth as a mirror; (*Wasser*) unrippled, glassy; **~gleich** *a math* symmetric(al); **~~heit** *f math* mirror symmetry; **~händler** *m* dealer in looking-glasses; **~ig** *a* specular, smooth and bright; **~karpfen** *m* mirror (*od* shining) carp; **~n** *itr* to shine, to glitter; to sparkle; *tr* to reflect; to mirror; *sich ~n* to be reflected; to look into the glass; **~pfeiler** *m arch* pier; **~reflexkamera** *f phot* (mirror-) reflex camera; **~scheibe** *f* plate-glass pane; **~schrank** *m* wardrobe with mirror; **~schrift** *f* mirror writing; **~skala** *f* mirror scale; **~stein** *m* specular stone; **~sucher** *m phot* mirror view finder; **~teleskop** *n* reflecting telescope; reflector; **~tisch** *m* pier-table, toilet-table; dressing-table; **~ung** *f* reflexion; (*Luft~~, Fata Morgana*) mirage; **~zimmer** *n* mirror-room.

Spieke *f bot* lavender, spikenard.

Spiel *n* play; (*Karten, Billard, Sport*) game; (*körperliche ~e im Freien*) sport; *sport* (*Wettkampf*) match; *Auswärts~* away match; *Heim~* home match; *die Olympischen ~e* the Olympic games; *theat* (*~ der Schauspieler*) acting, playing; (*Darstellung*) performance; (*Puppen~*) puppetry; (*Hör~*) (radio) play; (*Vergnügen*) pastime, amusement; *mus* (manner of) playing; (*Anschlag*) touch; (*Glücks~*) gambling; (*einzelnes*) game; (*~ Karten*) pack of cards, *Am* deck of cards; (*Schach~, Kegel~*) set; (*Glocken~*) carillon; *tech* (*Gang e-r Maschine*) working, action; (*Arbeits~*) working cycle; trip; time cycle; (*Maßunterschied von zus.gehörenden Maschinenteilen*) free space, free motion; floating looseness; backlash; play; slackness; (*~raum, Toleranz*) clearance, allowance; *Kolben~* play of the piston; *~ der Ventile* valve clearance; *fig* plaything; sport; child's play; scope; *ein* (*seltsames*) *~ der Natur* (*z. B. Kalb mit 2 Köpfen*) freak; *das ~ des Lebens* the game of life; *das ~ der Muskeln* the action of the muscles; *ein ~ des Zufalls* a whim of chance; *sein Glück im ~ versuchen* to try o.'s luck at gambling; *abgekartetes ~* get-

-up, *Am* frame-up; prearranged plan; *ehrliches* ~ fair play; *falsches* ~ foul play; underhand game; cheating; *ein gewagtes* ~ a bold (*od* risky) game; *hohes* ~ (to play) a high game; *Katz- u. Maus*~ cat and mouse game; *mit klingendem* ~ with drums (beating) and trumpets sounding; *leichtes* ~ walkover; *fig* easy task; *stummes* ~ (*Pantomime*) dumb-show; *unfaires, unehrliches* ~ foul play; *jds* ~ *durchschauen fig* to see through s. o.'s tricks; *aus dem* ~ *bleiben* to take no part in s. th.; to be left out of the question; *jdm freies* ~ *geben* to give s. o. a fair chance; ~ *haben tech* to be slack, to work loose; *leichtes* ~ *haben* to have no difficulty; to walk over the course; *gewonnenes* ~ *haben* to have gained o.'s point (*od* the day); *Glück im* ~ *haben* to be in a vein of luck; to play with luck; *die Hand im* ~ *haben* to have a finger in the pie; to have a hand in s. th.; *aus dem* ~ *lassen* to let alone; to leave out of the question; *lassen Sie mich aus dem* ~ leave me out of it; *jdm freies* ~ *lassen* to give s. o. full play; to give free scope to s. o.; *gute Miene zum bösen* ~ *machen prov* to grin and bear it; *sich ins* ~ *mischen* to interfere; *du bist am* ~ it is your turn; *im* ~ *sein* to be involved (in the case), to be at the bottom of s. th.; *ein* ~ *der Wellen sein* to be at the mercy of the waves; *aufs* ~ *setzen* to stake, to venture, to risk; to jeopardize; to hazard; *auf dem* ~ *stehen* to be at stake; *seine Ehre steht auf dem* ~ his hono(u)r is at stake; *sein Leben steht auf dem* ~ his life is at stake; *ein falsches* ~ *treiben* to act in an underhand manner; *sein* ~ *mit jdm treiben* to trifle with s. o.; to make game of s. o.; *jdm das* ~ *verderben* to put a spoke in s. o.'s wheel; *das* ~ *verlieren* to lose the game; *das* ~ *verloren geben* to give up the game as lost; to throw up the sponge; *ins* ~ *ziehen fig* to compromise; *wie steht das* ~? *sport* how is the score going? what's the score? **~abbruch** *m* breaking-off; **~ablauf** *m* expiration of the game; **~anzug** *m* jumpers *pl*, rompers *pl*; **~art** *f* manner of playing; *mus* touch; *zoo, bot* (*Abart*) variety; **~austragung** *f sport* tournament; **~automat** *m* slot machine; **~bahn** *f* (*Kegeln, Tennis*) alley; **~ball** *m* ball; (*Billard*) ball in play; *fig* plaything; sport; toy; *fig* (*Werkzeug*) tool; *ein* ~~ *der Winde* (*der Wellen*) *sein* to be at the mercy of the winds (of the waves); **~bar** *a* playable; *mus leicht* ~~ easy to play; **~bank** *f* gaming table; casino; **~bein** *n* (*Statue*) leg taking no weight; **~brett** *n* draught-board; dress-board; **~chen** *n* (a quiet) little game; **~dauer** *f* length of game, time; (*e-s Films*) box-office life; **~dose** *f* musical box; **~eifer** *m* ardo(u)r; **~einlage** *f*, **~einsatz** *m* stake; **~en** *tr, itr* to play; *um Geld* ~~ to play for money; *ein Spiel* ~~ to play at a game; *ein Instrument* ~~ to play on an instrument; *vom Blatt* ~~ to play at sight; *in der Lotterie* ~~ to invest in the lottery; to try o.'s chance in the lottery; *e-e Rolle* ~~ to play a part, to take the part of; (*vom Schauspieler*) to act a part; to perform; *Billard* ~~ to play (at) billiards; *Karten* ~~ to play at cards; *jdm e-n Streich* (*e-n Possen*) ~~ to play s. o. a trick, to play off a trick upon; *mit dem Gedanken* ~~ to toy with the idea; (*sich ab*~~, *stattfinden*) to take place; *das Stück* ~*t in Paris* the scene is laid in Paris; *den großen Herrn* ~~ to do the swell; *falsch* ~~ to cheat at play; *mus* to play wrong notes; *mit Worten* ~~ to play (up)on words; *jdm etw in die Hände* ~~ to play s. o.'s game; to help s. o. to s. th.; (*sich belustigen*) to sport; to toy; to dally; (*mit Einsatz* ~~) to gamble; (*an der Börse* ~~) to job; (*Komödie* ~~, *simulieren*) to feign, to simulate; to pretend; ~~ *lassen* (*in Gang setzen*) to set going; *mit etw* ~~ to trifle with; *sie läßt nicht mit sich* ~~ she is not to be trifled with; (*glitzern, funkeln von Edelsteinen*) to sparkle, to flash; to glitter; *ins Grüne* ~~ to incline to green; *der Apparat spielt mit Batterie u. Wechselstrom* the set works on battery and on AC; **~end** *a* playing; *adv* easily; with the utmost ease; **~er** *m* player; *sport auch* fielder; (*Schau*~~) actor, performer; (~*erin f*) actress; (*Puppen*~~) puppeteer; (*Glücks*~~) gambler; (*Berufs*~~) professional; **~erei** *f* play(ing); sport; pastime; silly trick; *fig* trifle; child's play; **~ergebnis, ~resultat** *n* (*Fußball etc*) score(s *pl*); *wie steht das* ~~? what's the score? **~erisch** *a* playful; sportive; amateurish; **~feld** *n* (playing) field; ground; boundary; (*Tennis*) (tennis-)court; *Am* (*Fußball*) gridiron; *Am* (*Baseball, Softball*) diamond; **~film** *m* feature (film); feature-length film; **~fläche** *f* (*Eis*) surface; **~folge** *f* program(me); **~frei** *a* idle; *es ist heute* ~~ (*theat*) the theatre is closed to-night; *tech* free from play; **~führer** *m sport* (team) captain; **~gefährte** *m* playmate, playfellow; *sport* team-mate; **~geld** *n* play-money; (*Einsatz*) stake; pool; **~genosse** *m* playmate, playfellow; **~gesellschaft** *f* card-party; **~gewinn** *m* gambling profit; winnings *pl*; **~glück** *n* luck in play; **~hahn** *m zoo* heath-cock; blackcock; **~hälfte** *f* (*Fußball*) half; **~haus** *n* gambling-house; **~hölle** *f* gambling-hell; *Am sl* flat joint; deadfall; crib; **~kamerad** *m* playmate, playfellow; **~karte** *f* playing card; **~kasino** *n* gambling casino, gambling palace; **~kasse** *f* cash for playing; **~klub** *m* playing club; card club; **~leiter** *m theat* stage-manager, director; *film, radio, tele* producer; **~mann** *m* musician; street-player; *hist* minstrel; *mil* bandsman; fifer; (~*leute pl*) bandsmen, band; **~mannschaft** *f sport* team; **~marke** *f* chip; counter; **~oper** *f* grand opera; **~passung** *f tech* clearance fit; **~plan** *m theat, radio, tele* program(me); (*Repertoir*) repertory, répertoire; (*Lotterie*) scheme for a lottery; **~platz** *m* (*Schule*) playground; *Am* campus; *sport* ground; recreation ground; *Am* (*Fußball*) gridiron; *Am* (*Baseball, Softball*) diamond; **~ratte** *f* gambler; **~raum** *m* room for action; *fig* elbow-room, free hand, free play; latitude; scope; range; swing; *com* margin; *tech* play; clearance; backlash; tolerance; allowance; free motion, free space; (*e-s Geschosses im Lauf*) windage; *freien* ~~ *haben* to have elbow-room; ~~ *lassen* to leave a margin; **~regel** *f* rule (of a game); **~rolle** *f* list; **~sachen** *f pl* toys *pl*, playthings *pl*; **~saison** *f* season; **~satz** *m* (*Tennis*) set; **~schar** *f* amateur-players; amateur-company; **~schuld** *f* gambling-debt; **~schule** *f* infant-school; kindergarten; **~stark** *a sport* powerful; **~sucht** *f* passion for gambling; **~teufel** *m* demon of gambling; **~tisch** *m* gaming table; card table; **~trieb** *m* instinct of play; **~uhr** *f* musical box (with clock); musical clock; **~unterbrechung** *f* time-out; **~verbot** *n* play interdiction; **~verderber** *m* kill-joy; marplot; spoil-sport; *Am* wet blanket; **~verlängerung** *f* overtime; **~verlust** *m* loss (at play); **~vertrag** *m* contract; **~waren** *f pl* toys *pl*, playthings *pl*; **~~geschäft** *n*, **~~handlung** *f* toy-shop; **~~händler** *m* toy-merchant; toyman; **~weise** *f* manner of playing; manner of acting; **~werk** *n* (*e-s Instruments*) action; (*Uhr*) chime; **~wut** *f* passion for gambling; **~zeit** *f* play-time; *theat, sport* season; **~zeug** *n* toy; plaything; **~~kasten** *m* box of toys; **~zimmer** *n* play-room; gambling room, card room; (*Kinder*~~) nursery.

Spier|e *f mar* spar, boom; spindle; *aero* rib; **~entonne** *f mar* spindle buoy; mast buoy; **~staude** *f bot* spiræa.

Spieß *m* spear; (*Lanze*) lance; (*Pike*) pike; (*Brat*~) spit; (*spitze Stange*) pointed bar, poker; (*lange Nadel*) long needle; *geol* spicule; *typ* (*Ausschuß*) pick, black; *mil sl* (*Hauptfeldwebel*) company sergeant-major (*Abk* C. S. M.), *sl* kissem, *Am* first sergeant, *Am sl* topkick; *am* ~ *braten* to roast on a spit, *Am* to barbecue; *den* ~ *umkehren* to turn the tables on; *Am* to get back at; **~bürger** *m* Philistine, bourgeois; narrow-minded townsman; *Am* (Mr.) Babbit, John Citizen; low-brow; **~~lich** *a* Philistine; narrow-minded; commonplace; bourgeois; *Am* low-brow; **~~tum** *n* narrow-mindedness, *Am* Babbit(t)ry; **~en** *tr* to spear; to spit; (*auf Gabel*) to stick on a fork; (*durchbohren*) to pierce, to transfix; (*auf*~~, *pfählen*) to impale (*auf* on); **~er** *m* (*Hirsch*) stag (*od* buck) in the first head; (*im zweiten Jahr*) brocket; *fam* = *Spießbürger*; **~gesell** *m* accomplice; **~glanz** *m* antimony sulphide; **~~artig** *a* antimonial; **~~erz** *n* antimony ore; stibnite; **~glas** *n* antimony; **~ig** *a*, **~erisch** *a* philistine, narrow-minded, prosaic; **~rute** *f*: ~~*n laufen* to run the gauntled; (*Am meist* gantlet); **~träger** *m* lancer.

Spiker *m* spike.

Spill *m mar* capstan; winch; windlass; air lead; **~e** *f siehe Spindel*; **~en** *tr mar* to operate a winch, to capstan.

spinal *a* spinal; ~*e Kinderlähmung* infantile spinal paralysis, (anterior) poliomyelitis, *Am fam* polio; **~lähmung** *f* spinal paralysis; **~punktion** *f* lumbar puncture.

Spinat *m* spinach.

Spind *m* (*Schrank*) wardrobe; cupboard; press; *mil* locker.

Spindel *f* spindle; (*Dorn, Docke*) mandrel; (*Spinnrocken, Kunkel*) distaff; (*Zapfen*) pivot, pinion; (*Welle*) arbor, axle; (*Uhr*~) verge; fusee; (*Heber*) lifting jack, screw jack; (*Hydrometer*) hydrometer; *anat* modiolus (of cochlea); **~baum** *m* spindle-tree; **~beine** *n pl* spindle-legs *pl*, spindle-shanks *pl*; **~beinig** *a* spindle-legged, spindle-shanked; **~drehbank** *f* chuck lathe; **~dürr** *a* lean as a rake; extremely slender; *Am* (*knochig*) scrawny; **~förmig** *a* spindle-shaped; fusiform; **~getriebe** *n* spindle gearing; **~kopf** *m* spindlehead; **~presse** *f* screw press; **~trieb** *m* worm drive; **~ung** *f* hydrometry; **~zelle** *f anat* spindle-shaped cell.

Spinett *n* spinet, harpsichord.

Spinn|e *f* spider; (*Wege*~~) road junction; *fig* venomous person; **~efeind** *a*: *jdm* ~~ *sein* to be bitterly hostile to; **~en** *tr* to spin; *fig* to plot, to intrigue; *Ränke* ~~ to hatch a plot; *e-n Gedanken weiter*~~ to spin out a thought; *itr phys* (*rasch rotieren, bes. von Atomen*) to spin (round), to whirl round; (*Faden ziehen bei Flüssigkeiten*) to draw threads; *fam fig* (*leicht geistesgestört sein*) to be crazy; (*Katze*) to purr; **~en** *n* spinning; **~engewebe** *n* cobweb; spider web; **~er** *m*, **~erin** *f* spinner; *zoo* bombyx; **~erei** *f* spinning; (*Fabrik*) spinning-mill; **~düse** *f* spinning nozzle; spinneret; **~faden** *m* spider thread; **~fäden** *m pl* (*Altweibersommer*) gossamer; floating cobwebs *pl*; **~faser** *f* spinning (*od* textile) fibre (*Am* fiber); synthetic fibre, spun rayon; **~fehler** *m* spinning defect; **~flüssigkeit** *f* spinning solution; **~kokon** *m* reelable cocoon; **~maschine** *f* spinning frame (*od* machine); **~rad** *n* spinning-wheel; **~rocken** *m* distaff; **~schema** *n* spinning arrangement; **~stoff** *m* spinning material; fibrous material; textile fibre; **~~industrie** *f* textile industry; **~~waren** *f pl* textiles *pl*; **~stube** *f* spinning-room; spinning-party; **~~nerzählung** *f* old wive's tale; cock-and-bull story; **~stuhl** *m* spinning frame; **~stutzen** *m* gooseneck; **~topf** *m* spinning can; **~warze** *f* spinneret; **~webe** *f* cobweb; spider web; **~~nartig** *a* cobweblike; arachnoid; **~webhaut** *f* arachnoid; arachnoid membrane; **~webfaden** *m* spider-web thread; thin thread; **~wolle** *f* wool for spinning.

Spion *m* spy, intelligencer; *Am fam* (*Späher, Aufpasser, Detektiv*) spotter; (*Polizeispitzel*) police informer; *sl* nark; *Am sl* gum-shoe, *Am fam* sleuth; **~age** *f* spying, espionage; **~~abwehr** *f* counter-espionage, *Am* counter-intelligence; **~~abwehrdienst** *m* counter-espionage service, *Am* counter-intelligence corps (*Abk* C. I. C.); **~~organisation** *f* spy ring; **~~prozeß** *m* spy trial; **~ieren** *itr* to spy; to play the spy; *fig* (*neugierig herumstöbern*) to pry into; to spy upon.

Spiral|bohrer *m* twist drill; auger; **~draht** *m* spiral (*od* coiled) wire; **~drehung** *f* spiral torsion; **~e** *f* spiral (line); (*Draht~~*) coil; (*Schraube*) helix; (*Turbinen~~*) scroll case; (*Gehäuse*) volute; **~feder** *f* spiral spring; coil; **~förmig** *a* spiral; helical; spirally; **~gleitflug** *m* spiral (glide); **~ig** *a* spiral; helical; **~kegel** *m* spiral bevel; **~linie** *f* spiral line; spiral; spiral curve; **~rohr** *n*, **~rohrschlange** *f* pipe coil; **~verzahnt** *a* spirally grooved; **~zahnrad** *n* spiral gear.

Spirit|ismus *m* spiritism; spiritualism; **~ist** *m* spiritualist; **~istisch** *a* spiritualistic; **~uosen** *f pl* spirits *pl*; (spirituous) liquors *pl*; **~us** *m* alcohol, spirit; (*denaturierter*) methylated spirit(s *pl*); *gram* breathing; **~~brennerei** *f* distillery; **~~dampf** *m* alcohol vapo(u)r; **~~kocher** *m* spirit (*od* primus) stove; **~~lampe** *f* spirit lamp, *Am* alcohol lamp; **~~löslich** *a* soluble in alcohol; **~~lötlampe** *f* alcohol blow torch; **~~mischung** *f* alcoholic mixture.

Spirochäten *f pl* spirochetes *pl*.

Spital *n*, ***Spittel*** *n* (*Krankenhaus*) hospital, infirmary; (*Altersheim*) old people's home.

spitz *a* (*spitzig*) pointed; peaked; (*scharf*) sharp, tapering; (*dünn*) thin, delicate; *math* acute; *fig* (*beißend*) biting, keen; sharp; pointed; (*verletzend*) cutting; caustic; (*sarkastisch*) sarcastic; *~ auslaufen* to end in a point; to taper; *etw ~ kriegen* to find out, to understand; *etw ~ nehmen* to take offence at s. th.; **~** *m* (*Hund*) Pomeranian dog; spitz (-dog); (*Rausch*) slight tipsiness; *e-n ~ haben Am* to be slightly elevated; **~bart** *m* pointed beard; *Am* goatee; **~bogen** *m* Gothic arch, pointed arch; **~~fenster** *n* lancet-window; **~bohrer** *m* pointed drill, drill bit; **~bube** *m* rascal, rogue, knave; *sl* spiv; (*Schwindler*) swindler; (*Dieb*) thief, pickpocket; **~~ngesicht** *n* hangdog appearance; **~~nstreich** *m*, **~büberei** *f* roguery, knavery; **~bübin** *f* wag; female thief; **~bübisch** *a* knavish, roguish; rascally; **~e** *f* point, spike; (*Ende*) end, tip; (*Gipfel*) top, summit, peak; (*Feder~~*) nib; (*Turm~~*) spire; (*Ähren~~*) beard; (*Baum~~, Haus~~*) top; (*Finger~~, Nasen~~, Zungen~~*) tip; (*Zehen~~*) toe; (*Lanzen~~, Schuh~~*) point; (*Zigaretten~~, Zigarren~~*) holder; (*Pfeifen~~*) mouthpiece; (*Zacke, Zinke*) prong; (*äußerstes Ende*) extremity; (*Gewebe~~, Kleider~~*) lace; *Brüsseler ~en* Brussels lace; *echte ~en* real lace; (*vorderste Stelle, oberste Leitung bei Betrieb, Partei etc, mil Vorhut*) head; *an der ~~ des Zuges* at the head of the parade; *fig* (*~~ gegen jdn*) point, sting; (*spitze Bemerkung*) pointed remark; (*beißende Anspielung*) nasty allusion, sarcastic observation; (*Höhepunkt*) climax; *bot* apex; *math* (*Dreieck*) vertex; (*Pyramide*) apex; *tech* (*Dorn*) spur; (*Drehbank~~*) centre, *Am* center; *die ~~ abbrechen fig* to mitigate; *jdm die ~~ bieten* to defy s. o.; to make head against, to face; *an der ~~ stehen* to be at the head of; (*zuoberst stehen*) to top; (*führen*) to lead; *sich an die ~~ stellen* to place o. s. at the head of; *auf der ~~ stehen* to stand upright; *auf die ~~ treiben* to carry to extremes; to carry things too far; *das war e-e ~~ gegen mich fig* that was aimed at me; **~el** *m* (*Spion*) spy; agent; (*Schnüffler*) snooper; trap; (*Polizei~~*) police spy; police informer; *sl* nark; (*Geheimpolizist*) secret police agent; plain-clothes man; *Am* FBI Agent; G-man; *Am* (*Detektiv*) *fam* sleuth(-hound), *Am sl* gum-shoe, flat(foot), smeller, sneaker; **~eln** *itr* to spy upon; **~eltum** *n allg* police spies *pl*; **~en** *tr* to point; (*schärfen*) to sharpen, (*Feder*) to nib; (*die Ohren*) to prick up (o.'s ears); *den Mund ~~* to purse o.'s lips; *sich ~en auf* to reckon upon, to anticipate; to count on; **~en** ... (*in Zssg*) top-ranking; topnotch; topflight; **~enarbeit** *f* lace work; **~enband** *n* lace edging; **~enbeanspruchung** *f* maximum stress; **~enbelastung** *f* peak load, capacity load; peak charge; maximum demand; **~enbesatz** *m* lace trimming; **~enbetrag** *m* highest amount; **~enbluse** *f* lace blouse; **~endrehbank** *f* centre lathe; engine lathe; **~endrehzahl** *f* top speed; **~eneinsatz** *m* (lace) insertion; **~enentladung** *f el* point discharge; **~enfahrzeug** *n* (*e-r Kolonne*) leading vehicle; **~enfilm** *m* top picture; **~enflieger** *m aero* flying ace; **~enform** *f sport* top form; **~engehalt** *n* top salary; **~engeschwindigkeit** *f* top speed; **~engruppe** *f sport* leading group; **~enkandidat** *m* top candidate; **~enkatarrh** *m med* pulmonary apicitis; **~enkleid** *n* lace dress; **~enklöppel** *m* lace-bobbin; **~enklöppelei** *f* pillow-lace making; **~enklöpplerin** *f* lace-maker; **~enkompanie** *f* advance party; **~enkraftwerk** *n el* peak-load power station; **~enkragen** *m* lace-collar; **~enlagerung** *f tech* point suspension; pivot jewel; **~enlast** *f* peak load; **~enleistung** *f* (*Rekord*) record; record achievement; peak capacity; (*Leistung*) maximum (*od* top *od* peak) performance; (*Maschine*) maximum (*od* peak) capacity (*od* output); *el* peak power; **~enlohn** *m* maximum pay; **~enmannschaft** *f sport* top team; leading team; **~enmuster** *n* lace pattern; **~enorganisation** *f* head (*od* top *od* central) organization; (*Dachorganisation*) roof organization; **~enschiff** *n* (*in Geleitzug etc*) leading ship; **~enschleier** *m* lace veil; **~enspannung** *f el* peak voltage; **~enspieler** *m sport* top-ranking player; topnotcher; **~nstoß** *m med* cardiac apex beat; **~enstrom** *m el* peak current; **~entanz** *m* toe dance; **~entänzerin** *f* toe dancer; **~entuch** *n* lace scarf; lace shawl; **~enverband** *m com* head (*od* top *od* central) organization; *mil* (*Vorhut*) advance party; **~enverkehr** *m* peak traffic; **~enweite** *f tech* distance between centres; **~enwert** *m* peak (*od* maximum) value; **~er** *m* (*Bleistift~~*) pencil-sharpener; *fam* (*Hund*) spitz (-dog); **~feile** *f* tapered file; **~findig** *a* (*fein*) subtle; (*scharf*) sharp; (*gerissen*) cunning, shrewd; cavil(l)ing; (*haarspaltend*) hair-splitting; **~~keit** *f* subtlety; sophistry; (*Schlauheit*) sharpness; craftiness; (*Kniff*) trick, cunning; **~geschoß** *n* pointed bullet; **~gras** *n* rye grass; **~hacke, ~haue** *f* pick-ax(e); pick; **~ig** *a* pointed; (*scharf*) sharp; (*~~ zulaufend*) tapering; *fig* sarcastic, caustic; *fig* (*Zunge*) lashing; **~kehre** *f* reversing curve; **~keil** *m* wedge; **~köpfig** *a* long-headed; **~marke** *f typ* heading; **~maus** *f* shrew-mouse; **~name** *m* nickname; (*Kosename*) pet name; **~nase** *f* pointed nose; **~säule** *f* obelisk; **~wegerich** *m bot* ribwort; **~winklig** *a* acute-angled; **~zange** *f* pointed pliers *pl*; **~zirkel** *m* compass; divider.

Spleiße *f* splinter; **~n** *irr tr* to split, to cleave.

Spließ *m* (*Schindel*) shingle.

Splint *m* peg; split pin; cotter; (*~holz*) alburnum, sap(wood); **~bolzen** *m* eyebolt; **~draht** *m* pin wire; **~e** *f* split pin; **~en** *tr* to cotter; **~holz** *n* sap(wood); **~verschluß** *m* cotter lock.

Spliß *m* splice; (*Splitter*) splinter.

Splitt *m* broken stone; fine gravel, stone chips *pl*.

Splitter *m* splinter; (*Span*) chip; (*Bruchstück*) fragment; shiver; sliver; (*Knochen~*) splinter (of bone); (*Metall~*) scale; (*Bibel*) mote; **~bombe** *f* splinter bomb; fragmentation bomb, *Am mil sl* frag bomb; antipersonnel bomb; *Flugzeuge griffen Brücken, Truppenbewegungen u. Nachschublager mit Raketen, ~~n u. Benzinbrandbomben an* airplanes struck bridges, troop convoys and supply dumps with rockets, frag bombs and fiery napalm; **~boxe** *f* blast bay; **~bruch** *m med* splintered fracture; **~dichte** *f* splinter density; **~(faser)nackt** *a* stark naked; **~frei** *a* splinter-proof; shatterproof; **~graben** *m mil* slit trench; **~granate** *f* fragmentation shell; **~gruppe** *f* splinter group; **~ig** *a* splintery; **~n** *itr* to splinter; to shatter; (*spalten*) to split; to shiver; (*in Bruchstücke*) to break into fragments; **~partei** *f* splinter party; **~richter** *m* fault-finder; carper; censorious critic; cavil(l)er; **~schutzgraben** *m* A. R. P trench; slit trench; **~sicher** *a* splinter-proof; non-splintering; *~~es Glas* safety glass; triplex glass; **~wirkung** *f mil* splinter(ing) effect; *Am* fragmentation.

Spondeus *m* spondee.

spontan *a* spontaneous; automatic.

sporadisch *a* sporadic(al).

Spore *f bot* spore; **~nbehälter** *m* spore case; **~nbildung** *f* formation of spores; sporulation; **~npflanze** *f* sporophyte; **~ntiere** *n pl* sporozoa.

Sporn (*pl Sporen*) *m* spur; *bot* spur, calcar; *arch* buttress; spur; *aero* tail skid; tail spade; *fig* spur, inducement; incentive; stimulus; *e-m Pferd die Sporen geben* to set spurs to a horse; *sich die Sporen verdienen* to win o.'s spurs; **~förmig** *a* spur-shaped; *bot* calcariform; **~en** *tr* to spur; *fig* to stimulate; **~kufe** *f aero* tail skid; **~rad** *n aero* tail wheel; *einziehbares, lenkbares ~~* retractable, steerable tail wheel; **~rädchen** *n* rowel; **~streichs** *adv* post-haste; immediately, at once; at full gallop, quickly.

Sport *m* sport; (*Leichtathletik*) athletics *pl*; (*Liebhaberei, Steckenpferd*) hobby; *~ treiben* to go in for sports; *~ treibend* sporting; **~abzeichen** *n* sports badge; badge for achievement in sports; **~amt** *n* athletic office; **~angelegenheiten** *f pl* sporting matters *pl*; **~angler** *m* angler; **~anlage** *f* recreation ground; playing ground; **~anzug** *m* sports suit; sports *pl*; **~art** *f* kind of sport; **~artikel** *m pl* sports articles *pl*; sports goods *pl*; **~~geschäft** *n* sporting-goods store; **~arzt** *m* sports doctor (*od* physician); **~ausrüstung** *f* sports equipment; **~begeistert** *a* sports-minded; **~begeisterte(r)** *m* sporting enthusiast, sports fan; **~beilage** *f* (*Presse*) sport section; **~bericht** *m* sporting news; sporting report; **~~er, ~~erstatter** *m* (*Presse*) sports writer, sports reporter, *Am fam* sports hack, scribe; *radio* sports broadcaster, *Am* sportscaster; **~eln** *f pl* fees *pl*; perquisites *pl*; *~~ itr* (*~ treiben*) to go in for sports; **~ereignis** *n* sporting event; **~feld** *n* sports ground, sports field; **~fest** *n* sports tournament; **~flieger** *m* sports pilot; **~~schule** *f* flying school; **~flugplatz** *m* club aerodrome; **~flugzeug** *n* sporting airplane; (*für Sport u. Reise*) sporting and touring plane; **~freund** *m* sportsman, sports fan; **~funk** *m* radio sports news, *Am* sportcast; **~geist** *m* sporting mind; sporting spirit; **~gerät** *n* sports equipment, sports requisites *pl*, *Am* sporting goods *pl*; **~geschäft** *n* sporting-goods store; **~gürtel** *m* (*mit Strumpfhalter für Damen*) garter belt; **~hemd** *n* sport-shirt; (*mit kurzen Ärmeln*) *Am* T-shirt; **~herz** *n med* athletic heart; **~jacke** *f* sports jacket, blazer; **~kabriolett** *n mot* sports convertible; **~kleidung** *f* sportwear; **~klub** *m* sporting club, athletic club; **~lehrer** *m* trainer, coach; **~leibchen** *n* athletic shirt; **~ler** *m* sportsman; **~lerin** *f* sportswoman; **~lich** *a* sporting, sportsmanlike; (*schnittig*) sporty; **~liebhaber** *m* sporting fan; **~mädel** *n* sports girl; **~mannschaft** *f* (sporting) team; **~mantel** *m* sports coat; **~mütze** *f* tweed cap, sporting cap; **~nachrichten** *f pl* (*Zeitung*) sporting news *pl*; **~nation** *f* sport-loving nation; **~offizier** *m mil* athletic officer; **~platz** *m* athletic field, *Am* stadium, sporting ground; playground; (*Fußball*) field, *Am* ball park; **~preis** *m* trophy; **~presse** *f* sporting press; **~schuhe** *m pl* gym-shoes *pl*; **~(s)kanone** *f* star, champ(ion), ace, crack-hand; **~smann** *m* sportsman, *Am fam* sport; **~smäßig** *a* sportsmanlike, sporting; *nicht ~~* unsportsmanlike; **~strumpf** *m* sports stockings *pl*, sports hose; (*Socken*) gym socks *pl*, hunting socks *pl*; **~sucher** *m phot* sports finder; **~veranstaltung** *f* sport(ing) event; meeting, meet; **~verband** *m* federation of sportsmen, sport association; **~verein** *m* athletic club, sports club; **~wagen** *m mot* sports car, (*Zweisitzer*) two seater, *Am* roadster; (*Kinderwagen*) folding pram; *Am* stroller; **~warenhändler** *m* sportsoutfitter; **~wart** *m* trainer, coach; **~welt** *f* sports world, sporting world; **~wettkampf** *m* sporting contest; **~zeitschrift** *f* sports review; **~zeitung** *f* sporting news *pl*, sporting paper; **~zweig** *m* branch of sport.

Spott *m* mockery; (*Hohn*) mock; (*Verachtung ausdrückend*) derision; (*Verachtung*) scorn; scoff; jeer; (*Lächerlichkeit*) ridicule; (*Sarkasmus*) sarcasm; (*Hänselei*) banter; raillery; chaff; (*Zielscheibe des ~s*) butt; (*Gegenstand des ~s*) laughing-stock; *seinen ~ treiben mit* to make sport of s. o.; to mock at; to scoff at; (*zum Narren haben*) *fam* to pull s. o.'s leg; **~bild** *n* caricature; **~billig** *a* dirt-cheap; ridiculously cheap; **~drossel** *f orn* mocking-bird; **~en** *itr* to mock, to rail, to rally; (*lächerlich machen*) to ridicule; *fam* to make fun of, to make a fool of; (*hänseln*) to tease; to chaff, to banter; (*spaßen*) to joke, to jest; to make sport of; (*verächtlich*) to deride; to sneer; to gibe; to jeer; to scoff at; (*höhnen*) to taunt; to flout; to fleer; *fig* to defy; *jeder Beschreibung ~~* to beggar description; **~gebot** *n com* ridiculous (*od* preposterous) offer; **~geburt** *f* (*Mißgeburt*) monstrosity; abortion; **~gedicht** *n* satirical poem; satire, squib; **~geist** *m* scoffer; **~gelächter** *n* derisive (*od* mocking) laughter; **~geld** *n* trifling sum; *um ein ~~* for a mere song; **~lied** *n* satirical song; **~lust** *f* mocking spirit; **~name** *m* nickname; **~preis** *m* ridiculous price, bargain price; trifle; **~rede** *f* satirical speech; **~schrift** *f* satire, lampoon; **~sucht** *f* love of ridicule, mania for ridicule; spirit of mockery; **~vogel** *m* mocking-bird; *fig* mocker; quiz.

Spött|elei *f* mockery; raillery; (*Hohn*) jeering; gibe; (*Fopperei*) banter; (*Stichelei*) taunt; chaff; (*Ironie*) irony; **~eln** *itr* (*lachen über*) to laugh at; (*höhnisch*) to jeer at; to sneer at; to gibe at; to chaff; **~er** *m*, **~erin** *f* mocker; scoffer; jeerer; derider; **~erei** *f* mockery; derision; **~isch** *a* mocking; (*höhnisch*) jeering; scoffing; scornful; (*beißend*) biting; (*verletzend scharf*) caustic; (*ironisch*) ironical; (*satirisch*) satirical.

*

Sprach|e *f* (*die menschliche ~~, die ~~ e-s Volkes; Redeweise*) language; tongue; (*Sprechvermögen*) speech; talk; (*Ausdrucksweise*) diction; (*Stil*) style; (*Aus~~*) articulation; accent; pronunciation; (*Stimme*) voice; (*Eigentümlichkeiten e-r ~~*) idiom; (*Dialekt*) dialect; (*Diskussion*) discussion; (*Klassen~~, Berufs~~, Sonder~~*) slang; (*Landes~~, Mutter~~, Volks~~*) vernacular; (*Berufs~~, Jargon, scheinheilige ~~*) cant; (*Kauderwelsch*) lingo; (*Zunft~~, Jargon*) jargon; (*Mundart*) patois; (*Diebes~~*) argot; (*Gauner~~*) patter; (*Augen~~*) language of the eyes; (*Blumen~~*) language of flowers; (*Mutter~~*) native tongue, mother tongue; (*Umgangs~~*) colloquial language; *die ~~ der Wissenschaft* the language of science; *alte ~~n* ancient languages; *lebende ~~* living language; *neuere ~~n* modern languages; *tote ~~* dead language; *deutliche ~~* clear voice, articulated voice; *in offener ~~* (*nicht verschlüsselt*) in plain language; *heraus mit der ~~!* speak out! out with it! *fam* speak up! *e-e ~~ beherrschen* to know a language thoroughly; to have a perfect command of a language; *die ~~ benehmen* to strike s. o. dumb; *etw zur ~~ bringen* to broach (a subject); *die ~~ bringen auf* to bring up; *mit der ~~ herausrücken* to speak freely; to speak out (*od* up); to make a clean breast of; *nicht mit der ~~ herauswollen* to refuse to answer; to be shy of speaking out; *zur ~~ kommen* to be touched on; to be mentioned; to come up; *die ~~ verlieren* (*Sprechfähigkeit*) to lose o.'s speech; *e-e ~~ verstehen* to understand a language; *die ~~ wiedergewinnen* to recover o.'s speech; to find o.'s tongue; **~eigen** *a* idiomatic; **~~heit, ~~tümlichkeit** *f* idiom; idiomatic expression; *amerikanische ~~heit* Americanism; *deutsche ~~heit* Germanism; *englische ~~heit* Anglicism; *französische ~~* Gallicism; **~enatlas** *m*, **~enkarte** *f* atlas of languages; linguistic map; **~enfrage** *f* question of language; **~engewirr** *n* confusion of languages; **~fähigkeit** *f* faculty of speech, power of speech; **~fehler** *m gram* grammatical mistake; (*falscher Satzbau*) solecism; (*ungebräuchlicher Ausdruck*) barbarism; *med* (*~störung*) defect of speech; impediment in speech; **~feinheit** *f* linguistic subtlety; **~fertigkeit** *f* fluency; *fam* gift of the gab; (*Beherrschung e-r ~e*) command of a language; **~forscher** *m* linguist; philologist; **~forschung** *f* philology; linguistics *pl mit sing*; **~frequenz** *f radio* audio frequency; **~führer** *m* phrase-book; guide; **~gebiet** *n* linguistic area; **~gebrauch** *m* (colloquial) usage; *der heutige ~~* the language of the present day; **~gefühl** *n* linguistic instinct; **~gelehrte(r)** *m* philologist; linguist; **~genie** *n* born linguist; **~gewandt** *a* fluent; **~~heit** *f* fluency; **~gewirr** *n* confusion of languages; **~grenze** *f* linguistic frontier; **~heilkunde** *f med* logopedics *pl mit sing*; **~insel** *f* isolated district speaking a dialect of its own; **~kenner** *m* linguist; grammarian; **~kenntnisse** *f pl* linguistic attainments *pl*; knowledge of a language; *Bewerber mit Fremd~~n* applicants with a knowledge of foreign languages; **~kundig** *a* versed in languages; proficient in languages; **~~e(r)** *m* linguist; **~lehre** *f* grammar; **~lehrer** *m* teacher (*od* professor) of languages; **~lich** *a* linguistic; grammatical; **~los** *a* speechless; *fig* (*stumm*) dumb; mute; *einfach ~~ sein* to be simply speechless; *jdn ~~ machen* to strike s. o. dumb; **~~igkeit** *f* speechlessness; *fig* dumbness; **~melodie** *f* intonation, speech-melody; **~mittler** *m* (*Dolmetscher*) interpreter; **~neuerung** *f* neologism; **~organ** *n* organ of speech; **~regel** *f* rule of grammar; **~registrierung** *f* (*Band- od Plattenaufnahme*) speech (*od* voice) recording; **~reinheit** *f* purity of language; purity of speech; **~reiniger** *m* purist; **~reinigung** *f* purification of a language; **~richtig** *a* correct; grammatical; **~rohr** *n* speaking-tube (*od* -trumpet), megaphone; *fig* mouthpiece; **~schatz** *m* vocabulary; **~schnitzer** *m* (grammatical) blunder; **~stamm** *m* family of languages; **~störung** *f* speech defect (*od* disorder); impediment in speech; **~studium** *n* linguistic study; study of languages; **~talent** *n* (*~begabung*) talent (*od* gift) for languages; **~tum** *n* language; **~unterricht**

m teaching of languages; instruction in a language; ~**verbesserer** *m* reformer of a language; ~**verderber** *m* corrupter of a language; ~**verein** *m* language society; ~**vergleichend** *a* referring to comparative philology; ~**vergleichung** *f* comparative philology; ~**vermögen** *n* faculty of speech; ~**verschandelung** *f* corruption of a language; ~**verstärkeranlage** *f* (*durch Lautsprecher*) public-address system; ~**verstoß** *m* blunder; solecism; ~**verwandtschaft** *f* affinity between languages; ~**werkzeug** *n* organ of speech; ~**wiedergabe** *f radio* voice reproduction; ~**widrig** *a* ungrammatical, contrary to grammar; incorrect; ~**verwirrung** *f* confusion of languages, Tower of Babel; ~**wissenschaft** *f* philology; linguistics *pl mit sing*; science of language; *vergleichende* ~~ comparative philology; ~**wissenschaftler** *m* philologist; linguist; ~**wissenschaftlich** *a* philological; linguistic; ~**zentrum** *n med* speech centre.

Sprech|apparat *m* (*Grammophon*) talking machine; speaking instrument; gramophone, *Am* phonograph; *tele* receiver; telephone; ~**art** *f* manner of speaking; diction; dialect; ~**aufnahme** *f* speech (*od* voice) recording; ~**chor** *m* speaking chorus; *Am sport* yell; *im* ~~ *rufen* to shout slogans, *Am sport* to yell; ~**en** *irr tr, itr* to speak (*mit* to, *auch* with: *über* of, about); (*sich unterhalten*) to talk (*mit* with, to; *von* about, of, over); (*Konversation treiben*) to converse; (*plaudern*) to chat; (*erörtern*) to discourse; (*diskutieren*) to discuss; (*be~en*) to talk over; (*sagen*) to say; (*aus~en*) to pronounce; *fig* (*für sich selbst*) to be evident; (*aus dem Gesicht*) to be written in; *jdn ~en* to have a conference with s. o.; *~en Sie Englisch?* do you speak English? *dafür ~en* to speak in favo(u)r of; (*unterstützen*) to support; *alles spricht dafür, daß* . . . there is every reason to believe that; *das spricht dagegen* that tells against it; *gut zu ~en sein auf* to be kindly disposed (to); *nicht gut auf jdn zu ~en sein* to bear s. o. ill-will; to be displeased with s. o.; *für jdn ~en* to speak in s. o.'s favo(u)r; *das spricht für ihn* that speaks in his favo(u)r; *mit jdm ~en über etw* to speak to (*od* with) s. o. about s. th.; *groß ~en* to brag; *sich herum~en* to be the talk of the town; *sich mit jdm aus~en* to have a heart-to-heart talk with s. o. on s. th.; *mit sich ~en lassen* to be easy of access; to listen to reason; to be open to a bargain; *sie ~en nicht miteinander* they are not on speaking terms; *unter uns gesprochen* between ourselves; *vor Gericht* ~~ to plead; *fließend ~en* to speak fluently; *laut ~en* to speak loud; *von etw anderem ~en* to change the topic; *eindringlich ~en* to speak home; *er ist nicht zu ~en* he is not to be seen, he is not at home; he is not in; he is engaged; he is busy; *wen wünschen Sie zu ~en?* who(m) do you want to see? *kann ich Sie, bitte, für e-n Augenblick ~en?* May I see you for a moment? *~en wir nicht davon* don't mention it; *ein Gebet ~en* to say a prayer; *zur Geschäftsordnung ~en* to rise to order; *Recht ~en* to administer justice; *den Segen ~en über* to give a benediction on; *e-e Sprache (fließend) ~en* to speak a language (fluently); *Urteil ~en* to pronounce judg(e)ment; to give (*od* to render) judg(e)ment against; to adjudicate; to pass sentence; *das Tischgebet ~en* to say grace; *die Wahrheit ~en* to speak the truth; *kein Wort ~en* not to open o.'s mouth; *heilig ~en* to canonize s. o.; *jdn schuldig ~en* to find s. o. guilty; *hier spricht Herr X.! tele* This is Mr. X. speaking! *~en Sie noch? tele* have you finished? *Am* are you thru? *diese Tat spricht Bände* this action speaks volumes; *Taten ~en lauter als Worte* actions speak louder than words; *laßt Blumen ~en!* say it with flowers! *frei ~en* (*offen*) to speak frankly; (*ohne Unterlagen*) to speak extempore; *zum ~en ähnlich* (of a) speaking likeness; *nicht zum ~en aufgelegt sein* not to be in a talkative mood; ~**end** *a* speaking; (*auffallend*) striking(ly); ~~ *ähnlich* of a speaking likeness; *das Bild ist ~~ ähnlich* the portrait speaks (*od* is a speaking likeness); *~~e Augen* eloquent eyes; *~~er Beweis* conclusive evidence; *~~e Bogenlampe* speaking arc; ~**ende(r)** *m* talker; ~**er** *m* (*Redner*) speaker; talker; orator; (*offizieller* ~~) spokesman; *radio* (*Ansager*) announcer; *allg* speaker (at the microphone); broadcaster; (*bei Schallplattensendungen*) *Am* disk jockey; *parl* (*Unterhaus, Am Repräsentantenhaus*) Speaker; ~**fehler** *m* slip of the tongue; ~**film** *m* (*Tonfilm*) talking film; vocal film; *Am* talking (motion) picture; *Am* talkie; ~**frequenz** *f radio* voice frequency, audio frequency; ~**gebühr** *f tele* message rate, call fee; ~**hörer** *m tele* transceiver; ~**gesang** *m* recitative; ~**kunst** *f* rhetoric; ~**leitung** *f tele* speaker wire, call wire; ~**maschine** *f* talking machine; gramophone, *Am* phonograph; ~**melodie** *f* speech-melody; intonation; ~**oper** *f* comic opera; ~**probe**, ~**prüfung** *f* voice test(ing); ~**reichweite** *f* speaking range; ~**rolle** *f theat, film* speaking role (*od* part); ~**saal** *m* hall for speaking; forum; ~**schalter** *m tele* speaking key, *Am* talking key; ~**sprache** *f* spoken language; ~**stelle** *f tele* telephone station, call station; telephone extension; *öffentliche* ~~ public station; ~**stunde** *f* (*Empfangsstunde*) reception-hour; calling hour; (*Bürostunde*) office hour; (*Geschäftsstunde*) business hour; (*Arzt*) consultation hour, consulting hour; counselling hours; *~~ samstags von . . . bis* . . . there will be a surgery from . . . to . . . on Saturdays; ~~**nhilfe** *f* receptionist; assistant; ~**taste** *f tele* talk-listen button; *radio* microphone switch; ~**technik** *f* method of speaking; ~**trichter** *m tele* mouthpiece; ~**übung** *f* exercise in speaking; ~**verbindung** *f* telephone connection; telephone line; *aero* (*an Bord*) interphone; *in ~~ stehen mit* (*aero*) to be in oral contact with; ~**verkehr** *m* radio-telephony traffic; ~**verständigung** *f* talking range; intelligibility; ~**weise** *f* manner of speaking; diction; ~**werkzeug** *n* organ of speech; ~**zelle** *f tele* call box, *Am* (tele)phone booth; ~**zimmer** *n* parlo(u)r; drawing-room; (*Arzt*) surgery, consulting (*od* consultation) room, *Am* doctor's office; (*Zahnarzt*) dental surgery, *Am* dental parlor; (*Kloster*) locutory.

Spreißel *m* (*Splitter*) splinter.

spreiten *tr* to extend, to spread.

Spreiz|e *f* prop, stay; strut; spreader; spacer; (*Ausleger*) outrigger; boom; ~**en** *tr* to spread asunder, to spread out, to stretch out; to force apart; to open; *die Beine* ~~ to straddle; *r* to sprawl out; *fig* to boast of, to ride the high horse; to be affected; *sich ~~ gegen* to strive against, to resist; ~**fuß** *m med* spread foot; metatarsus latus; ~**kamera** *f phot* extension camera; strut camera; ~**klappe** *f aero* wing flap; *mot* controllable gill; ~**lafette** *f mil* split trail (carriage); ~**ring** *m* spreader ring; ~**schritt** *m* straddle; ~**sprung** *m* leap with straddled legs.

Spreng|apparat *m* (*für Wasser*) sprinkling apparatus; sprinkler; sparger; ~**arbeit** *f* blasting; shooting; ~**befehl** *m* order to blast; ~**bohrloch** *n* blasthole; ~**bombe** *f aero mil* high explosive bomb, H. E. bomb; blasting bomb; demolition bomb; ~~**nwirkung** *f* explosive-bomb effect; ~**büchse** *f* blasting charge; *hist* petard; ~**eisen** *n* (*Glasfabrikation*) cracking ring; ~**en** *tr* (*aufbrechen, erbrechen*) to burst open; (*Fesseln*) to break; (*Tür*) to force; (*Mine, Bergbau*) to spring; (*in die Luft* ~~) to blow up; to explode; (*Felsen* ~~) to blast; (*Spielbank*) to break (the bank), *Am fam* to hit the jackpot; *med* (*Blutgefäß etc*) to rupture; *fig* (*zerstreuen*) to disperse; (*Bündnis*) to split up; (*Versammlung*) to break up, to dissolve (a meeting); (*mit Wasser od Flüssigkeit*) to sprinkle; to spray; (*gießen*) to water; *itr* (*schnell gallopieren*) to gallop; to dash (along), to ride fast; *über e-n Graben* ~~ to take a ditch; ~**er** *m* (*für Wasser*) sprinkler; spray; (*mit Explosivstoffen*) blaster; ~**falle** *f mil* booby trap; ~**flüssigkeit** *f* explosive liquid; ~**füllung** *f* explosive charge; ~**geschoß** *n* explosive projectile (*od* missile); ~**granate** *f* high explosive shell, H. E. shell; anti-personnel shell; ~**kabel** *n* blasting ignition cable; ~**kammer** *f* mine chamber; ~**kapsel** *f* (*Zünder*) detonator; primer cap; booster charge; ~**kegel** *m* cone of burst; ~**kolonne** *f* dynamiters *pl*; ~**kommando** *n* demolition party; (*für Bombenblindgänger*) bomb disposal unit (*od* squad *od* party), unexploded bomb squad (*Abk* U. X. B.); ~**kopf** *m* (*Torpedo, V-Bombe etc*) warhead; ~**körper** *m* explosive slab; explosive charge; ~**kraft** *f* explosive force (*od* power); ~**ladung** *f* explosive (*od* bursting) charge; demolition charge; *mar* scuttling charge; *verborgene* ~~ booby trap; ~**loch** *n* blasthole; shothole; ~**luft** *f* liquid-oxygen explosive (*Abk* LOX); ~**mittel** *n* blasting agent; ~**munition** *f* explosive ammunition; ~**niete** *f tech* explosive rivet; ~**öl** *n* nitroglycerin; ~**patrone** *f* blasting (*od* explosive) cartridge; ~**pulver** *n* blasting powder; ~**röhre** *f* Bangalore torpedo; ~**ring** *m tech* spring (*od* snap) ring; ~**schuß** *m* shot; ~**stoff** *m* (high-) explosive; dynamite; ~~**lager** *n* explosive dump; ~**stück** *n* splinter; ~**trichter** *m* explosive crater; (*Mine*) mine crater; (*Granate*) shell crater; (*Bombe*) bomb crater; ~**trupp** *m* blasting detachment; (*für Bombenblindgänger*) bomb disposal squad; unexploded bomb squad (*Abk* U. X. B.); ~**ung** *f* blowing up; blasting; explosion; (*mit Wasser*) watering; sprinkling; (*e-r Versammlung*) breaking, dispersion; ~**wagen** *m* (*für Wasser*) watering-cart; *Am* water wagon; sprinkler; ~**wedel**, ~**wisch** *m* sprinkler; ~**wirkung** *f* explosive (*od* splitting) effect; ~**wolke** *f* burst cloud; ~**zünder** *m* fuse, fuze.

Sprengel *m* (*Amtsbezirk e-s Geistlichen*) diocese; parish; (*Bezirk*) district; (*Weihwasserwedel*) sprinkling-brush; (*eingeschlossenes Gebiet*) enclave.

Sprenkel *m* (*Vogelschlinge*) springe, snare; (*Tüpfel*) spot, speckle; freckle;

~ig *a* speckled, spotted; **~n** *tr* to speckle, to spot; to mottle; to dapple; (*Haut*) to freckle; (*Wasser*) to sprinkle; **~ung** *f* mottling.

sprenzen *tr fam* to water, to drench.

Spreu *f* chaff; *den Weizen von der ~ sondern* to sift the chaff from the wheat.

Sprich|wort *n* proverb; adage; saying; *wie es im ~~ heißt* as the saying is; **~wörtlich** *a* proverbial.

Sprieße *f* (*Stütze*) prop, stay; buttress; **~n** *tr* (*abstützen*) to prop, to support; to buttress.

sprießen *irr itr* to sprout; to bud; (*keimen*) to germinate; (*herausschießen*) to shoot, to spring up.

Spriet *n mar* sprit.

Spring|bein *n* saltatorial leg; **~bock** *m zoo* springbok; **~brett** *n* spring board; **~bombe** *f aero* skid bomb; **~brunnen** *m* fountain; jet (of water); **~en** *irr itr* (*weit~~*) to leap; (*auf~~, hoch~~, ab~~*) to jump; (*hüpfen*) to hop; (*Seil~~*) to spring; (*hochschnellen*) to bounce; (*rennen*) to run; (*ins Wasser beim Baden*) to dive; (*über e-n Graben*) to clear; (*hervor~~*) to bound; (*sprudelnd*) to spout, to gush; to play; (*platzen*) to burst, to break, to snap; to split; (*entzwei~~*) to burst asunder; to crack; to fracture; *über die Klinge ~~ lassen* to put to the edge; *in die Augen ~~* to strike the eye; to be obvious; to be self-evident; to become apparent; *e-e Mine ~~ lassen* to spring a mine; *etw ~~ lassen* to treat (to); to stand; to spend (money); *das ist gehupft wie gesprungen fam* it's as broad as it's long; *der Kopf will mir ~~* my head is going to burst; *auf die Füße ~~* to spring to o.'s feet; *auf e-n Wagen ~~* to jump on to a vehicle; *Am* to hop a vehicle; *in die Bresche ~~* to throw o. s. into the breach; *vor Freude ~~* to leap for joy; *die Lokomotive sprang aus den Schienen* the engine jumped the track; **~end** *a* leaping; jumping; bursting; salient; *der ~~e Punkt* the salient point; the crucial point; the crux of the matter; **~er** *m* jumper; leaper; vaulter; (*Fallschirm~~*) parachute jumper; (*Schach*) knight; (*Ölquelle*) gusher (oil well); **~feder** *f* (elastic) spring; **~~waage** *f* spring balance; **~flut** *f* spring tide; bore; **~hengst** *m* stallion; **~insfeld** *m* young harum-scarum; giddy fellow; (*Mädchen*) hoyden; romp; **~käfer** *m* spring beetle; **~kraft** *f* springiness; elasticity; resiliency; power of recoil; **~maus** *f* jumping rat; **~mine** *f mil* anti-personnel mine; **~pferd** *n* jumper; **~quell** *m*, **~quelle** *f* fountain; spring; *heiße ~~* hot spring; geyser; **~reiter** *m sport* jumping rider; **~schreiber** *m* teletype; **~seil** *n* skipping-rope; *Am* jumping-rope; **~stab** *m* (*Hochsprung*) leaping pole; **~turm** *m* (*Sprungturm im Bad*) diving platform; (*Fallschirmturm*) parachute tower; **~welle** *f* bore.

Sprit *m* spirit, alcohol; spirits *pl*; *fam* (*Benzin, Betriebstoff*) (liquid) fuel; petrol; juice; **~essig** *m* spirit vinegar; **~fabrikant** *m* distiller; **~haltig** *a* containing spirit; spirituous; **~löslich** *a* soluble in spirit; alcohol-soluble; **~nachschub** *m mil* fresh supply of petrol (*od* fuel); **~raffinerie** *f* spirit refinery.

Spritz|apparat *m* sprinkler; sprayer; **~arbeit** *f* (*Buchbinderei*) marbled work; **~bad** *n* shower-bath, douche; **~beton** *m* gun concrete; **~bewurf** *m* rough plaster(ing); **~brett** *n* (*Wagen*) splash board; dashboard; **~düse** *f* spray(ing) nozzle; injector; **~e** *f med* syringe; squirt; (*Einspritzung*) injection, shot; *med* (*zweite ~~*) booster; *tech* spray, sprayer; injector; *mil sl* M.(achine) G.(un); (*Feuer~~*) fire-engine; *e-e ~~ geben* to administer an injection; **~en** *tr* (*heraus~~*) to squirt; to spout; to spurt (out *od* forth); *med* to inject, to syringe; (*besprühen*) to spray; (*sprengen*) to sprinkle; (*be~~, beschmutzen*) to splash; to bespatter; (*Wasser*) to throw water into; *tech* (*Spritzguß*) to die-cast; *itr* (*Feder*) to sputter; (*sprühen*) to splutter; (*hervorsprudeln*) to gush forth; to spurt up; to spout; (*Feuerspritze*) to play; **~enboot** *n* fire tug, *Am* fire float; **~enhaus** *n* fire-station; fire-engine house; **~enleute** *pl*, firemen *pl*; **~enrohr** *n* tube of a fire-engine; **~enschlauch** *m* hose (of a fire-engine); fire-hose; **~er** *m* splash; spatter; squirt; *tech* sprue; **~fahrt** *f* trip; excursion; **~flasche** *f chem* washing bottle; **~guß** *m tech* injection die-casting; **~~form** *f* die, die mo(u)ld; **~~masse** *f* injection mo(u)lding compound; **~~maschine** *f* die-casting machine; **~~metall** *n* die-cast metal; **~~verfahren** *n* die-casting process; injection mo(u)lding; **~ig** *a* prickling; lively; deft; **~kopf** *m* spraying nozzle; **~kuchen** *m* fritter; **~kur** *f med* injection treatment; **~lack** *m* spraying varnish; **~lackieren** *n* spray painting; **~lackiererei** *f* dope-spraying shop; **~leder** *n* (*am Wagen*) dash leather; splash leather; splasher; **~loch** *n* spout hole; **~masse** *f* spraying compound; **~pistole** *f* spray(ing) gun; air gun; **~pumpe** *f* jet pump; spraying pump; **~regen** *m* drizzle; **~ring** *m* oil ring, splash ring; **~verfahren** *n* spraying method; method of injection; mo(u)lding; **~vergaser** *m* spray carburet(t)or; **~wand** *f* dashboard; **~wasser** *n* spray (water).

spröd|e *a* brittle, *Am* brash; (*Eisen*) cold-short, dry; (*hart*) hard; (*nicht biegsam*) inflexible; (*Haut*) rough; chapped; *fig* (*zurückhaltend*) reserved; demure; (*bescheiden, verschlossen*) coy; modest; (*verschämt*) bashful; (*scheu*) shy; (*prüde*) prudish, *fam* prim; *~e tun* to play the prude; **~igkeit** *f* brittleness; roughness; shortness; inflexibility; *fig* (*von Personen*) reserve; demureness; prudery; *fam* primness.

Sproß *m* shoot, sprout; scion; (*Keim*) germ; *fig* (*Abkömmling*) offspring, descendant, scion.

Sprosse *f* (*Leiter*) step, round, rung, rundle, stave; (*Geweih*) tine, prong, point, branch; **~n** *itr* to sprout, to shoot, to germinate; *fig* to descend (from); **~end** *a* prolific; **~enrad** *n* stave-wheel; **~enwand** *f sport* wall bar.

Sprößling *m* shoot; sprout; *fig* (*Abkömmling*) offspring; descendant, scion.

Sprotte *f* sprat; *Kieler ~n* smoked sprats.

Spruch *m* (*Ausspruch*) saying; (*Bibel*) (bible-) text; passage; (*Lehrspruch, Sentenz*) aphorism; (*Lebensregel*) maxim; axiom; (*Motto*) motto; (*Kern~*) apophthegm; (*Orakel*) oracle; *jur* (*Strafsachenurteil*) sentence; conviction; finding; (*Richter~*) judg(e)ment; (*Entscheidung*) (final) decision; (*bei Ehescheidung*) decree; (*Geschworenen~*) verdict; (*Schieds~*) award; *e-n ~ fällen jur* to pronounce a sentence; to give a verdict; *die Sprüche Salomonis* Proverbs *pl*; **~band** *n* banderol; scroll; *Am* banner, bannerline; **~gedicht** *n* aphoristic poem; **~kammer** *f* trial tribunal; denazification board (*od* court *od* panel), spruchkammer; **~~entscheid** *m* decision (of as pruchkammer); **~reif** *a* ripe for decision; **~reim** *m* rhymed proverb; **~sammlung** *f* collection of aphorisms; **~weisheit** *f* wisdom contained in aphorisms.

Sprudel *m* bubbling source (*od* well), hot spring; (*Mineralwasser*) mineral water; **~bad** *n* shower-bath; **~brunnen** *m* gusher; **~kopf** *m* hotspur, spitfire; **~n** *itr* (*heraus~~*) to gush forth; to flow; to bubble (up); (*überstürzt reden*) to sputter (forth); *von Humor ~~* to sparkle with wit; (*übersprühen*) to prim over (with); **~nd** *a* bubbling; *fig* sparkling; scintillating; brimming.

sprüh|en *tr, itr* to sparkle, to scintillate; (*Funken*) to spark, to emit sparks; (*spritzen*) to spray; to fly; to spit; to scatter; to sprinkle; (*Regen*) to drizzle; (*vor Wut*) to flash with anger; (*Feuer ~*) to shoot forth fire; **~regen** *m* drizzle, drizzling rain; (*Spritzwasser*) spray, shower; **~rohr** *n* spray tube; **~teufel** *m* (*Person*) hotspur, spitfire.

Sprung *m* leap, jump, spring; (*Satz*) bound; bounce; *mil* dash, rush; (*ins Wasser*) dive; (*übers Pferd*) vault; *~ mit Anlauf* flying jump; *~ aus dem Stand* standing jump; (*kurze Strecke*) short distance, short hop; stone's throw; (*kurze Zeit*) short while; (*Riß*) crack, fissure; (*im Holz*) split; (*in Edelstein*) flaw, fault; (*in Mauer*) chink, crevice; (*Paarung*) copulation, pairing; *auf dem ~ sein* to be on the point of; to be on o.'s toes; to be on the alert; *hinter jds Sprünge kommen* to find s. o. out; *sich auf die Sprünge machen* to cut and run; *keine großen Sprünge machen können* to be forced to keep within bounds; *jdm auf die Sprünge helfen* to put in the right way; *e-n ~ haben* to be cracked; *~ ins Ungewisse* leap in the dark; *sie kommt auf e-n ~ herüber* she will drop in for a minute; **~bein** *n* ankle-bone; saltatorial leg; **~bildung** *f* fissure formation; cracking; **~bock** *m sport* wooden horse; **~brett** *n sport* spring-board; (*Bad*) diving board; *fig* stepping-stone; **~feder** *f* (elastic) spring; spiral spring; **~~matratze** *f* spring mattress; **~gelenk** *n anat* ankle joint; (*Pferd*) hock; **~grube** *f sport* pit; **~haft** *a* by leaps and bounds; jerky; jumpy; (*unregelmäßig*) irregular; *fig* erratic; desultory; **~~igkeit** *f* violent fluctuation; **~kraft** *f* elasticity; **~lauf** *m* (*Schi*) jumping run; **~riemen** *m* martingale; straps *pl*; **~schanze** *f* (*Schi*) ski-jump; **~seil** *n* skipping-rope, *Am* jumping-rope; **~stange** *f* jumping-pole; **~start** *m aero* (*Hubschrauber*) jumping take-off; jump start, quick start; **~tuch** *n* (*Feuerwehr*) jumping sheet; **~turm** *m sport* (*Bad*) high-diving board; *aero* (*Fallschirm~~*) parachute tower; **~weise** *adv* by leaps and bounds; by steps and stages; (*unregelmäßig*) by fits and starts; *fig* abruptly; intermittently; **~weite** *f* leaping range; **~wettbewerb** *m sport* jumping test; **~zeit** *f* transit(ion) time; **~zone** *f aero mil* (*Fallschirmspringer, Lastenabwurf*) drop zone (*Abk* D. Z.).

Spuck|e *f* spittle; saliva; **~en** *itr* to spit; *tr* to spit out; to expectorate; **~napf** *n* spittoon, *Am* cuspidor.

Spuk *m* (*Erscheinung, Gespenst*) apparition, spectre, spook, ghost; *fam* (*Ärger*) trouble; mischief; (*Lärm, Aufruhr*) noise; uproar; **~en** *itr* to haunt; *es ~t* the house is haunted; **~geist** *m* hobgoblin, imp; **~geschichte** *f* ghost-story; **~haft** *a* ghostly, ghostlike; weird.

Spul|e *f* (*Web∼∼*) bobbin, spool; (*Feder∼∼*) quill; (*Nähfaden∼∼*) reel, *Am* spool; *el* coil; (*Walze, Trommel*) drum; **∼en** *tr* to spool; to wind; to reel; *el* to coil up; **∼enantenne** *f radio* coil aerial; **∼engalvanometer** *n* coil galvanometer; **∼enkern** *m el* core of a coil; core of a spool; **∼enwicklung** *f* coil winding; **∼maschine** *f* spooling machine; winding machine; bobbin-frame; **∼rad** *n* spooling-wheel; **∼spindel** *f* spool pin; **∼winde** *f* winch; **∼wurm** *m* mawworm.

spül|en *tr* to wash, to rinse, to cleanse; to flush; *hinunter∼∼* to wash s. th. down; *an Land ∼∼* to wash ashore; *über Bord ∼∼* to wash overboard; *itr* (*Wellen*) to undulate; **∼eimer** *m* slop-pail, *Am* slop-jar; **∼faß** *n* wash-tub; **∼frau** *f* scullery maid, dish-washer; **∼icht** *n* dishwater; slops *pl*; swill; **∼lappen** *m* dish-cloth, *Am* dish rag; **∼maschine** *f* automatic dish-washer; **∼mittel** *n* (*Haar*) hair rinse; **∼napf** *m* rinsing-basin; **∼stein** *m* (*Küche*) sink; **∼ung** *f* rinsing; cleansing; (*Zylinder*) circulation; scavenging; (*Wasser∼∼*) flush cleaning; flush-pipe; **∼wasser** *n* dishwater, (*schmutziges*) slops *pl*.

Spund *m* bung, plug, spigot, stopper, stopple; tap; **∼bohrer** *m* tap-borer; **∼en** *tr* to bung; (*Tischlerei*) to join by means of grooves; **∼loch** *n* bung-hole; **∼wand** *f* sheet piling; cutoff wall; bulkhead.

Spur *f* track, trace; (*Fährte*) trail; (*Fuß∼*) footprint; footstep; (*Wagen∼*) rut; *tech* gutter; channel; groove; *fig* (*Merkmal*) mark, (*Anzeichen*) sign, (*Überrest*) vestige; (*Wild∼*) scent; (*∼ im Wasser*) wake; *fam* (*kleine Menge*) small quantity; *e-e ∼ Salz* a pinch of salt; *keine ∼! fam* not at all! not in the least! not a chance! *jdm auf die ∼ helfen* to give s. o. a clue; *es war keine ∼ davon zu sehen* there was no trace of it to be seen; *jdm auf die ∼ kommen* to get upon s. o.'s track; **∼anzeiger** *m* (*radioaktiver*) radioactive tracer; **∼en** *itr* to follow on the same track; (*∼ halten*) to keep the track; **∼∼element** *n* tracer element; **∼geschoß** *n* tracer bullet; **∼los** *a* traceless; *adv* without (leaving) a trace; **∼stange** *f* track rod; **∼weite** *f* (*Fahrgestell*) wheel track; (*des Geleises*) ga(u)ge; *normale ∼∼* normal ga(u)ge; *Schmal∼* narrow ga(u)ge.

spür|en *tr* (*nachspüren*) to trace; to search for; (*folgen*) to follow the track of; to be on s. o.'s track; to track; to trail; (*merken*) to notice; to perceive; to experience; (*fühlen*) to feel; **∼hund** *m* bloodhound, limer; pointer; track-hound; *fig* spy, detective; *Am fam* sleuth; **∼nase** *f* scenting nose; *fig* prying fellow; **∼sinn** *m* sagacity; flair (for); shrewdness; *∼∼ haben für* to have a scent (*od* flair) for.

sputen *r* to make haste, to be quick; to hurry, to hurry up; *sl* to get cracking; *spute dich!* make haste! hurry up! *Am fam* make it snappy!

st! *interj* (*leise*) hist! hush! peace! silence!

Staat *m* (*Staatswesen*) state; (*Gemeinwesen*) commonwealth; (*Regierung*) government; public authorities *pl*; (*Prunk*) pomp; show; parade; (*Putz*) finery; dress; *die Vereinigten ∼en* (*von Nordamerika*) the United States of America *pl mit sing* (*Abk* U. S. A.); the States; the Union; America; *in vollem ∼* in full dress; in full feather; *mit etw ∼ machen* to make a show of; to parade; to show off; to boast of; *damit kann man nicht viel ∼ machen* that is not worth much; *großen ∼ machen fam* to cut a dash; *bester ∼* (*fam*) dress-togs *pl*, *Am sl* glad rags *pl*; **∼enbildung** *f* formation of states; **∼enbund** *m* confederacy; confederation (of states); federation; *Engl* commonwealth; **∼engeschichte** *f* political history; **∼enkunde** *f* political science; **∼enlos** *a* stateless; having no nationality; **∼∼e(r)** *m* stateless person; **∼∼igkeit** *f* statelessness; **∼lich** *a* state- ...; (*politisch*) politic(al); (*öffentlich*) public; (*national*) national; *mit ∼∼er Genehmigung* under the authority of the state; *∼∼ anerkannt* state registered; *∼∼es Hoheitsgebiet* state territory; *∼∼e Unterstützung* state allowance.

Staats|abgabe *f* government taxes *pl*; **∼akt** *m* state ceremony; act of state; **∼akten** *m pl* state papers *pl*; **∼aktion** *f* political event; **∼allgewalt** *f* statism; **∼amt** *n* public office; government appointment; **∼angehörige(r)** *m* subject (of a state); national, *Am* citizen; **∼angehörigkeit** *f* nationality, *Am meist* citizenship; *die ∼∼ aberkennen* to deprive of nationality; **∼angelegenheit** *f* state-affair; **∼angestellte(r)** *m* state employee; **∼anleihe** *f* government loan; public loan, *Am* government bonds *pl* (*od* securities); **∼anstellung** *f* public appointment; **∼anwalt** *m* public prosecutor; (*General∼∼*) Attorney-General, *Am* prosecuting attorney, State's attorney; district attorney, circuit attorney; **∼∼schaft** *f* public prosecutor's office; **∼anzeiger** *m* official gazette; **∼archiv** *n* public record office; (*Dokumente*) state archives *pl*; **∼aufsicht** *f* state supervision; state control; **∼auftrag** *m* government contract; **∼ausgaben** *f pl* public expenditures *pl*; **∼bahn** *f* state railway, *Am* state railroad; **∼bank** *f* national bank; state bank; **∼bankerott** *m* national bankruptcy; **∼bauten** *m pl* public works *pl*; **∼beamte(r)** *m* civil servant; government official; public functionary; public official; *Am* (*Amtsinhaber*) office-holder; (*höherer ∼∼*) *Am* statesman; **∼begräbnis** *n* national funeral; **∼begriff** *m* conception of the state; **∼behörde** *f* government authority, public authority; **∼betrieb** *m* government enterprise; state service; **∼bibliothek** *f* state library; **∼bürger** *m* citizen; national; **∼∼kunde** *f* civics *pl*; **∼∼lich** *a* civic; **∼∼schaft** *f* citizenship; **∼diener** *m* civil servant; **∼dienst** *m* civil service, *Am* public service; *im ∼∼* in the service of the state; **∼druckerei** *f* government printing office; **∼eigen** *a* state-owned; **∼eigentum** *n* state property; public (*od* national) property; **∼eingriff** *m* state interference; **∼einkünfte** *f pl* public revenue(s *pl*); **∼feind** *m* public enemy; **∼finanzen** *f pl* finances of the state; public finance; **∼form** *f* form of government; **∼gebäude** *n* public building; *fig* state; **∼gebiet** *n* territory of state; **∼grenze** *f* boundary of state; **∼gefährlich** *a* dangerous to the state; **∼gefangene(r)** *m* prisoner of state; state prisoner; **∼gefühl** *n* national feeling; **∼geheimnis** *n* state secret; **∼gelder** *n pl* public money; **∼gesetz** *n* statute law; **∼gespräch** *n* government call, *Am* government message; *dringendes ∼∼* government priority call; **∼gewalt** *f* supreme power; executive power; **∼grundgesetz** *n* constitution; basic law; **∼haushalt** *m* budget; finances *pl* (of the state); ways and means *pl*; (*Plan*) *Engl* Estimates *pl*; **∼hoheit** *f* sovereignty; **∼interesse** *n* public interest; **∼kanzlei** *f* chancery (of state); **∼kanzler** *m Engl* Lord Chancellor; chancellor of state; **∼kapitalismus** *m* state capitalism; **∼kasse** *f* (public) treasury; exchequer; **∼∼nanweisung** *f* treasury warrant; **∼kerl** *m* fine fellow; **∼kirche** *f* state church; (*in England*) Church of England; Established Church; **∼kleid** *n* gala dress; robes of state; **∼klug** *a* politic; diplomatic; **∼∼heit** *f* political wisdom; policy; **∼kommissar** *m* state commissioner; **∼kommunismus** *m* state communism; **∼konkurs** *m* national bankruptcy; **∼körper** *m* body politic; **∼kosten** *pl* public expenses *pl*; *auf ∼∼* at public expense; **∼kunde** *f* politics *pl*, civics *pl*; **∼kunst** *f* statecraft; statesmanship; political science; politics *pl*; **∼lasten** *f pl* public burdens *pl*; **∼leben** *n* political life; politics *pl*; **∼lehre** *f* political science; **∼lotterie** *f* state lottery; **∼mann** *m* statesman; politician; **∼männisch** *a* statesman-like; political; **∼minister** *m* minister (of state); *Engl* Secretary of State; **∼ministerium** *n* state ministry; **∼monopol** *n* government monopoly; **∼notwendigkeit** *f* national emergency; **∼oberhaupt** *n* head of a state; (*Präsident*) president; (*Herrscher*) sovereign; (*Monarch*) monarch; **∼papiere** *n pl* government stocks *pl*, government securities *pl*, *Am* government bonds *pl*; **∼polizei** *f* state police; *geheime ∼∼* secret state police; **∼präsident** *m* President of the State; **∼prozeß** *m* state trial; **∼raison** *f* reason of state; **∼rat** *m* Privy Council; (*Person*) Privy Councillor; **∼recht** *n* constitutional law; public law; **∼regierung** *f* government; **∼rente** *f* government annuity; **∼schatz** *m* public treasury; exchequer; **∼schiff** *n fig* ship of state; **∼schuld** *f* national debt; public debt; **∼∼schein** *m* (treasury) bond; **∼sekretär** *m* Secretary of State; **∼sicherheitsdienst** *m* state security service; **∼siegel** *n* Great Seal; **∼sozialismus** *m* state socialism; **∼streich** *m* coup d'état; overthrow of the government; **∼telegramm** *n* government message; **∼treu** *a* loyal; **∼umwälzung** *f* (political) revolution; **∼unterstützung** *f* state subsidy; **∼verbrechen** *n* political crime; **∼verbrecher** *m* state (*od* political) criminal; **∼verfassung** *f* constitution; **∼vermögen** *n* public property; **∼verschuldung** *f* state indebtedness; **∼vertrag** *m* international treaty; convention; **∼verwaltung** *f* administration of the state; public administration; government; **∼verweser** *m* administrator; **∼voranschlag** *m* estimates *pl*; **∼werft** *f* government ship yard; **∼wesen** *n* state, commonwealth; **∼wirt** *m* economist; **∼wirtschaft** *f* political economy; **∼wissenschaften** *f pl* political science; politics *pl*; **∼wohl** *n* public weal, common weal; **∼zimmer** *n* state room; **∼zugehörigkeit** *f* nationality; **∼∼sabzeichen** *n* nationality mark; **∼zuschuß** *m* government grant; government subsidy; state subsidy; **∼zweck** *m* purpose of state.

Stab *m* staff; (*Stock*) stick; (*Rute, Stange*) rod; (*Gitter∼, Stange*) bar; (*dünner Holz- od Metall∼*) slat; (*Pfahl*) stake; (*Pfosten*) post; (*Schirm∼*) rib; (*Maß∼*) yardstick; (*Bischofs∼*) crosier; (*Schäfer∼*) crook; (*Marschall∼*) baton; (*Dirigenten∼*) baton; (*Szepter, eccl Amts∼*) mace; (*Zauber∼*) wand; *mil* staff; (*Hauptquartier*) headquarters *pl*; (*Personal des Hauptquartiers*) headquarters personnel; *fig* (*Mitarbeiter∼*) collaborators *pl*; (*∼ von Sach-*

verständigen) panel; *den ~ über jdm brechen* to pronounce sentence of death on; *fig* (*jdn verurteilen*) to condemn s. o.; **~antenne** *f radio* rod aerial, rod antenna; stub aerial; whip antenna; (*Dipol*) dipole aerial; **~batterie** *f el* torch battery; **~brandbombe** *f* rod-like incendiary bomb; **~eisen** *n* bar iron; steel bar; **~~profil** *n* bar section; **~~straße** *f* bar-rolling train; **~~walzwerk** *n* bar-rolling mill; **~(hoch)sprung** *m* pole-jump, *Am* pole vault(-ing); **~förmig** *a* bar- (*od* rod-) shaped; **~führung** *f mus* (*Dirigent*) conductor; conductorship; **~heuschrecke** *f* walking-stick insect; **~holz** *n* staves *pl*; **~magnet** *m* bar magnet; **~mühle** *f* rod mill; **~profil** *n* bar section; **~reim** *m* alliteration; **~sarzt** *m* captain (Medical Corps); *mar* staff-surgeon; **~sbatterie** *f mil* headquarters battery; **~sbootsmann** *m* boatswain; **~schef** *m* Chief of Staff; **~sfeldwebel** *m* staff sergeant-major; **~sgefreiter** *m* lance-corporal; **~shelfer** *m* staff assistant; **~skommandant** *m* headquarters commandant; **~skompanie** *f* headquarters company; **~soffizier** *m* field (-grade) officer; *mar* superior officer; (*Offizier in e-m ~*) staff officer; **~~srang** *m* field rank; **~squartier** *n* headquarters *pl*; **~springen** *irr itr* to pole-jump; **~stahl** *m* round bar steel; **~sveterinär** *m* veterinary officer; **~swache** *f* headquarters company; **~swagen** *m* staff car; **~szahlmeister** *m* paymaster; **~tierchen** *n* bacillus; **~träger** *m*(*Amts~*) mace-bearer; **~walzwerk** *n* bar-rolling mill; **~wechsel** *m sport* (*Staffellauf*) baton changing.

Stäbchen *n* little rod, rodlet; (*Bakterie*) bacillus; *anat* (*Auge*) rod of retina; *sl* (*Zigarette*) cigarette, cigaret; **~bakterie** *f* bacillus; **~form** *f* rod form; **~förmig** *a* rod-shaped; **~schicht** *f anat* (*Auge*) layer of rods; **~zelle** *f* rod cell; stab cell; band form.

stabil *a* stable; (*steif*) rigid; (*fest*) firm; (*stetig*) steady; (*stark*) strong; (*kräftig*) sturdy; (*hart*) rugged; (*solide, dauerhaft*) substantial; **~isator** *m* stabilizer; **~isieren** *tr* to stabilize; to steady; to make constant (*od* normal); (*Macht*) to consolidate; **~isierung** *f* stabilization; stability; steadying; (*Macht*) consolidation; **~~sfläche** *f* stabilizing surface; **~~sflosse** *f aero* stabilizer; horizontal fin; **~ität** *f* stability; steadiness; (*Steifheit*) rigidity.

Stachanowarbeiter *m* Stakhanovite.

Stachel *m* prick, prickle; (*Dorn*) thorn; (*bei Insekten*) sting; dart; *bot* spine; (*des Igels*) spine; (*des Stachelschweins*) quill; (*zum Antreiben von Tieren*) goad; (*Zinke, Zacke, Spitze*) prong; (*e-r Schnalle*) tongue; (*des Sporns*) prong; (*Spitze*) (sharp) point; (*unter Rennschuhen*) spike; *fig* sting; (*Ansporn, Antrieb*) spur, stimulus; incentive; *der ~ des Gewissens* the sting (*od* prick) of conscience; *ein ~ im Fleisch* (*Bibel*) a thorn in the flesh; *wider den ~ löcken* (*Bibel*) to kick against the prick; **~beere** *f* gooseberry; **~beerstrauch** *m* gooseberry-bush; **~draht** *m* barbed wire; dannert wire; **~~verhau, ~~zaun** *m* barbed-wire entanglement; barbed-wire fence; **~flosser** *m pl* (*Fische*) spine-finned fishes *pl*; acanthopterygii *pl*; **~haarig** *a* wiry-haired; **~halsband** *n* (*für Hunde*) spicked dog-collar; training collar; **~häuter** *m pl* echinodermata *pl* (*od* echinoderms *pl*); **~ig** *a* prickly, thorny, spiny; *fig* pungent; (*beißend*) biting; stinging; sarcastic; caustic; **~n** *itr* to sting; to prick; (*stechen, stoßen*) to prod; (*auf~*) to goad; *fig* (*an~~*) to spur; to urge, to stimulate; **~palme** *f* bactris; **~raupe** *f* spined caterpillar; **~rede** *f fig* sarcasm; stinging remarks *pl*; **~rochen** *m* thornback; **~scheibe** *f* pin-pointed disk; **~schwein** *n* porcupine.

Stadel *m* (*Scheune, Schuppen*) barn, shed; *tech* (*Erzröstofen*) open kiln.

Stadion *n sport* stadium, arena.

Stadium *n* (*Phase*) phase; (*Stufe der Entwicklung*) stage.

Stadt *f* town, *Am* (*schon von 8000 Einwohnern ab*) city; *Engl* (*Groß~*) city; *Innen~* (*Am Geschäftsbezirk*) downtown district; *Außen~* uptown district; *wir sind aus der gleichen ~* we are of the same place; *die ganze ~ spricht über sie* she is the talk of the town; *in der ~ aufgewachsen* town--bred; *in die ~ gehen* to go to town; *in der ~ sein* to be in town; **~abgabe** *f* town dues *pl*, municipal taxes *pl*; **~amt** *n* municipal office; **~anleihe** *f* municipal loan, *Am* city bonds *pl*; **~bahn** *f* city railway; (*London*) metropolitan railway; **~bank** *f* municipal bank; **~bann** *m* precincts *pl* (of the town); **~baumeister** *m* municipal architect; **~behörde** *f* municipal authorities *pl*; **~bekannt** *a* notorious (*od* known) all over the town; *es ist ~~* it is the talk of the town; **~bevölkerung** *f* population of a town; **~bewohner** *m* city dweller; *Am fam* city-slicker; **~bezirk** *m* ward; district of a city; quarter; *Am* section (of a city); **~bibliothek** *f* city library; **~bild** *n* panorama (of a town); site; townscape; **~brief** *m* local letter; **~bürger** *m* citizen; freeman of town; **~~recht** *n* citizenship; **~büro** *n* city office, *Am* metropolitan office; **~chronik** *f* chronicle of a town; *fig* person who knows all the gossip of a town; **~flughafen** *m aero* municipal airport; **~flugverkehr** *m* inter-city airline service; **~gas** *n* (*Klärgas*) sewer gas; **~gebiet** *n* urban area, city area; built-up area; **~gefängnis** *n* city jail; **~gemeinde** *f* municipality; township, *Am* city; **~gericht** *n* municipal court; **~gespräch** *n* town talk; **~graben** *m* town-moat; **~haus** *n* (*Rathaus*) townhall, *Am* city hall; (*im Gegensatz zu Landhaus*) town house; **~kasse** *f* city treasury; **~klatsch** *m* local gossip; **~koffer** *m* suit-case; (*kleiner*) overnight bag; **~kommandant** *m* governor of a city; (*Ortskommandant*) town-major; **~kreis** *m* district; (*selbständiger*) borough; **~kundig** *a* knowing o.'s way about a town; *siehe*: *~bekannt*; **~kupee** *n mot* brougham, *Am* town coupé; **~leben** *n* town life, city life; **~leute** *pl* townspeople, townsfolk *pl*; **~mauer** *f* town wall, city wall; **~musikant** *m* town musician; **~nebel** *m* urban fog; smog; **~neuigkeit** *f* local news *pl mit sing*; **~obrigkeit** *f* municipal authorities *pl*; **~park** *m* municipal park; **~pfarrer** *m* clergyman of a town; **~plan** *m* town plan, city map; **~planung** *f* town (*Am* city) planning; **~polizei** *f* municipal police, town police, city police; **~post** *f* town--post; **~rand** *m* outskirts *pl* of a city; **~~siedlung** *f* settlement on the outskirts of a town; suburban settlement; **~rat** *m* town council, *Am* city council; (*Person*) town councillor, alderman; *Am* member of the city council; **~recht** *n* freedom of the city; **~reisende(r)** *m* town travel(l)er; **~säckel** *n hum* city--treasury; **~schreiber** *m* town-clerk; recorder; **~schule** *f* town-school, board-school; **~teil** *m*, **~viertel** *n* quarter, ward; *Am* section (of a city); **~tor** *n* town gate, city gate; **~väter** *m pl* city fathers *pl*; **~verordnete(r)** *m* town councillor; **~~nversammlung** *f* town council; **~verwaltung** *f* city (*od* local) administration; **~waage** *f* public scales *pl*; **~wache** *f* municipal guard; **~wappen** *n* city-arms *pl*; **~wohnung** *f* town residence; **~zoll** *m* excise.

Städt|chen *n* small town; market town; **~ebau** *m* town planning; **~emannschaft** *f sport* town team; **~eordnung** *f* statute for the government of towns; *Engl* Municipal Corporation Act; **~er** *m* townsman, city dweller; citizen; *Am sl* dude, mucker; **~erin** *f* townswoman; **~etag** *m* association of communes; **~isch** *a* municipal, urban; (*Benehmen etc*) urbane; **~~e** *Werke* municipal public works *pl*.

Stafette *f* express; messenger relay service; courier; (*Sport*) relay; **~nlauf** *m* relay-race; **~nläufer** *m* relay-runner.

Staff|age *f* (*Ausstattung*) accessories *pl*; (*Dekoration*) decoration; (*in Landschaft*) figures in landscape, staffage; **~ieren** *tr* to garnish; (*Tuch*) to dress; to equip; to prepare; (*Hut*) to trim; **~ierung** *f* decoration; trim.

Staffel *f* (*Leiterstufe*) step; rung; *fig* (*Stufe*) degree; *mil* (*Gruppe*) echelon; (*Einheit*) party; detachment; *aero* squadron (= unit of 9 aircraft); *sport* relay; *motorisierte ~* (*mil*) motorized rear-echelon service; **~aufstellung** *f* echelon; **~ei** *f* (*Malerei*) easel; **~flug** *m* staggered flight; **~form** *f aero* squadron formation; **~förmig** *a* in (*od* by) echelons; **~führer, ~kapitän** *m aero* O. C. the squadron; **~gebühr** *f* graduated rate; **~keil** *m aero* V-formation of a flight; squad wedge; **~lauf** *m sport* relay race; **~n** *tr* to graduate, *Am oft* to grade; to differentiate; to rise by steps; *mil* to echelon; *aero* (*Tragflächen, Flugzeuge*) to stagger; *gestaffelte Flugformation* echelon formation; **~preis** *m com* graduated price; **~tarif** *m* (*Löhne, Preise etc*) adjustable (*od* graduated) tariff; graded wage scale; graduated scale of charges; **~ung** *f* graduation; gradation; grading; differentiation; *mil* echelon formation; *aero* stagger (of aircraft wings); **~winkel** *m aero* open squadron angle.

Stag *m mar* stay; **~segel** *n mar* staysail; (*großes*) mainstay-sail.

stagn|ieren *itr* to stagnate; to be at a standstill; **~ierung, ~ation** *f* stagnation, stagnancy; standstill, inactivity.

Stahl *m* steel; *fig* (*Schwert, Dolch*) sword, dagger; *Nerven von ~* iron nerves; (*Dreh~*) tool; (*Edel~*) refined steel; (*mit hoher Festigkeit*) high-grade steel; *korrosionsbeständiger ~* stainless steel; *legierter ~* alloy steel; *nichtrostender ~* stainless steel; *rostbeständiger ~* rustless (*od* non-corroding) steel; **~abfall** *m* waste steel, steel scrap; **~ähnlich, ~artig** *a* steel-like, steel(y); **~bad** *n* chalybeate bath (*od* spa); **~band** *n* steel band; *radio* tape; **~~aufnahme** *f* magnetic steel-tape recording; **~bau** *m* steel construction; **~bereitung** *f* steel-making; **~beton** *m* steel concrete; **~blau** *a* steel-blue; **~blech** *n* steel-plate, sheet steel; sheet iron; **~block** *m* steel ingot; **~draht** *m* steel wire; **~~aufnahme** *f* sound on wire-recording system; **~erz** *n* steel ore; **~erzeuger** *m* steel-maker; **~feder** *f* (*Schreib~~*) steel point, pen point; (*Sprungfeder*) steel spring; **~flasche** *f* steel cylinder; **~geschoß** *n* steel projectile; steel bullet; **~gießerei** *f* steel foundry; **~grau** *a* steel-gray;

~guß *m* cast steel; **~hart** *a* as hard as steel; **~helm** *m* steel helmet, *fam* tin-hat; **~kammer** *f* strong-room, *Am* steel vault; **~kern** *m* steel core; **~konstruktion** *f* structural steel (work); **~kugel** *f* steel ball; steel bullet; **~legierung** *f* steel alloy; **~mantel** *m* steel jacket; **~mast** *m* iron tower; **~meßband** *n* steel measuring tape; **~möbel** *n pl* steel (*od* tubular) furniture; **~platte** *f* steel plate; **~plattenpanzerung** *f* steel plate lining; **~quelle** *f* chalybeate spring; **~rahmen** *m* steel frame; **~rohr** *n*, **~röhre** *f* steel pipe, *Am* steel tube; **~rohrmöbel** *pl* tubular furniture; **~rohrrahmen** *m* tubular steel frame; **~roß** *n hum fam* bike; **~schiene** *f* steel rail; **~schrott** *m* steel scrap; **~seil** *n* steel cable; **~späne** *m pl* steel wool; **~spitze** *f* steel tip; **~stange** *f* steel bar; **~stecher** *m* steel engraver; **~stich** *m* steel engraving; **~träger** *m* steel girder; **~trosse** *f* wire rope; **~waren** *f pl* cutlery, *Am* hardware; **~~handlung** *f* cutlery, *Am* hardware store; **~walzwerk** *n* steel rolling mill; **~welle** *f* shaft; **~werk** *n* steelworks *pl*, steel plant, steel mill; **~werkzeug** *n* steel tool; **~wolle** *f* steel wool; steel shavings *pl*; **~zylinder** *m* steel cylinder.

Stake *f mar* (*Bootshaken*) grappling hook; **~n** *m* stake, pole; (*Bootshaken*) grappling hook; **~n** *itr* to pole, to punt; (*stelzen*) to stride.

Staket *n* stockade, fence; palisade; paling, railing.

Stalaktit *m* stalactite.

Stalinorgel *f mil* (*Raketenwerfer auf Kfz*) multiple rocket launcher.

Stall *m* stable, *Am oft* barn; (*Pferdestand*) stall; (*Kuh~*) cowshed, *Am* cow barn; (*Schweine~*) pigsty, *Am* hog-pen; (*Hunde~*) kennel; (*Schuppen*) shed; *in den ~ stellen* to stable; *fam* (*schlechte Wohnung od elendes Zimmer*) hole, pigsty; **~baum** *m* stable-bar; **~dienst** *m* stable-work, *mil* stable duty; **~dünger** *m* stable-manure; **~en** *itr* to stand in a stable, to stall; *itr* (*harnen*) to stale; **~fütterung** *f* stall-feeding; **~geld** *n* stallage, stable-money; **~halfter** *n* halter, headstall; **~junge** *m* stable boy; **~knecht** *m* horsekeeper, groom, (h)ostler; **~(l)eine** *f* stable halter; picket line; **~magd** *f* dairy maid; **~meister** *m* equerry; **~raum** *m*, **~ung** *f* stable-room; stabling; stables *pl*; mews *pl mit sing*; **~wache** *f* stable guard.

Stamm *m* (*Baum~*) trunk; stem; bole; (*schlanker Baum~, Stiel*) shaft; (*Stengel*) stalk; (*Wort~, Wurzel*) stem, root; *com* (*Kundschaft*) good will; *mil* (*Stammannschaft e-r Einheit etc*) cadre; permanent staff; (*Sippe, Familie*) family; (*in Schottland*) clan; (*Haus*) house; (*Abstammung e-s Geschlechts*) line; lineage; (*Volks~, Eingeborenen~*) tribe; (*Rasse*) race; *bot, zoo* phylum; (*von Vieh*) breed; (*Bestand*) stock; (*Spieleinsatz*) stakes *pl*; *fig* (*Hauptteil*) main part (*od* body); *der Apfel fällt nicht weit vom ~* (*fig prov*) like father, like son; **~aktie** *f* ordinary share, *Am* common stock; **~bataillon** *n mil* skeleton battalion; **~baum** *m* family tree, genealogical tree; *bot, zoo* phylogenetic tree; (*von Tieren*) pedigree; (*von Pferden*) stud-book; **~besatzung** *f mar* skeleton crew; **~buch** *n* album, remembrance-book; *zoo* herdbook; (*Pferde, Hunde*) stud-book; **~burg** *f* ancestral castle; **~einlage** *f com* original investment; **~eltern** *pl* first parents *pl*; ancestors *pl*; progenitors *pl*; **~en** *itr* (*her~~, ab~~, kommen aus*) to come from; to spring from; to originate at (*od* in), to proceed; *Am* to stem from; to descend from; to be descended from; (*zeitlich*) to date from; *gram* to be derived (*von* from); *woher ~~ Sie?* where do you come (*od* hail) from? *das Buch stammt aus dem 16. Jahrhundert* the book dates from the 16th century; **~ende** *n* stump (of a tree); butt (-end); **~endung** *f gram* termination; **~esbewußtsein** *n* clan spirit; **~esentwicklung** *f* evolution; **~esgenosse** *m* fellow tribesman; clansman; **~esgeschichtlich** *a* relating to racial history; **~eshäuptling** *m* chieftain; **~farbe** *f* primary colo(u)r; **~folge** *f* line of descent; **~form** *f* primitive form; cardinal form; prototype; **~gast** *m* regular customer; steady customer; regular guest, regular patron; habitué; **~gut** *n* family estate; ancestral seat; **~halter** *m* first-born male; eldest son; son and heir; **~haus** *n* ancestral mansion; principal line; *com* principal house; head firm; **~holz** *n* trunk wood, stem wood, heartwood, stem timber; log; **~kapital** *n com* original capital, *Am* capital stock; **~karte** *f* (*bei Rationierung*) basic ration card; **~kneipe** *f*, **~lokal** *n* favo(u)rite pub; **~körper** *m* parent substance; **~kunde** *m* regular (*od* steady) customer; **~land** *n* mother country; **~leser** *m* (*Zeitung*) constant reader; **~linie** *f* lineage; main line; **~(m)utter** *f* ancestress; **~personal** *n mil* cadre; permanent staff; *Angehöriger des ~~s mil* cadreman; **~register** *n* genealogical register; **~reis** *n bot* root; **~rolle** *f mil* (unit) nominal roll, nominal register, muster roll; personnel roster; **~~nnummer** *f* army number, *Am* serial number; **~schloß** *n* ancestral castle; **~silbe** *f* root syllable; stem; **~sitz** *m* ancestral seat; *theat* subscribed place; **~tafel** *f* genealogical table; **~tisch** *m* table reserved for regular customers; **~~stratege** *m hum* armchair strategist; **~truppe** *f mil* permanent staff; **~~nteil** *m mil* cadre unit, original unit, parent unit; **~vater** *m* ancestor; progenitor; predecessor; **~volk** *n* aborigines *pl*; **~verwandt** *a* kindred, cognate; of the same origine; of the same race; **~~schaft** *f* kinship; identity of origine; relationship; (*Bluts~~*) consanguinity; (*durch Heirat*) affinity; **~volk** *n* ancestral race; **~wappen** *n* family arms *pl*; **~werk** *n* parent plant; **~wort** *n* root word, primitive word; stem; **~würze** *f* (*Brauerei*) original wort.

stamm|eln *tr, itr* to stammer, to stutter; *fig* to falter; **~ler** *m*, **~lerin** *f* stammerer, stutterer.

stämmig *a fig* (*stark*) strong; (*kräftig*) sturdy, burly; robust; *Am* husky; (*untersetzt*) square-built, stocky, stumpy; **~keit** *f* robustness, stoutness, sturdiness.

Stampf|asphalt *m* compressed asphalt; **~beton** *m* compressed concrete; **~bewegung** *f mar, aero* pitching motion; **~boden** *m* tamped floor; **~e** *f* (*Ramme*) rammer, ram, beetle; (*Stempel*) stamp; (*Stößel*) pestle; (*Stanze, Stempel*) punch; **~en** *tr, itr* (*mit dem Fuß; tech stanzen*) to stamp; to trample; (*zermalmen, schlagen, hämmern*) to pound; to bray; (*schlagen*) to beat; (*Kartoffeln*) to mash; (*zer~~*) to crush; (*Trauben*) to press; (*rammen*) to ram; (*abdämmen, fest~~*) to tamp; (*pflastern*) to pave; (*mühsam gehen*) to trudge; (*Pferd*) to paw the ground; *mar aero* to pitch; *mar* to heave and set; **~er** *m tech* tamper; (*Ramme*) ram, rammer; (*Schlegel*) stamper; beater; **~erde** *f* stamped clay; **~hammer** *m* bumping hammer; **~kartoffeln** *f pl* mashed potatoes *pl*; **~schicht** *f* rammed layer; **~werk** *n* stamping mill; pounding machine; **~~zeug** *n* ramming tool.

Stand *m* (*das Stehen*) standing; (*aufrechter ~*) upright position; (*Standpunkt*) standing-place, stand; position; (*für den Fuß, fester Halt*) foothold, footing; (*Bude, Markt~*) stall, booth, stand, pitch; (*Wasser~*) level, height (of water etc); (*Geschütz~*) emplacement; *astr* (*der Gestirne*) constellation, position; (*der Sonne*) height, position; (*Barometer*) height; (*Thermometer etc*) reading; *com* (*Preis~*) level; rate; *sport* (*~ e-s Spieles*) score; (*Tabellen~*) standings *pl*; (*Zustand*) state, condition; (*Lage*) situation; (*Stadium*) stage; status, state; phase; (*Beruf, Gewerbe*) profession, trade; (*soziale Stellung*) social standing; status; (*Rang, Klasse*) rank, class; position; *die Stände* states *pl*, estates *pl*; *die höheren* (*niederen*) *Stände* the upper (lower) classes; *Leute aus allen Ständen* people from all walks of life; *seinen ~ behaupten* to hold o.'s ground; *im ~ halten* to keep up; to keep in repair; *jdn in den ~ setzen* to enable s. o. to; *in~ setzen* to repair; *gut im ~* in good condition (*od* repair); *nach dem heutigen ~* up-to-date; *festen ~ fassen* to obtain a firm footing; *e-n schweren ~ haben* to have a tough job, to labo(u)r under a difficulty; *mit jdm e-n schweren ~ haben* to have a hard battle to fight with; *sie hatte e-n schweren ~, ihn zu überzeugen* she had a hard time convincing him; *zu~ bringen* to accomplish, to bring about; **~anzeige** *f* deadbeat indication; **~~r** *m* level indicator; **~bein** *n* (*Bildhauerei*) leg bearing main weight of body; **~bild** *n* statue; *phot, film* inanimate picture, still-film picture; **~e** *f* tub; vat; **~entwicklung** *f phot* tank development; **~er** *m mar* (*Flagge*) pennant; **~esamt** *n* registrar's office; register office; *~~liche Trauung* marriage before the registrar; *~~lich trauen* to perform the civil marriage; **~esbeamte(r)** *m* registrar; **~esbewußtsein** *n* class feeling, caste feeling; **~esehe** *f* marriage for position (*od* rank); **~esehre** *f* professional hono(u)r; **~esgemäß** *adv* in accordance with o.'s rank; *~~ leben* to live according to o.'s rank; **~esgenosse** *m* equal in rank; compeer; **~esinteresse** *n* class interest; **~esperson** *f* person of rank (*od* position); dignitary; **~esrücksichten** *f pl* considerations of rank; **~esunterschied** *m* class distinction; **~esvorurteil** *n* class prejudice; **~fest** *a* (*stabil*) stable, firm; steady; strong, rigid, sturdy, substantial; **~~igkeit** *f* stabililty, rigidity, steadiness, solidity; **~geld** *n* stallage; stall money; (*Schiff*) demurrage; **~gericht** *n mil jur* (drum-head) court martial; **~glas** *n* level ga(u)ge; **~haft** *a* steadfast; (*beständig*) constant; (*fest*) firm; (*entschlossen*) resolute; (*stetig*) steady; *etw ~~ aushalten* to bear s. th. stoutly; **~~igkeit** *f* steadfastness; constancy; steadiness; firmness; resolution; perseverance; **~halten** *irr itr* to hold out; to hold o.'s ground; (*widerstehen*) to resist; to stand against; to withstand; to stand firm; *sport* to stay; **~licht** *n mot* parking light; **~linie** *f* base line; datum line; **~motor** *m* stationary engine; **~ort** *m* station; (*Funkpeilung*) position; stand; *aero* position of aircraft in flight; *mil* (*Garnison*) garrison;

~~älteste(r) *m mil* O. C. the garrison **~~bestimmung** *f* position (*od* location) finding; fix; **~~bezirk** *m mil* garrison district; **~~lazarett** *n* garrison hospital; **~~peilung** *f* position finding; **~~sbezeichnung** *f* (*Bibliothek*) shelf mark; **~~skatalog** *m* shelf list; **~~swechsel** *m* change of position; **~pauke** *f* rebuke, severe reprimand; *sl* telling-off; **~platz** *m* (*Taxi*) taxi-rank, *Am* taxi-stand; cab-rank, *Am* cab-stand; **~punkt** *m* point of view; *fig* (*Ansicht*) standpoint; (*Gesichtspunkt*) point of view, *Am* slant, angle; *überwundener* ~~ exploded idea (*od* notion); *jdm den* ~~ *klarmachen* to give s. o. a piece of o.'s mind; to tell s. o. the plain truth; *auf dem* ~~ *stehen* to take up the same ground; *auf e-m höheren* ~~ *stehen* to stand on a higher level; **~quartier** *n mil* permanent quarters *pl*; station; cantonment; *sein* ~~ *haben* to be stationed; **~recht** *n mil* martial law; *das* ~~ *verhängen* to establish martial law; **~~lich** *a* according to martial law; *~~lich erschießen* to shoot by sentence of the court-martial; **~rede** *f* harangue; **~rohr** *n tech* ga(u)ge pipe; **~sicher** *a* stable, rigid; **~uhr** *f* grandfather's clock; pendulum-clock; **~visier** *n mil* fixed sight; **~ziel** *n mil* fixed target.

Standard *m* standard; criterion; **~abweichung** *f* standard deviation; **~ausführung** *f* normal (*Am* conventional) design; **~isieren** *tr* to standardize; **~isierung** *f* standardization; **~lösung** *f* standard solution; **~typ** *m* standard (*Am* conventional) type; **~wert** *m* standard value.

Standarte *f* standard; ensign; *die* ~ *des Präsidenten* the president's flag; **~nträger** *m* standard-bearer.

Ständ|chen *n* serenade; morning music; *jdm ein* ~~ *bringen* to serenade s. o.; **~er** *m* (*Gestell*) stand; frame; trestle; (*Pfosten, Pfeiler*) pillar; post; stud; support; (*Stange*) pole; (*Noten~~*) music-desk; (*Kleider~~*) clothes-horse; *die* ~~ *fam* (*Beine*) stumps *pl*; **~erlampe** *f* floor lamp; **~ig** *a* (*dauernd*) permanent; steady; (*laufend*) constant; continual; (*fest*) fixed; stationary; settled; ~~ *adv* continuously; constantly; *~~es Einkommen* fixed income; ~~ *wechselnder Wind* fishtail wind; *sie hat e-n ~~en Freund Am sl* she is going steady; **~isch** *a parl* belonging to the estates.

Stange *f* pole; (*Gardinen, Eisen*) rod, bar; (*Siegellack*) stick (of sealing-wax); (*Hühner~*) perch; roost; (*Geweih~*) branch; (*kleiner Pfahl*) stake; (*Pfosten*) post; (~ *im Pferdegebiß*) bar; *bei der* ~ *bleiben* to persevere (with); *Am fam* to stick to o.'s guns; *jdm die* ~ *halten* to take s. o.'s part; to stand up for s. o.; *jdn bei der* ~ *halten fig* to bring s. o. up to scratch; *e-e* ~ *Geld fig* a mint of money; *ein Anzug von der* ~ (*fam*) a ready-made suit; a reach-me-down, *Am fam* a hand-me-down; *ich habe den Anzug von der* ~ *gekauft* I bought this suit ready-made; *e-e* ~ *Zigaretten fam* a carton of cigarettes; **~nbohne** *f* climbing bean; runner bean; **~nblitzableiter** *m* pole lightning arrester; **~neisen, ~ngold** *n* bar-iron, bar-gold; **~nholz** *n* pole-wood; **~npferd** *n* thiller; wheeler; **~nspargel** *m* asparagus served whole; **~nvisier** *n mil* tangent sight, bar sight.

Stänker *m* stinker; *fig* (*Zänker*) quarrelsome person, trouble-maker; **~ei** *f* stink; *fig* quarrel; squabble; **~n** *itr* to smell bad, to stink; *fig* to quarrel; to squabble; to sow discord; (*schnüffeln*) to smell about, to ferret about.

Stanniol *n* tinfoil; (*Silberpapier*) silver-paper; **~papier** *n* tinfoil paper; **~streifen** *m* tinfoil, (*Düppeln, Radar*) window; **~überzug** *m* tinfoil covering.

Stanz|automat *m* automatic stamping (*od* punching) machine; **~blech** *n* punching sheet (*od* steel); **~e** *f tech* stamp, punch; die; matrix; punching (*od* stamping) machine; **~en** *tr* to stamp; to punch; to perforate; **~er** *m* press operator; perforator; **~form** *f* matrix, mo(u)ld; **~maschine** *f* punching (*od* stamping) machine; punch press; **~stempel** *m* die; punch; **~werkzeug** *n* punching (*od* stamping) tool; cutting tool; blanking tool.

Stanze *f* (*Strophe*) stanza.

*

Stapel *m* (*Haufen*) pile, heap; stack; file; (*Platz*) staple; depot; dump; warehouse; (*Vorrat*) stock; *mar* (*Schiffsbaugerüst*) stocks *pl*, slip; (*Wolle*) staple; *auf* ~ *legen* to lay down; *auf* ~ *liegend* lying in drydock; shored up; *vom* ~ *lassen* to launch; *fig* to publish; *vom* ~ *laufen* to be launched; **~artikel** *m* staple article; **~faser** *f* rayon staple, rayon fibre; staple fibre; **~lauf** *m mar* launch(ing); **~n** *tr* to pile up, to stack up; **~platz** *m* depot, dump; stockyard; (*Handelsplatz*) emporium; **~wagen** *m* stacking truck; **~waren** *f pl* staple commodities *pl*.

Stapfe *f* track, footstep; **~n** *itr* to stamp, to tread; to plod.

Star[1] *m med* (*grauer* ~) cataract; *grüner* ~ glaucoma; *schwarzer* ~ black cataract; *den* ~ *stechen* to operate on s. o. for cataract; *fig* to open s. o.'s eyes; **~operation** *f* cataract operation; **~stechen** *n* needling of a cataract.

Star[2] *m orn* starling; *film, theat* star; *als* ~ *auftreten* (*od gastieren*), *als* ~ *vorstellen* to star; *als* ~ *vorgestellt* starred; *zusammen mit e-m andern als* ~ *auftreten* (*od vorstellen*) to co-star; *zum ersten Mal als* ~ *in New York auftreten* to make a star debut in New York; **~besetzung** *f film, theat* star cast; **~kasten** *m* (*Nistkasten*) nesting box; **~reklame** *f film, theat* star-billing; **~rolle** *f* star role; *e-e* ~~ *vor der Fernsehkamera* a starring role before the television camera; **~tum** *n*, **~welt** *f* stardom.

stark *a* strong, vigorous; robust; *Am* husky; (*leistungsfähig*) powerful; (*fest*) stout, sturdy; (*mächtig*) mighty; (*groß*) large, big; great; (*schwer*) heavy; (*intensiv*) intense; (*laut*) loud; (*scharf*) keen, sharp; (*dick*) thick; (*beträchtlich*) considerable; (*zahlreich*) numerous; (*beleibt*) corpulent, stout, obese; (*stämmig*) burly, sturdy; (*massig*) bulky; (*fett*) fat; (*heftig*) violent; *~e Auflage e-s Buches* large edition; *~er Band* big volume; *~e Brille* strong glasses; *~e Erkältung* bad cold; *~er Esser* hearty eater; *~es Fieber* high fever; *~er Frost* hard frost; *das ~e Geschlecht* the stronger sex; *~er Grog* stiff grog; *~e Meile* good mile; *~e Kälte* severe cold; *~er Motor* high-powered engine; *~e Seite fig* strong point; *e-e ~e Stunde* a full hour; *~er Sturm* strong wind; gale; *~er Tabak* strong tobacco; *das ist ~er Tabak fig fam* that's rather strong; *~er Verkehr* heavy traffic; *~er Wein* strong wine; *~er Wind* strong (*od* high) wind; *das ist ein ~es Stück* that is too bad; *das ist denn doch zu ~!* that's going too far! that's too much! that beats everything! that's a bit too stiff! *adv* very; much; hard; ~ *auftragen fig* to exaggerate, to boast; ~ *besetzt* crowded; ~ *bewaffnet* heavily armed; ~ *gesucht* in great demand; ~ *regnen* to rain hard; **~bier** *n* strong beer; **~gläubig** *a* of strong faith; **~knochig** *a* strong-boned; **~leibig** *a* stout; corpulent; obese; **~motorig** *a* high-powered; **~mut** *m* fortitude; courage; **~strom** *m el* power current; high-tension (*od* high-voltage) current; **~~anlage** *f* power plant; **~~leitung** *f* power line; power circuit; **~~netz** *n* power-supply system; mains *pl*; **~~technik** *f* power engineering; **~wandig** *a* thick-walled.

Stärke *f* strength, force; *Am* vim; (*Macht*) power; (*Energie*) energy; (*Kraft*) vigo(u)r; (*Gewalt*) violence; (*Beleibtheit*) corpulence; stoutness; (*Dicke von Sachen*) thickness; (*Festigkeit*) firmness; (*Größe*) greatness; largeness; (*Anzahl*) number; (*Heftigkeit*) intensity; (*Nachdruck*) stress; *fig* (*starke Seite*) strong point; forte; *chem* (*Mehl~*) starch; **~fabrik** *f* starch-factory; **~gehalt** *m* starch content; **~grad** *m* intensity; degree of strength; degree of concentration; **~haltig** *a* starchy; containing starch; **~körner** *n pl* starch granules *pl*; **~mehl** *n* starch-flour; **~n** *tr* to strengthen, to brace up; to invigorate; to comfort; to refresh; (*bestärken*) to corroborate; to confirm; (*Wäsche*) to starch; *r* to take some refreshment; to fortify o. s.; **~nd** *a* strengthening; invigorating; restorative; **~nachweis** *m* statement of actual strength; **~zucker** *m* starch sugar.

Stärkung *f* strengthening; (*Erfrischung*) refreshment, recreation; (*Kräftigung*) invigoration; (*Trost*) consolation; (*Bekräftigung*) confirmation; **~smittel** *n med* restorative, tonic; *fam* pick-me-up.

starr *a* (*steif*) stiff; (*unbeweglich*) fixed; rigid; motionless; (*in ~em Zustand*) torpid; (*unbeugsam*) stern, obstinate; stubborn, austere; (*leblos*) inert, lethargic; (*vor Kälte*) numb (with cold); (*unelastisch*) inflexible; inelastic; (*vor Staunen*) dumbfounded; *jdn* ~ *ansehen* to stare at; ~ *vor Kälte* stiff with cold; ~ *vor Schrecken* paralysed with terror; *~e Aufhängung* rigid suspension; *~e Kanone aero* fixed gun; *~es Maschinengewehr* fixed machine gun; **~e** *f* stiffness, numbed state; (*Leichen~~*) cadaverous rigidity; **~en** *itr* (*an~~*) to stare at; (*er~~*) to stiffen, to get numb, to be benumbed; (~ *dastehen*) to stand out, to project; to tower; ~~ *vor* (*strotzen*) to be covered with; to be crowded with; to bristle with (difficulties,guns, gold); *vor Schmutz ~en* to be filthy; **~heit** *f* stiffness; numbed state; obstinacy; rigidity; **~kopf** *m* headstrong fellow; stubborn fellow; **~köpfig** *a*, **~sinnig** *a* headstrong; (*hartnäckig*) stubborn, obstinate; **~krampf** *m* tetanus; **~luftschiff** *n aero* rigid airship; **~schlepp** *m aero* (*Segelflugschlepp*) non-flexible connection for glider towing; **~sinn** *m* obstinacy, stubbornness; mulishness; **~sucht** *f* catalepsy; **~süchtig** *a* cataleptic.

Start *m* start; *aero* take-off; (*vom Wasser*) water take-off; (*von Rakete*) launching; *fliegender* ~ flying start; *stehender* ~ dead (*od* standing) start; ~ *mit Seitenwind* cross-wind take-off; ~ *mit ~hilfe* assisted take-off; ~ *mit Hilfe zusätzlicher Strahlmotoren* jet assisted take-off (*Abk* Jato); take-off with auxiliary jet motors; ~ *mit*

Schubraketen rocket assisted take-off (*Abk* Rato); *zum ~ rollen* to taxi to the take-off point; **~art** *f aero* take-off method; **~bahn** *f aero* (take-off) runway; tarmac; flight strip; *befestigte ~~* paved (*od* hard-surfaced) runway; *der leichte Bomber brummte die ~~ hinab, erhob sich u. verschwand* the light bomber roared down the runway, took off and disappeared; **~~feuer** *n* runway lights *pl*; **~befehl** *m aero* order to take off; **~bereit** *a aero* ready to take off; **~deck** *n aero* (*auf Schiff*) starting deck; **~einrichtung** *f* starting device; **~en** *itr* to start; *aero* to take off, to take to the air, *sl* to go upstairs; (*Veranstaltung etc*) to tee off; *tr* to launch; **~er** *m mot* (automatic) starter; **~~batterie** *f mot* starter battery; **~~klappe** *f mot* choke; **~erlaubnis** *f* permission to take off; take-off clearance; **~flagge** *f aero* starter flag; **~geld** *n sport* entrance-stake; **~genehmigung** *f* starting permit; **~hilfe** *f* starting assistance; (*Katapult*) catapult; *Abflug mit ~~* assisted take-off; *~~ mit Hilfsstrahlwerk* jet assisted take-off (*Abk* Jato); *~~ durch Schubraketen* rocket assisted take-off (*Abk* Rato); **~katapult** *n* launching catapult; **~klar** *a aero* ready for the take-off; **~kommando** *n* starting (*od* take-off) signal; **~länge** *f* take-off distance; **~leistung** *f* take-off power (*od* performance); engine output at take-off; **~loch** *n sport* starting-pit; **~mannschaft** *f* launching crew, starting crew; **~meldung** *f aero* notification of departure; **~platz** *m aero* air base; starting point; **~punkt** *m* starting point; take-off point; **~rakete** *f* booster rocket; **~schiene** *f* (*für Raketen*) starting rail; **~schleuder** *f* catapult; **~schub** *m* take-off thrust; **~schuß** *m sport* starting shot; **~seil** *n aero* (*Segelflug*) tow-rope for glider; launching rope; **~signal** *n* starting signal, take-off signal, *Am fam* go-sign; *der Kontrollturm gibt der Maschine das ~~* the tower gives the airplane the go-sign; **~strecke** *f* take-off run; **~~ u. Landebahn** *f* runway; airstrip; **~~ u. Landezone** *f aero* approach zone; runway funnel; **~verbot** *n* take-off restriction; *e-m Flugzeug ~~ geben* (*od auferlegen*) to ground an airplane; **~vermögen** *n* take-off quality (*od* performance); **~vorrichtung** *f* catapult mechanism; **~wagen** *m* starting carriage; **~weg** *m* taxi (*od* take-off) strip; **~zeichen** *n* starting signal; take-off signal; **~zeit** *f* unstick time; **~zone** *f* take-off area.

stät, **~ig** *siehe*: *stet.*

Stat|ik *f* statics (*mit sing = phys Statik, mit pl = atmosphärische Störungen im Rundfunk*); **~isch** *a* static(al).

Station *f* stage; (*Eisenbahn*) station, terminus; *Am* depot; (*Halt*) stop; *radio* station; (*im Krankenhaus*) ward; *freie ~* board and lodging; **~är** *a* stationary; static; steady; fixed; **~ieren** *tr* to station; **~sansage** *f radio* station identification; (network) signature; (*am Anfang*) sign on; (*am Schluß der Sendungen*) sign off; **~sarzt** *m* house physician; **~smelder** *m radio* station indicator; **~svorsteher** *m rail* station-master, *Am* station agent; **~swagen** *m mot* estate wagon, *Am* station car (*od* wagon); beach wagon.

Statist *m theat* supernumerary (actor); walker-on; mute; *fam* super; *film* extra; **~ik** *f* statistics *pl*; **~iker** *m* statistician; **~isch** *a* statistical; *~~e Angaben* statistical returns (*od* data).

Stativ *n* stand, foot, support; (*Dreifuß*) tripod; **~gewinde** *n* tripod socket; **~kammer** *f phot* camera on tripod; **~kopf** *m* head of tripod.

Statt *f* place, stead; *an Eides ~* in lieu of oath; *an Kindes ~ annehmen* to adopt; *vonstatten gehen* to proceed, to come off; *zustatten kommen* to be of use to, to stand in good stead.

statt *prp* instead of; in lieu of; *~ meiner* in my place.

Stätte *f* place, stead, room; *keine bleibende ~ haben* to have no fixed abode.

statt|finden, **~haben** *irr itr* to take place, to happen; **~geben** *irr itr* to allow, to permit; **~haft** *a* admissible, allowable; (*rechtlich*) lawful, legal; **~halter** *m* governor; viceroy; (*im Orient*) satrap; **~~ei** *f* government; dignity of a governor; **~~schaft** *f* governorship; **~lich** *a* fine, stately; (*ansehnlich*) commanding, imposing; comely; (*würdevoll*) portly; (*prächtig*) grand; magnificent; (*beträchtlich*) considerable; **~~keit** *f* stateliness, portliness; magnificence; dignity.

Stat|ue *f* statue; **~uieren** *tr* to maintain, to tolerate; *ein Exempel ~~* to make an example (*an* of); **~ur** *f* stature, height; figure; size; **~ut** *n* statute; regulations *pl*; *~~en pl* (*e-r Gesellschaft*) articles *pl*; *Besatzungs~~* occupation statute.

Stau *m* dynamic air pressure; (*~ung*) deceleration; stagnation; **~becken** *n* reservoir; static tank; **~damm** *m* dam; **~~böschung** *f* spill-way; **~druck** *m* pressure head; ramming pressure; atmospheric pressure; **~~düse** *f aero* air intake pipe; **~~fahrtmesser** *m aero* velocity-head speed indicator; **~~rohr** *n* pressurizing pipe; **~mauer** *f* earth damm; **~punkt** *m aero* stagnation point; **~rohr** *n aero* pitot tube; **~see** *m* reservoir; **~strahldüse** *f aero* (*Lorindüse, Strahlrohr*) athodyd; aero-thermo-dynamic duct; *Am* ramjet; **~strahlmotor, ~strahlrohr** *m aero* athodyd, *Am* ramjet; flying stovepipe; **~wasser** *n* dammed up water; static water.

Staub *m* dust, powder; (*Blüten~*) pollen; *sich aus dem ~ machen* to run off, to decamp; to make off; *Am* to beat it, *Am fam* to skedaddle; *viel ~ aufwirbeln fig* to make a great stir; to cause a flutter; *in den ~ ziehen* to degrade; **~ablagerung** *f* dust deposit; **~belästigung** *f* dust nuisance; **~besen** *m* duster; **~beutel** *m bot* anther; **~blatt** *n bot* stamen; **~bö** *f* dust squall; **~decke** *f* dust cover; **~deckel** *m* dust cap; **~dicht** *a* dustproof; **~en** *itr* to make dust; **~faden** *m* filament; *bot* stamen; **~fänger** *m* dust collector; **~filter** *n* dust filter; **~flocke** *f* fluff; **~frei** *a* dust-free, dustless; **~gefäß** *n bot* stamen; **~ig** *a* dusty, powdery; **~kamm** *m* small-tooth comb; **~kappe** *f* dust cover; **~korn** *n* dust particle; **~lappen** *m* dust cloth; **~lawine** *f* avalanche of dry snow; dust avalanche; **~luft** *f* dust-laden air; **~mantel** *m* dust-cloak, *Am* duster; **~mehl** *n* mill-dust; **~nebel** *m* dust haze; **~plage** *f* dust nuisance; **~regen** *m* spray, drizzling rain, Scotch mist; **~sauger** *m* vacuum cleaner (*od* sweeper); Hoover; cleaner; *Am fam* vac; *e-n ~~ benützen* to vacuum; **~säule** *f* sand pillar; **~sicher** *a* dustproof; **~tuch** *n* dustcloth; duster; **~wedel** *m* whisk; feather-duster; **~wolke** *f* dust cloud; **~zucker** *m* castor sugar.

stäuben *tr* to dust; to powder; (*Flüssigkeiten zer~*) to spray; *fig* (*auseinander~*) to disperse; *itr* to raise dust; to throw off spray.

stauch|en *tr* (*mit dem Fuß*) to kick, to knock; (*stoßen*) to toss, to shake; (*von Fahrzeug*) to jolt; (*Getreide*) to stook; *tech* to upset; to compress; to cobble; to forge; to beat; (*Nieten*) to clinch; **~hammer** *m* jumper; **~maschine** *f* upsetting machine; **~ung** *f tech* upsetting; shortening; cobbling; slaving.

Staude *f*, **~ngewächs** *n* bush, shrub; perennial herb; **~nartig** *a* shrublike; **~nsalat** *m* cabbage-lettuce.

stau|en *tr* (*Wasser*) to dam up, to stem; to bank up; (*Waren*) to stow (away); (*drosseln, hemmen*) to choke, to pack; to impound; *sich ~~* to be banked up, to be blocked; to be jammed, to be stopped; to jam; to block; (*Menschen*) to mass; (*Wasser*) to be dammed up, to rise; *der Verkehr ~t sich* there is a stoppage; **~er** *m* stower; *mar* stevedore; **~ung** *f* stowing; stoppage obstruction; damming up; (*Engpaß*) bottle-neck.

Stauffer|büchse *f* grease box; grease cup; **~fett** *n* cup grease.

staunen *itr* to be astonished, to wonder at; to be amazed at; *~ n* astonishment, wonder; amazement; **~swert** *a* astonishing, wonderful.

Staup|besen *m* rod, scourge; **~e** *f* (*Züchtigung*) flogging, whipping; (*Hundekrankheit*) distemper.

stäupen *tr* to whip, to scourge; to flog.

Stearin *n* stearin; **~kerze** *f* stearin-candle; **~säure** *f* stearic acid.

Stech|apfel *m* thorn-apple; **~bahn** *f* tilt-yard; **~becken** *n* (*für Kranke*) bed-pan; **~beutel** *m* (ripping) chisel; **~eisen** *n* chisel; (*Pfriem*) punch; **~kontakt** *m el* connector; **~en** *irr tr, itr* to prick, to prod; (*von Insekten*) to sting; (*von Floh, Schlangen*) to bite; (*mit Waffe*) to stab; (*Faß an~~*) to tap (cask); (*auf~~*) to puncture; (*im Kartenspiel*) to trump; *tr* (*Spargel, Torf*) to cut; (*schlachten*) to kill, to slaughter; (*Schweine*) to stick; (*in Kupfer ~~*) to engrave; (*Löcher ~~*) to pierce (holes); *es sticht mich in der Seite* I have stitches in my side; *itr* (*Sonne*) to burn; to scorch; (*Turnier*) to joust, to tilt; *in See ~~* to put to sea; *in die Augen ~~* to strike o.'s eyes; to take o.'s fancy; *Silben ~~* to be punctilious; **~end** *a fig* (*Blick*) piercing; (*Schmerz*) shooting; (*Geruch*) stinging; penetrating; **~er** *m* pricker, engraver; (*am Gewehr*) hair-trigger; **~fliege** *f* cleg, horse-fly; stinging-fly; stable-fly; **~ginster** *m bot* furze, gorse, whin; **~heber** *m* siphon; pipette; **~kahn** *m* (*Punt*) punt; **~mücke** *f* gnat, mosquito; **~palme** *f bot* holly; Christ's thorn; **~rüssel** *m* proboscis; beak; promuscis; **~schloß** *n* hair-trigger lock; **~schritt** *m mil* goose-step; **~uhr** *f* control clock; **~walze(nknopf)** *m* variable line spacer (button); **~zirkel** *m* compasses *pl*, dividers *pl*.

Steck|buchse *f el* connector socket; *tech* sleeve, bush; **~brief** *m* warrant of arrest; **~~lich** *verfolgen* to take out a warrant against s. o.; **~dose** *f* wall plug, (plug) socket; wall socket, plug box; (wall *od* electric) outlet; **~~nverbindung** *f* socket-switch connection; **~en** *m* stick, staff; **~en** *tr* to stick; to put, to place; (*pflanzen*) to set, to plant; to dibble; (*befestigen*) to fix; to pin (up); (*zusammen~~*) to fasten together; (*hinein~~*) to insert; *in Brand ~~* to set s. th. on fire, to set fire to s. th.; *mit jdm unter e-r Decke ~~* to be in cahoots; to have a secret agreement with; *ins Gefängnis* ~~ to put in prison; *Geld in etw* ~~ to invest money in; *Grenzen* ~~ to set bounds; *seine Nase in alles* ~~ to poke o.'s nose into everything; *jdn in den Sack* ~~ (*fig*) to nonplus s. o.; to outdo s. o.; *an den Spieß* ~~ to put on the spit; *in die Tasche* ~~ to put in the pocket; *sich Watte in die Ohren* ~~ to stuff cotton in o.'s ears; *jdm ein Ziel* ~~ to set s. o. an aim; to set limits to; *sich ein Ziel* ~~ to aim at; *es jdm* ~~ (*fig*) to give s. o. a hint; *es hinter jdn* ~~ to make a tool of s. o.; *itr* (*fam irr: stak*) (*sich befinden*) to be; (*verwickelt sein in*) to be involved in; (*drinnen* ~~) to be in(side); (*fest* ~~) to stick fast; (*verborgen sein*) to be hidden; to be hiding; *im Elend* ~~ to be in distress; *tief in Schulden* ~~ to be deeply (*od* up to o.'s ears) in debts; *wo* ~~ *Sie denn?* where are you? *immer zu Hause* ~~ to shut o. s. up; *da steckt's!* there's the rub! *dahinter steckt etw* I smell a rat; there's s. th. at the bottom of it; *es steckt mir in allen Gliedern* I feel sore all over; *gesteckt voll* crammed (full); **~enbleiben** *irr itr* to stick fast; to be stuck; to get stuck; to come to a standstill (*od* dead stop); (*in e-r Rede*) to break down; **~enlassen** *irr tr* (*Schlüssel im Schloß*) to leave (key in the door); *fig* to leave in the lurch; **~enpferd** *n* hobby-horse; *fig* hobby, specialty; fad, whim; crotchet; **~er** *m el* plug; *Doppel~~* two-way plug, biplug; double; *Sicherheits~~* shockproof plug; **~~schnur** *f* cord and plug; **~fassung** *f* lamp jack; **~kissen** *n* (*Tragkissen*) cushion for carrying infant; **~kontakt** *m* plug point; plug (contact); **~ling** *m*, **~reis** *n bot* cutting; shoot; layer, slip; **~nadel** *f* pin; *jdn wie e-e* ~~ *suchen* to look for s. o. high and low; **~rübe** *f* (Swedish) turnip, swede, *Am* rutabaga; **~schlüssel** *m* box-spanner; socket wrench; **~schuß** *m mil med* retained missile; (*Wunde*) lodging wound; **~stift** *m* guide pin; **~zwiebel** *f* bulb for planting.

Steg *m* (*Weg*) footpath; *Am* walkway; (*Fußgängerbrücke*) footbridge; overpass; passage; *aero* (*Holm*) web; (*Brett*) plank; *mar* (*Landungs~*) gangboard, *Am* gangplank; (*Geigen~*) bridge; (*Hosen~*) strap; *arch* fillet; *rail* (*Schienen~*) web, stem; *typ* stick; furniture; (*Brillen~*) nose saddle; bridge; **~reif** *m*; *aus dem* ~~ off-hand; off the cuff; on the spur of the moment; *aus dem* ~~ *sprechen* to speak extempore, to extemporize, *Am* to adlib; *Einschaltung aus dem* ~~ *theat* gag; **~~dichter** *m* improvisator; **~~gedicht** *n* impromptu, improvisation; **~~rede** *f* extempore speech, *Am* off-the-cuff speech.

Steh|auf *m* ,**~aufmännchen** *n* tumbler; **~bierhalle** *f* pub, (public) bar; *Am* saloon; **~bild** *n phot* still picture; **~bolzen** *m tech* stud, stay bolt; **~en** *irr itr* to stand, to be; (*von Kleidern*) to become, to suit; (*in Garnison*) to be in garrison, to be quartered; *Modell* ~~ to (serve as a) model (to); (*Schildwache*) to stand sentry; *an der Seite von etw* ~~ to stand close to s.th.; ~~ *auf* to point to; to show; to be at; *auf dieses Verbrechen steht Todesstrafe* this crime is punishable by death; *auf den Zehen* ~~ to stand on tiptoe; *es steht bei ihm* it rests with him; *in Arbeit bei jdm* ~~ to be in s. o.'s employ; *Geld bei jdm* ~~ *haben* to have deposited money with s. o.; *in Gefahr* ~~ to run a risk; *in Verdacht* ~~ to be under suspicion, to be suspected; *für etw* ~~ to vouch for, to guarantee; to answer; to be responsible for; *es steht dir frei* you are at liberty to; *offen* ~~ to be open; *still* ~~ to pause; *mil* to stand at attention; *Stillgestanden!* Attention! 'shun! *da steht mir der Verstand still* I am at my wits' end; to stand still, to stop; *die Uhr steht* the watch has stopped; *zu* ~~ *kommen* to cost; *wie steht's?* how do you do? how are you? *wie steht das Spiel?* what's the score? *wie er geht u. steht* true to life; *wie steht's damit?* what of that? *das steht Ihnen gut* it becomes you well; *es steht zu befürchten* it is to be feared; *es steht dahin* it is yet uncertain; *es steht fest, daß* ... it is beyond doubt that ...; *sich gut* ~~ to be well off, to be in easy circumstances; *sich mit jdm gut* ~~ to be in good terms with; *seinen Mann* ~~ to hold o.'s own against; *so wie die Dinge* ~~ ... as things stand; *ich weiß nicht wo mir der Kopf steht* I don't know whether I am coming or going; I am over head and ears in business; *Rede u. Antwort* ~~ to give an account; *es steht geschrieben* it is written; *was steht zu Diensten?* what can I do for you? *jdm zur Seite* ~~ to stand by s. o.; *ich stehe zu meinem Wort* I won't go back on my word; *zur Debatte* ~~ to be at issue; **~en** *n* standing; *zum* ~~ *bringen* to stop, to arrest; **~enbleiben** *irr itr* to come to a standstill; to stand still; to stop; *mot* (*Motor*) to stall; (*beim Lesen etc*) to leave off; (*nicht umfallen*) to remain standing; *der Motor blieb ~en* the engine stalled; the engine died; *Ihre Uhr ist ~engeblieben* your watch has stopped; *ich bin auf Seite 16 ~engeblieben* I left off on page 16; **~end** *a* standing; (*ständig*) permanent; regular; (*aufrecht*) upright; (*senkrecht*) vertical; (*fest*) stationary; fixed; *~~er Ausdruck* standing phrase; *~~en Fußes* at once; immediately; on the spot; *~~es Heer* standing army, regular army; *~~er Motor* vertical engine; *~~er Preis* fixed price; *~~e Redensart* hackneyed phrase, stock phrase; *~~er Satz typ* standing matter; *~~es Wasser* stagnant water; **~enlassen** *irr tr* to leave (standing); (*vergessen*) to forget, to leave; (*verlassen*) to give s. o. the slip; to walk away; (*warten lassen*) to keep standing; (*Teig, Tee etc*) to allow to stand; (*aufgeben*) to give up; *alles liegen u. ~en lassen* to drop everything; **~er** *m sport* stayer; **~~rennen** *n* stayer-race; **~kragen** *m* stand-up collar; **~lampe** *f* standard lamp, *Am* floor lamp; **~leiter** *f* step-ladder; **~platz** *m* standing-place; standing-room; *nur* ~~*!* standing-room only! (*Abk* S. R. O.); **~~inhaber** *m Am* standee; (*in Bus, U-Bahn etc*) *fam* strap-hanger; **~pult** *n* high desk, standing-desk; **~schoppen** *m* glass of beer taken at a bar; **~umlegekragen** *m* turn-down collar; **~vermögen** *n* stamina, staying power.

steh|len *irr tr, itr allg* to steal; (*wegnehmen*) to take away; to remove; to make (*od* run) off with; *jur* (*e-n Diebstahl begehen*) to commit a theft; (*sich aneignen*) to appropriate; to misappropriate; (*mit raschem Griff einstecken*) to bag; (*Menschen, bes. Kinder entführen*) to kidnap; (*geistiges Eigentum* ~~, *abschreiben*) to plagiarize, to crib; (*entwenden*) to purloin (*aus* from); (*in kleinen Mengen* ~~, *mausen*) to pilfer; (*stibitzen*) to filch; (*wegnehmen, mausen*) to lift; *fam* (*klauen* to pinch; to scrounge; *sl* to snitch; *Am sl* (*stibitzen*) to swipe; to bum; to finger; (*bes. Vieh* ~~) to rustle; *sl* to cop; (*lange Finger haben*) to have light fingers; (*gewohnheitsmäßig Diebereien begehen*) to thieve; (*unter Gewaltanwendung* ~~) to rob; (*plündern*) to plunder; to loot; to ransack; (*ausrauben*) to rifle; (~~ *durch Einbruch*) to burglarize; (*Geld etc unterschlagen*) to embezzle; *sich davon*~~ to steal away (*od* off); to sneak away (*od* off); to slink away; *sich aus dem Haus* ~~ to steal out of the house; *sich in das Zimmer* ~~ to steal into the room; *sich stillschweigend weg*~~ to steal away silently; *das gestohlene Gut* stolen goods *pl*; *Am sl* hot goods *pl*; *sie kann mir gestohlen bleiben fig fam* I will have nothing to do with her; she can go and be hanged; *Am fam* you can have her for all I care; she can go jump in the lake; *das kann mir gestohlen werden fig* I don't care two straws for it; *e-n Blick von jds Augen* ~~ to catch a look from s. o.'s eyes; *jdm das Herz* ~~ to steal away s. o.'s heart; *jdm die Ruhe* ~~ to rob s. o. of his rest; *jdm den Wind aus den Segeln* ~~ (*fig*) to steal s. o.'s thunder; *jdm die Zeit* ~~ to make s. o. lose his time; *dem lieben Gott die Zeit* ~~ to idle away o.'s time; to kill time; *du sollst nicht* ~~*!* thou shalt not steal! ~~ *wie ein Rabe* to be as thievish as a magpie; **~en** *n* stealing; theft; pilfering; robbery; (*Einbruch*) burglary; *jur* larcency; **~er** *m* thief; pilferer; robber; *jur* larcenar, larcenist; *fam* lifter; (*Einbrecher*) burglar; **~sucht** *f*, **~trieb** *m* kleptomania **~süchtig** *a* kleptomaniac: **~süchtige(r)** *m* kleptomaniac.

steier|isch *a* Styrian; **~land** *n*, **~mark** *f* Styria; **~märker** *m*, **~märkisch** *a* Styrian.

steif *a* (*straff, starr, unbeweglich*) stiff; (*bes. phys*) rigid; (*nicht biegsam*) inflexible; (*fest*) firm; non-yielding; (*erstarrt*) numb, benumbed; (*Flüssigkeit, Teig etc*) thick; (*männliches Glied*) erect; (*hölzern, unbeweglich*) wooden; (*linkisch*) awkward; (*schwerfällig*) heavy; (*geziert*) strained; (*zurückhaltend, reserviert*) reserved; (*pedantisch*) pedantic; (*förmlich*) formal, ceremonious; ~ *u. fest* obstinately, firmly, stubbornly, strongly; ~ *u. fest behaupten* to persist in saying; to maintain obstinately, *Am fam* to swear up and down (that); *die Ohren* ~ *halten fig sl* to keep o.'s peckers up; to pluck up courage; ~ *machen*, ~ *werden* to stiffen; ~ *sein vor Kälte* to be stiff with cold; ~ *wie ein Bock* as stiff as a poker; *sich in allen Gliedern* ~ *fühlen* to be stiff all over; *~es Auftreten* stiff manner; *~e Brise* strong breeze; *~e Finger* (*vor Kälte*) benumbed fingers; (*dauernd*) stiff fingers; *~er Grog* strong (*od* stiff) grog; *~e Haltung* stiff bearing; *~er Hals med* stiff-neck, wryneck; *~er Hut* bowler (hat), *Am* derby; *~er Kragen* stiff collar; *~es Lächeln* forced smile; *~er Nacken fig* stiff neck; *~er Wind* stiff breeze, strong gale; **~e** *f* stiffness; rigidity; (*Stärke*) starch; *tech* (*Stempel, Stütze*) prop; strut; brace; stay; supporter; **~en** *tr* to stiffen; (*Wäsche*) to starch; (*stützen*) to prop; *jdm den Rücken* ~~ *fig* to back s. o. up; *sich auf etw* ~~ to insist on, to persist in, to make it a point to; **~heit** *f* stiffness; rigidity; stability; inflexibility; *fig* formality, constraint; **~leinen** *a* buckram; stiffening; *fig* (*Person*) strait-laced; dull; **~leinen** *n*, **~leinwand** *f* buckram;

~nackig *a* stiff-necked; *fig* stubborn; **~ung** *f* stiffening; *tech* prop; **~werden** *n* stiffening, hardening; (*Glied*) erection.

Steig *m* (*Pfad*) path; footpath; **~bö** *f aero* bump; ascending (*od* rising) gust; **~~enanzeiger** *m* vertical gust recorder; **~brunnen** *m* artesian well; **~bügel** *m* stirrup; **~~riemen** *m* stirrup-strap; **~e** *f* (*steile Stiege, Treppe*) steep staircase; steep stairs *pl*; (*Leiter*) ladder; (*steiler Weg*) ascent, ascending road; gradient, *Am* grade; (*Zauntritt*) stile; (*Hühner~~*) hen-roost; **~eigenschaft** *f* climbing quality; **~eisen** *n* (*zum Klettern*) climbing iron; crampon; (*Haken*) grapnel; **~en** *irr itr* (*hinaufklettern, aero*) to climb; (*hinauf~~*) to ascend; (*sich nach oben bewegen: Barometer, Temperatur, Preise, Wasser etc*) to rise; (*auf~~*) to mount; to go up; to scale; (*anwachsen, zunehmen*) to increase; to grow; to advance; (*Wasser*) to swell, to rise; (*Preise*) to rise, to go up; to run up; to move upward; to improve; to advance; (*schnell u. hoch an~~*) *Am fam* to rocket, to skyrocket; (*hinab~~*) to get down; to descend; (*sich bäumen von Pferden*) to prance, to rear; (*Teig*) to swell, to rise; (*Blut in den Kopf*) to rush; (*in die Luft ~~*) to fly, to soar; (*in Schiff, Flugzeug, Wagen ~~*) to board, to enter; (*vom Nebel*) to lift, to dissipate; *fig* (*zornig werden*) to lose o.'s temper; *~~ lassen* (*Drachen*) to fly (a kite); (*Rakete*) to launch (a rocket); *die Aktien ~~* the shares rise; *aus dem Bett ~~* to get out of bed; *jdm aufs Dach ~~* (*fam*) to come down upon s. o.; *in den* (*od zu*) *Kopf ~~* to go to o.'s head; *an Land ~~* to go ashore; *zu Pferd ~~* to mount a horse; *vom Pferd ~~* to dismount; *aus dem Wagen ~~* to descend from, to get out of, to step out of (a car); **~en** *n* (*der Preise*) rise, advance, increase (in prices); (*in die Höhe*) climb, climbing; (*Aufstieg*) ascent; (*Kurse*) upward movement; *auf ~~ spekulieren* to go in (*od* to buy) for a rise; (*Wasser*) swell, rise, rising; (*Flug nach oben*) upward flight; *aero* climbing; *das ~~ u. Fallen* (*Preise, Kurse*) fluctuation, ups and downs; *fig* the rise and fall; (*Zunahme*) increase, augmentation; (*Tendenz nach oben*) upward tendency; *ihr Stern ist im ~~* (*fig*) her star is in the ascendant; **~end** *a* (*an~~, wachsend*) growing; rising; increasing; gradient; *~~e Tendenz* upward tendency; *~~e Potenz* ascending power; **~er** *m min* mine inspector, deputy, foreman, captain, *Am* district boss; overman; (*Feuerwehr*) fireman; *tech* riser (gate); vent; **~erer** *m* (*bei Auktion*) bidder; (*Börse*) bull; **~ern** *tr* (*Preise*) to raise, to increase; to advance; (*verstärken*) to enhance; to push up; to run up; to drive up; (*erhöhen*) to heighten; (*intensivieren, hochtreiben*) to intensify; to force up; to step up; to screw up; (*zufügen*) to add to; (*bei Auktionen*) to bid; to outbid; to buy at an auction; *gram* (*Eigenschaftswort ~~*) to compare; *sich ~~* to go up; to increase; to run up to; to work up; to intensify; **~erung** *f* raising; rise; increase; advance; heightening; intensification; boost; (*rednerisch*) climax; gradation; (*Wert~~*) increment; *gram* comparison; **~~sgrad** *m gram* degree of comparison; **~fähigkeit** *f* climbing ability (*od* power *od* capacity *od* quality); **~flug** *m aero* climbing flight; climb; zooming; *steiler ~~* steep climb; (*Aufstieg*) ascent; **~geschwindigkeit** *f aero* climbing speed; rate of climb; **~~smesser** *m aero* rate-of-climb indicator; **~höhe** *f aero* height of climb; ceiling; (*Geschoß*) vertical range; **~kurve** *f* climb curve; **~leistung** *f* climb power; rate of climb; **~leiter** *f* ladder; **~leitung** *f* (*Wasser etc*) ascending pipe-line, feedpipe, standpipe; *el* rising main, *Am* riser; **~messer** *m aero* climb indicator; **~rad** *n* (*Uhr*) ratchet wheel; **~rohr** *n* ascending pipe-line, feedpipe, standpipe; rising main, *Am* riser; **~stromvergaser** *m mot* updraft carburet(t)or; **~ung** *f* rise, rising; increase; (*Anstieg*) ascent; (*Hang*) slope, hill; (*Neigung*) inclination; (*e-r Straße, Bahn etc*) gradient, *Am* grade; upgrade; (*Feder, Schraube, Luftschraube*) lead; pitch; **~~smesser** *m* (in)clinometer; gradient indicator; **~~swinkel** *m* angle of inclination; climbing angle; (*Schraube*) helix angle; pitch angle; **~vermögen** *n aero* climbing ability; **~winkel** *m* angle of climb; *aero* flight-path angle; **~zeit** *f* rate of climb.

steil *a* steep; (*~ abfallend*) precipitous; abrupt; *~ abfallen* to plunge; *~er Abhang* steep slope (*od* gradient); *~es Dach* high roof; *~er Kurvenflug aero* steep (climbing) turn; *~es Ufer* steep coast, bluff; (*felsig*) steep rocky shore; **~abfall** *m* abrupt drop; steep gradient; **~aufnahme** *f aero phot* low-oblique photograph; **~feuer** *n mil* high-angle fire; **~~geschütz** *n*, **~~kanone** *f* high-angle gun; **~flug** *m aero* climbing flight; vertical flight; **~hang** *m* steep (*od* abrupt) slope; **~heit** *f* steepness; (*e-r Kurve*) slope; *radio* (*e-r Röhre*) mutual conductance; slope of the emission, *Am* transconductance; (*Film*) contrast; **~kurve** *f aero* steep turn: vertical bank; sharp curve; (*in Bodennähe*) ground loop; *e-e ~~ fliegen* (*od sl drehen*) to make a steep turn; **~küste** *f* steep coast; shelving coast; **~schrift** *f* vertical writing; **~strahlung** *f* space radiation; **~trudeln** *n aero* spin; **~ufer** *n* steep bank, bluff shore.

Stein *m* stone; *Am* (*~ jeglicher Größe*) rock; *Engl* (*Felsgestein, großer ~*) rock; (*Edel~*) precious stone; gem; jewel; (*Spiel~*) piece; man; domino; (*künstlicher ~, Bau~, Ziegel~*) brick; (*Feuer~*) flint; *tech* (*Kulisse*) block; (*Schwefelverbindung mit Erz*) matte; *med* calculus; gravel; (*Grab~*) gravestone; (*Denkmal, Ehrenmal*) memorial; *bot* kernel, stone; (*Bierkrug*) mug, *Am* stein; *der ~ des Anstoßes fig* stumbling-block; *der ~ der Weisen* philosophers' stone; *e-e Uhr mit 10 ~en* a watch with ten jewels; *über Stock u. ~* through thick and thin; *~ u. Bein frieren* to freeze hard; *~ u. Bein schwören* to swear by all that is sacred (*od* by all the Gods); *Am fam* to swear on a stack of bibles; *bei jdm e-n ~ im Brett haben* to be in s. o.'s good books; to be in good with s. o.; *e-n ~ auf dem Herzen haben* to have s. th. weighing on o.'s mind; *es fällt mir ein ~ vom Herzen* a great weight is taken off my mind; that takes a load off my mind; *den ~ ins Rollen bringen fig* to start the ball rolling; *keinen ~ auf dem anderen lassen* not to leave one stone upon another; *jdm ~e in den Weg legen fig* to put obstacles in s. o.'s way; *~e nach jdm werfen* to throw stones at s. o.; *den ersten ~ auf jdn werfen* to cast the first stone at s. o.; *in ~ verwandeln, zu ~ werden* to petrify; *das ist wie ein Tropfen auf e-n heißen ~ fig* that is altogether insufficient; that is only a drop in the bucket; *wer im Glashaus sitzt, soll nicht mit ~en werfen prov* people (who live) in glass-houses shouldn't throw (with) stones; **~abdruck** *m typ* lithographic print; **~acker** *m* stony field; **~adler** *m* golden eagle; **~alt** *a* very old; old as the hills; **~artig** *a* stony; stone-like; **~axt** *f hist* stone-axe; **~bank** *f* stone bench; **~bau** *m* stone structure; **~~kasten** *m* box of bricks; **~bearbeitung** *f* stone-working; **~beschreibung** *f* petrography; **~beschwerden** *f pl med* calculous disease; **~bettung** *f* stone bedding; roadbed; **~bild** *n* statue; **~bildung** *f* stone formation; *med* lithiasis; **~bock** *m* ibex; *astr* Capricorn; **~boden** *m* stony soil; (*im Haus*) stone floor; **~bohrer** *m* rock drill; stone bit; wall chisel; **~brech** *bot m* stonebreak, saxifrage; **~brecher** *m* (*Maschine*) crushing machine, jaw (*Am* rock) crusher; (*Person*) quarryman; **~bruch** *m* quarry; stone-pit; **~~arbeiter** *m* quarryman; **~butt** *m* turbot; **~chen** *n* little stone; pebble; **~damm** *m mar* pier, mole; paved road; **~druck** *m* lithography; (*Bild*) lithograph; **~drucker** *m* lithographer; **~~ei** *f* lithography; lithographic printing; **~eiche** *f* holm-oak; **~erbarmen** *n*: *das ist zum ~~* it is enough to melt a heart of stone; **~ern** *a* stone, *fig* stony; **~flachs** *m* asbestos; **~frucht** *f*, **~obst** *n* stone-fruit, drupe; **~galle** *f min* stone-gall; (*bei Pferden*) vessignon, windgall; **~garten** *m* rock-garden; **~gerölle** *n* rubble; **~gut** *n* earthenware, crockery; stoneware; **~hagel** *m* shower of stones; **~hart** *a* hard as stone, stone-hard; **~hauer** *m* stone-mason; **~haufen** *m* heap of stones; (*Steingrab*) cairn; **~holz** *n* xylolith; **~hügel** *m* stony hill; (*Grab*) cairn; **~ig** *a* stony, rocky; **~igen** *tr* to stone; **~igung** *f* stoning; **~kenner** *m* mineralogist; **~kies** *m* sulphurous pyrites *pl*; **~kitt** *m* mastic cement; **~klopfer** *m* stone-breaker, crusher; **~kohle** *f* pit-coal, hard coal, mineral coal, bituminous coal, stone coal, sea coal, *Am auch* soft coal; **~~nbergwerk** *n*, **~~ngrube** *f* coal-mine, coal-pit, coal-works *pl*; colliery; **~~nfeld** *n* coal-field; **~~nflöz** *n* coal-bed, coal-seam; **~~ngas** *n* coal-gas; **~~nkraftwerk** *n* pit-coal power station; **~~nlager** *n* coal-deposit; **~~nöl** *n* coal-tar oil; **~~nschacht** *m* shaft of a coal-mine; **~~nschicht** *f* coal-seam; **~~nschwelung** *f* coal carbonization; **~~nstaub** *m* coal-dust; **~~nteer** *m* coal-tar; **~~nverkokung** *f* coal carbonization; **~~nvorkommen** *n* coal-deposit (*od* -area *od* -region); **~krug** *m* stone bottle (*od* jar *od* pitcher); **~marder** *m* beech-marten; **~mark** *n* stone-marrow; **~meißel** *m* tooler; stone-mason's chisel; **~metz** *m* stone-mason; **~öl** *n* petroleum; **~pflaster** *n* (stone) pavement; **~pilz** *m* yellow boletus; **~platte** *f* slab, flag; **~quader** *m* dressed stone; **~reich** *a fig* enormously rich; *~~ sein* to roll in riches (*od* wealth); *~~ n* mineral kingdom; **~salz** *n* mineral salt, rock-salt; **~schicht** *f* layer, stratum; **~schlag** *m* avalanche of stones; (*Straßenschotter*) broken stone, riprap; crushed rock; **~schleifer** *m* stone-polisher; **~schloß** *n* flint-lock; **~schmerzen** *pl* stone-colic; **~schneider** *m* lapidary; **~schnitt** *m med* lithotomy; **~schotter** *m* macadam; *mit ~~ belegen* to macadamize; **~schrift** *f* lapidary inscription; **~setzer** *m* stone-layer, paviour, paver; **~stoßen** *n sport* putting the stone; **~tafel** *f* slab; **~verkleidung** *f* facing; **~weg** *m* causeway;

-wein *m* Franconian wine; **-wurf** *m* stone's throw; **-zeichnung** *f typ* lithograph; **-zeit** *f* stone age; *ältere* ~~ pal(a)eolithic period; *jüngere* ~~ neolithic period; **-zeug** *n* = *-gut.*

Steiper *m dial* support, prop; stay; **-n** *tr* to prop, to stay; to support.

Steiß *m* backside, posteriors *pl*; buttocks *pl*; (*von Vögel*) rump; **-bein** *n* coccyx; **~-wirbel** *m anat* coccygeal vertebra; **-geburt** *f med* breech delivery; **-lage** *f med* breech presentation.

Stell|age *f* stand, frame; rack; contrivance; (*Börse*) straddle; *Am* spread eagle; **-bar** *a* movable, regulating; **-dichein** *n* meeting, rendezvous; appointment; *Am fam* date; ~~ *mit e-m* (*od e-r*) *Unbekannten Am fam* blind date; ~~ *von zwei Paaren Am fam* double date; *ein wichtiges* ~~ (*Am fam*) a heavy (date) *Partner e-s* ~~ (*Am fam*) date, datee, date-up, meetee; *ein* ~~ *mit jdm verabreden Am fam* to date (a girl); to date up, to have a date, to make a date; *ein* ~~ *nicht einhalten* not to keep an appointment, *Am fam* to break a date, to stand s. o. up.

Stell|e *f* place; (*Fleck*) spot; (*Standpunkt*) stand; point; (*Lage*) position; location; (*Bau*~~) site; (*Arbeits*~~) post; job; place; employment; appointment; occupation; (*Rang*) rank; position; (*Dienstboten*~~) situation; (*Buch*~~) passage (in book); (*Zitat*) quotation; quote; (*Behörde*) office, authority, *Am* agency; *math* digit; figure; *e-e angenehme* ~~ a soft job; *e-e schlechte* ~~ (*an etw*) defect; fault; flaw; *schwache* ~~ weak spot; *ein Bericht von Ort u.* ~~ on-the-scene report; *an meiner* ~~ in my place; *wenn ich an Ihrer* ~~ *wäre* if I were you; if I were in your position; *an* ~~ *von* instead of, in place of; in lieu of; *an Ort u.* ~~ *sein* to be on the spot; *an jds* ~~ *treten* to take the place of; to replace s. o.; *an e-r beliebigen* ~~ at any point; *auf der* ~~ at once, immediately; there and then, then and there; on the spot; right this minute; straight (*Am* right) away; *gerade auf dieser* ~~ in this very place; *auf der* ~~ *treten* to mark time; *ohne* ~~ *sein* to be unemployed, to be out of work; *fam* to be (*od* to go) on the dole; *sich um e-e* ~~ *bewerben* to apply for a situation; *sich nicht von der* ~~ *rühren* not to stir; *von der* ~~ *kommen* to get on, to make progress; *zur* ~~ *schaffen* to produce; *zur* ~~ *sein* to be present; to be at hand; to be available; *zur* ~~*!* here! *an erster* ~~ in the first place, first and foremost; *offene* ~~, *freie* ~~ vacancy; vacant post (*od* situation); open position; ~~ *gesucht* position desired; situation wanted; appointment wanted; **-en** *tr* to put; to set; to place; to stand; (*auf*~~) to arrange; to range; (*besorgen, zur Verfügung* ~~, *liefern*) to furnish, to provide; to supply; (*bereit*~~) to prepare; to get ready; (*regulieren, ein*~~) to regulate; to adjust; (*fest*~~) to establish; to ascertain; (*herausfordern*) to challenge; (*Feind* ~~) to engage; (*anhalten*) to stop; (*verhaften*) to arrest; (*abfangen bes. von feindlichen Flugzeugen*) to intercept; (*in die Enge treiben*) to corner; *sicher*~~ to guarantee; to warrant; to secure; *zufrieden*~~ to satisfy s. o., to content s. o.; *sich* ~~ to stand; to place o. s.; to present o. s.; to come forward; to take up o.'s stand; (*der Polizei*) to give o. s. up (to the police); *mil* (*den Rekrutierungsstellen*) to enlist; (*sich* ~~ *als ob, sich ver*~~, *vorgeben*) to feign, to sham; to pretend; to make believe; to make a show of; *sich krank* ~~ to feign sickness; *sich* ~~ *auf* (*com*) to cost; to amount to; to come to; *der Preis stellt sich auf* ... the price is ...; *sich jdm an die Seite* ~~ to side with s. o.; *sich gut* (*schlecht*) ~~ *mit jdm* to be on good (bad) terms with s. o.; to get on well (badly) with s. o.; *sich feindlich* ~~ *gegen jdn* to take up a hostile attitude towards s. o.; *sich dem Gericht* ~~ to surrender to justice; *sich* ~~ *zu* to behave towards; *sich zur Verfügung* ~~ to put o. s. at s. o.'s disposal; *auf sich selbst gestellt sein* to be dependent on o. s.; *gut gestellt sein* to be well off, *Am fam* to be well fixed; *in Abrede* ~~ to deny, to disclaim; *e-n Antrag* ~~ (*parl*) to put a motion; to move; *e-e Aufgabe* ~~ to set a task; *jdm ein Bein* ~~ to trip s. o. up; *Bedingungen* ~~ to make conditions; *Bürgen* ~~ to find bail (*od* security); *e-e Falle* ~~ to lay a snare; to set a trap; *e-e Frage* ~~ to ask a question; *in Frage* ~~ to call in question; *Kaution* ~~ to put up bail; *auf den Kopf* ~~ to turn upside down; *auf die Probe* ~~ to put to test; *nach dem Leben* ~~ to attempt s. o.'s life; *Preise* ~~ to fix (*od* to quote) prices; *in Rechnung* ~~ to put to account, to charge, to debit; *zur Rede* ~~ to call to account; *Sicherheit* ~~ to provide security; *Termin* ~~ to fix a time (*od* date), to appoint a day (*od* time); *die Uhr* ~~ to set the watch; *zur Verfügung* ~~ to place at o.'s disposal; *zum Verkauf* ~~ to offer (*od* to expose) for sale; *Zeugen* ~~ to produce witnesses; **-enangebot** *n* position (*od* situation) offered; vacancy; **-enanzeige** *f* (*in der Presse*) advertisement for a situation, *Am* advertisement for a position; **-enbewerber** *m* applicant; **-engesuch** *n* application for a place (*od* situation *od* post *od* job); **-enjagd** *f* place-hunting, *Am* job hunting; **-enjäger** *m* place-hunter, *Am* office-seeker; job hunter; **-enlos** *a* unemployed, out of work; *Am auch* jobless; **-enmarkt** *m* employment market; **-ennachweis** *m* employment agency; employment exchange; **-envermittler** *m* employment agent; **-envermittlung** *f* Labour Exchange; (*für Dienstboten*) registry-office; **-enweise** *adv* here and there, in places; sporadically; in parts; **-enzahl** *f math* number of digits; atomic number; **-hebel** *m* switch lever; **-macher** *m* wheelwright; wainwright, cartwright; **~-ei** *f* wheelwright's shop; **-marke** *f* marker; index; **-mutter** *f* lock-nut; adjusting nut; **-netz** *n* anchored net; **-schlüssel** *m tech* adjusting-spanner (*od* key); adjusting wrench; **-schraube** *f* adjusting screw; set screw; **-stift** *m* (*bei Regal*) shelf-peg; **-ung** *f* position; (*Lage*) situation; station; (*Ansehen*) standing; (*Beruf*) place; employment, job, situation; position; *dienstliche* ~~ official capacity; (*Rang*) rank, status; (*Haltung, Körper*~~) posture; attitude; *mil* (*Front*~~) line; position; trenches *pl*; *mil* (*Geschütz*~~) emplacement; *mil* (*rückwärtige* ~~) rearward position; (*vorgeschobene* ~~) advanced position; (*Anordnung*) arrangement; *seine* ~~ *behaupten* to stand o.'s ground; to hold a position; ~~ *beziehen* to move into a position; *in* ~~ *bringen* to (bring into) position; ~~*nehmen zu* to express o.'s opinion on; **~-nahme** *f* (*Äußerung*) comment; (*Ansicht*) opinion expressed; (*Haltung*) attitude; (*Entscheid*) decision; **~-sbau** *m* construction of a position; **~-sbauten** *pl mil* fortifications *pl*; **~-sbefehl** *m mil* call-up; calling-up; enlisting order; **~-sgesuch** *n* application for a post; (*in Zeitung*) *pl* situations wanted; **~-skampf** *m mil* position warfare; **~-skrieg** *m* trench warfare, war of position; static warfare, positional warfare; **~-slos** *a* unemployed, without a job; **~-spflichtig** *a* liable to enlistment; **~-swechsel** *m* change (*od* shift) of position; **-vertretend** *a* vicarious; delegated; (*amtlich*) acting, deputy, vice-; ~~*er Vorsitzender* vice-chairman; ~~*er Geschäftsführer* deputy managing director; **-vertreter** *m* representative; *mil* second in command; (*amtlicher*) deputy; (*Bevollmächtigter*) proxy; (*Ersatzmann*) substitute; **-vertretung** *f* representation; deputyship; substitution; agency; *in* ~~ in place of, as deputy; by proxy; **-vorrichtung** *f* adjusting gear (*od* device); **-wagen** *m* coach; omnibus, bus; **-werk** *n rail* signal box, *Am* switchtower; switch operating station.

Stelz|bein *n* (*Holzbein*) wooden leg; very long and thin leg; **-beinig** *a* with a wooden leg; stiff-legged; **-e** *f* stilt; *auf -en gehen* to walk on stilts; **-en** *itr* to walk on stilts; *fam* (*lang ausschreiten*) to stalk along; **-enläufer** *m* stilt-walker; **-enwurzel** *f bot* stilt (*od* prop) root; **-fuß** *m* wooden leg; **-vögel** *m pl* grallatores *pl*.

Stemm|bogen *m* (*Schisport*) stem turn; **-eisen** *n* (*zum Heben von Lasten etc*) crowbar; (*Holzbearbeitung*) (mortise) chisel; ca(u)lking iron; **-en** *tr* (*stützen, abstützen*) to prop, to support; (*hoch*~~) to lever up; (*Gewicht* ~~) to lift; *tech* (*Löcher*) to chisel (out); to ca(u)lk; (*Wasser etc abdämmen*) to stem; to dam up; *die Hände in die Seiten* ~~ to set o.'s arms akimbo; *sich* ~~ *gegen* (*dagegendrücken*) to lean firmly against; to brace o. s. against; (*sich auflehnen*) to oppose; to resist; **-fahren** *n* (*Schisport*) stemming; **-schwung** *m* (*Schisport*) stem christiania.

Stempel *m allg* stamp; (*Datum*~) date stamp; (*Gummi*~) rubber stamp; (*Präge*~, *Münz*~) die; (*Loch*~) punch; (*Post*~) postmark; (*Stößel*) pestle; (*Abstützbalken*) post, strut; *min* prop, stay; stemple, stanchion; (*eingebrannter* ~) brand; (*Echtheits*~ *auf Gold, Silber*) hall-mark; (*Pumpen*~, *Pressen*~) piston; ram; *bot* pistil; *fig* (*Abdruck, Eindruck, Zeichen*) mark, impression; stamp; *nicht gültig ohne* ~ not valid without stamp; **-abdruck** *m* impression of a stamp; **-abgabe** *f* (*Gebühr*) stamp duty; **-amt** *n* stamp-office; **-bogen** *m* stamped sheet of paper; **-farbe** *f* stamping ink; **-frei** *a* free from stamp duty, *Am* tax exempt; **-gebühr** *f* stamp duty; **-holz** *n min* pit prop; **-kissen** *n* ink-pad, stamp-pad; stamp-ink cushion; **-marke** *f* (duty) stamp; **-n** *tr* to stamp, to mark; (*mit Zeichen versehen*) to letter, to brand, to mark; *-n gehen fam* to be (*od* go) on the dole; **-papier** *n* stamped paper; **-pflichtig** *a* subject to stamp duty; **-schneider** *m* stamp-cutter, die-sinker; **-ung** *f* stamping; **-zeichen** *n* stamp; mark.

Stengel *m* stalk, stem.

Steno|gramm *n* shorthand report (*od* note); ~~ *aufnehmen* to take down in shorthand; **-graph** *m* shorthand writer, *Am* stenographer; **~-ie** *f* stenography, shorthand; **-graphieren** *tr, itr* to write shorthand; to write in shorthand; to take shorthand; **~graphiermaschine** *f* stenotype, stenograph; **~graphisch** *a* shorthand, stenographic; *adv* in shorthand; **~typist** *m*, **~~in** *f* (shorthand) typist, *Am* stenographer (*Abk* stenog).

Stentorstimme *f* stentorian voice.

Step *m* (*Tanzschritt*) step; **~pen** *tr* to step; **~tanz** *m* step dance; **~tänzer** *m*, **~~in** *f* step dancer, *Am sl* stepper; hoofer.

Stepp|decke *f* (*wattierte ~~*) wadded quilt, *Am* comforter, comfortable; *elektrisch beheizte ~~* electric comforter; **~en** *tr* to quilt, to stitch; **~erei** *f* quilting, stitched work; **~nadel** *f* quilting-needle; **~naht** *f* quilting-seam; **~stich** *m* quilting-stitch; (*Nähmaschine*) backstitch, lockstitch.

Steppe *f* steppe; *Am* prairie; **~enbewohner** *m* inhabitant of the steppes; **~enwolf** *m* coyote; prairie wolf.

Sterb|ealter *n* age of the deceased person; **~ebeihilfe** *f* death grant; **~ebett** *n* death-bed; **~efall** *m* a death; decease; **~egebet** *n* prayer for a dying person; **~egeld** *n* death benefit; funeral allowance; **~egesang** *m* funeral hymn; **~egewand** *n* winding-sheet, shroud; **~eglocke** *f* funeral bell; **~ehaus** *n* house of mourning; **~ehemd** *n siehe: ~egewand*; **~ejahr** *n* year of s. o.'s death; **~ekasse** *f* burial fund, burial club; **~eliste** *f* register of deaths; bill of mortality; **~en** *irr itr* to die (*an* of; *für* for; *durch* by; *vor* with); to decease; to expire; to depart; to pass away; to breathe o.'s last; *fam* to go off, *Am fam* to step out; *sl* to pop off, *sl* to push up daisies, *sl* to kick the bucket; (*euphemistisch*) to go the way of all flesh, *Am* to go to the long rest; to go West; *e-s natürlichen Todes ~~* to die a natural death; *Hungers ~~* to die of hunger; *an Krebs ~~* to die of cancer; *aus Gram ~~* to die with grief; *in Armut u. Elend ~~* to die in misery; *vor Langeweile ~~* to be bored to death; *~~ vor Lachen* to die with laughing; **~en** *n* death, dying; decease; mortality; epidemic; *das große ~~* the great plague; *im ~~ liegen* to be dying; *es ist zum ~~ zuviel u. zum Leben zuwenig* it's just enough to keep the wolf from the door; **~end** *a* dying; **~ensangst** *f* terrible agony; **~enskrank** *a* dangerously ill; **~ensmüde** *a* tired to death; **~enswort, ~enswörtchen** *n*: *kein ~~* not a single word, not a syllable; **~esakramente** *n pl* last sacraments *pl*; **~estunde** *f* hour of s. o.'s death **~etag** *m* death-day, dying day; **~eurkunde** *f* death certificate; **~ezeit** *f* time of s. o.'s death; **~ezimmer** *n* death-chamber; **~lich** *a* mortal; *~~ verliebt* desperately in love; head over ears in love; *fam* madly in love with; crazy about; *Am fam* dead gone on; **~~keit** *f* mortality; **~~keitsziffer** *f* death-rate.

Stereo|aufnahme *f phot* stereo-(photo)graph; **~chemie** *f* stereochemistry; **~graphie** *f* descriptive geometry; **~kamera** *f phot* stereoscopic camera; **~metrie** *f* stereometry; solid geometry; **~photographie** *f* stereoscopic photography; **~skop** *n* stereoscope; **~skopisch** *a* stereoscopic; **~telemeter** *n* stereoscopic range finder; **~typ** *a* stereotype; *fig* stereotyped; *~~e Wendung gram* cliché; **~typausgabe** *f typ* stereotype edition; **~typieren** *tr* to stereotype.

steril *a* sterile; **~isation** *f* sterilization; **~isator** *m* sterilizer; **~isierapparat** *m* sterilizer; **~isieren** *tr* to sterilize; (*Milch*) to heat-treat; **~isierung** *f* sterilization; **~ität** *f* sterility.

Stern *m* star; (*Augen~*) pupil; *fig* destination, fate; (*Ordens~*) cross; *typ* asterisk; (*Bühnen~, Film~*) star; (*Straßenkreuzung vieler Straßen*) circus; (*des Schiffes*) stern; *auf die ~e bezüglich* stellar; sidereal; *mit ~en besät* glittering with stars; starry; *unter e-m glücklichen ~ geboren sein* to be born unter a lucky star; *~e schießen* (*Navigation*) to take bearings on the stars; **~anbeter** *m* star-worshipper; **~besät** *a* starry; **~bild** *n* constellation, sign (of the zodiac); **~blume** *f* aster; **~chen** *n* little star, starlet; *typ* asterisk; **~deuter** *m* astrologer; **~deuterkunst, ~deutung** *f* astrology; **~enbanner** *n* star-spangled banner; stars and stripes *pl*; *Am fam* Old Glory, Old Flag; **~enzelt** *n poet* starry sky; **~fahrt** *f mot* motor rally; **~flug** *m aero* aviation rally, star flight; **~förmig** *a* radial; star-shaped; stellar; **~gucker** *m* stargazer; **~hagelbesoffen, ~hagelvoll** *a fam* dead drunk; **~haufen** *m* star cluster; **~hell, ~klar** *a* star-light, starlit, starry; **~himmel** *m* starry sky; **~jahr** *n* sidereal year; **~karte** *f* celestial chart; **~kunde** *f* astronomy; **~kundige(r)** *m* astronomer; **~kundlich** *a* astronomical; **~leuchtkugel** *f mil* star shell; **~licht** *n* starry light; astral rays *pl*; **~motor** *m* radial engine; **~punkt** *m* neutral point; **~rad** *n* star wheel; turnstile; **~schaltung** *f el* R connection; **~schnuppe** *f* shooting star, falling star; **~~nschwarm** *m* meteor shower; **~stunde** *f* sidereal hour; **~tag** *m* sidereal day; **~übersät** *a* studded with stars; **~warte** *f* observatory; **~zeit** *f* sidereal time.

Sterz *m*, **~e** *f* (*Schwanz, Steiß*) tail, rump; (*Pflug~*) plough-tail, plough-handle.

stet, **~ig** *a* steady, fixed, stable; continual, constant; perpetual; **~igkeit** *f* steadiness, constancy; continuity; **~s** *adv* (*immer*) always, ever, for ever; (*ständig*) constantly, continually.

Steuer[1] *n mar* (*Ruder*) rudder, helm; *mot* (*Lenkrad*) steering wheel, wheel; *aero* controls *pl*, control surface; *Höhen~* elevator; *Seiten~* rudder; **~anlage** *f* steering mechanism; **~ausschlag** *m* control deflection; **~bar** *a* (*lenkbar, leitbar*) steerable, controllable; manageable; manœuvrable, *Am* maneuverable; **~~keit** *f* manœuvrability, *Am* maneuverability; handling; **~betätigung** *f* actuating mechanism; **~bord** *a* starboard; **~~motor** *m* starboard motor (*od* engine); right side (*od* right hand) engine; **~bühne** *f* platform; **~diagramm** *n* (*für Ventile*) valve-timing diagram; **~drossel** *f radio* modulating choke; **~druck** *m aero* control pressure; **~eigenschaften** *f pl* handling qualities *pl*; **~fläche** *f aero* control surface; stabilizing surface; rudder surface; vane; **~~n** *pl* flying controls *pl*, *Am* surface controls *pl*; **~flosse** *f* fin, *Am* vertical stabilizer; **~flügel** *m* (*bei Bombe, Rakete*) control fin, bomb fin; **~gelenk** *n* steering knuckle; **~gerät** *n* steering gear, control gear; *aero* (*Selbst~~*) gyropilot, auto-pilot, automatic pilot; **~gitter** *n radio* control grid; shield; **~hebel** *m* operating lever, control lever, steering lever; *aero* stick; **~knüppel** *m aero* control column, *Am* control stick; *fam* (joy-) stick; **~kolben** *m* control piston; **~kompaß** *m* steering compass; **~kurs** *m* compass course, steered course; **~lastig** *a aero* control heavy; **~leistung** *f mot* rating horsepower; **~mann** *m* helmsman; man at the wheel, *Am* wheelman; (*als Titel*) mate; **~n** *tr mar* to steer; to navigate; *mar, aero* to pilot; *mot* to drive; (*regulieren*) to control; to regulate; *e-e Sache ~~* to check s. th.; to repress s. th.; to prevent s. th.; **~nocken** *m* cam; **~organ** *n* control; control surface; **~rad** *n mot* (steering) wheel; *das ~~ übernehmen* to take the wheel; *aero* control wheel; **~rose** *f aero* pointer of auto-pilot; **~ruder** *n* rudder; helm; **~~ausschlag** *m* deflection; **~säule** *f aero* control column; *mot* steering column; **~schalter** *m* control switch; controller; **~schwanz** *m aero* (tail) fin; **~stange** *f* steering rod; **~strom** *m el* controlling current; steering-control current; **~tisch** *m* pulpit; platform; **~ung** *f* (*Lenkung*) steering (gear); control; *elektrische ~~* electric control; *mot* driving; *aero* piloting, pilotage; *automatische ~~* (*aero*) gyropilot, auto-pilot; automatic pilot; (*Dampfmaschine*) steam distributor; (*Mechanismus e-r ~~*) steering mechanism; steering gear; controlling device; (*Ventil~~*) valve gear; timing (gear); **~~sgitter** *n radio* control grid; **~~shebel** *m* control lever; **~ventil** *n* control valve; **~vorrichtung** *f* control appliance; **~welle** *f mot* camshaft; control shaft; *radio* pilot wave; control wave; **~werk** *n aero* (flying) controls *pl*.

Steuer[2] *f* (*Staats~*) tax; (*Waren~, Zoll*) duty; (*städtische ~*) rate, *Am* tax; (*Beitrag, Abgabe*) contribution; *hist* impost; *~ auf* tax on, duty on; *~n auferlegen* to impose taxes, to tax; to establish duties; *~n eintreiben* to collect taxes; *~n erheben* to levy taxes; to collect taxes; to tax; *~n hinterziehen* to evade taxes; **~abschnitt** *m* fiscal period; **~abzug** *m* tax deduction; **~amnestie** *f* tax amnesty; **~amt** *n* inland revenue office, *Am* tax office; **~anlage** *f*, **~anschlag** *m* assessment (of taxes); rate; **~aufkommen** *n* tax receipts *pl*; inland (*Am* internal) revenue; **~bar** *a* taxable, rateable; **~beamte(r)** *m* tax collector, *Am* revenue officer; **~befreiung** *f* tax exemption; **~behörde** *f* board of assessment; **~beitreibung** *f* tax collection; **~belastung** *f* tax load; **~berater** *m* tax expert; tax adviser; **~bescheid** *m* tax assessment; **~betrug** *m* fraudulent tax evasion; **~einnahmen** *f pl* inland revenue, *Am* internal revenue, tax receipts *pl*; **~einnehmer** *m* tax collector; **~einschätzung** *f* tax assessment; **~~skommission** *f* board of assessment; **~erhebung** *f* collection of taxes; levying of taxes; **~erhöhung** *f* increase in taxation; **~erklärung** *f* (income-) tax return; *die ~~ abgeben* to file a return; **~erlaß** *m* tax provision, tax remission; **~erleichterung, ~ermäßigung** *f* tax abatement; tax reduction; allowance; **~ersparnis** *f* saving of taxes; **~frei** *a* exempt from taxation; tax-free, tax-exempt; (*von Waren*) duty-free; **~~heit** *f* exemption from taxation (*od* taxes); exemption from duty; **~gesetz** *n* finance bill; **~hinterziehung** *f* tax avoidance *od* evasion; **~jahr** *n* fiscal year, *Am* taxable year; **~kasse** *f* receiver's office, tax-collector's office; **~klasse** *f* tax group; **~marke** *f* revenue stamp; **~mittel** *n pl* tax money; **~n** *itr* (*bei~~ zu*) to contribute to; **~nachlaß** *m* remission of taxes; **~pflichtig** *a* subject to taxation; liable to pay taxes; taxable; **~~e(r)** *m* tax-payer, rate-payer, *Am* taxpayer; **~politik** *f* fiscal policy; **~quelle** *f* source of taxation; **~rechtlich** *a* fiscal; **~reform** *f* fiscal reform; taxation reform; **~satz** *m* rate (of assessment), rate of taxation; **~schätzung** *f* rating; **~schein** *m* receipt; **~stufe** *f* tax bracket; **~veranlagung** *f* assessment; **~verwaltung** *f* administration of taxes; **~wesen** *n* finances *pl*, taxes *pl*; **~zahler** *m* tax-payer, rate-payer, *Am nur* taxpayer; **~zettel** *m* bill of taxes; demand-note; **~zuschlag** *m* surtax, supertax; additional (*od* supplementary) tax.

Steven *m mar* (*Vorder~*) stem; (*Achter~*) stem-post, stem.

Steward *m* steward; **~eß** *f* stewardess; *aëro* air hostess, airline hostess.

stibitzen *tr* to filch, to pilfer, to crib; to purloin, to sneak, *Am fam* to snitch, to swipe.

Stich *m* (*Nadel~*) prick; (*Wanzen~*) bite; (*Insekten~*) sting; (*Näh~*) stitch; (*Degen~*) stab; (*Stoß*) thrust; (*Schmerz*) twitch, pang; (*Seitenstechen*) stitch (in the side); *med* (*Ein~*) puncture; (*Spaten~*) cut; (*Kupfer~*) engraving, cut; (*Karten~*) trick; (*Art Seemannsknoten*) knot, hitch; *fig* (*Stichelei*) hit; gibe, taunt; sarcasm; pointed remark; *e-n ~ haben* (*Bier, Milch etc*) to go bad, to turn sour; (*Wein*) to be on the turn; *fam* (*betrunken sein*) to be tipsy; *fam* (*etw verrückt sein*) to be mad; to be touched in the head; *~ halten* to hold good, to stand the test; to wear well; *das hält nicht ~* that doesn't hold water; *im ~ lassen* to leave in the lurch, to forsake, to desert; to let (s. o.) down; *Am* to go back on s. o.; *e-n ~ machen* to make a trick; *das gibt mir e-n ~ ins Herz fig* it cuts me to the quick; *ein ~ ins Grüne* a touch (*od* a tinge) of green; **~bahn** *f* branch-line; **~ballon** *m* (*Metereologie*) sounding balloon; **~blatt** *n* (*des Degens*) guard, sword-shell; (*Kartenspiel*) trump; *fig* butt; **~el** *m* graver, burin, graving tool; **~elei** *f fig* taunt, sneer, gibe; **~eln** *tr, itr* (*nähen*) to stitch, to sew; *fig* to jeer, to sneer, to banter (at); **~elrede** *f*, **~elwort** *n* raillery, taunt; squib, sarcasm; gibe; **~entscheid** *m* casting vote; **~flamme** *f* darting-flame; jet of flame; **~graben** *m mil* communication trench; **~haltig** *a* standing the test; (*begründet*) solid; (*gültig*) valid; *~~e Gründe* sound arguments, solid reasons; *es ist nicht ~~* it won't hold water; **~~keit** *f* validity, soundness; **~ler** *m* taunter; **~ling** *m* (*Fisch*) stickleback; **~loch** *n* tap hole, tapping hole; **~maß** *n* ga(u)ge; inside micrometer; **~ofen** *m* blast-furnace; **~probe** *f* sample taken at random; random sample; random test; *Am* spot check; **~säge** *f* compass saw; **~tag** *m* fixed day; key-date, key-day; settling-day; **~torf** *m* dug peat; **~verletzung** *f* injury caused by stab; **~waffe** *f* pointed weapon, thrust weapon; foil; **~wahl** *f* final (*od* second) ballot; **~wort** *n* catchword; key-word; (*im Wörterbuch*) head-word; *theat* cue; (*Schlüssel*) code (word); party-cry; **~~katalog** *m* (*Bibliothek*) alphabetical subject catalogue; **~~verzeichnis** *n* list of subjects; subject index; key-word index; **~wunde** *f* punctured wound, stab (wound); **~zahl** *f* test number.

stick|en *tr, itr* to embroider; (*er~~*) to suffocate; **~er** *m*, **~erin** *f* embroiderer; **~erei** *f* embroidery; **~fluß** *m* suffocating catarrh; **~garn** *n* embroider-cotton; **~gas** *n* suffocating gas; **~gaze** *f* canvas; **~husten** *m* hooping-cough; **~ig** *a* suffocating; (*Luft*) stuffy, close; **~luft** *f* stuffy air, mephitic air, close air; **~muster** *n* pattern (for embroidering); **~nadel** *f* embroidery-needle; **~rahmen** *m* embroidery-frame; **~stoff** *m* nitrogen; **~~gewinnung** *f* production of nitrogen; **~~haltig** *a* nitrogenous; **~~oxyd** *n* nitric oxide; **~~verbindung** *f* nitrogen compound; **~tuch** *n* sampler; **~wolle** *f* Berlin wool, embroidery-wool.

stieben *irr itr* to fly about; (*Flüssigkeit*) to spray; (*auseinander~*) to disperse; to scatter.

Stief|bruder *m* stepbrother, half-brother; **~eltern** *pl* step-parents *pl*; **~geschwister** *pl* stepbrothers and sisters *pl*; **~kind** *n* stepchild; **~mutter** *f* stepmother; **~mütterchen** *n bot* pansy; **~mütterlich** *a* like a stepmother; *~~ behandeln* to neglect; **~schwester** *f* stepsister; **~sohn** *m* stepson; **~tochter** *f* stepdaughter; **~vater** *m* stepfather.

Stiefel *m* boot; *Am* shoe; *tech* pump-barrel; **~absatz** *m* boot-heel; **~anzieher** *m* shoe-horn; **~appell** *m mil* boot inspection; **~bürste** *f* blacking-brush; **~chen** *n* small boot; **~hose** *f* riding breeches *pl*; **~knecht, ~zieher** *m* boot-jack; **~n** *itr fam* to walk, to march; **~putzer** *m* (*auf der Straße*) shoeblack; shoe-shiner, *Am* bootsblack; (*im Hotel*) boots *pl mit sing*; **~schaft** *m* leg of boot; **~sohle** *f* boot-sole; **~spanner** *m* boot-tree; **~strippe** *f* boot-strap; **~wichse** *f* blacking; *Am* shoe-shine.

Stiege *f* staircase; stairs *pl*, flight of stairs; (*Zaunübergang*) stile; (*20 Stück*) score.

Stieglitz *m orn* thistle-finch; goldfinch.

Stiel *m* handle, haft; (*Besen~*) stick; *bot* stalk; peduncle; (*Stengel*) stem; *tech* (*Stempel, Ständer*) post; strut; stud; column; *mit Stumpf u. ~ ausrotten* to exterminate; to extirpate; to root out; **~äugig** *a* stalk-eyed; **~en** *tr* to furnish with a handle; **~hammer** *m* chop hammer; **~handgranate** *f* stick handgrenade; **~strahler** *m radio* rod antenna.

stier *a* (*Blick, Augen*) staring, fixed; glassy; (*Blick*) vacant; **~en** *itr* to stare, to look fixedly (at); to look with a vacant gaze.

Stier *m* bull; *astr* Taurus; *junger ~* bullock; **~fechter, ~kämpfer** *m* bull-fighter, toreador; **~gefecht** *n* bull-fight; **~hetze** *f* bull-baiting; **~nackig** *a* bull-necked; thick-necked.

Stift[1] *m* (*Holz~*) peg; tag; (*Pflock*) pin; (*Nagel*) tack, nail; brad; (*Blei~*) pencil; (*Farb~*) crayon; (*Zahn~*) stump (of a tooth); *fam* (*Lehrjunge*) office boy; apprentice; youngster; **~bolzen** *m* stud bolt; **~lagerung** *f* pin suspension; **~zahn** *m* china crown.

Stift[2] *n* charitable institution; (charitable) foundation; (*Bistum*) bishopric; (*Domkapitel*) chapter; (*Kloster*) monastery; (*Schule*) (training) college; (*Altersheim*) home for old people, Eventide home; **~en** *tr* (*schenken, geben*) to donate, to give; (*gründen*) to found; (*errichten*) to establish, to institute; (*verursachen*) to cause, to make; to bring about; *Frieden ~~* to make peace; *Nutzen ~~* to be useful; *Händel ~~* to stir up a brawl; *Unfrieden ~~* to sow discord; to make trouble; *~~ gehen fam* to run away; **~er** *m*, **~erin** *f* (*Schenkende(r)* donor; (*Gründer*) founder, originator; (*Urheber*) author; **~sdame** *f* canoness; **~sherr** *m* canon, prebendary; **~shütte** *f* (*Bibel*) tabernacle; **~skirche** *f* collegiate church; cathedral; **~sschule** *f* foundation school; **~ung** *f* (charitable) foundation; charitable endowment; *milde ~~* pious bequest; (*Gründung*) establishment, foundation; **~~sbrief** *m* deed of foundation; **~~sfeier** *f*, **~~sfest** *n* founder's day; commemoration day; foundation-festival; anniversary; **~~surkunde** *f* charter of foundation.

Stigma *n* stigma; **~tisieren** *tr* to stigmatize.

Stil *m* style; *fig* manner; (*Art u. Weise*) kind, way; (*Geschmack*) taste; *alten ~s* (*Zeit*) old style; *im großen ~* on a large scale; **~blüte** *f* pun; (Irish) bull; **~gerecht** *a* in good style; in good taste; **~gefühl** *n* stilistic sense; **~isieren** *tr* to write, to compose, to word; to stylize; **~istik** *f* art of composition; theory of style; **~istisch** *a* relating to style; stylistic; **~los** *a* without style; in bad style; **~~igkeit** *f* want of style; **~möbel** *n pl* period furniture; **~voll** *a* in good taste; stylish.

Stilett *n* stiletto.

still *a* (*ohne Bewegung*) still, motionless; (*Luft, See, Gefühle*) calm; (*unbelebt*) inanimate; lifeless; (*ruhig*) quiet; (*geräuschlos*) noiseless; (*leise*) soft, low; (*bescheiden*) modest, gentle; mild; (*unauffällig*) unobtrusive; (*friedlich*) peaceful, peaceable; placid; *com* (*Börse*) flat, dull, inactive; (*Handel, Geschäft*) dull, dead, calm, slack; quiet; *~! interj* silence! peace! whist! mum! (*pst!*) hush! hist! *sei ~!* be quiet! *~ davon!* don't mention it! cut that! *wir bitten um ~es Beileid* we request your silent sympathy; *~e Beteiligung* sleeping partnership; *~er Freitag* Good Friday; *~es Gebet* silent prayer; *~es Hinbrüten* brown study; *~er Gesellschafter* sleeping partner, *Am* silent partner; *~e Hochzeit* quiet wedding; *~e Hoffnung* secret hope(s); *ein ~es Leben führen* to lead a quiet life; *~e Liebe* unavowed love; *ein ~er Mensch* a quiet (*od* silent) man; *~e Messe* low mass; *der ~e Ozean* the Pacific (Ocean); *~e Reserve* passive reserve, hidden assets *pl*; *~er Schmerz* silent grief; *~er Teilhaber* sleeping partner, *Am* silent partner; *sich dem ~en Trunk* (*vulg Suff*) *ergeben* to drink on the sly; *~er Verehrer* secret admirer; *~er Vorbehalt* mental reserve; *~es Wasser* stagnant (*od* smooth) water; *~e Wasser sind tief prov* still waters run deep; *~e Woche eccl* Holy Week; *~e Wut* dumb madness; *~e Zeit com* dull (*od* dead) season; *~ sein, sich ~ verhalten* to keep quiet; *verhalte dich ganz ~!* keep still! *~ werden* (*Wind*) to calm down; (*schweigen*) to grow silent; *im ~en* in silence, secretely; privately; *e-m Laster im ~en frönen* to indulge a vice in secret; *sich im ~en sein Teil denken* to keep o.'s own counsel about s. th.; *sich im ~en denken* to think to o. s.; **~amme** *f* wet nurse; **~beglückt** *a* enjoying a quiet bliss; **~bleiben** *irr itr* to be still, to remain silent; to keep quiet, to keep silence; **~e** *f* stillness; (*Schweigen*) silence; (*Ruhe*) quietness; quiet; tranquillity; (*Frieden*) peace; (*Wind*) lull; (*der See*) calmness; (*Pause*) pause; *com* (*Geschäft, Handel*) dul(l)ness; stagnation; flatness; stagnant condition; *in aller ~~* in secret, secretely; underhand; privately; silently; quietly; **~en** *tr* to still; (*zum Schweigen bringen*) to silence; (*beruhigen*) to calm; to quiet; (*anhalten*) to stop; to stay; (*befriedigen*) to satisfy; (*Begierde, Wunsch*) to gratify; (*Schmerz*) to allay, to soothe; to comfort; (*Hunger, Zorn*) to appease; (*Durst*) to quench; (*Blut*) to staunch;

(*Kind*) to nurse, to suckle; to (breast-) feed; **~end** *a* (*Schmerz~~*) sedative; allaying; lenitive; calming; **~geschäft** *n* (*der Mütter*) nursing; suckling; lactation; **~halteabkommen** *n* *com* standstill agreement; **~halten** *irr tr, itr* to keep still; to refrain from action; (*anhalten*) to stop; to pause; (*mit Fahrzeug*) to pull up; (*ruhig halten, ruhig sein*) to be quiet, to keep quiet; **~(l)eben** *n* (*Malerei*) still life; **~(l)egen** *tr* (*Betrieb*) to shut down, to close down; (*Verkehr einstellen*) to suspend; to stop; (*Fahrzeug*) to lay up; (*Schiff*) to put out of service, to put out of commission; **~(l)egung** *f* shutting-down, shut-down; closing-up; (*Arbeits-, Verkehrseinstellung*) stoppage; **~(l)iegen** *irr itr* (*Verkehr etc*) to be suspended; (*eingestellt sein*) to be at a standstill; to be stopped; (*Fabrik*) to be idle, to lie idle; to be out of production; **~periode** *f* (*der Mütter*) lactation; **~schweigen** *irr itr* to be silent, to keep silence; to hold o.'s tongue; (*zu etw ~~*) to take no notice of; *~~ n* silence; (*Ergebung, Zustimmung*) acquiescence; (*Geheimhaltung*) secrecy; *~~ beobachten* to observe strict silence; to keep mum (*über* about); *das ~~ brechen* to break silence; *mit ~~ übergehen* to pass over in silence; *zum ~~ bringen* to silence; **~schweigend** *a* silent; quiet, calm; *fig* tacit, implicit; implied; *~~es Einvernehmen* tacit understanding; *~~es Übereinkommen* tacit agreement; **~setzen** *tr* (*schließen*) to shut down; (*anhalten, ausschalten*) to stop; to cut out; **~setzung** *f* stopping, arresting; **~sitzen** *irr itr* to sit quiet; to remain inactive; **~stand** *m* (*Halt*) standstill, stop; (*Aufhören, Einstellen*) cessation; stopping; (*Nachlassen, Pause*) let-up; *Am* (*~~ der Geschäfte, des Verkehrs etc infolge Katastrophen, Streiks, Unfällen etc*) tie-up; (*Innehalten, Pause*) pause; (*Unterbrechung*) suspension; *fig* (*Stokkung, com Flaute*) stagnation; stagnancy; (*völlige Stockung*) deadlock; (*Sackgasse, Stocken*) stalemate; (*vorübergehender ~~*) lull; (*Betriebs~~*) shut-down; *astr* (*scheinbarer ~~*) station; *zum ~~ bringen* to arrest; (*völlig*) to deadlock; to stalemate; *zum ~~ kommen* to come to rest; to come to a standstill; (*Motor*) to stall; **~stehen** *irr itr* to stand still; (*anhalten*) to stop; to arrest; (*an Ort u. Stelle bleiben*) *Am* to stay put; (*unbeweglich sein*) to be stationary; (*Handel*) to be at a standstill; to be stagnant; (*Betrieb*) to be closed; (*Maschinen*) to be idle; to lie still; *mil* to stand at attention; *~gestanden!* (*Kommando*) Attention! 'Shun! (= attention); *da steht e-m der Verstand still* that's beyond comprehension; **~stehend** *a* standing still; motionless; (*stationär*) stationary; fixed; (*von Wasser u. fig stagnierend*) stagnant; (*Maschine*) idle; (*Verkehr*) tied-up; **~ung** *f* stilling; (*Blut*) staunching; (*Kind*) nursing, suckling; lactation; **~vergnügt** *a* calm and serene; quietly happy; **~wasser** *n* slack water; **~wein** *m* (*Gegensatz: Schaumwein*) still wine.

Stimm|abgabe *f* voting, vote; polling; **~band** *n* vocal cord; **~begabt** *a* endowed with a good voice; **~berechtigt** *a* entitled to vote; *nicht ~~* non-voting; *~~e(r) m* voter; **~berechtigung** *f* right to vote; voting power, suffrage; **~bildung** *f* formation of the voice; voice production; phonation; **~block** *m* *Am* (*Kongreß*) bloc; **~bruch** *m* breaking of the voice; **~e** *f* voice; (*Wahl*) vote; suffrage; *mus* (*Noten*) (musical) part; (*Ton*) sound; (*Orgel~~*) stop; (*Presse~~*) (newspaper) comment; (*Meinung*) opinion; *die erste ~~* soprano; *die zweite ~~* alto; *die ~~ des Gewissens* the voice of conscience; *die ~~ der Natur* the voice of nature; *die innere ~~* the inward voice; *Volkes ~~ ist Gottes ~~* the voice of the people is the voice of God; *Sitz u. ~~ haben* to have a seat and vote in; *auf die ~~ bezüglich* vocal; (*gut*) *bei ~~* in (good) voice; *ausschlaggebende* (*od entscheidende*) *~~* casting vote; *mit gedämpfter* (*od leiser*) *~~* in a low voice; low-voiced; *~~ abgeben* to vote; to cast o.'s vote, to record o.'s vote; to give o.'s vote *jdm seine ~~ geben* to vote for s. o.; *e-e gute ~~ haben* to have a good voice; *die meisten ~~n haben* to be at the head of the poll; *e-e ~~ haben in* (*od bei*) to have a voice in; *keine ~~ in e-r Sache haben* to have no voice (*od* say) in a matter; *die ~~ erheben* to raise (*od* to lift up) o.'s voice; *die ~~ sinken lassen* to drop o.'s voice; *~~n sammeln* to collect votes, to go canvassing; *~~n werben* to canvass; *die ~~n zählen* to count the votes; *wieviel ~~n wird X. bei der Wahl bekommen?* how many votes will X. poll; **~en** *tr* (*Instrument*) to tune (*nach* to); to put in tune; *höher* (*niedriger*) *~~* to raise (to lower) the pitch of an instrument; *jdn gegen etw* (*od jdn*) *~~* to prejudice s. o. against s. th. (*od* s. o.); *jdn* (*günstig*) *für etw* (*od jdn*) *~~* to prejudice s. o. in favo(u)r of s. th. (*od* s. o.); to dispose s. o. for s. th.; *jdn gut* (*schlecht*) *~~* to put s. o. in (a) good (bad) humo(u)r (*od* in good (bad) spirit); *jdn zu etw ~~* to induce s. o. to do s. th.; *traurig* (*froh*) *~~* to make sad (glad); *gut gestimmt sein* to be in good humo(u)r, to be in a good mood; *schlecht gestimmt sein* to be ill-humo(u)red; to be in a bad mood; *seine Forderungen hoch ~~* to pitch o.'s demands high; *itr* to vote; to put to the vote; *dagegen ~~* to vote against; to veto, *Am* to negative; *dafür od dagegen ~~* to vote for or against; *nur für Kandidaten e-r Partei ~~* to vote for the candidates of one party, *Am* to vote a straight ticket; *bei der* (*gleichen*) *Wahl für Kandidaten verschiedener Parteien ~~* to vote for candidates of different parties (at the same election), *Am* to split o.'s ticket; *jem, der widerrechtlich, mehr als einmal bei e-r Wahl stimmt* one who votes more than once in an election (in violation of law), *Am* repeater; *für etw ~~* to vote for s. th., to agree to s. th.; (*im Ton, bei Farben*) to harmonize; to be in tune; (*überein~~*) to accord, to be in accord; (*überein~~, zu etw ~~*) to agree with; to be in keeping with; to correspond to; to tally with; (*passen*) to suit; *com* (*richtig sein*) to be correct, to be right; to be in order; to be all right; *das stimmt!* that's all right! (that's) right! that's correct! check! that's true enough! *das stimmt nicht* there's s. th. wrong; that doesn't check; *die Rechnung stimmt* the account is correct (*od* square); **~enabgabe** *f* voting, vote; **~enanzahl** *f* number of votes; **~eneinheit** *f* unanimity; *mit ~~* unanimously; **~enfang** *m* canvassing; **~enfänger** *m* (*Werber*) canvasser; *Am* (*zugkräftiger Kandidat*) vote-getter; **~engewirr** *n* confused din of voices; jumble of voices; **~engleichheit** *f* equality of votes, parity of votes; same number of votes; *parl* tie; *bei ~~ den Ausschlag geben* to give the casting vote; *bei ~~ entscheidet die ~e des Vorsitzenden* the vote of the chairman shall be decisive in the event of a tie; **~enkauf** *m* buying of votes; **~enmehrheit** *f* majority of votes; *Am* plurality of votes; *einfache ~~* bare (*od* mere) majority; **~enminderheit** *f* minority of votes; **~enprüfung** *f* scrutiny of votes; **~enrutsch** *m* landslip, *Am* landslide; **~ensammler** *m* (*nach der Wahl*) counter of votes; (*Werber vor der Wahl*) canvasser; **~enteilung** *f* splitting of votes; division; **~enthaltung** *f* abstention (from voting); **~enverhältnis** *n* proportion of votes; **~enwerber** *m* canvasser; *Am auch* solicitor; **~enwerbung** *f* canvassing, electioneering; **~enzahl** *f* number of votes; **~enzähler** *m* counter of votes; *parl* teller; **~enzählung** *f* counting of votes; inspection of the ballot-box; **~er** *m mus* tuner; **~fähig** *a* entitled to vote; **~~keit** *f* right to vote; **~fall** *m* drop of the voice; inflection of the voice; **~falte** *f anat* fold of vocal cord; **~färbung** *f* timbre; (*Klang*) sound; ring of a voice; **~flöte** *f* tuning pipe; **~führer** *m* (*e-r Partei etc*) spokesman; **~gabel** *f* tuning-fork; **~~steuerung** *f* tuning-fork control; **~geber** *m* voter; **~gewaltig** *a* full-throated; **~haft** *a* voiced; *~~e Konsonanten* voiced (*od* sonant *od* vocal) consonants; **~hammer** *m*, **~horn** *n* tuning-key, tuning-hammer; **~holz** *n* (*Geige*) sounding-post; . . . **~ig** *a* (*in Zssg*): *fünf~~* in five parts, for five voices; **~klang** *m* timbre; ring of a voice; **~lage** *f* register; voice; pitch (of the voice); **~lich** *a* relating to the voice; **~liste** *f* voting list; **~los** *a* voiceless; *gram* unvoiced; nonvocal (*od* breathed *od* surd) consonants; **~(m)ittel** *n pl* compass of voice; **~organ** *n* vocal organ; **~pfeife** *f* tuning pipe, pitch pipe; **~recht** *n* right to vote; suffrage; franchise; *allgemeines ~~* universal suffrage; general vote; *aktives* (*passives*) *~~* active (passive) right to vote; *sein ~~ ausüben* to exercise o.'s right to vote; *~~ haben* to have a vote; **~rechtlerin** *f* suffragist; *fam* suffragette; **~ritze** *f anat* glottis; glottic catch (*od* cleft); **~schein** *m* voting certificate; **~schlüssel** *m* tuning-key; **~ton** *m* voice; tuning pitch; **~übung** *f* exercising the voice; **~umfang** *m* range of the voice, volume of the voice; **~ung** *f mus* tuning, tune; (*e-s Instruments*) pitch; key; tone; (*Gemüts~~*) mood; (*Temperament, Gleichmut*) temper; (*Gemütsanlage*) disposition; (*Geistes-, Gemütsverfassung*) frame of mind; (*Laune*) humo(u)r; spirits *pl*; (*Einklang*) harmony; (*Empfindung, Gefühl*) feeling; (*~~ e-s Bildes*) tone; *mil* (*Moral der Truppe*) morale; (*öffentliche Meinung*) prevailing (*od* public) opinion; (*Milieu, Atmosphäre*) atmosphere; (*Sinneseindruck*) impression; *com* (*Börse*) tone, tendency; disposition; *Ferien~~* holiday spirit; *Fest~~* festive mood; *die allgemeine ~~* the general feeling; *in freudiger ~~* in a cheerful frame of mind; *in guter* (*schlechter*) *~~ sein* to be in good (bad) humo(u)r; *fam* in high (*od* full) feather; *in gedrückter ~~* in low spirits, out of spirits; *fam* down in the mouth; *in gehobener ~~* in high spirits; *~~ machen für* to make propaganda for; to canvass; *jdn in gute ~~ versetzen* to put into good humo(u)r;

⁓⁓sbild *n* sentiment picture; key picture; **⁓⁓skapelle** *f* cheery band; **⁓⁓slage** *f* (*Psychologie*) affectivity; **⁓⁓smache** *f* creating of a special atmosphere; political agitation; **⁓⁓smensch** *m* moody person; **⁓⁓sumschwung, ⁓⁓swechsel** *m* (*Börse, Markt*) change of tendency, change of tone; **⁓⁓svoll** *a* impressive, appealing to the emotions; **⁓⁓swerte** *m pl* imponderable values *pl*; imponderabilia *pl*; **⁓vieh** *n fam* herd of voters; **⁓wechsel** *m* breaking ot the voice, mutation; **⁓werkzeug** *n* vocal organ; **⁓zettel** *m* voting-paper; ballot(-paper); *Wahl durch ⁓⁓* ballot.

Stimul|ans *n med* stimulant; **⁓ieren** *tr med* to stimulate; **⁓us** *m* (*Reizmittel, Reiz, Antrieb*) stimulus.

Stink|asant *m bot* asafetida; **⁓bock** *m* stinking he-goat; *fig* stinking fellow; **⁓bombe** *f* stench bomb; (*Tränengasbombe*) tear-gas bomb; **⁓drüse** *f* stink (*od* stench) gland; **⁓en** *irr itr* to stink; to have a bad smell; to smell foul; to be fetid; *zum Himmel ⁓⁓* (*fig*) to cry to heaven; to stink to high heaven; *die ganze Angelegenheit stinkt mir fam* I'm sick of the whole affair; *er stinkt vor Faulheit* he is bone-lazy; **⁓end, ⁓ig** *a* stinking; malodorous; (*mit Gestank behaftet*) fetid; (*faulend*) putrid; **⁓faul** *a fam* bone-lazy; **⁓tier** *n zoo* skunk; **⁓topf** *m hist mil* smudge pot; **⁓wut** *f fam* violent anger, bad temper.

Stint *m* (*Fisch*) smelt.

Stipend|iat *m* (*auf Grund e-s Wettbewerbs*) exhibitioner; (*Universität*) scholar; **⁓ium** *n* scholarship; exhibition.

stipp|en *tr* to dip, to steep; **⁓angriff** *m aero mil* hit-and-run raid; **⁓visite** *f fam* short call, *fam* pop-visit.

Stirn *f* forehead, brow; *arch* (*Vorderseite*) front; *fig* (*Frechheit, Unverschämtheit*) impudence, insolence, audacity, face, *fam* cheek; *hohe* (*niedrige*) ⁓ high (low) forehead; *die ⁓ bieten* to show a bold front; to face; to defy; *es steht ihm an der ⁓ geschrieben fig* it is written in his face; *die ⁓ haben* (*zu*) to have the cheek (to); to have the audacity (to); *die ⁓ runzeln* to frown; **⁓ader** *f anat* frontal vein; **⁓ansicht** *f* front view, front elevation; **⁓band** *n* headband; head-strap; (*mit Edelsteinen*) diadem; (*der Juden*) frontlet; **⁓bein** *n anat* frontal bone; **⁓⁓höhle** *f* frontal sinus; **⁓⁓naht** *f* frontal suture; **⁓binde** *f* headband; (*der Juden*) frontlet; **⁓bogen** *m arch* frontal arch; **⁓e** *f* forehead; **⁓falte** *f* wrinkle on the forehead; **⁓fläche** *f* face, front; end (*od* front) surface; frontal area; **⁓fräser** *m tech* front-milling tool; **⁓gegend** *f* frontal region; **⁓getriebe** *n* spur pinion, spur gear; **⁓haar** *n* front hair; **⁓höcker** *m* frontal eminence (*od* protuberance); **⁓höhle** *f* frontal cavity; frontal sinus; **⁓⁓nentzündung** *f* frontal sinusitis, prosopantritis; **⁓kühler** *m mot* front radiator; **⁓leiste** *f aero* leading edge; *anat* frontal ridge; **⁓locke** *f* forelock; **⁓moräne** *f* terminal moraine; **⁓muskel** *m* frontal muscle; **⁓rad** *n* spur wheel, spur gear; **⁓⁓getriebe** *n* spur-gear system; **⁓reif** *m* headband; **⁓reihe** *f* front row; **⁓riemen** *m* (*Geschirr*) frontlet (*od* headpiece) of bridle; brow-band; **⁓runzeln** *n* frown(ing); **⁓schutz** *m* brow-pad; **⁓seite** *f* front, façade, face; front side, front end; interface; **⁓wand** *f* front wall; front plate; **⁓welle** *f* front wave, bow wave; (*Explosions⁓⁓*) impact wave; **⁓wetter** *n* frontal weather; **⁓widerstand** *m* head resistance; frontal resistance; **⁓wunde** *f* frontal wound.

•

stöber|n *itr* to hunt, to rummage (for *od* about); to poke (around); (*suchen*) to search; (*Schnee, feiner Regen*) to drift; to be drifted; to blow about; *es ⁓t* a fine snow is falling; there is sleet falling; it drizzles; **⁓schnee** *m* drifting snow; **⁓wetter** *n* snowy weather; snow-drift, raining (*od* sleety) weather.

Stocher *m* (*Feuer⁓*) poker; (*Zahn⁓*) tooth-pick; **⁓n** *itr* to poke (about), to stir, to rake; (*in den Zähnen*) to pick o.'s teeth.

Stock *m allg* stick; (*Stab*) staff; (*Herrscherstab, Rute*) rod; (*Amtsstab, Kommandostab, Zauberstab*) wand; (*Spazier⁓*) cane; (*Prügel⁓*) cudgel; (*Keule*) club; *sport* bat; club; mallet; (*Billard⁓*) cue; (*Takt⁓*) baton; (*Anker⁓*) anchor-stock; (*Schaft*) shaft; (*Holz⁓*) block (*od* log) of wood; (*Gebirgs⁓*) (mountain-) mass; (*Zahn⁓*) body; stump; (*Druck⁓*) *typ* cliché, stereotype, block; plate;(*Armen⁓*) poor-box; (*Blumen⁓*) pot; (*Pflanzen⁓*) stem; (*Wein⁓*) vine; (*Baum⁓*) trunk, stock, stump; (*⁓werk*) floor, stor(e)y; (*Bienen⁓*) beehive; (*Grund⁓*) capital, funds *pl*; (*Folterinstrument*) stocks *pl*; *fig* blockhead; *stock ... in Zssg mit Nationennamen* (= *wahr, echt, typisch*); *mit Adjektiven* (= *ganz u. gar, vollständig, radikal*); *am ⁓ gehen* to walk with a stick; *im ersten ⁓* on the first floor, *Am* on the second floor; *über ⁓ u. Stein* up hill and down dale; **⁓amerikaner** *m* thorough Yankee; regular Yankee; **⁓blind** *a* stone-blind; **⁓degen** *m* tuck, sword-cane; **⁓dumm** *a* block-headed; utterly stupid; **⁓dummheit** *f* utter stupidity; **⁓dunkel** *a* pitch-dark; **⁓en** *tr* to prop (vines); *itr* (*anhalten*) to stop, to stop short; to arrest; to hold up; to stand still; to cease (moving); to get stuck; to come to a deadlock; (*pausieren*) to pause; (*langsamer werden*) to slacken (off); (*verzögern*) to delay; (*Flüssigkeiten*) to stagnate; to clog; (*gerinnen*) to coagulate; (*dick werden*) to thicken; (*Farbe*) to cake; (*Milch*) to curdle; (*schimmeln*) to turn mo(u)ldy; (*in Reden*) to hesitate; to falter; (*stammeln*) to stammer; *com* (*Geschäft, Absatz*) to be slack, to slacken off; to be dull; to be stagnant, to stagnate; to languish; (*Zahlungen*) to be in arrears (*mit* with); (*Unterhaltung, Gespräch*) to flag; (*Unterhandlungen*) to be suspended; to come to a standstill; (*Verkehr*) to stop; to come to a standstill; to get tied; *der Verkehr stockt* there is a traffic block (*od* traffic congestion *od* traffic jam *od Am* traffic snarl); **⁓en** *n* stopping; hesitation; deadness (of trade); *ins ⁓⁓ bringen* to tie up; *ins ⁓⁓ geraten* to stagnate; to come to a standstill; to come to a dead stop; to come to a deadlock; (*Verkehr*) to get tied up; (*mit Zahlungen*) to be in arrears with; **⁓end** *a* stagnant; (*ermattend*) flagging; **⁓engländer** *m* true-born (*od* typical) Englishman; regular John Bull; **⁓ente** *f* mallard; common wild duck; **⁓erbse** *f* common field-pea; **⁓fäule** *f* (*bei Trauben*) rot of the vine; **⁓finster** *a* pitch-dark; **⁓fisch** *m* stockfish; dried cod; *fam* blockhead; **⁓fleck** *m* damp stain; (*Mehltau*) mildew; **⁓fleckig** *a* stained by stamp; mildewy, foxy; **⁓flinte** *f* cane-gun; **⁓holz** *n* stump wood; **⁓ig** *a* fusty; mo(u)ldy; rotten, decayed; **⁓jobber** *m* stock-jobber; **⁓laterne** *f* cresset; **⁓makler** *m* stock-broker; **⁓presse** *f* bookbinder's large press; **⁓prügel** *m pl* sound thrashing; flogging; **⁓punkt** *m phys* setting point; freezing point; point of congelation; **⁓reis** *n* shoot; **⁓republikaner** *m Am* a straight-out Republican; **⁓schere** *f* bench shears *pl*; **⁓schläge** *m pl* cudgelling, thrashing; **⁓schnupfen** *m* chronic nasal catarrh; **⁓steif** *a* stiff as a poker; **⁓taub** *a* stone-deaf; **⁓träger** *m* (*Golf*) caddie; **⁓ung** *f* (*Halt*) stop, stopping, stoppage; check; cessation; standstill; *fig* deadlock; (*Unterbrechung*) interruption; suspension; (*Hindernis*) impediment, obstruction; (*Verzögerung*) delay; hold up; (*Verkehrs⁓⁓*) block, congestion, traffic-jam, interruption of traffic, *Am* tie-up, traffic snarl; *med* (*Blut⁓⁓*) (blood-) stasis; stagnation; (*Kongestion*) congestion; **⁓werk** *n* stor(e)y, floor; *im oberen ⁓⁓* upstairs; **⁓zahn** *m* molar, grinder; **⁓zwinge** *f* ferrule.

Stöckel *m* (*hoher Absatz*) (high) heel; *tech* (*Amboß*) anvil inset stake; **⁓schuh** *m* high-heeled shoe.

Stoff *m* (*natürlicher ⁓, Materie*) matter; (*Substanz*) substance; (*Grund-*) element; principle; *chem* component; (*Körper*) elementary body; (*Betriebs⁓*) fuel; (*Zeug, Material*) material, stuff; (*gewebter ⁓*) fabric; tissue; textile; texture; web; (*Tuch*) cloth; (*Papier⁓*) pulp, stuff; (*Redegegenstand*) subject, subject-matter; (*Thema*) theme, topic; (*Unterlagen, Daten*) data *pl*; *⁓ u. Form* matter and form; matter and manner; *⁓ für ein Buch* material for a book; *e-e Medizin mit schädlichen ⁓en* a medicine with harmful substances; *⁓ zu etw geben* to furnish matter for; *⁓ zum Lachen* s. th. to laugh about; laughing-matter; **⁓aufwand** *m* expenditure of material, requirement of material; **⁓bahn** *f* (*Tuch*) web of cloth; **⁓ballen** *m* bale of cloth; **⁓behang** *m* draping; **⁓bespannt** *a aero* fabric covered; **⁓fehler** *m* flaw of material; defect; **⁓gebiet** *n* range of subjects; **⁓gewicht** *n* specific gravity; **⁓kunde** *f* (*Warenkunde*) knowledge of goods; **⁓lehre** *f* chemistry; **⁓lich** *a* material; with regard to the subject-matter; **⁓los** *a* immaterial; **⁓mangel** *m* shortage of material; **⁓puppe** *f* moppet; **⁓reich** *a* substantial; **⁓teil** *m* (*Gasmaske*) facepiece; **⁓teilchen** *n* particle; corpuscle; **⁓überzug** *m* cloth covering; **⁓verwandtschaft** *f* chemical affinity; **⁓wahl** *f* selection of subject; **⁓wechsel** *m* metabolism; **⁓⁓störung** *f* disturbance of metabolism; **⁓zerfall** *m* decay; decomposition; **⁓zustand** *m* state of aggregation.

Stoffel *m fam* boor, cad; yokel; duffer; **⁓ig** *a* uncouth, unmannerly.

stöhnen *itr* to groan; *⁓ n* groans *pl*.

Stoi|ker *m* Stoic; **⁓isch** *a* stoical; **⁓zismus** *m* Stoicism.

Stol|a, **⁓e** *f* stole, surplice; **⁓gebühren** *f pl* surplice-fees *pl*.

Stolle *f*, **⁓n** *m* loaf-shaped cake; fruit loaf; stollen.

Stollen *m* (*Pfosten*) prop, post; (*am Hufeisen*) calk; *mil* (*gegen schweren Beschuß*) deep dug-out; (*Luftschutz*) underground shelter; *min* tunnel; mine gallery; drift; adit; (*Röhren⁓*) duct; **⁓bergbau** *m* drift mine; **⁓holz** *n* pit timber; props *pl*.

stolpern *itr* to stumble, to trip (over); *⁓ n* tripping.

Stolz *m* pride; (*Ruhm*) glory; (*Hochmut, Anmaßung*) arrogance; (*Einbildung*) conceit; haughtiness; *seinen ~ setzen in* to take a pride in; to pride o. s. on; *~ a* proud, haughty; *zu ~, um zu kämpfen* too proud to fight; (*anmaßend*) arrogant, insolent; (*eitel*) vain, conceited; (*großartig*) noble, majestic; stately; *~ machen* to make proud; *~ sein auf* to be proud of; **~ieren** *itr* to flaunt, to strut; (*von Pferden*) to prance.

Stopf|büchse *f tech* packing (*od* stuffing) box; **~dichtung** *f tech* packing washer; **~ei** *n* darner; **~en** *m siehe: Stöpsel*; **~en** *tr* (*aus~~*) to stuff; (*hinein~~, voll~~*) to cram; (*Pfeife ~~, Loch füllen*) to fill; (*Polsterung, Geflügel*) to stuff; (*Strümpfe etc ausbessern*) to darn; to mend; (*mit Stöpsel etc zu~~, Leck ~~*) to plug; to stop up; *mil* (*Feuer einstellen*) to cease (firing); *med* (*ver~~*) to constipate; to bind; *itr* to fill up; to be filling; *med* to cause constipation; to be constipating; *sich voll~~* to cram o. s. with food; *jdm den Mund ~~* to stop s. o.'s mouth; to silence; **~garn** *n* darning cotton, darning yarn; mending thread; **~haar** *n* hair for stuffing; **~nadel** *f* darning-needle; **~naht** *f* darn; **~nudel** *f* flour-ball.

Stoppel *f* stubble; *~n pl* young feathers *pl*; **~bart** *m* stubbly beard; **~feld** *n* stubble-field; **~gans** *f* stubble-goose; **~ig** *a* stubbly; **~n** *itr* to glean; *fig* (*zusammen~~*) to patch.

stopp|en *tr mar, mot* (*anhalten*) to stop; (*plötzlich ~~*) to stop short; (*mit der Uhr ab~~*) to clock; *der Rennwagen wurde mit 111 Stunden/Meilen gestoppt* the speedster has been clocked at 111 miles an hour; **~licht** *n* (*Brems- u. Schlußlicht*) stop tail lamp; (*Verkehrssignal*) red light; **~signal** *n* stop signal; **~uhr** *f* stopwatch.

Stöpsel *m* stopper; stopple; (*Kork~*) cork; (*Zapfen, bes. auch el Stecker*) plug; (*Stift*) peg; (*Spund, Zapfen*) bung; *fig* (*kleine Person*) stumpy person; tub; **~kontakt** *m el* plug contact; **~n** *tr* (*verkorken*) to cork; (*zu~~*) to stopper; (*bes. el*) to plug; *ein~~* (*el*) to plug in; to insert a plug; (*verspunden*) to bung; **~schalter** *m el* plug switch; **~sicherung** *f el* plug (*od* cartridge) fuse.

Stör *m* (*Fisch*) sturgeon; **~rogen** *m* sturgeon's roe; caviar(e).

Stör|abschirmung *f* screening; **~anfälligkeit** *f* susceptibility to trouble; **~angriff** *m mil* harassing raid, nuisance raid; **~einsatz** *m mil* harassing operation; *radio* jamming; **~en** *tr* to disturb; (*Unannehmlichkeiten bereiten*) to trouble; (*plagen, behelligen*) to annoy; to vex; (*lästig fallen*) to inconvenience, to bother; (*unterbrechen*) to interrupt; (*hindern*) to prevent; (*aus der Ordnung bringen*) to derange; (*sich jdm aufdrängen*) to intrude (upon s.o.); (*im Wege sein*) to be in the way; (*durcheinander bringen*) to upset; *radio* (*durch Störsender*) to jam; to interfere; to cause interference; *mil* to harass; (*mit Feuer bestreichen*) to rake; *jds Pläne* (*od Absichten*) *~~* to cross s. o.'s plans; *die Ruhe ~~, den Frieden ~~* to break the peace; *jds Vergnügen ~~* to spoil s. o.'s pleasure; *~~ wir Sie?* are we disturbing you? *~~ Sie mich nicht!* don't bother me! *lassen Sie sich nicht ~~!* don't let me disturb you! *hoffentlich ~e ich nicht!* I hope I'm not intruding! *wir müssen Sie leider noch einmal ~~* we are sorry, but we will have to trouble you again; **~end** *a* (*belästigend*) disturbing; troublesome; (*lästig*) inconvenient; (*unterbrechend*) interrupting; (*beunruhigend*) vexing, annoying; **~enfried** *m* kill-joy; mischief-maker; marplot; intruder; **~er** *m* disturber; *radio* jamming station, disturbing station; **~filter** *m* noise filter; **~flieger** *m aero* nuisance raider; **~flug** *m* nuisance raid; **~~zeug** *n* nuisance raider; sneak raider; **~frei** *a radio* immune to interference; undisturbed; **~~heit** *f* immunity from interference (*od* disturbance); **~frequenz** *f radio* interfering frequency; **~funk** *m radio* jamming; **~funkstelle** *f* jamming station; **~gebiet** *n* disturbed area; **~geräusch** *n* background noise; surface noise; interfering noise; interference; jamming; **~jäger** *m aero* nuisance raider; **~klappe** *f aero* spoiler; disruptor flap; **~lautstärke** *f radio* noise level; **~pegel, ~spiegel** *m* noise level; **~schutz** *m* noise suppression; radio shielding; **~sender** *m* jamming station; radio jammer; **~sperre** *f* noise gate; **~stelle** *f* fault; *radio* jamming station; **~ung** *f* disturbance; (*Unannehmlichkeit*) inconvenience; trouble; (*Unordnung*) disorder; derangement; (*Durcheinander*) upset; (*Hindernis*) obstruction; hitch; (*Unterbrechung*) interruption; (*Aufdringlichkeit*) intrusion; (*Zerstörung*) destruction; *radio* (*~~ durch Sender*) jamming; interference (with wireless reception); (*atmosphärische ~~*) atmospherics *pl*, strays *pl*, static; (*der Magnetnadel*) (magnetic) perturbation; *el, tele* (*Fehler*) fault, break-down; (*geistige ~~*) mental disorder; *ohne ~~* without accident; *entschuldigen Sie bitte die ~~!* pardon the intrusion! *e-e ~~ beseitigen tele* to clear a fault; **~~saktion** *f mil* harassing (operation); **~~sangriff** *m mil* nuisance raid; **~~sbericht** *m tele* fault report, *Am* trouble record; **~~sbeseitigung** *f tele* trouble shooting; clearing of a fault; **~~sdienst** *m tele* fault-complaint service; **~~sfeuer** *n mil* harassing fire; **~~sflugzeug** *n* (*Einzelmaschine*) sneak raider; **~~sfrei** *a radio* static-free; **~~smeldung** *f tele* fault docket; **~~spersonal** *n tele* fault staff; **~~sstelle** *f tele* fault section, *Am* trouble desk; **~~ssuche** *f* interference location; **~~ssucher** *m tele* lineman, faultsman, troubleman; trouble-shooter; **~~strupp** *m tele* break-down squad, break-down tracing detachment; repair gang; **~~swelle** *f radio* jamming wave.

Storch *m* stork; *fam da brat' mir e-r e-n ~!* that beats everything! **~beinig** *a* spindle-legged; **~ennest** *n* stork's nest; **~schnabel** *m bot* stork's bill, crane's bill; geranium; *tech* (*Zeichengerät*) pantograph; diagraph; **Störchin** *f* female stork.

stornier|en *tr com* (*Buchung*) to reverse (an entry); (*Auftrag*) to countermand; to cancel; (*Scheck sperren*) to stop (a cheque); **~ung** *f com* (*Buchung*) reversal; (*Auftrag*) countermanding; (*Scheck*) stopping (of a cheque).

störr|ig, **~isch** *a* (*halsstarrig*) stubborn; headstrong; obstinate; (*mürrisch*) cross; (*Pferd*) restive; **~igkeit** *f* obstinacy; stubborness.

Stoß *m* push, shove; (*bes. mil Vor~, tech Schub, Druck*) thrust; *phys* (*Einschlag*) impact; (*Impuls*) impulse; (*Erschütterung*) shock; vibration; (*schlagartiger ~*) percussion; (*Zus.~*) collision; clash; (*Bumser, Puff*) bump; (*Schlag*) blow, hit, knock; (*leichter Schlag*) nudge; (*Rippen~*) poke (in the ribs); dig; (*Stich*) stab; (*Saum an Kleid*) seam; lining (at the bottom of a dress); (*Billard*) stroke; impact; (*Rück~*) recoil; kick; *Erdbeben~*) shock, concussion; (*Faustschlag*) punch, box; (*Fecht~*) pass, thrust; (*Fuß~, Gewehr~*) kick; (*~ mit den Hörnern*) butt; *mil* (*Feuer~*) burst (of fire); (*Wind~*) gust; blast; (*~ des Wagens*) jolt, jog, jerk; (*Schwimm~*) stroke; (*Trompeten~*) blast, sound; (*Haufen*) pile, heap; (*~ von Banknoten*) *Am fam* wad; (*Akten~*) file (of deeds); (*Papier~*) bundle; *min* face of work; wall-face; *rail* (*Verbindung*) joint; junction; *Gnaden~* finishing stroke; *~ u. Schlag* shock and impact; *jdm e-n ~ versetzen* to deal s. o. a blow; *Geben Sie Ihrem Herzen e-n ~!* come on! get a move on! **~beanspruchung** *f* impact (*od* shock) stress; **~dämpfer** *m* cushion; pad; *aero, mot* shock-absorber; **~degen** *m*, **~rapier** *n* rapier; foil; **~druck** *m* impact; pressure; **~en** *irr tr* (*nach vorwärts*) to push; (*schieben*) to shove; (*puffen, schlagen*) to buffet; to hit; to strike; (*leicht an~~*) to jog, to jostle; (*mit dem Ellbogen*) to nudge (with the elbow); (*mit e-r Waffe*) to thrust; (*stechen*) to stab; (*mit dem Fuß*) to kick; to hit; *Am* to buck; (*mit der Faust*) to punch; (*mit dem Kopf*) to butt; (*mit dem Glas an~~*) to clink; (*einrammen, hineintreiben*) to ram (*in* into); *tech* (*auskerben, ausstanzen*) to slot out; (*zerstoßen*) to pound; to crush; to bray; (*pulverisieren*) to pulverize, to powder; *aneinander ~~* to touch, (*stark*) to bump together; *auf Widerstand ~~* to meet with (*od* to encounter) opposition; *Am* to run into stiff (*od* strong) opposition from; *jdn aus dem Haus ~~* to turn (*fam* to kick) s. o. out; *ins Elend ~~* to ruin; *über den Haufen ~~* to run down; to overturn: to overthrow; *jdn vor den Kopf ~~* (*fig*) to affront s. o.; to offend s. o.; to give offence to s. o.; *wie vor den Kopf ge~~ sein fig* to be off o.'s head; *von sich ~~* to push away; *weg~~* to reject; to discard; *~~ aus* (*vertreiben aus*) to expel from, to oust; to turn out from; to drive out; *sich ~~ an* to bump o. s. on; to knock (o. s.) against; to strike o.'s foot against; (*sich verletzen*) to hurt o. s.; *fig* (*Anstoß nehmen*) to scruple, to stick at; to take offence at; *muß ich Sie mit der Nase darauf ~~?* do I have to stick it under your nose? *sich an jds Bemerkung ~~* to take offence at s. o.'s remark; *itr* (*vom Wagen*) to jog; to jolt; to bump; (*Bock*) to butt; (*Gewehr etc*) to recoil; (*mit e-m Messer*) to stab at; *an etw an~~* to dash against; to strike against; to run against; to knock against; (*angrenzen an*) to border on; to be next to; to adjoin; *nieder~~ auf* (*Raubvogel, Flugzeug*) to swoop down upon; *zufällig auf jdn* (*od etw*) *~~* to come across s. o. (*od* s. th.), to chance upon, to happen to meet; to encounter; to run into; *Am* to happen on s. o. (*od* s. th.); *nach etw ~~* to make a pass at; *zu jdm ~~* to join; to join up with; *ins Horn ~~* to blow (*od* to sound) a horn; *in die Trompete ~~* to sound the trumpet; *mit jdm ins gleiche Horn ~~* to be hand and glove with s. o.; *ans Land ~~* to get ashore, to land; *vom Land ~~* to set sail, to go out; **~fänger** *m mot* bumper; buffer, ram; (*~dämpfer*) shock-absorber; **~feile** *f* sharp file; **~fest** *a* shockproof; **~~igkeit** *f* resistance to shock; **~frei** *a* (*glatt*) smooth; steady; without shock, without jolt;

~gebet *n* short and fervent prayer; **~hobel** *m* jointer; **~kante** *f* seam; hem; edge; lining; **~keil** *m mil* spearhead; **~klinge** *f* small-sword blade; **~kraft** *f* impact (force), impetus; impulsive force; motive power; **~maschine** *f* shaping machine, shaper; slotting machine; **~mine** *f mil* contact mine; **~naht** *f* butt-joint; **~punkt** *m mil* point of attack; *tech* point of impact; **~seufzer** *m* deep sigh (*od* groan); ejaculation; **~stange** *f mot* bumper; *hintere* (*vordere*) **~~** rear (front) bumper; (*Ventilsteuerung*) push-rod; *rail* buffer-bar; **~trupp** *m mil* raiding party; assault (*od* shock) detachment; **~~en** *m pl* assault troops *pl* shock troops *pl*; (*für Sondereinsatz*) commando(s *pl*), *Am* rangers *pl*; **~~kämpfer** *m* commando, *Am* ranger; **~~ u. Hiebwaffen** *pl* cut and thrust weapons *pl*; **~verkehr** *m* heavy traffic during rush hours; **~weise** *adv* by jerks; by fits and starts; in gushes; intermittent(ly); fitfully; **~welle** *f* shock wave; percussion wave; surge; **~wind** *m* squall; gust (of wind); **~zahn** *m* tusk.

Stößel *m* (*in Mörser*) pestle, pounder; (*e-r Presse*) slide; rammer, ram; plunger; striker; (*Ventil~*) (valve) tappet, *Am* push-rod; stem; **~führung** *f* tappet guide; **~spiel** *n* tappet clearance.

Stößer *m* thruster, pounder; (*Stampfer*) stamper, rammer; (*Ventil~*) stem; *Am* push-rod; driver rod; (*Habicht*) hawk, bird of prey.

Stotter|er *m* stutterer; stammerer; **~n** *itr*, *tr* to stutter; to stammer; *fam* (*auf Abzahlung kaufen*) to pay by instalments; **~n** *n* stuttering.

Stotz, ~en *m dial* (*Baumstumpf*) stump.

*

stracks *adv* (*direkt*) direct(ly); (*geradeaus*) straight (ahead); (*sofort*) immediately; exactly.

Straf|änderung *f* commutation of sentence; **~androhung** *f* punishment laid down in the law; sanction; *unter* **~~** under a penalty; *jdn unter* **~~** *vorladen* to subpœna; **~anstalt** *f* house of correction; penal institution; (*Besserungsanstalt, Am Staatsgefängnis*) penitentiary; (*Jugendgefängnis*) reformatory; (*Gefängnis*) prison; jail; *militärische* **~~** military prison; **~antrag** *m* sentence demanded by the public prosecutor; **~antritt** *m* beginning of imprisonment; **~anzeige** *f* penal report; **~arbeit** *f* (*Schule*) imposition, *fam* lines *pl*, *sl* impot; *Am* extra-work; **~arrest** *m* detention; **~aufschub** *m* reprieve; suspension of the sentence; *5 Jahre* **~~** 5 years suspended; **~~** *auf Bewährung* to grant suspension of sentence on probation; **~aussetzung** *f* suspension of the execution of a sentence; **~bar** *a* punishable; liable to punishment; (*schuldig*) culpable; criminal; **~~** *nach* punishable under; **~~** *sein* to be an offence; **~~e** *Handlung* offence, *Am* offense; crime; punishable act; *sich* **~~** *machen* to be liable to prosecution; to incur a penalty; **~~keit** *f* punishableness; liability to punishment; culpability; criminality; **~bataillon** *n mil* delinquent battalion; **~befehl** *m* penal (*od* summary) court order; **~befugnis** *f* punitive power; power of sentence; **~bestimmung** *f* penal regulation (*od* provision); penal clause; penalty; **~bully** *n* (*Hockey*) penalty bully; **~dienst** *m mil* extra duty; **~e** *f* punishment; (*Züchtigung*) chastisement; (*Geld~~*) fine; mulct; *jdn mit Geld~~ belegen* to fine; to mulct; (*Freiheits~~*) imprisonment; *auferlegte* **~~** (*auch sport, fig*) penalty; *gerichtliche* **~~** legal punishment; (*Urteil*) judg(e)ment; (*Verurteilung*) sentence; *bei* **~~** *von* on pain of; on penalty of; *bei* **~~** *vorladen* to subpœna; *seine* **~~** *abbüßen* (*od absitzen*) to serve o.'s time; to serve o.'s term (*od* sentence); **~~** *auferlegen* (*od verhängen*) to inflict a penalty; to impose a sentence; **~~** *aufheben* to set aside a penalty; **~~** *aufschieben* to suspend a penalty; *mit e-r* **~~** *belegen* to punish with; **~~** *erhöhen* to increase the sentence; **~~** *herabsetzen* to reduce the sentence; **~~** *umwandeln* to commute a sentence; **~~** *vollstrecken* to execute a punishment; **~~** *zahlen* to pay a fine; **~en** *tr* to punish; (*züchtigen*) to chastise *Am* chastize; *Lügen* **~~** to belie; to give one the lie; *am Leben* **~~** to punish capitally; *mit Worten* **~~** to reprove; *um Geld* **~~** to fine; **~end** *a* (*Blick*) reproachful; **~entlassene(r)** *m* ex-convict; **~erlaß** *m allg* (*Amnestie*) amnesty; (*durch Gnadenakt*) pardon; remission of a punishment; **~erleichterung** *f* mitigation of punishment; **~ermäßigung** *f* remission of part of the punishment; **~expedition** *f* punitive expedition; **~fall** *m* penal case, criminal case; **~fällig** *a* punishable; liable to punishment; finable; liable to be fined; (*schuldig*) culpable; delinquent; **~~keit** *f* punishableness, culpability; **~frei** *a* exempt from punishment; unpunished; **~~heit** *f* impunity; immunity from criminal prosecution; **~gebühr** *f* fine; **~gefangene(r)** *m* convict; prisoner; **~geld** *n* fine; **~gericht** *n* punishment; (*Züchtigung*) chastisement; (**~~** *Gottes*) judg(e)ment (of God); (*Gerichtshof*) criminal court; tribunal; **~~sbarkeit** *f* criminal jurisdiction; **~gesetz** *n* penal (*od* criminal) law; **~~buch** *n* penal (*od* criminal) code; **~~gebung** *f* penal legislation; **~gewalt** *f* penal authority; power of sentence; (*disziplinarisch*) disciplinary authority; **~haft** *f* punitive arrest; *in* **~~** *behalten* to detain s. o.; **~kammer** *f* criminal court; (*bei e-m Landgericht*) criminal chamber (of landgericht); **~kolonie** *f* convict settlement; penal settlement; **~lager** *n* concentration camp; **~los** *a* unpunished; exempt from punishment; with impunity; without punishment; **~~** *ausgehen* to come off clear; **~~igkeit** *f* impunity; immunity; indemnity; **~mandat** *n* penalty; *Am* (*bei Verkehrsübertretung etc*) ticket; **~maß** *n* amount of punishment; **~maßnahme** *f* restriction; measure of punishment; sanction; **~milderungsgrund** *m* extenuating circumstances *pl*; **~mittel** *n* means of punishment; **~mündig** *a* of a responsible age; liable for crime; **~~keit** *f* age of discretion; **~porto** *n* (*Post*) surcharge; extra (*od* additional) postage; postage due; extra charge; **~predigt** *f* severe lecture; reprimand; *jdm e-e* **~~** *halten* to blow s. o. up; **~prozeß** *m* criminal case; criminal suit; criminal proceedings *pl*; **~~ordnung** *f* code of criminal procedure; **~punkt** *m sport* point deducted, bad point; penalty; **~raum** *m sport* penalty area; **~recht** *n* criminal law; penal law; **~~lich** *a* criminal; penal; **~rede** *f* lecture, reprimand; **~register** *n* penal register; criminal records *pl*; *Auszug aus dem* **~~** excerpt from the criminal records; extract from the criminal register; **~richter** *m* criminal judge; **~senat** *m* criminal senate; **~sache** *f* criminal case; **~~** *gegen* (criminal) case pending against; **~stoß** *m sport* penalty kick; **~summe** *f* penalty, fine; **~tat** *f* punishable act, offence, *Am* offense; **~umwandlung** *f* commutation of punishment; **~verfahren** *n* criminal procedure (*od* proceedings *pl*); **~verfolgung** *f* prosecution; **~verfügung** *f* (*der Polizei*) police penal order; **~verschärfung** *f* increasing a sentence; **~versetzung** *f* disciplinary transfer; **~verteidiger** *m* trial lawyer; **~vollstreckung**, **~vollziehung** *f*, **~vollzug** *m* execution of punishment; execution of sentences; **~würdig** *a* punishable; indictable; deserving punishment; **~zeit** *f* term of confinement; period of sentence; **~zumessung** *f* award of punishment; **~zuschlag** *m* surcharge.

straff *a* (*gestreckt*) stretched; (*gespannt*) tense; (*Seil*) taut; (*eng, angespannt*) tight; (*aufrecht, stramm*) straight; erect; *fig* (*strikt, exakt*) strict; rigid; (*streng*) stern, severe, austere; *~e Haltung* straight military carriage; *~ spannen* to tighten; **~en** *tr* to tighten; to stretch; (*Seil*) to tauten; **~heit** *f* tightness; straitness; tenseness; tautness; strictness.

sträf|lich *a* punishable, criminal; culpable; (*tadelnswert*) blamable; (*unverzeihlich*) unpardonable; **~ling** *m* (*Gefängnis~~*) prisoner; (*Zuchthäusler*) convict; *Am sl* stiff, lag; *mehrere in Ketten zus.geschlossene* **~~e** (*Am*) chain gang of convicts; *entflohener* **~~** escaped convict; **~~sjacke**, **~~skleidung** *f* convict's garb.

Strahl *m* (*Licht~*) ray; (*Elektronen~, Licht~*) beam; (*Blitz~*) flash; (*Wasser~*) jet; spout; *math* radius; straight line; (*Hufkrankheit*) frog; *Kriegführung mit radioaktiven ~en* radiological warfare; *infrarote ~en* infrared rays; *kosmische ~en* cosmic rays; *ultraviolette ~en* ultraviolet rays; **~antrieb** *m aero* jet propulsion; **~bomber** *m* jet bomber; **~düse** *f* blast nozzle; **~en** *itr* (*aus~~*) to radiate; to emit rays; *radio* (*mit Richtstrahler senden*) to beam (*nach* at); *fig* (*Gesicht*) to beam; (*leuchten*) to shine; *vor Freude* **~~** to beam with joy; *Programm, das mit Richtstrahler nach Südafrika gestrahlt wird* program beamed at South Africa; **~enbrechend** *a* refractive; **~enbrechung** *f* refraction (*od* diffraction) of rays; **~enbündel**, **~enbüschel** *n* beam (*od* pencil) of rays; cone of rays; **~end** *a* radiant; radiating; shining; beaming; **~eneinfall** *m* incidence of rays; **~enförmig** *a* ray-shaped; radiate; radial; radiant; **~enforscher** *m* radiologist; **~enforschung** *f* radiology; **~engang** *m* path of rays; **~enkrieg** *m* radiological warfare; **~enkrone** *f* glory; aureole; halo; corona; nimbus; **~enmesser** *m* radiometer, actinometer; **~enpilz** *m* ray fungus; **~enschutz** *m* protective screen; **~entherapie** *f* radiotherapy; actinotherapy; **~enwerfer** *m radio* directional aerial; array; **~er** *m* (*Aus~~*) emitter; radiator; *aero* (*Düsenflugzeug*) jet-propelled aircraft; jet craft; jet plane; (*kurz*) jet; (*Düsenjäger*) jet fighter, *Am sl* squirt (plane); *sl* blow job; *sl* zizz plane; whizz plane; *sl* jaypee; (= *Abk* jet propelled); **~erplatz** *m* airfield for jet aircraft; **~flugzeug** *n* jet-propelled aircraft, jet plane; **~ig** *a* radiating; radiant; **~jäger** *m aero* jet fighter, jet pursuit plane; **~motor** *m* jet propulsion engine; jet (engine); *mit Antrieb durch* **~~** jet-propelled; *Flugzeug mit zwei* **~~en** twin jet; *Ver-*

kehrsflugzeug mit 4 ~~en four-jet airliner; *~~en brauchen nicht warmzulaufen* jets need no warm-up; **~~antrieb** *m* jet propulsion; **~nachtjäger** *m* jet night fighter; **~ofen** *m* radiator; **~rohr** *n* jet pipe; blast gun; **~rücklauf** *m* (*Radar*) flyback; **~sendestelle** *f radio* (*Richtstrahler*) beam transmitter, unidirectional transmitter; **~triebwerk** *n* jet (power plant); jet unit; jet engine; **~turbine** *f aero* turbine jet unit, *Am* turbojet; **~ung** *f* radiation; emission; *atomare ~~* atomic radiation; **~~sdichte** *f* radiation density; **~~sdruck** *m* radiation pressure; **~~senergie** *f* radiated energy; **~~sforscher** *m* radiologist; **~~shöhe** *f* radiation height; **~~sintensität** *f* intensity of radiation; **~~smesser** *m* radiometer; actinometer; **~~squant** *n* photon; **~~sverlust** *m* radiation loss; **~~svermögen** *n* radiating power; **~~swärme** *f* radiation heat; **~vortrieb** *m* jet propulsion.

strählen *tr* (*kämmen*) to comb.

Strähn|e *f* (*Haar~~*) lock, strand (of hair); (*Garnmaß*) hank, skein; **~ig** *a* wispy; in strands; of strands.

Stramin *m* (fine) canvas.

stramm *a* (*straff*) tight; taut; close; (*stark*) robust; strong; strapping; (*scharf, streng*) stiff; severe; (*aufrecht, steif*) erect; *~er Junge* strapping youngster; *~es Mädel* bouncing girl, bouncer; *~er Soldat* smart soldier; *~e Zucht* strict discipline; *jdm die Hosen ~ ziehen* to give s. o. a good hiding; *sie haben ~ arbeiten müssen* they had to work like beavers; *~ stehen mil* to stand at attention.

strampel|n *itr* to kick; to trample, to tread; to toss about; *sich bloß ~~* to kick the bed-clothes off; **~höschen** *n* rompers *pl*.

Strand *m* (*Ufer*) sea-shore, shore; (*sandiger ~, Bade~*) beach; *poet* strand; (*Küste*) coast; (*Gestade*) littoral; *am ~* on the beach; *an den ~ gehen* to go to the beach; *auf dem ~* (*Schiff*) high and dry; *auf* (*den*) *~ laufen* to strand; *auf den ~ laufen lassen, auf ~ setzen, auf ~ ziehen* to beach; **~ablagerung** *f* sea-shore deposit; **~anzug** *m* beach suit; beach wear; *Oberteil e-s zweiteiligen ~~es* (*für Damen*) halter; **~artig** *a* beachy; **~bad** *n* bathing beach; seaside resort; **~batterie** *f* shore-battery; **~besucher** *m* beachgoer; **~bewohner** *m* coast-dweller; **~burg** *f* sand castle; **~dieb** *m* wrecker; **~en** *itr* to be beached; to be stranded; to run aground (*od* ashore); to make the land; *fig* (*scheitern*) to go to wreck; to fail; **~fischer** *m* coast-fisherman; **~gebiet** *n* shoreland; **~gewächse** *n pl bot* littoral plants *pl*; **~gut** *n* stranded goods *pl*; jetsam; (*treibendes ~~*) flotsam; *fig* waif; **~gutjäger** *m* beach-comber; **~hafen** *m* dry harbo(u)r; **~hafer** *m bot* bent; lame-grass; dune grass; **~hose** *f* beach slacks *pl*; **~hotel** *n* seaside hotel; casino; **~kleidung** *f* beach wear; **~korb** *m* canopied beach-chair; **~krabbe** *f* shore-crab; **~läufer** *m orn* sand-piper; **~linie** *f* shore line; **~los** *a* beachless; **~mauer** *f* sea wall; **~nixe** *f* seaside girl; **~promenade** *f* promenade (of the bathing resort); *Am* boardwalk; **~raub** *m* wrecking; **~räuber** *m* wrecker; **~recht** *n* right of salvage; salvage law; **~schirm** *m* beach umbrella; **~schuhe** *m pl* sand-shoes *pl*, beach-shoes *pl*; **~see** *m* lagoon; **~tasche** *f* beach bag; **~ung** *f* stranding; shipwreck; running ashore; **~vogt** *m* wreck-master; inspector of the sea-shore; **~wache** *f* coast-guard; **~wächter** *m* coast-guardsman; **~wärter** *m* (*Badewärter*) life-guard, *Am* life-saver; **~welle** *f* (*große*) breaker, roller, *Am* beachcomber, comber; **~zelt** *n* beach tent.

Strang *m* (*Seil*) rope, cord; (*Strick zum Aufhängen*) halter; (*Zugseil amWagen*) trace; (*Strippe*) strap; (*Glocken~*) bell-rope; *rail* (*Schienen~*) track, rail; line; *gerader ~* (*rail*) straight line; *krummer ~* curved line; *min* (*Flöz*) vein, stratum, bed, layer, seam; (*Ader*) artery, vein; *anat* cord; funiculus; tract; (*Garn~, Seiden~*) hank, skein; *über die Stränge schlagen* (*od hauen*) *fig* to kick over the traces; to run riot; *wenn alle Stränge reißen fig* if the worst comes to the worst; *am gleichen ~ ziehen* to act in concert; *zum ~ verurteilen* to sentence to death by hanging; to condemn to the gallows; **~ulation, ~ulierung** *f* strangulation; **~ulieren** *tr* (*erdrosseln*) to strangle; **~zelle** *f anat* funicular cell.

Strapaz|e *f* exertion, hardship; drudgery; toil; **~ieren** *tr* to tire, to harass; to knock up; (*abnützen*) to wear hard; **~ierfähig** *a* long-wearing, hard-wearing; **~iös** *a* tiring; fatiguing.

Straße *f* (*in Stadt, Dorf etc*) street; (*Großstadt~ mit Bäumen, in USA mit starkem Verkehr*) boulevard; *Am* (*breite Quer~ in Großstadt*) avenue; (*Haupt~*) principal street, *Am* main street; (*Land~*) road; (*Verkehrs~*) highway; (*bes. für mot Verkehr*) high-road; (*Durchgangs~*) thoroughfare, *Am* artery; (*Neben~*) byway; (*Gäßchen, Sträßchen*) lane; (*Durchgangsgasse zu Rückgebäude*) alley(way); (*Reichs~*) national highway; (*Alleen~*) parkway; (*Meerenge*) strait, (*bei Namen*) Straits *pl*; (*~nblock*) block of buildings, *Am* block; *e-e ~ weiter* a block further on; *tech* (*Walzen~*) rolling mill train; *Oxford~* Oxford St.(reet); *die ~ nach Oxford* Oxford Road; *belebte ~* busy (*od* crowded) street (*od* road); *gepflasterte ~* paved road; *kurvenreiche ~* winding road; *öffentliche ~* public road; *nicht befestigte ~* not macadamized or paved road, *Am* dirt road; *~ mit Parkverbot*, yellow-band street; *an der ~* by the wayside; *auf der ~* in the street, *Am* on the street; *auf die ~ setzen* to turn out; to put out (in the street); to send packing; *der Mann auf der ~* the man in the street; *das Geld auf die ~ werfen* to throw o.'s money around; *in e-r ~ wohnen* to live in a street; *in welcher ~ wohnen Sie?* which street do you live in? *er wohnt über der ~* he lives just across the street.

Straßen|abzweigung *f* road diversion, deviation; branching off; **~anlage** *f* line of a road; **~anzug** *m* lounge-suit, sack-suit, *Am* business suit; **~arbeit** *f* road work; **~arbeiter** *m* road-man, navvy, *Am* road laborer; **~aufseher** *m* road-surveyor; **~aufsicht** *f* supervision of the highroads; **~ausrufer** *m* (street) crier; **~bagger** *m* bulldozer; **~bahn** *f* tramway, tram, *Am* trolley line; (*Wagen*) tram-car, *Am* trolley, streetcar; *mit der ~~ befördern* to convey on a tram-car; *mit der ~~ fahren* to ride on a tram-car; **~~depot** *n* tramway depot, *Am* car barn; **~~er** *m* tramwayman, tramway official; **~~fahrpreis** *m* tram (*Am* car) fare; **~~führer** *m* tramdriver, *Am* motorman; **~~haltestelle** *f* tramway stop, *Am* streetcar stop; **~~linie** *f* tramway line, *Am* trolley (*od* streetcar) line; **~~netz** *n* tramway system; **~~oberleitung** *f* tramway overhead line; **~~reklame** *f* tram-car advertising; **~~schaffner** *m* (tram-) conductor; **~~schiene** *f* tramway rail, *Am* street-car line; **~~verkehr** *m* tramway traffic; **~~wagen** *m* tram (-car), *Am* streetcar, trolley (car); (*in New York*) surface car; (*Motorwagen*) rail motor-car; (*Anhänger*) trailer; **~bau** *m* road construction (*od* building), highway engineeering; **~befestigung** *f* road surface; **~bekanntschaft** *f fam* pick-up; **~belag** *m* road surface; **~beleuchtung** *f* lighting of the streets, street lighting; (*verminderte*) star lighting; **~bengel, ~flegel** *m* ragamuffin; hooligan; **~benutzer** *m* user of roads; **~beschaffenheit** *f* road condition; **~beschotterung** *f* road metal; **~bett** *n* road bed; **~biegung** *f* road turn, road curve; **~block** *m* block of buildings, *Am* block; **~brücke** *f* viaduct, highway (*od* road) bridge; **~damm** *m* causeway, roadway; **~decke** *f* highway (*od* road) surface; **~dirne** *f* street-walker, prostitute; *fam* tart, *Am sl* street sister, gutter slut, sidewalk susie; **~~nunwesen** *n* prostitution, streetwalking; **~disziplin** *f* road discipline; **~dorf** *n* village built on either side of main road; **~dreieck** *n* triangular road junction; **~ecke** *f* street corner; *an der ~~* at the corner of the street; **~einmündung** *f* road (*od* street) junction; **~fahrzeug** *n* road vehicle; **~feger** *m* scavenger; **~fläche** *f* road surface; **~front** *f* street front; face, façade; **~gabel** *f* road fork; **~gabelung** *f* bifurcation; **~gesindel** *n* mob, rabble; **~graben** *m* road ditch; road drain; **~handel** *m* street hawking (*od* trading *od* peddling); **~händler** *m* street-vendor, street-hawker, street-seller, *Am* corner facer; **~hilfsdienst** *m* road service; **~höhe** *f* street level; **~insel** *f* refuge, island; **~instandhaltung** *f* road maintenance; **~junge** *m* street arab; street-urchin; *Am fam* dead-end kid; (*Bengel*) ragamuffin; **~kaffee** *n Am* sidewalk café; **~kampf** *m mil* street-fighting; **~kanal** *m* sewer; **~kante** *f* curbstone; **~karte** *f* road map; **~kehre** *f* (*Kurve*) road bend; sharp turn; **~kehrer** *m* street- (*od* road-)sweeper, *Am* street-cleaner; **~kehricht** *m* street sweepings *pl*; **~kehrmaschine** *f* street-sweeper, *Am* street cleanser, motor sweeper; **~kiosk** *m* street kiosk; **~kleid** *n* out-door dress; **~knie** *n* sharp road curve; **~kot** *m* street mud; **~krach** *m* street-brawl; **~kreuz** *n*, **~kreuzung** *f* cross-roads *pl mit sing*; crossing; traverse; **~kundgebung** *f* demonstration, manifestation (in the street); **~kundig** *a* knowing o.'s way about a town; **~lage** *f mot* road holding; **~lärm** *m* street noise; **~laterne** *f* street-lamp; **~leben** *n* street life; **~lümmel** *m* hooligan; **~mädchen** *n* (*Hure*) street-walker, prostitute; *Am sl* alley cat; molly; street sister; pavement pretty; gutter slut; sidewalk susie; **~musikant** *m* itinerant musician, strolling musician; **~netz** *n* road system, road network; **~oberfläche** *f* road surface; **~ordnung** *f* rule of the road; **~panzerwagen** *m* armo(u)red scout car; **~pflaster** *n* pavement; **~pöbel** *m* mob, rabble; **~polizei** *f* traffic police; **~rand** *m* verge of the road; road border; **~rasthaus** *n* road-house; **~raub** *m* highway robbery; **~räuber** *m* highwayman; bandit; robber; *Am* road agent; *hum* knight of the road; **~redner** *m* street orator, *Am fam* soapbox orator; soapboxer; **~~podium** *n Am fam* soapbox; **~reinigung** *f* street cleaning; scavenging; **~rennen** *n* road-race; **~rinne** *f* (side) gutter, drain, sewer; **~sammlung** *f* street collection; **~sänger** *m* street singer; **~schild** *n* street-sign; name plate; **~schmutz** *m* mud; **~schotter** *m* road ballast; street macadam; **~schuhe** *m pl* walking shoes *pl*; **~schwein** *n mot* (*rücksichtsloser Fahrer*) road hog, *Am fam* scortcher; **~seite** *f* roadside; **~sperre** *f* street barricade; road block; barrier; **~sperrung** *f* blocking of streets; (*Schild*) road closed for traffic; **~spinne** *f* road junction; **~sprengwagen** *m* watering-cart; **~streife** *f* (*Polizei*) highway patrol; **~szene** *f* street scene; **~transport(verkehr)** *m* road transport, road haulage; **~überführung** *f* viaduct, road overpass, road crossing; **~übergang** *m* street crossing; **~umleitung** *f* diversion, detour; **~umzug** *m* procession; (*politisch*) demonstration; **~unfall** *m* road accident; **~~ziffer** *f* toll of the road; **~unterführung** *f* tunnel, subway; underpassage; **~unterhaltung** *f* road maintenance; **~verengung** *f* road bottleneck; **~verkauf** *m* street sale; **~verkäufer** *m* street-vendor, costermonger, hawker; **~verkehr** *m* road (*od* highway) traffic; (*Stadt*) street traffic; **~~samt** *n* Road Traffic Office; **~~sordnung** *f* traffic regulations *pl*; **~~sunfall** *m* highway traffic accident; **~verstopfung** *f* road (*od* traffic) jam; **~verzeichnis** *n* street directory; **~walze** *f* road roller; (*Dampfwalze*) steam-roller; (*mit Dieselmotor*) Diesel roller; **~wärter** *m* road attendant; **~zug** *m* row, line of streets; **~zustand** *m* street condition.

Strateg|e *m* strategist; **~em** *n* (*Kriegslist*) stratagem; artifice; ruse; (*Trick*) trick, subterfuge; machination; **~ie** *f* strategy; strategics *pl*; **~isch** *a* strategic(al); *~~e Aufklärung* strategical reconnaissance; *~~e Bombardierung* strategic bombing; *~~e Luftkriegführung* strategic air warfare; *~~e Reserve* strategic reserve; *~~e Rohmaterialien* strategic material.

Strat|okumulus *m* strato-cumulus clouds *pl*; **~osphäre** *f* stratosphere; **~~naufstieg** *m* ascent into the stratosphere; **~~nballon** *m* stratosphere balloon, *fam* skyhook; **~~nbomber** *m* stratosphere bomber; **~~ndüsenbomber** *m Am* stratojet bomber; **~~nflug** *m* stratosphere flight; **~~nflugzeug** *n* stratosphere plane, *Am* stratoplane (*Abk* strat); *Am* (*Verkehrsflugzeug*) stratoliner, stratocruiser; **~~nmotor** *m aero* stratosphere engine; **~~nrakete** *f* stratospheric rocket; high altitude rocket; **~~nstrahlflugzeug** *n Am* stratojet (plane); **~uswolke** *f* stratus cloud.

*

sträuben *tr* to ruffle up, to bristle; *r* to bristle, to stand up; to stand on end; *fig* to resist, to oppose s. th.; to struggle (*od* to strive) against; *die Haare des Hundes sträubten sich* the dog's hair bristled; *der Vogel sträubte seine Federn* the bird ruffled up its feathers; *~ n* reluctance.

Strauch *m* shrub; (*Busch*) bush; (*Gesträuch*) shrubbery; **~artig** *a* shrub-like; bush-like; shrubby; **~birke** *f* dwarf birch tree; **~dieb** *m* footpad; highwayman; **~holz** *n* brushwood, underwood; **~ig** *a* bushy, shrubby; **~maske** *f* shrubbery screen; **~ritter** *m* highway robber; ruffian; **~werk** *n* shrubs *pl*, shrubbery, copse; (*Unterholz*) brushwood, underwood; **~wuchs** *m* shrubby growth.

straucheln *itr* (*auch fig*) to stumble (*über* over); to trip; to make a false step; *fig* to fail (in o.'s duty); to make a foolish mistake; (*wanken*) to totter; *er strauchelte über e-e Baumwurzel* he tripped over the root of a tree; *~ n* stumbling; trip.

Strauß *m* (*Blumen*) nosegay, bunch; (*kunstvoll gebunden*) bouquet; *ein herrlicher ~ Rosen* a beautiful bouquet of roses; *e-n ~ binden* to make a nosegay; (*Kampf*) struggle, strife; combat; *ein harter ~* a hot fight; *e-n ~ ausfechten* to fight a severe struggle; (*Vogel*) ostrich; (*südamerikanische Art*) rhea; *Vogel-~-Politik treiben* to hide o.'s head in the sand; **~binderin** *f* flower-girl; **~enei** *n* ostrich egg; **~enfeder** *f* ostrich feather; plume; **~enzucht** *f* ostrich farming.

Strazze *f* daybook.

Streb|e *f* (*Stütze, Pfeiler*) prop; (*Träger, Halt, Stütze*) support; (*Stützstange*) stay; (*Stütz~~*) shore; (*Verstrebung*) strut; **~ebalken** *m* strut; brace; buttress; **~ebogen** *m* flying buttress; **~emauer** *f* counterfort; pier; **~en** *itr* to strive (*nach* for *od* after) (*suchen nach*) to seek after; (*hinzielen auf*) to aim at; (*sich bemühen zu bekommen*) to endeavour (to get); (*trachten nach*) to aspire (to *od* after); (*hin ~~ zu*) to tend (towards); (*vorwärts ~~*) to push (*od* to press) forward; (*ringen um*) to struggle (for); **~en** *n* (*Bemühung*) endeavo(u)r; (*Anstrengung*) effort; exertion; striving (after *od* for); (*trachten nach*) aspiration (for, after); (*Ziel*) aim; (*Hang, Richtung*) tendency; **~enlos** *a* unsupported; unpropped; **~epfeiler** *m* buttress; pier; spur; counterfort; **~er** *m* pusher, pushing person; *Am* climber; *Am fam* (*in der Schule*) grind; grade-grabber; (*Speichellecker*) toady; (*verächtlich*) place-hunter; office-hunter; **~~tum** *n* place-hunting; **~sam** *a* (*ausdauernd*) assiduous; (*unternehmend*) active; (*fleißig*) industrious; (*nach Höherem trachtend*) aspiring; (*eifrig*) zealous; **~~keit** *f* (*Ausdauer*) assiduity; (*eifrige Tätigkeit*) activity; (*Tüchtigkeit, Energie*) strenuousness; (*Eifer*) zeal; (*Fleiß*) industry.

streck|bar *a* extensible; (*dehnbar*) ductile; **~~keit** *f* extensibility; ductility; **~bett** *n* orthop(a)edic bed; extension bed; **~e** *f* (*Stück*) stretch; (*Entfernung*) distance; stage, *Am* leg; (*Weg*) way; road; route; (*Weglänge*) length; (*Zwischenraum*) interval; (*Gegend, Land*) tract; extent; (*Raum*) space; (*Eisenbahn~~*) section; *Am* division; *rail, aero* (*Linie*) line; (*Ausdehnung*) extent; (*Fluß*) reach (of a river); (*Jagdbeute*) all the game killed; the bag; (*Bergbau*) gallery; drift; (gang)way; (*Geometrie*) straight line; *e-e ~~ fahren* to ride a way, to drive a way, to take a route; *e-e ~~ überbrücken* to span a distance; *e-e ~~ zurücklegen* to cover a distance; *e-e ~~ Weges* some distance; *auf ~~* while cruising; *auf freier ~~* (*rail*) on the open track; on the open line; (*bei Straße*) on the road; *auf der ~~ bleiben* to perish; *auf dieser ~~ ist reger Verkehr* there's heavy traffic on that line; *zur ~~ bringen* (*Jagd*) to bag; to kill; to shoot down; to finish off; **~en** *tr* (*dehnen*) to stretch, to stretch out; to extend; to elongate; (*durch Hämmern*) to hammer out; (*Metallwalzen*) to roll; (*ziehen*) to draw (out); to laminate; (*Glasfabrikation*) to spread, to flatten; *fig* to make last, to lengthen; to go slow; *sich ~~* to stretch (o. s.); to extend; *sich nach der Decke ~~* to cut o.'s coat according to o.'s cloth; *die Beine ~~* to stretch o.'s legs; *die Butter mit Margarine ~~* to stretch the butter with margarine; *alle Viere von sich ~~* to lie sprawling; *jdn zu Boden ~~* to knock s. o. down; to fell (to the ground); to floor; *die Hände gegen den Himmel ~~* to lift o.'s hands towards heaven; *die Waffen ~~* to lay down o.'s arms; *die Zunge aus dem Mund ~~* to put out o.'s tongue; *im gestreckten Galopp* at full speed; **~enabschnitt** *m* sector; track section; **~enapparat** *m rail tele* portable telephone set (*od* station); **~enarbeiter** *m* plate-layer; trackman; section-hand; *Am* construction laborer; **~enbau, ~enbetrieb** *m min* drifting; drift mining; **~enbefeuerung** *f aero* airway lighting; **~enfernsprecher** *m rail* portable telephone set (*od* station); **~enfeuer** *n* airway beacon; **~enflug** *m aero* distance flight, commercial flight; **~enförderung** *f min* underground hauling; **~enfunkfeuer** *n* range beacon; **~enkarte** *f* (*Straße*) road map; *aero* air-route map; **~enleitstrahl** *m aero* route avigation beam; **~ennavigation** *f aero* route avigation; **~ennetz** *n aero* air-lines network; **~enpilot** *m aero* route pilot; **~enrekord** *m* long-distance record; **~enwärter** *m rail* linekeeper, lineman, linesman, surface man, *Am* trackwalker, trackman; **~enweise** *adv* here and there; **~enwetterberatung** *f* airway weather forecast; **~festigkeit** *f* resistance to stretching; **~grenze** *f* yield(ing) point (*od* strength); elastic limit; **~mittel** *n* filler; **~muskel** *m anat* extensor (muscle); **~ung** *f* stretching, extending, lengthening; extension; **~~smittel** *n chem* diluent; **~verband** *m med* traction (*od* extension) bandage.

Streich *m* (*Hieb, Schlag*) stroke; blow; (*mit Peitsche*) lash; *Staats~* coup (d'état); *fig* (*Possen, Schabernack*) prank, trick; (*derber ~*) skylark; (*lustiger ~*) joke; *dummer ~* stupid (*od* silly) trick; blunder; folly; *schlechter ~* mean trick, *Am* dirty trick; *auf e-n ~* at one blow; *auf den ersten ~* at the first attempt; *jdm e-n ~ spielen* to play a trick (*od* joke) on s. o.; to play s. o. a mean trick; *Am fam* to take s. o. for a ride; *ohne e-n ~ zu tun* without striking a blow; **~eln** *tr* (*liebkosen, zärtlich darüberfahren*) to caress; to pet; (*tätscheln*) to pat; (*schmeicheln*) to coax; (*streichen*) to stroke; **~en** *irr tr* to stroke; (*reiben*) to rub; (*leicht berühren*) to touch gently; (*darüber ~~*) to pass lightly over; (*Butter etc*) to spread; (*Flagge*) to lower; to strike; to haul down; *fig* to give in; (*Geige*) to play; (*Messer*) to whet; (*Segel*) to haul down, to furl, to lower; (*mit Ruten*) to flog, to scourge; (*Ziegel*) to make (bricks); to mo(u)ld; (*Zündholz*) to strike (*an* against); *ab~~* to deduct; *an~~* to paint; to colo(u)r; to varnish; *aus~~* to strike out; to cross out; (*ausradieren, auslöschen*) to erase; (*tilgen*) to expunge (s. o.'s name from a list); (*durch~~, annullieren*) to cancel, to annul; (*entwerten, tilgen*) to obliterate; *sport* (*von Liste, Meldung*) to scratch; *der Posten ist gestrichen worden* the item has been cancel(l)ed; *das Haar aus der Stirne ~~* to push o.'s hair out of o.'s eyes; *glatt ~~* to smooth; to polish; to burnish; *itr* (*vorbei~~*) to pass; to move; to rush; (*über etw mit d.*

Hand ~~) to pass (*od* to stroke) one's hand over; (*fliegen*) to fly, to sweep; (*Zugvögel*) to migrate; (*Schiff durch die Wellen*) to plough (*od* to cut) through waves; (*wandern*) to stroll, to wander; (*umher~~*) to roam, to ramble; (*sich erstrecken*) to extend; to stretch; to run out; *frisch gestrichen!* wet paint! *gestrichen voll* full to the brim; **~en** *n* (*von Vögeln*) passage of (birds); (*Ab~~*) cancellation, crossing off; *typ* deletion; **~er** *m pl mus* the strings *pl*; **~garn** *n* carded wool; worsted yarn; **~~gewebe** *n* woolen goods *pl*; **~~spinnerei** *f* carded-wool spinning mill; **~holz, ~hölzchen** *n* match; match-stick; strike; **~~schachtel** *f* match-box; *Am* matchsafe; (*flache Packung mit Ziehzünder*) match folder; **~instrument** *n mus* string(ed) instrument; **~käse** *m* spread cheese; **~lack** *m* brushing lacquer; **~massage** *f med* effleurage; **~musik** *f* string music; **~orchester** *n* string-band; **~quartett** *n* string quartet; **~riemen** *m* razor-strop; **~ung** *f* cancel(l)ing, cancellation; nullification; **~~zeichen** *n typ* dele(atur).

Streif *m* stripe; (*Strich*) streak; band; **~abteilung** *f* raiding party; **~band** *n* (newspaper) wrapper; cover; *unter ~~* by book post; **~e** *f* (*Razzia*) razzia; raid; raiding; (*Ronde*) beat; *mil* patrol; raiding-party; *aero* sweep; **~en** *m* stripe, streak; band; (*Land~~*) strip, sector; (*Licht~~*) streak (of light); (*Papier~~*) slip (of paper), strip (of paper); **~en** *tr* (*mit Streifen versehen*) to stripe, to streak; (*leicht berühren*) to graze, to scrape, to touch slightly; to skim; to brush; *fig* to skirt; (*hinweg~~*) to glide (*über* over); (*seitlich ~~*) to sideswipe; (*ab~~*) to strip off; (*Ring*) to take off; (*auf~~*) to tuck up; to turn up; (*Ärmel*) to turn down; (*über~~*) to put on; *itr* (*im Gespräch*) to touch (upon); *ein Problem ~~* to touch a problem; *fig* (*angrenzen*) to border (up)on; to verge (upon); (*umher~~*) to ramble, to wander; to stroll; to rove; to roam; *mil* to reconnoitre; to patrol; **~enaufnahme** *f* strip photograph; **~enbildung** *f* striation; **~endrucker** *m* tape printer; **~enrolle** *f* tape roll; **~enwagen** *m* (*der Polizei*) police patrol car; *Am* (*mit Funk*) squad car, prowl car, cruiser; **~enweise** *adv* in strips; **~erei** *f* excursion, ramble; *mil* incursion, raid; **~ig** *a* striped; (*Speck*) streaky; (*geädert*) veined; **~jagd** *f* shooting expedition; **~kommando** *n* raiding party; scouting party; flying column; **~licht** *n* side-light; spotlight; *ein ~~ auf etw werfen* to throw a side-light on s. th.; **~schuß** *m* grazing shot; glancing shot; *e-n ~~ bekommen* to be grazed by a bullet; **~ung** *f* striation, stria; striping; **~wache** *f* patrol; **~wunde** *f* skin-wound; (*Kratzer*) scratch; **~zug** *m* incursion; expedition; inroad; (scouting) raid.

Streik *m* (*Arbeitsniederlegung*) strike, *Am fam* walk out; walk off; *Am sl* go-out; *e-n ~ abbrechen* to call off a strike; *e-n ~ ausrufen* to call a strike; *in den ~ treten* to (go on) strike, *Am fam* to walk out (on); to stage a walk-out; to turn out; *Arbeits- od Betriebseinstellung wegen e-s ~s* tie-up; *General~* general strike; *Sitz~* sit-down strike; *Sympathie~* sympathetic strike; *wilder ~* unauthorized strike; *Am* wildcat strike; **~abstimmung** *f* strike vote; **~ausschuß** *m* strike committee; **~bewegung** *f* strike movement; **~brecher** *m* strike-breaker, blackleg; *Am sl* scab, *Am sl* fink; rat; *als ~~ auftreten Am sl* to scab; **~dauer** *f* duration of strike; **~drohung** *f* threat of strike; **~en** *itr* to go on strike; to strike; to lay down tools; to come out on strike; *Am fam* to walk out; to be out; **~ende(r), ~er** *m* striker; *Am sl* walk-outer, *Am sl* turnout; **~kasse** *f* striking-funds *pl*; **~lage** *f* strike situation; **~posten** *m* picket; *Am sl* picketeer; *~~ stehen* to picket; **~~kette, ~~sperre** *f* picket line; **~recht** *n* freedom to strike; **~unterstützung** *f* strike pay; **~verkündung** *f* calling of a strike; **~versicherung** *f* strike insurance.

Streit *m* (*Kampf*) fight; combat; struggle; (*Krieg*) war; (*heftiger ~*) altercation; (*Reiberei, Konflikt*) conflict; (*Gezänk, bes. zwischen Kindern*) squabble; (*Zwist*) bicker, bickering; (*fortwährender, lauter ~*) wrangle, wrangling; (*Unstimmigkeit*) disagreement, dissension, difference, *fam* spat, tiff; (*Rechts~*) litigation, lawsuit; (*gelehrter ~*) controversy; (*Wett~*) contest, competition; (*Wort~*) debate, dispute; argument; (*Wortwechsel*) contest; (*Erörterung*) discussion; (*mit Handgemenge od Schlägerei*) brawl, row; fracas; mix-up; *fam* rumpus; *fam* set-to; *sl* scrap; (*Rauferei*) tussle, scuffle; *mit jdm ~ anfangen, e-n ~ vom Zaun brechen* to pick a quarrel with s.o.; to kick up a row; *e-n ~ beilegen* to settle a dispute; to arrange a dispute; to decide a quarrel; to put an end to a dispute; (*schlichten*) to arbitrate; *in ~ geraten* to differ from, to fall out; to come to words with s. o.; to get into a quarrel; *mit jdm im ~ liegen* to be at variance with s. o.; to be at loggerheads with s. o.; **~axt** *f* battle-axe; *die ~~ begraben* to bury the hatchet; **~bar** *a* fighting; pugnacious; (*kriegerisch*) martial; warlike; (*tapfer*) valiant; **~en** *irr itr* (*mit jdm über etw*) to contend (with s. o. for s. th.); (*kämpfen*) to fight; to combat; (*zanken*) to quarrel; to squabble (with); (*mit Worten ~~*) to dispute; to debate; to argue (*mit jdm über* with s. o. about); (*be~~, in Abrede stellen*) to contest; to deny; *sich ~~* to dispute; to quarrel; to wrangle; *sich um des Kaisers Bart ~~* to dispute about trifles; *darüber läßt sich ~~* that's open to question; *darüber will ich nicht ~~* I won't argue about that; **~end** *a* quarrel(l)ing; contending; disputing; *die ~~en Parteien jur* the litigant parties; **~er** *m* (*Kämpfer*) fighter, combatant; (*Krieger*) warrior; *fig* (*Verfechter*) champion; (*Zanksüchtiger*) quarreller; (*im Wortstreit*) disputant; *jur* contestant (to a suit); litigant; **~fall** *m* case at issue, question at issue; dispute, quarrel; controversy; **~frage** *f* point of controversy, point in debate; point at issue, *Am* issue; matter in dispute; moot point; contested case; argument; *jur* matter at bar; **~gegenstand** *m* matter in dispute; contention; **~hammel** *m fam* squabbler; brawler; **~handel** *m* dispute; **~ig** *a* contested; contestable; debatable; (*fraglich*) controversial; in dispute; disputed; (*zweifelhaft*) doubtful; *jdm etw ~~ machen* to dispute; to contest o.'s right to s. th.; *jdm den Rang ~~ machen* to compete with s. o.; **~~keit** *f* dispute; controversy; contention; quarrel; difference; **~kräfte** *f pl* military forces *pl*; (*Truppen*) troops *pl*; **~lust** *f* quarrelsome disposition; **~lustig** *a* pugnacious; eager to fight; **~objekt** *n* bone of contention; **~punkt** *m* point in dispute; point at issue; *Am* issue; moot point; **~roß** *n hist* steed; charger; **~sache** *f* matter in dispute; contested (*od* controversial) matter; **~satz** *m* thesis; **~schrift** *f* polemical pamphlet (*od* treatise); **~sucht** *f* quarrelsomeness; *jur* litigiousness; **~süchtig** *a* quarrelsome; cranky; litigious; disputatious; **~wagen** *m hist* war-chariot; **~wert** *m jur* money involved (in the case); value of claim.

streng *a* (*hart*) hard; (*unnachsichtlich*) severe; (*unnachgiebig, ernst*) stern; (*unbeugsam, hart*) rigid; (*unerbittlich, peinlich, unfreundlich*) rigorous; (*bestimmt*) strict; (*Kälte*) intense; biting; (*scharf*) harsh; (*genau*) exacting; (*schwierig, unbeugsam*) stiff; (*Regeln*) stringent; (*starr, unerbittlich*) inflexible; (*unzugänglich, fest*) adamant; (*rauh*) rough; (*Charakter, Sitten*) austere; (*asketisch ~*) ascetic; (*Disziplin, Strafe, Kritik, Probe*) severe; (*Geschmack*) sharp; *~er Arrest* close confinement; *jdm e-n ~en Blick zuwerfen* to give s. o. a stern look; *~e Maßnahmen ergreifen* to take stringent measures; *~ gegen jdn sein* to deal harshly with s. o.; *~ bestrafen* to punish s. o. severely; *im ~en Sinne* strictly speaking; *~ verboten!* strictly forbidden! *Rauchen ~ verboten!* smoking strictly prohibited! positively no smoking! **~e** *f* severity; (*Ernst*) sternness; (*Starrheit, Schärfe*) rigo(u)r; (*Härte, Derbheit*) harshness; (*Sitten, Charakter*) austerity; (*Rauhheit, Härte*) roughness; (*Bestimmtheit*) strictness; (*Schärfe, zwingende Kraft*) stringency; (*Heftigkeit*) sharpness; *~ genommen adv* in the strict sense of the word; strictly speaking; **~gläubig** *a* orthodox; **~~keit** *f* orthodoxy.

Strepto|kokkeninfektion *f med* streptococcal infection; **~kokkus** *m* streptococcus; **~mycin** *n* streptomycin.

Streu *f* (*für das Vieh*) litter; (*Strohlager*) shake-down; bed of straw; **~bereich** *m* dispersion; spread; **~büchse** *f* sand-box; (*für Gewürz*) castor; (*für Mehl*) dredger; (*für Zucker*) sugar-box; (*für Pfeffer*) pepper-box; **~düse** *f* spray nozzle; **~en** *tr* to strew; (*umherstreuen*) to scatter; (*verbreiten*) to spread; (*bestreuen, besprengen*) to sprinkle; (*besprengen*) to spray; (*bestäuben, bestreuen*) to dust; (*aus~~*) to disseminate; *Blumen auf den Weg ~~* to strew flowers on the way; *jdm Sand in die Augen ~~* to throw dust in s. o.'s eyes; *Am fam* to pull the wool over s. o.'s eyes; *etw in den Wind ~~* to scatter s. th. to the winds; *Zucker auf etw ~~* to sugar s. th.; *itr* (*vom Gewehr*) to spread (the shot); (*dem Vieh*) to litter; **~er** *m* (*für Zucker etc*) castor, dredger; **~faktor** *m* dispersion coefficient; **~feld** *n* stray field; **~feuer** *n mil* searching and sweeping fire; **~flugzeug** *n* spraying airplane; **~garbe** *f* cone of dispersion; **~gold** *n* gold dust; **~kegel** *m* cone of dispersion; **~licht** *n* stray light; floodlight; **~mine** *f mil* uncontrol(l)ed mine; floating mine; **~pulver** *n* dusting powder; powder for strewing; **~sand** *m* writing-sand, blotting-sand; dry sand; **~~büchse** *f* sand-box; powder-box; **~sel** *m od n* litter; dust; fine crumbs sprinkled upon a cake; **~selkuchen** *m* kind of cake strewn with fine crumbs, sugar and almonds; **~ung** *f* (*Ausstreuung*) scattering; spreading; spread; (*Ablen-*

kung) deviation; (*Geschütz*) dispersion; (*Diffusion*) diffusion effect; **~~sbereich** *m* zone of dispersion; **~~sgarbe** *f* cone of dispersion; **~vermögen** *n* scattering power; **~winkel** *m* angle of spread; **~zucker** *m* castor sugar, powdered sugar.

streunen *itr* (*herum~*) to roam about, to loaf about; to rove.

Strich *m* (*Pinsel~, Feder~, Feilen~*) stroke; (*Linie*) line; (*kurzer ~, Gedanken~*) dash; (*Bogen~*) bow; bowing; (*feiner Pinsel~*) touch; (*~ der Vögel*) passage; flight; (*Land~*) tract, country; district; zone; reg on; *unfruchtbarer Land~* barrens *pl*; (*Streifen*) stripe; streak; (*Kompaß~*) compass point; (*beim Holz*) grain; mark; (*~ vom Gewebe*) nap; right way of fabric; *mil* (*~ im Fadenkreuz*) graticule, graticulate; reticule; cross wires *pl*; (*Maßeinheit*) mil; *nach ~ u. Faden* thoroughly; *jdn nach ~ u. Faden besiegen* to knock spots out of s. o.; *wider den ~* against the grain; cross-grained to; *es geht mir gegen den ~* (*fig*) it goes against my grain; *~ fliegen aero* to fly on a straight course; *auf den ~ gehen fam* to walk the streets; *jdn auf dem ~ haben* to bear s. o. a grudge; to have a spite against; *e-n ~ machen unter* to underline s. th.; *fig* to put an end to; *~ drunter! fam* let's call it quits! *jdm e-n ~ durch die Rechnung machen* to cross (*od* to balk) s. o.'s plans; to upset s. o.'s plans; *sl* to put a crimp in s. o.'s plans; *keinen ~ an etw tun* not to do a stroke of work on s. th.; **~ätzung** *f typ* line etching, line block, *Am* line engraving, line cut; **~einteilung** *f* (*Fadenkreuz*) graduation (in mils); graduation scale; **~eln** *tr* to mark with little lines; (*schraffieren*) to hatch; to shade; to streak; **~kreuzplatte** *f* cross-hair plate, graticule; **~linie** *f* dotted line; **~punkt** *m* semicolon; **~~ieren** *tr* to chain-dot, to dash-dot; **~~iert** *a* indicated by a dot-dash line; **~regen** *m* local rain (*od* shower); **~vogel** *m* migratory bird, bird of passage; **~weise** *a* local; *adv* here and there; line by line; **~zeichnung** *f* line drawing; **~zeit** *f* (*der Vögel*) time of flight.

Strick *m* cord; (*dicker*) rope; string; (*Leine*) line; (*Strippe*) strap; (*zum Hängen*) halter; (*Fall~*) snare; *fig* (*Tunichtgut, Spitzbube*) good-for-nothing; young rascal; rogue; *am ~ führen* to lead by a rope; *wenn alle ~e reißen fig fam* if everything else fails; **~arbeit** *f* knitting; **~beutel** *m* knitting-bag; **~chen** *n* small cord; **~en** *tr, itr* to knit; *mit der Hand ~~* to knit by hand; **~er** *m*, **~erin** *f* knitter; **~erei** *f* knitting; **~~industrie** *f* knitting industry; **~garn** *n* knitting-yarn; **~handschuh** *m* knitted glove; **~jacke** *f* jersey; cardigan (jacket); **~kleid** *n* knitted dress; **~~ung** *f* knitted wear; **~leiter** *f* rope-ladder; **~masche** *f* mesh; **~maschine** *f* knitting machine; **~muster** *n* pattern for knitting; **~nadel** *f* knitting-needle; **~strumpf** *m* knitting (of stocking); **~waren** *f pl* knit (-ted) goods *pl*; knitwear; knitted fabrics *pl*; *fam* runnables *pl;* **~werk** *n* net-work, cordage; **~weste** *f* jersey; cardigan (jacket); cardigan sweater; **~wolle** *f* knitting wool; **~zeug** *n* knitting; knitting things *pl*.

Striegel *m* (*Pferde~*) curry-comb, horse-comb; **~n** *tr* (*Pferd*) to curry (a horse); *fig* to ill-use; to censure; *gestriegelt u. gebügelt* well groomed and dressed.

Striem|e *f* stripe, streak; band; (*in der Haut*) wale, weal; mark; **~ig** *a* striped; marked (*od* covered) with weals.

Striez|el *m* (*Gebäck*) cruller, friedcake; *fig* (*Lausbub*) youngster; **~en** *tr* to annoy, to chafe.

strikt *a* strict; severe; **~e** *adv* strictly.

Strippe *f* string, band; (*am Stiefel*) tab; (*in der Straßenbahn; an der Hose*) strap; *mil sl* telephone wire, telephone line; **~nzieher** *m mil sl* string-puller; wire-layer; signal man.

strittig *a* debatable; in dispute; at issue; *siehe: streitig.*

*

Stroh *n* straw; (*Dach~*) thatch; *leeres ~ dreschen* to waste o.'s words; to waste o.'s labo(u)r *~ im Kopf haben* to be empty-headed; *Am sl* to be dead from the neck up; *auf ~ schlafen* to sleep on straw; **~abstimmung** *f Am* straw-vote; **~artig** *a* strawy; straw-like; **~bett** *n* straw bed, pallet; **~blond** *a* straw-colo(u)red; **~blume** *f* everlasting flower, immortelle; **~boden** *m* straw loft; **~bund** *m* truss of straw; **~dach** *n* thatched roof; thatch; **~decke** *f* (*Gärtnerei*) cover of straw; (*Matte*) straw-mat; **~ern** *a* strawy; *fig* dull; insipid; **~feuer** *n* straw fire; *fig* short-lived passion; **~flechter** *m* straw-plaiter; **~flechterei** *f* straw-plaiting; **~geflecht** *n* straw-plaiting; straw-work; **~gelb** *a* straw-colo(u)red; straw-yellow; **~halm** *m* (a) straw; *sich an e-n ~~ klammern* to catch a straw; to clutch at any straw; **~haufen** *m* heap of straw; **~hülse** *f* straw envelope (*od* cover); **~hut** *m* straw hat, straw bonnet; **~hütte** *f* thatched hut; **~ig** *a* strawy; chaffy; **~kopf** *m fig* blockhead; dunce; **~lager** *n* straw-bed; layer of straw; **~mann** *m* man of straw; (*Vogelscheuche*) scarecrow; (*Whist*) dummy; (*vorgeschobene Person*) lay-figure; dummy, *Am sl* stooge; **~matratze** *f* straw-mattress; **~matte** *f* straw-mat; **~miete** *f* stack of straw; **~pappe** *f* straw-board; **~puppe** *f* dummy figure; scarecrow; **~sack** *m* palliasse; straw-mattress; *heiliger ~~! interj* Great Scott! **~schober** *m* straw-stack; (*Schuppen*) straw-shed; **~schütte** *f* layer of straw; **~seil** *n* straw-band; **~wisch** *m* wisp (*od* whisk) of straw; **~witwe** *f* grass-widow, *Am* sod widow; **~~r** *m* grass-widower; *ich bin ~~r* my wife is away from home.

Strolch *m* vagabond, loafer; tramp, scamp,rogue,street ruffian, *sl* hooligan, *Am fam* bum, *Am fam* hoodlum; **~en** *itr* to stroll about, to vagabondize, to roam about; to tramp, *Am fam* to bum; (*faulenzen*) to idle.

Strom *m* (*Fluß*) large river, stream; (*Berg~*) torrent; (*Flut*) tide; (*Strömung*) current; *el* (electric) current, (*Kraft~*) power; *sl* juice; *mit ~ versorgen* to deliver current to; to power; *Gleich~* direct current; *Wechsel~* alternating current; (*Menschen~*) throng, crowd; rush (of people); (*Worte*) flow; torrent (of words); flood; *im ~ der Zeit* in the flow of time; *den ~ einschalten* (*ausschalten*) *el* to turn on (turn off) the electric current; *der elektrische ~ fiel aus* power failed; *gegen den ~ schwimmen fig* to swim against the current (*od* stream *od* tide); *mit dem ~ schwimmen fig* to swim with the tide; *das Blut floß in Strömen* blood flowed in streams; *es regnet in Strömen* it's raining cats and dogs; **~ableitung** *f el* shunt; **~abnehmer** *m el* (*Kollektor*) collector; (*Bürste*) brush; (*Person*) current consumer; **~ab(wärts)** *adv* downstream; down the river; **~abzweigung** *f el* branch circuit; **~angabe** *f* current data *pl*; **~anschluß** *m el* current junction; **~anzeiger** *m* current indicator; **~art** *f* kind of current; **~aufnahme** *f* electric current consumption; **~auf(wärts)** *adv* upstream; up the river; **~ausbeute** *f el* current yield; **~belastung** *f el* current load; **~bett** *n* river-bed, stream-bed; **~bezug** *m* purchase of current; **~dichte** *f* current density; **~durchgang** *m* passage of current; **~einheit** *f* unit of current; **~einschränkung** *f* (*Licht~*) *Am* brown-out; **~enge** *f* gorge of a river, narrows *pl*; **~entnahme** *f* consumption of current; **~er** *m* vagabond, vagrant; tramp, *Am fam* bum, hoodlum; **~erzeuger** *m el* dynamo; (current) generator; **~erzeugung** *f* generation of current; **~feld** *n* field (of current); **~führend** *a* current-carrying; alive; **~~e** *Leitung* live wire; **~führung** *f* power supply; **~gebiet** *n* (river-)basin; (*Einzugsgebiet*) catchment area; **~gefälle** *n* (*bei Fluß*) slope (*od* fall) of a river; **~kontrollkommission** *f* (*in England*) conservancy; **~kreis** *m el* circuit; line; **~leiter** *m el* (current) conductor; **~lieferung** *f* current supply, electric power supply; **~linie** *f* streamline; flow line; **~~naufbau** *m* streamlined body; **~~nform** *f* streamline(d) shape; **~~nförmig** *a* streamline(d); *~~förmig ausbilden* (*od verkleiden*) to streamline; **~los** *a* without current, currentless, dead; de-energized; *~~er Draht* dead wire; **~messer** *m* ammeter; amperemeter; **~mitte** *f* midstream; **~netz** *n* electric circuit; **~~ausfall** *m* power failure; **~polizei** *f* river-police; **~quelle** *f* source of current; **~regler** *m* rheostat; **~richter** *m el* transformer, converter; **~sammler** *m* accumulator, storage battery; **~schiene** *f* live rail; bus bar; **~schnelle** *f* rapid, short; cataract; *Am* riffle; **~schwankung** *f* fluctuation of current; **~sicherung** *f* cut-out fuse; **~spannung** *f el* voltage; tension; **~sperre** *f* stoppage of current, cut; power interruption; **~stärke** *f* intensity of current; **~~messer** *m el* galvanometer; **~stoß** *m* current impulse; **~strahler** *m* electric beam transmitter; **~unterbrecher** *m* circuit-breaker, cut-out; interrupter; **~unterbrechung** *f* power failure; **~verbrauch** *m* (electric) current consumption; **~~er** *m* current (*od* power)- consumer; **~verlust** *m* current loss; leakage; **~versorgung** *f* power supply, current supply; **~wache** *f* (*Fluß*) river-police; **~wandler** *m* current transformer; **~wechsel** *m el* current reversal; **~weise** *adv* in torrents, in gushes; **~wender** *m el* commutator, current reversing key; current reverser; **~zähler** *m* electric meter; **~zuführung** *f* current supply; power supply; leads *pl*; (*Röhre*) conduit.

ström|en *itr* to stream; (*fließen*) to flow; (*laufen*) to run; (*Regen*) to pour (down); (*Menschen*) to rush, to flock, to crowd; **~ung** *f* current; stream; flood, flow; flux; drift; (*Zirkulation*) circulation; *fig* (*Tendenz, Richtung*) tendency; trend; spirit; **~~senergie** *f* kinetic energy; energy of flow; **~~sgeschwindigkeit** *f* velocity of flow; **~~sgetriebe** *n mot* hydro-matic gear; **~~shaube** *f aero* cowling ring; **~~skanal** *m* wind tunnel.

Strophe *f* strophe, stanza; verse.

strotzen *itr* to be swelled, to bunch out, to exuberate; to abound in, to teem with; to superabound (*von* with) to be full of; *vor Gesundheit* ~ to be in the full bloom of health; ~**d** *a* (*Gesundheit*) vigorous, robust; distended; exuberant.

strubbel|ig *a* unkempt, tousled, dishevel(l)ed, shaggy; ~**kopf** *m* unkempt hair.

Strudel *m* whirlpool, eddy, gulf; vortex, rapids *pl*; maelstrom; ~**kessel** *m* pothole; ~**kopf** *m* hotspur; ~**n** *itr* to whirl, to eddy, to swirl; (*sprudeln*) to bubble, to boil.

Struktur *f* structure; (*Gewebe*) texture (composition); (*Gefüge*) grain; ~**ell** *a* structural; ~**formel** *f* structural formula; ~**los** *a* structureless; amorphous; ~**wandel** *m* change in structure.

Strumpf *m* stocking; *ein Paar Strümpfe* a pair of stockings; (*lange Strümpfe*) hose *pl*; longs *pl*; (*Socke*) sock; (*ganz kurze Söckchen*) anklets *pl*; slack socks *pl*; *sehr dünne u. durchsichtige* (*Damen-*)*Strümpfe* sheers *pl*; *Strümpfe mit verstärkten Fersen u. Zehen* stockings reinforced in heels and toes; *nahtlose Strümpfe* seamless stockings; *Baumwollstrümpfe* cotton stockings *pl*, cottons *pl*; *Damen~* ladies' stocking, women's stocking; *Gummi~* elastic stocking; *Herren~* sock, half hose; *Knie~* mid-length; *Kunstseide~* rayon(s *pl*); *Nylon~* nylon; *Seiden~* silk stocking, silk hose; *Woll~* wool(l)en stocking; *die Strümpfe anziehen* (*ausziehen*) to put on o.'s stockings (to take off o.'s stockings); *auf bloßen Strümpfen* in stockings; *sich auf die Strümpfe machen* to make off; (*Licht~*) mantle; ~**band** *n* garter; ~**fabrik** *f* stocking (*od* hosiery) factory; ~~**ant** *m* stocking maker (*od* manufacturer); ~**ferse** *f* heel; ~**form** *f* leg of stocking; ~**garn** *n* stocking (*od* hosiery) yarn; stocking cotton; ~**gewebe** *n* hosiery fabric; ~**halter** *m* suspender; *Am* garter; ~~**befestiger** *m* strap; ~~**gürtel** *m* suspender belt; *Am* (*für Damen*) garter belt, girdle; panty girdle; garter bra; ~**spitze** *f* toe; ~**stricker** *m*, ~~**in** *f* stocking-knitter; ~**waren** *f pl* hosiery; ~~**handel** *m* hosier's trade; ~~**händler** *m* hosier; haberdasher; ~**wirker** *m* stocking-weaver; ~~**ei** *f* manufacture of stockings; ~~**stuhl** *m* stocking loom; ~**wolle** *f* wool for knitting stockings.

Strunk *m* (*Baum~*) stump, trunk; (*Kohl~*) stalk.

struppig *a* rough, unkempt, hirsute; rugged, shaggy, bristly.

Struwwelpeter *m* shock-headed Peter.

Strychnin *n* strychnine.

Stubbe *f*, ~**n** *m* (*Baumwurzelstumpf*) stump; ~**nholz** *n* stumps *pl*; ~**nrodung** *f* stump grubbing.

Stübchen *n* little chamber.

Stube *f* chamber, room; apartment; *gute* ~ drawing-room, *Am* living room; ~**nälteste(r)** *m* senior soldier of a barrack room; ~**narbeit** *f* indoor work; ~**narrest** *m* confinement to quarters, *Am* arrest in quarters; ~~ *haben* to be confined to quarters; ~**ndecke** *f* ceiling; ~**nfliege** *f* common housefly; ~**ngelehrte(r)** *m* bookworm, bookman; ~**ngenosse** *m* fellow-lodger; chum; *Am* room-mate; ~**nhocker**, ~**nsitzer** *m* home-bird, stay-at-home; ~~**ei** *f* staying-at-home; ~**nluft** *f* indoor air; stuffy air; ~**nmädchen** *n* housemaid, *Am* chambermaid; ~**nmaler** *m* decorator, house-painter; ~**nrein** *a* (*Hund etc*) house-trained, *Am* housebroke(n).

Stüber *m* (*Nasen~*) fillip; (*Münze*) stiver.

Stub(s)nase *f* snub-nose; turned-up nose.

Stuck *m* stucco; ~**arbeit** *f* stuccowork; plastering; ~~**er** *m* stuccoworker; ~**decke** *f* ceiling of raised plaster work; ~**gips** *m* plaster of Paris; ~**waren** *f pl* stucco works *pl*.

Stück *n* piece; (*Theater~*) play; show; *wie hat Ihnen das ~ gefallen?* how did you like the show? (*Bissen*) morsel; (*Bißchen*) bit; (*Teil*) part; (*Bruch~*) fragment; (*Vieh*) head; (*Brot*) slice; (*Butter*) pat; (*Land*) lot, plot; patch; (*Flick~*) patch; (*Seife*) cake; (*Wurst*) hunk; (*Brocken*) chunk; (*Abschnitt, Auszug aus Buch, Rede etc*) passage, extract; (~ *Weg*) part of the way; distance; (*Exemplar e-s Buches*) copy; (*Geld~*) coin, piece of money; (*Musik~*) piece of music; tune; melody; (*Klumpen*) lump; *20, 40, 80 etc* ~ a score, twoscore, fourscore etc; *ein starkes ~* (*fig*) a bit thick; *er kam ein ~ mit* he came along part of the way; *jdn ein ~ im Wagen mitnehmen* to give s. o. a lift; *pro ~* apiece; *2 DM das ~* 2 DMarks apiece (*od* each); *ein ~ Arbeit* a stiff job; *~ für ~* piece by piece; *aus e-m ~* all of a piece; *in allen ~en* in all points; in all (*od* every) respect; *in e-m ~* (*dauernd*) on and on; without a break; *in ~en zu* in denominations of; *aus freien ~en* of o.'s own accord; of o.'s own free-will; *ein gutes ~ Weg* a considerable distance, *in ~e schlagen* to break to pieces, to smash; *in ~e fliegen* to fall to pieces; *in ~e gehen* to break in pieces; *sich große ~e einbilden* to be very conceited; *große ~e halten auf* to make much of; to hold in high esteem; to have a high opinion of s. o., to think a lot of, to think much of (s. o.); *ein schönes ~ Geld* a nice little sum; ~**arbeit** *f* piece-work; jobbing; ~**arbeiter** *m* piece-worker, jobber; ~**chen** *n* bit, morsel; snatch; lump; welt; (*Holz*) chip; (*Papier*) scrap (of paper); *mus* air, tune; (*Streich*) trick; ~**eln** *tr* to cut into pieces; (*flicken*) to patch up; ~**en** *tr* to piece (together); to patch; (*zer~~*) to chop; to cut into pieces; ~**enzucker** *m* lump sugar; ~**erz** *n* lump (*od* coarse) ore; ~**faß** *n* large cask, butt; ~**fracht** *f* mixed cargo; ~**größe** *f* size of lump; ~**gut** *n com* goods in packets or bales; *Am* less-than-carload lot; piece goods; parcel, bale, bundle; ~**güter** *n pl* piece-goods *pl*, mixed goods *pl*; ~**ig** *a* lumpy, in lumps; ~**kohle** *f* lump coal; ~**kosten** *pl* piece-cost; ~**leistung** *f* capacity; ~**liste** *f* specification; ~**lohn** *m* wage(s) for piecework; ~~**arbeiter** *m* pieceworker; ~~**satz** *m* wage for piece-work; ~**metall** *n mil* gun metal; ~**preis** *m* price by the piece; ~**verzeichnis** *n* inventory; specification; ~**weise** *adv* (*einzeln*) piece by piece; piecemeal; (*im Kleinverkauf*) by retail; by the piece; ~**werk** *n* piece-work, jobbing; job-work; *fig* imperfect work; bungled work; patchwork; *unser Wissen ist ~~* we know in part; our knowledge is fragmentary; ~**zahl** *f* number of pieces; *Akkord nach ~~* agreement by piece; ~**zeit** *f* wage for piece-work; ~**zinsen** *m pl* interim interest; accrued interest.

Student *m* (*e-r Universität*) student; undergraduate; (*in England auch*) collegian; *~ im 1.* (*Studien-*) *Jahr* first-year-man, *Am* freshman; *~ im 2. Jahr* student in the second year, *Am* sophomore, *fam* soph; *im 3. Jahr* student in the third year, *Am* junior; *~ im letzten Studienjahr* *Am* senior; *~en e-s Jahrganges* class; *früherer ~ e-r Universität* (*od e-s College*) *Am* alumnus (*pl* -i), (*weiblich*) alumna (*pl* -ae); ~**enheim**, ~**enwohnhaus** *n* hostel (*od* hall of residence) for students, *Am* dormitory, dorm; ~**enjahrgang** *m Am* class; ~**enleben** *n* student's life, college life; ~**enschaft** *f* students *pl*, undergraduates *pl*; ~**ensprache** *f* students' slang; ~**enstreich** *m* student's prank; ~**enverbindung** *f* student's society (*od* club *od* association), *Am* fraternity; (*Abk* frat), *Am fam* Greek-letter-society; (*für Studentinnen*) sorority; *Anwärter e-r ~~* (*Am*) pledge, pledgee; ~**enviertel** *n* student's quarter; ~**enzeit** *f* years spent at the university; college time; ~**in** *f* woman (*od* girl) student, girl undergraduate, *Am* (*in College*) co-ed; ~~**enklub** *m* girl student's club, *Am* sorority, *Am fam* Greek-letter-society; ~**isch** *a* student-like.

Stud|ie *f* (*Malerei*) study; (*literarisch*) essay; sketch; ~**ienausschuß** *m* study group; ~**iendirektor** *m* headmaster (of a secondary school), *Am* principal; ~**ienfach** *n* branch of study; **ienfahrt** *f* study trip; excursion; ~**iengang** *m* course of study; ~**iengemeinschaft** *f* study seminar; ~**iengenosse** *m* fellow-student; ~**ienhalber** *adv* for the purpose of studying; ~**ienplan** *m* curriculum; schedule of studies; ~**ienreferendar** *m* teacher-trainee; ~**ienrat** *m* assistant master of a secondary school; ~**ienreise** *f* educational trip; ~**ienzeit** *f* undergraduate days *pl*; ~**ieren** *itr tr* to study; to con; (*auf die Hochschule gehen*) to be at college; to go to college; ~~ *lassen* to send to a university; *Medizin ~~* to study medicine; *Jura ~~* to read for the bar; *an der Universität ~~* to study at the university; *bis tief in die Nacht hinein ~~* to burn the midnight oil; ~**ierende(r)** *m siehe Student*; ~**ierstube** *f*, ~**ierzimmer** *n* study; library; *fam* den; ~**iert** *a* educated; (*affektiert*) affected, studied; *ein ~~er* (*Mann*) a university man; ~**io**, ~**iosus** *m siehe Student*; ~**ium** *n* study; studies *pl*, pursuits *pl*; higher education, university education; (*wissenschaftliche Forschung*) scientific research.

Stuf|e *f* (*Treppen~~*) step, stair; (*e-r Leiter*) rung; (*Ton~~*) interval; *fig* (*Grad*) degree; grade; stage; *Am* notch; (*Rang~~*) rank; (*Niveau*) level; (*Phase*) phase; (*Mittel, Sprungbrett*) stepping-stone (*zu* to); (*Farbschattierung*) hue; nuance; shade; *auf gleicher ~e stehen* to be on a level with; *die höchste ~e* summit; ~**enartig** *a* step-like; graduated, graded; ~**enbahn** *f* escalator; ~**enfolge** *f*, ~**engang** *m* gradation; gradual progress (*od* development); (*Folge*) succession; ~**enformation** *f* step formation; ~**enleiter** *f* (progressive) scale; gradation; *Am* progression; *fig* gamut; (*Leiter mit Stufen*) stepladder; ~**enlos** *a* ridgeless; steady; (*regelbar*) infinitely variable; ~**enschalter** *m el* step switch; ~**enweise** *adv* by steps, by degrees; in stages; gradually; progressively; ~**ung** *f aero* (*Formationsflug*) difference of altitude; staggering.

Stuhl *m* chair; (*ohne Lehne*) stool; (*Sitz*) seat; (*Dach~*) roofing; (*Glokken~*) belfry; (*Kirchen~*) pew; (*Lehn~*) easy chair; (*Lehr~*) chair; (*Richter~*) tribunal; (*Web~*) loom; *med* (*~gang*) evacuation of the bowels, stool, feces; *elektrischer ~* the electric chair; *der Heilige ~* The Holy See; *Meister* *vom* ~ master of the Lodge; *auf dem elektrischen* ~ *hinrichten Am* to electrocute; *jdm den* ~ *vor die Tür setzen* (*od stellen*) to turn s. o. out; to give s. o. the sack; *sich zwischen zwei Stühle setzen fig* to fall between two stools; **~bein** *n* leg of a chair; **~drang** *m* urgent need to relieve the bowels; **~entleerung** *f med* defecation; **~flechte** *f* wattling; **~flechter** *m* chair-bottomer; **~gang** *m med* stool; evacuation of the bowels, discharge from the bowels; **~lehne** *f* back of a chair; **~verstopfung** *f med* constipation; **~zäpfchen** *n med* suppository; **~zwang** *m* obstruction of the bowels, *med* (rectal) tenesmus.

Stuka *m* (= *Sturzkampfflugzeug*) dive bomber, dive fighter airplane; stuka; *mit ~s angreifen u. bombardieren* to divebomb; **~angriff** *m* dive-bomber attack.

Stulle *f* slice of bread and butter; sandwich.

Stulp|e *f* (*am Stiefel*) (boot-) top; (*Ärmel~~*) cuff; (*Fecht~~*) fencing-glove; **~enstiefel** *m pl* top-boots *pl*, wellingtons *pl*, *Am* boots *pl*; **~handschuhe** *m pl* gauntlet gloves *pl*, gauntlets *pl*; (*zum Fechten*) fencing gloves *pl*.

stülp|en *tr* (*über~~, auf~~*) to put on, to clap on; (*Hut*) to cock; (*umdrehen, kippen*) to turn upside down; to put in inverted position; to turn inside out; to tilt, to turn up; **~nase** *f* snub-nose; turned-up nose.

stumm *a* (*ohne Sprache*) dumb; (*stimmlos*) mute; speechless; *fig* (*schweigend*) silent; *fam* mum; *~er Diener* dumb-waiter; *~er Film* silent film; *~es h* silent h; *~es Spiel theat* dumb-show; pantomime; *~er Zorn* speechless rage; ~ *wie ein Fisch* mute as a fish (*od* maggot); *Am fam* close as a clam; *er war* ~ *vor Schrecken* he was struck dumb with horror; *das „e" in „late" ist* ~ the "e" in "late" is mute; **~abstimmung** *f radio* quiet automatic volume control; quiet tuning; **~e(r)** *m*, **~e** *f* mute person; a mute; **~film** *m* silent film; silent screen; *ein Filmstar aus der ~~zeit* a star of the silent era; **~heit** *f* muteness, dumbness; speechlessness; *fig* (*Schweigsamkeit*) taciturnity.

Stummel *m* (*Zigaretten~, Zigarren~*) (cigar-)end; fag-end; *Am* butt; stub; (*Arm~, Baum~, Zahn~*) stump; (*Überrest*) remnant; **~pfeife** *f* short pipe; **~wort** *n* abbreviation, abbreviated term.

Stumpen *m* (*Hut~*) (felt) body; (*Zigarre*) Swiss cheroot; (*kleiner* ~) whiff.

Stümper *m* (*Pfuscher*) botcher; bungler, blunderer; (*Amateur*) amateur; (*Dummkopf*) duffer; **~ei** *f* (*Pfuschertum*) bungling, botching; amateurism; **~haft** *a* bungling; (*ungeschickt*) unskilful; clumsy; *~~e Arbeit* a botchy job; **~n** *itr* (*pfuschen*) to botch; to huddle; to bungle; *auf e-r Gitarre ~~* to strum (on) a guitar.

Stumpf *m* (*Arm~, Baum~*) stump; trunk; stub; *mit ~ u. Stiel* root and branch; ~ *a* (*ohne Ecke*) blunt; (*Winkel*) obtuse; *fig* (*geistig*) stupid; dull; spiritless; obtuse; soggy; (*apathisch*) apathetic; indifferent; *~er Kegel* truncated cone; *~er Winkel* obtuse angle; ~ *werden* to grow blunt; **~eckig** *a* blunt-cornered; obtuse-angled; **~heit** *f* bluntness; *fig* (*Dummheit*) dul(l)ness; obtuseness; **~kantig** *a* blunt-edged; **~näschen** *n*, **~nase** *f* snub-nose, turned-up nose; **~schwanz** *m* bob-tail; **~sinn** *m* stupidity; dul(l)ness; doldrums *pl*; (*Apathie*) apathy, indifference; **~~ig** *a* stupid, dull; (*langsam*) slow-witted; sottish; *~~ige Person* dullard; **~wink(e)lig** *a* obtuse-angled; blunt-edged.

Stund|e *f* hour; (*Weg~~*) league; (*Unterrichts~~*) lesson; (*Zeitabschnitt*) period; *~~ X mil* zero-hour; *~en starken Verkehrsandrangs* rush hours; *ganze 2 ~en* for 2 hours at a stretch; *e-e halbe ~e* half an hour, *Am* a half hour; *e-e starke ~e* a good hour; *englische ~en geben* to give English lessons; *das Flugzeug erreichte e-n Durchschnitt von 450 Meilen in der ~e* the plane averaged 450 miles an hour; *es sind gute 5 ~en bis zur Stadt* it's a good five hours to the town; *von ~ an* from this very moment; ever since then; *von ~e zu ~e* from hour to hour; *zur ~e* presently, at the present hour; *zur rechten ~e* at the right moment; **~en** *tr* to grant a respite, to allow time to pay; *e-e Zahlung ~~* to grant delay for payment; **~enbuch** *n* prayer-book; book of hours; **~endurchschnitt** *m* speed of . . . km p.(er) h.(our); **~engeld** *n* fee for lessons; **~engeschwindigkeit** *f* (average) speed per hour; **~englas** *n* hour-glass; **~enkilometer** *m pl* kilometers per hour; **~enlang** *adv* (lasting) for hours; **~leistung** *f* output per hour; (*Arbeiter*) hourly output (*od* efficiency); **~enlohn** *m* wages for one hour work, hourly wage; **~enplan** *m* time-table; curriculum; *Am* schedule; syllabus; assignment of hours; **~ensatz** *m* hour rate; **~enschlag** *m* striking of the hour, stroke (of the clock); *mit dem ~~* punctually as the clock strikes; **~enverdienst** *m* hourly wages; **~enweise** *adv* by the hour; hourly; *~~ Beschäftigung* part-time job; **~enzeiger** *m* hour-hand; **~ung** *f* indulgence, delay; extension of time; (term of) respite; delay of payment; *~~ verlangen* to apply for a term of respite; **~~sfrist** *f com* days of grace; respite; time allowed for payment; **~~sgesuch** *n* petition (*od* request) for a respite.

stünd|ig *a* for an hour; of an hour's duration; **~lein, ~chen** *n* (*dim von Stunde*) short hour; *letztes ~~* last (*od* appointed) hour; **~lich** *a* hourly, per hour; *~~ adv* hourly, every hour, from hour to hour.

Stunk *m fam* (*Zänkerei*) bickering; (*Lüge, Verleumdung*) falsehood; backbiting; slander; ~ *machen fig fam* to make mischief.

stupfen *tr* to touch; to nudge.

stupid(e) *a* stupid, *Am* dumb.

Stups *m* nudge; **~en** *tr* to nudge; **~nase** *f* snub-nose, turned-up nose.

stur *a fam* (*stier*) staring, fixed; (*eigensinnig, begriffsstutzig*) stubborn, obdurate; self-willed; ~ *Kurs fliegen aero sl* to stick to a course; **~heit** *f* (*Eigensinn*) obstinacy, stubbornness, obtuseness.

Sturm *m* strong wind; gale (= *Windstärke 6—10*); whole gale (= *Windstärke 8—10*); (**Orkan**) hurricane (= *Windstärke 10—12*); (*Wirbel~*) whirlwind; tornado, *Am fam* twister; (*Tiefdruck~*) cyclone; (*Taifun*) typhoon; (*Unwetter*) storm; tempest; (*Windstoß, ~bö*) gust, blast, flaw; squall; *mil* (*Erstürmung, Angriff*) storm; assault; *sport* (*Fußball*) forward line, forwards *pl*; *fig* (~ *der Leidenschaft*) rage; fury; (*Aufruhr*) storm; (*Aufregung, Lärm*) tumult; turmoil; alarm; (*Andrang der Menge*) rush, onset; *Beifalls~* storm of applause; *ein ~ im Wasserglas* a storm in a tea-cup; ~ *u. Drang* storm and stress; ~ *laufen* to (make an) assault; to storm, to attack; ~ *läuten* to ring the alarm; *im ~e* with rushing speed; *im ~e nehmen* to take by storm; **~abteilung** *f mil* assault detachment; **~abzeichen** *n mil* assault badge; **~angriff** *m mil* assault; **~ausgangsstellung** *f mil* jump-off position; **~bahn** *f* storm track; **~ball** *m* storm ball; **~band** *n* hat-guard; elastic; **~bataillon** *n* shock battalion; **~bö** *f* squall; **~bock** *m hist* battering-ram; **~boot** *n* assault boat, storm boat; landing barge; **~feld** *n* storm area; **~fest** *a* storm-proof; **~flut** *f* high tide raised by a storm, storm tide; tidal wave; **~frei** *a* unassailable; *~~e Bude fam* rented furnished room with special entrance; **~gepäck** *n mil* combat pack, light pack; skeleton equipment; **~gepeitscht** *a* lashed by storm; **~geschütz** *n* assault gun (on armo(u)red self-propelled mount); tractor gun; **~~e** *n pl*, self-propelled artillery; **~gewehr** *n* automatic rifle; **~glocke** *f* tocsin; alarm bell; **~haube** *f hist* head-piece; helmet, morion; **~kompanie** *f* assault company; **~laterne** *f* hurricane lamp; **~laufen** *n* assault; **~leiter** *f* scaling-ladder; **~regiment** *n* assault regiment; **~reif** *a* softened up for assault; *~~ machen* (*durch Bombardierung*) to soften up for assault (by bombing); **~riemen** *m* chin-strap; **~schaden** *m* damage by storm, storm damage; **~schritt** *m* double quick pace; double march; quickened step for assault; **~schwalbe** *f orn* storm-petrel; **~segel** *n* lug-sail; **~segler** *m mil* assault glider; **~signal** *n* storm signal; **~trupp** *m* assault party, storming party; **~vogel** *m orn* stormy petrel; **~wagen** *m mil* tank; **~warngerät** *n* (*mit Radar*) *Am* sferics *pl u. sing*; **~warnung** *f* storm (*od* gale) warning; weather warning; **~~sdienst** *m* storm-warning service; **~~szeichen** *n* storm-warning signal; **~welle** *f* wave of assault; **~wetter** *n* stormy weather; **~wind** *m* storm; tempest; (whole) gale; heavy gale; hurricane; **~wolke** *f* storm cloud; **~zentrum** *n* storm centre; eye of a hurricane.

stürm|en *tr* to take by storm; to make an assault; to attack; *itr* (*dahin~~*) to rush along; to dash, to tear along; (*toben*) to rage, to roar; (*Sturm läuten*) to ring the tocsin; (*Unwetter*) to be stormy (weather); *es ~t* it blows a gale; **~er** *m* (*Angreifer*) assailant, assaulter; *sport* (*Fußball*) forward; **~~reihe** *f sport* forward line; **~isch** *a* stormy; tempestuous; (*die See*) rough, choppy (sea); *fig* (*ungestüm*) impetuous; (*polternd*) rumbustious, *Am* rambunctious; (*unruhig*) turbulent; (*wild*) wild; violent; (*lebhaft*) agitated, vivid; *~~es Wetter* stormy weather; *nicht so ~~!* not so fast! *Am* take it easy!

Sturz *m* (*auch fig*) fall; tumble; sudden drop; (*Ab~*) chute; (~ *gegen etw*) crash; *tech* (*Autoräder*) camber; *arch* (*Fenster~, Tür~*) lintel; (*Kopf~ ins Wasser*) plunge; dive; (*Ruin*) ruin; down-fall; (*Mißerfolg*) business failure; (*Börsen~, Preis~*) slump; collapse; (*Zus.Bruch*) collapse; break-down; (*Umfallen*) upset; *parl* (*e-r Regierung*) overthrow; (*Ungnade*) disgrace; (*Wasser~*) cataract; (*Kassen~*) audit (of accounts); *zum ~ bringen* to overthrow; **~acker** *m* land ploughed for the first time; newly ploughed field; *Am* plowed land; **~angriff** *m* *aero* diving attack; dive-bombing attack; **~bach** *m* torrent; waterfall; **~bad** *n* plunge (bath); **~bett** *n* downstream apron; tumble bay; **~blech** *n* thin sheet; **~bombenangriff** *m* dive-bombing attack; *e-n ~~ machen* to dive-bomb; **~bomber** *m* dive bomber; *die ~~ hatten e-e 250-kg-Bombe u. Raketen* the dive bombers were carrying a 500-pound bomb and rockets; **~flug** *m aero* nose-dive, vertical dive; diving flight; (*mit vollaufendem Motor*) power dive; *~~ ausführen* to dive, to nose-dive; to take a nose-dive; *Am aero sl* to scream downhill; *~~ abfangen* to pull out of a dive; **~~bremse** *f aero* dive brake; **~~geschwindigkeit** *f aero* diving speed; **~~klappen** *f pl aero* diving flaps *pl*; **~güter** *n pl com* bulk goods *pl*; **~helm** *m* crash helmet; **~kampfbomber** *m* dive bomber; **~kampfflieger** *m* dive bomber pilot; **~kampfflugzeug** *n* dive bomber; stuka; **~regen** *m* intense rain; **~see** *f* heavy sea; *e-e ~~ überbekommen* to ship a sea; **~spirale** *f aero* spirale nose-dive spin; **~visier** *n aero mil* dive bomber's bomb-sight; **~welle** *f* heavy sea; breakers *pl*; **~wind** *m* strong downcurrent; gust of wind.

Stürze *f* (*Deckel*) cover, lid; **~n** *tr* (*nieder~~*) to throw (down); (*um~~*) to upset, to tilt (over); to overturn; to tip, to dump; *parl* (*Regierung etc*) to overthrow; (*herab~~*) to hurl down; (*hinein~~*) to hurl in; (*Acker*) to plough; (*Kasse*) to audit the accounts; to count the cash; *ins Elend ~~* to ruin; to undo; *jdn ins Verderben ~~* to undo s. o.; *itr* (*fallen*) to fall (down), to tumble; (*treffen auf*) to fall upon; (*hinein~~*) to plunge into; (*herausströmen*) to stream out; (*vorwärts~~*) to rush, to dash; (*eilen*) to hurry; *aero* (*im Sturzflug*) to dive (*auf* upon); (*nieder~~*) to crash; *ins Meer ~~* to fall into the sea; *sich ~~ auf* to rush upon; to pounce upon; to attack; *fig* to engulf o. s. in; *sich in Schulden ~~* to plunge into debt; *sich in sein Schwert ~~* to rush on o.'s sword; *sich ins Unglück ~~* to plunge into misery; *sich in Unkosten ~~* to go to expenses; *nicht ~~!* (*Aufschrift*) this side up! handle with care!

Stuß *m fam* (*Unsinn, Narrheit*) nonsense, bosh, *Am sl* baloney; *~ reden* to talk nonsense.

Stute *f* mare; **~nfohlen**, **~nfüllen** *n* foal, filly; **~rei** *f* stud.

Stutz *m* anything curtailed; (*Feder~*) tuft of feathers, plume; (*Stoß*) push; thrust; punch; **~ärmel** *m* short sleeve; **~bart** *m* trimmed beard; **~büchse** *f*, **~en** *m* (*Jägerbüchse*) short rifle; **~en** *tr* (*abschneiden*) to cut short; to curtail; (*Flügel*) to clip; (*Ohren*) to crop; (*Bäume*) to lop; to prune; (*Bart*) to trim; (*Schwanz*) to dock; (*in Form bringen*) to shape; to (give a) start; (*zögern, stocken*) to hesitate; *über etw ~~* to be startled at; to be taken aback; to be baffled; to be perplexed; *itr* to stop short; **~en** *m* (*Jägerbüchse*) short rifle; *tech* (*Düse*) nozzle; (*Verbindungs~~*) connecting piece; socket; **~er** *m* dandy; fop; masher; spark; swell; *Am* dude; (*halblange Sportjacke*) sport coat, hip-length surcoat, *Am* Mackinaw (coat); **~erhaft** *a* foppish, stylish, *Am* dudish; **~ertum** *n* foppishness; **~flügel** *m mus* baby grand (piano); **~glas** *n* low tumbler; **~ig** *a* startled (*über* at), puzzled; taken aback; (*überrascht*) surprised; (*ganz verwirrt*) perplexed; (*verblüfft*) flabbergasted; *~~ machen* to startle; to puzzle, to nonplus; **~ohr** *n* cropped ear; **~schwanz** *m* bob-tail crop; **~uhr** *f* timepiece; mantelpiece clock.

Stütz|balken *m* joist, rest (*od* supporting *od* reinforcing) beam; brace; (*Stempel*) prop, shore; **~e** *f allg* support; (*Stempel*) prop, stay; truss; shore; (*Pfeiler*) pillar; *fig* (*Hilfe*) help; support(er); pillar; *~~ der Familie* bread-winner; *~~ der Hausfrau* mother's help(er), lady-help; **~en** *tr allg* to support; (*ab~~*) to stay, to prop (up); to shore up; to buttress; *sich ~~ auf* to rely on; to depend on; to base on; (*sich anlehnen an*) to lean (up)on; (*Behauptung*) to base; to be founded on; to be based on; to uphold; **~er** *m tech* pin; **~mauer** *f* supporting (*od* retaining) wall; **~pfeiler** *m* (supporting) pillar (*od* column); buttress; support; bedding pile; **~pfosten** *m* supporting post; **~punkt** *m* (*Base*) base; *mil* strong point; support; (*fester Halt*) footing; *tech* (*Hebel~~*) fulcrum; (*Luft~~*) air base; (*Flotten~~*) naval base; *schwimmender ~~* (*aero*) floating base; **~~system** *n mil* web defence; **~säule** *f* supporting pillar; **~schwimmer** *m aero* (*an den Flügelenden*) wing-tip float; sponson; **~weite** *f* span; width between support; **~wort** *n gram* propword.

subaltern *a* subordinate; (*untergeordnet*) inferior; *mil* subaltern; **~beamte(r)** *m* subordinate (*od* inferior) official; **~offizier** *m* junior officer.

Subhast|ation *f* public sale, auction; **~ieren** *tr* to sell by public auction.

Subjekt *n* subject, person, creature; **~iv** subjective; **~ivität** *f* subjectivity; subjectiveness; **~skasus** *m* nominative case.

subkutan *a med* subcutaneous; hypodermic; **~spritze** *f* subcutaneous syringe.

Subli|mat *n* sublimate; mercuric chlorid; **~~ion** *f* sublimation; **~~lösung** *f* sublimate solution; **~mieren** *tr* to sublimate; to sublime; **~mierung** *f* sublimation.

Submission *f* (*Ausschreibung*) submission; invitation for tenders; contract (for public works), *Am auch* public bidding; (*Gebot auf ~*) tender; **~sbedingungen** *f pl* conditions on which a public work is given out in tender; terms of contract; **~sgebot** *n*, **~sofferte** *f* tender; *ein(e) ~~ einreichen* to make a tender; **~svergebung** *f* sale upon sealed tenders; **~sweg** *m*: *im* (*od auf dem*) *~~ vergeben* to entrust the execution of public works by tender; **Submittent** *m* contractor, tenderer.

sub|ordinieren *tr* to subordinate; **~sidiär** *a* subsidiary; **~sidien** *pl* subsidies *pl*; *com* bounty; *durch ~~ unterstützen* to subsidize; **~sistenz** *f* subsistence; **~skribent** *m* subscriber; **~skribieren** *tr* to subscribe (for); **~skription** *f* subscription; **~~sanzeige**, **~~seinladung** *f* invitation to subscribe; **~~sliste** *f* list of subscribers.

sub|stantiell *a* substantial; **~stantiv** *n* substantiv, noun; **~~ieren** *tr* to use as a noun; **~~isch** *a* substantive; **~stanz** *f* substance, matter; essence; stuff; material; *von der ~~ leben* to live from the capital; **~sumieren** *tr* (*einschließen*) to comprise in; to subsume.

substit|uieren *tr* to substitute; **~ution** *f* substitution; **~~smethode** *f* substitution method.

Substratosphäre *f* substratosphere.

subtil *a* subtile; (*zart*) delicate; (*fein*) fine; (*spitzfindig*) subtle.

Subtrah|end *m* subtrahend; **~ieren** *tr* to subtract; **Subtraktion** *f* subtraction.

subtropisch *a* subtropical; semi-tropical.

Subvention *f* (*von privater Seite*) subvention; (*vom Staat*) subsidy; **~ieren** *tr* to subsidize; *staatlich ~iert* state-subsidized.

Such|aktion *f* search; tracing; **~anker** *m mar* grapnel; **~anzeige** *f* (*Zeitung*) classified ad, *Am* want ad; **~büro** *n* tracing office; **~dienst** *m* missing persons service, tracing service; **~e** *f* search; quest; (*Jagd*) tracking; *vergebliche ~~* wild goose chase; *auf der ~~ nach* on the lookout for, in search of (*od* for); in quest of, on the hunt for; *auf die ~~ gehen* to go in search of; **~en** *tr, itr* to seek (for *od* after); to look for; to hunt for; to search for; to try to find; (*jdn ausfindig machen*) to trace s. o.; to track (down); (*in der Zeitung*) to advertise for; (*tasten nach*) to grope for; (*ver~~*) to try (to), to attempt; (*sich bemühen*) to endeavo(u)r, to try hard; to strive for; (*wollen, wünschen*) to want, to desire; to be in want of; (*auswählen*) to select; *etw ~~ in* to pride o. s. upon; to take a pride in; *~~ gehen* to fetch; *sie sucht in allem etw* she is easily offended; *er hat hier nichts zu ~~* he has no business here; *die Gefahr ~~* to court danger; *e-e gute Gelegenheit ~~* to pick o.'s opportunity; *e-n Fehler ~~* to trace an error; *Streit* (*od Händel*) *~~* to pick a quarrel (with s. o); *das Weite ~~* to run away; *nach Worten ~~* to be at a loss for words; *gesuchte Stelle* situation required (*od* wanted); **~er** *m* seeker, searcher; *tech* (*Werkzeug*) selector; locator; (*Sonde, Nadel*) probe; detector; *opt* finder; *phot* view-finder; (*Fernrohr~~*) telescopic finder; (*Bleilot*) plummet; (*Scheinwerfer*) spotlight; **~~bild** *n* seeker picture; **~~ei** *f* searching, rummaging; **~~schacht** *m* focussing (*od* light) hood; **~gerät** *n* search-gear; locating equipment; **~strahlen** *m pl* directional rays *pl*.

Sucht *f* (*Krankheit*) sickness; disease; (*Epidemie*) epidemic; (*Vorliebe*) preference; special liking for; (*Leidenschaft*) passion, rage; (*krankhafte Gewohnheit*) addiction, habit.

süchtig *a* (*Betäubungsmitteln, Rauschgiften etc verfallen*) addicted to (*z. B.* addicted to morphine); (*krank*) sickly; suffering from a chronic disease; (*manisch*) manic, maniacal; **~e(r)** *m* addict (*z. B.* drug addict).

suckeln *tr, itr* to suck, to suckle.

Sud *m* boiling; (*Brauerei*) brewing; (*Ab~*) decoction; **~haus** *n* (*Brauerei*) brewing house.

Süd *m* (*der ~*) south; *poet* south-wind; **~afrika** *n* South Africa; **~afrikaner** *m*, **~afrikanisch** *a* South African; *~~e Union* Union of South Africa; **~amerika** *n* South America; **~amerikaner** *m*, **~amerikanisch** *a* South American; **~breite** *f* south latitude; **~deutsch** *a*, **~deutsche(r)** *m* South German; **~deutschland** *n* South Germany; **~en** *m* south; *im ~~* (to the) south (of); in the south of; *nach ~~* south; towards the south; *das Fenster geht nach ~~* the window faces south; *nach ~~ gehen* to go south; *der sonnige ~~* (*von Europa*) the (sunny) south; *der Wind kam aus ~~* the wind was south; **~england** *n* southern England; **~früchte** *f pl* fruits from the south, tropical fruit; **~fruchthandlung** *f* Italian warehouse; **~halbkugel** *f* southern hemisphere; **~kreuz** *n astr* the Southern Cross; **~küste** *f* south coast; **~lage** *f* southern exposure; southern aspect; **~länder** *m*, **~~in** *f* inhabitant of the south; southerner; **~lich** *a* south (*von* of), to the south (of); lying towards the south; southern; southerly, southward; meridional; *~~e Breite* south latitude; *~~e Erdhälfte*, *~~e Halbkugel* southern hemisphere; *~~e Richtung* southing; **~lichst** *a* southernmost; **~licht** *n* southern lights *pl*, aurora australis; **~ost(en)** *m* southeast; (*Wind*) southeast wind; **~östlich** *a* southeast(ern); *~~ von* to the southeast of; **~ostwärts** *a* southeasterly; **~ostwind** *m* southeaster; **~pol** *m* South Pole; Antarctic Pole; **~polargebiet** *n* antarctic region; **~punkt** *m* south (point); **~richtung** *f* southing; **~see** *f* (South) Pacific Ocean; (*früher*) South-Sea; **~seeländer** *n pl* Australasia; **~seite** *f* sunny side, south side; **~slawe** *m*, **~slawisch** *a* Jugoslav(ian); **~slawien** *n* Jugo-Slavia, Jugoslavia; Yugoslavia; **~sonne** *f mar* noon; **~staaten** *m pl* southern states *pl*; *Am fam* down south; Dixie (Land); *Am* the Southland; *Krieg gegen die ~~* (*Am hist*(War of Secession; **~staatler** *m Am* southern(er); **~wärts** *adv* southward(s), to the south; **~wein** *m* sweet wine; **~west(en)** *m* southwest; **~westafrika** *n* (German) South-West Africa; **~wester** *m* (*Hut*) southwester, sou'wester; **~westlich** *a* southwest(ern); **~weststaat** *m* (*Baden u. Württemberg*) South-West State; **~westwind** *m* southwest; **~wind** *m* southwind; souther.

Sudan *m* Sudan, Soudan; **~ese** *m*, **~esisch** *a* Sudanese.

Sud|elarbeit, ~elei *f* slovenly work, dirty work; (*Malerei*) daub(ing); (*beim Schreiben*) scribbling; **~elig** *a* slovenly; dirty; **~elkoch** *m* sluttish cook; **~eln** *itr* (*pfuschen*) to bungle, to do in a slovenly way; (*beim Schreiben*) to scribble; (*Malerei*) to daub; (*auf Papier Männchen malen*) to doodle; (*be~~*) to befoul; to drag in the mud; **~elwetter** *n* muggy weather; **~ler** *m* (*Pfuscher*) bungler; (*schlechter Maler*) dauber; (*im Schreiben*) scribbler.

Suff *m. vulg* (*Trunksucht*) tippling; boozing.

Süff|el *m vulg* tippler; **~eln** *tr, itr* to tipple; to sip; **~ig** *a* (*gut trinkbar*) palatable, bibulous; nice to drink; tasty; (*köstlich*) delicious.

Suffix *n* suffix.

sugge|rieren *tr* to suggest; **~stion** *f* suggestion; **~stiv** *a* suggestive; **~~frage** *f* leading question.

sühn|bar *a* expiable; atoneable; **~e** *f* (*Genugtuung*) atonement; (*Buße*) expiation; *jur* conciliation; **~ebescheid** *m* notice of sanction; **~efestsetzung** *f* sanction to be imposed; **~emaßnahme** *f* sanction; **~en** *tr* to atone (*für* for); to expiate; **~etermin** *m* day fixed for reconciliation; **~everfahren** *n* conciliation proceedings *pl*; **~eversuch** *m* attempt at reconciliation; **~opfer** *n* atonement; expiatory sacrifice; (*Bibel, fig*) peace-offering; **~ung** *f* atonement; expiation.

Suhle *f* muddy pool; slough, puddle; **~n** *itr* to wallow in the mire.

Suite *f* (*Gefolge*) suite, retinue; train; *mus* suite; *fam* (*Streich*) prank, trick; *fam* lark.

Sukkurs *m* succour.

Sukzess|ion *f* succession; **~iv** *a* successive; **~ive** *adv* gradually.

Sulf|anilsäure *f* sulfanilic acid; **~at** *n* sulphate; **~id** *n* sulphide; **~it** *n* sulphite; **~onamid** *n* sulfonamide; sulfa (drug); **~osäure** *f* sulpho acid; **~ur** *m* sulphur.

Sultan *m* sultan; **~in** *f* sultana; **~ine** *f* (*Rosine*) sultana, *Am* seedless raisin.

Sulze, Sülze *f* (*Lake*) brine; (*Speise*) brawn, jelly; jellied meat; **~fleisch** *n* pickled meat; **~n** *tr* (*Fleisch*) to jelly (meat); **sulzig, sülzig** *a* gelatinous.

Summ|a *f siehe Summe*; *in ~~*, *~~ summarum* in short, in brief; taking it all in all; when all is said and done; **~and** *m math* term of a sum; item; **~arisch** *a* summary; (*kurz*) brief; (*bündig*) succinct; *~~ verfahren* to take summary proceedings; **~e** *f* sum; *Gesamt~~* sum-total, grand total, total; (*Betrag*) total amount; (*Gesamtheit von etw*) totality; *die ~~ ziehen* to sum (*od* cast) up; **~ieren** *tr* to add up; to cast up; to totalize; *sich ~~* to amount to; to run up to; **~ierung** *f* summing up; summarizing; accumulation; summation.

summ|en *tr, itr* (*trällern*) to hum; to sing (*od* murmur) in a low tone; (*Melodie*) to croon; (*laut ~~*) to zoom; (*Insekt, Motor*) to buzz; (*Ohren*) to tingle; **~er** *m el* buzzer; oscillator; vibrator; **~~knopf** *m tele* buzzer key; **~~ton** *m* buzzing (*od* humming) tone; **~~zeichen** *n* buzzer signal, humming tone; **~ton** *m tele* dial hum.

Sumpf *m* swamp; marsh; bog; (*sumpfiges Land*) fen; (*Pfütze*) pool; (*Morast*) morass; (*Moor*) moor; *fig* den; *tech* (*Motor~*) sump; **~ablaß** *m mot* sump plug; **~boden** *m* swampy ground; **~dotterblume** *f* marsh-marigold; *Am* cowslip; **~en** *itr fam* to lead a dissolute life; **~fieber** *n* marsh-fever; (*Malaria*) malaria; **~gas** *n* marsh-gas; **~gebiet** *n*, **~gegend** *f* marshy country (*od* areas); marshland; **~huhn** *n* moorhen; marsh-hen, rail; *fig* (*Säufer*) boozer; (*Liederjan*) debauchee; **~ig** *a* boggy, marshy, swampy; **~land** *n* marshland; **~loch** *n* muddy pool; mud hole, *Am* slough; **~moor** *n* low moor; marshy ground; bog; **~otter** *f* mink; **~pflanze** *f* marsh plant; **~vogel** *m* aquatic bird, wader; **~wald** *m* bog; **~wasser** *n* stagnant pool; boogy water; marsh-water; **~wiese** *f* swamp meadow.

Sums *m fam* (*Lärm, viel Aufhebens*) fuss, twaddle; *viel ~ machen über* to make a great fuss about s. th.; **~en** *itr, tr* (*= summen*) to buzz; to hum.

Sünd|e *f* sin; (*Übertretung*) transgression; trespass; (*Fehler*) fault; (*Verstoß, Verbrechen*) offence; *kleine ~~* light offence, peccadillo; **~enbekenntnis** *n* confession of sins; **~enbock** *m* (scape)goat; *Am auch* stooge; **~enerlaß** *m* remission of sins; absolution; **~enfall** *m* the fall (of man); Adam's sin; **~engeld** *n* ill-gotten money; (*sehr viel Geld*) enormous sum; **~enleben** *n* sinful life; **~enpfuhl** *m fig* cesspool of sin; **~enregister** *n* list of sins committed; **~envergebung** *f* absolution; remission of sins; **~er** *m*, **~erin** *f* sinner; offender; delinquent; *armer ~~* criminal under sentence of death; *hum* poor chap; **~erbank** *f Am* mourner's bench; **~ergesicht** *n* guilty face; **~flut** *f* deluge; the Flood; **~haft, ~ig** *a* sinful; criminal; **~igen** *itr* to (commit a) sin; (*fehlen*) to trespass; to transgress; **~lich** *a* sinful, impious; **~~keit** *f* iniquity; **~los** *a* innocent.

Sund *m* sound, strait(s *pl*).

Super *m radio* (*Superheterodynempfänger*) superhet (radio receiving set); superheterodyne; **~(atom)bombe** *f* super atomic bomb; (*Wasserstoffbombe*) hydrogen bomb, H-bomb; *Am fam* hell bomb, super duper; **~dividende** *f com* extra dividend, *Am* bonus; **~fein** *a* superfine; **~festung** *f Am aero* Superfortress, *Abk* Superfort; **~heterodynempfänger** *m radio* superheterodyne receiver; **~intendent** *m* superintendent; **~kargo** *m mar* supercargo; **~klug** *a* overwise; pert; **~lativ** *m* superlative; **~numerar** *m* supernumerary; **~oxyd** *n* peroxide; **~phosphat** *n* superphosphate.

Suppe *f* soup; (*Brühe*) broth; (*Fleischbrühe*) clear soup, bouillon; consommé; *die ~ auslöffeln müssen fig* to have to face the music; *jdm e-e schöne ~ einbrocken fig* to do s. o. an ill turn; *jdm die ~ versalzen fig* to spoil s. o.'s sport; **~nfleisch** *n* meat to make soup of; boiled beef; **~ngrün, ~nkraut** *n* pot-herb; **~nküche** *f* soup--kitchen; **~nlöffel** *m* (*Schöpflöffel*) soup-ladle; dipper; (*Eßlöffel*) tablespoon **~nnapf** *m* (*bes. für Kinder*) porringer; **~nschüssel, ~nterrine** *f* (soup-)tureen; **~nteller** *m* soup-plate; **~ntopf** *m* stock-pot; pot of soup; **~nwürfel** *m* soup cube.

Supplement *n* supplement; **~band** *m* supplementary volume; **~winkel** *m* supplementary angle.

Support *m tech* (*Schlitten*) slide, rest, tool carriage; head.

Suppositorium *n med* suppository.

Supremat *n*, **~ie** *f* supremacy.

surren *itr* to hum, to buzz.

Surrogat *n* substitute; (*Notbehelf*) makeshift.

suspen|dieren *tr* to suspend; **~dierung, ~sion** *f* suspension; *jur* suspense; (*Einstellung*) discontinuance; **~sorium** *n med* suspensory.

süß *a* sweet; (*gezuckert*) sugared; (*frisch*) fresh; *fig* (*lieblich*) lovely; pleasant; (*reizend*) charming; (*lieb*) dear, sweet; *~e Butter* fresh butter, *Am* sweet butter; **~e** *f* sweetness; **~en** *tr* to sweeten; **~holz** *n* liquorice; *~~ raspeln fig* to spoon; to flirt; to say soft things; **~~raspler** *m* spoon; flirt; **~igkeit** *f* sweetness; *fig* suavity; complaisance; **~~en** *f pl* sweets *pl*, sweeties *pl*, lollipops *pl*, *Am* candy; *~~en lieben fam* to have a sweet tooth; *sich nichts aus ~~en machen* not to care for sweets; **~kirsche** *f* sweet cherry, black-heart; **~lich** *a* sweetish; *fig* (*widerlich*) mawkish; (*Lob*) fulsome; (*rührselig*) maudlin; *Am* sugar-coated; **~~keit** *f* sweetishness; *fig* mawkishness; **~maul** *n fam* sweet-tooth; **~säuerlich** *a* sourish-sweet; bitter-sweet; **~speise** *f* sweet; pudding; *Am* dessert; **~stoff** *m* saccharin(e); sweetening agent; dulcifiant; **~waren** *f pl* sweets *pl*, *Am* candy; **~~laden** *m* sweet shop, *Am* candy store, candy shop; **~wasser** *n* fresh water; **~~behälter** *m* fresh-water storage tank; **~~fisch** *m* fresh-water fish; **~~krebs** *m* crayfish, *Am* crawfish; **~wein** *m* sweet wine.

Swing *m mus* hot jazz, swing (music); *Am sl* jive; *~ spielen* to play hot jazz, to swing, *Am sl* to jive; *~ tanzen Am sl* to jitterbug; **~enthusiast** *m* swing fan, *Am sl* hepcat; jitterbug; **~kapelle** *f* swing band; **~musik** *f* swing (music), hot jazz, *Am sl* jive; **~~er** *m Am sl* hepcat, jammer, swingster.

Sylphe *f* sylph.

Sylvester, ~abend *m siehe Silvester*

Sym|bol *n* symbol; (*Zeichen*) sign; (*Zahl*) figure; (*Figur*) emblem; **~bolik** *f* symbolism; **~bolisch** *a* symbolic(al); figurative; **~bolisieren** *tr* to symbolize;

~**metrie** *f* symmetry; ~**metrisch** *a* symmetrical; ~**pathie** *f* sympathy; ~~**streik** *m* sympathetic strike; ~**pathisch** *a* likable; congenial; *sie war mir gleich* ~~ I liked her at once, I took to her right away; ~**pathisieren** *itr* to sympathize (*mit* with); to like; *jem, der mit dem Kommunismus* ~*pathisiert* fellow-travel(l)er; ~**phonie** *f* symphony; ~~**konzert** *n* symphony concert; ~~**orchester** *n* symphony orchestra; ~**phonisch** *a* symphonic; symphonious; ~**ptom** *n* symptom; (*Andeutung*) indication; ~~**atisch** *a* symptomatic(al) (*für* of).

Syn|agoge *f* synagogue; ~**chron** *a* synchronous; ~~**getriebe** *n mot* synchromesh; synchronizing gear; ~~**isieren** *tr* to synchronize; to bring into step; (*Tonfilm*) to dub; ~~**isierung** *f* synchronization; (*Tonfilm*) dub(bing); ~~**ismus** *m* synchronism; ~~**motor** *m* synchronous motor; ~~**zyklotron** *n* synchro-cyclotron; ~**chrotron** *n* synchrotron; ~**dikat** *n* syndicate; ~**dikus** *m* syndic; *Am* corporation lawyer; legal adviser; ~**kope** *f* syncope; ~**kopieren** *tr* to syncopate; ~**kopierung** *f mus* syncopation; ~**kopisch** *a* syncopic; ~**ode** *f eccl* synod; convention; ~**odisch** *a* synodic(al); ~**onym** *n* synonym; ~~ *a* synonymous; ~**onymik** *f* synonymy; ~**opsis** *f* synopsis (*pl* -ses); ~**optisch** *a* synoptic(al); ~**taktisch** *a* syntactic(al); ~**tax** *m* syntax; ~**these** *f* synthesis (*pl* -ses); ~**thetisch** *a* synthetic; ~~*es Benzin* synthetic petrol (*Am* gasoline); ~~*e Farbstoffe* synthetic dyestuffs; *voll*~~*e Faser* synthetics *pl*; ~**thetisieren** *tr* (~~ *herstellen*) to synthetize.

Syphil|is *f* syphilis; *fam* pox; ~**itiker** *m* syphilitic, luetic; ~**itisch** *a* syphilitic.

Syr|ien *n* Syria; ~**ier** *m*, ~**isch** *a* Syrian.

System *n* system; (*Methode*) method, scheme; (*Lehre*) doctrine; *Sonnen*~ solar system; *Nerven*~ nervous system; ~**atik** *f* systematology; ~**atiker** *m* systematist; ~**atisch** *a* systematic(al); ~~*er Katalog* classed catalog(ue); ~**atisieren** *tr* to systematize; ~**atisierung** *f* systematization; ~**erkrankung** *f med* system-disease; ~**los** *a* unsystematic; unmethodical; ~ **zahl** *f* file number.

*

Szen|arium *n* (*Bühnenbuch, Drehbuch*) scenario; ~**e** *f* (*Bühne*) stage; (*Schauplatz, Auftritt; Dekoration; Vorgang; Zank*) scene; *film* shot, set; *in* ~~ *setzen* to stage (*od* to mount) a play; to enact; *hinter der* ~~ behind the scenes, *Am* backstage; *sich in* ~~ *setzen* to show off; ~**enaufnahme** *f film* shot, take; ~**enbild** *n* stage setting; set; ~**enwechsel** *m* change of scenes; ~**erie** *f* scenery; décor; (*Bühnenaufbau*) props *pl*, *Am sl* set-stuff; ~**isch** *a* (*bühnenmäßig*) scenic.

Szepter *n* sceptre, *Am* scepter.

T

T *Abk mit* ***T*** *siehe Liste der Abk.*

Tabak *m* tobacco; (*Schnupf*~) snuff; (*Grobschnitt*) shag; (*Kau*~) chewing-tabacco; (*in Rollen*) pig-tail; *fam* (*Kraut*) weed; *leichter* ~ mild tabacco; *das ist starker* ~ (*fig fam*) that's too strong; ~ *rauchen* (*kauen*) to smoke (to chew) tabacco; ~**bau** *m* cultivation of tobacco; ~**beize** *f* sauce (for tobacco); ~**fabrik** *f* tobacco factory; ~**geruch** *m* tobacco smell; ~**händler** *m* tobacconist; ~**industrie** *f* tobacco industry; ~**laden** *m* tobacconist's (shop), *Am* cigar-store; ~**monopol** *n* tobacco monopoly; ~**pflanze** *f* tobacco plant; ~~**r** *m* tobacco grower; ~**pflanzung** *f* tobacco plantation; ~**qualm** *m* tobacco smoke; ~**regie** *f* tobacco monopoly; ~**sbeutel** *m* tobacco-pouch; tobacco box; ~**sdose** *f* snuff-box; ~ **s)pfeife** *f* tobacco pipe; ~**steuer** *f* duty on tobacco, tobacco tax; ~**verbrauch** *m* tobacco consumption; ~**waren** *f pl* tobacco and tobacco products *pl*.

tabell|arisch *a* tabular, tabulated; ~**arisieren** *tr* to tabulate, to tabularize; ~**e** *f* table; (*Register*) index; (*Liste*) schedule; (*vergleichende Übersicht*) synopsis; (*amtliches Verzeichnis*) register; (*Zus.stellung*) card; tabulation; ~**enform** *f*: *in* ~~ tabular, tabulated, in tabulated form.

Tabernakel *m, n* tabernacle.

Tablett *n* tray; (*Metall*) salver; ~**e** *f* tablet, lozenge.

tabu *a* taboo.

Tabulator *m* tabulator; ~**(lösch)taste** *f* tabulator set (key).

Taburett *n* tabouret, stool.

Tachometer *m* speedometer.

Tadel *m* blame; (*Vorwurf*) reproof, rebuke, reproach; (*Verweis*) reprimand; (*Rüge*) censure; (*Ermahnung*) admonition; (*Fehler*) fault; (*Ausschelten*) scolding, rating, *fam* wigging; (*Makel*) blemish; (*Schule*) bad mark; *fam* set-down, dressing down; *ohne* ~ blameless, without a blemish; ~**frei**, ~**los** *a* irreproachable; (*vollkommen*) perfect; (*fehlerlos*) flawless; (*ausgezeichnet*) excellent; ~**losigkeit** *f* blamelessness; ~**n** *tr* to blame, to find fault with; (*rügen*) to censure, *Am* to score; (*zurechtweisen*) to rebuke, to lecture, to reprimand; (*bekritteln*) to carp (*über* at), to nag; (*mahnen*) to admonish; (*mißbilligen*) to reprove, *Am fam* to call down; (*brandmarken*) to brand; (*Einwendungen machen*) to challenge; (*anfechten*) to impugn; (*in Frage stellen*) to impeach; (*kritisieren*) to criticize; (*vorwerfen*) to reproach; (*schelten*) to snub, to scold, *fam* to trim, to dress down; ~**nswert** *a* deserving of blame, blameworthy; faulty; reprehensible; ~**sucht** *f* censoriousness; ~**süchtig** *a* censorious, nagging, fault-finding.

Tadler *m* fault-finder, critic.

Tafel *f* table; (*Schul*~) blackboard; (*Anschlag*~) poster board, *Am* bill board; (*Metall*~) plate, sheet (of metal); (*Platte*) slab; (*Schmuck*~) plaque; (*Schreib*~) tablet; (*Schiefer*~) slate; (*Schokolade*) cake, tablet, bar; (*Holz*~)panel; (*Glas*) pane; (*Illustration*) plate; (*Diagramm*) chart; diagram; (*Tabelle*) index, list; (*Tisch*) (dinner-) table; (*Mahlzeit*) meal, banquet; *die* ~ *decken* to lay the cloth, to set the table; *sich an die* ~ *setzen* to sit down to table; *die* ~ *aufheben* to rise from table; ~**apfel** *m* dessert-apple; ~**artig**, ~**förmig** *a* tabular; ~**aufsatz** *m* centre-piece; ~**berg** *m* table mountain; ~**besteck** *n* knife, fork, and spoon; ~**bier** *n* table beer; ~**birne** *f* dessert-pear; ~**blei** *n* sheet lead; ~**brötchen** *n* roll; ~**butter** *f* best butter; ~**freuden** *f pl* pleasures of the table; ~**geschirr** *n* table service, tableware; ~**glas** *n* sheet glass; (*Spiegel*) plate-glass; ~**klavier** *n* square piano; ~**land** *n* table-land, plateau; terrace; ~**linnen** *n* table-linen; ~**musik** *f* table-music; ~**n** *itr* to dine, to sup, to feast; ~**obst** *n* dessert (fruit); ~**öl** *n* salad oil; ~**runde** *f* Round Table; (*Gäste*) guests (at table); ~**schiefer** *m* roofing plate; ~**silber** *n* table-silver, *Am* flatware, flat silver; ~**tuch** *n* table-cloth; ~**waage** *f* counter scales, platform scales *pl*.

täfel|n *tr* to floor; (*Wand*) to wainscot; (*einlegen*) to inlay; (*Fußboden*) to floor with boards; ~**ung** *f* (*Fußboden*) inlaying; wainscot(t)ing; panelling.

Taf(fe)t *m* taffeta.

Tag *m* day; (*Tageslicht*) daylight; (*Lebenszeit*) lifetime; (*Helle*) brilliance, brightness; (*Licht*) light; *der Jüngste* ~ the Last Day, Doomsday; *bei* (*od am*) ~*e* in the daytime, during the day, by daylight; *es ist* ~ it is daylight; *es wird* ~ it is beginning to get light, the day breaks; ~ *für* ~ from day to day; *acht* ~*e* a week; *in acht* ~*en* this day week; *alle acht* ~*e* every week; *vor acht* ~*en* a week ago; *vierzehn* ~*e* a fortnight, *Am* two weeks; *in vierzehn* ~*en* in a fortnight; *alle* ~*e* every day; *jeden zweiten* ~ every other day; day and day about; *zweimal am* ~*e* twice a day; *den ganzen* ~ all day long; *den lieben langen* ~ the livelong day; *am hellen* ~ in broad daylight; *auf ein paar* ~*e* for a few days; *dieser* ~*e* one of these days; (*kürzlich*) recently, lately; ~ *für* (*od um*) ~ day by day, day after day; *den andern* ~, *am folgenden* ~ the next day; *Jahr u.* ~ for ever so long; *e-s schönen* ~*es* one fine day; *in seinen alten* ~*en* in his old age; *guten* ~*!* (*morgens*) good morning! (*nachmittags*) good afternoon! (*allgemein*) how do you do? *fam* hallo! hullo! *Am* hello! (*bei Verabschiedung*) good day! *fam* see you again! *ein glücklicher* ~ a red letter day; *Bedürfnisse des* ~*es* present day needs; ~ *des Inkrafttretens* effective date; ~*s darauf* the next day; ~*s zuvor* the day before; *trüber* ~ overcast day; *über* ~ (*min*) open workings; aboveground; in the open; *unter* ~ (*min*) below ground; *sich e-n guten* ~ *machen* to make quite a day of it; *an den* ~ *bringen* (*kommen*) to bring (to come) to light; *in den* ~ *hinein leben* to live one day at a time, not to worry about to-morrow; *in den* ~ *hinein reden* to talk at random; *e-n* ~ *frei bekommen* to be allowed a day off; *es ist noch nicht aller* ~*e Abend* we have not seen the last day of it yet; *ob in guten, ob in schlechten ~en* for better, for worse; *unter ~e arbeiten min* to work underground; *zu ~ fördern* to unearth; **~aus, ~ein** *adv* day in day out; **~blind** *a* seeing best at night; **~~heit** *f* day blindness; **~bomber** *m* day(light) bomber; **~earbeit** *f* day labo(u)r; **~~er** *m* day-labo(u)rer, day-wage man; **~ebau** *m min* opencast (coal)mining; surface mining; *Am* strip-mining; **~blatt** *n* daily paper, journal; **~ebuch** *n* diary, journal; *com* daybook; *mar* log; *mil* file of orders; *med* medical report book; **~(e)dieb** *m* idler, *fam* lazy-bone; **~(e)geld** *n* day travel(l)ing allowance, per diem allowance; **~elang** *adv* for days (on end); **~(e)lohn** *m* daily wage, day's pay; *im ~~ arbeiten* to work by the day; **~(e)löhner** *m* day-labo(u)rer, *Am* hired man; **~en** *itr* to dawn, to get light; (*beraten*) to meet, to hold a meeting, to sit, to confer; (*Gericht*) to be in session; **~esanbruch** *m* daybreak; *bei ~~* at daybreak, at dawn, at the break (*od* peep) of day; **~esangabe** *f* date; **~esangriff** *m aero* daylight raid; **~esarbeit** *f* day's work; **~esausflug** *m* day trip; **~esausflügler** *m* day tripper; **~esbefehl** *m mil* Order of the Day; routine order; **~esbelastung** *f el, tele* daily load; **~esbericht** *m* daily report (*od* return), bulletin; **~esdienstplan** *m* daily schedule; **~eseinnahme** *f* daily receipts *pl* (*od* takings *pl*); **~eseinteilung** *f* agenda; **~esereignis** *n* event of the day; **~esfrage** *f* question of the day; **~esgebühr** *f* day rate; **~esgespräch** *n* topic of the day; **~esgrauen** *n* dawn, daybreak; **~eshelle** *f* light of day; **~eskarte** *f* ticket for the day; **~eskasse** *f theat* booking (*od* box)-office; *com* receipts *pl* of the day; **~eskurs** *m* current rate, day's rate of exchange, quotation; **~esleistung** *f* daily output; (*Maschine*) daily capacity; **~eslicht** *n* daylight; *das ~~ erblicken* to be born; to come to light; to come out; *das ~~ scheuen* to shun daylight; *ans ~~ kommen* to come to light, to transpire, *Am* to develop; **~~aufnahme** *f* daylight shot; **~~entwickler** *m* daylight developer; **~~farbfilm** *m* daylight type colo(u)r film; **~~kassette** *f film* daylight loading magazine; **~~spule** *f* daylight spool; **~esmädchen** *n* daily; **~esmarsch** *m* day's march; **~esmeldung** *f* daily report (*od* return); **~esnachrichten** *f pl* the day's news *pl*; **~esordnung** *f* agenda, program(me) of a meeting; *parl* order-paper, *Am* calendar; *auf die ~~ setzen* to place on the agenda; *zur ~~ übergehen* to deal with the agenda; to get down to business; to pass to the order of the day; **~espost** *f* day's mail; **~espreis** *m* current (*od* ruling) price; **~espresse** *f* daily press; **~(es)reise** *f* day's journey; **~essatz** *m* daily rate, daily-ration quantity; **~(es)schicht** *f* day-turn; day shift; **~esstempel** *m* date-stamp; **~esstunden** *f pl* hours of daylight; **~esumsatz** *m* daily turnover; **~esverdienst** *m* daily earnings *pl*; **~eswert** *m* market-value; **~eszeit** *f* time of day, daytime; hour of the day; *zu jeder ~~* at any hour; **~eszeitung** *f* daily paper; **~eszuteilung** *f* daily ration; **~eweise** *adv* by the day; **~ewerk** *n* day's work, daily task; (*Arbeitseinheit*) man-day; **~falter** *m* butterfly; **~flug** *m* day flight; **~hell** *a* as light as day, clear; **~jäger** *m* day fighter (aircraft); **~süber** *adv* during the day; **~täglich** *a* daily, everyday; **~~ und Nachtdienst** *m* day and night service; **~~ und Nachtgleiche** *f* equinox; **~ung** *f* conference, session, meeting; *parl, jur* sitting; (*offiziell*) congress, *Am* convention; *e-e ~~ einberufen* to call a meeting **~~sbericht** *m* proceedings *pl*; **~~sort** *m* meeting place; **~~steilnehmer** *m* member of a meeting.

täglich *a, adv* daily, day-to-day, every day, quotidian, diurnal, per day (*od* diem); *~es Geld* call-money.

Taifun *m* typhoon.

Taille *f* waist; (*Kleid*) bodice.

Takel *n* tackle; **~age, ~ung** *f*, **~werk** *n* rigging, tackle; cordage; **~n** *tr* to tackle, to rig.

Takt *m mus* time, measure; (*Arbeits~*) strokes *pl* per working cycle, cycle; (*Rhythmus*) cadence, rhythm; *fig* tact, discretion; *im ~* in time; (*Tanz*) in step; *~ halten* to keep time, to play in time; *aus dem ~ kommen* to play out of time; *den ~ schlagen* to beat time; *aus dem ~ bringen* to put out of time; $^3/_4$~ three-four time; **~bezeichnung** *f* time signature; **~fest** *a* keeping good time; (*zuverlässig*) reliable, sound; **~gefühl** *n* tact; tactfulness; **~ieren** *tr itr* to beat time; **~ik** *f* tactics *pl*; *~~ der verbrannten Erde* scorched earth tactics; **~~er** *m* tactician; **~isch** *a* tactical; *~~es Zeichen* military symbol, tactical call-sign; **~los** *a* tactless; (*ungeschickt*) maladroit, awkward, clumsy; **~~igkeit** *f* tactlessness, want of tact; indiscretion; *e-e ~~igkeit begehen* to commit an indiscretion, to act in bad form; **~messer** *m* metronome; **~stock** *m* baton; **~strich** *m mus* bar(-line); **~voll** *a* tactful, discreet; **~zeichen** *n* cadence signal.

Tal *n* valley; (*kleines ~*) dale; (*enges ~*) gorge, glen; dell; *poet* dale; (*Wellen~*) wave trough; **~(ab)wärts** *adv* down-hill; valleywards; down-stream; **~aufwärts** *adv* uphill; **~bildung** *f* valley formation; **~boden** *m* valley floor; **~einschnitt** *m geol* section of a valley; **~fahrt** *f* descent; **~hänge** *m pl* slopes *pl* of a valley; **~kessel** *m*, **~mulde** *f* hollow, basin (of a valley); (*steil*) gorge; **~senke** *f* depression of a valley, hollow (of a valley); **~sohle** *f* bed (*od* bottom) of a valley; **~sperre** *f* river dam, barrage; (*Staubecken*) catchment area (*od* basin); **~~rbombe** *f* dam-buster; **~wärts** *adv* downstream; **~weg** *m* road along a valley; (*Fluß*) channel; *geol* thalweg.

Talar *m* gown, robe.

Talent *n* talent, gift; (*Fähigkeit*) ability, faculty, aptitude (**zu** for); (*Fertigkeiten*) attainments *pl*; (*Geschick*) knack; (*Person*) talented person; **~iert, ~voll** *a* talented, gifted.

Talg *m* (*roh*) suet; (*ausgelassen*) tallow; *anat* sebum; **~drüse** *f* sebaceous gland; **~fett** *n* stearin; **~ig** *a* suety; tallowy; **~kerze** *f*, **~licht** *n* tallow-candle.

Talisman *m* talisman, amulet; charm; mascot.

Talje *f mar* (long)tackle; **~reep** *n* lanyard.

Talk *m* talc(cum); **~erde** *f* magnesia; **~puder** *m* talcum powder.

Talmigold *n* talmi-gold; pinchbeck; *Am* gold brick.

Tamb|our *m* drummer; **~~major** *m* drum-major; **~urin** *n* tambourine.

Tampon *m* plug (of cotton-wool); **~ieren** *tr* to plug (a wound).

Tamtam *n* tomtom; *fig* noise, fuss, *Am fam* stunt; *~ schlagen fig* to make a great noise.

Tand *m* trumpery, knicknacks *pl*, trifles *pl*, bauble, gewgaw, gimcrack, trinket; (*Spielzeug*) toy.

Tänd|elei *f* trifling, dallying, toying; (*Liebelei*) flirtation, *sl* spooning; (*Trödelei*) dawdling; **~eln** *itr* to dally, to trifle; *fig* to flirt; (*Zeit vergeuden*) to dawdle; **~ler** *m* trifler, dawdler; *com* second-hand dealer.

Tandem|anordnung *f* tandem (*od* compound) arrangement; **~flugzeug** *n* tandem aircraft; **~schraube** *f* tandem propeller.

Tang *m* seaweed.

Tang|ente *f* tangent; **~ieren** *tr* to touch.

Tango *m* tango; **~jüngling** *m fam* pansy.

Tank *m* (*Behälter*) tank, receptacle; (*Kampfwagen*) tank, *Am* combat car; (*leichter*) whippet, light tank; (*Abwurf~*) *aero* slip tank; **~abwehr** *f* anti-tank defence; **~~geschütz** *n* anti-tank gun; **~anlage** *f* fuel tank, fuel-storage depot; **~ausweis** *m* fuel permit; **~büchse** *f* anti-tank rifle; **~dampfer, ~er** *m*, **~schiff** *n* tanker; **~en** *itr* to take in petrol, to fill up, to refuel, *Am* to gas up (a car); *in der Luft ~~* to gas up (*od* to fuel in) in mid-air; *~~n* refuel(l)ing; **~fahrer** *m* tank driver; **~falle** *f* tank trap; **~flugzeug** *n* tanker plane; **~holz** *n* producer gas wood; **~landungsschiff** *n* tank-landing craft; **~pfeiler** *m mil* asparagus beds *pl*; **~raum** *m* tank space; **~schutz** *m* anti-tank protection; **~stelle** *f* service (*od* filling) station, petrol-point, refuelling point, *Am* gas station; **~~nautomat** *m Am* gas-a-teria; **~truppen** *f pl* tank troops *pl*; **~wagen** *m* petrol tender, tank lorry (*od Am* truck), *rail* tank car; **~~behälter** *m* truck tank; **~wart** *m* petrol-pump attendant, *mil* petrol point orderly.

Tann, ~enwald *m* pine forest; **~e** *f* fir; (*Rot~~*) spruce; **~en** *a* fir; **~~baum** *m* fir tree; **~~holz** *n* fir-wood, deal; **~~nadeln** *f pl* fir-needles *pl*; **~~wald** *m* fir-wood, pine forest; **~~zapfen** *m* fir-cone.

Tannin *n chem* tannin, tannic acid.

Tante *f* aunt.

Tantieme *f* percentage, premium, bonus; (*Gewinnanteil*) share, dividend; (*für Autoren, Erfinder*) royalty.

Tanz *m* dance; ball; *fam* hop; *fig* row, quarrel; *zum ~ aufspielen* to strike up for a dance; *jetzt geht der ~ los!* now the fun begins! *darf ich Sie um den nächsten ~ bitten?* may I have the next dance? **~bär** *m* dancing-bear; **~bein** *n*: *das ~~ schwingen* to dance; **~boden** *m*, **~diele** *f*, **~platz** *m*, **~saal** *m* ball-room, dancing-room; **~en** *itr tr* to dance; *fam* to hop, to prance; (*schaukeln*) to rock; (*wirbeln*) to spin, to go round; **~erei** *f* dance, hop; **~fanatikerin** *f Am sl* (*Swing*) hepcat; **~fest** *n* ball; **~fläche** *f* dance floor; **~gesellschaft** *f* dancing party; **~girl** *n* chorus-girl, show-girl; **~kapelle** *f* dance band; **~kränzchen** *n* dancing-club; **~kurs** *m*, **~stunde** *f* dancing lesson; **~lehrer** *m* dancing-master; **~lied** *n* dancing song; **~lokal** *n* public ball-room, dancing saloon, *Am* dance hall; **~lust** *f* love of dancing; **~~ig** *a* fond of dancing; **~musik** *f* dance music; **~palast** *m* dance palace; **~partner** *m* partner; **~platte** *f* dancing record; **~schritt** *m* step; **~schuh** *m* pump, *Am* step-in; **~schule** *f* dance school; **~tee** *m* dance tea; **~tournier** *n* dancing contest; **~vergnügen** *n* ball; **~wut** *f* dancingmania.

tänze|ln *itr* to trip, to frisk, to skip about; to caper; (*Pferd*) to amble; **~r** *m*, **~rin** *f* dancer; (*Mit~~*) partner; (*Ein~~*) gigolo; (*Spielzeug*) peg-top, whip-top; (*Ballett~rin*) ballerina.

Tapet *n*: *etw aufs ~ bringen* to introduce (*od* to broach) a subject; **~e** *f*

wall-paper, (paper) hangings *pl*; (*gewirkte*) tapestry; **~enhändler** *m* dealer in wall-paper; **~enmuster** *n* design; **~entür** *f* jib-door, hidden door.
Tapezier, ~er *m* paper-hanger; (*Anstreicher u.* ~) decorator; (*Polsterer*) upholsterer; **~geschäft** *n* upholstery; **~en** *tr* to paper; ~~ *n* papering.
tapfer *a* valiant, brave; (*mutig*) courageous, bold; (*kühn*) audacious; (*furchtlos*) dauntless, undaunted; (*unerschrocken*) intrepid; (*heroisch*) valiant, valorous, heroic, gallant; (*tüchtig*) doughty; (*beherzt*) plucky, gritty; **~keit** *f* valour, bravery; gallantry.
Tapisseriewaren *f pl* tapestry goods *pl*.
tappen *itr* to grope about; to fumble.
täppisch *a* awkward, clumsy.
Taps *m* clumsy fellow, gawk, hobbledehoy; **~en** *itr* to walk clumsily, to gawk; **~ig** *a* awkward, gawky.
Tar\|a *f* tare; **~ieren** *tr* to tare; **~ierwaage** *f* tare (*od* pharmaceutical) balance.
Tarantel *f* tarantula; *wie von der ~ gestochen* like mad; in a frenzy.
Tarif *m* (*Lohn*) wage scale (*od* schedule); *rail* tariff, railway rates *pl*, list of fares; (*Zoll*) tariff; (*Post*) postal rates *pl*; (*Preis*) scale of prices, list of charges; **~bestimmungen** *f pl* tariff regulations *pl*; **~erhöhung** *f* increase in rates; **~ermäßigung** *f* reduction in tariff; **~lich, ~mäßig** *a* in accordance with the tariff; according to scale; **~lohn** *m* standard wages *pl*; **~ordnung** *f* tariff agreement; **~politik** *f rail* rate policy, (*Zoll*) tariff policy; **~satz** *m* standard rate; **~verhandlungen** *f pl* collective bargaining; **~vertrag** *m* wage agreement, tariff treaty, *Am* collective agreement; **~vorteile** *m pl* (*Zoll*) tariff advantages *pl*; **~widrig** *a* not according to contract.
Tarn\|anstrich *m* shadow (*od* dazzle) painting; **~bezug** *m* camouflage covering; **~decke** *f* camouflage screen; **~en** *tr* to camouflage, to mask; to disguise; to screen; **~farbe** *f* drab painting; **~kappe** *f* magic hood; **~maßnahmen** *f pl* camouflage measures *pl*; **~netz** *n* screen, camouflage net; **~scheinwerfer** *m* screened head-lamp; masked headlight; **~ung** *f* camouflage; screening, masking; **~vorschrift** *f* camouflage instruction; **~zahl** *f* code number; **~zeltbahn** *f* camouflage cape.
Täschchen *n* little pocket; pouch; bag.
Tasche *f* (*Rock~*) pocket; (*Beutel*) pouch, bag; (*Hand~*) hand-bag; (*Schul~*) satchel; (*Akten~*) brief case, portfolio; (*Etui*) case; (*Brief~*) wallet, *Am* pocketbook; (*Geldbeutel*) purse; *med, zoo* bursa; *tech* trap; *~ mit Tragriemen* shoulder bag; *in die ~ stecken* to pocket; *so gut wie in der ~ haben* to be as good as in the bag; *so gut wie seine eigene ~ kennen* to know inside out; *jdm immer noch auf der ~ liegen* to be still living off s. o., to be a financial drain on s. o.; **~napotheke** *f* pocket medicine-chest; **~nausgabe** *f* pocket-edition; **~nbuch** *n* pocket-book, *Am* memo-book; **~ndieb** *m* pickpocket, *Am sl* dip; *vor ~~en wird gewarnt!* beware of pickpockets! **~~stahl** *m* pocket-picking; **~nfahrplan** *m* pocket time-table; time table pocket edition; **~nfeuerzeug** *n* pocket lighter; **~nformat** *n* pocket-size; **~ngeld** *n* pocket money, allowance, spending money; **~nkalender** *m* pocket almanac; **~nkamm** *m* pocket-comb; **~nklappe** *f* pocket flap; **~nkrebs** *m* common crab; **~nlampe** *f* electric torch, *Am* flashlight; **~nmesser** *n* pocket-knife, *Am* jackknife; (*kleines*) penknife; **~nnähzeug** *n* housewife; **~npuderdose** *f* compact; **~nspiegel** *m* pocket-mirror; **~nspieler** *m* conjurer, juggler; **~~ei** *f* jugglery, legerdemain, sleight of hand; **~ntuch** *n* handkerchief, *fam* hanky; (*buntes*) bandan(n)a; **~nuhr** *f* pocket watch, *fam* ticker; **~nwörterbuch** *n* pocket dictionary.
Täschner *m* purse-maker, trunk-maker.
Tasse *f* cup; (*Unter~*) saucer.
Tast\|atur *f* keyboard, keys *pl*; **~e** *f* key; **~en** *itr* to feel; to touch; (*tappen*) to grope; *tele* to key, to control; *sich ~~* to feel o.'s way; **~~brett** *n* finger board; **~~feld** *n* key set; **~~hebel** *m* key lever; **~~knopf** *m* key button; **~~reihe** *f* row of keys; **~er** *m* feeler antenna; *tele* key; *tech* cal(l)ipers *pl*; *radio* keying device; *tele* scanner, explorer; **~~schenkel** *m* cal(l)iper leg; **~sinn** *m* sense of touch; **~ung** *f* control, keying; **~versuch** *m* tentative experiment, preliminary experiment; **~werkzeug** *n* feeler, organ of touch.
Tat *f* action, deed, act; (*gewandte*) feat; (*Groß~*) achievement; (*Tatbestand, Handlung*) fact; (*Verbrechen*) crime; (*Helden~*) exploit; *Mann der ~* man of action; *auf frischer ~ ertappen* to catch in the very act, to catch red-handed; *in der ~* indeed, in fact, as a matter of fact; *in die ~ umsetzen* to give effect (to); to implement; **~bereit** *a* ready to act; **~bericht** *m* summary of evidence; **~bestand** *m* facts *pl* of the case, factual findings *pl*; **~~saufnahme** *f* official statement, summary of evidence; **~beweis** *m* practical proof; **~christentum** *n* practical Christianity; **~einheit** *f jur* coincidence; **~endrang, ~endurst** *m* thirst for action, desire to do great things; **~enlos** *a* inactive, idle; **~form** *f gram* active voice; **~kraft** *f* energy; strength; might, vigo(u)r; *sl* pep, *fam* go, vim; **~kräftig** *a* energetic; *ein ~~er Mensch Am* a live wire; **~ort** *m* place of action; **~sache** *f* fact, *Am* data *pl*; *grundlegende ~~n* basic data; *den ~~n ins Auge blicken* to face the facts; *~~n auf den Kopf stellen* to stand facts on their head; **~~nbericht** *m* first-hand account, factual account, eye-witness account; **~~nkenntnisse** *pl* factual knowledge; **~~nmaterial** *n* factual material; *~~nmaterial liefern* to furnish evidence (for), to substantiate s. th.; **~~nmensch** *m* matter-of-fact (*od* unimaginative) person; **~sächlich** *a* real, actual, factual; (*wirksam*) effective; *adv* really, actually, in reality, seriously, right enough, *Am* for fair.
Tät\|er *m* author; perpetrator; culprit; **~~schaft** *f* perpetration (of a crime); (*Schuld*) guilt; **~ig** *a* active, busy; (*wirksam*) efficacious, working; *~~ sein* (*als*) to officiate (as); to be active, to work; *immer ~* on the run; **~~en** *tr* to carry out; (*Geschäft*) to effect; (*Abschluß*) to conclude; **~igkeit** *f* activity; (*Handlung*) action; (*Beruf*) occupation, profession, job; (*Beschäftigung*) pursuits *pl*; (*Funktion*) function; (*Bewegung*) operation; *außer ~~ setzen* to set aside, to suspend; *in ~~ setzen* to set in motion, to put in action; *die ~~ einstellen* (*fam*) to close up shop; *e-e ~~ entfalten* to activate; *e-e ~~ wieder aufnehmen* to resume activity; **~~sbereich** *m* sphere of action, field of business; **~~sbericht** *m* progress report; business report; **~~sform** *f* active voice; **~igung** *f com* conclusion; **~lich** *a* active; (*gewaltsam*) violent; *~~ werden* to come to blows; to assault s. o.; *~~e Beleidigung* assault and battery; **~lichkeit** *f* violence, assault (and battery); *zu ~~ gelangen* to come from words to blows.
tätowieren *tr* to tattoo; *~ n* tattooing.
Tatsche *f* paw, clap; **~n** *tr* to clap, to flap.
tätscheln *tr* to caress, to pet, to stroke.
Tatterich *m* trembling, *Am sl* jitters *pl*.
Tatze *f* paw, claw; **~nhieb** *m* blow with a paw.
Tau *n* cable, rope, hawser, line; (*Geschirr*) trace; *~ m* dew; serein; **~en** *itr* to fall as dew; (*schmelzen*) to melt, to thaw; *es taut* the dew is falling; it is thawing; **~ende** *n* rope end; **~fall** *m* dew-fall; **~feucht** *a* wet with dew, dew-drenched; **~frisch** *a* dewy-fresh; **~luft** *f* soft air; **~öse** *f* ear of a cord; **~punkt** *m* dew point; thawing point; **~tropfen** *m* dewdrop; **~werk** *n* cordage, rigging; **~wetter** *n* thaw; **~wind** *m* mild breeze; **~ziehen** *n sport* tug of war.
taub *a* (*~ auf*) deaf of; (*~ gegen*) deaf to; (*~ vor*) deaf with; *fig* unfeeling, callous; (*leer*) empty, hollow; (*unfruchtbar*) barren, sterile, dead; (*betäubt*) numb; *~es Gestein* barren-ground, deads *pl*; *~e Ähre* empty ear; *~en Ohren predigen* to talk to the winds; *gegen jds Bitten ~ sein* to turn a deaf ear to s.o.'s request; *~e Nuß* empty nut; *~e Nessel* deadnettle, henbit; *~er Hafer* wild oats; **~heit** *f* deafness; (*Leere*) emptiness; (*Erstarrung*) numbness; **~nessel** *f* dead-nettle; **~stumm** *a* deaf and dumb; **~~enanstalt** *f* institute for the deaf and dumb; **~~e(r)** *m* deaf-mute.
Täub\|chen *n* little dove; **~erich** *m* cock-pigeon.
Taube *f* pigeon; dove; *ein Flug ~n* a flight of pigeons; *die ~ girrt* the pigeon coos; (*Brief~*) carrier pigeon; **~nhaus** *n*, **~nschlag** *m* dovecot; **~nmist** *m* pigeon's dung; **~npaar** *n* pair of pigeons; **~nschießen** *n* pigeon-shooting; **~nzüchter** *m* pigeon-breeder; **~r** *m* cock-pigeon.
Tauch\|boot *n* submarine; **~brenner** *m* immersion heater; **~en** *itr* to plunge, to dive, to dip; (*U-Boot*) to submerge, to dive, (*schnell*) to crash-dive; *tr* to plunge, to dip, to steep, to immerse, to douse; (*plötzlich*) to duck; **~er** *m* diver; **~~anzug** *m* diving dress; diving-bell suit; **~~apparat** *m* diving apparatus; **~~glocke** *f* diving bell; **~~helm** *m* diver's helmet; **~~leine** *f* diving line; **~fähig** *a* submersible; **~filter** *n* immersion filter; **~gerät** *n* diving apparatus; **~klar** *a mar* ready to submerge; **~retter** *m* life-saving apparatus; **~schmierung** *f mot* splash lubrication; **~schwimmer** *m* float; *mil* (*Kampfschwimmer*) frog-man; **~sieder** *m el* immersion-heater; **~spule** *f* moving coil; **~stab** *m* dip stick; **~tank** *m* ballast tank; **~tiefe** *f* diving depth; depth of immersion; **~waage** *f* areometer, hydrometer.
Tauf\|akt *m*, ***~handlung*** *f* christening ceremony; **~becken** *n*, **~stein** *m* baptismal font; **~buch, ~register** *n* parish register; **~e** *f* baptism; (*Vorgang*) christening; *aus der ~~ heben* to be godfather (*od* godmother) to a child, to stand sponsor to a child;

fig to originate, to initiate; **~en** *tr* to baptize, (*allg*) to christen; (*Wein*) to adulterate; (*bekehren*) to convert; *ein Schiff* **~~** to name a ship; **~formel** *f* form of baptism; **~gelübde** *n* baptismal vow; **~kapelle** *f* baptistry; **~name** *m* Christian name, *Am* given name; **~pate** *m* godfather; **~patin** *f* godmother; **~schein** *m* certificate of baptism; **~schmaus** *m* christening-feast; **~wasser** *n* baptismal water; **~zeuge** *m* sponsor.

Täuf|er *m* baptizer; *Johannes der ~* John the Baptist; **~ling** *m* child to be baptized; candidate for baptism, (*Neubekehrter*) neophythe.

taug|en *itr* to be worth; to be of use; to be useful, to be of value; *zu etw* **~~** to be fit (*od* good) for; *zu nichts* **~~** to be good for nothing; **~enichts** *m* good-for-nothing, scamp, bad fellow, *fam* bad lot, *Am fam* bad egg, skeezicks *pl*, scalawag; **~lich** *a* good (for), able, fit; (*geistig*) qualified (for); (*fähig*) capable; (*nützlich*) useful; (*geeignet*) suitable (to, for); *mil* fit (for service); (*Schiff*) seaworthy; **~~keit** *f* fitness; ability; usefulness; qualification.

Taumel *m* reeling, staggering; (*Schwindel*) giddiness; (*Rausch*) intoxication; *fig* transport, frenzy; (*Leidenschaft*) passion; (*Ekstase*) ecstasy; **~ig** *a* reeling; (*schwindlig*) giddy; **~n** *itr* to stagger, to reel; to wobble; (*schwindlig sein*) to be giddy; **~scheibe** *f tech* wobble plate; swash plate.

Tausch *m* exchange, *fam* swap (*od* swop); (*~handel*) barter, trading, *Am* truck; *im ~ gegen* in exchange for; *e-n ~ machen* to effect an exchange; *in ~ nehmen* to take in exchange; to trade in; *e-n guten ~ machen* to make a good exchange; *im ~ hergeben* to barter away; **~abkommen** *n* barter agreement; **~en** *tr* to exchange for; to barter, *fam* to swap; **~geschäft** *n* barter deal; **~handel** *m* barter, truck(age); exchange-trade; **~mittel, ~objekt** *n* article of exchange; **~verkehr** *m* exchange; **~wert** *m* exchange value.

täusch|en *tr* to deceive, to delude; (*anführen*) to dupe; (*betrügen*) to cheat, to deceit, to trick, to take in, to fool (*um* out of); (*irreführen*) to mislead; to delude; (*hintergehen*) to impose (upon); (*umgehen*) to elude; (*verraten*) to betray; (*vereiteln*) to baffle; (*ent~~*) to disappoint; *r* to be mistaken in, to be wrong; to deceive o. s., to fool o. s. (*über* about); *sich ~~ lassen* to let o. s. be deceived (*od* fooled); *wir haben uns in ihr sehr getäuscht* she was a great disappointment to us; **~end** *a* deceptive, delusive, illusory; *~~e Ähnlichkeit* striking resemblance; **~ung** *f* deception, deceit; (*Fehler*) mistake; (*Betrug*) fraud, cheat; (*Schwindel*) imposture; (*Selbsttäuschung*) illusion, delusion; **~~sangriff** *m mil* feint (*od* mock) attack; **~~smanöver** *n mil* deception tactics *pl*; **~~sversuch** *m* attempt to deceive.

tausend *a* (a) thousand; *viele Tausende* thousands of; *~ u. e-e Nacht* the Arabian Nights *pl*; **~er** *m* thousand; figure marking the thousands; banknote of 1000 (marks); **~erlei** *a* of a thousand different sorts, ever so many things; a thousand kind; *~~ Dinge* a thousand different things; **~fach, ~fältig** *a* thousandfold; *adv* in a thousand ways; **~fuß** *m* millipede; (*od* millepede); myriapod; wireworm; **~güldenkraut** *n* centaury; **~jährig** *a* a thousand years old, millennial; **~künstler, ~sasa** *m* Mr. Fixit, conjurer, juggler, Jack-of-all-trades; **~mal** *adv* a thousand times; **~schönchen** *n bot* daisy; **~ste** *a*, **~stel** *n* thousandth; **~weise** *adv* by thousands.

Tax|ameter *m* (*Fahrpreisanzeiger*) taximeter; (*Autodroschke*) taximeter cab, taxi(cab); **~ator** *m*, **~ierer** *m* valuer, appraiser; **~e** *f* (*Schätzung*) estimate; (*Steuer*) tax; rate, tariff; (*Zoll*) duty; (*Gebühr*) fee; (*Fahrzeug*) taxi(cab), cab, *Am fam* hack; *mit e-r ~~ fahren* to ride in a taxicab, *Am* to taxi; **~enhaltestelle** *f* taxi-rank, *Am* taxi-stand; cab-rank, *Am* cab-stand; **~gebühren** *f pl* appraiser's fees *pl*; **~i** *n* taxi(cab), cab, *Am fam* hack; **~ieren** *tr* to value, to appraise, to tax, to fix the price; (*Steuer*) to assess; *zu hoch ~~* to over-rate; *zu niedrig ~~* to under-rate; *~iert auf* valued at; **~ierung** *f* appraisal; taxation; valuation; **~ifahrer** *m* taxi-driver; cab-driver (*od* operator); **~iflugzeug** *n* taxiplane; **~uhr** *f* taximeter; **~wert** *m* valuation, appraised value; (*Steuer*) assessed value.

Taxus *m* yew(-tree).

Techn|ik *f* technics *pl*, technical science; (*Fertigkeit*) skill, workmanship, dexterity; *mus* technique, execution; (*Ingenieurwissenschaft*) engineering; (*Verfahren*) technique, practice; (*Kunstlehre*) technics *pl*; (*Lehre von der ~~*) technology; (*Industrie*) industry; **~iker** *m* (technical) engineer, technician; **~ikum** *n* technical school; **~isch** *a* technical, practical; (*mechanisch*) mechanical; engineering; industrial; *~~e Angelegenheit* technicality; *~~e Artikel* technical goods; *~~er Chemiker* chemical engineer; *~~e Hochschule* institute of technology, polytechnic academy, technical college; *~~e Nothilfe* engineering emergency service; *Am* technical emergency corps; *~~es Personal* technical staff; *~~e Störung radio* breakdown; *~~er Offizier der Luftwaffe Am aero mil* engineering officer; **~ologe** *m* technologist; **~ologie** *f* technology; **~ologisch** *a* technological.

Techtelmechtel *n* love affair, flirtation.

Teckel *m* dachshund, dachs.

Tee *m* tea; (*Aufguß*) infusion; *e-e Tasse ~* a cup of tea; *den ~ einnehmen mit* to sit at tea with; *Fünf-Uhr-~* five o'clock tea; *der ~ muß noch ziehen* the tea has not stood long enough; *abwarten u. ~ trinken!* just wait and see! *~ mit kalter Küche* meat (*od* high) tea; **~blatt** *n* tea-leaf; **~brett** *n* tea-tray; **~büchse** *f* tea-caddy; **~ei** *n* tea-egg, infuser; **~gebäck** *n* small cakes *pl*, *Am* cookies *pl*; biscuit; tea-cake; **~gedeck** *n* tea-set; **~geschirr, ~service** *n* tea-service; tea-set; tea-things *pl*; **~gesellschaft** *f* tea-party; **~glas** *n* tea-glass; **~haube** *f* tea-cosy; **~kanne** *f* tea-pot; **~kessel** *m* tea-kettle; **~löffel** *m* tea-spoon; **~löffelvoll** *m* tea-spoonful; **~maschine** *f* tea-urn, samovar; **~mischung** *f* blend of tea; **~rose** *f* tea-rose; **~satz** *m* tea-leaves *pl*; **~sieb** *n* tea-strainer; **~sorten** *f pl* teas *pl*, kinds *pl* of tea; **~staude** *f* tea-shrub; **~stunde** *f* tea-time; **~tasse** *f* tea-cup; **~tisch** *m* tea-table; **~topf** *m* tea-pot; **~ wagen** *m* tea-wagon; tea-cart; tea-trolley; **~wärmer** *m* tea-cosy; **~wasser** *n* hot water for tea.

Teer *m* tar; pitch; *mit ~ bestreichen* to tar; **~anstrich** *m* coat(ing) of tar; **~arbeiter** *m* tarrer; **~artig** *a* tarry; **~asphalt** *m* tar asphalt; **~benzin** *n* benzene, benzol; **~bildung** *f* formation of tar; **~brennerei** *f* tar factory; **~decke** *f* (*Straße*) tar surface; (*Leinwand*) tarpaulin; **~en** *tr* to tar; **~farbe** *f* coal-tar colo(u)r; **~jacke** *f fig mar* Jack Tar; **~ig** *a* tarry; **~kessel** *m* tar kettle; **~papier** *n* tarred paper; **~pappe** *f* tarboard; **~straße** *f* tarred street; **~ung** *f* tarring; tar spraying; **~werg** *n* tarred oakum.

Teich *m* pond, pool; artificial lake; *über dem großen ~* (*Ozean*) across the big pond; **~rose** *f* water lily.

Teig *m* (*Brot~*) dough; (*Eier~*) batter; (*Kuchen~*) paste; (*Blätter~*) puff-paste; **~ig, ~icht** *a* doughy; pasty; (*knetbar*) kneadable; plastic; (*Obst*) over-ripe, mellow; **~mulde** *f* baker's trough; **~waren** *f pl* macaroni, spaghetti, noodles etc.

Teil *m* part; (*Stück*) piece; component; element; (*Glied*) member; (*Anteil*) share; (*Portion*) portion, proportion; (*Abschnitt, Strecke*) section, division; (*~haber*) party; *ein wesentlicher ~* part and parcel of; *zum ~* in part(s), partly; *der größte ~* the greater part; *zum größten ~* for the most part; *einesteils adv* on the one hand; *ich für meinen ~* I for my part, as for me; *andernteils* on the other hand; *großenteils* in some measure; *größtenteils* to a large extent, in a great measure; *meistenteils* for the most part; *edle ~e* vital parts *pl*; *sich seinen ~ denken* to have o.'s own thoughts (about); *ein ~ der Leute* part of the people; *in zwei ~e zerschneiden* to cut in two; *zuteil werden* to fall to s. o.'s share; **~abschnitt** *m* sector, segment; leg (of a journey); **~angriff** *m mil* local attack; **~bar** *a* divisible; **~~keit** *f* divisibility; **~bericht** *m* partial report; **~betrag** *m* partial amount; (*Quote*) quota; (*Abzahlung*) instal(l)ment; **~chen** *n* particle; small part; corpuscle; *math* element; **~einheit** *f* component; *mil* element (of a unit); **~en** *tr* (*ein~~, ver~~*) to divide (*in* into; *unter* among, between); (*etw ~~*) to share (*unter* among; *mit* with s. o.); (*aus~~*) to portion out, to parcel out, to pass out, to deal out, to distribute; to dispense, to dole out; (*An~ haben*) to share (*an* with); (*gemeinsam haben*) to participate in, to go shares in, to partake; (*zu~~*) to allot, to allocate, to assign; (*trennen*) to separate, to part, to sever, to diverse; (*zerstückeln*) to dismember; (*ab~~*) to partition off; (*in Grade ein~~*) to graduate; (*in Anspruch nehmen*) to take up; (*Leiden*) to sympathize with; to partake in; *r* to divide; (*untereinander*) to share in, to go shares (in with s. o.); to split (s. th.); (*abzweigen*) to fork, to branch off; (*auseinandergehen*) to diverge; *geteilte Axe aero* split axle; *geteilte Gefühle* mixed feelings; *geteilter Meinung sein* to be of a different opinion; **~er** *m* divider; *math* divisor; (*ohne Rest*) submultiple; **~erfolg** *m* partial success; partial result; **~ersatz** *m* partial replacement; **~film** *m* episode; **~frequenz** *f el* component frequency; **~gebiet** *n* section; portion; branch; **~gruppe** *f* subgroup; **~haben** *irr itr* to participate (*an* in), to share (in), to have a share (in), to partake (of), to take part (in); **~haber** *m* (*Gesellschafter*) partner, associate, *Am auch* copartner, *sl* pard; (*Beteiligter*) participant, partner, sharer; shareholder; (*Miteigentümer*) joint (*od* part) owner; *persönlich haf-*

tender ~~ responsible partner; *tätiger* ~~ active (*od* working) partner; *geschäftsführender* ~~ managing partner; *stiller* ~~ sleeping (*od* dormant, *Am* silent) partner; *als* ~~ *eintreten* to join a firm as partner; ~~**schaft** *f* partnership; ~~**vertrag** *m* partnership agreement; ~**haftig** *a*: *etw* ~~ *werden* to be participating in, to be sharing in; ~**kessel** *m tech* sectional boiler; *mil* partial encirclement, round-up of small bodies of troops; ~**kraft** *f tech* component force; ~**kreis** *m* graduated circle; pitch circle; ~**ladung** *f* (*Treibladung*) boosting charge; ~**last** *f* partial load; ~**linie** *f* parting line; ~**marke** *f* index; ~**montage** *f* subassembly; ~**motorisiert** *a* partly motorized; ~**nahme** *f* participation; (*An*~) share; (*Mitarbeit*) co-operation; (*Interesse*) interest; (*Mitgefühl*) sympathy; (*Beileid*) condolence(s *pl*); (*Mitschuld*) complicity (*an* in); *seine* ~~ *ausdrücken* to condole (with); ~**nahmslos** *a* indifferent, apathetic, (*gegen* towards), listless; ~~**igkeit** *f* apathy, indifference; ~**nahmsvoll,** ~**nehmend** *a* full of sympathy, sympathetic; interested (in); ~**nehmen** *irr itr* to take part (*an* in), to participate (in), to share (in), to partake (of); (*mitwirken*) to co-operate, to collaborate; (*sich vereinigen*) to join (*mit jdm* with, to; *an etw* in); (*sich interessieren*) to take an interest (in), to interest o. s. (in); (*beitragen*) to contribute (to); (*anwesend sein*) to be present (*bei* at), to attend; (*mitfühlen*) to sympathize (with); *an e-m Lehrgang* ~~ to take a course; *an e-m Wettbewerb* ~~ to partake in a competition; ~**nehmer** *m* sharer, participant, partner; (*Mitglied*) member; *tele* user; (public) subscriber, party; (*Mitschuldiger*) accomplice; accessory (to); *sport* competitor, partner; ~~ *meldet sich nicht* party does not answer; there is no reply; *den* ~~ *trennen* to cut off the subscriber; *anrufender* ~~ calling party, caller; *verlangter* ~~ called subscriber, wanted party; ~~**anschluß** *m* subscriber's station, *Am* substation; ~~**apparat** *m* subscriber's set; ~~**fernschreibdienst** *m* telex service, *Am* teletypewriter service; ~~**gebühr** *f* rate (of subscription); ~~**leitung** *f* subscriber's line; ~~**liste** *f* list of participants; (*sport*) competitors *pl*; ~~**nebenanschluß** *m* subscriber's extension station; ~~**nummer** *f tele* number; ~~**verzeichnis** *n* telephone directory; ~~**zahl** *f* number of participants; *sport* number of entrants; *tele* number of subscribers; ~**pächter** *m* share tenant; ~**ring** *m* graduated ring; micrometer ring; ~**s** *adv* partly, in part; ~**schaden** *m com* part damage; ~**sendung** *f com* consignment in part, partial shipment; ~**strecke** *f rail* section; stage; ~**streik** *m* sectional strike; ~**strich** *m* (*Skala*) graduation (mark); ~**überholung** *f* partial overhaul; top overhaul; ~**ung** *f* (*Aufteilung*) division; (*Grade*) graduation, scale; (*mit Zwischenraum*) spacing; (*Verteilung*) distribution; (*Anteile*) sharing; (*Trennung*) separation; (*Land*) parcel(l)ing out; (*Zerstückelung*) dismemberment; (*Zell*~~) segmentation; (*Weg*) bifurcation, fork(ing); (*gleichmäßige Zuteilung*) apportionment; ~~**sartikel** *m* partitive article; ~~**skoeffizient** *m* distribution coefficient; ~~**smasse** *f com* property divisible among the creditors; ~~**sstrich** *m* mark of division; ~~**sverfahren** *n* partition procedure; ~~**svertrag** *m* treaty of partition; ~~**szahl** *f* dividend; ~**verlust** *m* partial loss; ~**weise** *adv* partly, in part(s), to some extent; *a* partial; ~**zahl** *f* quotient; ~**zahlung** *f* part(ial) payment; (*Rate*) instal(l)ment, time-payment; *auf* ~~ *kaufen* to buy on the instal(l)ment plan; ~~*en leisten* to pay by insta(l)ments; ~~**ssystem** *n* instal(l)ment plan, time-payment plan.

Teint *m* complexion.

T-Eisen *n* T-iron, tee-iron.

Telautograph *m* telautograph, telewriter.

Telefon *n siehe Telephon.*

Tele|gramm *n* telegram, message; *Am* wire; (*Bild*~~) picture telegram; (*Brief*~~) letter telegram; *Am* night telegraph letter; letter wire; (*Chiffre*~~) cipher(ed) telegram; (*Funk*~~) radiogram, wireless message; (*Glückwunsch*~~) greetings (*pl*) telegram, *Am* congratulation telegram; (*Kabel*~~) cablegram; *ein* ~~ *aufgeben* to hand in a telegram; *ein* ~~ *aufnehmen* to copy a message; *ein* ~~ *dringend durchgeben* to rush a telegram; ~~ *zu ermäßigten Gebühren* deferred (rate) telegram; *dringendes* ~~ urgent message; *zugesprochenes* ~~ phonogram; ~~**adresse,** ~~**anschrift** *f* telegraphic address; ~~**annahmestelle** *f* collecting office; ~~**aufgabe** *f* handing-in of telegrams; ~~**bote** *m* messenger; ~~**formblatt,** ~~**formular** *n* telegraph form (*Am* blank), *Am* message blank; ~~**gebühren** *f pl* telegram rates *pl*; ~~**kopf** *m* preface, preamble; ~~**(kurz)-anschrift** *f* registered address; ~~**schalter** *m* telegram counter; ~~**schlüssel** *m* code; ~~**verstümmelung** *f* mutilation of a telegram; ~~**zusteller** *m* messenger; ~~**zustellung** *f* delivery of telegrams; ~**graph** *m* telegraph; *optischer* ~~ semaphore, optical telegraph; (*Bild*~~) phototelegraphic apparatus; (*Funk*~~) radio telegraph; (*Maschinen*~~) machine (*od* automatic) telegraph; (*Zeiger*~~) pointer (*od* needle) telegraph; ~~**enamt** *n* telegraph office (*od* station); ~~**enanlage** *f* telegraph plant; ~~**enarbeiter** *m* line(s)man, wireman; ~~**enbau** *m* telegraph construction; ~~**enbauamt** *n* telegraph construction office; ~~**enbautrupp** *m* telegraph construction gang; ~~**enbote** *m* telegraph messenger; ~~**endraht** *m* telegraph wire; ~~**enkabel** *n* telegraph cable; ~~**enleitung** *f* telegraph circuit; ~~**enlinie** *f* telegraph line; ~~**ennetz** *n* telegraph network; ~~**enschlüssel** *m* telegraph code; ~~**enstange** *f* line pole; ~~**entruppe** *f mil* Signal Corps; ~~**enübertragungsamt** *n* repeater station; ~**graphie** *f* telegraphy; *drahtlose* ~~, *Funk*~~ radio (*od* wireless) telegraphy; (*Bild*~~) picture (*od* photo) telegraphy; (*Gegensprech*~~) duplex telegraphy; (*Morse*~~) Morse code telegraphy; (*Übersee*~~) transatlantic telegraphy; ~~**ren** *itr* to telegraph, to wire; (*Kabel*) to cable; ~~**sender** *m* radio telegraphic transmitter; ~**graphisch** *a* telegraphic(al). by telegram (*od* wire); ~~ *anfragen* to wire for; ~~ *überweisen* to wire, to cable; ~~*es Bild* telephotograph; ~**graphist** *m* telegraphist, telegraph operator, *Am* telegrapher; ~**meter** *n* range finder; telemeter; ~**objektiv** *n phot* telephoto lens; ~**pathie** *f* telepathy.

Telephon *n* (*siehe auch*: *Fernsprecher*) (tele)phone; telephone receiver; *ich habe* ~ I am on the phone; *am* ~ *bleiben* to hold the line; *das* ~ *bedienen* to answer the phone; *Gesprächspartner am* ~ telephonee; ~**amt** *n* telephone-exchange, *Am* telephone central office; ~**anlage** *f* telephone installation; ~**anruf** *m* (tele)phone-call; ~**anschluß** *m* telephone-connection; (*Nebenanschluß*) extension; ~~ *haben* to be on the (tele)phone; ~**apparat** *m* telephone set; ~**auskunft** *f* (telephone) information; ~**buch** *n* (tele)phone directory; ~**draht** *m* telephone wire; ~**gebühren** *f pl* telephone-fees *pl*, telephone-rates *pl*, telephone-charges *pl*; ~**gespräch** *n* (telephone) call; telephone conversation; *ein* ~~ *zustande bringen* to put through a call; ~~ *mit Herbeiruf Am* messenger call; *Unterbrechung e-s* ~~*s* disconnection; ~**hörer** *m* telephone receiver, handset; ~**ie** *f* telephony; *drahtlose* ~~ radio telephony; ~**ieren** *itr* to (tele)phone, to ring up, *Am* to call up, to call on the (tele)phone; (*wählen*) to dial; (*sprechen*) to talk on the phone; *nach auswärts* ~~ to call out-of-town; ~**ierender** *m* radio telephone transmitter; ~**isch** *a* by (tele)-phone, on the (tele)phone; over the telephone, telephonic; ~~*e Durchsage* delivery by telephone; ~~ *anfragen* to inquire by telephone; ~~ *anrufen* to ring up, *Am* to call up; ~**ist(in)** *m* (*f*) (tele)phone operator, *fam* op; (tele)-phone girl, *Am fam* hello-girl, switchboard-girl; ~**leitung** *f* telephone line; ~**netz** *n* telephone network; ~**nummer** *f* telephone(-call) number; *e-e* ~~ *wählen* to dial; ~**(sprech)zelle** *f* call-box, *Am* telephone-booth; *öffentliche* ~~ public call station; ~**verbindung** *f* telephone connection; telephone communication; *e-e* ~~ *herstellen* to put through a call; ~**vermittlung,** ~**zentrale** *f* (telephone-) exchange, *Am* telephone central office, *Am* (telephone-) central.

Teleskop *n* telescope; ~**gabel** *f* telescopic fork; ~**mast** *m* telescopic mast.

Teller *m* plate; *flacher* ~ shallow plate; *tiefer* ~, *Suppen*~ soup-plate; (*Präsentier*~) tray; (*Holz*~) platter, trencher; (*Hand*) palm; (*Ventil*) head; (*Scheibe*) disk; ~**brett** *n* plate-rack; plate-drainer; ~**eisen** *n* trap; ~**förmig** *a* plate-shaped; ~**fuß** *m* plate-shaped base; ~**gericht** *n* one course meal, stew; ~**mine** *f* plate-mine, anti-tank (*Abk* A. T.) mine; ~**mütze** *f* flat peaked cap; ~**tuch** *n* dish-towel; ~**rad** *n mot* bevel wheel; ~**schrank** *m* sideboard; ~**ventil** *n* disk valve; pipe valve; ~**voll** *m*: *ein* ~~ a plateful; ~**wärmer** *m* plate-warmer; ~**wäscher** *m* plate-scrubber, *Am* dishwasher; ~**zinn** *n* plate pewter.

Tellur *n* tellurium; ~**nickel** *n* nickel telluride.

Tempel *m* temple; ~**herr,** ~**ritter** *m* Knight-Templar; ~**raub** *m,* ~**schändung** *f* sacrilege.

Tempera(farbe) *f* distemper; tempera.

Temperament *n* temper, temperament; (*Feuer*) spirits *pl*, mettle; (*Lebhaftigkeit*) vivacity; (*Wesensart*) character, constitution, disposition, frame of mind; (*Gemütsart*) humo(u)r; *er hat kein* ~ he has no life in him; ~**los** *a* spiritless; ~**voll** *a* high-spirited, lively, full of spirits; (*lebhaft*) vivacious, eager; (*leidenschaftlich*) passionate; (*feurig*) ardent.

Temperatur *f* temperature; *bei* ~*en unter Null* at sub-zero temperature; *jds* ~ *messen* to take s. o.'s temperature; ~**abfall** *m* drop in temperature; ~**abhängig** *a* temperature dependent (*od* responsive); **~änderung** *f* change in temperature; **~anstieg** *m* rise of temperature; **~ausgleich** *m* temperature balance; **~beobachtung** *f* temperature observation; **~beständigkeit** *f* temperature stability (*od* constancy); **~einfluß** *m* influence of temperature; **~erhöhung** *f* rise in temperature; **~jahresmittel** *n* mean annual temperature; **~maximum** *n* maximum temperature; **~messung** *f* temperature measurement; **~mittel** *n* mean temperature; **~regelung** *f* air-conditioning; **~schwankung** *f* variation of temperature; **~steigerung, ~zunahme** *f* rise in temperature; **~sturz** *m* slump of temperature; **~umkehr** *f* inversion of temperature; **~unterschied** *m* difference of (*od* in) temperature; **~veränderung** *f*, **~wechsel** *m* change of temperature.

Temper|enzler *m* teetotaller; total abstainer; **~guß** *m* malleable cast iron; **~ieren** *tr* to temper; to give temperature (to); **~ofen** *m* annealing (*od* tempering) furnace; **~verfahren** *n* annealing process; **~wirkung** *f* annealing action.

Tempo *n mus* time, measure, tempo; (*Gangart*) pace; (*verhältnismäßige Geschwindigkeit*) rate; (*Geschwindigkeit*) speed; *mil* movement, pace; *das ~ angeben* to set the pace; *nun aber ~* (*mot*) now, step on it; **~rär** *a* temporary; **~schwung** *m* (*Schilaufen*) speed swing.

Tendenz *f* tendency, trend, drift; (*Neigung*) inclination, propensity; (*Wetter~*) weather outlook; **~iös** *a* tendentious; (*voreingenommen*) prejudiced, bias(s)ed; (*nicht unparteiisch*) not impartial; *~~ färben* (*Bericht, Nachricht*) to angle; **~lüge** *f* partisan lie; **~meldung** *f* information with a distinct tendency; **~roman** *m* novel with a purpose; **~stück** *n* drama with a strong bias.

Tender *m rail* tender; *mar* advice-boat, tender; **~lokomotive** *f* tank (*od* tender)locomotive; **~maschine** *f* tender.

Tenne *f* threshing-floor; barn-floor.

Tennis *n* (lawn-)tennis; (*Tisch~*) table-tennis, ping-pong; *~ spielen* to have a game of tennis; **~ball** *m* tennis ball; **~kleid** *n* tennis-dress; **~klub** *m* lawn-tennis club; **~~wettkampf** *m* club match; **~meisterschaft** *f* tennis championship; **~platz** *m* lawn-court; **~schläger** *m* tennis-racket; **~schuhe** *m pl* tennis-pumps *pl*; **~spiel** *n* tennis game; **~spieler** *m* tennis player; (*Kanone*) tennis crack; **~turnier** *n* tennis tournament.

Tenor, **~ist** *m*, **~stimme** *f* tenor.

Teppich *m* carpet; *Am* rug; (*Vorleger*) rug; (*Wand~*) tapestry; (*Tisch~*) (table) cover; (*Läufer*) runner; (*Decke*) blanket; **~belegt** *a* carpeted; **~händler** *m* carpet-dealer; **~kehrmaschine** *f* carpet-sweeper; **~schoner** *m* drugget; **~weber, ~wirker** *m* carpet-manufacturer.

Termin *m* fixed day, limit, last day, closing date, *Am* deadline; (*Datum*) date; (*Zeit*) time; (*Frist*) term; *jur* term, summons *pl*, court-day, date of trial; (*Zahlungs~*) date of payment; *sport* fixture; *e-n ~ anberaumen* to set a day (*od* date) for; to fix a time; *e-n ~ einhalten* to observe a fixed date; *zum ~ nicht erscheinen jur* to default; **~gemäß** *adv* in due time; **~geschäft** *n com* (dealing in) futures *pl*; time bargain; **~kalender** *m* date-book, memo(randum) book, *Am* tickler; almanac of deadlines; *jur* cause-list, *Am* calendar of a court; **~kurs** *m com* forward rate (of exchange); **~lieferung** *f* forward delivery; **~markt** *m* future market; **~ologie** *f* terminology; **~preis** *m com* future price; **~schluß** *m com* time bargain; **~weise** *adv* by instal(l)ments; **~zahlung** *f* payment by instal(l)ments.

Termite *f* termite, white ant.

Terpentin *n* turpentine; **~öl** *n* oil of turpentine; **~(~)ersatz** *m* turpentine substitute, white spirit.

Terrain *n* ground, plot of land; **~aufnahme** *f* ground survey; **~stufe** *f* scarp.

Terrasse *f* terrace; **~ndach** *n* platform roof; **~nförmig** *a* terraced.

Terrine *f* tureen.

Territor|ialtruppen *f pl* territorials *pl*; **~ium** *n* territory.

Terror *m* terror; **~angriff** *m* terror attack; **~isieren** *tr* to terrorize.

Tertia *f* third class; (*England*) fourth form, *Am* seventh grade.

Tertiär *n* tertiary, tertiary period.

Terz *f mus* third; *kleine ~* minor third; *große ~* major third; (*Fechten*) tierce; **~ett** *n* trio.

Terzerol *n* pocket-pistol.

Tesching *n* small rifle.

Test *m* test; (*Versuchstiegel*) *chem* cupel; (*Anzeiger*) indicator; **~ament** *n* (last) will, testament; *Altes* (*Neues*) *~~* Old (New) Testament; *eigenhändiges ~~* holograph will; *gemeinschaftliches ~~* joint will; *Eröffnung e-s ~~* opening (*od* proving) of a will; *ein ~~ machen* (*hinterlassen*) to make (to leave) a will; *jdn im ~~ bedenken* to remember (*od* include) s. o. in a will; *durch ~~ bestimmen* (*od vermachen*) to will; *ohne Hinterlassung e-s ~~s sterben* to die intestate; *ein ~~ widerrufen* to revoke a will; **~~arisch** *a* testamentary; *adv* by will; *~~arische Einsetzung* settlement; *~~arische Verfügung* testamentary disposition, disposition by will; *~~arisch vermachen* to leave (*od* dispose) by will, to bequeath; **~~seröffnung** *f* opening (*od* proving) of a will; **~~svollstrecker** *m* executor; (*gerichtlich*) administrator; **~at** *n* certificate; (*Unterschrift*) signature; **~ator** *m* testator; bequeather; **~ieren** *tr* to make a will, to bequeath; (*bezeugen*) to testify, to certify; (*Hochschule*) to sign the certificate of regular attendance.

teuer *a* dear; (*kostspielig*) costly, expensive; (*wertvoll*) valuable; (*kostbar*) precious; (*lieb*) dear, cherished, beloved; *~ zu stehen kommen* to cost dearly; *wie ~ ist es?* how much is it? what is the price? *~ kaufen* to pay a lot (for); *sein Leben ~ verkaufen* to sell o.'s life dearly; *da ist guter Rat ~* it's hard to know what to do in a case like that; **~ung** *f* increasing cost of living, high level of prices; (*Knappheit*) scarcity, dearth; (*teurer Preis*) dearness; **~~swelle** *f* wave of high prices; **~~szulage** *f* cost-of-living bonus (*od* allowance); **~~szuschlag** *m* price increment.

Teufe *f min* depth; **~n** *tr* to sink; to deepen; to bore.

Teuf|el *m* devil; (*Dämon*) demon; deuce, dickens, old Nick; (*der böse Feind, die Furie*) fiend; *pfui ~~!* how disgusting! *zum ~~ gehen* to go to the devil, to go to rack and ruin; *in der Not frißt der ~~ Fliegen* beggars can't be choosers; *des ~~s sein* to be mad; *mal den ~~ nicht an die Wand!* talk of the devil and he will appear! *er hat den ~~ im Leibe* he is a devil of a fellow; *der ~~ ist los* the fat is in the fire; *zum ~~!* hang it! dickens! **~~ei** *f* devilry, *Am* deviltry; devilish trick; **~~skerl** *m* devil of a fellow; **~~sweib** *n* shrew, witch, *sl* vamp; **~lisch** *a* devilish, diabolical, fiendish, infernal, hellish.

Text *m* text; (*Lied*) words *pl*; *typ* double pica; (*Oper*) libretto; *film* caption; (*Schreibmaschine*) script, manuscript; *radio* (*Sprecher*) continuity; *redaktioneller ~* editorial matter; *weiter im ~!* go on! *aus dem ~ kommen* to lose the thread, to be put out, to break down; **~abbildung** *f* illustration in the text; **~berichtigung** *f* emendation of a text; **~buch** *n* words *pl*, libretto; **~dichter** *m* (*Oper*) librettist; *film* scenario writer; **~er** *m* (*Anzeigen*) ad writer; copywriter; **~~abteilung** *f* copy department; **~gemäß** *adv* textual; **~kritik** *f* textual criticism; **~schrift** *f typ* double pica; paragon.

Textil|arbeiter *m* text ileworker; **~fabrik** *f* textile factory (*od* mill); **~ien** *pl*, **~waren** *f pl* textiles *pl*; **~faser** *f* spun rayon; **~industrie** *f* textile industry; **~schule** *f* textile trade school.

Theater *n* theatre, *Am* theater; (*Bühne*) stage; (*Rampe*) footlights *pl*; *mach kein ~!* don't make a fuss! *ins ~ gehen* to go to the theatre; *er führt immer das gleiche ~ auf* he always gives me the same song and dance; *~ spielen* (*fig*) to play little games; *ich war gestern im ~* I was yesterday at the theatre; *das ~ beginnt um ...* the play begins at ...; *heute ist kein ~* there is no performance to-day; **~aufführung** *f* performance; **~bericht** *m* stage report; **~besuch** *m* playgoing; **~~er** *m* playgoer; **~dekoration** *f* scenery; **~dichter** *m* dramatist, playwright; **~direktor** *m* manager of a theatre; stage director; **~effekt** *m* stage-effect; **~fimmel** *m*: *er hat den ~~* he is a theatre fan; **~karte** *f* ticket; **~kasse** *f* box-office, *Am* ticket-office (*od* window); **~kniff** *m* claptrap; **~loge** *f* box; **~maler** *m* scene-painter; **~maschinist** *m* scene-shifter; **~probe** *f* rehearsal; **~stück** *n* play, drama; **~unternehmer** *m* impresario; **~vorstellung** *f* theatrical performance; **~zettel** *m* play-bill.

theatralisch *a* theatrical; *~e Wirkung* stage effect.

Theke *f* bar, *Am* counter.

Thema *n* subject, theme, topic; *übliches ~* (*fam*) standing dish.

Themse *f* Thames.

Theolog(e) *m* theologian; **~ie** *f* theology; **~isch** *a* theological.

Theor|etiker *m* theorist; **~etisch** *a* theoretical; calculated; **~etisieren** *itr* to theorize; **~ie** *f* theory; *e-e ~~ aufstellen* to put forward a theory.

Theosophie *f* theosophy.

Therap|eutik, **~ie** *f* therapeutics *pl mit sing*.

Therm|alquelle *f* thermal spring; hot spring; **~ik** *f* heat; *aero* thermal; updraft of warm air; warm air current; **~~flug** *m* thermic flight; **~~segelflug** *m* thermal gliding; **~isch** *a* thermal, thermic; *~~er Aufwind* thermal upcurrent; *~~e Behandlung* hot-treatment; *~~er Segelflug* thermal soaring; **~it** *n* thermit; **~~brandbombe** *f* thermite incendiary bomb; **~~schweißung** *f* thermite welding; **~odynamisch** *a* thermodynamic; **~oelektrisch** *a* thermoelectric; **~okernreaktion** *f phys* thermo-nuclear reaction; **~ometer** *n* thermometer; *Am* mercury; **~~kugel** *f* thermometer bulb; **~~röhre, ~~säule** *f* thermometer column (*od* stem);

~~**stand** *m* thermometer reading; ~**osflasche** *f* thermos (*od* vacuum) flask, *Am* thermos (*od* vacuum) bottle; ~**ostat** *m* constant-temperature control.
These *f* thesis.
Thomas|eisen *n* Thomas iron; ~**mehl** *n* Thomas meal; ~**stahl** *m* Thomas steel, basic steel; ~**verfahren** *n* Thomas process, basic process.
Thrombose *f med* thrombosis.
Thron *m* throne; *den ~ besteigen* to ascend the throne, to succeed to; ~**besteigung** *f* accession to the throne; ~**en** *itr* to be enthroned; *fig* to reign; ~**entsagung** *f* abdication, demise; ~**erbe** *m* hereditary prince, heir to the throne; ~**folge** *f* succession to the throne; ~**folger** *m* successor to the throne; ~**himmel** *m* baldachin, canopy; ~**rede** *f parl* King's speech; ~**saal** *m* throne room; ~**sessel** *m* chair of state; ~**wechsel** *m* change of sovereigns.
Thunfisch *m* tunny.
Thüring|en *n* Thuringia; ~**er** *m*, ~**erin** *f*, ~**isch** *a* Thuringian.
Thymian *m* thyme.
Tick *m med* tic; (*Schrulle*) fancy, whim, *fam* fad; ~**en** *itr* to tick; to click; ~**tack** *n* tick-tack, tick-tock, pitapat; ~**zeichen** *n* ticking signal.
tief *a* deep, profound; (*niedrig gelegen*) low; (*Ton*) bass; (*Farbe*) dark; (*Schlaf*) sound, profound; (*Schweigen*) dead; (*äußerst*) extreme, utter, utmost; (*innerst*) innermost; (*Stille*) dead; *~ in jds Schuld stehen* to be deeply indebted (to); *~ in die Nacht hinein arbeiten* to work far into the night; *zu ~ singen* to sing flat; *in ~er Nacht* in the dead of night; *~er stimmen* to lower the pitch; *im ~sten Elend* in extreme misery; *im ~sten Frieden* in the lap of peace; *im ~sten Winter* in the depth of winter; *aus ~stem Herzen* from the bottom of o.'s heart; *~ atmen* to draw a deep breath; *~ fliegen aero* to hedgehop; *~ verletzen* to cut to the quick; *das läßt ~ blicken* that is very significant; *~ n* barometric depression, low; low pressure area; ~**angriff** *m aero* low level (*od* flying) attack; ground strafing; ~~**sflugzeug** *n* low attack plane, ground fighter, *Am* strafer plane; ~**ausgeschnitten** *a* (*Kleid*) deep-cut; ~**bau** *m* underground building (*od* engineering); ~**betrübt** *a* deeply grieved; ~**bettfelge** *f* drop-base rim; ~**bewegt** *a* deeply moved; ~**blau** *a* dark (*od* deep) blue; ~**blick** *m* insight; ~**bohrer** *m* auger; ~**bunker** *m* underground air raid shelter; ~**decker** *m aero* low-wing monoplane; ~**druck** *m* low pressure; *typ* copper plate printing; rotogravure; ~~**gebiet** *n* low-pressure area; ~**e** *f* depth; deepness; *fig* profundity, profoundness; (*Senkung*) low altitude; *Am* draw; (*Schlucht*) gorge; (*Abgrund*) abyss; (*Schiff*) draught; *aus der ~~ meines Herzens* from the bottom of my heart; *e-e ~~ abmessen* to fathom; ~**ebene** *f* plain, lowland(s *pl*); ~**einbruch** *m mil* penetration in depth; ~**en** *f pl mus* bass notes *pl*, low-pitch notes *pl*; (*Bild*) dark-picture portions *pl*; ~**enanzeiger** *m mar* depth ga(u)ge; ~**enbereich** *m* depth of field; ~**enbewegung** *f* movement in depth; ~**enfeuer** *n* searching fire; ~**engestein** *n* plutonic rock; ~**engliederung** *f mil* distribution in depth; ~**enmesser** *m* depth ga(u)ge, bathometer; ~**enmessung** *f* measuring of depths; ~**enruder** *n mar* hydroplane, low rudder, elevator; ~**enschärfe** *f phot* depth of focus (*od* field); ~**enstaffelung** *f* echelonment in depth; ~**enstreuung** *f mil* range dispersion on horizontal target; ~**enstufe** *f* gradient; ~**enunschärfe** *f phot* lack of depth of focus; ~**enverteidigung** *f* defence in depth; ~**enwahrnehmung** *f* perception of depth (*od* relief); ~**enwirkung** *f mil* depth effect; (*Bild*) plastic (*od* stereoscopic) effect; ~**ernst** *a* very grave, solemn; ~**erstellung** *f* lowering; ~**flieger** *m* low-flying aircraft, strafer; ~~**angriff** *m* low-level attack; ~~**beschuß** *m* strafing; ~**flug** *m* low-level flight, contour flight, hedgehopping; dragging; ~**gang** *m mar* draught; ~**gebeugt** *a fig* deeply afflicted; ~**gefühlt** *a* heart-felt; ~**gehend** *a* profound; thorough-going; *mar* deep-drawing; ~**gekühlt** *a* quick-frozen; ~**gestaffelt** *a* echeloned in depth; ~**greifend** *a* penetrating, far-reaching; radical;deep-seated; ~**gründig** *a* deep, profound; ~**hängend** *a* low; ~**kühlen** *tr* to quick-freeze; ~**kühlschrank** *m Am* (home) freezer; freeze box; ~**kühlung** *f* quick freezing; low (*od* intense) cooling; ~**land** *n* lowland(s *pl*); ~**liegend** *a* low-lying; deap-seated; (*Augen*) sunken; ~**punkt** *m* low mark, bottom; ~**rot** *a* deep red; ~**schlag** *m* hit below the belt; ~**schürfend** *a* profound, thorough; ~**schwarz** *a* deep black; ~**see** *f* deep sea; ~~**forschung** *f* deep-sea research; ~~**kabel** *n* deep-sea cable; ~~**lot** *n* deep-sea lead; ~~**lotung** *f* deep-sea sounding; ~~**tauchkugel** *f* bathysphere; ~**sinnig** *a* pensive; profound; (*schwermütig*) melancholy, wistful; ~**stand** *m* low level, lowness; (*Kurs*) low point; *fig* low-water mark; depression; *Am* hardpan; ~**stehend** *a* low-lying; *fig* inferior; ~**stgrenze** *f* minimum; ~**stwert** *m* lowest value; ~**unterst** *a* nethermost; ~**wurzelnd** *a* deep-rooted.
Tiegel *m* saucepan, stew-pan; (*Schmelz~*) crucible; *typ* platen; ~**guß** *m* casting in crucibles; ~**stahl** *m* crucible steel.
Tier *n* animal; (*Vierbeiner*) beast; brute; (*Reit~*) horse; *vierfüßiges ~* quadruped; *Last~* beast of burden; *ein reißendes ~* a beast of prey; *fig großes* (*od hohes*) *~* big noise, big gun, *Am* big bug, big shot, tycoon; ~**art** *f* species of animal; ~**arzneikunde** *f* veterinary science; ~**arzt** *m* veterinarian, veterinary; ~**bändiger** *m* tamer of wild beasts; ~**chen** *n* little animal; (*mikroskopisch klein*) animalcule; ~**fabel** *f* fable; ~**garten**, ~**park** *m* zoological garden(s *pl*); ~**geschichte** *f* story about animals; ~**halterhaftung** *f* liability for animals; ~**haut** *f* hide; ~**isch** *a* animal, animal-like; *fig* (*roh*) brute, brutal, bestial; ~**kohle** *f* animal charcoal; ~**körper** *m* animal body; ~**kreis** *m* zodiac; ~**kunde** *f* zoology; ~**leben** *n* animal life; ~**maler** *m* painter of animals; ~**pflanze** *f* zoophyte; ~**quäler** *m* tormentor of animals; ~~**ei** *f* cruelty to animals; ~**reich** *n*, ~**welt** *f* animal kingdom; ~**schau** *f* menagerie; ~**schutzverein** *m* Society for the Prevention of Cruelty to Animals; ~**stimmenimitator** *m* animal impersonator; ~**versuch** *m* experiment on an animal; ~**zucht** *f* animal-breeding.
Tiger *m* tiger; ~**farbig**, ~**fleckig** *a* spotted like a tiger; tabby, brindled; ~**fell** *n* tiger skin; ~**katze** *f* tiger-cat; ~**in** *f*, ~**weibchen** *n* tigress; ~**n** *tr* to spot, to speckle.
Tilde *f* tilde, sign of repetition (~).
tilg|bar *a* extinguishable; (*Schuld*) redeemable; ~**en** *tr* to extinguish; (*auswischen*) to efface, to erase, to blot out, to obliterate; (*zerstören*) to destroy; (*ausrotten*) to eradicate; *typ* to delete; (*streichen*) to cancel, to annul; (*Schuld*) to discharge, to pay off; (*Staatsschuld*) to redeem; (*amortisieren*) to amortize; (*Eintragung*) to strike out; *e-e Hypothek ~~* to pay off a mortgage; ~**ung** *f* (*Schulden*) discharge, settlement, liquidation, repayment; (*Einlösung*) redemption; (*Amortisation*) amortization, sinking; (*Auslöschen*) blotting out, effacement; (*Streichung*) cancelling; (*Zerstörung*) destruction; (*Ausrottung*) extermination; ~~**sdauer** *f* period of redemption; ~~**fonds** *m* sinking-fund; ~~**splan** *m* scheme of redemption; ~~**srate** *f* redemption instal(l)ment.
Tingeltangel *m* low music-hall.
Tinktur *f* tincture.
Tinnef *m* trash, *Am* junk, *fam* gold brick.
Tinte *f* ink; (*Färbung*) tint; *unverlöschliche ~* marking (*od* indelible) ink; *in der ~ sitzen* to be in a nice mess, to be in the soup; ~**nfaß** *n* inkpot, inkwell; inkstand; ~**nfisch** *m* cuttle-fish; ~**nfleck**, ~**nklecks** *m* blot, ink-stain; ~**ngummi** *m* ink-eraser; ~**nkuli** *m* hack writer; ~**nlöscher** *m* blotter; ~**nstift** *m* indelible pencil.
Tip *m* tip, hint, suggestion; (*Geheim~*, *Warnung*) *Am* tip-off; *jdm e-n* (*warnenden*) *~ geben* to tip; *Am* to tip off s. o.; ~**pelbruder** *m* tramp; ~**peln** *itr* to tramp, to walk the roads; ~**pen** *tr* to type(write); (*leicht berühren*) to tap, to touch lightly; (*wetten*) to bet; to tip; *daran kannst du nicht ~~* that's over your reach; ~**pfehler** *m* error in typing; ~**pfräulein** *n* (girl) typist; ~**ptopp** *a fam* elegant.
Tirol *n* Tyrol; ~**er** *m*, ~**erin** *f* Tyrolese.
Tisch *m* table; (*Kost*) board; (*Mahlzeit*) meal, dinner, supper; *bei ~* during the meal, at dinner (*od* supper); *den ~ decken* to set (*od* to lay) the table, to lay the cloth; *den ~ abräumen* to clear the table; *zu ~ gehen* to go out to lunch (dinner *etc*); *sich zu ~ setzen* to sit down to eat; *Gäste zu ~ haben* to have guests for dinner; *unter den ~ fallen* to be ignored, not to come under consideration;to get lost in the shuffle; *reinen ~ machen* to make a clean sweep of it; *am grünen ~* by red tape; *zum ~ des Herrn gehen* to partake of the Lord's Supper; ~**apparat** *m* table set, table model; ~**bein** *n* leg of a table; ~**besen** *m* crumb-brush; ~**besteck** *n* cover; knife and fork; ~**blatt** *n*, ~**platte** *f* table-top, table-board; ~**chen** *n* small table; ~**dame** *f*, ~**herr** *m* neighbo(u)r at dinner; ~**decke** *f* table-cover; ~**gast** *m* guest; ~**gebet** *n* grace; *das ~~ sprechen* to say grace; ~**gesellschaft** *f* dinner-party; ~**gespräch** *n* table-talk; ~**geschirr** *n* utensils *pl* for the table, *Am* tableware; ~**glocke** *f* dinner-bell; ~**karte** *f* place card; ~**kasten** *m* table-drawer; ~**klammer** *f* table-clamp; ~**klemme** *f* table terminal; ~**klopfen** *n* table-rapping; ~**lampe** *f* desk lamp; ~**läufer** *m* table-centre; ~**ler** *m* joiner; (*Kunst~~*) cabinet-maker; (*Bau~~*) carpenter; ~~**arbeit** *f* joiner's work, joinery, carpentry; ~~**ei**, ~~**werkstatt** *f* joiner's workshop, carpenter's shop; ~~**handwerk** *n* joinery; ~~**leim** *m* joiner's glue; ~~**meister** *m* master joiner; ~~**n** *tr*, *itr* to carpenter, to do joiner's work; ~**nachbar** *m* neighbo(u)r

at table; ~**rede** *f* after-dinner speech; ~**rücken** *n* table-turning; ~**telephon** *n* table telephone set; ~**tennis** *n* table tennis, ping-pong; ~~**ball** *m* table tennis ball; ~~**schläger** *m* table tennis bat; ~**tuch** *n* table-cloth; ~**wein** *m* table wine; ~**zeit** *f* meal-time, dinner-time.

Titan *m* Titan; ~**isch** *a* titanic.

Titel *m* title; (*Anspruch*) claim; *e-n ~ innehaben* to hold a title; ~**anwärter** *m* title expectant; ~**bild** *n* frontispiece; (*auf Umschlag*) cover; ~**blatt** *n* title-page; ~**bogen** *m*, ~**ei** *f* title-sheet; ~**halter** *m* (*Sport*) title-holder; ~**kampf** *m sport* title bout; ~**kopf** *m* heading; ~**rolle** *f* title role, title part; ~**sucht** *f* mania for titles; ~**verteidiger** *m* title defender, title-holder.

titul|ar *a* titulary, nominal; ~**atur** *f* titles *pl*; ~**ieren** *tr* to give the title of, to style, to call.

Toast *m* health, toast; (*Brot*) toasted bread; *e-n ~ ausbringen* to propose a toast; ~**en** *itr* to drink toasts.

tob|en *itr* to roar, to rave; (*wüten*) to storm, to rage, to bluster; (*Kinder*) to romp, to be wild; ~**en** *n* (*Wut*) rage; (*Lärm*) noise; ~**end** *a* roaring, boisterous; ~**sucht** *f* insanity, madness, frenzy; ~**süchtig** *a* raving mad; frantic, seized with frenzy.

Tochter *f* daughter; ~**gesellschaft** *f* subsidiary company; ~**kirche** *f* filial church; ~**kind** *n* daughter's child; ~**mann** *m* son-in-law; ~**sprache** *f* derivative language; ~**unternehmen** *n* subsidiary enterprise.

Töchter|chen *n* little daughter; ~**schule** *f*: (*höhere* ~~) High-school for girls.

Tod *m* death; (*Abscheiden*) decease; *e-s leichten ~es sterben* to die an easy death; *e-s elenden ~es sterben* to die a dog's death; *des ~es sein* to be doomed; *zu ~e erschrocken sein* to be frightened to death; *sich zu ~e lachen* to die with laughter; *sich auf den ~ erkälten* to catch o.'s death of cold; *zu ~e betrübt sein* to be heart-broken; *zu ~e langweilen* to bore to death; *etw zu ~e hetzen* (*fig*) to do s. th. to death; *zum ~e verurteilen* to sentence to death; *Kampf auf Leben u. ~* life-and-death struggle; *ein Kind des ~es sein* to be a dead man; ~**bringend** *a* fatal, deadly; ~**ernst** *a* very serious; ~**esahnung** *f* presentiment of death; ~**esangst** *f* death-agony; mortal fear; ~**esanzeige** *f* death notice; obituary; ~**esart** *f* manner of death; ~**eserklärung** *f* official declaration of death; ~**esfall** *m* death; *mil* casualty; ~**esfurcht** *f* fear of death; ~**esgefahr** *f* peril of o.'s life, imminent danger; ~**esjahr** *n* year of s. o.'s death; ~**eskampf** *m* death-agony; ~**eskandidat** *m* doomed man, dying man; ~**esnachricht** *f* news of s. o.'s death; ~**esopfer** *n pl* death toll; ~**esqualen** *f pl* pangs *pl* of death; ~**esröcheln** *n* death-rattle; ~**esschauer** *m* horrors of death; ~**esschweiß** *m* cold sweat of death; ~**esstoß** *m* death-blow; ~**esstrafe** *f* capital punishment; ~**esstunde** *f* hour of death; ~**estag** *m* anniversary (*od* day) of s. o.'s death; ~**esurteil** *n* death sentence; ~**esverachtung** *f* contempt of death; ~**eswunde** *f* mortal wound; ~**eswürdig** *a* deserving death; ~**feind** *m* deadly enemy; ~~**schaft** *f* deadly hatred; ~**krank** *a* dangerously ill; ~**müde** *a* dead-beat, dead tired, knocked-up, done-up; ~**schick** *a fam* very stylish; dashing; swell; ~**sicher** *a* death certain, cock-sure; *ein ~·er Schütze* a dead shot; *e-e ~~e Sache sl* cinch; ~**sünde** *f* mortal sin; ~**wund** *a* mortally wounded.

tödlich *a* deadly, mortal; (*Waffe, Dosis*) lethal; (*Unfall*) fatal; *sich ~ langweilen*, to be bored to death; (*mörderisch*) murderous.

Toilette *f* (*Anzug*) dress, clothes *pl*, toilet(te), *fam* rig-out; (*Tisch*) dressing-table; washstand, *Am* dresser, bureau, vanity; (*Abort*) lavatory, W.C., *Am* toilet; *~ machen* to wash; to dress, to get dressed, to dress up; *in großer ~* in full dress; ~**nartikel** *m pl* utensils *pl* for the toilet, *Am* toiletry; ~**ngarnitur** *f* toilet-set; ~**ngeheimnisse** *n pl* mystery of the toilet; ~**nmilch** *f* skin milk; ~**npapier** *n* toilet-paper; ~**nseife** *f* toilet soap; ~**nspiegel** *m* dressing-glass; ~**ntisch** *m* dressing-table, *Am* dresser, bureau, vanity.

toler|ant *a* tolerant (of); ~**anz** *f* toleration; *tech* tolerance, allowable variation, permissible limits *pl*; ~**ieren** *tr* to tolerate.

toll *a* (*verrückt*) mad, insane; (*rasend*) frantic (with), raving (*über* about, at; *gegen* against); (*begeistert*) mad (after), crazy (about), wild (with); (*ausgelassen*) wild, exuberant, wanton; (*wütend*) furious; (*unsinnig*) nonsensical; (*übermäßig*) excessive; (*riesig*) awful; *es ist zu ~* it goes too far; *es ist zum ~ werden* it is enough to drive one mad; *das wird noch ~er kommen* the worst is yet to come; *~ u. voll* dead drunk; *er treibt es etwas zu ~* he's carrying on a little too much; *bist du ~?* are you out of your senses? ~**e** *f* tuft; topknot; ~**en** *itr* (*Kinder*) to romp, to fool (*od* to ass) about, to gambol about; ~**haus** *n* madhouse, lunatic asylum; ~**häusler** *m* madman; ~**heit** *f* madness, frenzy, fury; (*toller Streich*) mad trick, piece of folly; ~**kirsche** *f* deadly nightshade, belladonna; ~**kopf** *m* madcap; ~**kühn** *a* foolhardy, rash; ~~**heit** *f* rashness, foolhardiness, temerity; ~**wut** *f* (canine) hydrophobia, rabies.

Tolpatsch *m* blockhead, clumsy fellow, lout, boor.

Tölpel *m* dunce, booby, dolt, mooncalf, *Am* boob, *Am sl* hayseed, mut(t); ~**ei** *f* awkwardness; ~**haft** *a* awkward, clumsy, *Am* dumb; *sich ~~ benehmen* to gawk; ~~**igkeit** *f* clumsiness, awkwardness.

Tomate *f* tomato.

Tombola *f* tombola, lottery.

Ton *m* (*Erde*) potter's earth, clay; (*feuerfester ~*) fire-clay; (*Laut*) sound; *mus* tone, note; (*Tonart*) key; (*Stimme*) tone; (*Melodie*) tune, melody; (*bei Zeitsignal*) *radio* pip; (*~folge*) strain; (*Klangfarbe*) timbre; (*Betonung*) stress, accent; (*Tönung*) tint, shade, colo(u)r; (*Mode*) fashion, tone; (*Art*) style, manner; (*guter ~*) good fashion; *hoher* (*reiner, tiefer, unreiner*) *~* high-pitched (pure, low-pitched, ragged) note; *keinen ~ von sich geben* not to utter a sound; *der ~ macht die Musik* it's the tone that makes the music; *Stummfilm mit ~ versehen* to dub; *ich verbitte mir diesen ~* I won't have you talk to me in that tone of voice; *zum guten ~ gehören* to be the fashion; *keinen ~ mehr* I will hear no more of it; *den ~ legen auf* to put the stress on; *den ~ angeben* to pitch the key, to give the note; *fig* to set the fashion; *in spöttischem ~* jeeringly; *große Töne reden* to talk big; *den ~ steuern radio* to modulate, to mix sounds; ~**abnehmer** *m* pick-up; ~**abstand** *m* interval; ~**abstimmung** *f* tone tuning; *tele* tuning note; ~**abstufung** *f* grading of tones; ~**abtaststelle** *f* sound gate; ~**angebend** *a* setting the fashion, leading; (*einflußreich*) influential; ~**angeber** *m* leader of fashion, *Am* topnotcher; ~**arm** *m* (*Grammophon*) tone arm; ~**art** *f* key, tune, mode; (*Erde*) kind of clay; *e-e andere ~~ anschlagen* to change o.'s tone of voice; ~**artig** *a* clayey, argillaceous; ~**atelier** *n* studio, sound stage, teletorium; ~**aufnahme** *f* recording; transcription; ~~**gerät** *n* (wire; tape) recorder, sound recording equipment; ~**bad** *n phot* toning bath; ~**band** *n* tape; *auf ~~ aufnehmen* to record on tape; ~~**aufnahme** *f* tape recording; ~**bereich** *m* range of tune; ~**beständigkeit** *f* syntony; ~**bezeichnung** *f* accentuation; ~**bild** *n* tonal pattern; ~~**rundfunk** *m* television-telephone broadcasting, sound-sight broadcasting; ~~**wand** *f film* transoral screen; ~**blende** *f* bass-treble control, tone control; (*Entzerrung*) variable correction unit; *radio* fader; ~**boden** *m* clay soil (*od* ground); ~**brei** *m* clay slip; ~**darbietung** *f* sound entertainment; ~**decke** *f* clay cover; ~**dichtung** *f* musical composition; ~**en** *tr phot* to tone; ~**erde** *f* alumina; argillaceous earth; *essigsaure ~~* alumina acetate; ~**fall** *m* intonation, speech-melody; *mus* inflexion; (*Stimme*) cadence; ~**farbe** *f* timbre, tone quality; ~**fenster** *n* sound gate; ~**figuren** *f pl* clay figures *pl*; ~**film** *m* sound film, sound motion picture; *fam* talkie, sound movie, talking film; ~~**atelier** *n* studio for sound film; ~~**kino** *n* talking picture theatre; ~~**schallaufzeichnungsgerät** *n film* sound recorder; ~~**vorführgerät** *n* sound projector; ~**filter** *n* clay filter; ~**fixierbad** *n phot* toning and fixing bath; ~**folge** *f* scale, strains *pl*, succession of tones; melody; ~**frequenz** *f* acoustic (*od* audio) frequency, voice frequency; ~**führung** *f* modulation; (*Lautsprecher*) labyrinth; ~**fülle** *f* volume of sound; sonority; ~**gefäß** *n* clay (*od* earthenware) vessel; ~**gemälde** *n* symphony; ~**geschirr**, ~**gut** *n* pottery, earthenware; ~**grube** *f* clay-pit; ~**halle** *f* concert-hall; ~**haltig** *a* argillaceous; ~**höhe** *f* pitch; *tele* tuning note; ~**industrie** *f* clay industry; ~**isch** *a* tonic; ~**kalk** *m* argillaceous limestone; ~**kamera** *f* sound (recording) camera; ~**krug** *m* earthenware jar; ~**kulisse** *f radio* sound effect, background; ~**kunst** *f* music, musical art; ~**künstler** *m* musician; ~**lage** *f* pitch, compass; ~**lager** *n* clay bed, stratum of clay; ~**leiter** *f* scale, gamut; ~**los** *a* soundless; silent; voiceless; (*unbetont*) unaccented; ~**malerei** *f* onomatopoeia; ~**masse** *f* (*Keramik*) paste; ~**meister** *m radio* sound engineer; ~**mergel** *m* clay marl; loam; ~**messer** *m* volume indicator; sonometer; ~**mischer** *m* tone fader, tone mixer; (*Erdmischer*) clay maker; ~**modulation** *f* sound modulation; ~**ofen** *m* clay-kiln; ~**papier** *n* tinted paper; ~**pfeife** *f* clay pipe; ~**reinheit** *f* purity of sound (*od* tone); ~**röhre** *f* earthenware pipe; clay tube; ~**rundfunk** *m* audio and video film broadcasting; ~**satz** *m mus* phrase; ~**schicht** *f* layer (*od* stratum) of clay; ~**schiefer** *m* clay slate, argillite; ~**schirm** *m* sound screen; ~**schlamm** *m* clay slip; ~**schneider** *m* pug mill; clay cutter; ~**schwingung** *f* sound vibration; ~**schwund** *m radio* fading;

~senkung *f radio* drop in level; **~setzer** *m* composer; **~sieb** *n* acoustic network, audio filter; **~silbe** *f* accented (*od* stressed) syllable; **~spur** *f* (*Grammophon, Film*) sound track; **~stärke** *f* intensity of sound; **~~messer** *m* sound level meter; **~stein** *m* clay stone; **~streifen** *m film* sound track; **~stufe** *f mus* pitch; degree; **~system** *n* musical system; **~taube** *f* clay pigeon; **~techniker** *m* sound man, *Am* arranger; **~träger** *m* sound carrier; **~~welle** *f* sound carrier wave; **~trickfilm** *m* sound animated cartoon; **~treue** *f radio* definition; **~überlagerung** *f radio* modulation at audible frequency; **~umfang** *m* compass, range, volume; band width; **~veränderung** *f* change of tone; modulation; **~veredler** *m* tone corrector (*od* clarifier); **~verstärker** *m* sound amplifier, note magnifier; **~verstärkung** *f* sound amplification, note magnification; **~vorführgerät** *n film* sound equipment; **~wagen** *m* sound truck, location truck; **~wahrnehmung** *f* acoustical perception; **~waren** *f pl* pottery, earthenware; **~welle** *f* sound wave; **~wiedergabe** *f radio* tonal output; tone (*od* sound) reproduction; **~~gerät** *n* sound-reproducing equipment; **~zeichen** *n* accent; note; **~zeug** *n* vitreous clayware, stoneware; **~ziegel** *m* clay tile.

tön|en *itr* (*erklingen*) to sound, to resound; (*läuten*) to ring; *tr* (*schattieren*) to shade (off); (*färben*) to tint, to tone; **~ung** *f* shading; (*Färbung*) tinge; **~~sskala** *f tele* tone control aperture.

tönern *a* earthen, of clay.

Tonika *f* tonic.

Tönnchen *n* small cask, keg.

Tonne *f* tun, cask, keg; (*Bier~*) barrel; (*Seezeichen*) buoy; (*Gewicht, mar*) ton; *1000 kg* = metric ton; *2240 engl. Pfund* (*gebräuchl. in Engl.*) = long ton; *2000 engl. Pfund* (*gebr. in Amerika*) = short ton; (*Wasserverdrängung*) displacement ton; (*Raumgehalt*) measurement (freight) ton; **~ngehalt** *m* tonnage; **~ngewölbe** *n* barrel-vault (*od* -arch); **~nweise** *adv* by tuns.

Tonsur *f* tonsure.

Topas *m* topaz.

Topf *m* pot; container; can; (*Krug*) jar, crock; **~gucker** *m* inquisitive person, nosy parker; **~lappen** *m* oven-cloth, kettle-holder; **~pflanze** *f* pot-plant; potted plant; **~scherbe** *f* piece of a broken pot, potsherd.

Töpfer *m* potter; (*Ofensetzer*) stove-fitter; **~arbeit** *f* pottery, ceramics *pl*; **~ei** *f* (*Geschäft*) potter's workshop, potter's trade; (*Arbeit*) pottery; **~erde** *f* potter's earth (*od* clay); **~ofen** *m* potter's kiln; **~scheibe** *f* potter's wheel; **~ware** *f* pottery, crockery, earthenware.

top|isch *a* topical; **~ographie** *f* topography; **~ographisch** *a* topographical.

topp! *interj* done! agreed! *sl* right oh!

Topp *m* top, head; **~laterne** *f*, **~licht** *n* masthead light; **~mast** *m* topmast; **~reep** *n* guy; **~segel** *n* topsail.

Tor[1] *n* gate; door; *sport* goal, score; (*~weg*) gateway; (*Pforte*) portal; (*rückwärtiges ~*) postern; *ein ~ erzielen* to score a goal; **~(ein)fahrt** *f* gateway; **~flügel** *m* wing of a gate; **~hüter** *m* gatekeeper, porter; *sport* goal-keeper; **~latte** *f sport* cross-bar; **~lauf** *m* ski-slalom; **~linie** *f sport* goal-line; **~netz** *n* goal net; **~pfosten** *m* door-post; *sport* goal-post; **~raum** *m* goal space; **~schluß** *m* closing of the gate(s); closing-up time; *kurz vor ~~* at the eleventh hour; **~schuß, ~stoß** *m* goal-kick; **~schütze** *m* scorer; **~turm** *m* gate-tower; **~wart** *m sport* goal-keeper; **~weg** *m* gateway, archway.

Tor[2] *m* fool; **~heit** *f* folly, foolishness.

Torf *m* peat; turf; *~ stechen* to dig peat; **~boden** *m* peat-soil; **~eisenerz** *n* bog iron ore; **~erde** *f* peat soil; **~kohle** *f* peat charcoal; **~lager, ~moor** *n* peat-bog; **~moos** *n* peat moss; **~mull** *m* peat-dust (*od* -litter); **~stecher** *m* peat-cutter; **~stich** *m* peat-cutting; **~streu** *f* peat-litter.

tör|icht *a* foolish, silly; **~in** *f* foolish girl, foolish woman.

torkeln *itr* to stagger, to reel; to tumble; to wobble; to shamble.

Tornado *m* tornado, whirlwind, *Am* twister.

Tornister *m* knapsack; *mil* (field) pack, kit bag; **~empfänger** *m radio* portable receiver, pack receiver radio, kit bag receiver; **~funkgerät** *n* knapsack transmitter; **~gerät** *n* portable set; **~sprechfunkgerät** *n Am* walkie-talkie.

torped|ieren *tr* to torpedo; **~o** *m* torpedo, *sl* tin fish; *~~ mit Zielsucher* homing torpedo, *sl* Chase-me-Charlie; **~~abwehrnetz** *n* crinoline; **~~bomber** *m* torpedo bomber; **~~boot** *n* torpedo-boat; (*Zerstörer*) torpedo-boat destroyer, torpedo-catcher; **~~flugzeug** *n* torpedo plane (*od* bomber); **~~rohr** *n* torpedo tube; **~~überwasserausstoßrohr** *n* torpedo tube on deck; **~~wulst** *m* torpedo bulge.

Torsion *f* torsion, twist; **~saufhängung** *f* torsion suspension; **~sbeanspruchung** *f* torsional stress; **~sfeder** *f* torsion spring; **~swaage** *f* torsion balance; **~swiderstand** *m* twisting resistance.

Torso *m* torso.

Tort *m* wrong, injury.

Törtchen *n* tartlet.

Torte *f* fancy cake; (*Frucht~*) tart, *Am* pie, layer cake; **~nbäcker** *m* pastry-cook; **~nheber, ~nschaufel** *f* cake server; **~nplatte** *f* cake plate; (*Papier*) paper doily; **~nschachtel** *f* cake-box; **~nteig** *m* paste for a tart.

Tortur *f* torture.

tosen *itr* to roar, to rage.

tot *a* dead; (*verstorben*) deceased, late; (*leblos*) lifeless, inanimate, inert; (*empfindungslos*) insensible, benumbed, hardened (against); (*glanzlos*) lustreless, dull; (*erloschen*) extinct, past, obsolete; (*abgestanden*) stagnant; (*unproduktiv*) idle; *~e Hand* mortmain; *~es Kapital* unemployed capital; *~er Punkt tech* dead centre, *fig* deadlock; *~es Geleise* dead-end siding; *~er Winkel* dead ground, shielded angle; *mil* blind spot; *~es Rennen* dead heat; *~e Zeit* dead season; *~es Feld* dead zone; *~e Zone* blind spot; skip distance; *~er Gang* lost motion; backlash, play; *das ~e Meer* the Dead Sea; *plötzlich ~ umfallen* to drop dead, to die in o.'s boots, *Am* to die in o.'s tracks; *~schlagen* to kill; **~arbeiten** *r* to kill o. s. with work; **~e(r)** *m*, **~e** *f* the deceased, dead person; *mil* casualty; **~enacker** *m* graveyard, churchyard; **~enbahre** *f* bier; **~beschwörer** *m* necromancer; **~enbett** *n* death-bed; **~enblaß, ~enbleich** *a* pale as death; **~enblässe** *f* deadly pallor; **~enfarbe** *f* livid colo(u)r; pallor of death; **~enfeier** *f* obsequies *pl*; **~enfrau** *f* layer-out; **~engeläut(e)** *n* knell; **~engeleit** *n* funeral procession; **~engerippe** *n* skeleton; **~engesang** *m* funeral chant; **~englocke** *f* funeral bell, passing bell; **~engottesdienst** *m* funeral service, requiem; **~engräber** *m* grave-digger; *zoo* burying-beetle; **~engruft** *f* vault; **~enhalle** *f* mortuary; **~enhaus** *n* dead-house; **~enhemd** *n* shroud, winding-sheet; **~enklage** *f* lamentation for the dead; **~enkopf, ~enschädel** *m* death's head; skull; (*Symbol*) skull and cross-bones; **~enkranz** *m* funeral wreath; **~enliste** *f* death-roll; list of casualties; **~enmal** *n* funeral monument; **~enmarsch** *m* funeral march; **~enmaske** *f* death-mask; **~enmesse** *f* mass for the dead; **~enopfer** *n* sacrifice to the dead; **~enreich** *n* realm of the dead; **~enschau** *f* coroner's inquest; post mortem examination; **~enschein** *m* death certificate; **~ensonntag** *m* memorial Sunday for the dead; **~enstadt** *f* necropolis; **~enstarre** *f* rigor mortis; **~enstill** *a* still as death; **~enstille** *f* death silence; **~entanz** *m* the dance of death; **~enuhr** *f zoo* death-watch; **~enurne** *f* funerary urn; **~enverbrennung** *f* cremation, incineration; **~envogel** *m* bird of death; **~enwache** *f* death-watch; wake; **~enwagen** *m* hearse; **~fahren** *irr tr* to kill by running over; **~geboren** *a* still-born; **~geburt** *f* death-birth, still-birth; **~lachen** *r* to split o.'s sides with laughter, to die laughing, *Am* to be tickled to death; **~lage** *f* dead centre; *aero* blind spot; **~last** *f* dead load; **~lauf** *m* dead travel; **~laufen** *irr r* to come to nought; to fail; **~punkt** *m* dead centre; **~schießen** *irr tr* to shoot dead, *Am* to shoot to death; **~schlag** *m* homicide, manslaughter; **~~en** *irr tr* to kill, to slay; (*Zeit*) to waste, to kill; (*Fliege*) to slap, *fam* to swat; **~schläger** *m* murderer; killer; (*Knüppel*) life-preserver, cosh, *sl* knuckle-duster, *Am* blackjack; **~schweigen** *irr tr* to hush up; **~stechen** *irr tr* to stab to death; **~stellen** *r* to feign death.

total *a* total, complete, altogether; *~er Krieg* total war(fare); **~ansicht** *f* general view; **~ausverkauf** *m* clearance sale; **~ertrag** *m* total proceeds *pl*; **~isator** *m* totalizer, totalizator; **~itär** *a* totalitarian; **~ität** *f* totality; **~~sanspruch** *m* totalitarianism; **~verlust** *m* clear (*od* total) loss.

töt|en *tr* to kill, to put to death, to slay; (*liquidieren*) to liquidate; (*Nerv*) to deaden; (*ab~*) to mortify (the flesh); *r* to (commit) suicide; **~ung** *f* killing, slaying.

Toto *m* (*Fußball~*) football pool; **~spieler** *m* pool player.

Tour *f* tour, excursion, trip, journey; (*Tanz*) figure, set; (*Umdrehung*) revolution, round; turn; *in e-r ~ reden* to talk a blue streak; *auf ~ gehen* to go on the road; *auf ~en kommen mot* to pick up; *die nächste ~* the next set; *in e-r ~* at a stretch; **~enrad** *n* roadster; **~enwagen** *m* touring-car; tourer; **~enzahl** *f* number of turns (*od* revolutions); **~enzähler** *m* revolution (*od* speed) indicator, tachometer; **~ist** *m* tourist; *Am fam* dude; **~~farm** *f Am fam* dude ranch; **~~enklasse** *f* (*Dampfer*) tourist class; **~~enverkehr** *m* tourist traffic; **~nee** *n theat* tour.

Trab *m* trot; *im ~* at a trot; *jdn auf den ~ bringen* to make s. o. speed up; **~en** *itr* to trot; **~er** *m* trotter; **~rennbahn** *f* trotting course; **~rennen** *n* trotting-race.

Trabant *m astr* satellite.

Tracht *f* (*Last*) carriage, load; (*~ Junge*) litter; (*Kleidung*) (national) costume; dress, fashion; *~ Prügel* a sound thrashing; **~en** *itr* to make efforts, to try; *nach etw* ~~ to aspire to, to seek after; to strive for, to endeavour to; *jdm nach dem Leben* ~~ to make an attempt on s. o. 's life; ~**en** *n* endeavo(u)r, aim, aspiration; ~~**fest** *n* show of national costumes.

trächtig *a* pregnant, with young; ~ *sein* to go with young; ~**keit** *f* pregnancy, gestation.

Tradition *f* tradition.

Trag|bahre *f* stretcher, litter; (hand-) barrow; ~**balken** *m* beam, transom; (*Decke*) joist; ~**band** *n tech* strap; *arch* brace; (*Schlinge*) sling; (*Hosenträger*) braces *pl*, *Am* suspenders *pl*; (*Suspensorium*) suspensory (bandage); ~**bar** *a* portable; (*erträglich*) bearable, supportable; (*vernünftig*) reasonable; (*Kleid*) wearable, fit to wear; (*Farbe*) fast to wearing; (*ertragreich*) productive, bearing; (*annehmbar*) possible, acceptable; ~**deck** *n aero* wing; ~**e** *f* litter; stretcher; (hand-)barrow; ~**en** *irr tr* to carry; (*Namen, Kosten, Schulden, Früchte*) to bear; (*hervorbringen*) to bear, to yield, to produce; (*Kleider*) to wear, to have on; (*Brille*) to wear; (*Paket, Stock, Stimme*) to carry; (*bringen*) to take; (*befördern*) to transport, to convey; (*erdulden*) to endure, to suffer; to support, to brook, *fam* to stomach; (*Junge bekommen*) to be with young; *itr* (*Entfernung*) to carry, to reach, to range; (*Eis*) to bear; *r* to dress; to wear; *den Kopf hoch* ~~ to carry o.'s head high; *e-e Last* ~~ to bear a burden; *die Kosten* ~~ to bear the expenses; *die Verantwortung* ~~ to bear the responsibility; *das Risiko* ~~ to run the risk; *Zinsen* ~~ to yield (*od* to bear) interest; *e-e Brille* ~~ to wear glasses; *den Verlust* ~~ to stand the loss; *die Folgen* ~~ to take the consequences; *Trauer* ~~ to be in mourning; *die Schuld tragen* to be to blame (*an* for); *zur Schau* ~~ to show off; *Bedenken* ~~ to doubt, to hesitate; *Sorge* ~~ to take care (of); *zu Grabe* ~~ to bury; *bei sich* ~~ to have about one; *sich mit dem Gedanken* ~~ to be thinking (of), to be intending (to); ~**fähig** *a* capable of carrying (*od* bearing); ~~**keit**, ~**kraft** *f* load capacity; bearing strength; (*Schwimmkraft*) buoyancy; *mar* tonnage; (*Kleider*) wearability; (*Boden*) productiveness; (*Brücke*) load limit; ~**fläche** *f*, ~**flügel** *m aero* wing; lifting surface; airfoil; ~**flächenbelastung** *f aero* wing load; ~**flächeninhalt** *m aero* wing area; ~**gestell** *n* support, rack, supporting structure; ~**himmel** *m* canopy; ~**korb** *m* pannier; hamper; (*Kiepe*) back-basket; ~**lager** *n tech* journal bearing; ~**last** *f* load; (*Gepäck*) hand-luggage; ~**leine** *f aero* shroud line; ~**pfeiler** *m* pillar; ~**riemen** *m* carrying strap; *mil* sling; ~**sattel** *m* packsaddle; ~**schraube** *f aero* lifter propeller; ~~**r** *m* gyroplane, hoverplane, autogiro; ~**seil** *n tele* suspending wire; ~**sessel**, ~**stuhl** *m* sedan-chair; ~**tier** *n* pack-animal; ~~**kolonne** *f Am* pack train; ~**vorrichtung** *f* supporting structure; *aero* stowing device; ~**weite** *f* (*Entfernung*) range; *arch* bearing; (*Bedeutung*) significance; importance; moment, purport, bearing; ~**werk** *n aero* wing-unit, supporting surface; ~**zeit** *f* (*Tiere*) time of gestation.

träg|e *a* lazy, idle; (*untätig*) inert; (*bequem*) indolent; (*langsam*) dull, sluggish, slow; *com* dull, sluggish; ~**er** *m* carrier; (*Kleider*) wearer; (*Inhaber*) bearer, holder; (*Gepäck*~~) porter; (*Balken*) beam; (*Eisen*~~) girder; (*Stütze*) support, prop; (*Pfeiler*) pillar, post; *arch* bracket; *anat* atlas; (*Preis*~~) prizeman; *aero* (*Flugzeug*~~) carrier; *Am* flattop; *Schlacht*~~ battle carrier; *leichter* ~~ light carrier; *Geleit*~~ escort carrier; (*Kranken*~~) stretcher-bearer; body snatcher; ~~**flugzeug** *n* carrier (based) aircraft, shipboard plane; ~~**frequenz** *f el* carrier frequency; ~~**gruppe** *f aero* carrier--born group; ~~**jagdstaffel** *f aero* carrier-born fighter flight; ~~**lager** *n* set of supporting girders; ~~**lohn** *m* porterage; ~~**los** *a* strapless; ~~**schürze** *f* apron with shoulder straps; ~~**welle** *f* carrier wave; ~**heit** *f* laziness, idleness, indolence; (*Langsamkeit*) slowness; *phys, chem* inertia, inertness; *chem* inactivity; (*zeitlich*) time lag; ~~**sgesetz** *n* law of inertia; ~~**smoment** *n* momentum of inertia.

Trag|ik *f* tragic art; (*Unglück*) calamity; ~**iker** *m* (*Dichter*) tragic poet, tragedian; (*Schauspieler*) tragic actor; ~**ikomisch** *a* tragicomic; ~**ikomödie** *f* tragicomedy; ~**isch** *a* tragic(al); *es* ~~ *nehmen* to take it to heart; (*traurig*) sad; (*unglaublich*) calamitous; ~**öde** *m* tragic actor; ~**ödie** *f* tragedy, tragic drama; (*Unglück*) calamity, sad event; ~**ödin** *f* tragic actress.

Train|er *m sport* trainer, coach; instructor; ~**ieren** *tr, itr* to train, to coach (*zu* for); to work out; *e-e Mannschaft* ~~ to train a team; ~**ing** *n* training; *Am* work-out; (~~ *beim Boxen*) sparring; ~~**sanzug** *m* training suit; *mil* smock; fatigue suit; ~~**sflugzeug** *n* trainer airplane; ~~**shosen** *f pl* training trousers *pl*; ~~**schüler** *m Am* coachee; ~~**slager** *n* training camp.

Trajekt *m, n* passage; moving ferry; ferry bridge; ~**schiff** *n* train-ferry; ferryboat, railway ferry.

Trakt|at *m* treatise; *eccl* tract; treaty; ~**ieren** *tr* to treat; ~**or** *m* tractor; (*Landwirtschaft*) agrimotor; ~~**anhängevorrichtung** *f* tractor hitch; ~~**pflug** *m* tractor plough (*Am* plow).

trällern *itr, tr* to hum, to trill, to warble.

Tram(bahn) *f* tramway, tram, *Am* trolley line; (*Wagen*) tram (-car), *Am* streetcar, trolley (car); (*in New York*) surface car.

trampel|n *itr* to trample, to stamp; ~**pfad**, ~**weg** *m* beaten path (*od* track); (*im Schnee*) path stamped in snow; ~**tier** *n* dromedary; *fig* clumsy person.

Tran *m* train-oil, whale-oil, blubber; ~**ig** *a* oily; greasy; *fig fam* slow, dull; ~**lampe** *f* trainoil lamp; *fig* dullard, mope.

Trance|schlaf *m* trance, hypnotic sleep; ~**zustand** *m* trance, cataleptic (*od* hypnotic) condition.

Tranchier|besteck *n* carvers *pl*, carving-knife and fork; ~**en** to carve, to cut up; ~**messer** *n* carving-knife.

Träne *f* tear; *in* ~**n** *ausbrechen* to burst into tears; *in* ~*n zerfließen* to melt into tears; *zu* ~*n rühren* to move s. o. to tears; ~*n vergießen* to shed tears; *unter* ~*n lächeln* to smile through o.'s tears; ~**n** *itr* to water; to be full of tears; ~~**absonderung** *f* lachrimal secretion; ~~**benetzt** *a* bedewed with tears; ~~**drüse** *f* lachrymal gland; ~~**erregend** *a* tear-exciting; ~~**erstickt** *a* choked with tears; ~~**fistel** *f* lachrymal fistula; ~~**gas** *n* tear gas; tear smoke; ~~**kanal** *m* lachrymal duct; ~~**reich** *a* lachrymose; ~~**reiz** *m* eye irritation; ~~**reizend** *a* lachrymatory; ~~**sack** *m* lachrymal sac; ~~**strom** *m* flood (*od* flow) of tears; ~~**überströmt** *a* tear-stained, tearful.

Trank *m* drink, beverage; (*kräftiger, giftiger* ~) drench; (*Trunk, Schluck*) potation, draught; *med* potion; ~**opfer** *n* libation, drink-offering.

Tränke *f* watering-place; ~**n** *tr* to water; (*durchtränken*) to soak, to impregnate, to steep, to saturate.

Trans|aktion *f* transaction; ~**atlantikflug** *m* transatlantic flight (*od fam* hop); ~~**boot** *n Am* clipper; ~~**verkehr** *m aero* transatlantic aviation; ~~**zeug** *n* transatlantic plane, *Am* stratocruiser; ~**atlantikkabel** *n* transatlantic cable; ~**atlantikverkehr** *m* transatlantic traffic; ~**atlantisch** *a* transatlantic; ~**fer** *m* transfer; ~~**ieren** *tr* to transfer; ~~**ierung** *f* transfer; ~**figuration** *f* transfiguration; ~**formation** *f* transformation; ~**formator** *m* transformer; ~**formieren** *tr* to transform; (*herunter*) to step down; (*hinauf*) to step up.

Transit *m* transit; ~**güter** *n pl* transit goods *pl*; ~**hafen** *m* port of transit; ~**handel** *m* transit-trade; ~**iv** *a* transitive; ~**lager** *n* bonded warehouse; ~**orisch** *a* transitory; ~**verkehr** *m* transit trade, through-traffic; ~**zoll** *m* transit-duty.

Trans|mission *f* transmission, belt--gearing; ~~**sanlage** *f* power transmission plant; ~~**swelle** *f* connecting--shaft; ~**ozeanisch** *a* transoceanic; ~**parent** *a* transparent; diaphanous; ~~ *n* transparency, *Am* translight; ~**piration** *f* transpiration, perspiration; ~**pirieren** *itr* to perspire; ~**plantation** *f* transplantation; ~**ponieren** *tr* to transpose; ~**port** *m* transport, transportation, carriage; forwarding; conveyance; transfer; (*Versand*) shipment, dispatch; (*Straße*) haulage; ~~**abel** *a* transportable; ~~**agentur** *f* carriers *pl*, transportation agency; ~~**anweisung** *f* shipping instructions *pl*; ~~**arbeiter** *m* transport worker; ~~**arbeiterverband** *m* transport workers union; ~~**auftrag** *m* shipping order; ~~**band** *n* conveyer; ~~**betrieb** *m* carrying trade; ~~**er** *m mar* transport ship; *aero* transport plane; cargo carrier; ~~**eur** *m* transporter, carrier; *math* protractor; ~~**fähig** *a* transportable; ~~**fähigkeit** *f* transportability; ~~**firma** *f*, ~~**geschäft** *n* carrier; carrier's business; ~~**flugzeug** *n* transport (*od* freight) aircraft, freighter, *Am* cargo (air)plane, C plane, carrier (*od* transport) plane, transport, *Am sl* sky truck; *mil* troop-carrier plane; ~~**führer** *m rail* train conducting officer; ~~**gefährdung** *f* impairing of transport; ~~**gesellschaft** *f* haulage (*od* transport) company, carriers *pl*; ~~**gewicht** *n* shipping weight; ~~**gleiter** *aero* motorless troop-carrier; ~~**ieren** *tr* to transport, to ship to convey; to haul; (*Fuhrwerk*) to cart, to carry; (*Schiff*) to ship, to carry; ~~**kolonne** *f* transport-column; ~~**kosten** *pl* transport(ation) charges *pl*; carriage, haulage; *rail* freight; (*Fuhrlohn*) cartage; ~~**mittel** *n* means *pl* of conveyance, transportation; ~~**möglichkeiten** *f pl* transport facilities *pl*; ~~**offizier** *m mil* transportation officer (*Abk* TO); ~~**problem** *n* conveying problem; ~~**raum** *m* shipping space; ~~**schadensforderung** *f* loss and damage claim; ~~**schiff** *n* transport; *mil* troop-transport; ~~**schwierigkeiten** *f pl* transport difficulties *pl*; ~~**spesen** *pl* shipping charges *pl*; ~~**stockung** *f* transport hold-up; ~~**unternehmung** *f* carriers *pl*, transport(ation) agency; ~~**versicherung** *f* transportation insurance; *mar* marine insurance;

~~wesen *n* transport services *pl*; transportation system; **~~zug** *m* transport-train; **~versale** *f* transversal line; **~zendent(al)** *a* transcendental.

Trapez *n math* trapezium: trapezoid; (*Turngerät*) trapeze; **~flügel** *m aero* tapered wing; **~künstler** *m* trapeze artist; aerialist, aerial acrobat; **~rahmen** *m* frame of trapezoidal shape.

Trappe *m u. f* bustard; (*Spur*) footstep; **~ln** *itr* (*Pferd*) to tramp, to trot; **~n** *itr* (*Kind*) to patter, to toddle.

Trara *n* sound of a trumpet; *fig* fuss; display, parade; humbug.

Trass|ant *m* drawer; **~at** *m* drawee; **~e** *f* line; **~ieren** *tr* to draw on; (*Strecke*) to trace, to mark out, to lay-out.

Tratsch *m am* twaddle; gossip, tittle-tattle; **~en** *itr* to twaddle, to prate, to prattle, to gabble.

Tratte *f* draft, bill of exchange.

*

Trau|altar *m* marriage-altar; **~en** *tr* to marry, to give in marriage, to unite in wedlock; *itr* (*vertrauen*) to trust (in), to rely upon, to give credit (to), to have confidence (*auf* in), to confide (in), (*glauben*) to believe (*an* in); *r* (*wagen*) to dare, to venture; *sich ~~ lassen* to get married; *kirchlich getraut werden* to be married in church; *ich ~te meinen Ohren nicht* I couldn't believe my ears; *~, schau, wem!* look twice before you leap! *jdm nicht über den Weg ~~* not to trust s. o. farther than one can see him; **~lich** *a* familiar; intimate; cosy, snug; **~register** *n* marriage register; **~ring** *m* wedding-ring; **~schein** *m* marriage lines *pl*, certificate of marriage; **~ung** *f* wedding, marriage ceremony; **~zeuge** *m* witness to a marriage.

Traube *f* bunch of grapes; grape; (*Büschel, Haufen, Gruppe*) cluster; bunch; (*Wein~*) **~nbeere** *f* grape; **~nförmig** *a* grapelike, botryoidal; *bot* aciniform, racemose; **~ngitter** *n* vine-trellis; **~nhaut** *f anat* uvea; **~nkelter** *f* wine-press; **~nkern** *m* grape seed, grapestone; **~nkrankheit** *f* vine-disease; **~nkur** *f* grape-cure; **~nlese** *f* vintage; **~nmost** *m* grape must; **~nsaft** *m* grape juice; **~nsauer** *a* racemate (of); **~nsäure** *f* racemic acid; **~nstock** *m* vine; **~nzucker** *m* grape sugar, dextrose; glucose.

Trauer *f* (*Gram*) sorrow, affliction, grief, pain; (*um e-n Toten*) mourning, mourning-dress; *~ anlegen* to put on mourning, *fam* to go into black (*od* into mourning); *~ tragen* to wear mourning; *~ haben* to be in mourning; **~anzeige** *f* announcement of a death; **~binde** *f* mourning-band, crape; **~botschaft** *f* mournful news *pl mit sing*; **~esche** *f* weeping ash; **~fahne** *f* black flag; **~farbe** *f* mourning colo(u)r; black; **~fall** *m* death, mournful event; **~flor** *m* mourning-crape; **~geläute** *n* knell; **~geleit** *n* funeral procession; **~gerüst** *n* catafalque; **~gottesdienst** *m* funeral service, *Am* funeral; **~haus** *n* house of mourning; **~jahr** *n* year of mourning; **~kleid** *n* mourning-suit; mourning-dress, weeds *pl*; **~kloß** *m fam* stick-in-the-mud; duffer, silly fellow; **~mantel** *m* (*Schmetterling*) Camberwell Beauty; **~marsch** *m* funeral march; **~musik** funeral music; **~n** *itr* to mourn (*um* for), to grieve (for); to wear mourning; **~nachricht** *f* mournful news *pl mit sing*; **~rand** *m* black edge; **~rede** *f* funeral oration; **~schleier** *m* mourning-veil; **~spiel** *n* tragedy; **~weide** *f bot* weeping willow; **~zeit** *f* time of mourning; **~zug** *m* funeral procession.

Trauf|dach *n* weather-moulding; **~e** *f* eaves *pl*, gutter; *aus dem Regen in die ~e kommen* to come from bad to worse (*od* out of the frying pan into the fire); **~en, träufeln** *tr* to drop; *itr* to drip, to trickle; to shower down; **~faß** *n* water-tub; **~rinne** *f* gutter; **~röhre** gutter-pipe.

Traum *m* dream; (*Täuschung*) illusion, fancy; (*~gesicht*) vision; (*Wach~*) reverie; *mein ~ ging in Erfüllung* my dream came true; *nicht im ~ daran denken etw zu tun* not to dream of doing s. th.; *Träume sind Schäume* dreams are empty; **~bild, ~gesicht** *n* vision, phantom; **~deuter** *m* interpreter of dreams; **~gestalt** *f* phantom, phantasm, fantasy; **~haft** *a* dreamlike; **~verloren, ~versunken** *a* lost in dreams; **~welt** *f* dreamland, world of fancy; **~zustand** *m* trance.

träum|en *itr, tr* to dream (of); (*wach ~~*) to daydream; (*tief nachdenken*) to think deeply, to muse; (*sich einbilden*) to imagine; (*meinen*) to believe; *das hätte ich mir nicht ~~ lassen* I would never have dreamed that; **~er** *m* dreamer, visionary; **~erei** *f* dreaming, idle fancy; brown study, reverie; **~erisch** *a* dreamy, fanciful, visionary; (*sinnend*) musing; (*geistesabwesend*) absent-minded, preoccupied.

traun! *interj* surely! certainly! forsooth!

traurig *a* sad; (*beklagenswert*) deplorable; (*elend*) wretched, dismal; (*betrübt*) afflicted; (*sorgenvoll*) sorrowful; (*trübe*) dull; (*düster*) mournful; (*niedergeschlagen*) depressed in spirits, *Am* blue; *in ~en Verhältnissen* in reduced circumstances; *ein ~er Anblick* a deplorable sight; *das ~e daran ist* ... the sad part of it is ...; **~keit** *f* sadness, melancholy; depression; (*Elend*) wretchedness; (*Sorge*) sorrow.

traut *a* beloved, dear; (*angenehm*) comfortable, cosy, snug; **~e** *f* (*Mut*) *fam* pluck.

Treber *pl* (*Bier~*) draff, grains *pl*; (*Trauben*) skins of grapes.

Treck *m* (*Auszug*) marching out; departure; emigration; **~en** *tr* (*ausziehen*) to march out; (*ziehen*) to haul; **~er** *m* tractor.

Treff *n* club(s *pl*); **~as** *n* ace of clubs; **~en** *irr tr, itr* to hit, to strike; (*an~~*) to meet (with), to find; (*begegnen*) to meet, to encounter, (*zufällig ~~*) to light on: (*stoßen auf*) to come upon, to run into, to hit upon, to fall in with; (*zustoßen*) to befall, to fall upon; (*be~~*) to concern, to affect, to touch; *nicht ~~* to fail, to miss; (*phot, Malerei*) to achieve a good likeness; (*zu~~*) to apply (to); *r* to happen, to chance; *e-e Entscheidung ~~* to come to a decision; *Maßnahmen* (*Vorsichtsmaßregeln*) *~~* to take measures (precautions); *Vorbereitungen ~~* to make preparations (*od* arrangements) (for); *e-e Wahl ~~* to make a choice; *den Nagel auf den Kopf ~~* to hit the nail right on the head; *vom Blitz getroffen werden* to be struck by lightning; *vom Blitz getroffen* thunderstruck; *er hat es schlecht getroffen* he picked the wrong day to come; *den rechten Ton ~~* to strike the right keynote; *ins Schwarze ~~* to hit the mark; *der Vorwurf trifft ihn* the blame rests on him; *Vorsorge ~~* to provide, to make provisions; *empfindlich ~~* (*fig*) to cut to the quick; *die Reihe trifft mich* it is my turn; *das Los traf ihn* the lot fell on him; *das trifft sich gut* (*schlecht*) that is lucky (bad); *wie es sich gerade trifft* as chance will have it; *sich getroffen fühlen* to feel hurt; **~en** *n* action, battle, encounter; (*Zus.~~*) meeting, assembly, gathering, *Am rally*; **~end** *a* (*Bemerkung*) to the point, pertinent; (*Ähnlichkeit*) striking; (*wohlgezielt*) well-aimed; (*passend*) appropriate; *~~ bemerken* to quip; **~er** *m* (*Schuß*) direct hit; good shot; (*Lotterie*) lucky hit; prize, winning ticket; (*Glücksfall*) lucky chance, luck; (*Haupt~~*) first prize; (*Erfolg*) success; *e-n ~~ erzielen* to score a hit; *~~ u. Nieten* prizes and blanks; **~ergebnis** *n* score; **~erraum** *m* zone of dispersion; **~erzahl** *f* number of impacts (*od* shots); **~genauigkeit** *f* accuracy of fire; **~lich** *a* excellent, choice, first-rate; **~~keit** *f* excellence; **~punkt** *m* meeting point, rendezvous; *mil* point of impact; **~~entfernung** *f* range of target; **~sicher** *a* accurate, well-aimed; *fig* pertinent, to the point; (*Urteil*) sound; **~~heit** *f* accuracy of fire; **~wahrscheinlichkeit** *f* expectancy of hitting; **~weite** *f* (*Elektronen*) focal length.

Treib|anker *m* drag (*od* sea-) anchor; **~eis** *n* drift-ice; floating ice; **~en** *irr tr* (*in Bewegung setzen*) to drive, to propel, to set in motion; (*drängen*) to urge, to press; (*aufreizen*) to incite; (*an~~*) to impel; (*hinaus~~*) to drive out, to expel from; (*Teig, Häute*) to raise; (*Metall*) to work, to hammer, to emboss, to chase; (*Pflanzen*) to force; (*Blätter*) to put forth; (*Fußball*) to dribble; (*Sport*) to go in for; (*tun*) to do, to be up to; (*Geschäft*) to carry on, to work at; (*Musik*) to practise; (*Beruf*) to profess; (*hervorbringen*) *med* to produce, to promote; *itr* (*Wasser*) to float, to drift; (*Blüte*) to blossom forth; *bot* to shoot, to sprout; (*gären*) to ferment; *med* to act as a diuretic; *auf die Spitze ~~* to carry things to the breaking point; *zur Verzweiflung ~~* to drive to despair; *es zu weit ~~* to carry it too far; *zu etw ~~* to prompt; *Sprachen ~~* to study languages; *vor Anker ~~* to drag the anchor; **~en** *n* doings *pl*; (*Tätigkeit*) activity; (*lustiges ~~*) *Am* shivaree; (*Aufregung*) stir; *tech* cupeling, swelling; *fam* goings-on; **~~d** *a* floating, drifting; (*Kraft*) driving, motive; *~~des Wrack* derelict hulk; *~~es Rad* pinion; **~er** *m* driver; (*Vieh~*) drover; (*Jagd*) beater; *tech* refiner, drift punch; **~gas** *n* propellent (*od* fuel) gas; (*Holzgas*) wood gas; **~~motor** *m* wood-gas engine; **~hammer** *m* chasing hammer; **~haus** *n* hothouse, conservatory; **~~pflanze** *f* hothouse plant; **~holz** *n* driftwood; **~jagd** *f* battue, *Am* surround; **~kraft** *f* motive power, moving force; **~ladung** *f* propelling charge; **~mine** *f* floating mine; **~öl** *n* motor oil; **~rad** *n* driving wheel; **~rakete** *f* booster rocket; **~riemen** *m* driving-belt; **~sand** *m* quicksand; **~satz** *m* (*Raketen~~*) rocket composition; **~stoff** *m* fuel, petrol; propellent; *Am* gas; **~~behälter** *m* fuel tank; **~~lager** *n* fuel dump; **~welle** *f tech* main (*od* work) shaft.

treidel|n *itr mar* to tow; **~pfad** tow(ing)-path.

tremulieren *itr* to quaver, to shake.

trenn|bar *a* separable; (*teilbar*) divisible; (*abnehmbar*) detachable; **~~keit** *f* separability; **~en** *tr* to separate, to sever, to sunder; to divide (from), to disjoin; (*entzweien*) to disunite; (*auflösen*) to dissolve; (*Naht*) to undo, to rip; *el, tele* to disconnect, to cut off, to interrupt; *r* to part (*von jdm* from, with; *von etw* with); (*dauernd*) to separate from; to become divorced; (*sich absondern*) to dissociate o. s. from; (*Weg*) to branch off; **~scharf** *a radio* selective; *nicht ~~* unselective; **~schärfe** *f radio* selectivity; sharp tuning; **~~regelung** *f* automatic band-width selection; **~schnitt** *m* cross section; **~stelle** *f tech* disconnecting point; **~taste** *f* disconnecting knob; **~ung** *f* separation, disunion; (*Silben~*) division; (*Auflösung*) dissolution; (*Scheiden*) parting; *el* disconnection, breaking, isolation; (*Ehescheidung*) divorce; (*Uneinigkeit*) disunion; **~~slinie** *f* line of demarcation; *mil* formation boundary; **~~sschmerz** *m* pain of separation; **~~sstrich** *m*, **~~szeichen** *n* dash; division; di(a)eresis; **~~sstunde** *f* hour of separation (*od* parting); **~~sverfahren** *n* process of separation; **~~svermögen** *n* selectivity; **~~swand** *f* partition wall; **~zeichen** *n tele* cut-off signal; **~~zulage** *f* separation allowance.

Trense *f* snaffle, bridoon.

trepp|ab *adv* downstairs; **~auf** *adv* upstairs; **~e** *f* staircase, stairs *pl mit sing*; flight of steps (*od* of stairs), *Am* stairway; *die ~~ hinauffallen fig* to be kicked upstairs; *vier ~en hoch* four flights up; *zwei ~en hoch* on the second floor; **~enabsatz** *m* landing; **~enbelag** *m* step planking; **~enbeleuchtung** *f* automatic device for lighting of staircase; **~engeländer** *n* banisters *pl*, railing; **~enhaus** *n* well of a staircase; entrance-hall; **~enläufer** *m* stair-carpet; **~enstufe** *f* step, stair; **~enwitz** *m* after-wit.

Tresor *m* treasury; safe.

Tresse *f* galloon, lace; *mil* stripe.

Trester *m pl* husks *pl*, grounds *pl*.

Tret|anlasser *m mot* kick-starter; foot-starter; **~en** *irr itr* to tread; to step, to walk; (*Radfahrer*) to pedal; (*Fußhebel*) to treadle; (*gehen*) to go; (*eintreten*) to step in, to enter; *tr* to tread, to trample, to kick; (*be~~*) to step on, to walk on; (*Pedal*) to pedal; (*Fußhebel*) to treadle; (*Orgel*) to blow; (*zer~~*) to crush; *fig* (*mahnen*) to dun, to press; *ins Haus ~~* to enter; *aus~~* to withdraw; *näher~~* to draw near, to approach; (*e-r Frage*) to consider; *an die Stelle ~~* to succeed, to take o.'s place; *auf jds Seite ~~* to side with; *zutage ~~* to appear, to come to light; *über die Ufer ~~* to overflow; *in Kraft ~~* to come into force, to become effective, to go into effect; *auf der Stelle ~~* (*mil*) to mark time, *Am* to saw wood; *in den Ehestand ~~* to get married; *dazwischen ~~* to intercede, to interfere, to intervene; *in jds Fußstapfen ~~* to follow in s. o.'s footsteps; *jdm zu nahe ~~* to hurt s. o.'s feelings; *das Glück mit Füßen ~~* to be blind to o.'s own good fortune; *ins Mittel ~~* to interpose, to mediate; *in Verbindung ~~* to enter into connection, to get in touch (with); *jdm vor die Augen ~~* to face s. o.; *mit Füßen ~~* to trample upon; *die Orgel ~~* to blow the bellows; **~fahrrad** *n* pedal cycle, push-bicycle; **~hebel** *m* treadle; **~mine** *f mil* contact mine; **~mühle** *f* treadmill; *fig* daily routine, humdrum round; **~schalter** *m* foot switch.

treu *a* faithful; loyal; true; (*beständig*) constant; (*aufrecht*) sta(u)nch, upright; (*ergeben*) devoted; (*zuverlässig*) trustworthy, trusty; (*aufrichtig*) sincere; (*genau*) accurate, exact, correct; (*Gedächtnis*) retentive; *e-m Vorsatz ~ bleiben* to stick to o.'s purpose; *zu ~en Händen* in trust; **~bruch** *m* breach of faith (*od* trust); (*Untreue*) disloyalty; (*Tücke*) perfidy; **~brüchig** *a* perfidious, faithless; **~e** *f* faith, faithfulness, fidelity, (*Ergebenheit*) loyalty; (*Genauigkeit*) accuracy; *auf ~ u. Glauben* in good faith; *jdm die ~~ brechen* to break o.'s faith with s. o.; *jdm die ~~ halten* to keep faith with s. o.; **~eid** *m* oath of allegiance; **~hand** *f* trust; **~~gesellschaft** *f* trust company; **~händer** *m* custodian, fiduciary, trustee; **~herzig** *a* true-hearted, frank; guileless; candid; **~~keit** *f* frankness; **~lich** *adv* truly, faithfully, loyally; **~los** *a* faithless, perfidious, disloyal; (*verräterisch*) treacherous; **~~igkeit** *f* faithlessness; (*Tücke*) perfidy; (*Abfall*) defection; (*Verrat*) treacherous deed; (*Ehe*) infidelity.

Trib|un *m* tribune; **~unal** *n* tribunal; **~üne** *f* (*Rednerbühne*) platform, rostrum; (*Zuschauer*) stand, gallery, (*offene ~~*) *Am* bleacher; **~~nkarte** *f* stand-ticket.

Tribut *m* tribute; **~pflichtig** *a* tributary.

Trichine *f* trichina; **~nkrankheit** *f* trichinosis.

Trichter *m* funnel; (*Granat~*) crater; (*Mühlen~*) tunnel; (*Lautsprecher*) horn; **~einlage** *f* filter cone; **~feld** *n* shell-torn (*od* shell-pitted) ground; **~förmig** *a* funnel-shaped, infundibular; **~gelände** *n* crater-area; **~lautsprecher** *m* horn-type speaker; **~mündung** *f* crater; (*Fluß*) estuary; *tech* gate opening; **~rohr** *n* funnel tube; **~wagen** *m rail* (*für Schüttgut*) hopper car.

Trick *m* trick, stunt, dodge; artifice; stratagem; sleight of hand; (*Wortspiel*) *Am fam* gag; **~aufnahme** *f* fake photo; **~film** *m* stunt film; trick film; (*gezeichneter ~~*) animated cartoon film; cartoon motion picture; **~~zeichner** *m* animator; **~~zeichnungen** *f pl film* animated cartoons *pl*.

Trieb *m* driving; force; (*Schößling*) sprout, shoot; (*Neigung*) inclination; (*Antrieb*) spur, impulse, bent; (*treibende Kraft*) moving force, motive power; (*Beweggrund*) motive; (*Instinkt*) instinct, impulse; (*Bier*) life; (*Vieh*) drove; *aus eigenem ~e* of o.'s own accord, spontaneously; **~achse** *f* motor-shaft; **~artig**, **~haft** *a* instinctive; unbridled; **~feder** *f* driving (*od* main) spring; *fig* motive; **~kette** *f* drive chain; **~kraft** *f* motive power, momentum; *bot* germinating power; **~ladung** *f* propellent charge; **~leben** *n* instinctive life; **~mäßig** *a* impulsive; **~rad** *n* driving wheel; **~sand** *m* quicksands *pl*; **~scheibe** *f* knob; micrometer head; **~wagen** *m rail* motor (rail) coach, *Am* motor railcar; rail-motor; Diesel (-electric rail coach); rail Diesel car; *mot* (*Zugwagen*) tractor vehicle; (*Straßenbahn*) motor car(riage), tramcar; **~~lokomotive** *f* battery car; **~~zug** *m* motor-coach (train), *Am* multiple-unit train; **~welle** *f* connecting-rod; **~werk** *n* machinery, mechanism, gear(ing); *aero* engine; power unit (*od* plant); **~~anlage** *f* power plant; transmission machinery.

Trief|auge *n* blear-eye; **~äugig** *a* blear-eyed; **~en** *irr itr* to trickle, to drip with, to drop, (*Auge*) to run; *vor Nässe ~~* to be soaking wet; *von Weisheit ~~* to overflow with wisdom; **~~d** *a* dropping, dripping; **~nasig** *a* snivelling; **~naß** *a* dripping wet, sopping.

triezen *tr fam* to worry, to vex, to bother.

Trift *f* pasturage, pasture land; (*Weg*) cattle-track, drove; (*Holz~*) floating; *geol* drift; (*Strömung*) drift; **~ig** *a* valid; important, weighty, urgent; (*einleuchtend*) evident; (*überzeugend*) convincing conclusive; (*glaubwürdig*) authentic; plausible; (*zwingend*) cogent; (*vernünftig*) sound; *mar* drifting, adrift; **~igkeit** *f* cogency, validity.

Trigonometr|ie *f* trigonometry; **~isch** *a* trigonometrical; **~~er** *Punkt* triangulation point.

Trikot *m u. n* (*Stoff*) stockinet; (*Zirkus*) tights *pl*; (*fleischfarben*) fleshings *pl*; **~agen** *pl* hosiery; **~fabrik** *f* hosiery manufacturing plant; **~gewebe** *n* knitting; **~hemd** *n* knitted shirt; **~stoff** *m* tricot tissue; **~waren** *pl* knitted goods *pl*, hosiery; **~wäsche** *f* tricot lingerie; **~wirkerei** *f* tricot weaving mill.

Triller *m* shake, trill; *mus* quaver; **~n** *itr, tr* to shake, to trill; *mus* to quaver; (*Vögel*) to warble; **~pfeife** *f* alarm-whistle.

trimm|en *tr* (*stutzen*) to trim; *mar, aero* to trim; **~er** *m mar* trimmer; **~fläche** *f* (*auch ~blech, ~kante*) *aero* trim(ming) tab; **~klappe** *f aero* trimming flap; **~ruder** *n aero* trimming tab; (*Rakete*) external control vane; **~tank** *m mar* trimming tank.

trink|bar *a* drinkable, potable; **~becher** *m* drinking-cup; mug; **~branntwein** *m* potable spirit(s *pl*); **~en** *irr tr, itr* to drink; (*Tee, Kaffee*) to take, to have; (*in sich aufnehmen*) to imbibe, to absorb; (*zechen*) to tipple, to carouse; (*in großen Zügen*) to quaff; (*nippen*) to sip; (*zu~~*) to drink to, to toast; **~er** *m* drinker; drunkard; **~~heilanstalt** *f* asylum for drunkards; **~fest** *a* able to stand alcohol; **~gelage** *n* drinking-bout, carouse; **~geld** *n* tip, gratuity; *ein ~~ geben* to tip s. o.; **~glas** *n* drinking glass, tumbler; **~halle** *f* (*Kurort*) pump-room; (*Straße*) refreshment-stall; **~halm** *m* drinking straw; **~kur** *f*: *e-e ~~ machen* to drink the waters; **~lied** *n* drinking-song; **~schale** *f* drinking-cup; **~spruch** *m* toast; **~stube** *f* tap-room; bar; **~wasser** *n* drinking-water, potable water; **~~versorgung** *f* drinking-water supply; **~~bereiter** *m* water-purification unit; **~~leitung** *f* drinking-water line; **~~zelle** *f mar* fresh-water tank; **~zwang** *m* obligation to drink spirits.

Trio *n* trio; **~blechstraße** *f* three-high plate-mill train; **~blockstraße** *f* three-high blooming-mill train; **~le** *f mus* triplet.

trippeln *itr* to trip.

Tripper *m* gonorrh(o)ea, *vulg* clap.

Tritt *m* step, tread; (*Spur*) trace, footprint, track; (*Fuß~*) kick; (*Stufe*) step; (*Wagen~*) carriage-step; (*Leiter*) small step-ladder; (*Orgel~*) pedal; (*Schritt*) pace; (*Geräusch des ~es*) footfall; *ohne ~* route step; *in falschem ~* out of step; *~ halten* to keep in step; **~brett** *n* foot-board; *mot* running-board; **~fläche** *f* tread; **~hebel** *m* foot lever; **~leiste** *f* floorboard, kick plate; **~leiter** *f* a pair of steps, step-ladder; **~stufe** *f* treadboard; **~wechsel** *m* change of step.

Triumph *m* triumph; **~ator** *m* victor, conquering hero; **~bogen** *m* triumphal arch; **~geheul**, **~geschrei** *n* howl of triumph; **~ieren** *itr* to triumph; (*frohlocken*) to exult (in), to boast; (*siegen*) to vanquish, to conquer, to score off s.o.; **~ierend** *a* triumphant, in triumph; **~zug** *m* triumphal procession.

trivial *a* trivial, trite; (*abgedroschen*) stale, thrashed-out; *~e Bemerkung* platitude, truism; **~ität** *f* triviality, platitude.

trocken *a* dry; (*dürr*) arid, parched; (*Husten*) hacking; *fig* (*nüchtern*) jejune; (*langweilig*) tedious, boring, dull; *~es Brot* plain bread; *~ werden* to dry off (*od Am* out); *~er Wechsel* promissory note; *auf dem ~en sein* to be under cover; *sein Schäfchen ins ~ene bringen* to feather o.'s nest; *auf dem ~en sitzen* to be hard up; to be in low water; *~legen* (*Kind*) to put a clean diaper on; (*Boden*) to drain; *noch nicht ~ hinter den Ohren sein* to be green; **~anlage** *f* drying establishment; **~apparat** *m* drying apparatus, drier, desiccator; **~bagger** *m* excavator; **~batterie** *f* dry battery; **~boden** *m* drying-loft; **~darre** *f* drying kiln; **~dock** *n* dry-dock; **~ei** *n* dried (*od* dehydrated) egg; **~eis** *n* dry ice; **~element** *n* dry cell; **~fäule** *f* dry rot; **~futter** *n* dry food; **~gemüse** *n* dehydrated vegetables *pl*; **~gerüst** *n* drying frame, hack; **~gestell** *n* drying-stand, towel-horse, clothes-horse; **~gewicht** *n* dry weight; **~hefe** *f* dry yeast; **~heit** *f* dryness; (*Dürre*) drought, *Am* drouth; (*Unfruchtbarkeit*) aridity; (*Langweile*) dul(l)ness, tediousness; **~kammer** *f* drying chamber; **~kartoffeln** *f pl* dehydrated potatoes *pl*; **~legen** *r* (*Land*) to drain; (*Kind*) to change napkins (*od* diapers); **~legung** *f* drainage; **~leine** *f* clothes-line; **~milch** *f* dried (*od* powdered) milk; **~mittel** *n* drying agent, drier, siccative; **~obst** *n* dried fruit; **~ofen** *m* drying oven (*od* kiln); **~periode** *f* dry spell; **~platte** *f phot* dry plate; **~platz** *m* drying-ground; **~präparat** *n* dry preparation; **~pulver** *n* drying powder; **~rasierapparat** *m* dry-shaver; **~raum** *m* drying room, drier; **~reinigung** *f* dry cleaning; **~schleuder** *f* centrifugal drier; **~schwimmen** *n sport* dry swimming; **~skikurs** *m* dry ski instructions *pl*; **~ständer** *m* drying rack; **~stange** *f* linen-pole; **~trommel** *f* drying drum, rotary drier; **~verfahren** *n* drying process; **~verlust** *m* loss on drying; **~vorrichtung** *f* drying apparatus; **~zeit** *f* drying time; (*Wetter*) drought(iness).

trockn|en *tr, itr* to dry; (*aus~*) to desiccate, to dry up; (*ausdörren*) to sear; (*entwässern*) to drain; (*ab~*) to wipe dry; (*lagern*) to season; (*Wäsche*) to air; (*in e-n Zustand bringen*) to condition; (*Heu*) to cure; (*dörren*) to bake; *mil* (*Gebäude, Schiffe*) to dehumidify; **~er** *m* drier, desiccator; **~ung** *f* drying, seasoning, desiccating; **~~sanlage** *f* drying plant.

Troddel *f* bob, tassel.

Tröd|el *m* second-hand articles *pl*; (*Gerümpel*) lumber, rubbish, trash, *Am* junk; **~~bude** *f* old-clothes shop; **~~ei** *f* dawdling, lingering; **~~fritz** *m fam* slow-coach; **~~kram** *m* lumber, rubbish; **~~markt** *m* rag-fair; **~~n** *itr* to deal in second-hand goods; (*sich langsam bewegen*) to be slow, to dawdle, to linger, to potter; **~~waren** *f pl* second-hand goods; **~ler** *m* dealer in second-hand goods, junk-dealer; (*Herumlungerer*) dawdler.

Trog *m* trough; vat; (*Mörtel~*) hod.

T-Rohr *n* T-tube, T-pipe.

trollen *itr* to toddle along (*od* off), to stroll away, to saunter on; to cut and run, to decamp; *r* to be off.

Tromm|el *f* drum; *tech* barrel, sleeve, cylinder; canister; *anat* tympanum; *die ~~ schlagen* to play the drum; *die ~~ wirbelt* the drum beats; **~~fell** *n* drum-head; *anat* tympanic membrane; **~~feuer** *n* drumfire, intense bombardment; barrage; **~~n** *itr, tr* to (beat the) drum; (*Finger*) to beat the devil's tattoo; **~~revolver** *m* revolver, *Am fam* six-shooter; **~~schlag** *m* beat of the drum; *bei gedämpftem ~~schlag* with muffled drums; **~~schlegel** *m* drum-stick; **~~trockner** *m* rotary drier; **~~wirbel** *m* roll of drums; (*leiser*) ruffle; **~ler** *m* drummer.

Trompete *f* trumpet; *anat* tube; **~n** *itr* to trumpet, to blow (*od* to sound) the trumpet; **~ngeschmetter** *n* blare (*od* blast) of trumpets; **~nsignal** *n* bugle call; **~nstoß** *m* flourish of trumpet; **~r** *m* trumpeter.

Trop|en *pl* tropics *pl*; *jem, der in den ~~ gelebt hat sl* sunshiner; **~~anzug** *m* tropical uniform; **~~ausführung** *f* tropical finish; **~~ausrüstung** *f* tropical kit; **~~beständig, ~~fest** *a* suitable for tropics; **~~beständigkeit, ~~festigkeit** *f* resistance to tropical conditions; **~~fieber** *n* tropical fever; **~~frucht** *f* tropical fruit; **~~gewächs** *n*, **~pflanze** *f* tropical plant; **~~helm** *m* pith (*od* sun) helmet, topee; **~~klima** *n* tropical climate; **~~koller** *m* tropical frenzy; **~~krankheit** *f* disease of tropical climates; tropical disease; **~~verwendungsfähig** *a* fit for service in tropical climate; **~isch** *a* tropical.

Tropf *m* simpleton, dunce, duffer; *armer ~* poor wretch; **~bad** *n* shower-bath; **~en** *m* drop; (*Schweiß*) bead; *ein ~~ auf den heißen Stein* a drop in the bucket; *ein guter ~~* a capital wine; *steter ~~ höhlt den Stein* constant dropping wears away the stone; **~en, tröpfeln** *itr, tr* to drop, to drip, to trickle; (*Wasserhahn*) to leak; **~~bildung** *f* drop formation; **~~fänger** *m* drip-catcher; **~~förmig** *a* drop-shaped, guttiform; **~~glas** *n* dropping glass (*od* tube); **~~messer** *m* drop counter, dropper; burette; **~~weise** *adv* drop by drop; **~~zähler** *m* dropping bottle; dropper; **~flasche** *f* dropping bottle; **~hahn** *m* dropping (*od* dripping) cock; **~naß** *a* dripping wet; **~rohr** *n* dropping tube; **~schale** *f* dripping dish (*od* basin); **~stein** *m* (*hängend*) stalactite; (*von unten*) stalagmite; **~~höhle** *f* stalactite cavern.

Trophäe *f* trophy.

Troposphäre *f* troposphere.

Troß *m* baggage, transport, impedimenta *pl*; supply lines *pl*; (*Anhänger*) gang, followers *pl*; **~schiff** *n* supply ship; **~wagen** *m* baggage wag(g)on.

Trosse *f* cable; *mar* hawser.

Trost *m* consolation, comfort; (*Erquickung*) solace; (*Erleichterung*) relief; *schlechter ~* cold (*od* small) comfort, poor consolation; *jdm ~ zusprechen* to console s. o.; *~ schöpfen aus* to take comfort from; *nicht recht bei ~ sein* not to be in o.'s right mind, to be off o.'s head, *Am* to have wheels in o.'s head; **~bedürftig** *a* in need of consolation; **~brief** *m* consolatory letter; (*Beileid*) letter of condolence; **~bringend** *a* comforting, consolatory; **~los** *a* disconsolate, sad; (*untröstlich*) inconsolable; (*hoffnungslos*) hopeless; (*freudlos*) cheerless; (*elend*) wretched; (*öde*) desolate, bleak; **~~igkeit** *f* despair; desolation; hopelessness; dreariness; **~preis** *m* consolation- (*od* booby-) -prize; **~reich** *a* consoling, comforting; **~spruch** *m* words of comfort.

tröst|en *tr* to comfort, to console, to solace, to cheer up; *r* to console o. s. with, to take comfort in, to cheer up; to be comforted, to be consoled; *~~ Sie sich!* take comfort! cheer up! **~er** *m* comforter, consoler; **~lich** *a* comforting, consolatory, consoling; cheering; **~ung** *f* consolation, comfort.

Trott *m* trot; (*leichter ~, Schlendrian*) jog-trot; **~el** *m* idiot, fool, booby, dolt, ninny, dope; **~eln, ~en** *itr* to trot; (*zu Fuß*) to trudge; **~oir** *n* pavement, *Am* sidewalk; *Am* (*in Louisiana*) banquette.

Trotz *m* defiance; (*Störrigkeit*) obstinacy, stubbornness, refractoriness; (*Frechheit*) insolence; (*Bosheit*) spite; *jdm zum ~* in defiance of s. o.; *etw aus ~ tun* to do s. th. for spite; *jdm ~ bieten* to defy s. o., to brave s. o.; *~ prp* in spite of, notwithstanding, despite; **~dem, ~alledem** *adv* for all that, notwithstanding; *conj* although, even though, in spite of the fact (that), despite the fact (that), nevertheless; **~en** *itr* to defy s. o.; (*Gefahren*) to brave; (*schmollen*) to sulk; (*störrig sein*) to be obstinate; **~ig, ~köpfig** *a* defiant; (*widerspenstig*) refractory; (*schmollend*) sulky; (*eigensinnig*) obstinate; **~kopf** *m* stubborn (*od* pig-headed) person; obstinate child.

trüb|e *a* (*glanzlos*) dim, dull; (*Flüssigkeit*) turbid, muddy, thick; (*Himmel*) cloudy, overcast; (*düster*) dusky, dark; sombre; (*finster*) gloomy; (*unangenehm*) unpleasant; (*Erfahrung*) sad; (*Stimmung*) melancholic, low-spirited, gloomy, dismal; *es sieht ~ aus* things are looking black; *es wird ~e* the sky is getting overcast; *im ~en fischen* to fish in troubled waters; **~en** *tr* to render turbid, to trouble, to make muddy; (*verdunkeln*) to dim, to darken; (*abstumpfen*) to dull; (*matt machen*) to tarnish; (*bewölken*) to cloud; (*stören*) to disturb, to trouble; (*Stimmung*) to render gloomy; (*verderben*) to spoil, to ruffle, to annoy; (*verwirren*) to upset; *r* to grow cloudy (*od* gloomy *od* dull *od* damp); *der Himmel trübt sich* the sky is getting overcast; **~sal** *f* affliction; (*Elend*) misery; (*Leid*) trouble; (*Kummer*) sorrow; (*Not*) distress; (*Drangsal*) tribulation; *~~ blasen* to be in the dumps, to mope; **~selig** *a* (*düster*) gloomy, dismal, dreary; (*traurig*) sad; (*jammervoll*) woeful; (*elend*) wretched; (*niedergeschlagen*) dejected; (*kummervoll*) mournful; **~~keit** *f* affliction, sadness, gloominess, melancholy, low spirits *pl*; **~sinn** *m* sadness, dejection, melancholy, gloom; **~~ig** *a* sad, dejected, melancholy, gloomy; **~ung** *f* rendering turbid; (*Zustand*) turbidity, turbidness; (*Mattheit, Verdunkelung*) dimming, darkening, tarnishing; (*Glas*) clouding, blur(ring); opacity; milkiness; (*Stimmung*) ruffling, spoiling; **~~spunkt** *m* turbidity point.

Trubel *m* bustle, racket; disturbance; (*Verwirrung*) confusion; (*Erregung*) excitement; *sich an den ~ gewöhnen* to get accustomed to the hustle and bustle.

trubenisieren *tr* (*Stoff*) to Trubenize.

Truchseß *m* Lord High Steward.

trudeln *itr* to spin, to trundle; *ins ~ kommen aero* to get into a flat spin; to fall into a spin; *ins ~ bringen aero* to put the machine into a spin; *unfreiwilliges ~* uncontrollable spin; *sich ab~ lassen* to go into a spin.

Trüffel *f* truffle.

Trug *m* deceit, fraud, imposture; (*Sinne*) delusion, illusion, deception; (*Lüge*) lie; (*Falschheit*) falsehood; (*Heuchelei*) hypocrisy; **~bild** *n* phantom, vision; (*optische Täuschung*) optical illusion, mirage; **~schluß** *m*

fallacy, false conclusion, erroneous conclusion; fallacious argument.
trüg|en *irr tr* to deceive; *itr* to be deceptive; to prove fallacious; *wenn mich mein Gedächtnis nicht ~t* if my memory serves me right; *wenn nicht alle Zeichen ~~* unless all signs fail; **~erisch, ~lich** *a* deceitful, deceptive, fallacious, delusive; (*verräterisch*) treacherous; (*hinterhältig*) insidious; (*blendend*) specious, illusive; illusory; (*unbegründet*) unfounded; (*falsch*) false; (*irreführend*) misleading (to); *der Schein ~t* appearances are deceitful.
Truhe *f* chest, trunk.
Trulle *f vulg* hussy, wench.
Trumm *n* (*Ende, Stück*) stump, end(-piece); fragment.
Trümmer *pl* ruins *pl* (*einzelne Steine u. geol*) debris *pl*; (*unvollendet, zerbrochen*) fragments *pl*; (*Stücke*) pieces *pl*; (*roh zugehauen, Schutt*) rubble; (*Überreste*) remains *pl*; remnant; *mar* wreck(age); *in ~n liegen* to be (*od* lie) in ruins; *~ beseitigen* to take away the debris; *in ~ gehen* to be shattered; *in ~ schlagen* to smash to pieces; **~besät** *a* strewn with debris; **~beseitigung, ~räumung** *f* removal of debris, clearing of rubble; rubble removal; **~~skommando** *n* rubble and debris detail; **~feld** *n* field covered with ruins; **~gestein** *n geol* breccia; conglomerate; **~haft** *a* ruinous; (*zerfallen*) decayed; **~haufen** *m* heap of ruins; **~räumungsbulldog** *m* power blade grader, *Am* motor patrol grader; bulldozer; **~stätte** *f* ruins *pl*.
Trumpf *m* trump, trump-card; *was ist ~?* what are trumps? *Herz ist ~* hearts are trumps; *alle Trümpfe in der Hand haben* to hold all the trumps; *mit ~ stechen* to take a trick with a trump; **~en** *tr, itr* to trump.
Trunk *m* drink; (*Arznei, Gift*) potion; (*Schluck*) draught; (*das Trinken*) drinking; *dem ~ ergeben* addicted to drinking; *sich dem ~ ergeben* to take to drinking; **~en** *a* drunk, intoxicated; *fig* elated (with), wild (with); **~enbold** *m* drunkard; **~enheit** *f* drunkenness, inebriety, intoxication; *fig* elation; **~sucht** *f* intemperance, inebriety, dipsomania; **~süchtig** *a* given to drink(-ing), dipsomaniac; **~süchtiger** *m* dipsomaniac.
Trupp *m* troop, band, set, squad, gang; (*Herde*) herd, flock; *mil* section, party, squad; **~e** *f* (*Schauspieler*) company, troupe; *mil* (*Einheit*) unit; detail; men; personnel; arm of service; branch of the service; *kämpfende ~~* combat element; **~en** *pl* troops *pl*, forces *pl*; **~~abteilung** *f* detachment, unit, detail; force; section; **~~ansammlung** *f* concentration of troops; **~~arzt** *m* medical officer; **~~aushebung** *f* levy of troops; **~~befehlshaber** *m* commander of troops; **~~bereitstellung** *f* assembly of troops; *pl* troops held in readiness; **~~bestand** *m* (*e-r Einheit*) strength; **~~betreuung** *f* troops comforts and welfare, army welfare service, *Am* moral branch; **~~bewegungen** *f pl* troop movements *pl*; **~~bezeichnung** *f* numbering and designation of units; **~~einheit** *f* unit; (*kleine*) element; **~~ersatz** *m* reserves *pl*; **~~führer** *m* military leader, commander, C.O.; commander of a task force; **~~führung** *f* applied tactics *pl*; generalship, handling of troops; conduct of field operations; leadership; **~~gattung** *f* branch of the service, arm; **~~gliederung** *f* order of battle; **~~kommandeur** *m* commander; **~~körper** *m* body; corps; **~~lager** *n* troop camp; **~~schau** *f* military review; **~~schleier** *m mil* screen; **~~standort** *m* garrison; **~~teil** *m* unit; **~~transport** *m* conveyance of troops; **~~transporter** *m aero* troop transport plane (*od* carrier); *mar* troopship, trooper, *Am* transport; **~~transportfahrzeug** *n* troop-carrier; **~~transportflugzeug** *n* troop carrying aircraft, troop plane (*od* -carrier); **~~übung** *f* manœuvres *pl*, *Am* maneuver; field exercise; **~~übungsplatz** *m* training area, permanent military camp; drill ground, troop training grounds; **~~unterkunft** *f* barracks *pl*, quarters *pl*; billet; **~~verband** *m* formation of various arms; task force; unit; **~~verbandplatz** *m med* regimental aid station (*od* post); advanced dressing station; **~~verladung** *f* entraining of troops; **~~verlegung, ~~verschiebung** *f* dislocation of troops; changes in the disposition of troops; **~~verpflegung** *f* provisioning of troops; **~~verstärkung** *f* reinforcements *pl*; **~~zeichen** *n* unit's badge; unit insignia; **~~zug** *m* troop train; **~führer** *m* squad leader; **~weise** *adv* in troops; in bands.
Trust *m* trust, *Am fam* combine.
Trut|hahn *m* turkey(-cock); **~henne** *f* turkey-hen.
Trutschel *f fam* squab woman.
Trutz *m* defiance; offensive; **~bündnis** *n* offensive alliance; **~ig** *a* defiant; **~waffen** *f pl* weapons for attack.
Tschech|e *m* Czech; **~isch** *a* Czech; **~oslowakei** *f* Czechoslovakia.
T-Träger *m*, T-girder, T, tee.
Tube *f* tube.
Tuberk|el *m, f* tubercle; **~~bildung** *f* tuberculation; **~ulös** *a* tuberculous, tubercular; **~ulose** *f* tuberculosis; (*Lungen~*) (pulmonary) phthisis, consumption.
Tuch *n* cloth; (*Gewebe*) fabric, web; (*Stoff*) stuff, material; (*Staub~*) duster, rag; (*Umschlag~*) shawl, kerchief, scarf; (*Hals~*) muffler; (*Taschen~*) handkerchief; *wie ein rotes ~ wirken* to be a red rag to; **~artig** *a* cloth-like; **~ballen** *m* bale of cloth; **~en** *a* of cloth; **~fabrik** *f* cloth-factory (*od* -mill); **~färberei** *f* cloth dyeing; **~fühlung** *f* close touch; **~geschäft** *n*, **~laden** *m* fabric shop; **~handel** *m* cloth-trade, drapery; **~händler** *m* cloth-merchant, draper; **~handlung** *f* draper's shop; **~hosen** *f pl* cloth trousers *pl*; **~lager** *n* cloth-warehouse; cloth department; **~lappen** *m* rags *pl*, bits *pl* of cloth; **~macher** *m* clothmaker, clothier; **~nadel** *f* shirt-pin, breast-pin; **~streifen** *m* list (of cloth); patch; **~waren** *f pl* cloths *pl*, drapery; **~zeichen** *n aero* (*Signal*) ground panel; code panel.
tüchtig *a* (*fähig*) qualified, able, fit (for); (*leistungsfähig*) efficient, capable; (*gründlich*) thorough; proper; (*anstellig*) smart; (*fleißig*) hard; (*erfahren*) experienced; (*gediegen*) sound, solid; (*klug*) clever; (*geschickt*) skil(l)ful; (*kräftig*) vigorous, strong; (*ausgezeichnet*) excellent; (*beträchtlich*) considerable; *adv* much; thoroughly; *jdn ~ verprügeln* to give s. o. a good thrashing; *~ arbeiten* to work hard, to do a good day's work; *ein ~er Mensch sein* to be a capable person; **~keit** *f* ability, fitness; proficiency, excellence, excellency; efficiency.
Tück|e *f* malice, spite; (*Bösartigkeit*) malignity; (*Hinterlist*) perfidy, *Am* skulduggery; (*Falschheit*) falseness; (*Bosheit*) viciousness; (*Streich*) mischievous trick; *~~ des Objekts* cussedness of the inanimate; **~isch** *a* (*boshaft*) mischievous, malicious, spiteful; *med* malignant; (*hinterlistig*) insidious; tricky; (*verräterisch*) treacherous; (*verschmitzt*) trickish; (*Hund*) vicious.
Tuff, **~stein** *m* tuff; (*Kalk~*) calcareous tufa.
tüft|eln *itr* to puzzle (over); to split hairs; to make subtle distinctions; **~elei** *f* hair-splitting, subtleties *pl*; **~elig** *a* very punctilious; **~ler** *m* punctilious person.
Tugend *f* virtue; (*Reinheit*) purity; (*Keuschheit*) chastity; *aus der Not e-e ~ machen* to make a virtue of necessity; **~bold** *m* paragon of virtue; **~haft, ~sam, ~reich** *a* virtuous; **~haftigkeit** *f* virtue, virtuousness; **~prediger** *m* moralizer; **~richter** *m* moralist, censor.
Tüll *m* tulle, maline(s *pl*); bobbin net; (*glatter ~*) plain net; **~spitze** *f* net-lace. machine made lace.
Tülle *f* socket; (*Schnauze*) spout, nozzle; mouthpiece; lip; funnel.
Tulpe *f* tulip; **~nzwiebel** *f* tulip-bulb.
tummel|n *tr* to put in motion; (*Pferd*) to exercise; *r* (*sich beeilen*) to make haste, to hurry; (*sich regen*) to bestir o. s.; (*geschäftig sein*) to bustle about; *Am* to hustle; (*umhertollen*) to romp; **~platz** *m* playground; *fig* scene.
Tümmler *m* porpoise.
Tümpel *m* pool, puddle.
Tumult *m* tumult; (*Aufruhr*) uproar, riot, commotion, turmoil, row; (*Unruhe*) bustle; (*Lärm*) noise; (*Wirrwarr*) hubbub; **~uant** *m* rioter; **~uarisch** *a* tumultuary, riotous.
tun *irr tr, itr* to do; (*ausführen*) to perform, to make, to execute; (*handeln*) to act; (*arbeiten*) to be busy, to work; (*stellen*) to put; (*an~, verletzen*) to hurt, to harm; *dick ~* (*fam*) to give o. s. airs; *spröde ~* to play the prude; *vertraut ~* to affect intimacy; *not~* to be necessary; *alle Hände voll zu ~ haben* to have (got) o.'s hands full; *weh ~* to hurt; *nur so ~* to pretend, to make as if, to affect, to feign; *e-e Äußerung ~* to make a statement; *stolz ~* to put on airs, to show off; *schön ~* to flatter s. o.; to cajole s. o., to be gallant (to); *nichts damit zu ~ haben wollen* to wash o.'s hands of it; *jdm Unrecht ~* to do s. o. wrong, not to be fair to; *gut daran ~* to act wisely (in that); *mit jdm etw zu ~ haben* to have dealings with s. o.; *sein möglichstes ~* to do o.'s best (*od* utmost); *seine Schuldigkeit ~* to do o.'s duty; *des Guten zuviel ~* to overdo s. th.; *es zu ~ bekommen mit* to have trouble with; *hinein~* to put into; *zu ~ haben* to have to do, to be busy; to have trouble with; *zu ~ geben, machen* to employ, to undertake; *~ als ob* to make a show of, to pretend to; *groß ~, sich ~* to talk big, to boast; *er tut es ungern* he hates to do it; *das tut ihm nichts* that does not affect him, that makes no difference to him; *das tut nichts* that doesn't matter; *das tut nicht gut* no good will come of it; *es tut mir sehr leid* I am very sorry; *er tut mir leid* I am sorry for him; *es tut sich was* something is going on; *~ Sie, als ob Sie zu Hause wären* make yourself at home; *~ Sie, was Sie wollen* do as you like; *ihm ist es nur um ihr Geld zu ~* he is only interested in her money; *er täte besser daran* he had better; *Sie täten am besten* you had best; *was ist da zu ~?* what is to be done? *gesagt, getan* no sooner said than done; *was tut's?* what does it matter? *es ist mir darum zu ~* I am anxious about it; *~ n* doings *pl*, action, conduct; deal-

ings *pl*; ~ *u. Treiben* ways and doings; **~lich** *a* (*durchführbar*) practicable, feasible; (*ratsam*) advisable; (*zweckmäßig*) expedient; (*passend*) convenient; **~~st** *a* utmost; *adv* if possible.
Tünch|e *f* whitewash; parget, plaster; *fig* varnish, veneer; **~en** *tr* to whitewash; to rough-cast, to plaster; **~er** *m* whitewasher.
Tunichtgut *m* good-for-nothing, scamp, ne'er-do-well.
Tunk|e *f* sauce; (*Braten~*) gravy; **~en** *tr* to dip, to steep, to sop; **~enschale** *f* sauce-boat.
Tunnel *m* tunnel; (*Unterführung*) subway, underground passage; underpass; *Am* cut; *min* gallery; **~bau** *m* tunnelling.
Tüpfel *m, n,* **~chen** *n* dot; spot; **~ig** *a* dotted; **~n** *tr* to dot; to spot; to stipple.
tupf|en *tr* to tip, to touch lightly; to dab; to dot; **~en** *m* dot, spot; **~er** *m* *med* swab.
Tür *f* door; (*~eingang*) door-way; *vor der ~* at the door; *vor der ~ stehen fig* to be imminent, to be just around the corner; *mit der ~ ins Haus fallen* to blurt out; *jdm die ~ vor der Nase zuschlagen* to slam the door in o.'s face; *jdm die ~ weisen* to show s. o. the door, to turn s. o. out; *vor seiner ~ kehren* to mind o.'s own business, to put o.'s own house in order, to sweep before o.'s own door; *jdn an die ~ begleiten* to see s. o. to the door; **~angel** *f* door-hinge; **~band** *n* loop; **~beschlag** *m* mounting; **~bogen** *m* ogee arch; **~drücker** *m,* **~klinke** *f* door handle, door knob, latch; **~einfassung** *f* door-frame; **~falz** *m* door folding; **~feld** *n* door bay; **~flügel** *m* wing, leaf; fold; **~fries** *m* head casing; **~füllung** *f* door panel; **~futter** *n* sleeper, jamb linings *pl*; **~gesims** *n* cornice of a door; **~griff** *m* door-handle; **~hüter** *m* doorkeeper, porter; *jur* usher; **~öffner** *m* door opener; **~öffnung** *f* opening of a door, bay; **~pfosten** *m* door post, jamb; **~rahmen** *m* door-case; **~riegel** *m* door bolt; (*selbsttätig*) snap-bolt; **~ritze** *f* chink of a door; **~schild** *n* door-plate, brass- (*od* name-) plate; **~schloß** *n* door lock; **~schwelle** *f* door sill, step stone, threshold; **~sturz** *m* lintel; **~verkleidung** *f* jamb lining.
Turb|ine *f* turbine; **~~nanlage** *f* turbine plant; **~~nantrieb** *m* turbine drive; **~~nauto** *n* turbocar; **~~ndampfer** *m* turbine steamer; **~~nflugzeug** *n* turbine airplane; **~~ngebläse** *n* turbine blower; **~~njäger** *m aero mil* turbo-jet fighter (plane); **~~nmotor** *m* turbine engine; *aero* jet-propulsion engine, *Am* turbojet; **~~nreaktionsmotor** *aero* turboreactor; **~~nrückstoßtriebwerk** *n* turbo-jet engine; **~odüse(nmotor)** *f* (*m*) turbojet; **~ohöhenlader** *m aero* turbosupercharger; **~opropellerstrahlmotor** *m* turboprop(jet); **~ostrahltriebwerk** *n* turbine jet unit, *Am* turbojet; **~ostrahljäger** *m* turbo-jet fighter; **~ostrahlmotor** *m* turbo-jet engine; **~ostrahltriebwerk** *n* turbine jet unit, *Am* turbojet.
Türk|e *m* Turk; **~ei** *f* Turkey; **~isch** *a* Turkish; *~~er Honig* Turkish delight.
Türkis *m* turquoise.
Turm *m* tower; (*Kirch~*) steeple, (*Verlies*) dungeon; (*Glocken~*) belfry; (*Geschütz~*) turret; (*Schachfigur*) castle, rook; **~bau** *m* building of a tower; **~dach** *n* (*Tank*) turret roof; **~decke** *f* (*Tank*) turret top; **~fahne** *f* vane; **~falke** *m* kestrel; **~geschütz** *n* turret gun; **~hals** *m* (*Tank*) turret base; **~haus** *n* sky-scraper; **~hoch** *a fig* very high; miles above; beyond; **~kran** *m* tower crane; **~kugellager** *n* (*Tank*) turret ball race; **~lafette** *f* turret mount(ing); **~lukendeckel** *m* turret door; **~schwalbe** *f* swift; **~schwenkwerk** *n* turret traversing gear; **~spitze** *f* spire; **~springen** *n sport* high diving; **~uhr** *f* church-clock; **~verlies** *n* dungeon; **~zinne** *f* battlement of a tower.
Türm|chen *n* turret; **~en** *tr, itr* to pile up; (*flüchten*) *fam* to bundle out, to buzz off, to decamp, to scamper off, *fam* to skedaddle; to skidoo; **r** to tower, to rise high; **~er** *m* watchman on a tower, warder.
turn|en *itr* to do gymnastics; to drill; **~en** *n* gymnastics *pl*, gym, drill; (*Freiübungen*) cal(l)isthenics *pl*; **~er** *m* gymnast; **~erisch** *a* gymnastic, athletic; **~erschaft** *f* athletic club; the gymnasts *pl*; **~fest** *n* gymnastic festival; **~gerät** *n* gymnastic apparatus; **~halle** *f* gym(nasium); **~hose** *f* shorts *pl*; **~kleidung** *f* gymnast's dress; **~lehrer** *m* teacher of gymnastics; **~platz** *m* athletic grounds *pl*; **~riege** *f* squad of gymnasts; **~schuhe** *f* gym-shoes *pl*, *Am fam* sneakers *pl*; **~spiele** *n pl* athletics *pl*, athletic sports *pl*; **~stunde** *f* lesson in gymnastics; **~übung** *f* gymnastic exercise; **~unterricht** *m* instruction in gymnastics; **~verein** *m* gymnastic (*od* athletic) club; **~wart** *m* superintendent of gymnastics.
Turnier *n* tournament; tourney; *hist* joust; **~en** *itr* to tilt, to joust; **~platz** *m* tilt-yard, jousting field, lists *pl*; **~richter** *m* umpire; **~schranken** *f pl* lists *pl.*
Turnus *m* cycle, rotation.
Turteltaube *f* turtle-dove, *Am* mourning dove.
Tusch *m* flourish.
Tusch|e *f* Indian ink; **~en** *tr* to wash, to paint with Indian ink; **~kasten** *m* paint-box; **~pinsel** *m* water-colo(u)r brush; **~zeichnung** *f* water-colo(u)r drawing.
tusch|eln *itr* to whisper; **~elei** *f* whisper.
Tüte *f* paper-bag.
tuten *itr, tr* to toot, to honk, to blow a horn.
Tüttel *m,* **~chen** *n* dot; *fig* jot.
Twist *m* twist; cotton waste.
Typ, ~us *m* type; model; **~e** *f* type, printing-letter; **~enbezeichnung** *f* model designation; **~endruck** *m* type printing; **~~er** *m* type printer; **~engießmaschine** *f* type-casting machine; **~enhebel** *m* type-lever (*od* bar); **~enmuster** *n* standard sample; **~nummer** *f* model number; **~enschild** *n* name-plate; **~ensetzmaschine** *f* typesetting machine; **~isch** *a* typic(al) (*für* of); **~isieren** *tr* to standardize; **~isierung** *f* standardization; **~ograph** *m* typographer; **~ographie** *f* typography; **~ographisch** *a* typographic(al).
typh|ös *a* typhoid; **~us** *m* typhoid fever; **~~artig** *a* typhoid, typhous; **~~bazillus** *m* typhoid bacillus; **~~kranke(r)** *m* typhus patient; **~~zunge** *f* baked tongue.
Tyrann *m* tyrant; **~ei** *f* tyranny; **~enmord** *m* tyrannicide; **~isch** *a* tyrannical, tyrannous; **~isieren** *tr* to tyrannize (over); (*unterdrücken*) to oppress.

U

*U Abk mit **U** siehe Liste der Abk.*
U-Bahn *f* underground (railway), tube, *Am* underground railroad.
Übel *n* evil; (*Unheil*) mischief; (*Krankheit*) disease, ailment, malady; (*Leiden*) complaint; (*Schaden*) injury (*für* to), sore; (*Verletzung*) hurt; (*Mißgeschick*) misfortune; (*Mißstand*) grievance; (*Beunruhigung*) annoyance; (*Plage*) nuisance, pest; *~ a* evil, bad; (*unrecht*) wrong; (*unrichtig*) improper; (*unwohl*) ill, sick, queasy; (*unzureichend*) bad; (*böse*) perverse; (*schlecht*) wicked; (*stinkend*) foul; *ein notwendiges ~* a necessary evil; *das ist vom ~* that is a nuisance; *e-m ~ abhelfen* to redress wrongs; *von zwei ~n das kleinste wählen* to change a bad for a worse; *nicht ~* not bad; rather nice; pretty good; *~ daran sein* to be in a bad way, to be in a fix; *ein übler Geselle sein* to be a bad lot; *davon kann e-m ~ werden* it's really enough to make you sick; *wohl od ~* willy-nilly; *er wird es wohl od ~ tun müssen* he'll have to do it whether he likes it or not; *~ aufgenommen werden* to be ill received; *~ auslegen* to misconstrue; *~ ergehen* to fare badly; *~ gelaunt sein* to be in bad humo(u)r, to be in a bad temper; *das wäre gar nicht ~* that wouldn't be a bad thing; *nicht ~ Lust haben, etw zu tun* to have a good mind to do s. th.; *mir wird ~, wenn ich daran denke* it makes me sick to think of it; *es ist mir ~* I feel sick; *~ aussehen* to look ill; *~ riechen* to smell badly; *~ nehmen* to take amiss, to take ill, to be offended at; *jdm ~ wollen* to bear s. o. a grudge; **~befinden** *n* indisposition; **~gelaunt, ~launig** *a* ill-humo(u)red; (*mürrisch*) cross, grumpy; **~gesinnt** *a* evil-minded; **~keit** *f* sickness, qualm, nausea; **~klingend** *a* dissonant; **~nehmen** *irr tr* to take amiss (*od* in bad part), to resent; to be offended at; *Sie nehmen es mir nicht ~, daß ich jetzt gehe* you don't mind my leaving now; *ich nehme es Ihnen nicht ~* I do not blame you for it; *nehmen Sie es mir nicht ~* I meant no harm; **~~d, ~nehmerisch** *a* touchy, huffy, resentful; **~riechend** *a* malodorous, malodorant; evil-smelling, ill-smelling, foul, fetid; **~sein** *n* sickness, nausea; **~stand** *m* (*Ungelegenheit*) inconvenience; (*Beeinträchtigung*) draw-

back (to); (*Nachteil*) disadvantage; (*Ärger*) annoyance; (*Übergriff*) abuse; (*Gebrechen*) defect; **~tat** *f* misdeed, offence, crime; **~täter** *m* evil-doer, malefactor, criminal; **~wollen** *itr* to wish ill (to); **~~** *n* malevolence, ill-will; **~wollend** *a* malevolent, spiteful.

üben *tr, itr* to exercise, to practise, *Am* to practice; (*ausüben*) to exert; *sport* to train; *mil* to drill; *mus* to play exercises, to practise; *geübt sein* to be skilled, to be clever (at); to be experienced; *Barmherzigkeit* ~ to show s. o. mercy; *Nachsicht* ~ to make allowance for; *Geduld* ~ to be patient; *Gewalt* ~ to use force; *Verrat* ~ to commit treason; *Rache* ~ to take vengeance on.

über *prp* over; (*oberhalb*) above, on top of; (*höher*) higher (than), superior (to); (*darüber hinaus*) beyond, across, on the other side; (*auf*) on, upon; (*während*) while, during; (*betreffend*) concerning, about; (*von*) about, of; (*mehr als*) more than; (*nach*) past; (*auf dem Weg*) via (*od* by way of); ~ ... *hin* over; (*quer~*) across; ~ *u.* ~ all over; *Fehler* ~ *Fehler* mistake upon mistake; ~ *drei Wochen* three weeks to-day; *heute* ~ *acht Tage* this day week; *den Tag* ~ all day long; ~ *alle Maßen* beyond measure; ~ *Leichen gehen* to stop at nothing; *jdm* ~ *sein* to beat s. o. (in); ~ *fünfzig Jahre alt sein* to be past fifty; *bis* ~ *die Ohren* over head and ears; ~ *Bord* overboard; ~ *jdn lachen* to laugh at s. o.; *heute* ~*s Jahr* a year from to-day; *es geht nichts* ~ ... there is nothing better than ...; ~ *Gebühr* more than was due; ~ *alles* more than anything; ~ *Nacht* during the night; ~ *meine Fassungskraft* past (*od* beyond) my comprehension; ~ *jedem Verdacht* above suspicion; *10 Minuten* ~ *10* ten minutes past ten; *adv* ~ *u.* ~ over and over; *mil Gewehr* ~*!* slope arms! ~ *kurz od lang* sooner or later; *die Sache ist mir* ~ I am tired of it; *nichts* ~ *haben* to have nothing left.

über|all *adv* everywhere, *Am* all over; throughout; **~allher** *adv* from all quarters; **~allhin** *adv* everywhere, in all directions; **~altert** *a* outmoded; grown too old; **~alterung** *f* superannuation; **~angebot** *n* excessive supply; over-supply; **~~** *an Arbeitskräften* over-supply of labo(u)r; **~ängstlich** *a* over-anxious, *Am* overly anxious; **~an'strengen** *tr* to over-exert, to overwork, to overstrain; **~an'strengung** *f* over-exertion, overstrain; **~ant'worten** *tr* to deliver up, to surrender; **~anzug** *m* overall (*Am* -s *pl*); **~ar'beiten** *tr* to do over again, to revise, to touch up; **~'~** *itr* to work overtime; *r* to overwork o. s.; **~ar'beiter** *m Am* rewrite man; **~ar'beitung** *f* revision, touching up; modified text; (*zuviel Arbeit*) overwork, overstrain; *med* stress disease; **~ärmel** *m* oversleeve; **~aus** *adv* exceedingly, extremely.

Über|bau *m* superstructure; **~bau'en** *tr* to build over; **~beanspruchen** *tr arch* to overstress; *fig* to overload, to overstrain; **~beanspruchung** *f* overstrain(-ing), overload; *arch* overstress; *el* overvoltage; **~bein** *n* node; exostosis; **~belasten** *tr* to overload; **~belastung** *f* overload; **~belegt** *a* overcrowded; **~belichten** *tr phot* to overexpose; **~belichtung** *f* overexposure; *tele Am sl* blooming; **~besteuern** *tr* to overtax; **~betonung** *f* overaccentuation; **~bett** *n* coverlet, quilt; **~bevölkerung** *f* overpopulation; **~bewerten** *tr* to overvalue; **~bie'ten** *irr* to outbid s. o.; *fig* to surpass; **~bleibsel** *n* remnants *pl*; (*Restbestände*) remains *pl*, remainder; *chem* residue, residuum; (*Rest*) rest; (*Speiserest*) left-over; (*aus früherer Zeit*) survival, *Am fam* hangover; **~blen'den** *tr film* to superimpose, to fade-over; to mix, to lap; **~blen'dung** *f* fading; **~blick** *m* general view, survey; *fig* summary, synopsis; sketch; **~bli'cken** *tr* to overlook, to survey; **~bombe** *f* superbomb; **~brettl** *n* cabaret, variety-theatre; **~brin'gen** *irr tr* to bear, to deliver, to convey, to carry; **~brin'ger** *m* bearer; **~brü'cken** *tr* to bridge, to span; *fig* to bridge over; *e-e Kluft* **~~** to bridge a gulf; **~brü'ckung** *f* culvert; bridging; **~~sdraht** *m el* jumper; **~~skredit** *m* stop-gap loan; emergency credit; **~bür'den** *tr* to overload; to encumber; **~bür'dung** *f* overburdening; **~chlorsäure** *f* perchloric acid.

über|da'chen *tr* to roof in; (*Stroh*) to thatch; (*schützen*) to shelter; **~dau'ern** *tr* to outlast, to outlive; to survive; **~de'cken** *tr* to cover, to lay over; to spread over; (*teilweise*) to overlap; (*mit Wasser*) to swamp; (*verbergen*) to conceal, to eclipse, to blanket; **~de'hnen** *tr* to elongate excessively; **~den'ken** *irr tr* to ponder on, to reflect upon; to think over, to consider; (*grübeln*) to brood, to muse; **~dies** *adv* besides, moreover; **~dre'hen** *tr* (*Uhr*) to overwind; (*Gewinde*) to strip; **~'druck** *m* overprint; *tech* excess pressure; (*Briefmarke*) surcharge; **~'~en** *tr* to overprint; **~~anzug** *m* high-pressure diving suit; **~~kabine** *f* high-pressure cabin; *aero* pressurized cabin; **~~turbine** *f* reaction turbine; **~~windkanal** *m* compressed-air tunnel; **~druß** *m* (*Langweile*) boredom, ennui; (*Übersättigung*) satiety; (*Ekel*) disgust; *zum* **~~** *werden* to become boring; *bis zum* **~~** to satiety; **~drüssig** *a* sick of, disgusted with, tired of, weary of; **~~** *werden* to get tired of; **~durchschnittlich** *a* above average; **~e'ck** *adv* across, diagonally; (*schräg*) obliquely; **~eifer** *m* overgreat zeal; **~eifrig** *a* too zealous; **~~e(r)** *m Am sl* eager beaver; **~ei'gnen** *tr* to assign, to transfer, to convey, to alienate; **~eignung** *f* assignment, transfer, conveyance, alienation; **~ei'len** *tr* to precipitate; to hurry too much; to rush; (*Arbeit*) to scamp; *r* to be in a great hurry, to be in too big a hurry, to rush (o. s.); to act rashly; **~~** *Sie sich nicht!* don't rush; *er* **~***eilt sich nicht* he is rather slow; **~ei'lt** *a* hasty, rash; *fig* precipitate, inconsiderate; **~ei'lung** *f* precipitance, rashness, hastiness.

überein|ander *adv* one upon another; **~~greifen** *irr itr* to overlap; **~~lagerung** *f* superposition; **~~legen** *tr* to superpose; **~~liegend** *a* superposed, superjacent; **~~schieben** *irr tr* to overlap, to lap over, to cover and extend beyond; **~~schlagen** *irr tr* (*Beine*) to cross; **~~setzen** *tr* to superpose; **~kommen** *irr itr* to agree (about), to come to an agreement, to come to terms; **~~** *n*, **~kunft** *f* agreement, understanding, settlement; (*Vergleich*) compromise; (*Gläubiger*) composition; (*Beilegung*) arrangement; (*stillschweigende* **~~**, *Vertrag*) convention; (*Pakt*) compact; *stillschweigendes* **~~** tacit agreement; *ein* **~~** *treffen* to come to (*od* to reach) an agreement; *laut* **~~** as agreed upon; **~stimmen** *itr* to agree, to concur; (*Sachen*) to correspond, to harmonize; (*zusammenfallen*) to coincide; (*in Einklang bringen*) to square; (*passen*) to tally (*zu* with), *Am* to check with; *nicht* **~~** to disagree, to differ; **~~d** *a* agreeing, corresponding, consistent, concordant; (*einstimmig*) unanimous; (*identisch*) identical; *adv* in conformity with; in accordance; **~stimmung** *f* agreement; (*Einmütigkeit*) accord; (*Gleichförmigkeit*) conformity; (*Einklang*) harmony; (*Gleichklang*) unison; (*Einverständnis*) concert; *in* **~~** *mit* in harmony with, in accordance with; *in* **~~** *sein mit* to be in harmony (with), *Am* to be in line with; *in* **~~** *bringen* to accommodate, to conform; to synchronize; to tune.

über|empfindlich *a* oversensitive; touchy; **~~keit** *f* hypersensitiveness; *med* allergy; **~entwicklung** *f* overdevelopment; *bot* hypertrophy; **~erfüllen** *tr* (*Norm*) to overfulfil(l); **~erregen** *tr* to overexcite; **~erregung** *f* overexcitation; **~erzeugung** *f* overproduction; **~essen** *irr r* to overeat o.s.

über'|fahren *itr, tr* to drive over, to pass over, to cross; (*zu weit*) to run past; (*hinüberbringen*) to convey over, to ferry over; *ein Signal* **~~'** to overrun (*od* to go through) a signal; *jdn* **~~'** to run over s. o.; **~~'** *werden* to be run over; **~'fahrt** *f* passage; crossing; ferrying over; **~~sgeld** *n* passage, fare; (*Fähre*) ferriage; **~'fall** *m* sudden (*od* surprise) attack, *Am* hold-up; (*Einfall*) raid, inroad; *tech* (*Wasser*) overfall weir; **~~'en** *tr* to attack suddenly, *Am* to hold-up, *mil* to surprise; (*Nacht*) to overtake; (*Schrecken*) to seize; (*Schlaf*) to steal (upon); (*Regen*) to catch; **~~hosen** *f pl* knickerbockers *pl*; **~~kommando** *n* flying squad, *Am* riot-squad; *mil* raiding party; **~~rohr** *n* overflow pipe; **~~wagen** *m* Q--car; **~'fällig** *a* overdue; **~fein** *a* superfine; over-refined; (*wählerisch*) fastidious; **~~ern** *tr* to over-refine; **~~erung** *f* over-refinement, daintiness; **~fetten** *tr* (*Leder*) to overstuff; (*Seife*) to superfat; **~flie'gen** *irr tr* to fly over; *fig* to glance over, to skim through; **~'fließen** *irr itr* to flow over, to overflow; **~~d** *a* profuse; redundant; **~flü'geln** *tr mil* to outflank; *fig* to surpass, to outdo, to outstrip; **~fluß** *m* plenty, abundance; (*Überschüssiges*) surplus, superfluity, excess, overflow; (*Fülle*) exuberance; (*Übersättigung*) glut; (*Worte*) redundancy; (*Reichtum*) wealth; (*Luxus*) luxury; *tech* overflow; **~~** *haben an* to abound (in), to have plenty (of), *Am* to have s. th. to burn; *zum* **~~** unnecessarily, needlessly; *im* **~~** abundantly; **~flüssig** *a* useless, superfluous; (*unnötig*) unnecessary; (*überschüssig*) surplus, leftover; **~flu'ten** *tr* to overflow, to inundate, to flood, to swamp; **~flu'tet** *a* awash; **~fo'rdern** *tr* to overcharge; **~fo'rderung** *f* excessive charge; **~fracht** *f* overweight; excess luggage; **~fre'mdung** *f* foreign infiltration; foreign influence; control by foreign capital; **~fre'ssen** *irr r* to overeat o. s.; **~füh'ren** *tr* to carry over, to transport, to transfer, to convey, to transmit; *aero* to ferry; *jur* to convict (of); (*überzeugen*) to convince (of), to bring s. th. home to s. o.; *chem* to convert; **~führung** *f* (*Transport*) transport(ation), conveyance; (*Überweisung*) transfer; (*Brücke*) bridge, viaduct; (*Übergang*) overpass, crossing; *jur* conviction; *chem* conversion; **~~sflug** *m aero* ferrying flight; **~'fülle** *f* superabundance, excess, repletion; **~fü'llen** *tr* (*Last*) to overload; (*hineinstopfen*) to cram;

(*überfließen lassen*) to overfill; (*Menschen*) to overcrowd, to cram, to jam, to congest; (*Markt*) to overstock, to glut; (*Magen*) to glut; (*übersättigen*) to surfeit; **-fü'llt** *a* overcrowded, packed, jammed, crowded to overflowing, cram-full, filled up, congested; **-fü'llung** *f* overfilling, cramming, overloading; (*Übermaß*) surfeit; (*Andrang*) congestion; (*Menschen*) overcrowding; (*Magen*) glut; (*Markt*) overstock.

Über|gabe *f* delivery; (*Ablieferung*, *mil*) surrender; (*Einhändigung*) handing over; (*Übertragung*) transfer; (*Vorlage*) submitting; (*Eröffnung*) opening; **--verhandlung** *f* negotiation for surrender; **-gang** *m* passage; (*zu e-r Partei*) going over; *mil* desertion; *radio* change-over; (*Zeit*) transition, change; *jur* transmission, transfer; (*Farbe*) blending, shading off; *rail* crossing, (*schienengleich*) level crossing, *Am* grade crossing, crossing at grade; **--sbeihilfe** *f* severance pay; **--sbestimmungen** *f pl* transitionary provisions *pl;* provisional regulations *pl*; **--sfarbe** *f* transition colo(u)r; **--smantel** *m* interseasonal coat; **--smaßnahme** *f* transitional measure; **--speriode** *f*, **--sstadium** *n* transition stage; **--spunkt** *m* transition point; **--srente** *f* temporary pension; **--sstation** *f rail* branching-off station; **--sstelle** *f* place of crossing; **--sverkehr** *m* interchange of traffic; **--svorschrift** *f* temporary (*od* transitional) provision; **--swiderstand** *m* transition resistance; **--szeit** *f* transition period; **--szustand** *m* transition(al) state; **-ge'ben** *tr* (*abliefern*) to deliver up; (*einhändigen*) to hand over; (*übermitteln*) to offer, to present, *Am* to extend; (*einreichen*) to file (in), to hand (in), to submit; (*übertragen*) to transfer; (*eröffnen*) to open; *mil* to surrender; *dem Verkehr* -- to open for traffic; *r* (*erbrechen*) to vomit, to throw up; **-gebot** *n* outbidding; **-'gehen** *irr itr* (*hinübergehen*) to pass over, to cross; (*weitergehen*) to go on; (*zu e-r Partei*) to go over, *sl* to rat, *Am* to flop; (*verändern*) to change (into), to turn over (to); (*Farben*) to shade; (*überfließen*) to overflow; (*werden*) to turn, to grow; *zum nächsten Punkt* -- to go on to the next point; *in andere Hände* -- to change hands; *in jds Besitz* -- to pass to; *in Fäulnis* -- to grow rotten; *zum Angriff* -- to take the offensive; *zur Verteidigung* -- to change over to defence; **--'** *tr* (*auslassen*) to leave out, to omit; (*übersehen*) to pass over (*od* by), to overlook; *mit Stillschweigen* -- to pass in silence; **-ge'hung** *f* passing over; (*Auslassung*) omission; (*Nichtbeachtung*) overlooking; (*Vernachlässigung*) neglect; **-genug** *adv* more than enough, ample; **-geschnappt** *a fam* cracked; **-gewicht** *n* overweight; *fig* superiority; preponderance; *das -- bekommen* to lose o.'s equilibrium, to get top-heavy; *fig* to get the upper hand (of); **-gie'ßen** *tr* to pour over; (*verschütten*) to spill; (*bedecken mit*) to pour on, to cover (with); (*Licht*) to blaze; *mit Licht übergossen* bathed in light; (*Zucker*) to candy; **-gla'sen** *tr* to glaze; to vitrify; to varnish; to ice; **-glücklich** *a* overhappy; -- *sein* to be overjoyed; **-go'lden** *tr* to gild; **-greifen** *irr itr* to overlap; (*unberechtigt eindringen*) to encroach (on), to infringe; **-griff** *m* encroachment, infringement, inroad (*auf* on); *sich --e erlauben* to infringe (on); **-groß** *a* huge, immense; oversize; **-größe** *f* (*Kleidung*) outsize; (*Reifen*) oversize; **-guß** *m* crust.

über|haben *irr tr* (*übrig haben*) to have left; (*angezogen haben*) to have on; (*genug haben*) to be fed up with; to be weary of s. th.; **-ha'ndnahme** *f* increase, prevalence; **-ha'ndnehmen** *irr itr* to prevail, to increase; to spread; **-hang** *m* (*Geld*) surplus money; (*Fels*) overhanging rock, projecting ledge; (*Vorhang*) curtain, hanging(s *pl*); *arch* cantilever; **--en** *irr itr* to hang over; **-hängen** *tr* to hang over, to impend, to project; **-ha'sten** *tr* to precipitate, to hurry too much; **-häu'fen** *tr* to overwhelm (with); to load with, to swamp; *-häuft werden von* to be snowed under; **-hau'pt** *adv* in general, at all; on the whole; altogether; -- *nicht* not at all; -- *kein* no . . . at all; *wenn* -- if at all; **-he'ben** *irr tr* to exempt (from); to spare, to save; (*befreien*) to relieve (from); *jdn e-r Mühe* -- to spare s. o. a trouble; to dispense (with); *r* to strain o. s. (by lifting); (*stolz sein*) to be overbearing, to be proud (of), to boast (of); **-he'blich** *a* overbearing, presumptuous; **--keit**, **-he'bung** *f* presumption, arrogance; **-hei'zen** *tr*, *itr* to overheat: **-hi'tzen** *tr* to overheat; *tech* to superheat; **-hi'tzer** *m* superheater; **-hö'hen** *tr* (*Schienen*, *Kurve*) to superelevate; (*Preise*) to raise excessively, *Am* to jack up; **-hö'ht** *a* superelevated; *Am* banked; increased; surmounted; **-hö'hung** *f* increased price; (*Kurve*) bank, cant; *rail* superelevation; **-ho'len** *tr* to overtake; to outdistance, to outrun; (*hinter sich lassen*) to outstrip; (*ausbessern*) to overhaul, to recondition, *Am* to service; (*übertreffen*) to surpass, to outstrip; -- *verboten!* no passing! **-'-** *tr* to fetch over; *itr mar* to heel; **-ho'lt** *a* obsolete, out of date, antiquated; (*repariert*) overhauled, reconditioned; **-ho'lung** *f* overtaking; *mot* overhauling; **-hö'ren** *tr* to miss, not to hear; to hear s. o. a lesson; (*absichtlich*) to ignore; *etw* -- to misunderstand; **-irdisch** *a* celestial, heavenly; supernatural; **-kippen** *itr* to tilt over; to lose o.'s equilibrium; **-kle'ben** *tr* to paste over; **-kleid** *n* upper garment, overdress; (*Schutzanzug*) overall; **-klei'den** *tr* to cover over, to clothe; **-kleidung** *f* outerwear; **-klei'stern** *tr* to glue over; **-kle'ttern** *tr*, **-'-** *itr* to climb over; **-klug** *a* overwise; priggish; *--er Mensch* wiseacre; **-kochen** *itr* to boil over; **-ko'mmen** *tr* to obtain, to receive; (*befallen*) to befall, to be seized (with); to happen to; (*Sitten*) to be transmitted; **-kompensieren** *tr* to overcompensate; **-komprimiert** *a* supercompressed; **-konfessionell** *a* inter-confessional; **-kopieren** *tr phot* to overprint; **-kra'gung** *f* overhang; **-kritisch** *a* overcritical; **-kultur** *f* over-refinement; **-künsteln** *tr* to overdo.

über|la'den *irr tr*, *itr* to overload; (*Kunst*) to overdo, to adorn profusely; *mot* to supercharge; *el* to overcharge; (*Magen*) to overeat o. s.; *fig* to surfeit (with); (*Waren*) to transship; **-la'dung** *f* overloading; *el* overcharge; **-la'gerer** *m radio* heterodyne oscillator; **-la'gern** *tr tele*, *radio* to heterodyne (with), to superpose (on); **-la'gerung** *f* super(im)position, superheterodyne; (*Schwingungen*) overlapping; -- *e-r Störung* interference; **--sempfänger** *m* heterodyne receiver; **--sschaltung** *f radio*, *tele* superimposed connection; **--sröhre** *f* ballast tube, *Am* barretter.

Überland|autobus *m* cross-country bus, *Am* motor coach, motorbus; **-bahn** *f* interurban railway; **-flug** *m* cross-country flight; **-leitung** *f tele* rural subscriber line; **-transportgesellschaft** *f* long-distance carriers *pl*; **-verkehr** *m Am* truck service; **-zentrale** *f el* long-distance power station; *tele* long-distance telephone exchange.

über|la'ppen *r* to overlap; **-la'ssen** *irr tr* to let have; (*anheimstellen*) to leave (to); (*aufgeben*) to give up, to relinquish; (*abtreten*) to cede, to yield; (*verzichten*) to resign; (*verkaufen*) to sell; (*übertragen*) to transfer; (*anvertrauen*) to (en)trust; *r* to give o. s. up (to), to give way (to); **-la'ssung** *f* leaving; (*Abtretung*) cession, transfer; (*Übergabe*) surrender; (*Aufgabe*) abandonment; **-last** *f* overweight; *fig* molestation; **--'en** *tr* to overload, to overcharge; to operate above capacity; *fig* to overburden, to harass with overwork, *Am* to haze; **--'ung** *f* overload, overcharge; *fig* heavy load of work; **-lauf** *m tech* overflow; **-'laufen** *irr itr* to run over, to flow over; *mil* to desert; *parl* to rat, *eccl* to vert, *Am* to flop; *zum -- voll* chokeful, brimful; **--'** *tr -- sein* to be besieged by, to be deluged with, to be swamped; *jdn mit Besuchen* -- to pester s. o. with visits; *es überläuft mich* I am seized with, I am overcome with; *mir läuft die Galle* - I get boiling mad; *dieser Beruf ist* -- this profession is overcrowded; *es überläuft mich kalt* my flesh creeps; **-läufer** *m* deserter, runaway; *parl* turncoat, *Am* flopper; **-laut** *a* overloud; too noisy; *-- schreien* to clamo(u)r; **-le'ben** *tr* to survive;(*jdn*) to outlive; **--de(r)** *m* survivor; **--sgroß** *a* bigger than life-size; **-lebt** *a* disused; out of date; *sich -- haben* to be antiquated (*od* old-fashioned); **-le'gen** *itr* to reflect upon, to think over, to consider, *Am* to figure on; *reiflich* -- to consider well; *es sich anders* -- to change o.'s mind; **-'-** to lay over; **--'a** superior; prevalent; -- *sein* to be better than; to be more than a match for; *tu bloß nicht so --!* don't act so superior! *er ist allem weit* -- he is head and shoulders above the rest; **-le'genheit** *f* superiority; preponderance; **-legt** *a* considerate; *wohl* -- deliberate; **-le'gung** *f* reflection, consideration; *nach reiflicher* -- on mature deliberation; **-leiten** *tr* to lead over, to conduct over, to pass over; *tech* to convert from ... to; *fig* to form a transition; (*Blut*) to transfuse; **-le'sen** *irr tr* to read over, to peruse; to overlook; **-li'chten** *tr phot* to overexpose; **-lie'fern** *tr* to deliver; (*der Nachwelt*) to hand down, to transmit; *mil* to surrender; **-lie'ferung** *f* delivery; *mil* surrender; *fig* tradition; **-li'sten** *tr* to outwit, to dupe, *Am* to outsmart; **-li'stung** *f* outwitting.

über|ma'chen *tr* to send, to transmit; (*vermachen*) to bequeath; **-'macht** *f* predominance, superiority; superior force; **-mächtig** *a* predominant; too powerful, overwhelming; (*ausschlaggebend*) paramount; **-ma'chung** *f* remittance; **-'malen** *tr* to paint over; **--'** to paint out; **-mangansauer** *a* permanganate (of); **-ma'nnen** *tr* to overpower; **-maß** *n* excess; (*Überfluß*) profuseness; (*Maßlosigkeit*) immoderateness; (*Unmäßigkeit*) intemperance; *im* -- to excess, excessively; **-mäßig** *a* excessive, immoderate, to excess; (*ungeheuer*) exorbitant; **~mensch** *m* superman; **~~lich** *a* superhuman; **~mi'tteln** *tr* to transmit; to convey; **~mittlung** *f* transmission, forwarding; **~morgen** *adv* the day after to-morrow; **~mü'den** *tr* to overtire; **~mü'det** *a* overtired, tired out, fagged out, *Am fam* all-in; **~mü'dung** *f* over-fatigue; **~mut** *m* haughtiness, insolence; (*Überhebung*) presumption; (*Mutwille*) wantonness; (*Ausgelassenheit*) high spirits *pl*, frolicsomeness; **~'mütig** *a* in high spirits; (*Kind*) wild; (*mutwillig*) wanton; (*keck*) cocky; (*eingebildet*) presumptuous; (*anmaßend*) insolent.

über|nächst *a* the next but one; *~~e Woche* the week after next, the next week but one; *am ~~en Tage* the day after to-morrow; **~na'chten** *itr* to pass the night, to stay over night; **~nächtig** *a* seedy, blear-eyed; **~na'chtung** *f* spending the night; **~~sgeld** *n* night-lodging allowance; **~~sköfferchen** *n* overnighter; **~'nahme** *f* (*Amt*) taking over; (*Besitznahme*) taking possession of; (*Annahme*) acceptance; (*Arbeit*) undertaking, taking in hand; (*Verpflichtung*) assumption; *die ~~ e-s Amtes ablehnen* to decline an appointment; **~~bedingung** *f* condition of acceptance; **~~bericht** *m* taking-over report; **~~kommando** *n* taking-over detachment; **~~vertrag** *m* indenture of assumption; **~national** *a* supranational; **~natürlich** *a* supernatural; **~ne'hmen** *irr tr* to take over; (*Besitz ergreifen*) to seize, to take possession of; (*annehmen*) to accept, to receive; (*Amt*) to enter upon; to succeed to; (*Arbeit*) to undertake, to take over; (*Verantwortung*) to assume, to accept; (*Last*) to take upon o. s.; *ein Risiko ~~* to take a risk; *r* to overwork; (*Essen*) to overeat; **~ne'hmer** *m* (*Empfänger*) receiver; (*Unternehmer*) contractor; undertaker; (*Warensendung*) consignee; (*Wechsel*) acceptor; **~ordnen** *tr* to place over, to set over; **~parteilich** *a* non-partisan, impartial; **~pfla'nzen** *tr* to transplant; to plant (with); **~pi'nseln** *tr* to paint over, to daub over; **~planmäßig** *a* in excess of authorized strength (*od* allowance); **~preis** *m* excessive price; **~produktion** *f* over-production; surplus output; **~prü'fen** *tr* to reconsider, to check, to verify; (*Personen*) to screen, to vet; (*Bücher*) to audit, to examine; (*überarbeiten*) to revise; (*untersuchen*) to investigate; **~prü'fung** *f* checking, verification, *Am* check-up; (*Bücher*) auditing, examination; (*Überarbeitung*) revision; (*Untersuchung*) investigation; **~~sausschuß** *m* vetting panel, *Am* screening committee.

über|quer *adv* across, crossways; **~~'en** *tr* to cross, to traverse; (*unvorsichtig Straße*) *Am* to jaywalk; **~~ung** *f* march (over); (*Ozean*) crossing; **~ra'gen** *itr, tr* to surpass, to outstrip; (*höher sein*) to overtop; **~ra'schen** *tr* to surprise; to come upon; to astonish; **~~d** *a* surprising; **~ra'schung** *f* surprise; **~~sangriff** *m* surprise attack; *aero* hit-and-run attack; **~re'chnen** *tr* to count over, to calculate; **~re'den** *tr* to persuade to, to prevail on, to talk into: to argue into; *Am* to sell s. o. on s. th.; **~re'dend** *a* persuasive; **~re'dung** *f* persuasion; **~~sgabe** *f* power of persuasion, *Am* salesmanship; **~reich** *a* too rich; abounding (in), teeming (in); **~~lich** *a* superabundant; **~rei'chen** *tr* to hand over; to present; **~rei'chung** *f* presentation; delivery; **~reif** *a* over-ripe; **~rei'ten** *tr* to run down; (*Pferd*) to override; (*überholen*) to outride; **~rei'zen** *tr* to over-excite; (*Nerven*) to overstrain; **~rei'zung** *f* overexcitement, excess of irritation; **~re'nnen** *irr tr* to run over; to overrun; to outrun; to run down; **~rest** *m* remainder, remnant; remains *pl*; relics *pl*; scraps *pl*, leavings *pl*, leftover; (*Restbetrag, chem Rückstand*) residue; **~rock** *m* top-coat; overcoat; (*Gehrock*) frock-coat; **~ru'mpeln** *tr* to surprise, to take by surprise; **~ru'mpelung** *f* surprise; unexpected attack; **~ru'nden** *tr* to outrun, to overround; *das ganze Feld ~~* to overround the whole field.

über|sä'en *tr* to sow over; *fig* to dot (with), to strew (with); **~sä'ttigen** *chem* to supersaturate; *fig* to surfeit; **~sä'ttigung** *f chem* supersaturation; *fig* satiety; **~sä'uern** *tr* to overacidify; to peroxidize; **~schall** *m* ultrasound; (*in Zssg*) supersonic, ultrasonic; **~~geschwindigkeit** *f* supersonic speed; *Flugzeug mit ~~geschwindigkeit* supersonic plane, faster-than-sound aircraft; *ferngesteuertes Geschoß mit ~~geschwindigkeit* supersonic guided missile; **~~jagdflugzeug** *n* supersonic fighter; **~~rakete** *f* supersonic rocket; **~~raketenflugzeug** *n* supersonic rocket-propelled airplane; **~~raketenjäger** *m* supersonic rocket-propelled fighter; **~~windkanal** *m* supersonic wind canal, *Am* supersonic wind tunnel; **~scha'tten** *tr* to overshadow; *fig* to eclipse; **~schä'tzen** *tr* to overrate, to over-estimate; **~schä'tzung** *f* overrating, over-estimation; (*Selbsttäuschung*) self-conceit; **~schau'en** *tr* to overlook; to survey; **~schäumen** *itr* to foam over; to froth over; *fig* to be exuberant, to exuberate; **~schicht** *f* extra shift; *e-e ~~ machen* to work overtime; **~~'en** *tr* to stratify, to arrange in layers; **~schi'cken** *tr* to send, to consign to; **~schie'ßen** *irr tr* to shoot over; to fire beyond the target; *fig* to exceed; (*Ziel*) to overshoot; *~~der Betrag* surplus; **~schlächtig** *a* overshot; **~schla'fen** *irr tr* to sleep on s. th., to take pillow counsel; *~~ Sie die Sache!* sleep on it!; **~schlag** *m* calculation, estimate; (*Schneiderei*) facing; (*Purzelbaum*) somersault; *aero* (*beim Landen*) nose-over; ground loop; (*in der Luft*) loop; *el* flash-over, spark-over, *Am* arc-over; *tech* covering; *e-n ~~ machen* to make an estimate; *aero* to loop the loop; (*beim Landen*) to groundloop; **~~'en** *irr tr* to calculate roughly, to make a rough estimate; (*überlegen*) to consider; (*weglassen*) to omit, to pass over; (*umdrehen*) to turn over; (*Seite*) to skip; (*Wasser*) to become lukewarm, *~'~en* (*Beine*) to cross; *el* to flash-over, to spark-over; *tele* to drown (a sound); *r ~~'en* to tumble over (one another), *Am* to fall over (one another); to capsize; (*Purzelbaum*) to throw (*od* turn) a somersault; *aero* to nose over; to loop the loop; *a* lukewarm, tepid; **~~srechnung** *f* rough estimate; **~schmie'ren** *tr* to besmear; **~schnappen** *itr* (*Stimme*) to squeak; *fam fig* to go mad, to turn crazy; **~geschnappt** *a fam* cracked, crazy, insane; **~schnei'den** *irr tr, r* to overlap; to intersect; **~schnei'dung** *f* overlapping; (point of) intersection; **~schnell** *a* superfast; **~schrei'ben** *irr tr* (*beschriften*) to address, to direct, to superscribe; (*Vermerk, Etikett*) to docket, to label; (*mit Überschrift versehen*) to entitle, to head; (*übertragen*) to transfer, to convey; (*Bank*) to pass to (the account of); **~schrei'bung** *f* transfer; superscription; **~~surkunde** *f jur* deed of conveyance; **~schrei'en** *irr tr* to cry down; *r* to overstrain o.'s voice; **~schrei'ten** *irr tr* to cross, to overstep; (*guten Geschmack*) to transgress; (*Gesetz*) infringe; (*Maß*) to exceed; (*Kredit*) to overdraw (o.'s balance); **~schrei'tung** *f* crossing, overstepping; (*Norm*) exceeding; transgression, violation; **~schrift** *f* title; head(-ing); (*Kopfzeile*) headline, guide line; *fam* head; (*Anschrift*) address; *film* caption; **~schuhe** *m pl* overshoes *pl*: (*Gummi~~*) galoshes, rubbers, *Am* gums *pl*, arctics *pl*; **~schu'ldet** *a* deeply (involved) in debts; **~schu'ldung** *f* heavy indebtedness; **~schuß** *m* surplus, overplus, (*negativ*) surplusage; (*Übertrag*) carry-over; (*Mehrbetrag, math*) excess; (*Rest*) remainder; (*Saldo*) balance; (*Gewinn*) profit; (*Verdienstspanne*) margin; (*Restbetrag*) residue; *~~ abwerfen* to yield a profit; **~~gebiet** *n* surplus area; **~~produkte** *n pl* surplus products *pl*; **~schüssig** *a* surplus; remaining; excess, in excess; *~~er Gewinn* surplus profit; **~schü'tten** *tr* to cover (with); *fig* to overwhelm (with); (*Geschenke*) to shower (with); **~schwang** *m* rapture, exuberance, exaltation; **~schwe'mmen** *tr* to overflow, to submerge; to inundate, to flood, to swamp; (*Markt*) *com* to overstock, to glut; (*Angebote*) to deluge (with), *Am* to snow under (with); (*Briefe*) to swamp (with); **~schwe'mmung** *f* overflow; inundation; (*auch fig*) flood, spate, freshet; *com* overstocking, glut(ting); **~~sgebiet** *n* inundated area; flooded area; **~schwenglich** *a* enthusiastic; exuberant; (*verzückt*) rapturous; (*übertrieben*) extravagant; (*übermäßig*) excessive; (*schwärmerisch*) sentimental; (*Stil*) high-flown; *~~ reden* to rhapsodize (*über* on); **~~keit** *f* exuberance; extravagance; enthusiasm; **~schwer** *a* exceedingly heavy; very heavy.

Über|see *f* oversea(s *pl*); **~~bank** *f* overseas bank; **~~dampfer** *m* ocean liner, transoceanic steamer; **~~flugboot** *n* ocean-going flying boat; **~~flugzeug** *n* seagoing (*od* oversea) plane; **~~handel** *m* oversea(s) trade; **~~isch** *a* transoceanic, oversea(s); (*Lage*) transmarine; **~~kabel** *n* transmarine cable; **~~luftlinie** *f* overseas airline; **~~markt** *m* foreign market; **~~telegramm** *n* cablegram; **~~verbindung** *f tele* transoceanic communication; **~~verkehr** *m* transoceanic (*od* oversea) traffic; *drahtloser ~~verkehr* transoceanic radio service; **~se'geln** *tr* to sail over; (*überholen*) to beat; **~se'hbar** *a* visible at a glance; surveyable; **~se'hen** *irr tr* (*überblicken*) to overlook, to survey; (*nicht bemerken*) to overlook, not to notice, to miss; (*absichtlich*) to disregard, to neglect; *das kann ich noch nicht genau ~~* I can't tell yet exactly; **~selig** *a* overjoyful; blissful; **~se'nden** *irr tr* to send, to transmit, to forward, *com* to consign; (*Geld*) to remit (to); **~se'nder** *m* sender; **~se'ndung** *f* conveyance; transmission, forwarding, *com* consignment; (*Geld*) remittance; **~~skosten** *pl* expenses of transportation; **~se'tzbar** *a* translatable; **~'setzen** *itr* to pass over, to cross; *tr* to ferry over; *~~' tr* to translate (into); *tech* to gear; (*Farbe*) to top; (*Ofen, Preise*) to overcharge; **~se'tzer** *m* translator; *tele* decoder; **~se'tzt** *a* translated; (*Preis*) overcharged; **~se't-zung** *f* translation; *tech* gear, transmission; **~~sbüro** *n* translation-bureau; **~~sfehler** *m* wrong translation; **~~sverhältnis** *n tech* gear (*od* transmission) ratio; **~sicht** *f* (*Überblick*) survey, review; (*Auszug*) compend(ium) syllabus; (*Abriß*) abstract, epitome, abridg(e)ment; (*kurze Darlegung*) analysis; (*Zusammenfassung*) summary, digest, condensation, summing up; (*vergleichend*) synopsis; (*Umriß*) outline; (*Aufsicht*) control; (*Ausblick*) perspective; *jede ~~ verlieren* to lose all perspective; **~~ig** *a* farsighted, hyperopic; **~~igkeit** *f* farsightedness, hyperopia; **~~lich** *a* clear, distinct, clearly arranged; (*verständlich*) easily understandable, easily followed up; (*Gelände*) open; **~~lichkeit** *f* clearness; (*Stil*) lucidity; (*Geist*) perspicuity; **~~sbild** *n* general view; *aero phot* index map; **~~skarte** *f* large (*od* general) map; **~~splan** *m* general plan; **~~skizze** *f* general sketch; synoptical sketch; scheme; **~~stabelle** *f* synoptic table; tabular summary; **~~stafel** *f* synoptical table; **~siedeln** *itr* to (re)move (to); to emigrate; **~sied(e)lung** *f* removal; emigration; **~sinnlich** *a* transcendental; abstract; metaphysical; **~spa'nnen** *tr* to overstrain; to force; (*sich ausdehnen*) to stretch over; (*bedecken*) to cover, to spread over; (*Hand*) to span; (*übertreiben*) to exaggerate; (*übersteigen*) to overexcite; (*Phantasie*) to heat; **~spa'nnt** *a* eccentric; extravagant; (*gekünstelt*) *Am fam* arty; **~~heit** *f* eccentricity, extravagance; **~spa'nnung** *f* overstraining; *el* excess (*od* boosting) voltage; *fig* exaggeration; **~~ssicherung** *f el* excess voltage cutout; **~spie'len** *tr sport* (*umspielen*) to pass, to play over; (*überwinden*) to outnumber; **~spi'nnen** *irr tr* to spin over, to cover; **~spo'nnen** *a* covered; **~spi'tzen** *tr* to exaggerate; **~spi'tzt** *fig* too subtle; exaggerated; **~spre'chen** *irr tr radio* to crosstalk; **~'springen** *irr itr el* to flash-over (*od* across); **~~'** *tr* (*Graben*) to leap over, to jump across; (*auslassen*) to skip, to omit; **~'spritzen** *itr* to spurt over; **~~'** *tr* to spray; **~sprudeln** *itr* to bubble (over), to gush (over); **~~d** *a* overflowing; *fig* exuberant.

über|staatlich *a* cosmopolitical; **~ste'chen** *tr* to overtrump; **~'stehen** *itr* to jut out, to project; **~~'** *tr* (*überwinden*) to overcome; (*erdulden*) to endure; (*überleben*) to survive, to get over; (*Operation*) to come (*od* to pull) through, *Am* to get around; **~'steigen** *irr itr* to step over; **~~'** *tr* to surmount; to surpass; (*hinausgehen*) to exceed; (*Berg*) to cross, to pass; (*Schwierigkeit*) to overcome; *Erwartungen ~~* to exceed o.'s expectations; **~stei'gern** *tr* (*Auktion*) to overbid, to outbid; (*in die Höhe treiben*) to force up; **~steu'ern** *tr* to override; to overmodulate; **~steu'erung** *f* overmodulation; *radio* overloading; (*Mikrophon*) blasting; **~sti'mmen** *tr* to outvote, to vote down, to overrule, to defeat (by a majority of); **~stra'hlen** *tr* to shine upon; (*verdunkeln*) to outshine, to eclipse; to surpass in splendo(u)r; **~strei'chen** *irr tr* to spread over; to paint over; **~'streifen** *tr* to put on; (*Ärmel*) to draw over; to slip over; **~streu'en** *tr* to strew over; **~'strömen** *itr* to overflow (with), to abound; **~~'** *tr* to inundate, to flood, to deluge; **~'stülpen** *tr* to put on, to tilt over, to cover over; **~stunden** *f pl* overtime (hours); *~~ machen* to work overtime; **~~vergütung** *f* extra duty allowance; **~stü'rzen** *tr* to hurry, to precipitate, to rush; *r* to rush (o. s.), to be in too big a hurry; to act rashly; (*Ereignisse*) to press upon each other; **~stü'rzt** *a* hasty, precipitate; **~stü'rzung** *f* precipitation; precipitancy; *nur keine ~~!* don't hurry!; take it easy! **~'süß** *a* too sweet; luscious.

über|täu'ben *tr* to deafen; (*Laut*) to drown; (*unterdrücken*) to stifle; **~teu'ern** *tr* to overcharge, *Am sl* to sting; **~teu'erung** *f* overcharge; **~tö'lpeln** *tr* to cheat, to dupe, to take in, to impose (upon); **~tö'nen** *tr* to drown; *alles ~~* (*Am*) to beat the band; **~'trag** *m* carrying over; (*Summe*) sum carried forward; (*Umbuchung*) transfer; (*Saldo*) balance; **~tra'gbar** *a* transferable, alienable, assignable; (*begebbar*) negotiable; (*indossierbar*) endorsable; (*übersetzbar*) translatable; (*Stenogramm*) transcribable; *med* infectious, contagious, catching; **~~'keit** *f* transferability; negotiability; **~tra'gen** *irr tr* (*befördern*) to transport; (*Hauptbuch*) to carry over, to bring forward; (*eintragen*) to enter; (*auf e-n Namen*) to register in (s. o.'s name); (*Besitz*) to transfer, to give up (to); (*abtreten*) to convey, to assign, to alienate; (*Geld*) to transfer; (*Vollmacht*) to delegate; (*Rechte*) to vest (in s. o.); (*Amt*) to confer; (*Patent*) to assign; (*Arbeit*) to entrust (with); (*Besorgung*) to charge; (*Titel*) to transmit; *radio* to broadcast, to transmit, (*mit Relais*) to relay; (*abschreiben*) to copy; (*Kurzschrift*) to transcribe, to transliterate; (*Sprache*) to translate, to put into; *med* to spread, to infect (with), to transmit, to communicate, to carry; *a* figurative, metaphorical; **~tra'gung** *f* (*Buchung*) transfer; carrying over; (*Eigentum*) transfer, transference, conveyance; (*Abtretung*) transfer, alienation, assignment, conveyance, cession; (*Vollmacht*) delegation; (*Amt*) conferring; (*Auftrag*) charging; *radio* transmission, broadcast; relay(ing); (*Abschrift*) copy; (*Kurzschrift*) transcription; (*Sprache*) translation, version; *med* infection, transmission, spreading; **~~sapparat** *m* broadcasting apparatus; **~~sbeleg** *m* transfer voucher; **~~serklärung** *f jur* deed of transfer; **~~sfunkstelle** *f* relay station; **~~sgüte** *f* transmission performance; **~~sleitung** *f* transmission line; **~~sraum** *m radio* studio; **~~surkunde** *f* deed of transfer; **~~sverfügung** *f* vesting order; **~~svermerk** *m* endorsement; **~~swagen** *m radio* mobile transmission van; **~~sweg** *m* channel; **~tre'ffen** *irr tr* to surpass, to excel, to top, to exceed, *fam* to beat, *Am fam* to take the cake; (*in der Leistung*) to outperform; *Erwartungen ~~* to exceed expectations; *das übertrifft alles* that beats all; **~trei'ben** *irr tr* to exaggerate; (*zu weit treiben*) to overdo; (*überschätzen*) to overestimate; (*stark auftragen*) to trowel; **~trei'bung** *f* exaggeration, excess; overstatement; **~tre'ten** *irr tr* to break, to violate; (*Besitz*) to trespass on (*od* against); (*Gesetz*) to act in contravention of; to trespass on (*od* against); to offend (against); (*Rechte*) to infringe on, to violate, to transgress, (*Sitte*) to offend (against); **~'~** *itr* to step over; (*austreten*) to overflow; (*Grenze*) to cross; (*zu e-r Partei*) to go over (to), to change over (to); (*Glauben*) to change; (*Fuß*) to sprain (o.'s ankle); *zum Protestantismus ~'~* to turn Protestant; **~tre'ter** *m* transgressor, trespasser, offender; **~tre'tung** *f* transgression, violation, contravention; (*Patent*) infringement; (*Übergriff*) encroachment; infringement; **~trie'ben** *a* exaggerated, magnified, piled up; (*Handlung*) overdone, overwrought; (*Preis*) excessive, exorbitant; (*überspannt*) extravagant; (*äußerst*) extreme; (*überschätzt*) overestimated, overstated; (*Rede*) hyperbolical; excessive, exaggerated; **~tritt** *m* going over; change (of religion); conversion; (*Partei*) joining; **~tru'mpfen** *tr* to overtrump; *fig* to outdo; **~tü'nchen** *tr* to whitewash; *fig* to gloss over.

übervö'l|kern *tr* to overpopulate; **~vö'lkerung** *f* overpopulation; **~voll** *a* too full; brimful; crowded; **~vor'teilen** *tr* to take advantage of, to overreach, to impose upon, *fam* to take in, to steal a march on, to palm off on; (*täuschen*) to deceive, *Am sl* to sting; (*betrügen*) to cheat, to defraud, to trick, to gull, to hoax, *Am sl* to hornswoggle.

über|wa'chen *tr* to watch over; to superintend, to supervise; (*kontrollieren*) to control; to inspect; to check; *radio* to monitor; (*beobachten*) to shadow; (*bewachen*) to guard; **~wa'chsen** *irr tr* to overgrow; **~wa'chung** *f* superintendence; inspection; supervision; control; **~~'sausschuß** *m* supervisory committee, *Am* vigilance committee; **~~'sbezirk** *m* observation area; **~~'sdienst** *m* investigation service; **~~'sflugzeug** *n* patrol aircraft; **~~'sliste** *f* check list; control roster; **~~'sstelle** *f* control office; **~wallen** *itr* to boil over; *fig* to effervesce, to run over; **~wä'ltigen** *tr* to overcome, to overpower, to subdue, to conquer; *fig* to overwhelm; **~~d** *a* stunning, imposing; **~wä'ltigung** *f* overpowering; conquering; subjugation, overwhelming; **~wasserfahrzeug** *n* surface craft; **~wasserstreitkräfte** *f pl* surface forces *pl*; **~wei'sen** *irr tr* to assign; to transfer; (*zur Entscheidung*) to refer to; (*Kommission*) to devolve (upon); (*Bank*) to remit, to transfer; (*Post*) to transmit; *telegraphisch ~~* to cable, to wire; **~wei'sung** *f* (*Geld*) remittance; (*Post*) transmission; (*Eigentum*) transfer, assignment; *jur* change of venue; *parl* devolution; (*Zuweisung*) assignment; **~~sabschnitt** *m* postal cheque; **~~sauftrag** *m* remittance order; **~~sformular** *n* transfer form; **~~sscheck** *m* transfer check (*od* ticket); **~wei'ßen** *tr* to whitewash; **~weltlich** *a* ultramundane; **~wendlich** *a* whipped; *~~ nähen* to whip, to oversew; *~~e Naht* overhand seam; **~'werfen** *irr tr* to throw over; (*Kleidungsstück*) to slip on, (*schnell*) to huddle on; **~~'** *r* to fall out (with), to quarrel; **~wie'gen** *irr itr* (*den Sieg davontragen*) to prevail (*über* over); (*Vorteil*) to outweigh; (*Gewinn*) to overbalance; (*Einfluß*) to preponderate, to predominate; **~'~** *itr* to have overweight; **~~d** *a* preponderant, dominant; *adv* (*hauptsächlich*) chiefly, mainly; *~~de Mehrheit* overwhelming (*od* clear) majority; **~wi'nden** *irr tr* to conquer, to subdue; (*Schwierigkeiten*) to overcome; *r* (*sich dahin bringen*) to bring o. s. (to); (*Leidenschaften*) to overcome o. s., to carry a victory over o. s.; *ein ~wundener Standpunkt* an out-of-date view; **~wi'nder** *m* conqueror; **~wi'ndlich** *a* conquerable; surmountable; **~wi'ndung** *f* conquest; overcoming; surmounting; (*Wider-*

streben) reluctance; (*Anstrengung*) effort; (*Selbst*~~) self-command, self-control; *es gehört viel* ~~ *dazu* it requires great self-restraint; *das hat mich* ~~ *gekostet* it cost me an effort; ~**wi'ntern** *itr* to winter (at); (*Tiere*) to hibernate; *tr* to winter; ~**wi'nterung** *f* hibernation; ~**wö'lben** *tr* to overarch; to vault over; ~**wu'chern** *tr* to overgrow, to overrun; (*ersticken*) to choke (up); *fig* to stifle; *itr* to grow luxuriantly; to teem; ~**wurf** *m* wrapper, shawl; *tech* (*Schloß*) hasp; ~~**mutter** *f* screw cap; clamping nut; ~~**ring** *m* screw collar ring.

Über|zahl *f* numerical superiority; (*Mehrheit*) majority; (*Übermacht*) odds *pl*; *mil* superior forces *pl*; ~**zä'hlen** *tr* to count over; ~**zählig** *a* supernumerary, surplus; (*über e-e runde Zahl*) odd; ~**zahn** *m* projecting tooth; ~**zei'chnen** *tr* to oversubscribe; ~**zeu'gen** *tr* to convince of; (*überreden*) to persuade, to induce (to), to prevail (up)on; (*zufriedenstellen*) to satisfy (of); *r* to be convinced (*od* satisfied) of; to ascertain s. th.; ~~ *Sie sich selbst davon* go and see for yourself; ~~**d** *a* convincing; carrying conviction; persuasive; (*durchschlagend*) telling; (*zwingend*) cogent; (*wohlbegründet*) valid; (*stichhaltig*) sound; (*entscheidend*) conclusive; ~**zeu'gt** *a* convinced, positive; ~~ *sein* to feel sure of, to be satisfied that; ~**zeu'gung** *f* conviction; (*feste Überzeugung*) certainty (of, that); (*Zuversicht*) assurance; (*innere Sicherheit*) certitude; (*fester Glaube*) belief, persuasion; (*Schlußfolgerung*) conclusion; *es ist meine feste* ~~ it's my firm conviction; *der* ~~ *sein* to be convinced; ~~**skraft** *f* persuasive power; ~**zie'hen** *irr tr* to cover (with), to put over; (*Farbe*) to coat; (*Konto*) to overdraw; *aero* to stall; to fly nose high; (*füttern*) to line; (*Metall*) to plate; to overlay; (*Schmutz*) to incrust, to encrust; *ein Bett* ~~ to put fresh sheets on a bed; *mit Krieg* ~~ to invade with war; *r* (*Wetter*) to become overcast; ~'~ *tr* to draw over, to cover (with); to put on; to pull over; ~'**zieher** *m* overcoat; greatcoat; (*loser, leichter*) topcoat; *Am* duster; ~'**ziehhose** *f* overalls *pl*; ~'**zoll** *m* surtax; ~**zu'ckern** *tr* to sugar over; (*Kuchen*) to ice; (*Früchte*) to candy; (*Pille*) to gild; ~**zug** *m* (*Schicht*) coat (-ing); film; (*Decke*) covering, cover; (*Hülle*) case; (*Kissen*) slip, case; (*Bett*) bed-tick; (*Plattierung*) plating; (*Kruste*) crust; (*Belag, Kesselstein*) incrustation; (*Schale, Rinde, Holz-, Eisenbekleidung*) skin; (*Anzugbesatz*) lining; (*Reifen*) cover, *Am* casing; ~**zwe'rch** *a* across, athwart.

üblich *a* customary, usual, in use; common, normal; conventional, ordinary; ~*er Art* standard make; ~*e Größe* standard size; *nicht* ~ unusual; *nicht mehr* ~ out of fashion, out of use, obsolete.

U-Boot *n* submarine; U-boat; *fam* sub, *Am sl* pigboat; ~**abwehr** *f* anti-submarine defence; ~**bunker** *m* submarine pen; ~**falle** *f* Q-ship, decoy; ~**jäger** *m* submarine chaser, corvette, *Am* subchaser; *aero* anti-submarine aircraft, *Am sl* sub hunter (*od* killer); (*Überwacher*) patrol craft (*Abk* PC.); ~**krieg** *m* submarine warfare; ~**ortungsgerät** *n* detecting gear, asdic; *Am* sonar; ~**rudel** *n* submarine pack; ~**schutz** *m* anti-submarine defence; ~~**geleit** *n* anti-submarine convoy; ~**stützpunkt** *m* submarine base.

übrig *a* left (over), remaining, rest of; (*überflüssig*) superfluous; (*über e-e Zahl hinaus*) odd; *das* ~*e* the remainder; *ein* ~*es tun* to stretch a point; *die* ~*en* the others, the rest; *im* ~*en* otherwise; ~**behalten** *irr tr* to keep, to spare; ~**bleiben** *irr tr* to be left (over); *es bleibt ihm nichts anderes* ~ he has no other choice; ~**ens** *adv* moreover, besides; (*jedoch*) however; (*bei alldem*) after all; (*nebenbei*) by the way; ~**haben** *irr tr* to have ... left, to have ... to spare; *nichts* ~~ *für* to have no use for; to care little for, to think little of; *für jdn ein paar Minuten* ~~ to spare s. o. a few minutes; ~**lassen** *irr tr* to leave (over); *zu wünschen* ~~ to leave much to be desired; ~**sein** *irr itr* to be left.

Übung *f* exercise; (*Gewohnheit*) use; *mil* drilling, training; dry run; *mus* study, exercise; (*praktische Ausübung*) practice; (*Gewandtheit*) dexterity; (*üblicher Gang*) routine; ~ *macht den Meister* practice makes perfect; *in der* ~ *bleiben* to keep in training, to keep o.'s hand in; *aus der* ~ out of practice; ~**saufgabe** *f* exercise; ~**sbeispiel** *n* paradigm; ~**sbuch** *n* exercise-book, *Am* composition book; ~**sflug** *m* practice flight; ~~**platz** *m* training airport (*od* field); ~~**zeug** *n* trainer, training plane; ~**sgelände** *n* training ground; (*für Bomben*) target area; ~**sgeschwader** *n* manœuvring squadron; ~**shandgranate** *f* practice hand grenade; ~**shang** *m* (*Ski*) nursery slope; ~**sheft** *n* exercise-book, *Am* composition book; ~**skurs** *m* refresher course; ~**slager** *n* training camp; ~**smarsch** *m* training-march; military march; ~**smunition** *f* practice (*od* training) ammunition; ~**sschießen** *n* practice firing; ~**ssegelflugzeug** *n* training glider; ~**splatz** *m* drill-ground.

Ufer *n* (*Fluß*~) bank; (*See*~) shore, beach; *am* ~ ashore; (~*einfassung*) embankment; ~**bewohner** *m* riparian; ~**böschung** *f*, ~**damm** *m*, ~**mauer** *f* embankment, quay; slope of river banks; ~**gelände** *n* riparian state; ~**linie** *f* shore line; (*Fluß*) bank line; ~**los** *a fig* (*grenzenlos*) boundless, limitless; (*überspannt*) extravagant; (*maßlos*) immoderate; ~**schutzbauten** *pl* (*Fluß*) embankment; (*Meer*) dikes *pl*; ~**staat** *m* riparian state; ~**strömung** *f* littoral current, coastal stream.

Uhr *f* clock; (*Taschen*~) watch; (*Stutz*~) timepiece; (*Schiffs*~) chronometer; (*Armband*~) wrist-watch; (*Wekker*) alarm-clock; (*Sand*~) sand glass; (*Stopp*~) stop watch; (*Sonnen*~) sun dial; (*Zeit*) time; (*allg*) time indicator; *wieviel* ~ *ist es?* what time is it? *um wieviel* ~? at what time? *es ist halb drei* (~) it's half past two; *um 12* ~ at twelve o'clock, at noon; *die* ~ *ist abgelaufen* the clock (*od* watch) has run down; *die* ~ *aufziehen* to wind up the watch; *meine* ~ *geht vor* (*nach*) my watch is fast (slow); my watch is gaining (losing) time; *die* ~ *stellen nach* ... to regulate (*od* to set) the watch by ...; *meine* ~ *geht genau* my watch keeps exact time; *nach meiner* ~ by my watch; ~**armband** *n* (wrist-) watch band; strap (*od* cord *od* link *od* expansion) band; (*Damen*~~) cord and snake chain band; ~**dekkel** *m* watch-cap; ~**enfabrik** *f* watch-manufactory; ~**enhandel** *m* trade in clocks and watches; ~**engeschäft** *n* watchmaker's shop; ~**enindustrie** *f* watch-and clock-making industry; ~**feder** *f* watch spring; ~**gehänge** *n* trinkets *pl*; ~**gehäuse** *n* clock-case; ~**getriebe** *n* pinion of a watch; ~**gewicht** *n* clock-weight; ~**glas** *n* clock- (*od* watch-) glass, *Am* (watch-) crystal; ~**kette** *f* watch-chain, watch-guard; ~**macher** *m* watchmaker; ~**werk** *n* clockwork; works *pl* of a watch; ~**zeiger** *m* hand; ~~**sinn** *m* clockwise direction; *im entgegengesetzten* ~~*sinn* counter-clockwise; ~**zeit** *f* (*gesetzliche*) legal time; ~~**angabe** *f* time announcement.

Uhu *m* eagle-owl.

Ukrain|e *f* Ukraine; (*offiziell*) Ukrainian Soviet Socialist Republic; ~**er** *m*, ~**isch** *a* Ukrainian.

Ulan *m* u(h)lan, lancer.

Ulk *m* fun, joke, lark, spree, hoax; ~**en** *itr* to make fun, to lark; ~**ig** *a* funny, amusing; (*seltsam*) strange, curious.

Ulme *f*, ~**nbaum** *m* elm(-tree).

Ultimo *m* last day (*od* end) of the month; ~**abschluß** *m* monthly settlement; ~**bedarf** *m* monthly requirements *pl*; ~**fälligkeiten** *f pl* maturities *pl* of the end of the month.

Ultra|kurzwelle *f* (*UKW*) ultra-short wave; ~~**nempfänger** *m* ultrahigh-frequency receiver; ~~**ngerät** *n* ultrashort-wave apparatus; ~~**nsender** *m* ultra-short-wave transmitter; ~~**nsuchgerät** *n* radar; ~~**nteil** *m* ultrashort-wave part; ~~**nübertragung** *f* ultrasbort-wave transmission; ~**marin** *a* ultramarine; ~**mikroskopisch** *a* ultra-microscopic; ~**montan** *a* ultramontane; ~**nuklear** *a* ultranuclear; ~**rot** *a* ultra-red, infrared; ~~**abtaster** *m* noctovisor scan; ~~**undurchlässig** *a* opaque to infrared; ~**schall** *m* ultrasonics *pl mit sing*; ~~**frequenz** *f* supersonic frequency; ~~**welle** *f* supersonic wave; ~**violett** *a* ultra-violet; ~~*e Strahlen* ultra-violet rays; ~~**bestrahlung** *f* treatment by ultra-violet radiation.

um *prep* (*räumlich*) round, (*unbestimmter*) around, about; ~ *e-n Garten* around a garden; ~ *die Ecke kommen* to come round the corner; ~ *die Welt reisen* to travel round the world; *die Erde dreht sich* ~ *die Sonne* the earth goes round the sun; ~ *e-n Tisch sitzen* to sit round a table; *er wickelte die Decke* ~ *sich herum* he wrapped the blanket around him; *besorgt sein* ~ to feel anxious about; *unbekümmert sein* ~ to be careless about; *sich ängstigen* ~ to be worried about; (*Maßangaben*) at, for, by, toward(s), about; *sich* ~ *6 Uhr treffen* to meet at six (o'clock); ~ *jeden Preis* at any rate; at any cost; ~ *keinen Preis* not at any price; *verkaufen* ~ to sell for; *kaufen* ~ to buy for; *eintauschen* ~ to change for; *ich würde es nicht* ~ *alles in der Welt tun* I would not do it for anything in the world; *er sollte* ~ *diese Zeit hier sein* he ought to be here by this time; ~ *e-n Kopf größer* taller by a head; *der Stein hätte mich* ~ *ein Haar getroffen* the stone missed me by a hair; *etwa* ~ *6 Uhr* towards six; ~ *Mitternacht* about midnight; ~ *die Hälfte mehr* half as much again; ~ *ein Jahr älter* a year older; ~ *so besser* so much the better, all the better; ~ *so weniger* all the fewer, all the less; (*Grund*) because of, for, on account of, for the sake of; ~ *des lieben Friedens willen* for the sake of peace; ~ *Himmels willen* for heaven's sake; *darf ich Sie* ~ *ein Zündholz bitten?* may I trouble you for a match? ~ *die Wette laufen* to race s. o.; *ich beneide sie* ~ *ihren Erfolg* I envy them their success; *schade* ~ *ihn!* I'm very sorry for him!

wie steht es ~ die Sache? what about it? *ich bitte ~ Entschuldigung* I beg your pardon; *ich bitte ~s Wort!* may I have the floor? *Tag ~ Tag* every day; *Jahr ~ Jahr* year after year; *e-n Tag ~ den andern* every other day; *e-r ~ den andern* one after another, every other; *Stück ~ Stück* piece by piece; *je länger ich sie kenne, ~ so weniger verstehe ich sie* the longer I know her the less I understand her; *conj* (in order) to; *~ den Zug zu erreichen, beeilte er sich mit seiner Arbeit* in order to catch the train, he hurried through his work; *ich brauche mehr Leute, ~ rechtzeitig fertig zu werden* I need more people in order to finish in time; *adv deine Zeit ist ~* your time is up; *~ und ~* round about; from (*od* on) all sides; *~ sein* to be over, to expire, to be gone.

um|ackern *tr* to plough up; **~adressieren** *tr* to redirect; **~ändern** *tr* to change, to alter; to modify; (*Gesetzentwurf*) to amend; **~änderung** *f* change, alteration; conversion; (*geringfügige*) modification; (*Abänderungsantrag*) amendment; **~arbeiten** *tr* to work over; (*Metall, Satz*) to recast; (*Meinung, Buch*) to revise; (*Schriftstück*) to rewrite; (*erweitern*) to work up; (*Haus, Kleid*) to remodel; (*berichtigen*) to correct, to rectify, to emend; (*verbessern*) to improve, to better, to ameliorate; **~arbeitung** *f* working over; recast(ing); revision; remodelling; correction; improvement; **~a'rmen** *tr* to embrace, to hug; **~a'rmung** *f* embrace, hug.

Um|bau *m* (*neu*) rebuilding, reconstruction; (*Umgestaltung*) remodelling; (*Änderungen*) alterations *pl*; (*Verwaltung*) reorganization, reform; **~~en** *tr* to rebuild, to reconstruct; to reorganize, to reform; to remodel; to make alterations (in); **~~'** (*herumbauen*) to build round; **~behalten** *irr tr* to keep on; **~besetzen** *tr theat* to recast; (*Posten*) to reshuffle, *Am* to cause a shake-up; **~besetzung** *f* reshuffle, shake-up; change; **~betten** *tr* to put into another bed; **~biegen** *irr tr* to bend; to turn up (*od* down *od* back); to deflect; to camber; **~bilden** *tr* (*umwandeln*) to transform; (*neu gestalten*) to remodel; (*wieder aufbauen*) to reconstruct; (*Verwaltung*) to reorganize, to reform; (*Regierung*) to reshuffle; **~bildung** *f* transformation; remodelling; reconstruction; reorganization, reform; reshuffle, *Am* shake-up; **~'binden** *irr tr* to put on; to tie round; (*Buch*) to rebind; **~~'** to bind round; **~blasen** *irr tr* to blow down (*od* over); **~blättern** *tr, itr* to turn over (a leaf), *Am* to leaf; **~blick** *m* panorama; survey; (*Rückblick*) look back; **~~en** *r* to look round; to look about; **~bö'rdeln** *tr* to turn over; *tech* to flange, to bead; **~'brechen** *irr tr* to break down; (*Feld*) to plough up, to break up; **~~'** *typ* to make up (into pages); **~bringen** *irr tr* to kill, to slay, to murder, to destroy, to liquidate, *fam* to do for, *Am sl* to take for a ride, to bump off; *ich hätte ihn ~~ können* I could have killed him; **~bruch** *m* revolutionary change, change-over; *Am parl* landslide; *typ* making up into pages; page-proof; (*Zeitung*) makeup; **~~redakteur** *m Am* makeup-man; **~buchen** *tr* to effect a transfer; **~buchung** *f* transfer in the books.

um|dä'mmen *tr* to embank; to surround with dikes; **~decken** *tr* to cover again; (*Tisch*) to lay the table again; (*Dach*) to re-tile; **~deuten** *tr* to give a new interpretation; (*falsch*) to misinterpret; **~dichten** *tr* (*Gedicht*) to recast, to remodel; **~disponieren** *tr* to re-arrange; **~drä'ngen** *tr* to throng, to press; **~drehbar** *a* reversible, rotatable; **~drehen** *tr* to turn round; (*Hals*) to wring; (*Worte*) to twist around; *r* to turn (a)round, to rotate, to revolve, to twirl, to twist, to spin, to whirl; *den Spieß ~~* to turn the tables (upon), *Am* to get back (at); **~drehung** *f* turn(ing round); *phys* rotation; revolution; *mot fam* rev; (*Kreisbewegung*) circuit; **~~sachse** *f* axis of rotation (*od* revolution); **~~sbewegung** *f* rotatory motion; **~~sgeschwindigkeit** *f* speed of rotation; **~~szahl** *f* number of revolutions; *die ~~szahl erhöhen mot fam* to rev up; **~~szähler** *m* revolution counter; **~druck** *m typ* transfer; reprint; **~~en** *tr* to reprint; **~~farbe** *f* reprinting ink; **~~papier** *n* transfer paper; **~dü'stern** *tr* to darken, to cloud, to overshadow; **~dü'stert** *a* dark, gloomy; **~einander** *adv* round each other; **~erziehen** *tr* to re-educate; **~erziehung** *f* re-education.

um|fa'hren *tr* to drive round; *mar* to sail round; (*Kap*) to double; (*Welt*) to circumnavigate; **~'~** to run down; *itr* to take the round-about way; **~fahrt** *f* circular tour (of), circuit; circumnavigation; doubling; **~fall** *m* fall, tumble; (*Meinung*) sudden change of opinion; **~~en** *irr itr* to fall down (*od Am* over), to tumble, to drop, *fam* to keel over; (*nachgeben*) to give in (*od* way); *parl* to change sides; *ich könnte vor Müdigkeit ~~* I am so tired I could drop; **~fang** *m* (*Kreis*) circumference, circuit; (*Umkreis*) periphery, perimeter; (*Bereich*) radius, range, compass, sphere; (*Ausmaß, Ausdehnung*) extent; (*Spielraum*) scope; (*Größe*) size; (*stattliche Größe, Bedeutung*) magnitude; (*Stimme, Geschäft*) volume; (*Masse*) bulk; (*Maßstab*) scale; (*Ausmaß*) proportion; (*Fassungsvermögen*) capacity, volume, bulk; (*Leibes~~*) girth; (*mus*) diapason, volume, range; **~~'en** *irr tr* to encircle; to surround; (*umarmen*) to embrace; **~fänglich, ~fangreich** *a* extensive; (*umfassend*) comprehensive; (*ausgedehnt, groß*) voluminous, bulky; (*geräumig*) spacious; **~färben** *tr* to redye; **~fa'ssen** *tr* (*einfassen, umringen*) to enclose, to surround; *mil* to outflank, to envelop; (*einschließen*) to comprise, to comprehend, to include; (*umklammern*) to clasp; (*umschließen, in sich begreifen*) to embrace; (*umspannen*) to span; **~end** *a* comprehensive; extensive; (*mit größter Stärke*) all-out; (*vollständig*) complete, full; overall; (*weitreichend*) far-reaching; **~fa'ssung** *f* embrace; (*Fassungskraft*) grasp; (*Griff*) grip; (*Einfriedigung*) enclosure; *mil* envelopment, surrounding; **~~sbewegung** *f mil* outflanking movement; **~~smauer** *f* enclosure-wall, outerwall; **~~soperation** *f mar* investment; **~fla'ttern** *tr* to flutter around; **~fle'chten** *irr tr* to twist about; to plait round; **~flie'gen** *irr tr* to fly round; **~'~** *itr fam* to fall over; (*Umweg*) to fly a round-about way; (*zerstören*) to destroy by flying against; **~flie'ßen** *irr, ~flu'ten tr* to flow round; *von Licht ~flossen* in a blaze of light; **~flort** *a* (*Stimme*) muffled; (*tränenerstickt*) dim; **~formen** *tr* to remodel, to transform, to recast; *el* to transform, to convert; (*umgestalten*) to reform; **~former** *m el* converter, transformer; **~~anlage** *f* conversion plant; **~~satz** *m* motor generator; converter unit; **~~werk** *n* rotary substation; **~formung** *f* transformation; conversion (into); change; reform; modification; remodel(l)ing; **~~sverhältnis** *n* transformation ratio; **~frage** *f* inquiry (round); (*zur Erforschung der öffentlichen Meinung*) poll; **~frie'digen** *tr* to fence in; to enclosure; **~füllen** *tr* to transfuse, to decant.

Um|gang *m* (*Windung*) convolution; (*Drehung*) rotation, turn, round, circuit; (*feierlicher*) procession; *fig* acquaintance; (*Verkehr*) intercourse; relations *pl* with, association; (*Chor~~*) ambulatory; (*Verhalten*) deportment, treatment; **~~sformen** *f pl* manners *pl*; **~~ssprache** *f* colloquial speech; **~gänglich** *a* sociable, companionable; (*lustig*) jolly; **~~keit** *f* sociableness, affability; **~ga'rnen** *tr* to ensnare, to trap, to enmesh; **~gau'keln** *tr* to flit around, to hover around, to dance around; **~ge'ben** *irr tr* to surround; **~'~** *tr* to put round; **~ge'bung** *f* surroundings *pl*; environs *pl*; (*Nachbarschaft*) neighbo(u)rhood; (*Gesellschaft*) company, society, associates *pl*; (*Milieu*) environment; (*Hintergrund*) background; **~gegend** *f* environs *pl*, vicinity, neighbo(u)rhood; **~'gehen** *irr itr* (*e-n Umweg machen*) to go a round-about way, to make a detour (*od* by-pass); (*sich im Kreis bewegen*) to circulate; (*beschäftigt sein*) to work, to be occupied (with); (*planen*) to intend, to plan, to contemplate; (*Sache, Personen*) to deal with, to manage, to handle; (*mit jdm*) to associate (with); (*Geister*) to haunt; *mit dem Gedanken ~~* to be thinking of; *mit jdm hart ~~* to treat s. o. harshly; **~~'** *tr* to go round; *mil* to outflank, to turn (a position); *jur* to evade; (*Verordnung*) to circumvent; (*Hindernis*) to by-pass; (*Steuer*) to dodge, to evade; (*entkommen*) to elude, to slip away from; (*vermeiden*) to evade; **~'gehend** *a* by return of post; **~ge'hung** *f* circuit; flank-movement, flanking manoeuvre; (*Straße*) detouring, by-passing; *fig* elusion; *jur* evasion; **~~sbewegung** *f* flanking movement; **~~sstraße** *f* by-pass; (*Umleitung*) detour.

um|gekehrt *a* inverted; opposite; reverse; contrary; *~~!* just the reverse! the other way round! *adv* on the contrary; vice versa; *~~ proportional* inversely proportional; *~~es Verhältnis* inverse ratio; **~gestalten** *tr* to transform, to alter, to modify; (*Verwaltung*) to reorganize; (*verbessern*) to reform; *tech* to recast, to remodel; **~gestülpt** *a* overturned, inverted; **~gießen** *irr tr* (*Flüssigkeit*) to decant; (*Metall*) to recast; **~gi't-tern** *tr* to surround with a railing; **~gliedern** *tr* to reorganize; **~gliederung** *f* reorganization; regrouping, redistribution of forces; **~graben** *irr tr* to dig up; (*Boden*) to break up; **~gre'nzen** *tr* to bound, to encircle, to enclose; (*einfrieden*) to fence; (*begrenzen*) to limit, to circumscribe; **~grenzung** *f* boundary; *fig* definition; **~~slinie** *f* boundary line; contour; circumferential line; **~gruppieren** *tr* to shift, to regroup, to reshape; (*neu verteilen*) to redistribute; **~gruppierung** *f* regrouping, shifting, *Am* shake-up; **~gucken** *itr fam* to look about; **~gü'rten** *tr* to gird (about); (*Schwert*) to buckle on; (*umgeben*) to encircle, to surround; **~guß**

m (*Übertragung*) transfusion; (*Flüssigkeit*) decantation; (*Umformung*, *Metall*) recast.

um|haben *irr tr* to have on; **~hacken** *tr* to hoe up; **~ha'lsen** *tr* to hug, to embrace; **~hang** *m* wrap, cape; shawl; **~hängen** *irr tr* to hang in another place; **~~** (*anziehen*) to put on; (*Gewehr*) to sling; (*Gepäck*) to take up; **~hängeriemen** *m* shoulder strap; **~hängetasche** *f* shoulder-bag; **~hauen** *tr* to fell, to cut down; **~her'** *adv* about; around; here and there; *rund ~~*, *rings ~~* round about; **~~blicken** *itr* to look about, to glance round; **~~gehen** *irr itr* to walk about; **~~irren**, **~~schweifen** *itr* to wander, to rove; **~~schlendern** *itr* to lounge about; **~~streichen** *itr* to prowl; **~~streifen** *itr*, **~~ziehen** *irr itr* to gad about; **~~treiben** *irr r* to knock about; **~hin'** *adv*: *ich kann nicht ~~ zu lachen* I cannot help laughing; I cannot but laugh; **~hü'llen** *tr* to wrap, to cover; (*Nebel*) to enshroud; (*Schleier*) to veil; (*umkleiden*) to case; (*bekleiden*) to sheathe; **~hüllung** *f* wrapper, casing, cover, veil; wrapping; coating; envelope; sheathing.

Um|kehr *f* return; (*Änderung*) complete change; (*Umschlag*) reversal; (*Gefühl*) revulsion; (*Bekehrung*) conversion; **~~bar** *a* reversible, invertible; **~~barkeit** *f* reversibility, invertibility; **~kehren** *itr* to turn back, to return; *tr* to turn round; to turn inside out; (*umdrehen*) to turn upside down; (*umstoßen*) to overturn, to subvert; *math, mus, gram* to invert; *el* to reverse; *r* to turn round; **~kehrung** *f* overturning; reversal; conversion; *gram* inversion; **~kippen** *tr* to turn over, to upset; *itr* to tilt over; to tip over, to turn over; to lose o.'s equilibrium; **~kla'mmern** *tr* to clasp; (*halten an*) to cling (to); (*Boxen*) to clinch; **~klammerung** *f* clasping; (*Boxen*) clinch; *mil* pincer-movement; **~klappbar** *a* collapsible; **~klappen** *tr* to turn down; to collapse; to drop down; **~'kleiden** *tr* to change s. o.'s clothes; *r* to change o.'s clothes; **~~'** *tr* to cover (*od* hang) with; (*Schicht*) to coat; (*Gehäuse*) to case, to jacket; **~kleideraum** *m* dressing-room; **~knicken** *tr* to break down, to snap off; **~kommen** *irr itr* to perish, to die; (*verderben*) to spoil, to go bad, to go to waste; **~krä'nzen** *tr* to wreathe; **~kreis** *m* circumference; (*Ausdehnung*) compass, extent, circuit; (*Kreis*) circle; (*Zone*) zone; (*Nähe*) neighbo(u)rhood, vicinity; *math* perimeter, periphery; *im ~~* within a radius of; **~krei'sen** *tr* to circle, to encircle; to rotate, to gyrate; *astr* to revolve round; **~krempe(l)n** *tr* to tuck up, to turn up; (*umwenden*) to turn inside; *alles ~~* to turn everything topsy-turvy.

um|laden *irr tr* to reload, to trans-ship, to shift; **~ladespesen** *pl* reloading charges *pl*; **~ladevorrichtung** *f* unloading plant; **~ladestation** *f* shunting station; *rail* transfer station; **~ladung** *f* reloading; transshipment; **~lage** *f* (*Steuer*) apportioned tax; (*Abgabe*) levy, contribution, impost; (*Gemeindeabgaben*) rates *pl*; (*Besteuerung*) assessment; **~la'gern** *tr mil* to besiege; *fig* to beset; **~'~** (*Güter*) to re-store, to rearrange, to regroup; **~lagerung** *f* rearrangement; **~lauf** *m* turning; (*Erde*) rotation; (*Geld*) circulation; currency; (*Umdrehung*) rotation; revolving; revolution, turn; (*Schreiben*) circular; *rail* (*Wagen*) turn-round; *in ~~ bringen* to put into circulation, to circulate; (*Gerüchte*) to spread, to start; *im ~~ sein* to circulate; **~~en** *irr tr* to run down; *itr* (*Blut*) to circulate; to revolve; to rotate; (*e-n Umweg machen*) to take a roundabout way; **~~'** *tr* to run around; **~~end** *a* rotary; rotating; circular; gyrating; **~~geschwindigkeit** *f* rotational speed; **~~getriebe** *n* sun-and-planet gear; **~~regler** *m* speed control(l)ing device; **~~schmierung** *f* circulated lubrication; **~~schreiben** *n* circular (letter); **~~zahl** *f* rotation number; **~~szeit** *f astr* revolution period; *com* period of circulation; **~laut** *m* umlaut, vowel-mutation; modification of a vowel; **~legbar** *a* reversible; inclinable; hinged; **~leg(e)kragen** *m* turn-down collar; **~'legen** *tr* to put on; to lay round; *mar* to put a ship about; (*Schienen*) to re-lay; (*Verband*) to apply; (*Kosten*) to apportion; (*Steuern*) to assess; (*weglegen*) to change the position of; (*verschieben*) to shift; *sl* (*töten*) to kill; *tele* (*Leitung*) to divert, to transfer; (*Schalter*) to throw, to tilt; *itr* (*Wind*) to change; **~~'** (*mit*) *tr* to lay round; **~legung** *f* transfer; shifting; **~leiten** *tr* (*Verkehr*) to divert; *tele* to divert, to deviate; **~leitung** *f* (*Verkehr*) diversion, loopway, deviation, roundabout way, by-pass, detour; *tele* diversion, deviation; **~lenken** *tr*, *itr* to turn round; **~lernen** *tr* to learn anew; (*Ansichten ändern*) to change o.'s views; to re-orientate o. s., to readjust o.'s views; **~lernling** *m* retrainee; **~leu'chten** *tr* to surround with light; **~liegend** *a* surrounding, neighbo(u)ring; *~~e Gegend* environs *pl*.

um|mau'ern *tr* to wall in; **~modeln** *tr* to remodel, to alter.

um|na'chtet *a* wrapped in darkness; (*geistig*) deranged; **~na'chtung** *f* mental derangement; **~nä'hen** *tr* to sew round; to hem; **~ne'beln** *tr* to cloud; *fig* to fog, to obfuscate; **~nehmen** *irr tr* to take about, to put on.

um|packen *tr* to repack; **~pa'nzern** *tr* to cover with a coat of mail; to plate; **~'pflanzen** *tr* to transplant; **~~'** to plant round (with); **~pflastern** *tr* to pave anew; to pave round; **~'pflügen** *tr* to plough up; **~polen** *tr el* to change the polarity; **~prägen** *tr* to recoin; **~prägung** *f* recoinage.

umquartieren *tr* to remove to other quarters; *mil* to re-billet; (*verpflanzen*) to displace, to evacuate, to dislocate.

*

um|ra'hmen *tr* to frame; (*umgeben*) to surround; **~rahmung** *f* frame, framing; *typ* box; **~ra'nden**, **~rä'ndern** *tr* to border, to edge; **~randung** *f* border, edge, rim; **~ra'nken** *tr* to twine round; *mit Efeu ~rankt* ivy-clad; **~räumen** *tr* (*Möbel*) to move about; to remove; to furnish differently; **~rau'schen** *tr* to rustle round; **~rechnen** *tr* to reduce to; to convert, to change; (*ausrechnen*) to figure out; *tele* to translate; **~rechnung** *f* reduction, conversion; *tele* translation; **~~skurs** *m* conversion rate, rate of change; **~~sschlüssel** *m* conversion key; **~~stabelle** *f* conversion table; **~~swert** *m* exchange value; **~'reißen** *irr tr* to pull down; (*umstoßen*) to knock down; **~~'** to outline; **~'reiten** *tr* to ride down; **~~'** *tr* to ride round; **~rennen** *irr tr* to run over, to run down; **~ri'ngen** *tr* to surround; **~riß** *m* outline, contour; (*e-r Stadt*) *Am* skyline; *e-n ~~ machen* to sketch; **~~'en** *a* defined, *nicht fest ~~en* undefined; **~~karte** *f* contour map; **~~linie** *f* outline; (*e-r Stadt*) *Am* skyline; **~~zeichnung** *f* (out)line drawing, sketch; **~rühren** *tr* to stir up.

um|satteln *tr* to resaddle; *itr fig* to change o.'s profession (*od* studies); *parl* to change sides; **~satz** *m com* turnover; (*Einnahme*) returns *pl*, receipts *pl*; (*Verkäufe*) sales *pl*; (*Börse*) transactions *pl*, business; *schneller ~~* ready sale, quick returns; **~~geschwindigkeit** *f* rate (*od* speed) of turnover; **~~höhe** *f* (amount of) turnover; **~~kapital** *n* working capital; **~~kurve** *f* sales curve (*od* fluctuations *pl*); **~~provision** *f* turnover provision; **~~steuer** *f* purchase tax; **~~ziffer** *f* turnover rate; **~säu'men** *tr* to hem; (*umgeben*) to surround; (*Platz*) to line; **~schalten** *tr el* to switch over; to reverse, to commutate; **~schalter** *m* commutator, reverser, selector switch; throw-over; switch; switch-board; (*Schreibmaschine*) shift-key; **~~hebel** *m el* switch lever; *tech* change-over; switch handle, change-lever; **~~schrank** *m* switch-board; **~~stöpsel** *m* switch-plug; **~~taste** *f tele* reversing key; (*Schreibmaschine*) shift-key; **~schaltung** *f* shifting; switch-over; switching; changing over; commutation; *~~ auf Empfang* change of connections for receiving; *~~ auf Sender* change of connections for transmitting; **~scha'nzen** *tr* to entrench; **~scha'tten** *tr* to shade; **~schau** *f* looking round; survey, review; *~~ halten* to look round, to muster o.'s surroundings; **~schauen** *itr* to look back; *r* to look round; **~schaufeln** *tr* to turn up with a shovel; (*Getreide*) to stir up; **~schichten** *tr* to pile anew; *fig* to shift, to regroup, to reshuffle; **~schichtig** *adv* in layers; *fig* in turns, in shifts; **~schi'ffen** *tr* to sail round, to circumnavigate; (*Kap*) to double; **~schlag** *m* (*Brief*) envelope; (*Buch*) wrapper, cover, jacket; (*Kragen*) collar; (*Einfassung*) hem; (*Hose, Ärmel*) cuff; turn-up; (*Wetter*) change; (*Veränderung*) alteration, turn; *med* compress, poultice; *com* turnover; (*Umladung*) transfer (*od* reshipment) of load; **~~bild** *n* cover picture (*od* photo); **~~en** *irr tr* to knock down, to fell; (*herumlegen*) to put on; (*Seite*) to turn over; (*Saum*) to turn up; (*Ärmel*) to tuck up; (*Kragen*) to turn down; *com* (*umladen*) to reload, to trans-ship; (*umsetzen*) to turn over; *itr* (*umfallen*) to fall down, to tilt over; to capsize; (*Wind*) to shift, to veer (round), to change; (*Boot*) to capsize; (*Stimme*) to break; **~~geschwindigkeit** *f* rate (*od* speed) of turnover; **~~hafen** *m* port of trans-shipment; **~~kapazität** *f* handling capacity; **~~papier** *n* wrapping paper; **~~platz** *m* transfer point; port (*od* place) of reshipment; **~~seite** *f* cover sheet; *innere ~~seite* inner cover; **~~tuch** *n* wrap, shawl; **~~zeit** *f com* period of turnover; (*beim Warentransport*) transit time; **~~zeichnung** *f* cover design; **~schlei'chen** *irr tr* to creep round; **~schlie'ßen** *irr tr* to enclose, to surround; (*umfassen*) to clasp; (*umarmen*) to embrace; *mil* to invest; **~schli'ngen** *irr tr* to twist about; to embrace, to clasp, to cling (to); **~schmeißen** *irr itr fam com* to go bankrupt, *Am* to go broke; *tr* to upset; to overthrow; **~schmelzen** *irr tr* to melt again; to remelt; to refound; to recast; **~schmelzung** *f* recast(ing), remelting; refounding; *fig* reorganization, reform; **~~sprozeß** *m*: *sich in e-m ~~sprozeß befinden* to be in the melting pot; **~schnallen** *tr* to buckle on; **~schnü'ren** *tr* to lace round; **~'schreiben** *irr tr* to rewrite; (*abschreiben*) to transcribe; (*Besitz*) to transfer; (*Wechsel*) to re-indorse; **~~'** to circumscribe; *fig* to paraphrase; **~schrei'bung** *f math* description; *fig* paraphrase; **~'~** transcription; transfer; rewriting; **~schrift** *f* inscription; (*Münzen*) legend; (*phonetische*) transcription; **~schulden** *tr* to convert a debt; **~schuldung** *f* conversion of a debt; **~~skredit** *m* conversion credit; **~schulen** *tr* to remove from one school to another; (*neu lernen*) to retrain, to re-educate; to train on different lines; **~schüler** *m* retrainee; **~schulung** *f* re-education, reorientation; retraining; **~schütteln** *tr* to shake (up), to agitate, to stir up, to mix; **~'schütten** *tr* (*ausschütten*) to spill, to upset; (*auflockern*) to loosen; (*in ein anderes Gefäß*) to pour into another vessel, to decant; **~schwä'rmen** *tr* to swarm round, to harass; *fig* to adore; **~schwe'ben** *tr* to hover around, to flutter round; **~schweif** *m* circumlocution; (*Abschweifung*) digression; *ohne ~~e* bluntly, point-blank, plainly; **~schwenken** *itr* to turn round, to wheel round; *fig* to change o.'s mind; **~schwi'rren** *tr* to buzz round; **~schwung** *m tech* revolution, rotation; (*Änderung*) change; (*Gefühle*) revulsion; (*völliger ~~*) about-face; *sport* (*nach vorn*) forward grand circle; (*Glückswechsel*) turn of the tide.

um|se'geln *tr* to sail round; (*Vorgebirge*) to double; (*Erde*) to circumnavigate; **~sehen** *irr r* to look round; (*zurück*) to look back; (*umher*) to take a look round; (*neugierig*) *Am sl* to rubberneck; *sich in der Welt ~~* to see s. th of the world; *sich nach etw ~~* to look out for; *im ~~* in a twinkling, in a trice; **~seitig** *a* overleaf, on the other page; **~setzbar** *a com* marketable, sal(e)able; *med* metabolizable; **~setzen** *tr* to transpose; (*Waren*) to sell; to dispose (of); (*zu Geld machen*) to realize; (*Umsatz haben*) to turn over; *mus* to transpose; (*Pflanze*) to transplant; (*in Taten ~~*) to translate (into deeds); *el* to transform, to convert; *tele* to reproduce; (*an e-e andere Stelle*) to place in a fresh position; *typ* to reset; **~setzung** *f* transposition; change, conversion; transformation; transplantation; *com* exchange, sale, business; double decomposition; **~sichgreifen** *n* spreading; **~sicht** *f* circumspection, prudence, caution; discretion; (*Behutsamkeit*) wariness; **~~ig** *a* cautious, circumspect, prudent; **~siedeln** *tr* to resettle; *itr* to settle somewhere else; **~siedler** *m* resettler; evacuee; **~siedlung** *f* resettlement; **~~slager** *n* relocation centre (*Am* center); **~sinken** *irr itr* to sink down; (*ohnmächtig werden*) to faint, to swoon; *vor Müdigkeit ~~* to drop down with fatigue; **~ so mehr** *adv* so much the more, the more; **~so'nst** *adv* (*zwecklos*) in vain, to no purpose; (*ohne Bezahlung*) gratis, free of charge, for nothing; (*grundlos*) without a reason, causelessly; **~'spannen** *tr* to change horses; (*Strom*) to transform; **~~'** to span; to encompass, to enclose; (*einschließen*) to comprise, to include; (*ergründen*) to fathom; **~'spanner** *m el* transformer; **~'spannstation** *f el* transformer station; **~'spannwerk** *n* transformer substation; **~spie'len** *tr sport Am* to outmaneuver; **~'~** (*Aufnahme*) to rerecord; **~spi'nnen** *irr tr* to spin round; (*Draht*) to braid, to cover, to whip; **~spri'ngen** *irr tr* to jump round; **~'~** *itr* (*Wind*) to change, to veer; *mit etw ~~* to manage, to handle; *mit jdm ~~* to deal with, to treat; **~spulen** *tr film* to rewind; **~spuler** *m*, **~spulvorrichtung** *f film* rewind; **~spü'len** to wash, to play around.

Um|stand *m*, **~stände** *pl* circumstance(s *pl*); (*Lage, Zustand*) condition, state; (*Tatsache*) fact; (*Förmlichkeit*) formalities *pl*, ceremonies *pl*; (*Aufheben*) fuss, trouble, ado; *besondere ~~* particulars *pl*; *ohne ~~* without ceremony; *entscheidender ~~* deciding factor; *unter ~ständen* in certain circumstances, circumstances permitting, possibly; *unter keinen ~ständen* on no account, under no circumstances; *unter allen ~ständen* by all means, in any case, at all events; *mildernde ~stände jur* extenuating circumstances; *~~ machen* to make (a) fuss, to bother; *sich ~stände machen* to go to trouble, to put o. s. out; *in anderen ~ständen sein* to be in the family way, to expect a baby, to be pregnant; **~stände halber** *adv* owing to circumstances; **~ständlich** *a* circumstantial; (*förmlich*) ceremonious, formal; (*verwickelt*) complicated, intricate, involved; (*verwirrt*) fussy; (*im einzelnen*) detailed; *~~ erzählen* to go into detail; **~~keit** *f* circumstantiality, formality; (*Verwirrtheit*) fussiness; **~standskleid** *n* maternity garment (*od* dress); **~standskrämer** *m* fussy person; **~standswort** *n* adverb; **~'stechen** *irr tr* to stir up; to re-engrave; **~stecken** *tr* to pin differently; to rearrange; **~ste'hen** *irr tr* to stand round; **~'stehend** *a* standing around; on the next page; *wie ~~* as stated overleaf; *die ~~en* the bystanders; **~steigebahnhof** *m rail* station for changing cars; **~steigefahrkarte** *f* transfer(-ticket); **~steigen** *irr itr* to change (*nach* for), *Am* to transfer; *alles ~~!* all change! *Am* all out! **~'stellen** *tr* to put into a different place, to rearrange; (*anpassen*) to adapt, to readjust; (*Betrieb*) to convert *auf* to); to reorganize; (*auf Friedensproduktion*) to reconvert; (*Erzeugung*) to switch (to); (*Währung*) to convert; *tech* to reverse; *gram* to invert, to transpose; *sport* (*Mannschaft*) to shift; *auf Maschinenbetrieb ~~* to mechanize; **~~'** to surround, to encircle; *r* to adapt o. s. (to); (*Haltung ändern*) to assume a different attitude; **~stellung** *f* (*Änderung*) change; (*Anpassung*) readjustment, adaptation; (*Fabrik*) conversion; (*auf Friedensproduktion*) reconversion; *gram* inversion; **~steuern** *tr tech* to reverse; to change over; to change direction; **~steuerung** *f* reversing gear; reversal; **~stimmen** *tr mus* to tune to another pitch; *fig* to make s. o. change his mind, to talk s. o. over, to bring s. o. round; **~stoßen** *irr tr* to knock down (*od* over), to tip over, to overturn; to push over, to overthrow; (*Pläne*) to upset; (*Befehl*) to override; (*Vertrag*) to annul, to invalidate, to cancel; **~stra'hlen** *tr* to surround with rays; **~stri'cken** *tr* to ensnare, to entangle; **~stri'tten** *a* disputed, controversial; *sport* contested; **~stülpen** *tr* to turn upside down (*od* inside out); to tilt over, to overturn, to invert; **~sturz** *m* downfall, overthrow; *fig* subversion, revolution; **~~partei** *f* revolutionary party; **~stürzen** *tr* to upset, to overturn; *itr* to fall down; **~stürzler** *m* revolutionary; **~~isch** *a* revolutionary, subversive.

um|taufen *tr* to rename; to rebaptize; to change s. o.'s name; **~tausch** *m* exchange, truck; barter, bartering; (*Börse*) swap; (*Wertpapiere*) conversion; **~~bar** *a* (*Papiergeld*) convertible; **~~en** *tr* to change for, to exchange, (*austauschen*) to barter, to truck (*gegen* for); (*Börse*) to swap; (*Wertpapiere*) to convert; **~~möglichkeit** *f* exchange allowed; exchange willingly; **~~recht** *n* (*Wertpapiere*) conversion privilege; **~to'ben, ~to'sen** *tr* to rage round; to storm round, to roar round; **~topfen** *tr bot* to repot; **~treiben** *irr tr* to drive round; *fig* to worry; **~trieb** *m* circulation; **~~e** *m pl* machinations *pl*; intrigues *pl*; **~triebsam** *a* active, assiduous, *Am sl* rustling; *~~ sein* to work vigorously, *Am sl* to rustle; *~~er Mensch* an energetic person, *Am sl* rustler; **~trunk** *m* drinking all round; **~tun** *irr tr* to put on; *sich nach etw ~~* to look about for, to apply for.

•

um|wa'chsen *irr tr* to overgrow, to entwine; **~~'** *a* covered; **~wa'llung** *f* circumvallation; **~wälzen** *tr* to roll round; *fig* to revolutionize; *r* to whirl round, to rotate; **~~d** *a* revolutionary, epoch-making; **~wälzung** *f* revolution, upheaval, *Am* overturn; (*Umschichtung*) *parl Am* landslide; **~wandelbar** *a* convertible, transformable, transmutable; **~~keit** *f* transmutability, convertibility, transformability; **~'wandeln** *tr* to change, to transform; (*Zinsfuß*) to convert; (*Gesellschaft*) to change; *jur* to commute; *tech* to transmute; *el* to convert, to transform; *gram* to inflect; *sich ~~ in chem* to be converted into; **~wandler** *m* converter, *el* transformer; **~wandlung** *f* change; conversion; transformation; transmutation; metamorphosis; *gram* inflection; **~~sanlage** *f* reactor; **~~senergie** *f* energy of transmutation; **~~sfähig** *a* convertible, transformable; **~~sprodukt** *n* transformation product; **~~sspannung** *f el* transformation potential; **~~stabelle** *f* conversion table; **~~sverfahren** *n* process of conversion; **~~swärme** *f* transformation heat; **~wechseln** *tr* to exchange for; (*Geld*) to change; (*Devisen*) to convert; **~weg** *m* roundabout way, detour; *auf ~~en* indirectly; *auf ~~en erfahren* to learn in a roundabout way, to hear through a side-channel; *e-n ~~ machen* to go out of o.'s way; **~'wehen** *tr* to blow down; **~~'** *itr* to blow round, to fan; **~welt** *f* environment; **~~einflüsse** *m pl* environmental influences *pl*; **~wenden** *irr tr* to turn over; *r* to turn round (*od* back); **~we'rben** *irr tr* to court, to seek eagerly; **~werfen** *irr tr* to overturn, to upset; (*Kleidungsstück*) to throw round (*od* over), to put on; (*besiegen*) to overthrow; (*Hürden*) to knock down; **~wertegerät** *n* instrument to convert data; **~werten** *tr* to revalue; **~wertung** *f* revaluation; **~wi'ckeln** *tr* to lap, to whip, (*Band*) to tape; (*einwickeln*) to wrap up; **~wi'nden** *irr tr* to wind round; **~wi'ttern** *tr fig* to envelop, to surround; **~wo'gen** *tr* to wash; to flow round; **~wohnend** *a* surrounding, neighbo(u)ring; **~wohner** *m pl* neighbo(u)rs *pl*, inhabitants of the vicinity; **~wö'lken** *tr* to overcast; *fig* to darken; to cloud; **~wo'rben** *a* sought after, courted; **~wühlen** *tr* to root up, to turn over.

um|zäu'nen *tr* to fence in, to enclose; **~zäu'nung** *f* hedge, fence, enclosure; **~'ziehen** *tr* to pull down; (*Kleider*) to change s. o.'s clothes; (*bedecken*) to cover, to wrap, to draw round; *r* to change o.'s clothes; *itr* to move (to), to change address, **~~'** to walk round; (*umgeben*) to surround; (*Wolken*) to overcast; **~zi'ngeln** *tr* to encompass, to surround; to encircle, to envelop; to invest; **~zug** *m* procession; (*Wohnungswechsel*) remove, removal; *pol* demonstration; **~zugskosten** *f pl* costs of removal; moving expenses *pl*; **~~zuschuß** *m* removal allowances *pl*; **~zü'ngeln** *tr* (*Flammen*) to play about, to envelop.

unab|änderlich *a* unalterable; invariable, immutable; (*unwiderruflich*) irrevocable; **~~keit** *f* unalterableness; **~dinglich, ~dingbar** *a* unalterable, final; inalienable; **~gefertigt** *a* undispatched, not dealt with; **~hängig** *a* independent (of); self-contained; **~~** *von* irrespective of; (*Schriftsteller*) freelance; **~~keit** *f* independence; **~kömmlich** *a* indispensable, reserved, keyed; **~~** *gestellt mil* deferred from military service; **~lässig** *a* incessant, unceasing, unremitting, continual, constant, uninterrupted; **~lösbar** *a* (*Hypotheken*) irredeemable; (*Renten*) perpetual; **~sehbar** *a* immeasurable; incalculable, immense, unbounded; **~setzbar** *a* irremovable; **~sichtlich** *a* unintentional; undesigned, unvoluntary; (*unachtsam*) inadvertent; **~weisbar, ~weislich** *a* imperative, pressing; (*entschieden*) peremptory; (*unvermeidlich*) unavoidable; **~wendbar** *a* inevitable; fatal.

unachtsam *a* inattentive, careless, negligent, inadvertent; **~keit** *f* carelessness, heedlessness, inadvertency; *aus* **~~** through inadvertency.

unähnlich *a* dissimilar, unlike; **~keit** *f* unlikeness, dissimilarity.

unan|fechtbar *a* indisputable, incontestable; **~~keit** *f* indisputability, incontestability; **~gebracht** *a* out of place, unsuitable, inopportune; **~gefochten** *a* (*unbestritten*) undisputed, *sport* unchallenged; (*unbelästigt*) unmolested; (*ungehindert*) unhindered, unhampered; **~gemeldet** *a* unannounced, without previous notice; (*Polizei*) unregistered; (*Vermögen*) not returned, not reported; **~gemessen** *a* unsuitable; (*unschicklich*) improper; (*unzulänglich*) inadequate, insufficient, incommensurate; (*unpassend*) incongruous; **~~heit** *f* (*Ungenügen*) inadequacy; (*Mißverhältnis*) incongruity; (*Ungeeignetheit*) unsuitability; **~genehm** *a* disagreeable (to), unpleasant, distasteful, *Am sl* lemon; (*unerwünscht*) undesirable; (*störend, lästig*) troublesome; **~gerührt, ~getastet** *a* untouched; **~greifbar** *a* unassailable; **~nehmbar** *a* unacceptable; **~nehmlichkeit** *f* annoyance, inconvenience; (*Schwierigkeit*) trouble, difficulty; **~sehnlich** *a* mean-looking; unsightly; (*Personen*) plain, insignificant; (*unauffällig*) inconspicuous; (*belanglos*) inconsiderable; **~~keit** *f* plainness; (*Ärmlichkeit*) paltriness; (*Äußeres*) meanness; **~ständig** *a* indecent; improper; **~~keit** *f* indecency; (*Ungehörigkeit*) impropriety; **~stößig** *a* harmless, inoffensive; (*einwandfrei*) unobjectionable, correct; **~tastbar** *a* unimpeachable, unviolable, unassailable; **~~keit** *f* inviolability, impeachability; **~wendbar** *a* inapplicable, unsuitable, impracticable.

un|appetitlich *a* unsavoury, distasteful, nasty, not appetizing; (*abstoßend*) repellent; (*reizlos*) uninviting; **~art** *f* bad (*od* ill *od* improper) behavio(u)r; (*Unfug*) mischief; (*schlechte Sitten*) bad manners *pl*; (*Rohheit*) rudeness, ill breeding; (*Kinder*) naughtiness; **~~** *m* naughty child; **~artig** *a* ill-bred; (*Kinder*) naughty, badly behaved; (*roh*) rude; **~~keit** *f* bad conduct; rudeness; (*Unhöflichkeit*) incivility; **~artikuliert** *a* inarticulate; **~ästhetisch** *a* not (a)esthetic.

unauf|fällig *a* without attracting attention; inconspicuous; (*Kleidung*) conservative; (*bescheiden*) modest, unassuming; **~findbar** *a* undiscoverable, not to be located (*od* found); **~gefordert** *a* unbidden, uncalled for, unasked; **~geklärt** *a* unexplained, mysterious; **~haltbar, ~haltsam** *a* irresistible; (*unaufhörlich*) incessant; (*andauernd*) continual, without stopping; (*heftig*) impetuous; **~hörlich** *a* incessant; **~lösbar, ~löslich** *a* indissoluble; insoluble; (*unerklärlich*) inexplicable; **~~keit** *f* insolubility; **~merksam** *a* inattentive; **~~keit** *f* inattention; **~richtig** *a* insincere; **~~keit** *f* insincerity; **~schiebbar** *a* urgent, pressing; not to be postponed.

unaus|bleiblich *a* infallible, inevitable; (*sicher*) sure, certain; **~führbar** *a* impracticable, not feasible; (*unmöglich*) impossible; **~gebildet** *a* uncultivated; *mil* untrained; (*unentwickelt*) undeveloped; **~geführt** *a* not carried out; (*Auftrag*) open, unexecuted; **~gefüllt** *a* not filled up (*Am* in); void; **~geglichen** *a* unbalanced; uneven; uncompensated; out-of-balance; **~~heit** *f* unbalance; **~gesetzt** *a* continual, constant, uninterrupted; **~löschlich** *a* (*Schrift*) indelible; inextinguishable; **~rottbar** *a* ineradicable; **~sprechlich** *a* ineffable, unspeakable, unutterable, inexpressible; **~stehlich** *a* insupportable, insufferable, intolerable; **~tilgbar** *a* ineradicable; ineffaceable; **~weichlich** *a* unavoidable, inevitable.

un|bändig *a* intractable, unruly, indomitable; (*übermäßig*) excessive; (*ungeheuer*) tremendous; **~barmherzig** *a* merciless, pitiless, unmerciful; **~~keit** *f* mercilessness, pitilessness.

unbe|absichtigt *a* unintentional; **~achtet** *a* unnoticed, neglected, not taken into account; (*absichtlich*) disregarded; ignored; **~anstandet** *a* not objected to; uncontested, unopposed, unhampered; **~antwortet** *a* unanswered; **~arbeitet** *a* (*Metall*) raw; unwrought; unmachined; unfinished; in blank form; (*Häute*) raw, undressed; (*Land*) untilled; (*Thema*) not treated before; (*Geschäftsvorgang*) not yet taken up; (*schwebend*) pending; **~aufsichtigt** *a* without supervision; **~baut** *a* (*Acker*) uncultivated, untilled; (*Baugelände*) undeveloped, vacant; **~dacht, ~~sam** *a* inconsiderate, thoughtless; (*übereilt*) rash; (*taktlos*) indiscreet; **~dachtsamkeit** *f* inconsiderateness; (*Fahrlässigkeit*) inadvertency, carelessness; (*Gedankenlosigkeit*) thoughtlessness; imprudence; (*Übereilung*) rashness; **~deckt** *a* uncovered, bare; *mit* **~~em** *Haupte* bare-headed; **~denklich** *a* (*Person*) unhesitating; (*Sache*) unobjectionable; (*unschuldig*) harmless; *adv* without scruples, without hesitation; **~~keitsvermerk** *m* permit, licence; **~deutend** *a* insignificant, of no importance, trifling; **~~er** *Mensch* small fry, *Am* small potatoes; **~~heit** *f* insignificance; **~dingt** *a* absolute; (*völlig*) complete; (*ganz bestimmt*) without fail; (*bedingungslos*) unconditional; (*Gehorsam*) unquestioning; (*Glaube*) implicit; **~einflußt** *a* not influenced; unaffected (by); (*objektiv*) unbiased, unprejudiced; **~einträchtigt** *a* unimpaired; **~endigt** *a* unfinished; **~fähigt** *a* incompetent; unqualified; **~fahrbar** *a* impracticable; impassable; **~fangen** *a* free, natural; (*harmlos*) ingenuous; (*unparteiisch*) unprejudiced, impartial; (*nicht verlegen*) unembarrassed; **~~heit** *f* impartiality; unaffectedness; ease, unrestrainedness; cando(u)r; **~festigt** *a* unfortified, open; **~fleckt** *a* unspotted; *fig* immaculate; **~~heit** *f* purity; spotlessness; **~friedigend** *a* unsatisfactory; **~friedigt** *a* unsatisfied, dissatisfied; (*enttäuscht*) disappointed; **~fugt** *a* unauthorized; incompetent; *Land* **~~** *betreten* to trespass; **~~e(r)** *m* intruder; unauthorized person; **~gabt** *a* untalented; **~greiflich** *a* inconceivable, incomprehensible; *das ist mir* **~~** I can't understand; **~~keit** *f* incomprehensibility; incomprehensible thing; **~glaubigt** *a* unauthenticated; **~glichen** *a* unsettled, unpaid, outstanding; **~grenzt** *a* unbounded, unlimited; **~gründet** *a* unfounded, groundless; **~gütert** *a* without means, not well off; **~haart** *a* without hair; hairless; (*kahl*) bald, glabrous; *bot* smooth-leaved; **~hagen** *n* discomfort, uneasiness; **~haglich** *a* uneasy, uncomfortable; **~~keit** *f* uneasiness; **~hauen** *a* unhewn; **~helligt** *a* unmolested; undisturbed; **~hilflich, ~holfen** *a* clumsy, awkward; **~holfenheit** *f* awkwardness; **~hindert** *a* unimpeded; unrestrained; unprevented; **~irrbar** *a* not to be put out, imperturbable; **~kannt** *a* unknown; unacquainted (with), ignorant (of); **~~e** *Ursache* unexplained cause; *das ist mir* **~~** I don't know that; *er ist hier* **~~** he is a stranger here; **~~e** *f* unknown (quantity); **~kehrbar** *a* inconvertible; **~kleidet** *a* undressed; **~kümmert** *a* careless (of); unconcerned; (*sorglos*) happy-go-lucky; (*rücksichtslos*) reckless; **~~heit** *f* carelessness; **~laden** *a* unladen, without cargo; **~lastet** *a* (*Grundstück*) unencumbered; (*Wagen*) not loaded; *pol* with clear records; **~lästigt** *a* unmolested; **~laubt** *a* leafless; **~lebt** *a* inanimate; (*Straße*) unfrequented; (*Markt*) dull, slack, sluggish; (*leblos*) lifeless; **~leckt** *a*: *von der Kultur* **~~** uncivilized; **~lehrbar** *a* unteachable; **~~e** *Person Am* big stiff; **~lesen** *a* illiterate; **~lichtet** *a* unexposed; **~liebt** *a* disliked, unpopular (*bei* with); **~~heit** *f* unpopularity; **~mannt** *a* unmanned; *aero* pilotless; **~merkbar** *a* imperceptible; **~merkt** *a* unobserved, unnoticed, unperceived; **~mittelt** *a* (*arm*) poor; (*mittellos*) without means; **~nannt** *a* undefined; unnamed; anonymous; (*Zahl*) indefinite; **~nommen** *a* permitted; *es bleibt Ihnen* **~~** you are quite at liberty (to); **~nützbar** *a* unavailable; unserviceable; **~nutzt** *a* unused; **~obachtet** *a* unobserved; **~quem** *a* inconvenient; uncomfortable; incommodious; **~~lichkeit** *f* inconvenience; discomfort; **~rechenbar** *a* incalculable; incomputable; (*launisch*) wayward; **~~keit** *f* incalculability; **~rechnet** *a* free of charge; **~rechtigt** *a* unauthorized, not entitled (to); (*ungerechtfertigt*) unjustified; (*ungesetzlich*) unlawful; **~rücksichtigt** *a* disregarded, neglected; not taken into account; **~rufen** *a* uncalled for, unbidden; without the inward call; *~~!* touch wood! **~rührt** *a* untouched; intact; (*Wald*) virgin; (*Mädchen*) chaste, innocent; *etw ~~ lassen* to pass over in silence; **~schadet** *prp* without prejudice (to), without detriment (to); (*ungeachtet*) notwithstanding; **~schädigt** *a* unhurt, uninjured; undamaged; **~schäftigt** *a* unemployed, out of work; **~scheiden** *a* immodest; (*anmaßend*) arrogant, presumptuous; (*Preis*) unreasonable, exorbitant; **~~heit** *f* lack of modesty; presumption; **~schnitten** *a* (*Buch*) uncut; (*Münze*) unclipped; (*Mensch*) uncircumcised; (*Hecke*) untrimmed; **~scholten** *a* irreproachable, stainless; of good reputation; **~~heit** *f* blamelessness, integrity; stainless character; **~schränkt** *a* unlimited, unbounded; absolute; **~schreiblich** *a* indescribable; **~schrieben** *a* (*Papier*) blank; **~schuht** *a* without shoes; **~schützt** *a* unprotected; **~schwert** *a* light, unburdened; **~seelt** *a* soulless; (*leblos*) inanimate, lifeless; **~sehen** *adv* unseen; unexamined; (*ohne Zögern*) without hesitation; **~setzt** *a* unoccupied; vacant, free; **~siegbar** *a* invincible; **~siegt** *a* unvanquished; *sport* unbeaten; **~soldet** *a* unsalaried, unpaid; **~sonnen** *a* thoughtless, rash, inconsiderate; light-minded; **~~heit** *f* thoughtlessness, inconsiderateness; (*Unvorsichtigkeit*) imprudence; (*Hast*) rashness; (*Unklugheit*) indiscretion; **~sorgt** *a* easy, carefree; (*unbeteiligt*) unconcerned (*über* about); *seien Sie ~~!* don't worry! don't trouble yourself! **~stand** *m* instability, inconstancy, changeableness; **~ständig** *a* inconstant, unstable; (*veränderlich*) changeable; (*wankelmütig*) fickle; (*Markt*) unsteady, unsettled; (*Preise*) fluctuating; **~~keit** *f* inconsistency, inconstancy; instability; (*Wankelmut*) fickleness; **~stätigt** *a* unconfirmed; **~stechlich** *a* incorruptible; **~~keit** *f* incorruptibility; **~steigbar** *a* unclimbed; (*unzugänglich*) inaccessible; **~stellbar** *a* undeliverable; (*Brief*) dead; *Abteilung für ~~e Briefe* (*Post*) Dead Letter Office; **~steuert** *a* untaxed; **~stimmbar** *a* undefinable, indeterminable; **~stimmt** *a* indeterminate; (*unklar*) vague, undefined; (*unsicher*) uncertain; *gram* indefinite; (*unentschieden*) undecided; (*undeutlich*) indistinct; *es ist noch ~~* it's still a tossup; *auf ~~e Zeit vertagen* to adjourn sine die; **~~heit** *f* indefiniteness; uncertainty; vagueness; indeterminateness; **~straft** *a* unpunished; **~streitbar** *a* incontestable, indisputable; **~stritten** *a* uncontested, undisputed, undoubted, unquestioned; **~teiligt** *a* not interested in, unconcerned, non-participating; (*gleichgültig*) indifferent; (*unbefangen*) impartial; **~~e(r)** *m* outsider; **~tont** *a* unstressed, unaccented; **~trächtlich** *a* inconsiderable, trifling; **~treten** *a* untrodden, unbeaten.

unbeugsam *a* inflexible; stubborn; obstinate; unyielding, uncompromising, *Am fam* hard-shell; **~~keit** *f* inflexibility; obstinacy.

unbe|wacht *a* unwatched, unguarded; **~waffnet** *a* unarmed; (*Auge*) naked; **~wandert** *a* not versed (in), inexperienced; **~weglich** *a* immovable; (*feststehend*) stationary, fix; (*bewegungslos*) motionless; *~~e Sachen* immovables *pl*; *~~es Gut* real estate; **~~keit** *f* immovableness, immobility; **~wehrt** *a* unarmed, defenceless; **~weibt** *a* unmarried, single, bachelor; **~weint** *a* unwept, unlamented; **~weisbar** *a* undemonstrable; **~wiesen** *a* not proven; **~wohnbar** *a* uninhabitable; **~wohnt** *a* uninhabited; **~wölkt** *a* cloudless; **~wußt** *adv* unconscious (of); unknown (to s. o.); *mir ~~* without my knowledge; **~zahlbar** *a* priceless; *fig* invaluable; **~zahlt** *a* unpaid, unsettled; (*Forderung*) outstanding; (*Wechsel*) dishono(u)red; **~zähmbar** *a* untamable, indomitable; uncontrollable; **~zeugt** *a* unattested; not witnessed; **~zweifelbar** *a* unquestionable; **~zwingbar, ~zwinglich** *a* unconquerable, invincible; **~zwungen** *a* unconquered.

un|biegsam *a* inflexible, unbending; **~bilden** *f pl: die ~~ des Wetters* inclemency of weather; **~bildung** *f* lack of education, illiteracy; **~bill** *f* injury, wrong; **~billig** *a* unjust, unfair, inequitable; (*Preis*) unreasonable; **~~keit** *f* unfairness, injustice; **~blutig** *a* bloodless; *eccl* unbloody; **~botmäßig** *a* unruly, refractory; (*widersetzlich*) insubordinate; **~~keit** *f* insubordination; **~brauchbar** *a* useless, of no use; (*Gegenstand*) unserviceable; (*nicht mehr reparierbar*) non-recoverable; (*Abfall*) waste; *~~ machen* to render unserviceable; **~~machung** *f* making useless; destruction; (*Geschütz*) dismounting; **~~keit** *f* uselessness; **~bußfertig** *a* impenitent, unrepentant; (*verstockt*) obdurate; **~~keit** *f* impenitence; **~christlich** *a* unchristian.

*

und *conj* and; *und?* so what? *~ so weiter* and so on, and so forth; *~ dann?* and then? and afterwards? *zwei ~ zwei ist vier* two and (*od* plus) two is four; *der ~ der* so and so; *da ~ da* at such and such a place; *~ ich auch nicht* nor I either; *~ wenn* even if; *~ das tat ich auch* which I did; *~ ich auch* and so do I; *seien Sie so gut ~* be so kind as to, have the kindness to.

Undank *m* ingratitude; **~bar** *a* ungrateful (*gegen* to); (*ohne Dank*) thankless; **~barkeit** *f* ingratitude; thanklessness.

un|datiert *a* undated; **~definierbar** *a* indefinable; **~dehnbar** *a* inextensible, nonductile; **~deklinierbar** *a* indeclinable; **~denkbar** *a* unthinkable, inconceivable; **~denklich** *a* immemorial; *seit ~~en Zeiten* from times immemorial; **~deutlich** *a* indistinct; (*Laut*) inarticulate; (*dunkel*) obscure, vague; (*verwirrt*) confused; (*unverständlich*) unintelligible; **~~keit** *f* indistinctness; inarticulateness; unintelligibility; **~deutsch** *a* un-German, contrary to German ideas; **~dicht** *a* not tight, pervious, permeable, leaky; *~~ sein* to leak; **~~igkeit** *f* perviousness, leakiness; porosity; leak; **~dienlich** *a* unserviceable, unsuitable; **~ding** *n* absurdity; (*Unsinn*) nonsense; (*unbedeutende Person od Sache*) nonentity; (*Unmöglichkeit*) impossibility; **~diszipliniert** *a* undisciplined; **~dramatisch** *a* undramatic; **~duldsam** *a* intolerant; **~~keit** *f* intolerance; (*Vorurteil*) prejudice.

undurch|dringlich, **~lässig** *a* impenetrable (*für* to); impermeable, impervious (*für* to); (*unerforschlich*) inscrutable; *~~e Miene Am sl* poker face, *Am sl* deadpan; **~~keit** *f* impenetrability; **~führbar** *a* impracticable, not feasible, *Am* impractical; **~sichtig** *a* opaque, not transparent; impervious to light, nondiaphanous; (*im Fluß*) fluid; **~~keit** *f* opacity.

un|eben *a* uneven; (*ungleich*) unequal; (*rauh*) rough, rugged; *nicht ~~* not bad, not amiss; **~~bürtig** *a* not equal in birth; **~~heit** *f* unevenness; roughness, ruggedness; inequality; **~echt** *a* false, not genuine, sham, spurious; (*nachgemacht*) counterfeit, bogus, *Am sl* phon(e)y; (*künstlich*) artificial, imitation; (*unrichtig*) *math* improper; (*unehelich*) illegitimate; (*flüchtig*) fugitive; (*Farbe*) loose, not fast; (*verfälscht*) adulterated; **~~heit** *f* falseness; spuriousness; **~edel** *a* ignoble; (*Metall*) base; (*gemein*) vulgar; **~ehelich** *a* illegitimate; **~ehrbar, ~ehrenhaft** *a* dishono(u)rable; (*unanständig*) indecent; (*entehrend*) disgraceful; **~ehre** *f* dishono(u)r, disgrace; **~ehrerbietig** *a* disrespectful, irreverent; **~~keit** *f* irreverence; disrespect; **~ehrlich** *a* dishonest; (*unaufrichtig*) insincere; (*treulos*) disloyal; (*falsch*) false, underhand, not straightforward; **~~keit** *f* dishonesty; (*Unaufrichtigkeit*) insincerity; **~eigennützig** *a* disinterested; unselfish; **~~keit** *f* disinterestedness; **~eigentlich** *a* not literal, figurative.

unein|bringlich *a* irrevocable; (*Verlust*) irretrievable; **~gedenk** *a* forgetful (of), unmindful (of); **~gelöst** *a* uncollected; (*Wechsel*) unredeemed, not taken up; **~geschränkt** *a* unlimited, unrestrained, unrestricted, unconditioned; **~geweiht** *a* uninitiated; **~heitlich** *a* (*unregelmäßig*) irregular; (*ungleichartig*) inhomogeneous, nonuniform.

un|einig, **~eins** *a* disagreeing, discordant, disunited; *~~ sein* to be at odds, to be at variance; *~~ werden* to fall out; **~~keit** *f* disharmony, discord, disagreement; **~einlöslich** *a* irredeemable.

un|einnehmbar *a* inexpugnable, impregnable, invincible; **~elastisch** *a* inelastic, unelastic; **~elegant** *a* not elegant, unfashionable; **~empfänglich** *a* unimpressionable, unreceptive, unsusceptible (*für* to); (*stumpfsinnig*) dull, apathetic; (*unzugänglich*) impervious (*für* to); **~empfindlich** *a* insensible; (*gleichgültig*) cold, indifferent (to); *~~ gegen* insensitive (to), not affected (*od* unaffected) by; (*teilnahmslos*) apathetic (towards); (*stumpf, träge*) inert; *~~ machen* to desensitize; **~~keit** *f* insensibility; indifference (to); **~endlich** *a* infinite, endless; (*ewig*) eternal; (*weit*) vast; *ins ~~e* to infinity, ad infinitum; *~~ klein math* infinitesimal; *~~ viele* an infinity (of); *~~ lang* endless; *auf ~~ eingestellt* focused for infinity; **~~keit** *f* infinity, endlessness; infinite space.

unent|behrlich *a* indispensable; necessary; **~~keit** *f* indispensableness; **~geltlich** *a* gratis, free (of charge), gratuitous; **~haltsam** *a* intemperate; incontinent; **~~keit** *f* intemperance; incontinence; **~rinnbar** *a* ineluctable; **~schieden** *a* undecided; (*unentschlossen*) irresolute; (*Spiel*) drawn; *~~es Spiel* tie game, draw; *torgleiches ~~es Spiel* score tie; *torloses ~~es Spiel* scoreless tie; *~~er Kampf* (*Fechten*) tie bout; *~~es Rennen* dead heat; *das Rennen war ~~* the race was a tie; **~~heit** *f* irresolution, indecision; **~schlossen** *a* irresolute; *~~ sein* to vacillate, to waver, to hesitate, to shilly-shally, *Am fam* to back and fill; (*gegenüber e-r Partei*) *fam* to sit on a fence, *Am fam* to straddle; **~~heit** *f* irresolution; **~schuldbar** *a* inexcusable; *es ist ~~* (*fam*) it allows of no excuse; **~wegt** *a* unflinching, unswerving; **~~e(r)** *m parl* die-hard, stalwart; **~wickelt** *a* undeveloped; **~wirrbar** *a* inextricable; **~zifferbar** *a* undecipherable.

uner|bittlich *a* inexorable; *die ~~en Tatsachen* the stubborn facts; **~~keit** *f* inexorability; **~fahren** *a* inexperienced, inexpert, green, callow, untrained, unskilled; **~~e(r)** *m* inexperienced person, novice, *Am fam* tenderfoot; **~~heit** *f* inexperience; *~~heit vorgeben* to plead infancy (as a legal defence), *Am* to plead the baby act; **~findlich** *a* undiscoverable; (*unverständlich*) incomprehensible; **~forschlich** *a* inscrutable, impenetrable; **~forscht** *a* unexplored; **~freulich** *a* unpleasant; (*unbefriedigend*) unsatisfactory; **~füllbar** *a* unrealizable; (*unerreichbar*) unattainable; (*unmöglich*) impossible to fulfil; **~füllt** *a* unfulfilled; **~giebig** *a* unproductive, unyielding; (*nicht lohnend*) unprofitable; **~gründlich** *a* unfathomable; impenetrable; **~~keit** *f* unfathomableness; impenetrability; **~heblich** *a* trifling; irrelevant (to), insignificant, inconsiderable; **~~keit** *f* inconsiderableness; irrelevance; **~'hört** *a* unheard of, unprecedented; (*abscheulich*) outrageous; (*empörend*) shocking; (*Preis*) exorbitant; **~~'** (*nicht gewährt*) ungranted; **~kannt** *a* unrecognized; **~kennbar** *a* unrecognizable; **~kenntlich** *a* ungrateful; **~klärlich** *a* inexplicable; unaccountable; **~läßlich** *a* indispensable; **~laubt** *a* illicit; (*ungesetzlich*) unlawful, illegal; (*nicht gestattet*) not permitted; *~~e Handlung* (action in) tort, wrongful act; *~~e Entfernung mil* absence without leave (*Abk* AWOL); *sich ~~* (*von der Truppe*) *entfernen* to go AWOL; **~ledigt** *a* unsettled, not finished; **~löst** *a* not redeemed; **~meßlich** *a* immeasurable, immense; (*grenzenlos*) boundless; (*unendlich*) infinite; (*riesig*) huge, vast; **~~keit** *f* immeasurableness; immensity; **~müdlich** *a* indefatigable; (*Bemühung*) untiring, tireless; **~~keit** *f* indefatigableness; **~öffnet** *a* not opened; **~örtert** *a* undiscussed; **~quicklich** *a* unpleasant, uncomfortable; **~reichbar** *a* unattainable; out of reach; (*unzugänglich*) inaccessible; (*Tennis*) pass; **~reicht** *a* unequalled, unrival(l)ed; (*Leistung*) record; **~sättlich** *a* insatiable; **~schlossen** *a* (*Gelände*) undeveloped; **~schöpflich** *a* inexhaustible; **~schrocken** *a* intrepid; (*furchtlos*) fearless, undaunted; **~~heit** *f* intrepidity; **~schütterlich** *a* imperturbable, unshakeable; (*fest*) firm, unflinching, steady; **~schwinglich** *a* unattainable; (*Preis*) exorbitant, prohibitive; **~setzlich** *a* (*Verlust*) irreparable; (*Sache*) irreplaceable; irrecoverable; **~sprießlich** *a* unpleasant; (*vergeblich*) fruitless, unprofitable; **~träglich** *a* intolerable; insufferable; unbearable; **~wachsen** *a* immature; (*jung*) young; **~wähnt** *a* unmentioned; *~~lassen* not to mention, to pass over (in silence); **~wartet** *a* unexpected; **~weislich** *a* indemonstrable; not to be proved; **~widert** *a* (*Brief*) unanswered, (*Liebe*) unreturned; **~wiesen** *a* unproved; **~wünscht** *a* unwelcome, unwished for, undesired; **~zogen** *a* uneducated; ill-bred; **~explodierbar** *a* non-explosive.

un|fähig *a* incapable (of); unable (to do); (*untauglich*) unfit (*zu* for), inefficient, incompetent; **~~keit** *f* incapacity; inability (for); (*geringe Leistungsfähigkeit*) inefficiency; (*Unzulänglichkeit*) incompetence; *~~ zur Bekleidung öffentlicher Ämter* unfitness to hold public office; **~fahrbar** *a* impracticable; **~fall** *m* accident; (*Unglück*) disaster; (*Mißgeschick*) misfortune; **~~bericht** *m* accident report; **~~entschädigung** *f* accident compensation; **~~fürsorge** *f* accident welfare-work; **~~häufigkeit** *f* accident frequency; **~~hilfstrupp** *m*, **~~kommando** *n mot* breakdown gang; **~~meldedienst** *m Am* accident reporting service; **~~meldung** *f* accident report; emergency call; **~~merkblatt** *n* accident-report sheet; **~~risiko** *n* risk of accident; **~~skizze** *f* diagram of accident; **~~station** *f* first aid station; **~~statistik** *f* accident statistics *pl*; **~~stelle** *f* scene of accident; **~~untersuchung** *f* accident investigation; **~~unterstützung** *f* accident relief; **~~verhütung** *f* accident prevention; **~~verhütungsvorschrift** *f* safety regulations *pl*; **~~verletzung** *f* accidental injury; **~~versicherung** *f* accident insurance; **~~wagen** *m* motor ambulance; *aero* crash wagon; **~~ziffer** *f* accident rate; **~faßbar, ~faßlich** *a* inconceivable; (*unverständlich*) incomprehensible, unintelligible; **~fehlbar** *a* infallible, sure, unfailing; *adv* surely, certainly; **~~keit** *f* infallibility; **~fein** *a* indelicate; (*unhöflich*) impolite, unmannerly; (*grob*) coarse; **~fern** *a* near; *prp* not far from; **~fertig** *a* not ready; unfinished; (*unreif*) immature; **~flat** *m* dirt, filth; **~flätig** *a* dirty, nasty, filthy; **~folgsam** *a* disobedient; **~~keit** *f* disobedience; **~förmig, ~förmlich** *a* shapeless, misshapen; (*mißgestaltet*) deformed; (*ohne Maße*) disproportionate; (*ungeheuer*) monstruous; **~~keit** *f* deformity; monstrosity; **~frankiert** *a* not prepaid; **~frei** *a* not free; (*nicht bezahlt*) unpaid; (*in Verlegenheit*) embarrassed; **~freiwillig** *a* involuntary; (*gezwungen*) compulsory; *~~er Passagier* unwilling passenger; **~freundlich** *a* unkind, unfriendly, unamiable; (*unangenehm*) unpleasant, *Am* mean; (*grämlich*) morose; (*barsch*) rude, rough; (*Wetter*) inclement; **~~keit** *f* unfriendliness; (*Wetter*) inclemency; (*Grobheit*) rudeness; **~friede** *m* discord, disunion, dissension; **~frisiert** *a* (*Haare*) uncombed, unkempt; *fig* (*Bericht*) authentic; not doctored; **~froh** *a* not glad; unhappy; **~fruchtbar** *a* barren, sterile; *fig* fruitless; (*nutzlos*) unproductive; **~~keit** *f* barrenness, sterility; **~fug** *m* nuisance; (*Unsinn*) nonsense, *Am fam* shenanigan; (*Unordnung*) disorder, disturbance; (*schlechtes Benehmen*) misdemeano(u)r; (*Unrecht*) wrong, offence; *grober ~~* gross misdemeano(u)r; **~fügsam** *a* unmanageable, intractable; **~galant** *a* uncourteous; (*unhöflich*) impolite; **~gangbar** *a* unusual; (*Weg*) impassable; (*Ware*) unsal(e)able; (*Münze*) not current; **~gastlich** *a* inhospitable.

Ungar *m* Hungarian; **~isch** *a* Hungarian; **~n** *n* Hungary.

unge|achtet *a* not esteemed; *prp* notwithstanding, in spite of; *conj* although; **~ahndet** *a* unpunished; **~ahnt** *a* unexpected, unanticipated, undreamt of; **~bahnt** *a* unbeaten, trackless, untrodden; **~bärdig** *a* unmannered; unruly; refractory; **~beten** *a* uninvited, unbidden; *~~er Gast* intruder, *sl* gate-crasher; **~beugt** *a* unbent, uncurbed; **~bildet** *a* uneducated, uncivilized; (*roh*) rude; (*schlecht erzogen*) ill-bred; (*Benehmen*) unpolished; **~bleicht** *a* unbleached; **~boren** *a* unborn; **~brannt** *a* unburnt; **~bräuchlich** unusual; (*veraltet*) antiquated, obsolete; **~braucht** *a* unused; **~brochen** *a* unbroken; (*Strahlen*) not refracted; **~bühr** *f* indecency, impropriety, misdemeano(u)r; **~bührlich** *a* unseemly, indecent, improper, unbecoming; **~~keit** *f* indecency; **~bunden** *a* unbound; (*Buch*) in sheets; *fig* free, unrestrained; (*Bestandteile*) uncombined; (*ausschweifend*) dissolute; *~~e Rede* prose; **~~heit** *f* freedom, lack of restraint; (*Zügellosigkeit*) licentiousness; **~dämpft** *a* (*Schwingung*) undamped; (*Welle*) continuous; **~deckt** *a* uncovered; (*Rechnung*) unpaid; (*Scheck*) dishono(u)red; (*Tisch*) not yet laid; **~druckt** *a* unprinted; in manuscript; **~duld** *f* impatience; **~duldig** *a* impatient (at); *~~ werden* to get impatient; **~eignet** *a* unfit (for), unsuitable, improper; **~~heit** *f* unsuitableness, unfitness, inappropriateness; **~erdet** *a* ungrounded; unearthed; **~fähr** *adv* about, *Am* around; in the neighbourhood of; (*etwa*) roughly; approximately; *a* (*Bild*) rough; (*wahrscheinlich*) probable; (*etwa*) approximate; *Sie müssen ~~ 30 Jahre alt sein* you must be thirty or thereabouts; *~ n* chance; accident; *von ~~* by chance; **~fährdet** *a* safe; out of danger; **~fährlich** *a* not dangerous; harmless; inoffensive; **~fällig** *a* disobliging, unkind; **~~keit** *f* disobligingness; discourtesy; **~färbt** *a* uncolo(u)red; *fig* unfeigned; **~faßt** *a* frameless; (*Glas*) rimless; **~federt** *a* without springs; **~fragt** *a* without being asked; *~~ dreinreden fam* to chip in; **~frierbar** *a* incongealable; **~füge** *a* misshapen, monstrous; **~fügig** *a* unpliant, unwieldy; unmanageable; **~füttert** *a* unfed; (*Kleider*) unlined; **~gerbt** *a* untanned; *~~es Leder* rawhide; **~goren** *a* unfermented; **~halten** *a* angry, indifferent (*über* at); (*Versprechen*) unfulfilled, unkept; **~härtet** *a* soft, unhardened; **~heilt** *a* uncured; **~heißen** *a* unasked for, unbidden; *adv* of o.'s own accord, spontaneously, voluntarily; **~heizt** *a* unfired; (*Zimmer*) cold; **~hemmt** *a* unchecked, unhampered; without restraint; **~heuchelt** *a* unfeigned; (*aufrichtig*) sincere; **~heuer** *a* huge, immense, tremendous, enormous; (*ausgedehnt*) vast; (*riesig*) monstrous; *adv* exceedingly; *ein ungeheurer Erfolg* a huge success; *ein ungeheures Wissen* vast knowledge; *~~ n* monster; **~~lich** *a* monstrous; **~~lichkeit** *f* monstrosity; (*Verbrechen*) enormity; **~hindert** *a* unchecked; **~hobelt** *a* not planed; *fig* unpolished, rude, rough-and-ready; (*grob*) coarse; *ein ~~er Mensch* an ill-bred man, a churl; **~hörig** *a* undue; improper; impertinent; **~~keit** *f* impropriety; **~horsam** *m* disobedience, insubordination; *~~ a* disobedient; *~~ sein* to disobey s. o.; **~klärt** *a* unclear, obscure; **~kocht** *a* unboiled; **~kühlt** *a* uncooled; **~kündigt** *a* not discharged; **~künstelt** *a* artless, unaffected; simple, natural; **~kürzt** *a* unabridged; **~laden** *a* uninvited; (*Gewehr*) unloaded; *el* uncharged, nonloaded; (*Wagen*) not loaded; **~leckt** *a* unlicked; **~legen** *a* inconvenient, inopportune, untimely; *~~ kommen* to inconvenience s. o., to intrude on s. o.; **~~heit** *f* inconvenience; trouble; *~~heiten machen* to give trouble to s. o., to molest s. o.;

-**lehrig** *a* indocile; -**lehrt** *a* illiterate, unlearned; -**lenk** *a* stiff; clumsy, awkward; -**lernt** *a* unskilled; -**löscht** *a* unquenched; *--er Kalk* unslaked lime; -**mach** *n* discomfort; hardship, trouble, adversity; -**mein** *a* extraordinary, uncommon; *-- viel* plenty of; -**messen** *a* unmeasured; *fig* unlimited; -**mildert** *a* unmitigated; -**mischt** *a* unmixed; -**münzt** *a* uncoined; *--es Gold* bullion; -**mütlich** *a* uncomfortable, dreary; (*Person*) nasty, unsociable, unpleasant; --**keit** *f* discomfort; -**nannt** *a* anonymous; -**nau** *a* inaccurate, inexact; *-- werden* to get out of true; --**igkeit** *f* inaccuracy, inexactitude; discrepancy.

*

ungeniert *a* free and easy, unceremonious.

unge|nießbar *a* not eatable; *auch fig* unpalatable; (*unerträglich*) unbearable; *-- machen* to denaturate; -**nügend** *a* insufficient; unsatisfactory, below standard; -**nügsam** *a* insatiable; --**keit** *f* insatiableness, greediness; -**nützt** *a* unused; unutilized, not made use of; *-- vorübergehen lassen* to let slip by; -**ordnet** *a* unsettled, unarranged; *--e Verhältnisse* disorder; -**pflastert** *a* unpaved; *--er Fußboden* unpaved (*od* earth) floor, *Am* dirt floor; -**pflegt** *a* neglected, untidy; -**prüft** *a* unexamined; -**rächt** *a* unavenged; -**rade** *a* not straight, out of line, uneven; (*gekrümmt*) crooked; (*Zahl*) odd; -**raten** *a* stunted; *fig* undutiful, degenerate; (*Kind*) spoiled; -**rechnet** *a* not counted; (*nicht einbegriffen*) not taken into account, not included; *prp* exclusively of; -**recht** *a* unjust, unfair, iniquitous; --**igkeit** *f* injustice; (*grobe*) iniquity; *schreiende --* burning shame; --**fertigt** *a* unjustified; unwarranted; -**regelt** *a* not regulated; *ein --es Leben führen* to lead a disorderly life; -**reimt** *a* unrhymed, blank; *fig* absurd; *--e Rede* nonsense; --**heit** *f* absurdity, preposterousness; -**richtet** *a radio* nondirectional. nondirective, equiradial; -**rinnbar** *a* uncoagulable; -**rn** *adv* unwillingly, reluctantly, with reluctance; -**röstet** *a* unroasted; -**rufen** *a* uncalled, unbidden; -**rührt** *a fig* unmoved, untouched, unaffected; -**rupft** *a* unplucked; *-- davonkommen* to get off without being fleeced.

unge|sagt *a* unsaid; -**salzen** *a* unsalted; (*Fische*) fresh; *fig* insipid; -**sättigt** *a* unsatiated; *chem* unsaturated; -**säuert** *a* unleavened; -**säumt** *a* unseamed; (*sofort*) immediate, prompt; *adv* without delay; -**schehen** *a* undone; -**schichtlich** *a* unhistorical; -**schick** *n*, --**lichkeit** *f* clumsiness, awkwardness; -**schickt** *a* clumsy, awkward, maladroit; *sl* ham-handed; *--er Mensch fam* big stiff; -**schlacht** *a* uncouth, rude; (*ungesittet*) barbarous, uncivilized; -**schlagen** *a* unbeaten, undefeated, unconquered; -**schliffen** *a* unpolished; (*Messer*) blunt; (*Edelstein*) rough; *fig* ill-bred, uncouth; --**heit** *f* want of polish; *fig* impoliteness; coarseness; -**schmälert** *a* undiminished, whole, unimpaired; -**schminkt** *a* not rouged, not done up; *fig* unvarnished; plain; -**schoren** *a* unshorn; *fig* unmolested; *jdn -- lassen* to let s. o. alone; -**geschützt** *a* unprotected, exposed; -**schwächt** *a* unweakened; unimpaired; -**sehen** *adv* unseen; -**sellig** *a* unsociable; --**keit** *f* unsociableness; -**setzlich** *a* illegal, unlawful; *für -- erklären* to outlaw; --**keit** *f* illegality; -**sittet** *a* impolite; uncivilized; (*unmanierlich*) unmannerly; -**stalt**, -**staltet** *a* deformed, ill-shaped, misshapen; -**stärkt** *a* not strengthened; (*Wäsche*) unstarched; -**steuert** *a* uncontrolled; -**stillt** *a* (*Hunger*) unappeased; (*Durst*) unquenched; (*Blut*) unstarched; -**stört** *a* undisturbed; uninterrupted; -**straft** *a* unpunished; *adv* with impunity; -**stüm** *a* violent, impetuous, fierce, blustering; *-- m u. n* violence, impetuosity; -**sucht** *a* unsought for; *fig* unaffected, artless; -**sund** *a* (*Person*) unhealthy; (*Ort, Essen*) unwholesome; *fig* unsound; fallacious; unreliable.

unge|teilt *a* undivided; -**treu** *a* perfidious, faithless; *--er Beamter Am sl* grafter; -**trübt** *a* cloudless; clear; untroubled; -**tüm** *n* monster; -**übt** *a* unexercised, unpracticed, untrained; (*Arbeiter*) inexperienced; -**wandt** *a* unskil(l)ful, awkward, clumsy; -**walkt** *a* rough; -**waschen** *a* unwashed; -**weiht** *a* profane; -**wiß** *a* uncertain; doubtful of; problematic; (*zweifelhaft*) precarious; *jdn im --en lassen* to leave s. o. in the air, to keep s. o. in suspense (*od* on tenterhooks); *Am* to keep s. o. guessing; --**heit** *f* uncertainty; incertitude; *in -- lassen* to keep in suspense; -**witter** *n* thunderstorm, violent storm; -**wöhnlich** *a* uncommon, unusual, strange; -**wohnt** *a* unwonted; (*Person*) unaccustomed (to), unfamiliar; (*Sache*) unusual; --**heit** *f* unwontedness; want of practice; -**wollt** *a* unintentional; -**zählt** *a* unnumbered, innumerable, untold; -**zähmt** *a* untamed; *fig* uncurbed; -**zähnt** *a* toothless; (*Briefmarke*) unperforated; -**zäumt** *a* unbridled; -**ziefer** *n* vermin; bugs *pl*, insects *pl*; --**vertilgungsmittel** *n* vermin destroyer; -**ziemend** *a* unseemly, unbecoming; (*frech*) impudent; -**zogen** *a* ill-bred, uncivil, rude; (*Kind*) naughty; *--er Bengel* brat; --**heit** *f* naughtiness; impertinence; -**zügelt** *a* unbridled; (*zügellos*) unrestrained; -**zwungen** *a* unconstrained, unforced; *fig* (*natürlich*) easy, unaffected; --**heit** *f* unconstraint; *fig* unaffectedness, ease, naturalness, spontaneity.

Un|glaube *m* (*Mißtrauen*) unbelief; *eccl* infidelity; -**gläubig** *a* incredulous; *eccl* unbelieving; (*heidnisch*) infidel; --**keit** *f* incredulity; unbelief; -**glaublich** *a* incredible; --**keit** *f* incredibility; -**glaubwürdig** *a* untrustworthy; *fam* fishy; (*unzuverlässig*) unreliable; (*unverbürgt*) unauthenticated.

ungleich *a* unequal, uneven; (*unähnlich*) dissimilar, unlike; (*verschieden*) different, varying, unmatched; (*Zahl*) odd; *adv* (*vor Komparativ*) by far, much; -**artig** *a* heterogeneous, different, dissimilar, nonuniform; --**keit** *f* heterogeneity, dissimilarity; -**förmig** *a* unlike; unequal; irregular; --**keit** *f* irregularity, discontinuity, asymetry; -**heit** *f* unequality; dissimilarity; diversity; unevenness; -**mäßig** *a* unequal, disproportionate; unsymmetrical; --**keit** *f* heterogeneity, discontinuity, nonuniformity; -**namig** *a el* opposite; -**schenklig** *a* unequal-sided; -**seitig** *math* (*Dreieck*) scalene.

Unglimpf *m* harshness; (*Schimpf*) insult; (*Ungerechtigkeit*) injustice, wrong; -**lich** *a* ungentle, harsh, rigorous.

Unglück *n* misfortune, adversity; (*Unfall*) accident, mishap, disaster; (*Schaden*) calamity, mischief; (*Elend*) misery, distress, reverse, calamity, disaster; (*Pech*) bad luck; (*unerwarteter Vorfall*) emergency; (*Mißgeschick*) misadventure; (*seelisch*) unhappiness; *zum -* unfortunately; *er ist ein Häufchen -* he's looking as if he had lost his last friend; *Glück im - haben* to be lucky at that; *vom - verfolgt* dogged by misfortune; -**lich** *a* unfortunate, unlucky; hapless, unhappy; (*verhängnisvoll*) ill-starred, ill-fated; (*erfolglos*) unsuccessful; (*elend*) miserable; (*Liebe*) unrequitted; --**erweise** *adv* unfortunately; -**selig** *a* (*Sache*) disastrous; (*Person*) wretched, miserable; -**sbote** *m* bearer of ill news; -**sbringer** *m Am* hoodoo; -**sfall** *m* accident, calamity, misadventure; (*Todesfall*) casualty; -**sgefährte** *m* fellow-sufferer; -**skind** *n* unhappy person; -**srabe** *m* croaker, *Am fam* jinx; -**svogel** *m* bird of ill omen; poor devil; -**szeichen** *n* ill omen.

Un|gnade *f* disgrace, displeasure; *in -- fallen* to fall into disgrace; to incur s. o.'s displeasure; *in -- sein Am fam* to be in the doghouse; -**gnädig** *a* ungracious, unkind; *etw -- aufnehmen* to take s. th. amiss; -**gültig** *a* null, void, invalid; (*Münze*) not current; (*Fahrkarte*) not available; *für -- erklären* to annul, to invalidate, to void, to nullify, to abolish, to declare null and void; *-- machen* to quash, to cancel, to set aside; --**keit** *f* invalidity; nullity; --**keitserklärung** *f* annulment; -**gunst** *f* disfavo(u)r; unpropitiousness; disadvantage; *-- der Witterung* inclemency; -**günstig** *a* unfavo(u)rable; (*nachteilig*) disadvantageous; *-- einwirken* to penalize; *--er Wind* head wind; -**gut** *a* unfriendly, unkind; *adv* not well, ill; *etw für -- nehmen* to take s. th. amiss; *nichts für --!* no offence! no harm meant!

un|haltbar *a* untenable; not durable; frivolous; -**handlich** *a* unwieldy; -**harmonisch** *a* inharmonious, discordant; -**heil** *n* mischief, harm, trouble; calamity, disaster; -**heilbar** *a* incurable; irreparable; --**keit** *f* incurableness; -**heilbringend** *a* fatal, unlucky, ominous; -**heilig** *a* unholy; profane; -**heilschwanger** *a* fraught with disaster; -**heilstifter** *m* mischief-maker; -**heilverkündend** *a* ominous, portentous; -**heilvoll** *a* disastrous, calamitous; pernicious; -**heimlich** *a* uncomfortable; (*Ort*) haunted; (*nicht geheuer*) uncanny; (*schlimm*) sinister (*für* to); -**höflich** *a* impolite, rude; incivil; --**keit** *f* impoliteness, rudeness; incivility; -**hold** *a* unkind; ill-disposed; *-- m* fiend, monster; -**hörbar** *a* inaudible; -**hygienisch** *a* insanitary.

Uniform *f* uniform; regimentals *pl*; (*Feld-*) battledress; -**ieren** *tr* to (dress in) uniform.

Unikum *n* unique object; original person.

uninteress|ant *a* uninteresting; -**iert** *a* uninterested.

universal *a* universal; -**erbe** *m* sole heir, (*nach Abzug der Schulden etc*) residuary legatee; -**mittel** *n* sovereign (*od* universal) remedy, panacea, cure-all; -**schlüssel** *m* universal screw wrench, *Am* monkey spanner; -**schraubenschlüssel** *m* skeleton key, *Am* monkey wrench; -**werkzeug** *n* all-purpose tool.

Univers|ität *f* university; college; --**sauswahlmannschaft** *f* varsity; --**sgelände** *n* college grounds *pl*; *Am* campus; --**sprofessor** *m* university professor; --**szeit** *f* college-years *pl*; -**um** *n* universe.

Unke *f* toad; -**n** *itr fam* to prophesy evil; -**nruf** *m* croaking.

un|kenntlich *a* indiscernible, unrecognizable; ~~ *machen* to disguise; **~kenntnis** *f* ignorance; **~keusch** *a* unchaste, lewd; **~~heit** *f* unchastity, lewdness; **~kindlich** *a* unchildlike; (*frühreif*) precocious; **~kirchlich** *a* unclerical; (*weltlich*) secular, worldly; **~klar** *a* not clear; (*trübe*) muddy; turbid; (*nebelig*) hazy, misty; (*undeutlich*) indistinct; *fig* obscure, unintelligible; *tech* not ready for use; *über etw im ~~en sein* to be uncertain about; to be in the dark about; **~~heit** *f* want of clearness; obscurity; **~klug** *a* imprudent; **~~heit** *f* imprudence, foolish action; **~kompliziert** *a* straightforward; **~kontrollierbar** *a* uncontrollable; **~körperlich** *a* incorporeal; immaterial; spiritual; **~kosten** *pl* charges *pl*, expenses *pl*, costs *pl*; *allgemeine ~~* overhead expenses; *laufende ~~* running costs; *sich in ~~ stürzen* to put o. s. to charge; *nach Abzug aller ~~* charges deducted; *jdm ~~ machen* to put s. o. to expenses; **~kraut** *n* weed; *~~ vergeht nicht* ill weeds grow apace; **~~bekämpfung** *f* weed control; **~~jäter** *m* weeder; **~~vertilgungsmittel** *n* weed killer; **~kündbar** *a* irredeemable; consolidated; (*Renten*) perpetual; (*Stellung*) permanent; **~kundig** *a* unacquainted with; *~~ sein* to be ignorant of.

un|längst *adv* lately, recently, not long ago, the other day; **~lauter** *a* impure; unfair, dishonest; *~~er Wettbewerb* unfair competition; **~leidlich** *a* intolerable, unbearable; **~lenksam** *a* unmanageable, unruly; *fig* indocile; **~leserlich** *a* illegible, unreadable; **~leugbar** *a* indisputable, evident, undeniable; **~lieb, ~~sam** *a* disagreeable; **~liebenswürdig** *a* unkind, unamiable; **~liniiert** *a* unruled; **~logisch** *a* illogical; **~lösbar** *a* insoluble; *chem* indissoluble; **~lust** *f* disgust, displeasure; (*Abneigung*) dislike, aversion, disinclination; *com* dul(l)ness, flatness; **~lustig** *a* listless, reluctant (to), disinclined.

un|magnetisch *a* unmagnetized, nonmagnetic; **~manierlich** *a* unmannerly; awkward; **~männlich** *a* unmanly, effeminate; **~masse, ~menge** *f* enormous number; **~maßgeblich** *a* without authority; open to correction; unpresuming; **~mäßig** *a* immoderate, excessive; (*im Trinken*) intemperate; **~~keit** *f* immoderateness; intemperance; excess; **~menge** *f* enormous quantity; **~mensch** *m* barbarian, brute; **~menschlich** *a* inhuman, barbarous; *fam* terrible, tremendous; **~~keit** *f* inhumanity; cruelty; **~merklich** *a* imperceptible, insensible; **~meßbar** *a* immeasurable; **~methodisch** *a* unmethodical; **~militärisch** *a* unmilitary; **~mißverständlich** *a* evident, unequivocal, *fam* sharp; **~mittelbar** *a* direct, immediate, just off, *Am* right off, right next to; **~möbliert** *a* unfurnished; **~modern** *a* old-fashioned, out of fashion, antiquated; **~moduliert** *a* unmodulated; **~möglich** *a* impossible; **~~keit** *f* impossibility; **~moralisch** *a* immoral; **~motiviert** *a* without motive; not sufficiently motivated; (*unbegründet*) unfounded; **~mündig** *a* not of age, minor; **~~keit** *f* minority; **~musikalisch** *a* unmusical; **~mut** *m* ill humo(u)r; displeasure; **~mutig** *a* ill-humo(u)red, angry, annoyed.

unnach|ahmlich *a* inimitable; **~giebig** *a* unyielding, relentless, tough, inflexible; uncompromising; **~~keit** *f* rigidity; **~sichtig** *a* unrelenting, pitiless; (*streng*) strict, severe.

un|nahbar *a* unapproachable, inaccessible; **~natürlich** *a* unnatural; (*geziert*) affected; **~~keit** *f* unnaturalness; affectation; **~nennbar** *a* ineffable, unutterable, inexpressible; **~nötig** *a* unnecessary, needless; **~nütz** *a* useless, unprofitable; (*überflüssig*) superfluous; (*nichtig*) idle; (*fruchtlos*) vain.

un|ordentlich *a* disorderly, careless, untidy; (*schäbig*) shabby, dowdy, *Am* tacky; (*schlampig*) slipshod; (*verwirrt*) confused; (*unsauber*) messy; **~ordnung** *f* disorder, confusion, untidiness, *Am fam* muss; (*Durcheinander*) mess; *in ~~* in a mess, out of order, out of gear, topsy-turvy; *in ~~ bringen* to derange, to throw into a confusion, to mess up; *in ~~ sein* to be in a muddle; *in ~~ kommen* to fall into disorder; **~organisch** *a* inorganic; **~orthographisch** *a* unorthographical, misspelt.

un|paar *adv* (*Zahl*) not even; (*Handschuhe*) odd; **~paarwertig** *a* of odd valence; **~parlamentarisch** *a* unparliamentary; **~parteiisch** *a* impartial, disinterested, unbias(s)ed; **~~e(r)** *m* umpire; **~parteilich** *a* unbias(s)ed; **~~keit** *f* impartiality; **~passend** *a* unsuitable; (*unschicklich*) improper, indecorous, unbecoming; (*unzeitgemäß*) inopportune, untimely; (*ungehörig*) inappropriate; (*unangebracht*) misplaced, misfitting; **~päßlich** *a* indisposed, unwell, ailing, ill; **~~keit** *f* indisposition, illness; **~passierbar** *a* impassable; **~patriotisch** *a* unpatriotic; **~periodisch** *a* nonperiodic, nonrecurrent; **~persönlich** *a* impersonal; **~pfändbar** *a* unseizable; **~poliert** *a* unpolished; **~politisch** *a* non-political; **~praktisch** *a* unpractical; *Am* impractical; (*unerfahren*) inexpert, unskil(l)ful; **~produktiv** *a* unproductive; **~pünktlich** *a* unpunctual, inexact, irregular; **~qualifiziert** *a* unqualified.

un|rasiert *a* unshaven; **~rast** *f* restlessness; **~rat** *m* dirt, rubbish, refuse; *~~ wittern* to smell a rat; **~rationell** *a* wasteful; **~ratsam** *a* unadvisable; **~recht** *a* wrong, injust, unfair; (*unrichtig*) incorrect; (*schlecht*) bad, evil; (*unpassend*) unsuitable; (*ungeeignet*) improper; (*ungelegen*) inopportune; *an den ~~en kommen* to pick the wrong man, to catch a Tartar; *am ~~en Ort* out of place; **~~ n** wrong, injustice; (*Schaden*) injury; *jur* tort; *jdm ~~ tun* to do s. o. an injustice; *im ~~ sein* to be in the wrong, to be mistaken; *zu ~~* unjustly, unlawfully, illegally; *jdm ~~ geben* to decide against s. o.; **~~mäßig** *a* illegal, unlawful; **~~mäßigkeit** *f* illegality, unlawfulness; **~redlich** *a* dishonest; **~~keit** *f* dishonesty; **~reell** *a* (*unlauter*) unfair; (*unehrlich*) dishonest; (*unzuverlässig*) unreliable; **~regelmäßig** *a* irregular, anomalous, erratic; *jur* informal; **~~keit** *f* irregularity, anomaly; **~reif** *a* unripe, green; *fig* immature; **~reife** *f* unripeness, immaturity; **~rein** *a* unclean; *fig* impure; (*roh*) crude; (*schmutzig*) dirty; (*Flüssigkeit*) muddy; (*Luft*) vitiated; (*Stil*) incorrect; *ins ~~e schreiben* to jot down, to make a rough copy; **~~heit** *f* uncleanness; *fig* impurity; **~reinlich** *a* unclean; dirty, filthy; **~~keit** *f* uncleanliness; **~rentabel** *a* unprofitable, not paying; **~rettbar** *a* irrecoverable; past help, past saving; *~~ verloren* irretrievably lost; **~richtig** *a* incorrect, wrong; (*irrtümlich*) erroneous; **~~keit** *f* incorrectness; **~ritterlich** *a* unchivalrous; **~rühmlich** *a* inglorious; **~ruh** *f* (*Uhr*) balance; **~ruhe** *f* restlessness, uneasiness, unrest; (*Beklemmung*) anxiety; (*Störung*) disturbance, trouble, *Am fam* worriment; (*Sorge*) disquiet; (*Aufruhr*) commotion, riot, alarm; (*Unsicherheit*) instability, unsteadiness; error; (*Uhr*) balance; **~ruhig** *a* restless; uneasy; troublesome; (*ungleichmäßig*) unsteady, uneven; (*laut*) noisy, unquiet; (*aufbrausend*) effervescent; (*Pferd*) restive, skittish; (*lärmend*) turbulent; (*Meer*) choppy; (*besorgt*) worried; (*zappelig*) fidgety; (*nervös*) jumpy, nervous, jittery; (*erschreckt*) panicky (*über* at); (*Schlaf*) unsound; **~ruhstifter** *m* disturber; agitator; troublemaker, troubler; *Am fam* hellion; (*Wirrkopf*) *Am sl* screwball; **~rühmlich** *a* inglorious; **~rund** *a* out of true, out of round; noncircular.

uns *prn acc* us, *dat* (to) us; (*reflexiv*) (to) ourselves.

un|sachgemäß *adv* improperly, incorrectly; (*ungeschickt*) unskil(l)fully; **~sachlich** *a* subjective, not objective, (*nicht zur Sache gehörig*) not to the point, not pertinent; **~sagbar, ~säglich** *a* unspeakable, ineffable, unutterable; *fig* immense; **~sanft** *a* ungentle; **~sauber** *a* untidy; (*schmutzig*) dirty, filthy; (*unlauter*) unfair; (*schmierig*) smudgy; **~~keit** *f* uncleanliness; **~schädlich** *a* harmless; innocuous; *~~ machen* to render harmless; to disarm; (*Gift*) to neutralize; **~scharf** *a* (*Bild*) blurred, hazy; (*Apparat*) out of focus; (*Begriff*) poorly defined; **~schärfe** *f* (*Bild*) lack of definition; **~schätzbar** *a* inestimable, invaluable; **~scheinbar** *a* (*unbedeutend*) insignificant; (*schlicht*) plain, homely, unpretending; **~schicklich** *a* improper, indecent, unseemly, unbecoming; **~~keit** *f* impropriety, indecency; **~schlitt** *n* tallow; **~schlüssig** *a* irresolute, wavering; *~~ sein* to hesitate, to hang on; **~~keit** *f* irresolution, indecision, hesitation; **~schmackhaft** *a* unpalatable; **~schmelzbar** *a* infusible; **~schön** *a* unpleasant, plain; ugly; *Am* homely; *fig* unfair; **~schuld** *f* innocence; *ich wasche meine Hände in ~~* I wash my hands of it; *e-e ~~ vom Lande* a rube; **~~ig** *a* innocent (of); (*jungfräulich*) virgin; (*harmlos*) harmless; (*keusch*) chaste; *für ~~ig erklären* to declare innocent; *sich für ~~ig erklären* to plead not guilty; **~schwer** *a* easy, not difficult; **~segen** *m* adversity; (*Fluch*) curse; **~selbständig** *a* dependent on others, helpless; non-self-sustaining; nonspontaneous; **~~keit** *f* dependence (on others); lack of independence; (*Hilflosigkeit*) helplessness; **~selig** *a* unfortunate, fatal; (*verflucht*) accursed.

unser *prn* our; of us; ours; **~ige, unsrige** *a* ours; *die ~~n* our people; **~einer, ~eins** *prn* like me, the like of us; **~sgleichen** *a* our equals; **~thalben, ~twegen, ~twillen** *adv* for our sake, on account of us.

un|sicher *a* unsafe; (*Hand*) unsteady; (*auf den Beinen*) shaky, wabbly; (*gefährlich*) precarious; (*unentschlossen*) irresolute; (*seelisch*) not sure of o. s.; (*zweifelhaft*) doubtful, dubious, uncertain; *jdn ~~ machen Am* to rattle s. o.; *die Wege ~~ machen* to infest the ways; **~~heit** *f* insecurity; unsteadiness; shakiness; uncertainty; precariousness; **~~heitsfaktor** *m* instability factor; **~sichtbar** *a* invisible; **~~keit** *f* invisibility; **~sichtig** *a* of zero visibility; hazy; **~sinn** *m* nonsense, tricks *pl*; rubbish, *Am* boloney; absurdity; foolishness, *sl* bilge; *~~!* nonsense! fiddlesticks! rubbish! *sl* nuts! *Am* fudge! applesauce! razzberries! rats! **~~** *reden* to talk nonsense, to blather; **~sinnig** *a* nonsensical, absurd; insensate; foolish, stupid, *Am fam* poppycockish; *Am sl* screwy; **~~keit** *f* insanity, madness; **~sitte** *f* bad habit; (*Mißbrauch*) abuse; **~sittlich** *a* immoral; **~~keit** *f* immorality; indecency; **~solid** *a* not solid; unreliable; (*Lebensweise*) loose, dissipated; **~sortiert** *a* unscreened; **~sozial** *a* unsocial, antisocial; unsociable; **~sportlich** *a* unsportsmanlike; **~ständig** *a* impermanent; **~~** *Beschäftigte(r)* casual worker; **~~e** *Beschäftigung* casual employment; **~starr** *a* nonrigid, flexible; **~~es** *Luftschiff* nonrigid airship; (*kleines*) blimp; **~statthaft** *a* inadmissible; (*ungesetzlich*) illegal, illicit; **~sterblich** *a* immortal; **~~keit** *f* immortality; **~stern** *m* unlucky star; *fig* disaster, mischance; **~stet** *a* unsteady; inconstant; (*wanderlustig*) vagrant; (*unruhig*) restless; (*veränderlich*) changeable; (*unterbrochen*) discontinuous, intermittent; (*unbeständig*) labile, unstable; **~igkeit** *f* unsteadiness; (*Unbeständigkeit*) inconstancy; (*Unruhe*) restlessness; (*Wanderlust*) vagrancy; (*Lage*) unsettled condition; **~stillbar** *a* unappeasable; (*Blut*) not to be stanched; (*Durst*) unquenchable; (*unersättlich*) insatiable; **~stimmigkeit** *f* discrepancy; (*innerer Widerspruch*) inconsistency; (*Unterschied*) difference; (*Widerspruch*) disagreement; (*Unvereinbarkeit*) variance; (*Ungleichheit*) disparity; **~strafbar** *a*, **~sträflich** *a* irreproachable, blameless; **~~keit** *f* irreprehensibleness; **~streitig** *a* indisputable, incontestable; **~sühnbar** *a* inexpiable; **~summe** *f* enormous sum; **~symmetrisch** *a* unsymmetrical, unbalanced; **~sympathisch** *a* unpleasant, distasteful, disagreeable; *er ist mir* **~~** I don't like him.

*

un|tadelhaft *a*, **~tadelig** *a* blameless, irreproachable; (*Material*) faultless, flawless; **~tat** *f* crime; **~tätig** *a* inactive, idle; **~~keit** *f* inactivity, idleness; **~tauglich** *a* unfit, unapt; (*Personen*) incompetent; (*unpassend*) unsuitable; (*nutzlos*) useless; (*unbrauchbar*) unserviceable; (*leistungsunfähig*) inefficient; *mil* unfit, disabled; **~~** *machen* to disqualify; *mil* to disable; **~~keit** *f* unfitness, unaptness; incompetence; disqualification; **~teilbar** *a* indivisible; **~~keit** *f* indivisibility.

unten *adv* below, beneath; (*im Hause*) downstairs; (*unterhalb*) underneath; (*am Grunde von*) at the bottom of; (*am Fuße von*) at the foot of; *von* **~** *nach oben* from the bottom toward the top; *von oben bis* **~** from head to foot, up and down; from top to bottom; *von* **~** *her* from underneath; *er ist bei mir* **~** *durch* I'm through with him; *hier* **~** here below; *von* **~** *auf* from below; *von* **~** *auf dienen* to serve from the ranks; **~** *genannt* undermentioned; **~***stehend* as below.

unter *prp* under, beneath, below; (*unterhalb, darunter*) underneath; (*zwischen*) among, amongst, between; (*zeitlich*) during; (*Preis*) for less than, for under; **~** *dem Preis* for less than the value; **~** *der Hand* secretly; **~** *dem Vorwand* under pretence; **~** *der Bedingung* on condition that; **~** *Freunden* among friends; **~** *seiner Regierung* in his reign; **~** *seiner Würde* beneath his dignity; **~** *Tag* underground workings; **~** *uns gesagt* between you and me; *Geld* **~** *die Leute bringen* to make the money go round; **~** *a* lower, inferior; **~** *m* (*Kartenspiel*) knave.

Unter|abteilung *f* subdivision; branch; sub-unit; subsection; **~arm** *m* forearm; **~art** *f* subvariety, subspecies; **~arzt** *m* junior surgeon; surgeon-ensign; **~ausschuß** *m* subcommittee; **~bau** *m* substructure; infra-structure; (*Weg*) foundation; *rail* formation level; (*Stütze*) support, base; *arch* underpinning; (*Erdbau*) earthwork; (*Grundierung*) groundwork; **~bau'en** *tr* to underpin; *fig* to lay the basis of; **~beinkleid** *n* drawers *pl*; (*Männer*) pants *pl*; (*Frauen*) knickers *pl*; **~belegt** *a* (*Wohnung*) not fully utilized (accommodation); **~belichten** *tr* to underexpose; **~belichtung** *f* underexposure; **~bett** *n* feather-bed; **~bewerten** *tr* to undervalue; to hold in mean estimation; **~bewußtsein** *n* the subconscious; **~bie'ten** *irr tr* to underbid; to undersell; (*Preise*) to undercut, to dump; (*Rekord*) to lower; **~bilanz** *f* short (*od* adverse) balance, deficit; **~binden** *irr tr* to tie up, **~~'** to ligature; (*Angriff*) to neutralize; *fig* to prevent, to cut off, to paralyse; to stop; (*vorbeugen*) to forestall; **~bi'ndung** *f* ligature; preventing, choking off, forestalling; **~blei'ben** *irr itr* to be left undone; (*Veranstaltung*) to be cancelled, not to take place; (*aufhören*) to cease, to be discontinued; **~bre'chen** *irr tr* to interrupt, to shut off, to disconnect; *Am aero mil* to interdict; *el* to switch off; (*Reise*) to break, *Am* to stop over (*od* off); (*Rede*) to cut short; (*Verhandlung*) to stay; (*aussetzen*) to discontinue; (*einstellen*) to suspend; **~bre'cher** *m* interrupter; break, cutout, circuit breaker, commutator; **~bre'chung** *f* interruption, break, disconnection, intermission; stop; (*Unfall*) accident; (*Verzögerung*) delay; (*Fahrt*) *Am* stopover; *Am aero mil* interdiction; **~~sfunke** *m* break spark; **~~skontakt** *m* break contact; **~~sstelle** *f* point of interruption; **~~sstrom** *m* current of break; **~'breiten** *tr* to spread under; **~~'** to lay before, to submit (to); **~bringen** *irr tr* to place, (*beherbergen*) to lodge, to house, to accommodate, to shelter; (*Truppen*) to billet, to quarter; (*in e-r Stelle*) to provide (a place) for; (*Anleihe*) to place, to dispose of; (*Kapital*) to invest; (*Waren*) to sell, to find a market for; (*Wechsel*) to negotiate, to discount; (*lagern*) to store, to stow; *untergebracht sein* to be taken care of; **~bringung** *f* lodgings *pl*; accommodation, housing; billet; *aero* hangarage; (*Anleihe*) placing; (*Kapital*) investment; (*Verkauf*) sale; **~~sgebiet** *n* quartering area; **~~skosten** *pl* costs of housing; **~~smöglichkeit** *f* accommodation; **~bro'chen** *a* interrupted, broken, intermittent, discontinuous; **~deck** *n* lowerdeck; **~derhand** *adv* secretly, in secret; **~de'ssen** *adv* in the meantime, meanwhile; **~druck** *m* underpressure, reduced pressure; **~~förderer** *m* vacuum fuel pump; **~~gebiet** *n* low-pressure area; **~~kammer** *f* pressure-testing chamber, low-pressure chamber; **~drü'cken** *tr* to suppress; (*bedrücken*) to oppress; (*Aufstand*) to crush; to quell; (*Seufzer*) to repress; (*ersticken*) to smother, to stifle, to choke down; **~drü'cker** *m* oppressor, suppressor; **~drü'ckung** *f* oppression; suppression; repression; **~durchschnittlich** *a* subaverage.

untere *a* low, inferior.

unter|einander *adv* among one another, mutually, reciprocally; (*miteinander*) together; (*in Unordnung*) in confusion; **~entwickelt** *a* underdeveloped; **~ernährt** *a* underfed, undernourished; **~ernährung** *f* underfeeding, undernourishment, malnutrition; **~fa'ngen** *irr r* to attempt, to dare, to venture (to), to presume (to); **~~** *n* venture, bold attempt; enterprise, undertaking; **~fassen** *tr* to take the arm of s. o.; **~feldwebel** *m* staff sergeant; **~fe'rtigen** *tr* to sign; **~fe'rtigte(r)** *m* the undersigned; **~feurung** *f* undergrate firing; **~führer** *m* subordinate commander; **~führung** *f* subway; (*Straße*) undercrossing structure; *Am auch rail* underpass; **~futter** *n* lining; **~fü'ttern** *tr* to line; **~gang** *m astr* setting; decline; *fig* ruin; fall; (*Schiff*) shipwreck; (*Sonne*) sunset; (*Zerstörung*) destruction; (*Aussterben*) extinction; **~gärig** *a* bottom-fermented; **~gattung** *f* subspecies **~ge'ben** *a* subject, inferior; under a person's control; **~~e** *Stelle* lower command; **~~e(r)** *m* subordinate; **~gehen** *irr itr* to sink, to founder; *fig* to perish; (*Sonne*) to set; *mit Mann u. Maus* **~~** to go down with all hands; **~geordnet** *a* subordinate, inferior; secondary, minor; immaterial; subsidiary; **~geschoben** *a* supposititious; (*Kind*) foisted; (*Dokument*) forged; **~geschoß** *n* ground-floor, *Am* first floor; **~gestell** *n* undercarriage; base; underframe; **~gewicht** *n* underweight; **~gra'ben** *irr tr* to undermine, to sap; *fig* to corrupt; to be subversive (to); *den Grund* **~~** to sap the foundation; **~gra'bung** *f* undermining; **~griff** *m* (*Ringen*) undersnatch; (*Rad*) single flange; **~grund** *m* substratum, subsoil; (*auch fig*) bedrock; (*fester* **~~**) *Am* hardpan; (*Malerei*) ground; **~~bahn** *f* underground (railway), tube, *Am* subway; **~~bewegung** *f* underground (organization *od* movement), resistance movement; **~gruppe** *f* subgroup, detachment; **~gurt** *m aero* bottom flange; **~guß** *m phot* substratum; **~haken** *tr fam* to take s. o.'s arm; **~halb** *prp* below, under, at the lower end of; downstream.

Unter|halt *m* support; (*Lebens-*) subsistence, livelihood, maintenance; upkeep; *für den* **~~** *sorgen* to provide for; **~'halten** *irr tr* to hold under; **~~'** *tr* to maintain; (*ergötzlich*) to amuse, to divert, to enjoy, to entertain; (*Feuer*) to feed, to replenish; (*Briefwechsel*) to keep up; *sich mit jdm* **~~** to converse with, to talk to; *sich* **~~** to enjoy o. s., to have a good time, to amuse o. s.; **~~d, ~ha'ltsam** *a* amusing, entertaining; **~***haltsame Weisen* light music; **~haltsanspruch** *m* right to alimony; **~haltsberechtigter** *m* dependent; **~haltskosten** *pl* living expense; **~haltspflicht** *f* liability for maintenance; **~haltszuschuß** *m* maintenance allowance; **~ha'ltung** *f* amusement, entertainment, *Am* bee; (*Gespräch*) conversation; (*Aufrechterhaltung*) maintenance, upkeep, keeping up; (*Unterstützung*) support; **~~sbeilage** *f* literary supplement; **~~skosten** *pl* maintenance (costs *pl*), cost of upkeep; (*Gebäude*) cost of repairs; **~~sliteratur** *f* light reading, fiction; **~~sprogramm** *n radio* light program; (*Kino: Beiprogramm*) supporting program(me); **~ha'ndeln** *itr* to negotiate, to treat with, *mil* to parley; **~'händler** *m* negotiator; agent; *com* broker; (*Vermittler*) mediator, go-between; *mil* bearer of a flag of truce, parliamentary; **~handlung** *f* negotiation; parley; *in ~~ stehen mit* to carry on negotiations with; *in ~~ treten mit* to enter into negotiation with; **~haus** *n* House of Commons, Lower House; *Am* House of Representatives; **~hemd** *n* vest, *Am* undershirt ; *~~ mit kurzen Ärmeln* T-style undershirt; **~hitze** *f* lower heating; **~hö'hlen** *tr* to undermine, to hollow out; **~holz** *n* underwood, copse, brushwood, undergrowth; **~hose** *f* (a pair of) pants *pl;* shorts *pl, Am* (under)drawers *pl;* **~irdisch** *a* subterraneous; underground; **~jacke** *f* undervest; (*wollen*) singlet; **~jo'chen** *tr* to subjugate, to subdue; **~jo'chung** *f* subjugation; **~ke'llern** *tr* to provide with a cellar; **~kiefer** *m* lower jaw; **~kleid** *n* slip; **~kleidung** *f* underwear; (*Frauen*) *fam* undies *pl;* **~kommen** *irr itr* to find lodgings (*od* accommodation); (*Beschäftigung*) to find employment (*od* a situation); *~~ n,* **~kunft** *f* (*Wohnung*) abode, dwelling; (*Wohnraum*) housing space; (*Räumlichkeit*) accommodation; (*Obdach*) shelter, place to stay; (*Untermiete*) lodgings *pl;* (*Etagenwohnung*) flat, flatlet; (*Zimmer*) room, *Am* apartment; *mil* billet, quarters *pl,* cantonment; (*Bude*) diggings *pl, fam* digs *pl;* (*Arbeitsstelle*) situation, place, employment; *~kunft u. Verpflegung* board and lodging; **~kunftsraum** *m* shelter; *rail* shed; **~kopieren** *tr phot* to underprint; **~körper** *m* lower part of the body; **~kriegen** *tr* to get the better of, to get s. o. down; *sich nicht ~~ lassen* to hold o.'s ground; **~kü'hlt** *a* undercooled; **~kü'hlung** *f* undercooling.

Unter|lage *f tech* base plate, foundation, support; rubble bed; *arch* underpin; *geol* substratum; (*Stütze*) rest; (*Schreib~~*) (blotting-) pad; (*Kleinkinder*) waterproof sheet; (*Futter*) lining; (*Beweis*) evidence; (*Beleg*) proof, voucher; (*Schriftstücke*) records *pl,* documents *pl;* (*Angaben*) data *pl;* **~land** *n* lowland; **~laß** *m* intermission; *ohne ~~* without intermission, incessantly, continually; **~la'ssen** *irr tr* to omit; (*versäumen*) to fail; (*vernachlässigen*) to neglect; (*sich enthalten*) to abstain from, to refrain from, to leave off; to forbear; **~la'ssung** *f* omission; neglect; **~~sklage** *f* action for injunction; **~~s-sünde** *f* sin of omission; **~lauf** *m* lower river, lower course; **~'laufen** *irr itr* to run under; to slip in; *mit ~~* to occur; *a* (*mit Blut ~~'*) bloodshot; **~legen** *tr* to put under; *e-n anderen Sinn ~~* to put another construction upon, to give another meaning to; *Worte ~~* to set words (to); *~~' a* overcome, beaten; *~~ sein* to be inferior; **~~e(r)** *m* underdog; **~legkeil** *m* wedge; **~legring** *m* washer; **~leib** *m* abdomen; **~~s...** abdominal; **~lie'gen** *irr itr* to be overcome, to succumb; (*verpflichtet sein*) to be liable to, to be subject to; *keinem Zweifel ~~* to admit of no doubt; **~lippe** *f* lower lip.

unter|ma'len *tr* to prime, to put on the ground colo(u)r; **~mau'ern** *tr* to underpin, to build a foundation to, to underset; **~me'ngen, ~mi'schen** *tr* to intermingle, to intermix; **~mensch** *m* gangster; **~~lich** *a* subhuman; **~mieter** *m* subtenant, lodger, *Am* roomer; **~minie'ren** *tr* to undermine.

unterne'hm|en *irr tr* to undertake; (*versuchen*) to attempt; (*wagen*) to venture, to risk, to hazard; *~~ n* enterprise, undertaking, firm, *Am* operation; (*Wagnis*) venture; (*Versuch*) attempt; (*gewagtes ~~*) adventure; *mil* operation; *ein schwindelhaftes ~~* a bogus enterprise, *Am* a wildcat business; *gemeinnütziges ~~* a non--profit making enterprise; **~end** *a* enterprising, bold; **~er** *m* manager; (*vertraglich*) contractor; (*Arbeitgeber*) employer; *com* enterpreneur; **~~gewinn** *m* employer's profit; **~~organisation** *f* employers' organization; **~~tum** *n* business, free enterprise; **~~verbände** *m pl* employers' associations *pl;* **~ung** *f* enterprise, undertaking; **~~sgeist** *m* spirit of enterprise, *Am fam* go-aheadativeness; *keinen ~~ haben sl* to have no guts; **~~slustig** *a* enterprising, *Am sl* full of pep.

Unter|offizier *m* non-commissioned officer, N. C. O., *Am* non-com; (*Dienstgrad*) corporal; **~ordnen** *tr* to subordinate, to make secondary; *r* to submit (to); *von ~geordneter Bedeutung sein* to be of secondary importance; **~ordnung** *f* subordination; **~pacht** *f* sublease; **~pächter** *m* subtenant; **~pfand** *n* pledge; *zum ~ geben* to pledge; **~pflügen** *tr* to plough (*Am* plow) under; **~prima** *f* lower Sixth; **~re'den** *r* to converse, to confer with; **~re'dung** *f* conference, conversation; (*zu Pressezwecken*) interview.

Unterricht *m* instruction, lessons *pl,* school; (*im Freien*) outdoor classes *pl;* (*Privat-*) tuition; (*Erziehung*) education; (*Lehren*) teaching; *~ geben* to teach; **~'en** *tr* to instruct, to teach, to train; (*erziehen*) to educate; (*e-e Stunde geben*) to give a lesson; (*einweisen*) to brief; (*benachrichtigen*) to inform (*über* of), to acquaint (with), to advise (of), *Am* to put s. o. wise (to); **~sbriefe** *m pl* correspondence--lessons *pl;* **~sfilm** *m* documentary film; **~sministerium** *n* Board of Education; **~sstoff** *m* subject matter; **~sstunde** *f* lesson, *Am* period; **~swesen** *n* education, public instruction, educational matters *pl;* **~ung** *f* information; *nur zur ~~* for information only.

Unterrock *m* petticoat, (*modern*) slip.

unter|sa'gen *tr* to forbid (to), to prohibit (from); **~sa'gung** *f* interdiction, prohibition; **~satz** *m* support, supporter; (*Gestell*) stand, base, pedestal; *arch* socle; (*Topf*) saucer; (*Rhetorik*) minor; **~schale** *f* saucer; (*Elektron*) subshell; **~schallgeschwindigkeit** *f* subsonic velocity; **~schä'tzen** *tr* to undervalue; to underrate; **~schei'den** *irr tr* to distinguish, to discern, to differentiate, to discriminate; to tell (from); *r* to differ (from); **~~d** *a* distinctive; **~schei'dung** *f* distinction, discrimination; (*Unterschied*) difference; **~~s-merkmal** *n* distinguishing feature, distinctive mark; **~~svermögen** *n* power of discrimination; **~schenkel** *m* shank; **~schicht** *f* lower stratum; **~schieben** *irr tr* to shove under; (*an die Stelle setzen*) to substitute; *fig* to attribute falsely; to foist (on), to father (upon); (*zur Last legen*) to impute (to); (*hineinschmuggeln*) to insinuate (into); (*Testament*) to forge a will; **~schied** *m* difference; distinction; (*unterschiedliche Behandlung*) discrimination; (*Schwankung*) variation; *zum ~~ von* as distinguished from; *es macht wenig ~~* it matters little; *ohne ~~* alike; irrespective of; **~~lich** *a* different, diverse; distinct; (*veränderlich*) variable; **~~slos** *a* indiscriminate; *adv* without exception; **~schlächtig** *a* undershot; **~'schlagen** *irr tr* to cross o.'s arms; *~~'* (*Geld*) to embezzle; (*Brief*) to intercept; (*Testament*) to suppress; (*veruntreuen*) to defalcate; **~schla'gung** *f* embezzlement; interception; suppression; **~schleif** *m* fraud, embezzlement; **~schlupf** *m* shelter, refuge; dugout; hiding place; **~schrei'-ben** *irr tr* to sign, to subscribe to; **~schrei'ten** *irr tr* to fall short (*od* below); to keep within; **~schrie'bene(r)** *m* signed; **~schrift** *f* signature; *film* caption; *e-e ~~ leisten* to subscribe; **~~enmappe** *f* signature blotting-book; due-date portfolio; **~~sber echtigt** *a* authorized to sign; **~~sprobe** *f* specimen signature; **~~svollmacht** *f* authorization to sign; *pol* signatory power.

Unter|seeboot *n* (*siehe auch: U-Boot*) submarine; U-boat; *sl* sub; **~~abwehr** *f* anti-sub-marine defence; **~~falle** *f* Q-ship, Q-boat; **~~jäger** *m* submarine chaser; **~~streitkräfte** *f pl* submarine force; **~~sstützpunkt** *m* submarine base; **~seeisch** *a* submarine; **~seekabel** *n* submarine cable; **~seite** *f* lower side, bottom side; *mit der ~~ nach oben* upside down; **~sekunda** *f* lower Fifth; **~'setzen** *tr* to set under; *mit etw ~~'* to mix; **~'setzer** *m* saucer; flowerpot-stand; **~se'tzt** *a* thick-set; square-built, dumpy, squat, stocky; *tech* geared down; **~se'tzung** *f* reduction (gearing); **~sie'geln** *tr* to seal; **~'sinken** *irr itr* to sink, to go down; **~spü'len** *tr* to wash away, to hollow out from below.

unterst *a* lowest, undermost; bottom; (*niedrigst*) nethermost; (*letzt*) last; *das Unterste zuoberst kehren* to turn everythink topsy-turvy.

Unter|staatssekretär *m* Under-Secretary of State; **~stand** *m mil* dug--out; **~'stehen** *irr itr* to stand below; to find shelter; *~~'* (*gehören*) to pertain; *jdm ~~* to be subordinate to, to be under s. o.'s control; *r* to dare, to venture; **~'stellen** *tr* to place under, to put under cover; *mot* to garage; *r* to seek shelter (from); *jdm ~~'* to place under the command; (*zur Last legen*) to impute (to), to insinuate; *~stellt sein* to be attached to; **~stellung** *f* imputation, insinuation; subordination, putting under the command of; **~strei'chen** *irr tr* to underline, to underscore; **~stufe** *f* sublevel; (*Schule*) lower grade; **~stü'tzen** *tr* to prop, to support, to back, *Am* to get behind; (*helfen*) to help, to assist, to sustain; (*begünstigen*) to favo(u)r; (*finanziell*) to subsidize; (*fördern*) to sponsor; **~stü'tzung** *f* support, aid; assistance; help; (*Beihilfe*) benefit payment; (*Zuschuß*) subsidy; (*Armen~~*) relief; **~~sbedürftig** *a* needy; **~~sempfänger** *m* person on benefit; **~~sfeuer** *n* supporting fire; **~sfonds** *m* relief fund; **~~sgelder** *n pl* subsidies *pl;* **~~skasse** *f* endowment (*od* benevolent) fund; **~~sleistungen** *f pl* benefits *pl;* **~~spunkt** *m* point of suspension; **~~ssatz** *m* benefit rate; **~~sverein** *m* relief society.

untersu'ch|en *tr* (*prüfen*) to examine; to inspect; (*genau prüfen*) to scrutinize; (*erproben*) to test; (*nachforschen*) to investigate, to inquire into; (*wissenschaftlich*) to study, to explore; (*aufspüren*) to trace; *jur* to try; *chem* to analyze; *tech* to overhaul; (*nachprüfen*) *Am* to screen, *Am* to check up; (*durchsuchen*) to search; **~su'chung** *f* examination; inquiry; investigation; testing; research, study; experiment; *chem* analysis; exploration; inspection; *jur* trial, *Am* probe; *tech* overhauling; *e-e ~~ anstellen* to investigate; *ärztliche ~~* medical examination; *ge-*

naue ~~ scrutinizing; *e-e* ~~ *an Ort u. Stelle* an on-the-spot investigation, *Am* field study; *bei näherer* ~~ on investigation; ~~**sabschnitt** *m* testing section; ~~**sanstalt** *m* research institution; ~~**sbereich** *m* range of investigation; ~~**sgefangene(r)** *m* prisoner upon trial; ~~**shaft** *f* detention for investigation, imprisonment on remand pre-trial confinement; *die* ~~*shaft anrechnen* to compensate the detention; *in* ~~*shaft nehmen* to commit for trial (*wegen* on a charge of); ~~**skommission** *f* fact-finding committee; court of inquiry; ~~**smethode** *f* research method; method of investigation; ~~**sobjekt** *n* test specimen; ~~**srichter** *m* examining magistrate.

Unter|tagbau *m* underground mining; ~**tagearbeiter** *m* workman underground; ~**tags** *adv* below-ground, underground; ~**tagstreik** *m* stay-down strike; ~**tan** *m* subject; ~**tänig** *a* subject; *fig* obsequious, submissive, humble; ~~**keit** *f* submission; humility; ~**tänigst** *a* most obedient; ~**tasse** *f* saucer; *fliegende* ~~ flying saucer; ~**tauchen** *tr* to dip, to duck, to immerse, to submerge; *itr* to dive; (*verschwinden*) to disappear, to be lost; ~**teil** *m* lower part, bottom, base; ~~**bar** *a* divisible; ~~**en** *tr* to subdivide, to section; (*in Felder*) to panel; ~~**ung** *f* subdivision; partition; ~**titel** *m* subtitle, subheading; *film* caption; ~**ton** *m* undertone; ~**treten** *irr itr* to seek shelter; ~**tu'nneln** *tr* to (drive a) tunnel under; ~**vermieten** *tr* to sublet; ~**vermieter** *m* underletter; *jur* sublessor; ~**verteilerstelle** *f* subsidiary distributing point; ~**vertrag** *m* subcontract; ~**wa'chsen** *a* (*Fleisch*) streaky; ~**wärts** *adv* downward(s); ~**wäsche** *f* underwear, underclothing, *fam* undie(s *pl*); ~**wa'schen** *tr* to undermine, to underscour; ~**wasser** *a* below water surface; ~~**anstrich** *m* antifouling painting; ~~**bombe** *f* depth bomb; ~~**bombenwerfer** *m* hedgehog; squid; Y-gun; ~~**brenner** *m* underwater cutting torch; ~~**geschwindigkeit** *f* submerged speed; ~~**horchgerät** *n* hydrophone; ~~**kabel** *n* submarine cable; ~~**ortungsgerät** *n* under-water sound detector; asdic, *Am* sonar; ~~**schneidebrenner** *m* underwater cutting burner; ~**we'gs** *adv* on the way, *Am* on the go; ~~ *abfangen* to intercept; ~**wei'sen** *irr tr* to teach, to instruct; ~**wei'sung** *f* instructions *pl*; information; indoctrination; ~**welt** *f* underworld; lower world; *poet* Hades; ~**we'rfen** *irr tr* to subdue, to subject, to subjugate; *r* to submit, to yield, to resign o. s., to surrender (to); (*sich fügen*) to toe the line; ~**we'rfung** *f* subduing, subjection; (*Unterwürfigkeit*) submission; (*Verzicht*) surrender, resignation (to); (*Ergebung*) acquiescence (in); ~**wo'rfen** *a* subject to, liable to; ~**wü'hlen** *tr* to undermine; ~**'würfig** *a* submissive; (*kriecherisch*) obsequious; ~~**keit** *f* submission, submissiveness, obsequiousness; ~**zei'chnen** *tr* to sign, to subscribe; *pol* to ratify; ~**zei'chner** *m* signer, subscriber; (*Vertrag*) signatory; ~**zei'chnete(r)** *m* undersigned; ~**zei'chnung** *f* subscription; signature; (*Vertrag*) ratification; ~**zie'hen** *tr* to subject to, to submit to; *r* to undertake s. th.; *sich der Mühe* ~~ to bother; *sich e-r Operation* ~~ to undergo an operation; *sich e-r Prüfung* ~~ to go in for an examination; ~'~ *tr* to put on underneath.

un|tief *a* low, shallow; ~**tiefe** *f* shallowness; shoal; shelf; bank; ~**tier** *n* monster; ~'**tilgbar** *a* inextinguishable; (*unverwischbar*) indelible; (*Anleihe*) irredeemable; ~**tragbar** *a* intolerable, unbearable; past endurance; (*Kleidung*) unwearable; ~~*e Kosten* prohibitive cost; ~**trennbar** *a* inseparable, undetachable, unseverable; ~~ *verbunden* inherent; ~~**keit** *f* inseparability; ~**treu** *a* unfaithful, perfidious; *seinem Versprechen* ~~ unfaithful to o.'s promise; *e-r Partei* ~~ *werden* to desert o.'s party, *Am* to bolt the ticket; ~**treue** *f* faithlessness, unfaithfulness; disloyalty, breach of trust; (*Tücke*) perfidy; ~**tröstlich** *a* inconsolable, disconsolate; ~**trüglich** *a* infallible, unerring; ~~**keit** *f* infallibility; ~**tüchtig** *a* unfit, incapable; (*geringe Leistung*) inefficient; (*unzulänglich*) incompetent; (*Schiff*) unseaworthy; ~~**keit** *f* unfitness; inefficiency; incompetence; ~**tugend** *f* vice, bad habit; ~**tunlich** *a* impracticable, unfeasable.

unüber|legt *a* inconsiderate, unwise, ill-considered, thoughtless; (*schlecht beraten*) ill-advised; (*übereilt*) rash, *Am* snap; ~~**heit** *f* thoughtlessness; ~**sehbar** *a* vast, immense; (*verwirrt*) intricate; (*unverständlich*) incomprehensible; (*unberechenbar*) incalculable; (*unkontrollierbar*) uncontrollable; hard to follow up; ~**setzbar** *a* untranslatable; ~**setzt** *a* not translated; *tech* ungeared; ~**sichtlich** *a* badly arranged; complex; hard to follow up; ~~*e Ecke mot* blind corner; ~**steiglich** *a* insurmountable; insuperable; ~**tragbar** *a* not transferable; inalienable; unassignable; (*Wertpapiere*) non-negotiable; ~**trefflich** *a* unsurpassable, unrival(l)ed, unequal(l)ed; ~**troffen** *a* unsurpassed; unexcelled; ~**wacht** *a* unattended, unguarded; ~**windlich** *a* invincible; (*Schwierigkeiten*) insurmountable; ~**wunden** *a* unconquered.

unum|gänglich *a* indispensable, absolutely necessary; imperative; ~**schränkt** *a* unlimited; *pol* absolute; ~**stößlich** *a* irrevocable, irrefutable; ~**stritten** *a* uncontested, undisputed; ~**wunden** *a* artless; (*offen*) plain, open, frank; point-blank.

ununter|brochen *a* uninterrupted, unbroken; continuous, incessant; *adv* continually; ~**scheidbar** *a* undistinguishable, undiscernible; ~**sucht** *a* unexamined; ~**zeichnet** *a* unsigned.

unver|änderlich *a* unalterable, unchangeable, invariable; constant; ~~**keit** *f* invariability, immutability; ~**ändert** *a* unchanged; ~**antwortlich** *a* irresponsible; (*unentschuldbar*) inexcusable; ~~**keit** *f* irresponsibility; ~**arbeitet** *a* unwrought; ~**äußerlich** *a* inalienable; ~**besserlich** *a* incorrigible; ~~**keit** *f* incorrigibleness; ~**bindlich** *a* not binding, without obligation; not obligatory; *Am* noncommittal; (*unfreundlich*) unkind; disobliging; ~**blümt** *a* plain, frank, open; ~**brannt** *a* unburned; ~**braucht** *a* unused; ~**brennbar**, ~**brennlich** *a* incombustible, fireproof; ~~**keit** *f* incombustibility; ~**brieft** *a* unchartered; ~**brüchlich** *a* inviolable; ~**bürgt** *a* unwarranted; (*Nachricht*) unconfirmed; ~**dächtig** *a* unsuspected; ~**daulich** *a* indigestible; ~~**keit** *f* indigestibleness; ~**daut** *a* not digested; ~**dient** *a* undeserved, unmerited; ~~**erweise** *adv* undeservedly; ~**dorben** *a* unspoiled; (*moralisch*) uncorrupted; ~**drossen** *a* indefatigable, unwearied; assiduous; ~~**heit** *f* indefatigableness; ~**dünnt** *a* undiluted; ~**ehelicht** *a* unmarried, single; ~**eidigt** *a* unsworn; ~**einbar** *a* incompatible, inconsistent with; contradictory; ~**fälscht** *a* unadulterated; *fig* pure, genuine; ~**fänglich** *a* harmless; ~**froren** *a* unabashed, imperturbable, brazen-faced, cheeky; *adv* impudently; ~~**heit** *f* impudence, cheek; ~**gänglich** *a* imperishable; (*unsterblich*) immortal; ~**geßlich** *a* unforgettable, not to be forgotten, ever memorable; ~**gleichlich** *a* incomparable; unequal(l)ed, unparalleled, matchless; (*einzigartig*) unique; ~**hältnismäßig** *a* disproportionate; ~**heiratet**, ~**mählt** *a* unmarried, single; ~**hofft** *a* unexpected, unhoped--for; unforeseen; ~**hohlen** *a* unconcealed; (*offen*) open, frank; ~**hüttbar** *a* unsmeltable; ~**jährbar** *a* imprescriptible; ~**käuflich** *a* unsal(e)able, not for sale; unmarketable; ~~*e Ware* dead stock; ~**kennbar** *a* unmistakable; *adv* evidently; ~**kürzt** *a* uncurtailed; (*Text*) unabridged; (*ohne Abzug*) without deduction; ~**langt** *a* unsolicited; ~**letzbar**, ~**letzlich** *a* invulnerable; *fig* inviolable; ~**letzbarkeit**, ~**letzlichkeit** *f* invulnerability; inviolability, sanctity; ~**letzt** *a* safe and sound; (*Personen*) unhurt, uninjured; (*Sachen*) undamaged; ~**lierbar** *a* not to be lost; inalienable; unforgettable; ~**löschlich** *a* unextinguishable; ~**mählt** *a* unmarried; ~**meidlich** *a* inevitable, unavoidable; ~**merkt** *a* unperceived; *adv* insensibly; ~**mindert** *a* undiminished, unabated; unimpaired; ~**mischbar** *a* immiscible; ~**mischt** *a* unmixed; unalloyed; ~**mittelt** *a* abrupt, sudden; ~**mögen** *n* inability, incapacity, impotence; insolvency; ~~**d** *a* powerless, unable, incapable (*zu* of); (*kraftlos*) impotent; (*ohne Geld*) penniless, impecunious, poor; ~**mutet** *a* unexpected; ~**nehmlich** *a* inaudible, indistinct; ~**nunft** *f* unreasonableness; (*Torheit*) folly; (*Albernheit*) absurdity; ~**nünftig** *a* unreasonable; (*töricht*) foolish, silly; senseless; ~ **keit** *f* unreasonableness; ~**öffentlicht** *a* unpublished; ~**packt** *a* unpacked, loose; in bulk; ~**pfändbar** *a* not subject to distraint; ~**richtet** *a* unperformed; ~~*er Sache* unsuccessfully; ~**schämt** *a* impertinent, impudent; insolent, saucy, *Am sl* fresh, gally, smart-alecky; (*Preis*) exorbitant; unconscionable; ~~**heit** *f* impertinence, impudence, cheek, sauciness; *die* ~~ *haben zu* to have the face to; *so e-e* ~~*!* *Am sl* can you beat it! ~**schuldet** *a* (*ohne Schulden*) not in debt; (*Grundstück*) unencumbered; (*unverdient*) unmerited, undeserved; ~**sehens** *adv* unexpectedly; unawares, by surprise; ~**sehrt** *a* unhurt, uninjured; safe, intact; (*Sachen*) undamaged; ~**sichert** *a* uninsured; ~**siegbar** *a* inexhaustible; ~**siegelt** *a* unsealed; ~**söhnlich** *a* irreconcilable; implacable; ~**sorgt** *a* unprovided for, without means; destitute; ~**stand** *m* want of judg(e)ment; (*Torheit*) folly; ~**ständig** *a* unwise, injudicious, foolish; ~**ständlich** *a* unintelligible, incomprehensible; indistinct; ~~**keit** *f* unintelligibility; ~**stärkt** *a* not reinforced; unamplified; ~**stellbar** *a* fixed; ~**stellt** *a* unfeigned; ~**steuert** *a* duty unpaid; ~**strebt** *a* unbraced; ~**sucht** *a* untried, unattempted; *nichts* ~~ *lassen* to leave no stone unturned, to leave nothing undone; ~**tilgbar** *a* ineradicable, indelible; ~**träglich** *a* unsociable; (*streitsüchtig*) quarrelsome; ~~ *mit fig* incompatible with; ~~**keit** *f* unsociableness; incompatibility; ~**wandt** *a* fixed, unmoved, steadfast; (*unermüdlich*) unflinching; ~**wechselbar** *a* noninterchangeable; **~wehrt** *a* not forbidden; *es ist Ihnen ~~* you are at liberty to; **~weilt** *adv* immediately, without delay, forthwith; **~welklich** *a* unfading; **~wendbar** *a* unusable; **~wertbar** *a* inconvertible; unusable; unrealizable; **~weslich** *a* imputrescible; **~wundbar** *a* invulnerable; **~wüstlich** *a* indestructible; *fig* irrepressible; (*Stoff*) everlasting; (*unermüdlich*) indefatigable, inexhaustible; (*kräftig*) robust; **~zagt** *a* undaunted, intrepid; **~zeihlich** *a* unpardonable; **~zerrt** *a* undistorted; **~zinslich** *a* without interest; *~~es Darlehen* free loan; **~zollt** *a* duty unpaid; **~züglich** *a* immediate, prompt, forthwith, right away, *Am* right now.

unvoll|endet *a* unfinished, uncompleted; **~kommen** *a* imperfect, defective, incomplete; **~~heit** *f* imperfection; **~ständig** *a* incomplete, imperfect; **~~keit** *f* incompleteness; **~zählig** *a* incomplete; **~ziehbar** *a* unpracticable.

unvor|bereitet *a* unprepared; *adv* (*reden*) extempore; **~denklich** *a* immemorial; *seit ~~en Zeiten* from time immemorial; **~eingenommen** *a* unbias(s)ed, unprejudiced, objective; **~hergesehen** *a* unforeseen, unexpected; **~sätzlich** *a* undesigned, unintentional; **~schriftsmäßig** *a* contrary to regulations, not regularly prescribed; **~sichtig** *a* incautious; (*unüberlegt*) inconsiderate; (*unklug*) imprudent; (*sorglos*) careless; **~~erweise** *adv* inadvertently; **~sichtigkeit** *f* imprudence; incautiousness; carelessness; *aus ~~* inadvertently; **~teilhaft** *a* unprofitable, disadvantageous; (*Kleid*) unbecoming; *~~ aussehen* not to look o.'s best.

un|wägbar *a* imponderable, unweighable; **~wählbar** *a* ineligible; **~wahr** *a* untrue, false; **~~haftig** *a* untruthful; (*unaufrichtig*) insincere; **~~haftigkeit** *f* untruthfulness; **~wahrscheinlich** *a* improbable, unlikely; **~~keit** *f* improbability; **~wandelbar** *a* unchangeable, immutable, invariable; **~wegsam** *a* impracticable, impassable; pathless; **~weiblich** *a* unwomanly; **~weigerlich** *a* unrefusing; unhesitating; unresisting; *adv* without fail; **~weise** *a* unwise, imprudent; **~weit** *adv* not far (off); *prp* not far from; near, close to; **~wert** *a* unworthy; *~~ m* unworthiness; **~wesen** *n* disorder, confusion; nuisance; mischief, tricks *pl*; *sein ~~ treiben* to do mischief; **~wesentlich** *a* unessential; immaterial (*für* to); (*unwichtig*) unimportant; (*unbedeutend*) insignificant; *das ist ~~* that doesn't matter; **~wetter** *n* stormy weather, thunderstorm, tempest; **~~warnung** *f* weather warnings *pl*; **~wichtig** *a* unimportant; insignificant; **~~keit** *f* insignificance.

unwider|legbar *a* irrefutable; **~ruflich** *a* irrevocable; **~stehlich** *a* irresistible; **~~keit** *f* irresistibility.

unwiederbringlich *a* irrecoverable, irretrievable.

Unwill|e *m* indignation; (*Widerwille*) reluctance; (*Ungeduld*) impatience (at s. th., with s. o.); **~ig** *a* indignant (at); *~~ werden* to get angry with; (*widerstrebend*) unwilling; *adv* reluctantly; **~kommen** *a* unwelcome; **~kürlich** *a* involuntary; instinctive; *ich mußte ~~ lachen* I couldn't help laughing.

un|wirklich *a* unreal; **~~keit** *f* unreality, fictitiousness; **~wirksam** *a* ineffective, inefficacious; ineffectual, inoperative; inefficient; inactive, inert; *jur* null, void; **~~keit** *f* inefficacy; ineffectiveness, inefficiency; **~wirsch** *a* cross; morose, angry, testy; **~wirtlich** *a* inhospitable; (*Ort*) desolate, dreary; **~wirtschaftlich** *a* not economical, unthrifty, inefficient; (*nicht lohnend*) unremunerative; **~~keit** *f* wastefulness; (*Verschwendung*) extravagance; **~wissend** *a* ignorant; *sich ~~ stellen* to make the ignorant; **~wissenheit** *f* ignorance; **~wissenschaftlich** *a* unscientific; **~wissentlich** *a* unconsciously; **~wohl** *a* unwell, indisposed; **~~sein** *n* indisposition; (*Frau*) menses *pl*; **~wohnlich** *a* uninhabitable; (*unbehaglich*) uncomfortable; **~würdig** *a* unworthy (of); **~~keit** *f* unworthiness.

Un|zahl *f* endless number; legion; **~zählbar, ~zählig** *a* countless, innumerable; **~zähmbar** *a* untamable; indomitable; **~zart** *a* indelicate; **~~heit** *f* indelicacy.

Unze *f* ounce.

Unzeit *f* wrong time; *zur ~* inopportunely, out of season; **~gemäß** *a* out-of-date, untimely, behind times; inopportune, unpropitious; **~ig** *a* untimely, unseasonable; (*vorzeitig*) premature; (*unreif*) immature.

unzer|brechlich *a* unbreakable, non-breakable; **~legbar** *a* indivisible, indecomposable; **~reißbar** *a* untearable; **~setzbar** *a* indecomposable; **~störbar** *a* indestructible; imperishable; non-corrodible; **~trennlich** *a* inseparable, indissoluble; *sie sind ~~* they are hand and glove together.

un|ziemend, **~ziemlich** *a* unseemly, unbecoming; **~zivilisiert** *a* uncivilized, barbarous; **~zucht** *f* unchastity; (*gewerbsmäßige*) prostitution; **~züchtig** *a* unchaste, lascivious; (*liederlich*) lewd.

unzu|frieden *a* dissatisfied, discontented; displeased; **~~heit** *f* discontent, dissatisfaction; **~gänglich** *a* inaccessible; (*zurückhaltend*) reserved; **~länglich** *a* insufficient, inadequate; **~~keit** *f* insufficiency, inadequacy; (*Mangel*) shortcomings *pl*; **~lässig** *a* inadmissible, unallowable; (*verboten*) prohibited; *tech* undue; *für ~~ erklären* to rule out; **~rechnungsfähig** *a* irresponsible; (*schwachsinnig*) imbecile; (*wahnsinnig*) insane; **~~keit** *f* irresponsibility; imbecility; insanity; **~reichend** *a* insufficient, inadequate, short; **~sammenhängend** *a* incoherent, disjointed, disconnected; (*lose*) detached, loose; (*planlos*) desultory; **~träglich** *a* disadvantageous; (*ungesund*) unhealthy, unwholesome; (*nicht geeignet*) unsuitable, not good (for); **~~keit** *f* inconvenience; (*Nachteil*) disadvantage; (*Mangel*) failure; (*Streit*) dissension, discord; **~verlässig** *a* unreliable, untrustworthy; (*Wetter, Eis, Gedächtnis*) treacherous; (*unsicher*) uncertain, precarious; **~~keit** *f* untrustworthiness, unreliability, unreliableness.

un|zweckmäßig *a* inexpedient, unsuitable, impracticable, improper; **~~keit** *f* unsuitableness, inexpediency; **~zweideutig** *a* unequivocal, unambiguous; explicit, plain; **~zweifelhaft** *a* undoubted, indubitable; *~~ adv* doubtless.

*

üppig *a* luxurious; *fig* luxuriant, exuberant; (*sinnlich*) voluptuous; (*übermütig*) presuming; (*reichlich*) plentiful, abundant; (*prächtig*) sumptuous; (*~ bewachsen*) rank; (*saftig*) lush; (*~ wuchernd*) rampant; *e-e ~e Figur* a well-developed (*od* full) figure; **~keit** *f* luxuriant growth; luxury, exuberance; voluptuousness; presumption.

Ur *m* aurochs; **~abstimmung** *f* plebiscite; **~ahn** *m* great-grandfather; (*Vorfahre*) ancestor; **~~e** *f* great-grandmother; ancestress; *die ~~en* ancestors *pl*; **~alt** *a* very old, very ancient.

Uran *n chem* uranium (*Abk* U *od* Ur); **~atom** *n* uranium atom; **~bergwerk** *n* uranium mine; **~bombe** *f* uranium bomb; **~brenner** *m* uranium pile; **~erz** *n* uranium ore; **~glimmer** *m* torbernite; **~haltig** *a* uraniferous; **~isotop** *n* uranium isotope (*Abk* U 235); **~lager, ~vorkommen** *n* uranium deposit; **~pechblende** *f* pitchblende; **~spaltung** *f* uranium fission; **~strahlen** *m pl* uranium rays *pl*; **~umwandlungsanlage** *f* uranium reactor; **~verbindung** *f* uranium compound.

Ur|anfang *m* first beginning; **~anfänglich** *a* original, primeval; **~atom** *n* primordial atom; **~aufführen** *tr* to première; **~aufführung** *f* first night (*od* performance); (*e-s Films*) release; **~bar** *a* arable; *~~ machen* to clear, to cultivate; **~~machung** *f* cultivation; **~bedeutung** *f* original meaning; **~bewohner** *m pl* aborigines *pl*; **~begriff** *m* primitive idea; **~bild** *n* prototype; *fig* ideal; **~christentum** *n* primitive Christianity; the early Church; **~eigen** *a* original; **~einwohner** *m* original inhabitant; *die ~~* aborigines *pl*; **~eltern** *pl* ancestors *pl*; **~enkel** *m* great-grandson; **~~in** *f* great-granddaughter; **~erzeugung** *f* primary production; **~fehde** *f* oath to refrain from vengeance; **~fide'l** *a* very jolly; **~form** *f* master pattern; prototype; **~gebirge** *n* primary rock; **~gemütlich** *a* exceedingly comfortable; **~geschichte** *f* primeval history; prehistory; **~geschichtlich** *a* prehistoric; **~gestein** *n* mother rock; **~großeltern** *pl* great-grandparents *pl*; **~großmutter** *f* great-grandmother; **~großvater** *m* great-grandfather; **~heber(in)** *m* (*f*) author; originator; founder; creator; **~~recht** *n* copyright; privilege of the author; **~~schaft** *f* parentage; authorship.

Urin *m* urine; **~flasche** *f* urinal; **~ieren** *itr* to urinate; **~treibend** *a* diuretic; **~untersuchung** *f med* urinalysis.

ur|komisch *a* extremely comical, screamingly funny; **~kraft** *f* original power; **~kunde** *f* document, deed; (*Beleg*) record, voucher; (*Beweis*) proof, evidence; (*Vertrag*) instrument; *e-e ~~ ausfertigen* to execute a document; *zu Urkund dessen* in witness whereof; **~~nbeweis** *m* documentary evidence; **~~nfälscher** *m* forger of document; **~~nfälschung** *f* falsification (*od* forgery) of documents; (*Freibrief*) charter; **~kundlich** *a* documentary; (*verbürgt*) authentic; *~~ belegt* documented; *~~ dessen* in proof of which; in writing, *Am* over o.'s signature; **~kundsbeamter** *m* certificating official; **~laub** *m* leave of absence; *mil* furlough; (*Freizeit*) time off; (*Ferien*) vacation; holidays *pl*; *auf ~~* on leave; *auf ~~ sein Am* to vacationize; *~~ nehmen* to take a holiday, *Am* to vacation; *den ~~ verbringen* to spend o.'s holidays, *Am* to vacation; **~~er** *m* holiday maker, *Am* vacationer, vacationist; *mil* soldier on leave; **~~sanspruch** *m* vacation privilege; **~~sberechtigt** *a* eligible for leave; **~~sbestimmungen** *f pl* vacation provisions *pl*; **~~sgesuch** *n* application for a leave; **~~ssaison** *f* vacation season; **~~sschein** *m* furlough certificate, *Am* pass; **~~süberschreitung** *f* absence without leave *Abk* (AWOL); **~~sverlängerung** *f* extension of leave; **~maß** *n* standard ga(u)ge; **~mensch** *m* primitive man; **~meter** *m* standard metre.

Urne *f* urn; casket.
ur|plötzlich *a* sudden; *adv* all of a sudden; **~quell** *m* fountain-head; original source; **~sache** *f* cause; reason; (*Beweggrund*) motive; *~~ haben* I have a cause for; *keine ~~!* don't mention it! not at all! *Am* you're welcome! *man hat ~~ zu zweifeln* there is reason to doubt; **~sächlich** *a* causal, causative; **~~keit** *f* causality, causation; **~schrift** *f* original (text); **~~lich** *a* (in the) original; **~sprache** *f* primitive language; (*e-r Übersetzung*) original language; **~sprung** *m* origin, source; (*Anfang*) beginning; (*Ursache*) cause; (*Herkunft*) extraction; *seinen ~~ nehmen* to originate in; **~~sbescheinigung** *f* certificate of origin; **~~sbezeichnung** *f* indication of origin; **~~sbild** *n* original subject copy; **~~sland** *n* country of origin; **~~szeugnis** *n* certificate of origin; **~sprünglich** *a* original; primitive; first; primary; parent; *adv* at first; **~stoff** *m* element; parent (*od* primary) material.

*

Urteil *n* judg(e)ment; (*Entscheidung*) decision; (*Ansicht*) opinion, view; *jur* verdict, (*Strafmaß*) sentence; (*Schiedsgericht*) award; (*Schuldfrage*) finding; (*Erlaß*) decree; (*Gottes ~*) ordeal; *sich ein ~ bilden* to form an opinion (*über* of *od* on *od* about); *ein ~ anerkennen* to confess a judg(e)ment; *ein ~ anfechten* to appeal against a decision; *ein ~ aufheben* to quash (*od* to set aside) a judg(e)ment; *ein ~ aussprechen* to pronounce a judg(e)ment; *ein ~ bestätigen* to confirm a judg(e)ment; to uphold a sentence; *ein ~ fällen* to render (*od* to pass) a judg(e)ment (on); to sentence; *ein ~~ verkünden* to pronounce a judg(e)ment; *ein ~ vollstrecken* to enforce (*od* to execute) a judg(e)ment; **~en** *itr* to judge (*über* of; *nach* by); to give o.'s opinion; *jur* to sentence (*über* upon); to give judg(e)ment against; **~saufhebung** *f* quashing of a sentence; **~saussetzung** *f* arrest of judg(e)ment; **~sbegründung** *f* opinion; **~sbestätigung** *f* confirmation of a judg(e)ment; **~seröffnung** *f* publication of a judg(e)ment; pronouncement of a decree; **~sfähig** *a* judicious; discriminating, competent to judge; **~sfällung** *f* passing of sentence; **~skraft** *f*, **~svermögen** *n* power of judg(e)ment; discernment; **~smilderung** *f* mitigation of a judg(e)ment; **~sspruch** *m* sentence; verdict; judg(e)ment; award; **~svollstreckung** *f* execution of a sentence.

Ur|text *m* original text; **~tier** *n* protozoon; **~tümlich** *a* original; native; **~urgroßvater** *m* great-great-grandfather; **~väterzeit** *f* olden times *pl*; **~volk** *n* primitive people; aborigines *pl*; **~wahl** *f* preliminary election; **~wähler** *m* primary elector; **~wald** *m* primeval forest; jungle; **~~krieg** *m* jungle warfare; **~welt** *f* primeval world; **~~lich** *a* primeval; antediluvian; **~wesen** *n* primordial being; **~wüchsig** *a* original; native; *fig* racy; (*grob*) rough (-and--ready); (*barsch*) blunt; **~zeit** *f* remote antiquity; primitive times *pl*; **~zelle** *f* primitive cell, ovum; **~zeugung** *f* abiogenesis; **~zustand** *m* primitive state, original condition.

*

Us|ance *f com* usage; **~owechsel** *m* bill at usance.
Usurp|ator *m* usurper; **~ieren** *tr* to usurp.
Utensilien *pl* utensils *pl*, implements *pl*.
Utop|ie *f* Utopian scheme, chimera; **~isch** *a* Utopian, utopian; visionary; impractical.
uzen *tr fam* to mock, to banter, to chaff, to quiz, to tease, *Am* to haze.

V

V *Abk mit* ***V*** *siehe Liste der Abk.*
V1: flying bomb, *fam* doodle-bug; *V1 u. V2 Geschosse* V1 and V2 projectiles; *V2* rocket bomb; *V2-Abschußbasis f* V2-launching site; *V-Waffe f* V-weapon; *V-Waffenbasis f* V-weapon site.
vag *a fam* vague.
Vagabund *m* vagabond, tramp, vagrant, *Am sl* vag, hobo, stiff, bum; **~entum** *n* vagabondage; vagrancy; **~ieren** *itr* to tramp about, to roam; to lead a vagabond life; *~~der Strom el* stray (*od* vagrant) current.
vak|ant *a* vacant; **~anz** *f* vacancy; (*Ferien*) holidays *pl*, vacation; **~ublitz** *m phot* flash-bulb; **~uum** *n* vacuum; **~~glocke** *f* vacuum-bell jar; **~~glühlampe** *f* incandescent lamp; **~~meter** *n* vacuum ga(u)ge; **~~röhre** *f* vacuum (*od* electron) tube; **~~trockner** *m* vacuum drier.
Valuta *f* value; (*Währung*) currency; foreign exchange; (*Kurs*) rate of exchange; (*feste*) standard; **~notierungen** *f pl* quotations of foreign exchange rates; **~schwach** *a* having a soft currency; **~stark** *a* having a high monetary standard.
Vampir *m* vampire.
Vandal|e *m*, **~isch** *a* Vandal; **~ismus** *m* vandalism.
Vanille *f* vanilla; **~eis** *n* vanilla ice--cream.
Varia|nte *f* variant; **~tion** *f* variation.
Vari|etät *f* variety; **~ete** *n* variety theatre, music-hall, *Am* burlesque, vaudeville theater; **~~künstler** *m* music-hall entertainer; **~~nummer** *f* variety act; **~~programm** *n* bill; **~~vorstellung** *f* variety show; **~ieren** *tr, itr* to vary.
Vasall *m* vassal; **~enstaat** *m* tributary state.
Vase *f* vase; **~lin** *n* vaseline.
Vater *m* father; (*Züchterausdruck*) sire; (*Vater oder Mutter*) parent; **~freude** *f* paternal joy; **~haus** *n* parental house; home; **~land** *n* native country, fatherland; *mein ~~* my country; **~ländisch** *a* national; *~~ gesinnt* patriotic; **~landsfreund** *m* patriot; **~landsliebe** *f* patriotism; **~los** *a* fatherless; **~mord** *m* parricide; **~mörder** *m* parricide; **~sbruder** *m* uncle; **~schaft** *f* paternity, fatherhood; **~~sklage** *f* affiliation case; **~sschwester** *f* aunt; **~sname** *m* surname; patronymic; **~stadt** *f* native town; **~stelle** *f* place of a father; *bei jdm ~~ vertreten* to be a father to; **~teil** *n* patrimony; **~unser** *n* the LORD's Prayer.
Väter|chen *n*, ***Vati*** *m* dad(dy), pa(pa); **~lich** *a* fatherly, paternal; *~~es Erbteil* patrimony; **~~erseits** *adv* on the father's side; **~sitte** *f* manners of our forefathers.

*

Veget|abilien *pl* vegetables *pl*; **~abilisch** *a* vegetable; **~arier** *m*, **~arisch** *a* vegetarian; **~ation** *f* vegetation; **~ieren** *itr* to vegetate.
Veilchen *n* violet; **~blau** *a* violet; **~stock** *m* violet-plant.
Veitstanz *m* St. Vitus's dance.
Velinpapier *n* vellum(-paper).
Vene *f* vein; **~nentzündung** *f* phlebitis; **~ risch** *a* venereal.
Ventil *n* valve; **~ation** *f* ventilation; **~ator** *m* ventilator; electric fan; blower; exhauster; **~~flügel** *m* fan baffle; **~~gebläse** *n* fan blower; **~einstellung** *f* valve adjustment; **~ieren** *tr* to ventilate; *fig* (*erörtern*) to discuss; **~klappe** *f* clack; **~steuerung** *f* valve timing; **~stößel** *m* valve tappet.
verabfolg|en *tr* to deliver up, to hand over, to let s. o. have s. th.; **~ung** *f* delivery.
verab|reden *tr* to concert, to agree upon; (*Zeitpunkt*) to fix; *~redet* (*vertraglich*) stipulated; *~redet sein fam* to have a date; *r* to make an appointment; (*sich treffen*) to meet; **~redetermaßen** *adv* as agreed upon; **~redung** *f* appointment, agreement; engagement; *fam* date; *frühere ~~* previous engagement; *der ~~ gemäß* as agreed upon; **~reichen** *tr* to deliver, to give, to hand over; (*Medizin*) to dispense; **~säumen** *tr* to neglect; to omit; (*fehlschlagen*) to fail; **~scheuen** *tr* to hate, to detest, to abhor, to abominate; (*abgeneigt sein*) to loathe; **~~swert, ~~swürdig** *a* abominable, detestable; **~schieden** *tr* to dismiss, to discharge; to pension off; *mil* to disband; (*Gesetz*) to pass, to ratify; *r* to say good-by(e), to retire, to take leave of; **~schiedung** *f* dismissal; discharge; farewell.
ver|achten *tr* to despise; (*tadeln*) to condemn; (*verschmähen*) to scorn, to disdain; *das ist nicht zu ~~* that's not to be sneezed at; **~ächter** *m* despiser; **~ächtlich** *a* contemptuous, disdainful; (*verachtungswert*) contemptible despicable; **~~keit** *f* contemptibleness; **~achtung** *f* disdain, contempt, scorn.
verallgemeiner|n *tr* to generalize; **~ung** *f* generalization.
ver|alten *itr* to become obsolete, to antiquate; to go out of date (*od* fashion); **~altet** *a* (*überlebt*) antiquated; (*ungebräuchlich*) obsolete; (*aus der Mode*) out-of-date, outmoded, old--fashioned; (*Leiden*) inveterate; *~~er Ausdruck* archaism.
Veranda *f* veranda(h), *Am* porch; stoop.

veränder|lich *a* changeable; *gram, math* variable; (*schwankend*) unsettled; (*fließend*) fluctuating; (*nicht stabil*) unstable, unsteady; (*unbeständig*) inconstant; (*wankelmütig*) fickle, vacillating; **~~e** *f* variable (quantity); **~~keit** *f* changeableness; variability; unsteadiness; fluctuation; instability; fickleness; **~n** *tr* to change, to alter; (*abwechseln*) to vary; (*Kleider*) to alter, *Am* to bushel; *r* to change, to vary, to alter; *die Gestalt ~~* to deform; **~ung** *f* change, alteration; variation; modification; (*Wendung*) turn.

verängstigt *a* nervous, jumpy, intimidated, scared, browbeat, *Am sl* jittery.

ver|ankern *tr* to anchor, to moor; (*Stange*) to stay, to guy; (*festbinden*) to tie; *fig* to establish firmly; **~ankerung** *f* anchoring, mooring; anchor tie; *tech* stay(ing); tying; **~~stau** *n* mooring rope.

veran|lagen *tr* (*Steuern*) to assess; **~lagt** *a* talented; *gut ~~* highly gifted; *künstlerisch ~~* artistically inclined; *sparsam ~~ sein* to have an economic turn of mind; **~lagung** *f* assessment; talents *pl*; disposition; turn; **~lassen** *tr* to cause, to occasion; to make; (*entstehen lassen*) to give rise (to); (*anordnen*) to arrange; (*jdn bereden*) to prevail upon, to induce s. o.; (*bitten um*) to solicit s. th. of s. o.; *das Nötige ~~* to take the necessary steps; **~lasser** *m* causer, author; **~lassung** *f* occasion, cause; inducement; motive; (*Grund*) reason; (*Anregung*) suggestion; (*Empfehlung*) recommendation; (*Betreiben*) instigation; (*Befehl*) order; (*Bitte*) request; *auf ~~ von* at the request of, at the instigation of, on behalf of; *~~ geben* to give rise (to); *es liegt keine ~~ vor zu* there is no need for; *ohne jede ~~* without any provocation; **~schaulichen** *tr* to render clear, to illustrate; **~schlagen** *irr tr* to value, to rate, to estimate (at); (*Steuer*) to assess; *zu hoch ~~* to overrate; *zu niedrig ~~* to underestimate; *~schlagter Preis* (*bei Auktion*) reserve price; **~schlagung** *f* estimate; valuation; **~stalten** *tr* to dispose, to arrange, to organize; (*Empfang*) to give; (*Versammlung*) to hold; *fam* to get up, *Am* to take up; *e-e Sammlung ~~* to open a subscription; to take up a collection; **~stalter** *m* organizer, arranger, manager, promoter; **~staltung** *f* arrangement, management; (*Sport*) event; (*Versammlung*) meeting; (*Unterhaltung*) entertainment, *fam* show, performance, presentation, *Am sl* pitch; (*Angelegenheit*) affair; *ohne gesellschaftliche ~~* without social engagements, *Am* dateless.

verantwort|en *tr* to answer for, to (render) account for; (*verteidigen*) to defend; *r* to defend o. s., to justify o. s.; **~lich** *a* responsible, answerable (for), liable, chargeable; **~~keit** *f* responsibility; **~ung** *f* responsibility; (*Rechtfertigung*) justification; *zur ~~ ziehen* to call to account, to take s. o. to task; to hold responsible; *die ~~ aufgehalst bekommen* to be left holding the baby; *tun Sie es auf meine ~~* do it and let me be answerable for it; *auf Ihre ~~* at your risk; *die ~~ abwälzen* to shift the responsibility on to, *fam* to pass the buck; *keine ~~ übernehmen* to accept no responsibility; **~~sbewußtsein** *n* sense of responsibility; **~~sfreudigkeit** *f* willingness to accept responsibility; **~~slos** *a* without responsibility; (*rücksichtslos*) reckless; **~~svoll** *a* involving great responsibility; responsible.

verarbeit|en *tr* to manufacture, to work up; to use (up), to machine, to handle, to fabricate, *Am* to process (*zu* into); (*gestalten*) to fashion; (*abnutzen*) to wear out; *fig* to digest, to assimilate; **~et** *a* (*abgearbeitet*) toil-worn; **~ung** *f* working (up), using up, manufacturing, machining, fashioning, *Am* processing; *fig* assimilation, digestion; **~~sindustrie** *f* finishing industry; **~~skosten** *pl* processing cost, *Am* process costs *pl*.

ver|argen *tr* to reproach s. o. for, to blame s. o. for, to find fault with; **~ärgern** *tr* to annoy, to vex, to irk, to mortify; to get on s. o.'s nerves; *Am fam* to peeve; **~armen** *itr* to become impoverished, to grow poor; **~armung** *f* impoverishment, pauperization; **~arzten** *tr fam* to doctor, to physic; **~ästeln** *tr, r* to branch out, to ramify; **~ästelung** *f* branching, ramification; **~auktionieren** *tr* to sell by public auction; **~ausgaben** *tr* to spend, to pay out; *r* to run short of money; (*Kräfte*) to exhaust o. s.; **~auslagen** *tr* to advance; **~äußerlich** *a* alienable; sal(e)able; **~äußern** *tr* to alienate; to sell; **~äußerung** *f* alienation; sale.

*

Verb *n* verb; **~al** *a* verbal; **~~injurie** *f* insult, libel.

verballhornen *tr* to bowdlerize.

Verband *m med* surgical dressing, bandage; *arch* binding, fastening; *mil* task force; unit; *aero, mar* formation; (*Vereinigung*) union, association, federation; *fliegender ~* flying unit; *gemischter ~* composite force, combined arms unit; *motorisierter ~* motorized unit; *sich aus dem ~ lösen aero* to peel off; **~kasten** *m* first-aid box, medicine chest; **~päckchen** *n* field-dressing, first-aid kit; **~platz** *m* field-dressing station; **~schere** *f* bandage scissors *pl*; **~smitglied** *n* member of a society; **~stoff** *m* bandage, dressing; **~watte** *f* surgical wool, compressed wadding; **~zeug** *n* bandaging material, first-aid outfit.

verbann|en *tr* to banish, to exile (from); **~te(r)** *m* exile, outlaw; **~ung** *f* banishment; (*Ort*) exile.

ver|barrikadieren *tr* to barricade, to block; **~bauen** *tr* to build up; to obstruct; (*falsch bauen*) to build badly; (*Geld*) to spend in building; **~bauern** *itr* to become countrified; **~beißen** *irr tr* to suppress, to swallow; (*Lachen*) to bite o.'s lips, to choke (*od* stifle) o.'s laughter; *sich in etw ~~* (*fig*) to stick obstinately to, to be mad after; **~bergen** *irr tr* to hide, to conceal; *r* to hide (from).

Verbesser|er *m* improver; reformer; (*Fehler*) corrector; **~lich** *a* corrigible; amendable, improvable, reformable; **~n** *tr* to improve; (*berichtigen*) to correct; (*e-e Tatsache*) to rectify; (*Gesetz*) to amend; *r* to better o. s.; **~ung** *f* improvement; (*Fehler~~*) correction; (*Gesetz*) amendment; (*Fortschritt*) advance, refinement.

verbeug|en *r* to bow to; **~ung** *f* bow; (*Knicks*) curts(e)y.

ver|beulen *tr* to crush, to bump, to bruise; **~beult** *a* battered.

ver|biegen *irr tr* to bend, to distort, to deform; *r* (*Holz*) to warp; **~bieten** *irr tr* to forbid, to prohibit s. th., s. o. from; *Am jur* to enjoin; **~bilden** *tr* to form wrongly; (*falsch lehren*) to educate badly, to spoil; **~bildlichen** *tr* to symbolize, to illustrate; **~billigen** *tr* to reduce the price of, to cheapen.

verbind|en *irr tr* to tie together, to couple, to pin; (*verknüpfen*) to connect; to gear to; (*verketten*) to link; (*vereinigen*) to unite, to join, to associate; (*kombinieren*) *chem* to combine; *tele* to put through (to, *Am* with); *med* to dress, to bandage; (*anschließen*) to affiliate (to, with); (*passend ~~*) to match; (*Augen*) to blindfold; *fig* to pledge (to), to oblige (to); *r* to unite, to ally o. s.; (*ehelich*) to marry; *ich bin Ihnen sehr verbunden* I am greatly obliged to you; *Sie haben mich falsch verbunden* you gave me the wrong number; **~lich** *a* obliging; (*bindend*) obligatory, binding; (*zwingend*) compulsory; *~~en Dank!* my best thanks! thank you ever so much! **~~keit** *f* (*Höflichkeit*) civility, courtesy; (*Schmeichelei*) compliment; (*Verpflichtung*) liability, obligation, commitment; *~~keiten pl* liabilities *pl*; *seinen ~~keiten nachkommen* to meet o.'s liabilities; *seinen ~~keiten nicht nachkommen* to make default; *e-e ~~keit eingehen* to incur a liability.

Verbindung *f* union; (*Zusammenschluß, Menschen, Zahlen*) combination; (*Vereinigung*) association, club; (*Bindung*) *fig* bond(s *pl*); (*Beziehung*) relation, *Am* affiliation; associations *pl*, acquaintanceships *pl*, *Am* contacts *pl*; (*Staatenbund*) confederation; (*Bündnis, Gemeinschaft*) alliance; (*Studenten*) association, fraternity; (*Standesgesellschaft, Verein, com*) society; (*Versammlung*) assembly; (*Berührung*) contact; touch; (*enge Zusammenarbeit, mil*) liaison; (*Verknüpfung*) linkage; (*Verkehr*) communication; (*Zusammenhang, tel, rail Anschluß, tech verbindender Teil*) connexion, connection; (*Synthese*) composition; (*Wechselbeziehung*) correlation; (*harmonische ~*) harmony; (*Koalition*) coalition; (*Gemeinschaft*) communion; (*Gemeinsamkeit, Körperschaft*) community; (*Zusammenkommen*) juncture, joining; (*eheliche ~*) matrimony; marriage; (*Verschmelzung*) amalgamation; *com* (*Fusion*) consolidation; *chem* compound; combination; (*Farbe*) blending; *gram, typ* composition; (*Fuge, Gelenk, Verspleißung*) joint; (*Band, arch, mus, fig*) tie; (*Glied, tech Verbindungsstück, fig*) link; *el* contact; *tele* connection; junction; (*Ruf*) call; (*Fernruf*) trunk call; *radio* (*Zusammenstellung der Einzelteile, Schema*) hookup; *e-e enge ~~ anknüpfen* to fraternize, *Am* to affiliate; *sich in ~ setzen mit* to get in(to) touch with; to communicate with; *Am* to contact s. o.; *mil sl* to liaise; *in ~ sein mit* to be in touch with; *mit jdm in ~ bleiben* to keep in touch with s. o.; *die ~ verlieren mit* to lose touch with; *in geschäftlicher ~ stehen* to have business relations; (*Briefe*) to correspond with s. o.; *e-e ~ eingehen chem* to enter into combination, to form a compound; *e-e ~ herstellen tele* to set up (*od* to complete) a call, to establish a connection; *e-e ~ lösen* (*tele*) to disconnect, to cut a connection; *nicht zustandegekommene ~* (*tele*) ineffective call, *Am* uncompleted call; *drahtlose ~* radio (*od* wireless) communication; *geschäftliche ~* business relation; *biegsame ~* (*tech*) flexible coupling; *einfache ~* simplex; *rückwärtige ~en* lines of communication; *in ~ mit*

in connection with; (*jur*) in conjunction with.
Verbindungs|aufbau *m tele* trunking scheme; **~bahn** *f* connecting line, junction line; **~bolzen** *m* connecting (*od* tie) bolt; **~dose** *f* connection box; **~draht** *m* connection wire; **~flieger** *m* liaison pilot; **~flugzeug** *n* communication plane, liaison (air)plane; *Am mil sl* grasshopper; **~gang** *m* connecting passage; **~gleis** *n* junction rails *pl*; **~glied** *n* connecting (*od* coupling) link; **~graben** *m mil* communication trench; **~kabel** *n* junction cable; **~kanal** *m* junction canal; connecting culvert; **~klammer** *f* splicing clamp; brace; *el* slip connector; **~klemme** *f el* connector; **~kommando** *n* liaison detachment; **~leitung** *f tele* junction circuit, interposition trunk; **~~sklappe** *f* junction indicator; **~~snetz** *n* junction network; **~~sschrank** *m* junction board; **~leute** *pl* liaison agents *pl*; **~linie** *f* line of communication; connecting line; **~mann** *m com* contact (man); *mil* liaison man, (*Vermittler*) mediator; **~muffe** *f* splicing sleeve, union socket; **~offizier** *m* liaison officer; *als ~~ tätig sein sl* to liaise; **~organ** *n* connecting device; **~punkt** *m* connection point, junction, juncture; **~rohr** *n* connecting pipe (*od* tube); **~schnur** *f tele* connecting cord; **~stange** *f* connecting rod, tie rod; **~steg** *m* walkway; **~stelle** *f* point of connection, junction, juncture; **~stück** *n* connecting piece, tie, bond, fitting, joint, coupling; **~tür** *f* communication door; **~welle** *f* driving shaft.
ver|bissen *a* suppressed; (*ingrimmig*) crabbed, soured; (*hartnäckig*) obstinate, grim, dogged; (*eifrig*) passionate; *~~ sein in fig* to stick doggedly to; **~~heit** *f* crabbed temper; (*Hartnäckigkeit*) doggedness, obstinacy, grimness; **~bitten** *irr r tr* to decline, not to permit, not to stand; (*mißbilligen*) to deprecate, to protest against; *sich etw ~* to refuse to be talked to; *ich verbitte mir diesen Ton!* I refuse to be talked to in that tone of voice! *das verbitte ich mir!* I won't stand that! **~bittern** *itr* to embitter; **~bitterung** *f* exasperation; bitterness (of heart); **~blassen** *itr* to grow pale; (*Farbe, Stoffe*) to lose colo(u)r, to fade; **~blättern** *tr* (*Buch*) to lose o.'s place.
Verbleib *m* the whereabouts *pl*; **~en** *irr itr* to remain, to abide, to stay; (*bei der Meinung*) to persist in, to stick to; *es dabei ~~ lassen* to let the matter rest.
ver|bleichen *irr itr* to grow pale; (*Stoff, Farbe, fig*) to fade; **~bleien** *tr* to lead; **~blenden** *tr* to dazzle, to blind; (*Mauer*) to face; (*Licht*) to screen; *mil* to mask, to screen, to camouflage; *fig* to delude; **~blendung** *f* blindness, infatuation, delusion; *arch* facing; (*Gebäude*) dressing; *mil* masking, camouflage; **~blichen** *a* faded; (*gestorben*) deceased; **~blöden** *itr* to become afflicted with imbecility; to become besotted; **~blödet** *a* imbecile; idiotic; **~blödung** *f* imbecility; idiocy; **~blüffen** *tr* to amaze, to dumbfound, to stupefy, to startle, *fam* to flabbergast, to nonplus, to puzzle, to stump; **~blüfft** *a* startled, *fam* taken aback; **~blüffung** *f* perplexity, stupefaction, dumbfoundedness, amazement; **~blühen** *itr* to wither, to fade; **~blümt** *a* figurative, allegorical; veiled; **~bluten** *itr, r* to bleed to death; **~blutung** *f* bleeding to death; **~bocken** *tr fam* to forget;(*durcheinanderbringen*) to make a mess of, to bungle; **~bohren** *r* to be mad on; **~bohrt** *a* (*eigensinnig*) stubborn, obdurate; (*schrullig*) cranky, faddy; (*seltsam*) odd, queer; **~borgen** *tr* to lend out; *~~ a* hidden, secret, latent, occult; *im V~~en* secretly; **~~heit** *f* secrecy; concealment; (*Zurückgezogenheit*) seclusion, retirement; **~bot** *n* prohibition, interdiction; *jur* injunction; *eccl* inhibition; (*Einschränkung*) restriction; (*öffentliches ~~*) ban; *ein ~~ aufheben* to lift a ban; **~boten** *a* forbidden, prohibited; (*ungesetzlich*) illicit; *Eintritt ~~!* keep out! no admittance! *Rauchen ~~!* no smoking! *Plakatankleben ~~!* stick no bills! *Stehenbleiben ~~!* no loitering! *Zutritt ~~* off limits; **~botswidrig** *a* illegal; **~botszeichen** *n* prohibiting sign; **~brämen** *tr* to edge, to border; **~brämung** *f* border, edging; **~brannt** *a* burnt (to death); (*sehr heiß*) torrid; *Politik der ~~en Erde* policy of scorched earth.
Verbrauch *m* consumption; (*Gebrauch*) use; (*Ausgaben*) expenditure; *zum ~ bestimmt mil* expendable; **~en** *tr* to consume, to use up; (*aufarbeiten*) to work up; (*benutzen*) to employ; (*abnutzen*) to wear out; (*vertun*) to dissipate, to spend; to squander, to waste; (*erschöpfen*) to exhaust; **~er** *m* consumer; (*Kunde*) customer, buyer; (*Benützer*) user; (*Empfänger*) receiver; (*große Masse*) *fam* load; *Aufnahmewilligkeit des ~ers* consumer acceptance; **~erbedarf** *m* consumer demand; **~erbezirk** *m* area of consumption; **~ergenossenschaft** *f* cooperative society; **~erhöchstpreis** *m* retail ceiling price; **~erkreis** *m el* receiver circuit; **~erseite** *f el* receiver end; **~erstreik** *m* consumers' strike; **~sgüter** *n pl* consumer goods *pl*; (daily) commodities *pl*; **~sgüterindustrie** *f* consumer-goods industries *pl*; **~slenkung** *f* consumption control; **~sregelung** *f* rationing; **~srückgang** *m* consumption decrease; **~ssteuer** *f* excise tax; **~sziffern** *f pl* consumption figures *pl*; **~t** *a* used up, exhausted, worn out; (*Geld*) spent; (*Material*) consumed; (*Luft*) stale; (*durch Zeit*) timeworn.
verbrech|en *irr tr* to commit (a crime); to perpetrate; *was habe ich verbrochen?* what wrong have I done? *~~ n* crime; (*Kapital~~*) felony; **~er** *m* criminal; offender; delinquent; felon; culprit; gangster; *rückfälliger ~~* recidivist; **~~album** *n* rogues' gallery; **~~isch** *a* criminal; **~~kolonie** *f* convict settlement; **~~tum** *n* outlawry; delinquency; *organisiertes ~~tum* racketeering; **~~viertel** *n*, **~~welt** *f* slumdom.
verbreit|en *tr* to spread, to diffuse; (*ausstreuen*) to disseminate; to propagate; (*verteilen*) to distribute; (*bekanntmachen*) to spread abroad, to circulate, to divulge; *r* (*Nachricht, Krankheit*) to spread; *sich ~~ über* to enlarge upon, to expatiate upon; **~er** *m* spreader, propagator; **~ern** *tr* to broaden, to widen; **~erung** *f* broadening, widening, expansion; **~breitet** *a* (*volkstümlich*) popular; (*wohlbekannt*) well-known; (*Zeitung*) having a large circulation; (*Meinung*) common, general, universal; **~ung** *f* distribution; dissemination; spread(ing), diffusion; circulation; propagation.
verbrenn|bar *a* combustible, inflammable; **~~keit** *f* combustibility; **~en** *tr* to burn; (*schnell*) to deflagrate; (*Sonne*) to tan; (*Nesseln*) to sting; (*raketenartig*) to fuse; (*verbrühen*) to scald; (*Leichen*) to cremate;(*versengen*) to scorch; *itr* to be consumed by fire; to be burnt down; **~lich** *a* combustible; **~ung** *f* burning, combustion; (*Leichen~~*) cremation, incineration; *chem* oxidation; *med* burn; **~~skammer** *f* combustion chamber; **~~smaschine** *f*, **~~smotor** *m* internal-combustion engine; **~~sofen** *m* combustion furnace, incinerator; **~~sprodukt** *n* product of combustion; **~~sraum** *m tech* combustion chamber; **~~svorgang** *m* process of combustion; **~~swärme** *f* heat of combustion.
ver|briefen *tr* to promise by writ, to confirm; *~brieftes Recht* vested interest; **~bringen** *irr tr* to spend, to pass; (*befördern*) to transport; (*wegbringen*) to remove; **~brüdern** *r* to fraternize (with); **~brüderung** *f* fraternization; **~brühen** *tr* to scald; **~buchen** *tr* to book, to record, to make an entry of; (*aufzeichnen*) to register; **~buchung** *f* booking; **~buhlt** *a* meretricious, debauched, wanton.
ver|bummeln *tr* (*versäumen*) to neglect, to forget; (*Zeit*) to idle away; (*Geld*) to waste, to squander; *itr* to go to the dogs; **~bummelt** *a* (*liederlich*) dissolute; (*verlumpt*) disreputable, raffish; *~~er Kerl* scamp; **~bunden** *a* connected; united; *zu Dank ~~* obliged; *untereinander ~~* interconnected; *falsch ~~! tele* sorry, wrong number! **~~heit** *f* connexion; union; harmony; (*Bindung*) tie, bond; **~bundmotor** *m* compound-wound motor; **~bundverfahren** *n* duplexing process; **~bünden** *r* to enter into a league (with), to ally o. s. (with); **~bündete(r)** *m* ally, confederate; **~bürgen** *tr* to warrant; *sich für etw ~~* to answer, to guarantee (for), to vouch (for); **~bürgt** *a* authentic, confirmed; **~büßen** *tr* to serve o.'s time; **~chromen** *tr* to chrome-plate, to chromium-plate; **~chromung** *f* chromium plating.

•

Ver|dacht *m* suspicion; (*Mißtrauen*) distrust; *~~ erregen* to arouse suspicion; *~~ hegen, im ~~ haben* to suspect; to distrust s. o.; **~~sgrund** *m* ground for suspicion; **~~smoment** *m* suspicious fact; **~dächtig** *a* suspected of, suspicious; (*unglaubhaft*) bogus, spurious, *Am sl* phony; **~~en** *tr* to throw suspicion (on), to suspect s. o. of; (*mißtrauen*) to distrust; (*verleumden*) to slander, to calumniate; *jdn e-r Sache ~~* to impute s. th. to; **~~ung** *f* calumny, insinuation; (*falsche Anschuldigung*) false charge.
verdamm|en *tr* to condemn; *eccl* to damn (for);**~enswert, ~lich** *a* condemnable; damnable; **~nis** *f* damnation; perdition; **~t!** *interj* confound it! damn! darn! doggone! gosh-darn! **~ung** *f* condemnation; damnation.
verdampf|en *tr* to evaporate, to vaporize, to volatilize; **~ung** *f* vaporization, volatilization, evaporation; **~~stemperatur** *f* volatilization temperature; **~~swärme** *f* heat of vaporization.
verdanken *tr: zu ~~ haben* to owe s. th. (to); to be indebted to s. o. (for).
verdattert *a fam* in a dither; staggered.
verdau|en *tr* to digest; **~lich** *a* digestible; **~~keit** *f* digestibility; **~ung** *f* digestion; **~~sbeschwerden** *f pl*, **~~sstörung** *f* indigestion; **~~swerkzeuge** *f pl* digestive organs *pl*.
Verdeck *n mar* deck; (*Plane*) awning; *mot* hood; top (of a bus); **~en** *tr* to cover; to hide, to conceal, to mask, to camouflage; **~hülle** *f* dust hood;

~sitz *m* roof seat; **~t** *a* camouflaged, masked, screened; concealed.

verdenken *irr itr* to find fault with, to blame s. o. for; *jdm etw ~* to take s. th. amiss.

Verderb *m* ruin, decay; **~en** *irr tr, itr* (*Geschäft, Spaß*) to spoil; (*ruinieren*) to ruin; (*verführen*) to corrupt; to deprave, to pervert; (*beschädigen*) to damage; (*verfälschen*) to adulterate; (*in Verfall geraten*) to decay; (*vernichten*) to mar; (*verfaulen*) to rot; (*umkommen*) to perish; (*Luft; beeinträchtigen*) to vitiate; (*schlecht werden*) to be spoiled; *sich den Magen ~~* to upset o.'s stomach; *es mit jdm ~~* to incur another's displeasure, to get in wrong with s. o.; *sich die Augen ~~* to ruin o.'s sight; *jdm die Freude ~~* to spoil (*od* to mar) s. o.'s joy; **~en** *n* ruin, destruction; corruption; *jdn ins ~~ stürzen* to ruin s. o.; *ins ~~ rennen* to go to o.'s ruin; **~lich** *a* destructive, ruinous; contaminating; (*Waren*) perishable; **~~keit** *f* (*Waren*) perishableness; (*Schädlichkeit*) perniciousness; (*moralisch*) corruptibility; **~nis** *f* corruption, depravity; **~t** *a* corrupt, depraved; **~~heit** *f* corruptness; depravity.

ver|deutlichen *tr* to explain, to illustrate, to elucidate, to make clear, to make evident; **~deutschen** *tr* to translate into German; **~dichten** *tr* to condense; to compress; to concentrate; to consolidate; to solidify; to pack, to squeeze; **~dichter** *m* compressor, condenser; **~dichtung** *f* concentration, consolidation; **~~sring** *m* packing ring; **~dicken** *tr* to thicken, to concentrate; *chem* to inspissate; (*Milch*) to curdle; *r* to thicken; to become viscous; (*gerinnen*) to coagulate, to curd; **~dickung** *f* thickening; **~dienen** *tr* (*Geld*) to earn, to gain, to make money; (*wert sein*) to deserve, to merit; *sich verdient machen um* to deserve well of; **~dienst** *m* gain, profit; (*Lohn*) earnings *pl*; wages *pl*; (*Nutzen*) profit; *~~ n* merit; *es ist hauptsächlich sein ~~, daß ...* it's largely owing to him that ...; **~~ausfall** *m* loss of wages; **~~lich, ~~voll** *a* meritorious, deserving; **~~möglichkeit** *f* earning opportunity; **~~spanne** *f* margin of profits; **~dient** *a* deserving; well-deserved; worthy of estimation; meritorious; **~~ermaßen** *adv* deservedly, according to o.'s deserts.

verding|en *tr* to put out, to hire out; *sich ~~* to bind o. s.

verdolmetsch|en *tr* to interpret, to translate.

ver|donnern *tr fam* to condemn; **~doppeln** *tr* to double, to redouble; **~doppelung** *f* doubling, duplication; **~dorben** *a* spoiled, deteriorated; (*beschädigt*) damaged; (*Waren*) spoiled, (*Fleisch*) tainted; (*Magen*) disordered; (*Luft*) foul, vitiated; (*Wasser*) putrid; (*moralisch*) corrupt, depraved; **~~heit** *f* corruption, depravity; **~dorren** *itr* to dry up; **~drängen** *tr* to push away (*od* aside); to displace, to dislocate, to dislodge; (*vertreiben*) to drive out, *Am* to crowd out; to oust, to evict; (*unterdrücken*) to suppress; (*seelisch*) to inhibit; *fig* to supersede; (*durch List*) to supplant; **~drängung** *f* removal, displacement; suppression; inhibition; supplantation; **~drehen** *tr* to twist, to distort; (*Augen, Gesicht*) to roll o.'s eyes; (*Glieder*) to contort; (*Tatsachen*) to misrepresent, to distort; *jur* to pervert; *tech* to twist, to distort, to wrench; *jdm den Kopf ~~* to turn s. o.'s head; *~dreht sein* to be crazy (*od* mad *od* cracked); **~drehtheit** *f* craziness; **~drehung** *f* distortion, perversion; *fig* misrepresentation; **~dreifachen** *tr* to triple; **~drießen** *irr tr* to vex, to annoy, to exasperate, to jar upon o.'s feelings, to go against the grain; *es verdrießt mich* I'm sick and tired of it; *sl* I'm fed up; *sich nichts ~~ lassen* not to be discouraged; *sich keine Mühe ~~ lassen* to grudge no pains; **~drießlich** *a* (*mürrisch*) morose; (*schlecht gelaunt*) sullen, sulky, bad-tempered, peevish; (*verärgert*) annoyed, vexed (at), *Am* stuffy; (*Arbeit*) tiresome, unpleasant; (*beschwerlich*) irksome; (*langweilig*) soggy; **~~keit** *f* peevishness; annoyance; vexation; irksomeness; **~drossen** *a* displeased, unwilling, sulky, peevish, *Am* peeved, grouchy; (*lustlos*) listless; (*verärgert*) annoyed; (*faul*) lazy, slow; **~~heit** *f* unwillingness, sulkiness; **~drucken** *tr* to misprint; **~drücken** *tr fam* to eat up; *r* to slink away; **~druß** *m* displeasure, vexation, annoyance; *~~ bereiten* to give trouble, to vex; *jdm etw zum ~~ tun* to do s. th. to spite s. o.; **~duften** *itr* to evaporate; *fig* to take French leave, to slip away, *Am sl* to beat it; *verdufte!* get out! *Am sl* scram! **~dummen** *itr* to become stupid; *tr* to make stupid; **~dunkeln** *tr* to darken, to obscure; *fig* to cloud; *astr* to eclipse; *mil* to blackout; (*teilweise*) to brownout; to dim out; (*Farben*) to deepen; **~dunkelung** *f* darkening; obscuration; *astr* eclipse; *mil* blackout; brownout; dim-out; **~~seinrichtung** *f* screening apparatus; **~~smaßnahme** *f* blackout measure; **~~spapier** *n* blackout paper; **~~sübung** *f* trial blackout; **~dünnen** *tr* to thin; *mit Wasser ~~* to dilute; (*Gase*) to rarefy; **~dünnung** *f* attenuation; (*Luft*) rarefaction; dilution; **~dunsten** *itr* to evaporate, to volatilize; **~dunstung** *f* evaporation; **~dursten** *itr* to die of thirst; **~düstern** *tr, r* to darken, to obscure; **~dutzen** *tr* to disconcert, to nonplus; **~dutzt** *a* disconcerted, puzzled, taken aback.

veredel|n *tr* to ennoble; (*Tiere*) to improve; (*verfeinern*) to refine; (*Pflanzen*) to cultivate; (*aufpfropfen*) to graft; (*Textilien*) to finish, to dress, to process; (*anreichern*) to enrich; **~ung** *f* improvement; refinement; purification; enrichment; finishing, processing; **~~sindustrie** *f* processing industry; **~~sverfahren** *n* refining process.

verehelich|en *tr, r* to marry; **~ung** *f* marriage.

verehr|en *tr* (*anbeten*) to worship; *fig* to adore; to venerate, to revere; *jdm etw ~~* to present s. o. with; *~te Anwesende!* Ladies and Gentlemen! **~er** *m* worshipper; (*Liebhaber*) adorer, admirer; **~lich** *a* reverend, hono(u)red; **~ung** *f* reverence, veneration; (*Gottes*) worship, adoration; **~~swürdig** *a* venerable.

vereid|en, **~igen** *tr* to swear in, to put on oath; **~igung** *f* swearing in; taking the oath.

Verein *m* union; (*Gesellschaft*) association; (*geselliger ~*) club; society; **~bar** *a* compatible, reconcilable, concordant; consistent (with); **~baren** *tr* to agree upon, to arrange; to come to an agreement; (*vertraglich*) to make a contract; (*schriftlich*) to stipulate in writing; *sich ~~ mit* to arrange with; **~barkeit** *f* compatibility; **~barung** *f* agreement, arrangement; terms *pl*; *e-e ~~ treffen* to make an agreement; *nur nach ~~* by appointment only; **~en** *tr* to join, to unite; **~fachen** *tr* to simplify; to short-circuit; *math* to reduce; **~fachung** *f* simplification; **~einheitlichen** *tr* to standardize, to unify; **~einheitlichung** *f* standardization, unification; (*Gleichschaltung*) coordination; making for uniformity; (*Normalisierung*) normalization; (*Regulierung*) regularization; **~igen** *tr, r* to unite, to join; (*verbinden*) to combine, to connect, to link; (*verschmelzen*) to merge, to mix, to blend; (*zusammenstellen*) to put together; (*fusionieren*) to amalgamate; (*anschließen*) to affiliate (*an* to, *Am* with); (*vergesellschaften*) to associate; (*in Beziehung bringen*) to relate; (*zusammenfassen*) to integrate (*in* into); (*verketten*) to concatenate; (*Glieder zusammenfügen*) to articulate; (*verbünden*) to ally (o. s.) with; (*versammeln*) to assemble; (*Truppen, Kräfte*) to rally; (*in Einklang bringen*) to reconcile (with); (*an e-m Punkt*) to centralize; **~(ig)t** *a* united; (*Ausschuß*) joint; (*Geld*) concentrated; *die Vereinigten Staaten* (*von Nordamerika*) the United States (of North America) *Abk* US(A) *mit sing*; *die Vereinten Nationen* the United Nations; **~igung** *f* (*Bund*) union; (*Zusammenschluß, Kartell*) combination; (*Gesellschaft*) society, association; (*Bündnis*) alliance; (*Organisation*) organization; (*Verschmelzung, Fusionierung*) fusion, merger, amalgamation, consolidation; (*Übereinstimmung*) agreement; (*staatliche ~~, Verband*) federation; (*Einheit*) unity; (*gesellige*) club; (*Knotenpunkt*) junction; **~~sfreiheit** *f* freedom of association; **~~spunkt** *m* junction, meeting point, joining; rallying point; **~nahmen** *tr* (*Geld*) to receive; **~samen** *tr* to isolate; *itr* to become isolated, to live more and more alone; **~samt** *a* solitary, lonely, desolate; **~samung** *f* isolation; loneliness, solitariness.

vereinzel|n *tr* to isolate, to separate; **~t** *a* isolated; single, solitary; sporadic; **~ung** *f* isolation, separation.

ver|eisen *itr* to cover with ice, to freeze, to frost; *aero* to take on ice, to ice up; *~~ n* freezing; (*glasartig*) glaze, clear ice; **~eisung** *f* ice-formation; *aero* icing up; *geol* glaciation; **~~sgefahr** *f* danger of ice-formation; **~~sschutz** *m* anti-icer fluid; (*Gerät*) anti-icing device; **~eiteln** *tr* to frustrate, to thwart, to baffle; **~eit(e)lung** *f* frustration; **~eitern** *itr* to suppurate, to fester; **~eiterung** *f* suppuration; **~ekeln** *tr* to disgust with; to spoil s. th. for; **~elenden** *itr* to sink into poverty; **~elendet** *a* pauperized; **~elendung** *f* pauperization; **~enden** *itr* to die, to perish; **~enge(r)n** *tr* to straiten, to narrow; (*zusammenziehen*) to contract; **~eng(er)ung** *f* straitening; contraction; **~erben** *tr* to leave (to), to bequeath; (*Krankheit*) to transmit; (*übermitteln*) to hand down; *r* to be hereditary, to run in the family; *sich ~~ auf* to devolve upon; **~erbt** *a* inherited; hereditary; **~erbung** *f* inheritance; transmission, *med* heredity; **~~sgesetz** *n* law of heredity; **~~slehre** *f* genetics *pl*; **~~ssubstanz** *f* idioplasm; **~ewigen** *tr* to perpetuate; (*unsterblich machen*) to immortalize; **~ewigt** *a* deceased, late, departed.

verfahren *irr itr* to proceed; to act, to work, to manage, to deal; *tr* (*Geld*) to spend (in driving about); (*verwirren*) to muddle, to bungle; *r* to take the wrong road, to lose o.'s way; *fig* to blunder, to be on the wrong tack; ~*a* bungled; ~ *n* (*Art u. Weise*) method, manner, dealing; *jur* (*Gang*) proceeding(s *pl*), (*als Einrichtung*) procedure; *tech* process, technique; (*Vorgang*) operation, mode of action; (*Handhabung*) treatment, management, conduct; (*Grundsatz*) principle; system; *das ~ einleiten gegen* to take (*od* to institute) proceedings against; *das ~ einstellen* to quash (*od* to drop) the proceedings; to dismiss the case; *e-m ~ unterwerfen* to process; **~sbestimmung** *f* rules of procedure; **~svorschlag** *m* tentative procedure; **~sweise** *f* mode of proceeding.

Verfall *m* decay, ruin; (*Niedergang*) decline; decadence; (*Entartung*) deterioration; (*Zusammenbruch*) failure; (*e-s Rechtes*) lapse, forfeiture; (*Hypothek*) foreclosure; (*Wechsel*) maturity, expiration; *in ~ geraten* to decay, to go to ruin; *bei ~* when due, at maturity; **~en** *irr itr* to go to ruin; (*körperlich*) to decline, to grow weaker; (*Wechsel*) to fall due, to mature; (*ablaufen*) to expire; (*Recht*) to lapse, to cease to be valid; (*Pfand*) to be forfeited; (*e-r Strafe*) to incur; (*Fehler, Gewohnheit*) to fall in, to slip back (into), to run (into); (*zufällig stoßen auf*) to chance; *auf e-n Gedanken ~~* to hit upon an idea; *darauf wäre er nie ~~* that would never have entered his mind; *jdm ~~* to become the property of; to become s. o.'s slave; *auf jdn ~~* to take a fancy to; *~~ lassen* to let lapse; (*Eintrittskarte*) to let go to waste; **~en** *a* dilapidated; ruinous; (*Gesichtszüge*) worn, wasted; (*Gebäude*) decayed, tumble-down; (*Laster*) addicted to; *jur* forfeited, lapsed; *com* due, payable; (*beschlagnahmt*) confiscated; (*Hypothek*) foreclosed; (*Patent*) void; **~serscheinung** *f* symptom of decline; **~tag** *m* day of payment, due date; *bis zum ~~* until maturity, till due; **~zeit** *f* time of maturity.

ver|fälschen *tr* to falsify; (*Urkunde*) to forge, to tamper with, *fam* to doctor; (*Geld*) to counterfeit; (*Wein*) to adulterate; **~fälscher** *m* falsifier, forger; (*Wein*) adulterator; **~fälschung** *f* falsification; adulteration; **~fangen** *irr itr* to take effect, to tell (*bei* on); *nicht ~~ bei* not to go down with; *r* to become entangled, to get ensnared; *fig* to betray o. s.; **~fänglich** *a* (*Frage*) captious, insidious; (*unbequem*) embarrassing, awkward; (*unschicklich*) indecent; (*Lage*) risky; **~färben** *r* to change colo(u)r; (*blaß werden*) to grow pale; (*erröten*) to blush.

verfass|en *tr* to compose, to write, to pen; **~er** *m* author, writer; **~~korrektur** *f* author's proof; **~~schaft** *f* authorship.

Verfassung *f* (*Staats~*) constitution; (*Zustand*) state, condition, *fam* shape, trim, *fig Am* fix, *sl* whack; (*Gemüts~*) frame of mind, disposition; **~gebend** *a* constituent; **~sausschuß** *m* constitutional committee; **~sgemäß, ~smäßig** *a* constitutional; **~stag** *m* Constitution Day; **~surkunde** *f* charter of the constitution; (*in England*) Magna Charta; **~swidrig** *a* unconstitutional.

ver|faulen *itr* to rot, to decay, to mo(u)lder; to putrefy; **~fechten** *irr tr* to defend, to maintain, to stand up for; (*e-e Sache*) to advocate, to champion; **~fechter** *m* champion, advocate, stalwart, steadfast partisan, staunch supporter; **~fehlen** *tr* (*nicht begegnen*) not to meet; (*Ziel*) to miss; (*unterlassen, fehlschlagen*) to fail (to); (*Weg*) to lose; *ich werde nicht ~~ zu* I shall not fail to; **~fehlt** *a* (*erfolglos*) unsuccessful; (*falsch*) wrong, false; (*unpassend*) unsuited, misplaced; (*schlecht gemacht*) bungled; *~~e Sache* failure; **~fehlung** *f* (*Fehler*) mistake; (*Vergehen*) offence; **~feinden** *tr* to embroil one with; *r* to fall out with; **~feinern** *tr* to refine, to improve, to purify; to subtilize; to polish; *r* to become refined; **~feinerung** *f* refinement, subtilization, improvement; **~femen** *tr* to outlaw.

verfertig|en *tr* to manufacture, to make, to fabricate, to prepare; to compose; **~er** *m* maker, manufacturer; **~ung** *f* manufacture, fabrication, preparation.

ver|festigen *tr* to make firm, to strengthen, to solidify, to consolidate; **~festigung** *f* strengthening, consolidation, stiffening, stabilization.

Ver|fettung *f med* fatty degeneration; *med* adiposis; **~feuern** *tr* to fire, to burn, to consume; (*unnütz vergeuden*) to waste fuel; **~filmen** *tr* to make a screen version of, to adapt to the screen; to film(ize), to picture, to screen; **~filmung** *f* screening, adaptation to the screen, film-version; **~~srecht** *n* screen rights *pl*; **~filzen** *r* to felt; (*Haare*) to mat; *r* to get entangled; **~finstern** *tr* to darken; to eclipse; to obscure; **~finsterung** *f* darkening; *astr* eclipse; **~flachen** *tr* to flatten, to level off; *itr, r* to become level; *fig* to become shallow; **~flechten** *irr tr* to interlace, to interweave; *fig* to implicate, to involve; *in etw ~flochten sein* to be entangled in, to be engaged in; **~flechtung** *f* interlacing, involving; *fig* entanglement, complexity, complication; **~fliegen** *irr itr* to fly off; *fig* to vanish, to disappear; (*Zeit*) to pass, to fly; (*verflüchtigen*) to evaporate; *chem* to volatilize; *r aero* to lose o.'s bearings; **~fließen** *irr itr* to flow off; (*Zeit*) to elapse, to pass, to expire; (*Farbe*) to blend, to run (into); **~flixt** *a fam* confounded, infernal; *~~! interj* that's too bad! *Am* darn it! **~flossen** *a* past; late; ex-.

verfluch|en *tr* to curse, to detest; **~t** *a* cursed, confounded; *~~! interj* confound it! *fam* dash it!

verflüchtig|en *tr, itr* to volatilize; *r* to evaporate; *fig* to vanish; **~ung** *f* evaporation; volatilization.

verflüssig|en *tr* to liquefy; *r* to become liquid; *~tes Gas* fixed gas; **~ung** *f* liquefaction; condensation; (*Metall*) thinning; (*Kohle*) hydrogenation; **~~sanlage** *f* liquefying plant.

Verfolg *m* continuation, progress, course; pursuance; **~en** *tr* to pursue; (*gerichtlich*) to prosecute; (*grausam*) to persecute; *fig* to follow up; to watch; (*Interessen*) to look out for; (*Spur*) to trace; (*Wild*) to trail; *heimlich ~~* to shadow; **~er** *m* pursuer; persecutor; **~te(r)** *m* persecutee; **~ung** *f* pursuit; *jur* prosecution; persecution; **~~sflugzeug** *n* (*Jäger*) pursuit plane; **~~skampf** *m* rear-guard engagement; **~~swahn** *m* persecution mania.

Verform|barkeit *f* deformability; malleability, plasticity; **~t** *a* shaped, deformed; **~ung** *f* deformation, distortion, warping; **~~sfähigkeit** *f* ductility.

verfracht|en *tr* (*Schiff*) to charter; (*Waren*) to freight, to load, to ship; **~er** *m* freighter, forwarding-agent, *Am* freight-agent; charterer; **~ung** *f* freighting, chartering, shipping.

verfranzen *r aero sl* to lose o.'s way, to wander off course.

verfrüht *a* premature.

verfüg|bar *a* disposable, available, at s. o.'s disposal; **~~keit** *f* availability; **~en** *tr* to order, to decree, to arrange; *itr über etw ~~* to dispose of, to have at o.'s disposal; *letzwillig ~~* to will; *r sich wohin ~~* to go (*nach* to), to proceed (to); **~ung** *f* (*Erlaß*) decree, ordinance, regulation, order; (*Anweisung*) instruction; (*Anordnung*) arrangement; (*freie ~~*) disposal, disposition; *zur besonderen ~~* at disposal for special duty; *einstweilige ~~* (*jur*) injunction; *~~en treffen* to make arrangements; *jdm zur ~~ stehen* to be at s. o.'s disposal; *zur ~~ stellen* to place at s. o.'s disposal; **~~sbefugnis** *f* right of disposal; **~~sberechtigt** *a* authorized to dispose; **~~sgewalt** *f* control; **~~struppen** *f pl* reserves *pl*.

verführ|en *tr* to lead astray, to mislead; *fig* to seduce; (*Mädchen*) to seduce, to ruin; (*verlocken*) to entice, to allure, to delude, to ensnare, to win over; (*bestechen*) to bribe, to suborn; (*überreden*) to induce; (*in Versuchung führen*) to tempt; **~er** *m* seducer, corrupter; **~erisch** *a* seductive, tempting, alluring; fascinating, bewitching, charming, prepossessing; **~ung** *f* seduction; enticement, allurement, ensnaring; (*Versuchung*) temptation; (*Verleitung*) bribing, subornation.

ver|fünffachen *tr* to quintuple; **~füttern** *tr* to use as fodder.

ver|gaffen *r* to fall in love (with); **~gällen** *tr* to embitter; to make loathsome, to spoil; *chem* to denature; **~galoppieren** *r* to overshoot the mark, to blunder; **~gangen** *a* past, last; bygone; (*verblüht*) faded, withered; **~~heit** *f* past; (*persönliche*) background; *gram* past tense; **~gänglich** *a* transitory, transient, fleeting; perishable; **~~keit** *f* transitoriness; perishableness; **~gären** *tr* to ferment; **~gasen** *tr* to gasify, to vaporize; *mil* to gas; *mot* to carburet; **~gaser** *m* carbure(t)tor; **~~brand** *m* fire in the carburet(t)or; **~~einstellung** *f* adjustment of the carburet(t)or; **~~filter** *n* carburet(t)or filter; **~~motor** *m* petrol engine, *Am* gasoline engine; **~~vereisung** *f* carburet(t)or icing; **~gasung** *f* gasification; carburetion; **~gattern** *tr* to grate; **~gatterung** *f* lattice-work; *mil* change of the guard.

vergeb|en *irr tr* to give away, to dispose (of); (*Auftrag*) to place; to commission; to confer, to bestow (on); (*verzeihen*) to forgive, to pardon; (*Karten*) to misdeal; (*Tochter*) to give in marriage; *~~ sein* to have a previous engagement; *sich etw ~~* to prejudice o.'s right; to derogate from o.'s dignity; *seiner Ehre nichts ~~* to be jealous of o.'s hono(u)r; **~ens** *adv* in vain, vainly; **~lich** *a* idle, futile, fruitless; *adv* in vain; **~~keit** *f* uselessness; **~ung** *f* pardon, forgiveness; (*Arbeit*) giving; (*Auftrag*) placing; (*Amt*) appointment, conferring; (*Gewährung*) bestowal.

vergegenwärtig|en *tr* to represent, to figure; *r* to imagine, to realize, to visualize; to bear in mind; *sich etw ~~* to realize a thing; **~ung** *f* realization.

vergehen *irr itr* to pass, to fly, to elapse; (*langsam*) to wear away, to draw to a close; (*verlieren*) to lose; (*aufhören*) to stop, to cease; (*verschwinden*) to disappear; (*vor Gram*) to pine away; (*dahinschwinden*) to waste away; (*allmählich*) to fade; (*verschmachten*) to perish, to die (of); *r* to commit an offence, to offend (against); to injure s. o., to insult s. o.; (*schwer*) to assault; *sich ~ an* to violate s. o.; *sich gegen das Gesetz ~* to violate (*od* to break) the law; *vor Neugier ~* to die of curiosity; *es verging ihm Hören u. Sehen* his hair stood on end; *~ n* fault, trespass; sin; (*Rechtsverletzung*) offence, crime, misdemeano(u)r.

vergeistigen *tr* to spiritualize.

vergelt|en *irr tr* to repay, to pay back, to return; (*Unrecht ~~*) to retort; (*heimzahlen*) to requite, to make reprisal, to pay home, *fam* to hit back at, to turn the tables upon; (*Vergeltung üben*) to retaliate; (*belohnen*) to reward (*für* for); (*Gegenbeschuldigung vorbringen*) to recriminate; *Gleiches mit Gleichem ~~* to return like for like, to give tit for tat; *Gutes mit Bösem ~~* to return good for evil; **~ung** *f* requital, retribution; (*feindliche*) retaliation, reprisals *pl*; recompense; **~~sangriff** *m* retaliatory attack; **~~smaßnahme** *f* reprisal; **~~swaffe** *f* V weapon, flying bomb.

vergesellschaft|en *tr* to convert into an association; (*verstaatlichen*) to socialize, to nationalize; **~ung** *f* converting into an association; socialization, nationalization.

vergessen *irr tr* to forget; (*übersehen*) to overlook; (*auslassen*) to omit; (*versäumen*) to neglect; (*vergeben*) to forgive for; *r* to forget o. s., to act unbecomingly, to lose selfconsciousness; (*seinen Vorteil ~*) to neglect o.'s own interests; **~heit** *f* forgetfulness; *in ~~ geraten* to fall into oblivion.

vergeßlich *a* forgetful; unmindful; **~keit** *f* forgetfulness.

vergeud|en *tr* to waste, to squander, to dissipate; to fool away (time); **~er** *m* squanderer, spendthrift; **~ung** *f* dissipation; extravagance; wastefulness, waste, squandering.

vergewaltig|en *tr* to violate, to (commit a) rape (on); (*gewalttätig sein*) to offer violence, to use force; **~ung** *f* oppression, violence; (*tätliche Drohung*) assault; (*Frau*) rape.

ver|gewissern *r* to make sure (of), to ascertain; **~gießen** *irr tr* to shed, to spill; *tech* to cast, to run in, to fill up; *Tränen ~~* to shed tears; **~giften** *tr* to poison; to embitter; **~giftung** *f* poisoning; *fig* infection; (*Ansteckung*) contamination; **~~serscheinung** *f* symptom of poisoning; **~gilben** *itr* to turn yellow; **~gilbt** *a* yellow(ed); **~gipsen** *tr* to plaster; **~gißmeinnicht** *n* forget-me-not; **~gittern** *tr* to grate, to lattice; (*Draht*) to wire in; to screen; **~gitterung** *f* grating, grid; lattice; grill(e); **~glasen** *tr* to glaze; (*in Glas verwandeln*) to vitrify; **~glasung** *f* glazing; vitrification.

Vergleich *m* comparison; (*Verständigung*) agreement, arrangement; (*Ausgleich*) settlement; (*gütlich*) compromise; *im ~ zu* compared to, in comparison with; *kein ~ mit* nothing in comparison with, *Am* not a circumstance to; *e-n ~ anstellen* to make a comparison (*zwischen* between); *er hält mit ihm keinen ~ aus* he doesn't bear comparison with him; *e-n ~ treffen* to come to an arrangement; **~bar** *a* comparable; **~en** *tr* to compare (*mit* with, *bei Gleichstellung* to); (*gegenüberstellen*) to contrast; (*kritisch*) to collate; (*prüfen*) to check; (*bereinigen*) to settle, to adjust; *r* (*sich verständigen*) to come to terms with; *verglichen mit* compared to; as against; as opposed to; **~sabkommen** *n* composition agreement; **~sgrundlage** *f* comparison basis; **~sjahr** *n* base year; **~smaßstab** *m* standard of comparison; **~smessung** *f* comparison measuring; **~spunkt** *m* article of arrangement; **~sverfahren** *n* comparison method; *jur* settlement sub judice; **~svorschlag** *m* offer of compromise; **~sweise** *adv* comparatively, by way of comparison; by way of agreement; **~swert** *m* relative value; **~szahl** *f* comparative figure; **~ung** *f* comparison; contrasting; matching; **~~sgrad** *m* degree of comparison; **~~spunkt** *m* check point.

ver|gletschern *tr* to turn into glacier-ice; **~glimmen** *irr itr* to die away, to go out; **~glühen** *itr* to cease glowing.

vergnüg|en *tr* to enjoy, to please, to amuse, to entertain, to divert; *r* to delight (in), to amuse o. s., to enjoy o. s.; to take pleasure (in); **~en** *n* pleasure, joy, enjoyment, amusement, *Am fam* jollification; (*Spaß*) fun; (*Erholung*) relaxation; (*Unterhaltung*) entertainment; (*Ablenkung*) diversion; (*Kurzweil*) sport; (*Zeitvertreib*) pastime; *es aus ~~ tun* to do it just for fun; *ich komme mit ~~* I'll be delighted to come; *das wird ein teures ~~* that's going to be an expensive proposition; *viel ~~!* have a good time! enjoy yourself! *an etw ~~ finden* to take pleasure in; **~lich** *a* pleasing, pleasant; **~t** *a* (*fröhlich*) merry; (*froh*) glad, happy, lighthearted; (*lebhaft*) vivacious, lively, sprightly; (*freudig*) joyful, joyous, cheerful; (*erfreut*) pleased (with), delighted (at); **~ung** *f* pleasure, enjoyment, joy, delight, delectation; (*Unterhaltung*) amusement, diversion, entertainment, recreation; **~~sdampfer** *m* pleasure-boat; **~~sfahrt** *f* pleasure drive; *e-e ~~sfahrt machen mot* to go for a run, *Am* to go for a joy ride; **~~sflug** *m* pleasure flight, *fam* flip; **~~slokal** *n* place of entertainment; **~~sreise** *f* pleasure trip; **~~sreisende(r)** *m* tourist; **~~sstätte** *f* place of amusement; **~~ssteuer** *f* entertainment tax, *Am* admission tax; **~~ssucht** *f* love of pleasure; **~~ssüchtig** *a* pleasure-seeking, pleasure-loving; **~~szentrum** *n* amusement centre; **~~szug** *m* excursion train.

vergold|en *tr* to gild; **~er** *m* gilder; **~ung** *f* gilding.

ver|gönnen *tr* not to grudge; (*gewähren*) to grant, to allow; **~göttern** *tr* to deify, *fig* to idolize; (*verehren*) to adore, to worship; **~götterung** *f* deification, apotheosis; *fig* adoration, worship; **~graben** *tr* to hide in the ground, to bury, to entrench; **~grämt** *a* care-worn, grief-stricken; woe-begone; **~greifen** *irr r* to mistake; to touch by mistake; *mus* to touch the wrong note; *sich an jdm ~~* to seize hold of, to attack, to violate; *sich an etw ~~* to steal, (*unterschlagen*) to embezzle; **~greisen** *itr* to become senile; **~griffen** *a* (*Waren*) bought up, out of stock, sold out; (*Bücher*) out of print, exhausted.

vergröbern *tr* to coarsen, to make coarser.

vergrößer|n *tr, r* to enlarge; (*Lupe*) to magnify; (*an Zahl, Umfang*) to increase; (*ausdehnen*) to expand, to extend; *phot* to enlarge; (*übertreiben*) to exaggerate, *fam* to blow up; (*verschlimmern*) to aggravate; **~ung** *f* enlargement; increase; magnification; extension; *phot* enlargement, blowup; exaggeration; **~~sapparat** *m* enlarging camera, enlarger; (*mit selbsttätiger Einstellung*) autofocus enlarger; **~~sbereich** *m* range of magnification; **~~sgerät** *n* enlarger; **~~sglas** *n* magnifying-glass; **~~szahl** *f* coefficient of magnification, enlargement factor.

Vergünstigung *f* (*Erlaubnis*) permission; (*Ermäßigung*) abatement, deduction, allowance; (*Rabatt*) rebate (*auf* on); (*Zugeständnis*) concession; (*Vorzugsbehandlung*) preferential treatment; (*Vorrecht*) privilege, favo(u)r.

vergüt|en *tr* to compensate; (*Auslagen*) to reimburse, to refund, to pay back; (*entschädigen*) to indemnify; to make good; *tech* to temper, to harden; (*Qualität*) to improve; (*Linse*) to coat; **~et** *a* (*Stahl*) heat-treated; (*Holz*) improved; (*Linse*) (hard) coated; **~ung** *f* indemnity, compensation; reimbursement; allowance; remuneration; *tech* tempering, heat-treatment, annealing; (*Linse*) coating.

verhaft|en *tr* to arrest, to take into custody; (*vorläufig*) to apprehend; *~et werden* to get arrested; *~et sein fig* to be dependent on, to be closely connected with; **~ung** *f* arrest; apprehension; (*Ergreifen*) capture; **~~sbefehl** *m* warrant (of apprehension).

verhageln *itr* to be damaged by hail.

verhallen *itr* to die away, to fade away.

verhalten *irr tr* to keep back, to stop, to retain; (*Atem*) to hold in; (*unterdrücken*) to suppress; (*in Schranken halten*) to restrain; *r* (*sich benehmen*) to behave, to act, to conduct o. s.; (*Zustand*) to be, to be the case; *math* to be in the ratio of; to be in proportion to; *sich gut ~* to get along with; *sich ruhig ~* to keep quiet; *wie verhält sich die Sache?* how is the matter? *die Sache verhält sich ganz anders* the matter is different; *~ n* behavio(u)r, conduct; attitude; **~ungsmaßregeln** *f pl* instructions *pl*, orders *pl*; rules of conduct.

Verhältnis *n* relation, proportion, rate, ratio; (*Lage*) situation, position, status, condition; (*Umstände*) circumstances *pl*; (*Mittel*) means *pl*; (*Liebes~*) (love-)affair; (*Geliebte*) mistress, girl-friend; *nach ~* in proportion to; *in keinem ~ stehend zu* unequal; *umgekehrtes ~* inverse ratio; *im quadratischen ~* in proportion to the square (of); *das ~ ist 3 zu 5* the ratio is three to five; *in guten ~sen* in easy circumstances, *Am* on easy street; *er lebt über seine ~se* he lives beyond his means; *in freundschaftlichem ~ mit* on friendly terms with; **~anteil** *m* proportion, quota; **~mäßig** *a* proportional, proportionate; *adv* comparatively; relatively; reasonably; **~maßstab** *m* scale; **~wahl** *f* proportional representation; **~widrig** *a* disproportionate; **~wort** *n* preposition; **~zahl** *f* proportionality factor, ratio, index figure, proportionate figure.

verhand|eln *tr* to discuss; (*erörtern*) to debate, to argue; *jur* to plead, to try (a case); (*verkaufen*) to sell, to barter away; *itr* to negotiate, to treat (*wegen* for); to parley, to confer, to consult, to advise; **~lung** *f* discussion; negotiation, transaction; *jur* pleading, trial, hearing, proceedings *pl*; (*Debatte*) debate; (*Besprechung*) conference; (*Erörterung*) argument; *~~en aufnehmen* to enter into negotiations; **~~sbereit** *a* ready for negotiations; **~~sbericht** *m* record on the proceedings; **~~sort** *m jur* venue; **~~sprotokoll** *n* minutes *pl*; record of proceedings; **~~stermin** *m* date of trial; **~~stisch** *m* round table.

verhäng|en *tr* to cover (over), to curtain off; (*bestimmen*) to decree, to proclaim; (*Strafe*) to impose, to inflict, to assess; *mit ~tem Zügel* at full speed; **~nis** *n* fate, destiny; (*Unglück*) disaster; **~~voll** fatal, fateful; (*unselig*) disastrous.

ver|härmt *a* care-worn; **~harren** *itr* to persist in, to remain; *fam* to stick (to), to hold out, to cling (to), *fam* to keep the ball rolling, *fam* to see it through; **~harschen** *itr* (*Schnee*) to (get a) crust; (*Wunde*) to close; **~härten** *itr, r* to harden, to grow hard; (*Herz*) to indurate; (*Zement*) to set; **~härtung** *f* (*der Haut*) callosity; *fig* induration; (*Verstocktheit*) obduration; **~harzen** *tr* to resinify; **~haspeln** *r* to tangle; *fig* to get muddled; **~haßt** *a* hated, odious; **~hätscheln** *tr* to coddle, to pamper, to spoil; **~hau** *m* abat(t)is; **~hauen** *tr* to thrash, *fam* to lick, to give a dressing, *Am* to shingle, to flax; *sl* to ribroast, to towel, to beat up; (*Ball*) to muff; *r fig fam* to blunder; (*Arbeit*) to fail (in), *Am* to flunk (in); **~heben** *irr r* to hurt o. s. by lifting; **~heddern** *r* to tangle; *fig* to break down; **~heeren** *tr* to lay waste, to devastate; to ravage; **~~d** *a* devastating; *fam* (*schrecklich*) awful; **~heerung** *f* devastation; **~hehlen** *tr* to conceal, to hide; **~hehlung** *f* concealment; **~heilen** *itr* to heal up; **~heimlichen** *tr* to conceal, to keep secret; **~heimlichung** *f* concealment; **~heiraten** *tr, r* to marry; *r* to get married (*mit* to); *seine Tochter ~~* to give o.'s daughter away; **~heiratung** *f* marrying, marriage; **~heißen** *irr tr* to promise; **~heißung** *f* promise; *Land der ~~* the Land of Promise; **~~svoll** *a* promising; **~helfen** *irr itr: jdm zu etw ~~* to help s. o. to; **~herrlichen** *tr* to glorify; **~herrlichung** *f* glorification; **~hetzen** *tr* to instigate, to incite; *jdn ~~ gegen* to set one against; **~hetzung** *f* instigation; **~hexen** *tr* to bewitch; **~hexung** *f* bewitchment; **~himmeln** *tr* to praise up to the skies.

verhinder|n *tr* to prevent, to hinder, to embarrass, to hamper; to keep from, to cut off, *Am* to filibuster; **~ung** *f* hindrance, prevention; (*Hindernis*) impediment, handicap, holdback; stumbling block.

verhohlen *a* hidden, concealed.

verhöhn|en *tr* to scoff at, to jeer at, to jibe, to taunt; to ridicule, to make fun of; to catcall; to deride; *Am sl* to give the Bronx cheer, to razz; **~ung** *f* derision, mockery, scoffing, jeer, jibe, scoff, *Am sl* jab, rab, razz.

Verhör *n* examination; trial, hearing, questioning; (*Zeugen*) interrogation; **~en** *tr* to examine, to hear, to try; to interrogate, to question; (*scharf ~~*) *Am fam* to grill; *sich ~~* to misunderstand.

ver|hudeln, **~hunzen** *tr* to spoil, to bungle, to foozle; **~hüllen** *tr* to cover, to wrap up, to veil, to cloud, to mask; **~hüllung** *f* cover(ing), veil(ing), disguise; **~hundertfachen** *tr* to centuple; **~hungern** *itr* to die of hunger, to starve; *~~ lassen* to starve to death; **~hüten** *tr* to prevent, to avert, to keep off, to ward off, to sidetrack, to obviate; (*bewahren*) to preserve (from), to protect, to safeguard; (*untersagen*) to inhibit s. o. from; **~~d** *a* preventive; **~hütten** *tr* to smelt (ores); **~hüttung** *f* smelting, working off; **~hütung** *f* prevention, averting; *med* prophylaxis; **~~smittel** *n* preventive (*gegen* of), prophylactic; inhibitor; **~hutzelt** *a* shrivel(l)ed, wizened.

verinnerlich|en *tr* to intensify, to deepen; **~ung** *f* intensification; profundity.

verirr|en *r* to lose o.'s way, to go astray; **~ung** *f* losing o.'s way, going astray; *fig* error, mistake; aberration.

verjagen *tr* to drive away, to expel.

verjähr|bar *a* prescriptible; **~en** *itr* to grow old (*od* obsolete); *jur* to fall under the statute of limitation; **~t** *a* stale, out of date, superannuated; *jur* prescriptive, statute-barred; **~ung** *f jur* limitation; prescription; superannuation; **~~sfrist** *f* limitation (period).

ver|jubeln *tr* to spend merry-making, to squander, to lavish, (*Geld*) *sl* to blue; **~juden** *itr* to come under Jewish influence; **~jüngen** *tr* to rejuvenate; (*erneuern*) to renew; (*regenerieren*) to regenerate; (*spitz zulaufen*) to taper; (*Zeichnung*) to reduce; (*verkürzen*) to contract; *r* to be rejuvenated, to grow young again; to taper, to narrow; **~jüngt** *a* rejuvenated; *tech* tapered, conic(al), converging; *in ~~em Maßstab* on a reduced scale; **~jüngung** *f* rejuvenescence; *arch* tapering; reduction; **~~skur** *f* rejuvenating cure; **~~smaßstab** *m* scale of reduction.

ver|kalken *itr* to calcine; *r* to calcify; **~kalkulieren** *tr* to miscalculate; **~kalkung** *f* calcination; calcification; *med* arteriosclerosis; **~kannt** *a* misunderstood; undervalued; unappreciated; **~kanten** *tr* to tilt, to twist, to cant; **~kantet** *a* swung; **~kappen** *tr* to disguise, to mask; **~kappt** *a* disguised, secret; **~kapseln** *r* to encyst; **~kapselung** *f* encystment; **~katert** *a fam* suffering from a hang-over.

Verkauf *m* sale; **~en** *tr* to sell, to dispose of; *zu ~~* for sale, to be sold; *gegen bar ~~* to sell for cash; *mit Gewinn ~~* to sell at a profit; *unter der Hand ~~* to sell privately; *leicht ~~* to find a ready market; **~sabrechnung** *f* sales account; **~sabteilung** *f* sales department; **~sangebot** *n* sales offer; **~sanzeige** *f Am* for-sale ad; **~sautomat** *m* vendor; vending machine; mechanical seller; **~sbedingungen** *f pl* conditions of sale, *Am* sales terms *pl*; **~sbüro** *n* sales office; **~serlös** *m* realization proceeds *pl*; **~sfeldzug** *m* selling campaign; **~skontrolle** *f* sales control; **~skosten** *pl* marketing expenses *pl*; **~sleiter** *m* sales manager; **~smethode** *f* sales method; **~sorganisation** *f* selling organization; **~spersonal** *n* sales personnel; **~spolitik** *f* sales angle, sales approach, *Am* merchandizing; **~spreis** *m* sales price; **~sprovision** *f* selling commission; **~sschlager** *m* best-seller; (*billige Ware zur Anlockung*) loss leader; **~ssteigerung** *f* sales promotion; **~ssteuer** *f* sales tax; **~sunkosten** *pl* selling expenses *pl*; **~surkunde** *f* bill of sales; **~svertrag** *m* sales agreement; **~svertretung** *f* selling agency; **~swerber** *f Am* sales promoter; **~swerbung** *f* sales promotion; **~swirkung** *f* sales effectiveness; **~sziffer** *f* sales figure; **~t** *a* sold; *~~ ab Lager* sold ex warehouse; *~~ für Rechnung von* sold for account of; *~~ franko Waggon* sold free on board; *meistbietend ~~* sold by auction.

Verkäuf|er *m*, **~~in** *f* seller; (*im kleinen*) retailer; (*Ladengehilfe*) salesman, attendant, shop assistant, *Am* clerk; sales-woman, shopgirl, salesgirl; *jur* vendor; *als ~~ tätig sein Am* to clerk; **~ermarkt** *m* sellers' market; **~lich** *a* sal(e)able, marketable, vendible; *leicht ~~* commanding a ready sale; *schwer ~~* hard to sell, unsal(e)able; **~~keit** *f* sal(e)ableness, vendibility.

Verkehr *m* traffic; (*Verbindung*) communication; (*Handel*) trade, commerce; (*Verkehrsdienst*) *rail, aero* service; (*Brief~~*) correspondence; (*Beziehung*) connection; (*Bewegung*) circulation; (*persönlicher, geschlechtlicher*) intercourse; *in brieflichem ~ stehen mit* to be corresponding with; to communicate; *dem ~ übergeben* to open to traffic; *den ~ umleiten* to detour; *den ~ vermitteln zwischen* to ply between; *abgehender* (*ankommender*) *~* outgoing (incoming) traffic; *einseitiger* (*doppelseitiger*) *~* one-way (two-way) traffic; *aus dem ~ ziehen* to withdraw from circulation; **~en** *itr* (*Fahrzeug*) to run, to ply (between), to be operated; (*in Beziehung stehen*) to communicate, to intercommunicate; (*besuchen*) to frequent, to visit; to associate (with); to see each other; (*in e-r Wirtschaft*) to patronize; (*Handel treiben*) to traffic, to trade; (*geschlechtlich*) to have sexual intercourse with; *tr* to invert, to reverse; to turn the wrong way; (*umkehren*) to turn upside down, to turn the tables, to turn topsy-turvy; (*verwandeln*) to turn (into), to convert (into), to resolve (into); *fig* pervert; **~t** *a* reversed, inverted; (*falsch*) wrong; (*unsinnig*) absurd; (*verführt*) perverted, perverse; **~~heit** *f* absurdity, folly.

Verkehrs|abwicklung *f* handling of traffic; **~ader** *f* thoroughfare, main artery, arterial road, *Am* boulevard; **~ampel** *f* traffic light; stop-go sign; **~amt** *n* traffic office; **~andrang** *m* rush; **~anhäufung** *f* accumulation of traffic; **~bedürfnisse** *n pl* traffic requirements *pl*; *den ~~n Rechnung tragen* to provide for traffic requirements; **~belastung** *f* traffic load; **~betrieb** *m* transport undertaking; **~bewegung** *f* distribution of traffic; **~dezernent** *m rail* goods manager, *Am* freight traffic manager; **~dichte** *f* density of traffic; **~einrichtungen** *f pl* transport facilities *pl*; **~entflechtung** *f* disentanglement of traffic; **~entwicklung** *f* development of transportation; **~erleichterung** *f* new facilities for traffic; **~erschwerung** *f* traffic restrictions *pl*; **~erziehung** *f* kerb drill; **~~swoche** *f* safety traffic week; **~fähig** *a* marketable; (*begebbar*) negotiable; **~flieger** *m* commercial aviator; **~~el** *f* air transport; **~~schule** *f* transport-pilots' school; **~flughafen** *m* aerodrome, *Am* airport; **~flugzeug** *n* commercial plane, passenger plane, airliner; jet liner; **~~führer** *m* transport pilot; **~geschwindigkeit** *f* commercial speed; **~gesetz** *n* traffic law; **~gewerbe** *n* conveyance; **~insel** *f* traffic island, safety zone, (street-) refuge, *Am* safety isle; **~knotenpunkt** *m* railroad junction, centre of traffic; **~leistung** *f* traffic load; **~lenkung** *f* traffic control; **~luftfahrt** *f* commercial aviation, civil aviation; **~lufthafen** *m* commercial airport; **~minister** *m* Minister of Transport; **~~ium** *n* Ministry of Transport; **~mittel** *n* vehicle, conveyance, means of communication; transport, *Am* transportation; **~netz** *n* communication system; transport system, *Am* traction system; **~ordnung, ~regelung** *f* traffic regulation; **~polizist** *m* traffic policeman, *Am fam* speed-cop; **~problem** *n* traffic problem; **~reich** *a* crowded; **~rückgang** *m* reduction of traffic; **~schwach** *a* having little traffic; **~schwankungen** *f pl* traffic fluctuations *pl*; **~sicherheit** *f* traffic safety; **~signal** *n* traffic signal; **~sperre** *f* block, *Am* blockade; **~spitze** *f* peak of traffic; **~stark** *a* busy; *~~e Zeit* rush hours, *Am* heavy hours; **~stärke** *f* traffic-load; **~stockung, ~störung** *f* interruption of traffic, traffic jam (*od* snarl), *Am* tie-up; break-down; block, *Am* blockade; **~straße** *f* main road, traffic route, highway; **~streifenpolizist** *m Am* highway patrolman; **~tafel** *f* traffic sign; **~umfang** *m* traffic volume; **~umleitung** *f* detour; **~unfall** *m* street accident; **~unfälle** *m pl* (*Opfer*) the toll of the road; **~unternehmen** *n* transport firm; **~verbesserung** *f* traffic improvement; **~verbot** *n* 'do not enter'; **~verein** *m* tourist bureau; **~verstopfung** *f* traffic congestion, *Am* traffic snarl; **~vorschriften** *f pl* traffic regulations *pl*; **~weg** *m* traffic route; public road; **~welle** *f* traffic wave; **~wesen** *n* traffic, transport(ation); **~zählung** *f* traffic count; **~zeichen** *n* traffic sign(al), road sign; **~zunahme** *f* traffic increase.

ver|keilen *tr* to fasten with edges, to quoin, to spline; *fig fam* to thrash; **~kennen** *tr* (*Person*) to mistake, to misjudge; (*unterschätzen*) to undervalue; (*Sache*) to misunderstand; **~kennung** *f* mistaking, lack of appreciation; misunderstanding; **~ketten** *tr* to chain together; *fig* to link together; **~kettung** *f* chaining together; concatenation; bonding; coincidence; *el* interlinkage; *fig* linkage, *fig* connection; **~ketzern** *tr* to charge with heresy; **~kitten** *tr* to cement; to putty; to seal; to lute; **~kittung** *f* cementing, luting, bond(ing); **~klagen** *tr* to accuse; *jur* to sue for, to bring an action against, to take legal steps; **~klagte(r)** *m* accused, defendant; **~klären** *tr* to clarify, to glorify, to transfigure; **~klärt** *a* transfigured; glorified; (*strahlend*) radiant; **~klarung** *f com* ship's protest; **~klärung** *f* glorification, transfiguration; ecstasy; **~klatschen** *tr* to calumniate, to slander; (*anzeigen*) to inform against; **~klauseln, ~klausulieren** *tr* to guard by clauses, to limit by provisos; **~kleben** *tr* to stick over, to plaster (over), to glue (over); to gum up; to agglutinate; to cement, to lute; **~kleiden** *tr* to disguise; *mil* to mask, to camouflage; (*mit Farbe*) to coat; *aero* to fair; (*mit Brettern*) to line; to case, to cover; (*täfeln*) to wainscot; (*mit Stein*) to revet; **~kleidung** *f* disguise; *mil* camouflage; (*Täfelung*) wainscot(t)ing; casing, lining; *aero* fairing; planking; revetment; **~kleinern** *tr* to lessen, to diminish; *math* to reduce; *fig* to derogate, to belittle; (*Verdienste*) to disparage; *maßstäblich ~~* to scale down; **~kleinert** *a* reduced, scaled down; **~kleinerung** *f* diminution, reduction; *fig* derogation, detraction; **~~swort** *n* diminutive; **~kleistern** *tr* to glue up, to paste; (*zusammenflicken*) *fig* to patch up; **~klingen** *irr itr* to die away, to expire; **~knappen** *tr* to render insufficient; **~knappung** *f* shortage, scarcity; **~kneifen**: *sich etw ~~* to deny o. s. s. th.; *verkniffenes Gesicht* wry face; **~knöchern** *itr* to ossify; *fig* to grow pedantic, to fossilize; **~knöchert** *a fig* hide-bound; **~knöcherung** *f* ossification; **~knorpeln** *itr* to become cartilaginous; **~knoten** *tr* to snarl, to knot, to tie up; **~knüpfen** *tr* to knot, to tie together, to join, to link; (*vereinigen*) to unite; (*nach sich ziehen*) to involve, to entail; *fig* to connect, to combine; *mit Kosten ~knüpft* attended with expense; **~knüpfung** *f* knotting; *fig* connection, combination; **~kochen** *tr* to boil down, to concentrate; **~kohlen** *tr* to carbonize, to char; *fig fam* to chaff; to banter, to hoax, to pull s. o.'s leg; *itr* to turn into coal; **~koken** *tr* to coke, to char, to carbonize; **~kokung** *f* coking; **~~sanlage** *f* coking plant; **~kommen** *irr itr* (*umkommen*) to perish; (*zugrundegehen*) to be ruined; to go to wrack and ruin, to go to the dogs, to come down in the world; (*Gegenstände*) to decay; (*ausarten*) to degenerate; *~~ a* depraved, demoralized; disreputable; (*verfallen*) decayed; **~~heit** *f* depravity; (*Entartung*) degeneracy; **~koppeln** *tr* to couple, to join, to tie together; **~korken** *tr* to cork (up); **~körpern** *tr* to embody; (*personifizieren*) to personify, to impersonate; (*darstellen*) to represent; (*verwirklichen*) to incarnate; (*als Typ*) to typify; **~körperung** *f* embodiment; personification; incarnation; **~köstigen** *tr* to board, to feed; **~krachen** *itr* to become bankrupt; *sich mit jdm ~~* (*fam*) to fall out with s. o., to break squares with s. o.; **~kramen** *tr* to mislay; **~krampft** *a* cramped; **~kriechen** *irr r* to hide, to creep into a hiding-place; **~krümeln** *tr* to crumble away, to fritter away; *r fig* to make off, to disappear, to take a French leave, *fam* to clear out, to skedaddle, to skip out; **~krümmen** *tr* to crook, to curve, to bend, to warp; **~krümmung** *f* crookedness; *med* curvature; warping; (*Verzerrung*) distortion; **~krüppeln** *tr* to cripple; (*verunstalten*) to deform; (*verkümmern*) to stunt; *itr* to become crippled (*od* stunted); **~krusten** *tr* to (in)crust, to form a crust; **~krustung** *f* incrustation; **~kühlen** *tr* to cool down; *r* to catch (a) cold; **~kümmern** *tr* to embitter (s. o.'s life); (*Rechte*) to encroach upon s. o.'s rights; (*Vergnügen, Freude*) to spoil; to interfere with; *itr* to be stunted; (*zusammenschrumpfen, auch fig*) to shrivel, to shrink, to dry up; (*verblühen*) to wither, to fade; *med* to atrophy; (*dahinsiechen*) to pine away, to waste away; (*körperlich*) to fall away; **~kümmerung** *f* embittering; stunted growth, atrophy; *jur* curtailment; **~künd(ig)en** *tr* to proclaim, to publish; (*bekanntmachen*) to announce, to make known; (*verbreiten*) to circulate; (*predigen*) to preach; (*wahrsagen*) to prophesy; (*Urteil*) to pronounce; (*Gesetze*) to promulgate; **~künd(ig)ung** *f* announcement; publication, proclamation; prophecy; preaching; *Mariä ~~* Annunciation, Lady Day; **~kupfern** *tr* to copper(plate); **~kuppeln** *tr* to couple; (*Frau*) to pander, to pimp, to procure; **~kuppelung** *f* coupling; pandering; **~kürzen** *tr* to shorten; (*vermindern*) to diminish, to lessen; (*verkürzen*) to contract; (*abkürzen*) to abridge, to abbreviate; (*beschneiden*) to clip; (*zusammenfassen*) to condense; (*beschränken, herabsetzen*) to curtail, to cut; (*Zeit*) to beguile, to pass away; **~kürzung** *f* shortening, abridg(e)ment; (*Lohn*) reduction; (*Recht*) curtailment; (*Verminderung*) diminution; (*Zus.-ziehung*) contraction; (*Zeichnung*) foreshortening; *mit perspektivischer ~~ zeichnen* to foreshorten.

ver|lachen *tr* to laugh at, to deride.

Verlade|anlage *f* handling machinery, loading plant; **~bahnhof** *m* loading station; **~band** *n* loading belt; **~bedingungen** *f pl* shipping conditions *pl*; **~einrichtung** *f* loading arrangement; **~n** *tr* to load (on to), to ship; (*verfrachten*) to freight; *rail* to entrain; *mot* to entruck; *mar* to embark, to ship; (*verschicken*) to forward, to consign, to dispatch; **~gebühr** *f* loading charges *pl*: **~gerüst** *n* handling platform; **~greifer** *m* loading grab; **~hafen** *m* loading port; **~kai** *m* loading wharf; **~kommando** *n mil* entraining command post; **~kran** *m* loading crane; pillar crane; **~offizier** *m* entraining officer; **~ort, ~platz** *m* loading (*od* entraining) point; **~papiere** *n pl* shipping documents *pl*; **~plan** *m* entraining table; **~r** *m* loader, shipper; **~rampe** *f* loading ramp; **~schein** *m* bill of lading; **~stelle** *f* entraining (*od* loading) point; entrucking point; point of embarcation; **~vorrichtung** *f* loading plant; **~zeit** *f* entraining time.

Verladung *f* loading, shipment, entraining, embarkation; consignment.

Verlag *m* publication; publishing-firm, publishing-house; publishers *pl*; *im ~ von* published by; **~sanzeige** *f* publisher's advertisement; **~sartikel** *m* publication; **~sbuchhandel** *m* publishing business; **~sbuchhändler** *m* publisher; **~sbuchhandlung** *f*, **~shaus** *n* firm of publishers, publishing house, *Am* book concern; **~skatalog** *m* publisher's catalogue; **~srecht** *n* copyright; **~szeichen** *n* publisher's mark.

verlager|n *tr* to shift, to displace, to dislocate, to evacuate; (*Gewicht*) to unweight; (*überführen*) to transfer; *r* to move; **~ung** *f* shift, displacement, dislocation; (*Evakuierung*) evacuation, removal; (*Industrie*) relocation.

verlande|n *itr* to silt up; **~ung** *f* silting-up.

verlangen *tr* (*fordern*) to demand; (*erfordern*) to require; (*wünschen*) to desire; (*haben wollen*) to want, to ask; (*beanspruchen*) to claim; *itr* to ask (*nach* for); (*sich sehnen*) to long (*nach* for), to hanker (after); *das ist zu viel verlangt* that's asking too much; *was ~ Sie von ihr?* what do you want of her? *verlangt werden* to be wanted; *~ n* demand; request; (*Forderung*) claim; (*Wunsch*) desire, wish; (*Sehnsucht*) longing, hankering, yearning, *Am fam* yen; (*Streben*) aspiration; (*Eifer*) eagerness, zeal, ardo(u)r; *auf ~* on demand, by request, on application; *~ erwecken* (*Reklame*) to spark the urge.

*

verlänger|n *tr* to lengthen, to elongate; *geom* to produce; (*Frist*) to prolong, to extend; (*Wechsel*) to renew; **~ung** *f* lengthening, extension, elongation; *math* production; (*Frist*) prolongation; (*Vorsprung*) projection; **~~sgebühr** *f* renewal fee; **~~sleitung** *f* extension circuit; **~~sschnur** *f* flex, *Am* extension-wire (*od* cord); **~~sstück** *n* lengthening piece.

verlangsam|en *tr* to retard; *mot* to slow down; *aero* to damp; *r* to slacken; **~ung** *f* retardation; slowdown; deceleration.

ver|läppern *tr* to trifle away, to fritter away; *r* to dawdle away; **~laß** *m* reliance; *es ist kein ~~ auf ihn* he is not to be relied on, there is no relying on him.

verlassen *irr tr* to leave, to quit; (*im Stich lassen*) to abandon, to forsake, to desert; (*überlassen*) to relinquish; (*davoneilen*) to rush away, to bolt from; *sich ~ auf* to rely on, to depend on, to count on, to reckon on, to build on, to trust s.o. *Am fam* to bank on, to figure on; *Sie können sich darauf ~* you can count on that; *~ a* forsaken, abandoned, deserted; (*öde*) desolate; **~heit** *f* dereliction, abandonment; solitude; loneliness.

ver|läßlich *a* reliable, to be relied on (*od* depended upon); **~lastet** *a mil* lorry-borne; **~lästern** *tr* to slander, to calumniate; **~lästerung** *f* calumniation; **~laub** *m: mit ~~* by your leave, with your permission.

Verlauf *m* (*Zeit*) course, lapse; (*Vorgang*) progress, course, development, process; (*Linie*) run, curve; (*Faser*) flow; (*Gestalt*) shape; (*Tendenz*) trend; (*Modell*) pattern; (*geradlinige Strecke*) reach; (*Art*) character, nature; *e-n schlimmen ~ nehmen* to take a bad turn; *nach ~ von* after a lapse of; *~en irr itr* (*Zeit*) to pass, to elapse; (*vorgehen*) to take a course, to proceed, to run; (*sich entwickeln*) to develop; (*ablaufen*) to turn out, to come off, to go off; *r* (*Wasser*) to disperse; (*Menge*) to scatter, to disperse; (*den Weg verlieren*) to lose o.'s way, to go the wrong way; (*fortlaufen*) to run off; *im Sande ~~* (*fam*) to peter out; *~~ a* stray, lost.

ver|lautbaren *tr* to divulge, to make known; *itr* to transpire; **~lauten** *itr* to be heard, to transpire; *~~ lassen* to give to understand, to hint; *nichts ~~ lassen* to betray nothing; *es ~lautet* it is reported, there is a rumo(u)r; **~leben** *tr* to pass, to spend; **~lebt** *a* decrepit; worn out, broken down.

verleg|en *tr* to mislay, to misplace, to displace; (*befördern*) to transport, to transfer; (*Platz verändern*) to remove, to shift; *mil* to transfer, *Am* to redeploy; (*zeitlich*) to postpone, to put off, to delay; (*Sitzung*) to adjourn, to change (to); (*Ort der Handlung*) to locate; (*Weg versperren*) to bar, to obstruct, to cut off; (*Buch*) to publish, to bring out; (*Draht*) to string; (*Kabel*) to lay; (*Straße*) to relocate; (*Rohrleitung*) to assemble; *Feuer rückwärts* (*vorwärts*) *~~* to shorten (to lengthen) range; *sich ~~ auf* to go in for, to take up; to apply o. s. to, to devote o.s. to; **~en** *n* shift, change of position; **~en** *a* embarrassed, self-conscious, confused; *um etw ~~ sein* to be at a loss for; *um Geld ~~ sein* to be short of money; *~~ werden* to get embarrassed; **~~heit** *f* embarrassment; (*Schwierigkeit*) predicament, difficulty, dilemma; (*Klemme*) fix; *in ~~heit sein* to be at a loss (*um* for); *jdn in ~~heit bringen* to put s. o. in a predicament; *in ~~heit kommen* to get embarrassed; *sich geschickt aus der ~~heit ziehen* to get o. s. out of the predicament very neatly; **~er** *m* publisher; **~ung** *f* transfer; removal; relocation; (*Kabel*) laying; (*Röhren*) bedding; (*Verschiebung*) postponement, adjournment; (*Buch*) publication.

ver|leiden *tr* to disgust s.o. with s. th.; to spoil; **~leih** *m* letting out; *film* film lending; **~leihen** *irr tr* to lend (out), to let out, *Am* to loan, to rent; (*gewähren*) to bestow, to confer (on), to endow; (*Gunst*) to grant; (*Auszeichnung*) to award; (*Recht*) to vest (a right in s. o.); (*Eigenschaft*) to impart; (*belehnen*) to invest (with); *den Offiziersrang ~~* to commission an officer; **~leiher** *m,* **~~in** *f* lender; bestower; **~leihkopie** *f film* distributing print; **~leihung** *f* lending; grant; bestowal; conferring; investiture; *min* concession; **~~surkunde** *f* document conveying the licence; **~leiten** *tr* to mislead, to lead astray; (*verführen*) to seduce; (*veranlassen*) to induce, *Am fam* to put up; **~leitung** *f* misleading; seduction; *jur* subornation; **~lernen** *tr* to unlearn, to forget; **~lesen** *irr tr* to recite, to read aloud (*od* out); (*Namen*) to call over; (*auslesen*) to pick, to sort; *r* to read wrong, to make a slip in reading; **~letzbar, ~letzlich** *a* vulnerable; (*leicht gekränkt*) susceptible, touchy; (*beschädigt*) damageable; **~~keit** *f* vulnerability; susceptibility; **~letzen** *tr* to hurt, to injure; *fig* to hurt s. o.'s feelings, to offend; (*Gesetze*) to trespass, to violate, to contravene; (*Recht*) to infringe (upon); to encroach (upon); (*beeinträchtigen*) to prejudice; *seine Pflicht ~~* to fail in o.'s duty; **~~d** offensive; **~letzt** *a* injured; **~letzung** *f* violation; offence; (*Wunde*) lesion, injury; hurt; trauma; (*Rechte*) infringement; (*Vertrag*) breach; **~leugnen** *tr* to deny; (*Kind*) to disown; (*Glauben*) to renounce; (*ableugnen*) to disavow; (*nicht anerkennen*) to disclaim; (*nichts zu tun haben wollen*) to refuse to have anything to do with, to set at nought; *sich ~~ lassen* (*vor*) to have o. s. denied; not to be at home (to); **~leugnung** *f* denial; disavowal; renunciation; **~leumden** *tr* to calumniate, to slander, to speak ill of, *Am fam* to run down, to backcap, to smear; **~leumder** *m* calumniator, slanderer; **~~isch** *a* calumnious, slanderous, disparaging, defamatory, vilipenditory; **~leumdung** *f* calumny, slander, disparagement, defamation; (*Schrift*) libel, lampoon; **~lieben** *r* to fall in love (with); **~liebt** *a* in love (with), enamoured (of); *~~ sein* to be in love (with), *Am* to be sweet on; *sterblich ~~ sein* to be madly in love with; *bis über beide Ohren ~~ sein* to be head over heels in love; *Am fam* to be dead stuck on; **~~heit** *f* amorousness, infatuation; **~lierbar** *a* liable to be lost, amissible; **~lieren** *irr tr, itr* to lose; (*Zeit*) to waste; (*Blätter, Haare*) to shed; (*an Wert*) to fall off; (*Hoffnung*) to give up; (*Bewußtsein*) to faint; *r* to lose o.'s way; (*verschwinden*) to disappear; (*Menge*) to disperse; (*Farben*) to fade; (*Schmerzen*) to subside; *~loren gehen* to be lost; *den Verstand ~~* to be out of o.'s mind; *auf ~lorenem Posten kämpfen* to fight a losing battle; *an ihm ist Hopfen u. Malz verloren* he's a hopeless case; *wir wollen kein Wort mehr darüber ~~* let's not waste another word on it; *~~ Sie den Kopf nicht* keep your head, *Am fam* keep your shirt on; **~lies** *n* dungeon, keep.

ver|loben *tr* to betroth (with); to affiance (to); *r* to become engaged (to); **~löbnis** *n,* **~lobung** *f* engagement, betrothal; *e-e ~ auflösen* to break an engagement; **~~sanzeige** *f* announcement of an engagement; **~~sring** *m* engagement-ring; *fam* engaged-ring; **~lobte** *f,* **~~(r)** *m* betrothed, intended, fiancé, fiancée (*f*); **~locken** *tr* to allure, to entice; *Am sl* to rope in(to); (*verführen*) to seduce; (*versuchen*) to tempt; **~~d** *a* tempting, enticing, enchanting, entrancing, *Am fam* killing; **~lockung** *f* allurement; enticement; temptation; seduction; **~logen** *a* mendacious, given to lying; **~~heit** *f* mendacity; **~lohnen** *tr* to pay (for); *es ~lohnt sich nicht der Mühe* it is not worth while, it is not worth the trouble; **~loren** *a* lost; (*einsam*) lonely; (*hilflos*) forlorn; *~~e Eier* poached eggs; *~~e Form* sand mo(u)ld; *~~er Kopf* (*tech*) feedhead, topend; *der ~~e Sohn* the Prodigal Son; *~~e Partie* losing game; *~~er Posten* forlorn hope; *~~ geben* to give up for lost; *~~ gehen* to be lost, *mar sl* to go adrift; **~löschen** *tr* to extinguish; (*Geschriebenes*) to efface; *itr* to be extinguished, to go out; **~losen** *tr* to dispose of by lot, to raffle for, to draw lots for; **~losung** *f* raffle, lottery; **~löten** *tr* to solder.

ver|lottern, ~lumpen *itr* to go to the dogs; (*Sache*) to go to ruin; *tr* (*verschwenden*) to waste, to squander; (*ruinieren*) to ruin; **~lottert** *a* dissipated, dissolute; ruined; **~lötung** *f* soldering.

Verlust *m* loss; (*Entziehung*) privation; (*Beraubung*) bereavement; (*Schaden*) damage, detriment; (*Einbuße*) forfeiture; (*Abnahme*) waste; (*Defizit*) deficit; (*Entweichen, Ausfluß*) escape, leakage; (*Verschwendung an Energie*) dissipation; (*an Licht*) absorption; *~e m pl mil* casualties *pl*; (*Spiel*) losings *pl*; *mit ~* at a loss; *bei ~ von* under pain of, with forfeiture of; *mit ~ arbeiten* to operate at a loss; *fam* to run in the red; *für e-n ~ aufkommen* to be liable for a loss; *e-n beträchtlichen ~ erleiden* to suffer a heavy loss; *in ~ geraten* to get lost; **~anzeige** *f* notice of loss; **~ausgleich** *m* loss adjustment; **~bringend** *a* involving a loss, detrimental; **~höhe** *f* amount of loss; **~ig** *a* deprived of; *e-r Sache ~~ gehen* to lose (*od* forfeit) s. th.; *jdn e-r Sache für ~~ erklären* to declare s. o. to have forfeited s. th.; **~konto** *n*: *Gewinn- u. ~konto* profit and loss account; **~liste** *f* casualty list, death roll; **~los** *a* without loss (*od* waste); **~quote** *f* percentage of losses; **~reich** *a* causing heavy losses; bloody; **~verkäufe** *m pl* lost sales *pl*; **~ziffer** *f mil* casualties *pl*; *el* phase angle difference; *tele* percentage of lost calls.

ver|machen *tr* to bequeath; **~mächtnis** *n* legacy, bequest; (*Testament*) testament, will; **~mahlen** *tr* to grind up; **~mählen** *tr, r* to marry; to get married (to); **~mählung** *f* marriage, wedding; **~mahnen** *tr* to admonish, to exhort; **~mahnung** *f* admonition, exhortation; **~maledeien** *tr* to execrate, to curse; **~mannigfachen** *tr* to multiply; **~männlichen** *tr* to make a man of; **~manschen** *tr* to make a mess of; **~masseln** *tr* to (make a) muff (of); **~massen** *itr* to lose o.'s individuality; *tr* to deprive s. o. of his individuality; **~massung** *f* disappearance of individualism; **~mauern** *tr* to wall up, to wall in.

ver|mehren *tr* to augment, to multiply, to increase; (*ausdehnen*) to extend; (*vergrößern*) to enlarge; (*fortpflanzen*) to propagate; *r* (*an Zahl*) to multiply; **~mehrung** *f* increase, multiplication; propagation; **~meiden** *irr tr* to avoid, to shun, to shirk, to elude, to keep away from, *fam* to steer clear of, to get around; *es läßt sich nicht ~~* it cannot be helped; **~meidlich** *a* avoidable; **~meidung** *f* avoidance, forbearance; *bei ~~ von* under pain of; **~meinen** *itr* to suppose, to think, to believe, to presume; to deem; **~meint(-lich)** *a* supposed, alleged; (*angeblich*) pretended; (*erdacht*) imaginary; (*nur angenommen*) supposititious; (*Erbe*) presumptive; **~melden** *tr* to mention, to announce, to inform; **~mengen** *tr* to mingle, to mix, to blend; (*durcheinanderwerfen*) to jumble; (*verwechseln*) to confound; *r* (*mit*) to meddle with, to interfere in; **~menschlichen** *tr* to humanize; to represent in a human form; **~merk** *m* remark, note, notice, entry; (*Notizen*) notation, jotting; **~merken** *tr* to note down, to record; (*beobachten*) to observe, to remark; (*abhaken*) to tick off; *übel ~~* to take amiss; **~messen** *irr tr* to measure; (*Land*) to survey; *r* to measure wrong; (*sich erdreisten*) to presume (to), to venture; *~~ a* bold, audacious; (*frech*) insolent; (*eingebildet*) presumptuous; **~~heit** *f* temerity, audacity, boldness, daring; (*Einbildung*) presumption; **~messung** *f* measuring; (*Land*) survey; *e-e ~~ durchführen* to conduct a survey; **~~sabteilung** *f* survey detachment; **~~samt** *n* surveyor's office; **~~sbatterie** *f* survey battery; **~~sflugzeug** *f* survey plane; **~~sgerät** *n* measuring instrument; **~~sinstrument** *n* surveyor's transit; **~~skunde** *f* geodesy; **~~strupp** *m* survey detachment; **~mietbar** *a* rentable, to let; **~mieten** *tr* to let, *Am* to rent; to hire out; (*Grundstück*) to lease, to let; *Zimmer ~~* to let rooms; *Zimmer zu ~~* rooms to let, *Am* rooms for rent; *Möbel zu ~~* furniture on hire; *r* to hire o. s. out; **~mieter** *m* landlord; *jur* lessor; **~mietung** *f* hiring, letting out; **~mindern** *tr* to diminish, to lessen, to decrease; (*senken*) to lower; (*beeinträchtigen*) to impair; (*beschränken*) to reduce, *Am* to cut; *r* to fall off, to go down, to decrease; **~minderung** *f* diminution, lessening, decrease; impairment; reduction, *Am* cut; fall, decline; abatement; **~minen** *tr* to mine; **~mischen** *tr, r* to mix, to mingle; to blend; (*zus.setzen*) to compound; (*verfälschen*) to adulterate; (*verschmelzen*) to amalgamate; (*legieren*) to alloy; (*einverleiben*) to incorporate; **~mischt** *a* mixed; *~~e Nachrichten* miscellaneous news; *~~e Aufsätze* miscellany; **~mischung** *f* mixture; commingling; alloy; adulteration; (*Mischmasch*) medley; **~missen** *tr* to miss; (*ermangeln*) to lack; (*bedauern*) to regret; **~mißt** *a mil* missing in action; *~~ werden* to be greatly missing; **~~e(r)** *m* missing person.

vermitt|eln *tr* to mediate; (*Zwist*) to arrange, to compose, to settle; (*Anleihe*) to negotiate; (*sich einmischen*) to intervene; (*zustande bringen*) to bring about; (*ausgleichen*) to adjust; (*beschaffen*) to get, to procure, to obtain; *itr* to mediate (*bei* in); to intercede (*zwischen* between); *tele* to repeat a message; to connect, to put through; **~els, ~elst** *prp* by means of, through, by help of; **~ler** *m,* **~~in** *f* mediator, intermediary; agent; go-between; *Am pol* troubleshooter; **~lung** *f* mediation; (*Handel*) agency; (*Makler*) brokerage; (*Anleihe*) negotiation; (*Beilegung*) settlement, adjustment; (*Einmischung*) intervention; (*Fürsprache*) intercession; (*Eingreifen*) interposition; (*Überbringung*) conveyance (to); (*Mittel*) means, agency; (*Versorgung*) supplying, providing, procuring; *tele* exchange, operator('s room); **~~sagent** *m* agent; **~~samt** *n* (telephone) exchange, *Am* central office; **~~sbeamter** *m* trunk operator; **~~sfunkstelle** *f* radio-relay station; **~~sgebühr** *f* commission; (*Makler*) brokerage; **~~skästchen** *n* switch box; **~~sprovision** *f* commission; (*Makler*) brokerage; **~~sschnur** *f* patching cord; **~~sschrank** *m* switchboard; **~~sstelle** *f* exchange, *Am* central office; agency; **~~svorschlag** *m* offer of mediation, proposal for settlement, proposed compromise.

vermöbeln *tr fam* to give s. o. a good thrashing.

vermodern *itr* to mo(u)lder away, to rot, to decay.

vermög|e *prp* by virtue of, by dint of; **~en** *tr* to be able; *jdn zu etw ~~* to prevail upon, to induce s. o. to; *etw ~~* to have influence (*über* over, *bei* with); (*Macht haben*) to have (the) power; **~en** *n* (*Fähigkeit*) ability, capacity, power, faculty; (*Besitz*) property; (*Geld*) fortune, means *pl*, funds *pl*; (*Reichtum*) wealth; (*Nachlaß*) estate; (*Aktiva*) *com* assets *pl*; *nach bestem ~~* to the best of o.'s ability; **~~d** *a* wealthy, rich; (*wohlhabend*) well-off, well-to-do; **~~sabgabe** *f* capital levy; **~~sabschätzung** *f* (*Steuer*) assessment of property; **~~sanmeldung** *f* declaration of property; **~~santeil** *m* share in property; **~~saufsicht** *f* property control; **~~sbeschlagnahme** *f* seizure of property; *jur* attachment of property; **~~sbestand** *m* assets *pl*; **~~sbesteuerung** *f* property taxation; **~~seinziehung** *f* confiscation of property; **~~slage** *f* financial condition; **~~smasse** *f* assets *pl*; (*Nachlaß*) estate; **~~ssteuer** *f* property tax; **~~sübertragung** *f* transfer of property; **~~sverhältnisse** *n pl* pecuniary circumstances *pl*; *gute* (*schlechte*) *~~sverhältnisse* easy (bad) circumstances; **~~sverwalter** *m* custodian; (*Nachlaß*) administrator; (*Treuhänder*) trustee; **~~swert** *m* value; property, assets *pl*; property values *pl*; **~~szuwachs** *m* increment value.

ver|mooren *itr* to moor; **~morscht** *a* rotten; **~mottet** *a* moth-eaten.

vermumm|en *tr* (*einhüllen*) to wrap up, to muffle up; (*verkleiden*) to disguise, to mask; **~ung** *f* disguise.

vermut|en *tr* (*annehmen*) to suppose, to presume, *Am* to reckon, to calculate; (*mutmaßen*) to suspect, to conjecture, *Am* to guess; (*sich vorstellen*) to imagine; **~lich** *a* likely, probable; presumable; (*Erbe*) presumptive; *adv* (as) I suppose, probably; **~ung** *f* conjecture, supposition, surmise, guesswork, assumption.

•

ver|nachlässigen *tr* to neglect; to be careless of; to disregard, to leave out, to omit; to slight; *seine Pflicht ~~* to fail in o.'s duty, *Am* to be derelict in o.'s duty; **~nachlässigung** *f* neglect; omission; oversight; **~nageln** *tr* to nail up; **~nähen** *tr* to sew up; (*verbrauchen*) to use in sewing; **~narben** *itr* to heal up; *r* to cicatrize; **~narbung** *f* cicatrization; **~narrt** *a* infatuated (*in* with), struck (on), *Am sl* stuck on; **~~heit** *f* infatuation; **~naschen** *tr* to spend on sweets; **~nebeln** *tr* to screen (by smoke), to smokescreen; (*unter Druck*) to atomize; **~nebelung** *f* smoke screening; fine dispersion; **~~sapparat** *m* atomizer; *mil* smoke generator.

vernehm|bar *a* audible, perceptible, within ear-shot; (*klar*) distinct; **~en** *irr tr* to perceive, to become aware of; (*unterscheiden*) to distinguish; (*erfahren*) to understand, to hear, to learn; *jur* to interrogate, to examine, to question; *sich ~~ lassen* to express an opinion; **~en** *n* intelligence; (*Verständnis*) understanding; *dem ~~ nach* according to rumo(u)r; **~lich** *a* perceptible, audible; **~ung** *f jur* examination, trial, interrogation, hearing, question; **~~soffizier** *m* interrogation officer.

verneig|en *r* to curts(e)y, to bow to; **~ung** *f* curts(e)y, bow.

vernein|en *tr* to deny, to disavow; to say no (to), to answer in the negative; **~end** *a* negative; **~ung** *f* negation, denial, disavowal; *gram* negative.

vernicht|en *tr* to annihilate, to extirpate, to eradicate, to do away with; *fam* to wipe out, *Am sl* to spif(f)licate, to kibosh; (*zerstören*) to destroy, to annul, to overthrow, to ruin, to lay waste, to wreck, to smash; *Am sl* to flinderate; *fam* to break to smithers; **~~d** *a* crushing; **~ung** *f* destruction, annihilation, extermination, extirpation, *Am sl* kibosh, washout; **~~sbombe** *f* demolition bomb; **~~sfeuer** *n* annihilating fire; **~~skrieg** *m* war of extermination; **~~sschlacht** *f* battle of destruction; **~~sstrategie** *f* strategy of destruction; **~~strupp** *m* mopping-up party.

vernick|eln *tr* to plate with nickel; **~elt** *a* nickel-plate(d); **~(e)lung** *f* nickel-plating.

verniet|en *tr* to clinch, to rivet; **~ung** *f* clinching, riveting.

Vernunft *f* reason, good sense, senses *pl*; (*Verständnis*) understanding; (*Einsicht*) intelligence; (*Urteilskraft*) judg(e)ment; *die gesunde ~* common sense; *~ annehmen* to listen to reason; *zur ~ bringen* to bring s. o. to o.'s senses; **~ehe** *f* marriage de convenance; **~gemäß, ~mäßig** *a* reasonable; rational; **~glaube** *m* rationalism; **~los** *a* senseless, unreasonable; **~widrig** *a* contrary to reason; unreasonable.

Vernünft|elei *f* subtlety; **~eln** *itr* to subtilize; **~ig** *a* reasonable, (*vernunftbegabt u. vernunftgemäß*) rational; (*verständig*) sensible, judicious, wise, level-headed; **~ler** *m* subtile reasoner, hair-splitter.

ver|öden *tr* to lay waste; *itr* to become desolate; **~ödet** *a* deserted, desolate; waste; **~ödung** *f* desolation; devastation; **~öffentlichen** *tr* to publish; to promulgate; (*ankündigen*) to announce; to advertise; **~öffentlichung** *f* publication; promulgation; announcement; advertisement; *nicht zur ~~ bestimmt* (*Am*) off the record; **~ölen** *itr mot* to oil up; **~ordnen** *tr* to order; *med* to prescribe; (*gesetzlich*) to decree; **~ordnung** *f* order; prescription; decree, directive; ordinance; **~~sblatt** *n* official gazette.

ver|pachten *tr* to farm out; (*Haus*) to rent; *jur* to lease; *~pachtet sein* to be under lease; **~pächter** *m,* **~~in** *f* lessor; **~pachtung** *f* farming out; *jur* leasing; **~packen** *tr* to pack up, to wrap up; (*in ein Paket*) to package; **~packung** *f* packing up, wrapping in; package; (*Sack*) bagging; (*Faß*) casking; **~~sgewicht** *n* dead weight; **~~skiste** *f* packing case; **~~skosten** *pl* packing charges *pl*, packaging costs *pl*; **~~smaterial** *n* packing material; **~~ssack** *m* (*Fallschirm*) parachute pack; **~~spapier** *n* wrapping paper; **~~sraum** *m* wrapping room.

ver|passen *tr* to let slip; (*Zug*) to miss; to lose by delay; (*Kleidungsstück*) to fit, to adjust; **~patzen** *tr* to bungle, to boggle, to make sad work; to hash up, to blunder, to spoil, *fam* to bobble, to foozle, *Am sl* to bugger, to bull; *mil sl* to snafu; **~pesten** *tr* to infest, to poison, to taint; **~petzen** *tr* to inform against, *fam* to peach (up)on; (*Schule*) to sneak against;

~pfänden *tr* to pawn, to pledge; (*Hypothek*) to mortgage; (*versetzen*) to pawn, *Am fam* to put in hock; **~pfändung** *f* pledging; mortgaging; pawning; **~pfeifen** *irr tr sl* to inform against; **~pflanzen** *tr* to transplant; **~pflanzung** *f* transplanting; transplantation.

verpfleg|en *tr* to take care of, to tend, to nurse; (*ernähren*) to feed, to board, to maintain; (*Lebensmittel liefern*) to cater for; (*verproviantieren*) to victual; **~ung** *f* care, nursing; food, feeding, board, rations *pl*, maintenance; food supply; *mil* messing; **~~samt** *n* food office; **~~sausgabe(-stelle)** *f* commissary distributing point; **~~sbasis** *f* supply base; **~~sempfang** *m* receipt of rations; **~~sgeld** *n* subsistence allowance; maintenance; **~~skolonne** *f* commissary train; supply column; **~~skosten** *pl* cost(s *pl*) of maintenance; **~~slager** *n* commissary depot; **~~slastwagen** *m* commissary truck; **~~snachschub** *m* supply replacement; **~~soffizier** *m* mess officer, commissary officer; **~~sstärke** *f* ration strength; **~~sunteroffizier** *m* quartermaster-sergeant; **~~swesen** *n* logistics *pl*; **~~szug** *m* supply train; canteen train.

ver|pflichten *tr* to engage; to oblige, to pledge; *eidlich ~~* to swear in; *zu Dank ~~* to lay s. o. under an obligation; *r* to bind o. s. (to), to pledge o. s.; to obligate o. s.; **~pflichtet** *a* obligated, bound, under obligation; liable; *~~ sein* to have to, to be obligated, to be under obligation; *zu Dank ~~ sein* to be obliged (*od* indebted) to; **~pflichtung** *f* obligation, duty; (*übernommene*) engagement; (*Verbindlichkeit*) liability, obligation; (*finanziell*) commitments *pl*; *e-e ~~ eingehen* to assume an obligation; *e-e ~~ erfüllen* to meet a liability; *seinen ~~en nicht nachkommen* to default; *~~en nach sich ziehen* to involve liabilities; *sich der ~~ zum Dienst in der Wehrmacht entziehen* to evade the draft; **~~sschein** *m* surety bond, promissory note; **~pfuschen** *tr* to waste, to botch, to spoil by careless work, to bungle, to muff; to make a mess of; **~pichen** *tr* to pitch; **~plappern, ~plaudern** *tr* to prattle away; *r* to blab out a secret; to give o. s. away; **~plempern** *tr* to spend foolishly; **~pönt** *a* prohibited, tabooed; **~prassen** *tr* to dissipate, to squander in luxury; **~proviantieren** *tr* to victual, to supply, to provision; **~proviantierung** *f* victualling, provisioning; **~prügeln** *tr* to thrash, to wallop, *fam* to lick, to trounce; **~puffen** *itr* to detonate, to explode, to crackle; *fig* to fizzle out; to be lost (upon), to produce no effect (upon); **~pulvern** *tr fam* to waste, to squander, to fritter away; **~pumpen** *tr fam* to lend out; **~puppen** *r* to change into a chrysalis; **~pusten** *r* to recover o.'s breath; **~putz** *m* finishing; plaster, plasterwork; **~~en** *tr* to plaster; to roughcast, to coat; *fam* (*Geld vergeuden*) to squander; *jdn nicht ~~en können fam* not to like s. o.

ver|qualmt *a* filled with smoke; **~quellen** *itr* to swell up by moisture; to warp; **~quer** *adv*: *das geht mir ~~* that upsets my plan; **~quicken** *tr* to bind up intimately, to amalgamate; *fig* to mix up; **~quickung** *f* fusion, amalgamation; mixing up; **~quollen** *a* (*Holz*) warped; (*Gesicht*) bloated.

ver|rammeln *tr* to bar, to barricade; **~ramschen** *tr* to sell at a loss; **~rannt** *a* obstinate, stubborn as a mule; untractable; **~~heit** *f* stubbornness; stubborn adherence; **~rat** *m* treachery; treason; betrayal; **~~en** *tr* to betray; (*ausplaudern*) to tattle, to blab, *Am sl* to sell out, to nark, to rat; (*ungetreu sein*) to be faithless, to sell on s. o.; *Am sl* to play one false, to doublecross; *e-e Stellung ~~* to disclose a position; *ein Geheimnis ~~* to give away a secret, *Am fam* to spill the beans; **~räter** *m* traitor (*an* to); betrayer; informer; *pol* fifth-columnist, quisling; **~~in** *f* traitress; **~räterisch** *a* treacherous, traitorous; (*heimtückisch*) perfidious; (*treulos*) faithless; (*aufschlußreich*) revealing; (*verdachterregend*) suspicious; (*doppelzüngig*) double-dealing, double-tongued; **~~erweise** *adv* faithlessly; **~rauchen** *itr* to evaporate; to go off in smoke; *fig* to cool down; *~~ lassen* to let pass away; *tr* to spend on tobacco; **~räuchern** *tr* to fill with smoke; **~räuchert** *a* smoky; **~rauschen** *itr* to pass away; **~rechnen** *tr* to reckon up; (*verbuchen*) to place to s. o.'s account; (*als Gegenrechnung*) to set off against; (*belasten*) to charge to account; *r* to miscalculate; *fig* to make a mistake, to figure wrong, to be off; *sich gründlich ~~* to be sadly mistaken; **~rechnung** *f* (*Belastung*) charging to account; (*zus.rechnen*) reckoning up; (*Ausgleich*) settling of account, clearing; **~~sabkommen** *n* clearing agreement; **~~sbank** *f* clearing bank; **~~skonto** *n* credit account; (*Gegenkonto*) offset-account; **~~ssatz** *m* rate applied; **~~sscheck** *m* crossed cheque (*od* check); not-negotiable cheque; **~~sverkehr** *m* clearing; **~recken** *itr* (*Tiere*) to die; (*umkommen*) to perish, *sl* to croak; **~regnen** *tr* to spoil by rainy weather; **~regnet** *a* spoiled by rain; **~reisen** *itr* to go out of town, to go away, to go on a journey; *~reist sein* to be away; **~reißen** *irr tr fam* to criticize sharply, to excoriate; **~renken** *tr* to dislocate, to sprain; **~renkung** *f* sprain, dislocation; luxation; **~rennen** *irr r* to adhere stubbornly (to), *fam* to get stuck (in); **~richten** *tr* to do, to perform, to execute; **~richtung** *f* performance, achievement; (*Arbeit*) work, duty; (*Dienst*) maintenance; (*Geschäft*) business; (*der Organe*) function; **~riegeln** *tr* to bolt; to latch, to lock, to bar; *mil* to cut off; to barricade; **~riegelung** *f* locking mechanism; barricade; **~ringern** *tr* to diminish, to reduce, to lessen, to decrease, to minimize; to slow up; **~ringerung** *f* diminution, reduction; decrease, lessening; **~rinnen** *irr itr* to run off, to pass; (*Zeit*) to elapse, to pass away; **~rohen** *itr* to become brutal; **~rosten** *itr* to rust; **~rostet** *a* rusty; **~rottet** *a* rotten; **~rucht** *a* profligate, villainous, wicked; infamous; **~ruchtheit** *f* profligacy, villainy, wickedness; **~rücken** *tr* to displace, to remove; (*verschieben*) to shift; **~rückt** *a* crazy, mad, lunatic, deranged, *Am* bughouse; (*erpicht*) *fam* mad (*nach* on, about); crazy (*nach* for, over, about), struck (with), *sl* keen (about), stuck on, wild (about); *du bist ~~* you are crazy; *sl* you are nuts (*od* cuckoo); you have bats in the belfry; *~~e Idee* (*Am*) crackpot idea; *jdn ~~ machen* to drive s. o. mad; *ein(e) ~~e(r)* lunatic, madman, madwoman; **~~heit** *f* craziness, madness; (*Handlung*) foolish action; **~rückung** *f* displacement, removing; **~ruf** *m* bad repute; *in ~~ bringen* to bring into discredit; *in ~~ erklären* to declare infamous; to boycott; *in ~~ sein* to be under a cloud; **~rufen** *a* ill-reputed, notorious, disreputable; **~rühren** *tr* to mix, to stir (into); **~rußen** *tr* to soot; **~rußt** *a* sooty.

Vers *m* verse, line; (*Strophe*) stanza; (*~absatz*) strophe; (*Reimpaar*) couplet; *in ~e bringen* to put into verse; *sich keinen ~ machen können aus* not to make head or tail of; **~bau** *m* versification; **~fuß** *m* foot.

versacken *itr* to give way, to sink; to get bogged (*od* ditched).

versag|en *tr* to deny, to refuse; *itr* to fail, to break down, to come to grief; *Am* to fall down, to give out; (*zurückbleiben*) to fall short in, *Am* to slip up on; (*Gewehr*) to miss fire, to fail to go off; (*Bremse*) to fail; *r* to deprive o. s. of, to deny o. s., to forgo; **~er** *m* breakdown, *Am* slip-up; (*Mensch*) failure, unsuccessful person, *Am* washout; (*Unsozialer*) misfit; *mil* misfire; dud shell; **~ung** *f* denial, refusal.

Versalien *pl* capital letters *pl*.

ver|salzen *tr* to oversalt; *fig* to spoil; **~sammeln** *tr* to gather, to assemble, to bring together; (*einberufen*) to convoke, to convene, to hold a meeting; (*sammeln*) to muster, to collect; to draw together; *r* to meet, to assemble; to flock together; to crowd, to throng; **~sammlung** *f* meeting, assembly; gathering; convention; convocation; session; concourse; conflux; *Am* caucus, *fam* powwow; *e-e ~~ abhalten* to hold a meeting; *e-e ~~ einberufen* (*vertagen*) to convene (to adjourn) a meeting; **~~sfreiheit** *f* freedom of public meeting; **~~shalle** *f* convention hall; **~~sort** *m* meeting-place; **~sand** *m* dispatch, consignment, *Am* shipment; (*Lieferung*) delivery; (*durch Post*) posting, mailing; (*ins Ausland*) export(ation); **~~abteilung** *f* forwarding department; **~~anweisung** *f* shipping instruction; **~~bereit** *a* ready for dispatch; **~~fähig** *a* fit for shipment; **~~geschäft** *n* export business; distributing house, *Am* mail order house; **~~liste** *f* mailing list; **~~papiere** *n pl* shipping papers *pl*; **~sanden** *itr* to get covered with sand; *fig* to break down; **~satz** *m* pawning; *tech* stowing; *min* gobbing; (*Leder*) layer; (*Keramik*) batch; **~~amt** *n* pawn-shop; **~~berg** *m* dirt; **~~kran** *m* shifting crane; **~~mauer** *f* partition wall; **~~stück** *n theat* set; **~sauern** *itr fig* to get rusty (*od* seedy), to become morose; **~säuern** *tr* to sour; **~saufen** *irr tr sl* to waste in drinking; **~säumen** *tr* to omit, to neglect; to fail (to); (*Stunde*) to miss; (*Zug*) to lose; **~säumnis** *f od n* neglect, omission; loss of time, delay; **~~urteil** *n* judg(e)ment by default; **~schachern** *tr* to barter away; **~schachteln** *tr* to insert into one another; **~schachtelung** *f* (*Industrie*) agglomeration; **~schaffen** *tr* to offer, to procure; *r* to obtain, to get, to get hold of s. th.; **~schalen** *tr* to encase, to board, to plank, to lag; **~schalung** *f* planking, boarding, casing; **~schämt** *a* bashful, shame-faced; **~~heit** *f* bashfulness; **~schandeln** *tr* to disfigure, to spoil; **~schanzen** *tr* to fortify, to entrench; *r fig* to (take) shelter behind; **~schanzung** *f* entrenchment, fortification; **~schärfen** *tr* to heighten, to intensify; (*verschlimmern*) to aggravate, to make worse; (*vermehren*) to increase; (*verstärken*) to sharpen; (*Vorschriften*) to tighten up; (*Tempo*) to speed up, *Am* to step up; **~schärfung** *f* aggravation; increase; intensification; tightening up; **~scharren** *tr* to hide in the ground; to bury.

ver|scheiden *irr itr* to expire, to die; **~~** *n* decease; **~schenken** *tr* to give away, to make a present of; (*ausschenken*) to retail; **~scherzen** *tr* to trifle away; to forfeit; **~scheuchen** *tr* to frighten away, to scare away, to drive off; *fig* (*Furcht*) to banish; **~scheuern** *tr fam* to sell, to dispose of.

ver|schicken *tr* to send off, to dispatch, to forward; (*übermitteln*) to transmit; (*Sträfling*) to deport; **~schickung** *f* dispatch(ing); transportation; forwarding; shipment; evacuation; deportation.

verschieb|bar *a* displaceable; (*beweglich*) movable, sliding; (*regulierbar*) adjustable; (*posaunenartig*) telescoping; **~~keit** *f* movability, displaceability; **~eanlage** *f* shunting installation; **~ebahnhof** *m* marshalling (*od* shunting) yard, *Am* switching yard; **~egleis** *n* shunting track, *Am* switching track; **~en** *irr tr* (*aufschieben*) to postpone, to put off, to defer; (*Ort verändern*) to displace, to shift, to (re)move; (*hineinschieben*) to slide (into); to telescope; *rail* to shunt, *Am* to switch; (*in der Phase*) to dephase; (*Waren*) to sell illicitly, to black-market; *r* to get out of place; **~ung** *f* displacement, shifting, moving; (*zeitlich*) postponement; (*Waren*) illicit sale; *el* lag; *geol* dislocation, slip.

verschieden *a* different (*von* from); distinct (from); **~** *sein* to be different, to vary, to differ; **~es** *a* (*gemischt*) miscellaneous; *pl* various, several, diverse, varied; (*unähnlich*) dissimilar, unlike; (*getrennt*) separate; (*Boden*) unclassified; *jur* sundry; **~artig, ~erlei** *a* of a different kind, various, heterogeneous; **~artigkeit** *f* heterogeneity; **~e(s)** *n* miscellany; **~farbig** *a* varicolo(u)red; **~heit** *f* difference; (*Mannigfaltigkeit*) diversity, variety; (*Unähnlichkeit*) dissimilarity, disparity; (*in der Meinung*) discrepancy; **~tlich** *adv* occasionally, at times; repeatedly.

ver|schießen *irr tr* to use up ammunition; *itr* (*Farbe*) to fade, to change colo(u)r, to lose colo(u)r; **~schiffen** *tr* to export; to ship; **~schiffung** *f* exportation; shipment; **~~spapiere** *n pl* shipping documents *pl*; **~~shafen** *m* port of loading; **~schimmeln** *itr* to get mo(u)ldy.

ver|schlacken *itr* to be reduced to scoria (*od* slag *od* clinker *od* scale); **~schlackt** *a* scorious; **~schlafen** *irr tr* to sleep away; to lose (*od* miss) by sleeping; *tr, itr* to oversleep; **~~** *a* sleepy, drowsy; **~~heit** *f* drowsiness; **~schlag** *m* partition; (*Koje*) box, booth; (*hölzerner*) planking; (*Abteilung*) compartment; (*Hürde*) pen; (*Schuppen*) shed; **~schlagen** *irr tr* (*abteilen*) to partition, to cross off; (*mit Brettern*) to board; (*Seite in e-m Buch*) to lose o.'s place; (*Schiff*) to drive out of her course; to drive away; (*überschlagen*) to take the chill off; *e-m den Atem* **~~** to take away o.'s breath; *itr es verschlägt nichts* it doesn't matter; **~~** *a* cunning, crafty, sly, wily; (*Flüssigkeit*) lukewarm, tepid; **~~heit** *f* cunning, craftiness, slyness; **~schlammen** *itr*: *die Wege* **~~** the roads become morasses; **~schlammung** *f* mudding-up of roads; **~schlämmen** *tr* to clog with mud, to silt up; **~schlampen** *tr* to bring into disorder; to take no care of; (*verlieren*) to lose.

ver|schlechtern *tr* to make worse, to impair; *r* to deteriorate, to change for the worse; **~schlechterung** *f* deterioration; degeneration; debasement; vitiation; **~schleiern** *tr* to veil; (*verbergen*) to conceal; *mil* to camouflage, to screen; (*trüben*) to make cloudy; *die Bilanz* **~~** *sl* to cook accounts; **~schleiert** *a* (*Himmel, Bier*) hazy, slightly clouded; (*Blick*) veiled; (*Stimme*) husky; **~schleierung** *f mil* camouflaging, masking, concealment, screening; veiling; *film* foggy condition; (*Lichtbild*) glare; *jur* concealment, disguise; **~schleifen** *tr* (*Silben*) to slur; **~schleifung** *f* slurring; **~schleimen** *tr* to fill with slime; to choke up with mucus; **~schleimung** *f* choking with mucus; **~schleiß** *m* (*Abnutzung*) wear and tear, attrition; (*Zerfressung*) corrosion; (*durch Abschaben*) abrasion; **~~en** *tr* to wear out; **~~fest** *a* wear-resistant; **~~festigkeit** *f* wearing quality, resistance to wear (and tear); **~schleppen** *tr* (*an e-n falschen Ort*) to misplace, to take to a wrong place; (*wegtragen*) to carry off; (*Menschen*) to displace, to deport, to abduct; (*Krankheit*) to spread, to carry; (*verzögern*) to put off, to postpone, to delay; (*hinausschieben*) to protract; **~schleppung** *f* carrying off; mislaying; deportation; spreading; delaying; (*Verzögerung*) procrastination; (*Behinderung*) obstruction; **~~staktik** *f* obstructionism; **~schleudern** *tr* to waste, to squander; to sell below cost price, to sell dirt-cheap (*od* at rock-bottom prices); **~schleuderung** *f* dissipation, wasting, squandering; *com* selling at ruinous prices, (*Export*) dumping.

ver|schließbar *a* fitted with lock and key; **~schließen** *irr tr* to shut, to close; (*versiegeln*) to seal up; (*dichten*) *tech* to lute; (*mit e-m Schlüssel*) to lock; *sich e-r Sache* **~~** to shut o.'s eyes to, to keep aloof from; **~schlimmern** *tr* to make worse; *fig* to aggravate; *r* to get worse, to go from bad to worse; **~schlimmerung** *f* growing worse; change for the worse; deterioration; aggravation; **~schlingen** *irr tr* (*verflechten*) to entangle, to twist, to intertwine; (*eng*) to interlace; (*verschlucken*) to devour, to swallow; (*gierig*) to gobble (up); **~schlissen** *a* worn-out, threadbare; **~schlossen** *a* closed, shut; locked up; (*luftdicht*) sealed; *fig* taciturn, reserved; **~~heit** *f* reserve, taciturnity; **~schlucken** *tr* to swallow; to absorb; (*unterdrücken*) to suppress; *r* to swallow the wrong way; (*ersticken*) to choke; **~schlungen** *a* sinuous; twisted; **~schluß** *m* closing, fastening; (*Mechanismus*) breech (mechanism), breechblock, cutoff; (*Flasche*) stopper; *phot* shutter; (*luftdicht*) seal; (*Zoll*) seal, bond; (*Wasser*) trap; (*Klammer*) clasp; (*Schnappschloß*) snap; *unter* **~~** under lock and key; **~~auslöseknopf** *m phot* shutter release button; **~~auslösung** *f phot* shutter release; **~~geschwindigkeit** *f phot* shutter speed; **~~haken** *m* locking hook; **~~klammer** *f* locking clamp; **~~knopf** *m* lock knob; **~~laut** *m* explosive; **~~mutter** *f* lock nut; **~~stück** *n* plug, stopper; seal; lid; **~schlüsseln** *tr* to (en)code, to encipher; **~schlüsselt** *a* in code, coded; **~schlüsselung** *f* coding, cryptography.

ver|schmachten *itr* to pine (away); to languish, to die (of); *vor Durst* **~~** to be parched with thirst; **~schmähen** *tr* to disdain, to scorn, to despise; **~schmähung** *f* scorn, disdain; **~schmälern** *tr* to narrow; to diminish; to constrict; **~schmausen** *tr* to eat up; to spend in feasting; **~schmelzen** *tr* to melt (together), to fuse; (*Farben*) to blend; (*legieren*) to alloy; (*löten, auch fig*) to solder; (*zus.schließen*) to amalgamate, to merge, *Am* to meld; *itr* (*zus.wachsen*) to coalesce; (*aufgehen in*) to merge, to blend; (*zerschmelzen*) to melt (away); **~schmelzung** *f* blending; coalescence; fusion, merger, amalgamation, consolidation; alloy; **~schmerzen** *tr* to get over; to make the best of, to put up with; **~schmieren** *tr* to smear, to daub; *chem* to lute; (*beschmutzen*) to soil; (*verwischen*) to blur; (*Papier*) to waste in writing; *r* to become foggy (*od* fouled); **~schmitzt** *a* sly, crafty, wily, cunny; **~~heit** *f* craftiness, slyness, wiliness; **~schmoren** *tr* to scorch; *el* to freeze together; **~schmort** *a* charred; **~schmutzen** *tr* to soil; (*verunreinigen*) to contaminate; (*beflecken*) to pollute; (*Gewehr*) to defile, to foul; *itr* to get dirty; **~schmutzt** *a* dirty, filthy, foul.

ver|schnappen *r fam* to blab, to blurt it out, to give the show away; **~schnauben, ~schnaufen** *itr u. r* to stop for breath; **~schneiden** *irr tr* to cut away, to clip; (*Bäume*) to prune; (*Tiere*) to castrate; (*Haare*) to cut; (*Wein*) to adulterate, to mix; (*verderben*) to cut wrong, to spoil; **~schneien** *itr* to be snowed up; **~schneit** *a* covered with snow, snowed up (*od* under); **~schnitt** *m* mixed wine; (*Tabak*) blend; (*Holz*) waste of timber; (*Späne*) cuttings *pl*, chips *pl*; **~schnittene(r)** *m* eunuch; **~schnörkeln** *tr* to adorn with flourishes; **~schnupfen** *tr* to nettle, to annoy; *~schnupft sein* to have a cold; *fig* to be piqued; **~schnüren** *tr* to cord; to lace; to tie up.

ver|schoben *a* displaced; (*zeitlich*) postponed, delayed; **~schollen** *a* missing; *jur* presumed dead; (*vergessen*) long past, forgotten; **~~heit** *f* presumptive death; (*Schiff*) presumptive loss; **~schonen** *tr* to spare; *jdn mit etw* **~~** not to trouble with; to exempt s. o. from; **~schönern** *tr* to embellish, to beautify, to adorn; (*verbessern*) to improve; **~schönerung** *f* embellishment; improvement; **~schossen** *a* faded, discolo(u)red; *fig* smitten with love, to be madly in love with, *fam* to be spoons on, to be gone on.

ver|schränken *tr* to interlace; (*Arme*) to cross, to fold; (*Säge*) to set; (*Balken*) to joggle; **~schrauben** *tr* to screw up; **~schreiben** *irr tr* to use in writing; (*Arznei*) to prescribe; (*kommen lassen*) to order, to write for; (*vermachen*) to make over (to); (*falsch schreiben*) to write incorrectly; *r* to make a slip (in writing *od* of the pen); *fig* to sell o. s. to; to set o.'s heart upon, to devote o. s. to; **~schreibung** *f* (*Bestellung*) order; *med* prescription; *jur* bond, obligation; **~schreien** *irr tr* to decry, to cry down; **~schrien** *a* ill-reputed; **~schroben** *a* eccentric, queer, odd; **~~heit** *f* queerness, eccentricity, crankiness; **~schrotten** *tr* to scrap; **~schrottung** *f* scrapping; **~schrumpfen** *itr* to shrink, to shrivel.

ver|schüchtern *tr* to intimidate; **~schulden** *tr* to involve in debt; *etw* **~~** to be guilty of; *fig* to be the cause of; **~~** *n* wrong, fault; **~schuldet** *a* indebted, encumbered; **~~** *sein* to be in debt; **~schuldung** *f* offence, fault; (*Verschuldetsein*) indebtedness;

-schütten *tr* (*Wasser*) to spill, to shed; (*ausfüllen*) to fill up; (*versperren*) to block; (*Menschen*) to bury alive.

ver|schwägert *a* related by marriage; **-schwägerung** *f* relationship by marriage; **-schwatzen** *tr* (*Zeit*) to gossip away; **-schweigen** *irr tr* to keep secret, to suppress, to conceal (from), to keep (from); **-schweigung** *f* concealment, suppression; **-schweißen** *tr* to weld together; **-schwelen** *tr* to carbonize; **-schwenden** *tr* to waste; to squander, to dissipate, to lavish, *sl* to blow in; (*Geld*) *fam* to put down the drain; to burn the candle at both ends; **-schwender** *m*, **--in** *f* prodigal, spendthrift, squanderer; **--isch** *a* spendthrift, prodigal, wasteful, dissipated, extravagant; (*reich*) profuse, lavish (*mit* of); **-schwendung** *f* dissipation, prodigality, extravagance; **--ssucht** *f* lavishness; squandermania; **-schwiegen** *a* close, discreet; (*zurückhaltend*) reticent, reserved; **--heit** *f* taciturnity; secrecy; discretion; reticence; **-schwimmen** *irr itr* to dissolve, to fade away, to vanish; (*Farben*) to blend; (*undeutlich werden*) to become blurred; to grow hazy; **-schwinden** *irr itr* to disappear, to vanish, to fade, to evanesce; *das Ziel -- lassen* to lower target; *-- n* disappearance; **-schwindfahrgestell** *n aero* retractable undercarriage (*Am* landing gear); **-schwistert** *a* brother and sister; *fig* closely united; **-schwitzen** *tr* to spoil by perspiration; *fig fam* to forget; **-schwollen** *a* swollen; (*Augen*) *fam* bunged up; (*Gesicht*) bloated; **-schwommen** *a* indefinite, vague; blurred, foggy, bleary; **-schwören** *irr tr* to adjure, to forswear; *r* to plot, to conspire; **-schworene(r)**, **-schwörer** *m* conspirator; **-schwörergruppe** *f* undercover group; **-schwörung** *f* conspiracy, plot; *e-e -- anzetteln* to form (*od* to hatch) a plot.

versehen *irr tr* (*liefern*) to provide, to supply, to furnish, to assort (with); (*mit Zähnen*) to tooth; (*mit Saiten*) to string; (*Stellung*) to fill; (*mit Vollmacht*) to invest (with); (*mit Unterschrift*) to sign; (*Pflichten*) to perform, to discharge; (*Amt*) to administer, to attend (to); (*Haushalt*) to look after, to keep; *eccl* to administer the last sacrament; (*übersehen*) to overlook, to neglect; *r* to make a mistake, to be in error; (*erwarten*) to expect, to be aware, to look for; (*versorgen*) to provide o. s. with; *ehe man es sich versieht* suddenly, unexpectedly; *- n* mistake, slip; (*beim Sprechen*) slip of the tongue; (*Irrtum*) error; (*Unachtsamkeit*) inadvertance; (*Übersehen*) oversight, negligence; *aus -* by mistake, unintentionally; by accident; **-tlich** *adv* inadvertently, erroneously, by mistake.

versehr|en *tr* to hurt, to injure, to damage; **-te(r)** *m* disabled person; **-tenrente** *f* disablement pension; **-tenstufe** *f* degree of disablement.

ver|senden *irr tr* to send off, to dispatch, to forward; to ship; (*konsignieren*) to consign; (*übersenden*) to transmit; (*ins Ausland*) to export; **-sendung** *f* dispatch, forwarding, shipment; transmission; transport; exportation; **-sengen** *tr* to singe, to scorch, to parch; **-senkbar** *a* submersible; *--e Nähmaschine* table (sewing) machine; **-senken** *tr* to sink, to send to the bottom; to lower, to let down; (*U-Boot*) to kill; (*untertauchen*) to submerge; (*Schraube*) to countersink; (*Kabel*) to lay; (*durch Anbohren*) to scuttle; *r* to become absorbed (in); **-senkt** *a* sunk; (*Schraube*) countersunk; (*liegend*) immerged; submerged; (*Linie*) underground; **-senkung** *f* sinking; submersion; *theat* trap-door; **-sessen** *a*: *auf etw --* mad after (*od* about), bent on; *-- sein auf sl* to be nuts on, *Am sl* to be stuck on.

versetz|bar *a* transportable, removable; (*Pfand*) pawnable; **-en** *tr* to displace; (*Schüler*) to remove, to move up, *Am* to promote; (*von e-r Stelle zu e-r andern*) to move, to shift; (*vertauschen*) to transpose; (*Bäume*) to transplant; (*Personen*) to transfer; (*verpfänden*) to pawn, to pledge; (*versperren*) to obstruct; (*vermischen*) to mix, to compound, to treat; (*Metall*) to alloy; (*Schlag*) to give, to deal; (*Beamten*) to transfer; *typ* to transpose; (*zickzackförmig anordnen*) to stagger; (*hinzufügen*) to add; (*im Stich lassen*) *fam* to leave in the lurch, *Am* to stand s. o. up; *in höchstes Erstaunen --* to amaze s. o.; *in den Ruhestand --* to pension off; *in die Notwendigkeit --* to put under a necessity; *in Angst --* to terrify; *itr* (*erwidern*) to reply; *r* to place o. s. (in a position), to imagine; *-- Sie sich in meine Lage* put yourself in my place; **-setzt** *a* displaced, dislocated, shifted; misplaced; *tech* (*gestaffelt*) staggered; joggled; *el* dephased; **-ung** *f* displacing; remove; transposition; promotion; pawning; alloy; pledging; transplanting; (*Beamter*) transfer; pensioning off, superannuation; *math* permutation; *tech* staggering; joggle; *mar* deviation from course, drift; **--szeichen** *n mus* accidental.

verseuch|en *tr* (*verpesten, infizieren*) to infect; (*vergiften*) to poison; (*Luft*) to vitiate; (*mit Gas, radioaktiv*) to contaminate; *für verseucht erklären* to declare infected; **-ung** *f* infection, contamination.

Versich|erer *m* insurer; (*bei Lebensversicherung*) assurer; **-ern** *tr* to declare, to affirm, to assure; to assert; to aver, *Am fam* to allow; (*Leben*) to assure, to take out a life policy; (*Sache*) to insure; *r* to make sure of, to ascertain; **-ert** *a* insured; **--e(r)** *m* insured person; **-erung** *f* (*des Eigentums*) insurance; (*Leben*) assurance; (*Bestätigung*) affirmation, assertion, statement, declaration, confirmation; *eidesstattliche --* affirmation in lieu of oath, statutory declaration; *eidliche --* affidavit, sworn statement; **--sagent** *m* insurance agent; **--sanspruch** *m* insurance claim; **--sanstalt** *f* insurance company; **--sbeitrag** *m* premium; **--sbetrag** *m* amount insured; **--sbetrug** *m* insurance fraud; **--sgesellschaft** *f* insurance company; **--shöhe** *f* amount of insurance; **--sleistung** *f* insurance benefit; **--snehmer** *m* insured, assured, policy holder; **--spolice** *f* insurance policy; **--sprämie** *f* insurance premium; **--ssumme** *f* sum insured; **--svertrag** *m* insurance contract; **--svertreter** *m* insurance agent; **--swert** *m* insurable value; **--swesen** *n* insurance.

ver|sickern *itr* to ooze away, to seep away; **-sickerung** *f* seepage; **-siegeln** *tr* to seal up; **-siegen** *itr* to dry up, to be exhausted; **-silbern** *tr* to silver, to plate; *fig* to realize, to convert into money; **-silberung** *f* silver coating; *fig* realization; **-sinken** *irr itr* to sink; to founder; *fig* to immerse (in), to involve deeply (in), to be absorbed (in); **-sinnbildlichen** *tr* to symbolize, to express (*od* represent) by symbols, to illustrate; **-sintern** *itr* to sinter; **-sippt** *a* closely related; **-sittlichen** *tr* to civilize.

versklaven *tr* to enslave.

versoffen *a vulg* drunk(en); *min* drowned.

versohlen *tr fam* to thrash.

versöhn|en *tr* to reconcile (*mit* to), to conciliate (*mit* to), to restore to friendship, to arrange matters (between), to patch up a quarrel, *fam* to fix up; (*beruhigen*) to appease, to placate, to propitiate; *r* to get reconciled, to make up a quarrel, to come round, to bury the hatchet, *Am sl pol* to mend o.'s fences; **-lich** *a* conciliatory, forgiving, placatory, propitiating; *-- stimmen Am* to placate; **--keit** *f* placability; **-ung** *f* reconciliation, reconcilement, placation, propitiation, accommodation; **--sfest** *n eccl* Day of Atonement.

versonnen *a* lost in thought, wistful.

versorg|en *tr* (*sich kümmern um*) to take care of, to look after, to nurse; (*beliefern*) to supply (with), to provide (with), to furnish (with); (*unterhalten*) to maintain, to provide for, to feed; **-er** *m* provider, bread-winner; (*Hauptstütze*) mainstay, support; **-sorgt** *a* provided for; **-sorgung** *f* supply, provision; (*Familie*) maintenance, care for, social security; (*Stelle*) situation; **--sanspruch** *m* claim to maintenance; *mil* preferential status of ex-servicemen; **--sbehörde** *f mil Am* veterans' administration; **--sberechtigt** *a* entitled to maintenance; **--sbetriebe** *m pl* public utilities *pl*; **--sbombe** *f aero* container with supplies; **--sgebiet** *n* supply district; **--slage** *f* supply situation; **--sstützpunkt** *m* supply centre.

ver|spannen *tr* to brace, to stay, to guy; **-sparen** *tr* to put off; *tr* to spare; to defer, to delay; to reserve; **-späten** *r* to be late, to be behind time; *tr* to delay; **-spätet** *a* late, belated; delayed; **-spätung** *f* delay, tardiness, lateness, retardation, lag; *rail* delay; *-- haben* to be late, to be overdue; **-speisen** *tr* to eat up; **-spekulieren** *tr* to lose by speculation; *r* to ruin o. s. by speculation; *fig* to be out in o.'s calculations; **-sperren** *tr* to bar, to block up, to barricade, to obstruct; (*verschließen*) to lock up, to close; **-spielen** *tr* to lose (at play); (*Zeit*) to gamble away; *es bei jdm --* to get into s. o.'s bad books, to lose s. o.'s favo(u)r; *itr* to lose the game; **-spleißen** *tr* to splice, to joint; **-splinten** *tr* to cotter; **-spotten** *tr* to deride, to ridicule, to mock, to scoff (at); **-spottung** *f* derision, scoffing; **-sprechen** *irr tr* to promise, to pledge, to become bound to; *goldene Berge --* to promise mountains and marvels; *r* to make a mistake in speaking (*od* a slip of the tongue); (*sich verloben*) to engage o. s.; *sich etw -- von* to expect much of; *-- n*, **-sprechung** *f* promise; **-sprengen** *tr mil* to disperse, to scatter; **-sprengte(r)** *m* straggler; **-sprengtensammelstelle** *f mil* straggler collecting point; **-spritzen** *tr* to squirt away, to splash, to spatter; (*verschütten*) to spill; (*sein Blut*) to shed; **-spunden** *tr* to bung up; **-spüren** *tr* to perceive, to feel, to be aware (of).

ver|staatlichen *tr* to nationalize: **-staatlicht** *a* nationalized; taken over by the government; **-staatlichung** *f* nationalization; *die ~~ wieder aufheben* to denationalize: **~städtern** *itr* to become urban; **~städterung** *f* urbanization; **~stählt** *a* steel-plated.

Verstand *m* (*Verständnis, Denkkraft*) understanding; comprehension; (*Denkfähigkeit, Auffassungsgabe*) intelligence, intellect, brains *pl*; (*Vernunft*) reason; (*Geist*) mind; (*praktischer ~~*) sense; (*Urteilsfähigkeit*) judg(e)ment; *ein sehr scharfer ~* a very keen mind; *nicht bei ~ sein* to be out of o.'s mind; *den ~ verlieren* to go out of o.'s mind; *mehr Glück als ~ haben* to have more luck than brains; *das geht über meinen ~* this is beyond me; that's over my head; *bei klarem ~ sein* to be of sound mind; **~eskraft** *f* intellectual faculty; **~esmäßig** *a* rational; **~esmensch** *m* matter-of-fact person; **~esschärfe** *f* sagacity.

verständ|ig *a* intelligent; (*vernünftig*) reasonable, sensible; (*richtig urteilend*) judicious; (*klug*) prudent, wise; (*vorsichtig*) cautious; **~igen** *tr* to inform, to notify (*von* of), to transmit; *sich mit jdm ~~* to come to an understanding with s. o., to arrange with; **~igung** *f* information; (*Übereinkunft*) agreement, arrangement; *tele* communication, transmission, reception; *tele* audibility, quality of reception; (*Botschaft*) message; **~~sanlage** *f* communication system; **~lich** *a* intelligible, understandable, comprehensible; (*klar*) clear, distinct; *jdm etw ~~ machen* to make s. o. understand s. th.; *sich ~~ machen* to make o. s. understood, *fam* to get o. s. across; **~~keit** *f* intelligibleness; clearness; *tele* articulation, transmission audibility; **~nis** *n* intelligence, comprehension; (*Einverständnis*) agreement; (*Scharfsinn*) discernment; (*Einsicht*) insight, discrimination; (*Mitgefühl*) sympathy; (*Würdigung*) appreciation; *etw mit ~~ behandeln* to handle s. th. intelligently; *~~ haben für* to appreciate s. th.; **~~innig** *a* full of deep understanding; **~~los** *a* unappreciative; **~~voll** *a* sympathetic; understanding, appreciative.

ver|stärken *tr* to strengthen, to fortify, to reinforce; *radio* to amplify; (*steigern*) to intensify; (*vermehren*) to augment, to increase; (*Batterie*) to boost; (*Träger*) to truss; (*konzentrieren*) to concentrate; **~stärker** *m radio* amplifier; (*Mittel*) reinforcing agent; activator; **~~amt** *n* repeater station; **~~anlage** *f* amplifier installation; **~~betrieb** *m* repeater operation; **~~röhre** *f* amplifier valve; **~~stufe** *f* intensifier stage; **~stärkt** *a* strengthened; (*Erzeugung*) increased; (*Werkstoff*) reinforced; (*Träger*) trussed; *radio* amplified; **~stärkung** *f* reinforcement, support(s *pl*); *radio* amplification; strengthening; intensification; aggravation; (*Textilien*) splicing; (*Zunahme*) gain; (*zuverlässiger Helfer*) stand-by; **~~sbatterie** *f* auxiliary battery; **~~sbereich** *m* amplification range; **~~spfeiler** *m* counterfort; **~~sstreifen** *m* stiffener; **~~sstufe** *f* amplifier stage; **~statten** *tr* to permit, to allow; **~stauben** *itr* to get dusty; **~stauchen** *tr* to sprain; **~stauchung** *f* sprain; strain; **~stauen** *tr* to stow away.

Versteck *n* hiding-place, *Am bes. jur* hideout; **~en** *tr* to hide (from), to conceal; *r* to hide; *fig* to be ashamed (of); **~spiel** *n* hide-and-seek, *Am* hide-and--coop; **~t** *a* hidden, concealed; latent; (*unaufrichtig*) insincere; (*verschleiert*) veiled, covert; (*verstohlen*) secretive; *~e Absichten* ulterior motives.

verstehen *irr tr* to understand, to comprehend, to make out, *Am* to get; (*erfassen*) to appreciate; (*begreifen*) to conceive, to realize, to catch, *Am* to catch on (to), to grasp, *fam* (*geistig wahrnehmen*) to envisage; to take in; (*deuten*) to interpret; (*ergründen*) to penetrate; (*tief eindringen*) to probe (into); (*einsehen*) to see; (*können*) to know (how, *über* about); *falsch ~* to misunderstand, to get s. o. wrong; *zu ~ geben* to give to understand, to intimidate (to); *zu ~ beginnen* to begin to realize (*od* understand), *Am* to get on to; *verstanden?* do you understand me? *fam* got the idea? *Am sl* O. K.? *radio* roger; *ich verstehe!* I see! *e-n Spaß ~* to see a joke; *was ~ Sie darunter?* what do you mean by it? *sie versteht ihn nicht zu nehmen* she doesn't know how to take him; *r* to understand one another; *sich ~ zu* to agree, to consent, to accede to; *sich ~ auf* to know well; to be skilled in, *fam* to be an old hand at; *das versteht sich* that's understood; *das versteht sich von selbst* that goes without saying, that's a matter of course; *ich verstehe mich gut mit ihm* I get on well with him.

versteif|en *tr* to stiffen; *tech* to strut, to stay, to brace, to prop, to reinforce; *sich ~~ auf* to insist on, to make a point of; **~ung** *f* stiffening, strengthening; reinforcement, propping; strut.

versteig|en *irr r* to lose o.'s way (in the mountains); *fig* to have the presumption to, to go so far as to; **~erer** *m* auctioneer; **~ern** *tr* to sell by auction (*Am* at auction), to put up for sale; *zwangsweise ~~* to auction under compulsion; **~erung** *f* auction, public sale, *Am* auction sale; **~~stermin** *m* date of receipt of tenders.

versteiner|n *itr* to turn (in)to stone, to petrify; **~ung** *f* petrifaction; fossil.

verstell|bar *a* movable; adjustable; variable; controllable; **~~keit** *f* adjustability; **~bereich** *m* pitch range, range of adjustment; **~brett** *n* adjuster board; **~einrichtung** *f* setting mechanism; **~en** *tr* to displace, to remove; to misplace, to put in the wrong place; *tech* to shift, to adjust; (*versperren*) to block; (*Stimme, Handschrift*) to disguise, to change; *r* to dissemble, to feign; to sham, *Am* to put on an act; **~getriebe** *n* control gear; **~luftschraube** *f* controllable(-pitch) propeller; **~t** *a* out of adjustment; *fig* feigned, fictitious; **~ung** *f* dissimulation; (*Schein*) pretence, make-believe; (*Heuchelei*) hypocrisy; *tech* adjustment, regulation; shift, displacement; **~vorrichtung** *f* adjusting device, shifter; pitch-control mechanism; **~winkel** *m* angle of adjustment.

ver|steuern *tr* to pay duty on; **~steuert** *a* duty paid; taxed; **~steuerung** *f* payment of duty (*od* taxes); **~stiegen** *a fig* eccentric; high-flown; **~stimmen** *tr* to untune; *fig* to put out of humo(u)r, to annoy; **~stimmt** *a* out of tune; ill--humo(u)red, cross (*über* with); (*Magen*) upset; **~stimmung** *f* ill-humo(u)r; (*zwischen zweien*) ill-feeling, discord; *mus* detuning, mistuning; **~stockt** *a* stubborn, obdurate; (*unbußfertig*) impenitent, hardened; **~~heit, ~stokkung** *f* obduracy; stubbornness; hardness of heart; *eccl* impenitence; **~stohlen** *a* secret, surreptitious; furtive, stealthy; **~stopfen** *tr* to stop up, to obstruct, to block, to clog, to choke; (*Straße*) to block, to fill up, to jam; (*Leib*) to constipate; **~stopfung** *f* obstruction; stopping (up), clogging; blocking, jam; *med* constipation; **~storben** *a* defunct, late, deceased, *jur* decedent; **~stört** *a* (*verwirrt*) disconcerted, troubled; (*geistig*) disordered, crazy; (*Aussehen*) haggard, wild; **~~heit** *f* disorder, trouble; (*Verwirrung*) confusion; (*Zerrüttung*) distraction; (*Aussehen*) bewildered look, haggardness; **~stoß** *m* violation, offence (*gegen* against), infringement, infraction; (*Fehler*) mistake, fault; (*Irrtum*) error; (*Schnitzer*) blunder; **~stoßen** *irr tr* to reject, to expel, to cast off, to put away; (*Frau*) to repudiate; *itr* to offend (against), to infringe, to transgress; **~~e(r)** *m* outcast; **~stoßung** *f* rejection; repulsion; repudiation; **~streben** *tr* to stay, to prop, to brace, to reinforce; **~strebung** *f* strut(ting), prop, bracing; **~streichen** *irr itr* to pass away, to elapse; to slip by, to expire; *tr* to coat over, to spread over; (*Fuge*) to stop up; **~streuen** *tr* to scatter, to disperse; **~stricken** *tr* to entangle, to ensnare; **~stümmeln** *tr* to mutilate; **~stümmelung** *f* mutilation; **~stummen** *itr* to grow dumb (*od* speechless), to become silent.

Versuch *m* (*Probe*) trial, test, practice, *Am fam* try(out); (*Bemühung*) effort, attempt; (*wissenschaftlich*) experiment; (*Forschung*) research; (*Erprobung, Metall*) assay; (*literarisch*) essay; *machen Sie noch e-n ~* try again; *e-n ~ anstellen* to experiment; *alle ~e scheiterten* all attempts were defeated; **~en** *tr* to attempt, to try; (*sich bemühen*) to strive; (*ausprobieren*) to test; (*kosten*) to taste, to sample; (*in Versuchung führen*) to entice, to tempt; *es ~~ mit* to give a trial (to), to put to the test; to try o.'s hand at, *fam* to have a go at s. th.; *sein Glück ~~* to seek o.'s fortune; **~er** *m* tempter, seducer; **~sabteilung** *f* experimental department; **~sanlage** *f* testing (*od* pilot) plant; **~sanordnung** *f* procedure, experimental arrangement; **~sanstalt** *f* testing laboratory, experiment station, research institute; **~saufbau** *m* test setup; **~sauswertung** *f* test evaluation; **~sballon** *m* sounding balloon; *fig* kite; trial balloon; **~sbedingungen** *f pl* test conditions *pl*; **~sbericht** *m* test sheet; **~sdauer** *f* duration of test; **~seinrichtung** *f* testing installation; **~sergebnis** *n* test result; **~sfahrt** *f* trial run; **~sfeld** *n* proving ground; **~sflieger** *m* test pilot; **~sflug** *m* test flight; **~~zeug** *n* test plane; experimental airplane; **~sgrundlage** *f* basis of experiment; **~skaninchen** *n* guinea-pig; **~slaboratorium** *n* research laboratory; **~smäßig** *a* experimental; **~smethode** *f* method of testing, experimental method; **~smodell** *n* test model; **~smuster** *n* experimental type; **~sperson** *f* patient; **~sprotokoll** *n* log sheet, test log; **~sreihe** *f* series of experiments; **~sstrecke** *f* trial track; **~sstadium** *n* experimental (*od* laboratory) stage; **~sstück** *n* test specimen; **~stier** *n* experimental animal; **~sweise** *adv* experimentally, tentatively; on approval; **~swert** *m* experimental datum, test result; **~szweck** *m* experimental purpose; **~ung** *f* trial, temptation; *in ~~ führen* to lead into temptation; *in ~~ geraten* to be tempted.

ver|sudeln *tr* to soil; **~sumpfen** *itr* to become boggy (*od* marshy); *fig* to grow rusty; to grow dissolute, to go to the bad; **~sumpft** *a* swampy, boggy; *fig* dissolute; **~sündigen** *r* to sin (against), to wrong, to offend; **~sündigung** *f* sin, offence; **~sunken** *a* absorbed; *~~ sein in* to be lost (*od* absorbed) in; **~~heit** *f* absorption, preoccupation; **~süßen** *tr* to sweeten.

ver|tagen *tr r* to adjourn; *parl* to prorogue; to (take a) recess; *Am* to table; (*aufschieben*) to shelve, to postpone, to defer; *auf unbestimmte Zeit ~~* to recess sine die (*Am* without date); **~tagung** *f* adjournment; prorogation; **~tändeln** *tr* to trifle away; **~täuen** *tr mar* to moor; (*am Land*) to make fast to shore; **~tauschen** *tr* to exchange for; to mistake for; (*auswechseln*) to interchange; *math* to substitute, to permute; *ich habe meinen Hut vertauscht* I have got a wrong hat; **~tauschung** *f* exchange; bartering; interchange; permutation.

verteidig|en *tr* to defend; *sein Recht ~~* to maintain o.'s right; **~er** *m* defender; (*Befürworter, Anwalt*) advocate; *jur* counsel for the defence, *Am* attorney for the defense; (*Sport*) back; **~ung** *f* defence, *Am* defense; **~~sanlagen** *f pl* defence works *pl*, defences *pl*; **~~sausgaben** *f pl* defence expenditures *pl*; **~~sbeitrag** *m* defence contribution; **~~sgemeinschaft** *f* defence community; **~~skrieg** *m* defensive warfare; **~~slinie** *f* line of defence; **~~srede** *f* counsel's speech; **~~sschrift** *f* argued statement of defence; **~~sstellung** *f* defensive position; **~~swaffe** *f* defensive weapon.

ver|teilbar *a* distributable; **~teilen** *tr* to distribute, to pass out; to dispense; (*zuteilen*) to apportion; to allot (to); (*e-e Aufgabe*) to assign; (*ausstreuen*) to diffuse, to spread, to disseminate, to scatter; (*zerteilen*) to divide; *r* to disperse; to spread; **~teiler** *m* distributor; (*Gewerbe*) retail trade; *tech* distribution frame, check table; (*Liste*) distribution list; **~~antrieb** *m* universal drive; **~~getriebe** *n* distributor gear; **~~leitung** *f* distribution conduit; **~~schrank** *m* distributing switchboard; **~ung** *f* distribution; dissemination; allotment, allocation, apportionment; partition; dispersion; division; (*Ausgabe*) issuance; **~~sapparat** *m* distributive facilities *pl*; **~~skosten** *pl* distribution costs *pl*; **~~sschlüssel** *m* ratio of distribution; **~~sstelle** *f* distributing agency.

ver|teuern *tr* to make dearer, to raise the price of; **~teufelt** *a* devilish; a devil of; **~tiefen** *tr* to deepen, to hollow, to dish; *r* to be deeply engaged, to be engrossed (in), to bury o. s. (in), to be lost (*od* absorbed) in; to plunge into; **~tieft** *a* sunk; *fig* absorbed; **~tiefung** *f* deepening; (*Loch*) hole; *fig* absorption; (*Höhlung*) hollow, cavity, depression; (*Nische*) recess, niche; (*kleine ~~*) dimple; (*Einschnitt*) indentation; **~tieren** *itr* to grow brutish; **~tikal** *a* vertical; **~tilgen** *tr* (*verzehren*) to make away with, to consume; (*ausrotten*) to exterminate, to extirpate, to eradicate; (*zerstören*) to destroy; (*vernichten*) to annihilate; **~tilger** *m* exterminator, destroyer; **~tilgung** *f* extermination, extirpation; destruction; **~~smittel** *n* eradicator, destroyer; **~tonen** *tr* to compose, to set to music; **~tonung** *f* musical arrangement; composition; **~torft** *a* peaty; **~trackt** *a* odd, strange; difficult; *fam* confounded.

Vertrag *m* agreement, contract; *pol* treaty; *e-n ~ schließen* to make a treaty (*com* contract); *com* bargain; (*Übereinkommen*) musical arrangement; composition; treaty; (*Vereinbarung*) arrangement; (*feierlich*) compact, pact; (*zur Verteidigung des Glaubens, e-s Prinzips*) covenant; (*Lehr~*) indenture; **~en** *irr tr* (*Kleidung*) to wear out; (*ertragen*) to endure, to bear, to stand, to tolerate, to suffer; (*wegtragen*) to carry away; (*e-n Spaß*) to take; *etw ~~ können* (*fam*) to be able to stand it; (*Magen*) to digest; *ich kann die Speise nicht ~~* this food does not agree with me; *sich ~~* to agree; to get on well together; to harmonize, to get along; (*vereinbar sein*) to be compatible, to be consistent; *sich wieder ~~* to make it up, to settle o.'s differences; *wir wollen uns wieder ~~* let's be friends again; **~lich** *a* stipulated, contractual, agreed (upon); *~~ verpflichtet* indentured; *e-e ~~e Verpflichtung haben* to be bound by contract (*gegenüber* with); **~sabschluß** *m* contract of agreement; **~sabschrift** *f* copy of contract; **~saufhebung** *f* rescission of contract; **~sbedingungen** *f pl* conditions of contract; **~sbestandteile** *m pl* elements of a contract; **~bestätigung** *f pol* ratification of treaty; **~sbestimmungen** *f pl* terms of contract; **~sbruch** *m* breach of contract; **~sbrüchig** *a* defaulting; *~~ werden* to break a contract; **~schließend** *a*: *~~de Partei* contracting party; **~~e(r)** *m* contractor; **~sentwurf** *m* draft agreement; **~serfüllung** *f* performance of contract; **~sgemäß, ~smäßig** *a* stipulated, agreed (upon); according to contract; **~sgegenstand** *m* object of the contract; **~spartei** *f* party to contract; contractant; **~spflicht** *f* contractual duty; **~spunkte** *m pl* clauses of agreement; **~sschluß** *m* concluding of contract; **~sunterzeichnung** *f* execution of contract; **~surkunde** *f* deed; instrument; **~sverletzung** *f* violation of contract; **~sverpflichtung** *f* contractual obligation; **~swidrig** *a* contrary to an agreement; **~szeit** *f* life of contract.

verträglich *a* sociable, peaceable; friendly, amicable; good-natured; **~keit** *f* good nature, peaceable disposition; (*Sachen*) compatible (with); **~keit** *f* sociability; compatibility.

vertrauen *itr* to trust, to confide (in), to rely upon, to have confidence (in), to put o.'s trust (in), to set store by, *Am* to take stock (in); **~** *n* confidence (*auf* in); trust, reliance; *im ~ (gesagt)* confidentially, in confidence, between ourselves; *im ~ auf* trusting to, relying on; *zu jdm ~ haben* to trust s. o.; *das ~ verlieren zu* to lose faith in; *jdn ins ~ ziehen* to admit (*od* to take) s. o. into o.'s confidence; **~erweckend** *a* inspiring confidence; **~sarzt** *m* company doctor; **~sbruch** *m* breach of trust; **~skrise** *f* crisis of public confidence; **~smann** *m* confidant; trusted agent; secret-service man; (*Fabrik*) trade union organizer; shop steward; **~sposten** *m* position of confidence; **~srat** *m* workers' council; **~ssache** *f* confidential matter; **~sschüler(in)** *m* (*f*) monitor (monitress); **~sselig** *a* rashly trustful, gullible; **~~keit** *f* blind confidence; **~sstellung** *f* position of trust; **~svoll** *a* confident, full of confidence; **~svotum** *n* vote of confidence; **~swürdig** *a* trustworthy; reliable; sound; **~~keit** *f* trustworthiness.

vertrauern *tr* to pass in mourning.

vertrau|lich *a* familiar, intimate; private; *parl* off the record; *~~e Mitteilung* confidential communication, *Am sl* dope; **~~keit** *f* confidence; (*im Verkehr*) familiarity, intimacy; **~t** *a* intimate, close, familiar; well acquainted (with), well versed (in), conversant (with, in); *~~ machen* to become familiar, to familiarize, to acquaint; *~~ sein mit* to be at home with (on, in); **~te(r)** *m* intimate friend; confidant(e); **~theit** *f* familiarity, intimacy; thorough knowledge (of).

verträumen *tr* to dream away.

vertreib|en *irr tr* to drive away, to expel from, to dispel, to remove, to dislodge; (*aus dem Lande*) to banish; (*aus dem Hause*) to turn out; (*Waren*) to sell; to distribute, to market; (*sich*) *die Zeit ~~* to while away (*od* to pass away) the time; *jdm die Zeit ~~* to amuse s. o.; **~ung** *f* expulsion; banishment; (*aus Stellung*) ejection.

vertret|bar *a* capable of being attended to; (*ersetzbar*) replaceable; **~en** *tr* (*als Bevollmächtigter*) to represent; (*ersetzen*) to replace; to deputize (for), to act as a substitute (for); (*einstehen*) to answer for; (*eintreten*) *jur* to plead for, to intercede for; (*Interessen*) to attend (to), to see (to); (*Ansicht*) to advocate; (*Fuß*) to sprain (o.'s foot); (*Beine*) to stretch (o.'s legs); (*Weg*) to stop s. o., to stand in s. o.'s way, to obstruct; *parl* to sit for; **~er** *m* representative; (*Stell~~*) deputy, substitute, proxy, (*bei Ärzten, Geistlichen*) locum tenens; (*im Amt; eccl, parl*) substitute, *Am* alternate, substitute delegate; (*Fürsprecher*) advocate; intercessor; (*Vorkämpfer*) champion; (*Handels~~*) agent, *Am* solicitor; distributor; salesman; (*Allein~~*) concessionaire, sole agent; *film* double, *Am* stand-in; **~~provision** *f* agent's commission; **~~tätigkeit** *f* agency work; **~~versammlung** *f pol* meeting, *Am* caucus; **~ung** *f* representation; (*Ersatz*) replacement; (*Amt*) substitution; *com* agency; (*Interessen*) safeguarding; *in ~~* signed for; *e-e ~~ übernehmen* to take the place of; to deputize for; **~~svollmacht** *f* power of attorney.

Ver|trieb *m* sale, market; (*Verteilung*) distribution; (*Räumung*) clearance; *film* releasing; **~~ene(r)** *m* banished, exiled; (*Flüchtling*) expellee; **~~sabteilung** *f* marketing department; **~~sapparat** *m* marketing organization; **~~kosten** *pl* sales expense; **~~srecht** *n* monopoly; copyright; **~~sstelle** *f* distributor; **~~sunternehmen** *n* distributing agency (*od* enterprise); **~~sweg** *m* channel of distribution; **~trinken** *tr* to spend in drinking; **~trocknen** *itr* to dry up, to wither; **~trödeln** *tr* to trifle away, to waste, to idle away, to fritter away; **~trösten** *tr* to feed with hopes, to give hope; to console; *von e-m Tag zum anderen ~~* to put off from day to day; **~tröstung** *f* empty promises (*od* hopes *pl*); **~trusten** *tr* to pool; **~tun** *irr tr* to spend, to squander; **~tuschen** *tr* to hush up, to gloss over.

ver|übeln *tr* to take amiss; *jdm etw ~~* to blame s. o. for; **~üben** *tr* to commit; to perpetrate; **~übung** *f* perpetration; **~ulken** *tr* to make fun of, to tease, to jeer at, *sl* to guy.

verun|ehren *tr* to dishono(u)r, to disgrace; **~einigen** *tr* to disunite, to set at variance; *r* to fall out, to quarrel; **~einigung** *f* disunion, discord; **~glimpfen** *tr* to defame, to calumniate, to tarnish, to backbite, to disparage, to revile; **~glücken** *itr* (*Person*) to meet with an accident; (*tödlich*) to perish; (*Sache*) to fail; **~glückte(r)** *m* casualty; *pl* the injured; the killed; the victims *pl*; **~krautet** *a* overgrown with weeds; ~**krautung** *f* weed infestation; ~**reinigen** *tr* to soil; (*Wasser*) to contaminate; to pollute; (*Luft*) to vitiate, to infect; (*verfälschen*) to adulterate; ~**reinigung** *f* impurity, contamination; pollution; ~~ *der Luft* atmospheric pollution; ~**stalten** *tr* to disfigure, to deface; ~**staltung** *f* disfigurement; ~**treuen** *tr* to embezzle; ~**treuung** *f* embezzlement; ~**zieren** *tr* to disfigure, to mar.

verur|sachen *tr* to cause, to occasion, to produce, to bring about; (*zur Folge haben*) to result in; to entail, to involve; (*hervorrufen*) to give rise to, to provoke; ~**teilen** *tr* to condemn, to sentence, to convict, to pass judg(e)ment against; (*Geldstrafe*) to fine; (*richten*) to adjudicate (*über* on); ~**teilung** *f* condemnation, sentence.

verviel|fachen *tr* to multiply; (*anwachsen*) to snowball; ~**fachung** *f* multiplication; ~**fältigen** *tr* to multiply; (*nachbilden*) to reproduce; (*Schriftsatz*) to manifold, to duplicate, to copy; to mimeograph; ~**fältigung** *f* multiplication; reproduction, mimeographed copy, accurate duplication; copying; *film* printing; *photomechanische* ~~ photoengraving; ~~**sapparat** *m* duplicating apparatus, duplicator; hectograph; mimeograph; (*graphisch*) manifold writer; ~~**sarbeit** *f* manifolding work; ~~**sfarbe** *f* duplicating (*od* printing) ink; ~~**smatrize** *f* stencil.

vervierfachen *tr* to quadruple.

vervoll|kommnen *tr* to perfect, to improve (on); ~**kommnung** *f* perfection, improvement; ~~**sfähig** *a* perfectible; ~**ständigen** *tr* to complete; ~**ständigung** *f* completion.

verwachs|en *irr itr* to grow together; to become deformed; (*überwachsen*) to become overgrown; (*binden*) to tie (*an* to); *med* to heal up; ~~ *a* deformed, humpbacked, stunted; (*dicht*) dense, thick; ~**ung** *f* intergrowth, intercrescence; deformity; healing up.

verwackeln *tr phot* to jump.

verwahr|en *tr* to keep (from), to hold in trust, to have in safe-keeping; (*schützen*) to preserve; *sich* ~~ *gegen* to protest against; ~**er** *m* keeper; preserver; (*Treuhänder*) custodian; ~**losen** *tr* to neglect; *itr* to be neglected; to go to the bad; ~**lost** *a* uncared-for; (*Person*) unkempt; neglected; (*verdorben*) depraved, degenerate; (*Garten*) overgrown with weeds; ~~*e Kinder* waifs and strays; ~**losung** *f* neglect; demoralization; ~**ung** *f* keeping; custody; preservation; care; (*Kaution*) depositing, bailment; *in* ~~ *geben* to give into s. o.'s charge, to deposit; *in* ~~ *haben* to hold; *in* ~~ *nehmen* to take charge of; ~~ *einlegen* to (enter a) protest against; ~~**sort** *m* depository, custody deposit.

ver|waisen *itr* to become an orphan; ~**waist** *a* orphaned; *fig* deserted.

verwalt|en *tr* to administer; (*Fabrik*) to manage, to conduct; (*beaufsichtigen*) to superintend, to supervise; (*Amt*) to hold; (*lenken, leiten*) to govern, to rule; (*als Treuhänder*) to act as trustee; ~**er** *m* administrator; manager, head; superintendent; trustee, custodian; (*Haus*) steward; ~**ung** *f* administration; management; ~~**sabteilung** *f* management department; ~~**sapparat** *m* administrative organization; ~~**saufwand** *m* administrative expense; ~~**sausschuß** *m* executive committee; ~~**sbeamter** *m* civil servant; administrative official; ~~**sbehörde** *f* administrative authority; ~~**sbezirk** *m* administrative district; ~~**sbüro** *n* administrative office; ~~**sdienst** *m* civil service; ~~**sgebäude** *n* administration building; ~~**sgebiet** *n* administrative area; ~~**sgebühren** *f pl* fees *pl*; ~~**sgericht** *n* administrative court; ~~**skosten** *pl* management expenses *pl*; ~~**smaßnahme** *f* administrative action; ~~**smethoden** *f pl* methods of management; ~~**soffizier** *m* supply officer; ~~**spersonal** *n* administrative personnel; ~~**spolitik** *f* (*Betrieb*) managerial policy; ~~**srat** *m* advisory board; executive committee; (*Aktiengesellschaft*) board of directors; (*Institut*) board of trustees; ~~**sratsversammlung** *f* board meeting; ~~**sstellen** *f pl* administrative authorities (*od* agencies) *pl*; ~~**svorschrift** *f* administrative regulations *pl*; ~~**szimmer** *n* administration office.

verwand|eln *tr* to change; to transform; to turn, to convert; (*umwandeln, jur, el*) to commute; (*artmäßig*) to transmute; to metamorphose; *r* to turn (in)to; ~**lung** *f* change, transformation; conversion; reduction; metamorphosis; *eccl* transubstantiation; ~~**skünstler** *m* quick-change artist; ~~**sszene** *f* transformation-scene.

verwandt *a* related, akin (to); *fig* kindred, congenial, cognate; ~**e** *f*, ~**e(r)** *m* relation, relative; kinsman; (*angeheiratete*) in-laws *pl*; ~**schaft** *f* relationship, relations *pl*; *fig* congeniality; *chem* affinity; ~~**lich** allied, congenial, kindred; ~~**sgrad** *m* family connection.

ver|wanzt *a* buggy; ~**warnen** *tr* to warn, to caution; (*ermahnen*) to admonish; ~**warnung** *f* warning, caution; admonition; ~**waschen** *irr tr* to use up in washing; (*wegwaschen*) to wash out; (*Kunst*) to blend; ~~ *a* washed out; faded; *fig* indistinct, vague, blurred; ~**wässern** *tr* to water; to dilute, to weaken.

ver|weben *tr* to interweave; ~**wechseln** *tr* to exchange; to (mis)take (for); (*durcheinanderbringen*) to mix up, to confuse, to confound (with); *den Hut* ~~ to take the wrong hat; ~**wechslung** *f* confusion; exchange; mistake; mix-up; ~**wegen** *a* audacious, daring, bold; ~~**heit** *f* temerity, boldness, audacity; ~**wehen** *tr* to blow away; (*Schnee*) to drift; (*zudecken*) to cover up; *itr* to blow over; (*zerstreuen*) to be scattered; ~**wehung** *f* (*Schnee*) drift of snow; ~**wehren** *tr* to keep s. o. from, to prevent from, to hinder from; (*verbieten*) to prohibit, to forbid; (*verweigern*) to refuse; ~**weichlichen** *tr* to effeminate, to coddle; *itr* to grow flabby; ~**weichlicht** *a* effeminate; flabby, soft; ~**weichlichung** *f* effeminacy; ~**weigern** *tr* to deny, to refuse; ~**weigerung** *f* denial, refusal; ~**weilen** *itr* to linger, to stop, to stay (at); *fig bei etw* ~~ to dwell on; ~**weint** *a* red with weeping; ~**weis** *m* reproof, reprimand, rebuke; (*schärfer*) set-down, *Am fam* roast; (*Hinweis*) reference; (*Bibliothek*) cross-reference; *jdm e-n* ~~ *geben* to reprove s. o.; ~**weisen** *tr* (*verbannen*) to banish; (*Schüler*) to expel; *auf etw* ~~ to refer to; *jdm etw* ~~ to reprimand s. o. for, to rebuke; ~**weisung** *f* banishment, exile; (*Hin*~~) reference (to); ~~**szeichen** *n* mark of reference; ~**welken** *itr* to wither, to fade; ~**weltlichen** *tr* to secularize; ~**weltlichung** *f* secularization; ~**wendbar** *a* available; usable, applicable; (*praktisch*) practical; ~~**keit** *f* availability, usability, utilization, adaptability; usefulness, utility; *vielseitige* ~~*keit* versatility of service; ~**wenden** *irr tr* to apply to; to employ (in), to use, to utilize; (*ausgeben*) to spend, to expend; (*anlegen*) to invest; *viel Zeit* ~~ *auf* to spend (*od fam* to put in) a lot of time on; *nützlich* ~~ to turn to account; *sich bei jdm* ~~ *für* to put in a good word for, to intervene, to mediate, to intercede with s. o. for; ~**wendung** *f* application; use, employment, utilization; (*Anlage*) investment; (*Zuteilung*) appropriation; *mil* duty; (*Fürsprache*) intercession; ~~**sfähigkeit** *f* usefulness; usability, employability, applicability; ~~**smöglichkeit** *f* range (*od* possibility) of use; ~~**szweck** *m* purpose, use, applicability; ~**werfen** *irr tr* to reject, to refuse, to repudiate, to abandon; *geol* to dislocate; *die Berufung* ~~ to dismiss the appeal; *jur* to quash; *r* (*Holz*) to warp; *geol* to be dislocated; ~**werflich** *a* blam(e)able, objectionable; reprehensible; ~~**keit** *f* blam(e)ableness; ~**werfung** *f* rejection; warping; *geol* fault, dislocation; ~~**slinie** *f* fault line; ~~**stal** *n* fault valley; ~**werten** *tr* to turn to account, to convert into money; to utilize; (*zu Geld machen*) to realize; (*Altmaterial*) to recover, to retrieve; ~**wertung** *f* realization; utilization; (*Gebrauch*) use, employment; (*Verkauf*) realization, sale; ~~**sanlage** *f* utilizing plant; ~**wesen** *tr* (*verwalten*) to administer; *itr* (*in Fäulnis übergehen*) to putrify, to rot, to decompose, to decay; ~**weser** *m* administrator; ~**weslich** *a* perishable, corruptible; ~~**keit** *f* perishableness; ~**wesung** *f* management, administration; (*Fäulnis*) decay, putrefaction, decomposition; ~**wetten** *tr* to bet, to stake; (*verlieren*) to lose by betting; ~**wettert** *a* weather-beaten; *fig* bewildered, confused.

ver|wichen *a* past, last, former; ~**wickeln** *tr* to entangle (in); to complicate; *r* to engage in; to get involved in; ~**wickelt** *a* complicated, intricate; complex; ~~ *werden in* to get involved; to get mixed up (in); ~**wicklung** *f* entanglement; (*Gewirr, fig Verwirrung*) tangle, snarl; (*Kniffligkeit*) intricacy; (*Verflechtung*) complexity; complication; ~**wiegen** *irr tr* to weigh out; *r* to weigh wrongly; ~**wildern** *itr* (*Gärten*) to run wild; (*wild werden*) to grow savage; (*Kinder*) to be neglected; (*Haar*) to snarl; *fig* to become depraved; to degenerate; ~**wildert** *a* wild, savage, uncultivated; (*Garten*) weed-grown; *fig* intractable; ~**wilderung** *f* growing wild; return to barbarism; degeneration; demoralization; ~**winden** *irr tr* to get over, to overcome; to recover from; *tech* to twist, to subject to torsional force; to warp; ~**windung** *f tech* torsion; twist, warping; ~~**sklappe** *f aero* wing flap; ~**wirken** *itr* to forfeit; (*Strafe*) to incur; ~**wirklichen** *tr* to realize, to materialize, to accomplish; (*bewahrheiten*) to come true; ~**wirklichung** *f* realization, materialization; practical embodiment; ~**wirkung** *f* forfeiture, loss; ~**wirren** *tr* to throw into disorder; to puzzle, to perplex, to bewilder, to disconcert, to confuse, to stupefy, to befuddle, to snarl, to mix up; *Am* to muss up; ~**wirrt** *a* entangled; *fig* puzzled, crazed; disconcerted; confused, distracted; complicated, complex; ~**wirrung** *f* entanglement; *fig* complication, confusion, embarrassment; disorder; trouble; *fam* mix-up, *Am fam* muss, mash; *in ~~ geraten* to get into disorder; to get puzzled; *fam* to be at sixes and sevens; **~wirtschaften** *tr* to squander away; **~wischen** *tr* to wipe out, to blot out; (*undeutlich sprechen od schreiben*) to slur; (*Zeichnung*) to smudge; (*beschmutzen*) to smear; (*verschwimmen lassen*) to blur; (*undeutlich machen*) to obscure; *fig* to obliterate, to efface; **~wittern** *itr* to become weather-beaten; (*Fels*) to weather; (*zerfallen*) to disintegrate, to crumble away; (*Kalk*) to air-slake; *chem* to effloresce; **~wittert** *a* weather-beaten; dilapidated; **~witterung** *f* decomposition, decay; weathering; surface disintegration; *chem* efflorescence; (*stufenförmig*) degradation; **~~sschicht** *f* layer of weather-worn material; **~witwet** *a* widowed; *~~e Königin* the Queen Dowager; *~~ sein* to be (left) a widow (*od* widower).

ver|wogen *siehe: verwegen*; **~wohnen** *tr* to injure a house by living in it; **~wohnt** *a* showing wear and tear; **~wöhnen** *tr* to spoil; (*verzärteln*) to pamper, to coddle, to featherbed; **~wöhnung** *f* spoiling, coddling; pampering; **~worfen** *a* depraved, vile, abject; **~~heit** *f* depravity, abjectness; **~worren** *a* (*Lage*) intricate, tangled; (*Gedanken*) confused; **~~heit** *f* confusion; intricacy.

ver|wundbar *a* vulnerable; **~wunden** *tr* to wound, to hurt, to injure; *~~ a* twisted; **~wunderlich** *a* astonishing, surprising; *es ist nicht ~~, daß* it is small wonder that; **~wundern** *tr* to astonish; *r* to wonder, to be surprised (at); **~wundert** *a* surprised, astonished; **~wunderung** *f* astonishment, surprise; **~wundet** *a* wounded; **~~enabzeichen** *n mil* wound stripe; *Am* Purple Heart; **~~ensammelstelle** *f* collecting point; **~~entransport** *m* transportation of wounded; **~~e(r)** *m* wounded (*od* injured) person; *mil auch* casualty; **~wundung** *f* wound(ing); injury; **~wunschen** *a* enchanted; **~wünschen** *tr* to curse, to execrate, to wish ill (to); (*verhexen*) to bewitch, to cast a spell on; **~wünscht** *a* cursed, confounded; *~~!* confound it! **~wünschung** *f* curse, malediction, imprecation; **~wurzeln** *itr* to become deeply rooted; **~wüsten** *tr* to ravage, to lay waste, to devastate; to ruin; **~wüster** *m* devastator, destroyer; **~wüstung** *f* devastation.

ver|zagen *itr* to lose courage (*od* heart), to despair, to be despondent (of); **~zagt** *a* despondent, discouraged, disheartened; (*kleinmütig*) faint-hearted; **~~heit** *f* despondency; despair; timidity; **~zählen** *r* to count wrong(ly), to miscount; **~zahnen** *tr* to tooth; (*Rad*) to cog; (*Balken*) to indent, to dovetail; *fig* to link together; **~zahnung** *f* toothing, indentation, toothed gearing, cogging; **~zapfen** *tr* (*Bier*) to sell on draught; *tech* to mortise, to join; *Unsinn ~~* (*fam*) to tell nonsense; **~zärteln** *tr* to pamper, to coddle; **~zärtelung** *f* coddling, pampering; (*Zustand*) effeminacy; **~zaubern** *tr* to enchant, to charm, to bewitch; **~zauberung** *f* enchantment; **~zäunen** *tr* to hedge in, to fence in; **~zäunung** *f* hedging, fence.

ver|zehnfachen *tr* to decuple; **~zehrbar** *a* expendable; **~zehren** *tr* to consume, to eat (up); *r* to pine away with, to be dying with, to eat o.'s heart out; **~zehrung** *f* consumption; **~zeichnen** *tr* (*falsch zeichnen*) to draw badly; (*Optik*) to distort; (*einschreiben*) to book, to enter; (*aufzeichnen*) to record, to make a list, to catalog(ue), to write down, to specify; **~zeichnis** *n* list, catalog(ue); (*Register*) register; (*Inventar*) inventory; (*Buch*) index, table of contents; (*Einzelaufstellung*) specification; (*Tabelle*) schedule; (*Namensliste*) roll; *tele* directory; *~~ der Vorlesungen* syllabus; *~~ versandter Waren* invoice; **~zeichnung** *f phot* distortion; (*schlechte Zeichnung*) poor drafting; faulty delineation; **~zeihen** *irr tr* to pardon, to forgive; *~~ Sie!* pardon me! excuse me! (I) beg (your) pardon! **~zeihlich** *a* pardonable, excusable; (*Sünde*) venial; **~zeihung** *f* pardon, forgiveness; *bitte um ~~!* I beg your pardon! **~zerren** *tr* to distort, to contort; to strain; **~zerrung** *f* contortion, distortion; (*Zerrbild*) caricature; (*Gesicht*) grimace; **~~sfrei** *a* distortionless; **~zetteln** *tr* to scatter, to disperse; (*verschwenden*) to squander, to dissipate; (*katalogisieren*) to catalog(ue); **~zettelung** *f* scattering; (*für Katalog*) cataloguing.

Ver|zicht *m* renunciation, resignation; *auf etw ~~ leisten* to renounce, to resign; **~zichten** *itr* to give up, to renounce, to resign, to abandon, to drop, to disclaim, to dispense with, to forgo; *fam* to do without; (*Anspruch*) to waive; **~zichterklärung** *f* letter of renunciation; **~zichtleistung** *f* renunciation, abandonment; resignation; disclaimer, waiver (*auf* of); **~ziehen** *irr tr* (*Kind*) to spoil; (*Mund*) to draw, to screw up; (*verzerren*) to distort, to contract; *er verzog keine Miene* he didn't bat an eye; *ohne e-e Miene zu ~~* without betraying the least emotion; *itr* (*zögern*) to delay, to tarry; (*aus e-r Wohnung*) to move; *r* (*Holz*) to warp, to be twisted; (*Stahl*) to shrink; (*durch Hitze, Druck*) to buckle; (*überanstrengen*) to strain; (*Kleid*) to drag; (*Lippen, Stirn*) to pucker; (*sich zurückziehen*) to withdraw; (*sich hinziehen*) to stay; (*verschwinden*) to disappear, to vanish, to make off; (*Volksmenge, Wolken*) to disperse; (*beim Spiel*) to make a false move; (*Nebel*) to dissolve; **~zieren** *tr* to decorate, to adorn, to ornament; (*verschönern*) to embellish; **~zierung** *f* decoration; (*Schmuck*) ornament; (*Verschönerung*) embellishment; *mus* flourish; **~zimmern** *tr* to timber; *mar* to repair; **~zinken** *tr* to galvanize; (*Holz*) to dovetail **~zinnen** *tr* to tin; **~zinsen** *tr* to pay interest (for *od* on); *r* to bear (*od* yield) interest; **~zinslich** *a* bearing interest; *~~es Darlehen* loan on interest; *~~ anlegen* to put out at interest; **~zinsung** *f* (payment of) interest.

ver|zogen *a tech* distorted; warped; (*Kind etc*) spoiled; (*aus Wohnort*) moved away; **~zögern** *tr* to delay, to retard, to put off, *Am* to hold up; *r* to be late; to be deferred; **~zögerung** *f* delay, retardment, retardation, lag, deceleration; braking, checking; **~~ssatz** *m mil* delay composition; **~~szünder** *m* delay-action fuse; **~zollen** *tr* to pay duty on; *mar* to clear; *haben Sie etw zu ~~?* have you anything to declare? **~zollt** *a* duty paid; **~zollung** *f mar* clearance; payment of duty.

ver|zuckern *tr* to sugar over, to ice; (*versüßen*) to sweeten; *fig* to sugar (the pill); **~zückt** *a* enraptured, in ecstasy; **~zückung** *f* rapture, ecstasy; **~zug** *m* delay; (*in der Leistung*) default; *ohne ~~* without delay, forthwith, immediately; *in ~~ geraten* to come in default; *es ist Gefahr im ~~* there is imminent danger; there is no time to be lost; **~~skosten** *pl* demurrage; **~~sstrafe** *f* penalty for delayed delivery; **~~szeit** *f* dead time; **~~szinsen** *m pl* interest payable on arrears; **~zweifeln** *itr* to despair (*an* of), to despond (of); *es ist zum ~~* it's enough to drive o. to despair; **~zweifelt** *a* despairing; (*aussichtslos, rücksichtslos*) desperate; **~zweiflung** *f* despair; desperation; *zur ~~ bringen* to drive to despair; **~zweigen** *r* to ramify, to branch off; *verzweigtes Röhrensystem* manifold; **~zweigung** *f* ramification, branching; **~zwickt** *a* complicated; knotty, intricate; awkward; (*seltsam*) queer, odd, strange.

Vesper *f* a light meal; (*Kirche*) vespers *pl*; **~n** *itr* to have a light meal.

Vestibül *n* vestibule, hall, lobby.

Veteran *m* veteran, ex-service man, *Am fam* vet.

Veterinär, ~arzt *m* veterinary surgeon, veterinarian, *sl* vet; **~dienst** *m* veterinary service; **~kompanie** *f* veterinary company.

Veto *n* veto; *ein ~ einlegen gegen* to veto s. th.

Vettel *f* strumpet; old hag; slut.

Vetter *m* cousin **~nwirtschaft** *f* nepotism.

Vexier|bild *n* picture-puzzle; **~en** *tr* to quiz, to tease; (*foppen*) to puzzle; **~schloß** *n* combination-lock, puzzle-lock; **~spiegel** *m* distorting mirror.

V|-Form *f aero* dihedral; **~-Formation** *f aero* Vee formation; Vic; **~-förmig** *a* V-shape(d); *aero* dihedral.

Viadukt *m* viaduct.

vibrieren *itr* to vibrate; *aero* (*Propeller*) to flutter.

Vieh *n* beast, brute; (*in Herden*) cattle; **~ausstellung** *f* cattle show; **~bestand** *m* live stock; **~bremse** *f* (*Insekt*) gadfly; **~futter** *n* fodder, provender; **~fütterung** *f* livestock feeding; **~handel** *m* cattle-trade; **~händler** *m* cattle-dealer; **~hirt** *m* herdsman, *Am* cowboy, *fam* cowpuncher; **~hof** *m* stock-yard; **~isch** *a* beastly, bestial, brutal; **~magd** *f* dairymaid; **~markt** *m* cattle-market; **~salz** *n* cattle salt; **~seuche** *f* cattle-plague; murrain; foot-and-mouth disease; **~stall** *m* cow-house; **~stand** *m* live-stock; **~tränke** *f* watering-place for cattle; **~treiber** *m* drover; **~wagen** *m rail* stock car; cattletruck; **~weide** *f* pasture; **~zucht** *f* cattle-breeding; **~züchter** *m* cattle-breeder, stock-farmer; grazier.

viel *a u. adv* much, a great deal, a lot of, *fam* lots of; numerous; *~e* many, plenty, a quantity; *so viel(e)* so much, so many; *sehr ~(e)* very many, a great many; a considerable amount, a good deal, *Am* considerable (of); *ein bißchen ~* a little too much; *noch einmal so ~* as much again; *~ besser* much better; *mehr als zu ~* more than enough; *ziemlich ~* a good deal (of); *ziemlich ~e* a good many; *das ~e Geld* all that money; *in ~em* in many respects; *sich nicht ~ machen aus* not to make much of; *wie ~(e)?* how much? how many? *zu ~(e)* too much, too many; *~ Vergnügen!* have a good time! *~ Glück!* good luck! lots of luck! *~en Dank!* many thanks! thanks a lot! **~adrig** *a* multicore; **~ästig** *a* with many branches; **~bedeutend** *a* significant; **~beschäftigt** *a* very busy; **~deutig** *a* ambiguous;

~eck *n* polygon; **~eckig** *a* polygonal; **~erlei** *a* of many kinds, different, various; **~fach, ~fältig** *a* manifold, multifarious, multiple; *adv* frequently, in many cases; **~~abstimmgerät** *n radio* multiple tuner; **~~antenne** *f radio* multiple antenna; **~~schaltung** *f el* multiple connection; **~~stecker** *m* manifold plug; **~fältigkeit** *f* multiplicity, variety; **~farbendruck** *m* polychromy; **~farbig** *a* many-colo(u)red; **~fraß** *m* glutton; **~geliebt** *a* dearly beloved; **~genannt** *a* often-mentioned; **~geprüft** *a* much tried; **~gereist** *a* travelled; **~gestaltig** *a* multiform, of many shapes; manifold, diverse; polymorphic; **~gliederig** *a* many-membered; *math* polynomial; **~götterei** *f* polytheism; **~heit** *f* multiplicity, multitude; **~jährig** *a* of many years; many years old; **~köpfig** *a* many-headed, polycephalous; (*zahlreich*) numerous; **~leicht** *adv* perhaps, possibly, maybe; **~liebchen** *n* philippine; **~mal(s)** *adv* many times, frequently, often; very much, a lot, *fam* loads; *ich bitte ~~ um Entschuldigung* I'm awfully sorry; *ich danke Ihnen ~~* many thanks; **~malig** *a* often repeated; **~mehr** *adv* rather; much more; *conj* rather, on the contrary; **~sagend** *a* significant, expressive, full of meaning; highly suggestive; **~schichtig** *a* multiple; **~schreiber** *m* prolific writer, quilldriver; **~seitig** *a* many-sided; (*Personen*) versatile; all-round, *Am* all-around; *geom* polyhedral; (*umfassend*) comprehensive; *auf ~~en Wunsch* by popular request; **~~keit** *f* many-sidedness; *fig* versatility; **~silbig** *a* polysyllabic; **~sprachig** *a* polyglot; **~stimmig** *a* polyphonic; **~stufig** *a* multiple-stage; *~~er Schalter* multipoint switch; **~teilig** *a* of many parts; *math* polynomial; **~verheißend, ~versprechend** *a* most promising, of great promise; **~weiberei** *f* polygamy; **~wisser** *m* erudite man, polyhistor; *fam* pundit, walking encyclopedia; **~zahl** *f* plurality; **~zellig** *a* multicellular; **~zweckflugzeug** *n* general purpose aircraft.

vier *a* four; *unter ~ Augen* face to face, confidentially, privately; *zu ~t* four of (us); *zu je ~en* in fours; *auf allen Vieren* on all fours; **~beinig** *a* four-legged; **~blätterig** *a* four-leaved; **~dimensional** *a* four-dimensional; **~düsenbomber** *m aero* four-jet bomber; **~(e)** *f* four, quart; **~eck** *n* quadrangle, square; **~eckig** *a* quadrangular, square, four-cornered, rectangular; **~er** *m* (*Rudern*) four; **~erlei** *a* of four different sorts; four kinds of; **~fach, ~fältig** *a* fourfold, quadruple; **~farbendruck** *m* four-colo(u)r printing; **~füßler** *m* quadruped; **~füßig** *a* quadruped; **~gespann** *n* team of four (horses); **~gestrichen** *a mus* four-tailed; **~gleisig** *a* with four rails; **~gliederig** *a* four-membered; *math* quadrinomial; (*Kristall*) tetragonal; **~händig** *a* four-handed; *zoo* quadrumanous; *~~ spielen* to play a duet; **~hundert** *a* four hundred; **~jahresplan** *m* four-year plan; **~jährig** *a* quadrennial; lasting four years; of four years; **~kanteisen** *n* square-bar iron; **~kantig** *a* square, four-cornered; **~linge** *m pl* quads *pl*, quadruplets *pl*; **~lingsflak** *f* four-barrelled pom-pom, quadruple anti-aircraft gun; **~mächteausschuß** *m* Quadripartite Committee; **~mächtebesprechung** *f* four-power talk; **~mächte-Kontrollrat** *m* Quadripartite Control Council; **~kantig** *a* square, four-cornered; **~mal** *adv* four times; **~malig** *a* four times repeated; **~motorig** *a* four-engined; **~punktaufhängung** *f* four-point attachment; **~radbremse** *f mot* four-wheel brake; **~räderig** *a* four-wheeled; **~schrötig** *a* stout, square-built, thick-set; **~seitig** *a* quadrilateral; four-sided; **~silbig** *a* tetrasyllabic, of four syllables; **~sitzer** *m mot* four-seater; **~spänner** *m* four-in-hand; **~sitzig** *a* with four seats; **~spännig** *a* drawn by four horses; four-in-hand; **~stellig** *a* of four places, of four digits; *~~e Zahl* four-figure number; **~stimmig** *a* for four voices; **~stöckig** *a* four-storied; **~stufig** *a* four-stage; **~takt** *m* four-stroke cycle; **~~motor** *m* four-stroke engine; **~tägig** *a* of four days; *~~es Fieber* quartan ague; **~tausend** *a* four thousand.

vierte *a* fourth.

vierteil\|en *tr* to quarter, to divide into four parts; **~ig** *a* consisting of four parts, four-point; **~ung** *f* quadripartition.

Viertel *n* fourth (part); (*Maß; Stadt~, Mond~*) quarter; (*Gegend*) section; quarter; *ein ~ auf zwölf* a quarter past eleven; *drei ~ auf zwölf* a quarter to twelve; **~drehung** *f* quarter turn; **~jahr** *n* quarter (of a year), three months; **~~esschrift** *f* quarterly (periodical); **~jährig** *a* quarterly; **~jährlich** *a* quarterly, every three months; **~kreis** *m aero* quadrant, quarter circle; **~n** *tr* to quarter, to divide into four parts; **~note** *f* crotchet, *Am* quarter note; **~pause** *f* crotchet-rest; **~stunde** *f* quarter of an hour, *Am* a quarter hour; *e-e ~~ vor acht* a quarter to eight (*Am* of eight); **~stündlich** *a* every quarter of an hour.

Vier\|ung *f arch* crossing, intersection of the nave; **~vierteltakt** *m* common time; **~wertig** *a* quadrivalent; **~zehn** *a* fourteen; *~~ Tage* a fortnight, *Am* two weeks; **~~te** *a* fourteenth; **~~tel** *n* fourteenth; **~zeiler** *m* poem consisting of four lines; **~zig** *a* forty; **~zigste** *a* fortieth.

Vignette *f* vignette.

Vikar *m* curate.

Vill\|a *f* villa, *Am* home; **~enkolonie** *f* garden-city; **~enviertel** *n* residential district.

Viol\|a *f mus* viola; viol; *bot* viola; viol; **~e** *f bot* viola, violet; **~ett** *a* violet(-blue); **~ine** *f* violin, fiddle; **~inist** *m* violinist, violin-player; **~inkasten** *m* violin-case; **~inschlüssel** *m* trebleclef; **~oncell(o)** *n* (violon)cello.

Viper *f* viper, adder.

Virtuos\|e *m*, **~in** *f* artist, virtuoso; **~enhaft** *a* masterly; **~ität** *f* virtuosity, mastery, artistic perfection.

Virusforschung *f* virus research; virology.

*

Visier *n* (*Helm*) visor; (*Gewehr*) sight; view finder; *das ~ einstellen* to adjust the sight; *starres ~* fixed sight; **~achse** *f* line of sight; **~ebene** *f* plane of sighting; **~einrichtung** *f* sighting device, view finder; **~einschnitt** *m* notch; **~einteilung** *f* readings on the sight; **~en** *tr tech* to adjust; (*eichen*) to ga(u)ge; (*Paß*) to endorse, to visé; (*Richtung*) to take bearings; (*Gewehr*) to sight, to point, to aim; *itr* to take aim (at); **~feder** *f* rear-sight base spring; **~fernrohr** *n* sighting telescope; **~kimme** *f* rear-sight notch; **~klappe** *f* sight leaf; **~latte** *f* level(l)ing board; **~linie** *f* line of sight; **~maß** *n* ga(u)ge; **~stab** *m* ga(u)ging-rod; (*Feldmeßkunst*) surveying-pole; **~weite** *f* range of sight; **~winkel** *m* angle of dispart.

Vision *f* dream, phantom; phantasm; **~är** *a* visionary.

Visit\|ation *f* (*Durchsuchung*) search; (*Besichtigung*) inspection; **~enkarte** *f* visiting-card, *Am* calling card; **~ieren** *tr* to search; to inspect.

viskos *a* viscous; **~e** *f* viscose; **~~zellwolle** *f* spun viscose rayon; **~ität** *f* viscosity.

visuell *a* visual.

Visum *n* visé, visa.

Vitamin *n* vitamin(e); **~mangel** *m* vitamin deficiency.

Vitrine *f* show-case, glass case.

Vitriol *n* vitriol; **~artig** *a* vitriolic.

Vivat! *interj* long live ...!, three cheers for ...! **~** *n* cheer.

Vize\|admiral *m* vice-admiral; **~könig** *m* viceroy; **~konsul** *m* vice-consul; **~präsident** *m* vice-president; deputy-chairman.

Vlies *n* fleece.

*

Vogel *m* bird; *e-n ~ haben fam* to have a bee in o.'s bonnet, *fam* to have a kink; *den ~ abschießen* to carry off the prize, to steal the show; *friß ~ od stirb!* do or die! **~bauer** *m* bird-cage; **~beerbaum** *m* mountain-ash, rowan; **~beere** *f* berry of the mountain-ash; **~beize** *f* hawking; **~dunst** *m* small shot; **~ei** *n* bird's egg; **~fang** *m* fowling, bird-catching; **~fänger** *m* fowler, bird-catcher; **~flinte** *f* fowling-piece; **~flug** *m* bird flight; **~frei** *a* outlawed; *für ~~ erklären* to outlaw; **~futter** *n* bird-seed; **~gesang** *m* song of (the) birds; **~händler** *m* bird-seller, bird-fancier; **~haus** *n* aviary; **~hecke** *f* breeding-cage; **~herd** *m* fowling-floor; **~kirsche** *f* bird-cherry; **~kunde** *f* ornithology; **~leim** *m* bird-lime; *mit ~~ bestreichen* to lime; **~mist** *m* bird-dung; **~napf** *m* seed-box; **~nest** *n* bird's nest; **~perspektive, ~schau** *f* bird's-eye view; **~pfeife** *f* bird-call; **~scheuche** *f* scarecrow; **~stange** *f* perch, roost; **~steller** *m* bird-catcher; **~strich, ~zug** *m* migration of birds of passage; **~warte** *f* ornithological station; **~zucht** *f* breeding of birds.

Vög\|elchen, **~lein** *n* little bird.

Vogesen *pl* Vosges Mountains *pl*.

Vogt *m* overseer; (*Amtmann*) bailiff; (*Statthalter*) governor; (*e-s Gutes*) steward; **~ei** *f* office of a bailiff.

Vok\|abel *f* word; **~al** *m* vowel; **~almusik** *f* vocal music; **~ativ** *m* vocative.

Volant *m* frill, flounce; *mot* steering-wheel.

Volk *n* people; (*Nation*) nation; (*Rasse*) race; (*Masse*) masses *pl*, common people; (*Menge*) crowd; (*die unteren Schichten*) the lower classes *pl*; (*Stamm, Sippe*) tribe; (*verächtlich*) mob; (*Kriegs~*) troops *pl*, forces *pl*; *mar* crew; (*Bienen*) swarm; (*Rebhühner*) covey; (*Herde*) flock; *kleines ~* small fry; *das arbeitende ~* the working classes; *das gemeine ~* the mob, the rabble; *viel ~s* a large crowd; *der Mann aus dem ~* the man in the street; *das ganze ~ umfassend* nation-wide.

Völker\|bund *m* League of Nations; **~~ssatzung** *f* Covenant of the League of Nations; **~friede** *m* international peace; **~gemeinschaft** *f* community of nations; **~kunde** *f* ethnology; **~mord** *m Am* genocide; **~recht** *n* international law; **~~lich** *a* relating to international law; **~schaft** *f* people; (*Stamm*) tribe; **~schlacht** *f* battle of (the) nations; **~wanderung** *f* migration of nations.

volkreich *a* populous.

Volks|abstimmung *f* plebiscite; referendum; **~aufstand** *m* revolution, rising; **~aufwiegler** *m* demagogue, *Am* rabble rouser; **~ausdruck** *m* popular expression; **~ausgabe** *f* popular edition; **~ausrottung** *f Am* genocide; **~befragung** *f* plebiscite; referendum; *Am* public opinion poll; **~begehren** *n* initiative; **~bewaffnung** *f* mobilization of the entire people; **~bibliothek, ~bücherei** *f* public library, free library; **~bildung** *f* adult education; **~~swerk** *n* adult education scheme; **~charakter** *m* national character; **~demokratie** *f* people's democracy; **~deutsche(r)** *m* ethnic German; **~dichter** *m* popular poet; national poet; **~empfinden** *n* popular feeling; **~entscheid** *m* plebiscite; referendum; **~epos** *n* national epic; **~fest** *n* national festival; public merry-making; **~freund** *m* friend of the people; **~front** *f* people's front; **~gemeinschaft** *f* community of the people; **~genosse** *m* fellow country-man; comrade; **~gesundheit** *f* public health; **~glaube** *m* popular belief; **~gruppe** *f* organized corporate racial minority; **~gunst** *f* popularity; **~haufen** *m*, **~menge** *f* crowd; populace, mob; **~herrschaft** *f* democracy; **~hochschule** *f* University Extension; adult education courses *pl*; **~justiz** *f* mob-justice; lynch-law; **~kongreß** *m* People's Congress; **~körper** *m* racial corpus; **~küche** *f* soup-kitchen; **~kunde** *f* folklore; **~lied** *n* folk-song; **~märchen** *n* popular fairy-tale; **~mäßig** *a* popular; **musik** *f* popular music; **~nah** *a* popular; **~partei** *f* people's party; **~rat** *m* people's council; **~redner** *m* popular speaker; (*Agitator*) mob (*od* stump) orator, *Am sl* soapbox orator; **~sage** *f* folk-tale; **~schädling** *m* wrongdoer against the people; **~schicht** *f* class (*od* stratum) of society; **~schlag** *m* race; **~schule** *f* primary school, elementary (*od* common) school; *Am* grade(d) school; **~schüler** *m* pupil of an elementary school; **~schullehrer** *m* primary teacher; **~sitte** *f* national custom; **~sprache** *f* vernacular language, popular tongue **~staat** *m* peopl'es (*od* free) state; republic; **~stamm** *m* tribe; race; **~stimme** *f* voice of the people; **~stimmung** *f* feeling of the people; **~tanz** *m* folk-dance; **~tracht** *f* national costume; **~tum** *n* nationality; national characteristics *pl*; **~~sfragen** *f pl* ethnological problems *pl*; **~tümlich** *a* national; (*beim Volk beliebt*) popular, *Abk fam Am* pop; **~~keit** *f* popularity; **~verbunden** *a* closely bound up with o.'s nation; **~versammlung** *f* public meeting; **~vertreter** *m* representative of the people, deputy; **~vertretung** *f* parliament; **~wagen** *m* people's car; **~wehr** *f* militia; **~wirt** *m* economist; **~wirtschaft, ~~slehre** *f* political economy; **~wohlfahrt** *f* public welfare; **~wohlstand** *m* national wealth, national prosperity; **~zählung** *f* census.

voll *a* full of; (*ganz*) entire, whole, complete; (*~zählig*) complete; (*gefüllt*) filled, replete; (*betrunken*) intoxicated; (*gedrängt*) crowded; (*massiv*) massive, solid; (*höchst*) maximum; *ein ~er Tag* a whole day; *die ~e Summe* the entire sum; *drei ~e Jahre* three whole years; *~e acht Tage* a whole week; *die ~e Wahrheit* the whole truth; *aus ~em Herzen* from the bottom of o.'s heart, heartily; *aus ~er Kehle* at the top of o.'s voice; *in ~er Fahrt* at full speed; *mit ~em Recht* with perfect justice; *im ~en Sinne des Wortes* in every sense of the word; *aus dem ~en schöpfen* to draw freely from the store of; to have plenty of; *jdn für ~ ansehen* to take s. o. seriously; *um das Maß ~ zu machen* to fill up the measure; *um das Unglück ~ zu machen* to make things worse; *den Mund ~ nehmen* to brag, to boast; *das Lokal war ~* the place was crowded; *vor ~en Häusern spielen* to play to capacity audiences; *~ besetzt!* full up! occupied! **~auf'** *adv* in abundance, abundantly, plentifully; **~automatisch** *a* fully automatic; **~bad** *n* full bath; complete bath; **~bahn** *f* standard-ga(u)ge railway; **~bart** *m* beard; **~berechtigt** *a* fully authorized (*od* entitled); **~beschäftigt** *a* fully employed; **~beschäftigung** *f* full-time job; (*für alle*) full employment; **~besitz** *m* full possession; **~betriebsfähig** *a* in complete working order; **~bier** *n* entire beer; **~blut** *n* (*Pferd*) thorough-bred (horse), *Am* blooded horse; **~blütig** *a* full-blooded; *med* plethoric; (*blutrot*) sanguine; **~bri'ngen** *irr tr* to accomplish, to achieve, to perform; to carry out, to effectuate, to bring about, to fulfil(l), to realize, *fam* to knock off; **~bringung** *f* accomplishment, achievement; **~busig** *a* full-bosomed; **~dampf** *m* full steam; *mit ~~* (*fig*) in full blast; **~e'nden** *tr* to finish, to terminate, to end, to close, to discontinue, to stop, *fam* to wind up; (*vervollständigen*) to complete, to accomplish, to finish off, to give the final touch (to); (*vervollkommnen*) to perfect, to bring to perfection, to elaborate, to mature; **~endet** *a fig* accomplished; **~ends** *adv* quite, entirely, wholly; (*obendrein*) besides; (*völlig*) completely; (*gänzlich*) altogether; (*schließlich*) finally; *~~ sagen* to say moreover; **~e'ndung** *f* finishing, termination; (*letzter Schliff*) finish; (*Fertigstellung*) completion; (*Vollendung*) perfection; *fig* accomplishment.

Völlerei *f* gluttony, intemperance.

voll|fü'hren *tr* to execute, to carry out, to accomplish; **~fü'hrung** *f* execution; **~gas** *n* full throttle; *mit ~~* with full throttle, *Am* opened up; at full speed; *~~ geben* to give full throttle, *Am* to open the engine full out, *fam* to step on the gas; *aero* to give the gun; **~gefühl** *n* (full) consciousness; **~genuß** *m* full enjoyment; **~gepfropft** *a* crowded, crammed, *fam* packed; **~gießen** *irr tr* to fill (up); **~gültig** *a* of full value, valid; **~gummi** *m* solid rubber; **~~reifen** *m* solid-rubber tyre; **~heit** *f* ful(l)ness, completeness.

völlig *a* complete, entire, full, *Am* fair, straight-out; through; *adv* quite; thoroughly, *Am* good and ...

voll|jährig *a* of age; **~~keit** *f* full age, majority; **~kettenfahrzeug** *n* full-track vehicle; **~ko'mmen** *a* perfect; accomplished; **~~heit** *f* perfection; **~korn** *n mil* full sight; **~kornbrot** *n* wholemeal bread; **~körnig** *a* full-grained; **~kraft** *f* full vigo(u)r; **~machen** *tr* to fill (up); *fig* to complete; (*beschmutzen*) to dirty; **~macht** *f* full power; *jur* power of attorney; authority, warrant; (*Urkunde*) proxy; *e-e ~~ ausstellen* (*ausüben, erteilen*) to execute (to exercise, to confer) a power of attorney; **~~geber** *m* constituent, mandator; **~~übertragung** *f* delegation of authority; **~matrose** *m* able-bodied seaman; **~milch** *f* full cream (*od* rich *od* unskimmed) milk; **~~pulver** *n* whole milk powder; **~mond** *m* full moon; **~motorisiert** *a* full motorized (*od* mechanized); **~netzanschluß** *m* mains supply; **~~gerät** *n radio* all electric set; **~saftig** *a* juicy, succulent; **~saugen** *tr* to suck full; **~schiff** *n* full-rigged ship; **~schlank** *a* well developed; pleasantly plump; **~selbsttätig** *a* fully automatic; **~sichtkanzel** *f aero* full-view cockpit, *Am* turret with all--around visibility; **~sitzung** *f* plenary session; **~spur** *f* standard-ga(u)ge; **~~ig** *a* of standard ga(u)ge; **~stampfen** *tr* to ram up, to tamp full; **~ständig** *a* complete; entire, total, whole; integral; *adv* quite, perfectly; *~~ machen* to complete; **~~keit** *f* completeness; **~stopfen** *tr* to gorge, to stuff, *Am* to fill up; **~streckbar** *a* enforceable, executable, executory; **~~keit** *f* execution; **~stre'kken** *tr* to execute, to carry out; **~strecker** *m* executor; **~~in** *f* executrix; **~stre'ckung** *f* execution; **~~sanordnung** *f* writ of execution; **~~sbeamte(r)** *m* executory officer; **~~sbefehl** *m* writ of execution; **~~sschutz** *m* order suspending executions; **~synchronisiert** *a phot* fully (flash-) synchronized; **~tönend** *a* sonorous, full-toned, rich in tone; **~treffer** *m* direct hit; **~versammlung** *f* plenary meeting; **~wertig** *a* up to standard, perfect, complete; **~wichtig** *a* of full weight; **~~keit** *f* full weight; **~zählig** *a* complete, integral; full strength; *adv* in full force; **~~keit** *f* completeness; **~zie'hen** *irr tr* to execute, to fulfil(l), to carry out, to accomplish, to effect; (*Vertrag*) to ratify; (*Ehe*) to consummate; *eccl* to solemnize; *r* to take place; **~~d** *a* executive; **~zie'her** *m* executor; **~zie'hung** *f*, **~zug'** *m* execution, accomplishment; **~zugsausschuß** *m* executive committee; **~zugsmeldung** *f* report of execution of orders.

Volont|är *m* volunteer; *com* unsalaried (*od* supernumerary) clerk; **~ieren** *itr* to volunteer; to work as voluntary helper.

Volt *n* volt; **~aisch** *a* voltaic; **~ampere** *n* volt-ampere; **~e** *f* volt; slight of hand; **~igieren** *itr* to vault; **~meter** *n* voltmeter; **~spannung, ~zahl** *f* voltage.

Volum|en *n* volume; size, bulk; capacity, content; **~gewicht** *n* volume weight; **~inös** *a* voluminous; **~minderung** *f* decrease in volume; **~regler** *m radio* volume control; **~teil** *m* part by volume; **~veränderung** *f* change in volume; **~verhältnis** *n* volume ratio; **~verlust** *m* loss in volume.

•

von *prp* of; by; from; about; against; upon, on; with; *von ... an* from, beginning, starting; *~ nun an* henceforth; *~ morgen an* from to-morrow; *~ hinten* from behind; *~ Montag bis Freitag* from Monday to (*Am* through) Friday; *~ selbst* automatically; by myself, by yourself, *etc*; *~ mir aus* I don't mind, as far as I am concerned; if you like; *~ vornherein* from the (very) beginning; *~ London nach Manchester* from L. to M.; *~ fern* from afar; *~ Zeit zu Zeit* from time to time; *~ klein auf* from childhood (on); *~ morgens bis abends* from morning to night; *~ Holz* (made) of wood; *~ wem ist das Buch?* by whom is that book? *das hängt ~ dem Wetter ab* that depends on the weather; *sich nähren ~* to feed on; *wimmeln ~* to crawl with; *sie haben ~ dir gesprochen* they were talking about you; *~ Angesicht zu Angesicht* face to face; *grüßen Sie ihn ~ mir* my best regards to him; **~einander** *adv* from each other; of each other; (*auseinander*) separate, apart; **~nöten** *adv* necessary, needful; **~statten** *adv*: *~~*

gehen to proceed, to pass off, to progress.

vor *prp* (*Zeit, Ort*) before; (*Zeit*) before, previous, prior to; ago; since; to; of; (*Ort*) in front of, ahead of; (*Abwehr*) from, against; of; (*Freude, Schmerz*) with, for; (*Vorsilbe*) fore-, pre-, pro-; prior, previous, preliminary, first; ~ *allem* above all, first of all; *nach wie* ~ still; as usual; *nicht* ~ not till; *zwei Stunden* ~ *der Zeit* two hours before time (*Am* ahead of time); *fünf Minuten* ~ *zehn* five minutes to (*Am* of) ten; ~ *3 Wochen* three weeks ago; *warnen* ~ to warn against; ~ *Aufregung* for excitement; *sich fürchten* ~ to be afraid of; ~ *Wut zittern* to tremble with rage; ~ *Zeugen* in presence of witnesses; ~ *unserm Haus* in front of our house; ~ *sich hin* to o. s.; *etw* ~ *sich haben* to be in for s. th.; ~ *sich gehen* to occur, to take place.

vor|ab *adv* first of all, above all; tentatively; **~abdruck** *m* preprint; (*Exemplar*) advance copy; **~abend** *m* eve; **~abzug** *m typ* advance sheet; **~ahnen** *tr* to have a presentiment; **~ahnung** *f* presentiment, foreboding, premonition; misgiving; *Am fam* hunch; (*Erkenntnis*) intuition, subconscious perception; inspiration; **~alpen** *pl* the Lower Alps *pl*; **~an** *adv* at the head of, in front of, ahead of; before; (*vorwärts*) on, onwards; *~~! interj* go ahead! go on! **~~gehen** *irr itr* to walk at the head of, to go on ahead; *fig* to take the lead; (*zeitlich, örtlich*) to precede; *mit gutem Beispiel ~~ gehen* to set a good example; **~~gehend** *a* preceding, leading, antecedent; **~~kommen** *irr itr* to get on, to make headway, to progress, to advance; (*Fortschritt erzielen*) to make progress; *im Leben ~~ kommen* to make o.'s way; **~~kündigung** *f* advance notice; *film* trailer; **~~laufen** *irr itr* to run on before; **~~meldung** *f* preadvice; *tele* (*Gespräch*) preadvice call; **~~schicken** *tr* to send on before.

Vor|anschlag *m* (rough *od* provisional) estimate, preliminary calculation; **~antreiben** *irr tr* to push; **~anzeige** *f* preliminary announcement; **~arbeit** *f* preparatory work, preliminary operation, preparation, ground work; spade work; **~arbeiten** *itr* to prepare s. th.; to prepare the ground for; *jdm ~~* to pave the way for; *r* to work o.'s way up; (*mit Mühe*) to forge ahead; **~arbeiter** *m* foreman; leading hand, chief operator, *Am* gang boss; **~~in** *f* forewoman; **~auf** *adv* before, ahead, in front.

vorau's *adv* (*örtlich*) before, foremost; ahead (of), forward; (*zeitlich*) beforehand; *im* ~ beforehand, by anticipation, in advance; *weit* ~ (*Am*) way ahead of; *im* ~ *etw tun* to anticipate; *etw* ~ *haben vor* to have an advantage over s. o.; *nicht im* ~ *bestimmbar* unpredictable; *seinem Alter* ~ *sein* to be forward for o.'s age; **~abteilung** *f* advance force, spearhead; reconnaissance force; **~bedingen** *irr tr* to stipulate beforehand; **~berechnen** *tr* to predetermine; **~berechnet** *a* calculated; **~berechnung** *f* preliminary calculation; predetermination **~bestellen** *tr* to book in advance, to order beforehand, *Am* to make reservations for; (*Veröffentlichung*) to subscribe (to); **~bestellung** *f* advance order; subscription; **~bestimmen** *tr* to predetermine; **~bestimmung** *f* predetermination; **~bezahlen** *tr* to pay in advance, to prepay; **~bezahlung** *f* payment in advance, prepayment; **~datiert** *a* antedated; **~eilen** *itr* to hurry on in advance (of); **~flugzeug** *n* advance plane; **~gesetzt** *pp*: ~~ *daß* assuming that, provided that; **~haben** *irr tr* to have an advantage over s. o.; **~gehen** *irr itr* to go before, to precede (one), to walk in front, to lead the way; **~~d** *a* preceding, leading, anteceding; previous, prior; **~nahme** *f* anticipation; **~nehmen** *irr tr* to anticipate; **~sage, ~sagung** *f* prediction; (*Prophezeiung*) prophecy; (*Wink*) tip; *sport* selection(s *pl*); (*Wetter*) forecast; **~sagen** *tr* to predict, to foretell, to tell in advance; to prophesy; (*Wetter*) to forecast; **~schauend** *a* far-sighted; **~schicken** *tr* to premise; (*Sachen*) to send on before; **~sehbar** *a* foreseeable; **~sehen** *irr tr* to foresee, to anticipate; **~setzen** *tr* to presume, to (pre)suppose, to postulate, to take for granted; **~setzung** *f* supposition, assumption; hypothesis; (*erste* ~~) prerequisite, prior condition; (*Bedingung*) condition, stipulation; *unter der* ~~ on the premises; with the understanding (that); **~sicht** *f* foresight, prudence; *aller ~~ nach* in all probability; **~~lich** *a* probable, presumptive, prospective, to be expected; *adv* presumably, as is anticipated, in all likelihood, so far as one can see, the way it looks; *treffe ich ihn ~~? Am* am I apt to meet him? **~truppen** *f pl* advanced detachment; **~zahlung** *f* prepayment, payment in advance (*od* by anticipation); *Am* anticipated payment.

Vorbau *m* front structure; (*Vorhalle*) porch; **~en** *tr* to build out; to build in front of; *itr* (*vorbeugen*) to guard against, to prevent, to take precautions against, to obviate; (*vorsorgen*) to provide for.

vorbe|arbeiten *tr* to rough; **~arbeitung** *f* preliminary working; **~dacht** *m* forethought, premeditation; *mit ~~* deliberately, on purpose; ~~ *a* premeditated; **~deuten** *tr* to forebode, to presage; **~deutung** *f* foreboding, omen; **~dingung** *f* prerequisite, preliminary condition; **~griff** *m* preliminary notion; **~halt** *m* reservation, reserve, proviso; *geheimer* (*innerer*) ~~ mental reservation: *unter* ~ reservedly; *unter dem ~~, daß* on the proviso that; *unter ~~ aller Rechte* all rights reserved; *ohne ~~* unconditionally; **~halten** *irr tr* to reserve; *r* to reserve to o. s.; **~hältlich** *adv* with the reservation of (*od* as to), on condition that, with the proviso that; subject to, reserving; **~haltlos** *a* unconditional; **~haltsgut** *n jur* separate estate; **~haltsklausel** *f* proviso clause; **~handeln** *tr* to pretreat; **~handlung** *f* primary treatment.

vorbei *adv* (*örtlich*) by, along, past; (*zeitlich*) past, over, gone; done; **~eilen** *itr* to hasten past; **~fahren** *irr itr* to drive past; **~fliegen** *irr itr* to fly past; **~fließen** *irr itr* to flow past; **~gehen** *irr itr* to pass by (*an* s. o.), to go past, to walk along; (*aufhören*) to cease, to stop, to pass; (*scheitern*) to go wrong, to miscarry; (*nicht treffen*) to miss the mark; (*vermeiden*) to evade, to steer clear of, *Am* to side-step; **~kommen** *irr itr* to go past, to go by; (*besuchen*) to call, to look in, *Am* to come by; **~lassen** *irr tr* to let pass; **~marsch** *m* march(ing) past, *Am* street parade; **~~ieren** *itr* to march past (*an* s. o.); **~reden** *itr: aneinander ~~* to be at cross-purposes; **~reiten** *irr itr* to ride past; **~schießen, ~schlagen, ~treffen** *irr itr* to miss the mark; **~sehen** *irr itr* not to look straight at each other; **~streifen** *itr* to pass, to skirt, to brush (against); **~ziehen** *irr tr* to draw past; *itr* to pass by.

vorbe|lastet *a* compromised; **~merkung** *f* preliminary note (*od* remark); prefatory notice; (*Gesetz*) preamble; **~nannt** *a* aforesaid; **~reiten** *tr* to prepare, to get ready; *r* (*Schule, Examen*) to prepare, *fam* to prep, *Am* to fit; to specialize (*auf* in, *Am* on); *e-e vorbereitete Rede* a prepared speech, *Am* a set speech; **~~d** *a* preparatory; **~reitung** *f* preparation; preparatory training; preliminaries *pl*; (*Aufstellung*) line-up, readying; **~~sdienst** *m* term of probation; **~~sschule** *f* preparatory school, *Am* fitting school; **~richt** *m* preliminary report, advertisement; (*Zeitung*) *Am* flash; (*Einleitung*) introduction, preface; **~scheid** *m* preliminary decision; interim action; **~sitzer** *m* previous possessor; **~sprechung** *f* preliminary discussion; **~stellen** *tr* to order in advance; to book, *Am* to make reservations; **~stellt** *a: ~~er Platz* booked seat, *Am* reservation; **~stellung** *f* advance order; booking, *Am* reservation; **~straft** *a* previously convicted; *nicht ~~er* first offender.

vor|beten *itr* to lead in prayer; **~beter** *m* precentor; **~beugen** *itr* to prevent, to preclude, to obviate; *r* to bend forward, to crane (forward); **~~d** *a* preventive, prophylactic; **~beugung** *f* prevention; *med* prophylaxis; **~smaßregel** *f* preventive (*od* prophylactic) measure; **~smittel** *n* preservative; preventive; *med* prophylactic; **~bild** *n* pattern, model, standard, exemplar; (*Ausbund*) paragon; (*Maßstab*) *fig* yardstick; (*Urbild*) prototype, original; **~~en** *tr* to train; to prepare; **~~lich** *a* exemplary, model; typical, representative (*für* of); **~bildung** *f* preparatory training; **~binden** *irr tr* to put on, to tie on; **~bohren** *tr* to rough-drill; **~bohrer** *m* auger, gimlet; **~bote** *m* forerunner, precursor; *fig* harbinger; **~bringen** *irr tr* (*äußern*) to say, to put forward; (*aussprechen*) to utter; (*Plan*) to propose; (*Wunsch*) to express, to state; (*Meinung*) to advance; (*Gründe*) to bring up, to allege; (*erörtern*) to argue, to reason; (*Beweis*) to plead; (*Entschuldigung*) to make; (*zitieren*) to bring forward; (*vorzeigen, vorlegen*) to produce; **~buchstabieren** *tr* to spell out (for); **~bühne** *f theat* proscenium.

vorchristlich *a* pre-Christian.

Vor|dach *n* penthouse; **~datieren** *tr* to antedate; **~dem** *adv* formerly, in former times, of old.

vorder *a* front, fore, anterior, forward, in the front.

Vorder|achse *f* front-axle; **~~nantrieb** *m* front-axle drive; **~~nschenkel** *m* stub axle; **~~nzapfen** *m* steering-knuckle pivot; **~ansicht** *f* front view (*od* elevation); **~arm** *m* forearm; **~asien** *n* Near East; **~bein** *n* foreleg; **~deck** *n* fore-deck; **~front** *f* front; **~fuß** *m* forefoot; **~e** *a* anterior; **~ende** *n* front (*od* fore) end; **~feder** *f* front spring; **~fläche** *f* front face; **~gebäude, ~haus** *n* front building; **~gestell** *n mot* forecarriage; **~grund** *m* foreground; *im ~~* in the foreground, conspicuous, prominent, striking, noticeable; *im ~~ stehen* to be well to the fore, to hold the spotlight; *im ~~ des Interesses stehen* to be much in the news, to hit the headlines; **~hand** *f* forehand; *adv* at first, for the beginning, for the present, provisionally; **~kipper** *m* front tipper; **~lader** *m* muzzle-loader; **~lastig** *a* nose-heavy; **~~keit** *f* nose-heaviness; **~lauf** *m* (*Jagd*) foreleg; **~mann** *m* man in front; front rank man; file leader; *mar* ship next ahead; **~mast** *m* foremast; **~rad** *n* front wheel; **~~achse** *f* front axle; **~~antrieb** *m* front-wheel drive; **~~bremse** *f* front-wheel brake; **~~nabe** *f* front hub; **~rand** *m* anterior end; **~reihe** *f* front row, front rank; **~satz** *m* antecedent; *die ~sätze* premises *pl*; **~seite** *f* front, face; (*Münze*) obverse; (*Buch*) odd page; **~sitz** *m* front seat; **~st** *a* foremost; **~steven** *m* stem; **~teil** *m* front, front part; *tech* head, nosepiece; *mar* prow; **~tür** *f* front door; **~wagen** *m* fore carriage; (*Protze*) limber; **~zähne** *m pl* front teeth *pl*; **~zimmer** *n* front room, *Am* foreroom.

vor|drängen *tr, r* to push (*od* to press) forward; **~dringen** *irr itr* to advance, to forge ahead, to gain ground; **~dringlich** *a* urgent; (*lästig*) intrusive; obtrusive; *~~e Aufgabe* priority task; **~~keitsliste** *f* priority list; **~druck** *typ* first impression; (*Formular*) form, *Am* blank; schedule.

vor|ehelich *a* prenuptial; **~eilen** *itr* to run fast, to slip forward, to hasten forward, to outrun; *fig* to anticipate; **~eilig** *a* hasty, rash, precipitate, premature; *~~e Schlüsse ziehen* to jump to conclusions; **~~keit** *f* hastiness, precipitation, precipitancy, rashness; **~einflugzeichen** *n aero* foremarker, warning signal; **~eingenommen** *a* bias(s)ed, prejudiced (*für* in favour of); **~~heit** *f* bias, prejudice; **~eltern** *pl* forefathers *pl*, ancestors *pl*; **~empfinden** *tr* to foresee, to anticipate; **~empfindung** *f* foreboding, anticipation; **~enthalten** *irr tr* to keep back (from), to withhold (*jdm* from s. o.); **~enthaltung** *f* withholding; *jur* detention; **~entwarnung** *f* immediate danger past; **~erklärung** *f* preliminary declaration; **~erst** *adv* first of all, before all; for the time being, in the meantime; **~erwähnt** *pp* before-mentioned, aforesaid; **~erzeugnis** *n* semifinished product.

Vor|fabrikation *f* prefabrication; **~fabriziert** *a* prefabricated; *attr* prefab; **~fahr** *m* forefather, ancestor; **~fahren** *irr itr* to drive up (*bei* to), to stop (at); *~~ lassen* let to pass; **~fahrt(s)recht** *n* right of way, priority (in traffic); **~fahrt(s)zeichen** *n* sign to pass; priority sign; **~fall** *m* occurrence, incident; (*Begebenheit*) event, incident; *med* prolapsus; **~fallen** *irr itr fig* to occur, to happen, to take place; **~feier** *f* preliminary celebration; **~feld** *n* area on immediate front; *aero* (*der Flughallen*) apron; **~~batterie** *f* outlying battery; **~fenster** *n* outer window; **~fertigen** *tr* to prefabricate; **~finanzierung** *f* prefinancing; **~finden** *irr tr* to find, to meet with, to come upon; **~frage** *f* preliminary question; *parl* previous question; **~formen** *tr* to preform; **~fräsen** *tr* to rough-ream; **~freude** *f* anticipated joy; **~frühling** *m* early spring; **~fühlen** *itr* to feel o.'s way forward; *fig* to try, to attempt; **~führdame** *f* mannequin; model; **~führen** *tr* to bring forward, to produce, to present, to demonstrate, to display; (*Kleider*) to model; (*Film*) to project, to exhibit; (*Pferd*) to trot out; **~führer** *m* projectionist, motion-picture operator; **~führgerät** *n* projector; **~führraum** *m* operating room; **~führung** *f* bringing forth; production; demonstration, experiment; presentation; (*Vorstellung*) show; act; performance; **~~sapparat** *m* apparatus for demonstration; projector; **~~sflug** *m* demonstration flight; **~~skabine** *f* projection booth; **~~swagen** *m* demonstration car.

Vor|gabe *f sport* points (*od* odds) given; allowance; (*Rennen*) handicap; *min* burden; *ohne ~~ starten* to start from scratch; **~~zeit** *f* advance time; **~~rennen, ~~spiel** *n* handicap; **~gang** *m* occurrence, event, incident, phenomenon; (*Verfahren*) process, procedure, operation; (*Akte*) subject; (*Hergang*) proceedings *pl*; (*Präzedenzfall*) precedent; **~gänger** *m*, **~~in** *f* predecessor; **~garten** *m* front garden, backyard, *Am* dooryard; **~gaukeln** *tr* to buoy up with false hopes; to lead s. o. to believe; **~gearbeitet** *a* prepared; **~geben** *irr tr* to give an advantage (to); (*behaupten*) to allege, to pretend; (*vorschützen*) to feign; *itr* (*Spiel*) to give odds (to); to allow s. o. points; **~gebildet** *a* trained; **~gebirge** *n* foothills *pl*; (*am Meer*) cape, promontory; **~geblich** *a* pretended, would-be, so-called; ostensible; **~gefaßt** *a* preconceived; *~~e Meinung* prejudice; **~gefühl** *n* presentiment, anticipation, *Am* hunch; (*böse Ahnung*) misgiving; **~gehen** *irr itr* to advance, to go before; to go forward, to go on ahead; (*führen*) to lead, to go first, to take the lead; to come first; (*handeln*) to act, to take action, to proceed; *jur* to proceed (against); (*Rang*) to take precedence (of), to have the precedence; (*Wichtigkeit*) to be of special importance; (*sich ereignen*) to occur, to happen, to go on; (*Uhr*) to be fast; *was geht hier vor?* what's up? **~gehen** *n* advance; (*Handlungsweise*) proceeding; procedure; *jur* action; *gemeinschaftliches ~~* concerted action; *abschnittweises ~~* advance by bounds; **~gelagert** *a* put up in front of; **~gelände** *n* foreground, outlying lands *pl*; **~gelege** *n* back-gearing arrangement; **~gemischt** *a* premixed; **~gericht** *n* first dish, entree; **~gerüst** *n* roughing stand; **~geschichte** *f* prehistory, prehistoric times *pl*; history of a preceding period; (*Person*) antecedents *pl*; **~geschichtlich** *a* prehistoric; **~geschlagen** *a* proposed; *ein ~~er* a nominee; **~geschmack** *m* foretaste; **~geschoben** *a* advanced; forward; *~~e Stellung mil* advance position; **~geschrieben** *a* prescribed, specified, positive; stipulated; **~gesehen** *a* intended, provided; *wie ~~* as arranged, *Am* as scheduled, according to schedule; **~gesetzte(r)** *m* superior, chief, *Am* boss; *mil* senior (officer); **~gesetztenverhältnis** *n* authority; **~gestern** *adv* the day before yesterday; **~gestrig** *a* of the day before yesterday; **~getäuscht** *a* simulated; **~gewärmt** *a* preheated; **~greifen** *irr itr* to anticipate, to forestall; **~griff** *m* anticipation.

vor|haben *irr tr* to have s. th. on, to have before; (*beabsichtigen*) to intend, to plan, to mean, to purpose, to have in mind; (*prüfen*) to examine; (*beschäftigt sein*) to be busy with, to be engaged on; (*ausfragen*) to question (*jdn* s. o.); (*im Begriff sein*) to be about to; (*schelten*) to reprimand; *nichts ~~* to be at a loose end; *haben Sie morgen etw vor?* do you have any plans for tomorrow? what are your plans for tomorrow? *was hat sie jetzt vor?* what's she up to now? *wenn Sie nichts anderes ~~* unless you are otherwise engaged; **~haben** *n* (*Plan*) plan, design, (*Absicht*) purpose, intention; **~halle** *f* entrance-hall, vestibule, lobby, porch; *theat* lounge, *Am* lobby; **~halt** *m* aiming-off allowance; **~halten** *irr tr* to hold before; *fig* to reproach, to throw up to, to rebuke; *itr* to last, to hold out; **~haltewinkel** *m aero mil* bombing angle; **~haltung** *f* remonstrance, reproach; **~hand** *f* (*Kartenspiel*) lead; forehand; *com* first claim; first option; **~handen** *a* existing, available; at hand, present; *com* in stock; *~~ sein* to be on hand, to exist; *es ist nichts ~~* there is nothing left; *nicht ~~* out of stock; *reichlich ~~* abundant; **~~sein** *n* presence, existence; **~handschlag** *m* (*Tennis*) forehand (stroke); **~hang** *m* curtain, *Am* shade; (*Drapierung*) drapery; *theat* (drop) curtain, (*Herausruf*) *Am* curtain call; *der Eiserne ~~* the Iron Curtain; **~~blende** *f phot* curtain-fading shutter; **~~halter** *m* curtain clasp; **~hängen** *tr* to hang before; **~hängeschloß** *n* padlock; **~haut** *f* foreskin, prepuce; **~hemd(chen)** *n* shirt-front, dicky.

vorher *adv* before(hand), in advance; previously; *kurz ~* a short time before; **~bedenken** *irr tr* to premeditate; **~bestimmen** *tr* to arrange (*od* determine) beforehand; *eccl* to predestine; **~bestimmung** *f eccl* predestination; **~gehen** *irr itr* to precede s. o.; **~~d, ~ig** *a* preceding, foregoing, previous, anterior, prior, former; (*letzt*) last; **~sage** *f* prediction; (*Prophezeiung*) prophecy; (*Wetter*) forecast; prognosis; **~sagen, ~verkündigen** *tr* to foretell, to predict; to prophesy; (*Wetter*) to forecast; **~sehbar** *a* foreseeable; **~sehen** *irr tr* to foresee; **~wissen** *irr tr* to foreknow.

Vor|herrschaft *f* predominance; prevalence; preponderance; **~herrschen** *itr* to prevail; to predominate; **~~d** *a* predominant; prevailing, prevalent; **~hin** *adv* before; a little while ago; just now; **~hof** *m* foreyard; vestibule, forecourt, entry; **~hut** *f mil* vanguard, advance guard; **~~gefecht** *n* advance-guard engagement; **~ig** *a* former, preceding, previous; (*letztvergangen*) last; **~jahr** *n* preceding year; **~jährig** *a* last year's, of last year.

Vor|kalkulation *f* preliminary calculation; **~kammer** *f mot* antechamber, precombustion chamber; **~kampf** *m sport* heat; (*Boxen*) *Am* prelim(inary); **~kämpfer** *m* pioneer; protagonist; *sport* champion; **~kauen** *tr* to chew (for); *fig* to spoon-feed, to repeat over and over; **~kauf** *m* pre-emption; **~käufer** *m* forestaller; **~kaufsrecht** *n* right of pre-emption, first refusal; *das ~~ haben* to have the first refusal of; **~kehrung** *f* precaution, preparation, provision, arrangement; precautionary measure, preventive measure; *die nötigen ~~en treffen* to take the necessary precautions; to make arrangements for; **~kenntnis** *f* preliminary knowledge (of); **~~se** *pl* elements *pl*, rudiments *pl*; *~~se nicht erforderlich* no previous experience necessary; *er hat gute ~~se in* he's grounded in the elements of; **~klage** *f* previous complaint; **~kommando** *n* advance party.

vorkommen *irr itr* to be found, to be met (with); (*zuvorkommen*) to prevent; (*geschehen*) to happen, to occur, to take place; (*stoßen auf, erleben*) to come across, to come up against, to experience; (*scheinen*) to appear, to seem; (*vorgelassen werden*) to be admitted; (*zu Besuch*) to call on; (*zur Verhandlung*) to be proposed, to be brought forward; *jur* to be tried; (*erörtert werden*) to be pleaded; *es kommt mir vor* it seems to me, I have an impression that; *so etw ist mir noch nicht vorgekommen* well, I never; I've never heard of such a thing; *es kommt dir nur so vor* you are just imagining that; *sie kam sich dumm vor* she felt silly; *bei ~der Gelegenheit* when occasion offers; ~ *n* occurrence, presence, existence; *min* deposit, occurrence.

Vor|kommnis *n* occurrence, event; **~konferenz** *f* preconference; **~kost** *f* first course; (*Krankenbrei*) spoon-meat; **~krieg** *m* prewar period; **~~szeit** *f* prewar days *pl*; **~kühlen** *tr* to precool; **~kühlung** *f* primary cooling; **~laden** *irr tr* to cite, to summon; *jur* to serve a writ on s. o.; (*unter Strafandrohung*) to subpoena; **~ladung** *f* notice, notification, appointment; *jur* summons; subpoena; writ; citation; **~lage** *f* (*Einreichung*) filing, submission, presentation; (*Muster*) pattern, model; (*Schreib~~, Zeichen~~*) original copy; *parl* bill; (*Fußball*) pass forward; (*Ski*) leaning; *tech* receiver; condenser; (*Gas*) collecting main; (*Kanone*) flash hider; *zur ~~* for submission (to); **~lagern** *tr* to extend in front of; to protrude; to store before using; **~längst** *adv* long ago, long since; **~lassen** *irr tr* to let pass before, to give precedence (to); (*zulassen*) to admit, to give access to, to show in; **~lassung** *f* access, admission, admittance; **~lauf** *m* *sport* start; heat; preliminary round; eliminating race; *chem* first runnings *pl*; **~laufen** *irr itr* to run before; (*vorkommen*) to outrun; **~läufer** *m* forerunner, precursor; pioneer; *fig* harbinger; (*Berg*) spur; (*Zeichen*) indication, sign, clue; **~läufig** *a* provisional, preliminary, preparatory, introductory, tentative, temporary, advance; *adv* for the present, (in the) meantime, provisionally; **~laut** *a* pert, forward, presumptuous, *Am sl* fresh; *~~es Wesen* pertness; **~leben** *n* former life, antecedents *pl*; background; **~legebesteck** *n* carvers *pl*, **~legegabel** *f* carving-fork; **~legelöffel** *m* soup-ladle; **~legemesser** *n* carving knife; **~legen** *tr* to put before; (*bei Tisch*) to serve with, to help to; (*zeigen*) to show, to display, to exhibit; (*Schriftstück*) to submit, to file; *parl* to table; (*unterbreiten*) to produce, to present; (*Schloß*) to put on, to apply; (*vorschlagen*) to propose; *r* to lean forward; **~leger** *m* mat, rug; **~legeschloß** *n* padlock; **~lesen** *irr tr* to read to s. o., to read aloud, *Am* to read out loud; **~leser** *m* reader; **~lesung** *f* reading; (*akademische*) lecture; *~~en halten* to lecture (on), to deliver (*od* give) a lecture (to); *e-e ~~ hören* to attend a lecture; **~~sverzeichnis** *n* syllabus of lectures, university calendar (*Am* catalog); **~letzt** *a* last but one, before last; *gram* penultimate (syllable); **~liebe** *f* predilection, preference, special liking (for), fondness, partiality (for, to); **~liebnehmen** *irr itr* to be satisfied with, to put up with; *Sie müssen ~~ mit dem, was wir haben* you'll have to take pot luck; **~liegen** *irr itr* to lie before (one); (*in Bearbeitung*) to be in (*od* at, *Am* on) hand, to be under consideration; (*vorhanden sein*) to be existent, to be present; (*vorgelegt sein*) to be submitted (to), to be put forward; **~liegend** *a* in question; in hand, present; *die ~~e Angelegenheit* the matter in hand; *der ~~e Fall* the case in question, the case under review; *im ~~en Falle* in the present case; **~lügen** *irr tr* to tell lies (*über* about).

vor|machen *tr* to put before; *jdm etw ~~* to show s. o. how to do s. th.; (*täuschen*) to impose upon s. o., to deceive, to humbug s. o., to fool, to hoodwink; *machen Sie sich nichts vor* don't fool yourself; *Am fam* don't kid yourself; **~macht** *f* leading power; **~~stellung** *f* supremacy, predominance; **~malen** *tr* to paint s. th. as a pattern; *fig* to describe, to depict; **~malig** *a* former; **~mals** *adv* formerly; **~mann** *m* foreman; (*beim Rudern*) stroke; *com* previous endorser; **~marsch** *m* advance, onward march; *~~ zum Gefecht* development for combat; **~~linie** *f* axis of advance; **~~straße** *f* line of advance, approach road; **~marssegel** *n* *mar* fore-topsail; **~mast** *m* *mar* foremast; **~meldung** *f* warning; preliminary report.

Vormerk|buch *n* memorandum-book, *fam* memo-book; notebook; engagement book, promptbook; **~en** *tr* to put down, to note down, to jot down, to make a note of; to enter on a list; *e-n Platz ~~* to book a seat, *Am* to reserve a seat; *sich ~~ lassen* to have reserved for; **~gebühr** *f* booking-fee; **~liste** *f* waiting list; **~schein** *m* priority; **~ung** *f* entry; reservation; notice; note, memorandum; caveat.

vormilitärisch *a* premilitary.

Vormittag *m* morning, forenoon; **~s** *adv* in the forenoon, in the morning, a. m.; **~sstunde** *f* morning hour; **~szeit** *f* morning time.

Vormund *m* guardian; **~schaft** *f* guardianship; tutelage; **~~lich** *a* tutelary, of a guardian; **~~sgericht** *n* guardianship court.

vorn *adv* before, in front, ahead, at the head, in the forepart; (*am Anfang*) at the beginning; (*Buch*) on the front; *nach ~* forward; *~ u. hinten* before and behind; *von ~(e)herein* from the first, to begin with, from the outset; *ganz ~* right in the front; *von ~* from before, from the front; (*von neuem*) anew, afresh, from the beginning; *noch einmal von ~* all over again; *von ~ anfangen* to begin at the beginning; *von ~ nach hinten* from front to back; *wieder von ~ anfangen* to begin all over again; *~ heraus* forward; *nach ~ heraus wohnen* to live in the front part of a house; *nach ~ liegen* to face the front; **~an** *adv* in the front; **~liegend** *a* ahead; **~über** *adv* (bent)forward; **~weg** *adv* at the beginning; from the outset.

Vor|nahme *f* undertaking, taking in hand, taking up; **~name** *m* Christian name, *Am* first name, given name.

vornehm *a* of superior rank; of gentle birth; noble, select, distinguished; (*Sachen*) fashionable, stylish, elegant, *Am fam* exclusive; distinguished; *~e Gesinnung* high mind; *~es Äußere* distinguished appearance; *~e Welt* polite world; *~ste(r)* principal, chief; *~ tun* to give o. s. airs, to put on airs; *die ~e Welt* rank and fashion; *die ~ste Pflicht* the first (*od* principle) duty; **~en** *irr tr* to take before one; (*Schürze*) to put on; *fig* to undertake, to conduct, to deal with, to take up; (*machen*) to make; (*ins Auge fassen*) to consider, to face; *jdn ~~* to reprimand; to examine; *r* to intend, to purpose; to resolve, to make up o.'s mind; (*planen*) to plan; (*Arbeit*) to take up, to occupy o. s. with; *sich jdn ~~* to take s. o. to task; **~heit** *f* distinction, high rank; (*Verhalten*) distinguished bearing; **~lich** *adv* chiefly, especially, particulary; **~ste** *a* principal, first; chief, foremost.

Vorort *m* suburb; (*e-s Bundes*) administrative centre (of an association); **~sgebiet** *n* suburban area; **~sgespräch** *n* suburban call; **~snetz** *n* tandem area; **~sverkehr** *m* junction traffic, suburban traffic; **~swagen** *m* inter urban car; **~szug** *m* suburban train, *Am* shuttle train.

vor|planen *tr* to pre-plan; **~plappern** *tr* to chat; **~platz** *m* hall, vestibule, *Am* stoop; court; (*Treppenabsatz*) landing; *aero* (*Hallenvorfeld*) apron; **~plaudern** *tr* to tattle to; **~posten** *m* outpost; **~~aufstellung** *f* outpost disposition; **~~boot** *n* patrol boat; **~~dienst** *m* outpost duty; **~~gefecht** *n* outpost skirmish; **~~linie** *f* outpost line; **~~sicherungslinie** *f* outpost line of resistance; **~~stellung** *f* outpost position; **~predigen** *tr* to preach to; **~probe** *f* preliminary test; **~produkt** *n* initial product; crude product; **~prüfung** *f* previous (*od* preliminary) examination; (*Universität*) *sl* little go; *sport* trial; (*Pferde*) beforehand test; **~pumpe** *f* auxiliary pump; (*Brauerei*) circulator; **~quellen** *irr itr* to presoak, to presteep; (*herausragen*) to be prominent; **~raffinieren** *tr* to prerefine; (*Blei*) to soften, to improve.

*

vor|ragen *itr* to be prominent, to stand out, to project, to protrude; **~~d** *a* prominent, projecting; **~rang** *m* (*Vordringlichkeit*) priority; (*Reihenfolge*) precedence (of), superiority (to, over), first rank, pre-eminence; *den ~~ vor jdm haben* to have the precedence of; **~rat** *m* store, stock, provision, supply, reserve; (*Ersatzteile*) spare parts *pl*; (*Material*) *Am* stockpile; *e-n ~~ anlegen* to lay in stocks; (*von Rohmaterial, Atombomben etc*) to stockpile; *mit Vorräten überhäuft* overstocked; *auf ~~* in stock; **~~sbehälter** *m* stock bin, storage bunker; **~~skammer** *f* storeroom, pantry; **~~slager** *n* storage dump, *mil* commissary; **~~sraum** *m* storeroom, warehouse, magazine, stockhouse; **~~sschrank** *m* pantry, *Am* safe; **~~stank** *m* storage tank; **~~swirtschaft** *f* stockpiling; **~raum** *m* anteroom, outer chamber; **~rätig** *a* in store, in stock, on hand; *nicht ~~* out of stock; **~rechnen** *tr* to enumerate to; to reckon up (to); to give an account of; **~recht** *n* privilege; prerogative; (*Vordringlichkeit*) priority; exclusive right; (*Bevorzugung*) preference; *dieselben ~~e genießen Am com* to get in on the ground floor; **~rede** *f* preface, foreword; prologue; introduction; (*Vorspruch*) preamble; **~reden** *tr* to make s. o. believe s. th., to tell s. o. tales (about); **~redner** *m* previous speaker; **~reiten** *irr itr* to ride before; *tr* to ride (a horse) through its paces; *jdm etw ~~* (*fig*) to parade s. th. before s. o.; **~reiter** *m* outrider; **~richten** *tr* to prepare, to fit up; **~richtung** *f* arrangement, preparation; (*Apparat*) apparatus, appliance, contrivance; (*tech Gerät*) device, fixture, mechanism; *Am* notion(s *pl*); (*Ausrüstung*) outfit, equipment, installation; *leicht zu be-*

dienende ~~ easy-to-operate device; ~**rücken** *tr* to move forward, to advance; (*Uhr*) to put on; *itr* to advance, to progress; to step forward; (*im Dienst*) to be promoted; ~~ *n* advance; ~**rufen** *irr tr* to call forth; ~**runde** *f sport* preliminary round.

Vor|saal *m* anteroom, entrance-hall; ~**sagen** *tr* to tell, to rehearse (to); *itr* (*zuflüstern*) to prompt s. o.; ~**sager** *m* prompter; ~**saison** *f* early season; ~**sänger** *m eccl* precentor, *Am auch* chorister; ~**satz** *m* design, purpose; intention, plan, premeditation; (*Entschluß*) resolution; (*Apparat*) attached device; *mit* ~~ on purpose, deliberately, intentionally; *seinen* ~~ *ausführen* to gain o.'s end(s); ~~**blatt** *n* (*Buch*) end paper; fly-leaf; ~~**gerät** *n* converter; *radio* adapter; (*Film*) head; ~~**linse** *f* front (*od* supplementary) lens; ~~**papier** *n* book lining paper; ~**sätzlich** *a* intentional, designed, deliberate, wil(l)ful, premeditated; ~~*er Mord* premeditated murder; ~~*e Beschädigung* sabotage.

vor|schalten *tr el* to connect in series, *tech* to add; ~**schaltwiderstand** *m* series resistance, rheostat resistance; ~**schau** *f film* trailer, preview, *Am* prevue; ~**schein** *m* appearance; *zum* ~~ *kommen* to come to light, to appear, to emerge; *zum* ~~ *bringen* to bring to light, to produce; ~**schicken** *tr* to send to the front, to send forward; ~**schieben** *irr tr* to push forward, to shove forward; (*Riegel*) to slip, to bolt; *tech* to feed; (*Entschuldigung*) to pretend, to plead as an excuse; *e-n Riegel* ~~ *fig* to obviate, to prevent; ~**schießen** *irr tr* to advance, to lend (money); ~**schiff** *n* forecastle; ~**schlag** *m* proposal; *Am* proposition; (*Anregung*) suggestion; (*Empfehlung*) recommendation; (*Antrag*) motion; (*Metall*) flux, fusion; (*Buch*) blank space on the first page *auf meinen* ~~ at my suggestion; *Vorschläge ausarbeiten* to draw up proposals; (*Anerbieten*) offer; *mus* grace-note; ~**schlagen** *irr tr* to propose, to propound, to suggest; (*anbieten*) to offer; (*Antrag*) to move (a resolution); (*empfehlen*) to recommend; ~**schlaghammer** *m* sledge hammer; ~**schlußrunde** *f sport* semi-final; ~**schneidebrett** *n* trencher; ~**schneidemesser** *n* carving-knife; ~**schneiden** *irr tr* (*bei Tische*) to carve; ~**schneider** *m* carver; *tech* (wire) cutter; taper tap; ~**schnell** *a* precipitate, hasty, rash; ~**schreiben** *irr tr* to set a copy of; (*anordnen*) to prescribe, to order, to command, to direct; (*im einzelnen*) to specify; (*e-e Grenze setzen*) to limit; (*gebieten*) to dictate (to); ~~ *lassen* to take orders; ~**schreiten** *irr itr* to step forward, to advance; (*weitergehen*) to march on.

Vorschrift *f* copy(-head); (*ärztliche*) prescription; (*Befehl*) order, command; (*Anweisung*) direction, instruction; (*genaue Angabe*) specification; (*Richtschnur*) rule, precept; (*Verordnung*) decree, regulation; (*Muß*~~) mandatory regulation; (*Soll*~~) guidance rule, recommendable rule; (*Kann*~~) discretionary regulation; *technische* ~~*en* specifications *pl*, instructions *pl*; ~**smäßig** *a* as prescribed, according to regulations (*od* instructions); (*formell*) in due form; ~~*e Länge* regulation length; ~**swidrig** *a* contrary to regulations.

Vor|schub *m* assistance, aid, support, furtherance; *tech* feed, traverse, conveyance; *jdm* ~~ *leisten* to help, to assist, to further, *jur* to (aid and) abet; ~~ *geben* (*tech*) to feed; ~**schuh** *m* upper leather, vamp; ~**schuhen** *tr* to new-front, to re-vamp; ~**schulalter** *n* pre-school age; ~**schule** *f* preparatory school, *Am fam* prep school; elementary course; ~**schuß** *m* money advanced, advance, deposit; (*auf Lohn*) advance against wages; (*für den Rechtsanwalt*) retaining fee; *jdm* ~~ *geben* to grant an advance; ~~**dividende** *f* interim dividend; ~~**zahlung** *f* payment in advance; ~**schützen** *tr* to pretend, to plead; ~**schützung** *f* pretence, excuse; ~**schwatzen** *tr* to prattle about (to); ~**schweben** *itr: jdm* ~~ to be present in o.'s mind; to have a notion (*od* dim recollection) of; ~**schwindeln** *tr: jdm etw* ~~ to humbug s. o. about; to tell lies (to).

vor|sehen *irr tr* to foresee, to consider; (*zuweisen*) to earmark for, to assign for, to mark out; (*planen*) to plan, to set down definitely, *Am* to schedule; (*sorgen*) to provide for; *r* to take care, to take heed, to be careful; (*sich schützen*) to guard (against), to beware (of); ~*gesehen!* take care! look out! ~**sehung** *f* providence; (*Gott*) Providence.

vorsetzen *tr* to put forward; to place before, to set before; (*Nahrungsmittel*) to serve; (*Silbe*) to prefix; (*e-m andern*) to set over; (*anbieten*) to offer; (*vornehmen*) to resolve upon, to intend, to determine (to), to propose (to o. s.).

Vorsicht *f* caution, prudence; (*Voraussicht*) foresight; providence; (~*smaßregel*) precaution; (*Sorgfalt*) care; (*Besonnenheit*) discretion; (*auf Kisten*) with care! ~*!* take care! look out! watch out! beware! ~, *Stufe!* mind the step! *mit* ~ *hinnehmen* to discount; ~**ig** *a* cautious, careful, prudent; *fam* cagey; ~**shalber** *adv* as a precaution; ~**smaßregel** *f* precautionary measure, precaution; safety order.

Vor|signal *n rail* warning signal, outer marking signal; ~**silbe** *f gram* prefix; ~**singen** *irr tr* to sing to; *itr* to lead (the choir); ~**sintflutlich** *a* antediluvian; ~**sitz** *m* presidency, chairmanship, the chair; *den* ~~ *führen* to be in the chair, to preside; *den* ~~ *übernehmen* to take the chair; *unter dem* ~~ *von* under the chairmanship of, with . . . in the chair; ~**sitzende(r)**, ~**sitzer** *m* chairman, president, *Am oft* chair; *f* chairwoman; *das Wort an den* ~~*n richten* to address the chair; *den* ~~*n unterstützen* to support the chair; ~**sorge** *f* care; providence, foresight; provision (against), precaution; ~~ *treffen* to take precautions; ~~**en** *itr* to provide (for), to make provisions (for), to take care (that); to take precautions; ~**sorglich** *a* provident, careful; *adv* as a precaution; ~**spann** *m* relay, trace horses *pl*; (*Film* leader; *typ* label; ~**spannen** *tr* to put horses (to); *el* to bias; to stretch in front of; *e-e Lokomotive* ~~ to put an additional locomotive to; ~**speise** *f* hors d'œuvre, appetizer, entree, relish; ~**spiegeln** *tr* to pretend (to); (*täuschen*) to deceive, to simulate; (*falsche Hoffnungen erwecken*) to awake false hopes; *jdm etw* ~~ to delude s. o. with false hopes; ~**spiegelung** *f* pretence, sham; (*Täuschung*) deceiving, shamming; ~~ *falscher Tatsachen* misrepresentation of facts, false pretences; ~**spiel** *n* prelude; *theat* introductory piece, curtain raiser; (*auf der Orgel*) voluntary; (*zur Oper*) overture; *sport* prelim; ~**spielen** *tr* to prelude; *jdm etw* ~~ to play to; *theat* to audition for; ~**sprechen** *irr tr* to teach s. o. how to pronounce a word; to pronounce to; *itr bei jdm* ~~ to call on, to drop in (*bei* at, upon, on); ~**springen** *irr itr* to leap forward; (*hervorragen*) to project, to protrude, to be prominent, to be salient, to jut out; ~~**d** *a* projecting; prominent; (*Augen*) *Am* pop-eyed; (*Winkel*) salient; ~**sprung** *m arch* projection; (*Vorteil*) advantage (*über* of); *sport* head start, lead; (*Sims*) ledge; (*Brüstung*) shoulder; (*Bosse*) boss; (*Überhang*) overhang; (*Zapfen*) tenon; *in der ersten Runde hatte er 10 m* ~~ he was in the lead by ten meters in the first lap.

Vor|stadt *f* suburb; ~~**bewohner(in)**, ~**städter(in** *f*) *m* suburban, suburbanite; ~**stadtjargon** *m* suburbanese; ~**städtisch** *a* suburban.

Vorstand *m* board of directors, directory, directorate, managing committee, executive committee; board of trustees; (*Person*) head, principal, director; chairman of the board; ~~**smitglied** *n* member of the executive board; managing director; ~~**ssitzung** *f* meeting of the executive board.

vorsteck|en *tr* to put before; (*Nadel*) to pin on; *sich ein Ziel* ~~ to propose to o. s. an aim; ~**nadel** *f* breast (*od* scarf)-pin, *Am* stickpin; ~**splint** *m* cotter split pin.

vorsteh|en *irr itr* (*hervorragen*) to project, to protrude; (*vorangehen*) to precede; (*vertreten*) to represent (a firm); (*leiten*) to be at the head of; to administer, to manage, to direct ~**end** *adv* protruding, prominent; last, above, preceding, aforesaid, pending; ~**er** *m* director, manager, principal, chief, superintendent; (*Schule*) head-master, *Am* principal; ~~**drüse** *f* prostate gland; ~**hund** *m* pointer; (*langhaariger*) setter.

vorstell|en *tr* to put forward, to put ahead, to place in front of; (*Uhr*) to put on, to set ahead; (*einführen*) to introduce, to present; (*unterbreiten*) to submit; (*darstellen*) to represent; (*bedeuten*) to mean, to signify; (*erläutern*) to make clear, to explain; (*darstellen*) to represent, to act; (*hinstellen*) to pose (*als* as); (*verkörpern*) to personate, to play; (*anschaulich zeigen*) to demonstrate; (*hinweisen*) to point out s. th. to s. o.; (*mahnen*) to remonstrate, to protest, to expostulate (with); *r* to realize, to conceive, to imagine, to fancy, to suppose, *Am* to envision; to picture; to think; (*sich bekannt machen*) to introduce o. s. to; *stell dir vor!* fancy that! *darf ich Ihnen Herrn X.* ~~ allow me to introduce Mr. X., *Am* I'd like you to meet Mr. X.; ~**ig** *a:* ~~ *werden* to present a case (*od* petition) to s. o.; to protest; ~**ung** *f theat* performance, show; (*Gedanke*) conception, idea, notion, imagination; (*Bild*) picture; representation; (*Einführung*) introduction, presentation; (*Einspruch*) remonstrance, expostulation; (*Vorhaltung*) representation; (*Darlegung*) demonstration, display; (*Unterredung*) interview; *räumliche* ~~ impression of space; ~~**svermögen** *n* conceptual (*od* imaginative) power.

Vor|stoß *m* (*Litze*) edging; (*Uniform*) piping; (*Ziegel*) lap; (*Baukunst*) eking-piece, projection; *mil* (*Angriff*) attack, drive, advance, push, dash; (*Sport*) rush; ~**stoßen** *irr tr* to push forward; *itr* to advance suddenly; (*Saum*) to edge; ~**strafe** *f* previous conviction; **~~nregister** *n* punishment record; **~strecken** *tr* to stretch forward; (*Hals*) to protrude; (*Geld*) to lend, to advance; *tech* to rough down, to bloom, to break down; **~studie** *f* preliminary study; **~stufe** *f* first step; (*Anfangsgründe*) first elements *pl*; primer; *el* input stage; **~~nschalter** *m* protection switch with resistance; **~stürmen** *itr* to assault, to rush forward; **~synchronisieren** *tr* to prescore.

Vor|tag *m* day before; **~~sanmeldung** *f* carried-forward call; **~tanzen** *itr* to dance before s. o.; to lead off the dance; **~tänzer(in** *f*) *m* leader of a dance; **~täuschen** *tr* to simulate, to mislead, to feign; to delude, to deceive; to make believe, to pretend, to put on.

Vorteil *m* advantage; (*Nutzen*) benefit, interest; (*Gewinn*) profit, gain; (*Kniff*) knack; (*Tennis*) (ad)vantage; *~ bringen* to be advantageous; *~ ziehen* to profit by, to turn to account; *großen ~ ziehen aus* to derive great benefit from; *zu Ihrem ~* in your interest; *er weiß, wo sein ~ liegt* he knows on which side his bread is buttered; *ungerechtfertigter ~* privilege, franchises *pl*, *Am sl* graft; *nach zwei Seiten seinen ~ wahrnehmen Am sl* to whip-saw; *Vor- u. Nachteile kennen* to know the ins and outs; **~haft** *a* advantageous; profitable; lucrative (*für* to); beneficial; remunerative; favo(u)rable; *~~ aussehen* to look o.'s best.

Vortrab *m* vanguard.

Vortrag *m* paper, essay, address, speech, performance; (*Vortragsweise*) delivery, utterance; (*Gedicht*) recitation; (*~sart*) delivery, enunciation, elocution, *Am* diction; *mus* execution; (*Vorlesung*) discourse, lecture; (*Bericht*) report, statement; *radio* talk; *com* balance carried forward; *e-n ~ halten über* to read a paper on; to (give a) lecture; **~en** *irr tr* to carry forward; (*Gedicht*) to recite, to declaim; (*Rede*) to lecture on; *mus* to execute, to perform, to play; (*berichten*) to report on (to); (*Meinung*) to express (o.'s opinion); (*vorschlagen*) to propose, to submit; (*Rede*) to deliver; *den Saldo ~~* to carry forward the balance; **~ende(r)** *m* lecturer; speaker; performer; **~skunst** *f* art of reciting (*od* lecturing *od* delivery); **~skünstler** *m* elocutionist; *mus* executant, performer; **~~ssaal** *m* lecture hall, *Am* auditorium; **~stisch** *m* lecture table.

vor|trefflich *a* excellent, exquisite, splendid, admirable; **~~keit** *f* excellence, superiority; **~treiben** *irr tr* to drive; *e-n Stollen ~~* to drive a gallery on; **~treten** *irr itr* to step forth, to come forward; (*vorragen*) to project, to protrude; **~trieb** *m* propulsion, forward thrust, positive drive; **~~sdüse** *f* propulsion nozzle; **~~sgeschwindigkeit** *f* forward speed; **~~skraft** *f* propulsive force; **~tritt** *m* precedence; *jdm den ~~ lassen* to give precedence to; *den ~~ haben Am* to rank; *unter ~~* preceded by; **~trupp** *m* vanguard; advance unit; **~turner** *m* leader of a gym squad, team leader.

vorüber *adv* along, past, by, over; (*zeitlich*) past, over, gone, after; **~fahren** *irr itr* to go past, to go by; *~~ an* to drive past (*od* by); **~gehen** *irr itr* to pass; (*räumlich*) to pass (*od* go by), to go past; (*nicht beachten*) to pass over, to pass by, to neglect; (*zu Ende gehen*) to pass away, to be over; to cease, to stop; **~gehend** *a* passing, transitory, temporary; (*schnell*) transient; **~~e(r)** *m* passer-by; **~ziehen** *irr itr* to march past; (*Gewitter*) to pass.

Vor|übung *f* previous exercise, initiatory lesson; **~untersuchung** *f* preliminary examination; *jur* preliminary inquiry; **~urteil** *n* prejudice, preconception, bias; *ein ~~ haben gegen* to be prejudiced against, to have a prejudice against; **~~sfrei** *a* unprejudiced, impartial, unbias(s)ed; **~~svoll** *a* prejudiced.

Vor|väter *pl* ancestors *pl*, forefathers *pl*, progenitors *pl*; **~verdichten** *tr* to supercharge, **~verdichter** *m* supercharger, compressor; **~verfahren** *n* preliminary procedure; **~verkauf** *m* advance sale; *theat* booking in advance; *im ~~ zu haben* bookable; **~~sstelle** *f* booking-office; **~verlegen** *tr* to advance; *mil* (*Feuer*) to lift (fire); **~verlegt** *a* advanced; **~verstärker** *m* input amplifier; **~versuch** *m* preliminary test; **~vertrag** *m* provisional agreement; **~vorgestern** *adv* three days ago; **~vorig** *a* last but one; penultimate; **~vorletzt** *a* last but two.

vor|wagen *r* to venture forward; **~wahl** *f* preliminary election, *Am* primary; *tele* preselection; *radio* assigned frequency; **~wähler** *m tele* preselector, individual line switch; *mot* preselector gear; **~walten** *itr* to prevail, to predominate; **~wand** *m* pretext, pretence, *Am* pretense, plea, excuse, subterfuge; *unter dem ~~* on the plea of, under the pretence; *unter dem ~~e* under pretence of; *zum ~~ nehmen* to make s. th. a pretext; **~wärmen** *tr* to preheat; **~wärmer** *m* preheater, economizer, water-feed heater; **~warnung** *f* (*Luftschutz*) early warning, alert signal; **~wärts** *adv* forward, onward, on, ahead; *~~!* go on! go ahead! forward! **~~bewegung** *f* forward motion; *film* active stroke; **~~bringen** *irr tr* to promote, to advance; **~~gang** *m* forward speed; **~~gehen** *irr itr* to advance, to go on, to progress; **~~kommen** *irr itr fig* to get on, to prosper; to get ahead; (*räumlich*) to make headway; **~~schalten** *tr* to step on, to step up (to); **~~strebend** *a* going-ahead; **~~treiben** *irr tr* to propel, to impel; **~we'g** *adv* before, beforehand; **~~nehmen** *tr* to anticipate, to forestall; **~~nehmend** *a* anticipatory; **~weihnachtlich** *a Am* pre-Yule; **~weisen** *irr tr* to show, to produce, to exhibit; **~welt** *f* former ages *pl*; prehistoric world; **~~lich** *a* primeval; **~werfen** *irr tr* to throw forward (*od* before); to throw to; (*tadeln*) to reproach, to upbraid with, to blame for, to throw up to; *fam* to cast s. th. in s. o.'s teeth, to tax s. o. with; **~werk** *n* farm; outwork; **~wiegen** *irr itr* to predominate, to prevail, to preponderate; **~~d** *a* preponderant, predominant; *adv* for the most part, especially, chiefly, mostly; **~wind** *m* head wind; **~wissen** *n* prescience, previous knowledge; *ohne jds ~~* unknown to s. o.; **~witz** *m* pertness, forwardness; (*Neugier*) curiosity, inquisitiveness; **~~ig** *a* pert, forward; inquisitive, prying; **~wort** *n* preface, foreword; *gram* preposition; **~wurf** *m* reproach, blame, reproof, *Am* scorcher; (*Gegenstand*) object; (*e-s Dramas*) subject, motif; *Vorwürfe machen* to blame (for), to throw up to, *fam* to cast s. th. in s. o.'s teeth; **~~sfrei** *a* free from blame, irreproachable; **~~svoll** *a* reproachful.

vor|zählen *tr* to enumerate; **~zeichen** *n* omen, prognostic, symptom; *mus* signature, accidental; *math* sign; *med* preliminary symptom; **~zeichnen** *tr* to draw before; to trace out; *mus* to prefix; (*angeben*) to indicate, to mark; **~zeichner** *m* tracer; **~zeichnung** *f* drawing, pattern; *mus* signature; **~zeigen** *tr* to show, to produce; (*zeigen, darlegen*) to exhibit, to display; (*Wechsel*) to present; **~zeiger** *m* bearer, presenter; **~zeigung** *f* showing, producing, production; exhibition; presentation; **~zeit** *f* remote antiquity; times of old, olden times; **~~en** *adv* in olden times, formerly; once upon a time; **~zeitig** *a* precocious; premature; **~ziehen** *irr tr* to draw forth; *fig* to prefer; **~zimmer** *n* antechamber, anteroom; **~zug** *m* preference; (*Vorteil*) advantage; (*Überlegenheit*) superiority; (*Vorrang*) priority (to); (*gute Eigenschaft*) merit, good qualities *pl*; (*Vorzüglichkeit*) excellence; (*Vorrecht*) privilege; (*Vortritt*) precedence; *rail* relief train; *den ~~ haben* to surpass, to excel; **~~saktie** *f* preference share; *Am* preferred stock; **~~sbedingungen** *f pl* preferential terms *pl*; **~~sbehandlung** *f* preferential treatment; **~~sgläubiger** *m* preferential creditor; **~~spreis** *m* special price, preferential rate; **~~srecht** *n* priority; privilege; **~~srente** *f* preference rent, priority-pension; **~~sweise** *adv* preferably, chiefly, by preference; **~~szoll** *m* preferential tariff; **~züglich** *a* excellent, superior, exquisite; *adv* (*vornehmlich*) especially, above all, particularly; **~~keit** *f* excellence, superiority; (*Auserlesenheit*) choiceness; **~zündung** *f* premature ignition, spark advance.

Vot|ivbild *n* votive picture; **~ivkirche** *f* votive church; **~ivtafel** *f* votive tablet; **~um** *n* vote, suffrage.

*

vulgär *a* vulgar, common.

Vulkan *m* volcano; **~ausbruch** *m* eruption; **~faser, ~fiber** *f* vulcanized fibre; **~isation** *f* vulcanization; **~isch** *a* volcanic, igneous; **~isierapparat** *m* vulcanizer; **~isieren** *tr* to vulcanize; (*Gummi*) to cure; *fam* (*Reifen runderneuern*) to recap; to retread; **~isierung** *f* vulcanization; **~ismus** *m geol* vulcanism, vulcanisity.

W

***W** Abk mit **W** siehe Liste der Abk.*

Waage *f* balance, (a pair of) scales *pl*, scale; (*Brücken~, Tafel~*) weighing machine; (*öffentliche ~*) weigh-house; (*Wasser~*) level; (*für das spezifische Gewicht von Flüssigkeiten*) hydrometer; *astr* the Scales *pl*, the Libra, the Balance; *sport* horizontal position (on parallel bars); *auf die ~ legen* to put on the scale; *die ~ halten* to be a match for; (*e-r Sache*) to counterbalance; **~balken** *m* (scale-)beam; swingletree; **~bühne** *f* weighing platform; **~gegengewicht** *n* counterpoise; **~meister** *m* inspector of weights and measures; **~recht** *a* horizontal, level; **~~bombenwurf** *m* level-flight bombardment; **~~einstellung** *f* horizontal adjustment; **~schale** *f* balance pan, scale.

wabbelig *a* flabby.

Wabe *f* honeycomb; **~nartig, ~nförmig** *a* honeycombed, pitted; **~nhonig** *m* comb honey; **~nkühler** *m mot* honeycomb radiator.

wabern *itr* to flicker.

wach *a*, *pred* awake, astir; (*lebhaft*) brisk, alive, quick, animated, stirring; (*auf der Hut*) on the alert; *ganz ~* wide awake; *~ werden* to awake; **~bataillon** *n* guards *pl*, guard battalion; **~boot** *n* patrol vessel; **~buch** *n* guard book; **~dienst** *m* guard duty; *~~ haben* to be on watch; **~e** *f* watch, guard; (*Wachlokal*) guard-house, guardroom; (*Polizei~~*) police station; (*Feuer~~* fire-guard; (*Wächter*) watchman; (*Schild~~*) sentry, sentinel; *~~ haben* to keep watch, to be on guard; *~~ stehen* to be on duty, to stand sentry, *Am* to stand guard; *~ stehen vor e-m Gebäude* to keep the door of ...; *auf ~~ ziehen* to mount guard; *die ~ ablösen* to relieve the guard; *von der ~~ kommen* to come off duty; *die ~~ herausrufen* to turn out the guard; **~en** *itr* to be awake, to remain wake; (*aufpassen*) to watch (*über* over), to keep an eye on; *bei jdm ~~* to sit up with s. o.; **~gebäude** *n* guardhouse; **~habend** *a* on duty; **~~e(r)** *m* commander of the guard; **~hund** *m* watchdog; **~kompanie** *f* guard company; **~lokal** *n* guard-room; **~mann** *m* guard; **~~schaft** *f* guard detail; **~offizier** *m* officer on duty, watch officer; **~posten** *m* sentry (post); **~regiment** *n* guard regiment; **~rufen** *irr tr* to wake; *fig* to call forth, to rouse; **~sam** *a* vigilant, watchful; (*vorsichtig, munter*) alert, wide-awake; (*aufmerksam*) attentive, sharp; *ein ~~es Auge auf etw haben* to keep a watchful eye upon; **~~keit** *f* vigilance; **~traum** *m* day-dream; **~vergehen** *n* negligence while on guard duty; **~vorgesetzte(r)** *m* commander of the guard; **~zeiten** *f pl* hours of duty.

Wacholder *m* juniper; **~baum** *m* juniper-tree; **~beere** *f* juniper-berry; **~branntwein** *m* gin.

Wachs *n* wax; **~abdruck** *m* wax impression; **~bild** *n* wax image; **~draht** *m* wax-insulated wire; **~drüse** *f* ceruminous gland; **~farben** *a* wax-colo(u)red; **~figurenkabinett** *n* waxworks *pl*; **~gelb** *a* wax-yellow; **~kerze** *f* taper, (wax) candle; **~matrize** *f* stencil; **~modell** *n* wax pattern; **~papier** *n* wax paper; **~platte** *f* wax disk, wax master; **~~naufnahme** *f radio* wax master record; **~pauspapier** *n* waxed tracing paper; **~streichhölzchen** *n* wax match, vesta; **~tuch** *n* oilcloth; **~~futteral** *n* case of wax cloth; **~überzug** *m* wax(y) coating; **~weich** *a* soft like wax.

wachs|en *irr itr* to grow; *fig* to increase, to augment, to extend, to expand; (*quellen*) to swell; (*gedeihen*) to thrive; (*entwickeln*) to develop; (*Wasser*) to rise; *tr* to wax; *ans Herz ~~* to become very attached to, to get fond of; *jdm gewachsen sein* to be a match for; *e-r Sache gewachsen sein* to be equal to a task; *er ist mir über den Kopf gewachsen* he's become too much for me; I can't handle him any more; *lassen Sie sich darüber keine grauen Haare ~~* don't let that give you any grey hair; **~en** *n* growth; fanning-out; swelling; waxing; **~~d** *a* growing, increasing; **~tum** *n* growth; *fig* increase; *im ~~ hindern* to stunt; *im ~~ zurückgeblieben* undersized; **~~sfördernd** *a* growth-promoting; **~~sgeschwindigkeit** *f* rate of growth; **~~shemmend** *a* growth-checking, growth-inhibiting; **~~sspitze** *f* strategic outpost, expansion base; **~~svorgang** *m* growth process.

wächsern *a* wax; *fig* waxen, waxy.

Wacht *f* guard; **~dienst** *m* guard-duty; **~feuer** *n* watch-fire; **~habend** *a* on duty; **~mannschaft** *f* guard, picket; **~meister** *m* sergeant-major; *Am* first sergeant; **~stube** *f* guard room; **~truppe** *f* guard detachment; **~turm** *m* guard turret.

Wächte *f* (*Schnee*) (snow) cornice.

Wachtel *f* quail; **~hund** *m* spaniel.

Wächter *m* watchman; *mar* look-out man; (*Hüter*) keeper, warder; (*Hausmeister*) care-taker; *el* controller; **~kontrolluhr** *f* watchman's control clock, telltale watch.

wackel|ig *a* tottering, shaky; (*Zahn*) loose; (*Möbel*) rickety; (*schwankend*) wabbly; **~kontakt** *m el* loose contact, variable connection; **~n** *itr* to totter, to shake; *mit dem Kopf ~n* to shake o.'s head; (*wanken*) to rock; (*taumeln*) to reel, to totter, to stagger; (*schwanken*) to wabble, to wobble; (*hin u. her ~~*) to wiggle; (*wedeln*) to wag; (*Zähne*) to be loose.

wacker *a* gallant, brave; (*anständig*) decent; *adv* bravely; heartily.

Wade *f* calf (of the leg); **~nbein** *n* fibula; peroneal bone; **~nkrampf** *m* cramp in the leg; **~nstrumpf** *m* long stocking.

*

Waffe *f* weapon, arm; *blanke ~* side-arm; (*~ngattung*) arm, branch of service; *~n u. Gerät* ordnance material; *unter den ~n stehen* to be under arms; *zu den ~n rufen* to call to arms; *zu den ~n!* at arms! *zu den ~n greifen* to take up arms; **~namt** *n* ordnance department; **~nausrüstung** *f* armament; **~nbehälter** *m* (*Abwurf*) *aero* container; **~nbruder** *m* brother in arms, comrade; ally; **~ndienst** *m* military service; **~nfabrik** *f* (manu)factory of arms, *Am* armory; **~nfähig** *a* fit to bear arms; **~nfarbe** *f* colo(u)r on uniform; **~nfeldwebel** *m* technical sergeant; **~nführung** *f* tactics and technique; **~ngang** *m* passage of arms; armed conflict; **~ngattung** *f* arm, branch of the service; **~ngebrauch** *m* use of arms; **~ngewalt** *f* force of arms; **~nglück** *n* fortune of war; **~nhilfsprogramm** *n* arms-aid program; **~ninspektion** *f* ordnance inspectorate; **~nlager** *n* ordnance depot; **~nlehrgang** *m* special training course; **~nlos** *a* unarmed; **~nmeister** *m* ordnance sergeant, armo(u)rer-artificer official; **~~ei** *f* maintenance section; armory ordnance shop; **~nöl** *n* gun oil; **~noffizier** *m mil mar* ordnance officer; *aero Am* armament officer; **~pflege** *f* gun maintenance; **~nplatz** *m* large fortress; **~nrock** *m* uniform blouse, tunic; **~nruhe** *f* truce, suspension of hostilities; **~nsammelstelle** *f* salvage dump; **~nschein** *m* licence to carry fire-arms, *Am* gun-license; **~nschmied** *m* armo(u)rer; **~nschmuck** *m* full armo(u)r; **~nschmuggel** *m* gun-running; **~nschule** *f* branch-of-service school for young officers and officer aspirants; **~nstillstand** *m* armistice; truce; **~~sbedingungen** *f pl* armistice terms *pl*; **~nstreckung** *f* surrender, capitulation; **~ntat** *f* feat of arms; **~ntragend** *a* bearing arms; **~nträger** *m* arms bearer; **~nüberlegenheit** *f* superiority of arms and equipment; **~nübung** *f* military exercise; **~n u. Gerätenachweis** *m* property book; **~nunteroffizier** *m* ordnance sergeant; **~nwart** *m* armo(u)rer-artificer; **~nwerkstatt** *f* ordnance shop; **~nwirkung** *f* effectiveness of a weapon.

Waffel *f* (*in Fett gebacken*) waffle; (*Eis~*) wafer; **~eisen** *n* waffle-iron.

waffnen *tr* to arm.

wäg|bar *a* ponderable, weighable; **~en** *irr tr* to weigh; *fig* to consider.

Wage *f siehe* **Waage**.

Wag|ehals *m* dare-devil; **~(e)halsig** *a* reckless, foolhardy, daring; **~~keit** *f* foolhardiness, daredevilry; **~emut** *m* daring, gallantry, **~en** *tr* to risk, to venture; (*aufs Spiel setzen*) to hazard, to jeopard(ize), to stake; (*sich getrauen*) to dare; (*sich erdreisten*) to presume; (*es darauf ankommen lassen*) to take a chance; to trust, to luck; *wer wagt, gewinnt* nothing ventured, nothing gained: *sich an e-e Arbeit ~~ Am sl* to take a whack at a job; *gewagt* daring, risky; **~estück** *n* risk, dangerous enterprise; **~nis** *n* risk, venture, hazardous enterprise, jeopardy.

Wagen *m* carriage; (*Kutsche*) coach; *mot* car, auto(mobile); (*Last~*) lorry, truck; (*Taxi*) taxi, cab; (*Karren*) cart; (*Fracht~*) wag(g)on; (*Gefährt*) vehicle, conveyance; (*Gepäck~, Möbel~*) van; *rail* railway carriage, *Am* railroad car; *geschlossener ~* (*mot*) limousine; closed lorry, *Am* truck; *der Große ~* the Plough (*Am* Plow), Charles's Wain, *fam* the (Big) Dipper; **~abteil** *n rail* compartment; **~achse** *f* car axle; **~aufbau** *m* car body; **~auslösetaste** *f* (*Schreibmaschine*) carriage-release key; **~bauer** *m* carriage builder; **~burg** *f* barricade of wag(g)ons; laager; **~decke** *f* tarpaulin, tilt; (*um sich zuzudecken*) carriage rug, *Am* lap-robe; **~deichsel** *f* wag(g)on tongue; **~einstellhalle** *f* garage; **~feder** *f* wag(g)on spring; **~feststeller** *m* carriage lock; **~fett** *n* axle grease; **~führer** *m el* driver, *Am* motorman; **~gestell** *n* car frame; **~halle** *f* garage, car shed;

~halteplatz *m* wag(g)on stop; **~heber** *m* (lifting) jack; (*Schreibmaschine*) carriage lever; **~kasten** *m* car body, *Am* wagon-box; **~kipper** *m* car dumper; **~kolonne** *f* vehicular convoy; **~kran** *m* derrick-wag(g)on crane; **~kuppelung** *f* railway coupling; **~ladung** *f* wag(g)on-load, truckload, *Am* carload; **~laterne** *f* carriage lantern; **~mangel** *m rail* shortage of rolling-stock; **~meister** *m* wag(g)on-inspector; **~park** *m* wag(g)on park, car park, fleet; **~plane** *f* tarpaulin, tilt, awning; **~rad** *n* cart wheel; **~schlag** *m* carriage-door, car-door; **~schmiere** *f* carriage grease; lubricant; **~schuppen** *m* car shed; **~spur** *f* wheel track, rut; **~tritt** *m* step; **~umlauf** *m* wag(g)on circulation; **~untergestell** *n* chassis, car truck; **~vermieter** *m* car hire operator; **~vermietungsdienst** *m* (motor) car hire service; **~wäscher** *m Am* car-washer; **~winde** *f* jack; **~zug** *m* train (of carriages).

Waggon *m* wagon; truck; railway carriage, *Am* railroad car.

Wagner *m* cartwright.

Wahl *f* choice; (*Auslese*) selection; (*freie ~*) option; *parl* election; (*~stimme*) vote, voting; (*~ zwischen zwei Dingen*) alternative; *engere ~* second ballot; *in die engere ~ kommen* to be on the short list; *e-e ~ treffen* to make o.'s choice; *vor die ~ stellen* to let s. o. choose; *angefochtene ~* disputed (*Am* contested) election; **~berechtigt** *a* entitled to vote, eligible; **~bericht** *m* return; **~beteiligung** *f* voting; **~bezirk** *m* constituency, division, *Am* district; *sich um seinen ~~ bekümmern* to nurse o.'s constituency, *Am* to look after o.'s fences; **~ergebnis** *n* poll, election returns *pl*; **~fach** *n* optional (subject), *Am* elective (subject); **~fähig** *a* (*aktiv*) having a vote; (*passiv*) eligible; **~~keit** *f* franchise; eligibility; **~feldzug** *m* canvass, *Am* campaign; **~fonds** *m* campaign-fund, *Am* barrel; **~gang** *m* ballot; **~geometrie** *f*: *~~ treiben* to gerrymander; **~gesetz** *n* electoral law; **~handlung** *f* poll; **~heimat** *f* country of o.'s choice; **~kampf** *m* election contest (*od* campaign); **~kollegium** *n Am* electoral college; **~kommissar** *m* returning officer; **~kreis** *m* constituency, ward, division, *Am* district; **~leiter** *m Am* campaign-manager; **~liste** *f* register of electors; (*Kandidaten*) *Am* ticket, slate; **~lokal** *n* polling station, *Am* polls *pl*, ward-room; **~los** *adv* indiscriminately, at random, haphazardly; without guiding principle; **~mann** *m Am* elector; **~programm** *n* platform, *Am* ticket; **~prüfer** *m* scrutineer; **~prüfung** *f* scrutiny; **~recht** *n* right to vote, franchise; (*passiv*) eligibility; *allgemeines ~~* universal suffrage; **~rede** *f* election speech, *Am* campaign speech; *~~ halten* to electioneer, *Am* to stump; **~redner** *m* stump orator, *Am* campaign-orator, (campaign) spellbinder; **~reform** *f* electoral reform; **~schlacht** *f* campaign; **~spruch** *m* motto, device; **~stimme** *f* vote; **~tag** *m* election-day; **~urne** *f* ballot-box; **~versammlung** *f* election meeting, electoral assembly, *Am* caucus; **~verwandtschaft** *f* elective affinity; congeniality; **~vorschlag** *m* party-ticket; **~weise** *adv* at will, as one chooses; *tele* selective; **~zelle** *f* polling-booth, voting-booth; **~zettel** *m* voting-paper, ballot.

wähl|bar *a* eligible; **~~keit** *f* eligibility; **~betrieb** *m tele* dial service; **~en** *tr* to choose, to single out, to make a choice; (*sich festlegen auf*) to fix upon, to decide upon, to settle upon; (*annehmen*) to adopt, to take up, to embrace, *fam* to go in for; (*vorziehen*) to prefer, to have rather, to like better, to think fit; *parl* to elect, to vote, to poll, to ballot; to go to the polls; (*auslesen*) to select, to pick out; (*bestimmen*) to appoint; *tele* to dial; **~er** *m* elector, voter, constituent, *Am nur* voter; (*fluktuierender*) *Am* floater; *tele* switch, dial, selector; **~~amt** *n tele* dial central office; **~~anlage** *f tele* selector plant; **~~betrieb** *m* dial service; **~~in** *f* electress; **~~isch** *a* particular, fastidious; choosy; **~~liste** *f* poll, electoral register (*od* poll); **~~raum** *m tele* switchroom; **~~scheibe** *f tele* selector dial; **~~schaft** *f* body of electors, constituency.

Wahn *m* delusion, illusion; (*Irrtum*) error; (*Täuschung*) fallacy, chimera, hallucination; (*eingebildete Vorstellung*) fancy; (*Verrücktheit*) madness, craziness, folly; **~bild** *n* chimera, phantom, delusion; **~sinn** *m* insanity; (*Raserei*) delirium, frenzy; (*Verrücktheit*) madness, craziness; **~~ig** *a* insane, mad, crazy (*vor* with); (*rasend*) frantic; *fam* terrific; **~~ige(r)** *m* madman; (*f*) madwoman; **~vorstellung** *f* fixed idea; **~witz** *m* insanity; madness; (*Torheit*) absurdity.

wähnen *itr* to fancy, to think, to believe, to imagine, to suppose.

wahr *a* true, sincere; (*echt, wirklich*) real, genuine; (*eigentlich*) proper, veritable, real; (*richtig*) correct; *nicht ~?* is it not so? don't you think so? *~ ist, daß* the truth is that; *es ist kein Wort daran ~* there is not word of truth in the whole story; *~ machen* to carry into effect; *~ werden* to come true; *nicht ~ haben wollen* not to admit s. th.; *das Wahre* the true, the real, the truth; *so ~ ich lebe!* as sure as I live; *so ~ mir Gott helfe!* So help me God! **~en** *tr* (*schützen*) to keep, to preserve, to take care of, to look after, to watch over; (*aufrechterhalten*) to keep up, to maintain; (*verteidigen*) to defend, to guard; *den Schein ~~* to keep up appearances; **~haft, ~haftig** *a* true, correct; (*echt*) genuine; (*wirklich*) real, actual; (*wahrheitsliebend*) veracious; (*wahrheitsgemäß*) truthful; (*aufrichtig*) sincere; *adv* truly, really, actually; **~haftigkeit** *f* sincerity, veracity; **~heit** *f* truth; *jdm die ~~ sagen* to give s. o. a piece of o.'s mind, *fam* to tell s. o. off; *ungeschminkte ~~* unvarnished truth; **~~sgetreu** *a* truthful, true; *adv* truly, in accordance with the true facts; **~~sliebe** *f* love of truth; **~~sliebend** *a* truthful, veracious; **~~swidrig** *a* contrary to the truth; **~lich** *adv* truly, in truth; verily; surely; *interj* upon my word; **~nehmbar** *a* noticeable, perceptible, discernible; *mit dem Auge ~~* visible; *mit dem Ohr ~~* audible; *durch Fühlen nicht ~~* impalpable; **~~keit** *f* perceptibility, noticeability, observability; visibility, discernability; audibility; **~nehmen** *irr tr* to perceive, to observe, to notice, to sense; (*benützen*) to make use of, to avail o. s. of, to attend to, to profit by; (*Interessen*) to look after, to protect; **~nehmung** *f* observation; perception; sensation; (*Schutz*) protection, maintenance; attention; **~~svermögen** *n* perceptive faculty; power of observation; **~sagen** *tr* to prophesy, to predict, to divine; (*aus Karten*) to tell fortunes; *sich ~~ lassen* to have o.'s fortunes told; **~sager** *m*, **~~in** *f* fortune-teller; soothsayer; **~sagerei, ~sagung** *f* fortune-telling; prophecy; prediction; **~scheinlich** *a* probable, likely; *ich gehe ~~* (*Am*) I'm apt to go; **~~keit** *f* probability, likelihood; plausibility; *aller ~~keit nach* in all probability; *es ist mit aller ~~keit anzunehmen, daß* the chances are that; **~~keitsrechnung** *f* theory of probabilities, probability calculus; **~spruch** *m* verdict; **~ung** *f* preservation, maintenance; (*Schutz*) protection; **~zeichen** *n* landmark; distinctive sign (*od* mark); (*Anzeichen*) token; (*Vorzeichen*) omen, symptom.

währen *itr* to last, to continue; **~d** *prp* during; in the course of; *jur* pending; *conj* while, whilst; (*bei Gegensätzen*) whereas.

Währung *f* currency; standard, value; *harte* (*weiche*) *~* hard (soft) currency; **~sabkommen** *n* monetary agreement; **~sabwertung** *f* devaluation; **~sausgleichfonds** *m* exchange equalization fund; **~seinheit** *f* monetary unit; **~sfonds** *m* monetary fund; **~sfrage** *f* currency problem; **~sreform** *f* currency (*od* monetary) reform; **~sschwach** *a* having a soft currency; **~sschwierigkeiten** *f pl* currency difficulties *pl*; **~sstabilisierung** *f* stabilization of currency; **~sumrechnungstabelle** *f* currency-conversion table; **~sumstellung** *f* currency change-over; **~svorteile** *m pl* advantages of exchange; **~szusammenbruch** *m* collapse of currency.

Waise *f* orphan; **~nhaus** *n* orphanage; **~knabe** *m* orphan boy.

Wal, ~fisch *m* whale; **~fang** *m* whaling; **~~flotte** *f* whaling fleet; **~fänger** *m* whaler; **~(fisch)tran** *m* train-oil, *Am* speck; **~rat** *m u. n* spermaceti; **~roß** *n* walrus.

Wald *m* wood, forest; (*klein*) grove; (*Gelände*) woodland; *den ~ vor Bäumen nicht sehen* to miss the wood for the trees; **~arm** *a* destitute of forests; **~baum** *m* forest tree; **~bestand** *m* forest stand; (*Bauholz*) timber; **~blöße** *f* forest clearing; **~boden** *m* soil for forest growth; **~brand** *m* forest fire; **~~bekämpfung** *f* forest fire fighting; **~erdbeere** *f* wild strawberry; **~frevel** *m* mischief done in a wood; **~gebirge** *n* woody mountains *pl*; **~gegend** *f* wooded country; **~gelände** *n* woodland; **~horn** *n* bugle; French horn; **~hüter** *m* forest-keeper, ranger; **~ig** *a* woody, wooded; **~lichtung** *f* clearing, glade; **~meister** *m bot* woodruff; **~rand** *m* edge of the forest; **~reich** *a* well-wooded, rich in forests; **~~tum** *m* abundance of forests; **~säge** *f* wood saw; **~saum** *m* fringe of a wood; **~schlucht** *f* dingle; **~schneise** *f* forest lane, aisle (*od* vista) in a forest, firebreak; **~schnepfe** *f* wood-cock; **~schonung** *f* young forest plantation; **~schrat(t)** *m* forest-sprite; **~ung** *f* woodland, forest; **~weg** *m* forest road; **~wiese** *f* glade; **~wirtschaft** *f* forestry, forest culture.

Walk|e *f* fullery; (*Maschine*) fulling-machine; **~mühle** *f* fulling-mill; **~en** *tr* to full; *fam* to thrash; **~er, ~müller** *m* fuller; **~erde** *f*, **~erton** *m* fulling-clay.

Walküre *f* Valkyrie.

Wall *m mil* rampart; (*Damm*) dam, embankment; (*Deich*) dike; *mar* coast, shore; (*Erde*) mound; **~graben** *m* moat, ditch of rampart.

Wallach *m* gelding.

wall|en *itr* (*kochen*) to boil, to bubble; (*wogen*) to undulate; (*brodeln*) to simmer; (*sich kräuseln*) to flutter; (*e-e Pilgerfahrt machen*) to go on a pilgrimage; (*reisen*) to travel, to wander;

(*erregt sein*) to be agitated; **~fahren** *itr* to go on a pilgrimage; **~fahrer** *m* pilgrim; **~fahrt** *f* pilgrimage; **~~sort** *m* place of pilgrimage; **~ung** *f* boiling, ebulition; simmering; undulation; *fig* agitation, excitement, flutter.
Walmdach *n* hip roof.
Walnuß *f* walnut; **~baum** *m* walnut-tree.
Walstatt *f* battle-field.
walten *itr* to rule, to govern, to dispose; ~ *u. schalten* to govern, to lord it; *Gnade ~ lassen* to show mercy; *das walte Gott!* God grant it! amen! ~ *n* working, rule, government; *das ~ der Vorsehung* the hand of Providence.
Walz|bahn *f* path of rolling; **~bar** *a* rollable; **~~keit** *f* rolling property; **~betrieb** *m* rolling-mill operation; **~blech** *n* rolled sheet, sheet metal; **~e** *f* roller, roll; cylinder, drum; (*Schreibmaschine*) platen; (*in Musikinstrumenten*) record, barrel; **~en** *tr* to roll; to mill; (*zermahlen*) to grind, to crush, to pulverize; *itr* (*tanzen*) to waltz; **~enförmig** *a* cylindrical; **~er** *m* waltz; **~erzeugnis** *n* roller product; **~straße** *f* roll train; **~werk** *n* rolling-mill.
wälz|en *tr* to roll; to turn about; (*wegschieben*) to shove off; *die Schuld auf jdn ~~* to lay the blame upon s. o.; *etw von sich ~~* to release o. s. from s. th.; *r* to roll; to revolve; (*in Wasser*) to wallow; (*im Blute*) to welter; (*sich hin u. her ~~*) to toss; *sich vor Lachen ~~* to be convulsed with laughter, to be rolling; **~er** *m* heavy volume.
Wamme *f* (*des Rindviehs*) dewlap.
Wams *n* jacket, doublet, jerkin.
Wand *f* wall; (*Scheide~*) partition; (*Gefäß*) side; *med* coat; *tech* side, cheek, baffle, panel, screen; *spanische ~* folding-screen; *mit dem Kopf gegen die ~ rennen* to butt o.'s head against a stone wall; **~apparat** *m* wall telephone set; **~arm** *m* wall-bracket; **~bekleidung** *f* wainscot(t)ing, wall facing, panelling; **~belag** *m* wall coating; **~bewurf** *m* plastering; **~dicke** *f* wall thickness; **~fliese** *f* wall flag; **~gestell** *n* wall bracket; **~haken** *m* wall hook; **~kalender** *m* sheet almanac; **~karte** *f* wall map; **~leuchter** *m* sconce, bracket; **~malerei** *f* mural painting; **~pfeiler** *m* pilaster; **~photo** *n* photomural; **~schild** *n* wall sign; **~schirm** *m* folding screen; **~schrank** *m* wall chest; cupboard; *Am* closet; **~spiegel** *m* pier-glass; **~stärke** *f* thickness of wall; **~stecker** *m* wall plug; **~tafel** *f* blackboard; wall diagram; **~täfelung** *f* wainscot(t)ing; **~teppich** *m* hangings *pl*, tapestry; **~uhr** *f* wall-clock; **~ung** *f* wall; thickness; partition; **~waschbecken** *n* wall hand basin.
Wandel *m* mutation, change; alteration; (*Lebens~*) behavio(u)r, conduct, habits *pl*, mode of life; *Handel u. ~* trade and traffic, business, commerce; *~ schaffen* to bring about a change; **~bar** *a* changeable, variable; (*unbeständig*) inconstant; (*launisch*) fickle; (*vergänglich*) perishable; **~~keit** *f* changeableness, inconstancy; **~gang** *m*, **~halle** *f* *parl*, *theat* lobby; *Am parl* cloak-room; **~n** *tr* to change; *itr* to walk, to travel, to wander; *r* to change, to turn into; **~stern** *m* planet.
Wander|arbeiter *m* seasonal (*Am* migratory) worker; **~ausstellung** *f* itinerant (*od* flying) exhibition; **~bewegung** *f* hiking-movement; **~bibliothek** *f* circulating library; **~bühne** *f* travel(l)ing theatre; **~bursche** *m* travel(l)ing journeyman; tramp; **~düne** *f* shifting dune; **~er** *m* travel(l)er, wanderer; hiker; **~geschwindigkeit** *f* speed of travel; velocity of advance; **~heuschrecke** *f* migratory locust; **~jahre** *n pl* years spent in travel; **~leben** *n* roving life; **~lust** *f* wanderlust; **~n** *itr* to wander, to travel, to hike; (*umherschweifen*) to roam; (*Sand*) to shift; (*el Strom*) to creep; (*kriechen*) to crawl; (*verbreiten*) to diffuse; (*Vögel*) to migrate; **~~d** *a* moving, travel(l)ing; running; flying; migratory; **~niere** *f* floating kidney; **~prediger** *m* itinerant preacher; **~preis** *m* challenge trophy; **~ratte** brown rat; **~schaft** *f* travel(l)ing, travels *pl*, tour; *auf ~~* on the tramp; *auf die ~~ gehen* to go on o.'s travels; **~smann** *m* travel(l)er; (*zu Fuß*) wayfarer; **~stab** *m* walking-stick; *den ~~ ergreifen* to set out on o.'s travels; **~tisch** *m tech* platform conveyer; **~trieb** *m* roving spirit; migratory instinct; **~truppe** *f* *theat* strolling players *pl*; **~ung** *f* trip, walking-tour, wandering; excursion; hike; migration; shifting; *tech* creeping, diffusion; conveyance, transfer; **~~sgeschwindigkeit** *f* migration velocity, travel velocity; *tele* crawl, creep; **~welle** *f* moving wave; **~vogel** *m* bird of passage; (*Mensch*) rover; (*Verein*) Ramblers *pl*.
Wandlung *f* change, transformation; *eccl* transsubstantiation.
Wange *f* cheek; *tech* side piece, end piece, frame; **~nbein** *n* cheek bone, zygoma; malar.
Wankel|mut *m* fickleness, inconstancy; **~mütig** *a* fickle, inconstant; *~~ sein* (*Am*) to straddle; **~~keit** *f* fickleness.
wanken *itr* to shake, to totter, to stagger, to reel, to sway; *fig* to be irresolute, to waver; *nicht ~* not to yield; ~ *n* staggering.
wann *conj* when; ~ *immer* when ever; *dann u. ~* now and then; sometimes; *von ~en* whence; *seit ~?* how long? since what time?
Wanne *f* tub; (*Bade~*) bath; *Am* tub; (*Getreide~*) van; (*Bottich*) vat; (*Trog*) trough; (*Behälter*) tank; *aero* underfuselage tunnel; (*Öl~*) *mot* oil sump (*Am* pan); **~nbad** *n* sponge-bath; tub-bath.
Wanst *m* belly, paunch.
Wanten *f pl* shrouds *pl*.
Wanze *f* bug, *Am* bedbug, *sl* chinch.
Wappen *n* (coat of) arms, armorial bearings *pl*; **~bild** *n* heraldic figure; **~buch** *n* armorial; **~herold** *m* herald; **~könig** *m* king-of-arms; **~kunde** *f* heraldry; **~schild** *m* escutcheon; **~schmuck** *m* blazonry; **~spruch** *m* heraldic motto, device; **~tier** *n* heraldic animal.
wappnen *itr* to arm.
Ware *f* (*Artikel*) article; commodity; ware; (*Erzeugnis*) product; make; (*Web~*) fabric; (*Güter*) goods *pl*; (*Börse*) offer; (*Waren*) commodities *pl*; merchandise, *Am* wares *pl*; *~n in Herstellung* goods in process; *verbotene ~n* contraband articles *pl*.
Waren|absatz *m* selling, sale; commodity marketing; **~absatzorganisation** *f* merchandising organization; **~absender** *m* consigner; shipper; **~akkreditiv** *n* commercial letter of credit; **~akzept** *n* trade acceptance; **~angebot** *n* supply of goods; **~aufzug** *m* hoist; *Am* freight-elevator; **~ausfuhr** *f* export(ation) of goods; export trade; **~ausgabe** *f* (*im Laden*) wrapping counter; **~ausgangsbuch** *n* sales ledger; sales journal; **~auslage** *f* display of goods; **~automat** *m* (penny-in-the-) slot-machine; **~ballen** *m* ball (of goods); **~bedarf** *m* want, demand; **~bestand** *m* stock (on *od* in hand); inventory; **~~sanmeldung** *f* declaration of stocks; **~~saufnahme** *f* stock-taking; **~bestellbuch** *n* order book; **~bezeichnung** *f* description of commodities; **~börse** *f* commodity exchange; **~deckung** *f* commodity coverage; **~einfuhr** *f* import(ation of goods); **~eingang** *m* receipt of goods; goods received; **~~sbuch** *n* purchases journal; **~einzelhandel** *m* retail trade; **~empfänger** *m* consignee; **~entnahme** *f* withdrawal of commodities; **~gattung** *f* kind (*od* class) of goods; **~handel** *m* trade, commerce; **~haus** *n* (*Kaufhaus*) stores *pl*; *Am* department store; (*in Zssg*) warehouse; **~inventur** *f* inventory of goods; **~kenntnis** *f* knowledge of articles of commerce; **~knappheit** *f* commodity shortage; **~konto** *n* goods account; **~kredit** *m* credit on goods, *Am* trade loan; **~kunde** *f* knowledge of goods; **~lager** *n* (*Vorrat*) stock-in-trade, assortment of goods; (*Raum*) warehouse, magazine; storehouse; depot; *Am* stockroom; **~lieferant** *m* purveyor, contractor; furnisher; **~makler** *m* commission-agent; broker; **~mangel** *m* scarcity of goods; **~markt** *m* commodity market; **~muster** *n* design; **~niederlage** *f* magazine; warehouse; store-house; **~posten** *m* item, lot; **~preis** *m* quotation; commodity price; **~probe** *f* sample, pattern; **~sendung** *f* consignment, shipment; **~stapel** *m* pile, stack; staple; **~stempel** *m* trade-mark; **~tausch** *m* barter; trading; **~umsatz** *m* goods turnover; **~~steuer** *f* (*Abk*: ***Wust***) turnover tax on commodities; **~verkehr** *m* exchange of goods; goods traffic; **~vertrieb** *m* commodity marketing; **~verzeichnis** *n* list of goods; inventory; (*Faktur*) invoice; **~vorrat** *m* stock (-in-trade); **~wechsel** *m* commercial (*od* trade) bill; *Am* business paper; **~zeichen** *n* trade-mark; *eingetragenes ~~* registered trade-mark; **~zettel** *m* label; docket; **~zoll** *m* customs duty; **~zugang** *m* commodities received.
warm *a* warm; (*heiß*) hot; *mir ist ~* I am warm; *~ machen* to warm; *die Sonne scheint ~* the sun is hot; *jdm den Kopf ~ machen* to worry s.o.; *sich jdn ~ halten* to keep up o.'s contact with; *ich werde nicht mit ihm ~* I can't warm up to him; *etw ~es essen* to have a hot meal; *~ sitzen* to be sitting pretty; *~ stellen* to keep hot; *~ laufen lassen* to warm up (the engine); *das Lager läuft sich ~* the bearing runs hot; *~e Luftschicht* layer of warm air; **~bad** *n* warm bath; (*Quelle*) thermal springs *pl*; **~behandlung** *f* hot-treatment; **~blüter** *m* warm-blooded animal; **~blütig** *a* warm-blooded; **~halter** *m* plate-warmer; **~haus** *n* hothouse; **~herzig** *a* warm-hearted; **~luft** *f* warm air; **~~eintritt** *m* hot-air intake; **~~enteisung** *f* *aero* thermal ice elimination; **~~front** *f* warm front; **~~heizung** *f* hot air heating; **~~klappe** *f* heater valve; **~~masse** *f* warm air mass; **~wasserbereiter** *m* boiler; electric water heater; geyser; *Am* (hot water) heater; **~wasserheizung** *f* central heating; **~wasserspeicher** *m* geyser, *Am* hot water tank.
Wärme *f* warmth; warmness; temperature; *phys* heat; (*Herzens~*) cordiality; *~ abgeben* to give out (*od* to radiate) heat; *~ ableiten* to

carry off heat; ~ *aufspeichern* to store heat; ~ *erzeugend* calorific, exothermic; **~abfall** *m* heat drop; **~abgabe** *f* loss of heat; **~abnahme** *f* decrease in temperature; **~aufnahmefähigkeit** *f* heat-absorption capacity; **~ausdehnung** *f* thermal expansion; **~ausnützung** *f* heat utilization; **~austausch** *m* heat exchange; **~ausstrahlung** *f* radiation of heat; **~bedarf** *m* heat requirement; **~beständig** *a* heatproof, heat-resisting; **~~keit** *f* heatproof quality, resistance to heat; **~durchlässig** *a* diathermic; **~einheit** *f* thermal (*od* heat) unit; **~einstrahlung** *f* heat absorption; **~empfindlich** *a* sensitive to heat; **~entwicklung** *f* development of heat; **~erzeugung** *f* heat production; **~flasche** *f* hot-water bottle; **~fortpflanzung** *f* propagation of heat; **~gleiche** *f* isotherm; **~grad** *m* degree of heat, temperature; **~halle** *f* warming centre; **~lehre** *f* theory of heat; **~leistung** *f* thermal efficiency; **~leiter** *m* conductor of heat; **~leit(ungs)vermögen** *n* thermal (*od* heat) conductivity; **~leitzahl** *f* coefficient of thermal conductivity; **~liefernd** *a* exothermal; **~mechanik** *f* thermodynamics *pl mit sing*; **~menge** *f* amount (*od* quantity) of heat; **~messer** *m* calorimeter, thermometer; **~messung** *f* calorimetry, heat measurement; **~n** *tr* to warm, to heat; *r* to warm o. s., to bask; **~quelle** *f* heat source; **~regler** *m* heat regulator, thermostat; **~rückstrahlung** *f* heat reflection; **~schutz** *m* insulation against loss of heat; **~~mittel** *n* heat insulator; **~schwankung** *f* heat fluctuation; **~sicher** *a* heatproof, heat-resisting; **~speicher** *m* heat accumulator, heat storage; **~strahlung** *f* heat radiation; **~strom** *m* heat flow; **~strömung** *f* heat convection; **~stube** *f* warming centre; **~träger** *m* heat carrier; **~überschuß** *m* heat surplus; **~undurchlässig** *a* athermanous, impervious to heat; **~unterschied** *m* drop (*od* difference) in heat; **~verbrauch** *m* heat consumption; **~~end** *a* heat consuming, endothermal; **~verlust** *m* heat (*od* thermal) loss; **~verteilung** *f* distribution of temperature; **~wert** *m* calorific value, thermal coefficient; **~wirkung** *f* effect of heat; **~zufuhr** *f* heat input; **~zunahme** *f* increase in temperature; **~zustand** *m* thermal condition.

Warn|anlage *f* warning indicator; **~boje** *f* fairway buoy; **~dienst** *m* air-raid warning service; **~en** *tr* to warn (of), to caution (against); *vor Taschendieben wird gewarnt* beware of pickpockets; **~er** *m* warner; admonisher; **~flagge** *f* danger flag; **~gebiet** *n* danger zone, banned area; **~gerät** *n* monitor; **~lampe** *f* pilot lamp; **~licht** *n* warning light; **~meldung** *f* warning notice; **~netz** *n* warning net; (*mit Radar*) radar screen; **~ruf** *m* warning cry; **~signal** *n* air-raid alarm; caution signal; *rail* level-crossing signal; **~stelle** *f* (district) warning station; lookout post; **~ung** *f* alarm, warning (*vor* of, *für* to); (*Mahnung*) admonition; (*Hinweis*) tip-off; **~~sschild** *n* danger signal, warning plate; **~~sschuß** *m* warning shot; **~~ssignal** *n* warning (*od* danger) signal; **~~stafel** *f* notice-board, danger board; **~~szeichen** *n* warning sign; **~vorrichtung** *f* alarm apparatus; **~zentrale** *f* control centre.

Warschau *n* Warsaw.

Wart *m* warden; *aero* ground-mechanic maintenance man; **~e** *f* observation tower, watch-tower, observatory; look-out; **~efrau** *f* nurse, attendant; **~egeld** *n* half-pay; *mar* demurrage; **~eliste** *f* waiting list; **~en** *itr* to wait (*auf* for, *fam* (up)on), to lie in wait (for), to stay (for), to tarry (for); (*erwarten*) to await, to expect; (*bevorstehen*) to be in store for, to be imminent; (*den Atem anhalten*) to hold o.'s breath; *tr* (*pflegen*) to nurse; to tend; (*seines Amtes*) to attend to; (*Kinder*) to look after; **~~** *lassen* to keep waiting; *jeder muß* **~~**, *bis er an der Reihe ist* everybody has to wait his turn; **~~** *Sie hier!* wait here! *Am* stick around! **~eraum** *m* waiting-room; *radio* stand-by area; **~esaal** *m rail* waiting-room; **~ezeichen** *n* waiting signal; **~ezeit** *f* delay, waiting-time; (*Versicherung*) gap; *mar* demurrage; **~ezimmer** *n* waiting-room; **~ung** *f tech* maintenance, service, upkeep; (*Pflege*) care, attendance, nursing; **~~skosten** *pl* maintenance cost; **~~svorschrift** *f* servicing schedule.

Wärter *m* (male) nurse, attendant; (*Hüter*) keeper; guard; (*Aufseher*) care-taker; (*Gefängnis~*) (prison-) warder; *rail* pointsman, signalman; **~häuschen** *n* watchman's (*od* pointsman's *od* lineman's) hut; **~in** *f* nurse; care-taker; **~wohnung** *f* watchman's dwelling.

warum *adv* why; for what reason; wherefore; ~ *nicht?* why not? I don't mind; ~ *nicht gar!* certainly not!

Warz|e *f* wart; (*Brust~*) nipple, teat; pimple; (*Auswuchs*) excrescence, tubercle; **~enförmig** *a* mammilated; *bot* papillary; **~enkraut** *n* marigold; **~ig** *a* nodular, warty, verrucose.

was *pron* (*Frage*) what; (*Beziehung*) that which; which; that; (*verallgemeinernd*) what(so)ever; no matter what; (*etwas*) something; ~ *für ein!* what a! (*Frage*) what sort of a? what kind of? ~ *mich betrifft* as far as I'm concerned; as for me; ~ *Sie nicht sagen!* you don't say! *ach ~!* stuff and nonsense! go on! ~ *haben sie gelacht!* how they laughed! *nein, so ~!* well, I never! *das ist so sicher wie nur ~!* that's as sure as anything! *ich will dir ~ sagen* I'll tell you what; ~ *ist mit ...?* how about ...? ~ *weiter?* what of it? *Am* so what?

Wasch|anstalt *f* laundry; **~apparat** *m* washing apparatus; **~bar** *a* washable; (*Farbe*) fast; **~~e** *Kleidungsstücke* washables *pl*; **~~keit** *f* washability; **~bär** *m* (rac)coon; **~becken** *n* washing (*od* hand)-basin; **~behälter** *m* washing tank; **~benzin** *n* gasoline for cleaning; **~beständig** *a* wash-proof; **~blau** *n* washing-blue; **~bottich** *m* washing vat; **~brett** *n Am* wash-board; **~bürste** *f* washing brush; **~bütte** *f* wash-tub; **~echt** *a* fast to washing, washfast; (colo(u)r) fast; *fig* genuine; **~~heit** *f* bleaching resistance; **~einrichtung** *f* washing accommodation; **~en** *irr tr* to wash; (*reinigen*) to clean, to purify; (*Wäsche*) to wash, to launder; (*abreiben*) to scrub, to scour; (*Haare*) to shampoo; *r, itr* to wash; *e-e Hand wäscht die andere* one good turn deserves another; *die Wäsche* **~~** *lassen* to send o.'s laundry out; *jdm gründlich den Kopf* **~~** to scold s. o., to pick a crow with s. o., *Am fam* to give s. o. a good bawling-out; *er ist mit allen Wassern gewaschen* he's cunning, *fam* he's as shrewd as they come; **~erzeugnisse** *n pl* laundry products *pl*; **~faß** *n* wash-tub; **~frau** *f* washerwoman, laundress, *Am* wash-woman, washlady; **~geschirr** *n* wash-stand set; **~kessel** *m* wash-boiler, copper; **~kleid** *n* print dress, cotton frock; **~korb** *m* clothes-basket; **~küche** *f* wash-house; laundry; *aero sl* thick fog, thick cloud; **~lappen** *m* face-cloth, *Am* washrag; *fig* molly-coddle, jellyfish; **~lauge** *f* washing liquor; lye; **~leder** *n* wash-leather, chamois-leather; **~lösung** *f* wash solution; **~maschine** *f* washing machine; (automatic) washer; **~mittel** *n* washing agent, detergent; *med* lotion; **~pulver** *n* washing powder; **~raum** *m* cloak room, lavatory; ladies' room; *Am* washroom; **~schüssel** *f* hand-basin, *Am* wash-bowl; **~seide** *f* washing silk; **~seife** *f* laundry-soap, plain (*od* yellow) soap; **~tag** *m* washing day, *Am* wash-day; **~tisch** *m* washstand; **~trog** *m* washing trough; **~trommel** *f* washing drum; **~ung** *f* washing; *med* ablution; *pharm* lotion, wash; **~wasser** *n* water for washing, washing water, *Am* wash-water; **~weib** *n fig* gossip; **~zettel** *m* laundry list; *typ* publisher's note, *Am* blurb; **~zuber** *m* wash(ing) tub.

Wäsche *f* washing, laundry; (*Bett~*) linen; (*Unter~*) underclothing, underwear; *min* dressing floor; *schmutzige ~* soiled linen; dirty clothes; *in die ~ geben* to send to the laundry; *in der ~ sein* to be at the wash; *große ~ haben* to have washing day; **~besatz** *m* trimming for linen; **~beutel** *m* soiled-linen bag; **~fabrik** *f* lingerie factory; **~glanzstärke** *f* brilliant starch for linen; **~geschäft** *n* lingerie, linen warehouse; **~kasten** *m* washing tank; **~klammer** *f* clothes-peg; (*mit Feder*) spring clip, *Am* clothes-pin; **~leine** *f* clothes-line; **~leinen** *n* linen; **~mangel** *f* mangle; **~r** *m* washer; **~rei** *f* laundry; **~~anlage** *f* laundry plant; **~rin** *f* washerwoman, laundress, *Am* wash-woman, washlady; **~rlohn** *m* charge for washing; **~sack** *m* laundry bag, *mil* barracks bag; **~schrank** *m* linen-cupboard; **~ständer** *m* clothes-horse; **~tasche** *f* laundry pocket; **~tinte** *f* marking ink; **~trockner** *m* (automatic) clothes dryer; **~wechsel** *m* change of underclothing.

Wasser *n* water; ~ *entziehen* to dehydrate; ~ *nachgießen* to pour water again; *auf dem ~ treiben* to float; *kohlensaures ~* aerated water; *fließendes ~* running water; *stehendes ~* stagnant water; *unter ~ setzen* to flood, to submerge; *zu ~ u. zu Lande* by land and sea; ~ *einnehmen mar* to water; ~ *lassen* to make water; ~ *ziehen* to leak; *mir läuft das ~ im Mund zusammen* my mouth is watering; *ins ~ fallen, zu ~ werden fig* to come to naught; to end in smoke, to fall through; *das ist ~ auf seine Mühle* that's grist to his mill; *auf beiden Achseln ~ tragen* to favo(u)r both sides, *Am* to straddle; *von reinstem ~* of the first water; *sich mühsam über ~ halten fig* to keep o.'s head above water; *er ist mit allen ~n gewaschen* he's cunning, *Am* he's as shrewd as they come; **~abfluß** *m* water discharge; **~ablaßhahn** *m* water-drawoff cock; **~ablaßrohr** *n* water drain pipe; **~ableitung** *f* drainage; **~abstoßend** *a* water-repellent; **~abzug** *m* culvert; **~~sgraben** *m* catch pit; **~ader** *f* water-spring; **~anlage** *f* waterworks *pl*; **~anschluß** *m* water connection; **~anziehend** *a* hygroscopic; **~arm** *a* of low humidity; **~~** *m* arm of a river; channel; **~armut** *f* scarcity of water; **~artig** *a* watery, like water; aqueous; **~aufnahme** *f* absorption of water; ~~**fähigkeit** *f* absorptive capacity; ~**aufsaugend** *a* water-absorbing; ~**austritt** *m* water outlet; ~**bad** *n* water bath; ~**bahn** *f* shoot-the-chute; ~**ball** *m* water-polo; ~**ballast** *m* water ballast; ~**bauunternehmung** *f* enterprise of hydraulic structure; ~**becken** *n* water basin (*od* tank); ~**bedarf** *m* water requirement; ~**behälter** *m* reservoir, tank, cistern; ~**berieselung** *f* water-irrigation, water-jet scrubbing, water spraying; ~**beständig** *a* water-resistant; waterproof; ~**bindend** *a* water-absorbent; ~**blase** *f* bubble of water; vesicle; ~**blau** *a* sea-blue; ~**bombe** *f* depth-charge; ~**bunker** *m* submarine pen; ~**dampf** *m* water vapo(u)r; *der* ~~ *schlägt sich nieder* the water vapo(u)r condenses; ~**dicht** *a* watertight; waterproof; impermeable; ~~*er Abschluß* water seal; ~**druck** *m* hydraulic pressure, water pressure; ~~**presse** *f* hydraulic press; ~**durchbruch** *m* water burst; ~**durchlässig** *a* pervious to water; ~~**keit** *f* permeability; ~**eimer** *m* water bucket; ~**einbruch** *m* water breaking-in; ~**eintritt** *m* water inlet; ~**enthärtung** *f* water softening; ~**entnahme** *f* intake; ~**entziehend** *a* removing water; dehydrating; desiccating; ~**entziehung** *f* removal of water, dehydration; desiccation; ~**erguß** *m* watery effusion, edema; ~**ersparnis** *f* water saving; ~**fahrzeug** *n* watercraft, vessel; ~**fall** *m* waterfall; (*kleiner od künstlicher*) cascade; (*großer*) cataract; ~**farbe** *f* water colo(u)r; distemper; ~**fest** *a* waterproof, watertight, resistant to water; ~**fläche** *f* surface of water; water-level; sheet of water; ~**flasche** *f* water bottle; ~**fleck** *m* water stain; ~**floh** *m* water-fly; ~**flughafen** *m* marine airport, seadrome; ~**flugzeug** *n* seaplane, hydroplane; ~~**schleppwagen** *m* seaplane beaching trolley; ~**förderung** *f* raising of water; ~**frei** *a* dehydrated, desiccated, anhydrous; ~**führend** *a* water-bearing; ~**gefäß** *n* water vat; ~**gehalt** *m* water content; ~**gekühlt** *a* water-cooled; ~**gewinnung** *f* water procuring; ~**glas** *n auch chem* water-glass; (*Gefäß*) tumbler, *Am* water glass; ~**graben** *m* ditch; moat; ~**hahn** *m* water-cock (*od* -tap, *Am* -faucet); *Am* spigot; ~**haltig** *a* containing water, aqueous; hydrous; hydrated; ~**hebewerk** *n* water-supply and -pumping station; ~**heilanstalt** *f* hydropathic establishment; ~**hell** *a* clear as water, transparent; ~**höhe** *f* depth of water; ~**hose** *f* waterspout; ~**huhn** *n* coot; ~**jungfer** *f* mermaid, water-nymph; ~**kanne** *f* waterjug; ewer; ~**kessel** *m* cauldron, copper, tank; boiler; kettle; ~**kopf** *m* hydrocephalus; ~**kraft** *f* hydraulic power, water power; ~~**anlage** *f* water-power plant, hydraulic power station; ~~**werk** *n* hydroelectric generating station; ~**kran** *m rail* feeding crane; ~**kreislauf** *m* water circulation; ~**krug** *m* (water-) pitcher; water pot; ~**kühlung** *f* water cooling; ~**kunst** *f* artificial fountain; ~**kur** *f* water-cure; ~**lache** *f* pool; ~**landflugzeug** *n* amphibian (plane); ~**landpanzerwagen** *m* amphibian tank; ~**lauf** *m* watercourse; river, stream; channel, canal; ~**leitung** *f* water supply, water pipes *pl*, water conduit, water main; aqueduct; ~~**shahn** *m* water tap (*od* spout), *Am* faucet; ~~**srohr** *n* water pipe; ~~**swasser** *n* city water; ~**lilie** *f* water-lily; ~**linie** *f* water mark; ~**loch** *n* drain hole; ~**los** *a* without water, arid; ~**mangel** *m* scarcity of water; ~**mann** *m astr* the Water Bearer, Aquarius; ~**mantel** *m mot* water jacket; ~**melone** *f* water melon; ~**menge** *f* volume (*od* quantity) of water; ~**messer** *m* water ga(u)ge, hydrometer; ~**motor** *m* hydraulic engine; ~**mühle** *f* water-mill; ~**n** *itr* to alight upon the water; ~**pflanze** *f* aquatic plant; ~**pfuhl** *m* pool; ~**pocken** *f pl* chicken-pox; ~**rad** *n* water wheel; *oberschlächtiges* ~~ overshot water wheel; *unterschlächtiges* ~~ undershot water wheel; ~**ratte** *f* water-rat; *fig* sea-dog, old salt; ~**recht** *n* water right; ~**reich** *a* rich in water; of high humidity; ~**reinigung** *f* water purification; ~~**sanlage** *f* water purification plant; ~**rinne** *f* gutter, water channel; ~**rohr** *n* water pipe; ~**rose** *f* water-lily; ~**rutschbahn** *f* water-chute; ~**sack** *m* canvas bucket; ~**säule** *f* column of water; ~**schaden** *m* damage caused by water; ~**schallsender** *m mil* submarine oscillator; ~**scheide** *f* watershed; *Am* water divide; ~**scheu** *f* dread of water; hydrophobia; ~~ *a* afraid of water, hydrophobic; ~**schlange** *f* water-snake; ~**schlauch** *m* water hose; ~**snot** *f* distress caused by water; ~**speicher** *m* reservoir, tank; ~~**ung** *f* storage of water; ~**speier** *m* gargoyle; ~**spiegel** *m* water level, water-surface; sea level; pool elevation; ~**sport** *m* aquatic sports *pl*; ~**sprengwagen** *m* watering car, sprinkling wag(g)on; ~**sprühregen** *m* water spray; ~**spülung** *f* flushing; ~**stand** *m* water level, water ga(u)ge, water line; sea level; pool elevation; state of the tide; flood stage; ~~**sänderung** *f* change of water level; ~~**sanzeiger** *m* water-level indicator, water ga(u)ge; ~~**smarke** *f* watermark; ~~**szeichen** *n* tidal signal; ~**start** *m aero* rise off water; ~**stein** *m* scale from water; ~~ *entfernen* to descale; ~**stiefel** *m pl* waterproof boots *pl*, waders *pl*; ~**stoff** *m* hydrogen; *schwerer* ~~ heavy hydrogen, deuterium; ~~**behälter** *m* hydrogen tank; ~~**blondine** *f Am* peroxide blonde; ~~**bombe** *f* hydrogen bomb, H-bomb, *sl Am* superduper; ~~**haltig** *a* hydrogenous; ~~**superoxyd** *n* hydrogen peroxide; ~~**verbindung** *f* hydrogen compound; ~**strahl** *m* water jet; ~~**gebläse** *n* blowers actuated by water power; ~**straße** *f* canal, waterway; navigable river; ~**sucht** *f* dropsy; ~**süchtig** *a* dropsical; ~**suppe** *f* gruel; ~**tank** *m* water tank; ~**temperatur** *f* water temperature; ~**tiefe** *f* depth of water, draft; ~**tier** *n* aquatic animal; ~**träger** *m* water-carrier; ~**transport** *m* water transportation; ~**tropfen** *m* water drop (*od* particle); ~**turbine** *f* water turbine; ~**turm** *m* water tower; ~**überlauf** *m* water overflow; ~**überschwemmung** *f* water flood; ~**uhr** *f* water-clock; ~**umlauf** *m* water circulation; ~**undurchlässig** *a* impervious; ~**ung** *f* alighting on water; ~**unlöslich** *a* waterproof, insoluble in water; ~**verbrauch** *m* water consumption; ~**verdampfung** *f* evaporation of water; ~**verdrängung** *f* displacement of water; *aero* draft of water; ~**versorgung** *f* water supply; ~**verteilungsstelle** *f* water-supply point; ~**vögel** *m pl* water fowl; ~**vorrat** *m* water supply; ~**waage** *f* water-level, ga(u)ge; *phys* hydrostatic balance; ~**weg** *m* waterway; *auf dem* ~~ by waterway; ~**welle** *f* waterwave; ~**werk** *n* waterworks *pl*; ~**zeichen** *n* water-mark; ~**ziehen** *n* (*Sonne*) sun's eye lashes *pl*, *mar* sun's backstays *pl*; ~**zins** *m* water rent; ~**zuleitungsrohr** *n* water-supply pipe.

Wässer|chen *n*: *er sieht aus, als ob er kein* ~~ *trüben könnte* he looks as if butter would not melt in his mouth; ~**ig** *a* watery, aqueous, hydrous; *med* serous; *jdm den Mund* ~~ *machen* to make s. o.'s mouth water; ~~**keit** *f* wateriness; *med* serosity; ~**n** *tr* to water, to dilute with water; (*bewässern*) to irrigate; (*hydrieren*) to hydrate; *phot* to wash; (*ausspülen*) to rinse; ~**ung** *f* watering; irrigation; soaking; hydration; washing.

waten *itr* to wade (through).

watschel|ig *a* waddling; ~**n** *itr* to waddle.

Watt *n* shore belt, mud flat; *el* watt; ~**leistung** *f* wattage; ~**messer** *m* wattmeter; ~**stunde** *f* watt-hour; ~**verbrauch** *m* watt consumption; ~**zahl** *f* number of watts, wattage.

Watt|e *f* wadding, cotton wool; *Am* absorbent cotton; *blutstillende* ~~ styptic cotton; ~~**bausch** *m* pad of cotton-wool, cotton plug; ~~**filter** *n* cotton filter; ~~**kugel** *f* cotton-wool ball; ~~**pfropfen** *m* wad; ~**ieren** *tr* to pad, to line with wadding; (*polstern*) to quilt, to wad.

*

Web|ebaum *m* weaver's beam, warp-beam; ~**eeinlage** *f* lay; ~**ekante** *f* selvage; ~**en** *irr tr, itr* to weave; *poet* to move, to be active; (*schweben*) to float; ~**er(in)** *m* (*f*) weaver; ~~**baum** *m* loom beam; ~~**ei** *f* weaving-mill, textile mill; (*Gewerbe*) weaver's trade; (*Tuch*) woven material, texture; ~~**eierzeugnis** *n* weaving product; ~~**eimechaniker** *m* mule fitter; ~~**glas** *n* cloth prover; ~~**knecht** *m zoo* daddy-long-legs; ~~**knoten** *m* weaver's knot; ~~**schiffchen** *n* shuttle; ~~**vogel** *m* weaver-bird; ~**fehler** *m* flaw (*od* fault) in weaving; ~**stuhl** *m* (weaver's) loom; ~**vogel** *m* picker; ~**waren** *f pl* woven goods *pl*; ~~**fabrik** *f* weaving factory.

Wechsel *m* change, alteration, variation, shift; (*Austausch*) exchange; (*Geld*) change; (*Aufeinanderfolge*) alternation, succession, turn; (*Ernte*) rotation; (*Umkehrung*) inversion; reversal; (*Schwankung*) fluctuation; (*des Glücks*) vicissitude; (*Jagd*) runway, *Am* trace; (*Gewebe*) doff; *com* bill of exchange; *gezogener* ~ draft; *eigener* (*trockener*) ~ note of hand, promissory note; *offener* ~ letter of credit; *fälliger* ~ matured bill; *kurzer* ~ short bill; *ungedeckter* ~ uncovered bill; *an den Inhaber zahlbarer* ~ bill payable to bearer; ~ *auf Sicht* bill payable at sight; *e-n* ~ *ausstellen* to draw a draft; *e-n* ~ *einlösen* to hono(u)r a bill; *e-n* ~ *unterschreiben* to sign a bill; *e-n* ~ *verlängern* to renew a bill; *e-n* ~ *auf jdn ziehen* to draw a bill on s. o.; ~**abteilung** *f* discount department; ~**agent** *m* bill broker; ~**agio** *n* exchange; ~**akzept** *n* acceptance of a bill; ~**anhang** *m* allonge; ~**arbitrage** *f* arbitrage; arbitration of exchange; ~**aussteller** *m* maker of a bill; ~**balg** *m* changeling; ~**bank** *f* discount house; ~**bestand** *m* bill holdings *pl*; ~**betrieb** *m* shifting operation; ~**bewegung** *f* intermittent motion; ~**beziehung** *f* mutual relation(ship), correlation; interrelation; ~**buch** *n* discount register; ~**bürge** *m* guarantor of a bill of exchange; ~**bürgschaft** *f* security given by bill; bill; ~**diskont** *m* bill discount; ~~**ierung** *f* discounting of bills; ~**einlösung** *f* cashing of a bill; ~**farbig** *a* iridescent; ~**fälle** *m pl* vicissitudes *pl*, ups and downs *pl*; ~**fälscher** *m* forger of a bill; ~**fälschung** *f* forgery of bills; ~**feld** *n* alternating field; ~**fieber** *n* malaria, intermittent fever; ~**folge** *f* alternation; ~**forderung** *f* claim based upon a bill of exchange; ~**formular** *n* draft form; ~**frist** *f* days of grace; ~**geld** *n* change, agio; (*Kleingeld*) small change; ~**gesang** *m* antiphony, amœbæan song; glee; ~**geschäft** *n* banking business; exchange office; ~**gespräch** *n* dialogue; ~**getriebe** *n* change(-speed) gear, variable gear; ~**gläubiger** *m* holder of a bill; ~**haft** *a* changing; ~**haftung** *f* indorser's liability; ~**inhaber** *m* holder of a bill; ~**inkassogeschäft** *n* collection of bills; ~**jahre** *n pl* climacteric; ~**kassette** *f phot* (film-) changing magazine; ~**klage** *f* lawsuit relating to bills of exchange; ~**klappe** *f* butterfly valve; ~**kredit** *m* paper credit, acceptance credit; ~**kurs** *m* rate of exchange; ~**lager** *n* ball-thrust bearing; ~**laufzeit** *f* currency of a bill; ~**makler** *m* bill-broker; ~**n** *tr, itr* to change, to exchange; to interchange; (*abwechseln*) to vary; to alternate; (*ändern*) to alter; (*Szene*) to shift; (*umdrehen*) to reverse; (*Zähne*) to cut; (*Jagd*) to pass; (*Stimme*) to break; *die Kleider* ~ to change o.'s clothes; *Worte* ~~ *mit jdm* to dispute with s. o.; *den Besitzer* ~~ to change hands; *seinen Wohnort* ~~ to remove, to go elsewhere; ~~**d** *a* changing; alternating; varying, variable; ~**nehmer** *m* taker of a bill; ~**notierungen** *f pl* foreign exchange rates *pl*; ~**ordnung** *f* codified law of bills of exchange; ~**pari** *n* par of exchange; ~**protest** *m* protest of a bill; ~**rad** *n* change gear; ~**recht** *n* law of exchange; ~**rede** *f* dialogue; ~**reiter** *m* bill-jobber; ~**reiterei** *f* bill-jobbing; ~**richter** *m tech* inverted converter, mutator; ~**ring** *m* changing ring; ~**schalter** *m* double-throw switch; ~**schaltung** *f* alternating switch; ~**schuld** *f* debt founded on a bill of exchange; ~**seitig** *a* mutual, reciprocal; alternate; interchangeable; *tele* two-way; ~~**keit** *f* reciprocity; ~**spiel** *n* alternate play, fluctuation; ~**ständig** *a bot* alternate; ~**stempelsteuer** *f* exchange stamp tax; ~**strom** *m* alternating current, *Abk* A.C.; ~~**empfänger** *m* alternating-current mains receiver; ~~**generator** *m* alternating-current generator; ~~**gleichrichter** *m* alternating-current rectifier; ~~**technik** *f* alternating-current engineering; ~~**wecker** *m* magneto bell; ~**stube** *f* money changer's office, exchange office; ~**taste** *f* shift key; ~**tierchen** *n* amœba; ~**verhältnis** *n* reciprocal relation; ~**verkehr** *m* two-way communication, intercommunication; ~**verlängerung** *f* prolongation of a bill; ~**voll** *a* fluctuating; ~**weise** *adv* alternately, by turns; (*gegenseitig*) mutually, reciprocally; ~**winkel** *m pl* alternate angles *pl*; ~**wirkung** *f* reciprocal action, alternating effect, reciprocation; *in* ~~ *stehen* to reciprocate; ~**wirtschaft** *f* (*Feld*) rotation of crops; ~**zahl** *f* frequency, cycle; ~**zeichen** *n* shift signal.

Wechsler *m* money-changer.

Weck|anruf *m* call bell; ~**en** *tr* to wake, to awaken, to call, to rouse (up); ~~ *n* ringing, reveille; ~**(en)** *m* (*Brötchen*) roll; ~**er** *m* alarm-clock; *tele* call bell, ringer, buzzer; (*Radar*) bell set; (*Person*) knockerup, *Am* call-boy; ~~**ausschalter** *m* bell stop; ~~**uhr** *f* alarm clock; ~~**werk** *n* alarm mechanism; ~**ruf** *m* reveille; call; ~**strom** *m* ringing current.

Wedel *m* brush, whisk; (*Fächer*) fan; (*Staub*~) duster; (*Fliegen*~) fly-flap; (*Weih*~) aspergillum; (*Schwanz*) tail, brush; *bot* frond; palm-leaf; ~**n** *itr* to fan; *mit dem Schwanze* ~*n* to wag the tail; *fig* to fawn, to cringe.

weder ... ***noch*** *conj* neither ... nor, not ... either ... or.

Weg *m* way; (*Pfad*) path; (*Straße*) street, road; (*Gang*) walk; (*Durchgang*) passage; (*Verkehrsstraße*) thoroughfare; (*Reise, Verlauf, Kurs*) course; (*Botengang*) errand; (*Reise*~) route; (*Weise*) manner; (*Mittel*) means *pl*, channel; (*Verfahren*) method; *tech* displacement; *geschlossener* ~ closed path; *öffentlicher* ~ public road; *holperiger* ~ bumpy road; *unbefestigter* ~ gravel road; *geteerter* ~ tar road; *auf halbem* ~*e* half-way, midway; *am* ~*e* by the roadside; *verbotener* ~*!* no thoroughfare! private! *wohin des* ~*es?* where are you off to? *aus dem* ~*e gehen* to shun; *auf gütlichem* ~*e* amicably, in a friendly way; *woher des* ~*s?* where do you come from? *aus dem* ~*e gehen* to stand aside, to make way for; *fig* to evade, to shirk; *fam* to stear clear of; *e-r Entscheidung aus dem* ~ *gehen Am* to side-step a decision; *er steht mir im* ~*e* he's in my way; *aus dem* ~*e räumen* to remove; (*töten*) to kill, *sl* to bump off; *in die* ~*e leiten* to pave the way for, to prepare; *jdm auf halbem* ~*e entgegenkommen* to meet s. o. half-way; *das hat gute* ~*e* there is no hurry; *sich auf den* ~ *machen* to start, to set out; *seiner* ~*e gehen* to go o.'s way, to go for o.'s walk; *den* ~ *abschneiden* to intercept s. o.; ~ *u. Steg kennen* to know every fork in the road; *auf dem richtigen* ~ *sein* to be on the beam; ~**abkürzung** *f* short cut, by-pass, *Am* cut-off; ~**abschnitt** *m* fraction of path; ~**arm** *a* lacking in roads; ~**bereiter** *m* forerunner, pioneer; ~**ebau** *m* road-making; ~**ebiegung** *f* road curve (*od* bend); ~**edreieck** *n* triangular road junction; ~**egabel** *f* road fork; ~**einmündung** *f* junction of side road with main road, V fork; ~**elagerer** *m* highwayman; ~**emeister** *m* road surveyor; ~**emesser** *m* odometer; ~**enetz** *n* road network; ~**eenge** *f* narrow defile; ~**erich** *m bot* plantain; ~**erkundung** *f* road reconnaissance; ~**espinne** *f* road junction; ~**karte** *f* road map; ~**kreuzung** *f* crossroad, junction; ~**krümmung** *f* curvature of a road; ~**länge** *f* length of path; ~**markierung** *f* trail mark; ~**sam** *a* practicable, passable; ~**scheide** *f* cross roads *pl*, road fork; ~**schild** *n* road sign; ~**schnecke** *f* slug; ~**schranke** *f* railway gate; ~**skizze** *f* strip map, sketched road map; ~**sperre** *f* road block, road barricade; ~**spur** *f* track; ~**strecke** *f* stretch of road; length of path; distance; ~**steuer** *f* toll; ~**stunde** *f* league; ~**überführung** *f* overhead crossing; viaduct; ~**übergang** *m* line crossing; ~**unterführung** *f* underground crossing, underpass; ~**verhältnisse** *n pl* road conditions *pl*; ~**warte** *f bot* chicory; ~**weiser** *m* sign post, road sign; (*Person, Buch*) guide; ~**zehrung** *f* provisions taken on a journey; *eccl* viaticum; (*Geld*) travelling-expenses *pl*; ~**zeitkurve** *f* trajectory.

weg *adv* away; (*verschwunden*) gone, disappeared, lost; (*fort*) off; ~ *da!* get away! be off! get out! ~ *damit!* take it away! ~ *mit ihm!* take him away! *Hände* ~*!* hands off! *er wohnt weit* ~ he lives far away; *der Schnee ist* ~ the snow is gone; *mein Hut ist* ~ my hat is gone; *er ist endlich* ~ he's gone for good; *ich muß* ~ I must be off; I have to go; *ich kann nicht* ~ I can't leave; *er wollte nicht* ~ he didn't want to go (away); *ganz* ~ *sein fam* to be in raptures (about); ~**begeben** *irr r* to go away, to leave, to absent o. s.; ~**beizen** *tr* to remove by caustics; ~**bekommen** *irr tr* to get away; (*lernen*) to get the knack of; ~**blasen** *irr tr* to blow off; *wie weggeblasen* without leaving a trace; ~**bleiben** *irr itr* to stay away; (*ausgelassen werden*) to be omitted; ~**blicken** *itr* to look away; ~**brechen** *irr tr, itr* to break off; *tr* to pull down; ~**brennen** *irr tr, itr* to burn down; ~**bringen** *irr tr* to take away; (*Sachen*) to remove; (*Flecken*) to take out; ~**denken** *irr tr* to imagine to be absent; ~**drängen** *tr* to push away; ~**dürfen** *itr* to be allowed to go away.

wegen *prp* because of, on account of, by reason of; (*um ... willen*) for, for the sake of; (*mit Rücksicht auf*) in consideration of, with regard to, regarding; (*infolge*) in consequence of, owing to; *ich konnte* ~ *des Regens nicht kommen* I couldn't come because of the rain; *der Kürze* ~ to be short; *von Amts*~ officially; *von Rechts*~ by right.

weg|fahren *irr tr* to carry away, to cart away, to remove; *itr* to leave; to drive away; *über etw* ~~ to pass over; ~**fall** *m* omission; *in* ~~ *kommen* to be abolished; not to take place; ~**fallen** *irr itr* to fall away; (*aufhören*) to cease; (*ausgelassen werden*) to be omitted; (*abgeschafft werden*) to be abolished; (*ausfallen*) not to take place; ~~ *lassen* to discard; ~**fangen** *irr tr* to catch away; (*Briefe*) to intercept; ~**fegen** *tr* to sweep away; ~**fischen** *tr* to snatch away; ~**fliegen** *irr itr* to fly away; ~**fließen** *irr itr* to flow off; ~**fressen** *irr tr* to eat off, to devour; ~**führen** *tr* to lead away.

Weg|gang *m* going away, departure; *bei seinem* ~~ on his leaving; ~**geben** *irr tr* to give away; ~**gehen** *irr itr* to go off, to leave, to depart, *Am sl* to scram; *beim* ~~ on leaving; *über etw* ~~ to pass over; ~**gießen** *irr tr* to pour away.

weg|haben *irr tr* to have got; *fig* (*gut verstehen*) to understand, to have got the knack of; *fam e-n* ~~ to be tipsy; ~**hängen** *irr tr* to hang away; ~**haschen** *tr* to snatch away; ~**hauen** *tr* to cut off; ~**heben** *irr tr* to lift away; *hebe dich* ~*!* be gone! go away! ~**helfen** *irr tr* to help s. o. to get away; ~**holen** *tr* to fetch away; ~**jagen** *tr* to drive away, to expel.

weg|kehren *tr* to sweep away, to turn off; ~**kommen** *irr itr* to get away, to come off; *gut* ~~ to come off well; (*abhanden kommen*) to be (*od* get) lost; ~**kratzen** *tr* to scratch out; ~**kurven** *itr mil aero sl* to weave.

weg|lassen *irr tr* to let go; (*auslassen*) to omit, to leave out; ~**lassung** *f* omission; ~**laufen** *irr itr* to run off; ~**legen** *tr* to put away, to lay aside, to discard; ~**leugnen** *tr* to deny flatly, to disavow.

weg|machen *tr* to remove; (*Flecken*) to take out; *r* to withdraw; ~**meißeln** *tr* to cut away with the chisel; ~**müssen** *itr* to be obliged to go; *ich muß* ~ I must be off; ~**nahme** *f jur* seizure; confiscation; *mil, mar* capture; ~**nehmen** *irr tr* to take away; (*mit Beschlag belegen*) to seize; to confiscate; (*Gas*) *mot* to close (the throttle); (*Zeit, Raum*) to take up, to occupy; *mil,* *mar* to capture; **~packen** *tr* to pack away; *r* to pack off.

weg|radieren *tr* to erase; **~raffen** *tr* to snatch away, to carry off; **~räumen** *tr* to remove, to clear away; (*Schwierigkeiten*) to remove obstacles; **~reisen** *itr* to set out, to depart; **~reißen** *irr tr* to tear, to pull, to snatch away; (*Häuser*) to pull down; **~rücken** *tr* to move away, to remove.

weg|schaffen *tr* to remove, to put away; *math* to eliminate; **~scheren** *tr* to clip; (*Bart*) to shave off, to shear; *r* to be off, to decamp, to pack off; **~schicken** *tr* to send off; to let go; *fam* to send s. o. packing; (*abschicken*) to dispatch, to send away; **~schieben** *tr* to shove away; **~schießen** *irr tr* to shoot away; **~schlagen** *irr tr* to beat off; **~schleichen** *itr, r* to steal away, to sneak away; **~schleppen** *tr* to drag off; **~schleudern** *tr* to fling away; **~schmeißen** *irr tr* to throw away; **~schmelzen** *irr tr* to melt away (*od* off); **~schnappen** *tr* to snatch away (from); **~schneiden** *irr tr* to cut off; (*an Bäumen*) to lop off; **~schütten** *tr* to pour away; **~sehen** *irr itr* to look away, to overlook; *über etw* ~~ to shut o.'s eye to; **~sehnen** *r* to long to get away; **~sein** *irr itr* to be absent; (*gegangen*) to be gone; *über etw* ~~ to be above s. th., to have passed s. th.; (*nicht zu finden sein*) to be lost; **~setzen** *tr* to put away; *itr über e-n Graben* ~~ to clear a ditch; *sich über etw* ~~ not to mind s. th., to disregard s. th.; **~stecken** *tr* to put away; (*verstecken*) to hide; **~stehlen** *irr tr* to steal, to purloin; *r* to steal off; **~stellen** *tr* to put aside; **~sterben** *irr itr* to die off; **~stoßen** *irr tr* to push away; **~streichen** *irr tr* to rub away; to erase, to cancel; (*abhaken*) to tick off, *Am* to check off.

weg|tragen *irr tr* to bear, to carry away; **~treiben** *irr tr* to drive away; *itr* to drift away; **~treten** *irr itr* to step aside; *mil* to break (the) ranks, to fall out; ~~ *lassen* to dismiss; *~getreten! mil* dismiss! **~tun** *irr tr* to put aside; to remove.

weg|weisen *irr tr* to turn off s. o.; **~wenden** *irr tr, r* to turn away, to avert; **~werfen** *irr tr* to cast (*od* throw) away; *r* to degrade o.s.; **~~d** *a* disdainful, disparaging, flippant, contemptuous; **~wischen** *tr* to wipe away.

weg|ziehen *irr tr* to pull away; to pull aside; *itr* (*die Wohnung wechseln*) to remove; (*Truppen*) to march away; **~zug** *m* removal; departure.

weh, ~e! *interj* woe! alas! oh dear! oh my! oh my goodness! dear me! ~ *a* sore, painful, aching; *mir ist ~ ums Herz* I am sick at heart; ~ *tun* to cause pain, to ache; (*beleidigen*) to offend; *der Kopf tut mir ~* my head aches; *sich ~ tun* to hurt o. s.; ~ *n* pain; (*seelisch*) grief, pang; **~en** *pl* labo(u)r pains *pl*, travail; (*Schnee-, Sand~~*) drifts *pl*; ~~ *itr* to blow; (*weg~~*) to blow away; (*Fahne*) to flutter, to wave; ~~ *n* blowing, waving; **~geschrei** *n* lamentations *pl*, wailings *pl*; **~klage** *f* wail, lamentation; **~klagen** *itr* to lament (*um* for, *über* over), to wail; **~leidig** *a* woe-begone, plaintive, lackadaisical; **~mut** *f* sadness, melancholy; **~mütig** *a* wistful, melancholy, sad; sorrowful; **~mutter** *f* midwife.

Wehr *n* weir; dam, dike; (*Stau~*) barrage; ~ *f* (*Schutz*) protection, defence, bulwark; (*Widerstand*) resistance; (*Waffe*) weapon, arm; (*Ausrüstung*) equipment; (*Brüstung*) parapet; *sich zur ~ setzen* to show fight, to offer resistance, *fam* to put up a fight; **~anlage** *f* weir plant; *mil* military establishment; **~ausbildung** *f* military training; **~bereitschaft** *f* preparedness; **~bezirk** *m* recruiting district; military district subarea; **~~skommandeur** *m* commanding officer of recruiting district; **~~skommando** *n* recruiting-district headquarters *pl*; **~dienst** *m* service with the colo(u)rs, military service; **~~beschädigung** *f* nonbattle injury; **~~verhältnis** *n* service status; **~en** *itr* to restrain, to hinder, to keep from, to forbid; (*zügeln*) to check; to arrest; *r* to resist, to put up a fight; to fight (against), to defend o. s.; *sich seiner Haut ~~* to fight for o.'s life; **~ersatz** *m* recruiting and replacements for the armed forces; **~~bezirk** *m* recruiting district; **~~dienststelle** *f* recruiting office; **~~inspekteur** *m* recruiting-area commander; **~~inspektion** *f* recruiting-district headquarters *pl*; **~ertüchtigung** *f* pre-military training; **~fähig** *a* fit to serve, able-bodied, eligible for military service; **~gehänge** *n* sword-belt; **~geographie** *f* military geography; **~gesetz** *n* compulsory service law; **~haft** *a* capable of bearing arms, able-bodied; strong, full of fight; ~~ *machen* to train, to arm; **~höhe** *f* height of weir; **~hoheit** *f* military sovereignty; **~kraft** *f* total defence potential; **~~zersetzung** *f* undermining the fighting spirit and the will to serve; impairing military discipline; **~kreis** *m* corps area; **~~befehlshaber** *m* military-area commander; **~~kommando** *n* corps-area-headquarters *pl*; **~krone** *f* crest of the weir; **~los** *a* defenceless, weak; (*waffenlos*) unarmed; ~~ *machen* to disarm; **~losigkeit** *f* defencelessness; **~macht** *f* The Armed Forces *pl*; **~~angehörige(r)** *m* member of the armed forces; **~~auskunftstelle** *f* armed forces information office; **~~beamte(r)** *m* civilian official of armed forces; **~~befehlshaber** *m* military district commander in occupied area; **~~sbericht** *m* army communiqué; **~~sbevollmächtigte(r)** *m* armed-forces plenipotentiary; **~~seigentum** *n* service property; **~~sfahrkarte** *f* soldiers' reduced-rate railway ticket; **~~sgefängnis** *n* military prison; **~~sgeistliche(r)** *m* chaplain; **~~sgelände** *n* military reservation; **~~sgesundheitsdienst** *m* military-hygiene service; **~~srundfunkempfänger** *m* standard broadcast receiver issued to armed forces personnel; **~~sseelsorger** *m* chaplain; **~~sführerschein** *m* military motor-vehicle operator's permit; **~~spsychologe** *m* military psychologist; **~~sstandort** *m* military post; **~~sstrafgesetzbuch** *n* military penal code; **~~teil** *m* branch of the armed forces; **~mauer** *f* water stop wall; **~meldeamt** *n* recruiting classification headquarters *pl, Am* draft board; **~meldebezirk** *m* recruiting classification area; **~mittelbeschädigung** *f* sabotage; **~nummer** *f* personal (*od* service *od* serial) number; **~ordnung** *f* conscription regulations *pl*; **~paß** *m* service-record book; **~pflicht** *f* obligation to serve in armed forces, compulsory military service, conscription; *allgemeine ~~* universal conscription, *Am* universal military training (*Abk* UMT); **~~ig** *a* liable to military service; **~~ige(r)** *m* man subject to military service; **~sohle** *f* sill, foundation; **~sold** *m* army pay; **~stammblatt** *n* document giving personal data; **~stammbuch** *n* service-record book; **~stammkarte** *f* service-record card; **~stammrolle** *f* roster of draftees by age groups; **~stand** *m* the military profession; **~strafrecht** *n* military penal and disciplinary code; **~tauglich** *a* fit for military service; **~überlauf** *m* overflow weir; **~überwachung** *f* counterespionage service; **~unwürdig** *a* unworthy to serve in the armed forces; **~vergehen** *n* military offence; **~verrat** *m* military treason; **~versammlung** *f* yearly meeting of reservists; **~vorbereitung** *f* defence preparation; **~vorlage** *f* army bill; **~wichtig** *a* important for defence; *~~e Nachricht* military information; **~wille** *m* desire for military preparedness; **~wirtschaft** *f* war economy, military economics *pl* (*u. sing*); **~wissenschaft** *f* military science; **~würdig** *a* worthy to bear arms; **~~keit** *f* qualification to bear arms.

Weib *n* woman; (*Gattin*) wife; (*weibliches Wesen*) female; **~chen** *n* little woman; wife; (*Tiere*) female, mate; **~erart** *f* women's ways *pl*; **~erfeind** *m* woman-hater, misogynist; **~ergeschwätz** *n* gossip of women; **~erheld** *m* lady-killer, lady's man; **~erherrschaft** *f* petticoat-government; **~erlaune** *f* woman's caprice; **~erlist** *f* woman's trick; **~ernarr** *m* dangler after women; **~ervolk** *n fam* womenfolk; **~isch** *a* womanish, effeminate; *~~er Mann Am fam* sissy, pansy; **~lich** *a* female, womanly, feminine; *das ewig ~~e* the Eternal Woman; **~~keit** *f* womanliness, feminine charm, womanhood; feminine nature; **~sbild** female; (*verächtlich*) hussy, wench; **~svolk** *n*, **~sleute** *pl* women, females *pl*; womenfolk.

weich *a* soft; (*zart*) tender; (*schwach*) weak; (*schwächlich, mild*) mild; (*mürbe*) mellow; (*gelinde, sanft*) gentle; (*Leder*) limp; (*Haar*) sleek; (*Ton*) sonorous; (*formbar*) plastic; (*hämmerbar*) malleable; (*biegsam*) supple; (*nachgebend*) yielding; (*geschmeidig*) pliant, pliable; (*reibungslos, weich*) smooth; (*feinfühlig*) sensitive; *~ machen* (*durch Bomben*) to soften up; *~ werden* (*auch fig*) to soften; (*nachgiebig werden*) to relent; (*gerührt werden*) to be moved; *~gekochtes Ei* soft-boiled egg; *~es Wasser* soft water; **~e** *f* flank, side; (*Leiste*) groin; (*~heit*) softness; **~eisen** *n* soft iron, mild steel; **~~kern** *m* soft-iron core; **~fluß** *m* porous white pig; **~gummi** *m* soft rubber, caoutchouc; **~guß** *m* malleable iron; **~heit** *f* softness; (*Reife, Milde*) mellowness; (*Zartheit*) tenderness; (*Schwachheit*) weakness; (*Sanftheit*) gentleness; *tech* elasticity, pliableness, resilience; **~herzig** *a* tender-hearted; **~~keit** *f* tender-heartedness; **~holz** *n* soft wood; **~käse** *m* soft cheese; **~kohle** *f* soft coal; **~lich** *a* soft, tender; (*schlapp*) sloppy, flabby; (*verweichlicht*) effeminate; (*weibisch*) *Am fam* sissy; (*lässig*) indolent; (*zimperlich*) supersensitive; prim, prudish; **~~keit** *f* softness; tenderness; weakness; effeminacy; flabbiness; indolence; mellowness; **~ling** *m* molly-coddle, weakling, milksop, *Am fam* sissy, prissy, cot betty, goody-goody, effie, softy; **~stahl** *m* soft steel; **~teile** *m pl* soft parts *pl*; belly, abdomen; **~tier** *n* mollusc; **~tönend** *a* sonorous; **~ werden** *itr* to soften; **~zeichner** *m phot* soft-focus lens.

Weichbild *n* precincts *pl*, environs *pl*, outskirts *pl*; municipal area.

Weiche *f rail* shunt, points *pl*, *Am* switch; turnout; *tele* filter; separator; (*Nebengleis*) siding; **~nhebel** *m* switch lever; **~nlaterne** *f* switch lamp;

~**nrost** *m* switch and crossing tie; ~**nschiene** *f* movable rail, *Am* switch tongue; ~**nschwelle** *f* switch tie; ~**nsicherung** *f* point locking; ~**nsignal** *n* point indicator, switch signal; ~**nsteller** *m* pointsman, *Am* switchman; ~**nstellwerk** *n* switch-stand; ~**nstraße** *f* set of points.

weichen *irr itr* to give way (*od* ground), to fall back, to retreat, to budge; (*nachgeben*) to yield, to give in; (*Preise*) to decline, to fall, to drop, to ease off; *zum* ~ *bringen* to push back, to repel; *von jdm* ~ to leave, to abandon; *jdm nicht von der Seite* ~ not to budge from s. o.'s side.

Weichsel *f* Vistula; ~**kirsche** *f* mahaleb cherry, morello cherry; ~**rohr** *n* cherry-wood tube; ~**zopf** *m med* Polish plait.

Weide *f* pasture; (*Vieh~*) pasture-ground, pasturage; (*Baum*) willow, osier; ~**n** *itr* to pasture, to graze; *tr* to feed; to drive to pasture; *r* to feast (o.'s eyes on), to delight in; to gloat over; ~**nband** *n* withe; ~**nbaum** *m* willow-tree; ~**nbusch** *m*, ~**ngebüsch** *n* willow-bush, willow-plot; ~**nflechter** *m* osier plaiter; ~**ngeflecht** *n* wicker-work; ~**ngerte**, ~**nrute** *f* willow-twig, osier-switch; ~**nkätzchen** *n* catkin; ~**nkorb** *m* wicker-basket; ~**nröschen** *n* willow-herb; ~**nzweige** *m pl* wicker; ~**platz** *m* pasture-ground; ~**recht** *n* right of pasture; ~**rich** *m* willow-herb.

weid|lich *a* greatly, thoroughly; properly; ~**mann** *m* sportsman, huntsman; ~~**heil!** good sport! ~~**ssprache** *f* hunter's slang; ~**männisch** *a* sportsmanlike; ~**messer** *n* hunting-knife; ~**werk** *n* the chase, hunt(ing), sport; ~**wund** *a* shot in the intestines.

Weife *f* reel; ~**n** *tr* to reel, to wind.

weiger|n *r* to refuse, to decline, to deny; (*zurückweisen*) to reject; (*einwenden*) to object; ~**ung** *f* refusal, denial, rejection; *Am sl* brush-off; ~~ *zu kaufen* buyer's resistance.

Weih *m*, ~**e** *f* (*Vogel*) kite; ~**altar** *m* consecrated altar; ~**becken** *n* holy-water font; ~**bischof** *m* suffragan bishop; ~**e** *f* consecration; (*Einweihung*) inauguration; (*Priester~*) ordination; (*Einführung*) initiation; (*Widmung*) dedication; ~**en** *tr* (*salben*) to consecrate; (*Priester*) to ordain; (*widmen*) to devote, to dedicate; (*segnen*) to bless; *r* to devote o. s. (to); *dem Tode geweiht* doomed to death; ~**estunde** *f* hour of commemoration; ~**evoll** *a* solemn, pathetic; (*heilig*) holy, hallowed; ~**egabe** *f* votive offering; ~**geschenk** *n* oblation; ~**nacht** *f*, ~~**en** *f pl* Christmas, *Abk* Xmas; *fröhliche* ~~! merry Christmas! ~~**lich** *a* Christmas; ~~**sabend** *m* Christmas Eve; ~~**sbaum** *m* Christmas tree; tannenbaum; *aero sl* airfield lights *pl*; ~~**sbescherung** *f* distribution of Christmas presents; ~~**seinkaufszeit** *f* Christmas shopping season; ~~**sfeiertag** *m* Christmas Day; ~~**sfest** *n* Christmas; ~~**sgeschenk** *n* Christmas present (*Am* gift); (*für Dienstboten*) Christmas-box; ~~**sgratifikation** *f* Christmas gratuity; ~~**skerze** *f* Christmas candle; ~~**slied** *n* carol; ~~**smann** *m* Father Christmas; Santa Claus; ~~**smarkt** *m* Christmas shopping; Christmas fair; ~~**stag** *m* Christmas Day; *zweiter* ~~*stag* Boxing-day; ~~**szeit** *f* Christmas-tide, Yuletide; ~**rauch** *m* incense; ~~**faß** *n* censer, thurible; ~**wasser** *n* holy water; ~~**bekken** *n* font; stoup; ~~**kessel** *m* aspersorium, font; ~(~)**wedel** *m* aspergillum.

Weiher *m* pond.

weil *conj* because, since.

weil|and *adv* formerly, of old, once; *a* (*Person*) late, defunct; ~**chen** *n* little while, *fam* spell; *warte ein* ~~ wait a bit; ~**e** *f* a space of time, while; (*Muße*) leisure; *Eile mit* ~*e* more haste, less speed; haste makes waste; *damit hat es gute* ~~ there's no hurry; *vor e-r ganzen* ~~ quite a while ago; ~**en** *itr* to tarry, to stay, to linger.

Weiler *m* hamlet.

Wein *m* wine; (*Pflanze*) vine; (*Trauben*) grapes *pl*; *wilder* ~ Virginia creeper; *der* ~ *ist ihm in den Kopf gestiegen* the wine has gone to his head; *jdm klaren* ~ *einschenken* to tell s. o. the plain truth; ~**artig** *a* vinous, winy; ~**ausschank** *m* retail of wine; ~**bau** *m* wine-growing, viticulture; ~**bauer** *m* wine-grower, vinedresser; ~**beere** *f* grape; ~**berg** *m* vineyard; ~~**besitzer** *m* proprietor of a vineyard; ~~**schnecke** *f* edible snail; ~**blume** *f* bouquet; ~**blüte** *f* vine blossom; ~**brand** *m* brandy, cognac; ~**drossel** *f* thrush, redwing; ~**ernte** *f* vintage; ~**essig** *m* wine vinegar; ~**fabrik** *f* winery; ~**farbe** *f* wine colo(u)r; ~**faß** *n* wine-cask; ~**flasche** *f* winebottle; ~**garten** *m* vineyard; ~**gärtner** *m* vinedresser; ~**gärung** *f* vinous fermentation; ~**gegend** *f* wine-district; ~**gehalt** *m* vinosity; ~**geist** *m* spirit of wine, alcohol; ~~**firnis** *m* spirit varnish; ~~**messer** *m* alcoholmeter; ~**gelb** *a* wine-yellow; ~**geruch** *m* smell of wine; ~**glas** *n* wineglass; ~**gut** *n* vineyard; ~**handel** *m* wine-trade; ~**händler** *m* wine-merchant; ~**handlung** *f* wine-merchant's shop; ~**haus** *n* wine-tavern; ~**heber** *m* siphon for drawing wine; ~**hefe** *f* dregs (*pl*) of wine; ~**icht**, ~**ig** *a* vinous; ~**jahr** *n* year's wine crop, vintage; ~**kanne** *f* wine-jug; ~**karte** *f* wine-list; ~**keller** *m* wine-cellar, wine-vault; (*Ausschank*) wine-tavern; ~**kelter** *f* winepress; ~**kenner** *m* judge of wines; ~**kneipe**, ~**schenke** *f* wine-shop; ~**krug** *m* wine-jug, tankard; ~**küfer** *m* cooper; ~**kühler** *m* wine-cooler; ~**lager** *n* stock of wine(s); (*Kelter*) wine-vaults *pl*; ~**land** *n* wine-country; ~**laub** *n* vine-leaves *pl*; ~**laube** *f* vine-arbour; ~**laune** *f* merry mood produced by wine-drinking; ~**lese** *f* grape-gathering, vintage; ~**leser** *m*, ~~**in** *f* vintager; ~**most** *m* must; ~**panscher** *m* adulterator of wine; ~**pfahl** *m* vine-prop; ~**presse** *f* winepress; ~**probe** *f* sample of wine; tasting of wine; ~**prüfer** *m* wine-taster; ~**ranke** *f* vine-branch, tendril; ~**rausch** *m* intoxication caused by wine; ~**rebe** *f* vine-branch, vine; grape-vine; ~**reich** *a* vinous; ~**reisende(r)** *m* travel(l)er for a wine-firm; ~**rot** *a* ruby; ~**sauer** *a* tartaric; ~**säure** *f* acidity of wine; *chem* tartaric acid; ~**schank** *m* retail of wine; ~**schenk** *m* tavern-keeper, vintner; ~**schlauch** *m* wine-skin; (*Trinker*) winebibber; ~**schröter** *m* wine-porter; ~**sorte** *f* kind of wine; ~**stein** *m* tartar; ~**steuer** *f* duty (*od* tax) on wine; ~**stock** *m* vine; ~**stube** *f* wine-room, wine-shop; ~**traube** *f* bunch of (*Am* wine-) grapes; ~~**nkur** *f* grape-cure; ~**treber** *m pl*, ~**trester** *m pl* skins (*pl*) of pressed grapes; ~**trinker** *m* winebibber; ~**umrankt** *a* vine-clad; ~**verfälschung** *f* adulteration of wine; ~**waage** *f* wine-ga(u)ge; ~**zieher** siphon, pipette; ~**zwang** *m* obligation to order wine.

wein|en *itr* to weep (*um* for), to cry, to shed tears; *sich die Augen aus dem Kopf* ~~ to weep o.'s eyes out; *bittere Tränen* ~~ to weep bitter tears; *heftig* ~~ to burst into tears; *heiße Tränen* ~~ to shed hot tears; *vor Freude* ~~ to weep for joy; *dem* ~~ *nahe* on the verge of tears; ~~**d** *a* crying, weeping; sobbing; ~**erlich** *a* inclined to weep; whining; ~**krampf** *m* crying-fit, convulsive sobbing.

Weise *f* mode, manner, way; (*Form*) fashion, method; (*Melodie*) melody, tune; (*Gewohnheit*) habit, custom; *auf diese* ~ in this way; by this means; *auf diese* ~ *erreichen Sie nichts* you won't get anywhere that way; *in der* ~, *daß* in such a way that; so that; *das ist wirklich keine Art u.* ~ (*fam*) that's really no way to behave; *auf welche* ~? in what way? *auf keine* ~ by no means, not at all; *jeder nach seiner* ~ every one in his own way.

weise *a* wise; (*klug*) prudent, sage; ~ *m* wise man.

Weisel *m* queen-bee.

weis|en *irr tr* to show, to point out, to indicate; *jdn* ~~ *nach* to direct to; *an jdn* ~~ to refer to; *von sich* ~~ to refuse, to reject, to decline; ~~ *aus* to expel; *aus dem Hause* ~~ to show the door; *aus dem Lande* ~~ to banish, to exile; *itr* to point (*auf* at); ~**er** *m* pointer; indicator; (*Uhr*) hand; (*Führer*) guide; (*Weg~~*) signpost; ~**ung** *f* order, instruction, direction; directive; ~~**sgemäß** *a* as instructed; ~~**srecht** *n* right to give orders.

Weis|heit *f* wisdom, knowledge, prudence; *behalte deine* ~~ *für dich!* keep your advice to yourself*! seine* ~~ *auskramen* to display o.'s learning; *ich bin mit meiner* ~~ *zu Ende* I am at my wits' end; ~~**szahn** *m* wisdom-tooth; ~**lich** *adv* wisely, prudently; ~**machen** *tr: jdm etw* ~~ to make s. o. believe; to fool, to hoax; *lassen Sie sich nichts* ~~! don't be taken in! *das machen Sie e-m anderen* ~ tell that to the marines; ~**sagen** *tr* to predict, to prophesy, to foretell; ~**sager(in)** *m* (*f*) prophet, prophetess; fortune-teller; ~**sagung** *f* prophecy, prediction.

weiß *a* white; (*sauber*) clean; (*unbeschrieben*) blank; (*weißgrau, bereift*) hoary; *das* ~*e Haus* the White House; ~*es Eisenblech* tin plate; ~*er Fluß* leucorrh(o)ea; ~*er Sonntag* Sunday after Easter, Low Sunday; *die* ~*en* the white races; ~*e Woche* white sale; *etw schwarz auf* ~ *zeigen* to show s. th. in black and white; ~ *machen* to whiten; *sich* ~ *waschen* to exculpate (*od* white-wash) o. s.; ~ *färben* to dye white; ~**bäcker** *m* baker of wheaten bread; ~~**ei** *f* baker and confectioner's shop; ~**bier** *n* pale beer; ~**blech** *n* tin-plate; ~~**dose** *f* tin can, tin box; ~~**waren** *f pl* tinware; ~**blei** *n* tin; ~~**erz** *n* white lead ore; ~**bleiche** *f* full bleach; ~**brot** *n* white bread; ~**buch** *n* white-paper; ~**buche** *f* beech-tree; (*Hain~*) hornbeam; ~**dorn** *m* hawthorn; (*Blüte*) May-flower; ~**en** *tr* to whiten; (*tünchen*) to whitewash; ~**fisch** *m* bleak, blay; (*kleinerer*) white-bait; ~**fleckig** *a* white-speckled; ~**fluß** *m* leucorrh(o)ea; ~**fuchs** *m zoo* white fox; (*Pferd*) light sorrel horse; ~**gekleidet** *a* dressed in white; ~**gelb** *a* pale yellow; ~**gerben** *tr* to taw; ~**gerber** *m* tawer; ~~**ei** *f* tawery; ~**glühend** *a* white-hot, incandescent; ~**glut** *f* white heat, incandescence; ~**gold** *n* white gold, platinum; ~**grau** *a* whitish-gray; hoary; ~**guß** *m* white cast iron; ~**haarig** *a* white-haired; ~**kohl** *m*, ~**kraut** *n* white cabbage; ~**lich** *a* whitish; ~**metall** *n* white metal;

babbit metal; **~näherei** *f* plain (needle)-work; **~näherin** *f* needlewoman; **~tanne** *f* silver fir; **~waren** *f pl* linen goods *pl*, drapery; **~~geschäft** *n* linen-drapery; **~~händler** *m* linen-draper; **~wein** *m* white wine; hock; *Am* Rhine wine; **~wurst** *f* Bavarian sausage; **~zeug** *n* (household-)linen.

weit *a* (*Gegensatz eng*) wide; (*geräumig*) ample, large, spacious; (*umfassend*) capacious; (*breit*) broad; (*ausgedehnt*) extensive; (*unermeßlich*) vast, immense; (*entfernt*) remote; far, far away, *Am* way off; a long way, *Am* away; (*lose*) loose; *bei ~em* by far, much; *bei ~em nicht* by no means; not nearly; *von ~em* from a distance; *~ voraus* far ahead, *Am* way ahead; *~ hergeholt* far-fetched; distant; *wie ~* how far on; *so ~* so far; *~ entfernt von* far from; *~ u. breit* far and wide; *das geht zu ~* that is beyond me; that's going too far; *~ zurück* as long as, *Am* away back; *von ~em* from a distance, from afar; *ein ~er Weg* a long way; *~ von hier* far from here; *fünf Meter ~* a distance of five metres; *es ~ bringen* to get on (well); to go far; *nicht ~ her sein* not to be worth much; *ich bin so ~* I'm ready; *wenn alles so ~ ist* when everything is ready; *~ vom Ziel sein fam* to be off the beam; *das Kleid ist dir viel zu ~* that dress is much too big for you; *das ~e suchen* to decamp; *~es Gewissen* elastic conscience; *~er Satz typ* driving-out; *~ gefehlt!* far from it! **~ab** *adv* far away; **~aus** *adv* by far, much; **~blick** *m* far-sightedness, fore--sight; vision; **~~end** *a* far-sighted.

Weit\|e *f* width; wideness; (*Größe*) size; largeness; (*Breite*) breadth; (*Entfernung*) distance; (*Länge*) length; (*Spielraum*) range; (*Ausdehnung*) extent; (*Fassungsvermögen*) capacity; (*Durchmesser*) diameter; *astr, math, phys* amplitude; *mar* beam; *fig* range, scope, comprehensiveness, breadth; *lichte ~~* inside diameter, inside width; bore; lumen; **~en** *tr* to enlarge, to extend, to widen, to expand; (*Schuhe*) to stretch; *r* to broaden out, to widen (into); *fig* to broaden; **~gehend** *a* far-reaching, far-stretched, far-embracing, far-flying, far-ranging; (*umfassend*) extensive; wholesale; sweeping; (*sehr*) much; (*Verständnis*) full; **~geöffnet** *a* wide-opened; **~gereist** *a* having travel(l)ed far; **~greifend** *a* far-reaching; **~her** *adv* from afar; **~~geholt** *a* far-fetched; **~herzig** *a* broad-minded; **~hin** *adv* far away, far off; **~läufig** *a* extensive, lengthy, wide; (*entfernt*) distant; (*geräumig*) spacious, roomy, vast; (*zerstreut*) scattered, widespread, straggling; diffuse; (*umständlich*) circumstantial; (*eingehend*) detailed; (*verwickelt*) complicated; *adv* at great length; **~maschig** *a* wide-meshed, coarse-meshed; **~reichend** *a* far-reaching; long-range; **~schuß** *m mil* over; **~schweifig** *a* detailed, circumstantial; (*mühsam*) tedious; (*wortreich*) prolix; diffuse; (*langwierig*) lengthy; **~~keit** *f* prolixity, verbosity; lengthiness; diffuseness; **~sichtig** *a* long-sighted; *fig* far--sighted; **~~keit** *f* long-sightedness, presbyopia; *fig* far-sightedness; (*Scharfsichtigkeit*) perspicacity; **~sprung** *m* long jump; **~spurig** *a* wide--tracked; **~streckenflug** *m* far-distance flight; **~tragend** *a* long-range; *fig* far-reaching; (*wichtig*) important, portentous; **~umfassend** *a* comprehensive, extensive; **~ung** *f* widening; **~verbreitet** *a* widespread; (*Zeitung*) widely circulated; (*vorherrschend*) prevalent; (*allgemein*) general; **~verzweigt** *a* widely ramified, widely extended; **~winkelaufnahme** *f phot* wide--angle photograph; **~winkelbild** *n* wide-angle picture; **~winkelobjektiv** *n* wide-angle lens; **~winklig** *a* wide--angle(d).

weiter *a* farther; (*bes. fig*) further; (*entfernter*) more distant; (*ausgedehnter*) more extensive, wider; (*zusätzlich*) additional; *adv* farther; further; (*sonst*) else; (*voran*) forward, on; (*ferner*) furthermore, moreover; *~!* go on! proceed! *nichts ~* nothing more, not ... anything else; *was ~?* what else? *~ nichts?* is that all? *bis auf ~es* until further notice, for the present; *des ~en* furthermore, moreover; *ohne ~es* without more ado, immediately, off-hand; (*bereitwillig*) readily; (*mühelos*) without any trouble; *wenn es ~ nichts ist* if that's all there is to it; *nur ~ so!* keep going! *er will nicht ~ hier bleiben* he doesn't want to stay any longer; *er kann nicht ~* he can't go any further; *was geschah ~?* what happened next? *u. so ~* and so on, and so forth, et cetera (*Abk* etc.); *~e Angaben* further particulars; *~e Begründung* substantiation; **~bearbeitung** *f* further treatment; **~befördern** *tr* to forward, to retransmit, to send on; (*umadressieren*) to redirect; **~beförderung** *f* transmittal, retransmission; **~begeben** *irr tr com* to negotiate further; **~behandlung** *f* subsequent treatment; **~bestehen** *irr itr* to continue to exist, to survive, to go on; **~bestand** *m* continued existence; continuance; **~bewegen** *tr* to move on; *tech* to feed; **~bilden** *tr* to develop; *r* to continue o.'s studies; **~bildung** *f* advanced training; in-service training; further development; (*Biologie*) evolutionary development; **~bringen** *irr tr* to help on; *itr es ~~* to get on, to make progress; **~denkend** *a* (*bedacht*) mindful (of); (*vorsorglich*) provident; (*vorausschauend*) far-sighted; **~drehen** *tr* to step round; **~empfehlung** *f* recommendation; **~entwickeln** *tr* to develop; **~entwicklung** *f* development; advancement; **~e(s)** *n* the rest; (*genaueres*) further details *pl*; **~existenz** *f* survival; **~fliegen** *irr itr* to continue the flight; **~flug** *m* continuation of a flight; **~führen** *tr* to continue, to carry on; (*Leitung*) to extend; **~führung** *f* continuation; **~gabe** *f tele* retransmission; (*Brief*) forwarding; **~~stelle** *f* distribution point; **~geben** *irr tr* to pass on, to forward, to retransmit; (*wiederholen*) to repeat; *radio, tele* to relay; **~gehen** *irr itr* to go on, to continue; to walk on; *~~!* keep moving! move on! **~~d** *a* comprehensive, extensive; (*fühlbar*) perceptible; (*weittragend*) far-reaching; **~greifen** *irr itr* to extend; **~helfen** *irr itr* to help on; **~hin** *adv* furthermore, moreover; in future, after that; **~kommen** *irr itr* to get on, to get ahead; to (make) progress, to advance; **~~ n** getting on; making o.'s way; **~können** *irr itr* to be able to go on; **~laufen** *irr itr* to go on, to continue; **~leiten** *tr* to forward, to pass on, to transmit; **~leitung** *f* forwarding, transmission; **~~stelle** *f rail* forwarding station; **~lesen** *irr itr, tr* to go on reading, to continue reading; **~marsch** *m* resumed march; **~reise** *f* continuation of a journey; **~sagen** *tr* to repeat, to tell others; **~schalten** *tr* to step up (*od* on); **~schieben** *irr tr* to push forward, to shuffle; **~senden** *irr tr* to send on, to forward; (*an neue Anschrift*) to redirect; **~sendung** *f* retransmission; forwarding; redirection; **~ungen** *f pl* difficulties *pl*; complications *pl*; formalities *pl*; red tape; **~verarbeitet** *a* worked subsequently (into); **~verarbeitung** *f* subsequent treatment, machining, processing; **~~sbetrieb** *m* finishing plant; **~veräußerung** *f* resale; **~verbreiten** *tr* to hawk about, to spread; **~verbreitung** *f* communication, spreading, propagation.

Weizen *m* wheat; (*oft*) corn; **~brot** *n* wheaten bread; **~flocken** *f pl* squashed wheat; **~gries** *m* wheat grits *pl*; **~mehl** *n* wheaten flour; **~schrot** *n* shredded wheat.

welch *prn* who, which, what, some, any; *~ ein Unglück!* what a misfortune! **~er, ~e, ~es** *prn, a* (*auswählend*) which; (*relativ*) who, which, that; *~er von beiden* which of the two; *derjenige, ~er* he who; *diejenigen, ~e* those who, such as; *~er auch immer* whoever, whichever, whatever; *mit ~em Recht sagt er das?* what right has he to say that? **~erlei** *adv* of what kind.

welk *a* withered, decayed, faded; (*schlaff*) limp, flabby; (*schlapp*) languid; *~ werden,* **~en** *itr* to wither, to fade.

Well\|baum *m* arbo(u)r, axletree, shaft; **~blech** *n* corrugated iron; **~~decke** *f* corrugated-iron cover; **~~hütte** *f* corrugated-iron shelter, *mil Am* Quonset hut; **~e** *f* (*Wasser*) wave, billow; (*Brandung*) surge, surf; *radio* wave (-length), frequency; beam; *tech* axle, arbo(u)r, shaft, spindle, vertical capstan, roll(er); (*im Glas*) stria; (*Holz*) fagot, bundle; (*Hitze~~*) heat-wave, hot spell; *sport* circling round the horizontal bar, *fam* grinder; *durchgehende ~~* throughgoing wave; *einfallende ~~* incident wave; *gedämpfte ~~* decadent wave; *kurze ~~* short wave; *liegende ~~* horizontal wave; *modulierte ~~* modulated wave; *ungedämpfte ~~* continuous wave; *verzerrte ~~* deformed wave; *zurücklaufende ~~* backwash; *~~n schlagen* to rise in waves; *die ~~n schlagen gegen die Felsen* the waves beat against the rocks; **~en** *tr* to wave; (*Blech*) to corrugate; (*kochen*) to boil, to simmer; (*rollen*) to roll; **~~abgrenzung** *f* frequency and wave-band designation; **~~änderung** *f* frequency shift; **~~antrieb** *m* shaft drive; **~~anzeiger** *m* wave detector, cymoscope; **~~artig** *a* wavelike, wavy, ondulatory; **~~aufzeichner** *m* oscillograph; **~~ausbreitung** *f* wave propagation; **~~ausschlag** *m* wave extent; **~~bad** *n* bathe; swimming-bath with artificial waves; **~~band** *n* wave (*od* frequency) band; **~~bauch** *m* loop, bulge, antinode; **~~bereich** *m* wave range (*od* band), frequency band; **~~bereichschalter** *m* wave-band switch; **~~berg** *m* (wave) crest; **~~bewegung** *f* undulation, wave motion; **~~bildung** *f* waving; **~~brecher** *m* breakwater, breaker, jetty; **~~bündel** *n* wave packet, beam of electrons and ions; **~~einstellknopf** *m* wave-passage button; **~~einteilung** *f* classification of waves; **~~empfänger** *m* wave receiver; **~~filter** *n* (wave) filter; **~~förmig** *a* wave-like, wavy, undulating; **~~fortpflanzung** *f* wave propagation; **~~gang** *m* dashing of waves; **~~gipfel, ~~kamm** *m* crest (*od* hump) of a wave; **~~lager** *n* main bearing; **~~länge** *f* wave length; **~~lehre** *f* undulating mechanics *pl*;

~~leiter *m* wave guide; **~~linie** *f* wavy line, undulatory (*od* sinuous) line; **~~messer** *m* frequency meter; **~~reiten** *irr itr* to aquaplane; **~~reiter** *m* surf rider; **~~saugkreis** *m* wave trap; **~~schalter** *m* wave-range switch; **~~schieber** *m* phase shifter; **~~schlag** *m* shock of waves, dashing (*od* breaking) of waves; **~~sieb** *n* filter, wave screen; **~~sittich** *m* budgerigar; **~~tal** *n* wave trough; **~~theorie** *f* undulatory theory; **~~umschalter** *m* wave-length changing switch; **~~verteilung** *f* allocation of frequencies; **~~wechsel** *m* frequency change; **~~weite** *f* amplitude of waves; **~~widerstand** *m* surge impedance; (*Seeflugzeug*) hump resistance; (*Überschall*) impact wave resistance; **~~zahl** *f* wave number; **~~zug** *m* wave train, beat; **~fleisch** *n* boiled pork; **~ig** *a* undulating, rolling, wavy; (*bauschig*) baggy; (*gekräuselt, el*) rippled; **~~keit** *f* waviness; rippled condition; pulsation factor; **~karton** *m*, **~pappe** *f* corrugated paper; **~rad** *n* front wheel; **~sand** *m* shifting sand.

Welpe *f* whelp.

Wels *m* sheat-fish.

welsch *a* Italian; French; (*wallisisch*) Welsh; (*fremdländisch*) foreign.

Welt *f* world; (*Weltall*) universe; *alle ~* everybody, all the world; *die elegante ~* the smart set; *auf der ~, in aller ~* on earth; *auf die ~ kommen* to come into the world; to be born; *so geht es in der ~* such is the life; *um alles in der ~* by all means; *aus der ~ schaffen* to settle a matter, to do away with, to put out of the way; *in die ~ setzen, zur ~ bringen* to give birth to, to bring into the world; *in der ganzen ~ herumgekommen sein* to have been all over the world; **~abgewandt** *a* detached from the world; **~all** *n* universe; **~alter** *n* age, period in history; **~anschaulich** *a* ideological; **~anschauung** *f* (philosophical) conception of the world; world-outlook, views *pl*; (*Glaube*) creed; ideology; **~ausmaß** *n*: *im ~~* on a global scale; **~ausstellung** *f* international exhibition; **~bekannt, ~berühmt** *a* world-famous, world-renowned; **~beschreibung** *f* cosmography; **~bild** *n* conception of the world; **~blatt** *n* newspaper of a world-wide circulation; **~brand** *m* universal conflagration; **~bummler** *m* globetrotter; **~bund** *m* international union; **~bürger** *m* cosmopolitan, citizen of the world; **~~lich** *a* cosmopolitan; **~dame** *f* fashionable lady; **~enraum** *m* universe; interstellar space; **~entrückt** *a* isolated, detached; **~ereignis** *n* event of world-wide importance; **~erfahren** *a* worldly-wise; **~erfahrung** *f* worldly wisdom; **~erschütternd** *a* world-shaking; **~flucht** *f* flight from the world; **~flug** *m* round-the-world flight; **~fremd** *a* solitary, secluded; ignorant of the world; **~friede** *m* world peace; **~~nsrat** *m* World Peace Council; **~funknetz** *n* world radio network; **~gebäude** *n* cosmic system; **~gegend** *f* region; **~geistliche(r)** *m* secular priest; **~gericht** *n* last judg(e)ment; **~geltung** *f* international reputation; **~geschichte** *f* universal history; **~gewandt** *a* knowing the ways of the world; **~handel** *m* international commerce, world trade; **~händel** *m pl* worldly affairs *pl*; **~herrschaft** *f* empire of the world; world domination; **~höchstleistung** *f* world record; **~karte** *f* map of the world, globular chart, planisphere; **~kenntnis** *f* worldly wisdom, knowledge of the world; **~kind** *n*, **~mensch** *m* worldling; **~klug** *a* worldly-wise, politic; prudent; **~~heit** *f* worldly wisdom; **~körper** *m* heavenly body, sphere; **~kreis** *m* universe; **~krieg** *m* World War (I, II); Armageddon; **~~teilnehmer** *m* veteran of the First World War; **~kugel** *f* globe; **~lage** *f* state of political affairs; general political situation; **~lauf** *m* course of the world; **~lich** *a* worldly; mundane; (*diesseitig*) secular, temporal; (*nicht kirchlich*) profane; **~~keit** *f* worldliness; secularity, temporality; **~literatur** *f* universal literature; **~luftstreitkräfte** *f pl* global air striking force; **~luftverkehr** *m* world air traffic; **~lust** *f* worldly pleasure; **~macht** *f* world power; **~~politik** *f* imperialist policy, imperialism; **~mann** *m* man of the world, society man; **~männisch** *a* well-bred, gentlemanly; **~markt** *m* world market; international trade; **~~preise** *m pl* world-market prices *pl*; **~meer** *n* ocean; **~meinung** *f* world opinion; **~meister** *m* world champion; **~~schaft** *f* world's championship; **~monopol** *n* global monopoly; **~ordnung** *f* invariable laws of nature; *pol* system of the world; **~politik** *f* world politics *pl*; foreign policy on the grand scale; **~postverein** *m* Postal Union; **~raum** *m* interstellar space; **~~bewohner** *m* space man; **~~fahrer, ~~reisende(r)** *m* space travel(l)er; **~~fahrt** *f* astronautics *pl;* space travel; **~~schiff** *n* space ship; **~~strahlen** *m pl* cosmic rays *pl*; **~reich** *n* universal empire; **~reise** *f* journey round the world; **~~nde(r)** *m* globetrotter; **~rekord** *m* world record; *aero* air speed record; **~ruf** *m* world-wide reputation; **~schmerz** *m* world-weariness; sentimental pessimism; **~schöpfer** *m* Creator; **~sicherheitsrat** *m* U.N. Security Council; **~sinn** *m* worldliness; **~sprache** *f* universal language; **~stadt** *f* metropolis; **~teil** *m* continent; part of the world; **~telegraphenverein** *m* international telegraphic union; **~umfassend** *a* global; world-wide; **~umsegler** *m* circumnavigator of the globe; **~umseglung** *f* circumnavigation of the globe; **~umspannend** *a* world-wide, universal; **~untergang** *m* end of the world; **~verkehr** *m* international traffic, world traffic; **~weisheit** *f* philosophy; **~weit** *a* world-wide; **~wende** *f* turning point in world's history; **~wirtschaft** *f* world trade and industry; **~~skonferenz** *f* international economic conference; **~~skrise** *f* world depression, international economic crisis; **~wunder** *n* wonder of the world; **~zeituhr** *f* universal time clock.

Weltergewicht *n* (*Boxen*) welter-weight (=147 lbs.).

wem *prn dat* to whom; **~fall** *m* dative case, objective case.

wen *prn acc* whom; **~fall** *m* accusative case, objective case.

Wend|e *f* turn; turning-point; (*Änderung*) change; (*Zeit~~*) new epoch, new era; *sport* face vault; **~~getriebe** *n* reversing gear; **~~hals** *m* wryneck; **~~kreis** *m geog* tropic; *tech* radius of turn; **~~kurve** *f aero* turn in landing; **~~l** *f* helix, spiral, coil; **~~ltreppe** *f* (*e-e* a flight of) winding-stairs *pl*; **~~marke** *f* turning point; *aero* pylon; **~~maschine** *f* hay tedder; **~~n** (*auch irr*) *tr* to turn (round); *el* to reverse; (*schwanken, gieren*) to yaw; (*Wind*) *mar* to veer; (*Geld*) to spend (*an* on); *bitte ~~n!* (please) turn over! *Abk* P.T.O.; *kein Auge ~~n von* not to take o.'s eyes off; *r* (*umdrehen*) to roll over, to turn round; (*ändern*) to change; *sich ~~n an* to apply to, to turn to; (*ansprechen*) to address o. s. to; (*aufsuchen*) to see, to contact s. o.; *sich zum Guten ~~n* to turn out for the best; *sich ~~n gegen* to turn towards (*od* on); to head towards; *das Blatt hat sich gewendet* the tables are turned; **~~n** *n* turning over; *mar* turning (*od* swinging) round; **~~pflug** *m* hillside plough (*Am* plow); **~~platz** *m mar* turning basin; **~~pol** *m* reversing pole; **~~punkt** *m* turning point; crisis, critical moment; *astr* solstitial point; *math* point of inflection; *el* reversing point, cusp; **~~r** *m tech* turning lever, rotator; *el* reverser; **~~schalter** *m* reversing switch; **~~turm** *m aero* pylon; **~~zeiger** *m aero* turn-and-bank indicator; **~ig** *a* (*behend*) nimble; (*leicht zu handhaben*) man(o)euvrable; *mot* easily steered; (*findig*) resourceful; (*wandlungsfähig*) versatile; **~~keit** *f* manageableness, man(o)euvrability; mobility; adaptability; *aero* handling; *fig* versatility; **~ung** *f* turn; turning; (*Änderung*) change; turning-point; crisis; *mil* facing (about); wheeling; *aero* bank, turning in; *el* reversal; *gram* idiomatic expression, saying, phrase.

wenig *a* little; **~e** few, some; *ein ~* a little, a bit; *mit ~ Worten* in a few words; *vor ~en Tagen* some days ago; *das W~e* the little; *das ist zu ~* that's too little; **~er** *a* less; (*von mehreren*) fewer; *immer ~~* less and less; *nichts ~~ als* anything but; *nicht ~~ als* no less than; *fünf ~~ drei* five minus three; **~keit** *f* smallness; pittance; fewness; (*Kleinigkeit*) trifle; *meine ~~* my own little self; **~ste** *a* least; fewest; *zum ~sten* at the least; *am ~sten* least of all; *die ~~n Leute* only a very few people; **~stens** *adv* at least.

wenn *conj* (*bedingend*) if, in case; *auch ~* even if; *selbst ~* even if, even supposing that, though; *immer ~* whenever; *außer ~* unless, except when (*od* if); *~ anders* provided that, if indeed, if really; *~ auch noch so* however; if ever so; *~ nicht* unless, except when (*od* if); *~ ... schon* as long as; *~ etwa* if by chance; *~ das so ist!* in that case! *na, ~ schon!* well, what of it! *~ ... nicht gewesen wäre* but for; **~gleich, ~schon** *conj* although, though.

wer *prn* (*relativ*) who; he who; (*fragend*) who; (*auswählend*) which; (*jemand*) somebody, anyone; *~ anders* who else; *~ auch immer* whoever, whosoever; *~ da?* who goes there? **~fall** *m* nominative (case).

Werbe|abteilung *f* advertising department; **~agent** *m* canvasser; publicity man; **~artikel** *m* advertising article; **~berater** *m* advertising expert, public relations counsel; **~brief** *m* publicity letter; **~büro** *n* advertising service, *Am* bureau of publicity; *mil* recruiting office; **~drucksache** *f* advertising printed matter; (*einzelnes Blatt*) broadsheet, broadside; **~druckschrift** *f* prospectus; **~erfolg** *m* advertising success; **~fachmann** *m* advertising expert, publicity specialist; **~feldzug** *m* publicity campaign (*od* drive); stunt; **~film** *m* advertising film; **~fläche** *f* advertising space; **~graphik** *f* commercial art; **~idee** *f* advertising idea; **~kosten** *pl* advertising expenses *pl*; **~kraft** *f* advertising appeal, *Am* attention value; **~leiter** *m* manager of the advertising department; **~material** *n* advertising material; **~n** *irr tr* to recruit, to enlist, to enrol(l), to levy; (*gewaltsam*) to press; (*einstellen*) to engage (*zu* for); *itr* to make propaganda for; to advertise for; to canvass for; *~~ um* to court, to woo, to make love to, to sue for; to ask for (a girl's hand in marriage); (*sich bemühen*) to strive (for); *um jds Wohlwollen ~~* to enlist s. o.'s sympathy; **~nummer** *f* complimentary copy; **~plakat** *n* advertising poster; **~prospekt** *m* booklet, leaflet, handbill, prospectus; **~r** *m* suitor; *mil* recruiting officer; (*Bittsteller*) petitioner, *Am* solicitor; *com* canvasser; *Am sl* plugger; **~schreiben** *n* prospectus; **~schrift** *f* publication; (*klein*) small pamphlet, *Am* folder; **~~steller** *m* ad(vertisement) writer; **~seite** *f* advertising page; **~stelle** *f* advertising agency; **~text** *m* copy; **~thema** *n* advertising theme, slogan; **~trommel** *f*: *die ~~ rühren* to beat up recruits; *fig* to make propaganda; **~wirksam** *a* effective in advertising; **~woche** *f* propaganda week; **~zeichner** *m* advertising artist; **~zeichnung** *f* propaganda drawing; **~zweck** *m* advertising aim.

Werbung *f mil* recruiting, levying; (*Mädchen*) wooing, courting; *com* propaganda; advertising; (*Aufträge, Wähler*) canvassing; *Am* publicity; **~skosten** *pl* advertising expenses *pl*, publicity costs *pl*; (*beruflich*) professional expenditure; **~smaterial** *n Am* promotion matter; **~smittler** *m* advertising agent.

Werdegang *m* career, background; (*Entwicklung*) development; (*Wachstum*) growth; (*Entfaltung*) evolution; *tech* process of production.

werden *itr* to become, to get; (*allmählich*) to grow; (*plötzlich*) to turn; (*ausfallen*) to turn out, to prove; (*entstehen*) to come into existence, to arise, to originate; (*sich ereignen*) to happen; *~ zu* to change into, to turn into; *alt ~* to grow old; *jünger ~* to grow young; *krank ~* to fall ill; *reich ~* to become rich, to grow rich; *böse ~* to grow angry; *schlimmer ~* to grow worse, to impair; *zu Wasser ~* to be frustrated; *Arzt ~* to become a doctor; *was ist aus ihm geworden?* what has become of him? *was will er ~?* what is he going to be? *sauer ~* to turn sour; *zu nichts ~* to come to nought; *es wurde nichts daraus* nothing came of it; *zu Staub ~* to fall to dust; *sich einig ~* to come to terms, *fam* to get together; *es wird kalt* it is getting cold; *es wird Nacht* it is growing dark; *es werde Licht* let there be light; (*Hilfszeitwort*) *ich werde gehen* I shall go; *geliebt ~* to be loved; *es wird uns gesagt* we are told; *~de Mutter* expectant mother; *~ n* becoming, growing, development; genesis; (*Herkunft*) origin; (*Entstehung*) formation, evolution; (*Wachstum*) growth; *im ~ sein* to be in process of development; *große Dinge sind im ~* great things are preparing.

Werder *m* small river-islet, holm.

werf|en *irr tr, itr* to throw (*nach* at); (*Anker, Blick, Licht, Schatten*) to cast; (*schleudern*) to fling; (*heftig*) to hurl; (*hin u. her, in die Höhe*) to toss; (*hin~*) to pitch; (*auf ein Ziel*) to sling; (*vorwärts, Schatten, Bild*) to project; (*auswerfen*) to emit; (*Junge*) to bring forth young, to whelp; (*Pferd*) to foal; (*Schwein*) to litter; (*Raubtier*) to cub; (*Blasen*) to throw up, to form; (*Bomben*) to drop; *r* (*Holz*) to warp; to distort, to deform; (*Linoleum*) to buckle; *sich ~~ auf* to throw o. s. upon, to apply o. s. to, to engage vigorously in; *über Bord ~~* to dump overboard, to jettison; *über den Haufen ~~* to upset; *die Flinte ins Korn ~~* to throw up the sponge; *sich in die Brust ~~* to put out o.'s chest; *sich jdm zu Füßen ~~* to throw o. s. at s. o.'s feet; **~er** *m mil* trench mortar; rocket projector; *Am sport* pitcher; *mar* (*Wasserbomben ~~*) hedgehog; squid; Y-gun; *~~ einsetzen mil* to mortar; **~~abteilung** *f* rocket-projector battalion; chemical battalion; **~~geschoß** *n* projector missile; **~~rahmen** *m* frame-type rocket projector.

Werft wharf; shipyard, dockyard; *aero* workshops *pl*; **~anlage** *f* shipbuilding installation; **~arbeiter** *m* dock labo(u)rer; docker; **~besitzer** *m* wharfinger; **~hafenbecken** *n* careening basin; **~halle** *f aero* repair hangar; **~kran** *m* shipyard crane.

Werg *n* tow; (*gezupftes, geteertes*) oakum; *mit ~ zustopfen* to tow; **~dichtung** *f* hemp packing; **~leinwand** *f* tow linen.

Werk *n* work, labo(u)r; (*das Hergestellte*) workmanship; (*Leistung*) performance; (*Tun*) doing; (*Erzeugnis*) production; (*Tat*) action, deed; (*Unternehmen*) undertaking; (*Fabrik*) factory, manufacturing plant, mill, workshop, works *pl*; (*Hütten~*) forge; (*Mechanismus*) mechanism, gear; (*Metall*) pig of raw lead; (*Papier*) stuff; (*Uhr~*) clock-work; *ins ~ setzen* to set going; *zu ~e gehen* to set about, to begin, to go about it; to proceed; *im ~e sein* to be on foot; *ans ~ gehen* to set to work; *das muß sein ~ sein* that must be his doing; *ans ~!* go to it! **~anlage** *f* plant, works *pl mit sing*; work equipment; **~bahn** *f* works railway; **~bank** *f* (work)bench; **~besitzer** *m* manufacturer, mill-owner; **~druckerei** *f* book-printing establishment; **~en** *itr* to operate, to handle, to manage, to manipulate; to be busy; **~fremd** *a* outside; **~führer, ~meister** *m* foreman, overseer; *Am* superintendent; **~leitung** *f* management; **~luftschutz** *m* factory passive air-defence system; **~nummer** *f* factory serial number; **~pause** *f* rest, recess, work interval; **~photo** *n* studio still; **~platz** *m* block yard; **~probe** *f* sample of metal; **~sangehörige(r)** *m* employe(e) of the firm; **~sausrüstung** *f* plant equipment; **~schrift** *f* staff magazine; **~schutz** *m* industrial police; **~skantine** *f* staff canteen; **~siedlung** *f* workmen's dwellings *pl*; **~sleiter** *m* works (*od* mill) manager; **~spionage** *f* industrial spying (system); **~statt, ~stätte** *f* workshop; plant, factory, mill; **~~arbeit** *f* workmanship; **~~auftrag** *m* work order; **~~bank** *f* mechanical bench; **~~halle** *f* workshop hall; **~~kompanie** *f* repair-shop company; **~~montage** *f* shop assembly; **~~trupp** *m* repair-shop detachment, maintenance party; **~~wagen** *m* maintenance truck; **~~zeichnung** *f* work drawing; **~~zug** *m* maintenance platoon; **~stein** *m* freestone, quarry stone; **~stoff** *m* material, raw materials *pl*, stock; (*künstlich*) substitute fabric; synthetic plastics *pl*; *e-n ~~ verarbeiten* to work with a material; **~~bestellung** *f* material requisition; **~~(f)orschung** *f* materials research; **~~liste** *f* specification; **~~prüfung** *f* testing of materials; **~~verbrauch** *m* material consumption; **~~verfeinerung** *f* processing of any construction material; **~~zuführung** *f* feed of material; **~stück** *n* workpiece, work(ing part), blank to be machined; **~student** *m* student who earns his livings; *~~ sein* (*Am*) to work o.'s way; **~stufe** *f* operation; **~tag** *m* work(ing) day; **~tägig** *a* workaday, commonplace; **~tags** *adv* on week-days; **~tätig** *a* labo(u)ring; active, operative; (*praktisch*) practical; *~~e Bevölkerung* working classes *pl*; *die ~~en* the working people; **~tisch** *m* work-table; **~vertrag** *m* contract of manufacture; **~vertreter** *m* work's representative; **~wohnung** *f* company-dwelling; **~zeichnung** *f* working drawing; **~zeitschrift** *f* house organ, shop news; works magazine; **~zeug** *n* tool, implement, instrument; *fig* organ; **~~abteilung** *f* toolroom; **~~ausgabe** *f* distribution of tools; **~~ausrüstung** *f* tool kit, tool equipment; **~~besteck** *n* set of tools; **~~kasten** *m* tool-box; **~~macher** *m* toolmaker, die-maker; **~~maschine** *f* machine tool; **~~maschinenbau** *m* machine-tool industry; **~~maschinenbauer** *m* machine-tool builder; **~~maschineneinrichter** *m* set-up man; **~~schlitten** *m* tool carrier; **~~schlosser** *m* toolmaker; **~~schlüssel** *m* tool wrench; **~~schrank** *f* tool cabinet; **~~stahl** *m* tool steel; **~~tasche** *f* tool bag, kit.

Wermut *m bot* wormwood; (**Wein**) verm(o)uth.

Wert *m* value, (*bes. innerer*) worth; (*Preis*) price, rate; (*Gegen~*) equivalent; (*Verdienst*) merit; (*Wichtigkeit*) importance; (*Schätzung*) appreciation; (*Nachdruck*) stress; (*Nutzen*) use; *chem* valence; *~ a* valuable; worth (*etw* s. th); (*würdig*) worthy (of); (*lieb*) dear; (*geehrt*) hono(u)red, esteemed; (*gleichwertig*) tantamount (to); *höchstzulässiger ~* maximum safe value; *äußerer ~* face value; *großen ~ legen auf* to make much of, to care much about, to set great store by, *Am* to be very choice of; *im ~ von* at a price of; to the value of; *im ~ sinken* to depreciate; *an ~ übertreffen* to outvalue; *jdn über den ~ e-r Sache aufklären Am* to sell s. o. on the value of s. th.; *nichts ~ sein* to be no good, to be worthless; *es ist nicht der Mühe ~* it isn't worth the trouble; *es ist nicht der Rede ~* it's not worth mentioning; it's nothing to speak of; *nicht viel ~ sein* not to be up to much, not to be worth o.'s salt; *keinen Deut ~ sein* not to be worth a fig, not to be worth a straw; **~angabe** *f* declaration of value, valuation; **~arbeit** *f* workmanship; **~ausgleich** *m* compensation; **~berechnung** *f* valuation, estimation; **~berichtigung** *f* adjustment of value; **~beständig** *a* (of) stable (value), of fixed value; **~~keit** *f* fixed value; **~bestimmung** *f* valuation, evaluation, appraisal, estimate; *chem* determination of valence; **~brief** *m* registered letter, insured letter; **~e** *m pl* (*Wertpapiere*) securities *pl*; (*Aktiva*) assets *pl*; (*Anlagen*) investments *pl*; (*Artillerie*) data *pl*; **~en** *tr* to value, to appraise, to evaluate; **~ersatz** *m* compensation, indemnification, equivalent; **~gegenstand** *m* article of value, valuable; **~geschätzt** *a* esteemed; **~grenze** *f* maximum value; **~ig** *a* valent; **~~keit** *f chem* valence; **~los** *a* worthless, valueless, *Am* no-account; (*nutzlos*) useless; (*unnütz*) trashy; (*vergeblich*) futile; (*unbedeutend*) trifling; (*armselig*) paltry; (*erbärmlich*) trumpery; (*nichtig*) *fam* gimcracky; *fig* not worth mentioning, not worth a straw (*od* a rap); **~~igkeit** *f* worthlessness;

(*Nutzlosigkeit*) uselessness; (*Vergeblichkeit*) futility; **~maßstab, ~messer** *m* standard (of values); **~minderung** *f* depreciation, deterioration in value; **~paket** *n* registered parcel; *als ~~* by insured parcel post; **~papier** *n* security, bond; *festverzinsliches ~~* security at regular interest; **~~anlage** *f* investment in securities; **~~börse** *f* stock market; **~~hinterlegung** *f* deposit of securities; **~schaffend** *a* productive; **~schätzen** *tr* to value, to esteem highly; **~schätzung** *f* esteem, value, appreciation (of); (*Abschätzung*) valuation, appraisal, estimate; **~schwankungen** *f pl* fluctuations in value; **~sendung** *f* consignment of valuables; **~ung** *f* valuation, evaluation, estimate, appraisal; *sport* classification; **~urteil** *n* judg(e)ment as to value; **~verlust** *m*, **~verminderung** *f* depreciation, drop in value; **~voll** *a* valuable, precious; **~zeichen** *n* paper money; (*Briefmarke*) stamp; **~zoll** *m* ad valorem duty; **~zuwachs** *m* accretion in (*od* incremental) value; **~~steuer** *f* increased value tax.

Werwolf *m* wer(e)wolf.

wes, wessen *prn* whose; **~halb, ~wegen** *adv, conj* why, wherefore; on account of which; (*deshalb*) therefore, so; **~fall** *m* genitive (case); possessive case.

Wesen *n* being, creature; (*das Wesentliche*) essence; (*Natur*) nature; (*Beschaffenheit*) character; (*Sinnesart*) disposition; (*~tlicher Zug*) essential feature; (*Persönlichkeit*) personality; (*Stoff*) substance; (*Wirklichkeit*) reality; (*wirkende Kraft*) intrinsic virtue; (*Zustand*) condition; (*Aufbau*) organization, system; (*Betragen*) conduct, manners *pl*, demeano(u)r, bearing, way, air; (*Getue*) fuss, ado; (*philosophisch*) entity; *höchstes ~* Supreme Being; *ein einnehmendes ~ haben* to have a pleasing personality; *sein ~ treiben* to go about; (*Geist*) to haunt a place; *mach nicht so viel ~s davon* don't make such a fuss about it; *das entspricht ganz seinem ~* that's just like him; **~haft** *a* real, substantial; schematic; **~los** *a* incorporeal; (*unwirklich*) unreal, shadowy; **~seigen** *a* characteristic; **~seinheit** *f* identity; **~sgleich** *a* consubstantial; homogeneous; **~szug** *m* characteristic feature; **~tlich** *a* essential; (*bemerkenswert*) remarkable; (*wirklich*) real; (*eigentlich*) intrinsic; (*beträchtlich, ~haft*) substantial; (*wichtig*) important; (*lebenswichtig*) vital; (*bedeutsam*) material (to); *adv* very much, considerably; *im ~en* essentially, in the main.

Wespe *f* wasp; **~nnest** *n* wasps' nest; *in ein ~~ greifen fig* to bring a hornets' nest about o.'s ears, *Am* to wake snakes; **~nstich** *m* wasp's sting; **~ntaille** *f* wasp waist.

West|(en) *m* west, occident; *poet* west wind; **~deutschland** *n* Western Germany; **~europäische Union** *f* Western European Union; **~europäische Gemeinschaft** *f* Western European community; **~falen** *n* Westphalia; **~lich** *a* west(ern); westerly, occidental, westward; **~mächte** *f* Western Powers *pl*; **~union** *f* Western Union; **~wind** *m* west wind; **~wärts** *adv* westward; **~zone** *f* Western zone.

Weste *f* waistcoat, *Am* vest; *e-e reine ~* (*fig*) a clean slate; **~ntasche** *f* waistcoat-pocket.

wett *a* even, equal, *fam* quits; *~ sein* to be quits; **~bewerb** *m* competition; *Am* contest; (*Rennen*) race; (*Treffen*) meet; (*Kampf, Streit*) contest; (*Schule*) *Am* exhibition; *sport* event; *in ~~ treten* to enter into competition, to compete (*mit* with, *bei* in); *außer ~~* non-competitive; **~~er** *m* competitor, rival; **~~sbestimmung** *f* contest rules *pl*; **~~steilnehmer** *m* competitor; **~e** *f* bet, wager; *um die ~~ laufen* to race; *was gilt die ~~?* what do you bet? *e-e ~~ eingehen* to bet; *um die ~~ ...* to vie with one another; **~eifer** *m* emulation, rivalry, competition; **~~n** *itr* to emulate; to vie (with s. o. in s. th.), to contend with, to cope with, to rival s. o.; **~einsatz** *m* stake; **~en** *itr, tr* to bet, to wager; (*setzen*) to bet (*auf* on), to back (a horse); (*e-e ~e machen*) to lay (*od* to make) a bet (*auf* on); *ich ~e mit Ihnen zwei gegen eins* I bet you two to one; *mit jdm ~~, daß* to wager s. o. that; **~er** *m* better; **~fahrt** *f* race; **~flug** *m* air race; **~kampf** *m* competition, event, contest, match, prize-fighting; (*kurz*) short and sharp contest, *Am* brush; **~kämpfer** *m* champion, athlete, competitor; prize-fighter; **~lauf** *m* race, foot-race, running match; (*kurze Strecke*) sprint; **~~en** *irr itr* to run a race; *mit jdm ~~en* to run s. o.; **~läufer** *m* runner; **~machen** *tr* to make up for, to square up, to make good, to compensate for; **~rennen** *n* race, racing; (*mit Hindernissen*) to steeple-chase; **~rudern** *n* pulling race, boat-race; regatta; **~rüsten** *n* armament race, competition in armaments; **~schwimmen** *n* swimming match; *an e-m ~~ teilnehmen* to swim a race; **~segeln** *n* sailing race; **~spiel** *n* match, *Am* game; (*Turnier*) tournament; **~steuer** *f* betting-tax; **~streit** *m* game; (*Turnier*) tournament; emulation; competition; contest; *sport* match, race; **~zettel** *m* betting-slip.

Wetter *n* weather; (*Un~*) tempest, storm, bad weather; *min* damp; air, ventilation; *das ~ hält sich* the weather keeps up; *es ist schönes ~* it is fair weather; *schlagende ~* fire-damp; *alle ~!* my word! by Jove! you don't say so! **~amt** *n* meteorological office, *Am* weather bureau; **~änderung** *f* weather change; **~ansage** *f* weather forecast; **~beobachtung** *f* meteorological observation, weather research; **~bericht** *m* meteorological report, weather forecast; **~beständig** *a* weatherproof, weather-resistant; **~dach** *n* penthouse; **~damm** *m min* ventilation; **~dienst** *m* meteorological service, weather service; **~~stelle** *f* meteorological station; **~dynamit** *m min* permissible dynamite; **~erkundung** *f* weather reconnaissance; **~fahne** *f* vane, weathercock; *aero* wind sack; **~fest** *a* weatherproof; **~flug** *m* weather flight; **~~zeug** *n* meteorological airplane; **~führung** *f min* ventilation service; **~funkmeldung** *f* meteorological message; **~glas** *n* aneroid barometer; **~hahn** *m* weathercock; **~karte** *f* meteorological chart, weather chart; **~kunde** *f* meteorology; aerology; **~lage** *f* weather conditions *pl*, atmospheric conditions *pl*; **~lampe** *f min* safety lamp; **~leitung** *f min* air-channel; **~leuchten** *n* sheet-lightning, heat-lightning; **~mantel** *m* weather-coat, trenchcoat; **~meldung** *f* weather report (*od* message); **~n** *itr* to be stormy, to thunder and lighten; *fig* to curse and swear; to inveigh (*gegen* against); **~nachrichten** *f pl* weather report; **~prophet** *m* weather prophet; **~regel** *f* weather maxim; **~schacht** *m min* air shaft; **~schaden** *m* damage done by the weather; **~scheide** *f* weather limit; **~seite** *f* weather side; **~signaldienst** *m* weather signal service; **~stelle** *f* weather station; **~~nnetz** *n* meteorological network, reseau; **~sturz** *m* sudden fall of temperature; **~übersicht** *f* weather bulletin; **~umschlag, ~wechsel** *m* change of weather; **~verhältnisse** *n pl* weather conditions *pl*, atmospheric conditions *pl*; **~vorhersage** *f* weather forecast; **~warte** *f* meteorological (*od* weather) station; **~wendisch** *a* fickle, capricious, changeable; **~wolke** *f* thunder cloud; **~zeichen** *n* sign of storm; **~zone** *f* zone of bad weather *Flug oberhalb der ~~* overweather flight; **~zug** *m mil* weather platoon.

wetz|en *tr* to sharpen, to whet, to grind; **~stahl** *m* whet steel; **~stein** *m* whetstone, hone.

Whisky *m* whisk(e)y; *Am sl* tangle-foot; *~ ohne Zutaten* neat whiskey, *Am* straight whiskey; *~ mit Soda* whiskey and soda, *Am* highball; **~punsch** *m* whiskey-toddy.

Wichs *m* full dress; **~bürste** *f* blacking-brush.

Wichse *f* blacking; polish(ing paste); (*Prügel*) thrashing; **~n** *tr* to black, to polish, *Am* to shine; *fam* (*prügeln*) to thrash.

Wicht *m* wight; child; chap; (*unreife Person*) chit; (*Geschöpf*) creature; *elender ~* wretch; *armer ~* poor fellow; **~elmännchen** *n* brownie; (*Kobold*) (hob)goblin, imp; (*Elf*) pixie.

wichtig *a* important (to), weighty, momentous; (*wesentlich*) essential; (*hervorragend*) salient; (*zutreffend*) to the point; (*folgenreich*) consequential; (*denkwürdig*) memorable; (*erheblich*) substantial, considerable; (*hervorstechend*) conspicuous, outstanding, distinguished; (*eindrucksvoll*) impressive, striking, imposing, commanding; *~ tun* to assume an air of importance, to give o. s. airs, to act important; **~keit** *f* importance, moment, weight, import; consequence; significance; consideration; seriousness; outstanding feature; essential matter; **~tuer** *m* pompous person; **~~ei** *f* pomposity, self-importance; swanking.

Wicke *f bot* vetch; sweet peas *pl*.

Wickel *m* roll(er); (*Eis~*) ice-pack; (*Haar~*) curler; (*Garn*) ball; (*der Zigarre*) filler; *beim ~ fassen* to collar s. o., to catch hold of; **~band** *n* baby's binder; **~gamasche** *f* puttee; **~kind** *n* baby; child in swaddling-clothes; **~n** *tr* to wind (round), to roll (up), to coil, to twist, to spool; (*ein~~*) to wrap up; (*Zigaretten*) to roll, to make; (*Haar*) to put in curlers; (*Kind*) to put on a baby's clothes, to swathe, to swaddle; *jdn um den Finger ~~* to twist s. o. round o.'s finger; *schief gewickelt sein fam* to be on the wrong track; **~zeug** *n* swaddling-clothes *pl*.

Wick|ler *m* coil winder, wrap; **~lung** *f* winding, coiling; wrapping; casing.

Widder *m* ram; *astr* Aries.

wider *prp* against, contrary to; versus; *in Zssg*: counter-, contra-, anti-, re-, with-; *~ meinen Willen* in spite of my wishes; *für u. ~* pro and con; **~borstig** *a* cross-grained, intractable; **~druck** *m* reaction, counterpressure; *typ* backing up; **~fahren** *irr itr* to happen, to befall, to meet with; *~~ lassen* to do, to mete out to; *jdm Gerechtigkeit ~~ lassen* to give s. o. his due; **~haarig** *a* cross-grained, refractory; **~~keit** *f* repulsiveness; unpleasantness; **~haken** *m* barbed hook;

(*Angel, Pfeil*) barb; **~hall** *m* echo, reverberation; *fig* response; **~hallen** *itr* to echo, to resound with; **~halt** *m* support, hold, prop, grip; *el* resistance; **~klage** *f* countersuit; **~kläger** *m* cross claim (*od* counteraction) plaintiff; **~lager** *n* abutment; support; dolly; **~legbar** *a* refutable, confutable; **~legen** *tr* to disprove, to refute, to confute; **~legung** *f* refutation, confutation, rebuttal, disproof; **~lich** *a* repugnant, disgusting, disagreeable, repulsive, loathsome, nauseous; **~~keit** *f* repulsiveness; loathsomeness; **~natürlich** *a* unnatural, contrary to nature; **~~keit** *f* unnaturalness; **~part** *m* opposition; (*Person*) opponent, adversary; **~raten** *irr tr* to dissuade from; **~rechtlich** *a* illegal, unlawful, contrary to law; *~~ betreten* to trespass (upon); **~~keit** *f* illegality, unlawfulness; **~rede** *f* contradiction, objection; *ohne ~~* unquestionably; **~rist** *m* withers *pl*.

Widerruf *m* revocation, recantation, disavowal; retractation; *jur* disclaimer; *com* cancellation, countermand, withdrawal; *bis auf ~* until recalled, unless countermanded; **~en** *irr tr* to revoke; (*Gesetz*) to repeal, to abolish; (*Ansicht*) to retract; (*Vertrag*) to cancel; (*Befehl*) to countermand; (*Auftrag*) to cancel, to revoke, to withdraw; **~lich** *a* revocable; **~ung** *f* revocation.

Wider|sacher *m* adversary, opponent, antagonist; **~schein** *m* reflection, reverberation; **~setzen** *r* to oppose, to resist; **~setzlich** *a* refractory; (*im Dienste*) insubordinate; **~~keit** *f* refractoriness; (*im Dienste*) insubordination; obstinacy; **~setzung** *f* opposition; repugnance; **~sinn** *m* wrong sense; absurdity, nonsense; **~sinnig** *a* contrary to common sense, nonsensical, absurd; **~spenstig** *a* refractory, recalcitrant; (*eigensinnig*) obstinate, stubborn; (*im Dienste*) insubordinate; **~~keit** *f* refractoriness; obstinacy; **~spiegeln** *tr* to reflect, to mirror; *r* to be reflected; **~spiel** *n* contrary, reverse, counterpart; **~sprechen** *irr itr* to contradict, to gainsay; (*e-m Vorschlag*) to oppose; **~~d** *a* contradictory; (*unvereinbar*) inconsistent (with); (*entgegengesetzt*) contrary (to); conflicting; **~spruch** *m* contradiction; opposition; conflict; (*Text*) inconsistence; *math* discrepancy; (*Gegenrede*) *Am* back talk; *im ~~ stehen mit* to disagree, to clash; to be contradictory to; to be inconsistent with; *keinen ~~ dulden Am* not to stand for back talk; *auf jds scharfen ~~ stoßen* to run into stiff opposition from; **~~sgeist** *m* spirit of contradiction.

Wider|stand *m* (*auch el*) resistance; (*Material~*) drag, strength; (*Wellen~*) impedance; (*gegenüberstehen*) opposition, stand, withstanding; (*Zurückweisung*) repulse, repulsion, rebuff; (*Widerwille*) repugnance; (*Feindseligkeit*) hostility, antagonism; *den ~~ einschalten* to switch in resistance; *den ~~ ausschalten* to cut out resistance; *~~ leisten* to oppose, to offer (*od* put up) resistance; *~~ aufgeben* to give in; *auf jds scharfen ~~ stoßen* to run into stiff opposition from; *hinhaltender ~~* delaying resistance; **~~sbewegung** *f* resistance movement; **~~sfähig** *a* resistant, refractory; **~~sfähigkeit** *f* capability of resisting; strength, stability; load-bearing capacity; **~~skraft** *f* power of resistance; defensive power; *tech* interference drag, strength; **~~slinie** *f* line of resistance; **~~slos** *a* resistanceless, without resistance; **~~smessung** *f* measurement of resistance; **~~smoment** *n* moment of resistance; **~~snest** *n mil* island (*od* pocket) of resistance; **~~sschwankung** *f* resistance variation; **~~sstellung** *f mil* delaying position; **~~svermögen** *n* defensive (*od* resistance) power; **~stehen** *irr itr* to resist, to withstand, to hold out, to stand; (*widerlich sein*) to be repugnant (to); **~streben** *itr* to oppose, to resist, to struggle against; (*zuwider sein*) to be repugnant to, to go against the grain; *~~ n* reluctance; resistance, opposition; repugnance; **~~d** *a* reluctant, opposing; repugnant; **~streit** *m* opposition, antagonism; conflict, clash; **~~en** *irr itr* to be contrary (to), to conflict (with), to clash (with); to resist, to oppose; (*streiten*) to militate (*gegen* against); **~wärtig** *a* disagreeable, disgusting, unpleasant, *fam* nasty; (*widerlich*) vile; offensive, odious, repugnant; (*ärgerlich*) annoying; (*verdrießlich*) tiresome; (*ekelhaft*) distasteful; (*widrig*) adverse; **~~keit** *f* unpleasantness, disagreeableness; (*Unfug*) nuisance; (*Benachteiligung*) handicap; (*Schwierigkeit*) difficulty; (*Ekelhaftigkeit*) loathsomeness, repulsiveness; (*Unglück*) calamity, adversity; *er muß gegen viele ~~keiten ankämpfen* he is up against heavy odds; **~wille** *m* aversion (*gegen* to), dislike (to, of, for); (*Ekel*) disgust (for), repugnance; (*Widerstreben*) reluctance; *mit ~~n* reluctantly; **~willig** *a* unwilling, reluctant; (*abgeneigt*) disinclined, indisposed (*gegen* to); (*ungern gegeben*) grudging; (*abwehrend*) demurring; (*scheu*) shrinking, shy (of).

widm|en *tr* (*zueignen*) to dedicate; (*Buch*) to inscribe (to), to address (to); (*weihen*) to devote; *r* to devote o. s. to, to give o. s. up to; **~ung** *f* dedication; **~~sstück** *n* presentation copy, inscribed copy.

widrig *a* contrary; adverse; (*ungünstig*) unfavo(u)rable; (*feindlich*) inimical, hostile; (*widerwärtig*) disgusting, repugnant; **~enfalls** *adv* failing this, in default of which, otherwise, else; **~keit** *f* contrariety; (*~er Zufall*) adversity.

wie *adv, conj* (*fragend*) what, how; (*vergleichend*) like, such as, as; (*zeitlich*) as; *~ breit* how wide; *~ lang* how long; *~ oft* how often; *~ alt sind Sie?* how old are you? *~ geht's Ihnen?* how are you? how do you do? *~ schön!* how beautiful! *~ wäre es mit ...?* how about ...? *u. ~!* and how! *~ viele?* how many? *ich möchte wissen ~* I'd like to know how; *~ bitte?* what did you say? (I beg your) pardon? *~ heißt er?* what's his name? *~ verstehen Sie das?* what do you mean by that? *~ ist es mit ...?* what about ...? *~ gesagt* as has been said; *~ zuvor* as before; *~ oben* as above; *~ gewöhnlich* as usual; *so ... ~* as ... as; *nicht so ... ~* not so (*auch* as) ... as; *~ man sagt* as people say; *~ Sie wollen* as you wish; *~ in den folgenden Beispielen* as in the following examples; *laß es, ~ es ist* leave it as it is; *er sieht ~ ein Künstler aus* he looks like an artist; *Tiere, ~ (z. B.) Katzen* animals like (*od* such as) cats; *er ist genau ~ jeder andere* he is just like everybody else; *es sieht ~ Schnee aus* it looks like snow; *~ auch (immer)* however, no matter how; *~ wir es auch machen, es wird falsch* however we do it, it will be wrong; *~ oft er es auch tut* however often he does it; *~ dem auch sei* be that as it may; *~ du mir, so ich dir* tit for tat; **~so** *adv* why; **~viel** *adv* how much; *~~e* how many; *den ~~ten haben wir heute?* what day of the month is it? what's today's date? *~~ Uhr ist es?* what time is it? **~wohl** *conj* although.

Wiedehopf *m* hoopoe.

wieder *adv* again, anew, afresh; once more; (*zurück*) back; (*als Vergeltung*) in return for; *immer ~* again and again, time and again, over and over again; *hin u. ~* now and then, from time to time; to and fro; *unsere Arbeit war für nichts u. ~ nichts* our work has been absolutely for nothing; *es ist ~ ein Jahr vorbei* another year has passed; *~ in Dienst stellen* to recommission; *~ gut machen* to redress; *da haben wir es schon ~* there it goes again.

Wiederab|druck *m typ* reprint; **~drucken** *tr* to reprint; **~reisen** *itr* to depart again; **~treten** *irr tr* to retrocede; **~tretung** *f* retrocession.

Wiederan|fang *m* recommencement; (*Schule*) reopening; **~fangen** *irr tr* to begin anew, to restart, to resume; (*Fabrik*) to reopen; **~gehen** *irr itr* to begin anew, to recommence; **~kleiden, ~ziehen** *irr tr* to dress again; **~knüpfen** *tr* to renew; **~meldung** *f* reissue; **~nähern** *r* to near again; **~nehmen** *irr tr* to reassume; **~stellen** *tr* to reappoint, to reinstall; **~stellung** *f* reappointment; **~wärmen** *tr* to reheat; **~zünden** *tr* to rekindle.

Wiederauf|bau *m* reconstruction; rebuilding; rehabilitation; **~~programm** *n* recovery program(me); *europäisches ~~programm* European Recovery Program, *Abk* E. R. P.; **~bauen** *tr* to rebuild, to reconstruct; **~blühen** *itr* to flourish anew; **~erstehen** *irr itr* to rise from the dead; **~erstehung** *f* resurrection; **~finden** *irr tr* to find, to recover, to retrieve; **~frischen** *tr* to refresh again; **~heben** *irr tr chem* to neutralize; **~kommen** *irr itr* (*Kranker*) to recover (o.'s health); (*Mode*) to come into fashion again; **~laden** *irr tr* to recharge; **~leben** *itr* to revive; *~~ n* revival; **~lösen** *tr* to redissolve; **~machen** *tr* to reopen; **~nahme** *f* resumption, retake; *jur* reopening; **~~verfahren** *n jur* retrial; **~nehmen** *irr tr* to resume, to take up again; **~richten** *tr* to raise again; *fig* to consolate; **~rüstung** *f* rearmament; **~stehen** *irr itr* to rise again; **~tauchen** *itr mar* to re-surface; **~tauen** *n* thawing; **~wachen** *itr* to awake again; **~wärmen** *tr* to warm again; **~werten** *tr* to revaluate, to revalorize; **~wertung** *f* revaluation, revalorization; **~ziehen** *irr tr* to draw up again.

wiederaus|bessern *tr* to mend again; **~brechen** *irr itr* to break out again; **~fuhr** *f* re-exportation; **~führen** *tr* to re-export; **~strahlen** *tr* to reradiate; **~strahlung** *f* reradiation.

wieder|bekommen *irr tr* to get back, to recover; **~beleben** *tr* to reanimate, to revive, to revivify; to reactivate; to regenerate; *med* to resuscitate; **~belebung** *f* revival, reanimation; regeneration; **~~sapparat** *m* life-restoring apparatus; **~~smittel** *n* restorative; **~~sversuch** *m* attempt at resuscitation; **~beschaffen** *tr* to replace; **~beschaffungspreis** *m* cost of replacement; **~beschicken** *tr* to recharge, to reload; (*Kongreß*) to delegate; **~besetzen** *tr* to reoccupy; **~bezahlen** *tr* to repay; **~brauchbarmachen** *n chem* regeneration; **~bringen** *irr tr* to

bring back; (*~geben*) to restore, to return to.
wiederein|bauen *tr* to reinstall; **~bringen** *irr tr* to make up for, to retrieve; **~finden** *irr itr r* to turn up again; **~führen** *tr* to re-introduce; (*Gebrauch*) to re-establish; **~führung** *f* reintroduction; reinsertion, restoration; re-establishment; **~holen** *tr* to overtake again; **~lösen** *tr* to redeem; **~lösung** *f* redemption; **~nahme** *f* recapture; **~nehmen** *irr tr* to recapture; **~packen** *tr* to pack up again; **~schalten** *tr* to reclose, to connect in circuit again; **~schiffen** *tr* to re-embark; **~schiffung** *f* re-embarkation; **~schlafen** *irr itr* to fall asleep again; **~schmelzen** *irr tr* to remelt; **~setzen** *tr* to replace; *fig* to restore; (*Amt*) to reinstate (in); *jur* to rehabilitate; **~setzung** *f* restoration; *jur* rehabilitation; **~spannen** *tr tech* to reclamp, to rechuck; **~stellen** *tr* (*Amt*) to reinstate; *tech* to readjust; **~stellung** *f* reinstatement; readjustment; **~treten** *irr itr* to re-enter; **~tritt** *m* re-entry.
wieder|ergreifen *irr tr* (*Flüchtling*) to reseize; **~ergreifung** *f* reseizure; **~erhalten** *irr tr* to retrieve, to recover; **~erhitzen** *tr* to reheat; **~erinnern** *r* to remember; **~erkennen** *irr tr* to recognize; **~erkennung** *f* recognition; **~erlangen** *tr* to recover, to get back, to retrieve; **~erlangung** *f* recovery; **~erobern** *tr* to reconquer; **~eröffnen** *tr* to reopen; **~eröffnung** *f* reopening, resumption; **~ersetzen** *tr* to restore: **~erstatten** *tr* to restore, to return; (*Kosten*) to reimburse, to refund; (*Maschinen*) to restitute; **~erstattung** *f* restitution; (*Kosten*) reimbursement, repayment; **~erwärmen** *tr* to rewarm, to reheat; **~erzählen** *tr* to repeat; to retell; **~finden** *irr tr* to find, to recover.
Wieder|gabe *f* restitution, return; (*Bild*) reproduction; *fig* rendering; reading; (*Übersetzung*) translation; (*Nacherzählung*) reproduction; *genaue ~~* faithful reproduction; *getreue ~~* (*Bild, Ton*) good definition; (*Ton*) orthophonic reproduction; **~~dose** *f* gramophone (*Am* phonograph) pickup; **~~güte** *f* quality of reproduction; **~~röhre** *f tele* electronic picture reproducing tube; **~~treue** *f* fidelity (*od* realism) of reproduction; **~geben** *irr tr* to give back, to return; to render; (*Gesundheit, Ehre*) to restore; (*übersetzen*) to translate; to reproduce; (*Bild*) to project, to reproduce; **~geburt** *f* regeneration, rebirth; **~genesen** *irr itr* to recover; **~genesung** *f* recovery; **~gewinnen** *irr tr* to recover, to regain, to recuperate; to reclaim; to retrieve; **~gewinnung** *f* recovery; regeneration; **~grüßen** *tr, itr* to return a bow, to resalute; **~gutmachen** *tr* to make amends for, to repair; to compensate; to restitute; **~gutmachung** *f* restoration; restitution; *jur* redress; *parl* reparation; **~haben** *irr tr* to get back, to have recovered; **~herstellen** *tr* to restore; (*Kranke*) to cure; to repair; to re-establish; to rebuild, to reconstruct; **~herstellung** *f* restoration; (*Kranker*) recovery; repair; re-establishment, reconstruction; **~~sarbeit** *f* repair work; **~~strupp** *m* repair squad; **~hervorbringung** *f* reproduction; **~holbar** *a* reproducible, repeatable; **~ho'len** *tr* to repeat, to say (over) again; (*tun od sagen*) to reiterate; (*erneuern*) to renew; *r* to say (over and over) again; to recur; **'~~** *tr* to fetch back, to bring back; **~ho'lt** *adv* repeatedly, again and again, often; **~ho'lung** *f* repetition; reiteration; (*Weben*) round of pattern; *radio* repeat; **~~saufnahme** *f radio* retake, repeat; **~~skurs** *m* refresher course; **~~szeichen** *n mus* repeat; ditto-marks *pl*; **~hören** *itr* to hear again; *auf ~~!* good-by(e)! **~instandsetzen** *tr* to repair, to reinstate, to recondition; **~instandsetzung** *f* reconditioning; **~käuen** *tr* to ruminate; *fig* to repeat over and over; **~käuer** *m* ruminant; **~kauf** *m* repurchase, redemption; **~~en** *tr* to repurchase, to redeem; **~kehr** *f* return, coming back (*od* home); (*Wiederholung*) repetition, recurrence; (*Periode*) period; *regelmäßige ~~* periodicity; **~~en** *itr* to return, to come back; **~~end** *a* recurrent; returning; **~kommen** *irr itr* to come back; **~kunft** *f* return, coming back; *eccl* advent; **~machen** *tr* to do (*od* make) again; **~nehmen** *irr tr* to take back; *mil* to recapture, to retake; **~sagen** *tr* to repeat, to tell again; **~sammeln** *tr* to reassemble, to rally; **~sehen** *irr tr* to see again, to meet again; *~~ n* meeting again; *auf ~~!* good-by(e)! so long! *Am* see you again! *fam* cheerio! **~taufen** *tr* to rebaptize; **~täufer** *m* anabaptist; **~tun** *irr tr* to do again, to repeat; **~um** *adv* again, anew, afresh; on the other hand; **~umkehren** *itr* to turn back again, to retrace o.'s step; **~vereinigen** *tr* to reunite; (*aussöhnen*) to reconcile; **~vereinigung** *f* reunion; reunification; *chem* recombination; *phys* focussing; **~vergelten** *irr tr* to retaliate, to requite; **~vergeltung** *f* retaliation; **~verheiraten** *r* to marry again, to remarry; **~verheiratung** *f* remarriage; **~verkaufen** *tr* to resell, to retail; **~verkäufer** *m* re-seller; (*Detail*) retailer; (*Mittelsmann*) middleman; *Lieferung nur an ~~* supplied to trade only; **~~preis** *m* trade price; (*Einzelhandelspreis*) retail price; **~~rabatt** *m* trade discount; **~vermieten** *tr* to sublet; to underlet; **~versöhnen** *tr* to reconcile; **~versöhnung** *f* reconciliation; **~verteilen** *tr* to redistribute; **~verteilung** *f* redistribution; **~verwendung** *f* reuse; **~verwertung** *f* reutilization, further utilization; **~vorlage** *f* renewed submission; **~wahl** *f* re-election; **~wählbar** *a* re-eligible; **~wählen** *tr* to re-elect; **~zulassen** *irr tr* to re-admit; **~zulassung** *f* re-admission; **~zusammenbau** *m* reassembly; **~zusammentreten** *itr* to reassemble, *Am* to reconvene; **~zustellen** *tr* to return; **~zustellung** *f* return.
Wiege *f* cradle; rocking device; **~balken** *m* movable beam; **~fehler** *m* error in weighing; **~kufe** *f* rocker; **~messer** *n* mincing-knife; **~n** *irr tr* (*wägen*) to weigh; *~~ tr* (*schaukeln*) to rock, to move to and fro; (*bewegen*) to sway; (*zerkleinern*) to chop, to mince; *r sich in Hoffnungen ~~* to indulge in hopes; **~~druck** *m* incunabulum, incunable; **~~fest** *n* birthday; **~~kind** *n* infant; **~~lied** *n* lullaby, cradle song.
wiehern *itr* to neigh; (*lachen*) *fam* to hee-haw; *~des Gelächter* horse-laugh; *~ n* neighing.
Wien *n* Vienna; **~er(in)** *m* (*f*) Viennese; *~er Schnitzel* veal cutlet; *~er Würstchen Am* wienies *pl*.
Wiese *f* meadow; (*Rasen*) lawn; (*Weide*) grassland, pasture; **~nblume** *f* meadow-flower; **~nerz** *n* bog iron ore; **~ngrund** *m* grassy valley, meadow-land; **~nschaumkraut** *n bot* lady's smock, cuckoo-flower.
Wiesel *n* weasel.
wie|so, **~viel**, **~wohl** *siehe wie*.
wild *a* wild; (*unzivilisiert*) savage, uncivilized; (*heftig*) impetuous, violent; (*rauh*) rough, rude, rough-and-tumble; (*roh*) barbarous, brutish, brutal, bestial; (*unbändig*) intractable; unruly; (*grimmig*) fierce; (*grausam*) ferocious; (*verrückt*) mad (*auf* about); (*zornig*) angry, furious, enraged, rabid, infuriated; (*leidenschaftlich*) passionate; (*lärmend*) turbulent, tempestuous, riotous, uproarious, boisterous; *fam* harum-scarum, rampacious; *Am* rambunctious; (*unordentlich aussehend*) untidy, unkempt, dishevel(l)ed; (*ungeschlacht*) uncouth, coarse, unlicked; (*zügellos*) licentious; (*unbebaut*) uncultivated; *~e Ehe* concubinage; *~es Fleisch* proud flesh; *~er Streik* lightning-strike; *~er Wein* Virginia creeper; *~e Flucht* headlong flight, rout; *~ machen* to enrage; (*Tier*) to frighten; *~ sein auf* to be mad (on, after, for); *~ werden* to get furious, to turn wild, *fam* to see red; (*Pferd*) to shy; *seid nicht so ~* don't make so much noise; don't be so wild; *~ n* deer, game; (*Fleisch*) venison; **~bach** *m* torrent; **~bad** *n* hot springs *pl*; **~bahn** *f* preserve, hunting ground; **~braten** *m* (roast) venison; **~bret** *n* game, venison; **~dieb** *m* poacher; **~dieberei** *f* poaching; **~ente** *f* wild duck; **~e(r)** *m* savage; **~erer** *m* poacher; **~ern** *itr* to poach; **~fang** *m* (*Knabe*) madcap; (*Mädchen*) romp; **~fremd** *a* quite strange; **~garten, ~park** *m* preserve, park; **~geruch, ~geschmack** *m* smell of game, taste of venison; **~heit** *f* wildness; barbarity; ferocity, fierceness; savageness; **~hüter** *m* gamekeeper; **~leder** *n* deerskin, buckskin, doeskin; chamois-leather; suede; **~~schuhe** *m pl* suede shoes *pl*; **~ling** *m* wildtree; **~nis** *f* wilderness; desert; **~reich** *a* abounding in game; **~schaden** *m* damage done by game; **~schütz(e)** *m* poacher; **~schwein** *n* wild boar, sow; **~spur** *f* track; **~stand** *m* stock of game; **~wachsend** *a* wild; **~wasser** *n* torrent; **~westfilm** *m Am film* western (picture); *sl* horse opera.
Wille *m* will; (*Wollen*) volition; (*Willenssphäre*) conation; (*Absicht*) design, intention, intent, purpose; (*Bestimmtheit*) determination; decision; (*Wunsch*) wish; (*Wahl*) choice, election, preference; (*Erlaubnis*) consent, permission, leave; (*Belieben*) pleasure; (*Befehl*) order, direction; (*Einverständnis*) consent; *letzter ~* last will and testament; *guter ~* kind intention; *aus freiem ~n* of o.'s own accord, voluntarily; *mit ~n* on purpose, purposely, intentionally; *wider ~n* unwillingly; unintentionally, involuntarily; in spite of s. o.; *jdm seinen ~n lassen* to let s. o. have his own way; *jdm zu ~n sein* to comply with s. o.'s wishes; *um meines Bruders ~n* for my brother's sake; *~ns sein* to be willing to, to be ready to; *sie will ihren ~n durchsetzen* she's determined to have her way; *es geht beim besten ~n nicht* it just can't be done; *ich kann mich beim besten ~n nicht erinnern* I can't for the life of me remember; *wo ein ~ ist, ist ein Weg* where there's a will there's a way; **~nlos** *a* irresolute; lacking will-power; (*zögernd*) hesitating; (*nervös*) fidgety; (*schwankend*) vacillating, shilly-shally, wabbly; (*verzagt*) half-hearted; (*lau*) lukewarm; (*unsicher*) unsure, doubtful, at a loss; **~~igkeit** *f* lack of will-power; weakness; abul(oman)ia; in-

decision, irresolution; instability; vacillation; hesitation; demur; fickleness; **~nsakt** *m* act of volition; **~nsänderung** *f* change of mind; **~nsanspannung** *f* exertion of will-power; **~nsäußerung** *f* expression of o.'s wish; volition; **~nserklärung** *f* declaration of legal intent; **~nsfreiheit** *f* free will, freedom of will; **~nskraft** *f* will-power, strength of mind; faculty of volition; **~nslähmung** *f* abul(oman)ia; **~nsmeinung** *f* will, mind; expression of o.'s wish; **~nsschwach** *a* lacking will-power, weak; **~nsschwäche** *f* weak will; **~nsstark** *a* strong-willed, energetic; **~nsstärke** *f* strength of will; **~ntlich** *a* intentional, wil(l)ful.

will|fahren *itr* to comply with, to accede (to); (*Wunsch*) to gratify, to grant; (*jdm*) to humo(u)r s. o., to please s. o.; **~fährig** *a* compliant, complaisant, accommodating; (*unterwürfig*) obsequious; **~~keit** *f* compliance, complaisance; **~ig** *a* willing, ready; **~igen** *itr*: *~~ in etw* to consent, to agree to, to comply with; **~igkeit** *f* willingness, readiness; (*Eifer*) zeal, zest; **~kommen** *n u. m* welcome; reception; *~~ a* welcome; (*angenehm*) acceptable; (*gelegen*) opportune; (*wünschenswert*) desirable; *~~ heißen* to welcome, to extend a welcome (to); **~kür** *f* arbitrary action; arbitrariness; (*Belieben*) discretion; (*Wahl*) choice, option; **~~akt** *m* arbitrary act; **~~herrschaft** *f* despotism; **~~lich** *a* arbitrary, high-handed; despotic; (*aufs Geratewohl*) haphazard, (at) random; **~~lichkeit** *f* arbitrariness; arbitrary act.

wimmeln *itr* to swarm (with), to crowd (with), to teem (with).

wimmern *itr* to whimper, to moan.

Wimpel *m* pennon, pennant, streamer.

Wimper *f* eyelash; *ohne mit der ~ zu zucken* without batting an eyelash.

Wind *m* wind; (*leichter ~*) breeze; (*frischer ~*) gale; (*~stoß*) blast; (*Sturm*) storm; (*Luftzug*) air; (*Blähung*) wind; flatulence; *starker ~* strong (*od* high) wind; *guter ~* fair wind; *unbeständiger ~* shifting (*od* chopping) wind; *bei ~ u. Wetter* in storm and rain, in all weathers; *~ von hinten aero* tail wind; *in den ~ reden* to talk in vain; *in den ~ schlagen* to disregard, to make light of; *~ bekommen fig* to get scent (*od* wind) of; *jdm den ~ aus den Segeln nehmen* to steal s. o.'s thunder, to take the wind out of s. o.'s sails; *in alle vier ~e zerstreuen* to scatter to the four winds; *daher weht also der ~* that's where the wind blows; *~ machen fig* to brag, to boast; *den Mantel nach dem ~ hängen* to turn o.'s coat; *in alle ~e zerflattern* to be thrown to the winds; *dem ~ entgegendrehen* to head into the wind; *mit dem ~* before the wind; down (*od* off) the wind; *dem ~ entgegen* in the eye (*od* teeth) of the wind; into the wind; *was für ~ haben wir?* where is the wind from? *der ~ kommt von Osten* the wind is in the east; *am ~ liegen* to be to windward; *unter ~ liegen* to be to leeward; *draußen weht ein starker ~* there's a strong wind blowing outside; *der ~ blies mir den Hut vom Kopf* the wind blew my hat off; **~angriffsfläche** *f* wind surface; **~anker** *m* downstream anchor; *el* transversal stay; **~antrieb** *m* impeller drive; **~anzeiger** *m* wind indicator, windicator; **~ausnutzung** *f* utilization of the wind; **~bahn** *f* wind course; **~beutel** *m* cream puff; éclair; *aero, fig* wind-bag; **~~ei** *f* boasting; humbug; **~bewegung** *f* motion of the wind; **~bluse** *f* anarak; windcheater; **~bö** *f* squall, gust; **~bruch** *m* windfall; rolled timber; **~büchse** *f* wind gun; **~dicht** *a* air-tight; **~druck** *m* wind pressure; **~~messer** *m* wind-pressure ga(u)ge; **~ei** *n* wind-egg; **~einwirkung** *f* action of wind; **~en** *itr*: *es ~et* there's a wind blowing; **~eseile** *f* lightning speed; **~fächer** *m* fan; **~fahne** *f* weather vane; **~fang** *m* vent hole; ventilator; *arch* porch; **~flügel** *m* fan blade; **~geschützt** *a* sheltered; **~geschwindigkeit** *f* wind velocity; wind component; **~~smesser** *m* anemometer; **~harfe** *f* Aeolian harp; **~haube** *f* cowl; **~hauch** *m* puff of wind; **~hose** *f* whirlwind, tornado; **~hund** *m* greyhound; whippet; borzoi; *fig* wind-bag; **~~rennen** *n* greyhound racing; **~ig** *a* windy, breezy; (*unzuverlässig*) unreliable; (*eitel*) vain, empty; (*Sache*) precarious; *~~es Wetter* windy weather; **~jacke** *f* windproof jacket, double-breasted field jacket; **~kammer** *f* air chamber; **~kanal** *m* wind tunnel (*od* channel); **~~messung** *f* wind-tunnel measurements *pl*; **~~modell** *n* wind-tunnel model; **~~untersuchung** *f* wind-tunnel investigation; **~~versuch** *m* wind-tunnel test; **~karte** *f* wind chart; **~kasten** *m* (*Orgel*) wind chest; **~licht** *n* storm lantern; **~messer** *m* anemometer; **~motor** *m* windmill motor; **~mühle** *f* windmill; **~~nflügel** *m* vane; **~~nflugzeug** *n* gyroplane, helicopter, autogiro; **~pocken** *f pl* chicken-pox; **~richtung** *f* wind direction; **~~sanzeiger** *m* wind indicator; **~röschen** *n bot* anemone; **~rose** *f* compass card, wind rose; **~sack** *m aero* wind-sleeve, wind cone, wind sock; **~sbraut** *f* gale, whirlwind, hurricane; **~schacht** *m* air-shaft; **~schatten** *m* lee; **~scheibe** *f* windscreen; **~schief** *a* warped, twisted, deformed; *arch* skew; **~schirm** *m* windscreen; **~schnittig** *a* streamlined, aerodynamic; **~schutz** *m* wind guard, front shield; (*Hecken*) *Am* windbreak; **~~kappe** *f* wind cap; **~~scheibe** *f* windscreen, *Am* windshield; **~seite** *f* weather side; **~spiel** *n* whippet; **~stärke** *f* wind force (*od* intensity); **~~messer** *m* anemometer, wind ga(u)ge; **~still** *a* calm; **~~e** *f* calm, lull; **~stoß** *m* gust (of wind), blast; **~strich** *m* rhumb, lubber line; **~strom** *m* air current; **~strömung** *f* air flow; **~veränderung** *f* wind shift; **~verhältnisse** *n pl* wind conditions *pl*; **~wärts** *adv* windward; **~widerstand** *m* wind resistance; **~winkel** *m aero* angle of drift; **~zufluß** *m* air supply; **~zug** *m* air current, draught; gust.

Wind|e *f* windlass, crane; (*Gangspill*) capstan; (*Flaschenzug*) hoist; (*Heber*) lifting jack; crab; worm; (*Wagen~*) winch; (*Garn~*) reel, winder; *bot* bind-weed, convolvulus; **~en** *irr tr* to wind (on); (*aufwickeln*) to coil; (*zus. drehen*) to twist; (*flechten*) to wreathe; (*spulen*) to reel; (*rollen*) to roll; (*verstricken*) to wrap; (*in die Höhe*) to hoist; (*Kranz*) to make, to bind; (*ent~~*) to wrest (from), to wrench (from); *r* to turn, to wind, to wriggle; (*lavieren*) to tack; (*herum~~*) to twine (round); (*in Schmerz*) to writhe; (*Fluß*) to meander; (*Weg*) to wind; **~~bock** *m* lifting jack; **~~trommel** *f* hoisting drum; **~ung** *f* winding, twisting; convolution; (*Kurve*) bend, turn; (*Tau, Schlange*) coil; (*Schraube*) worm, thread; (*e-r Wicklung*) spire; (*Spirale*; *Muschel~~*) whorl; **~~sganghöhe** *f* pitch; **~~szahl** *f* number of turns.

Windel *f* diaper, baby's napkin, swaddle; (*Wickeltuch*) pilch; **~n** *pl* swaddling-clothes *pl*; **~höschen** *n* rubber pants *pl*; **~kind** *n* infant; **~n** *tr* to swaddle, to swathe; **~weich** *a* quite soft, compliant, yielding; *~~ schlagen* to beat to a jelly.

Wink *m* sign; (*durch Nicken*) nod; (*zublinzeln*) wink; (*mit der Hand*) wave, beckoning; *fig* hint, suggestion; (*sachkundiger ~*) tip; *Am* pointer, tip-off; *jdm e-n ~ geben* to give s. o. a tip (*od* hint); *sie hat den ~ nicht verstanden* she didn't take the hint; *jds ~ gewärtig sein* to be at beck and call; *~ mit dem Zaunpfahl* broad hint; **~en** *itr* to make a sign; to signal with flags and rods, to semaphore, to flag; (*Hand*) to beckon, to wave; (*Kopf*) to nod; (*Augen*) to wink; (*Belohnung*) to be in store; *mit dem Taschentuch ~~* to wave o.'s handkerchief; **~er** *m* signal light, blinker light; (*Mann*) flag signalman; *mot* direction indicator; trafficator; signal arm, signal light; **~~dienst** *m* wigwagging; **~~flagge** *f* signal(l)ing flag; **~~zeichen** *n* flag signal; signal; **~spruch** *m* semaphore message; **~verbindung** *f* visual communication by flag.

Winkel *m math* angle; (*Ecke*) corner, nook; (*Werkzeug*) square; *aero* wedge formation; *mil* stripe (on sleeve), chevron; *spitzer, stumpfer, rechter ~* acute, obtuse, right angle; *toter ~* dead angle (*od* space); *vorspringender ~* salient; **~abstand** *m* angular distance; **~advokat** *m* pettifogger, *Am sl* shyster; **~blatt** *n* local rag, obscure newspaper; **~eisen** *n* angle iron; **~förmig** *a* angular; **~haken** *m tech* square; *typ* composing stick; **~ig** *a* angular; (*Straße*) crooked; **~maß** *n* (carpenter's) square; angle measuring instrument; **~messer** *m* goniometer, clinometer; protractor; theodolite; **~messung** *f* goniometry; **~summe** *f* sum of the angles; **~zug** *m* trick, dodge, subterfuge, shift; (*Ausflucht*) evasion; *~züge machen* to use shifts, to prevaricate; to shuffle.

winseln *itr* to whimper, to whine, to wail.

Winter *m* winter; *im ~* in winter; *mitten im ~* in the depth of winter; *für den ~ herrichten* to winterize; **~abend** *n* winter evening; **~aufenthalt** *m* winter abode; (*Ort*) winter resort; **~ausrüstung** *f* winter equipment; **~birne** *f* winter pear; **~fest** *a* wintertight; (*Pflanze*) hardy; *~~ machen* to winterize; **~flugplan** *m* winter schedules *pl*; **~frische** *f* winter resort; **~früchte** *f pl* winter fruit; **~garten** *m* conservatory; winter-garden; **~getreide, ~korn** *n* winter corn; **~gewächs** *n* perennial plant; **~grün** *n* periwinkle; **~hart** *a* hardy; **~kleid** *n* winter garment; **~kohl** *m* kale; **~krieg** *m* winter warfare; **~lich, ~mäßig** *a* wintry; **~märchen** *n* winter's tale; **~n** *itr* to get wintry; **~quartier** *m* winter quarters *pl*; **~saat** *f* winter corn; **~schlaf** *m* winter-sleep; hibernation; *~~ halten* to hibernate; **~schlußverkauf** *m* winter clearance sale; **~seite** *f* north side; **~sonnenwende** *f* winter solstice; **~sport** *m* winter sports *pl*; **~~ler** *m* winter sportsman; **~~platz** *m* winter sport centre; **~überzieher** *m* winter overcoat; **~vorrat** *m* winter stock; **~weizen** *m* winter wheat; **~zeit** *f* winter time; *zur ~~* during winter; **~zeug** *n* winter cloth.

Winzer *m* vinedresser, wine-grower; (*Traubenleser*) vintager.

winzig *a* tiny, diminutive; minute; (*unbedeutend*) petty; **~keit** *f* diminutiveness, extreme smallness, tininess; minuteness.

Wipfel *m* tree-top.

Wipp|e *f* balance, seesaw, counterpoise; rocker; *el* tumbler switch; **~en** *itr, tr* to balance, to seesaw; **~kran** *m* whipping crane; **~säge** *f* jig saw; **~tisch** *m* tilting table.

wir *prn* we.

Wirbel *m* (*Drehung*) whirl, rotatory motion; (*Wasser~*) eddy, whirlpool; maelstrom; (*Strudel*) vortex; (*Fenster~*) joint; (*Trommel~*) roll; (*Rücken~*) vertebra; (*Scheitel*) crown; (*Violin~*) peg, pin; (*Wind*) whirlwind; (*Rauch*) wreath, curl; (*Schwindel*) vertigo; *tech* spigot, swivel, collar, button; *e-n ~ machen* (*fam*) to make a row, *Am* to raise hell; **~bewegung** *f* vortex motion, eddying whirl; **~bildung** *f* eddying, turbulence; **~frei** *a* irrotational; (*Strömung*) parallel (flow); **~ig** *a* whirling; *fig* giddy; (*ungestüm*) impetuous, wild; **~kasten** *m* (*Violine*) neck for pegs; **~knochen** *m* vertebra, *pl* -ae; **~los** *a* spineless, invertebrate; (*Wasser*) free from eddies; **~n** *itr* to whirl (round), to eddy, to swirl round, to spin; (*Trommel*) to roll; (*Lerche*) to warble; (*spiralförmig*) to spiral; *mir ~t der Kopf* my head is swimming; **~säule** *f* vertebral column, spine; **~sturm** *m* cyclone, tornado; hurricane; twister: **~tier** *n* vertebrate animal; **~wind** *m* whirlwind.

wirk|en *itr, tr* (*arbeiten, vollbringen*) to work, to do, to perform, to produce, to bring about, to effect; (*Strümpfe*) to weave; (*Teig*) to knead; (*stricken, fig verknüpfen*) to knit; *itr* to work, to be active; (*e-e Wirkung haben*) to take effect; to have an effect; to go home; (*funktionieren*) to function; (*in Betrieb sein*) to run; (*hinauslaufen auf*) to result in; *auf jdn ~~* to have an effect on, to tell on; to influence s. o.; to impress s. o.; *Wunder ~~* to work wonders; *das Bild ~t viel besser aus der Ferne* the picture looks much better at a distance; *das ~t bei ihm nicht* this has no effect on him; this cuts no ice with him; *sie ~t auf ihn wie ein rotes Tuch* she makes him see red; *auf die Sinne ~~* to effect the senses; **~en** *n* performance, action; functioning, operation; **~end** *a* acting, active, operating, operative; effective; *~~es Mittel* agent; **~erei** *f* knitting trade; **~leistung** *f* actual efficiency; **~lich** *a* real, actual; (*echt*) true, genuine; (*~sam*) effective; *adv* really, actually, truly; *~~?* really? indeed? *Am* you don't say so? is that so? *das ist ~~ zuviel* that's really too much; *glaubst du diese Geschichte ~~?* do you actually believe that story? *es ist ~~ zum Wahnsinnigwerden* it's enough to drive you crazy; **~~keit** *f* actuality, reality; *Flucht aus der ~~keit* escapi sm; **~~keitsnah** *a* realistic; objective; **~maschine** *f* knitting (*od* weaving) frame; hosiery machine; **~sam** *a* active, efficacious, effective; (*Personen*) efficient; (*mächtig*) powerful; (*brauchbar*) practicable; *chem* actinic; (*tätig*) operative; (*eindrucksvoll*) impressive; *~~ machen* to activate; *~~ werden* to become effective, to take effect, to come into force; to become valid; **~~keit** *f* efficacy, effectiveness, operation; activity; effect, virtue; efficiency; impressiveness; (*Gültigkeit*) validity; *in ~~keit treten* to come into force (*od* operation), to take effect; *in ~~keit setzen* to render operative; *tech* to start, to throw in gear; **~schema** *n* working diagram; **~spannung** *f el* active voltage; **~stoff** *m* active substance; vitamin; hormone; **~strom** *m el* active current; **~stuhl** *m* knitting frame; **~~u. Strickwaren** *f pl* woven and knitted goods *pl*; **~ung** *f* effect; (*Tätigkeit*) action, operation; (*Wirksamkeit*) working, agency; (*~~skraft*) effectiveness, efficacy; (*starke ~~*) kick, powerful effect; (*Ergebnis*) result, consequence; (*Gegen~~*) reaction; (*Einfluß*) influence; (*Eindruck*) impression; *psychologische ~~* moral effect; *mit ~~ vom heutigen Tag* effective this date; *mit sofortiger ~~* with immediate effect; *~~ erzielen* to produce effect; *seine ~~ verfehlen* to fail to work; to prove ineffectual; *die ~~ blieb aus* the effect failed to materialize; *e-e ~~ aufheben* to negate an effect, to neutralize; **~~sart** *f* kind of action; mode of operation; **~~sbereich** *m* radius of action, scope; effective range; *mil* zone of fire; **~~sdauer** *f* duration of effect; persistency; **~~sfähig** *a* active, effective, efficient; **~~sfähigkeit** *f* effectiveness, efficiency; **~~sfeuer** *n mil* fire for effect; **~~sgehalt** *m* active content; **~~sgrad** *m* effectiveness, efficiency, effect; output; *chem* strength; **~~sgröße** *f* action quantity; **~~skraft** *f* effective force, working power, efficiency; **~~skreis** *m* radius (*od* sphere) of action, sphere of influence; **~~slinie** *f phys* line of application; **~~slos** *a* ineffectual, inefficient; inactive, inert; **~~slosigkeit** *f* ineffectiveness, inefficacy, inefficiency; inactivity; **~~smöglichkeit** *f* possible effect; **~~squantum** *n* action quantum; **~~squerschnitt** *m* effective cross section; **~~srichtung** *f* positive direction; **~~sschießen** *n mil* effective fire; **~~svermögen** *n* working power, power of action; **~~svoll** *a* effective, efficacious; **~~sweise** *f* mode of action, operation; **~~swert** *m* effective value; **~~swinkel** *m* angle of action; **~waren** *f pl* knitwear, woven goods *pl*; **~~fertigung** *f* hosiery manufacture; **~widerstand** *m* effective resistance; **~zeit** *f* reaction time.

wirr *a* confused, entangled; (*verworren*) chaotic; (*Haar*) dishevelled; **~en** *f pl* disorders *pl*, troubles *pl*; **~kopf** *m* muddle-headed fellow, *Am sl* screw ball; **~nis** *f*, **~sal** *n* confusion; chaos; error; perplexity; **~warr** *m* hurly-burly, muddle, disorder, confusion, jumble, *fam* mix up, mess, *Am* mish-mash; (*Unruhe*) turmoil, perturbation, *fam* row, rumpus, *Am* callithump; (*Chaos*) chaos, anarchy.

Wirsing *m* savoy.

Wirt *m* host; (*Haus~*) landlord; (*Gast~*) innkeeper; proprietor, *Am* saloon-keeper; (*Verwalter*) manager; **~in** *f* hostess; innkeeper; landlady, proprietrix; **~lich** *a* hospitable; (*bewohnbar*) habitable; **~schaft** *f* (*Haushaltung*) housekeeping, domestic economy; (*Hauswesen*) household; (*Land~~*) husbandry; (*Bauernhof*) farm; (*Welt~~*) economic system, economy, economics *pl u. sing*; (*Verwaltung*) management; (*Industrie*) industry; (*Wirtshaus*) public house, inn, hotel, tavern, bar, *fam* pub, *Am* saloon; (*Vorgang*) goings-on, to-do; (*Durcheinander*) mess; (*Lärm*) hubbub, bustle; *die ~~ führen* to keep house, to run the household; *gelenkte ~~* planned economy; *die ~~ lenken* to control economic life; *die ~~ ankurbeln* to foster trade, to boost business; *die ~~ umstellen* to reconvert industry; **~~en** *itr* to keep house, to run the household; (*sparsam*) to economize, to manage (well); (*schlecht*) to mismanage; to run o.'s business to the ground; (*herumhantieren*) to bustle about, to rummage about; **~~er(in)** *m (f)* manager(-ess); housekeeper, steward; **~~lich** *a* (*sparsam*) economical; thrifty; (*volkswirtschaftlich*) economic; (*leistungsfähig*) efficient; (*vorteilhaft*) profitable, paying; (*industriell*) industrial; *~~lich gestalten* to rationalize; **~~lichkeit** *f* economy; profitability; *~~lichkeit im Betrieb* economy of operation; **~~sabkommen** *n* trade agreement; **~~sablauf** *m* trading process; economic cycle; **~~sabteilung** *f* trade section; industry branch; **~~sankurbelung, ~~sbelebung** *f* economic recovery; promotion of trade; (*durch den Staat*) pump priming; **~~saufbau** *m* economic reconstruction; **~~sbeihilfe** *f* subsidy, grant; **~~sbelange** *pl* trade concerns *pl*; **~~sberater** *m* economic adviser; **~~sbeziehungen** *f pl* economic relations *pl*; **~~sblockade** *f* economic blockade; **~~sbuch** *n* housekeeping book; **~~sdepression** *f* business depression; **~~seinheit** *f* economic unit; **~~sentwicklung** *f* commercial development; **~~sfortschritt** *m* economic progress; **~~sfragen** *f pl* economic problems *pl*; **~~sführer** *m* captain of industry; **~~sführung** *f* management; exploitation; **~~sgebäude** *n* farm building, outhouses *pl*; **~~sgebiet** *n* economic field; *geog* economic district; **~~sgeld** *n* housekeeping money; **~~sgeographie** *f* economic geography; **~~sgeschichte** *f* economic history; **~~sgruppe** *f* corporation; trust; **~~sgüter** *n pl* economic goods *pl*; **~~shilfe** *f* economic support; **~~sinteressen** *n pl* business interests *pl*; **~~sjahr** *n* financial year; **~~skampf** *m* trade competition; **~~skenntnis** *f* trade knowledge; **~~skonferenz** *f* trade conference; **~~skontrolle** *f* industrial control; **~~skonzern** *m* business group, combine; **~~skraft** *f* economic power; economic resources *pl*; **~~skrieg** *m* economic warfare; **~~skrise** *f* economic crisis, business depression, slump; **~~slage** *f* economic situation; **~~sleben** *n* economic life; **~~slenkung** *f* control of economy; **~~smacht** *f* economic power; **~~sminister** *m* Minister of Economics; **~~sministerium** *n* Ministry of Economics, *Am* Department of Commerce; **~~snormen** *f pl* trade standards *pl*; **~~sordnung** *f* economic system; **~~sorganisation** *f* economic organization; **~~splanung** *f* economic planning; **~~spolitik** *f* economic policy, economics *sing u. pl*; **~~spotential** *n* economic potential; **~~sprogramm** *n* trade program(me); **~~sprozeß** *m* trading process; **~~sprüfer** *m* chartered accountant; *Am* certified public accountant; **~~srat** *m* economic council, board of trade; **~~sraum** *m* economic domain; **~~sräume** *m pl* offices *pl*; outhouses *pl*; **~~ssabotage** *f* economic sabotage; **~~ssachverständiger** *m* economic expert; **~~sstruktur** *f* business structure; **~~ssystem** *n* economic system; **~~steil** *m* (*Zeitung*) financial columns *pl*; **~~stheorie** *f* economic theory; **~~sunion** *f* economic union; **~~sunternehmen** *n* business enterprise (*od* undertaking); concern; **~~sverband** *m*, **~~svereinigung** *f* trade association; **~~sverhältnisse** *n pl* economic conditions *pl*; **~~sverhandlungen** *f pl* trade negotiations *pl*; **~~sverkehr** *m* economic relations *pl*; **~~svorteile** *m pl* trade advantages *pl*; **~~swissenschaft** *f* political economy, economics *pl u. sing*; **~~szentrum** *n* commercial centre;

~~szusammenschluß *m* economic merger; **~~szwecke** *m pl* commercial purposes *pl*; **~~szweig** *m* branch of trade; line of business; **~shaus** *n* inn, public house, restaurant; tavern; bar; *Am* saloon; **~sleute** *pl* host and hostess; landlord and landlady; innkeeper and innkeeper's wife; **~sstube** *f* inn parlo(u)r, coffee-room.

Wisch *m* (*Stoff~*) cloth, clout; (*Stroh~*) wisp of straw; (*Papier~*) scrap of paper; (*Zettel*) slip, note; (*Gekritzel*) scrawl; **~en** *tr* to wipe, to rub; (*scheuern*) to mop; (*Zeichnung*) to stump; **~er** *m* wiper, rubber; (*zum Zeichnen*) stump; (*Verweis*) wigging, rebuke; *mot* windscreen-wiper, *fam* wiper; *Am* windshieldwiper; **~lappen** *m*, **~tuch** *n* (*Staub*) duster; (*Geschirr*) dish-cloth; (*für Fußboden*) house-flannel; mop.

Wisent *m* bison, aurochs.

Wismut *m* bismuth.

wispern *tr, itr* to whisper.

Wißbegier|(de) *f* craving for knowledge; (*Neugier*) curiosity; **~ig** *a* anxious to learn, eager for knowledge; (*neugierig*) curious, inquisitive.

wissen *irr itr* to know, to be aware of; (*vertraut sein mit*) to be acquainted with, to understand; (*sicher ~*) to be positive about; *nicht ~* not to know, to be ignorant of; *ich weiß wohl* I am sure of; *um etw ~* to know about; *zu ~ geben* to send word; *~ lassen* to let know; to acquaint s. o. with; *auswendig ~* to know by heart; *Dank ~* to be thankful to; *so viel ich weiß* for aught I know; *er weiß weder aus noch ein* he is at his wits' end; *ich möchte gerne ~* I should like to know, I wonder (whether *od* if); *man kann nie ~* you never know; *nicht daß ich wüßte* not that I am aware of; *Mittel u. Wege ~* to know means; *ich weiß darin Bescheid* I'm well acquainted with it; I'm at home in it; *er weiß mit den Leuten umzugehen* he knows how to manage people; *was weiß ich, wo sie hingegangen ist* how do I know where she went; *ich will nichts mehr von ihr ~* (*fam*) I'm through with her, I don't want to have anything to do with her; *~ Sie noch?* do you remember? *was ich nicht weiß, macht mich nicht heiß* what I don't know won't hurt me; what the eye does not see the heart does not grieve over; *~ n* knowing, knowledge, learning; *tech* (*wie man etw macht*) *Am* know-how; (*Gelehrsamkeit*) scholarship, erudition; *meines ~s* as far as I know, to my knowledge; *nach bestem ~ u. Gewissen* to the best of o.'s knowledge and belief; most conscientiously; *mit meinem ~* with my knowledge; *ohne mein ~* without my knowledge; *wider besseres ~* against o.'s better judg(e)ment; **~schaft** *f* science; learning, knowledge, scholarship; *angewandte ~~* applied science; **~~ler** *m* scientist; scholar; research worker; **~~lich** *a* scientific; scholarly, learned; *~~licher Versuch* experiment; **~~lichkeit** *f* scientific method; **~~slehre** *f* theory of science; **~sdrang, ~sdurst, ~strieb** *m* thirst (*Am fam* yen) for knowledge; **~sgebiet** *n* field (*od* department) of knowledge; **~swert** *a* worth knowing, interesting; **~szweig** *m* branch of knowledge; **~tlich** *a* knowing; (*bewußt*) conscious; (*absichtlich*) wil(l)ful, deliberate; *adv* deliberately, on purpose, knowingly.

Witfrau *f* widow.

wittern *tr* to scent; *fig* to suspect, to perceive; *Unrat ~* to smell a rat.

Witterung *f* weather; (*Geruch*) scent; (*Köder*) scented bait; *bei günstiger ~* weather permitting; **~sbedingungen** *f pl* atmospheric conditions *pl*; **~sbeständig** *a* weather-resisting; (*Stahl*) rust-resisting; **~~keit** *f* resistance to weathering; **~seinfluß** *m* atmospheric influence; **~sumschlag** *m* sudden change of weather; **~sunbilden** *f pl* inclemency of the weather; **~sverhältnisse** *n pl* weather conditions *pl*; **~svorhersage** *f* weather forecast; *langfristige ~~* long period weather forecast.

Wit|we, **~frau** *f* widow; *Königin~~* Queen-Dowager; *Herzogin~~* dowager-duchess; **~~ngeld** *n* widow's allowance; **~~nkleider** *n pl* widow's weeds *pl*; **~~npension** *f* widow's pension; **~~nstand** *m* widowhood; **~~nverbrennung** *f* suttee; **~wer** *m* widower.

Witz *m* wit, wittiness; (*Spaß*) joke, pleasantry, witticism, pun, *Am sl* wisecrack, gag; (*witziger Einfall*) quip, quirk; (*Neckerei*) quiz; (*Wortspiel*) crank; play upon words; (*Streich*) prank, practical joke; (*Mutter~*) mother wit, common sense; *alter ~* old (*od* trite) joke, hoary-headed joke, *sl* old chestnut; *Am sl* bromide; *schlechter ~* bad joke, *fam* corny joke; *er hat viel ~* he's very witty; *dieser ~ ist sehr schwach* that joke is cold turkey; *mach keine ~e!* quit joking! *e-n ~ machen* to crack a joke; **~blatt** *n* comic paper; **~bold** *m* witty fellow, wag, *Am* wisecracker; **~elei** *f* witticism, witty chaffing; **~eln** *itr* to joke, to poke fun (*über* at); to joke mildly; **~ig** *a* witty; (*spaßhaft*) funny, facetious; (*klug*) smart, clever, brilliant; *fam* cute; (*erfinderisch*) ingenious; (*wunderlich*) whimsical; (*drollig*) droll; (*schelmisch*) waggish; **~seite** *f Am* the funnies *pl*; **~sprühend** *a* sparkling with wit; **~zeichnung** *f* cartoon; *e-e Serie von ~~en Am* comic strip.

wo *adv* where, in which; (*zeitlich*) when; *~ nicht* if not, unless; *~ auch, ~ nur* wherever, whithersoever; (*irgend~*) somewhere; *~ möglich* if possible; *ach ~!* oh no! *~ denkst du hin!* what ideas you get! *~ fehlt's?* what's the trouble? **~anders** *adv* elsewhere, somewhere else; **~bei** *adv* whereby, whereat; *prn* (*Frage*) at what? up(on) what? (*relativ*) at which; in which; where; in the course of which; through which.

Woche *f* week; *heute in e-r ~* to-day week, this day week; *Sonntag in e-r ~* (on) Sunday week; *in e-r ~* in a week; *letzte ~* last week; *nächste ~* next week; *heute vor drei ~n* this day three weeks; *vor e-r ~* a week ago; *er blieb e-e ~* he stayed (for) a week; *~ um ~* week in, week out; week by week; *weiße ~* white sale; *in den ~n sein* to be lying in; to be confined; *in die ~n kommen* to be delivered of; **~nausweis** *m* weekly statement; **~nbeginn** *m* week's start; **~nbeihilfe** *f* maternity benefit; **~nbericht** *m* weekly report; **~nbett** *n* childbett; *im ~~ liegen* to be confined; **~~fieber** *n* puerperal fever; **~nblatt** *n* weekly paper; **~nende** *n* week-end; *zum ~~* at week's end; *er ist zum ~~ weggefahren* he's gone away for the week-end; *ein Besuch zum ~~* a week-end visit; **~nendhaus** *n* week-end house; **~nlang** *a* for weeks; **~nlohn** *m* weekly wage; **~~empfänger** *m* weekly wage earner; **~nmarkt** *m* weekly market; **~nschau** *f* weekly review; *Am film* newsreel; **~~photograph** *m* newsreel operator; newsreel camera man; **~nschrift** *f* weekly publication; **~nspielplan** *m theat* weekly program(me); **~nstube** *f* lying-in-room; **~ntag** *m* week-day; (*bestimmter*) day of the week; **~~s** *adv* on week-days; *~~s bin ich beschäftigt* I'm busy on week-days; **~nübersicht** *f* weekly report; **~nverdienst** *m* weekly earnings *pl*; **~nweise** *adv* by the week; **~nzeitung** *f* weekly (paper).

wöchentlich *a* weekly; *adv* every week, a week; by the week; *~ bezahlen* to pay by the week; *einmal ~* once a week.

Wöchnerin *f* woman in childbed; **~nenheim** *n* maternity home.

Wocken *m* (*Rocken*) distaff.

wo|durch *adv* whereby; *prn* (*Frage*) by what? how? by which means? (*relativ*) by which, whereby, through which; **~fern** *conj* if, provided that; (in) so far as; in case; *~~ nicht* unless; **~für** *adv* wherefore; what for; *prn* (*Frage*) what ... for? for what? (*relativ*) for which, for what; *~~ ist das gut?* what is that good for? *~~ halten Sie mich?* what do you take me for? *ich weiß nicht ~~* I don't know what for.

Wog|e *f* billow, wave; **~en** *itr* to surge; (*Getreide*) to wave; (*schwellend*) to heave; (*wellenförmig bewegen*) to undulate; (*hin u. her*) to fluctuate.

wo|gegen *conj* whereas, whilst, on the other hand; *adv* against what, what ... against; in return for what (*od* which); **~her** *adv* whence; from what place; how; from where, where ... from; *~~ wissen Sie das?* how do you know that? *ich weiß nicht, ~~ die Nachricht stammt* I don't know where this news comes from; *ach, ~!* oh, no! I should say not! **~hin** *adv* whither; where ... (to); to what place; *~~ ... auch* wherever; *~~ gehst du heute abend?* where are you going to-night? **~~aus** *adv* which way; to what place; where; **~~gegen** *conj* whereas.

wohl *adv* well; (*zwar, freilich*) to be sure, it is true, all right; (*in der Tat*) indeed, doubtless; (*einräumend, vermutend*) I suppose, I presume, *Am* I guess; possibly, probably; very likely; (*vielleicht*) perhaps; (*fragend*) I wonder; *~ bekomm's!* may it do you good! *sich ~ fühlen* to feel well; to feel at home; *zu Hause fühle ich mich am ~sten* I like it best at home; *~tun* to do good; (*richtig handeln*) to act well; *sich's ~ sein lassen* to enjoy o. s.; to have a good time; *~ dem, der ...* happy he who...; *~ od übel* willy-nilly, come what may; *er wird ~ od übel mit müssen* he'll have to go along whether he likes it or not; *nun ~!* now then! well! *leben Sie ~!* good-by(e)! farewell! *es mag ~ sein* it may be (so), *fam* it is very likely; *ob sie ~ noch dort ist?* I wonder whether she is still there; *ich kann ~ sagen* I dare say; *er hat ~ zehnmal dasselbe gesagt* he must have said the same thing ten times; *ich habe es mir ~ gedacht* I thought so; *es wird sich ~ nicht machen lassen* it will hardly be feasible; *es ist ~ fertig, aber wie!* it's done, all right, but how! *ich verstehe ~, warum ...* I can well understand why...; *Sie sind ~ zufrieden* I suppose you are satisfied; *nicht so~ als* (*vielmehr*) not so much as; *~ n* well-being, good health; (*Wohlfahrt*) welfare; (*Gedeihen*) prosperity; (*Nutzen*) interest; *öffentliches ~* public weal; *auf Ihr ~!* your health! here's to you! good luck! cheers!

wohl|an! *interj* come on! well! now then! **~anständig** *a* proper, decent; **~~keit** *f* propriety, decency; **~auf!** *interj* well then! come on! cheer up! *adv* well, in good health; *~~ sein* to be in good health; **~bedacht** *a* well-considered; **~befinden** *n* good health; well-being; **~behagen** *n* comfort, ease; **~behalten** *a* safe and sound; **~bekannt** *a* well known, familiar; **~beleibt** *a* corpulent; **~~heit** *f* corpulence; **~beschaffen** *a* in good condition; **~bestallt** *a* duly appointed; **~erfahren** *a* expert, experienced; **~ergehen** *n* welfare, prosperity; well-being; health and happiness; **~erwogen** *a* well-considered; **~erworben** *a* duly acquired; **~erzogen** *a* well-bred, well brought up; **~fahrt** *f* welfare, prosperity; (*Unterstützung*) relief; **~~samt** *n* relief-office; Department of Welfare; **~~sausschuß** *m* public welfare committee; **~~sbriefmarke** *f* charity stamp; **~~sfonds** *m* benefit fund; **~~sorganisation** *f* charitable institution, nonprofit-making organization; **~~spflege** *f* welfare work; **~~sstaat** *m* welfare state; **~~sunterstützung** *f* poor-relief, public relief; **~feil** *a* cheap; **~~heit** *f* cheapness; **~geartet** *a* well-disposed; (*~erzogen*) well-bred; **~gebildet** *a* well-made, well-formed; **~geboren** *a* well-born; (*in Briefen*) *Ew. W~~* Sir; (*auf Briefumschlag, hinter dem Namen*) Esquire, Esq.; **~gefallen** *n* pleasure, delight, satisfaction; (*Beifall*) approval; *~~ an etw finden* to take pleasure in; *sich in ~~ auflösen* to end satisfactorily; to come to nothing; **~gefällig** *a* agreeable, pleasant; (*selbstgefällig*) complacent; **~geformt** *a* well-formed, shapely; **~gelitten** *a* popular, much liked; **~gemeint** *a* well-meant; **~gemerkt** *adv* nota bene; take notice; observe what follows; **~gemut** *a* cheerful, merry, light-hearted; **~genährt** *a* well-fed, corpulent; **~geneigt** *a* affectionate; well-affected; **~geordnet** *a* well-arranged; **~geraten** *a* well-done; (*Kinder*) good; **~geruch** *m* perfume; sweet scent, fragrance; **~geschmack** *m* agreeable taste, flavo(u)r; **~gesetzt** *a* well-worded; **~gesinnt** *a* well-minded; **~gesittet** *a* well-mannered; **~gestaltet** *a* well-shaped, shapely; **~getroffen** *a* striking; **~gewogen** *a* kind, benevolent; **~~heit** *f* kindness, benevolence; **~gezogen** *a* well-educated; **~habend** *a* well-to-do, well-off, wealthy, prosperous, pecunious, opulent, moneyed; *fam* well set up; *Am sl* well-heeled, oofy, tinny, well fixed, forehanded; **~habenheit** *f* easy circumstances *pl*, wealth, affluence, opulence, riches *pl*, *fam* money-bags *pl*; **~ig** *a* comfortable; happy, content; **~klang, ~laut** *m* harmony, melodious sound, euphony; **~klingend, ~lautend** *a* harmonious, melodious, sweet-sounding, sonorous, euphonious; **~leben** *n* life of pleasure, good living, luxury; **~meinend** *a* well-meaning; **~riechend** *a* sweet-scented, fragrant; perfumed; **~schmeckend** *a* savoury, tasty, palatable; **~sein** *n* prosperity, welfare; (*gesundheitlich*) good health; *zum ~~!* your health! **~stand** *m* well-being; (*Reichtum*) wealth, fortune; (*wirtschaftlich*) prosperity; **~tat** *f* benefit; (*Gunst*) boon, kindness; (*Mildtätigkeit*) charity, benefaction; *fig* (*Erfrischung*) comfort, blessing; **~täter** *m* benefactor; **~~in** *f* benefactress; **~tätig** *a* charitable; (*wohltuend*) beneficent (to); (*von Dingen*) salutary, wholesome; **~tätigkeit** *f* beneficence; charity; **~~sbazar** *m* charity bazaar, fancy fair; **~~seinrichtung** *f* charitable institution; **~~sfonds** *m Am* community chest; **~~sveranstaltung** *f* charity performance; **~~sverein** *m* charitable society, fraternal society; **~tuend** *a* beneficial; comforting, pleasant; **~tun** *irr tr* to do good, to dispense charity; to be comforting, to be pleasant; **~überlegt** *a* well-considered; (*Rede*) set; **~unterrichtet** *a* well-informed; **~verdient** *a* well-deserved; of great merit; **~verhalten** *n* good conduct; **~verstanden** *a* well-understood; *~~!* you must understand! **~weislich** *adv* prudently, very wisely; **~wollen** *itr* to wish s. o. well, to befriend s. o.; *~~ n* goodwill, benevolence; (*Gunst*) favo(u)r, patronage; **~~d** *a* kind, benevolent (to).

Wohn|anhänger *m* caravan, *Am* (house-) trailer; **~bevölkerung** *f* resident population; **~bezirk** *m* residential quarter (*Am* section); (residential) neighbo(u)rhood; **~block** *m* block of flats; **~~knacker** *m aero fam* block-buster; **~en** *itr* to live, to dwell, to reside; to stay (with); *Am* to room, to bunk, to keep, *sl* to hang out; *zur Miete ~~* to lodge; **~fläche** *f* housing space; **~gebäude** *n* dwelling house, residential premises *pl*; (*Miethaus*) block of flats, *Am* apartment house; **~~steuer** *f* house tax; **~gegend** *f* residential district; **~gelegenheit** *f* accommodation; **~grundstück** *n* residential site (*Am* lot); **~haus** *n* dwelling-house, *Am* apartment house; (*der Studenten*) hostel, hall of residence for students, *Am* dormitory; **~hotel** *n* block of service-flats, *Am* apartment hotel; **~küche** *f* parlo(u)r kitchen; **~lich** *a* comfortable, snug, cosy; *fam* livable; *~~er Ort* snuggery; **~~keit** *f* cosiness; **~möglichkeiten** *f pl* housing facilities *pl*; **~ort, ~sitz** *m* place of residence, domicile; *com* office; *ständiger ~~* permanent residence; *seinen ~~ nehmen* to establish o. s. in a place, *fam* to locate; *ohne festen ~~* unsettled; of no fixed abode; **~~veränderung** *f* change of residence, removal; **~raum** *m* housing space; living quarters *pl*; **~schlafzimmer** *n* bed-sitting room; **~straße** *f* residential street; **~stube** *f* sitting-room; **~ung** *f* dwelling, habitation, residence; (*Miet~~*) flat, rooms *pl*, lodgings *pl*, *Am* apartment; (*Klein~~*) flatlet; (*Unterbringung*) accommodation, housing; (*Heim*) home; *jdm die ~~ kündigen* to give s. o. notice to quit; *e-e ~~ beziehen* to move in; *e-e ~~ vermieten* to let lodgings; *unterbelegte ~~* not fully utilized accommodation; *zweckentfremdete ~~* accommodation used for purposes other than originally intended; **~~samt** *n* housing administration, housing office; **~~sänderung** *f* change of address; **~~sanschluß** *m* residence telephone; **~~sanzeiger** *m* directory; **~~sbau** *m* housing-construction, home-building; **~~sbaufinanzierung** *f* financing of housing; **~~sbauprogramm** *n* building program(me); **~~sbedarf** *m* housing requirements *pl*; **~~sbewirtschaftung** *f* housing control; **~~seinheit** *f* dwelling unit; **~~sfrage** *f* housing problem; **~~sgeld** *n* lodging allowance; allowance for housing; **~~sinhaber** *m* lodger, *Am* roomer; **~~smangel** *m* housing shortage; **~~smangelgebiet** *n* critical housing area; **~~smiete** *f* residential rent; **~~snachweis** *m* house-agency; **~~snot** *f* housing shortage; **~~sproblem** *n* housing problem; **~~sräumung** *f* eviction; **~~ssuche** *f*: *auf der ~~ssuche sein* to be house-hunting; **~~stausch** *m* exchange of dwellings; **~~sverhältnisse** *n pl* housing conditions *pl*; **~~swechsel** *m* change of residence; **~~szuschuß** *m* rent allowance; **~~szwangswirtschaft** *f* housing control; **~viertel** *n* residential quarter (*Am* section *od* district); **~vorort** *m* (residential) neighbo(u)rhood; **~wagen** *m* caravan, *Am* trailer; **~~parkplatz** *m Am* trailer park; **~zimmer** *n* sitting-room, *Am* livingroom.

Woilach *m* saddle blanket; horse-rug.

wölb|en *tr* to vault, to arch, to camber; *r* to arch (over); **~ung** *f* vault, vaulting; (*gewölbte Form*) curvature; (*Gewölbe*) arch; (*Kuppel*) dome; (*Biegung*) camber; **~~sradius** *m* radius of crown.

Wolf *m* wolf; *med* excoriation, chafe; *der ~ im Schafspelz* the wolf in a sheep's clothing; *tech* (*Spinnerei*) willow; (*Metall*) devil; (*Luppe*) bloom; (*Fleisch*) (meat) mincer; **~ram** *n* tungsten, wolframite; **~seisen** *n*, **~sfalle** *f* wolf-trap; *hist* caltrop; **~sgrube** *f* wolf-trap; *mil* obstacle pit; **~shund** *m* Alsatian dog; **~shunger** *m* ravenous appetite; **~smilch** *f bot* spurge; **~spelz** *m* wolfskin; **~srudel** *n* wolf pack.

Wölf|in *f* she-wolf; **~isch** *a* wolfish.

Wolk|e *f* cloud; *~en ziehen* clouds are drifting; *tiefliegende ~en aero* low ceiling; *über den ~en fliegen aero sl* to fly over the top; *Flug über den ~en* over-the-top flight; *Mächtigkeit der ~e* density of cloud; **~enbank** *f* cloud bank; **~enbildung** *f* cloud formation; **~enbruch** *m* cloud-burst; **~endecke** *f* cloud-cover (*od* pall); **~enfetzen** *m* scud, tattered cloud; **~enflug** *m* cloud flight; **~enformen** *f pl* cloud forms *pl;* **~enfrei** *a* cloudless; **~enhöhe** *f* cloud height, ceiling; **~enkappe** *f* cloud cap; **~enkratzer** *m* skyscraper; **~enlandschaft** *f* sky-scape; **~enlos** *a* clear, cloudless; **~enmeer** *n* sea of clouds; **~enmessung** *f* cloud measurement; **~enschatten** *m* cloud shadow (*od* bank); **~enscheinwerfer** *m* cloud searchlight; **~enschicht** *f* cloud layer, stratum of cloud; **~enschleier** *m* clouds *pl*, haze, cloud veil; **~ensegeln** *n aero* cloud soaring; **~enstreifen** *m* cloud banner; **~enuntergrenze** *f* base of cloud; **~enwand** *f* bank of clouds; **~enzone** *f* troposphere; **~enzug** *m* cloud train; **~ig** *a* cloudy, clouded; broken.

Woll|abfall *m* wool waste; **~arbeiter** *m* wool-dresser (*od*-picker); **~artig** *a* wool-like, woolly; **~atlas** *m* woolen satin; **~aufbereitungsmaschine** *f* wool-dressing machine; **~decke** *f* wool blanket; **~e** *f* wool; *in der ~~ gefärbt* dyed in the grain; *in der ~~ sitzen* to live in clover; *viel Geschrei u. wenig ~~* much ado about nothing; *~~ lassen müssen fig* to get fleeced; **~en** *a* wool(l)en; (*Strümpfe*) worsted; **~faser** *f* wool fibre; **~fett** *n* wool grease; **~filz** *m* wool felt; **~garn** *n* wool(l)en yarn; **~handel** *m* wool-trade; **~händler** *m* wool-merchant; wool-stapler; **~ig** *a* woolly; (*weich*) fleecy; (*flockig*) cottony; (*kraus*) curly; (*plüschartig*) plushy, shaggy; **~industrie** *f* wool(l)en industry; **~jacke** *f* jersey; **~kleidung** *f* wool(l)en clothing; **~kraut** *n* mulle(i)n; **~krempelmaschine** *f* carding-machine; **~schur** *f* sheep-shearing; **~schweiß** *m* (wool) yolk, suint; **~spinnerei** *f* wool(l)en mill, wool-spinning factory; **~staub** *m* wool flock; **~stoff** *m* wool(l)en stuff; **~waren** *f pl* wool(l)en articles (*od* goods) *pl*; **~~händler** *m* wool(l)en draper; **~wäsche** *f chem* wool scouring.

wollen *irr tr, itr* (*Willensäußerung*) to be willing (to); to want; (*Hilfszeit-*

wort) will; (*bereit sein*) to be ready; (*entschlossen sein*) to be determined; (*wünschen*) to wish, to want, to desire; (*beabsichtigen*) to intend; to mean; (*auswählen*) to choose; (*bevorzugen*) to prefer; (*gern haben*) to like; (*im Begriff sein*) to be going to, to be about to, to be on the point of; *unbedingt* ~ to insist (on); *lieber* ~ to prefer; *nicht* ~ to be unwilling; (*sich weigern*) to refuse; *tun Sie, was Sie* ~ do what you want; *sie hat es so gewollt* she wanted it that way; *was* ~ *Sie?* what do you want? *was* ~ *Sie damit sagen?* what do you mean by it? *er weiß, was er will* he knows what he wants; he knows his mind; *er will das Geld nicht annehmen* he won't accept the money; ~ *Sie lieber nach Hause gehen?* would you rather go home? *ich wollte, sie wären schon da* I wish they were here already; *er wollte anrufen, hat es aber vergessen* he meant to call, but he forgot; *das will ich meinen!* I should think so! rather! I should say so! *das will etwas heißen!* that means something! that's really something! *er will gehört haben* he pretends (*od* maintains) he has heard; *was will er jetzt tun?* what does he intend to do now? what is he going to do now? *wo will er hinaus?* what is he aiming (*od* driving) at? *er soll machen, was er will* let him do his worst; *das will überlegt sein* that requires some thinking; *so Gott will!* please God! *wie Sie* ~ as you like; as you wish; suit yourself; *er mag* ~ *od nicht* whether he likes it or not; *wir* ~ *gehen* let us go; *ohne es zu* ~ in spite of myself (himself *usw*); *dem sei, wie ihm wolle* be that as it may; *was wollte ich sagen?* what was I going to say? *was ich noch sagen wollte* ... and another thing ...; *das wolle Gott!* would to God! *er wollte schon immer hoch hinaus* he always aimed high; ~ *n* will; (*Absicht*) intention; (*Willensentschluß*) volition.

Wol|lust *f* voluptuousness; lust; **~lüstig** *a* voluptuous; **~lüstling** *m* voluptuary, (*stärker*) libertine, debauchee.

wo|mit *adv* with which; with what, by which, wherewith; (*Frage*) with what, what ... with; *~~ kann ich dienen?* what can I do for you? *~~ soll ich anfangen?* what shall I start with? **~möglich** *adv* if possible, possibly; **~nach** *adv* after what, after which; whereupon, whereafter; (*zufolge*) according to which.

Wonne *f* delight, bliss; (*Entzücken*) rapture; (*Vergnügen*) great pleasure; (*Freude*) joy; **~gefühl** *n* feeling of delight; **~monat, ~mond** *m* month of May; **~schauer** *m* thrill of delight; **~sam** *a* delightful, blissful; **~trunken** *a* enraptured; **~voll** *a* blissful.

wonnig *a* delightful, blissful.

wo|ran *prn* (*Frage*) at what? about what? what ... about? how? what ... of? of what? (*relativ*) at what; on what; whereon; whereat; by what; *~~ denken Sie?* what are you thinking of (*od* about)? *~~ arbeitet er?* what is he working at? *ich weiß, ~~ es liegt* I know what is the cause; *~~ erinnert Sie das?* what does that remind you of? *man weiß bei ihm nie, ~~ man ist* with him you never know where you are at; **~rauf** *adv* (*Frage*) (up)on what? what ... on? for what? what ... for? (*relativ*) upon what, upon which; whereupon; *~~ warten Sie?* what are you waiting for? *~~ alle gingen* whereupon all went away; **~raus** *adv* (*Frage*) (out) of what? from what? what ... of; (*relativ*) out of which, from which, whence; *~~ ist das gemacht?* what's it made of? *~~ schließen Sie das?* from what do you infer that? **~rein, ~rin** *adv* into which, into what; with which; *~rin besteht der Unterschied?* where does the difference lie?

worf|eln *tr* to winnow, to fan; **~schaufel** *f* winnowing-shovel.

Wort *n* word; (*Ausdruck*) expression, term; (*Ausspruch*) saying; (*Ehren~*) word of hono(u)r; (*Versprechen*) promise; *geflügelte ~e* familiar quotations; ~ *für* ~ word for word, literally; *auf mein* ~ upon my word; *auf ein ~!* can I have a word with you? *aufs* ~ *gehorchen* to obey to the letter; *ein Mann von* ~ *sein* to be as good as o.'s word; *ein Mann, ein ~!* word of honour! honour bright! *mit anderen ~en* in other words; *kein* ~ *mehr!* not another word! *das* ~ *ergreifen* to begin to speak; *parl* to rise to speak; to address the House; *Am* to take the floor; to take the lift; *jdm das* ~ *erteilen* to allow s. o. to speak; *das* ~ *haben, das* ~ *erhalten* to have leave to speak, to be allowed to speak; *parl* to catch the Speaker's eye; to be in possession of the House; *Sie haben das* ~ it is your turn to speak; *ums* ~ *bitten* to beg permission to speak; to ask leave to speak; *Ich bitte ums* ~ (*Am*) may I have the floor? *e-r Sache das* ~ *reden* to speak for (*od* in favo(u)r of); *das* ~ *führen* to be the spokesman; *das große* ~ *führen* to monopolize the conversation; (*aufschneiden*) to brag, to swagger; *jdm ins* ~ *fallen* to interrupt s. o., to cut short; *fam* to chip in; *viele ~e machen* to talk too much; to make a fuss; *sein* ~ *halten* to keep o.'s word; *sein* ~ *brechen* to break o.'s word; *jdn beim ~e nehmen* to take s. o. at o.'s word; *jdm das* ~ *entziehen* to stop s. o. from speaking; *jdm das* ~ *abschneiden* to stop s. o. short; *sein* ~ *geben* to pledge o.'s word, to give o.'s word; *das entscheidende* ~ *haben bei* to have the final say (in); *es ist kein wahres* ~ *daran* there isn't a word of truth in it; *Sie dürfen mir aufs* ~ *glauben* you may take my word for it; you can believe every word I say; *für Geld u. gute ~e* for love or money; *er läßt uns überhaupt nicht zu* ~ *kommen* he doesn't let us get a word in edgewise; *ich lege ein gutes* ~ *für Sie ein* I'll put in a good word for you; *hast du ~e! fam* what do you say to that! *ich habe kein* ~ *davon gewußt* I didn't know a thing about it; *spare deine ~e!* save your breath! *in ~en* in writing; *ein schwer aussprechbares* ~ a tongue twister; *bei diesem Lärm kann man sein eigenes* ~ *nicht verstehen* you can't hear your own voice in this noise; you can't hear yourself think in this noise; *ein* ~ *gab das andere* one word led to another; *er verlor kein* ~ *über* he wasted no words about; *er macht nicht viel ~e* he is a man of few words; **~ableitung** *f* derivation of words; etymology; **~ähnlichkeit** *f* synonymy; **~akzent** *m* word-stress; **~anfang** *m* beginning of a word; **~arm** *a* deficient in vocabulary; **~armut** *f* poverty of language; **~art** *f gram* part of speech; **~auslaut** *m* final sound at the end of a word; **~bedeutung** *f* lexical meaning; **~~slehre** *f* semantics *pl*; **~beugung** *f* inflection; **~bildung** *f* word-formation; **~~slehre** *f* morphology; **~bruch** *m* breach of o.'s word; **~brüchig** *a* having broken o.'s word; disloyal; treacherous; perfidious; *~~ werden* to break o.'s word; **~~keit** *f* breach of faith, perfidiousness; **~emacher** *m* idle talker, verbose speaker; **~familie** *f* family of words; **~folge** *f* word-order; **~formverweisung** *f* cross reference from one form of subject heading to another; **~forscher** *m* etymologist; **~forschung** *f* etymologism; **~fügung** *f* syntax; construction; **~führer** *m* speaker; spokesman; **~fülle** *f* verbosity; **~gebühr** *f* word rate, fee; **~gedächtnis** *n* verbal memory; **~gefecht** *n* dispute, debate; **~geklingel** *n* jingle of words; **~getreu** *a* word for word, literal; **~karg** *a* taciturn, laconic; **~~heit** *f* taciturnity; **~klauber** *m* stickler for words; quibbler, hair-splitter; **~~ei** *f* hair-splitting; **~kunde** *f* lexicology; **~kunst** *f* style; **~laut** *m* wording; (*Inhalt*) text; *jur* tenor; *nach dem ~~ des Vertrags* by the terms of the contract; **~los** *a* speechless, wordless; (*stumm*) mute; **~meldung** *f*: *~~en liegen nicht vor* there is nobody who asked leave to speak; **~rätsel** *n* logogriph; **~register** *n* index (of words), glossary; **~reich, ~überladen** *a* abundant in words; verbose, wordy, voluble; **~~tum** *m* abundance in words; (*Geschwätzigkeit*) verbosity; **~schatz** *m* vocabulary; **~schwall** *m* torrent of words; long rigmarole; verbosity, bombast; **~sinn** *m* meaning of a word; literal sense; **~spiel** *n* pun, play upon words; **~stamm** *m* radical, root stem; **~stellung** *f* word-order, order of words; **~streit** *m* dispute; **~ton** *m* word-stress; **~verdrehung** *f* distortion of words; **~verkürzung** *f* syncope; **~verständlichkeit** *f* word intelligibility; **~verstümmelung** *f tele* clipping; **~vorrat** *m* stock of words; **~wechsel** *m* dispute, debate; (high) words *pl*; argument; (*Zank*) altercation; *e-n ~~ haben* to have words; **~witz** *m* pun, play upon words; **~wörtlich** *a* word for word, literally, exactly like that; **~zähler** *m tele* word counter; **~zusammenziehung** *f* portmanteau word; **~zwischenraum** *m* space between words.

Wört|erbuch *n* dictionary; **~erverzeichnis** *n* list of words, vocabulary; **~lich** *a* verbal, verbatim; word for word, literal.

wor|über *adv* whereat, whereof, at which; (*fragend*) about which? over which? what ... over? over what? about what? what... about? **~um** *adv* about what, what ... about, about; *~~ handelt es sich?* what's it all about? **~unter** *adv* among which; (*Frage*) among what? under what? what ... under?

wo|selbst *adv* where; **~von** *adv* of which, from which; whereof; (*Frage*) about what? what ... about? from what? what ... from? *~~ spricht er?* what is he talking about? *~~ kann dieser Ausschlag kommen?* what can this rash come from? **~vor** *adv* before which; of which; (*Frage*) of what? what ... of? *~~ fürchtest du dich?* what are you afraid of? **~zu** *adv* to which; (*warum*) why; (*Frage*) for what? what ... for? *~~ soll das gut sein?* what is that supposed to be good for? *~~ soll ich hingehen?* what should I go there for?

Wrack *n* wreck; **~guß** *m tech* spoiled casting; **~gut** *n* wreckage, wrecked goods *pl*.

wring|en *tr* to wring; **~maschine** *f* wringing-machine, wringer.

Wucher *m*, **~ei** *f* usury; (*Waren~*) profiteering; ~ *treiben* to practise usury; **~blume** *f* golden daisy; **~er** *m* usurer, money-lender; profiteer; **~gesetz** *n* law against usury (*od* profiteering); **~gewinn** *m* excess profit; **~haft, ~isch** *a* usurious; profiteering; *~~ aufkaufen* to forestall; **~handel** *m* usurious trade; **~miete** *f* rack-rent; **~n** *itr* to practise usury (*od* profiteering), to profiteer; *fig* to make the most of; (*Fleisch*) to form proud flesh; (*Pflanzen*) to grow exuberantly (*od* rankly); to pullulate; **~pflanze** *f* parasite; **~ung** *f med* growth, tumo(u)r; *bot* exuberance, rank growth; **~zins** *m* usurious interest.

Wuchs *m* growth; (*Trieb*) rankness; (*Körper~*) shape, stature, figure, form; (*Größe*) height; size; (*Entwicklung*) development; (*Holz*) grain.

Wucht *f* weight, burden; (*Gewalt*) force; (*Anstoß*) impetus; (*Druck*) pressure; *tech* kinetic energy; inertia force; *mit voller ~* (*Am*) in a big way; **~en** *itr* to weigh heavy; *tr* to lever up; **~ig** *a* weighty, heavy; (*kräftig*) vigoro(u)s, powerful.

Wühl|arbeit *f fig* insidious agitation, subversive activity; **~en** *itr, tr* to dig, to turn up; (*Tier*) to burrow; (*Schwein*) to root up; (*zernagen*) to gnaw (at); (*zerreißen*) to tear; (*durchstöbern*) to rummage, to rake about (in); *fig* to stir up, to agitate; *im Gelde ~~* to wallow (*od* to be rolling) in money; **~er** *m* agitator, demagogue; **~erei** *f* agitation; **~erisch** *a* demagogic, revolutionary, inflammatory, incendiary; **~maus** *f* vole.

Wulst *m* roll, pad; (*Haar~*) puff; *med* pad; (*Falte*) fold; (*Kissen*) cushion; (*Vorsprung*) swelling, enlargement; *arch* torus; **~eisen** *n* bulb iron; **~felge** *f* clincher rim; **~förmig** *a* doughnut-shaped; roll-shaped; **~ig** *a* stuffed, padded; thick; (*aufgedunsen*) puffed up; (*Lippen*) protruding, pouting; (*angeschwollen*) swelled; **~lippen** *f pl* thick lips *pl*, blubber lips *pl*; **~los** *a* ridgeless; **~naht** *f* reinforced seam; **~rand** *m* beaded edge; **~reifen** *m* clincher (*od* heel) tyre; **~schutzstreifen** *m* chafer.

wund *a* sore; (*verwundet*) wounded; (*~ gerieben*) chafed; *mit ~en Füßen* footsore; *~er Punkt fig* sore spot (*od* point); *die ~e Stelle* sore, gall, raw; *sich ~ liegen* to become bed-sore, to get bed-sores; *sich ~ reiben* to gall, to chafe; *sich ~ reiten* to lose leather; **~arzneikunst** *f* surgery; **~arzt** *m* surgeon; **~ärztlich** *a* surgical; **~balsam** *m* vulnerary balsam; **~brand** *m* gangrene; **~e** *f* wound, cut; (*Verletzung*) injury, hurt; (*wunde Stelle*) sore; (*Brand~~*) burn, scald; (*Schnitt~~*) cut, gash; (*Quetschung*) contusion, bruise; (*schwärende ~~*) ulcer; *die Zeit heilt ~en* time is a great healer; *alte ~en wieder aufreißen fig* to open old sores; **~eisen** *n* sound; **~eiterung** *f* suppuration of a wound; **~fieber** *n* wound fever; **~gelaufen** *a* footsore; **~klammer** *f* wound-clamp, suture clip; **~liegen** *n* bed-sore; **~mal** *n* scar; *~~e Christi* stigmata *pl*; **~naht** *f* wound-suture; **~pulver** *n* vulnerary powder; **~rand** *m* lip of wound; **~salbe** *f* ointment for wounds; **~schorf** *m* scab; **~sein** *n* being sore; chafe, excoriation; **~starrkrampf** *m* (traumatic) tetanus; lockjaw; **~verband** *m* dressing; bandage; *erster ~~* first aid.

Wunder *n* wonder, marvel; (*übernatürliches*) miracle; (*Person*) prodigy; *es ist kein ~* no wonder; *es nimmt mich ~* I wonder, I am surprised at; *~ tun* to work wonders (*od* miracles); *sein blaues ~ erleben* to be amazed; *es geschehen Zeichen u. ~* wonders will never cease; *sich ~ was einbilden* to be full of conceit, to be very cocky; **~bar** *a* wonderful, marvellous, wondrous; *fam* smashing; (*seltsam*) strange; (*übernatürlich*) miraculous; **~~erweise** *adv* strange to say; **~bild** *n* miracle-working image; **~ding** *n* wonderful thing, prodigy; **~doktor** *m* quack; **~geschichte** *f* marvellous story; **~glaube** *m* belief in miracles; **~horn** *n*: *des Knaben ~~* the Youth's Magic Horn; **~hübsch** *a* lovely; **~kind** *n* infant prodigy; **~kraft** *f* miraculous power; **~kur** *f* miraculous cure; **~land** *n* Fairyland; **~lich** *a* strange, odd, quaint; (*launisch*) whimsical; (*überspannt*) eccentric; (*eigenartig*) peculiar, singular; **~~keit** *f* oddity, peevishness; whimsicalness; eccentricity; **~n** *tr* to wonder; *es ~t mich* I wonder at it, I am surprised; *es soll mich ~n, ob* I wonder if; *r* to wonder (at), to be surprised (*od* astonished) (at); **~sam** *a* wonderful, wondrous; **~schön** *a* awfully nice, exceedingly beautiful; exquisite; **~spiegel** *m* magic mirror; **~tat** *f* wonderful (*od* miraculous) deed; **~täter** *m* worker of miracles; **~tätig** *a* performing miracles, miraculous; **~tier** *n* monster; *fig* prodigy; **~voll** *a* wonderful, admirable, marvellous; **~welt** *f* world of wonders, enchanted world; **~werk** *n* miracle; **~zeichen** *n* miraculous sign, prodigy.

Wunsch *m* wish, desire; (*Sehnsucht*) longing, *Am* yen; (*Bestreben*) aspiration; (*Absicht*) intention; *auf ~* by request; *com* if desired, on application; *nach ~* as desired, according to o.'s wish; *auf jds ~* at s. o.'s request; *den ~ hegen* to entertain a wish; *mit den besten Wünschen zum Fest* with the compliments of the season; *alles ging nach seinen Wünschen* everything turned out the way he wanted it; *das war nur ein frommer ~* that was only wishful thinking; *haben Sie noch e-n ~?* is there anything else you'd like? will there be anything else? **~gemäß** *adv* according to s.o.'s wishes; as requested; **~konzert** *n* request program(me); **~traum** *m* wish dream, *Am* pipe-dream; **~zettel** *m* list of things desired; letter to Santa Claus.

Wünsch|elrute *f* dowsing-rod, divining-rod; **~~ngänger** *m* dowser; **~en** *tr* to wish, to desire, to want; (*sehnen*) to wish for, to long for; *jdm Glück ~~* to congratulate s. o. (*zu* on); to wish s. o. luck; to wish s. o. well; *ich ~e ihm alles Gute* I wish him all the best; *was ~~ Sie?* may I help you? *das läßt zu ~~ übrig* that could be better; *was ~~ Sie sich zum Geburtstag?* what would you like for your birthday? *ich ~e Ihnen ein glückliches Neujahr* I wish you a happy New Year; *wie Sie ~~* as you please; just as you wish; *Am* right you are; *das will ich keinem ~~* (*Am*) it shouldn't happen to a dog; **~enswert** *a* desirable.

*

Würd|e *f* dignity; (*Ehre*) honour; (*Amt*) post; office; (*Rang*) rank, title; *akademische ~~* academic degree; *in Amt u. ~en* holding office; *unter jds ~~* beneath s.o.'s dignity; not quite in keeping with o.'s position; *unter aller ~e* beneath contempt; **~elos** *a* undignified; **~enträger** *m* dignitary; **~evoll** *a* dignified, full of dignity; **~ig** *a* worthy of; (*verdient*) deserving (of); (*angesehen*) respectable; (*würdevoll*) dignified; **~igen** *tr* (*schätzen*) to appreciate, to value; *e-r Sache ~~* to deign; *jdn e-s Wortes ~~* to deign to speak to; *nicht e-s Wortes ~~* not to vouchsafe a word to; *ein Ereignis ~~* to keynote an event; *er hat mich keines Blickes gewürdigt* he didn't so much as look at me; **~igkeit** *f* worthiness; (*Verdienst*) merit; (*würdiges Äußere*) dignified appearances *pl*; **~igung** *f* valuation, appreciation; estimation.

Wurf *m* throw, cast, fling; (*Tiere*) litter, brood; (*Schwung*) sling; (*Schleudern*) hurl; (*rascher ~*) chuck; (*Ball~*) pitch; *tech* projection; (*Bomben*) bomb release, salvo; *zum ~ ausholen* to get ready to show; *ein gelungener ~* (*fig*) a lucky hit; (*Meister~*) *Am fam* tenstrike; **~anker** *m* kedge, grapnel; **~bahn** *f* trajectory, flight path; **~bewegung** *f* projectile motion; **~feuer** *n* mortar fire; **~gerät** *n* projector; **~geschoß** *m* missile, projectile; **~gitter** *n* screen; **~granate** *f* mortar shell; **~hebel** *m mil aero* bomb-release lever; **~höhe** *f* height of projection; **~kraft** *f* projectile force; **~ladung** *f* propelling charge; **~leine** *f* heaving line; **~linie** *f* trajectory, line of projection; **~mine** *f* thrown mine; **~rad** *n* scoop wheel; **~schaufel** *f* casting shovel; winnowing shovel; **~scheibe** *f* discus; quoit; **~sendung** *f* mass of circulars sent out; direct mail; **~speer** *m* javelin, dart; **~taube** *f* clay pigeon; **~taubenschießstand** *m* skeet range; **~weite** *f* range (of projection).

Würfel *m* die (*pl* dice); *math* (*Kubus*) cube; hexahedron; (*Kapsel*) capsule, pellet; *der ~ ist gefallen* the die is cast; *~ spielen* to play at dice; **~becher** *m* dice-box; **~brikett** *n* cube-shaped briquet(te); **~eck** *n* corner of a cube; **~festigkeit** *f* crushing strength of a cube; **~förmig** cubic(al), cuboidal, cube-shaped; **~ig** *a* cubic; (*Muster*) chequered, check(er)ed; (*Boden*) tessellar; **~inhalt** *m* cubic contents *pl*; **~kohle** *f* cobbles *pl*; **~muster** *n* checkered pattern; **~n** *itr* to play at dice, to throw dice; to raffle (*um* for); *tr* (*in Stückchen schneiden*) to cut into little squares; (*Stoff*) to chequer, to check(er); *durcheinander ~~* to jumble up; **~spat** *m* anhydrite; **~spiel** *n* game at dice; **~~er** *m* dice-player; **~zucker** *m* lump (*od* cube *od* tablet) sugar.

würg|en *itr* to choke, to stick in o.'s throat; (*beim Erbrechen*) to retch; *tr* to throttle, to strangle; (*auch tech*) to choke; (*an der Kehle packen*) to seize by the throat; *hinunter~~* to gulp, to swallow; *r* to choke; to struggle hard; *am Essen ~~* to gag on o.'s food; *mit Hängen u. ~~* with the greatest difficulty; **~engel** *m* destroying angel; **~er** *m* strangler, killer, murderer; (*Vogel*) shrike, butcher-bird.

Wurm *m* worm; (*Made, Larve*) maggot, grub; (*Ungeziefer*) vermin; (*Reptil*) reptile, snake; (*Drache*) dragon; *tech* worm; (*am Finger*) whitlow, panaris; (*Kind*) *fam ~ n* little mite, poor little thing; *jdm die Würmer aus der Nase ziehen fam* to draw s. o. out, to pump s.o.; *von Würmern zerfressen* worm-eaten; **~abtreibend** *a* vermifuge, anthelmintic; **~artig** *a* worm-like, vermiform; **~en** *tr* to vex, to annoy, to fret; *es ~t mich* it annoys me, *fam* it riles me; **~farn** *m* male fern; **~förmig** *a* worm-shaped, vermicular, vermiform; **~fortsatz** *m* appendix; **~fraß** *m* damage done by worms; ~**fräßig** *a* worm-eaten; ~**getriebe** *n* worm gear; ~**ig** *a* maggoty; (*zerfressen*) worm-eaten; ~**krankheit** *f* worm disease; ~**kuchen** *m* wormcake; ~**mehl** *n* worm-dust; ~**mittel** *n* vermifuge; ~**stich** *m* worm-hole; ~~**ig** *a* worm-eaten; ~**treibend** *a* anthelmintic.

Würmchen *n* vermicule; *fig* poor little wretch, little (*od* tiny) mite.

Wurst *f* sausage; (*Blut*~) black pudding; (*Frankfurter*) frankfurt(er), (*heiße mit Brot*) *Am fam* hot dog; (*Wiener*) wiener, *Am sl* wienie(s *pl*); (*Leber*~) liverwurst; (*Bologneser* ~) bologna, *fam* boloney; *mit der* ~ *nach der Speckseite werfen* to give a sprat to catch a herring; ~ *wider* ~ tit for tat; *fam das ist mir* ~ it is all the same to me; I don't care a rap, *Am* I don't give a hang; ~**darm** *m* gut for sausages; ~**eln** *itr fam* to muddle along; ~**fabrik** *f* sausage factory; ~**förmig** *a* toric, tyre-shaped; ~**füllmaschine** *f* sausage machine; ~**händler** *m* pork-butcher; ~**haut** *f* skin for sausages; sausage casing; ~**ig** *a fam* quite indifferent; ~~**keit** *f* complete indifference; ~**kessel** *m* sausage-boiler; ~**laden** *m* pork-butcher's shop; ~**suppe** *f* pudding broth; ~**vergiftung** *f* sausage-poisoning, botulism; ~**waren** *f pl* sausages *pl*; ~**zipfel** *m* sausage-end.

Würstchen *n* (small) sausage; *heiße* ~ hot sausages, (*mit Brötchen*) *Am fam* hot dogs; *kleines* ~ (*fig*) small fry; ~**stand** *m Am* hot-dog stand.

Würz|e *f* seasoning, flavo(u)r; (*Bier*~) wort; (*Gewürz, Beigeschmack*) spice; (*Zutat*) condiment; (*Duft*) fragrance, smell; *fig* zest; ~**en** *tr* to season, to spice; *gewürzt* spiced; aromatic; ~**epfanne** *f* (*Bier*~~) wort kettle; ~**ig** *a* well-seasoned, spicy; piquant; fragrant, aromatic; ~**los** *a* unspiced, unseasoned, flat; ~**mittel** *n* condiment; ~**nelke** *f* clove; ~**stoff** *m* aromatic essence; ~**wein** *m* spiced wine.

Wurzel *f* root; *gram* stem, radical; (*Haar*) bulb; (*Zahn*) root; (*Stumpen*) stump; (*Rübe*) carrot; ~ *fassen* (*od schlagen*) to take root; *mit der* ~ *ausreißen* to uproot; *die* ~ *ziehen* to extract the root; ~**behandlung** *f med* root-treatment; ~**chen** *n* radicle; ~**ende** *n* root end; ~**exponent** *m math* radical index; ~**faser** *f* root fibre, rootlet; ~**fäule** *f* root rot; ~**gewächs** *n* root plant (*od* crop), bulbous plant; ~**größe** *f math* radical quantity; ~**haar** *n bot* root hair; ~**haut** *f* dental periosteum, tooth-socket; ~~**entzündung** *f* periodontitis; ~**keim** *m* radicle; ~**knollen** *m* tuber, bulb; ~**los** *a* without roots; ~**n** *itr* to (take) root, to be rooted; ~**reis** *n* shoot, sucker; ~**schößling** *m* sucker, runner, layer; ~**ständig** *a* radical; ~**stock** *m* root-stock; ~**werk** *n* roots *pl*; ~**wort** *n* radical word, stem; ~**zange** *f* stump forceps; ~**zeichen** *n math* radical sign.

Wust *m* (*Durcheinander*) confused mass, chaos; (*Plunder*) rubbish, trash; filth.

wüst *a* waste, desert; deserted, desolate; (*unbebaut*) uncultivated; (*verwahrlost*) overrun with weeds; (*vernachlässigt*) neglected, unkempt; (*verworren*) confused; (*liederlich*) wild, disorderly, depraved, dissolute; (*roh*) coarse, vulgar, brutal, rude; ~ *u. leer* waste and void; ~*er Traum* nightmare; ~**e**, ~**enei** *f* waste, desert, wilderness; ~**en** *itr* to waste, to squander; (*verderben*) to spoil, to ruin; ~**engebiet** *n* desert belt; ~**enkrieg** *m* desert warfare; ~**ensand** *m* desert sand; ~**enschiff** *n* camel; ~**ensturm** *m* desert storm; ~**ling** *m* libertine, debauchee, dissolute person.

Wut *f* rage, fury; madness (*über* at); (*Wahnsinn*) mania; (*Tollwut*) rabies; *er kochte vor* ~ he was boiling with rage; *bring ihn nicht in* ~*! Am* don't get him mad! *wenn ihn die* ~ *packt* ... when he gets in(to) a rage ...; *er schäumte vor* ~ he foamed with rage; *er ließ seine* ~ *an mir aus* he vented his rage on me; *in* ~ *geraten* to fly into a passion; ~**anfall**, ~**ausbruch** *m* fit of rage; *Am fam* conniption; ~**entbrannt**, ~**erfüllt** *a* infuriated, furious, enraged; ~**geschrei** *n*, ~**schrei** *m* yell of rage ~**krankheit** *f* rabies, lyssa; hydrophobia; ~**schäumend**, ~**schnaubend** *a* foaming with rage; infuriated; in a towering passion.

wüt|en *itr* to rage, to be furious, to be in a fury, *Am* to be mad; (*toben, tosen*) to rave; (*brüllen*) to roar; (*lärmen*) to riot; (*aufgebracht sein*) to fume; (*schurigeln*) to ride roughshod over s. o.; (*Spektakel machen*) to kick up a row; ~**end**, ~**ig** *a* furious, enraged; *Am* mad (*auf* at); (*wild*) fierce; (*tobend*) blustering; (*lärmend*) riotous, boisterous; ~*end werden* to turn mad, enraged; *das* ~*ende Heer* the Wild Huntsman and his train; ~**erich** *m* blood-thirsty villain; madman; tyrant; savage fellow.

X

X; ~ *math* (*Unbekannte*) X (= the unknown quantity); *jdm ein* ~ *für ein U vormachen* to throw dust in s. o.'s eyes, to bamboozle s. o., to hoodwink s. o.

X-Achse *f* X axis, axis of the abscissas.

Xanthippe *f fig* (*zänkisches Weib*) shrew, termagant, *Am* scold, *sl* battle-ax(e).

X-Beine *n pl* turned-in legs *pl*, knock-knees *pl*; **x-beinig** *a* bandy-legged, knock-kneed.

x-beliebig *a* any, whoever, whatever (you like); *jeder* ~*e* every Tom, Dick and Harry.

X-Chromosom *n* (*Geschlechtschromosom*) X chromosome.

Xenie *f* epigram.

Xereswein *m* sherry.

X-Haken *m* X-hook.

*

x-mal *adv* many times, hundreds of times; *fam* umpteen times.

X-Strahlen *m pl* Röntgen-rays *pl*, X-rays *pl*.

X-Tag *m* M-Day, mobilization day.

xte (*Numerale*): *fam zum* ~*n Mal* for the umpteenth time.

X-Uhr *f mil* zero hour, *Am* H hour.

*

Xylograph *m* xylographer, wood-cutter; ~**ie** *f* xylography, wood-carving.

Xylophon *n* xylophone.

Y

Y-Achse *f* Y axis, transverse axis.

Yacht *f* (*siehe: Jacht*) yacht.

Yak *m zoo* (*tibet. Grunzochse*) yak, longhaired wild ox of the Tebetan highlands.

Yalta *n* Yalta; ~-**Konferenz** *f* Yalta Conference (*4.-12. Febr. 1945*); ~-**Formel** *f* Yalta Formula.

Yam(s)wurzel *f bot* yam (= *dioscorea batatas*).

Yankee *m* Yank(ee); ~**tum** *n* Yankeedom, Yankeeism.

Yard *n* yard; ~**maß** *n* yardstick.

Y-Chromosom *n* Y chromosome.

Yerbastrauch *m bot* maté, Paraguay tea.

y-förmig *a* y-shaped.

Y-Legierung *f* (*hochschmelzende Alulegierung*) hiduminium.

Yoghurt *n* yogurt, yoghurt.

Yperit *n mil* (*Lost*) mustard gas; yperite.

Ysop *m bot* hyssop.

Yttererde *f* yttria; yttrium oxide.

Z

Z *Abk mit* **Z** *siehe Liste der Abk.*
Zäckchen *n* small prong (*od* tooth *od* dent); (*Spitzen~*) purl.
Zack|e *f*, **~en** *m* (*Gabel*) prong; (*Kamm*) tooth; (*Mauer~~*) spike; (*vorspringender Punkt*) point; (*Gipfel*) peak; (*Eis*) icicle; (*Fels~~*) jag; (*Geweih*) crocket, knag; (*Kleid*) scallop; (*Litze*) edging; *bot* crenature; (*Zweig*) twig, bough; (*Metall*) plate; (*Auszackung*) indentation, serration; **~en** *tr* to indent, to tooth; to notch; (*Kleidersäume*) to scallop; **~enförmig** *a* toothed, pronged; **~enreihe** *f* line of teeth; **~ig** *a* toothed; (*Felsen*) jagged; (*Blätter*) crenate, serrate, dentated; (*gekerbt*) jaggy, jagged; (*spitz*) pointed; *tech* notched, indented, toothed; (*Gabel*) pronged; (*Baum*) branched; (*Kleid*) scalloped; (*Bruch*) hackly; (*zerfetzt*) ragged; (*Mensch*) *fam* alert; smart; glamorous; spirited; *Am* snappy; (*famos*) *fam* ripping.
zag *a* faint-hearted; **~en** *itr* to quail; (*zurückschrecken*) to shrink, to flinch; (*Angst haben*) to be afraid; (*zögern*) to hesitate; *~~ n* (*Zurückweichen*) quailing; (*Zurückschrecken*) shrinking, flinching; (*Furcht*) fear; (*Schüchternheit*) timidity; (*Zögern*) hesitation; **~haft** *a* timid, faint-hearted, timorous; **~~igkeit** *f* faint-heartedness, timidity, fear.
zäh|(e) *a* tough; tenacious; (*widerstandsfähig*) resistant, robust, refractory; (*halsstarrig*) stubborn; (*beharrlich*) persistent, persevering; (*Fleisch*) stringy; tough; (*fest zus.-hängend*) cohesive; (*dehnbar*) ductile; (*klebrig*) clammy, viscous, ropy; *ein ~es Leben haben* to be tenacious of life; **~egrad** *m* (*Flüssigkeit*) viscosity; **~flüssig** *a* viscous, thickly liquid; (*feuerfest*) refractory; **~~keit** *f* viscosity; refractoriness; **~igkeit** *f* toughness; tenacity; (*Ausdauer*) perseverance, *Am* stick-to-it-iveness; (*Lebenskraft*) vitality; (*Hartnäckigkeit*) pertinacity; (*Flüssigkeit*) viscosity, viscidity; (*Dehnbarkeit*) ductility; **~~ziffer** *f* toughness index; **~lebig** *a* tenacious of life.
Zahl *f* number; (*Ziffer*) figure; (*Zahlzeichen*) cipher; numeral; (*einstellige ~*) digit; (*Nummer*) number; *math* factor; coefficient; (*Betrag*) figure, amount; *ganze, gerade, ungerade gebrochene ~* integer, even, odd, fractional number; *eingeklammerte ~* number in brackets; *dreistellige ~* three-figure number; *der ~ nach* numerical; in number; *e-e ~ abrunden* to express in round numbers; *an ~ übertreffen* to outnumber; *~en zusammenzählen* to add up numbers; **~bar** *a* payable; (*fällig*) due; (*Wechsel*) domiciled; *am 1. d. M. ~~* payable on the first of the month; *~~ bei Lieferung* cash on delivery; *~~ bei Verfall* payable at maturity; *~~ an Überbringer* payable to bearer; *~~ sein* to fall (*od* become) due; **~blatt** *n* payroll; **~brett** *n* money-tray; **~en** *tr, itr* to pay; (*Schuld*) to pay off, to liquidate; (*Rechnung*) to settle (accounts with), to make accounts square; (*Anteil ~~*) *Am* to ante up; *bar ~~* to pay (in) cash, to pay ready money, *sl* to pay down on the nail; *nach Empfang ~~* to pay cash on delivery (*Abk* C.O.D.); *auf Abschlag ~~* to pay by instalments; *bei Sicht ~~* to pay at sight; *~~ müssen* to be charged; *im voraus ~~* to pay in advance; *zurück ~~* to repay, to refund, to reimburse; *Ober, bitte ~~!* waiter, the bill (*Am* check), please! *Kinder ~~ die Hälfte* children half-price; **~~angaben** *f pl* figures *pl*; numerical data *pl*; **~~beispiel** *n* numerical example; **~~d** *a* paying; *~~de Last* paying load; **~~folge** *f* numerical order; **~~gedächtnis** *n* memory for numbers; **~~größe** *f* numerical quantity; **~~gruppe** *f* group of numbers; **~~index** *m* numerical index; **~~mäßig** *a* numerical; quantitative; *~~mäßig ausdrücken* to evaluate; *~~mäßige Aufstellung* tabulation; **~~material** *n* numerical data *pl*; **~~reihe** *f* numerical series; **~~schloß** *n* combination lock; **~~tafel** *f* table of figures, numerical table; *in e-r ~~tafel zusammengestellte Werte* tabular data; **~~verhältnis** *n* numerical relation (*od* ratio); **~~wert** *m* numerical value; **~er** *m* payer; *pünktlicher ~~* prompt payer; *säumiger ~~* dilatory payer, defaulter; **~karte** *f* money-order form; **~kasse** *f* cash register; **~kellner** *m* head-waiter; **~los** *a* countless, numberless, innumerable; **~meister** *m* paymaster, *mar* purser; **~~ei** *f* paymaster's office; **~reich** *a* numerous; a great many; **~stelle** *f* pay-office, cashier's office; **~tag** *m* pay-day; **~~tüte** *f* pay envelope; **~tisch** *m* counter; **~ung** *f* payment; (*Schuld*) clearance, liquidation, settlement; *an ~~s Statt* in lieu of cash; *ausstehende, einmalige, vierteljährliche ~~* outstanding, single, quarterly payment; *rückständige ~~* arrears *pl*; *überfällige ~~* overdue payment; *zur ~~ auffordern* to press for payment, to dun; *in ~~ nehmen* to take in part payment; *in ~~ geben* to offer as payment; *zur ~~ vorlegen* to present for payment; *~~ gegen Lieferung* cash on delivery; *~~ für Rechnung* payment to account; *~~ bescheinigen* to receipt a payment; *~~ einstellen* to stop payment; *~~ hinausschieben* to postpone payment; *~~ leisten* to make payments; *~~ stunden* to grant a respite in payment; *~~ verweigern* to refuse payment; **~~sabkommen** *n* payments agreement; **~~sangebot** *n* offer to pay; (*Kauf*) bid; (*Kostenanschlag*) tender, *Am* bid; **~~sanspruch** *m* demand for payment; **~~sanweisung** *f* order to pay; draft; (*Bank*) cheque, order; (*Post*) post-office order (*Abk* P.O.O.); **~~sanzeige** *f* advice of payment; **~~sart** *f* mode of payment; **~~saufschub** *m* delay of payment, respite; **~~sausgleich** *m* balance of payments in clearing; **~~sbedingungen** *f pl* terms of payment; **~~sbefehl** *m* order to pay, *jur* writ of execution; **~~sbestätigung** *f* acquittance, receipt, acknowledg(e)ment of payment; **~~sbilanz** *f* balance of payments; *aktive, passive ~~sbilanz* favo(u)rable, unfavo(u)rable balance of payments; **~~seingänge** *m pl* payments received; **~~seinstellung** *f* suspension of payment; **~~sempfänger** *m* payee; **~~serleichterungen** *f pl* facilities of payment; **~~sfähig** *a* solvent, able to pay; **~~sfähigkeit** *f* solvency; **~~sfrist** *f* term of payment; (*Aufschub*) respite; **~~smittel** *n* (legal) tender, *Am* lawful money; currency; **~~smittelumlauf** *m* currency in circulation; **~~sort** *m* place of payment; (*Wechsel*) domicile; **~~spflicht** *f* obligation to pay; **~~spflichtige(r)** *m* debtor; **~~splan** *m* (*Raten*) instal(l)ment plan; settlement (*od* payment) plan; (*Tilgung*) terms of redemption; **~~sschwierigkeit** *f* financial difficulty; **~~ssperre** *f* stoppage of payments; blockage; **~~sstundung** *f* delay of payment, respite; **~~stermin** *m* date of payment; (*Wechsel*) day of maturity; (*vierteljährlich*) quarter day; **~~süberweisung** *f* remittance; bank transfer; **~~sunfähig** *a* insolvent; **~~sunfähigkeit** *f* insolvency; **~~sverbindlichkeit** *f* liability to pay; **~~sverbot** *n* prohibition of payment; (*an Drittschuldner*) garnishee order, *Am* trustee-process; **~~svereinbarungen** *f pl* financial payments *pl*; **~~sverkehr** *m* clearing system; **~~sverpflichtung** *f* liability, financial obligation; **~~sversprechen** *n* promise of pay; (*schriftlich*) promissory note; **~~sverweigerung** *f* non-payment, refusal to pay; **~~svollmacht** *f* authority to pay; **~~sweise** *f* mode of payment; **~~szertifikat** *n* scrip money; **~wert** *m* numerical value; **~wort** *n* numeral; **~zeichen** *n* numeral, figure.
Zähl|ader *f* pilot wire; **~apparat** *m* counter, numerator; **~bar** *a* countable, computable, calculable; **~einrichtung** *f* counting device; **~en** *tr, itr* to count, to number; (*rechnen*) to reckon; to class among; (*berechnen*) to calculate; (*abmessen*) to meter, to record; (*Tennis*) to score; (*Volkszählung*) to take the census (of); (*Stimmzettel*) to tell; (*gehören zu*) to belong (to); (*sich belaufen auf*) to amount to, to number; *~~ auf* to count on, to rely on; *sie sind zu ~~* they can be counted on the fingers; *er sieht aus, als könne er nicht auf 3 ~~* he looks as if he could not say boo to a goose; *sie zählte 6 Jahre* she was six years of age; *seine Tage sind gezählt* his days are numbered; **~er** *m* counter; *math* numerator; (*Registrierapparat*) recorder; register; (*Gas, el*) meter; *sport* marker; (*Stimmenzähler*) *parl* teller; **~~ableser** *m* meter reader; **~~ablesung** *f* meter reading; **~~gehäuse** *n* meter case; **~~standsaufnahme** *f* end of billing period; **~~tafel** *f* meter board; **~gerät** *n* integrating apparatus; **~karte** *f sport* scoring card; (*Volks~~*) census-paper; **~rad** *n* notch wheel; **~rohr** *n phys* Geiger counter; **~scheibe** *f* recording disk; **~tafel** *f* differential counting chart; **~taste** *f* meter (*od* register) key; **~ung** *f* counting; calculation; computation; numeration; *tech* metering, registering; (*Auf~~*) enumeration; (*Volks~~*) census; (*zeitlich*) timing; **~vorrichtung** *f* counting device; **~werk** *n* counter, register, meter.
zahm *a* tame; (*häuslich*) domestic; (*gefügig*) tractable; (*sanft*) gentle; (*friedlich*) peaceful; (*gutmütig*) good-natured; **~heit** *f* tameness.
zähm|bar *a* tamable; **~en** *tr* to tame, to domesticate; (*Pferd*) to break in; (*abrichten*) to train; *fig* to subdue, to check, to restrain; (*mäßigen*) to moderate; (*Leidenschaft*) to control; **~ung** *f* taming; domestication.

Zahn *m* tooth, *pl* teeth; (*Gift~, Hauer*) fang; (*Stoß~*) tusk; *tech* (*Rad*) cog; (*Eck~*) eye-tooth; (*Backen~*) molar; (*Schneide~*) incisor; *e-n süßen ~ haben fig* to be fond of delicacies; *falscher ~* artificial (*Am* store) tooth; *mit Zähnen versehen* toothed; studded; *jdm auf den ~ fühlen* to sound s. o.; *Haare auf den Zähnen haben* to be a Tartar; *sie hat Haare auf den Zähnen* (*Am fam*) she's a tough baby; *Zähne bekommen* to cut o.'s teeth; *Zähne ziehen* to extract (*od* pull out) teeth; *e-n ~ plombieren* to stop (*od* fill) a tooth; *sich die Zähne dabei ausbrechen* to come to grief over it; *beiß die Zähne zusammen u. laß dir nichts anmerken* grin and bear it; *mit den Zähnen knirschen* to grind o.'s teeth; *bis an die Zähne bewaffnet* armed to the teeth; *die Zähne putzen* to brush (*od* clean) o.'s teeth; *der ~ der Zeit* the ravages of time; **~arzt** *m* dentist, dental surgeon; **~ärztlich** *a* dental; **~ausziehen** *n* extraction of teeth; **~bein** *n* dentine; **~behandlung** *f* dental treatment; **~belag** *m* film (*od* crusts) on o.'s teeth, sordes; **~bogen** *m* dental arch; *tech* tooth sector; **~breite** *f tech* tooth pitch; **~bürste** *f* tooth brush; **~chirurgie** *f* dental surgery; **~creme, ~pasta** *f* tooth-paste, dentifrice; **~defekt** *m* dental defect; **~durchbruch** *m* cutting of a tooth; **~en** *itr* to cut teeth, to teethe; *tr* to dent, to tooth; *gezahnt a* toothed, dentate(d), indented; **~~** *n* dentition, cutting of a tooth; **~ersatz** *m* artificial teeth; denture; **~fach** *n* tooth socket, alveolus; **~fäule** *f* caries; **~fistel** *f* dental fistula; **~fleisch** *n* gum, gingiva; **~~blutung** *f* hemorrhage from gums; **~~entzündung** *f* gingivitis; **~form** *f tech* tooth profile; **~förmig** *a* tooth-shaped, dentiform; **~füllung** *f* stopping, filling; **~geschwür** *n* gumboil, parulis; **~gewebe** *n* dental tissue; **~hals** *m* neck of tooth; **~heilkunde** *f* dental surgery; **~höhle** *f* socket of a tooth; pulp-cavity; **~ig** *a* toothed; **~keim** *m* dental pulp; **~kettenrad** *n* sprocket wheel; **~kitt** *m* dental cement; **~klinik** *f* dental hospital; **~krankheit** *f* disease of the teeth; **~kranz** *m tech* gear rim; **~krone** *f* crown, jacket; **~kuppelung** *f tech* jaw clutch coupling; **~laut** *m* dental (sound); **~los** *a* toothless; **~lücke** *f* gap between teeth; *tech* space of tooth; gullet; **~meißel** *m* dental chisel; **~mittel** *n* remedy for toothache; **~naht** *f* dentate suture; **~nerv** *m* dental nerve; **~pasta** *f* tooth-paste, dentifrice; **~pflege** *f* dental care; care for o.'s teeth; **~plombe** *f* filling, stopping; **~pulpa** *f* tooth-pulp; **~pulver** *n* tooth powder; **~rad** *n* cog wheel, gear; pinion; **~~antrieb** *m* gear drive; **~~bahn** *f* rack (*od* cog) railway; **~~getriebe** *n* gear drive, toothed-wheel gearing; **~~kasten** *m* gear box; **~~pumpe** *f* geared pump; **~~scheibe** *f* sprocket-wheel washer; **~~übersetzung** *f* transmission gear; **~~welle** *f* pinion spindle; **~~winde** *f* windlass; **~reihe** *f* row of teeth; **~reinigungsmittel** *n* dentifrice; **~ritzel** *n* pinion; **~scheibe** *f* ratched wheel, face gear; **~schlüssel** *m* alligator grip wrench; *med* tooth-key; **~schmelz** *m* dental enamel; **~schmerz** *m* toothache; **~schnitt** *m arch* denticulation; **~spiegel** *m* dental mirror; **~spitze** *f* tip of a tooth; **~stange** *f tech* rack; **~~ngetriebe** *n* rack-and-pinion gear; **~station** *f* dental centre; **~stein** *m* tartar (on teeth), odontolith; **~stocher** *m* tooth-pick; **~techniker** *m* mechanical dentist; **~teilung** *f tech* tooth pitch; **~trieb** *m tech* rack-and-pinion drive; **~trommel** *f tech* sprocket; **~ung** *f* dentation, serration; *tech* toothing; **~verlust** *m* loss of teeth; **~wasser** *n* tooth-wash, dental lotion; **~wechsel** *m* teething, dentition, cutting of teeth; **~weh** *n* toothache; **~wurzel** *f* root of a tooth; **~~haut** *f* dental periosteum; **~zange** *f* dental forceps *pl*; **~zement** *m* dental cement; **~zerfall** *m* tooth decay; **~ziehen** *n* tooth-extraction.

Zähne|fletschen *n* showing o.'s teeth; **~klappern** *n* chattering of teeth.

Zähre *f poet* tear.

Zain *m* bar, ingot.

Zander *m* perch-pike, pike-perch.

Zange *f* (*Pinzette*) tweezers *pl*; (*Beiß~*) pliers *pl*; (*Kneif~*) nippers *pl*, pincers *pl*; (*Klampe*) stirrup, clamp; (*Draht~*) clippers *pl*; (*Feuer~*) tongs *pl*; (*medizinische ~*) forceps *sing u. pl*; *e-e ~* a pair of pincers; **~narm** *m* tongarm; **~nbewegung** *f mil* pincer movement; **~ngeburt** *f* forceps delivery; **~ngriff** *m* handle of tongs; **~nmaul** *n* mouth of tongs.

Zank *m* quarrel, brawl, row; **~apfel** *m* bone of contention; apple of discord; **~en** *itr* to quarrel, to wrangle; *r* to quarrel, to dispute; to bicker: *sich ~~ mit* to have words with; *tr* to scold; **~sucht** *f* quarrelsomeness; **~süchtig, zänkisch** *a* quarrelsome, contentious; **~teufel** *m* quarrelsome person; shrew.

Zänker *m* quarrel(l)er, wrangler; **~ei** *f* quarrel, altercation; **~in** *f* quarrelsome person; shrew, termagant.

Zäpfchen *n* little peg; *med* uvula; (*Auge*) cones *pl*; (*Einführ~*) suppository; **~~r** *n* uvular (*od* guttural) r.

Zapf|en *m* (*Pflock*) pin, peg; (*Dübel*) plug; (*Bolzen*) gudgeon; (*Stift*) stud; (*Drehpunkt, Tür~~*) pivot; (*Drehlager*) trunnion; (*Balken*) tenon; (*Well~~*) journal; (*Faß~~*) tap, spigot, bung, *Am* faucet; (*Tannen~~*) cone, apple; (*Eis~~*) icicle; **~en** *tr* to tap; **~~bohrer** *m* tap borer, teat drill; **~~förmig** *a* peg-shaped, cone-shaped; *bot* strobiliform; **~~lager** *n* trunnion bed; pivot bearing; socket, bush, collar; **~~loch** *n* peg hole, pivot hole; (*Balken*) mortise; (*Faß*) bung (*od* tap) hole; **~~streich** *m* tattoo, retreat, taps *pl*, *Am* retreat to quarters; **~~tragend** *a bot* coniferous; **~er** *m* feeder, delivery mechanism; **~grube** *f* fuel(l)ing pit; **~hahn** *m* discharge nozzle, tap; **~loch** *n* tap-hole, bung-hole; **~rohr** *n* discharge pipe; **~schlauch** *m* delivery (*od* filling) hose; **~stelle** *f* tap connection; *el* wiring point; (*Ausschank*) dispenser; (*Tankstelle*) petrol station, refuel(l)ing point; *Am* gasoline (*od* filling) station; **~ung** *f* tapping, drawing.

zappel|ig *a* fidgety, sprawling; (*unruhig*) restless; **~n** *itr* to struggle; (*vor Unruhe*) to fidget; (*auffahren*) to jerk; (*im Wasser*) to flounder; (*sich rekeln*) to sprawl; (*hin- u. her werfen*) to toss about; *~~ lassen* to keep in suspense; to tantalize; **~philipp** *m fam* fidget.

Zar *m* czar; **~in** *f* czarina.

Zarge *f* border, rim; (*Rahmen*) frame; sash.

zart *a* tender; (*Haut, Farbe, Ton*) soft; (*Gesundheit*) delicate; (*zerbrechlich*) fragile, frail; (*empfindlich*) sensitive; (*dünn*) slender, slim; fine; (*Farbe*) pale, subdued; (*jung*) young, fresh; (*zärtlich*) fond, loving; **~besaitet** *a* sensitive, tender-hearted; **~fühlend** *a* of delicate feeling; sensitive; tactful; **~gefühl** *n* delicacy of feeling; **~heit** *f* tenderness; softness; delicacy; (*Schwachheit*) frailty, delicateness; (*Empfindlichkeit*) sensitiveness.

zärt|lich *a* tender, fond, loving, affectionate; **~~keit** *f* softness, tenderness; fondness; caress.

Zaser *f* filament, fibre.

Zaster *m fam* (*Geld*) brass, tin; *Am* dough.

Zäsur *f* caesura.

Zauber *m* (*Verzauberung*) enchantment; (*Anziehungskraft*) charm, attractiveness, allure, glamo(u)r, spell, fascination; *fauler ~* humbug, bosh, *Am* punk; *der ganze ~* (*fam*) the whole concern; *durch e-n ~ gebannt* spell-bound; *den ~ lösen* to break the spell; **~ei** *f* magic, witchcraft, sorcery; *Am* (*Neger*) voodoo; (*Geisterbannung*) necromancy; (*Taschenspielerei*) legerdemain; **~er** *m* magician, sorcerer, enchanter, wizard, *Am Abk* wiz; (*Taschenspieler*) conjurer, juggler; **~flöte** *f* magic flute; **~formel** *f* magic formula, incantation, spell; **~haft, ~isch** *a* magic(al); bewitching, glamo(u)rous, enchanting; (*feenhaft*) fairy-like; (*wunderbar*) marvel(l)ous, miraculous; **~kraft** *f* magic power; **~kräftig** *a* magic(al); **~kreis** *m* magic circle; **~kunst** *f* magic art; **~~stück** *n* conjuring trick; **~künstler** *m* conjurer, juggler; **~land** *n* enchanted land, Fairyland; **~laterne** *f* magic lantern; **~lehrling** *m* magician's apprentice; **~n** *itr* to practise magic; *tr* to conjure, to produce by magic; **~schloß** *n* enchanted castle; **~spruch** *m* spell, incantation; **~stab** *m* magic wand; **~trank** *m* philtre, magic potion; **~werk** *n* witchcraft; **~wort** *n* magic word.

Zauder|ei *f* delay, tarrying; **~er** *m* loiterer, lingerer, tarrier; **~n** *itr* to linger, to delay; (*zögern*) to hesitate; (*schwanken*) to waver; (*sich sträuben*) to hang back; (*Zeit zu gewinnen suchen*) to temporize; **~en** *n* lingering; hesitation; delay; temporizing.

Zaum *m* bridle, rein; *im ~e halten fig* to bridle, to check, to restrain, to keep a tight rein on; **~zeug** *n* head-gear, bridle.

zäumen *tr* to bridle; *fig* to restrain.

Zaun *m* hedge, fence; (*lebender ~*) quickset (hedge); *e-n Streit vom ~e brechen* to pick a quarrel (with); **~draht** *m* fence wire; **~gast** *m* non-paying spectator, deadhead, *Am* fence-rider; **~gitter** *n* wire fencing, fence netting; **~könig** *m* wren; **~latte** *f* pale, stake; **~pfahl** *m* fence-post; *mit dem ~~ winken* to give a broad hint; **~rebe** *f bot* Virginia creeper; **~rübe** *f* bryony.

zäunen *tr* to fence in.

zausen *tr* to pull about, to tug; (*Haar*) to tousle.

Zebra *n* zebra.

Zech|bruder *m* tippler, toper; boon-companion; **~e** *f* (*Wirtshausrechnung*) bill, reckoning, score; (*Bergwerk*) mine, colliery, coal pit; (*Bergwerksgesellschaft*) mining company; *die ~e bezahlen* to stand treat, to pay for all; **~en** *itr* to drink, to carouse, to tipple; **~enhaus** *n* mine house; **~enkohle** *f* mine coal; **~enkoks** *m* furnace coke, by-product coke; **~enteer** *m* coke tar; **~er** *m* tippler, toper; revel(l)er; **~frei** *a* scot-free; **~gelage** *n* carouse, drinking-bout, spree; **~kumpan** *m* boon-companion; **~preller** *m* guest who evades paying bill, bilk(er); **~~ei** *f* evading payment of bill, bilking; **~schuld** *f* debt for drink.

Zecke *f zoo* tick.

Zeder *f bot* cedar; **~nholz** *n* cedar wood.

zedieren *tr* to cede, to transfer; to assign (to).
Zehe *f* toe; *große* ~ big toe; *vom Scheitel bis zur* ~ from top to toe; *jdm auf die* ~*n treten* to step on s.o.'s toes; **~nballen** *m* ball of the toes; **~ngänger** *m pl* digitigrades *pl*; **~ngelenk** *n* toe-joint; **~nglied** *n* phalanx of a toe; **~nnagel** *m* toe-nail; **~nspitze** *f* point of the toe; *auf den* ~~*n gehen* to walk on tiptoe.
zehn *a* ten; ~ *Jahre* decade; *Stücker* ~ (*fam*) ten or so; *zwischen* ~ *u. 20* in o.'s teens; *etwa* ~ about ten; decade; **~eck** *n*, **~eckig** *a* decagonal; **~ender** *m* stag with ten points; **~er** *m math* ten; number of ten; **~~lei** *a* of ten different sorts; **~~potenz** *f* tenth power; **~~ringscheibe** *f* decimal target; **~~satz** *m* tens digit; **~~stelle** *f* decimal place; **~~system** *n* decimal system; **~fach** *a* tenfold; **~fingersystem** *n* touch system; **~flächner** *m* decahedron; **~jährig** *a* ten-year-old; **~kampf** *m sport* decathlon; **~mal** *adv* ten times; **~~ig** *a* ten times repeated; **~pfennigroman** *m* shilling-shocker, yellow-back, *Am* dime novel; **~pfünder** *m* ten-pounder; **~silbig** *a* decasyllabic; **~tägig** *a* of ten days, lasting ten days; **~tausend** *a* ten thousand; *die oberen* ~~ the upper ten, *Am* the four hundred; *e-r von den oberen* ~~ *Am* a socialite; **~te** *a* tenth; *am* ~~*n Mai* on the tenth of May; **~~** *m* (*Abgabe*) tithe; **~tel** *n* tenth (part); **~~grad** *m* tenth of a degree; **~tens** *adv* tenthly; in the tenth place.
zehr|en *itr* (*leben*) to live (*von* on), to feed (on); (*Appetit geben*) to give an appetite; (*verzehren*) to consume; (*abmagern*) to emaciate; (*abnehmen*) to waste; (*nagen*) *fig* to gnaw (*an* at), to prey (upon); *von der Erinnerung* ~~ to enjoy o.'s memories; *von seinen Vorräten* ~~ to draw on o.'s supplies; *seine Lebensweise* ~*t an seiner Gesundheit* his life undermines his health; **~end** *a med* consumptive; **~geld** *n*, **~pfennig** *m* travel(l)ing allowance; **~ung** *f* expenses *pl*; consumption; (*Verlust*) loss, waste; (*Vorräte*) provisions *pl*; *eccl* viaticum.
Zeichen *n* sign, signal; (*Merkmal*) token, distinguishing mark; (*Waren*~) brand, stamp; (*Beweis*) proof; evidence; *med* indication, symptom; (*Vor*~) omen; (*Ab*~) badge; (*Buch*~) mark; (*Wunder*~) miraculous sign, miracle; *mar* sea-mark; *astr* sign; *gram* punctuation; *mil* symbol; *radio* interval, call sign; *ein* ~ *der Freundschaft* a token of friendship; *ein* ~ *geben* to give a sign, to signal, to motion; *zum* ~ *daß* as a proof that; *seines* ~*s Tischler* a joiner by trade; **~apparat** *m* drawing apparatus; **~block** *m* sketch block; **~brett** *n* drawing board; **~buch** *n* sketch-book; **~büro** *n* drawing-office; *Am* drafting room; **~deutung** *f* interpretation of signs; astrology; **~ebene** *f* drawing plane; **~erklärung** *f* list of conventional signs; letters of reference; explanation of symbols; legend; **~farbe** *f* drawing colo(u)r; **~feder** *f* drawing-pen; **~film** *m* animated cartoon(s *pl*); **~gabe** *f* transmission of signals; **~garn** *n* marking-thread; **~geber** *m* signal transmitter; **~gerät** *n* drawing instrument; **~kohle** *f* drawing charcoal; carbon pencil; **~kreide** *f* drawing chalk; **~kunst** *f* art of drawing; **~lehrer** *m* drawing-master; **~lineal** *n* drawing rule; **~mappe** *f* portfolio; **~material** *n* drawing materials *pl*; **~netz** *n* drawing grid, canvas reticulation; **~papier** *n* drawing paper; **~saal** *m* drawing room; art-room; **~schule** *f* school of design; **~setzung** *f* punctuation; **~sprache** *f* language of signs; **~stift** *m* drawing pencil; stylus; crayon; **~stunde** *f* drawing-lesson; **~tinte** *f* drawing ink; marking ink; **~tisch** *m* drawing table, drawing board; (*großer* ~~) loft floor; **~trickfilm** *m* animated cartoon (film); **~unterricht** *m* drawing lessons *pl*; **~verbindung** *f* visual (*od* signal) communication; **~vorlage** *f* drawing pattern (*od* copy); **~wechsel** sign change.
zeichn|en *tr, itr* to draw; (*Muster*) to design; (*flüchtig*) to sketch; (*Wäsche*) to mark, to initial; (*auf*~~, *entwerfen*) to plot; to delineate; (*in groben Umrissen*) to outline; (*Karte* ~~) to map; (*brandmarken*) to brand; (*mit e-m Zettel aus* ~~) to label; (*Beitrag*) to subscribe (*für* to); (*Anleihe*) to subscribe (for); (*Staatspapiere*) to fund; (*Aktien*) to take up shares, to subscribe for shares; (*unter*~~) to sign; *nach dem Leben* ~~ to draw from life; *maßstäblich* ~~ to draw to scale; *perspektivisch* ~~ to foreshorten; *e-e Kurve* ~~ to plot a curve, to map a graph; *in unserem Namen zu* ~~ to sign on our behalf; *ich* ~*e hochachtungsvoll* I remain yours truly; **~en** *n* drawing, design; sketch; subscription; **~er** *m* draughtsman, *Am* draftsman, drawer, designer; (*technischer* ~~) tracer; *film* (*Trickfilm*~~) animator; (*Unter*~~) signer; (*Anleihe*) subscriber; **~~isch** *a* graphic, diagrammatic; *~~ische Begabung* talent for drawing; **~ung** *f* drawing; design; (*Skizze*) sketch; (*Plan*) plan; (*Muster*) pattern, design; (*Bild*) picture; illustration; (*erläuternde Figur*) diagram; (*Entwurf*) delineation; draught; (*Anlage*) layout, arrangement; (*Paus*~~) tracing, blueprint; (*Tusch*~~) washed drawing; (*Unterschrift*) signature; (*Anleihe*) subscription; *schematische* ~~ skeleton sketch; *schraffierte* ~~ hatched drawing; *zur* ~~ *auflegen* to invite subscriptions for a loan; **~~sangebot** *n com* tender; **~~sberechtigt** *a* authorized to sign; **~~sberechtigung, ~~sbefugnis** *f* authorization to sign; **~~sbetrag** *m* amount of subscription; **~~sformular** *n* subscription form; **~~sfrist** *f* subscription time; **~~skurs** *m* subscription rate; **~~sliste** *f* subscription list; **~~sstelle** *f* subscription office; **~~svollmacht** *f* authorization to sign.
Zeig|efinger *m* forefinger, index; **~en** *tr* to show, to point (at), to indicate; (*dartun*) to demonstrate; (*beweisen*) to prove; (*zur Schau stellen*) to display, to exhibit; (*vor*~~) to present; to produce; (*offenbaren*) to manifest; (*verwirklichen*) to materialize; (*erläutern*) to set forth; (*sichtbar machen*) to bring to view, to visibilize; to expose to view, to make visible; (*darlegen*) to lay open; (*enthüllen*) to unveil, to uncover, to unscreen, to unfold, to uncloak; *r* to appear, to put in appearance, to show up; to show itself; (*sich erweisen*) to turn out, to prove; (*plötzlich*) to turn up; (*prahlerisch*) to show off; (*bemerkbar*) to be noticeable; (*offensichtlich werden*) to become evident; (*herauskommen*) to be found out; *sich erkenntlich* ~~ to show o.'s appreciation; *ich werde es ihm schon* ~~! I'll show him! *das wird sich* ~~ we'll soon see; that remains to be seen; *jetzt muß er* ~~, *was er kann* that'll make him or break him; *nun zeigt sich's, daß* ... now it turns out that; **~er** *m* pointer; indicator; index; (*Uhr*) hand; (*Nadel*) needle; *math* index; vector; (*Inhaber*) bearer; *der* ~~ *schlägt aus* the pointer moves; **~~ablesung** *f* pointer reading; **~~ausschlag** *m* deflection of pointer; **~~barometer** *n* wheel barometer; **~~galvanometer** *n* needle galvanometer; **~~hebel** *m* pointing lever; **~~platte** *f* dial; **~~stellung** *f* hand setting; **~~telegraph** *m* pointer telegraph; **~estock** *m* pointer.
Zeile *f* (*Druck*~, *Schreib*~) line; *tele* scanning line; (*Reihe, Häuser*~) row; **~nweise** *adv* by the line; in lines; by rows; **... zeilig** *a*: *zwei*~ two-lined.
Zeisig *m orn* siskin; greenfinch.
Zeit *f* time; (*Epoche*) epoch; (~*raum*) period; space of time; (~*alter*) age; era; (*Jahres*~) season; (*Stadium*) stage; (*Datum*) date; (*Augenblick*) moment; minute; (*Stunde*) hour; (~*spanne*) span; (*Frist*) term; (*Arbeits*~, *kurze* ~, *längere Periode*) spell; (~*dauer*) duration; (~*en*) times *pl*, days *pl*; *gram* tense; (*Gezeit*) tide; (*Zwischen*~) interval, interim, meantime; (*freie* ~) leisure; spare time, off-time; *flaue* ~ slack time; *schlechte* ~*en* hard times; *verkehrsstarke* ~ rush hours; *bes. tele* busy (*od* heavy) hours; *verkehrsschwache* ~ light (*od* slack) hours; *du liebe* ~! Good heavens! *höchste* ~! high time! ~ *seines Lebens* so long as he lives, during life; *e-e* ~*lang* for a time; *auf* ~ (*com*) on credit, on account; *auf kurze* ~ for a short time; *außer der* ~ out of season; *für alle* ~*en* for all time; *in der letzten* ~ lately; *in jüngster* ~ quite recently; *in kurzer* ~ in a short time, shortly; *mit der* ~ gradually; in the course of time, in time; *nach einiger* ~ some time afterwards; *seit dieser* ~ since that time; *seit langer* ~ for a long time; *um welche* ~? at what time? *von* ~ *zu* ~ from time to time; now and then; once in a while; *vor der* ~ prematurely; *vor einiger* ~ some time ago; *vor langer* ~ long ago; a long time ago; *Am fam* way back; *vor* ~*en* once upon a time, formerly, in olden times; *zu der* ~ at that time; *zu* ~*en* now and then; *zu gleicher* ~ at the same time; *zu meiner* ~ in my time; *zur* ~ at present, now; in the time of; in time; *zur rechten* ~ in the nick of time; in due course of time; *Am* on time; *die* ~ *abstoppen* to time, to stop the time; *das braucht* ~ that will take time; *e-e* ~ *festsetzen* to fix a date; *mit der* ~ *gehen* to keep pace with the times; *jdm* ~ *geben* to give s. o. time; *das hat* ~ there is plenty of time for that; *es hat* ~ *bis morgen* it can wait till to-morrow; *keine* ~ *haben für* to have no time for; *haben Sie e-n Augenblick* ~ *für mich?* can you spare me a moment? *es ist die höchste* ~ it is high time; *die* ~ *ist um* time is up; ~ *ist Geld* time is money; *kommt* ~, *kommt Rat* time brings wisdom; *lassen Sie sich* ~! take your time! *die* ~ *nützen* to take time by the forelock; ~ *sparen* to save time; *die* ~ *totschlagen* to kill time; *die* ~ *verbringen* to pass o.'s time; *die* ~ *vergleichen* to check the time of day; ~ *verschwenden* to waste time, *Am sl* to boondoggle; *die* ~ *vertreiben* to while away the time; *das wird sich mit der* ~ *zeigen* that will show; *ich wußte es die ganze* ~ I have known it all the time (*od* all along); **~abnahme** *f* timing; **~abschnitt** *m* epoch, period; interval of time; **~abstand** *m* time interval,

range, period; **~alter** *n* age; era; generation; **~angabe** *f* time; date; statement of time; exact date and hour; **~ansage** *f radio* time-signal; **~aufnahme** *f phot* time exposure; **~aufwand** *m* loss of time; time spent (on); **~auslöser** *m phot* self-timing release; **~ball** *m* time ball; **~berechnung, ~bestimmung** *f* determination of time; **~bombe** *f* time-bomb; **~dauer** *f* duration, period of time, term; **~dehneraufnahme** *f phot* slow-motion picture; **~differenz** *f* time lag; **~dokument** *n* document of time; **~einheit** *f* unit-(of) time; **~einteilung** *f* time-table, *Am* time-schedule; timing; **~enfolge** *f gram* sequence of tenses; **~ereignis** *n* event; **~ersparnis** *f* time-saver; (cutting and) economy of time; **~faktor** *m* time factor; **~fern** *a* antiquated, obsolete; **~film** *m* newsreel; **~folge** *f* chronological order; time interval, time sequence; **~form** *f* tense; **~frage** *f* modern problem; **~funk** *m* timely topic, outside broadcast; **~gebunden** *a* seasonable; **~geist** *m* spirit of the age; **~gemäß** *a* timely; opportune; seasonable; up-to-date, modern, streamlined; (*zur ~ wichtig*) actual; **~genosse** *m* contemporary; **~genössisch** *a* contemporary; **~gerecht** *a* timely, *adv* in time; **~geschäft** *n com* time-bargain; forward exchange bargain; **~geschichte** *f* contemporary history; **~geschmack** *m* prevailing taste; **~gewinn** *m* economy of time; **~gleichung** *f* equation of time; **~ig** *a* (*früh*) early; (*recht~~*) timely; (*reif*) mature, ripe; (*der Zeit gemäß*) opportune; *adv* early, in (*Am* on) time; **~igen** *tr, itr* (*hervorbringen*) to produce, to effect; (*reifen*) to ripen, to mature; **~karte** *f* season-ticket, *Am* commutation ticket; **~~ninhaber** *m* (*Pendler*) season-ticket holder; *Am* commuter; **~lage** *f* state of affairs, juncture; **~lang**: *e-e ~~* for some time; **~lauf** *m* course of time, period; **~läufte** *pl* conjunctures *pl*, times *pl*; **~lebens** *adv* during life, for life; **~lich** *a* temporary; temporal; in time; *~~ aufeinanderfolgend* chronological; *~~ veränderlich* variable with time; *~~e Reihenfolge* chronological sequence; *~~e(r) Verlauf* time slope; *~~ zusammenfallen* to coincide; *das ~~e segnen* to die; **~~keit** *f* temporal state, temporality; **~los** *a* timeless; **~losigkeit** *f* timelessness; **~lupe** *f* time-lens; slow-motion camera; **~~naufnahme** *f* slow-motion picture; **~~ntempo** *n* slow motion; **~mangel** *m* want (*od* lack) of time; **~maß** *n* measure of time; *mus* time; (*Vers*) quantity; (*Rhythmus*) rhythm; **~~stab** *m* scale of time; **~messer** *m* chronometer, time-keeper; metronome; **~messung** *f* measurement of time; timing; (*Vers*) prosody; **~nah(e)** *a* current; **~nehmer** *m* time-keeper, timer; **~ordnung** *f* chronological order; **~problem** *n* modern problem; **~punkt** *m* (point of) time, moment, instant; *günstiger ~~* occasion; **~raffer** *m phot* quick-motion apparatus, time accelerator; time-lapse camera; **~~aufnahme** *f* quick-motion picture; **~raubend** *a* time-consuming; (*ermüdend*) wearisome, tedious; (*in die Länge gezogen*) protracted; **~raum** *m* space of time; period, age, interval; **~rechnung** *f* chronology; era; *christliche ~~* Christian era; **~regler** *m* time regulator; **~schrift** *f* magazine, journal, periodical, review; *Am fam* (*schlechte ~~, auf billigem Papier*) pulp; (*vornehme ~~, auf sehr gutem Papier*) slick; **~~enlesesaal** *m* periodical room; **~~enschau** *f* digest, **~sichtwechsel** *m com* after sight bill; **~signal** *n* time-signal; **~~geber** *m* time-signal transmitter; **~spanne** *f* period of time; **~sparend** *a* time-saving; **~stempel** *m* time stamp; **~studie** *f tech* time study; **~tafel** *f* chronological table; **~überschreitung** *f radio* overrun; **~umstände** *m pl* circumstances *pl* (of the time), times *pl*; **~unterschied** *m* difference of time; **~vergeudung, ~verschwendung** *f* waste of time; **~verhältnisse** *n pl* circumstances *pl* (of the time); coincidences *pl*; *bei den jetzigen ~~n* in the present state of affairs; **~verkürzend** *a* time-shortening; (*unterhaltend*) entertaining; **~verlust** *m* loss of time; delay; *fam* woolgathering; **~vermerk** *m* date; **~verschluß** *m phot* time shutter; **~vertreib** *m* pastime, amusement; *sie tut es nur zum ~~* it's just a pastime with her; **~weilig** *a* temporary, at times; (*aussetzend*) intermittent; periodic; (*nicht ganztägig*) part-time; **~weise** *adv* at times; from time to time; for a time; **~wende** *f* turn of time; new epoch, new era; **~wort** *n* verb; **~zähler** *m* time recorder; **~zeichen** *n* time-signal; **~zünder** *m* time-fuse, delay igniter; (*Bombe*) delayed-action bomb.

Zeitung *f* newspaper, paper; journal; (*kleinformatig*) tabloid; (*amtlich*) gazette; *kopflose ~* partly printed sheets *pl*; *e-e ~ halten* (*beziehen*) to take in (*od* to subscribe to) a newspaper; **~sabonnent** *m* subscriber; **~sabonnement** *n* subscription to a newspaper; **~sablage** *f* newspaper stand; **~sabsatz** *m* par; **~sanzeige** *f*, **~sinserat** *n* press advertisement, announcement, insertion; advert, *Am* ad; **~sarchiv** *n* reference library, *Am* morgue; **~sartikel** *m* newspaper article; (*kurzer ~~*) item; **~sausrufer** *m* (newspaper) crier; **~sausschnitt** *m* press cutting, *Am* newspaper clipping, *fam* clip; **~~büro** *n* press cutting agency, *Am* clipping agency; **~sausträger** *m* newsvendor; **~sbeilage** *f* supplement; **~sberichterstatter** *m* reporter; (*ohne Vertrag*) free lance; **~sblatt** *n* newspaper; **~sdienst** *m* news work; **~sdruck** *m* newspaper printing; **~~erei** *f* newspaper printing plant; **~sente** *f* canard; hoax; **~sexpedition** *f* newspaper office; **~sfalzmaschine** *f* journal folding machine; **~sfeldzug** *m* crusade; **~sflugzeug** *n* newspaper-service plane; **~sfrau** *f* newsvendor; **~shalter** *m* newspaper holder; **~shändler** *m* newsagent, *Am* newsdealer; **~sjunge** *m* newsboy, *Am* newsy; **~skiosk** *m* news-stall, *Am* newsstand; **~skorrespondent** *m* press correspondent; **~sleser** *m* newspaper reader; **~slesesaal** *m* newspaper-room, newsroom; **~smann** *m* pressman, *Am* newspaper man; **~snachricht** *f* (piece of) news; (*falsche*) hoax; **~~enbüro** *n* press association; **~snotiz** *f* press item, notice, paragraph; **~snummer** *f* copy; (*alte*) back-number; **~spapier** *n* newsprint; **~sredakteur** *m* editor of a newspaper; **~sredaktion** *f* editorial office; **~sreklame** *f* newspaper advertising; **~sreporter** *m* newspaper reporter; **~srotationsmaschine** *f* newspaper rotary machine; **~sschreiber** *m* journalist, columnist; reporter; **~ssensation** *f Am* (*Erstmeldung*) scoop; beat; **~ssprache** *f*, **~sstil** *m* journalese; **~sstand** *m* kiosk, news-stall, *Am* newsstand; **~sverkäufer** *m* newsvendor; newsagent; *Am* newsdealer; **~sverleger** *m* newspaper proprietor, *Am* publisher; **~svertreter** *m* newspaper representative; **~swerbung** *f* press advertising, *Am* magazine and newspaper advertising; **~swesen** *n* journalism; the (daily) press; **~swissenschaft** *f* science of journalism.

zelebrieren *tr* to celebrate.

Zell\|e *f* (*phys, bot, parl, Gefängnis, Kloster*) cell; *el* cell, element, battery; *tele* booth; *aero* airframe, structure; *schalldichte ~~* soundproof cabinet; *verstrebte ~~* (*aero*) strut-braced wing; **~enartig** *a* cell-like, celloid, cytoid; *~~e Struktur* cellular structure, honeycomb; **~enaufbau** *m* cell structure; **~enbildung** *f* cell formation; **~eneinbau** *m* cellular arrangement; **~enförmig** *a* cellular; **~engenosse** *m* cellmate; **~engewebe** *n* cellular tissue; **~enkühler** *m* honeycomb radiator; **~enrad** *n tech* bucket wheel; **~enschalter** *m el* cell switch; **~faser** *f* synthetic cellulose fibre; **~förmig** *a* cellular; **~gewebe** *n* cellular tissue; **~~entzündung** *f med* cellulitis; **~glas** *n* cellophane; **~haut** *f bot* cell membrane; *tech* cellophane; **~horn** *n* celluloid; **~ig** *a* cellular, celled, honeycombed; vesicular; **~kern** *m* cell nucleus; **~~teilung** *f bot* nuclear division; **~körper** *m* cellular body; **~masse** *f* cellular substance; **~onlack** *m* cellulose acetate lacquer; **~ophan** *n* cellophane; **~stoff** *m* cellulose; (*Papier*) pulp; **~~(f)abrikation** *f* cellulose manufacture; **~~(f)aser** *f* cellulose fibre (*Am* fiber); **~~seide** *f* cellulose silk, rayon; **~~watte** *f* cellulose wadding; cellucotton; **~tätigkeit** *f* cell activity; **~uloid** *n* celluloid; **~ulose** *f* cellulose; **~~fabrik** *f* woodpulp works *pl*; **~verschmelzung** *f* cell fusion; **~wand** *f* cell membrane (*od* wall); **~wolle** *f* spun rayon, rayon staple.

Zelot *m* zealot; **~isch** *a* fanatical.

Zelt *n* tent; (*groß*) pavilion, marquee; (*mar Sonnen~*) awning; *ein ~ aufschlagen* (*abschlagen*) to pitch (to strike) a tent; **~ausrüstung** *f* tent equipment; **~bahn** *f* tent section, *Am* shelter half; **~dach** *n* tent roof; **~en** *itr* to tent; to camp; **~lager** *n* tent camp; **~leinwand** *f* canvas, tent cloth; **~pfahl** *m* tent pole; **~pflock** *m* tent pin, tent peg; **~schnur** *f* tent guy-rope; **~stange** *f* tent pole.

*

Zement *m* (*auch med*) cement; *mit ~ ausgießen* to grout with cement; **~beton** *m* cement concrete; **~bewurf** *m* cement plaster; **~brei** *m* cement grout; **~fabrik** *f* cement factory; **~fußboden** *m* concrete floor; **~gußwaren** *f pl* compressed-concrete articles *pl*; **~ieren** *tr* to cement; to caseharden; to carburize; **~ierung** *f* cementation; carburization; **~ierverfahren** *n* cementation process; **~it** *m* cementite; **~kalk** *m* hydraulic lime; **~~beton** *m* cement-lime concrete; **~klinker** *m* cement clinker; **~kupfer** *n* cement copper; **~platte** *f* slab of cement; **~pulver** *n* cementing powder, carburizer; **~sack** *m* cement bag; **~sockel** *m* cement foundation; **~stahl** *m* blister (*od* cemented) steel; **~verputz** *m* cement plaster; **~werk** *n* cement plant.

Zenit *m* zenith.

zens\|ieren *tr* to censor; (*tadeln*) to censure, to find fault with, to blame; (*prüfen*) to examine; (*Schule*) to give marks; **~or** *m* censor; **~ur** *f* censoring, censorship; (*Schule*) report; certificate; marks *pl*; *Am* credit, grade; point; *gute ~~* good mark; *von der ~~ geöffnet!* Opened by Censor!

Zentimeter *n* centimetre; *Am* centimeter (*1 cm* = 0.3937 inch).
Zentner *m* hundredweight; (*metrischer* ~) quintal; **~last** *f fig* heavy weight; **~schwer** *a* very heavy.
zentral *a* central; **~abteilung** *f* central office; **~anlage** *f* central station (*od* plant); **~anmeldeamt** *n* central filing agency; **~bahnhof** *m* central station, *Am* (*für verschiedene Eisenbahngesellschaften*) union station; **~e** *f* central office, centre, *Am* headquarters *pl*, main office; *tele* (telephone) exchange, chief operator('s room), switchboard; *tech* control room; *mot* car shed; traction station; *mar* (*U-Boot*) control station; *el* electric power house; **~forschungsinstitut** *n* research centre; **~heizung** *f* central heating; **~~sanlage** *f* central heating plant; **~~skessel** *m* boiler for central heating; **~~srohr** *n* radiator pipe; **~isieren** *tr* to centralize; **~isierung** *f* centralization; **~kartei** *f* master file; **~körperchen** *n med* centrosome; **~nervensystem** *n* central nervous system; **~schmierung** *f* central (*od* one-shot) lubrication; **~uhrenanlage** *f* time-electrical distribution system; **~verschluß** *m phot* central shutter; **~verwaltung** *f* central administration; **~wasserversorgung** *f* central water supply.
Zentrier|ansatz *m* spigot; **~en** *tr* to centre, *Am* to center, to spot; **~vorrichtung** *f* centering device.
Zentrifugal|bewegung *f* centrifugal motion; **~gebläse** *n* centrifugal blower; **~kraft** *f* centrifugal force; **~pumpe** *f* centrifugal pump; **~regler** *m* centrifugal governor; **~wirkung** *f* centrifugal action.
Zentrifuge *f* centrifuge, (*Trockner*) hydroextractor; (*Milch*) cream separator.
zentri|petal *a* centripetal; **~sch** *a* concentric, central.
Zentrum *n* centre, *Am* center; *ins* ~ *treffen* to hit the bull's eye; *im* ~ *Neu Yorks* in midtown New York.
Zephir *m* zephyr.
Zepter *n* sceptre.

*

zer|beißen *irr tr* to bite to pieces, to crack, to crunch; **~bersten** *irr itr* to burst asunder; to split in pieces; **~bomben** *tr* to destroy (*od* wreck) by bombs; to bomb-destroy; **~bombt** *a* bomb-shattered; (*Stadt*) bomb-wrecked; **~brechen** *irr tr, itr* to break to pieces; to shatter, to smash, to rupture, to fracture; *sich den Kopf* ~~ to rack o.'s brains (over), *Am* to ransack o.'s brains; **~brechlich** *a* fragile; brittle, breakable, *Am* slimsy; (*bröcklig*) friable; ~~ ! with care! **~~keit** *f* fragility; brittleness; **~bröckeln** *tr, itr* to crumble; **~drücken** *tr* to crush, to crumple, to mash, to grind; (*Hut*) to squash; (*Kragen*) to wrinkle; (*Kleider*) to crease.
Zeremon|ie *f* ceremony; **~iell** *n* ceremonial; ~~ *a* ceremonial, formal; **~lös** *a* ceremonious.
zer|fahren *irr tr* to crush, to ruin (by driving); *a* (*Weg*) rutted; (*Geist*) absent-minded, thoughtless; (*unbesonnen*) giddy; (*konfus*) scatter-brained; **~~heit** *f* giddiness, thoughtlessness; (*Geistesabwesenheit*) absent-mindedness; (*Sorglosigkeit*) carelessness; **~fall** *m* ruin, decay; (*geistig*) decadence; (*Auflösung*) disintegration, dissociation, decomposition; **~~en** *irr itr* to fall to pieces, to fall into ruin, to decay; *mit jdm* ~~ to fall out with; *mit jdm* ~~ *sein* to be at variance with, to be on bad terms with; (*in Teile* ~~) to be divided (into); (*auflösen*) to decompose, to dissociate, to disintegrate; (*zus.fallen*) to collapse; (*zu Staub*) to crumble; (*Atom*) to split, to undergo fission, to decay; **~~geschwindigkeit** *f* velocity of decomposition; **~~produkt** *n* decomposition (*od* disintegration) product; **~~prozeß** *m* decomposition process; **~~zeit** *f* decay time; disintegration time; **~fasern** *tr* to separate into fibres; to rag; to pulp; to unravel; **~fetzen** *tr* to tear in pieces, to tear up, to shred; (*mit e-m Messer ~fleischen*) to slash; (*verstümmeln*) to mutilate; **~fetzt** *a* ragged, tattered; **~fleischen** *tr* to lacerate; to mangle; **~fließen** *irr itr* to dissolve, to melt; *in Tränen* ~~ to melt away (*od* to dissolve) in tears; *chem* to deliquesce; (*Farben*) to run; (*~streuen*) to disperse; **~fressen** *irr tr* to gnaw; *chem* to corrode, to erode; (*ausbrennen*) to cauterize; **~~d** *a* corrosive; **~furcht** *a* wrinkled, furrowed; **~gehen** *irr itr* to dissolve, to melt; (*schwinden*) to dwindle; **~gliedern** *tr* to dismember; *anat* to dissect; *fig* to analyse; **~gliederung** *f* dismemberment; dissection; *fig* analysis; **~hakken, ~hauen** *tr* to cut to pieces; (*Holz*) to chop; (*Fleisch*) to mince.
zer|kauen *tr* to chew; **~kleinern** *tr* to reduce to small pieces; (*Holz*) to chop; (*in Pulver*) to pulverize; (*zermalmen*) to crush; (*zerreiben*) to grind; **~kleinerungsmaschine** *f* crusher; pulverizer; **~klopfen** *tr* to pound to pieces; **~klüftet** *a* cleft, fissured, riven; **~knacken** *tr* to crack; **~knallen** *itr* to detonate, to explode; **~knautschen, ~knüllen** *tr* to crush, to crumple; **~knicken** *tr* to break, to crush, to crack; **~knirscht** *a* contrite; **~knirschung** *f* contrition; **~knittern** *tr* to (c)rumple, to wrinkle; to crease; to ruffle; **~knüllen** *tr* to rumple; **~kochen** *itr* to boil to pieces; **~kratzen** *tr* to scratch; **~krümeln** *tr, itr* to crumb(le).
zer|lassen *irr tr* to dissolve; to melt, to liquefy; **~legbar** *a* collapsible; detachable; decomposable; **~~keit** *f* decomposability; collapsibility; detachability; **~legen** *tr* (*zerteilen*) to part, to separate, to divide; (*zersetzen*) to decompose; (*absondern*) to dissociate; (*zerstückeln*) to cut up; (*in Gruppen aufteilen*) to split up; (*in Einzelteile* ~~) to take apart, to disassemble; *med* to dissect; *chem u. fig* to analyse, *Am* to analyze; *chem, math, mus* to resolve; *tech* to dismount, to dismantle, *Am* to knock down; (*Licht*) to disperse, to diffract, to split up; *el* to scan; (*Waffe*) to strip; (*dezentralisieren*) to decentralize; (*Braten*) to carve; **~legung** *f* carving; taking to pieces; analysis; splitting up; dissection; decomposition; dissociation; disintegration; (*Kräfte*) resolution; (*in Bestandteile*) dismantling, *Am* tear-down; **~lesen** *a* (*Buch*) well-thumbed; **~löchern** *tr* to perforate; **~löchert** *a* full of holes; **~lumpt** *a* ragged, tattered; **~mahlen** *tr* to grind; **~malmen** *tr* to bruise, to crush; **~martern** *tr* to torture, to torment; *den Kopf* ~~ to rack o.'s brains (over), *Am* to ransack o.'s brains (over); **~mürben** *tr* to wear down; **~mürbungskrieg** *m* war of attrition; **~nagen** *tr* to gnaw, to eat away; *chem* to corrode; (*Boden, Metall*) to erode; **~nieren** *tr* to blockade; **~pflücken** *tr* to pluck to pieces; **~platzen** *itr* to burst asunder, to explode; **~quetschen** *tr* to crush, to bruise, to squash.
Zerr|bild *n* distorted picture; caricature; **~en** *tr* to pull, to drag, to tug, to tear; (*Sehne*) to strain; **~ung** *f* pulling, dragging; tensile strength.
zer|reiben *irr tr* to grind, to powder, to pulverize, to triturate; **~reibung** *f* attrition, trituration; comminution; **~reiblich** *a* triturable; friable; pulverizable; **~reißbar** *a* tearable, capable of being torn; **~reißbelastung** *f* breaking stress (*od* load); **~reißen** *irr tr* to tear up; to rend; (*zerstückeln*) to dismember; (*zerfleischen*) to lacerate; (*auseinanderreißen*) to sever; (*Gefäß*) *med* to rupture; *itr* (*Kleider*) to wear out; (*Papier, Stoff*) to tear; (*zersplittern*) to split; (*in Fetzen, Stückchen*) to shred; **~reißfestigkeit** *f* ultimate (*od* tensile) strength; **~reißgrenze** *f* breaking limit; **~reißprobe** *f* breaking test; **~rinnen** *irr itr* to vanish away, to disappear; to melt away; *wie gewonnen, so ~ronnen* money lightly gained is lightly spent; **~rissenheit** *f* tattered condition; (*Zerlumptheit*) raggedness; (*Uneinigkeit*) want of union, disunion; (*Streit*) inner strife; (*seelisch*) confusion of the mind; **~rupfen** *tr* to pick to pieces; **~rütten** *tr* to ruin; (*Nerven, Gesundheit*) to shatter, to disorder; (*Einrichtung*) to disorganize; (*Geist*) to derange, to unhinge; **~rüttung** *f* disorganization; disorder, confusion; ruin; (*des Geistes*) derangement.
zer|sägen *tr* to saw to pieces; **~schellen** *tr* to dash, to smash; *itr* to be dashed (*od* smashed *od* wrecked), to be battered to pieces; **~schießen** *irr tr* to shoot to pieces; **~schlagen** *irr tr* to beat to pieces, to break (in pieces), to smash, to shatter, to batter; *r fig* to come to nothing, to be broken off; ~~ *a* battered, shattered, broken; (*Anstrengung*) knocked up; **~schmeißen** *irr tr* to dash to pieces; **~schmelzen** *tr, itr* to melt; **~schmettern** *tr* to dash (to pieces), to smash, to shatter, to crush; (*zerstören*) to destroy; **~schneiden** *irr tr* to cut up; (*in Stücke*) to mince, to shred; *med* to dissect; (*durch Einschnitte*) to carve; **~setzen** *tr* to decompose, to dissolve; (*in Teile*) to disintegrate, to break up, to dissociate; *chem, fig* to analyse, (-lyze); *el* to electrolyze; *fig* to undermine; **~setzend** *a fig* subversive; undermining; demoralizing; **~setzung** *f* decomposition; disintegration splitting up; dissociation; (*Erdöl*) cracking; (*Verfall*) decay; *fig* demoralization, undermining; **~~sprodukt** *n* decomposition product; **~~svorgang** *m* decomposition process; **~~swärme** *f* heat of decomposition; **~spalten, ~spellen** *tr* to cleave, to split; **~splittern** *tr* to splinter, to split up, to shiver, to break to pieces; (*Menge, Wolken, Soldaten*) to disperse; *fig* to dissipate; *seine Kräfte* ~~, *sich* ~~ to fritter away o.'s powers; **~splitterung** *f* shivering; splintering; *fig* dissipation; **~sprengen** *tr* to burst open, to blow up; (*Menschenmenge*) to disperse; *mil* to rout; **~springen** *irr itr* to fly into pieces; to explode, to burst; (*Glas*) to crack; (*Kopf*) to split; **~stampfen** *tr* to crush; *tech* to bray; to pound; (*mit Füßen*) to trample down; **~stäuben** *tr* to reduce to dust, to pulverize; (*Flüssigkeit*) to spray; (*spritzen*) to spatter, to sputter; (*in kleinste Teile*) to atomize; *fig* to disperse, to scatter; **~stäuber** *m* pulverizer; (*Flüssigkeiten*) sprayer; *med* atomizer; (*Verdampfer*) vapo(u)rizer; (*Parfüm*) scent-spray, *Am* atomizer; **~stäubungsdüse** *f* spray diffuser;

~stechen *irr tr* to pierce, to prick; **~stieben** *irr itr* to fly away; to disperse, to vanish; **~störangriff** *m mil* destruction raid, hit-and-run raid; **~störbar** *a* destructible; **~stören** *tr* to destroy; to demolish; to ruin, to shatter, to break down; (*verwüsten*) to devastate; (*untergraben*) *fig* to be subversive; **~~d** *a* destroying; **~störer** *m* destroyer; *aero* large fighter aircraft; interceptor plane; **~~flugzeug** *n* destroyer plane, long-range fighter bomber; **~~sicherung** *f mar* destroyer escort; **~stört** *a* wrecked; **~störung** *f* destruction, demolition; ruin; (*Verfall*) decay; (*Gewebe~~*) corrosion; (*Glauben*) subversion; **~~sbombe** *f* demolition bomb; **~~sfeuer** *n* destruction fire, fire for effect; **~~swut** *f* vandalism; **~stoßen** *irr tr* to bruise; to pound; to break; to powder, to pulverize; **~streuen** *tr* to scatter, to disperse; (*Bedenken*) to dissipate; (*Zweifel*) to dispel; (*Furcht, Unwissenheit, Nebel*) to dissipate; (*Wissen, Licht, Hitze, Duft*) to diffuse; (*ausbreiten*) to spread; (*Gedanken*) to divert; *r* to amuse o. s., to divert o. s., to distract o. s.; **~streut** *a* dispersed; (*Licht*) diffused; *fig* absent-minded, preoccupied; **~~heit** *f* absent-mindedness, distraction; **~streuung** *f* dispersion, scattering, dissipation; diffusion; (*Entspannung*) relaxation; (*Erholung*) diversion, amusement; (*Zerstreutheit*) absence of mind; **~stückeln** *tr* to dismember; to chop to pieces, to cut up; (*zerdrücken*) to crush; (*zersetzen*) to disintegrate; (*Gebiet aufteilen*) to partition; (*ab-, aufteilen*) to parcel out (into); **~stückelung** *f* dismemberment; partition; cutting up; parcel(l)ing out.

zer|teilen *tr* to divide, to separate; (*zerstreuen*) to disperse; *chem, med* to dissolve, to resolve; (*in Stücke*) to cut up; **~teilung** *f* division, separation; dismemberment; *med* dissolution; **~trampeln** *tr* to trample down; **~trennen** *tr* to sever, to disjoin; (*Kleid*) to rip up; **~trennlich** *a* separable, dissoluble; **~trennung** *f* separation, disruption; ripping up; **~treten** *irr tr* to trample down, to tread under foot; (*~malmen*) to crush; (*Feuer, fig*) to stamp out; **~trümmerbar** *a* fissionable, disintegrable; **~trümmern** *tr* to lay in ruins, to wreck, to demolish; (*in kleine Stücke*) to smash; (*zerstören*) to destroy; (*vernichten*) to ruin; (*zerbrechen*) to break (up); (*Atome*) to split; **~trümmerung** *f* destruction, demolition; shattering, smashing; disintegration; (*Atome*) fission, splitting.

Zervelatwurst *f* saveloy.

zer|wühlen *tr* to root up; (*Haar*) to dishevel; **~würfnis** *n* discord, difference, disunion, disagreement, dissension; (*Streit*) quarrel; **~zausen** *tr* to tousle, to rumple; *jdn ~~* to pull about; *die Haare ~~* to dishevel; **~zaust** *a* untidy.

*

Zeter *n*: *~ schreien* to cry murder; **~geschrei, ~mordio** *n* yell, loud outcry, clamo(u)r; **~n** *itr* to raise a loud outcry, to kick up a shindy.

Zettel *m* scrap of paper, slip; (*beschriebener*) note; (*zum Ankleben*) ticket, *Am* sticker; (*Anschlag*) poster, bill, placard; (*zum Anhängen*) label, *Am* tag; (*Theater~*) play-bill; (*Weberei*) warp; *~ ankleben verboten!* stick (*Am* post) no bills! **~ankleber** *m* bill-sticker, bill-poster; **~bank** *f* bank of issue; **~kasten, ~katalog** *m* filing-cabinet; box for slips; card index (catalogue); **~verteiler** *m* bill distributor; **~wahl** *f* scrutiny.

Zeug *n* material, stuff; (*Stoff*) cloth, fabric; (*Webwaren*) textiles *pl*; (*Dinge*) things *pl*; (*Sache*) matter; (*Waren*) goods *pl*; (*Wäsche*) linen; (*Anzug*) clothes *pl*; (*Werk~*) utensils *pl*, implements *pl*, tools *pl*; (*Plunder*) rubbish, junk; (*vielerlei*) all sorts of things; (*Papier*) stuff, pulp; (*Brauerei*) yeast; (*Geschirr*) harness; *mar* rigging; *fig dummes ~* humbug, stuff and nonsense; *er hat nicht das ~ dazu* it is not in him, *Am* he hasn't got what it takes; *was das ~ hält* as much as possible, with might and main, *fam* hell for leather; *sich ins ~ legen* to set to work with a will; to put o.'s shoulders to the wheel; *jdm etw am ~ flicken* to pick holes in s. o.; **~amt** *n* ordnance department; **~druck** *m* cloth printing; **~~erei** *f* cloth printing factory; **~haus** *n* arsenal, armo(u)ry.

Zeuge *m* witness; (*beeideter*) deponent, sworn witness; *Vernehmung e-s ~n* examination (*od* hearing) of a witness; *jdn als ~n anrufen* to call s. o. in evidence; *als ~ aussagen* to (bear) witness, to testify; to give evidence of; *~n laden* to call evidences in court; *als ~ vernommen werden* to be put into the witness-box; **~n** *itr* to give (*od* bear) testimony, to testify, to bear witness; to give evidence (of); to prove; *tr* to beget, to procreate, to generate, to produce, to create; **~naussage** *f* evidence, deposition; **~nbeeinflussung** *f* suborning (*od* corruption) of witnesses; **~nbeweis** *m* evidence of a witness; proof of evidence; **~neid** *m* oath of a witness; **~ngebühren** *f pl* witness fee; **~ngeld** *n* conduct money; **~nstand** *m* witness-box, *Am* witness-stand; **~nvereidigung** *f* swearing-in of a witness; **~nvernehmung** *f* hearing (*od* examination) of witness.

Zeugnis *n* (*Beweis*) evidence, testimony, proof; (*Bezeugung*) witness; (*Zeugenaussage*) deposition; (*schriftliche Bescheinigung*) certificate, testimonial; (*für Hausgehilfen*) character; (*Gewährsmann*) authority; (*Schule*) school report, *Am* credit, mark, grade, report card; (*bei Bewerbungen*) (letter of) reference, letter of recommendation; *~ ablegen* to bear witness; to give testimony (to); *zum ~ dessen* in witness of this; *ärztliches ~* medical certificate; *ein ~ geben* to mark, *Am* to grade; **~abschrift** *f* copy of testimonial; **~verweigerung** *f* refusal to give evidence.

Zeugung *f* procreation, generation, begetting; breeding; **~sfähig** *a* capable of begetting, procreative; **~sglied** *n* penis; **~skraft** *f* generative power; **~sorgane** *n pl* genital organs *pl*; **~strieb** *m* sexual instinct; **~sunfähig** *a* impotent.

Zichorie *f* chicory, *Am* endive.

Zick|e *f*, **~lein** *n* kid.

Zickzack *m* zigzag; **~blitz** *m* fork-lightning; **~kurs** *m*: *im ~~ fahren* to zigzag; *im ~~ fliegen* to snake; **~linie** *f* zigzag line.

Ziege *f* goat; she-goat; **~nbart** *m* goat's beard; *Am* (*beim Menschen*) goatee; **~nbock** *m* he-goat; **~nfell** *n* goatskin; **~nhirt** *m* goatherd; **~nkäse** *m* goat-cheese; **~leder** *n* goatskin; kid leather; **~nmilch** *f* goat's milk; **~npeter** *m med* mumps *pl*, parotitis.

Ziegel *m* (*Mauer~*) brick; (*Dach~*) tile; (*lufttrocken*) *Am* adobe; **~arbeit** *f* brick-work; **~brenner** *m* tilemaker; brickmaker; **~dach** *n* tiled roof; **~decker** *m* tiler; **~ei** *f* brickworks *pl*, brickyard; **~erde** *f* brick clay; **~mehl** *n* brick-dust; **~ofen** *m* brick-kiln; **~rot** *a* brick-red; **~stein** *m* brick; **~~schicht** *f* course of bricks; **~~verkleidung** *f* brickwork casing.

Zieh|bank *f* draw bench; (*Röhren~~*) skelp mill; **~brunnen** *m* draw-well.

ziehen *irr tr* to pull, to draw; (*zerren*) to tug; (*schleppen*) to haul; (*schleifen*) to drag; (*Schiff*) to tow; (*saugen, Nutzen ~*) to suck; (*Zahn*) to pull out, to extract; (*Parallele*) to draw out; (*Vergleich*) to make; (*Hand weg~*) to remove; (*züchten*) *bot* to cultivate; (*Tiere*) to breed, to raise; (*er~*) to educate, to rear, to train; *math* to extract; (*Kreis*) to describe; (*Gewehr*) to rifle; (*Hut*) to take off; (*Schach*) to move; (*Mauer*) to build, to erect; (*Graben*) to dig; (*Faß ab~*) to broach; (*Draht*) to string; (*Los*) to draw; *den Steuerknüppel ~* (*aero*) to pull the control column back; *itr* to draw, to pull; (*aus~*) to (re)move, to quit, to leave; (*Tee, Ofen, Pfeife*) to draw; (*Luftzug*) to be draughty; (*sich bewegen*) to move, to go; (*Dienstboten*) to go out of service; to quit a place; (*an e-r Zigarette*) to have a whiff (*od* puff); (*schmerzen*) to ache; (*an~*) to attract, to draw; *theat* to catch on; (*von Wert sein*) to weigh, to be of value; (*wirken*) to have effect; *sich ~* to extend, to stretch; (*Holz*) to warp; (*Stahl*) to distort; (*aufsaugen*) to soak, to penetrate; (*Flüssigkeit*) to be ropy; *die Bilanz ~* to balance accounts, to strike the balance; *Blasen ~* to raise blisters; *Grimassen ~* to make faces; *den kürzeren ~* to come off the loser, to get the worst of it; *das große Los ~* to hit the jackpot; *Nutzen ~* to derive profit (from); *die Stirn kraus ~* to frown, to knit the brows; *Wasser ~* to suck up water; (*Schiff*) to leak; *e-n Wechsel ~* to draw a bill; *am gleichen Strang ~* to be in the same boat; *an den Haaren ~* to pull by the hair; *ans Land ~* to haul ashore; *Saiten auf e-e Geige ~* to string a violin; *auf seine Seite ~* to win over to o.'s side; *auf Flaschen ~* to bottle; *aller Augen auf sich ~* to attract universal attention; *aufs Land ~* to go to live in the country; *auf Wache ~* to mount guard; *sich aus der Schlinge ~* to get o. s. out of a tight spot; to slip the collar; *in den Krieg ~* to go to war; *in den Schmutz ~* to drag through the mud; *in Erwägung ~* to take into consideration, to contemplate; *ins Lächerliche ~* to turn into ridicule; *in die Länge ~* to delay, to protract, to put off; to be dragging on; (*Erzählung*) to spin out; *in e-e andere Wohnung ~* to move to other lodgings; *in Zweifel ~* to doubt, to call in question; *nach sich ~* to have consequences; to entail, to involve; *das Fell über die Ohren ~* (*fam*) to fleece s. o.; *zu Rate ~* to consult s. o.; *zu jdm ~* to go to live with s. o.; *zur Rechenschaft ~* to call to account; *es zieht hier* there is a draught (*Am* draft) here; *dieser Grund zieht bei mir nicht* this reason does not weigh with me; *~ n* drawing; pulling; dragging; haulage; breeding; cultivation; (*Vögel*) migration; (*Flüssigkeit*) ropiness; (*Um~*) move; *phys* coupling-hysteresis effect; *med* rheumatic pain.

Zieh|fähigkeit *f* drawing quality; **~harmonika** *f* accordion, concertina, *fam* squeeze-box; **~kind** *n* foster-child; **~mutter** *f* foster-mother; **~schnur** *f* draw cord; **~tag** *m* moving day; ~**ung** *f* (*Lotterie*) drawing; (*Zug*) draught; (*Zugkraft*) traction; ~~**sliste** *f* list of prize-winners.

Ziel *n* aim; (*Reise~*) destination; (*Grenze*) limit, boundary; (*Rennsport*) winning-post; (*Ende*) end; (*Frist*) term; *fig* mark; (*Zweck*) aim, end, object; (*Lebens~*, ~ *der Wünsche*) goal; (*Streben*) aspiration; (~ *der Kritik*) target; *mil* objective, (*Geschoß*) target; (*Bereich*) scope; (~*scheibe*) butt; *das ~ treffen* to hit the mark; *ein ~ setzen* to limit; *sich ein ~ setzen* to aim at; *jdm ein ~ setzen* to put a stop to, to check; *ins ~ gehen* to come on aim; *durch das ~ gehen* to breast the tape; *das ~ verfehlen* to miss the mark; *über das ~ hinausschießen* to overshoot the mark; *Maß u. ~ halten* to keep within bounds; *sein ~ erreichen* to gain o.'s end(s), to reach o.'s goal, *Am* to get there; *ohne Zweck u. ~* without aim or end; *gegen 3 Monate ~* at three months' credit; *bewegliches* (*festes*) ~ moving (stationary) target; ~**abschnitt** *m mil* sector of fire; ~**anflug** *m aero mil* flight toward object, bomb run; ~~**gerät** *n aero* homing-approach set, beacon-receiver set; ~**ansprache** *f mil* target designation; ~**auffassung** *f mil* target pick-up; ~**aufklärung** *f* target reconnaissance; ~**band** *n sport* tape; ~**bewußt** *a* methodical, systematic; purposeful; resolute; with an object in view; ~**einrichtung** *f* aiming mechanism; ~**en** *itr* to aim (*auf* at, *Am* to *mit Infinitiv*), to take aim; (*anvisieren*) to sight, to point, to adjust sight; (*streben nach*) to strive for, to direct to, to tend to; (*anspielen auf*) to allude to, to refer to; (*hin~~ auf*) to drive at; ~**entfernung** *f* distance of the target; ~**fehler** *m* sighting error; fault of aim; ~**fernrohr** *n* telescopic sight; ~**flug** *m* homing flight; ~~**gerät** *n* direction finder; ~~**zeug** *n* target airplane; ~**genauigkeit** *f* accuracy of sighting; ~**gerade** *f* home stretch; (*Rennen*) straight; ~**gerät** *n* (*Gewehr*) sight; *aero* bombsight; ~**geschwindigkeit** *f* target speed; ~**gevierttafel** *f* protractor and scale; ~**höhe** *f* altitude of target; ~**karte** *f* range table; *aero* target map; ~**kopfsteuerung** *f* electronic target-detecting control; ~**kreis** *m* target circle; ~**kurs** *m* course; ~**landung** *f aero* precision landing; ~**linie** *f* line of collimation; *sport* finishing line; ~**los** *a* aimless; erratic; ~**marke** *f* measuring mark; ~**markierung** *f* target marking for bombers; ~**peilung** *f aero* destination bearing; ~**photographie** *f* photofinish; ~**punkt** *m* aiming point; objective; goal; (*Zielscheibe*) bull's eye, mark; ~**raum** *m aero* target area; (*Golf*) teeing ground; ~**richter** *m sport* judge; ~**scheibe** *f* practice target, sighting disk; ~~ *des Spottes sein* to be a laughing stock; ~**schiff** *n* target ship; ~**setzung** *f* fixing of an aim; setting of an objective; ~**sicher** *a* sure of o.'s aim; steady; ~**strebig** *a* purposive; ~**sucher** *m* (*bei Raketengeschoß*) (automatic) aiming device; homing device; ~**unterlagen** *f pl* target data *pl*; ~**vorrichtung** *f* sight; (*Rakete*) launching rack; (*Bomben*) aerial-bomb aiming device; ~**wechsel** *m* change of target; ~**weisungsschießen** *n* target-indication fire; ~**zeichen** *n* (*Radar*) target blip; ~**zuweisung** *f* assignment of target.

ziem|en *itr, r* to become, to be seemly; (*passend sein*) to be proper, to be suitable, to be fitting; ~**lich** *a* (*passend*) suitable, fit; (*leidlich*) middling, passable; (*mäßig*) moderate, fair; (~~ *gut*) tolerable; (*beträchtlich*) rather considerable, *adv* pretty, fairly, rather, tolerably; ~~ *weit* a rather long way (off); quite a distance; ~~ *gut* tolerably well; ~~ *spät* rather late; ~~ *lange Zeit* a pretty long time; ~~ *klein* rather small; ~~ *viele* a good many, quite a few; *es ist so ~~ dasselbe* it's about the same.

Ziemer *m* (*Wildbret*) haunch, hind-quarter; (*Peitsche*) whip, cat.

Zier *f* ornament, decoration, embellishment; ~**affe** *m* fop, coxcomb; ~**at** *m* ornament, finery, decoration; (*unnötige*) showy accomplishments *pl*, unnecessary adornments *pl*, *Am* frills *pl*; ~**de** *f* ornament, decoration; *fig* hono(u)r (to); ~**en** *tr* to ornament, to adorn; to be an ornament (to); (*verschönern*) to embellish, to decorate; *r* to be affected; (*Frauen*) to be prim (*od* coy); (*beim Essen*) to need pressing to eat; (*Umstände machen*) to stand on ceremony; (*sich sträuben*) to refuse; ~**erei** *f* affectation, airs *pl*; ~**garten** *m* flower-garden; ornamental garden; ~**knopf** *m* knurled knob; ~**leiste** *f* border, edging; *typ* vignette, tailpiece; ~**lich** *a* graceful, elegant; (*nett*) neat; (*hübsch*) pretty, nice; (*niedlich*) dainty, delicate; (*fein*) fine; ~~**keit** *f* elegance; daintiness; neatness, nicety; ~**pflanze** *f* ornamental plant; ~**puppe** *f* dressy woman; ~**schrift** *f* ornamental type; ~**strauch** *m* ornamental shrub; ~**stück** *n* ornament.

Ziffer *f* figure, numeral, number, digit; coefficient; (*Schriftzeichen*) cipher; *mit ~n schreiben* to write in ciphers; ~**blatt** *n* dial, (*Uhr*) face; ~**nmäßig** *a* numerical, by figures; ~**nscheibe** *f* figure dial; ~**schrift** *f* ciphers *pl*.

Zigarette *f* cigaret(te); *fam* fag, cigs *pl*; *e-e ~ drehen* to make a cigarette; *e-e ~ an der andern anbrennen* to chainsmoke cigaret(te)s; *e-e ~ schnorren Am sl* to bum a cigarette; *heftig an e-r ~ ziehen* to puff fiercely on a cigarette; ~**nautomat** *m* cigarette slot-machine; ~**ndreher** *m* cigarette-maker; ~**netui** *n* cigarette-case; ~**npackung** *f* cigarette package; ~**nspitze** *f* cigarette-holder; ~**nstummel** *m* cigarette-end, *Am* cigaret(te)-butt.

Zigarillo *m* whiff.

Zigarre *f* cigar; ~**nabschneider** *m* cigar-cutter; ~**nanzünder** *m* cigar lighter; ~**ndeckblatt** *n* wrapper; ~**ngeschäft** *n*, ~**nhändler** *m* tobacconist; ~**nkiste** *f* cigar-box; ~**nladen** *m* tobacconist's, *Am* cigar store; ~**nspitze** *f* (*Mundstück*) cigar-holder; (*abgeschnittene*) cigar-tip; ~**nstummel** *m* cigar-end (*Am* -butt); ~**ntasche** *f* cigar-case.

Zigeuner *m*, ~**in** *f* gipsy; ~**bande** *f* gang of gipsies.

Zikade *f* cicada.

Zille *f* river-boat, skiff.

Zimbel *f* cymbal.

Zimmer *n* room, chamber, apartment; *möbliertes ~* furnished apartment; *das ~ hüten* to keep the room; *das ~ liegt nach dem Garten* the room looks into the garden; ~**antenne** *f radio* indoor aerial; ~**arbeit** *f* carpenter's work; ~**axt** *f* carpenter's axe; ~**chen** *n* little room, closet; ~**decke** *f* ceiling; ~**dekoration** *f* upholstery; ~**dienst** *m* room service, *Am* valet service; ~**einrichtung** *f* furnishing; (*Möbel*) furniture, interior; ~**ei** *f* carpenter's trade, carpentry; ~**flucht** *f* suite (of rooms); ~**geselle** *m* journeyman carpenter; ~**gymnastik** *f* indoor gymnastics *pl*; ~**herr** *m* lodger; ~**hof**, ~**platz** *m* timber-yard; ~**holz** *n* timber; ~**mädchen** *n* chamber-maid; (*Hotel*) room-maid, housemaid; ~**mann** *m* carpenter; ~**meister** *m* master carpenter; ~**n** *tr* to carpenter; to timber, to fabricate; *itr fig* to frame; ~**reihe** *f* suite of apartments; ~**temperatur** *f* normal room temperature; ~**ung** *f* timbering, frame-work; ~**vermieter** *m*, ~~**in** *f* lodging-house keeper; private hotel-keeper; ~**werk** *n* carpenter's work.

zimperlich *a* prim, *fam* kid-glove, *Am* finicky; (*überempfindlich*) supersensitive; (*geziert*) affected, finical; (*übertrieben sittsam*) prudish; ~ *tun* to mince it; ~**keit** *f* primness; prudery; affectation, finicalness; supersensitiveness.

Zimt *m* cinnamon.

Zink *m u. n* zinc, spelter; ~**artig** *a* zincky, like zinc; ~**asche** *f* zinc ash (*od* dross); ~**ätze** *f* zinc-etching solution; ~**ätzung** *f* zincography; ~**auflage** *f* zinc coat; ~**bedachung** *f* zinc roofing; ~**blech** *n* sheet zinc; ~**blende** *f* zinc blende; ~**blüte** *f* zinc bloom; ~**druckverfahren** *n* zinc printing; ~**eisenerz** *n* franklinite; ~**folie** *f* zinc foil; ~**salbe** *f* zinc ointment; ~**weiß** *a* zinc white.

Zinke *f* peak; prong; spike; (*Kamm*) tooth; (*Zapfen*) tenon, dovetail; *mus* cornet; (*Karten*) secret mark; ~**n** *m vulg* (*Nase*) proboscis.

Zinn *n* tin; (*Hart~*) pewter; ~**ader** *f* tin load (*od* vein); ~**barren** *m* tin bar (*od* slab); ~**bergwerk** *n*, ~**grube** *f* tin mine; ~**blech** *n* tin plate, sheet tin; ~**e(r)n** *a* of tin (*od* pewter); ~**farbe** *f* vermilion; ~**folie** *f* tin foil; ~**geschirr** *n* tin (*od* pewter) vessels *pl*; ~**gießer** *m* tin founder; ~**haltig** *a* containing tin, stanniferous; ~**kraut** *n* horsetail; ~**legierung** *f* tin alloy; ~**metall** *n* metallic tin; ~**soldat** *m* tin soldier.

Zinne *f* pinnacle, battlement.

Zinnober *m* cinnabar; ~**rot** *a* vermilion.

Zins *m* (*Miete*) rent; (*Zinsen pl: Geld*) interest; *hoher ~* (*Am*) shave; (*Abgabe*) tax, duty; *aufgelaufene ~en* accumulated interest; *rückständige ~en* arrears of interest; *hohe ~en* dear interest; *laufende ~en* running interest; *schuldige ~en* interest due; *~en zum Satz von* interest at the rate of; *~en tragen* to bear interest; *auf ~en anlegen* to put out at interest; *~en berechnen* to charge interest; *~en geben* to grant an interest of . . . per cent; *Geld auf ~en ausleihen* to lend out money at (*od* on) interest; *~en zum Kapital schlagen* to add the interest to the principal; *mit ~ u. ~eszins* (*fig*) in full measure; *von den ~en seines Kapitals leben* to live on the interest from his capital; ~**abschnitt** *m* coupon; ~**abzug** *m* discount; ~**bar** *a* interest-bearing; ~**bogen** *m* coupon sheet; ~**bringend** *a* interest-bearing; ~~ *anlegen* to put out at interest; ~**einkommen** *n* interest income; ~**en** *tr, itr* to pay interest; to pay rent; to pay tribute; ~**enausfall** *m* loss of interest; ~**enbelastung**, ~**enlast** *f* interest charge; ~**enberechnung** *f* computation of interest; ~**endienst** *m* (*Anleihe*) loan service; ~**enzuwachs** *m* accrued interest; ~**erhöhung** *f* increase in the interest rate; ~**ermäßigung** *f* reduction in the rate of interest; ~**erneuerungsschein** *m* talon; ~**erträgnisse** *pl* interest proceeds *pl*; ~**eszinsen** *m pl* compound interest; ~**frei** *a* free of interest; (*ohne Miete*) rent-free; ~**fuß**,

-satz *m* rate of interest; bank rate; *gesetzlicher --* legal rate of interest; **-haus** *n* apartment house; **-herabsetzung** *f* reduction in the rate of interest; **-höhe** *f* amount of interest; **-knechtschaft** *f* interest serfdom; **-los** *a* free of interest; **-pflichtig** *a* interest-bearing; (*Pacht*) subject to rent; subject to tax; tributary; **-rechnung** *f* interest account; calculation of interest; **-rückstände** *m pl* arrears of interest; **-saldo** *n* balance of interest; **-schein** *m* (interest) coupon; (*Aktien*) dividend warrant; **-senkung** *f* reduction of interest; **-tabelle** *f* interest table; **-tragend** *a* interest-bearing; **-umwandlung** *f* conversion of the rate of interest; **-verlust** *m* loss of interest; **-zahlungen** *f pl* interest payments *pl*.

Zionis|mus *m* Zionism; **-t** *m* Zionist.

Zipfel *m* tip, edge, point, end; (*Ohr*) lobe; (*Ecke*) corner; (*Rock-*) lappet; flap; *phys* secondary beams *pl*; **-ig** *a* pointed, peaked; **-mütze** *f* jelly-bag cap, tassel(l)ed cap, night-cap.

Zipperlein *n* gout.

Zirbel|drüse *f* pineal gland; **-kiefer** *f* stone pine; **-nuß** *f* cedar-nut, pine-cone.

Zirkel *m* (*Kreis*) circle; (*Instrument*) a pair of compasses; *- mit Reißfeder* inking compass; **-n** *tr* to move in a circle; to measure with compasses; **-rund** *a* circular; **-spitze** *f* point of the compass; **-verlängerung** *f* lengthening bar of compass.

Zirkul|ar *n* circular; **-ation** *f* circulation; **--spumpe** *f* circulating pump; **-ieren** *itr* to circulate; *-- lassen fig* to put in circulation.

Zirkumflex *m* circumflex.

Zirkus *m* circus; **-reiterin** *f* circus-rider; **-vorstellung** *f* circus-performance; **-wagen** *m* circus wag(g)on; **-zelt** *n* circus-tent; *Am* Big Top.

zirpen *itr* to chirp, to cheep.

Zirr|okumulus *m* cirro-cumulus; **-ostratus** *m* cirro-stratus; **-uswolke** *f* cirrus cloud.

zisch|eln *itr* to whisper; **-en** *itr* to hiss, to sizzle; (*brodeln*) to bubble; (*schwirren*) to whiz(z); (*Ruhe gebieten*) to cry hush; **-en** *n* hissing, sizz, sizzle, fizz; **-hahn** *m* compression tap; relief cock; **-laut** *m* hissing sound; (*Lautlehre*) sibilant.

Ziselier|arbeit *f* chasing; chisel(l)ed work; **-en** *tr* to chase; to carve, to engrave; **-werkzeug** *n* engraving tool.

Zisterne *f* cistern, tank; **-nflugzeug** *n* chemical-spraying plane; **-nwagen** *m* cistern car, tank car.

Zitadelle *f* citadel.

Zit|at *n* quotation, quote; *Anfang* (*Ende*) *e-s --s* begin (end) quote; **--enschatz** *m* book of quotations; **-ieren** *tr* (*vorladen*) to summon, to call up; (*anführen*) to cite, to quote; (*beschwören*) to raise (spirits).

Zither *f* zither; **-spieler** *m* zither-player.

Zitron|at *n* candied lemon peel; **-e** *f* lemon; **-enbaum** *m* lemon (*od* citron)-tree; **-enblüte** *f* lemon blossom; **-enfalter** *m* brimstone butterfly; **-enfarbe** *f* lemon (*od* citron) colo(u)r; **-enfarbig** *a* lemon-colo(u)red; **-engelb** *a* lemon-yellow, citrine; **-enlimonade** *f* lemon squash; **-enpresse** *f* lemon-squeezer; **-ensaft** *m* lemon juice; (*Getränk*) lemon-squash; **-ensauer** *a* citrate of; **-ensäure** *f* citric acid; **-enschale** *f* lemon peel; **-enscheibe** *f* slice of lemon; **-enwasser** *n* still lemonade.

Zitter|aal *m* electric eel; **-gras** *n* quaking-grass; **-ig** *a* trembling, shaky; (*Stimme*) faltering; **-n** *itr* (*Wut, Furcht, Kälte*) to tremble (*vor* with); (*Schwäche*) to shake (with); (*Kälte*) to shiver (with); (*Erde, Furcht*) to quake; (*Blatt, Stimme*) to quiver; (*vibrieren*) to vibrate; (*Zähne*) to chatter; **-n** *n* tremor; quivering, trembling, shivering; **-pappel** *f* aspen; **-roche(n)** *m* electric ray, torpedo fish; **-sieb** *n* vibrating screen.

Zitz *m* chintz, calico.

Zitze *f* teat, dug, nipple.

Zivil *n* civil (body), civilians *pl*; *in -* in plain clothes, in mufti, *sl* in civvies; *Am sl* in cits; *- a* civil; (*Preise*) reasonable, moderate; **-angestellte(r)** *m* civil employee; **-anzug** *m* civilian suit; **-arzt** *m* civilian physician; **-behörde** *f* civil authority; **-bevölkerung** *f* civilian population; **-courage** *f* civilian courage; **-dienstpflicht** *f* civil-service duty; **-ehe** *f* civil marriage; **-flugzeug** *n* commercial plane; private plane, **-gericht** *n* civil court; **-isation** *f* civilization; **-isator** *m* civilizer; **-isatorisch** *a* civilizing; **-isieren** *tr* to civilize; **-ist** *m* civilian, *Am* citizen; **-kammer** *f* civil chamber; **-klage** *f* civil case; **-kleidung** *f* civilian clothes *pl*, mufti, *sl* civ(v)ies *pl*; *Am sl* cits *pl;* **-leben** *n* civilian life; **-luftfahrt** *f* civil aviation; **-luftverkehr** *m* civil air traffic; **-person** *f* civilian; **-prozeß** *m* civil action (*od* suit); **--ordnung** *f* Civil Practice Act, *Am* Rules of Civil Procedure; **-rechtlich** *a* by civil law; **-sache** *f* civil case; **-trauung** *f* marriage before the registrar; **-versorgung** *f* guaranty (*Am* guarantee) of civil employment for ex-servicemen; **-verwaltung** *f* civil administration.

Zobel *m* sable; *Am* marten; **-fell** *n* sable-skin; **-pelz** *m* sable-fur.

Zofe *f* lady's maid.

zöger|n *itr* to linger, to tarry, to delay; (*schwanken*) to hesitate; (*trödeln*) to loiter; **-n** *n*, **-ung** *f* tarrying, delay, hesitation.

Zögling *m* pupil, scholar.

Zölibat *m, n* celibacy.

Zoll *m* (*Maß*) inch; (*Abgabe*) (import) duty, customs *pl*; (*-tarif, pl Zölle*) tariff; (*-amt, -behörde*) Customs *pl*; (*Brücken-*) toll; (*Zins u. fig*) tribute; **-abfertigung** *f* clearance, permit; **-abgaben** *f pl* custom-duties *pl*; **-amt** *n* custom-house; **--lich** *a*: *--liche Untersuchung* customs inspection; **-angabe** *f* bill of entry; **-aufschlag** *m* additional duty; **-beamte(r)** *m* custom-house officer, customs officer, *Am auch* collector; **-begleitschein** *m* bond note; **-deklaration** *f* customs declaration; *mar* entry; **-einfuhrbescheinigung** *f* bill of entry; certificate of clearance inwards; **-einnahmen** *f pl* customs receipts *pl*; **-einnehmer** *m* toll collector; customs receiver; **-en** *tr* to pay, to give; *jdm Dank --* to thank; *jdm Beifall --* to applaud; *jdm Achtung --* to show respect; **-erhebungsverfahren** *n* method of levying duty; **-erhöhung** *f* tariff increase; **-ermäßigung** *f* tariff reduction; **-fahndungsbeamter** *m* preventive officer; **-flughafen** *m* customs airport; **-frei** *a* duty-free; **--heit** *f* exemption from duty; **-gebiet** *n* customs-district; **-gebühr** *f* duty; **-gesetz** *n* tariff law; **-grenze** *f* customs-frontier; **-hafen** *m* customs port; **-haus** *n* customs-house; **-hinterziehung** *f* defraudation of the customs; *-- begehen* to evade customs duty; **-inspektor** *m* customs official; **-kontrolle** *f* customs examination; **-krieg** *m* tariff-war, war of taxes; **-maß** *n* inch-measure, measure in inches; **-papiere** *n pl* customs documents *pl*; clearance papers *pl*; **-pflichtig** *a* liable to duty, *Am* customable; **-plombe** *f* seal; **-politik** *f* customs policy; **-revision** *f* customs examination; **-satz** *m* customs tariff rate; **-schein** *m* customs receipt; certificate of clearance; **-schiff** *n* revenue cutter; **-schranke** *f* customs (*od* tariff) barrier; turnpike; **-schutz** *m* tariff protection; **-speicher** *m* bonded warehouse; **-stab, -stock** *m* rule; inch scale; **-stempel** *m* duty mark; **-tarif** *m* tariff; **- u. Paßabfertigung** *f* customs and passport clearing; **-untersuchung** *f* customs inspection (*od* examination); **-verband, -verein** *m* tariff-union; **-vergünstigungen** *f pl* preferential tariff; **-verschluß** *m* bond; customs seal; *unter --* in bond; **-vertrag** *m* tariff agreement; **-verwaltung** *f* administration of customs; **-wesen** *n* customs service.

Zöllner *m* customs collector; (*Bibel*) publican.

Zone *f* zone; (*Landstrich*) region, *Am* belt; *tele Am* zone; (*Abschnitt*) section; (*Klima*) climate; (*Gebiet*) district; *heiße -* torrid zone; *gemäßigte -* temperate zone; *befestigte -* fortified zone; *neutrale -* neutral zone; *aero* apron; *stille -* (*radio*) skip (*od* dead) zone; *verbotene -* prohibited zone; *- der Passatwinde* trade-wind belt; *- der Windstillen* doldrums *pl*; **-neinteilung** *f* division into zones; **-nförmig** *a* zonal; **-ngrenze** *f* zonal boundary; **-ntarif** *m* zone-tariff; **-nzusammenschluß** *m* zone merger.

Zoolog|e *m* zoologist; **-ie** *f* zoology; **-isch** *a* zoological.

Zopf *m* plait, tress; pigtail; *fig* pedantry, formality; red tape; *falscher -* switch; *sie trägt Zöpfe* she wears her hair plaited (*od* in plaits); **-band** *n* pigtail-ribbon; **-ig** *a fig* pedantic; old-fashioned.

Zorn *m* anger; (*heftiger -*) wrath; (*Wut*) rage; (*Erbitterung*) ranco(u)r (*über* of); (*Gereiztheit*) temper, *Am fam* dander; (*Entrüstung*) resentment (*über* at); *in - versetzen* to enrage; *in - geraten* to get angry, to fly into a passion; *seinen - auslassen* to vent o.'s anger upon; *zum - reizen* to make angry, to provoke; **-anfall, -ausbruch** *m* fit of anger; **-entbrannt** *a* boiling with rage; **-ig** *a* angry, *fam* mad (*über* at, *auf* with); in a passion; **-röte** *f* angry flush, flush of anger.

Zot|e *f* obscenity, smutty joke; *-en reißen* to talk smut; **-enhaft, -ig** *a* smutty, obscene, filthy, *Am* racy; **-enreißer** *m* obscene talker.

Zott|e(l) *f* rag, tuft, lock; **-eln** *itr* to toddle, to loiter, to shuffle along; **-(el)ig** *a* shaggy; (*verfilzt*) matted.

zu *prp* (*Ruhe*) at; (*Richtung, Ziel*) in, on, to; (*hinzutretend*) along with, in addition to; (*neben*) beside, next to; (*für*) for; (*Verhältnis*) by; (*bis zu*) up to; (*mit*) with; *- Hause* at home; *zur rechten Zeit* at the right time; *- e-m Preise* at a price; *zur Ansicht schicken* to send on approval; *möchtest du zum Kaffee etw essen?* would you like s. th. with your coffee? *- Fuß* on foot; *- Wasser* by water; at sea; *- Bett* to bed; *zum Beispiel* for instance; *zum letzten Mal* for the last time; *zum Essen einladen* to invite for dinner; *was essen Sie zum Frühstück?* what do you eat for breakfast? *zum Glück* fortunately; *- Hunderten* by hundreds; *das Blatt* *ist 4 ~ 6* the sheet is four by six; *setzen Sie sich ~ mir* sit down beside me; *~ fürchten haben* to have to fear; *da ist nichts ~ machen* there's nothing you can do; *es ist zum Weinen* it's enough to make you cry; *~ zweien* two of us; by (*od* in) twos, in couples; *~ Ende sein* to be over; *ich habe Lust zum Singen* I feel like singing; *zum Präsidenten wählen* to elect president; *ab u. ~* now and then; *zum mindesten* at least; *zum Teil* partly; *zur Genüge* only too well; *zum Ersten, zum Zweiten, zum Dritten!* going, going, gone! *sich jdn zum Feinde machen* to make an enemy of s. o.; *~ Gesicht bekommen* to catch a sight of; *zur Hälfte* by half; *adv* (*allzu*) too; (*Richtung*) towards; to; (*geschlossen*) shut, closed; *gar ~* far too; *~ sehr, ~ viel* too much; *~ wenig* too little; *immer ~!* go on! on! *Tür ~!* shut the door, please!

zu|allererst *adv* first of all, before all; **~allerletzt** *adv* last of all; **~bauen** *tr* to wall up (*od* in); **~behör** *n, m* accessories *pl*, appurtenances *pl*, fixture, fittings *pl*, *Am* fixings *pl*; mountings *pl*; belongings *pl*; trimmings *pl*; (*Zugabe*) appendage; (*Vorhänge usw*) soft furnishings *pl*; (*Wasserleitung, Drähte*) *Am* furnishings *pl*; *ohne ~~* plain, bare; *Wohnung von 4 Zimmern mit ~~* four-roomed flat with all conveniences; **~~industrie** *f* accessories industry; **~~teil** *m* accessory part; attachment; component; spare part; **~beißen** *irr itr* to bite (at); (*Hund*) to snap (at); (*tüchtig essen*) to eat away, to tuck in; **~bekommen** *irr tr* to get in addition.

Zuber *m* tub.

zu|bereiten *tr* to prepare; (*Speise*) to cook, to dress; (*Getränk*) to mix; *tech* to finish, to make ready; to dress; **~bereitung** *f* preparation; dressing; cooking; mixing; **~biegen** *irr tr* to close by bending; **~billigen** *tr* to grant, to concede; to allow; **~binden** *irr tr* to tie up; *jdm die Augen ~~* to blindfold s. o.; **~blasen** *irr tr: jdm etw ~~* to suggest s. th. to s. o.; **~bläser** *m* prompter; **~bleiben** *irr itr* to remain closed (*od* shut); **~blinzeln** *itr* to wink at; **~bringen** *irr tr* to bring to; to take to; *die Zeit mit etw ~~* to spend (*od* pass) the time; **~bringer** *m tech* feeder, conveyer; *attr* feeder; **~~dienst** *m* feeder service; **~~flugzeug** *n* feeder-service airplane; feeder-liner; **~~förderband** *n* delivery-belt conveyer; **~~linie** *f* auxiliary field railway; *aero* feeder line; **~~pumpe** *f* transfer pump; **~~wagen** *m* transfer car, travel(l)ing hopper; **~~zug** *m Am* shuttle-train; **~buße** *f* contribution.

Zucht *f* (*Tätigkeit*) breeding, rearing; (*Bienen*) culture; (*Pflanzen*) cultivation; (*Rasse*) breed, race, stock; (*Bakterien*) culture; (*Heranziehen*) growing; (*Erziehung*) education; (*Manns~*) discipline; drill; training; (*Züchtigkeit*) decency, propriety, decorum; (*Bescheidenheit*) modesty; *in ~ halten* to keep in hand; to keep strict discipline; **~buch** *n* stud-book; **~bulle** *m* bull; **~haus** *n* house of correction; jail; bridewell; *Am* penitentiary; (*Strafe*) penal servitude; imprisonment with (*Am* at) hard labo(u)r; **~häusler** *m*, **~~in** *f* convict; **~hausstrafe** *f* penal servitude; **~hengst** *m* stud-horse, stallion; **~los** *a* undisciplined; (*liederlich*) dissolute; (*unordentlich*) disorderly; (*widersetzlich*) insubordinate; **~~igkeit** *f* want of discipline; licentiousness; insubordination; **~meister** *m* task-master, disciplinarian; **~mittel** *n* means of correction; **~rute** *f* scourge, rod (of correction); **~sau** *f* brood-sow; **~schaf** *n* ewe (for breeding); **~stier** *m* bull (for breeding); **~stute** *f* brood-mare; **~vieh** *n* breeding cattle; **~wahl** *f* (natural) selection.

zücht|en *tr* (*Tiere*) to breed; to rear; to raise; (*Pflanzen*) to cultivate, to grow; to rear; **~er** *m* (*Vieh etc*) breeder; (*Pflanzen*) grower, cultivator; (*Bienen*) keeper; **~ung** *f* (*Vieh etc*) breeding; (*Pflanzen*) cultivation, growing; (*Zuchtwahl*) selection.

zücht|ig *a* modest, chaste; **~~keit** *f* chastity; modesty; **~igen** *tr* to correct, to punish, to chastise, to lash; (*körperlich*) to flog; **~igung** *f* chastisement, correction, punishment; flogging.

zuck|en *itr* to twitch; (*auffahren*) to jerk, *Am fam* to yank; (*ausschlagen*) to kick; (*heftig klopfen*) to palpitate; (*krankhaft*) to move convulsively; (*vor Schmerz*) to wince; (*Blitz*) to flash; (*flackern*) to flicker; (*zittern*) to quiver; to quake; (*zerren*) to tweak; (*ruckweise ziehen*) to pluck (at); (*hastig zugreifen*) to snatch; *tr: die Achsel ~* to shrug o.'s shoulders; *es zuckte ihm in allen Gliedern* (*fig*) he was itching (to do s. th.); *sie zuckte mit keiner Wimper* she didn't blink an eye, *Am* she didn't bat an eyelash; *ohne zu ~~* without wincing; **~~d** *a* convulsive, spasmodic; **~en** *n*, **~ung** *f* convulsion, twitch; quiver.

zücken *tr: den Degen ~* to draw the sword (upon).

Zucker *m* sugar; *gestoßener ~* pounded sugar; **~artig** *a* sugary; **~ausbeute** *f* yield of sugar; **~bäcker** *m* confectioner; **~bäckerei** *f* confectioner's shop, sugar pastry; **~bestimmung** *f* determination of sugar; **~bildung** *f* formation of sugar, saccharification; (*biologisch*) glycogenesis; **~brezel** *f* sweet cracknel; **~brot** *n* sweet rusk; sugar loaf; sweet bread; **~büchse, ~dose** *f* sugar-basin, sugar-box, *Am* sugar bowl; **~dicksaft** *m* molasses *pl*, treacle; **~erbse** *f* sweet pea, sugar-pea; (*~kügelchen*) sugar-plum, sweet, comfit; **~fabrik** *f* sugar-mill, sugar-factory; **~~ation** *f* sugar manufacture; **~form** *f* sugar mo(u)ld; **~gärung** *f* fermentation of sugar; **~gebackene(s)** *n* confectionery; **~gehalt** *m* sugar content; **~~messer** *m* saccharimeter; **~geschmack** *m* sugary taste; **~gewinnung** *f* extraction of sugar, sugar manufacture; **~guß** *m* crust of sugar, sugar-icing; **~haltig** *a* containing sugar, sacchariferous; **~hut** *m* sugar-loaf; **~ig** *a* sugary; **~kandis** *m* sugar-candy; **~krank** *a*, **~kranke(r)** *m* diabetic; **~krankheit** *f* diabetes *pl mit sing*; **~lösung** *f* sugar solution; syrup; **~mandel** *f* sugared almond; **~melone** *f* musk-melon; **~n** *tr* to sugar, to sweeten; **~pflanzung** *f* sugar-plantation; **~plätzchen** *n* lozenge, drop; **~raffinerie** *f* sugar refinery; **~rohr** *n* sugar-cane; **~~melasse** *f* cane molasses *pl*; **~~rückstände** *m pl* bagasse; **~~saft** *m* cane juice; **~rübe** *f* (*weiße*) sweet turnip; (*rote*) beet-root, sugar-beet; **~~nsaft** *m* sugar-beet juice; **~~nschnitzel** *n* sugar-beet cossette; **~~nzucker** *m* beet(-root) sugar; **~saft** *m* syrup; **~säure** *f* saccharic acid; **~schale** *f* sugar-basin, *Am* sugar bowl; **~sieden** *n* sugar-refining; **~sieder** *m* sugar-refiner; **~~ei** *f* sugar-refinery; **~sirup** *m* treacle, *Am* molasses *pl*; **~stoff** *m* saccharine matter; **~süß** *a* sweet as sugar, sugared; **~umwandlung** *f* sugar metabolism; **~ware** *f*, **~werk**, **~zeug** *n* confectionery, comfits *pl*, sweets *pl*, sweet meats *pl*, *Am* candy; **~wasser** *n* sugared-water; **~zange** *f* sugar-tongs *pl*.

zu|dämmen *tr* to dam up; **~decken** *tr* to cover (up); to put a lid on; (*verbergen*) to conceal; **~dem** *adv* besides, moreover, in addition; **~denken** *irr tr* to destine, to design (for); *jdm etw ~~* to intend s. th. as a present for s. o.; **~diktieren** *tr* (*Strafe*) to inflict (on), to impose (on); **~drang** *m* crowding, rush (to), run (*zu* on); **~drehen** *tr* to turn off; *el* to switch out; *den Rücken ~~* to turn o.'s back (up)on; **~dringlich** *a* importunate; intruding; obtrusive; (*naseweis*) forward; (*aufdringlich*) officious; *Am sl* fresh; *sei nicht so ~~* don't be such a pest; **~~keit** *f* importunity; obtrusiveness; officiousness; forwardness; **~drücken** *tr* to close; to shut; *ein Auge ~~* to **wink at** s. th., to connive at, to overlook, to let it pass.

zu|eignen *tr* (*Buch*) to dedicate; *sich etw ~~* to appropriate, to seize to o. s.; (*widerrechtlich*) to usurp; **~eignung** *f* dedication; appropriation; **~~sschrift** *f* dedicatory letter, dedication; **~eilen** *itr* to run up to, to run towards; to hasten to; **~einander** *adv* to each other; **~erkennen** *irr tr* to decree; to adjudicate; (*verleihen*) to confer (up)on; to allot; (*zumessen*) to allot; (*zusprechen*) to adjudge, to award; *e-e Entschädigung ~~* to award damages; *jdm e-e Strafe ~~* to sentence s. o. to; **~erkennung** *f* award, adjudg(e)ment, adjudication; **~erst** *adv* (*als erster*) first; (*zunächst*) at first; firstly, in the first place; first of all; above all; *wer ~~ kommt, mahlt ~~* first come, first served; **~erteilen** *tr* to award, to allot; to assign.

zu|fächeln *tr* (*Kühlung*) to fan to s. o.; **~fahren** *irr itr* to drive on, to go on; *auf jdn ~~* to rush at s. o.; to drive towards; **~fahrt** *f* drive in; **~~srampe** *f* approach ramp; **~~sstraße** *f* approach (road), access road; **~fall** *m* chance; accident; (*reiner ~~*) *fig* toss-up; (*Pech*) tough (*od* bad) break; (*Ereignis*) occurrence, event; (*Zusammentreffen*) coincidence; (*zufälliger Todesfall*) casualty; *durch ~~* by accident, accidentally; at (*od* by) haphazard, by chance; casually; *durch e-n glücklichen ~~* (*fam*) by a fluke; *ein glücklicher ~~* a lucky hit; *ein unglücklicher ~~* misfortune; **~fallen** *irr itr* (*Tür*) to shut (of) itself; to close; (*zuteil werden*) to fall to, to fall on; *jdm ~~* to fall to s. o.'s share; (*~fließen*) to accrue to; (*Aufgabe*) to devolve upon; *die Augen fallen mir zu* I cannot keep my eyes open; **~fällig** *a* (*unwesentlich*) accidental; incidental; (*gelegentlich*) casual, by chance; (*unerwartet*) fortuitous; *adv* by chance; at random; at (*od* by) haphazard; *~~ treffen Am* to run into; *ich war ~~ da* I happened to be there; **~~erweise** *adv* by chance; **~~keit** *f* chance; casualness; accidentalness; casualty; fortuitousness; contingency; **~~keitsfehler** *m* accidental error; **~fallsergebnis** *n* fortuitous result; **~fallsstimme** *f parl* snap-vote; **~fallstreffer** *m* chance (*od* accidental) hit; **~falten** *tr* to fold up; **~fassen** *itr* to seize s. th., to catch on to s. th.; *fig* to set to work, to lend a hand; **~flicken** *tr* to patch up; **~fliegen** *irr itr* to fly to; (*Tür*) to slam, to bang; **~fließen** *irr itr* to flow to (*od* towards); to flow into; (*Worte*) to come readily (to); *~~ lassen* to grant, to afford, to bestow on; **~flucht** *f* refuge, shelter, recourse; *seine ~~ zu etw nehmen* to resort to, to have recourse to, to take refuge with; **~~sort** *m* retreat, asylum, place of refuge (*od* resort), *Am* hangout, *sl* funk-hole; **~fluß** *m* influx; supply (of goods); (*Nebenfluß*) tributary; (*Eintritt*) admission; *tech* feed; **~~behälter** *m* feed tank; **~~gebiet** *n* basin; **~~menge** *f* rate of flow; **~~regler** *m* flow regulator; **~~rohr** *n* feed pipe; **~flüstern** *itr* to whisper to; (*soufflieren*) to prompt; **~folge** *prp* according to; in consequence of, owing to; on the strength of; **~frieden** *a* satisfied, content(ed); *jdn ~~ lassen* to let alone, to leave in peace, to leave undisturbed; *sich ~~ geben* to acquiesce (in), to rest content with; **~~heit** *f* satisfaction, contentment; **~~stellen** *tr* to content, to satisfy; *schwer ~zustellen* difficult to please; **~~stellend** *a* satisfactory; **~~stellung** *f* satisfaction; **~frieren** *irr itr* to freeze up (*od* over); **~fügen** *tr* to add (to); (*antun*) to cause, to do; (*Böses*) to inflict pain upon; **~fuhr** *f* supply, supplies *pl*; (*Zuwachs*) addition; (*Lebensmittel*) provisions *pl*; (*Einfuhr*) importation; (*Transport*) conveyance; *tech* feed; *el* input; *jdm die ~~ abschneiden* to cut off supplies; **~~gleis** *n* leading-in line; **~~regler** *m* supply valve; **~~stockung** *f* interruption of supply; **~~straße** *f* road approach, supply road; **~führen** *tr* to lead to, to bring to; (*Waren*) to supply; (*beschaffen*) to procure; (*transportieren*) to carry into, to convey; (*hinzufügen*) to add; (*liefern*) to deliver; *phys* to conduct; (*Draht*) to lead in; *tech* to feed; **~führer** *m* feed mechanism; **~führung** *f* supply; provision, conveyance; *el* lead; *tech* feed; inlet; (*Linie*) supply line; **~~sdraht** *m el* lead wire; **~~skabel** *n* leading-in cable; **~~sleitung** *f* supply main; **~~srohr** *n* supply pipe; **~~sschiene** *f* conductor bar; **~~svorrichtung** *f* feeding device; **~füllen** *tr* (*Loch*) to fill up; (*hinzugießen*) to pour to.

Zug *m* pull, tug; stress; (*ziehen*) drawing, pulling; stretch; (*~kraft*) traction, tension; propelling force; (*Spannung*) tension; strain; (*Schub*) thrust; (*Schnur*) strap; (*Schornstein*) flue; (*Ofen*) draught, *Am* draft; (*Bewegung*) motion; *rail* train, *Am* the cars *pl*; *abfahrender, fahrplanmäßiger ~* starting, regular (*od* scheduled) train; *verspäteter ~* delayed train; *durchgehender ~* direct (*od* through) train; (*Geleit*) *mil* escort; *mar* convoy; (*Leichen~*) funeral procession; (*Fest~*) festive procession; (*Reihe, Gruppe*) file; succession; row; group; flock; team; (*Um~*) procession; *pol* manifestation, demonstration; (*Fahrzeuge*) procession; *mil* (*Feld~*) campaign, expedition; (*Infanterie*) platoon; (*Kavallerie*) troup; (*Artillerie*) section; (*Trupp*) section, squad; (*Arbeiter*) gang; (*Schar, mus*) band; (*Gewehr*) groove; rifling; (*Marsch*) march(ing); (*Vögel*) passage, flight, migration; flock; (*Rudel*) troop, pack; herd; (*Häuser*) row; (*Richtung*) trend, direction; tendency; (*~ der Wolken*) drift; (*Luft~*) draught, *Am* draft, current of air; (*Orgel*) stop, register; (*Schrift*) stroke, dash; (*Schnörkel*) flourish; (*Berg~*) range; (*Schluck*) draught, *Am* draft; gulp; (*Rauchen*) whiff, puff, pull; (*Schach~*) move; (*Gesichts~*) feature, trait; (*Anwandlung*) impulse, bent; (*Neigung*) inclination; disposition; (*Einfall*) idea, brain-wave; whim; (*Geste*) gesture; (*Charakter~*) trait; characteristic; (*Hauptzüge, Umriß*) outlines *pl*; *der ~ der Zeit* the sign of the time; *das ist ein ~ unserer Zeit* that's characteristic of our times; *auf e-n ~* at one draught; *im ~e* in the course of; *in e-m ~* (*fig*) at one stroke, straight off; uninterruptedly; at a stretch; *mit dem ~ abfahren* to leave by train; *in e-m ~* in (*Am* on) a train; *in e-n ~ einsteigen* to board (*od* to enter, to get (on) the train; *der ~ hat Verspätung* the train is late (*od* overdue); *jdn zum ~ begleiten* to see s. o. off; *im ~e sein* to be in full swing; *er ist jetzt gut im ~* (*Am fam*) he's going strong now; *~ in etw bringen* to set going, to start; *~ um ~* without delay, uninterruptedly; *in vollen Zügen* thoroughly, deeply; *in den letzten Zügen liegen* to be at o.'s last gasp, to breathe o.'s last; **~abfertigungsdienst** *m* train dispatch service; **~abteil** *n* railway compartment; **~anker** *m* tie rod (*od* bar); through bolt; **~artikel** *m com* popular article, draw; **~band** *n* draw-string; (*Fallschirm*) shock cord; **~beanspruchung** *f* tensile stress, stretching strain; **~begleitpersonal** *n* train-staff, *Am* train crew; **~beleuchtung** *f* train lighting; **~bereich** *m mil* platoon sector; **~bolzen** *m* set bolt; **~brücke** *f* drawbridge; **~dienst** *m* train service; **~~leiter** *m* train dispatcher; **~druckverhältnis** *n* ratio of tension and thrust; **~elastizität** *f* elasticity of extension; **~entgleisung** *f* derailment, *Am* train wreck; **~fähre** *f* cable ferry; *rail* train ferry; **~feder** *f* bolt (*od* tension) spring; (*Uhr*) barrel spring; **~festigkeit** *f* breaking (*od* tensile) strength; **~~suntersuchung** *f* tensile-strength test; **~flugzeug** *n* tractor airplane; **~folge** *f* block system; order of marching; **~frei** *a* non-draught; **~führer** *m rail* guard, *Am* conductor; *mil* platoon (*od* section) commander (*od* leader); **~gespräch** *n* train call; **~gitter** *n* space-charge grid; **~graben** *m* drainage ditch; **~gurt** *f* trace; tension flange (*od* chord); **~haken** *m* trace hook, pintle; **~hebel** *m* draw (*od* traction) lever; **~ig** *a* (*Fläche*) windy; (*Zimmer*) draughty, *Am* drafty; **~kanal** *m* (*Schornstein*) flue; **~kette** *f* drag (*od* hauling) chain; **~knopf** *m* pull knob, push button; **~kraft** *f* tensile force; tractive power; propeller thrust; *fig* attraction; (*Reklame*) attention value; **~~wagen** *m* half-track carrier; **~kräftig** *a* attractive; with box-office value; **~leine** *f* towing-rope, drag-rope; **~leistung** *f* tractive power; (*Tiere*) draught efficiency; **~linie** *f* tractrix; **~loch** *n* air hole, air vent; **~luft** *f* draught, current of air; **~maschine** *f* prime mover, traction engine, tractor; **~messer** *m* tension dynamometer; **~mittel** *n* tension medium; *fig* attraction, draw, means of attraction; **~ochse** *m* draught ox; **~personal** *n* railway personnel (*od* staff), train crew; **~pferd** *n* draught horse, *Am* drafter; **~pflaster** *n* blister; **~regler** *m* draught regulator; **~richtung** *f* direction in which the train runs; *tech* trajectory motion; **~ring** *m* tugging ring; **~schaffner** *m* train conductor; **~scheit** *n* swingletree; **~schieber** *m* chimney damper; **~schnur** *f* draw (*od* pull) cord; **~schranke** *f* railway gate, barrier; **~schraube** *f* tractor screw (*od* *Am* propeller); **~seil** *n* traction rope; *mar* hawser; **~stange** *f* pull rod; **~stiefel** *m pl* elastic-sided boots *pl*; **~streife** *f* train patrol; **~stück** *n* popular play, draw, *Am* hit; **~telephon** *n* train telephone; **~tier** *n* draught animal; **~trupp** *m mil* platoon headquarters personnel; platoon command group personnel; **~unfall** *m* train accident; **~verkehr** *m* railway (*Am* railroad) traffic; **~versuch** *m* tensile test; **~vieh** *n* draught-cattle; **~vogel** *m* bird of passage; **~wache** *f* train guard; **~wagen** *m* tractor; **~weise** *adv mil* by platoons; **~widerstand** *m* tractional resistance; **~wind** *m* draught, *Am* draft; **~winde** *f* tackle; pulley, windlass; **~wirkung** *f* pulling action; **~zünder** *m* pull igniter.

Zu|gabe *f* addition, adjunct; (*zum Gewicht*) makeweight, surplus; *theat* repetition, encore; *com Am* lagn(i)appe; (*Zuschlag*) extra; (*Ergänzung*) supplement; (*Prämie*) premium; (*Bonus*) bonus; (*beim Tausch*) boot money; *als ~~* into the bargain; **~gang** *m* access, approach; (*Weg*) avenue; (*Tür*) entry, entrance, door; (*Zunahme*) increase; (*Waren*) incoming stocks *pl*; (*Bücher*) accessions *pl*; *~gänge eintragen* to enter books on a list of accessions; *~~ haben zu* to have accession to; **~~sgraben** *m* approach trench; **~~sleiter** *f* approach ladder; **~~snummer** *f* accession number; **~~sregister** *n* accession book; **~~sweg** *m* approach; **~gänglich** *a* accessible; (*benutzbar*) available; (*Personen*) affable, of easy access; approachable, open to, get-at-able.

zu|geben *irr tr* to add; *com* to give into the bargain; (*erlauben*) to allow. to permit; (*eingestehen*) to confess; (*anerkennen*) to admit, to recognize, *Am* to concede; **~gegen** *a* present (*bei* at); **~gehen** *irr itr* to go on, to walk faster; (*sich schließen*) to shut; (*geschehen*) to happen, to take place; *auf jdn ~~* to move towards, to go up to; to reach s. o.; *mir ist ein Brief ~gegangen* a letter came to my hand; *~~ lassen* to transmit, to forward to; *so geht es in der Welt zu* that is the way of the world; *es geht nicht mit rechten Dingen zu* this is not all fair and aboveboard, there's something fishy around here; *hier geht es lustig zu* there are fine goings-on; you are having a good time; **~gehören** *itr* to belong to; *jdm ~~* to appertain to; **~gehörig** *a* belonging to, appertaining; accompanying, inherent, proper; respective; **~~keit** *f* membership (*zu* of), affiliation (to); *fig* relationship; **~geklinkt sein** to be on the latch; **~geknöpft** *a* reserved, uncommunicative; **~gelassen** *a* (*Rechtsanwalt*) called (*Am* admitted) to the bar.

Zügel *m* rein; (*des Reitpferdes*) bridle; *fig* curb, restraint, check; *im ~ halten* to keep in check; *die ~ schießen lassen* to give (a horse) his head; to let loose (o.'s passions); **~los** *a* unbridled; *fig* unrestrained; (*ausschweifend*) licentious; **~losigkeit** *f* licentiousness, dissoluteness; **~n** *tr* (*auch fig*) to bridle, to curb; to check.

zuge|sellen *tr, r* to join, to associate with; **~sprochen** *a* awarded; assigned; *~~es Telegramm* phonogram; **~standenermaßen** *adv* admittedly, *Am* concededly; **~ständnis** *n* admission; concession; compromise; **~stehen** *irr tr* to admit, to concede, to grant; **~tan** *a* attached to, devoted to, fond of; **~wanderte(r)** *m* immigrant.

zu|gießen *irr itr* to pour on; *tr* to fill up with; **~gittern** *tr* to rail in; **~gleich** *adv* at the same time; along with, together with.

zu|graben *irr tr* to cover with earth; **~greifen** *irr itr* to seize, to take hold of, to grasp (at), *fam* to grab; (*helfen*) to help, to lend a hand, to take a hand at; (*Gelegenheit*) to take the opportunity; (*bei Tisch*) to help o. s.; ~**griff** *m* grip, clutch; *sicher vor unbefugtem* ~~ tamperproof.

zugu'nsten *adv* (*von od mit Genitiv*) in favo(u)r of, for the benefit of.

zugu'te *adv:* ~ *halten* to allow for; to take into consideration; (*jdm etw*) to account to s. o. for s. th.; (*verzeihen*) to pardon s. o. s. th.; *jdm* ~ *kommen* to be an advantage to; to stand in good stead; *Am* to inure to s. o.; *jdm etw* ~ *kommen lassen* to give s. o. the benefit of; *sich etw* ~ *tun* (*od halten*) *auf* to be proud of; to pique o. s. on s. th; to make a merit of.

zu|haben *irr itr* to have shut (*od* closed); to be closed; *der Laden hat schon zu* the shop has closed already; *sie hatte die Augen zu* her eyes were closed; (*Rock*) to have (his coat) buttoned up; *noch etw* ~~ *wollen* to want s. th. besides (*od* into the bargain *od* thrown in); ~**haken,** ~**häkeln** *tr* to hook (up); ~**halten** *irr tr* to keep closed (*od* shut); to close; *jdm den Mund* ~~ to stop s. o.'s mouth; *die Hand* ~~ to clench o.'s fist; *sich die Ohren* ~~ to stop o.'s ears; *sich die Augen* ~~ to close o.'s eyes; *itr* ~~ *auf* to make for; to go straight to; *mar* to steer for; ~**hälter** *m* souteneur, procurer, *sl* pimp, bully, fancy (man); free holder; ~~**ei** *f* pandering; ~~**in** *f* procuress; *Am sl* assignator, flesh peddler, auntie; ~**haltung** *f* (*beim Schloß*) tumbler; bolt keeper; ~~**sfeder** *f* tumbler spring; ~~**sschloß** *n* tumbler lock; ~**hämmern** *tr* to hammer down; ~**ha'nden** *adv* (close) at hand; ready, in readiness; in hand, to hand; ~**hängen** *tr* to hang over; to hang (*od* to cover) with a curtain; ~**hauen** *tr* to form, to shape by hewing; (*Schwein*) to cut up; (*Stein*) to carve; (*zurichten*) to trim; *itr* to strike (at), to thrash; *hau zu!* strike hard! *fam* give it them! ~**hau'f** *adv poet* together; ~**hause** *n* a home of o.'s own; (at) home; ~**heften** *tr* to stitch up; ~**heilen** *itr* to heal up, to close; ~**hilfenahme** *f: unter* (*ohne*) ~~ *von* with (without) the help of; ~**hinterst** *adv* at the end, at the very end, last of all; ~**hören** *itr* to listen to, to attend to; *nun hören Sie mal zu!* now listen! *sie hat nicht zugehört* she wasn't listening; *sehr genau* ~~ to be all ears; ~**hörer** *m* auditor, hearer; listener; *die* ~~ audience, attendance; ~~**raum** *m* auditory, lecture-room; ~~**schaft** *f* audience; *ein Rundfunkansager hat e-e* ~~ *von Millionen* a radio announcer has an audience of millions; ~**innerst** *adv* quite inside, innermost; ~**jagen** *itr* to speed (*od* to rush) towards; ~**jauchzen,** ~**jubeln** *itr* to shout to, to hail, to applaud, to cheer.

zu|kehren *tr* to turn to (*od* towards); *jdm das Gesicht* ~~ to face s. o.; *jdm den Rücken* ~~ to turn o.'s back (up)on s. o.; ~**ketteln** *tr* to chain up; ~**kitten** *tr* to cement up; ~**klappen** *tr* to slam, to bang (to); to close (with a clap); ~**klatschen** *itr: jdm Beifall* ~~ to applaud s. o. (by clapping o.'s hands); ~**kleben,** ~**kleistern** *tr* to paste up; to glue up; to gum, to fasten down; (*Brief*) to seal; ~**klemmen** *tr* to squeeze together; ~**klinken** *tr* to latch (up); ~**knöpfen** *tr* to button up; *er ist sehr zugeknöpft fig* he is very reserved; ~**knüpfen** *tr* to tie up; ~**kommen** *irr itr* (*hinkommen, erreichen*) to come to s. o.; to come to hand; (*zuteil werden, angehören*) to belong to, to accrue to; to fall to o.'s share; (*gebühren, geziemen*) to befit, to become, to be due to; to be suitable to; *ihr kommt es zu zu handeln* it is for her to act; *dieser Titel kommt ihm nicht zu* he has no right to this title; ~~ *auf* to approach, to come to; to step up to; *jdm etw* ~~ *lassen* to let s. o. have s. th.; (*schenken*) to make a present of; (*senden*) to forward s. th. to s. o.; *jedem geben, was ihm* ~*kommt* to give every one his due; ~**korken** *tr* to cork (up), to stop; ~**kost** *f* (*Gemüse etc*) vegetables *pl* etc; preserves *pl.*

Zu|kunft *f* future; time to come; *gram* future tense; *für die* ~~ for the future; *in* ~~ in future; after this, henceforth; eventually; *in naher* ~~ in the near future; *der Mann der* ~~ the coming man; *e-e große* ~~ *haben* to have a great future; *die* ~~ *lesen* to read the future; *in die* ~~ *sehen* to look into the future; *die* ~~ *voraussagen* to predict (*od* to foretell *od* to prophesy) the future; *die* ~~ *trägt* (*od birgt od hat*) *Freud od Leid im Schoße* the future holds (*od* contains *od* has in store) good or evil; ~**künftig** *a* future; (*voraussichtlich*) prospective; (*nächst*) next; *mein* ~~*er, meine* ~~*e* my intended; *an ein* ~~*es Leben glauben* to believe in a future life; ~~ *adv* in future; for the future; ~~**hin** *adv* for the future; ~**kunftsfreudig** *a* optimistic; ~**kunftskrieg** *m* war of the future; ~**kunftsmöglichkeiten** *f pl* prospects *pl*; ~**kunftsmusik** *f fig* dreams of the future; castles in the air; ~**kunftspläne** *m pl* plans for the future; ~**kunftsroman** *m* novel of the future.

zu|lächeln *itr* to smile at (*od* on); *tr jdm Beifall* ~~ to smile approval to s. o.; ~**ladung** *f mot, aero* useful load, pay load, safe load; *aero mil* service load; *größte* ~~ maximum load; ~**lage** *f* addition; (*Gehaltszuschuß*) increase (of salary), *Am* raise; (*Gratifikation, auch mil*) extra pay, bonus; extra allowance; *Flieger*~~ flying allowance, flying pay; *Front*~~ combat pay, front-line pay; *Lebensmittel*~~ supplementary rations; *er hat e-e* ~~ *bekommen* (*zum Gehalt*) he got an increase, *Am* he got a raise; *jdm* ~~ *geben* to raise s. o.'s salary; ~**lande** *adv: bei uns* ~~ in my (native) country; ~**langen** *itr* to stretch out o.'s hand; (*bei Tisch*) to help o. s.; *langen Sie zu!* help yourself! (*genügen*) to be sufficient; *tr jdm etw* ~~ to reach (*od* to hand) s. th. to s. o.; to give (*od* to pass) s. o. s. th.; ~**länglich** *a* adequate, sufficient; ~~**keit** *f* adequacy; sufficiency; ~**lassen** *irr tr* (*Tür*) to leave shut; *jdn* ~~ to admit; (*erlauben*) to admit; (*geschehen lassen*) to allow, to permit, to let; to grant; to tolerate; *e-e günstige Deutung* ~~ to admit of a favo(u)rable construction; *wieder* ~~ to readmit; (*bei Gericht*) to call (to the bar), *Am* to admit (to the bar); (*staatlich* ~~, *Arzt etc*) to qualify; (*Konzession geben, Fahrzeug* ~~) to license; ~*gelassenes Flugzeug* certificated aircraft; ~**lässig** *a* admissible, permissible, permitted; allowable; safe; *das ist nicht* ~~ that is not allowed; ~~*e Abweichung* tolerance, allowance; ~~*e Beanspruchung* safe stress; safe load; ~~**keit** *f* admissibility; allowableness; ~**lassung** *f* admission; permission; (*amtliche Genehmigung*) licence, *Am* license; approval; ~~**sbescheinigung** *f aero* certificate of air-worthiness; ~~**sfähigkeit** *f* acceptability; ~~**skarte** *f* admission ticket; ~~**sprüfung** *f* acceptance test; ~~**sschein** *m* licence, *Am* license; ~~**szeichen** *n* registration mark; ~**lauf** *m* (*von Kunden*) run; (*von Menschen*) crowd, concourse; rush (of people); *tech* (*Zuführung*) feed; supply; intake; ~~ *haben* to be much sought after; to be in great demand; to be popular; to be run after; to draw crowds; (*von Arzt*) to have an extensive practice; (*von Theaterstück*) to have a long run; to have a long box-office life; ~**laufen** *irr itr* to run up to, to run on; to run towards; to run faster; *lauf zu!* run on! quick! *spitz* ~~ to taper (off); (*zusammenlaufen*) to crowd, to flock; ~**laufkanal** *m* air-inlet conduit; ~**laufrohr** *n* intake pipe; feed line; ~**legen** *tr* to cover, to shut; (*hinzufügen*) to add, to increase; to put more to; *e-m Gehalt etw* ~~ to increase a salary by; *sich etw* ~~ to get, to provide o. s. with; to procure s. th.; (*kaufen*) to buy, to purchase; *sich e-n Bauch* ~~ to get stout; *sich e-e Frau* ~~ to take a wife; ~**lei'de** *adv: jdm etw* ~~ *tun* to hurt s. o., to do harm to s. o., to harm s. o.; to wrong s. o.; *er tut keiner Fliege was* ~~ he wouldn't harm a fly; *was hat er dir* ~~ *getan?* what harm has he done you? ~**leimen** *tr* to glue up, to paste up, to cement; ~**leiten** *tr* (*Wasser*) to let in, to lead to; to direct to; to supply, to lead in; to pipe into; to route; ~**leitung** *f* (*Röhre*) delivery pipe; feed pipe; supply line; *el* conductor; lead (wire); ~~**sdraht** *m* lead-in wire; ~~**skabel** *n* conducting cable; feeder; ~~**srohr** *n* feed pipe; ~**lernen** *tr* to learn in addition; to add to o.'s stock of knowledge; to go on learning; ~**le'tzt** *adv* (*als letzter*) last; (*endlich*) at last, lastly, finally, ultimately; in the end; after all; (*zum letztenmal*) for the last time; ~~ *kommen* to arrive last; ~**lie'be** *adv: jdm* ~~ for s. o.'s sake; to please s. o.; *jdm etw* ~~ *tun* to oblige s. o.; *tun Sie es mir* ~~*!* do it for my sake! ~**löten** *tr* to solder up.

Zulu *m.* ~**kaffer** *m* Zulu; ~**land** *n* Zululand; ~**sprache** *f* Zulu (language).

zum = *zu dem*; ~ *Beispiel* for instance; ~ *Glück* fortunately; ~ *Teil* partially; ~ *mindesten* at the least.

zu|machen *tr* to shut, to close; to fasten; (*Brief*) to fold; to seal; (*Loch*) to stop up; (*Rock*) to button; (*Schirm*) to shut up; (*Flasche*) to cork up; *kein Auge* ~~ *können* not to sleep a wink; *itr* (*sich beeilen*) to hurry, to make haste; *itr: mach zu!* be quick! make haste! ~**ma'l** *adv* especially (as); principally, chiefly; all the more, particularly (because); so much the more so as; ~**mauern** *tr* to wall up; to brick up; ~**mei'st** *adv* mostly, for the most part; ~**messen** *tr* to measure out; to mete out; (*Aufgabe, Tätigkeit*) to assign; (*Teil*) to apportion; *e-e Zeit* ~~ to allot a time; ~**mi'ndest** *adv* at least; ~**mu'te** *adv*: *mir ist wohl* ~~ I feel well; *mir ist nicht zum Lachen* ~~ I am not in the mood for laughing; ~**muten** *tr* to expect of s. o.; to impute; *jdm etw* ~~ to expect s. th. of s. o.; *jdm zuviel* ~~ to expect too much of s. o.; *sich zuviel* ~~ to overtask o.'s strength; to attempt too much; ~**mutung** *f* (unreasonable) demand; imputation; *das ist e-e* ~~ that's an imposition.

zu|nä'chst *adv* (*vor allem*) first, first of all; above all; (*in erster Linie*) in the first instance, to begin with; *prp* next to; close to; **~nageln** *tr* to nail up; to nail down; **~nähen** *tr* to sew up; to sew together; **~nahme** *f* increase; (*Wachstum*) growth; (*Ansteigen*) rise; (*des Mondes*) increment; (*Fortschritt*) progress, advance; **~name** *m* family name, *Am* last name; (*Beiname*) surname.

Zünd|anlage *f* ignition device, ignition system; *Abschirmung der ~~* ignition system shielding; **~anode** *f* ignition anode; **~apparat** *m* igniter; primer; (*Magnet*) magneto; **~bar** *a* inflammable; ignitable, combustible; **~~keit** *f* inflammability; **~batterie** *f* ignition battery; B battery; **~blättchen** *n pl aero mil* incendiary leaves *pl*; **~büchse** *f* fire lighter; **~dynamo** *m* ignition dynamo; **~einrichtung** *f* ignition device; **~einstellung** *f* (spark) timing; **~en** *itr, tr* to set fire to, to set on fire; to kindle, to ignite; to fire; to catch fire; *fig* (*ent~~*) to inflame; to take, to catch on; to arouse enthusiasm; *wieder ~~* to re-ignite; **~end** *a* taking, stirring, fetching; inflammatory; *~~e Rede* spirit-stirring speech; **~er** *m* (*Geschoß*) fuse; (*Sprengstoff*) detonator; (*Vorrichtung*) igniter; lighter; (*Streichholz*) match; *den ~~ einstellen* to set the fuse; *~~ scharf machen* (*bei Bomben*) to make a bomb live; **~~einstellung** *f* fuse setting; **~~empfindlichkeit** *f* sensitivity of a fuse; **~~gehäuse** *n*, **~~hülse** *f* fuse body; **~~kappe** *f* fuse cap; **~~satz** *m* fuse composition; **~~stellung** *f* fuse setting; **~fähig** *a* ignitable; **~~keit** *f* ignitability; **~flämmchen** *n* (*Gasofen*) pilot flame (*od* light); **~folge** *f mot* firing order; **~funke(n)** *m* ignition spark; **~hebel** *m* ignition lever; spark control; **~holz, ~hölzchen** *n* match; (*Sicherheits~~*) safety-match; *Holz für ~hölzer* match-wood; **~holzschachtel** *f* match-box; **~hub** *m* ignition stroke; **~hütchen** *n* percussion cap; primer; **~kabel** *n* ignition lead (*od* cable); ignition wire; detonator cable; spark(ing)-plug wire; **~kanal** *m* detonating canal, flash hole; **~kapsel** *f* detonator (cap); **~kerze** *f* sparking-plug, *Am* spark-plug, ignition plug; **~~ndichtung** *f* spark(ing)-plug washer; **~~nelektrode** *f* spark(-ing)-plug electrode; **~~nkabel** *n* ignition wire; **~~nprüfer** *m* plug tester; **~ladung** *f* detonating charge, primer charge; ignition charge; explosive charge; **~leine** *f* slow-match; **~leitung** *f* firing circuit; **~lichtmaschine** *f* magneto generator; **~loch** *n* (*Geschütz*) (flash) vent; *min* touch-hole; **~magnet** *m* (ignition) magneto; **~maschine** *f* *mot* magneto; *min* mine priming machine; **~masse** *f* inflammable composition; **~nadel** *f* primer; **~~gewehr** *n* needle-gun; **~patrone** *f* ignition cartridge; **~pfanne** *f* touch-pan; **~pulver** *n* priming-powder; **~punkt** *m* ignition point; flash point; **~~einstellung** *f* ignition timing; **~~verstellung** *f* timing; **~rohr** *n* (*bei Düsenmotor*) interconnector; **~satz** *m* detonator (*od* primer) composition; **~schalter** *m* ignition switch; **~schlüssel** *m* ignition key; **~schnur** *f* fuse (cord), (quick-) match; firing tape; **~~anzünder** *m* fuse lighter; **~schwamm** *m* amadou; tinder, spunk; **~spannung** *f* ignition tension, ignition voltage; **~spule** *f* ignition coil, ignition unit; **~~unterbrecher** *m* trembler coil; **~~nzündung** *f* coil ignition; **~stab** *m* ignition rod; **~stein** *m* flint; **~stift** *m* (*bei ~kerze*) centre (*Am* center) electrode; **~stoff** *m* combustible matter; fuel; *fig* inflammable material; **~störung** *f* ignition interference; **~strom** *m* ignition current; **~~kreis** *m* ignition circuit; **~totpunkt** *m* ignition dead centre; **~ung** *f* *min* priming; *mot* ignition; (*Explosivladung*) detonation; (*Zünder*) fuse; primer; detonator; *Doppel~~* (*aero*) dual ignition system; *~~ ausschalten* to switch off ignition; *~~ einschalten* to turn on (the) ignition; to contact; *~~ einstellen* to time the ignition; *die ~~ versagt* the ignition fails; **~~saussetzung** *f* spark failure; **~~seinstellung** *f* timing of ignition; **~~sschalter** *m* ignition switch; **~~sstörung** *f* ignition trouble; **~verstellhebel** *m* ignition lever; **~verstellung** *f* timing (of the ignition); spark adjustment; **~verteiler** *m* ignition distributor; **~vorrichtung** *f* ignition device (*od* system *od* mechanism); **~vorgang** *m* ignition process; **~zeitfolge** *f* ignition order; **~zeitpunkt** *m* ignition point; **~~verstellung** *f* ignition timing adjustment.

Zunder *m* (*Schwamm*) tinder, touchwood, spunk.

zunehmen *irr itr* (*wachsen*) to grow (larger); (*anwachsen*) to increase (*an* in); (*größer werden*) to augment; (*Fortschritte machen*) to improve, to progress; (*an Jahren*) to advance (in years); (*an Größe*) to increase (in size); (*an Kräften*) to grow stronger; to gather strength; (*an Umfang*) to grow in bulk; (*an Zahl*) to increase in number; (*länger werden*) to grow longer; to lengthen; (*dicker werden*) to put on weight (*od* flesh); to grow stouter; (*schwerer werden*) to grow heavier; to gain; (*steigen*) to rise; (*etw Übles, schlimmer werden*) to grow worse; *die Bevölkerung nimmt zu* the population is increasing; *~de Geschwindigkeit* accelerated velocity; *~de Jahre* advancing years; *~der Mond* crescent (*od* waxing) moon; *der Mond nimmt zu* the moon is getting fuller; *der Mond ist im ~* the moon is on the increase, the moon is waxing.

zuneig|en *itr* to incline to; to lean toward; *sich dem Ende ~~* to draw to a close; **~ung** *f* inclination, liking (to), attachment, affection, good will; sympathy; *~~ zu jdm fassen* to take a liking to s. o.; to feel affection for s. o.

Zunft *f* company, guild, corporation; (*im schlimmen Sinn*) clique; **~gemäß** *adv* according to the statutes of a guild; **~genosse** *m* member of a guild, freeman; **~meister** *m* head of a guild.

zünftig *a* belonging to a guild; *fig* (*erfahren*) competent, skilled; proper, thorough.

Zunge *f* tongue; (*e-r Schnalle*) catch; (*e-r Waage*) tongue; (*Fisch*) sole; (*Sprache*) tongue, language; *rail* (*Weichen~*) switch blade (*od* tongue); (*Blasinstrument*) mouthpiece, reed; *e-e belegte ~* a dirty (*od* coated) tongue; *böse ~en behaupten* malicious tongues maintain; *sie hat e-e sehr spitze ~* she has a sharp tongue; *sie hat e-e lose ~* she has a very loose tongue; *hüten Sie Ihre ~!* mind your tongue! *e-e böse ~* a wicked tongue; *e-e geläufige ~ haben* to have a glib tongue; *geräucherte ~* smoked tongue; *mir klebt die ~ am Gaumen* my throat is parched; *seine ~ im Zaum halten* to keep o.'s tongue in check; *etw auf der ~ haben* to have s. th. on the tip of o.'s tongue; *mit der ~ anstoßen* to lisp; to stutter; *das Fleisch zergeht auf der ~* the meat is so tender that it melts on the tongue; *sie läßt ihrer ~ freien Lauf* she is very outspoken; *die ~ lösen* to make s. o. speak; *das Herz auf der ~ haben* to wear o.'s heart on o.'s sleeve; *e-e feine ~ haben* to have a delicate taste; to be a gourmet; *auf die ~ bezüglich* lingual; **~nband** *n* ligament (*od* frenulum) of the tongue; **~nbein** *n* tongue bone; hyoid bone; **~nbelag** *m* fur of tongue; **~nbrecher** *m* (*Wort*) crack-jaw; **~ndrescher** *m* babbler; **~nfehler** *m* slip of the tongue; **~nfertig** *a* voluble; flippant, glib; **~~keit** *f* volubility; glib tongue; gift of the gab; **~nförmig** *a* tongue-shaped; **~nheld** *m* braggart, braggadocio; **~nlaut** *m* lingual (sound); **~nmuskel** *m* lingual muscle; **~npfeife** *f* reed-pipe; **~nrücken** *m* dorsal surface (*od* back) of tongue; **~nschiene** *f rail* switch point; **~nspitze** *f* tip of the tongue; **~nwärzchen** *n* papilla (*pl* -ae) of the tongue; **~nwurst** *f* tongue sausage; **~nwurzel** *f* base (*od* root) of the tongue; **~nzäpfchen** *n* epiglottis, uvula.

züng|eln *itr* to dart out the tongue; to shoot out the tongue; (*Schlange*) to hiss; (*Flamme*) to lick, to leap up; **~~d** *a* lambent; **~lein** *n* little tongue, tonguelet; *das ~~ an der Waage* tongue of the balance.

zu|ni'chte *adv: ~~ machen* to ruin, to destroy; (*e-n Plan*) to frustrate; *~~ werden* to come to nothing; **~nicken** *itr* to nod to; *tr Beifall ~~* to nod o.'s assent to; **~nu'tze** *adv: sich etw ~~ machen* to profit by, to avail o. s. of, to utilize s. th.; to turn to account; **~o'berst** *adv* (quite) at the top, uppermost; **~ordnen** *tr* to attach to, to appoint to; to associate with; **~packen** *itr* to grasp at; (*bei der Arbeit*) to set to (work); **~pa'ß** *adv: ~~ kommen* to come at the right moment, to come in the nick of time.

zupf|en *tr* to pull, to twitch, to tug; (*Wolle*) to pick; *jdn am Ärmel ~~* to pull s. o. by the sleeve; **~geige** *f* guitar; **~seide** *f* unravel(l)ed silk; **~wolle** *f* wood-pickings *pl*.

zu|pflöcken *tr* to peg up; **~pfropfen** *tr* to cork up; **~pichen** *tr* to pitch up.

zur = *zu der*; *~ Ansicht* on approval; *~ See* at sea, to sea.

zu|raten *itr* to advise (strongly); (*empfehlen*) to recommend; *auf ihr ~~* at her suggestion, by her advice; **~raunen** *tr* to whisper (into s. o.'s ear); to suggest; **~rechnen** *tr* to add; *jdm ~~* to attribute to; to ascribe to; (*einschließen*) to include, to class; (*Schlechtes*) to impute to; **~rechnung** *f* addition; imputation, attribution; **~~sfähig** *a* accountable; of sound mind; responsible; **~~sfähigkeit** *f* accountability, responsibility; sound state of mind; *erheblich verminderte ~~sfähigheit* considerably lessened responsibility.

zure'cht *adv* right, in (due) order, in good order; with reason, rightly; as it should (*od* ought to) be; in (due) time, in good time; ready; **~bringen** *irr tr* to put to rights, to restore; to adjust; to arrange; **~finden** *irr* (*sich*) to find o.'s way about (*Am* around); *fig* to see o.'s way in s. th.; to begin to know; *sich nicht ~~* to be lost; **~fragen**: *sich ~~* to ask o.'s way; **~helfen** *irr itr* to help; **~kommen** *irr itr* to arrive in (the nick of) time; *mit jdm ~~* to get on (well) with s. o.; *mit etw ~~* to succeed in; **~legen** *tr* to arrange; to put out, to put ready, to get out; *sich etw ~~* to figure out s. th.; *ich muß mir erst ~~, was ich sagen will* I have to figure out first what I am going to say; ~**machen** *tr* to prepare; *Am* to fix; (*für e-n Zweck*) to adapt to (*od* for); *r* to get ready; (*sich anziehen*) to dress; (*sich zurichten*) to make up; ~**rücken** *tr* to put (*od* to push *od* to move) (in)to the right place; ~**setzen** *tr* to set right; *jdm den Kopf* ~~ to bring s. o. to reason; ~**weisen** *irr tr* to direct; to show s. o. the (right) way; (*tadeln*) to set s. o. right, to put in o.'s place; to reprimand; to reprove; ~**weisung** *f* instruction; (*Tadel*) reprimand, reproof, rebuke; *fam* wigging.

zu|reden *itr* to advise, to coax; to urge (s. o. to do s. th.); (*ermutigen*) to encourage, to persuade; ~~ *n* encouragement, persuasion; (*Ermahnung*) admonition; (*Bitten*) entreaty; *auf vieles* ~~ by dint of urgent persuasion (*von* of); at the urgent request of; *bei ihr hilft kein* ~~ with her, talking doesn't do any good; ~**reichen** *tr* to reach, to hand to; *itr* to suffice; ~~**d** *a* sufficient; ~**reiten** *irr tr* to break in a horse; *itr* (*auf etw od jdn* ~~) to ride up to; (*weiterreiten*) to ride on; to ride faster; ~**reiter** *m* rough-rider; trainer, groom; *Am sl* (*für halbwilde Pferde*) broncobuster; ~**richten** *tr* (*vorbereiten*) to prepare; (*fertig machen*) to get ready; to finish; (*Essen etc*) to cook, to dress; to do; to prepare dinner; *tech* to dress; to fit; to set; (*Holz etc*) to cut, to square; to trim; (*Leder*) to dress; (*Steine*) to hew; *typ* to make ready; (*Stoff*) to finish; *übel* (*od schlimm*) ~~ to ill-treat; to use badly; to handle roughly; ~**richter** *m tech* dresser, finisher; ~**richterei** *f* dressing (*od* adjusting) shop; ~**richtung** *f* preparation; *tech* dressing, adjustment; fitting; finishing; *typ* making ready; ~**riegeln** *tr* to bolt up; ~**rollen** *tr*, *itr* to roll towards; ~**rosten** *itr* to be covered with rust.

zürnen *itr* to be angry with (*über* at).

zurren *tr mar* (*festbinden*) to lash; to tie; to clamp.

Zurschaustellung *f* display; *fig* parading.

zurü'ck *adv* back; (*hinten*) behind, (*rückwärts*) backward(s); (*Bezahlung*) in arrears; late; ~ *sein* to have come back; (*in Kenntnissen*) to be backward; ~*! interj* stand back! out of the way! ~**beben** *itr* to shrink (*od* to start) back (*vor* from); to recoil; ~**begeben** *irr r* to return, to go back; ~**begehren** *tr* to demand back; ~**begleiten** *tr* to conduct back; to see home; ~**behalten** *irr tr* to keep back, to retain; ~**bekommen** *irr tr* to get back; to recover; to retrieve; ~**berufen** *irr tr* to call back; (*absetzen*) to recall; ~**berufung** *f* (*Absetzung*) recall; ~**bewegen** *tr* to move back; *sich* ~~ to back; ~**bezahlen** *tr* to repay, to reimburse; to refund; to pay back; ~**biegen** *irr tr* (*sich*) to bend back; ~**bilden** *tr* to re-form; to form again; ~**bildung** *f* involution; ~**bleiben** *irr itr* to stay (*od* to remain) behind; to fall behind; to be left behind; (*allmählich*) to lag behind; *sport* to be outdistanced; to drop away; (*Kenntnisse*) to be backward; to fall short of the standard; (*Uhr*) to be slow; *geistig* ~*geblieben* mentally deficient; ~**blicken** *itr* to look back; ~**bringen** *irr tr* to bring back, to return; (*ins Leben*) to recall (to life); (*verzögern*) to retard; (*math*) to reduce (*auf* to); ~**datieren** *tr* to date back, to antedate; ~**denken** *irr itr* to think back (on); to reflect on the past; to recall to memory; ~**drängen** *tr* to drive (*od* to force *od* to press *od* to roll *od* to push) back; *fig* to repress; ~**drehen** *tr* to turn back; to put back; ~**drücken** *tr* to press back; to compress; ~**dürfen** *irr itr* to be allowed to return; ~**eilen** *itr* to hasten back; ~**erbitten** *irr tr* to ask for the return; to ask back; *ich erbitte es* ~ I beg to return it; ~**erobern** *tr* to reconquer; ~**erstatten** *tr* to return, to restore, to reimburse; to refund; to give back; ~**erstattung** *f* return, restitution, reimbursement; ~**fahren** *irr itr* to drive back; to go back; (*mit dem Zug*) to go back by train; *fig* (*plötzlich* ~*weichen*) to start back, to recoil; *tr* to convey back (in a carriage, boat, etc); ~**fallen** *irr itr* to fall back; (*in e-n Fehler, in ein Laster etc*) to relapse (*in* into); (*von Strahlen*) to be reflected; *jur* to revert to, to return to; ~**finden** *irr r* to find o.'s way back; ~**fließen** *irr itr* to flow back; to recede; to ebb; ~**fordern** *tr* to reclaim, to recall; ~**forderung** *f* reclamation; ~**führen** *tr* to lead back; *math* to reduce; (*Ursache, Grund*) to attribute (to); (*auf etw* ~~) to trace back (to); to refer (to); to ascribe (to); (*auf e-n bestimmten Ort*) to localize; (*auf das kleinste Maß*) to minimize; *auf fremden Einfluß* ~*zuführen* traceable to foreign influence; ~**gabe** *f* return, restitution; restoration; giving back; ~**geben** *irr tr* to give back, to return, to restore; ~**gehen** *irr itr* to go back; to fall back; (~*weichen*) to recede; (*sich* ~*ziehen*) to retreat; (~*kehren*) to return; (*Preise*) to fall, to drop; to decline; to decrease; (*nachgeben*) to give way; (*Geschäft*) to go down; (*auf den Ursprung od die Quelle* ~~) to trace back (to); to originate in (*od* from *od* with), to have its origin (*od* source) in; (*sich vermindern*) to diminish; to get smaller; to fall off; to subside; (*Kauf, Abmachung, Verlöbnis*) to be broken off; to come to nought, to be cancel(l)ed; ~~ *lassen* (*Waren etc*) to send back; to return; *auf e-e vorbereitete Stellung* ~~ (*mil*) to fall back upon a prepared position; *der Kauf ist* ~*gegangen* the bargain is off; ~**geleiten** *tr* to lead back; ~**gelegt** *a* (*Weg, Strecke*) walked, gone; made, covered, attained; ~~*e Meilenzahl Am* mileage; ~~*e Strecke* distance covered; ~**gesetzt** *a* cast off; ~~*er Preis* reduced price, *Am* cut rate; ~~*e Waren* old stock *mit sing*; (*Ausschußwaren*) damaged goods *pl*; *zu* ~~*en Preisen* at reduced prices; *sie fühlte sich* ~~ she felt slighted; ~**gezogen** *a* (*Leben*) retired, secluded; solitary, lonely; ~~**heit** *f* retirement, seclusion; privacy; solitude; solitary life; ~~ *leben* to live in seclusion; ~**greifen** *irr itr* to fall back upon; to go back to; to refer to; ~**haben** *irr tr* to have back; *sein Wort* ~~ *wollen* to want to be released from o.'s promise; ~**halten** *irr tr* (*nicht fortlassen*) to hold back, to keep back; to retain, to stop; (*hindern, hemmen*) to retard; to inhibit; (*Tränen*) to restrain; (*festhalten*) to keep in, to detain; (*hindern*) to prevent from; (*bändigen, zügeln*) to curb; (*Gefühle* ~~) to check, to repress; (*Atem*) to hold (o.'s breath); *itr* to refrain from; (*im Urteil*) to reserve (judg(e)ment); (*etw verbergen*) to conceal s. th.; to hide s. th.; to keep back; *sich* ~~ to be reserved; to hold aloof; to keep to o. s.; ~**haltend** *a* (*Benehmen*) reserved; (*nicht mitteilsam*) uncommunicative; (*vorsichtig*) cautious; (*verschwiegen*) discreet; (*Mädchen*) coy, shy, demure; ~**haltung** *f* reserve, reservedness; (*Bescheidenheit*) modesty; discretion; (~~ *der Gefühle*) check, restraint; holding back, keeping back; ~**holen** *tr* to fetch back; ~**jagen** *tr* to drive back; *itr* to rush back; ~**kaufen** *tr* to buy back, to repurchase; ~**kehren** *itr* to come back, to go back, to return; ~**kommen** *irr itr* to come back, to recur to; to return; (*in der Arbeit*) to get behindhand (with); *in die Ruhelage* ~~ to return to normal; *auf etw* ~~ to revert to; *von seiner Meinung* ~~ to give up o.'s opinion; *sehr* ~*gekommen* greatly reduced; ~**können** *irr itr* to be able to return (*od* to recede); ~**kunft** *f* return; ~**lassen** *irr tr* to leave, to leave behind; (*verlassen*) to abandon; *Nachricht* ~~ to leave word; ~**laufen** *irr itr* to return, to run back; (*Geschütz*) to recoil; ~**legen** *tr* (*Geld*) to lay aside; to lay (*od* to put) by; to save; (*durchqueren*) to traverse; (*Jahre erleben*) to attain, to accomplish, to complete; (*Weg*) to cover; *ein gutes Stück Weg* ~~ to cover a distance; (*durchlaufen*) to go through; *sich* ~~ to lie back; *können Sie es mir* ~~*?* could you put it aside for me? ~**lehnen** *r* to lean back; ~**leiten** *tr* to redirect, to lead back; to return; to feed back; ~**liefern** *tr* to send back; ~**liegen** *irr itr* to belong to the past; ~**marschieren** *itr* to march back; *mil* to fall back; ~**melden** *tr* to report back; *r* to report o.'s return; ~**müssen** *irr itr* to be obliged to return; *der Tisch muß* ~ the table must be moved back; ~**nahme** *f* taking back; (*e-r Bestellung, e-r Beleidigung*) withdrawal; (*e-r Anordnung, der Zustimmung*) revocation; (*e-r Beschuldigung*) retraction; (*Widerrufung*) recantation; *jur* (*e-r Klage*) nonsuit; discontinuance (*od* withdrawal) of an action; ~**nehmen** *irr tr* to take back; (*Behauptung*) to withdraw; (*Gesetz, Anordnung*) to revoke; (*aufheben, widerrufen*) to recall; (*Auftrag*) to cancel, to countermand; (*Vorwurf*) to retract; *sport* (*Meldung*) to scratch; *sein Wort* ~~ to withdraw (*od* to retract) o.'s promise; *er mußte seine Worte* ~~ (*fam*) he had to eat his words; *das Gas* ~~ (*mot*) to throttle back; ~**prallen** *itr* to rebound, to recoil (from); (*Ball*) to ricochet; to shrink (*od* to start) back; ~**rechnen** *tr* to count back; ~**reisen** *itr* to travel back, to return; ~**reiten** *irr itr* to ride back; ~**rollen** *itr*, *tr* to roll back; ~**rudern** *itr* to row back; ~**rufen** *irr tr* to call back; to recall; (*ins Gedächtnis*) to call (to mind), to recall to o.'s memory; ~**rufung** *f* recall; ~**sacken** *itr* to backslide; ~**sagen** *tr* to reply; ~~ *lassen* to send back word; ~**schaffen** *tr* to take back, to haul back; to convey back; ~**schaudern** *itr* to recoil, to shrink back (from); ~**schauen** *itr* to look back; ~**scheuchen** *tr* to scare away; ~**schicken** *tr* to send back; ~**schlagen** *irr tr* to beat back; (*Feind*) to repel; to repulse; (*Ball*) to return; (*Mantel*) to throw open; (*Decke*) to throw off; *itr* to strike back, to hit back; (*Flamme*) to flash back; ~**schnellen** *tr* to rebound, to fling back; *itr* to fly back; to jump back; to recoil; ~**schrecken** *itr* to shrink (from); to start back; *tr* to frighten away; (*abhalten*) to deter (*von* from); *sie schreckt vor nichts* ~ she stops at nothing; ~**schreiben** *irr tr*, *itr* to write back; ~**schreiten** *irr itr* to stride back; ~**sehen** *irr itr* to look back; to reflect on (the past); ~**sehnen** *tr* to sigh for; *r* to long to return, to wish o. s. back; **~senden** *irr tr* to send back; **~setzen** *tr* to put back; to set aside; to replace; (*Preis*) to reduce (the price of); to lower; *Am* to roll back; (*Waren*) to cast off; *fig* (*jdn ~~*) to neglect, to disregard, to slight, to snub s. o.; **~setzung** *f* disregard, neglect, slight; (*Preise*) reduction, *Am* rollback (of prices); **~sinken** *irr itr* to fall back; *fig* to relapse into; **~spiegeln** *tr* to reflect; **~springen** *irr itr* to rebound; to jump back; (*Bauwerk*) to recede; **~stecken** *tr* to put back; *e-n Pflock ~~* (*fig*) to make an allowance; to come down a peg or two; **~stehen** *irr itr* to stand back; *fig* to be inferior to; **~stellen** *tr* (*allg; Uhr*) to put back; to set back; to replace; (*aufsparen*) to reserve; (*beiseite stellen*) to put aside, to shelve; *Am* to side-track; *mil* to defer, to exempt from service; **~stellung** *f* putting back; *mil* deferment, exemption (from service); **~~santrag** *m* request for deferment; **~stoßen** *irr tr* to push back; *fig* to repulse, to repel; **~~d** *a* repulsive; **~strahlen** *tr* to reflect; to radiate back, to reverberate; *itr* to be reflected; **~strahlung** *f* reflection; reverberation; **~strömen** *itr* to flow back, to reflux; **~stufen** *tr* to downgrade; **~stürzen** *itr* to rush back; **~treiben** *irr tr* to drive back, to repel, to repulse; **~treten** *irr itr* to step back, to stand back; to draw back; (*Berge, Bauwerk, Wasser*) to recede; (*sich ~ziehen*) to withdraw, to retreat, (*vom Amt*) to resign; (*ins Privatleben*) to retire; *das Kabinett ist ~getreten* the cabinet resigned; to stand back; *fig* to withdraw; **~tun** *irr tr* to put back (into its place); **~übersetzen** *tr* to retranslate; **~verlangen** *tr* to reclaim, to demand back; **~versetzen** *tr* to put back; to restore (to a former) state; (*Schüler*) to send back to a lower form; *r* to turn o.'s thoughts back (to a former period); to go back to a time; **~verweisen** *irr tr* to refer back (to); **~weichen** *irr itr* to recede; to fall back, to retreat, to give ground; (*nachgeben*) to yield; to give in, to give way; **~weisen** *irr tr* to send away, to send back; *fig* (*ablehnen*) to decline, to refuse; (*als falsch*) to disapprove; (*verwerfen*) to reject, to turn down; to dismiss; to dissallow; to overrule; (*abwimmeln*) to brush off; *mil* (*Angriff*) to repel, to repulse; *itr* (*auf e-e Anmerkung*) to refer to; **~weisung** *f* refusal, repulsion, repulse; rejection, rebuttal, dismissal; brush-off; **~werfen** *irr tr* to throw back, to repulse; (*Licht ~~*) to reflect; (*Strahlen*) to reverberate, to bend back; (*Ton*) to echo back; **~werfung** *f* reflection; refraction; reverberation; **~wirken** *itr* to react (upon); **~zahlen** *tr* to pay back, to repay; to refund, to reimburse; **~zahlung** *f* repayment; refunding; reimbursement; **~ziehbar** *a* retractable; **~ziehen** *irr tr* to draw back; to take back; (*etw ~~, Antrag, Gesuch etc*) to withdraw; *sport, parl* (*Nennung, Antrag*) to scratch; (*Geld*) to call in, to withdraw; (*einziehen*) to retract; (*Truppen*) to retire; to re-deploy; *itr* (*umziehen an früheren Platz*) to move back; *mil* to fall back, to retreat; (*Zugvögel*) to return; *sich ~~* to retire; to withdraw; *Am* to back out, to take the back track; *mil* to retreat; *sich vom öffentlichen Leben ~~* to retire into obscurity; *sie lebt ~gezogen* she lives a retired life; **~ziehung** *f* drawing back; withdrawal; retirement; retreat; retraction.

Zu|ruf *m* call; shout; (*Beifall*) acclamation, cheerings *pl*; **~rufen** *irr tr, itr: jdm ~~* to call to; to shout to; *jdm Beifall ~~* to cheer, to applaud; **~rüsten** *tr* to prepare; to get ready; (*ausrüsten*) to fit out, to equip; to rig out; to arm; **~rüstung** *f* preparation; fitting out, equipment; **~sage** *f* promise, word; (*Zustimmung*) acceptance, consent, assent; **~sagen** *tr* to promise; *jdm etw auf den Kopf ~~* to tell s. o. s. th. to his face; *itr* (*auf Einladung*) to promise to come, to accept; (*entsprechen*) to answer to; (*behagen, gefallen*) to suit s. o., to please s. o.; (*Speisen, Klima*) to agree with; **~~d** *a* pleasant, suitable.

zusa'mmen *adv* together; (*alles~*) in all, all told; all together; (*alle ~*) in a body; (*zur gleichen Zeit*) at the same time; (*gemeinschaftlich*) jointly; in common; **~addieren** *tr* to sum up; **~arbeit** *f* (close) co-operation; collaboration; mutual support; (*e-r Gemeinschaft*) team-work; *im Geiste freundschaftlicher ~~* in a spirit of friendship and collaboration; *Verwaltung für Wirtschaftliche ~~* Economic Co-operation Administration (*Abk* ECA); **~arbeiten** *itr* to work together, to co-operate; to collaborate, *Am fam* to collab; to interwork; **~backen** *tr, itr* to cake, to frit (*od* to stick) together; to conglomerate; to agglomerate; **~ballen** *tr* to roll into a ball; to ball up; (*Faust*) to clench (o.'s fist); (*sich häufen*) to agglomerate; (*zus.häufen*) to conglomerate; (*sich konzentrieren*) to concentrate; (*sich massieren*) to mass; *sich ~~* (*Wolken*) to gather; *fig* to draw near; **~ballung** *f* balling up; bunching; (*Anhäufung*) agglomeration; conglomeration; **~bau** *m tech* assembly, assemblage; erection; fitting; **~bauen** *tr tech* to mount; to assemble; to set up; to erect; **~beißen** *irr tr: die Zähne ~~* to set o.'s teeth; *Am* to grit o.'s teeth; **~berufen** *irr tr* to assemble; to convene, to summon; **~berufung** *f* convocation; **~binden** *irr tr* to tie together, to bundle up; to tie up; **~brechen** *irr tr* to break down, to collapse; to crumble; *Am* to go out; *vor Erschöpfung ~~* to drop from exhaustion; **~bringen** *irr tr* to collect, to assemble; (*Geld*) to raise; (*Vermögen*) to amass; (*Leute*) to bring together; (*versöhnen*) to reconcile; **~bruch** *m* breakdown, collapse; failure; ruin; *fam* smash; **~drängen** *tr* (*sich*) to crowd together, to huddle together; (*auf engen Raum*) to compress; to press together; (*kürzen*) to abridge, to condense; (*konzentrieren*) to concentrate; **~drehen** *tr* to twist together; **~drücken** *tr* to compress; **~drückung** *f* compression; **~fahren** *irr itr* to bring together; (*erschrecken*) to shrink, to start at; to wince; (*gegeneinander stoßen*) to collide (with); to rush against one another; *tr* (*e-n Wagen ~~*) to crash (a car); **~fallen** *irr itr* to fall down, to collapse; to coincide (*mit* with); (*auf dieselbe Zeit od denselben Tag fallen*) to come at the same time, to come on the same day; (*Person*) to lose in flesh; *phys* to synchronize; **~falten** *tr* to fold (up); **~fassen** *tr* (*mit der Hand*) to grasp, to gather up; to seize; (*mit einschließen*) to comprehend, to comprise; (*sammelnd ~~*) to collect; to combine; to collate; to unite; (*zentral ~~*) to concentrate; to condense; (*Bericht, Meinung etc kurz ~~*) to sum up, to summarize; to abridge, to reduce; *fam* to boil down; (*noch einmal kurz ~~*) to recapitulate; **~fassend** *a* comprehensive; summary; *~~er Bericht* survey; summarizing report; summary; **~fassung** *f* summing up; summary; (*Übersicht*) résumé, recapitulation; (*~~ziehung*) concentration; condensation; (*Sammlung*) compilation (*aus* from); (*Verschmelzung*) fusion; (*~~schau*) synopsis; (*Abriß, Auszug*) abstract; *mil* (*von Truppen*) combined arms; **~finden** *irr r* to find together, to meet; **~flechten** *irr tr* to plait together, to twine; **~flicken** *tr* to patch up; **~fließen** *irr itr* to flow together, to join their waters; to meet; **~fluß** *m* confluence, junction; conflux; (*von Farben*) fusion; (*von Menschen*) concourse; **~frieren** *irr itr* to freeze, to congeal; **~fügen** *tr* to join, to unite; to combine; **~fügung** *f* adjoining, conjunction; **~führen** *tr* to bring together; **~geben** *irr tr* to join in wedlock, to marry; **~gehen** *irr itr* to go together; (*sich schließen*) to close; (*zus.passen*) to suit one another, to match; (*weniger werden, schrumpfen*) to get lower; to diminish; to shrink; (*begleitet sein von, nach sich ziehen*) to be attended with; **~gehören** *itr* to belong together, to be pairs; to be of the same kind; (*passen*) to match; (*in Wechselbeziehung stehen*) to be correlated; **~gehörig** *a* belonging together; homogeneous; correlated; **~gehörigkeit** *f* (*von Personen*) solidarity; intimate connexion; unity; homogeneousness; correlation; **~~sgefühl** *n* (*e-r Gruppe*) team-spirit; **~geraten** *irr itr fig* to collide; (*in Streit geraten*) to quarrel, to fall out; to have words with; **~gesetzt** *a* composed; (*aus mehreren Stoffen*) compound; *math* composite; (*kombiniert*) combined; (*aus Einzelteilen*) assembled; (*verwickelt*) complex; complicated; *~~ aus* consisting of, composed of; *~~es Glas* laminated glass; *~~er Satz gram* complex sentence; *~~es Wort gram* compound (word); **~gewürfelt** *a* mixed, motley; **~gießen** *irr tr* to mix; to pour together; **~grenzen** *itr* to confine (with); **~halt** *m* holding together; (*Übereinstimmung, Dichtigkeit, Grad der Festigkeit*) consistence, consistency; *phys* cohesion; *fig* (*Einheit*) union; (*Einigkeit*) unity; (*gegenseitiges Verstehen*) understanding; agreement; concord; (*Bindung*) tie, bond; **~halten** *irr tr* to hold together; (*vergleichen mit*) to compare, to collate, to confront with; *itr* to hold together; *fig* to assist one another; to assist; to support, to maintain; (*als Freunde*) to stick together, to be staunch friends; **~hang** *m* connexion, *Am* connection; (*Übereinstimmung*) coherence; (*~~ des Textes*) context; (*Beziehung*) relation; (*Wechselbeziehungen*) interrelation (*zwischen* between); correlation; (*Zus.-halt*) consistency; (*fortlaufender ~~*) continuity; sequence; (*ursächlicher ~~*) cause; (*Ideenverbindung*) association (of ideas); *phys* cohesion; (*durch Flächenanziehung*) adhesion; *Mangel an ~~* incoherence; *ohne ~~* incoherent, loose; *aus dem ~~ reißen* to detach from the context; *im ~~ mit* in connexion with; *im ~~ stehen mit* to relate to, to have reference to; *in diesem ~~* in this connexion; *keinen ~~ haben mit* to have no connexion with; *das ist nur* *im ~~ verständlich* that is clear only in context; **~hangen** *irr*, **~hängen** *itr* to cohere, to hang together; *fig* to be connected with; *das hängt nicht mit dem Blutdruck ~* that has nothing to do with the blood-pressure; *wie hängt das ~?* how is that? **~~d** *a* coherent; (*ununterbrochen*) continuous; **~hang(s)-los** *a* disconnected; incoherent; loose; disjointed; (*Rede*) rambling; (*planlos*) desultory; **~hangslosigkeit** *f* incoherence; disconnectedness; inconsistency; **~hauen** *irr tr* to cut up; *fam* to thrash soundly; **~häufen** *tr* to pile up, to heap up, to accumulate; **~häufung** *f* accumulation; **~heften** *tr* to stitch together; (*Buch*) to sew; **~heilen** *tr*, *itr* to heal up, to close; **~hetzen** *tr* to set by the ears; **~holen** *tr* to fetch from all sides; **~kauern**: *sich ~~* to squat down, to cower o. s. up; **~kaufen** *tr* to buy up; **~ketten** *tr* to chain together; *fig* to link together; **~kitten** *tr* to cement together; (*Glaserei*) to putty, to lute; **~klang** *m* accord, harmony; **~klappbar** *a* folding, foldable, collapsible; *~~er Sitz* folding seat, tip-up seat; *~~es Verdeck* folding roof; **~klappen** *tr* to fold up; *itr* to break down; to collapse; **~kleben** *tr* to paste together; **~knoten** *tr* to knot; **~knüllen** *tr* to crumple (up); **~kommen** *irr itr* to meet, to assemble, to come together; **~koppeln** *tr* to couple; **~krachen** *itr* to break down with a crash, to crash; (*in Stücke zerbrechen*) to crack up; **~kratzen** *tr* to rake together, to scrape together; **~kriechen** *irr itr* to creep together; **~kunft** *f* meeting, gathering, assembly; convention; reunion; (*von zwei Personen*) interview; (*Verabredung*) appointment, rendezvous, *Am* date; (*zur Beratung*) conference; *astr* conjunction; *gesellige ~~* social gathering (*od* party), *Am* sociable; **~~sort** *m* place of meeting; trysting-place; **~lauf** *m* concourse; (*Auflauf*) riot, mob; **~laufen** *irr itr* to run together; to come together, to crowd together; to flock; to raise a tumult, to riot; (*sich sammeln*) to congregate, to collect; (*Farbe*) to run; (*sich mischen*) to blend; (*einschrumpfen*) to shrink up; (*Milch*) to curdle; *geom* to converge; **~leben** *itr* to live together; *~~ n* social life; **~legbar** *a* foldable, collapsible; **~legen** *tr* (*aufhäufen*) to put (*od* to lay) together; to pile up; (*vereinigen*) to combine, to unite; (*zentralisieren*) to centralize, to concentrate; (*verschmelzen*) to fuse; to merge; (*Briefe, Fallschirm, Wäsche etc ~falten*) to fold (up); (*~klappen*) *Am* to collapse; (*Geld*) to club together; to pool; to contribute; **~legung** *f* (*Vereinigung*) uniting, union; (*Fusion*) fusion, merger; (*Zentralisierung*) concentration, centralization; **~leimen** *tr* to glue together; to agglutinate; **~lesen** *irr tr* to collect, to glean, to compile; **~löten** *tr* to solder up; **~nähen** *tr* to sew up; **~nehmen** *irr tr* to take together, to gather; *seine Gedanken ~~* to collect o.'s thoughts; to pay attention; to look out, to watch; to take care; (*sich anstrengen*) to make an effort; (*im Benehmen*) to control o. s., to restrain o. s., to pull o. s. together; *nimm dich ~!* pull yourself together! take care! *Am fam* snap out of it! **~packen** *tr* to pack up; **~passen** *tr* to adjust, to fit; to match, to adapt; *itr* to agree; to harmonize, to go well together; to be matched; **~pferchen** *tr* (*Leute*) to crowd, to pack, to squeeze (together); *Am sl* to sardine; (*Vieh*) to pen up; **~prall** *m* collision; *fig* impact (*mit* on); **~prallen** *itr* to collide; **~pressen** *tr* to compress, to squeeze together; (*fest ~~*) to clench; (*verdichten*) to condense; *die Zähne ~~* to set o.'s teeth; **~pressung** *f* compression; (*Verdichtung*) condensation; **~raffen** *tr* to scrape together; to collect in haste (*od* hurriedly); (*Kleider*) to tuck up; (*ein Vermögen*) to amass; (*seine Kräfte*) to summon up (o.'s strength); *sich ~~* to pull o. s. together; (*Mut fassen*) to pluck up courage; (*sich anstrengen*) to make an effort; **~rechnen** *tr* to add up; to reckon up; to compute; to figure up, *fam* to tot up; to sum up, to total; *alles ~gerechnet* taking everything into account; **~reimen** *tr* to make out; (*verstehen*) to understand; (*auf den Grund gehen*) to get to the bottom of; *sich ~~* to make sense; to fit in; *wie reimt sich das ~?* how does it fit in? **~reißen** *irr tr* (*etw*) to pull down; to demolish; *sich ~~* (*fam*) to pull o. s. together; **~rollen** *tr* to roll up; **~rotten** *r* to band together, to form a gang, to cause a riot; **~rottung** *f* riot; riotous mob; unlawful assembly; **~rücken** *tr* to move together; *itr* to draw nearer; to move nearer (to); to sit closer, to close up; *mil* to close the ranks; to make room; *fam* to squeeze up; **~rufen** *irr tr* to call together, to convene, to convoke; *parl* to summon; **~rufung** *f* convocation; **~scharen** *r* to assemble, to band together; **~scharren** *tr* to scrape (*od* rake) together; (*Geld*) to hoard; **~schau** *f* synopsis; **~schießen** *irr tr* to shoot down; to knock out; (*mit Kanonen*) to batter down; (*Geld*) to club money together; **~schlagen** *irr tr* (*zerschlagen*) to smash up; to knock down; (*Hände*) to clap; to clasp; (*die Absätze*) to click; (*etw mit Nägeln*) to nail together; (*Kosten zus.zählen*) to lump; *die Hände über dem Kopf ~~* to hold up o.'s arms in astonishment; *itr* (*von Wasser*) to close (*od* dash) over; to engulf; **~schließen** *irr tr* to join closely; to link together; to chain together; to interlock; *sich ~~* to unite; *Am* to gang; to close the ranks; (*fusionieren*) to amalgamate; **~schluß** *m* union, federation; merger, fusion; amalgamation; combine; consolidation; combination; aggregation, organization; **~schmelzen** *irr tr*, *itr* to melt together, to fuse; to dissolve; *fig* to diminish, to dwindle; **~schmieden** *tr* to weld together; **~schmieren** *tr* to compile carelessly; to huddle together; **~schnüren** *tr* to lace up, to tie up; to cord (up); (*Herz*) to wring; *das schnürt mir die Kehle ~* it makes me choke; **~schrauben** *tr* to bolt together; to screw; **~schreiben** *irr tr* to compile, to scribble; **~schrumpfen** *itr* to shrivel up; to shrink; to contract; to wrinkle; to dwindle; to collapse; **~schütten** *tr* to pour together; **~schweißen** *tr* to weld together (*zu* into); **~sein** *n* meeting; **~setzen** *tr* to put together, to compound, to compose; to make up; to join; (*die Waffen*) to pile (arms); (*aus Teilen*) to fabricate, to assemble, to fit; *r* to sit down together; (*bestehen aus*) to consist of; to be composed of; **~setzung** *f* composition; combination; (*von Maschinen*) construction; *chem*, *gram* compound; (*Synthese*) synthesis; analysis; (*Bau, Struktur*) structure; (*Bildung*) formation; **~sinken** *irr itr* to sink down; **~spiel** *n* playing together; concerted acting; *theat*, *sport* team-work; **~stecken** *tr* to put together; *itr* to be always together; to conspire together; **~stehen** *irr itr* to stand together; to side with one another; to stick together; **~stellen** *tr* to put together; (*ordnend u. vergleichend*) to collate; (*~tragen*) to compile; (*~setzen*) to compose; (*nach Sorten*) to assort; (*zu Gruppen*) to group; (*zu Klassen*) to classify; (*aus einzelnen Teilen*) to make up; (*Maschine, Apparat ~~*) to set up; (*vergleichend*) to compare; (*vereinigend*) to combine; (*passend*) to match; **~stellung** *f* composition, arrangement, combination; (*~tragung*) compilation; (*Liste*) list; (*~fassung*) summary; digest; synopsis; (*Vergleich*) comparison; juxtaposition; (*Aufstellung*) statement; inventory; (*Gruppierung*) grouping; (*in Klassen*) classification; association; (*Sammlung*) assembly; (*Montage*) assemblage; *typ* (*~~ e-r Druckseite*) (page) make up, *Am* (page) lay-out; **~stimmen** *itr* to chime in, to agree, to accord, to harmonize; **~stoppeln** *tr* to patch up, to compile badly; **~stoß** *m* (*Auto, Zug, Schiff etc, auch fig*) collision, *fam* smash-up, crack up; *phys* impact; (*der Meinungen*) clash, clashing; (*Konflikt*) conflict; (*Schlag*) shock; *mil* (*mit dem Feind*) engagement; (*Treffen*) encounter; **~stoßen** *irr tr* to push against; to knock together; to smash; *itr* (*mit Gläsern*) to clink; to collide; to run into; (*treffen auf*) to clash; to conflict; to encounter; (*berühren*) to touch; (*angrenzen*) to adjoin (each other); to border upon; **~strömen** *itr* to flow together; (*von Menschen*) to flock together, to throng, to crowd together; **~stürzen** *itr* to tumble down, to collapse, to fall in; **~suchen** *tr* to gather, to collect; **~tragen** *irr tr* to carry together; (*Gedanken*) to compile; (*mühsam*) to glean; **~treffen** *irr itr* to meet (each other); (*feindlich*) to encounter; (*gleichzeitig geschehen*) to coincide; *~~ n* meeting; encounter; coincidence; **~treten** *irr itr* to come together, to meet; to unite; *tr* to trample down; **~tritt** *m* meeting, association, congress; **~tun** *irr tr* to put together; *r* to associate, to unite; to join; to combine; **~wickeln** *tr* to wrap up; **~wirken** *itr* to act together, to work together; to interact; to collaborate; to co-operate; to concur; *~~ n* co-operation; **~würfeln** *tr* to jumble up; to mix up confusedly; *~gewürfelte Gesellschaft* motley company; **~zählen** *tr* to sum up, to add up, to count up; *fam* to tot up, *Am* to foot up; **~ziehen** *irr tr* to draw together, to contract, to assemble; to concentrate; (*Lippen*) to purse up; (*Brauen*) to pucker; (*Text*) to abridge, to condense; (*Herz*) to wring, to oppress; *med* to a(d)stringe; (*Truppen*) to gather, to concentrate; *sich ~~* to gather; to shrink up; to collect; to contract; *fig* to draw nearer; *ein Gewitter zieht sich ~* a storm is gathering; **~ziehend** *a* contractive; astringent; **~ziehung** *f* contraction, constriction; shrinking; concentration; (*Text*) condensing; *med* (*Herz*) systole.

Zu|satz *m* addition; (*Ergänzung*) supplement; (*Beimischung*) admixture; (*von Metallen*) alloy, dash; (*Anhang*) appendix; (*Nachschrift*) postscript, (*zum Testament*) codicil; (*zu e-m Vertrag*) clause; (*Beigabe, gram Attribut*) adjunct, (*Hilfsmittel*) auxiliary; (*~~gerät*) booster set; *typ* (*zu e-m Artikel*) add, *Am* insert; *pl* (*~sätze*) finishing metals *pl*; loading agents *pl*; *unter* ~~ *von* with addition of; ~~**abkommen** *n* supplementary agreement; ~~**aggregat** *n* additional set; *el* booster aggregate; ~~**annahme** *f* (*Folgesatz*) corollary; ~~**antrag** *m* (*zu Gesetz*) amendment; *parl* additional motion; ~~**artikel** *m* additional article; (*bei Gesetz*) extra clause; ~~**batterie** *f* booster battery; ~~**behälter** *m aero* additional (*od* spare *od* jettisonable) tank; *Am* (*für Luftfracht*) speedpack; ~~**bestimmung** *f* supplementary rule (*od* regulation); ~~**betriebsstofftank** *m* extra fuel tank, *Am* auxiliary gas tank, *Am sl* Tokyo tank; ~~**fallschirm** *m* pilot parachute; ~~**gebühr** *f* additional charge; (*Post*) supplementary fee; ~~**gerät** *n* attachment, accessory; adapter; ~~**gewicht** *n* additional weight; ~~**ladung** *f* supercharge; ~~**linse** *f phot* supplementary lens; ~~**material** *n* (*Metall*) filler metal; ~~**verbrennung** *f* stepped-up combustion; ~~**versicherung** *f* additional (*od* supplementary) insurance; ~~**vertrag** *m* supplementary agreement; ~**sätzlich** *a* additional; extra; supplementary; ~**scha'nden** *adv*: ~~ *hauen* to knock to pieces; ~~ *jagen* (*Pferd*) to work to death; ~~ *machen* to ruin, to thwart; to foil; ~~ *werden* to fail, to come to nothing, to be ruined; ~**schanzen** *tr* to secure, *sl* to wangle; (*zuschieben*) to make s. th. come s.o.'s way; ~**schärfen** *itr* to cut to a point, to sharpen; ~**scharren** *tr* to fill up, to cover by scraping; ~**schauen** *itr* to look on s. th.; to watch s.o.; ~**schauer** *m* spectator, onlooker, looker-on; (*umstehender* ~~) bystander; (*Beobachter*) observer; beholder; (*Zeuge*) witness; (*Augenzeuge*) eyewitness; (*im Kino*) patron; (*beim Kartenspiel*) kibitzer; *die* ~~ *pl* the public, the audience; the spectators *pl*; (*bei Konzerten etc*) the auditors *pl*; ~~**plätze** *m pl* places for the spectators; ~~**raum** *m theat* house; auditorium; seats *pl*; ~~**tribüne** *f* (grand-) stand; gallery; *Am* (*offene*) bleachers *pl*; ~**schaufeln** *tr* to fill up; ~**schenken** *tr* (*in Glas*) to fill up; *darf ich* ~~? may I fill up your glass? ~**schicken** *tr* to send on (to); *Am* (*mit Post*) to mail; (*Geld*) to remit; (*Waren*) to forward; to consign; ~**schieben** *irr tr* to push (*od* to shove) towards; (*jdm etw zuspielen*) to pass s. th. on to s. o.; (*Fenster*) to close; (*Schublade*) to shut; *den Riegel* ~~ to draw the bolt; *jdm den Eid* ~~ to give s. o. the oath; to put s. o. upon his oath; *jdm die Schuld* ~~ to put (*od* to lay) the blame on; *die Schuld auf den Falschen* ~~ (*fig*) to put the saddle on the wrong horse; *jdm die Verantwortung* ~~ to saddle the responsibility upon s. o.; ~**schießen** *irr tr, itr* (*auf etw*) to rush (at); (*zu etw beitragen*) to add to; to contribute, to supply; to subsidize.

Zuschlag *m* (*Zusatz*) increase, addition; (*Preis*~) extra charge; surcharge; increase; (*zum Fahrpreis*) additional (*od* excess) fare; (*Metall*) flux; (*Beimischung*) admixture; (*Steuer*~) surtax, additional tax; (*Teuerungs*~) bonus; (*Auktion*) knocking down; *jur* adjudication; ~**en** *irr itr* to strike (hard); to hit out; *tr* (*Tür*) to bang, to slam; (*Auktion*) to knock down; (*Buch*) to shut up; ~**erz** *n* fluxing ore; ~**frei** *a* without surcharge; ~**gebühr** *f* additional fee; excess fare; ~**hammer** *m* sledge hammer; ~**karte** *f* extra ticket; additional ticket; ~**material** *n* flux material; ~**porto** *n* excess postage, surcharge; ~**spflichtig** *a* liable to additional payment; ~**steuer** *f* surtax; ~**zoll** *m* additional duty.

zu|schließen *irr tr* to lock (up), to shut, to close; ~**schmeißen** *irr tr* (*Türe*) to slam, to bang; *jdm etw* ~~ to throw to, to fling to; ~**schmieren** *tr* to smear up (*mit* with); ~**schnallen** *tr* to buckle; to fasten, to strap up; ~**schnappen** *itr* to snap (to), to shut with a snap; (*zubeißen*) to snap up; ~**schneiden** *irr tr* to cut; (*Kleid*) to cut out (*od* up); ~**schneider** *m* cutter; ~**schnitt** *m* cut; *fig* style; ~**schnüren** *tr* to lace (up); to tie up; (*Ballen*) to cord up; (*Hals*) to strangle; *es schnürt mir die Kehle zu* that makes me choke; ~**schrauben** *tr* to screw up (*od* tight); ~**schreiben** *irr tr* (*jdm etw* ~~) to attribute to; to impute to; (*verdanken*) to thank (it) to; to owe; (*Schuld*) to blame s. o. for; (*Handlung*) to ascribe to; *com* (*übertragen*) to transfer to; to place to credit of; *er hat es sich selbst zuzuschreiben* he has himself to thank for it; *itr* to accept an invitation; ~**schreien** *irr itr, tr* to shout to; to call out to; ~**schreiten** *irr itr* to step up to; (*lebhaft ausschreiten*) to step out well, to walk along, to walk briskly; ~**schrift** *f* notice, letter; communication; ~**schu'lden** *adv*: *sich etw* ~~ *kommen lassen* to be guilty of doing s. th.; ~**schuß** *m* (*Gehalts*~~) rise; extra pay; (*für Kosten*) extra allowance; (*staatlicher* ~~) subsidy; government grant; (*Not*~~) grant-in-aid; (*Beitrag*) contribution; *typ* overplus; (*bei Buch*) waste; (*Baukosten* ~~) key money; ~~**bedarf** *m* subsidy requirement; ~~**betrieb** *m* subsidized establishment; ~~**bogen** *m typ* extra sheet; ~~**gebiet** *n* deficiency area; ~**schütten** *tr* to fill up with; (*zugießen*) to pour on; to add to; ~**schwören** *irr tr* to swear to, to assure on oath.

zu|sehen *irr itr* to look on; (*beobachten*) to watch; (*als Zeuge*) to witness; *Am* (*bei etw*) to sit in on s. th.; (*zuwarten*) to wait; to be patient; (*dulden*) to suffer, to stand, to endure; (*Sorge tragen*) to take care, to look out for; to pay attention to; to see to (it); *da müssen Sie selber* ~~ you must see to it yourself; ~~**ds** *adv* visibly; noticeably; manifestly; obviously; ~**senden** *irr tr* to send on to; to forward to; *Am* to ship; ~**setzen** *tr* (*hinzufügen*) to add to; (*Geld*) to lose; *itr jdm* ~~ to press, to attack, to urge s. o.; (*jdm sehr* ~~) to ride s. o. roughshod, *Am* to ride hard on s. o.; (*Gesundheit*) to wear out; *jdm mit Fragen* ~~ to ply s. o. with questions; *jdm mit Bitten* ~~ to importune s. o.; to be urgent with s. o.; ~**sichern** *tr* to assure of, to give assurance of, to promise; ~**sicherung** *f* assurance, promise; ~**siegeln** *tr* to seal up.

Zuspätkommende *pl theat* late-comers *pl*.

zu|sperren *tr* to bar, to close, to shut, to lock; ~**spielen** *tr* to play into s. o.'s hands; *sport* to pass to s. o.; ~**spitzen** *tr* to tip; (*Bleistift etc*) to sharpen; *fig* to bring to a point; *sich* ~~ (*spitz zulaufen*) to taper, to end in a point; *fig* (*Lage etc*) to come to a crisis; to get critical; to come to a head; ~**spitzung** *f* point, tapering; *fig* (*der Lage etc*) increasing gravity of the situation; ~**sprechen** *irr itr* to speak to; (*Getränken*) to drink copiously; *dem Essen wacker* ~~ to eat heartily; *dem Glas* ~~ to imbibe freely; *tr Mut* ~~ to encourage; *Trost* ~~ to comfort, to console; *gerichtlich* ~~ to adjudge, to award; (*Telegramm*) to telephone (a message), to phonogram; ~**sprechgebühr** *f* (*Telegramm*) additional charge for telephoning of telegram; ~**sprechung** *f jur* adjudication; ~**springen** *irr itr* (*von Schlössern*) to snap to, to shut suddenly; *auf jdn* ~~ to run towards; to jump up (at); ~**spruch** *m* consolation, encouragement; (*Kunden*) run (of customers), customers *pl*; (*Kundschaft*) clientele, custom; *großer* ~~ plenty of customers; *viel* ~~ *haben* to have a good custom, to be much frequented; (*Zustimmung, Lob*) approval, praise; ~**spunden** *tr* to bung up.

Zu|stand *m* (*Beschaffenheit*) condition; *Am fam* fix; (*dauernder* ~~) state; (*Lage*) situation; (*Anlage, Einrichtung*) disposition; (*Stellung*) position; (*Ordnung, Grad*) order; (*rechtliche, politische Lage, Stand*) status; (*Beschaffenheit*) habit; (*Entwicklungsstufe*) phase; (*Umstände*) circumstance (-s *pl*); (*Zustände*) state of things, state of affairs, conditions *pl*; *med* (*Nervenzustände*) attack (of nerves); fit (of hysteria); *epileptischer* ~~ status epilepticus; *gegenwärtiger* ~~ status quo; ~~, *in dem sich etw bis zu e-m bestimmten Ereignis befand* status quo ante; *betriebsfähiger* ~~ working order (*od* condition); *in gutem* (*schlechtem*) ~~ in good (bad) shape; (*Gebäude*) in good (out of) repair; *mobiler* ~~ (*mil*) on a war footing; ~**stande** *adv*: ~~ *bringen* to bring about, to bring off; to achieve, to accomplish, to effect; (*durchsetzen*) to succeed in accomplishing, *Am* to get away with; to get done; to put across; ~~ *kommen* to come about, to come off, *Am* to come out; *Am* to go over; to be accomplished, to be realized; (*Vertrag*) to come into existence; (*geschehen*) to take place, to happen, to occur; to mature; (*Gesetz*) to pass; *nicht* ~~ *kommen* to fail, not to come off; to come to nought; ~**standekommen** *n* formation; occurrence, taking place; ~**ständig** *a* (*gehörig*) belonging to; appertaining to; (*zukommend*) due to; (*passend, angemessen*) appropriate (*zu, für* to, for); (*qualifiziert*) competent, (duly) qualified; (*verantwortlich*) responsible; authorized; (*maßgebend*) proper; *jur* (*Gericht*) having jurisdiction over; *nicht* ~~ incompetent; *jur* (*Gericht*) to have no jurisdiction over; *dafür bin ich nicht* ~~ that's not in my department; ~~ *sein jur* to have jurisdiction over; (*für Berufung*) to have appellate jurisdiction over; ~~*es Gericht* court of competent jurisdiction (*od* venue); ~~*er Gerichtsort* venue; ~~*er Richter* competent judge; ~~**keit** *f* competence; (*des Gerichts*) jurisdiction (over); *der* ~~*keit entziehen jur* to withdraw from the jurisdiction; ~~**keitsbereich** *m* sphere of responsibility; ~~**keitsgebiet** *n* area of competence; ~**statten** *adv*: ~~ *kommen* to be of use to, to be useful to; to prove (*od* to come in) useful; ~**stecken** *tr* to pin up; *jdm etw* (*heimlich*) ~~ to provide s. o. secretly with s. th., to convey secretly, to slip s. th. into s. o.'s hand; *sie steckte ihm etw Geld zu* she slipped him some money; ~**stehen** *irr itr* (*rechtlich*) to be due to; (*passen*) to become to, to suit; (*sich schicken, sich ziemen*) to behove; *es steht mir zu* it behoves me; (*gehören*) to belong to; *es steht ihm nicht zu* he has no right to; ~**stellen** *tr* (*Waren zuschicken*) to deliver to, to forward to; (*übersenden*) to send;

(*überreichen*) to hand to; *jur* to serve (upon); (*etw verbarrikadieren*) to barricade, to block up, to obstruct; **~stellung** *f* (*Übersendung*) forwarding, sending on; (*Post; Lieferung*) delivery; (*Aushändigung*) handing (in); *jur* service, writ; **~~sdienst** *m* delivery service; **~~sgebühr** *f* charges for conveyance, *Am* cartage; **~~surkunde** *f* notice of delivery; *jur* writ of summons; **~steuern** *itr mar* to bear down on; to head for; **~stimmen** *itr* to assent, to consent, to agree (to); to comply (with); *Am fam* to jibe; **~~denfalls** *adv* in case of agreement; **~stimmung** *f* assent, agreement, consent; (*Einwilligung, Ergebung*) acquiescence; (*Erlaubnis*) permission; (*Beifall*) approval; (*Billigung*) endorsement; *~~ finden* to get through, to pass muster, *Am* to get by; **~~serklärung** *f* declaration of consent; **~stopfen** *tr* to stop up; to plug; (*ausbessern*) to darn, to mend; **~stöpseln** *tr* to cork, to stopper; **~stoßen** *irr tr* (*Tür etc heftig schließen*) to slam, to shut, to close; to push to; *itr* (*mit dem Schwerte*) to lunge; (*voranstoßen*) to thrust forward; (*Unglück, Unfall*) to meet with; to happen (to), to befall (s. o.); **~streben** *itr* to aim (for); to hasten (toward); *fig* (*streben nach*) to make for, to strive for; to aim (at); **~strom** *m* (*Zufluß*) arriving current; influx; (*von Leuten*) crowd, throng, multitude; **~strömen** *itr* (*hineinfließen*) to flow in(to); (*Menschen*) to throng to, to flock; to crowd in (upon); (*in Richtung*) to stream towards, to blow towards; **~stürzen** *itr* to rush (*auf* towards, *auf jdn* upon s. o.); (*angreifen*) to assault, to attack; **~stutzen** *tr* to dock, to trim; to cut; (*Baum*) to lop; (*zurichten*) to fit up; (*Stück für die Bühne*) to adapt.

zu|ta'ge *adv* to light; at day; on the surface; *~~ fördern* to bring to light; *~~ kommen, ~~ treten* to come to light; *~~ liegen* to be evident, to be manifest; **~tat** *f* (*meist pl ~taten*) ingredient(s *pl*); (*Würze*) seasoning; (*Zufügung*) addition, complement; (*zu e-m Kleid*) trimmings *pl*, *Am* (*Knöpfe etc*) findings *pl*; (*Rohmaterial*) raw material; **~tei'l** *adv: ~~ werden* to fall to o.'s share; *~~ werden lassen* to allot to, to administer; to bestow on; **~teilen** *tr* (*jdm etw zuweisen*) to allot to, to assign to; (*Geld, Sache, Gebiet, Macht*) to allocate; (*in festgelegten Teilen ~~*) to apportion; to give a share of; (*sehr reichlich ~~*) to lavish on; (*gewähren*) to grant; (*austeilen*) to distribute; (*ausgeben*) to issue; (*rationieren*) to ration; (*ein Amt*) to confer on; (*e-n Titel*) to bestow on; (*bestimmen für*) to appropriate; (*Vollmacht übertragen*) to delegate; (*zusprechen, zuerkennen*) to adjudicate, to award; *tech* (*Material zuführen*) to feed; (*liefern*) to supply; *mil* to attach; to post to; to appoint to; **~teiler** *m* allocator; **~teilung** *f* allotment; allocation; assignment; appropriation; apportionment; (*Verteilung*) distribution; (*Ausgabe*) issue; (*Ration*) ration; (*Rationierung*) rationing; (*Quote*) quota; (*Zuschuß*) allowance; *tech* (*Zufuhr*) feed; *mil* attachment; posting; appointment; (*e-s Titels*) bestowal; **~~sempfänger** *m* allocatee; **~~skürzung** *f* (*Rationierung*) ration cut; **~~snachricht** *f* letter of allotment; **~~speriode** *f* (*Rationierung*) ration(ing) period; **~~ssätze** *m pl* ration scales *pl*; **~~ssystem** *n* quota system; **~tiefst** *adv* at bottom; deeply; **~tragen** *irr tr* to carry (to), (*Neuigkeiten*) to report; (*Klatsch*) to tell, to repeat; *r* to happen, to come to pass; to take place; **~träger** *m* tale-bearer, tell-tale, informer; gossip, scandal-monger; **~trägerei** *f* talebearing, gossip; **~träglich** *a* advantageous; conducive, useful; (*der Gesundheit*) wholesome; *jdm ~~ sein* to agree with s. o.; **~~keit** *f* usefulness; wholesomeness; **~trauen** *tr* (*jdm etw ~~*) to credit s. o. with; to give s. o. credit for; (*für fähig halten*) to believe s. o. capable of; *jdm nicht viel ~~* to have no high opinion of s. o.; *~~ n* trust, confidence (in); *~~ zu jdm haben, ~~ in jdn setzen* to rely on s. o.; **~traulich** *a* confiding, trustful, trusting; unsuspicious; friendly; **~~keit** *f* trustfulness; friendliness; confidingness; reliance; intimacy; **~treffen** *irr itr* to prove right, to prove true, to come true; to be right, to hold true; to be conclusive; *das trifft besonders auf Sie zu* that applies especially to you; *das trifft hier nicht zu* that doesn't hold true in this case; **~treffend** *a* right, correct; just; to the point; (*anwendbar*) applicable; **~treiben** *irr tr, itr* to drive on (*od* towards); **~trinken** *irr itr* to drink to, to drink o.'s health; **~tritt** *m* admission (to), entrance; admittance; (free) access; (*freier ~~ zu den Buchbeständen e-r Bibliothek*) open shelves; *kein ~~! ~~ verboten!* no admittance! no entrance! *fam* keep out! (*für Militär*) off limits! *~~ frei!* admission free! *jdm den ~~ verwehren* to bar from admittance; *bei jdm ~~ haben* to be admitted; **~'tun** *tr* to shut, to close; (*hinzufügen*) to add; *~~ n* (*Hilfe, Beistand, Eingreifen*) assistance, help; agency, inference; *ohne mein ~~* without my agency; **~tu(n)lich** *a* attentive; not timid; (*zutraulich*) friendly, confiding; **~~keit** *f* attentiveness, complaisance.

zu|verlässig *a* (*Nachricht*) authentic, certain, sure; (*von Personen*) trusty, reliable; trustworthy; dependable; *ein ~~er Tip fam* a straight tip; **~~keit** *f* authenticity; certainty; reliability; trustworthiness; **~~keitsprobe, ~~keitsprüfung** *f* reliability (*od* dependability) test; **~versicht** *f* confidence, assurance, trust; **~~lich** *a* confident, sure; **~~lichkeit** *f* confidence, trust; (self-) assurance; **~viel** *adv* too much; **~vor** *adv* before; previously; beforehand; first; formerly; *allem ~~* above all; *kurz ~~* shortly before; **~vörderst** *adv* first of all, before all; **~vorkommen** *irr itr* to anticipate, to forestall; to come first; *jdm ~~* to outdo s. o.; to get the start of s. o., *Am fam* to get the jump on s. o.; (*e-r Sache vorbeugen*) to prevent; **~~d** *a* (*gefällig*) obliging, complaisant; (*höflich*) polite; courteous; **~vorkommenheit** *f* complaisance, civility, politeness; **~vortun** *irr u. imp: es jdm ~~ an* to outdo, to surpass s. o. (in).

Zu|wachs *m* (*Vermehrung, Zunahme*) increase, increment; augmentation; (*Wachstum*) growth; accretion; (*Ausdehnung*) expansion; (*in e-r Bibliothek*) accession(s *pl*); (*e-n Rock*) *auf ~~ machen* to make so as to allow for growing; **~wachsen** *irr itr* to grow together; (*Wunde*) to heal up; (*mit Pflanzen*) to become (*od* to get) overgrown; *jdm ~~* to accrue to s. o.; **~wachsnummer** *f* (*Bibliothek*) accession number; **~wachssteuer** *f* increment tax; **~wachsverzeichnis** *n* (*Bibliothek*) accession book; **~wägen** *irr tr* to weigh out; **~wandern** *itr* to immigrate; **~warten** *itr* (*abwarten*) to wait; **~we'ge** *adv: ~~ bringen* to bring about, to effect, to accomplish; to produce; **~wehen** *tr* to blow to; *itr* to get closed by the wind; **~wei'len** *adv* sometimes, at times; (*gelegentlich*) occasionally; (*hie u. da*) now and then; now and again; **~weisen** *irr tr* to allot to; to apportion to; to appropriate, to assign to; (*Kunden*) to introduce; to recommend to; **~weisung** *f* assignment, appropriation, allotment; *radio* (*Wellenlänge*) allocation of frequency; **~wenden** *irr tr* to turn towards; *jdm etw ~~* to procure for s. o.; (*Gabe*) to let s. o. have; to make a present of; (*geben*) to give; (*seine Liebe etc*) to bestow upon; (*sich widmen*) to devote to; *e-r Sache seine Aufmerksamkeit ~~* to attend to; **~wendung** *f* (*Gabe*) gift; (*Schenkung*) donation; (*Unterstützung*) allowance; (*Geld~~*) gratuity; gratification; (*von Gefühlen*) bestowal; **~werfen** *irr tr* (*jdm ~~*) to throw to; (*Grube*) to fill up; (*Tür*) to slam.

zuwi'der *adv* contrary to; against; (*verhaßt*) repugnant, distasteful; odious; offensive; *die Sache ist mir ~* I dislike it; **~handeln** *itr* to act contrary (*od* in opposition to); to act in contravention of; to counteract; (*nicht gehorchen*) to disobey; (*gegen Anordnungen, Gesetze etc verstoßen*) to contravene, to infringe; to offend (against); (*brechen, verletzen*) to break, to violate; **~handlung** *f* infringement; contravention, violation; non-compliance; *~~en werden bestraft* violations will be punished; **~laufen** *irr itr* to run counter to, to be contrary to; **~sein** *irr tr* to be repugnant to, to be loathsome to.

zu|winken *itr* (*nickend*) to nod to; to beckon to, to make a sign to; **~zahlen** *tr* to pay extra; **~zählen** *tr* to allot to; (*hinzurechnen*) to add to; *jdm etw ~~* to count out to; **~zei'ten** *adv* now and then; at times; **~ziehen** *irr tr* (*Knoten*) to draw together; to tighten; to pull together; (*Vorhang*) to shut, to draw; *jdn zu etw ~~* to invite, to call in; (*als Beirat*) to consult; *sich etw ~~* (*Krankheit*) to catch, to contract; to get; (*Feinde*) to make; (*Strafe*) to incur; *itr* (*als Mieter*) to move in; (*einwandern*) to immigrate; **~ziehung** *f* (*e-s Beirats*) consultation; consulting (of); calling in; (*Hilfe*) assistance, help; *unter ~~ von* by the advice of, with the aid of; (*einschließlich*) including; **~zug** *m* (*Einwanderung*) immigration; influx; (*der Bevölkerung*) increase; (*Ankunft*) arrival; *mil* (*Verstärkung*) auxiliary troops *pl*, reinforcements *pl*; **~~sbewilligung** *f* permission to take up residence; **~~sgenehmigung** *f* (*für Staat od Stadt*) entry permit; (*für Wohnung*) permit of residence.

zuzüglich *adv* plus; adding, with the addition of; (*einschließlich*) including.

*

Zwang *m* compulsion, coercion; (*moralischer ~*) restraint; constraint; check; (*Verpflichtung*) obligation; (*Gewalt*) force; violence; (*Anspannung, Druck*) stress; *jur* (*unter Drohung*) duress; *med* pressure; *unter ~* under (*od* upon) compulsion; *sich ~ antun* to restrain o. s.; to impose restraint on o. s.; *sich keinen ~ antun* to be quite free and easy; *seinen Gefühlen ~ antun* to check o. s.; **~los** *a* unconstraint; unconventional; (*ungezwungen*) free and easy; unceremonious; informal; **~~igkeit** *f* ease; (*Freiheit*) freedom; familiarity.

zwängen *tr* to press (into), to force (into).

Zwangs|anleihe *f* forced loan; **~arbeit** *f* (*Zuchthaus*) hard labo(u)r; (*staatliche Maßnahme*) forced labo(u)r; **~~slager** *n* forced labo(u)r camp; **~beitreibung** *f* forcible collection; **~bewirtschaftet** *a* under economic control; **~dienst** *m* compulsory service; **~einquartierung** *f* compulsory billeting; **~enteignung** *f* compulsory expropriation; **~ernährung** *f* forcible feeding; **~erziehungsanstalt** *f* Borstal, reformatory, *Am* reform school; **~evakuierung** *f* *mil* relocation; **~innung** *f* obligatory guild; **~jacke** *f* strait waistcoat; strait jacket; **~lage** *f* distress, necessity; embarrassing situation, dilemma; *sich in e-r ~~ befinden* to be hard pressed; to be under the necessity of; **~landung** *f* *aero* forced landing; **~läufig** *adv* inevitably; necessarily; automatically; *a tech* guided; positive; **~läufigkeit** *f* *tech* guided motion; **~maßregel** *f* compulsory (*od* coercive) measure; **~mieter** *m* assigned tenant; **~mittel** *n* means of coercion; **~verfahren** *n* coercive proceedings *pl*; coercive measures *pl*; **~vergleich** *m* forced settlement; **~verkauf** *m* forced sale; **~verpflichtet** *a* conscript; **~verschleppte(r)** *m* displaced person, D. P.; **~versteigerung** *f* forced sale; compulsory sale by auction; bankrupt sale; **~verwaltung** *f* compulsory administration; sequestration; **~vollstreckung** *f* distraint, execution; distress; **~~sbefehl** *m* writ of execution; **~vorstellung** *f* hallucination; **~weise** *adv* by force, by compulsion; compulsory; forcible; *~~ Ernährung* forcible feeding; **~wirtschaft** *f* government control; (*Planwirtschaft*) planned economy; (*Rationierung*) rationing (system); *~~ aufheben* to decontrol; *Aufhebung der ~~* decontrol.

zwanzig *a* twenty; *20 Stück* a score; **~er** *m* man in the twenties; man of twenty; *in den ~ern sein* to be in o.'s twenties; **~erlei** *a* of twenty kinds; **~fach, ~fältig** *adv* twentyfold; **~jährig** *a* twenty-year-old; **~ste** *a* twentieth; **~stel** *n* twentieth part.

zwar *adv* indeed, to be sure, it is true; *u. ~* and that; namely; in fact; that is.

Zweck *m* (*bestimmter ~*) purpose; (*Ziel*) aim, goal; (*objektiv*) object; (*End~*) end (in view); (*Sinn, Nutzen*) sense, point, use; (*Plan, Absicht*) design, intention; (*Grund*) reason; *Mittel zum ~* a means to an end; *keinen ~ haben* to be of no use; there is no point in doing; *es hat keinen ~ aufzuhören* there is no point in stopping; *zu dem ~* for the purpose of; with a view to; *zu diesem ~* toward this end, for this purpose; *seinen ~ erreichen* to attain (*od* to achieve) o.'s aim; *den ~ verfehlen* to fall flat; *seinen ~ verfehlen* to miss o.'s aim; *e-n ~ verfolgen* to pursue an object; *der ~ heiligt die Mittel* the end justifies the means; *zu welchem ~?* what for? why? for what purpose? **~dienlich** *a* serviceable; expedient; answering the purpose; (*wirksam*) efficient; pertinent; convenient; **~~keit** *f* serviceableness; expediency; **~entsprechend** *a* appropriate, proper; answering the purpose; efficient; **~leuchte** *f* working lamp; **~los** *a* (*ziellos*) purposeless; aimless; to no purpose; (*unnütz*) useless; **~mäßig** *a* suitable; expedient; reasonable; practical; proper; fit; *es für ~~ halten* to think it proper; to deem expedient (*od* appropriate); **~~keit** *f* suitableness; expediency; **~~keitsgründe** *m pl* interest of expediency; **~verband** *m* association, combine for a common purpose; **~widrig** *a* inexpedient; unsuitable; inappropriate.

Zweck|e *f* (*Reißnagel*) drawing-pin, tack; (*Holz~~*) wooden peg; (*Schuh~~*) (hob)nail; **~en** *tr* to peg, to tack.

zwecks *prp* for the purpose of.

zwei *a u. f* two; *alle ~* both; the two; *die ~* (*im Spiel*) deuce; *zu ~en* two by two, in twos, in pairs; *zu ~en hintereinander* in double file; **~achser** *m mot* four-wheel vehicle; two-axle vehicle; **~achsig** *a* biaxial; *mot* four-wheel(ed); **~adrig** *a el* (*Litze*) two-stranded, twin; bifilar; **~armig** *a* two-armed; **~atomig** *a* diatomic; **~äugig** *a* binocular; *~~e Kamera phot* twin-lens camera; **~bändig** *a* in two volumes; **~basisch** *a* dibasic; **~bein** *n* bipod; **~beinig** *a* two-legged; **~bettig** *a* with two beds; **~blättrig** *a bot* bifoliate; **~bund** *m* double-alliance; **~decker** *m mar* two-decker; *aero* biplane; **~deutig** *a* ambiguous, equivocal; (*unklar*) doubtful; double-meaning; (*obszön*) obscene, smutty; *~~ reden* to equivocate; *~~es Verhalten* double-dealing; **~~keit** *f* ambiguity, equivocation; obscurity; **~dimensional** *a* two-dimensional; **~drittelmehrheit** *f* two thirds majority; **~er** *m mar* (*mit Steuermann*) pair with coxy, *Am* double scull; (*ohne Steuermann*) pair without coxy; **~erzelt** *n* two-man shelter tent; **~erlei** *a* of two kinds, two kinds of; (*verschieden*) of two different sorts, different; *aus ~~ Leder* of two kinds of leather; *das ist ~~* (*fam*) that's two different things; **~fach, ~fältig** *a* twofold, double; dual; twice; *in ~facher Ausfertigung* in duplicate; **~fachsteuerung** *f* dual control; **~familienhaus** *n Am* duplex house; **~farbendruck** *m typ* two-colo(u)r print(ing); **~farbig** *a* two-colo(u)red; two-tone; **~felderwirtschaft** *f* rotation of crops; **~flügelig** *a* two-winged; (*Tür*) two-leaf; *~~e Türe* folding door; *~~e Luftschraube aero* two bladed airscrew (*Am* propeller); **~flügler** *m pl* diptera *pl*; **~füßler** *m* biped; **~ganggetriebe** *n tech* two-ratio gear; **~geschlechtig** *a* of two sexes, bisexual; androgynous; **~gestirn** *n* double constellation; **~gestrichen** *a mus* twice accented; **~gleisig** *a* double-track(ed); *~~e Bahn* double-track railway; **~händig** *a* two-handed; *mus* for two hands; **~heit** *f* duality; **~höckerig** *a* two-humped; **~hufer** *m* cloven-footed animal; **~hundert** *a* two hundred; **~~jahrfeier** *f* bicentenary; *Am* bicentennial; **~jährig** *a* two-year-old; *bot* biennial; **~jährlich** *a* every two years; **~kammersystem** *n* two-chamber system; **~kampf** *m* single combat, duel; **~kindersystem** *n* two--child system; **~lebig** *a* amphibious; **~mächteausschuß** *m* Bipartite Board; **~mal** *adv* twice; *sich etw nicht ~~ sagen lassen* not to need to be told a thing twice; **~~ig** *a* done twice; (*wiederholt*) repeated; **~master** *m mar* two-master; brig; **~monatlich** *a* bi-monthly; every two month; **~motorig** *a* twin-engined; *~~es Düsenflugzeug* twin-jet; **~parteiensystem** *n* bi--partisan system, two-party system; **~polig** *a* bipolar; **~punktlandung** *f aero* two-point landing, *Am sl* French landing; **~rad** *n* bicycle, *fam* bike; **~rädrig** *a* two-wheeled; **~reihig** *a* double-rowed; with two rows; (*Sakko*) double--breasted; **~röhrenempfänger** *m radio* two-valve receiver; **~rud(e)rig** *a* two--oared; **~rumpfflugzeug** *n* double fuselage airplane, *Am* twin-boom aircraft; **~schenk(e)lig** *a* having two legs, two-legged; **~schläf(e)rig** *a* (*Bett*) double (bed); **~schneidig** *a* two-edged; *fig* (*Bemerkung*) ambiguous; **~schraubenschiff** *n* twin-screw ship; **~seitig** *a* two-sided; bilateral; (*Stoff*) reversible; *~~e Anzeige* double page spread; **~silbig** *a* dis(s)yllabic; *~~es Wort* di(s)-syllable; **~sitzer** *m* two-seater; *aero* two-seater (*od* two-place) airplane; *mot* (*Sport~~*) roadster; (*geschlossener*) coupé; (*Fahrrad*) tandem; **~sitzig** *a* two-seat(ed); **~spaltig** *a typ* in double columns; with two columns; *bot* two--cleft, bifid; **~spänner** *m* carriage and pair; **~spännig** *a* drawn by two horses; **~sprachig** *a* bilingual; in two languages; **~stärkenglas** *n opt* bifocal lens; (*Brille*) bifocal glasses *pl*, *fam* bifocals *pl*; **~stimmig** *a mus* for two voices; *~~er Gesang* duet; **~stöckig** *a* two-storied; two-stor(e)y; **~stufig** *a* two-stage; two-step; **~stündig** *a* lasting two hours; of two hours; **~stündlich** *a* every two hours; **~takter, ~taktmotor** *m* two-stroke engine, *Am* two-cycle engine; **~teilig** *a* in two pieces; two--piece; two-part; double; bipartite; **~teilung** *f* bipartition, bisection; **~unddreißigsteInote** *f* demisemiquaver; **~viertelnote** *f* minim; **~vierteltakt** *m* two-four time; **~weghahn** *m* two-way tap; **~wertig** *a* bivalent, divalent; **~~keit** *f* bivalence; **~wöchentlich** *a* fortnightly; **~zackig** *a* two-forked; two-pronged; **~zeiler** *m* couplet; **~zeilig** *a* of two lines, two-lined; **~zinkig** *a* two-pronged; **~zonen-** *in Zssg:* bizonal; **~~verwaltung** *f* bizonal administration; **~züngig** *a* two--tongued; *fig* double-tongued; *~~er Mensch* double dealer; **~zylindermotor** *m* two-cylinder engine.

Zweifel *m* doubt (*an* of); (*Verdacht*) suspicion; (*Frage*) question; (*Ungewißheit*) uncertainty; (*Befürchtung, böse Ahnung*) misgiving; (*Bedenken*) scruple; (*Zweifelsucht*) scepticism; (*Zögern*) hesitation, wavering; *ohne ~* without doubt, no doubt, doubtless, *es unterliegt keinem ~* there is no doubt; *darüber besteht nicht der geringste ~* there's not a shadow of a doubt about it; *außer ~* beyond (all) doubt; *~ stiegen in ihr auf* she had misgivings (*über* as to); *in ~ stehen* to be in two minds (about it); *in ~ ziehen* to call in question; **~haft** *a* doubtful; (*stärker*) dubious; (*ungewiß*) uncertain; (*fraglich*) questionable; (*verdächtig*) suspicious; equivocal; *ein ~~es Kompliment* a left-handed compliment; *e-e ~~e Persönlichkeit* a suspicious character; **~~igkeit** *f* doubtfulness; **~los** *a* doubtless, indubitable, undoubted; *adv* without doubt; decidedly; **~n** *itr* to doubt (*an etw* s. th.); to be in doubt (*über* about); (*fragen*) to question; (*schwanken*) to waver; to hesitate; (*Verdacht hegen*) to suspect; to be distrustful; *ich zweifle nicht daran* I don't doubt it; **~nd** *a* doubting; doubtful; sceptical; **~sfall** *m* case of doubt; doubtful case; **~sfrei** *a* free from doubt; **~sohne** *adv* without doubt, doubtless; **~sucht** *f* scepticism; **~süchtig** *a* sceptical.

Zweifler *m* doubter, sceptic.

Zweig *m* (*auch fig*) branch; bough; (*kleiner ~*) twig; (*Blumen~*) spray; (*Abteilung, Linie*) section; department; line; *er wird nie auf e-n grünen ~ kommen* he'll never get anywhere; **~anstalt** *f* branch establishment; **~bahn** *f* branch(--line); **~bank** *f* branch bank; **~bibliothek** *f* branch library; **~fabrik** *f* branch works *pl*; **~geschäft** *n* branch (of a shop etc); **~gesellschaft** *f* affiliated company; **~ig** *a* branchy; **~kabel** *n* branch cable; **~linie** *f* branch line, junction line; *aero* feeder line; **~niederlassung** *f* branch establishment; **~station** *f rail* junction; **~stelle** *f* branch office; **~verein** *m* branch-society; **~werk** *n* branch factory.

zweit *a* second, next; *~er* (*sport*) runner-up; *mein ~es Ich* my other self, my alter ego; *das ~e Gesicht* the second sight; *ein ~er Demosthenes* another Demosthenes; *aus ~er Hand* (*kaufen*) second-hand; *~e Kompanie* B company; *zu ~* two by two; two (of us), by twos; *wir sind zu ~* we are two of us; **~ältest** *a* second eldest; **~ausfertigung** *f* duplicate; **~best** *a* second-best; **~ens** *adv* secondly; in the second place; **~geboren** *a* second, younger; **~höchst** *a* second in height, highest but one; **~jüngst** *a* youngest but one; **~klassig** *a* second-rate; *ein ~~es Hotel* a second-rate hotel; *~~e Waren* seconds *pl*; **~letzt** *a* last but one; next to last; **~mädchen** *n* second maid; between-maid, *fam* tweeny; **~nächst** *a* next but one; **~rangig** *a* of secondary importance; second-rate; **~schrift** *f* duplicate.

zwerch *adv* (*über~*) across; **~fell** *n* diaphragm; midriff; *das ~~ erschüttern* to make s. o. split with laughing; **~~erschütternd** *a* side-splitting.

Zwerg *m*, **~in** *f* dwarf, pygmy; (*außerordentlich klein*) midget; little mite; *fam* shrimp; (*Heinzelmännchen*) manikin; brownie; **~apfelsine** *f* tangerine; mandarin; **~artig** *a* (of) diminutive (size); dwarfish, dwarf-like; pygmy; (*sehr klein*) midget; **~baum** *m* dwarf-tree, stunted tree; **~bildung** *f* dwarfishness; **~(en)haft** *a* diminutive; stunted; undersized, dwarfish, tiny; **~kiefer** *f* dwarf pine; **~könig** *m* dwarf king; **~lampe** *f el* pea lamp; **~maus** *f* harvest-mouse; **~mensch** *m* pygmy; **~obst** *n* dwarf-tree fruit; **~palme** *f* dwarf-palm; **~röhre** *f radio* midget valve; **~völker** *n pl* dwarf tribes *pl*; **~wuchs** *m* stunted growth.

Zwetsch(g)e *f* plum; (*gedörrt*) prune; **~nschnaps** *m*, **~nwasser** *n* plum spirits *pl*, plum schnaps.

*

Zwickel *m* (*im Strumpf*) clock; (*Hemd, Kleider*) gusset, gore; *arch* spandrel; (*Keil*) wedge; **~bart** *m* imperial; **~naht** *f* gore-seam.

zwick|en *tr* to pinch, to nip; to tweak; to gripe; **~er** *m* eye-glasses *pl*, pince-nez; **~mühle** *f* double-mill; (*ein Spiel*) whip-saw; *fig* dilemma; **~zange** *f* pincers *pl*, nippers *pl*, *Am* cutter.

Zwieback *m* biscuit, rusk, *Am* cracker, zwieback.

Zwiebel *f* onion; (*Blumen~*) bulb; *fam* (*dicke od schlechte Uhr*) turnip; **~artig** *a* bulbous; **~beet** *n* onion-bed; **~fische** *m pl typ* pies *pl*; **~geruch** *m* smell of onions; **~gewächs** *n* bulbous plant; **~n** *tr* to rub (*od* season) with onions; *fam* to maltreat, to treat s. o. harshly, to sweat; to worry, to torment; **~schale** *f* onion-peel; **~suppe** *f* onion-soup; **~turm** *m* onion-shaped dome; **~wurzel** *f* bulb.

zwie|fach, ~fältig *a* double, two-fold; **~gespräch** *n* dialogue; (*Unterhaltung*) conversation, talk; colloquy; (*Unterredung*) interview; **~licht** *n* twilight; (*Dämmerung*) dusk; *im ~~* at twilight, in the dusk; **~spalt** *m* dissension, discord, disunion; schism; **~spältig** *a* disunited; (*geteilt*) divided, (*widerstreitend*) conflicting; **~tracht** *f* discord, dissension; **~trächtig** *a* discordant, at variance.

Zwiesel *f* forked branch; bifurcation.

Zwil(l)ich *m* ticking; **~weber** *m* ticking-weaver.

Zwilling|e *m pl* twins *pl*; (*Knabe, Mädchen*) twin-boy, twin-girl; *eineiige ~~* identical twins; *zweieiige ~~* fraternal twins; *astr* Gemini *pl*; the Twins *pl*, *mil* (*Waffe*) twin-barrel(l)ed weapon; **~sachse** *f* twin axis; **~sbereifung** *f* double tyres (*Am* tires); **~sbildung** *f* twin formation; **~sbruder** *m* twin brother; **~sflugzeug** *n aero* composite aircraft; **~sgeschwister** *pl* twins *pl*; **~spaar** *n* pair (*od* set) of twins; **~sschwester** *f* twin sister; **~sstecker** *m el* biplug; **~striebwerk** *n aero* twin engine; **~swaffe** *f* twin-barrel(l)ed weapon.

Zwing|burg *f* stronghold; fortified castle; **~e** *f* (*Werkzeug*) clamp, cramp, holder; (*Endring*) ferrule, collar; (*Schraubstock*) vice(-pin); **~en** *irr tr* to force, to compel; (*nötigen*) to oblige; to bring pressure to bear on; to push; *Am* to crowd, *Am fam* to bulldoze; (*erledigen, besiegen*) to overcome; to finish; to get through; *sich ~~* to force o. s. to, to constrain o. s.; to make a great effort; **~end** *a* forcible, cogent; compulsory, mandatory; coercive; **~er** *m* (*Hof*) outer court(yard); (*Gefängnishof*) prison-yard; (*Tier~~*) den, cage; arena; (*Hunde~~*) kennel; (*Bären~~*) bear-pit; (*Turm*) tower, keep; dungeon; **~herr** *m* despot, tyrant; **~~schaft** *f* despotism, tyranny.

zwinkern *itr* to twinkle, to wink, to blink.

Zwirn *m* (*Faden*) thread; twine; sewing-cotton; yarn; **~band** *n* tape; **~en** *a* of thread; of yarn; *~~ tr* to twine, to twist; (*doppelt ~~*) to throw; **~faden** *m* thread; **~knäuel** *m* ball of thread; **~rolle** *f* reel (*Am* spool) of thread.

zwischen *prp* (*in der Mitte von zwei Dingen*) between; *poet* betwixt; (*unter e-r Anzahl*) among, amongst; *es ist ein Unterschied ~ ihm u. mir* there is a difference between him and me; *ein Mann ~ 50 u. 60* a man between fifty and sixty; *~ zwei Dingen befindlich* interjacent; *~ den Papieren* among the papers; **~akt** *m* entr'acte; interval; *im ~~* between the two acts; **~~smusik** *f* entr'acte music; **~bemerkung** *f* incidental remark; (*Unterbrechung*) interruption; (*Abschweifung*) digression; *theat* (*Aparte*) aside; **~bescheid** *m jur* interlocutory decree; **~bilanz** *f* interim balance (*od* statement); **~deck** *n mar* steerage, between-decks *pl*, lower deck; **~decke** *f* inserted ceiling; false floor; **~ding** *n* intermediate thing; mixture; combination; cross; **~durch** *adv* through; (*inmitten*) in the midst; (*zuzeiten*) at times; now and then; in between; between-while; **~ergebnis** *n sport* provisional result; **~essen, ~gericht** *n* side-dish, extra dish; **~fall** *m* incident; episode; *ohne ~~* uneventful; (*ganz glatt*) without a hitch; **~feld** *n* intermediate area; **~form** *f* temporary type; **~frequenzempfang** *m radio* superheterodyne reception; **~frage** *f* question interjected in speech (*od* thrown in); **~gerade** *f sport* straight between two curves; **~gericht** *n* entrée; extra-dish; **~gesang** *m* interlude of song; **~geschoß** *n* entresol; mezzanine; **~gewinn** *m* middleman's profit; **~glied** *n* connecting link; intermediate; **~hafen** *m* trading-port; emporium; **~handel** *m* middleman's business; carrying trade; intermediate trade; commission business; **~händler** *m* middleman; agent; intermediary; jobber; commission-agent; **~handlung** *f* episode, entr'acte; **~hirn** *n* diencephalon; betweenbrain; **~lage** *f* intermediate layer; inset; interposition; **~landung** *f aero* intermediate landing; stop; *Am* stopover; *ohne ~~* non-stop; *ohne ~~ um die Welt fliegen* **to fly non-stop** around the world; **~~splatz** *m aero* intermediate landing field; **~liegend** *a* intermediate; intervening; **~linie** *f* middle line; **~lösung** *f* solution for the time being; **~mahlzeit** *f* lunch; collation; **~mauer** *f* partition-wall; party-wall; **~pause** *f* (time) interval; break, interlude; **~person** *f* go-between; intermediary; **~raum** *m* interval; interstice; *typ* space (between); (*im Druck etc*) blank space; (*Weite*) clearance; (*Lücke*) gap; **~~taste** *f* (*Schreibmaschine*) space-bar, *Am* space key; **~rede** *f* interruption; **~regierung** *f* interregnum; **~ruf** *m* interruption; **~~er** *m* (*durch störende Fragen*) heckler; **~runde** *f sport* semi-final; **~satz** *m* parenthesis; **~schalten** *tr* to interpose; to insert; **~sender** *m radio* relay transmitter (*od* station); repeater station; **~sockel** *m radio* adapter; **~spiel** *n* interlude, intermezzo; **~staatlich** *a* international; *Am* interstate; **~station** *f rail* intermediate station; *Am rail* way station; **~stecker** *m el, radio* adapter; **~stellung** *f.* intermediate position; **~stock** *m* mezzanine; entresol; **~stück** *n* (*Einsatz*) inset; (*Verbindung*) connection; *el* adapter; *theat* interlude; **~stufe** *f* intermediate stage; **~stunde** *f* intermediate hour; *pl* odd hours *pl*; (*Schulpause*) recreation; **~titel** *m* sub-title; **~träger** *m* talebearer; telltale; scandal-monger; **~~ei** *f* talebearing; back-biting; **~verkehr** *m* intercommunication; **~vertreter** *m* intermediate agent; **~vorhang** *m theat* drop-scene; **~wand** *f* partition (-wall); (*Schott*) bulkhead; **~wasserung** *f aero* stop (*Am* stopover) of a seaplane; **~wirt** *m med* intermediate host; **~zeile** *f* intermediate line; interline, interlace; *typ* space line; **~zeit** *f* interval, interim; intervening time; *in der ~~* in the mean time; meanwhile; **~zone** *f* intermediate zone; **~zonen-** *in Zssg* interzonal; **~zustand** *m* intermediate stage (*od* state).

Zwist *m*, **~igkeit** *f* discord; dissension; (*Streit*) quarrel; dispute; **~ig** *a* at variance; in dispute, questionable; **~igkeit** *f* dissension, quarrel.

zwitschern *itr* to chirp, to twitter, to warble; *Am* to chipper; *~ n* chirping.

Zwitter *m allg* hybrid; cross; (*Mensch*) hermaphrodite; (*Bastard*) mongrel; **~bildung** *f* hybridization; hermaphroditism; **~fahrzeug** *n mil* half-track vehicle; **~haft** *a* hybrid; hermaphrodite; **~wort** *n* hybrid (word).

zwo = *zwei* (*nur beim Telephonieren gebraucht*).

zwölf *a* twelve; *~ Stück* a dozen; *~ Uhr mittags* at noon, *nachts* at midnight; *um halb ~* at half past eleven; **~eck** *n* dodecagon; **~ender** *m* stag with twelve antlers; **~erlei** *a* of twelve different sorts; **~fach** *a* twelvefold; **~fingerdarm** *m* duodenum; **~~geschwür** *n med* duodenal ulcer; **~flach** *n* dodecahedron; **~jährig** *a* twelve-year-old; **~malig** *a* repeated twelve times; **~pfünder** *m* twelve-pounder; **~seitig** *a* twelve-sided; **~tägig** *a* of twelve days, twelve days'; **~te** *a* twelfth; *in ~ter Stunde* at the last moment; **~teilig** *a* consisting of twelve parts; **~tel** *n* twelfth part; **~tens** *adv* in the twelfth place.

*

Zyan *n* cyanogen; **~eisen** *n* iron cyanide; **~kali(um)** *n* potassium cyanide; **~salz** *n* cyanide; **~verbindung** *f* cyanogen compound.
Zyklon *m* cyclone, tornado, hurricane; **~e** *f* area of low pressure.
Zyklop *m* Cyclops (*pl* Cyclopes); **~isch** *a* cyclopean.
Zyklotron *n phys* cyclotron; *Am sl* whirligig atomic gun; *Synchro~* synchro-cyclotron.
Zyk\|lus *m* cycle; (*von Vorlesungen*) set, course, series (of lectures); **~lisch** *a* cyclic(al).
Zylind\|er *m tech* (*mot, Walze, Trommel*) cylinder; (*Lampen~~*) chimney, glass; (*~~hut*) top-hat, silk hat; *Am* high hat, *Am fam* stovepipe hat, *Am fam* plug; **~erblock** *m mot* cylinder block, motor block; **~erbohrung** *f mot* cylinder bore; **~erdeckel** *m mot* cylinder cover; **~erdichtungsring** *m* packing ring; **~erhub** *m mot* length of stroke; **~erhut** *m* top-hat, silk hat; **~erinhalt** *m mot* cylinder volume (*od* displacement); **~erkopf** *m mot* cylinder head; **~erpresse** *f tech* roller-press; **~drisch** *a* cylindric(al).
Zyn\|iker *m* (*Philosoph*) Cynic; (*zynischer Mensch*) cynic, cynical person; **~isch** *a* cynical; (*schamlos*) shameless; impudent; **~ismus** *m* Cynicism; cynicism; shamelessness; impudence.
Zypern *n* (*Insel*) Cyprus.
Zypresse *f* cypress; **~nhain** *m* grove of cypresses.
Zyste *f med* cyst.

Abkürzungen – Abbreviations

A		
a	*Ar*	are (= 100 square meters)
a.	*an; an der; am; asymmetrisch*	on; on the; asymmetric
	aus	of
A.	*Alkohol; Ampere*	alcohol; ampere
Ä	*Äther*	ether
A. A.	*Auswärtiges Amt*	Foreign Office
a. a. O.	*am angeführten Ort*	(opere citato) in the work cited;
	am angegebenen Ort;	(loco citato) in the place cited
	an anderen Orten	elsewhere
Abb.	*Abbildung*	illustration, figure, cut, portrait
abds.	*abends*	in the evening, p. m.
Abf.	*Abfahrt*	departure
Abg.	*Abgeordnete(r)*	member
abh.	*abhängig*	dependent
Abh.	*Abhandlung*	papers, treatise
Abk.	*Abkürzung*	abbreviation
Abs.	*Absatz*	paragraph
	Absender	sender
abs.	*absolut*	absolute
Abschn.	*Abschnitt*	section, paragraph, chapter
abstr.	*abstrakt*	abstract
Abt.	*Abteilung*	department, section, part, division
Acc.	*Akzept*	acceptance, accepted bill
a. Chr.	*ante Christum (vor Christus)*	before Christ, B. C.
a. d.	*an der*	at the, on, on the
a. D.	*außer Dienst; an der Donau*	retired; on the Danube
Adr.	*Adresse*	address
Afl.	*Artillerieflieger*	artillery spotting pilot
afr.	*afrikanisch*	African
A. G.	*Atomgewicht*	atomic weight
	Aktiengesellschaft	joint-stock company, corporation;
	Arbeitsgemeinschaft	study group;
	Arbeitsgericht	labo(u)r court
A. H.	*Alter Herr*	former member of a (students') club
Ah	*Amperestunde*	ampere hour
ahd.	*althochdeutsch*	Old High German
Ak.	*Akademie*	academy
Akku.	*Akkumulator*	accumulator
Akt.-Ges.	*Aktiengesellschaft*	joint-stock company, corporation
Alk.	*Alkohol*	alcohol
allg.	*allgemein*	general, commonly
am	*an dem*	at the, to the, on the
Am.	*Amerikanismus*	Americanism
am.	*amerikanisch*	American
Amp.	*Ampere*	ampere
amtl.	*amtlich*	official
anerk.	*anerkannt*	recognized
Anf.	*Anfang*	beginning
Anfr.	*Anfrage*	inquiry
Ang., Angeb.	*Angebot*	application, offer
Angekl.	*Angeklagte(r)*	the accused, prisoner, defendant
Angest.	*Angestellte(r)*	employee
Anh.	*Anhang*	appendix
Ank.	*Ankunft*	arrival
Anl.	*Anlage*	inclosure, installation
Anm.	*Anmerkung*	remark, note
anorg.	*anorganisch*	inorganic
Anspr.	*Anspruch*	requirement
Anst.	*Anstalt*	institution; *med* asylum
Ant.	*Anteil(e)*	part(s)
Antw.	*Antwort*	answer, reply
Anw.	*Anwendung*	application
	Anwalt	lawyer, counsel, solicitor, attorney, advocate
	Anwärter	candidate
	Anweisung	instruction, direction, order, cheque, draft, money-order
Anz.	*Anzeiger*	announcer
a. o. Prof.	*außerordentlicher Professor*	assistant professor; university lecturer
AOK	*Armeeoberkommando*	Army High Command
	Allgemeine Ortskrankenkasse	Local Health Insurance
App.	*Apparat*	apparatus
Apr.	*April*	April
A. R.	*Aufsichtsrat*	board of directors
Arch.	*Archiv*	archive
Art.	*Artikel*	article
Ass.	*Assistent*	assistent
asymm.	*asymmetrisch*	asymmetric
A.T.	*Altes Testament*	Old Testament
at, Atm.	*Atmosphäre*	atmosphere
äth.	*ätherisch*	etheral
At.-Gew.	*Atomgewicht*	atomic weight
Atom-gew., Atgw.	*Atomgewicht*	atomic weight
Atü	*Atmosphäre Überdruck*	atmospheres absolute pressure
a. u. a.	*auch unter andern*	also among others
Aufg.	*Aufgang*	ascent, staircase
	Aufgabe	task, problem, lesson
Aufl.	*Auflage*	edition
Aufst.	*Aufstellung*	statement
Aug.	*August (Monat)*	August (month)
Ausg.	*Ausgabe*	edition (of book)
Ausl.	*Ausland, ausländisch*	foreign, export
Aussch.	*Ausschuß*	committee, board
ausschl.	*ausschließlich*	exclusive(ly)
Ausspr.	*Aussprache*	pronunciation
autom.	*automatisch*	automatic
a. Z.	*auf Zeit*	on credit, on account

B		
b.	*bei, beim, bei dem*	at, with, by
B.	*Beobachtung*	observation
	Brief (Kurszettel)	bills, papers
	Beispiel	example
Bch.	*Buch*	book
Bd.	*Band*	volume
Bde.	*Bände*	volumes
Bdtg.	*Bedeutung*	meaning
Bed.	*Bedeutung*	significance
bed.	*bedeutet*	signifies
beh.	*behandeln*	treat, handle
Beibl.	*Beiblätter*	supplements
beif.	*beifolgend*	(sent) herewith
Beil.	*Beilage*	enclosure, supplement
beil.	*beiliegend*	enclosed
bek.	*bekannt*	(well-)known
Bekl.	*Beklagte(r)*	accused, defendant
Bem.	*Bemerkung*	remark, note, comment
Beob.	*Beobachter*	observer
	Beobachtung	observation
ber.	*berechnet*	calculated
Ber.	*Bericht*	report
bes.	*besonders*	particularly, especially
best.	*bestimmt*	definite, determined, destined
Best.	*Bestimmung*	determination
	Bestellung	order
	Bestand	amount
betr.	*betreffend, betreffs*	concerned, said, in question, concerning
bev.	*bevollmächtigt*	authorized
bez.	*beziehungsweise*	respectively, or
	bezahlt	paid
	bezüglich	with reference to
bezl.	*bezüglich*	with reference to
Bez.	*Bezirk*	district
	Bezeichnung	mark, name
Bg.	*Bogen*	sheet
BGB	*Bürgerliches Gesetzbuch*	Code of Civil Law
B.H.	*Büstenhalter*	bra(ssière)
Bhf.	*Bahnhof*	station
bibl.	*biblisch*	biblical
bildl.	*bildlich*	figuratively, metaphorically
bisw.	*bisweilen*	sometimes
Bl.	*Blatt (Papier)*	paper
Bln.	*Berlin*	Berlin
Br.	*Bruder*	brother
br.	*breit*	wide
	broschiert	stitched
	brutto	gross weight
B.-G.	*Bruttogewicht*	gross weight
briefl.	*brieflich*	by letter
brit.	*britisch*	British
brosch.	*broschiert*	in paper covers
BRT.	*Bruttoregistertonnen*	gross register tons
b. w.	*bitte wenden*	please turn (page)
Bz.	*Bestellzettel*	order form
Bz., Bzn.	*Benzol*	benzene
bzw.	*beziehungsweise*	respectively, or

C

C	*Celsius*	centigrade
ca., cca.	*circa, zirka*	about, approximately, nearly
cal.	(*Gramm-*) *Kalorie*	gram calorie, small calorie
Cal.	(*Kilogramm-*) *Kalorie*	kilogram calorie, large calorie
cbm	*Kubikmeter*	cubic metre
ccm	*Kubikzentimeter*	cubic centimetre
cg	*Zentigramm*	centigram(s)
Chm.	*Chemie*	chemistry
chem.	*chemisch*	chemical
Chem.	*Chemiker*	chemist
Cie.	*Kompagnie, Gesellschaft*	company
cm	*Zentimeter*	centimetre
corr.	*corrigiert, korrigiert*	corrected
Cos	*Kosinus*	cosine

D

d.	*das, dem, den, der, des, die*	the, of the, to the, etc.
D.	*Dichte*	density, specific gravity
dad. gek.	*dadurch gekennzeichnet*	thereby characterized
Darst.	*Darstellung*	preparation
dch.	*durch*	through, by
dergl.	*dergleichen*	the like, such, same, similar
Deriv.	*Derivat*	derivative
d. s.	*das sind*	i. e., that is, namely
dsgl.	*desgleichen*	the like, such, same, similar
deut.	*deutsch*	German
dg	*Dezigramm*	decigram
d. Gr.	*der Große*	the Great
d. h.	*das heißt*	namely, that is, that is to say, i. e. which mean
d. i.	*das ist*	namely, that is
Dipl.-Ing.	*Diplomingenieur*	graduate engineer
Diss.	*Dissertation*	dissertation
d. m.	*dieses Monats*	of this month, instant
dm	*Dezimeter*	decimetre
Dm.	*Durchmesser*	diameter
DM	*Deutsche Mark*	German Mark
DIN, D.I.N.	*Deutsche Industrie Normen*	German Industry Standards
d. O.	*der Obige*	the above-mentioned
D. P. a.	*Deutsche Patentanmeldung*	German Patent Application
d. u.	*dienstuntauglich*	unfit for service
durchschn.	*durchschnittlich*	on the average
Dutz.	*Dutzend*	dozen
dz	*Doppelzentner (100 kg)*	hundredweight, cwt (100 kg)

E

E.	*Erstarrungspunkt*	freezing point, solidification point
	elektromotorische Kraft	electromotive force
ebd.	*ebenda*	at the same place
e. g.	*zum Beispiel*	for instance
e. h.	*ehrenhalber*	honorary
ehem., ehm.	*ehemals*	formerly
eidg.	*eidgenössisch*	Federal
eig.	*eigene*	own
Eigg. Eigsch.	*Eigenschaft(en)*	properties, property
eigtl.	*eigentlich*	properly speaking, true, especially
Einfl.	*Einfluß*	influence
einschl.	*einschließlich*	including, inclusive of
Einw.	*Einwirkung*	influence, action, effect
E. K.	*Eisernes Kreuz*	iron cross
el.	*elektrisch*	electric
Elekt.	*Elektrizität*	electricity
elektrol.	*elektrolytisch*	electrolytic
EMK	*elektromotorische Kraft*	electromotive force, EMF
enth.	*enthaltend*	containing
engl.	*englisch*	English
entspr.	*entsprechend*	corresponding
Entsteh.	*Entstehung*	origin
entw.	*entweder*	either
	entwickelt	developed
Entw.	*Entwicklung*	development, evolution
Erg.Bd.	*Ergänzungsband*	supplementary volume
Erh.	*Erhitzung*	heating
Erk.	*Erkennung*	recognition, detection
etc.	*et cetera, und so weiter*	et cetera, and so on, and so forth
etw.	*etwas*	something
e. V.	*eingetragener Verein*	incorporated
ev.	*evangelisch*	Protestant
ev., event., evtl.	*eventuell*	perhaps, possibly
EVG	*Europäische Verteidigungs-Gemeinschaft*	European Defense Community (*Abk* EDC)
exkl.	*exklusive*	excepted, not included
exp.	*experimentell*	experimental
Expl.	*Exemplar*	copy
Extr.	*Extrakt*	extract
E-Zug	*Eilzug*	fast passenger train

F

F	*Fernsprecher*	telephone
F, F.	*Fahrenheit*	Fahrenheit, F.
F.	*Fusionspunkt*	fusion point, melting point
f.	*fast*	almost
	fest	solid
	fein	fine
	folgende	the following, onward
	für	for
Fam.	*Familie*	family
farbl.	*farblos*	colo(u)rless
FD-Zug	*Fern-D-Zug*	long-distance express
ff., fff.	*sehr fein*	very fine, extra fine
ff., f. f.	*und folgende*	and following
F. f.	*Fortsetzung folgt*	to be continued
Fig.	*Figur*	figure
fl.	*flüssig*	liquid, fluid
Fl.	*Flüssigkeit*	liquid, fluid
Flak.	*Flugabwehrkanone*	anti-aircraft gun
Flugschr.	*Flugschrift*	pamphlet
Fol.	*Folio*	page, folio
folg.	*folgend*	following
Forts.	*Fortsetzung*	continuation
Forts. f.	*Fortsetzung folgt*	to be continued
fr.	*frei*	post free, post paid
Fr.	*Frau*	Mrs.
frakt.	*fraktioniert*	fractionated
franz.	*französisch*	French
Frhr.	*Freiherr*	Baron
Frl.	*Fräulein*	Miss, fraulein
frz.	*französisch*	French
FS	*Fernsehen*	television
F.T.	*Funkentelegraphie*	radiotelegraphy
Frzbd.	*Franzband*	calf binding

G

G	*Geld (gefragt)*	mainly buyers, in demand but not available
g	*Gramm*	gram(me)
G. E.	*Gewichtseinheit*	unit of weight, standard of weight
Geb.	*Gebirge*	mountain(s), range
geb.	*gebildet*	formed, educated
	geboren	born
	gebunden	bound
Gbf.	*Güterbahnhof*	goods station, *Am* freight yard
Gebr.	*Gebrüder*	Brothers
gebr.	*gebräuchlich*	used commonly
	gebräunt	burned
gef.	*gefunden*	found
	gefälligst	kindly
gefl.	*gefälligst*	kindly
Gef. P.	*Gefrierpunkt*	freezing point
geg.	*gegen*	against
Gegenw.	*Gegenwart*	presence
gegr.	*gegründet*	founded
geh.	*geheftet*	sewn, paper-bound
Geh.	*Gehilfe*	assistant, help
gek.	*gekocht*	boiled
gel.	*gelöst*	dissolved
gem.	*gemahlen*	ground, powdered, pulverized
	gemischt	mixed
	gemäß	according to, in consequence of
Gen.	*Genossenschaft*	association, company, co-operative society
	Genitiv	genitive
gen.	*genannt*	mentioned
Gen.-Dir.	*Generaldirektor*	chief manager
geolog.	*geologisch*	geological
Ges.	*Gesellschaft*	company, society
ges.	*gesamt*	total
	gesetzlich	by law
	gesättigt	saturated
gesch.	*geschieden*	divorced
Geschst.	*Geschäftsstelle*	office, bureau
Geschw.	*Geschwister*	brother(s) and sister(s)
ges. gesch.	*gesetzlich geschützt*	patented, protected by law; registered trademark
gespr.	*gesprochen*	spoken
gest.	*gestorben*	died
gew.	*gewöhnlich*	usual, ordinary
Gew.-T.	*Gewichtsteil*	part by weight
gez.	*gezeichnet*	signed
g. g.	*gegen*	against

Ggw.	*Gegenwart*	presence
G. K.	*Geschlechtskrankheit*	venereal disease, V. D.
Gl.	*Gleichung*	equation
	Gletscher	glacier
Gldr.	*Ganzleder*	leather
gl. N.	*gleichen Namens*	of the same name
GM.	*Gebrauchsmuster*	registered trademark
G. m. b. H.	*Gesellschaft mit beschränkter Haftung*	limited (liability) company, *Am* Incorperated
g-Mol.	*Grammolekül*	gram(me) molecule
g. R.	*gegen Rückgabe*	please return
gr	*Gramm*	gram(me)
	groß	great, large
gr. 8°	*groß 8°*	large 8°
gründl.	*gründlich*	entirely, fundamentally
GV.	*Generalversammlung*	general meeting
	Gerichtsvollzieher	sheriff, bailiff

H

H.	*Haben*	credit
	Heizwert	calorific value
	Härte	hardness
	Höhe	height, altitude
	el Henry	*el* henry
	Hydrogenium	hydrogen
h.	*heiß*	hot
	hoch	high
h	hora, *Stunde*	hour
ha	*Hektar*	hectare
Hbf.	*Hauptbahnhof*	main station, central station
H.D.	*Hochdruck*	high pressure
Hdb.	*Handbuch*	manual, handbook, compendium
Heilk.	*Heilkunde*	medical science, therapeutics
Hekt	*Hektoliter*	hectoliter
herg.	*hergestellt*	produced
Herst.	*Herstellung*	production, construction, manufacture
HF	*Hochfrequenz*	high frequency
HK	*Hefner-Kerze(n)*	Hefner candle(s)
Hl.	*Halbleder*	half leather
hl	*Hektoliter*	100 litre
hl.	*heilig*	holy
Hlw.	*Halbleinwand*	half cloth
HO	*Handelsorganisation*	trade-organization
Hochsch.	*Hochschule*	university, college
Hp.	*rail Haltepunkt*	stop, station
Hr.	*Herr*	Mr.
hrsg.	*herausgegeben*	edited
Hyp.	*Hypothek*	mortgage
hypothek.	*hypothekarisch*	hypothecary

I

i.	*in*	in
	im	
i. A.	*im Auftrag*	by order, on behalf of
i. allg.	*im allgemeinen*	in general
i.Durchschn.	*im Durchschnitt*	on the average
i. J.	*im Jahre*	in the year
inakt.	*inaktiv*	inactive
Inaug. Diss.	*Inaugural Dissertation*	thesis for doctor's degree
Ind.	*Industrie*	industry
Inh.	*Inhalt*	content, capacity
inkl.	*inklusiv*	inclusive, including
insb.	*insbesondere*	in particular
Inst.	*Institut*	institute
i. R.	*im Ruhestand*	retired, emeritus
i. V.	*in Vertretung*	by order, on behalf of
I. W.	*innere Weite*	inside diameter
i. W. v.	*im Werte von*	amounting to

J

J.	*Journal*	journal
	Jahrbuch	annual
	Jahresbericht	annual report
	Jahr	year
Jb	*Jahrbuch*	annual
Jg.	*Jahrgang*	year's set, class
Jhrb.	*Jahrbuch*	annual
jun., jr.	*junior*	junior

K

K	*Konstante*	constant
K.	*Kalorie*	calorie
k.	*kaiserlich*	imperial
	königlich	royal
	kalt	cold
Ka.	*Kathode*	cathode
Kap.	*Kapitel*	chapter
kart.	*kartoniert*	bound in boards
kath.	*katholisch*	Roman-Catholic
K. G.	*Kommanditgesellschaft*	limited partnership
Kg, kg	*Kilogramm*	kilogram(s)
kgl.	*königlich*	royal
Kl.	*Klasse*	class
k. M.	*kommenden Monats*	of next month
km	*Kilometer*	kilometre
Kn, kn	*Knoten*	knot
Koeffiz.	*Koeffizient*	coefficient
Komp.	*Kompanie*	company
kompr.	*komprimiert*	compressed
Konj.	*Konjunktiv*	subjunctive mood
konst.	*konstant*	constant
konz.	*konzentriert*	concentrated
korr.	*korrigiert*	corrected
Kr.	*Kran*	crane
krist.	*kristallisiert, kristallinisch*	crystallized, crystalline
krit.	*kritisch*	critical
Kryst.	*Kristall*	crystal
kub.	*kubisch*	cubic
kW, kw	*Kilowatt*	kilowatt
KWst.' kWh	*Kilowattstunde*	kilowatt hour
K. Z.	*Konzentrationslager*	concentration camp

L

L.	*Lösung*	solution
l.	*lies*	read
	löslich	soluble
	Liter	liter
	links	left
	linksdrehend	levorotatory
lab.	*labil*	labile, unstable
landw.	*landwirtschaftlich*	agricultural
langj.	*langjährig*	for many years
Ldrbd	*Lederband*	leather binding
Lebensl.	*Lebenslauf*	career
Legg.	*Legierungen*	alloys
leichtl.	*leichtlöslich*	easily soluble
lfd.	*laufend*	current, running, consecutive, regular
lfd. Nr.	*laufende Nummer*	serial number, current number, running number
Lfg.	*Lieferung*	issue, number, part
lg.	*lang*	long, in length
Lit.	*Literatur*	literature
l. J.	*laufenden Jahres*	of the current year
lösl.	*löslich*	soluble
LS	*Luftschutz*	A. R. P.
LS-Keller		bombproof cellar, shelter, S.
lt.	*laut*	in accordance with
Lw., Lwd.	*Leinwand*	linen, cloth, canvas
l. w.	*lichte Weite*	inside diameter, width in the clear
L-Zug	*Luxuszug*	train de luxe

M

M	*Mark*	mark(s)
M.	*Masse*	mass
	Molekulargewicht	molecular weight
	Monat	month
m	*Meter*	metre, *Am* meter
m.	*Minute*	minute
	mit	with
	Meta	meta
mA	*Milliampere*	milliampere
magnet.	*magnetisch*	magnetic
m. A. n.	*meiner Ansicht nach*	in my opinion
m. a. W.	*mit anderen Worten*	in other words
max	*maximum*	maximum
m. b. H.	*mit beschränkter Haftung*	with limited liability, limited
M. d. B.	*Mitglied des Bundestags*	member of the Bundestag
M. d. L.	*Mitglied des Landtags*	member of the Diet
M. E.	*Mache-Einheit*	Mache unit
m. E.	*meines Erachtens*	in my opinion
mechan.	*mechanisch*	mechanical(ly)
metall.	*metallisch*	metallic
Meth.	*Methode*	method
M. E. Z.	*Mitteleuropäische Zeit*	Central European Time
M. G.	*Maschinengewehr*	machine gun
	Molekulargewicht	molecular weight
mg	*Milligramm*	milligram
mhd.	*mittelhochdeutsch*	Middle High German
Mill.	*Million*	million
Min.	*Minute(n)*	minute(s)
min.	*minimal, minimum*	minimum
Mitt.	*Mitteilung*	communication, report
mitt.	*mittels*	by means of
Mk	*Mark*	mark(s)
mkr.	*mikroskopisch*	microscopic
Mm, mm	*Millimeter*	millimetre
möbl.	*möbliert*	furnished
mögl.	*möglich*	possible

Mol. *Molekül(e)* molecule(s)
mol. *molekular* molecular
Mol.-Gew. *Molekulargewicht* molecular weight
Mo-natsh. *Monatshefte* monthly number (of a publication)
Ms. *Manuskript* manuscript
m. W. *meines Wissens* as far as I know
mx. *Maximum* maximum

N

N. *nachts* at night, p. m.
nachmittags afternoon, p. m.
Leistung output, load
n. *nach* after
neutral neutral
nördlich northern
normal normal
Nutzeffekt efficiency
Nachf. *Nachfolger* successors
n. Chr. *nach Christus* after Christ, A. D.
Nd. *Niederschlag* precipitate
neutr. *neutralisiert* neutralized
nhd. *neuhochdeutsch* New High German
n. J. *nächstes Jahr* next year
Nm. *nachmittags* afternoon, p.m.
n. M. *nächsten Monats* of next month, proximo
NN *Normalnull* sea-level
No. *Numero, Nummer* number
Norm. *Normen* standards
Nr. *Nummer* number
N. T. *Neues Testament* New Testament

O

O *Ost* east
o. *oben* above
oder or
ohne without
ordinär ordinary grade
ortho ortho
o. B. *ohne Befund* without findings
Obb. *Oberbayern* South Bavaria
od. *oder* or
o. dgl. o.drgl. *oder dergleichen* or the like, or similar
OEZ *Osteuropäische Zeit* time of the east European zone
OG *Ortsgruppe* local branch
o. J. *ohne Jahr* no date
o. O. *ohne Ort* no date
o. O. u. J. *ohne Ort und Jahr* without place or date
opt. *optisch* optical
Ord. *Ordnung* order
org. *organisch* organic
Ostpr. *Ostpreußen* East Prussia

P

P. *Pater* Father
Pastor Minister
p. *pro* per
p. A. *per Adresse* care of, c/o
pa. *prima* first-class
Pf. *Pfennig* pfennig
Pfund pound
Pferd(e) horse(power)
Pfl. *Pflanze* plant
phys. *physikalisch* physical
P. K. *Pferdekraft* horsepower
Pkt. *Punkt* point
P.K.W. Pkw. *Personenkraftwagen* motor car
pl. *Plural* plural
p. m. *pro Minute* per minute, per min.
p. p., ppa. *per procura* by proxy, per pro
Ppbd. *Pappband* (bound in) boards
prakt. *praktisch* practical, applied
prim. *primär* primary
Prod. *Produkt* product
Prof. *Professor* (University) professor
Progr. *Programm* program(me)
prot. *protestantisch* Protestant
Prov. *Provinz* province
Proz. *Prozent, prozentig* per cent, percentage
PS, P.S. *Postskriptum* postscript
PS *Pferdestärke* horsepower

Q

q *Quadrat* square
qcm *Quadratzentimeter* square centimetre
qkm *Quadratkilometer* square kilometre
qm *Quadratmeter* square metre

R

R *Reaumur, el. Widerstand* Reaumur, electrical resistance
r. *Radius* radius
rechtsdrehend dextro-rotatory
Rab. *Rabatt* discount, rebate, reduction
raff. *raffiniert* refined
rd. *rund* about, approximately, nearly
Red. *Reduktion* reduction
Ref. *Referat* report, abstract
Reg.-Bez. *Regierungsbezirk* administrative district
Rep. *Report* report
resp. *respektive* respectively, or, or rather
rglm. *regelmäßig* regular(ly)
Rh. *Rhein* Rhine
RM *Reichsmark* Reichsmark(s)
rm *Raummeter* cubic metre
R. P. *Reichspatent* state patent
R.T. *Raumteil* part by volume

S

S. *Säure* acid
Seite page
Sekunde second
s. *Sekunde* second
siehe see
symmetrisch symmetric(al)
SA *Sonderabdruck* reprint
Sa. *Summa* total, together
s. a. *siehe auch* see also
s. a. S. *siehe auch Seite* see also page
schr. *schriftlich* in writing
Schw. *schwedisch* Swedish
schweizerisch Swiss
sd. *siedend* boiling
s. d. *siehe dies* see this
siehe dort see there
sec *Sekunde* second
s.g. *sogenannt* so-called
sied. *siedend* boiling
sk. *Sekunde* second
s. o. *siehe oben* see above
sof. *sofort* immediate
sog., sogen. *sogenannt* so-called
spez. *speziell* especially
spezifisch specific
spez. Gew. *spezifisches Gewicht* specific gravity, specific weight
Spl. *Supplement* supplement
S. S. *Sommersemester* summer term
s. S. *siehe Seite* see page
St. *Stahl* steel
Stunde hour
Stück each, in number
Std., Stde., Stdn *Stunde(n)* hour(s)
std. *stündig* for hour(s)
Str. *Straße* street
s. u. *siehe unten* see below
subcut. *subkutan* subcutaneous, hypodermic
subl. *sublimiert* sublimes
Subst. *Substanz* substance
s. w. u. *siehe weiter unten* see below
s. Z., s. Zt. *seiner Zeit* in due time, at that time, then

T

T. *Tausend* thousand
Teile parts
Tonnen tons
T *absolute Temperatur* absolute temperature
t *Tonne(n)* ton(s)
t *Celsiusgrad* centigrade
Tab. *Tabelle* table
tägl. *täglich* daily, everyday
Tato *Tagestonnen* tons per day
Tbc. *Tuberkulose* tuberculosis
techn. *technisch* technical
Teilh. *Teilhaber* partner
teilw. *teilweise* partly
Tel. *Telephon, Telefon* telephone
Tel.-Adr. *Telegramm-Adresse* telegraphic address, cable address
Temp. *Temperatur* temperature
tert. *tertiär* tertiary
Tfl. *Tafel* table
tgl. *täglich* daily, everyday
TH *Technische Hochschule* technical university (*od* college), central engineering school
t/h *Stundentonne* tons per hour
Tit. *Titel* title
tkm *Tonnenkilometer* tons per km
Tl(e) *Teil(e)* part(s) by weight
T-Mine *Tellermine* A.T. mine
Tonk. *Tonkunst* music, musical art
Toto *Totalisator* totalizator, totalizer, tote
Trafo *Transformator* transformer
Tragk. *Tragkraft* carrying capacity
tschech. *tschechisch* Czech

U

U *Uran(ium)* Uranium
U. *Umdrehung* revolution
Uhr hour, o'clock

u.	*und*	and
	unten	below
	unter	under, among
u. a.	*und andere*	and others, and other things
	unter andern	among others, moreover
	unter anderem	among other things
u. a. a.	*und an anderen Orten*	and elsewhere
u. a. m.	*und andere mehr*	and many others
	und anderes mehr	and so forth, and so on
u. ä. m.	*und ähnliches mehr*	and the like, and so on
u. a. O.	*und andere Orte*	and elsewhere
	unter anderen Orten	among other places
u. A. w. g.	*um Antwort wird gebeten*	an answer is requested, R. S. V. P., please, reply
U-Bahn	*Untergrundbahn*	underground, tube, *Am* subway
übers.	*übersetzt*	translated
übertr.	*übertragen*	figurative sense
U-Boot	*Unterseeboot*	submarine
u. d. f.	*und die folgenden*	and those following
u. dgl. (m.)	*und dergleichen (mehr)*	and the like
u. d. L.	*unter der Leitung*	under the direction, under the management
u. d. M.	*unter dem Meeresspiegel*	below sea-level
ü. d. M.	*über dem Meeresspiegel*	above sea-level
UdSSR	*Union der Sozialistischen Sowjetrepubliken*	Union of Soviet Socialist Republics
u. E.	*unseres Erachtens*	in our opinion
u. e. a.	*und einige andere*	and some others
u. f.	*und folgende*	and the following, onward
u. ff.	*und folgende*	and the following, onward
UKW	*Ultrakurzwelle*	ultra-short wave
UKW FM	*Ultrakurzwellen-Frequenzmodulation*	ultra-short wave frequency modulation
ult.	*ultimo, am letzen des Monats*	on the last day of the month
Umwandl.	*Umwandlung*	transformation, conversion
unb.	*unbekannt*	unknown
unbest.	*unbestimmt*	uncertain
ung.	*ungefähr*	about, approximately
ungebr.	*ungebräuchlich*	unusual
Univ.	*Universität*	university
unpers.	*unpersönlich*	impersonal
Unters.	*Untersuchung*	examination, investigation
u. R.	*unter Rückerbittung*	to be returned
urspr.	*ursprünglich*	original, first, primary
Urt.	*Urteil*	view, opinion, *jur* judgement, decision, sentence
u. s. f.	*und so fort*	and so on, and so forth, etc.
u. s. w.	*und so weiter*	and so forth, and so on, etc.
u. U.	*unter Umständen*	on occasion, under certain conditions, perhaps, circumstances permitting
u. ü. V.	*unter üblichem Vorbehalt*	with the usual reserves
u. zw.	*und zwar*	namely, that is

V

V.	*Volt*	volt(s)
	vormittags	in the forenoon
	Vorkommen	occurrence
	Vers	line, verse
	Verfasser	author
	Verfügung	order
	Verordnung	ordinance
v.	*vom*	by
	von	from, of
	vormals	formerly
	vide, siehe	see
vb.	*verbessert*	revised
v. Chr.	*vor Christus*	before Christ, B. C.
ver.	*vereinigt*	united
Verb.	*Verbindung*	compound
verb.	*verbessert*	revised, improved
verbr.	*verbraucht*	consumed, used
Verf.	*Verfasser*	author
Vergl.	*Vergleich*	comparison
vergl.	*vergleiche*	refer, see, compare
Vergr.	*Vergrößerung*	magnification
Verh.	*Verhalten*	behavio(u)r
	Verhältnis	condition, proportion, ration
verh.	*verheiratet*	married
verkl.	*verkleinert*	reduced
Verl.	*Verlag*	publishing house
	Verleger	publisher
verm.	*vermehrt*	increased
	vermählt	married
Vers.	*Versuch*	test, trial, experiment
	Versammlung	meeting
versch.	*verschieden*	different
verst.	*verstorben*	deceased, late
verw.	*verwandt*	related
	verwitwet	widowed
vgl.	*vergleiche*	compare, see, refer
v., g., u.	*vorgelesen, genehmigt, unterschrieben*	read, confirmed, signed
v. H.	*vom Hundert*	per cent
v. J.	*vorigen Jahres*	(of) last year
v. M.	*vorigen Monats*	of last month, ultimo
vm.	*vormittags*	in the forenoon, in the morning
	vormals	formerly
Vol.	*Volumen*	volume
vor.	*vorig*	former, preceding
vorm.	*vormittags*	in the forenoon, a. m.
	vormals	previously, formerly
Vors.	*Vorsitzender*	chairman
V. St. A.	*Vereinigte Staaten von Amerika*	U.S.A.
v. T.	*von Tausend, pro Mille*	per thousand
v. u.	*von unten*	from below, from the bottom
VW	*Volkswagen*	people's car
Vw.	*Verwaltung*	administration

W

W	*Widerstand*	electric resistance;
	West(en)	West
	Watt	Watt(s)
W.	*Wasser*	water
	Watt	watt(s)
	Wechsel	bill of exchange
	wenden	please turn over
w.	*warm*	warm, hot
Wb.	*Wörterbuch*	dictionary
W. E.	*Wärmeeinheit*	heat unit
Wewa	*Wetterwarte*	meteorological observatory (*od* station)
WEZ	*Westeuropäische Zeit*	Western European Time
Wirk.	*Wirkung*	effect, action
wirtschaftl.	*wirtschaftlich*	economic(al)
wiss.	*wissenschaftlich*	scientific
wktgs.	*werktags*	on week-days
w. L.	*westliche(r) Länge*	west longitude
w. o.	*weiter oben*	above
	wie oben	as above
W. S.	*Wintersemester*	winter term
Württ.	*Württemberg*	Württemberg
Wwe.	*Witwe*	widow

Z

Z.	*Zahl*	number
	Zeile	line
	Zeit	time
	Zeitschrift	journal
	Zoll	inch
z.	*zu, zum, zur*	at, to, for, by
zahlr.	*zahlreich*	numerous
z. B.	*zum Beispiel*	for example, for instance, e. g.
z. b. V.	*zur besonderen Verwendung*	for special use, unattached
Zeitschr.	*Zeitschrift*	journal, periodical
Zers.	*Zersetzung*	decomposition
z. H.	*zu Händen*	attention of, care of, c/o
z. S.	*zur See*	of the navy
z. s. Z.	*zu seiner Zeit*	in due time, at its time
z. T.	*zum Teil*	partly, in part
Ztg.	*Zeitung*	journal, newspaper
Ztr.	*Zentner*	hundredweight
Ztschr.	*Zeitschrift*	journal, periodical
Ztw.	*Zeitwort*	verb
Zus.	*Zusatz*	addition
	Zusammensetzung	composition
zus.	*zusammen*	together, total(l)ing
zuw.	*zuweilen*	sometimes
zw.	*zwar*	true, no doubt
	zwischen	between
Zyl.	*Zylinder*	cylinder
z. Z., z. Zt.	*zur Zeit*	at the time being, at present. presently; acting

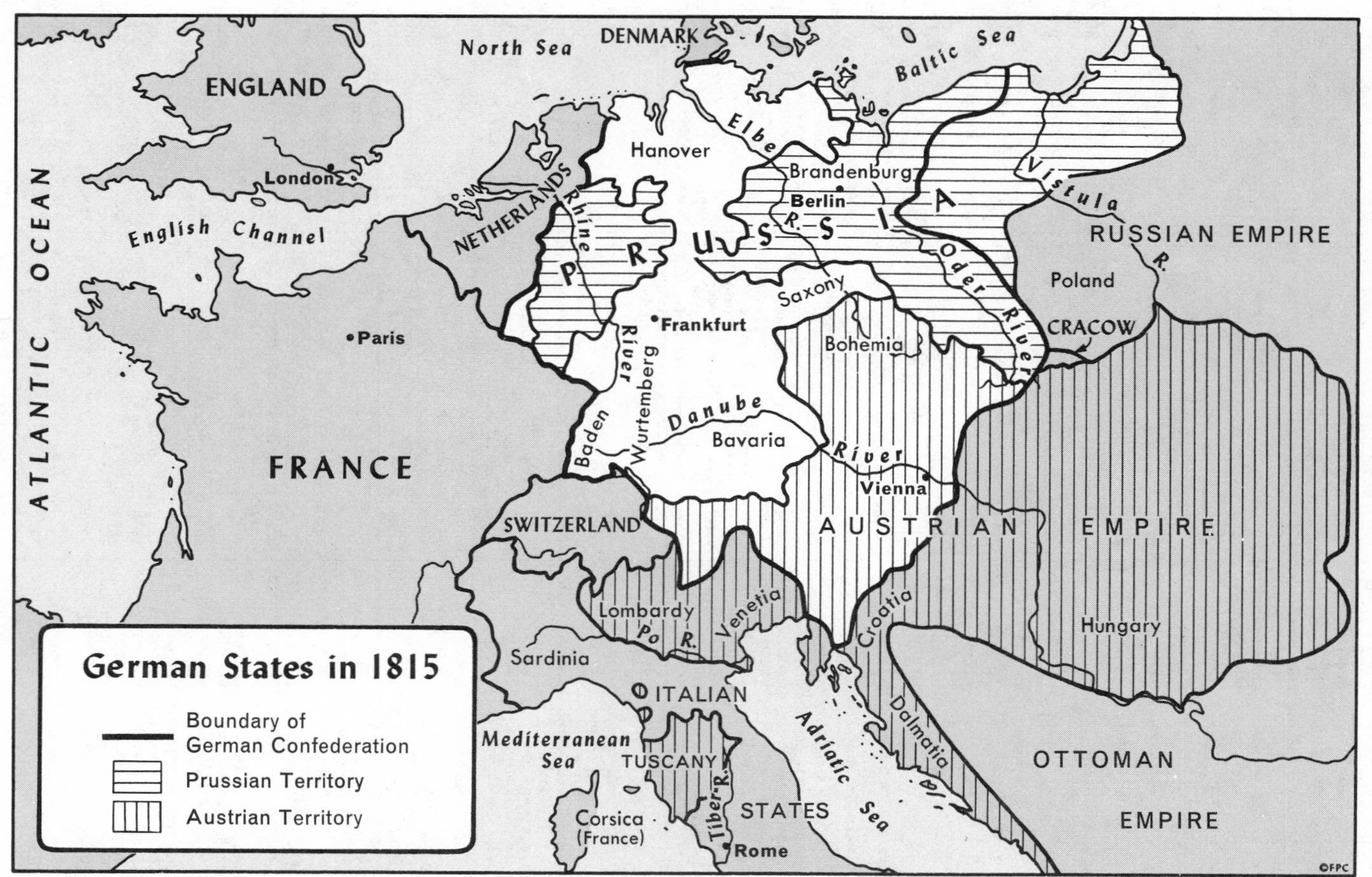
German States in 1815
Boundary of German Confederation
Prussian Territory
Austrian Territory
ATLANTIC OCEAN
North Sea
DENMARK
Baltic Sea
ENGLAND
London
English Channel
NETHERLANDS
Hanover
Elbe
Brandenburg
Berlin
R.
PRUSSIA
Vistula
RUSSIAN EMPIRE
R.
Poland
CRACOW
Oder River
Rhine
Saxony
Frankfurt
Paris
River
Bohemia
Wurtemberg
Danube
Baden
Bavaria
River
Vienna
FRANCE
SWITZERLAND
AUSTRIAN EMPIRE
Lombardy
Po R.
Venetia
Croatia
Hungary
Sardinia
ITALIAN STATES
Mediterranean Sea
TUSCANY
Tiber R.
Corsica (France)
Rome
Adriatic Sea
Dalmatia
OTTOMAN EMPIRE
©FPC

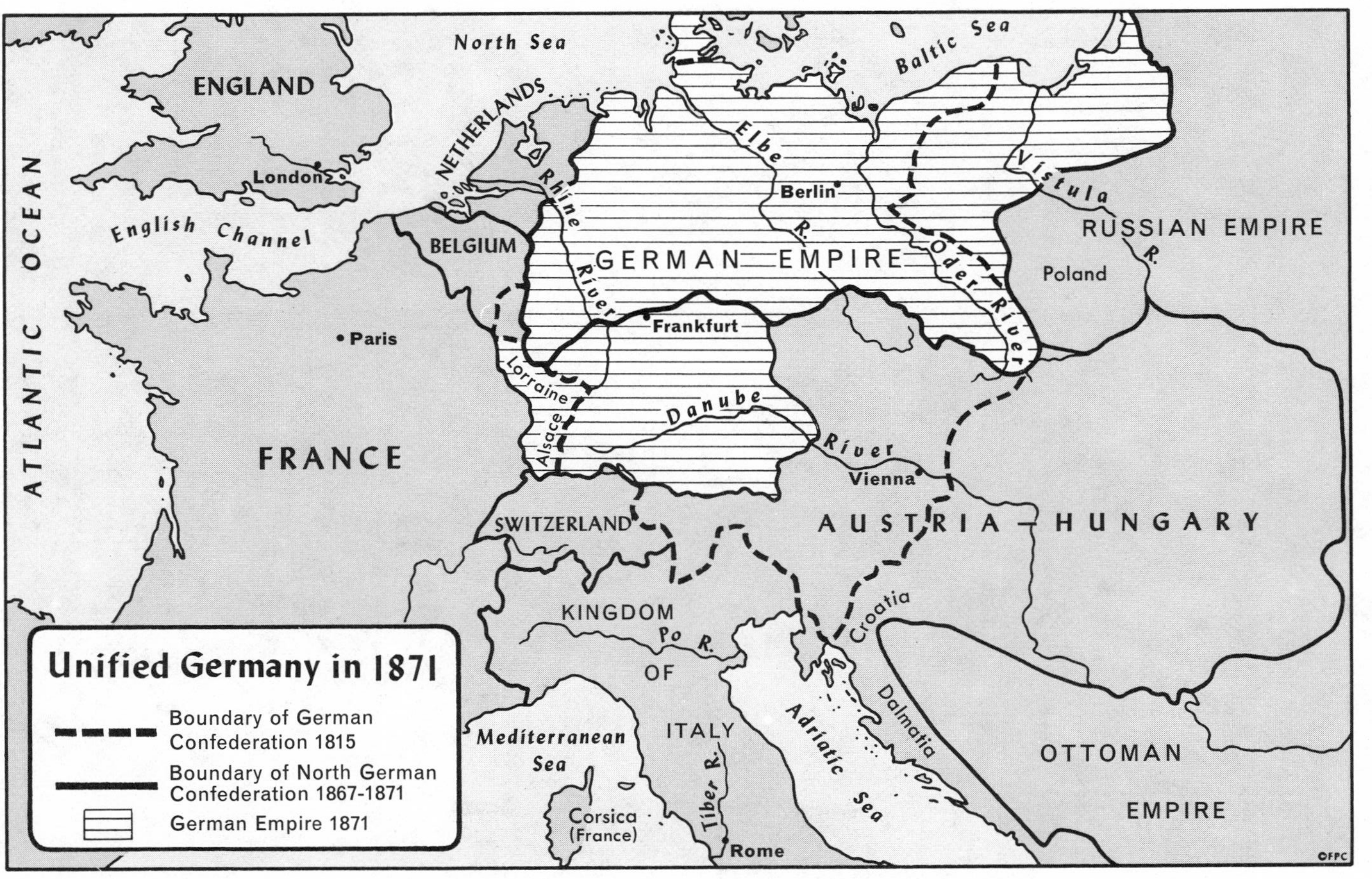
Unified Germany in 1871
Boundary of German Confederation 1815
Boundary of North German Confederation 1867-1871
German Empire 1871
ATLANTIC OCEAN
North Sea
Baltic Sea
ENGLAND
London
English Channel
NETHERLANDS
BELGIUM
Paris
FRANCE
Rhine River
Elbe R.
Berlin
GERMAN EMPIRE
Oder River
Vistula R.
RUSSIAN EMPIRE
Poland
Frankfurt
Lorraine
Alsace
Danube River
Vienna
AUSTRIA-HUNGARY
SWITZERLAND
KINGDOM OF ITALY
Po R.
Croatia
Dalmatia
Adriatic Sea
Mediterranean Sea
Corsica (France)
Tiber R.
Rome
OTTOMAN EMPIRE
©FPC

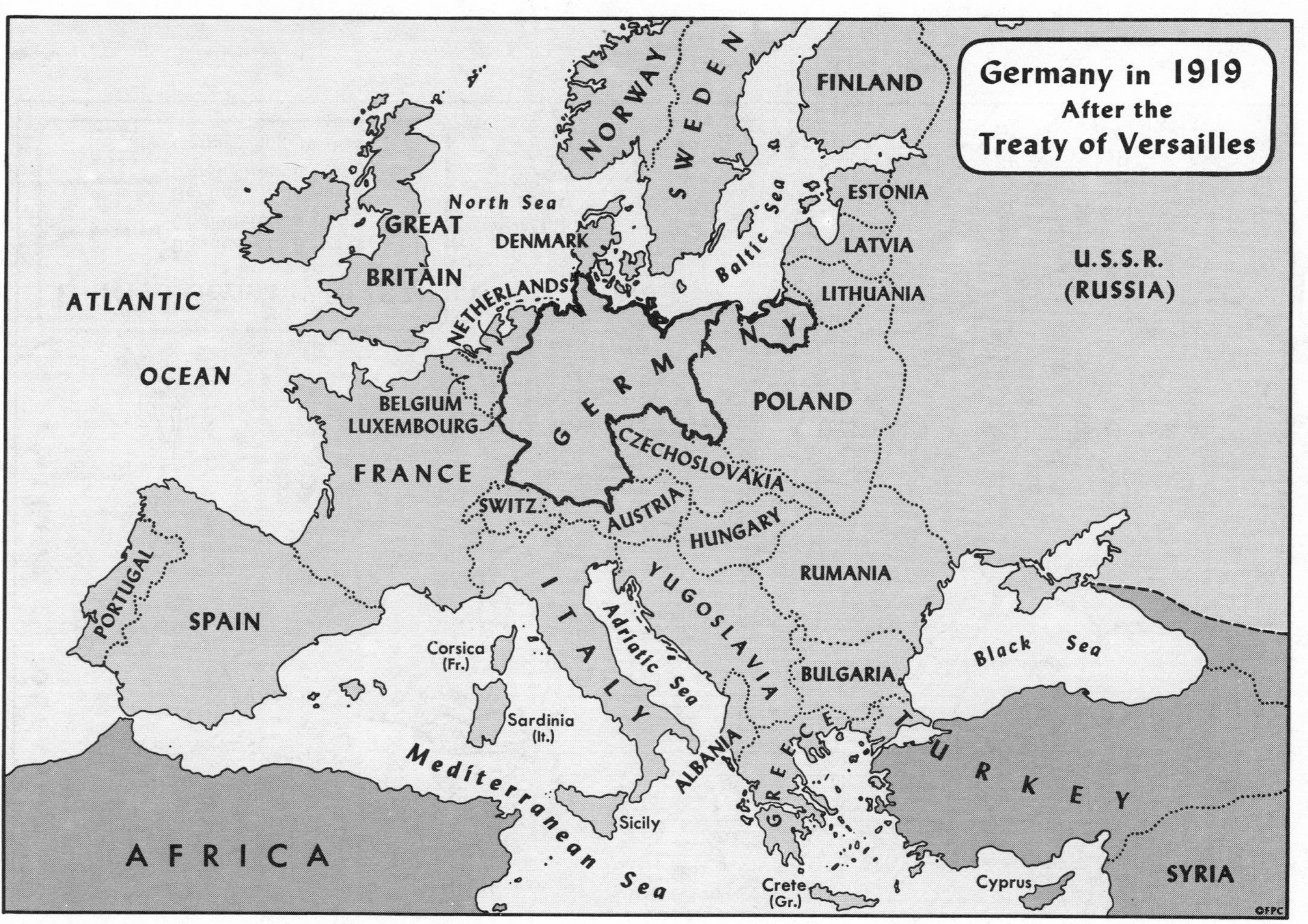

Germany in 1919
After the
Treaty of Versailles
FINLAND
NORWAY
SWEDEN
ESTONIA
LATVIA
LITHUANIA
U.S.S.R.
(RUSSIA)
North Sea
GREAT
BRITAIN
DENMARK
Baltic Sea
ATLANTIC
OCEAN
NETHERLANDS
GERMANY
POLAND
BELGIUM
LUXEMBOURG
FRANCE
CZECHOSLOVAKIA
SWITZ.
AUSTRIA
HUNGARY
RUMANIA
PORTUGAL
SPAIN
ITALY
YUGOSLAVIA
Adriatic Sea
Corsica
(Fr.)
Sardinia
(It.)
BULGARIA
Black Sea
ALBANIA
GREECE
TURKEY
Mediterranean Sea
Sicily
AFRICA
Crete
(Gr.)
Cyprus
SYRIA
©FPC

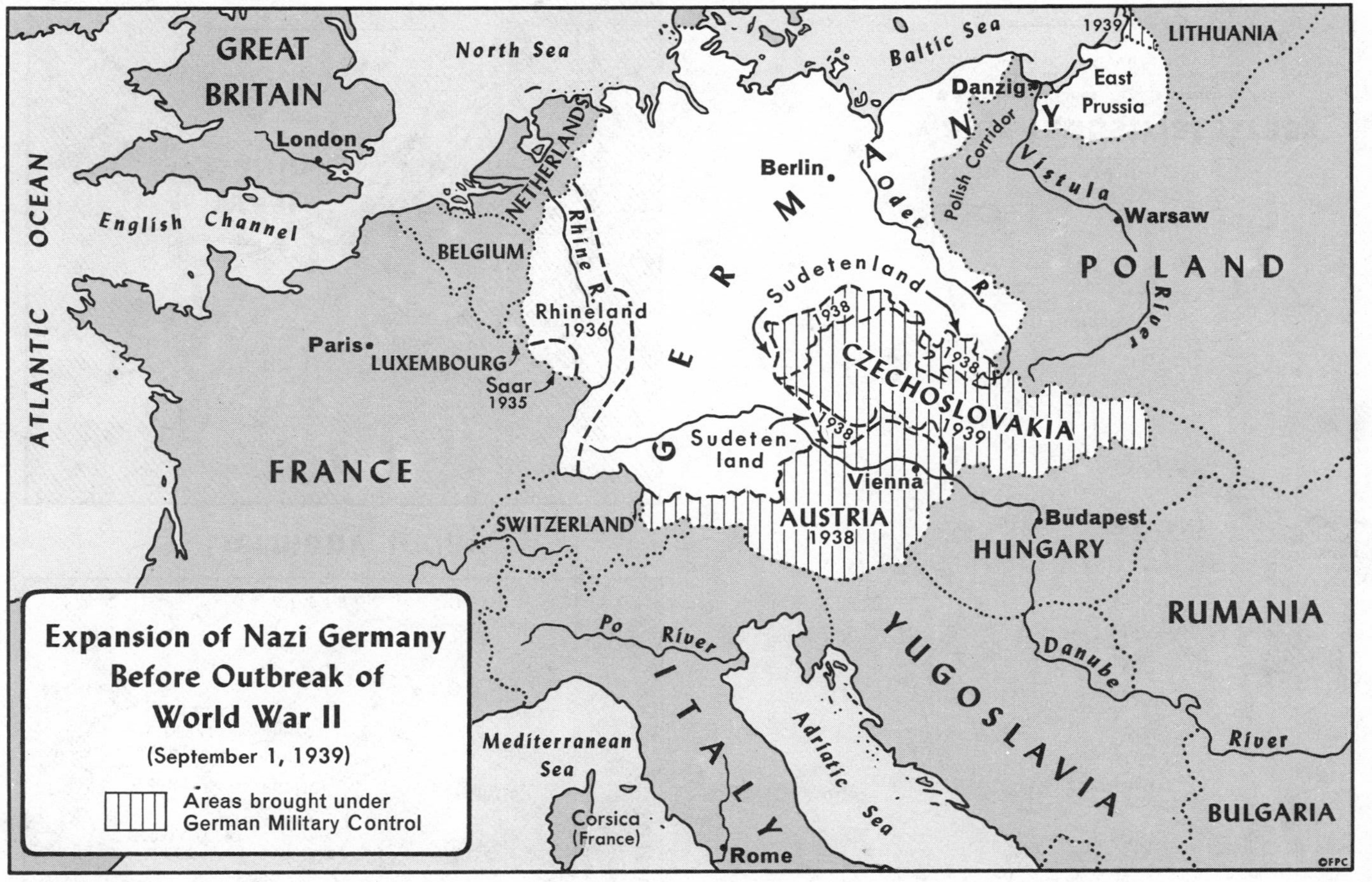

Expansion of Nazi Germany Before Outbreak of World War II (September 1, 1939)

Germany Today

Berlin Today

Major Industrial Areas